Visit *Norton Topics Online*

at www.wwnorton.com/nael

Prepared by the Norton Anthology editors, *Norton Topics Online*, a freely accessible Web resource for *The Norton Anthology of English Literature*, Seventh Edition, offers:

- Annotated **Texts and Contexts** grouped by topic
- Over **1000 Illustrations**
- **250 Explorations** to stimulate critical thinking and generate paper topics
- **Annotated Links** to related sites
- **Cross-References** to the *Norton Anthology*
- A student-friendly **"How to Use This Site"** section

"Thanks for *The Norton Anthology of English Literature* companion Web site; it is what my students like and what I need in the way of an 'electronic T.A.'!"
– Jesse Airaudi, Baylor University

"As an English major in college, I find the resources, guides, and links within your Web site to be a useful supplement to assigned readings and class lectures."
– Kevin Coats, student

Coming in January 2000: *The Norton Online Archive*, an electronic library of over 180 literary texts, annotated by the editors, to supplement *The Norton Anthology of English Literature*, Seventh Edition.

W. W. Norton & Company ⊠ Electronic Media
www.wwnorton.com/college/english

The Norton Anthology
of English Literature

SEVENTH EDITION
VOLUME 1

The Norton Anthology
of English Literature

SEVENTH EDITION

VOLUME 1

M. H. Abrams, *General Editor*

CLASS OF 1916 PROFESSOR OF ENGLISH EMERITUS,
CORNELL UNIVERSITY

Stephen Greenblatt, *Associate General Editor*

HARRY LEVIN PROFESSOR OF LITERATURE,
HARVARD UNIVERSITY

W • W • NORTON & COMPANY • *New York* • *London*

The text of this book is composed in Fairfield Medium
with the display set in Bernhard Modern.
Composition by Binghamton Valley Composition.
Manufacturing by R. R. Donnelley, Inc.
Cover illustration: The Ditchley portrait of Elizabeth I (ca. 1592), by Marcus Gheeraerts.
Courtesy of the National Portrait Gallery, London.

Editor: Julia Reidhead
Developmental Editor/Associate Managing Editor: Marian Johnson
Production Manager: Diane O'Connor
Manuscript and Project Editors: Candace Levy, Barry Katzen, David Hawkins,
Ann Tappert, Will Rigby
Editorial Assistant: Christa Grenawalt
Permissions Manager: Kristin Sheerin
Cover and Text Design: Antonina Krass
Art Research: Neil Ryder Hoos

Library of Congress Cataloging-in-Publication Data

The Norton anthology of English literature / M. H. Abrams, general
editor : Stephen Greenblatt, associate general editor. — 7th ed.
p.   cm.
Includes bibliographical references and index.

ISBN 0-393-97486-3 (v. 1). — ISBN 0-393-97487-1 (pbk.: v. 1).
ISBN 0-393-97490-1 (v. 2). — ISBN 0-393-97491-X (pbk.: v. 2).

1. English literature.   2. Great Britain—Literary collections.
I. Abrams, M. H. (Meyer Howard), 1912–   .   II. Greenblatt, Stephen, 1943–
III.   Title: Anthology of English literature.
PR1109.A2   1999
820.8—dc21   99-43298
CIP

W. W. Norton & Company, Inc., 500 Fifth Avenue, New York, N.Y. 10110
www.wwnorton.com

W. W. Norton & Company Ltd., 10 Coptic Street, London WC1A 1PU

3 4 5 6 7 8 9 0

Contents

On the Late Massacre in Piedmont   1814
Methought I Saw My Late Espousèd Saint   1815

Paradise Lost   1815

The Restoration and the Eighteenth Century
(1660–1785)   2045

CONTENTS

Preface to the Seventh Edition

The outpouring of English literature overflows all boundaries, including the capacious boundaries of *The Norton Anthology of English Literature*. But these pages manage to contain many of the most remarkable works written in English during centuries of restless creative effort. We have included epic poems and short lyrics; love songs and satires; tragedies and comedies written for performance on the commercial stage and private meditations meant to be perused in silence; prayers, popular ballads, prophecies, ecstatic visions, erotic fantasies, sermons, short stories, letters in verse and prose, critical essays, polemical tracts, several entire novels, and a great deal more. Such works generally form the core of courses that are designed to introduce students to the history of English literature, a history not only of gradual development, continuity, and dense internal echoes, but also of radical contingency, sudden change, and startling innovation.

One of the joys of literature in English is its spectacular abundance. Even from within the geographical confines of Great Britain and Ireland, where the majority of texts brought together in this collection originated, there are more than enough distinguished and exciting works to fill the pages of this anthology many times over. The abundance is all the greater if one takes, as the editors of these volumes do, a broad understanding of the term *literature*. The meaning of the term has in the course of several centuries shifted from the whole body of writing produced in a particular language to a subset of that writing consisting of works that claim special attention because of their formal beauty or expressive power. But any individual text's claim to attention is subject to constant debate and revision; established texts are jostled both by new arrivals and by previously neglected claimants; and the boundaries between the literary and whatever is thought to be "non-literary" are constantly challenged and redrawn. The heart of this collection consists of poems, plays, and prose fiction, but these categories are themselves products of ongoing historical transformations, and we have included many texts that call into question any conception of literature as denoting only a limited set of particular kinds of writing.

The designation "English" provides some obvious limits to the unwieldy, unstable, constantly shifting field of literature, but these limits are themselves in constant flux, due in part to the complexity of the territory evoked by the term (as explained in our appendix on "Geographical Nomenclature") and in part to the multinational, multicultural, and hugely expansive character of the language. As Geoffrey Nunberg's informative essay "The Persistence of English" (p. xlvii), commissioned for this Seventh Edition, makes clear, the variations in the forms of the spoken language that all go by the

call into question the very notion of a
...istory and diffusion of the language have
...e is enormous. In the momentous process that
...Great Britain and eventually into the center of a
...d more writers from outside England, beginning with
...d Scottish presence in the eighteenth century and grad-
...ut into the colonies, were absorbed into "English literature."
...English has constantly interacted with other languages and has
...ansformed by this interaction. The scope of the cross-currents may
...gauged by our medieval section, which includes selections in Old Irish
and Middle Welsh, along with works by Bede, Geoffrey of Monmouth, Wace,
and Marie de France—all of them authors living in the British Isles writing
in languages other than English. Their works are important in themselves
and also provide cultural contexts for understanding aspects of what we have
come to think of as "English literature." Certain literary texts—many of them
included in these volumes—have achieved sufficient prominence to serve as
widespread models for other writers and as objects of enduring admiration,
and thus to constitute a loose-boundaried canon. But just as there have never
been academies in English-speaking countries established to regulate the
use of language, so too there have never been firm and settled guidelines for
canonizing particular texts. English literature as a field arouses not a sense
of order but what the poet Yeats calls "the emotion of multitude."

The term "English Literature" in our title designates two different things.
First, it refers to all the literary productions of a particular part of the world:
the great preponderance of the works we include were written by authors
living in England, Scotland, Wales, and Ireland. Second, it refers to literary
works in the English language, a language that has extended far beyond the
boundaries of its point of origin. Following the lead of most college courses,
we have separated off, for purposes of this anthology, English literature from
American literature, but in the selections for the latter half of the twentieth
century we have incorporated a substantial number of texts by authors from
other countries.

The linguistic mobility and cultural intertwining reflected in these twentieth-century texts are not new. It is fitting that among the first works in this
anthology is *Beowulf*, a powerful epic written in the Germanic language
known as Old English about a singularly restless Scandinavian hero, an epic
newly translated for this edition by the Irish poet Seamus Heaney. Heaney,
who was awarded the Nobel Prize for Literature in 1995, is one of the contemporary masters of English literature, but it would be potentially misleading to call him an "English poet," for he was born in Northern Ireland and
is not in fact English. It would be still more misleading to call him a "British
poet," as if his having been born in a country that was part of the British
Empire were the most salient fact about the language he speaks and writes
or the culture by which he was shaped. What does matter is that the language
in which Heaney writes is English, and this fact links him powerfully with
the authors assembled in these volumes, a linguistic community that stubbornly refuses to fit comfortably within any firm geographical or ethnic or
national boundaries. So too, to glance at authors and writings included in
the anthology, in the sixteenth century William Tyndale, in exile in the Low
Countries and inspired by German religious reformers, translated the New

Testament from Greek and thereby changed the course of ...
guage; in the seventeenth century Aphra Behn touched her readers
story that moves from Africa, where its hero is born, to South America, where
she may have witnessed some of the tragic events she describes; and early
in the twentieth century Joseph Conrad, born in Ukraine of Polish parents,
wrote in eloquent English a celebrated novella whose vision of European
empire was trenchantly challenged at the century's end by the Nigerian-born
writer in English, Chinua Achebe.

A vital literary culture is always on the move. The Seventh Edition of *The
Norton Anthology of English Literature* has retained the body of works that
have traditionally been taught as the principal glories of English literature,
but many of our new selections reflect the fact that the *national* conception
of literary history, the conception by which English Literature meant the
literature of England or at most of Great Britain, has begun to give way to
something else. Writers like William Butler Yeats (born in Dublin), Hugh
MacDiarmid (born in Dumfriesshire, Scotland), Virginia Woolf (born in
London), and Dylan Thomas (born in Swansea, Wales) are now being taught,
and are here anthologized, alongside such writers as Nadine Gordimer (born
in the Transvaal, South Africa), Alice Munro (born in Wingham, Ontario),
Derek Walcott (born on Saint Lucia in the West Indies), Chinua Achebe
(born in Ogidi, Nigeria), and Salman Rushdie (born in Bombay, India).
English literature, like so many other collective enterprises in our century,
has ceased to be principally the product of the identity of a single nation; it
is a global phenomenon.

A central feature of *The Norton Anthology of English Literature*, established by its original editors, was a commitment to provide periodic revisions
in order to take advantage of newly recovered or better-edited texts, reflect
scholarly discoveries and the shifting interests of readers, and keep the
anthology in touch with contemporary critical and intellectual concerns. To
help us honor this commitment we have, as in past years, profited from a
remarkable flow of voluntary corrections and suggestions proposed by students, as well as teachers, who view the anthology with a loyal but critical
eye. Moreover, we have again solicited and received detailed information on
the works actually assigned, proposals for deletions and additions, and suggestions for improving the editorial matter, from over two hundred reviewers
from around the world, almost all of them teachers who use the books in a
course. In its evolution, then, this anthology has been the product of an
ongoing collaboration among its editors, teachers, and students.

The active participation of an engaged community of readers has been
crucial as the editors grapple with the challenging task of retaining (and
indeed strengthening) the selection of more traditional texts even while adding many texts that reflect the transformation and expansion of the field
of English studies. The challenge is heightened by the wish to keep each
volume manageable, in size and weight, so that students will actually carry
the book to class. The final decisions on what to include were made by
the editors, but we were immeasurably assisted, especially in borderline
cases, by the practical experience and the detailed opinions of teachers and
scholars.

In addition to the new translation of *Beowulf* and to the greatly augmented
global approach to twentieth-century literature in English, several other fea-

...rit special mention. We have greatly
...g by women in all of the historical periods.
...nolars in recent years has recovered dozens of
...had been marginalized or neglected by a male-
...dition and has deepened our understanding of those
...o had managed, against considerable odds, to claim a place
...n. The First Edition of the *Norton Anthology* was ahead of its
...cluding six women writers; this Seventh Edition includes sixty, of
...twenty-one are newly added and twenty are reselected or expanded.
...ets and prose writers whose names were scarcely mentioned even in the
specialized literary histories of earlier generations—Isabella Whitney, Aemilia Lanyer, Lady Mary Wroth, Elizabeth Cary, Margaret Cavendish, Mary
Leapor, Anna Letitia Barbauld, Charlotte Smith, Letitia Elizabeth Landon,
and many others—now appear in the company of their male contemporaries.
There are in addition three complete long prose works by women: Aphra
Behn's *Oroonoko,* Mary Shelley's *Frankenstein,* and Virginia Woolf's *A Room
of One's Own.*

The novel is, of course, a stumbling block for an anthology. The length
of many great novels defies their incorporation in any volume that hopes
to include a broad spectrum of literature. At the same time it is difficult
to excerpt representative passages from narratives whose power often
depends upon amplitude or upon the slow development of character or
upon the on-rushing urgency of the story. Therefore, better to represent
the remarkable achievements of novelists, the publisher is making available, in inexpensive and well-edited Norton Anthology Editions, a range
of novels, including Jane Austen's *Pride and Prejudice,* Charles Dickens's
Hard Times, Charlotte Brontë's *Jane Eyre,* and Emily Brontë's *Wuthering
Heights.*

A further innovation in the Seventh Edition is our inclusion of new and
expanded clusters of texts that resonate with one another culturally and the-
matically. Using the "Victorian Issues" section long featured in *The Norton
Anthology of English Literature* as our model, we devised for each period
groupings that serve to suggest some ways in which the pervasive concepts,
images, and key terms that haunt major literary works can often be found in
other written traces of a culture. Hence, for example, the adventures of
Edmund Spenser's wandering knights resonate with the excerpts from Elizabethan travel accounts brought together in "The Wider World": Frobisher's
violent encounters with the Eskimos of Baffin Island, Drake's attempt to lay
claim to California, Amadas and Barlowe's idealizing vision of the Indians as
the inhabitants of the Golden Age, and Hariot's subtle attempt to analyze
and manipulate native beliefs. Similarly, the millenarian expectations voiced
in the texts grouped in "The French Revolution and the 'Spirit of the Age' "
helped shape the major writings of poets from William Blake to Percy Bysshe
Shelley, while the historical struggles reflected in texts by Jawaharlal Nehru
and others in "The Rise and Fall of Empire" echo in the fiction of Chinua
Achebe, V. S. Naipaul, and J. M. Coetzee. We supplement the clusters for
each period with several more topical groupings of texts and copious illustrations on the *Norton Anthology* Web site.

Period-by-Period Revisions

The scope of the revisions we have undertaken, the most extensive in t t long publishing history of *The Norton Anthology of English Literature*, can be conveyed more fully by a list of some of the principal additions.

The Middle Ages. Better to represent the complex multilingual situation of the period, the section has been reorganized and divided into three parts: Anglo-Saxon England, Anglo-Norman England, and Middle English Literature of the Fourteenth and Fifteenth Centuries. Nearly fifteen years in the making, Seamus Heaney's translation of *Beowulf* comes closer to conveying the full power of the Anglo-Saxon epic than any existing rendering and will be of major interest as well to students of modern poetry. The selection of Anglo-Saxon poems has also been augmented by *The Wife's Lament*. We have added a new section, Anglo-Norman England, which provides a key bridge between the Anglo-Saxon period and the time of Chaucer, highlighting a cluster of texts that trace the origins of Arthurian romance. This section includes selections from the chronicle account of the Norman conquest; legendary histories by Geoffrey of Monmouth, Wace, and Layamon; Marie de France's *Lanval* (a Breton lay about King Arthur's court, here in a new verse translation by Alfred David), along with two of her fables; a selection from the *Ancrene Riwle* (Rule for Anchoresses); and two Celtic narratives: the Irish *Exile of the Sons of Uisliu* and the Welsh *Lludd and Lleuelys*. To Chaucer's works we have added *The Man of Law's Epilogue* and *Troilus's Song*; we have added to the grouping of Late Middle English lyrics and strengthened the already considerable selection from the revelations of the visionary anchoress Julian of Norwich; and we have included for the first time a work by Robert Henryson, *The Cock and the Fox*.

The Sixteenth Century. Shakespeare's magnificent comedy of cross-dressing and cross-purposes, *Twelfth Night*, is for the first time included in the *Norton Anthology*, providing a powerful contrast with his bleakest tragedy, *King Lear*. The raucous *Tunning of Elinour Rumming* has been added to Skelton's poems and the somber *Stand whoso list* to Wyatt's, while Gascoigne is now represented by his poem *Woodmanship*. Additions in poetry and prose works have similarly been made to Roger Ascham, Henry Howard, Earl of Surrey, Sir Walter Ralegh, Fulke Greville, Samuel Daniel, Thomas Campion, and Thomas Nashe. Along with the grouping of travel texts described above, another new cluster, "Literature of the Sacred," brings together contrasting Bible translations; writings by William Tyndale and Richard Hooker; Anne Askew's account, smuggled from the Tower, of her interrogation and torture, along with the martyrologist John Foxe's account of her execution; selections from the Book of Common Prayer and the Book of Homilies; and an Elizabethan translation of John Calvin's influential account of predestination. In addition to Anne Askew, another Elizabethan woman writer, Isabella Whitney, makes her appearance in the *Norton Anthology*, along with a new selection of texts by Mary Herbert and a newly added speech and letters by Queen Elizabeth.

The Early Seventeenth Century. In response to widespread demand and to our own sense of the work's commanding importance, both in its own time and in the history of English literature, we have for the first time included the whole of Milton's *Paradise Lost*. Other substantial works that newly

···son's *Masque of Blackness* and Andrew
···extensive selections from Elizabeth Cary's
··· y and prose by Aemilia Lanyer and Margaret
··· been made to the works of John Donne, Jonson,
···rge Herbert, Henry Vaughan, Richard Crashaw, Rob-
···n Suckling. The "Voices of the War" cluster, introduced
···ion, now includes Anna Trapnel's narrative of her eventful
··· London to Cornwall; and a new cluster, "The Science of Self
···nd," brings together meditative texts, poems, and essays by Francis
···n, Martha Moulsworth, Robert Burton, Rachel Speght, Sir Thomas
Browne, Izaak Walton, and Thomas Hobbes.

The Restoration and the Eighteenth Century. John Gay's *The Beggar's Opera*—familiar to modern audiences as the source of Bertolt Brecht's *Threepenny Opera*—makes its appearance in the *Norton Anthology,* along with William Hogarth's illustration of a scene from the play. Hogarth's "literary" graphic art is represented by his satiric *Marriage A-la-Mode.* Two new clusters of texts enable readers to engage more fully with key controversies in the period. "Debating Women: Arguments in Verse" presents the war between the sexes in spirited poems by Jonathan Swift, Lady Mary Wortley Montagu, Alexander Pope, Anne Finch, Anne Ingram, and Mary Leapor. The period's sexual politics is illuminated as well in added texts by Samuel Pepys, John Wilmot, Second Earl of Rochester, and Aphra Behn. "Slavery and Freedom" brings together the disquieting exchange on the enslavement of African peoples between Ignatius Sancho and Laurence Sterne, along with Olaudah Equiano's ground-breaking history of his own enslavement. The narrative gifts of Frances Burney, whose long career spans this period and the next, are newly presented by six texts, including her famous, harrowing account of her mastectomy.

The Romantic Period. The principal changes here center on the greatly increased representation of women writers in the period: Mary Robinson and Letitia Elizabeth Landon are included for the first time, and there are substantially increased selections by Anna Letitia Barbauld, Charlotte Smith, Joanna Baillie, Dorothy Wordsworth, and Felicia Hemans; to Mary Wollstonecraft's epochal *Vindication of the Rights of Women,* we have now added a selection from her *Letters Written in Sweden.* Conjoined with Mary Shelley's *Frankenstein,* presented here in its entirety, these texts restore women writers, once marginalized in literary histories of the period, to the significant place they in fact occupied. A new thematic cluster focusing on the period's cataclysmic event, the French Revolution, brings together texts in prose and verse by Richard Price, Edmund Burke, Mary Wollstonecraft, Thomas Paine, Elhanan Winchester, Joseph Priestley, William Black, Robert Southey, William Wordsworth, Samuel Taylor Coleridge, and Percy Bysshe Shelley. The selection of poems by the peasant poet John Clare has been expanded and is printed in a new text prepared for this edition. We have also added to Sir Walter Scott the introductory chapter of his *Heart of Midlothian,* and to William Wordsworth his long and moving lyrical ballad *The Thorn.*

The Victorian Age. The important novelist, short story writer, and biographer Elizabeth Gaskell makes her appearance in the *Norton Anthology,* along with two late-nineteenth-century poets, Michael Field and Mary Elizabeth Coleridge. Rudyard Kipling's powerful story *The Man Who Would Be King* is a significant new addition, as is the selection from Oscar Wilde's prison writings, *De Profundis*. Dickens's somber reflection *A Visit to Newgate* has been added. There are new texts in the selections of many authors as well, including John Henry Cardinal Newman, Elizabeth Barrett Browning, Alfred, Lord Tennyson, Elizabeth Gaskell, George Eliot, Dante Gabriel Rossetti, William Morris, and Gerard Manley Hopkins. Bernard Shaw's play *Mrs. Warren's Profession* has been moved to its chronological place in this section. New texts have also been added to the "Victorian Issues" clusters on evolution, industrialism, and the debate about gender.

The Twentieth Century. The principal addition here, in length and in symbolic significance, is Chinua Achebe's celebrated novel *Things Fall Apart*, presented in its entirety, and, with Joseph Conrad's *Heart of Darkness* and Virginia Woolf's *A Room of One's Own*, the third complete prose work in this section. But there are many other changes as well, in keeping with a thoroughgoing rethinking of this century's literary history. We begin with Thomas Hardy (now shown as fiction writer as well as poet) and Joseph Conrad, both liminal figures poised between two distinct cultural worlds. These are followed by groupings of texts that articulate some of the forces that helped pull these worlds asunder. A cluster on "The Rise and Fall of Empire" brings together John Ruskin, John Hobson, the Easter Proclamation of the Irish Republic, Richard Mulcahy, James Morris, Jawaharlal Nehru, and Chinua Achebe, and these texts of geo-political crisis in turn resonate with "Voices from World War I" and "Voices from World War II," both sections newly strengthened by prose texts. We have added selections to E. M. Forster, James Joyce, and T. S. Eliot, among others, and for the first time present the work of the West Indian writer Jean Rhys and the Irish poet Paul Muldoon. Samuel Beckett is now represented by the complete text of his masterful tragicomedy, *Endgame*. Above all, the explosion of writing in English in "postcolonial" countries around the world shapes our revision of this section, not only in our inclusion of Achebe but also in new texts by Derek Walcott, V. S. Naipaul, Anita Desai, Les Murray, J. M. Coetzee, Eavan Boland, Alice Munro, and Salman Rushdie. Seamus Heaney's works, to which another poem has been added, provide the occasion to look back again to the beginning of these volumes with Heaney's new translation of *Beowulf*. This translation is a reminder that the history of literature is not a straightforward sequence, that the most recent works can double back upon the distant past, and that the words set down by men and women who have crumbled into dust can speak to us with astonishing directness.

Editorial Procedures

The scope of revisions to the editorial apparatus in the Seventh Edition is the most extensive ever undertaken in *The Norton Anthology of English Literature*. As in past editions, period introductions, headnotes, and annotation are designed to give students the information needed, without imposing an interpretation. The aim of these editorial materials is to make the anthology self-sufficient, so that it can be read anywhere—in a coffeehouse, on a bus, or under a tree. In this edition, this apparatus has been thoroughly revised in response to new scholarship. The period introductions and many headnotes have been either entirely or substantially rewritten to be more helpful to students, and all the Selected Bibliographies have been thoroughly updated.

Several new features reflect the broadened scope of the selections in the anthology. The new introductory essay, "The Persistence of English" by Geoffrey Nunberg, Stanford University and Xerox Palo Alto Research Center, explores the emergence and spread of English and its apparent present-day "triumph" as a world language. It provides a lively point of departure for the study of literature in English. The endpaper maps have been reconceived and redrawn. New timelines following each period introduction help students place their reading in historical and cultural context. So that students can explore literature as a visual medium, the anthology introduces visual materials from several periods—Hogarth's *Marriage A-la-Mode*, engravings by Blake, and Dante Gabriel Rossetti's illustrations for poems by Tennyson, Christina Rossetti, and Rossetti himself. These illustrations can be supplemented by the hundreds of images available on Norton Topics Online, the Web companion to the *Norton Anthology*.

Each volume of the anthology includes an appendix, "Poems in Process," which reproduces from manuscripts and printed texts the genesis and evolution of a number of poems whose final form is printed in that volume. Both volumes contain a useful section on "Poetic Forms and Literary Terminology," much revised in the Seventh Edition, as well as brief appendices on the intricacies of English money, the baronage, and religions. A new appendix, "Geographic Nomenclature," has been added to clarify the shifting place-names applied to regions of the British Isles.

Students, no less than scholars, deserve the most accurate texts available; in keeping with this policy, we continue to introduce improved versions of the selections where available. In this edition, for example, in addition to Seamus Heaney's new verse translation of *Beowulf*, we introduce Alfred David's new verse translation of Marie de France's *Lanval*, the Norton/Oxford text of *Twelfth Night*; and Jack Stillinger's newly edited texts of the poems of John Clare. To ease a student's access, we have normalized spelling and capitalization in texts up to and including the Victorian period to follow the conventions of modern English; we leave unaltered, however, texts in which modernizing would change semantic or metrical qualities and those texts for which we use specially edited versions (identified in a headnote or footnote); these include Wollstonecraft's *Vindication*, William Wordsworth's *Ruined Cottage* and *Prelude*, Dorothy Wordsworth's *Journals*, the verse and prose of P. B. Shelley and Keats, and Mary Shelley's *Frankenstein*. In The Twentieth Century, we have restored original spelling and punctuation to selections retained from the previous edition in the belief that the authors' choices, when they pose no difficulties for student readers, should be respected.

We continue other editorial procedures that have proved useful in the past. After each work, we cite (when known) the date of composition on the left and the date of first publication on the right; in some instances, the latter is followed by the date of a revised edition for which the author was responsible. We have used square brackets to indicate titles supplied by the editors for the convenience of readers. Whenever a portion of a text has been omitted, we have indicated that omission with three asterisks. If the omitted portion is important for following the plot or argument, we have provided a brief summary within the text or in a footnote. We have extended our longstanding practice of providing marginal glossing of single words and short phrases from medieval and dialect poets (such as Robert Burns) to all the poets in the anthology. Finally, we have adopted a bolder typeface and redesigned the page, so as to make the text more readable.

The Course Guide to Accompany "The Norton Anthology of English Literature," by Alfred David, Indiana University, Philip Schwyzer, University of Oxford, and Kelly Hurley, University of Colorado at Boulder, based on an earlier version by Alfred David, has been thoroughly revised and expanded; it contains detailed syllabi for a variety of approaches to the course, thematic teaching notes on periods and works, study and essay questions, and cross references that facilitate integrating the printed texts with material on the Norton Web site and recordings on the Audio Companion. A copy of the *Guide* may be obtained on request from the publisher.

Two cardinal innovations, one print and one electronic, greatly increase the anthology's flexibility: The book is now available both in the traditional two-volume format, in clothbound and paperback versions, and in a new six-volume paperback version comprised of volume 1A, *The Middle Ages*, volume 1B, *The Sixteenth Century/The Early Seventeenth Century*, volume 1C, *The Restoration and the Eighteenth Century*, volume 2A, *The Romantic Period*, volume 2B, *The Victorian Age*, and volume 2C, *The Twentieth Century*. By maintaining the same pagination as in the original two volumes, the six-volume format offers a more portable option for students in survey courses and allows the individual volumes to be used in period courses.

Extending beyond the printed page, the Norton Topics Online Web site (*www.wwnorton.com/nael*) augments the anthology's already broad representation of the sweep of English literature. For students who wish to extend their exploration of literary and cultural contexts, the Web site offers a huge range of related texts, prepared by the anthology editors, and by Myron Tuman, University of Alabama, and Philip Schwyzer, University of Oxford. An ongoing venture, the Web site currently offers twenty-one thematic clusters—three per period—of texts and visual images, cross-referenced to the anthology, together with overviews, study explorations, and annotated links to related sites. In addition, the Audio Companion to *The Norton Anthology of English Literature* is available without charge upon request by teachers who adopt the anthology. It consists of two compact discs of readings by the authors of the works represented in the anthology, readings of poems in Old and Middle English and in English dialects, and performances of poems that were written to be set to music.

The editors are deeply grateful to the hundreds of teachers worldwide who have helped us to improve *The Norton Anthology of English Literature*. A list of the advisors who prepared in-depth reviews and of the instructors who replied to a detailed questionnaire follows on a separate page, under Acknowledgments. The editors would like to express appreciation for their assistance to Tiffany Beechy (Harvard University), Mitch Cohen (Wissenschaftskolleg zu Berlin), Sandie Byrne (Oxford University), Sarah Cole (Columbia University), Dianne Ferriss (Cornell University), Robert Folkenflik (University of California, Irvine), Robert D. Fulk (Indiana University), Andrew Gurr (The University of Reading), Wendy Hyman (Harvard University), Elissa Linke (Wissenschaftskolleg zu Berlin), Joanna Lipking (North-western University), Linda O'Riordan (Wissenschaftskolleg zu Berlin), Ruth Perry (M.I.T.), Leah Price (Harvard University), Ramie Targoff (Yale University), and Douglas Trevor (Harvard University). The editors give special thanks to Paul Leopold, who drafted the appendix on Geographic Nomenclature and revised the appendix on Religions in England, and to Philip Schwyzer (University of Oxford), whose wide-ranging contributions include preparing texts and study materials for the Web site, assisting with the revision of numerous headnotes, updating appendices on the British baronage and British money, and co-authoring the Course Guide. We also thank the many people at Norton who contributed to the Seventh Edition: Julia Reidhead, who served not only as the inhouse supervisor but also as an unfailingly wise and effective collaborator in every aspect of planning and accomplishing this Seventh Edition; Marian Johnson, developmental editor, who kept the project moving forward with a remarkable blend of focused energy, intelligence, and common sense; Candace Levy, Ann Tappert, Barry Katzen, David Hawkins, and Will Rigby, project and manuscript editors; Anna Karvellas and Kirsten Miller, Web site editors; Diane O'Connor, production manager; Kristin Sheerin, permissions manager; Toni Krass, designer; Neil Ryder Hoos, art researcher; and Christa Grenawalt, editorial assistant and map coordinator. All these friends provided the editors with indispensable help in meeting the challenge of representing, justly and in only two volumes, the unparalleled range and variety of English literature.

M. H. ABRAMS
STEPHEN GREENBLATT

Acknowledgments

Among our many critics, advisors, and friends, the following were of especial help toward the preparation of the Seventh Edition, either with advice or by providing critiques of particular periods of the anthology: Judith H. Anderson (Indiana University), Paula Backsheider (Auburn University), Elleke Boehmer (Leeds University), Rebecca Brackmann (University of Illinois), James Chandler (University of Chicago), Valentine Cunningham (Oxford University), Lennard Davis (SUNY Binghamton), Katherine Eggert (University of Colorado), P. J. C. Field (University of Wales), Vincent Gillespie (Oxford University), Roland Greene (University of Oregon), A. C. Hamilton (Queen's University), Emrys Jones (Oxford University), Laura King (Yale University), Noel Kinnamon (Mars Hill College), John Leonard (University of Western Ontario), William T. Liston (Ball State University), F. P. Lock (Queen's University), Lee Patterson (Yale University), Jahan Ramazani (University of Virginia), John Regan (Oxford University), John Rogers (Yale University), Herbert Tucker (University of Virginia), Mel Wiebe (Queen's University).

The editors would like to express appreciation and thanks to the hundreds of teachers who provided reviews: Porter Abbott (University of California, Santa Barbara), Robert Aguirre (University of California, Los Angeles), Alan Ainsworth (Houston Community College Central), Jesse T. Airaudi (Baylor University), Edward Alexander (University of Washington), Michael Alexander (University of St. Andrews), Gilbert Allen (Furman University), Jill Angelino (George Washington University), Linda M. Austin (Oklahoma State University), Sonja S. Baghy (State University of West Georgia), Vern D. Bailey (Carleton College), William Barker (Fitchburg State University), Carol Barret (Northridge Campus, Austin Community College), Mary Barron (University of North Florida), Jackson Barry (University of Maryland), Dean Bevan (Baker University), Carol Beran (St. Mary's College), James Biester (Loyola University, Chicago), Nancy B. Black (Brooklyn College), Alan Blackstock (Wharton Community Junior College), Alfred F. Boe (San Diego State University), Cheryl D. Bohde (McLennan Community College), Karin Boklund-Lagopouloou (Aristotle University of Thessaloniki), Scott Boltwood (Emory and Henry College), Troy Boone (University of California, Santa Cruz), James L. Boren (University of Oregon), Ellen Brinks (Princeton University), Douglas Bruster (University of Texas, San Antonio), John Bugge (Emory University), Maria Bullon-Fernandez (Seattle University), John J. Burke (University of Alabama), Deborah G. Burks (Ohio State University), James Byer (Western Carlonia University), Gregory Castle (Arizona State University), Paul William Child (Sam Houston State University), Joe R. Christopher (Tarleton State University), A. E. B. Coldiron (Towson State University), John Constable (University of Leeds), C. Abbott Conway (McGill University), Patrick Creevy (Mississippi State University), Thomas M. Curley (Bridgewater State College), Clifford Davidson (Western Michigan University), Craig R. Davis (Smith College), Frank Day (Clemson University), Marliss Desens (Texas Tech University), Jerome Donnelly (University of Central Florida), Terrance Doody (Rice University), Max Dorsinville (McGill University), David Duff (University of Aberdeen), Alexander Dunlop (Auburn University), Richard J. DuRocher (St. Olaf College), Dwight Eddins (University of Alabama), Caroline L. Eisner (George Washington University), Andrew Elfenbein (University of Minnesota), Doris Williams Elliott (University of Kansas), Nancy S. Ellis (Mississippi State University), Kevin Eubanks (University of Tennessee), Gareth Euridge (Denison University), Deanna Evans (Bemidji State University), Julia A. Fesmire (Middle Tennessee State University), Michael Field (Bemidji State University), Judith L. Fisher (Trinity University), Graham Forst (Capilano College), Marilyn Francus (West Virginia University), Susan S. Frisbie (Santa Clara University), Shearle Furnish (West Texas A&M University), Arthur Ganz (City College of CUNY; The New School), Stephanie Gauper (Western Michigan University), Donna A. Gessell (North Georgia College and State University), Reid Gilbert (Capilano College), Jonathan C. Glance (Mercer University), I. Gopnik (McGill University), William Gorski (Northwestern State University of Louisiana), Roy Gottfried (Vanderbilt University), Timothy Gray (University of California, Santa Barbara), Patsy Griffin (Georgia Southern University), M. J. Gross (Southwest Texas State University), Gillian Hanson (University of Houston), Linda Hatchel (McLennan Community College), James Heldman (Western Kentucky University), Stephen Hemenway (Hope College), Michael Hennessy (Southwest Texas State University), Peter C. Herman (San Diego State University), James Hirsh (Georgia State University), Diane Long Hoeveler (Marquette University), Jerrold E. Hogle (University of Arizona), Brian Holloway (College of West Virginia), David Honick (Bentley College), Catherine E. Howard (University of Houston), David Hudson (Augsburg College), Steve Hudson (Portland Community College), Clark Hulse (University of Illinois, Chicago), Jefferson Hunter (Smith College), Vernon Ingraham (University of Massachusetts, Dartmouth), Thomas Jemielity (University of Notre Dame), R. Jothiprakash (Wiley College), John M. Kandl (Walsh University), David Kay (University of Illinois, Urbana-Champaign), Richard Kelly (University of Tennessee), Elizabeth Keyser (Hollins College), Gail Kienitz (Wheaton College), Richard Knowles (University of Wisconsin, Madison), Deborah Knuth (Colgate University), Albert Koinm (Sam Houston State University), Jack Kolb (University of California, Los Angeles), Valerie Krishna (City College, CUNY), Richard Kroll (University of California, Irvine), Jameela Lares (University of Southern Mississippi), Beth Lau (California State University, Long Beach), James Livingston (Northern Michigan University), Christine Loflin (Grinnell College), W. J. Lohman Jr. (University of Tampa), Suzanne H. MacRae (University of Arkansas, Fayettesville), Julia Maia (West Valley College), Sarah R. Marino (Ohio Northern University), Louis Martin (Elizabethtown College), Irene Martyniuk (Fitchburg State College), Frank T. Mason (University of South Florida), Mary Massirer (Baylor University), J. C. C. Mays (University College, Dublin), James McCord (Union College), Brian McCrea (University of Florida), Claie McEachern (University of California, Los Angeles), Joseph McGowan (University of San Diego), Alexander Menocal (University of North Florida), John Mercer (Northeastern State University),

Teresa Michals (George Mason University), Michael Allen Mikolajezak (University of St. Thomas), Jonathan Middlebrook (San Francisco State University), Sal Miroglotta (John Carroll University), James H. Morey (Emory University), Maryclaire Moroney (John Carroll University), William E. Morris (University of South Florida), Charlotte C. Morse (Virginia Commonwealth University), Alan H. Nelson (University of California, Berkeley), Jeff Nelson (University of Alabama, Huntsville), Richard Newhauser (Trinity University), Ashton Nichols (Dickinson College), Noreen O'Connor (George Washington University), Peter Okun (Davis and Elkins College), Nora M. Olivares (San Antonio College), Harold Orel (University of Kansas), Sue Owen (University of Sheffield), Diane Parkin-Speer (Southwest Texas State University), C. Patton (Texas Tech University), Paulus Pimoma (Central Washington University), John F. Plummer (Vanderbilt University), Alan Powers (Bristol Community College), William Powers (Michigan Technological University), Nicholas Radel (Furman University), Martha Rainbolt (DePauw University), Robert L. Reid (Emory and Henry College), Luke Reinsina (Seattle Pacific University), Cedric D. Reverand II (University of Wyoming), Mary E. Robbins (Georgia State University), Mark Rollins (Ohio State University, Athens), Charles Ross (Purdue University), Donelle R. Ruwe (Fitchburg State College), John Schell (University of Central Florida), Walter Scheps (SUNY Stony Brook), Michael Schoenfeldt (University of Michigan), Robert Scotto (Baruch College), Asha Sen (University of Wisconsin, Eau Claire), Lavina Shankar (Bates College), Michael Shea (Southern Connecticut State University), M. P. A. Sheaffer (Millersville University), R. Allen Shoaf (University of Florida), Michael N. Stanton (University of Vermont), Massie C. Stinson Jr. (Longwood College), Andrea St. John (University of Miami), Donald R. Stoddard (Anne Arundel Community College), Joyce Ann Sutphen (Gustavas Adolphus College), Max K. Sutton (University of Kansas), Margaret Thomas (Wilberforce University), John M. Thompson (U.S. Naval Academy), Dinny Thorold (University of Westminster), James B. Twitchell (University of Florida), J. K. Van Dover (Lincoln University), Karen Van Eman (Wayne State University), Paul V. Voss (Georgia State University), Leon Waldoff (University of Illinois, Urbana-Champaign), Donald J. Weinstock (California State University, Long Beach), Susan Wells (Temple University), Winthrop Wetherbee (Cornell University), Thomas Willard (University of Arizona), J. D. Williams (Hunter College), Charles Workman (Stanford University), Margaret Enright Wye (Rockhurst College), R. O. Wyly (University of Southern Florida), James J. Yoch (University of Oklahoma), Marvin R. Zirker (Indiana University, Bloomington).

The Persistence of English

If you measure the success of a language in purely quantitative terms, English is entering the twenty-first century at the moment of its greatest triumph. It has between 400 and 450 million native speakers, perhaps 300 million more who speak it as a second language—well enough, that is, to use it in their daily lives—and somewhere between 500 and 750 million who speak it as a foreign language with various degrees of fluency. The resulting total of between 1.2 billion and 1.5 billion speakers, or roughly a quarter of the world's population, gives English more speakers than any other language (though Chinese has more native speakers). Then, too, English is spoken over a much wider geographical area than any other language and is the predominant lingua franca of most fields of international activity, such as diplomacy, business, travel, science, and technology.

But figures like these can obscure a basic question: what exactly do we mean when we talk about the "English language" in the first place? There is, after all, an enormous range of variation in the forms of speech that go by the name of English in the various parts of the world—or often, even within the speech of a single nation—and it is not obvious why we should think of all of these as belonging to a single language. Indeed, there are some linguists who prefer to talk about "world Englishes," in the plural, with the implication that these varieties may not have much more to unite them than a single name and a common historical origin.

To the general public, these reservations may be hard to understand; people usually assume that languages are natural kinds like botanical species, whose boundaries are matters of scientific fact. But as linguists observe, there is nothing in the forms of English themselves that tells us that it is a single language. It may be that the varieties called "English" have a great deal of vocabulary and structure in common and that English-speakers can usually manage to make themselves understood to one another, more or less (though films produced in one part of the English-speaking world often have to be dubbed or subtitled to make them intelligible to audiences in another). But there are many cases where we find linguistic varieties that are mutually intelligible and grammatically similar, but where speakers nonetheless identify separate languages—for example, Danish and Norwegian, Czech and Slovak, or Dutch and Afrikaans. And on the other hand, there are cases where speakers identify varieties as belonging to a single language even though they are linguistically quite distant from one another: the various "dialects" of Chinese are more different from one another than the Latin offshoots that we identify now as French, Italian, Spanish, and so forth.

Philosophers sometimes compare languages to games, and the analogy is apt here, as well. Trying to determine whether American English and British English or Dutch and Afrikaans are "the same language" is like trying to determine whether baseball and softball are "the same game"—it is not something you can find out just by looking at their rules. It is not surprising, then, that linguists should throw up their hands when someone asks them to determine on linguistic grounds alone whether two varieties belong to a single language. That, they answer, is a political or social determination, not a linguistic one, and they usually go on to cite a well-known quip: "a language is just a dialect with an army and a navy."

There is something to this remark. Since the eighteenth century, it has been widely believed that every nation deserved to have its own language, and declarations of political independence have often been followed by declarations of linguistic independence. Until recently, for example, the collection of similar language varieties that were spoken in most of central Yugoslavia was regarded as a single language, Serbo-Croatian, but once the various regions became independent, their inhabitants began to speak of Croatian, Serbian, and Bosnian as separate languages, even though they are mutually comprehensible and grammatically almost identical.

The English language has avoided this fate (though on occasion it has come closer to breaking up than most people realize). But the unity of a language is never a foregone conclusion. In any speech-community, there are forces always at work to create new differences and varieties: the geographic and social separation of speech-communities, their distinct cultural and practical interests, their contact with other cultures and other languages, and, no less important, a universal fondness for novelty for its own sake, and a desire to speak differently from one's parents or the people in the next town. Left to function on their own, these centrifugal pressures can rapidly lead to the linguistic fragmentation of the speech-community. That is what happened, for example, to the vulgar (that is, "popular") Latin of the late Roman Empire, which devolved into hundreds or thousands of separate dialects (the emergence of the eight or ten standard varieties that we now think of as the Romance languages was a much later development).

Maintaining the unity of a language over an extended time and space, then, requires a more or less conscious determination by its speakers that they have certain communicative interests in common that make it worthwhile to try to curb or modulate the natural tendency to fragmentation and isolation. This determination can be realized in a number of ways. The speakers of a language may decide to use a common spelling system even when dialects become phonetically distinct, to defer to the same set of literary models, to adopt a common format for their dictionaries and grammars, or to make instruction in the standard language a part of the general school curriculum, all of which the English-speaking world has done to some degree. Or in some other places, the nations of the linguistic community may establish academies or other state institutions charged with regulating the use of the language, and even go so far as to publish lists of words that are unacceptable for use in the press or in official publications, as the French government has done in recent years. Most important, the continuity of the language rests on speakers' willingness to absorb the linguistic and cultural influences of other parts of the linguistic community.

THE EMERGENCE OF THE ENGLISH LANGUAGE

To recount the history of a language, then, is not simply to trace the development of its various sounds, words, and constructions. Seen from that exclusively linguistic point of view, there would be nothing to distinguish the evolution of Anglo-Saxon into the varieties of modern English from the evolution of Latin into modern French, Italian, and so forth—we would not be able to tell, that is, why English continued to be considered a single language while the Romance languages did not. We also have to follow the play of centrifugal and centripetal forces that kept the language always more or less a unity—the continual process of creation of new dialects and varieties, the countervailing rise of new standards and of mechanisms aimed at maintaining the linguistic center of gravity.

Histories of the English language usually put its origin in the middle of the fifth century, when several Germanic peoples first landed in the place we now call England and began to displace the local inhabitants, the Celts. There is no inherent linguistic reason why we should locate the beginning of the language at this time, rather than with the Norman Conquest of 1066 or in the fourteenth century, say, and in fact the determination that English began with the Anglo-Saxon period was not generally accepted until the nineteenth century. But this point of view has been to a certain extent self-justifying, if only because it has led to the addition of Anglo-Saxon works to the canon of English literature, where they remain. Languages are constructions over time as well as over space.

Wherever we place the beginnings of English, though, there was never a time when the language was not diverse. The Germanic peoples who began to arrive in England in the fifth century belonged to a number of distinct tribes, each with its own dialect, and tended to settle in different parts of the country—the Saxons in the southwest, the Angles in the east and north, the Jutes (and perhaps some Franks) in Kent. These differences were the first source of the distinct dialects of the language we now refer to as Anglo-Saxon or Old English. As time went by, the linguistic divisions were reinforced by geography and by the political fragmentation of the country, and later, through contact with the Vikings who had settled the eastern and northern parts of England in the eighth through eleventh centuries.

Throughout this period, though, there were also forces operating to consolidate the language of England. Over the centuries, cultural and political dominance passed from Northumbria in the north to Mercia in the center and then to Wessex in the southwest, where a literary standard emerged in the ninth century, owing in part to the unification of the kingdom and in part to the singular efforts of Alfred the Great (849–899), who encouraged literary production in English and himself translated Latin works into the language. The influence of these standards and the frequent communication between the regions worked to level many of the dialect differences. There is a striking example of the process in the hundreds of everyday words derived from the language of the Scandinavian settlers, which include *dirt*, *lift*, *sky*, *skin*, *die*, *birth*, *weak*, *seat*, and *want*. All of these spread to general usage from the northern and eastern dialects in which they were first introduced, an indication of how frequent and ordinary were the contacts among the

Anglo-Saxons of various parts of the country—and initially, between the Anglo-Saxons and the Scandinavians themselves. (By contrast, the Celtic peoples that the Anglo-Saxons had displaced made relatively few contributions to the language, apart from place-names like *Thames, Avon,* and *Dover.*)

The Anglo-Saxon period came to an abrupt end with the Norman Conquest of 1066. With the introduction of a French-speaking ruling class, the written use of English was greatly reduced for 150 years. English did not reappear extensively in written records until the beginning of the thirteenth century, and even then it was only one of the languages of a multilingual community: French was widely used for another two hundred years or so (Parliament was conducted in French until 1362), and Latin was the predominant language of scholarship until the Renaissance. The English language that re-emerged in this period was considerably changed from the language of Alfred's period. Its grammar was simplified, continuing a process already under way before the Conquest, and its vocabulary was enriched by thousands of French loan words. Not surprisingly, given the preeminent role of French among the elite, these included the language of government (*majesty, state, rebel*); of religion (*pastor, ordain, temptation*); of fashion and social life (*button, adorn, dinner*); and of art, literature, and medicine (*painting, chapter, paper, physician*). But the breadth of French influence was not limited to those domains; it also provided simple words like *move, aim, join, solid, chief, clear, air,* and *very.* All of this left the language sufficiently different from Old English to warrant describing it with the name of Middle English, though we should bear in mind that language change is always gradual and that the division of English into neat periods is chiefly a matter of scholarly convenience.

Middle English was as varied a language as Old English was: Chaucer wrote in *Troilus and Criseyde* that "ther is so gret diversite in Englissh" that he was fearful that the text would be misread in other parts of the country. It was only in the fifteenth century or so that anything like a standard language began to emerge, based in the speech of the East Midlands and in particular of London, which reflected the increased centralization of political and economic power in that region. Even then, though, dialect differences remained strong; the scholar John Palsgrave complained in 1540 that the speech of university students was tainted by "the rude language used in their native countries [i.e., counties]," which left them unable to express themselves in their "vulgar tongue."

The language itself continued to change as it moved into what scholars describe as the Early Modern English period, which for convenience's sake we can date from the year 1500. Around this time, it began to undergo the Great Vowel Shift, as the long vowels engaged in an intricate dance that left them with new phonetic values. (In Chaucer's time, the word *bite* had been pronounced roughly as "beet," *beet* as "bate," *name* as "nahm," and so forth.) The grammar was changing as well; for example, the pronoun *thee* began to disappear, as did the verbal suffix-*eth,* and the modern form of questions began to emerge: in place of "See you that house?" people began to say "Do you see that house?" Most significantly, at least so far as contemporary observers were concerned, the Elizabethans and their successors coined thousands of new words based on Latin and Greek in an effort to make English an adequate replacement for Latin in the writing of philosophy, science, and literature. Many of these words now seem quite ordinary to us—for example, *accommodation*, *frugal*, *obscene*, *premeditated*, and *submerge*, all of which are recorded for the first time in Shakespeare's works. A large proportion of these linguistic experiments, though, never gained a foothold in the language—for example, *illecebrous* for "delicate," *deruncinate* for "to weed," *obtestate* for "call on," or Shakespeare's *disquantity* to mean "diminish." Indeed, some contemporaries ridiculed the pretension and obscurity of these "inkhorn words" in terms that sound very like modern criticisms of bureaucratic and corporate jargon—the rhetorician Thomas Wilson wrote in 1540 of the writers who affected "outlandish English" such that "if some of their mothers were alive, they were not able to tell what they say." But this effect was inevitable: The additions to the standard language that made it a suitable vehicle for art and scholarship could only increase the linguistic distance between the written language used by the educated classes and the spoken language used by other groups.

DICTIONARIES AND RULES

These were essentially growing pains for the standard language, which continued to gain ground in the sixteenth and seventeenth centuries, abetted by a number of developments: the ever-increasing dominance of London and the Southeast, the growth in social and geographic mobility, and in particular the introduction and spread of print, which led both to higher levels of literacy and schooling and to the gradual standardization of English spelling. But even as this process was going on, other developments were both creating new distinctions and investing existing ones with a new importance. For one thing, people were starting to pay more attention to accents based on social class, rather than region, an understandable preoccupation as social mobility increased and speech became a more important indicator of social background. Not surprisingly, the often imperfect efforts of the emerging middle class to speak and dress like their social superiors occasioned some ridicule; Thomas Gainsford wrote in 1616 of the "foppish mockery" of commoners who tried to imitate gentlemen by altering "habit, manner of life, conversation, and even their phrase of speech." Yet even the upper classes were paying more attention to speech as a social indicator than they had in previous ages; as one writer put it, "it is a pitty when a Noble man is better distinguished from a Clowne by his golden laces, than by his good language." (Shakespeare plays on this theme in *1 Henry IV* [3.1.250, 257–58] when he has Hotspur tease his wife for swearing too daintily, which makes her sound like "a comfitmaker's wife," rather than "like a lady as thou art," who swears with "a good mouth-filling oath.")

Over the course of the seventeenth and eighteenth centuries, print began to exercise a paradoxical effect on the perception of the language: even as it was serving to codify the standard, it was also making people more aware of variation and more anxious about its consequences. This was largely the result of the growing importance of print, as periodicals, novels, and other new forms became increasingly influential in shaping public opinion, together with the perception that the contributors to the print discourse were drawn from a wider range of backgrounds than in previous periods. As Samuel Johnson wrote: "The present age . . . may be styled, with great propriety, the Age of Authors; for, perhaps, there was never a time when men of all degrees of ability, of every kind of education, of every profession and employment were posting with ardor so general to the press. . . . "

This anxiety about the language was behind the frequent eighteenth-century lamentations that English was "unruled," "barbarous," or, as Johnson put it, "copious without order, and energetick without rule." Some writers looked for a remedy in public institutions modeled on the French Academy. This idea was advocated by John Dryden, Daniel Defoe, Joseph Addison, and most notably by Jonathan Swift, in a 1712 pamphlet called *A Proposal for Correcting, Improving, and Ascertaining* [i.e., "fixing"] *the English Tongue*, which did receive some official attention from the Tory government. But the idea was dropped as a Tory scheme when the Whigs came to power two years later, and by the middle of the eighteenth century, there was wide agreement among all parties that an academy would be an unwarranted intervention in the free conduct of public discourse. Samuel Johnson wrote in the Preface to his *Dictionary* of 1775 that he hoped that "the spirit of English liberty will hinder or destroy" any attempt to set up an academy; and the scientist and radical Joseph Priestly called such an institution "unsuitable to the genius of a *free nation*."

The rejection of the idea of an academy was to be important in the subsequent development of the language. From that time forward, it was clear that the state was not to play a major role in regulating and reforming the language, whether in England or in the other nations of the language community—a characteristic that makes English different from many other languages. (In languages like French and German, for example, spelling reforms can be introduced by official commissions charged with drawing up rules which are then adopted in all textbooks and official publications, a procedure that would be unthinkable in any of the nations of the English-speaking world.) Instead, the task of determining standards was left to private citizens, whose authority rested on their ability to gain general public acceptance.

The eighteenth century saw an enormous growth in the number of grammars and handbooks, which formulated most of the principles of correct English that, for better or worse, are still with us today—the rules for using *who* and *whom*, for example, the injunction against constructions like "very unique," and the curious prejudice against the split infinitive. Even more important was the development of the modern English dictionary. Before 1700, English speakers had to make do with alphabetical lists of "hard-words," a bit like the vocabulary improvement books that are still frequent today; it was only in the early 1700s that scholars began to produce anything like a comprehensive dictionary in the modern sense, a process that culminated in the publication of Samuel Johnson's magisterial *Dictionary* of 1755. It would be hard to argue that these dictionaries did much in fact to reduce variation or to arrest the process of linguistic change (among the words that Johnson objected to, for example, were *belabor, budge, cajole, coax, doff, gambler*, and *job*, all of which have since become part of the standard language). But they did serve to ease the sense of linguistic crisis, by providing a structure for describing the language and points of reference for resolving disputes about grammar and meaning. And while both the understanding of language and the craft of lexicography have made a great deal of progress since Johnson's time, the form of the English-language dictionary is still pretty much as he laid it down. (In this regard, Johnson's *Dictionary* is likely to present a much more familiar appearance to a modern reader than his poetry or periodical essays.)

THE DIFFUSION OF ENGLISH

The Modern English period saw the rise of another sort of variation, as well, as English began to spread over an increasingly larger area. By Shakespeare's time, English was displacing the Celtic languages in Wales, Cornwall, and Scotland, and then in Ireland, where the use of Irish was brutally repressed on the assumption—in retrospect a remarkably obtuse one—that people who were forced to become English in tongue would soon become English in loyalty as well. People in these new parts of the English-speaking world—a term we can begin to use in this period, for English was no longer the language of a single country—naturally used the language in accordance with their own idiom and habits of thought and mixed it with words drawn from the Celtic languages, a number of which eventually entered the speech of the larger linguistic community, for example, *baffle, bun, clan, crag, drab, galore, hubbub, pet, slob, slogan,* and *trousers.*

The development of the language in the New World followed the same process of differentiation. English settlers in North America rapidly developed their own characteristic forms of speech. They retained a number of words that had fallen into disuse in England (*din, clod, trash,* and *fall* for *autumn*) and gave old words new senses (like *corn,* which in England meant simply "grain," or *creek,* originally "an arm of the sea"). They borrowed freely from the other languages they came in contact with. By the time of the American Revolution, the colonists had already taken *chowder, cache, prairie,* and *bureau* from French; *noodle* and *pretzel* from German; *cookie, boss,* and *scow* and *yankee* from the Dutch; and *moose, skunk, chipmunk, succotash, toboggan,* and *tomahawk* from various Indian languages. And they coined new words with abandon. Some of these answered to their specific needs and interests—for example, *squatter, clearing, foothill, watershed, congressional, sidewalk*—but there were thousands of others that had no close connection to the American experience as such, many of which were ultimately adopted by the other varieties of English. *Belittle, influential, reliable, comeback, lengthy, turn down, make good*—all of these were originally American creations; they and other words like them indicate how independently the language was developing in the New World.

This process was repeated wherever English took root—in India, Africa, the Far East, the Caribbean, and Australia and New Zealand; by the late nineteenth century, English bore thousands of souvenirs of its extensive travels. From Africa (sometimes via Dutch) came words like *banana, boorish, palaver, gorilla,* and *guinea*; from the aboriginal languages of Australia came *wombat* and *kangaroo*; from the Caribbean languages came *cannibal, hammock, potato,* and *canoe*; and from the languages of India came *bangle, bungalow, chintz, cot, dinghy, jungle, loot, pariah, pundit,* and *thug.* And even lists like these are misleading, since they include only words that worked their way into the general English vocabulary and don't give a sense of the thousands of borrowings and coinages that were used only locally. Nor do they touch on the variation in grammar from one variety to the next. This kind of variation occurs everywhere, but it is particularly marked in regions like the Caribbean and Africa, where the local varieties of English are heavily influenced by English-based creoles—that is, language varieties that use English-based vocabulary with grammars largely derived from spoken—in this case, African—languages. This is the source, for example, of a number of the distinctive syntactic features of the variety used by many inner-city African Americans, like the "invariant *be*" of sentences like *We be living in Chicago*, which signals a state of affairs that holds for an extended period. (Some linguists have suggested that Middle English, in fact, could be thought of as a kind of creolized French.)

The growing importance of these new forms of English, particularly in America, presented a new challenge to the unity of the language. Until the eighteenth century, English was still thought of as essentially a national language. It might be spoken in various other nations and colonies under English control, but it was nonetheless rooted in the speech of England and subject to a single standard. Not surprisingly, Americans came to find this picture uncongenial, and when the United States first declared its independence from Britain, there was a strong sentiment for declaring that "American," too, should be recognized as a separate language. This was the view held by John Adams, Thomas Jefferson, and above all by America's first and greatest lexicographer, Noah Webster, who argued that American culture would naturally come to take a distinct form in the soil of the New World, free from what he described as "the old feudal and hierarchical establishments of England." And if a language was naturally the product and reflection of a national culture, then Americans could scarcely continue to speak "English." As Webster wrote in 1789: "Culture, habits, and language, as well as government should be national. America should have her own distinct from the rest of the world. . . ." It was in the interest of symbolically distinguishing American from English that Webster introduced a variety of spelling changes, such as *honor* and *favor* for *honour* and *favour*, *theater* for *theatre*, *traveled* for *travelled*, and so forth—a procedure that new nations often adopt when they want to make their variety of a language look different from its parent tongue.

In fact Webster's was by no means an outlandish suggestion. Even at the time of American independence, the linguistic differences between America and Britain were as great as those that separate many languages today, and the differences would have become much more salient if Americans had systematically adopted all of the spelling reforms that Webster at one time proposed, such as *wurd, reezon, tung, iz,* and so forth, which would ultimately have left English and American looking superficially no more similar than German and Dutch. Left to develop on their own, English and American might soon have gone their separate ways, perhaps paving the way for the separation of the varieties of English used in other parts of the world.

In the end, of course, the Americans and British decided that neither their linguistic nor their cultural and political differences warranted recognizing distinct languages. Webster himself conceded the point in 1828, when he entitled his magnum opus *An American Dictionary of the English Language.* And by 1862 the English novelist Anthony Trollope could write:

An American will perhaps consider himself to be as little like an Englishman as he is like a Frenchman. But he reads Shakespeare through
the medium of his own vernacular, and has to undergo the penance of
a foreign tongue before he can understand Molière. He separates himself from England in politics and perhaps in affection; but he cannot
separate himself from England in mental culture.

ENGLISH AND ENGLISHNESS

This was a crucial point of transition, which set the English language on a
very different course from most of the European languages, where the association of language and national culture was being made more strongly than
ever before. But the detachment of English from Englishness did not take
place overnight. For Trollope and his Victorian contemporaries, the "mental
culture" of the English-speaking world was still a creation of England, the
embodiment of English social and political values. "The English language,"
said G. C. Swayne in 1862, "is like the English constitution . . . and perhaps
also the English Church, full of inconsistencies and anomalies, yet flourishing in defiance of theory." The monumental *Oxford English Dictionary* that
the Victorians undertook was conceived in this patriotic spirit. In the words
of Archbishop Richard Chevenix Trench, one of the guiding spirits of the
OED project:

> We could scarcely have a lesson on the growth of our English tongue,
> we could scarcely follow upon one of its significant words, without
> having unawares a lesson in English history as well, without not merely
> falling upon some curious fact illustrative of our national life, but learn-
> ing also how the great heart which is beating at the centre of that life,
> was being gradually shaped and moulded.

It was this conception of the significance of the language that led, too, to
the insistence that the origin of the English language should properly be
located in Anglo-Saxon, rather than in the thirteenth or fourteenth century,
as scholars argued that contemporary English laws and institutions could be
traced to a primordial "Anglo-Saxon spirit" in an almost racial line of descent,
and that the Anglo-Saxon language was "immediately connected with the
original introduction and establishment of their present language and their
laws, their liberty, and their religion."

This view of English as the repository of "Anglo-Saxon" political ideals had
its appeal in America, as well, particularly in the first decades of the twentieth
century, when the crusade to "Americanize" recent immigrants led a number
of states to impose severe restrictions on the use of other languages in
schools, newspapers, and public meetings, a course that was often justified
on the grounds that only speakers of English were in a position to fully
appreciate the nuances of democratic thought. As a delegate to a New York
State constitutional convention in 1916 put the point: "You have got to learn
our language because that is the vehicle of the thought that has been handed
down from the men in whose breasts first burned the fire of freedom at the
signing of the Magna Carta."

But this view of the language is untenable on both linguistic and historical grounds. It is true that the nations of the English-speaking world have a common political heritage that makes itself known in similar legal systems and an (occasionally shaky) predilection for democratic forms of government. But while there is no doubt that the possession of a common language has helped to reinforce some of these connections, it is not responsible for them. Languages do work to create a common worldview, but not at such a specific level. Words like *democracy* move easily from one language to the next, along with the concepts they name—a good thing for the English-speaking world, since a great many of those ideals of "English democracy," as the writer calls it, owe no small debt to thinkers in Greece, Italy, France, Germany, and a number of other places, and those ideals have been established in many nations that speak languages other than English. (Thirteenth-century England was one of them. We should bear in mind that the Magna Carta that people sometimes like to mention in this context was a Latin document issued by a French-speaking king to French-speaking barons.) For that matter, there are English-speaking nations where democratic institutions have not taken root—nor should we take their continuing health for granted even in the core nations of the English-speaking world.

In the end, the view of English as the repository of Englishness has the effect of marginalizing or disenfranchising large parts of the English-speaking world, particularly those who do not count the political and cultural imposition of Englishness as an unmixed blessing. In most of the places where English has been planted, after all, it has had the British flag flying above it. And for many nations, it has been hard to slough off the sense of English as a colonial language. There is a famous passage in James Joyce's *Portrait of the Artist as a Young Man*, for example, where Stephen Daedelus says of the speech of an English-born dean, "The language in which we are speaking is his not mine," and there are still many people in Ireland and other parts of the English-speaking world who have mixed feelings about the English language: they may use and even love English, but they resent it, too.

Today the view of English as an essentially English creation is impossible to sustain even on purely linguistic grounds; the influences of the rest of the English-speaking world have simply been too great. Already in Trollope's time there were vociferous complaints in England about the growing use of Americanisms, a sign that the linguistic balance of payments between the two communities was tipping westward, and a present-day English writer would have a hard time producing a single paragraph that contained no words that originated in other parts of the linguistic community. Nor, what is more important, could you find a modern British or North American writer whose work was not heavily influenced, directly or indirectly, by the literature of the rest of the linguistic community, particularly after the extraordinary twentieth-century efflorescence of the English-language literatures of other parts of the world. Trying to imagine modern English literature without the contributions of writers like Yeats, Shaw, Joyce, Beckett, Heaney, Walcott, Lessing, Gordimer, Rushdie, Achebe, and Naipaul (to take only some of the writers who are included in this collection) is like trying to imagine an "English" cuisine that made no use of potatoes, tomatoes, corn, noodles, eggplant, olive oil, almonds, bay leaf, curry, or pepper.

THE FEATURES OF "STANDARD ENGLISH"

Where should we look, then, for the common "mental culture" that English-speakers share? This is always a difficult question to answer, partly because the understanding of the language changes from one place and time to the next, and partly because it is hard to say just what sorts of things languages are in the abstract. For all that we may want to think of the English-speaking world as a single community united by a common worldview, it is not a social group comparable to a tribe or people or nation—the sorts of groups that can easily evoke the first-person plural pronoun *we*. (Americans and Australians do not travel around saying "We gave the world Shakespeare," even though one might think that as paid-up members of the English-speaking community they would be entirely within their rights to do so.)

But we can get some sense of the ties that connect the members of the English-speaking community by starting with the language itself—not just in its forms and rules, but in the centripetal forces spoken of earlier. Forces like these are operating in every language community, it's true, but what gives each language its unique character is the way they are realized, the particular institutions and cultural commonalties which work to smooth differences and create a basis for continued communication—which ensure, in short, that English will continue as a single language, rather than break up into a collection of dialects that are free to wander wherever they will.

People often refer to this basis for communication as "Standard English," but that term is misleading. There are many linguistic communities that do have a genuine standard variety, a fixed and invariant form of the language that is used for certain kinds of communication. But that notion of the standard would be unsuitable to a language like English, which recognizes no single cultural center and has to allow for a great deal of variation even in the language of published texts. (It is rare to find a single page of an English-language novel or newspaper that does not reveal what nation it was written in.) What English does have, rather, is a collection of standard features—of spelling, of grammar, and of word use—which taken together ensure that certain kinds of communication will be more or less comprehensible in any part of the language community.

The standard features of English are as notable for what they don't contain as for what they do. One characteristic of English, for example, is that it has no standard pronunciation. People pronounce the language according to whatever their regional practice happens to be, and while certain pronunciations may be counted as "good" or "bad" according to local standards, there are no general rules about this, the way there are in French or Italian. (Some New Yorkers may be stigmatized for pronouncing words like *car* and *bard* as 'kah' and 'bahd', but roughly the same *r*-less pronunciation is standard in parts of the American South and in England, South Africa, Australia, and New Zealand.) In this sense, "standard English" exists only as a written language. Of course there is some variation in the rules of written English, as well, such as the American spellings that Webster introduced, but these are relatively minor and tend to date from earlier periods. A particular speech-community can pronounce the words *half* or *car* however it likes, but it can't unilaterally change the way the words are spelled. Indeed, this is one of the unappreciated advantages of the notoriously irregular English spelling system—it is so plainly *un*phonetic that there's no temptation to take it as codifying any particular spoken variety. When you want to define a written standard in a linguistic community that embraces no one standard accent, it's useful to have a spelling system that doesn't tip its hand.

The primacy of the written language is evident in the standard English vocabulary, too, if only indirectly. The fact is that English as such does not give us a complete vocabulary for talking about the world, but only for certain kinds of topics. If you want to talk about vegetables in English, for example, you have to choose among the usages common in one or another region: Depending on where you do your shopping, you will talk about *rutabagas*, *scallions*, and *string beans* or *Swedes*, *spring onions*, and *French beans*. That is, you can only talk about vegetables in your capacity as an American, an Englishman, or whatever, not in your capacity as an English-speaker in general. And similarly for fashion (*sweater* vs. *jumper*, *bobby pin* vs. *hair grip*, *vest* vs. *waistcoat*), for car parts (*hood* vs. *bonnet*, *trunk* vs. *boot*), and for food, sport, transport, and furniture, among many other things.

The English-language vocabulary is much more standardized, though, in other areas of the lexicon. We have a large common vocabulary for talking about aspects of our social and moral life—*blatant*, *vanity*, *smug*, *indifferent*, and the like. We have a common repertory of grammatical constructions and "signpost" expressions—for example, adverbs like *arguably*, *literally*, and *of course*—which we use to organize our discourse and tell readers how to interpret it. And there is a large number of common words for talking about the language itself—for example, *slang*, *usage*, *jargon*, *succinct*, and *literate*. (It is striking how many of these words are particular to English. No other language has an exact synonym for *slang*, for example, or a single word that covers the territory that *literate* covers in English, from "able to read and write" to "knowledgeable or educated.")

The common "core vocabulary" of English is not limited to these notions, of course—for example, it includes as well the thousands of technical and scientific terms that are in use throughout the English-speaking world, like *global warming* and *penicillin*, which for obvious reasons are not particularly susceptible to cultural variation. Nor would it be accurate to say that the core vocabulary includes all the words we use to refer to our language or to our social and moral life, many of which have a purely local character. But the existence of a core vocabulary of common English words, as fuzzy as it may prove to be, is an indication of the source of our cultural commonalities. What is notable about words like *blatant*, *arguably*, and *succinct* is that their meanings are defined by reference to our common literature, and in particular to the usage of what the eighteenth-century philosopher George Campbell described as "authors of reputation"—writers whose authority is determined by "the esteem of the public." We would not take the usage of Ezra Pound or Bernard Shaw as authoritative in deciding what words like *sweater* or *rutabaga* mean—they could easily have been wrong about either— but their precedents carry a lot of weight when we come to talking about the meaning of *blatant* and *succinct*. In fact the body of English-language "authors of reputation" *couldn't* be wrong about the meanings of words like these, since it is their usage by these authors that collectively determines what these words mean. And for purposes of defining these words it does not matter where a writer is from. The *American Heritage Dictionary*, for example, uses citations from the Irish writer Samuel Beckett to illustrate the meanings of *exasperate* and *impulsion*, from the Persian-born Doris Lessing, raised in southern Africa, to illustrate the meaning of *efface*, and from the Englishman E. M. Forster to illustrate the meaning of *solitude*; and dictionaries from other communities feel equally free to draw on the whole of English literature to illustrate the meanings of the words of the common vocabulary.

It is this strong connection between our common language and our common literature that gives both the language and the linguistic community their essential unity. Late in the eighteenth century, Samuel Johnson said that Britain had become "a nation of readers," by which he meant not just that people were reading more than ever before, but that participation in the written discourse of English had become in some sense constitutive of the national identity. And while the English-speaking world and its ongoing conversation can no longer be identified with a single nation, that world is still very much a community of readers in this sense. Historically, at least, we use the language in the same way because we read and talk about the same books—not *all* the same books, of course, but a loose and shifting group of works that figure as points of reference for our use of language.

This sense of the core vocabulary based on a common literature is intimately connected to the linguistic culture that English-speakers share—the standards, beliefs, and institutions that keep the various written dialects of the language from flying apart. The English dictionary is a good example. It is true that each part of the linguistic community requires its own dictionaries, given the variation in vocabulary and occasionally in spelling and the rest, but they are all formed on more or less the same model, which is very different from that of the French or the Germans. They all organize their entries in the same way, use the same form of definitions, include the same kind of information, and so on, to the point where we often speak of "*the* dictionary," as if the book were a single, invariant text like "the periodic table." By the same token, the schools in every English-speaking nation generally teach the same principles of good usage, a large number of which date from the grammarians of the eighteenth century. There are a few notable exceptions to this generality (Americans and most other communities outside England abandoned some time ago the effort to keep *shall* and *will* straight and seem to be none the worse off for it), but even in these cases grammarians justify their prescriptions using the same terminology and forms of argument.

THE CONTINUITY OF ENGLISH

To be sure, our collective agreement on standards of language and literature is never more than approximate and is always undergoing redefinition and change. Things could hardly be otherwise, given the varied constitution of the English-speaking community, the changing social background, and the insistence of English-speakers that they must be left to decide these matters on their own, without the intervention of official commissions or academies. It is not surprising that the reference points that we depend on to maintain the continuity of the language should often be controversial, even within a single community, and even less so that different national communities should have different ideas as to who counts as authority or what kinds of texts should be relevant to defining the common core of English words. The most we can ask of our common linguistic heritage is that it give us a general format for adapting the language to new needs and for reinterpreting its significance from one time and place to another.

This is the challenge posed by the triumph of English. Granted, there is no threat to the hegemony of English as a worldwide medium for practical communication. It is a certainty that the nations of the English-speaking community will continue to use the various forms of English to communicate with each other, as well as with the hundreds of millions of people who speak English as a second language (and who in fact outnumber the native speakers of the language by a factor of two or three to one). And with the growth of travel and trade and of media like the Internet, the number of English-speakers is sure to continue to increase.

But none of this guarantees the continuing unity of English as a means of cultural expression. What is striking about the accelerating spread of English over the past two centuries is not so much the number of speakers that the language has acquired, but the remarkable variety of the cultures and communities who use it. The heterogeneity of the linguistic community is evident not just in the emergence of the rich new literatures of Africa, Asia, and the Caribbean, but also in the literatures of what linguists sometimes call the "inner circle" of the English-speaking world—nations like Britain, the United States, Australia, and Canada—where the language is being asked to describe a much wider range of experience than ever before, particularly on behalf of groups who until recently have been largely excluded or marginalized from the collective conversation of the English-speaking world.

Not surprisingly, the speakers of the "new Englishes" use the language with different voices and different rhythms and bring to it different linguistic and cultural backgrounds. The language of a writer like Chinua Achebe reflects the influence not just of Shakespeare and Wordsworth but of proverbs and other forms of discourse drawn from West African oral traditions. Indian writers like R. K. Narayan and Salman Rushdie ground their works not just in the traditional English-language canon but in Sanskrit classics like the epic *Rāmāyana*. The continuing sense that all English-speakers are engaged in a common discourse depends on the linguistic community's being able to accommodate and absorb these new linguistic and literary influences, as it has been able to do in the past.

In all parts of the linguistic community, moreover, there are questions posed by the new media of discourse. Over the past hundred years, the primacy of print has been challenged first by the growth of film, recordings, and the broadcast media, and more recently by the remarkable growth of the Internet, each of which has had its effects on the language. With film and the rest, we have begun to see the emergence of spoken standards that coexist with the written standard of print, not in the form of a standardized English pronunciation—if anything, pronunciation differences among the communities of the English-speaking world have become more marked over the course of the century—but rather in the use of words, expressions, and rhythms that are particular to speech (there is no better example of this than the universal adoption of the particle *okay*). And the Internet has had the effect of projecting what were previously private forms of written communication, like the personal letter, into something more like models of public discourse, but with a language that is much more informal than the traditional discourse of the novel or newspaper.

It is a mistake to think that any of these new forms of discourse will wholly replace the discourse of print (the Internet, in particular, has shown itself to be an important vehicle for marketing and diffusing print works with much greater efficiency than has ever been possible before). It seems reasonable to assume that a hundred years from now the English-speaking world will still be at heart a community of readers—and of readers of books, among other things. And it is likely, too, that the English language will still be at heart a means of written expression, not just for setting down air schedules and trade statistics, but for doing the kind of cultural work that we have looked for literature to do for us in the past; a medium, that is, for poetry, criticism, history, and fiction. But only time will tell if English will remain a single language—if in the midst of all the diversity, cultural and communicative, people will still be able to discern a single "English literature" and a characteristic English-language frame of mind.

GEOFFREY NUNBERG
Stanford University and Xerox Palo Alto Research Center

The Norton Anthology
of English Literature

SEVENTH EDITION

VOLUME 1

The Middle Ages
to ca. 1485

43–ca. 420:	Roman invasion and occupation of Britain
ca. 450:	Anglo-Saxon Conquest
597:	St. Augustine arrives in Kent; beginning of Anglo-Saxon conversion to Christianity
871–899:	Reign of King Alfred
1066:	Norman Conquest
1154–1189:	Reign of Henry II
ca. 1200:	Beginnings of Middle English literature
1360–1400:	Geoffrey Chaucer; *Piers Plowman; Sir Gawain and the Green Knight*
1485:	William Caxton's printing of Sir Thomas Malory's *Morte Darthur*. one of the first books printed in England

The Middle Ages designates the time span roughly from the collapse of the Roman Empire to the Renaissance. The adjective "medieval," coined from Latin *medium* (middle) and *aevum* (age), refers to whatever was made, written, or thought during the Middle Ages. The Renaissance was so named by nineteenth-century historians and critics because they associated it with an outburst of creativity attributed to a "rebirth" or revival of Latin and, especially, of Greek learning and literature. The Renaissance was seen as spreading from Italy in the fourteenth and fifteenth centuries to the rest of Europe. The very idea of a "rebirth," however, implies something dormant or lacking in the preceding era. More recently, there has been a tendency to emphasize the continuities between the Middle Ages and the later time now often called the Early Modern period. Medieval authors, of course, did not think of themselves as living in the "middle"; they sometimes expressed the idea that the world was growing old and that theirs was a declining age, close to the end of time. Yet art, literature, and science flourished during the Middle Ages, rooted in the Christian culture that preserved, transmitted, and transformed classical tradition.

The works covered in this section of the anthology encompass a period of more than eight hundred years, from Cædmon's *Hymn* at the end of the seventh century to *Everyman* at the beginning of the sixteenth. The date 1485, the year of the accession of Henry VII and the beginning of the Tudor dynasty, is an arbitrary but convenient one to mark the "end" of the Middle Ages.

Although the Roman Catholic Church provided continuity, the period was one of enormous historical, social, and linguistic change. To emphasize these changes and the events underlying them, we have divided the period into three primary sections: Anglo-Saxon England, Anglo-Norman England, and

1

Middle English Literature in the Fourteenth and Fifteenth Centuries. The Anglo-Saxon invaders, who began their conquest of the southeastern part of Britain around 450, spoke an early form of the language we now call Old English. Old English displays its kinship with other Germanic languages (German or Dutch, for example) much more clearly than does contemporary British and American English, of which Old English is the remote ancestor. As late as the tenth century, part of an Old Saxon poem written on the Continent was transcribed and transliterated into the West Saxon dialect of Old English without presenting problems to its English readers. In form and content Old English literature also has much in common with other Germanic literatures with which it shared a body of heroic as well as Christian stories. The major characters in *Beowulf* are pagan Danes and Geats, and the only connection to England is an obscure allusion to the ancestor of one of the kings of the Angles.

The changes already in progress in the language and culture of Anglo-Saxon England were greatly accelerated by the Norman Conquest of 1066. The ascendancy of a French-speaking ruling class had the effect of adding a vast number of French loan words to the English vocabulary. The conquest resulted in new forms of political organization and administration, architecture, and literary expression. In the twelfth century, through the interest of the Anglo-Normans in British history before the Anglo-Saxon Conquest, not only England but all of Western Europe became fascinated with a legendary hero named Arthur who makes his earliest appearances in Celtic literature. King Arthur and his knights became a staple subject of medieval French, English, and German literature. Selections from French, Old Irish, and Middle Welsh as well as from Early Middle English have been included here to give a sense of the cross-currents of languages and literatures in Anglo-Norman England and to provide background for later English literature in all periods.

Literature in English was performed orally and written throughout the Middle Ages, but the awareness of and pride in a uniquely *English* literature does not actually exist before the late fourteenth century. In 1336 Edward III began a war to enforce his claims to the throne of France; the war continued intermittently for one hundred years until finally the English were driven from all their French territories except for the port of Calais. One result of the war and these losses was a keener sense on the part of England's nobility of their English heritage and identity. Toward the close of the fourteenth century English finally began to displace French as the language for conducting business in Parliament and in the courts of law. Although the high nobility continued to speak French by preference, they were certainly bilingual, whereas some of the earlier Norman kings had known no English at all. It was becoming possible to obtain patronage for literary achievement in English. Chaucer's decision to emulate French and Italian poetry in his own vernacular is an indication of the change taking place in the status of English, and Chaucer's works were greatly to enhance the prestige of English as a vehicle for important literature. He was acclaimed by fifteenth-century poets as the embellisher of the English tongue; later writers called him the English Homer and the father of English poetry. His friend John Gower (1325?–1408) wrote long poems in French and Latin before producing his last major work, the *Confessio Amantis* (The Lover's Confession), which in spite of its Latin title is composed in English. The third and longest of the three primary sections, Middle English Literature in the Fourteenth and Fifteenth Centuries, is thus not only a chronological and linguistic division but implies a new sense of English as a literary medium that could compete with French and Latin in elegance and seriousness.

Texts in Old English, Early Middle English, and the more difficult texts in later Middle English (*Sir Gawain and the Green Knight, Piers Plowman*) and other languages are given in translation. Chaucer and other Middle English works may be read in the original, even by the beginner, with the help of marginal glosses and notes. These texts have been spelled in a way that is intended to aid the reader. Analyses of the sounds and grammar of Middle English and of Old and Middle English prosody are discussed on pages 15–20.

ANGLO-SAXON ENGLAND

From the first to the fifth century, England was a province of the Roman Empire and was named Britannia after its Celtic-speaking inhabitants, the Britons. The Britons adapted themselves to Roman civilization, of which the ruins survived to impress the poet of *The Wanderer*, who refers to them as "the old works of giants." The withdrawal of the Roman legions during the fifth century, in a vain attempt to protect Rome itself from the threat of Germanic conquest, left the island vulnerable to seafaring Germanic invaders. These belonged primarily to three related tribes, the Angles, the Saxons, and the Jutes. The name *English* derives from the Angles, and the names of the counties Essex, Sussex, and Wessex refer to the territories occupied by the East, South, and West Saxons.

The Anglo-Saxon occupation was no sudden conquest but extended over decades of fighting against the native Britons. The latter were finally confined to the mountainous region of Wales, where the modern form of their language is spoken alongside English to this day. The Britons had become Christians in the fourth century after the conversion of Emperor Constantine along with most of the rest of the Roman Empire, but for about 150 years after the beginning of the invasion, Christianity was maintained only in the remoter regions where the as yet pagan Anglo-Saxons failed to penetrate. In the year 597, however, a Benedictine monk (afterward St. Augustine of Canterbury) was sent by Pope Gregory as a missionary to King Ethelbert of Kent, the most southerly of the kingdoms into which England was then divided, and about the same time missionaries from Ireland began to preach Christianity in the north. Within 75 years the island was once more predominantly Christian. Before Christianity there had been no books. The impact of Christianity on literacy is evident from the fact that the first extended written specimen of the Old English (Anglo-Saxon) language is a code of laws promulgated by Ethelbert, the first English Christian king.

In the centuries that followed the conversion, England produced many distinguished churchmen. One of the earliest of these was Bede, whose Latin *Ecclesiastical History of the English People*, which tells the story of the conversion and of the English church, was completed in 731; this remains one of our most important sources of knowledge about the period. In the next generation Alcuin (735–804), a man of wide culture, became the friend and adviser of the Frankish emperor Charlemagne, whom he assisted in making the Frankish court a great center of learning; thus by the year 800 English culture had developed so richly that it overflowed its insular boundaries.

In the ninth century the Christian Anglo-Saxons were themselves subjected to new Germanic invasions by the Danes who in their longboats repeatedly ravaged the coast, sacking Bede's monastery among others. Such a raid in the tenth century inspired *The Battle of Maldon*, the last of the Old English heroic poems. The Danes also occupied the northern part of the island, threatening to overrun the rest. They were stopped by Alfred, king of the West Saxons from 871 to 899, who for a time united all the kingdoms of southern England. This most active king was also an enthusiastic patron of literature. He himself translated various works from Latin, the most important of which was Boethius's *Consolation of Philosophy*, a sixth-century Roman work also translated in the fourteenth century by Chaucer. Alfred probably also instigated a translation of Bede's *History* and the beginning of the *Anglo-Saxon Chronicle*: this year-by-year record in Old English of important events in England was maintained at one monastery until the middle of the twelfth century. Practically all of Old English poetry is preserved in copies made in the West Saxon dialect after the reign of Alfred.

Old English Poetry

The Anglo-Saxon invaders brought with them a tradition of oral poetry (see "Bede and Cædmon's *Hymn*," p. 23). Because nothing was written down before the conversion to Christianity, we have only circumstantial evidence of what that poetry must have been like. Aside from a few short inscriptions on small artifacts, the earliest records in the English language are in manuscripts produced at monasteries and other religious establishments, beginning in the seventh century. Literacy was mainly restricted to servants of the church, and so it is natural that the bulk of Old English literature deals with religious subjects and is mostly drawn from Latin sources. Manuscripts were costly and time-consuming to produce, because they required the copying of texts word by word onto parchment, a durable material made from the prepared skins of domestic animals (paper would not be used in Europe before the twelfth century). Under these difficult circumstances, few texts were written down that did not pertain directly to the work of the church. Most of Old English poetry is contained in just four manuscripts.

Germanic heroic poetry continued to be performed orally in alliterative verse and was at times used to describe current events. *The Battle of Brunanburh*, which celebrates an English victory over the Danes in traditional alliterative verse, is preserved in the *Anglo-Saxon Chronicle*. *The Battle of Maldon* commemorates a Viking victory in which the Christian English invoke the ancient code of honor that obliges a warrior to avenge his slain lord or to die beside him.

These poems show that the aristocratic heroic and kinship values of Germanic society continued to inspire both clergy and laity in the Christian era. As represented in the relatively small body of Anglo-Saxon heroic poetry that survives, this world shares many characteristics with the heroic world described by Homer. Nations are reckoned as groups of people related by kinship rather than by geographical areas, and kinship is the basis of the heroic code. The tribe is ruled by a chieftain who is called *king*, a word that has "kin" for its root. The *lord* (a word derived from Old English *hlaf*, "loaf," plus *weard*, "protector") surrounds himself with a band of retainers (many of them his blood kindred) who are members of his household. He leads his men in battle and rewards them with the spoils; royal generosity was one of the most important aspects of heroic behavior. In return, the retainers are obligated to fight for their lord to the death, and if he is slain, to avenge him or die in the attempt. Blood vengeance is regarded as a sacred duty, and in poetry, everlasting shame awaits those who fail to observe it.

Even though the heroic world of poetry could be invoked to rally resistance to the Viking invasions, it was already remote from the Christian world of Anglo-Saxon England. Nevertheless, Christian writers like the *Beowulf* poet were fascinated by the distant culture of their pagan ancestors and by the inherent conflict between the heroic code and a religion that teaches that we should "forgive those who trespass against us" and that "all they that take the sword shall perish with the sword." The *Beowulf* poet looks back on that ancient world with admiration for the courage of which it was capable and at the same time with elegiac sympathy for its inevitable doom.

For Anglo-Saxon poetry, it is difficult and probably futile to draw a line between "heroic" and "Christian," for the best poetry crosses that boundary. Much of the Christian poetry is also cast in the heroic mode: although the Anglo-Saxons adapted themselves readily to the ideals of Christianity, they did not do so without adapting Christianity to their own heroic ideal. Thus Moses and St. Andrew, Christ and God the Father are represented in the style of heroic verse. In the *Dream of the Rood*, the Cross speaks of Christ as "the young hero, . . . strong and stouthearted." In Cædmon's *Hymn* the creation of heaven and earth is seen as a mighty deed, an "establishment of wonders." Anglo-Saxon heroines, too, are portrayed in the heroic manner. St. Helena, who leads an expedition to the Holy Land to discover the true Cross, is described as a "battle-queen." Christian and heroic ideals are poignantly blended in *The Wanderer*, which laments the separation from one's lord and kinsmen and the transience of all earthly treasures. Love between man and woman, as described by the female speaker of *The Wife's Lament*, is disrupted by separation, exile, and the malice of kinfolk.

The world of Old English poetry is predominantly harsh. Men are said to be cheerful in the mead hall, but even there they think of struggle in war, of possible triumph but more possible failure. Romantic love—one of the principal topics of later literature—appears hardly at all. Even so, at some of the bleakest moments, the poets powerfully recall the return of spring. The blade of the magic sword with which Beowulf has killed Grendel's mother in her sinister underwater lair begins to melt, "as ice melts / when the Father eases the fetters off the frost / and unravels the water ropes, He who wields power."

The poetic diction, formulaic phrases, and repetitions of parallel syntactic structures, which are determined by the versification, are difficult to reproduce in modern translation. A few features may be anticipated here and studied in the text of Cædmon's *Hymn*, printed below (pp. 24–25) with interlinear translation.

Poetic language is created out of a special vocabulary that contains a multiplicity of terms for *lord, warrior, spear, shield*, and so on. Synecdoche and metonymy are common figures of speech as when *keel* is used for "ship" or *iron*, for "sword." A particularly striking effect is achieved by the kenning, a compound of two words in place of another as when *sea* becomes "whale-road" or *body* is called "life-house." The figurative use of language finds playful expression in poetic riddles, of which about one hundred survive. Common (and sometimes uncommon) creatures, objects, or phenomena are described in an enigmatic passage of alliterative verse, and the reader must guess their identity. Sometimes they are personified and ask, "What is my name?"

Because special vocabulary and compounds are among the chief poetic effects, the verse is constructed in such a way as to show off such terms by creating a series of them in apposition. In the second sentence of Cædmon's *Hymn*, for example, God is referred to five times appositively as "he," "holy Creator," "mankind's Guardian," "eternal Lord," and "Master Almighty." This use of parallel and appositive expressions, known as *variation*, gives the verse a highly structured and musical quality.

The overall effect of the language is to formalize and elevate speech. Instead of being straightforward, it moves at a slow and stately pace with steady indirection. A favorite mode of this indirection is irony. A grim irony pervades heroic poetry even at the level of diction where *fighting* is called "battle-play." A favorite device, known by the rhetorical term *litotes*, is ironic understatement. After the monster Grendel has slaughtered the Danes in the great hall Heorot, it stands deserted. The poet observes, "It was easy then to meet with a man / shifting himself to a safer distance."

More than a figure of speech, irony is also a mode of perception in Old English poetry. In a famous passage, the Wanderer articulates the theme of *Ubi sunt* (where are they now): "Where has the horse gone? Where the young warrior? Where the giver of treasure? . . ." *Beowulf* is full of ironic balances and contrasts—between the aged Danish king and the youthful Beowulf, and between Beowulf, the high-spirited young warrior at the beginning, and Beowulf, the gray-haired king at the end, facing the dragon and death.

The formal and dignified speech of Old English poetry was always distant from the everyday language of the Anglo-Saxons, and this poetic idiom remained remarkably uniform throughout the roughly three hundred years that separate Cædmon's *Hymn* from *The Battle of Maldon*. This clinging to old forms—grammatical and orthographic as well as literary—by the Anglo-Saxon church and aristocracy conceals from us the enormous changes that were taking place in the English language and the diversity of its dialects. The dramatic changes between Old and Middle English did not happen overnight or over the course of a single century. The Normans displaced the English ruling class with their own barons and clerics, whose native language was a dialect of Old French that we call Anglo-Norman. Without a ruling literate class to preserve English traditions, the custom of transcribing vernacular texts in an earlier form of the West-Saxon dialect was abandoned, and both language and literature were allowed to develop unchecked in new directions.

ANGLO-NORMAN ENGLAND

The Normans, who took possession of England after the decisive Battle of Hastings (1066), were, like the Anglo-Saxons, descendants of Germanic adventurers who at the beginning of the tenth century had seized a wide part of northern France. Their name is actually a contraction of "Norsemen." A highly adaptable people, they had adopted the French language of the land they had settled in and its Christian religion. Both in Normandy and in Britain they were great builders of castles, with which they enforced their political dominance, and magnificent churches. Norman bishops, who held land and castles like the barons, wielded both political and spiritual authority. The earlier Norman kings of England, however, were often absentee rulers, as much concerned with defending their Continental possessions as with ruling over their English holdings. The English Crown's French territories were enormously increased in 1154 when Henry II, the first of England's Plantagenet kings, ascended the throne. Through his marriage with Eleanor of Aquitaine, the divorced wife of Louis VII of France, Henry had acquired vast provinces in the south of France.

The presence of a French-speaking ruling class in England created exceptional opportunities for linguistic and cultural exchange. Four languages coexisted in the realm of Anglo-Norman England: Latin, as it had been for Bede, remained the international language of learning, used for theology, science, and history. It was not by any means a written language only but a lingua franca by which different nationalities communicated in the church and the newly founded universities. The Norman aristocracy for the most part spoke French, but intermarriage with the native English nobility and the business of daily life between masters and servants encouraged bilingualism. Different branches of the Celtic language group were spoken in Ireland, Wales, Cornwall, and Brittany.

Inevitably there was also literary intercourse among the different languages. The Latin Bible and Latin saints' lives provided subjects for a great deal of Old English as well as Old French poetry and prose. The first medieval drama in the vernacular, *The Play of Adam*, with elaborate stage directions in Latin and realistic dialogue in the Anglo-Norman dialect of French, was probably produced in England during the twelfth century.

The Anglo-Norman aristocracy was especially attracted to Celtic legends and tales that had been circulating orally for centuries. The twelfth-century poets Marie de France and Chrétien de Troyes both claim to have obtained their narratives from Breton storytellers, who were probably bilingual performers of native tales for French audiences. "Breton" may indicate that they came from Brittany, or it may have been a generic term for a Celtic bard. Marie speaks respectfully of the storytellers; Chrétien accuses them of marring their material, which, he boasts, he has retold with an elegant fusion of form and meaning. Marie wrote a series of short romances, which she refers to as "lays" originally told by Bretons. Her versions are the most original and sophisticated examples of the genre that came to be known as the Breton lay, represented here by Marie's *Lanval*. It is very likely that Henry II is the "noble king" to whom she dedicated her lays and that they were written for his court. Chrétien is the principal creator of the romance of chivalry in which knightly adventures are a means of exploring psychological and ethical dilemmas that the knights must solve, in addition to displaying martial prowess in saving ladies from monsters, giants, and wicked knights. Chrétien, like Marie, is thought to have spent time in England at the court of Henry II. Both Marie de France and Chrétien de Troyes were innovators of the genre that has become known as "romance." The word *roman* was initially applied in French to a work written in the French vernacular. Thus the thirteenth-century *Roman de Troie* is a long poem about the Trojan War in French. While this work deals mainly with the siege of Troy, it also includes stories about the love of Troilus for Cressida and of Achilles for the Trojan princess Polyxena. Eventually "romance" acquired the generic associations it has for us as a story about love and adventure. In the late twelfth century, Andreas Capellanus (Andrew the Chaplain) wrote a Latin treatise, the title of which may be translated *The Art of Loving Correctly* [*honeste*]. In one part, Eleanor of Aquitaine, her daughter, the countess Marie de Champagne, and other noble women are cited as a supreme court rendering decisions on difficult questions of love—for example, whether there is greater passion between lovers or between married couples. Whether such "courts of love" were purely imaginary or whether they represent some actual court entertainment, they imply that the literary taste and judgment of women had a significant role in determining the rise of romance in France and Anglo-Norman England.

In Marie's *Lanval* and in Chrétien's romances, the court of King Arthur had already acquired for French audiences a reputation as the most famous center of chivalry. That eminence is owing in large measure to a remarkable book in Latin, *The History of the Kings of Britain*, completed by Geoffrey of Monmouth, ca. 1136–38. Geoffrey claimed to have based his "history" on a book in the British tongue (i.e., Welsh), but no one has ever found such a book. He drew on a few earlier Latin chronicles, but the bulk of his history was probably fabricated from Celtic oral tradition, his familiarity with Roman history and literature, and his own fertile imagination. The climax of the book is the reign of King Arthur, who defeats the Roman armies but is forced to turn back to Britain to counter the treachery of his nephew Mordred. Geoffrey's Latin was rendered into French rhyme by an Anglo-Norman poet called Wace, and Wace's poem was turned by Layamon, an English priest, into a much longer poem that combines English alliterative verse with sporadic rhyme.

Layamon's work is one of many instances where English receives new material directly through French sources, which may be drawn from Celtic or Latin sources. There are two Middle English versions of Marie's *Lanval*, and the English romance called *Yvain and Gawain* is a cruder version of Chrétien's *Le Chevalier au Lion* (The Knight of the Lion). There is a marvelous English lay, *Sir Orfeo*, a version of the Orpheus story in which Orpheus succeeds in rescuing his wife from the other world, for which a French original, if there was one, has never been found. Romance, stripped of its courtly, psychological, and ethical subtleties, had an immense popular appeal for English readers and listeners. Many of these romances are simplified adaptations of more aristocratic French poems and recount in a rollicking and rambling style the adventures of heroes like Guy of Warwick, a poor steward who must prove his knightly worth to win the love of Fair

Phyllis. The ethos of many romances, aristocratic and popular alike, involves a knight proving his worthiness through nobility of character and brave deeds rather than through high birth. In this respect romances reflect the aspirations of a lower order of the nobility to rise in the world, as historically some of these nobles did. William the Marshall, for example, the fourth son of a baron of middle rank, used his talents in war and in tournaments to become tutor to the oldest son of Henry II and Eleanor of Aquitaine. He married a great heiress and became one of the most powerful nobles in England and the subject of a verse biography in French, which often reads like a romance.

Of course not all writing in Early Middle English depends on French sources or intermediaries. The *Anglo-Saxon Chronicle* continued to be written at the monastery of Peterborough. It is an invaluable witness for the changes taking place in the English language and allows us to see Norman rule from an English point of view. *The Owl and the Nightingale* is a witty and entertaining poem in which these two birds engage in a fierce debate about the benefits their singing brings to humankind. The owl grimly reminds his rival of the sinfulness of the human condition, which his mournful song is intended to amend; the nightingale sings about the pleasures of life and love when lord and lady are in bed together. The poet, who was certainly a cleric, is well aware of the fashionable new romance literature; he specifically has the nightingale allude to Marie de France's lay *Laüstic*, the Breton word, she says, for "rossignol" in French and "nightingale" in English. The poet does not side with either bird; rather he has amusingly created a dialectic between the discourses of religion and romance that is carried on throughout medieval literature.

There is also a body of Early Middle English religious prose aimed at women. Three saints' lives celebrate the heroic combats of virgin martyrs who suffer dismemberment and death; a tract entitled "Holy Maidenhead" paints the woes of marriage not from the point of view of the husband, as in standard medieval antifeminist writings, but from that of the wife. Related to these texts, named the Katherine Group after one of the virgin martyrs, is a religious work also written for women but in a very different spirit. The *Ancrene Riwle* (Anchoresses' Rule), or *Ancrene Wisse* (Anchoresses' Guide) as it is called in another manuscript, is one of the finest works of English religious prose in any period. It is a manual of instruction written at the request of three sisters who have chosen to live as religious recluses. The author, who may have been their personal confessor, addresses them with affection, with kindness, and, at times, with humor. He is also profoundly serious in his analyses of sin, penance, and love. In the selection included here from his chapter on love, he, too, tells a tale of romance in a strikingly different way.

MIDDLE ENGLISH LITERATURE IN THE FOURTEENTH AND FIFTEENTH CENTURIES

The styles of *The Owl and the Nightingale* and *Ancrene Riwle* show that around the year 1200 both poetry and prose were being written for sophisticated and well-educated readers whose primary language was English. Throughout the thirteenth and early fourteenth centuries, there are many kinds of evidence that, although French continued to be the principal language of Parliament, law, business, and high culture, English was gaining ground. Several authors of religious and didactic works in English state that they are writing for the benefit of those who do not understand Latin or French. Anthologies are made of miscellaneous works adapted from French for English readers and original pieces in English. Most of the nobility are by now bilingual, and the author of an English romance written early in the fourteenth century declares that he has seen many nobles who cannot speak French. Children of the nobility and the merchant class are now learning French as a second language. By the 1360s the linguistic, political, and cultural climate had been prepared for the flowering of Middle English literature in the writings of Chaucer, Langland, and the *Gawain* poet.

The Fourteenth Century

War and disease were prevalent throughout the Middle Ages but never more devastatingly than during the fourteenth century. In the wars against France, the gains of two spectacular English victories, at Crécy in 1346 and Poitiers in 1356, were gradually frittered away in futile campaigns that ravaged the French countryside without obtaining any clear advantage for the English. In 1348 the first and most virulent epidemic of the bubonic plague—the Black Death—swept Europe, wiping out a quarter to a third of the population. The toll was higher in crowded urban centers. Giovanni Boccaccio's description of the plague in Florence, with which he introduces the *Decameron*, vividly portrays its ravages: "So many corpses would arrive in front of a church every day and at every hour that the amount of holy ground for burials was certainly insufficient for the ancient custom of giving each body its individual place; when all the graves were full, huge trenches were dug in all of the cemeteries of the churches and into them the new arrivals were dumped by the hundreds; and they were packed in there with dirt, one on top of another, like a ship's cargo, until the trench was filled." The resulting scarcity of labor and a sudden expansion of the possibilities for social mobility fostered popular discontent. In 1381 attempts to enforce wage controls and to collect oppressive new taxes provoked a rural uprising in Essex and Kent that dealt a profound shock to the English ruling class. The participants were for the most part tenant farmers, day laborers, apprentices, and rural workers not attached to the big manors. A few of the lower clergy sided with the rebels against their wealthy church superiors; the priest John Ball was among the leaders. The movement was quickly suppressed, but not before sympathizers in London had admitted the rebels through two city gates, which had been barred against them. The insurgents burned down the palace of the hated duke of Lancaster, and they summarily beheaded the archbishop of Canterbury and the treasurer of England, who had taken refuge in the Tower of London. The church had become the target of popular resentment because it was among the greatest of the oppressive landowners and because of the wealth, worldliness, and venality of many of the higher clergy.

These calamities and upheavals nevertheless did not stem the growth of international trade and the influence of the merchant class. In the portrait of Geoffrey Chaucer's merchant, we see the budding of capitalism based on credit and interest. Cities like London ran their own affairs under politically powerful mayors and aldermen. Edward III, chronically in need of money to finance his wars, was obliged to negotiate for revenues with the Commons in the English Parliament, an institution that became a major political force during this period. A large part of the king's revenues depended on taxing the profitable export of English wool to the Continent. The Crown thus became involved in the country's economic affairs, and this involvement led to a need for capable administrators. These were no longer drawn mainly from the church, as in the past, but from a newly educated laity that occupied a rank somewhere between that of the lesser nobility and the upper bourgeoisie. The career of Chaucer, who served Edward III and his successor Richard II in a number of civil posts, is typical of this class—with the exception that Chaucer was also a great poet.

In the fourteenth century, a few poets and intellectuals achieved the status and respect formerly accorded only to the ancients. Marie de France and Chrétien de Troyes had dedicated their works to noble patrons and, in their role as narrators, address themselves as entertainers and sometimes as instructors to court audiences. Dante (1265–1321) made himself the protagonist of *The Divine Comedy*, the sacred poem, as he called it, in which he revealed the secrets of the afterlife. After his death, manuscripts of the work were provided with lengthy commentaries as though it were Scripture, and public readings and lectures were devoted to it. Francesco Petrarch (1304–1374) won an international reputation as a man of letters. He wrote primarily in Latin and contrived to have himself crowned "poet laureate" in emulation of the Roman poets whose works he imitated, but his most famous work is the sonnet sequence he wrote in Italian. Giovanni Boccaccio (1313–1375) was among Petrarch's most ardent admirers and carried on a literary correspondence with him.

Chaucer read these authors along with the ancient Roman poets and drew on them in his own works. Chaucer's *Clerk's Tale* is based on a Latin version Petrarch made from the last tale in Boccaccio's *Decameron*; in his prologue, the Clerk refers to Petrarch as "lauriat poete" whose sweet rhetoric illuminated all Italy with his poetry. Yet in his own time, the English poet Chaucer never attained the kind of laurels that he and others accorded to Petrarch. In his earlier works, Chaucer portrayed himself comically as a diligent reader of old books, as an aspiring apprentice writer, and as an eager spectator on the fringe of a fashionable world of courtiers and poets. In *The House of Fame*, he relates a dream of being snatched up by a huge golden eagle (the eagle and many other things in this work were inspired by Dante), who transports him to the palace of the goddess of Fame. There he gets to see phantoms, like the shades in Dante's poem, of all the famous authors of antiquity. At the end of his romance *Troilus and Criseyde*, Chaucer asks his "litel book" to kiss the footsteps where the great ancient poets had passed before. Like Dante and Petrarch, Chaucer had an ideal of great poetry and, in his *Troilus* at least, strove to emulate it. But in *The House of Fame* and in his final work, *The Canterbury Tales*, he also views that ideal ironically and distances himself from it. The many surviving documents that record Geoffrey Chaucer's career as a civil servant do not contain a single word to show that he was also a poet. Only in the following centuries would he be canonized as the father of English poetry.

Chaucer is unlikely to have known his contemporary William Langland, who says in an autobiographical passage (see p. 346), added to the third and last version of his great poem *Piers Plowman*, that he lived in London on Cornhill (a poor area of the city) among "lollers." "Loller" was a slang term for the unemployed and transients; it was later applied to followers of the religious and social reformer John Wycliffe (see p. 252), some of whom were burned at the stake for heresy in the next century. Langland assailed corruption in church and state, but he was certainly no radical. It is thought that he may have written the third version of *Piers Plowman*, which tones down his attacks on the church, after the rebels of 1381 invoked Piers as one of their own. Although Langland does not condone rebellion and his religion is quite orthodox, he nevertheless presents the most clear-sighted vision of social and religious issues in the England of his day. *Piers Plowman* is also a painfully honest search for the right way that leads to salvation. Though learned himself, Langland and the dreamer who represents him in the poem arrive at the insight that learning can be one of the chief obstacles on that way.

Langland came from the west of England, and his poem belongs to the "Alliterative Revival," a final flowering in the late fourteenth century of the verse form that goes all the way back to Anglo-Saxon England. Native traditions held out longest in the west and north, away from London, where Chaucer and his audience were more open to literary fashions from the Continent. Admiration for Chaucer's poetry and the controversial nature of Langland's writing assured the survival of their work in many manuscripts. The work of a third major fourteenth-century English poet, who remains anonymous, is known only through a single manuscript, which contains four poems all thought to be by a single author: *Cleanness* and *Patience*, two biblical narratives in alliterative verse; *Pearl*, a moving dream vision in which a grief-stricken father is visited and consoled by his dead child, who has been transformed into a queen in the kingdom of heaven; and *Sir Gawain and the Green Knight*, the finest of all English romances. The plot of *Gawain* involves a folklore motif of a challenge by a supernatural visitor, first found in an Old Irish tale. The poet has made this motif a challenge to King Arthur's court and has framed the tale with allusions at the beginning and end to the legends that link Arthur's reign with the Trojan War and the founding of Rome and of Britain. The poet has a sophisticated awareness of romance as a literary genre and plays a game with both the hero's and the readers' expectations of what is supposed to happen in a romance. One could say that the broader subject of *Sir Gawain and the Green Knight* is "romance" itself, and in this respect the poem resembles Chaucer's *Canterbury Tales* in its author's interest in literary form.

The Fifteenth Century

In 1399 Henry Bolingbroke, the duke of Lancaster, deposed his cousin Richard II, who was murdered in prison. As Henry IV, he successfully defended his crown against several insurrections and passed it on to Henry V, who briefly united the country once more and achieved one last apparently decisive victory over the French at the Battle of Agincourt (1415). The premature death of Henry V, however, left England exposed to the civil wars known as the Wars of the Roses, the red rose being the emblem of the house of Lancaster; the white, of York. These wars did not end until 1485, when Henry Tudor defeated Richard III at Bosworth Field and acceded to the throne as Henry VII.

Social, economic, and literary life continued as they had throughout all of the previous wars. The prosperity of the towns was shown by performances of the mystery plays—a sequence or "cycle" of plays based on the Bible and produced by the city guilds, the organizations representing the various trades and crafts. The cycles of several towns are lost, but those of York, Wakefield, and Chester have been preserved. Under the guise of dramatizing biblical history, playwrights such as the Wakefield Master manage to comment satirically on the social ills of the times. The century also saw the development of the morality play, in which personified vices and virtues struggle for the soul of "Mankind" or "Everyman." Performed by strolling players, the morality plays were precursors of the professional theater in the reign of Elizabeth I.

While religious works of all kinds continued to be produced, the fourteenth and fifteenth centuries are notable (both in England and on the Continent) for mystical writings in which the authors, many of whom were women, tell of their direct personal experience of God. The anchoress Julian of Norwich spent her life meditating and writing about a series of visions, which she called "showings," that she had received in 1373, when she was thirty years old. Early in the fifteenth century she was still in her cell, attached to a church in Norwich, when she was consulted by Margery Kempe, whom a series of visions had directed to lead a spiritual life. Kempe, a controversial figure, made a pilgrimage to the Holy Land and during the 1430s dictated the first autobiography in English. Both Julian of Norwich and Margery Kempe, in highly individual ways, allow us to see the medieval church and its doctrines from female points of view.

The most prolific poet of the fifteenth century was the monk John Lydgate (1370?–1451?), who produced dream visions; a life of the Virgin; translations of French religious allegories; a *Troy Book; The Siege of Thebes*, which he framed as a "new" Canterbury tale; and a thirty-six-thousand-line poem called *The Fall of Princes*, a free translation of a French work, itself based on a Latin work by Boccaccio. The last illustrates the late medieval idea of tragedy, namely that emperors, kings, and other famous men enjoy power and fortune only to be cast down in misery. Lydgate shapes these tales as a "mirror" for princes, i.e., as object lessons to the powerful men of his own day, several of whom were his patrons. A self-styled imitator of Chaucer, Lydgate had a reputation almost equal to Chaucer's in the fifteenth century. The best of Chaucer's imitators was the "Scottish Chaucerian," Robert Henryson (1425?–1508?), who wrote *The Testament of Cressid*, a continuation of Chaucer's great poem *Troilus and Criseyde*. He also wrote the *Moral Fabilis of Esope*, among which *The Cock and the Fox*, included here, is a remake of Chaucer's *Nun's Priest's Tale*. The works of Sir Thomas Malory gave the definitive form in English to the saga of King Arthur and his knights. Malory spent years in prison Englishing a series of Arthurian romances that he translated and abridged chiefly from several enormously long thirteenth-century French prose romances. Malory was a passionate devotee of chivalry, which he personified in his hero Sir Lancelot. In the jealousies and rivalries that finally break up the round table and destroy Arthur's kingdom, Malory saw a distant image of the civil wars of his own time. A manuscript of Malory's works fell into the hands of William Caxton (1422?–1491), who had introduced the new art of printing by movable type to England in 1476. Caxton divided Malory's tales into the chapters and books of a single long work, as though it were a chronicle history, and gave it the title *Morte Darthur*, which has stuck to it ever since. Caxton also printed *The Canterbury Tales*, some of Chaucer's earlier works, and Gower's *Confessio Amantis*. Caxton himself translated many of the works he printed for English readers: a history of Troy, a book on chivalry, Aesop's fables, and *The Game and Playe of Chesse*. The new technology extended literacy and made books more easily accessible to new classes of readers. Printing made the production of literature a business and made possible the bitter political and doctrinal disputes that, in the sixteenth century, were waged in print as well as on the field of battle.

MEDIEVAL ENGLISH

The medieval works in this book were composed in different states of our language. Old English, the language that took shape among the Germanic settlers of England, preserved its integrity until the Norman Conquest radically altered English civilization. Middle English, the earliest records of which date from the early twelfth century, was continually changing. Shortly after the introduction of printing at the end of the fifteenth century, it attained the form designated as Early Modern English. Old English is a very heavily inflected language. (That is, the words change form to indicate changes in usage, such as person, number, tense, case, mood, and so on. Most languages have some inflection—for example, the personal pronouns in Modern English have different forms when used as objects—but a "heavily inflected" language is one in which almost all classes of words undergo elaborate patterns of change.) The vocabulary of Old English is almost entirely Germanic. In Middle English, the inflectional system was weakened, and a large number of words were introduced into it from French, so that many of the older native words disappeared. Because of the difficulty of Old English, all selections from it in this book have been given in translation. So that the reader may see an example of the language, Cædmon's *Hymn* and a passage from *The Battle of Maldon* have been printed in the original, together with interlinear translations. The present discussion, then, is concerned primarily with the relatively late form of Middle English used by Chaucer and the East Midland dialect in which he wrote.

The chief difficulty with Middle English for the modern reader is caused not by its inflections so much as by its spelling, which may be described as a rough-and-ready phonetic system, and by the fact that it is not a single standardized language, but consists of a number of regional dialects, each with its own peculiarities of sound and its own systems for representing sounds in writing. The Midland dialect—the dialect of London and of Chaucer, which is the ancestor of our own standard speech—differs greatly from the dialect spoken in the west of England (the original dialect of *Piers Plowman*), from that of the northwest (*Sir Gawain* and *the Green Knight*), and from that of the north (*The Second Shepherds' Play*). In this book, the long texts composed in the more difficult dialects have been translated or modernized, and those that—like Chaucer, *Everyman*, the lyrics, and the ballads—appear in the original, have been re-spelled in a way that is designed to aid the reader. The remarks that follow apply chiefly to Chaucer's Midland English, although certain non-Midland dialectal variations are noted if they occur in some of the other selections.

I. *The Sounds of Middle English: General Rules*

The following general analysis of the sounds of Middle English will enable the reader who has not time for detailed study to read Middle English aloud so as to preserve some of its most essential characteristics, without, however, giving heed to many important details. The next section, "Detailed Analysis," is designed for the reader who wishes to go more deeply into the pronunciation of Middle English.

Middle English differs from Modern English in three principal respects: (1) the pronunciation of the long vowels *a, e, i* (or *y*), *o*, and *u* (spelled *ou, ow*); (2) the fact that Middle English final *e* is often sounded; and (3) the fact that all Middle English consonants are sounded.

1. LONG VOWELS

Middle English vowels are long when they are doubled (*aa, ee, oo*) or when they are terminal (*he, to, holy*); *a, e,* and *o* are long when followed by a single consonant plus a vowel (*name, mete, note*). Middle English vowels are short when they are followed by two consonants.

Long *a* is sounded like the *a* in Modern English "father": *maken, madd.*

Long *e* may be sounded like the *a* in Modern English "name" (ignoring the distinction between the close and open vowel): *be, sweete.*

Long *i* (or *y*) is sounded like the *i* in Modern English "machine": *lif, whit; myn, holy.*

Long *o* may be sounded like the *o* in Modern English "note" (again ignoring the distinction between the close and open vowel): *do, soone.*

Long *u* (spelled *ou, ow*) is sounded like the *oo* in Modern English "goose": *hous, flowr.*

Note that in general Middle English long vowels are pronounced like long vowels in modern European languages other than English. Short vowels and diphthongs, however, may be pronounced as in Modern English.

2. FINAL E

In Middle English syllabic verse, final *e* is sounded like the *a* in "sofa" to provide a needed unstressed syllable: *Another Nonnë with hire haddë she.* But (cf. *hire* in the example) final *e* is suppressed when not needed for the meter. It is commonly silent before words beginning with a vowel or *h*.

3. CONSONANTS

Middle English consonants are pronounced separately in all combinations—*gnat*: g-nat; *knave*: k-nave; *write*: w-rite; *folk*: fol-k. In a simplified system of pronunciation the combination *gh* as in *night* or *thought* may be treated as if it were silent.

II. *The Sounds of Middle English: Detailed Analysis*

1. SIMPLE VOWELS

Sound	Pronunciation	Example
long *a* (spelled *a, aa*)	*a* in "father"	*maken, maad*
short *a*	*o* in "hot"	*cappe*
long *e* close (spelled *e, ee*)	*a* in "name"	*be, sweete*

long *e* open (spelled *e, ee*)	*e* in "there"	*mete, heeth*
short *e*	*e* in "set"	*setten*
final *e*	*a* in "sofa"	*large*
long *i* (spelled *i, y*)	*i* in "machine"	*lif, mym*
short *i*	*i* in "wit"	*wit*
long *o* close (spelled *o, oo*)	*o* in "note"	*do, soone*
long *o* open (spelled *o, oo*)	*oa* in "broad"	*go, goon*
short *o*	*o* in "oft"	*pot*
long *u* when spelled *ou, ow*	*oo* in "goose"	*hous, flowr*
long *u* when spelled *u*	*u* in "pure"	*vertu*
short *u* (spelled *u, o*)	*u* in "full"	*ful, love*

Doubled vowels and terminal vowels are always long, whereas single vowels before two consonants other than *th, ch* are always short. The vowels *a*, *e*, and *o* are long before a single consonant followed by a vowel: *nāmë, sēkë* (sick), *hōly*. In general, words that have descended into Modern English reflect their original Middle English quantity: *lĭven* (to live), but *līf* (life).

The close and open sounds of long *e* and long *o* may often be identified by the Modern English spellings of the words in which they appear. Original long close *e* is generally represented in Modern English by *ee*: "sweet," "knee," "teeth," "see" have close *e* in Middle English, but so does "be"; original long open *e* is generally represented in Modern English by *ea*: "meat," "heath," "sea," "great," "breath" have open *e* in Middle English. Similarly, original long close *o* is now generally represented by *oo*: "soon," "food," "good," but also "do," "to"; original long open *o* is represented either by *oa* or by *o*: "coat," "boat," "moan," but also "go," "bone," "foe," "home." Notice that original close *o* is now almost always pronounced like the *oo* in "goose," but that original open *o* is almost never so pronounced; thus it is often possible to identify the Middle English vowels through Modern English sounds.

The nonphonetic Middle English spelling of *o* for short *u* has been preserved in a number of Modern English words ("love," "son," "come"), but in others *u* has been restored: "sun" (*sonne*), "run" (*ronne*).

For the treatment of final *e*, see "General Rules," "Final *e*."

2. DIPHTHONGS

Sound	Pronunciation	Example
ai, ay, ei, ay	between *ai* in "aisle" and *ay* in "day"	*saide, day, veine, preye*
au, aw	*ou* in "out"	*chaunge, bawdy*
eu, ew	*ew* in "few"	*newe*
oi, oy	*oy* in "joy"	*joye, point*
ou, ow	*ou* in "thought"	*thought, lowe*

Note that in words with *ou, ow* that in Modern English are sounded with the *ou* of "about," the combination indicates not the diphthong but the simple vowel long *u* (see "Simple Vowels").

3. CONSONANTS

In general, all consonants except *h* were always sounded in Middle English, including consonants that have become silent in Modern English, such as the *g* in *gnaw*, the *k* in *knight*, the *l* in *folk*, and the *w* in *write*. In noninitial *gn*, however, the *g* was silent as in Modern English "sign." Initial *h* was silent in short common English words and in words borrowed from French and may have been almost silent in all words. The combination *gh* as in *night* or *thought* was sounded like the *ch* of German *ich* or *nach*. Note that Middle English *gg* represents both the hard sound of "dagger" and the soft sound of "bridge."

III. Parts of Speech and Grammar

1. NOUNS

The plural and possessive of nouns end in *es*, formed by adding *s* or *es* to the singular: *knight, knightes; roote, rootes*; a final consonant is frequently doubled before *es: bed, beddes*. A common irregular plural is *yën*, from *yë*, eye.

2. PRONOUNS

The chief differences from Modern English are as follows:

Modern English	Middle English
I	*I, ich* (*ik* is a northern form)
you (singular)	*thou* (subjective); *thee* (objective)
her	*hir(e), her(e)*
its	*his*
you (plural)	*ye* (subjective); *you* (objective)
their	*hir*
them	*hem*

In formal speech, the second person plural is often used for the singular. The possessive adjectives *my, thy* take *n* before a word beginning with a vowel or *h: thyn yë, myn host*.

3. ADJECTIVES

Adjectives ending in a consonant add final *e* when they stand before the noun they modify and after another modifying word such as *the, this, that*, or nouns or pronouns in the possessive: *a good hors*, but *the (this, my, the kinges) goode hors*. They also generally add *e* when standing before and modifying a plural noun, a noun in the vocative, or any proper noun: *goode men, oh goode man, faire Venus*.

Adjectives are compared by adding *er(e)* for the comparative, *est(e)* for the superlative. Sometimes the stem vowel is shortened or altered in the process: *sweete, swettere, swettest; long, lenger, lengest*.

4. ADVERBS

Adverbs are formed from adjectives by adding *e, ly*, or *liche*; the adjective *fair* thus yields *faire, fairly, fairliche*.

5. VERBS

Middle English verbs, like Modern English verbs, are either "weak" or "strong." Weak verbs form their preterites and past participles with a *t* or *d* suffix and preserve the same stem vowel throughout their systems, although it is sometimes shortened in the preterite and past participle: *love, loved; bend, bent; hear, heard; meet, met.* Strong verbs do not use the *t* or *d* suffix, but vary their stem vowel in the preterite and past participle: *take, took, taken; begin, began, begun; find, found, found.*

The inflectional endings are the same for Middle English strong verbs and weak verbs except in the preterite singular and the imperative singular. In the following paradigms, the weak verbs *loven* (to love) and *heeren* (to hear), and the strong verbs *taken* (to take) and *ginnen* (to begin) serve as models.

	Present Indicative	Preterite Indicative
I	*love, heere*	*loved(e), herde*
	take, ginne	*took, gan*
thou	*lovest, heerest*	*lovedest, herdest*
	takest, ginnest	*tooke, gonne*
he, she, it	*loveth, heereth*	*loved(e), herde*
	taketh, ginneth	*took, gan*
we, ye, they	*love(n) (th), heere(n) (th)*	*loved(e) (en), herde(n)*
	take(n) (th), ginne(n) (th)	*tooke(n), gonne(n)*

The present plural ending *eth* is southern, whereas the *e(n)* ending is Midland and characteristic of Chaucer. In the north, *s* may appear as the ending of all persons of the present. In the weak preterite, when the ending *e* gave a verb three or more syllables, it was frequently dropped. Note that in certain strong verbs like *ginnen* there are two distinct stem vowels in the preterite; even in Chaucer's time, however, one of these had begun to replace the other, and Chaucer occasionally writes *gan* for all persons of the preterite.

	Present Subjunctive	Preterite Subjunctive
Singular	*love, heere*	*lovede, herde*
	take, ginne	*tooke, gonne*
Plural	*love(n), heere(n)*	*lovede(n), herde(n)*
	take(n), ginne(n)	*tooke(n), gonne(n)*

In verbs like *ginnen*, which have two stem vowels in the indicative preterite, it is the vowel of the plural and of the second person singular that is used for the preterite subjunctive.

The imperative singular of most weak verbs is *e*: *(thou) love*, but of some weak verbs and all strong verbs, the imperative singular is without termination: *(thou) heer, taak, gin*. The imperative plural of all verbs is either *e* or *eth*: *(ye) love(th), heere(th), take(th), ginne(th)*.

The infinitive of verbs is *e* or *en*: *love(n), heere(n), take(n), ginne(n)*.

The past participle of weak verbs is the same as the preterite without inflectional ending: *loved, herd.* In strong verbs the ending is either *e* or *en*: *take(n), gonne(n).* The prefix *y* often appears on past participles: *yloved, yherd, ytake(n).*

OLD AND MIDDLE ENGLISH PROSODY

All the poetry of Old English is in the same verse form. The verse unit is the single line, because rhyme was not used to link one line to another, except very occasionally in late Old English. The organizing device of the line is alliteration, the beginning of several words with the same sound ("Foemen fled"). The Old English alliterative line contains, on the average, four principal stresses and is divided into two half-lines of two stresses each by a strong medial caesura, or pause. These two half-lines are linked to each other by the alliteration; at least one of the two stressed words in the first half-line, and often both of them, begin with the same sound as the first stressed word of the second half-line (the second stressed word is generally nonalliterative). The fourth line of *Beowulf* is an example (*sc* has the value of modern *sh*; þ is a runic symbol with the value of modern *th*):

Oft Scyld Scefing   sceaþena þreatum.

For further examples, see Cædmon's *Hymn* and the passage from *The Battle of Maldon*. It will be noticed that any vowel alliterates with any other vowel. In addition to the alliteration, the length of the unstressed syllables and their number and pattern is governed by a highly complex set of rules. When sung or intoned—as it was—to the rhythmic strumming of a harp, Old English poetry must have been wonderfully impressive in the dignified, highly formalized way that aptly fits both its subject matter and tone.

The majority of Middle English verse is either in alternately stressed rhyming verse, adapted from French after the conquest, or in alliterative verse that is descended from Old English. The latter preserves the caesura of Old English and in its purest form the same alliterative system, the two stressed words of the first half-line (or at least one of them) alliterating with the first stressed word in the second half-line. But most of the alliterative poets allowed themselves a number of deviations from the norm. All four stressed words may alliterate, as in the first line of *Piers Plowman*:

In a summer season   when soft was the sun.

Or the line may contain five, six, or even more stressed words, of which all or only the basic minimum may alliterate:

A *f*air *f*ield *f*ull of   *f*olk *f*ound I therebetween.

There is no rule determining the number of unstressed syllables, and at times some poets seem to ignore alliteration entirely. As in Old English, any vowel may alliterate with any other vowel; furthermore, since initial *h* was silent or lightly pronounced in Middle English, words beginning with *h* are treated as though they began with the following vowel.

There are two general types of stressed verse with rhyme. In the more common, stressed and unstressed syllables alternate regularly as x X x X x X or, with two unstressed syllables intervening as x x X x x X x x X or a combination of the two as x x X x X x x X (of the reverse patterns, only X x X x X x is common in English). There is also a line that can only be defined as containing a predetermined number of stressed syllables but an irregular number and pattern of unstressed syllables. Much Middle English verse has to be read without expectation of regularity; some of this was evidently composed in the irregular meter, but some was probably originally composed according to a strict metrical system that has been obliterated by scribes careless of fine points. One receives the impression that many of the lyrics— as well as the *Second Shepherds' Play*—were at least composed with regular syllabic alternation. In the play *Everyman*, only the number of stresses is generally predetermined but not the number or placement of unstressed syllables.

In pre-Chaucerian verse the number of stresses, whether regularly or irregularly alternated, was most often four, although sometimes the number was three and rose in some poems to seven. Rhyme in Middle English (as in Modern English) may be either between adjacent or alternate lines, or may occur in more complex patterns. Most of the *Canterbury Tales* are in rhymed couplets, the line containing five stresses with regular alternation—technically known as iambic pentameter, the standard English poetic line, perhaps introduced into English by Chaucer. In reading Chaucer and much pre-Chaucerian verse one must remember that the final *e*, which is silent in Modern English, could be pronounced at any time to provide a needed unstressed syllable. Evidence seems to indicate that it was also pronounced at the end of the line, even though it thus produced a line with eleven syllables. Although he was a very regular metricist, Chaucer used various conventional devices that are apt to make the reader stumble until he or she understands them. Final *e* is often not pronounced before a word beginning with a vowel or *h*, and may be suppressed whenever metrically convenient. The same medial and terminal syllables that are slurred in Modern English are apt to be suppressed in Chaucer's English: *Canterb'ry* for *Canterbury*; *ev'r* (perhaps *e'er*) for *evere*. The plural in *es* may either be syllabic or reduced to *s* as in Modern English. Despite these seeming irregularities, Chaucer's verse is not difficult to read if one constantly bears in mind the basic pattern of the iambic pentameter line.

THE MIDDLE AGES

TEXTS	CONTEXTS
	43–ca. 420 Romans conquer Britons; Brittania a province of the Roman Empire
	307–37 Reign of Constantine the Great leads to adoption of Christianity as official religion of the Roman Empire
ca. 405 St. Jerome completes *Vulgate*, Latin translation of the Bible that becomes standard for the Roman Catholic Church	
	432 St. Patrick begins mission to convert Ireland
	ca. 450 Withdrawal of Roman legions; Anglo-Saxon conquest of Britons begins
523 Boethius, *Consolation of Philosophy* (Latin)	
	597 St. Augustine of Canterbury's mission to Kent begins conversion of Anglo-Saxons to Christianity
ca. 658–80 *Cædmon's Hymn*, earliest poem recorded in English	
731 Bede completes *Ecclesiastical History of the English People*	
? ca. 750 *Beowulf* composed	
	ca. 787 First Viking raids on England
	871–99 Reign of King Alfred
ca. 1000 Unique *Beowulf* manuscript written	
	1066 Norman Conquest by William I establishes French-speaking ruling class in England
	1095–1221 Crusades
ca. 1135–38 Geoffrey of Monmouth's Latin *History of the Kings of Britain* gives pseudohistorical status to Arthurian and other legends	
	1152 Future Henry II marries Eleanor of Aquitaine, bringing vast French territories to the English crown
1154 End of *Peterborough Chronicle*, last branch of the *Anglo-Saxon Chronicle*	
? ca. 1165–80 Marie de France, *Lais* in Anglo-Norman French from Breton sources	
ca. 1170–91 Chrétien de Troyes, chivalric romances about knights of the Round Table	**1170** Archbishop Thomas Becket murdered in Canterbury Cathedral
	1182 Birth of St. Francis of Assisi
? ca. 1200 Layamon's *Brut*	
? ca. 1215–25 *Ancrene Riwle*	**1215** Fourth Lateran Council requires annual confession. English barons force King John to seal Magna Carta (the Great Charter) guaranteeing baronial rights

TEXTS	CONTEXTS
ca. 1304–21 Dante Alighieri writing *Divine Comedy*	
	ca. 1337–1453 Hundred Years' War
	1348 Black Death ravages Europe
	1362 English first used in law courts and Parliament
1368 Chaucer, *Book of the Duchess*	
	1372 Chaucer's first journey to Italy
ca. 1375–1400 *Sir Gawain and the Green Knight*	
	1376 Earliest record of performance of drama at York
1377–79 William Langland, *Piers Plowman* (B-Text)	
ca. 1380 John Wycliffe and his followers begin first complete translation of the Bible into English	
	1381 People's uprising briefly takes control of London before being suppressed
ca. 1385–87 Chaucer, *Troilus and Criseyde*	
ca. 1387–89 Chaucer working on *The Canterbury Tales*	
ca. 1390–92 John Gower, *Confessio Amantis*	
	1399 Richard II deposed by his cousin, who succeeds him as Henry IV
	1400 Richard II murdered
	1401 Execution of William Sawtre, first Lollard burned at the stake under new law against heresy
	1415 Henry V defeats French at Agincourt
	1431 English burn Joan of Arc at Rouen
ca. 1432–38 Margery Kempe, *The Book of Margery Kempe*	
ca. 1450–75 Wakefield mystery cycle, *Second Shepherds' Play*	
	1455–85 Wars of the Roses
ca. 1470 Sir Thomas Malory in prison working on *Morte Darthur*	
	1476 William Caxton sets up first printing press in England
1485 Caxton publishes *Morte Darthur,* one of the first books in English to be printed	1485 The earl of Richmond defeats the Yorkist king, Richard III, at Bosworth Field and succeeds him as Henry VII, founder of the Tudor dynasty
ca. 1510 *Everyman*	1575 Last performance of mystery plays at Chester

Anglo-Saxon England

BEDE (ca. 673–735) and CÆDMON'S HYMN

The Venerable Bede (the title by which he is known to posterity) became a novice at the age of seven and spent the rest of his life at the neighboring monasteries of Wearmouth and Jarrow. Although he may never have traveled beyond the boundaries of his native district of Northumbria, he achieved an international reputation as one of the greatest scholars of his age. Writing in Latin, the learned language of the era, Bede produced many theological works as well as books on science and rhetoric, but his most popular and enduring work is the *Ecclesiastical History of the English People* (completed 731). The *History* tells about the Anglo-Saxon conquest and the vicissitudes of the petty kingdoms that comprised Anglo-Saxon England; Bede's main theme, however, is the spread of Christianity and the growth of the English church. The latter were the great events leading up to Bede's own time, and he regarded them as the unfolding of God's providence. The *History* is, therefore, also a moral work and a hagiography—that is, it contains many stories of saints and miracles meant to testify to the grace and glory of God.

The story we reprint preserves what is probably the earliest extant Old English poem (composed sometime between 658 and 680) and the only biographical information, outside of what is said in the poems themselves, about any Old English poet. Bede tells how Cædmon, an illiterate cowherd employed by the monastery of Whitby, miraculously received the gift of song, entered the monastery, and became the founder of a school of Christian poetry. Cædmon was clearly an oral-formulaic poet, one who created his work by combining and varying formulas—units of verse developed in a tradition transmitted by one generation of singers to another. In this respect he resembles the singers of the Homeric poems and oral-formulaic poets recorded in the twentieth century, especially in the Balkan countries. Although Bede tells us that Cædmon had never learned the art of song, we may suspect that he concealed his skill from his fellow workmen and from the monks because he was ashamed of knowing "vain and idle" songs, the kind Bede says Cædmon never composed. Cædmon's inspiration and the true miracle, then, was to apply the meter and language of such songs, presumably including pagan heroic verse, to Christian themes.

Although most Old English poetry was written by lettered poets, they continued to use the oral-formulaic style. The *Hymn* is, therefore, a good short example of the way Old English verse, with its traditional poetic diction and interwoven formulaic expressions, is constructed. Eight of the poem's eighteen half-lines contain epithets describing various aspects of God: He is *Weard* (Guardian), *Meotod* (Measurer), *Wuldor-Fæder* (Glory-Father), *Drihten* (Lord), *Scyppend* (Creator), and *Frea* (Master). God is *heofonrices Weard* or *mancynnes Weard* (heaven's or mankind's Guardian), depending on the alliteration required. This formulaic style provides a richness of texture and meaning difficult to convey in translation. As Bede said about his own Latin paraphrase of the *Hymn*, no literal translation of poetry from one language to another is possible without sacrifice of some poetic quality.

Several manuscripts of Bede's *History* contain the Old English text in addition to Bede's Latin version. The poem is given here in a West Saxon form with a literal

23

interlinear translation. In Old English spelling, æ (as in Cædmon's name and line 3) is a vowel symbol that represents the vowel of Modern English *cat*; þ (line 2) and ð (line 7) both represented the sound *th*. The spelling *sc* (line 1) = *sh*; ġ (line 1) = *y* in *yard*; ċ (line 1) = *ċ* in *chin*; *c* (line 2) = *k*. The large space in the middle of the line indicates the caesura. The alliterating sounds that connect the half-lines have been italicized.

From An Ecclesiastical History of the English People

[THE STORY OF CÆDMON]

Heavenly grace had especially singled out a certain one of the brothers in the monastery ruled by this abbess,[1] for he used to compose devout and religious songs. Whatever he learned of holy Scripture with the aid of interpreters, he quickly turned into the sweetest and most moving poetry in his own language, that is to say English. It often happened that his songs kindled a contempt for this world and a longing for the life of Heaven in the hearts of many men. Indeed, after him others among the English people tried to compose religious poetry, but no one could equal him because he was not taught the art of song by men or by human agency but received this gift through heavenly grace. Therefore, he was never able to compose any vain and idle songs but only such as dealt with religion and were proper for his religious tongue to utter. As a matter of fact, he had lived in the secular estate until he was well advanced in age without learning any songs. Therefore, at feasts, when it was decided to have a good time by taking turns singing, whenever he would see the harp getting close to his place,[2] he got up in the middle of the meal and went home.

Once when he left the feast like this, he went to the cattle shed, which he had been assigned the duty of guarding that night. And after he had stretched himself out and gone to sleep, he dreamed that someone was standing at his side and greeted him, calling out his name. "Cædmon," he said, "sing me something."

And he replied, "I don't know how to sing; that is why I left the feast to come here—because I cannot sing."

"All the same," said the one who was speaking to him, "you have to sing for me."

"What must I sing?" he said.

And he said, "Sing about the Creation."

At this, Cædmon immediately began to sing verses in praise of God the Creator, which he had never heard before and of which the sense is this:

| Nu sculon   *heriġean* | *heo*fonrices Weard |
| Now we must praise | heaven-kingdom's Guardian, |

| *Meo*todes   *mea*hte | and his *mod*ġeþanc |
| the Measurer's might | and his mind-plans, |

---

1. Abbess Hilda (614–680), a grandniece of the first Christian king of Northumbria, founded Whitby, a double house for monks and nuns, in 657 and ruled over it for twenty-two years.

2. Oral poetry was performed to the accompaniment of a harp; here the harp is being passed from one participant of the feast to another, each being expected to perform in turn.

weorc Wuldor-Fæder
the work of the Glory-Father,

swa he wundra ġehwæs
when he of wonders of every one,

eċe Drihten
eternal Lord,

or onstealde
the beginning established.[3]

5 He ærest sceop
He first created

ielda[4] bearnum
for men's sons

heofon to hrofe
heaven as a roof,

haliġ Scyppend
holy Creator;

ða middanġeard
then middle-earth

moncynnes Weard
mankind's Guardian,

eċe Drihten
eternal Lord,

æfter teode
afterwards made—

firum foldan
for men earth,

Frea ælmihtiġ
Master almighty.

This is the general sense but not the exact order of the words that he sang in his sleep;[5] for it is impossible to make a literal translation, no matter how well-written, of poetry into another language without losing some of the beauty and dignity. When he woke up, he remembered everything that he had sung in his sleep, and to this he soon added, in the same poetic measure, more verses praising God.

The next morning he went to the reeve,[6] who was his foreman, and told him about the gift he had received. He was taken to the abbess and ordered to tell his dream and to recite his song to an audience of the most learned men so that they might judge what the nature of that vision was and where it came from. It was evident to all of them that he had been granted the heavenly grace of God. Then they expounded some bit of sacred story or teaching to him, and instructed him to turn it into poetry if he could. He agreed and went away. And when he came back the next morning, he gave back what had been commissioned to him in the finest verse.

Therefore, the abbess, who cherished the grace of God in this man, instructed him to give up secular life and to take monastic vows. And when she and all those subject to her had received him into the community of brothers, she gave orders that he be taught the whole sequence of sacred history. He remembered everything that he was able to learn by listening, and turning it over in his mind like a clean beast that chews the cud,[7] he converted it into sweetest song, which sounded so delightful that he made his teachers, in their turn, his listeners. He sang about the creation of the

3. I.e., established the beginning of every one of wonders.
4. The later manuscript copies read eorþan, "earth," for ælda (West Saxon ielda), "men's."
5. Bede is referring to his Latin translation for which we have substituted the Old English text with interlinear translation.

6. Superintendent of the farms belonging to the monastery.
7. In Mosaic law "clean" animals, those that may be eaten, are those that both chew the cud and have a cloven hoof (cf. Leviticus 11.3 and Deuteronomy 14.6).

world and the origin of the human race and all the history of Genesis; about the exodus of Israel out of Egypt and entrance into the promised land; and about many other stories of sacred Scripture, about the Lord's incarnation, and his passion,[8] resurrection, and ascension into Heaven; about the advent of the Holy Spirit and the teachings of the apostles. He also made many songs about the terror of the coming judgment and the horror of the punishments of hell and the sweetness of the heavenly kingdom; and a great many others besides about divine grace and justice in all of which he sought to draw men away from the love of sin and to inspire them with delight in the practice of good works.[9] * * *

8. The suffering of Christ on the Cross and during his trial leading up to the Crucifixion.
9. The great majority of extant Old English poems are on religious subjects like those listed here, but most are thought to be later than Cædmon.

THE DREAM OF THE ROOD

The *Dream of the Rood* (i.e., of the Cross) is the finest of a rather large number of religious poems in Old English. Neither its author nor its date of composition is known. It appears in a late tenth-century manuscript located in Vercelli in northern Italy, a manuscript made up of Old English religious poems and sermons. The poem may antedate its manuscript, because some passages from the Rood's speech were carved, with some variations, in runes on a stone cross at some time after its construction early in the eighth century; this is the famous Ruthwell Cross, which is preserved near Dumfries in southern Scotland. The precise relation of the poem to this cross is, however, uncertain.

The experience of the Rood—its humiliation at the hands of those who changed it from tree to instrument of punishment for criminals, its humility when the young hero Christ mounts it, and its pride as the restored "tree of glory"—has a suggestive relevance to the condition of the sad, lonely, sin-stained Dreamer. His isolation and melancholy is typical of exile figures in Old English poetry. For the Rood, however, glory has replaced torment, and at the end, the Dreamer's description of Christ's triumphant entry into heaven with the souls He has liberated from hell reflects the Dreamer's response to the hope that has been brought to him.

The Dream of the Rood[1]

Listen, I will speak of the best of dreams, of what I dreamed at midnight when men and their voices were at rest. It seemed to me that I saw a most rare tree reach high aloft, wound in light, brightest of beams. All that beacon[2] was covered with gold; gems stood fair where it met the ground, five were above about the crosspiece. Many hosts of angels gazed on it, fair in the form created for them. This was surely no felon's gallows, but holy spirits beheld it there, men upon earth, and all this glorious creation. Wonderful was the triumph-tree, and I stained with sins, wounded with wrongdoings. I saw the

1. This prose translation, by E. T. Donaldson, has been based in general on the edition of the poem by John C. Pope, *Seven Old English Poems* (1966).

2. The Old English word *beacen* also means token or sign and battle standard.

tree of glory shine splendidly, adorned with garments, decked with gold: jewels had worthily covered the Lord's tree. Yet through that gold I might perceive ancient agony of wretches, for now it began to bleed on the right side.[3] I was all afflicted with sorrows, I was afraid for that fair sight. I saw that bright beacon change in clothing and color now it was wet with moisture, drenched with flowing of blood, now adorned with treasure. Yet I, lying there a long while troubled, beheld the Saviour's tree until I heard it give voice: the best of trees began to speak words.

"It was long ago—I remember it still—that I was hewn down at the wood's edge, taken from my stump. Strong foes seized me there, hewed me to the shape they wished to see, commanded me to lift their criminals. Men carried me on their shoulders, then set me on a hill; foes enough fastened me there. Then I saw the Lord of mankind hasten with stout heart, for he would climb upon me. I dared not bow or break against God's word when I saw earth's surface tremble. I might have felled all foes, but I stood fast. Then the young Hero stripped himself—that was God Almighty—strong and stouthearted. He climbed on the high gallows, bold in the sight of many, when he would free mankind. I trembled when the Warrior embraced me, yet I dared not bow to earth, fall to the ground's surface; but I must stand fast. I was raised up, a cross; I lifted up the Mighty King, Lord of the Heavens: I dared not bend. They pierced me with dark nails: the wounds are seen on me, open gashes of hatred. Nor did I dare harm any of them. They mocked us both together. I was all wet with blood, drenched from the side of that Man after he had sent forth his spirit. I had endured many bitter happenings on that hill. I saw the God of Hosts cruelly racked. The shades of night had covered the Ruler's body with their mists, the bright splendor. Shadow came forth, dark beneath the clouds. All creation wept, bewailed the King's fall; Christ was on Cross.

"Yet from afar some came hastening to the Lord.[4] All that I beheld. I was sore afflicted with griefs, yet I bowed to the men's hands, meekly, eagerly. Then they took Almighty God, lifted him up from his heavy torment. The warriors left me standing, covered with blood. I was all wounded with arrows. They laid him down weary of limb, stood at the body's head, looked there upon Heaven's Lord; and he rested there a while, tired after the great struggle. Then warriors began to build him an earth-house in the sight of his slayer,[5] carved it out of bright stone; they set there the Wielder of Triumphs. Then they began to sing him a song of sorrow, desolate in the evening. Then they wished to turn back, weary, from the great Prince; he remained with small company.[6] Yet we[7] stood in our places a good while, weeping. The voice of the warriors departed. The body grew cold, fair house of the spirit. Then some began to fell us to earth—that was a fearful fate! Some buried us in a deep pit. Yet thanes[8] of the Lord, friends, learned of me there. . . . decked me in gold and silver.[9]

3. The wound Christ received on the Cross was supposed to have been on the right side.
4. According to John 19.38–39, it was Joseph of Arimathea and Nicodemus who received Christ's body from the Cross.
5. I.e., the Cross.
6. I.e., alone (an understatement).
7. I.e., Christ's Cross and those on which the two thieves were crucified.
8. Members of the king's body of warriors.
9. A number of lines describing the finding of the Cross have apparently been lost here. According to the legend, St. Helen, the mother of Constantine the Great, the first Christian emperor, led a Roman expedition that discovered the true Cross in the 4th century.

"Now you might understand, my beloved man, that I had endured the work of evildoers, grievous sorrows. Now the time has come that men far and wide upon earth honor me—and all this glorious creation—and pray to this beacon. On me God's Son suffered awhile; therefore I tower now glorious under the heavens, and I may heal every one of those who hold me in awe. Of old I became the hardest of torments, most loathed by men, before I opened the right road of life to those who have voices. Behold, the Lord of Glory honored me over all the trees of the wood, the Ruler of Heaven, just as also he honored his mother Mary, Almighty God for all men's sake, over all woman's kind.

"Now I command you, my beloved man, that you tell men of this vision. Disclose with your words that it is of the tree of glory on which Almighty God suffered for mankind's many sins and the deeds Adam did of old. He tasted death there; yet the Lord arose again to help mankind in his great might. Then he climbed to the heavens. He will come again hither on this earth to seek mankind on Doomsday, the Lord himself, Almighty God, and his angels with him, for then he will judge, he who has power to judge, each one just as in this brief life he has deserved. Nor may any one be unafraid of the word the Ruler will speak. Before his host he will ask where the man is who in the name of the Lord would taste bitter death as he did on the Cross. But then they will be afraid, and will think of little to begin to say to Christ. There need none be afraid who bears on his breast the best of tokens, but through the Cross shall the kingdom be sought by each soul on this earthly journey that thinks to dwell with the Lord."

Then I prayed to the tree, blithe-hearted, confident, there where I was alone with small company. My heart's thoughts were urged on the way hence. I endured many times of longing. Now is there hope of life for me, that I am permitted to seek the tree of triumph, more often than other men honor it well, alone. For it my heart's desire is great, and my hope of protection is directed to the Cross. I do not possess many powerful friends on earth, but they have gone hence from the delights of the world, sought for themselves the King of Glory. They live now in the heavens with the High Father, dwell in glory. And every day I look forward to when the Lord's Cross that I beheld here on earth will fetch me from this short life and bring me then where joy is great, delight in the heavens, where the Lord's folk are seated at the feast, where bliss is eternal. And then may it place me where thenceforth I may dwell in glory, fully enjoy bliss with the saints. May the Lord be my friend, who once here on earth suffered on the gallows-tree for man's sins: he freed us and granted us life, a heavenly home. Hope was renewed, with joys and with bliss, to those who endured fire.[1] The Son was victorious in that foray, mighty and successful. Then he came with his multitude, a host of spirits, into God's kingdom, the Almighty Ruler; and the angels and all the saints who dwelt then in glory rejoiced when their Ruler, Almighty God, came where his home was.

---

1. This and the following sentences refer to the Harrowing (i.e., pillaging) of Hell; after His death on the Cross, Christ descended into Hell, from which He released the souls of certain of the patriarchs and prophets, conducting them triumphantly to Heaven.

BEOWULF

Beowulf, the oldest of the great long poems written in English, may have been composed more than twelve hundred years ago, in the first half of the eighth century, although some scholars would place it as late as the tenth century. As is the case with most Old English poems, the title has been assigned by modern editors, for the manuscripts do not normally give any indication of title or authorship. Linguistic evidence shows that the poem was originally composed in the dialect of what was then Mercia, the Midlands of England today. But in the unique late-tenth-century manuscript preserving the poem, it has been converted into the West-Saxon dialect of the southwest in which most of Old English literature survives. In 1731, before any modern transcript of the text had been made, the manuscript was seriously damaged in a fire that destroyed the building in London that housed the extraordinary collection of medieval English manuscripts made by Sir Robert Bruce Cotton (1571–1631). As a result of the fire and subsequent deterioration, a number of lines and words have been lost from the poem.

It is possible that *Beowulf* may be the lone survivor of a genre of Old English long epics, but it must have been a remarkable and difficult work even in its own day. The poet was reviving the heroic language, style, and pagan world of ancient Germanic oral poetry, a world that was already remote for his contemporaries and that is stranger to the modern reader, in many respects, than the epic world of Homer and Virgil. With the help of *Beowulf* itself, a few shorter heroic poems in Old English, and later poetry and prose in Old Saxon, Old Icelandic, and Middle High German, we can only conjecture what Germanic oral epic must have been like when performed by the Germanic *scop*, or bard. The *Beowulf* poet himself imagines such oral performances by having King Hrothgar's court poet recite a heroic lay at a feast celebrating Beowulf's defeat of Grendel. Many of the words and formulaic expressions in *Beowulf* can be found in other Old English poems, but there are also an extraordinary number of what linguists call *hapax legomena*—that is, words recorded only once in a language. The poet may have found them elsewhere, but the high incidence of such words suggests that he was an original wordsmith in his own right.

Although the poem itself is English in language and origin, it deals not with native Englishmen but with their Germanic forebears, especially with two south Scandinavian tribes, the Danes and the Geats, who lived on the Danish island of Zealand and in southern Sweden. Thus the historical period the poem concerns—insofar as it may be said to refer to history at all—is some centuries before it was written—that is, a time after the initial invasion of England by Germanic tribes in the middle of the fifth century but before the Anglo-Saxon migration was completed. The one datable fact of history mentioned in the poem is a raid on the Franks in which Hygelac, the king of the Geats and Beowulf's lord, was killed, and this raid occurred in the year 520. Yet the poet's elliptical references to quasihistorical and legendary material show that his audience was still familiar with many old stories, the outlines of which we can only infer, sometimes with the help of later analogous tales in other Germanic languages. This knowledge was probably kept alive by other heroic poetry, of which little has been preserved in English, although much may once have existed.

It is now widely believed that *Beowulf* is the work of a single poet who was a Christian and that his poem reflects well-established Christian tradition. The conversion of the Germanic settlers in England had been largely completed during the seventh century. The Danish king Hrothgar's poet sings a song about the Creation (lines 87–98) reminiscent of Cædmon's *Hymn*. The monster Grendel is said to be a descendant of Cain. There are allusions to God's judgment and to fate (*wyrd*) but none to pagan deities. References to the New Testament are notably absent, but Hrothgar and Beowulf often speak of God as though their religion is monotheistic. With sadness the poet relates that, made desperate by Grendel's attacks, the Danes pray for help at heathen shrines—apparently backsliding as the children of Israel and the earliest Anglo-Saxon Christians had sometimes done.

Although Hrothgar and Beowulf are portrayed as morally upright and enlightened pagans, they fully espouse and frequently affirm the values of Germanic heroic poetry. In the poetry depicting this warrior society, the most important of human relationships was that which existed between the warrior—the thane—and his lord, a relationship based less on subordination of one man's will to another's than on mutual trust and respect. When a warrior vowed loyalty to his lord, he became not so much his servant as his voluntary companion, one who would take pride in defending him and fighting in his wars. In return, the lord was expected to take care of his thanes and to reward them richly for their valor; a good king, one like Hrothgar or Beowulf, is referred to by such poetic epithets as "ring-giver" and as the "helmet" and "shield" of his people.

The relationship between kinsmen was also of deep significance to this society. If one of his kinsmen had been slain, a man had a moral obligation either to kill the slayer or to exact the payment of *wergild* (man-price) in compensation. Each rank of society was evaluated at a definite price, which had to be paid to the dead man's kin by the killer if he wished to avoid their vengeance—even if the killing had been an accident. In the absence of any legal code other than custom or any body of law enforcement, it was the duty of the family (often with the lord's support) to execute justice. The payment itself had less significance as wealth than as proof that the kinsmen had done what was right. The failure to take revenge or to exact compensation was considered shameful. Hrothgar's anguish over the murders committed by Grendel is not only for the loss of his men but also for the shame of his inability either to kill Grendel or to exact a "death-price" from the killer. "It is always better / to avenge dear ones than to indulge in mourning" (lines 1384–85), Beowulf says to Hrothgar, who has been thrown back into despair by the revenge-slaying of his old friend Aeschere by Grendel's mother.

Yet the young Beowulf's attempt to comfort the bereaved old king by invoking the code of vengeance may be one of several instances of the poet's ironic treatment of the tragic futility of the never-ending blood feuds. The most graphic example in the poem of that irony is the Finnsburg episode, the lay sung by Hrothgar's hall-poet. The Danish princess Hildeburh, married to the Frisian king Finn—probably to put an end to a feud between those peoples—loses both her brother and her son when a bloody fight breaks out in the hall between a visiting party of Danes and her husband's men. The bodies are cremated together on a huge funeral pyre: "The glutton element flamed and consumed / the dead of both sides. Their great days were gone" (lines 1124–25).

Such feuds, the staple subject of Germanic epic and saga, have only a peripheral place in the poem. Instead, the poem turns on Beowulf's three great fights against preternatural evil, which inhabits the dangerous and demonic space surrounding human society. He undertakes the fight against Grendel to save the Danes from the monster and to exact vengeance for the men Grendel has slain. Another motive is to demonstrate his strength and courage and thereby to enhance his personal glory. Hrothgar's magnificent gifts become the material emblems of that glory. Revenge and glory also motivate Beowulf's slaying of Grendel's mother. He undertakes his last battle against the dragon, however, only because there is no other way to save his own people.

A somber and dignified elegiac mood pervades *Beowulf*. The poem opens and closes with the description of a funeral and is filled with laments for the dead. Our first view of Beowulf is of an ambitious young hero. At the end, he has become an old king, facing the dragon and death. His people mourn him and praise him, as does the poet, for his nobility, generosity, courage, and, what is less common in Germanic heroes, kindness to his people. The poet's elegiac tone may be informed by something more than the duty to "praise a prince whom he holds dear / and cherish his memory when that moment comes / when he has to be convoyed from his bodily home" (lines 3175–

77). The entire poem could be viewed as the poet's lament for heroes like Beowulf who went into the darkness without the light of his own Christian faith.

The present verse translation is by the Irish poet Seamus Heaney, who received the Nobel Prize for literature in 1995. Selections from Heaney's own poems appear in Volume 2 of the anthology. His *Beowulf* is both a translation of one of the oldest English poems and a personal response to a work that speaks to a modern poet about the violence of our own century and the courage with which some men and women have faced up to it.

TRIBES AND GENEALOGIES

1. *The Danes (Bright-, Half-, Ring-, Spear-, North-, East-, South-, West-Danes; Shield-ings, Honor-, Victor-, War-Shieldings; Ing's friends)*

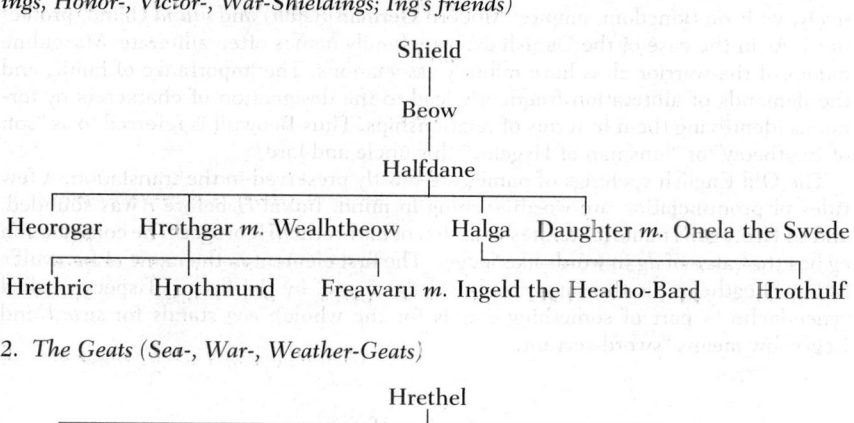

2. *The Geats (Sea-, War-, Weather-Geats)*

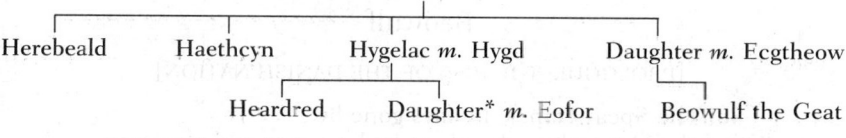

3. *The Swedes*

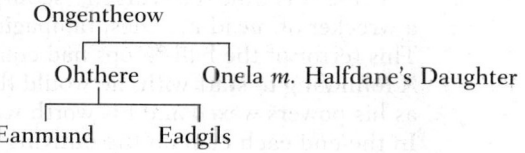

4. *Miscellaneous*

A. The Half-Danes (also called Shieldings) involved in the fight at Finnsburg may represent a different tribe from the Danes described above. Their king Hoc had a son, Hnaef, who succeeded him, and a daughter Hildeburh, who married Finn, king of the Jutes.

B. The Jutes or Frisians are represented as enemies of the Danes in the fight at Finnsburg and as allies of the Franks or Hugas at the time Hygelac the Geat made the attack in which he lost his life and from which Beowulf swam home. Also allied with the Franks at this time were the Hetware.

* The daughter of Hygelac who was given to Eofor may have been born to him by a former wife, older than Hygd.

C. The Heatho-Bards (i.e., "Battle-Bards") are represented as inveterate enemies of the Danes. Their king Froda had been killed in an attack on the Danes, and Hrothgar's attempt to make peace with them by marrying his daughter Freawaru to Froda's son Ingeld failed when the latter attacked Heorot. The attack was repulsed, although Heorot was burned.

A NOTE ON NAMES

Old English, like Modern German, contained many compound words, most of which have been lost in Modern English. Most of the names in *Beowulf* are compounds. Hrothgar is a combination of words meaning "glory" and "spear"; the name of his older brother, Heorogar, comes from "army" and "spear"; Hrothgar's sons Hrethric and Hrothmund contain the first elements of their father's name combined, respectively, with *ric* (kingdom, empire; Modern German *Reich*) and *mund* (hand, protection). As in the case of the Danish dynasty, family names often alliterate. Masculine names of the warrior class have military associations. The importance of family and the demands of alliteration frequently lead to the designation of characters by formulas identifying them in terms of relationships. Thus Beowulf is referred to as "son of Ecgtheow" or "kinsman of Hygelac" (his uncle and lord).

The Old English spellings of names are mostly preserved in the translation. A few rules of pronunciation are worth keeping in mind. Initial *H* before *r* was sounded, and so Hrothgar's name alliterates with that of his brother Heorogar. The combination *cg* has the value of *dg* in words like "edge." The first element in the name of Beowulf's father "Ecgtheow" is the same word as "edge," and, by the figure of speech called synecdoche (a part of something stands for the whole), *ecg* stands for *sword* and Ecgtheow means "sword-servant."

Beowulf

[PROLOGUE: THE RISE OF THE DANISH NATION]

So. The Spear-Danes[1] in days gone by
and the kings who ruled them had courage and greatness.
We have heard of those princes' heroic campaigns.
There was Shield Sheafson,[2] scourge of many tribes,
5   a wrecker of mead-benches, rampaging among foes.
This terror of the hall-troops had come far.
A foundling to start with, he would flourish later on
as his powers waxed and his worth was proved.
In the end each clan on the outlying coasts
10   beyond the whale-road had to yield to him
and begin to pay tribute. That was one good king.
    Afterward a boy-child was born to Shield,
a cub in the yard, a comfort sent
by God to that nation. He knew what they had tholed,[3]

---

1. There are different compound names for tribes, often determined by alliteration in Old English poetry. Line 1 reads, *"Hwæt, we Gar-dena in geardagum,"* where alliteration falls on *Gar* (spear) and *gear* (year). Old English hard and soft *g* (spelled *y* in Modern English) alliterate. The compound *geardagum* derives from "year," used in the special sense of "long ago," and "days" and survives in the archaic expression "days of yore."

2. Shield is the name of the founder of the Danish royal line. Sheafson translates *Scefing*, i.e., *sheaf* + the patronymic suffix *-ing*. Because Sheaf was a "foundling" (line 7: *feasceaft funden*, i.e., found destitute) who arrived by sea (lines 45–46), it is likely that as a child Shield brought with him only a sheaf, a symbol of fruitfulness.

3. Suffered, endured.

15   the long times and troubles they'd come through
     without a leader; so the Lord of Life,
     the glorious Almighty, made this man renowned.
     Shield had fathered a famous son:
     Beow's name was known through the north.
20   And a young prince must be prudent like that,
     giving freely while his father lives
     so that afterward in age when fighting starts
     steadfast companions will stand by him
     and hold the line. Behavior that's admired
25   is the path to power among people everywhere.
       Shield was still thriving when his time came
     and he crossed over into the Lord's keeping.
     His warrior band did what he bade them
     when he laid down the law among the Danes:
30   they shouldered him out to the sea's flood,
     the chief they revered who had long ruled them.
     A ring-whorled prow rode in the harbor,
     ice-clad, outbound, a craft for a prince.
     They stretched their beloved lord in his boat,
35   laid out by the mast, amidships,
     the great ring-giver. Far-fetched treasures
     were piled upon him, and precious gear.
     I never heard before of a ship so well furbished
     with battle-tackle, bladed weapons
40   and coats of mail. The massed treasure
     was loaded on top of him: it would travel far
     on out into the ocean's sway.
     They decked his body no less bountifully
     with offerings than those first ones did
45   who cast him away when he was a child
     and launched him alone out over the waves.[4]
     And they set a gold standard up
     high above his head and let him drift
     to wind and tide, bewailing him
50   and mourning their loss. No man can tell,
     no wise man in hall or weathered veteran
     knows for certain who salvaged that load.
       Then it fell to Beow to keep the forts.
     He was well regarded and ruled the Danes
55   for a long time after his father took leave
     of his life on earth. And then his heir,
     the great Halfdane,[5] held sway
     for as long as he lived, their elder and warlord.
     He was four times a father, this fighter prince:
60   one by one they entered the world,
     Heorogar, Hrothgar, the good Halga,
     and a daughter, I have heard, who was Onela's queen,

---

4. See n. 2, above. Since Shield was found destitute, "no less bountifully" is litotes or understatement; the ironic reminder that he came with
nothing (line 43) emphasizes the reversal of his
fortunes.

5. Probably named so because, according to one
source, his mother was a Swedish princess.

a balm in bed to the battle-scarred Swede.
　　The fortunes of war favored Hrothgar.
65　Friends and kinsmen flocked to his ranks,
young followers, a force that grew
to be a mighty army. So his mind turned
to hall-building: he handed down orders
for men to work on a great mead-hall
70　meant to be a wonder of the world forever;
it would be his throne-room and there he would dispense
his God-given goods to young and old—
but not the common land or people's lives.[6]
Far and wide through the world, I have heard,
75　orders for work to adorn that wallstead
were sent to many peoples. And soon it stood there
finished and ready, in full view,
the hall of halls. Heorot was the name[7]
he had settled on it, whose utterance was law.
80　Nor did he renege, but doled out rings
and torques at the table. The hall towered,
its gables wide and high and awaiting
a barbarous burning.[8] That doom abided,
but in time it would come: the killer instinct
85　unleashed among in-laws, the blood-lust rampant.[9]

[HEOROT IS ATTACKED]

　　Then a powerful demon,[1] a prowler through the dark,
nursed a hard grievance. It harrowed him
to hear the din of the loud banquet
every day in the hall, the harp being struck
90　and the clear song of a skilled poet
telling with mastery of man's beginnings,
how the Almighty had made the earth
a gleaming plain girdled with waters;
in His splendor He set the sun and the moon
95　to be earth's lamplight, lanterns for men,
and filled the broad lap of the world
with branches and leaves; and quickened life
in every other thing that moved.
　　So times were pleasant for the people there
100　until finally one, a fiend out of hell,
began to work his evil in the world.
Grendel was the name of this grim demon
haunting the marches, marauding round the heath
and the desolate fens; he had dwelt for a time
105　in misery among the banished monsters,

6. The king could not dispose of land used by all, such as a common pasture, or of slaves.
7. I.e., "Hart," from antlers fastened to the gables or because the crossed gable-ends resembled a stag's antlers; the hart was also an icon of royalty.
8. An allusion to the future destruction of Heorot by fire, probably in a raid by the Heatho-Bards.

9. As told later (lines 2020–69), Hrothgar plans to marry a daughter to Ingeld, chief of the Heatho-Bards, in hopes of resolving a long-standing feud. See previous note.
1. The poet withholds the name for several lines. He does the same with the name of the hero as well as others.

Cain's clan, whom the Creator had outlawed
and condemned as outcasts.[2] For the killing of Abel
the Eternal Lord had exacted a price:
Cain got no good from committing that murder
110 because the Almighty made him anathema
and out of the curse of his exile there sprang
ogres and elves and evil phantoms
and the giants too who strove with God
time and again until He gave them their reward.
115   So, after nightfall, Grendel set out
for the lofty house, to see how the Ring-Danes
were settling into it after their drink,
and there he came upon them, a company of the best
asleep from their feasting, insensible to pain
120 and human sorrow. Suddenly then
the God-cursed brute was creating havoc:
greedy and grim, he grabbed thirty men
from their resting places and rushed to his lair,
flushed up and inflamed from the raid,
125 blundering back with the butchered corpses.
    Then as dawn brightened and the day broke,
Grendel's powers of destruction were plain:
their wassail was over, they wept to heaven
and mourned under morning. Their mighty prince,
130 the storied leader, sat stricken and helpless,
humiliated by the loss of his guard,
bewildered and stunned, staring aghast
at the demon's trail, in deep distress.
He was numb with grief, but got no respite
135 for one night later merciless Grendel
struck again with more gruesome murders.
Malignant by nature, he never showed remorse.
It was easy then to meet with a man
shifting himself to a safer distance
140 to bed in the bothies,[3] for who could be blind
to the evidence of his eyes, the obviousness
of the hall-watcher's hate? Whoever escaped
kept a weather-eye open and moved away.
    So Grendel ruled in defiance of right,
145 one against all, until the greatest house
in the world stood empty, a deserted wallstead.
For twelve winters, seasons of woe,
the lord of the Shieldings[4] suffered under
his load of sorrow; and so, before long,
150 the news was known over the whole world.
Sad lays were sung about the beset king,
the vicious raids and ravages of Grendel,
his long and unrelenting feud,
nothing but war; how he would never

2. See Genesis 4.9–12.
3. Huts, outlying buildings. Evidently Grendel wants only to dominate the hall.
4. The descendants of Shield, another name for the Danes.

155 parley or make peace with any Dane
nor stop his death-dealing nor pay the death-price.[5]
No counselor could ever expect
fair reparation from those rabid hands.
All were endangered; young and old
160 were hunted down by that dark death-shadow
who lurked and swooped in the long nights
on the misty moors; nobody knows
where these reavers from hell roam on their errands.
        So Grendel waged his lonely war,
165 inflicting constant cruelties on the people,
atrocious hurt. He took over Heorot,
haunted the glittering hall after dark,
but the throne itself, the treasure-seat,
he was kept from approaching; he was the Lord's outcast.
170   These were hard times, heartbreaking
for the prince of the Shieldings; powerful counselors,
the highest in the land, would lend advice,
plotting how best the bold defenders
might resist and beat off sudden attacks.
175 Sometimes at pagan shrines they vowed
offerings to idols, swore oaths
that the killer of souls[6] might come to their aid
and save the people. That was their way,
their heathenish hope; deep in their hearts
180 they remembered hell. The Almighty Judge
of good deeds and bad, the Lord God,
Head of the Heavens and High King of the World,
was unknown to them. Oh, cursed is he
who in time of trouble has to thrust his soul
185 in the fire's embrace, forfeiting help;
he has nowhere to turn. But blessed is he
who after death can approach the Lord
and find friendship in the Father's embrace.

[THE HERO COMES TO HEOROT]

        So that troubled time continued, woe
190 that never stopped, steady affliction
for Halfdane's son, too hard an ordeal.
There was panic after dark, people endured
raids in the night, riven by the terror.
        When he heard about Grendel, Hygelac's thane
195 was on home ground, over in Geatland.
There was no one else like him alive.
In his day, he was the mightiest man on earth,
highborn and powerful. He ordered a boat
that would ply the waves. He announced his plan:
200 to sail the swan's road and seek out that king,

5. I.e., *wergild* (man-price); monetary compensation for the life of the slain man is the only way,
according to Germanic law, to settle a feud peacefully.
6. I.e., the devil. Heathen gods were thought to be
devils.

the famous prince who needed defenders.
Nobody tried to keep him from going,
no elder denied him, dear as he was to them.
Instead, they inspected omens and spurred
205 his ambition to go, whilst he moved about
like the leader he was, enlisting men,
the best he could find; with fourteen others
the warrior boarded the boat as captain,
a canny pilot along coast and currents.
210   Time went by, the boat was on water,
in close under the cliffs.
Men climbed eagerly up the gangplank,
sand churned in surf, warriors loaded
a cargo of weapons, shining war-gear
215 in the vessel's hold, then heaved out,
away with a will in their wood-wreathed ship.
Over the waves, with the wind behind her
and foam at her neck, she flew like a bird
until her curved prow had covered the distance,
220 and on the following day, at the due hour,
those seafarers sighted land,
sunlit cliffs, sheer crags
and looming headlands, the landfall they sought.
It was the end of their voyage and the Geats vaulted
225 over the side, out on to the sand,
and moored their ship. There was a clash of mail
and a thresh of gear. They thanked God
for that easy crossing on a calm sea.
    When the watchman on the wall, the Shieldings' lookout
230 whose job it was to guard the sea-cliffs,
saw shields glittering on the gangplank
and battle-equipment being unloaded
he had to find out who and what
the arrivals were. So he rode to the shore,
235 this horseman of Hrothgar's, and challenged them
in formal terms, flourishing his spear:
"What kind of men are you who arrive
rigged out for combat in your coats of mail,
sailing here over the sea-lanes
240 in your steep-hulled boat? I have been stationed
as lookout on this coast for a long time.
My job is to watch the waves for raiders,
any danger to the Danish shore.
Never before has a force under arms
245 disembarked so openly—not bothering to ask
if the sentries allowed them safe passage
or the clan had consented. Nor have I seen
a mightier man-at-arms on this earth
than the one standing here: unless I am mistaken,
250 he is truly noble. This is no mere
hanger-on in a hero's armor.
So now, before you fare inland

as interlopers, I have to be informed
about who you are and where you hail from.
255   Outsiders from across the water,
I say it again: the sooner you tell
where you come from and why, the better."
      The leader of the troop unlocked his word-hoard;
the distinguished one delivered this answer:
260   "We belong by birth to the Geat people
and owe allegiance to Lord Hygelac.
In his day, my father was a famous man,
a noble warrior-lord named Ecgtheow.
He outlasted many a long winter
265   and went on his way. All over the world
men wise in counsel continue to remember him.
We come in good faith to find your lord
and nation's shield, the son of Halfdane.
Give us the right advice and direction.
270   We have arrived here on a great errand
to the lord of the Danes, and I believe therefore
there should be nothing hidden or withheld between us.
So tell us if what we have heard is true
about this threat, whatever it is,
275   this danger abroad in the dark nights,
this corpse-maker mongering death
in the Shieldings' country. I come to proffer
my wholehearted help and counsel.
I can show the wise Hrothgar a way
280   to defeat his enemy and find respite—
if any respite is to reach him, ever.
I can calm the turmoil and terror in his mind.
Otherwise, he must endure woes
and live with grief for as long as his hall
285   stands at the horizon on its high ground."
      Undaunted, sitting astride his horse,
the coast-guard answered: "Anyone with gumption
and a sharp mind will take the measure
of two things: what's said and what's done.
290   I believe what you have told me, that you are a troop
loyal to our king. So come ahead
with your arms and your gear, and I will guide you.
What's more, I'll order my own comrades
on their word of honor to watch your boat
295   down there on the strand—keep her safe
in her fresh tar, until the time comes
for her curved prow to preen on the waves
and bear this hero back to Geatland.
May one so valiant and venturesome
300   come unharmed through the clash of battle."
      So they went on their way. The ship rode the water,
broad-beamed, bound by its hawser
and anchored fast. Boar-shapes[7] flashed

---

7. Carved images of boars were placed on helmets, probably as good luck charms to protect the warriors.

above their cheek-guards, the brightly forged
305 work of goldsmiths, watching over
those stern-faced men. They marched in step,
hurrying on till the timbered hall
rose before them, radiant with gold.
Nobody on earth knew of another
310 building like it. Majesty lodged there,
its light shone over many lands.
So their gallant escort guided them
to that dazzling stronghold and indicated
the shortest way to it; then the noble warrior
315 wheeled on his horse and spoke these words:
"It is time for me to go. May the Almighty
Father keep you and in His kindness
watch over your exploits. I'm away to the sea,
back on alert against enemy raiders."
320   It was a paved track, a path that kept them
in marching order. Their mail-shirts glinted,
hard and hand-linked; the high-gloss iron
of their armor rang. So they duly arrived
in their grim war-graith[8] and gear at the hall,
325 and, weary from the sea, stacked wide shields
of the toughest hardwood against the wall,
then collapsed on the benches; battle-dress
and weapons clashed. They collected their spears
in a seafarers' stook, a stand of grayish
330 tapering ash. And the troops themselves
were as good as their weapons.
                           Then a proud warrior
questioned the men concerning their origins:
"Where do you come from, carrying these
decorated shields and shirts of mail,
335 these cheek-hinged helmets and javelins?
I am Hrothgar's herald and officer.
I have never seen so impressive or large
an assembly of strangers. Stoutness of heart,
bravery not banishment, must have brought you to Hrothgar."
340   The man whose name was known for courage,
the Geat leader, resolute in his helmet,
answered in return: "We are retainers
from Hygelac's band. Beowulf is my name.
If your lord and master, the most renowned
345 son of Halfdane, will hear me out
and graciously allow me to greet him in person,
I am ready and willing to report my errand."
    Wulfgar replied, a Wendel chief
renowned as a warrior, well known for his wisdom
350 and the temper of his mind: "I will take this message,
in accordance with your wish, to our noble king,
our dear lord, friend of the Danes,
the giver of rings. I will go and ask him

---

8. "Graith": archaic for apparel.

about your coming here, then hurry back
355 with whatever reply it pleases him to give."
With that he turned to where Hrothgar sat,
an old man among retainers;
the valiant follower stood foursquare
in front of his king: he knew the courtesies.
360 Wulfgar addressed his dear lord:
"People from Geatland have put ashore.
They have sailed far over the wide sea.
They call the chief in charge of their band
by the name of Beowulf. They beg, my lord,
365 an audience with you, exchange of words
and formal greeting. Most gracious Hrothgar,
do not refuse them, but grant them a reply.
From their arms and appointment, they appear well born
and worthy of respect, especially the one
370 who has led them this far: he is formidable indeed."
Hrothgar, protector of Shieldings, replied:
"I used to know him when he was a young boy.
His father before him was called Ecgtheow.
Hrethel the Geat[9] gave Ecgtheow
375 his daughter in marriage. This man is their son,
here to follow up an old friendship.
A crew of seamen who sailed for me once
with a gift-cargo across to Geatland
returned with marvelous tales about him:
380 a thane, they declared, with the strength of thirty
in the grip of each hand. Now Holy God
has, in His goodness, guided him here
to the West-Danes, to defend us from Grendel.
This is my hope; and for his heroism
385 I will recompense him with a rich treasure.
Go immediately, bid him and the Geats
he has in attendance to assemble and enter.
Say, moreover, when you speak to them,
they are welcome to Denmark."
At the door of the hall,
390 Wulfgar duly delivered the message:
"My lord, the conquering king of the Danes,
bids me announce that he knows your ancestry;
also that he welcomes you here to Heorot
and salutes your arrival from across the sea.
395 You are free now to move forward
to meet Hrothgar in helmets and armor,
but shields must stay here and spears be stacked
until the outcome of the audience is clear."
The hero arose, surrounded closely
400 by his powerful thanes. A party remained
under orders to keep watch on the arms;
the rest proceeded, led by their prince
under Heorot's roof. And standing on the hearth

---

9. Hygelac's father and Beowulf's grandfather.

in webbed links that the smith had woven,
405 the fine-forged mesh of his gleaming mail-shirt,
resolute in his helmet, Beowulf spoke:
"Greetings to Hrothgar. I am Hygelac's kinsman,
one of his hall-troop. When I was younger,
I had great triumphs. Then news of Grendel,
410 hard to ignore, reached me at home:
sailors brought stories of the plight you suffer
in this legendary hall, how it lies deserted,
empty and useless once the evening light
hides itself under heaven's dome.
415 So every elder and experienced councilman
among my people supported my resolve
to come here to you, King Hrothgar,
because all knew of my awesome strength.
They had seen me boltered[1] in the blood of enemies
420 when I battled and bound five beasts,
raided a troll-nest and in the night-sea
slaughtered sea-brutes. I have suffered extremes
and avenged the Geats (their enemies brought it
upon themselves; I devastated them).
425 Now I mean to be a match for Grendel,
settle the outcome in single combat.
And so, my request, O king of Bright-Danes,
dear prince of the Shieldings, friend of the people
and their ring of defense, my one request
430 is that you won't refuse me, who have come this far,
the privilege of purifying Heorot,
with my own men to help me, and nobody else.
I have heard moreover that the monster scorns
in his reckless way to use weapons;
435 therefore, to heighten Hygelac's fame
and gladden his heart, I hereby renounce
sword and the shelter of the broad shield,
the heavy war-board: hand-to-hand
is how it will be, a life-and-death
440 fight with the fiend. Whichever one death fells
must deem it a just judgment by God.
If Grendel wins, it will be a gruesome day;
he will glut himself on the Geats in the war-hall,
swoop without fear on that flower of manhood
445 as on others before. Then my face won't be there
to be covered in death: he will carry me away
as he goes to ground, gorged and bloodied;
he will run gloating with my raw corpse
and feed on it alone, in a cruel frenzy
450 fouling his moor-nest. No need then
to lament for long or lay out my body:[2]
if the battle takes me, send back
this breast-webbing that Weland[3] fashioned

---

1. Clotted, sticky.
2. I.e., for burial. Hrothgar will not need to give

Beowulf an expensive funeral.
3. Famed blacksmith in Germanic legend.

and Hrethel gave me, to Lord Hygelac.
455 Fate goes ever as fate must."
     Hrothgar, the helmet of Shieldings, spoke:
"Beowulf, my friend, you have traveled here
to favor us with help and to fight for us.
There was a feud one time, begun by your father.
460 With his own hands he had killed Heatholaf
who was a Wulfing; so war was looming
and his people, in fear of it, forced him to leave.
He came away then over rolling waves
to the South-Danes here, the sons of honor.
465 I was then in the first flush of kingship,
establishing my sway over the rich strongholds
of this heroic land. Heorogar,
my older brother and the better man,
also a son of Halfdane's, had died.
470 Finally I healed the feud by paying:
I shipped a treasure-trove to the Wulfings,
and Ecgtheow acknowledged me with oaths of allegiance.
     "It bothers me to have to burden anyone
with all the grief that Grendel has caused
475 and the havoc he has wreaked upon us in Heorot,
our humiliations. My household-guard
are on the wane, fate sweeps them away
into Grendel's clutches—but God can easily
halt these raids and harrowing attacks!
480   "Time and again, when the goblets passed
and seasoned fighters got flushed with beer
they would pledge themselves to protect Heorot
and wait for Grendel with their whetted swords.
But when dawn broke and day crept in
485 over each empty, blood-spattered bench,
the floor of the mead-hall where they had feasted
would be slick with slaughter. And so they died,
faithful retainers, and my following dwindled.
Now take your place at the table, relish
490 the triumph of heroes to your heart's content."

[FEAST AT HEOROT]

     Then a bench was cleared in that banquet hall
so the Geats could have room to be together
and the party sat, proud in their bearing,
strong and stalwart. An attendant stood by
495 with a decorated pitcher, pouring bright
helpings of mead. And the minstrel sang,
filling Heorot with his head-clearing voice,
gladdening that great rally of Geats and Danes.
     From where he crouched at the king's feet,
500 Unferth, a son of Ecglaf's, spoke
contrary words. Beowulf's coming,
his sea-braving, made him sick with envy:

he could not brook or abide the fact
that anyone else alive under heaven
505 might enjoy greater regard than he did:
"Are you the Beowulf who took on Breca
in a swimming match on the open sea,
risking the water just to prove that you could win?
It was sheer vanity made you venture out
510 on the main deep. And no matter who tried,
friend or foe, to deflect the pair of you,
neither would back down: the sea-test obsessed you.
You waded in, embracing water,
taking its measure, mastering currents,
515 riding on the swell. The ocean swayed,
winter went wild in the waves, but you vied
for seven nights; and then he outswam you,
came ashore the stronger contender.
He was cast up safe and sound one morning
520 among the Heatho-Reams, then made his way
to where he belonged in Bronding country,
home again, sure of his ground
in strongroom and bawn.⁴ So Breca made good
his boast upon you and was proved right.
525 No matter, therefore, how you may have fared
in every bout and battle until now,
this time you'll be worsted; no one has ever
outlasted an entire night against Grendel."
       Beowulf, Ecgtheow's son, replied:
530 "Well, friend Unferth, you have had your say
about Breca and me. But it was mostly beer
that was doing the talking. The truth is this:
when the going was heavy in those high waves,
I was the strongest swimmer of all.
535 We'd been children together and we grew up
daring ourselves to outdo each other,
boasting and urging each other to risk
our lives on the sea. And so it turned out.
Each of us swam holding a sword,
540 a naked, hard-proofed blade for protection
against the whale-beasts. But Breca could never
move out farther or faster from me
than I could manage to move from him.
Shoulder to shoulder, we struggled on
545 for five nights, until the long flow
and pitch of the waves, the perishing cold,
night falling and winds from the north
drove us apart. The deep boiled up
and its wallowing sent the sea-brutes wild.
550 My armor helped me to hold out;
my hard-ringed chain-mail, hand-forged and linked,

4. Fortified outwork of a court or castle. The word was used by English planters in Ulster to describe
fortified dwellings they erected on lands confiscated from the Irish [Translator's note].

a fine, close-fitting filigree of gold,
kept me safe when some ocean creature
pulled me to the bottom. Pinioned fast
555 and swathed in its grip, I was granted one
final chance: my sword plunged
and the ordeal was over. Through my own hands,
the fury of battle had finished off the sea-beast.
   "Time and again, foul things attacked me,
560 lurking and stalking, but I lashed out,
gave as good as I got with my sword.
My flesh was not for feasting on,
there would be no monsters gnawing and gloating
over their banquet at the bottom of the sea.
565 Instead, in the morning, mangled and sleeping
the sleep of the sword, they slopped and floated
like the ocean's leavings. From now on
sailors would be safe, the deep-sea raids
were over for good. Light came from the east,
570 bright guarantee of God, and the waves
went quiet; I could see headlands
and buffeted cliffs. Often, for undaunted courage,
fate spares the man it has not already marked.
However it occurred, my sword had killed
575 nine sea-monsters. Such night dangers
and hard ordeals I have never heard of
nor of a man more desolate in surging waves.
But worn out as I was, I survived,
came through with my life. The ocean lifted
580 and laid me ashore, I landed safe
on the coast of Finland.
               Now I cannot recall
any fight you entered, Unferth,
that bears comparison. I don't boast when I say
that neither you nor Breca were ever much
585 celebrated for swordsmanship
or for facing danger on the field of battle.
You killed your own kith and kin,
so for all your cleverness and quick tongue,
you will suffer damnation in the depths of hell.
590 The fact is, Unferth, if you were truly
as keen or courageous as you claim to be
Grendel would never have got away with
such unchecked atrocity, attacks on your king,
havoc in Heorot and horrors everywhere.
595 But he knows he need never be in dread
of your blade making a mizzle of his blood
or of vengeance arriving ever from this quarter—
from the Victory-Shieldings, the shoulderers of the spear.
He knows he can trample down you Danes
600 to his heart's content, humiliate and murder
without fear of reprisal. But he will find me different.
I will show him how Geats shape to kill

in the heat of battle. Then whoever wants to
may go bravely to mead, when the morning light,
605   scarfed in sun-dazzle, shines forth from the south
and brings another daybreak to the world."
    Then the gray-haired treasure-giver was glad;
far-famed in battle, the prince of Bright-Danes
and keeper of his people counted on Beowulf,
610   on the warrior's steadfastness and his word.
So the laughter started, the din got louder
and the crowd was happy. Wealhtheow came in,
Hrothgar's queen, observing the courtesies.
Adorned in her gold, she graciously saluted
615   the men in the hall, then handed the cup
first to Hrothgar, their homeland's guardian,
urging him to drink deep and enjoy it
because he was dear to them. And he drank it down
like the warlord he was, with festive cheer.
620   So the Helming woman went on her rounds,
queenly and dignified, decked out in rings,
offering the goblet to all ranks,
treating the household and the assembled troop,
until it was Beowulf's turn to take it from her hand.
625   With measured words she welcomed the Geat
and thanked God for granting her wish
that a deliverer she could believe in would arrive
to ease their afflictions. He accepted the cup,
a daunting man, dangerous in action
630   and eager for it always. He addressed Wealhtheow;
Beowulf, son of Ecgtheow, said:
"I had a fixed purpose when I put to sea.
As I sat in the boat with my band of men,
I meant to perform to the uttermost
635   what your people wanted or perish in the attempt,
in the fiend's clutches. And I shall fulfill that purpose,
prove myself with a proud deed
or meet my death here in the mead-hall."
This formal boast by Beowulf the Geat
640   pleased the lady well and she went to sit
by Hrothgar, regal and arrayed with gold.
    Then it was like old times in the echoing hall,
proud talk and the people happy,
loud and excited; until soon enough
645   Halfdane's heir had to be away
to his night's rest. He realized
that the demon was going to descend on the hall,
that he had plotted all day, from dawn-light
until darkness gathered again over the world
650   and stealthy night-shapes came stealing forth
under the cloud-murk. The company stood
as the two leaders took leave of each other:
Hrothgar wished Beowulf health and good luck,
named him hall-warden and announced as follows:

655 "Never, since my hand could hold a shield
have I entrusted or given control
of the Danes' hall to anyone but you.
Ward and guard it, for it is the greatest of houses.
Be on your mettle now, keep in mind your fame,
660 beware of the enemy. There's nothing you wish for
that won't be yours if you win through alive."

[THE FIGHT WITH GRENDEL]

Hrothgar departed then with his house-guard.
The lord of the Shieldings, their shelter in war,
left the mead-hall to lie with Wealhtheow,
665 his queen and bedmate. The King of Glory
(as people learned) had posted a lookout
who was a match for Grendel, a guard against monsters,
special protection to the Danish prince.
And the Geat placed complete trust
670 in his strength of limb and the Lord's favor.
He began to remove his iron breast-mail,
took off the helmet and handed his attendant
the patterned sword, a smith's masterpiece,
ordering him to keep the equipment guarded.
675 And before he bedded down, Beowulf,
that prince of goodness, proudly asserted:
"When it comes to fighting, I count myself
as dangerous any day as Grendel.
So it won't be a cutting edge I'll wield
680 to mow him down, easily as I might.
He has no idea of the arts of war,
of shield or sword-play, although he does possess
a wild strength. No weapons, therefore,
for either this night: unarmed he shall face me
685 if face me he dares. And may the Divine Lord
in His wisdom grant the glory of victory
to whichever side He sees fit."
Then down the brave man lay with his bolster
under his head and his whole company
690 of sea-rovers at rest beside him.
None of them expected he would ever see
his homeland again or get back
to his native place and the people who reared him.
They knew too well the way it was before,
695 how often the Danes had fallen prey
to death in the mead-hall. But the Lord was weaving
a victory on His war-loom for the Weather-Geats.
Through the strength of one they all prevailed;
they would crush their enemy and come through
700 in triumph and gladness. The truth is clear:
Almighty God rules over mankind
and always has.
Then out of the night

came the shadow-stalker, stealthy and swift.
The hall-guards were slack, asleep at their posts,
705   all except one; it was widely understood
that as long as God disallowed it,
the fiend could not bear them to his shadow-bourne.
One man, however, was in fighting mood,
awake and on edge, spoiling for action.
710   In off the moors, down through the mist-bands
God-cursed Grendel came greedily loping.
The bane of the race of men roamed forth,
hunting for a prey in the high hall.
Under the cloud-murk he moved toward it
715   until it shone above him, a sheer keep
of fortified gold. Nor was that the first time
he had scouted the grounds of Hrothgar's dwelling—
although never in his life, before or since,
did he find harder fortune or hall-defenders.
720   Spurned and joyless, he journeyed on ahead
and arrived at the bawn.[5] The iron-braced door
turned on its hinge when his hands touched it.
Then his rage boiled over, he ripped open
the mouth of the building, maddening for blood,
725   pacing the length of the patterned floor
with his loathsome tread, while a baleful light,
flame more than light, flared from his eyes.
He saw many men in the mansion, sleeping,
a ranked company of kinsmen and warriors
730   quartered together. And his glee was demonic,
picturing the mayhem: before morning
he would rip life from limb and devour them,
feed on their flesh; but his fate that night
was due to change, his days of ravening
had come to an end.
735   Mighty and canny,
Hygelac's kinsman was keenly watching
for the first move the monster would make.
Nor did the creature keep him waiting
but struck suddenly and started in;
740   he grabbed and mauled a man on his bench,
bit into his bone-lappings, bolted down his blood
and gorged on him in lumps, leaving the body
utterly lifeless, eaten up
hand and foot. Venturing closer,
745   his talon was raised to attack Beowulf
where he lay on the bed, he was bearing in
with open claw when the alert hero's
comeback and armlock forestalled him utterly.
The captain of evil discovered himself
750   in a handgrip harder than anything
he had ever encountered in any man

5. See p. 43, n. 4.

on the face of the earth. Every bone in his body
quailed and recoiled, but he could not escape.
He was desperate to flee to his den and hide
755   with the devil's litter, for in all his days
he had never been clamped or cornered like this.
Then Hygelac's trusty retainer recalled
his bedtime speech, sprang to his feet
and got a firm hold. Fingers were bursting,
760   the monster back-tracking, the man overpowering.
The dread of the land was desperate to escape,
to take a roundabout road and flee
to his lair in the fens. The latching power
in his fingers weakened; it was the worst trip
765   the terror-monger had taken to Heorot.
And now the timbers trembled and sang,
a hall-session[6] that harrowed every Dane
inside the stockade: stumbling in fury,
the two contenders crashed through the building.
770   The hall clattered and hammered, but somehow
survived the onslaught and kept standing:
it was handsomely structured, a sturdy frame
braced with the best of blacksmith's work
inside and out. The story goes
775   that as the pair struggled, mead-benches were smashed
and sprung off the floor, gold fittings and all.
Before then, no Shielding elder would believe
there was any power or person upon earth
capable of wrecking their horn-rigged hall
780   unless the burning embrace of a fire
engulf it in flame. Then an extraordinary
wail arose, and bewildering fear
came over the Danes. Everyone felt it
who heard that cry as it echoed off the wall,
785   a God-cursed scream and strain of catastrophe,
the howl of the loser, the lament of the hell-serf
keening his wound. He was overwhelmed,
manacled tight by the man who of all men
was foremost and strongest in the days of this life.
790   But the earl-troop's leader was not inclined
to allow his caller to depart alive:
he did not consider that life of much account
to anyone anywhere. Time and again,
Beowulf's warriors worked to defend
795   their lord's life, laying about them
as best they could, with their ancestral blades.
Stalwart in action, they kept striking out
on every side, seeking to cut
straight to the soul. When they joined the struggle
800   there was something they could not have known at the time,

---

6. In Hiberno-English the word "session" (*seissiún* in Irish) can mean a gathering where musicians and
singers perform for their own enjoyment [Translator's note].

that no blade on earth, no blacksmith's art
could ever damage their demon opponent.
He had conjured the harm from the cutting edge
of every weapon.[7] But his going away
805   out of this world and the days of his life
would be agony to him, and his alien spirit
would travel far into fiends' keeping.
    Then he who had harrowed the hearts of men
with pain and affliction in former times
810   and had given offense also to God
found that his bodily powers failed him.
Hygelac's kinsman kept him helplessly
locked in a handgrip. As long as either lived,
he was hateful to the other. The monster's whole
815   body was in pain; a tremendous wound
appeared on his shoulder. Sinews split
and the bone-lappings burst. Beowulf was granted
the glory of winning; Grendel was driven
under the fen-banks, fatally hurt,
820   to his desolate lair. His days were numbered,
the end of his life was coming over him,
he knew it for certain; and one bloody clash
had fulfilled the dearest wishes of the Danes.
The man who had lately landed among them,
825   proud and sure, had purged the hall,
kept it from harm; he was happy with his nightwork
and the courage he had shown. The Geat captain
had boldly fulfilled his boast to the Danes:
he had healed and relieved a huge distress,
830   unremitting humiliations,
the hard fate they'd been forced to undergo,
no small affliction. Clear proof of this
could be seen in the hand the hero displayed
high up near the roof: the whole of Grendel's
835   shoulder and arm, his awesome grasp.

[CELEBRATION AT HEOROT]

    Then morning came and many a warrior
gathered, as I've heard, around the gift-hall,
clan-chiefs flocking from far and near
down wide-ranging roads, wondering greatly
840   at the monster's footprints. His fatal departure
was regretted by no one who witnessed his trail,
the ignominious marks of his flight
where he'd skulked away, exhausted in spirit
and beaten in battle, bloodying the path,
845   hauling his doom to the demons' mere.[8]
The bloodshot water wallowed and surged,

7. Grendel is protected by a charm against metals.
8. A lake or pool, although we learn later that it has an outlet to the sea. Grendel's habitat.

there were loathsome upthrows and overturnings
of waves and gore and wound-slurry.
With his death upon him, he had dived deep
850 into his marsh-den, drowned out his life
and his heathen soul: hell claimed him there.
    Then away they rode, the old retainers
with many a young man following after,
a troop on horseback, in high spirits
855 on their bay steeds. Beowulf's doings
were praised over and over again.
Nowhere, they said, north or south
between the two seas or under the tall sky
on the broad earth was there anyone better
860 to raise a shield or to rule a kingdom.
Yet there was no laying of blame on their lord,
the noble Hrothgar; he was a good king.
    At times the war-band broke into a gallop,
letting their chestnut horses race
865 wherever they found the going good
on those well-known tracks. Meanwhile, a thane
of the king's household, a carrier of tales,
a traditional singer deeply schooled
in the lore of the past, linked a new theme
870 to a strict meter.[9] The man started
to recite with skill, rehearsing Beowulf's
triumphs and feats in well-fashioned lines,
entwining his words.
                              He told what he'd heard
repeated in songs about Sigemund's exploits,[1]
875 all of those many feats and marvels,
the struggles and wanderings of Waels's son,[2]
things unknown to anyone
except to Fitela, feuds and foul doings
confided by uncle to nephew when he felt
880 the urge to speak of them: always they had been
partners in the fight, friends in need.
They killed giants, their conquering swords
had brought them down.
                              After his death
Sigemund's glory   grew and grew
885 because of his courage   when he killed the dragon,
the guardian of the hoard.   Under gray stone
he had dared to enter   all by himself
to face the worst   without Fitela.
But it came to pass   that his sword plunged
890 right through   those radiant scales
and drove into the wall.   The dragon died of it.

---

9. I.e., an extemporaneous heroic poem in alliterative verse about Beowulf's deeds.
1. Tales about Sigemund, his nephew Sinfjotli
(Fitela), and his son Sigurth are found in a 13th-
century Old Icelandic collection of legends known

as the *Volsung Saga*. Analogous stories must have
been known to the poet and his audience, though
details differ.
2. Waels is the father of Sigemund.

His daring had given him   total possession
of the treasure-hoard,   his to dispose of
however he liked.   He loaded a boat:
895   Waels's son   weighted her hold
with dazzling spoils.   The hot dragon melted.
      Sigemund's name   was known everywhere.
He was utterly valiant   and venturesome,
a fence round his fighters   and flourished therefore
900   after King Heremod's[3]   prowess declined
and his campaigns slowed down.   The king was betrayed,
ambushed in Jutland,   overpowered
and done away with.   The waves of his grief
had beaten him down,   made him a burden,
905   a source of anxiety   to his own nobles:
that expedition   was often condemned
in those earlier times   by experienced men,
men who relied   on his lordship for redress,
who presumed that the part   of a prince was to thrive
910   on his father's throne   and defend the nation,
the Shielding land   where they lived and belonged,
its holdings and strongholds.   Such was Beowulf
in the affection of his friends   and of everyone alive.
But evil entered   into Heremod.
915   Meanwhile, the Danes kept racing their mounts
down sandy lanes. The light of day
broke and kept brightening. Bands of retainers
galloped in excitement to the gabled hall
to see the marvel; and the king himself,
920   guardian of the ring-hoard, goodness in person,
walked in majesty from the women's quarters
with a numerous train, attended by his queen
and her crowd of maidens, across to the mead-hall.
      When Hrothgar arrived at the hall, he spoke,
925   standing on the steps, under the steep eaves,
gazing toward the roofwork and Grendel's talon:
"First and foremost, let the Almighty Father
be thanked for this sight. I suffered a long
harrowing by Grendel. But the Heavenly Shepherd
930   can work His wonders always and everywhere.
Not long since, it seemed I would never
be granted the slightest solace or relief
from any of my burdens: the best of houses
glittered and reeked and ran with blood.
935   This one worry outweighed all others—
a constant distress to counselors entrusted
with defending the people's forts from assault
by monsters and demons. But now a man,
with the Lord's assistance, has accomplished something
940   none of us could manage before now

3. Heremod was a bad king, held up by the bard as the opposite of Beowulf, as Sigemund is held up as a
heroic prototype of Beowulf.

for all our efforts. Whoever she was
who brought forth this flower of manhood,
if she is still alive, that woman can say
that in her labor the Lord of Ages
945   bestowed a grace on her. So now, Beowulf,
I adopt you in my heart as a dear son.
Nourish and maintain this new connection,
you noblest of men; there'll be nothing you'll want for,
no worldly goods that won't be yours.
950   I have often honored smaller achievements,
recognized warriors not nearly as worthy,
lavished rewards on the less deserving.
But you have made yourself immortal
by your glorious action. May the God of Ages
955   continue to keep and requite you well."
    Beowulf, son of Ecgtheow, spoke:
"We have gone through with a glorious endeavor
and been much favored in this fight we dared
against the unknown. Nevertheless,
960   if you could have seen the monster himself
where he lay beaten, I would have been better pleased.
My plan was to pounce, pin him down
in a tight grip and grapple him to death—
have him panting for life, powerless and clasped
965   in my bare hands, his body in thrall.
But I couldn't stop him from slipping my hold.
The Lord allowed it, my lock on him
wasn't strong enough; he struggled fiercely
and broke and ran. Yet he bought his freedom
970   at a high price, for he left his hand
and arm and shoulder to show he had been here,
a cold comfort for having come among us.
And now he won't be long for this world.
He has done his worst but the wound will end him.
975   He is hasped and hooped and hirpling with pain,
limping and looped in it. Like a man outlawed
for wickedness, he must await
the mighty judgment of God in majesty."
    There was less tampering and big talk then
980   from Unferth the boaster, less of his blather
as the hall-thanes eyed the awful proof
of the hero's prowess, the splayed hand
up under the eaves. Every nail,
claw-scale and spur, every spike
985   and welt on the hand of that heathen brute
was like barbed steel. Everybody said
there was no honed iron hard enough
to pierce him through, no time-proofed blade
that could cut his brutal, blood-caked claw.
990   Then the order was given for all hands
to help to refurbish Heorot immediately:
men and women thronging the wine-hall,

getting it ready. Gold thread shone
in the wall-hangings, woven scenes
995   that attracted and held the eye's attention.
But iron-braced as the inside of it had been,
that bright room lay in ruins now.
The very doors had been dragged from their hinges.
Only the roof remained unscathed
1000   by the time the guilt-fouled fiend turned tail
in despair of his life. But death is not easily
escaped from by anyone:
all of us with souls, earth-dwellers
and children of men, must make our way
1005   to a destination already ordained
where the body, after the banqueting,
sleeps on its deathbed.
                              Then the due time arrived
for Halfdane's son to proceed to the hall.
The king himself would sit down to feast.
1010   No group ever gathered in greater numbers
or better order around their ring-giver.
The benches filled with famous men
who fell to with relish; round upon round
of mead was passed; those powerful kinsmen,
1015   Hrothgar and Hrothulf, were in high spirits
in the raftered hall. Inside Heorot
there was nothing but friendship. The Shielding nation
was not yet familiar with feud and betrayal.[4]
        Then Halfdane's son presented Beowulf
1020   with a gold standard as a victory gift,
an embroidered banner; also breast-mail
and a helmet; and a sword carried high,
that was both precious object and token of honor.
So Beowulf drank his drink, at ease;
1025   it was hardly a shame to be showered with such gifts
in front of the hall-troops. There haven't been many
moments, I am sure, when men exchanged
four such treasures at so friendly a sitting.
An embossed ridge, a band lapped with wire
1030   arched over the helmet: head-protection
to keep the keen-ground cutting edge
from damaging it when danger threatened
and the man was battling behind his shield.
Next the king ordered eight horses
1035   with gold bridles to be brought through the yard
into the hall. The harness of one
included a saddle of sumptuous design,
the battle-seat where the son of Halfdane
rode when he wished to join the sword-play:
1040   wherever the killing and carnage were the worst,

4. Probably an ironic allusion to the future usurpation of the throne from Hrothgar's sons by Hrothulf, although no such treachery is recorded of
Hrothulf, who is the hero of other Germanic stories.

he would be to the fore, fighting hard.
Then the Danish prince, descendant of Ing,
handed over both the arms and the horses,
urging Beowulf to use them well.
1045   And so their leader, the lord and guard
of coffer and strongroom, with customary grace
bestowed upon Beowulf both sets of gifts.
A fair witness can see how well each one behaved.
     The chieftain went on to reward the others:
1050   each man on the bench who had sailed with Beowulf
and risked the voyage received a bounty,
some treasured possession. And compensation,
a price in gold, was settled for the Geat
Grendel had cruelly killed earlier—
1055   as he would have killed more, had not mindful God
and one man's daring prevented that doom.
Past and present, God's will prevails.
Hence, understanding is always best
and a prudent mind. Whoever remains
1060   for long here in this earthly life
will enjoy and endure more than enough.
     They sang then and played to please the hero,
words and music for their warrior prince,
harp tunes and tales of adventure:
1065   there were high times on the hall benches,
and the king's poet performed his part
with the saga of Finn and his sons, unfolding
the tale of the fierce attack in Friesland
where Hnaef, king of the Danes, met death.[5]

     Hildeburh
1070   *had little cause*
       to credit the Jutes:
                 son and brother,
       she lost them both
                 on the battlefield.
       She, bereft
                 and blameless, they
       foredoomed, cut down
                 and spear-gored. She,
       the woman in shock,
1075   *waylaid by grief,*
       Hoc's daughter—
                 how could she not

5. The bard's lay is known as the Finnsburg Episode. Its allusive style makes the tale obscure in
many details, although some can be filled in from
a fragmentary Old English lay, which modern editors have entitled *The Fight at Finnsburg*. Hildeburh, the daughter of the former Danish king Hoc,
was married to Finn, king of Friesland, presumably
to help end a feud between their peoples. As the
episode opens, the feud has already broken out
again when a visiting party of Danes, led by Hildeburh's brother Hnaef, who has succeeded their
father, is attacked by a tribe called the Jutes. The
Jutes are subject to Finn but may be a clan distinct
from the Frisians, and Finn does not seem to have
instigated the attack. In the ensuing battle, both
Hnaef and the son of Hildeburh and Finn are
killed, and both sides suffer heavy losses.

lament her fate
>> when morning came
and the light broke
>> on her murdered dears?
And so farewell
>> delight on earth,
war carried away
1080 >> Finn's troop of thanes
all but a few.
>> How then could Finn
hold the line
>> or fight on
to the end with Hengest,
>> how save
the rump of his force
>> from that enemy chief?
So a truce was offered
1085 >> as follows:[6] first
separate quarters
>> to be cleared for the Danes,
hall and throne
>> to be shared with the Frisians.
Then, second:
>> every day
at the dole-out of gifts
>> Finn, son of Focwald,
should honor the Danes,
1090 >> bestow with an even
hand to Hengest
>> and Hengest's men
the wrought-gold rings,
>> bounty to match
the measure he gave
>> his own Frisians—
to keep morale
>> in the beer-hall high.
Both sides then
1095 >> sealed their agreement.
With oaths to Hengest
>> Finn swore
openly, solemnly,
>> that the battle survivors
would be guaranteed
>> honor and status.
No infringement
>> by word or deed,
no provocation
1100 >> would be permitted.
Their own ring-giver
>> after all

---

6. The truce was offered by Finn to Hengest, who succeeded Hnaef as leader of the Danes.

was dead and gone,
                    they were leaderless,
in forced allegiance
                    to his murderer.
So if any Frisian
                    stirred up bad blood
1105 with insinuations
                    or taunts about this,
the blade of the sword
                    would arbitrate it.
A funeral pyre
                    was then prepared,
effulgent gold
                    brought out from the hoard.
The pride and prince
                    of the Shieldings lay
1110 awaiting the flame.
                    Everywhere
there were blood-plastered
                    coats of mail.
The pyre was heaped
                    with boar-shaped helmets
forged in gold,
                    with the gashed corpses
of wellborn Danes—
                    many had fallen.
1115 Then Hildeburh
                    ordered her own
son's body
                    be burnt with Hnaef's
the flesh on his bones
                    to sputter and blaze
beside his uncle's.
                    The woman wailed
and sang keens,
                    the warrior went up.[7]
1120 Carcass flame
                    swirled and fumed,
they stood round the burial
                    mound and howled
as heads melted,
                    crusted gashes
spattered and ran
                    bloody matter.
The glutton element
                    flamed and consumed
1125 the dead of both sides.
                    Their great days were gone.
Warriors scattered

7. The meaning may be, the warrior was placed up on the pyre, or went up in smoke. "Keens": lamentations or dirges for the dead.

               to homes and forts
all over Friesland,
               fewer now, feeling
loss of friends.
               Hengest stayed,
lived out that whole
               resentful, blood-sullen
winter with Finn,

1130   *homesick and helpless.*
No ring-whorled prow
               could up then
and away on the sea.
               Wind and water
raged with storms,
               wave and shingle
were shackled in ice
               until another year
appeared in the yard

1135   *as it does to this day,*
the seasons constant,
               the wonder of light
coming over us.
               Then winter was gone,
earth's lap grew lovely,
               longing woke
in the cooped-up exile
               for a voyage home—
but more for vengeance,

1140   *some way of bringing*
things to a head:
               his sword arm hankered
to greet the Jutes.
               So he did not balk
once Hunlafing
               placed on his lap
Dazzle-the-Duel,
               the best sword of all,[8]
whose edges Jutes

1145   *knew only too well.*
Thus blood was spilled,
               the gallant Finn
slain in his home
               after Guthlaf and Oslaf[9]
back from their voyage
               made old accusation:
the brutal ambush,
               the fate they had suffered,
all blamed on Finn.

---

8. Hunlafing may be the son of a Danish warrior called Hunlaf. The placing of the sword in Hengest's lap is a symbolic call for revenge.
9. It is not clear whether the Danes have traveled home and then returned to Friesland with reinforcements, cr whether the Danish survivors attack once the weather allows them to take ship.

1150
                        The wildness in them
had to brim over.
                        The hall ran red
with blood of enemies.
                                Finn was cut down,
the queen brought away
                        and everything
the Shieldings could find
                        inside Finn's walls—
1155   *the Frisian king's*
                        gold collars and gemstones—
swept off to the ship.
                        Over sea-lanes then
back to Daneland
                        the warrior troop
bore that lady home.

                        The poem was over,
the poet had performed, a pleasant murmur
1160   started on the benches, stewards did the rounds
with wine in splendid jugs, and Wealhtheow came to sit
in her gold crown between two good men,
uncle and nephew, each one of whom
still trusted the other;[1] and the forthright Unferth,
1165   admired by all for his mind and courage
although under a cloud for killing his brothers,
reclined near the king.
                        The queen spoke:
"Enjoy this drink, my most generous lord;
raise up your goblet, entertain the Geats
1170   duly and gently, discourse with them,
be open-handed, happy and fond.
Relish their company, but recollect as well
all of the boons that have been bestowed on you.
The bright court of Heorot has been cleansed
1175   and now the word is that you want to adopt
this warrior as a son. So, while you may,
bask in your fortune, and then bequeath
kingdom and nation to your kith and kin,
before your decease. I am certain of Hrothulf.
1180   He is noble and will use the young ones well.
He will not let you down. Should you die before him,
he will treat our children truly and fairly.
He will honor, I am sure, our two sons,
repay them in kind, when he recollects
1185   all the good things we gave him once,
the favor and respect he found in his childhood."
She turned then to the bench where her boys sat,
Hrethric and Hrothmund, with other nobles' sons,

1. See n. 4, p. 53.

all the youth together; and that good man,
1190 Beowulf the Geat, sat between the brothers.
    The cup was carried to him, kind words
spoken in welcome and a wealth of wrought gold
graciously bestowed: two arm bangles,
a mail-shirt and rings, and the most resplendent
1195 torque of gold I ever heard tell of
anywhere on earth or under heaven.
There was no hoard like it since Hama snatched
the Brosings' neck-chain and bore it away
with its gems and settings to his shining fort,
1200 away from Eormenric's wiles and hatred,[2]
and thereby ensured his eternal reward.
Hygelac the Geat, grandson of Swerting,
wore this neck-ring on his last raid;[3]
at bay under his banner, he defended the booty,
1205 treasure he had won. Fate swept him away
because of his proud need to provoke
a feud with the Frisians. He fell beneath his shield,
in the same gem-crusted, kingly gear
he had worn when he crossed the frothing wave-vat.
1210 So the dead king fell into Frankish hands.
They took his breast-mail, also his neck-torque,
and punier warriors plundered the slain
when the carnage ended; Geat corpses
covered the field.
                Applause filled the hall.
1215 Then Wealhtheow pronounced in the presence of the company:
"Take delight in this torque, dear Beowulf,
wear it for luck and wear also this mail
from our people's armory: may you prosper in them!
Be acclaimed for strength, for kindly guidance
1220 to these two boys, and your bounty will be sure.
You have won renown: you are known to all men
far and near, now and forever.
Your sway is wide as the wind's home,
as the sea around cliffs. And so, my prince,
1225 I wish you a lifetime's luck and blessings
to enjoy this treasure. Treat my sons
with tender care, be strong and kind.
Here each comrade is true to the other,
loyal to lord, loving in spirit.
1230 The thanes have one purpose, the people are ready:
having drunk and pledged, the ranks do as I bid."
    She moved then to her place. Men were drinking wine

---

2. The necklace presented to Beowulf is compared to one worn by the goddess Freya in Germanic mythology. In another story it was stolen by Hama from the Gothic king Eormenric, who is treated as a tyrant in Germanic legend, but how Eormenric came to possess it is not known.
3. Later we learn that Beowulf gave the necklace to Hygd, the queen of his lord Hygelac. Hygelac is here said to have been wearing it on his last expedition. This is the first of several allusions to Hygelac's death on a raid up the Rhine, the one incident in the poem that can be connected to a historical event documented elsewhere.

at that rare feast; how could they know fate,
the grim shape of things to come,
1235 the threat looming over many thanes
as night approached and King Hrothgar prepared
to retire to his quarters? Retainers in great numbers
were posted on guard as so often in the past.
Benches were pushed back, bedding gear and bolsters
1240 spread across the floor, and one man
lay down to his rest, already marked for death.
At their heads they placed their polished timber
battle-shields; and on the bench above them,
each man's kit was kept to hand:
1245 a towering war-helmet, webbed mail-shirt
and great-shafted spear. It was their habit
always and everywhere to be ready for action,
at home or in the camp, in whatever case
and at whatever time the need arose
1250 to rally round their lord. They were a right people.

[ANOTHER ATTACK]

They went to sleep. And one paid dearly
for his night's ease, as had happened to them often,
ever since Grendel occupied the gold-hall,
committing evil until the end came,
1255 death after his crimes. Then it became clear,
obvious to everyone once the fight was over,
that an avenger lurked and was still alive,
grimly biding time. Grendel's mother,
monstrous hell-bride, brooded on her wrongs.
1260 She had been forced down into fearful waters,
the cold depths, after Cain had killed
his father's son, felled his own
brother with a sword. Branded an outlaw,
marked by having murdered, he moved into the wilds,
1265 shunned company and joy. And from Cain there sprang
misbegotten spirits, among them Grendel,
the banished and accursed, due to come to grips
with that watcher in Heorot waiting to do battle.
The monster wrenched and wrestled with him,
1270 but Beowulf was mindful of his mighty strength,
the wondrous gifts God had showered on him:
he relied for help on the Lord of All,
on His care and favor. So he overcame the foe,
brought down the hell-brute. Broken and bowed,
1275 outcast from all sweetness, the enemy of mankind
made for his death-den. But now his mother
had sallied forth on a savage journey,
grief-racked and ravenous, desperate for revenge.
She came to Heorot. There, inside the hall,
1280 Danes lay asleep, earls who would soon endure
a great reversal, once Grendel's mother

attacked and entered. Her onslaught was less
only by as much as an amazon warrior's
strength is less than an armed man's
1285 when the hefted sword, its hammered edge
and gleaming blade slathered in blood,
razes the sturdy boar-ridge off a helmet.
Then in the hall, hard-honed swords
were grabbed from the bench, many a broad shield
1290 lifted and braced; there was little thought of helmets
or woven mail when they woke in terror.
    The hell-dam was in panic, desperate to get out,
in mortal terror the moment she was found.
She had pounced and taken one of the retainers
1295 in a tight hold, then headed for the fen.
To Hrothgar, this man was the most beloved
of the friends he trusted between the two seas.
She had done away with a great warrior,
ambushed him at rest.
                Beowulf was elsewhere.
1300 Earlier, after the award of the treasure,
the Geat had been given another lodging.
    There was uproar in Heorot. She had snatched their trophy,
Grendel's bloodied hand. It was a fresh blow
to the afflicted bawn. The bargain was hard,
1305 both parties having to pay
with the lives of friends. And the old lord,
the gray-haired warrior, was heartsore and weary
when he heard the news: his highest-placed adviser,
his dearest companion, was dead and gone.
1310   Beowulf was quickly brought to the chamber:
the winner of fights, the arch-warrior,
came first-footing in with his fellow troops
to where the king in his wisdom waited,
still wondering whether Almighty God
1315 would ever turn the tide of his misfortunes.
So Beowulf entered with his band in attendance
and the wooden floorboards banged and rang
as he advanced, hurrying to address
the prince of the Ingwins, asking if he'd rested
1320 since the urgent summons had come as a surprise.
    Then Hrothgar, the Shieldings' helmet, spoke:
"Rest? What is rest? Sorrow has returned.
Alas for the Danes! Aeschere is dead.
He was Yrmenlaf's elder brother
1325 and a soul-mate to me, a true mentor,
my right-hand man when the ranks clashed
and our boar-crests had to take a battering
in the line of action. Aeschere was everything
the world admires in a wise man and a friend.
1330 Then this roaming killer came in a fury
and slaughtered him in Heorot. Where she is hiding,
glutting on the corpse and glorying in her escape,

I cannot tell; she has taken up the feud
because of last night, when you killed Grendel,
1335   wrestled and racked him in ruinous combat
since for too long he had terrorized us
with his depredations. He died in battle,
paid with his life; and now this powerful
other one arrives, this force for evil
1340   driven to avenge her kinsman's death.
Or so it seems to thanes in their grief,
in the anguish every thane endures
at the loss of a ring-giver, now that the hand
that bestowed so richly has been stilled in death.
1345   "I have heard it said by my people in hall,
counselors who live in the upland country,
that they have seen two such creatures
prowling the moors, huge marauders
from some other world. One of these things,
1350   as far as anyone ever can discern,
looks like a woman; the other, warped
in the shape of a man, moves beyond the pale
bigger than any man, an unnatural birth
called Grendel by the country people
1355   in former days. They are fatherless creatures,
and their whole ancestry is hidden in a past
of demons and ghosts. They dwell apart
among wolves on the hills, on windswept crags
and treacherous keshes, where cold streams
1360   pour down the mountain and disappear
under mist and moorland.
                        A few miles from here
a frost-stiffened wood waits and keeps watch
above a mere; the overhanging bank
is a maze of tree-roots mirrored in its surface.
1365   At night there, something uncanny happens:
the water burns. And the mere bottom
has never been sounded by the sons of men.
On its bank, the heather-stepper halts:
the hart in flight from pursuing hounds
1370   will turn to face them with firm-set horns
and die in the wood rather than dive
beneath its surface. That is no good place.
When wind blows up and stormy weather
makes clouds scud and the skies weep,
1375   out of its depths a dirty surge
is pitched toward the heavens. Now help depends
again on you and on you alone.
The gap of danger where the demon waits
is still unknown to you. Seek it if you dare.
1380   I will compensate you for settling the feud
as I did the last time with lavish wealth,
coffers of coiled gold, if you come back."

[BEOWULF FIGHTS GRENDEL'S MOTHER]

Beowulf, son of Ecgtheow, spoke:
"Wise sir, do not grieve. It is always better
1385   to avenge dear ones than to indulge in mourning.
For every one of us, living in this world
means waiting for our end. Let whoever can
win glory before death. When a warrior is gone,
that will be his best and only bulwark.
1390   So arise, my lord, and let us immediately
set forth on the trail of this troll-dam.
I guarantee you: she will not get away,
not to dens under ground nor upland groves
nor the ocean floor. She'll have nowhere to flee to.
1395   Endure your troubles today. Bear up
and be the man I expect you to be."
    With that the old lord sprang to his feet
and praised God for Beowulf's pledge.
Then a bit and halter were brought for his horse
1400   with the plaited mane. The wise king mounted
the royal saddle and rode out in style
with a force of shield-bearers. The forest paths
were marked all over with the monster's tracks,
her trail on the ground wherever she had gone
1405   across the dark moors, dragging away
the body of that thane, Hrothgar's best
counselor and overseer of the country.
So the noble prince proceeded undismayed
up fells and screes, along narrow footpaths
1410   and ways where they were forced into single file,
ledges on cliffs above lairs of water-monsters.
He went in front with a few men,
good judges of the lie of the land,
and suddenly discovered the dismal wood,
1415   mountain trees growing out at an angle
above gray stones: the bloodshot water
surged underneath. It was a sore blow
to all of the Danes, friends of the Shieldings,
a hurt to each and every one
1420   of that noble company when they came upon
Aeschere's head at the foot of the cliff.
    Everybody gazed as the hot gore
kept wallowing up and an urgent war-horn
repeated its notes: the whole party
1425   sat down to watch. The water was infested
with all kinds of reptiles. There were writhing sea-dragons
and monsters slouching on slopes by the cliff,
serpents and wild things such as those that often
surface at dawn to roam the sail-road
1430   and doom the voyage. Down they plunged,
lashing in anger at the loud call
of the battle-bugle. An arrow from the bow
of the Geat chief got one of them

as he surged to the surface: the seasoned shaft
1435   stuck deep in his flank and his freedom in the water
got less and less. It was his last swim.
He was swiftly overwhelmed in the shallows,
prodded by barbed boar-spears,
cornered, beaten, pulled up on the bank,
1440   a strange lake-birth, a loathsome catch
men gazed at in awe.
                          Beowulf got ready,
donned his war-gear, indifferent to death;
his mighty, hand-forged, fine-webbed mail
would soon meet with the menace underwater.
1445   It would keep the bone-cage of his body safe:
no enemy's clasp could crush him in it,
no vicious armlock choke his life out.
To guard his head he had a glittering helmet
that was due to be muddied on the mere bottom
1450   and blurred in the upswirl. It was of beaten gold,
princely headgear hooped and hasped
by a weapon-smith who had worked wonders
in days gone by and adorned it with boar-shapes;
since then it had resisted every sword.
1455   And another item lent by Unferth
at that moment of need was of no small importance:
the brehon[4] handed him a hilted weapon,
a rare and ancient sword named Hrunting.
The iron blade with its ill-boding patterns
1460   had been tempered in blood. It had never failed
the hand of anyone who hefted it in battle,
anyone who had fought and faced the worst
in the gap of danger. This was not the first time
it had been called to perform heroic feats.
1465   When he lent that blade to the better swordsman,
Unferth, the strong-built son of Ecglaf,
could hardly have remembered the ranting speech
he had made in his cups. He was not man enough
to face the turmoil of a fight under water
1470   and the risk to his life. So there he lost
fame and repute. It was different for the other
rigged out in his gear, ready to do battle.
      Beowulf, son of Ecgtheow, spoke:
"Wisest of kings, now that I have come
1475   to the point of action, I ask you to recall
what we said earlier: that you, son of Halfdane
and gold-friend to retainers, that you, if I should fall
and suffer death while serving your cause,
would act like a father to me afterward.
1480   If this combat kills me, take care
of my young company, my comrades in arms.

---

4. One of an ancient class of lawyers in Ireland [Translator's note]. The Old English word for Unferth's office, *thyle,* has been interpreted as "orator" and "spokesman."

And be sure also, my beloved Hrothgar,
to send Hygelac the treasures I received.
Let the lord of the Geats gaze on that gold,
1485   let Hrethel's son take note of it and see
that I found a ring-giver of rare magnificence
and enjoyed the good of his generosity.
And Unferth is to have what I inherited:
to that far-famed man I bequeath my own
1490   sharp-honed, wave-sheened wonder-blade.
With Hrunting I shall gain glory or die."
    After these words, the prince of the Weather-Geats
was impatient to be away and plunged suddenly:
without more ado, he dived into the heaving
1495   depths of the lake. It was the best part of a day
before he could see the solid bottom.
    Quickly the one who haunted those waters,
who had scavenged and gone her gluttonous rounds
for a hundred seasons, sensed a human
1500   observing her outlandish lair from above.
So she lunged and clutched and managed to catch him
in her brutal grip; but his body, for all that,
remained unscathed: the mesh of the chain-mail
saved him on the outside. Her savage talons
1505   failed to rip the web of his war-shirt.
Then once she touched bottom, that wolfish swimmer
carried the ring-mailed prince to her court
so that for all his courage he could never use
the weapons he carried; and a bewildering horde
1510   came at him from the depths, droves of sea-beasts
who attacked with tusks and tore at his chain-mail
in a ghastly onslaught. The gallant man
could see he had entered some hellish turn-hole
and yet the water there did not work against him
1515   because the hall-roofing held off
the force of the current; then he saw firelight,
a gleam and flare-up, a glimmer of brightness.
    The hero observed that swamp-thing from hell,
the tarn-hag in all her terrible strength,
1520   then heaved his war-sword and swung his arm:
the decorated blade came down ringing
and singing on her head. But he soon found
his battle-torch extinguished; the shining blade
refused to bite. It spared her and failed
1525   the man in his need. It had gone through many
hand-to-hand fight, had hewed the armor
and helmets of the doomed, but here at last
the fabulous powers of that heirloom failed.
    Hygelac's kinsman kept thinking about
1530   his name and fame: he never lost heart.
Then, in a fury, he flung his sword away.
The keen, inlaid, worm-loop-patterned steel
was hurled to the ground: he would have to rely

on the might of his arm. So must a man do
1535   who intends to gain enduring glory
in a combat. Life doesn't cost him a thought.
Then the prince of War-Geats, warming to this fight
with Grendel's mother, gripped her shoulder
and laid about him in a battle frenzy:
1540   he pitched his killer opponent to the floor
but she rose quickly and retaliated,
grappled him tightly in her grim embrace.
The sure-footed fighter felt daunted,
the strongest of warriors stumbled and fell.
1545   So she pounced upon him and pulled out
a broad, whetted knife: now she would avenge
her only child. But the mesh of chain-mail
on Beowulf's shoulder shielded his life,
turned the edge and tip of the blade.
1550   The son of Ecgtheow would have surely perished
and the Geats lost their warrior under the wide earth
had the strong links and locks of his war-gear
not helped to save him: holy God
decided the victory. It was easy for the Lord,
1555   the Ruler of Heaven, to redress the balance
once Beowulf got back up on his feet.
     Then he saw a blade that boded well,
a sword in her armory, an ancient heirloom
from the days of the giants, an ideal weapon,
1560   one that any warrior would envy,
but so huge and heavy of itself
only Beowulf could wield it in a battle.
So the Shieldings' hero hard-pressed and enraged,
took a firm hold of the hilt and swung
1565   the blade in an arc, a resolute blow
that bit deep into her neck-bone
and severed it entirely, toppling the doomed
house of her flesh; she fell to the floor.
The sword dripped blood, the swordsman was elated.
1570   A light appeared and the place brightened
the way the sky does when heaven's candle
is shining clearly. He inspected the vault:
with sword held high, its hilt raised
to guard and threaten, Hygelac's thane
1575   scouted by the wall in Grendel's wake.
Now the weapon was to prove its worth.
The warrior determined to take revenge
for every gross act Grendel had committed—
and not only for that one occasion
1580   when he'd come to slaughter the sleeping troops,
fifteen of Hrothgar's house-guards
surprised on their benches and ruthlessly devoured,
and as many again carried away,
a brutal plunder. Beowulf in his fury
1585   now settled that score: he saw the monster

in his resting place, war-weary and wrecked,
a lifeless corpse, a casualty
of the battle in Heorot. The body gaped
at the stroke dealt to it after death:
1590   Beowulf cut the corpse's head off.
     Immediately the counselors keeping a lookout
with Hrothgar, watching the lake water,
saw a heave-up and surge of waves
and blood in the backwash. They bowed gray heads,
1595   spoke in their sage, experienced way
about the good warrior, how they never again
expected to see that prince returning
in triumph to their king. It was clear to many
that the wolf of the deep had destroyed him forever.
1600   The ninth hour of the day arrived.
The brave Shieldings abandoned the cliff-top
and the king went home; but sick at heart,
staring at the mere, the strangers held on.
They wished, without hope, to behold their lord,
Beowulf himself.
1605   Meanwhile, the sword
began to wilt into gory icicles
to slather and thaw. It was a wonderful thing,
the way it all melted as ice melts
when the Father eases the fetters off the frost
1610   and unravels the water-ropes, He who wields power
over time and tide: He is the true Lord.
     The Geat captain saw treasure in abundance
but carried no spoils from those quarters
except for the head and the inlaid hilt
1615   embossed with jewels; its blade had melted
and the scrollwork on it burned, so scalding was the blood
of the poisonous fiend who had perished there.
Then away he swam, the one who had survived
the fall of his enemies, flailing to the surface.
1620   The wide water, the waves and pools,
were no longer infested once the wandering fiend
let go of her life and this unreliable world.
     The seafarers' leader made for land,
resolutely swimming, delighted with his prize,
1625   the mighty load he was lugging to the surface.
His thanes advanced in a troop to meet him,
thanking God and taking great delight
in seeing their prince back safe and sound.
Quickly the hero's helmet and mail-shirt
1630   were loosed and unlaced. The lake settled,
clouds darkened above the bloodshot depths.
     With high hearts they headed away
along footpaths and trails through the fields,
roads that they knew, each of them wrestling
1635   with the head they were carrying from the lakeside cliff,
men kingly in their courage and capable

of difficult work. It was a task for four
to hoist Grendel's head on a spear
and bear it under strain to the bright hall.
1640 But soon enough they neared the place,
fourteen Geats in fine fettle,
striding across the outlying ground
in a delighted throng around their leader.
In he came then, the thanes' commander,
1645 the arch-warrior, to address Hrothgar:
his courage was proven, his glory was secure.
Grendel's head was hauled by the hair,
dragged across the floor where the people were drinking,
a horror for both queen and company to behold.
1650 They stared in awe. It was an astonishing sight.

[ANOTHER CELEBRATION AT HEOROT]

Beowulf, son of Ecgtheow, spoke:
"So, son of Halfdane, prince of the Shieldings,
we are glad to bring this booty from the lake.
It is a token of triumph and we tender it to you.
1655 I barely survived the battle under water.
It was hard-fought, a desperate affair
that could have gone badly; if God had not helped me,
the outcome would have been quick and fatal.
Although Hrunting is hard-edged,
1660 I could never bring it to bear in battle.
But the Lord of Men allowed me to behold—
for He often helps the unbefriended—
an ancient sword shining on the wall,
a weapon made for giants, there for the wielding.
1665 Then my moment came in the combat and I struck
the dwellers in that den. Next thing the damascened
sword blade melted; it bloated and it burned
in their rushing blood. I have wrested the hilt
from the enemies' hand, avenged the evil
1670 done to the Danes; it is what was due.
And this I pledge, O prince of the Shieldings:
you can sleep secure with your company of troops
in Heorot Hall. Never need you fear
for a single thane of your sept or nation,
1675 young warriors or old, that laying waste of life
that you and your people endured of yore."
Then the gold hilt was handed over
to the old lord, a relic from long ago
for the venerable ruler. That rare smithwork
1680 was passed on to the prince of the Danes
when those devils perished; once death removed
that murdering, guilt-steeped, God-cursed fiend,
eliminating his unholy life
and his mother's as well, it was willed to that king
1685 who of all the lavish gift-lords of the north

was the best regarded between the two seas.
    Hrothgar spoke; he examined the hilt,
that relic of old times. It was engraved all over
and showed how war first came into the world
1690 and the flood destroyed the tribe of giants.
They suffered a terrible severance from the Lord;
the Almighty made the waters rise,
drowned them in the deluge for retribution.
In pure gold inlay on the sword-guards
1695 there were rune-markings correctly incised,
stating and recording for whom the sword
had been first made and ornamented
with its scrollworked hilt. Then everyone hushed
as the son of Halfdane spoke this wisdom:
1700 "A protector of his people, pledged to uphold
truth and justice and to respect tradition,
is entitled to affirm that this man
was born to distinction. Beowulf, my friend,
your fame has gone far and wide,
1705 you are known everywhere. In all things you are even-tempered,
prudent and resolute. So I stand firm by the promise of friendship
we exchanged before. Forever you will be
your people's mainstay and your own warriors'
helping hand.
               Heremod was different,
1710 the way he behaved to Ecgwela's sons.
His rise in the world brought little joy
to the Danish people, only death and destruction.
He vented his rage on men he caroused with,
killed his own comrades, a pariah king
1715 who cut himself off from his own kind,
even though Almighty God had made him
eminent and powerful and marked him from the start
for a happy life. But a change happened,
he grew bloodthirsty, gave no more rings
1720 to honor the Danes. He suffered in the end
for having plagued his people for so long:
his life lost happiness.
                  So learn from this
and understand true values. I who tell you
have wintered into wisdom.
                 It is a great wonder
1725 how Almighty God in His magnificence
favors our race with rank and scope
and the gift of wisdom; His sway is wide.
Sometimes He allows the mind of a man
of distinguished birth to follow its bent,
1730 grants him fulfillment and felicity on earth
and forts to command in his own country.
He permits him to lord it in many lands
until the man in his unthinkingness
forgets that it will ever end for him.

1735 He indulges his desires; illness and old age
  mean nothing to him; his mind is untroubled
  by envy or malice or the thought of enemies
  with their hate-honed swords. The whole world
  conforms to his will, he is kept from the worst
1740 until an element of overweening
  enters him and takes hold
  while the soul's guard, its sentry, drowses,
  grown too distracted. A killer stalks him,
  an archer who draws a deadly bow.
1745 And then the man is hit in the heart,
  the arrow flies beneath his defenses,
  the devious promptings of the demon start.
  His old possessions seem paltry to him now.
  He covets and resents; dishonors custom
1750 and bestows no gold; and because of good things
  that the Heavenly Powers gave him in the past
  he ignores the shape of things to come.
  Then finally the end arrives
  when the body he was lent collapses and falls
1755 prey to its death; ancestral possessions
  and the goods he hoarded are inherited by another
  who lets them go with a liberal hand.
   "O flower of warriors, beware of that trap.
  Choose, dear Beowulf, the better part,
1760 eternal rewards. Do not give way to pride.
  For a brief while your strength is in bloom
  but it fades quickly; and soon there will follow
  illness or the sword to lay you low,
  or a sudden fire or surge of water
1765 or jabbing blade or javelin from the air
  or repellent age. Your piercing eye
  will dim and darken; and death will arrive,
  dear warrior, to sweep you away.
   "Just so I ruled the Ring-Danes' country
1770 for fifty years, defended them in wartime
  with spear and sword against constant assaults
  by many tribes: I came to believe
  my enemies had faded from the face of the earth.
  Still, what happened was a hard reversal
1775 from bliss to grief. Grendel struck
  after lying in wait. He laid waste to the land
  and from that moment my mind was in dread
  of his depredations. So I praise God
  in His heavenly glory that I lived to behold
1780 this head dripping blood and that after such harrowing
  I can look upon it in triumph at last.
  Take your place, then, with pride and pleasure,
  and move to the feast. Tomorrow morning
  our treasure will be shared and showered upon you."
1785 The Geat was elated and gladly obeyed
  the old man's bidding; he sat on the bench.

And soon all was restored, the same as before.
Happiness came back, the hall was thronged,
and a banquet set forth; black night fell
and covered them in darkness.
1790   Then the company rose
for the old campaigner: the gray-haired prince
was ready for bed. And a need for rest
came over the brave shield-bearing Geat.
He was a weary seafarer, far from home,
1795   so immediately a house-guard guided him out,
one whose office entailed looking after
whatever a thane on the road in those days
might need or require. It was noble courtesy.

[BEOWULF RETURNS HOME]

That great heart rested. The hall towered,
1800   gold-shingled and gabled, and the guest slept in it
until the black raven with raucous glee
announced heaven's joy, and a hurry of brightness
overran the shadows. Warriors rose quickly,
impatient to be off: their own country
1805   was beckoning the nobles; and the bold voyager
longed to be aboard his distant boat.
Then that stalwart fighter ordered Hrunting
to be brought to Unferth, and bade Unferth
take the sword and thanked him for lending it.
1810   He said he had found it a friend in battle
and a powerful help; he put no blame
on the blade's cutting edge. He was a considerate man.
And there the warriors stood in their war-gear,
eager to go, while their honored lord
1815   approached the platform where the other sat.
The undaunted hero addressed Hrothgar.
Beowulf, son of Ecgtheow, spoke:
"Now we who crossed the wide sea
have to inform you that we feel a desire
1820   to return to Hygelac. Here we have been welcomed
and thoroughly entertained. You have treated us well.
If there is any favor on earth I can perform
beyond deeds of arms I have done already,
anything that would merit your affections more,
1825   I shall act, my lord, with alacrity.
If ever I hear from across the ocean
that people on your borders are threatening battle
as attackers have done from time to time,
I shall land with a thousand thanes at my back
1830   to help your cause. Hygelac may be young
to rule a nation, but this much I know
about the king of the Geats: he will come to my aid
and want to support me by word and action
in your hour of need, when honor dictates

1835 that I raise a hedge of spears around you.
Then if Hrethric should think about traveling
as a king's son to the court of the Geats,
he will find many friends. Foreign places
yield more to one who is himself worth meeting."

1840   Hrothgar spoke and answered him:
"The Lord in his wisdom sent you those words
and they came from the heart. I have never heard
so young a man make truer observations.
You are strong in body and mature in mind,
1845 impressive in speech. If it should come to pass
that Hrethel's descendant dies beneath a spear,
if deadly battle or the sword blade or disease
fells the prince who guards your people
and you are still alive, then I firmly believe
1850 the seafaring Geats won't find a man
worthier of acclaim as their king and defender
than you, if only you would undertake
the lordship of your homeland. My liking for you
deepens with time, dear Beowulf.
1855 What you have done is to draw two peoples,
the Geat nation and us neighboring Danes,
into shared peace and a pact of friendship
in spite of hatreds we have harbored in the past.
For as long as I rule this far-flung land
1860 treasures will change hands and each side will treat
the other with gifts; across the gannet's bath,
over the broad sea, whorled prows will bring
presents and tokens. I know your people
are beyond reproach in every respect,
1865 steadfast in the old way with friend or foe."
Then the earls' defender furnished the hero
with twelve treasures and told him to set out,
sail with those gifts safely home
to the people he loved, but to return promptly.
1870 And so the good and gray-haired Dane,
that highborn king, kissed Beowulf
and embraced his neck, then broke down
in sudden tears. Two forebodings
disturbed him in his wisdom, but one was stronger:
1875 nevermore would they meet each other
face to face. And such was his affection
that he could not help being overcome:
his fondness for the man was so deep-founded,
it warmed his heart and wound the heartstrings
tight in his breast.
1880   The embrace ended
and Beowulf, glorious in his gold regalia,
stepped the green earth. Straining at anchor
and ready for boarding, his boat awaited him.
So they went on their journey, and Hrothgar's generosity
1885 was praised repeatedly. He was a peerless king
until old age sapped his strength and did him

mortal harm, as it has done so many.
    Down to the waves then, dressed in the web
of their chain-mail and war-shirts the young men marched
1890   in high spirits. The coast-guard spied them,
thanes setting forth, the same as before.
His salute this time from the top of the cliff
was far from unmannerly; he galloped to meet them
and as they took ship in their shining gear,
1895   he said how welcome they would be in Geatland.
Then the broad hull was beached on the sand
to be cargoed with treasure, horses and war-gear.
The curved prow motioned; the mast stood high
above Hrothgar's riches in the loaded hold.
1900   The guard who had watched the boat was given
a sword with gold fittings, and in future days
that present would make him a respected man
at his place on the mead-bench.
                    Then the keel plunged
and shook in the sea; and they sailed from Denmark.
1905   Right away the mast was rigged with its sea-shawl;
sail-ropes were tightened, timbers drummed
and stiff winds kept the wave-crosser
skimming ahead; as she heaved forward,
her foamy neck was fleet and buoyant,
1910   a lapped prow loping over currents,
until finally the Geats caught sight of coastline
and familiar cliffs. The keel reared up,
wind lifted it home, it hit on the land.
    The harbor guard came hurrying out
1915   to the rolling water: he had watched the offing
long and hard, on the lookout for those friends.
With the anchor cables, he moored their craft
right where it had beached, in case a backwash
might catch the hull and carry it away.
1920   Then he ordered the prince's treasure-trove
to be carried ashore. It was a short step
from there to where Hrethel's son and heir,
Hygelac the gold-giver, makes his home
on a secure cliff, in the company of retainers.
1925   The building was magnificent, the king majestic,
ensconced in his hall; and although Hygd, his queen,
was young, a few short years at court,
her mind was thoughtful and her manners sure.
Haereth's daughter behaved generously
1930   and stinted nothing when she distributed
bounty to the Geats.
                Great Queen Modthryth
perpetrated terrible wrongs.[5]

---

5. The story of Queen Modthryth's vices is abruptly introduced as a foil to Queen Hygd's virtues. A transitional passage may have been lost, but the poet's device is similar to that of using the earlier reference to the wickedness of King Heremod to contrast with the good qualities of Sigemund and Beowulf.

If any retainer ever made bold
to look her in the face, if an eye not her lord's[6]
1935 stared at her directly during daylight,
the outcome was sealed: he was kept bound,
in hand-tightened shackles, racked, tortured
until doom was pronounced—death by the sword,
slash of blade, blood-gush, and death-qualms
1940 in an evil display. Even a queen
outstanding in beauty must not overstep like that.
A queen should weave peace, not punish the innocent
with loss of life for imagined insults.
But Hemming's kinsman[7] put a halt to her ways
1945 and drinkers round the table had another tale:
she was less of a bane to people's lives,
less cruel-minded, after she was married
to the brave Offa, a bride arrayed
in her gold finery, given away
1950 by a caring father, ferried to her young prince
over dim seas. In days to come
she would grace the throne and grow famous
for her good deeds and conduct of life,
her high devotion to the hero king
1955 who was the best king, it has been said,
between the two seas or anywhere else
on the face of the earth. Offa was honored
far and wide for his generous ways,
his fighting spirit and his farseeing
1960 defense of his homeland; from him there sprang Eomer,
Garmund's grandson, kinsman of Hemming,[8]
his warriors' mainstay and master of the field.

    Heroic Beowulf and his band of men
crossed the wide strand, striding along
1965 the sandy foreshore; the sun shone,
the world's candle warmed them from the south
as they hastened to where, as they had heard,
the young king, Ongentheow's killer
and his people's protector,[9] was dispensing rings
1970 inside his bawn. Beowulf's return
was reported to Hygelac as soon as possible,
news that the captain was now in the enclosure,
his battle-brother back from the fray
alive and well, walking to the hall.
1975 Room was quickly made, on the king's orders,
and the troops filed across the cleared floor.

---

6. This could refer to her husband or her father before her marriage. The story resembles folktales about a proud princess whose unsuccessful suitors are all put to death, although the unfortunate victims in this case seem to be guilty only of looking at her.

7. I.e., Offa I, a legendary king of the Angles. We know nothing about Hemming other than that Offa was related to him. Offa II (757–96) was king of Mercia, and although the story is about the second Offa's ancestor on the Continent, this is the only English connection in the poem and has been taken as evidence to date its origins to 8th-century Mercia.

8. I.e., Eomer, Offa's son. See previous note. Garmund was presumably the name of Offa's father.

9. I.e., Hygelac. Ongentheow was king of the Swedish people called the Shylfings. This is the first of the references to wars between the Geats and the Swedes. One of Hygelac's war party named Eofer was the actual slayer of Ongentheow.

After Hygelac had offered greetings
to his loyal thane in a lofty speech,
he and his kinsman, that hale survivor,
1980   sat face to face. Haereth's daughter
moved about with the mead-jug in her hand,
taking care of the company, filling the cups
that warriors held out. Then Hygelac began
to put courteous questions to his old comrade
1985   in the high hall. He hankered to know
every tale the Sea-Geats had to tell:
"How did you fare on your foreign voyage,
dear Beowulf, when you abruptly decided
to sail away across the salt water
1990   and fight at Heorot? Did you help Hrothgar
much in the end? Could you ease the prince
of his well-known troubles? Your undertaking
cast my spirits down, I dreaded the outcome
of your expedition and pleaded with you
1995   long and hard to leave the killer be,
let the South-Danes settle their own
blood-feud with Grendel. So God be thanked
I am granted this sight of you, safe and sound."
Beowulf, son of Ecgtheow, spoke:
2000   "What happened, Lord Hygelac, is hardly a secret
any more among men in this world—
myself and Grendel coming to grips
on the very spot where he visited destruction
on the Victory-Shieldings and violated
2005   life and limb, losses I avenged
so no earthly offspring of Grendel's
need ever boast of that bout before dawn,
no matter how long the last of his evil
family survives.
When I first landed
2010   I hastened to the ring-hall and saluted Hrothgar.
Once he discovered why I had come,
the son of Halfdane sent me immediately
to sit with his own sons on the bench.
It was a happy gathering. In my whole life
2015   I have never seen mead enjoyed more
in any hall on earth. Sometimes the queen
herself appeared, peace-pledge between nations,
to hearten the young ones and hand out
a torque to a warrior, then take her place.
2020   Sometimes Hrothgar's daughter distributed
ale to older ranks, in order on the benches:
I heard the company call her Freawaru
as she made her rounds, presenting men
with the gem-studded bowl, young bride-to-be
2025   to the gracious Ingeld,[1] in her gold-trimmed attire.
The friend of the Shieldings favors her betrothal:

---

1. King of the Heatho-Bards; his father, Froda, was killed by the Danes.

the guardian of the kingdom sees good in it
and hopes this woman will heal old wounds
and grievous feuds.
                                But generally the spear
2030   is prompt to retaliate when a prince is killed,
no matter how admirable the bride may be.
        "Think how the Heatho-Bards are bound to feel,
their lord, Ingeld, and his loyal thanes,
when he walks in with that woman to the feast:
2035   Danes are at the table, being entertained,
honored guests in glittering regalia,
burnished ring-mail that was their hosts' birthright,
looted when the Heatho-Bards could no longer wield
their weapons in the shield-clash, when they went down
2040   with their beloved comrades and forfeited their lives.
Then an old spearman will speak while they are drinking,
having glimpsed some heirloom that brings alive
memories of the massacre; his mood will darken
and heart-stricken, in the stress of his emotion,
2045   he will begin to test a young man's temper
and stir up trouble, starting like this:
'Now, my friend, don't you recognize
your father's sword, his favorite weapon,
the one he wore when he went out in his war-mask
2050   to face the Danes on that final day?
After Withergeld[2] died and his men were doomed,
the Shieldings quickly claimed the field;
and now here's a son of one or other
of those same killers coming through our hall
2055   overbearing us, mouthing boasts,
and rigged in armor that by right is yours.'
And so he keeps on, recalling and accusing,
working things up with bitter words
until one of the lady's retainers lies
2060   spattered in blood, split open
on his father's account.[3] The killer knows
the lie of the land and escapes with his life.
Then on both sides the oath-bound lords
will break the peace, a passionate hate
2065   will build up in Ingeld, and love for his bride
will falter in him as the feud rankles.
I therefore suspect the good faith of the Heatho-Bards,
the truth of their friendship and the trustworthiness
of their alliance with the Danes.
                                But now, my lord,
2070   I shall carry on with my account of Grendel,
the whole story of everything that happened
in the hand-to-hand fight.
                                After heaven's gem

2. One of the Heatho-Bard leaders.
3. I.e., the young Danish attendant is killed
because his father killed the father of the young

Heatho-Bard who has been egged on by the old
veteran of that campaign.

had gone mildly to earth, that maddened spirit,
the terror of those twilights, came to attack us
2075 where we stood guard, still safe inside the hall.
There deadly violence came down on Hondscio
and he fell as fate ordained, the first to perish,
rigged out for the combat. A comrade from our ranks
had come to grief in Grendel's maw:
2080 he ate up the entire body.
There was blood on his teeth, he was bloated and dangerous,
all roused up, yet still unready
to leave the hall empty-handed;
renowned for his might, he matched himself against me,
2085 wildly reaching. He had this roomy pouch,
a strange accoutrement, intricately strung
and hung at the ready, a rare patchwork
of devilishly fitted dragon-skins.
I had done him no wrong, yet the raging demon
2090 wanted to cram me and many another
into this bag—but it was not to be
once I got to my feet in a blind fury.
It would take too long to tell how I repaid
the terror of the land for every life he took
2095 and so won credit for you, my king,
and for all your people. And although he got away
to enjoy life's sweetness for a while longer,
his right hand stayed behind him in Heorot,
evidence of his miserable overthrow
2100 as he dived into murk on the mere bottom.
      "I got lavish rewards from the lord of the Danes
for my part in the battle, beaten gold
and much else, once morning came
and we took our places at the banquet table.
2105 There was singing and excitement: an old reciter,
a carrier of stories, recalled the early days.
At times some hero made the timbered harp
tremble with sweetness, or related true
and tragic happenings; at times the king
2110 gave the proper turn to some fantastic tale,
or a battle-scarred veteran, bowed with age,
would begin to remember the martial deeds
of his youth and prime and be overcome
as the past welled up in his wintry heart.
2115   "We were happy there the whole day long
and enjoyed our time until another night
descended upon us. Then suddenly
the vehement mother avenged her son
and wreaked destruction. Death had robbed her,
2120 Geats had slain Grendel, so his ghastly dam
struck back and with bare-faced defiance
laid a man low. Thus life departed
from the sage Aeschere, an elder wise in counsel.
But afterward, on the morning following,

2125 the Danes could not burn the dead body
nor lay the remains of the man they loved
on his funeral pyre. She had fled with the corpse
and taken refuge beneath torrents on the mountain.
It was a hard blow for Hrothgar to bear,
2130 harder than any he had undergone before.
And so the heartsore king beseeched me
in your royal name to take my chances
underwater, to win glory
and prove my worth. He promised me rewards.
2135 Hence, as is well known, I went to my encounter
with the terror-monger at the bottom of the tarn.
For a while it was hand-to-hand between us,
then blood went curling along the currents
and I beheaded Grendel's mother in the hall
2140 with a mighty sword. I barely managed
to escape with my life; my time had not yet come.
But Halfdane's heir, the shelter of those earls,
again endowed me with gifts in abundance.
  "Thus the king acted with due custom.
2145 I was paid and recompensed completely,
given full measure and the freedom to choose
from Hothgar's treasures by Hrothgar himself.
These, King Hygelac, I am happy to present
to you as gifts. It is still upon your grace
2150 that all favor depends. I have few kinsmen
who are close, my king, except for your kind self."
Then he ordered the boar-framed standard to be brought,
the battle-topping helmet, the mail-shirt gray as hoar-frost,
and the precious war-sword; and proceeded with his speech:
2155 "When Hrothgar presented this war-gear to me
he instructed me, my lord, to give you some account
of why it signifies his special favor.
He said it had belonged to his older brother,
King Heorogar, who had long kept it,
2160 but that Heorogar had never bequeathed it
to his son Heoroward, that worthy scion,
loyal as he was. Enjoy it well."
  I heard four horses were handed over next.
Beowulf bestowed four bay steeds
2165 to go with the armor, swift gallopers,
all alike. So ought a kinsman act,
instead of plotting and planning in secret
to bring people to grief, or conspiring to arrange
the death of comrades. The warrior king
2170 was uncle to Beowulf and honored by his nephew:
each was concerned for the other's good.
  I heard he presented Hygd with a gorget,
the priceless torque that the prince's daughter,
Wealhtheow, had given him; and three horses,
2175 supple creatures brilliantly saddled.
The bright necklace would be luminous on Hygd's breast.

Thus Beowulf bore himself with valor;
he was formidable in battle yet behaved with honor
and took no advantage; never cut down
2180 a comrade who was drunk, kept his temper
and, warrior that he was, watched and controlled
his God-sent strength and his outstanding
natural powers. He had been poorly regarded
for a long time, was taken by the Geats
2185 for less than he was worth:[4] and their lord too
had never much esteemed him in the mead-hall.
They firmly believed that he lacked force,
that the prince was a weakling; but presently
every affront to his deserving was reversed.
2190 The battle-famed king, bulwark of his earls,
ordered a gold-chased heirloom of Hrethel's[5]
to be brought in; it was the best example
of a gem-studded sword in the Geat treasury.
This he laid on Beowulf's lap
2195 and then rewarded him with land as well,
seven thousand hides; and a hall and a throne.
Both owned land by birth in that country,
ancestral grounds; but the greater right
and sway were inherited by the higher born.

[THE DRAGON WAKES]

2200 A lot was to happen in later days
in the fury of battle. Hygelac fell
and the shelter of Heardred's shield proved useless
against the fierce aggression of the Shylfings:[6]
ruthless swordsmen, seasoned campaigners,
2205 they came against him and his conquering nation,
and with cruel force cut him down
so that afterwards
                    the wide kingdom
reverted to Beowulf. He ruled it well
for fifty winters, grew old and wise

4. There is no other mention of Beowulf's unpromising youth. This motif of the "Cinderella hero" and others, such as Grendel's magic pouch, are examples of folklore material, probably circulating orally, that made its way into the poem.
5. Hygelac's father and Beowulf's grandfather.
6. There are several references, some of them lengthy, to the wars between the Geats and the Swedes. Because these are highly allusive and not in chronological order, they are difficult to follow and keep straight. This outline, along with the Genealogies (p. 31), may serve as a guide. *Phase 1:* After the death of the Geat patriarch, King Hrethel (lines 2462–70), Ohthere and Onela, the sons of the Swedish king Ongentheow, invade Geat territory and inflict heavy casualties in a battle at Hreosnahill (lines 2472–78). *Phase 2:* The Geats invade Sweden under Haethcyn, King

Hrethel's son who has succeeded him. At the battle of Ravenswood, the Geats capture Ongentheow's queen, but Ongentheow counterattacks, rescues the queen, and kills Haethcyn. Hygelac, Haethcyn's younger brother, arrives with reinforcements; Ongentheow is killed in savage combat with two of Hygelac's men; and the Swedes are routed (lines 2479–89 and 2922–90). *Phase 3:* Eanmund and Eadgils, the sons of Ohthere (presumably dead), are driven into exile by their uncle Onela, who is now king of the Swedes. They are given refuge by Hygelac's son Heardred, who has succeeded his father. Onela invades Geatland and kills Heardred; his retainer Weohstan kills Eanmund; and after the Swedes withdraw, Beowulf becomes king (lines 2204–8, which follow, and 2379–90). *Phase 4:* Eadgils, supported by Beowulf, invades Sweden and kills Onela (lines 2391–96).

2210 as warden of the land
                        until one began
to dominate the dark, a dragon on the prowl
from the steep vaults of a stone-roofed barrow
where he guarded a hoard; there was a hidden passage,
unknown to men, but someone[7] managed
2215 to enter by it and interfere
with the heathen trove. He had handled and removed
a gem-studded goblet; it gained him nothing,
though with a thief's wiles he had outwitted
the sleeping dragon. That drove him into rage,
2220 as the people of that country would soon discover.
    The intruder who broached the dragon's treasure
and moved him to wrath had never meant to.
It was desperation on the part of a slave
fleeing the heavy hand of some master,
2225 guilt-ridden and on the run,
going to ground. But he soon began
to shake with terror;[8] . . . . . . in shock
the wretch . . . .
. . . . panicked and ran
2230 away with the precious . . . . . .
metalwork. There were many other
heirlooms heaped inside the earth-house,
because long ago, with deliberate care,
somebody now forgotten
2235 had buried the riches of a highborn race
in this ancient cache. Death had come
and taken them all in times gone by
and the only one left to tell their tale,
the last of their line, could look forward to nothing
2240 but the same fate for himself: he foresaw that his joy
in the treasure would be brief.
                        A newly constructed
barrow stood waiting, on a wide headland
close to the waves, its entryway secured.
Into it the keeper of the hoard had carried
2245 all the goods and golden ware
worth preserving. His words were few:
"Now, earth, hold what earls once held
and heroes can no more; it was mined from you first
by honorable men. My own people
2250 have been ruined in war; one by one
they went down to death, looked their last
on sweet life in the hall. I am left with nobody
to bear a sword or to burnish plated goblets,
put a sheen on the cup. The companies have departed.
2255 The hard helmet, hasped with gold,

---

7. The following section was damaged by fire. In lines 2215–31 entire words and phrases are missing or indicated by only a few letters. Editorial attempts to reconstruct the text are conjectural and often disagree.
8. Lines 2227–30 are so damaged that they defy guesswork to reconstruct them.

will be stripped of its hoops; and the helmet-shiner
who should polish the metal of the war-mask sleeps;
the coat of mail that came through all fights,
through shield-collapse and cut of sword,
2260 decays with the warrior. Nor may webbed mail
range far and wide on the warlord's back
beside his mustered troops. No trembling harp,
no tuned timber, no tumbling hawk
swerving through the hall, no swift horse
2265 pawing the courtyard. Pillage and slaughter
have emptied the earth of entire peoples."
And so he mourned as he moved about the world,
deserted and alone, lamenting his unhappiness
day and night, until death's flood
brimmed up in his heart.
2270   Then an old harrower of the dark
happened to find the hoard open,
the burning one who hunts out barrows,
the slick-skinned dragon, threatening the night sky
with streamers of fire. People on the farms
2275 are in dread of him. He is driven to hunt out
hoards under ground, to guard heathen gold
through age-long vigils, though to little avail.
For three centuries, this scourge of the people
had stood guard on that stoutly protected
2280 underground treasury, until the intruder
unleashed its fury; he hurried to his lord
with the gold-plated cup and made his plea
to be reinstated. Then the vault was rifled,
the ring-hoard robbed, and the wretched man
2285 had his request granted. His master gazed
on that find from the past for the first time.
    When the dragon awoke, trouble flared again.
He rippled down the rock, writhing with anger
when he saw the footprints of the prowler who had stolen
2290 too close to his dreaming head.
So may a man not marked by fate
easily escape exile and woe
by the grace of God.
                          The hoard-guardian
scorched the ground as he scoured and hunted
2295 for the trespasser who had troubled his sleep.
Hot and savage, he kept circling and circling
the outside of the mound. No man appeared
in that desert waste, but he worked himself up
by imagining battle; then back in he'd go
2300 in search of the cup, only to discover
signs that someone had stumbled upon
the golden treasures. So the guardian of the mound,
the hoard-watcher, waited for the gloaming
with fierce impatience; his pent-up fury
2305 at the loss of the vessel made him long to hit back

and lash out in flames. Then, to his delight,
the day waned and he could wait no longer
behind the wall, but hurtled forth
in a fiery blaze. The first to suffer
2310 were the people on the land, but before long
it was their treasure-giver who would come to grief.
    The dragon began to belch out flames
and burn bright homesteads; there was a hot glow
that scared everyone, for the vile sky-winger
2315 would leave nothing alive in his wake.
Everywhere the havoc he wrought was in evidence.
Far and near, the Geat nation
bore the brunt of his brutal assaults
and virulent hate. Then back to the hoard
2320 he would dart before daybreak, to hide in his den.
He had swinged the land, swathed it in flame,
in fire and burning, and now he felt secure
in the vaults of his barrow; but his trust was unavailing.
    Then Beowulf was given bad news,
2325 the hard truth: his own home,
the best of buildings, had been burned to a cinder,
the throne-room of the Geats. It threw the hero
into deep anguish and darkened his mood:
the wise man thought he must have thwarted
2330 ancient ordinance of the eternal Lord,
broken His commandment. His mind was in turmoil,
unaccustomed anxiety and gloom
confused his brain; the fire-dragon
had razed the coastal region and reduced
2335 forts and earthworks to dust and ashes,
so the war-king planned and plotted his revenge.
The warriors' protector, prince of the hall-troop,
ordered a marvelous all-iron shield
from his smithy works. He well knew
2340 that linden boards would let him down
and timber burn. After many trials,
he was destined to face the end of his days,
in this mortal world, as was the dragon,
for all his long leasehold on the treasure.
2345   Yet the prince of the rings was too proud
to line up with a large army
against the sky-plague. He had scant regard
for the dragon as a threat, no dread at all
of its courage or strength, for he had kept going
2350 often in the past, through perils and ordeals
of every sort, after he had purged
Hrothgar's hall, triumphed in Heorot
and beaten Grendel. He outgrappled the monster
and his evil kin.
                    One of his cruelest
2355 hand-to-hand encounters had happened
when Hygelac, king of the Geats, was killed

in Friesland: the people's friend and lord,
Hrethel's son, slaked a sword blade's
thirst for blood. But Beowulf's prodigious
2360 gifts as a swimmer guaranteed his safety:
he arrived at the shore, shouldering thirty
battle-dresses, the booty he had won.
There was little for the Hetware[9] to be happy about
as they shielded their faces and fighting on the ground
2365 began in earnest. With Beowulf against them,
few could hope to return home.
    Across the wide sea, desolate and alone,
the son of Ecgtheow swam back to his people.
There Hygd offered him throne and authority
2370 as lord of the ring-hoard: with Hygelac dead,
she had no belief in her son's ability
to defend their homeland against foreign invaders.
Yet there was no way the weakened nation
could get Beowulf to give in and agree
2375 to be elevated over Heardred as his lord
or to undertake the office of kingship.
But he did provide support for the prince,
honored and minded him until he matured
as the ruler of Geatland.
                Then over sea-roads
2380 exiles arrived, sons of Ohthere.[1]
They had rebelled against the best of all
the sea-kings in Sweden, the one who held sway
in the Shylfing nation, their renowned prince,
lord of the mead-hall. That marked the end
2385 for Hygelac's son: his hospitality
was mortally rewarded with wounds from a sword.
Heardred lay slaughtered and Onela returned
to the land of Sweden, leaving Beowulf
to ascend the throne, to sit in majesty
2390 and rule over the Geats. He was a good king.
    In days to come, he contrived to avenge
the fall of his prince; he befriended Eadgils
when Eadgils was friendless, aiding his cause
with weapons and warriors over the wide sea,
2395 sending him men. The feud was settled
on a comfortless campaign when he killed Onela.
    And so the son of Ecgtheow had survived
every extreme, excelling himself
in daring and in danger, until the day arrived
2400 when he had to come face to face with the dragon.
The lord of the Geats took eleven comrades
and went in a rage to reconnoiter.
By then he had discovered the cause of the affliction
being visited on the people. The precious cup
2405 had come to him from the hand of the finder,

9. A tribe of the Franks allied with the Frisians.   1. See p. 79. n. 6, Phases 3 and 4.

the one who had started all this strife
and was now added as a thirteenth to their number.
They press-ganged and compelled this poor creature
to be their guide. Against his will
2410   he led them to the earth-vault he alone knew,
an underground barrow near the sea-billows
and heaving waves, heaped inside
with exquisite metalwork. The one who stood guard
was dangerous and watchful, warden of the trove
2415   buried under earth: no easy bargain
would be made in that place by any man.
        The veteran king sat down on the cliff-top.
He wished good luck to the Geats who had shared
his hearth and his gold. He was sad at heart,
2420   unsettled yet ready, sensing his death.
His fate hovered near, unknowable but certain:
it would soon claim his coffered soul,
part life from limb. Before long
the prince's spirit would spin free from his body.
2425   Beowulf, son of Ecgtheow, spoke:
"Many a skirmish I survived when I was young
and many times of war: I remember them well.
At seven, I was fostered out by my father,
left in the charge of my people's lord.
2430   King Hrethel kept me and took care of me,
was openhanded, behaved like a kinsman.
While I was his ward, he treated me no worse
as a wean[2] about the place than one of his own boys,
Herebeald and Haethcyn, or my own Hygelac.
2435   For the eldest, Herebeald, an unexpected
deathbed was laid out, through a brother's doing,
when Haethcyn bent his horn-tipped bow
and loosed the arrow that destroyed his life.
He shot wide and buried a shaft
2440   in the flesh and blood of his own brother.
That offense was beyond redress, a wrongfooting
of the heart's affections; for who could avenge
the prince's life or pay his death-price?
It was like the misery felt by an old man
2445   who has lived to see his son's body
swing on the gallows. He begins to keen
and weep for his boy, watching the raven
gloat where he hangs: he can be of no help.
The wisdom of age is worthless to him.
2450   Morning after morning, he wakes to remember
that his child is gone; he has no interest
in living on until another heir
is born in the hall, now that his first-born
has entered death's dominion forever.
2455   He gazes sorrowfully at his son's dwelling,

2. A young child [Northern Ireland; Translator's note].

the banquet hall bereft of all delight,
the windswept hearthstone; the horsemen are sleeping,
the warriors under ground; what was is no more.
No tunes from the harp, no cheer raised in the yard.
2460 Alone with his longing, he lies down on his bed
and sings a lament; everything seems too large,
the steadings and the fields.
                                          Such was the feeling
of loss endured by the lord of the Geats
after Herebeald's death. He was helplessly placed
2465 to set to rights the wrong committed,
could not punish the killer in accordance with the law
of the blood-feud, although he felt no love for him.
Heartsore, wearied, he turned away
from life's joys, chose God's light
2470 and departed, leaving buildings and lands
to his sons, as a man of substance will.
        "Then over the wide sea Swedes and Geats
battled and feuded and fought without quarter.
Hostilities broke out when Hrethel died.[3]
2475 Ongentheow's sons were unrelenting,
refusing to make peace, campaigning violently
from coast to coast, constantly setting up
terrible ambushes around Hreosnahill.
My own kith and kin avenged
2480 these evil events, as everybody knows,
but the price was high: one of them paid
with his life. Haethcyn, lord of the Geats,
met his fate there and fell in the battle.
Then, as I have heard, Hygelac's sword
2485 was raised in the morning against Ongentheow,
his brother's killer. When Eofor cleft
the old Swede's helmet, halved it open,
he fell, death-pale: his feud-calloused hand
could not stave off the fatal stroke.
2490   "The treasures that Hygelac lavished on me
I paid for when I fought, as fortune allowed me,
with my glittering sword. He gave me land
and the security land brings, so he had no call
to go looking for some lesser champion,
2495 some mercenary from among the Gifthas
or the Spear-Danes or the men of Sweden.
I marched ahead of him, always there
at the front of the line; and I shall fight like that
for as long as I live, as long as this sword
2500 shall last, which has stood me in good stead
late and soon, ever since I killed
Dayraven the Frank in front of the two armies.
He brought back no looted breastplate
to the Frisian king but fell in battle,

3. See p. 79, n. 6, Phases 1 and 2.

2505 their standard-bearer, highborn and brave.
No sword blade sent him to his death:
my bare hands stilled his heartbeats
and wrecked the bone-house. Now blade and hand,
sword and sword-stroke, will assay the hoard."

[BEOWULF ATTACKS THE DRAGON]

2510   Beowulf spoke, made a formal boast
for the last time: "I risked my life
often when I was young. Now I am old,
but as king of the people I shall pursue this fight
for the glory of winning, if the evil one will only
2515 abandon his earth-fort and face me in the open."
    Then he addressed each dear companion
one final time, those fighters in their helmets,
resolute and highborn: "I would rather not
use a weapon if I knew another way
2520 to grapple with the dragon and make good my boast
as I did against Grendel in days gone by.
But I shall be meeting molten venom
in the fire he breathes, so I go forth
in mail-shirt and shield. I won't shift a foot
2525 when I meet the cave-guard: what occurs on the wall
between the two of us will turn out as fate,
overseer of men, decides. I am resolved.
I scorn further words against this sky-borne foe.
    "Men-at-arms, remain here on the barrow,
2530 safe in your armor, to see which one of us
is better in the end at bearing wounds
in a deadly fray. This fight is not yours,
nor is it up to any man except me
to measure his strength against the monster
2535 or to prove his worth. I shall win the gold
by my courage, or else mortal combat,
doom of battle, will bear your lord away."
    Then he drew himself up beside his shield.
The fabled warrior in his war-shirt and helmet
2540 trusted in his own strength entirely
and went under the crag. No coward path.
    Hard by the rock-face that hale veteran,
a good man who had gone repeatedly
into combat and danger and come through,
2545 saw a stone arch and a gushing stream
that burst from the barrow, blazing and wafting
a deadly heat. It would be hard to survive
unscathed near the hoard, to hold firm
against the dragon in those flaming depths.
2550 Then he gave a shout. The lord of the Geats
unburdened his breast and broke out
in a storm of anger. Under gray stone

his voice challenged and resounded clearly.
Hate was ignited. The hoard-guard recognized
2555 a human voice, the time was over
for peace and parleying. Pouring forth
in a hot battle-fume, the breath of the monster
burst from the rock. There was a rumble under ground.
Down there in the barrow, Beowulf the warrior
2560 lifted his shield: the outlandish thing
writhed and convulsed and viciously
turned on the king, whose keen-edged sword,
an heirloom inherited by ancient right,
was already in his hand. Roused to a fury,
2565 each antagonist struck terror in the other.
Unyielding, the lord of his people loomed
by his tall shield, sure of his ground,
while the serpent looped and unleashed itself.
Swaddled in flames, it came gliding and flexing
2570 and racing toward its fate. Yet his shield defended
the renowned leader's life and limb
for a shorter time than he meant it to:
that final day was the first time
when Beowulf fought and fate denied him
2575 glory in battle. So the king of the Geats
raised his hand and struck hard
at the enameled scales, but scarcely cut through:
the blade flashed and slashed yet the blow
was far less powerful than the hard-pressed king
2580 had need of at that moment. The mound-keeper
went into a spasm and spouted deadly flames:
when he felt the stroke, battle-fire
billowed and spewed. Beowulf was foiled
of a glorious victory. The glittering sword,
2585 infallible before that day,
failed when he unsheathed it, as it never should have.
For the son of Ecgtheow, it was no easy thing
to have to give ground like that and go
unwillingly to inhabit another home
2590 in a place beyond; so every man must yield
the leasehold of his days.
                                        Before long
the fierce contenders clashed again.
The hoard-guard took heart, inhaled and swelled up
and got a new wind; he who had once ruled
2595 was furled in fire and had to face the worst.
No help or backing was to be had then
from his highborn comrades; that hand-picked troop
broke ranks and ran for their lives
to the safety of the wood. But within one heart
2600 sorrow welled up: in a man of worth
the claims of kinship cannot be denied.
    His name was Wiglaf, a son of Weohstan's,
a well-regarded Shylfing warrior

related to Aelfhere.[4] When he saw his lord
2605 tormented by the heat of his scalding helmet,
he remembered the bountiful gifts bestowed on him,
how well he lived among the Waegmundings,
the freehold he inherited from his father[5] before him.
He could not hold back: one hand brandished
2610 the yellow-timbered shield, the other drew his sword—
an ancient blade that was said to have belonged
to Eanmund, the son of Ohthere, the one
Weohstan had slain when he was an exile without friends.
He carried the arms to the victim's kinfolk,
2615 the burnished helmet, the webbed chain-mail
and that relic of the giants. But Onela returned
the weapons to him, rewarded Weohstan
with Eanmund's war-gear. He ignored the blood-feud,
the fact that Eanmund was his brother's son.[6]
2620 Weohstan kept that war-gear for a lifetime,
the sword and the mail-shirt, until it was the son's turn
to follow his father and perform his part.
Then, in old age, at the end of his days
among the Weather-Geats, he bequeathed to Wiglaf
innumerable weapons.
2625   And now the youth
was to enter the line of battle with his lord,
his first time to be tested as a fighter.
His spirit did not break and the ancestral blade
would keep its edge, as the dragon discovered
2630 as soon as they came together in the combat.
    Sad at heart, addressing his companions,
Wiglaf spoke wise and fluent words:
"I remember that time when mead was flowing,
how we pledged loyalty to our lord in the hall,
2635 promised our ring-giver we would be worth our price,
make good the gift of the war-gear,
those swords and helmets, as and when
his need required it. He picked us out
from the army deliberately, honored us and judged us
2640 fit for this action, made me these lavish gifts—
and all because he considered us the best
of his arms-bearing thanes. And now, although
he wanted this challenge to be one he'd face
by himself alone—the shepherd of our land,
2645 a man unequaled in the quest for glory
and a name for daring—now the day has come
when this lord we serve needs sound men
to give him their support. Let us go to him,

---

4. Although Wiglaf is here said to be a Shylfing
(i.e., a Swede), in line 2607 we are told his family
are Waegmundings, a clan of the Geats, which is
also Beowulf's family. It was possible for a family
to owe allegiance to more than one nation and to
shift sides as a result of feuds. Nothing is known
of Aelfhere.
5. I.e., Weohstan, who, as explained below, was
the slayer of Onela's nephew Eanmund. Possibly,

Weohstan joined the Geats under Beowulf after
Eanmund's brother, with Beowulf's help, avenged
Eanmund's death on Onela and became king of the
Shylfings. See p. 79, n. 6, Phase 2.
6. An ironic comment: since Onela wanted to kill
Eanmund, he rewarded Weohstan for killing his
nephew instead of exacting compensation or
revenge.

help our leader through the hot flame
2650 and dread of the fire. As God is my witness,
I would rather my body were robed in the same
burning blaze as my gold-giver's body
than go back home bearing arms.
That is unthinkable, unless we have first
2655 slain the foe and defended the life
of the prince of the Weather-Geats. I well know
the things he has done for us deserve better.
Should he alone be left exposed
to fall in battle? We must bond together,
2660 shield and helmet, mail-shirt and sword."
Then he waded the dangerous reek and went
under arms to his lord, saying only:
"Go on, dear Beowulf, do everything
you said you would when you were still young
2665 and vowed you would never let your name and fame
be dimmed while you lived. Your deeds are famous,
so stay resolute, my lord, defend your life now
with the whole of your strength. I shall stand by you."
After those words, a wildness rose
2670 in the dragon again and drove it to attack,
heaving up fire, hunting for enemies,
the humans it loathed. Flames lapped the shield,
charred it to the boss, and the body armor
on the young warrior was useless to him.
2675 But Wiglaf did well under the wide rim
Beowulf shared with him once his own had shattered
in sparks and ashes.
Inspired again
by the thought of glory, the war-king threw
his whole strength behind a sword stroke
2680 and connected with the skull. And Naegling snapped.
Beowulf's ancient iron-gray sword
let him down in the fight. It was never his fortune
to be helped in combat by the cutting edge
of weapons made of iron. When he wielded a sword,
2685 no matter how blooded and hard-edged the blade,
his hand was too strong, the stroke he dealt
(I have heard) would ruin it. He could reap no advantage.
Then the bane of that people, the fire-breathing dragon,
was mad to attack for a third time.
2690 When a chance came, he caught the hero
in a rush of flame and clamped sharp fangs
into his neck. Beowulf's body
ran wet with his life-blood: it came welling out.
Next thing, they say, the noble son of Weohstan
2695 saw the king in danger at his side
and displayed his inborn bravery and strength.
He left the head alone,[7] but his fighting hand
was burned when he came to his kinsman's aid.

---

7. I.e., he avoided the dragon's flame-breathing head.

He lunged at the enemy lower down
2700 so that his decorated sword sank into its belly
and the flames grew weaker.
                            Once again the king
gathered his strength and drew a stabbing knife
he carried on his belt, sharpened for battle.
He stuck it deep in the dragon's flank.
2705 Beowulf dealt it a deadly wound.
They had killed the enemy, courage quelled his life;
that pair of kinsmen, partners in nobility,
had destroyed the foe. So every man should act,
be at hand when needed; but now, for the king,
2710 this would be the last of his many labors
and triumphs in the world.
                            Then the wound
dealt by the ground-burner earlier began
to scald and swell; Beowulf discovered
deadly poison suppurating inside him,
2715 surges of nausea, and so, in his wisdom,
the prince realized his state and struggled
toward a seat on the rampart. He steadied his gaze
on those gigantic stones, saw how the earthwork
was braced with arches built over columns.
2720 And now that thane unequaled for goodness
with his own hands washed his lord's wounds,
swabbed the weary prince with water,
bathed him clean, unbuckled his helmet.
Beowulf spoke: in spite of his wounds,
2725 mortal wounds, he still spoke
for he well knew his days in the world
had been lived out to the end—his allotted time
was drawing to a close, death was very near.
"Now is the time when I would have wanted
2730 to bestow this armor on my own son,
had it been my fortune to have fathered an heir
and live on in his flesh. For fifty years
I ruled this nation. No king
of any neighboring clan would dare
2735 face me with troops, none had the power
to intimidate me. I took what came,
cared for and stood by things in my keeping,
never fomented quarrels, never
swore to a lie. All this consoles me,
2740 doomed as I am and sickening for death;
because of my right ways, the Ruler of mankind
need never blame me when the breath leaves my body
for murder of kinsmen. Go now quickly,
dearest Wiglaf, under the gray stone
2745 where the dragon is laid out, lost to his treasure;
hurry to feast your eyes on the hoard.
Away you go: I want to examine
that ancient gold, gaze my fill

on those garnered jewels; my going will be easier
2750 for having seen the treasure, a less troubled letting-go
of the life and lordship I have long maintained."
    And so, I have heard, the son of Weohstan
quickly obeyed the command of his languishing
war-weary lord; he went in his chain-mail
2755 under the rock-piled roof of the barrow,
exulting in his triumph, and saw beyond the seat
a treasure-trove of astonishing richness,
wall-hangings that were a wonder to behold,
glittering gold spread across the ground,
2760 the old dawn-scorching serpent's den
packed with goblets and vessels from the past,
tarnished and corroding. Rusty helmets
all eaten away. Armbands everywhere,
artfully wrought. How easily treasure
2765 buried in the ground, gold hidden
however skillfully, can escape from any man!
    And he saw too a standard, entirely of gold,
hanging high over the hoard,
a masterpiece of filigree; it glowed with light
2770 so he could make out the ground at his feet
and inspect the valuables. Of the dragon there was no
remaining sign: the sword had dispatched him.
Then, the story goes, a certain man
plundered the hoard in that immemorial howe,
2775 filled his arms with flagons and plates,
anything he wanted; and took the standard also,
most brilliant of banners.
                                         Already the blade
of the old king's sharp killing-sword
had done its worst: the one who had for long
2780 minded the hoard, hovering over gold,
unleashing fire, surging forth
midnight after midnight, had been mown down.
    Wiglaf went quickly, keen to get back,
excited by the treasure. Anxiety weighed
2785 on his brave heart—he was hoping he would find
the leader of the Geats alive where he had left him
helpless, earlier, on the open ground.
    So he came to the place, carrying the treasure
and found his lord bleeding profusely,
2790 his life at an end; again he began
to swab his body. The beginnings of an utterance
broke out from the king's breast-cage.
The old lord gazed sadly at the gold.
    "To the everlasting Lord of all,
2795 to the King of Glory, I give thanks
that I behold this treasure here in front of me,
that I have been allowed to leave my people
so well endowed on the day I die.
Now that I have bartered my last breath

2800 to own this fortune, it is up to you
to look after their needs. I can hold out no longer.
Order my troop to construct a barrow
on a headland on the coast, after my pyre has cooled.
It will loom on the horizon at Hronesness[8]
2805 and be a reminder among my people—
so that in coming times crews under sail
will call it Beowulf's Barrow, as they steer
ships across the wide and shrouded waters."
        Then the king in his great-heartedness unclasped
2810 the collar of gold from his neck and gave it
to the young thane, telling him to use
it and the war-shirt and gilded helmet well.
"You are the last of us, the only one left
of the Waegmundings. Fate swept us away,
2815 sent my whole brave highborn clan
to their final doom. Now I must follow them."
        That was the warrior's last word.
He had no more to confide. The furious heat
of the pyre would assail him. His soul fled from his breast
2820 to its destined place among the steadfast ones.

[BEOWULF'S FUNERAL]

        It was hard then on the young hero,
having to watch the one he held so dear
there on the ground, going through
his death agony. The dragon from underearth,
2825 his nightmarish destroyer, lay destroyed as well,
utterly without life. No longer would his snakefolds
ply themselves to safeguard hidden gold.
Hard-edged blades, hammered out
and keenly filed, had finished him
2830 so that the sky-roamer lay there rigid,
brought low beside the treasure-lodge.
        Never again would he glitter and glide
and show himself off in midnight air,
exulting in his riches: he fell to earth
2835 through the battle-strength in Beowulf's arm.
There were few, indeed, as far as I have heard,
big and brave as they may have been,
few who would have held out if they had had to face
the outpourings of that poison-breather
2840 or gone foraging on the ring-hall floor
and found the deep barrow-dweller
on guard and awake.
                        The treasure had been won,
bought and paid for by Beowulf's death.
Both had reached the end of the road
through the life they had been lent.
2845   Before long

8. A headland by the sea. The name means "Whalesness."

the battle-dodgers abandoned the wood,
the ones who had let down their lord earlier,
the tail-turners, ten of them together.
When he needed them most, they had made off.
2850 Now they were ashamed and came behind shields,
in their battle-outfits, to where the old man lay.
They watched Wiglaf, sitting worn out,
a comrade shoulder to shoulder with his lord,
trying in vain to bring him round with water.
2855 Much as he wanted to, there was no way
he could preserve his lord's life on earth
or alter in the least the Almighty's will.
What God judged right would rule what happened
to every man, as it does to this day.
2860 Then a stern rebuke was bound to come
from the young warrior to the ones who had been cowards.
Wiglaf, son of Weohstan, spoke
disdainfully and in disappointment:
"Anyone ready to admit the truth
2865 will surely realize that the lord of men
who showered you with gifts and gave you the armor
you are standing in—when he would distribute
helmets and mail-shirts to men on the mead-benches,
a prince treating his thanes in hall
2870 to the best he could find, far or near—
was throwing weapons uselessly away.
It would be a sad waste when the war broke out.
Beowulf had little cause to brag
about his armed guard; yet God who ordains
2875 who wins or loses allowed him to strike
with his own blade when bravery was needed.
There was little I could do to protect his life
in the heat of the fray, but I found new strength
welling up when I went to help him.
2880 Then my sword connected and the deadly assaults
of our foe grew weaker, the fire coursed
less strongly from his head. But when the worst happened
too few rallied around the prince.
    "So it is good-bye now to all you know and love
2885 on your home ground, the open-handedness,
the giving of war-swords. Every one of you
with freeholds of land, our whole nation,
will be dispossessed, once princes from beyond
get tidings of how you turned and fled
2890 and disgraced yourselves. A warrior will sooner
die than live a life of shame."
    Then he ordered the outcome of the fight to be reported
to those camped on the ridge, that crowd of retainers
who had sat all morning, sad at heart,
2895 shield-bearers wondering about
the man they loved: would this day be his last
or would he return? He told the truth

and did not balk, the rider who bore
news to the cliff-top. He addressed them all:
2900 "Now the people's pride and love,
the lord of the Geats, is laid on his deathbed,
brought down by the dragon's attack.
Beside him lies the bane of his life,
dead from knife-wounds. There was no way
2905 Beowulf could manage to get the better
of the monster with his sword. Wiglaf sits
at Beowulf's side, the son of Weohstan,
the living warrior watching by the dead,
keeping weary vigil, holding a wake
for the loved and the loathed.
2910   Now war is looming
over our nation, soon it will be known
to Franks and Frisians, far and wide,
that the king is gone. Hostility has been great
among the Franks since Hygelac sailed forth
2915 at the head of a war-fleet into Friesland:
there the Hetware harried and attacked
and overwhelmed him with great odds.
The leader in his war-gear was laid low,
fell among followers: that lord did not favor
2920 his company with spoils. The Merovingian king
has been an enemy to us ever since.
      "Nor do I expect peace or pact-keeping
of any sort from the Swedes. Remember:
at Ravenswood,[9] Ongentheow
2925 slaughtered Haethcyn, Hrethel's son,
when the Geat people in their arrogance
first attacked the fierce Shylfings.
The return blow was quickly struck
by Ohthere's father.[1] Old and terrible,
2930 he felled the sea-king and saved his own
aged wife, the mother of Onela
and of Ohthere, bereft of her gold rings.
Then he kept hard on the heels of the foe
and drove them, leaderless, lucky to get away
2935 in a desperate rout into Ravenswood.
His army surrounded the weary remnant
where they nursed their wounds; all through the night
he howled threats at those huddled survivors,
promised to axe their bodies open
2940 when dawn broke, dangle them from gallows
to feed the birds. But at first light
when their spirits were lowest, relief arrived.
They heard the sound of Hygelac's horn,
his trumpet calling as he came to find them,
2945 the hero in pursuit, at hand with troops.

---

9. The messenger describes in greater detail the
Battle of Ravenswood. See the outline of the Swedish wars on p. 79, n. 6.
1. I.e., Ongentheow.

"The bloody swathe that Swedes and Geats
cut through each other was everywhere.
No one could miss their murderous feuding.
Then the old man made his move,
2950 pulled back, barred his people in:
Ongentheow withdrew to higher ground.
Hygelac's pride and prowess as a fighter
were known to the earl; he had no confidence
that he could hold out against that horde of seamen,
2955 defend his wife and the ones he loved
from the shock of the attack. He retreated for shelter
behind the earthwall. Then Hygelac swooped
on the Swedes at bay, his banners swarmed
into their refuge, his Geat forces
2960 drove forward to destroy the camp.
There in his gray hairs, Ongentheow
was cornered, ringed around with swords.
And it came to pass that the king's fate
was in Eofor's hands,[2] and in his alone.
2965 Wulf, son of Wonred, went for him in anger,
split him open so that blood came spurting
from under his hair. The old hero
still did not flinch, but parried fast,
hit back with a harder stroke:
2970 the king turned and took him on.
Then Wonred's son, the brave Wulf,
could land no blow against the aged lord.
Ongentheow divided his helmet
so that he buckled and bowed his bloodied head
2975 and dropped to the ground. But his doom held off.
Though he was cut deep, he recovered again.
"With his brother down, the undaunted Eofor,
Hygelac's thane, hefted his sword
and smashed murderously at the massive helmet
2980 past the lifted shield. And the king collapsed,
the shepherd of people was sheared of life.
Many then hurried to help Wulf,
bandaged and lifted him, now that they were left
masters of the blood-soaked battle-ground.
2985 One warrior stripped the other,
looted Ongenteow's iron mail-coat,
his hard sword-hilt, his helmet too,
and carried the graith[3] to King Hygelac,
he accepted the prize, promised fairly
2990 that reward would come, and kept his word.
For their bravery in action, when they arrived home,
Eofor and Wulf were overloaded
by Hrethel's son, Hygelac the Geat,

2. I.e., he was at Eofor's mercy. Eofor's slaying of
Ongetheow was described in lines 2486–89, where
no mention is made of his brother Wulf's part in
the battle. They are the sons of Wonred. *Eofor*
means boar, and *Wulf* is the Old English spelling
of wolf.
3. Possessions, apparel.

with gifts of land and linked rings
2995 that were worth a fortune. They had won glory,
so there was no gainsaying his generosity.
And he gave Eofor his only daughter
to bide at home with him, an honor and a bond.
"So this bad blood between us and the Swedes,
3000 this vicious feud, I am convinced,
is bound to revive; they will cross our borders
and attack in force when they find out
that Beowulf is dead. In days gone by
when our warriors fell and we were undefended,
3005 he kept our coffers and our kingdom safe.
He worked for the people, but as well as that
he behaved like a hero.
                    We must hurry now
to take a last look at the king
and launch him, lord and lavisher of rings,
3010 on the funeral road. His royal pyre
will melt no small amount of gold:
heaped there in a hoard, it was bought at heavy cost,
and that pile of rings he paid for at the end
with his own life will go up with the flame,
3015 be furled in fire: treasure no follower
will wear in his memory, nor lovely woman
link and attach as a torque around her neck—
but often, repeatedly, in the path of exile
they shall walk bereft, bowed under woe,
3020 now that their leader's laugh is silenced,
high spirits quenched. Many a spear
dawn-cold to the touch will be taken down
and waved on high; the swept harp
won't waken warriors, but the raven winging
3025 darkly over the doomed will have news,
tidings for the eagle of how he hoked and ate,
how the wolf and he made short work of the dead."[4]
    Such was the drift of the dire report
that gallant man delivered. He got little wrong
in what he told and predicted.
3030   The whole troop
rose in tears, then took their way
to the uncanny scene under Earnaness.[5]
There, on the sand, where his soul had left him,
they found him at rest, their ring-giver
3035 from days gone by. The great man
had breathed his last. Beowulf the king
had indeed met with a marvelous death.
    But what they saw first was far stranger:
the serpent on the ground, gruesome and vile,

4. The raven, eagle, and wolf—the scavengers who will feed on the slain—are "the beasts of battle," a common motif in Germanic war poetry. "Hoked": rooted about [Northern Ireland, Translator's note].

5. The site of Beowulf's fight with the dragon. The name means "Eaglesness."

3040 lying facing him. The fire-dragon
was scaresomely burned, scorched all colors.
From head to tail, his entire length
was fifty feet. He had shimmered forth
on the night air once, then winged back
3045 down to his den; but death owned him now,
he would never enter his earth-gallery again.
Beside him stood pitchers and piled-up dishes,
silent flagons, precious swords
eaten through with rust, ranged as they had been
3050 while they waited their thousand winters under ground.
That huge cache, gold inherited
from an ancient race, was under a spell—
which meant no one was ever permitted
to enter the ring-hall unless God Himself,
3055 mankind's Keeper, True King of Triumphs,
allowed some person pleasing to Him—
and in His eyes worthy—to open the hoard.
    What came about brought to nothing
the hopes of the one who had wrongly hidden
3060 riches under the rock-face. First the dragon slew
that man among men, who in turn made fierce amends
and settled the feud. Famous for his deeds
a warrior may be, but it remains a mystery
where his life will end, when he may no longer
3065 dwell in the mead-hall among his own.
So it was with Beowulf, when he faced the cruelty
and cunning of the mound-guard. He himself was ignorant
of how his departure from the world would happen.
The highborn chiefs who had buried the treasure
3070 declared it until doomsday so accursed
that whoever robbed it would be guilty of wrong
and grimly punished for their transgression,
hasped in hell-bonds in heathen shrines.
Yet Beowulf's gaze at the gold treasure
3075 when he first saw it had not been selfish.
    Wiglaf, son of Weohstan, spoke:
"Often when one man follows his own will
many are hurt. This happened to us.
Nothing we advised could ever convince
3080 the prince we loved, our land's guardian,
not to vex the custodian of the gold,
let him lie where he was long accustomed,
lurk there under earth until the end of the world.
He held to his high destiny. The hoard is laid bare,
3085 but at a grave cost; it was too cruel a fate
that forced the king to that encounter.
I have been inside and seen everything
amassed in the vault. I managed to enter
although no great welcome awaited me
3090 under the earthwall. I quickly gathered up
a huge pile of the priceless treasures

handpicked from the hoard and carried them here
where the king could see them. He was still himself,
alive, aware, and in spite of his weakness
3095　　he had many requests. He wanted me to greet you
and order the building of a barrow that would crown
the site of his pyre, serve as his memorial,
in a commanding position, since of all men
to have lived and thrived and lorded it on earth
3100　　his worth and due as a warrior were the greatest.
Now let us again go quickly
and feast our eyes on that amazing fortune
heaped under the wall. I will show the way
and take you close to those coffers packed with rings
3105　　and bars of gold. Let a bier be made
and got ready quickly when we come out
and then let us bring the body of our lord,
the man we loved, to where he will lodge
for a long time in the care of the Almighty."
3110　　　　Then Weohstan's son, stalwart to the end,
had orders given to owners of dwellings,
many people of importance in the land,
to fetch wood from far and wide
for the good man's pyre:
　　　　　　　　　　　"Now shall flame consume
3115　　our leader in battle, the blaze darken
round him who stood his ground in the steel-hail,
when the arrow-storm shot from bowstrings
pelted the shield-wall. The shaft hit home.
Feather-fledged, it finned the barb in flight."
3120　　　　Next the wise son of Weohstan
called from among the king's thanes
a group of seven: he selected the best
and entered with them, the eighth of their number,
under the God-cursed roof; one raised
3125　　a lighted torch and led the way.
No lots were cast for who should loot the hoard
for it was obvious to them that every bit of it
lay unprotected within the vault,
there for the taking. It was no trouble
3130　　to hurry to work and haul out
the priceless store. They pitched the dragon
over the cliff-top, let tide's flow
and backwash take the treasure-minder.
Then coiled gold was loaded on a cart
3135　　in great abundance, and the gray-haired leader,
the prince on his bier, borne to Hronesness.
　　　　The Geat people built a pyre for Beowulf,
stacked and decked it until it stood foursquare,
hung with helmets, heavy war-shields
3140　　and shining armor, just as he had ordered.
Then his warriors laid him in the middle of it,
mourning a lord far-famed and beloved.

On a height they kindled the hugest of all
funeral fires; fumes of woodsmoke
3145   billowed darkly up, the blaze roared
and drowned out their weeping, wind died down
and flames wrought havoc in the hot bone-house,
burning it to the core. They were disconsolate
and wailed aloud for their lord's decease.
3150   A Geat woman too sang out in grief;
with hair bound up, she unburdened herself
of her worst fears, a wild litany
of nightmare and lament: her nation invaded,
enemies on the rampage, bodies in piles,
3155   slavery and abasement. Heaven swallowed the smoke.
    Then the Geat people began to construct
a mound on a headland, high and imposing,
a marker that sailors could see from far away,
and in ten days they had done the work.
3160   It was their hero's memorial; what remained from the fire
they housed inside it, behind a wall
as worthy of him as their workmanship could make it.
And they buried torques in the barrow, and jewels
and a trove of such things as trespassing men
3165   had once dared to drag from the hoard.
They let the ground keep that ancestral treasure,
gold under gravel, gone to earth,
as useless to men now as it ever was.
Then twelve warriors rode around the tomb,
3170   chieftains' sons, champions in battle,
all of them distraught, chanting in dirges,
mourning his loss as a man and a king.
They extolled his heroic nature and exploits
and gave thanks for his greatness; which was the proper thing,
3175   for a man should praise a prince whom he holds dear
and cherish his memory when that moment comes
when he has to be convoyed from his bodily home.
So the Geat people, his hearth-companions,
sorrowed for the lord who had been laid low.
3180   They said that of all the kings upon earth
he was the man most gracious and fair-minded,
kindest to his people and keenest to win fame.

THE WANDERER

The lament of *The Wanderer* is an excellent example of the elegiac mood so common
in Old English poetry. The loss of a lord, of companions in arms, of a mead hall (in
which Anglo-Saxon life realized itself to the full) are themes that enhance the melancholy tone of *Beowulf* as they are the emotional basis for such a poem as the present
one. But nowhere more poignantly expressed than in *The Wanderer* is the loneliness
of the exile in search of a new lord and hall; this is what Beowulf's father, Ecgtheow,

would have suffered, had it not been for Hrothgar's hospitality. To the wretched seeker all weather is wintry, for nature seems to conspire to match a man's mood as he moves over the water from one land to another, yearning for a home and kin to replace those vanished ones that still fill his thoughts.

As is true of most Old English elegiac laments, both the language and the structure of *The Wanderer* are difficult. At the beginning the speaker (whom the poet identifies as an "earth-walker") voices hope of finding comfort after his many tribulations. After the poet's interruption, the wanderer continues to speak—to himself—of his long search for a new home, describing how he must keep his thoughts locked within him while he makes his search. But these thoughts form the most vivid and moving part of his soliloquy—how, floating on the sea, dazed with sorrow and fatigue, he imagines that he sees his old companions, and how, as he wakens to reality, they vanish over the water like seabirds. The second part of the poem, beginning with the seventh paragraph ("Therefore I cannot think why . . ."), expands the theme from one man to all human beings in a world wasted by war and time, and the speaker draws philosophical implications from his harsh experiences (presumably now in the past). He derives such cold comfort as he can from asking the old question *Ubi sunt?*—where are they who were once so glad to be alive? And he concludes with the thought that "all this earthly habitation shall be emptied" of humankind. The narrator, "wise in heart," communes with himself in private, apparently as an indication of his detachment from life. The poem concludes with a characteristic Old English injunction to practice restraint on earth, place hope only in heaven.

The Wanderer is preserved only in the Exeter Book, a manuscript copied about 975, which contains the largest surviving collection of Old English poetry.

The Wanderer[1]

"He who is alone often lives to find favor, mildness of the Lord, even though he has long had to stir with his arms the frost-cold sea, troubled in heart over the water-way had to tread the tracks of exile. Fully-fixed is his fate."

So spoke the earth-walker, remembering hardships, fierce war-slaughters—the fall of dear kinsmen.

"Often before the day dawned I have had to speak of my cares, alone: there is now none among the living to whom I dare clearly express the thought of my heart. I know indeed that it is a fine custom for a man to lock tight his heart's coffer, keep closed the hoard-case of his mind, whatever his thoughts may be. Words of a weary heart may not withstand fate, nor those of an angry spirit bring help. Therefore men eager for fame shut sorrowful thought up fast in their breast's coffer.

"Thus I, wretched with care, removed from my homeland, far from dear kinsmen, have had to fasten with fetters the thoughts of my heart—ever since the time, many years ago, that I covered my gold-friend in the darkness of the earth; and from there I crossed the woven waves, winter-sad, downcast for want of a hall, sought a giver of treasure—a place, far or near, where I might find one in a mead-hall who should know of my people, or would comfort me friendless, receive me with gladness. He who has experienced it

1. This translation by E. T. Donaldson is based on the text as edited by John C. Pope in *Seven Old English Poems* (1966).

knows how cruel a companion sorrow is to the man who has no beloved protectors. Exile's path awaits him, not twisted gold—frozen thoughts in his heart-case, no joy of earth. He recalls the hall-warriors and the taking of treasure, how in youth his gold-friend made him accustomed to feasting. All delight has gone.

"He who has had long to forgo the counsel of a beloved lord knows indeed how, when sorrow and sleep together bind the poor dweller-alone, it will seem to him in his mind that he is embracing and kissing his liege lord and laying his hands and his head on his knee, as it some times was in the old days when he took part in the gift-giving. Then he wakens again, the man with no lord, sees the yellow waves before him, the sea-birds bathe, spread their feathers, frost and snow fall, mingled with hail.

"Then the wounds are deeper in his heart, sore for want of his dear one. His sorrow renews as the memory of his kinsmen moves through his mind: he greets them with glad words, eagerly looks at them, a company of warriors. Again they fade, moving off over the water; the spirit of these fleeting ones brings to him no familiar voices. Care renews in him who must again and again send his weary heart out over the woven waves.

"Therefore I cannot think why the thoughts of my heart should not grow dark when I consider all the life of men through this world—with what terrible swiftness they forgo the hall-floor, bold young retainers. So this middle-earth each day fails and falls. No man may indeed become wise before he has had his share of winters in this world's kingdom. The wise man must be patient, must never be too hot-hearted, nor too hasty of speech, nor too fearful, nor too glad, nor too greedy for wealth, nor ever too eager to boast before he has thought clearly. A man must wait, when he speaks in boast, until he knows clearly, sure-minded, where the thoughts of his heart may turn.

"The wise warrior must consider how ghostly it will be when all the wealth of this world stands waste, just as now here and there through this middle-earth wind-blown walls stand covered with frost-fall, storm-beaten dwellings. Wine-halls totter, the lord lies bereft of joy, all the company has fallen, bold men beside the wall. War took away some, bore them forth on their way; a bird carried one away over the deep sea; a wolf shared one with Death; another a man sad of face hid in an earth-pit.

"So the Maker of mankind laid waste this dwelling-place until the old works of giants[2] stood idle, devoid of the noise of the stronghold's keepers. Therefore the man wise in his heart considers carefully this wall-place and this dark life, remembers the multitude of deadly combats long ago, and speaks these words: 'Where has the horse gone? Where the young warrior? Where is the giver of treasure? What has become of the feasting seats? Where are the joys of the hall? Alas, the bright cup! Alas, the mailed warrior! Alas, the prince's glory! How that time has gone, vanished beneath night's cover, just as if it never had been! The wall, wondrous high, decorated with snake-likenesses, stands now over traces of the beloved company. The ash-spears' might has borne the earls away—weapons greedy for slaughter, Fate the mighty; and storms beat on the stone walls, snow, the herald of winter, falling thick binds the earth when darkness comes and the night-shadow falls, sends

2. Probably a reference to Roman ruins.

harsh hailstones from the north in hatred of men. All earth's kingdom is wretched, the world beneath the skies is changed by the work of the fates. Here wealth is fleeting, here friend is fleeting, here man is fleeting, here woman is fleeting—all this earthly habitation shall be emptied.' "

So spoke the man wise in heart, sat apart in private meditation. He is good who keeps his word; a man must never utter too quickly his breast's passion, unless he knows first how to achieve remedy, as a leader with his courage. It will be well with him who seeks favor, comfort from the Father in heaven, where for us all stability resides.

THE WIFE'S LAMENT

In modern English translation, the speaker of this poem sounds much like the speaker in *The Wanderer*, lamenting his exile, isolation, and the loss of his lord. But in Old English the grammatical gender of the pronouns reveals that this speaker is a woman; the man she refers to as "my lord" must, therefore, be her husband. The story behind the lament remains obscure. All that can be made out for certain is that the speaker was married to a nobleman of another country; that her husband has left her (possibly forced into exile as a result of a feud); that his kinsmen are hostile to her; and that she is now living alone in a wilderness. Although the circumstances are shadowy, it is reasonable to conjecture that the wife may have been a "peace-weaver" (a woman married off to make peace between warring tribes), like Hildeburh and Freawaru, whose politically inspired marriages only result in further bloodshed (see *Beowulf*, pp. 54 and 75). The obscurity of the Old English text has led to diametrically opposed interpretations of the husband's feeling toward his wife. One interpretation holds that, for unexplained reasons, possibly because of his kinsmen's hostility to her, he has turned against her. The other, which is adopted in this translation, is that, in her mind at least, they share the suffering of his exile and their separation. Thus in the line here rendered "I must suffer the feud of my much-beloved," *fæðu* (feud) is read by some as the technical term for a blood feud—the way it is used in *Beowulf* when Hrothgar says he settled a great feud started by Beowulf's father with *feo* (fee), i.e., monetary compensation (p. 40). Others take the word in a more general sense as referring to the man's enmity toward his wife. In either case, the woman's themes and language resemble those of male "wræccas" (outcasts or exiles; the Old English root survives in modern *wretch* and *wretched*) in the Old English poems called "elegies" because of their elegiac content and mood.

The Wife's Lament[1]

Full of grief, I make this poem about myself, my own fate. I have the right to say what miseries I have endured since I grew up, new or old—never greater than now. Endlessly I have suffered the wretchedness of exile.

First my lord went away from his people here across the storm-tossed sea. At daybreak I worried in what land my lord might be. Then I set out—a

---

1. Translated by Alfred David.

friendless exile—to seek a household to shelter me against wretched need. Hiding their thoughts, the man's kinfolk hatched a plot to separate us so that we two should live most unhappy and farthest from one another in this wide world. And I felt longing.

My lord commanded me to stay in this place. I had few dear ones, faithful friends, in this country; that is why I am sad. Then I found my husband like-minded—luckless, gloomy, hiding murderous thoughts in his heart. With glad countenance, how often we vowed that death alone—nothing else—would drive us apart. That vow has been overthrown. Our friendship is as if it had never been. Far and near, I must suffer the feud of my much-beloved.

I was told to live in an earth-cave beneath an oak tree amid the forest. This earthen hall is old. I am overcome with longing. These dales are dark, and hills high, bitter bulwarks overgrown with briers, a joyless dwelling. Here very often my lord's going away has wrenched me. There are couples on earth, lovers lying together in bed, while at dawn I come out of this cave to sit under the oak tree the summerlong day alone. There I weep my exile, the many burdens. Therefore I can never set my cares at rest, nor still all this life's longing, which is my lot.

Should a young person ever be sad, harsh care at heart, he must then at one and the same time have heartache and a glad countenance, although he suffers endless surging sorrows. Whether my friend has all the world's joy at his bidding or whether, outlawed from his homeland, he sits covered with storm-frost beneath a rocky cliff—my weary-minded friend, drenched in some dreary hall—he suffers great anguish. Too often he remembers a happier place. Woe is the one who, languishing, waits for a lover.

THE BATTLE OF MALDON

The *Battle of Maldon* celebrates an event of the year 991, when a large party of Scandinavian raiders met the English defense forces on the estuary of the Blackwater River (the Pant of the poem), near Maldon in Essex. The Vikings had made a number of successful raids on seaports in the vicinity, after which they had encamped on an island near the mouth of the river. The island, because it was accessible from the mainland by a causeway that might be used only at low tide, provided a natural base from which the Vikings could continue their hit-and-run depredations on the countryside. Birhtnoth, the earl of Essex, who was leader of the English militia, took up his position at the end of the causeway and from there was able to prevent the enemy from crossing to the mainland. As the poem relates, however, in his "overconfidence" he allowed them free passage so that a battle might take place. As a result, he was himself killed, and many of the defenders took to their heels, but the members of the earl's retinue—his close associates and retainers—continued to fight bravely until they were overwhelmed. In the incomplete form in which the poem has come down to us, we do not hear of the ultimate defeat of the English, although the grim tone and in particular the famous speech of Birhtwold prepare us for the disaster.

The unknown poet of late Anglo-Saxon times was apparently well versed in heroic English poetry of the type of *Beowulf*, and he does a brilliant job of adapting traditional epic mannerisms to his description of a local battle of no particular historical importance, which involved people with whom he was acquainted. The defense forces were actually no more than a home guard: inexperienced farmers and laborers conscripted for the local defense, together with a small group of aristocrats who were acquainted with heroic martial tradition. Godric and his brothers, who, according to the poem, fled from the battle, are representative of those Englishmen who preferred to pay tribute rather than to fight. But Birhtnoth and his retinue are of the traditional tough fiber, and it is especially in their speeches and single combats that the poet uses the epic style. After Birhtnoth is killed, his loyal companions make speeches that express the heroic ethic, each in his own way. Last and most eloquent, Birhtwold, an old retainer, speaks these memorable lines, set down here, as Cædmon's *Hymn* was, in the original with interlinear translation that, where possible, provides the modern form of the Old English word. For the pronunciation of the consonants as marked, see page 24.

"Hyġe sceal þy heardra,   heorte þy cenre,
Spirit must be by as much the harder,   heart by as much the keener,

Mod sceal þy mare   þy ure mæġen lytlaþ.
Mood must be by as much the more,   by as much as our strength lessens.

Her liġeþ ure ealdor   eall forheawen,
Here lieth our elder   all hewn to pieces,

god on greote.   A mæg gnornian
good (man) on (the) sand.   Ever may he be sorry

se-þe nu fram þys wiġ-plegan   wendan þenċeþ
who now from this battle-play   thinks to turn.

Iċ eom frod feores;   fram iċ ne wille
I am old of life;   I do not want (to go away) from (here),

Ac iċ me be healfe   minum hlaforde,
But I myself beside   my lord,

be swa leofum menn,   licgan þenċe.
By so beloved (a) man,   think to lie (dead)."

Birhtnoth's decision to let the Vikings cross the river is treated in the epic manner as an instance of heroic overconfidence, like Beowulf's refusal to use his sword against the unarmed Grendel—but in this case it is a gesture that leads to tragic doom. Probably Birhtnoth had a practical motive for his rashness: if the Vikings were prevented from raiding here, they would simply sail along the coast to a less well-defended spot to continue their depredations. Only their destruction would ensure general peace, but from the local point of view, Birhtnoth's permitting the enemy to come where he could fight with them might well appear as the rashly noble act of a traditional hero.

The poem was written down in a manuscript that was reduced to charred fragments in the same fire that damaged the *Beowulf* manuscript. Fortunately, a transcript had been made of it before the fire, and on this modern editions depend. Even before the manuscript was burned, the poem must have lacked a number of lines at its beginning and end, although most scholars believe that nothing very substantial has been lost.

The Battle of Maldon[1]

Then he[2] commanded each of his warriors to leave his horse, drive it far away, and walk forward, trusting in his hands and in his good courage. When Offa's kinsman[3] understood that the earl would not put up with cowardice, he let his beloved hawk fly from his hand toward the woods and advanced to the battle: by this men might know that the youth would not weaken in the fight once he had taken up his weapons. Eadric wished also to serve his lord the earl in the battle; he carried his spear forward to the conflict. He was of good heart as long as he might hold shield and broadsword in his hands; he carried out the vow that he had made, now that he was to fight before his lord.

Then Birhtnoth began to place his men at their stations; he rode about and advised them, taught the troops how they should stand and hold the place and bade them grasp their shields aright, firm in their hands, and have no fear. When he had arranged his folk properly, he alighted among them where it seemed best to him, where he knew his retainers to be most loyal.

Then the Vikings' herald stood on the river bank, cried out loudly, spoke words, boastfully proclaimed the seafarers' message to the earl where he stood on the shore: "Bold seamen have sent me to you, have commanded me to say to you that you must quickly send treasure in order to protect yourself; and it is better for you to buy off this spear-assault with tribute than to have us give you harsh war. There is no need for us to destroy one another, if you are rich enough to pay. With the gold we will confirm truce. If you that are highest here decide upon this, that you will ransom your people, and in return for peace give the seamen money in the amount they request, and receive peace from us, we will go to ship with the tribute, set sail on the sea, and keep peace with you."

Birhtnoth spoke, raised his shield, his slender ash-spear, uttered words, angry and resolute gave him answer: "Do you hear, seafarer, what this folk says? They will give you spears for tribute, poisoned point and old sword, heriot[4] that avails you not in battle. Sea-wanderers' herald, take back our answer, speak to your people a message far more hateful, that here stands with his host an undisgraced earl who will defend this country, my lord Æthelred's[5] homeland, folk and land. Heathen shall fall in the battle. It seems to me too shameful that you should go unfought to ship with our tribute, now that you have come thus far into our land. Not so easily shall you get treasure: point and edge shall first reconcile us, grim battle-play, before we give tribute."

Then he ordered the men to bear their shields, go forward so that they all stood on the river bank. Because of the water neither band could come to the other: after the ebb, the floodtide came flowing in; currents met and

---

1. In this prose translation by E. T. Donaldson, a few liberties have been taken with the text to make clear the references of some of the loosely used Old English terms for *warrior*. The translation is in general based on the text in John C. Pope's *Seven Old English Poems* (1966).
2. Earl Birhtnoth, commander of the English defense forces.

3. Offa is mentioned later in the poem as one of Birhtnoth's principal retainers; his young kinsman is not otherwise identified.
4. The weapons a tenant received from his lord; they were returned to the lord upon the tenant's death.
5. King Ethelred reigned from 978 to 1016.

crossed. It seemed to them too long a time before they might bear their spears together. On the river Pant they stood in proud array, the battle-line of the East Saxons and the men from the ash-ships. Nor might any of them injure another, unless one should receive death from the flight of an arrow.

The tide went out. The seamen stood ready, many Vikings eager for war. The earl, protector of men, bade a war-hard warrior—he was named Wulfstan, of bold lineage—to hold the bridge:[6] he was Ceola's son, who with his spear pierced the first man bold enough to step upon the bridge. There stood with Wulfstan fearless fighters, Ælfhere and Maccus, bold men both who would not take flight from the ford, but defended themselves stoutly against the enemy as long as they might wield weapons.

When the loathed strangers saw that, and understood clearly that they would face bitter bridge-defenders there, they began to prefer words to deeds,[7] prayed that they might have access to the bank, pass over the ford and lead their forces across. Then in his overconfidence the earl began to yield ground—too much ground—to the hateful people: Birhthelm's son began to call over the cold water while warriors listened: "Now the way is laid open for you. Come straightway to us, as men to battle. God alone knows which of us may be master of the field."

The slaughter-wolves advanced, minded not the water, a host of Vikings westward over the Pant, over the bright water bore their shields: sailors to land brought shields of linden. Opposite stood Birhtnoth with his warriors, ready for the fierce invaders. He ordered his men to form a war-hedge[8] with their shields and to hold the formation fast against the enemy. Now was combat near, glory in battle. The time had come when doomed men should fall. Shouts were raised; ravens circled, the eagle eager for food. On earth there was uproar.

They let the file-hard spears fly from their hands, grim-ground javelins. Bows were busy, shield felt point. Bitter was the battle-rush. On either side warriors fell, young men lay dead. Wulfmær was wounded, chose the slaughter-bed: kinsman of Birhtnoth—his sister's son—he was cruelly hewn down with swords. Then requital was made to the Vikings: I have heard that Eadweard struck one fiercely with his sword, withheld not the stroke, so that the warrior fell doomed at his feet; for this his lord gave the chamberlain[9] thanks when he had opportunity. Thus men stood firm in the battle, stern of purpose. Eagerly all these armed fighters contended with one another to see who could be the first with his weapon's point to take life from doomed man. The slain fell, carrion, to the earth. The defenders stood fast; Birhtnoth urged them on, bade each man who would win glory from the Danes to give his whole heart to the battle.

A war-hard Viking advanced, raised up his weapon, his shield to defend himself, moved against Birhtnoth. As resolute as the churl,[1] the earl advanced toward him. Each of them meant harm to the other. Then the seaman threw his southern-made[2] spear so that the fighters' chief was

---

6. Not a bridge in the modern sense, but probably a stone causeway, underwater even at low tide; immediately below, it is called a ford.
7. Literally, "to practice deception"—an overstatement due to the poet's scorn for fighters who refused to do things the hard heroic way.
8. A wall of shields (a common defensive formation).
9. I.e., Eadweard.
1. A common soldier, in contrast to "earl" Birhtnoth.
2. Apparently the Vikings preferred weapons made in England or France—the "south."

wounded. But he thrust the spear with his shield so that the shaft split and the spearhead broke off and sprang away.[3] The war-chief was maddened; with his spear he stabbed the proud Viking that had given him the wound. Wise in war was the host's leader: he let his spear go through the man's neck, guided his hand so that he mortally wounded the raider. Then he quickly stabbed another, breaking through the mail-shirt: in the breast, quite through the corselet, was this one wounded; at his heart stood the deadly point. The earl was the blither; the bold man laughed, gave thanks to God that the Lord had given him this day's work.

One of the Vikings loosed a javelin from his hand, let it fly from his fist, and it sped its way through Æthelred's noble thane. By the earl's side stood a lad not yet grown, a boy in the battle, son of Wulfstan, Wulfmær the young, who plucked full boldly the bloody spear from the warrior. He sent the hard spear flying back again: its point went in, and on the earth lay the man who had sorely wounded his lord. Then an armed Viking stepped toward the earl. He wished to seize the earl's war-gear, make booty of rings and ornamented sword. Then Birhtnoth took his sword from its sheath, broad and bright-edged, and struck at his assailant's coat of mail. Too soon one of the seafarers hindered him, wounded the earl in his arm. Then the gold-hilted sword fell to the earth: he might not hold the hard blade, wield his weapon. Yet he spoke words, the hoar battle-leader, encouraged his men, bade them go forward stoutly together. He might no longer stand firm on his feet. He looked toward Heaven and spoke: "I thank thee, Ruler of Nations, for all the joys that I have had in the world. Now, gentle Lord, I have most need that thou grant my spirit grace, that my soul may travel to thee—under thy protection, Prince of Angels, depart in peace. I beseech thee that fiends of hell harm it not." Then the heathen warriors slew him and both the men who stood by him; Ælfnoth and Wulfmær both were laid low; close by their lord they gave up their lives.

Then there retired from the battle those who did not wish to be there. The son of Odda was the first to flee: Godric went from the fight and left the good man that had given him many a steed. He leaped upon the horse that his lord had owned, upon trappings that he had no right to, and both his brothers galloped with him, Godwine and Godwig cared not for battle, but went from the war and sought the wood, fled to its fastness and saved their lives—and more men than was in any way right, if they remembered all the favors he had done for their benefit. So Offa had said to him that day at the meeting he had held in the place, that many there spoke boldly who would not remain firm at need.

The folk's leader had fallen, Æthelred's earl: all his hearth-companions saw that their lord lay dead. Then the proud thanes advanced; men without fear pressed eagerly on. They all desired either of two things, to leave life or avenge the man they loved. Thus Ælfric's son urged them on; the warrior young of winters spoke words; Ælfwine it was who spoke, and spoke boldly: "Remember the speeches we have spoken so often over our mead,[4] when we raised boast on the bench, heroes in the hall, about hard fighting. Now may the man who is bold prove that he is. I will make my noble birth known to

3. The maneuver described frees the spear from the wounded man's body and enables him to take retaliatory action.

4. Boasting of prowess while drinking is a common element in Old English poetry.

all, that I was of great kin in Mercia. My grandfather was named Ealhelm, a wise earl, worldly-prosperous. Thanes among that people shall not have reason to reproach me that I would go from this band of defenders, seek my home, now that my lord lies hewn down in battle. To me that is greatest of griefs: he was both my kinsman and my lord." Then he went forward, bent on revenge, and with the point of his spear pierced one of the pirate band, so that he lay on the earth, destroyed by the weapon. Then Ælfwine began to encourage his comrades, friends and companions, to go forward.

Offa spoke, shook his ash-spear: "Lo, you, Ælfwine, have encouraged us all, thanes in need. Now that our lord the earl lies on the earth, there is need for us all that each one of us encourage the other, warriors to battle, as long as he may have and hold weapon, hard sword, spear and good blade. The coward son of Odda, Godric, has betrayed us all; when he rode off on that horse, on that proud steed, many a man thought that he was our lord. Therefore here on the field folk were dispersed, the shield-wall broken. Curses on his action, by which he caused so many men here to flee."

Leofsunu spoke, raised the linden buckler, his shield to defend himself; he answered the warrior: "I promise that I will not flee a footstep hence, but I will go forward, avenge my dear lord in the fight. Steadfast warriors about Sturmer[5] need not reproach me with their words that now that my patron is dead I would go lordless home, abandon the battle. But weapon, point and iron, shall take me." Full wrathful he went forward, fought fiercely; flight he despised.

Then Dunnere spoke, shook his spear; humble churl,[6] he cried over all, bade each warrior avenge Birhtnoth: "He who intends to avenge his lord on the folk may not hesitate nor care for life." Then they advanced: they cared not for life. The retainers began to fight hardily, fierce spear-bearers, and prayed God that they might avenge their patron and bring destruction to their enemies.

The hostage[7] began to help them eagerly. He was of bold kin among the Northumbrians, the son of Ecglaf: his name was Æscferth. He did not flinch at the war-play, but threw spears without pause. Now he hit shield, now he pierced man: each moment he caused some wound, as long as he might wield weapons.

Eadweard the Long still stood in the line, ready and eager, spoke boasting words, how he would not flee a footstep nor turn back, now that his chief lay dead. He broke the shield-wall and fought against the foe until he had worthily avenged his treasure-giver on the seamen—before he himself lay on the slaughter-bed.

So also did Æthelric, noble companion, eager and impetuous; he fought most resolutely, this brother of Sibirht, as did many another: they split the hollow shield and defended themselves boldly.[8] . . . The shield's rim broke and the mail-shirt sang one of horror's songs. Then in the battle Offa struck the seafarer so that he fell on the earth, and there Gadd's kinsman himself sought the ground: Offa was quickly hewn down in the fight. He had, however, performed what he had promised his lord, what he had vowed before

---

5. The Essex village where the speaker lived.
6. I.e., freeman of the lowest rank.
7. Among Germanic peoples, hostages of high rank generally fought on the side of the warriors

who held them in hostage.
8. Apparently a description of a Viking's attack on Offa has been lost.

to his ring-giver, that they should either both ride to the town, hale to their home, or fall among the host, die of wounds in the slaughter-place. He lay as a thane should, near his lord.

Then there was a crash of shields. The seamen advanced, enraged by the fight. Spear oft pierced life-house of doomed man. Then Wistan advanced: Thurstan's son fought against the men. He was the slayer of three of them in the throng before the son of Wighelm[9] lay dead in the carnage. There was stubborn conflict. Warriors stood fast in the fight. Fighting men fell, worn out with wounds: slain fell among slain.

All the while Oswold and Eadwold, brothers both, encouraged the men, with their words bade their dear kinsmen that they should stand firm at need, wield their weapons without weakness.

Birhtwold spoke, raised his shield—he was an old retainer—shook his ash spear; full boldly he exhorted the men: "Purpose shall be the firmer, heart the keener, courage shall be the more, as our might lessens. Here lies our lord all hewn down, good man on ground. Ever may he lament who now thinks to turn from war-play. I am old of life; from here I will not turn, but by my lord's side, by the man I loved, I intend to lie."

So also the son of Æthelgar encouraged them all to the battle: this Godric oft let spear go, slaughter-shaft fly on the Vikings: thus he advanced foremost among the folk, hewed and laid low until he died in the fighting: he was not that Godric who fled the battle.

9. Identification uncertain.

Anglo-Norman England

THE ANGLO-SAXON CHRONICLE

The Anglo-Saxon Chronicle is a historical record in English, which takes the form of annals—that is, an annual summary of important events. Entries begin with variations of the formula "Ðis gear" (This year) and may be brief or, occasionally, extended narratives. Copies of the original *Chronicle*, which was started in 891, were distributed to centers of learning where they were carried on independently. Seven manuscripts survive. The following selections are from the *Peterborough Chronicle* (named for the monastery where it was kept), which was continued until 1154.

The *Peterborough Chronicle* provides an English perspective on the rule of the Normans after the conquest. In recording the death of William the Conqueror, the chronicler begins with conventional pious observations about the transitory nature of fortune in this world and the expected eulogy of the late king. But the rhetorical praise of the great man shifts into criticism and finally into doggerel rhyme satirizing William's greed and arbitrary exercise of power—especially his cruel game laws.

Since the *Chronicle* was written by monks, much space is devoted to church politics. The resentment of English monks at French exploitation clearly shows in the chronicler's barbed account of Henry of Poitou, an enterprising French churchman who pulled strings to get himself appointed abbot of Peterborough even though he was already abbot of a monastery in Normandy.

The Conqueror's iron rule, which, according to the *Chronicle*, provided a measure of peace and security, did not last. After the death of Henry I in 1135, Henry's nephew, Stephen of Blois, crossed the English Channel and succeeded in having himself crowned. He thus displaced his cousin Matilda, Henry's daughter, who had been the designated heir. Matilda had been married at the age of twelve to the emperor Henry V and, upon the latter's death, was remarried to Geoffrey Plantagenet, count of Anjou, whose raids in Normandy made him extremely unpopular with the Anglo-Norman barons who owned lands in that province. Stephen, however, soon managed to alienate his supporters, and a bitter civil war ensued. The chronicler gives an apocalyptic account of King Stephen's reign. Although people unquestionably suffered greatly during this period, the chronicler's descriptions of torture, famine, and robbery perhaps reflect a rhetorical excess considered appropriate to descriptions of evil times, the other side of which may be seen in the idealization of a legendary past in the twelfth-century Arthurian chronicles of Geoffrey of Monmouth, Robert Wace, and Layamon (see pp. 115–26).

The Anglo-Saxon Chronicle[1]

[OBITUARY FOR WILLIAM THE CONQUEROR]

[1087] In the same year, before the feast of the Assumption of Saint Mary,[2] King William went from Normandy into France with an army and made war

---

1. Translated by Alfred David.　　　　　2. August 15.

on his own lord King Philip,[3] and killed a great number of his men, and burned down the city of Mantes and all the holy churches that were in the city; and two holy men, who served God, living there in an anchorite's cell, were burned to death. When he had done this, King William returned to Normandy. He did a wretched thing, and one more wretched happened to him. In what way more wretched? He got sick and suffered severely. Bitter death, which spares neither the powerful nor the lowly, seized him. He died in Normandy the day after the feast of the birth of Saint Mary,[4] and they buried him in Caen at the abbey of St. Stephen. He had had it built and then endowed it richly. Oh, how false and how fickle is the wealth of this world! He who had been a powerful king and lord of many lands, of all the land then held no more than seven feet. He who was once clothed in gold and gems, now lay covered with earth. He left three sons: the oldest was called Robert, who succeeded him as duke of Normandy; the second was called William who bore the crown of England after him; the third was called Henry to whom the father bequeathed countless treasures.

If anyone wishes to know what kind of man he was, or what honor he possessed, or how many lands he was lord of, we will write about him just as he appeared to us, who beheld him and formerly lived in his court. This King William we are speaking about was a very wise man, and very powerful, and worthier and stronger than any of his predecessors. He was mild to good men who loved God and extremely harsh to men who crossed his will. On that site where God had granted him to gain possession of England, he established a famous monastery[5] and set up monks in it and endowed it well. In his days the famous church of Canterbury was built and also many others throughout England. Moreover, this land was filled with a great many monks, and they led their life according to the rule of St. Benedict. And Christianity was such in his day that every man who wished was able to perform the duties that pertained to his religious order. Also he attached great importance to ceremony: he wore his crown three times a year as often as he was in England—at Easter he wore it at Winchester, at Pentecost at Westminster, and at Christmas at Gloucester. And at those times all the powerful men in England attended him—archbishops and bishops, abbots and earls, thanes and knights. He was also a very harsh and violent man so that no one dared do anything against his will. He put earls who acted against his will in fetters; he removed bishops from their bishoprics and abbots from their abbacies; and he threw thanes into prison. And he did not spare even his own brother, who was called Odo. The latter was a very powerful bishop in Normandy— his see was at Bayeux—and he was the foremost man next to the king. He had an earldom in England, and when the king was in Normandy, then he was master in this land. The king threw him in prison. Among other things, one must not forget the good peace that he made in this land so that any man of property might travel safely throughout the kingdom with his purse full of gold. No man dared to kill another, no matter how much harm that one had done to him. And if a man raped a woman, he immediately lost those parts with which he took pleasure.

He ruled over England and because of his management contrived that

3. The king of France was lord of the dukes of Normandy.
4. September 9.

5. Battle Abbey where the Battle of Hastings took place.

there was not a hide of land in England that he did not know who owned it and what it was worth; and he set it down in his record.[6] The land of the Britons[7] was in his power, and he built castles in it and completely dominated that people. Likewise he subjected Scotland because of his great strength. Normandy was his by inheritance, and he ruled over the county called Maine.[8] And if he had lived another two years, he would have conquered Ireland with no weapon other than astute diplomacy. Truly in his time men suffered much hardship and very many injuries.

> He built fortresses
> And caused poor men great distress.
> This king was very hard.
> He took many a gold mark
> From his subjects and did purloin
> Hundreds more of silver coin.
> He extorted it by pounds
> On most illegal grounds.
> His people he would bleed,
> Not from any need.
> Into avarice he fell
> And loved greed above all.
> He laid laws severe
> To protect the deer.
> Whoever killed a hart or hind
> Was to be made blind.
> The harts were forbidden, and
> The wild boars were also banned.
> He loved the tall deer
> As if he were their father.
> And the hares, he made a decree,
> That they should go free.
> His rich men lamented it,
> And his poor men resented it,
> But so stern a man was he
> He cared not for all their enmity.
> But they must in everything
> Follow the will of the king
> If they wished to live or planned
> To own any land—
> Estates or goods to embrace
> And to remain in his good grace.
> Alas, that any man should be
> So filled with arrogance that he
> Exalts himself above all the rest
> And holds himself to be the highest.
> May almighty God be merciful
> And grant forgiveness to his soul.

We have written these things about him, both the good and the bad, so that good men may take after the good and shun the bad in every respect and follow the path that leads us to the kingdom of heaven.

---

6. Reference to the Domesday Book, a census and survey of land ordered by William. A hide of land is roughly equivalent to 120 acres.

7. Wales.
8. Province in France adjoining Normandy.

[HENRY OF POITOU BECOMES ABBOT OF PETERBOROUGH]

[1127] This same year [King Henry I] gave the abbacy of Peterborough to an abbot called Henry of Poitou, who held the abbey of St. Jean d'Angely[9] in his possession. And all the archbishops and bishops said that it was illegal and that he might not hold two abbacies. But this same Henry gave the king to understand that he had given up his abbey because of the great unrest that was in that country, and that he did this on the advice and with the consent of the pope of Rome and the abbot of Cluny, and because he was the papal tax collector.[1] But it was no more true for all he said, but he wanted to have both monasteries in his possession, and so he had it as long as it was God's will. As a priest, he had been bishop of Soissons; then he became a monk at Cluny and afterwards prior of that same monastery; and then he became prior at Savigny. Thereupon, because he was related to the king of England and to the count of Poitou, the count made him abbot of St. Jean d'Angely. Then, as a result of his elaborate stratagems, he got the archbishopric of Besançon and held it for three days; then he justly lost it because he had obtained it unjustly. Then he got the bishopric of Saintes, which is five miles from the monastery of which he was abbot. He had that for almost a week. The abbot of Cluny got him out of there, as he had previously out of Besançon. Then he considered that if he could put down roots in England, he could have all his will. He sought out the king and told him that he was a broken-down old man, and that he could not put up with great injustices and strife in their land. Then he asked specifically for the abbey of Peterborough on his own behalf and that of all his friends. And the king granted it to him because he was his kinsman and had been the chief cleric to swear an oath and bear witness when the son of the count of Normandy and daughter of the count of Anjou were divorced because of consanguinity.[2]

Thus miserably was the abbacy given away between Christmas and Candlemas at London. And so he traveled with the king to Winchester and then he came to Peterborough. And there he lived like the drones in the hive. All that the bees drag in the drones devour and drag out—so did he. All that he might take, inside and outside, from churchmen or laymen, he sent across the sea. He did no good there and left nothing good there.

Let no one think strange the truth that we declare, for it was well-known throughout the entire country that as soon as he arrived there—that is, on the Sunday on which one sings, "Exurge, quare obdormis, Domine?"[3] immediately thereafter many men saw and heard many huntsmen hunting. These hunters were black and big and ugly, and all their dogs were black and ugly with wide eyes, and they rode on black horses and black goats.[4] This was seen in the deer park itself in the town of Peterborough and in all the woods between Peterborough and Stamford. And the monks heard the horns blowing, which they blew at night. Reliable witnesses observed them at night. They said it seemed to them there might well have been twenty to thirty

9. Monastery in Normandy.
1. For the tax popularly known in England as "Peter's Pence."
2. The divorce was promoted by Henry I to allow the count's son (Henry's nephew) to marry the sister of the king of France, who, in return, made him count of Flanders. Such a divorce or annulment required the endorsement of the church, usually

on grounds that the marriage had violated the permissible degree of kinship between the partners.
3. Awake, why sleepest thou, Oh Lord? (Latin); Psalm 43 [44].23, sung at the beginning of the mass on the second Sunday before Lent, February 6 in 1127.
4. The Wild Hunt, a motif in Germanic mythology, is here given a diabolical twist.

blowing horns. This was seen and heard from the time he came here all that
Lent up to Easter. This was his arrival. Of his departure we cannot yet speak.
May God provide!

[THE REIGN OF KING STEPHEN]

[1135] In [King Stephen's] time all was warfare, wickedness, and robbery,
for right away all the powerful men who were traitors rose up against him[5]
* * * [1137] When the traitors discovered that he was a mild man, and gentle
and good, and did not enforce justice they committed every sort of atrocity.
They had done homage to him and sworn oaths, but they kept no faith. They
were all forsworn and broke their oaths, for every powerful man built castles
and held them against him. And they filled the land full of castles.

They oppressed the wretched people greatly with forced labor on castle
works. When the castles were built, they filled them with devils and evil men.
Night and day they seized anyone who they thought possessed any wealth
(both men and women), and put them in prison, and tortured them with
unspeakable tortures to get their gold and silver. For never were any martyrs
so tortured as these were. They were hung up by the feet and smoked with
foul smoke. They were hung up by the thumbs or by the head with armor
attached to the feet. Knotted cords were tied around their heads and twisted
till they cut into the brain. They were incarcerated with adders, snakes, and
toads and killed in that way. Some were put into a torture box—that is, in a
chest that was short, narrow, and shallow—into which they put sharp stones,
and pressed the man in it so that all his limbs were broken. Many of the
castles had a "strangle-trap": that was a device made up of chains so heavy
that it was all two or three men could do to carry one of them. It worked like
this—they fitted a sharp iron, which was fastened to a beam, around a man's
throat and neck so that he could not move in any direction, nor sit, nor lie
down, nor sleep but had to bear up all that iron. Many thousands they starved
to death.

I do not know how nor would it be possible to tell all the atrocities and
tortures they inflicted upon the wretched people of this land. And that lasted
nineteen winters for as long as Stephen was king. And the whole time it went
from bad to worse. They were constantly making the villages pay taxes, which
they called "protection money." When the wretched people had nothing
more to give, they pillaged and burned all the villages so that you could easily
do a day's journey without ever seeing an inhabitant in a village or land under
cultivation. Then grain was expensive, and meat and cheese and butter, for
there was none in the land. Wretched people starved to death. Some, who
had once been wealthy, went begging. Some fled the country. Never before
in the land had there been more misery, nor did ever heathens do worse
things than they did.

Contrary to civilized behavior, they spared neither church nor churchyard
but took all the valuables therein and then burned church and all together.
They did not spare bishop's land, nor abbot's nor priest's, but robbed monks
and clerics, and every man robbed the other if he was the stronger. If two or

5. Though dated the year of Stephen's accession,
these entries, which later refer to the entire reign
of nineteen years, were written after 1154. In fact,
Stephen at first had considerable support from the
city of London and among the baronage. Many of
the barons—traitors according to this chronicler,
who regards Stephen as an ineffectual but legitimate monarch—soon switched to Matilda's cause.

three men rode into a village, the entire village would flee them because they thought they were robbers. The bishops and clergy kept excommunicating them, but they did not care about that since they were all totally accursed, perjured, and abandoned.

Wherever the ground was tilled, the earth bore no grain, for the land was ruined by such acts. It was openly said that Christ and his saints were asleep. Such things—and more than we can tell—we suffered nineteen winters for our sins.

LEGENDARY HISTORIES OF BRITAIN

During the twelfth century, three authors, who wrote in Latin, Anglo-Norman French, and Middle English, respectively, created a mostly legendary history of Britain for their Norman overlords (see pp. 7–8). This "history" was set in the remote past, beginning with a foundation myth—a heroic account of national origins—modeled on Virgil's *Aeneid* and ending with the Anglo-Saxon conquest of the native islanders, the Britons, in the fifth and sixth centuries. The chief architect of the history is Geoffrey of Monmouth, who was writing his *History of the Kings of Britain* in Latin prose ca. 1136–38. His work was freely translated into French verse by Wace in 1155, and Wace in turn was translated into English alliterative poetry by Layamon.

Geoffrey of Monmouth and Wace wrote their histories of Britain primarily for an audience of noblemen and prelates who were descendants of the Norman conquerors of the Anglo-Saxons. Geoffrey wrote several dedications of his *History*, first to supporters of Matilda, the heiress presumptive of Henry I, and, when the Crown went instead to Stephen of Blois, to the new king's allies and to Stephen himself. Layamon tells us that Wace wrote his French version for Eleanor of Aquitaine, queen of Stephen's successor, Henry II. The prestige and power of ancient Rome still dominated the historical and political imagination of the feudal aristocracy, and the legendary history of the ancient kings of the Britons, especially of King Arthur, who had defeated Rome itself, served to flatter the self-image and ambitions of the Anglo-Norman barons. Perhaps the destruction of Arthur's kingdom also provided a timely object lesson of the disastrous consequences of civil wars such as those over the English succession in which these lords were engaged.

The selections from Geoffrey of Monmouth and Wace are translated by Alfred David. The Layamon selections are translated by Rosamund Allen.

GEOFFREY OF MONMOUTH

The author of the *History of the Kings of Britain* was a churchman, probably of Welsh or Breton ancestry, who spent much of his life at Oxford. One of his motives in writing the work was undoubtedly to obtain advancement in the church. In the dedications of the *History*, Geoffrey claims that it is merely a translation into Latin of "a very old book in the British language [i.e., Welsh]," which had been loaned to him by his friend Walter, archdeacon of Oxford, but scholars have discounted this story as another one of Geoffrey's many fictions.

Geoffrey began his history with a British foundation myth modeled upon Virgil's

Aeneid. Out of legends that Rome had been founded by refugees from the fall of Troy, the poet Virgil had created his epic poem the *Aeneid* for Augustus Caesar. Aeneas, carrying his father upon his back, had escaped from the ruins of Troy and, fulfilling prophecies, became the founding father of a new Troy in Italy. The Britons had developed an analogous foundation myth in which a great-grandson of Aeneas called Brutus had led another band of Trojan exiles to establish another Troy, which was named Britain after him. Geoffrey drew upon earlier Latin chronicles and Welsh oral tradition, but he himself provided his history with a chronology, a genealogy, a large cast of both historical and legendary characters (among many other stories, he is the first to tell of King Lear and his daughters), and a cyclical sense of the rise and fall of empires. The longest and most original part of the work (over one-fifth of the *History*) is devoted to the birth and reign of King Arthur. In the first part of Arthur's reign, he defeats and drives out the pagan Anglo-Saxon invaders. At the end of his reign the Saxons return at the invitation of the traitor Mordred and, though defeated again by Arthur in his last battle, they ultimately triumph over his successors.

The historicity of Geoffrey's book, although questioned by some of Geoffrey's contemporary historians, was widely accepted and not fully discredited until the seventeenth century. In the course of time Arthur was adopted as a national and cultural hero by the English against whose ancestors he had fought, and his court became the international ideal of a splendid chivalric order in the past of which contemporary knighthood was only a faint imitation. Geoffrey of Monmouth himself already declares that in Arthur's time, "Womenfolk became chaste and more virtuous and for their love the knights were ever more daring."

In the following selections, Geoffrey relates the British foundation myth, which he historicizes, amplifies, and fleshes out with details that he regards as classical.

From The History of the Kings of Britain

[THE STORY OF BRUTUS AND DIANA'S PROPHECY]

After the Trojan War, Aeneas with his son Ascanius fled from the destruction of the city and sailed to Italy. Although King Latinus would have received him there with honor, Turnus, the king of the Rutuli, was envious and made war on him. In their rivalry Aeneas prevailed and, having slain Turnus, obtained the kingdom of Italy and Latinus's daughter, Lavinia.

At the end of Aeneas's days, Ascanius was elevated to royal power and founded the city of Alba on the banks of the Tiber. He fathered a son whose name was Silvius. The latter had a secret love affair with a niece of Lavinia's whom he married and got with child. When his father Ascanius learned about this he ordered his wise men to find out the sex of the child that the girl had conceived. When the wise men had made sure of the truth, they said that she would bear a son who would be the death of his father and mother. After travelling through many lands as an exile, he would nevertheless attain to the highest honor. Their prophecies did not turn out to be mistaken. For when her time had come, the woman bore a boy and died in childbirth. The boy was handed over to the midwife and named Brutus. At last, after fifteen years had gone by, the boy went hunting with his father and killed him with a misdirected bowshot. For as the servants were driving some stags into their path, Brutus, believing that he was aiming at them, hit his father below the breast. On account of this death, his relatives, outraged that he should have done such a deed, drove him from Italy.* * *

[The exiled Brutus travels to Greece, where he discovers descendants of Trojan prisoners of war living in slavery. He organizes a successful rebellion against their Greek masters and, like Aeneas before him, leads them on a quest for a new homeland.]

Driven by favorable winds, the Trojans sailed for two days and one night until they made land on an island called Leogetia, which was uninhabited because long ago it had been devastated by pirate raids. So Brutus sent three hundred armed men to explore the island and see whether anything was living on it. They found no one but they killed several kinds of wild animals that they came across in the woods and thickets.

They came to a deserted city where they found a temple of Diana in which a statue of the goddess rendered oracles if someone should consult it. At last they returned to their ships, loaded down with game, and told their comrades about the land and the city. They suggested to their chief that he go to the temple and, after making propitiatory sacrifices, inquire of the goddess what land might afford them a permanent home. When everyone agreed, Brutus with the soothsayer Gero and twelve elders set out for the temple, taking along everything necessary for the sacrifice. When they got there, they bound their brows with headbands and, in preparation of the most ancient rite, they erected three hearths to three gods, namely to Jupiter, Mercury, and Diana. They poured out libations to each one in turn. Before the altar of the goddess, Brutus himself, holding a sacrificial vessel filled with wine and the blood of a white doe in his right hand, raised his face to her statue and broke the silence with these words:[1]

> Mighty goddess of woodlands, terror of the wild boar,
> Thou who art free to traverse the ethereal heavens
> And the mansions of hell, disclose my rights on this earth
> And say what lands it is your wish for us to inhabit,
> What dwelling-place where I shall worship you all my life,
> Where I shall dedicate temples to you with virgin choirs.

After he had spoken this prayer nine times, he walked four times around the altar and poured out the wine he was holding upon the hearth. Then he spread out the hide of the doe before the altar and lay down on it. He tried to doze off and finally fell asleep. It was now the third hour of the night when sweetest slumber overcomes mortals. Then it seemed to him that the goddess was standing before him and speaking to him like this:

> Brutus, where the sun sets beyond the kingdoms of Gaul
> Is an isle in the ocean, closed all around by the sea.
> Once on a time giants lived on that isle in the ocean,
> But now it stands empty and fit to receive your people.
> Seek it out, for it shall be your homeland forever;
> It shall be a second Troy for your descendants.
> There kings shall be born of your seed and to them
> All nations of the round earth shall be subject.

When the vision vanished, Brutus remained in doubt whether what he had seen was only a phantom or whether the actual voice of the goddess had

1. Brutus's prayer and Diana's prophecy are written as Latin poetry and employ a more formal diction than the prose narrative. The entire episode is meant to show off Geoffrey's classical learning and familiarity with pagan ritual.

foretold the homeland to which he was to travel. Finally he called his comrades and told them point by point what had happened to him while he slept. Waves of great joy swept over them, and they urged that they return to the ships and, while the wind blew behind them, head with swiftest sail toward the ocean to seek out what the goddess had promised. Without delay they rejoined their comrades and set out on the high seas.

WACE

Wace (ca. 1110–ca. 1180) was a Norman cleric, born on the island of Jersey in the English Channel, which was then part of the dukedom of Normandy. Although educated for the church, he seems to have served the laity, perhaps in a secretarial function. All of his extant works, which include saints' lives, *Le Roman de Brut*, and *Le Roman de Rou*, were written in French verse for a lay audience that would have included women like Eleanor of Aquitaine, to whom he dedicated the *Brut*, and Marie de France, who drew on that work in her lays. *Roman* in these titles refers to the fact that they are, respectively, chronicles in French verse about the dynasties of Brutus (first of the kings of Britain) and Rollo (first of the dukes of Normandy).

The *Roman de Brut* is a very free translation in eight-syllable couplets of Geoffrey of Monmouth's Latin prose *History of the Kings of Britain*. Wace has cut some details and added a good deal, including the first mention of the Round Table. He is far more interested than Geoffrey in creating an atmosphere of courtliness—in the way his characters dress, think, speak, and behave. The following selection covers a challenge delivered to Arthur by the Roman emperor Lucius and Arthur's response. This climactic sequence follows an elaborate coronation scene attended by a large gathering of kings and dukes from Britain and overseas who owe allegiance to Arthur and whose lands comprise what might be called the Arthurian Empire. At the feast following his coronation, Arthur's authority is challenged by ambassadors who present an insulting letter from Lucius. Arthur's reply is a masterpiece of feudal rhetoric that would have been admired by Wace's audience.

From Le Roman de Brut

[THE ROMAN CHALLENGE]

Arthur was seated on a dais surrounded by counts and kings when a dozen white-haired, very well-dressed men came into the hall in pairs, one holding the other's hand. Each held an olive branch. They crossed the hall very slowly in an orderly and solemn procession, approached the king and hailed him. They said they had come from Rome as messengers. They unfolded a letter, which one of them gave to Arthur on behalf of the Roman emperor. Listen to what it said:

"Lucius who holds Rome in his domain and is sovereign lord of the Romans, proclaims to King Arthur, his enemy, what he has deserved. I am disdainful in amazement and am amazed with disdain at the inordinate and insane pride with which you have set your sights on Rome. With disdain and amazement I ask myself at whose prompting and from what quarters you have undertaken to pick a quarrel with Rome as long as a single Roman remains alive. You have acted with great recklessness in attacking us who have the right to rule the world and hold supremacy over it. You still don't know, but we shall teach you; you are blind, but we shall make you see what a great thing it is to anger Rome, which has the power to rule over everything. You have presumed beyond your place and crossed the bounds of your authority! Have you any idea who you are and where you come from—you who are taking and holding back the tribute that belongs to us? You are taking our tribute and our lands: why do you hold them, why don't you turn them over, why do you keep them, what right do you have to them? If you keep them any longer, you will be acting most recklessly. And if you are capable of holding them without our forcing you to give them up, you might as well say—an unprecedented miracle!—that the lion flees from the lamb, the wolf from the goat, the greyhound from the hare. But that could never happen, for Nature would not suffer it. Julius Caesar, our ancestor—but maybe you have little respect for him—conquered Britain and imposed a tribute that our people have collected since that time. And we have also been receiving tribute for a long time from the other islands surrounding you. And you have foolishly presumed to take tribute from both of them. Already you were guilty of senseless behavior, but you have committed an even greater insult that touches us still more closely than the losses we have sustained: you killed our vassal Frollo[1] and illegally occupied France. Therefore, since you are not afraid of Rome nor its great power, the Senate summons and orders you—for the summons is an order—to come before it in mid-August, ready, at whatever cost, to make full restitution of what you have taken from them. And thus you will give satisfaction for the wrongs of which we accuse you. But if you delay in any fashion to do what I command you, I will cross the Alps with an army and will deprive you of Britain and France. But I can't imagine that you will await my coming or will defend France against me. I don't think you will dare to face me on this side of the Channel. And even if you stay over there, you will never await my coming. You won't know a place to hide where I won't flush you out. I'll lead you to Rome in chains and hand you over to the Senate."

At these words there was a great uproar, and all were greatly enraged. You could have heard the Britons shouting loudly, calling God as witness and swearing by his name that they were going to punish the messengers. They would have showered them with abuse and insults, but the king rose to his feet and called out to them, "Silence! Silence! Don't lay a hand on these men. They are messengers; they have a master, they are bringing his message; they can say whatever they like. No one shall do them the slightest harm."

When the noise quieted down and the retainers recovered their composure, the king ordered his dukes and counts and his personal advisers to accompany him to a stone tower called the Giant Tower. There he wanted to seek advice on what to reply to the messengers. Side by side the barons and counts were already mounting the stairs, when Cador, the duke of Cornwall, with a smile spoke to the king, who was in front of him, as follows: "I've been afraid," he said, "and have often thought that leisure and peace might spoil the Britons, for leisure is conducive to bad habits and causes many a man to become lazy. Leisure diminishes prowess, leisure promotes lechery, leisure kindles clandestine love affairs. Through prolonged repose and leisure

1. Roman governor of France.

youth gets preoccupied with entertainment and pleasure and backgammon and other games of diversion. By staying put and resting for a long time, we could lose our reputation. Well, we've been asleep, but God has given us a little wake-up call—let us thank him for encouraging the Romans to challenge our country and the others we have conquered. Should the Romans find it in themselves to carry out what they say in that letter, the Britons will still retain their reputation for valor and strength. I never like peace for long, nor shall I love a peace that lasts a long time."

"My lord," said Gawain, "in faith, you're getting upset over nothing. Peace after war is a good thing. The land is better and more beautiful on account of it. It's very good to amuse oneself and to make love. It's for love and for their ladies that knights perform chivalrous deeds."

While bantering in this way, they entered the tower and took their seats. When Arthur saw them sitting down and waiting in silence with full attention, he paused for a moment in thought, then raised his head and spoke:

"Barons," he said, "you who are here, my companions and friends, you have stood by me in good times and bad; you have supported me when I had to go to war; you have taken my part whether I won or lost; you have been partners in my loss, and in my gain when I conquered. Thanks to you and your help, I have won many a victory. I have led you through many dangers by land and by sea, in places near and far. I have found you loyal in action and in counsel. I have tested your mettle many times and always found it good. Thanks to you the neighboring countries are subject to me. You have heard the Romans' order, the tenor of the letter, and the overbearingness and arrogance of their demands. They have provoked and threatened us enough, but if God protects us, we shall do away with the Romans. They are rich and have great power, and now we must carefully consider what we can properly and reasonably say and do. Trouble is dealt with better when a strategy has been worked out in advance. If someone sees the arrow in flight, he must get out of the way or shield himself. That is how we must proceed. The Romans want to shoot at us, and we must get ready so that they cannot wound us. They demand tribute from Britain and must have it, so they tell us; they demand the same from the other islands and from France.

"But first I shall reply how matters stand with regard to Britain. They claim that Caesar conquered it; Caesar was a powerful man and carried out his will by force. The Britons could not defend themselves against him, and he exacted tribute from them by force. But might is not right; it is force and superior power. A man does not possess by right what he has taken by force. Therefore, we are allowed to keep by right what they formerly took by force. They have held up to us the damages, losses, humiliations, the sufferings and fears that they inflicted on our ancestors. They boasted that they conquered them and extorted tribute and rents from them. We have all the more right to make them suffer; they have all the more restitution to make to us. We ought to hate those who hated our ancestors and to injure those who injured them. They remind us that they made them suffer, got tribute from them, and demand tribute from us. They want us to suffer the same shame and extortion as our ancestors. They once got tribute from Britain, and so they want to get it from us. By the same reason and with equal cause we can challenge the Romans and dispute our rights. Belinus, who was king of the

Britons, and Brennus,[2] duke of the Burgundians, two brothers born in Britain, valiant and wise knights, marched on Rome, laid siege to the city, and took it by assault. They hanged twenty-four hostages in plain sight of their families. When Belinus returned from Rome, he entrusted the city to his brother.

"I won't dwell on Belinus and Brennus but will speak of Constantine. He was British by birth, the son of Helen; he held Rome in his own right. Maximian, king of Britain, conquered France and Germany, crossed the Alps and Lombardy and reigned over Rome. These were my ancestors by direct descent, and each one held Rome in his possession. Now you may hear and understand that we have just as much right to possess Rome as they do to possess Britain. The Romans had our tribute, and my ancestors had theirs. They claim Britain, and I claim Rome. This is the gist of my counsel: that they may have the land and tribute who can take it away from another. As for France and the other lands we have taken from them, they have no right to dispute them since they would not or could not defend them, or perhaps had no right to them because they held them in bondage through force and greed. So let he who can hold all. There is no need to look for any other kind of right. The emperor threatens us. God forbid that he should do us any harm. He says that he will take away our lands and lead me to Rome as a prisoner. He has small regard or fear of me. But, God willing, if he comes to this land, before he leaves again he'll have no stomach to make threats. He defies me, and I defy him: may he possess the lands who is able to take them!"

When King Arthur had spoken what he wanted to his barons, the others spoke in turn while the rest listened. Hoël, king of Brittany, spoke next: "Sire," he said, "in faith, you have spoken many just words; none could have said it better. Send after and mobilize your forces along with us who are here at court. Without delay pass over the sea, pass through Burgundy and France, pass the Alps, conquer Lombardy! Throw the emperor who is defying you into confusion and panic so that he will not have the chance to cause you harm. The Romans have begun a suit that will ruin them. God wants to exalt you: don't hold back and lose any time! Make yourself master of the empire, which is ready to surrender to you of its own will. Remember what is written in the Sibyl's prophecies.[3] Three Britons will be born in Britain who shall conquer Rome by might. Two have already lived and been sovereigns over Rome. The first was Belinus and the second, Constantine. You shall be the third to possess Rome and conquer it by force; in you the Sibyl's prophecy will be fulfilled. Why delay to seize that which God wants to bestow on you? Increase your glory and ours to which we aspire. We may say truly that we are not afraid of blows or wounds or death or hardship or prison so

2. Brennus was not a Briton but a Gaulish chieftain who sacked Rome in the 4th century. Belinus is fictional. Constantine I, who adopted Christianity as the official religion of the Roman Empire, was believed to be British. Maximian (Maximus) was a 5th-century Roman general serving in Britain who abandoned the island when his army proclaimed him emperor and usurped the imperium in civil wars that weakened Rome and left Britain at the mercy of attacks by the Picts, Scots, and Germanic tribes. Geoffrey of Monmouth's earlier accounts of these personages had conflated a tiny amount of fact with a great deal of fiction.
3. Reference to the Sibylline books containing prophecies of the Roman Sibyl of Cumae, but these no longer existed and could have been known only by reputation. This prophecy was probably invented by Geoffrey of Monmouth.

long as we strive for honor. As long as you are in danger, I will lead ten
thousand armed knights in your host, and if that should not be enough, I
shall mortgage all my lands and give you the gold and silver. I won't keep
back a farthing so long as you have need of it!"

LAYAMON

Layamon, an English priest, adapted Wace's *Roman de Brut* into Middle English
alliterative verse. His *Brut* (ca. 1190) runs to 16,095 lines, expanding on Wace and
adding much new material.

After winning the continental campaign against Lucius, Arthur is forced to return
to Britain upon learning that his nephew, Mordred, whom he had left behind as
regent, has usurped Arthur's throne and queen. The following selection, a passage
added by Layamon, presents Arthur's dream of Mordred's treachery.

Layamon employs a long alliterative line that harks back to Old English poetry, but
the two halves of his line are often linked by rhyme as well as by alliteration. Layamon
reveals his ties with Germanic literary tradition in other ways. In Arthur's nightmare,
the king and Gawain are sitting astride the roof beam of a building like the mead hall
Heorot in *Beowulf*—a symbol of the control a king wields over his house and kingdom.
On the ground below, Mordred is chopping away at the foundations like the gigantic
rodent in Norse mythology that is gnawing away at the roots of Yggdrasil, the great
tree, which holds together earth, heaven, and hell.

From Brut

[ARTHUR'S DREAM]

Then came to pass what Merlin spoke of long before,
13965 That the walls of Rome would fall down before Arthur;
This had already happened there in relation to the emperor
Who had fallen in the fighting with fifty thousand men:
That's when Rome with her power was pushed to the ground.
      And so Arthur really expected to possess all of Rome,
13970 And the most mighty of kings remained there in Burgundy.
      Now there arrived at this time a bold man on horseback;
News he was bringing for Arthur the king
From Modred, his sister's son: to Arthur he was welcome,
For he thought that he was bringing very pleasant tidings.
13975 Arthur lay there all that long night, talking with the young knight,
Who simply did not like to tell him the truth of what had happened.
The next day, as dawn broke, the household started moving,
And then Arthur got up, and, stretching his arms,
He stood up, and sat down again, as if he felt very sick.
      Then a good knight questioned him: "My Lord, how did you get on
13980   last night?"
Arthur responded (his heart was very heavy):
"Tonight as I was sleeping, where I was lying in my chamber,

There came to me a dream which has made me most depressed:
I dreamed someone had lifted me right on top of some hall
13985 And I was sitting on the hall, astride, as if I was going riding;
All the lands which I possess, all of them I was surveying,
And Gawain sat in front of me, holding in his hands my sword.
Then Modred came marching there with a countless host of men,
Carrying in his hand a massive battle-axe.
13990 He started to hew, with horrible force,
And hacked down all the posts which were holding up the hall.
I saw Guinevere there as well, the woman I love best of all:
The whole roof of that enormous hall with her hands she was
        pulling down;
The hall started tottering, and I tumbled to the ground,
13995 And broke my right arm, at which Modred said 'Take that!'
Down then fell the hall and Gawain fell as well,
Falling on the ground where both his arms were broken,
So with my left hand I clutched my beloved sword
And struck off Modred's head and it went rolling over the ground,
14000 And I sliced the queen in pieces with my beloved sword,
And after that I dropped her into a dingy pit.
And all my fine subjects set off in flight,
And what in Christendom became of them I had no idea,
Except that I was standing by myself in a vast plain,
14005 And then I started roaming all around across the moors:
There I could see griffins and really gruesome birds.
    "Then a golden lioness came gliding over the downs,
As really lovely a beast as any Our Lord has made.
The lioness ran up to me and put her jaws around my waist,
14010 And off she set, moving away towards the sea,
And I could see the waves, tossing in the sea,
And taking me with her, the lioness plunged into the water.
When we two were in the sea, the waves swept her away from me;
Then a fish came swimming by and ferried me ashore.
14015 Then I was all wet and weary, and I was sick with sorrow.
And upon waking, I started quaking,
And then I started to shudder as if burning up with fire,
And so all night I've been preoccupied with my disturbing dream,
For I know of a certainty this is the end of my felicity,
14020 And all the rest of my life I must suffer grief.
O alas that I do not have here my queen with me, my Guinevere!"
    Then the knight responded: "My Lord, you are mistaken;
Dreams should never be interpreted as harbingers of sorrow!
You are the most mighty prince who has rule in any land,
14025 And the most intelligent of all inhabitants on the earth.
If it should have happened—as may Our Lord not allow it—
That your sister's son, Lord Modred, your own queen might have
        wedded,
And all your royal domains might have annexed in his own name,
Those which you entrusted to him when you intended going to
        Rome,
14030 And if he should have done all this by his treacherous deeds,
Even then you might avenge yourself honorably with arms,

And once again possess your lands and rule over your people,
And destroy your enemies who wish you so much evil,
And slay them, every one alive, so that there is none who survives!"
14035   Then Arthur answered him, most excellent of all kings:
"For as long as is for ever, I have no fear whatever,
That Modred who is my relative, the man I love best,
Would betray all my trust, not for all of my realm,
Nor would Guinevere, my queen, weaken in her allegiance,
14040   She will not begin to, for any man in the world!"
Immediately after these words, the knight gave his answer:
"I am telling you the truth, dear king, for I am merely your
     underling:
Modred has done these things: he has adopted your queen,
And has placed in his own hands your lovely land;
14045   He is king and she is queen; they don't expect your return,
For they don't believe it will be the case that you'll ever come back
     from Rome.
I am your loyal liegeman, and I did see this treason,
And so I have come to you in person to tell you the truth.
Let my head be as pledge of what I have told you,
14050   The truth and no lie, about your beloved queen,
And about Modred, your sister's son, and how he has snatched
     Britain from you."
     Then everything went still in King Arthur's hall;
There was great unhappiness for the excellent king,
And because of it the British men were utterly depressed;
14055   Then after a while came the sound of a voice;
All over could be heard the reactions of the British
As they started to discuss in many kinds of expression
How they wished to condemn Modred and the queen
And destroy all the population who had supported Modred.
14060   Most courteous of all Britons, Arthur then called out aloud,
"Sit down quietly, my knights in this assembly,
And then I shall tell you some very strange tales.
Now tomorrow when daylight is sent by our Lord to us,
I wish to be on my way toward entering Britain,
14065   And there I shall kill Modred and burn the queen to death,
And I shall destroy all of them who gave assent to the treason."

THE MYTH OF ARTHUR'S RETURN

Folklore and literature provide examples of a recurrent myth about a leader or hero
who has not really died but is asleep somewhere or in some state of suspended life
and will return to save his people. Evidently, the Bretons and Welsh developed this
myth about Arthur in oral tradition long before it turns up in medieval chronicles.
Geoffrey of Monmouth, Wace, and Layamon, and subsequent writers about Arthur,
including Malory (see p. 434), allude to it with varying degrees of skepticism.

GEOFFREY OF MONMOUTH: *From* History of the Kings of Britain

But also the famous King Arthur himself was mortally wounded. When he was carried off to the island of Avalon to have his wounds treated, he bestowed the crown on his cousin Constantine, the son of Duke Cador in the year 542 after the Incarnation of our lord. May his soul rest in peace.

WACE: *From* Roman de Brut

Arthur, if the story is not false, was mortally wounded; he had himself carried to Avalon to be healed of his wounds. He is still there and the Britons expect him as they say and hope. He'll come from there if he is still alive. Master Wace, who made this book, won't say more about Arthur's end than the prophet Merlin rightly said once upon a time that one would not know whether or not he were dead. The prophet spoke truly: ever since men have asked and shall always ask, I believe, whether he is dead or alive. Truly he had himself taken to Avalon 542 years after the Incarnation. It was a pity that he had no offspring. He left his realm to Constantine, the son of Cador of Cornwall, and asked him to reign until his return.

LAYAMON: *From* Brut

Arthur was mortally wounded, grievously badly;
To him there came a young lad who was from his clan,
He was Cador the Earl of Cornwall's son;
The boy was called Constantine; the king loved him very much.
14270 Arthur gazed up at him, as he lay there on the ground,
And uttered these words with a sorrowing heart:
"Welcome, Constantine; you were Cador's son;
Here I bequeath to you all of my kingdom,
And guard well my Britons all the days of your life
14275 And retain for them all the laws which have been extant in my days
And all the good laws which there were in Uther's days.
And I shall voyage to Avalon, to the fairest of all maidens,
To the Queen Argante, a very radiant elf,
And she will make quite sound every one of my wounds,
14280 Will make me completely whole with her health-giving potions.
And then I shall come back to my own kingdom
And dwell among the Britons with surpassing delight."
    After these words there came gliding from the sea
What seemed a short boat, moving, propelled along by the tide
14285 And in it were two women in remarkable attire,
Who took Arthur up at once and immediately carried him
And gently laid him down and began to move off.
And so it had happened, as Merlin said before:

That the grief would be incalculable at the passing of Arthur.
14290 The Britons even now believe that he is alive
And living in Avalon with the fairest of the elf-folk,
And the Britons are still always looking for when Arthur comes
     returning.
Yet once there was a prophet and his name was Merlin:
He spoke his predictions, and his sayings were the truth,
14295 Of how an Arthur once again would come to aid the English.

MARIE DE FRANCE

Much of twelfth-century French literature was composed in England in the Anglo-Norman dialect (see pp. 7–8). Prominent among the earliest poets writing in the French vernacular, who shaped the genres, themes, and styles of later medieval European poetry, is the author who, in an epilogue to her *Fables*, calls herself Marie de France. That signature tells us only that her given name was Marie and that she was born in France, but circumstantial evidence from her writings shows that she spent much of her life in England. A reference to her in a French poem written in England around 1180 speaks of "dame Marie" who wrote "lais" much loved and praised, read, and heard by counts, barons, and knights and indicates that her poems also appealed to ladies who listened to them gladly and joyfully.

Three works can be safely attributed to Marie, probably written in the following order: the *Lais* [English "lay" refers to a short narrative poem in verse], the *Fables*, and *St. Patrick's Purgatory*. Marie's twelve lays are short romances (they range from 118 to 1,184 lines), each of which deals with a single event or crisis in the affairs of noble lovers. In her prologue, Marie tells us that she had heard these *performed*, and in several of the lays she refers to the Breton language and Breton storytellers—that is, professional minstrels from the French province of Brittany or the Celtic parts of Great Britain. Because no sources of Marie's stories have survived, it is not possible to determine the exact nature of the materials she worked from, but they were probably oral and were presented with the accompaniment of a stringed instrument. Marie's lays provide the basis of the genre that came to be known as the "Breton lay." In the prologue Marie dedicates the work to a "noble king," who is most likely to have been Henry II of England, who reigned from 1154 to 1189.

In an epilogue to her *Fables*, Marie claims to have translated the stories into "romance" (i.e., French) from an English version by King Alfred, who translated them from a Latin translation that was translated from the Greek by Aesop, for whom the book is named. No such collection in English or any other vernacular prior to Marie's time is known, but of course fables have been transmitted from time immemorial in oral tradition as well as in translations. In the Middle Ages the classical fables, ascribed to the legendary Aesop, were used for teaching elementary Latin. *St. Patrick's Purgatory* is a verse translation for the laity of a moralistic twelfth-century monastic poem in Latin about a knight's descent to the underworld through an entryway first found by St. Patrick.

The portrait of the author that emerges from the combination of these works is of a highly educated noblewoman, proficient in Latin and English as well as her native French, with ideas of her own and a strong commitment to writing. Scholars have proposed several Maries of the period who fit this description to identify the author. A likely candidate is Marie, abbess of Shaftesbury, an illegitimate daughter of Geoffrey of Anjou and thus half-sister of Henry II. Correct or not, such an identification points to the milieu in which Marie moved and to the kind of audience she was addressing.

Many of Marie's lays contain elements of magic and mystery. Medieval readers would recognize that *Lanval* is about a mortal lover and a fairy bride, although the word "fairy" is not used in the tale. In the Middle Ages fairies were not thought of as the small creatures they became in Elizabethan and later literature. Fairies are supernatural, sometimes dangerous, beings who possess magical powers and inhabit another world. Their realm in some respects resembles the human (fairies have kings and queens), and fairies generally keep to themselves and disappear when humans notice them. But the tales are often about crossovers between the human and fairy worlds. Chaucer's *Wife of Bath's Tale* is such a story. In *Lanval* the female fairy world eclipses King Arthur's chivalric court (which Marie had read about in Wace's *Roman de Brut*) in splendor, riches, and generosity.

With Chrétien de Troyes, Marie is among the twelfth-century writers who made love the means of analyzing the individual's relation to his or her society. The only woman writer known to be among the creators of this literature, Marie explores both female and male desire. Her lays portray different kinds of love relationships, both favorably and unfavorably, with both happy and tragic resolutions. They resist reduction to a pattern.

In fables, animals stand for types of human characters, and a succinct moral is spelled out at the end. Some of Marie's fables, like the two printed here, are exceptional in the way they criticize feudal society and sympathize with the female against the male animals.

Two Middle English versions of Marie's *Lanval* exist, but we prefer to offer a modern verse translation of the original. Marie wrote in eight-syllable couplets, which was the standard form of French narrative verse, employed also by Wace and Chrétien de Troyes. Here is what the beginning of Marie's prologue to the *Lais* says about her view of a writer's duty and, implicitly, of her own talent:

Ki Deu ad duné escïence	He to whom God has given knowledge
E de parler bon' eloquence	And the gift of speaking eloquently,
Ne s'en deit taisir ne celer,	Must not keep silent nor conceal the gift,
Ainz se deit volunters mustrer.	But he must willingly display it.

Lanval[1]

Another lay to you I'll tell,
Of the adventure that befell
A noble vassal whom they call
In the Breton tongue Lanval.
5   Arthur, the brave and courtly king,
At Carlisle was sojourning
Because the Scots and Picts allied
Were ravaging the countryside;
Of Logres° they had crossed the border   *Arthur's kingdom*
10 Where often they caused great disorder.
He had come there with his host
That spring to hold the Pentecost.
He lavished ample patronage
On all his noble baronage—

---

1. The translation is by Alfred David and is based on *Marie de France: Lais*, edited by Alfred Ewert (1947).

That is the knights of the Round Table
(In all the world none are so able).
Lands and wives he gave outright
To all his servants save one knight:
20 That was Lanval; him he forgot.
His men disliked him, too; the lot
Were envious of his handsomeness,
His strength, his courage, his largesse.
There were a few who friendship feigned,
25 But would by no means have complained
Had Lanval met some evil fate.
He was a prince of great estate,
But all his personal property
He gave away for amity,
30 And he got nothing from the king,
Nor would he ask for anything.
Now Lanval is much preoccupied,
Gloomy, seeing the darker side.
My lords, please do not think it rare:
35 A foreigner is filled with care
And sadness in a distant land,
Finding no help at any hand.
        The knight of whom I'm telling you,
In the king's service tried and true,
40 Mounting upon his steed one day,
For pleasure's sake set on his way.
Outside the town he went to ride
Alone into the countryside.
He got off by a running brook,
45 But there his horse trembled and shook.
He unlaced the saddle, set it free,
And let it ramble on the lee.
He folded up his riding gown
To make a pillow and lay down.
Much troubled by his luck's declining,
50 He can't see any silver lining.
There as he lay without a clue,
Two damoiselles hove into view,
The fairest he had ever eyed,
Riding along the riverside.
55 Their clothes were in expensive taste,
Close-fitting tunics, tightly laced,
Made of deep-dyed purple wool.
Their faces most beautiful.
The elder bore a well-made pair
60 Of basins; of purest gold they were.
My lords, I swear that I'm not lying!
The other held a towel for drying.
The two of them went straightaway
Right to the spot where the knight lay.
65 Lanval, the soul of courtesy,
Rose to his feet immediately.

They greeted him first by his name
And told the reason why they came.
"Sir Lanval, our damoiselle,
70   Who is so worthy, wise, and *belle*,[2]
Dispatched us to come after you,
For she has come here with us, too.
We shall bring you safely to her:
See, her pavillion's over there."
75   The knight followed without regard
For the horse left grazing on the sward.
The tent to which they bring the knight
Was fairly pitched, a beauteous sight.
Not Queen Semiramis of yore,
80   Had she been owner of even more
Wealth, power, and *savoir*,°   *wisdom, know-how*
Nor Octavian, the emperor,
Could have afforded to pay for
The right-hand flap of the front door.
85   On top was set an eagle of gold,
The cost of which cannot be told,
Nor of the cords and poles which brace
That structure and hold it in place.
No earthly king could own this tent
90   For any treasure that he spent.
Inside the tent the maiden was:
Not rose nor lily could surpass
Her beauty when they bloom in May.
The sumptuous bed on which she lay
95   Was beautiful. The drapes and tassel,
Sheets and pillows were worth a castle.
The single gown she wore was sheer
And made her shapely form appear.
She'd thrown, in order to keep warm,
100 An ermine stole over her arm,
White fur with the lining dyed
Alexandrian purple. But her side,
Her face, her neck, her bosom
Showed whiter than the hawthorn blossom.
105 The knight moved toward the bed's head.
She asked him to sit down and said,
"Lanval, fair friend, for you I've come,
For you I've traveled far from home.
If you are brave and courteous,
110 You'll be more glad and prosperous
Than ever was emperor or king,
For I love you over everything."
Her loveliness transfixed his gaze.
Love pierced his eyes with its bright rays,
115 Set fire to and scorched his heart.

---

2. Beautiful. Several words and phrases are in French, partly for the sake of rhyme but also as an indication of the great influence that the French language exercised on English. Most of these words can be found in a modern English dictionary.

He gave fair answer on his part.
"Lady," he said, "if this should be
Your wish (and such joy meant for me),
To have me for your paramour,
120 There's no command, you may be sure,
Wise or foolish, what you will,
Which I don't promise to fulfill.
I'll follow only your behest.
For you I'll give up all the rest."
125 When the lady heard him say
That he would love her in this way,
She bestowed on him her heart
And her body, every part.
Now Lanval is on easy street!
130 Whatever his needs are she will meet:
As a gift to him she granted
He should get whatever he wanted—
Money, as fast as he can spend it,
No matter how much, she will send it.
135 The more largesse he gives, the more
Gold and silver in his store.
Now Sir Lanval is harbored well.
To him then spoke the damoiselle:
"Ami,"³ she said, "please understand,
140 I warn and pray you and command:
You must never tell anyone
About the love that you have won.
The consequence I shall declare:
Should people learn of this affair,
145 You shall never again see me,
Nor have my body in your fee."
He promised her that he would do
Whatever thing she told him to.
He lay beside her on the bed:
150 Now is Lanval well bestead.
He stayed with her all afternoon
Until it would be evening soon
And gladly would have stayed all night
Had she consented that he might.
155 But she told him, "Rise up, Ami.
You may no longer stay with me.
Get on your way; I shall remain.
But one thing I will tell you plain:
When you would like to talk to me
160 At any rendezvous that's free
Of blame or of unseemliness,
Where one his true love may possess,
I shall attend you at your will
All your wishes to fulfill."
165 These words gave him great happiness.

---

3. Literally "friend," but used as a term of endearment for a lover. The feminine form is *amie*.

He kissed her, then got up to dress.
The damsels who had brought him there
Gave him expensive clothes to wear.
This world has no such comely squire
170 As Lanval in his new attire.
He was no simpleton or knave.
Water to wash his hands they gave,
Also the towel with which he dried,
And next he was with food supplied.
175 His love ate supper with Lanval,
A thing he did not mind at all.
They served him with great courtesy,
Which he accepted with much glee.
There were many special dishes
180 That the knight found most delicious.
And many times the gallant knight
Kissed his love and held her tight.
After they had cleared the table,
They fetched his horse out of the stable,
185 Harnessed just as it should be.
He had been served luxuriously.
He took his leave, mounted the horse,
And toward town he held his course,
Oftentimes looking to his rear.
190 Lanval was very much in fear
As he went thinking about the maiden,
And his heart with doubts was laden.
What to believe he's all astir;
He thinks he's seen the last of her.
195 Arrived back home, Sir Lanval sees
His men dressed in new liveries.
That night the lavish host he plays,
But no one knows from whence he pays.
In town there is no *chevalier*[4]
200 Who badly needs a place to stay
Whom Lanval doesn't make his guest
And serves him richly of the best.
Lanval gives expensive presents;
Lanval remits the captive's sentence;
205 Lanval puts minstrels in new dress;
Lanval does honors in excess.
There's no stranger nor private friend
On whom Lanval does not spend.
He lives in joy and in delight,
210 Whether it be by day or night.
He sees his lady often, and
Has all the world at his command.
   That same summer, I would say,
After the feast of St. John's Day,
215 Thirty knights made an excursion,

---

4. Knight. Rhymes with -*ay* in French pronunciation.

For the sake of their diversion,
To a garden beneath the tower
In which the queen had her bower.
Among that party was Gawain
220 And his cousin, the good Yvain.
Sir Gawain spoke, brave and sincere,
Whom everybody held so dear,
"By God, my lords, we've not done right
By our companion, that good knight—
225 Lanval, so free, courtly, and loyal,
Son of a king who's rich and royal—
To leave that nobleman behind."
And straightway they turn back and find
Sir Lanval at his residence
230 And beg that they might take him thence.
     From a window with fine molding
The queen herself leaned out beholding
(Waited on by damsels three)
King Arthur's festive company.
235 She gazed at Lanval and knew him well.
She called out to one damoiselle
And sent her for her maids-in-waiting,
The fairest and most captivating.
With her into the garden then
240 They went to relax with the men.
Thirty she took along and more,
Down the stairs and out the door.
Rejoiced to have the ladies meet them,
The *chevaliers* advance to greet them.
245 Each girl by a knight's hand is led:
Such pleasant talk is not ill-bred.
Lanval goes off alone and turns
Aside from all the rest. He yearns
To hold his love within his arms,
250 To kiss, embrace, and feel her charms.
The joy of others is less pleasant
To him, his own not being present.
When she perceives him stand alone,
The queen straightway to him has gone
255 To sit beside him and reveals
All the passion that she feels:
"Lanval, I've honored you sincerely,
Have cherished you and loved you dearly.
All my love is at your disposal.
260 What do you say to my proposal?
Your mistress I consent to be;
You should receive much joy from me."
"Lady," he said, "hold me excused
Because your love must be refused.
265 I've served the king for many a day;
My faith to him I won't betray.
Never for love, and not for you,

Would I be to my lord untrue."
Made angry by these words, the queen
270 Insultingly expressed her spleen.
"Lanval," she said, "It's evident
That to such pleasures you have no bent.
Often I have heard men aver
That women are not what you prefer.
275 But you have many pretty boys
With whom you like to take your joys.
Faithless coward of low degree,
My lord was badly served when he
Suffered your person to come near.
280 For that he could lose God, I fear."
    Hearing this, Lanval was dismayed;
His answer was not long delayed.
With spite, as he was much upset,
He spoke what soon he would regret.
285 "My lady queen," was his retort,
"I know nothing about that sport.
But I love one, and she loves me;
From every woman I know of, she
Deserves to bear the prize away.
290 And one more thing I wish to say,
So that you may know it plain:
Each serving-maid in her domain,
The poorest girl of the whole crew,
My lady, is worth more than you
295 In beauty of both figure and face,
In good breeding and bounteous grace."
In tears the queen at once repairs
Back to her chamber up the stairs.
Dolorous she is and mortified
300 To be by him thus villified.
She goes to bed where sick she lies,
Vowing never again to rise,
Unless the king grants her redress
For that which caused her such distress.
305 The king had come back from the wood
Cheerful because the day was good.
To the queen's bedroom he attained;
As soon as she saw him, she complained.
Fallen at his feet, she cried, "Merci!5
310 Lanval has done me infamy."
To be her lover he had affected.
When his advances were rejected,
He had reviled her shamefully
And boasted he had an amie
315 So chic, noble, and proud, he said,
That even her lowliest chambermaid,
The poorest one that might be seen,

5. Exclamation appealing for compassion and favor.

Was worthier than she—the queen.
The king grew marvelously wroth,
320 And solemnly he swore an oath:
Unless the knight proved what he'd boasted,
The king would have him hanged or roasted.
Leaving the chamber, the king then
Summoned three of his noblemen.
325 After Lanval they were to go,
Who, feeling enough of grief and woe,
Had returned to his habitation,
Well aware of his situation.
Since he had told of their *amour*,
330 He had lost his love for sure.
In his room alone he languished,
Melancholy and sorely anguished.
He calls his love time and again,
But all his pleadings are in vain.
335 Sighs he utters and complaints,
And from time to time he faints.
A hundred times he cries *merci*
And begs her speak to her *ami*.
He curses both his heart and tongue;
340 A wonder 'tis he lives so long
Without committing suicide.
However much he roared and cried,
Fought with himself and scratched his face,
She would not show him any grace—
345 Even to see her once again.
Alas, how can he bear the pain?
    The king's men have arrived to say
He must to court without delay.
The king had summoned him for this reason:
350 The queen had charged the knight with treason.
Lanval went with them very sadly.
Should he be killed, he'd bear it gladly.
The knight was brought before the king,
Grief-stricken, not saying anything,
355 Like someone in great misery.
The king spoke out indignantly:
"Vassal, you've done lèse-majesté.[6]
You have begun a churlish play,
Me to dishonor and demean
360 And to speak slander of the queen.
It was a foolish boast to call
Your love the noblest one of all,
And her servant—to declare her
Worthier than the queen and fairer.
365   Lanval protested, word for word,
Any dishonor done to his lord
Respecting the queen's accusation

6. Treason against the highest authority.

Of a guilty solicitation.
But of his speech—to give her due—
370 He confessed that it was true.
The mistress he had boasted of
He mourned, for he had lost her love.
Regarding that, he said he'd do
Whatever the court told him to.
375 This put the king in a great fury.
He summoned his knights to act as jury
To tell how to proceed by law
So none might catch him in a flaw.[7]
They obeyed him—the entire lot,
380 Whether they wanted to or not.
They met together to consult
And deemed and judged with this result:
A court day set, Lanval goes free
But must find pledges to guarantee
385 His lord that judgment he'll abide.
Return to court and there be tried
By Arthur's entire baronage,
Not just the palace entourage.[8]
Back to the king the barons bring
390 The judgment of their parleying.
The king demands his sureties,
Thus putting Lanval ill at ease.
A foreigner, he felt chagrin
Since he had neither friend nor kin.
395 Gawain stepped forth and pledged that he
Would stand as Lanval's surety.
And his companions in succession
Each one made the same profession.
The king replied, "He's in your hands
400 At risk to forfeit all your lands
And fiefs, whatever they may be,
Which each of you obtained from me."
The pledges made, the court adjourned,
And Lanval to his place returned.
405 The knights escort him on his way.
They blame and warn him, and they say
To shun excessive melancholy;
And they lay curses on love's folly.
Worried about his mental state,
410 Each day they go investigate
Whether he's taking nourishment
Or to himself is violent.
    On the day that had been set,
All King Arthur's barons met.

7. The trial of Lanval shows precise knowledge of 12th-century legal procedure concerning the respective rights of the king and his barons. So as not to violate baronial rights, Arthur asks the knights of his household to determine the proper ways to proceed against one of their own.
8. The case is important enough to require judgment by all of Arthur's vassals, not just the immediate household. Hence the delay of the trial.

415 Attending were the king and queen;
Pledges brought Lanval on the scene.
They were all sad on his account—
A hundred of them I could count
Who would have done their best to see
420 Him without trial go scot-free,
For he'd been wrongfully arraigned.
On the charge, the king maintained,
And his response, he must be tried:
And now the barons must decide.
425 To the judgment they go next
Greatly worried and perplexed,
Since the noble foreign guest
In their midst is so hard-pressed.
Some were willing to condemn
430 To oblige their sovereign.
The Duke of Cornwall counselled thus:
"No fault shall be ascribed to us:
Though some may weep and some may play,
Justice must take its lawful way.
435 A vassal by the king denounced,
Whose name—"Lanval"—I heard pronounced,
Has been accused of felony
And charged that mischievously he
To a mistress had pretended
440 And Madame the Queen offended.
By the faith I owe you duly,
In this case, should one speak truly,
The king being the sole adversary,
No defense were necessary,
445 Save for the sake of his lord's name
A man must never speak him shame.
Sir Lanval by his oath must stand,
And the king quitclaim our land,
If the knight can guarantee
450 The coming here of his *amie*.
Should it prove true what he has claimed,
By which the queen felt so defamed,
Of that he'll be judged innocent,
Since he spoke without base intent.
455 But if he cannot prove it so,
In that case we must let him know,
All the king's service he must lose
And banished say his last adieus.
The knight was sent the court's decree
460 And informed by them that he
Must summon his *amie* and send her
To be his witness and defender.
The knight responded that he could not:
To his rescue come she would not.
465 To the judges they made report
That he looked for no support.

The king pressed them to make an ending
And not to keep the queen attending.
   When they came to lay down the law,
470 Two maidens from afar they saw
On two fine steeds, riding apace,
Who were extremely fair of face.
Of purple taffeta a sheath
They wore with nothing underneath.
475 The men took pleasure in the view.
Sir Gawain and three of his crew
Went to Sir Lanval to report
And show the girls coming to court.
Happy, he asked him earnestly
480 If one of them were his *amie.*
He told them that he knew not who
They were, where from, or going to.
The damoiselles rode on withal
Upon their mounts into the hall,
485 And they got off before the dais
There where the king sat at his place.
Their features were of beauty rare;
Their form of speech was debonair:
"King, clear your chambers, if you please,
490 And hang them with silk draperies,
Where my lady may make arrest,
For she wishes to be your guest.
The king gladly gave his consent.
Two of his courtiers he sent
495 To show them to their rooms upstairs.
No more was said of these affairs.
   The king ordered his retinue
To render up their judgment due.
The long procrastination had,
500 He said, made him extremely mad.
"My lord," they answered, "we have acted.
But our attention was distracted
By those ladies we have seen.
But now the court shall reconvene."
505 They reassembled much perturbed,
By too much noise and strife disturbed.
   While they engaged in this debate,
Two damoiselles of high estate—
In silks produced in Phrygia,
510 On mules from Andalusia—
Came riding up the street just then.
This gave great joy to Arthur's men,
Who told each other this must be
The worthy Lanval's remedy.
515 To him there hastened Sir Gawain
With his companions in his train.
"Sir knight," he said, "be of good cheer.
For God's sake speak to us! See here,

Two maidens are approaching us,
520 Most beautiful and decorous;
Surely one must be your *amie*."
Lanval made answer hastily.
He said that he recognized neither.
He didn't know or love them either.
525 Meanwhile the damoiselles had gone
And dismounted before the throne
Where the king was sitting on the dais.
From many there they won great praise
For figure, visage, and complexion.
530 They came much nearer to perfection
Than did the queen, so people said.
The elder was courteous and well-bred.
She spoke her message with much flair:
"King, tell your household to prepare
535 A suite to lodge my lady, who
Is coming here to speak with you."
The king had them conducted where
His men had lodged the previous pair.
As soon as they were from him gone,
540 He told his barons to have done
And give their verdict right away.
There had been far too much delay;
The queen had found it most frustrating
That they so long had kept her waiting.
545   When they were just about to bring
Judgment, a girl was entering
The town, whose beauty, it was clear,
In all the world could have no peer.
She rode upon a milkwhite horse,
550 Which bore her gently down the course.
Its neck and head were shapeliest;
Of all creatures, it was the best.
Splendidly furnished was this mount:
Beneath the heavens, no king or count
555 Could have afforded gear so grand
Unless he sold or pawned his land.
And this is how she was arrayed:
A white linen shift displayed—
There where it was with laces tied—
560 Her slender flanks on either side.
Slim-hipped, her form was *comme il faut*;[9]
Her neck, whiter than branch in snow;
Her eyes were gray; her face was bright;
Her mouth, lovely; nose, set just right;
565 Eyebrows black, forehead fair;
Blonde and curly was her hair.
Golden wire sheds no such ray
As did her locks against the day.

9. As required, perfectly correct.

A mantle was around her drawn,
570 A cloak of deep-dyed purple lawn.
A falcon on her wrist sat still;
A greyhound followed her at will.
In town was neither high nor low,
Old man or child, who did not go
575 And line the streets along the way
To watch as she made her entrée.
And as they stood gazing at her,
Her beauty was no laughing matter.
She rode up to the castle slowly.
580 The judges, seeing her, were wholly
Astonished at that spectacle
And held it for a miracle.
The heart of every single knight
Among them warmed with sheer delight.
585 Those who loved Sir Lanval well
Quickly went to him to tell
About the maiden who perchance,
Please God, brought him deliverance.
"Comrade," they said, "here comes one,
590 Who is neither swart nor dun.
Of all women by land and sea,
She is the fairest that may be.
Lanval heard and raised his eye;
He knew her well and gave a sigh.
595 The blood shot up into his cheeks,
And somewhat hastily he speaks:
"In faith," he said, "that's my *amie*!
Now I don't care if they kill me
If but her mercy is assured,
600 For when I see her, I am cured."
The maid rode through the palace door,
So fair came never there before.
In front of Arthur she got down
With the whole company looking on.
605 Softly she let her mantle fall,
The better to be seen by all.
King Arthur, who was most discreet,
To greet her got up on his feet.
In turn, to honor her the rest
610 Offered their service to the guest.
When they had satisfied their gaze
And greatly sung her beauty's praise,
She made her speech in such a way
As she did not intend to stay:
615 "King, I have loved one of your band—
It's Lanval, there you see him stand.
I would not have the man ill-used—
In your court he has been accused
Of lies he spoke. Take it from me,
620 The queen committed perjury;

He never asked her for her love.
As for the things he boasted of,
If I may be his warranty,
Your barons ought to speak him free."
625 The king agreed he would abide
By what they lawfully decide.
Among them there was no dissent;
Lanval was pronounced innocent.
The damoiselle set off again,
630 Though the king asked her to remain.
Outside there stood a marble rock
With steps to make a mounting block,
From which armed men would get astride
When they from court set out to ride.
635 Lanval climbed up on it before
The damoiselle rode out the door.
Swiftly he sprang the horse to straddle
And sat behind her on the saddle.
To Avalon they came away,
640 Which Breton storytellers say
An island is, most ravishing,
There Lanval has gone, vanishing.
No man has heard more of his fate;
I've nothing further to relate.

FINIS

FABLES[1]

The Wolf and the Lamb

This tells of wolf and lamb who drank
Together once along a bank.
The wolf right at the spring was staying
While lambkin down the stream was straying.
5 The wolf then spoke up nastily,
For argumentative was he,
Saying to lamb, with great disdain,
"You give me such a royal pain!"
The lamb made this reply to him,
10 "Pray sir, what's wrong?"—"Are your eyes dim!
You've so stirred up the water here,
I cannot drink my fill, I fear.
I do believe I should be first,
Because I've come here dying of thirst."
15 The little lamb then said to him,
"But sir, 'twas you who drank upstream.
My water comes from you, you see."
"What!" snapped the wolf. "You dare curse me?"
"Sir, I had no intention to!"

1. The translation is by Harriet Spiegel, *Fables* (1987).

20 The wolf replied, "I know what's true.
Your father treated me just so
Here at this spring some time ago—
It's now six months since we were here."
"So why blame me for that affair?
25 I wasn't even born, I guess."
"So what?" the wolf responded next;
"You really are perverse today—
You're not supposed to act this way."
The wolf then grabbed the lamb so small,
30 Chomped through his neck, extinguished all.
  And this is what our great lords do,
The viscounts and the judges too,
With all the people whom they rule:
False charge they make from greed so cruel.
35 To cause confusion they consort
And often summon folk to court.
They strip them clean of flesh and skin,
As the wolf did to the lambkin.

The Wolf and the Sow

Once long ago a wolf strolled down
A path and chanced to come upon
A sow who was with piglets big.
He hastily approached the pig.
5 He'd give her peace, he told the sow,
If quickly she'd bear piglets now—
Her piglet babes he wished to have.
With wisdom, this response she gave:
"My lord, how can you hurry me?
10 When you, so close to me I see,
I cannot bear my young outright;
I'm so ashamed when in your sight.
Do you not sense the implication?
All women suffer degradation
15 If male hands should dare to touch
At such a time, or even approach!"
With this the wolf hid in retreat
Who'd sought the baby pigs to eat.
The mother pig could now proceed
20 Who through her cleverness was freed.
  All women ought to hear this tale
And should remember it as well:
Merely to avoid a lie,
They should not let their children die!

CELTIC CONTEXTS

The changes European literature underwent during the twelfth and thirteenth centuries are greatly indebted to Celtic influences. The legends about King Arthur and his knights, although they were assimilated to the feudal culture of the Anglo-Normans and transmitted by texts written in Latin, French, and English (see pp. 7–8), were originally products of Celtic myth and legend. The folkloric otherworld elements and the major role played by women in those stories profoundly shaped and colored the literature we now think of as "romance." The French Tristan romances, the romances of Marie de France and Chrétien de Troyes, and even the legends of the Holy Grail could not have been imagined without their Celtic components.

The Celts overran central Europe, Spain, and the British Isles during the first millennium B.C.E. On the Continent and in Great Britain, south of the wall built by the emperor Hadrian (see the map inside the front cover), they were absorbed into the Roman Empire. However, the Celtic vernacular continued to be spoken as the native language, and Ireland never became a Roman province. The Anglo-Saxon invasions in the fifth and early sixth centuries, and the Danish invasions after the eighth, displaced Celtic in England, but Celtic language and culture continued to flourish in Wales (Welsh), in Cornwall (Cornish), across the English Channel in Brittany (Breton), and, of course, in Ireland (Gaelic). While still part of the Roman Empire, Britain and, in consequence, Ireland had been converted to Christianity. As portrayed in the Arthurian legend, the Christian Britons fought against barbaric Germanic invaders. Irish and Welsh missionaries, along with Roman ones, brought about the conversion of the Anglo-Saxons.

The earliest Celtic literature, like that of the Anglo-Saxons, was transmitted orally and little was copied down before the twelfth century. Nevertheless, the surviving monuments indicate its richness and its significance for the development of French and English medieval literature.

EXILE OF THE SONS OF UISLIU

The Old Irish tale of the *Exile of the Sons of Uisliu* [ísh-lu] is believed on linguistic grounds to date back to at least the eighth century, although the earliest text is found in a mid-twelfth-century manuscript known as the Book of the Dun Cow. As is typical in Old Irish narrative, many of the characters' speeches are in verse that is probably even older. The *Exile* is one of several tales leading up to the epic *Táin Bó Cuailnge* (The Cattle Raid of Cooley), which tells of the war between the kingdoms of Connacht and Ulster. Its heroine Derdriu [dér-dru] is one of the passionate and strong-willed women, whose prototypes may have been ancient divinities, for which Old Irish literature is noted. In some respects the triangle of Derdriu, Conchobor [kón-chor: *ch* is guttural as in Scots *loch*], and Noisiu [nói-shu] resembles that of Isolt, King Mark, and Tristan, told in twelfth-century poetic versions by Thomas, who probably wrote for the court of Henry II, and by the Norman Béroul. The Tristan story has antecedents in Irish, Welsh, and Breton. The story of Derdriu is the source of modern plays by William Butler Yeats and John Millington Synge and a novel by James Stephens.[1]

---

1. The translation and notes 2, 4, 6–8 are by Thomas Kinsella, *The Táin* (1969).

Exile of the Sons of Uisliu

What caused the exile of the sons of Uisliu? It is soon told.
The men of Ulster were drinking in the house of Conchobor's storyteller,
Fedlimid mac Daill. Fedlimid's wife was overseeing everything and looking
after them all. She was full with child. Meat and drink were passed round,
and a drunken uproar shook the place. When they were ready to sleep the
woman went to her bed. As she crossed the floor of the house the child
screamed in her womb and was heard all over the enclosure. At that scream
everyone in the house started up, staring at each other. Sencha mac Ailella
said:
"No one move! Bring the woman here. We'll see what caused this noise."
So the woman was brought before them. Her husband Fedlimid said:

> Woman,
> what was that fierce shuddering sound
> furious in your troubled womb?
> The weird uproar at your waist
> hurts the ears of all who hear it.
> My heart trembles at some great terror
> or some cruel injury.

She turned distracted to the seer Cathbad:

> Fair-faced Cathbad, hear me
> —prince, pure, precious crown,
> grown huge in druid spells.
> I can't find the fair words
> that would shed the light of knowledge
> for my husband Fedlimid,
> even though it was the hollow
> of my own womb that howled.
> No woman knows what her womb bears.

Then Cathbad said:

> A woman with twisted yellow tresses,
> green-irised eyes of great beauty
> and cheeks flushed like the foxglove
> howled in the hollow of your womb.
> I say that whiter than the snow
> is the white treasure of her teeth;
> Parthian-red,[2] her lip's luster.
> Ulster's chariot-warriors
> will deal many a blow for her.
> There howled in your troubled womb
> a tall, lovely, long-haired woman.
> Heroes will contend for her,
> high kings beseech on her account;

2. A word of doubtful meaning. It has been suggested that it derives from "Parthica"—Parthian leather
dyed scarlet.

> then, west of Conchobor's kingdom
> a heavy harvest of fighting men.
> High queens will ache with envy
> to see those lips of Parthian-red
> opening on her pearly teeth,
> and see her pure perfect body.

Cathbad placed his hand on the woman's belly and the baby wriggled under it.

"Yes," he said, "there is a girl there. Derdriu shall be her name. She will bring evil."

Then the daughter was born and Cathbad said:

> Much damage, Derdriu, will follow
> your high fame and fair visage:
> Ulster in your time tormented,
> demure daughter of Fedlimid.
>
> And later, too, jealousy
> will dog you, woman like a flame,
> and later still—listen well—
> the three sons of Uisliu exiled.
>
> Then again, in your lifetime,
> a bitter blow struck in Emain.
> Remorse later for that ruin
> wrought by the great son of Roech;[3]
>
> Fergus exiled out of Ulster
> through your fault, fatal woman,
> and the much-wept deadly wound
> of Fiachna, Conchobor's son.
>
> Your fault also, fatal woman,
> Gerrce felled, Illadan's son,
> and a crime that no less cries out,
> the son of Durthacht, Eogan, struck.
>
> Harsh, hideous deeds done
> in anger at Ulster's high king,
> and little graves everywhere
> —a famous tale, Derdriu.

"Kill the child!" the warriors said.

"No," Conchobor said. "The girl will be taken away tomorrow. I'll have her reared for me. This woman I'll keep to myself."

The men of Ulster didn't dare speak against him.

And so it was done. She was reared by Conchobor and grew into the loveliest woman in all Ireland. She was kept in a place set apart, so that no

---

3. Fergus, a great hero of Ulster. One consequence of this episode is that he will side with Connacht in the war against Ulster.

Ulsterman might see her until she was ready for Conchobor's bed. No one was allowed in the enclosure but her foster-father and her foster-mother, and Leborcham, tall and crooked, a satirist, who couldn't be kept out.[4]

One day in winter, the girl's foster-father was skinning a milk-fed calf on the snow outside, to cook it for her. She saw a raven drinking the blood on the snow. She said to Leborcham:

"I could desire a man who had those three colors there: hair like the raven, cheeks like blood and his body like snow."

"Good luck and success to you!" Leborcham said. "He isn't too far away, but close at hand—Noisiu, Uisliu's son."

"I'll be ill in that case," she said, "until I see him." This man Noisiu was chanting by himself one time near Emain,[5] on the rampart of the stronghold. The chanting of the sons of Uisliu was very sweet. Every cow or beast that heard it gave two-thirds more milk. Any person hearing it was filled with peace and music. Their deeds in war were great also: if the whole province of Ulster came at them at once, they could put their three backs together and not be beaten, their parrying and defense were so fine. Besides this they were swift as hounds in the chase, killing the wild beasts in flight.

While Noisiu was out there alone, therefore, she slipped out quickly to him and made as though to pass him and not recognize him.

"That is a fine heifer going by," he said.

"As well it might," she said. "The heifers grow big where there are no bulls."

"You have the bull of this province all to yourself," he said, "the king of Ulster."

"Of the two," she said, "I'd pick a game young bull like you."

"You couldn't," he said. "There is Cathbad's prophecy."

"Are you rejecting me?"

"I am," he said.

Then she rushed at him and caught the two ears of his head.

"Two ears of shame and mockery," she said, "if you don't take me with you."

"Woman, leave me alone!" he said.

"You will do it," she said, binding him.[6]

A shrill cry escaped him at that. The men of Ulster nearby, when they heard it, started up staring at each other. Uisliu's other sons went out to quieten their brother.

"What is wrong?" they said. "Whatever it is, Ulstermen shouldn't kill each other for it."

He told them what had happened.

"Evil will come of this," the warriors said. "But even so, you won't be shamed as long as we live. We can bring her with us to some other place. There's no king in Ireland who would deny us a welcome."

They decided on that. They left that night, with three times fifty warriors and three times fifty women and the same of hounds and menials. Derdriu was among them, mingling with the rest.

4. Through fear that her verses might bring harm. Leborcham, as a satirist, would have more than usual freedom.
5. Emain Macha [év-in-má-cha], Conchobor's royal stronghold.
6. The words "binding him" are not in the text. Her words put Noisiu under bond, or *geasa*, to do what she asked.

They traveled about Ireland for a long time, under protection. Conchobor tried to destroy them often with ambushes and treachery. They went round southwestward from the red cataract at Es Ruaid, and to the promontory at Benn Etair, northeastward. But still the men of Ulster pursued them until they crossed the sea to the land of Alba.[7]

They settled there in the waste places. When the mountain game failed them they turned to take the people's cattle. A day came when the people of Alba went out to destroy them. Then they offered themselves to the king of Alba, who accepted them among his people as hired soldiers. They set their houses on the green. They built their houses so that no one could see in at the girl in case there might be killing on her account.

It happened that a steward came looking around their house early one morning. He saw the couple sleeping. Then he went and woke the king:

"I never found a woman fit for you until today," he said. "There is a woman with Noisiu mac Uislenn who is fit for a king over the Western World. If you have Noisiu killed, you can have the woman to sleep with," the steward said.

"No," the king said, "but go and ask her every day in secret."

He did this, but every day he came she told Noisiu about it that night. Since nothing could be done with her, the sons of Uisliu were ordered into all kinds of traps and dangerous battles to have them killed. But they were so hard in the carnage that nothing came of it.

They tried her one last time. Then the men of Alba were called together to kill them. She told Noisiu this.

"Go away from here," she said. "If you don't leave here this night, you will be dead tomorrow."

So they left that night and reached an island in the sea.

This news reached Ulster.

"Conchobor," everyone said, "it would be shameful if the sons of Uisliu fell in enemy lands by the fault of a bad woman. Better to forgive and protect them—to save their lives and let them come home—than for enemies to lay them low."

"Let them come," Conchobor said. "Send for them, with guarantees of safety."

This news was brought to them.

"It is welcome," they said. "We'll go if Fergus comes as a pledge of safety, and Dubthach and Conchobor's son Cormac."

Then they went down with the messengers to the sea.

So they were brought back to Ireland. But Fergus was stopped through Conchobor's cunning. He was invited to a number of ale feasts and, by an old oath, couldn't refuse. The sons of Uisliu had sworn they would eat no food in Ireland until they ate Conchobor's food first, so they were bound to go on. Fiacha, Fergus's son, went on with them, while Fergus and Dubthach stayed behind. The sons of Uisliu came to the green at Emain. Eogan mac Durthacht, king of Fernmag, was there: he had come to make peace with Conchobor, with whom he had long been at enmity. He had been chosen to kill them. Conchobor's hired soldiers gathered around him so that the sons of Uisliu couldn't reach him. They stood in the middle of the green. The women settled on the ramparts of Emain.

7. This means Britain generally.

Eogan crossed the green with his men. Fergus's son came and stood at Noisiu's side. Eogan welcomed Noisiu with the hard thrust of a great spear that broke his back. Fergus's son grasped Noisiu in his two arms and pulled him down and threw himself across him, and Noisiu was finished off through Fergus's son's body. Then the slaughter broke out all over the green. No one left except by spike of spear or slash of sword. Derdriu was brought over to Conchobor and stood beside him with her hands bound at her back.

Fergus was told of this, and Dubthach and Cormac. They came at once and did mighty deeds. Dubthach killed Maine, Conchobor's son. Fiachna, son of Conchobor's daughter Fedelm, was killed with a single thrust. Fergus killed Traigthrén, Traiglethan's son, and his brother. Conchobor was outraged, and on a day soon afterward battle was joined between them, and three hundred among the men of Ulster fell. Before morning Dubthach had massacred the girls of Ulster and Fergus had burned Emain.

Then they went to Connacht, to Ailill and Medb—not that this was a home for Ulstermen, but that they knew these two would protect them. A full three thousand the exiles numbered. For sixteen years they made sure that weeping and trembling never died away in Ulster; there was weeping and trembling at their hands every single night. She was kept a year by Conchobor. In that time she never gave one smile, nor took enough food or sleep, nor lifted up her head from her knees. If they sent musicians to her, she would say this following poem:

> Sweet in your sight the fiery stride
> of raiding men returned to Emain.
> More nobly strode the three proud.
> sons of Uisliu toward their home:
>
> Noisiu bearing the best mead
> —I would wash him by the fire—
> Ardán, with a stag or a boar,
> Anle, shouldering his load.
>
> The son of Nes, battle-proud,
> drinks, you say, the choicest mead.
> Choicer still—a brimming sea—
> I have taken frequently.
>
> Modest Noisiu would prepare
> a cooking-pit in the forest floor.
> Sweeter then than any meat
> the son of Uisliu's, honey-sweet.
>
> Though for you the times are sweet
> with pipers and with trumpeters,
> I swear today I can't forget
> that I have known far sweeter airs.
>
> Conchobor your king may take delight
> in pipers and in trumpeters
> —I have known a sweeter thing,
> the three sons' triumphant song.

Noisiu's voice a wave roar,
a sweet sound to hear forever;
Ardán's bright baritone;
Anle, the hunter's, high tenor.

Noisiu: his grave-mound is made
and mournfully accompanied.
The highest hero—and I poured
the deadly potion when he died.

His cropped gold fleece I loved,
and fine form—a tall tree.
Alas, I needn't watch today,
nor wait for the son of Uisliu.

I loved the modest, mighty warrior,
loved his fitting, firm desire,
loved him at daybreak as he dressed
by the margin of the forest.

Those blue eyes that melted women,
and menaced enemies, I loved;
then, with our forest journey done,
his chanting through the dark woods.

I don't sleep now,
nor redden my fingernails.
What have I to do with welcomes?
The son of Indel[8] will not come.

I can't sleep,
lying there half the night.
These crowds—I am driven out of my mind.
I can neither eat nor smile.

What use for welcome have I now
with all these nobles crowding Emain?
Comfortless, no peace nor joy,
nor mansion nor pleasant ornament.

If Conchobor tried to soothe her, she would chant this following poem:

Conchobor, what are you thinking, you
that piled up sorrow over woe?
Truly, however long I live,
I cannot spare you much love.

The thing most dear to me in the world,
the very thing I most loved,
your harsh crime took from me.
I will not see him till I die.

8. The mother of the three sons.

I feel his lack, wearily,
the son of Uisliu. All I see—
black boulders on fair flesh
so bright once among the others.

Red-cheeked, sweet as the river-brink;
red-lipped; brows beetle-black;
pearly teeth gleaming bright
with a noble snowy light.

His figure easiest to find,
bright among Alba's fighting-men
—a border made of red gold
matched his handsome crimson cloak.

A soft multitude of jewels
in the satin tunic—itself a jewel:
for decoration, all told,
fifty ounces of light gold.

He carried a gold-hilted sword
and two javelins sharply tipped,
a shield rimmed with yellow gold
with a knob of silver at the middle.

Fergus did an injury
bringing us over the great sea.
How his deeds of valor shrank
when he sold honor for a drink!

If all Ulster's warriors
were gathered on this plain, Conchobor,
I would gladly give them all
for Noisiu, son of Uisliu.

Break my heart no more today.
In a short while I'll be no more.
Grief is heavier than the sea,
if you were but wise, Conchobor.

"What do you see that you hate most?" Conchobor said.

"You, surely," she said, "and Eogan mac Durthacht!"

"Go and live for a year with Eogan, then," Conchobor said.

Then he sent her over to Eogan.

They set out the next day for the fair of Macha. She was behind Eogan in
the chariot. She had sworn that two men alive in the world together would
never have her.

"This is good, Derdriu," Conchobor said. "Between me and Eogan you are
a sheep eyeing two rams."

A big block of stone was in front of her. She let her head be driven against
the stone, and made a mass of fragments of it, and she was dead.

LLUDD AND LLEUELYS

The Welsh tale of *Lludd and Lleuelys* is preserved in a collection of stories contained in two manuscripts, the English titles of which are the White Book of Rhydderch (written ca. 1300–25) and the Red Book of Hergest (ca. 1375–1425). The stories are thought to be much older, some dating back to the latter part of the eleventh century. The traditional but inaccurate title, given to the collection by its nineteenth-century translator, is *The Mabinogion*, a mistake for *Mabinogi*, which has been interpreted as a generic term for the youthful exploits of a hero but probably refers to a group of interconnected traditional stories. A group of the *Mabinogi* deals with characters who are related through crossovers between the human world and a supernatural other-world; *Lludd and Lleuelys*, however, is one of several independent tales. Lludd is among the kings of Britain mentioned by Geoffrey of Monmouth, where he appears (as in the tale below) as a restorer of the walls of London and builder of many towers in that city. Geoffrey says that the city's original name Trinovantum (New Troy), given to it by its eponymous founder Brutus (see pp. 116–18), was changed to Caer Lludd (Lludd's city or stronghold), which became Caer Llundein, and finally London. The tale here has the same etymology for London though nothing about a change of names. Geoffrey probably took the etymology from a Welsh source, and the redactor of *Lludd and Lleuelys* could have taken it from Geoffrey's *History*, which was translated into Welsh. Either way, the etymology is not convincing but typifies a characteristic of both Irish and Welsh literature to explain place names with stories. *Lludd and Lleuelys* gives us an idea of the kind of material Geoffrey of Monmouth must have been dealing with and what he may have chosen to omit. The three plagues of which King Lludd rids his land on the advice of his brother are the stuff of folktales, which Geoffrey may have regarded as too far-fetched to belong in a history book even though he did not draw that line at Merlin's magic.

Ll in Welsh represents a sound that does not exist in English and may be approximated by an aspirated *l* [hl] or simply pronounced as [1]. Welsh *u* may represent short or long *i*. The double consonant *dd* corresponds to *th* in see*the*. Thus Lludd in Welsh is pronounced something like *hleethe*, but when his name is anglicized, it is spelled and pronounced as Lud.

Lludd and Lleuelys[1]

Beli Mawr son of Mynogan had three sons: Lludd, Caswallawn, and Ninniaw; according to the lore about him, Lleuelys was a fourth son. After Beli died, the kingdom of the isle of Britain fell into the hands of Lludd, his eldest son, and Lludd ruled it successfully. He refurbished the walls of London, and surmounted them with countless towers. After that he ordered the citizens to build houses of such quality that no kingdom would have houses as splendid as were in London.

And besides that, he was a good warrior and generous, and he gave food and drink freely to all who sought it, and although he had many forts and cities, he loved this one more than any other, and dwelt there most of the year. For that reason it was called Caer Lludd, and finally Caer Llundein. After the foreign people came it was called Llundein or Londres.

Lludd loved Lleuelys best of all his brothers, for he was a wise and prudent

---

1. The translation is by Patrick K. Ford, *The Mabinogi and Other Medieval Welsh Tales* (1977).

man. When Lleuelys heard that the king of France had died leaving no heir save a daughter, and that he had left his realm in her hands, he came to his brother Lludd seeking counsel and encouragement from him. And not only for personal advantage, but to try to add honor, dignity, and merit to their race, if he could go to the kingdom of France to seek that woman for his wife. His brother agreed with him immediately, and he was pleased with that counsel. Without delay ships were made ready and filled with armed horsemen, and they set out for France. As soon as they disembarked, they sent messengers to announce to the nobles of France the nature of the business they had come to attempt. And by joint counsel of the nobles of France and her princes, the maiden was given to Lleuelys, and the realm's crown along with her. After that, he ruled the land wisely, prudently, and in good fortune, as long as he lived.

After some time had passed, three oppressions came upon the isle of Britain, such that none of the islands had ever seen before. The first of these was the advent of a people called the Coraniaid; so great was their knowledge that there was no utterance over the face of the land—however low it was spoken—that, if the wind met it, they didn't know. For that reason, one could do them no harm.

The second oppression was a cry that resounded every May Day eve above every hearth in Britain; it went through the hearts of men and terrified them so much that men lost their color and their strength, women miscarried, sons and daughters lost their senses and all animals, forests, earth and waters were left barren.

The third oppression was that despite how extensive the preparations and provisions were that were readied in the king's courts, even though it be a year's provision of food and drink, nothing was ever had of it except what could be consumed on the very first night.

The first oppression was evident and clear enough, but no one knew the meaning of the other two oppressions. There was greater hope, therefore, of deliverance from the first than from the second or third.

Lludd, the king, grew anxious and worried then, for he didn't know how he could get relief from those oppressions. He summoned all the nobles of his realm, and sought advice from them concerning what they could do against those oppressions. With the unanimous counsel of the nobles, Lludd son of Beli determined to go to his brother Lleuelys, king of France, for he was a man of great and wise counsel, from whom to seek advice. And they prepared a fleet—secretly and quietly, lest that people or anyone else know the meaning of their business except the king and his counselors. When they had been prepared, Lludd and those whom he had selected went to their ships and began to plough the seas toward France.

When news of that came to Lleuelys—since he did not know the reason for his brother's fleet—he came from the other side to meet him, with an enormous fleet. When Lludd saw that, he left all his ships out at sea except one, and in that he went to meet his brother. The other did the same. After they came together, each put his arms around the other's neck, and they greeted each other with brotherly affection. When Lludd had told his brother the purpose of his mission, Lleuelys said that he knew the meaning of his arrival in those lands. Then they conspired to conduct their business differently, in order that the wind might not carry their speech, lest the Coraniaid know what they said. So Lleuelys had a long brass horn made, and they talked through that. But whatever speech one of them uttered through the horn, only adverse, contrary speech was heard by the other. When Lleuelys saw that, and that a demon was obstructing them and creating turmoil in the horn, he had wine poured into the horn to cleanse it. By virtue of the wine, the demon was driven out.

When their speech was unobstructed, Lleuelys told his brother that he would give him some vermin, and that he should let some of them live to breed, in case by chance that sort of oppression came again. The others he should take and break up in water. That, he affirmed, would be good to destroy the race of Coraniaid, as follows: after he came home to his realm, he should summon all the people together—his people and the Coraniaid people in the same assembly, with the pretext of making peace between them. When they were all together, he should take that charged water and sprinkle it on everyone universally. And he affirmed that that water would poison the Coraniaid people, but that it would neither kill nor injure any of his own people.

"The second oppression in your realm," he said, "is a dragon. A dragon of foreign blood is fighting with him and seeking to overthrow him. Because of that, your dragon utters a horrible scream. This is how you shall be instructed regarding that: after you return home, have the length and width of the island measured. Where you discover the exact center, have that place dug up. Then, have a vatful of the best mead that can be made put into that hole, with a cover of silk brocade over the top of the vat. And then you yourself stand watch, and you will see the dragons fighting in the shape of horrible animals. Finally, they will assume the form of dragons in the air. Last of all, after they cease their violent and fierce battle, being tired, they will fall in the shape of two young pigs onto the coverlet. They will sink the sheet with them and draw it down to the bottom of the vat; they will drink all the mead, and after that they will sleep. Then immediately wrap the cover around them. In the strongest place you can find in your kingdom, deposit them in a stone chest, and hide it in the ground. And as long as they remain in that secure place, no oppression shall visit the isle of Britain from another place."

"The cause of the third oppression," he said, "is a powerful magician who carries off your food, your drink, and your provisions, and by his sorcery and his magic he puts everyone to sleep. And so you yourself must stand guard over your banquets and your feasts. And lest he induce sleep in you, have a vat of cold water at hand, and when sleep weighs you down, get into the vat."

Lludd returned to his country then, and without delay summoned every single one of his own people and the Coraniaid. He broke the vermin up in the water, as Lleuelys had taught him, and sprinkled it generally over everyone. All the Coraniaid folk were destroyed instantly without injury to any of the Britons.

Some time after that, Lludd had the island measured in length and breadth; the middle point was found to be in Oxford. There he had the earth dug up, and in that hole he put a vat full of the best mead that could be made, with a silk veil over the surface. He himself stood watch that night. As he was thus, he could see the dragons fighting. When they grew weary and exhausted, they fell onto the screen and dragged it down with them to the bottom of the vat. After they drank the mead they slept; as they slept, Lludd wrapped the veil about them. In the safest place he could find in Eryri, he secluded them in a stone chest. After that the place was called Dinas Emrys; before that it was known as Dinas Ffaraon Dandde. He was one of three stewards whose hearts broke from sorrow.

Thus was stopped the tempestuous scream that was in the realm.

When that was done, Lludd the king had a feast of great magnitude prepared. When it was ready, he put a vat full of cold water beside him and he personally stood guard. And as he stood there fully armed, about the third watch of the night, he heard much magnificent music and songs of different kinds, and drowsiness driving him to sleep. What he did then—lest his plan be thwarted and he be overcome by sleep—was to leap into the water frequently. At last a man of enormous stature, armed with powerful, heavy weapons, came in carrying a basket. As was his custom, he put all the preparations and the provisions of food and drink into the basket and started out with it. Nothing astounded Lludd more than such a quantity as that fitting into that basket. Thereupon, Lludd the King set out after him, and shouted; "Stop! Stop!" he said, "though you have committed many outrages and have been responsible for many losses before this, you'll do it no more—unless your prowess proves you stronger than I or more valiant."

Immediately, he set the basket on the floor and waited for him. They fought ferociously, until sparks flew from their weapons. Finally, Lludd took hold of him, and fate took care that the victory fell to Lludd, casting the tyrant to the ground beneath him. When he had conquered him through force and violence, the fellow sought protection from him.

"How could I give you protection," said the King, "after how much loss and injury you have perpetrated against me?"

"All the losses I have ever caused you," said the other, "I will restore to you, as well as I have carried them off, and I will not do the like from this moment on, but will be your faithful man henceforth."

And the King accepted that from him. Thus did Lludd ward off the three oppressions from the isle of Britain. From then until the end of his life, Lludd ruled the isle of Britain successfully and peacefully.

This tale is called the Adventure of Lludd and Lleuelys, and so it ends.

ANCRENE RIWLE (RULE FOR ANCHORESSES)

In the twelfth and thirteenth centuries, there was a movement toward a more solitary religious life and a more personal encounter with God. In the early days of Christianity, monasticism had originated with the desert fathers, men who withdrew to the wilderness in order to lead a life of prayer and meditation. The fifth and sixth centuries saw the growth and spread of religious orders, men and women living in religious communities, especially the Benedictine order, founded in Italy by St. Benedict. New orders founded in the eleventh and twelfth centuries—the Cistercians, for example—emphasized a more actively engaged and individual spirituality. The Dominican and

Franciscan orders were not confined to their houses but were preaching and teaching orders who staffed the newly founded universities.

Along with the new orders, a number of both men and women chose to become anchorites or hermits, living alone or in small groups. In his *Rule*, St. Benedict had described such solitaries with a military metaphor: "They have built up their strength and go from the battle line in the ranks of their brothers to the single combat of the desert. Self-reliant now, without the support of another, they are ready with God's help to grapple single-handed with the vices of body and mind." Benedict's battle imagery anticipates the affinities between this solitary kind of spirituality and the literary form of romance, both of which were developing in the twelfth and thirteenth centuries. The individual soul confined in its enclosure fights temptation as Sir Gawain rides out alone in the wilderness to seek the Green Chapel and encounters temptation along the way (see pp. 173–99). The wilderness in romance often contains hermits, who may be genuinely holy men, or they may be enchanters like Archimago, disguised as a holy hermit, in the *Faerie Queene*. The influence of romance on religion and of religion on romance is also strikingly seen in portrayals of Christ as a knight who jousts for the love and salvation of human souls, which is a motif common to *Ancrene Riwle*, William Herebert's poem *What is he, this lordling, that cometh from the fight* (pp. 352–53), and *Piers Plowman* (see pp. 336–38).

Anchoress (the feminine form of *anchorite*, from the Greek *anachoretes*, "one who lives apart") refers to a religious recluse who, unlike a hermit, lives in an enclosure, attached to a church, from which she never emerges. Anchoresses and anchorites might live singly, like Julian of Norwich (see pp. 355–56) or in small groups. *Ancrene Riwle* (ca. 1215) was originally written for three young sisters, who, the author says in an aside in one manuscript, come from a noble family with ample means to support them. The author of *Ancrene Riwle* addresses the sisters in a colloquial, urbane, and personal prose style that distinguishes the guide both as a book of religious instruction and as a literary achievement of Early Middle English.

The excerpt comes from Part 7, to which the author gave the title "Love."[1]

From Ancrene Riwle

[THE PARABLE OF THE CHRIST-KNIGHT]

A lady was completely surrounded by her enemies, her land laid waste, and she herself quite destitute, in a castle of clay. But a powerful king had fallen in love with her so inordinately that to win her love he sent her his messengers, one after another, often many together; he sent her many splendid presents of jewelry, provisions to support her, help from his noble army to hold her castle. She accepted everything as if it meant nothing to her, and was so hard-hearted that he could never come closer to gaining her love. What more do you want? At last he came himself; showed her his handsome face, as the most supremely handsome of men; spoke so very tenderly, and with words so beguiling that they could raise the dead to life; worked many wonders and did great feats before her eyes; showed her his power; told her about his kingdom; offered to make her queen of all that he owned. All this had no effect. Was not this scorn surprising?—for she was never fit to be his maidservant. But because of his gentle nature love had so overcome him that at last he said: "You are under attack, lady, and your enemies are so strong that without my help there is no way that you can escape falling into their

1. The translation is from *Medieval English Prose for Women*, edited by Bella Millett and Jocelyn Wogan-Browne (1990).

hands, and being put to a shameful death after all your troubles. For your love I am willing to take on that fight, and rescue you from those who are seeking your death. But I know for certain that in fighting them I shall receive a mortal wound; and I will accept it gladly in order to win your heart. Now, therefore, I beg you, for the love I am showing towards you, to love me at least when this is done, after my death, although you refused to during my life." This king did just as he had promised; he rescued her from all her enemies, and was himself shamefully ill-treated and at last put to death. But by a miracle he rose from death to life. Would not this lady have a base nature if she did not love him after this above all things?

This king is Jesus, Son of God, who in just this way wooed our soul, which devils had besieged. And he, like a noble suitor, after numerous messengers and many acts of kindness came to prove his love, and showed by feats of arms that he was worthy of love, as was the custom of knights once upon a time. He entered the tournament and, like a bold knight, had his shield pierced through and through in battle for love of his lady. His shield, which hid his divinity, was his dear body, which was stretched out on the cross: broad as a shield above in his extended arms, narrow below, where the one foot (as many people think) was fixed above the other. That this shield has no sides is to signify that his disciples, who should have stood by him and been his sides, all fled from him and abandoned him like strangers, as the Gospel says: *They all abandoned him and fled* [Matthew 26.56]. This shield is given to us against all temptations, as Jeremiah testifies: *You will give your labor as a shield for the heart* [Lamentations 3.65]. This shield not only protects us against all evils, but does still more: it crowns us in heaven. *With the shield of good will* [Psalms 5.12]—"Lord," says David, "you have crowned us with the shield of your good will." He says "shield of good will" because he suffered willingly all that he suffered. Isaiah says: *He was offered because he wished to be* [Isaiah 53.7].

"But, master," you say, "what was the point? Could he not have saved us without so much suffering?" Yes, indeed, very easily; but he did not wish to. Why? To deprive us of any excuse for denying him our love, since he had paid so dearly for it. You buy cheaply what you do not value highly. He bought us with his heart's blood—a higher price was never paid—to attract our love, which cost him so much suffering. In a shield there are three things: the wood, and the leather, and the painted design. So it was in this shield: the wood of the cross, the leather of God's body, the painting of the red blood which colored it so brightly. The third reason, then: after a brave knight's death, his shield is hung high in the church in his memory. Just so this shield—that is, the crucifix—is placed in church where it can be seen most easily, to be a reminder of the knightly prowess of Jesus Christ on the cross. His beloved should see in this how he bought her love: he let his shield be pierced, his side opened up, to show her his heart, to show her openly how deeply he loved her, and to attract her heart.

Middle English Literature in the Fourteenth and Fifteenth Centuries

SIR GAWAIN AND THE GREEN KNIGHT
ca. 1375–1400

The finest Arthurian romance in English survives in only one manuscript, which also contains three religious poems—*Pearl*, *Patience*, and *Purity*—generally believed to be by the same poet. Nothing is known about the author except what can be inferred from the works. The dialect of the poems locates them in a remote corner of the northwest midlands between Cheshire and Staffordshire, and details of Sir Gawain's journey north show that the author was familiar with the geography of that region. But if author and audience were provincials, *Sir Gawain* and the other poems in the manuscript reveal them to have been highly sophisticated and well acquainted both with the international culture of the high Middle Ages and with ancient native traditions.

    Sir Gawain belongs to the so-called Alliterative Revival. After the Norman Conquest, alliterative verse doubtless continued to be recited by oral poets. At the beginning, the *Gawain* poet pretends that this romance is an oral poem and asks the audience to "listen" to a story, which he has "heard." Alliterative verse also continued to appear in Early Middle English texts. Layamon's *Brut* (see pp. 122–24) is the outstanding example. During the late fourteenth century there was a renewed flowering of alliterative poetry, especially in the north and west of Britain, which includes *Piers Plowman* and a splendid poem known as *The Alliterative Morte Darthur*.

    The *Gawain* poet's audience evidently valued the kind of alliterative verse that Chaucer's Parson caricatures as "Rum-Ram-Ruf by lettre" (see p. 312, line 43). They would also have understood archaic poetic diction surviving from Old English poetry such as *athel* (noble) and words of Scandinavian origin such as *skete* (quickly) and *skifted* (alternated). They were well acquainted with French Arthurian romances and the latest fashions in clothing, armor, and castle building. In making Sir Gawain, Arthur's sister's son, the preeminent knight of the Round Table, the poet was faithful to an older tradition. The thirteenth-century French romances, which in the next century became the main sources of Sir Thomas Malory, had made Sir Lancelot the best of Arthur's knights and Lancelot's adultery with Queen Guinevere the central event on which the fate of Arthur's kingdom turns. In *Sir Gawain* Lancelot is only one name in a list of Arthur's knights. Arthur is still a youth, and the court is in its springtime. Sir Gawain epitomizes this first blooming of Arthurian chivalry, and the reputation of the court rests upon his shoulders.

    Ostensibly, Gawain's head is what is at stake. The main plot belongs to a type folklorists classify as the "Beheading Game," in which a supernatural challenger offers to let his head be cut off in exchange for a return blow. The earliest written occurrence of this motif is in the Middle Irish tale of *Bricriu's Feast*. The *Gawain* poet could have encountered it in several French romances as well as in oral tradition. But the outcome of the game here does not turn only on the champion's courage as it does in

Bricriu's Feast. The *Gawain* poet has devised another series of tests for the hero that link the beheading with his truth, the emblem of which is the pentangle—a five-pointed star—displayed on Gawain's coat of arms and shield. The word *truth* in Middle English, as in Chaucer's ballade of that name (see p. 315), means not only what it still means now—a fact, belief, or idea held to be "true"—but what is conveyed by the old-fashioned variant from the same root: *troth*—that is, faith pledged by one's word and owed to a lord, a spouse, or anyone who puts someone else under an obligation. In this respect, Sir Gawain is being measured against a moral and Christian ideal of chivalry. Whether or not he succeeds in that contest is a question carefully left unresolved—perhaps as a challenge for the reader.

The poet has framed Gawain's adventure with references in the first and last stanzas to what are called the "Brutus books," the foundation stories that trace the origins of Rome and Britain back to the destruction of Troy. See, for example, the selection from Geoffrey of Monmouth's *History of the Kings of Britain* (p. 115). A cyclical sense of history as well as of the cycles of the seasons of the year, the generations of humankind, and of individual lives runs through *Sir Gawain and the Green Knight.*

The poem is written in stanzas that contain a group of alliterative lines (the number of lines in a stanza varies). The line is longer and does not contain a fixed number or pattern of stresses like the classical alliterative measure of Old English poetry. Each stanza closes with five short lines rhyming *a b a b a.* The first of these rhyming lines contains just two (rarely three) syllables and is called the "bob"; the four three-stress lines that follow are called the "wheel." For details on alliterative verse, see "Old and Middle English Prosody" (pp. 19–20). The opening stanza is printed below in Middle English with an interlinear translation. The alliterating sounds, which should be stressed, have been italicized.

Sithen the sege and the assaut was sesed at Troye,
After the siege and the assault was ceased at Troye,

The borgh brittened and brent to brondes and askes,
The city crumbled and burned to brands and ashes,

The tulk that the trammes of tresoun ther wroght
The man who the plots of treason there wrought

Was tried for his tricherie, the trewest on erthe.
Was tried for his treachery, the truest on earth.

Hit was Ennias the athel and his highe kynde,
It was Aeneas the noble and his high race,

That sithen depreced provinces, and patrounes bicome
Who after subjugated provinces, and lords became

Welneghe of al the wele in the west iles.
Wellnigh of all the wealth in the west isles.

Fro riche Romulus to Rome ricchis hym swythe,
Then noble Romulus to Rome proceeds quickly,

With gret bobbaunce that burghe he biges upon fyrst
With great pride that city he builds at first

And nevenes hit his aune nome, as hit now hat;
And names it his own name, as it now is called;

Ticius to Tuskan and teldes bigynnes,
Ticius (goes) to Tuscany and houses begins,

Langaberde in Lumbardie lyftes up homes,
Longbeard in Lombardy raises up homes,

And *fer* over the French *flod, Felix Brutus*
And far over the English Channel, Felix Brutus

On mony *bonkkes* ful *brode* Bretayn he settes
On many banks very broad Brittain he sets

> *Wyth wynne,*
> With joy,

Where werre and wrake and wonder
Where war and revenge and wondrous happenings

Bi sythes has wont therinne,
On occasions have dwelled therein

And oft *bothe blysse and blunder*
And often both joy and strife

Ful skete has skyfted synne.
Very swiftly have alternated since.

Sir Gawain and the Green Knight[1]

Part 1

Since the siege and the assault was ceased at Troy,
The walls breached and burnt down to brands and ashes,
The knight that had knotted the nets of deceit
Was impeached for his perfidy, proven most true,[2]
5   It was high-born Aeneas and his haughty race
That since prevailed over provinces, and proudly reigned
Over well-nigh all the wealth of the West Isles.[3]
Great Romulus[4] to Rome repairs in haste;
With boast and with bravery builds he that city
10 And names it with his own name, that it now bears.
Ticius to Tuscany, and towers raises,
Langobard[5] in Lombardy lays out homes,
And far over the French Sea, Felix Brutus[6]
On many broad hills and high Britain he sets,
15   most fair.

---

1. The Modern English translation is by Marie Borroff (1967), who has reproduced the alliterative meter of the original as well as the "bob" and "wheel," the five-line rhyming group that concludes each of the long irregular stanzas.
2. The treacherous knight is Aeneas, who was a traitor to his city, Troy, according to medieval tradition, but Aeneas was actually tried ("impeached") by the Greeks for his refusal to hand over to them his sister Polyxena.
3. Perhaps Western Europe.
4. The legendary founder of Rome is here given Trojan ancestry, like Aeneas.
5. The reputed founder of Lombardy. "Ticius": not otherwise known.
6. Great-grandson of Aeneas and legendary founder of Britain; not elsewhere given the name Felix (Latin "happy").

Where war and wrack and wonder
By shifts have sojourned there,
And bliss by turns with blunder
In that land's lot had share.

20 And since this Britain was built by this baron great,
Bold boys bred there, in broils delighting,
That did in their day many a deed most dire.
More marvels have happened in this merry land
Than in any other I know, since that olden time,
25 But of those that here built, of British kings,
King Arthur was counted most courteous of all,
Wherefore an adventure I aim to unfold,
That a marvel of might some men think it,
And one unmatched among Arthur's wonders.
30 If you will listen to my lay but a little while,
As I heard it in hall, I shall hasten to tell
                              anew.
              As it was fashioned featly
              In tale of derring-do,
35   And linked in measures meetly
              By letters tried and true.

This king lay at Camelot[7] at Christmastide;
Many good knights and gay his guests were there,
Arrayed of the Round Table[8] rightful brothers,
40 With feasting and fellowship and carefree mirth.
There true men contended in tournaments many,
Joined there in jousting these gentle knights,
Then came to the court for carol-dancing,
For the feast was in force full fifteen days,
45 With all the meat and the mirth that men could devise,
Such gaiety and glee, glorious to hear,
Brave din by day, dancing by night.
High were their hearts in halls and chambers,
These lords and these ladies, for life was sweet.
50 In peerless pleasures passed they their days,
The most noble knights known under Christ,
And the loveliest ladies that lived on earth ever,
And he the comeliest king, that that court holds,
For all this fair folk in their first age
55   were still.
              Happiest of mortal kind,
              King noblest famed of will;
              You would now go far to find
              So hardy a host on hill.

60 While the New Year was new, but yesternight come,
This fair folk at feast two-fold was served,

7. Capital of Arthur's kingdom, presumably located in southwest England or southern Wales.
8. According to legend, Merlin made the Round Table after a dispute broke out among Arthur's knights about precedence: it seated one hundred knights. The table described in the poem is not round.

When the king and his company were come in together,
The chanting in chapel achieved and ended.
Clerics and all the court acclaimed the glad season,
65   Cried Noel anew, good news to men;
Then gallants gather gaily, hand-gifts to make,
Called them out clearly, claimed them by hand,
Bickered long and busily about those gifts.
Ladies laughed aloud, though losers they were,
70   And he that won was not angered, as well you will know.[9]
All this mirth they made until meat was served;
When they had washed them worthily, they went to their seats,
The best seated above, as best it beseemed,
Guenevere the goodly queen gay in the midst
75   On a dais well-decked and duly arrayed
With costly silk curtains, a canopy over,
Of Toulouse and Turkestan tapestries rich,
All broidered and bordered with the best gems
Ever brought into Britain, with bright pennies
80   to pay.
          Fair queen, without a flaw,
          She glanced with eyes of grey.
          A seemlier that once he saw,
          In truth, no man could say.

85   But Arthur would not eat till all were served;
So light was his lordly heart, and a little boyish;
His life he liked lively—the less he cared
To be lying for long, or long to sit,
So busy his young blood, his brain so wild.
90   And also a point of pride pricked him in heart,
For he nobly had willed, he would never eat
On so high a holiday, till he had heard first
Of some fair feat or fray some far-borne tale,
Of some marvel of might, that he might trust,
95   By champions of chivalry achieved in arms,
Or some suppliant came seeking some single knight
To join with him in jousting, in jeopardy each
To lay life for life, and leave it to fortune
To afford him on field fair hap or other.
100 Such is the king's custom, when his court he holds
At each far-famed feast amid his fair host
                         so dear.
          The stout king stands in state
          Till a wonder shall appear;
105   He leads, with heart elate,
          High mirth in the New Year.

So he stands there in state, the stout young king,
Talking before the high table of trifles fair.
There Gawain the good knight by Guenevere sits,

9. The dispensing of New Year's gifts seems to have involved kissing.

110 With Agravain à la dure main on her other side,
   Both knights of renown, and nephews of the king.
   Bishop Baldwin above begins the table,
   And Yvain, son of Urien, ate with him there.
   These few with the fair queen were fittingly served;
115 At the side-tables[1] sat many stalwart knights.
   Then the first course comes, with clamor of trumpets
   That were bravely bedecked with bannerets bright,
   With noise of new drums and the noble pipes.
   Wild were the warbles that wakened that day
120 In strains that stirred many strong men's hearts.
   There dainties were dealt out, dishes rare,
   Choice fare to choose, on chargers so many
   That scarce was there space to set before the people
   The service of silver, with sundry meats,
125   on cloth.
      Each fair guest freely there
      Partakes, and nothing loth;
      Twelve dishes before each pair;
      Good beer and bright wine both.

130 Of the service itself I need say no more,
   For well you will know no tittle was wanting.
   Another noise and a new was well-nigh at hand,
   That the lord might have leave his life to nourish;
   For scarce were the sweet strains still in the hall,
135 And the first course come to that company fair,
   There hurtles in at the hall-door an unknown rider,
   One the greatest on ground in growth of his frame:
   From broad neck to buttocks so bulky and thick,
   And his loins and his legs so long and so great,
140 Half a giant on earth I hold him to be,
   But believe him no less than the largest of men,
   And that the seemliest in his stature to see, as he rides,
   For in back and in breast though his body was grim,
   His waist in its width was worthily small,
145 And formed with every feature in fair accord
         was he.
      Great wonder grew in hall
      At his hue most strange to see,
      For man and gear and all
150   Were green as green could be.

   And in guise all of green, the gear and the man:
   A coat cut close, that clung to his sides,
   And a mantle to match, made with a lining
   Of furs cut and fitted—the fabric was noble,
155 Embellished all with ermine, and his hood beside,
   That was loosed from his locks, and laid on his shoulders.

1. The side tables are on the main floor and run along the walls at a right angle with the high table, which is on a dais.

With trim hose and tight, the same tint of green,
His great calves were girt, and gold spurs under
He bore on silk bands that embellished his heels,
160 And footgear well-fashioned, for riding most fit.
And all his vesture verily was verdant green;
Both the bosses on his belt and other bright gems
That were richly ranged on his raiment noble
About himself and his saddle, set upon silk,
165 That to tell half the trifles would tax my wits,
The butterflies and birds embroidered thereon
In green of the gayest, with many a gold thread.
The pendants of the breast-band, the princely crupper,
And the bars of the bit were brightly enameled;
170 The stout stirrups were green, that steadied his feet,
And the bows of the saddle and the side-panels both,
That gleamed all and glinted with green gems about.
The steed he bestrides of that same green
                    so bright.
175   A green horse great and thick;
              A headstrong steed of might;
              In broidered bridle quick,
              Mount matched man aright.

Gay was this goodly man in guise all of green,
180 And the hair of his head to his horse suited;
Fair flowing tresses enfold his shoulders;
A beard big as a bush on his breast hangs,
That with his heavy hair, that from his head falls,
Was evened all about above both his elbows,
185 That half his arms thereunder were hid in the fashion
Of a king's cap-à-dos,[2] that covers his throat.
The mane of that mighty horse much to it like,
Well curled and becombed, and cunningly knotted
With filaments of fine gold amid the fair green,
190 Here a strand of the hair, here one of gold;
His tail and his foretop twin in their hue,
And bound both with a band of a bright green
That was decked adown the dock with dazzling stones
And tied tight at the top with a triple knot
195 Where many bells well burnished rang bright and clear.
Such a mount in his might, nor man on him riding,
None had seen, I dare swear, with sight in that hall
                    so grand.
              As lightning quick and light
200   He looked to all at hand;
              It seemed that no man might
              His deadly dints withstand.

Yet had he no helm, nor hauberk neither,
Nor plate, nor appurtenance appending to arms,

---

2. The word *capados* occurs in this form in Middle English only in *Gawain*, here and in line 572. The translator has interpreted it, as the poet apparently did also, as *cap-à-dos*, i.e., a garment covering its wearer "from head to back," on the model of *cap-à-pie*, "from head to foot," referring to armor.

205 Nor shaft pointed sharp, nor shield for defense,
But in his one hand he had a holly bob
That is goodliest in green when groves are bare,
And an ax in his other, a huge and immense,
A wicked piece of work in words to expound:
210 The head on its haft was an ell long;
The spike of green steel, resplendent with gold;
The blade burnished bright, with a broad edge,
As well shaped to shear as a sharp razor;
Stout was the stave in the strong man's gripe,
215 That was wound all with iron to the weapon's end,
With engravings in green of goodliest work.
A lace lightly about, that led to a knot,
Was looped in by lengths along the fair haft,
And tassels thereto attached in a row,
220 With buttons of bright green, brave to behold.
This horseman hurtles in, and the hall enters;
Riding to the high dais, recked he no danger;
Not a greeting he gave as the guests he o'erlooked,
Nor wasted his words, but "Where is," he said,
225 "The captain of this crowd? Keenly I wish
To see that sire with sight, and to himself say
                    my say."
                He swaggered all about
                To scan the host so gay;
230   He halted, as if in doubt
                Who in that hall held sway.

There were stares on all sides as the stranger spoke,
For much did they marvel what it might mean
That a horseman and a horse should have such a hue,
235 Grow green as the grass, and greener, it seemed,
Than green fused on gold more glorious by far.
All the onlookers eyed him, and edged nearer,
And awaited in wonder what he would do,
For many sights had they seen, but such a one never,
240 So that phantom and faerie the folk there deemed it,
Therefore chary of answer was many a champion bold,
And stunned at his strong words stone-still they sat
In a swooning silence in the stately hall.
As all were slipped into sleep, so slackened their speech
245   apace.
                Not all, I think, for dread,
                But some of courteous grace
                Let him who was their head
                Be spokesman in that place.

250 Then Arthur before the high dais that entrance beholds,
And hailed him, as behooved, for he had no fear,
And said "Fellow, in faith you have found fair welcome;
The head of this hostelry Arthur am I;
Leap lightly down, and linger, I pray,
255 And the tale of your intent you shall tell us after."

"Nay, so help me," said the other, "He that on high sits,
To tarry here any time, 'twas not mine errand;
But as the praise of you, prince, is puffed up so high,
And your court and your company are counted the best,
260 Stoutest under steel-gear on steeds to ride,
Worthiest of their works the wide world over,
And peerless to prove in passages of arms,
And courtesy here is carried to its height,
And so at this season I have sought you out.
265 You may be certain by the branch that I bear in hand
That I pass here in peace, and would part friends,
For had I come to this court on combat bent,
I have a hauberk at home, and a helm beside,
A shield and a sharp spear, shining bright,
270 And other weapons to wield, I ween well, to boot,
But as I willed no war, I wore no metal.
But if you be so bold as all men believe,
You will graciously grant the game that I ask
                                by right."
275   Arthur answer gave
                    And said, "Sir courteous knight,
                    If contest bare you crave,
                    You shall not fail to fight."

"Nay, to fight, in good faith, is far from my thought;
280 There are about on these benches but beardless children,
Were I here in full arms on a haughty steed,
For measured against mine, their might is puny.
And so I call in this court for a Christmas game,
For 'tis Yule and New Year, and many young bloods about;
285 If any in this house such hardihood claims,
Be so bold in his blood, his brain so wild,
As stoutly to strike one stroke for another,
I shall give him as my gift this gisarme noble,
This ax, that is heavy enough, to handle as he likes,
290 And I shall bide the first blow, as bare as I sit.
If there be one so wilful my words to assay,
Let him leap hither lightly, lay hold of this weapon;
I quitclaim it forever, keep it as his own,
And I shall stand him a stroke, steady on this floor,
295 So you grant me the guerdon to give him another,
                                sans blame.
                    In a twelvemonth and a day
                    He shall have of me the same;
                    Now be it seen straightway
300   Who dares take up the game."

If he astonished them at first, stiller were then
All that household in hall, the high and the low;
The stranger on his green steed stirred in the saddle,
And roisterously his red eyes he rolled all about,
305 Bent his bristling brows, that were bright green,

Wagged his beard as he watched who would arise.
When the court kept its counsel he coughed aloud,
And cleared his throat coolly, the clearer to speak:
"What, is this Arthur's house," said that horseman then,
310   "Whose fame is so fair in far realms and wide?
Where is now your arrogance and your awesome deeds,
Your valor and your victories and your vaunting words?
Now are the revel and renown of the Round Table
Overwhelmed with a word of one man's speech,
315   For all cower and quake, and no cut felt!"
With this he laughs so loud that the lord grieved;
The blood for sheer shame shot to his face,
                and pride.
        With rage his face flushed red,
320   And so did all beside.
        Then the king as bold man bred
        Toward the stranger took a stride.

And said "Sir, now we see you will say but folly,
Which whoso has sought, it suits that he find.
325   No guest here is aghast of your great words.
Give to me your gisarme, in God's own name,
And the boon you have begged shall straight be granted."
He leaps to him lightly, lays hold of his weapon;
The green fellow on foot fiercely alights.
330   Now has Arthur his ax, and the haft grips,
And sternly stirs it about, on striking bent.
The stranger before him stood there erect,
Higher than any in the house by a head and more;
With stern look as he stood, he stroked his beard,
335   And with undaunted countenance drew down his coat,
No more moved nor dismayed for his mighty dints
Than any bold man on bench had brought him a drink
                of wine.
        Gawain by Guenevere
340   Toward the king doth now incline:
        "I beseech, before all here,
        That this melee may be mine."

"Would you grant me the grace," said Gawain to the king,
"To be gone from this bench and stand by you there,
345   If I without discourtesy might quit this board,
And if my liege lady misliked it not,
I would come to your counsel before your court noble.
For I find it not fit, as in faith it is known,
When such a boon is begged before all these knights,
350   Though you be tempted thereto, to take it on yourself
While so bold men about upon benches sit,
That no host under heaven is hardier of will,
Nor better brothers-in-arms where battle is joined;
I am the weakest, well I know, and of wit feeblest;
355   And the loss of my life would be least of any;

That I have you for uncle is my only praise;
My body, but for your blood, is barren of worth;
And for that this folly befits not a king,
And 'tis I that have asked it, it ought to be mine,
360 And if my claim be not comely let all this court judge,
              in sight."
                    The court assays the claim,
                    And in counsel all unite
                    To give Gawain the game
365   And release the king outright.

Then the king called the knight to come to his side,
And he rose up readily, and reached him with speed,
Bows low to his lord, lays hold of the weapon,
And he releases it lightly, and lifts up his hand,
370 And gives him God's blessing, and graciously prays
That his heart and his hand may be hardy both.
"Keep, cousin," said the king, "what you cut with this day,
And if you rule it aright, then readily, I know,
You shall stand the stroke it will strike after."
375 Gawain goes to the guest with gisarme in hand,
And boldly he bides there, abashed not a whit.
Then hails he Sir Gawain, the horseman in green:
"Recount we our contract, ere you come further.
First I ask and adjure you, how you are called
380 That you tell me true, so that trust it I may."
"In good faith," said the good knight, "Gawain am I
Whose buffet befalls you, what'er betide after,
And at this time twelvemonth take from you another
With what weapon you will, and with no man else
385   alive."
                    The other nods assent:
                    "Sir Gawain, as I may thrive,
                    I am wondrous well content
                    That you this dint shall drive."

390 "Sir Gawain," said the Green Knight, "By God, I rejoice
That your fist shall fetch this favor I seek,
And you have readily rehearsed, and in right terms,
Each clause of my covenant with the king your lord,
Save that you shall assure me, sir, upon oath,
395 That you shall seek me yourself, wheresoever you deem
My lodgings may lie, and look for such wages
As you have offered me here before all this host."
"What is the way there?" said Gawain. "Where do you dwell?
I heard never of your house, by him that made me,
400 Nor I know you not, knight, your name nor your court.
But tell me truly thereof, and teach me your name,
And I shall fare forth to find you, so far as I may,
And this I say in good certain, and swear upon oath."
"That is enough in New Year, you need say no more,"
405 Said the knight in the green to Gawain the noble,

"If I tell you true, when I have taken your knock,
And if you handily have hit, you shall hear straightway
Of my house and my home and my own name;
Then follow in my footsteps by faithful accord.
410 And if I spend no speech, you shall speed the better:
You can feast with your friends, nor further trace
                    my tracks.
              Now hold your grim tool steady
              And show us how it hacks."
415   "Gladly, sir; all ready,"
              Says Gawain; he strokes the ax.

The Green Knight upon ground girds him with care:
Bows a bit with his head, and bares his flesh:
His long lovely locks he laid over his crown,
420 Let the naked nape for the need be shown.
Gawain grips to his ax and gathers it aloft—
The left foot on the floor before him he set—
Brought it down deftly upon the bare neck,
That the shock of the sharp blow shivered the bones
425 And cut the flesh cleanly and clove it in twain,
That the blade of bright steel bit into the ground.
The head was hewn off and fell to the floor;
Many found it at their feet, as forth it rolled;
The blood gushed from the body, bright on the green,
430 Yet fell not the fellow, nor faltered a whit,
But stoutly he starts forth upon stiff shanks,
And as all stood staring he stretched forth his hand,
Laid hold of his head and heaved it aloft,
Then goes to the green steed, grasps the bridle,
435 Steps into the stirrup, bestrides his mount,
And his head by the hair in his hand holds,
And as steady he sits in the stately saddle
As he had met with no mishap, nor missing were
                    his head.
440   His bulk about he haled,
              That fearsome body that bled;
              There were many in the court that quailed
              Before all his say was said.

For the head in his hand he holds right up.
445 Toward the first on the dais directs he the face,
And it lifted up its lids, and looked with wide eyes,
And said as much with its mouth as now you may hear:
"Sir Gawain, forget not to go as agreed,
And cease not to seek till me, sir, you find,
450 As you promised in the presence of these proud knights.
To the Green Chapel come, I charge you, to take
Such a dint as you have dealt—you have well deserved
That your neck should have a knock on New Year's morn.
The Knight of the Green Chapel I am well-known to many,
455 Wherefore you cannot fail to find me at last;

Therefore come, or be counted a recreant knight."
With a roisterous rush he flings round the reins,
Hurtles out at the hall-door, his head in his hand,
That the flint-fire flew from the flashing hooves.
460 Which way he went, not one of them knew
Nor whence he was come in the wide world
        so fair.
        The king and Gawain gay
        Make game of the Green Knight there,
465   Yet all who saw it say
        'Twas a wonder past compare.

Though high-born Arthur at heart had wonder,
He let no sign be seen, but said aloud
To the comely queen, with courteous speech,
470 "Dear dame, on this day dismay you no whit;
Such crafts are becoming at Christmastide,
Laughing at interludes, light songs and mirth,
Amid dancing of damsels with doughty knights.
Nevertheless of my meat now let me partake,
475 For I have met with a marvel, I may not deny."
He glanced at Sir Gawain, and gaily he said,
"Now, sir, hang up your ax,[3] that has hewn enough,"
And over the high dais it was hung on the wall
That men in amazement might on it look,
480 And tell in true terms the tale of the wonder.
Then they turned toward the table, these two together,
The good king and Gawain, and made great feast,
With all dainties double, dishes rare,
With all manner of meat and minstrelsy both,
485 Such happiness wholly had they that day
        in hold.
        Now take care, Sir Gawain,
        That your courage wax not cold
        When you must turn again
490   To your enterprise foretold.

Part 2

This adventure had Arthur of handsels[4] first
When young was the year, for he yearned to hear tales;
Though they wanted for words when they went to sup,
Now are fierce deeds to follow, their fists stuffed full.
495 Gawain was glad to begin those games in hall,
But if the end be harsher, hold it no wonder,
For though men are merry in mind after much drink,
A year passes apace, and proves ever new:
First things and final conform but seldom.
500 And so this Yule to the young year yielded place,

3. A colloquial expression equivalent to "bury the
hatchet," but here with an appropriate literal sense   also.
    4. New Year's presents.

And each season ensued at its set time;
After Christmas there came the cold cheer of Lent,
When with fish and plainer fare our flesh we reprove;
But then the world's weather with winter contends:
505   The keen cold lessens, the low clouds lift;
Fresh falls the rain in fostering showers
On the face of the fields; flowers appear.
The ground and the groves wear gowns of green;
Birds build their nests, and blithely sing
510   That solace of all sorrow with summer comes
               ere long.
            And blossoms day by day
            Bloom rich and rife in throng;
            Then every grove so gay
515   Of the greenwood rings with song.

And then the season of summer with the soft winds,
When Zephyr sighs low over seeds and shoots;
Glad is the green plant growing abroad,
When the dew at dawn drops from the leaves,
520   To get a gracious glance from the golden sun.
But harvest with harsher winds follows hard after,
Warns him to ripen well ere winter comes;
Drives forth the dust in the droughty season,
From the face of the fields to fly high in air.
525   Wroth winds in the welkin wrestle with the sun,
The leaves launch from the linden and light on the ground,
And the grass turns to gray, that once grew green.
Then all ripens and rots that rose up at first,
And so the year moves on in yesterdays many,
530   And winter once more, by the world's law,
               draws nigh.
            At Michaelmas° the moon   *September 29*
            Hangs wintry pale in sky;
            Sir Gawain girds him soon
535   For travails yet to try.

Till All-Hallows' Day[5] with Arthur he dwells,
And he held a high feast to honor that knight
With great revels and rich, of the Round Table.
Then ladies lovely and lords debonair
540   With sorrow for Sir Gawain were sore at heart;
Yet they covered their care with countenance glad:
Many a mournful man made mirth for his sake.
So after supper soberly he speaks to his uncle
Of the hard hour at hand, and openly says,
545   "Now, liege lord of my life, my leave I take;
The terms of this task too well you know—
To count the cost over concerns me nothing.
But I am bound forth betimes to bear a stroke

5. All Saints' Day, November 1.

From the grim man in green, as God may direct."
550 Then the first and foremost came forth in throng:
Yvain and Eric and others of note,
Sir Dodinal le Sauvage, the Duke of Clarence,
Lionel and Lancelot and Lucan the good,
Sir Bors and Sir Bedivere, big men both,
555 And many manly knights more, with Mador de la Porte.
All this courtly company comes to the king
To counsel their comrade, with care in their hearts;
There was much secret sorrow suffered that day
That one so good as Gawain must go in such wise
560 To bear a bitter blow, and his bright sword
lay by.
He said, "Why should I tarry?"
And smiled with tranquil eye;
"In destinies sad or merry,
565 True men can but try."

He dwelt there all that day, and dressed in the morning;
Asked early for his arms, and all were brought.
First a carpet of rare cost was cast on the floor
Where much goodly gear gleamed golden bright;
570 He takes his place promptly and picks up the steel,
Attired in a tight coat of Turkestan silk
And a kingly cap-à-dos, closed at the throat,
That was lavishly lined with a lustrous fur.
Then they set the steel shoes on his sturdy feet
575 And clad his calves about with comely greaves,
And plate well-polished protected his knees,
Affixed with fastenings of the finest gold.
Fair cuisses enclosed, that were cunningly wrought,
His thick-thewed thighs, with thongs bound fast,
580 And massy chain-mail of many a steel ring
He bore on his body, above the best cloth,
With brace burnished bright upon both his arms,
Good couters and gay, and gloves of plate,
And all the goodly gear to grace him well
585 that tide.
His surcoat blazoned bold;
Sharp spurs to prick with pride;
And a brave silk band to hold
The broadsword at his side.

590 When he had on his arms, his harness was rich,
The least latchet or loop laden with gold;
So armored as he was, he heard a mass,
Honored God humbly at the high altar.
Then he comes to the king and his comrades-in-arms,
595 Takes his leave at last of lords and ladies,
And they clasped and kissed him, commending him to Christ.
By then Gringolet was girt with a great saddle
That was gaily agleam with fine gilt fringe,
New-furbished for the need with nail-heads bright;

600 The bridle and the bars bedecked all with gold;
The breast-plate, the saddlebow, the side-panels both,
The caparison and the crupper accorded in hue,
And all ranged on the red the resplendent studs
That glittered and glowed like the glorious sun.
605 His helm now he holds up and hastily kisses,
Well-closed with iron clinches, and cushioned within;
It was high on his head, with a hasp behind,
And a covering of cloth to encase the visor,
All bound and embroidered with the best gems
610 On broad bands of silk, and bordered with birds,
Parrots and popinjays preening their wings,
Lovebirds and love-knots as lavishly wrought
As many women had worked seven winters thereon,
      entire.
615   The diadem costlier yet
     That crowned that comely sire,
     With diamonds richly set,
     That flashed as if on fire.

Then they showed forth the shield, that shone all red,
620 With the pentangle[6] portrayed in purest gold.
About his broad neck by the baldric he casts it,
That was meet for the man, and matched him well.
And why the pentangle is proper to that peerless prince
I intend now to tell, though detain me it must.
625 It is a sign by Solomon sagely devised
To be a token of truth, by its title of old,
For it is a figure formed of five points,
And each line is linked and locked with the next
For ever and ever, and hence it is called
630 In all England, as I hear, the endless knot.
And well may he wear it on his worthy arms,
For ever faithful five-fold in five-fold fashion
Was Gawain in good works, as gold unalloyed,
Devoid of all villainy, with virtues adorned
635   in sight.
     On shield and coat in view
     He bore that emblem bright,
     As to his word most true
     And in speech most courteous knight.

6. A five-pointed star, formed by five lines that are drawn without lifting the pencil from the paper, supposed to have mystical significance; as Solomon's sign (line 625) it was enclosed in a circle.

640 And first, he was faultless in his five senses,
Nor found ever to fail in his five fingers,
And all his fealty was fixed upon the five wounds
That Christ got on the cross, as the creed tells;
And wherever this man in melee took part,
645 His one thought was of this, past all things else,
That all his force was founded on the five joys[7]
That the high Queen of heaven had in her child.
And therefore, as I find, he fittingly had
On the inner part of his shield her image portrayed,
650 That when his look on it lighted, he never lost heart.
The fifth of the five fives followed by this knight
Were beneficence boundless and brotherly love
And pure mind and manners, that none might impeach,
And compassion most precious—these peerless five
655 Were forged and made fast in him, foremost of men.
Now all these five fives were confirmed in this knight,
And each linked in other, that end there was none,
And fixed to five points, whose force never failed,
Nor assembled all on a side, nor asunder either,
660 Nor anywhere at an end, but whole and entire
However the pattern proceeded or played out its course.
And so on his shining shield shaped was the knot
Royally in red gold against red gules,
That is the peerless pentangle, prized of old
665   in lore.
                    Now armed is Gawain gay,
                    And bears his lance before,
                    And soberly said good day,
                    He thought forevermore.

670 He struck his steed with the spurs and sped on his way
So fast that the flint-fire flashed from the stones.
When they saw him set forth they were sore aggrieved,
And all sighed softly, and said to each other,
Fearing for their fellow, "Ill fortune it is
675 That you, man, must be marred, that most are worthy!
His equal on this earth can hardly be found;
To have dealt more discreetly had done less harm,
And have dubbed him a duke, with all due honor.
A great leader of lords he was like to become,
680 And better so to have been than battered to bits,
Beheaded by an elf-man,° for empty pride!   supernatural being
Who would credit that a king could be counseled so,
And caught in a cavil in a Christmas game?"
Many were the warm tears they wept from their eyes
685 When goodly Sir Gawain was gone from the court
                                        that day.
                    No longer he abode,

---

7. Most commonly in Middle English literature, the Annunciation, Nativity, Resurrection, Ascension, and Assumption, although the list varies. These overlap but are not identical with the Five Joyful Mysteries of the Rosary, which were not formally established until the 16th century.

But speedily went his way
Over many a wandering road,
690   As I heard my author say.

Now he rides in his array through the realm of Logres,[8]
Sir Gawain, God knows, though it gave him small joy!
All alone must he lodge through many a long night
Where the food that he fancied was far from his plate;
695 He had no mate but his mount, over mountain and plain,
Nor man to say his mind to but almighty God,
Till he had wandered well-nigh into North Wales.
All the islands of Anglesey he holds on his left,
And follows, as he fares, the fords by the coast,
700 Comes over at Holy Head, and enters next
The Wilderness of Wirral[9]—few were within
That had great good will toward God or man.
And earnestly he asked of each mortal he met
If he had ever heard aught of a knight all green,
705 Or of a Green Chapel, on ground thereabouts,
And all said the same, and solemnly swore
They saw no such knight all solely green
in hue.
Over country wild and strange
710   The knight sets off anew;
Often his course must change
Ere the Chapel comes in view.

Many a cliff must he climb in country wild;
Far off from all his friends, forlorn must he ride;
715 At each strand or stream where the stalwart passed
'Twere a marvel if he met not some monstrous foe,
And that so fierce and forbidding that fight he must.
So many were the wonders he wandered among
That to tell but the tenth part would tax my wits.
720 Now with serpents he wars, now with savage wolves,
Now with wild men of the woods, that watched from the rocks,
Both with bulls and with bears, and with boars besides,
And giants that came gibbering from the jagged steeps.
Had he not borne himself bravely, and been on God's side,
725 He had met with many mishaps and mortal harms.
And if the wars were unwelcome, the winter was worse,
When the cold clear rains rushed from the clouds
And froze before they could fall to the frosty earth.
Near slain by the sleet he sleeps in his irons
730 More nights than enough, among naked rocks,
Where clattering from the crest the cold stream ran
And hung in hard icicles high overhead.
Thus in peril and pain and predicaments dire
He rides across country till Christmas Eve,

8. One of the names for Arthur's kingdom.
9. Gawain went from Camelot north to the northern coast of Wales, opposite the islands of Anglesey; there he turned east across the Dee to the
forest of Wirral in Cheshire.

735

our knight.
And at that holy tide
He prays with all his might
That Mary may be his guide
Till a dwelling comes in sight.

740 By a mountain next morning he makes his way
Into a forest fastness, fearsome and wild;
High hills on either hand, with hoar woods below,
Oaks old and huge by the hundred together.
The hazel and the hawthorn were all intertwined
745 With rough raveled moss, that raggedly hung,
With many birds unblithe upon bare twigs
That peeped most piteously for pain of the cold.
The good knight on Gringolet glides thereunder
Through many a marsh and mire, a man all alone;
750 He feared for his default, should he fail to see
The service of that Sire that on that same night
Was born of a bright maid, to bring us his peace.
And therefore sighing he said, "I beseech of Thee, Lord,
And Mary, thou mildest mother so dear,
755 Some harborage where haply I might hear mass
And Thy matins tomorrow—meekly I ask it,
And thereto proffer and pray my pater and ave

and creed."
He said his prayer with sighs,

760

Lamenting his misdeed;
He crosses himself, and cries
On Christ in his great need.

No sooner had Sir Gawain signed himself thrice
Than he was ware, in the wood, of a wondrous dwelling,
765 Within a moat, on a mound, bright amid boughs
Of many a tree great of girth that grew by the water—
A castle as comely as a knight could own,
On grounds fair and green, in a goodly park
With a palisade of palings planted about
770 For two miles and more, round many a fair tree.
The stout knight stared at that stronghold great
As it shimmered and shone amid shining leaves,
Then with helmet in hand he offers his thanks
To Jesus and Saint Julian,[1] that are gentle both,
775 That in courteous accord had inclined to his prayer;
"Now fair harbor," said he, "I humbly beseech!"
Then he pricks his proud steed with the plated spurs,
And by chance he has chosen the chief path
That brought the bold knight to the bridge's end
780

in haste.
The bridge hung high in air;
The gates were bolted fast;

---

1. Patron saint of hospitality.

The walls well-framed to bear
The fury of the blast.

785 The man on his mount remained on the bank
Of the deep double moat that defended the place.
The wall went in the water wondrous deep,
And a long way aloft it loomed overhead.
It was built of stone blocks to the battlements' height,
790 With corbels under cornices in comeliest style;
Watch-towers trusty protected the gate,
With many a lean loophole, to look from within:
A better-made barbican the knight beheld never.
And behind it there hoved a great hall and fair:
795 Turrets rising in tiers, with tines° at their tops,   *spikes*
Spires set beside them, splendidly long,
With finials° well-fashioned, as filigree fine.   *gable ornaments*
Chalk-white chimneys over chambers high
Gleamed in gay array upon gables and roofs;
800 The pinnacles in panoply, pointing in air,
So vied there for his view that verily it seemed
A castle cut of paper for a king's feast.[2]
The good knight on Gringolet thought it great luck
If he could but contrive to come there within
805 To keep the Christmas feast in that castle fair
         and bright.
      There answered to his call
      A porter most polite;
      From his station on the wall
810   He greets the errant knight.

"Good sir," said Gawain, "Wouldst go to inquire
If your lord would allow me to lodge here a space?"
"Peter!" said the porter, "For my part, I think
So noble a knight will not want for a welcome!"
815 Then he bustles off briskly, and comes back straight,
And many servants beside, to receive him the better.
They let down the drawbridge and duly went forth
And kneeled down on their knees on the naked earth
To welcome this warrior as best they were able.
820 They proffered him passage—the portals stood wide—
And he beckoned them to rise, and rode over the bridge.
Men steadied his saddle as he stepped to the ground,
And there stabled his steed many stalwart folk.
Now come the knights and the noble squires
825 To bring him with bliss into the bright hall.
When his high helm was off, there hied forth a throng
Of attendants to take it, and see to its care;
They bore away his brand° and his blazoned shield;   *sword*
Then graciously he greeted those gallants each one,
830 And many a noble drew near, to do the knight honor.

2. A common table decoration at feasts.

All in his armor into hall he was led,
Where fire on a fair hearth fiercely blazed.
And soon the lord himself descends from his chamber
To meet with good manners the man on his floor.
835 He said, "To this house you are heartily welcome:
What is here is wholly yours, to have in your power
and sway."
"Many thanks," said Sir Gawain;
"May Christ your pains repay!"
840 The two embrace amain
As men well met that day.

Gawain gazed on the host that greeted him there,
And a lusty fellow he looked, the lord of that place:
A man of massive mold, and of middle age;
845 Broad, bright was his beard, of a beaver's hue,
Strong, steady his stance, upon stalwart shanks,
His face fierce as fire, fair-spoken withal,
And well-suited he seemed in Sir Gawain's sight
To be a master of men in a mighty keep.
850 They pass into a parlor, where promptly the host
Has a servant assigned him to see to his needs,
And there came upon his call many courteous folk
That brought him to a bower where bedding was noble,
With heavy silk hangings hemmed all in gold,
855 Coverlets and counterpanes curiously wrought,
A canopy over the couch, clad all with fur,
Curtains running on cords, caught to gold rings,
Woven rugs on the walls of eastern work,
And the floor, under foot, well-furnished with the same.
860 Amid light talk and laughter they loosed from him then
His war-dress of weight and his worthy clothes.
Robes richly wrought they brought him right soon,
To change there in chamber and choose what he would.
When he had found one he fancied, and flung it about,
865 Well-fashioned for his frame, with flowing skirts,
His face fair and fresh as the flowers of spring,
All the good folk agreed, that gazed on him then,
His limbs arrayed royally in radiant hues,
That so comely a mortal never Christ made
870 as he.
Whatever his place of birth,
It seemed he well might be
Without a peer on earth
In martial rivalry.

875 A couch before the fire, where fresh coals burned,
They spread for Sir Gawain splendidly now
With quilts quaintly stitched, and cushions beside,
And then a costly cloak they cast on his shoulders
Of bright silk, embroidered on borders and hems,
880 With furs of the finest well-furnished within,
And bound about with ermine, both mantle and hood;

And he sat at that fireside in sumptuous estate
And warmed himself well, and soon he waxed merry.
Then attendants set a table upon trestles broad,
885 And lustrous white linen they laid thereupon,
A saltcellar of silver, spoons of the same.
He washed himself well and went to his place,
Men set his fare before him in fashion most fit.
There were soups of all sorts, seasoned with skill,
890 Double-sized servings, and sundry fish,
Some baked, some breaded, some broiled on the coals,
Some simmered, some in stews, steaming with spice,
And with sauces to sup that suited his taste.
He confesses it a feast with free words and fair;
895 They requite him as kindly with courteous jests,
                              well-sped.
                    "Tonight you fast[3] and pray;
                    Tomorrow we'll see you fed."
                    The knight grows wondrous gay
900   As the wine goes to his head.

Then at times and by turns, as at table he sat,
They questioned him quietly, with queries discreet,
And he courteously confessed that he comes from the court,
And owns him of the brotherhood of high-famed Arthur,
905 The right royal ruler of the Round Table,
And the guest by their fireside is Gawain himself,
Who has happened on their house at that holy feast.
When the name of the knight was made known to the lord,
Then loudly he laughed, so elated he was,
910 And the men in that household made haste with joy
To appear in his presence promptly that day,
That of courage ever-constant, and customs pure,
Is pattern and paragon, and praised without end:
Of all knights on earth most honored is he.
915 Each said solemnly aside to his brother,
"Now displays of deportment shall dazzle our eyes
And the polished pearls of impeccable speech;
The high art of eloquence is ours to pursue
Since the father of fine manners is found in our midst.
920 Great is God's grace, and goodly indeed,
That a guest such as Gawain he guides to us here
When men sit and sing of their Savior's birth
                              in view.
                    With command of manners pure
925   He shall each heart imbue;
                    Who shares his converse, sure,
                    Shall learn love's language true."

When the knight had done dining and duly arose,
The dark was drawing on; the day nigh ended.

---

3. Gawain is said to be "fasting" because the meal, although elaborate, consisted only of fish dishes, appropriate to a fasting day.

930 Chaplains in chapels and churches about
Rang the bells aright, reminding all men
Of the holy evensong of the high feast.
The lord attends alone: his fair lady sits
In a comely closet, secluded from sight.
935 Gawain in gay attire goes thither soon;
The lord catches his coat, and calls him by name,
And has him sit beside him, and says in good faith
No guest on God's earth would he gladlier greet.
For that Gawain thanked him; the two then embraced
940 And sat together soberly the service through.
Then the lady, that longed to look on the knight,
Came forth from her closet with her comely maids.
The fair hues of her flesh, her face and her hair
And her body and her bearing were beyond praise,
945 And excelled the queen herself, as Sir Gawain thought.
He goes forth to greet her with gracious intent;
Another lady led her by the left hand
That was older than she—an ancient, it seemed,
And held in high honor by all men about.
950 But unlike to look upon, those ladies were,
For if the one was fresh, the other was faded:
Bedecked in bright red was the body of one;
Flesh hung in folds on the face of the other;
On one a high headdress, hung all with pearls;
955 Her bright throat and bosom fair to behold,
Fresh as the first snow fallen upon hills;
A wimple the other one wore round her throat;
Her swart chin well swaddled, swathed all in white;
Her forehead enfolded in flounces of silk
960 That framed a fair fillet, of fashion ornate,
And nothing bare beneath save the black brows,
The two eyes and the nose, the naked lips,
And they unsightly to see, and sorrily bleared.
A beldame, by God, she may well be deemed,
965   of pride!
                    She was short and thick of waist,
                    Her buttocks round and wide;
                    More toothsome, to his taste,
                    Was the beauty by her side.

970 When Gawain had gazed on that gay lady,
With leave of her lord, he politely approached;
To the elder in homage he humbly bows;
The lovelier he salutes with a light embrace.
He claims a comely kiss, and courteously he speaks;
975 They welcome him warmly, and straightway he asks
To be received as their servant, if they so desire.
They take him between them; with talking they bring him
Beside a bright fire; bade then that spices
Be freely fetched forth, to refresh them the better,
980 And the good wine therewith, to warm their hearts.

The lord leaps about in light-hearted mood;
Contrives entertainments and timely sports;
Takes his hood from his head and hangs it on a spear,
And offers him openly the honor thereof
985 Who should promote the most mirth at that Christmas feast;
"And I shall try for it, trust me—contend with the best,
Ere I go without my headgear by grace of my friends!"
Thus with light talk and laughter the lord makes merry
To gladden the guest he had greeted in hall
990   that day.
                    At the last he called for light
                    The company to convey;
                    Gawain says goodnight
                    And retires to bed straightway.

995 On the morn when each man is mindful in heart
That God's son was sent down to suffer our death,
No household but is blithe for his blessed sake;
So was it there on that day, with many delights.
Both at larger meals and less they were lavishly served
1000 By doughty lads on dais, with delicate fare;
The old ancient lady, highest she sits;
The lord at her left hand leaned, as I hear;
Sir Gawain in the center, beside the gay lady,
Where the food was brought first to that festive board,
1005 And thence throughout the hall, as they held most fit,
To each man was offered in order of rank.
There was meat, there was mirth, there was much joy,
That to tell all the tale would tax my wits,
Though I pained me, perchance, to paint it with care;
1010 But yet I know that our knight and the noble lady
Were accorded so closely in company there,
With the seemly solace of their secret words,
With speeches well-sped, spotless and pure,
That each prince's pastime their pleasures far
1015   outshone.
                    Sweet pipes beguile their cares,
                    And the trumpet of martial tone;
                    Each tends his affairs
                    And those two tend their own.

1020 That day and all the next, their disport was noble,
And the third day, I think, pleased them no less;
The joys of St. John's Day° were justly praised,   *December 27*
And were the last of their like for those lords and ladies;
Then guests were to go in the gray morning,
1025 Wherefore they whiled the night away with wine and with mirth,
Moved to the measures of many a blithe carol;
At last, when it was late, took leave of each other,
Each one of those worthies, to wend his way.
Gawain bids goodbye to his goodly host
1030 Who brings him to his chamber, the chimney beside,

And detains him in talk, and tenders his thanks
And holds it an honor to him and his people
That he has harbored in his house at that holy time
And embellished his abode with his inborn grace.
1035 "As long as I may live, my luck is the better
That Gawain was my guest at God's own feast!"
"Noble sir," said the knight, "I cannot but think
All the honor is your own—may heaven requite it!
And your man to command I account myself here
1040 As I am bound and beholden, and shall be, come
                                    what may."
                        The lord with all his might
                        Entreats his guest to stay;
                        Brief answer makes the knight:
1045   Next morning he must away.

Then the lord of that land politely inquired
What dire affair had forced him, at that festive time,
So far from the king's court to fare forth alone
Ere the holidays wholly had ended in hall.
1050 "In good faith," said Gawain, "you have guessed the truth:
On a high errand and urgent I hastened away,
For I am summoned by myself to seek for a place—
I would I knew whither, or where it might be!
Far rather would I find it before the New Year
1055 Than own the land of Logres, so help me our Lord!
Wherefore, sir, in friendship this favor I ask,
That you say in sober earnest, if something you know
Of the Green Chapel, on ground far or near,
Or the lone knight that lives there, of like hue of green.
1060 A certain day was set by assent of us both
To meet at that landmark, if I might last,
And from now to the New Year is nothing too long,
And I would greet the Green Knight there, would God but allow,
More gladly, by God's Son, than gain the world's wealth!
1065 And I must set forth to search, as soon as I may;
To be about the business I have but three days
And would as soon sink down dead as desist from my errand."
Then smiling said the lord, "Your search, sir, is done,
For we shall see you to that site by the set time.
1070 Let Gawain grieve no more over the Green Chapel;
You shall be in your own bed, in blissful ease,
All the forenoon, and fare forth the first of the year,
And make the goal by midmorn, to mind your affairs,
                                    no fear!
1075   Tarry till the fourth day
                        And ride on the first of the year.
                        We shall set you on your way;
                        It is not two miles from here."

Then Gawain was glad, and gleefully he laughed:
1080 "Now I thank you for this, past all things else!

Now my goal is here at hand! With a glad heart I shall
Both tarry, and undertake any task you devise."
Then the host seized his arm and seated him there;
Let the ladies be brought, to delight them the better,
1085 And in fellowship fair by the fireside they sit;
So gay waxed the good host, so giddy his words,
All waited in wonder what next he would say.
Then he stares on the stout knight, and sternly he speaks:
"You have bound yourself boldly my bidding to do—
1090 Will you stand by that boast, and obey me this once?"
"I shall do so indeed," said the doughty knight;
"While I lie in your lodging, your laws will I follow."
"As you have had," said the host, "many hardships abroad
And little sleep of late, you are lacking, I judge,
1095 Both in nourishment needful and nightly rest;
You shall lie abed late in your lofty chamber
Tomorrow until mass, and meet then to dine
When you will, with my wife, who will sit by your side
And talk with you at table, the better to cheer
1100   our guest.
              A-hunting I will go
              While you lie late and rest."
              The knight, inclining low,
              Assents to each behest.

1105 "And Gawain," said the good host, "agree now to this:
Whatever I win in the woods I will give you at eve,
And all you have earned you must offer to me;
Swear now, sweet friend, to swap as I say,
Whether hands, in the end, be empty or better."
1110 "By God," said Sir Gawain, "I grant it forthwith!
If you find the game good, I shall gladly take part."
"Let the bright wine be brought, and our bargain is done,"
Said the lord of that land—the two laughed together.
Then they drank and they dallied and doffed all constraint,
1115 These lords and these ladies, as late as they chose,
And then with gaiety and gallantries and graceful adieux
They talked in low tones, and tarried at parting.
With compliments comely they kiss at the last;
There were brisk lads about with blazing torches
1120 To see them safe to bed, for soft repose
                   long due.
              Their covenants, yet awhile,
              They repeat, and pledge anew;
              That lord could well beguile
1125   Men's hearts, with mirth in view.

Part 3

Long before daylight they left their beds;
Guests that wished to go gave word to their grooms,
And they set about briskly to bind on saddles,

Tend to their tackle, tie up trunks.
1130 The proud lords appear, appareled to ride,
Leap lightly astride, lay hold of their bridles,
Each one on his way to his worthy house.
The liege lord of the land was not the last
Arrayed there to ride, with retainers many;
1135 He had a bite to eat when he had heard mass;
With horn to the hills he hastens amain.
By the dawn of that day over the dim earth,
Master and men were mounted and ready.
Then they harnessed in couples the keen-scented hounds,
1140 Cast wide the kennel-door and called them forth,
Blew upon their bugles bold blasts three;
The dogs began to bay with a deafening din,
And they quieted them quickly and called them to heel,
A hundred brave huntsmen, as I have heard tell,
1145   together.
          Men at stations meet;
          From the hounds they slip the tether;
          The echoing horns repeat,
          Clear in the merry weather.

1150 At the clamor of the quest, the quarry trembled;
Deer dashed through the dale, dazed with dread;
Hastened to the high ground, only to be
Turned back by the beaters, who boldly shouted.
They harmed not the harts, with their high heads,
1155 Let the bucks go by, with their broad antlers,
For it was counted a crime, in the close season,
If a man of that demesne should molest the male deer.
The hinds were headed up, with "Hey!" and "Ware!"
The does with great din were driven to the valleys.
1160 Then you were ware, as they went, of the whistling of arrows;
At each bend under boughs the bright shafts flew
That tore the tawny hide with their tapered heads.
Ah! they bray and they bleed, on banks they die,
And ever the pack pell-mell comes panting behind;
1165 Hunters with shrill horns hot on their heels—
Like the cracking of cliffs their cries resounded.
What game got away from the gallant archers
Was promptly picked off at the posts below
When they were harried on the heights and herded to the streams:
1170 The watchers were so wary at the waiting-stations,
And the greyhounds so huge, that eagerly snatched,
And finished them off as fast as folk could see
                          with sight.
          The lord, now here, now there,
1175   Spurs forth in sheer delight.
          And drives, with pleasures rare,
          The day to the dark night.

So the lord in the linden-wood leads the hunt
And Gawain the good knight in gay bed lies,

1180 Lingered late alone, till daylight gleamed,
Under coverlet costly, curtained about.
And as he slips into slumber, slyly there comes
A little din at his door, and the latch lifted,
And he holds up his heavy head out of the clothes;
1185 A corner of the curtain he caught back a little
And waited there warily, to see what befell.
Lo! it was the lady, loveliest to behold,
That drew the door behind her deftly and still
And was bound for his bed—abashed was the knight,
1190 And laid his head low again in likeness of sleep;
And she stepped stealthily, and stole to his bed,
Cast aside the curtain and came within,
And set herself softly on the bedside there,
And lingered at her leisure, to look on his waking.
1195 The fair knight lay feigning for a long while,
Conning in his conscience what his case might
Mean or amount to—a marvel he thought it.
But yet he said within himself, "More seemly it were
To try her intent by talking a little."
1200 So he started and stretched, as startled from sleep,
Lifts wide his lids in likeness of wonder,
And signs himself swiftly, as safer to be,
                                with art.
                    Sweetly does she speak
1205   And kindling glances dart,
                    Blent white and red on cheek
                    And laughing lips apart.

"Good morning, Sir Gawain," said that gay lady,
"A slack sleeper you are, to let one slip in!
1210 Now you are taken in a trice—a truce we must make,
Or I shall bind you in your bed, of that be assured."
Thus laughing lightly that lady jested.
"Good morning, good lady," said Gawain the blithe,
"Be it with me as you will; I am well content!
1215 For I surrender myself, and sue for your grace,
And that is best, I believe, and behooves me now."
Thus jested in answer that gentle knight.
"But if, lovely lady, you misliked it not,
And were pleased to permit your prisoner to rise,
1220 I should quit this couch and accoutre me better,
And be clad in more comfort for converse here."
"Nay, not so, sweet sir," said the smiling lady;
"You shall not rise from your bed; I direct you better:
I shall hem and hold you on either hand,
1225 And keep company awhile with my captive knight.
For as certain as I sit here, Sir Gawain you are,
Whom all the world worships, whereso you ride;
Your honor, your courtesy are highest acclaimed
By lords and by ladies, by all living men;
1230 And lo! we are alone here, and left to ourselves:
My lord and his liegemen are long departed,

The household asleep, my handmaids too,
The door drawn, and held by a well-driven bolt,
And since I have in this house him whom all love,
1235 I shall while the time away with mirthful speech
                              at will.
                    My body is here at hand,
                    Your each wish to fulfill;
                    Your servant to command
1240   I am, and shall be still."

"In good faith," said Gawain, "my gain is the greater,
Though I am not he of whom you have heard;
To arrive at such reverence as you recount here
I am one all unworthy, and well do I know it.
1245 By heaven, I would hold me the happiest of men
If by word or by work I once might aspire
To the prize of your praise—'twere a pure joy!"
"In good faith, Sir Gawain," said that gay lady,
"The well-proven prowess that pleases all others,
1250 Did I scant or scout it, 'twere scarce becoming.
But there are ladies, believe me, that had liefer far
Have thee here in their hold, as I have today,
To pass an hour in pastime with pleasant words,
Assuage all their sorrows and solace their hearts,
1255 Than much of the goodly gems and gold they possess.
But laud be to the Lord of the lofty skies,
For here in my hands all hearts' desire
                              doth lie."
                    Great welcome got he there
1260   From the lady who sat him by;
                    With fitting speech and fair
                    The good knight makes reply.

"Madame," said the merry man, "Mary reward you!
For in good faith, I find your beneficence noble.
1265 And the fame of fair deeds runs far and wide,
But the praise you report pertains not to me,
But comes of your courtesy and kindness of heart."
"By the high Queen of heaven" (said she) "I count it not so,
For were I worth all the women in this world alive,
1270 And all wealth and all worship were in my hands,
And I should hunt high and low, a husband to take,
For the nurture I have noted in thee, knight, here,
The comeliness and courtesies and courtly mirth—
And so I had ever heard, and now hold it true—
1275 No other on this earth should have me for wife."
"You are bound to a better man," the bold knight said,
"Yet I prize the praise you have proffered me here,
And soberly your servant, my sovereign I hold you,
And acknowledge me your knight, in the name of Christ."
1280 So they talked of this and that until 'twas nigh noon,
And ever the lady languishing in likeness of love.

With feat words and fair he framed his defense,
For were she never so winsome, the warrior had
The less will to woo, for the wound that his bane
1285   must be.
He must bear the blinding blow,
For such is fate's decree:
The lady asks leave to go;
He grants it full and free.

1290   Then she gaily said goodbye, and glanced at him, laughing,
And as she stood, she astonished him with a stern speech:
"Now may the Giver of all good words these glad hours repay!
But our guest is not Gawain—forgot is that thought."
"How so?" said the other, and asks in some haste,
1295   For he feared he had been at fault in the forms of his speech.
But she held up her hand, and made answer thus:
"So good a knight as Gawain is given out to be,
And the model of fair demeanor and manners pure,
Had he lain so long at a lady's side,
1300   Would have claimed a kiss, by his courtesy,
Through some touch or trick of phrase at some tale's end."
Said Gawain, "Good lady, I grant it at once!
I shall kiss at your command, as becomes a knight,
And more, lest you mislike, so let be, I pray."
1305   With that she turns toward him, takes him in her arms,
Leans down her lovely head, and lo! he is kissed.
They commend each other to Christ with comely words,
He sees her forth safely, in silence they part,
And then he lies no later in his lofty bed,
1310   But calls to his chamberlain, chooses his clothes,
Goes in those garments gladly to mass,
Then takes his way to table, where attendants wait,
And made merry all day, till the moon rose
in view
1315   Was never knight beset
'Twixt worthier ladies two:
The crone and the coquette;
Fair pastimes they pursue.

And the lord of the land rides late and long,
1320   Hunting the barren hind over the broad heath.
He had slain such a sum, when the sun sank low,
Of does and other deer, as would dizzy one's wits.
Then they trooped in together in triumph at last,
And the count of the quarry quickly they take.
1325   The lords lent a hand with their liegemen many,
Picked out the plumpest and put them together
And duly dressed the deer, as the deed requires.
Some were assigned the assay of the fat:
Two fingers' width fully they found on the leanest.
1330   Then they slit the slot open and searched out the paunch,
Trimmed it with trencher-knives and tied it up tight.

They flayed the fair hide from the legs and trunk,
Then broke open the belly and laid bare the bowels,
Deftly detaching and drawing them forth.
1335   And next at the neck they neatly parted
The weasand° from the windpipe, and cast away the guts.   *esophagus*
At the shoulders with sharp blades they showed their skill,
Boning them from beneath, lest the sides be marred;
They breached the broad breast and broke it in twain,
1340   And again at the gullet they begin with their knives,
Cleave down the carcass clear to the breach;
Two tender morsels they take from the throat,
Then round the inner ribs they rid off a layer
And carve out the kidney-fat, close to the spine,
1345   Hewing down to the haunch, that all hung together,
And held it up whole, and hacked it free,
And this they named the numbles,[4] that knew such terms
of art.
They divide the crotch in two,
1350   And straightway then they start
To cut the backbone through
And cleave the trunk apart.

With hard strokes they hewed off the head and the neck,
Then swiftly from the sides they severed the chine,
1355   And the corbie's bone[5] they cast on a branch.
Then they pierced the plump sides, impaled either one
With the hock of the hind foot, and hung it aloft,
To each person his portion most proper and fit.
On a hide of a hind the hounds they fed
1360   With the liver and the lights,° the leathery paunches,   *lungs*
And bread soaked in blood well blended therewith.
High horns and shrill set hounds a-baying,
Then merrily with their meat they make their way home,
Blowing on their bugles many a brave blast.
1365   Ere dark had descended, that doughty band
Was come within the walls where Gawain waits
at leisure.
Bliss and hearth-fire bright
Await the master's pleasure;
1370   When the two men met that night,
Joy surpassed all measure.

Then the host in the hall his household assembles,
With the dames of high degree and their damsels fair.
In the presence of the people, a party he sends
1375   To convey him his venison in view of the knight.
And in high good-humor he hails him then,
Counts over the kill, the cuts on the tallies,
Holds high the hewn ribs, heavy with fat.

4. The other internal organs.
5. A bit of gristle assigned to the ravens ("corbies").

"What think you, sir, of this? Have I thriven well?
1380 Have I won with my woodcraft a worthy prize?"
"In good earnest," said Gawain, "this game is the finest
I have seen in seven years in the season of winter."
"And I give it to you, Gawain," said the goodly host,
"For according to our convenant, you claim it as your own."
1385 "That is so," said Sir Gawain, "the same say I:
What I worthily have won within these fair walls,
Herewith I as willingly award it to you."
He embraces his broad neck with both his arms,
And confers on him a kiss in the comeliest style.
1390 "Have here my profit, it proved no better;
Ungrudging do I grant it, were it greater far."
"Such a gift," said the good host, "I gladly accept—
Yet it might be all the better, would you but say
Where you won this same award, by your wits alone."
1395 "That was no part of the pact; press me no further,
For you have had what behooves; all other claims
                    forbear."
               With jest and compliment
               They conversed, and cast off care;
1400   To the table soon they went;
               Fresh dainties wait them there.

And then by the chimney-side they chat at their ease;
The best wine was brought them, and bounteously served;
And after in their jesting they jointly accord
1405 To do on the second day the deeds of the first:
That the two men should trade, betide as it may,
What each had taken in, at eve when they met.
They seal the pact solemnly in sight of the court;
Their cups were filled afresh to confirm the jest;
1410 Then at last they took their leave, for late was the hour,
Each to his own bed hastening away.
Before the barnyard cock had crowed but thrice
The lord had leapt from his rest, his liegemen as well.
Both of mass and their meal they made short work:
1415 By the dim light of dawn they were deep in the woods
                    away.
               With huntsmen and with horns
               Over plains they pass that day;
               They release, amid the thorns,
1420   Swift hounds that run and bay.

Soon some were on a scent by the side of a marsh;
When the hounds opened cry, the head of the hunt
Rallied them with rough words, raised a great noise.
The hounds that had heard it came hurrying straight
1425 And followed along with their fellows, forty together.
Then such a clamor and cry of coursing hounds
Arose, that the rocks resounded again.
Hunters exhorted them with horn and with voice;

Then all in a body bore off together
1430 Between a mere in the marsh and a menacing crag,
To a rise where the rock stood rugged and steep,
And boulders lay about, that blocked their approach.
Then the company in consort closed on their prey:
They surrounded the rise and the rocks both,
1435 For well they were aware that it waited within,
The beast that the bloodhounds boldly proclaimed.
Then they beat on the bushes and bade him appear,
And he made a murderous rush in the midst of them all;
The best of all boars broke from his cover,
1440 That had ranged long unrivaled, a renegade old,
For of tough-brawned boars he was biggest far,
Most grim when he grunted—then grieved were many,
For three at the first thrust he threw to the earth,
And dashed away at once without more damage.
1445 With "Hi!" "Hi!" and "Hey!" "Hey!" the others followed,
Had horns at their lips, blew high and clear.
Merry was the music of men and of hounds
That were bound after this boar, his bloodthirsty heart
                    to quell.
1450   Often he stands at bay,
               Then scatters the pack pell-mell;
               He hurts the hounds, and they
               Most dolefully yowl and yell.

Men then with mighty bows moved in to shoot,
1455 Aimed at him with their arrows and often hit,
But the points had no power to pierce through his hide,
And the barbs were brushed aside by his bristly brow;
Though the shank of the shaft shivered in pieces,
The head hopped away, wheresoever it struck.
1460 But when their stubborn strokes had stung him at last,
Then, foaming in his frenzy, fiercely he charges,
Hies at them headlong that hindered his flight,
And many feared for their lives, and fell back a little.
But the lord on a lively horse leads the chase;
1465 As a high-mettled huntsman his horn he blows;
He sounds the assembly and sweeps through the brush,
Pursuing this wild swine till the sunlight slanted.
All day with this deed they drive forth the time
While our lone knight so lovesome lies in his bed,
1470 Sir Gawain safe at home, in silken bower
                    so gay.
               The lady, with guile in heart,
               Came early where he lay;
               She was at him with all her art
1475   To turn his mind her way.

She comes to the curtain and coyly peeps in;
Gawain thought it good to greet her at once,

And she richly repays him with her ready words,
Settles softly at his side, and suddenly she laughs,
1480 And with a gracious glance, she begins on him thus:
"Sir, if you be Gawain, it seems a great wonder—
A man so well-meaning, and mannerly disposed,
And cannot act in company as courtesy bids,
And if one takes the trouble to teach him, 'tis all in vain.
1485 That lesson learned lately is lightly forgot,
Though I painted it as plain as my poor wit allowed."
"What lesson, dear lady?" he asked all alarmed;
"I have been much to blame, if your story be true."
"Yet my counsel was of kissing," came her answer then,
1490 "Where favor has been found, freely to claim
As accords with the conduct of courteous knights."
"My dear," said the doughty man, "dismiss that thought;
Such freedom, I fear, might offend you much;
It were rude to request if the right were denied."
1495 "But none can deny you," said the noble dame,
"You are stout enough to constrain with strength, if you choose,
Were any so ungracious as to grudge you aught."
"By heaven," said he, "you have answered well,
But threats never throve among those of my land,
1500 Nor any gift not freely given, good though it be.
I am yours to command, to kiss when you please;
You may lay on as you like, and leave off at will."
                    With this,
            The lady lightly bends
1505   And graciously gives him a kiss;
            The two converse as friends
            Of true love's trials and bliss.

"I should like, by your leave," said the lovely lady,
"If it did not annoy you, to know for what cause
1510 So brisk and so bold a young blood as you,
And acclaimed for all courtesies becoming a knight—
And name what knight you will, they are noblest esteemed
For loyal faith in love, in life as in story;
For to tell the tribulations of these true hearts,
1515 Why, 'tis the very title and text of their deeds,
How bold knights for beauty have braved many a foe,
Suffered heavy sorrows out of secret love,
And then valorously avenged them on villainous churls
And made happy ever after the hearts of their ladies.
1520 And you are the noblest knight known in your time;
No household under heaven but has heard of your fame,
And here by your side I have sat for two days
Yet never has a fair phrase fallen from your lips
Of the language of love, not one little word!
1525 And you, that with sweet vows sway women's hearts,
Should show your winsome ways, and woo a young thing,
And teach by some tokens the craft of true love.

How! are you artless, whom all men praise?
Or do you deem me so dull, or deaf to such words?
1530   Fie! Fie!
     In hope of pastimes new
     I have come where none can spy;
     Instruct me a little, do,
     While my husband is not nearby."

1535 "God love you, gracious lady!" said Gawain then;
"It is a pleasure surpassing, and a peerless joy,
That one so worthy as you would willingly come
And take the time and trouble to talk with your knight
And content you with his company—it comforts my heart.
1540 But to take to myself the task of telling of love,
And touch upon its texts, and treat of its themes
To one that, I know well, wields more power
In that art, by a half, than a hundred such
As I am where I live, or am like to become,
1545 It were folly, fair dame, in the first degree!
In all that I am able, my aim is to please,
As in honor behooves me, and am evermore
Your servant heart and soul, so save me our Lord!"
Thus she tested his temper and tried many a time,
1550 Whatever her true intent, to entice him to sin,
But so fair was his defense that no fault appeared,
Nor evil on either hand, but only bliss
      they knew.
     They linger and laugh awhile;
1555   She kisses the knight so true,
     Takes leave in comeliest style
     And departs without more ado.

Then he rose from his rest and made ready for mass,
And then a meal was set and served, in sumptuous style;
1560 He dallied at home all day with the dear ladies,
But the lord lingered late at his lusty sport;
Pursued his sorry swine, that swerved as he fled,
And bit asunder the backs of the best of his hounds
When they brought him to bay, till the bowmen appeared
1565 And soon forced him forth, though he fought for dear life,
So sharp were the shafts they shot at him there.
But yet the boldest drew back from his battering head,
Till at last he was so tired he could travel no more,
But in as much haste as he might, he makes his retreat
1570 To a rise on rocky ground, by a rushing stream.
With the bank at his back he scrapes the bare earth,
The froth foams at his jaws, frightful to see.
He whets his white tusks—then weary were all
Those hunters so hardy that hoved round about
1575 Of aiming from afar, but ever they mistrust
      his mood.
     He had hurt so many by then

That none had hardihood
To be torn by his tusks again.
1580   That was brainsick, and out for blood.

Till the lord came at last on his lofty steed,
Beheld him there at bay before all his folk;
Lightly he leaps down, leaves his courser,
Bares his bright sword, and boldly advances;
1585 Straight into the stream he strides towards his foe.
The wild thing was wary of weapon and man;
His hackles rose high; so hotly he snorts
That many watched with alarm, lest the worst befall.
The boar makes for the man with a mighty bound
1590 So that he and his hunter came headlong together
Where the water ran wildest—the worse for the beast,
For the man, when they first met, marked him with care,
Sights well the slot, slips in the blade,
Shoves it home to the hilt, and the heart shattered,
1595 And he falls in his fury and floats down the water,
                     ill-sped.
                Hounds hasten by the score
                To maul him, hide and head;
                Men drag him in to shore
1600   And dogs pronounce him dead.

With many a brave blast they boast of their prize,
All hallooed in high glee, that had their wind;
The hounds bayed their best, as the bold men bade
That were charged with chief rank in that chase of renown.
1605 Then one wise in woodcraft, and worthily skilled,
Began to dress the boar in becoming style:
He severs the savage head and sets it aloft,
Then rends the body roughly right down the spine;
Takes the bowels from the belly, broils them on coals,
1610 Blends them well with bread to bestow on the hounds.
Then he breaks out the brawn in fair broad flitches,
And the innards to be eaten in order he takes.
The two sides, attached to each other all whole,
He suspended from a spar that was springy and tough;
1615 And so with this swine they set out for home;
The boar's head was borne before the same man
That had stabbed him in the stream with his strong arm,
                   right through.
                He thought it long indeed
1620   Till he had the knight in view;
                At his call, he comes with speed
                To claim his payment due.

The lord laughed aloud, with many a light word,
When he greeted Sir Gawain—with good cheer he speaks.
1625 They fetch the fair dames and the folk of the house;
He brings forth the brawn, and begins the tale

Of the great length and girth, the grim rage as well,
Of the battle of the boar they beset in the wood.
The other man meetly commended his deeds
1630   And praised well the prize of his princely sport,
For the brawn of that boar, the bold knight said,
And the sides of that swine surpassed all others.
Then they handled the huge head; he owns it a wonder,
And eyes it with abhorrence, to heighten his praise.
1635   "Now, Gawain," said the good man, "this game becomes yours
By those fair terms we fixed, as you know full well."
"That is true," returned the knight, "and trust me, fair friend,
All my gains, as agreed, I shall give you forthwith."
He clasps him and kisses him in courteous style,
1640   Then serves him with the same fare a second time.
"Now we are even," said he, "at this evening feast,
And clear is every claim incurred here to date,
                             and debt."
                  "By Saint Giles!" the host replies,
1645   "You're the best I ever met!
                  If your profits are all this size,
                  We'll see you wealthy yet!"

Then attendants set tables on trestles about,
And laid them with linen; light shone forth,
1650   Wakened along the walls in waxen torches.
The service was set and the supper brought;
Royal were the revels that rose then in hall
At that feast by the fire, with many fair sports:
Amid the meal and after, melody sweet,
1655   Carol-dances comely and Christmas songs,
With all the mannerly mirth my tongue may describe.
And ever our gallant knight beside the gay lady;
So uncommonly kind and complaisant was she,
With sweet stolen glances, that stirred his stout heart,
1660   That he was at his wits' end, and wondrous vexed;
But he could not rebuff her, for courtesy forbade,
Yet took pains to please her, though the plan might
                             go wrong.
                  When they to heart's delight
1665   Had reveled there in throng,
                  To his chamber he calls the knight,
                  And thither they go along.

And there they dallied and drank, and deemed it good sport
To enact their play anew on New Year's Eve,
1670   But Gawain asked again to go on the morrow,
For the time until his tryst was not two days.
The host hindered that, and urged him to stay,
And said, "On my honor, my oath here I take
That you shall get to the Green Chapel to begin your chores
1675   By dawn on New Year's Day, if you so desire.
Wherefore lie at your leisure in your lofty bed,

And I shall hunt hereabouts, and hold to our terms,
And we shall trade winnings when once more we meet,
For I have tested you twice, and true have I found you;
1680 Now think this tomorrow: the third pays for all;
Be we merry while we may, and mindful of joy,
For heaviness of heart can be had for the asking."
This is gravely agreed on and Gawain will stay.
They drink a last draught and with torches depart
1685   to rest.
                 To bed Sir Gawain went:
                 His sleep was of the best;
                 The lord, on his craft intent,
                 Was early up and dressed.

1690 After mass, with his men, a morsel he takes;
Clear and crisp the morning; he calls for his mount;
The folk that were to follow him afield that day
Were high astride their horses before the hall gates.
Wondrous fair were the fields, for the frost was light;
1695 The sun rises red amid radiant clouds,
Sails into the sky, and sends forth his beams.
They let loose the hounds by a leafy wood;
The rocks all around re-echo to their horns;
Soon some have set off in pursuit of the fox,
1700 Cast about with craft for a clearer scent;
A young dog yaps, and is yelled at in turn;
His fellows fall to sniffing, and follow his lead,
Running in a rabble on the right track,
And he scampers all before; they discover him soon,
1705 And when they see him with sight they pursue him the faster,
Railing at him rudely with a wrathful din.
Often he reverses over rough terrain,
Or loops back to listen in the lee of a hedge;
At last, by a little ditch, he leaps over the brush,
1710 Comes into a clearing at a cautious pace,
Then he thought through his wiles to have thrown off the hounds
Till he was ware, as he went, of a waiting-station
Where three athwart his path threatened him at once,
               all gray.
1715   Quick as a flash he wheels
                 And darts off in dismay;
                 With hard luck at his heels
                 He is off to the wood away.

Then it was heaven on earth to hark to the hounds
1720 When they had come on their quarry, coursing together!
Such harsh cries and howls they hurled at his head
As all the cliffs with a crash had come down at once.
Here he was hailed, when huntsmen met him;
Yonder they yelled at him, yapping and snarling;
1725 There they cried "Thief!" and threatened his life,
And ever the harriers at his heels, that he had no rest.

Often he was menaced when he made for the open,
And often rushed in again, for Reynard was wily;
And so he leads them a merry chase, the lord and his men,
1730 In this manner on the mountains, till midday or near,
While our hero lies at home in wholesome sleep
Within the comely curtains on the cold morning.
But the lady, as love would allow her no rest,
And pursuing ever the purpose that pricked her heart,
1735 Was awake with the dawn, and went to his chamber
In a fair flowing mantle that fell to the earth,
All edged and embellished with ermines fine;
No hood on her head, but heavy with gems
Were her fillet and the fret° that confined her tresses;   *ornamental net*
1740 Her face and her fair throat freely displayed;
Her bosom all but bare, and her back as well.
She comes in at the chamber-door, and closes it with care,
Throws wide a window—then waits no longer,
But hails him thus airily with her artful words,
1745   with cheer:
          "Ah, man, how can you sleep?
          The morning is so clear!"
          Though dreams have drowned him deep,
          He cannot choose but hear.

1750 Deep in his dreams he darkly mutters
As a man may that mourns, with many grim thoughts
Of that day when destiny shall deal him his doom
When he greets his grim host at the Green Chapel
And must bow to his buffet, bating all strife.
1755 But when he sees her at his side he summons his wits,
Breaks from the black dreams, and blithely answers.
That lovely lady comes laughing sweet,
Sinks down at his side, and salutes him with a kiss.
He accords her fair welcome in courtliest style;
1760 He sees her so glorious, so gaily attired,
So faultless her features, so fair and so bright,
His heart swelled swiftly with surging joys.
They melt into mirth with many a fond smile,
Nor was fair language lacking, to further that hour's
1765   delight.
          Good were their words of greeting;
          Each joyed in other's sight;
          Great peril attends that meeting
          Should Mary forget her knight.

1770 For that high-born beauty so hemmed him about,
Made so plain her meaning, the man must needs
Either take her tendered love or distastefully refuse.
His courtesy concerned him, lest crass he appear,
But more his soul's mischief, should he commit sin
1775 And belie his loyal oath to the lord of that house.
"God forbid!" said the bold knight. "That shall not befall!"

With a little fond laughter he lightly let pass
All the words of special weight that were sped his way;
"I find you much at fault," the fair one said,
1780 "Who can be cold toward a creature so close by your side,
Of all women in this world most wounded in heart,
Unless you have a sweetheart, one you hold dearer,
And allegiance to that lady so loyally knit
That you will never love another, as now I believe.
1785 And, sir, if it be so, then say it, I beg you;
By all your heart holds dear, hide it no longer
     with guile."
      "Lady, by Saint John,"
      He answers with a smile,
1790   "Lover have I none,
      Nor will have, yet awhile."

"Those words," said the woman, "are the worst of all,
But I have had my answer, and hard do I find it!
Kiss me now kindly: I can but go hence
1795 To lament my life long like a maid lovelorn."
She inclines her head quickly and kisses the knight,
Then straightens with a sigh, and says as she stands,
"Now, dear, ere I depart, do me this pleasure:
Give me some little gift, your glove or the like,
1800 That I may think on you, man, and mourn the less."
"Now by heavens," said he, "I wish I had here
My most precious possession, to put it in your hands,
For your deeds, beyond doubt, have often deserved
A repayment far passing my power to bestow.
1805 But a love-token, lady, were of little avail;
It is not to your honor to have at this time
A glove as a guerdon from Gawain's hand.
And I am here on an errand in unknown realms
And have no bearers with baggage with becoming gifts,
1810 Which distresses me, madame, for your dear sake.
A man must keep within his compass: account it neither grief
     nor slight."
      "Nay, noblest knight alive,"
      Said that beauty of body white,
1815   "Though you be loath to give,
      Yet you shall take, by right."

She reached out a rich ring, wrought all of gold,
With a splendid stone displayed on the band
That flashed before his eyes like a fiery sun:
1820 It was worth a king's wealth, you may well believe.
But he waved it away with these ready words:
"Before God, good lady, I forgo all gifts;
None have I to offer, nor any will I take."
And she urged it on him eagerly, and ever he refused,
1825 And vowed in very earnest, prevail she would not.
And she sad to find it so, and said to him then,

"If my ring is refused for its rich cost—
You would not be my debtor for so dear a thing—
I shall give you my girdle; you gain less thereby."
1830 She released a knot lightly, and loosened a belt
That was caught about her kirtle, the bright cloak beneath,
Of a gay green silk, with gold overwrought,
And the borders all bound with embroidery fine,
And this she presses upon him, and pleads with a smile,
1835 Unworthy though it were, that it would not be scorned.
But the man still maintains that he means to accept
Neither gold nor any gift, till by God's grace
The fate that lay before him was fully achieved.
"And be not offended, fair lady, I beg,
1840 And give over your offer, for ever I must
                              decline.
                  I am grateful for favor shown
                  Past all deserts of mine,
                  And ever shall be your own
1845   True servant, rain or shine."

"Now does my present displease you," she promptly inquired,
"Because it seems in your sight so simple a thing?
And belike, as it is little, it is less to praise,
But if the virtue that invests it were verily known,
1850 It would be held, I hope, in higher esteem.
For the man that possesses this piece of silk,
If he bore it on his body, belted about,
There is no hand under heaven that could hew him down,
For he could not be killed by any craft on earth."
1855 Then the man began to muse, and mainly he thought
It was a pearl for his plight, the peril to come
When he gains the Green Chapel to get his reward:
Could he escape unscathed, the scheme were noble!
Then he bore with her words and withstood them no more,
1860 And she repeated her petition and pleaded anew,
And he granted it, and gladly she gave him the belt,
And besought him for her sake to conceal it well,
Lest the noble lord should know—and, the knight agrees
That not a soul save themselves shall see it thenceforth
1865   with sight.
                  He thanked her with fervent heart,
                  As often as ever he might;
                  Three times, before they part,
                  She has kissed the stalwart knight.

1870 Then the lady took her leave, and left him there,
For more mirth with that man she might not have.
When she was gone, Sir Gawain got from his bed,
Arose and arrayed him in his rich attire;
Tucked away the token the temptress had left,
1875 Laid it reliably where he looked for it after.
And then with good cheer to the chapel he goes,

Approached a priest in private, and prayed to be taught
To lead a better life and lift up his mind,
Lest he be among the lost when he must leave this world.
1880 And shamefaced at shrift he showed his misdeeds
From the largest to the least, and asked the Lord's mercy,
And called on his confessor to cleanse his soul,
And he absolved him of his sins as safe and as clean
As if the dread Day of Doom were to dawn on the morrow.
1885 And then he made merry amid the fine ladies
With deft-footed dances and dalliance light,
As never until now, while the afternoon wore
              away.
        He delighted all around him,
1890   And all agreed, that day,
        They never before had found him
        So gracious and so gay.

Now peaceful be his pasture, and love play him fair!
The host is on horseback, hunting afield;
1895 He has finished off this fox that he followed so long:
As he leapt a low hedge to look for the villain
Where he heard all the hounds in hot pursuit,
Reynard comes racing out of a rough thicket,
And all the rabble in a rush, right at his heels.
1900 The man beholds the beast, and bides his time,
And bares his bright sword, and brings it down hard,
And he blenches from the blade, and backward he starts;
A hound hurries up and hinders that move,
And before the horse's feet they fell on him at once
1905 And ripped the rascal's throat with a wrathful din.
The lord soon alighted and lifted him free,
Swiftly snatched him up from the snapping jaws,
Holds him over his head, halloos with a will,
And the dogs bayed the dirge, that had done him to death.
1910 Hunters hastened thither with horns at their lips,
Sounding the assembly till they saw him at last.
When that comely company was come in together,
All that bore bugles blew them at once,
And the others all hallooed, that had no horns.
1915 It was the merriest medley that ever a man heard,
The racket that they raised for Sir Reynard's soul
              that died.
        Their hounds they praised and fed,
        Fondling their heads with pride,
1920   And they took Reynard the Red
        And stripped away his hide.

And then they headed homeward, for evening had come,
Blowing many a blast on their bugles bright.
The lord at long last alights at his house,
1925 Finds fire on the hearth where the fair knight waits.
Sir Gawain the good, that was glad in heart.

With the ladies, that loved him, he lingered at ease;
He wore a rich robe of blue, that reached to the earth
And a surcoat lined softly with sumptuous furs;
1930 A hood of the same hue hung on his shoulders;
With bands of bright ermine embellished were both.
He comes to meet the man amid all the folk,
And greets him good-humoredly, and gaily he says,
"I shall follow forthwith the form of our pledge
1935 That we framed to good effect amid fresh-filled cups."
He clasps him accordingly and kisses him thrice,
As amiably and as earnestly as ever he could.
"By heaven," said the host, "you have had some luck
Since you took up this trade, if the terms were good."
1940 "Never trouble about the terms," he returned at once,
"Since all that I owe here is openly paid."
"Marry!" said the other man, "mine is much less,
For I have hunted all day, and nought have I got
But this foul fox pelt, the fiend take the goods!
1945 Which but poorly repays such precious things
That you have cordially conferred, such kisses three
                    so good."
            "Enough!" said Sir Gawain;
            "I thank you, by the rood!"
1950   And how the fox was slain
            He told him, as they stood.

With minstrelsy and mirth, with all manner of meats,
They made as much merriment as any men might
(Amid laughing of ladies and light hearted girls;
1955 So gay grew Sir Gawain and the goodly host)
Unless they had been besotted, or brainless fools.
The knight joined in jesting with that joyous folk,
Until at last it was late; ere long they must part,
And be off to their beds, as behooved them each one.
1960 Then politely his leave of the lord of the house
Our noble knight takes, and renews his thanks:
"The courtesies countless accorded me here,
Your kindness at this Christmas, may heaven's King repay!
Henceforth, if you will have me, I hold you my liege,
1965 And so, as I have said, I must set forth tomorrow,
If I may take some trusty man to teach, as you promised,
The way to the Green Chapel, that as God allows
I shall see my fate fulfilled on the first of the year."
"In good faith," said the good man, "with a good will
1970 Every promise on my part shall be fully performed."
He assigns him a servant to set him on the path,
To see him safe and sound over the snowy hills,
To follow the fastest way through forest green
                    and grove.
1975   Gawain thanks him again,
            So kind his favors prove,
            And of the ladies then
            He takes his leave, with love.

Courteously he kissed them, with care in his heart,
1980 And often wished them well, with warmest thanks,
Which they for their part were prompt to repay.
They commend him to Christ with disconsolate sighs;
And then in that hall with the household he parts—
Each man that he met, he remembered to thank
1985 For his deeds of devotion and diligent pains,
And the trouble he had taken to tend to his needs;
And each one as woeful, that watched him depart,
As he had lived with him loyally all his life long.
By lads bearing lights he was led to his chamber
1990 And blithely brought to his bed, to be at his rest.
How soundly he slept, I presume not to say,
For there were matters of moment his thoughts might well
              pursue.
            Let him lie and wait;
1995   He has little more to do,
            Then listen, while I relate
            How they kept their rendezvous.

Part 4

Now the New Year draws near, and the night passes,
The day dispels the dark, by the Lord's decree;
2000 But wild weather awoke in the world without:
The clouds in the cold sky cast down their snow
With great gusts from the north, grievous to bear.
Sleet showered aslant upon shivering beasts;
The wind warbled wild as it whipped from aloft,
2005 And drove the drifts deep in the dales below.
Long and well he listens, that lies in his bed;
Though he lifts not his eyelids, little he sleeps;
Each crow of the cock he counts without fail.
Readily from his rest he rose before dawn,
2010 For a lamp had been left him, that lighted his chamber.
He called to his chamberlain, who quickly appeared,
And bade him get him his gear, and gird his good steed,
And he sets about briskly to bring in his arms,
And makes ready his master in manner most fit.
2015 First he clad him in his clothes, to keep out the cold,
And then his other harness, made handsome anew,
His plate-armor of proof, polished with pains,
The rings of his rich mail rid of their rust,
And all was fresh as at first, and for this he gave thanks
2020   indeed.
            With pride he wears each piece,
            New-furbished for his need:
            No gayer from here to Greece;
            He bids them bring his steed.

2025 In his richest raiment he robed himself then:
His crested coat-armor, close-stitched with craft,
With stones of strange virtue on silk velvet set;

All bound with embroidery on borders and seams
And lined warmly and well with furs of the best.
2030 Yet he left not his love-gift, the lady's girdle;
Gawain, for his own good, forgot not that:
When the bright sword was belted and bound on his haunches,
Then twice with that token he twined him about.
Sweetly did he swathe him in that swatch of silk,
2035 That girdle of green so goodly to see,
That against the gay red showed gorgeous bright.
Yet he wore not for its wealth that wondrous girdle,
Nor pride in its pendants, though polished they were,
Though glittering gold gleamed at the tips,
2040 But to keep himself safe when consent he must
To endure a deadly dint, and all defense
                              denied.
                    And now the bold knight came
                    Into the courtyard wide;
2045   That folk of worthy fame
                    He thanks on every side.

Then was Gringolet girt, that was great and huge,
And had sojourned safe and sound, and savored his fare;
He pawed the earth in his pride, that princely steed.
2050 The good knight draws near him and notes well his look,
And says sagely to himself, and soberly swears,
"Here is a household in hall that upholds the right!
The man that maintains it, may happiness be his!
Likewise the dear lady, may love betide her!
2055 If thus they in charity cherish a guest
That are honored here on earth, may they have his reward
That reigns high in heaven—and also you all;
And might I live in this land but a little while,
I should willingly reward you, and well, if I might."
2060 Then he steps into the stirrup and bestrides his mount;
His shield is shown forth; on his shoulder he casts it;
Strikes the side of his steed with his steel spurs,
And he starts across the stones, nor stands any longer
                              to prance.
2065   On horseback was the swain
                    That bore his spear and lance;
                    "May Christ this house maintain
                    And guard it from mischance!"

The bridge was brought down, and the broad gates
2070 Unbarred and carried back upon both sides;
He commended him to Christ, and crossed over the planks;
Praised the noble porter, who prayed on his knees
That God save Sir Gawain, and bade him good day,
And went on his way alone with the man
2075 That was to lead him ere long to that luckless place
Where the dolorous dint must be dealt him at last.
Under bare boughs they ride, where steep banks rise,

Over high cliffs they climb, where cold snow clings;
The heavens held aloof, but heavy thereunder
2080 Mist mantled the moors, moved on the slopes.
Each hill had a hat, a huge cape of cloud;
Brooks bubbled and broke over broken rocks,
Flashing in freshets that waterfalls fed.
Roundabout was the road that ran through the wood
2085 Till the sun at that season was soon to rise,
                         that day.
                    They were on a hilltop high;
                    The white snow round them lay;
                    The man that rode nearby
2090   Now bade his master stay.

"For I have seen you here safe at the set time,
And now you are not far from that notable place
That you have sought for so long with such special pains.
But this I say for certain, since I know you, sir knight,
2095 And have your good at heart, and hold you dear—
Would you heed well my words, it were worth your while—
You are rushing into risks that you reck not of:
There is a villain in yon valley, the veriest on earth,
For he is rugged and rude, and ready with his fists,
2100 And most immense in his mold of mortals alive,
And his body bigger than the best four
That are in Arthur's house, Hector[6] or any.
He gets his grim way at the Green Chapel;
None passes by that place so proud in his arms
2105 That he does not dash him down with his deadly blows,
For he is heartless wholly, and heedless of right,
For be it chaplain or churl that by the Chapel rides,
Monk or mass-priest or any man else,
He would as soon strike him dead as stand on two feet.
2110 Wherefore I say, just as certain as you sit there astride,
You cannot but be killed, if his counsel holds,
For he would trounce you in a trice, had you twenty lives
                         for sale.
                    He has lived long in this land
2115   And dealt out deadly bale;
                    Against his heavy hand
                    Your power cannot prevail.

"And so, good Sir Gawain, let the grim man be;
Go off by some other road, in God's own name!
2120 Leave by some other land, for the love of Christ,
And I shall get me home again, and give you my word
That I shall swear by God's self and the saints above,
By heaven and by my halidom[7] and other oaths more,
To conceal this day's deed, nor say to a soul

6. Either the Trojan hero or one of Arthur's   7. Holiness or, more likely, patron saints.
knights.

2125 That ever you fled for fear from any that I knew."
"Many thanks!" said the other man—and demurring he speaks—
"Fair fortune befall you for your friendly words!
And conceal this day's deed I doubt not you would,
But though you never told the tale, if I turned back now,
2130 Forsook this place for fear, and fled, as you say,
I were a caitiff coward; I could not be excused.
But I must to the Chapel to chance my luck
And say to that same man such words as I please,
Befall what may befall through Fortune's will
2135   or whim.
        Though he be a quarrelsome knave
        With a cudgel great and grim,
        The Lord is strong to save:
        His servants trust in him."

2140 "Marry," said the man, "since you tell me so much,
And I see you are set to seek your own harm,
If you crave a quick death, let me keep you no longer!
Put your helm on your head, your hand on your lance,
And ride the narrow road down yon rocky slope
2145 Till it brings you to the bottom of the broad valley.
Then look a little ahead, on your left hand,
And you will soon see before you that self-same Chapel,
And the man of great might that is master there.
Now goodbye in God's name, Gawain the noble!
2150 For all the world's wealth I would not stay here,
Or go with you in this wood one footstep further!"
He tarried no more to talk, but turned his bridle,
Hit his horse with his heels as hard as he might,
Leaves the knight alone, and off like the wind
2155   goes leaping.
        "By God," said Gawain then,
        "I shall not give way to weeping;
        God's will be done, amen!
        I commend me to his keeping."

2160 He puts his heels to his horse, and picks up the path;
Goes in beside a grove where the ground is steep,
Rides down the rough slope right to the valley;
And then he looked a little about him—the landscape was wild,
And not a soul to be seen, nor sign of a dwelling,
2165 But high banks on either hand hemmed it about,
With many a ragged rock and rough-hewn crag;
The skies seemed scored by the scowling peaks.
Then he halted his horse, and hoved there a space,
And sought on every side for a sight of the Chapel,
2170 But no such place appeared, which puzzled him sore,
Yet he saw some way off what seemed like a mound,
A hillock high and broad, hard by the water,
Where the stream fell in foam down the face of the steep
And bubbled as if it boiled on its bed below.

2175 The knight urges his horse, and heads for the knoll;
Leaps lightly to earth; loops well the rein
Of his steed to a stout branch, and stations him there.
He strides straight to the mound, and strolls all about,
Much wondering what it was, but no whit the wiser;
2180 It had a hole at one end, and on either side,
And was covered with coarse grass in clumps all without,
And hollow all within, like some old cave,
Or a crevice of an old crag—he could not discern
aright.
2185 "Can this be the Chapel Green?
Alack!" said the man, "here might
The devil himself be seen
Saying matins at black midnight!"

"Now by heaven," said he, "it is bleak hereabouts;
2190 This prayer-house is hideous, half-covered with grass!
Well may the grim man mantled in green
Hold here his orisons, in hell's own style!
Now I feel it is the Fiend, in my five wits,
That has tempted me to this tryst, to take my life;
2195 This is a Chapel of mischance, may the mischief take it!
As accursed a country church as I came upon ever!"
With his helm on his head, his lance in his hand,
He stalks toward the steep wall of that strange house.
Then he heard, on the hill, behind a hard rock,
2200 Beyond the brook, from the bank, a most barbarous din:
Lord! it clattered in the cliff fit to cleave it in two,
As one upon a grindstone ground a great scythe!
Lord! it whirred like a mill-wheel whirling about!
Lord! it echoed loud and long, lamentable to hear!
Then "By heaven," said the bold knight, "that business
2205   up there
Is arranged for my arrival, or else I am much
misled.
Let God work! Ah me!
All hope of help has fled!
2210 Forfeit my life may be
But noise I do not dread."

Then he listened no longer, but loudly he called,
"Who has power in this place, high parley to hold?
For none greets Sir Gawain, or gives him good day;
2215 If any would a word with him, let him walk forth
And speak now or never, to speed his affairs."
"Abide," said one on the bank above over his head,
"And what I promised you once shall straightway be given."
Yet he stayed not his grindstone, nor stinted its noise,
2220 But worked awhile at his whetting before he would rest,
And then he comes around a crag, from a cave in the rocks,
Hurtling out of hiding with a hateful weapon,
A Danish° ax devised for that day's deed,   *i.e., long-bladed*

With a broad blade and bright, bent in a curve,
2225 Filed to a fine edge—four feet it measured
By the length of the lace that was looped round the haft.
And in form as at first, the fellow all green,
His lordly face and his legs, his locks and his beard,
Save that firm upon two feet forward he strides,
2230 Sets a hand on the ax-head, the haft to the earth;
When he came to the cold stream, and cared not to wade,
He vaults over on his ax, and advances amain
On a broad bank of snow, overbearing and brisk
                                        of mood.
2235   Little did the knight incline
                   When face to face they stood;
                   Said the other man, "Friend mine,
                   It seems your word holds good!"

"God love you, Sir Gawain!" said the Green Knight then,
2240 "And well met this morning, man, at my place!
And you have followed me faithfully and found me betimes,
And on the business between us we both are agreed:
Twelve months ago today you took what was yours,
And you at this New Year must yield me the same.
2245 And we have met in these mountains, remote from all eyes:
There is none here to halt us or hinder our sport;
Unhasp your high helm, and have here your wages;
Make no more demur than I did myself
When you hacked off my head with one hard blow."
2250 "No, by God," said Sir Gawain, "that granted me life,
I shall grudge not the guerdon, grim though it prove;
Bestow but one stroke, and I shall stand still,
And you may lay on as you like till the last of my part
                                        be paid."
2255   He proffered, with good grace,
                   His bare neck to the blade,
                   And feigned a cheerful face:
                   He scorned to seem afraid.

Then the grim man in green gathers his strength,
2260 Heaves high the heavy ax to hit him the blow.
With all the force in his frame he fetches it aloft,
With a grimace as grim as he would grind him to bits;
Had the blow he bestowed been as big as he threatened,
A good knight and gallant had gone to his grave.
2265 But Gawain at the great ax glanced up aside.
As down it descended with death-dealing force,
And his shoulders shrank a little from the sharp iron.
Abruptly the brawny man breaks off the stroke,
And then reproved with proud words that prince among knights.
2270 "You are not Gawain the glorious," the green man said,
"That never fell back on field in the face of the foe,
And now you flee for fear, and have felt no harm:
Such news of that knight I never heard yet!

I moved not a muscle when you made to strike,
2275 Nor caviled at the cut in King Arthur's house;
My head fell to my feet, yet steadfast I stood,
And you, all unharmed, are wholly dismayed—
Wherefore the better man I, by all odds,
                              must be."
2280   Said Gawain, "Strike once more;
                       I shall neither flinch nor flee;
                       But if my head falls to the floor
                       There is no mending me!"

"But go on, man, in God's name, and get to the point!
2285 Deliver me my destiny, and do it out of hand,
For I shall stand to the stroke and stir not an inch
Till your ax has hit home—on my honor I swear it!"
"Have at thee then!" said the other, and heaves it aloft,
And glares down as grimly as he had gone mad.
2290 He made a mighty feint, but marred not his hide;
Withdrew the ax adroitly before it did damage.
Gawain gave no ground, nor glanced up aside,
But stood still as a stone, or else a stout stump
That is held in hard earth by a hundred roots.
2295 Then merrily does he mock him, the man all in green:
"So now you have your nerve again, I needs must strike;
Uphold the high knighthood that Arthur bestowed,
And keep your neck-bone clear, if this cut allows!"
Then was Gawain gripped with rage, and grimly he said,
2300 "Why, thrash away, tyrant, I tire of your threats;
You make such a scene, you must frighten yourself."
Said the green fellow, "In faith, so fiercely you speak
That I shall finish this affair, nor further grace
                              allow."
2305   He stands prepared to strike
                       And scowls with both lip and brow;
                       No marvel if the man mislike
                       Who can hope no rescue now.

He gathered up the grim ax and guided it well:
2310 Let the barb at the blade's end brush the bare throat;
He hammered down hard, yet harmed him no whit
Save a scratch on one side, that severed the skin;
The end of the hooked edge entered the flesh,
And a little blood lightly leapt to the earth.
2315 And when the man beheld his own blood bright on the snow,
He sprang a spear's length with feet spread wide,
Seized his high helm, and set it on his head,
Shoved before his shoulders the shield at his back,
Bares his trusty blade, and boldly he speaks—
2320 Not since he was a babe born of his mother
Was he once in this world one-half so blithe—
"Have done with your hacking—harry me no more!
I have borne, as behooved, one blow in this place;

If you make another move I shall meet it midway
2325 And promptly, I promise you, pay back each blow
      with brand.
    One stroke acquits me here;
    So did our covenant stand
    In Arthur's court last year—
2330   Wherefore, sir, hold your hand!"

He lowers the long ax and leans on it there,
Sets his arms on the head, the haft on the earth,
And beholds the bold knight that bides there afoot,
How he faces him fearless, fierce in full arms,
2335 And plies him with proud words—it pleases him well.
Then once again gaily to Gawain he calls,
And in a loud voice and lusty, delivers these words:
"Bold fellow, on this field your anger forbear!
No man has made demands here in manner uncouth,
2340 Nor done, save as duly determined at court.
I owed you a hit and you have it; be happy therewith!
The rest of my rights here I freely resign.
Had I been a bit busier, a buffet, perhaps,
I could have dealt more directly, and done you some harm.
2345 First I flourished with a feint, in frolicsome mood,
And left your hide unhurt—and here I did well
By the fair terms we fixed on the first night;
And fully and faithfully you followed accord:
Gave over all your gains as a good man should.
2350 A second feint, sir, I assigned for the morning
You kissed my comely wife—each kiss you restored.
For both of these there behooved two feigned blows
      by right.
    True men pay what they owe;
2355   No danger then in sight.
    You failed at the third throw,
    So take my tap, sir knight.

"For that is my belt about you, that same braided girdle,
My wife it was that wore it; I know well the tale,
2360 And the count of your kisses and your conduct too,
And the wooing of my wife—it was all my scheme!
She made trial of a man most faultless by far
Of all that ever walked over the wide earth;
As pearls to white peas, more precious and prized,
2365 So is Gawain, in good faith, to other gay knights.
Yet you lacked, sir, a little in loyalty there,
But the cause was not cunning, nor courtship either,
But that you loved your own life; the less, then, to blame."
The other stout knight in a study stood a long while,
2370 So gripped with grim rage that his great heart shook.
All the blood of his body burned in his face
As he shrank back in shame from the man's sharp speech.
The first words that fell from the fair knight's lips:

"Accursed be a cowardly and covetous heart!
2375 In you is villainy and vice, and virtue laid low!"
Then he grasps the green girdle and lets go the knot,
Hands it over in haste, and hotly he says:
"Behold there my falsehood, ill hap betide it!
Your cut taught me cowardice, care for my life,
2380 And coveting came after, contrary both
To largesse and loyalty belonging to knights.
Now am I faulty and false, that fearful was ever
Of disloyalty and lies, bad luck to them both!
                            and greed.
2385   I confess, knight, in this place,
                 Most dire is my misdeed;
                 Let me gain back your good grace,
                 And thereafter I shall take heed."

Then the other laughed aloud, and lightly he said,
2390 "Such harm as I have had, I hold it quite healed.
You are so fully confessed, your failings made known,
And bear the plain penance of the point of my blade,
I hold you polished as a pearl, as pure and as bright
As you had lived free of fault since first you were born.
2395 And I give you, sir, this girdle that is gold-hemmed
And green as my garments, that, Gawain, you may
Be mindful of this meeting when you mingle in throng
With nobles of renown—and known by this token
How it chanced at the Green Chapel, to chivalrous knights.
2400 And you shall in this New Year come yet again
And we shall finish out our feast in my fair hall,
                            with cheer."
                 He urged the knight to stay,
                 And said, "With my wife so dear
2405   We shall see you friends this day,
                 Whose enmity touched you near."

"Indeed," said the doughty knight, and doffed his high helm,
And held it in his hands as he offered his thanks,
"I have lingered long enough—may good luck be yours,
2410 And he reward you well that all worship bestows!
And commend me to that comely one, your courteous wife,
Both herself and that other, my honoured ladies,
That have trapped their true knight in their trammels so quaint.
But if a dullard should dote, deem it no wonder,
2415 And through the wiles of a woman be wooed into sorrow,
For so was Adam by one, when the world began,
And Solomon by many more, and Samson the mighty—
Delilah was his doom, and David thereafter
Was beguiled by Bathsheba, and bore much distress;
2420 Now these were vexed by their devices—'twere a very joy
Could one but learn to love, and believe them not.
For these were proud princes, most prosperous of old,
Past all lovers lucky, that languished under heaven,

bemused.

And one and all fell prey

To women that they had used;

If I be led astray,

Methinks I may be excused.

"But your girdle, God love you! I gladly shall take

And be pleased to possess, not for the pure gold,

Nor the bright belt itself, nor the beauteous pendants,

Nor for wealth, nor worldly state, nor workmanship fine,

But a sign of excess it shall seem oftentimes

When I ride in renown, and remember with shame

The faults and the frailty of the flesh perverse,

How its tenderness entices the foul taint of sin;

And so when praise and high prowess have pleased my heart,

A look at this love-lace will lower my pride.

But one thing would I learn, if you were not loath,

Since you are lord of yonder land where I have long sojourned

With honor in your house—may you have His reward

That upholds all the heavens, highest on throne!

How runs your right name?—and let the rest go."

"That shall I give you gladly," said the Green Knight then;

"Bercilak de Hautdesert this barony I hold,

Through the might of Morgan le Faye,[8] that lodges at my house,

By subtleties of science and sorcerers' arts,

The mistress of Merlin,[9] she has caught many a man,

For sweet love in secret she shared sometime

With that wizard, that knows well each one of your knights

and you.

Morgan the Goddess, she,

So styled by title true;

None holds so high degree

That her arts cannot subdue.

"She guided me in this guise to your glorious hall,

To assay, if such it were, the surfeit of pride

That is rumored of the retinue of the Round Table.

She put this shape upon me to puzzle your wits,

To afflict the fair queen, and frighten her to death

With awe of that elvish man that eerily spoke

With his head in his hand before the high table.

She was with my wife at home, that old withered lady,

Your own aunt[1] is she, Arthur's half-sister,

The Duchess' daughter of Tintagel, that dear King Uther

Got Arthur on after, that honored is now.

And therefore, good friend, come feast with your aunt;

Make merry in my house; my men hold you dear,

---

8. Arthur's half-sister, an enchantress who sometimes abetted him, sometimes made trouble for him.
9. The wise magician who had helped Arthur become king.

1. Morgan was the daughter of Igraine, duchess of Tintagel, and her husband the duke; Igraine conceived Arthur when his father, Uther, lay with her through one of Merlin's trickeries.

And I wish you as well, sir, with all my heart,
2470 As any man God ever made, for your great good faith."
But the knight said him nay, that he might by no means.
They clasped then and kissed, and commended each other
To the Prince of Paradise, and parted with one
assent.
2475   Gawain sets out anew;
    Toward the court his course is bent;
    And the knight all green in hue,
    Wheresoever he wished, he went.

Wild ways in the world our worthy knight rides
2480 On Gringolet, that by grace had been granted his life.
He harbored often in houses, and often abroad,
And with many valiant adventures verily he met
That I shall not take time to tell in this story.
The hurt was whole that he had had in his neck,
2485 And the bright green belt on his body he bore,
Oblique, like a baldric, bound at his side,
Below his left shoulder, laced in a knot,
In betokening of the blame he had borne for his fault;
And so to court in due course he comes safe and sound.
2490 Bliss abounded in hall when the high-born heard
That good Gawain was come; glad tidings they thought it.
The king kisses the knight, and the queen as well,
And many a comrade came to clasp him in arms,
And eagerly they asked, and awesomely he told,
2495 Confessed all his cares and discomfitures many,
How it chanced at the Chapel, what cheer made the knight,
The love of the lady, the green lace at last.
The nick on his neck he naked displayed
That he got in his disgrace at the Green Knight's hands,
2500   alone.
    With rage in heart he speaks,
    And grieves with many a groan;
    The blood burns in his cheeks
    For shame at what must be shown.

2505 "Behold, sir," said he, and handles the belt,
"This is the blazon of the blemish that I bear on my neck;
This is the sign of sore loss that I have suffered there
For the cowardice and coveting that I came to there;
This is the badge of false faith that I was found in there,
2510 And I must bear it on my body till I breathe my last.
For one may keep a deed dark, but undo it no whit,
For where a fault is made fast, it is fixed evermore."
The king comforts the knight, and the court all together
Agree with gay laughter and gracious intent
2515 That the lords and the ladies belonging to the Table,
Each brother of that band, a baldric should have,
A belt borne oblique, of a bright green,
To be worn with one accord for that worthy's sake.

So that was taken as a token by the Table Round,
2520 And he honored that had it, evermore after,
As the best book of knighthood bids it be known.
In the old days of Arthur this happening befell;
The books of Brutus' deeds bear witness thereto
Since Brutus, the bold knight, embarked for this land
2525 After the siege ceased at Troy and the city fared
                        amiss.
                    Many such, ere we were born,
                    Have befallen here, ere this.
                    May He that was crowned with thorn
2530   Bring all men to His bliss! Amen.

Hony Soyt Qui Mal Pense[2]

2. "Shame be to the man who has evil in his mind." This is the motto of the Order of the Garter, founded ca. 1350: apparently a copyist of the poem associated this order with the one founded to honor Gawain.

GEOFFREY CHAUCER
ca. 1343–1400

Medieval social theory held that society was made up of three "estates": the nobility, composed of a small hereditary aristocracy, whose mission on earth was to rule over and defend the body politic; the church, whose duty was to look after the spiritual welfare of that body; and everyone else, the large mass of commoners who were supposed to do the work that provided for its physical needs. By the late fourteenth century, however, these basic categories were layered into complex, interrelated, and unstable social strata among which birth, wealth, profession, and personal ability all played a part in determining one's status in a world that was rapidly changing economically, politically, and socially. Chaucer's life and his works, especially *The Canterbury Tales*, were profoundly influenced by these forces. A growing and prosperous middle class was beginning to play increasingly important roles in church and state, blurring the traditional class boundaries, and it was into this middle class that Chaucer was born.

Chaucer was the son of a prosperous wine merchant and probably spent his boyhood in the mercantile atmosphere of London's Vintry, where ships docked with wines from France and Spain. Here he would have mixed daily with people of all sorts, heard several languages spoken, become fluent in French, and received schooling in Latin. Instead of apprenticing Chaucer to the family business, however, his father was apparently able to place him, in his early teens, as a page in one of the great aristocratic households of England, that of the countess of Ulster who was married to Prince Lionel, the second son of Edward III. There Chaucer would have acquired the manners and skills required for a career in the service of the ruling class, not only in the role of personal attendant in royal households but in a series of administrative posts.

We can trace Chaucer's official and personal life in a considerable number of surviving historical documents, beginning with a reference, in Elizabeth of Ulster's household accounts, to an outfit he received as a page (1357). He was captured by the French and ransomed in one of Edward III's campaigns during the Hundred Years

War (1359). He was a member of King Edward's personal household (1367) and took part in several diplomatic missions to Spain (1366), France (1368), and Italy (1372). As controller of customs on wool, sheepskins, and leather for the port of London (1374–85), Chaucer audited and kept books on the export taxes, which were one of the Crown's main sources of revenue. During this period he was living in a rent-free apartment over one of the gates in the city wall, probably as a perquisite of the customs job. He served as a justice of the peace and knight of the shire (the title given to members of Parliament) for the county of Kent (1385–86) where he moved after giving up the controllership. As clerk of the king's works (1389–91), Chaucer was responsible for the maintenance of numerous royal residences, parks, and other holdings; his duties included supervision of the construction of the nave of Westminster Abbey and of stands and lists for a celebrated tournament staged by Richard II. While the records show Chaucer receiving many grants and annuities in addition to his salary for these services, they also show that at times he was being pressed by creditors and obliged to borrow money.

These activities brought Chaucer into association with the ruling nobility of the kingdom, with Prince Lionel and his younger brother John of Gaunt, duke of Lancaster, England's most powerful baron during much of Chaucer's lifetime; with their father, King Edward; and with Edward's grandson, who succeeded to the throne as Richard II. Near the end of his life Chaucer addressed a comic *Complaint to His Purse* to Henry IV—John of Gaunt's son, who had usurped the crown from his cousin Richard—as a reminder that the treasury owed Chaucer his annuity. Chaucer's wife, Philippa, served in the households of Edward's queen and of John of Gaunt's second wife, Constance, daughter of the king of Castile. A Thomas Chaucer, who was probably Chaucer's son, was an eminent man in the next generation, and Thomas's daughter Alice was married successively to the earl of Salisbury and the duke of Suffolk. The gap between the commoners and the aristocracy would thus have been bridged by Chaucer's family in the course of three generations.

None of these documents contains any hint that this hardworking civil servant wrote poetry, although poetry would certainly have been among the diversions cultivated at English courts in Chaucer's youth. That poetry, however, would have been in French, which still remained the fashionable language and literature of the English aristocracy, whose culture in many ways had more in common with that of the French nobles with whom they warred than with that of their English subjects. Chaucer's earliest models, works by Guillaume de Machaut (1300?–1377) and Jean Froissart (1333?–1400?), the leading French poets of the day, were lyrics and narratives about courtly love, often cast in the form of a dream in which the poet acted as a protagonist or participant in some aristocratic love affair. The poetry of Machaut and Froissart derives from the thirteenth-century *Romance of the Rose*, a long dream allegory in which the dreamer suffers many agonies and trials for the love of a symbolic rosebud. Chaucer's apprentice work may well have been a partial translation of the twenty-one-thousand-line *Romance*. His first important original poem is *The Book of the Duchess*, an elegy in the form of a dream vision commemorating John of Gaunt's first wife, the young duchess of Lancaster, who died in 1368.

The diplomatic mission that sent Chaucer to Italy in 1372 was in all likelihood a milestone in his literary development. Although he may have acquired some knowledge of the language and literature from Italian merchants and bankers posted in London, this visit and a subsequent one to Florence (1378) brought him into direct contact with the Italian Renaissance. Probably he acquired manuscripts of works by Dante, Petrarch, and Boccaccio—the last two still alive at the time of Chaucer's visit, although he probably did not meet them. These writers provided him with models of new verse forms, new subject matter, and new modes of representation. *The House of Fame*, still a dream vision, takes the poet on a journey in the talons of a gigantic eagle to the celestial palace of the goddess Fame, a trip that at many points affectionately parodies Dante's journey in the *Divine Comedy*. In his dream vision *The*

Parliament of Fowls, all the birds meet on St. Valentine's Day to choose their mates; their "parliament" humorously depicts the ways in which different classes in human society think and talk about love. Boccaccio provided sources for two of Chaucer's finest poems—although Chaucer never mentions his name. *The Knight's Tale*, the first of *The Canterbury Tales*, is based on Boccaccio's romance *Il Teseida* (The Story of Theseus). His longest completed poem, *Troilus and Criseyde* (ca. 1385), which tells the story of how Trojan Prince Troilus loved and finally lost Criseyde to the Greek warrior Diomede, is an adaptation of Boccaccio's *Il Filostrato* (The Love-Stricken). Chaucer reworked the latter into one of the greatest love poems in any language. Even if he had never written *The Canterbury Tales*, *Troilus* would have secured Chaucer a place among the major English poets.

A final dream vision provides the frame for Chaucer's first experiment with a series of tales, the unfinished *Legend of Good Women*. In the dream, Chaucer is accused of heresy and antifeminism by Cupid, the god of love himself, and ordered to do penance by writing a series of "legends," i.e., saints' lives, of Cupid's martyrs, women who were betrayed by false men and died for love. Perhaps a noble patron, possibly Queen Anne, asked the poet to write something to make up for telling about Criseyde's betrayal of Troilus.

Throughout his life Chaucer also wrote moral and religious works, chiefly translations. Besides French, which was a second language for him, and Italian, Chaucer also read Latin. He made a prose translation of the Latin *Consolation of Philosophy*, written by the sixth-century Roman statesman Boethius while in prison awaiting execution for crimes for which he had been unjustly condemned. The *Consolation* became a favorite book for the Middle Ages, providing inspiration and comfort through its lesson that worldly fortune is deceitful and ephemeral and through the platonic doctrine that the body itself is only a prison house for the soul that aspires to eternal things. The influence of Boethius is deeply ingrained in *The Knight's Tale* and *Troilus*. The ballade *Truth* compresses the Boethian and Christian teaching into three stanzas of homely moral advice.

Thus long before Chaucer conceived of *The Canterbury Tales*, his writings were many faceted: they embrace prose and poetry; human and divine love; French, Italian, and Latin sources; secular and religious influences; comedy and philosophy. Moreover, different elements are likely to mix in the same work, often making it difficult to extract from Chaucer simple, direct, and certain meanings.

This Chaucerian complexity owes much to the wide range of Chaucer's learning and his exposure to new literary currents on the Continent but perhaps also to the special social position he occupied as a member of a new class of civil servants. Born into the urban middle class, Chaucer, through his association with the court and service of the Crown, had attained the rank of "esquire," roughly equivalent to what would later be termed a "gentleman." His career brought him into contact with overlapping bourgeois and aristocratic social worlds, without his being securely anchored in either. Although he was born a commoner and continued to associate with commoners in his official life, he did not live as a commoner; and although his training and service at court, his wife's connections, and probably his poetry brought him into contact with the nobility, he must always have been conscious of the fact that he did not really belong to that society of which birth alone could make one a true member. Situated at the intersection of these social worlds, Chaucer had the gift of being able to view with both sympathy and humor the behaviors, beliefs, and pretensions of the diverse people who comprised the levels of society. Chaucer's art of being at once involved in and detached from a given situation is peculiarly his own, but that art would have been appreciated by a small group of friends close to Chaucer's social position—men like Sir Philip de la Vache, to whom Chaucer addressed the humorous envoy to *Truth*. Chaucer belongs to an age when poetry was read aloud. A beautiful frontispiece to a manuscript of *Troilus* pictures the poet's public performance before a magnificently dressed royal audience, and he may well have been invited at times to read his poems at court. But besides addressing a listening audience, to whose allegedly superior taste and sensibility the poet often ironically defers (for example, *The General Prologue,* lines 745–48), Chaucer has in mind discriminating readers whom he might expect to share his sense of humor and his complex attitudes toward the company of "sondry folk" who make the pilgrimage to Canterbury.

The text given here is from E. T. Donaldson's *Chaucer's Poetry: An Anthology for the Modern Reader* (1958, 1975) with some modifications. For *The Canterbury Tales* the Hengwrt Manuscript has provided the textual basis. The spelling has been altered to improve consistency and has been modernized in so far as is possible without distorting the phonological values of the Middle English. A discussion of Middle English pronunciation, grammar, and prosody is included in the introduction to "The Middle Ages" (pp. 14–20).

The Canterbury Tales

Chaucer's original plan for *The Canterbury Tales*—if we assume it to be the same as that which the fictional Host proposes at the end of *The General Prologue*—projected about one hundred twenty stories, two for each pilgrim to tell on the way to Canterbury and two more on the way back. Chaucer actually completed only twenty-two and the beginnings of two others. He did write an ending, for the Host says to the Parson, who tells the last tale, that everyone except him has told "his tale." Indeed, the pilgrims never even get to Canterbury. The work was probably first conceived in 1386, when Chaucer was living in Greenwich, some miles east of London. From his house he might have been able to see the pilgrim road that led toward the shrine of the famous English saint, Thomas à Becket, the archbishop of Canterbury who was murdered in his cathedral in 1170. Medieval pilgrims were notorious tale tellers, and the sight and sound of the bands riding toward Canterbury may well have suggested to Chaucer the idea of using a fictitious pilgrimage as a framing device for a number of stories. Collections of stories linked by such a device were common in the later Middle Ages. Chaucer's contemporary John Gower had used one in his *Confessio Amantis.* The most famous medieval framing tale besides Chaucer's is Boccaccio's *Decameron,* in which ten different narrators each tell a tale a day for ten days. Chaucer could have known the *Decameron,* which contains tales with plots analogous to plots found also in *The Canterbury Tales,* but these stories were widespread, and there is no proof that Chaucer got them from Boccaccio.

Chaucer's artistic exploitation of the device is, in any case, altogether his own. Whereas in Gower a single speaker relates all the stories, and in Boccaccio the ten speakers—three young gentlemen and seven young ladies—all belong to the same sophisticated social elite, Chaucer's pilgrim narrators represent a wide spectrum of ranks and occupations. This device, however, should not be mistaken for "realism." It is highly unlikely that a group like Chaucer's pilgrims would ever have joined together and communicated on such seemingly equal terms. That is part of the fiction, as is the tacit assumption that a group so large could have ridden along listening to one another tell tales in verse. The variety of tellers is matched by the diversity of their tales: tales are assigned to appropriate narrators and juxtaposed to bring out contrasts in genre, style, tone, and values. Thus the Knight's courtly romance about the rivalry of two noble lovers for a lady is followed by the Miller's fabliau of the seduction of an old carpenter's young wife by a student. In several of *The Canterbury Tales* there is a fascinating accord between the narrators and their stories, so that the story takes on rich overtones from what we have learned of its teller in *The General Prologue* and elsewhere, and the character itself grows and is revealed by the story. Chaucer conducts two fictions simultaneously—that of the individual tale and that of the pilgrim to whom he has assigned it. He develops the second fiction not only through *The General Prologue* but also through the "links," the interchanges among pilgrims connecting the stories. These interchanges sometimes lead to quarrels. Thus *The Miller's Tale* offends the Reeve, who takes the figure of the Miller's foolish, cuckolded carpenter as directed personally at himself, and he retaliates with a story satirizing an arrogant miller very much like the pilgrim Miller. The antagonism of the two tellers provides comedy in the links and enhances the comedy of their tales. The links also offer interesting literary commentary on the tales by members of the pilgrim audience, especially the Host, whom the pilgrims have declared "governour" and "juge" of the storytelling. Further dramatic interest is created by the fact that several tales respond to topics taken up by previous tellers. The Wife of Bath's thesis that women should have sovereignty over men in marriage gets a reply from the Clerk, which in turn elicits responses from the Merchant and the Franklin. The tales have their own logic and interest quite apart from the framing fiction; no other medieval framing fiction, however, has such varied and lively interaction between the frame and the individual stories.

The composition of none of the tales can be accurately dated; most of them were written during the last fourteen years of Chaucer's life, although a few were probably written earlier and inserted into *The Canterbury Tales*. The popularity of the poem in late medieval England is attested by the number of surviving manuscripts: more than eighty, none from Chaucer's lifetime. It was also twice printed by William Caxton, who introduced printing to England in 1476, and often reprinted by Caxton's early successors. The manuscripts reflect the unfinished state of the poem—the fact that when he died Chaucer had not made up his mind about a number of details and hence left many inconsistencies. The poem appears in the manuscripts as nine or ten "fragments" or blocks of tales; the order of the poems within each fragment is generally the same, but the order of the fragments themselves varies widely. The fragment containing *The General Prologue;* the Knight's, Miller's, and Reeve's tales; and the Cook's unfinished tale, always comes first, and the fragment consisting of *The Parson's Tale* and *The Retraction* always comes last. But the others, such as that containing the Wife of Bath, the Friar, and the Summoner or that consisting of the Physician and Pardoner or the longest fragment, consisting of six tales concluding with the Nun's Priest's, are by no means stable in relation to one another. The order followed here, that of the Ellesmere manuscript, has been adopted as the most nearly satisfactory.

THE GENERAL PROLOGUE

Chaucer did not need to make a pilgrimage himself to meet the types of people that his fictitious pilgrimage includes, because most of them had long inhabited literature as well as life: the ideal Knight, who had taken part in all the major expeditions and battles of the crusades during the last half-century; his fashionably dressed son, the Squire, a typical young lover; the lady Prioress, the hunting Monk, and the flattering Friar, who practice the little vanities and larger vices for which such ecclesiastics were conventionally attacked; the prosperous Franklin; the fraudulent Doctor; the lusty and domineering Wife of Bath; the austere Parson; and so on down through the lower orders to that spellbinding preacher and mercenary, the Pardoner, peddling his paper indulgences and phony relics. One meets all these types throughout medieval literature, but particularly in a genre called estates satire, which sets out to expose and pillory typical examples of corruption at all levels of society. A remarkable number of details in *The General Prologue* could have been taken straight out of books as well as drawn from life. Although it has been argued that some of the pilgrims are portraits of actual people, the impression that they are drawn from life is more likely to be a function of Chaucer's art, which is able to endow types with a reality we generally associate only with people we know. The salient features of each pilgrim leap out randomly at the reader, as they might to an observer concerned only with what meets the eye. This imitation of the way our minds actually perceive reality may make us fail to notice the care with which Chaucer has selected his details to give an integrated sketch of the person being described. Most of these details give something more than mere verisimilitude to the description. The pilgrims' facial features, the clothes they wear, the foods they like to eat, the things they say, the work they do are all clues not only to their social rank but to their moral and spiritual condition and, through the accumulation of detail, to the condition of late-medieval society, of which, collectively, they are representative. What uniquely distinguishes Chaucer's prologue from more conventional estates satire, such as the *Prologue* to *Piers Plowman*, is the suppression in all but a few flagrant instances of overt moral judgment. The narrator, in fact, seems to be expressing chiefly admiration and praise at the superlative skills and accomplishments of this particular group, even such dubious ones as the Friar's begging techniques or the Manciple's success in cheating the learned lawyers who employ him. The reader is left free to draw out the ironic implications of details presented with such seeming artlessness, even while falling in with the easygoing mood of "felaweship" that pervades Chaucer's prologue to the pilgrimage.

FROM THE CANTERBURY TALES
The General Prologue

Whan that April with his° showres soote°   its / fresh
The droughte of March hath perced to the roote,
And bāthed every veine[1] in swich° licour,[2]   such / liquid
Of which vertu[2] engendred is the flowr;
5   Whan Zephyrus eek° with his sweete breeth   also
Inspired[3] hath in every holt° and heeth°   grove / field
The tendre croppes,° and the yonge sonne[4]   shoots
Hath in the Ram his halve cours yronne,
And smale fowles° maken melodye   birds
10 That sleepen al the night with open yë°—   eye
So priketh hem° Nature in hir corages°—   them
Thanne longen folk to goon° on pilgrimages,   go
And palmeres for to seeken straunge strondes
To ferne halwes,[6] couthe° in sondry° londes;   known / various
15 And specially from every shires ende
Of Engelond to Canterbury they wende,
The holy blisful martyr[7] for to seeke
That hem hath holpen° whan that they were seke.°   helped / sick
    Bifel° that in that seson on a day,   It happened
20 In Southwerk[8] at the Tabard as I lay,
Redy to wenden on my pilgrimage
To Canterbury with ful° devout corage,   very
At night was come into that hostelrye

1. I.e., in plants.
2. By the power of which.
3. Breathed into. "Zephyrus": the west wind.
4. The sun is young because it has run only half-way through its course in Aries, the Ram—the first sign of the zodiac in the solar year.
5. Their hearts.
6. Far-off shrines. "Palmeres": palmers, wide-ranging pilgrims—especially those who sought out the "straunge strondes" (foreign shores) of the Holy Land.
7. St. Thomas à Becket, murdered in Canterbury Cathedral in 1170.
8. Southwark, site of the Tabard Inn, was then a suburb of London, south of the Thames River.

neen
29

Wel nine and twenty in a compaignye
25 Of sondry folk, by aventure° yfalle *E-falla*   *chance*
    In felaweshipe, and pilgrimes were they alle *alla*
    That toward Canterbury wolden° ride. *reed-a*   *would*
    The chambres and the stables weren wide, *weed-a*
    And wel we weren esed° at the beste.[9] *a-sad*   *accommodated*
30 And shortly,° whan the sonne was to reste,[1]   *in brief*
    So hadde I spoken with hem everichoon°   *every one*
    That I was of hir felaweshipe anoon,°   *at once*
    And made forward[2] erly for to rise, *rees-a*
    To take oure way ther as[3] I you devise.°   *describe*
35   But nathelees,° whil I have time and space,[4]   *nevertheless*
    Er° that I ferther in this tale pace,°   *before/proceed*
    Me thinketh it accordant to resoun[5]
    To telle you al the condicioun
    Of eech of hem, so as it seemed me,
40 And whiche they were, and of what degree,°   *social rank*
    And eek° in what array that they were inne: *also*
    And at a knight thanne° wol I first biginne.   *then*
       A Knight ther was, and that a worthy man,
    That fro the time that he first bigan

he was viewed as valliant b/c he is preserving christianity

45 To riden out, he loved chivalrye,
    Trouthe and honour, freedom and curteisye.[6]
    Ful worthy was he in his lordes werre,°   *war*
    And therto hadde he riden, no man ferre,°   *farther*
    As wel in Cristendom as hethenesse,°   *heathen lands*
50 And[7] evere honoured for his worthinesse.
       At Alisandre[8] he was whan it was wonne;
    Ful ofte time he hadde the boord bigonne[9]
    Aboven alle nacions in Pruce;

he provided everything for himself

    In Lettou had he reised,° and in Ruce,   *campaigned*
55 No Cristen man so ofte of his degree;
    In Gernade° at the sege eek hadde he be   *Granada*
    Of Algezir, and riden in Belmarye;
    At Lyeis was he, and at Satalye,
    Whan they were wonne; and in the Grete See[1]
60 At many a noble arivee° hadde he be.   *military landing*
       At mortal batailes[2] hadde he been fifteene,
    And foughten for oure faith at Tramissene
    In listes[3] thries,° and ay° slain his fo.   *thrice/always*
       This ilke° worthy Knight hadde been also   *same*
65 Sometime with the lord of Palatye[4]

---

9. In the best possible way.
1. Had set.
2. I.e., (we) made an agreement.
3. Where.
4. I.e., opportunity.
5. It seems to me according to reason.
6. Courtesy. "Trouthe": integrity. "Freedom": generosity of spirit.
7. I.e., and he was.
8. The Knight has taken part in campaigns fought against three groups who threatened Christian Europe during the 14th century: the Moslems in the Near East, from whom Alexandria was seized

after a famous siege; the northern barbarians in Prussia, Lithuania, and Russia; and the Moors in North Africa. The place names in the following lines refer to battlegrounds in these continuing wars.
9. Sat in the seat of honor at military feasts.
1. The Mediterranean.
2. Tournaments fought to the death.
3. Lists, tournament grounds.
4. A Moslem: alliances of convenience were often made during the Crusades between Christians and Moslems.

[handwritten: he went straight to Canterbury]

Again° another hethen in Turkye; — *against*
And everemore he hadde a soverein pris.° — *reputation*
And though that he were worthy, he was wis,[5]
And of his port° as meeke as is a maide. — *demeanor*
[handwritten: he is gentle and honorable]

70 He nevere yit no vilainye° ne saide — *rudeness*
[handwritten: 3 neg.]
In al his lif unto no manere wight:[6]
He was a verray,° parfit,° gentil° knight. — *true/perfect/noble*
But for to tellen you of his array,
His hors° were goode, but he was nat gay.[7] — *horses*

75 Of fustian° he wered° a gipoun[8] — *thick cloth/wore*
Al bismotered with his haubergeoun,[9]
[handwritten: he wore humble clothes]
For he was late° come from his viage,° — *lately/expedition*
And wente for to doon his pilgrimage.

— With him ther was his sone, a yong Squier,[1]
80 A lovere and a lusty bacheler,
With lokkes crulle° as° they were laid in presse. — *curly/as if*
[handwritten: he is vain]
Of twenty yeer of age he was, I gesse.
[handwritten: and loves life, he is learning]
Of his stature he was of evene° lengthe, — *moderate*
And wonderly delivere,° and of greet° strengthe. — *agile/great*
[handwritten: ...ning]
85 And he hadde been som time in chivachye[2] *[handwritten: his from]*
In Flandres, in Artois, and Picardye, *[handwritten: he is father]*
And born him wel as of so litel space,[3] *[handwritten: courting]*
In hope to stonden in his lady° grace. — *lady's*
Embrouded° was he as it were a mede.[4] — *embroidered*
90 Al ful of fresshe flowres, white and rede;° — *red*
Singing he was, or floiting,° al the day: — *whistling*
He was as fressh as is the month of May.
Short was his gowne, with sleeves longe and wide.
Wel coude he sitte on hors, and faire ride;
95 He coude songes make, and wel endite,° — *compose verse*
Juste[5] and eek° daunce, and wel portraye° and write. — *also/sketch*
So hote° he loved that by nightertale[6] — *hotly*
He slepte namore than dooth a nightingale.
Curteis he was, lowely,° and servisable, — *humble*
[handwritten: he is a good man. he is learning to be a good knight]
100 And carf biforn his fader at the table.[7]
— A Yeman hadde he[8] and servants namo° — *no more*
At that time, for him liste[9] ride so;
And he[1] was clad in cote and hood of grene.
A sheef of pecok arwes,° bright and keene, — *arrows*
105 Under his belt he bar° ful thriftily;° — *bore/properly*
Wel coude he dresse° his takel° yemanly.[2] — *tend to/gear*
His arwes drouped nought with fetheres lowe.

5. I.e., he was wise as well as bold.
6. Any sort of person. In Middle English, negatives
are multiplied for emphasis, as in these two lines:
"nevere," "no," "ne," "no."
7. I.e., gaily dressed.
8. Tunic worn underneath the coat of mail.
9. All rust-stained from his hauberk (coat of mail).
1. The vague term "Squier" (Squire) here seems
to be the equivalent of "bacheler" (line 80), a
young knight still in the service of an older one.
2. On cavalry expeditions. The places in the next
line are sites of skirmishes in the constant warfare
between the English and the French.

3. I.e., considering the little time he had been in
service.
4. Mead, meadow.
5. Joust, fight in a tournament.
6. At night.
7. It was a squire's duty to carve his lord's meat.
8. I.e., the Knight. The "Yeman" (Yeoman) is an
independent commoner who acts as the Knight's
military servant.
9. It pleased him to.
1. I.e., the Yeoman.
2. In a workmanlike way.

And in his hand he bar a mighty bowe.
A not-heed° hadde he with a brown visage.   *close-cut head*
110 Of wodecraft wel coude° he al the usage.   *knew*
Upon his arm he bar a gay bracer,[3]
And by his side a swerd° and a bokeler,[4]   *sword*
And on that other side a gay daggere,
Harneised° wel and sharp as point of spere;   *mounted*
115 A Cristophre[5] on his brest of silver sheene;°   *bright*
An horn he bar, the baudrik[6] was of greene.
A forster° was he soothly,° as I gesse.   *forester / truly*

Ther was also a Nonne, a Prioresse,
That of hir smiling was ful simple and coy.[7]
120 Hir gretteste ooth was but by sainte Loy!°   *Eloi*
And she was cleped° Madame Eglantine.   *named*
Ful wel she soong° the service divine,   *sang*
Entuned° in hir nose ful semely;[8]   *chanted*
And Frenssh she spak ful faire and fetisly,°   *elegantly*
125 After the scole° of Stratford at the Bowe[9]—   *school*
For Frenssh of Paris was to hire unknowe.
At mete° wel ytaught was she withalle:°   *meals / besides*
She leet° no morsel from hir lippes falle,   *let*
Ne wette hir fingres in hir sauce deepe;
130 Wel coude she carye a morsel, and wel keepe°   *take care*
That no drope ne fille° upon hir brest.   *should fall*
In curteisye was set ful muchel hir lest.[1]
Hir over-lippe° wiped she so clene   *upper lip*
That in hir coppe° ther was no ferthing° seene   *cup / bit*
135 Of grece,° whan she dronken hadde hir draughte;   *grease*
Ful semely after hir mete she raughte.°   *reached*
And sikerly° she was of greet disport,[2]   *certainly*
And ful plesant, and amiable of port,°   *mien*
And pained hire to countrefete cheere[3]
140 Of court, and to been statlich° of manere,   *dignified*
And to been holden digne[4] of reverence.
But, for to speken of hir conscience,
She was so charitable and so pitous°   *merciful*
She wolde weepe if that she saw a mous
145 Caught in a trappe, if it were deed° or bledde.   *dead*
Of[5] smale houndes hadde she that she fedde
With rosted flessh, or milk and wastelbreed;°   *fine white bread*
But sore wepte she if oon of hem were deed,
Or if men smoot it with a yerde smerte;[6]
150 And al was conscience and tendre herte.
Ful semely hir wimpel° pinched° was,   *headdress / pleated*
Hir nose tretis,° hir yën° greye as glas,   *well-formed / eyes*

---

3. Wrist guard for archers.
4. Buckler (a small shield).
5. St. Christopher medal.
6. Baldric (a supporting strap).
7. Sincere and shy. The Prioress is the mother superior of her nunnery.
8. In a seemly, proper manner.
9. The French learned in a convent school in Stratford-at-the-Bow, a suburb of London, was evidently not up to the Parisian standard.
1. I.e., her chief delight lay in good manners.
2. Of great good cheer.
3. And took pains to imitate the behavior.
4. And to be considered worthy.
5. I.e., some.
6. If someone struck it with a rod sharply.

Hir mouth ful smal, and therto° softe and reed,° *moreover / red*
But sikerly° she hadde a fair forheed: *certainly*
155 It was almost a spanne brood,[7] I trowe,° *believe*
For hardily,° she was nat undergrowe. *assuredly*
Ful fetis° was hir cloke, as I was war;° *becoming / aware*
Of smal° coral aboute hir arm she bar *dainty*
A paire of bedes, gauded all with greene,[3]
160 And theron heeng° a brooch of gold ful sheene,° *hung / bright*
On which ther was first writen a crowned A,[9]
And after, *Amor vincit omnia.*[1]
　Another Nonne with hire hadde she
That was hir chapelaine,° and preestes three.[2] *secretary*
165 　A Monk ther was, a fair for the maistrye,[3]
An outridere[4] that loved venerye,° *hunting*
A manly man, to been an abbot able.° *worthy*
Ful many a daintee° hors hadde he in stable, *fine*
And whan he rood,° men mighte his bridel heere *rode*
170 Ginglen° in a whistling wind as clere *jingle*
And eek° as loude as dooth the chapel belle *also*
Ther as this lord was kepere of the celle.[5]
The rule of Saint Maure or of Saint Beneit,
By cause that it was old and somdeel strait[6]—
175 This ilke° Monk leet olde thinges pace,° *same / pass away*
And heeld° after the newe world the space.° *held / course*
He yaf° nought of that text a pulled hen[7] *gave*
That saith that hunteres been° nought holy men, *are*
Ne that a monk, whan he is recchelees,[8]
180 Is likned til° a fissh that is waterlees— *to*
This is to sayn, a monk out of his cloistre:
But thilke° text heeld he nat worth an oystre. *that same*
And I saide his opinion was good:
What° sholde he studye and make himselven wood° *why / crazy*
185 Upon a book in cloistre alway to poure,° *pore*
Or swinke° with his handes and laboure, *work*
As Austin bit?[9] How shal the world be served?
Lat Austin have his swink to him reserved!
Therefore he was a prikasour° aright. *hard rider*
190 Grehoundes he hadde as swift as fowl in flight.
Of priking° and of hunting for the hare *riding*
Was al his lust,° for no cost wolde he spare. *pleasure*
I sawgh his sleeves purfiled° at the hand *fur lined*
With gris,° and that the fineste of a land; *gray fur*
195 And for to festne his hood under his chin
He hadde of gold wrought a ful curious[1] pin:

7. A handsbreadth wide.
8. Provided with green beads to mark certain prayers. "A paire": string (i.e., a rosary).
9. An *A* with an ornamental crown on it.
1. "Love conquers all."
2. The three get reduced to just one nun's priest.
3. I.e., a superlatively fine one.
4. A monk charged with supervising property distant from the monastery. Monasteries obtained income from large landholdings.
5. Prior of an outlying cell (branch) of the monastery.
6. Somewhat strict. St. Maurus and St. Benedict were authors of monastic rules.
7. He didn't give a plucked hen for that text.
8. Reckless, careless of rule.
9. I.e., as St. Augustine bids. St. Augustine had written that monks should perform manual labor.
1. Of careful workmanship.

A love-knotte in the grettere° ende ther was. *greater*

His heed was balled,° that shoon as any glas, *bald*

And eek his face, as he hadde been anoint:

200 He was a lord ful fat and in good point;[2]

His yën steepe,° and rolling in his heed, *protruding*

That stemed as a furnais of a leed,[3]

His bootes souple,° his hors in greet estat° *supple / condition*

Now certainly he was a fair prelat.[4]

205 He was nat pale as a forpined° gost: *wasted away*

A fat swan loved he best of any rost.

His palfrey° was as brown as is a berye. *saddle horse*

— A Frere ther was, a wantoune° and a merye, *jovial*

A limitour,[5] a ful solempne° man. *ceremonious*

210 In alle the ordres foure is noon that can° *knows*

So muche of daliaunce° and fair langage: *sociability*

He hadde maad ful many a mariage

Of yonge wommen at his owene cost;

Unto his ordre he was a noble post.[6]

215 Ful wel biloved and familier was he

With frankelains over al[7] in his contree,

And with worthy wommen of the town—

For he hadde power of confessioun,

As saide himself, more than a curat,° *parish priest*

220 For of° his ordre he was licenciat.[8] *by*

Ful swetely herde he confessioun,

And plesant was his absolucioun.

He was an esy man to yive penaunce

Ther as he wiste to have[9] a good pitaunce;° *donation*

225 For unto a poore ordre for to yive

Is signe that a man is wel yshrive,[1]

For if he yaf, he dorste make avaunt° *boast*

He wiste° that a man was repentaunt; *knew*

For many a man so hard is of his herte

230 He may nat weepe though him sore smerte:[2]

Therfore, in stede of weeping and prayeres,

Men mote° yive silver to the poore freres.[3] *may*

His tipet° was ay farsed° ful of knives *hood / stuffed*

And pinnes, for to yiven faire wives;

235 And certainly he hadde a merye note;

Wel coude he singe and playen on a rote;° *fiddle*

Of yeddinges he bar outrely the pris.[4]

His nekke whit was as the flowr-de-lis;° *lily*

Therto he strong was as a champioun.

---

2. In good shape, plump.

3. That glowed like a furnace with a pot in it.

4. Prelate (an important churchman).

5. The "Frere" (Friar) is a member of one of the four religious orders whose members live by begging; as a "limitour" he has been granted by his order exclusive begging rights within a certain limited area.

6. I.e., pillar, a staunch supporter.

7. I.e., with franklins everywhere. Franklins were well-to-do country men.

8. I.e., licensed to hear confessions.

9. Where he knew he would have.

1. Shriven, absolved.

2. Although he is sorely grieved.

3. Before granting absolution, the confessor must be sure the sinner is contrite; moreover, the absolution is contingent on the sinner's performance of an act of satisfaction. In the case of Chaucer's Friar, a liberal contribution served both as proof of contrition and as satisfaction.

4. He absolutely took the prize for ballads.

240　He knew the tavernes wel in every town,
　　And every hostiler° and tappestere,°　　　　　　　　　*innkeeper/barmaid*
　　Bet° than a lazar or a beggestere.⁵　　　　　　　　　*better*
　　For unto swich a worthy man as he
　　Accorded nat, as by his facultee,⁶
245　To have with sike° lazars aquaintaunce:　　　　　　　*sick*
　　It is nat honeste,° it may' nought avaunce,°　　　　　*dignified/profit*
　　For to delen with no swich poraile,⁷
　　But al with riche, and selleres of vitaile;°　　　　　*foodstuffs*
　　And over al ther as⁸ profit sholde arise,
250　Curteis he was, and lowely of servise.
　　Ther was no man nowher so vertuous:°　　　　　　　*effective*
　　He was the beste beggere in his hous.°　　　　　　　*friary*
　　And yaf a certain ferme for the graunt:°
　　Noon of his bretheren cam ther in his haunt.¹
255　For though a widwe° hadde nought a sho,°　　　　　*widow/shoe*
　　So plesant was his *In principio*²
　　Yit wolde he have a ferthing° er he wente;°　　　　　*small coin*
　　His purchas was wel bettre than his rente.³
　　And rage he coude as it were right a whelpe;⁴
260　In love-dayes⁵ ther coude he muchel° helpe,　　　　*much*
　　For ther he was nat lik a cloisterer,
　　With a thredbare cope, as is a poore scoler,
　　But he was lik a maister⁶ or a pope.
　　Of double worstede was his semicope,°　　　　　　　*short robe*
265　And rounded as a belle out of the presse.°　　　　　*bell mold*
　　Somwhat he lipsed° for his wantounesse°　　　　　　*lisped/affectation*
　　To make his Englissh sweete upon his tonge;
　　And in his harping, whan he hadde songe,°　　　　　*sung*
　　His yën twinkled in his heed aright
270　As doon the sterres° in the frosty night.　　　　　*stars*
　　This worthy limitour was cleped Huberd.
　　　　A Marchant was ther with a forked beerd,
　　In motelee,⁷ and hye on hors he sat,
　　Upon his heed a Flandrissh° bevere hat,　　　　　　*Flemish*
275　His bootes clasped faire and fetisly.°　　　　　　　*elegantly*
　　His resons° he spak ful solempnely,　　　　　　　　*opinions*
　　Souning° alway th' encrees of his winning.°　　　　*implying/profit*
　　He wolde the see were kept for any thing⁸
　　Bitwixen Middelburgh and Orewelle.
280　Wel coude he in eschaunge sheeldes⁹ selle.

---

5. "Beggestere": female beggar. "Lazar:" leper.
6. It was not suitable because of his position.
7. I.e., poor trash. The oldest order of friars had been founded by St. Francis to administer to the spiritual needs of precisely those classes the Friar avoids.
8. Everywhere.
9. And he paid a certain rent for the privilege of begging.
1. Assigned territory.
2. A friar's usual salutation: "In the beginning [was the Word]" (John 1.1).
3. I.e., the money he got through such activity was more than his proper income.

4. And he could flirt wantonly, as if he were a puppy.
5. Days appointed for the settlement of lawsuits out of court.
6. A man of recognized learning.
7. Motley, a cloth of mixed color.
8. I.e., he wished the sea to be guarded at all costs. The sea route between Middelburgh (in the Netherlands) and Orwell (in Suffolk) was vital to the Merchant's export and import of wool—the basis of England's chief trade at the time.
9. Shields were units of transfer in international credit, which he exchanged at a profit.

This worthy man ful wel his wit bisette:°   *employed*
Ther wiste° no wight° that he was in dette,   *knew/person*
So statly° was he of his governaunce,[1]   *dignified*
With his bargaines,° and with his chevissaunce.° *bargainings/borrowing*
285 Forsoothe° he was a worthy man withalle;   *in truth*
But, sooth to sayn, I noot° how men him calle.   *don't know*
   A Clerk[2] ther was of Oxenforde also
That unto logik hadde longe ygo.[3]
As lene was his hors as is a rake,
290 And he was nought right fat, I undertake,
But looked holwe,° and therto sobrely.   *hollow*
Ful thredbare was his overeste courtepy,
For he hadde geten him yit no benefice,[4]
Ne was so worldly for to have office.°   *secular employment*
295 For him was levere[5] have at his beddes heed
Twenty bookes, clad in blak or reed,
Of Aristotle and his philosophye,
Than robes riche, or fithele,° or gay sautrye.[6]   *fiddle*
But al be that he was a philosophre[7]
300 Yit hadde he but litel gold in cofre;°   *coffer*
But al that he mighte of his freendes hente,°   *take*
On bookes and on lerning he it spente,
And bisily gan for the soules praye
Of hem that yaf him wherwith to scoleye.°   *study*
305 Of studye took he most cure° and most heede.   *care*
Nought oo° word spak he more than was neede,   *one*
And that was said in forme[8] and reverence,
And short and quik,° and ful of heigh sentence:[9]   *lively*
Souning° in moral vertu was his speeche,   *resounding*
310 And gladly wolde he lerne, and gladly teche.
   A Sergeant of the Lawe, war and wis,[1]
That often hadde been at the Parvis[2]
Ther was also, ful riche of excellence.
Discreet he was, and of greet reverence—
315 He seemed swich, his wordes weren so wise.
Justice he was ful often in assise°   *circuit courts*
By patente[3] and by plein° commissioun.   *full*
For his science° and for his heigh renown   *knowledge*
Of fees and robes hadde he many oon.
320 So greet a purchasour° was nowher noon;   *speculator in land*
Al was fee simple[4] to him in effect—
His purchasing mighte nat been infect.[5]

---

1. The management of his affairs.
2. The Clerk is a student at Oxford; to become a student, he would have had to signify his intention of becoming a cleric, but he was not bound to proceed to a position of responsibility in the church.
3. Who had long since matriculated in philosophy.
4. Ecclesiastical living, such as the income a parish priest receives. "Courtepy": outer cloak.
5. He would rather.
6. Psaltery (a kind of harp).
7. The word may also mean alchemist, someone who tries to turn base metals into gold. The Clerk's

"philosophy" does not pay either way.
8. With decorum.
9. Elevated thought.
1. Wary and wise. The Sergeant is not only a practicing lawyer but one of the high justices of the nation.
2. The Paradise, the porch of St. Paul's Cathedral, a meeting place for lawyers and their clients.
3. Royal warrant.
4. Owned outright without legal impediments.
5. Invalidated on a legal technicality.

Nowher so bisy a man as he ther nas;°   *was not*
And yit he seemed bisier than he was.
325   In termes hadde he caas and doomes⁶ alle
That from the time of King William⁷ were falle.
Therto he coude endite and make a thing,⁸
Ther coude no wight pinchen° at his writing;   *cavil*
And every statut coude° he plein° by rote.⁹   *knew/entire*
330   He rood but hoomly° in a medlee cote,¹   *unpretentiously*
Girt with a ceint° of silk, with barres² smale.   *belt*
Of his array telle I no lenger tale.
    A Frankelain³ was in his compaignye:
Whit was his beerd as is the dayesye;°   *daisy*
335   Of his complexion he was sanguin.⁴
Wel loved he by the morwe a sop in win.⁵
To liven in delit° was evere his wone,°   *sensual delight/wont*
For he was Epicurus⁶ owene sone,
That heeld opinion that plein° delit   *full*
340   Was verray° felicitee parfit.°   *true/perfect*
An housholdere and that a greet was he:
Saint Julian⁷ he was in his contree.
His breed, his ale, was always after oon;⁸
A bettre envined° man was nevere noon.   *wine-stocked*
345   Withouten bake mete was nevere his hous,
Of fissh and flessh, and that so plentevous°   *plenteous*
It snewed° in his hous of mete° and drinke,   *snowed/food*
Of alle daintees that men coude thinke.
After° the sondry sesons of the yeer   *according to*
350   So chaunged he his mete° and his soper.°   *dinner/supper*
Ful many a fat partrich hadde he in mewe,°   *cage*
And many a breem,° and many a luce° in stewe.⁹   *carp/pike*
Wo was his cook but if his sauce were
Poinant° and sharp, and redy all his gere.   *spicy*
355   His table dormant in his halle alway
Stood redy covered all the longe day.¹
At sessions ther was he lord and sire.
Ful ofte time he was Knight of the Shire.²
An anlaas° and a gipser° al of silk   *dagger/purse*
360   Heeng at his girdel,³ whit as morne° milk.   *morning*
A shirreve° hadde he been, and countour.⁴   *sheriff*
Was nowhere swich a worthy vavasour.⁵

---

6. Law cases and decisions. "By termes": i.e., by heart.
7. I.e., the Conqueror (reigned 1066–87).
8. Compose and draw up a deed.
9. By heart.
1. A coat of mixed color.
2. Transverse stripes.
3. The "Frankelain" (Franklin) is a prosperous country man, whose lower-class ancestry is no impediment to the importance he has attained in his county.
4. A reference to the fact that the Franklin's temperament, "humor," is dominated by blood as well as to his red face (see p. 225, n.8).
5. I.e., in the morning he was very fond of a piece of bread soaked in wine.

6. The Greek philosopher whose teaching is popularly believed to make pleasure the chief goal of life.
7. The patron saint of hospitality.
8. Always of the same high quality.
9. Fishpond.
1. Tables were usually dismounted when not in use, but the Franklin kept his mounted and set ("covered"), hence "dormant."
2. County representative in Parliament. "Sessions": i.e., sessions of the justices of the peace.
3. Hung at his belt.
4. Auditor of county finances.
5. Feudal landholder of lowest rank; a provincial gentleman.

An Haberdasshere and a Carpenter,
A Webbe,° a Dyere, and a Tapicer°—   *weaver/tapestry maker*
365 And they were clothed alle in oo liveree[6]
Of a solempne and greet fraternitee.
Ful fresshe and newe hir gere apiked° was;   *trimmed*
Hir knives were chaped° nought with bras,   *mounted*
But al with silver; wrought ful clene and weel
370 Hir girdles and hir pouches everydeel.°   *altogether*
Wel seemed eech of hem a fair burgeis°   *burgher*
To sitten in a yeldehalle° on a dais.   *guildhall*
Everich, for the wisdom that he can,[7]
Was shaply° for to been an alderman.   *suitable*
375 For catel° hadde they ynough and rente,°   *property/income*
And eek hir wives wolde it wel assente—
And elles certain were they to blame:
It is ful fair to been ycleped° "Madame,"   *called*
And goon to vigilies all bifore,[8]
380 And have a mantel royalliche ybore.[9]
A Cook they hadde with hem for the nones,[1]
To boile the chiknes with the marybones,°   *marrowbones*
And powdre-marchant tart and galingale.[2]
Wel coude he knowe° a draughte of London ale.   *recognize*
385 He coude roste, and seethe,° and broile, and frye,   *boil*
Maken mortreux,° and wel bake a pie.   *stews*
But greet harm was it, as it thoughte° me,   *seemed to*
That on his shine a mormal° hadde he,   *ulcer*
For blankmanger,[3] that made he with the beste.
390 A Shipman was ther, woning° fer by weste—°   *dwelling/in the west*
For ought I woot,° he was of Dertemouthe.[4]   *know*

he is a pirate

He rood upon a rouncy° as he couthe,[5]   *large nag*
In a gowne of falding° to the knee.   *heavy wool*
A daggere hanging on a laas° hadde he   *strap*
395 Aboute his nekke, under his arm adown.
The hote somer hadde maad his hewe° al brown;   *color*
And certainly he was a good felawe. *sarcastic*

stole things

Ful many a draughte of win hadde he drawe[6]
Fro Burdeuxward, whil that the chapman sleep:[7]
400 Of nice° conscience took he no keep;°   *fastidious/heed*

ne killed his prisoners

If that he faught and hadde the hyer° hand,   *upper*
By water he sente hem hoom to every land.[8]
But of his craft, to rekene wel his tides,
His stremes° and his daungers° him bisides,[9]   *currents/hazards*
405 His herberwe° and his moone, his lodemenage,[1]   *anchorage*

---

6. In one livery, i.e., the uniform of their "frater-nitee" or guild, a partly religious, partly social organization.
7. Was capable of.
8. I.e., at the head of the procession. "Vigiles": feasts held on the eve of saints' days.
9. Royally carried.
1. For the occasion.
2. "Powdre-marchant" and "galingale" are flavoring materials.

3. A white stew or mousse.
4. Dartmouth, a port in the southwest of England.
5. As best he could.
6. Drawn, i.e., stolen.
7. Merchant slept. "Fro Burdeuxward": from Bordeaux; i.e., while carrying wine from Bordeaux (the wine center of France).
8. He drowned his prisoners.
9. Around him.
1. Pilotage, art of navigation.

There was noon swich from Hulle to Cartage.[2]
Hardy he was and wis to undertake;[3]
With many a tempest hadde his beerd been shake;
He knew alle the havenes° as they were   *harbors*
410   Fro Gotlond to the Cape of Finistere,[4]
And every crike° in Britaine° and in Spaine.   *inlet/Brittany*
His barge ycleped was the Maudelaine.°   *Magdalene*
—   With us ther was a Doctour of Physik:°   *medicine*
In al this world ne was ther noon him lik
415   To speken of physik and of surgerye.
For° he was grounded in astronomye,°   *because/astrology*
He kepte° his pacient a ful greet deel[5]   *tended to*
In houres by his magik naturel.[6]
Wel coude he fortunen the ascendent
420   Of his images[7] for his pacient.
He knew the cause of every maladye,
Were it of hoot or cold or moiste or drye,
And where engendred and of what humour:[8]
He was a verray parfit praktisour.[9]
425   The cause yknowe,° and of his° harm the roote,   *known/its*
Anoon he yaf the sike man his boote.°   *remedy*
Ful redy hadde he his apothecaries
To senden him drogges° and his letuaries,°   *drugs/medicines*
For eech of hem made other for to winne:
430   Hir frendshipe was nought newe to biginne.
Wel knew he the olde Esculapius,[1]
And Deiscorides and eek Rufus,
Olde Ipocras, Hali, and Galien,
Serapion, Razis, and Avicen,
435   Averrois, Damascien, and Constantin,
Bernard, and Gatesden, and Gilbertin.
Of his diete mesurable° was he,   *moderate*
For it was of no superfluitee,
But of greet norissing° and digestible.   *nourishment*
440   His studye was but litel on the Bible.
In sanguin° and in pers° he clad was al,   *blood red/blue*
Lined with taffata and with sendal;°   *silk*
And yit he was but esy of dispence;°   *expenditure*

2. From Hull (in northern England) to Cartagena (in Spain).
3. Shrewd in his undertakings.
4. From Gotland (an island in the Baltic) to Finisterre (the westernmost point in Spain).
5. Closely.
6. Natural—as opposed to black—magic. "In houres": i.e., the astrologically important hours (when conjunctions of the planets might help his recovery).
7. Assign the propitious time, according to the position of stars, for using talismanic images. Such images, representing either the patient himself or points in the zodiac, were thought to be influential on the course of the disease.
8. Diseases were thought to be caused by a disturbance of one or another of the four bodily "humors," each of which, like the four elements, was a compound of two of the elementary qualities

mentioned in line 422: the melancholy humor, seated in the black bile, was cold and dry (like earth); the sanguine, seated in the blood, hot and moist (like air); the choleric, seated in the yellow bile, hot and dry (like fire); the phlegmatic, seated in the phlegm, cold and moist (like water).
9. True perfect practitioner.
1. The Doctor is familiar with the treatises that the Middle Ages attributed to the "great names" of medical history, whom Chaucer names: the purely legendary Greek demigod Aesculapius; the Greeks Dioscorides, Rufus, Hippocrates, Galen, and Serapion; the Persians Hali and Rhazes; the Arabians Avicenna and Averroës; the early Christians John (?) of Damascus and Constantine Afer; the Scotsman Bernard Gordon; the Englishmen John of Gatesden and Gilbert, the former an early contemporary of Chaucer.

He kepte that he wan in pestilence.[2]
445 For° gold in physik is a cordial,[3]   *because*
Therfore he loved gold in special.
   A good Wif was ther of biside Bathe,
But she was somdeel deef,° and that was scathe.°   *a bit deaf/a pity*
Of cloth-making she hadde swich an haunt,°   *skill*
450 She passed° hem of Ypres and of Gaunt.[4]   *surpassed*
In al the parissh wif ne was ther noon
That to the offring[5] bifore hire sholde goon,
And if ther dide, certain so wroth° was she   *angry*
That she was out of alle charitee.
455 Hir coverchiefs° ful fine were of ground°—   *headcovers/texture*
I dorste° swere they weyeden° ten pound   *dare/weighed*
That on a Sonday weren° upon hir heed.   *were*
Hir hosen° weren of fin scarlet reed,°   *leggings/red*
Ful straite yteyd,[6] and shoes ful moiste° and newe.   *supple*
460 Bold was hir face and fair and reed of hewe.
She was a worthy womman al hir live:
Housbondes at chirche dore[7] she hadde five,
Withouten° other compaignye in youthe—   *not counting*
But therof needeth nought to speke as nouthe.°   *now*
465 And thries hadde she been at Jerusalem;
She hadde passed many a straunge° streem;   *foreign*
At Rome she hadde been, and at Boloigne,
In Galice at Saint Jame, and at Coloigne:[8]
She coude° muchel of wandring by the waye: *knew*
470 Gat-toothed[9] was she, soothly for to saye.
Upon an amblere[1] esily she sat,
Ywimpled° wel, and on hir heed an hat   *veiled*
As brood as is a bokeler or a targe,[2]
A foot-mantel° aboute hir hipes large,   *riding skirt*
475 And on hir feet a paire of spores° sharpe.   *spurs*
In felaweshipe wel coude she laughe and carpe:°   *talk*
Of remedies of love she knew parchaunce,°   *as it happened*
For she coude of that art the olde daunce.[3]
   A good man was ther of religioun,
480 And was a poore Person° of a town,   *parson*
But riche he was of holy thought and werk.
He was also a lerned man, a clerk,
That Cristes gospel trewely° wolde preche;   *faithfully*
His parisshens° devoutly wolde he teche.   *parishioners*
485 Benigne he was, and wonder° diligent,   *wonderfully*
And in adversitee ful pacient,

---

2. He saved the money he made during the plague time.
3. A stimulant. Gold was thought to have some medicinal properties.
4. Ypres and Ghent ("Gaunt") were Flemish cloth-making centers.
5. The offering in church, when the congregation brought its gifts forward.
6. Tightly laced.
7. In medieval times, weddings were performed at the church door.
8. Rome, Boulogne (in France), St. James (of Compostella) in Galicia (Spain), and Cologne (in Germany) were all sites of shrines much visited by pilgrims.
9. Gap-toothed, thought to be a sign of amorousness.
1. Horse with an easy gait.
2. "Bokeler" and "targe": small shields.
3. I.e., she knew all the tricks of that trade.

[Handwritten marginalia: "if she made this she wouldn't be able to travel, she is probably a business woman." / "she likes to be the center of attention" / "she dresses very well vain" / "5 husbands" / "even though she isn't perfect, he likes her, she isn't false" / "she rode stradled" / "he was devout, taught others, had patience"]

And swich he was preved° ofte sithes.°   *he would* proved/times
Ful loth were him to cursen for his tithes,[4]   *excommunicate people.*
But rather wolde he yiven, out of doute,[5]
490   Unto his poore parisshens aboute
Of his offring[6] and eek of his substaunce:°   *he would give people money* property
He coude in litel thing have suffisaunce.°   *sufficiency*
Wid was his parissh, and houses fer asonder,
But he ne lafte° nought for rain ne thonder,   neglected
495   In siknesse nor in meschief,° to visite   misfortune
The ferreste° in his parissh, muche and lite,[7]   farthest
Upon his feet, and in his hand a staf.
This noble ensample° to his sheep he yaf   example
That first he wroughte,[8] and afterward he taughte.   *practice*
500   Out of the Gospel he tho° wordes caughte,°   *what you preach* those/took
And this figure° he added eek therto: metaphor
That if gold ruste, what shal iren do?
For if a preest be foul, on whom we truste,
No wonder is a lewed° man to ruste.   *if the holy* uneducated
505   And shame it is, if a preest take keep,°   *don't set the* heed
A shiten° shepherde and a clene sheep.   *example, what* befouled
Wel oughte a preest ensample for to yive   *will the commoners do.*
By his clennesse how that his sheep sholde live.
He sette nought his benefice[9] to hire
510   And leet° his sheep encombred in the mire   left
And ran to London, unto Sainte Poules,[1]
To seeken him a chaunterye[2] for soules,
Or with a bretherhede to been withholde,[3]
But dwelte at hoom and kepte wel his folde,
515   So that the wolf ne made it nought miscarye:
He was a shepherde and nought a mercenarye.
And though he holy were and vertuous,
He was to sinful men nought despitous,°   scornful
Ne of his speeche daungerous° ne digne,°   disdainful/haughty
520   But in his teching discreet and benigne,
To drawen folk to hevene by fairnesse
By good ensample—this was his bisinesse.
But it° were any persone obstinat,   if there
What so he were, of heigh or lowe estat,
525   Him wolde he snibben° sharply for the nones:[4]   scold
A bettre preest I trowe° ther nowher noon is.   believe
He waited after[5] no pompe and reverence,
Ne maked him a spiced conscience,[6]

4. He would be most reluctant to invoke excommunication in order to collect his tithes.
5. Without doubt.
6. The offering made by the congregation of his church was at the Parson's disposal.
7. Great and small.
8. I.e., he practiced what he preached.
9. I.e., his parish. A priest might rent his parish to another and take a more profitable position.
1. St. Paul's Cathedral.
2. Chantry, i.e., a foundation that employed

priests for the sole duty of saying masses for the souls of wealthy persons. St. Paul's had many of them.
3. Or to be employed by a brotherhood; i.e., to take a lucrative and fairly easy position as chaplain with a parish guild (see p. 224, 1st n. 6).
4. On the spot, promptly.
5. I.e., expected.
6. Nor did he assume an overfastidious conscience, a holier-than-thou attitude.

But Cristes lore° and his Apostles twelve   *teaching*
530   He taughte, but first he folwed it himselve.
     With him ther was a Plowman, was his brother,
  That hadde ylad° of dong° ful many a fother.[7]   *carried / dung*
  A trewe swinkere° and a good was he,   *worker*
  Living in pees° and parfit charitee.   *peace*
535   God loved he best with al his hoole° herte   *whole*
  At alle times, though him gamed or smerte,[8]
  And thanne his neighebor right as himselve.
  He wolde thresshe, and therto dike° and delve,°   *work hard / dig*
  For Cristes sake, for every poore wight,
540   Withouten hire, if it laye in his might.
  His tithes payed he ful faire and wel,
  Bothe of his propre swink[9] and his catel.°   *property*
  In a tabard° he rood upon a mere.°   *workman's smock / mare*
     Ther was also a Reeve° and a Millere,   *estate manager*
545   A Somnour, and a Pardoner[1] also,
  A Manciple,° and myself—ther were namo.   *steward*
     The Millere was a stout carl° for the nones.   *fellow*
  Ful big he was of brawn° and eek of bones—   *muscle*
  That preved[2] wel, for overal ther he cam
550   At wrastling he wolde have alway the ram.[3]
  He was short-shuldred, brood,° a thikke knarre.[4]   *broad*
  Ther was no dore that he nolde heve of harre,[5]
  Or breke it at a renning° with his heed.°   *running / head*
  His beerd as any sowe or fox was reed,°   *red*
555   And therto brood, as though it were a spade;
  Upon the cop right[6] of his nose he hade
  <u>A werte,° and theron stood a tuft of heres,</u>   *wart*
  <u>Rede as the bristles of a sowes eres;°</u>   *ears*
  His nosethirles° blake were and wide.   *nostrils*
560   A swerd and a bokeler° bar° he by his side.   *shield / bore*
  His mouth as greet was as a greet furnais.°   *furnace*
  He was a janglere° and a Goliardais,[7]   *chatterer*
  And that was most of sinne and harlotries.°   *obscenities*
  Wel coude he stelen corn and tollen thries[8]—
565   And yit he hadde a thombe[9] of gold, pardee.°   *by heaven*
  A whit cote and a blew hood wered° he.   *wore*
  A baggepipe wel coude he blowe and soune,°   *sound*
  And therwithal° he broughte us out of towne.   *therewith*
     A gentil Manciple[1] was ther of a temple,
570   Of which achatours° mighte take exemple   *buyers of food*
  For to been wise in bying of vitaile;°   *victuals*
  For wheither that he paide or took by taile,[2]

---

7. Load.
8. Whether he was pleased or grieved.
9. His own work.
1. "Somnour" (Summoner): server of summonses to the ecclesiastical court. "Pardoner": dispenser of papal pardons (see p. 230, 1st n. 8, and p. 231, n. 5).
2. Proved, i.e., was evident.
3. A ram was frequently offered as the prize in wrestling, a village sport.
4. Sturdy fellow.

5. He would not heave off (its) hinge.
6. Right on the tip.
7. Goliard, teller of ribald stories.
8. Take toll thrice—i.e., deduct from the grain far more than the lawful percentage.
9. Thumb. Ironic allusion to a proverb: "An honest miller has a golden thumb."
1. The Manciple is the business agent of a community of lawyers in London (a "temple").
2. By talley, i.e., on credit.

Algate he waited so in his achat[3]
That he was ay biforn and in good stat.[4]

575   Now is nat that of God a ful fair grace
That swich a lewed° mannes wit shal pace°   *uneducated / surpass*
The wisdom of an heep of lerned men?
Of maistres° hadde he mo than thries ten   *masters*
That weren of lawe expert and curious,°   *cunning*
580 Of whiche ther were a dozeine in that hous
Worthy to been stiwardes of rente° and lond   *income*
Of any lord that is in Engelond,
To make him live by his propre good[5]
In honour dettelees but if he were wood,[6]
585 Or live as scarsly° as him list° desire,   *economically / it pleases*
And able for to helpen al a shire
In any caas° that mighte falle° or happe,   *event / befall*
And yit this Manciple sette hir aller cappe![7]

read → again him 590   The Reeve was a sclendre° colerik[8] man; *a mean overseer*   *slender*
His beerd was shave as neigh° as evere he can;   *close*
His heer was by his eres ful round yshorn;
His top was dokked[9] lik a preest biforn;°   *in front*
Ful longe were his legges and ful lene,
Ylik a staf, ther was no calf yseene.°   *visible*
595 Wel coude he keepe° a gerner° and a binne—   *guard / granary*
Ther was noon auditour coude on him winne.[1]
Wel wiste° he by the droughte and by the rain   *knew*
The yeelding of his seed and of his grain.
His lordes sheep, his neet,° his dayerye,°   *cattle / dairy herd*
600 His swin, his hors, his stoor,° and his pultrye   *stock*
Was hoolly° in this Reeves governinge,   *wholly*
And by his covenant yaf[2] the rekeninge,
Sin° that his lord was twenty-yeer of age.   *since*
There coude no man bringe him in arrerage.[3]
605 Ther nas baillif, hierde, nor other hine,
That he ne knew his sleighte and his covine[4]—
They were adrad° of him as of the deeth.°   *afraid / plague*
His woning° was ful faire upon an heeth;°   *dwelling / meadow*
With greene trees shadwed was his place.
610 He coude bettre than his lord purchace.°   *acquire goods*
Ful riche he was astored° prively.°   *stocked / secretly*
His lord wel coude he plesen subtilly,
To yive and lene° him of his owene good,°   *lend / property*
And have a thank, and yit a cote and hood.
615 In youthe he hadde lerned a good mister:°   *occupation*
He was a wel good wrighte, a carpenter.
This Reeve sat upon a ful good stot°   *stallion*

---

3. Always he was on the watch in his purchasing.
4. Financial condition. "Ay biforn": i.e., ahead of the game.
5. His own money.
6. Out of debt unless he were crazy.
7. This Manciple made fools of them all.
8. Choleric describes a person whose dominant humor is yellow bile (choler)—i.e., a hot-tempered person. The Reeve is the superintendent of a large

farming estate.
9. Cut short; the clergy wore the head partially shaved.
1. I.e., find him in default.
2. And according to his contract he gave.
3. Convict him of being in arrears financially.
4. There was no bailiff (i.e., foreman), shepherd, or other farm laborer whose craftiness and plots he didn't know.

That was a pomely° grey and highte° Scot.   *dapple* / *was named*
A long surcote° of pers° upon he hade,[5]   *overcoat* / *blue*
620 And by his side he bar° a rusty blade.   *bore*
Of Northfolk was this Reeve of which I telle,
Biside a town men clepen Baldeswelle.°   *Bawdswell*
Tukked[6] he was as is a frere aboute,
And evere he rood the hindreste of oure route.[7]

625 A Somnour[8] was ther with us in that place
That hadde a fir-reed° cherubinnes[9] face,   *fire-red*
For saucefleem° he was, with yën narwe,   *wanted*   *pimply*
And hoot° he was, and lecherous as a sparwe,° *sex as*   *hot* / *sparrow*
With scaled° browes blake and piled[1] beerd: *much as a sparrow* *scabby*
630 Of his visage children were aferd.°   *afraid*
Ther nas quiksilver, litarge, ne brimstoon,
he has syphalus Boras, ceruce, ne oile of tartre noon,[2] *he looks scary*
Ne oinement that wolde clense and bite,
That him mighte helpen of his whelkes° white,   *pimples*
635 Nor of the knobbes° sitting on his cheekes.   *lumps*
Wel loved he garlek, oinons, and eek leekes,
he is an alcoholic And for to drinke strong win reed as blood.
Thanne wolde he speke and crye as he were wood;°   *mad*
And whan that he wel dronken hadde the win,
640 Thanne wolde he speke no word but Latin:
A fewe termes hadde he, two or three,
That he hadde lerned out of som decree;
No wonder is—he herde it al the day,
And eek ye knowe wel how that a jay°   *parrot*
645 Can clepen "Watte"[3] as wel as can the Pope—
But whoso coude in other thing him grope,°   *examine*
Thanne hadde he spent all his philosophye;[4]
Ay *Questio quid juris*[5] wolde he crye.

He was a gentil harlot° and a kinde;   *sarcastic*   *rascal*
650 A bettre felawe sholde men nought finde:
he would let someone sleep w/ her for a quart of wine He wolde suffre,° for a quart of win, *bribe* *permit*
A good felawe to have his concubin
A twelfmonth, and excusen him at the fulle;[6]
Ful prively° a finch eek coude he pulle.[7]   *secretly*
And if he foond° owher° a good felawe   *found* / *anywhere*
Chaucer is offended by this He wolde techen him to have noon awe
655 In swich caas of the Ercedekenes curs,[8]
But if[9] a mannes soule were in his purs,

---

5. He had on.
6. With clothing tucked up like a friar.
7. Hindmost of our group.
8. The "Somnour" (Summoner) is an employee of the ecclesiastical court, whose duty is to bring to court persons whom the archdeacon—the justice of the court—suspects of offenses against canon law. By this time, however, summoners had generally transformed themselves into corrupt detectives who spied out offenders and blackmailed them by threats of summonses.
9. Cherubs, often depicted in art with red faces.
1. Uneven, partly hairless.
2. These are all ointments for diseases affecting

the skin, probably diseases of venereal origin.
3. Call out: "Walter"—like modern parrots' "Polly."
4. I.e., learning.
5. "What point of law does this investigation involve?" A phrase frequently used in ecclesiastical courts.
6. Fully. Ecclesiastical courts had jurisdiction over many offenses that today would come under civil law, including sexual offenses.
7. "To pull a finch" (pluck a bird) is to have sexual relations with a woman.
8. Archdeacon's sentence of excommunication.
9. Unless.

For in his purs he sholde ypunisshed be.
660   "Purs is the Ercedekenes helle," saide he.
       But wel I woot he lied right in deede:
       Of cursing° oughte eech gilty man him drede,   *excommunication*
       For curs wol slee° right as assoiling° savith—   *slay/absolution*
       And also war him of a *significavit*.[1]
665   In daunger[2] hadde he at his owene gise°   *disposal*
       The yonge girles of the diocise,
       And knew hir conseil,° and was al hir reed.[3]   *secrets*
       A gerland hadde he set upon his heed
       As greet as it were for an ale-stake,[4]
670   A bokeler hadde he maad him of a cake.
       With him ther rood a gentil Pardoner[5]
       Of Rouncival, his freend and his compeer,°   *comrade*
       That straight was comen fro the Court of Rome.[6]
       Ful loude he soong,° "Com hider, love, to me."   *sang*
675   This Somnour bar to him a stif burdoun:[7]
       Was nevere trompe° of half so greet a soun.   *trumpet*
       This Pardoner hadde heer as yelow as wex,
       But smoothe it heeng° as dooth a strike° of flex;   *hung/hank/flax*
       By ounces[8] heenge his lokkes that he hadde,
680   And therwith he his shuldres overspradde,°   *overspread*
       But thinne it lay, by colpons,° oon by oon;   *strands*
       But hood for jolitee° wered° he noon,   *nonchalance/wore*
       For it was trussed up in his walet:°   *pack*
       Him thoughte he rood al of the newe jet.°   *fashion*
685   Dischevelee° save his cappe he rood al bare.   *with hair down*
       Swiche glaring yën hadde he as an hare.
       A vernicle[9] hadde he sowed upon his cappe,
       His walet biforn him in his lappe,
       Bretful° of pardon, come from Rome al hoot.°   *brimful/hot*
690   A vois he hadde as smal° as hath a goot;°   *high-pitched/goat*
       No beerd hadde he, ne nevere sholde have;
       As smoothe it was as it were late yshave:
       I trowe° he were a gelding[1] or a mare.   *believe*
       But of his craft, fro Berwik into Ware,[2]
695   Ne was ther swich another pardoner;
       For in his male° he hadde a pilwe-beer°   *bag/pillowcase*
       Which that he saide was Oure Lady veil;
       He saide he hadde a gobet° of the sail   *piece*
       That Sainte Peter hadde whan that he wente
700   Upon the see, til Jesu Crist him hente.°   *seized*

1. And also one should be careful of a *significavit* (the writ that transferred the guilty offender from the ecclesiastical to the civil arm for punishment).
2. Under his domination.
3. Was their chief source of advice.
4. A tavern was signalized by a pole ("ale-stake"), rather like a modern flagpole, projecting from its front wall; on this hung a garland, or "bush."
5. A Pardoner dispensed papal pardon for sins to those who contributed to the charitable institution that he was licensed to represent; this Pardoner purported to be collecting for the hospital of Roncesvalles ("Rouncival") in Spain, which had a London branch.
6. The papal court.
7. I.e., provided him with a strong bass accompaniment.
8. I.e., thin strands.
9. Portrait of Christ's face as it was said to have been impressed on St. Veronica's handkerchief, i.e., a souvenir reproduction of a famous relic in Rome.
1. A neutered stallion, i.e., a eunuch.
2. I.e., from one end of England to the other.

[handwritten margin note: he is cheating people / these people think they will go to heaven.]

He hadde a crois° of laton,° ful of stones, *cross/brassy metal*
And in a glas he hadde pigges bones,
But with thise relikes[3] whan that he foond° *found*
A poore person° dwelling upon lond,[4] *parson*
705 Upon° a day he gat° him more moneye *in/got*
Than that the person gat in monthes twaye;
And thus with feined° flaterye and japes° *false/tricks*
He made the person and the peple his apes.° *dupes*
But trewely to tellen at the laste,
710 He was in chirche a noble ecclesiaste;
Wel coude he rede a lesson and a storye,° *liturgical narrative*
But alderbest° he soong an offertorye,[5] *best of all*
For wel he wiste° whan that song was songe, *knew*
He moste° preche and wel affile° his tonge *must/sharpen*
715 To winne silver, as he ful wel coude—
Therefore he soong the merierly° and loude. *more merrily*
  Now have I told you soothly in a clause[6]
Th'estaat, th'array, the nombre, and eek the cause
Why that assembled was this compaignye
720 In Southwerk at this gentil hostelrye
That highte the Tabard, faste° by the Belle;[7] *close*
But now is time to you for to telle
How that we baren us[8] that ilke° night *same*
Whan we were in that hostelrye alight;
725 And after wol I telle of oure viage,° *trip*
And al the remenant of oure pilgrimage.
But first I praye you of youre curteisye
That ye n'arette it nought my vilainye[9]
Though that I plainly speke in this matere
730 To telle you hir wordes and hir cheere,° *behavior*
Ne though I speke hir wordes proprely;° *accurately*
For this ye knowen also wel as I:
Who so shal telle a tale after a man
He moot° reherce,° as neigh as evere he can, *must/repeat*
735 Everich a word, if it be in his charge,° *responsibility*
Al speke he[1] nevere so rudeliche and large,° *broadly*
Or elles he moot telle his tale untrewe,
Or feine° thing, or finde° wordes newe; *make up/devise*
He may nought spare[2] although he were his brother:
740 He moot as wel saye oo word as another.
Crist spak himself ful brode° in Holy Writ, *broadly*
And wel ye woot no vilainye° is it; *rudeness*
Eek Plato saith, who so can him rede,
The wordes mote be cosin to the deede.
745 Also I praye you to foryive it me
Al° have I nat set folk in hir degree *although*
Here in this tale as that they sholde stonde:

---

3. Relics, i.e., the pigs' bones that the Pardoner represented as saints' bones.
4. Upcountry.
5. Part of the mass sung before the offering of alms.
6. I.e., in a short space.

7. Another tavern in Southwark.
8. Bore ourselves.
9. That you do not attribute it to my boorishness.
1. Although he speak.
2. I.e., spare anyone.

My wit is short, ye may wel understonde.
  Greet cheere made oure Host[3] us everichoon,
750 And to the soper sette he us anoon.°   *at once*
He served us with vitaile° at the beste.   *food*
Strong was the win, and wel to drinke us leste.°   *it pleased*
A semely man oure Hoste was withalle
For to been a marchal[4] in an halle;
755 A large man he was, with yën steepe,°   *prominent*
A fairer burgeis° was ther noon in Chepe[5]—   *burgher*
Bold of his speeche, and wis, and wel ytaught,
And of manhood him lakkede right naught.
Eek therto he was right a merye man,
760 And after soper playen he bigan,
And spak of mirthe amonges othere thinges—
Whan that we hadde maad oure rekeninges[6]—
And saide thus, "Now, lordinges, trewely,
Ye been to me right welcome, hertely.°   *heartily*
765 For by my trouthe, if that I shal nat lie,
I sawgh nat this yeer so merye a compaignye
At ones in this herberwe° as is now.   *inn*
Fain° wolde I doon you mirthe, wiste I[7] how.   *gladly*
And of a mirthe I am right now bithought,
770 To doon you ese, and it shal coste nought.
  "Ye goon to Canterbury—God you speede;
The blisful martyr quite you youre meede.[8]
And wel I woot as ye goon by the waye
Ye shapen you[9] to talen° and to playe,   *converse*
775 For trewely, confort ne mirthe is noon
To ride by the waye domb as stoon;°   *stone*
And therefore wol I maken you disport
As I saide erst,° and doon you som confort;   *before*
And if you liketh alle, by oon assent,
780 For to stonden at[1] my juggement,
And for to werken as I shall you saye,
Tomorwe whan ye riden by the waye—
Now by my fader° soule that is deed,   *father's*
But° ye be merye I wol yive you myn heed!°   *unless/head*
785 Holde up youre handes withouten more speeche."
  Oure counseil was nat longe for to seeche;°   *seek*
Us thought it was not worth to make it wis,[2]
And graunted him withouten more avis,°   *deliberation*
And bade him saye his voirdit° as him leste.[3]   *verdict*
790 "Lordinges," quod he, "now herkneth for the beste;
But taketh it nought, I praye you, in desdain.
This is the point, to speken short and plain,
That eech of you, to shorte° with oure waye   *shorten*
In this viage, shal tellen tales twaye°—   *two*

3. The landlord of the Tabard Inn.   9. Intend.
4. Marshal, one who was in charge of feasts.   1. Abide by.
5. Cheapside, business center of London.   2. We didn't think it worthwhile to make an issue
6. Had paid our bills.   of it.
7. If I knew.   3. It pleased.
8. Pay you your reward.

795 To Canterburyward, I mene it so,
    And hoomward he shal tellen othere two,
    Of aventures that whilom° have bifalle;   *once upon a time*
    And which of you that bereth him best of alle—
    That is to sayn, that telleth in this cas
800 Tales of best sentence° and most solas°—   *meaning / delight*
    Shal have a soper at oure aller cost,[4]
    Here in this place, sitting by this post,
    Whan that we come again fro Canterbury.
    And for to make you the more mury°   *merry*
805 I wol myself goodly° with you ride—   *kindly*
    Right at myn owene cost—and be youre gide.
    And who so wol my juggement withsaye°   *contradict*
    Shal paye al that we spende by the waye.
    And if ye vouche sauf that it be so,
810 Telle me anoon, withouten wordes mo,°   *more*
    And I wol erly shape me[5] therefore."
        This thing was graunted and oure othes swore
    With ful glad herte, and prayden[6] him also
    That he wolde vouche sauf for to do so,
815 And that he wolde been oure governour,
    And of oure tales juge and reportour,°   *accountant*
    And sette a soper at a certain pris,°   *price*
    And we wol ruled been at his devis,°   *disposal*
    In heigh and lowe; and thus by oon assent
820 We been accorded to his juggement.
    And therupon the win was fet° anoon;   *fetched*
    We dronken and to reste wente eechoon°   *each one*
    Withouten any lenger° taryinge.   *longer*
        Amorwe° whan that day bigan to springe   *in the morning*
825 Up roos oure Host and was oure aller cok,[7]
    And gadred us togidres in a flok,
    And forth we riden, a litel more than pas,°   *walking pace*
    Unto the watering of Saint Thomas;[8]
    And ther oure Host bigan his hors arreste,°   *halt*
830 And saide, "Lordes, herkneth if you leste:°   *it please*
        Ye woot youre forward° and it you recorde:[9] *agreement*
    If evensong and morwesong° accorde,°   *morning song / agree*
    Lat see now who shal telle the firste tale.
    As evere mote° I drinken win or ale,   *may*
835 Who so be rebel to my juggement
    Shal paye for al that by the way is spent.
    Now draweth cut er that we ferrer twinne:[1]
    He which that hath the shorteste shal biginne.
        "Sire Knight," quod he, "my maister and my lord,
840 Now draweth cut, for that is myn accord.°   *will*
    Cometh neer," quod he, "my lady Prioresse,
    And ye, sire Clerk, lat be youre shamefastnesse°— *modesty*

4. At the cost of us all.
5. Prepare myself.
6. I.e., we prayed.
7. Was rooster for us all.

8. A watering place near Southwark.
9. You recall it.
1. Go farther. "Draweth cut": i.e., draw straws.

Ne studieth nought. Lay hand to, every man!"
Anoon to drawen every wight bigan,
845 And shortly for to tellen as it was
Were it by aventure, or sort, or cas,[2]
The soothe° is this, the cut fil° to the Knight;   *truth/fell*
Of which ful blithe and glad was every wight,
And telle he moste° his tale, as was resoun,   *must*
850 By forward and by composicioun,[3]
As ye han herd. What needeth wordes mo?
And whan this goode man sawgh that it was so,
As he that wis was and obedient
To keepe his forward by his free assent,
855 He saide, "Sin° I shal biginne the game,   *since*
What, welcome be the cut, in Goddes name!
Now lat us ride, and herkneth what I saye."
And with that word we riden forth oure waye,
And he bigan with right a merye cheere°   *countenance*
860 His tale anoon, and saide as ye may heere.

2. Whether it was luck, fate, or chance.   3. By agreement and compact.

[*The Knight's Tale* is a romance of 2,350 lines, which Chaucer had written before beginning *The Canterbury Tales*—one of several works assumed to be earlier that he inserted into the collection. It is probably the same story, with only minor revisions, that Chaucer referred to in *The Legend of Good Women* as "al the love of Palamon and Arcite." These are the names of the two heroes of *The Knight's Tale*, kinsmen and best friends who are taken prisoner at the siege and destruction of ancient Thebes by Theseus, the ruler of Athens. Gazing out from their prison cell in a tower, they fall in love at first sight and almost at the same moment with Theseus's sister-in-law, Emily, who is taking an early-morning walk in a garden below their window. After a bitter rivalry, they are at last reconciled through a tournament in which Emily is the prize. Arcite wins the tournament but, as he lies dying after being thrown by his horse, he makes a noble speech encouraging Palamon and Emily to marry. The tale is an ambitious combination of classical setting and mythology, romance plot, and themes of fortune and destiny.]

The Miller's Prologue and Tale

The Miller's Tale belongs to a genre known as the "fabliau": a short story in verse that deals satirically, often grossly and fantastically as well as hilariously, with intrigues and deceptions about sex or money (and often both these elements in the same story). These are the tales Chaucer is anticipating in *The General Prologue* when he warns his presumably genteel audience that they must expect some rude speaking (see lines 727–44). An even more pointed apology follows at the end of *The Miller's Prologue*. Fabliau tales exist everywhere in oral literature; as a literary form they flourished in France, especially in the thirteenth century. By having Robin the Miller tell a fabliau to "quit" (to requite or pay back) the Knight's aristocratic romance, Chaucer sets up a dialectic between classes, genres, and styles that he exploits throughout *The Canterbury Tales*.

The Prologue

Whan that the Knight hadde thus his tale ytold,
In al the route° nas° ther yong ne old   *group/was not*
That he ne saide it was a noble storye,
And worthy for to drawen° to memorye,   *recall*
5 And namely° the gentils everichoon.   *especially*
    Oure Hoste lough° and swoor, "So mote I goon,[1]   *laughed*
This gooth aright: unbokeled is the male.°   *pouch*
Lat see now who shal telle another tale.
For trewely the game is wel bigonne.
10 Now telleth ye, sire Monk, if that ye conne,°   *can*
Somwhat to quite° with the Knightes tale."   *repay*
    The Millere, that for dronken[2] was al pale,
So that unnethe° upon his hors he sat,   *with difficulty*
He nolde° avalen° neither hood ne hat,   *would not/take off*
15 Ne abiden no man for his curteisye,
But in Pilates vois[3] he gan to crye,
And swoor, "By armes[4] and by blood and bones,
I can° a noble tale for the nones,   *know*
With which I wol now quite the Knightes tale."
20 Oure Hoste sawgh that he was dronke of ale,
And saide, "Abide, Robin, leve° brother,   *dear*
Som bettre man shal telle us first another.
Abide, and lat us werken thriftily."°   *with propriety*
    "By Goddes soule," quod he, "that wol nat I,
25 For I wol speke or elles go my way."
    Oure Host answerde, "Tel on, a devele way![5]
Thou art a fool; thy wit is overcome."
    "Now herkneth," quod the Millere, "alle and some.[6]
But first I make a protestacioun°   *public affirmation*
30 That I am dronke: I knowe it by my soun.°   *tone of voice*
And therfore if that I misspeke° or saye,   *speak or say wrongly*
Wite it[7] the ale of Southwerk, I you praye;
For I wol telle a legende° and a lif   *saint's life*
Bothe of a carpenter and of his wif,
35 How that a clerk hath set the wrightes cappe."[8]
    The Reeve answerde and saide, "Stint thy clappe![9]
Lat be thy lewed° dronken harlotrye.°   *ignorant/obscenity*
It is a sinne and eek° a greet folye   *also*
To apairen° any man or him defame,   *injure*
40 And eek to bringen wives in swich fame.°   *reputation*
Thou maist ynough of othere thinges sayn."
    This dronken Millere spak ful soone again,
And saide, "Leve° brother Osewold,   *dear*
Who hath no wif, he is no cokewold.°   *cuckold*
45 But I saye nat therfore that thou art oon.

---

1. So might I walk—an oath.
2. I.e., drunkenness.
3. The harsh voice usually associated with the character of Pontius Pilate in the mystery plays.
4. I.e., by God's arms, a blasphemous oath.
5. I.e., in the devil's name.
6. Each and every one.
7. Blame it on.
8 I.e., how a clerk made a fool of a carpenter.
9. Stop your chatter.

Ther ben ful goode wives many oon,°   *a one*
And evere a thousand goode ayains oon badde.
That knowestou wel thyself but if thou madde.°   *rave*
Why artou angry with my tale now?
50 I have a wif, pardee,° as wel as thou,   *by God*
Yit nolde° I, for the oxen in my plough,   *would not*
Take upon me more than ynough°   *enough*
As deemen of myself that I were oon:[1]
I wol bileve wel that I am noon.
55 An housbonde shal nought been inquisitif
Of Goddes privetee,° nor of his wif.   *secrets*
So[2] he may finde Goddes foison° there,   *plenty*
Of the remenant° needeth nought enquere."°   *rest/inquire*
     What sholde I more sayn but this Millere
60 He nolde his wordes for no man forbere,
But tolde his cherles tale in his manere.
M'athinketh° that I shal reherce° it here,   *I regret/repeat*
And therefore every gentil wight I praye,
Deemeth nought, for Goddes love, that I saye
65 Of yvel entente, but for° I moot reherse   *because*
Hir tales alle, be they bet° or werse,   *better*
Or elles falsen° som of my matere.   *falsify*
And therfore, whoso list it nought yheere°   *hear*
Turne over the leef,° and chese° another tale,   *page/choose*
70 For he shal finde ynowe,° grete and smale,   *enough*
Of storial[3] thing that toucheth gentilesse,°   *gentility*
And eek moralitee and holinesse:
Blameth nought me if that ye chese amis.
The Millere is a cherl, ye knowe wel this,
75 So was the Reeve eek, and othere mo,
And harlotrye° they tolden bothe two.   *ribaldry*
Aviseth you,[4] and putte me out of blame:
And eek men shal nought maken ernest of game.

The Tale

     Whilom° ther was dwelling at Oxenforde   *once upon a time*
80 A riche gnof° that gestes heeld to boorde,[5]   *churl*
And of his craft he was a carpenter.
With him ther was dwelling a poore scoler,
Hadde lerned art,[6] but al his fantasye°   *desire*
Was turned for to lere° astrologye,   *learn*
85 And coude a certain of conclusiouns,
To deemen by interrogaciouns,[7]
If that men axed° him in certain houres   *asked*
Whan that men sholde have droughte or elles showres,
Or if men axed him what shal bifalle

1. To think that I were one (a cuckold).
2. Provided that.
3. Historical, i.e., true.
4. Take heed.
5. I.e., took in boarders.

6. Who had completed the first stage of university education (the trivium).
7. I.e., and he knew a number of propositions on which to base astrological analyses (which would reveal the matters in the next three lines).

90 Of every thing—I may nat rekene hem alle.
  This clerk was cleped° hende[8] Nicholas.   *called*
 Of derne love he coude, and of solas,[9]
 And therto he was sly and ful privee,°   *secretive*
 And lik a maide meeke for to see.
95 A chambre hadde he in that hostelrye
 Allone, withouten any compaignye,
 Ful fetisly ydight[1] with herbes swoote,°   *sweet*
 And he himself as sweete as is the roote
 Of licoris or any setewale.[2]
100 His *Almageste*[3] and bookes grete and smale,
 His astrelabye, longing for[4] his art,
 His augrim stones,[5] layen faire apart
 On shelves couched° at his beddes heed;   *set*
 His presse° ycovered with a falding reed;[6]   *storage chest*
105 And al above ther lay a gay sautrye,°   *psaltery (harp)*
 On which he made a-nightes melodye
 So swetely that al the chambre roong,°   *rang*
 And *Angelus ad Virginem*[7] he soong,
 And after that he soong the *Kinges Note:*[8]
110 Ful often blessed was his merye throte.
 And thus this sweete clerk his time spente
 After his freendes finding and his rente.[9]
  This carpenter hadde wedded newe° a wif   *lately*
 Which that he loved more than his lif.
115 Of eighteteene yeer she was of age;
 Jalous he was, and heeld hire narwe in cage,
 For she was wilde and yong, and he was old,
 And deemed himself been lik a cokewold.[1]
 He knew nat Caton,[2] for his wit was rude,
120 That bad men sholde wedde his similitude:[3]
 Men sholde wedden after hir estat,[4]
 For youthe and elde° is often at debat.   *age*
 But sith that he was fallen in the snare,
 He moste endure, as other folk, his care.
125 Fair was this yonge wif, and therwithal
 As any wesele° hir body gent and smal.[5]   *weasel*
 A ceint she wered, barred[6] al of silk;
 A barmcloth° as whit as morne° milk   *apron / morning*
 Upon hir lendes,° ful of many a gore;°   *loins / flounce*
130 Whit was hir smok,° and broiden° al bifore *undergarment / embroidered*
 And eek bihinde, on hir coler° aboute,   *collar*

---

8. Courteous, handy, attractive.
9. I.e., he knew about secret love and pleasurable practices.
1. Elegantly furnished.
2. Setwall, a spice.
3. The 2nd-century treatise by Ptolemy, still the standard astronomy textbook.
4. Belonging to. "Astrelabye": astrolabe, an astronomical instrument.
5. Counters used in arithmetic.
6. Red coarse woolen cloth.
7. "The Angel to the Virgin," an Annunciation

hymn.
8. Probably a popular song of the time.
9. In accordance with his friends' provision and his own income.
1. I.e., suspected of himself that he was like a cuckold.
2. Dionysius Cato, the supposed author of a book of maxims used in elementary education.
3. Commanded that one should wed his equal.
4. Men should marry according to their condition.
5. Slender and delicate.
6. A belt she wore, with transverse stripes.

Of° col-blak silk, withinne and eek withoute;   *with*
The tapes° of hir white voluper°   *ribbons/cap*
Were of the same suite of[7] hir coler;
135 Hir filet° brood° of silk and set ful hye; *headband/broad*
And sikerly° she hadde a likerous° yë; *certainly/wanton*
Ful smale ypulled[8] were hir browes two,
And tho were bent,° and blake as any slo.° *arching/sloeberry*
She was ful more blisful on to see
140 Than is the newe perejonette° tree,   *pear*
And softer than the wolle° is of a wether;° *wool/ram*
And by hir girdel° heeng° a purs of lether, *belt/hung*
Tasseled with silk and perled with latoun.[9]
In al this world, to seeken up and down,
145 Ther nis no man so wis that coude thenche° *imagine*
So gay a popelote° or swich° a wenche. *doll/such*
Ful brighter was the shining of hir hewe
Than in the Towr[1] the noble° yforged newe. *gold coin*
But of hir song, it was as loud and yerne° *lively*
150 As any swalwe° sitting on a berne.°   *swallow/barn*
Therto she coude skippe and make game°   *play*
As any kide or calf folwing his dame.°   *mother*
Hir mouth was sweete as bragot or the meeth,[2]
Or hoord of apples laid in hay or heeth.° *heather*
155 Winsing° she was as is a joly° colt, *skittish/high-spirited*
Long as a mast, and upright° as a bolt.° *straight/arrow*
A brooch she bar upon hir lowe coler
As brood as is the boos° of a bokeler;° *boss/shield*
Hir shoes were laced on hir legges hye.
160 She was a primerole,° a piggesnye,[3]   *primrose*
For any lord to leggen° in his bedde,   *lay*
Or yit for any good yeman to wedde.
  Now sire, and eft° sire, so bifel the cas *again*
That on a day this hende Nicholas
165 Fil° with this yonge wif to rage° and playe, *happened/flirt*
Whil that hir housbonde was at Oseneye[4]
(As clerkes been ful subtil and ful quainte),° *clever*
And prively he caughte hire by the queinte.[5]
And saide, "Ywis,° but° if ich° have my wille, *truly/unless/I*
170 For derne° love of thee, lemman, I spille,"° *secret/die*
And heeld hire harde by the haunche-bones,° *thighs*
And saide, "Lemman,° love me al atones,[6] *sweetheart*
Or I wol dien, also° God me save."   *so*
And she sproong° as a colt dooth in a trave.[7] *sprang*
175 And with hir heed she wried° faste away; *twisted*
She saide, "I wol nat kisse thee, by my fay.° *faith*
Why, lat be," quod she, "lat be, Nicholas!
Or I wol crye 'Out, harrow,° and allas!'   *help*

---

7. The same kind as, i.e., black.
8. Delicately plucked.
9. I.e., with brassy spangles on it.
1. The Tower of London, the Mint.
2. "Bragot" and "meeth" are honey drinks.
3. A pig's eye, a name for a common flower.

4. A town near Oxford.
5. Elegant (thing); a euphemism for the female genitals.
6. Right now.
7. Frame for holding a horse to be shod.

Do way youre handes, for your curteisye!"
180   This Nicholas gan mercy for to crye,
And spak so faire, and profred him so faste,[8]
That she hir love him graunted atte laste,
And swoor hir ooth by Saint Thomas of Kent[9]
That she wolde been at his comandement,
185   Whan that she may hir leiser[1] wel espye.
"Myn housbonde is so ful of jalousye
That but ye waite° wel and been privee   be on guard
I woot right wel I nam but deed,"[2] quod she.
"Ye moste been ful derne° as in this cas."   secret
190   "Nay, therof care thee nought," quod Nicholas.
"A clerk hadde litherly biset his while,[3]
But if he coude a carpenter bigile."
And thus they been accorded and ysworn
To waite° a time, as I have told biforn.   watch for
195   Whan Nicholas hadde doon this everydeel,°   every bit
And thakked° hire upon the lendes° weel,   patted/loins
He kiste hire sweete, and taketh his sautrye,
And playeth faste, and maketh melodye.
        Thanne fil° it thus, that to the parissh chirche,   befell
200   Cristes owene werkes for to wirche,°   perform
This goode wif wente on an haliday:°   holy day
Hir forheed shoon as bright as any day,
So was it wasshen whan she leet° hir werk.   left
        Now was ther of that chirche a parissh clerk,[4]
205   The which that was ycleped° Absolon: called
Crul° was his heer, and as the gold it shoon,   curly
And strouted° as a fanne[5] large and brode;   spread out
Ful straight and evene lay his joly shode.[6]
His rode° was reed, his yën greye as goos.°   complexion/goose
210   With Poules window corven[7] on his shoos,
In hoses° rede he wente fetisly.°   stockings/elegantly
Yclad he was ful smale° and proprely,   finely
Al in a kirtel° of a light waget°—   tunic/blue
Ful faire and thikke been the pointes[8] set—
215   And therupon he hadde a gay surplis,°   surplice
As whit as is the blosme upon the ris.°   bough
A merye child° he was, so God me save.   young man
Wel coude he laten blood, and clippe,[9] and shave,
And maken a chartre of land, or acquitaunce;[1]
220   In twenty manere° coude he trippe and daunce   ways
After the scole of Oxenforde tho,°   then
And with his legges casten° to and fro,   prance
And playen songes on a smal rubible;°   fiddle
Therto he soong somtime a loud quinible,[2]

8. I.e., made such vigorous advances.
9. Thomas à Becket.
1. I.e., opportunity.
2. I am no more than dead, I am done for.
3. Poorly employed his time.
4. Assistant to the parish priest, not a cleric or student.
5. Wide-mouthed basket for separating grain from chaff.

6. Parting of the hair.
7. Carved with intricate designs, like the tracery in the windows of St. Paul's.
8. Laces for fastening the tunic and holding up the hose.
9. Let blood and give haircuts. Bleeding was a medical treatment performed by barbers.
1. Legal release. "Chartre": deed.
2. Part requiring a very high voice.

225	And as wel coude he playe on a giterne:°	*guitar*
	In al the town nas brewhous ne taverne	
	That he ne visited with his solas,°	*entertainment*
	Ther any gailard tappestere³ was.	
	But sooth to sayn, he was somdeel squaimous°	*a bit squeamish*
230	Of° farting, and of speeche daungerous.⁴	*about*
	This Absolon, that joly° was and gay,	*pretty, amorous*
	Gooth with a cencer° on the haliday,	*incense burner*
	Cencing the wives of the parissh faste,	
	And many a lovely look on hem he caste,	
235	And namely° on this carpenteres wif:	*especially*
	To looke on hire him thoughte a merye lif.	
	She was so propre° and sweete and likerous,⁵	*neat*
	I dar wel sayn, if she hadde been a mous,	
	And he a cat, he wolde hire hente° anoon.	*pounce on*
240	This parissh clerk, this joly Absolon,	
	Hath in his herte swich a love-longinge°	*lovesickness*
	That of no wif ne took he noon offringe—	
	For curteisye he saide he wolde noon.	
	The moone, whan it was night, ful brighte shoon,°	*shone*
245	And Absolon his giterne° hath ytake—	*guitar*
	For paramours° he thoughte for to wake—	*love*
	And forth he gooth, jolif° and amorous,	*pretty*
	Til he cam to the carpenteres hous,	
	A litel after cokkes hadde ycrowe,	
250	And dressed him up by a shot-windowe⁶	
	That was upon the carpenteres wal.	
	He singeth in his vois gentil and smal,°	*dainty*
	"Now dere lady, if thy wille be,	
	I praye you that ye wol rewe° on me,"	*have pity*
255	Ful wel accordant to his giterninge.⁷	
	This carpenter awook and herde him singe,	
	And spak unto his wif, and saide anoon,	
	"What, Alison, heerestou nought Absolon	
	That chaunteth thus under oure bowres° wal?"	*bedroom's*
260	And she answerde hir housbonde therwithal,	
	"Yis, God woot, John, I heere it everydeel."°	*every bit*
	This passeth forth. What wol ye bet than weel?⁸	
	Fro day to day this joly Absolon	
	So woweth° hire that him is wo-bigoon:	*woos*
265	He waketh° al the night and al the day;	*stays awake*
	He kembed° his lokkes brode⁹ and made him gay;	*combed*
	He woweth hire by menes and brocage,¹	
	And swoor he wolde been hir owene page°	*personal servant*
	He singeth, brokking° as a nightingale;	*trilling*
270	He sente hire piment,° meeth,° and spiced ale,	*spiced wine/mead*
	And wafres° piping hoot out of the gleede;°	*pastries/coals*
	And for she was of towne,² he profred meede°—	*money*

3. Gay barmaid.
4. Prudish about (vulgar) talk.
5. Wanton, appetizing.
6. Took his position by a hinged window.
7. In harmony with his guitar playing.

8. Better than well.
9. I.e., wide-spreading.
1. By go-betweens and agents.
2. Because she was a town woman.

For som folk wol be wonnen for richesse,
And som for strokes,° and som for gentilesse.   *blows (force)*
275   Somtime to shewe his lightnesse and maistrye,[3]
He playeth Herodes[4] upon a scaffold° hye.   *platform, stage*
But what availeth him as in this cas?
She loveth so this hende Nicholas
That Absolon may blowe the bukkes horn;[5]
280   He ne hadde for his labour but a scorn.
And thus she maketh Absolon hir ape,[6]
And al his ernest turneth til° a jape.°   *to / joke*
Ful sooth is this proverbe, it is no lie;
Men saith right thus: "Alway the nye slye
285   Maketh the ferre leve to be loth."[7]
For though that Absolon be wood° or wroth,   *furious*
By cause that he fer was from hir sighte,
This nye° Nicholas stood in his lighte.   *nearby*
     Now beer° thee wel, thou hende Nicholas,   *bear*
290   For Absolon may waile and singe allas.
     And so bifel it on a Saterday
This carpenter was goon til Oseney,
And hende Nicholas and Alisoun
Accorded been to this conclusioun,
295   That Nicholas shal shapen° hem a wile°   *arrange / trick*
This sely[8] jalous housbonde to bigile,
And if so be this game wente aright,
She sholden sleepen in his arm al night—
For this was his desir and hire° also.   *hers*
300   And right anoon, withouten wordes mo,
This Nicholas no lenger wolde tarye,
But dooth ful softe unto his chambre carye
Bothe mete and drinke for a day or twaye,
And to hir housbonde bad hire for to saye,
305   If that he axed after Nicholas,
She sholde saye she niste° wher he was—   *didn't know*
Of al that day she sawgh him nought with yë:
She trowed° that he was in maladye,   *believed*
For for no cry hir maide coude him calle,
310   He nolde answere for no thing that mighte falle.°   *happen*
     This passeth forth al thilke° Saterday   *this*
That Nicholas stille in his chambre lay,
And eet,° and sleep,° or dide what him leste,[9]   *ate / slept*
Til Sonday that the sonne gooth to reste.
315   This sely carpenter hath greet mervaile
Of Nicholas, or what thing mighte him aile,
And saide, "I am adrad,° by Saint Thomas,   *afraid*
It stondeth nat aright with Nicholas.
God shilde° that he deide sodeinly!   *forbid*

---

3. Facility and virtuosity.
4. Herod, a role traditionally played as a bully in the mystery plays.
5. Blow the buck's horn, i.e., go whistle, waste his time.
6. I.e., thus she makes a monkey out of Absolon.
7. Always the sly man at hand makes the distant dear one hated.
8. Poor innocent.
9. He wanted.

320   This world is now ful tikel,° sikerly: *precarious*
        I sawgh today a corps yborn to chirche
        That now a° Monday last I sawgh him wirche.°   *on/work*
        Go up," quod he unto his knave° anoon,   *manservant*
        "Clepe° at his dore or knokke with a stoon.°   *call/stone*
325   Looke how it is and tel me boldely."
          This knave gooth him up ful sturdily,
        And at the chambre dore whil that he stood
        He cride and knokked as that he were wood,°   *mad*
        "What? How? What do ye, maister Nicholay?
330   How may ye sleepen al the longe day?"
        But al for nought: he herde nat a word.
        An hole he foond ful lowe upon a boord,
        Ther as the cat was wont in for to creepe,
        And at that hole he looked in ful deepe,
335   And atte laste he hadde of him a sighte.
          This Nicholas sat evere caping° uprighte   *gaping*
        As he hadde kiked° on the newe moone.   *gazed*
        Adown he gooth and tolde his maister soone
        In what array° he saw this ilke° man.   *condition/same*
340   This carpenter to blessen him[1] bigan,
        And saide, "Help us, Sainte Frideswide!
        A man woot litel what him shal bitide.
        This man is falle, with his astromye,°   *astronomy*
        In som woodnesse° or in som agonye.   *madness*
345   I thoughte ay° wel how that it sholde be: *always*
        Men sholde nought knowe of Goddes privetee.
        Ye, blessed be alway a lewed° man   *ignorant*
        That nought but only his bileve° can.°   *creed/knows*
        So ferde° another clerk with astromye: *fared*
350   He walked in the feeldes for to prye°   *gaze*
        Upon the sterres,° what ther sholde bifalle,   *stars*
        Til he was in a marle-pit[2] yfalle—
        He saw nat that. But yit, by Saint Thomas,
        Me reweth sore[3] for hende Nicholas.
355   He shal be rated of[4] his studying,
        If that I may, by Jesus, hevene king!
        Get me a staf that I may underspore,°   *pry up*
        Whil that thou, Robin, hevest° up the dore.   *heave*
        He shal[5] out of his studying, as I gesse."
360   And to the chambre dore he gan him dresse.[6]
        His knave was a strong carl° for the nones,°   *fellow/purpose*
        And by the haspe he haaf° it up atones: *heaved*
        Into° the floor the dore fil° anoon.   *on/fell*
        This Nicholas sat ay as stille as stoon,
365   And evere caped up into the air.
        This carpenter wende° he were in despair,   *thought*
        And hente° him by the shuldres mightily,   *seized*
        And shook him harde, and cride spitously,°   *vehemently*

1. Cross himself.   4. Scolded for.
2. Pit from which a fertilizing clay is dug.   5. I.e., shall come.
3. I sorely pity.   6. Took his stand.

"What, Nicholay, what, how! What! Looke adown!
370 Awaak and thenk on Cristes passioun![7]
I crouche[8] thee from elves and fro wightes."°   *wicked creatures*
Therwith the nightspel saide he anoonrightes[9]
On foure halves° of the hous aboute,   *sides*
And on the thresshfold° on the dore withoute: *threshold*
375 "Jesu Crist and Sainte Benedight,°   *Benedict*
Blesse this hous from every wikked wight!
For nightes nerye the White Pater Noster.[1]
Where wentestou,° thou Sainte Petres soster?°   *did you go / sister*
And at the laste this hende Nicholas
380 Gan for to sike° sore, and saide, "Allas,   *sigh*
Shal al the world be lost eftsoones° now?"   *again*
    This carpenter answerde, "What saistou?
What, thenk on God as we doon, men that swinke."°   *work*
    This Nicholas answerde, "Fecche me drinke,
385 And after wol I speke in privetee
Of certain thing that toucheth me and thee.
I wol telle it noon other man, certain."
    This carpenter gooth down and comth again,
And broughte of mighty° ale a large quart,   *strong*
390 And when that eech of hem hadde dronke his part,
This Nicholas his dore faste shette,°   *shut*
And down the carpenter by him he sette,
And saide, "John, myn hoste lief° and dere,   *beloved*
Thou shalt upon thy trouthe° swere me here   *word of honor*
395 That to no wight thou shalt this conseil° wraye;°   *secret / disclose*
For it is Cristes conseil that I saye,
And if thou telle it man,[2] thou art forlore,°   *lost*
For this vengeance thou shalt have therfore,
That if thou wraye me, thou shalt be wood."[3]
400 "Nay, Crist forbede it, for his holy blood,"
Quod tho this sely° man. "I nam no labbe,°   *innocent / tell-tale*
And though I saye, I nam nat lief to gabbe.[4]
Say what thou wilt, I shal it nevere telle
To child ne wif, by him that harwed helle."[5]
405   "Now John," quod Nicholas, "I wol nought lie.
I have yfounde in myn astrologye,
As I have looked in the moone bright,
That now a Monday next, at quarter night,[6]
Shal falle a rain, and that so wilde and wood,°   *furious*
410 That half so greet was nevere Noees° flood.   *Noah's*
This world," he saide, "in lasse° than an hour   *less*
Shal al be dreint,° so hidous is the showr.   *drowned*
Thus shal mankinde drenche° and lese° hir lif."   *drown / lose*

7. I.e., the Crucifixion.
8. Make the sign of the cross on.
9. The night-charm he said right away (to ward off evil spirits).
1. Pater Noster is Latin for "Our Father," the beginning of the Lord's Prayer. The line is obscure, but a conjectural reading would be, "May the White 'Our Father' (or 'Our White Father') [either a prayer or the personification of a protecting power] defend [nerye] (us) against nights." The "nightspel" is a jumble of Christian references and pagan superstition.
2. To anyone.
3. Go mad.
4. And though I say it myself, I don't like to gossip.
5. By Him that despoiled hell—i.e., Christ.
6. I.e., shortly before dawn.

This carpenter answerde, "Allas, my wif!
415 And shal she drenche? Allas, myn Alisoun."
For sorwe of this he fil almost⁷ adown,
And saide, "Is there no remedye in this cas?"
"Why yis, for⁸ Gode," quod hende Nicholas,
"If thou wolt werken after lore and reed⁹—
420 Thou maist nought werken after thyn owene heed;°   *head*
For thus saith Salomon that was ful trewe,
'Werk al by conseil and thou shalt nought rewe.'°   *be sorry*
And if thou werken wolt by good conseil,
I undertake, withouten mast or sail,
425 Yit shal I save hire and thee and me.
Hastou nat herd how saved was Noee
Whan that oure Lord hadde warned him biforn
That al the world with water sholde be lorn?"°   *lost*
"Yis," quod this carpenter, "ful yore° ago."   *long*
430 "Hastou nat herd," quod Nicholas, "also
The sorwe of Noee with his felaweshipe?
Er° that he mighte gete his wif to shipe,   *before*
Him hadde levere,¹ I dar wel undertake,
At thilke time than alle his wetheres² blake
435 That she hadde had a ship hirself allone.³
And therfore woostou° what is best to doone?   *do you know*
This axeth° haste, and of an hastif° thing   *requires / urgent*
Men may nought preche or maken tarying.
Anoon go gete us faste into this in°   *lodging*
440 A kneeding trough or elles a kimelin°   *brewing tub*
For eech of us, but looke that they be large,°   *wide*
In whiche we mowen swimme as in a barge,⁴
And han therinne vitaile suffisaunt⁵
But for a day—fy° on the remenaunt!   *fie*
445 The water shal aslake° and goon away   *diminish*
Aboute prime⁶ upon the nexte day.
But Robin may nat wite° of this, thy knave,   *know*
Ne eek thy maide Gille I may nat save.
Axe nought why, for though thou axe me,
450 I wol nought tellen Goddes privetee.°   *secrets*
Suffiseth thee, but if thy wittes madde,°   *go mad*
To han° as greet a grace as Noee hadde.   *have*
Thy wif shal I wel saven, out of doute.
Go now thy way, and speed thee heraboute.
455 But whan thou hast for hire° and thee and me   *her*
Ygeten us thise kneeding-tubbes three,
Thanne shaltou hangen hem in the roof ful hye,
That no man of oure purveyance° espye.   *preparations*
And whan thou thus hast doon as I have said,
460 And hast oure vitaile faire in hem ylaid,

7. Almost fell.
8. I.e., by.
9. Act according to learning and advice.
1. He had rather.
2. Rams. I.e., he'd have given all the black rams he had.

3. The reluctance of Noah's wife to board the ark is a traditional comic theme in the mystery plays.
4. In which we can float as in a vessel.
5. Sufficient food.
6. 9 A.M.

And eek an ax to smite the corde atwo,
Whan that the water comth that we may go,
And broke an hole an heigh[7] upon the gable
Unto the gardinward,[8] over the stable,
465 That we may freely passen forth oure way,
Whan that the grete showr is goon away,
Thanne shaltou swimme as merye, I undertake,
As dooth the white doke° after hir drake.   duck
Thanne wol I clepe,° 'How, Alison? How, John?   call
470 Be merye, for the flood wol passe anoon.'
And thou wolt sayn, 'Hail, maister Nicholay!
Good morwe, I see thee wel, for it is day!'
And thanne shal we be lordes al oure lif
Of al the world, as Noee and his wif.
475 But of oo thing I warne thee ful right:
Be wel avised° on that ilke night   warned
That we been entred into shippes boord
That noon of us ne speke nought a word,
Ne clepe, ne crye, but been in his prayere,
480 For it is Goddes owene heeste dere.[9]
Thy wif and thou mote hange fer atwinne,[1]
For that bitwixe you shal be no sinne—
Namore in looking than ther shal in deede.
This ordinance is said: go, God thee speede.
485 Tomorwe at night whan men been alle asleepe,
Into oure kneeding-tubbes wol we creepe,
And sitten there, abiding Goddes grace.
Go now thy way, I have no lenger space°   time
To make of this no lenger sermoning.
490 Men sayn thus: 'Send the wise and say no thing.'
Thou art so wis it needeth thee nat teche:
Go save oure lif, and that I thee biseeche."
      This sely carpenter gooth forth his way:
Ful ofte he saide allas and wailaway,
495 And to his wif he tolde his privetee,
And she was war,° and knew it bet° than he,   aware/better
What al this quainte cast was for to saye.[2]
But nathelees she ferde° as she wolde deye,   acted
And saide, "Allas, go forth thy way anoon.
500 Help us to scape,° or we been dede eechoon.   escape
I am thy trewe verray wedded wif:
Go, dere spouse, and help to save oure lif."
      Lo, which a greet thing is affeccioun!°   emotion
Men may dien of imaginacioun,
505 So deepe° may impression be take.   deeply
This sely carpenter biginneth quake;
Him thinketh verrailiche° that he may see   truly
Noees flood come walwing° as the see   rolling

7. On high.
8. Toward the garden.
9. Precious commandment.

1. Far apart.
2. What all this clever plan meant.

To drenchen° Alison, his hony dere.   *drown*
510 He weepeth, waileth, maketh sory cheere;
He siketh° with ful many a sory swough,°   *sighs/groan*
And gooth and geteth him a kneeding-trough,
And after a tubbe and a kimelin,
And prively he sente hem to his in,°   *dwelling*
515 And heeng° hem in the roof in privetee;   *hung*
His° owene hand he made laddres three,   *with his*
To climben by the ronges° and the stalkes°   *rungs/uprights*
Unto the tubbes hanging in the balkes,°   *rafters*
And hem vitailed,° bothe trough and tubbe,   *victualed*
520 With breed and cheese and good ale in a jubbe,°   *jug*
Suffising right ynough as for a day.
But er° that he hadde maad al this array,   *before*
He sente his knave, and eek his wenche also,
Upon his neede[3] to London for to go.
525 And on the Monday whan it drow to[4] nighte,
He shette° his dore withouten candel-lighte,   *shut*
And dressed° alle thing as it sholde be,   *arranged*
And shortly up they clomben° alle three.   *climbed*
They seten° stille wel a furlong way.[5]   *sat*
530   "Now, Pater Noster, clum,"[6] saide Nicholay,
And "Clum" quod John, and "Clum" saide Alisoun.
This carpenter saide his devocioun,
And stille he sit° and biddeth° his prayere,   *sits/prays*
Awaiting on the rain, if he it heere.°   *might hear*
535   The dede sleep, for wery bisinesse,
Fil° on this carpenter right as I gesse   *fell*
Aboute corfew time,[7] or litel more.
For travailing of his gost[8] he groneth sore,
And eft° he routeth,° for his heed mislay.[9]   *then/snores*
540   Down of the laddre stalketh Nicholay,
And Alison ful softe adown she spedde:
Withouten wordes mo they goon to bedde
Ther as the carpenter is wont to lie.
Ther was the revel and the melodye,
545 And thus lith° Alison and Nicholas   *lies*
In bisinesse of mirthe and of solas,°   *pleasure*
Til that the belle of Laudes[1] gan to ringe,
And freres° in the chauncel° gonne singe.   *friars/chancel*
This parissh clerk, this amorous Absolon,
550 That is for love alway so wo-bigoon,
Upon the Monday was at Oseneye,
With compaignye him to disporte and playe,
And axed upon caas a cloisterer[2]
Ful prively after John the carpenter;

3. On an errand for him.
4. Drew toward.
5. The time it takes to go a furlong (i.e., a few minutes).
6. Hush (?). "Pater Noster": Our Father.
7. Probably about 8 P.M.

8. Affliction of his spirit.
9. Lay in the wrong position.
1. The first church service of the day, before daybreak.
2. Here a member of the religious order of Osney Abbey. "Upon caas": by chance.

555 And he drow him apart out of the chirche,
And saide, "I noot:[3] I sawgh him here nought wirche°   *work*
Sith Saterday. I trowe that he be went
For timber ther oure abbot hath him sent.
For he is wont for timber for to go,
560 And dwellen atte grange[4] a day or two.
Or elles he is at his hous, certain.
Where that he be I can nought soothly sayn."
     This Absolon ful jolif was and light,[5]
And thoughte, "Now is time to wake al night,
565 For sikerly,° I sawgh him nought stiringe   *certainly*
Aboute his dore sin day bigan to springe.
So mote° I thrive, I shal at cokkes crowe   *may*
Ful prively knokken at his windowe
That stant° ful lowe upon his bowres° wal.   *stands/bedroom's*
570 To Alison now wol I tellen al
My love-longing,° for yet I shal nat misse   *lovesickness*
That at the leeste way[6] I shal hire kisse.
Som manere confort shal I have, parfay.°   *in faith*
My mouth hath icched al this longe day:
575 That is a signe of kissing at the leeste.
Al night me mette[7] eek I was at a feeste.
Therfore I wol go sleepe an hour or twaye,
And al the night thanne wol I wake and playe."
     Whan that the firste cok hath crowe, anoon
580 Up rist° this joly lovere Absolon,   *rises*
And him arrayeth gay at point devis.[8]
But first he cheweth grain[9] and licoris,
To smellen sweete, er he hadde kembd° his heer.   *combed*
Under his tonge a trewe-love[1] he beer,°   *bore*
585 For therby wende° he to be gracious.°   *supposed/pleasing*
He rometh° to the carpenteres hous,   *strolls*
And stille he stant° under the shot-windowe—   *stands*
Unto his brest it raughte,° it was so lowe—   *reached*
And ofte he cougheth with a semisoun.°   *small sound*
590 "What do ye, hony-comb, sweete Alisoun,
My faire brid,[2] my sweete cinamome?°   *cinnamon*
Awaketh, lemman° myn, and speketh to me.   *sweetheart*
Wel litel thinken ye upon my wo
That for your love I swete° ther I go.   *sweat*
595 No wonder is though that I swelte° and swete: *melt*
I moorne as doth a lamb after the tete.°   *teat*
Ywis, lemman, I have swich love-longinge,
That lik a turtle° trewe is my moorninge: *dove*
I may nat ete namore than a maide."
600   "Go fro the windowe, Jakke fool," she saide.
"As help me God, it wol nat be com-pa-me.°   *come-kiss-me*

---

3. Don't know.
4. The outlying farm belonging to the abbey.
5. Was very amorous and cheerful.
6. I.e., at least.
7. I dreamed.

8. To perfection.
9. Grain of paradise; a spice.
1. Sprig of a cloverlike plant.
2. Bird or bride.

I love another, and elles I were to blame,
Wel bet° than thee, by Jesu, Absolon.   *better*
Go forth thy way or I wol caste a stoon,
605   And lat me sleepe, a twenty devele way."[3]
    "Allas," quod Absolon, "and wailaway,
That trewe love was evere so yvele biset.[4]
Thanne kis me, sin that it may be no bet,
For Jesus love and for the love of me."
610   "Woltou thanne go thy way therwith?" quod she.
"Ye, certes, lemman," quod this Absolon.
"Thanne maak thee redy," quod she. "I come anoon."
And unto Nicholas she saide stille,°   *quietly*
"Now hust,° and thou shalt laughen al thy fille."   *hush*
615   This Absolon down sette him on his knees,
And said, "I am a lord at alle degrees,[5]
For after this I hope ther cometh more.
Lemman, thy grace, and sweete brid, thyn ore!"°   *mercy*
The windowe she undooth, and that in haste.
620   "Have do," quod she, "come of and speed thee faste,
Lest that oure neighebores thee espye."
    This Absolon gan wipe his mouth ful drye:
Derk was the night as pich or as the cole,
And at the windowe out she putte hir hole,
625   And Absolon, him fil no bet ne wers,[6]
But with his mouth he kiste hir naked ers,
Ful savourly,° er he were war of this.   *with relish*
Abak he sterte,° and thoughte it was amis,   *started*
For wel he wiste a womman hath no beerd.°   *beard*
630   He felte a thing al rough and longe yherd,°   *haired*
And saide, "Fy, allas, what have I do?"
    "Teehee," quod she, and clapte the windowe to.
And Absolon gooth forth a sory pas.[7]
    "A beerd, a beerd!"[8] quod hende Nicholas,
635   "By Goddes corpus,° this gooth faire and weel."   *body*
    This sely Absolon herde everydeel,°   *every bit*
And on his lippe he gan for anger bite,
And to himself he saide, "I shal thee quite."°   *repay*
    Who rubbeth now, who froteth° now his lippes   *wipes*
640   With dust, with sond,° with straw, with cloth, with chippes,   *sand*
But Absolon, that saith ful ofte allas?
"My soule bitake° I unto Satanas,°   *commit / Satan*
But me were levere[9] than all this town," quod he,
"Of this despit° awroken° for to be.   *insult / avenged*
645   Allas," quod he, "allas I ne hadde ybleint!"°   *turned aside*
His hote love was cold and al yqueint,°   *quenched*
For fro that time that he hadde kist hir ers
Of paramours he sette nought a kers,[1]
For he was heled° of his maladye.   *cured*

---

3. In the name of twenty devils.
4. Ill-used.
5. In every way.
6. It befell him neither better nor worse.

7. I.e., walking sadly.
8. A trick (slang), but with a play on line 629.
9. I had rather.
1. He didn't care a piece of cress for woman's love.

650   Ful ofte paramours he gan defye,°   *renounce*
       And weep° as dooth a child that is ybete.   *wept*
       A softe paas[2] he wente over the streete
       Until° a smith men clepen daun Gervais,[3]   *to*
       That in his forge smithed plough harneis:°   *equipment*
655   He sharpeth shaar and cultour[4] bisily.
       This Absolon knokketh al esily,°   *quietly*
       And saide, "Undo, Gervais, and that anoon."°   *at once*
          "What, who artou?" "It am I, Absolon."
       "What, Absolon? What, Cristes sweete tree!°   *cross*
660   Why rise ye so rathe?° Ey, benedicite,°   *early/bless me*
       What aileth you? Som gay girl, God it woot,
       Hath brought you thus upon the viritoot.[5]
       By Sainte Note, ye woot wel what I mene."
          This Absolon ne roughte nat a bene[6]
665   Of al his play. No word again he yaf:
       He hadde more tow on his distaf[7]
       Than Gervais knew, and saide, "Freend so dere,
       This hote cultour in the chimenee° here,   *fireplace*
       As lene[8] it me: I have therwith to doone.
670   I wol bringe it thee again ful soone."
          Gervais answerde, "Certes, were it gold,
       Or in a poke nobles alle untold,[9]
       Thou sholdest have, as I am trewe smith.
       Ey, Cristes fo,[1] what wol ye do therwith?"
675   "Therof," quod Absolon, "be as be may.
       I shal wel telle it thee another day."
       And caughte the cultour by the colde stele.°   *handle*
       Ful softe out at the dore he gan to stele,
       And wente unto the carpenteres wal:
680   He cougheth first and knokketh therwithal
       Upon the windowe, right as he dide er.°   *before*
          This Alison answerde, "Who is ther
       That knokketh so? I warante[2] it a thief."
          "Why, nay," quod he, "God woot, my sweete lief,°   *dear*
685   I am thyn Absolon, my dereling.°   *darling*
       Of gold," quod he, "I have thee brought a ring—
       My moder yaf it me, so God me save;
       Ful fin it is and therto wel ygrave:°   *engraved*
       This wol I yiven thee if thou me kisse."
690   This Nicholas was risen for to pisse,
       And thoughte he wolde amenden[3] al the jape:°   *joke*
       He sholde kisse his ers er that he scape.
       And up the windowe dide he hastily,
       And out his ers he putteth prively,
695   Over the buttok to the haunche-boon.
          And therwith spak this clerk, this Absolon,

---

2. I.e., quiet walk.
3. Master Gervais.
4. He sharpens plowshare and coulter (the turf cutter on a plow).
5. I.e., on the prowl.
6. Didn't care a bean.

7. I.e., more on his mind.
8. I.e., please lend.
9. Or gold coins all uncounted in a bag.
1. Foe, i.e., Satan.
2. I.e., wager.
3. Improve on.

"Speek, sweete brid, I noot nought wher thou art."
This Nicholas anoon leet flee[4] a fart
As greet as it hadde been a thonder-dent°   *thunderbolt*
700 That with the strook he was almost yblent,°   *blinded*
And he was redy with his iren hoot,°   *hot*
And Nicholas amidde the ers he smoot:°   *smote*
Of° gooth the skin an hande-brede° aboute;   *off/handsbreadth*
The hote cultour brende so his toute°   *buttocks*
705 That for the smert° he wende for to[5] die;   *pain*
As he were wood° for wo he gan to crye,   *crazy*
"Help! Water! Water! Help, for Goddes herte!"
   This carpenter out of his slomber sterte,
And herde oon cryen "Water!" as he were wood,
710 And thoughte, "Allas, now cometh Noweles[6] flood!"
He sette him up[7] withoute wordes mo,
And with his ax he smoot the corde atwo,
And down gooth al: he foond neither to selle
Ne breed ne ale til he cam to the celle,[8]
715 Upon the floor, and ther aswoune° he lay.   *in a faint*
   Up sterte hire[9] Alison and Nicholay,
And criden "Out" and "Harrow" in the streete.
The neighebores, bothe smale and grete,
In ronnen for to gauren° on this man   *gape*
720 That aswoune lay bothe pale and wan,
For with the fal he brosten° hadde his arm;   *broken*
But stonde he moste° unto his owene harm,   *must*
For whan he spak he was anoon bore down[1]
With° hende Nicholas and Alisoun: *by*
725 They tolden every man that he was wood—
He was agast so of Noweles flood,
Thurgh fantasye, that of his vanitee°   *folly*
He hadde ybought him kneeding-tubbes three,
And hadde hem hanged in the roof above,
730 And that he prayed hem, for Goddes love,
To sitten in the roof, *par compaignye*.[2]
   The folk gan laughen at his fantasye.
Into the roof they kiken° and they cape,°   *peer/gape*
And turned al his harm unto a jape,°   *joke*
735 For what so that this carpenter answerde,
It was for nought: no man his reson° herde;   *argument*
With othes grete he was so sworn adown,
That he was holden° wood in al the town,   *considered*
For every clerk anoonright heeld with other:
740 They saide, "The man was wood, my leve brother,"
And every wight gan laughen at this strif.°   *fuss*
Thus swived[3] was the carpenteres wif
For al his keeping° and his jalousye,   *guarding*

4. Let fly.
5. Thought he would.
6. The carpenter is confusing Noah and Noel (Christmas).
7. Got up.
8. He found time to sell neither bread nor ale until

he arrived at the foundation, i.e., he did not take time out.
9. Started.
1. Refuted.
2. For company's sake.
3. The vulgar verb for having sexual intercourse.

And Absolon hath kist hir nether° yë,   *lower*
745   And Nicholas is scalded in the toute:
This tale is doon, and God save al the route!°   *company*

The Man of Law's Epilogue

The Reeve has taken *The Miller's Tale* personally and retaliates with a fabliau about a miller whose wife and daughter are seduced by two clerks. Next the Cook begins yet another fabliau, which breaks off after fifty-five lines, thereby closing Fragment I of *The Canterbury Tales*. Chaucer may never have settled on a final order for the tales he completed, but all modern editors, following many manuscripts, agree in putting *The Man of Law's Tale* next. The Man of Law tells a long moralistic tale about the many trials of a heroine called Constance for the virtue she personifies. This tale is finished, but Fragment II shows that *The Canterbury Tales* reaches us as a work in progress, which Chaucer kept revising, creating many problems for its scribes and editors. In the link that introduces him, the Man of Law says he will tell a tale in prose, but the story of Constance turns out to be in a seven-line stanza called rhyme royal. That inconsistency has led to speculation that at one time the Man of Law was assigned a long prose allegory, which Chaucer later reassigned to his own pilgrim persona. In thirty-five manuscripts *The Man of Law's Tale* is followed by an *Epilogue* omitted in twenty-two of the manuscripts that contain more or less complete versions of *The Canterbury Tales*. The often-missing link begins with the Host praising the *Man of Law's Tale* and calling upon the Parson to tell another uplifting tale. The Parson, however, rebukes the Host for swearing. The Host angrily accuses the Parson of being a "Lollard," a derogatory term for followers of the reformist preacher John Wycliffe. This is Chaucer's only overt reference to an important religious and political controversy that anticipates the sixteenth-century English Reformation.
  A third speaker, about whose identity the manuscripts disagree (six read "Summoner"; twenty-eight, "Squire"; one, "Shipman"), interrupts with the promise to tell a merry tale. Several modern editions, including the standard one used by scholars, print *The Man of Law's Epilogue* at the end of Fragment II, and begin Fragment III with *The Wife of Bath's Prologue*. Because the third speaker in the former *sounds* like the Wife, an argument has been made that she is the pilgrim who refers to "My joly body" (line 23), who at one time told a fabliau tale in which the narrator speaks of married women in the first person plural ("we," "us," "our"). Chaucer, so the argument goes, later gave that story to the Shipman. If in fact the Wife of Bath did once tell what is now *The Shipman's Tale*, that would be an indication of the exciting new possibilities he discovered in the literary form he had invented.

              Oure Host upon his stiropes stood anoon
              And saide, "Goode men, herkneth everichoon,
              This was a thrifty° tale for the nones,°   *proper/occasion*
              Sire parissh Preest," quod he, "for Goddes bones,
5   Tel us a tale as was thy forward° yore.°   *agreement/earlier*
              I see wel that ye lerned men in lore°   *teaching*
              Can° muche good, by Goddes dignitee."   *know*
              The Person him answerde, "Benedicite,°   *bless me*
              What aileth the man so sinfully to swere?"
10   Oure Host answerede, "O Jankin, be ye there?[1]
              I smelle a lollere[2] in the wind," quod he.

---

1. Is that where you're coming from? "Jankin": Johnny; derogatory name for a priest.

2. Contemptuous term for a religious reformer considered radical; a heretic.

"Now, goode men," quod oure Hoste, "herkneth me:
Abideth, for Goddes digne° passioun,   *worthy*
For we shal have a predicacioun.°   *sermon*
15 This lollere here wol prechen us somwhat."
"Nay, by my fader soule, that shal he nat,"
Saide the [Wif of Bathe],³ "here shal he nat preche:
He shal no gospel glosen⁴ here ne teche.
We leven° alle in the grete God," quod [she].   *believe*
20 He wolde sowen som difficultee
Or sprengen cokkel in oure clene corn.⁵
And therfore, Host, I warne thee biforn,
My joly body shal a tale telle
And I shal clinken you so merye a belle
25 That I shal waken al this compaignye.
But it shal nat been of philosophye,
Ne physlias,⁶ ne termes quainte of lawe:
There is but litel Latin in my mawe."°   *stomach*

The Wife of Bath's Prologue and Tale

In creating the Wife of Bath, Chaucer drew upon a centuries-old tradition of anti-feminist writings that was particularly nurtured by the medieval church. In their conviction that the rational, intellectual, spiritual, and, therefore, higher side of human nature predominated in men, whereas the irrational, material, earthly, and, therefore, lower side of human nature predominated in women, St. Paul and the early Church fathers exalted celibacy and virginity above marriage, although they were also obliged to concede the necessity and sanctity of matrimony. In the fourth century, a monk called Jovinian wrote a tract in which he apparently presented marriage as a positive good rather than as a necessary evil. That tract is known only through St. Jerome's extreme attack upon it. Jerome's diatribe and other antifeminist and anti-matrimonial literature provided Chaucer with a rich body of bookish male "auctoritee" (authority) against which the Wife of Bath asserts her female "experience" and defends her rights and justifies her life as a five-time married woman. In her polemical wars with medieval clerks and her matrimonial wars with her five husbands, the last of whom was once a clerk of Oxenford, the Wife of Bath seems ironically to confirm the accusations of the clerks, but at the same time she succeeds in satirizing the shallowness of the stereotypes of women and marriage in antifeminist writings and in demonstrating how much the largeness and complexity of her own character rise above that stereotype.

The Prologue

Experience, though noon auctoritee
Were in this world, is right ynough for me
To speke of wo that is in mariage:
For lordinges,° sith I twelf yeer was of age—   *gentlemen*
5 Thanked be God that is eterne on live—
Housbondes at chirche dore¹ I have had five

---

3. On the speaker here, see discussion in head-note.
4. Gloss, with the sense of distorting the meaning of scripture.
5. Sow tares (impure doctrine) in our pure wheat.

6. No such word exists. The speaker is coining a professional-sounding term in philosophy, law, or medicine.
1. The actual wedding ceremony was celebrated at the church door, not in the chancel.

(If I so ofte mighte han wedded be),
And alle were worthy men in hir degree.
But me was told, certain, nat longe agoon is,
10 That sith that Crist ne wente nevere but ones°   once
To wedding in the Cane[2] of Galilee,
That by the same ensample° taughte he me   example
That I ne sholde wedded be but ones.
Herke eek,° lo, which° a sharp word for the nones,[3]   also/what
15 Biside a welle, Jesus, God and man,
Spak in repreve° of the Samaritan: reproof
"Thou hast yhad five housbondes," quod he,
"And that ilke° man that now hath thee   same
Is nat thyn housbonde." Thus saide he certain.
20 What that he mente therby I can nat sayn,
But that I axe° why the fifthe man   ask
Was noon housbonde to the Samaritan?[4]
How manye mighte she han in mariage?
Yit herde I nevere tellen in myn age
25 Upon this nombre diffinicioun.°   definition
Men may divine° and glosen° up and down,   guess/interpret
But wel I woot,° expres,° withouten lie,   know/expressly
God bad us for to wexe[5] and multiplye:
That gentil text can I wel understonde.
30 Eek wel I woot° he saide that myn housbonde   know
Sholde lete° fader and moder and take to me,[6]   leave
But of no nombre mencion made he—
Of bigamye or of octogamye:[7]
Why sholde men thanne speke of it vilainye?
35 Lo, here the wise king daun° Salomon: master
I trowe° he hadde wives many oon,[8]   believe
As wolde God it leveful° were to me   permissible
To be refresshed half so ofte as he.
Which yifte[9] of God hadde he for alle his wives!
40 No man hath swich° that in this world alive is.   such
God woot this noble king, as to my wit,°   knowledge
The firste night hadde many a merye fit°   bout
With eech of hem, so wel was him on live.[1]
Blessed be God that I have wedded five,
45 Of whiche I have piked out the beste,[2]
Bothe of hir nether purs[3] and of hir cheste.°   money box
Diverse scoles maken parfit° clerkes,   perfect
And diverse practikes[4] in sondry werkes
Maken the werkman parfit sikerly:°   certainly
50 Of five housbondes scoleying° am I.   schooling

---

2. Cana (see John 2.1).
3. To the purpose.
4. Christ was actually referring to a sixth man who was not married to the Samaritan woman (cf. John 4.6 ff.).
5. I.e., increase (see Genesis 1.28).
6. See Matthew 19.5.
7. I.e., of two or even eight marriages. The Wife of Bath is referring to successive, rather than simultaneous, marriages.
8. Solomon had seven hundred wives and three hundred concubines (1 Kings 11.3).
9. What a gift.
1. I.e., so pleasant a life he had.
2. Whom I have cleaned out of everything worthwhile.
3. Lower purse, i.e., testicles.
4. Practical experiences.

Welcome the sixte whan that evere he shal![5]
For sith I wol nat kepe me chast in al,
Whan my housbonde is fro the world agoon,
Som Cristen man shal wedde me anoon.°   right away
55 For thanne th'Apostle[6] saith that I am free
To wedde, a Goddes half, where it liketh me.[7]
He saide that to be wedded is no sinne:
Bet is to be wedded than to brinne.[8]
What rekketh me[9] though folk saye vilainye
60 Of shrewed° Lamech[1] and his bigamye?   cursed
I woot wel Abraham was an holy man,
And Jacob eek, as fer as evere I can,°   know
And eech of hem hadde wives mo than two,
And many another holy man also.
65   Where can ye saye in any manere age
That hye God defended° mariage   prohibited
By expres word? I praye you, telleth me.
Or where comanded he virginitee?
I woot as wel as ye, it is no drede,°   doubt
70 Th'Apostle, whan he speketh of maidenhede,°   virginity
He saide that precept therof hadde he noon:
Men may conseile a womman to be oon.°   single
But conseiling nis° no comandement.   is not
He putte it in oure owene juggement.
75 For hadde God comanded maidenhede,
Thanne hadde he dampned° wedding with the deede;[2]   condemned
And certes, if there were no seed ysowe,   _virgins can't_
Virginitee, thanne wherof sholde it growe?   _make more_
Paul dorste nat comanden at the leeste   _virgines._
80 A thing of which his maister yaf° no heeste.° _she is quite_ gave/command
                                               repetitive
The dart[3] is set up for virginitee:
Cacche whoso may, who renneth° best lat see.   runs
But this word is nought take of[4] every wight,°   person
But ther as[5] God list° yive it of his might.   it pleases
85 I woot wel that th'Apostle was a maide,°   virgin
But nathelees, though that he wroot and saide
He wolde that every wight were swich° as he,   such
Al nis but conseil to virginitee;
And for to been a wif he yaf me leve
90 Of indulgence; so nis it no repreve°   disgrace
To wedde me[6] if that my make° die,   mate
Withouten excepcion of bigamye[7]—
Al° were it good no womman for to touche[8]   although
(He mente as in his bed or in his couche.

5. I.e., shall come along.
6. St. Paul.
7. I please. "A Goddes half": on God's behalf.
8. "It is better to marry than to burn" (1 Corinthians 7.9). Many of the Wife's citations of St. Paul are from this chapter, often secondhand from St. Jerome's tract Against Jovinian.
9. What do I care.
1. The first man whom the Bible mentions as having two wives (Genesis 4.19–24); he is cursed, however, not for his marriages but for murder.
2. I.e., at the same time.
3. I.e., prize in a race.
4. Understood for, i.e., applicable to.
5. Where.
6. For me to marry.
7. I.e., without there being any legal objection on the score of remarriage.
8. "It is good for a man not to touch a woman" (1 Corinthians 7.1).

95   For peril is bothe fir° and tow° t'assemble—   *fire/flax*
     Ye knowe what this ensample may resemble).[9]
     This al and som,[1] he heeld virginitee
     More parfit than wedding in freletee.°   *frailty*
     (Freletee clepe I but if[2] that he and she
100   Wolde leden al hir lif in chastitee.)
     I graunte it wel, I have noon envye
     Though maidenhede preferre° bigamye:°   *excel/remarriage*
     It liketh hem to be clene in body and gost.°   *spirit*
     Of myn estaat ne wol I make no boost;
105   For wel ye knowe, a lord in his houshold
     Ne hath nat every vessel al of gold:
     Some been of tree,° and doon hir lord servise.   *wood*
     God clepeth° folk to him in sondry wise,   *calls*
     And everich hath of God a propre[3] yifte,
110   Som this, som that, as him liketh shifte.°   *ordain*
     Virginitee is greet perfeccioun,
     And continence eek with devocioun,
     But Crist, that of perfeccion is welle,°   *source*
     Bad nat every wight he sholde go selle
115   Al that he hadde and yive it to the poore,
     And in swich wise folwe him and his fore:°[4]   *footsteps*
     He spak to hem that wolde live parfitly°—   *perfectly*
     And lordinges, by youre leve, that am nat I.
     I wol bistowe the flour of al myn age
120   In th'actes and in fruit of mariage.
       Telle me also, to what conclusioun°   *end*
     Were membres maad of generacioun
     And of so parfit wis a wrighte ywrought?[5]
       Trusteth right wel, they were nat maad for nought.
125   Glose° whoso wol, and saye bothe up and down   *interpret*
     That they were maked for purgacioun
     Of urine, and oure bothe thinges smale
     Was eek° to knowe a femele from a male,   *also*
     And for noon other cause—saye ye no?
130   Th'experience woot it is nought so.
     So that the clerkes be nat with me wrothe,
     I saye this, that they been maad for bothe—
     That is to sayn, for office° and for ese°   *use/pleasure*
     Of engendrure,° ther we nat God displese.   *procreation*
135   Why sholde men elles in hir bookes sette
     That man shal yeelde[6] to his wif hir dette?°   *(marital) debt*
     Now wherwith sholde he make his payement
     If he ne used his sely° instrument?   *innocent*
     Thanne were they maad upon a creature
140   To purge urine, and eek for engendrure.
       But I saye nought that every wight is holde,°   *bound*
     That hath swich harneis° as I to you tolde,   *equipment*

[Handwritten marginal note beside lines 105–110: "she may not have been perfect, but she was a good wife."]

---

9. I.e., what this metaphor may apply to.
1. This is all there is to it.
2. Frailty I call it unless.
3. I.e., his own.

4. Matthew 19.21.
5. And wrought by so perfectly wise a maker.
6. I.e., pay.

To goon and usen hem in engendrure:
Thanne sholde men take of chastitee no cure.°   *heed*
145 Crist was a maide° and shapen as a man,   *virgin*
And many a saint sith that the world bigan,
Yit lived they evere in parfit chastitee.
I nil° envye no virginitee: *will not*
Lat hem be breed° of pured° whete seed,   *bread / refined*
150 And lat us wives hote° barly breed—   *be called*
And yit with barly breed, Mark telle can,
Oure Lord Jesu refresshed many a man.⁷
In swich estaat as God hath cleped us
I wol persevere: I nam nat precious.°   *fastidious*
155 In wifhood wol I use myn instrument
As freely° as my Makere hath it sent.   *generously*
If I be daungerous⁸, God yive me sorwe:
Myn housbonde shal it han both eve and morwe,°   *morning*
    Whan that him list⁹ come forth and paye his dette.
160 An housbonde wol I have, I wol nat lette,¹
Which shal be bothe my dettour° and my thral,°   *debtor / slave*
And have his tribulacion withal°   *as well*
Upon his flessh whil that I am his wif.
I have the power during al my lif
165 Upon his propre° body, and nat he: *own*
Right thus th'Apostle tolde it unto me,
And bad oure housbondes for to love us weel.
Al this sentence° me liketh everydeel.°   *sense / entirely*

[AN INTERLUDE]

    Up sterte° the Pardoner and that anoon: *started*
170 "Now dame," quod he, "by God and by Saint John,
Ye been a noble prechour in this cas.
I was aboute to wedde a wif: allas,
What° sholde I bye° it on my flessh so dere?   *why / purchase*
Yit hadde I levere° wedde no wif toyere."°   *rather / this year*
175   "Abid," quod she, "my tale is nat bigonne.
Nay, thou shalt drinken of another tonne,°   *tun, barrel*
Er° that I go, shal savoure wors than ale.   *before*
And whan that I have told thee forth my tale
Of tribulacion in mariage,
180 Of which I am expert in al myn age—
This is to saye, myself hath been the whippe—
Thanne maistou chese° wheither thou wolt sippe   *choose*
Of thilke° tonne that I shal abroche;°   *this same / open*
Be war of it, er thou too neigh approche,
185 For I shal telle ensamples mo than ten.
'Whoso that nil° be war by othere men,   *will not*
By him shal othere men corrected be.'

---

7. In the descriptions of the miracle of the loaves and fishes, it is actually John, not Mark, who mentions barley bread (6.9).
8. In romance *dangerous* is a term for disdainfulness with which a woman rejects a lover. The Wife means she will not withhold sexual favors, in emulation of God's generosity (line 156).
9. When he wishes to.
1. I will not leave off, desist.

Thise same wordes writeth Ptolomee:
Rede in his *Almageste* and take it there."[2]

190 "Dame, I wolde praye you if youre wil it were,"
Saide this Pardoner, "as ye bigan,
Telle forth youre tale; spareth for no man,
And teche us yonge men of youre practike."°   *mode of operation*
"Gladly," quod she, "sith it may you like;°   *please*

195 But that I praye to al this compaignye,
If that I speke after my fantasye,[3]
As taketh nat agrief° of that I saye,   *amiss*
For myn entente nis but for to playe."

[THE WIFE CONTINUES]

Now sire, thanne wol I telle you forth my tale.

200 As evere mote I drinke win or ale,
I shal saye sooth: tho° housbondes that I hadde,   *those*
As three of hem were goode, and two were badde.
The three men were goode, and riche, and olde;
Unnethe° mighte they the statut holde   *scarcely*

205 In which they were bounden unto me—
Ye woot wel what I mene of this, pardee.
As help me God, I laughe whan I thinke
How pitously anight I made hem swinke;°   *work*
And by my fay,° I tolde of it no stoor:[4]   *faith*

210 They hadde me yiven hir land and hir tresor;
Me needed nat do lenger diligence
To winne hir love or doon hem reverence.
They loved me so wel, by God above,
That I ne tolde no daintee of[5] hir love.

215 A wis womman wol bisye hire evere in oon[6]
To gete hire love, ye, ther as she hath noon.
But sith I hadde hem hoolly in myn hand,
And sith that they hadde yiven me al hir land,
What° sholde I take keep° hem for to plese,   *why/care*

220 But it were for my profit and myn ese?
I sette hem so awerke,° by my fay,   *awork*
That many a night they songen° wailaway.   *sang*
The bacon was nat fet° for hem, I trowe,   *brought back*
That some men han in Essexe at Dunmowe.[7]

225 I governed hem so wel after° my lawe   *according to*
That eech of hem ful blisful was and fawe°   *glad*
To bringe me gaye thinges fro the faire;
They were ful glade whan I spak hem faire,
For God it woot, I chidde° hem spitously.°   *chided/cruelly*

230 Now herkneth how I bar me[8] properly:

---

2. "He who will not be warned by the example of others shall become an example to others." The *Almagest*, an astronomical work by the Greek astronomer and mathematician Ptolemy (2nd century C.E.), contains no such aphorism.
3. If I speak according to my fancy.
4. I set no store by it.

5. Set no value on.
6. Busy herself constantly.
7. At Dunmow, a side of bacon was awarded to the couple who after a year of marriage could claim no quarrels, no regrets, and the desire, if freed, to remarry one another.
8. Bore myself, behaved.

Ye wise wives, that conne understonde.
Thus sholde ye speke and bere him wrong on honde[9]—
For half so boldely can ther no man
Swere and lie as a woman can.
235 I saye nat this by wives that been wise,
But if it be whan they hem misavise.[1]
A wis wif, if that she can hir good,[2]
Shal bere him on hande the cow is wood,[3]
And take witnesse of hir owene maide
240 Of hir assent.[4] But herkneth how I saide:
    "Sire olde cainard,° is this thyn array?[5]   *sluggard*
Why is my neighebores wif so gay?
She is honoured overal° ther she gooth: *wherever*
I sitte at hoom; I have no thrifty° cloth.   *decent*
245 What doostou at my neighebores hous?
Is she so fair? Artou so amorous?
What roune° ye with oure maide, benedicite?[6]   *whisper*
Sire olde lechour, lat thy japes° be.   *tricks, intrigues*
And if I have a gossib° or a freend   *confidant*
250 Withouten gilt, ye chiden as a feend,
If that I walke or playe unto his hous.
Thou comest hoom as dronken as a mous,
And prechest on thy bench, with yvel preef.[7]
Thou saist to me, it is a greet meschief°   *misfortune*
255 To wedde a poore womman for costage.[3]
And if that she be riche, of heigh parage,°   *descent*
Thanne saistou that it is a tormentrye
To suffre hir pride and hir malencolye.°   *bad humor*
And if that she be fair, thou verray knave,
260 Thou saist that every holour° wol hire have: *lecher*
She may no while in chastitee abide
That is assailed upon eech a side.
    "Thou saist som folk desiren us for richesse,
Som[9] for oure shap, and som for oure fairnesse,
265 And som for she can outher° singe or daunce,   *either*
And som for gentilesse and daliaunce,°   *flirtatiousness*
Som for hir handes and hir armes smale°—   *slender*
Thus gooth al to the devel by thy tale![1]
Thou saist men may nat keepe[2] a castel wal,
270 It may so longe assailed been overal.°   *everywhere*
And if that she be foul,° thou saist that she   *ugly*
Coveiteth° every man that she may see;   *desires*
For as a spaniel she wol on him lepe,
Til that she finde som man hire to chepe.°   *bargain for*
275 Ne noon so grey goos gooth ther in the lake,

9. Accuse him falsely.
1. Unless it happens that they make a mistake.
2. If she knows what's good for her.
3. Shall persuade him the chough has gone crazy.
The chough, a talking bird, was popularly supposed
to tell husbands of their wives' infidelity.
4. And call as a witness her maid, who is on her
side.

5. I.e., is this how you behave?
6. Bless me.
7. I.e., (may you have) bad luck.
8. Because of the expense.
9. "Som," in this and the following lines, means
"one."
1. I.e., according to your story.
2. I.e., keep safe.

As, saistou, wol be withoute make;°   mate
And saist it is an hard thing for to weelde°   possess
A thing that no man wol, his thankes, heelde.[3]
Thus saistou, lorel,° whan thou goost to bedde,   wretch
280   And that no wis man needeth for to wedde,
Ne no man that entendeth° unto hevene—   aims
With wilde thonder-dint° and firy levene°   thunderbolt/lightning
Mote thy welked nekke be tobroke![4]
Thou saist that dropping° houses and eek smoke   leaking
285   And chiding wives maken men to flee
Out of hir owene hous: a, benedicite,
What aileth swich an old man for to chide?
Thou saist we wives wil oure vices hide
Til we be fast,[5] and thanne we wol hem shewe—
290   Wel may that be a proverbe of a shrewe!°   rascal
Thou saist that oxen, asses, hors,° and houndes,   horses
They been assayed° at diverse stoundes;°   tried out/times
Bacins, lavours,° er that men hem bye,°   washbowls/buy
Spoones, stooles, and al swich housbondrye,°   household goods
295   And so be° pottes, clothes, and array°—   are/clothing
But folk of wives maken noon assay
Til they be wedded—olde dotard shrewe!
And thanne, saistou, we wil oure vices shewe.
Thou saist also that it displeseth me
300   But if° that thou wolt praise my beautee,   unless
And but thou poure° alway upon my face,   gaze
And clepe me 'Faire Dame' in every place,
And but thou make a feeste on thilke day
That I was born, and make me fressh and gay,
305   And but thou do to my norice° honour,   nurse
And to my chamberere within my bowr,[6]
And to my fadres folk, and his allies[7]—
Thus saistou, olde barel-ful of lies.
And yit of our apprentice Janekin,
310   For his crispe° heer, shining as gold so fin,   curly
And for° he squiereth me bothe up and down,   because
Yit hastou caught a fals suspecioun;
I wil° him nat though thou were deed° tomorwe.   want/dead
"But tel me this, why hidestou with sorwe[8]
315   The keyes of thy cheste° away fro me?   money box
It is my good° as wel as thyn, pardee.   property
What, weenestou° make an idiot of oure dame?[9]   do you think to
Now by that lord that called is Saint Jame,
Thou shalt nought bothe, though thou were wood,°   furious
320   Be maister of my body and of my good:
That oon thou shalt forgo, maugree thine yën.[1]
"What helpeth it of me enquere° and spyen?   inquire

---

3. No man would willingly hold.
4. May thy withered neck be broken!
5. I.e., married.
6. And to my chambermaid within my bedroom.
7. Relatives by marriage.

8. I.e., with sorrow to you.
9. I.e., me, the mistress of the house.
1. Despite your eyes, i.e., despite anything you can
do about it.

I trowe thou woldest loke° me in thy cheste.   *lock*
Thou sholdest saye, 'Wif, go wher thee leste.°   *it may please*
325   Taak youre disport.² I nil leve° no tales: *believe*
I knowe you for a trewe wif, dame Alis.'
We love no man that taketh keep or charge³
Wher that we goon: we wol been at oure large.⁴
Of alle men yblessed mote he be
330   The wise astrologen° daun Ptolomee,   *astronomer*
That saith this proverbe in his *Almageste*:
'Of alle men his wisdom is the hyeste
That rekketh° nat who hath the world in honde.'⁵   *cares*
By this proverbe thou shalt understonde,
335   Have thou⁶ ynough, what thar° thee rekke or care   *need*
How merily that othere folkes fare?
For certes, olde dotard, by youre leve,
Ye shal han queinte⁷ right ynough at eve:
He is too greet a nigard that wil werne°   *refuse*
340   A man to lighte a candle at his lanterne;
He shal han nevere the lasse° lighte, pardee.   *less*
Have thou ynough, thee thar nat plaine thee.⁸
"Thou saist also that if we make us gay
With clothing and with precious array,
345   That it is peril of oure chastitee,
And yit, with sorwe, thou moste enforce thee,⁹
And saye thise wordes in th' Apostles¹ name:
'In habit° maad with chastitee and shame   *clothing*
Ye wommen shal apparaile you,' quod he,
350   'And nat in tressed heer² and gay perree,°   *jewelry*
As perles, ne with gold ne clothes riche.'³
After thy text, ne after thy rubriche,⁴
I wol nat werke as muchel as a gnat.
Thou saidest this, that I was lik a cat:
355   For whoso wolde senge° a cattes skin,   *singe*
Thanne wolde the cat wel dwellen in his in;°   *lodging*
And if the cattes skin be slik° and gay,   *sleek*
She wol nat dwelle in house half a day,
But forth she wol, er any day be dawed,⁵
360   To shewe her skin and goon a-caterwawed.°   *caterwauling*
This is to saye, if I be gay, sire shrewe,
I wol renne° out, my borel° for to shewe.   *run/clothing*
Sir olde fool, what helpeth⁶ thee t'espyen?
Though thou praye Argus with his hundred yën⁷
365   To be my wardecors,° as he can best,   *bodyguard*
In faith, he shal nat keepe° me but me lest:⁸   *guard*

2. Enjoy yourself.
3. Notice or interest.
4. I.e., liberty.
5. Who rules the world.
6. If you have.
7. Elegant, pleasing thing; a euphemism for sexual enjoyment.
8. I.e., you need not complain.
9. Strengthen your position.
1. I.e., St. Paul's.

2. I.e., elaborate hairdo.
3. See 1 Timothy 2.9.
4. Rubric, i.e., direction.
5. Has dawned.
6. What does it help.
7. Argus was a monster whom Juno set to watch over one of Jupiter's mistresses. Mercury put all one hundred of his eyes to sleep and slew him.
8. Unless I please.

Yit coude I make his beerd,[9] so mote I thee.°   *prosper*
    "Thou saidest eek that ther been thinges three,
The whiche thinges troublen al this erthe,
370   And that no wight may endure the ferthe.°   *fourth*
O leve° sire shrewe, Jesu shorte° thy lif!   *dear/shorten*
Yit prechestou and saist an hateful wif
Yrekened° is for oon of thise meschaunces.[1]   *is counted*
Been ther nat none othere resemblaunces
375   That ye may likne youre parables to,[2]
But if° a sely° wif be oon of tho?   *unless/innocent*
    "Thou liknest eek wommanes love to helle,
To bareine° land ther water may nat dwelle;   *barren*
Thou liknest it also to wilde fir—
380   The more it brenneth,° the more it hath desir   *burns*
To consumen every thing that brent° wol be;   *burned*
Thou saist right° as wormes shende° a tree,   *just/destroy*
Right so a wif destroyeth hir housbonde—
This knowen they that been to wives bonde."°   *bound*
385   Lordinges, right thus, as ye han understonde,
Bar I stifly mine olde housbondes on honde[3]
That thus they saiden in hir dronkenesse—
And al was fals, but that I took witnesse
On Janekin and on my nece also.
390   O Lord, the paine I dide hem and the wo,
Ful giltelees, by Goddes sweete pine!°   *suffering*
For as an hors I coude bite and whine;°   *whinny*
I coude plaine° and° I was in the gilt,   *complain/if*
Or elles often time I hadde been spilt.°   *ruined*
395   Whoso that first to mille comth first grint.°   *grinds*
I plained first: so was oure werre stint.[4]
They were ful glade to excusen hem ful blive°   *quickly*
Of thing of which they nevere agilte hir live.[5]
Of wenches wolde I beren hem on honde,[6]
400   Whan that for sik[7] they mighte unnethe° stonde,   *scarcely*
Yit tikled I his herte for that he
Wende° I hadde had of him so greet cheertee.°   *thought/affection*
I swoor that al my walking out by nighte
Was for to espye wenches that he dighte.[8]
405   Under that colour[9] hadde I many a mirthe.
For al swich wit is yiven us in oure birthe:
Deceite, weeping, spinning God hath yive
To wommen kindely° whil they may live.   *naturally*
And thus of oo thing I avaunte me:[1]
410   At ende I hadde the bet° in eech degree,   *better*
By sleighte or force, or by som manere thing,
As by continuel murmur° or grucching;°   *complaint/grumbling*

---

9. I.e., deceive him.
1. For the other three misfortunes see Proverbs 30.21–23.
2. Are there no other (appropriate) similitudes to which you might draw analogies?
3. I rigorously accused my old husbands.
4. Our war brought to an end.

5. Of which they were never guilty in their lives.
6. Falsely accuse them.
7. I.e., sickness.
8. Had intercourse with.
9. I.e., pretense.
1. Boast.

Namely° abedde hadden they meschaunce: *especially*
Ther wolde I chide and do hem no plesaunce;[2]
415 I wolde no lenger in the bed abide
If that I felte his arm over my side,
Til he hadde maad his raunson° unto me;   *ransom*
Thanne wolde I suffre him do his nicetee.°   *foolishness (sex)*
And therfore every man this tale I telle:
420 Winne whoso may, for al is for to selle;
With empty hand men may no hawkes lure.
For winning° wolde I al his lust endure,   *profit*
And make me a feined° appetit—   *pretended*
And yit in bacon[3] hadde I nevere delit.
425 That made me that evere I wolde hem chide;
For though the Pope hadde seten° hem biside,   *sat*
I wolde nought spare hem at hir owene boord.°   *table*
For by my trouthe, I quitte° hem word for word.   *repaid*
As help me verray God omnipotent,
430 Though I right now sholde make my testament,
I ne owe hem nat a word that it nis quit.
I broughte it so aboute by my wit
That they moste yive it up as for the beste,
Or elles hadde we nevere been in reste;
435 For though he looked as a wood° leoun,   *furious*
Yit sholde he faile of his conclusioun.°   *object*
    Thanne wolde I saye, "Goodelief, taak keep,[4]
How mekely looketh Wilekin,[5] oure sheep!
Com neer my spouse, lat me ba° thy cheeke—   *kiss*
440 Ye sholden be al pacient and meeke,
And han a sweete-spiced° conscience,   *mild*
Sith ye so preche of Jobes pacience;
Suffreth alway, sin ye so wel can preche;
And but ye do, certain, we shal you teche
445 That it is fair to han a wif in pees.
Oon of us two moste bowen, doutelees,
And sith a man is more resonable
Than womman is, ye mosten been suffrable.°   *patient*
What aileth you to grucche° thus and grone?   *grumble*
450 Is it for ye wolde have my queinte° allone?   *sexual organ*
Why, taak it al—lo, have it everydeel.°   *all of it*
Peter,[6] I shrewe° you but ye° love it weel.   *curse / if you don't*
For if I wolde selle my bele chose,[7]
I coude walke as fressh as is a rose;
455 But I wol keepe it for youre owene tooth.°   *taste*
Ye be to blame. By God, I saye you sooth!"°   *the truth*
Swiche manere° wordes hadde we on honde.   *kind of*
Now wol I speke of my ferthe° housbonde.   *fourth*
    My ferthe housbonde was a revelour°   *reveler*
460 This is to sayn, he hadde a paramour°   *mistress*

---

2. Give them no pleasure.
3. I.e., old meat.
4. Good friend, take notice.
5. I.e., Willie.

6. By St. Peter.
7. French for "beautiful thing"; a euphemism for sexual organs.

And I was yong and ful of ragerye,°   *passion*
Stiborne° and strong and joly as a pie:°   *untamable / magpie*
How coude I daunce to an harpe smale,°   *gracefully*
And singe, ywis,° as any nightingale,   *indeed*
465 Whan I hadde dronke a draughte of sweete win.
Metellius, the foule cherl, the swin,
That with a staf birafte° his wif hir lif   *deprived*
For° she drank win, though I hadde been his wif,   *because*
Ne sholde nat han daunted° me fro drinke;   *frightened*
470 And after win on Venus moste° I thinke,   *must*
For also siker° as cold engendreth hail,   *sure*
A likerous° mouth moste han a likerous° tail: *greedy / lecherous*
In womman vinolent° is no defence—   *who drinks*
This knowen lechours by experience.
475   But Lord Crist, whan that it remembreth me[8]
Upon my youthe and on my jolitee,
It tikleth me aboute myn herte roote—
Unto this day it dooth myn herte boote°   *good*
That I have had my world as in my time.
480 But age, allas, that al wol envenime,°   *poison*
Hath me biraft[9] my beautee and my pith°—   *vigor*
Lat go, farewel, the devel go therwith!
The flour is goon, ther is namore to telle:
The bren° as I best can now moste I selle;   *bran*
485 But yit to be right merye wol I fonde.°   *strive*
Now wol I tellen of my ferthe housbonde.
    I saye I hadde in herte greet despit
That he of any other hadde delit,
But he was quit,° by God and by Saint Joce: *paid back*
490 I made him of the same wode a croce[1]—
Nat of my body in no foul manere—
But, certainly, I made folk swich cheere[2]
That in his owene grece I made him frye,
For angre and for verray jalousye.
495 By God, in erthe I was his purgatorye,
For which I hope his soule be in glorye.
For God it woot, he sat ful ofte and soong°   *sang*
Whan that his sho ful bitterly him wroong.°   *pinched*
Ther was no wight save God and he that wiste°   *knew*
500 In many wise how sore I him twiste.
He deide whan I cam fro Jerusalem,
And lith ygrave under the roode-beem,[3]
Al° is his tombe nought so curious[4]   *although*
As was the sepulcre of him Darius,
505 Which that Apelles wroughte subtilly:[5]
It nis but wast to burye him preciously.°   *expensively*
Lat him fare wel, God yive his soule reste;

---

8. When I look back.
9. Has taken away from me.
1. I made him a cross of the same wood. The proverb has much the same sense as the one quoted in line 493.
2. Pretended to be in love with others.

3. And lies buried under the rood beam (the crucifix beam running between nave and chancel).
4. Carefully wrought.
5. Accordingly to medieval legend, the artist Apelles decorated the tomb of Darius, king of the Persians.

He is now in his grave and in his cheste.° *coffin*
    Now of my fifthe housbonde wol I telle—
510 God lete his soule nevere come in helle—
And yit he was to me the moste shrewe:[6]
That feele I on my ribbes al by rewe,[7]
And evere shal unto myn ending day.
But in oure bed he was so fressh and gay,
515 And therwithal so wel coulde he me glose° *flatter, coax*
Whan that he wolde han my bele chose,
That though he hadde me bet° on every boon,° *beaten / bone*
He coude winne again my love anoon.° *immediately*
I trowe I loved him best for that he
520 Was of his love daungerous[8] to me.
We wommen han, if that I shal nat lie,
In this matere a quainte fantasye:[9]
Waite what[1] thing we may nat lightly° have, *easily*
Therafter wol we crye al day and crave;
525 Forbede us thing, and that desiren we;
Preesse on us faste, and thanne wol we flee.
With daunger oute we al oure chaffare:[2]
Greet prees° at market maketh dere° ware, *crowd / expensive*
And too greet chepe is holden at litel pris.[3]
530 This knoweth every womman that is wis.
    My fifthe housbonde—God his soule blesse!—
Which that I took for love and no richesse,
He somtime was a clerk at Oxenforde,
And hadde laft° scole and wente at hoom to boorde *left*
535 With my gossib,° dwelling in oure town *confidante*
God have hir soule!—hir name was Alisoun;
She knew myn herte and eek my privetee° *secrets*
Bet° than oure parissh preest, as mote I thee.° *better / prosper*
To hire biwrayed° I my conseil° al, *disclosed / secrets*
540 For hadde myn housbonde pissed on a wal,
Or doon a thing that sholde han cost his lif,
To hire,° and to another worthy wif, *her*
And to my nece which I loved weel,
I wolde han told his conseil everydeel;° *entirely*
545 And so I dide ful often, God it woot,
That made his face often reed° and hoot° *red / hot*
For verray shame, and blamed himself for he
Hadde told to me so greet a privetee.
    And so bifel that ones° in a Lente— *once*
550 So often times I to my gossib wente,
For evere yit I loved to be gay,
And for to walke in March, Averil, and May,
From hous to hous, to heere sondry tales—
That Janekin clerk and my gossib dame Alis
555 And I myself into the feeldes wente.

6. Worst rascal.
7. In a row.
8. I.e., he played hard to get.
9. Strange fancy.

1. Whatever.
2. (Meeting) with reserve, we spread out our merchandise.
3. Too good a bargain is held at little value.

Myn housbonde was at London al that Lente:
I hadde the better leiser for to playe,
And for to see, and eek for to be seye°   seen
Of lusty folk—what wiste I wher my grace°   luck
560 Was shapen° for to be, or in what place?   destined
Therfore I made my visitaciouns
To vigilies[4] and to processiouns,
To preching eek, and to thise pilgrimages,
To playes of miracles and to mariages,
565 And wered upon[5] my gaye scarlet gites°—   gowns
Thise wormes ne thise motthes ne thise mites,
Upon my peril,[6] frete° hem neveradeel: ate
And woostou why? For they were used weel.
     Now wol I tellen forth what happed me.
570 I saye that in the feeldes walked we,
Til trewely we hadde swich daliaunce,°   flirtation
This clerk and I, that of my purveyaunce°   foresight
I spak to him and saide him how that he,
If I were widwe, sholde wedde me.
575 For certainly, I saye for no bobaunce,°   boast
Yit was I nevere withouten purveyaunce
Of mariage n'of othere thinges eek:
I holde a mouses herte nought worth a leek
That hath but oon hole for to sterte° to,   run
580 And if that faile thanne is al ydo.[7]
I bar him on hand[8] he hadde enchaunted me
(My dame° taughte me that subtiltee);   mother
And eek I saide I mette° of him al night: dreamed
He wolde han slain me as I lay upright,°   on my back
585 And al my bed was ful of verray blood—
"But yit I hope that ye shul do me good;
For blood bitokeneth° gold, as me was taught."   signifies
And al was fals, I dremed of it right naught,
But as I folwed ay my dames° lore°   mother's / teaching
590 As wel of that as othere thinges more.
But now sire—lat me see, what shal I sayn?
Aha, by God, I have my tale again.
     Whan that my ferthe housbonde was on beere,°   funeral bier
I weep,° algate,° and made sory cheere,   wept / anyhow
595 As wives moten,° for it is usage,°   must / custom
And with my coverchief covered my visage;
But for I was purveyed° of a make.°   provided / mate
I wepte but smale, and that I undertake.°   guarantee
     To chirche was myn housbonde born amorwe;[9]
600 With neighebores that for him maden sorwe,
And Janekin oure clerk was oon of tho.
As help me God, whan that I saw him go
After the beere, me thoughte he hadde a paire
Of legges and of feet so clene[1] and faire,

4. Evening service before a religious holiday.
5. Wore.
6. On peril (to my soul), an oath.
7. I.e., the game is up.

8. I pretended to him.
9. In the morning.
1. I.e., neat.

605	That al myn herte I yaf unto his hold.°	possession
	He was, I trowe,° twenty winter old,	believe
	And I was fourty, if I shal saye sooth—	
	But yit I hadde alway a coltes tooth:[2]	
	Gat-toothed[3] was I, and that bicam me weel;	
610	I hadde the prente[4] of Sainte Venus seel.°	seal
	As help me God, I was a lusty oon,	
	And fair and riche and yong and wel-bigoon,°	well-situated
	And trewely, as mine housbondes tolde me,	
	I hadde the beste quoniam[5] mighte be.	
615	For certes I am al Venerien	
	In feeling, and myn herte is Marcien:[6]	
	Venus me yaf my lust, my likerousnesse,°	amorousness
	And Mars yaf me my sturdy hardinesse.	
	Myn ascendent was Taur[7] and Mars therinne—	
620	Allas, allas, that evere love was sinne!	
	I folwed ay° my inclinacioun	ever
	By vertu of my constellacioun;[8]	
	That made me I coude nought withdrawe	
	My chambre of Venus from a good felawe.	
625	Yit have I Martes° merk upon my face,	Mars's
	And also in another privee place.	
	For God so wis° be my savacioun,°	surely/salvation
	I loved nevere by no discrecioun,°	moderation
	But evere folwede myn appetit,	
630	Al were he short or long or blak or whit;	
	I took no keep,° so that he liked° me,	heed/pleased
	How poore he was, ne eek of what degree.	
	What sholde I saye but at the monthes ende	
	This joly clerk Janekin that was so hende°	courteous, nice
635	Hath wedded me with greet solempnitee,°	splendor
	And to him yaf I al the land and fee°	property
	That evere was me yiven therbifore—	
	But afterward repented me ful sore:	
	He nolde suffre no thing of my list.°	wish
640	By God, he smoot° me ones on the list°	struck/ear
	For that I rente° out of his book a leef,	tore
	That of the strook° myn ere weex° al deef.	blow/grew
	Stibourne° I was as is a leonesse,	stubborn
	And of my tonge a verray jangleresse,°	chatterbox
645	And walke I wolde, as I hadde doon biforn,	
	From hous to hous, although he hadde it[9] sworn;	
	For which he often times wolde preche,	
	And me of olde Romain geestes° teche,	stories
	How he Simplicius Gallus lafte° his wif,	left
650	And hire forsook for terme of al his lif,	
	Nought but for open-heveded he hire sey[1]	

2. I.e., youthful appetites.
3. Gap-toothed women were considered to be amorous.
4. Print, i.e., a birthmark.
5. Latin for "because"; another euphemism for a sexual organ.
6. Influenced by Mars. "Venerien": astrologically influenced by Venus.
7. My birth sign was the constellation Taurus, a sign in which Venus is dominant.
8. I.e., horoscope.
9. I.e., the contrary.
1. Just because he saw her bareheaded.

Looking out at his dore upon a day.
   Another Romain tolde he me by name
That, for his wif was at a someres° game   *summer's*
655   Withouten his witing,° he forsook hire eke;   *knowledge*
And thanne wolde he upon his Bible seke
That ilke proverbe of Ecclesiaste[2]
Where he comandeth and forbedeth faste°   *strictly*
Man shal nat suffre his wif go roule° aboute;   *roam*
660   Thanne wolde he saye right thus withouten doute:
"Whoso that buildeth his hous al of salwes,°   *willow sticks*
And priketh° his blinde hors over the falwes,[3]   *rides*
And suffreth° his wif to go seeken halwes,°   *allows/shrines*
Is worthy to be hanged on the galwes."°   *gallows*
665   But al for nought—I sette nought an hawe[4]
Of his proverbes n'of his olde sawe;
N' I wolde nat of him corrected be:
I hate him that my vices telleth me,
And so doon mo, God woot, of us than I.
670   This made him with me wood al outrely:°   *entirely*
I nolde nought forbere° him in no cas.   *submit to*
   Now wol I saye you sooth, by Saint Thomas,
Why that I rente° out of his book a leef,   *tore*
For which he smoot me so that I was deef.
675   He hadde a book that gladly night and day
For his disport° he wolde rede alway.   *entertainment*
He cleped it *Valerie*[5] *and Theofraste,*
At which book he lough° alway ful faste;   *laughed*
And eek ther was somtime a clerk at Rome,
680   A cardinal, that highte Saint Jerome,
That made a book[6] again° Jovinian;   *against*
In which book eek ther was Tertulan,
Crysippus, Trotula, and Helouis,[7]
That was abbesse nat fer fro Paris;
685   And eek the Parables of Salomon,
Ovides *Art,*[8] and bookes many oon—
And alle thise were bounden in oo volume.
And every night and day was his custume,
Whan he hadde leiser and vacacioun°   *free time*
690   From other worldly occupacioun,
To reden in this book of wikked wives.
He knew of hem mo legendes and lives
Than been of goode wives in the Bible.
For trusteth wel, it is an impossible°   *impossibility*
695   That any clerk wol speke good of wives,
But if it be of holy saintes lives,

2. Ecclesiasticus (25.25).
3. Plowed land.
4. I did not rate at the value of a hawthorn berry.
5. "Valerie": i.e., the *Letter of Valerius Concerning Not Marrying*, by Walter Map; "Theofraste": Theophrastus's *Book Concerning Marriage*. Medieval manuscripts often contained a number of different works, sometimes, as here, dealing with the same subject.

6. St. Jerome's antifeminist *Against Jovinian*.
7. "Tertulan": i.e., Tertullian, author of treatises on sexual modesty. "Crysippus": mentioned by Jerome as an antifeminist. "Trotula": a female doctor whose presence here is unexplained. "Helouis": i.e., Eloise, whose love affair with the great scholar Abelard was a medieval scandal.
8. Ovid's *Art of Love*. "Parables of Salomon": the biblical Book of Proverbs.

N'of noon other womman nevere the mo—
Who painted the leon, tel me who?[9]
By God, if wommen hadden writen stories,
700 As clerkes han within hir oratories,°   *chapels*
They wolde han writen of men more wikkednesse
Than al the merk[1] of Adam may redresse.
The children of Mercurye and Venus[2]
Been in hir werking° ful contrarious:°   *operation/opposed*
705 Mercurye loveth wisdom and science,
And Venus loveth riot° and dispence;°   *revelry/spending*
And for hir diverse disposicioun
Each falleth in otheres exaltacioun,[3]
And thus, God woot, Mercurye is desolat
710 In Pisces wher Venus is exaltat,[4]
And Venus falleth ther Mercurye is raised:
Therfore no womman of no clerk is praised.
The clerk, whan he is old and may nought do
Of Venus werkes worth his olde sho,°   *shoe*
715 Thanne sit° he down and writ° in his dotage   *sits/writes*
That wommen can nat keepe hir mariage.
    But now to purpose why I tolde thee
That I was beten for a book, pardee:
Upon a night Janekin, that was our sire,[5]
720 Redde on his book as he sat by the fire
Of Eva first, that for hir wikkednesse
Was al mankinde brought to wrecchednesse,
For which that Jesu Crist himself was slain
That boughte° us with his herte blood again—   *redeemed*
725 Lo, heer expres of wommen may ye finde
That womman was the los° of al mankinde.[6]   *ruin*
    Tho° redde he me how Sampson loste his heres: *then*
Sleeping his lemman° kitte° it with hir sheres,   *lover/cut*
Thurgh which treson loste he both his yën.
730 Tho redde he me, if that I shal nat lien,
Of Ercules and of his Dianire,[7]
That caused him to sette himself afire.
    No thing forgat he the sorwe and wo
That Socrates hadde with his wives two—
735 How Xantippa caste pisse upon his heed:
This sely° man sat stille as he were deed: *poor, hapless*
He wiped his heed, namore dorste° he sayn   *dared*
But "Er that thonder stinte,° comth a rain."   *stops*
    Of Pasipha[8] that was the queene of Crete—
740 For shrewednesse° him thoughte the tale sweete—   *malice*

[handwritten annotation: he read books about wicked women, probably to teach her a lesson]

9. In one of Aesop's fables, the lion, shown a picture of a man killing a lion, asked who painted the picture. Had a lion been the artist, of course, the roles would have been reversed.
1. Mark, sex.
2. I.e., clerks and women, astrologically ruled by Mercury and Venus, respectively.
3. Because of their contrary positions (as planets), each one descends (in the belt of the zodiac) as the other rises, hence one loses its power as the other

becomes dominant.
4. I.e., Mercury is deprived of power in Pisces (the sign of the Fish), where Venus is most powerful.
5. My husband.
6. The stories of wicked women Chaucer drew mainly from St. Jerome and Walter Map.
7. Dejanira unwittingly gave Hercules a poisoned shirt, which hurt him so much that he committed suicide by fire.
8. Pasiphaë, who had intercourse with a bull.

Fy, speek namore, it is a grisly thing
Of hir horrible lust and hir liking.°   *pleasure*
    Of Clytermistra⁹ for hir lecherye
That falsly made hir housbonde for to die,
745   He redde it with ful good devocioun.
    He tolde me eek for what occasioun
Amphiorax¹ at Thebes loste his lif:
Myn housbonde hadde a legende of his wif
Eriphylem, that for an ouche° of gold   *trinket*
750   Hath prively unto the Greekes told
Wher that hir housbonde hidde him in a place,
For which he hadde at Thebes sory grace.
    Of Livia tolde he me and of Lucie:²
They bothe made hir housbondes for to die,
755   That oon for love, that other was for hate;
Livia hir housbonde on an even late
Empoisoned hath for that she was his fo;
Lucia likerous° loved hir housbonde so   *lecherous*
That for° he sholde alway upon hire thinke,   *in order that*
760   She yaf him swich a manere love-drinke
That he was deed er it were by the morwe.³
And thus algates° housbondes han sorwe.   *in every way*
    Thanne tolde he me how oon Latumius
Complained unto his felawe Arrius
765   That in his garden growed swich a tree,
On which he saide how that his wives three
Hanged hemself for herte despitous.⁴
    "O leve° brother," quod this Arrius,   *dear*
"Yif me a plante of thilke blessed tree,
770   And in my gardin planted shal it be."
    Of latter date of wives hath he red
That some han slain hir housbondes in hir bed
And lete hir lechour dighte⁵ hire al the night,
Whan that the cors° lay in the floor upright;°   *corpse/on his back*
775   And some han driven nailes in hir brain
Whil that they sleepe, and thus they han hem slain;
Some han hem yiven poison in hir drinke.
He spak more harm than herte may bithinke,°   *imagine*
And therwithal he knew of mo proverbes
780   Than in this world ther growen gras or herbes:
"Bet° is," quod he, "thyn habitacioun   *better*
Be with a leon or a foul dragoun
Than with a womman using° for to chide."   *accustomed*
"Bet is," quod he, "hye in the roof abide
785   Than with an angry wif down in the hous:
They been so wikked° and contrarious,   *perverse*

---

9. Clytemnestra, who, with her lover, Aegisthus, slew her husband, Agamemnon.
1. Amphiaraus, betrayed by his wife, Eriphyle, and forced to go to the war against Thebes.
2. Livia murdered her husband in behalf of her lover, Sejanus. "Lucie": i.e., Lucilla, who was said

to have poisoned her husband, the poet Lucretius, with a potion designed to keep him faithful.
3. He was dead before it was near morning.
4. For malice of heart.
5. Have intercourse with.

They haten that hir housbondes loveth ay."
He saide, "A womman cast° hir shame away   *casts*
When she cast of° hir smok,"⁶ and ferthermo,   *off*
790 "A fair womman, but she be chast also,
Is like a gold ring in a sowes nose."
Who wolde weene,° or who wolde suppose   *think*
The wo that in myn herte was and pine?°   *suffering*
 And whan I sawgh he wolde nevere fine°   *end*
795 To reden on this cursed book al night,
Al sodeinly three leves have I plight°   *snatched*
Out of his book right as he redde, and eke
I with my fist so took⁷ him on the cheeke
That in oure fir he fil° bakward adown.   *fell*
800 And up he sterte as dooth a wood° leoun,   *raging*
And with his fist he smoot me on the heed°   *head*
That in the floor I lay as I were deed.°   *dead*
And whan he sawgh how stille that I lay,
He was agast, and wolde have fled his way,
805 Til atte laste out of my swough° I braide:°   *swoon/started*
"O hastou slain me, false thief?" I saide,
"And for my land thus hastou mordred° me?   *murdered*
Er I be deed yit wol I kisse thee."
And neer he cam and kneeled faire adown,
810 And saide, "Dere suster Alisoun,
As help me God, I shal thee nevere smite. *he hit her*
That I have doon, it is thyself to wite.° *so hard*   *blame*
Foryif it me, and that I thee biseeke."° *that she*   *beseech*
And yit eftsoones° I hitte him on the cheeke, *fell*   *another time*
815 And saide, "Thief, thus muchel am I wreke.° *over 8*   *avenged*
Now wol I die: I may no lenger speke." *he promised*
 But at the laste with muchel care and wo *never to hit*
We fille⁸ accorded by us selven two. *her again*
He yaf me al the bridel° in myn hand,   *bridle*
820 To han the governance of hous and land,
And of his tonge and his hand also;
And made⁹ him brenne° his book anoonright tho.   *burn*
And whan that I hadde geten unto me
By maistrye° al the sovereinetee,°   *skill/dominion*
825 And that he saide, "Myn owene trewe wif,
Do as thee lust° the terme of al thy lif;   *it pleases*
Keep thyn honour, and keep eek myn estat,"
After that day we hadde nevere debat.
God help me so, I was to him as kinde
830 As any wif from Denmark unto Inde,°   *India*
And also trewe, and so was he to me.
I praye to God that sit° in majestee,   *sits*
So blesse his soule for his mercy dere.
Now wol I saye my tale if ye wol heere.

6. Undergarment.   8. I.e., became.
7. I.e., hit.   9. I.e., I made.

[ANOTHER INTERRUPTION]

835   The Frere lough° whan he hadde herd all this: *laughed*
"Now dame," quod he, "so have I joye or blis,
This is a long preamble of a tale."
And whan the Somnour herde the Frere gale,°   *exclaim*
"Lo," quod the Somnour, "Goddes armes two,
840 A frere wol entremette him[1] everemo!
Lo, goode men, a flye and eek a frere
Wol falle in every dissh and eek matere.
What spekestou of preambulacioun?
What, amble or trotte or pisse or go sitte down!
845 Thou lettest° oure disport in this manere."   *hinder*
    "Ye, woltou so, sire Somnour?" quod the Frere.
"Now by my faith, I shal er that I go
Telle of a somnour swich a tale or two
That al the folk shal laughen in this place."
850   "Now elles, Frere, I wol bishrewe° thy face,"   *curse*
Quod this Somnour, "and I bishrewe me,
But if I telle tales two or three
Of freres, er I come to Sidingborne,[2]
That I shal make thyn herte for to moorne°—   *mourn*
855 For wel I woot thy pacience is goon."
    Oure Hoste cride, "Pees, and that anoon!"
And saide, "Lat the womman telle hir tale:
Ye fare as folk that dronken been of ale.
Do, dame, tel forth youre tale, and that is best."
860   "Al redy, sire," quod she, "right as you lest°—   *it pleases*
If I have licence of this worthy Frere."
"Yis, dame," quod he, "tel forth and I wol heere."

The Tale

As was suggested in the headnote to *The Man of Law's Epilogue,* Chaucer may have originally written the fabliau that became *The Shipman's Tale* for the Wife of Bath. If so, then he replaced it with a tale that is not simply appropriate to her character but that develops it even beyond the complexity already revealed in her *Prologue.* The story survives in two other versions in which the hero is Sir Gawain, whose courtesy contrasts sharply with the behavior of the knight in the Wife's tale. As Chaucer has the Wife tell it, the tale expresses her views about the relations of the sexes, her wit and humor, and her fantasies. Like Marie de France's lay *Lanval* (see pp. 126–40), the Wife's tale is about a fairy bride who seeks out and tests a mortal lover.

    In th'olde dayes of the King Arthour,
Of which that Britouns speken greet honour,
865 Al was this land fulfild of faïrye:[3]
The elf-queene° with hir joly compaignye   *queen of the fairies*
Daunced ful ofte in many a greene mede°—   *meadow*
This was the olde opinion as I rede;
I speke of many hundred yeres ago.

---

1. Intrude himself.
2. Sittingbourne (a town forty miles from Lon-don).
3. I.e., filled full of supernatural creatures.

870   But now can no man see none elves mo,
      For now the grete charitee and prayeres
      Of limitours,[4] and othere holy freres,
      That serchen every land and every streem,
      As thikke as motes° in the sonne-beem,   dust particles
875   Blessing halles, chambres, kichenes, bowres,
      Citees, burghes,° castels, hye towres,   townships
      Thropes, bernes, shipnes,[5] dayeries—
      This maketh that ther been no faïries.
      For ther as wont to walken was an elf
880   Ther walketh now the limitour himself,
      In undermeles° and in morweninges,°   afternoons / mornings
      And saith his Matins and his holy thinges,
      As he gooth in his limitacioun.[6]
      Wommen may go saufly° up and down: safely
885   In every bussh or under every tree
      Ther is noon other incubus[7] but he,
      And he ne wol doon hem but[8] dishonour.
          And so bifel it that this King Arthour
      Hadde in his hous a lusty bacheler,°   young knight
890   That on a day cam riding fro river,[9]
      And happed° that, allone as he was born,   it happened
      He sawgh a maide walking him biforn;
      Of which maide anoon, maugree hir heed,[1]
      By verray force he rafte° hir maidenheed;   deprived her of
895   For which oppression° was swich clamour,   rape
      And swich pursuite° unto the King Arthour,   petitioning
      That dampned was this knight for to be deed[2]
      By cours of lawe, and sholde han lost his heed—
      Paraventure° swich was the statut tho—   perchance
900   But that the queene and othere ladies mo
      So longe prayeden the king of grace,
      Til he his lif him graunted in the place,
      And yaf him to the queene, al at hir wille,
      To chese° wheither she wolde him save or spille.[3]   choose
905   The queene thanked the king with al hir might,
      And after this thus spak she to the knight,
      Whan that she saw hir time upon a day:
      "Thou standest yit," quod she, "in swich array°   condition
      That of thy lif yit hastou no suretee.°   guarantee
910   I graunte thee lif if thou canst tellen me
      What thing it is that wommen most desiren:
      Be war and keep thy nekke boon° from iren.   bone
      And if thou canst nat tellen me anoon,°   right away
      Yit wol I yive thee leve for to goon
915   A twelfmonth and a day to seeche° and lere°   search / learn
      An answere suffisant° in this matere,   satisfactory

---

4. Friars licensed to beg in a certain territory.
5. Thorps (villages), barns, stables.
6. I.e., the friar's assigned area. His "holy thinges"
are prayers.
7. An evil spirit that seduces mortal women.
8. "Ne . . . but": only.

9. Hawking, usually carried out on the banks of a
stream.
1. Despite her head, i.e., despite anything she
could do.
2. This knight was condemned to death.
3. Put to death.

And suretee wol I han er that thou pace,°   *pass*
Thy body for to yeelden in this place."
Wo was this knight, and sorwefully he siketh.°   *sighs*
920   But what, he may nat doon al as him liketh,
And atte laste he chees° him for to wende,   *chose*
And come again right at the yeres ende,
With swich answere as God wolde him purveye,°   *provide*
And taketh his leve and wendeth forth his waye.
925   He seeketh every hous and every place
Wher as he hopeth for to finde grace,
To lerne what thing wommen love most.
But he ne coude arriven in no coost[4]
Wher as he mighte finde in this matere
930   Two creatures according in fere.[5]
      Some saiden wommen loven best richesse;
Some saide honour, some saide jolinesse;°   *pleasure*
Some riche array, some saiden lust abedde,
And ofte time to be widwe and wedde.
935   Some saide that oure herte is most esed
Whan that we been yflatered and yplesed—
He gooth ful neigh the soothe, I wol nat lie:
A man shal winne us best with flaterye,
And with attendance° and with bisinesse°   *attention/solicitude*
940   Been we ylimed,° bothe more and lesse.   *ensnared*
      And some sayen that we loven best
For to be free, and do right as us lest,°   *it pleases*
And that no man repreve° us of oure vice,   *reprove*
But saye that we be wise and no thing nice.°   *foolish*
945   For trewely, ther is noon of us alle,
If any wight wol clawe° us on the galle,°   *rub/sore spot*
That we nil kike° for° he saith us sooth: *kick/because*
Assaye° and he shal finde it that so dooth.   *try*
For be we nevere so vicious withinne,
950   We wol be holden° wise and clene of sinne.   *considered*
      And some sayn that greet delit han we
For to be holden stable and eek secree,[6]
And in oo° purpos stedefastly to dwelle,   *one*
And nat biwraye° thing that men us telle—   *disclose*
955   But that tale is nat worth a rake-stele.°   *rake handle*
Pardee,° we wommen conne no thing hele:°   *by God/conceal*
Witnesse on Mida.° Wol ye heere the tale?   *Midas*
      Ovide, amonges othere thinges smale,
Saide Mida hadde under his longe heres,
960   Growing upon his heed, two asses eres,
The whiche vice° he hidde as he best mighte   *defect*
Ful subtilly from every mannes sighte,
That save his wif ther wiste° of it namo.   *knew*
He loved hire most and trusted hire also.
965   He prayed hire that to no creature
She sholde tellen of his disfigure.°   *deformity*

4. I.e., country.   6. Reliable and also closemouthed.
5. Agreeing together.

She swoor him nay, for al this world to winne,
She nolde do that vilainye or sinne
To make hir housbonde han so foul a name:
970 She nolde nat telle it for hir owene shame.
But nathelees, hir thoughte that she dyde°   would die
That she so longe sholde a conseil° hide;   secret
Hire thoughte it swal° so sore about hir herte   swelled
That nedely som word hire moste asterte,[7]
975 And sith she dorste nat telle it to no man,
Down to a mareis° faste° by she ran—   marsh/close
Til she cam there hir herte was afire—
And as a bitore bombleth[8] in the mire,
She laide hir mouth unto the water down:
980 "Biwray° me nat, thou water, with thy soun,"°   betray/sound
Quod she. "To thee I telle it and namo:°   to no one else
Myn housbonde hath longe asses eres two.
Now is myn herte al hool,[9] now is it oute.
I mighte no lenger keep it, out of doute."
985 Here may ye see, though we a time abide,
Yit oute it moot:° we can no conseil hide.   must
The remenant of the tale if ye wol heere,
Redeth Ovide, and ther ye may it lere.[1]
      This knight of which my tale is specially,
990 Whan that he sawgh he mighte nat come thereby—
This is to saye what wommen loven most—
Within his brest ful sorweful was his gost,°   spirit
But hoom he gooth, he mighte nat sojourne:°   delay
The day was come that hoomward moste° he turne.   must
995 And in his way it happed him to ride
In al this care under° a forest side,   by
Wher as he sawgh upon a daunce go
Of ladies foure and twenty and yit mo;
Toward the whiche daunce he drow ful yerne,[2]
1000 In hope that som wisdom sholde he lerne.
But certainly, er he cam fully there,
Vanisshed was this daunce, he niste° where.   knew not
No creature sawgh he that bar° lif,   bore
Save on the greene he sawgh sitting a wif°—   woman
1005 A fouler wight ther may no man devise.°   imagine
Again[3] the knight this olde wif gan rise,
And saide, "Sire knight, heer forth lith° no way.°   lies/road
Telle me what ye seeken, by youre fay.°   faith
Paraventure it may the better be:
1010 Thise olde folk conne° muchel thing," quod she.   know
      "My leve moder,"° quod this knight, "certain,   mother
I nam but deed but if that I can sayn
What thing it is that wommen most desire.
Coude ye me wisse,° I wolde wel quite youre hire."[4]   teach

---

7. Of necessity some word must escape her.
8. Makes a booming noise. "Bittore": bittern, a
heron.
9. I.e., sound.
1. Learn. The reeds disclosed the secret by whispering "aures aselli" (ass's ears).
2. Drew very quickly.
3. I.e., to meet.
4. Repay your trouble.

1015   "Plight° me thy trouthe here in myn hand," quod she,   *pledge*
    "The nexte thing that I requere° thee,   *require of*
    Thou shalt it do, if it lie in thy might,
    And I wol telle it you er it be night."
       "Have heer my trouthe," quod the knight. "I graunte."
1020   "Thanne," quod she, "I dar me wel avaunte°   *boast*
    Thy lif is sauf,° for I wol stande therby.   *safe*
    Upon my lif the queene wol saye as I.
    Lat see which is the pruddeste° of hem alle   *proudest*
    That wereth on⁵ a coverchief or a calle°   *headdress*
1025   That dar saye nay of that I shal thee teche.
    Lat us go forth withouten lenger speeche."
    Tho rouned° she a pistel° in his ere,   *whispered / message*
    And bad him to be glad and have no fere.
       Whan they be comen to the court, this knight
1030   Saide he hadde holde his day as he hadde hight,°   *promised*
    And redy was his answere, as he saide.
    Ful many a noble wif, and many a maide,
    And many a widwe—for that they been wise—
    The queene hirself sitting as justise,
1035   Assembled been this answere for to heere,
    And afterward this knight was bode° appere.   *bidden to*
    To every wight comanded was silence,
    And that the knight sholde telle in audience°   *open hearing*
    What thing that worldly wommen loven best.
1040   This knight ne stood nat stille as dooth a best,°   *beast*
    But to his question anoon answerde
    With manly vois that al the court it herde.
       "My lige° lady, generally," quod he,   *liege*
    "Wommen desire to have sovereinetee°   *dominion*
1045   As wel over hir housbonde as hir love,
    And for to been in maistrye him above.
    This is youre moste desir though ye me kille.
    Dooth as you list:° I am here at youre wille."   *please*
       In al the court ne was ther wif ne maide
1050   Ne widwe that contraried° that he saide,   *contradicted*
    But saiden he was worthy han° his lif.   *to have*
       And with that word up sterte° that olde wif,   *started*
    Which that the knight sawgh sitting on the greene;
    "Mercy," quod she, "my soverein lady queene,
1055   Er that youre court departe, do me right.
    I taughte this answere unto the knight,
    For which he plighte me his trouthe there
    The firste thing I wolde him requere°   *require*
    He wolde it do, if it laye in his might.
1060   Bifore the court thanne praye I thee, sire knight,"
    Quod she, "that thou me take unto thy wif,
    For wel thou woost that I have kept° thy lif.   *saved*
    If I saye fals, say nay, upon thy fay."
       This knight answerde, "Allas and wailaway,
1065   I woot right wel that swich was my biheeste.°   *promise*

5. That wears.

For Goddes love, as chees° a newe requeste: *choose*
Taak al my good and lat my body go."
    "Nay thanne," quod she, "I shrewe^c us bothe two.   *curse*
For though that I be foul and old and poore,
1070 I nolde for al the metal ne for ore
That under erthe is grave° or lith° above,   *buried/lies*
But if thy wif I were and eek thy love."
    "My love," quod he. "Nay, my dampnacioun!°   *damnation*
Allas, that any of my nacioun⁶
1075 Sholde evere so foule disparaged° be."   *degraded*
But al for nought, th'ende is this, that he
Constrained was: he needes moste hire wedde,
And taketh his olde wif and gooth to bedde.
    Now wolden some men saye, paraventure,
1080 That for my necligence I do no cure⁷
To tellen you the joye and al th'array
That at the feeste was that ilke day.
To which thing shortly answere I shal:
I saye ther nas no joye ne feeste at al;
1085 Ther nas but hevinesse and muche sorwe.
For prively he wedded hire on morwe,⁸
And al day after hidde him as an owle,
So wo was him, his wif looked so foule.
    Greet was the wo the knight hadde in his thought:
1090 Whan he was with his wif abedde brought,
He walweth° and he turneth to and fro.   *tosses*
His olde wif lay smiling everemo,
And saide, "O dere housbonde, benedicite,°   *bless me*
Fareth° every knight thus with his wif as ye?   *behaves*
1095 Is this the lawe of King Arthures hous?
Is every knight of his thus daungerous?°   *standoffish*
I am youre owene love and youre wif;
I am she which that saved hath youre lif;
And certes yit ne dide I you nevere unright.
1100 Why fare ye thus with me this firste night?
Ye faren like a man hadde lost his wit.
What is my gilt? For Goddes love, telle it,
And it shal been amended if I may."   *he is not being a gentleman!*
    "Amended!" quod this knight. "Allas, nay, nay,
1105 It wol nat been amended neveremo.
Thou art so lothly° and so old also,   *hideous*
And therto comen of so lowe a kinde,°   *lineage*
That litel wonder is though I walwe and winde.°   *turn*
So wolde God myn herte wolde breste!"°   *break*
1110   "Is this," quod she, "the cause of youre unreste?"
"Ye, certainly," quod he. "No wonder is."
    "Now sire," quod she, "I coude amende al this,
If that me liste, er it were dayes three,
So° wel ye mighte bere you⁹ unto me.   *provided that*
1115   "But for ye speken of swich gentilesse°   *nobility*

6. I.e., family.   8. In the morning.
7. I do not take the trouble.   9. Behave.

As is descended out of old richesse—
That therfore sholden ye be gentilmen—
Swich arrogance is nat worth an hen.
Looke who that is most vertuous alway,
1120 Privee and apert,[1] and most entendeth° ay°   *tries/always*
To do the gentil deedes that he can,
Taak him for the gretteste° gentilman.   *greatest*
Crist wol° we claime of him oure gentilesse,   *desires that*
Nat of oure eldres for hir 'old richesse.'
1125 For though they yive us al hir heritage,
For which we claime to been of heigh parage,°   *descent*
Yit may they nat biquethe for no thing
To noon of us hir vertuous living,
That made hem gentilmen ycalled be,
1130 And bad[2] us folwen hem in swich degree.
     "Wel can the wise poete of Florence,
That highte Dant,[3] speken in this sentence;°   *topic*
Lo, in swich manere rym is Dantes tale:
'Ful selde° up riseth by his braunches[4] smale   *seldom*
1135 Prowesse° of man, for God of his prowesse   *excellence*
Wol that of him we claime oure gentilesse.'
For of oure eldres may we no thing claime
But temporel thing that man may hurte and maime.
Eek every wight woot this as wel as I,
1140 If gentilesse were planted natureelly
Unto a certain linage down the line,
Privee and apert, thanne wolde they nevere fine°   *cease*
To doon of gentilesse the faire office°—   *function*
They mighte do no vilainye or vice.
1145   "Taak fir and beer° it in the derkeste hous   *bear*
Bitwixe this and the Mount of Caucasus,
And lat men shette° the dores and go thenne,°   *shut/thence*
Yit wol the fir as faire lye° and brenne°   *blaze/burn*
As twenty thousand men mighte it biholde:
1150 His° office natureel ay wol it holde,   *its*
Up° peril of my lif, til that it die.   *upon*
Heer may ye see wel how that genterye°   *gentility*
Is nat annexed° to possessioun,[5]   *related*
Sith folk ne doon hir operacioun
1155 Alway, as dooth the fir, lo, in his kinde.°   *nature*
For God it woot, men may wel often finde
A lordes sone do shame and vilainye;
And he that wol han pris of his gentrye,[6]
For he was boren° of a gentil° hous,   *born/noble*
1160 And hadde his eldres noble and vertuous,
And nil himselven do no gentil deedes,
Ne folwen his gentil auncestre that deed° is,   *dead*
He nis nat gentil, be he duc or erl—
For vilaines sinful deedes maken a cherl.

1. Privately and publicly.
2. I.e., they bade.
3. Dante (see his *Convivio*).
4. I.e., by the branches of a man's family tree.
5. I.e., inheritable property.
6. Have credit for his noble birth.

1165   Thy gentilesse[7] nis but renomee°   *renown*
       Of thine auncestres for hir heigh bountee,°   *magnanimity*
       Which is a straunge° thing for thy persone.   *external*
       For gentilesse[3] cometh fro God allone.
       Thanne comth oure verray gentilesse of grace:
1170   It was no thing biquethe us with oure place.
       Thenketh how noble, as saith Valerius,[9]
       Was thilke Tullius Hostilius
       That out of poverte° roos to heigh noblesse.   *poverty*
       Redeth Senek° and redeth eek Boece:°   *Seneca/Boethius*
1175   Ther shul ye seen expres that no drede° is   *doubt*
       That he is gentil that dooth gentil deedes.
       And therfore, leve housbonde, I thus conclude:
       Al° were it that mine auncestres weren rude,[1]   *although*
       Yit may the hye God—and so hope I—
1180   Graunte me grace to liven vertuously.
       Thanne am I gentil whan that I biginne
       To liven vertuously and waive° sinne.   *avoid*
       "And ther as ye of poverte me repreve,°   *reprove*
       The hye God, on whom that we bileve,
1185   In wilful° poverte chees° to live his lif;   *voluntary/chose*
       And certes every man, maiden, or wif
       May understonde that Jesus, hevene king,
       Ne wolde nat chese° a vicious living.   *choose*
       Glad poverte is an honeste° thing, certain;   *honorable*
1190   This wol Senek and othere clerkes sayn.
       Whoso that halt him paid of[2] his poverte,
       I holde him riche al hadde he nat a sherte.°   *shirt*
       He that coveiteth[3] is a poore wight,
       For he wolde han that is nat in his might;
1195   But he that nought hath, ne coveiteth° have,   *desires to*
       Is riche, although we holde him but a knave.
       Verray° poverte it singeth proprely.°   *true/appropriately*
       Juvenal saith of poverte, 'Merily
       The poore man, whan he gooth by the waye,
1200   Biforn the theves he may singe and playe.'
       Poverte is hateful good, and as I gesse,
       A ful greet bringere out of bisinesse;[4]
       A greet amendere eek of sapience°   *wisdom*
       To him that taketh it in pacience;
1205   Poverte is thing, although it seeme elenge,°   *wretched*
       Possession that no wight wol chalenge;[5]
       Poverte ful often, whan a man is lowe,
       Maketh[6] his God and eek himself to knowe;
       Poverte a spectacle° is, as thinketh me,   *pair of spectacles*
1210   Thurgh which he may his verray° freendes see.   *true*
       And therfore, sire, sin that I nought you greve,

---

7. I.e., the gentility you claim.
8. I.e., true gentility.
9. A Roman historian.
1. I.e., low born.
2. Considers himself satisfied with.

3. I.e., suffers desires.
4. I.e., remover of cares.
5. Claim as his property.
6. I.e., makes him.

Of my poverte namore ye me repreve.°   *reproach*
"Now sire, of elde° ye repreve me: *old age*
And certes sire, though noon auctoritee
1215   Were in no book, ye gentils of honour
Sayn that men sholde an old wight doon favour,
And clepe him fader for youre gentilesse—
And auctours[7] shal I finde, as I gesse.
     "Now ther ye saye that I am foul and old:
1220   Thanne drede you nought to been a cokewold,°   *cuckold*
For filthe and elde, also mote I thee,[8]
Been grete wardeins° upon chastitee.   *guardians*
But nathelees, sin I knowe your delit,
I shal fulfille youre worldly appetit.
1225   "Chees° now," quod she, "oon of thise thinges twaye: *choose*
To han me foul and old til that I deye
And be to you a trewe humble wif,
And nevere you displese in al my lif,
Or elles ye wol han me yong and fair,
1230   And take youre aventure° of the repair[9]   *chance*
That shal be to youre hous by cause of me—
Or in some other place, wel may be.
Now chees youreselven wheither° that you liketh."   *whichever*
     This knight aviseth him[1] and sore siketh;°   *sighs*
1235   But atte laste he saide in this manere:
"My lady and my love, and wif so dere,
I putte me in youre wise governaunce:
Cheseth° youreself which may be most plesaunce°   *choose / pleasure*
And most honour to you and me also.
1240   I do no fors the wheither[2] of the two,
For as you liketh it suffiseth° me."   *satisfies*
     "Thanne have I gete° of you maistrye," quod she,   *got*
"Sin I may chese and governe as me lest?"°   *it pleases*
     "Ye, certes, wif," quod he. "I holde it best."
1245   "Kisse me," quod she. "We be no lenger wrothe.
For by my trouthe, I wol be to you bothe—
This is to sayn, ye, bothe fair and good.
I praye to God that I mote sterven wood,[3]
But° I to you be al so good and trewe   *unless*
1250   As evere was wif sin that the world was newe.
And but I be tomorn° as fair to seene   *tomorrow morning*
As any lady, emperisse, or queene,
That is bitwixe the eest and eek the west,
Do with my lif and deeth right as you lest:
1255   Caste up the curtin,[4] looke how that it is."
     And whan the knight sawgh verraily al this,
That she so fair was and so yong therto,
For joye he hente° hire in his armes two;   *took*
His herte bathed in a bath of blisse;

7. I.e., authorities.   2. I do not care whichever.
8. So may I prosper.   3. Die mad.
9. I.e., visits.   4. The curtain around the bed.
1. Considers.

1260	A thousand time arewe° he gan hire kisse,	*in a row*
	And she obeyed him in every thing	
	That mighte do him plesance or liking.°	*pleasure*
	And thus they live unto hir lives ende	
	In parfit° joye. And Jesu Crist us sende	*perfect*
1265	Housbondes meeke, yonge, and fresshe abedde—	
	And grace t'overbide° hem that we wedde.	*outlive*
	And eek I praye Jesu shorte° hir lives	*shorten*
	That nought wol be governed by hir wives,	
	And olde and angry nigardes of dispence°—	*spending*
1270	God sende hem soone a verray° pestilence!	*veritable*

The Pardoner's Prologue and Tale

As with *The Wife of Bath's Prologue* and *Tale*, *The Pardoner's Prologue* and *Tale* develop in profound and surprising ways the portrait sketched in *The General Prologue*. In his *Prologue* the Pardoner boasts to his fellow pilgrims about his own depravity and the ingenuity with which he abuses his office and extracts money from poor and ignorant people.

The medieval pardoner's job was to collect money for the charitable enterprises, such as hospitals, supported by the church. In return for donations he was licensed by the pope to award token remission of sins that the donor should have repented and confessed. By canon law pardoners were permitted to work only in a prescribed area; within that area they might visit churches during Sunday service, briefly explain their mission, receive contributions, and in the pope's name issue indulgence, which was not considered to be a sale but a gift from the infinite treasury of Christ's mercy made in return for a gift of money. In practice, pardoners ignored the restrictions on their office, made their way into churches at will, preached emotional sermons, and claimed extraordinary power for their pardons.

The Pardoner's Tale is a bombastic sermon against gluttony, gambling, and swearing, which he preaches to the pilgrims to show off his professional skills. The sermon is framed by a narrative that is supposed to function as an *exemplum* (that is, an illustration) of the scriptural text, the one on which the Pardoner, as he tells the pilgrims, always preaches: "*Radix malorum est cupiditas*" (Avarice is the root of evil).

The Introduction

	Oure Hoste gan to swere as he were wood°	*insane*
	"Harrow,"° quod he, "by nailes and by blood,[1]	*help*
	This was a fals cherl and a fals justise.[2]	
	As shameful deeth as herte may devise	
5	Come to thise juges and hir advocats.	
	Algate° this sely° maide is slain, allas!	*at any rate / innocent*
	Allas, too dere boughte she beautee!	
	Wherfore I saye alday° that men may see	*always*
	The yiftes of Fortune and of Nature	
10	Been cause of deeth to many a creature.	

1. I.e., God's nails and blood.
2. The Host has been affected by the Physicians's sad tale of the Roman maiden Virginia, whose great beauty caused a judge to attempt to obtain her person by means of a trumped-up lawsuit in which he connived with a "churl" who claimed her as his slave; in order to preserve her chastity, her father killed her.

As bothe yiftes that I speke of now,
Men han ful ofte more for harm than prow.°   *benefit*
   "But trewely, myn owene maister dere,
This is a pitous tale for to heere.
15 But nathelees, passe over, is no fors:[3]
I praye to God to save thy gentil cors,°   *body*
And eek thine urinals and thy jurdones,[4]
Thyn ipocras and eek thy galiones,[5]
And every boiste° ful of thy letuarye°—   *box/medicine*
20 God blesse hem, and oure lady Sainte Marye.
So mote I theen,[6] thou art a propre man,
And lik a prelat, by Saint Ronian![7]
Saide I nat wel? I can nat speke in terme.[8]
But wel I woot, thou doost° myn herte to erme°   *make/grieve*
25 That I almost have caught a cardinacle.[9]
By corpus bones,[1] but if° I have triacle,°   *unless/medicine*
Or elles a draughte of moiste° and corny° ale,   *fresh/malty*
Or but I here anoon° a merye tale,   *at once*
Myn herte is lost for pitee of this maide.
30 "Thou bel ami,[2] thou Pardoner," he saide,
"Tel us som mirthe or japes° right anoon."   *jokes*
   "It shal be doon," quod he, "by Saint Ronion.
But first," quod he, "here at this ale-stake[3]
I wol bothe drinke and eten of a cake."°   *flat loaf of bread*
35   And right anoon thise gentils gan to crye,
"Nay, lat him telle us of no ribaudye.°   *ribaldry*
Tel us som moral thing that we may lere,°   *learn*
Som wit,[4] and thanne wol we gladly heere."
   "I graunte, ywis,"° quod he, "but I moot thinke   *certainly*
40 Upon som honeste° thing whil that I drinke."   *decent*

The Prologue

Lordinges—quod he—in chirches whan I preche,
I paine me[5] to han° an hautein° speeche,   *have/loud*
And ringe it out as round as gooth a belle,
For I can al by rote[6] that I telle.
45 My theme is alway oon,[7] and evere was:
Radix malorum est cupiditas.[8]
First I pronounce whennes° that I come,   *whence*
And thanne my bulles shewe I alle and some:[9]
Oure lige lordes seel on my patente,[1]

3. I.e., never mind.
4. Jordans (chamber pots): the Host is somewhat confused in his endeavor to use technical medical terms. "Urinals": vessels for examining urine.
5. A medicine, probably invented on the spot by the Host, named after Galen. "Ipocras": a medicinal drink named after Hippocrates.
6. So might I prosper.
7. St. Ronan or St. Ninian, with a possible play on "runnion" (sexual organ).
8. Speak in technical idiom.
9. Apparently a cardiac condition, confused in the Host's mind with a cardinal.
1. An illiterate oath, mixing "God's bones" with

corpus dei ("God's body").
2. Fair friend.
3. Sign of a tavern.
4. I.e., something with significance.
5. Take pains.
6. I know all by heart.
7. I.e., the same. "Theme": biblical text on which the sermon is based.
8. Avarice is the root of evil (1 Timothy 6.10).
9. Each and every one. "Bulles": papal bulls, official documents.
1. I.e., the pope's or bishop's seal on my papal license.

50   That shewe I first, my body to warente,°   keep safe
     That no man be so bold, ne preest ne clerk,
     Me to destourbe of Cristes holy werk.
     And after that thanne telle I forth my tales²—
     Bulles of popes and of cardinales,
55   Of patriarkes and bisshopes I shewe,
     And in Latin I speke a wordes fewe,
     To saffron with³ my predicacioun,°   preaching
     And for to stire hem to devocioun.
          Thanne shewe I forth my longe crystal stones,°   jars
60   Ycrammed ful of cloutes° and of bones   rags
     Relikes been they, as weenen° they eechoon.   suppose
     Thanne have I in laton° a shulder-boon   brass
     Which that was of an holy Jewes sheep.
     "Goode men," I saye, "take of my wordes keep:°   notice
65   If that this boon be wasshe in any welle,
     If cow, or calf, or sheep, or oxe swelle,
     That any worm hath ete or worm ystonge,⁴
     Take water of that welle and wassh his tonge,
     And it is hool⁵ anoon. And ferthermoor,
70   Of pokkes° and of scabbe and every soor°   pox, pustules / sore
     Shal every sheep be hool that of this welle
     Drinketh a draughte. Take keep eek° that I telle: also
     If that the goode man that the beestes oweth°   owns
     Wol every wike,° er° that the cok him croweth,   week / before
75   Fasting drinken of this welle a draughte—
     As thilke° holy Jew oure eldres taughte—   that same
     His beestes and his stoor° shal multiplye.   stock
          "And sire, also it heleth jalousye:
     For though a man be falle in jalous rage,
80   Lat maken with this water his potage,°   soup
     And nevere shal he more his wif mistriste,°   mistrust
     Though he the soothe of hir defaute wiste,⁶
     Al hadde she⁷ taken preestes two or three.
          "Here is a mitein° eek that ye may see: mitten
85   He that his hand wol putte in this mitein
     He shal have multiplying of his grain,
     Whan he hath sowen, be it whete or otes—
     So that he offre pens or elles grotes.⁸
          "Goode men and wommen, oo thing warne I you:
90   If any wight be in this chirche now
     That hath doon sinne horrible, that he
     Dar nat for shame of it yshriven° be,   confessed
     Or any womman, be she yong or old,
     That hath ymaked hir housbonde cokewold,°   cuckold
95   Swich° folk shal have no power ne no grace   such
     To offren to⁹ my relikes in this place;

2. I go on with my yarn.   6. Knew the truth of her infidelity.
3. To add spice to.   7. Even if she had.
4. That has eaten any worm or been bitten by any 8. Pennies, groats, coins.
snake.   9. To make gifts in reverence of.
5. I.e., sound.

And whoso findeth him out of swich blame,
He wol come up and offre in Goddes name,
And I assoile° him by the auctoritee   *absolve*
100 Which that by bulle ygraunted was to me."
By this gaude° have I wonne, yeer by yeer,   *trick*
An hundred mark¹ sith° I was pardoner.   *since*
I stonde lik a clerk in my pulpet,
And whan the lewed° peple is down yset,   *ignorant*
105 I preche so as ye han herd bifore,
And telle an hundred false japes° more.   *tricks*
Thanne paine I me² to strecche forth the nekke,
And eest and west upon the peple I bekke°   *nod*
As dooth a douve,° sitting on a berne;°   *dove/barn*
110 Mine handes and my tonge goon so yerne°   *fast*
That it is joye to see my bisinesse.
Of avarice and of swich cursednesse°   *sin*
Is al my preching, for to make hem free°   *generous*
To yiven hir pens, and namely° unto me,   *especially*
115 For myn entente is nat but for to winne,³
And no thing for correccion of sinne:
I rekke° nevere whan that they been beried°   *care/buried*
Though that hir soules goon a-blakeberied.⁴
For certes, many a predicacioun°   *sermon*
120 Comth ofte time of yvel entencioun:
Som for plesance of folk and flaterye,
To been avaunced° by ypocrisye,   *promoted*
And som for vaine glorye, and som for hate;
For whan I dar noon otherways debate,°   *fight*
125 Thanne wol I stinge him⁵ with my tonge smerte°   *sharply*
In preching, so that he shal nat asterte°   *escape*
To been defamed falsly, if that he
Hath trespassed to my bretheren⁶ or to me.
For though I telle nought his propre name,
130 Men shal wel knowe that it is the same
By signes and by othere circumstaunces.
Thus quite° I folk that doon us displesaunces;⁷   *pay back*
Thus spete° I out my venim under hewe°   *spit/false colors*
Of holinesse, to seeme holy and trewe.
135 But shortly myn entente I wol devise:°   *explain*
I preche of no thing but for coveitise;°   *covetousness*
Therfore my theme is yit and evere was
Radix malorum est cupiditas.
Thus can I preche again that same vice
140 Which that I use, and that is avarice.
But though myself be gilty in that sinne,
Yit can I make other folk to twinne°   *separate*
From avarice, and sore to repente—
But that is nat my principal entente:

1. Marks (pecuniary units).
2. I take pains.
3. My intent is only to make money.
4. Go blackberrying, i.e., go to hell.

5. An adversary critical of pardoners.
6. Injured my fellow pardoners.
7. Make trouble for us.

145 I preche no thing but for coveitise.
Of this matere it oughte ynough suffise.
　　Thanne telle I hem ensamples[8] many oon
Of olde stories longe time agoon,
For lewed° peple loven tales olde—　　　　　　　　　　　　*ignorant*
150 Swiche° thinges can they wel reporte and holde.[9]　　　　*such*
What, trowe° ye that whiles I may preche,　　　　　　　　*believe*
And winne gold and silver for° I teche,　　　　　　　　　*because*
That I wol live in poverte wilfully?°　　　　　　　　　　*voluntarily*
Nay, nay, I thoughte° it nevere, trewely,　　　　　　　　*intended*
155 For I wol preche and begge in sondry landes;
I wol nat do no labour with mine handes,
Ne make baskettes and live therby,
By cause I wol nat beggen idelly.[1]
I wol none of the Apostles countrefete:°　　　　　　　　　*imitate*
160 I wol have moneye, wolle,° cheese, and whete,　　　　　　*wool*
Al were it[2] yiven of the pooreste page,
Or of the pooreste widwe in a village—
Al sholde hir children sterve[3] for famine.
Nay, I wol drinke licour of the vine
165 And have a joly wenche in every town.
But herkneth, lordinges, in conclusioun,
Youre liking° is that I shal telle a tale:　　　　　　　　*pleasure*
Now have I dronke a draughte of corny ale,
By God, I hope I shal you telle a thing
170 That shal by reson been at youre liking;
For though myself be a ful vicious man,
A moral tale yit I you telle can,
Which I am wont to preche for to winne.
Now holde youre pees, my tale I wol biginne.

The Tale

175 　　In Flandres whilom° was a compaignye　　　　　　　　　*once*
Of yonge folk that haunteden° folye—　　　　　　　　　　*practiced*
As riot, hasard, stewes,[4] and tavernes,
Wher as with harpes, lutes, and giternes°　　　　　　　　*guitars*
They daunce and playen at dees° bothe day and night,　　*dice*
180 And ete also and drinke over hir might,[5]
Thurgh which they doon the devel sacrifise
Within that develes temple in cursed wise
By superfluitee° abhominable.　　　　　　　　　　　　　　*overindulgence*
Hir othes been so grete and so dampnable
185 That it is grisly for to heere hem swere:
Oure blessed Lordes body they totere[6]—
Hem thoughte that Jewes rente° him nought ynough.　　　*tore*
And eech of hem at otheres sinne lough.°　　　　　　　　　*laughed*

---

8. Exempla (stories illustrating moral principles).
9. Repeat and remember.
1. I.e., without profit.
2. Even though it were.
3. Even though her children should die.

4. Wild parties, gambling, brothels.
5. Beyond their capacity.
6. Tear apart (a reference to oaths sworn by parts of His body, such as "God's bones!" or "God's teeth!").

And right anoon thanne comen tombesteres,°   *dancing girls*
190   Fetis° and smale,° and yonge frutesteres,[7]   *shapely/slender*
     Singeres with harpes, bawdes,° wafereres[8]—   *pimps*
     Whiche been the verray develes officeres,
     To kindle and blowe the fir of lecherye
     That is annexed unto glotonye:[9]
195   The Holy Writ take I to my witnesse
     That luxure° is in win and dronkenesse.   *lechery*
     Lo, how that dronken Lot[1] unkindely°   *unnaturally*
     Lay by his doughtres two unwitingly:
     So dronke he was he niste° what he wroughte.°   *didn't know/did*
200   Herodes, who so wel the stories soughte,[2]
     Whan he of win was repleet° at his feeste,   *filled*
     Right at his owene table he yaf his heeste°   *command*
     To sleen° the Baptist John, ful giltelees.   *slay*
       Senek[3] saith a good word doutelees:
205   He saith he can no difference finde
     Bitwixe a man that is out of his minde
     And a man which that is dronkelewe,°   *drunken*
     But that woodnesse, yfallen in a shrewe,[4]
     Persevereth lenger than dooth dronkenesse.
210   O glotonye, ful of cursednesse!°   *wickedness*
     O cause first of oure confusioun!°   *downfall*
     O original of oure dampnacioun,°   *damnation*
     Til Crist hadde bought° us with his blood again!   *redeemed*
     Lo, how dere, shortly for to sayn,
215   Abought° was thilke° cursed vilainye;   *paid for/that same*
     Corrupt was al this world for glotonye:
     Adam oure fader and his wif also
     Fro Paradis to labour and to wo
     Were driven for that vice, it is no drede.°   *doubt*
220   For whil that Adam fasted, as I rede,
     He was in Paradis; and whan that he
     Eet° of the fruit defended° on a tree,   *ate/forbidden*
     Anoon he was out cast to wo and paine.
     O glotonye, on thee wel oughte us plaine!°   *complain*
225   O, wiste a man[5] how manye maladies
     Folwen of excesse and of glotonies,
     He wolde been the more mesurable°   *moderate*
     Of his diete, sitting at his table.
     Allas, the shorte throte, the tendre mouth,
230   Maketh that eest and west and north and south,
     In erthe, in air, in water, men to swinke,°   *work*
     To gete a gloton daintee mete° and drinke.   *food*
     Of this matere, O Paul, wel canstou trete:
     "Mete unto wombe,° and wombe eek unto mete,   *belly*
235   Shal God destroyen bothe," as Paulus saith.[6]

---

7. Fruit-selling girls.
8. Girl cake vendors.
9. I.e., closely related to gluttony.
1. See Genesis 19.30–36.
2. For the story of Herod and St. John the Baptist, see Mark 6.17–29. "Who so . . . soughte": i.e.,

whoever looked it up in the Gospel would find.
3. Seneca, the Roman Stoic philosopher.
4. But that madness, occurring in a wicked man.
5. If a man knew.
6. See 1 Corinthians 6.13.

Allas, a foul thing is it, by my faith,
To saye this word, and fouler is the deede
Whan man so drinketh of the white and rede[7]
That of his throte he maketh his privee°   *toilet*
240 Thurgh thilke cursed superfluitee.°   *overindulgence*
      The Apostle[8] weeping saith ful pitously,
"Ther walken manye of which you told have I—
I saye it now weeping with pitous vois—
They been enemies of Cristes crois,°   *cross*
245 Of whiche the ende is deeth—wombe is hir god!"[9]
O wombe, O bely, O stinking cod,°   *bag*
Fulfilled° of dong° and of corrupcioun!   *filled full / dung*
At either ende of thee foul is the soun.°   *sound*
How greet labour and cost is thee to finde!°   *provide for*
250 Thise cookes, how they stampe° and straine and grinde,   *pound*
And turnen substance into accident[1]
To fulfillen al thy likerous° talent!°   *greedy / appetite*
Out of the harde bones knokke they
The mary,° for they caste nought away   *marrow*
255 That may go thurgh the golet[2] softe and soote.°   *sweetly*
Of spicerye° of leef and bark and roote   *spices*
Shal been his sauce ymaked by delit,
To make him yit a newer appetit.
But certes, he that haunteth swiche delices°   *pleasures*
260 Is deed° whil that he liveth in tho° vices.   *dead / those*
      A lecherous thing is win, and dronkenesse
Is ful of striving° and of wrecchednesse.   *quarreling*
O dronke man, disfigured is thy face!
Sour is thy breeth, foul artou to embrace!
265 And thurgh thy dronke nose seemeth the soun
As though thou saidest ay,° "Sampsoun, Sampsoun."   *always*
And yit, God woot,° Sampson drank nevere win.[3]   *knows*
Thou fallest as it were a stiked swin;°   *stuck pig*
Thy tonge is lost, and al thyn honeste cure,[4]
270 For dronkenesse is verray sepulture°   *burial*
Of mannes wit° and his discrecioun.   *intelligence*
In whom that drinke hath dominacioun
He can no conseil° keepe, it is no drede.°   *secrets / doubt*
Now keepe you fro the white and fro the rede—
275 And namely° fro the white win of Lepe[5]   *particularly*
That is to selle in Fisshstreete or in Chepe:[6]
The win of Spaine creepeth subtilly
In othere wines growing faste° by,   *close*
Of which ther riseth swich fumositee°   *heady fumes*
280 That whan a man hath dronken draughtes three
And weeneth° that he be at hoom in Chepe,   *supposes*

---

7. I.e., white and red wines.
8. I.e., St. Paul.
9. See Philippians 3.18.
1. A philosophic joke, depending on the distinction between inner reality (substance) and outward
appearance (accident).
2. Through the gullet.

3. Before Samson's birth an angel told his mother
that he would be a Nazarite throughout his life;
members of this sect took no strong drink.
4. Care for self-respect.
5. A town in Spain.
6. Fishstreet and Cheapside in the London market
district.

He is in Spaine, right at the town of Lepe,
Nat at The Rochele ne at Burdeux town;[7]
And thanne wol he sayn, "Sampsoun, Sampsoun."
285   But herkneth, lordinges, oo° word I you praye,   *one*
That alle the soverein actes,[8] dar I saye,
Of victories in the Olde Testament,
Thurgh verray God that is omnipotent,
Were doon in abstinence and in prayere:
290   Looketh° the Bible and ther ye may it lere.°   *behold / learn*
    Looke Attila, the grete conquerour,[9]
Deide° in his sleep with shame and dishonour,   *died*
Bleeding at his nose in dronkenesse:
A capitain sholde live in sobrenesse.
295   And overal this, aviseth you[1] right wel
What was comanded unto Lamuel[2]—
Nat Samuel, but Lamuel, saye I—
Redeth the Bible and finde it expresly,
Of win-yiving° to hem that han[3] justise: *wine-serving*
300   Namore of this, for it may wel suffise.
    And now that I have spoken of glotonye,
Now wol I you defende° hasardrye:°   *prohibit / gambling*
Hasard is verray moder° of lesinges,°   *mother / lies*
And of deceite and cursed forsweringes,°   *perjuries*
305   Blaspheme of Crist, manslaughtre, and wast° also   *waste*
Of catel° and of time; and ferthermo,   *property*
It is repreve° and contrarye of honour   *disgrace*
For to been holden a commune hasardour,°   *gambler*
And evere the hyer he is of estat
310   The more is he holden desolat.[4]
If that a prince useth hasardrye,
In alle governance and policye
He is, as by commune opinioun,
Yholde the lasse° in reputacioun.   *less*
315   Stilbon, that was a wis embassadour,
Was sent to Corinthe in ful greet honour
Fro Lacedomye° to make hir alliaunce,   *Sparta*
And whan he cam him happede° parchaunce   *it happened*
That alle the gretteste° that were of that lond   *greatest*
320   Playing at the hasard he hem foond,°   *found*
For which as soone as it mighte be
He stal him[5] hoom again to his contree,
And saide, "Ther wol I nat lese° my name,   *lose*
N'I wol nat take on me so greet defame°   *dishonor*
325   You to allye unto none hasardours:
Sendeth othere wise embassadours,
For by my trouthe, me were levere[6] die
Than I you sholde to hasardours allye.

---

7. The Pardoner is joking about the illegal custom of adulterating fine wines of Bordeaux and La Rochelle with strong Spanish wine.
8. Distinguished deeds.
9. Attila was the leader of the Huns who almost captured Rome in the 5th century.
1. Consider.

2. Lemuel's mother told him that kings should not drink (Proverbs 31.4–5).
3. I.e., administer.
4. I.e. dissolute.
5. He stole away.
6. I had rather.

For ye that been so glorious in honours
330 Shal nat allye you with hasardours
     As by my wil, ne as by my tretee."°   *treaty*
     This wise philosophre, thus saide he.
         Looke eek that to the king Demetrius
     The King of Parthes,° as the book[7] saith us,   *Parthians*
335 Sente him a paire of dees° of gold in scorn,   *dice*
     For he hadde used hasard therbiforn,
     For which he heeld his glorye or his renown
     At no value or reputacioun.
     Lordes may finden other manere play
340 Honeste° ynough to drive the day away.   *honorable*
         Now wol I speke of othes false and grete
     A word or two, as olde bookes trete:
         Greet swering is a thing abhominable,
     And fals swering is yit more reprevable.°   *reprehensible*
345 The hye God forbad swering at al—
     Witnesse on Mathew.[8] But in special
     Of swering saith the holy Jeremie,[9]
     "Thou shalt swere sooth thine othes and nat lie,
     And swere in doom° and eek in rightwisnesse,°   *equity/righteousness*
350 But idel swering is a cursednesse."°   *wickedness*
         Biholde and see that in the firste Table[1]
     Of hye Goddes heestes° honorable   *commandments*
     How that the seconde heeste of him is this:
     "Take nat my name in idel or amis."
355 Lo, rather° he forbedeth swich swering   *sooner*
     Than homicide, or many a cursed thing.
     I saye that as by ordre thus it stondeth—
     This knoweth that[2] his heestes understondeth
     How that the seconde heeste of God is that.
360 And fertherover,° I wol thee telle al plat°   *moreover/plain*
     That vengeance shal nat parten° from his hous   *depart*
     That of his othes is too outrageous.
     "By Goddes precious herte!" and "By his nailes!"°   *fingernails*
     And "By the blood of Crist that is in Hailes,[3]
365 Sevene is my chaunce,° and thyn is cink and traye!"[4]   *winning number*
     "By Goddes armes, if thou falsly playe
     This daggere shal thurghout thyn herte go!"
     This fruit cometh of the bicche bones[5] two—
     Forswering, ire, falsnesse, homicide.
370 Now for the love of Crist that for us dyde,°   *died*
     Lete° youre othes bothe grete and smale.   *leave*
     But sires, now wol I telle forth my tale.
         Thise riotoures° three of whiche I telle,   *revelers*
     Longe erst er prime[6] ronge of any belle,
375 Were set hem in a taverne to drinke,

7. The book that relates this and the previous incident is the *Policraticus* of the 12th-century Latin
writer John of Salisbury.
8. "But I say unto you, Swear not at all" (Matthew
5.34).
9. Jeremiah 4.2.
1. I.e., the first three of the Ten Commandments.

2. I.e., he that.
3. An abbey in Gloucestershire supposed to possess some of Christ's blood.
4. Five and three.
5. I.e., damned dice.
6. Long before 9 A.M.

And as they sat they herde a belle clinke
Biforn a cors° was caried to his grave.   *corpse*
That oon of hem gan callen to his knave:°   *servant*
Go bet,"[7] quod he, "and axe° redily°   *ask/promptly*
380 What cors is this that passeth heer forby,
And looke° that thou reporte his name weel."°   *be sure/well*
    "Sire," quod this boy, "it needeth neveradeel:[8]
It was me told er ye cam heer two houres.
He was, pardee,° an old felawe of youres,   *by God*
385 And sodeinly he was yslain tonight,°   *last night*
Fordronke° as he sat on his bench upright;   *very drunk*
Ther cam a privee° thief men clepeth° Deeth,   *stealthy/call*
That in this contree al the peple sleeth,°   *slays*
And with his spere he smoot his herte atwo,
390 And wente his way withouten wordes mo.
He hath a thousand slain this° pestilence.   *during this*
And maister, er ye come in his presence,
Me thinketh that it were necessarye
For to be war of swich an adversarye;
395 Beeth redy for to meete him everemore:
Thus taughte me my dame.° I saye namore."   *mother*
    "By Sainte Marye," saide this taverner,
"The child saith sooth, for he hath slain this yeer,
Henne° over a mile, within a greet village,   *hence*
400 Bothe man and womman, child and hine[9] and page.
I trowe° his habitacion be there.   *believe*
To been avised° greet wisdom it were   *wary*
Er that he dide a man a dishonour."
    "Ye, Goddes armes," quod this riotour,
405 "Is it swich peril with him for to meete?
I shal him seeke by way and eek by streete,[1]
I make avow to Goddes digne° bones.   *worthy*
Herkneth, felawes, we three been alle ones:°   *of one mind*
Lat eech of us holde up his hand to other
410 And eech of us bicome otheres brother,
And we wol sleen this false traitour Deeth.
He shal be slain, he that so manye sleeth,
By Goddes dignitee, er it be night."
    Togidres han thise three hir trouthes plight[2]
415 To live and dien eech of hem with other,
As though he were his owene ybore° brother.   *born*
And up they sterte,° al dronken in this rage,   *started*
And forth they goon towardes that village
Of which the taverner hadde spoke biforn,
420 And many a grisly ooth thanne han they sworn,
And Cristes blessed body they torente:°   *tore apart*
Deeth shal be deed° if that they may him hente.°   *dead/catch*
    Whan they han goon nat fully half a mile,
Right as they wolde han treden° over a stile,   *stepped*

7. Better, i.e., quick.   1. By highway and byway.
8. It isn't a bit necessary.   2. Pledged their words of honor.
9. Farm laborer.

425 An old man and a poore with hem mette;
This olde man ful mekely hem grette,° *greeted*
And saide thus, "Now lordes, God you see."³
The pruddeste° of thise riotoures three *proudest*
Answerde again, "What, carl° with sory grace, *fellow*
430 Why artou al forwrapped° save thy face? *muffled up*
Why livestou so longe in so greet age?"
This olde man gan looke in his visage,
And saide thus, "For° I ne can nat finde *because*
A man, though that I walked into Inde,° *India*
435 Neither in citee ne in no village,
That wolde chaunge his youthe for myn age;
And therefore moot° I han myn age stille, *must*
As longe time as it is Goddes wille.
"Ne Deeth, allas, ne wol nat have my lif.
440 Thus walke I lik a restelees caitif,° *wretch*
And on the ground which is my modres° gate *mother's*
I knokke with my staf bothe erly and late,
And saye, 'Leve° moder, leet me in: *dear*
Lo, how I vanisshe, flessh and blood and skin.
445 Allas, whan shal my bones been at reste?
Moder, with you wolde I chaunge° my cheste⁴ *exchange*
That in my chambre longe time hath be,
Ye, for an haire-clout⁵ to wrappe me.'
But yit to me she wol nat do that grace,
450 For which ful pale and welked° is my face. *withered*
But sires, to you it is no curteisye
To speken to an old man vilainye,° *rudeness*
But° he trespasse° in word or elles in deede. *unless/offend*
In Holy Writ ye may yourself wel rede,
455 'Agains⁶ an old man, hoor° upon his heed, *hoar*
Ye shall arise.'⁷ Wherfore I yive you reed,° *advice*
Ne dooth unto an old man noon harm now,
Namore than that ye wolde men dide to you
In age, if that ye so longe abide.⁸
460 And God be with you wher ye go° or ride: *walk*
I moot go thider as I have to go."
"Nay, olde cherl, by God thou shalt nat so,"
Saide this other hasardour anoon.
"Thou partest nat so lightly,° by Saint John! *easily*
465 Thou speke° right now of thilke traitour Deeth, *spoke*
That in this contree alle oure freendes sleeth:
Have here my trouthe, as thou art his espye,° *spy*
Tel wher he is, or thou shalt it abye,° *pay for*
By God and by the holy sacrament!
470 For soothly thou art oon of his assent⁹
To sleen us yonge folk, thou false thief."
"Now sires," quod he, "if that ye be so lief° *anxious*

---

3. May God protect you.
4. Chest for one's belongings, used here as the
symbol for life—or perhaps a coffin.
5. Haircloth, for a winding sheet.

6. In the presence of.
7. Cf. Leviticus 19.32.
8. I.e., if you live so long.
9. I.e., one of his party.

To finde Deeth, turne up this crooked way,
For in that grove I lafte° him, by my fay,°   *left/faith*
475   Under a tree, and ther he wol abide:
Nat for youre boost° he wol him no thing hide.   *boast*
See ye that ook?° Right ther ye shal him finde.   *oak*
God save you, that boughte again[1] mankinde,
And you amende." Thus saide this olde man.
480   And everich of thise riotoures ran
Til he cam to that tree, and ther they founde
Of florins° fine of gold ycoined rounde   *coins*
Wel neigh an eighte busshels as hem thoughte—
Ne lenger thanne after Deeth they soughte,
485   But eech of hem so glad was of the sighte,
For that the florins been so faire and brighte,
That down they sette hem by this precious hoord.
The worste of hem he spak the firste word:
        "Bretheren," quod he, "take keep° what that I saye: *heed*
490   My wit is greet though that I bourde° and playe.   *joke*
This tresor hath Fortune unto us yiven
In mirthe and jolitee oure lif to liven,
And lightly° as it cometh so wol we spende.   *easily*
Ey, Goddes precious dignitee, who wende[2]
495   Today that we sholde han so fair a grace?
But mighte this gold be caried fro this place
Hoom to myn hous—or elles unto youres—
For wel ye woot that al this gold is oures—
Thanne were we in heigh felicitee.
500   But trewely, by daye it mighte nat be:
Men wolde sayn that we were theves stronge,°   *flagrant*
And for oure owene tresor doon us honge.[3]
This tresor moste ycaried be by nighte,
As wisely and as slyly as it mighte.
505   Therefore I rede° that cut° amonges us alle   *advise/straws*
Be drawe, and lat see wher the cut wol falle;
And he that hath the cut with herte blithe
Shal renne° to the town, and that ful swithe,°   *run/quickly*
And bringe us breed and win ful prively;
510   And two of us shal keepen° subtilly   *guard*
This tresor wel, and if he wol nat tarye,
Whan it is night we wol this tresor carye
By oon assent wher as us thinketh best."
That oon of hem the cut broughte in his fest°   *fist*
515   And bad hem drawe and looke wher it wol falle;
And it fil° on the yongeste of hem alle,   *fell*
And forth toward the town he wente anoon.
And also° soone as that he was agoon,°   *as/gone away*
That oon of hem spak thus unto that other:
520   "Thou knowest wel thou art my sworen brother;
Thy profit wol I telle thee anoon:
Thou woost wel that oure felawe is agoon,

---

1. Redeemed.   3. Have us hanged.
2. Who would have supposed.

And here is gold, and that ful greet plentee,
That shall departed° been among us three.   *divided*
525 But nathelees, if I can shape° it so   *arrange*
That it departed were among us two,
Hadde I nat doon a freendes turn to thee?"
    That other answerde, "I noot[4] how that may be:
He woot that the gold is with us twaye.
530 What shal we doon? What shal we to him saye?"
    "Shal it be conseil?"[5] saide the firste shrewe.°   *villain*
"And I shal telle in a wordes fewe
What we shul doon, and bringe it wel aboute."
    "I graunte," quod that other, "out of doute,
535 That by my trouthe I wol thee nat biwraye."°   *expose*
    "Now," quod the firste, "thou woost wel we be twaye,
And two of us shal strenger° be than oon: *stronger*
Looke whan that he is set that right anoon
Aris as though thou woldest with him playe,
540 And I shal rive° him thurgh the sides twaye,   *pierce*
Whil that thou strugelest with him as in game,
And with thy daggere looke thou do the same;
And thanne shal al this gold departed be,
My dere freend, bitwixe thee and me.
545 Thanne we may bothe oure lustes° al fulfille,   *desires*
And playe at dees° right at oure owene wille."   *dice*
And thus accorded been thise shrewes twaye
To sleen the thridde, as ye han herd me saye.
    This yongeste, which that wente to the town,
550 Ful ofte in herte he rolleth up and down
The beautee of thise florins newe and brighte.
"O Lord," quod he, "if so were that I mighte
Have al this tresor to myself allone,
Ther is no man that liveth under the trone°   *throne*
555 Of God that sholde live so merye as I."
And at the laste the feend oure enemy
Putte in his thought that he sholde poison beye,°   *buy*
With which he mighte sleen his felawes twaye—
Forwhy° the feend° foond him in swich livinge   *because/devil*
560 That he hadde leve° him to sorwe bringe:[6]   *permission*
For this was outrely° his fulle entente,   *plainly*
To sleen hem bothe, and nevere to repente.
    And forth he gooth—no lenger wolde he tarye—
Into the town unto a pothecarye,°   *apothecary*
565 And prayed him that he him wolde selle
Som poison that he mighte his rattes quelle,°   *kill*
And eek ther was a polcat[7] in his hawe°   *yard*
That, as he saide, his capons hadde yslawe,°   *slain*
And fain he wolde wreke him[8] if he mighte
570 On vermin that destroyed him[9] by nighte.
    The pothecarye answerde, "And thou shalt have

---

4. Don't know.
5. A secret.
6. Christian doctrine teaches that the devil may
not tempt people except with God's permission.

7. A weasellike animal.
8. He would gladly avenge himself.
9. I.e., were ruining his farming.

A thing that, also° God my soule save,   *as*
In al this world there is no creature
That ete or dronke hath of this confiture°   *mixture*
575 Nat but the mountance° of a corn° of whete— *amount/grain*
That he ne shal his lif anoon forlete.°   *lose*
Ye, sterve° he shal, and that in lasse° while   *die/less*
Than thou wolt goon a paas¹ nat but a mile,
The poison is so strong and violent."
580 This cursed man hath in his hand yhent°   *taken*
This poison in a box and sith° he ran   *then*
Into the nexte streete unto a man
And borwed of him large botels three,
And in the two his poison poured he—
585 The thridde he kepte clene for his drinke,
For al the night he shoop him² for to swinke°   *work*
In carying of the gold out of that place.
And whan this riotour with sory grace
Hadde filled with win his grete botels three,
590 To his felawes again repaireth he.
 What needeth it to sermone of it more?
For right as they had cast° his deeth bifore,   *plotted*
Right so they han him slain, and that anoon.
And whan that this was doon, thus spak that oon:
595 "Now lat us sitte and drinke and make us merye,
And afterward we wol his body berye."°   *bury*
And with that word it happed him par cas³
To take the botel ther the poison was,
And drank, and yaf his felawe drinke also,
600 For which anoon they storven° bothe two.   *died*
 But certes I suppose that Avicen
Wroot nevere in no canon ne in no *fen*⁴
Mo wonder signes⁵ of empoisoning
Than hadde thise wrecches two er hir ending:
605 Thus ended been thise homicides two,
And eek the false empoisonere also.
 O cursed sinne of alle cursednesse!
O traitours homicide, O wikkednesse!
O glotonye, luxure,° and hasardrye!   *lechery*
610 Thou blasphemour of Crist with vilainye
And othes grete of usage° and of pride!   *habit*
Allas, mankinde, how may it bitide
That to thy Creatour which that thee wroughte,
And with his precious herte blood thee boughte,° *redeemed*
615 Thou art so fals and so unkinde,° allas?   *unnatural*
 Now goode men, God foryive you youre trespas,
And ware° you fro the sinne of avarice: *guard*
Myn holy pardon may you alle warice°—   *save*
So that ye offre nobles or sterlinges,⁶

---

1. Take a walk.
2. He was preparing.
3. By chance.
4. The *Canon of Medicine,* by Avicenna, an 11th-

century Arabic philosopher, was divided into sections called "fens."
5. More wonderful symptoms.
6. "Nobles" and "sterlinges" were valuable coins.

620   Or elles silver brooches, spoones, ringes.
      Boweth your heed under this holy bulle!
      Cometh up, ye wives, offreth of youre wolle!°   *wool*
      Youre name I entre here in my rolle: anoon
      Into the blisse of hevene shul ye goon.
625   I you assoile° by myn heigh power—   *absolve*
      Ye that wol offre—as clene and eek as cleer
      As ye were born.—And lo, sires, thus I preche.
      And Jesu Crist that is oure soules leeche°   *physician*
      So graunte you his pardon to receive,
630   For that is best—I wol you nat deceive.

The Epilogue

      "But sires, oo word forgat I in my tale:
      I have relikes and pardon in my male°   *bag*
      As faire as any man in Engelond,
      Whiche were me yiven by the Popes hond.
635   If any of you wol of devocioun
      Offren and han myn absolucioun,
      Come forth anoon, and kneeleth here adown,
      And mekely receiveth my pardoun,
      Or elles taketh pardon as ye wende,°   *ride along*
640   Al newe and fressh at every miles ende—
      So that ye offre alway newe and newe[7]
      Nobles or pens whiche that be goode and trewe.
      It is an honour to everich° that is heer   *everyone*
      That ye have a suffisant° pardoner   *competent*
645   T'assoile you in contrees as ye ride,
      For aventures° whiche that may bitide: *accidents*
      Paraventure ther may falle oon or two
      Down of his hors and breke his nekke atwo;
      Looke which a suretee° is it to you alle   *safeguard*
650   That I am in youre felaweshipe yfalle
      That may assoile you, bothe more and lasse,[8]
      Whan that the soule shal fro the body passe.
      I rede° that oure Hoste shal biginne,   *advise*
      For he is most envoluped° in sinne.   *involved*
655   Com forth, sire Host, and offre first anoon,
      And thou shalt kisse the relikes everichoon,°   *each one*
      Ye, for a grote: unbokele° anoon thy purs."   *unbuckle*
      "Nay, nay," quod he, "thanne have I Cristes curs!
      Lat be," quod he, "it shal nat be, so theech!°   *may I prosper*
660   Thou woldest make me kisse thyn olde breech°   *breeches*
      And swere it were a relik of a saint,
      Though it were with thy fundament° depeint.°   *anus/stained*
      But, by the crois which that Sainte Elaine foond,[9]
      I wolde I hadde thy coilons° in myn hond,   *testicles*
665   In stede of relikes or of saintuarye.°   *relic-box*

---

7. Over and over.
8. Both high and low (i.e., everybody).
9. I.e., by the cross that St. Helena found. Helena,   mother of Constantine the Great, was reputed to have found the True Cross.

Lat cutte hem of: I wol thee helpe hem carye.
They shal be shrined in an hogges tord."°   *turd*
   This Pardoner answerde nat a word:
So wroth he was no word ne wolde he saye.
670 "Now," quod oure Host, "I wol no lenger playe
With thee, ne with noon other angry man."
   But right anoon the worthy Knight bigan,
Whan that he sawgh that al the peple lough,°   *laughed*
"Namore of this, for it is right ynough.
675 Sire Pardoner, be glad and merye of cheere,
And ye, sire Host that been to me so dere,
I praye you that ye kisse the Pardoner,
And Pardoner, I praye thee, draw thee neer,
And as we diden lat us laughe and playe."
680 Anoon they kiste and riden forth hir waye.

The Nun's Priest's Tale

In the framing story, *The Nun's Priest's Tale* is linked to a dramatic exchange that
follows *The Monk's Tale*. The latter consists of brief tragedies, the common theme of
which is the fall of famous men and one woman, most of whom are rulers, through
the reversals of Fortune. Like *The Knight's Tale*, this was probably an earlier work of
Chaucer's, one that he never finished. As the Monk's tragedies promise to go on and
on monotonously, the Knight interrupts and politely tells the Monk that his tragedies
are too painful. The Host chimes in to say that the tragedies are "nat worth a bot-
terflye" and asks the Monk to try another subject, but the Monk is offended and
refuses. The Host then turns to the Nun's Priest, that is, the priest who is accompanying the Prioress. The three priests said in *The General Prologue* to have been
traveling with her have apparently been reduced to one.

    The Nun's Priest's Tale is an example of the literary genre known as the "beast
fable," familiar from the fables of Aesop in which animals, behaving like human
beings, point a moral. In the Middle Ages fables often functioned as elementary texts
to teach boys Latin. Marie de France's fables in French are the earliest known vernacular translations (see pp. 140–41). This particular fable derives from an episode
in the French *Roman de Renard*, a "beast epic," which satirically represents a feudal
animal society ruled over by Noble the Lion. Reynard the Fox is a wily trickster hero
who is constantly preying upon and outwitting the other animals, although sometimes
Reynard himself is outwitted by one of his victims.

    In *The Nun's Priest's Tale*, morals proliferate: both the priest-narrator and his hero,
Chauntecleer the rooster, spout examples, learned allusions, proverbs, and sententious generalizations, often in highly inflated rhetoric. The simple beast fable is thus
inflated into a delightful satire of learning and moralizing and of the pretentious
rhetoric by which medieval writers sometimes sought to elevate their works. Among
them, we we may include Chaucer himself who in this tale seems to be making
affectionate fun of some of his own works like the tragedies which became *The Monk's
Tale*.

A poore widwe somdeel stape° in age   *advanced*
Was whilom° dwelling in a narwe¹ cotage,   *once upon a time*

---

1. I.e., small.

Biside a grove, stonding in a dale:
This widwe of which I telle you my tale,

5 Sin thilke° day that she was last a wif,   *that same*
In pacience ladde° a ful simple lif.   *led*
For litel was hir catel° and hir rente,°   *property/income*
By housbondrye° of swich as God hire sente   *economy*
She foond° hirself and eek hir doughtren two.   *provided for*

10 Three large sowes hadde she and namo,
Three kin,° and eek a sheep that highte° Malle. *cows/was called*
Ful sooty was hir bowr° and eek hir halle.   *bedroom*
In which she eet ful many a sclendre° meel;   *scanty*
Of poinant° sauce hire needed neveradeel:° *pungent/not a bit*

15 No daintee morsel passed thurgh hir throte—
Hir diete was accordant to hir cote.°   *cottage*
Repleccioun° ne made hire nevere sik: *overeating*
Attempre° diete was al hir physik,°   *moderate/medicine*
And exercise and hertes suffisaunce.°   *contentment*

20 The goute lette hire nothing for to daunce,[2]
N'apoplexye shente° nat hir heed.°   *hurt/head*
No win ne drank she, neither whit ne reed:°   *red*
Hir boord° was served most with whit and blak,[3] *table*
Milk and brown breed, in which she foond no lak;[4]

25 Seind bacon, and somtime an ey° or twaye,   *egg*
For she was as it were a manere daye.[5]
A yeerd° she hadde, enclosed al withoute   *yard*
With stikkes, and a drye dich aboute,
In which she hadde a cok heet° Chauntecleer: *named*

30 In al the land of crowing nas° his peer.   *was not*
His vois was merier than the merye orgon
On massedayes that in the chirche goon;[6]
Wel sikerer[7] was his crowing in his logge°   *dwelling*
Than is a clok or an abbeye orlogge;°   *timepiece*

35 By nature he knew eech ascensioun
Of th'equinoxial[8] in thilke town:
For whan degrees fifteene were ascended,
Thanne crew° he that it mighte nat been amended.° *crowed/improved*
His comb was redder than the fin coral,

40 And batailed° as it were a castel wal;   *battlemented*
His bile° was blak, and as the jeet° it shoon;   *bill/jet*
Like asure[9] were his legges and his toon;°   *toes*
His nailes whitter° than the lilye flowr,   *whiter*
And lik the burned° gold was his colour.   *burnished*

45 This gentil° cok hadde in his governaunce   *noble*
Sevene hennes for to doon al his plesaunce,°   *pleasure*
Whiche were his sustres and his paramours,[1]

---

2. The gout didn't hinder her at all from dancing.
3. I.e., milk and bread.
4. Found no fault.
5. I.e., a kind of dairywoman. "Seind": scorched (i.e., broiled).
6. I.e., is played.
7. More reliable.
8. I.e., he knew by instinct each step in the pro-

gression of the celestial equator. The celestial equator was thought to make a 360° rotation around the earth every twenty-four hours; therefore, a progression of 15° would be equal to the passage of an hour (line 37).
9. Blue (lapis lazuli).
1. His sisters and his mistresses.

And wonder like to him as of colours;
Of whiche the faireste hewed° on hir throte   *colored*
50 Was cleped° faire damoisele Pertelote: *called*
Curteis she was, discreet, and debonaire,°   *meek*
And compaignable,° and bar° hirself so faire,   *companionable / bore*
Sin thilke day that she was seven night old,
That trewely she hath the herte in hold
55 Of Chauntecleer, loken° in every lith.°   *locked / limb*
He loved hire so that wel was him therwith.[2]
But swich a joye was it to heere hem singe,
Whan that the brighte sonne gan to springe,
In sweete accord *My Lief is Faren in Londe*[3]—
60 For thilke time, as I have understonde,
Beestes and briddes couden speke and singe.
    And so bifel that in a daweninge,
As Chauntecleer among his wives alle
Sat on his perche that was in the halle,
65 And next him sat this faire Pertelote,
This Chauntecleer gan gronen in his throte,
As man that in his dreem is drecched° sore.   *troubled*
    And whan that Pertelote thus herde him rore,°   *roar*
She was agast, and saide, "Herte dere,
70 What aileth you to grone in this manere?
Ye been a verray slepere,[4] fy, for shame!"
    And he answerde and saide thus, "Madame,
I praye you that ye take it nat agrief.°   *amiss*
By God, me mette I was in swich meschief[5]
75 Right now, that yit myn herte is sore afright.
Now God," quod he, "my swevene recche aright,[6]
And keepe my body out of foul prisoun!
Me mette° how that I romed up and down   *dreamed*
Within oure yeerd, wher as I sawgh a beest,
80 Was lik an hound and wolde han maad arrest[7]
Upon my body, and han had me deed.[8]
His colour was bitwixe yelow and reed,
And tipped was his tail and bothe his eres
With blak, unlik the remenant° of his heres;°   *rest / hairs*
85 His snoute smal, with glowing yën twaye.
Yit of his look for fere almost I deye:°   *die*
This caused me my groning, doutelees."
    "Avoi,"° quod she, "fy on you, hertelees!°   *fie / coward*
Allas," quod she, "for by that God above,
90 Now han ye lost myn herte and al my love!
I can nat love a coward, by my faith.
For certes, what so any womman saith,
We alle desiren, if it mighte be,
To han housbondes hardy, wise, and free,°   *generous*

2. That he was well contented.
3. "My Love Has Gone Away," a popular song of the time. See p. 352.
4. Sound sleeper.
5. I dreamed that I was in such misfortune.
6. Interpret my dream correctly (i.e., in an auspicious manner).
7. Would have laid hold.
8. I.e., killed me.

95 And secree,° and no nigard, ne no fool,   *discreet*
    Ne him that is agast of every tool,°   *weapon*
    Ne noon avauntour.° By that God above,   *boaster*
    How dorste° ye sayn for shame unto youre love   *dare*
    That any thing mighte make you aferd?
100 Have ye no mannes herte and han a beerd?°   *beard*
    Allas, and conne° ye been agast of swevenes?°   *can / dreams*
    No thing, God woot, but vanitee[9] in swevene is!
    Swevenes engendren of replexiouns,[1]
    And ofte of fume° and of complexiouns,°   *gas / bodily humors*
105 Whan humours been too habundant in a wight.[2]
    Certes, this dreem which ye han met° tonight   *dreamed*
    Comth of the grete superfluitee
    Of youre rede colera,[3] pardee,
    Which causeth folk to dreden° in hir dremes   *fear*
110 Of arwes,° and of fir with rede lemes,°   *arrows / flames*
    Of rede beestes, that they wol hem bite,
    Of contek,° and of whelpes grete and lite[4]—   *strife*
    Right° as the humour of malencolye[5]   *just*
    Causeth ful many a man in sleep to crye
115 For fere of blake beres° or boles° blake,   *bears / bulls*
    Or elles blake develes wol hem take.
    Of othere humours coude I tell also
    That werken many a man in sleep ful wo,
    But I wol passe as lightly° as I can.   *quickly*
120 Lo, Caton,[6] which that was so wis a man,
    Saide he nat thus? 'Ne do no fors of[7] dremes.'
    Now, sire," quod she, "whan we flee fro the bemes,[8]
    For Goddes love, as take som laxatif.
    Up° peril of my soule and of my lif,   *upon*
125 I conseile you the beste, I wol nat lie,
    That bothe of colere and of malencolye
    Ye purge you; and for° ye shal nat tarye,   *in order that*
    Though in this town is noon apothecarye,
    I shal myself to herbes techen you,
130 That shal been for youre hele° and for youre prow,° *health / benefit*
    And in oure yeerd tho° herbes shal I finde,   *those*
    The whiche han of hir propretee by kinde°   *nature*
    To purge you binethe and eek above.
    Foryet° nat this, for Goddes owene love.   *forget*
135 Ye been ful colerik° of complexioun;   *bilious*
    Ware° the sonne in his ascencioun   *beware that*
    Ne finde you nat repleet° of humours hote;°   *filled / hot*
    And if it do, I dar wel laye° a grote   *bet*
    That ye shul have a fevere terciane,[9]

9. I.e., empty illusion.
1. Dreams have their origin in overeating.
2. I.e., when humors (bodily fluids) are too abundant in a person. Pertelote's diagnosis is based on
the familiar concept that an excess of one of the
bodily humors in a person affected his or her temperament (see p. 225, n. 8).
3. Red bile.

4. And of big and little dogs.
5. I.e., black bile.
6. Dionysius Cato, supposed author of a book of
maxims used in elementary education.
7. Pay no attention to.
8. Fly down from the rafters.
9. Tertian (recurring every other day).

140 Or an agu° that may be youre bane.°   ague/death
   A day or two ye shul han digestives
   Of wormes, er° ye take youre laxatives   before
   Of lauriol, centaure, and fumetere,[1]
   Or elles of ellebor° that groweth there,   hellebore
145 Of catapuce, or of gaitres beries,[2]
   Of herb-ive° growing in oure yeerd ther merye is[3]—   herb ivy
   Pekke hem right up as they growe and ete hem in.
   Be merye, housbonde, for youre fader° kin!   father's
   Dredeth no dreem: I can saye you namore."
150   "Madame," quod he, "graunt mercy of youre lore,[4]
   But nathelees, as touching daun° Catoun,   master
   That hath of wisdom swich a greet renown,
   Though that he bad no dremes for to drede,
   By God, men may in olde bookes rede
155 Of many a man more of auctoritee°   authority
   Than evere Caton was, so mote I thee,°   prosper
   That al the revers sayn of his sentence,°   opinion
   And han wel founden by experience
   That dremes been significaciouns
160 As wel of joye as tribulaciouns
   That folk enduren in this lif present.
   Ther needeth make of this noon argument:
   The verray preve[5] sheweth it in deede.
       "Oon of the gretteste auctour[6] that men rede
165 Saith thus, that whilom two felawes wente
   On pilgrimage in a ful good entente,
   And happed so they comen in a town,
   Wher as ther was swich congregacioun
   Of peple, and eek so strait of herbergage,[7]
170 That they ne founde as muche as oo cotage
   In which they bothe mighte ylogged° be;   lodged
   Wherfore they mosten° of necessitee   must
   As for that night departe° compaignye.   part
   And eech of hem gooth to his hostelrye,
175 And took his logging as it wolde falle.°   befall
   That oon of hem was logged in a stalle,
   Fer° in a yeerd, with oxen of the plough;   far away
   That other man was logged wel ynough,
   As was his aventure° or his fortune,   lot
180 That us governeth alle as in commune.
   And so bifel that longe er it were day,
   This man mette° in his bed, ther as he lay,   dreamed
   How that his felawe gan upon him calle,
   And saide, 'Allas, for in an oxes stalle
185 This night I shal be mordred° ther I lie!   murdered
   Now help me, dere brother, or I die!

---

1. Of laureole, centaury, and fumitory. These, and the herbs mentioned in the next lines, were all common medieval medicines used as cathartics.
2. Of caper berry or of gaiter berry.
3. Where it is pleasant.
4. Many thanks for your instruction.
5. Actual experience.
6. I.e., one of the greatest authors (perhaps Cicero or Valerius Maximus).
7. And also such a shortage of lodging.

In alle haste com to me,' he saide.
    "This man out of his sleep for fere abraide,°   *started up*
But whan that he was wakened of his sleep,
190   He turned him and took of this no keep:°   *heed*
       Him thoughte his dreem nas but a vanitee.°   *illusion*
       Thus twies in his sleeping dremed he,
       And atte thridde time yit his felawe
       Cam, as him thoughte, and saide, 'I am now slawe:°   *slain*
195   Bihold my bloody woundes deepe and wide.
       Aris up erly in the morwe tide,[8]
       And atte west gate of the town,' quod he,
       'A carte ful of dong° ther shaltou see,   *dung*
       In which my body is hid ful prively:
200   Do thilke carte arresten boldely.[9]
       My gold caused my mordre, sooth to sayn'
       —And tolde him every point how he was slain,
       With a ful pitous face, pale of hewe.
       And truste wel, his dreem he foond° ful trewe,   *found*
205   For on the morwe° as soone as it was day,   *morning*
       To his felawes in° he took the way,   *lodging*
       And whan that he cam to this oxes stalle,
       After his felawe he bigan to calle.
       "The hostiler° answerde him anoon,   *innkeeper*
210   And saide, 'Sire, youre felawe is agoon:°   *gone away*
       As soone as day he wente out of the town.'
       "This man gan fallen in suspecioun,
       Remembring on his dremes that he mette;°   *dreamed*
       And forth he gooth, no lenger wolde he lette,°   *tarry*
215   Unto the west gate of the town, and foond
       A dong carte, wente as it were to donge° lond,   *put manure on*
       That was arrayed in that same wise
       As ye han herd the dede° man devise;   *dead*
       And with an hardy herte he gan to crye,
220   'Vengeance and justice of this felonye!
       My felawe mordred is this same night,
       And in this carte he lith° gaping upright!°   *lies/on his back*
       I crye out on the ministres,' quod he,
       'That sholde keepe and rulen this citee.
225   Harrow,° allas, here lith my felawe slain!'   *help*
       What sholde I more unto this tale sayn?
       The peple up sterte° and caste the carte to grounde,   *started*
       And in the middel of the dong they founde
       The dede man that mordred was al newe.[1]
230   "O blisful God that art so just and trewe,
       Lo, how that thou biwrayest° mordre alway!   *disclose*
       Mordre wol out, that see we day by day:
       Mordre is so wlatsom° and abhominable   *loathsome*
       To God that is so just and resonable,
235   That he ne wol nat suffre it heled° be,   *concealed*

---

8. In the morning.   1. Recently.
9. Boldly have this same cart seized.

Though it abide a yeer or two or three.
Mordre wol out: this my conclusioun.
And right anoon ministres of that town
Han hent° the cartere and so sore him pined,[2]   *seized*
240 And eek the hostiler so sore engined,°   *racked*
That they biknewe° hir wikkednesse anoon,   *confessed*
And were anhanged° by the nekke boon.   *hanged*
Here may men seen that dremes been to drede.[3]
 "And certes, in the same book I rede—
245 Right in the nexte chapitre after this—
I gabbe° nat, so have I joye or blis—   *lie*
Two men that wolde han passed over see
For certain cause into a fer contree,
If that the wind ne hadde been contrarye
250 That made hem in a citee for to tarye,
That stood ful merye upon an haven° side—   *harbor's*
But on a day again° the even-tide   *toward*
The wind gan chaunge, and blewe right as hem leste:[4]
Jolif° and glad they wenten unto reste,   *merry*
255 And casten° hem ful erly for to saile.   *determined*
 "But to that oo man fil° a greet mervaile;   *befell*
That oon of hem, in sleeping as he lay,
Him mette[5] a wonder dreem again the day:
Him thoughte a man stood by his beddes side,
260 And him comanded that he sholde abide,
And saide him thus, 'If thou tomorwe wende,
Thou shalt be dreint:° my tale is at an ende.'   *drowned*
 "He wook and tolde his felawe what he mette,
And prayed him his viage° to lette;°   *voyage / delay*
265 As for that day he prayed him to bide.
 "His felawe that lay by his beddes side
Gan for to laughe, and scorned him ful faste.°   *hard*
'No dreem,' quod he, 'may so myn herte agaste°   *terrify*
That I wol lette for to do my thinges.°   *business*
270 I sette nat a straw by thy dreminges,[6]
For swevenes been but vanitees and japes:[7]
Men dreme alday° of owles or of apes,[8]   *constantly*
And of many a maze° therwithal—   *delusion*
Men dreme of thing that nevere was ne shal.[9]
275 But sith I see that thou wolt here abide,
And thus forsleuthen° wilfully thy tide,°   *waste / time*
God woot, it reweth me;[1] and have good day.'
And thus he took his leve and wente his way.
But er that he hadde half his cours ysailed—
280 Noot I nat why ne what meschaunce it ailed—
But casuelly the shippes botme rente,[2]

2. Tortured.
3. Worthy of being feared.
4. Just as they wished.
5. He dreamed.
6. I don't care a straw for your dreamings.
7. Dreams are but illusions and frauds.

8. I.e., of absurdities.
9. I.e., shall be.
1. I'm sorry.
2. I don't know why nor what was the trouble with it—but accidentally the ship's bottom split.

man under the water wente,

And sh there shippes it biside,

In sig m sailed at the same tide.

Tha e, faire Pertelote so dere,

nsamples olde maistou lere°   *learn*

285   an sholde been too recchelees°   *careless*

, for I saye thee doutelees

y a dreem ful sore is for to drede.

the lif of Saint Kenelm[3] I rede—

s Kenulphus sone, the noble king

cenrike°—how Kenelm mette a thing   *Mercia*

er he was mordred on a day.   *little*

ordre in his avision° he sey.°   *dream/saw*

rice° him expounded everydeel°   *nurse/every bit*

wevene, and bad him for to keepe him[4] weel

raison, but he nas but seven yeer old,

d therfore litel tale hath he told

Of any dreem,[5] so holy was his herte.

By God, I hadde levere than my sherte[6]

That ye hadde rad° his legende as have I.   *read*

   "Dame Pertelote, I saye you trewely,

Macrobeus,[7] that writ the *Avisioun*

In Affrike of the worthy Scipioun,

305   Affermeth° dremes, and saith that they been   *confirms*

Warning of thinges that men after seen.

   "And ferthermore, I praye you looketh wel

In the Olde Testament of Daniel,

If he heeld° dremes any vanitee.[8]   *considered*

310   "Rede eek of Joseph[9] and ther shul ye see

Wher° dremes be somtime—I saye nat alle—   *whether*

Warning of thinges that shul after falle.

   "Looke of Egypte the king daun Pharao,

His bakere and his botelere° also,   *butler*

315   Wher they ne felte noon effect in dremes.

Whoso wol seeke actes of sondry remes°   *realms*

May rede of dremes many a wonder thing.

   "Lo Cresus, which that was of Lyde° king,   *Lydia*

Mette° he nat that he sat upon a tree,   *dreamed*

320   Which signified he sholde anhanged° be?   *hanged*

   "Lo here Andromacha, Ectores° wif,   *Hector's*

That day that Ector sholde lese° his lif,   *lose*

She dremed on the same night biforn

How that the lif of Ector sholde be lorn,°   *lost*

325   If thilke° day he wente into bataile;   *that same*

She warned him, but it mighte nat availe:°   *do any good*

---

3. Kenelm succeeded his father as king of Mercia at the age of seven, but was slain by his aunt (in 821).
4. Guard himself.
5. Therefore he has set little store by any dream.
6. I.e., I'd give my shirt.
7. Macrobius wrote a famous commentary on Cic-

ero's account in *De Republica* of the dream of Scipio Africanus Minor; the commentary came to be regarded as a standard authority on dream lore.
8. See Daniel 7.
9. See Genesis 37.
1. See Genesis 39–41.

He wente for to fighte nathelees,
But he was slain anoon° of Achilles.   *right away*
But thilke tale is al too long to telle,
330 And eek it is neigh day, I may nat dwelle.
Shortly I saye, as for conclusioun,
That I shal han of this avisioun[2]
Adversitee, and I saye ferthermoor
That I ne telle of[3] laxatives no stoor,
335 For they been venimes,° I woot it weel:
I hem defye, I love hem neveradeel.°
     "Now lat us speke of mirthe and stinte° al this.
Madame Pertelote, so have I blis,
Of oo thing God hath sente me large grace:
340 For whan I see the beautee of youre face—
Ye been so scarlet reed° aboute youre yën—
It maketh al my drede for to dien.
For also siker° as *In principio*,[4]   *certain*
Mulier est hominis confusio.[5]
345 Madame, the sentence° of this Latin is,   *meaning*
'Womman is mannes joye and al his blis.'
For whan I feele anight youre softe side—
Al be it that I may nat on you ride,
For that oure perche is maad so narwe, allas—
350 I am so ful of joye and of solas°   *delight*
That I defye bothe swevene and dreem."
And with that word he fleigh° down fro the beem,   *flew*
For it was day, and eek his hennes alle,
And with a "chuk" he gan hem for to calle,
355 For he hadde founde a corn lay in the yeerd.
Real° he was, he was namore aferd:°   *regal / afraid*
He fethered[6] Pertelote twenty time,
And trad hire as ofte er it was prime.[7]
He looketh as it were a grim leoun,
360 And on his toes he rometh up and down:
Him deined[8] nat to sette his foot to grounde.
He chukketh whan he hath a corn yfounde,
And to him rennen° thanne his wives alle.   *run*
Thus royal, as a prince is in his halle,
365 Leve I this Chauntecleer in his pasture,
And after wol I telle his aventure.
     Whan that the month in which the world bigan,
That highte° March, whan God first maked man,   *is called*
Was compleet, and passed were also,
370 Sin March biran,° thritty days and two,[9]   *passed by*
Bifel that Chauntecleer in al his pride,
His sevene wives walking him biside,

2. Divinely inspired dream (as opposed to the more ordinary "swevene" or "dreem").
3. Set by.
4. Beginning of the Gospel of St. John that gives the essential premises of Christianity: "In the beginning was the Word."
5. Woman is man's ruination.
6. I.e., embraced.
7. 9 A.M. "Trad": trod, copulated with.
8. He deigned.
9. The rhetorical time telling yields the date May 3.

Caste up his yën to the brighte sonne,
That in the signe of Taurus hadde yronne
375 Twenty degrees and oon and somwhat more,
And knew by kinde,° and by noon other lore,   *nature*
That it was prime, and crew with blisful stevene.°   *voice*
"The sonne," he saide, "is clomben¹ up on hevene
Fourty degrees and oon and more, ywis.°   *indeed*
380 Madame Pertelote, my worldes blis,
Herkneth thise blisful briddes° how they singe,   *birds*
And see the fresshe flowers how they springe:
Ful is myn herte of revel and solas."
But sodeinly him fil° a sorweful cas,°   *befell/chance*
385 For evere the latter ende of joye is wo—
God woot that worldly joye is soone ago,
And if a rethor° coude faire endite,   *rhetorician*
He in a cronicle saufly° mighte it write,   *safely*
As for a soverein notabilitee.²
390 Now every wis man lat him herkne me:
This storye is also° trewe, I undertake,   *as*
As is the book of *Launcelot de Lake*,³
That wommen holde in ful greet reverence.
Now wol I turne again to my sentence.°   *main point*
395   A colfox⁴ ful of sly iniquitee,
That in the grove hadde woned° yeres three,   *dwelled*
By heigh imaginacion forncast,⁵
The same night thurghout the hegges° brast°   *hedges/burst*
Into the yeerd ther Chauntecleer the faire
400 Was wont, and eek his wives, to repaire;
And in a bed of wortes° stille he lay   *cabbages*
Til it was passed undren° of the day,   *midmorning*
Waiting his time on Chauntecleer to falle,
As gladly doon thise homicides alle,
405 That in await liggen to mordre⁶ men.
O false mordrour, lurking in thy den!
O newe Scariot! Newe Geniloun!⁷
False dissimilour!° O Greek Sinoun,⁸   *dissembler*
That broughtest Troye al outrely° to sorwe!   *utterly*
410 O Chauntecleer, accursed be that morwe°   *morning*
That thou into the yeerd flaugh° fro the bemes!   *flew*
Thou were ful wel ywarned by thy dremes
That thilke day was perilous to thee;
But what that God forwoot° moot° needes be,   *foreknows/must*
415 After° the opinion of certain clerkes: *according to*
Witnesse on him that any parfit° clerk is   *perfect*
That in scole is greet altercacioun

1. Has climbed.
2. Indisputable fact.
3. Romances of the courteous knight Lancelot of the Lake were very popular.
4. Fox with black markings.
5. Predestined by divine planning.
6. That lie in ambush to murder.

7. I.e., Ganelon, who betrayed Roland to the Saracens (in the medieval French epic *The Song of Roland*). "Scariot": Judas Iscariot.
8. Sinon, who persuaded the Trojans to take the Greeks' wooden horse into their city—with, of course, the result that the city was destroyed.

In this matere, and greet disputisoun,°   *disputation*
And hath been of an hundred thousand men.
420   But I ne can nat bulte it to the bren,[9]
As can the holy doctour Augustin,
Or Boece, or the bisshop Bradwardin[1]—
Wheither that Goddes worthy forwiting°   *foreknowledge*
Straineth me nedely[2] for to doon a thing
425   ("Nedely" clepe I simple necessitee),
Or elles if free chois be graunted me
To do that same thing or do it naught,
Though God forwoot° it er that I was wrought;   *foreknew*
Or if his witing° straineth neveradeel,   *knowledge*
430   But by necessitee condicionel[3]—
I wol nat han to do of swich matere:
My tale is of a cok, as ye may heere,
That took his conseil of his wif with sorwe,
To walken in the yeerd upon that morwe
435   That he hadde met° the dreem that I you tolde.   *dreamed*
Wommenes conseils been ful ofte colde,[4]
Wommanes conseil broughte us first to wo,
And made Adam fro Paradis to go,
Ther as he was ful merye and wel at ese.
440   But for I noot° to whom it mighte displese   *don't know*
If I conseil of wommen wolde blame,
Passe over, for I saide it in my game°—   *sport*
Rede auctours where they trete of swich matere,
And what they sayn of wommen ye may heere—
445   Thise been the cokkes wordes and nat mine:
I can noon harm of no womman divine.°   *guess*
    Faire in the sond° to bathe hire merily   *sand*
Lith° Pertelote, and alle hir sustres by,   *lies*
Again° the sonne, and Chauntecleer so free°   *in/noble*
450   Soong° merier than the mermaide in the see—   *sang*
For Physiologus[5] saith sikerly
How that they singen wel and merily.
    And so bifel that as he caste his yë
Among the wortes on a boterflye,°   *butterfly*
455   He was war of this fox that lay ful lowe.
No thing ne liste him[6] thanne for to crowe,
But cride anoon "Cok cok!" and up he sterte,°   *started*
As man that[7] was affrayed in his herte—
For naturelly a beest desireth flee
460   Fro his contrarye[8] if he may it see,

---

9. Sift it to the bran, i.e., get to the bottom of it.
1. St. Augustine, Boethius (6th-century Roman philosopher, whose *Consolation of Philosophy* was translated by Chaucer), and Thomas Bradwardine (archbishop of Canterbury, d. 1349) were all concerned with the interrelationship between people's free will and God's foreknowledge.
2. Constrains me necessarily.
3. Boethius's "conditional necessity" permitted a large measure of free will.
4. I.e., baneful.
5. Supposed author of a bestiary, a book of moralized zoology describing both natural and supernatural animals (including mermaids).
6. He wished.
7. Like one who.
8. I.e., his natural enemy.

Though he nevere erst° hadde seen it with his yë.   *before*
This Chauntecleer, whan he gan him espye,
He wolde han fled, but that the fox anoon
Saide, "Gentil sire, allas, wher wol ye goon?
465   Be ye afraid of me that am youre freend?
Now certes, I were worse than a feend
If I to you wolde° harm or vilainye.   *meant*
I am nat come youre conseil° for t'espye,   *secrets*
But trewely the cause of my cominge
470   Was only for to herkne how ye singe:
For trewely, ye han as merye a stevene°   *voice*
As any angel hath that is in hevene.
Therwith ye han in musik more feelinge
Than hadde Boece,[9] or any that can singe.
475   My lord your fader—God his soule blesse!—
And eek youre moder, of hir gentilesse,°   *gentility*
Han in myn hous ybeen, to my grete ese.
And certes sire, ful fain° wolde I you plese.   *gladly*
   "But for men speke of singing, I wol saye,
480   So mote I brouke[1] wel mine yën twaye,
Save ye, I herde nevere man to singe
As dide youre fader in the morweninge.
Certes, it was of herte° al that he soong.°   *heartfelt / sang*
And for to make his vois the more strong,
485   He wolde so paine him[2] that with bothe his yën
He moste winke,[3] so loude wolde he cryen;
And stonden on his tiptoon therwithal,
And strecche forth his nekke long and smal;
And eek he was of swich discrecioun
490   That ther nas no man in no regioun
That him in song or wisdom mighte passe.
I have wel rad° in *Daun Burnel the Asse*[4]   *read*
Among his vers how that ther was a cok,
For a preestes sone yaf him a knok[5]
495   Upon his leg whil he was yong and nice,°   *foolish*
He made him for to lese° his benefice.[6]   *lose*
But certain, ther nis no comparisoun
Bitwixe the wisdom and discrecioun
Of youre fader and of his subtiltee.[7]
500   Now singeth, sire, for sainte° charitee!   *holy*
Lat see, conne° ye youre fader countrefete?"°   *can / imitate*
   This Chauntecleer his winges gan to bete,
As man that coude his traison nat espye,
So was he ravisshed with his flaterye.
505   Allas, ye lordes, many a fals flatour°   *flatterer*
Is in youre court, and many a losengeour°   *deceiver*

9. Boethius also wrote a treatise on music.   Wireker.
1. So might I enjoy the use of.   5. Because a priest's son gave him a knock.
2. Take pains.   6. The offended cock neglected to crow so that his
3. He had to shut his eyes.   master, now grown to manhood, overslept, missing
4. Master Brunellus, a discontented donkey, was   his ordination and losing his benefice.
the hero of a 12th-century satirical poem by Nigel   7. His (the cock in the story) cleverness.

That plesen you wel more, by my faith,
Than he that soothfastnesse° unto you saith!   truth
Redeth Ecclesiaste[8] of flaterye.
510 Beeth war, ye lordes, of hir trecherye.
     This Chauntecleer stood hye upon his toos,
Strecching his nekke, and heeld his yën cloos,
And gan to crowe loude for the nones;°   occasion
And daun Russel the fox sterte° up atones,   jumped
515 And by the gargat° hente° Chauntecleer,   throat / seized
And on his bak toward the wode him beer,°   bore
For yit ne was ther no man that him sued.°   followed
     O destinee that maist nat been eschued!°   eschewed
Allas that Chauntecleer fleigh° fro the bemes!   flew
520 Allas his wif ne roughte nat of[9] dremes!
And on a Friday fil° al this meschaunce!   befell
     O Venus that art goddesse of plesaunce,
Sin that thy servant was this Chauntecleer,
And in thy service dide al his power—
525 More for delit than world[1] to multiplye—
Why woldestou suffre him on thy day[2] to die?
     O Gaufred,[3] dere maister soverein,
That, whan thy worthy king Richard was slain
With shot,[4] complainedest his deeth so sore,
530 Why ne hadde I now thy sentence and thy lore,[5]
The Friday for to chide as diden ye?
For on a Friday soothly slain was he.
Thanne wolde I shewe you how that I coude plaine°   lament
For Chauntecleres drede and for his paine.
535 Certes, swich cry ne lamentacioun
Was nevere of ladies maad when Ilioun°   Ilium, Troy
Was wonne, and Pyrrus[6] with his straite° swerd,   drawn
Whan he hadde hent° King Priam by the beerd   seized
And slain him, as saith us Eneidos,[7]
540 As maden alle the hennes in the cloos,°   yard
Whan they hadde seen of Chauntecleer the sighte.
But sovereinly° Dame Pertelote shrighte°   supremely / shrieked
Ful louder than dide Hasdrubales[8] wif
Whan that hir housbonde hadde lost his lif,
545 And that the Romains hadden brend° Cartage: burned
She was so ful of torment and of rage°   madness
That wilfully unto the fir she sterte,°   jumped
And brende hirselven with a stedefast herte.
     O woful hennes, right so criden ye
550 As, whan that Nero brende the citee
Of Rome, criden senatoures wives

---

8. The Book of Ecclesiasticus, in the Apocrypha.
9. Didn't care for.
1. I.e., population.
2. Friday is Venus's day.
3. Geoffrey of Vinsauf, a famous medieval rhetorician, who wrote a lament on the death of Richard
I in which he scolded Friday, the day on which the
king died.

4. I.e., a missile.
5. Thy wisdom and thy learning.
6. Pyrrhus was the Greek who slew Priam, king of
Troy.
7. As the Aeneid tells us.
8. Hasdrubal was king of Carthage when it was
destroyed by the Romans.

For that hir housbondes losten alle hir lives:[9]
Withouten gilt this Nero hath hem slain.
Now wol I turne to my tale again.

555   The sely° widwe and eek hir doughtres two   *innocent*
Herden thise hennes crye and maken wo,
And out at dores sterten° they anoon,   *leapt*
And sien° the fox toward the grove goon,   *saw*
And bar upon his bak the cok away,
560 And criden, "Out, harrow,° and wailaway,   *help*
Ha, ha, the fox," and after him they ran,
And eek with staves many another man;
Ran Colle oure dogge, and Talbot and Gerland,[1]
And Malkin with a distaf in hir hand,
565 Ran cow and calf, and eek the verray hogges,
Sore aferd° for berking of the dogges   *frightened*
And shouting of the men and wommen eke.
They ronne° so hem thoughte hir herte breke;[2]   *ran*
They yelleden as feendes doon in helle;
570 The dokes° criden as men wolde hem quelle;°   *ducks / kill*
The gees for fere flowen° over the trees;   *flew*
Out of the hive cam the swarm of bees;
So hidous was the noise, a, benedicite,°   *bless me*
Certes, he Jakke Straw[3] and his meinee°   *company*
575 Ne made nevere shoutes half so shrille
Whan that they wolden any Fleming kille,
As thilke day was maad upon the fox:
Of bras they broughten bemes° and of box,°   *trumpets / boxwood*
Of horn, of boon,° in whiche they blewe and pouped,°   *bone / tooted*
580 And therwithal they skriked° and they houped°—   *shrieked / whooped*
It seemed as that hevene sholde falle.
    Now goode men, I praye you herkneth alle:
Lo, how Fortune turneth° sodeinly   *reverses, overturns*
The hope and pride eek of hir enemy.
585 This cok that lay upon the foxes bak,
In al his drede unto the fox he spak,
And saide, "Sire, if that I were as ye,
Yit sholde I sayn, as wis° God helpe me,   *surely*
'Turneth ayain, ye proude cherles alle!
590 A verray pestilence upon you falle!
Now am I come unto this wodes side,
Maugree your heed,[4] the cok shal here abide.
I wol him ete, in faith, and that anoon.' "
    The fox answerde, "In faith, it shal be doon."
595 And as he spak that word, al sodeinly
The cok brak from his mouth deliverly,°   *nimbly*
And hye upon a tree he fleigh° anoon.   *flew*
    And whan the fox sawgh that he was agoon,

9. According to the legend, Nero not only set fire to Rome (in 64 C.E.) but also put many senators to death.
1. Two other dogs.
2. Would break.

3. One of the leaders of the Uprising of 1381, which was partially directed against the Flemings living in London.
4. Despite your head—i.e., despite anything you can do.

"Allas," quod he, "O Chauntecleer, allas!
600 I have to you," quod he, "ydoon trespas,
In as muche as I maked you aferd
Whan I you hente° and broughte out of the yeerd.   *seized*
But sire, I dide it in no wikke° entente: *wicked*
Come down, and I shal telle you what I mente.
605 I shal saye sooth to you, God help me so."
    "Nay thanne," quod he, "I shrewe° us bothe two: *curse*
But first I shrewe myself, bothe blood and bones,
If thou bigile me ofter than ones;
Thou shalt namore thurgh thy flaterye
610 Do° me to singe and winken with myn yëe.   *cause*
For he that winketh whan he sholde see,
Al wilfully, God lat him nevere thee."°   *prosper*
    "Nay," quod the fox, "but God yive him meschaunce
That is so undiscreet of governaunce°   *self-control*
615 That jangleth° whan he sholde holde his pees."   *chatters*
    Lo, swich it is for to be reccheless°   *careless*
And necligent and truste on flaterye.
But ye that holden this tale a folye
As of a fox, or of a cok and hen,
620 Taketh the moralitee, goode men.
For Saint Paul saith that al that writen is
To oure doctrine it is ywrit, ywis:[5]
Taketh the fruit, and lat the chaf be stille.[6]
Now goode God, if that it be thy wille,
625 As saith my lord, so make us alle goode men,
And bringe us to his hye blisse. Amen.

Close of *Canterbury Tales*

At the end of *The Canterbury Tales*, Chaucer invokes a common allegorical theme, that life on earth is a pilgrimage. As Chaucer puts it in his moral ballade *Truth* (p. 315), "Here is noon home . . . / Forth, pilgrim, forth!" In the final fragment, he makes explicit a metaphor that has been implicit all along in the journey to Canterbury. The pilgrims never arrive at the shrine of St. Thomas, but in *The Parson's Tale*, and in its short introduction and in the "Retraction" that follows it, Chaucer seems to be making an end for two pilgrimages that had become one, that of his fiction and that of his life.

In the introduction to the tale we find the twenty-nine pilgrims moving through a nameless little village as the sun sinks to within twenty-nine degrees of the horizon. The atmosphere contains something of both the chill and the urgency of a late autumn afternoon, and we are surprised to find that the pilgrimage is almost over, that there is need for haste to make that "good end" that every medieval Christian hoped for. This delicately suggestive passage, rich with allegorical overtones, introduces an extremely long penitential treatise, translated by Chaucer from Latin or French sources. Although often assumed to be an earlier work, it may well have been written by Chaucer to provide the ending for *The Canterbury Tales*.

In the "Retraction" that follows *The Parson's Tale*, Chaucer acknowledges, lists,

---

5. See Romans 15.4.
6. The "fruit" refers to the kernel of moral or doctrinal meaning; the"chaf," or husk, is the narrative containing that meaning. The metaphor was commonly applied to scriptural interpretation.

revokes, and asks forgiveness for his "giltes" (that is, his sins), which consist of having written most of the works on which his reputation as a great poet depends. He thanks Christ and Mary for his religious and moral works. One need not take this as evidence of a spiritual crisis or conversion at the end of his life. The "Retraction" seems to have been written to appear at the end of *The Canterbury Tales*, without censoring any of the tales deemed to be sinful. At the same time, one need not question Chaucer's sincerity. A readiness to deny his own reality before the reality of his God is implicit in many of Chaucer's works, and the placement of the "Retraction" within or just outside the border of the fictional pilgrimage suggests that although Chaucer finally rejected his fictions, he recognized that he and they were inseparable.

From The Parson's Tale

The Introduction

By that[1] the Manciple hadde his tale al ended,
The sonne fro the south line[2] was descended
So lowe, that he has nat to my sighte
Degrees nine and twenty as in highte.
5   Four of the clokke it was, so as I gesse,
For elevene foot, or litel more or lesse,
My shadwe was at thilke time as there,
Of swich feet as° my lengthe parted° were   *as if/divided*
In sixe feet equal of proporcioun.[3]
10 Therwith the moones exaltacioun[4]—
I mene Libra—always gan ascende,
As we were entring at a thropes° ende.   *village's*
For which oure Host, as he was wont to gie°   *lead*
As in this caas oure joly compaignye,
15 Saide in this wise, "Lordinges everichoon,
Now lakketh us no tales mo than oon:
Fulfild is my sentence° and my decree;   *purpose*
I trowe° that we han herd of ech degree;   *believe*
Almost fulfild is al myn ordinaunce.
20 I praye to God, so yive him right good chaunce
That telleth this tale to us lustily.
Sire preest," quod he, "artou a vicary,°   *vicar*
Or arte a Person? Say sooth, by thy fay.°   *faith*
Be what thou be, ne breek° thou nat oure play,   *break*
25 For every man save thou hath told his tale.
Unbokele and shew us what is in thy male!°   *bag*
For trewely, me thinketh by thy cheere°   *expression*
Thou sholdest knitte up wel a greet matere.
Tel us a fable anoon, for cokkes bones!"[5]
30   This Person answerde al atones,°   *immediately*
"Thou getest fable noon ytold for me,
For Paul, that writeth unto Timothee,
Repreveth° hem that waiven soothfastnesse,[6]   *reproves*

---

1. By the time that.
2. I.e., the line that runs some 28° to the south of the celestial equator and parallel to it.
3. This detailed analysis merely says that the shadows are lengthening.
4. I.e., the astrological sign in which the moon's influence was dominant.
5. Cock's bones, a euphemism for God's bones.
6. Depart from truth (see 1 Timothy 1.4).

And tellen fables and swich wrecchednesse.
35 Why sholde I sowen draf° out of my fest,°   *chaff/fist*
    Whan I may sowen whete if that me lest?[7]
    For which I saye that if you list to heere
    Moralitee and vertuous matere,
    And thanne that ye wol yive me audience,
40 I wol ful fain,° at Cristes reverence,   *gladly*
    Do you plesance leveful° as I can.   *lawful*
    But trusteth wel, I am a southren man:
    I can nat geeste Rum-Ram-Ruf by lettre[8]—
    Ne, God woot, rym holde° I but litel bettre.   *consider*
45 And therfore, if you list—I wol nat glose[9]—
    I wol you telle a merye tale in prose
    To knitte up al this feeste and make an ende.
    And Jesu for his grace wit me sende
    To shewe you the way in this viage°   *journey*
50 Of thilke parfit glorious pilgrimage
    That highte° Jerusalem celestial.   *is called*
    And if ye vouche sauf, anoon I shal
    Biginne upon my tale, for which I praye
    Telle youre avis:° I can no bettre saye.   *opinion*
55 But nathelees, this meditacioun
    I putte it ay under correccioun
    Of clerkes, for I am nat textuel:[1]
    I take but the sentence,° trusteth wel.   *meaning*
    Therefore I make protestacioun°   *public acknowledgment*
60 That I wol stonde to correccioun."
        Upon this word we han assented soone,
    For, as it seemed, it was for to doone[2]
    To enden in som vertuous sentence,°   *doctrine*
    And for to yive him space° and audience;   *time*
65 And bede[3] oure Host he sholde to him saye
    That alle we to telle his tale him praye.
        Oure Hoste hadde the wordes for us alle:
    "Sire preest," quod he, "now faire you bifalle:
    Telleth," quod he, "youre meditacioun.
70 But hasteth you; the sonne wol adown.
    Beeth fructuous,° and that in litel space,°   *fruitful/time*
    And to do wel God sende you his grace.
    Saye what you list, and we wol gladly heere."
    And with that word he saide in this manere.

---

7. It pleases me.
8. I.e., I cannot tell stories in the alliterative measure (without rhyme): this form of poetry was not
common in southeastern England.

9. I.e., speak in order to please.
1. Literal, faithful to the letter.
2. Necessary to be done.
3. I.e., we bade.

Chaucer's Retraction

Here taketh the makere of this book his leve[4]

Now praye I to hem alle that herkne this litel tretis[5] or rede, that if ther be any thing in it that liketh[6] hem, that therof they thanken oure Lord Jesu Crist, of whom proceedeth al wit[7] and al goodnesse. And if ther be any thing that displese hem, I praye hem also that they arrette it to the defaute of myn unconning,[8] and nat to my wil, that wolde ful fain have said bettre if I hadde had conning. For oure book saith, "Al that is writen is writen for oure doctrine,"[9] and that is myn entente. Wherfore I biseeke[1] you mekely, for the mercy of God, that ye praye for me that Crist have mercy on me and foryive me my giltes, and namely of my translacions and enditinges[2] of worldly vanitees, the whiche I revoke in my retraccions: as is the *Book of Troilus;* the Book also of *Fame;* the *Book of the Five and Twenty Ladies;*[3] the *Book of the Duchesse;* the *Book of Saint Valentines Day of the Parlement of Briddes;* the *Tales of Canterbury,* thilke that sounen into[4] sinne; the *Book of the Leon;*[5] and many another book, if they were in my remembrance, and many a song and many a leccherous lay: that Crist for his grete mercy foryive me the sinne. But of the translacion of Boece[6] *De Consolatione,* and othere bookes of legendes of saintes, and omelies,[7] and moralitee, and devocion, that thanke I oure Lord Jesu Crist and his blisful Moder and alle the saintes of hevene, biseeking hem that they from hennes[8] forth unto my lives ende sende me grace to biwaile my giltes and to studye to the salvacion of my soule, and graunte me grace of verray penitence, confession, and satisfaccion to doon in this present lif, thurgh the benigne grace of him that is king of kinges and preest over alle preestes, that boughte[9] us with the precious blood of his herte, so that I may been oon of hem at the day of doom that shulle be saved. *Qui cum patre et Spiritu Sancto vivis et regnas Deus per omnia saecula.*[1] Amen.

1386–1400

LYRICS AND OCCASIONAL VERSE

In addition to his narrative verse, Chaucer wrote lyric poetry on the models of famous French and Italian poets who made lyric into a medieval art form aimed at learned and aristocratic audiences, an audience that included fellow poets. Chaucer also embedded lyric in narrative poetry. As an example of courtly lyric, we print a "song" that Troilus, the hero of Chaucer's romance *Troilus and Criseyde,* makes up about his violent and puzzling emotions after falling in love. The "song" is actually Chaucer's

---

4. "Chaucer's Retraction" is the title given to this passage by modern editors. The heading, "Here . . . leve," which does appear in all manuscripts, may be by Chaucer himself or by a scribe.
5. Hear this little treatise, i.e., *The Parson's Tale.*
6. Pleases.
7. Understanding.
8. Ascribe it to the defect of my lack of skill.
9. Romans 15.4.
1. Beseech.

2. Compositions. "Namely": especially.
3. I.e., the *Legend of Good Women.*
4. Those that tend toward.
5. The *Book of the Lion* has not been preserved.
6. Boethius.
7. Homilies.
8. Hence.
9. Redeemed.
1. Who with the Father and the Holy Spirit livest and reignest God forever.

translation into rhyme royal of one of Petrarch's sonnets, more than a century before Sir Thomas Wyatt introduced the sonnet form itself to England. In the fifteenth century, Troilus's song was sometimes excerpted and included in anthologies of lyric poetry.

Chaucer also wrote homiletic ballades, one of which is entitled *Truth* by modern editors and called "ballade de bon conseil" (ballade of good advice) in some manuscripts. A ballade is a verse form of three or more stanzas, each with an identical rhyme scheme and the same last line, the refrain. Often a ballade ends with a shorter final stanza called an *envoy* in which the poem is addressed or sent to a friend or patron, or, conventionally, to a "prince" or "princes" in general. The good advice of *Truth* is to abandon worldly pursuits of wealth and power and to concentrate on the pilgrimage that leads to our true home in heaven. There are many copies of *Truth* with only this heartfelt advice. The one printed below contains a unique humorous *envoy*, addressed to a "Vache" (French for "cow"), who is probably a Sir Philip de la Vache.

A single stanza *To His Scribe Adam* comically conveys Chaucer's exasperation at the sloppy work of a professional copyist. The *Complaint to His Purse* is a parody of a lover's complaint to his lady: Ladies, like coins, should be golden, and, like purses, they should not be "light" (i.e., fickle). *Purse* survives both without and with an *envoy*. The addressee in the latter case is the recently crowned Henry IV, who is being wittily implored to restore payment of Chaucer's annuity, which had been interrupted by the new king's deposition of Richard II.

Troilus's Song[1]

	If no love is, O God, what feele I so?	
	And if love, is, what thing and which is he?	
	If love be good, from whennes cometh my wo?	
	If it be wikke,° a wonder thinketh° me,	*miserable / it seems to*
5	Whan every torment and adversitee	
	That cometh of him may to me savory° thinke,°	*pleasant / seem*
	For ay° thurste I, the more that ich° drinke.	*always / I*

	And if that at myn owene lust° I brenne,°	*desire / burn*
	From whennes cometh my wailing and my plainte?°	*complaint*
10	If harm agree° me, wherto plaine° I thenne?	*agrees with / complain*
	I noot,° ne why unwery° that I fainte.	*know not / not weary*
	O quikke° deeth, O sweete harm so quainte,°	*living / strange*
	How may° of thee in me swich quantitee,	*can there be*
	But if that I consente that it be?	

15	And if that I consente, I wrongfully	
	Complaine: ywis,° thus possed° to and fro	*indeed / tossed*
	All stereless° within a boot° am I	*rudderless / boat*
	Amidde the see, bitwixen windes two,	
	That in contrarye stonden everemo.	
20	Allas, what is this wonder maladye?	
	For hoot° of cold, for cold of hoot I die.	*hot*

---

1. *Troilus and Criseyde*, Book 1, lines 400–420. A translation of Petrarch's Sonnet 88, "S'amor non è."

Truth[1]

Flee fro the prees° and dwelle with soothfastnesse;	*crowd*
Suffise unto° thy thing, though it be smal;	*be content with*
For hoord hath[2] hate, and climbing tikelnesse;°	*insecurity*
Prees hath envye, and wele° blent° overal.	*prosperity/blinds*

5 Savoure° no more than thee bihoove shal;   *relish*
Rule wel thyself that other folk canst rede:°   *advise*
And Trouthe shal delivere,[3] it is no drede.°   *doubt*

Tempest thee nought al crooked to redresse[4]
In trust of hire[5] that turneth as a bal;
10 Muche wele stant in litel bisinesse;[6]
Be war therfore to spurne ayains an al.[7]
Strive nat as dooth the crokke° with the wal.   *pot*
Daunte° thyself that dauntest otheres deede: *master*
And Trouthe shal delivere, it is no drede.

15 That° thee is sent, receive in buxomnesse;°   *what/obedience*
The wrastling for the world axeth° a fal;   *asks for*
Here is noon hoom, here nis° but wildernesse: *is not*
Forth, pilgrim, forth! Forth, beest, out of thy stal!
Know thy countree, looke up, thank God of al.
20 Hold the heigh way and lat thy gost° thee lede: *spirit*
And Trouthe shal delivere, it is no drede.

Envoy

Therfore, thou Vache,[8] leve thyn olde wrecchednesse
Unto the world; leve° now to be thral.   *i.e., cease*
Crye him mercy° that of his heigh goodnesse   *thank him*
25 Made thee of nought, and in especial
Draw unto him, and pray in general,
For thee and eek for othere, hevenelich meede:[9]
And Trouthe shal delivere, it is no drede.

To His Scribe Adam[1]

Adam scrivain,° if evere it thee bifalle	*scribe*
Boece or *Troilus*[2] for to writen newe,	

1. Taking as his theme Christ's words to his disciples (in John 8.32), "And ye shall know the truth, and the truth shall make you free," Chaucer plays on the triple meaning that the Middle English word *trouthe* seems to have had for him: the religious truth of Christianity, the moral virtue of integrity, and the philosophical idea of reality. By maintaining one's faith and one's integrity, one rises superior to the vicissitudes of this world and comes eventually to know reality—which is not, however, of this world.
2. Hoarding causes.
3. I.e., truth shall make you free.
4. Do not disturb yourself to straighten all that's crooked.

5. Fortune, who turns like a ball in that she is always presenting a different aspect to people.
6. Peace of mind stands in little anxiety.
7. Awl, i.e., "don't kick against the pricks," wound yourself by kicking a sharp instrument.
8. Probably Sir Philip de la Vache, with a pun on the French for "cow."
9. Reward, with a pun on *meadow*.
1. Chaucer had fair copies of longer works made by a professional scribe. This humorous complaint about Adam's sloppy work is written in the verse form of Chaucer's great poem *Troilus and Criseyde*.
2. *Troilus and Criseyde*. "Boece": i.e., Chaucer's translation of Boethius's *De Consolatione*.

Under thy longe lokkes thou moste[3] have the scalle,°   *scurf*
But after my making thou write more trewe,[4]
5   So ofte a day I moot° thy werk renewe,   *must*
It to correcte, and eek to rubbe and scrape:
And al is thurgh thy necligence and rape.°   *haste*

Complaint to His Purse

To you, my purs, and to noon other wight,°   *person*
Complaine I, for ye be my lady dere.
I am so sory, now that ye be light,
For certes, but if° ye make me hevy cheere,   *unless*
5   Me were as lief[1] be laid upon my beere;°   *bier*
For which unto youre mercy thus I crye:
Beeth hevy again, or elles moot° I die.   *must*

Now voucheth sauf° this day er° it be night   *grant/before*
That I of you the blisful soun may heere,
10 Or see youre colour, lik the sonne bright,
That of yelownesse hadde nevere peere.°   *equal*
Ye be my life, ye be myn hertes steere,°   *rudder, guide*
Queene of confort and of good compaignye:
Beeth hevy again, or elles moot I die.

15 Ye purs, that been to me my lives light
And saviour, as in this world down here,
Out of this towne[2] helpe me thurgh your might,
Sith that ye wol nat be my tresorere;°   *treasurer*
For I am shave as neigh as any frere.[3]
20 But yit I praye unto youre curteisye:
Beeth hevy again, or elles moot I die.

Envoy to Henry IV

O conquerour of Brutus Albioun,[4]
Which that by line° and free eleccioun   *lineage*
Been verray° king, this song to you I sende: *true*
25 And ye, that mowen° alle oure harmes amende, *may*
Have minde upon my supplicacioun.

3. I.e., may you.
4. Unless you write more accurately what I've composed.
1. I'd just as soon.
2. Probably Westminster, where Chaucer had rented a house.

3. Shaved as close as any (tonsured) friar, an expression for being broke.
4. Britain (Albion) was supposed to have been founded by Brutus, the grandson of Aeneas, the founder of Rome.

WILLIAM LANGLAND
ca. 1330–1387

William Langland is agreed by most scholars to be the sole author of a long religious allegory in alliterative verse known as *The Vision of Piers Plowman* or more simply *Piers Plowman*, which survives in three distinct versions that scholars refer to as the A-, B-, and C-texts. The first, about twenty-four hundred lines long, breaks off at a rather inconclusive point in the action; the second is a revision of the first plus an extension of more than four thousand lines; and the third is a revision of the second. About Langland we know hardly anything except what can be inferred from the poem itself. He came from the west of England and was probably a native of the Malvern Hills area in which the opening of the poem is set. We can never identify the persona of the narrator of a medieval text positively or precisely with its author, especially when we are dealing with allegory. Nevertheless, a passage that was added to the C-text, the last of the selections printed here, gives the strong impression of being at one and the same time an allegory in which the narrator represents willful Mankind and a poignantly ironic self-portrait of the stubborn-willed poet who occasionally plays on his own name: "I have lived in *land* . . . my name is *Long Will*" (15.152). In this new episode the narrator tries to defend his shiftless way of life against Conscience and Reason, presumably his own conscience and reason. Conscience dismisses his specious argument that a clerical education has left him no "tools" to support himself with except for his prayer book and the Psalms with which he prays for the souls of those from whom he begs alms. The entire work conforms well with the notion that its author was a man who was educated to enter the church but who, through marriage and lack of preferment, was reduced to poverty and may well have wandered in his youth like those "hermits" he scornfully describes in the prologue.

Piers Plowman has the form of a dream vision, a common medieval type in which the author presents the story under the guise of having dreamed it. The dream vision generally involves allegory, not only because one expects from a dream the unrealistic, the fanciful, but also because people have always suspected that dreams relate the truth in disguised form—that they are natural allegories. Through a series of such visions it traces the Dreamer-narrator's tough-minded, persistent, and passionate search for answers to his many questions, especially the question he puts early in the poem to Lady Holy Church: "How I may save my soul." Langland's theme is nothing less than the history of Christianity as it unfolds both in the world of the Old and New Testaments and in the life and heart of an individual fourteenth-century Christian—two seemingly distinct realms between which the poet's allegory moves with dizzying rapidity.

The first selection, from the prologue to the poem, introduces the famous vision of the Field of Folk. The poet describes fourteenth-century English society in terms of its failure to represent an ideal society living in accord with Christian principles; hence the satirical poetry for which Langland is noted. Society's failure, of course, is attributable in part to the corruption of the church and ecclesiastics, and whenever he considers clerical corruption, he pours out savagely indignant satire. But he is equally angry with the failure of the wealthy laity—untaught by the church to practice charity—to alleviate the sufferings of the poor.

After his vision of the Field of Folk, the Dreamer in *Passus 1* (*Passus*, Latin for "step," is the word the poet uses for the sections of his poem) is approached by Lady Holy Church, who explains to him the fundamental principles of Christianity with which, presumably, he has been familiar since childhood. But mere knowledge is not enough for him: he must learn by experience and feel in his heart what he learns—a process that takes up the rest of the poem. The departure of Lady Holy Church is followed by the vision of Lady Meed whose name has the basically neutral meaning of "reward" or "pay" but who in Langland's often scathing satire represents "bribery" or "graft" in state and church. Lady Meed is about to be married to a figure named False over the protests of Conscience. The episode presents Langland's mordant view of a country being bled by a swarm of greedy and corrupt officials but holds out some hope that the king with the counsel of Conscience and Reason may yet bring about reforms.

At the beginning of *Passus 5* the Dreamer awakes for the first time, but after a very short interval he falls asleep again and dreams that Reason preaches a sermon to the whole kingdom, causing the people to confess their sins. Langland describes the confession by personifying the seven deadly sins and having each one relate to the personified figure Repentance how badly he behaves in society. The confessions of Envy and Gluttony, included in the second selection, display most clearly Langland's social realism.

In the third and fourth selections, which comprise the conclusion of *Passus 5* and most of *Passus 6*, the prayer of Repentance inspires Hope (personified as a trumpeter) to move the people to set out blindly in search of Truth, a figure for God or Christ, but there is no one to show them the way. At this point Piers Plowman, the titular hero, makes his first appearance. Piers explains that the "way" to Saint Truth leads through the two "great" commandments of Matthew 22.37–39 (to love God and thy neighbor) and the Ten Commandments, and he offers himself as the people's guide. First, however, all must help Piers plow his half acre. The episode is a brilliant allegory of how people in the ideal community should work together for the common good but how the actual society breaks down, especially in times of plenty. The only effective enforcer of social order is not the knight, who represents the ruling class, but Hunger, a grim figure that graphically portrays the ravages of famine during the fourteenth century.

Passus 18 describes the central event of Christianity, Christ's crucifixion, followed by an account of the descent into hell, traditionally called the "Harrowing of Hell." The Dreamer has come a long way in his personal search for Truth, and this vision is the most immediate and fulfilling answer to the questions he addressed to Lady Holy Church, although not a final answer, for in Langland's poem the search has no end in this life. Piers, who in earlier appearances had assumed aspects of Adam, Moses, and the Good Samaritan, is now partially identified with Christ. With this development his farm produce is no longer simple foodstuffs, but becomes the souls of the patriarchs and prophets, and of all humankind, which must be redeemed from the devil's power by Christ's sacrifice on the cross. In lines 20 and 33 these souls are referred to as the "fruit" of Piers Plowman, which Christ, having assumed Piers's human nature, will win back from hell, where it has been since Adam's sin. Langland describes the crucifixion as a literal, historical event, yet at the same time he speaks of it as if it were a medieval joust between the Christ-knight and an adversary. After Christ dies on the cross, the Dreamer hears an argument among the "Four Daughters of God" (personifications taken from Psalm 85.10) about the validity and efficacy of Christ's sacrifice: Righteousness and Truth maintain that the Old Law condemns mankind irredeemably, while Mercy and Peace prophesy that by Christ's New Law man will be saved. Christ appears before hell's gates as a great light, the devils are thrown into confusion, and the souls of the righteous are released from hell's power. The four Daughters of God are reconciled as the New Law fulfills the Old, and the Dreamer wakes to celebrate Easter with his family.

A large number of manuscripts and two sixteenth-century editions show that *Piers Plowman* was avidly read and studied by a great many people from the end of the fourteenth century to the reign of Elizabeth I. Some of these readers have left a record of their engagement with the poem in marginal comments. Almost from the first, it was a controversial text. Within four years of the writing of the second version— which scholars have good evidence to date 1377, the year of Edward III's death and Richard II's accession to the throne—it had become so well known that the leaders of the Uprising of 1381 used phrases borrowed from it as part of the rhetoric of the rebellion. Langland's sympathy with the sufferings of the poor and his indignant satire of official corruption undoubtedly made his poem popular with the rebels, although he himself, despite his interest in social reform, remained a fundamentally conservative and orthodox thinker. The passionate sympathy for the commoner, idealized in *Piers Plowman*, also appealed to reformers who felt that true religion was best represented not by the ecclesiastical hierarchy but by the humblest orders of society. Many persons reading his poem in the sixteenth century (it was first printed in 1550) saw in *Piers Plowman* a prophecy and forerunner of the English Reformation. Immersed as it is in thorny political and theological controversies of its own day, *Piers Plowman* is arguably the most difficult and, at times, even the most frustrating of Middle English texts, but its poetic, intellectual, and moral complexity and integrity also make it one of the most rewarding.

From The Vision of Piers Plowman[1]

From *The Prologue*

[THE FIELD OF FOLK]

In a summer season when the sun was mild
I clad myself in clothes as I'd become a sheep;
In the habit of a hermit unholy of works,[2]
Walked wide in this world, watching for wonders.
5 And on a May morning, on Malvern Hills,
There befell me as by magic a marvelous thing:
I was weary of wandering and went to rest
At the bottom of a broad bank by a brook's side,
And as I lay lazily looking in the water
10 I slipped into a slumber, it sounded so pleasant.
There came to me reclining there a most curious dream
That I was in a wilderness, nowhere that I knew;
But as I looked into the east, up high toward the sun,
I saw a tower on a hill-top, trimly built,
15 A deep dale beneath, a dungeon tower in it,
With ditches deep and dark and dreadful to look at.
A fair field full of folk I found between them,
Of human beings of all sorts, the high and the low,
Working and wandering as the world requires.
20 Some applied themselves to plowing, played very rarely,
Sowing seeds and setting plants worked very hard;
Won what wasters gluttonously consume.
And some pursued pride, put on proud clothing,
Came all got up in garments garish to see.
25 To prayers and penance many put themselves,
All for love of our Lord lived hard lives,
Hoping thereafter to have Heaven's bliss—
Such as hermits and anchorites that hold to their cells,

1. The translation is by E. T. Donaldson (1990) and is based on *Piers Plowman: The B Version*, edited by George Kane and E. T. Donaldson (1975).

2. For Langland's opinion of hermits, see lines 28–30 and 53–57. The sheep's clothing may suggest the habit's physical resemblance to sheep's wool as well as a false appearance of innocence.

Don't care to go cavorting about the countryside,
30 With some lush livelihood delighting their bodies.
And some made themselves merchants—they managed better,
As it seems to our sight that such men prosper.
And some make mirth as minstrels can
And get gold for their music, guiltless, I think.
35 But jokers and word jugglers, Judas' children,[3]
Invent fantasies to tell about and make fools of themselves,
And have whatever wits they need to work if they wanted.
What Paul preaches of them I don't dare repeat here:
Qui loquitur turpiloquium[4] is Lucifer's henchman.
40 Beadsmen[5] and beggars bustled about
Till both their bellies and their bags were crammed to the brim;
Staged flytings[6] for their food, fought over beer.
In gluttony, God knows, they go to bed
And rise up with ribaldry, those Robert's boys.°   *i.e., robbers*
45 Sleep and sloth pursue them always.
    Pilgrims and palmers[7] made pacts with each other
To seek Saint James[8] and saints at Rome.
They went on their way with many wise stories,
And had leave to lie all their lives after.
50 I saw some that said they'd sought after saints:
In every tale they told their tongues were tuned to lie
More than to tell the truth—such talk was theirs.
A heap of hermits with hooked staffs
Went off to Walsingham,[9] with their wenches behind them.
55 Great long lubbers that don't like to work
Dressed up in cleric's dress to look different from other men
And behaved as they were hermits, to have an easy life.
I found friars there—all four of the orders[1]—
Preaching to the people for their own paunches' welfare,
60 Making glosses° of the Gospel that would look good for   *interpretations*
    themselves;
Coveting copes,[2] they construed it as they pleased.
Many of these Masters[3] may clothe themselves richly,
For their money and their merchandise[4] march hand in hand.
Since Charity[5] has proved a peddler and principally shrives lords,
65 Many marvels have been manifest within a few years.
Unless Holy Church and friars' orders hold together better,
The worst misfortune in the world will be welling up soon.

---

3. Minstrels who entertain with jokes and fantastic stories are regarded as descendants of Christ's betrayer, Judas.
4. Who speaks filthy language. Not Paul, though cf. Ephesians 5.3–4.
5. Prayer sayers, i.e., people who offered to say prayers, sometimes counted on the beads of the rosary, for the souls of those who gave them alms.
6. Contests in which the participants took turns insulting each other, preferably in verse.
7. Virtually professional pilgrims who took advantage of the hospitality offered them to go on traveling year after year (see p. 215, n. 6).

8. I.e., his shrine at Compostela in Spain.
9. English town, site of a famous shrine to the Virgin Mary.
1. In Langland's day there were four orders of friars in England: Franciscans, Dominicans, Carmelites, and Augustinians.
2. Monks', friars', and hermits' capes.
3. I.e., masters of divinity.
4. The "merchandise" sold by the friars for money is shrift, that is, confession and remission of sins, which by canon law cannot be sold.
5. The ideal of the friars, as stated by St. Francis, was simply love, i.e., charity.

A pardoner[6] preached there as if he had priest's rights,
Brought out a bull[7] with bishop's seals,
70 And said he himself could absolve them all
Of failure to fast, of vows they'd broken.
Unlearned men believed him and liked his words,
Came crowding up on knees to kiss his bulls.
He banged them with his brevet and bleared their eyes,[8]
75 And raked in with his parchment-roll rings and brooches.
Thus you give your gold for gluttons' well-being,
And squander it on scoundrels schooled in lechery.
If the bishop were blessed and worth both his ears,
His seal should not be sent out to deceive the people.
80 —It's nothing to the bishop that the blackguard preaches,
And the parish priest and the pardoner split the money
That the poor people of the parish would have but for them.
    Parsons and parish priests complained to the bishop
That their parishes were poor since the pestilence-time,[9]
85 Asked for license and leave to live in London,
And sing Masses there for simony,[1] for silver is sweet.

* * *

Yet scores of men stood there in silken coifs
Who seemed to be law-sergeants[2] that served at the bar,
Pleaded cases for pennies and impounded[3] the law,
And not for love of our Lord once unloosed their lips:
215 You might better measure mist on Malvern Hills
Than get a "mum" from their mouths till money's on the table.
Barons and burgesses[4] and bondmen also
I saw in this assemblage, as you shall hear later;
Bakers and brewers and butchers aplenty.
220 Weavers of wool and weavers of linen,
Tailors, tinkers, tax-collectors in markets,
Masons, miners, many other craftsmen.
Of all living laborers there leapt forth some,
Such as diggers of ditches that do their jobs badly,
225 And dawdle away the long day with *"Dieu save dame Emme."*[5]
Cooks and their kitchen-boys crying, "Hot pies, hot!
Good geese and pork! Let's go and dine!"
Tavern-keepers told them a tale of the same sort:
"White wine of Alsace and wine of Gascony,

6. An official empowered to pass on from the pope temporal indulgence for the sins of people who contributed to charitable enterprises—a function frequently abused.
7. Papal license to act as a pardoner, endorsed with the local bishop's seals.
8. I.e., pulled the wool over their eyes. "Brevet": pardoner's license.
9. Since 1349 England had suffered a number of epidemics of the plague, the Black Death, which had caused famine and depopulated the countryside.
1. Buying and selling the functions, spiritual powers, or offices of the church. Wealthy persons, especially in London, set up foundations to pay

priests to sing masses for their souls and those of their relatives (see the portrait of Chaucer's Parson, p. 227, lines 509–12).
2. Important lawyers (see *The General Prologue* to *The Canterbury Tales*, p. 222, lines 311ff.). "Coifs": a silk scarf was a lawyer's badge of office.
3. Detained in legal custody. Pennies were fairly valuable coins in medieval England.
4. Town dwellers who had full rights as the citizens of a municipality. In contrast, barons were members of the upper nobility, and bondmen were peasants who held their land from a lord in return for customary services or rent.
5. "God save Dame Emma," presumably a popular song.

230 Of the Rhine and of La Rochelle, to wash the roast down with."
All this I saw sleeping, and seven times more.

From *Passus* 5

[THE CONFESSION OF ENVY]

75   Envy with heavy heart asked for shrift
And grieving for his guilt began his confession.
He was pale as a sheep's pelt, appeared to have the palsy.
He was clothed in a coarse cloth—I couldn't describe it—
A tabard[6] and a tunic, a knife tied to his side,
80 Like those of a friar's frock were the foresleeves.
Like a leek that had lain long in the sun
So he looked with lean cheeks, louring foully.
His body was so blown up for anger that he bit his lips
And shook his fist fiercely, he wanted to avenge himself
85 With acts or with words when he saw his chance.
Every syllable he spat out was of a serpent's tongue;
From chiding and bringing charges was his chief livelihood,
With backbiting and bitter scorn and bearing false witness.
This was all his courtesy wherever he showed himself.
90 "I'd like to be shriven," said this scoundrel, "if shame would let me.
By God, I'd be gladder that Gib had bad luck
Than if I'd won this week a wey[7] of Essex cheese.
I've a neighbor dwelling next door, I've done him harm often
And blamed him behind his back to blacken his name.
95 I've done my best to damage him day after day
And lied to lords about him to make him lose money,
And turned his friends into his foes with my false tongue.
His good luck and his glad lot grieve me greatly.
Between household and household I often start disputes
100 So that both life and limb are lost for my speech.
When I met the man in market that I most hated,
I fondled him affectionately as if I were a friend of his:
He is stronger than I am—I don't dare harm him.
But if I had might and mastery I'd murder him once for all.
105 When I come to kirk° and kneel before Christ's Cross   *church*
To pray for the people as the priest teaches,
For pilgrims, for palmers, for all the people after,
Then crouching there I call on Christ to give him sorrow
That took away my tankard and my torn sheet.[8]
110 Away from the altar I turn my eyes
And notice how Heinie has a new coat;
Then I wish it were mine and all the web[9] it came from.
And when he loses I laugh—that lightens my heart,
But when he wins I weep and wail the time.
115 I condemn men when they do evil, yet I do much worse;

---

6. A loose sleeveless jacket, worn over the tunic.
7. A very large measure.
8. The loss of Envy's tankard and torn sheet, and

his fury at it, have not been explained.
9. I.e., bolt of cloth.

Whoever upbraids me for that, I hate him deadly after.
I wish that every one were my servant,
And if any man has more than I, that angers my heart.
So I live loveless like a loathsome dog

120 So that all my breast is blown up for bitterness of spirit.
For many years I might not eat as a man ought
For envy and ill will are hard to digest.
Is there any sugar or sweet thing to assuage my swelling
Or any *diapenidion*[1] that will drive it from my heart,

125 Or any shrift or shame, unless I have my stomach scraped?"
    "Yes, readily," said Repentance, directing him to live better;
"Sorrow for sins is salvation for souls."
"I am sorry," said Envy. "I'm seldom anything else,
And that makes me so miserable, since I may not avenge myself.

130 I've been among burgesses buying at London
And made Backbiting a broker to blame men's wares.
When he sold and I didn't, then I was ready
To lie and lour at my neighbor and belittle his merchandise.
I will amend this if I may, by might of God almighty."

*   *   *

[THE CONFESSION OF GLUTTONY]

    Now Glutton begins to go to shrift
And takes his way towards the Church to tell his sins.
But Betty the brewer bade him good morning
And she asked him where he was going.

300 "To Holy Church," he said, "to hear Mass,
And then I shall be shriven and sin no more."
"I've got good ale, old friend," she said. "Glutton, will you try it?"
"Have you," he asked, "any hot spices?"
"I have pepper and peony and a pound of garlic,

305 A farthingworth of fennel seed[2] for fasting days."
Then Glutton goes in, and great oaths after.
Cissy the seamstress was sitting on the bench,
Wat the warren-keeper° and his wife too,   *game warden*
Tim the tinker and two of his servants,

310 Hick the hackneyman and Hugh the needle-seller,
Clarice of Cock's Lane and the clerk of the church,
Sir Piers of Pridie and Parnel[3] of Flanders,
Dave the ditch-digger and a dozen others,
A rebeck-player, a rat-catcher, a street-raker of Cheapside,

315 A rope-maker, a redingking,[4] and Rose the dish vendor,
Godfrey of Garlickhithe and Griffin the Welshman,
A heap of old-clothesmen early in the morning
Gladly treated Glutton to drinks of good ale.

---

1. A twist of medicinal sugar.
2. This herb was considered good for one drinking on an empty stomach. "Peony": considered a spice in the Middle Ages.
3. Parnel and Clarice are prostitutes.

4. What a "redingking" was is not known. "Rebeck-player": fiddler. "Street-raker": scavenger, hence street cleaner. "Cheapside": a section of London.

Clement the cobbler took the coat off his back
320 And put it up as a prize for a player of "New Fair."[5]
Then Hick the ostler[6] took off his hood
And bade Bart the butcher to be on his side.
Then peddlers were appointed to appraise the goods:
For his cloak Clement should get the hood plus compensation.
325 They went to work quickly and whispered together
And appraised these prize items apart by themselves.
There were heaps of oaths for any one to hear.
They couldn't in conscience come to an agreement
Till Robin the roper was requested to rise
330 And named as an umpire so no quarrel should break out.
Then Hick the ostler had the cloak
In covenant that Clement should have the cup filled
And have Hick the ostler's hood, and call it a deal;
The first to regret the agreement should get up straightway
335 And greet Sir Glutton with a gallon of ale.
There was laughing and louring and "Let go the cup!"
They began to make bets and bought more rounds
And sat so till evensong[7] and sang sometimes
Till Glutton had gulped down a gallon and a gill.°   *quarter pint*
340 His guts began to grumble like two greedy sows;
He pissed four pints in a Paternoster's length,[8]
And on the bugle of his backside he blew a fanfare
So that all that heard that horn held their noses after
And wished it had been waxed up with a wisp of gorse.[9]
345 He had no strength to stand before he had his staff in hand,
And then he made off moving like a minstrel's bitch,[1]
Some times sideways and some times backwards,
Like some one laying lines to lime birds with.[2]
But as he started to step to the door his sight grew dim;
350 He fumbled for the threshold and fell on the ground.
Clement the cobbler caught him by the waist
To lift him aloft and laid him on his knees.
But Glutton was a large lout and a load to lift,
And he coughed up a custard in Clement's lap.
355 There's no hound so hungry in Hertfordshire
That would dare lap up that leaving, so unlovely the taste.
    With all the woe of this world his wife and his maid
Brought him to his bed and bundled him in it.

5. This was a game in which two participants exchanged items in their possession that were not of equal value and hence involved a cash payment by the player who put up the less valuable object. Clement puts up his cloak and Hick, his hood; each chooses an agent to represent him in the evaluation of the objects, which is conducted by peddlers. Hick is represented by Bart, but because the evaluators are unable to agree, Robin is named as an umpire. It is decided that Hick should have Clement's cloak and Clement Hick's hood but that Clement should receive a cup of ale as well or perhaps the money for a cup of ale, which he would then share with all the participants. A fine of further ale would be placed on either of the men who grumbled at the exchange.
6. I.e., a stableman (called "hackneyman" above, implying that he keeps horses for hire).
7. Vespers, the evening prayer service said just before sunset.
8. I.e., the time it takes to say the Lord's Prayer.
9. A spiny shrub. "Waxed up": i.e., sealed.
1. I.e., a trained dog performing some feat (probably walking on her hind legs) with difficulty.
2. Birds were caught by smearing a sticky substance ("lime") on strings laid out on the ground. A bird catcher "laying lines" would move systematically right and left or forward and backward.

And after all this excess he had a fit of sloth
360 So that he slept Saturday and Sunday till the sun set.
When he was awake and had wiped his eyes,
The first word he spoke was, "Where is the bowl?"
His spouse scolded him for his sin and wickedness,
And right so Repentance rebuked him at that time.
365 "As with words as well as with deeds you've done evil in your life,
Shrive yourself and be ashamed, and show it with your mouth."
"I, Glutton," he began, "admit I'm guilty of this:
That I've trespassed with my tongue, I can't tell how often;
Sworn by God's soul and his sides and 'So God help me!'
370 When there was no need for it nine hundred times.
And over-stuffed myself at supper and sometimes at midday,
So that I, Glutton, got rid of it before I'd gone a mile,
And spoiled what might have been saved and dispensed to the hungry;
Over-indulgently on feast days I've drunk and eaten both;
375 And sometimes sat so long there that I slept and ate at once;
To hear tales in taverns I've taken more drink;
Fed myself before noon on fasting days."
"This full confession," said Repentance, "will gain favor for you."
Then Glutton began to groan and to make great lament
380 For the life he had lived in so loathsome a way,
And vowed he would fast, what for hunger or for thirst:
"Shall never fish on Friday be fed to my belly
Till Abstinence my aunt has given me leave.
And yet I have hated her all my lifetime."

[PIERS PLOWMAN SHOWS THE WAY TO SAINT TRUTH]

Then Hope took hold of a horn of *Deus tu conversus vivificabis nos*[3]
And blew it with *Beati quorum remissae sunt iniquitates*,[4]
So that all the saints sang for sinners at once,
*"Men and animals thou shalt save inasmuch as thou hast multiplied
thy mercy, O God."*[5]
510 A thousand men then thronged together,
Cried upward to Christ and to his clean mother
To have grace to go to Truth—God grant they might!
But there was no one so wise as to know the way thither,
But they blundered forth like beasts over banks and hills
515 Till they met a man, many hours later,
Appareled like a pagan[6] in pilgrims' manner.
He bore a stout staff with a broad strap around it,
In the way of woodbine wound all about.
A bowl and a bag he bore by his side.
520 A hundred holy water phials were set on his hat,
Souvenirs of Sinai and shells of Galicia,
And many a Cross on his cloak and keys of Rome,
And the vernicle in front so folk should know

3. O God, you will turn and give us life (from the Mass).
4. Blessed [are they] whose transgressions are forgiven (Psalms 32.1).
5. Psalms 36.6–7.
6. I.e., outlandishly. (Langland's word *paynym* was especially associated with Saracens, i.e., Arabs.)

By seeing his signs what shrines he'd been to.[7]
525 These folk asked him fairly from whence he came.
"From Sinai," he said, "and from the Holy Sepulchre.
Bethlehem, Babylon, I've been to both;
In Armenia, in Alexandria,[8] in many other places.
You can tell by the tokens attached to my hat
530 That I've walked far and wide in wet and in dry
And sought out good saints for my soul's health."
"Did you ever see a saint," said they, "that men call Truth?
Could you point out a path to where that person lives?"
"No, so God save me," said the fellow then.
535 "I've never known a palmer with knapsack or staff
To ask after him ere now in this place."
    "Peter!"[9] said a plowman, and put forth his head.
"We're as closely acquainted as a clerk and his books.
Conscience and Kind Wit[1] coached me to his place
540 And persuaded me to swear to him I'd serve him forever,
Both to sow and set plants so long as I can work.
I have been his follower all these forty winters,
Both sowed his seed and overseen his cattle,
Indoors and outdoors taken heed for his profit,
545 Made ditches and dikes, done what he bids.
Sometimes I sow and sometimes I thresh,
In tailor's craft and tinker's, whatever Truth can devise.
I weave wool and wind it and do what Truth says.
For though I say it myself, I serve him to his satisfaction.
550 I get good pay from him, and now and again more.
He's the promptest payer that poor men know.
He withholds no worker's wages so he's without them by evening.
He's as lowly as a lamb and lovely of speech.
And if you'd like to learn where that lord dwells,
555 I'll direct you on the road right to his palace."
"Yes, friend Piers,"[2] said these pilgrims, and proffered him pay.
"No, by the peril of my soul!" said Piers, and swore on oath:
"I wouldn't take a farthing's fee for Saint Thomas's shrine.[3]
Truth would love me the less a long time after.
560   But you that are anxious to be off, here's how you go:
You must go through Meekness, both men and women,
Till you come into Conscience[4] that Christ knows the truth

---

7. A pilgrim to Canterbury collected a phial of holy water from St. Thomas's shrine; collecting another every time one passed through Canterbury was a mark of a professional pilgrim. "Sinai": souvenirs from the Convent of St. Katharine on Sinai. "Shells": the emblem of St. James at Compostela, in Galicia. "Many a cross": commemorating trips to the Holy Land. "Keys": the sign of St. Peter's keys, from Rome. "Vernicle": a copy of the image of Christ's face preserved on a cloth, another famous relic from Rome. It was believed to have appeared after Veronica gave her head cloth to Christ, as he was going to execution, to wipe his face on.
8. "Babylon": near Cairo, where there was a church on the site where Mary lived during the Flight into Egypt. "Armenia": presumably to visit Mt. Ararat, where the Ark is said to have landed. "Alexandria": the site of the martyrdom of St. Catherine and St. Mark.
9. I.e., an oath "By St. Peter!"
1. Moral sense and natural intelligence (common sense).
2. I.e., Peter, hence the particular appropriateness of his swearing by St. Peter (line 537), a connection that Langland will exploit in a variety of ways.
3. The shrine of St. Thomas at Canterbury was famous for the gold and jewels offered by important pilgrims.
4. Consciousness, moral awareness, related to but not identical with the moral sense personified in line 539.

That you love our Lord God of all loves the most,
And next to him your neighbors—in no way harm them,
565   Otherwise than you'd have them behave to you.
And so follow along a brook's bank, Be-Modest-Of-Speech,
Until you find a ford, Do-Your-Fathers-Honor:
     Honor thy father and thy mother, etc.[5]
Wade in that water and wash yourselves well there
And you'll leap the lighter all your lifetime.
570   So you shall see Swear-Not-Unless-It-Is-For-Need-
And-Namely-Never-Take-In-Vain-The-Name-Of-God-Almighty.
Then you'll come to a croft,[6] but don't come into it:
The croft is called Covet-Not-Men's-Cattle-Nor-Their-Wives
And-None-Of-Your-Neighbor's-Serving-Men-So-As-To-Harm-Them.
575   See that you break no boughs there unless they belong to you.
Two wooden statues stand there, but don't stop for them:
They're called Steal-Not and Slay-Not: stay away from both;
Leave them on your left hand and don't look back.
And hold well your holiday until the high evening.[7]
580   Then you shall blench at a barrow,[8] Bear-No-False-Witness:
It's fenced in with florins and other fees aplenty.
See that you pluck no plant there for peril of your soul.
Then you shall see Speak-The-Truth-So-It-Must-Be-Done-
And-Not-In-Any-Other-Way-Not-For-Any-Man's-Asking.
585   Then you shall come to a castle shining clear as the sun.
The moat is made of mercy, all about the manor;
And all the walls are of wit° to hold will out.   *reason*
The crenelations are of Christendom to save Christiankind,
Buttressed with Believe-So-Or-You-Won't-Be-Saved;
590   And all the houses are roofed, halls and chambers,
Not with lead but with Love-And-Lowness-As-Brothers-Of-One-
     Womb.
The bridge is of Pray-Properly-You-Will-Prosper-The-More.
Every pillar is of penance, of prayers to saints;
The hooks are of almsdeeds that the gates are hanging on.
595   The gate-keeper's name is Grace, a good man indeed;
His man is called Amend-Yourself, for he knows many men.
Say this sentence to him: 'Truth sees what's true;
I performed the penance the priest gave me to do
And I'm sorry for my sins and shall be so always
600   When I think thereon, though I were a pope.'
Pray Amend-Yourself mildly to ask his master once
To open wide the wicket-gate that the woman shut
When Adam and Eve ate unroasted apples.

---

5. Exodus 20.12. Beginning in lines 563–64 with the two "great" commandments (Matthew 22.37–39), Piers's directions include most of the commandments of Exodus 20. The line numbering is that of the edition on which the translation is based. The indented lines printed in italics are translated from the Latin of the original and are generally quotations from the Bible, the liturgy, or the fathers of the church. Hence they are given the status of "a-lines" because they are not composed by Langland. Thus this line is numbered 567a.
6. A small enclosed field, or a small agricultural holding worked by a tenant.
7. A holiday (i.e., a holy day) lasted until sunset ("high evening"); it was not supposed to be used for work, and drinking and games were forbidden, at least until after attendance at church services.
8. A low hillock or a burial mound.

Through Eve it was closed to all and through the Virgin
Mary it was opened again.[9]

605 For he keeps the latchkey though the king sleep.
And if Grace grants you to go in in this way
You shall see in yourself Truth sitting in your heart
In a chain of charity as though you were a child again,[1]
To suffer your sire's will and say nothing against it."

* * *

630 "By Christ," cried a pickpocket, "I have no kin there."
"Nor I," said an ape-trainer, "for anything I know."
"God knows," said a cake-seller, "if I were sure of this,
I wouldn't go a foot further for any friar's preaching."
"Yes!" said Piers Plowman, and prodded him for his good.
635 "Mercy is a maiden there that has dominion over them all,
And she is sib to all sinners, and her son as well,
And through the help of these two—think nothing else—
You might get grace there if you go in time."
"By Saint Paul!" said a pardoner, "possibly I'm not known there;
640 I'll go fetch my box with my brevets and a bull with bishop's letters."
"By Christ!" said a common woman,[2] "I'll keep you company.
You shall say I am your sister." I don't know what became of them.

Passus 6

[THE PLOWING OF PIERS'S HALF-ACRE]

"This would be a bewildering way unless we had a guide
Who could trace our way foot by foot": thus these folk complained.
Said Perkin[3] the Plowman, "By Saint Peter of Rome!
I have a half-acre to plow by the highway;
5 If I had plowed this half-acre and afterwards sowed it,
I would walk along with you and show you the way to go."
"That would be a long delay," said a lady in a veil.
"What ought we women to work at meanwhile?"
"Some shall sew sacks to stop the wheat from spilling.
10 And you lovely ladies, with your long fingers,
See that you have silk and sendal to sew when you've time
Chasubles[4] for chaplains for the Church's honor.
Wives and widows, spin wool and flax;
Make cloth, I counsel you, and teach the craft to your daughters.
15 The needy and the naked, take note how they fare:
Keep them from cold with clothing, for so Truth wishes.
For I shall supply their sustenance unless the soil fails
As long as I live, for the Lord's love in Heaven.

9. From a service commemorating the Virgin
Mary.
1. Cf. Mark 10.15: "whosoever shall not receive
the kingdom of God as a little child, he shall not
enter therein." This childlike quality is here envis-
aged as total submissiveness (line 608). "In a chain
of charity": either Truth is bound by (that is, con-

strained by) *caritas* (love) or Truth is enthroned,
adorned with *caritas* like a chain of office.
2. Prostitute. "Brevets": pardoner's credentials.
3. A nickname for Piers, or Peter.
4. Garments worn by priests to celebrate Mass.
"Sendal": a thin, rich form of silk.

And all sorts of folk that feed on farm products,
20 Busily abet him who brings forth your food."
    "By Christ!" exclaimed a knight then, "your counsel is the best.
    But truly, how to drive a team has never been taught me.
    But show me," said the knight, "and I shall study plowing."
    "By Saint Paul," said Perkin, "since you proffer help so humbly,
25 I shall sweat and strain and sow for us both,
    And also labor for your love all my lifetime,
    In exchange for your championing Holy Church and me
    Against wasters and wicked men who would destroy me.
    And go hunt hardily hares and foxes,
30 Boars and bucks that break down my hedges,
    And have falcons at hand to hunt down the birds
    That come to my croft[5] and crop my wheat."
    Thoughtfully the knight then spoke these words:
    "By my power, Piers, I pledge you my word
35 To uphold this obligation though I have to fight.
    As long as I live I shall look after you."
    "Yes, and yet another point," said Piers, "I pray you further:
    See that you trouble no tenant unless Truth approves,
    And though you may amerce[6] him, let Mercy set the fine,
40 And Meekness be your master no matter what Meed° does.   *bribery*
    And though poor men proffer you presents and gifts,
    Don't accept them for it's uncertain that you deserve to have them.
    For at some set time you'll have to restore them
    In a most perilous place called purgatory.
45 And treat no bondman badly—you'll be the better for it;
    Though here he is your underling, it could happen in Heaven
    That he'll be awarded a worthier place, one with more bliss:
        Friend, go up higher.[7]
    For in the charnelhouse[8] at church churls are hard to distinguish,
    Or a knight from a knave: know this in your heart.
50 And see that you're true of your tongue, and as for tales—hate them
    Unless they have wisdom and wit for your workmen's instruction.
    Avoid foul-mouthed fellows and don't be friendly to their stories,
    And especially at your repasts shun people like them,
    For they tell the Fiend's fables—be very sure of that."
55 "I assent, by Saint James," said the knight then,
    "To work by your word while my life lasts."
    "And I shall apparel myself," said Perkin, "in pilgrims' fashion
    And walk along the way with you till we find Truth."
    He donned his working-dress, some darned, some whole,
60 His gaiters and his gloves to guard his limbs from cold,
    And hung his seed-holder behind his back instead of a knapsack:
    "Bring a bushel of bread-wheat for me to put in it,
    For I shall sow it myself and set out afterwards
    On a pilgrimage as palmers do to procure pardon.
65 And whoever helps me plow or work in any way
    Shall have leave, by our Lord, to glean my land in harvest-time,

5. A small enclosed field   7. Luke 14.10
6. Punish with a fine the amount of which is at   8. A crypt for dead bodies.
the discretion of the judge.

And make merry with what he gets, no matter who grumbles.
And all kinds of craftsmen that can live in truth,
I shall provide food for those that faithfully live,
70 Except for Jack the juggler and Jonette from the brothel,
And Daniel the dice-player and Denot the pimp,
And Friar Faker and folk of his order,
And Robin the ribald for his rotten speech.
Truth told me once and bade me tell it abroad:
75 *Deleantur de libro viventium:*[9] I should have no dealings with them,
For Holy Church is under orders to ask no tithes[1] of them.
    For let them not be written with the righteous.[2]
Their good luck has left them, the Lord amend them now."
    Dame-Work-When-It's-Time-To was Piers's wife's name;
His daughter was called Do-Just-So-Or-Your-Dame-Will-Beat-You;
80 His son was named Suffer-Your-Sovereigns-To-Have-Their-Will-
Condemn-Them-Not-For-If-You-Do-You'll-Pay-A-Dear-Price-
Let-God-Have-His-Way-With-All-Things-For-So-His-Word-Teaches.
"For now I am old and hoary and have something of my own,
To penance and to pilgrimage I'll depart with these others;
85 Therefore I will, before I go away, have my will written:
'*In Dei nomine, amen,*[3] I make this myself.
He shall have my soul that has deserved it best,
And defend it from the Fiend—for so I believe—
Till I come to his accounting, as my Creed teaches me—
90 To have release and remission I trust in his rent book.
The kirk° shall have my corpse and keep my bones,   *church*
For of my corn and cattle it craved the tithe:
I paid it promptly for peril of my soul;
It is obligated, I hope, to have me in mind
95 And commemorate me in its prayers among all Christians.
My wife shall have what I won with truth, and nothing else,
And parcel it out among my friends and my dear children.
For though I die today, my debts are paid;
I took back what I borrowed before I went to bed.'
100 As for the residue and the remnant, by the Rood of Lucca,[4]
I will worship Truth with it all my lifetime,
And be his pilgrim at the plow for poor men's sake.
My plowstaff shall be my pikestaff and push at the roots
And help my coulter to cut and cleanse the furrows."
105   Now Perkin and the pilgrims have put themselves to plowing.
Many there helped him to plow his half-acre.
Ditchers and diggers dug up the ridges;
Perkin was pleased by this and praised them warmly.
There were other workmen who worked very hard:
110 Each man in his manner made himself a laborer,

---

9. Let them be blotted out of the book of the living (Psalms 69.28).
1. Because the money they make is not legitimate income or increase derived from the earth; therefore, they do not owe the tithes, or 10 percent taxes, due the church.
2. Psalms 69.28.
3. "In the name of God, amen," customary beginning of a will.

4. An ornate crucifix at Lucca in Italy was a popular object of pilgrimage. "Residue and remnant": land had to be left to one's natural heirs, although up to one-third of personal property (the "residue and remnant") could be left to the church for Masses for the testator or other purposes; the other two-thirds had to go to the family, one to the widow and the other to the children. Piers's arrangements seem to leave the wife considerably more latitude.

And some to please Perkin pulled up the weeds.
At high prime⁵ Piers let the plow stand
To oversee them himself; whoever worked best
Should be hired afterward, when harvest-time came.
115 Then some sat down and sang over ale
And helped plow the half-acre with "Ho! trolly-lolly!"⁶
"Now by the peril of my soul!" said Piers in pure wrath,
"Unless you get up again and begin working now,
No grain that grows here will gladden you at need,
120 And though once off the dole you die let the Devil care!"
Then fakers were afraid and feigned to be blind;
Some set their legs askew as such loafers can
And made their moan to Piers, how they might not work:
"We have no limbs to labor with, Lord, we thank you;
125 But we pray for you, Piers, and for your plow as well,
That God of his grace make your grain multiply,
And reward you for whatever alms you will give us here,
For we can't strain and sweat, such sickness afflicts us."
"If what you say is so," said Piers, "I'll soon find out.
130 I know you're ne'er-do-wells, and Truth knows what's right,
And I'm his sworn servant and so should warn him
Which ones they are in this world that do his workmen harm.
You waste what men win with toil and trouble.
But Truth shall teach you how his team should be driven,
135 Or you'll eat barley bread and use the brook for drink;
Unless you're blind or broken-legged, or bolted° with iron—   *braced*
Those shall eat as well as I do, so God help me,
Till God of his goodness gives them strength to arise.
But you could work as Truth wants you to and earn wages and bread
140 By keeping cows in the field, the corn from the cattle,
Making ditches or dikes or dinging on sheaves,
Or helping make mortar, or spreading muck afield.
You live in lies and lechery and in sloth too,
And it's only for suffrance that vengeance has not fallen on you.
145 But anchorites and hermits that eat only at noon
And nothing more before the morrow, they shall have my alms,
And buy copes at my cost—those that have cloisters and churches.
But Robert Runabout shall have no rag from me,
Nor 'Apostles' unless they can preach and have the bishop's permission.
150 They shall have bread and boiled greens and a bit extra besides,
For it's an unreasonable religious life that has no regular meals."
Then Waster waxed angry and wanted to fight;
To Piers the Plowman he proffered his glove.
A Breton, a braggart, he bullied Piers too,
155 And told him to go piss with his plow, peevish wretch.
"Whether you're willing or unwilling, we will have our will
With your flour and your flesh, fetch it when we please,
And make merry with it, no matter what you do."
Then Piers the Plowman complained to the knight

---

5. 9 A.M., or after a substantial part of the day's
work has been done, because laborers start so
early.

6. Presumably the refrain of a popular song (note
similarly musical loafers in the *Prologue*, lines
224–25).

160 To keep him safe, as their covenant was, from cursed rogues,
"And from these wolfish wasters that lay waste the world,
For they waste and win nothing, and there will never be
Plenty among the people while my plow stands idle."
Because he was born a courteous man the knight spoke kindly to
     Waster
165 And warned him he would have to behave himself better:
"Or you'll pay the penalty at law, I promise, by my order!"
"It's not my way to work," said Waster, "I won't begin now!"
And made light of the law and lighter of the knight,
And said Piers wasn't worth a pea or his plow either,
170 And menaced him and his men if they met again.
     "Now by the peril of my soul!" said Piers, "I'll punish you all."
And he whooped after Hunger who heard him at once.
"Avenge me on these vagabonds," said he, "that vex the whole world."
Then Hunger in haste took hold of Waster by the belly
175 And gripped him so about the guts that his eyes gushed water.
He buffeted the Breton about the cheeks
That he looked like a lantern all his life after.
He beat them both so that he almost broke their guts.
Had not Piers with a pease loaf[7] prayed him to leave off
180 They'd have been dead and buried deep, have no doubt about it.
"Let them live," he said, "and let them feed with hogs,
Or else on beans and bran baked together."
Fakers for fear fled into barns
And flogged sheaves with flails from morning till evening,
185 So that Hunger wouldn't be eager to cast his eye on them.
For a potful of peas that Piers had cooked
A heap of hermits laid hands on spades
And cut off their copes and made short coats of them
And went like workmen to weed and to mow,
190 And dug dirt and dung to drive off Hunger.
Blind and bedridden got better by the thousand;
Those who sat to beg silver were soon healed,
For what had been baked for Bayard[8] was boon to many hungry,
And many a beggar for beans obediently labored,
195 And every poor man was well pleased to have peas for his wages,
And what Piers prayed them to do they did as sprightly as
     sparrowhawks.
And Piers was proud of this and put them to work,
And gave them meals and money as they might deserve.
     Then Piers had pity and prayed Hunger to take his way
200 Off to his own home and hold there forever.
"I'm well avenged on vagabonds by virtue of you.
But I pray you, before you part," said Piers to Hunger,
"With beggars and street-beadsmen[9] what's best to be done?
For well I know that once you're away, they will work badly;
205 Misfortune makes them so meek now,

7. The cheapest and coarsest grade of bread, the
food of those who cannot get better.
8. Generic name for a horse; a bread made of
beans and bran, the coarsest category of bread, was
used to feed horses and hounds, but was eaten by
people when need was great.
9. Paid prayer sayers.

And it's for lack of food that these folk obey me.
And they're my blood brothers, for God bought° us all.   *redeemed*
Truth taught me once to love them every one
And help them with everything after their needs.
210   Now I'd like to learn, if you know, what line I should take
And how I might overmaster them and make them work."
"Hear now," said Hunger, "and hold it for wisdom:
Big bold beggars that can earn their bread,
With hounds' bread and horses' bread hold up their hearts,
215   And keep their bellies from swelling by stuffing them with beans—
And if they begin to grumble, tell them to get to work,
And they'll have sweeter suppers once they've deserved them.
And if you find any fellow-man that fortune has harmed
Through fire or through false men, befriend him if you can.
220   Comfort such at your own cost, for the love of Christ in Heaven;
Love them and relieve them—so the law of Kind° directs.   *Nature*
    Bear ye one another's burdens.[1]
And all manner of men that you may find
That are needy or naked and have nothing to spend,
With meals or with money make them the better.
225   Love them and don't malign them; let God take vengeance.
Though they behave ill, leave it all up to God
    Vengeance is mine and I will repay.[2]
And if you want to gratify God, do as the Gospel teaches,
And get yourself loved by lowly men: so you'll unloose his grace."
    Make to yourselves friends of the mammon of unrighteousness.[3]
    "I would not grieve God," said Piers, "for all the goods on earth!
230   Might I do as you say without sin?" said Piers then.
"Yes, I give you my oath," said Hunger, "or else the Bible lies:
Go to Genesis the giant, engenderer of us all:[4]
In sudore[5] and slaving you shall bring forth your food
And labor for your livelihood, and so our Lord commanded.
235   And Sapience says the same—I saw it in the Bible.
Piger propter frigus[6] would plow no field;
He shall be a beggar and none abate his hunger.
Matthew with man's face[7] mouths these words:
'Entrusted with a talent, *servus nequam*[8] didn't try to use it,
240   And earned his master's ill-will for evermore after,
And he took away his talent who was too lazy to work,
And gave it to him in haste that had ten already;
And after he said so that his servants heard it,
He that has shall have, and help when he needs it,
245   And he that nothing has shall nothing have and no man help him,

---

1. Galatians 6.2.
2. Romans 12.19.
3. Luke 16.9.
4. This puzzling epithet has been explained on the grounds that Genesis is the longest book (except for Psalms) in the Bible and that it recounts the creation of humankind.
5. In the sweat [of thy face shalt thou eat bread] (Genesis 3.19).
6. The sluggard [will not plow] by reason of the cold (Proverbs 20.4). "Sapience": the biblical "Wis-

dom Books" attributed to Solomon.
7. Each of the four Evangelists had his traditional pictorial image, derived partly from the faces of the four creatures in Ezekiel's vision (Ezekiel 1.5–12) and partly from those of the four beasts of the Apocalypse (Revelation 4.7): Matthew was represented as a winged man; Mark, a lion; Luke, a winged ox; and John, an eagle.
8. The wicked servant (Luke 19.22; see 17–27). "Talent": a unit of money.

And what he trusts he's entitled to I shall take away.'
Kind Wit wants each one to work,
Either in teaching or tallying or toiling with his hands,
Contemplative life or active life; Christ wants it too.
250 The Psalter says in the Psalm of *Beati omnes*,[9]
The fellow that feeds himself with his faithful labor,
He is blessed by the Book in body and in soul."
　　The labors of thy hands, etc.[1]
　　"Yet I pray you," said Piers, "*pour charité*,° if you know　　for charity
Any modicum of medicine, teach me it, dear sir.
255 For some of my servants and myself as well
For a whole week do no work, we've such aches in our stomachs."
"I'm certain," said Hunger, "what sickness ails you.
You've munched down too much: that's what makes you groan,
But I assure you," said Hunger, "if you'd preserve your health,
260 You must not drink any day before you've dined on something.
Never eat, I urge you, ere Hunger comes upon you
And sends you some of his sauce to add savor to the food;
And keep some till suppertime, and don't sit too long;
Arise up ere Appetite has eaten his fill.
265 Let not Sir Surfeit sit at your table;
Love him not for he's a lecher whose delight is his tongue,
And for all sorts of seasoned stuff his stomach yearns.
And if you adopt this diet, I dare bet my arms
That Physic for his food will sell his furred hood
270 And his Calabrian[2] cloak with its clasps of gold,
And be content, by my troth, to retire from medicine
And learn to labor on the land lest livelihood fail him.
There are fewer physicians than frauds—reform them, Lord!—
Their drinks make men die before destiny ordains."
275 "By Saint Parnel,"[3] said Piers, "these are profitable words.
This is a lovely lesson; the Lord reward you for it!
Take your way when you will—may things be well with you always!"
　　"My oath to God!" said Hunger, "I will not go away
Till I've dined this day and drunk as well."
280 "I've no penny," said Piers, "to purchase pullets,
And I can't get goose or pork; but I've got two green cheeses,
A few curds and cream and a cake of oatmeal,
A loaf of beans and bran baked for my children.
And yet I say, by my soul, I have no salt bacon
285 Nor any hen's egg, by Christ, to make ham and eggs,
But scallions aren't scarce, nor parsley, and I've scores of cabbages,
And also a cow and a calf, and a cart-mare
To draw dung to the field while the dry weather lasts.
By this livelihood I must live till Lammass[4] time
290 When I hope to have harvest in my garden.

---

9. Blessed [are] all [who] (Psalms 128.1).
1. Psalms 128.2.
2. Of gray fur (a special imported squirrel fur).
3. Who St. Pernelle was is obscure; other manuscripts and editions read "By Saint Paul."

4. The harvest festival, August 1 (the name derived from Old English *hlaf*, "loaf"), when a loaf made from the first wheat of the season was offered at Mass.

Then I can manage a meal that will make you happy."
All the poor people fetched peasepods;[5]
Beans and baked apples they brought in their skirts,
Chives and chervils and ripe cherries aplenty,
295   And offered Piers this present to please Hunger with.
Hunger ate this in haste and asked for more.
Then poor folk for fear fed Hunger fast,
Proffering leeks and peas, thinking to appease him.
And now harvest drew near and new grain came to market.[6]
300   Then poor people were pleased and plied Hunger with the best;
With good ale as Glutton taught they got him to sleep.
Then Waster wouldn't work but wandered about,
And no beggar would eat bread that had beans in it,
But the best bread or the next best, or baked from pure wheat,
305   Nor drink any half-penny ale[7] in any circumstances,
But of the best and the brownest that barmaids sell.
Laborers that have no land to live on but their hands
Deign not to dine today on last night's cabbage.
No penny-ale can please them, nor any piece of bacon,
310   But it must be fresh flesh or else fried fish,
And that *chaud* or *plus chaud*[8] so it won't chill their bellies.
Unless he's hired at high wages he will otherwise complain;
That he was born to be a workman he'll blame the time.
Against Cato's counsel he commences to murmur:
315   *Remember to bear your burden of poverty patiently.*[9]
He grows angry at God and grumbles against Reason,
And then curses the king and all the council after
Because they legislate laws that punish laboring men.[1]
But while Hunger was their master there would none of them complain
320   Or strive against the statute,[2] so sternly he looked.
But I warn you workmen, earn wages while you may,
For Hunger is hurrying hitherward fast.
With waters he'll awaken Waster's chastisement;
Before five years are fulfilled such famine shall arise.
325   Through flood and foul weather fruits shall fail,
And so Saturn[3] says and has sent to warn you:
When you see the moon amiss and two monks' heads,
And a maid have the mastery, and multiply by eight,[4]
Then shall Death withdraw and Dearth be justice,
330   And Daw the diker[5] die for hunger,
Unless God of his goodness grants us a truce.

---

5. Peas in the pod. These, like most foods in the next lines, are early crops.
6. Presumably as the new harvest approaches, merchants who have been holding grain for the highest prices release it for sale, because prices are about to tumble.
7. Weak ale diluted with water; in line 309, laborers are too fussy and will no longer accept even penny ale.
8. "Hot" or "very hot."
9. From Cato's *Distichs*, a collection of pithy phrases used to teach Latin to beginning students.
1. Like so many governments, late-14th-century England responded to inflation and the bargaining power of the relatively scarce laborers with wage and price freezes, which had their usual lack of effect. One way landowners, desperate to obtain enough laborers, tried to get around the wage laws was by offering food as well as cash.
2. I.e., anti-inflationary legislation.
3. Planet thought to influence the weather, generally perceived as hostile.
4. This cryptic prophecy has never been satisfactorily explained; the basic point is that it is Apocalyptic.
5. A laborer who digs dikes and ditches.

Passus 18

[THE HARROWING OF HELL]

Wool-chafed[6] and wet-shoed I went forth after
Like a careless creature unconscious of woe,
And trudged forth like a tramp, all the time of my life,
Till I grew weary of the world and wished to sleep again,
5   And lay down till Lent, and slept a long time,
Rested there, snoring roundly, till *Ramis-Palmarum*.[7]
    I dreamed chiefly of children and cheers of "*Gloria, laus!*"
And how old folk to an organ sang "*Hosanna!*"
And of Christ's passion and pain for the people he had reached for.
10 One resembling the Samaritan[8] and somewhat Piers the Plowman
Barefoot on an ass's back bootless came riding
Without spurs or spear: sprightly was his look,
As is the nature of a knight that draws near to be dubbed,
To get himself gilt spurs and engraved jousting shoes.
15 Then was Faith watching from a window and cried, "*A, fili David!*"
As does a herald of arms when armed men come to joust.
Old Jews of Jerusalem joyfully sang,
    "*Blessed is he who cometh in the name of the Lord.*"
And I asked Faith to reveal what all this affair meant,
20 And who was to joust in Jerusalem. "Jesus," he said,
"And fetch what the Fiend claims, the fruit of Piers the Plowman."
"Is Piers in this place?" said I; and he pierced me with his look:
"This Jesus for his gentleness will joust in Piers's arms,
In his helmet and in his hauberk, *humana natura*,[9]
25 So that Christ be not disclosed here as *consummatus Deus*.[1]
In the plate armor of Piers the Plowman this jouster will ride,
For no dint will do him injury as *in deitate Patris*.[2]
"Who shall joust with Jesus," said I, "Jews or Scribes?"[3]
"No," said Faith, "but the Fiend and False-Doom°-To-Die.   *sentence*
30 Death says he will undo and drag down low
All that live or look upon land or water.
Life says that he lies, and lays his life in pledge
That for all that Death can do, within three days he'll walk
And fetch from the Fiend the fruit of Piers the Plowman,
35 And place it where he pleases, and put Lucifer in bonds,
And beat and bring down burning death forever.
    O death, I will be thy death."[4]

---

6. Scratchy wool was worn next to the body as an act of penance.
7. Palm Sunday (literally, "branches of palms"): the background of this part of the poem is the biblical account of Christ's entry into Jerusalem on this day, when the crowds greeted him crying, "Hosanna [line 8] to the son of David [line 15]: Blessed is he that cometh in the name of the Lord [line 17a]; Hosanna in the highest" (see Matthew 21.9). "*Gloria, laus*" [line 7] are the first words of an anthem, "Glory, praise, and honor," that was sung by children in medieval religious processions on Palm Sunday.
8. In the previous vision, the Dreamer has

encountered Abraham, or Faith (mentioned in lines 15, 18, 28, and 92); Moses, or Hope; and the Good Samaritan, or Charity, who was riding toward a "jousting in Jerusalem" and who now appears as an aspect of Christ.
9. Human nature, which Christ assumed in order to redeem humanity. "Hauberk": coat of mail.
1. The perfect (three-personed) God.
2. In the godhead of the Father: as God, Christ could not suffer but as man, he could.
3. People who made a very strict, literal interpretation of the Old Law and hence rejected Christ's teaching of the New.
4. Cf. Hosea 13.14.

Then Pilate came with many people, *sedens pro tribunali*,[5]
To see how doughtily Death should do, and judge the rights of both.
40 The Jews and the justice were joined against Jesus,
And all the court cried upon him, "*Crucifige!*"[6] loud.
Then a plaintiff appeared before Pilate and said,
"This Jesus made jokes about Jerusalem's temple,
To have it down in one day and in three days after
45 Put it up again all new—here he stands who said it—
And yet build it every bit as big in all dimensions,
As long and as broad both, above and below."
"*Crucifige!*" said a sergeant, "he knows sorcerer's tricks."
"*Tolle! tolle!*"[7] said another, and took sharp thorns
50 And began to make a garland out of green thorn,
And set it sorely on his head and spoke in hatred,
"*Ave, Rabbi*," said that wretch, and shot reeds[8] at him;
They nailed him with three nails naked on a Cross,
And with a pole put a potion up to his lips
55 And bade him drink to delay his death and lengthen his days,
And said, "If you're subtle, let's see you help yourself.
If you are Christ and a king's son, come down from the Cross!
Then we'll believe that Life loves you and will not let you die."
"*Consummatum est*,"[9] said Christ and started to swoon,
60 Piteously and pale like a prisoner dying.
The Lord of Life and of Light then laid his eyelids together.
The day withdrew for dread and darkness covered the sun;
The wall wavered and split and the whole world quaked.
Dead men for that din came out of deep graves
65 And spoke of why that storm lasted so long:
"For a bitter battle," the dead body said;
"Life and Death in this darkness, one destroys the other.
No one will surely know which shall have the victory
Before Sunday about sunrise"; and sank with that to earth.
70 Some said that he was God's son that died so fairly:
Truly this was the Son of God.[1]
And some said he was a sorcerer: "We should see first
Whether he's dead or not dead before we dare take him down."
Two thieves were there that suffered death that time
75 Upon crosses beside Christ; such was the common law.
A constable came forth and cracked both their legs
And the arms afterward of each of those thieves.
But no bastard was so bold as to touch God's body there;
Because he was a knight and a king's son, Nature decreed that time
80 That no knave should have the hardiness to lay hand on him.
     But a knight with a sharp spear was sent forth there
Named Longeus[2] as the legend tells, who had long since lost his
          sight;

---

5. Sitting as a judge (cf. Matthew 27.19).
6. Crucify him! (John 19.15).
7. Away with him, away with him! (John 19.15).
8. Arrows, probably small ones intended to hurt rather than to kill. "*Ave, Rabbi*": "Hail, master" (Matthew 26.49): these are actually Judas's words when he kissed Christ in order to identify him to the arresting officers.
9. It is finished (John 19.30).
1. Matthew 27.54.
2. Longeus (usually Longinus) appears in the apocryphal Gospel of Nicodemus, which provided Langland with the material for much of his account of Christ's despoiling of hell.

Before Pilate and the other people in that place he waited on his
    horse.
For all that he might demur, he was made that time
85   To joust with Jesus, that blind Jew Longeus.
For all who watched there were unwilling, whether mounted or afoot,
To touch him or tamper with him or take him down from the Cross,
Except this blind bachelor that bore him through the heart.
The blood sprang down the spear and unsparred[3] his eyes.
90   The knight knelt down on his knees and begged Jesus for mercy.
"It was against my will, Lord, to wound you so sorely."
He sighed and said, "Sorely I repent it.
For what I here have done, I ask only your grace.
Have mercy on me, rightful Jesu!" and thus lamenting wept.
95   Then Faith began fiercely to scorn the false Jews,[4]
Called them cowards, accursed forever.
"For this foul villainy, may vengeance fall on you!
To make the blind beat the dead, it was a bully's thought.
Cursed cowards, no kind of knighthood was it
100   To beat a dead body with any bright weapon.
Yet he's won the victory in the fight for all his vast wound,
For your champion jouster, the chief knight of you all,
Weeping admits himself worsted and at the will of Jesus.
For when this darkness is done, Death will be vanquished,
105   And you louts have lost, for Life shall have the victory;
And your unfettered freedom has fallen into servitude;
And you churls and your children shall achieve no prosperity,
Nor have lordship over land or have land to till,
But be all barren and live by usury,
110   Which is a life that every law of our Lord curses.
Now your good days are done as Daniel prophesied;
When Christ came their kingdom's crown should be lost:
    When the Holy of Holies comes your anointing shall cease."[5]
    What for fear of this adventure and of the false Jews
115   I withdrew in that darkness to *Descendit-ad-Inferna,*[6]
And there I saw surely *Secundum Scripturas*[7]
Where out of the west a wench,[8] as I thought,
Came walking on the way—she looked toward hell.
Mercy was that maid's name, a meek thing withal,
120   A most gracious girl, and goodly of speech.
Her sister as it seemed came softly walking
Out of the east, opposite, and she looked westward,
A comely creature and cleanly: Truth was her name.
Because of the virtue that followed her, she was afraid of nothing.
125   When these maidens met, Mercy and Truth,

3. Opened; in the original there is a play on words
with "spear." "Bachelor": knight.
4. The references in this passage (lines 92–110)
and in lines 258–60 appear to reflect a blind anti-
Semitism all too prevalent in late-medieval art and
literature, brought out especially in portrayals of
the Passion. Elsewhere Langland exhibits a more
enlightened attitude—for instance, in a passage in
which he holds up Jewish charity as an example to
Christians. In the present passage he may intend

a distinction between those who betrayed and condemned Jesus and the "old Jews of Jerusalem" who
welcomed him in the Palm Sunday procession
(lines 7–17).
5. Daniel 9.24.
6. He descended into hell (from the Apostles'
Creed).
7. According to the Scriptures.
8. The word is Langland's and had much the same
connotations in his time as it has in ours.

Each of them asked the other about this great wonder,
And of the din and of the darkness, and how the day lowered,
And what a gleam and a glint glowed before hell.
"I marvel at this matter, by my faith," said Truth,
130 "And am coming to discover what this queer affair means."
"Do not marvel," said Mercy, "it means only mirth.
A maiden named Mary, and mother without touching
By any kind of creature, conceived through speech
And grace of the Holy Ghost; grew great with child;
135 With no blemish to her woman's body brought him into this world.
And that my tale is true, I take God to witness,
Since this baby was born it has been thirty winters,
Who died and suffered death this day about midday.
And that is the cause of this eclipse that is closing off the sun,
140 In meaning that man shall be removed from darkness
While this gleam and this glow go to blind Lucifer.
For patriarchs and prophets have preached of this often
That man shall save man through a maiden's help,
And what a tree took away a tree shall restore,[9]
145 And what Death brought down a death shall raise up."
"What you're telling," said Truth, "is just a tale of nonsense.
For Adam and Eve and Abraham and the rest,
Patriarchs and prophets imprisoned in pain,
Never believe that yonder light will lift them up,
150 Or have them out of hell—hold your tongue, Mercy!
Your talk is mere trifling. I, Truth, know the truth,
For whatever is once in hell, it comes out never.
Job the perfect patriarch disproves what you say:
Since in hell there is no redemption."[1]
155 Then Mercy most mildly uttered these words:
"From observation," she said, "I suppose they shall be saved,
Because venom destroys venom, and in that I find evidence
That Adam and Eve shall have relief.
For of all venoms the foulest is the scorpion's:
160 No medicine may amend the place where it stings
Till it's dead and placed upon it—the poison is destroyed,
The first effect of the venom, through the virtue it possesses.
So shall this death destroy—I dare bet my life—
All that Death did first through the Devil's tempting.
165 And just as the beguiler with guile beguiled man first,
So shall grace that began everything make a good end
And beguile the beguiler—and that's a good trick:
A trick by which to trick trickery."[2]
"Now let's be silent," said Truth. "It seems to me I see
170 Out of the nip[3] of the north, not far from here,
Righteousness come running—let's wait right here,
For she knows far more than we—she was here before us both."

9. The first tree bore the fruit that Adam and Eve ate, thereby damning humankind; the second tree is the cross on which Christ was crucified, thereby redeeming humankind.
1. Cf. Job 7.9.
2. From a medieval Latin hymn.
3. The word is Langland's and the sense obscure; it probably meant "coldness" to him, although an Old English word similar to *nip* meant "gloom."

"That is so," said Mercy, "and I see here to the south
Where Peace clothed in patience[4] comes sportively this way.
175 Love has desired her long: I believe surely
That Love has sent her some letter, what this light means
That hangs over hell thus: she will tell us what it means."
When Peace clothed in patience approached near them both,
Righteousness did her reverence for her rich clothing
180 And prayed Peace to tell her to what place she was going,
And whom she was going to greet in her gay garments.
"My wish is to take my way," said she, "and welcome them all
Whom many a day I might not see for murk of sin.
Adam and Eve and the many others in hell,
185 Moses and many more will merrily sing,
And I shall dance to their song: sister, do the same.
Because Jesus jousted well, joy begins to dawn.
*Weeping may endure for a night, but joy cometh in the
        morning.*[5]
Love who is my lover sent letters to tell me
190 That my sister Mercy and I shall save mankind,
And that God has forgiven and granted me, Peace, and Mercy
To make bail for mankind for evermore after.
Look, here's the patent," said Peace: "*In pace in idipsum:*
And that this deed shall endure, *dormiam et requiescam.*"[6]
195 "What? You're raving," said Righteousness. "You must be really
        drunk.
Do you believe that yonder light might unlock hell
And save man's soul? Sister, don't suppose it.
At the beginning God gave the judgment himself
That Adam and Eve and all that followed them
200 Should die downright and dwell in torment after
If they touched a tree and ate the tree's fruit.
Adam afterwards against his forbidding
Fed on that fruit and forsook as it were
The love of our Lord and his lore too,
205 And followed what the Fiend taught and his flesh's will
Against Reason. I, Righteousness, record this with Truth,
That their pain should be perpetual and no prayer should help them,
Therefore let them chew as they chose, and let us not chide, sisters,
For it's misery without amendment, the morsel they ate."
210 "And I shall prove," said Peace, "that their pain must end,
And in time trouble must turn into well-being;
For had they known no woe, they'd not have known well-being;
For no one knows what well-being is who was never in woe,
Nor what is hot hunger who has never lacked food.
215 If there were no night, no man, I believe,
Could be really well aware of what day means.
Never should a really rich man who lives in rest and ease

---

4. What Langland envisioned clothes of patience to look like, aside from their "richness" (line 173), it is impossible to say; to him any abstraction could become a concrete allegory without visual identification.

5. Psalm 30.5.

6. The "patent" or "deed" is a document conferring authority: this one consists of phrases from Psalm 4.8: "In peace in the selfsame"; "I will sleep and find rest."

Know what woe is if it weren't for natural death.
So God, who began everything, of his good will
220 Became man by a maid for mankind's salvation
And allowed himself to be sold to see the sorrow of dying.
And that cures all care and is the first cause of rest,
For until we meet *modicum*,° I may well avow it,   small quantity
No man knows, I suppose, what 'enough' means.
225 Therefore God of his goodness gave the first man Adam
A place of supreme ease and of perfect joy,
And then he suffered him to sin so that he might know sorrow,
And thus know what well-being is—to be aware of it naturally.
And afterward God offered himself, and took Adam's nature,
230 To see what he had suffered in three separate places,
Both in Heaven and on earth, and now he heads for hell,
To learn what all woe is like who has learned of all joy.
So it shall fare with these folk: their folly and their sin
Shall show them what sickness is—and succor from all pain.
235 No one knows what war is where peace prevails,
Nor what is true well-being till 'Woe, alas!' teaches him."
      Then was there a wight with two broad eyes:
Book was that beaupere's[7] name, a bold man of speech.
"By God's body," said this Book, "I will bear witness
240 That when this baby was born there blazed a star
So that all the wise men in the world agreed with one opinion
That such a baby was born in Bethlehem city
Who should save man's soul and destroy sin.
And all the elements," said the Book, "hereof bore witness.
245 The sky first revealed that he was God who formed all things:
The hosts in Heaven took *stella comata*[8]
And tended her like a torch to reverence his birth.
The light followed the Lord into the low earth.
The water witnessed that he was God for he walked on it;
250 Peter the Apostle perceived his walking
And as he went on the water knew him well and said,
      'Bid me come unto thee on the water.'[9]
And lo, how the sun locked her light in herself
When she saw him suffer that made sun and sea.
255 The earth for heavy heart because he would suffer
Quaked like a quick° thing and the rock cracked all to pieces.   living
Lo, hell might not hold, but opened when God suffered,
And let out Simeon's sons[1] to see him hang on Cross.
And now shall Lucifer believe it, loath though he is,
260 For Jesus like a giant with an engine[2] comes yonder
To break and beat down all that may be against him,
And to have out of hell every one he pleases.

7. Fine fellow. The book s two broad eyes suggest the Old and New Testaments. "Wight": creature, person.
8. Hairy star, i.e., comet.
9. Matthew 14.28.
1. Simeon, who was present at the presentation of the infant Jesus in the temple, had been told by the Holy Ghost that "he should not see death"
before he had seen "the Lord's Christ" (Luke 2.26). The Apocryphal Gospel of Nicodemus echoes the incident in reporting that Simeon's sons were raised from death at the time of Jesus's crucifixion.
2. A device, probably thought of as a gigantic slingshot, although, of course, Christ needs nothing to break down his enemies but his own authority.

And I, Book, will be burnt unless Jesus rises to life
In all the mights of a man and brings his mother joy,
265 And comforts all his kin, and takes their cares away,
And all the joy of the Jews disjoins and disperses;
And unless they reverence his Rood and his resurrection
And believe on a new law be lost body and soul."
"Let's be silent," said Truth, "I hear and see both
270 A spirit speaks to hell and bids the portals be opened."
  Lift up your gates.[3]
A voice loud in that light cried to Lucifer,
"Princes of this place, unpin and unlock,
For he comes here with crown who is King of Glory."
275 Then Satan[4] sighed and said to hell,
"Without our leave such a light fetched Lazarus away:[5]
Care and calamity have come upon us all.
If this King comes in he will carry off mankind
And lead it to where Lazarus is, and with small labor bind me.
280 Patriarchs and prophets have long prated of this,
That such a lord and a light should lead them all hence."
"Listen," said Lucifer, "for this lord is one I know;
Both this lord and this light, it's long ago I knew him.
No death may do this lord harm, nor any devil's trickery,
285 And his way is where he wishes—but let him beware of the perils.
If he bereaves me of my right he robs me by force.
For by right and by reason the race that is here
Body and soul belongs to me, both good and evil.
For he himself said it who is Sire of Heaven,
290 If Adam ate the apple, all should die
And dwell with us devils: the Lord laid down that threat.
And since he who is Truth himself said these words,
And since I've possessed them seven thousand winters,
I don't believe law will allow him the least of them."
295 "That is so," said Satan, "but I'm sore afraid
Because you took them by trickery and trespassed in his garden,
And in the semblance of a serpent sat upon the apple tree
And egged them to eat, Eve by herself,
And told her a tale with treasonous words;
300 And so you had them out, and hither at the last."
"It's an ill-gotten gain where guile is at the root,
For God will not be beguiled," said Goblin, "nor tricked.
We have no true title to them, for it was by treason they were damned."
"Certainly I fear," said the Fiend,[6] "lest Truth fetch them out.
305 These thirty winters, as I think, he's gone here and there and preached.

---

3. The first words of Psalm 24.9, which reads in the Latin version, "Lift up your gates, O princes, and be ye lift up, ye everlasting doors, and the King of Glory shall come in."
4. Langland, following a tradition also reflected in Milton's *Paradise Lost*, pictures hell as populated by a number of devils: Satan; Lucifer (line 273 ff.), who began the war in heaven and tempted Eve; Goblin (line 293); Belial (line 321); and Ashtoreth (line 404). Lucifer the rebel angel naturally became identified with Satan, a word that in the Old Testament had originally meant an evil adversary; many of the other devils are displaced gods of pagan religions.
5. For Christ's raising of Lazarus from the dead, cf. John 11.
6. Here and in line 309 "the Fiend" is presumably Lucifer's most articulate critic, Satan, whom Christ names as his tempter in Matthew 4.10.

I've assailed him with sin, and sometimes asked
Whether he was God or God's son: he gave me short answer.
And thus he's traveled about like a true man these two and thirty
    winters.
And when I saw it was so, while she slept I went
310   To warn Pilate's wife what sort of man was Jesus,[7]
For some hated him and have put him to death.
I would have lengthened his life, for I believed if he died
That his soul would suffer no sin in his sight.
For the body, while it walked on its bones, was busy always
315   To save men from sin if they themselves wished.
And now I see where a soul comes descending hitherward
With glory and with great light; God it is, I'm sure.
My advice is we all flee," said the Fiend, "fast away from here.
For we had better not be at all than abide in his sight.
320   For your lies, Lucifer, we've lost all our prey.
Through you we fell first from Heaven so high:
Because we believed your lies we all leapt out.
And now for your latest lie we have lost Adam,
And all our lordship, I believe, on land and in hell."
325   *Now shall the prince of this world be cast out.*[8]
     Again the light bade them unlock, and Lucifer answered,
        "Who is that?[9]
What lord are you?" said Lucifer. The light at once replied,
    "The King of Glory.
The Lord of might and of main and all manner of powers:
    The Lord of Powers.
Dukes of this dim place, at once undo these gates
330   That Christ may come in, the Heaven-King's son."
And with that breath hell broke along with Belial's bars;
For° any warrior or watchman the gates wide opened.   *in spite of*
Patriarchs and prophets, *populus in tenebris,*[1]
Sang Saint John's song, *Ecce agnus Dei.*[2]
335   Lucifer could not look, the light so blinded him.
And those that the Lord loved his light caught away,
And he said to Satan, "Lo, here's my soul in payment
For all sinful souls, to save those that are worthy.
Mine they are and of me—I may the better claim them.
340   Although Reason records, and right of myself,
That if they ate the apple all should die,
I did not hold out to them hell here forever.
For the deed that they did, your deceit caused it;
You got them with guile against all reason.
345   For in my palace Paradise, in the person of an adder,

---

7. In Matthew 27.19 Pilate's wife warns Pilate to "have nothing to do with that just man [Jesus]," for she has been troubled by a dream about him. Langland has the Fiend admit to having caused the dream so that Pilate's wife should persuade her husband not to harm Jesus and thus keep him safe on earth and not come to visit hell and despoil it.
8. John 12.31. "Prince of this world" is a title for the devil.
9. This and the next two phrases translated from the Latin are from Psalm 24.8, following immediately on the words quoted in line 262a.
1. "People in darkness," the phrase is from Matthew 4.16, citing Isaiah 9.2, "The people that walked in darkness have seen a great light."
2. Behold the Lamb of God (John 1.36).

You stole by stealth something I loved.
Thus like a lizard with a lady's face[3]
Falsely you filched from me; the Old Law confirms
That guilers be beguiled, and that is good logic:
350   *A tooth for a tooth and an eye for an eye.*[4]
Ergo[5] soul shall requite soul and sin revert to sin,
And all that man has done amiss, I, man, will amend.
Member for member was amends in the Old Law,
And life for life also, and by that law I claim
355   Adam and all his issue at my will hereafter.
And what Death destroyed in them, my death shall restore
And both quicken° and requite what was quenched through   revitalize
   sin.
And that grace destroy guile is what good faith requires.
So don't believe it, Lucifer, against the law I fetch them,
360   But by right and by reason here ransom my liegemen.
   I have not come to destroy the law but to fulfill it.[6]
You fetched mine in my place unmindful of all reason
Falsely and feloniously; good faith taught me
To recover them by reason and rely on nothing else.
365   So what you got with guile through grace is won back.
You, Lucifer, in likeness of a loathsome adder
Got by guile those whom God loved;
And I, in likeness of a mortal man, who am master of Heaven,
Have graciously requited your guile: let guile go against guile!
370   And as Adam and all died through a tree
Adam and all through a tree return to life,
And guile is beguiled and grief has come to his guile:
   And he is fallen into the ditch which he made.[7]
And now your guile begins to turn against you,
375   And my grace to grow ever greater and wider.
The bitterness that you have brewed, imbibe it yourself
Who are doctor[8] of death, the drink you made.
   For I who am Lord of Life, love is my drink
And for that drink today I died upon earth.
380   I struggled so I'm thirsty still for man's soul's sake.
No drink may moisten me or slake my thirst
Till vintage time befall in the Vale of Jehoshaphat,[9]
When I shall drink really ripe wine, *Resurrectio mortuorum.*[1]
And then I shall come as a king crowned with angels
385   And have out of hell all men's souls.
Fiends and fiendkins shall stand before me
And be at my bidding, where best it pleases me.
But to be merciful to man then, my nature requires it.
For we are brothers of one blood, but not in baptism all.

3. In medieval art the devil tempting Eve was sometimes represented as a snake (see the "serpent" of line 288) and sometimes as a lizard with a female human face and standing upright.
4. See Matthew 5.38 citing Exodus 21.24.
5. Therefore. The Latin conjunction was used in formal debate to introduce the conclusion derived from a number of propositions.
6. See Matthew 5.17.

7. Psalm 7.15.
8. The ironical use of the word carries the sense both of "physician" and of "one learned in a discipline."
9. On the evidence of Joel 3.2, 12, the site of the Last Judgment was thought to be the Vale of Jehoshaphat.
1. The resurrection of the dead (from the Nicene Creed).

390   And all that are both in blood and in baptism my whole brothers
Shall not be damned to the death that endures without end.
        Against thee only have I sinned, etc.[2]
It is not the custom on earth to hang a felon
Oftener than once, even though he were a traitor.
395   And if the king of the kingdom comes at that time
When a felon should suffer death or other such punishment,
Law would he give him life if he looks upon him.[3]
And I who am King of Kings shall come in such a time
Where doom to death damns all wicked,
400   And if law wills I look on them, it lies in my grace
Whether they die or do not die because they did evil.
And if it be any bit paid for, the boldness of their sins,
I may grant mercy through my righteousness and all my true words;
And though Holy Writ wills that I wreak vengeance on those
        that wrought evil,
405   *No evil unpunished, etc.*[4]
They shall be cleansed and made clear and cured of their sins,
In my prison purgatory till *Parce!*° says 'Stop!'   *Spare!*
And my mercy shall be shown to many of my half-brothers,
For blood-kin may see blood-kin both hungry and cold,
410   But blood-kin may not see blood-kin bleed without his pity:
        I heard unspeakable words which it is not lawful for a man to
          utter.[5]
But my righteousness and right shall rule all hell
And mercy rule all mankind before me in Heaven.
For I'd be an unkind king unless I gave my kin help,
415   And particularly at such a time when help was truly needed.
        Enter not into judgment with thy servant.[6]
Thus by law," said our Lord, "I will lead from here
Those I looked on with love who believed in my coming;
And for your lie, Lucifer, that you lied to Eve,
420   You shall buy it back in bitterness"—and bound him with chains.
Ashtoreth and all the gang hid themselves in corners;
They dared not look at our Lord, the least of them all,
But let him lead away what he liked and leave what he wished.
    Many hundreds of angels harped and sang,
425   *Flesh sins, flesh redeems, flesh reigns as God of God.*[7]
Then Peace piped a note of poetry:
        As a rule the sun is brighter after the biggest clouds; After
          hostilities love is brighter.
"After sharp showers," said Peace, "the sun shines brightest;

2. Psalm 51.4. The psalm is understood to assign the sole power of judging the sinner to God, because it is only against God that the sinner has acted.
3. I.e., "Law dictates that the king pardon the felon if the king sees him."
4. [He is a just judge who leaves] no evil unpunished [and no good unrewarded]. Not from the Bible but from Pope Innocent III's tract *Of Contempt for the World* (1195).
5. In 2 Corinthians 12.4, St. Paul tells how in a vision he was snatched up to heaven where he heard things that may not be repeated among men.

Langland is apparently invoking a similar mystic experience when he puts into Christ's mouth a promise to spare many of his half-brothers, the unbaptized. The orthodox theology of the time taught that all the unbaptized were irredeemably damned, a proposition Langland refused to accept: in his vision he has heard words to the contrary that might not be repeated among men, because they would be held heretical.
6. Psalm 143.2.
7. From a medieval Latin hymn. The source of the two Latin verses immediately below is Alain of Lisle, a late 12th-century poet and philosopher.

No weather is warmer than after watery clouds;
430 Nor any love lovelier, or more loving friends,
Than after war and woe when Love and peace are masters.
There was never war in this world nor wickedness so sharp
That Love, if he liked, might not make a laughing matter.
And peace through patience puts an end to all perils."
435 "Truce!" said Truth, "you tell the truth, by Jesus!
Let's kiss in covenant, and each of us clasp other."
"And let no people," said Peace, "perceive that we argued;
For nothing is impossible to him that is almighty."
"You speak the truth," said Righteousness, and reverently kissed her,
440 Peace, and Peace her, *per saecula saeculorum:*[8]
  Mercy and Truth have met together; Righteousness and Peace
   have kissed each other.[9]
Truth sounded a trumpet then and sang *Te Deum Laudamus,*[1]
And then Love strummed a lute with a loud note:
  Behold how good and how pleasant, etc.[2]
445 Till the day dawned these damsels caroled.
When bells rang for the Resurrection, and right then I awoke
And called Kit my wife and Calote my daughter:
"Arise and go reverence God's resurrection,
And creep to the Cross on knees, and kiss it as a jewel,
450 For God's blessed body it bore for our good,
And it frightens the Fiend, for such is its power
That no grisly ghost may glide in its shadow."

From *The C-Text*

[THE DREAMER MEETS CONSCIENCE AND REASON][3]

Thus I awoke, as God's my witness, when I lived in Cornhill,[4]
Kit and I in a cottage, clothed like a loller,[5]
And little beloved, believe you me,
Among lollers of London and illiterate hermits.
5 For I wrote rhymes of those men as Reason taught me.
For as I came by Conscience I met with Reason,
In a hot harvest time when I had my health,
And limbs to labor with, and loved good living,
And to do no deed but to drink and sleep.
10 My body sound, my mind sane, a certain one accosted me;
Roaming in remembrance, thus Reason upbraided me:

8. For ever and ever (the liturgical formula).
9. Psalm 85.10.
1. We praise thee, O Lord.
2. Psalm 133.1. The verse continues, "it is for brothers to dwell together in unity."
3. In the C-text, the last of the three versions of *Piers Plowman,* Langland prefixed to the "Confession of the Seven Deadly Sins" (*Passus* 5 of the B-text) an apology by the Dreamer, "Long Will," who is at once long (or tall) and long on willing (or, arguably, willful). Although there is no conclusive historical evidence for doing so, readers of *Piers Plowman* have generally regarded this passage as a source of information about the real author, about

whom we otherwise know so little.
4. An area of London associated with vagabonds, seedy clerics, and people at loose ends.
5. Idler, vagabond. The term was eventually applied to the proto-Protestant followers of John Wycliffe. "Kit": refers to "Kit my wife and Calote [i.e., Colette] my daughter" (B-text, 18.426). The Dreamer seems to be someone with clerical training who has received consecration into minor clerical orders (such as that of deacon) but who is not a priest. Lesser clerics could marry, although marriage blocked their further advancement in the church.

"Can you serve," he said, "or sing in a church?
Or cock hay with my hay-makers, or heap it on the cart,
Mow it or stack what's mown or make binding for sheaves?
15   Or have a horn and be a hedge-guard and lie outdoors at night,
And keep my corn in my field from cattle and thieves?
Or cut cloth or shoe-leather, or keep sheep and cattle,
Mend hedges, or harrow, or herd pigs or geese,
Or any other kind of craft that the commons needs,
20   So that you might be of benefit to your bread-providers?"
    "Certainly!" I said, "and so God help me,
I am too weak to work with sickle or with scythe,
And too long,[6] believe me, for any low stooping,
Or laboring as a laborer to last any while."
    "Then have you lands to live by," said Reason, "or relations with
25   money
To provide you with food? For you seem an idle man,
A spendthrift who thrives on spending, and throws time away.
Or else you get what food men give you going door to door,
Or beg like a fraud on Fridays[7] and feastdays in churches.
30   And that's a loller's life that earns little praise
Where Rightfulness rewards men as they really deserve.
    He shall reward every man according to his works.[8]
Or are you perhaps lame in your legs or other limbs of your body,
Or maimed through some misadventure, so that you might be
    excused?"
    "When I was young, many years ago,
35   My father and my friends provided me with schooling,
Till I understood surely what Holy Scripture meant,
And what is best for the body as the Book tells,
And most certain for the soul, if so I may continue.
And, in faith, I never found, since my friends died,
40   Life that I liked save in these long clothes.[9]
And if I must live by labor and earn my livelihood,
The labor I should live by is the one I learned best.
    [Abide] in the same calling wherein you were called.[1]
And so I live in London and upland[2] as well.
The tools that I toil with to sustain myself
45   Are Paternoster and my primer, *Placebo* and *Dirige*,[3]
And sometimes my Psalter and my seven Psalms.
These I say for the souls of such as help me.
And those who provide my food vouchsafe, I think,
To welcome me when I come, once a month or so,
50   Now with him, now with her, and in this way I beg
Without bag or bottle but my belly alone.
    And also, moreover, it seems to me, sir Reason,

6. I.e., tall, perhaps a pun on "willfulness." The Dreamer is called "Long Will" in B-text, 15.152.
7. Fast days, because Christ was crucified on a Friday.
8. Matthew 16.27; cf. Psalm 62.12.
9. The long dress of a cleric, not limited to actual priests.
1. 1 Corinthians 7.20, with variations.
2. North of London, in rural country.

3. "I will please [the Lord]" and "Make straight [my way]" (Psalm 116.9 and 5.8, respectively). *Placebo* and *Dirige* are the first words of hymns based on two of the seven "penitential" Psalms that were part of the regular order of personal prayer. "Paternoster": the Lord's Prayer ("Our father"). The "primer" was the basic collection of private prayers for laypeople.

No clerk should be constrained to do lower-class work.
For by the law of Leviticus[4] that our Lord ordained
55 Clerks with tonsured crowns should, by common understanding,
Neither strain nor sweat nor swear at inquests,
Nor fight in a vanguard and defeat an enemy:
      Do not render evil for evil.[5]
For they are heirs of Heaven, all that have the tonsure,
And in choir and in churches they are Christ's ministers.
      The Lord is the portion of my inheritance. And elsewhere,
      Mercy does not constrain.[6]
60 It is becoming for clerks to perform Christ's service,
And untonsured boys be burdened with bodily labor.
For none should acquire clerk's tonsure unless he claims descent
From franklins[7] and free men and folk properly wedded.
Bondmen and bastards and beggars' children—
65 These belong to labor; and lords' kin should serve
God and good men as their degree requires,
Some to sing Masses or sit and write,
Read and receive what Reason ought to spend.
But since bondmen's boys have been made bishops,
70 And bastards' boys have been archdeacons,
And shoemakers and their sons have through silver become knights,
And lords' sons their laborers whose lands are mortgaged to them—
And thus for the right of this realm they ride against our enemies
To the comfort of the commons and to the king's honor—
75 And monks and nuns on whom mendicants must depend
Have had their kin named knights and bought knight's-fees,[8]
And popes and patrons have shunned poor gentle blood
And taken the sons of Simon Magus[9] to keep the sanctuary,
Life-holiness and love have gone a long way hence,
80 And will be so till this is all worn out or otherwise changed.
Therefore proffer me no reproach, Reason, I pray you,
For in my conscience I conceive what Christ wants me to do.
Prayers of a perfect man and appropriate penance
Are the labor that our Lord loves most of all.
85 "*Non de solo,*" I said, "forsooth *vivit homo,*
Nec in pane et in pabulo;[1] the Paternoster witnesses
Fiat voluntas Dei[2]—that provides us with everything."
      Said Conscience, "By Christ, I can't see that this lies;°   ° *is pertinent*
But it seems no serious perfectness to be a city-beggar,
90 Unless you're licensed to collect for prior or monastery."

---

4. Leviticus 21 sets restrictions on members of the priesthood.
5. 1 Thessalonians 5.15, with variations.
6. I.e., "mercy is not restricted," source unknown. The quotation above is from Psalm 16.5.
7. Freemen. By this date, the term did not just mean nonserfs but designated landowners who were becoming members of the gentry class yet were not knights. The distinction Langland seems to make in this line between franklins and freemen may reflect the rising status of certain families of "freedmen," the original meaning of the word *franklins.*
8. The estate a knight held from his overlord in return for military service was called his "fee."
9. Priests who obtained office through bribery or "simony," a term derived from Simon Magus, a magician who offered the apostles money for their power to perform miracles through the Holy Spirit (see Acts 8).
1. "Not solely [by bread] doth man live, neither by bread nor by food"; the verse continues, "but by every word that proceedeth out of the mouth of God": Matthew 4.4, with variations; cf. Deuteronomy 8.3.
2. "God's will be done." The Lord's Prayer reads, "Thy will be done" (Matthew 6.10).

"That is so," I said, "and so I admit
That at times I've lost time and at times misspent it;
And yet I hope, like him who has often bargained
And always lost and lost, and at the last it happened
95   He bought such a bargain he was the better ever,
That all his loss looked paltry in the long run,
Such a winning was his through what grace decreed.
    The kingdom of Heaven is like unto treasure hidden in a field.
    The woman who found the piece of silver, etc.[3]
So I hope to have of him that is almighty
A gobbet of his grace, and begin a time
100   That all times of my time shall turn into profit."
    "And I counsel you," said Reason, "quickly to begin
The life that is laudable and reliable for the soul."
    "Yes, and continue," said Conscience, and I came to the church.[4]

---

3. Matthew 13.44, Luke 15.9–10. Both passages come from parables that compare finding the kingdom of heaven to risking everything you have to get the one thing that matters most.
4. The four lines that follow this passage connect it to the beginning of the second dream (B-text, 5): "And to the church I set off, to honor God; before the Cross, on my knees, I beat my breast, sighing for my sins, saying my Paternoster, weeping and wailing until I fell asleep."

MIDDLE ENGLISH LYRICS

It was only late in the fourteenth century that English began to develop the kinds of aristocratic, formal, learned, and literary types of lyric that had long been cultivated on the Continent by the Troubador poets in the south of France, the Minnesänger in Germany (German *Minne* corresponds to French *fine amour*—that is, refined or aristocratic love), or the Italian poets whose works Dante characterized as the *dolce stil nuovo* (the sweet new style). Chaucer, under the influence of French poets, wrote lovers' complaints, homiletic poetry, and verse letters in the form of ballades, roundels, and other highly stylized lyric types (see pp. 313–16). In the fifteenth century, John Lydgate, Thomas Hoccleve, and others following Chaucer wrote lyrics of this sort, which were praised for embellishing the English language, and these along with Chaucer's were collected in manuscript anthologies that were produced commercially for well-to-do buyers.

Chaucer, his courtly predecessors, and their followers were of course familiar with and influenced by an ancient tradition of popular song from which only a small fraction survives. With one exception, the Middle English lyrics included in this section are the work of anonymous poets and are difficult to date with any precision. Some of these survive in a single manuscript, especially in anthologies of religious poetry and prose. The topics and language in these poems are highly conventional, yet the lyrics often seem remarkably fresh and spontaneous. Many are marked by strong accentual rhythms with a good deal of alliteration. Their pleasure does not come from originality or lived experience but from variations of expected themes and images. Some were undoubtedly set to music, and in a few cases the music has survived. Perhaps the earliest of those printed here, *The Cuckoo Song*, is a canon or round in which the voices follow one another and join together echoing the joyous cry, "Cuckou." The rooster and hen in *The Nun's Priest's Tale* sing *My Lief Is Faren in Londe* in "sweet accord." *I Am of Ireland* was undoubtedly accompanied by dancing as well as music.

A frequent topic that lyric shares with narrative is the itemization of the beloved's beauties. The Alisoun of the lyric and Alisoun of *The Miller's Tale* are both dark eyed, a quality that suggests a sexuality supressed in the conventional gray- or blue-eyed heroines of courtly romance. The lover in the lyric protests, as Nicholas does in *The Miller's Tale*, that he will die if he cannot obtain her love.

The joyous return of spring (the *reverdie*, spring song, or, literally, "regreening") is the subject of many lyrics. In love lyrics the mating of birds and animals in wild nature often contrasts with the melancholy of unrequited or forsaken lovers. These lovers are usually male. We know that some women wrote troubador and court poetry, but we do not know whether women composed popular lyrics; women certainly sang popular songs, just as they are portrayed doing in narrative poetry.

Many more religious lyrics were written down and preserved. These were mostly written by anonymous clerics, but in rare instances we know at least the name of an author. Seventeen poems by the Franciscan William Herebert are collected in a single manuscript. In his dramatic lyric printed here, the main speaker is the Christ-knight, returning from the Crucifixion, which is treated as a battle the way it is in *Dream of the Rood* and in Passus 18 of *Piers Plowman*. Christ in his bloodstained garments is compared in a famous image from Isaiah 63.2 to one who treads grapes in a winepress, a passage that is also the source of Julia Ward Howe's "grapes of wrath" in *The Battle Hymn of the Republic*.

The religious lyrics are for the most part devotional poems that depend on the Latin Bible and liturgy of the church. The passage from Isaiah adapted by Herebert was part of a lesson in a mass performed during Holy Week. But the diction of that poem, though there are a few French loan words, is predominantly of native English origin. Many of the poems, like Herebert's, contain an element of drama: *Ye that Pasen by the Weye* is spoken by Christ from the Cross to all wayfarers; similar verses are spoken by the crucified Christ to the crowd (as well as to the audience) in the mystery plays of the Crucifixion.

Among the most beautiful and tender lyrics are those about the Virgin Mary, who is the greatest of all queens and ladies. They celebrate Mary's joys, sorrows, and the mystery of her virgin motherhood. *Sunset on Calvary*, a tableau of Mary at the foot of the Cross, contains an implicit play upon English "sun," which is setting, and the "son," who is dying but, like the sun, will rise again. Like love songs the Marian lyrics often celebrate the mysteries of the natural world and thus defy any simple division of medieval lyric into "secular" or "religious" poetry. *I Sing of a Maiden* visualizes the conception of Jesus in terms of the falling dew, and he steals silently to her bower like a lover. *Adam Lay Bound* cheerfully treats the original sin as though it were a child's theft of an apple, which had the happy result of making Mary the Queen of Heaven. *The Corpus Christi Carol* has the form of a lullaby but penetrates by stages to the heart of a mystery similar to the Holy Grail, the chalice that contained Christ's blood, which continues to flow, as it does in this carol, for humanity's salvation.

The Cuckoo Song

> Sumer is ycomen in,
> Loude sing cuckou!
> Groweth seed and bloweth meed,[1]
> And springth the wode° now.   *wood*
> 5 Sing cuckou!
>
> Ewe bleteth after lamb,
> Loweth after calve cow,

1. The meadow blossoms.

Bulloc sterteth,° bucke verteth,°   *leaps/farts*
Merye sing cuckou!
10   Cuckou, cuckou,
Wel singest thou cuckou:
Ne swik° thou never now!   *cease*

Alison

Bitweene° Merch and Averil,   *in the seasons of*
When spray biginneth to springe,
The litel fowl hath hire wil°   *pleasure*
On hire leod[1] to singe.
5   Ich° libbe° in love-longinge   *I/live*
For semlokest° of alle thinge.   *seemliest, fairest*
Heo° may me blisse bringe: *she*
    Ich am in hire baundoun.°   *power*
    An hendy hap ich habbe yhent,[2]
10   Ichoot° from hevene it is me sent: *I know*
From alle[3] wommen my love is lent,°   *removed*
And light° on Alisoun.   *alights*

On hew° hire heer° is fair ynough,   *hue/hair*
Hire browe browne, hire yë° blake;   *eye*
15   With lossum cheere heo on me lough;[4]
With middel smal and wel ymake.
But° heo me wolle to hire take   *unless*
For to been hire owen make,°   *mate*
Longe to liven ichulle° forsake,   *I will*
20   And feye° fallen adown.   *dead*
    An hendy hap, etc.

Nightes when I wende° and wake,   *turn*
Forthy° mine wonges° waxeth wan: *therefore/cheeks*
Levedy,° al for thine sake   *lady*
25   Longinge is ylent me on.[5]
In world nis noon so witer° man   *clever*
That al hire bountee° telle can;   *excellence*
Hire swire° is whittere° than the swan,   *neck/whiter*
    And fairest may° in town.   *maid*
30   An hendy, etc.

Ich am for wowing° al forwake,°   *wooing/worn out from waking*
Wery so° water in wore.[6]   *as*
Lest any reve me[7] my make
Ich habbe y-yerned yore.[8]
35   Bettere is tholien° while° sore   *endure/for a time*
Than mournen evermore.
Geinest under gore,[9]

---

1. In her language.
2. A gracious chance I have received.
3. I.e., all other.
4. With lovely face she on me smiled.
5. Longing has come upon me.

6. Perhaps "millpond."
7. Deprive me.
8. I have been worrying long since.
9. Fairest beneath clothing.

Herkne to my roun:°   *song*
An hendy, etc.

My Lief Is Faren in Londe

My lief is faren in londel[1]—
Allas, why is she so?
And I am so sore bonde°   *bound*
I may nat come her to.
5 She hath myn herte in holde
Wherever she ride or go°—   *walk*
With trewe love a thousand folde.

Western Wind

Westron wind, when will thou blow?
The small rain down can rain.
Christ, that my love were in my arms,
And I in my bed again.

I Am of Ireland

Ich am of Irlonde,
And of the holy londe
Of Irlonde.
Goode sire, praye ich thee,
5 For of° sainte charitee,   *sake of*
Com and dance with me
In Irlonde.

What is he, this lordling, that cometh from the fight[1]

"What is he, this lordling,[2] that cometh from the fight
With blood-rede wede so grislich ydight,[3]
So faire ycointised,° so semelich in sight,[4]   *appareled*
So stiflich he gangeth,[5] so doughty° a knight?"   *valiant*

5 "Ich° it am, ich it am, that ne speke but right,[6]   *I*
Champioun to helen° mankinde in fight."   *save*

"Why then is thy shroud rede, with blood al ymeind,
As troddares in wringe with must al bespreind?"[7]

---

1. My beloved has gone away.
1. The poem, by William Herebert (d. 1333), paraphrases Isaiah 63.1–7, in which the "lordling" (lord's son) is a messianic figure returning from battle against the Edomites.
2. Who is this lord's son?
3. With blood-red garment, so terribly arrayed.

4. So fair to behold.
5. So boldly he goes.
6. Who speaks only what is right.
7. Why then is thy garment red, all stained with blood, like treaders in the winepress all spattered with must (the juice of the grapes).

"The wring ich have ytrodded al myself one°   *alone*
10   And of° al mankinde was none other wone.°   *for/hope*
Ich hem[8] have ytrodded in wrathe and in grame,°   *anger*
And al my wede is bespreind with here blood ysame,[9]
And al my robe yfouled° to here grete shame.   *soiled*
The day of th'ilke wreche[1] liveth in my thought;
15   The yeer of medes yelding ne foryet ich nought.[2]
Ich looked al aboute some helping mon;[3]
Ich soughte al the route,[4] but help nas ther non.
It was mine owne strengthe that this bote° wrought,   *remedy*
Mine owne doughtinesse that help ther me brought."[5]
20   Ich have ytrodded the folk in wrathe and in grame,
Adreint al with shennesse, ydrawe down with shame."[6]

"On Godes milsfulnesse° ich wil bethenche me,[7]   *mercy*
And herien° him in alle thing that he yeldeth° me."   *praise/gives*

Ye That Pasen by the Weye

Ye that pasen by the weye,
Abidet a little stounde.°   *while*
Beholdet, all my felawes,
Yif° any me lik is founde.   *if*
5   To the tre with nailes thre
Wol° fast I hange bounde;   *very*
With a spere all thoru my side
To mine herte is made a wounde.

Sunset on Calvary

Now gooth sunne under wode.[1]
Me reweth,[2] Marye, thy faire rode.°   *face*
Now gooth sunne under tree:
Me reweth, Marye, thy sone and thee.

I Sing of a Maiden

I sing of a maiden
     That is makelees:[1]
King of alle kinges
     To° her sone she chees.[2]   *as/chose*

8. Them, i.e., humankind symbolized by the grapes in the press. Cf. line 20.
9. And my garment is all spattered with their blood together.
1. That same vengeance (perhaps Judgment Day).
2. I do not forget the year of paying wages.
3. I looked all around for some man to help (me).
4. I searched the whole crowd.

5. My own valor brought help to me there.
6. All drowned with ignominy, pulled down with shame.
7. I will bethink myself.
1. Both the woods and the wooden Cross.
2. I pity.
1. Spotless, matchless, and mateless—a triple pun.

as

5   He cam also° stille
      Ther° his moder° was   *where / mother*
As dewe in Aprille
    That falleth on the gras.

He cam also stille
10   To his modres bowr
As dewe in Aprille
    That falleth on the flowr.

He cam also stille
    Ther his moder lay
15   As dewe in Aprille
    That falleth on the spray.

Moder and maiden
    Was nevere noon but she:
Wel may swich° a lady   *such*
20   Godes moder be.

Adam Lay Bound

Adam lay ybounden, bounden in a bond,
Four thousand winter thoughte he not too long;
And al was for an apple, an apple that he took,
As clerkes finden writen, writen in hire book.
5 Ne hadde[1] the apple taken been, the apple taken been,
Ne hadde nevere Oure Lady ybeen hevene Queen.
Blessed be the time that apple taken was:
Therfore we mown° singen *Deo Gratias*.[2]   *may*

The Corpus Christi Carol

Lully, lullay, lully, lullay,
The faucon° hath borne my make° away.   *falcon / mate*

He bare him up, he bare him down,
He bare him into an orchard brown.

5 In that orchard ther was an hall
That was hanged with purple and pall.°   *black velvet*

And in that hall ther was a bed:
It was hanged with gold so red.

And in that bed ther lith° a knight,   *lies*
10 His woundes bleeding by day and night.

---

1. Had not.   2. Thanks be to God.

By that beddes side ther kneeleth a may,°   *maid*
And she weepeth both night and day.

And by that beddes side ther standeth a stoon°   *stone*
   Corpus Christ[1] writen thereon.

1. Body of Christ.

JULIAN OF NORWICH
1342–ca.1416

The "Showings," or "Revelations" as they are also called, were sixteen mystical visions received by the woman known as Julian of Norwich. The name may be one that she adopted when she became an anchoress in a cell attached to the church of St. Julian that still stands in that town on the northeast coast of England. An anchorite (m.) or anchoress (f.) is a religious recluse confined to an enclosure, which he or she has vowed never to leave. At the time of such an enclosing the burial service was performed, signifying that the enclosed person was dead to the world and that the enclosure corresponded to a grave. The point of this confinement was, of course, to pursue more actively the contemplative or spiritual life.

Julian may well have belonged to a religious order at the time that her visions led her to choose the life of an anchoress. We know very little about her except what she tells us in her writings. She is, however, very precise about the date of her visions. They occurred, she tells us, at the age of thirty and a half on May 13, 1373. Four extant wills bequeath sums for Julian's maintenance in her anchorage. The most important document witnessing her life is *The Book of Margery Kempe* (see the headnote for Margery Kempe, p. 367). Kempe sought out Julian's advice whether there might be any deception in Kempe's own visions, "for the anchoress," she says, "was expert in such things." Kempe's description of Julian's conversation accords well with the doctrines and personality that emerge from Julian's own book.

A Book of Showings survives in a short and a long version. The longer text, from which the following excerpts are taken, was the product of fifteen and more years of meditation on the meaning of the visions in which much had been obscure to Julian. Apparently the mystical experiences were never repeated, but through constant study and contemplation the showings acquired a greater clarity, richness, and profundity as they continued to be turned over in a mind both gifted with spiritual insight and learned in theology. Her editors document her extensive use of the Bible and her familiarity with medieval religious writings in both English and Latin.

Julian's showings are, in her words, both "ghostly" (that is, spiritual) and "bodily." They embrace powerful visual phenomena such as blood drops running from the crown of thorns and revelations that take place in pure mind. The years of meditation on these showings led her ultimately to a personal, profound, and difficult understanding of the Trinity—the one God in the three persons of the father, the son, and the Holy Spirit—and humanity's participation in that oneness. For Julian, God the father generates the human soul (conceived of as immortal "substance," co-eternal with God); God the son is the mother who bears, nourishes, and redeems (through his own incarnation) sensual human nature; God the Holy Spirit binds deity and humanity in eternal love and grace. Julian expresses such sophisticated theological concepts in language that can be intricate in its logic yet at other times transparently simple. She herself is amazed that God, who is so great and awe inspiring, can be so "homely" (so direct, intimate, and familial) with "a sinful creature." The blood of Christ reminds her of water dripping from the eaves of a house and of the scales of herring. Her concept of Jesus as mother has antecedents in both the Old and New Testaments, in medieval theology, and in the writings of medieval mystics (both men and women). The idea is integral to Julian's complex metaphysical reasoning about the Trinity; she also vividly realizes it by analogy with the emotional experiences of mother and child: a sinner is like a frightened child running to its mother for comfort and help.

Julian is an accomplished prose stylist, inheriting a tradition of English religious prose that goes back to the Old English period. Her book is one of many distinguished devotional and mystical works, both English and Continental, composed during the late Middle Ages, such as the *Dialogue* of Catherine of Siena (translated into Middle English as *The Orchard of Syon*) or the anonymous *Cloud of Unknowing*. Julian wrote and rewrote *A Book of Showings* to come to terms with her visions, but, like other visionaries, she felt the visions were not only a personal gift but an obligation. "We are all one," she says, "and I am sure I saw it for the profit of many other."

From A Book of Showings to the Anchoress Julian of Norwich[1]

[THE FIRST REVELATION]

Chapter 3

And when I was thirty year old and a half, God sent me a bodily sickness in the which I lay three days and three nights; and on the fourth night I took all my rites of holy church, and went[2] not to have liven till day. And after this I lay two days and two nights; and on the third night I weened[3] oftentimes to have passed, and so weened they that were with me. And yet in this I felt a great loathsomeness[4] to die, but for nothing that was on earth that me liketh to live for, ne[5] for no pain that I was afraid of, for I trusted in God of his mercy. But it was for I would have lived to have loved God better and longer time, that I might by the grace of that living have the more knowing and loving of God in the bliss of heaven. For me thought[6] all that time that I had lived here so little and so short in regard of[7] that endless bliss, I thought: Good Lord, may my living no longer be to thy worship?[8] And I understood by my reason and by the feeling of my pains that I should die; and I assented fully with all the will of my heart to be at God's will.

Thus I endured till day, and by then was my body dead from the middes downward, as to my feeling.[9] Then was I holpen[1] to be set upright, underset[2] with help, for to have the more freedom of my heart to be at God's will, and thinking on God while my life lasted. My curate was sent for to be at my ending, and before he came I had set up my eyen[3] and might not speak. He

1. The text is based on that given by Edmund Colledge, O.S.A., and James Walsh, S. J., for the Pontifical Institute of Mediaeval Studies, Toronto (1978), but it has been freely edited and modern spelling has been used where possible.
2. Thought.
3. Supposed.
4. Reluctance.

5. Nor.
6. I thought, [it] thought me.
7. In comparison with.
8. Glory.
9. As it felt to me.
1. Helped.
2. Supported.
3. Eyes.

set the cross before my face and said: "I have brought the image of thy savior; look thereupon and comfort thee therewith." Me thought I was well, for my eyen was set upright into heaven, where I trusted to come by the mercy of God; but nevertheless I assented to set my eyen in the face of the crucifix, if I might, and so I did, for me thought I might longer dure to look even forth than right up.[4] After this my sight began to fail. It waxed as dark about me in the chamber as if it had been night, save in the image of the cross, wherein held a common light; and I wist[5] not how. All that was beside the cross was ugly and fearful to me as[6] it had been much occupied with fiends.

After this the over[7] part of my body began to die so farforth that unneth[8] I had any feeling. My most pain was shortness of breath and failing of life. Then went[9] I verily to have passed. And in this suddenly all my pain was taken from me, and I was as whole, and namely in the over part of my body, as ever I was before. I marvelled of this sudden change, for me thought that it was a privy working of God, and not of kind;[1] and yet by feeling of this ease I trusted never more to have lived, ne the feeling of this ease was no full ease to me, for me thought I had liever[2] have been delivered of this world, for my heart was willfully set thereto.

Then came suddenly to my mind that I should desire the second wound of our Lord's gift and of his grace, that my body might be fulfilled with mind and feeling of his blessed passion, as I had before prayed,[3] for I would that his pains were my pains, with compassion and afterward longing to God. Thus thought me that I might with his grace have the wounds that I had before desired; but in this I desired never no bodily sight ne no manner showing of God, but compassion as me thought that a kind soul might have with our Lord Jesu, that for love would become a deadly[4] man. With him I desired to suffer, living in my deadly body, as God would give me grace.

Chapter 4

And in this suddenly I saw the red blood running down from under the garland, hot and freshly, plenteously and lively, right as it was in the time that the garland of thorns was pressed on his blessed head. Right so, both God and man, the same that suffered for me, I conceived truly and mightily that it was himself that shewed it me without any mean.[5]

And in the same showing suddenly the Trinity fulfilled my heart most of joy, and so I understood it shall be in heaven without end to all that shall come there. For the Trinity is God, God is the Trinity. The Trinity is our maker, the Trinity is our keeper, the Trinity is our everlasting lover, the Trinity is endless joy and our bliss, by our Lord Jesu Christ, and in our Lord Jesu Christ. And this was showed in the first sight and in all, for where Jesu appeareth, the blessed Trinity is understand, as to my sight.[6] And I said, "Benedicite dominus."[7] This I said for reverence in my meaning,[8] with a

---

4. Endure to look straight ahead than straight up.
5. Knew.
6. As if.
7. Upper.
8. To the extent that scarcely.
9. Thought.
1. Nature.
2. Rather.
3. Julian had prayed for three gifts: direct experi-

ence of Christ's passion, mortal sickness, and the wounds of true contrition, loving compassion, and a willed desire for God.
4. Mortal.
5. Intermediary.
6. Is understood, as I see it.
7. Blessed be the Lord.
8. Intention.

mighty voice, and full greatly was I astoned[9] for wonder and marvel that I had, that he that is so reverend and so dreadful[1] will be so homely[2] with a sinful creature living in this wretched flesh.

Thus I took it for that time that our Lord Jesu of his courteous love would show me comfort before the time of my temptation; for me thought it might well be that I should by the sufferance of God and with his keeping be tempted of[3] fiends before I should die. With this sight of his blessed passion, with the godhead that I saw in my understanding, I knew well that it was strength enough to me, yea, and to all creatures living that should be saved, against all the fiends of hell, and against all ghostly[4] enemies.

In this he brought our Lady Saint Mary to my understanding; I saw her ghostly in bodily likeness, a simple maiden and a meek, young of age, a little waxen above a child,[5] in the stature as she was when she conceived. Also God showed me in part the wisdom and the truth of her soul, wherein I understood the reverend beholding, that she beheld her God, that is her maker, marvelling with great reverence that he would be born of her that was a simple creature of his making. And this wisdom and truth, knowing the greatness of her maker and the littlehead[6] of herself that is made, made her to say full meekly to Gabriel: "Lo me here, God's handmaiden."[7] In this sight I did understand verily that she is more than all that God made beneath her in worthiness and in fullhead;[8] for above her is nothing that is made but the blessed manhood of Christ, as to my sight.

Chapter 5

In this same time that I saw this sight of the head bleeding, our good Lord showed a ghostly sight of his homely loving. I saw that he is to us all thing that is good and comfortable to our help. He is our clothing that for love wrappeth us and windeth us, halseth us[9] and all becloses us, hangeth about us for tender love that[1] he may never leave us. And so in this sight I saw that he is all thing that is good, as to my understanding.

And in this he showed a little thing, the quantity of an hazelnut, lying in the palm of my hand, as me seemed, and it was as round as a ball. I looked thereon with the eye of my understanding, and thought: What may this be? And it was answered generally thus: It is all that is made. I marvelled how it might last, for me thought it might suddenly have fallen to nought for[2] littleness. And I was answered in my understanding: It lasteth and ever shall, for God loveth it; and so hath all thing being by the love of God.

In this little thing I saw three properties. The first is that God made it, the second that God loveth it, the third that God keepeth[3] it. But what beheld I therein? Verily, the maker, the keeper, the lover. For till I am substantially united to him[4] I may never have full rest ne very[5] bliss; that is to say that I be so fastened to him that there be right nought that is made between my God and me.

9. Astonished.
1. Awe-inspiring.
2. Familiar, intimate (the quality of being "at home").
3. By.
4. Spiritual.
5. Grown a little older than a child.
6. Littleness.
7. See Luke 1.38.

8. Perfection.
9. Envelops us and embraces us.
1. So that.
2. Because of.
3. Looks after.
4. Joined to him in "substance," which Julian regards as the eternal essence of being.
5. True.

This little thing that is made, me thought it might have fallen to nought for littleness. Of this needeth us to have knowledge, that us liketh nought all thing that is made, for to love and have God that is unmade.[6] For this is the cause why we be not all in ease of heart and of soul, for we seek here rest in this thing that is so little, where no rest is in, and we know not our God, that is almighty, all wise and all good, for he is very rest. God will be known, and him liketh that we rest us in him; for all that is beneath him suffiseth not to us. And this is the cause why that no soul is in rest till it is noughted of all things that is made.[7] When she is wilfully[8] noughted for love, to have him that is all, then is she able to receive ghostly rest.

And also our good Lord showed that it is full great pleasance to him that a sely[9] soul come to him naked, plainly and homely. For this is the kind[1] yearning of the soul by the touching of the Holy Ghost, as by the understanding that I have in this showing: God of thy goodness gave me thyself, for thou art enough to me, and I may ask nothing that is less that may be full worship to thee. And if I ask any thing that is less, ever me wanteth;[2] but only in thee I have all.

And these words of the goodness of God be full lovesome to the soul and full near touching the will of our Lord, for his goodness fulfilleth all his creatures and all his blessed works and overpasseth[3] without end. For he is the endlesshead and he made us only to himself and restored us by his precious passion, and ever keepeth us in his blessed love; and all this is of his goodness.

* * *

From *Chapter 7*

And in all that time that he showed this that I have now said in ghostly sight, I saw the bodily sight lasting of the plenteous bleeding of the head. The great drops of blood fell down fro under the garland like pellets, seeming as it had come out of the veins. And in the coming out they were brown red, for the blood was full thick; and in the spreading abroad they were bright red. And when it came at the brows, there they vanished; and not withstanding the bleeding continued till many things were seen and understood. Nevertheless the fairhead and livelihead continued in the same beauty and liveliness.

The plenteoushead is like to the drops of water that fall of the evesing[4] of an house after a great shower of rain, that fall so thick that no man may number them with no bodily wit.[5] And for the roundness they were like to the scale of herring in the spreading of the forehead.

These three things came to my mind in the time: pellets for the roundhead[6] in the coming out of the blood, the scale of the herring for the roundhead in the spreading, the drops of the evesing of a house for the plenteoushead unnumerable. This showing was quick[7] and lively and hideous and dreadful and sweet and lovely; and of all the sight that I saw this was most comfort

---

6. I.e., we need to know that we should not be attracted to earthly things, which are made, to love and possess God, who is not made, who exists eternally.
7. Emptied of (its attachment to) all created things.
8. Of its free will.
9. Innocent.

1. Natural.
2. I am forever lacking.
3. Surpasses.
4. Eaves.
5. Intelligence.
6. Roundness.
7. Vivid.

to me, that our good Lord, that is so reverend and dreadful, is so homely and so courteous, and this most fulfilled me with liking and sickerness[8] in soule.

And to the understanding of this he showed this open example. It is the most worship[9] that a solemn king or a great lord may do to a poor servant if he will be homely with him; and namely if he show it himself of a full true meaning[1] and with a glad cheer both in private and openly. Then thinketh this poor creature thus: "Lo, what might this noble lord do more worship and joy to me than to show to me that am so little this marvelous homeliness? Verily, it is more joy and liking to me than if he gave me great gifts and were himself strange in manner." This bodily example was showed so high that this man's heart might be ravished and almost forget himself for joy of this great homeliness.

Thus it fareth by our Lord Jesu and by us, for verily it is the most joy that may be, as to my sight, that he that is highest and mightiest, noblest and worthiest, is lowest and meekest, homeliest and courteousest. And truly and verily this marvelous joy shall be show us all when we shall see him. And this will our good Lord that we believe and trust, joy and like, comfort us and make solace as we may with his grace and with his help, into[2] the time that we see it verily. For the most fullhead of joy that we shall have, as to my sight, is this marvelous courtesy and homeliness of our fader, that is our maker, in our Lord Jesu Christ, that is our brother and oure saviour. But this marvelous homeliness may no man know in this life, but if he have it by special showing of our Lord, or of great plenty of grace inwardly given of the Holy Ghost. But faith and belief with charity deserve the meed,[3] and so it is had by grace. For in faith with hope and charity our life is grounded. The showing is made to whom that God will, plainly teacheth the same opened and declared, with many privy points belonging to our faith and belief which be worshipful to be known. And when the showing which is given for a time is passed and hid, then faith keepeth it by grace of the Holy Ghost into our life's end. And thus by the showing it is none other than the faith, ne less ne more, as it may be seen by our Lord's meaning in the same matter, by then[4] it come to the last end.

Chapter 27

And after this our Lord brought to my mind the longing that I had to him before; and I saw nothing letted[5] me but sin, and so I beheld generally in us all, and me thought that if sin had not been, we should all have been clean[6] and like to our Lord as he made us. And thus in my folly before this time often I wondered why, by the great foreseeing wisdom of God, the beginning of sin was not letted.[7] For then thought me that all should have been well.

This stering[8] was much to be forsaken; and nevertheless mourning and sorrow I made therefore without reason and discretion. But Jesu that in this vision informed me of all that me needed answered by this word and said: "Sin is behovely,[9] but all shall be well, and all manner of thing shall be

8. Security.
9. Honor.
1. Intent.
2. Until.
3. Reward. "Charity": love. See 1 Corinthians 13.13.

4. By the time that.
5. Hindered.
6. Pure.
7. Prevented.
8. Fretting.
9. Necessary.

well."[1] In this naked word "Sin," our Lord brought to my mind generally all
that is not good, and the shameful despite[2] and the uttermost tribulation
that he bore for us in this life, and his dying and all his pains, and passion[3]
of all his creatures ghostly and bodily. For we be all in part troubled, and we
shall be troubled, following our master Jesu, till we be fully purged of our
deadly[4] flesh which be not very good.

And with the beholding of this, with all the pains that ever were or ever
shall be, I understood the passion of Christ for the most pain and overpassing.[5] And with all, this was showed in a touch, readily passed over into
comfort. For our good Lord would not that the soul were afeared of this ugly
sight. But I saw not sin, for I believe it had no manner of substance, ne no
part of being,[6] ne it might not be known but by the pain that is caused
thereof. And this pain is something, as to my sight, for a time, for it purgeth
and maketh us to know ourself and ask mercy; for the passion of our Lord
is comfort to us against all this, and so is his blessed will. And for the tender
love that our good Lord hath to all that shall be saved, he comforteth readily
and sweetly, meaning thus: It is true that sin is cause of all this pain, but all
shall be well, and all manner of thing shall be well.

These words were showed full tenderly, showing no manner of blame to
me ne to none that shall be safe.[7] Then were it great unkindness of me to
blame or wonder on God of my sin, sithen[8] he blameth not me for sin. And
in these same words I saw an high marvelous privity[9] hid in God, which
privity he shall openly make and shall be known to us in heaven. In which
knowing we shall verily see the cause why he suffered sin to come, in which
sight we shall endlessly have joy.

[JESUS AS MOTHER]

From *Chapter* 58

God the blessedful Trinity, which is everlasting being, right as he is endless
fro without beginning,[1] right so it was in his purpose endless to make mankind,[2] which fair kind[3] first was dight to[4] for his own son, the second person;
and when he would,[5] by full accord of all the Trinity he made us all at once.[6]
And in our making he knit us and oned[7] us to himself, by which oneing we
be kept as clean[8] and as noble as we were made. By the virtue of that ilke[9]
precious oneing we love our maker and like[1] him, praise and thank him, and
endlessly enjoy[2] in him. And this is the working which is wrought continually
in each soul that shall be saved, which is the godly will before said.

And thus in our making God almighty is our kindly[3] father, and god all

---

1. T. S. Eliot quotes this statement, versions of
which appear several times in the *Showings*, in the
last movement of his *Four Quartets*.
2. Spite.
3. Suffering.
4. Mortal.
5. Exceeding (pain).
6. On "substance" and "being," see chapter 5,
p. 358, n. 4.
7. Saved.
8. Since.
9. Secret.
1. I.e., eternal.

2. I.e., his purpose to make humankind is also
eternal.
3. Nature.
4. Prepared for.
5. Wanted to.
6. All of us at one and the same time.
7. United. Julian sustains the idea of oneness in
the verb *oned* and the noun *oneing*.
8. Pure.
9. Same.
1. Please.
2. Rejoice.
3. Both "kind" and "natural."

wisdom is our kindly mother, with the love and the goodness of the Holy Ghost, which is all one God, one Lord. And in the knitting and in the oneing he is our very true spouse and we his loved wife[4] and his fair maiden, with which wife he was never displeased. For he sayeth: "I love thee and thou lovest me, and our love shall never part in two."

I beheld the working of all the blessed Trinity, in which beholding I saw and understood these three properties: The property of the fatherhood, and the property of the motherhood, and the property of the lordship in one God. In our father almighty we have our keeping[5] and our bliss as anemptis[6] our kindly substance which is to us by our making fro without beginning.[7] And in the second person in wit[8] and wisdom we have our keeping as anemptis our sensuality[9] our restoring and our saving, for he is our mother, brother and savior And in our good lord the Holy Ghost we have our rewarding and our yielding[1] for our living and our travail,[2] and endlessly overpassing[3] all that we desire in his marvelous courtesy of his high plenteous grace. For all our life is in three: in the first we have our being, and in the second we have our increasing, and in the third we have our fulfilling. The first is kind,[4] the second is mercy, the third is grace.

For the first[5] I saw and understood that the high might of the Trinity is our father, and the deep wisdom of the Trinity is our mother, and the great love of the Trinity is our lord; and all these have we in kind and in our substantial making. And furthermore I saw that the second person, which is our mother, substantially the same dearworthy person,[6] is now become our mother sensual,[7] for we be double of God's making, that is to say substantial and sensual. Our substance is the higher part, which we have in our father God almighty; and the second person of the Trinity is our mother in kind in our substantial making, in whom we be grounded and rooted, and he is our mother of mercy in our sensual taking.[8]

* * *

From *Chapter 59*

* * *

And thus is Jesu our very[9] mother in kind of our first making, and he is our very mother in grace by taking of our kind made. All the fair working and all the sweet kindly offices of dearworthy motherhood is impropered to[1] the second person, for in him we have this goodly will, whole and safe without end, both in kind and in grace, of his own proper goodness.

I understood three manner of beholdings of motherhood in God. The first is ground of our kind making, the second is taking of our kind, and there beginneth the motherhood of grace, the third is motherhood in working.[2]

---

4. The relationship between God and humanity is also conceived as a mystical marriage in which Christ is the bridegroom and the human soul his spouse.
5. Protection.
6. With regard to.
7. I.e., our natural created being, which is eternal. On *substance* see chapter 5, p. 358, n. 4.
8. Intelligence.
9. With regard to the nature of our sensual being (as opposed to substance).
1. Payment.

2. Life and labor.
3. Surpassing.
4. Nature.
5. For the first time.
6. The same beloved person with regard to our eternal being.
7. Mother of our physical being.
8. Taking on of sensuality.
9. True.
1. Appropriated to.
2. At work.

And therein is a forthspreading[3] by the same grace of length and breadth, of high and of deepness without end. And all is one love.

Chapter 60

But now me behooveth to say a little more of this forthspreading, as I understood, in the meaning of our Lord: how that we be brought again by the motherhood of mercy and grace into our kindly stead, where that we were in,[4] made by the motherhood of kind love, which kind love never leaveth us.

Our kind mother, our gracious mother (for he would[5] all wholly become our mother in all thing) he took the ground of his work full low[6] and full mildly in the maiden's womb. And that showed he first, where he brought that meek maiden before the eye of my understanding, in the simple stature as she was when she conceived;[7] that is to say our high god, the sovereign wisdom of all, in this low place he arrayed him and dight him[8] all ready in our poor flesh, himself to do the service, he and the office of motherhood in all thing. The mother's service is nearest, readiest, and surest: nearest for it is most of kind, readiest for it is most of love, and sikerest[9] for it is most of truth. This office ne might nor could never none doon to the full but he alone. We wit[1] that all our mothers bear us to pain and to dying. Ah, what is that? But our very Mother Jesu, he alone beareth us to joy and to endless living, blessed moot[2] he be. Thus he sustaineth us within him in love and travail, into the full time that he would suffer the sharpest thorns and grievous pains that ever were or ever shall be, and died at the last. And when he had done, and so borne us to bliss, yet might not all this make aseeth[3] to his marvelous love. And that showed he in these high overpassing words of love: "If I might suffer more I would suffer more."[4] He might no more die, but he would not stint[5] working.

Wherefore him behooveth to find[6] us, for the dearworthy love of motherhood hath made him debtor to us.[7] The mother may give her child sucken her milk, but our precious mother Jesu, he may feed us with himself, and doth full courteously and full tenderly with the blessed sacrament, that is precious food of very life; and with all the sweet sacraments he sustaineth us full mercifully and graciously, and so meant he in these blessed words, where he said: "I it am that holy church preacheth thee and teacheth thee." That is to say: All the health and the life of sacraments, all the virtue and the grace of my word, all the goodness that is ordained in holy church to thee, I it am.

The mother may lay her child tenderly to her breast, but our tender mother Jesu, he may homely lead us into his blessed breast by his sweet open side,[8] and show us therein in party of[9] the godhead and the joys of heaven with

3. (Infinite) spreading out, expansion.
4. The natural condition, i.e., the state of grace, that we were in originally.
5. Because he wanted to.
6. I.e., he laid the groundwork for his mission in a very humble place.
7. The appearance of the Virgin in Julian's first vision. See chapter 4, p. 358.
8. Arrayed and dressed himself.
9. Surest.
1. Know.

2. May.
3. Bring satisfaction.
4. These and other quotations refer back to Julian's earlier revelations.
5. Stop.
6. Nourish, feed.
7. As any mother is obligated to look after her child.
8. The wound inflicted by a soldier in John 19.34.
9. A part of.

ghostly sureness of endless bliss. And that showed he in the tenth revelation, giving the same understanding in this sweet word where he sayeth: "Lo, how I love thee." * * *

This fair lovely word "Mother," it is so sweet and so kind in itself that it may not verily be said of none ne to none but of him and to him[1] that is very mother of life and of all. To the property of motherhood longeth[2] kind love, wisdom, and knowing, and it is God. For though it be so that our bodily forthbringing be but little, low, and simple in regard[3] of our ghostly forth-bringing, yet it is he that doth it in the creatures by whom that it is done. The kind loving mother that woot and knoweth the need of her child, she keepeth it full tenderly as the kind and condition of motherhood will. And ever as it waxeth[4] in age and in stature, she changeth her works but not her love. And when it is waxed of more age, she suffereth it that it be chastised in breaking down of vices to make the child receive virtues and grace. This working with all that be fair and good, our Lord doth it in hem by whom it is done. Thus he is our mother in kind by the working of grace in the lower party for love of the higher. And he will[5] that we know it, for he will have all our love fastened to him; and in this I saw that all debt that we owe by God's bidding to fatherhood and motherhood is fulfilled in true loving of God, which blessed love Christ worketh in us. And this was showed in all, and namely in the words where he sayeth: "I it am that thou lovest."

Chapter 61

And in our ghostly forthbringing he useth more tenderness in keeping without any comparison, by as much as our soul is of more price in his sight. He kindleth our understanding, he prepareth our ways, he easeth our con-science, he comforteth our soul, he lighteth our heart and giveth us in party knowing and loving in his blessedful godhead, with gracious mind in his sweet manhood and his blessed passion, with courteous marveling in his high overpassing goodness, and maketh us to love all that he loveth for his love, and to be well apaid[6] with him and with all his works. And when we fall, hastily he raiseth us by his lovely becleping[7] and his gracious touching. And when we be strengthened by his sweet working, then we wilfully[8] choose him by his grace to be his servants and his lovers, lastingly without end.

And yet after this he suffereth some of us to fall more hard and more grievously than ever we did before, as us thinketh. And then ween[9] we (that be not all wise) that all were nought that we have begun. But it is not so, for it needeth us to fall, and it needeth us to see it; for if we fell not, we should not know how feeble and how wretched we be of ourself, nor also we should not so fulsomely[1] know the marvelous love of our maker.

For we shall verily see in heaven without end that we have grievously sinned in this life; and notwithstanding this we shall verily see that we were never hurt in his love, nor we were never the less of price in his sight. And by the assay of this falling we shall have an high and a marvelous knowing

---

1. Other manuscripts read "her," with reference to the Virgin.
2. Belongs.
3. In comparison with.
4. Grows.
5. Wants.
6. Pleased.
7. Calling (to us).
8. Gladly.
9. Suppose.
1. Fully.

of love in God without an end. For hard and marvelous is that love which may not nor will not be broken for[2] trespass.

And this was one understanding of profit; and other[3] is the lowness and meekness that we shall get by the sight of our falling, for thereby we shall highly be raised in heaven, to which rising we might never have come without that meekness. And therefore it needed us to see it; and if we see it not, though we fell it should not profit us. And commonly first we fall and sithen[4] we see it; and both is of the mercy of God.

The mother may suffer the child to fall sometime and be diseased[5] in diverse manner of peril come to her child for love. And though our earthly mother may suffer her child to perish, our heavenly mother Jesu may never suffer us that be his children to perish, for he is all mighty, all wisdom, and all love, and so is none but he, blessed mote he be.

But oft times when our falling and our wretchedness is showed to us, we be so sore adread and so greatly ashamed of ourself that unnethes[6] we wit where that we may hold us. But then will not our courteous mother that we flee away, for him were nothing loather;[7] for then he will that we use[8] the condition of a child. For when it is diseased and afeared, it runneth hastily to the mother; and if it may do no more, it crieth on the mother for help with all the might. So will he that we do as the meek child, saying thus: "My kind mother, my gracious mother, my dearworthy mother, have mercy on me. I have made myself foul and unlike to thee, and I may not nor can amend it but with thine help and grace."

And if we feel us not then eased, as soon be we sure that he useth[9] the condition of a wise mother. For if he see that it be for profit to us to mourn and to weep, he suffereth with ruth[1] and pity, into the best time,[2] for love. And he will then that we use the property of a child that ever more kindly trusteth to the love of the mother in weal and in woe. And he will that we take us mightily to the faith of holy church and find there our dearworthy mother in solace and true understanding with all the blessed common.[3] For one singular person may oftentimes be broken, as it seemeth to the self, but the whole body of holy church was never broken, nor never shall be without end. And therefore a sure thing it is, a good and a gracious, to willen meekly and mightily been fastened and oned to our mother holy church, that is Christ Jesu. For the flood of his mercy that is his dearworthy blood and precious water is plenteous to make us fair and clean. The blessed wounds of our savior be open and enjoy[4] to heal us. The sweet gracious hands of our mother be ready and diligent about us; for he in all this working useth the very office of a kind nurse that hath not else to do but to entend[5] the salvation of her child.

It is his office to save us, it is his worship to do it, and it is his will we know it; for he will we love him sweetly and trust in him meekly and mightily. And this showed he in these gracious words: "I keep thee full surely."

2. Because of.
3. Another.
4. Then.
5. Unhappy.
6. Scarcely.
7. Nothing would be more hateful to him.
8. He wants us to experience.

9. Right away we are sure he is practicing.
1. Compassion.
2. Until the right time.
3. Community.
4. Rejoice.
5. Be busy about.

[CONCLUSION]

Chapter 86

This book is begun by God's gift and his grace, but it is not yet performed,[6] as to my sight. For charity, pray we all together with God's working, thanking, trusting, enjoying, for thus will our good Lord be prayed, but the understanding that I took in all his own meaning, and in the sweet words where he sayeth full merrily: "I am ground of thy beseeching." For truly I saw and understood in our Lord's meaning that he showed it for he will have it known more than it is. In which knowing he will give us grace to love him and cleave to him, for he beheld his heavenly treasure with so great love on earth that he will give us more light, and solace in heavenly joy, in drawing of our hearts fro sorrow and darkness which we are in.

And fro the time that it was showed, I desired oftentimes to wit[7] in what was our Lord's meaning. And fifteen year after and more, I was answered in ghostly understanding, saying thus: "What, wouldst thou wit thy Lord's meaning in this thing? Wit it well, love was his meaning. Who showeth it thee? Love. What showed he thee? Love. Wherefore showeth he it thee? For love. Hold thee therein, thou shalt wit more in the same. But thou shalt never wit therein other withouten end."

Thus was I learned,[8] that love is our Lord's meaning. And I saw full surely in this and in all, that ere God made us he loved us, which love was never slaked[9] ne never shall. And in this love he hath done all his works, and in this love he hath made all things profitable to us, and in this love our life is everlasting. In our making we had beginning, but the love wherein he made us was in him fro without beginning. In which love we have our beginning, and all this shall we see in God withouten end.

Deo gracias. Explicit liber revelacionum Julyane anacorite Norwyche, cuius anime propicietur deus.[1]

ca. 1390

---

6. Completed.
7. Know.
8. Taught.
9. Abated.

1. Thanks be to God. Here ends the book of revelations of Julian, anchorite of Norwich, on whose soul may god have mercy.

MARGERY KEMPE *there were strong women*
ca. 1373–1438

The Book of Margery Kempe is the spiritual autobiography of a medieval laywoman, telling of her struggles to carry out instructions for a holy life that she claimed to have received in personal visions from Christ and the Virgin Mary. The assertion of such a mission by a married woman, the mother of fourteen children, was in itself sufficient grounds for controversy; in addition, Kempe's outspoken defense of her visions as well as her highly emotional style of religious expression embroiled her with fellow citizens and pilgrims and with the church, although she also won both lay and clerical supporters. Ordered by the archbishop of York to swear not to teach in his diocese, she courageously stood up for her freedom to speak her conscience.

Margery Kempe was the daughter of John Burnham, five-time mayor of King's Lynn, a thriving commercial town in Norfolk. At about the age of twenty she married John Kempe, a well-to-do fellow townsman. After the traumatic delivery of her first child—the rate of maternal mortality in childbirth was high—she sought to confess to a priest whose harsh, censorious response precipitated a mental breakdown, from which she eventually recovered through the first of her visions. Her subsequent conversion and strict religious observances generated a good deal of domestic strife, but she continued to share her husband's bed until, around the age of forty, she negotiated a vow of celibacy with him, which was confirmed before the bishop and left her free to undertake a pilgrimage to the Holy Land. There she experienced visions of Christ's passion and of the sufferings of the Virgin. These visions recurred during the rest of her life, and her noisy weeping at such times made her the object of much scorn and hostility. Her orthodoxy was several times examined, as in her encounter with the archbishop of York, but her unquestioning acceptance of the church's doctrines and authority, and perhaps also her status as a former mayor's daughter, shielded her against charges of heresy.

Like the Wife of Bath in *The Canterbury Tales*, Kempe was unable to read or write but acquired her command of Scripture and theology from sermons and other oral sources. Late in her life, she dictated her story in two parts to two different scribes; the latter of these was a priest who revised the whole text. Nevertheless, it seems likely that the work retains much of the characteristic form and expression of its author.

Kempe was an exceptional woman and was regarded by many of her contemporaries as an eccentric and even a heretic. The generally accepted way for a woman to follow a religious vocation was for her to enter a convent or to become a recluse like Julian of Norwich, author of a profound mystical treatise *A Book of Showings* (p. 355). Kempe tells of her visit to the famous anchoress; the two women talked, and Julian seems to have understood and approved of Kempe's way of life. Modern scholars have linked that way of life to patterns of late medieval religious experience. In particular, she exemplifies the affective piety advocated by the Franciscans, which emphasized the importance of love through a direct experiential knowledge of Christ by every Christian. *The Book of Margery Kempe* is a remarkable record of the powerful and potentially liberating effect this doctrine exercised on the fifteenth-century laity and on women in particular.

bombast: padding to accentuate certain areas of the body.

From The Book of Margery Kempe[1]

[THE BIRTH OF HER FIRST CHILD AND HER FIRST VISION]

When this creature[2] was twenty year of age or somedeal more, she was married to a worshipful burgess and was with child within short time, as kind[3] would. And after that she had conceived, she was labored with great accesses[4] till the child was born, and then, what for labor she had in childing and for sickness going before, she despaired of her life, weening[5] she might not live. And then she sent for her ghostly father,[6] for she had a thing in

1. The text is based on the unique manuscript, first discovered in 1934, edited by Sanford B. Meech and Hope Emily Allen, but has been freely edited. Spelling has been modernized. The selections here given are from Chapters 1, 2, 11, 18, 28, 52, and 76.
2. Throughout the book Kempe refers to herself

in the third person as "this creature," a standard way of saying "this person, a being created by God."
3. Nature.
4. Fits of pain.
5. Supposing.
6. Spiritual father, i.e., a priest.

conscience which she had never showed before that time in all her life. For she was ever letted[7] by her enemy, the Devil, evermore saying to her while she was in good heal[8] her needed no confession but [to] do penance by herself alone, and all should be forgiven, for God is merciful enow. And therefore this creature oftentimes did great penance in fasting bread and water and other deeds of alms with devout prayers, save she would not show it in confession. And when she was any time sick or diseased, the Devil said in her mind that she should be damned for she was not shriven of that default.[9] Wherefore after that her child was born she, not trusting her life, sent for her ghostly father, as said before, in full will to be shriven of all her lifetime as near as she could. And, when she came to the point for to say that thing which she had so long concealed, her confessor was a little too hasty and gan sharply to undernim[1] her ere that she had fully said her intent, and so she would no more say for nought he might do.

And anon for dread she had of damnation on that one side and his sharp reproving on that other side, this creature went out of her mind and was wonderly vexed and labored with spirits half year eight weeks and odd days. And in this time she saw, as her thought, devils open their mouths all inflamed with burning lows[2] of fire as they should 'a swallowed her in, sometime ramping[3] at her, sometime threating her, sometime pulling her and hauling her both night and day during the foresaid time. And also the devils cried upon her with great threatings and bade her she should forsake her Christendom, her faith, and deny her God, his Mother, and all the saints in Heaven, her good works and all good virtues, her father, her mother, and all her friends. And so she did. She slandered her husband, her friends, and her own self; she spoke many a reprevous word and many a shrewd[4] word; she knew no virtue nor goodness; she desired all wickedness; like as the spirits tempted her to say and do so she said and did. She would 'a fordone[5] herself many a time at their steering[6] and 'a been damned with them in Hell, and into witness thereof she bit her own hand so violently that it was seen all her life after. And also she rived[7] her skin on her body again her heart with her nails spiteously,[8] for she had none other instruments, and worse she would 'a done save she was bound and kept with strength both day and night that she might not have her will.

And when she had long been labored in this and many other temptations that men weened she should never 'a scaped[9] or lived, then on a time as she lay alone and her keepers were from her, our merciful Lord Christ Jesu, ever to be trusted (worshiped be his name) never forsaking his servant in time of need, appeared to his creature, which had forsaken him, in likeness of a man, most seemly, most beauteous, and most amiable that ever might be seen with man's eye, clad in a mantle of purple silk, sitting upon her bed's side, looking upon her with so blessed a cheer[1] that she was strengthened in all her spirits, said to her these words: "Daughter, why hast thou forsaken

7. Prevented.
8. Health.
9. Sin.
1. Rebuke. "Gan": began.
2. Blazes.
3. Raising their arms.
4. Wicked. "Reprevous": reproachful.

5. Destroyed.
6. Direction.
7. Tore.
8. Cruelly.
9. Escaped.
1. Expression.

me, and I forsook never thee?" And anon as he had said these words she saw verily how the air opened as bright as any levin,[2] and he sty[3] up into the air, not right hastily and quickly, but fair and easily that she might well behold him in the air till it was closed again. And anon the creature was stabled[4] in her wits and in her reason as well as ever she was before, and prayed her husband as so soon as he came to her that she might have the keys of the buttery[5] to take her meat and drink as she had done before.

[HER PRIDE AND ATTEMPTS TO START A BUSINESS]

And when this creature was thus graciously come again to her mind, she thought she was bound to God and that she would be his servant. Nevertheless, she would not leave her pride nor her pompous array that she had used beforetime, neither for her husband nor for none other man's counsel. And yet she wist full well that men said her full much villainy, for she wore gold pipes on her head and her hoods with the tippets were dagged.[6] Her cloaks also were dagged and laid with divers colors between the dags that it should be the more staring[7] to men's sight and herself the more be worshiped. And when her husband would speak to her for to leave her pride she answered shrewdly and shortly and said that she was come of worthy kindred—him seemed never for to 'a wedded her[8]—for her father was sometime mayor of the town N and sithen[9] he was alderman of the high Gild of the Trinity in N.[1] And therefore she would save[2] the worship of her kindred whatsoever any man said. She had full great envy at her neighbors that they should be arrayed as well as she. All her desire was for to be worshiped of the people. She would not beware by one's chastening nor be content with the good that God had sent her, as her husband was, but ever desired more and more.

And then, for pure covetise[3] and for to maintain her pride, she gan to brew and was one of the greatest brewers in the town N a three year or four till she lost much good,[4] for she had never ure[5] thereto. For though she had never so good servants and cunning[6] in brewing, yet it would never prove[7] with them. For when the ale was as fair standing under barm[8] as any man might see, suddenly the barm would fall down[9] that all the ale was lost every brewing after other, that her servants were ashamed and would not dwell with her. Then this creature thought how God had punished her beforetime and she could not beware, and now eftsoons[1] by losing of her goods, and then she left and brewed no more. And then she asked her husband mercy for she would not follow his counsel aforetime, and she said that her pride was cause of all her punishing and she would amend that she had trespassed with good will.

---

2. Flash of lightning.
3. Ascended.
4. Made stable.
5. Pantry.
6. I.e., her hoods were ornamented with loose bands of cloth ("tippets") and slashed according to high fashion of the time. "Pipes": tubular head ornaments.
7. Obtrusive.
8. It never became him to have married her.
9. Afterward.

1. The merchant guild of Lynn was the Guild of the Holy Trinity.
2. Maintain.
3. Avarice.
4. Wealth.
5. Experience [in brewing].
6. Skill.
7. Turn out well.
8. The froth or head.
9. I.e., go flat.
1. Again.

[MARGERY AND HER HUSBAND REACH A SETTLEMENT][2]

It befell upon a Friday on Midsummer Even in right hot weather, as this creature was coming from York-ward[3] bearing a bottle with beer in her hand and her husband a cake in his bosom, he asked his wife this question: "Margery, if there came a man with a sword and would smite off my head unless that I should commune kindly[4] with you as I have done before, say me truth of your conscience—for ye say ye will not lie—whether would ye suffer my head to be smit off or else suffer me to meddle with you again as I did sometime?" "Alas, sir," she said, "why move[5] ye this matter and have we been chaste this eight weeks?" "For I will wit[6] the truth of your heart." And then she said with great sorrow, "Forsooth, I had liefer[7] see you be slain than we should turn again to our uncleanness." And he said again, "Ye are no good wife."

And then she asked her husband what was the cause that he had not meddled with her eight weeks before, sithen[8] she lay with him every night in his bed. And he said he was so made afeared when he would 'a touched her that he durst no more do. "Now, good sir, amend you and ask God mercy, for I told you near three year sithen that ye should be slain suddenly, and now is this the third year, and yet I hope I shall have my desire. Good sir, I pray you grant me that I shall ask, and I shall pray for you that ye shall be saved through the mercy of our Lord Jesu Christ, and ye shall have more meed[9] in Heaven than if ye wore a hair or a habergeon.[1] I pray you, suffer me to make a vow of chastity in what bishop's hand that God will." "Nay," he said, "that will I not grant you, for now I may use you without deadly sin and then might I not so." Then she said again, "If it be the will of the Holy Ghost to fulfill that I have said, I pray God ye might consent thereto; and if it be not the will of the Holy Ghost, I pray God ye never consent thereto."

Then went they forth to-Bridlington-ward[2] in right hot weather, the foresaid creature having great sorrow and great dread for her chastity. And as they came by a cross, her husband set him down under the cross, cleping[3] his wife unto him and saying these words unto her, "Margery, grant me my desire, and I shall grant you your desire. My first desire is that we shall lie still together in one bed as we have done before; the second that ye shall pay my debts ere ye go to Jerusalem; and the third that ye shall eat and drink with me on the Friday as ye were wont to do."[4] "Nay, sir," she said, "to break the Friday I will never grant you while I live." "Well," he said, "then shall I meddle with you again."

She prayed him that he would give her leave to make her prayers, and he granted it goodly. Then she knelt down beside a cross in the field and prayed in this manner with great abundance of tears, "Lord God, thou knowest all

---

2. Despite her resolution, Kempe made one more attempt to run a profitable business: she set up a horse mill to grind grain, but the horses refused to draw, and the enterprise was as disastrous as her brewing had been. After that she did indeed reform.
3. The direction of York.
4. In the way of nature.
5. Bring up.
6. Learn.

7. Rather.
8. Since.
9. Reward.
1. Hair shirt or mail shirt.
2. In the direction of Bridlington.
3. Calling.
4. Christ had told her that keeping a strict Friday fast would allow her to have her wish to end further sexual relations with her husband.

thing; thou knowest what sorrow I have had to be chaste in my body to thee all this three year, and now might I have my will and I dare not for love of thee. For if I would break that manner of fasting which thou commandest me to keep on the Friday without meat[5] or drink, I should now have my desire. But, blessed Lord, thou knowest I will not contrary thy will, and mickle[6] now is my sorrow unless that I find comfort in thee. Now, blessed Jesu, make thy will known to me unworthy that I may follow thereafter and fulfil it with all my might." And then our Lord Jesu Christ with great sweetness spoke to this creature, commanding her to go again to her husband and pray him to grant her that she desired, "And he shall have that he desireth. For, my dearworthy daughter, this was the cause that I bade thee fast for thou shouldest the sooner obtain and get thy desire, and now it is granted thee. I will no longer thou fast, therefore I bid thee in the name of Jesu eat and drink as thy husband doth."

Then this creature thanked our Lord Jesu Christ of his grace and his goodness, sithen[7] rose up and went to her husband, saying unto him, "Sir, if it like[8] you, ye shall grant me my desire and ye shall have your desire. Granteth me that ye shall not come in my bed, and I grant you to quit your debts ere I go to Jerusalem. And maketh my body free to God so that ye never make no challenging in me[9] to ask no debt of matrimony after this day while ye live, and I shall eat and drink on the Friday at your bidding." Then said her husband again to her, "As free may your body be to God as it hath been to me." This creature thanked God greatly, enjoying that she had her desire, praying her husband that they should say three Pater Noster[1] in the worship of the Trinity for the great grace that he had granted them. And so they did, kneeling under a cross, and sithen they ate and drank together in great gladness of spirit. This was on a Friday on Midsummer Even.

[A VISIT WITH JULIAN OF NORWICH][2]

And then she was bidden by our Lord for to go to an anchoress in the same city, which hight[3] Dame Julian. And so she did and showed her the grace that God put in her soul of compunction, contrition, sweetness and devotion, compassion with holy meditation and high contemplation, and ful many holy speeches and dalliance[4] that our Lord spoke to her soul, and many wonderful revelations which she showed to the anchoress to wit[5] if there were any deceit in them, for the anchoress was expert in such things and good counsel could give.

The anchoress, hearing the marvelous goodness of our Lord, highly thanked God with all her heart for his visitation, counseling this creature to be obedient to the will of our Lord God and fulfill with all her mights whatever he put in her soul if it were not again[6] the worship of God and profit of her even-Christians,[7] for, if it were, then it were not the moving of a good

---

5. Food.
6. Much.
7. Afterward.
8. Please.
9. Make my body free to [be possessed by] God so that you never call me to account. Kempe uses legal terminology.

1. "Our Father," i.e, the Lord's Prayer.
2. See the headnote for Julian of Norwich (p. 355).
3. Who was called.
4. Conversation.
5. Know.
6. Against.
7. Fellow Christians.

spirit but rather of an evil spirit: "The Holy Ghost moveth never a thing again charity,[8] and, if he did, he were contrarious to his own self, for he is all charity. Also he moveth a soul to all chasteness, for chaste livers be cleped[9] the temple of the Holy Ghost, and the Holy Ghost maketh a soul stable and steadfast in the right faith and the right belief. And a double man in soul is ever unstable and unsteadfast in all his ways. He that is evermore doubting is like to the flood of the sea, the which is moved and borne about with the wind, and that man is not like to receive the gifts of God. What creature that hath these tokens, he must steadfastly believe that the Holy Ghost dwelleth in his soul. And much more, when God visiteth a creature with tears of contrition, devotion, or compassion, he may and ought to leve[1] that the Holy Ghost is in his soul. Saint Paul saith that the Holy Ghost asketh for us with mournings and weepings unspeakable,[2] that is to say, he maketh us to ask and pray with mournings and weepings so plentivously[3] that the tears may not be numbered. There may no evil spirit give these tokens, for Jerome saith that tears torment more the Devil than do the pains of Hell. God and the Devil been evermore contrarious, and they shall never dwell together in one place, and the Devil hath no power in a man's soul. Holy Writ saith that the soul of a rightful man is the seat of God, and so I trust sister that ye been. I pray God grant you perseverance. Set all your trust in God and fear not the language of the world, for the more despite, shame, and reproof that ye have in the world, the more is your merit in the sight of God. Patience is necessary unto you, for in that shall ye keep your soul."

Much was the holy dalliance that the anchoress and this creature had by communing in the lof[4] of our Lord Jesu Christ many days that they were together.

[PILGRIMAGE TO JERUSALEM]

* * * And so they[5] went forth into the Holy Land till they might see Jerusalem. And when this creature saw Jerusalem, riding on an ass, she thanked God with all her heart, praying him for his mercy that like as he had brought her to see this earthly city Jerusalem, he would grant her grace to see the blissful city Jerusalem above, the city of Heaven. Our Lord Jesu Christ, answering to her thought, granted her to have her desire. Then for joy that she had and the sweetness that she felt in the dalliance[6] of our Lord, she was in point to 'a fallen off her ass, for she might not bear the sweetness and grace that God wrought in her soul. Then twain[7] pilgrims of Dutchmen went to her and kept her from falling, of which the one was a priest. And he put spices in her mouth to comfort her, weening[8] she had been sick. And so they helped her forth to Jerusalem. And when she came there, she said, "Sirs, I pray you be not displeased though I weep sore in this holy place where our Lord Jesu Christ was quick[9] and dead."

Then went they to the Temple in Jerusalem, and they were let in that one day at evensong time and they abide there till the next day at evensong time.

8. Love.
9. Called (see 1 Corinthians 6.19).
1. Believe.
2. Inarticulate (Romans 8.26).
3. Plentifully.
4. Praise.

5. The company of pilgrims.
6. Conversation.
7. Two.
8. Thinking.
9. Living.

Then the friars lifted up a cross and led the pilgrims about from one place to another where our Lord had suffered his pains and his passions, every man and woman bearing a wax candle in their hand. And the friars always as they went about told them what our Lord suffered in every place.[1] And the foresaid creature wept and sobbed so plentivously[2] as though she had seen our Lord with her bodily eye suffering his Passion at that time. Before her in her soul she saw him verily by contemplation, and that caused her to have compassion. And when they came up onto the Mount of Calvary she fell down that she might not stand nor kneel but wallowed and wrested[3] with her body, spreading her arms abroad, and cried with a loud voice as though her heart should 'a burst asunder, for in the city of her soul she saw verily and freshly how our Lord was crucified. Before her face she heard and saw in her ghostly sight the mourning of our Lady, of St. John and of Mary Magdalene,[4] and of many other that loved our Lord. And she had so great compassion and so great pain to see our Lord's pain that she might not keep herself from crying and roaring though she should 'a been dead therefore.

And this was the first cry that ever she cried in any contemplation. And this manner of crying endured many years after this time for aught that any man might do, and therefore suffered she much despite and much reproof. The crying was so loud and so wonderful that it made the people astoned[5] unless that they had heard it before or else that they knew the cause of the crying. And she had them so oftentimes that they made her right[6] weak in her bodily mights, and namely if she heard of our Lord's Passion. And sometime when she saw the Crucifix, or if she saw a man had a wound or a beast whether[7] it were, or if a man beat a child before her or smote a horse or another beast with a whip, if she might see it or hear it, her thought she saw our Lord be beaten or wounded like as she saw in the man or in the beast, as well in the field as in the town, and by herself alone as well as among the people. First when she had her cryings at Jerusalem, she had them oftentimes, and in Rome also. And when she came home into England, first at her coming home it came but seldom as it were once in a month, sithen[8] once in the week, afterward quotidianly,[9] and once she had fourteen on one day, and another day she had seven, and so as God would visit her, sometime in the church, sometime in the street, sometime in the chamber, sometime in the field when God would send them, for she knew never time nor hour when they should come. And they came never without passing[1] great sweetness of devotion and high contemplation. And as soon as she perceived that she should cry, she would keep it in as much as she might that the people should not 'a heard it for noying[2] of them. For some said it was a wicked spirit vexed her; some said it was a sickness; some said she had drunken too much wine; some banned[3] her; some wished she had been in the haven;[4] some would she had been in the sea in a bottomless boat; and so each man as him thought. Other ghostly[5] men loved her and favored her the more.

[Marginal note, right:] she had visions of the lord.

[Marginal note, right:] empathy

[Marginal note, right:] people now fear her.

[Marginal note, right:] she is very compassionate.

[Marginal note, left:] "that" whatever lowliest creature / christ said to the lowiest to do

---

1. I.e., in Jerusalem.
2. Plentifully.
3. Twisted and turned.
4. Mary, St. John, and Mary Magdalene are traditionally portrayed at the foot of the Cross in medieval art. See John 19.25.
5. Astonished.
6. Especially.

7. Whichever.
8. After.
9. Daily.
1. Surpassing.
2. Annoying.
3. Cursed.
4. Harbor.
5. Spiritual.

Some great clerks[6] said our Lady cried never so, nor no saint in Heaven, but they knew full little what she felt, nor they would not believe but that she might 'a abstained her from crying if she had wished.

[EXAMINATION BEFORE THE ARCHBISHOP]

There was a monk should preach in York, the which had heard much slander and much evil language of the said creature. And when he should preach, there was much multitude of people to hear him, and she present with them. And so when he was in his sermon, he rehearsed[7] many matters so openly that the people conceived well that it was for cause of her, wherefore her friends that loved her well were full sorry and heavy thereof, and she was much the more merry, for she had matter to prove her patience and her charity wherethrough she trusted to please our Lord Christ Jesu. When the sermon was done, a doctor of divinity which loved her well with many other also came to her and said, "Margery, how have ye done this day?" "Sir," she said, "right well, blessed be God. I have cause to be right merry and glad in my soul that I may anything suffer for his love, for he suffered much more for me."

Anon after came a man which loved her right well of good will with his wife and other more and led her seven mile thence to the Archbishop of York,[8] and brought her into a fair chamber, where came a good clerk, saying to the good man which had brought her thither, "Sir, why have ye and your wife brought this woman hither? She shall steal away from you, and then shall ye have a villainy[9] of her." The good man said, "I dare well say she will abide and be at her answer[1] with good will."

On the next day she was brought into the Archbishop's Chapel, and there came many of the Archbishop's meinie, despising her, calling her "loller"[2] and "heretic," and swore many an horrible oath that she should be burnt. And she through the strength of Jesu said again to them, "Sirs, I dread me ye shall be burnt in hell without end, unless that ye amend you of your oaths-swearing, for ye keep not the commandments of God. I would not swear as ye do for all the good[3] of this world." Then they went away as they had been ashamed. She then, making her prayer in her mind, asked grace so to be demeaned[4] that day as was most pleasance[5] to God and profit to her own soul and good example to her even-Christians.[6] Our Lord, answering her, said it should be right well.

At the last the said Archbishop came into the Chapel with his clerks and sharply he said to her, "Why goest thou in white? Art thou a maiden?" She, kneeling on her knees before him, said, "Nay, sir, I am no maiden; I am a wife." He commanded his men to fetch a pair of fetters and said she should be fettered, for she was a false heretic. And then she said, "I am none heretic, nor ye shall none prove me." The Archbishop went away and let her stand alone. Then she made her prayers to our Lord God almighty for to help her

6. Clerics.
7. Repeated.
8. The archbishop was at this time residing not in York but at his palace in Cawood.
9. Slander.
1. Answer charges against her.

2. Lollard: a follower of the reformer John Wycliffe. "Meinie": household.
3. Property.
4. Treated.
5. Pleasing.
6. Fellow Christians.

and succor her against all her enemies, ghostly and bodily, a long while, and her flesh trembled and quaked wonderly that she was fain[7] to put her hands under her clothes that it should not be espied.

Sithen[8] the Archbishop came again into the Chapel with many worthy clerks, amongst which was the same doctor[9] which had examined her before and the monk that had preached again her a little time before in York. Some of the people asked whether she were a Christian woman or a Jew; some said she was a good woman, and some said nay. Then the Archbishop took his see,[1] and his clerks also, each of them in his degree, much people being present. And in the time while the people was gathering together and the Archbishop taking his see, the said creature stood all behind, making her prayers for help and succor against her enemies with high devotion so long that she melted all into tears. And at the last she cried loud therewith that the Archbishop and his clerks and much people had great wonder of her, for they had not heard such crying before.

When her crying was passed, she came before the Archbishop and fell down on her knees, the Archbishop saying full boistously[2] unto her, "Why weepest thou so, woman?" She answering said, "Sir, ye shall will some day that ye had wept as sore as I." And then anon after the Archbishop put to her the Articles of our Faith,[3] to the which God gave her grace to answer well and truly and readily without any great study so that he might not blame her, then he said to the clerks, "She knoweth her Faith well enough. What shall I do with her?" The clerks said, "We know well that she can[4] the Articles of the Faith, but we will not suffer her to dwell among us, for the people hath great faith in her dalliance, and peradventure[5] she might pervert some of them." Then the Archbishop said unto her, "I am evil informed of thee; I hear say thou art a right wicked woman." And she said again, "Sir, so I hear say that ye are a wicked man. And if ye be as wicked as men say, ye shall never come in Heaven unless that ye amend you while ye be here." Then said he full boistously, "Why, thou wretch, what say men of me?" She answered, "Other men, sir, can tell you well enow." Then said a great clerk with a furred hood, "Peace, thou speak of thyself and let him be."

Sithen said the Archbishop to her, "Lay thine hand on the book here before me and swear that thou shalt go out of my diocese as soon as thou may." "Nay, sir," she said, "I pray you, give me leave to go again into York to take my leave of my friends." Then he gave her leave for one day or two. She thought it was too short a time, wherefore she said again, "Sir, I may not go out of this diocese so hastily, for I must tarry and speak with good men ere I go, and I must, sir, with your leave, go to Bridlington and speak with my confessor, a good man, the which was the good Prior's confessor that is now canonized."[6] Then said the Archbishop to her, "Thou shalt swear that thou shalt not teach nor challenge the people in my diocese." "Nay, sir, I shall not swear," she said, "for I shall speak of God and undernim[7] them that swear great oaths wheresoever I go unto the time that the Pope and Holy Church

---

7. Glad.
8. Then.
9. Doctor of theology.
1. Throne.
2. Coarsely.
3. The twelve separate statements of the Apostles'

Creed.
4. Knows.
5. Perhaps. "Dalliance": conversation.
6. St. John of Bridlington, recently canonized.
7. Reprove.

hath ordained that no man shall be so hardy to speak of God, for God almighty forbids not, sir, that we shall speak of him. And also the Gospel maketh mention that when the woman had heard our Lord preach, she came before him with a loud voice and said, 'Blessed be the womb that thee bore and the teats that gave thee suck.' Then our Lord said again to her, 'Forsooth so are they blessed that hear the word of God and keep it.' And therefore, sir, me thinketh that the Gospel giveth me leave to speak of God." "Ah, sir," said the clerks, "here woot[8] we well that she hath a devil within her, for she speaks of the Gospel." As swithe[9] a great clerk brought forth a book and laid Saint Paul for his party[1] against her that no woman should preach. She answering thereto said, "I preach not, sir, I come in no pulpit. I use but communication and good words, and that will I do while I live." Then said a doctor which had examined her beforetime, "Sir, she told me the worst tales of priests that ever I heard." The Bishop commanded her to tell that tale.

"Sir, with your reverence, I spoke but of one priest by the manner of example, the which, as I have learned, went wil[2] in a wood through the sufferance of God for the profit of his soul till the night came upon him. He, destitute of his harbor,[3] found a fair arbor in the which he rested that night, having a fair pear tree in the midst, all flourished and belished,[4] and blooms full delectable to his sight, where came a bear, great and boisteous,[5] ugly to behold, shaking the pear tree and felling down the flowers. Greedily this grievous beast ate and devoured those fair flowers. And, when he had eaten 'em, turning his tail-end in the priest's presence, voided 'em out again at the hinder part. The priest having great abomination at that loathly sight, conceiving great heaviness[6] for doubt what it might mean, on the next day he wandered forth in his way, all heavy and pensive, whom it fortuned to meet with a seemly aged man like to a palmer or a pilgrim, the which inquired of the priest the cause of his heaviness. The priest, rehearsing the matter before-written, said he conceived great dread and heaviness when he beheld that loathly beast defoul and devour so fair flowers and blooms and afterward so horribly to devoid 'em before him at his tail-end, and he not understanding what this might mean. Then the palmer, showing himself the messenger of God, thus areasoned[7] him: 'Priest, thou thyself art the pear tree, somedeal[8] flourishing and flowering through thy service-saying and the sacraments-ministering, though thou do undevoutly, for thou takest full little heed how thou sayest thy matins and thy service, so it be[9] blabbered to an end. Then goest thou to thy mass without devotion, and for thy sin hast thou full little contrition. Thou receivest there the fruit of everlasting life, the sacrament of the altar, in full feeble disposition. Sithen[1] al the day after thou misspendest thy time, thou givest thee to buying and selling, chopping and changing[2] as it were a man of the world. Thou sittest at the ale, giving thee to gluttony and excess, to lust of thy body through lechery and uncleanness. Thou breakest the commandments of God through swearing, lying, detraction, and back-

8. Know.
9. At once.
1. Side of the argument.
2. Erring.
3. Lacking a place to put up.
4. Blossoming and embellished.
5. Rough.

6. Depression.
7. Addressed.
8. Somewhat.
9. As long as it is.
1. Then.
2. Bargaining and exchanging.

biting, and such other sins using. Thus be thy misgovernance, like unto the loathly bear: thou devourest and destroyest the flowers and blooms of virtuous living to thine endless damnation and many men's hindering, less than[3] thou have grace of repentance and amending.'"

Then the Archbishop liked well the tale and commended it, saying it was a good tale. And the clerk which had examined her beforetime in the absence of the Archbishop said, "Sir, this tale smiteth me to the heart." The foresaid creature said to the clerk, "Ah, worshipful doctor, sir, in place where my dwelling is most is a worthy clerk, a good preacher, which boldly speaketh again the misgovernance[4] of the people and will flatter no man. He sayeth many times in the pulpit, 'If any man be evil-pleased with my preaching, note him well, for he is guilty.' And right so, sir," said she to the clerk, "fare ye by me,[5] God forgive it you." The clerk wist not well what he might say to her. Afterward the same clerk came to her and prayed her of forgiveness that he had so been again her. Also he prayed her specially to pray for him.

And then anon[6] after the Archbishop said, "Where shall I have a man that might lead this woman from me?" As swithe there started up many young men, and every man said of them, "My Lord, I will go with her." The Archbishop answered, "Ye be too young; I will not have you." Then a good sad[7] man of the Archbishop's meinie asked his Lord what he would give him and[8] he should lead her. The Archbishop proffered him five shillings, and the man asked a noble.[9] The Archbishop answering said, "I will not ware[1] so much on her body." "Yes, good sir," said the said creature, "our Lord shall reward you right well again." Then the Archbishop said to the man, "See, here is five shillings, and lead her fast out of this country." She kneeling down on her knees asked his blessing. He, praying her to pray for him, blessed her and let her go. Then she going again to York was received of much people and of full worthy clerks, which enjoyed[2] in our Lord that had given her, not lettered, wit and wisdom to answer so many learned men without villainy or blame, thanking be to God.

[MARGERY NURSES HER HUSBAND IN HIS OLD AGE]

It happed on a time that the husband of the said creature, a man in great age passing three score year,[3] as he would 'a come down of his chamber barefoot and barelegged, he sledered[4] or else failed of his footing and fell down to the ground fro the greses,[5] and his head under him grievously broken and bruised, in so much that he had in his head five tents[6] many days while his head was in healing. And, as God would, it was known to some of his neighbors how he was fallen down of the greses, peradventure[7] through the din and the lushing[8] of his falling. And so they came to him and found him lying with his head under him, half alive, all rowed[9] with blood, never like to 'a spoken with priest ne with clerk but through high grace and miracle.[1]

3. Unless.
4. Against the misconduct.
5. You behave with me.
6. Straightway.
7. Sober.
8. If.
9. A coin worth six shillings and eight pence.
1. Spend.
2. Rejoiced.

3. Sixty years.
4. Slipped.
5. Steps.
6. Swabs for probing wounds.
7. Perchance.
8. Rushing.
9. Streaked.
1. I.e., unlikely to have confessed to a priest and received last rites except by grace.

Then the said creature, his wife, was sent for, and so she came to him. Then was he taken up and his head was sewed, and he was sick a long time after that[2] men weened[3] that he should be dead. And then the people said, if he died, his wife was worthy to be hanged for his death, forasmuch as she might 'a kept him and did not. They dwelled not together, ne they lay not together, for, as is written before, the both with one assent and with free will of their either[4] had made a vow to live chaste. And therefore to enchewen[5] all perils they dwelled and sojourned in diverse places where no suspicion should be had of their incontinence, for first they dwelled together after that they had made their vow, and then the people slandered 'em and said they used their lust and their liking as they did before their vow-making. And when they went out on pilgrimage or to see and speak with other ghostly creatures, many evil folk whose tongues were their own hurt, failing the dread and love of our Lord Jesu Christ,[6] deemed and said that they went rather to woods, groves, or valeys to use[7] the lust of their bodies that the people should not aspie it ne wit it. They, having knowledge of how prone the people was to deem evil of 'em, desiring to avoid all occasion, in as much as they might goodly, by their good will and their both consenting, they parted asunder as touching to their board and their chambers, and weened to board in diverse places. And this was the cause that she was not with him and also that she should not be letted[8] fro her contemplation. And therefore when he had fallen and grievously was hurt, as is said before, the people said if he died, it was worthy that she should[9] answer for his death.

Then she prayed to our Lord that her husband might live a year and she to be delivered out [of] slander if it were His pleasance.[1] Our Lord said to her mind, "Daughter, thou shalt have thy boon, for he shall live, and I have wrought a great miracle for thee that he was not dead. And I bid thee take him home and keep him for my love."

She said, "Nay, good Lord, for I shall then not tend to thee as I do now."

"Yes, daughter," said our Lord, "thou shalt have as much meed[2] for to keep him and help him in his need at home as if thou were in church to make thy prayers. And thou hast said many times that thou wouldst fain keep me. I pray thee now keep him for the love of me, for he hath sometime fulfilled thy will and my will both, and he hath made thy body free to me that thou shouldst serve me and live chaste and clean, and therfore I will that thou be free to help him at his need in my name."

"A, Lord," said she, "for thy mercy grant me grace to obey Thy will and fulfill Thy will and let never my ghostly enemies have no power to let me fro fulfilling of Thy will." Then she took home her husband to her and kept him years after as long as he lived and had full much labor with him, for in his last days he turned childish again and lacked reason, that[3] he could not do his own easement to go to a sege[4] or else he would not, but as a child voided his natural digestion in his linen clothes there he sat by the fire or at the table, whether it were,[5] he would spare no place. And therefore was her labor

---

2. So that.
3. Thought.
4. Each of them.
5. Avoid.
6. I.e., their gossip hurt themselves, [because] lacking in fear and love of Christ.
7. Practice.

8. Prevented.
9. She deserved to.
1. If he pleased.
2. Reward.
3. So that.
4. Stool.
5. Wherever it might be.

much the more in washing and wringing and her costage in firing[6] and letted her full much fro her contemplation that many times she should 'a irked[7] her labor save she bethought her how she in her young age had full many delectable thoughts, fleshly lusts, and inordinate loves to his person.[8] And therefore she was glad to be punished with the same person and took it much the more easily and served him and helped him, as her thought, as she would 'a done Christ himself.

1436–38

6. Expense in firewood.
7. Have resented.

8. Body.

MYSTERY PLAYS

The word *mystery*, as applied to medieval drama, refers to the spiritual mystery of Christ's redemption of humankind, and mystery plays are dramatizations of the Old Testament, which foretells that redemption, and of the New, which recounts it. In England the mysteries were generally composed in cycles containing as many as forty-eight individual plays: a typical cycle would begin with the Creation, continue with the Fall of Man, and proceed through the most significant events of the Old Testament, such as the Flood, to the New Testament, which provided plays on the Nativity, the chief events of Christ's life, the Crucifixion, the Harrowing of Hell (based on sources now deemed apocryphal), and the Last Judgment.

The church had its own drama in Latin, dating back to the tenth century, which developed through the dramatization and elaboration of the liturgy—the regular service—for certain holidays, the Easter morning service in particular. The vernacular drama was once thought to have evolved from the liturgical, passing by stages from the church into the streets of the town. However, even though the vernacular plays at times echo their Latin counterparts and although their authors may have been clerics, the mysteries represent an old and largely independent tradition of vernacular religious drama. As early as the twelfth century a *Play of Adam* in Anglo-Norman French was performed in England, a dramatization of the Fall with highly sophisticated dialogue, characterization, and stagecraft.

During the late fourteenth and the fifteenth centuries the great English mystery cycles, four of which have survived complete, were formed in the towns that, in spite of war and plague, became increasingly prosperous and independent. Most of our knowledge of the plays, apart from the texts themselves, comes through municipal and guild records. Every trade in urban society had its guild, an organization combining the functions of a modern trade union, club, religious society, and political action group. The guilds, which played a major role in the governance of the towns, produced the plays; each guild was responsible for putting on a traditional play during the holidays when the cycles were presented.

The town and guild documents tell us a great deal about the evolution, staging, and all aspects of the production of the cycles. In some of the towns each company had a wagon that served as a stage. The wagon would proceed from one strategic point in the city to another, and the play would be performed a number of times on the same day. The spectators gathered at any one place would never be without a play before them and might see the whole cycle without moving. In other towns, plays were probably acted out in sequence on a platform erected at a single location such as the main city square.

The cycles were performed every year at the time of one of two great early summer festivals—Whitsuntide, the week following the seventh Sunday after Easter, or Corpus Christi, a week later. They served as both religious instruction and entertainment for wide audiences, including unlearned folk like the carpenter in *The Miller's Tale* (lines 405–74), who recalls from them the trouble Noah had getting his wife aboard the ark, but also educated laypeople and clerics, who besides enjoying the sometimes boisterous comedy would find the plays acting out traditional interpretations of Scripture such as the ark as a type, or prefiguration, of the church.

Thus the cycles were public spectacles watched by every layer of society, and they paved the way for the professional theater in the age of Elizabeth I. The rainbow in *Noah's Flood* and the Angel's *Gloria* in the *Shepherds' Play*, with their messages of mercy and hope, unite actors and audience in a common faith. Yet the first shepherd's opening speech, complaining of taxation and the insolent exploitation of farmers by "gentlery-men," shows how the plays also served as vehicles of social criticism and reveal many of the rifts and tensions in the late-medieval social fabric.

The Chester Play of Noah's Flood

The most durable of the four surviving English mystery cycles was that of Chester, which was still occasionally performed when Shakespeare was a boy and was produced for the last time in 1575. The plays, however, remained of great interest to antiquarians and were a source of municipal pride. The five surviving manuscripts are all later than the final performance. Because the cycle had been extensively revised during the sixteenth century, we cannot know what it was like during the medieval period. The text we have is certainly very late. God's lengthy instructions to Noah concerning "clean" and "unclean" beasts reflect a new, probably Protestant, interest in Jewish law, also seen in other plays of the Chester cycle. But the revisers were also concerned to preserve what they felt to be traditional medieval features and, in the case of *Noah's Flood*, to introduce such a feature when it was missing. Thus the entertaining scene in which Noah and his wife quarrel and she gives him a box on the ear is an interpolation based on an old comic tradition that is well attested in the other cycle plays and in Chaucer's *The Miller's Tale*. The Chester play is a typical example of the composite authorship so characteristic of many medieval works, by which a text, passing through many hands and generations, carries with it traces of its past that blend in a rich, although not always smooth mixture. An interesting feature of the play is its stage directions, which show how such business as the animals on the ark was managed. A few additional stage directions are provided in braces.

Noah's Flood[1]

The Waterleaders and Drawers of Dee[2]

CAST OF CHARACTERS

GOD	NOAH'S WIFE
NOAH	SHEM'S WIFE
SHEM	HAM'S WIFE
HAM	JAPHET'S WIFE
JAPHETH	GOSSIPS

And first in some high place—or in the clouds, if it may be—God speaketh to Noah, standing without the ark[3] with all his family.

GOD   I, God, that[4] all this world hath wrought,
    Heaven and earth, and all of nought,
    I see my people in deed and thought
      Are set foully° in sin.   *are mired*
5   My ghost shall not leng in mon,
    That through flesh-liking is my fon,
    But till six score years be comen and gone,
      To look if they will blin.[5]

    Man that I made will I destroy,
10 Beast, worm, and fowl to fly;[6]
    For on earth they do me noy,°   *harm*
      The folk that are thereon.
    It harmes me so hurtfully,°   *grievously*
    The malice that doth now multiply,
15 That sore it grieves me inwardly
      That ever I made mon.

    Therefore Noah, my servant free,°   *noble*
    That righteous man art as I see,
    A ship soon thou shalt make thee
20   Of trees dry and light.
    Little chambers therein thou make
    And binding slitch also thou take;

1. The text is based on that of R. M. Lumiansky and David Mills in *The Chester Mystery Cycle* (1974), but has been freely edited. Spelling has been normalized except in some cases for the sake of rhyme and meter. Stage directions are original except for a few added in braces.
2. The guild responsible for the production of the play, the Waterleaders and Drawers, carted and sold water, a trade appropriate for the producers of Noah's flood.
3. Outside the ark. Evidently the ark is already on stage, although Noah and his family will simulate its building.
4. Who. *That* is used throughout as the relative pronoun.
5. My spirit shall remain with mankind, who through fleshly lust are my foes, only till six score [120] years be come and gone, to see if they will stop [sinning]. I.e., God allows the human race a probationary period to reform (cf. lines 149–50), probably a misunderstanding of Genesis 6.3, where God limits the human life span to 120 years. "Mon": man. In the West-Midland dialect, *a* is rounded before a nasal and rhymes with the vowel of *gone* and *on*. Both spellings *mon* and *man* occur in the manuscripts.
6. Animal, reptile, and bird flying.

Within and without thou ne slake
To annoint it through all thy might.[7]

25   Three hundred cubits it shall be long
And fifty broad to make it strong;
Of height sixty. The meet thou fong;[8]
     Thus measure thou it about.
One window work through thy wit;
30   A cubit of length and breadth make it.
Upon the side a door shall shut,
     For to come in and out.

Eating-places thou make also,
Three roofed chambers on a row,[9]
35   For with water I think to flow°   *drown*
     Man that I can° make.   *did*
Destroyed all the world shall be—
Save thou, thy wife, thy sonnes three,
And their wives also with thee—
40   Shall saved be for thy sake.

NOAH   A, Lord, I thank thee loud and still[1]
That to me art in such will
And spares me and my household to spill.[2]
     As now I soothly° find.   *truly*
45   Thy bidding, Lord, I shall fulfill
Nor never more Thee grieve ne grill,°   *offend*
That such grace has sent me till°   *to me*
     Amonges all mankind.

Have done, you men and women all,
50   Hie° you, lest this water fall,   *haste*
To work this ship, chamber and hall,
     As God hath bidden us do.
SHEM   Father, I am already boun:°   *prepared*
An ax I have, by my crown,[3]
55   As sharp as any in all this town,
     For to go thereto.

HAM   I have a hatchet wonder keen
To bite well, as may be seen;
A better ground,° as I ween,°   *sharpened/think*
60   Is not in all this town.
JAPHETH   And I can well make a pin°   *peg*
And with this hammer knock it in.

---

7. Do not slacken to smear it [to make it water-tight], inside and out, with all your might. "Slitch": mud (for caulking).
8. Take thou the measurement.
9. May refer to three decks, but the text is obscure.
1. Aloud and silent, i.e., at all times.
2. Who are so minded toward me and refrain from destroying me and my household.
3. By my head (an oath).

Go we work but° more din,°   *without/fuss*
        And I am ready boun.

65   NOAH'S WIFE   And we shall bring timber to,°   *thereto*
        For we mun° nothing else do—   *may*
        Woman been weak to underfo°   *undertake*
            Any great travail.°   *labor*
     SHEM'S WIFE   Here is a good hackestock;°   *chopping block*
70   On this you may hewe and knock,
        Shall none be idle in this flock,
            Ne now may no man fail.

     HAM'S WIFE   And I will go gather slitch,°   *pitch*
        The ship for to cleam° and pitch.   *caulk*
75   Annoint° it must be every stitch—   *smeared*
            Board, tree,° and pin.   *mast*
     JAPHETH'S WIFE   And I will gather chippes here
        To make a fire for you in fere,°   *together*
        And for to dighte° your dinner   *prepare*
80   Against° you come in.   *before*

[*Then they make signs as if they were working with different tools.*]

     NOAH   Now in the name of God I begin
        To make the ship that we shall in,°   *go in*
        That we may be ready for to swim°   *float*
            At the coming of the flood.
85   These boards I pin here together
        To bear us safe from the weather
        That we may row both hither and thither
            And safe be from this flood.

        Of this tree will I make a mast
90   Tied with cables that will last,
        With a sail-yard° for each blast,   *spar*
            And each thing in their kind.
        With topcastle⁴ and bowsprit,
        Both cords and ropes I have all meet°   *suitable*
95   To sail forth at the nexte wet;°   *rain*
            This ship is at an end.

     ⟨Wife, in this vessel we shall be kept;
        My children and thou, I would in ye leapt.⁵

4. An armed platform at the masthead. "And each thing in their kind": and each kind of thing (required).
5. I would like you to jump aboard. The behavior of Noah's Wife in the next two stanzas and in lines 193–252, both enclosed in angle brackets, is inconsistent with her cooperation and meek words in lines 65–68 and elsewhere. Nor does it make sense that Noah orders her to board the ark before God tells him to take his family inside. Stylistic evidence strongly suggests that these comic exchanges were added, probably in the early 16th century, to bring the Chester play in line with the tradition of the shrewish and recalcitrant Wife of the other mystery cycles.

NOAH'S WIFE   In faith, Noah, I had as lief thou slept.
100   For all thy frankish fare,
            I will not do after thy rede.[6]
    NOAH   Good wife, do now as I thee bid.
    NOAH'S WIFE   By Christ, not ere I see more need,
            Though thou stand all day and stare.

105   NOAH   Lord, that° women been crabbed ay,°   how/always
            And none are meek, I dare well say.
            That is well seen by me today
                In witness of you each one.[7]
            Good wife, let be all this bear°   behavior
110   That thou makest in this place here,
            For all they ween° that thou art master—   think
            And so thou art, by Saint John.⟩

        GOD   Noah, take thou thy meinie,°   household
            And in the ship hie° that ye be;   hasten
115   For none so righteous man to me
                Is now on earth living.
            Of clean beasts with thee thou take
            Seven and seven ere then thou slake;[8]
            He and she, make to make,°   mate with mate
120   Belive in that thou bring.[9]

            Of beasts unclean two and two,
            Male and female, but mo;°   no more
            Of clean fowls seven also
                The he and she together;
125   Of fowls unclean, twain and no more,
            As I of beasts said before,
            That shall be saved through my lore,°   teaching
                Against° I send this weather.   before

            Of meats° that may be eaten,   foods
130   Into the ship look they be gotten,
            For that may be no way forgotten.
                And do this al bedene.°   at once
            To sustain man and beasts therein.
            Ay till the water cease and blin.°   stop
135   This world is filled full of sin,
                And that is now well seen.

            Seven days been yet coming;°   are yet to come
            You shall have space° them in to bring.   time

6. I'd just as soon have you go to bed. In spite of
your polite ("Frenchified") manner, I won't follow
your direction.
7. As each one of you (i.e., in the audience) witnesses.

8. I.e., seven by seven before you leave off. See
Genesis 7.2–4, where God's instructions follow
Jewish dietary laws. According to Genesis 6.19–21,
Noah is to take only one pair of each.
9. [See] that you bring in quickly.

After that it is my liking
140   Mankind to annoy.°   *afflict*
Forty days and forty nights
Rain shall fall for their unrights,°   *sins*
And that I have made through mights[1]
    Now think I to destroy.

145 NOAH   Lord, at Your bidding I am bain.°   *ready*
Sithen° no other grace will gain,°   *since/avail*
It will I fulfill fain,°   *gladly*
    For gracious I Thee find.
An hundred winters and twenty
150   This ship-making tarried° have I,   *delayed*
If through amendment Thy mercy
    Would fall to mankind.[2]

Have done, ye men and women all;
Hie you lest this water fall,
155   That each beast were in his stall
    And into the ship brought.
Of clean beastes seven shall be,
Of unclean two; thus God bade me.
The flood is nigh, you may well see;
160   Therefore tarry you nought.

[*Then* NOAH *shall go into the ark with all his family, his wife except,
and the ark must be boarded[3] round about. And on the boards all the
beasts and fowls hereafter rehearsed must be painted, that their words
may agree with the pictures.*]

SHEM   Sir, here are lions, leopards in;
Horses, mares, oxen, and swine,
Goats, calves, sheep, and kine
    Here sitten thou may see.
165 HAM   Camels, asses, man may find,
Buck and doe, hart and hind.
All beasts of all manner kind
    Here been, as thinketh me.

JAPHETH   Take here cattes, dogges too,
170   Otters and foxes, fulmarts° also;   *polecats*
Hares hopping gaily can go
    Here have cole° for to eat.   *cabbage*
NOAH'S WIFE   And here are bears, wolves set,
Apes, owls, marmoset,
175   Weasels, squirrels, and ferret;
    Here they eat their meat.°   *food*

1. That [which] I have made through [my] power.
2. If through reform mankind would obtain Thy

mercy (cf. lines 7–8).
3. Supplied with boards.

SHEM'S WIFE   Here are beasts in this house;
　　Here cats maken it crouse;[4]
　　Here a raton,° here a mouse　　　　　　　　　　　*rat*
180　　　That standen near together.
　　HAM'S WIFE   And here are fowles less and more—
　　Herons, cranes, and bittor,°　　　　　　　　　*bittern*
　　Swanes, peacocks—and them before,
　　　Meat for this weather.

185　JAPHETH'S WIFE   Here are cockes, kites, crowes,
　　Rookes, ravens, many rowes,
　　Duckes, curlews, whoever knowes,
　　　Each one in this kind.
　　And here are doves, digges,° drakes,　　　　　　*ducks*
190　Redshanks running through the lakes;
　　And each fowl that leden° makes　　　　　　　　*song*
　　　In this ship man may find.

　　⟨NOAH   Wife, come in. Why stands thou there?
　　Thou art ever froward;[5] that dare I swear.
195　Come, in God's name! Time it were,
　　　For fear lest that we drown!
　　NOAH'S WIFE   Yea, sir, set up your sail
　　And row forth with evil hail;°　　　　　　　　*ill luck*
　　For withouten any fail°　　　　　　　　　　　*doubt*
200　　　I will not out of this town.

　　But° I have my gossips° every one,　　　　*unless/friends*
　　One foot further I will not gone.°　　　　　　　*go*
　　They shall not drown, by Saint John,
　　　And° I may save their life.　　　　　　　　　*if*
205　They loved me full well, by Christ.
　　But thou wilt let them into thy chist,°　　　*ark (chest)*
　　Else row forth, Noah, when thee list°　　　*you please*
　　　And get thee a new wife.

　　NOAH   Shem, son, lo thy mother is wrow;°　　*angry*
210　By God, such another I do not know.
　　SHEM   Father, I shall fetch her in, I trow,°　　*trust*
　　　Withouten any fail.
　　Mother, my father after thee send
　　And bids thee into yonder ship wend.°　　　　　*go*
215　Look up and see the wind,
　　　For we been ready to sail.

　　NOAH'S WIFE   Son, go again to him and say
　　　I will not come therein today.
　　NOAH   Come in, Wife, in twenty devils way,[6]

---

4. Have a merry time.　　　　　　　　　6. In the name of twenty devils.
5. Bold, presumptuous.

220   Or else stand there without.°   *outside*
    HAM   Shall we all fetch her in?
    NOAH   Yea, son, in Christ's blessing and mine,
        I would ye hied you betime,
            For of this flood I stand in doubt.[7]

Song

225   THE GOOD GOSSIPS   The flood comes fleeting in full fast,[8]
        On every side that spreadeth full far.
        For fear of drowning I am aghast;
        Good gossip, let us draw near.

        And let us drink ere we depart,
230   For oftentimes we have done so.
        For at one draught thou drink a quart,
        And so will I do ere I go.

    NOAH'S WIFE   Here is a pottle of Malmsey[9] good and strong;
        It will rejoice both heart and tongue.
235   Though Noah think us never so long,
        Yet we will drink atyte.°   *at once*

    JAPHETH   Mother, we pray you all together—
        For we are here, your own childer°—   *children*
        Come into the ship for fear of the weather,
240   For his love that you bought![1]
    NOAH'S WIFE   That will I not for all your call
        But° I have my gossips all.   *unless*
    SHEM   I° faith, mother, yet thou shall,   *in*
        Whether thou will or nought.   {*Drags her aboard.*}

245   NOAH   Welcome, wife, into this boat.
    NOAH'S WIFE   {*slaps him*} Have thou that for thy note!°   *trouble*
    NOAH   Aha, Mary,[2] this is hot!
        It is good for to be still.
        Ah, children, methinks my boat remeves.°   *moves off*
250   Our tarrying here me highly grieves.
        Over the land the water spreads;
            God do as He will.)

    [*Then they sing and* NOAH *shall speak again.*[3]]

    NOAH   Ah, great God that art so good,
        That° workes not thy will is wood.°   *whoever/crazy*

---

7. I want you to hurry before it's too late because
I'm afraid of the flood.
8. The flood comes flowing in very fast.
9. A sweet wine. "Pottle": two-quart measure.
1. For the love of him who redeemed you (i.e.,

Christ).
2. [By] Mary (an oath).
3. The manuscripts do not indicate what song
Noah and his family sing. A song might originally
have followed after line 192.

255 Now all this world is on a flood.
   As we see well in sight.
   The windows I will shut anon,
   And into my chamber I will gone.
   Till this water, so great one,
260   Is slaked° through Thy might.   *diminished*

[*Then shall* NOAH *shut the window of the ark, and for a little space within the boards he shall be silent; and afterward opening the window and looking round about saying:*]

   Now forty days are fully gone.
   Send a raven I will anon,
   If aughtwhere° earth, tree, or stone   *anywhere*
      Be dry in any place.
265 And if this fowl come not again,
   It is a sign, sooth to sayn,°   *truth to say*
   That dry it is on hill or plain,
      And God hath done some grace.

[*Then he shall send forth a raven, and taking a dove in his hands, let him say:*]

   Ah, Lord, wherever this raven be,
270 Somewhere is dry, well I see;
   But yet a dove, by my lewty,°   *faith*
      After I will send.
   Thou wilt turn again to me,
   For of all fowls that may fle°   *fly*
275   Thou art most meek and hend.°   *gentle*

[*Then he shall send forth the dove; and there shall be another dove in the ship, bearing an olive branch in its mouth, which someone shall let down from the mast into* NOAH's *hands with a rope; and then let* NOAH *say:*]

   Ah, Lord, blessed be thou ay,
   That me hast comfort° thus today.   *comforted*
   By this sight I may well say
      This flood begins to cease.
280 My sweet dove to me brought has
   A branch of olive from some place,
   This betokeneth God has done us some grace,
      And is a sign of peace.

   Ah, Lord, honored must Thou be;
285 All earth dries now I see.
   But yet till thou command me,
      Hence I will not hie.
   All this water is away;

Therefore, as soon as I may,
290   Sacrifice I shall do in fay°   *faith*
    To Thee devoutly.

GOD   Noah, take thy wife anon,
    And thy children every one;
    Out of the ship thou shalt gone,
295   And they all with thee.
    Beasts and all that can fly,
    Out anon they shall hie.
    On earth to grow and multiply.
        I will that it so be.

300 NOAH   Lord, I thank Thee through Thy might;
    Thy bidding shall be done in hight,°   *haste*
    And, as fast as I may dight,°   *get ready*
    I will do Thee honor.
    And to Thee offer sacrifice
305   Therefore comes in all wise,[4]
    For of these beasts that been His,
        Offer I will this store.°   *great number*

[Then, going out of the ark with his whole family he shall take his animals and birds and offer and sacrifice them.]

Lord God in majesty,
That such grace has granted me,
310   Where all was lorn,° safe to be,   *lost*
    Therefore now am I boun,°   *ready*
    My wife, my children, and my meinie,°   *household*
    With sacrifice to honor Thee
    Of beasts, fowls, as Thou mayst see,
315   And full devotioun.

GOD   Noah, to me thou art full able°   *very worthy*
    And thy sacrifice acceptable,
    For I have found thee true and stable,
        On thee now must I min.[5]
320   Wary° earth I will no more   *curse*
    For man's sins that grieve me sore;
    For of youth man full yore
        Has been inclined to sin.[6]

Ye shall now grow and multiply
325   And earth again to edify.°   *replenish*
    Each beast, and fowl that may fly,
        Shall be feared° of you;   *afraid*

4. Is, therefore, becoming in every way.
5. I must now be mindful of you.

6. Because for a very long time man, from his youth, has been inclined to sin.

And fish in sea, all that may flete,°   *swim*
Shall sustain you, I thee beheet;°   *promise*
330   To eat of them ye ne let
    That clean been you may know.[7]

Thereas° ye have eaten before   *whereas*
Trees and roots since ye were bore,°   *born*
Of clean beasts now, less and more,
335   I give you leave to eat—
Save blood and flesh both in fere.[8]
Of wrong dead carrion that is here,
Eat ye not of that in no manner,
    For that ay ye shall let.[9]

340   Manslaughter also ay ye shall flee,
For that is not pleasant unto me.
They that shed blood, he or she,
   Aughtwhere° amongst mankin,°   *anywhere/mankind*
That blood foully shed shall be
345   And vengeance have, that men shall see.
Therefore beware now all ye,
    Ye fall not into that sin.

A forward,° Noah, with thee I make   *covenant*
And all thy seed for thy sake,
350   Of such vengeance for to slake,[1]
    For now I have my will.
Here I beheet thee an hest[2]
That man, woman, fowl, ne beast,
With water while this world shall last
355   I will no more spill.°   *destroy*

My bow° between you and me   *rainbow*
In the firmament shall be
By very° tokening that you may see   *true*
    That such vengeance shall cease.
360   That man ne woman shall never more
Be wasted by water as hath before;[3]
But for sin that grieveth me sore,
    Therefore this vengeance was.

Where cloudes in the welkin° been,   *sky*
365   That ilke° bow shall be seen,   *same*
In tokening that my wrath and teen°   *anger*

---

7. Do not abstain from eating those you know to be clean (Genesis 9.1–3). The eating of meat will henceforth be permissible so long as the dietary laws are observed. "Ye": God speaks not just to Noah but to all the human race.
8. Except for blood and flesh both together (Genesis 9.4).

9. Of wrongly dead carrion (i.e., meat not killed according to dietary law), which is here, of that do not eat at all, for you must always leave that alone.
1. To give over such vengeance (as the flood).
2. Here I make you a promise.
3. Be destroyed by water as has happened.

Shall never thus wroken° be.   *avenged*
The string is turned towards you,
And towards me is bent the bow,[4]
370   That such weather shall never show;[5]
And this beheet° I thee.   *promise*

My blessing now I give thee here,
To thee, Noah, my servant dear,
For vengeance shall no more appear;
375   And now farewell, my darling dear.

The Wakefield Second Shepherds' Play

In putting on the stage biblical shepherds and soldiers, medieval playwrights inevitably and often quite deliberately gave them the appearance and characters of contemporary men and women. No play better illustrates this aspect of the drama than the *Second Shepherds' Play*, so called because it is the second of two Nativity plays that are part of the cycle believed to have been performed at Wakefield in Yorkshire. As the play opens, the shepherds complain about the cold, the taxes, and the high-handed treatment they get from the gentry—evils closer to shepherds on the Yorkshire moors than to those keeping their flocks near Bethlehem. The sophisticated dramatic intelligence at work in this and several other of the Wakefield plays belonged undoubtedly to one individual, who probably revised older, more traditional plays some time during the last quarter of the fifteenth century. His identity is not known, but because of his achievement scholars refer to him as the Wakefield Master. He was probably a highly educated cleric stationed in the vicinity of Wakefield, perhaps a friar of a nearby priory. The Wakefield Master had a genius for combining comedy, including broad farce, with religion in ways that make them enhance one another. In the *Second Shepherds' Play*, by linking the comic subplot of Mak and Gill with the solemn story of Christ's nativity, the Wakefield Master has produced a dramatic parable of what the Nativity means in Christian history and in Christian hearts. No one will fail to observe the parallelism between the stolen sheep, ludicrously disguised as Mak's latest heir, lying in the cradle, and the real Lamb of God, born in the stable among beasts. A complex of relationships based on this relationship suggests itself. But perhaps the most important point is that the charity twice shown by the shepherds—in the first instance to the supposed son of Mak and in the second instance to Mak and Gill when they decide to let them off with only the mildest of punishments—is rewarded when they are invited to visit the Christ Child, the embodiment of charity. The bleak beginning of the play, with its series of individual complaints, is ultimately balanced by the optimistic ending, which sees the shepherds once again singing together in harmony.

The *Second Shepherds' Play* is exceptional among the mystery plays in its development of plot and character. There is no parallel to its elaboration of the comic subplot and no character quite like Mak, who has doubtless been imported into religious drama from popular farce. Mak is perhaps the best humorous character outside of Chaucer's works in this period. A braggart of the worst kind, he has something of Falstaff's charm; and he resembles Falstaff also in his grotesque attempts to maintain the last shreds of his dignity when he is caught in a lie. Most readers will be glad that the shepherds do not carry out their threat to have the death penalty invoked for his crime.

Following the 1994 edition of the Early English Text Society, the stanza, tradition-

---

4. The rainbow is visualized as a bow aimed away   5. [A sign] that such a flood shall never appear.
from the earth at the sky.

ally printed as nine lines (with an opening quatrain of four long lines, the first halves of which rhyme with one another) is rendered here as "thirteeners," rhyming *a b a b a b a b c d d d c*.

The Second Shepherds' Play[1]

CAST OF CHARACTERS

COLL	GILL
GIB	ANGEL
DAW	MARY
MAK	

[A field.]

[Enter COLL]

COLL	Lord, what° these weathers are cold,	*how*
	And I am ill happed;°	*badly covered*
	I am nearhand dold,°	*numb*
	So long have I napped;	
5	My legs they fold,°	*give way*
	My fingers are chapped.	
	It is not as I wold,°	*would (wish)*
	For I am all lapped°	*wrapped*
	In sorrow:	
10	In storms and tempest,	
	Now in the east, now in the west,	
	Woe is him that has never rest	
	Midday nor morrow.	
	But we sely° husbands[2]	*hapless*
15	That walks on the moor,	
	In faith we are nearhands°	*nearly*
	Out of the door.°	*homeless*
	No wonder, as it stands	
	If we be poor,	
20	For the tilth of our lands	
	Lies fallow as the floor,[3]	
	As ye ken.°	*know*
	We are so hammed,	
	Fortaxed, and rammed,	

---

1. The text is based on the (1994) edition by A. C. Cawley and Martin Stevens, but has been freely edited. Spelling has been normalized except where rhyme makes changes impossible. Because the original text has no indications of scenes and only four stage directions, written in Latin, appropriate scenes of action and additional stage directions have been added; the four original stage directions are identified in the notes.
2. Farmers. The shepherds are also tenant farmers.
3. The arable part of our land lies fallow (as flat) as the floor. Landowners were converting farmland to pasture for sheep.

25 We are made hand-tamed
        With these gentlery-men.⁴

        Thus they reave° us our rest—   rob
        Our Lady them wary!°   curse
        These men that are lord-fest,°   attached to lords
30   They cause the plow tarry.⁵
        That, men say, is for the best—
        We find it contrary.
        Thus are husbands oppressed
        In point to miscarry.
35   On live.⁶
        Thus hold they us under,
        Thus they bring us in blunder,°   trouble
        It were a great wonder
            And° ever should we thrive.   if

40   There shall come a swain°   fellow
        As proud as a po:°   peacock
        He must borrow my wain,°   wagon
        My plow also;
        Then I am full fain°   glad
45   To grant ere he go.
        Thus live we in pain,
        Anger, and woe,
            By night and by day.
        He must have if he lang° it,   wants
50   If I should forgang it.⁷
        I were better be hanged
            Than once say him nay.⁸

        For may he get a paint-sleeve⁹
        Or brooch nowadays,
55   Woe is him that him grieve
        Or once again-says.°   gainsays
        Dare no man him reprieve,°   reprove
        What mastery he maes.¹
        And yet may no man lieve°   believe
60   One word that he says,
            No letter.
        He can make purveyance²
        With boast and bragance,°   bragging

4. We are so hamstrung, overtaxed, and beaten down [that] we are made to obey these gentry folk. Coll is complaining about the peasants' hard lot, at the mercy of retainers of the wealthy landowners.
5. Hold up the plow, i.e., interfere with the farm work.
6. In life. "In point to miscarry": to the point of ruin.
7. Even if I have to do without it.
8. In the manuscript, this stanza follows the next.
9. An embroidered sleeve, part of the livery worn by the landlord's officers as a badge of authority.
1. No matter what force he uses.
2. Requisition (of private property).

And all is through maintenance[3]
65   Of men that are greater.

It does me good, as I walk
Thus by mine one,°   *self*
Of this world for to talk
In manner of moan.
70   To my sheep I will stalk,
And hearken anon,
There abide on a balk,[4]
Or sit on a stone,
      Full soon;
75   For I trow,° pardie,°   *think/by God*
True men if they be,
We get more company
      Ere it be noon.[5]

[*Enter* GIB, *who at first does not see* COLL.]

GIB   Benste and Dominus,[6]
80   What may this bemean?°   *mean*
Why fares this world thus?
Such have we not seen.
Lord, these weathers are spiteous°   *cruel*
And the winds full keen,
85   And the frosts so hideous
They water mine een,°   *eyes*
      No lie.
Now in dry, now in wet,
Now in snow, now in sleet,
90   When my shoon° freeze to my feet   *shoes*
      It is not all easy.

But as far as I ken,°   *see*
Or yet as I go,°   *walk*
We sely° wedmen°   *hapless/married men*
95   Dree° mickle° woe;   *suffer/much*
We have sorrow then and then°—   *constantly*
It falls oft so.
Sely Copple, our hen,[7]
Both to and fro
100   She cackles;
But begin she to croak,
To groan or to cluck,

3. Practice of retaining servants under a noble-man's protection with the power to lord it over his tenants.
4. A raised strip of grassland dividing parts of a field.
5. I.e., if the other shepherds keep their promise to meet Coll.
6. Bless us and Lord.
7. Silly Copple, our hen, i.e., Gib's wife, who hen-pecks him.

Woe is him is our cock,
　For he is in the shackles.

105　These men that are wed
　　Have not all their will:
　　When they are full hard stead°　　　　　　　　　beset
　　They sigh full still;°　　　　　　　　　　　　　constantly
　　God wot° they are led　　　　　　　　　　　　knows
110　Full hard and full ill;
　　In bower nor in bed
　　They say nought theretill.°　　　　　　　　　against that
　　　This tide°　　　　　　　　　　　　　　　　time
　　My part have I fun;°　　　　　　　　　　　found, learned
115　I know my lesson:
　　Woe is him that is bun,°　　　　　　　　bound (in wedlock)
　　　For he must abide.

　　But now late in our lives—
　　A marvel to me,
120　That I think my heart rives°　　　　　　　　　splits
　　Such wonders to see;
　　What that destiny drives
　　It should so be[8]—
　　Some men will have two wives,
125　And some men three
　　　In store.[9]
　　Some are woe° that has any,　　　　　　　　　miserable
　　But so far can° I,　　　　　　　　　　　　　know
　　Woe is him that has many,
130　　For he feels sore.

　　But young men a-wooing,
　　For God that you bought,°　　　　　　　　　redeemed
　　Be well ware of wedding
　　And think in your thought:
135　"Had I wist"° is a thing　　　　　　　　　　known
　　That serves of nought.
　　Mickle° still° mourning　　　　　　　　　much/continual
　　Has wedding home brought,
　　　And griefs,
140　With many a sharp shower,°　　　　　　　　　fight
　　For thou may catch in an hour
　　That° shall sow° thee full sour°　　　　that which/vex/bitterly
　　　As long as thou lives.

　　For as ever read I 'pistle,[1]
145　I have one to my fere[2]

8. What destiny causes must occur.
9. I.e., by remarrying after being widowed.

1. Epistle, i e., part of the church service.
2. As my mate.

As sharp as a thistle,
As rough as a brere;°   *briar*
She is browed like a bristle,
With a sour-loten cheer;³
150 Had she once wet her whistle
She could sing full clear
    Her Pater Noster.⁴
She is great as a whale;
She has a gallon of gall:
155 By him that died for us all,
    I would I had run to° I lost her.   *till*

COLL   God look over the raw!⁵
[*to* GIB] Full deafly ye stand!
GIB   Yea, the devil in thy maw°   *guts*
160 So tariand!⁶
Saw thou awhere° of Daw?   *anywhere*
COLL   Yea, on a lea-land°   *pasture land*
Heard I him blaw.°   *blow (his horn)*
He comes here at hand,
165   Not far.
Stand still.
GIB   Why?
COLL   For he comes, hope° I.   *think*
GIB   He will make us both a lie
    But if° we be ware.   *unless*

[*Enter* DAW,⁷ *who does not see the others.*]

170 DAW   Christ's cross me speed
And Saint Nicholas!⁸
Thereof had I need:
It is worse than it was.
Whoso could take heed
175 And let the world pass,
It is ever in dread°   *doubt*
And brickle° as glass,   *brittle*
    And slithes.°   *slips away*
This world foor° never so,   *behaved*
180 With marvels mo° and mo,   *more*
Now in weal, now in woe,
    And all thing writhes.°   *changes*

Was never sin° Noah's flood   *since*
Such floods seen,

---

3. She has brows like pig's bristles and a sour-looking face.
4. "Our Father," or The Lord's Prayer.
5. I.e., God watch over the audience! Coll has been trying to get Gib's attention as the latter harangues the audience.
6. For being so late.
7. Daw (Davy) is a boy working for the older shepherds.
8. May Christ's cross and St. Nicholas help me.

185   Winds and rains so rude
      And storms so keen:
      Some stammered, some stood
      In doubt,[9] as I ween.°   *suppose*
      Now God turn all to good!
190   I say as I mean.
          For ponder: *consider (this)*
      These floods so they drown
      Both in fields and in town,
      And bears all down,
195   And that is a wonder.

      We that walk on the nights
      Our cattle to keep,°   *keep watch over*
      We see sudden° sights   *startling*
      When other men sleep.
200   Yet methink my heart lights:°   *feels lighter*
      I see shrews peep.[1]

      [*He sees the others, but does not hail them.*]

      Ye are two tall wights.°   *creatures*
      I will give my sheep
          A turn.
205   But full ill have I meant:[2]
      As I walk on this bent°   *field*
      I may lightly° repent,   *quickly*
          My toes if I spurn.°   *stub*

      Ah, sir, God you save,
210   And master mine!
      A drink fain° would I have,   *gladly*
      And somewhat to dine.
    COLL   Christ's curse, my knave,
      Thou art a lither° hine!°   *lazy/servant*
215   GIB   What, the boy list rave!
      Abide unto sine.[3]
         We have made it.°   *had dinner*
      Ill thrift on thy pate![4]
      Though the shrew° came late   *rascal*
220   Yet is he in state
         To dine—if he had it.

    DAW   Such servants as I,
      That° sweats and swinks,°   *who/toil*

---

9. Probably refers to people's consternation at the time of Noah's Flood.
1. I see rascals peeping. Daw is relieved to recognize the other shepherds aren't monstrous apparitions.

2. But that's a very poor idea (to give the sheep a turn).
3. The boy must be crazy! Wait till later.
4. Bad luck on thy head!

Eats our bread full dry,
225 And that me forthinks.°   *angers*
We are oft wet and weary
When master-men winks,°   *sleep*
Yet comes full lately°   *tardily*
Both dinners and drinks.
230   But nately°   *profitably*
Both our dame and our sire,⁵
When we have run in the mire,
They can nip at our hire,⁶
        And pay us full lately.

235 But here my troth, master,
For the fare° that ye make°   *food / provide*
I shall do thereafter:
Work as I take.⁷
I shall do a little, sir,
240 And among° ever lake,°   *betweentimes / play*
For yet lay my supper
Never on my stomach⁸
        In fields.
Whereto should I threap?°   *haggle*
245 With my staff can I leap,°   *run away*
And men say, "Light cheap
        Litherly foryields."⁹

      COLL   Thou were an ill lad
To ride a-wooing
250 With a man that had
But little of spending.¹
      GIB   Peace, boy, I bade—
No more jangling,
Or I shall make thee full rad,°   *quickly (stop)*
255 By the heaven's King!
          With thy gauds°—   *tricks*
Where are our sheep, boy?—we scorn.²
      DAW   Sir, this same day at morn
I left them in the corn°   *wheat*
260   When they rang Lauds.³

They have pasture good,
They cannot go wrong.
      COLL   That is right. By the rood,°   *cross*
These nights are long!
265   Yet I would, ere we yode,°   *went*

---

5. I.e., mistress and master.
6. They can deduct from our wages.
7. I.e., work (as little) as I am paid.
8. I.e., a full stomach has never weighed me down.
9. A cheap bargain repays badly (a proverb).

1. You would be a bad servant to take wooing for a man with little money to spend.
2. We scorn (your tricks).
3. The first church service of the day (morn) but performed while it is still dark.

One° gave us a song.   *someone*
GIB   So I thought as I stood,
      To mirth° us among.°   *cheer/meanwhile*
DAW   I grant.
270 COLL   Let me sing the tenory.°   *tenor*
GIB   And I the treble so hee.°   *high*
DAW   Then the mean° falls to me.   *middle part*
      Let see how you chant.   [*They sing.*]

[*Enter* MAK *with a cloak over his clothes.*]⁴

MAK   Now, Lord, for thy names seven,
275   That made both moon and starns°   *stars*
      Well mo than I can neven,°   *name*
      Thy will, Lord, of me tharns.⁵
      I am all uneven°—   *at odds*
      That moves oft my harns.⁶
280   Now would God I were in heaven,
      For there weep no barns.°   *children*
        So still.°   *continually*
COLL   Who is that pipes so poor?
MAK   [*aside*] Would God ye wist° how I foor!°   *knew/fared*
285   [*aloud*] Lo, a man that walks on the moor
        And has not all his will.

GIB   Mak, where has thou gane?°   *gone*
      Tell us tiding.
DAW. Is he come? Then ilkane
290   Take heed to his thing.⁷

[*Snatches the cloak from him.*]

MAK   What! Ich⁸ be a yeoman,
      I tell you, of the king,
      The self and the same,
      Sond° from a great lording   *messenger*
295   And sich.°   *suchlike*
      Fie on you! Goth° hence   *go*
      Out of my presence:
      I must have reverence.
        Why, who be ich?

300 COLL   Why make ye it so quaint?⁹
      Mak, ye do wrang.°   *wrong*
GIB   But, Mak, list ye saint?
      I trow that ye lang.¹

4. Stage direction in the original manuscript.
5. Thy will, Lord, falls short in regard to me.
6. That often disturbs my brains.
7. Each one look to his possessions (lest Mak steal them). The stage direction below is in the manuscript.
8. I (a southern dialect form in contrast with the northern dialect spoken by the Yorkshire shepherds). Mak pretends to be an important person from the south.
9. Why are you putting on such airs?
1. Do you want to play the saint? I guess you long (to do so).

DAW   I trow the shrew can paint[2]—
305   The devil might him hang!
MAK   Ich shall make complaint
       And make you all to thwang°   *be flogged*
          At a word,
       And tell even° how ye doth.   *exactly*
310 COLL   But Mak, is that sooth?
       Now take out that Southern tooth,[3]
          And set in a turd![4]

     GIB   Mak, the devil in your ee!°   *eye*
       A stroke would I lean° you!   *give*
315 DAW   Mak, know ye not me?
       By God, I could teen° you.   *vex*
     MAK   God look° you all three: *guard*
       Methought I had seen you.
       Ye are a fair company.
320 COLL   Can ye now mean you?[5]
     GIB   Shrew, peep![6]
       Thus late as thou goes,
       What will men suppose?
       And thou has an ill nose[7]
325   Of stealing sheep.

     MAK   And I am true as steel,
       All men wate.°   *know*
       But a sickness I feel
       That holds me full hate:°   *hot, feverish*
330   My belly fares not weel,
       It is out of estate.
     DAW   Seldom lies the de'el°   *devil*
       Dead by the gate.[8]
     MAK   Therefore[9]
335   Full sore am I and ill
       If I stand stone-still,
       I eat not a needill[1]
          This month and more.

     COLL   How fares thy wife? By my hood,
340   How fares sho?°   *she*
     MAK   Lies waltering,° by the rood,   *sprawling*
       By the fire, lo!
       And a house full of brood.°   *children*

2. I think the rascal knows how to put on false colors.
3. I.e., now stop pretending to speak like a southerner.
4. I.e., shut up!
5. Can you now remember (who you are)?
6. Rascal, watch out.
7. Noise, i.e., reputation.
8. Road, i.e., the devil is always on the move.
9. Mak ignores Daw and continues his speech from line 331.
1. As sure as I'm standing here as still as a stone, I haven't eaten a needle (i.e., a tiny bit).

345	She drinks well, too:	
	Ill speed other good	
	That she will do!²	
	But sho	
	Eats as fast as she can;	
	And ilk° year that comes to man	*every*
350	She brings forth a lakan°—	*baby*
	And some years two.	

	But were I now more gracious°	*prosperous*
	And richer by far,	
	I were eaten out of house	
355	And of harbar.°	*home*
	Yet is she a foul douce,°	*sweetheart*
	If ye come nar:³	
	There is none that trows°	*imagines*
	Nor knows a war°	*worse*
360	Than ken° I.	*know*
	Now will ye see what I proffer:	
	To give all in my coffer	
	Tomorn at next° to offer	*tomorrow*
	Her head-masspenny.⁴	

365	GIB I wot° so forwaked⁵	*know*
	Is none in this shire.	
	I would sleep if° I taked	*even if*
	Less to my hire.⁶	
	DAW I am cold and naked	
370	And would have a fire.	
	COLL I am weary forraked°	*from walking*
	And run in the mire.	
	Wake thou.⁷	[*Lies down.*]
	GIB Nay, I will lie down by,	
375	For I must sleep, truly.	[*Lies down beside him.*]
	DAW As good a man's son was I	
	As any of you.	

[*Lies down and motions to* MAK *to lie between them.*]

	But Mak, come hither, between	
	Shall thou lie down.	
380	MAK Then might I let you bedeen	
	Of that ye would rown,⁸	

2. I.e., that (drinking) is the only good she does.
3. I.e., near the truth.
4. The penny paid to sing a mass for her soul; i.e., I wish she were dead.
5. Exhausted from lack of sleep.
6. I should take a cut in wages.
7. Keep watch.
8. Then I might be in the way if you wanted to whisper together.

No dread.°   doubt
From my top to my toe,   [*Lies down and prays.*]
Manus tuas commendo
385   *Pontio Pilato.*[9]
      Christ's cross me speed!°   help

[*He gets up as the others sleep and speaks.*][1]

Now were time for a man
That lacks what he wold°   would, wants
To stalk privily than°   then
390   Unto a fold,°   sheepfold
And nimbly to work than,
And be not too bold,
For he might abuy° the bargan°   pay for/bargain
      At the ending.
395   Now were time for to reel:°   move fast
But he needs good counseel°   counsel
That fain would fare weel°   well
      And has but little spending.°   money

[*He draws a magic circle around the shepherds and recites a spell.*]

But about you a circill,°   circle
400   As round as a moon,
To° I have done that° I will,   until/what
Till that it be noon,
That ye lie stone-still
To° that I have done;   until
405   And I shall say theretill°   thereto
Of good words a foon:°   few
      "On hight,
Over your heads my hand I lift.
Out go your eyes! Fordo your sight!"[2]
410   But yet I must make better shift
      And it be right.[3]

Lord, what° they sleep hard—   how
That may ye all hear.
Was I never a shephard,
415   But now will I lear.°   learn
If the flock be scar'd,
Yet shall I nip near.[4]
How! Draws hitherward![5]   [*He catches one.*]
Now mends our cheer

---

9. "Thy hands I commend to Pontius Pilate." A parody of Luke 23.46, "Into thy hands I commend my spirit."
1. One of the original stage directions.
2. May your sight be rendered powerless.

3. If it is to turn out all right.
4. Even if the flock is alarmed, yet shall I grip (a sheep) close.
5. Stop! come this way.

420   From sorrow.
         A fat sheep, I dare say!
         A good fleece, dare I lay!°   bet
         Eft-quit° when I may,   repay
            But this will I borrow.

[Moves with the sheep to his cottage and calls from outside.]

425   How, Gill, art thou in?
         Get us some light.
      GILL   [*inside*] Who makes such a din
         This time of the night?
         I am set for to spin;
430   I hope not I might
         Rise a penny to win⁶—
         I shrew° them on height!   curse
            So fares
         A housewife that has been
435   To be raised thus between:
         Here may no note be seen
            For such small chares.⁷

      MAK   Good wife, open the hek!°   door
         Sees thou not what I bring?
440   GILL   I may thole thee draw the sneck.⁸
         Ah, come in, my sweeting.°   sweetheart
      MAK   Yea, thou thar not reck
         Of my long standing.⁹

      [She opens the door.]

      GILL   By the naked neck
445   Art thou like for to hing.°   hang
      MAK   Do way!°   let it be
         I am worthy° my meat,   worthy of
         For in a strait° I can get   pinch
         More than they that swink° and sweat   work
450   All the long day.

         Thus it fell to my lot,
         Gill, I had such grace.°   luck
      GILL   It were a foul blot
         To be hanged for the case.°   deed
455   MAK   I have 'scaped,° Jelot,°   escaped/Gill
         Of as hard a glase.°   blow
         GILL   But "So long goes the pot

6. I don't think I can earn a penny by getting up
(from my work).
7. So it goes with anyone who has been a housewife—to be interrupted like this: no work gets done
here because of such petty chores.
8. I'll let you draw the latch.
9. Sure, you needn't care about keeping me standing a long time.

To the water," men says,
"At last
460 Comes it home broken."
MAK   Well know I the token,°   saying
But let it never be spoken!
    But come and help fast.

I would he were flain,°   skinned
465 I list° well eat: wish
This twelvemonth was I not so fain
Of one sheep-meat.
    GILL   Come they ere he be slain,
    And hear the sheep bleat—
470 MAK   Then might I be ta'en°—   taken
That were a cold sweat!
    Go spar°   fasten
The gate-door.°   street door
    GIL   Yes, Mak,
    For and° they come at thy back—   if
475 MAK   Then might I buy, for all the pack,
    The devil of the war.[1]

GILL   A good bourd° have I spied,   trick
Sin° thou can° none.   since / know
Here shall we him hide
480 To° they be gone,   until
In my cradle. Abide!
Let me alone,
And I shall lie beside
In childbed and groan.
485 MAK   Thou red,°   get ready
And I shall say thou was light°   delivered
Of a knave-child° this night.   boy child
    GILL   Now well is me day bright
    That ever I was bred.[2]

490 This is a good guise°   method
And a far-cast:°   clever trick
Yet a woman's advice
Helps at the last.
I wot° never who spies: know
495 Again° go thou fast.   back
    MAK   But° I come ere they rise,   unless
    Else blows a cold blast.
        I will go sleep.   [Returns to the shepherds.]
    Yet sleeps all this meny,°   company
500 And I shall go stalk privily,

---

1. Then I might have to pay the devil the worse on   2. Now lucky for me the bright day I was born.
account of the whole pack of them.

As it had never been I
    That carried their sheep.   [*Lies down among them.*]

[*The shepherds are waking.*]

COLL   *Resurrex a mortruus!*[3]
    Have hold my hand!
505   *Judas carnas dominus!*[4]
    I may not well stand.
    My foot sleeps, by Jesus,
    And I walter° fastand.°   *stagger*/(*from*) *fasting*
    I thought we had laid us
510   Full near England.
   GIB   Ah, yea?
    Lord, what° I have slept weel!°   *how*/*well*
    As fresh as an eel,
    As light I me feel
515   As leaf on a tree.

   DAW   Benste° be herein!   (*God's*) *blessing*
    So my body quakes,
    My heart is out of skin,
    What-so° it makes.°   *whatever*/*causes*
520   Who makes all this din?
    So my brows blakes,[5]
    To the door will I win.[6]
    Hark, fellows, wakes!
       We were four:
525   See ye aywhere of Mak now?
   COLL   We were up ere thou.
   GIB   Man, I give God avow
       Yet yede he naw're.[7]

   DAW   Methought he was lapped°   *covered*
530   In a wolfskin.
   COLL   So are many happed°   *clad*
    Now, namely° within.   *especially*
   DAW   When we had long napped,
    Methought with a gin°   *snare*
535   A fat sheep he trapped,
    But he made no din.
   GIB   Be still!
    Thy dream makes thee wood.°   *crazy*
    It is but phantom, by the rood.°   *cross*
540   COLL   Now God turn all to good,
       If it be his will.

3. A garbled form of "resurrexit a mortuis" (he arose from the dead) from the Creed.
4. Judas, (in?)carnate lord.
5. My brow turns pale (with fear).
6. I'll head for the door. Still half-asleep, Daw thinks he's inside.
7. He's gone nowhere yet.

[They wake up MAK *who pretends to have been asleep.]*

GIB   Rise, Mak, for shame!
    Thou lies right lang.°   *long*
MAK   Now Christ's holy name
545   Be us amang!°   *among*
    What is this? For Saint Jame,
    I may not well gang.°   *walk*
    I trow° I be the same.   *think*
    Ah, my neck has lain wrang.°   *wrong*
    [One of them twists his neck.]
550   Enough!
    Mickle° thank! Sin° yestereven   *much/since*
    Now, by Saint Stephen,
    I was flayed with a sweven—
    My heart out of slough.[8]

555   I thought Gill began to croak
    And travail° full sad,°   *labor/hard*
    Well-near at the first cock,[9]
    Of a young lad,
    For to mend° our flock—   *increase*
560   Then be I never glad:
    I have tow on my rock[1]
    More than ever I had.
      Ah, my head!
    A house full of young tharms!°   *bellies*
565   The devil knock out their harns!°   *brains*
    Woe is him has many barns,°   *children*
      And thereto little bread.

    I must go home, by your leave,
    To Gill, as I thought.°   *intended*
570   I pray you look° my sleeve,   *examine*
    That I steal nought.
    I am loath you to grieve
    Or from you take aught.
DAW   Go forth! Ill might thou chieve!°   *prosper*
575   Now would I we sought
      This morn,
    That we had all our store.[2]
COLL   But I will go before.
    Let us meet.
GIB   Whore?°   *where*
580 DAW   At the crooked thorn.

---

8. I was terrified by a dream—my heart [jumped] out of [my] skin.
9. First cockcrow, i.e., midnight.
1. Flax on my distaff (i.e., trouble, mouths to feed).
2. Now I want us to make sure . . . we have all our stock.

[MAK's *house*. MAK *at the door*.]

MAK Undo this door!
GILL   Who is here?
MAK How long shall I stand?
GILL Who makes such a bere?°   clamor
      Now walk in the weniand!³
585 MAK Ah, Gill, what cheer?
      It is I, Mak, your husband.
      GILL   Then may we see here
      The devil in a band,⁴
          Sir Guile!
590 Lo, he comes with a lote°   sound
      As° he were holden in° the throat: as if / by
      I may not sit at my note°   work
      A hand-long° while.   short

      MAK Will ye hear what fare° she makes   fuss
595 To get her a glose?°   excuse
      And does nought but lakes°   plays
      And claws° her toes?   scratches
      GILL Why, who wanders? Who wakes?
      Who comes? Who goes?
600 Who brews? Who bakes?
      What makes me thus hose?⁵
          And than°   then
      It is ruth° to behold,   pity
      Now in hot, now in cold,
605 Full woeful is the household
          That wants° a woman.   lacks

      But what end has thou made
      With the herds,° Mak?   shepherds
      MAK The last word that they said
610 When I turned my back,
      They would look that they had
      Their sheep all the pack.
      I hope they will not be well paid⁶
      When they their sheep lack.
615   Pardie!°   by God
      But how-so the game goes,
      To me they will suppose,⁷
      And make a foul nose,°   noise
          And cry out upon me.

3. Waning of the moon (an unlucky time), i.e., "Go with bad luck!"
4. In a noose (?) Gill perhaps continues to remind Mak that sheep stealing is a hanging offense.
5. Hoarse (from shouting at her husband and children).
6. I expect they won't be well pleased.
7. They will suspect me.

620　But thou must do as thou hight.°　　　　　　　　　　*promised*
　　GILL　I accord me theretill.[8]
　　I shall swaddle him right
　　In my cradill.

[*She wraps up the sheep and puts it in the cradle.*]

　　If it were a greater sleight,
625　Yet could I help till.[9]
　　I will lie down straight.°　　　　　　　　　　　*immediately*
　　Come hap° me.　　　　　　　　　　　　　　　*cover*
　　MAK　　　　　I will.　　　　　　[*Covers her.*]
　　GILL　Behind
　　Come Coll and his marrow;[1]
630　They will nip° us full narrow.°　　　　　　*pinch / closely*
　　MAK　But I may cry "Out, harrow,"[2]
　　The sheep if they find.

　　GILL　Hearken ay when they call—
　　They will come anon.
635　Come and make ready all,
　　And sing by thine one.°　　　　　　　　　　　*self*
　　Sing "lullay"° thou shall,　　　　　　　　　*lullaby*
　　For I must groan
　　And cry out by the wall
640　On Mary and John
　　　For sore.°　　　　　　　　　　　　　　　　*pain*
　　Sing "lullay" on fast
　　When thou hears at the last,[3]
　　And but I play a false cast,[4]
645　　Trust me no more.

[*The shepherds meet again.*]

　　DAW　Ah, Coll, good morn.
　　Why sleeps thou not?
　　COLL　Alas, that ever I was born!
　　We have a foul blot:
650　A fat wether° have we lorn.°　　　　　　　*ram / lost*
　　DAW　Marry, God's forbot!°　　　　　　　*God forbid*
　　GIB　Who should do us that scorn?
　　That were a foul spot!°　　　　　　　　　　*disgrace*
　　COLL　Some shrew.°　　　　　　　　　　　*rascal*
655　I have sought with my dogs
　　All Horbury[5] shrogs,°　　　　　　　　　　*thickets*

8. I agree to that.
9. Even if it were a greater trick, I could still help with it.
1. Coll and his mate are coming on your tracks.

2. A cry of distress.
3. When at last you hear (them coming).
4. Unless I play a false trick.
5. A village near Wakefield.

And of fifteen hogs
Found I but one ewe.[6]

660 DAW Now trow° me, if ye will,   *believe*
    By Saint Thomas of Kent,
    Either Mak or Gill
      Was at that assent.[7]
  COLL Peace, man, be still!
    I saw when he went.
665 Thou slanders him ill—
    Thou ought to repent
      Good speed.°   *speedily*
  GIB Now as ever might I thee,°   *thrive*
    If I should even here dee,°   *die*
670 I would say it were he
      That did that same deed.

  DAW Go we thither, I read,°   *advise*
    And run on our feet.
    Shall I never eat bread
675 The sooth to I weet.[8]
  COLL Nor drink in my head,
    With him till I meet.[9]
  GIB I will rest in no stead°   *place*
    Till that I him greet,
680 My brother.
    One I will hight:[1]
    Till I see him in sight
    Shall I never sleep one night
      There I do another.[2]

[The shepherds approach MAK's *house.* MAK *and* GILL *within, she in bed, groaning, he singing a lullaby.]*

685 DAW Will ye hear how they hack?[3]
    Our sire list° croon.   *wants to*
  COLL Heard I never none crack°   *sing loudly*
    So clear out of tune.
    Call on him.
  GIB   Mak!
690 Undo your door soon!°   *at once*
  MAK Who is that spake,
    As° it were noon,   *as if*
      On loft?°   *loudly*

6. And with fifteen lambs I found only a ewe (i.e., the wether [ram] was missing).
7. Was a party to it.
8. Until I know the truth.
9. Nor take a drink till I meet with him.

1. One thing will I promise.
2. I'll never sleep in the same place two nights in a row.
3. Trill; a musical term used sarcastically, as also "crack" below

Who is that, I say?
695 DAW Good fellows, were it day.[4]
MAK As far as ye may,
[*opening*] Good,° speaks soft   *good men*

Over a sick woman's head
That is at malease.[5]
700 I had liefer° be dead   *rather*
Ere she had any disease.°   *distress*
GILL Go to another stead!°   *place*
I may not well wheeze:°   *breathe*
Each foot that ye tread
705 Goes through my nese.°   *nose*
So, hee![6]
COLL Tell us, Mak, if you may,
How fare ye, I say?
MAK But are ye in this town today?[7]
710 Now how fare ye?

Ye have run in the mire
And are wet yit.
I shall make you a fire
If you will sit.
715 A nurse would I hire.
Think ye on yit?[8]
Well quit is my hire—
My dream this is it—
A season.[9]
720 I have barns,° if ye knew,   *children*
Wel mo° than enew:°   *more/enough*
But we must drink as we brew,
And that is but reason.

I would ye dined ere ye yode.°   *went*
725 Methink that ye sweat.
GIB Nay, neither mends our mood,
Drink nor meat.[1]
MAK Why sir, ails you aught but good?[2]
DAW Yea, our sheep that we get°   *tend*
730 Are stolen as they yode:°   *wandered*
Our loss is great.
MAK Sirs, drinks!
Had I been thore,°   *there*

---

4. Good friends, if it were daylight (i.e., not friends, since it's still night).
5. Who feels badly.
6. So loudly, i.e., your tramping goes right through my head.
7. I.e., what brings you to this neighborhood today?
8. Do you still remember (my dream)?
9. Ironic: my season's wages are well paid—my dream (that Gill was giving birth) has come true.
1. Neither food nor drink will improve our mood.
2. Does anything other than good trouble you? I.e., what's wrong?

Some should have bought° it full sore.   *paid for*

735 COLL Marry, some men trows° that ye wore,°   *think/were*
And that us forthinks.°   *displeases*

GIB Mak, some men trows,
That it should be ye.
DAW Either ye or your spouse,
740   So say we.
MAK Now if you have suspouse°   *suspicion*
To Gill or to me,
Come and ripe° the house   *ransack*
And then ye see
745   Who had her³—
If I any sheep fot,°   *fetched, stole*
Either cow or stot⁴—
And Gill my wife rose not
Here sin she laid her.°   *lay down*

750 As I am true and leal,°   *honest*
To God here I pray
That this be the first meal
That I shall eat this day.
COLL Mak, as I have sele,⁵
755   Advise thee, I say:
He learned timely to steal
That could not say nay.⁶   [*They begin to search.*]
GILL I swelt!°   *die*
Out, thieves, from my wones!°   *dwelling*
760 Ye come to rob us for the nones.⁷
MAK Hear ye not how she groans?
Your hearts should melt.

GILL Out, thieves, from my barn!°   *child*
Nigh him not thore!⁸
765 MAK Wist ye how she had farn,⁹
Your hearts would be sore.
You do wrong, I you warn,
That thus comes before°   *in the presence*
To a woman that has farn°—   *been in labor*
770 But I say no more.
GILL Ah, my middill!°   *middle*
I pray to God so mild,
If ever I you beguiled,
That I eat this child
775   That lies in this cradill.

3. I.e., the sheep.
4. Either female or male.
5. As I hope to have salvation.
6. He learned early to steal who could not say no
(proverbial).
7. You come for the purpose of robbing us.
8. Don't come close to him there.
9. If you knew how she had fared (in labor).

MAK   Peace, woman, for God's pain,
    And cry not so!
    Thou spills° thy brain   *harm*
    And makes me full woe.
780 GIB   I trow our sheep be slain.
    What find ye two?
    DAW   All work we in vain;
    As well may we go.
      But hatters![1]
785 I can find no flesh,
    Hard nor nesh,°   *soft*
    Salt nor fresh,
      But two tome° platters.   *empty*

    Quick cattle but this,[2]
790 Tame nor wild,
    None, as I have bliss,
    As loud as he smiled.[3]   [*Approaches the cradle.*]
    GILL   No, so God me bliss,°   *bless*
    And give me joy of my child!
795 COLL   We have marked° amiss—   *aimed*
    I hold° us beguiled.   *consider*
    GIB   Sir, don!°   *totally*
    [*to* MAK]   Sir—Our Lady him save!—
    Is your child a knave?[4]
800 MAK   Any lord might him have,
    This child, to° his son.   *as*

    When he wakens he kips,°   *snatches, grabs*
    That joy is to see.
    DAW   In good time to his hips,
805 And in sely.[5]
    But who were his gossips,°   *godparents*
    So soon ready?
    MAK   So fair fall their lips[6]—
    COLL   Hark, now, a lee,°   *lie*
810 MAK   So God them thank,
    Perkin, and Gibbon Waller, I say,
    And gentle John Horne, in good fay°—   *faith*
    He made all the garray°   *quarrel*
    With the great shank.[7]

815 GIB   Mak, friends will we be,
    For we are all one.°   *in accord*

1. An expression of consternation.
2. Livestock other than this (the baby).
3. Smelled as strongly as he (the missing ram).
4. Boy (although Mak takes the alternate meaning of "rascal").

5. Good luck and happiness to him.
6. May good luck befall them.
7. An allusion to a dispute among the shepherds in the author's *First Shepherds' Play.*

MAK   We? Now I hold for me,
 For mends get I none.[8]
 Farewell all three,
820 All glad[9] were ye gone.
DAW   Fair words may there be,
 But love is there none
  This year.   [*They go out the door.*]
COLL   Gave ye the child anything?
825 GIB   I trow not one farthing.
DAW   Fast again will I fling.°   *dash*
 Abide ye me there.   [*He runs back.*]

 Mak, take it no grief
 If I come to thy barn.°   *child*
830 MAK   Nay, thou does me great reprief,°   *shame*
 And foul has thou farn.°   *behaved*
DAW   The child it will not grief,
 That little day-starn.°   *day star*
 Mak, with your leaf,°   *permission*
835 Let me give your barn
  But sixpence.
MAK   Nay, do way! He sleeps.
DAW   Methinks he peeps.°   *opens his eyes*
MAK   When he wakens he weeps.
840 I pray you go hence.

[*The other shepherds reenter.*]

DAW   Give me leave him to kiss,
 And lift up the clout.°   *cover*
 [*lifts the cover*]
 What the devil is this?
 He has a long snout!
845 COLL   He is marked amiss.
 We wot ill about.[1]
GIB   Ill-spun weft, ywis,
 Ay comes foul out.[2]
 Aye, so!
850 He is like to our sheep.
DAW   How, Gib, may I peep?
COLL   I trow kind will creep
 Where it may not go.[3]

GIB   This was a quaint gaud
855 And a far-cast.[4]

---

8. I'll look out for myself, for I'll get no compensation.
9. I.e., I would be glad.
1. He is deformed. We know something fishy is going on around here.
2. An ill-spun web, indeed, always comes out

badly (proverbial), i.e., ill work always comes to a bad end.
3. Nature will creep where it can't walk (proverbial), i.e., nature will reveal itself by hook or crook.
4. This was a cunning trick and a clever ruse.

It was high fraud.
DAW   Yea, sirs, was't.°   *it was*
    Let bren° this bawd   *burn*
    And bind her fast.
860   A false scaud°   *scold*
    Hang at the last:[5]
    So shall thou.
    Will you see how they swaddle
    His four feet in the middle?
865   Saw I never in the cradle
    A horned lad ere now.

MAK   Peace bid I! What,
    Let be your fare!°   *fuss*
    I am he that him gat.°   *begot*
870   And yond woman him bare.
COLL   What devil shall he hat?[6]
    Lo, God, Mak's heir!
GIB   Let be all that!
    Now God give him care°—   *sorrow*
875   I sawgh!°   *saw*
GILL   A pretty child is he
    As sits on a woman's knee,
    A dillydown,° pardie,°   *darling/by God*
    To gar° a man laugh.   *make*

880 DAW   I know him by the earmark—
    That is a good token.
MAK   I tell you, sirs, hark,
    His nose was broken.
    Sithen° told me a clerk   *later*
885   That he was forspoken.°   *bewitched*
COLL   This is a false wark.°   *work*
    I would fain be wroken.°   *avenged*
    Get wapen.°   *weapon*
GILL   He was taken with an elf[7]
890   I saw it myself—
    When the clock struck twelf
    Was he forshapen.°   *transformed*

GIB   Ye two are well feft
    Sam in a stead.[8]
895 DAW   Sin° they maintain their theft,   *since*
    Let do° them to dead.°   *put/death*
MAK   If I trespass eft,°   *again*

5. Will hang in the end.
6. What the devil shall he be named?
7. He was stolen by a fairy, i.e., the baby is a changeling.
8. You two are well endowed in the same place, i.e., you are two of a kind.

	Gird° off my head.	chop
	With you will I be left.⁹	
900	COLL Sirs, do my read:°	advice
	For this trespass	
	We will neither ban° ne flite,°	curse/quarrel
	Fight nor chite,°	chide
	But have done as tite,°	quickly
905	And cast him in canvas.	

[They toss MAK *in a blanket.]*

[The fields]

	COLL Lord, what° I am sore,	how
	In point for to brist!°	burst
	In faith, I may no more—	
	Therefore will I rist.°	rest
910	GIB As a sheep of seven score¹	
	He weighed in my fist:	
	For to sleep aywhore°	anywhere
	Methink that I list.°	want
	DAW Now I pray you	
915	Lie down on this green.	
	COLL On the thieves yet I mean.°	think
	DAW Whereto should ye teen?°	be angry
	Do as I say you. *[They lie down.]*	

[An ANGEL *sings* Gloria in Excelsis *and then speaks.]²*

	ANGEL Rise, herdmen hend,°	gracious
920	For now is he born	
	That shall take fro the fiend°	devil
	That Adam had lorn;³	
	That warlock° to shend,°	devil/destroy
	This night is he born.	
925	God is made your friend	
	Now at this morn,	
	He behestys.°	promises
	At Bedlem° go see:	Bethlehem
	There lies that free,°	noble one
930	In a crib full poorly,	
	Betwixt two bestys.°	beasts

[The ANGEL *withdraws.]*

	COLL This was a quaint° steven°	marvelous/voice
	That ever yet I hard.°	heard
	It is a marvel to neven°	tell of

9. I put myself at your mercy.
1. I.e., 140 pounds.
2. This is an original stage direction; "Glory [to

God] in the highest" (see Luke 2.14).
3. That [which] Adam had brought to ruin.

935   Thus to be scar'd.°   *scared*
     GIB   Of God's Son of heaven
        He spake upward.°   *on high*
        All the wood on a leven
        Methought that he gard
940   Appear.[4]
     DAW He spake of a barn°   *child*
        In Bedlem, I you warn.°   *tell*
     COLL That betokens yond starn.[5]
        Let us seek him there.

945   GIB Say, what was his song?
        Heard ye not how he cracked it?[6]
        Three breves° to a long?   *short notes*
     DAW Yea, marry, he hacked it.
        Was no crochet° wrong,   *note*
950   Nor nothing that lacked it.[7]
     COLL For to sing us among,
        Right as he knacked it,
        I can.°   *know how*
     GIB Let see how ye croon!
955   Can ye bark at the moon?
     DAW Hold your tongues! Have done!
     COLL Hark after, than!   [*Sings.*]

     GIB To Bedlem he bade
        That we should gang:°   *go*
960   I am full fard°   *afraid*
        That we tarry too lang.°   *long*
     DAW Be merry and not sad;
        Of mirth is our sang:
        Everlasting glad°   *joy*
965   To meed° may we fang.°   *reward/get*
     COLL Without nose°   *noise*
        Hie we thither forthy°   *therefore*
        To that child and that lady;
        If° we be wet and weary,   *though*
970   We have it not to lose.[8]

     GIB We find by the prophecy—
        Let be your din!—
        Of David and Isay,
        And mo than I min,[9]
975   That prophesied by clergy°   *learning*
        That in a virgin

4. I thought he made the whole woods appear in a flash of light.
5. That's what yonder star means.
6. Trilled it; a technical musical term, close in meaning to *hacked* and *knacked*: to break (notes), to sing in a lively or ornate manner (cf. lines 685 and 687).
7. That it lacked.
8. We must not neglect it.
9. Of David and Isaiah and more than I remember.

        Should he light° and lie,   *alight*

        To sloken° our sin   *quench*

        And slake° it,   *relieve*

980   Our kind,° from woe,   *humankind*

        For Isay said so:

        Ecce virgo

        Concipiet[1] a child that is naked.

    DAW   Full glad may we be

985   And° we abide that day   *if*

        That lovely to see,

        That all mights may.[2]

        Lord, well were me

        For once and for ay

990   Might I kneel on my knee,

        Some word for to say

           To that child.

        But the angel said

        In a crib was he laid,

995   He was poorly arrayed,

           Both meaner° and mild.   *very humbly*

    COLL   Patriarchs that has been,

        And prophets beforn,°   *before (our time)*

        That desired to have seen

1000   This child that is born,

        They are gone full clean—

        That have they lorn.[3]

        We shall see him, I ween,°   *think*

        Ere it be morn,

1005   To token.[4]

        When I see him and feel,

        Then wot° I full weel°   *know/well*

        It is true as steel

          That° prophets have spoken: *what*

1010   To so poor as we are

        That he would appear,

        First find and declare[5]

        By his messenger.

    GIB   Go we now, let us fare,

1015   The place is us near.

    DAW   I am ready and yare;°   *eager*

        Go we in fere°   *together*

          To that bright.°   *glorious one*

        Lord, if thy wills be—

1. Behold, a virgin shall conceive (Isaiah 7.14).
2. I.e., when we see that lovely one who is all-powerful.
3. That (sight) have they lost.
4. As a sign.
5. Find (us) first (of all), and make known (his birth).

1020   We are lewd° all three—   *ignorant*
       Thou grant us some kins glee⁶
       To comfort thy wight.°   *child*

       [*They go to Bethlehem and enter the stable.*]

       COLL   Hail, comely and clean!°   *pure*
       Hail, young child!
1025   Hail Maker, as I mean,°   *believe*
       Of° a maiden so mild!   *born of*
       Thou has waried,° I ween,°   *cursed / think*
       The warlock° so wild.   *devil*
       The false guiler of teen,⁷
1030   Now goes he beguiled.
           Lo, he merries!°   *is merry*
       Lo, he laughs, my sweeting!
       A well fair meeting!
       I have holden my heting:°   *promise*
1035   Have a bob° of cherries.   *bunch*

       GIB   Hail, sovereign Saviour,
       For thou has us sought!
       Hail freely food° and flour,°   *noble child / flower*
       That all thing has wrought!
1040   Hail, full of favour,
       That made all of nought!
       Hail! I kneel and I cower.°   *crouch*
       A bird have I brought
           To my barn.°   *child*
1045   Hail, little tiny mop!°   *baby*
       Of our creed thou art crop.°   *head*
       I would drink on thy cup,
           Little day-starn.   *day star*

       DAW   Hail, darling dear,
1050   Full of Godhead!
       I pray thee be near
       When that I have need.
       Hail, sweet is thy cheer°—   *face*
       My heart would bleed
1055   To see thee sit here
       In so poor weed,°   *clothing*
           With no pennies.
       Hail, put forth thy dall!°   *hand*
       I bring thee but a ball:
1060   Have and play thee withal,
           And go to the tennis.

---

6. Some kind of cheer.   7. The false grievous deceiver, i.e., the devil.

MARY   The Father of heaven,
      God omnipotent,
      That set all on seven,[8]
1065   His Son has he sent.
      My name could he neven,
      And light ere he went.[9]
      I conceived him full even
      Through might as he meant.[1]
1070   And now is he born.
      He° keep you from woe!   *(may) he*
      I shall pray him so.
      Tell forth as ye go,
      And min on° this morn.   *remember*

1075 COLL   Farewell, lady,
      So fair to behold,
      With thy child on thy knee.
     GIB   But he lies full cold.
      Lord, well is me.
1080   Now we go, thou behold.
     DAW Forsooth, already
      It seems to be told
        Full oft.
     COLL   What grace we have fun!°   *received*
1085 GIB   Come forth, now are we won!°   *redeemed*
     DAW   To sing are we bun:°   *bound*
      Let take on loft.[2]
      [They sing.]

---

8. Who created everything in seven (days).
9. My name did he name, and alighted (in me) before he went (see Luke 1.28).

1. I conceived him, indeed, through his power, just as he intended.
2. Let's raise our voices.

SIR THOMAS MALORY

ca. 1405–1471

Morte Darthur (Death of Arthur) is the title that William Caxton, the first English printer, gave to Malory's volume, which Caxton described more accurately in his Preface as "the noble histories of * * * King Arthur and of certain of his knights." The volume begins with the mythical story of Arthur's birth. King Uther Pendragon falls in love with the wife of one of his barons. Merlin's magic transforms Uther into the likeness of her husband, and Arthur is born of this union. The volume ends with the destruction of the Round Table and the deaths of Arthur, Queen Guinevere, and Sir Lancelot, who is Arthur's best knight and the queen's lover. The bulk of the work is taken up with the separate adventures of the knights of the Round Table.

On the evolution of the Arthurian saga, see the headnote to *Legendary Histories of Britain*, p. 115. During the thirteenth century the stories about Arthur and his knights had been turned into a series of enormously long prose romances in French, and it was these, as Caxton informed his readers, "Sir Thomas Malory did take out of certain books of French and reduced into English."

Little was known about the author until the early twentieth century when scholars began to unearth the criminal record of a Sir Thomas Malory of Newbold Revell in Warwickshire. In 1451 he was arrested for the first time to prevent his doing injury—presumably further injury—to a priory in Lincolnshire, and shortly thereafter he was accused of a number of criminal acts. These included escaping from prison after his first arrest, twice breaking into and plundering the Abbey of Coombe, extorting money from various persons, and committing rape. Malory pleaded innocent of all charges. The Wars of the Roses—in which Malory, like the formidable earl of Warwick (the "kingmaker"), whom he seems to have followed, switched sides from Lancaster to York and back again—may account for some of his troubles with the law. After a failed Lancastrian revolt, the Yorkist king, Edward IV, specifically excluded Malory from four amnesties he granted to the Lancastrians.

The identification of this Sir Thomas Malory (there is another candidate with the same name) as the author of the *Morte* was strengthened by the discovery in 1934 of a manuscript that differed from Caxton's text, the only version previously known. The manuscript contained eight separate romances. Caxton, in order to give the impression of a continuous narrative, had welded these together into twenty-one books, subdivided into short chapters with summary chapter headings. Caxton suppressed all but the last of the personal remarks the author had appended to individual tales in the manuscript. At the very end of the book Malory asks "all gentlemen and gentlewomen that readeth this book * * * pray for me while I am alive that God send me good deliverance." The discovery of the manuscript revealed that at the close of the first tale he had written: "this was drawyn by a knight presoner Sir Thomas Malleoré, that God sende him good recover." There is strong circumstantial evidence, therefore, that the book from which the Arthurian legends were passed on to future generations to be adapted in literature, art, and film was written in prison by a man whose violent career might seem at odds with the chivalric ideals he professes.

Such a contradiction—if it really is one—should not be surprising. Nostalgia for an ideal past that never truly existed is typical of much historical romance. Like the slave-owning plantation society of Margaret Mitchell's *Gone with the Wind*, whose southern gentlemen cultivate chivalrous manners and respect for gentlewomen, Malory's Arthurian world is a fiction. In our terms, it cannot even be labeled "historical," although the distinction between romance and history is not one that Malory would have made. Only rarely does he voice skepticism about the historicity of his tale; one such example is his questioning of the myth of Arthur's return. Much of the tragic power of his romance lies in his sense of the irretrievability of past glory in comparison with the sordidness of his own age.

The success of Malory's retelling owes much to his development of a terse and direct prose style, especially the naturalistic dialogue that keeps his narrative close to earth. And both he and many of his characters are masters of understatement who express themselves, in moments of great emotional tension, with a bare minimum of words.

In spite of its professed dedication to service of women, Malory's chivalry is primarily devoted to the fellowship and competitions of aristocratic men. Fighting consists mainly of single combats in tournaments, chance encounters, and battles, which Malory never tires of describing in professional detail. Commoners rarely come into view; when they do, the effect can be chilling—as when pillagers by moonlight plunder the corpses of the knights left on the field of Arthur's last battle. Above all, Malory cherishes an aristocratic male code of honor for which his favorite word is "worship." Men win or lose "worship" through their actions in war and love.

The most "worshipful" of Arthur's knights is Sir Lancelot, the "head of all Christian knights," as he is called in a moving eulogy by his brother, Sir Ector. But Lancelot is compromised by his fatal liaison with Arthur's queen and torn between the incompatible loyalties that bind him as an honorable knight, on the one hand, to his lord Arthur and, on the other, to his lady Guinevere. Malory loves his character Lancelot even to the point of indulging in the fleeting speculation, after Lancelot has been admitted to the queen's chamber, that their activities might have been innocent, "for love that time was not as love is nowadays." But when the jealousy and malice of two wicked knights forces the affair into the open, nothing can avert the breaking up of the fellowship of the Round Table and the death of Arthur himself, which Malory relates with somber magnificence as the passing of a great era.

From Morte Darthur[1]

[THE CONSPIRACY AGAINST LANCELOT AND GUINEVERE]

In May, when every lusty[2] heart flourisheth and burgeoneth, for as the season is lusty to behold and comfortable,[3] so man and woman rejoiceth and gladdeth of summer coming with his fresh flowers, for winter with his rough winds and blasts causeth lusty men and women to cower and to sit fast by the fire—so this season it befell in the month of May a great anger and unhap that stinted not[4] till the flower of chivalry of all the world was destroyed and slain. And all was long upon two unhappy[5] knights which were named Sir Agravain and Sir Mordred that were brethren unto Sir Gawain.[6] For this Sir Agravain and Sir Mordred had ever a privy[7] hate unto the Queen, Dame Guinevere, and to Sir Lancelot, and daily and nightly they ever watched upon Sir Lancelot.

So it misfortuned Sir Gawain and all his brethren were in King Arthur's chamber, and then Sir Agravain said thus openly, and not in no counsel,[8] that many knights might hear: "I marvel that we all be not ashamed both to see and to know how Sir Lancelot lieth daily and nightly by the Queen. And all we know well that it is so, and it is shamefully suffered of us all[9] that we should suffer so noble a king as King Arthur is to be shamed."

Then spoke Sir Gawain and said, "Brother, Sir Agravain, I pray you and charge you, move no such matters no more afore[1] me, for wit you well, I will not be of your counsel."[2]

"So God me help," said Sir Gaheris and Sir Gareth,[3] "we will not be known of your deeds."[4]

"Then will I!" said Sir Mordred.

"I lieve[5] you well," said Sir Gawain, "for ever unto all unhappiness, sir, ye will grant.[6] And I would that ye left all this and make you not so busy, for I know," said Sir Gawain, "what will fall of it."[7]

---

1. The selections given here are from the section that Caxton called book 20, chaps. 1–4, 8–10, and book 21, chaps. 3–7, 10–12, with omissions. In the Winchester manuscript this section is titled "The Most Piteous Tale of the Morte Arthur Saunz Guerdon" (i.e., the death of Arthur without reward or compensation). The text has been based on Winchester, with some readings introduced from the Caxton edition; spelling has been modernized and modern punctuation added.
2. Merry.
3. Pleasant.
4. Misfortune that ceased not.
5. On account of two ill-fated.
6. Gawain and Agravain are sons of King Lot of

Orkney and his wife Arthur's half-sister Morgause. Mordred is the illegitimate son of Arthur and Morgause.
7. Secret.
8. Secret manner.
9. Put up with by all of us.
1. Before. "Move": propose.
2. On your side. "Wit you well": know well, i.e., give you to understand.
3. Sons of King Lot and Gawain's brothers.
4. A party to your doings.
5. Believe.
6. You will consent to all mischief.
7. Come of it.

"Fall whatsoever fall may," said Sir Agravain, "I will disclose it to the King."

"Not by my counsel," said Sir Gawain, "for and[8] there arise war and wrack betwixt[9] Sir Lancelot and us, wit you well, brother, there will many kings and great lords hold with Sir Lancelot. Also, brother, Sir Agravain," said Sir Gawain, "ye must remember how often times Sir Lancelot hath rescued the King and the Queen. And the best of us all had been full cold at the heart-root[1] had not Sir Lancelot been better than we, and that has he proved himself full oft. And as for my part," said Sir Gawain, "I will never be against Sir Lancelot for[2] one day's deed, when he rescued me from King Carados of the Dolorous Tower and slew him and saved my life. Also, brother, Sir Agravain and Sir Mordred, in like wise Sir Lancelot rescued you both and three score and two[3] from Sir Tarquin. And therefore, brother, methinks such noble deeds and kindness should be remembered."

"Do as ye list,"[4] said Sir Agravain, "for I will layne[5] it no longer."

So with these words came in Sir Arthur.

"Now, brother," said Sir Gawain, "stint your noise."[6]

"That will I not," said Sir Agravain and Sir Mordred.

"Well, will ye so?" said Sir Gawain. "Then God speed you, for I will not hear of your tales, neither be of your counsel."

"No more will I," said Sir Gaheris.

"Neither I," said Sir Gareth, "for I shall never say evil by[7] that man that made me knight." And therewithal they three departed making great dole.[8]

"Alas!" said Sir Gawain and Sir Gareth, "now is this realm wholly destroyed and mischieved,[9] and the noble fellowship of the Round Table shall be disparbeled."[1]

So they departed, and then King Arthur asked them what noise they made. "My lord," said Sir Agravain, "I shall tell you, for I may keep[2] it no longer. Here is I and my brother Sir Mordred broke[3] unto my brother Sir Gawain, Sir Gaheris, and to Sir Gareth—for this is all, to make it short—how that we know all that Sir Lancelot holdeth your queen, and hath done long; and we be your sister[4] sons, we may suffer it no longer. And all we woot[5] that ye should be above Sir Lancelot, and ye are the king that made him knight, and therefore we will prove it that he is a traitor to your person."

"If it be so," said the King, "wit[6] you well, he is none other. But I would be loath to begin such a thing but[7] I might have proofs of it, for Sir Lancelot is an hardy knight, and all ye know that he is the best knight among us all. And but if he be taken with the deed,[8] he will fight with him that bringeth up the noise, and I know no knight that is able to match him. Therefore, and[9] it be sooth as ye say, I would that he were taken with the deed."

For, as the French book saith, the King was full loath that such a noise

---

8. If.
9. Strife between.
1. Would have been dead.
2. On account of.
3. I.e., sixty-two.
4. You please.
5. Conceal.
6. Stop making scandal.
7. About.
8. Lamentation.

9. Put to shame.
1. Dispersed.
2. Conceal.
3. Revealed.
4. Sister's.
5. Know.
6. Know.
7. Unless.
8. Unless he is caught in the act.
9. If.

should be upon Sir Lancelot and his queen. For the King had a deeming[1] of it, but he would not hear of it, for Sir Lancelot had done so much for him and for the Queen so many times that, wit you well, the King loved him passingly[2] well.

"My lord," said Sir Agravain, "ye shall ride tomorn[3] on hunting, and doubt ye not, Sir Lancelot will not go with you. And so when it draweth toward night, ye may send the Queen word that ye will lie out all that night, and so may ye send for your cooks. And then, upon pain of death, that night we shall take him with the Queen, and we shall bring him unto you, quick[4] or dead."

"I will well,"[5] said the King. "Then I counsel you to take with you sure fellowship."

"Sir," said Sir Agravain, "my brother, Sir Mordred, and I will take with us twelve knights of the Round Table."

"Beware," said King Arthur, "for I warn you, ye shall find him wight."[6]

"Let us deal!"[7] said Sir Agravain and Sir Mordred.

So on the morn King Arthur rode on hunting and sent word to the Queen that he would be out all that night. Then Sir Agravain and Sir Mordred got to them[8] twelve knights and hid themself in a chamber in the castle of Carlisle. And these were their names: Sir Colgrevance, Sir Mador de la Porte, Sir Guingalen, Sir Meliot de Logres, Sir Petipace of Winchelsea, Sir Galeron of Galway, Sir Melion de la Mountain, Sir Ascamore, Sir Gromore Somyr Jour, Sir Curselayne, Sir Florence, and Sir Lovell. So these twelve knights were with Sir Mordred and Sir Agravain, and all they were of Scotland, or else of Sir Gawain's kin, or well-willers[9] to his brother.

So when the night came, Sir Lancelot told Sir Bors[1] how he would go that night and speak with the Queen.

"Sir," said Sir Bors, "ye shall not go this night by my counsel."

"Why?" said Sir Lancelot.

"Sir," said Sir Bors, "I dread me[2] ever of Sir Agravain that waiteth upon[3] you daily to do you shame and us all. And never gave my heart against no going that ever ye went[4] to the queen so much as now, for I mistrust[5] that the King is out this night from the Queen because peradventure he hath lain[6] some watch for you and the Queen. Therefore, I dread me sore of some treason."

"Have ye no dread," said Sir Lancelot, "for I shall go and come again and make no tarrying."

"Sir," said Sir Bors, "that me repents,[7] for I dread me sore that your going this night shall wrath[8] us all."

"Fair nephew," said Sir Lancelot, "I marvel me much why ye say thus, sithen[9] the Queen hath sent for me. And wit you well, I will not be so much a coward, but she shall understand I will[1] see her good grace."

---

1. Suspicion.
2. Exceedingly.
3. Tomorrow.
4. Alive.
5. Readily agree.
6. Strong.
7. Leave it to us.
8. Gathered to themselves.
9. Partisans.
1. Nephew and confidant of Sir Lancelot.

2. I am afraid.
3. Lies in wait.
4. Never misgave my heart against any visit you made.
5. Suspect.
6. Perhaps he has set.
7. I regret.
8. Cause injury to.
9. Since.
1. Wish to.

"God speed you well," said Sir Bors, "and send you sound and safe again!"

So Sir Lancelot departed and took his sword under his arm, and so he walked in his mantel,[2] that noble knight, and put himself in great jeopardy. And so he passed on till he came to the Queen's chamber, and so lightly he was had[3] into the chamber. And then, as the French book saith, the Queen and Sir Lancelot were together. And whether they were abed or at other manner of disports, me list[4] not thereof make no mention, for love that time[5] was not as love is nowadays.

But thus as they were together there came Sir Agravain and Sir Mordred with twelve knights with them of the Round Table, and they said with great crying and scaring[6] voice: "Thou traitor, Sir Lancelot, now are thou taken!" And thus they cried with a loud voice that all the court might hear it. And these fourteen knights all were armed at all points, as[7] they should fight in a battle.

"Alas!" said Queen Guinevere, "now are we mischieved[8] both!"

"Madam," said Sir Lancelot, "is there here any armor within your chamber that I might cover my body withal? And if there be any, give it me, and I shall soon stint[9] their malice, by the grace of God!"

"Now, truly," said the Queen, "I have none armor neither helm, shield, sword, neither spear, wherefore I dread me sore our long love is come to a mischievous end. For I hear by their noise there be many noble knights, and well I woot they be surely[1] armed, and against them ye may make no resistance. Wherefore ye are likely to be slain, and then shall I be burned! For and[2] ye might escape them," said the Queen, "I would not doubt but that ye would rescue me in what danger that ever I stood in."

"Alas!" said Sir Lancelot, "in all my life thus was I never bestead[3] that I should be thus shamefully slain for lack of mine armor."

But ever in one[4] Sir Agravain and Sir Mordred cried: "Traitor knight, come out of the Queen's chamber! For wit thou well thou art beset so that thou shalt not escape."

"Ah, Jesu mercy!" said Sir Lancelot, "this shameful cry and noise I may not suffer, for better were death at once than thus to endure this pain." Then he took the Queen in his arms and kissed her and said, "Most noblest Christian queen, I beseech you, as ye have been ever my special good lady, and I at all times your poor knight and true unto[5] my power, and as I never failed you in right nor in wrong sithen the first day King Arthur made me knight, that ye will pray for my soul if that I be slain. For well I am assured that Sir Bors, my nephew, and all the remnant of my kin, with Sir Lavain and Sir Urry,[6] that they will not fail you to rescue you from the fire. And therefore, mine own lady, recomfort yourself,[7] whatsoever come of me, that ye go with Sir Bors, my nephew, and Sir Urry and they all will do you all the pleasure that they may, and ye shall live like a queen upon my lands."

---

2. Cloak. Lancelot goes without armor.
3. Quickly he was received.
4. I care. "Disports": pastimes.
5. At that time.
6. Terrifying.
7. Completely, as if.
8. Come to grief.
9. Stop.
1. Securely.

2. If.
3. Beset.
4. In unison.
5. To the utmost of.
6. The brother of Elaine, the Fair Maid of Astolat, and a knight miraculously healed of his wound by Sir Lancelot. "Remnant": rest.
7. Take heart again.

"Nay, Sir Lancelot, nay!" said the Queen. "Wit thou well that I will not live long after thy days. But and[8] ye be slain I will take my death as meekly as ever did martyr take his death for Jesu Christ's sake."

"Well, Madam," said Sir Lancelot, "sith it is so that the day is come that our love must depart,[9] wit you well I shall sell my life as dear as I may. And a thousandfold," said Sir Lancelot, "I am more heavier[1] for you than for myself! And now I had liefer[2] than to be lord of all Christendom that I had sure armor upon me, that men might speak of my deeds ere ever I were slain."

"Truly," said the Queen, "and[3] it might please God, I would that they would take me and slay me and suffer[4] you to escape."

"That shall never be," said Sir Lancelot. "God defend me from such a shame! But, Jesu Christ, be Thou my shield and mine armor!" And therewith Sir Lancelot wrapped his mantel about his arm well and surely; and by then they had gotten a great form[5] out of the hall, and therewith they all rushed at the door. "Now, fair lords," said Sir Lancelot, "leave[6] your noise and your rushing, and I shall set open this door, and then may ye do with me what it liketh you."[7]

"Come off,[8] then," said they all, "and do it, for it availeth thee not to strive against us all. And therefore let us into this chamber, and we shall save thy life until thou come to King Arthur."

Then Sir Lancelot unbarred the door, and with his left hand he held it open a little, that but one man might come in at once. And so there came striding a good knight, a much[9] man and a large, and his name was called Sir Colgrevance of Gore. And he with a sword struck at Sir Lancelot mightily. And he put aside[1] the stroke and gave him such a buffet[2] upon the helmet that he fell groveling dead within the chamber door. Then Sir Lancelot with great might drew the knight within[3] the chamber door. And then Sir Lancelot, with help of the Queen and her ladies, he was lightly[4] armed in Colgrevance's armor. And ever stood Sir Agravain and Sir Mordred, crying, "Traitor knight! Come forth out of the Queen's chamber!"

"Sirs, leave[5] your noise," said Sir Lancelot, "for wit you well, Sir Agravain, ye shall not prison me this night. And therefore, and[6] ye do by my counsel, go ye all from this chamber door and make you no such crying and such manner of slander as ye do. For I promise you by my knighthood, and ye will depart and make no more noise, I shall as tomorn appear afore you all and before the King, and then let it be seen which of you all, other else ye all,[7] that will deprove[8] me of treason. And there shall I answer you, as a knight should, that hither I came to the Queen for no manner of mal engine,[9] and that will I prove and make it good upon you with my hands."

"Fie upon thee, traitor," said Sir Agravain and Sir Mordred, "for we will have thee malgré thine head[1] and slay thee, and we list. For we let thee wit we have the choice of[2] King Arthur to save thee other slay thee."

"Ah, sirs," said Sir Lancelot, "is there none other grace with you? Then keep[3] yourself!" And then Sir Lancelot set all open the chamber door and mightily and knightly he strode in among them. And anon[4] at the first stroke he slew Sir Agravain, and after twelve of his fellows. Within a little while he had laid them down cold to the earth, for there was none of the twelve knights might stand Sir Lancelot one buffet.[5] And also he wounded Sir Mordred, and therewithal he fled with all his might.

And then Sir Lancelot returned again unto the Queen and said, "Madam, now wit you well, all our true love is brought to an end, for now will King Arthur ever be my foe. And therefore, Madam, and it like you[6] that I may have you with me, I shall save you from all manner adventurous[7] dangers."

"Sir, that is not best," said the Queen, "me seemeth, for[8] now ye have done so much harm, it will be best that ye hold you still with this. And if ye see that as tomorn they will put me unto death, then may ye rescue me as ye think best."

"I will well,"[9] said Sir Lancelot, "for have ye no doubt, while I am a man living I shall rescue you." And then he kissed her, and either of them gave other a ring, and so there he left the Queen and went until[1] his lodging.

[WAR BREAKS OUT BETWEEN ARTHUR AND LANCELOT][2]

Then said King Arthur unto Sir Gawain, "Dear nephew, I pray you make ready in your best armor with your brethren, Sir Gaheris and Sir Gareth, to bring my Queen to the fire, there to have her judgment and receive the death."

"Nay, my most noble king," said Sir Gawain, "that will I never do, for wit you well I will never be in that place where so noble a queen as is my lady Dame Guinevere shall take such a shameful end. For wit you well," said Sir Gawain, "my heart will not serve me for to see her die, and it shall never be said that ever I was of your counsel for her death."

"Then," said the King unto Sir Gawain, "suffer[3] your brethren Sir Gaheris and Sir Gareth to be there."

"My lord," said Sir Gawain, "wit you well they will be loath to be there present because of many adventures[4] that is like to fall, but they are young and full unable to say you nay."

Then spake Sir Gaheris and the good knight Sir Gareth unto King Arthur: "Sir, ye may well command us to be there, but wit you well it shall be sore against our will. But and[5] we be there by your straight commandment, ye shall plainly[6] hold us there excused—we will be there in peaceable wise and bear none harness of war upon us."

1. In spite of you.
2. From.
3. Defend.
4. Right away.
5. Withstand Sir Lancelot one blow.
6. If it please you.
7. Perilous.
8. Because.
9. Agree.
1. To.
2. Lancelot and Sir Bors mobilize their friends for the rescue of Guinevere. In the morning Mordred reports the events of the night to Arthur who, against Gawain's strong opposition, condemns the queen to be burned, for "the law was such in those days that whatsoever they were, of what estate or degree, if they were found guilty of treason there should be none other remedy but death."
3. Allow.
4. Chance occurrences.
5. If.
6. Openly. "Straight": strict.

"In the name of God," said the King, "then make you ready, for she shall have soon[7] her judgment."

"Alas," said Sir Gawain, "that ever I should endure[8] to see this woeful day." So Sir Gawain turned him and wept heartily, and so he went into his chamber.

And then the Queen was led forth without[9] Carlisle, and anon she was dispoiled into[1] her smock. And then her ghostly father[2] was brought to her to be shriven of her misdeeds.[3] Then was there weeping and wailing and wringing of hands of many lords and ladies, but there were but few in comparison that would bear any armor for to strengthen[4] the death of the Queen.

Then was there one that Sir Lancelot had sent unto that place, which went to espy what time the Queen should go unto her death. And anon as[5] he saw the Queen dispoiled into her smock and shriven, then he gave Sir Lancelot warning. Then was there but spurring and plucking up[6] of horses, and right so they came unto the fire. And who[7] that stood against them, there were they slain—there might none withstand Sir Lancelot. So all that bore arms and withstood them, there were they slain, full many a noble knight. * * * And so in this rushing and hurling, as Sir Lancelot thrang[8] here and there, it misfortuned him[9] to slay Sir Gaheris and Sir Gareth, the noble knight, for they were unarmed and unwares.[1] As the French book saith, Sir Lancelot smote Sir Gaheris and Sir Gareth upon the brain-pans, wherethrough[2] that they were slain in the field, howbeit[3] Sir Lancelot saw them not. And so were they found dead among the thickest of the press.

Then when Sir Lancelot had thus done, and slain and put to flight all that would withstand him, then he rode straight unto Queen Guinevere and made a kirtle[4] and a gown to be cast upon her, and then he made her to be set behind him and prayed her to be of good cheer. Now wit you well the Queen was glad that she was escaped from death, and then she thanked God and Sir Lancelot.

And so he rode his way with the Queen, as the French book saith, unto Joyous Garde,[5] and there he kept her as a noble knight should. And many great lords and many good knights were sent him, and many full noble knights drew unto him. When they heard that King Arthur and Sir Lancelot were at debate,[6] many knights were glad, and many were sorry of their debate.

Now turn we again unto King Arthur, that when it was told him how and in what manner the Queen was taken away from the fire, and when he heard of the death of his noble knights, and in especial Sir Gaheris and Sir Gareth, then he swooned for very pure[7] sorrow. And when he awoke of his swoon, then he said: "Alas, that ever I bore crown upon my head! For now have I lost the fairest fellowship of noble knights that ever held Christian king[8] together. Alas, my good knights be slain and gone away from me. Now within these two days I have lost nigh forty knights and also the noble fellowship

7. Right away.
8. Live.
9. Outside.
1. Undressed down to.
2. Spiritual father, i.e., her priest.
3. For her to be confessed of her sins.
4. Secure.
5. As soon as.
6. Urging forward.
7. Whoever.

8. Pressed. "Hurling": turmoil.
9. He had the misfortune.
1. Unaware.
2. Through which.
3. Although.
4. Petticoat.
5. Lancelot's castle in England.
6. Strife.
7. Sheer.
8. That Christian king ever held.

of Sir Lancelot and his blood,[9] for now I may nevermore hold them together with my worship.[1] Alas, that ever this war began!

"Now, fair fellows," said the King, "I charge you that no man tell Sir Gawain of the death of his two brethren, for I am sure," said the King, "when he heareth tell that Sir Gareth is dead, he will go nigh out of his mind. Mercy Jesu," said the King, "why slew he Sir Gaheris and Sir Gareth? For I dare say, as for Sir Gareth, he loved Sir Lancelot above all men earthly."[2]

"That is truth," said some knights, "but they were slain in the hurling,[3] as Sir Lancelot thrang in the thickest of the press. And as they were unarmed, he smote them and wist[4] not whom that he smote, and so unhappily[5] they were slain."

"Well," said Arthur, "the death of them will cause the greatest mortal war that ever was, for I am sure that when Sir Gawain knoweth hereof that Sir Gareth is slain, I shall never have rest of him[6] till I have destroyed Sir Lancelot's kin and himself both, other else he to destroy me. And therefore," said the King, "wit you well, my heart was never so heavy as it is now. And much more I am sorrier for my good knights' loss[7] than for the loss of my fair queen; for queens I might have enough, but such a fellowship of good knights shall never be together in no company. And now I dare say," said King Arthur, "there was never Christian king that ever held such a fellowship together. And alas, that ever Sir Lancelot and I should be at debate. Ah, Agravain, Agravain!" said the King, "Jesu forgive it thy soul, for thine evil will that thou and thy brother Sir Mordred haddest unto Sir Lancelot hath caused all this sorrow." And ever among these complaints the King wept and swooned.

Then came there one to Sir Gawain and told him how the Queen was led away with[8] Sir Lancelot, and nigh a four-and-twenty knights slain. "Ah, Jesu, save me my two brethren!" said Sir Gawain. "For full well wist I," said Sir Gawain, "that Sir Lancelot would rescue her, other else he would die in that field. And to say the truth he were not of worship but if he had[9] rescued the Queen, insomuch as she should have been burned for his sake. And as in that," said Sir Gawain, "he hath done but knightly, and as I would have done myself and I had stood in like case. But where are my brethren?" said Sir Gawain. "I marvel that I hear not of them."

Then said that man, "Truly, Sir Gaheris and Sir Gareth be slain."

"Jesu defend!"[1] said Sir Gawain. "For all this world I would not that they were slain, and in especial my good brother Sir Gareth."

"Sir," said the man, "he is slain, and that is great pity."

"Who slew him?" said Sir Gawain.

"Sir Lancelot," said the man, "slew them both."

"That may I not believe," said Sir Gawain, "that ever he slew my good brother Sir Gareth, for I dare say my brother loved him better than me and all his brethren and the King both. Also I dare say, an[2] Sir Lancelot had desired my brother Sir Gareth with him, he would have been with him against

---

9. Kin.
1. Glory.
2. Earthly men.
3. Turmoil.
4. Knew.
5. Unluckily.

6. He will never give me any peace.
7. The loss of my good knights.
8. By.
9. Of honor if he had not.
1. Forbid.
2. If.

the King and us all. And therefore I may never believe that Sir Lancelot slew my brethren."

"Verily, sir," said the man, "it is noised[3] that he slew him."

"Alas," said Sir Gawain, "now is my joy gone." And then he fell down and swooned, and long he lay there as he had been dead. And when he arose out of his swoon, he cried out sorrowfully and said, "Alas!" And forthwith he ran unto the King, crying and weeping, and said, "Ah, mine uncle King Arthur! My good brother Sir Gareth is slain, and so is my brother Sir Gaheris, which were two noble knights."

Then the King wept and he both, and so they fell on swooning. And when they were revived, then spake Sir Gawain and said, "Sir, I will go and see my brother Sir Gareth."

"Sir, ye may not see him," said the King, "for I caused him to be interred and Sir Gaheris both, for I well understood that ye would make overmuch sorrow, and the sight of Sir Gareth should have caused your double sorrow."

"Alas, my lord," said Sir Gawain, "how slew he my brother Sir Gareth? Mine own good lord, I pray you tell me."

"Truly," said the King, "I shall tell you as it hath been told me—Sir Lancelot slew him and Sir Gaheris both."

"Alas," said Sir Gawain, "they bore none arms against him, neither of them both."

"I woot not how it was," said the King, "but as it is said, Sir Lancelot slew them in the thickest of the press and knew them not. And therefore let us shape a remedy for to revenge their deaths."

"My king, my lord, and mine uncle," said Sir Gawain, "wit you well, now I shall make you a promise which I shall hold by my knighthood, that from this day forward I shall never fail[4] Sir Lancelot until that one of us have slain the other. And therefore I require you, my lord and king, dress[5] you unto the wars, for wit you well, I will be revenged upon Sir Lancelot; and therefore, as ye will have my service and my love, now haste you thereto and assay[6] your friends. For I promise unto God," said Sir Gawain, "for the death of my brother Sir Gareth I shall seek Sir Lancelot throughout seven kings' realms, but I shall slay him, other else he shall slay me."

"Sir, ye shall not need to seek him so far," said the King, "for as I hear say, Sir Lancelot will abide me and us all within the castle of Joyous Garde. And much people draweth unto him, as I hear say."

"That may I right well believe," said Sir Gawain, "but my lord," he said, "assay your friends and I will assay mine."

"It shall be done," said the King, "and as I suppose I shall be big[7] enough to drive him out of the biggest tower of his castle."

So then the King sent letters and writs throughout all England, both the length and the breadth, for to summon all his knights. And so unto King Arthur drew many knights, dukes, and earls, that he had a great host, and when they were assembled the King informed them how Sir Lancelot had bereft him his Queen. Then the King and all his host made them ready to lay siege about Sir Lancelot where he lay within Joyous Garde.

3. Reported.
4. Give up the pursuit of.
5. Prepare.
6. Appeal to
7. Strong.

[THE DEATH OF ARTHUR][8]

So upon Trinity Sunday at night King Arthur dreamed a wonderful dream, and in his dream him seemed that he saw upon a chafflet[9] a chair, and the chair was fast to a wheel, and thereupon sat King Arthur in the richest cloth of gold that might be made. And the King thought there was under him, far from him, an hideous deep black water, and therein was all manner of serpents, and worms, and wild beasts, foul and horrible. And suddenly the King thought that the wheel turned upside down, and he fell among the serpents, and every beast took him by a limb. And then the King cried as he lay in his bed, "Help, help!"

And then knights, squires, and yeomen awaked the King, and then he was so amazed that he wist[1] not where he was. And then so he awaked[2] until it was nigh day, and then he fell on slumbering again, not sleeping nor thoroughly waking. So the King seemed[3] verily that there came Sir Gawain unto him with a number of fair ladies with him. So when King Arthur saw him, he said, "Welcome, my sister's son. I weened ye had been dead. And now I see thee on-live, much am I beholden unto Almighty Jesu. Ah, fair nephew and my sister's son, what been these ladies that hither be come with you?"

"Sir," said Sir Gawain, "all these be ladies for whom I have foughten for when I was man living. And all these are tho[4] that I did battle for in righteous quarrels, and God hath given them that grace, at their great prayer, because I did battle for them for their right, that they should bring me hither unto you. Thus much hath given me leave God, for to warn you of your death. For and ye fight as tomorn[5] with Sir Mordred, as ye both have assigned,[6] doubt ye not ye must be slain, and the most party of your people on both parties. And for the great grace and goodness that Almighty Jesu hath unto you, and for pity of you and many mo other good men there[7] shall be slain, God hath sent me to you of his special grace to give you warning that in no wise ye do battle as tomorn, but that ye take a treatise for a month-day.[8] And proffer you largely,[9] so that tomorn ye put in a delay. For within a month shall come Sir Lancelot with all his noble knights and rescue you worshipfully and slay Sir Mordred and all that ever will hold with him."

Then Sir Gawain and all the ladies vanished. And anon the King called upon his knights, squires, and yeomen, and charged them wightly[1] to fetch his noble lords and wise bishops unto him. And when they were come the King told them of his avision,[2] that Sir Gawain had told him and warned him that, and he fought on the morn, he should be slain. Then the King commanded Sir Lucan the Butler[3] and his brother Sir Bedivere the Bold, with

---

8. The pope arranges a truce, Guinevere is returned to Arthur, and Lancelot and his kin leave England to become rulers of France. At Gawain's instigation Arthur invades France to resume the war against Lancelot. Word comes to the king that Mordred has seized the kingdom, and Arthur leads his forces back to England. Mordred attacks them upon their landing, and Gawain is mortally wounded and dies, although not before he has repented for having insisted that Arthur fight Lancelot and has written Lancelot to come to the aid of his former lord.

9. Scaffold. "Him seemed": it seemed to him.

1. Knew.

2. Lay awake.

3. It seemed to the king.

4. Those.

5. If you fight tomorrow.

6. Decided.

7. I.e., who there. "Mo": more.

8. For a month from today. "Treatise": treaty, truce.

9. Make generous offers.

1. Quickly.

2. Dream.

3. "Butler" here is probably only a title of high rank, although it was originally used to designate the officer who had charge of wine for the king's table.

two bishops with them, and charged them in any wise to take a treatise for a month-day with Sir Mordred. "And spare not: proffer him lands and goods as much as ye think reasonable."

So then they departed and came to Sir Mordred where he had a grim host of an hundred thousand, and there they entreated[4] Sir Mordred long time. And at the last Sir Mordred was agreed for to have Cornwall and Kent by King Arthur's days,[5] and after that, all England, after the days of King Arthur.

Then were they condescended[6] that King Arthur and Sir Mordred should meet betwixt both their hosts, and everich[7] of them should bring fourteen persons. And so they came with this word unto Arthur. Then said he, "I am glad that this is done," and so he went into the field.

And when King Arthur should depart, he warned all his host that, and they see any sword drawn, "Look ye come on fiercely and slay that traitor Sir Mordred, for I in no wise trust him." In like wise Sir Mordred warned his host that "And ye see any manner of sword drawn, look that ye come on fiercely, and so slay all that ever before you standeth, for in no wise I will not trust for this treatise." And in the same wise said Sir Mordred unto his host, "For I know well my father will be avenged upon me."

And so they met as their pointment[8] was and were agreed and accorded thoroughly. And wine was fetched and they drank together. Right so came an adder out of a little heath-bush, and it stung a knight in the foot. And so when the knight felt him so stung, he looked down and saw the adder. And anon he drew his sword to slay the adder, and thought[9] none other harm. And when the host on both parties saw that sword drawn, then they blew beams,[1] trumpets, and horns, and shouted grimly. And so both hosts dressed them[2] together. And King Arthur took his horse and said, "Alas, this unhappy day!" and so rode to his party, and Sir Mordred in like wise.

And never since was there never seen a more dolefuller battle in no Christian land, for there was but rushing and riding, foining[3] and striking; and many a grim word was there spoken of either to other, and many a deadly stroke. But ever King Arthur rode throughout the battle[4] of Sir Mordred many times and did full nobly, as a noble king should do, and at all times he fainted never. And Sir Mordred did his devoir[5] that day and put himself in great peril.

And thus they fought all the long day, and never stinted[6] till the noble knights were laid to the cold earth. And ever they fought still till it was near night, and by then was there an hundred thousand laid dead upon the down. Then was King Arthur wood-wroth[7] out of measure when he saw his people so slain from him. And so he looked about him and could see no mo[8] of all his host, and good knights left no mo on-live, but two knights: the t'one[9] was Sir Lucan the Butler and [the other] his brother Sir Bedivere. And yet they were full sore wounded.

"Jesu, mercy," said the King, "where are all my noble knights become?[1]

4. Dealt with.
5. During King Arthur's lifetime.
6. Agreed.
7. Each.
8. Arrangement.
9. Meant.
1. A kind of trumpet.
2. Prepared to come.

3. Lunging.
4. Battalion.
5. Knightly duty.
6. Stopped.
7. Mad with rage.
8. Others.
9. That one, i.e., the first.
1. What has become of all my noble knights?

Alas that ever I should see this doleful day! For now," said King Arthur, "I am come to mine end. But would to God," said he, "that I wist[2] now where were that traitor Sir Mordred that has caused all this mischief."

Then King Arthur looked about and was ware where stood Sir Mordred leaning upon his sword among a great heap of dead men.

"Now give me my spear," said King Arthur unto Sir Lucan, "for yonder I have espied the traitor that all this woe hath wrought."

"Sir, let him be," said Sir Lucan, "for he is unhappy.[3] And if ye pass this unhappy day ye shall be right well revenged upon him. And, good lord, remember ye of your night's dream, and what the spirit of Sir Gawain told you tonight, and yet God of his great goodness hath preserved you hitherto. And for God's sake, my lord, leave off by this,[4] for, blessed be God, ye have won the field: for yet we been here three on-live, and with Sir Mordred is not one on-live. And therefore if ye leave off now, this wicked day of destiny is past."

"Now, tide[5] me death, tide me life," said the King, "now I see him yonder alone, he shall never escape mine hands. For at a better avail[6] shall I never have him."

"God speed you well!" said Sir Bedivere.

Then the King got his spear in both his hands and ran toward Sir Mordred, crying and saying, "Traitor, now is thy deathday come!"

And when Sir Mordred saw King Arthur he ran until him with his sword drawn in his hand, and there King Arthur smote Sir Mordred under the shield, with a foin[7] of his spear, throughout the body more than a fathom.[8] And when Sir Mordred felt that he had his death's wound, he thrust himself with the might that he had up to the burr[9] of King Arthur's spear, and right so he smote his father King Arthur with his sword holden in both his hands, upon the side of the head, that the sword pierced the helmet and the tay[1] of the brain. And therewith Sir Mordred dashed down stark dead to the earth.

And noble King Arthur fell in a swough[2] to the earth, and there he swooned oftentimes, and Sir Lucan and Sir Bedivere ofttimes heaved him up. And so, weakly betwixt them, they led him to a little chapel not far from the seaside, and when the King was there, him thought him reasonably eased. Then heard they people cry in the field. "Now go thou, Sir Lucan," said the King, "and do me to wit[3] what betokens that noise in the field."

So Sir Lucan departed, for he was grievously wounded in many places. And so as he yede[4] he saw and harkened by the moonlight how that pillers[5] and robbers were come into the field to pill and to rob many a full noble knight of brooches and bees[6] and of many a good ring and many a rich jewel. And who that were not dead all out there they slew them for their harness[7] and their riches. When Sir Lucan understood this work, he came to the King as soon as he might and told him all what he had heard and seen. "Therefore by my read,"[8] said Sir Lucan, "it is best that we bring you to some town."

2. Knew.
3. I.e., unlucky for you.
4. I.e., with this much accomplished.
5. Betide.
6. Advantage.
7. Thrust.
8. I.e., six feet.
9. Hand guard.

1. Edge.
2. Swoon.
3. Let me know.
4. Walked.
5. Plunderers.
6. Bracelets.
7. Armor. "All out": entirely.
8. Advice.

"I would it were so," said the King, "but I may not stand, my head works[9] so. Ah, Sir Lancelot," said King Arthur, "this day have I sore missed thee. And alas that ever I was against thee, for now have I my death, whereof Sir Gawain me warned in my dream."

Then Sir Lucan took up the King the t'one party[1] and Sir Bedivere the other party; and in the lifting up the King swooned and in the lifting Sir Lucan fell in a swoon that part of his guts fell out of his body, and therewith the noble knight's heart burst. And when the King awoke he beheld Sir Lucan how he lay foaming at the mouth and part of his guts lay at his feet.

"Alas," said the King, "this is to me a full heavy[2] sight to see this noble duke so die for my sake, for he would have holpen[3] me that had more need of help than I. Alas that he would not complain him for[4] his heart was so set to help me. Now Jesu have mercy upon his soul."

Then Sir Bedivere wept for the death of his brother.

"Now leave this mourning and weeping, gentle knight," said the King, "for all this will not avail me. For wit thou well, and[5] I might live myself, the death of Sir Lucan would grieve me evermore. But my time passeth on fast," said the King. "Therefore," said King Arthur unto Sir Bedivere, "take thou here Excalibur[6] my good sword and go with it to yonder water's side; and when thou comest there I charge thee throw my sword in that water and come again and tell me what thou sawest there."

"My lord," said Sir Bedivere, "your commandment shall be done, and [I shall] lightly[7] bring you word again."

So Sir Bedivere departed. And by the way he beheld that noble sword, that the pommel and the haft[8] was all precious stones. And then he said to himself, "If I throw this rich sword in the water, thereof shall never come good, but harm and loss." And then Sir Bedivere hid Excalibur under a tree. And so, as soon as he might, he came again unto the King and said he had been at the water and had thrown the sword into the water.

"What saw thou there?" said the King.

"Sir," he said, "I saw nothing but waves and winds."

"That is untruly said of thee," said the King. "And therefore go thou lightly again and do my commandment; as thou art to me lief[9] and dear, spare not, but throw it in."

Then Sir Bedivere returned again and took the sword in his hand. And yet him thought[1] sin and shame to throw away that noble sword. And so eft[2] he hid the sword and returned again and told the King that he had been at the water and done his commandment.

"What sawest thou there?" said the King.

"Sir," he said, "I saw nothing but waters wap and waves wan."[3]

"Ah, traitor unto me and untrue," said King Arthur, "now hast thou betrayed me twice. Who would have weened that thou that has been to me so lief and dear, and thou art named a noble knight, and would betray me

---

9. Aches.
1. On one side.
2. Sorrowful.
3. Helped.
4. Because.
5. If.
6. The sword that Arthur had received as a young man from the Lady of the Lake; it is presumably she who catches it when Bedivere finally throws it

into the water.
7. Quickly.
8. Handle. "Pommel": rounded knob on the hilt.
9. Beloved.
1. It seemed to him.
2. Again.
3. The phrase seems to mean "waters wash the shore and waves grow dark."

for the riches of this sword. But now go again lightly, for thy long tarrying putteth me in great jeopardy of my life, for I have taken cold. And but if thou do now as I bid thee, if ever I may see thee I shall slay thee mine[4] own hands, for thou wouldest for my rich sword see me dead."

Then Sir Bedivere departed and went to the sword and lightly took it up, and so he went to the water's side; and there he bound the girdle[5] about the hilts, and threw the sword as far into the water as he might. And there came an arm and an hand above the water and took it and clutched it, and shook it thrice and brandished; and then vanished away the hand with the sword into the water. So Sir Bedivere came again to the King and told him what he saw.

"Alas," said the King, "help me hence, for I dread me I have tarried overlong."

Then Sir Bedivere took the King upon his back and so went with him to that water's side. And when they were at the water's side, even fast[6] by the bank hoved[7] a little barge with many fair ladies in it; and among them all was a queen; and all they had black hoods, and all they wept and shrieked when they saw King Arthur.

"Now put me into that barge," said the King; and so he did softly. And there received him three ladies with great mourning, and so they set them[8] down. And in one of their laps King Arthur laid his head, and then the queen said, "Ah, my dear brother, why have ye tarried so long from me? Alas, this wound on your head hath caught overmuch cold." And anon they rowed fromward the land, and Sir Bedivere beheld all tho ladies go froward him.

Then Sir Bedivere cried and said, "Ah, my lord Arthur, what shall become of me, now ye go from me and leave me here alone among mine enemies?"

"Comfort thyself," said the King, "and do as well as thou mayest, for in me is no trust for to trust in. For I must into the vale of Avilion[9] to heal me of my grievous wound. And if thou hear nevermore of me, pray for my soul."

But ever the queen and ladies wept and shrieked that it was pity to hear. And as soon as Sir Bedivere had lost the sight of the barge he wept and wailed and so took the forest, and went[1] all that night. And in the morning he was ware betwixt two holts hoar[2] of a chapel and an hermitage.[3]

* * *

Thus of Arthur I find no more written in books that been authorized,[4] neither more of the very certainty of his death heard I never read,[5] but thus was he led away in a ship wherein were three queens: that one was King Arthur's sister, Queen Morgan la Fée, the t'other[6] was the Queen of North Wales, and the third was the Queen of the Waste Lands. * * *

Now more of the death of King Arthur could I never find but that these

---

4. I.e., with mine.
5. Sword belt.
6. Close.
7. Waited.
8. I.e., they sat.
9. A legendary island, sometimes identified with the earthly paradise.
1. Walked. "Took": took to.
2. Ancient copses.
3. In the passage here omitted, Sir Bedivere meets

the former bishop of Canterbury, now a hermit, who describes how on the previous night a company of ladies had brought to the chapel a dead body, asking that it be buried. Sir Bedivere exclaims that the dead man must have been King Arthur and vows to spend the rest of his life there in the chapel as a hermit.
4. That have authority.
5. Tell.
6. The second.

ladies brought him to his burials,[7] and such one was buried there that the hermit bore witness that sometime was Bishop of Canterbury.[8] But yet the hermit knew not in certain that he was verily the body of King Arthur, for this tale Sir Bedivere, a Knight of the Table Round, made it to be written. Yet some men say in many parts of England that King Arthur is not dead, but had by the will of our Lord Jesu into another place. And men say that he shall come again and he shall win the Holy Cross. Yet I will not say that it shall be so, but rather I will say, Here in this world he changed his life. And many men say that there is written upon his tomb this verse: *Hic iacet Arthurus, rex quondam, rexque futurus.*[9]

[THE DEATHS OF LANCELOT AND GUINEVERE][1]

And thus upon a night there came a vision to Sir Lancelot and charged him, in remission[2] of his sins, to haste him unto Amesbury: "And by then[3] thou come there, thou shalt find Queen Guinevere dead. And therefore take thy fellows with thee, and purvey them of an horse-bier,[4] and fetch thou the corse[5] of her, and bury her by her husband, the noble King Arthur. So this avision[6] came to Lancelot thrice in one night. Then Sir Lancelot rose up ere day and told the hermit.

"It were well done," said the hermit, "that ye made you ready and that ye disobey not the avision."

Then Sir Lancelot took his eight fellows with him, and on foot they yede[7] from Glastonbury to Amesbury, the which is little more than thirty mile, and thither they came within two days, for they were weak and feeble to go. And when Sir Lancelot was come to Amesbury within the nunnery, Queen Guinevere died but half an hour afore. And the ladies told Sir Lancelot that Queen Guinevere told them all ere she passed that Sir Lancelot had been priest near a twelve-month:[8] "and hither he cometh as fast as he may to fetch my corse, and beside my lord King Arthur he shall bury me." Wherefore the Queen said in hearing of them all, "I beseech Almighty God that I may never have power to see Sir Lancelot with my worldly eyes."

"And thus," said all the ladies, "was ever her prayer these two days till she was dead."

Then Sir Lancelot saw her visage, but he wept not greatly, but sighed. And so he did all the observance of the service himself, both the *dirige*[9] and on the morn he sang mass. And there was ordained[1] an horse-bier, and so with an hundred torches ever burning about the corse of the Queen, and ever Sir Lancelot with his eight fellows went about[2] the horse-bier, singing and reading many an holy orison,[3] and frankincense upon the corse incensed.[4]

Thus Sir Lancelot and his eight fellows went on foot from Amesbury unto

---

7. Grave.

8. Of whom the hermit, who was formerly bishop of Canterbury, bore witness.

9. "Here lies Arthur, who was once king and king will be again."

1. Guinevere enters a convent at Amesbury where Lancelot, returned with his companions to England, visits her, but she commands him never to see her again. Emulating her example, Lancelot joins the bishop of Canterbury and Bedivere in their hermitage where he takes holy orders and is joined in turn by seven of his fellow knights.

2. For the remission.

3. By the time.

4. Provide them with a horse-drawn hearse.

5. Body.

6. Dream.

7. Went.

8. Nearly twelve months.

9. Funeral service.

1. Prepared.

2. Around.

3. Reciting many a prayer.

4. Burned frankincense over the body.

Glastonbury, and when they were come to the chapel and the hermitage, there she had a *dirige* with great devotion.[5] And on the morn the hermit that sometime[6] was Bishop of Canterbury sang the mass of requiem with great devotion, and Sir Lancelot was the first that offered, and then als[7] his eight fellows. And then she was wrapped in cered cloth of Rennes, from the top[8] to the toe, in thirtyfold, and after she was put in a web[9] of lead, and then in a coffin of marble.

And when she was put in the earth Sir Lancelot swooned and lay long still, while[1] the hermit came and awaked him, and said, "Ye be to blame, for ye displease God with such manner of sorrow-making."

"Truly," said Sir Lancelot, "I trust I do not displease God, for He knoweth mine intent—for my sorrow was not, nor is not, for any rejoicing of sin, but my sorrow may never have end. For when I remember of her beauté and of her noblesse[2] that was both with her king and with her,[3] so when I saw his corse and her corse so lie together, truly mine heart would not serve to sustain my careful[4] body. Also when I remember me how by my defaute and mine orgule[5] and my pride that they were both laid full low, that were peerless that ever was living of Christian people, wit you well," said Sir Lancelot, "this remembered, of their kindness and mine unkindness, sank so to mine heart that I might not sustain myself." So the French book maketh mention.

Then Sir Lancelot never after ate but little meat,[6] nor drank, till he was dead, for then he sickened more and more and dried and dwined[7] away. For the Bishop nor none of his fellows might not make him to eat, and little he drank, that he was waxen by a kibbet[8] shorter than he was, that the people could not know him. For evermore, day and night, he prayed, but sometime he slumbered a broken sleep. Ever he was lying groveling on the tomb of King Arthur and Queen Guinevere, and there was no comfort that the Bishop nor Sir Bors, nor none of his fellows could make him—it availed not.

So within six weeks after, Sir Lancelot fell sick and lay in his bed. And then he sent for the Bishop that there was hermit, and all his true fellows. Then Sir Lancelot said with dreary steven,[9] "Sir Bishop, I pray you give to me all my rights that longeth[1] to a Christian man."

"It shall not need you,"[2] said the hermit and all his fellows. "It is but heaviness of your blood. Ye shall be well mended by the grace of God tomorn."

"My fair lords," said Sir Lancelot, "wit you well my careful body will into the earth; I have warning more than now I will say. Therefore give me my rights."

So when he was houseled and annealed[3] and had all that a Christian man ought to have, he prayed the Bishop that his fellows might bear his body to Joyous Garde. (Some men say it was Alnwick, and some men say it was

5. Solemnity.
6. Once.
7. Also. "Offered": made his donation.
8. Head. "Cloth of Rennes": A shroud made of fine linen smeared with wax, produced at Rennes.
9. Afterward she was put in a sheet.
1. Until.
2. Her beauty and nobility.
3. That she and her king both had.

4. Sorrowful.
5. My fault and my haughtiness.
6. Food.
7. Wasted.
8. Grown by a cubit.
9. Sad voice.
1. Pertains. "Rights": last sacrament.
2. You shall not need it.
3. Given communion and extreme unction.

Bamborough.) "Howbeit," said Sir Lancelot, "me repenteth[4] sore, but I made mine avow sometime that in Joyous Garde I would be buried. And because of breaking[5] of mine avow, I pray you all, lead me thither." Then there was weeping and wringing of hands among his fellows.

So at a season of the night they all went to their beds, for they all lay in one chamber. And so after midnight, against[6] day, the Bishop that was hermit, as he lay in his bed asleep, he fell upon a great laughter. And therewith all the fellowship awoke and came to the Bishop and asked him what he ailed.[7]

"Ah, Jesu mercy," said the Bishop, "why did ye awake me? I was never in all my life so merry and so well at ease."

"Wherefore?" said Sir Bors.

"Truly," said the Bishop, "here was Sir Lancelot with me, with mo[8] angels than ever I saw men in one day. And I saw the angels heave[9] up Sir Lancelot unto heaven, and the gates of heaven opened against him."

"It is but dretching of swevens,"[1] said Sir Bors, "for I doubt not Sir Lancelot aileth nothing but good."[2]

"It may well be," said the Bishop. "Go ye to his bed and then shall ye prove the sooth."

So when Sir Bors and his fellows came to his bed, they found him stark dead. And he lay as he had smiled, and the sweetest savor[3] about him that ever they felt. Then was there weeping and wringing of hands, and the greatest dole they made that ever made men. And on the morn the Bishop did his mass of Requiem, and after the Bishop and all the nine knights put Sir Lancelot in the same horse-bier that Queen Guinevere was laid in tofore that she was buried. And so the Bishop and they all together went with the body of Sir Lancelot daily, till they came to Joyous Garde. And ever they had an hundred torches burning about him.

And so within fifteen days they came to Joyous Garde. And there they laid his corse in the body of the choir,[4] and sang and read many psalters[5] and prayers over him and about him. And ever his visage was laid open and naked, that all folks might behold him; for such was the custom in tho[6] days that all men of worship should so lie with open visage till that they were buried.

And right thus as they were at their service, there came Sir Ector de Maris that had seven year sought all England, Scotland, and Wales, seeking his brother, Sir Lancelot. And when Sir Ector heard such noise and light in the choir of Joyous Garde, he alight and put his horse from him and came into the choir. And there he saw men sing and weep, and all they knew Sir Ector, but he knew not them. Then went Sir Bors unto Sir Ector and told him how there lay his brother, Sir Lancelot, dead. And then Sir Ector threw his shield, sword, and helm from him, and when he beheld Sir Lancelot's visage, he fell down in a swoon. And when he waked, it were hard any tongue to tell the doleful complaints that he made for his brother.

4. I am sorry.
5. In order not to break.
6. Toward.
7. Ailed him.
8. More.
9. Lift.
1. Illusion of dreams.

2. Has nothing wrong with him.
3. Odor. A sweet scent is a conventional sign in saints' lives of a sanctified death.
4. The center of the chancel, the place of honor.
5. Psalms.
6. Those.

"Ah, Lancelot!" he said, "thou were head of all Christian knights. And now I dare say," said Sir Ector, "thou Sir Lancelot, there thou liest, that thou were never matched of earthly knight's hand. And thou were the courteoust[7] knight that ever bore shield. And thou were the truest friend to thy lover that ever bestrode horse, and thou were the truest lover, of a sinful man,[8] that ever loved woman, and thou were the kindest man that ever struck with sword. And thou were the goodliest person that ever came among press of knights, and thou was the meekest man and the gentlest that ever ate in hall among ladies, and thou were the sternest knight to thy mortal foe that ever put spear in the rest."[9]

Then there was weeping and dolor out of measure.

Thus they kept Sir Lancelot's corse aloft fifteen days, and then they buried it with great devotion. And then at leisure they went all with the Bishop of Canterbury to his hermitage, and there they were together more than a month.

Then Sir Constantine that was Sir Cador's son of Cornwall was chosen king of England, and he was a full noble knight, and worshipfully he ruled this realm. And then this King Constantine sent for the Bishop of Canterbury, for he heard say where he was. And so he was restored unto his bishopric and left that hermitage, and Sir Bedivere was there ever still hermit to his life's end.

Then Sir Bors de Ganis, Sir Ector de Maris, Sir Gahalantine, Sir Galihud, Sir Galihodin, Sir Blamour, Sir Bleoberis, Sir Villiars le Valiant, Sir Clarrus of Clermount, all these knights drew them to their countries. Howbeit[1] King Constantine would have had them with him, but they would not abide in this realm. And there they all lived in their countries as holy men.

And some English books make mention that they went never out of England after the death of Sir Lancelot—but that was but favor of makers.[2] For the French book maketh mention—and is authorized—that Sir Bors, Sir Ector, Sir Blamour, and Sir Bleoberis went into the Holy Land, theras Jesu Christ was quick[3] and dead, and anon as they had stablished their lands;[4] for the book saith so Sir Lancelot commanded them for to do ere ever he passed out of this world. There these four knights did many battles upon the miscreaunts,[5] or Turks, and there they died upon a Good Friday for God's sake.

Here is the end of the whole book of King Arthur and of his noble knights of the Round Table, that when they were whole together there was ever an hundred and forty. And here is the end of *The Death of Arthur*.[6]

I pray you all gentlemen and gentlewomen that readeth this book of Arthur and his knights from the beginning to the ending, pray for me while I am alive that God send me good deliverance. And when I am dead, I pray you all pray for my soul.

For this book was ended the ninth year of the reign of King Edward the

---

7. Most courteous.
8. Of any man born in original sin.
9. Support for the butt of the lance.
1. However.
2. The authors' bias.
3. Living. "Thereas": where.

4. As soon as they had put their lands in order.
5. Infidels.
6. By the "whole book" Malory refers to the entire work; the *Death of Arthur*, which Caxton made the title of the entire work, refers to the last part of Malory's book.

Fourth, by Sir Thomas Malory, knight, as Jesu help him for His great might,
as he is the servant of Jesu both day and night.

1469–70   1485

ROBERT HENRYSON
ca. 1425–ca. 1500

Robert Henryson is one of a group of Middle Scots poets sometimes referred to as
"Scottish Chaucerians." That term does less than justice to an older tradition of
Scottish literature that carries on into modern times but does indicate the great influence Chaucer exerted on both his English and his Scottish followers. That influence
is nowhere more apparent than in Henryson's *The Testament of Cresseid*, which is a
sequel to Chaucer's other major poem, *Troilus and Criseyde*, and relates the fate of
its heroine. In the sixteenth century, *The Testament* was printed as one of Chaucer's
works. *The Cock and the Fox*, one of fourteen fables that constitute another important
work by Henryson, is a highly original retelling of Chaucer's *Nun's Priest's Tale*.
Henryson clearly enjoyed and shared Chaucer's humor, and the animals in his fables
speak a wonderfully colloquial idiom. He is also a serious moralist: his earnest purpose
and that of his master Aesop, he explains in a *Prologue*, is to show in an entertaining
way how many men behave like beasts.

Very little is known for certain about Henryson's life. Because he is spoken of as
"master," he probably held a master's degree, and evidence points to his having been
headmaster of a grammar school founded by monks of the town Dunfermline. As a
schoolmaster, Henryson would have regularly used collections of fables to teach boys
their Latin. Such a Latin collection by Walter the Englishman served as Henryson's
main source for *The Fables*.

One of the chief attractions of Henryson's poetry is the language, which is no more
difficult than Chaucer's. The text here is based on the Oxford edition by Denton Fox
(1981), but spellings have occasionally been altered for easier comprehension. The
notes call attention to some of the main differences between Chaucer's East Midland
and Henryson's Scots dialect. The seven-line stanza of *The Fables* and *The Testament
of Cresseid*, known as rhyme royal, is the one Chaucer used in his *Troilus and Criseyde*
and most of the religious stories in *The Canterbury Tales*. It has been said to derive
its name from the fact that a royal poet, King James I of Scotland, wrote *The Kingis
Quair* (The King's Book) in that stanza.

The Cock and the Fox

Thogh brutal¹ beestes be irrational,
That is to say, wantand,² discretioun,
Yit ilk ane° in their³ kindes natural   *each one*
Has many divers inclinatioun:°   *natural disposition*

---

1. Brute, adj., in the sense of relating to animals,
as in "brute beasts."
2. Wanting, (i.e., lacking). In the Scottish dialect
the normal ending of the present participle is *-and*

instead of *-ing*.
3. Note that Scottish dialect uses *their* and *them*
where Chaucer's East Midland still has *hire* and
hem.

5 The bair° busteous,° the wolf, the wylde lyoun,   *bear/rough, rude*
   The fox fenyeit,° craftie and cautelous,°   *deceitful/cunning*
   The dog to bark on night and keep the hous.

   Sa⁴ different they are in properteis°   *qualities*
   Unknawin° unto man and infinite,   *unknown*
10 In kind havand sa fel° diversiteis,   *having so many*
   My cunning° it excedis⁵ for to dyte.°   *skill/write*
   Forthy° as now, I purpose for to wryte   *therefore*
   Ane case I fand whilk fell this other yeer⁶
   Betwix° ane fox and gentil° Chauntecleer.   *between/noble*

15 Ane widow dwelt intill ane drop they dayis⁷
   Whilk wan hir food off⁸ spinning on hir rok,°   *distaff*
   And na mair° had, forsooth, as the fabill sayis,   *no more*
   Except of hennes scho° had ane lyttel flok,   *she*
   And them to keep scho had ane jolie cok,
20 Right corageous, that to this widow ay°   *always*
   Divided night⁹ and crew before the day.

   Ane lyttel fra° this foresaid widow's hous,   *from*
   Ane thornie schaw° there was of greet defence,   *thicket*
   Wherein ane foxe, craftie and cautelous,°   *cunning*
25 Made his repair and daylie residence,
   Whilk° to this widow did greet violence   *which*
   In pyking off pultrie° baith° day and night,   *poultry/both*
   And na way be revengit on him scho might.

   This wylie tod,° when that the lark couth sing,¹   *fox*
30 Full sair° and hungrie unto the toun him drest,°   *sorely, painfully/proceeded*
   Where Chauntecleer, in to the gray dawing,°   *dawn*
   Werie for° night, was flowen fra his nest.   *weary of*
   Lowrence² this saw and in his mind he kest°   *cast, considered*
   The jeperdies, the wayes, and the wyle,³
35 By what menis° he might this cok begyle.   *means*

   Dissimuland in to countenance and cheer,⁴
   On knees fell and simuland thus he said,
   "Gude morne, my maister, gentil Chantecleer!"
   With that the cok start bakwart in ane braid.°   *with a start*
40 "Schir,"° by my saul,° ye need not be effraid,   *sir/soul*
   Nor yit for me to start nor flee abak;
   I come bot here service to you to mak.

---

4. So. Note that in Scottish dialect long *a* is pronounced for long *o*.
5. Note that the third person singular of verbs
ends in-*s* or-*is* instead of-*th* as in Chaucer.
6. A case I found which happened a year or two
ago. "Ane": a. The same word as *one*, which functions as the indefinite article.
7. In a village [in] those days.
8. Who made her living (literally: won her food)
by.

9. I.e., kept the hours at night by crowing. Cf. *The
Miller's Tale*, line 567, and *The Nun's Priest's Tale*,
lines 33–38.
1. When the lark could sing, i.e., at dawn.
2. Generic name for a fox, perhaps invented here
by Henryson.
3. The stratagems, the devices, and the trickery.
4. Dissimulating in facial expression and manner.

"Wald I not serve to you, it wer bot blame,[5]
As I have done to your progenitouris.
45 Your father oft fulfillit has my wame,°   *belly*
And sent me meit° fra midding° to the muris,°   *food / refuse pile / moors*
And at his end I did my besie curis°   *busy cares*
To held his heed and gif him drinkis warme,
Syne° at the last, the sweit° swelt° in my arme!"   *then / sweet (man) / died*

50 "Knew ye my father?" quad the cok, and leuch.°   *laughed*
"Yea, my fair son, forsooth I held his heed
When that he deit° under ane birkin beuch,°   *died / birch bough*
Syne said the Dirigie[6] when that he was deed.
Betwix us twa how suld there be ane feid?[7]
55 Wham suld ye traist° bot me, your servitour   *whom should you trust*
That to your father did so greet honour?

When I beheld your fedderis° fair and gent,   *feathers*
Your beck, your breast, your hekill,° and your kame°—   *hackle / comb*
Schir, by my saul, and the blissit sacrament,[8]
60 My heart warmis, me think I am at hame.
You for to serve, I wald creep on my wame°   *belly*
In froist and snaw, in wedder wan and weit°   *dark and wet*
And lay my lyart° lokkes under your feit."   *gray*

This fenyeit fox, fals and dissimulate,
65 Made to this cok ane cavillatioun:°   *a critical remark*
"Ye are, me think, changed and degenerate
Fra your father and his conditioun,
Of craftie crawing he might beer the croun,[9]
For he weld on his tais° stand and craw.   *toes*
70 This is no le;° I stude beside and saw."   *lie*

With that the cok, upon his tais° hie,   *toes*
Kest up his beek and sang with all his might.
Quod schir Lowrence, "Well said, sa mot I the.[1]
Ye are your fatheris son and heir upright,°   *rightful*
75 Bot of his cunning yit ye want ane slight."°   *trick*
"What?" quad the cok. "He wald, and have na dout,
Baith wink, and craw, and turne him thryis about."[2]

The cok, inflate with wind and fals vanegloir,°   *vainglory*
That mony puttes unto confusioun,
80 Traisting to win ane greet worship therefoir,
Unwarlie winkand[3] walkit up and doun,
And syne° to chant and craw he made him boun°—   *then / ready*

---

5. It would be just a shame if I were not to serve you. "Serve" has both the feudal sense of service and a second sense.
6. *Dirigie* (>modern "cirge"): the first word of the anthem beginning the funeral service, which designates the prayer itself or the whole Office for the Dead: *"Dirige Dominus Deus meus"*—Lead me O Lord my God (Psalm 5.9).

7. Between the two of us how should there be a feud? "Suld": should. The future of "shall" is "sall."
8. The Eucharist.
9. He might bear the crown of skilfull crowing.
1. So may I prosper.
2. Both shut his eyes, and crow, and turn himself around thrice.
3. Unwarily shutting his eyes.

And suddandlie, by° he had crawin ane note   *by the time that*
The fox was war, and hent° him be the throte.   *seized*

85 Syne to the wood but tarie° with him hyit,°   *without delay/hurried*
Of countermaund havand but lytil dout.[4]
With that Pertok, Sprutok, and Coppok cryit,
The widow heard, and with ane cry come out.
Seand the case scho sighit and gaif[5] ane schout,
90 "How, murther, reylok!"[6] with ane hiddeous beir,°   *noise*
"Allas, now lost is gentil Chauntecleer!"

As scho were wod° with mony yell and cry,   *mad*
Ryvand hir hair, upon hir breist can beit,[7]
Syne pale of hew,° half in ane extasy,°   *hue/frenzy*
95 Fell doun for care in swoning° and in sweit.°   *fainting/sweating*
With that the selie° hennes left their meit,°   *poor/food*
And whyle this wyfe was lyand thus in swoon,
Fell of that case in disputacioun.

"Allas," quod Pertok, makand sair murning,[8]
100 With teeris greet attour hir cheekis fell,[9]
"Yon was our drowrie° and our day's darling,   *beloved*
Our nightingal, and als° our orlege° bell,   *also/clock*
Our walkrife watch,° us for to warne and tell   *wakeful sentinel*
When that Aurora with hir curcheis° gray   *headcovers, scarves*
105 Put up hir heid° betwix the night and day.   *head*

"Wha sall° our lemman° be? Who sall us leid?°   *who shall/lover/lead*
When we are sad wha sall unto us sing?
With his sweet bill he wald breke us the breid;°   *bread*
In all this warld was there ane kynder thing?
110 In paramouris° he wald do us plesing,   *making love*
At his power, as nature list him geif.[1]
Now efter him, allas, how sall we leif?"°   *live*

Quod Sprutok than, "Ceis,° sister of your sorrow,   *cease*
Ye be too mad, for him sic murning mais.[2]
115 We sall fare well, I find Sanct John to borrow;[3]
The proverb sayis, 'Als gude lufe cummis as gais.'[4]
I will put on my haly-dayis clais°   *holiday clothes*
And mak me fresch agane this jolie May,
Syne chant this sang, 'Was never widow sa gay!'

120 "He was angry and held us ay in aw,°   *always in fear*
And wounded with the speir° of jelowsy.   *spear*
Of chalmerglew,[5] Pertok, full well ye knaw,
Wasted he was, of nature cauld and dry.[6]

4. Having but little fear of prevention.
5. Gave. Note the hard *g* where the Chaucerian form would be *yaf.* "Seand": seeing.
6. Ho [Stop], murder, robbery.
7. Tearing her hair did beat upon her breast.
8. Making sore mourning.
9. While great tears fell down over her cheeks.
1. To the extent of the potency nature was pleased to give him.

2. You are too silly—you make such mourning for him.
3. I take St. John to be my guarantor; an expression used at parting.
4. As good love comes as goes.
5. Chamber-joy, i.e., performance in the bedroom.
6. A preponderance of black bile, the humor that is cold and dry like earth, enfeebled his potency.

	Sen° he is gone, therefore, sister, say I,	since
125	Be blythe in baill,⁷ for that is best remeid.°	remedy
	Let quik° to quik, and deid° ga to the deid."	living/dead

	Than Pertok spak, that feinyeit° faith before,	pretended
	In lust but° lufe that set all hir delyte,	without
	"Sister, ye wait° of sic° as him ane score	know/such
130	Wald not suffice to slake our appetyte.	
	I hecht° you by my hand, sen ye are quyte,°	promise/free
	Within ane oulk,° for schame and I durst speik,	week
	To get ane berne suld better claw oure breik."⁸	

	Than Coppok like ane curate° spak full crous:°	priest/smugly
135	"Yon was ane verray vengeance from the hevin.	
	He was sa lous° and sa lecherous,	loose, dissolute
	Ceis coud he noght with kittokis ma than sevin,⁹	
	But righteous God, haldand the balance evin,¹	
	Smytis right sair,° thoght he be patient,	sore
140	Adulteraris° that list them not repent.	adulterers

	"Prydeful he was, and joyit of his sin,	
	And comptit° not for Goddis favor nor feid.°	cared/enmity
	Bot traisted ay to rax and sa to rin,²	
	Whil at the last his sinnis can° him leid°	did/lead
145	To schameful end and to yon suddand deid.°	sudden death
	Therefore it is the verray hand of God	
	That causit him be werryit° with the tod."°	seized by the throat/fox

	When this was said, this widow fra hir swoun	
	Start up on fute, and on hir kennettis° cryde,	small hunting dogs
150	"How,° Birkye, Berrie, Bell, Bawsie, Broun,	what
	Rype Schaw, Rin Weil, Curtes, Nuttieclyde!	
	Togidder all but grunching furth ye glyde!³	
	Reskew my nobil cok ere he be slane,°	slain
	Or ellis to me see ye come never agane!°	again

155	With that, but baid, they braidet over the bent,⁴	
	As fire off flint they over the feildis flaw,°	flew
	Full wichtlie° they through wood and wateris went,	swiftly
	And ceissit not, schir Lowrence while they saw.⁵	
	But when he saw the raches° come on raw,°	dogs/in a line
160	Unto the cok in mind° he said, "God sen°	thought/grant
	That I and thou were fairlie in my den."	

	Then spak the cok, with sum gude spirit inspyrit,	
	"Do my counsall⁶ and I sall warrand° thee.	guarantee
	Hungrie thou art, and for greet travel° tyrit,°	labor/tired

7. Be merry in misery.
8. If I dare speak, shame not withstanding, to get a man who should better claw our tail.
9. He could not stop [even] with more than seven wenches. "Kittock" is a Scots diminutive for Katherine (as -ok is a diminutive in the names of the hens), used here as a generic term for "girl."

1. Holding the scales (of judgment) level.
2. And trusted always to have rule and so to reign.
3. Glide forth all together without grumbling.
4. Without delay they rushed over the ground.
5. And did not stop as long as they saw sir Lowrence.
6. Take my advice.

165 Right faint of force° and may not ferther flee: *strength*
     Swyth° turn agane and say that I and ye *quickly*
     Freindes are made and fellowis for ane yeir.° *year*
     Than will they stint,° I stand for it, and not steir."[7] *stop*

     This tod, thogh he were fals and frivolous,° *untrustworthy*
170 And had fraudis, his querrel° to defend, *cause*
     Desavit° was by menis° right marvelous, *deceived / means*
     For falset° failis ay at the latter end. *falsehood*
     He start about, and cryit as he was kend°— *instructed*
     With that the cok he braid° unto a bewch.° *moved quickly / bough*
175 Now juge ye all whereat schir Lowrence lewch.[8]

     Begylit° thus, the tod under the tree *deceived*
     On knees fell, and said, "Gude Chauntecleer,
     Come doun agane, and I but meit or fee[9]
     Sall be your man and servant for ane yeir."
180 "Na, murther, theif, and revar, stand on reir.[1]
     My bludy hekill° and my nek sa bla° *bloody hackle / blue*
     Has partit love for ever betwene us twa.

     "I was unwise that winkit° at thy will, *shut my eyes*
     Wherethrough almaist I loissit° had my heid."° *lost / head*
185 "I was mair fule,"[2] quod he, "coud noght be still,
     Bot spake to put my pray into pleid."[3]
     "Fare on, fals theef, God keep me fra thy feid."° *enmity, feud*
     With that the cok over the feildis tuke his flight,
     And in at the widow's lewer[4] couth he light.

                    Moralitas° *moral*

190 Now worthie folk, suppose this be ane fabill,
     And overheillit with typis figural,[5]
     Yit may ye find ane sentence° right agreabill° *meaning / suitable*
     Under their fenyeit termis textual.[6]
     To our purpose this cok well may we call
195 Nyce° proud men, woid° and vaneglorious *foolish / mad*
     Of kin and blude, whilk is presumptuous.[7]

     Fy, puffed up pride, thou is full poysonabill!° *poisonous*
     Wha favoris thee, on force man have ane fall,[8]
     Thy strength is noght, thy stule° standis unstabill. *stool*
200 Tak witnes of the feyndes infernall,
     Whilk° houndit doun was fra that hevinlie° hall[9] *who / heavenly*

---

7. I guarantee it and [will] not move.
8. Laughed, i.e., he had no reason whatsoever to laugh.
9. Without board or wages.
1. No, murderer, thief, and robber, back off (literally, "stand in the rear").
2. The greater fool. (Said by the fox).
3. To make my prey a subject of a plea (i.e., a legal argument).
4. Louver, i.e., a hole in a roof for letting out smoke.

5. And covered over with figural symbols, i.e., a hidden allegory.
6. Beneath the feigned words of the text, i.e., referring to the interpretation of scripture allegorically, not by the "letter" but by the "spirit."
7. Of family and bloodline, which (pride) is arrogant.
8. Whoever favors thee necessarily must have a fall.
9. The fallen angels who were cast from heaven into hell because they rebelled against God.

To hellis hole and to that hiddeous hous,
Because in pride they were presumptous.

This fenyeit foxe may well be figurate°   *serve as a figure for*
To flatteraris with plesand wordis white,
With fals mening and mynd maist toxicate,°   *most poisonous*
To loif and le that settis their hail delyte.[1]
All worthie folk at sic suld haif despite[2]—
For where is there mair perrelous pestilence?—
205 Nor give to learis° haistelie credence.   *liars*

The wickit mind and adullatioun,°   *excessive praise*
Of sucker sweet haifand similitude,[3]
Bitter as gall and full of fell poysoun
To taste it is, wha cleirlie understude,[4]
210 Forthy° as now schortlie to conclude,   *therefore*
Thir° twa sinnis, flatterie and vanegloir.   *these*
Are venomous: gude folk, flee them thairfoir!

1. Who set their whole delight in lauding and lying.
2. Should have contempt for such people.
3. Having resemblance to sweet sugar.
4. Whoever clearly understands it.

EVERYMAN
after 1485

Everyman is a late example of a kind of medieval drama known as the morality play. Morality plays apparently evolved side by side with the mystery plays, although they were composed individually and not in cycles. They too have a primarily religious purpose, but their method of attaining it is different. The mysteries dramatized significant events in biblical and sacred history from the creation of the world to Judgment Day in order to bring out the meaning of God's scheme of salvation. The moralities, on the other hand, employed allegory to show this scheme in the lifespan of a representative figure called "Mankind" or "Everyman." *Everyman* is about the day of judgment that every individual human being must face eventually. The play represents allegorically the forces—both outside the protagonist and within—that can help to save Everyman and those that cannot or that obstruct his salvation.

Everyman lacks the broad (even slapstick) humor of some morality plays that portray as clowns the vices that try to lure the Everyman figure away from salvation. The play does contain a certain grim humor in showing the haste with which the hero's fair-weather friends abandon him when they discover what his problem is. The play inculcates its austere lesson by the simplicity and directness of its language and of its approach. A sense of urgency builds—one by one Everyman's supposed resources fail him as time is running out. Ultimately Knowledge teaches him the lesson that every Christian must learn in order to be saved.

The play was written near the end of the fifteenth century. It is probably a translation of a Flemish play, although it is possible that the Flemish play is the translation and the English *Everyman* the original.

Everyman[1]

CAST OF CHARACTERS

MESSENGER	KNOWLEDGE
GOD	CONFESSION
DEATH	BEAUTY
EVERYMAN	STRENGTH
FELLOWSHIP	DISCRETION
KINDRED	FIVE-WITS
COUSIN	ANGEL
GOODS	DOCTOR
GOOD DEEDS	

HERE BEGINNETH A TREATISE HOW THE HIGH FATHER OF HEAVEN
SENDETH DEATH TO SUMMON EVERY CREATURE TO COME AND GIVE
ACCOUNT OF THEIR LIVES IN THIS WORLD, AND IS IN MANNER OF A
MORAL PLAY

[*Enter* MESSENGER.]

MESSENGER   I pray you all give your audience,
　　And hear this matter with reverence,
　　By figure° a moral play.　　　　　　　　　　　　　　*in form*
　　The Summoning of Everyman called it is,
5　　That of our lives and ending shows
　　How transitory we be all day.°　　　　　　　　　　*always*
　　The matter is wonder precious,
　　But the intent of it is more gracious
　　And sweet to bear away.
10　　The story saith: Man, in the beginning
　　Look well, and take good heed to the ending,
　　Be you never so gay.
　　You think sin in the beginning full sweet,
　　Which in the end causeth the soul to weep,
15　　When the body lieth in clay.
　　Here shall you see how fellowship and jollity,
　　Both strength, pleasure, and beauty,
　　Will fade from thee as flower in May.
　　For ye shall hear how our Heaven-King
20　　Calleth Everyman to a general reckoning.
　　Give audience and hear what he doth say.

[*Exit* MESSENGER.—*Enter* GOD.]

GOD   I perceive, here in my majesty,
　　How that all creatures be to me unkind,°　　　　　*thoughtless*

---

1. The text is based on the earliest printing of the play (no manuscript is known) by John Skot about 1530, as reproduced by W. W. Greg (1904). The spelling has been modernized except where modernization would spoil the rhyme, and modern punctuation has been added. The stage directions have been amplified.

Living without dread in worldly prosperity.
25 Of ghostly° sight the people be so blind,   *spiritual*
Drowned in sin, they know me not for their God.
In worldly riches is all their mind:
They fear not of my righteousness the sharp rod;
My law that I showed when I for them died
30 They forget clean, and shedding of my blood red.
I hanged between two,[2] it cannot be denied:
To get them life I suffered to be dead.
I healed their feet, with thorns hurt was my head.
I could do no more than I did, truly—
35 And now I see the people do clean forsake me.
They use the seven deadly sins damnable,
As pride, coveitise,° wrath, and lechery[3]   *avarice*
Now in the world be made commendable.
And thus they leave of angels the heavenly company.
40 Every man liveth so after his own pleasure,
And yet of their life they be nothing sure.
I see the more that I them forbear,
The worse they be from year to year:
All that liveth appaireth° fast.   *degenerates*
45 Therefore I will, in all the haste,
Have a reckoning of every man's person.
For, and° I leave the people thus alone   *if*
In their life and wicked tempests,
Verily they will become much worse than beasts;
50 For now one would by envy another up eat.
Charity do they all clean forgeet.
I hoped well that every man
In my glory should make his mansion,
And thereto I had them all elect.°   *chosen*
55 But now I see, like traitors deject,°   *abased*
They thank me not for the pleasure that I to° them meant, *for*
Nor yet for their being that I them have lent.
I proffered the people great multitude of mercy,
And few there be that asketh it heartily.°   *sincerely*
60 They be so cumbered° with worldly riches   *encumbered*
That needs on them I must do justice—
On every man living without fear.
Where art thou, Death, thou mighty messenger?

   [*Enter* DEATH.]

  DEATH Almighty God, I am here at your will,
65   Your commandment to fulfill.
  GOD Go thou to Everyman,
   And show him, in my name,

---

2. I.e., the two thieves between whom Christ was crucified.

3. The other three deadly sins are envy, gluttony, and sloth.

A pilgrimage he must on him take,
Which he in no wise may escape;
70   And that he bring with him a sure reckoning
Without delay or any tarrying.
      DEATH   Lord, I will in the world go run over all,°   *everywhere*
And cruelly out-search both great and small.

        [*Exit* GOD.]

Everyman will I beset that liveth beastly
75   Out of God's laws, and dreadeth not folly.
He that loveth riches I will strike with my dart,
His sight to blind, and from heaven to depart°   *separate*
Except that Almsdeeds be his good friend—
In hell for to dwell, world without end.
80   Lo, yonder I see Everyman walking:
Full little he thinketh on my coming;
His mind is on fleshly lusts and his treasure,
And great pain it shall cause him to endure
Before the Lord, Heaven-King.

        [*Enter* EVERYMAN.]

85   Everyman, stand still! Whither art thou going
Thus gaily? Hast thou thy Maker forgeet?°   *forgotten*
      EVERYMAN   Why askest thou?
Why wouldest thou weet?°   *know*
      DEATH   Yea, sir, I will show you:
90   In great haste I am sent to thee
From God out of his majesty.
      EVERYMAN   What! sent to me?
      DEATH   Yea, certainly.
Though thou have forgot him here,
95   He thinketh on thee in the heavenly sphere,
As, ere we depart, thou shalt know.
      EVERYMAN   What desireth God of me?
      DEATH   That shall I show thee:
A reckoning he will needs have
100   Without any longer respite.
      EVERYMAN   To give a reckoning longer leisure I crave.
This blind° matter troubleth my wit.   *unexpected*
      DEATH   On thee thou must take a long journey:
Therefore thy book of count° with thee thou bring,   *accounts*
105   For turn again thou cannot by no way.
And look thou be sure of thy reckoning,
For before God thou shalt answer and shew
Thy many bad deeds and good but a few—
How thou hast spent thy life and in what wise,
110   Before the Chief Lord of Paradise.

Have ado that we were in that way,[4]
For weet thou well thou shalt make none attornay.[5]

EVERYMAN   Full unready I am such reckoning to give.
I know thee not. What messenger art thou?

115 DEATH   I am Death that no man dreadeth,[6]
For every man I 'rest,° and no man spareth;   *arrest*
For it is God's commandment
That all to me should be obedient.

EVERYMAN   O Death, thou comest when I had thee least in mind.

120 In thy power it lieth me to save:
Yet of my good° will I give thee, if thou will be kind,   *goods*
Yea, a thousand pound shalt thou have—
And defer this matter till another day.

DEATH   Everyman, it may not be, by no way.

125 I set nought by[7] gold, silver, nor riches,
Nor by pope, emperor, king, duke, nor princes,
For, and° I would receive gifts great,   *if*
All the world I might get.
But my custom is clean contrary:

130 I give thee no respite. Come hence and not tarry!

EVERYMAN   Alas, shall I have no longer respite?
I may say Death giveth no warning.
To think on thee it maketh my heart sick,
For all unready is my book of reckoning.

135 But twelve year and I might have a biding,[8]
My counting-book I would make so clear
That my reckoning I should not need to fear.
Wherefore, Death, I pray thee, for God's mercy,
Spare me till I be provided of remedy.

140 DEATH   Thee availeth not to cry, weep, and pray;
But haste thee lightly° that thou were gone that journay   *quickly*
And prove° thy friends, if thou can.   *test*
For weet° thou well the tide° abideth no man,   *know / time*
And in the world each living creature

145 For Adam's sin must die of nature.[9]

EVERYMAN   Death, if I should this pilgrimage take
And my reckoning surely make,
Show me, for saint° charity,   *holy*
Should I not come again shortly?

150 DEATH   No, Everyman. And thou be once there,
Thou mayst never more come here,
Trust me verily.

EVERYMAN   O gracious God in the high seat celestial,
Have mercy on me in this most need!

155 Shall I have company from this vale terrestrial
Of mine acquaintance that way me to lead?

---

4. I.e., let's get started at once.
5. I.e., none to appear in your stead.
6. That fears nobody.
7. I care nothing for.
8. If I might have a delay for just twelve years.
9. Naturally.

DEATH   Yea, if any be so hardy
       That would go with thee and bear thee company.
       Hie° thee that thou were gone to God's magnificence,   *hasten*
160   Thy reckoning to give before his presence.
       What, weenest° thou thy life is given thee,   *suppose*
       And thy worldly goods also?
       EVERYMAN   I had weened so, verily.
       DEATH   Nay, nay, it was but lent thee.
165   For as soon as thou art go,
       Another a while shall have it and then go therefro,
       Even as thou hast done.
       Everyman, thou art mad! Thou hast thy wits° five,   *senses*
       And here on earth will not amend thy live!¹
170   For suddenly I do come.
       EVERYMAN   O wretched caitiff! Whither shall I flee
       That I might 'scape this endless sorrow?
       Now, gentle Death, spare me till tomorrow,
       That I may amend me
175   With good advisement.°   *preparation*
       DEATH   Nay, thereto I will not consent,
       Nor no man will I respite,
       But to the heart suddenly I shall smite,
       Without any advisement.
180   And now out of thy sight I will me hie:
       See thou make thee ready shortly,
       For thou mayst say this is the day
       That no man living may 'scape away.

                    [*Exit* DEATH.]

       EVERYMAN   Alas, I may well weep with sighs deep:
185   Now have I no manner of company
       To help me in my journey and me to keep.°   *guard*
       And also my writing° is full unready—   *ledger*
       How shall I do now for to excuse me?
       I would to God I had never be geet!°   *been forgotten*
190   To my soul a full great profit it had be.
       For now I fear pains huge and great.
       The time passeth: Lord, help, that all wrought!
       For though I mourn, it availeth nought.
       The day passeth and is almost ago:°   *gone by*
195   I wot° not well what for to do.   *know*
       To whom were I best my complaint to make?
       What and I to Fellowship thereof spake,
       And showed him of this sudden chance?
       For in him is all mine affiance,°   *trust*
200   We have in the world so many a day
       Be good friends in sport and play.

       ---

1. In thy life.

I see him yonder, certainly.
I trust that he will bear me company.
Therefore to him will I speak to ease my sorrow.

[*Enter* FELLOWSHIP.]

205   Well met, good Fellowship, and good morrow!
    FELLOWSHIP   Everyman, good morrow, by this day!
      Sir, why lookest thou so piteously?
      If anything be amiss, I pray thee me say,
      That I may help to remedy.
210   EVERYMAN   Yea, good Fellowship, yea:
      I am in great jeopardy.
    FELLOWSHIP   My true friend, show to me your mind.
      I will not forsake thee to my life's end
      In the way of good company.
215   EVERYMAN   That was well spoken, and lovingly!
    FELLOWSHIP   Sir, I must needs know your heaviness.°   *sorrow*
      I have pity to see you in any distress.
      If any have you wronged, ye shall revenged be,
      Though I on the ground be slain for thee,
220   Though that I know before that I should die.
    EVERYMAN   Verily, Fellowship, gramercy.°   *many thanks*
    FELLOWSHIP   Tush! by thy thanks I set not a stree.°   *straw*
      Show me your grief and say no more.
    EVERYMAN   If I my heart should to you break,°   *disclose*
225   And then you to turn your mind fro me,
    And would not me comfort when ye hear me speak,
    Then should I ten times sorrier be.
    FELLOWSHIP   Sir, I say as I will do, indeed.
    EVERYMAN   Then be you a good friend at need.
230   I have found you true herebefore.
    FELLOWSHIP   And so ye shall evermore.
      For, in faith, and° thou go to hell,   *if*
      I will not forsake thee by the way.
    EVERYMAN   Ye speak like a good friend. I believe you well.
235   I shall deserve° it, and° I may.   *repay / if*
    FELLOWSHIP   I speak of no deserving, by this day!
      For he that will say and nothing do
      Is not worthy with good company to go.
      Therefore show me the grief of your mind,
240   As to your friend most loving and kind.
    EVERYMAN   I shall show you how it is:
    Commanded I am to go a journay,
    A long way, hard and dangerous,
    And give a strait° count,° without delay,   *strict / accounting*
245   Before the high judge Adonai.°   *God*
    Wherefore I pray you bear me company,
    As ye have promised, in this journay.
    FELLOWSHIP   This is matter indeed! Promise is duty—

But, and I should take such a voyage on me,
250   I know it well, it should be to my pain.
      Also it maketh me afeard, certain.
      But let us take counsel here, as well as we can—
      For your words would fear° a strong man.   *frighten*
EVERYMAN   Why, ye said if I had need,
255   Ye would me never forsake, quick ne dead,
      Though it were to hell, truly.
FELLOWSHIP   So I said, certainly,
      But such pleasures° be set aside, the sooth to say.   *jokes*
      And also, if we took such a journay,
260   When should we again come?
EVERYMAN   Nay, never again, till the day of doom.
FELLOWSHIP   In faith, then will not I come there!
      Who hath you these tidings brought?
EVERYMAN   Indeed, Death was with me here.
265 FELLOWSHIP   Now by God that all hath bought,°   *redeemed*
      If Death were the messenger,
      For no man that is living today
      I will not go that loath° journay—   *loathsome*
      Not for the father that begat me!
270   EVERYMAN   Ye promised otherwise, pardie.°   *by God*
FELLOWSHIP   I wot well I said so, truly.
      And yet, if thou wilt eat and drink and make good cheer,
      Or haunt to women the lusty company,[2]
      I would not forsake you while the day is clear,
275   Trust me verily!
EVERYMAN   Yea, thereto ye would be ready—
      To go to mirth, solace,° and play: *pleasure*
      Your mind to folly will sooner apply°   *attend*
      Than to bear me company in my long journay.
280 FELLOWSHIP   Now in good faith, I will not that way.
      But, and thou will murder or any man kill,
      In that I will help thee with a good will.
EVERYMAN   O that is simple° advice, indeed!   *foolish*
      Gentle fellow, help me in my necessity:
285   We have loved long, and now I need—
      And now, gentle Fellowship, remember me!
FELLOWSHIP   Whether ye have loved me or no,
      By Saint John, I will not with thee go!
EVERYMAN   Yet I pray thee take the labor and do so much for me,
290   To bring me forward,° for saint charity,   *escort me*
      And comfort me till I come without the town.
FELLOWSHIP   Nay, and° thou would give me a new gown,   *if*
      I will not a foot with thee go.
      But, and thou had tarried, I would not have left thee so.
295   And as now, God speed thee in thy journay!
      For from thee I will depart as fast as I may.

2. Or frequent the lusty company of women.

EVERYMAN   Whither away, Fellowship? Will thou forsake me?
FELLOWSHIP   Yea, by my fay!° To God I betake° thee.   *faith / commend*
EVERYMAN   Farewell, good Fellowship! For thee my heart is sore.
300   Adieu forever—I shall see thee no more.
FELLOWSHIP   In faith, Everyman, farewell now at the ending:
         For you I will remember that parting is mourning.

         [*Exit* FELLOWSHIP.]

EVERYMAN   Alack, shall we thus depart° indeed—   *part*
         Ah, Lady, help!—without any more comfort?
305   Lo, Fellowship forsaketh me in my most need!
         For help in this world whither shall I resort?
         Fellowship herebefore with me would merry make,
         And now little sorrow for me doth he take.
         It is said, "In prosperity men friends may find
310   Which in adversity be full unkind."
         Now whither for succor shall I flee,
         Sith° that Fellowship hath forsaken me?   *since*
         To my kinsmen I will, truly,
         Praying them to help me in my necessity.
315   I believe that they will do so,
         For kind will creep where it may not go.[3]
         I will go 'say°—for yonder I see them—   *assay*
         Where° be ye now my friends and kinsmen.   *whether*

         [*Enter* KINDRED *and* COUSIN.]

KINDRED   Here be we now at your commandment:
320   Cousin, I pray you show us your intent
         In any wise, and not spare.
COUSIN   Yea, Everyman, and to us declare
         If ye be disposed to go anywhither.
         For, weet° you well, we will live and die togither.   *know*
325 KINDRED   In wealth and woe we will with you hold,
         For over his kin a man may be bold.[4]
EVERYMAN   Gramercy,° my friends and kinsmen kind.   *much thanks*
         Now shall I show you the grief of my mind.
         I was commanded by a messenger
330   That is a high king's chief officer:
         He bade me go a pilgrimage, to my pain—
         And I know well I shall never come again.
         Also I must give a reckoning strait,°   *strict*
         For I have a great enemy that hath me in wait,[5]
335   Which intendeth me to hinder.
KINDRED   What account is that which ye must render?
         That would I know.

3. For kinship will creep where it cannot walk (i.e., kinsmen will suffer hardship for one another).
4. I.e., for a man may make demands of his kins-men.
5. I.e., Satan lies in ambush for me.

EVERYMAN   Of all my works I must show
How I have lived and my days spent;
340   Also of ill deeds that I have used
In my time sith life was me lent,
And of all virtues that I have refused.
Therefore I pray you go thither with me
To help me make mine account, for saint charity.
345   COUSIN   What, to go thither? Is that the matter?
Nay, Everyman, I had liefer fast[6] bread and water
All this five year and more!
EVERYMAN   Alas, that ever I was bore!°   *born*
For now shall I never be merry
350   If that you forsake me.
KINDRED   Ah, sir, what? Ye be a merry man:
Take good heart to you and make no moan.
But one thing I warn you, by Saint Anne,
As for me, ye shall go alone.
355   EVERYMAN   My Cousin, will you not with me go?
COUSIN   No, by Our Lady! I have the cramp in my toe:
Trust not to me. For, so God me speed,
I will deceive you in your most need.
KINDRED   It availeth you not us to 'tice.°   *entice*
360   Ye shall have my maid with all my heart:
She loveth to go to feasts, there to be nice,°   *wanton*
And to dance, and abroad to start.[7]
I will give her leave to help you in that journey,
If that you and she may agree.
365   EVERYMAN   Now show me the very effect° of your mind: *bent*
Will you go with me or abide behind?
KINDRED   Abide behind? Yea, that will I and I may!
Therefore farewell till another day.

[*Exit* KINDRED.]

EVERYMAN   How should I be merry or glad?
370   For fair promises men to me make,
But when I have most need they me forsake.
I am deceived. That maketh me sad.
COUSIN   Cousin Everyman, farewell now,
For verily I will not go with you;
375   Also of mine own an unready reckoning
I have to account—therefore I make tarrying.
Now God keep thee, for now I go.

[*Exit* COUSIN.]

EVERYMAN   Ah, Jesus, is all come hereto?°   *to this*
Lo, fair words maketh fools fain:°   *glad*

---

6. I.e., rather fast on.   7. To go gadding about.

380   They promise and nothing will do, certain.
         My kinsmen promised me faithfully
         For to abide with me steadfastly,
         And now fast away do they flee.
         Even so Fellowship promised me.
385   What friend were best me of to provide?
         I lose my time here longer to abide.
         Yet in my mind a thing there is:
         All my life I have loved riches;
         If that my Good° now help me might,   Goods
390   He would make my heart full light.
         I will speak to him in this distress.
         Where art thou, my Goods and riches?
    GOODS [within] Who calleth me? Everyman? What, hast thou haste?
         I lie here in corners, trussed and piled so high,
395   And in chests I am locked so fast—
         Also sacked in bags—thou mayst see with thine eye
         I cannot stir, in packs low where I lie.
         What would ye have? Lightly° me say.   quickly
    EVERYMAN Come hither, Good, in all the haste thou may,
400   For of counsel I must desire thee.

         [*Enter* GOODS.]

    GOODS Sir, and° ye in the world have sorrow or adversity,   if
         That can I help you to remedy shortly.
    EVERYMAN It is another disease° that grieveth me: distress
         In this world it is not, I tell thee so.
405   I am sent for another way to go,
         To give a strait count general
         Before the highest Jupiter° of all.   God
         And all my life I have had joy and pleasure in thee:
         Therefore I pray thee go with me,
410   For, peradventure, thou mayst before God Almighty
         My reckoning help to clean and purify.
         For it is said ever among°   now and then
         That money maketh all right that is wrong.
    GOODS Nay, Everyman, I sing another song:
415   I follow no man in such voyages.
         For, and° I went with thee,   if
         Thou shouldest fare much the worse for me;
         For because on me thou did set thy mind.
         Thy reckoning I have made blotted and blind,°   illegible
420   That thine account thou cannot make truly—
         And that hast thou for the love of me.
    EVERYMAN That would grieve me full sore
         When I should come to that fearful answer.
         Up, let us go thither together.
425 GOODS Nay, not so, I am too brittle, I may not endure.
         I will follow no man one foot, be ye sure.

EVERYMAN   Alas, I have thee loved and had great pleasure
    All my life-days on good and treasure.
GOODS   That is to thy damnation, without leasing,°   *lie*
430   For my love is contrary to the love everlasting.
    But if thou had me loved moderately during,°   *in the meanwhile*
    As to the poor to give part of me,
    Then shouldest thou not in this dolor be,
    Nor in this great sorrow and care.
435 EVERYMAN   Lo, now was I deceived ere I was ware,
    And all I may wite° misspending of time.   *blame on*
GOODS   What, weenest° thou that I am thine?   *suppose*
EVERYMAN   I had weened so.
GOODS   Nay, Everyman, I say no.
440   As for a while I was lent thee;
    A season thou hast had me in prosperity.
    My condition° is man's soul to kill;   *disposition*
    If I save one, a thousand I do spill.°   *ruin*
    Weenest thou that I will follow thee?
445   Nay, from this world, not verily.
EVERYMAN   I had weened otherwise.
GOODS   Therefore to thy soul Good is a thief;
    For when thou art dead, this is my guise°—   *custom*
    Another to deceive in the same wise
450   As I have done thee, and all to his soul's repreef.° *shame*
EVERYMAN   O false Good, cursed thou be,
    Thou traitor to God, that hast deceived me
    And caught me in thy snare!
GOODS   Marry, thou brought thyself in care,°   *sorrow*
455   Whereof I am glad:
    I must needs laugh, I cannot be sad.
EVERYMAN   Ah, Good, thou hast had long my heartly° love; *sincere*
    I gave thee that which should be the Lord's above.
    But wilt thou not go with me, indeed?
460   I pray thee truth to say.
GOODS   No, so God me speed!
    Therefore farewell and have good day.

      [*Exit* GOODS.]

EVERYMAN   Oh, to whom shall I make my moan
    For to go with me in that heavy° journey?   *sorrowful*
465 First Fellowship said he would with me gone:°   *go*
    His words were very pleasant and gay,
    But afterward he left me alone.
    Then spake I to my kinsmen, all in despair,
    And also they gave me words fair—
470   They lacked no fair speaking,
    But all forsake me in the ending.
    Then went I to my Goods that I loved best,
    In hope to have comfort; but there had I least,

For my Goods sharply did me tell
475 That he bringeth many into hell.
Then of myself I was ashamed,
And so I am worthy to be blamed:
Thus may I well myself hate.
Of whom shall I now counsel take?
480 I think that I shall never speed
Till that I go to my Good Deed.
But alas, she is so weak
That she can neither go° nor speak.   *walk*
Yet will I venture° on her now.   *gamble*
485 My Good Deeds, where be you?
GOOD DEEDS   [*speaking from the ground*] Here I lie, cold in the
     ground:
Thy sins hath me sore bound
That I cannot stear.°   *stir*
EVERYMAN   O Good Deeds, I stand in fear:
490 I must you pray of counsel,
For help now should come right well.
GOOD DEEDS   Everyman, I have understanding
That ye be summoned, account to make,
Before Messiah of Jer'salem King.
495 And you do by me,[8] that journey with you will I take.
EVERYMAN   Therefore I come to you my moan to make:
I pray you that ye will go with me.
GOOD DEEDS   I would full fain, but I cannot stand, verily.
EVERYMAN   Why, is there anything on you fall?°   *fallen*
500 GOOD DEEDS   Yea, sir, I may thank you of all:
If ye had perfectly cheered me,
Your book of count full ready had be.

[GOOD DEEDS *shows him the account book.*]

Look, the books of your works and deeds eke,°   *also*
As how they lie under the feet,
505 To your soul's heaviness.°   *distress*
EVERYMAN   Our Lord Jesus help me!
For one letter here I cannot see.
GOOD DEEDS   There is a blind° reckoning in time of distress!   *illegible*
EVERYMAN   Good Deeds, I pray you help me in this need,
510 Or else I am forever damned indeed.
Therefore help me to make reckoning
Before the Redeemer of all thing
That King is and was and ever shall.
GOOD DEEDS   Everyman, I am sorry of° your fall   *for*
515 And fain would help you and° I were able.   *if*
EVERYMAN   Good Deeds, your counsel I pray you give me.
GOOD DEEDS   That shall I do verily,

8. I.e., if you do what I say.

Though that on my feet I may not go;
I have a sister that shall with you also,
520   Called Knowledge, which shall with you abide
To help you to make that dreadful reckoning.

[*Enter* KNOWLEDGE.]

KNOWLEDGE   Everyman, I will go with thee and be thy guide,
In thy most need to go by thy side.
EVERYMAN   In good condition I am now in everything,
525   And am whole content with this good thing,
Thanked be God my Creator.
GOOD DEEDS   And when she hath brought you there
Where thou shalt heal thee of thy smart,°   *pain*
Then go you with your reckoning and your Good Deeds together
530   For to make you joyful at heart
Before the blessed Trinity.
EVERYMAN   My Good Deeds, gramercy!
I am well content, certainly,
With your words sweet.
535   KNOWLEDGE   Now go we together lovingly
To Confession, that cleansing river.
EVERYMAN   For joy I weep—I would we were there!
But I pray you give me cognition,°   *knowledge*
Where dwelleth that holy man Confession?
540   KNOWLEDGE   In the House of Salvation:
We shall us comfort, by God's grace.

[KNOWLEDGE *leads* EVERYMAN *to* CONFESSION.]

Lo, this is Confession: kneel down and ask mercy,
For he is in good conceit° with God Almighty.   *esteem*
545   EVERYMAN   [*kneeling*] O glorious fountain that all
            uncleanness doth clarify,°   *purify*
Wash from me the spots of vice unclean,
That on me no sin may be seen.
I come with Knowledge for my redemption,
Redempt° with heart and full contrition,   *redeemed*
550   For I am commanded a pilgrimage to take
And great accounts before God to make.
Now I pray you, Shrift,° mother of Salvation,   *confession*
Help my Good Deeds for my piteous exclamation.
CONFESSION   I know your sorrow well, Everyman:
555   Because with Knowledge ye come to me,
I will you comfort as well as I can,
And a precious jewel I will give thee,
Called Penance, voider° of adversity.   *expeller*
Therewith shall your body chastised be—
560   With abstinence and perseverance in God's service.
Here shall you receive that scourge of me,

Which is penance strong° that ye must endure,   *harsh*
To remember thy Saviour was scourged for thee
With sharp scourges, and suffered it patiently.
565   So must thou ere thou 'scape that painful pilgrimage.
Knowledge, keep° him in this voyage,   *guard*
And by that time Good Deeds will be with thee.
But in any wise be secure° of mercy—   *certain*
For your time draweth fast—and ye will saved be.
570   Ask God mercy and he will grant, truly.
When with the scourge of penance man doth him° bind,   *himself*
The oil of forgiveness then shall he find.
    EVERYMAN   Thanked be God for his gracious work,
For now I will my penance begin.
575   This hath rejoiced and lighted my heart,
Though the knots be painful and hard within.[9]
    KNOWLEDGE   Everyman, look your penance that ye fulfill,
What pain that ever it to you be;
And Knowledge shall give you counsel at will
580   How your account ye shall make clearly.
    EVERYMAN   O eternal God, O heavenly figure,
O way of righteousness, O goodly vision,
Which descended down in a virgin pure
Because he would every man redeem,
585   Which Adam forfeited by his disobedience;
O blessed Godhead, elect and high Divine,°   *divinity*
Forgive my grievous offense!
Here I cry thee mercy in this presence:
O ghostly Treasure, O Ransomer and Redeemer,
590   Of all the world Hope and Conduiter,°   *guide*
Mirror of joy, Foundator° of mercy,   *Founder*
Which enlumineth° heaven and earth thereby,   *lights up*
Hear my clamorous complaint, though it late be;
Receive my prayers, of thy benignity.
595   Though I be a sinner most abominable,
Yet let my name be written in Moses' table.[1]
O Mary, pray to the Maker of all thing
Me for to help at my ending,
And save me from the power of my enemy,
600   For Death assaileth me strongly.
And Lady, that I may by mean of thy prayer
Of your Son's glory to be partner—
By the means of his passion I it crave.
I beseech you help my soul to save.
605   Knowledge, give me the scourge of penance:
My flesh therewith shall give acquittance.°   *satisfaction for sins*
I will now begin, if God give me grace.

---

9. I.e., to my senses. "Knots": i.e., the knots on the
scourge (whip) of penance.
1. "Moses' table" is here the tablet on which are
recorded those who have been baptized and have
done penance.

KNOWLEDGE   Everyman, God give you time and space!°   *opportunity*
     Thus I bequeath you in the hands of our Saviour:
610   Now may you make your reckoning sure.
EVERYMAN   In the name of the Holy Trinity
     My body sore punished shall be:
     Take this, body, for the sin of the flesh!
     Also° thou delightest to go gay and fresh,   *as*
615   And in the way of damnation thou did me bring,
     Therefore suffer now strokes of punishing!
     Now of penance I will wade the water clear,
     To save me from purgatory, that sharp fire.
GOOD DEEDS   I thank God, now can I walk and go,
620   And am delivered of my sickness and woe.
     Therefore with Everyman I will go, and not spare:
     His good works I will help him to declare.
KNOWLEDGE   Now, Everyman, be merry and glad:
     Your Good Deeds cometh now, ye may not be sad.
625   Now is your Good Deeds whole and sound,
     Going° upright upon the ground.   *walking*
EVERYMAN   My heart is light, and shall be evermore.
     Now will I smite faster than I did before.
GOOD DEEDS   Everyman, pilgrim, my special friend,
630   Blessed be thou without end!
     For thee is preparate° the eternal glory.   *prepared*
     Ye have me made whole and sound
     Therefore I will bide by thee in every stound.°   *trial*
EVERYMAN   Welcome, my Good Deeds! Now I hear thy voice,
635   I weep for very sweetness of love.
KNOWLEDGE   Be no more sad, but ever rejoice:
     God seeth thy living in his throne above.
     Put on this garment to thy behove,°   *advantage*
     Which is wet with your tears—
640   Or else before God you may it miss
     When ye to your journey's end come shall.
EVERYMAN   Gentle Knowledge, what do ye it call?
KNOWLEDGE   It is a garment of sorrow;
     From pain it will you borrow:°   *redeem*
645   Contrition it is
     That getteth forgiveness;
     It pleaseth God passing° well.   *surpassingly*
GOOD DEEDS   Everyman, will you wear it for your heal?°   *welfare*
EVERYMAN   Now blessed be Jesu, Mary's son,
650   For now have I on true contrition.
     And let us go now without tarrying.
     Good Deeds, have we clear our reckoning?
GOOD DEEDS   Yea, indeed, I have it here.
EVERYMAN   Then I trust we need not fear.
655   Now friends, let us not part in twain.
KNOWLEDGE   Nay, Everyman, that will we not, certain.

GOOD DEEDS   Yet must thou lead with thee
   Three persons of great might.
EVERYMAN   Who should they be?
660   GOOD DEEDS   Discretion and Strength they hight,°   *are called*
   And thy Beauty may not abide behind.
KNOWLEDGE   Also ye must call to mind
   Your Five-Wits° as for your counselors.   *senses*
GOOD DEEDS   You must have them ready at all hours.
665   EVERYMAN   How shall I get them hither?
KNOWLEDGE   You must call them all togither,
   And they will be here incontinent.°   *at once*
EVERYMAN   My friends, come hither and be present,
   Discretion, Strength, my Five-Wits, and Beauty!

      [*They enter.*]

670   BEAUTY   Here at your will we be all ready.
   What will ye that we should do?
GOOD DEEDS   That ye would with Everyman go
   And help him in his pilgrimage.
   Advise you:° will ye with him or not in that voyage?   *take thought*
675   STRENGTH   We will bring him all thither,
   To his help and comfort, ye may believe me.
DISCRETION   So will we go with him all togither.
EVERYMAN   Almighty God, loved° might thou be!   *praised*
   I give thee laud that I have hither brought
680   Strength, Discretion, Beauty, and Five-Wits—lack I nought—
   And my Good Deeds, with Knowledge clear,
   All be in my company at my will here:
   I desire no more to my business.
STRENGTH   And I, Strength, will by you stand in distress,
685   Though thou would in battle fight on the ground.
FIVE-WITS   And though it were through the world round,
   We will not depart for sweet ne sour.
BEAUTY   No more will I, until death's hour,
   Whatsoever thereof befall.
690   DISCRETION   Everyman, advise you first of all:
   Go with a good advisement° and deliberation.   *preparation*
   We all give you virtuous° monition°   *confident / prediction*
   That all shall be well.
EVERYMAN   My friends, hearken what I will tell;
695   I pray God reward you in his heaven-sphere;
   Now hearken all that be here,
   For I will make my testament,
   Here before you all present:
   In alms half my good° I will give with my hands twain,   *goods*
700   In the way of charity with good intent;
   And the other half, still° shall remain,   *which still*
   I 'queath° to be returned there it ought to be.   *bequeath*

This I do in despite of the fiend of hell,
To go quit out of his perel,[2]
705   Ever after and this day.
    KNOWLEDGE   Everyman, hearken what I say:
    Go to Priesthood, I you advise,
    And receive of him, in any wise,°   *at all costs*
    The holy sacrament and ointment° togither;   *extreme unction*
710   Then shortly see ye turn again hither:
    We will all abide you here.
    FIVE-WITS   Yea, Everyman, hie you that ye ready were.
    There is no emperor, king, duke, ne baron,
    That of God hath commission
715   As hath the least priest in the world being:
    For of the blessed sacraments pure and bening°   *benign*
    He beareth the keys, and thereof hath the cure°   *care*
    For man's redemption—it is ever sure—
    Which God for our souls' medicine
720   Gave us out of his heart with great pine,°   *torment*
    Here in this transitory life for thee and me.
    The blessed sacraments seven there be:
    Baptism, confirmation, with priesthood° good,   *ordination*
    And the sacrament of God's precious flesh and blood,
725   Marriage, the holy extreme unction, and penance:
    These seven be good to have in remembrance,
    Gracious sacraments of high divinity.
    EVERYMAN   Fain° would I receive that holy body,   *gladly*
    And meekly to my ghostly° father I will go.   *spiritual*
730   FIVE-WITS   Everyman, that is the best that ye can do:
    God will you to salvation bring.
    For priesthood exceedeth all other thing:
    To us Holy Scripture they do teach,
    And converteth man from sin, heaven to reach;
735   God hath to them more power given
    Than to any angel that is in heaven.
    With five words[3] he may consecrate
    God's body in flesh and blood to make,
    And handleth his Maker between his hands.
740   The priest bindeth and unbindeth all bands,[4]
    Both in earth and in heaven.
    Thou ministers° all the sacraments seven;   *administer*
    Though we kiss thy feet, thou were worthy;
    Thou art surgeon that cureth sin deadly;
745   No remedy we find under God
    But all only priesthood.[5]
    Everyman, God gave priests that dignity

---

2. In order to go free of danger from him.
3. The five words ("For this is my body") spoken by the priest when he offers the wafer at communion.
4. A reference to the power of the keys, inherited

by the priesthood from St. Peter, who received it from Christ (Matthew 16.19) with the promise that whatever St. Peter bound or loosed on earth would be bound or loosed in heaven.
5. Except from priesthood alone.

And setteth them in his stead among us to be.
Thus be they above angels in degree.

[*Exit* EVERYMAN.]

750 KNOWLEDGE   If priests be good, it is so, surely.
But when Jesu hanged on the cross with great smart,°   *pain*
There he gave out of his blessed heart
The same sacrament in great torment,
He sold them not to us, that Lord omnipotent:
755 Therefore Saint Peter the Apostle doth say
That Jesu's curse hath all they
Which God their Saviour do buy or sell,[6]
Or they for any money do take or tell.[7]
Sinful priests giveth the sinners example bad:
760 Their children sitteth by other men's fires, I have heard;
And some haunteth women's company
With unclean life, as lusts of lechery.
These be with sin made blind.
FIVE-WITS   I trust to God no such may we find.
765 Therefore let us priesthood honor,
And follow their doctrine for our souls' succor.
We be their sheep and they shepherds be
By whom we all be kept in surety.
Peace, for yonder I see Everyman come,
770 Which hath made true satisfaction.
GOOD DEEDS   Methink it is he indeed.

[*Re-enter* EVERYMAN.]

EVERYMAN   Now Jesu be your alder speed![8]
I have received the sacrament for my redemption,
And then mine extreme unction.
775 Blessed be all they that counseled me to take it!
And now, friends, let us go without longer respite.
I thank God that ye have tarried so long.
Now set each of you on this rood° your hond   *cross*
And shortly follow me:
780 I go before there° I would be. God be our guide!   *where*
STRENGTH   Everyman, we will not from you go
Till ye have done this voyage long.
DISCRETION   I, Discretion, will bide by you also.
KNOWLEDGE   And though this pilgrimage be never so strong,°   *harsh*
785 I will never part you fro.
STRENGTH   Everyman, I will be as sure by thee
As ever I did by Judas Maccabee.[9]

6. To give or receive money for the sacraments is simony, named after Simon, who wished to buy the gift of the Holy Ghost and was cursed by St. Peter.
7. Or who, for any sacrament, take or count out money.

8. The prosperer of you all.
9. Judas Maccabaeus was an enormously powerful warrior in the defense of Israel against the Syrians in late Old Testament times.

EVERYMAN   Alas, I am so faint I may not stand—
    My limbs under me doth fold!
790   Friends, let us not turn again to this land,
    Not for all the world's gold.
    For into this cave must I creep
    And turn to earth, and there to sleep.
BEAUTY   What, into this grave, alas?
795 EVERYMAN   Yea, there shall ye consume,° more and lass.¹   *decay*
BEAUTY   And what, should I smother here?
EVERYMAN   Yea, by my faith, and nevermore appear.
    In this world live no more we shall,
    But in heaven before the highest Lord of all.
800 BEAUTY   I cross out all this! Adieu, by Saint John—
    I take my tape in my lap and am gone.²
EVERYMAN   What, Beauty, whither will ye?
BEAUTY   Peace, I am deaf—I look not behind me,
    Not and thou wouldest give me all the gold in thy chest.

        [*Exit* BEAUTY.]

805 EVERYMAN   Alas, whereto may I trust?
    Beauty goeth fast away fro me—
    She promised with me to live and die!
STRENGTH   Everyman, I will thee also forsake and deny.
    Thy game liketh° me not at all.   *pleases*
810 EVERYMAN   Why then, ye will forsake me all?
    Sweet Strength, tarry a little space.
STRENGTH   Nay, sir, by the rood of grace,
    I will hie me from thee fast,
    Though thou weep till thy heart tobrast.°   *break*
815 EVERYMAN   Ye would ever bide by me, ye said.
STRENGTH   Yea, I have you far enough conveyed!°   *escorted*
    Ye be old enough, I understand,
    Your pilgrimage to take on hand:
    I repent me that I hither came.
820 EVERYMAN   Strength, you to displease I am to blame,³
    Yet promise is debt, this ye well wot.°   *know*
STRENGTH   In faith, I care not:
    Thou art but a fool to complain;
    You spend your speech and waste your brain.
825   Go, thrust thee into the ground.

        [*Exit* STRENGTH.]

EVERYMAN   I had weened° surer I should you have found.   *supposed*
    He that trusteth in his Strength
    She him deceiveth at the length.

---

1. More and less (i.e., all of you).   3. I'm to blame for displeasing you.
2. I tuck my skirts in my belt and am off.

Both Strength and Beauty forsaketh me—
830　Yet they promised me fair and lovingly.
DISCRETION　Everyman, I will after Strength be gone:
　　As for me, I will leave you alone.
EVERYMAN　Why Discretion, will ye forsake me?
DISCRETION　Yea, in faith, I will go from thee.
835　For when Strength goeth before,
　　I follow after evermore.
EVERYMAN　Yet I pray thee, for the love of the Trinity,
　　Look in my grave once piteously.
DISCRETION　Nay, so nigh will I not come.
840　Farewell everyone!

　　　　　[*Exit* DISCRETION.]

EVERYMAN　O all thing faileth save God alone—
　　Beauty, Strength, and Discretion.
　　For when Death bloweth his blast
　　They all run fro me full fast.
845　FIVE-WITS　Everyman, my leave now of thee I take.
　　I will follow the other, for here I thee forsake.
EVERYMAN　Alas, then may I wail and weep,
　　For I took you for my best friend.
FIVE-WITS　I will no longer thee keep.°　　　　　*watch over*
850　Now farewell, and there an end!

　　　　　[*Exit* FIVE-WITS.]

EVERYMAN　O Jesu, help, all hath forsaken me!
GOOD DEEDS　Nay, Everyman, I will bide with thee:
　　I will not forsake thee indeed;
　　Thou shalt find me a good friend at need.
855　EVERYMAN　Gramercy, Good Deeds! Now may I true friends see.
　　They have forsaken me every one—
　　I loved them better than my Good Deeds alone.
　　Knowledge, will ye forsake me also?
KNOWLEDGE　Yea, Everyman, when ye to Death shall go,
860　But not yet, for no manner of danger.
EVERYMAN　Gramercy, Knowledge, with all my heart!
KNOWLEDGE　Nay, yet will I not from hence depart
　　Till I see where ye shall become.⁴
EVERYMAN　Methink, alas, that I must be gone
865　To make my reckoning and my debts pay,
　　For I see my time is nigh spent away.
　　Take example, all ye that this do hear or see,
　　How they that I best loved do forsake me,
　　Except my Good Deeds that bideth truly.
870　GOOD DEEDS　All earthly things is but vanity.

4. Till I see what shall become of you.

Beauty, Strength, and Discretion do man forsake,
Foolish friends and kinsmen that fair spake—
All fleeth save Good Deeds, and that am I.

EVERYMAN   Have mercy on me, God most mighty,
875   And stand by me, thou mother and maid, holy Mary!

GOOD DEEDS   Fear not: I will speak for thee.

EVERYMAN   Here I cry God mercy!

GOOD DEEDS   Short our end, and 'minish our pain.[5]
Let us go, and never come again.

880   EVERYMAN   Into thy hands, Lord, my soul I commend:
Receive it, Lord, that it be not lost.
As thou me boughtest,° so me defend,   *redeemed*
And save me from the fiend's boast,
That I may appear with that blessed host
885   That shall be saved at the day of doom.
In manus tuas, of mights most,
Forever *commendo spiritum meum.*[6]

[EVERYMAN *and* GOOD DEEDS *descend into the grave.*]

KNOWLEDGE   Now hath he suffered that we all shall endure,
The Good Deeds shall make all sure.
890   Now hath he made ending,
Methinketh that I hear angels sing
And make great joy and melody
Where Everyman's soul received shall be.

ANGEL   [*within*] Come, excellent elect° spouse to Jesu![7]   *chosen*
895   Here above thou shalt go
Because of thy singular virtue.
Now the soul is taken the body fro,
Thy reckoning is crystal clear:
Now shalt thou into the heavenly sphere—
900   Unto the which all ye shall come
That liveth well before the day of doom.

[*Enter* DOCTOR.[8]]

DOCTOR   This memorial° men may have in mind: *reminder*
Ye hearers, take it of worth,° old and young,   *prize it*
And forsake Pride, for he deceiveth you in the end.
905   And remember Beauty, Five-Wits, Strength, and Discretion,
They all at the last do Everyman forsake,
Save his Good Deeds there doth he take—
But beware, for and they be small,
Before God he hath no help at all—
910   None excuse may be there for Everyman.

5. I.e., make our dying quick and diminish our
pain.
6. Into thy hands, O greatest of powers, I commend my spirit forever.

7. The soul is often referred to as the bride of
Jesus.
8. The Doctor is the learned theologian who
explains the meaning of the play.

Alas, how shall he do than?°   *then*
For after death amends may no man make,
For then mercy and pity doth him forsake.
If his reckoning be not clear when he doth come,
915   God will say, *"Ite, maledicti, in ignem eternum!"*[9]
And he that hath his account whole and sound,
High in heaven he shall be crowned,
Unto which place God bring us all thither,
That we may live body and soul togither.
920   Thereto help, the Trinity!
Amen, say ye, for saint charity.

9. Depart, ye cursed, into everlasting fire.

The Sixteenth Century
1485–1603

1485:	Accession of Henry VII inaugurates Tudor dynasty
1509:	Accession of Henry VIII
1517:	Martin Luther's Wittenberg Theses; beginning of the Reformation
1534:	Henry VIII declares himself head of the English church
1557:	Publication of Tottel's *Songs and Sonnets,* containing poems by Sir Thomas Wyatt; Henry Howard, earl of Surrey; and others
1558:	Accession of Elizabeth I
1576:	Building of The Theater, the first permanent structure in England for the presentation of plays
1588:	Defeat of the Spanish Armada
1603:	Death of Elizabeth I, accession of James I, the first of the Stuart kings

The Ancient Roman poet Virgil characterized Britain as a wild, remote place set apart from all the world, and it must still have seemed so in the early sixteenth century to the cosmopolitan inhabitants of cities like Venice, Madrid, and Paris. To be sure, some venturesome travelers crossed the Channel and visited London, Oxford, or Cambridge, bringing home reports of bustling markets, impressive universities, and ambitious nobles vying for position at an increasingly powerful royal court. But these visitors were but a trickle compared with the flood of wealthy young Englishmen (and, to a lesser extent, Englishwomen) who embarked at the first opportunity for the Continent. English travelers were virtually obliged to learn some French, Italian, or Spanish, for they would encounter very few people who knew their language. On returning home, they would frequently wear foreign fashions— much to the disgust of moralists—and would pepper their speech with foreign phrases.

At the beginning of the sixteenth century, the English language had almost no prestige abroad, and there were those at home who doubted that it could serve as a suitable medium for serious, elevated, or elegant discourse. It is no accident that one of the first works in this selection of sixteenth-century literature, Thomas More's *Utopia,* was not written in English: More, who began his great book in 1515 when he was on a diplomatic mission in the Netherlands, was writing for an international intellectual community, and as such his language of choice was Latin. His work quickly became famous throughout Europe, but it was not translated into English until the 1550s. Evidently, neither More himself nor the London printers and booksellers thought it imperative to publish a vernacular *Utopia.* Yet by the century's end there were signs of a great increase in what we might call linguistic self-confidence, signs that at least some contemporary observers were aware that something extraordinary had happened to their language. Though in 1600 England still remained somewhat peripheral to the Continent, English had been fashioned into an immensely powerful expressive medium, one whose cadences in the works of Marlowe, Shakespeare, or the translators of the Bible continue after more than four centuries to thrill readers.

How did it come about that by the century's end so many remarkable poems, plays, and prose works were written in English? The answer lies in part in the spectacular creativity of a succession of brilliant writers, the best of whom are represented in these pages. Still, a vital literary culture is the product of a complex process, involving thousands of more modest, half-hidden creative acts sparked by a wide range of motives, some of which we will briefly explore.

THE COURT AND THE CITY

The development of the English language in the sixteenth century is linked at least indirectly to the consolidation and strengthening of the English state. Preoccupied by violent clashes between the thuggish feudal retainers of rival barons, England through most of the fifteenth century had rather limited time and inclination to cultivate rhetorical skills. The social and economic health of the nation had been severely damaged by the so-called Wars of the Roses, a vicious, decades-long struggle for royal power between the noble houses of York and Lancaster. The struggle was resolved by the establishment of the Tudor dynasty that ruled England from 1485 to 1603. The family name derives from Owen Tudor, an ambitious Welshman who himself had no claim to the throne but who married Catherine of Valois, widow of the Lancastrian king Henry V. Their grandson, the earl of Richmond, became the first Tudor monarch: he won the crown by leading the army that defeated and killed the reigning Yorkist king, Richard III, at the battle of Bosworth Field. The victorious Richmond, crowned King Henry VII in 1485, promptly consolidated his rather shaky claim to the throne by marrying Elizabeth of the house of York, hence effectively uniting the two rival factions.

England's barons, impoverished and divided by the dynastic wars, could not effectively oppose the new power of the crown, and the leaders of the church also generally supported the royal power. The wily Henry VII was therefore able to counter the multiple and competing power structures characteristic of feudal society and to impose a much stronger central authority and order on the nation. Initiated by the first Tudor sovereign, this consolidation progressed throughout the sixteenth century; by the reign of the last Tudor—Henry's granddaughter, Elizabeth I—though the ruler still needed the consent of Parliament on crucial matters (including the all-important one of raising taxes), the royal court had concentrated in itself much of the nation's power.

The court was a center of culture as well as power: court entertainments such as theater and masque (a sumptuous, elaborately costumed performance of dance, song, and poetry); court fashions in dress and speech; court tastes in painting, music, and poetry—all shaped the taste and the imagination of the country as a whole. Culture and power were not, in any case, easily separable in Tudor England. In a society with no freedom of speech as we understand it and with relatively limited means of mass communication, important public issues were often aired indirectly, through what we might now regard as entertainment, while lyrics that to us seem slight and nonchalant could serve as carefully crafted manifestations of rhetorical agility by aspiring courtiers.

Court culture simultaneously spawned an art of intrigue and one of ostentation. Ambitious men and women sought to call attention to themselves. They did so by the gorgeous, immensely costly clothes they wore—Elizabethan high fashion was among the most extravagantly ornamented in European history—and by the display of their artistic and social skills. A highly influential book, *Il Cortegiano* (The Courtier) by Count Baldassare Castiglione, provided subtle guidance in the performance of these skills. It was particularly important, Castiglione wrote, to conceal the effort that lay behind elegant accomplishments, so that they would seem natural. This art of concealing art—which he termed *sprezzatura*—was widely practiced (or at least attempted), along with techniques secretly memorized from the age's other great study of court life, Machiavelli's notorious *Il Principe* (The Prince). The goal was close proximity to the monarch's body (one of the coveted positions in the court of Henry VIII was Groom of the Stool, "close stool" being the Tudor term for toilet). The monarch's chief ministers and favorites were the primary channels through which patronage was dispensed to courtiers who competed for offices in the court, the government bureaucracies, the royal household, the army, the church, and the universities, or who sought titles, grants of land, leases, or similar favors. But if proximity held out the promise of wealth and power, it also harbored danger. Festive evenings with the likes of the ruthless Henry VIII were not occasions for relaxation. The court fostered paranoia—the principal character in John Skelton's poem about court life is aptly named "Dread"—and an attendant obsession with secrecy, spying, duplicity, and betrayal. Courtiers were highly gifted at crafting and deciphering graceful words with double or triple meanings. Sixteenth-century poets had much to learn from courtiers, the Elizabethan critic George Puttenham observed; indeed many of the best poets in the period, Sir Thomas Wyatt, Sir Philip Sidney, Sir Walter Ralegh, and others, *were* courtiers.

If court culture fostered performances for a small coterie audience, other forces in Tudor England pulled toward a more public sphere. Markets expanded significantly, international trade flourished, and cities throughout the realm experienced a rapid surge in size and importance. London's population in particular soared, from 60,000 in 1520 to 120,000 in 1550 to 375,000 a century later, making it the largest and fastest-growing city not only in England but in all of Europe. Every year in the first half of the seventeenth century about 10,000 people migrated to London from other parts of England—wages in London tended to be around 50 percent higher than in the rest of the country—and it is estimated that one in eight English people lived in London at some point in their lives.

About a decade before Henry VII won his throne, the art of printing from movable metal type, a German invention, had been introduced into England by William Caxton (ca. 1422–1491), who had learned and practiced it in the

Low Countries. Though reliable statistics are impossible to come by, literacy seems to have increased during the fifteenth century and still more during the sixteenth, when Protestantism encouraged a direct encounter with the Bible. Printing made books cheaper and more plentiful, providing more opportunity to read and more incentive to learn. The greater availability of books may also have reinforced the trend toward silent reading, a trend that gradually transformed what had been a communal experience into a more intimate encounter with a text.

Yet it would be a mistake to imagine these changes as sudden and dramatic. Manuscripts retained considerable prestige among the elite; throughout the sixteenth and well into the seventeenth centuries court poets in particular were wary of the "stigma of print" that might mark their verse as less exclusive. Although Caxton, who was an author and translator as well as a printer, introduced printed books, he attempted to cater to courtly tastes by translating works whose tone was more medieval than modern. The fascination with the old chivalric code of behavior is reflected as well in the jousts and tournaments that continued at court for a century, long after gunpowder had rendered them obsolete. As often in an age of spectacular novelty, many people looked back to an idealized past.

RENAISSANCE HUMANISM

During the fifteenth century a few English clerics and government officials had journeyed to Italy and had seen something of the extraordinary cultural and intellectual movement flourishing in the city-states there. That movement, generally known as the Renaissance, involved a rebirth of letters and arts stimulated by the recovery of texts and artifacts from classical antiquity, the development of techniques such as linear perspective, and the creation of powerful new aesthetic norms based on classical models. It also unleashed new ideas and new social, political, and economic forces that gradually displaced the otherworldly and communal values of the Middle Ages. In the brilliant, intensely competitive, and vital world of Leonardo da Vinci and Michelangelo, the submission of the human spirit to penitential discipline gave way to unleashed curiosity, individual self-assertion, and a powerful conviction that man was the measure of all things. To Renaissance intellectuals, the achievements of the pagan philosophers of antiquity came to seem more compelling than the subtle distinctions drawn by the Christian theologians of the Middle Ages. The perception spurred an impossibly ambitious attempt to assert the underlying unity of the truth found in all philosophical systems, along with an emphasis on the worth of life in this world and the remarkable malleability of the individual. "We have made thee neither of heaven nor of earth, neither mortal nor immortal," God tells Adam, in the Florentine Pico della Mirandola's *Oration on the Dignity of Man* (1486), "so that with freedom of choice and with honor, as though the maker and molder of thyself, thou mayest fashion thyself in whatever shape thou shalt prefer." "As though the maker and molder of thyself": this vision of self-fashioning may be glimpsed in the poetry of Petrarch, the sculpture of Donatello, and the statecraft of Lorenzo de' Medici. But in England it was not until Henry VII's reign brought some measure of political stability that the Renaissance could take root, and it was not until the accession of Henry VIII that it began to flower.

This flowering, when it occurred, came not, as in Italy, in the visual arts and architecture. It came rather in the spiritual and intellectual orientation known as humanism. More's *Utopia* (1516), with its dream of human existence entirely transformed by a radical change in institutional arrangements, is an extreme instance of a general humanist interest in education: in England and elsewhere, humanism was bound up with struggles over the purposes of education and curriculum reform. The great Dutch humanist Erasmus, who spent some time in England and developed a close friendship with More, was a leader in the assault on what he and others regarded as a hopelessly narrow and outmoded intellectual culture based on scholastic hair-splitting and a dogmatic adherence to the philosophy of Aristotle. English humanists, including John Colet (founder of St. Paul's School), Roger Ascham (tutor to Princess Elizabeth), and Sir Thomas Elyot, wrote treatises on education to promote the kind of learning they regarded as the most suitable preparation for public service. That education—predominantly male and conducted by tutors in wealthy families or in grammar schools— was ordered according to the subjects of the medieval *trivium* (grammar, logic, and rhetoric) and *quadrivium* (arithmetic, geometry, astronomy, and music), but its focus shifted from training for the church to the general acquisition of "literature," in the sense both of literacy and of cultural knowledge. For some of the more intellectually ambitious humanists, that knowledge extended to ancient Greek, whose enthusiastic adherents began to challenge the entrenched prestige of Latin.

Still, at the core of the curriculum remained the study of Latin, the mastery of which was in effect a prolonged male puberty rite involving pain as well as pleasure. Though some educators counseled mildness, punishment was an established part of the pedagogy of the age, and even gifted students could scarcely have escaped recurrent flogging. The purpose was to train the sons of the nobility and gentry to speak and write good Latin, the language of diplomacy, of the professions, and of all higher learning. Their sisters were always educated at home or in other noble houses. They chiefly learned modern languages, religion, music, and needlework, but they very seldom received the firm grounding in ancient languages and classical literature so central to Renaissance culture. Elizabethan schoolmasters sought to impart facility and rhetorical elegance, but the books their students laboriously pored over were not considered mere exhibitions of literary style: from the *Sententiae Pueriles* (Maxims for Children) for beginners on up through the dramatists Terence, Plautus, and Seneca, the poets Virgil and Horace, and the orator Cicero, the classics were also studied for the moral, political, and philosophical truths they contained. Though originating in pagan times, those truths could, in the opinion of many humanists, be reconciled to the moral vision of Christianity.

Humanists committed to classical learning were faced with the question of whether to write their own works in Latin or in English. To many learned men, influenced both by the humanist exaltation of the classical languages and by the characteristic Renaissance desire for eternal fame, the national languages seemed relatively unstable and ephemeral. Intellectuals had long shared a pan-European world of scientific inquiry, so that works by such

English scientists as William Gilbert, William Harvey, and Francis Bacon easily joined those by Nicolaus Copernicus, Johannes Kepler, and Andreas Vesalius on the common linguistic ground of Latin. But throughout Europe nationalism and the expansion of the reading public were steadily strengthening the power and allure of the vernacular. The famous schoolmaster Richard Mulcaster (ca. 1530–1611), teacher of the poet Edmund Spenser, captured this emergent sense of national identity in singing the praises of his native tongue:

> Is it not indeed a marvelous bondage, to become servants to one tongue for learning's sake the most of our time, with loss of most time, whereas we may have the very same treasure in our own tongue, with the gain of more time? our own bearing the joyful title of our liberty and freedom, the Latin tongue remembering us of our thralldom and bondage? I love Rome, but London better; I favor Italy, but England more; I honor the Latin, but I worship the English.

These two impulses—humanist reverence for the classics and English pride in the vernacular language—gave rise to many distinguished translations throughout the century: Homer's *Iliad* and *Odyssey* by George Chapman, Plutarch's *Lives of the Noble Grecians and Romans* by Sir Thomas North, and Ovid's *Metamorphoses* by Arthur Golding. Translators also sought to make available in English the most notable literary works in the modern languages: Castiglione's *Il Cortegiano* by Sir Thomas Hoby, Ariosto's *Orlando Furioso* (Orlando Mad) by Sir John Harington, and Montaigne's *Essais* by John Florio. The London book trade of the sixteenth century was a thoroughly international affair.

THE REFORMATION

There had long been serious ideological and institutional tensions in the religious life of England, but officially at least England in the early sixteenth century had a single religion, Catholicism, whose acknowledged head was the pope in Rome. For its faithful adherents the Catholic church was the central institution in their lives, a universal infallible guide to human existence from cradle to grave and on into the life to come. They were instructed by its teachings, corrected by its discipline, sustained by its sacraments, and comforted by its promises. At Mass, its most sacred ritual, the congregation could witness a miracle, as the priest held aloft the Host and uttered the words that transformed the bread and wine into the body and blood of God incarnate. A vast system of confession, pardons, penance, absolution, indulgences, sacred relics, and ceremonies gave the unmarried male clerical hierarchy great power, at once spiritual and material, over their largely illiterate flock. The Bible, the liturgy, and most of the theological discussions were in Latin, which few lay people could understand; however, religious doctrine and spirituality were mediated to them by the priests, by beautiful church art and music, and by the liturgical ceremonies of daily life—festivals, holy days, baptisms, marriages, exorcisms, and funerals.

Several of the key doctrines and practices of the Catholic church had been challenged in fourteenth-century England by the teachings of John Wycliffe and his followers, known as the Lollards. But the heretical challenge had been ruthlessly suppressed, and the embers of dissent lay largely dormant until they were ignited once again in Germany by Martin Luther, an Augustinian monk and professor of theology at the University of Wittenberg. What began in November 1517 as an academic disputation grew with amazing speed into a bitter, far-reaching, and bloody revolt that forever ruptured the unity of Western Christendom.

When Luther rose up against the ancient church, he did so in the name of private conscience enlightened by a personal reading of the Scriptures. A person of formidable intellectual energy, eloquence, and rhetorical violence, Luther charged that the pope and his hierarchy were the servants of Satan and that the church had degenerated into a corrupt, worldly conspiracy designed to bilk the credulous and subvert secular authority. Salvation depended upon destroying this conspiracy and enabling all of the people to regain direct access to the word of God by means of vernacular translations of the Bible. The common watchwords of the Reformation, as the movement Luther sparked came to be known, were *sola scriptura* and *sola fide*: only the Scriptures (not the church or tradition or the clerical hierarchy) have authority in matters of religion and should determine what an individual must believe and practice; only the faith of the individual (not good works or the scrupulous observance of religious rituals) can effect a Christian's salvation.

These tenets, heretical in the eyes of the Catholic Church, spread and gathered force, especially in Northern Europe, where major leaders like the Swiss pastor Ulrich Zwingli in Zurich and the French theologian John Calvin in Geneva, elaborating various and sometimes conflicting doctrinal principles, organized the populace to overturn the existing church and established new institutional structures. In England, however, the Reformation began less with popular discontent and theological disputation than with dynastic politics and royal greed. Henry VIII, who had received from Pope Leo X the title Defender of the Faith for writing a book against Luther, craved a legitimate son to succeed to the throne, and his queen, Catherine of Aragon, failed to give him one. (Catherine had borne six children, but only a daughter, Mary, survived infancy.) After lengthy negotiations, the pope, under pressure from Catherine's powerful Spanish family, refused to grant the king the divorce he sought in order to marry Anne Boleyn. A series of momentous events followed, as England lurched away from the Church of Rome. In 1531 Henry charged the entire clergy of England with having usurped royal authority in the administration of canon law (the law that governed such matters as divorce). Under extreme pressure, including the threat of mass confiscations and imprisonment, the Convocation of the Clergy begged for pardon and made a donation to the royal coffers of over one hundred thousand pounds.

In 1533 Henry's marriage to Catherine was officially declared null and void and Anne Boleyn was crowned queen. The king was promptly excommunicated by the pope, Clement VII. In the following year, a parliamentary Act of Succession required an oath from all adult male subjects confirming the new dynastic settlement. Thomas More and John Fisher, the bishop of Rochester, were among the small number who refused. The Act of Supremacy, passed later in the year, formally declared the king to be "Supreme Head of the Church in England" and again required an oath to this effect. In 1535 and 1536 further acts made it treasonous to refuse the oath of royal supremacy or, as More had tried to do, to remain silent. The first victims were three Carthusian monks who rejected the oath—"How could the king, a layman," said one of them, "be Head of the Church of England?"—and in May 1535 were duly hanged, drawn, and quartered. A few weeks later Fisher and More were convicted and beheaded. Between 1536 and 1539, under the direction of Henry's powerful secretary of state, Thomas Cromwell, England's monasteries were suppressed and their vast wealth seized by the crown.

Royal defiance of the authority of Rome was a key element in the Reformation but did not by itself constitute the establishment of Protestantism in England. On the contrary, in the same year that Fisher and More were martyred for their adherence to Roman Catholicism, twenty-five Protestants, members of a sect known as Anabaptists, were burned for heresy on a single day. Through most of his reign, Henry remained an equal-opportunity persecutor, pitiless to Catholics loyal to Rome and hostile to many of those who espoused Reformation ideas, though these ideas gradually established themselves on English soil.

Even when Henry (in his brief stint as Defender of the Faith) was eager to do so, it proved impossible to eradicate Protestantism, as it would later prove impossible for Protestant monarchs to eradicate Catholicism. In part this persistence in the face of ferocious persecution arose from the willingness of a small core of ardent believers to die for their faith; in part it arose from the ability of even a small number of clandestine printing presses to flood the country with texts that the authorities were unable to suppress. Hence in his role as Defender of the Faith, Henry had driven the great English translator of the Bible, William Tyndale, into exile on the Continent, where he was eventually seized and garroted by Catholic authorities. But Tyndale's eloquent—and distinctly Protestant—translation of the New Testament circulated widely in England, despite repeated attempts by officials to burn every copy. After Henry's break with Rome, Tyndale's version served as the core of the so-called Great Bible, the authorized translation that made the Scriptures available in English to anyone who could read.

Upon Henry's death in 1547, his son, Edward (by his third wife, Jane Seymour), came to the throne, with his maternal uncle, Edward Seymour, the duke of Somerset, as Lord Protector. Both the ten-year-old Edward and his uncle were staunch Protestants, and reformers hastened to transform the English church accordingly. During Edward's brief reign, Thomas Cranmer, the archbishop of Canterbury, formulated the forty-two articles of religion which became the core of Anglican orthodoxy and wrote the first *Book of Common Prayer*, which was officially adopted in 1549 as the basis of English worship services.

The sickly Edward died in 1553, only six years after his accession to the throne, and was succeeded by his half-sister Mary (Henry VIII's daughter by his first wife, Catherine), who immediately took steps to return her kingdom to Roman Catholicism. Though she was unable to get Parliament to agree to return church lands seized under Henry VIII, she restored the Catholic Mass, once again affirmed the authority of the pope, and put down a rebellion that sought to depose her. Seconded by her ardently Catholic husband, Philip II, king of Spain, she initiated a series of religious persecutions that earned her (from her enemies) the name Bloody Mary. Hundreds of Protestants took refuge abroad in cities like Calvin's Geneva; almost three hundred less fortunate Protestants were condemned as heretics and burned at the stake.

Mary died childless in 1558, and her younger half-sister, Elizabeth, became queen. Elizabeth's succession had been by no means assured. For if Protestants regarded Henry VIII's marriage to Catherine as invalid and hence deemed Mary illegitimate, so Catholics regarded his marriage to Anne Boleyn as invalid and hence deemed her daughter, Elizabeth, illegitimate. Henry VIII himself seemed to support both views, since only three years after divorcing Catherine, he beheaded Anne on charges of treason and adultery and urged Parliament to invalidate the marriage. Moreover, though during her sister's reign Elizabeth outwardly complied with the official Catholic religious observance, Mary and her advisers suspected her of Protestant leanings, and the young princess's life was in grave danger. Poised and circumspect, Elizabeth warily evaded the traps that were set for her. When she ascended the throne, her actions were scrutinized for some indication of the country's future course. During her coronation procession, when a girl in an allegorical pageant presented her with a Bible in English translation— banned under Mary's reign—Elizabeth kissed the book, held it up reverently, and laid it to her breast. England had returned to the Reformation.

Many English men and women, of all classes, remained loyal to the old Catholic faith, but English authorities under Elizabeth moved steadily, if cautiously, toward ensuring at least an outward conformity to the official Protestant settlement. Recusants, those who refused to attend regular Sunday services in their parish churches, were heavily fined. Anyone who wished to receive a university degree, to be ordained as a priest in the Church of England, or to be named as an officer of the state had to swear an oath to the royal supremacy. Commissioners were sent throughout the land to confirm that religious services were following the officially approved liturgy and to investigate any reported backsliding into Catholic practice or, alternatively, any attempts to introduce reforms more radical than the queen and her bishops had chosen to embrace, for the Protestant exiles who streamed back were eager not only to undo the damage Mary had done but also to carry the Reformation much further than it had gone. They sought to dismantle the church hierarchy, to purge the calendar of folk customs deemed pagan and the church service of ritual practices deemed superstitious, to dress the clergy in simple garb, and, at the extreme edge, to smash "idolatrous" statues, crucifixes, and altarpieces. Throughout her long reign, however, Elizabeth herself remained cautiously conservative and determined to hold religious zealotry in check.

In the space of a single lifetime, England had gone officially from Roman Catholicism, to Catholicism under the supreme headship of the English king, to a guarded Protestantism, to a more radical Protestantism, to a renewed and aggressive Roman Catholicism, and finally to Protestantism again. Each of these shifts was accompanied by danger, persecution, and death. It was enough to make people wary. Or skeptical. Or extremely agile.

THE ENGLISH AND OTHERNESS

Elizabethan London had a large population of resident aliens, mainly artisans and merchants and their families, from Portugal, Italy, Spain, Germany, and, above all, France and the Netherlands. Many of these people were Protestant refugees, and they were accorded some legal and economic protection by the government. But they were not always welcome to the local populace. Throughout the sixteenth century London was the site of repeated demonstrations and, on occasion, bloody riots against the communities of foreign artisans, who were accused of taking jobs away from Englishmen. There was widespread hostility as well toward the Welsh, the Scots, and above all the Irish, whom the English had for centuries been struggling unsuccessfully to subdue. The kings of England claimed to be rulers of Ireland, but in reality they effectively controlled only a small area known as the Pale, extending north from Dublin. The great majority of the population remained stubbornly Catholic and, despite endlessly reiterated English repression, burning of villages, destruction of crops, seizure of land, and massacres, incorrigibly independent.

Medieval England's Jewish population, the recurrent object of persecution, extortion, and massacre, had been officially expelled by King Edward I in 1290, but Elizabethan England harbored a tiny number of Jews or Jewish converts to Christianity. They were the objects of suspicion and hostility. Elizabethans appear to have been fascinated by Jews and Judaism but quite uncertain whether the terms referred to a people, a foreign nation, a set of strange practices, a living faith, a defunct religion, a villainous conspiracy, or a messianic inheritance. Protestant Reformers brooded deeply on the Hebraic origins of Christianity; government officials ordered the arrest of those "suspected to be Jews"; villagers paid pennies to itinerant fortunetellers who claimed to be descended from Abraham or masters of kabbalistic mysteries; and London playgoers enjoyed the spectacle of the downfall of the wicked Barabas in Christopher Marlowe's *The Jew of Malta* and the forced conversion of Shylock in Shakespeare's *The Merchant of Venice*. Jews were not officially permitted to resettle in England until the middle of the seventeenth century, and even then their legal status was ambiguous.

Sixteenth-century England also had a small African population whose skin color was the subject of pseudoscientific speculation and theological debate. Some Elizabethans believed that Africans' blackness resulted from the climate of the regions where they lived, where, as one traveler put it, they were "so scorched and vexed with the heat of the sun, that in many places they curse it when it riseth." Others held that blackness was a curse inherited from their forefather Cush, the son of Ham (who had, according to Genesis, wickedly exposed the nakedness of his drunken father, Noah). George Best, a proponent of this theory of inherited skin color, reported that "I myself have seen an Ethiopian as black as coal brought into England, who taking a fair English woman to wife, begat a son in all respects as black as the father was, although England were his native country, and an English woman his mother: whereby it seemeth this blackness proceedeth rather of some natural infection of that man."

As the word "infection" suggests, Elizabethans frequently regarded blackness as a physical defect, though the black people who lived in England and Scotland throughout the sixteenth century were also treated as exotic curiosities. At his marriage to Anne of Denmark, James VI of Scotland (the son of Mary, Queen of Scots; as James I of England, he succeeded Elizabeth in 1603) entertained his bride and her family by commanding four naked black youths to dance before him in the snow. (The youths died of exposure shortly afterward.) In 1594, in the festivities celebrating the baptism of James's son, a "Black-Moor" entered pulling an elaborately decorated chariot that was, in the original plan, supposed to be pulled by a lion. In England there was a black trumpeter in the courts of Henry VII and Henry VIII, while Elizabeth had at least two black servants, one an entertainer, the other a page. Africans became increasingly popular as servants in aristocratic and gentle households in the last decades of the sixteenth century.

Some of these Africans were almost certainly slaves, though the legal status of slavery in England was ambiguous. In Cartwright's Case (1569), the court ruled "that England was too Pure an Air for Slaves to breathe in," but there is evidence that black slaves were owned in Elizabethan and Jacobean England. Moreover, by the mid-sixteenth century the English had become involved in the profitable trade that carried African slaves to the New World. In 1562 John Hawkins embarked on his first slaving voyage, transporting some three hundred Africans from the Guinea coast to Hispaniola, where they were sold for ten thousand pounds. Elizabeth is reported to have said of this venture that it was "detestable, and would call down the Vengeance of Heaven upon the Undertakers." Nevertheless, she invested in Hawkins's subsequent voyages and loaned him ships.

Elizabeth also invested in other enterprises that combined aggressive nationalism and the pursuit of profit. In 1493 the pope had divided the New World between the Spanish and the Portuguese by drawing a line from pole to pole (hence Brazil speaks Portuguese today and the rest of Latin America speaks Spanish): the English were not in the picture. But by the end of Edward VI's reign the Company of Merchant Adventurers was founded, and Englishmen began to explore Asia and North America. Some of these adventurers turned to piracy, preying on Spanish ships that were returning laden with wealth extracted from their New World possessions. (The pope had ruled that the Indians were human beings—and hence could be converted to Christianity—but the ruling did nothing to prevent their enslavement and brutal exploitation.) English acts of piracy soon became a private undeclared war, with the queen and her courtiers covertly investing in the raids but accepting no responsibility for them. The greatest of many astounding exploits was the voyage of Francis Drake (1577–80): he sailed through the Strait of Magellan, pillaged Spanish towns on the Pacific, reached as far north as San Francisco, crossed to the Philippines, and returned around the Cape of Good Hope; he came back with a million pounds in treasure, and his investors earned a dividend of 5,000 percent. Queen Elizabeth knighted him on the deck of his ship, *The Golden Hind*.

A FEMALE MONARCH IN A MALE WORLD

In the last year of Mary's reign, the Scottish Calvinist minister John Knox thundered against what he called "the monstrous regiment of women." After the Protestant Elizabeth came to the throne the following year, Knox and his religious brethren were less inclined to denounce all female rulers, but in England, as elsewhere in Europe, there remained a widespread conviction that women were unsuited to wield power over men. Many men seem to have regarded the capacity for rational thought as exclusively male; women, they assumed, were led only by their passions. While gentlemen mastered the arts of rhetoric and warfare, gentlewomen were expected to display the virtues of silence and good housekeeping. Among upper-class males, the will to dominate others was acceptable and indeed admired; the same will in women was condemned as a grotesque and dangerous aberration.

Apologists for the queen countered these prejudices by appealing to historical precedent and legal theory. History offered inspiring examples of just female rulers, notably Deborah, the biblical prophetess who had judged Israel. In the legal sphere, crown lawyers advanced the theory of "the king's two bodies." As England's crowned head, Elizabeth's person was mystically divided between her mortal "body natural" and the immortal "body politic." While the queen's natural body was inevitably subject to the failings of human flesh, the body politic was timeless and perfect. In political terms, therefore, Elizabeth's sex was a matter of no consequence, a thing indifferent.

Elizabeth, who had received a fine humanist education and an extended, dangerous lesson in the art of survival, made it immediately clear that she intended to rule in more than name only. She assembled a group of trustworthy advisers, foremost among them William Cecil (later created Lord Burghley), but she insisted on making many of the crucial decisions herself. Like many Renaissance monarchs, Elizabeth was drawn to the idea of royal absolutism, the theory that ultimate power was quite properly concentrated in her person and indeed that God had appointed her to be His deputy in the kingdom. Opposition to her rule, in this view, was not only a political act but also a kind of impiety, a blasphemous grudging against the will of God. Apologists for absolutism contended that God commands obedience even to manifestly wicked rulers whom He has sent to punish the sinfulness of mankind. Such arguments were routinely made in speeches and political tracts and from the pulpits of churches, where they were incorporated in the *Book of Homilies* that clergymen were required to read out to their congregations.

In reality, Elizabeth's power was not absolute. The government had a network of spies, informers and *agents provocateurs*, but it lacked a standing army, a national police force, an efficient system of communication, and an extensive bureaucracy. Above all, the queen had limited financial resources and needed to turn periodically to an independent and often recalcitrant Parliament, which by long tradition had the sole right to levy taxes and to grant subsidies. Members of the House of Commons were elected from their boroughs, not appointed by the monarch, and though the queen had considerable influence over their decisions, she could by no means dictate policy. Under these constraints, Elizabeth ruled through a combination of adroit political maneuvering and imperious command, all the while enhancing her authority in the eyes of both court and country by means of an extraordinary cult of love.

"We all loved her," Elizabeth's godson Sir John Harington wrote, with just a touch of irony, a few years after the queen's death, "for she said she loved us." Ambassadors, courtiers, and parliamentarians all submitted to Elizabeth's cult of love, in which the queen's gender was transformed from a potential liability into a significant asset. Those who approached her generally did so on their knees and were expected to address her with the most extravagant compliments; she in turn spoke, when it suited her to do so, in a comparable language of love. The court moved in an atmosphere of romance, with music, dancing, plays, and the elaborate, fancy-dress entertainments called masques. The queen adorned herself in dazzling clothes and rich jewels. When she went on one of her summer "progresses," ceremonial journeys through her land, she looked like an exotic, sacred image in a religious cult of love, and her noble hosts virtually bankrupted themselves to lavish upon her the costliest pleasures. England's leading artists, such as the poet Spenser and the painter Nicholas Hilliard, enlisted themselves in the celebration of Elizabeth's mystery, likening her to the goddesses of mythology and the heroines of the Bible: Diana, Astraea, Cynthia, Deborah. Her cult drew its power from cultural discourses that ranged from the secular (her courtiers could pine for her as the cruelly chaste mistress celebrated in Petrarchan love poetry) to the sacred (the veneration that under Catholicism had been due to the Virgin Mary could now be directed toward England's semi-divine queen).

There was a sober, even grim aspect to these poetical fantasies: Elizabeth was brilliant at playing one dangerous faction off against another, now turning her gracious smiles on one favorite, now honoring his hated rival, now suddenly looking elsewhere and raising an obscure upstart to royal favor. And when she was disobeyed or when she felt that her prerogatives had been challenged, she was capable of an anger that, as Harington put it, "left no doubtings whose daughter she was." Thus when Sir Walter Ralegh, one of the queen's glittering favorites, married without her knowledge or consent, he found himself promptly imprisoned in the Tower of London. Or when the Protestant polemicist John Stubbs ventured to publish a pamphlet stridently denouncing the queen's proposed marriage to the French Catholic duke of Anjou, Stubbs and his publisher were arrested and had their right hands chopped off. (After receiving the blow, the now prudent Stubbs lifted his hat with his remaining hand and cried, "God save the Queen!")

The queen's marriage negotiations were a particularly fraught issue. When she came to the throne at twenty-five, speculation about a suitable match, already widespread, intensified and remained for decades at a fever pitch, for the stakes were high. If Elizabeth died childless, the Tudor line would come to an end. The nearest heir was her cousin Mary, Queen of Scots, a Catholic whose claim was supported by France and by the papacy and whose penchant for sexual and political intrigue confirmed the worst fears of English Protestants. The obvious way to avert the nightmare was for Elizabeth to marry and produce an heir, and the pressure upon her to do so was intense.

More than the royal succession hinged on the question of the queen's marriage; Elizabeth's perceived eligibility was a vital factor in the complex machinations of international diplomacy. A dynastic marriage between the queen of England and a foreign ruler would forge an alliance sufficient to alter the balance of power in Europe. The English court hosted a steady stream of ambassadors from kings and princelings eager to win the hand of the royal maiden, and Elizabeth, who prided herself on speaking fluent French and Italian (and on reading Latin and Greek), played her romantic part with exemplary skill, sighing and spinning the negotiations out for months and even years. Most probably, she never meant to marry any of her numerous foreign (and domestic) suitors. Such a decisive act would have meant the end of her independence, as well as the end of the marriage game by which she played one power off against another. One day she would seem to be on the verge of accepting a proposal; the next, she would vow never to forsake her virginity. "She is a princess," the French ambassador remarked, "who can act any part she pleases."

THE KINGDOM IN DANGER

Beset by Catholic and Protestant extremists, Elizabeth contrived to forge a moderate compromise that enabled her realm to avert the massacres and civil wars that poisoned France and other countries on the Continent. But menace was never far off, and there were continual fears of conspiracy, rebellion, and assassination. Many of the fears swirled around Mary, Queen of Scots, who had been driven from her own kingdom in 1567 and had taken refuge in England. Her presence, under a kind of house arrest, was the source of intense anxiety and helped generate continual rumors of plots, some of them real enough, others imaginary, still others fabricated by the secret agents of the government's intelligence service under the direction of Sir Francis Walsingham. The situation worsened greatly after Spanish imperial armies invaded the Netherlands in order to stamp out Protestant rebels (1567), after the St. Bartholomew's Day Massacre of Protestants (Huguenots) in France (1572), and after the assassination of Europe's other major Protestant leader, William of Orange (1584).

The queen's life seemed to be in even greater danger after Pope Gregory XIII's proclamation in 1580 that the assassination of the great heretic Elizabeth (who had been excommunicated a decade before) would not constitute a mortal sin. The immediate effect of the proclamation was to make life more difficult for English Catholics, most of whom were loyal to the queen but who fell under grave suspicion. Suspicion was intensified by the clandestine presence of English Jesuits, trained at seminaries abroad and smuggled back into England to serve the Roman Catholic cause. When, after several botched conspiracies had been disclosed, Elizabeth's spymaster Walsingham unearthed another assassination plot in the correspondence between the Queen of Scots and the Catholic Anthony Babington, the wretched Mary's fate was sealed. After vacillating, a very reluctant Elizabeth signed the death warrant, and her cousin was beheaded.

The long-anticipated military confrontation with Catholic Spain was now unavoidable. Elizabeth learned that Philip II, her former brother-in-law and one-time suitor, was preparing to send an enormous fleet against her island realm. The Armada was to sail to the Netherlands, where a Spanish army would be waiting to embark and invade England. Barring its way was England's small fleet of well-armed and highly maneuverable fighting vessels, backed up by ships from the merchant navy. The Invincible Armada reached English waters in July 1588, only to be routed in one of the most famous and decisive naval battles in European history. Then, in what many viewed as an Act of God on behalf of Protestant England, the Spanish fleet was dispersed and all but destroyed by violent storms.

As England braced itself to withstand the invasion that never came, Elizabeth appeared in person to review a detachment of soldiers assembled at Tilbury. Dressed in a white gown and a silver breastplate, she declared that though some among her councillors had urged her not to appear before a large crowd of armed men, she would never fail to trust the loyalty of her faithful and loving subjects. Nor did she fear the Spanish armies. "I know I have the body but of a weak and feeble woman," Elizabeth declared, "but I have the heart and stomach [i.e., valor] of a king, and of a king of England too." In this celebrated speech, Elizabeth displayed many of her most memorable qualities: her self-consciously theatrical command of grand public occasion, her subtle blending of magniloquent rhetoric and the language of love, her strategic appropriation of traditionally masculine qualities, and her great personal courage. "We princes," she once remarked, "are set on stages in the sight and view of all the world."

WRITERS, PRINTERS, AND PATRONS

The career of professional writer in sixteenth-century England was almost impossible: there was no such thing as author's copyright, no royalties paid to an author according to the sales of his book, and virtually no notion that anyone could make a decent living through the creation of works of literature. Writers sold their manuscripts to the printer or bookseller outright, for what now seem like ridiculously low prices. Freedom of the press did not exist. Writers and printers were supposed to abide by stringent government regulations concerning the publication of books and could be severely punished for failing to do so. The regulations provided that the number of printers (not booksellers) be strictly limited, that nothing could be legally printed except in the city of London and at the universities of Oxford and Cambridge, that everything published in London must be entered in the register of the Stationers' Company (the guild of the book trade), and that everything printed must receive the prior approval of official censors. The political, judicial, and ecclesiastical authorities that enforced these regulations could mete out severe punishments for breaches of censorship and other infractions: fines, interrogation, imprisonment; even branding, mutilation, and execution. Not surprisingly, therefore, literary texts sometimes bear traces of self-censorship and often deploy strategies of indirection designed to evade official scrutiny. It was potentially dangerous to put pen to paper and so unprofitable that it is a wonder that any serious original writing was published at all.

Fortunately, the system of state censorship was inefficient, and many men and women of the sixteenth century had a passionate determination to make themselves heard. The *Short-Title Catalogue* of the Bibliographical Society, which lists works published in English between 1475 and 1640, includes more than 26,000 items, and that is an incomplete list. To these we must add the many manuscripts in which poems and other literary texts were circulated, especially those by authors of higher rank, and the commonplace books in which people jotted down poems and prose passages they considered worth keeping.

Elizabethan writers of exalted social standing, like the earl of Surrey or Sir Philip Sidney, thought of themselves as courtiers, statesmen, and landowners; poetry was for them an indispensable social grace and a deeply pleasurable, exalted form of play. Writers of lower rank, such as Samuel Daniel and Michael Drayton, sought careers as civil servants, secretaries, tutors, and clerics; they might take up more or less permanent residence in a noble household, or, more casually, offer their literary work to actual or prospective patrons, in the hope of protection, career advancement, or financial reward. Ambitious authors eager to rise from threadbare obscurity often looked to the court for livelihood, notice, and encouragement, but their great expectations generally proved chimerical. "A thousand hopes, but all nothing," wailed John Lyly, alluding to his long wait for the office of Master of the Revels, "a hundred promises but yet nothing."

Financial rewards for writing prose or poetry came mostly in the form of gifts from wealthy patrons, who sought to enhance their status and gratify their vanity through the achievements and lavish praises of their clients. Some Elizabethan patrons, though, were well-educated humanists motivated by aesthetic interests, and with them, patronage extended beyond financial support to the creation of lively literary and intellectual circles. Poems by Daniel, Ben Jonson, Aemilia Lanyer, and others bear witness to the sustaining intelligence and sophistication, as well as the generosity, of their benefactors. But the experience of Robert Greene is perhaps equally revealing: the fact that he had sixteen different patrons for seventeen books suggests that he did not find much favor or support from any one of them. Indeed, a practice grew up of printing off several dedications to be inserted into particular copies of a book, so that an impecunious author could deceive each of several patrons into thinking that he or she was the fortunate person to be honored by the volume.

In addition to the court and the great families as dispensers of patronage, the city of London and the two universities also had a substantial impact on the period's literature. London was the center of the book trade, the nursery of a fledgling middle-class reading public, and, most important, the home of the public theaters. Before Elizabeth's time, the universities were mainly devoted to educating the clergy, and that remained an important part of their function. But in the second half of the century, the sons of the gentry and the aristocracy were going in increasing numbers to the universities and the Inns of Court (law schools), not in order to take religious orders or to practice law but to prepare for public service or the management of their estates. Other, less affluent students, such as Marlowe and Spenser, attended Oxford and Cambridge on scholarship. A group of graduates, including Thomas Nashe, Robert Greene, and George Peele, enlivened the literary scene in London in the 1590s, but the precarious lives of these so-called "university wits" testify to the difficulties they encountered in their quixotic attempt to survive by their writing skill. The diary of Philip Henslowe, a leading theatrical manager, has entry after entry showing university graduates in prison or in debt or at best eking out a miserable existence patching plays.

Women had no access to grammar schools, the universities, or the Inns of Court and, when not altogether illiterate, received for the most part only a rudimentary education. While Protestantism, with its emphasis on reading Scripture, certainly helped to improve female literacy in the sixteenth century, girls were rarely encouraged to pursue their studies. Indeed, while girls were increasingly taught to read, they were not necessarily taught to write, for the latter skill in women was considered to be at the very least useless, at the worst dangerous. When the prominent humanist Sir Thomas Smith thinks of how he should describe his country's social order, he declares that "we do reject women, as those whom nature hath made to keep home and to nourish their family and children, and not to meddle with matters abroad, nor to bear office in a city or commonwealth." Then, with a kind of nervous glance over his shoulder, he makes an exception of those few in whom "the blood is respected, not the age nor the sex": for example, the queen. Every piece of writing by a woman from this period is a triumph over nearly impossible odds.

TUDOR STYLE: ORNAMENT, PLAINNESS, AND WONDER

Renaissance literature is the product of a rhetorical culture, a culture steeped in the arts of persuasion and trained to process complex verbal signals. (The contemporary equivalent would be the ease with which we deal with complex visual signals, effortlessly processing such devices as fade-out, montage, crosscutting, and morphing.) In 1512, Erasmus published a work called *De copia* that taught its readers how to cultivate "copiousness," verbal richness, in discourse. The work obligingly provides, as a sample, a list of 144 different ways of saying "Thank you for your letter."

In Renaissance England, certain syntactic forms of patterns of words known as "figures" (also called "schemes") were shaped and repeated in order to confer beauty or heighten expressive power. Figures were usually known by their Greek and Latin names, though in an Elizabethan rhetorical manual, *The Arte of English Poesie*, George Puttenham made a valiant if short-lived attempt to give them English equivalents, such as "Hyperbole, or the Overreacher," "Ironia, or the Dry Mock," and "Ploce, or the Doubler." Those who received a grammar-school education throughout Europe at almost any point between the Roman Empire and the eighteenth century probably knew by heart the names of up to one hundred such figures, just as they knew by heart their multiplication tables. According to one scholar's count, William Shakespeare knew and made use of about two hundred.

As certain grotesquely inflated Renaissance texts attest, lessons from *De copia* and similar rhetorical guides could encourage prolixity and verbal self-display. Elizabethans had a taste for elaborate ornament in language as in clothing, jewelry, and furniture, and, if we are to appreciate their accomplishments, it helps to set aside the modern preference, particularly in prose, for unadorned simplicity and directness. When, in one of the age's most fashionable works of prose fiction, John Lyly wishes to explain that the vices of his young hero, Euphues, are tarnishing his virtues, he offers a small flood of synonymous images: "The freshest colors soonest fade, the teenest [i.e., keenest] razor soonest turneth his edge, the finest cloth is soonest eaten with moths." The euphistic multiplication of figures was soon ridiculed by Shakespeare and others, but its pleasure is deeply rooted in rhetorical culture, and most of the greatest Renaissance writers used to it extraordinary effect. Consider, for example, the succession of images in Shakespeare's sonnet 73:

> That time of year thou mayst in me behold
> When yellow leaves, or none, or few, do hang
> Upon those boughs which shake against the cold,
> Bare ruined choirs, where late the sweet birds sang.
> In me thou seest the twilight of such day
> As after sunset fadeth in the west;
> Which by and by black night doth take away,
> Death's second self that seals up all in rest.
> In me thou seest the glowing of such fire
> That on the ashes of his youth doth lie,
> As the deathbed whereon it must expire,
> Consumed with that which it was nourished by.
>> This thou perceiv'st, which makes thy love more strong,
>> To love that well, which thou must leave ere long.

What seems merely repetitious in Lyly here becomes a subtle, poignant amplification of the perception of decay, through the succession of images from winter (or late fall) to twilight to the last glow of a dying fire. Each of these images is in turn sensitively explored, so that, for example, the season is figured by bare boughs that shiver, as if they were human, and then these anthropomorphized tree branches in turn are figured as the ruined choirs of a church where services were once sung. No sooner is the image of singers in a church choir evoked than these singers are instantaneously transmuted back into the songbirds who, in an earlier season, had sat upon the boughs, while these sweet birds in turn conjure up the poet's own vanished youth. And this nostalgic gaze extends, at least glancingly, to the chancels of the Catholic abbeys reduced to ruins by Protestant iconoclasm and the dissolution of the monasteries. All of this within the first four lines: here and elsewhere Shakespeare, along with other poets of his time, contrives to freight the small compass and tight formal constraints of the sonnet—fourteen lines of iambic pentameter in three principal rhyming patterns—with remarkable emotional intensity, psychological nuance, and imagistic complexity. The effect is what Christopher Marlowe called "infinite riches in a little room."

Elizabethans were certainly capable of admiring plainness of speech—in *King Lear* Shakespeare contrasts the severe directness of the virtuous Cordelia to the "glib and oily art" of her wicked sisters—and such poets as George Gascoigne, Thomas Nashe, and, in the early seventeenth century, Ben Jonson wrote restrained, aphoristic, moralizing lyrics in a plain style whose power depends precisely on the avoidance of richly figurative verbal pyrotechnics. This power is readily apparent in the wintry spareness of Nashe's *A Litany in Time of Plague*, with its grim refrain:

> Wit with his wantonness
> Tasteth death's bitterness;
> Hell's executioner
> Hath no ears for to hear
> What vain art can reply.
> I am sick, I must die.
>> Lord, have mercy on us!

Here the linguistic playfulness beloved by Elizabethan culture is scorned as an ineffectual "vain art" to which the executioner, death, is utterly indifferent.

But here and in other plain-style poetry, the somber, lapidary effect depends on a tacit recognition of the allure of the suppleness, grace, and sweet harmony that the dominant literary artists of the period so assiduously cultivated. Poetry, writes Puttenham, is "more delicate to the ear than prose is, because it is more current and slipper upon the tongue [i.e., flowing and easily pronounced], and withal tunable and melodious, as a kind of Music, and therefore may be termed a musical speech or utterance." The sixteenth century was an age of superb vocal music. The renowned composers William Byrd, Thomas Morley, John Dowland, and others wrote a rich profusion of madrigals (part songs for two to eight voices, unaccompanied) and airs (songs for solo voice, generally accompanied by the lute). These works, along with hymns, popular ballads, rounds, catches, and other forms of song, enjoyed immense popularity, not only in the royal court, where musical skill was regarded as an important accomplishment, and in aristocratic households, where professional musicians were employed as entertainers, but also in less exalted social circles. In his *Plain and Easy Introduction to Practical Music* (1597), Morley tells a story of social humiliation at a failure to perform that suggests that a well-educated Elizabethan was expected to be able to sight-sing. Even if this is an exaggeration in the interest of book sales, there is evidence of impressively widespread musical literacy, a literacy reflected in a splendid array of music for the lute, viol, recorder, harp, and virginal, as well as vocal music.

Many sixteenth-century poems were written to be set to music, but even those that were not often aspire in their metrical and syllabic virtuosity to the complex pleasures of madrigals or to the sweet fluency of airs. In poetry and music, as in gardens, architecture and dance, Elizabethans had a taste for elaborate, intricate, but perfectly regular designs. They admired form, valued the artist's manifest control of the medium, and took pleasure in the highly patterned surfaces of things. Suspicion of surfaces, impatience with order, the desire to rip away the mask in order to discover a hidden core of experiential truth: these responses to art, highly characteristic of later periods, are far less in evidence in Renaissance aesthetics than is a delight in pattern. Indeed many writers of the time expressed the faith that the universe itself had in its basic construction the beauty, concord, and harmonious order of a poem or a piece of music. "The world is made by Symmetry and proportion," wrote Thomas Campion, who was both a poet and a composer, "and is in that respect compared to Music, and Music to Poetry." The design of an exquisite work of art is deeply linked in this view to the design of the cosmos.

Such an emphasis on conspicuous pattern might seem to encourage an art as stiff as the starched ruffs that ladies and gentlemen wore around their necks, but the period's fascination with order was conjoined with a profound interest in persuasively conveying the movements of the mind and heart. Syntax in the sixteenth century was looser, more flexible than our own and punctuation less systematic. If the effect is sometimes confusing, it also enabled writers to follow the twists and turns of thought or perception. Consider, for example, Roger Ascham's account, in his book on archery, of a day in which he saw the wind blowing the new-fallen snow:

> That morning the sun shone bright and clear, the wind was whistling aloft, and sharp according to the time of the year. The snow in the highway lay loose and trodden with horse feet: so as the wind blew, it took the loose snow with it, and made it so slide upon the snow in the field which was hard and crusted by reason of the frost overnight, that thereby I might see very well, the whole nature of the wind as it blew that day. And I had a great delight and pleasure to mark it, which maketh me now far better to remember it. Sometime the wind would be not past two yards broad, and so it would carry the snow as far as I could see. Another time the snow would blow over half the field at once. Sometime the snow would tumble softly, by and by it would fly wonderful fast. And this I perceived also that the wind goeth by streams and not whole together. . . . And that which was the most marvel of all, at one time two drifts of snow flew, the one of the West into the East, the other out of the North into the East: And I saw two winds by reason of the snow the one cross over the other, as it had been two highways. . . . The more uncertain and deceivable the wind is, the more heed must a wise Archer give to know the guiles of it.

What is delightful here is not only the author's moment of sharpened perception but his confidence that this moment—a glimpse of baffling complexity and uncertainty—can be captured in the restless succession of sentences and then neatly summed up in the pithy conclusion. A similar confidence emanates from Sir Walter Ralegh's deeply melancholy, deeply ironic apostrophe to Death at the close of *The History of the World*, written when he was a prisoner in the Tower:

> O eloquent, just, and mighty Death! Whom none could advise, thou hast persuaded; what none hath dared, thou hast done; and whom all the world hath flattered, thou only hast cast out of the world and despised; thou hast drawn together all the far-stretched greatness, all the pride, cruelty, and ambition of man, and covered it all over with these two narrow words: *Hic jacet!* [Here lies]

Death is triumphant here, but so is Ralegh's eloquent, just, and mighty language.

The sense of *wonder* that animates both of these exuberant prose passages—as if the world were being seen clearly and distinctly for the first time—characterizes much of the period's poetry as well. The mood need not always be solemn. One can sense laughter, for example, rippling just below the surface of Marlowe's admiring description of the beautiful maiden Hero's boots:

> Buskins of shells all silvered usèd she,
> And branched with blushing coral to the knee,
> Where sparrows perched, of hollow pearl and gold,
> Such as the world would wonder to behold;
> Those with sweet water oft her handmaid fills,
> Which, as she went, would chirrup through the bills.

Seashells were beloved by Renaissance collectors because their intricate designs, functionally inexplicable, seemed the works of an ingenious, infinitely playful craftsman. Typically, the shells did not simply stand by themselves in cabinets but were gilded or silvered and then turned into other objects: cups, miniature ships, or, in Marlowe's fantasy, boots further decorated with coral and mechanical sparrows made of conspicuously precious materials and designed, as he puts it deliciously, to "chirrup." The poet knows perfectly well that the boots would be implausible footwear in the real world, but he invites us into an imaginary world of passion, a world in which the heroine's costume includes a skirt "whereon was many a stain, / Made with the blood of wretched lovers slain" and a veil of "artificial flowers and leaves, / Whose workmanship both man and beast deceives." The veil reflects an admiration for an art of successful imitation—after all, bees are said to look in vain for honey amidst the artificial flowers—but it is cunning illusion rather than realism that excites Marlowe's wonder. Renaissance poetry is interested not in representational accuracy but in the magical power of exquisite workmanship to draw its readers into fabricated worlds.

In his *Defense of Poesy*, the most important work of literary criticism in sixteenth-century England, Sidney claims that this magical power is also a moral power. All other arts, he argues, are subjected to fallen, imperfect nature, but the poet alone is free to range "within the zodiac of his own wit" and create a second nature, superior to the one we are condemned to inhabit: "Her world is brazen, the poets only deliver a golden." The poet's golden world in this account is not an escapist fantasy; it is a model to be emulated in actual life, an ideal to be brought into reality as completely as possible. It is difficult to say, of course, how seriously this project of realization was taken—though the circumstances of Sidney's own death suggest that he may have been attempting to enact on the battlefield an ideal image of Protestant chivalry. A didactic role for poetry is, in any case, urged not by Sidney alone but by most Elizabethan poets. Human sinfulness has corrupted life, robbing it of the sweet wholesomeness that it had once possessed in Eden, but poetry can mark the way back to a more virtuous and fulfilled existence. And not only mark the way: poetry, Sidney and others argue, has a unique persuasive force that shatters inertia and impels readers toward the good they glimpse in its ravishing lines.

This force, attributed to the energy and vividness of figurative language, made poetry a fitting instrument not only for such high-minded enterprises as moral exhortation, prayer, and praise, and for such uplifting narratives as the legends of religious and national heroes, but also for such verbal actions as cursing, lamenting, flattering, and seducing. The almost inexhaustible range of motives was given some order by literary conventions that functioned as shared cultural codes, enabling poets to elicit particular responses from readers and to relate their words to other times, other languages, and other cultures. Among the most prominent of the clusters of conventions in the period were those that defined the major literary modes (or "kinds," as Sidney terms them): pastoral, heroic, lyric, satiric, elegiac, tragic, and comic. They helped to shape subject matter, attitude, tone, and values, and in some cases—sonnet, verse epistle, epigram, funeral elegy, and masque, to name a few—they also governed formal structure, meter, style, length, and occasion. We can glimpse a few of the ways in which these literary codes worked by looking briefly at the two that are, for modern readers, the least familiar: pastoral and heroic.

The conventions of the pastoral mode present a world inhabited by shepherds and shepherdesses who are chiefly concerned to tend their flocks, fall in love, and engage in friendly singing contests. The mode celebrated leisure, humility, and contentment, exalting the simple country life over the city and its business, the military camp and its violence, the court and its burdens of rule. Pastoral motifs could be deployed in different genres. Pastoral songs commonly expressed the joys of the shepherd's life or disappointment in love. Pastoral dialogues between shepherds might conceal serious, satiric comment on abuses in the great world under the guise of homely, local concerns. There were pastoral funeral elegies, pastoral dramas, pastoral romances (prose fiction), and even pastoral episodes within epics. Probably the most famous pastoral poem of the period is Marlowe's *The Passionate Shepherd to His Love*, an erotic invitation whose promise of gold buckles, coral clasps, and amber studs serves to remind us that, however much it sings of naïve innocence, the mode is ineradicably sophisticated and urban.

With its rustic characters, simple concerns, and modest scope, the pastoral mode was regarded as situated at the opposite extreme from heroic, with its values of honor, martial courage, loyalty, leadership, and endurance and its glorification of a nation or people. The chief genre here was the epic, typically a long, exalted poem in the high style, based on a heroic story from the nation's distant past and imitating Homer and Virgil in structure and motifs. Renaissance poets throughout Europe undertook to honor their nations and their vernacular languages by writing this most prestigious kind of poetry. In sixteenth-century England the major success in heroic poetry is Spenser's *Faerie Queene*, properly speaking, a romantic epic in that it draws more heavily on the romance conventions employed by the great Italian poets Ariosto and Tasso—tangled, episodic plots, exotic adventures and marvels, and a fundamental concern with love as well as war—than on the classical epics. To these basic elements Spenser also conjoins medieval allegory, pastoral, satire, mythological narrative, comedy, philosophical meditation, and many other literary conventions in a strange, wonderful blend. The spectacular mixing of genres in Spenser's poem is only an extreme instance of a general Elizabethan indifference to the generic purity admired by writers, principally on the Continent, who adhered to Aristotle's *Poetics*. Where such neoclassicists attempted to observe rigid stylistic boundaries, English poets tended to approach the different genres in the spirit of Sidney's inclusivism: "if severed they be good, the conjunction cannot be hurtful."

THE ELIZABETHAN THEATER

If Sidney welcomed the experimental intertwining of genres in both poetry and prose—and his own *Arcadia*, a prose romance incorporating both pastoral and heroic elements, confirms that he did—there was one place where he found it absurd: the theater. He condemned the conjunction of high and low characters in "mongrel" tragicomedies that mingled "kings and clowns." Moreover, in the spirit of neoclassical advocacy of the "dramatic unities," Sidney disliked the ease with which the action on the bare stage ("where you shall have Asia of the one side, and Afric of the other") violated the laws of time and space. "Now you shall have three ladies walk to gather flowers," he writes in *The Defense of Poesy*, "and then we must believe the stage to be a garden. By and by we hear news of shipwreck in the same place: and then we are to blame if we accept it not for a rock." The irony is that this mocking account, written probably in 1579, anticipates by a few years the stupendous achievements of Marlowe and Shakespeare, whose plays joyously break every rule that Sidney thought it essential to observe.

A permanent, freestanding public theater in England dates only from Shakespeare's own lifetime. A London playhouse, the Red Lion, is first mentioned in 1567, and James Burbage's playhouse, The Theater, was built in 1576. But it is quite misleading to identify English drama exclusively with the new, specially constructed playhouses, for in fact there was a rich and vital theatrical tradition in England stretching back for centuries. Several towns in late medieval England were the sites of annual festivals that mounted elaborate cycles of plays depicting the great biblical stories, from the creation of the world to Christ's Passion and its miraculous aftermath. Many of these plays have been lost, but the surviving cycles, as the selection in this anthology demonstrates, include magnificent and complex works of art. They are sometimes called "mystery plays," either because they were performed by the guilds of various crafts (known as "mysteries") or, more likely, because they represented the mysteries of the faith. The cycles were most often performed on the occasion of the annual feast day instituted in the early fourteenth century in honor of the Corpus Christi, the sacrament of the Lord's Supper that is perhaps the greatest of these religious mysteries. This feast helped give the play cycles their extraordinary cultural resonance, but it also contributed to their downfall, for they were closely identified with the Catholic church. Protestant authorities in the sixteenth century, eager to eradicate all remnants of popular Catholic piety, moved to suppress the annual procession of the Host, with its richly decorated banners, pageant carts, and cycle of visionary plays.

But early English theater was not restricted to these civic and religious festivals. Performers acted in town halls and the halls of guilds and aristocratic mansions, on scaffolds erected in town squares and marketplaces, on pageant wagons in the streets, and in innyards. By the fifteenth century, and probably earlier, there were organized companies of players traveling under noble patronage. Such companies earned a precarious living providing amusement, while enhancing the prestige of the patron whose livery they wore and whose protection they enjoyed. (Otherwise, by statutes enjoining productive labor, actors without another, ordinary trade could have been classified as vagabonds and whipped or branded.) This practice explains why the professional acting companies of Shakespeare's time, including Shakespeare's own, attached themselves to a nobleman and were technically his servants (the Lord Chamberlain's Men, the Lord Admiral's Men, etc.), even though virtually all their time was devoted to entertaining the public from whom most of their income derived.

Before the construction of the public theaters, the playing companies often performed short plays called "interludes" that were, in effect, staged dialogues on religious, moral, and political themes. Henry Medwall's *Fulgens and Lucrece* (ca. 1490–1501), for example, pits a wealthy but dissolute nobleman against a virtuous public servant of humble origins, while John Heywood's *The Play of the Weather* (ca. 1525–33) stages a debate among social rivals, including a gentleman, a merchant, a forest ranger, and two millers. The structure of such plays reflects the training in argumentation that students received in Tudor schools and, in particular, the sustained practice in examining both sides of a difficult question. Some of Shakespeare's amazing ability to look at critical issues from multiple perspectives may be traced back to this practice and the dramatic interludes it helped to inspire.

Another major form of theater that flourished in England in the fifteenth century and continued on into the sixteenth was the morality play. Like the mysteries, moralities addressed questions of the ultimate fate of the soul. They did so, however, not by rehearsing scriptural stories but by dramatizing allegories of spiritual struggle. Typically, a person named Human or Mankind or Youth is faced with a choice between a pious life in the company of such associates as Mercy, Discretion, and Good Deeds and a dissolute life among riotous companions like Lust or Mischief. Plays such as *Mankind* (ca. 1465–70) and *Everyman* (ca. 1495) show how powerful these unpromising-sounding dramas could be, in part because of the extraordinary comic vitality of the evil character, or Vice, and in part because of the poignancy and terror of an individual's encounter with death.

If such plays sound more than a bit like sermons, it is because they were. The church was a profoundly different institution from the theater, but its professionals shared some of the same rhetorical skills. It would be grossly misleading to regard churchgoing and playgoing as comparable entertainments, but clerical attacks on the theater sometimes make it sound as if ministers thought themselves to be in direct competition with professional players. The players, for their part, were generally too discreet to present themselves in a similar light, yet they almost certainly understood their craft as relating to sermons with an uneasy blend of emulation and rivalry.

By the later sixteenth century, many churchmen, particularly those with Puritan leanings, were steadfastly opposed to the theater, but early Protestant Reformers, such as John Bale, tried their hand at writing plays. Thomas Norton, who with a fellow lawyer, Thomas Sackville, wrote the first English tragedy, *Gorboduc, or Ferrex and Porrex* (1561), was also a translator of the great Reformer John Calvin. There is no evidence that Norton felt a tension between his religious convictions and his theatrical interests, nor was his play a private exercise. The five-act tragedy in blank verse, a grim vision of Britain descending into civil war, was performed at the Inner Temple (one of London's law schools) and subsequently acted before the queen.

A likely classical model for *Gorboduc* was the work of the Roman playwright Seneca, and Senecan influence—including violent plots, resounding rhetorical speeches, and ghosts thirsting for blood—remained pervasive in the Elizabethan period, giving rise to a subgenre of revenge tragedy, in which a wronged protagonist plots and executes revenge, destroying himself (or herself) in the process. An early, highly influential example is Thomas Kyd's *Spanish Tragedy* (1592), and, despite all its unprecedented psychological complexity, Shakespeare's *Hamlet* clearly participates in this kind. A related but distinct kind is the villain tragedy in which the protagonist is blatantly evil: if Thomas Preston's crude *Cambyses, King of Persia* (ca. 1560?) seems to bear out Aristotle's strictures, in his *Poetics*, against attempting to use a wicked person as the hero of a tragedy, Shakespeare's *Richard III* and *Macbeth* amply justify the general English indifference to classical rules. Some

Elizabethan tragedies, such as the fine *Arden of Feversham* (whose author is unknown), are concerned not with the fall of great men but with domestic violence; others, such as Christopher Marlowe's *Tamburlaine*, are concerned with "overreachers," larger-than-life heroes who challenge the limits of human possibility. Certain tragedies in the period, such as *Richard III*, intersect with another Elizabethan genre, the history play, in which dramatists staged the great events, most often conspiracies, rebellions, and wars, of the nation. Not all of the events commemorated in history plays were tragic, but they tend to circle back again and again on the act that epitomized what for this period was the ultimate challenge to authority: the killing of a king.

English schoolboys would read and occasionally perform comedies by the great Latin playwrights Plautus and Terence. Shortly before mid-century a schoolmaster, Nicholas Udall, used these as a model for a comedy in English, *Ralph Roister Doister*. At about the same time, another comedy, *Gammar Gurton's Needle*, which put vivid, native English material into classical form, was amusing the students at Cambridge. From the classical models English playwrights derived some elements of structure and content: plots based on intrigue, division into acts and scenes, and type characters such as the rascally servant and the *miles gloriosus* (cowardly braggart soldier). The latter type appears in *Ralph Roister Doister* and is a remote ancestor of Shakespeare's Sir John Falstaff in *1 Henry IV*.

Other kinds of comedy developed during the Elizabethan and Jacobean age, influenced by French and Italian examples as well as by classical models. The conventions of romantic comedy call for noble characters and a plot in which love triumphs over potentially tragic obstacles (as in Shakespeare's *As You Like It* and *Twelfth Night*). Domestic comedy centers on the household or the workshop (as in Thomas Dekker's *Shoemaker's Holiday*). City comedy typically has bourgeois characters, a London setting, and a satirical streak (as in Thomas Middleton's *A Chaste Maid in Cheapside*). Humor comedy (such as Ben Jonson's *Every Man in His Humor*) has type characters created on the medical theory that the predominance of a particular fluid, or humor, in the body creates a specific temperament (melancholic, choleric, splenetic, and phlegmatic). There are many other varieties, including the elegant mythological comedies by John Lyly, written for a company of children; slapstick comedies; comedies that feature knights, ladies, and magicians; and tragicomedies, whose plots veer perilously close to irreparable loss before happily righting themselves.

Play-acting, whether of tragedies, comedies, or any of the other Elizabethan forms, took its place alongside other forms of public expression and entertainment as well. Perhaps the most important, from the perspective of the theater, were music and dance, since these were directly and repeatedly incorporated into plays. Moreover, virtually all plays in the period, including Shakespeare's, apparently ended with a dance. Brushing off the theatrical gore and changing their expressions from woe to pleasure, the actors in plays like *Doctor Faustus* and *King Lear* would presumably have received the audience's applause and then bid for a second round by performing a stately pavane or a lively jig.

Plays, music, and dancing were by no means the only shows in town. There were jousts, tournaments, royal entries, religious processions, pageants in honor of newly installed civic officials or ambassadors arriving from abroad;

wedding masques, court masques, and costumed entertainments known as Disguisings or Mummings; juggling acts, fortune tellers, exhibitions of swordsmanship, mountebanks, folk healers, storytellers, magic shows; bear-baiting, bullbaiting, cockfighting, and other blood sports; folk festivals such as Maying, the Feast of Fools, Carnival, and Whitsun Ales. For several years, Elizabethan Londoners were delighted by a trained animal—Banks's Horse—that could, it was thought, do arithmetic and answer questions. And there was always the grim but compelling spectacle of public shaming, mutilation, and execution.

Most English towns had stocks and whipping posts. Drunks, fraudulent merchants, adulterers, and quarrelers could be placed in carts or mounted backward on asses and paraded through the streets for crowds to jeer and throw refuse at. Women accused of being scolds could be publicly muzzled by an iron device called a brank or tied to a "cucking stool" and dunked in the river. Convicted criminals could have their ears cut off, their noses slit, their foreheads branded. Public beheadings and hangings were common. In the worst cases, felons were sentenced to be "hanged by the neck, and being alive cut down, and your privy members to be cut off, and your bowels to be taken out of your belly and there burned, you being alive." In the dismemberment with which Marlowe's *Doctor Faustus* ends, the audience was witnessing the theatrical equivalent of the execution of criminals and traitors that they could have also watched in the flesh, as it were, nearby.

Doctor Faustus was performed by the Lord Admiral's Men at the Rose Theater, one of four major public playhouses that by the mid-1590s were feverishly competing for crowds of spectators. These playhouses (including Shakespeare's famous Globe Theater, which opened in 1599) each accommodated some two thousand spectators and generally followed the same design: they were oval in shape, with an unroofed yard in the center where stood the groundlings (apprentices, servants, and others of the lower classes) and three rising tiers around the yard for men and women able to pay a higher price for places to sit and a roof over their heads. A large platform stage jutted out into the yard, surrounded on three sides by spectators (see the conjectural drawing of an Elizabethan playhouse, in the appendices to this volume). These financially risky ventures relied on admission charges—it was an innovation of this period to have money advanced in the expectation of pleasure rather than offered to servants as a reward—and counted on habitual playgoing fueled by a steady supply of new plays. The public playhouses were all located outside the limits of the city of London and, accordingly, beyond the jurisdiction of city authorities generally hostile to dramatic spectacles. Eventually, indoor theaters, artificially lighted and patronized by a more select audience, were also built, secured under conditions that would allow them some protection from those who wished to shut them down.

Why should what we now regard as one of the undisputed glories of the age have aroused so much hostility? One answer, curiously enough, is traffic: plays drew large audiences, and residents objected to the crowds, the noise, and the crush of carriages. Other, more serious concerns were public health and crime. It was thought that many diseases, including the dreaded bubonic plague, were spread by noxious odors, and the packed playhouses were obvious breeding grounds for infection. (Patrons often tried to protect themselves by sniffing nosegays or stuffing cloves in their nostrils.) The large crowds drew pickpockets, cutpurses, and other scoundrels. On one memorable afternoon a pickpocket was caught in the act and tied for the duration of the play to one of the posts that held up the canopy above the stage. The theater was, moreover, a well-known haunt of prostitutes, and, it was alleged, a place where innocent maids were seduced and respectable matrons corrupted. It was darkly rumored that "chambers and secret places" adjoined the theater galleries, and, in any case, taverns, disreputable inns, and whorehouses were close at hand.

There were other charges as well. Plays were performed in the afternoon and therefore drew people, especially the young, away from their work. They were schools of idleness, luring apprentices from their trades, law students from their studies, housewives from their kitchens, and potentially pious souls from the sober meditations to which they might otherwise devote themselves. Moralists warned that the theaters were nests of sedition, and religious polemicists, especially Puritans, obsessively focusing on the use of boy actors to play the female parts, charged that theatrical transvestism excited illicit sexual desires, both heterosexual and homosexual.

But the playing companies had powerful allies, including Queen Elizabeth herself, and continuing popular support. One theater historian has estimated that between the late 1560s and 1642, when the playhouses were shut down by the English Civil War, well over fifty million visits were paid to the London theater, an astonishing figure for a city that had, by our standards, a very modest population. Plays were performed without the scene breaks and intermissions to which we are accustomed; there was no scenery and few props, but costumes were usually costly and elaborate. The players formed what would now be called repertory companies—that is, they filled the roles of each play from members of their own group, not employing outsiders. They performed a number of different plays on consecutive days, and the principal actors were shareholders in the profits of the company. Boys were apprenticed to actors just as they had been apprenticed to master craftsmen in the guilds; they took the women's parts in plays until their voices changed. The plays might be bought for the company from hack writers, or, as in Shakespeare's company, the group might include an actor-playwright who could supply it with some (though by no means all) of its plays. The script remained the property of the company, but a popular play was eagerly sought by the printers, and the companies, which generally tried to keep their plays from appearing in print, sometimes had trouble guarding their rights. The editors of the first collected edition of Shakespeare, the First Folio (1623), complain about the prior publication of "divers stolen and surreptitious copies" of his plays, "maimed and deformed by the frauds and stealths of injurious imposters."

SURPRISED BY TIME

All of the ways we cut up time into units are inevitably distortions. The dividing line between centuries was not, as far as we can tell, a highly significant one for people in the Renaissance, and many of the most important literary careers cross into the seventeenth century without a self-conscious moment of reflection. But virtually everyone must have been aware that the long reign of England's Queen Elizabeth was nearing its end, and this impending closure occasioned considerable anxiety. Childless, the last of her line, Elizabeth had steadfastly refused to name a successor. She continued to make brilliant speeches, to receive the extravagant compliments of her flatterers, and to exercise her authority—in 1601, she had her favorite, the headstrong earl of Essex, executed for attempting to raise an insurrection. But, as her seventieth birthday approached, she was clearly, as Ralegh put it, "a lady surprised by time." She suffered from bouts of ill health and melancholy; her godson, Sir John Harington, was dismayed to see her pacing through the rooms of her palace, striking at the tapestries with a sword. Her more astute advisers—among them Lord Burghley's son, Sir Robert Cecil, who had succeeded his father as her principal counselor—secretly entered into correspondence with the likeliest claimant to the throne, James VI of Scotland. Though the English queen had executed his Catholic mother, Mary, Queen of Scots, the Protestant James had continued to exchange polite letters with Elizabeth. It was at least plausible, as officially claimed, that in her dying breath, on March 24, 1603, Elizabeth designated James as her successor. A jittery nation that had feared a possible civil war lit bonfires to welcome its new king. But in a very few years, the English began to express nostalgia for the rule of "Good Queen Bess" and to look back on her reign as a magnificent high point in the history and culture of their nation.

THE SIXTEENTH CENTURY

TEXTS	CONTEXTS
	1485 Accession of Henry VII inaugurates Tudor dynasty
	1499 Desiderius Erasmus first visits England; meets Thomas More
ca. 1504 Amerigo Vespucci, *New World* and *Four Voyages*	**ca. 1504** Leonardo paints Mona Lisa
	1508–12 Michaelangelo paints Sistine Chapel ceiling
	1509 Death of Henry VII; accession of Henry VIII
1511 Erasmus, *Praise of Folly*	
	1513 James IV of Scotland killed at Battle of Flodden; succeeded by James V
1516 More, *Utopia*. Ludovico Ariosto, *Orlando furioso*	
ca. 1517 John Skelton, *The Tunning of Elinour Rumming*	**1517** Martin Luther's Ninety-Five Theses; beginning of the Reformation in Germany
	1519 Cortés invades Mexico. Magellen begins his voyage around the world
1520s–30s Thomas Wyatt's poems circulating in manuscript	**1521** Pope Leo X names Henry VIII "Defender of the Faith"
1525 William Tyndale's English translation of the New Testament	
1528 Baldessare Castiglione, *The Courtier*	
	1529–32 More is Lord Chancellor
1532 Nicolò Machiavelli, *The Prince* (written 1513)	**1532–34** Henry VIII divorces Catherine of Aragon to marry Anne Boleyn; Elizabeth I born; Henry declares himself head of the English church
	1535 More beheaded
1537 John Calvin, *The Institution of Christian Religion*	**1537** Establishment of Calvin's theocracy at Geneva
	1542 Roman Inquisition. James IV of Scotland dies; succeeded by daughter Mary
1543 Copernicus, *On the Revolution of the Spheres*	
1547 *Book of Homilies*	**1547** Death of Henry VIII; accession of Protestant Edward VI
1549 *Book of Common Prayer*	
	1553 Death of Edward VI; accession of Catholic Queen Mary, daughter of Catherine of Aragon
	1555–56 Archbishop Cranmer and former bishops Latimer and Ridley burned at the stake
1557 Tottel's *Songs and Sonnets* (printed poems by Wyatt, Surrey, and others)	
	1558 Mary dies; succeeded by Protestant Elizabeth I

TEXTS	CONTEXTS
1563 John Foxe, *Acts and Monuments*	
1565 Thomas Norton and Thomas Sackville, *Gorboduc*, first English blank-verse tragedy (acted in 1561)	
1567 Arthur Golding, translation of Ovid's *Metamorphoses*	**1567** Mary, Queen of Scots, abdicates; succeeded by her son James VI; Mary imprisoned in England
	1570 Elizabeth I excommunicated by Pope Pius V
	1576 James Burbage's playhouse, The Theater, built in London
	1576–77 Frobisher's voyage to North America
	1577–80 Drake's circumnavigation
1578 John Lyly, *Euphues*	
1579 Edmund Spenser, *Shepheardes Calender*	
1580 Montaigne, *Essays*	
	1583 Irish rebellion crushed
	1584–87 Sir Walter Ralegh's earliest attempts to colonize Virginia
	1586–87 Mary, Queen of Scots, tried for treason and executed
ca. 1587–90 Marlowe's *Tamburlaine* acted. Shakespeare begins career as actor and playwright	
1588 Thomas Hariot, *A Brief and True Report of Virginia*	**1588** Failed invasion of the Spanish Armada
1589 Richard Hakluyt, *The Principal Navigations . . . of the English Nation*	
1590 Sir Philip Sidney, *Arcadia* (posthumously published); Spenser, *The Faerie Queene*, Books 1–3	
1591 Sidney, *Astrophil and Stella*	
ca. 1592 John Donne's earliest poems circulating in manuscript	
1595 Sidney, *The Defense of Poesy*	**1595** Ralegh's voyage to Guiana
1596 Spenser, *The Faerie Queene*, Books 4–6 (with Books 1–3)	
1598 Ben Jonson, *Every Man in His Humor*	**1599** Globe Theater opens
	1603 Elizabeth I dies; succeeded by James VI of Scotland (as James I), inaugurating the Stuart dynasty

JOHN SKELTON
ca. 1460–1529

John Skelton was not a tame poet. There was something wild about him that continues to provoke, baffle, and fascinate readers. It is difficult to fit the varied pieces of his life together: gifted rhetorician, translator, Latin tutor to the young prince who became Henry VIII, disgruntled courtier, political pamphleteer, visionary, biting satirist, and ordained priest. He was also the major poet of the first quarter of the century, with the title of poet laureate from both Oxford and Cambridge. His poetic achievement, remarkable though it is, is equally difficult to place; as C. S. Lewis observes, Skelton had "no real predecessors and no important disciples." His poetry draws, to be sure, on a long tradition of medieval anticlerical satire and carnival-esque parody, but Skelton brings to his mature works a fresh, often extremely eccentric voice.

His early works were more routinely conventional—ornate compliments, dutiful elegies, pious hymns to the Trinity and the like—but in a satire written at the century's end, *The Bowge of Court*, Skelton gave unusually powerful expression to the anxiety of living in the dangerous, viciously competitive precincts of royal power. (The poem's main character is called "Dread.") A few years later, whether self-exiled or sent away by his enemies, Skelton was living far from the court: about 1503 he became the rector of the parish church at Diss, in Norfolk, where he remained for some eight years. By 1512 he had returned to the court, appointed king's orator. He moved to a house in the sanctuary of Westminster Abbey in 1518 and shortly thereafter began vituperative attacks on Cardinal Wolsey, the great prelate-statesman, in a series of satires, including *Speak, Parrot; Colin Clout;* and *Why Come Ye Not to Court* (1521–22). Wolsey had Skelton briefly imprisoned but released him and promptly hired his services for himself.

Skelton's poems gain some of their most startling effects by mixing high and low styles and by playing bawdy and scatological verbal games with the Catholic liturgy. The games are not necessarily sacrilegious, for the pre-Reformation church Skelton served as priest tolerated a wide latitude of expressions. but they seem risk-taking and obstreperous, an impression heightened by the way they are written. Skelton rejects the ornate rhetorical devices and aureate language that characterized his period's most ambitious poetry; he writes in short, rhymed lines, from two to five beats, and the lines can keep on rhyming helter-skelter until the resources of the language give out. To many of his poems, with their aggressive and restless energies, this strange verse form is singularly appropriate. *The Tunning of Elinour Rumming* is, for example, a wonderfully disordered, clattering portrait of an alewife, and the "skeltonics," as this way of writing has come to be called, contribute to the effect of disorder. The voice of the narrator of the satires has a breathless urgency much admired by Robert Graves and W. H. Auden, among other modern poets, while to contemporary ears it is strikingly reminiscent of rapping.

Many critics view Skelton as a transitional figure, uneasily poised between the Middle Ages and the Renaissance. His lyrics, like his satires, partake of traditional medieval modes but typically give these modes an unorthodox twist. To the three-part song *Mannerly Margery*, a conventional ballad of the clerk and the serving maid, he gives an ironic ending. His *Lullay, lullay* is a cynical, sexually suggestive burlesque of traditional lullabies in which the Virgin Mary rocks the Christ child in her lap. In 1523 Skelton published *The Garland of Laurel,* a long work in which the poet imagines himself praised as the Homer of his country and crowned with a laurel wreath by the countess of Surrey and her ladies; in gratitude he writes a poem to each of them. The dream of a central place in English poetry. of course, proved false, but

Skelton's voice continues to have surprising power precisely because of his strange, marginal position.

Mannerly Margery Milk and Ale[1]

Aye, beshrew° you, by my fay,°   *curse / faith*
These wanton clerks[2] be nice° alway,   *foolish*
Avaunt, avaunt, my popagay![3]
"What, will ye do nothing but play?"
5   Tilly vally straw, let be I say!
Gup,[4] Christian Clout, gup, Jack of the Vale!
With Mannerly Margery milk and ale.

"By God, ye be a pretty pode,°   *toad*
And I love you an whole cartload."
10 Straw, James Foder, ye play the fode,°   *deceiver, flatterer*
I am no hackney for your rod:°   *riding*
Go watch a bull, your back is broad!
Gup, Christian Clout, gup, Jack of the Vale!
With Mannerly Margery milk and ale.

15 Ywis° ye deal uncourteously;   *truly*
What, would ye frumple° me? now fie!   *rumple, tumble*
"What, and ye shall not be my pigsny?"[5]
By Christ, ye shall not, no hardily:
I will not be japed° bodily!   *tricked, deceived*
20 Gup, Christian Clout, gup, Jack of the Vale!
With Mannerly Margery milk and ale.

"Walk forth your way, ye cost me naught;
Now have I found that I have sought:
The best cheap flesh that ever I bought."
25 Yet, for his love that hath all wrought,
Wed me, or else I die for thought.
Gup, Christian Clout, gup, your breath is stale!
With Mannerly Margery milk and ale!
Gup, Christian Clout, gup, Jack of the Vale!
30 With Mannerly Margery milk and ale.

ca. 1495   1523

Lullay, lullay, like a child

With lullay, lullay, like a child,
Thou sleepest too long, thou art beguiled.°   *deceived*

---

1. The poem is a song for three voices. The seducer's lines are in quotation marks; Margery sings the rest, except the chorus, which is sung by a bass.
2. A *clerk* is an educated man: a student, scholar,
or clergyman.
3. Popinjay, parrot—i.e., vain fellow.
4. "Go on!" (usually applied to horses).
5. Pig's eye. Here used as a (rough) term of endearment.

"My darling dear, my daisy flower,
Let me," quod° he, "lie in your lap."　　　　　　　　　　*quoth*
5　"Lie still," quod she, "my paramour,
Lie still, hardily,° and take a nap."　　　　　　　　　　*confidently*
His head was heavy, such was his hap,
All drowsy dreaming, drowned in sleep,
That of his love he took no keep.
10　With hey, lullay, lullay, like a child,
Thou sleepest too long, thou art beguiled.

With ba, ba, ba! and bas, bas, bas![1]
She cherished him, both cheek and chin,
That he wist° never where he was;　　　　　　　　　　*knew*
15　He had forgotten all deadly sin.
He wanted wit[2] her love to win,
He trusted her payment and lost all his prey;
She left him sleeping and stale° away,　　　　　　　　　*stole*
With hey, lullay, lullay, like a child,
20　Thou sleepest too long, thou art beguiled.

The rivers rowth,° the waters wan,　　　　　　　　　　*rough*
She sparèd not to wet her feet;
She waded over, she found a man
That halsèd° her heartily and kissed her sweet—　　　　*embraced*
25　Thus after her cold she caught a heat.
"My lief,"° she said, "routeth° in his bed;　　　　　　*lover/snores*
Ywis° he hath an heavy head."　　　　　　　　　　　　*truly*
With hey, lullay, lullay, like a child,
Thou sleepest too long, thou are beguiled.

30　What dreamest thou, drunkard, drowsy pate?°　　　　*head*
Thy lust and liking[3] is from thee gone.
Thou blinkard blowboll,[4] thou wakest too late.
Behold thou liest, luggard,° alone!　　　　　　　　　　*sluggard*
Well may thou sigh, well may thou groan,
35　To deal with her so cowardly.
Ywis, pole-hatchet, she bleared thine eye.[5]

1495–1500　　　　　　　　　　　　　　　　　　　　　　1527

From The Tunning of Elinour Rumming[1]

Secundus Passus

Some have no money
That thither comey
For their ale to pay;

---

1. Kiss, kiss, kiss. "Ba" the "by" of *lullaby*.
2. Lacked sufficient intelligence.
3. Your pleasure and enjoyment.
4. Blink-eyed drunkard.
5. Deceived you. "Pole-hatchet": a soldier who carried a poleax.

1. This rowdy poem—whose titular heroine actually kept an alehouse in Surrey—recounts Elinour's brewing practices ("tunning") and the social life in her establishment.

That is a shrewd array!°   *sorry state of affairs*

5   Elinour sweared, "Nay,
Ye shall not bear away
My ale for nought,
By Him that me bought."
With, "Hey, dog, hey,
10   Have these hogs away!"
With, "Get me a staff,
The swine eat my draff!°   *refuse, dregs*
Strike the hogs with a club,
They have drunk up my swilling-tub!"°   *tub for stirring*
15   For, be there never so much prese,°   *crowd*
These swine go to the high dese;[2]
The sow with her pigs;
The boar his tail wrigs,°   *wriggles*
His rump also he frigs°   *rubs*
20   Against the high bench!
With, "Fo, there is a stench!
Gather up, thou wench;
Seest thou not what is fall?
Take up dirt and all,
25   And bear out of the hall:
God give it ill preving°   *ill success*
Cleanly as evil cheving!"°   *bad luck*
    But let us turn plain
There we left again.
30   For as ill a patch° as that   *poor piece of ground*
The hens run in the mash-fat;°   *mixing vat*
For they go to roost
Straight over the ale-joust,°   *ale pot*
And dung, when it comes,
35   In the ale tuns.°   *barrels*
Then Elinour taketh
The mash-bowl, and shaketh
The hens' dung away,
And skommeth° it in a tray   *skims*
40   Whereas the yeast is,
With her mangy fistis,°   *fists*
And sometime she blens
The dung of her hens
And the ale together;
45   And saith, "Gossip,° come hither,   *friend*
This ale shall be thicker,
And flower° the more quicker;   *froth*
For I may tell you,
I learned it of a Jew,
50   When I began to brew,
And I have found it true;
Drink now while it is new;
And ye may it brook,°   *tolerate*

2. Go to the dais—i.e., take the best place.

It shall make you look
55 Younger than ye be
Years two or three,
For ye may prove it by me.
Behold," she said, "and see
How bright I am of ble!°   *complexion*
60 Ich am not cast away,
That can my husband say,
Whan we kiss and play
In lust and in liking;
He calleth me his whiting,[3]
65 His mulling and his miting,
His nobs° and his cony,°   *dear/bunny*
His sweeting and his honey,
With, 'Bas,° my pretty bonny,   *kiss*
Thou art worth good and money!'
70 This make I my falyre fonny,°   *make my fellow foolish*
Till that he dream and dronny,°   *laze*
For, after all our sport,
Then will he rout° and snort;   *snore*
Then sweetly together we lie,
75 As two pigs in a sty."
     To cease me seemeth best,
And of this tale to rest,
And for to leave this letter,°   *text, subject*
Because it is no better,
80 And because it is no sweeter;
We will no farther rime,
Of it at this time;
But we will turn plain
Where we left again.[4]

1517?   ca. 1545

3. A small white fish—here a term of endearment,   4. I.e., go back to where we left off.
like "mulling" (meaning unclear) and "miting"
(mite).

SIR THOMAS MORE
1478–1535

Sir Thomas More is one of the most brilliant, compelling, and disturbing figures of
the English Renaissance. He has been the hero of people who, given the chance,
would (and on occasion did) tear each other apart: the Catholic church has made
him a saint; leading Communists have celebrated his book *Utopia* as a visionary forerunner of their plan to abolish private property; and middle-class liberals have admired
his vision of free public education, careers open to talents, and freedom of thought.
But at the same time each of these groups has been deeply troubled by aspects of
More's life and writings: the Catholic bishops of sixteenth-century Spain and Portugal

placed *Utopia* on their list of prohibited books; Karl Marx reserved his most bitter scorn for those impractical socialists he branded as "utopian"; and liberals have noticed uneasily that More (as Alexandr Solzhenitsyn observed bitterly) invented the idea of the forced labor camp.

More was born in London, the son of a prominent lawyer. As a boy he served as a page in the grand household of the archbishop of Canterbury, John Morton; it is reported that at Christmastime, when wandering actors would perform plays at the archbishop's palace, young More would step in among the players and improvise a part for himself. This early talent for improvisation characterized More throughout his life, as did a lingering sense that he was never quite at home in any of the parts he played.

He studied at Oxford and at the Inns of Court, but he did not automatically follow in his father's footsteps. He was torn between a career as a lawyer, with its promise of wealth and access to power, and a life of religious devotion. For some four years, according to his early biographers, he lived as a layman among the ascetic monks in London's Charterhouse, but deciding that he wanted to marry, he turned toward a secular career in public affairs. Still, amid his law practice, his position as undersheriff of London, his participation in Parliament and on the king's council, his service in diplomatic and commercial negotiations, and ultimately his three tumultuous years as lord chancellor of England, More constantly showed signs of reserving some part of himself for other realms. One of those realms was his growing family, to whom he was a devoted and loving father, but he himself spoke of his familial concerns as a kind of business that took him away from the life of the mind. Shortly after his law studies, he gave a series of public lectures on Saint Augustine's monumental work, *The City of God*, and theological and moral arguments continued to fascinate him until his death. He also had a passion for Greek and Latin literature, a passion he shared with the greatest humanist scholar of the Northern Renaissance, Desiderius Erasmus of Rotterdam (ca. 1466–1536).

Erasmus and More became close friends. They shared not only the profound classical learning that lay at the heart of the humanist movement but also an ardent Christian piety, a suspicion of scholastic hair-splitting, a delight in rhetoric, a taste for the ancient satirist Lucian, and a lively interest in experimental, unsettling wit. For Erasmus this interest bore fruit in his most enduring work, *The Praise of Folly*, which he composed as a guest in More's London house and dedicated to him. For More the love of playful, subversive wit culminated in *Utopia*, which he began in 1515 while in the Netherlands on a diplomatic mission for Henry VIII and completed the next year. Both works, written in Latin and quickly circulated among humanists throughout Europe, are daring intellectual games that call into question the period's most cherished assumptions.

Utopia displays the strong influence of Plato's *Republic*, with its radically communalistic reimagining of society, but it is also shaped by more contemporary influences: monastic communities, which forbade private property and required everyone to labor; emerging market societies, with their emphasis on education and social mobility over hereditary privilege and their dislike of the old warrior aristocracy; the recurrent outcries of peasant rebels demanding a more just distribution of wealth; and, explicitly, Amerigo Vespucci's published accounts of his voyages to the newly discovered lands across the Atlantic Ocean. Those voyages disclosed a whole world organized on principles utterly unlike those that governed European societies, a world seemingly free of the inequality, economic exploitation, dynastic squabbles, and legal chicanery that More observed everywhere around him.

Vespucci's letters, part sober reportage, part wild fantasy, helped More imagine an alternative to the world he inhabited. Book 2 of *Utopia* (the part of the work More composed first) describes in detail the laws and customs of a country that bears a striking geographical resemblance to England. But how unlike England it is! The abolition of money and private property has prevented any neurotic attachment to goods and status, and the parasitic classes—nobles, lawyers, idle priests, rapacious soldiers—have been eliminated. In Utopia, a well-ordered political democracy, education is free and universal. Instead of the misery of oppressed peasants, there are prosperous collective farms. Instead of stench and suffering in crowded, crooked streets, there are gleaming, rational cities, with free hospitals and child care. Since everyone works, no one is overburdened; and there is ample time for all citizens to pursue the arts of peace and the pleasures of the mind and the body.

Book 1 of *Utopia*, with its cold, hard look at the everyday reality of England— beggars in the streets, convicted petty thieves hanging from the gibbets, hungry farmers displaced from lands fenced off for more profitable sheep-rearing, cynical flatterers encouraging the king to embark on imperialistic wars—makes startlingly clear the devastating social and economic problems which the imaginary commonwealth of Book 2 addresses. Book 1 also makes clear that More's work is not a manifesto but a dialogue, not a political platform but a complex, often ambiguous meditation on the nature of the ideal commonwealth. Utopia is described by a strange traveler named Raphael Hythloday whose arguments for radical reform are countered by a character named More. The dialogue form not only allows the actual Thomas More some rhetorical cover for arguments that might otherwise have gotten him into serious trouble but also encourages the reader to register the disturbing underside to the dream of liberation: Utopia is a society that rests upon slavery, including enslavement for social deviance. There is no motive for individual initiative, no variety in dress or housing or cityscape, no privacy. Citizens are encouraged to value pleasure, but they are constantly monitored, lest their pursuit of pleasure pass the strict bounds set by "nature" or "reason"; there is nominal freedom of thought, but priests can punish people for "impiety"; the governors routinely condemn wars, but there is a mercenary army and a proto-imperialist foreign policy. It is very difficult to gauge More's attitude toward his imaginary commonwealth; perhaps he himself could not have said with any absolute certainty what it was.

If there is deep ambivalence in More's attitude toward Utopia, there is no comparable ambivalence in the other great work he wrote at approximately the same time, *The History of King Richard III*. In More's influential account, Richard III, the last Yorkist king, was a unmitigated monster, twisted in mind and body, subtle, hypocritical, and murderous. This characterization, obviously appealing to the Tudors whose dynasty was founded upon Richard's overthrow, was adopted verbatim by several sixteenth-century chroniclers and so came down to Shakespeare, whose *Richard III* (ca. 1592) fixed the portrait of Richard as a deformed, homicidal tyrant.

More wrote *Utopia* in Latin for an international audience of humanist intellectuals; he wrote *Richard III*, which he left unfinished, in both Latin and English versions. The English text, in prose of considerable energy and suppleness, suggests that he may with this highly charged account of the recent past have been trying to reach a different readership, more national in scope and interests. In his subsequent works, he continued to address both audiences on the matters that most concerned him, but he never repeated the mode of either playful speculation or historical narrative. Instead he focussed on theology, moral philosophy, and religious controversy, and though his wit and irony are everywhere evident in these writings, they are yoked to the service of an increasingly desperate struggle.

The struggle was against Lutheranism, which began to make inroads into England precisely during the period of More's rise to great power. More, an ardent Catholic, hated the central tenets of the Protestant Reformation and fought its adherents with every means at his disposal, including book burnings, imprisonment, and execution. As Henry VIII's confidant and lord chancellor, he played for a time a significant role in the war on heresy, but he resigned his high office when the king, seeking a divorce in order to marry Anne Boleyn, broke with the Roman Catholic Church. When More was required to take the oath for the Act of Succession and the Act of Supremacy, affirming that the king rather than the pope was the supreme head of the church in England, he declined. He attempted to remain silent, but the state treated his silence as a refusal and deemed this refusal to be treason. Against the pleadings of his family, More maintained his silence, choosing, as he put it, "to die the King's good servant, but God's first." In 1535 he was beheaded. Four hundred years later he was canonized by the Catholic church as Saint Thomas More.

From Utopia[1]

From Book 1

*The Best State of a Commonwealth,
A Discourse by the Extraordinary
Raphael Hythloday, as Recorded by
The Noted Thomas More,
Citizen and Sheriff[2]
of the Famous
City of Britain, London*

[MORE MEETS A RETURNED TRAVELER]

The most invincible king of England, Henry the Eighth of that name, a prince adorned with the royal virtues beyond any other, had recently some differences of no slight import with Charles, the most serene Prince of Castile,[3] and sent me into Flanders as his spokesman to discuss and settle them.

Cuthbert Tunstall   I was companion and associate to that incomparable man Cuthbert Tunstall, whom the king has recently created Master of the Rolls,[4] to everyone's great satisfaction. I will say nothing in praise of this man, not because I fear the judgment of a friend might be questioned, but because his integrity and learning are greater than I can describe and too well known everywhere to need my commendation—unless

Adage   I would, according to the proverb, "show the sun with a lantern."

Those appointed by the prince to deal with us, all excellent men, met us at Bruges by prearrangement. Their head man and leader was the Mayor of Bruges, a most distinguished person. But their main speaker and guiding spirit was Georges de Themsecke, the Provost of Cassel, a man eloquent by nature as well as by training, very learned in the law, and most skillful in diplomatic affairs through his ability and long practice. After we had met several times, certain points remained on which we could not come to agreement; so they adjourned the meeting and went to Brussels for some days to consult their prince in person.

Meanwhile, since my business required it, I went to Antwerp. Of those who visited me while I was there, Peter Giles was *Peter Giles*   more welcome to me than any of the others. He was

---

1. Our selections are taken from Thomas More, *Utopia*, ed. George M. Logan and Robert M. Adams (1989).

The marginal comments are not by More. Because he was in England while *Utopia* was being printed on the Continent, the details of publication were handled by several of his friends, including Peter Giles, who figures as a character in Book 1. Giles, perhaps assisted by Erasmus, added these marginal notes. Both a humanist scholar and a man of practical affairs, Giles was the city clerk of

Antwerp.

2. As undersheriff of London, More's chief duty was to serve as judge in the city court known as the Sheriff's Court.

3. Later Charles V (1500–1558), king of Spain and Holy Roman emperor. The differences were commercial ones, especially over tariffs.

4. Principal clerk of the Chancery Court. Tunstall (1474–1559) was later bishop of London and of Durham and was one of More's closest friends.

a native of Antwerp, a man of high reputation, already appointed to a good position and worthy of the very best: I hardly know a young man of more learning or better character. Apart from being cultured, virtuous, and courteous to all, with his intimates he is so open, trustworthy, loyal, and affectionate that it would be hard to find another friend like him anywhere. No man is more modest or more frank; none better combines simplicity with wisdom. His conversation is so pleasant, and so witty without malice, that the ardent desire I felt to see my native country, my wife, and my children (from whom I had been separated more than four months) was much eased by his agreeable company and pleasant talk.

One day after I had heard Mass at Nôtre Dame, the most beautiful and most popular church in Antwerp, I was about to return to my quarters when I happened to see him talking with a stranger, a man of quite advanced years. The stranger had a sunburned face, a long beard, and a cloak hanging loosely from his shoulders; from his face and dress, I took him to be a ship's captain. When Peter saw me, he approached and greeted me. As I was about to return his greeting, he drew me aside and, indicating the stranger, said, "Do you see that man? I was just on the point of bringing him to you."

"He would have been very welcome on your behalf," I answered.

"And on his own too, if you knew him," said Peter, "for there is no man alive today can tell you so much about strange peoples and unexplored lands; and I know that you're always greedy for such information."

"In that case," said I, "my guess wasn't a bad one, for at first glance I supposed he was a skipper."

"Then you're off the mark," he replied, "for his sailing has not been like that of Palinurus, but more that of Ulysses, or rather of Plato.[5] This man, who is named Raphael—his family name is Hythloday—knows a good deal of Latin and is particularly learned in Greek. He studied Greek more than Latin because his main interest is philosophy, and in that field he found that the Romans have left us nothing very valuable except certain works of Seneca and Cicero. Being eager to see the world, he bestowed on his brothers the patrimony to which he was entitled at home (for he is Portuguese by birth), and took service with Amerigo Vespucci.[6] He accompanied Vespucci on the last three of his four voyages, accounts of which are now common reading everywhere; but on the last voyage, he did not return home with the commander. After much persuasion and expostulation he got Amerigo's permission to be one of the twenty-four men who were left in a garrison at the farthest point of the last voyage. Being marooned in this way was altogether agreeable to him, as he was more eager to pursue his travels than afraid of death. He would often say, 'The man who has no grave is covered by the sky,' and 'The road to *Aphorism* heaven is equally short from all places.' Yet this frame of mind would have cost him dear, if God had not been gracious to him. After Vespucci's departure he traveled through many countries with five companions from the gar-

5. Palinurus, Aeneas's pilot, dozed at the helm, fell overboard, and drowned. Ulysses, by contrast, was a wily, alert traveler. According to an early biography, Plato traveled widely in the Mediterranean world; his *Republic* strongly influenced *Utopia*. Raphael Hythloday is an invented character.

His last name is coined from Greek words meaning "a skilled conveyor of nonsense."
6. Vespucci sailed for the king of Portugal (hence Hythloday's birthplace). His account of his voyages, published ca. 1504, made him more famous than Columbus.

rison. At last, by strange good fortune, he got via Ceylon to Calicut,[7] where by good luck he found some Portuguese ships; and so, beyond anyone's expectation, he returned to his own country."

When Peter had told me this, I thanked him for his kindness in introducing me to a man whose conversation he hoped I would enjoy, and then I turned toward Raphael. After greeting one another and exchanging the usual civilities of strangers upon their first meeting, we all went to my house. There in the garden we sat down on a bench covered with grassy turf to talk together.

He told us that after Vespucci sailed away, he and his companions who had stayed behind in the garrison often met with the people of the countryside, and by ingratiating speeches gradually won their friendship. Before long they came to dwell with them safely and even affectionately. The prince also gave them his favor (I have forgotten his name and that of his country), furnishing Raphael and his five companions not only with ample provisions, but with means for traveling—rafts when they went by water, wagons when they went by land. In addition, he sent with them a most trusty guide who was to introduce and recommend them to such other princes as they wanted to visit. After many days' journey, he said, they came to towns and cities, and to commonwealths that were both populous and not badly governed.

To be sure, under the equator and as far on both sides of the line as the sun moves, there lie vast empty deserts, scorched with the perpetual heat. The whole region is desolate and squalid, grim and uncultivated, inhabited by wild beasts, serpents, and men no less wild and dangerous than the beasts themselves. But as they went on, conditions gradually grew milder. The heat was less fierce, the earth greener, the creatures less savage. At last they reached people, cities, and towns which not only traded among themselves and with their neighbors, but even carried on commerce by sea and land with remote countries. After that, he said, they were able to visit different lands in every direction, for he and his companions were welcome as passengers aboard any ship about to make a journey.

The first vessels they saw were flat-bottomed, he said, with sails made of papyrus-reeds and wicker, occasionally of leather. Farther on they found ships with pointed keels and canvas sails, in every respect like our own. The seamen were skilled in managing wind and water; but they were most grateful to him, Raphael said, for showing them the use of the compass, of which they had been ignorant. For that reason they had formerly sailed with great timidity, and only in summer. Now they have such trust in the compass that they no longer fear winter at all, and tend to be rash rather than cautious. There is some danger that through their imprudence this discovery, which they thought would be so advantageous to them, may become the cause of much mischief.

It would take too long to repeat all that Raphael told us he had observed in various places, nor would it altogether serve our present purpose. Perhaps on another occasion we shall tell more about the things that are most profitable, especially the wise and sensible institutions that he observed among the civilized nations. We asked him many eager questions about such things,

---

7. A seaport on the west coast of India.

and he answered us willingly enough. We made no inquiries, however, about monsters, which are the routine of travelers' tales. Scyllas, ravenous Celaenos, man-eating Lestrygonians,[8] and that sort of monstrosity you can hardly avoid, but to find governments wisely established and sensibly ruled is not so easy. While he told us of many ill-considered usages in these new-found nations, he also described quite a few other customs from which our own cities, nations, races, and kingdoms might take lessons in order to correct their errors. These I shall discuss in another place, as I said. Now I intend to relate only what he told us about the manners and institutions of the Utopians, first explaining the occasion that led him to speak of that commonwealth. Raphael had been discoursing very thoughtfully on the many errors and also the wiser institutions found both in that hemisphere and in this (as many of both sorts in one place as in the other), speaking as shrewdly about the manners and governments of each place he had briefly visited as if he had lived there all his life. Peter was amazed.

"My dear Raphael," he said, "I'm surprised that you don't enter some king's service; for I don't know of a single prince who wouldn't be glad to have you. Your learning and your knowledge of various countries and men would entertain him while your advice and supply of examples would be helpful at the counsel board. Thus you might advance your own interest agreeably and be of great use at the same time to all your relatives and friends."

"About my relatives and friends," he replied, "I'm not much concerned, because I consider I've already done my duty by them. While still young and healthy, I distributed among my relatives and friends the possessions that most men do not part with till they're old and sick (and then only reluctantly, when they can no longer keep them). I think they should be content with this gift of mine, and not expect, far less insist, that for their sake I should enslave myself to any king whatever."

"Well said," Peter replied; "but I do not mean that you should be in servitude to any king, only in his service."

"The difference is only a matter of one syllable,"[9] Raphael replied.

"All right," said Peter, "but whatever you call it, I do not see any other way in which you can be so useful to your friends or to the general public, in addition to making yourself happier."

"Happier indeed!" exclaimed Raphael. "Would a way of life so absolutely repellent to my spirit make my life happier? As it is now, I live as I please, and I fancy very few courtiers, however splendid, can say that. As a matter of fact, there are so many men soliciting favors from the great that it will be no great loss if they have to do without me and a couple of others like me."

Then I said, "It is clear, my dear Raphael, that you seek neither wealth nor power, and indeed I prize and revere a man of your disposition no less than I do the greatest persons in the world. Yet I think if you would devote your time and energy to public affairs, you would be doing something worthy of a generous and truly philosophical nature, even if you did not much like it. You could best perform such a service by joining the council of some great prince, whom you would incite to just and noble actions. I'm sure you would

8. Gigantic cannibals in the *Odyssey*. "Scyllas": fabulous monsters, like the one who lived in a cave in the rock Scylla in the *Odyssey*. "Celaeno": leader of the harpies in the *Aeneid*, large birds with the faces of women, pale with hunger, and provided with long, sharp talons.
9. The play on words here depends on the Latin original: *inservias* and *servias*.

do this if you held such an office, and your influence would be felt, because a people's welfare or misery flows in a stream from their prince as from a never-failing spring. Your learning is so full, even if it weren't combined with experience, and your experience is so great, even apart from your learning, that you would be an extraordinary counselor to any king in the world."

"You are twice mistaken, my dear More," he replied, "first in me and then in the situation itself. I don't have the capacity you ascribe to me, and if I had it in the highest degree, the public would not be any better off if I bartered my peace of mind for some ruler's convenience. In the first place, most princes apply themselves to the arts of war, in which I have neither interest nor ability, instead of to the good arts of peace. They are generally more set on acquiring new kingdoms by hook or crook than on governing well those they already have. Moreover, the counselors of kings are so wise already that they don't need advice from anyone else—or at least they have that opinion of themselves. At the same time they endorse and flatter the most absurd statements of the prince's special favorites, through whose influence they hope to stand well with the prince. It's only natural, of course, that each man should think his own opinions best: the old crow loves his fledgling and the ape his cub.

"Now in a court composed of people who envy everyone else and admire only themselves, if a man should suggest something he had read of in other ages or seen in practice elsewhere, the other counselors would think their reputation for wisdom was endangered, and henceforth they would look like simpletons, unless they could find fault with his proposal. If all else failed, they would take refuge in some remark like this: 'The way we're doing it is the way we've always done it, this custom was good enough for our fathers, and I only hope we're as wise as they were.' And with this deep thought they would take their seats, as though they had said the last word on the subject— implying, forsooth, that it would be a very dangerous matter if a man were found to be wiser on any point than his forefathers were. As a matter of fact, we quietly neglect the best examples they have left us; but if something better is proposed, we seize the excuse of reverence for times past and cling to it desperately. Such proud, obstinate, ridiculous judgments I have encountered many times, and once even in England."

* * *

Summary Hythloday proceeds to recount a conversation in which he once took part at the dinner table of Cardinal John Morton, archbishop of Canterbury and lord chancellor of England. There follows an argument with More, who maintains that, despite the self-serving sycophancy of most royal counselors (to which Morton himself is a conspicuous exception), people like Hythloday can still accomplish some good at court. In Hythloday's reply, he asserts that social justice can be attained only through communism, and he offers a long account of Utopia, which he and his companions visited in their New World odyssey, in support of this claim.

From *Book 2*

[THE GEOGRAPHY OF UTOPIA]

The island of Utopia is two hundred miles across in the middle part where it is widest, and nowhere much narrower than this except toward the two ends, where it gradually tapers. These ends, curved round as if completing a circle *Site and shape of Utopia the new island* five hundred miles in circumference, make the island crescent-shaped, like a new moon. Between the horns of the crescent, which are about eleven miles apart, the sea enters and spreads into a broad bay. Being sheltered from the wind by the surrounding land, the bay is not rough, but placid and smooth instead, like a big lake. Thus, nearly the whole inner coast is one great harbor, across which ships pass in every direction, to the great advantage of the people. What with shallows on one side, and rocks on the other, entrance into the bay is very dangerous. Near midchannel, there is one rock that rises above the water, and so presents no danger in itself; a tower has been built on top of it, and a garrison is kept there. *Being naturally safe, the* Since the other rocks lie under the water, they are *entry is defended by a* very dangerous to navigation. The channels are *single fort* known only to the Utopians, so hardly any strangers enter the bay without one of their pilots; and even they themselves could not enter safely if they did not direct their course by some landmarks on the coast. Should these landmarks be shifted about, the *The trick of shifting landmarks* Utopians could lure to destruction an enemy fleet coming against them, however big it was.

On the outer side of the island, occasional harbors are to be found; but the coast is rugged by nature, and so well fortified that a few defenders could beat off the attack of a strong force. They say (and the appearance of the place confirms this) that their land was not always an island. But Utopus, who conquered the country and gave it his name (for it had previously been called Abraxa[1]), and who *Utopia named for king Utopus* brought its rude, uncouth inhabitants to such a high level of culture and humanity that they now excel in that regard almost every other people, also changed its geography. After subduing the natives, at his first landing, he *This was a bigger job than digging across the Isthmus[2]* promptly cut a channel fifteen miles wide where their land joined the continent, and thus caused the sea to flow around the country. He put not only the natives to work at this task, but all his own soldiers too, so that the vanquished would not think the labor a disgrace. With the work *Many hands make light work* divided among so many hands, the project was finished quickly. and the neighboring peoples, who at first had laughed at his folly, were struck with wonder and terror at his success.

There are fifty-four cities on the island, all spacious and magnificent, identical in language, customs, in- *The towns of Utopia*

---

1. The Greek Gnostic philosopher Basilides (second century C.E.) postulated 365 heavens, and gave the name "Abraxas" to the highest of them. The Greek letters that constitute the term have numerical equivalents summing to 365, but what

"Abraxas" actually means, nobody knows.
2. The Isthmus of Corinth joins the Peloponnesian peninsula to the rest of Greece. Various attempts to dig a canal across it failed.

stitutions, and laws. So far as the location permits, all of them are built on the same plan and have the same appearance. The nearest at least twenty-four miles apart, and the farthest are not so remote that a man cannot go on foot from one to the other in a day.

Likeness breeds concord

A middling distance between towns

Once a year each city sends three of its old and experienced citizens to Amaurot[3] to consider affairs of common interest to the island. Amaurot lies at the navel of the land, so to speak, and convenient to every other district, so it acts as a capital. Every city has enough ground assigned to it so that at least twelve miles of farm land are available in every direction, though where the cities are farther apart, their territories are more extensive. No city wants to enlarge its boundaries, for the inhabitants consider themselves good cultivators rather than landlords. At proper intervals all over the countryside they have built houses and furnished them with farm equipment. These houses are inhabited by citizens who come to the country by turns to occupy them. No rural household has fewer than forty men and women in it, besides two slaves[5] bound to the land. A master and mistress, serious and mature persons, are in charge of each household, and over every thirty households is placed a single phylarch.[6] Each year twenty persons from each rural household move back to the city after completing a two-year stint in the country. In their place, twenty others are sent out from town, to learn farm work from those who have already been in the country for a year, and who are better skilled in farming. They, in turn, will teach those who come the following year. If all were equally untrained in farm work and new to it, they might harm the crops out of ignorance. This custom of alternating farm workers is solemnly established so that no one will have to perform such heavy labor for more than two years; but many of them who take a natural pleasure in farm life are allowed to stay longer.

Distributon of land

But today this is the curse of all countries[4]

Farming is the prime occupation

The farm workers till the soil, feed the animals, hew wood, and take their produce to the city by land or water, as is convenient. They breed an enormous number of chickens by a most marvelous method. Men, not hens, hatch the eggs by keeping them in a warm place at an even temperature. As soon as they come out of the shell, the chicks recognize the men, follow them around, and are devoted to them instead of to their real mothers.

Farmers' jobs

A notable way of hatching eggs

They raise very few horses, and these full of mettle, which they keep only to exercise the young men in the art of horsemanship. For the heavy work of plowing and hauling they use oxen, which they agree are inferior to horses over the short haul, but which can hold out longer under heavy burdens, are less subject to disease (as they suppose), and besides can

Uses of the horse

Uses of oxen

---

3. Coined from a Greek word meaning "dark" or "dim"—a suitable name for the capital of a country whose name means "nowhere."
4. Although Utopia exists in the present, the glosses repeatedly refer to it as if it belonged to the

distant past, like classical Greece or Rome.
5. More provides for a few bondmen or slaves in Utopia, to perform tasks unfit for citizens, such as slaughtering.
6. From a Greek word meaning "head of a tribe."

be kept with less cost and trouble. Moreover, when oxen are too old for work, they can be used for meat.

Food and drink

Grain they use only to make bread.[7] They drink wine made of grapes, apple or pear cider, or simple water, which they sometimes mix with honey or licorice, of which they have plenty. Although they know very well, down to the last detail, how much food each city and its surrounding district will consume, they produce much more grain and cattle than they need for them-

Planned planting

selves, and share the surplus with their neighbors. Whatever goods the folk in the country need which cannot be produced there, they request of the town magistrates, and since there is nothing to be paid or exchanged, they get what they want at once without any haggling. They generally go to town once a month in any case, to observe the holy days. When harvest time approaches, the phylarchs in the country notify the town magistrates how many hands will be needed. Crews of harvesters come just when they're wanted, and in about one day of good weather they can get in the whole crop.

The value of collective labor

[THEIR GOLD AND SILVER]

For these reasons,[8] therefore, they have accumulated a vast treasure, but they do not keep it like a treasure. I'm really quite ashamed to tell you how they do keep it, because you probably won't believe me; I would not have believed it myself if someone had just told me about it, but I was there, and saw it with my own eyes. As a general rule, the more different anything is from what people are used to, the harder it is to accept. But considering that all their other customs are so unlike ours, a sensible man will perhaps not be surprised that they treat gold and silver quite differently from the way we do. After all, they never do use money among themselves, but keep it only for a contingency that may or may not actually arise. So in the meanwhile they take care that no one shall value gold and silver, of which money is made, beyond what the metals themselves deserve. Anyone can see, for example, that iron is far superior to either; men could not live without iron, by heaven, any more than without fire

O crafty fellow!

As far as utility goes, gold is inferior to iron

or water. But gold and silver have, by nature, no function with which we cannot easily dispense. Human folly has made them precious because they are rare. But in fact nature, like a most indulgent mother, has placed her best gifts out in the open, like air, water, and the earth itself; vain and unprofitable things she has hidden away in remote places.

If in Utopia gold and silver were kept locked up in some tower, smart fools among the common people might concoct a story that the governor and senate[9] were out to cheat ordinary folk and get some advantage for themselves. Of course, the gold and silver might be put into beautiful plate-ware and such rich handiwork, but then in case of necessity the people would not

---

7. I.e., they don't, like the English, use it to make beer and ale.

8. More has explained, in a section here omitted, that the Utopians, though living in a moneyless economy, have a huge treasury, kept in reserve especially to hire mercenary soldiers (and to buy

off their enemy's soldiers) in time of war.

9. The governor of each Utopian city, as More has earlier explained, is chosen for life by its senate, each of whose members is elected by a group of thirty households.

want to give up articles on which they had begun to fix their hearts—only to melt them down for soldiers' pay. To avoid these problems they thought of a plan which conforms with their institutions as clearly as it contrasts with our own. Unless one has actually seen it working, their plan may seem incredible, because we prize gold so highly and are so careful about guarding it. With them it's just the other way. While they eat from earthenware dishes and drink from glass cups, finely made but inexpensive, their chamber pots and all their humblest vessels, for use in common halls and even in private homes, are made of gold and silver. The chains and heavy fetters of slaves are also made of these metals. Finally, criminals who are to bear the mark of some disgraceful act are forced to wear golden rings in their ears and on their fingers, golden chains around their necks, even gold crowns on their heads. Thus they hold up gold and silver to scorn in every conceivable way. As a result, if they had to part with their entire supply of these metals, which other people give up with as much agony as if they were being disemboweled, the Utopians would feel it no more than the loss of a penny.

O magnificent scorn for gold!

Gold the mark of infamy

They pick up pearls by the seashore, diamonds and garnets from certain cliffs, but never go out of set purpose to look for them. If they happen to find some, they polish them and give them to the children, who feel proud and pleased with such gaudy decorations when they are small. But after, when they grow a bit older and notice that only babies like such toys, they lay them aside. Their parents don't have to say anything, they simply put these trifles away out of a shamefaced sense that they're no longer suitable, just as our children, when they grow up, put away their marbles, rattles, and dolls.

Gems the playthings of children

Different customs, different feelings: I never saw the adage better illustrated than in the case of the Anemolian[1] ambassadors, who came to Amaurot while I was there. Because they came to discuss important business, the national council had assembled ahead of time, three citizens from each city. The ambassadors from nearby nations, who had visited Utopia before and knew the local customs, realized that fine clothing was not much respected in that land, silk was despised, and gold a badge of contempt; therefore they always came in the very plainest of their clothes. But the Anemolians, who lived farther off and had had fewer dealings with the Utopians, had heard only that they all dressed alike and very simply; so they took for granted that their hosts had nothing to wear that they didn't put on. Being themselves rather more proud than wise, they decided to dress as splendidly as the very gods, and dazzle the eyes of the poor Utopians with their gaudy garb.

A neat tale

Consequently the three ambassadors made a grand entry with a suite of a hundred attendants, all in clothing of many colors, and most in silk. Being noblemen at home, the ambassadors were arrayed in cloth of gold, with heavy gold chains round their necks, gold jewels at their ears and on their fingers, and sparkling strings of pearls and gems on their caps. In fact, they were decked out in all the articles which in Utopia are used to punish slaves,

---

1. From Greek, "windy."

shame wrongdoers, or pacify infants. It was a sight to see how they strutted when they compared their finery with the dress of the Utopians who had poured out into the street to see them pass. But it was just as funny to see how wide they fell of the mark, and how far they were from getting the consideration they expected. Except for a very few Utopians who for some special reason had visited foreign countries, all the onlookers considered this splendid pomp a mark of disgrace. They therefore bowed to the humblest servants as lords, and took the ambassadors, because of their golden chains, to be slaves, passing them by without any reverence at all. You might have seen children, who had themselves thrown away their pearls and gems, nudge their mothers when they saw the ambassadors' jeweled caps, and say: "Look at that big lout, mother, who's still wearing pearls and jewels as if he were a little kid!" But the mother, in *The rascal!* all seriousness, would answer, "Quiet, son, I think he is one of the ambassadors' fools."

Others found fault with the golden chains as useless because they were so flimsy any slave could break them, and so loose that he could easily shake them off and run away whenever he wanted.

But after the ambassadors had spent a couple of days among the Utopians, they learned of the immense amounts of gold which were as thoroughly despised there as they were prized at home. They saw too that more gold and silver went into making chains and fetters for a single runaway slave than into costuming all three of them. Somewhat crestfallen, then, they put away all the finery in which they had strutted so arrogantly; but they saw the wisdom of doing so after they had talked with the Utopians enough to learn their customs and opinions.

[MARRIAGE CUSTOMS]

Women do not marry till they are eighteen, nor *Marriages* men till they are twenty-two. Clandestine premarital intercourse, if discovered and proved, brings severe punishment on both man and woman; and the guilty parties are forbidden to marry for their whole lives, unless the governor by his pardon mitigates the sentence. Also both the father and mother of the household where the offense occurred suffer public disgrace for having been remiss in their duty. The reason they punish this offense so severely is that they suppose few people would join in married love—with confinement to a single partner and all the petty annoyances that married life involves—unless they were strictly restrained from promiscuity.

In choosing marriage partners they solemnly and seriously follow a custom which seemed to us foolish and absurd in the ex- *Not very modest, but not* treme. Whether she be widow or virgin, the bride-to- *so impractical either* be is shown naked to the groom by a responsible and respectable matron; and similarly, some respectable man presents the groom naked to his prospective bride.[2] We laughed at this custom, and called it absurd; but they were just as amazed at the folly of all other peoples. When men go to buy a colt, where they are risking only a little money, they are so cautious that, though the animal is almost bare, they won't close the deal

2. Plato recommends a similar practice in his second dialogue on the ideal commonwealth, the *Laws*, with complete seriousness.

until saddle and blanket have been taken off, lest there be a hidden sore underneath. Yet in the choice of a mate, which may cause either delight or disgust for the rest of their lives, men are so careless that they leave all the rest of the woman's body covered up with clothes and estimate her attractiveness from a mere handsbreadth of her person, the face, which is all they can see. And so they marry, running great risk of bitter discord, if something in either's person should offend the other. Not all people are so wise as to concern themselves solely with character; even the wise appreciate physical beauty as a supplement to a good disposition. There's no doubt that a deformity may lurk under clothing, serious enough to make a man hate his wife when it's too late to be separated from her. If some disfiguring accident takes place after marriage, each person must bear his own fate; but the Utopians think everyone should be legally protected from deception beforehand.

There is extra reason for them to be careful, because in that part of the world they are the only people who practice monogamy, and because their marriages are seldom terminated except by death— *Divorce* though they do allow divorce for adultery or for intolerably offensive behavior. A husband or wife who is an aggrieved party to such a divorce is granted leave by the senate to take a new mate, but the guilty party suffers disgrace and is permanently forbidden to remarry. They absolutely forbid a husband to put away his wife against her will and without any fault on her part, just because of some bodily misfortune; they think it cruel that a person should be abandoned when most in need of comfort; and they add that old age, since it not only entails disease but is a disease itself, needs more than a precarious fidelity.

It happens occasionally that a married couple cannot get along, and have both found other persons with whom they hope to live more harmoniously. After getting approval of the senate, they may then separate by mutual consent and contract new marriages. But such divorces are allowed only after the senators and their wives have carefully investigated the case. Divorce is deliberately made difficult because they know that couples will have a hard time settling down if each has in mind that a new relation is easily available.

They punish adulterers with the strictest form of slavery. If both parties were married, both are divorced, and the injured parties may marry one another if they want, or someone else. But if one of the injured parties continues to love such an undeserving spouse, the marriage may go on, provided the innocent person chooses to share in the labor to which every slave is condemned. And sometimes it happens that the repentance of the guilty and the devotion of the innocent party so move the governor to pity that he restores both to freedom. But a second conviction of adultery is punished by death.

[RELIGIONS]

There are different forms of religion throughout the island, and in the different cities as well. Some worship as a god the sun, others the moon, still others one of the planets. There are some who worship a man of past ages, conspicuous either for virtue or glory; they consider him not only a god, but the supreme god. The vast majority of Utopians, however, and among these all the wisest, believe nothing of the sort: they believe in a single power, unknown, eternal, infinite, inexplicable, far beyond the grasp of the human mind, and diffused throughout the universe, not physically, but in influence. Him they call father, and to him alone they attribute the origin, increase, progress, change, and end of all visible things; they do not offer divine honors to any other.

Though the other sects differ from this group in various particular doctrines, they all agree in a single main head, that there is one supreme power, the maker and ruler of the universe; in their native tongue they all call him Mithra.[3] Different people define him differently, and each supposes the object of his worship is the special vessel of that great force which all people agree in worshipping. But gradually they are coming to forsake this mixture of superstitions and unite in that one religion which seems more reasonable than any of the others. And there is no doubt that the other religions would have disappeared long ago, had not various unlucky accidents, befalling certain Utopians who were thinking of changing their religion, been interpreted as a sign of divine anger, not chance—as if the deity who was being abandoned were avenging an insult against himself.

But after they heard from us the name of Christ, and learned of his teachings, his life, his miracles, and the no less marvelous devotion of the many martyrs whose blood, freely shed, had drawn nations far and near into the Christian fellowship, you would not believe how they were impressed. Either through the secret inspiration of God, or because Christianity seemed very like the belief that most prevails among them, they were well disposed toward it from the start. But I think they were also much influenced by the fact that Christ encouraged his disciples to practice community of goods, and that among the truest groups of Christians, the practice *Monasteries* still prevails.[4] Whatever the reason, no small number of them chose to join our communion and were washed in the holy water of baptism.

By that time, two of our group had died, and among us four survivors there was, I am sorry to say, no priest. So, though they received instruction in other matters, they still lack those sacraments which in our religion can be administered only by priests.[5] They do, however, understand what these are, and eagerly desire them. In fact, they dispute warmly whether a man chosen from among themselves could be considered a priest without ordination by a Christian bishop. Though they seemed about to select such a person, they had not yet done so when I left.

Those who have not accepted Christianity make no effort to restrain others from it, nor do they criticize new converts to it. While I was there, only one of the Christians got into trouble with the law. As soon as he was baptized, he took on himself to preach the Christian religion publicly, with more zeal than discretion. We warned him not to do so, but he soon worked himself up to a pitch where he not only preferred our religion, but condemned all others as profane, leading their impious and sacrilegious followers to the

3. In ancient Persian religion, Mithra or Mithras, the spirit of light, was the supreme force of good in the universe.
4. Many monastic orders of More's time disal-
lowed private property for their members.
5. In Catholic teaching, only baptism and matrimony among the seven sacraments can be conferred without a priest.

hell-fires they richly deserved. After he had been going on in this style for a
long time, they arrested him. He was tried on a

Men must be drawn to religion by its merits

charge, not of despising their religion, but of creating a public disorder, convicted, and sentenced to exile. For it is one of their oldest rules that no one should suffer for his religion.

Even before he took over the island, King Utopus had heard that the natives were continually squabbling over religious matters. Actually, he found it easy to conquer the country because the different sects were too busy fighting one another to oppose him. As soon as he had gained the victory, therefore, he decreed that every man might cultivate the religion of his choice, and proselytize for it too, provided he did so quietly, modestly, rationally, and without bitterness toward others. If persuasions failed, no man might resort to abuse or violence, under penalty of exile or slavery.

Utopus laid down these rules not simply for the sake of peace, which he saw was being destroyed by constant quarrels and implacable hatreds, but also for the sake of religion itself. In such matters he was not at all quick to dogmatize, because he suspected that God perhaps likes various forms of worship and has therefore deliberately inspired different men with different views. On the other hand, he was quite sure that it was arrogant folly for anyone to enforce conformity with his own beliefs by threats or violence. He supposed that if one religion is really true and the rest are false, the true one will sooner or later prevail by its own natural strength, if men will only consider the matter reasonably and moderately. But if they try to decide things by fighting and rioting, since the worst men are always most headstrong, the best and holiest religion in the world will be crowded out by foolish superstitions, like grain choked out of a field by thorns and briars. So he left the whole matter open, allowing each person to choose what he would believe. The only exception was a positive and strict law against anyone who should sink so far below the dignity of human nature as to think that the soul perishes with the body, or that the universe is ruled by blind chance, not divine providence.

Thus they believe that after this life vices will be punished and virtue rewarded. Anyone who denies this proposition they consider less than a man, since he has degraded the sublimity of his own soul to the base level of a beast's wretched body. Still less will they count him as one of their citizens, since he would openly despise all the laws and customs of society, if not prevented by fear. Who can doubt that a man who has nothing to fear but the law, and no hope of life beyond the grave, will do anything he can to evade his country's laws by craft or to break them by violence, in order to gratify his own personal greed? Therefore a man who holds such views is offered no honors, entrusted with no offices, and given no public responsibility; he is universally regarded as a low and sordid fellow. Yet they do not punish him, because they are persuaded that no man can choose to believe by a mere act of the will. They do not compel him by threats to dissemble his views, nor do they tolerate in the matter any deceit or lying, which they detest as next door to deliberate malice. The man may not argue with common people in behalf of his opinion; but in the presence of priests and other important persons, they not only permit but encourage it. For they are confident that in the end his madness will yield to reason.

There are some others, in fact no small number of them, who err the other way in supposing that animals too have immortal souls, though not comparable to ours in excellence nor destined to equal felicity. These men are not *A strange opinion on the souls of animals* thought to be evil, their opinion is not considered wholly unreasonable, and so they are not interfered with.

Almost all the Utopians are absolutely convinced that man's bliss after death will be enormous and eternal; thus they lament every man's sickness, but mourn over a death only if the man was torn from life wretchedly and against his will. Such behavior they take to be a very bad sign, as if the soul, despairing and conscious of guilt, dreaded death through a secret premonition of punishments to come. Besides, they suppose God can hardly be well pleased with the coming of one who, when he is summoned, does not come gladly, but is dragged off reluctantly and against his will. Such a death fills the onlookers with horror, and they carry off the corpse to the cemetery in melancholy silence. There, after begging God to have mercy on his spirit and to pardon his infirmities, they bury the unhappy man. But when someone dies blithely and full of good hope, they do not mourn for him, but carry the body cheerfully away, singing and commending the dead man's soul to God. They cremate[6] him in a spirit of reverence more than of grief, and erect a tombstone on which the dead man's honors are inscribed. As they go home, they talk of his character and deeds, and no part of his life is mentioned more frequently or more gladly than his joyful death.

They think that recollecting the good qualities of a man inspires the living to behave virtuously and is the most acceptable form of honor to the dead. For they think that dead persons are actually present among us, and hear what we say about them, though through the dullness of human sight they remain invisible. Given their state of bliss, the dead must be able to travel freely where they please, and it would be unkind of them to cast off every desire of seeing those friends to whom in life they had been joined by mutual affection and charity. Like other good qualities they think that after death charity is increased rather than diminished in all good men; and thus they believe the dead come frequently among the living, to observe their words and acts. Hence they go about their business the more confidently because of their trust in such protectors; and the belief that their forefathers are physically present keeps men from any secret dishonorable deed.

Fortune-telling and other vain, superstitious divinations, such as other peoples take very seriously, they consider ridiculous and contemptible. But they venerate miracles which occur without the help of nature, considering them direct and visible manifestations of the divinity. Indeed, they report that miracles have often occurred in their country. Sometimes in great and dangerous crises they pray publicly for a miracle, which they then anticipate with great confidence, and obtain.

They think the investigation of nature and the reverence arising from it are most acceptable to God. There are some people, however, and quite a few of them, who from religious motives reject literary and scientific pursuits, and refuse all leisure, but devote their full time to good works. Only by constant dedication to the of- *The active life*

---

6. Cremation was not practiced by Christians before the nineteenth century, because it was thought to be at odds with the doctrine of the resurrection of the body.

fices of charity, these people think, can happiness after death be earned; and so they are always busy. Some tend the sick; others repair roads, clean ditches, rebuild bridges, dig turf, sand, or stones; still others fell trees and cut them up, and transport wood, grain, or other commodities into the cities by wagon. They work for private citizens as well as for the public, and work even harder than slaves. With cheery good will they undertake any task that is so rough, hard, and dirty that most people refuse to tackle it because of the toil, tedium, and frustration involved. While constantly engaged in heavy labor themselves, they procure leisure for others, yet claim no credit for it. They neither criticize the way others live, nor boast of their own doings. The more they put themselves in the position of slaves, the more highly they are honored by everyone.

These people are of two sects. The first are celibates who abstain not only from sex, but also from eating meat, and some from any sort of animal food whatever. They reject all the pleasures of this life as harmful, and look forward only to the joys of the life to come, which they hope to merit by hard labor and all-night vigils. As they hope to attain it soon, they are cheerful and active in the here and now. The other kind are just as fond of hard work, but prefer to marry. They don't despise the comforts of marriage, but think as they owe nature their labor, so they owe children to their country. Unless it interferes with their labor, they avoid no pleasure, and gladly eat meat, precisely because they think it makes them stronger for any sort of heavy work. The Utopians regard the second sort as more sensible, but the first sort as holier. If anyone chose celibacy over marriage and a hard life over a comfortable one on grounds of reason alone, they would laugh at him; but as these men say they are motivated by religion, the Utopians respect and revere them. On no subject are they warier of jumping to conclusions than in this matter of religion. Such then are the men whom in their own language they call Buthrescas, a term which can be translated as "specially religious."

[CONCLUSION]

Now I have described to you as accurately as I could the structure of that commonwealth which I consider not only the best but indeed the only one that can rightfully claim that name. In other places men talk very liberally of the commonwealth, but what they mean is simply their own wealth; in Utopia, where there is no private business, every man zealously pursues the public business. And in both places men are right to act as they do. For elsewhere, even though the commonwealth may flourish, each man knows that unless he makes separate provision for himself, he may perfectly well die of hunger. Bitter necessity, then, forces men to look out for themselves rather than for the people, that is, for other people. But in Utopia, where everything belongs to everybody, no man need fear that, so long as the public warehouses are filled, he will ever lack for anything he needs. Distribution is not one of their problems; in Utopia no men are poor, no men are beggars, and though no man owns anything, everyone is rich.

For what can be greater riches than for a man to live joyfully and peacefully, free from all anxieties, and without worries about making a living? No man is bothered by his wife's querulous complaints about money, no man fears poverty for his son, or struggles to scrape up a dowry for his daughter.

Each man can feel secure of his own livelihood and happiness, and of his whole family's as well: wife, sons, grandsons, great-grandsons, great-great-grandsons, and that whole long line of descendants that the gentry are so fond of contemplating. Indeed, even those who once worked but can no longer do so are cared for just as well as if they were still productive.

At this point, I'd like to see anyone venture to compare this equity of the Utopians with the so-called justice that prevails among other nations—among whom let me perish if I can discover the slightest scrap of justice or fairness. What kind of justice is it when a nobleman, a goldsmith,[7] a moneylender, or someone else who makes his living by doing either nothing at all or something completely useless to the commonwealth, gets to live a life of luxury and grandeur, while in the meantime, a laborer, a carter, a carpenter, or a farmer works so hard and so constantly that even beasts of burden would scarcely endure it; and this work of theirs is so necessary that no commonwealth could survive for a year without it? Yet they earn so meager a living and lead such miserable lives that beasts would really seem to be better off. Beasts do not have to work every minute, and their food is not much worse; in fact they like it better, and besides, they do not have to worry about their future. But workingmen must not only sweat and suffer without present reward, but agonize over the prospect of a penniless old age. Their daily wage is inadequate even for present needs, so there is no possible chance of their saving for their declining years.

Now isn't this an unjust and ungrateful commonwealth? It lavishes rich rewards on so-called gentry, loan sharks, and the rest of that crew, who don't work at all or are mere parasites, purveyors of empty pleasures. And yet it makes no provision whatever for the welfare of farmers and colliers, laborers, carters, and carpenters, without whom the commonwealth would simply cease to exist. After society has taken the labor of their best years, when they are worn out by age, sickness, and utter destitution, then the thankless commonwealth, forgetting all their pains and services, throws them out to die a miserable death. What is worse, the rich constantly try to grind out of the poor part of their meager pittance, not only by private swindling but by public laws. It is basically unjust that people who deserve most from the commonwealth should receive least. But now they have distorted and debased the right even further by giving their extortion the form of law; and thus they have palmed injustice off as legal. When I run over in my mind the various commonwealths flourishing today, so help me God, I *Reader, note well!* can see in them nothing but a conspiracy of the rich, who are fattening up their own interests under the name and title of the commonwealth. They invent ways and means to hang onto whatever they have acquired by sharp practice, and then they scheme to oppress the poor by buying up their toil and labor as cheaply as possible. These devices become law as soon as the rich, speaking through the commonwealth—which, of course, includes the poor as well—say they must be observed.

And yet when these insatiably greedy and evil men have divided among themselves goods which would have sufficed for the entire people, how far

---

7. In addition to being the creators of objects that are, from the Utopian point of view, worthless, goldsmiths often functioned as bankers. As the inclusion of moneylenders in this list suggests, the idea that lending money at interest constituted sinful usury remained strong in More's time—though the sentence also makes it clear that the practice was firmly established.

they remain from the happiness of the Utopian Republic, which has abolished not only money but with it greed! What a mass of trouble was cut away
by that one step! What a thicket of crimes was uprooted! Everyone knows
that if money were abolished, fraud, theft, robbery, quarrels, brawls, sedi-
tions, murders, treasons, poisonings, and a whole set of crimes which are
avenged but not prevented by the hangman would at once die out. If money
disappeared, so would fear, anxiety, worry, toil, and sleepless nights. Even
poverty, which seems to need money more than anything else, would vanish
if money were entirely done away with.

Consider if you will this example. Take a barren year of failed harvests,
when many thousands of men have been carried off by hunger. If at the end
of the famine the barns of the rich were searched, I dare say positively
enough grain would be found in them to have kept all those who died of
starvation and disease from even realizing that a shortage ever existed—if
only it had been divided equally among them. So easily might men get the
necessities of life if that cursed money, which is supposed to provide access
to them, were not in fact the only barrier to our getting what we need to live.
Even the rich, I'm sure, understand this. They must know that it's better to
have enough of what we really need than an abundance of superfluities,
much better to escape from our many present troubles than to be burdened
with great masses of wealth. And in fact I have no doubt that every man's
perception of where his true interest lies, along with the authority of Christ
our Savior (whose wisdom could not fail to recognize the best, and whose
goodness would not fail to counsel it), would long ago have brought the whole
world to adopt Utopian laws, were it not for one single
monster, the prime plague and begetter of all others—
I mean Pride.

A *striking phrase*

Pride measures her advantages not by what she has but by what other
people lack. Pride would not deign even to be made a goddess if there were
no wretches for her to sneer at and domineer over. Her good fortune is
dazzling only by contrast with the miseries of others, her riches are valuable
only as they torment and tantalize the poverty of others. Pride is a serpent
from hell that twines itself around the hearts of men, acting like a suckfish[8]
to hold them back from choosing a better way of life.

Pride is too deeply fixed in human nature to be easily plucked out. So I
am glad that the Utopians at least have been lucky enough to achieve this
Republic which I wish all mankind would imitate. The institutions they have
adopted have made their community most happy, and, as far as anyone can
tell, capable of lasting forever. Now that they have torn up the seeds of
ambition and faction at home, along with most other vices, they are in no
danger from internal strife, which alone has been the ruin of many other
nations that seemed secure. As long as they preserve harmony at home, and
keep their institutions healthy, the Utopians can never be overcome or even
shaken by their envious neighbors, who have often attempted their ruin, but
always in vain.

When Raphael had finished his story, I was left thinking that quite a few
of the laws and customs he had described as existing among the Utopians

---

8. The remora, which attaches itself by a suction cup to larger fish or ships. It was fabled to be strong
enough to hold back a ship under sail.

were really absurd. These included their methods of waging war, their religious practices, as well as others of their customs; but my chief objection was to the basis of their whole system, that is, their communal living and their moneyless economy. This one thing alone utterly subverts all the nobility, magnificence, splendor, and majesty which (in the popular view) are the true ornaments and glory of any commonwealth. But I saw Raphael was tired with talking, and I was not sure he could take contradiction in these matters, particularly when I recalled what he had said about certain counselors who were afraid they might not appear knowing enough unless they found something to criticize in other men's ideas. So with praise for the Utopian way of life and his account of it, I took him by the hand and led him in to supper. But first I said that we would find some other time for thinking of these matters more deeply, and for talking them over in more detail. And I still hope such an opportunity will present itself some day.

Meantime, while I can hardly agree with everything he said (though he is a man of unquestionable learning and enormous experience of human affairs), yet I freely confess that in the Utopian commonwealth there are many features that in our own societies I would wish rather than expect to see.

1515–16   1516

From The History of King Richard III

[A KING'S MISTRESS][1]

Now then, by and by, as it were for anger not for covetise,[2] the Protector sent into the house of Shore's wife (for her husband dwelled not with her) and spoiled her of all that ever she had, above the value of two or three thousand marks,[3] and sent her body to prison. And when he had a while laid unto her for the manner' sake,[4] that she went about to bewitch him, and that she was of counsel with the Lord Chamberlain[5] to destroy him; in conclusion when that no color[6] could fasten upon these matters, then he laid heinously to her charge the thing that herself could not deny, that all the world wist was true, and that natheles[7] every man laughed at to hear it then so suddenly so highly taken, that she was naught of her body.[8] And for this cause (as a goodly continent prince clean and faultless of himself, sent out of heaven into this vicious world for the amendment of men's manners) he caused the Bishop of London to put her to open penance, going before the cross in procession upon a Sunday with a taper in her hand.[9] In which she went in countenance and pace demure, so womanly, and albeit she were out of all array save her kirtle only,[1] yet went she so fair and lovely, namely while the wondering of the people cast a comely rud in her checks (of which she before had most miss),[2] that her great shame won her much praise among those that were more amorous of her body than curious of[3] her soul. And many

---

1. Jane Shore, wife of a London merchant and mistress of the late king, Edward IV, persecuted by Richard, duke of Gloucester, "the Protector" during the minority of Edward's sons. After their mysterious death in the Tower of London he ascended the throne as Richard III.
2. Greed.
3. A monetary unit. "Spoiled": despoiled.
4. Accused her, to justify arrest.

5. Lord Hastings, beheaded by Richard.
6. Plausibility.
7. Nevertheless. "Wist": knew.
8. Unchaste.
9. The standard punishment for a harlot.
1. Dressed only in a loose gown.
2. Lack. "Namely" especially. "Rud": redness (i.e., blush).
3. Concerned about.

good folk also that hated her living and glad were to see sin corrected, yet pitied they more her penance than rejoiced therein, when they considered that the Protector procured it more of a corrupt intent than any virtuous affection.[4]

This woman was born in London, worshipfully friended,[5] honestly brought up, and very well married, saving somewhat too soon, her husband an honest citizen, young and goodly and of good substance.[6] But forasmuch as they were coupled ere she were well ripe, she not very fervently loved for whom she never longed. Which was haply[7] the thing that the more easily made her incline unto the king's appetite when he required[8] her. Howbeit, the respect of his royalty, the hope of gay apparel, ease, pleasure, and other wanton wealth was able soon to pierce a soft tender heart. But when the king had abused her, anon[9] her husband (as he was an honest man and one that could his good,[1] not presuming to touch a king's concubine) left her up to him altogether. When the king died, the Lord Chamberlain took her, which in the king's days, albeit he was sore[2] enamored upon her, yet he forbare her, either for reverence or for a certain friendly faithfulness.

Proper[3] she was, and fair: nothing in her body that you would have changed, but if you would have wished her somewhat higher. Thus say they that knew her in her youth, albeit some that now see her (for yet she liveth) deem her never to have been well visaged. Whose judgment seemeth me somewhat like as though men should guess the beauty of one long before departed by her scalp taken out of the charnel house;[4] for now is she old, lean, withered, and dried up, nothing left but rivelled[5] skin and hard bone. And yet, being even such, whoso well advise[6] her visage might guess and devise which parts how filled would make it a fair face.

Yet delighted not men so much in her beauty as in her pleasant behavior. For a proper wit[7] had she, and could both read well and write, merry in company, ready and quick of answer, neither mute nor full of babble, sometime taunting without displeasure and not without disport.[8] The king would say that he had three concubines, which in three divers[9] properties diversly excelled: one the merriest, another the wiliest, the third the holiest harlot in his realm, as one whom no man could get out of the church lightly[1] to any place but it were to his bed. The other two were somewhat greater personages, and natheles[2] of their humility content to be nameless and to forbear the praise of those properties. But the merriest was this Shore's wife, in whom the king therefore took special pleasure. For many he had, but her he loved, whose favor, to say the truth (for sin it were to belie the devil), she never abused to any man's hurt, but to many a man's comfort and relief. Where the king took displeasure, she would mitigate and appease his mind. Where men were out of favor, she would bring them in his grace. For many that had highly offended, she obtained pardon. Of great forfeitures[3] she gat men remission. And finally, in many weighty suits she stood many

---

4. Motive.
5. With worthy friends.
6. Wealth.
7. Perhaps.
8. Entreated.
9. Immediately.
1. Knew what was good for him.
2. Very.
3. Good-looking.

4. Common burial place.
5. Wrinkled.
6. Observe.
7. Good mind.
8. Playfulness.
9. Different.
1. Easily.
2. Notwithstanding.
3. Fines.

men in great stead, either for none or very small rewards, and those rather gay than rich, either for that she was content with the deed'[4] self well done, or for that she delighted to be sued unto and to show what she was able to do with the king; or for that wanton women and wealthy be not alway covetous.

I doubt not some shall think this woman too slight a thing to be written of and set among the remembrances of great matters, which they shall specially think that haply shall esteem her only by that[5] they now see her. But meseemeth the chance[6] so much the more worthy to be remembered, in how much she is now in the more beggarly condition, unfriended and worn out of acquaintance,[7] after good substance, after as great favor with the prince, after as great suit[8] and seeking to with all those that those days had business to speed, as many other men were in their times, which be now famous only by the infamy of their ill deeds. Her doings were not much less, albeit they be much less remembered because they were not so evil. For men use[9] if they have an evil turn to write it in marble; and whoso doth us a good turn, we write it in dust; which is not worst proved[1] by her; for at this day she beggeth of many at this day living, that at this day had begged if she had not been.

ca. 1514–18   1557

4. Deed's.
5. That which.
6. Story. "Meseemeth": I think.
7. Without friends.

8. Influence at court.
9. Are accustomed.
1. Illustrated.

SIR THOMAS WYATT THE ELDER
1503–1542

Thomas Wyatt made his career in the shifting, dangerous currents of Renaissance courts, and court culture, with its power struggles, sexual intrigues, and sophisticated tastes, shaped his remarkable achievements as a poet. The son of a gentleman who early linked his fortunes to the Tudor dynasty, Wyatt was educated at St. John's College, Cambridge, and then entered the service of Henry VIII, becoming clerk of the king's jewels, a member of diplomatic missions to France and the Low Countries, and, in 1537–39, ambassador to the court of the Emperor Charles V in Spain. The years he spent abroad as a diplomat had a significant impact upon his writing, most obvious in his translations and imitations of poems by Ronsard, Aretino, Sannazaro, Alamanni, and, above all, Petrarch. Diplomacy, with its veiled threats, subtle indirection, and cynical role-playing, may have had a more indirect impact as well, reinforcing the lessons in self-display and self-concealment that Wyatt would have received at the English court.

Life in the orbit of the ruthless, unpredictable Henry VIII was competitive and risky. When, in the late 1530s, Wyatt wrote to his son of the "thousand dangers and hazards, enmities, hatreds, prisonments, despites, and indignations" he had faced, he was not exaggerating. He probably came closest to the executioner's axe when in 1536 he was imprisoned in the Tower of London along with several others accused of having adulterous affairs with the queen, Anne Boleyn. As his poem *Who list his wealth and ease retain* implies, Wyatt may have watched from his cell the execution of the queen and her alleged lovers, but he himself was spared, as he was spared a few years later, when he was again imprisoned in the Tower on charges of high treason brought by his enemies at court. His death, at the age of thirty-nine, came from a fever.

It is not surprising, given his career, that many of Wyatt's poems, including his satires and his psalm translations, express an intense longing for "steadfastness" and an escape from the corruption, anxiety, and duplicity of the court. The praise, in his verse epistle to John Poins, of a quiet retired life in the country and the harsh condemnation of courtly hypocrisy derive from his own experience. But of course the eloquent celebration of simplicity and truthfulness can itself be a cunning strategy. Wyatt was a master of the game of poetic self-display. Again and again he represents himself as a plain-speaking and steadfast man, betrayed by the "doubleness" of a fickle mistress or the instability of fortune. At this distance it is impossible to know how much this account corresponds to reality, but we can admire, as Wyatt's contemporaries did, the rhetorical deftness of the performance.

In a move with momentous consequences for English poetry, Wyatt introduced into English the sonnet, a fourteen-line poem in pentameter with a complex, intertwining rhyme scheme. For the most part, he took his subject matter from Petrarch's sonnets, but his rhyme schemes came from other Italian models. The most common rhyme scheme in Wyatt's sonnets is *abba abba cddc ee*; the more typical Italian structure—an octave (the first eight lines) followed, after a turn in the sense, by a sestet (the last six lines)—was already beginning to change into the characteristic "English" structure for the sonnet, three quatrains and a couplet.

In his translations of Petrarchan sonnets, such as *Whoso list to hunt*, Wyatt tends to turn the idealizing of the woman into disillusionment and complaint. For the lover in Petrarch's poems, love is a transcendent experience; for the lover in Wyatt's poems, it is obsessive and embittering. The tone of bitterness carries over to many poems less closely linked to Italian and French models, poems with short stanzas and refrains in the manner of the native English "ballet" (pronounced to rhyme with *mallet*) or dancesong. Some of the ballets, to be sure, strike a note of jaunty independence, often tinged with misogyny, but melancholy complaint is rarely very distant. Perhaps the poem that most brilliantly captures Wyatt's blend of passion, anger, cynicism, longing, and pain is *They flee from me*.

Wyatt never published a collection of his own poems, and very little of his verse appeared in print during his lifetime. In 1557 (fifteen years after his death), the printer Richard Tottel included 97 poems attributed to Wyatt among the 271 poems in his miscellany, *Songs and Sonnets*. Wyatt was not primarily concerned with regularity of accent and smoothness of rhythm. By the time Tottel's collection was published, Wyatt's deliberately rough, vigorous, and expressive metrical practice was felt to be crude, and Tottel (or someone in his printing house) smoothed out the versification. We reprint *They flee from me* both in Tottel's "improved" version and in the version found in the Egerton Manuscript, a manuscript that contains poems in Wyatt's own hand and corrections in his hand of scribal copies of his poems. Unlike the Egerton Manuscript (E. MS.), the Devonshire Manuscript (D. MS.) was not apparently in the poet's possession, but some of its texts seem earlier than Egerton's, and it furnishes additional poems, as do the Blage Manuscript (B. MS.) and the Arundel Manuscript (A. MS.).

In the following selections we have indicated the manuscript from which each of the poems derives and divided the poems into three generic groups: sonnets, other lyrics, and finally a satire. Within each of the first two groups, the poems are printed in the order in which they appear in the manuscripts. There is no reason to think that this is a chronological ordering.

The long love that in my thought doth harbor[1]

The long love that in my thought doth harbor,
And in mine heart doth keep his residence,
Into my face presseth with bold pretense
And therein campeth, spreading his banner.[2]
5 She that me learneth to love and suffer
And will that my trust and lust's negligence[3]
Be reined by reason, shame,° and reverence,   *modesty*
With his hardiness taketh displeasure.
Wherewithal unto the heart's forest he fleeth,
10 Leaving his enterprise with pain and cry,
And there him hideth, and not appeareth.
What may I do, when my master feareth,
But in the field with him to live and die?
For good is the life ending faithfully.

              E. MS.

Whoso list to hunt[1]

Whoso list° to hunt, I know where is an hind,° *cares / female deer*
But as for me, alas, I may no more.
The vain travail hath wearied me so sore,
I am of them that farthest cometh behind.
5 Yet may I, by no means, my wearied mind
Draw from the deer, but as she fleeth afore,
Fainting I follow. I leave off, therefore,
Since in a net I seek to hold the wind.
Who list her hunt, I put him out of doubt,
10 As well as I, may spend his time in vain.
And graven with diamonds in letters plain
There is written, her fair neck round about,
"*Noli me tangere*, for Caesar's I am,
And wild for to hold, though I seem tame."

              E. MS.

1. Wyatt's version of poem 140 of Petrarch's *Rime sparse* (Scattered Rhymes); his younger friend, the earl of Surrey, also translated it (p. 571).
2. I.e., the speaker's blush. The first four lines of this sonnet introduce the "conceit" (or elaborately sustained metaphor) of Love as a warrior who, "with bold pretense" (i.e., making bold claim), flaunts his presence by means of the "banner." Elaborate metaphors of this kind are common in Petrarchan (and Elizabethan) love poetry, and often, as in this instance, an entire sonnet will turn on a single conceit.
3. I.e., my open and careless revelation of my love. "Learneth": teaches.
1. An adaptation of Petrarch's *Rima* 190, perhaps influenced by commentators on Petrarch, who said that *Noli me tangere quia Caesaris sum* ("Touch me not, for I am Caesar's") was inscribed on the collars of Caesar's hinds, which were then set free and were presumably safe from hunters. Wyatt's sonnet is usually supposed to refer to Anne Boleyn, in whom Henry VIII became interested in 1526.

Farewell, Love

Farewell, Love, and all thy laws forever,
Thy baited hooks shall tangle me no more;
Senec and Plato call me from thy lore,
To perfect wealth my wit for to endeavor.[1]
In blind error when I did persever,
Thy sharp repulse, that pricketh aye so sore,
Hath taught me to set in trifles no store
And 'scape forth since liberty is lever.°   *more pleasing, dearer*
Therefore farewell, go trouble younger hearts,
And in me claim no more authority;
With idle youth go use thy property,[2]
And thereon spend thy many brittle darts.
For hitherto though I have lost all my time,
Me lusteth° no longer rotten boughs to climb.   *I care*

E. MS.

My galley[1]

My galley charged° with forgetfulness   *freighted*
Thorough° sharp seas, in winter nights doth pass   *through*
'Tween rock and rock; and eke° mine enemy, alas,   *also*
That is my lord, steereth with cruelness;
And every oar a thought in readiness,
As though that death were light in such a case.[2]
An endless wind doth tear the sail apace
Of forced sighs and trusty fearfulness.°   *fear to trust*
A rain of tears, a cloud of dark disdain,
Hath done the wearied cords great hinderance;
Wreathed with error and eke with ignorance.
The stars be hid that led me to this pain.
Drowned is reason that should me consort,°   *accompany*
And I remain despairing of the port.

E. MS.

Divers doth use

Divers doth use,[1] as I have heard and know,
When that to change their ladies do begin,
To mourn and wail, and never for to lin,°   *cease*
Hoping thereby to pease° their painful woe.   *appease, relieve*
And some there be, that when it chanceth so

---

1. I.e., "Senec" (Seneca, the Roman moral philosopher and tragedian) and Plato call him to educate
his mind to perfect well-being ("wealth").
2. Do what you characteristically do.
1. Translated from Petrarch's *Rima* 189.

2. As though my destruction would not matter
much.
1. Are accustomed. "Divers": diverse—i.e., some
other men.

That women change and hate where love hath been,
They call them false and think with words to win
The hearts of them which otherwhere doth grow.
But as for me, though that by chance indeed
10 Change hath outworn the favor that I had,
I will not wail, lament, nor yet be sad,
Nor call her false that falsely did me feed,
But let it pass, and think it is of kind°   *nature*
That often change doth please a woman's mind.

D. MS.

Madam, withouten many words

Madam, withouten many words,
Once,° I am sure, ye will or no.   *sometime*
And if ye will, then leave your bordes,°   *jests*
And use your wit° and show it so.   *mind*

5 And with a beck ye shall me call.
And if of one that burneth alway
Ye have any pity at all,
Answer him fair with yea or nay.

If it be yea, I shall be fain.°   *glad*
10 If it be nay, friends as before.
Ye shall another man obtain,
And I mine own and yours no more.

E. MS.

They flee from me

They flee from me, that sometime did me seek
With naked foot stalking° in my chamber.   *walking softly*
I have seen them gentle, tame, and meek
That now are wild and do not remember
5 That sometime they put themself in danger
To take bread at my hand; and now they range,
Busily seeking with a continual change.

Thanked be fortune it hath been otherwise
Twenty times better; but once in special,
10 In thin array, after a pleasant guise,
When her loose gown from her shoulders did fall,
And she me caught in her arms long and small,°   *slender*
Therewithal sweetly did me kiss
And softly said, "Dear heart, how like you this?"

15 It was no dream, I lay broad waking.
But all is turned, thorough my gentleness,

Into a strange fashion of forsaking;
And I have leave to go, of her goodness,
And she also to use newfangleness.°   *fickleness*
20 But since that I so kindely[1] am served,
I fain would know what she hath deserved.

E. MS.

The Lover Showeth How He Is Forsaken of Such as He Sometime Enjoyed

[THEY FLEE FROM ME]

They flee from me, that sometime did me seek
With naked foot stalking within my chamber.
Once have I seen them gentle, tame, and meek
That now are wild and do not once remember
5   That sometime they have put themselves in danger
To take bread at my hand; and now they range,
Busily seeking in continual change.

Thankèd be fortune, it hath been otherwise
Twenty times better; but once especial,
10 In thin array, after a pleasant guise,
When her loose gown did from her shoulders fall,
And she me caught in her arms long and small,
And therewithal so sweetly did me kiss
And softly said, "Dear heart, how like you this?"

15 It was no dream, for I lay broad awaking.
But all is turned now, through my gentleness,
Into a bitter fashion of forsaking;
And I have leave to go, of her goodness,
And she also to use newfangleness.
20 But since that I unkindly so am served,
How like you this? What hath she now deserved?

TOTTEL, 1557

My lute, awake!

My lute, awake! Perform the last
Labor that thou and I shall waste,
And end that I have now begun;
For when this song is sung and past,
5   My lute, be still, for I have done.

As to be heard where ear is none,
As lead to grave in marble stone,[1]

---

1. Naturally, but with an ironic suggestion of the modern meaning of "kindly." In Wyatt's spelling, the word should presumably be pronounced as three syllables.

1. I.e., when sound may be heard with no ear to hear it or when soft lead is able to carve ("grave") hard marble.

My song may pierce her heart as soon.
Should we then sigh or sing or moan?
10   No, no, my lute, for I have done.

The rocks do not so cruelly
Repulse the waves continually
As she my suit and affectiön.
So that I am past remedy,
15   Whereby my lute and I have done.

Proud of the spoil that thou hast got
Of simple hearts, thorough love's shot,
By whom, unkind, thou hast them won,
Think not he hath his bow forgot,
20   Although my lute and I have done.

Vengeance shall fall on thy disdain
That makest but game on earnest pain.
Think not alone under the sun
Unquit° to cause thy lovers plain,°   *unrevenged / to complain*
25   Although my lute and I have done.

Perchance thee lie withered and old
The winter nights that are so cold,
Plaining in vain unto the moon.
Thy wishes then dare not be told.
30   Care then who list,° for I have done.   *likes*

And then may chance thee to repent
The time that thou hast lost and spent
To cause thy lovers sigh and swoon.
Then shalt thou know beauty but lent,
35   And wish and want as I have done.

Now cease, my lute. This is the last
Labor that thou and I shall waste,
And ended is that we begun.
Now is this song both sung and past;
40   My lute, be still, for I have done.

E. MS.

And wilt thou leave me thus?

And wilt thou leave me thus?
Say nay, say nay, for shame,
To save thee from the blame
Of all my grief and grame!°   *sorrow*
5   And wilt thou leave me thus?
Say nay, say nay!

And wilt thou leave me thus,
That hath loved thee so long

In wealth° and woe among?   *happiness*
10 And is thy heart so strong
As for to leave me thus?
    Say nay, say nay!

And wilt thou leave me thus,
That hath given thee my heart
15 Never for to depart,
Neither for pain nor smart?
And wilt thou leave me thus?
    Say nay, say nay!

And wilt thou leave me thus,
20 And have no more pity
Of him that loveth thee?
Alas, thy cruelty!
And wilt thou leave me thus?
    Say nay, say nay!

                                      D. MS.

Forget not yet

Forget not yet the tried intent
Of such a truth as I have meant,
My great travail so gladly spent,
    Forget not yet.

5 Forget not yet when first began
The weary life ye know since when,
The suit, the service[1] none tell can,
    Forget not yet.

Forget not yet the great essays,
10 The cruel wrong, the scornful ways,
The painful patience in denays,°   *denials, refusals*
    Forget not yet.

Forget not yet, forget not this,
How long ago hath been and is
15 The mind that never meant amiss,
    Forget not yet.

Forget not then thine own approved,
The which so long hath thee so loved,
Whose steadfast faith yet never moved,
20   Forget not this.

                                      D. MS.

---

1. Actions of a lover, often called the lady's "servant."

Blame not my lute

Blame not my lute, for he must sound
Of this or that as liketh° me: *pleases*
For lack of wit° the lute is bound   *intelligence*
To give such tunes as pleaseth me.
5 Though my songs be somewhat strange,
And speaks such words as touch thy change,° *unfaithfulness*
    Blame not my lute.

My lute, alas, doth not offend,
Though that perforce he must agree
10 To sound such tunes as I intend
To sing to them that heareth me.
Then though my songs be somewhat plain,
And toucheth some that use to feign,[1]
    Blame not my lute.

15 My lute and strings may not deny,
But as I strike they must obey:
Break not them then so wrongfully,
But wreak° thyself some wiser way.   *avenge*
And though the songs which I indite
20 Do quit thy change[2] with rightful spite,
    Blame not my lute.

Spite asketh spite, and changing change,
And falsèd faith must needs be known;
The fault so great, the case so strange,
25 Of right it must abroad be blown.
Then since that by thine own desert
My songs do tell how true thou art,
    Blame not my lute.

Blame but thyself, that hast misdone
30 And well deservèd to have blame;
Change thou thy way so evil begun,
And then my lute shall sound that same.
But if till then my fingers play
By thy desert their wonted° way,   *accustomed*
35   Blame not my lute.

Farewell, unknown, for though thou break
My strings in spite with great disdain,
Yet have I found out for thy sake
Strings for to string my lute again.
40 And if perchance this foolish rhyme

1. And comment on some who are accustomed to   2. Requite your unfaithfulness.
dissemble.

Do make thee blush at any time,
Blame not my lute.

D. MS.

Stand whoso list[1]

Stand whoso list° upon the slipper° top   *cares to / slippery*
Of court's estates,° and let me here rejoice   *high positions*
And use me quiet without let or stop,[2]
Unknown in court, that hath such brackish joys.
5   In hidden place so let my days forth pass
That when my years be done withouten noise,
I may die aged after the common trace.°   *way*
For him death grippeth right hard by the crop°   *throat*
That is much known of other, and of himself, alas,
10   Doth die unknown, dazed, with dreadful° face.   *fearful*

A. MS.

Who list his wealth and ease retain[1]

Who list° his wealth° and ease retain,   *desires / well-being*
Himself let him unknown contain.[2]
Press not too fast in at that gate
Where the return stands by disdain:
5   For sure, *circa Regna tonat*.[3]

The high mountains are blasted oft
When the low valley is mild and soft.
Fortune with Health stands at debate.[4]
The fall is grievous from aloft.
10   And sure, *circa Regna tonat*.

These bloody days have broken my heart.
My lust,° my youth did then depart,   *pleasure*
And blind desire of estate.
Who hastes to climb seeks to revert.°   *fall back*
15   Of truth, *circa Regna tonat*.

The Bell Tower showed me such sight
That in my head sticks day and night.
There did I learn out of a grate,°   *barred window*
For all favor, glory, or might,[5]
20   That yet *circa Regna tonat*.

1. A translation of Seneca, *Thyestes*, lines 391–403.
2. Comport myself quietly without hindrance or impediment from others.
1. This poem was almost certainly written at the time of Wyatt's imprisonment in 1536, during which he witnessed from the Bell Tower the execution of Anne Boleyn.

2. I.e., let him keep himself unknown.
3. "He [i.e., Jupiter] thunders around thrones" (Seneca, *Phaedra*, line 1140). The first two stanzas of Wyatt's poem paraphrase lines from that play. "The return stands by disdain": i.e., "you will be disdained as you make your (forced) exit."
4. I.e., fortune and well-being are always at odds.
5. I.e., whatever one's favor, glory, or might.

By proof,° I say, there did I learn: *experience*
Wit helpeth not defense to yerne,
Of innocence to plead or prate.[6]
Bear low, therefore, give God the stern,[7]
25   For sure, *circa Regna tonat.*

                                                                     B. MS.

Mine own John Poins[1]

Mine own John Poins, since ye delight to know
The cause why that homeward I me draw
(And flee the press of courts, whereso they go,
Rather than to live thrall under the awe
5   Of lordly looks) wrapped within my cloak,
To will and lust° learning to set a law;   *pleasure*
It is not for because I scorn or mock
The power of them to whom Fortune hath lent
Charge over us, of right to strike the stroke.[2]
10   But true it is that I have always meant
Less to esteem them than the common sort,
Of outward things that judge in their intent
Without regard what doth inward resort.
I grant sometime that of glory the fire
15   Doth touch my heart; me list not to report
Blame by honor, and honor to desire.[3]
But how may I this honor now attain
That cannot dye the color black a liar?[4]
My Poins, I cannot frame my tongue to feign,
20   To cloak the truth for praise, without desert,
Of them that list° all vice for to retain.   *desire*
I cannot honor them that sets their part
With Venus and Bacchus all their life long,[5]
Nor hold my peace of them although I smart.
25   I cannot crouch nor kneel nor do so great a wrong
To worship them like God on earth alone
That are as wolves these sely° lambs among.   *innocent*
I cannot with my words complain and moan
And suffer naught, nor smart without complaint,
30   Nor turn the word that from my mouth is gone;
I cannot speak and look like a saint,
Use wiles for wit° and make deceit a pleasure,   *wisdom*
And call craft counsel, for profit still to paint;

6. I.e., intelligence does not help one earn ("yerne") a defense, [nor does it help] to plead or prattle about one's innocence.
7. Let God do the steering. "Bear low": be humble.
1. A friend of Wyatt's. This verse epistle of informal satire is based on the tenth satire of the Italian Luigi Alamanni but is personalized and Anglicized in detail by Wyatt. It was apparently written during Wyatt's banishment from court in 1536. Lines 1–52 of the poem are missing from the authoritative Egerton Manuscript and are here supplied from the Devonshire Manuscript.
2. I.e., my retirement from court is not because I scorn great and powerful princes. But I esteem them less than do the "common sort" of people, who judge by externals only (lines 10–13).
3. I.e., I do not wish to attack honor or to call dishonorable desire honorable.
4. I.e., cannot pretend that black is not black.
5. I.e., I cannot honor those who devote themselves to Venus (goddess of love) and Bacchus (god of drinking).

I cannot wrest the law to fill the coffer,
35 With innocent blood to feed myself fat,
And do most hurt where most help I offer.
I am not he that can allow° the state   *approve*
Of high Caesar and damn Cato[6] to die,
That with his death did 'scape out of the gate
40 From Caesar's hands, if Livy[7] do not lie,
And would not live where liberty was lost,
So did his heart the common weal[8] apply.
I am not he such eloquence to boast
To make the crow singing as the swan,
45 Nor call the lion of coward beasts the most,
That cannot take a mouse as the cat can;
And he that dieth for hunger of the gold,
Call him Alexander,[9] and say that Pan
Passeth Apollo in music many fold;[1]
50 Praise Sir Thopas for a noble tale,
And scorn the story that the Knight told;[2]
Praise him for counsel that is drunk of ale;
Grin when he laugheth that beareth all the sway,°   *power*
Frown when he frowneth, and groan when he is pale;
55 On other's lust° to hang both night and day—   *pleasure*
None of these points would ever frame in me;°   *appeal to me*
My wit is naught: I cannot learn the way;
And much the less of things that greater be
That asken help of colors of device°   *tricks of rhetoric*
60 To join the mean with each extremity:
With the nearest virtue to cloak alway the vice,
And, as to purpose likewise it shall fall,[3]
To press the virtue that it may not rise;
As drunkenness, good fellowship to call;
65 The friendly foe, with his double face,
Say he is gentle and courteous therewithal;
And say that favel° hath a goodly grace   *flattery*
In eloquence; and cruelty to name
Zeal of justice, and change in time and place;
70 And he that suffereth offense without blame,
Call him pitiful, and him true and plain
That raileth reckless to every man's shame;
Say he is rude that cannot lie and feign,
The lecher a lover, and tyranny
75 To be the right of a prince's reign.
I cannot, I: no, no, it will not be.
This is the cause that I could never yet
Hang on their sleeves that weigh, as thou mayst see,
A chip of chance more than a pound of wit.

---

6. Cato the Younger, the famous Roman patriot
who committed suicide rather than submit to Caesar.
7. Titus Livius (59 B.C.E.–17 C.E.), the great
Roman historian.
8. The common good, or the state.
9. Alexander yearned for more worlds to conquer.

1. Pan's music was simple and rustic, played on
"Pan's pipes."
2. The silly tale of Sir Thopas, in Chaucer's *Canterbury Tales,* is told by Chaucer himself, until the
Host forces him to stop. *The Knight's Tale* is the
most courtly and dignified of the tales.
3. I.e., as will also be opportune.

80 This maketh me at home to hunt and hawk
    And in foul weather at my book to sit;
    In frost and snow then with my bow to stalk.
    No man doth mark whereso I ride or go.
    In lusty leas° at liberty I walk,   *pleasant fields*
85 And of these news I feel nor weal nor woe,
    Save that a clog doth hang yet at my heel.[4]
    No force° for that, for it is ordered so   *no matter*
    That I may leap both hedge and dike full well.
    I am not now in France, to judge the wine,
90 With sav'ry sauce the delicates° to feel;   *delicacies*
    Nor yet in Spain, where one must him incline,
    Rather than to be, outwardly to seem.
    I meddle not with wits that be so fine;
    Nor Flanders' cheer[5] letteth° not my sight to deem   *hinders*
95 Of black and white, nor taketh my wit away
    With beastliness, they, beasts, do so esteem.
    Nor am I not where Christ is given in prey
    For money, poison, and treason—at Rome[6]
    A common practice, usèd night and day.
100 But here I am in Kent and Christendom,
    Among the Muses, where I read and rhyme;
    Where if thou list, my Poins, for to come,
    Thou shalt be judge how I do spend my time.

D. MS., E. MS.

---

4. "I feel neither happiness nor unhappiness about current political affairs, except that a 'clog' (i.e., his confinement or parole to his estate) keeps me from traveling far." Note that "news" is a plural in Elizabethan English.
5. I.e., the drinking for which Flemings were noto-

rious in the 16th century.
6. In *Tottel's Miscellany*, published in the reign of the Catholic Queen Mary, these lines were altered as follows: "where *truth* is given in prey / For money, poison and treason; *of some*."

Literature of the Sacred

When, in the late 1520s, the Catholic authorities of England tried to burn all copies of William Tyndale's English translation of the New Testament, they were attempting to stop the spread of what they viewed as a dangerous new plague of heresies spreading out from Luther's Germany. The plague was the Protestant Reformation, a movement opposed to crucial aspects of both the belief system and the institutional structure of Roman Catholicism.

Many of the key tenets of the Reformation were not new: they had been anticipated in England by the teachings of John Wycliffe in the fourteenth century. But Wycliffe's ideas had been denounced as heretical, and many of his followers, known as Lollards, had been executed. Officially at least, England in the early sixteenth century had a single religion, Catholicism, whose acknowledged head was the pope in Rome. In 1517, drawing upon long-standing currents of dissent, Martin Luther, an Augustinian monk and professor of theology at the University of Wittenberg, challenged the authority of the pope and attacked several key doctrines of the Catholic church. According to Luther, the church, with its elaborate hierarchical structure centered in Rome, its rich monasteries and convents, and its enormous political influence, had become hopelessly corrupt, a conspiracy of venal priests who manipulated popular superstitions to enrich themselves and amass worldly power. Luther began by vehemently attacking the sale of indulgences—certificates promising the remission of punishments to be suffered in the afterlife by souls sent to Purgatory to expiate their sins. Purgatory, he argued, had no foundation in Scripture, which in his view was the only legitimate source of religious truth (*sola scriptura*). Christians would be saved not by scrupulously following the ritual practices fostered by the Catholic church— observing fast days, reciting the ancient Latin prayers, endowing chantries to say prayers for the dead, and so on—but by faith and faith alone (*sola fide*).

This challenge spread and gathered force, especially in Northern Europe, where major leaders like the Swiss pastor Zwingli and the French theologian Calvin transformed religious institutions and elaborated various and sometimes conflicting doctrinal principles. Calvin, whose thought came to be particularly influential in England, emphasized the obligation of governments to implement God's will in the world. He advanced too the doctrine of predestination by which, as he put it, "God adopts some to hope of life and sentences others to eternal death." God's "secret election" of the saved made Calvin uncomfortable, but his study of the Scriptures had led him to conclude that "only a small number, out of an incalculable multitude, should obtain salvation." It might seem that such a conclusion would lead to passivity or even despair, but for Calvin predestination was a mystery bound up with faith, confidence, and an active engagement in the fashioning of a Christian community.

The Reformation had a direct and powerful impact on those realms where it gained control. Monasteries were sacked, their possessions seized by princes or sold off to the highest bidder; monks and nuns, expelled from their cloisters, were encouraged to break their vows of chastity and find spouses, as Luther and his wife, a former nun, had done. In the great cathedrals and in hundreds of smaller churches and chapels, the elaborate altarpieces, bejewelled crucifixes, crystal reliquaries holding the bones of saints, venerated statues, and paintings were attacked as "idols" and often defaced or destroyed. Protestant congregations continued, for the most part, to celebrate the most sacred Christian ritual, the Eucharist or Lord's Supper, but they did so in a profoundly different spirit from the Catholic church, more as commemoration than as miracle, and the service was conducted not in the old liturgical Latin but in the vernacular.

The Reformation was at first vigorously resisted in England. Protestant writings were seized by officials of the church and the state and burned. Protestants who made their views known were persecuted, driven to flee the country or arrested, put on trial, and burned at the stake. But the situation changed drastically after Henry decided to seek a divorce from his first wife, Catherine of Aragon, in order to marry Anne Boleyn. When the Roman Catholic Church, under pressure from Catherine's powerful family, refused to grant the divorce, Henry defied papal authority, declared himself head of the church in England, seized the wealth of the monasteries, and unleashed Protestant energies, including fierce bursts of iconoclasm. On most doctrinal questions, however, Henry remained an orthodox Catholic, and in the latter part of his reign, his clerical authorities renewed the persecution of Protestants.

The turn toward the Reformation was more decisive in the reign (1547–53) of Henry's heir, Edward VI, and the attempt by Edward's successor, Mary (daughter of Catherine of Aragon), to reimpose Roman Catholicism as the national religion came to an end with her death in 1558. The long reign of Henry's daughter by Anne Boleyn, Elizabeth I (1558–1603), firmly established Protestantism as the faith of the Church of England. Reformation doctrine shaped the vernacular liturgy eloquently formulated in the officially sanctioned *Book of Common Prayer* and was reinforced in the homilies or sermons that ministers were commanded annually to deliver to their parishioners.

Once Protestantism began to take root in England, it proved impossible for authorities to eradicate it, as it would later prove impossible to eradicate Catholicism. In large part this tenacity arose from the passionate, often suicidal heroism of men and women who felt that their soul's salvation depended upon the precise character of their Christianity and who consequently embraced martyrdom rather than repudiate their beliefs. It arose too from a mid-fifteenth-century technological innovation that made it extremely difficult to suppress unwelcome ideas: the printing press. Early Protestants quickly grasped that with a few clandestine presses they could defy the Catholic authorities and flood the country with their texts. "How many printing presses there be in the world," wrote the Protestant polemicist and martyrologist John Foxe, "so many blockhouses there be against the high castle" of the pope in Rome, "so that either the pope must abolish knowledge and printing or printing at length will root him out." By the century's end it was the Catholics, as well as the more radical Protestants—known as Puritans—who were using the clandestine press to propagate their beliefs in the face of official persecution.

THE ENGLISH BIBLE

Protestantism required direct lay access to the Bible, which meant in practice the widespread availability of vernacular translations. The Roman Catholic Church had not always and everywhere opposed such translations, but it generally preferred that the populace encounter the Scriptures through the interpretations of the priests, trained to read the Latin translation known as the Vulgate. In times of great conflict this preference for clerical mediation hardened into outright prohibition of vernacular translation and into persecution and book burning.

Zealous Protestants set out, in the teeth of fierce opposition, to put the Bible into the hands of the laity. A remarkable translation of the New Testament, by an English Lutheran named William Tyndale, was printed on the Continent and smuggled into England in 1525; Tyndale's translation of the Pentateuch, the first five books of the Hebrew Bible, followed in 1530. Many copies of these translations were seized and destroyed, as was the translator himself, but the printing press made it extremely difficult for authorities to eradicate books for which there was a passionate demand. The English Bible was a force that could not be suppressed, and it became, in its various forms, the single most important book of the sixteenth century.

Tyndale's translation was completed by an associate, Miles Coverdale, whose rendering of the Psalms proved to be particularly influential. Their joint labor was the basis for the Great Bible (1539), the first authorized version of the Bible in English, a copy of which was ordered to be placed in every church in the kingdom. With the accession of Edward VI, many editions of the Bible followed, but the process was sharply reversed when Mary came to the throne in 1553. Along with people condemned as heretics, English Bibles were burned in great bonfires.

Marian persecution was indirectly responsible for what would become the most scholarly Protestant English Bible, the translation known as the Geneva Bible, prepared, with extensive, learned, and often fiercely polemical marginal notes, by English exiles in Calvin's Geneva and widely diffused in England after Elizabeth came to the throne. In addition, Elizabethan church authorities ordered a careful revision of the Great Bible, and this version, known as the Bishops' Bible, was the one read in the churches. The success of the Geneva Bible in particular prompted those Elizabethan Catholics who now in turn found themselves in exile to bring out a vernacular translation of their own, the Douay-Rheims version, in order to counter the Protestant readings and glosses.

After Elizabeth's death in 1603, King James I and his bishops ordered that a revised translation of the entire Bible be undertaken by a group of forty-seven scholars. The result was the Authorized Version, more popularly known as the King James Bible.

In the passage selected here, 1 Corinthians 13, Tyndale's use of the word "love," echoed by the Geneva Bible, is set against the Catholic "charity." The latter term would gesture toward the religious doctrine of "works," against the Protestant insistence on salvation by faith alone. It is a sign of the conservative, moderate Protestantism of the King James version that it too opts for "charity."

From Tyndale's Translation

Though I spake with the tongues of men and angels, and yet had no love, I were even as sounding brass: or as a tinkling cymbal. And though I could prophesy, and understood all secrets, and all knowledge: yea, if I had all faith, so that I could move mountains out of their places, and yet had no love, I were nothing. And though I bestowed all my goods to feed the poor, and though I gave my body even that I burned, and yet had no love, it profiteth me nothing.

Love suffereth long, and is courteous. Love envieth not. Love doth not frowardly,[1] swelleth not, dealeth not dishonestly, seeketh not her own, is not provoked to anger, thinketh not evil, rejoiceth not in iniquity: but rejoiceth in the truth, suffereth all things, believeth all things, hopeth all things, endureth in all things. Though that prophesying fail, other[2] tongues shall cease, or knowledge vanish away, yet love falleth never away.

1. Perversely, evilly.   2. Or.

For our knowledge is unperfect and our prophesying is unperfect. But when that which is perfect is come, then that which is unperfect shall be done away. When I was a child, I spake as a child, I understood as a child, I imagined as a child. But as soon as I was a man, I put away childishness. Now we see in a glass,[3] even in a dark speaking: but then shall we see face to face. Now I know unperfectly: but then shall I know even as I am known. Now abideth faith, hope, and love, even these three: but the chief of these is love.

1525, 1535

From The Geneva Bible[1]

Though I speak with the tongues of men and Angels, and have not love, I am as sounding brass, or a tinkling cymbal. [2]And though I had the gift of prophecy, and knew all secrets and all knowledge, yea, if I had all faith, so that I could remove mountains, and had not love, I were nothing. [3]And though I feed the poor with all my goods, and though I give my body, that I be burned, and have not love, it profiteth me nothing. [4]Love suffereth long: it is bountiful: love envieth not: love doth not boast itself: it is not puffed up: [5]It disdaineth not: it seeketh not her own things: it is not provoked to anger: it thinketh not evil: [6]It rejoiceth not in iniquity, but rejoiceth in the truth: [7]It suffereth all things: it believeth all things: it hopeth all things: it endureth all things. [8]Love doth never fall away, though that prophesyings be abolished, or the tongues cease, or knowledge vanish away. [9]For we know in part, and we prophesy in part. [10]But when that which is perfect is come, then that which is in part shall be abolished. [11]When I was a child, I spake as a child, I understood as a child, I thought as a child: but when I became a man, I put away childish things. [12]For now we see through a glass darkly:[2] but then shall we see face to face. Now I know in part: but then shall I know even as I am known. [13]And now abideth faith, hope, and love, even these three: but the chiefest of these is love.

1560, 1602

From The Douay-Rheims Version

If I speak with the tongues of men and of Angels, and have not charity, I am become as sounding brass, or a tinkling cymbal. [2]And if I should have prophecy, and knew all mysteries, and all knowledge, and if I should have all faith so that I could remove mountains, and have not charity, I am nothing. [3]And if I should distribute all my goods to be meat[1] for the poor, and if I should deliver my body so that I burn, and have not charity, it doth profit me nothing.

---

3. Mirror. "Dark": obscure, unclear. This metaphor of indirect and imperfect sight seems to derive from Plato's Allegory of the Cave (*Republic* 7).

1. The Geneva Bible is the earliest English version printed with verse divisions.
2. By means of a mirror, obscurely.
1. Food (in general).

[4]Charity is patient, is benign: charity envieth not, dealeth not perversely: is not puffed up, [5]is not ambitious, seeketh not her own, is not provoked to anger, thinketh not evil: [6]rejoiceth not upon iniquity, but rejoiceth with the truth: [7]suffereth all things, believeth all things, hopeth all things, beareth all things. [8]Charity never falleth away: whether prophecies shall be made void, or tongues shall cease, or knowledge shall be destroyed. [9]For in part we know, and in part we prophesy. [10]But when that shall come that is perfect, that shall be made void that is in part. [11]When I was a little one, I spake as a little one, I understood as a little one, I thought as a little one. But when I was made a man, I did away the things that belonged to a little one. [12]We see now by a glass in a dark sort: but then face to face. Now I know in part: but then I shall know as also I am known. [13]And now there remain faith, hope, charity, these three, but the greater of these is charity.

1582

From The Authorized (King James) Version

Though I speak with the tongues of men and of angels, and have not charity, I am become as sounding brass, or a tinkling cymbal. [2]And though I have the gift of prophecy, and understand all mysteries, and all knowledge; and though I have all faith, so that I could remove mountains, and have no charity, I am nothing. [3]And though I bestow all my goods to feed the poor, and though I give my body to be burned, and have not charity, it profiteth me nothing. [4]Charity suffereth long, and is kind; charity envieth not; charity vaunteth not itself, is not puffed up, [5]doth not behave itself unseemly, seeketh not her own, is not easily provoked, thinketh no evil; [6]rejoiceth not in iniquity, but rejoiceth in the truth; [7]beareth all things, believeth all things, hopeth all things, endureth all things. [8]Charity never faileth: but whether there be prophecies, they shall fail; whether there be tongues, they shall cease; whether there be knowledge, it shall vanish away. [9]For we know in part, and we prophesy in part. [10]But when that which is perfect is come, then that which is in part shall be done away. [11]When I was a child, I spake as a child, I understood as a child, I thought as a child: but when I became a man, I put away childish things. [12]For now we see through a glass, darkly; but then face to face: now I know in part; but then shall I know even as also I am known. And now abideth faith, hope, charity, these three; but the greatest of these is charity.

1611

WILLIAM TYNDALE

Educated at Oxford, William Tyndale (ca. 1490–1536) became a lecturer at Cambridge, where he was associated with a group of humanist scholars who met regularly at the White Horse Inn. Having become convinced that salvation depended upon direct access to the word of God, he sought support to undertake a translation of the Bible into English, but English church authorities, concerned about the spread of heresies, blocked this project. In 1524 Tyndale went to Germany, where with the financial assistance of wealthy London merchants, he completed a translation of the New Testament the following year. Deeply influenced by the writings of Martin Luther and other reformers, he also wrote a series of doctrinal and polemical works, such as *The Obedience of a Christian Man* (1527), that eloquently express the Protestant hope of salvation through faith alone and reject the principles and practices of Roman Catholicism. Because of their vitriolic assaults upon the Catholic church, Protestants like Tyndale were often accused of fomenting rebellion. *The Obedience of a Christian Man* attempts to answer the charge by insisting upon the subject's absolute secular obligation to obey the king. At Anne Boleyn's urging, Henry VIII read it and is reported to have remarked that "This is a book for me and for all kings to read." Notwithstanding this supposed endorsement, English Catholic authorities during Henry's reign managed to lure Tyndale into a trap and had him executed in Vilvorde, Flanders.

From The Obedience of a Christian Man

[THE FORGIVENESS OF SINS]

* * *For sin we through fragility never so oft, yet as soon as we repent and come into the right way again, and unto the testament which God hath made in Christ's blood, our sins vanish away as smoke in the wind, and as darkness at the coming of light; or as thou castest a little blood, or milk, into the main sea: insomuch that whosoever goeth about to make satisfaction for his sins to God-ward, saying in his heart, This much have I sinned, this much will I do again; or this-wise will I live to make amends withal; or this will I do, to get heaven withal; the same is an infidel, faithless, and damned in his deed-doing, and hath lost his part in Christ's blood; because he is disobedient unto God's testament, and setteth up another of his own imagination, unto which he will compel God to obey. If we love God, we have a commandment to love our neighbor also, as saith John in his epistle;[1] and if we have offended him, to make him amends; or if we have not wherewith, to ask him forgiveness, and to do and suffer all things for his sake, to win him to God, and to nourish peace and unity. But to God-ward Christ is an everlasting satisfaction, and ever sufficient.[2]

[SCRIPTURAL INTERPRETATION]

Thou shalt understand, therefore, that the Scripture hath but one sense, which is the literal sense. And that literal sense is the root and ground of all, and the anchor that never faileth, whereunto if thou cleave, thou canst never err or go out of the way. And if thou leave the literal sense, thou canst not but go out of the way. Neverthelater,[3] the Scripture useth proverbs, simili-

---

1. "If a man say, I love God, and hateth his brother, he is a liar: for he that loveth not his brother whom he hath seen, how can he love God whom he hath not seen? And this commandment have we from him, That he who loveth God love his brother also" (1 John 4.20–21).
2. To the ecclesiastical commissioners who exam-

ined Tyndale's works in 1530, this passage was clearly heretical. One of the commissioners, Sir Thomas More, lambasted it as constituting an encouragement to sin, since it made obtaining forgiveness seem such an easy matter.
3. Nevertheless.

tudes, riddles, or allegories, as all other speeches do; but that which the proverb, similitude, riddle, or allegory signifieth, is ever the literal sense, which thou must seek out diligently: as in the English we borrow words and sentences of one thing, and apply them unto another, and give them new significations. We say, "Let the sea swell and rise as high as he will, yet hath God appointed how far he shall go": meaning that the tyrants shall not do what they would, but that only which God hath appointed them to do. "Look ere thou leap": whose literal sense is, "Do nothing suddenly, or without advisement." "Cut not the bough that thou standest upon": whose literal sense is, "Oppress not the commons"; and is borrowed of hewers. When a thing speedeth[4] not well, we borrow speech, and say, "The bishop hath blessed it"; because that nothing speedeth well that they meddle withal. If the porridge be burned too, or the meat over-roasted, we say, "The bishop hath put his foot in the pot," or "The bishop hath played the cook"; because the bishops burn whom they lust,[5] and whosoever displeaseth them. "He is a pontifical fellow"; that is, proud and stately. "He is popish"; that is, super-stitious and faithless.

* * *

Beyond all this, when we have found out the literal sense of the Scripture by the process of the text, or by a like text of another place, then go we, and as the Scripture borroweth similitudes of worldly things, even so we again borrow similitudes or allegories of the Scripture, and apply them to our pur-poses; which allegories are no sense of the Scripture, but free things besides the Scripture, and altogether in the liberty of the Spirit. * * * This allegory proveth nothing, neither can do. For it is not the Scripture, but an ensample or a similitude borrowed of the Scripture, to declare a text or a conclusion of the Scripture more expressly, and to root it and grave it in the heart. For a similitude, or an ensample,[6] doth print a thing much deeper in the wits of a man than doth a plain speaking, and leaveth behind him as it were a sting to prick him forward, and to awake him withal. Moreover, if I could not prove with an open[7] text that which the allegory doth express, then were the allegory a thing to be jested at, and of no greater value than a tale of Robin Hood.

1527, 1528

4. Succeeds, prospers.
5. Whomever they please.

6. Example. "Grave": engrave.
7. Plain, clear.

JOHN CALVIN

Born to middle-class parents in Picardy, France, and trained as a lawyer, Calvin (1509–1564) was steeped in the Greek and Latin learning associated with Renais-sance humanism. He acquired as well a knowledge of Hebrew, so that he was powerfully equipped to respond to the call, from Erasmus and others, for a study of the Bible in its original languages. Drawn increasingly toward Protestantism, Calvin left Catholic France for Switzerland, where he eventually became the dominant figure in Geneva, establishing a stern theocratic rule. Through his voluminous writings, he also became the principal theologian of the Protestant Reformation, exercising immense influence in England as well as on the Continent. His major work, revised in successive Latin and French editions and widely translated, is *The Institution of Christian Religion*. The passage selected here is from Calvin's famous, deeply troubling account of the doctrine of predestination, according to which God has determined from eternity whom he will save and whom he will damn, regardless of the merits or defects of these individuals. The translation, closely adhering to the Latin original, is by Thomas Norton (1532–1584), a lawyer and member of Parliament and, with Thomas Sackville, the author of the earliest English tragedy in blank verse, *Gorboduc*—first performed in the same year (1561) that his translation of Calvin appeared.

From The Institution of Christian Religion, written in Latin by Master John Calvin, and translated into English according to the author's last edition

From *Book 3, Chapter 21*
Of the eternal election, whereby God hath predestinate some to salvation, and other some to destruction

But now whereas the covenant of life is not equally preached to all men, and with them to whom it is preached it doth not either equally or continually find like place: in this diversity the wondrous depth of the judgment of God appeareth. For neither is it any doubt but that this diversity also serveth the free choice of God's eternal election.[1] If it be evident that it is wrought by the will of God that salvation is freely offered to some, and other some are debarred from coming to it, here by and by[2] arise great and hard questions which cannot otherwise be discussed than if the godly minds have that certainly stablished which they ought to hold[3] concerning election and predestination. This is (as many think) a cumbersome[4] question: because they think nothing to be less reasonable than of the common multitude of men some to be foreordained to salvation, other some to destruction. But how they wrongfully encumber themselves shall afterward be evident by the framing of the matter together.[5] Beside that in the very same darkness which maketh men afraid, not only the profitableness of this doctrine but also the most sweet fruit showeth forth itself. We shall never be clearly persuaded as we ought to be, that our salvation floweth out of the fountain of the free mercy of God, till his eternal election be known to us, which by this comparison brightly setteth forth the grace of God, that he doth not without difference adopt all into the hope of salvation, but giveth to some that which he denieth to other. How much the ignorance of this principle diminisheth of the glory of God, how much it withdraweth from true humility, it is plain to see.

* * *

They which shut the gates, that none may be bold to come to the tasting of this doctrine, do no less wrong to men than to God: because neither shall

---

1. Choice—i.e., of whom to save.
2. Immediately.
3. Believe. "Stablished": established.

4. Troublesome.
5. I.e., from the following discussion.

any other thing suffice to humble us as we ought to be, neither shall we otherwise feel from our heart how much we are bound to God. Neither yet is there any otherwhere the upholding stay of sound affiance,[6] as Christ himself teacheth, which to deliver us from all fear, and to make us unvanquishable among so many dangers, ambushes, and deadly battles, promiseth that whatsoever he hath received of[7] his Father to keep shall be safe.[8] Whereof we gather that they shall with continual trembling be miserable, whosoever they be that know not themselves to be the proper possession of God; and therefore that they do very ill provide both for themselves and for all the faithful, which, in being blind at these three profits which we have touched,[9] would wish the whole foundation of our salvation to be quite taken from among us. Moreover, hereby the Church appeareth unto us, which otherwise (as Bernard rightly teacheth)[1] were not possible to be found nor to be known among creatures, because both ways in marvelous wise[2] it lieth hidden: within the bosom of blessed predestination, and within the mass of miserable damnation.

But ere I enter into the matter itself, I must beforehand in two sorts speak to two sorts of men.[3] That the entreating[4] of predestination, whereas of itself it is somewhat cumbersome, is made very doubtful, yea, and dangerous, the curiousness of men is the cause: which can by no stops be refrained from wandering into forbidden compasses,[5] and climbing up on high; which, if it may, will leave to God no secret which it will not search and turn over. Into this boldness and importunacy[6] forasmuch as we commonly see many to run headlong, and among those some that are otherwise not evil men, here is fit occasion to warn them what is in this behalf[7] the due measure of their duty. First, therefore, let them remember that when they inquire upon predestination, they pierce into the secret closets[8] of the wisdom of God: whereinto if any man too carelessly and boldly break in, he shall both not attain wherewith to satisfy his curiousness, and he shall enter into a maze whereof he shall find no way to get out again. For neither is it meet[9] that man should freely search those things which God hath willed to be hidden in himself, and to turn over from very eternity the height of wisdom,[1] which he willed to be honored and not to be conceived, that by it also he mought[2] be marvelous unto us. Those secrets of his will which he hath determined to be opened unto us, he hath disclosed in his Word:[3] and he hath determined, so far as he foresaw to pertain to us and to be profitable for us.[4]

* * *

6. Trust, faith. "Stay": support.
7. From.
8. "My sheep hear my voice, and I know them, and they follow me: And I give unto them eternal life; and they shall never perish, neither shall any man pluck them out of my hand. My Father, which gave them me, is greater than all; and no man is able to pluck them out of my Father's hand" (John 10.27–29).
9. I.e., God's free mercy, God's glory, and our true humility.
1. St. Bernard of Clairvaux (1090–1153), in his *Sermons on the Song of Songs*.
2. In a marvelous fashion.
3. I must first speak in two different ways about

two sorts of men.
4. Treating, discussing.
5. Places.
6. Pertinacity, stubborn persistence.
7. In this regard.
8. Inner chambers.
9. Fitting.
1. And to search out from eternity itself the sublimest wisdom.
2. Might. "Conceived": understood.
3. The Scriptures.
4. I.e., God has let us know, in the Scriptures, as much about these matters as he foresaw would be useful for us to know.

There be other which, when they have a will to remedy this evil,[5] do command all mention of predestination to be in a manner buried: at the least they teach men to flee from every manner of questioning thereof as from a rock. Although the moderation of these men be herein worthily to be praised, that they judge that mysteries should be tasted of with such sobriety, yet because they descend too much beneath the mean,[6] they little prevail with the wit[7] of man, which doth not lightly suffer itself to be restrained. Therefore, that in this behalf also we may keep a right end[8] we must return to the Word of the Lord, in which we have a sure rule of understanding. For the Scripture is the school of the Holy Ghost, in which as nothing is left out which is both necessary and profitable to be known, so nothing is taught but that which is behoveful[9] to learn. Whatsoever therefore is uttered in the Scripture concerning predestination, we must beware that we debar not the faithful from it, lest we should seem either enviously to defraud them of the benefit of their God, or to blame and accuse the Holy Ghost who hath published those things which it is in any wise[1] profitable to be suppressed.

* * *

That, therefore, which the Scripture clearly showeth, we say that God by eternal and unchangeable counsel hath once appointed whom in time to come he would take to salvation, and on the other side whom he would condemn to destruction. This counsel as touching the elect, we say to be grounded upon his free mercy, without any respect of the worthiness of man: but whom he appointeth to damnation, to them by his judgment (which is indeed just and irreprehensible but also incomprehensible) the entry of life is foreclosed. Now in the elect we set vocation to be the testimony of election; and then justification[2] to be another sign of the manifest showing of it, till they come to glory, wherein is the fulfilling of it. But as by vocation and election God maketh his elect, so by shutting out the reprobate either from the knowledge of his name or from the sanctification of his spirit, he doth as it were by these marks open what judgment abideth[3] for them. * * *

1561

5. I.e., the audacious attempt to learn more about predestination than Scripture teaches.
6. Descend to too low a level—i.e., go too far.
7. Intellect.
8. Keep within proper bounds.
9. Useful, advantageous.
1. In any way.
2. The state of being justified—i.e., freed from the penalty of sin and accounted righteous by God. The underlying Scriptural text for this passage is Romans 8.30: "whom he did predestinate, them he also called: and whom he called, them he also justified: and whom he justified, them he also glorified." "Testimony": evidence. "Vocation": a calling —a predisposition to the religious life.
3. Waits. "Open": reveal.

ANNE ASKEW

In the 1540s, Henry VIII sought to return the English church to a basically Catholic doctrinal position. and Protestants were subjected to persecution. The outspoken Protestant Anne Askew (1521–1546) was called in for questioning in 1545; the next year, she was tortured and burned at the stake. Askew's accounts of her two examinations were smuggled out of England and published in Germany (1546–47) by the reformer John Bale. The texts were later incorporated into John Foxe's *Acts and Monuments* (1563).

The theological controversies over the Eucharist, for which Askew and her companions along with many other Protestants and Catholics were willing to lay down their lives, require some explanation. Catholic doctrine held that sacraments properly performed were independent of the spiritual condition either of the priest or of the worshipper. Hence, for example, if the formula of consecration of the bread and wine was correctly spoken by a properly ordained priest, the miraculous transubstantiation of the Host into the body and blood of Christ would occur, whether or not the priest or the communicant was in a state of grace. Indeed, some Catholic theologians argued, since the bread had objectively been transformed into the body of God, even a mouse, nibbling on a consecrated host, would be receiving Christ's flesh. Protestants argued that the efficacy of certain key religious sacraments, including the Lord's Supper, depended on the spiritual state of the minister and the congregant. An evil priest, in such a conception, would not only be damning himself (as Catholics also believed) but would be turning the Lord's Supper into the Devil's Supper.

From The First Examination of Anne Askew

To satisfy your expectation, good people (sayeth she), this was my first examination in the year of our Lord 1545, and in the month of March. First, Christopher Dare examined me at Saddlers' Hall,[1] being one of the quest,[2] and asked if I did not believe that the sacrament hanging over the altar[3] was the very body of Christ really. Then I demanded this question of him: wherefore Saint Stephen was stoned to death.[4] And he said he could not tell. Then I answered that no more would I assoil[5] his vain question.

Secondly, he said that there was a woman which did testify that I should read[6] how God was not in temples made with hands. Then I showed him the seventh and the seventeenth chapters of the Acts of the Apostles, what Stephen and Paul had said therein.[7] Whereupon he asked me how I took those sentences. I answered that I would not throw pearls among swine,[8] for acorns were good enough.

Thirdly, he asked me wherefore I said that I had rather to read five lines in the Bible than to hear five masses in the temple. I confessed that I said no less. Not for the dispraise of either the Epistle or Gospel, but because the one did greatly edify me and the other[9] nothing at all. As Saint Paul doth witness in the fourteenth chapter of his first Epistle to the Corinthians, whereas he doth say: "If the trumpet giveth an uncertain sound, who will prepare himself to the battle?"

Fourthly, he laid unto my charge that I should say: "If an ill[1] priest ministered, it was the Devil and not God." My answer was that I never spake

---

1. Belonging to the guild of saddle-makers.
2. Inquest.
3. The holy wafers were sometimes held in a hanging vessel in the shape of a dove, symbolizing the Holy Ghost.
4. Stephen was martyred in Jerusalem after proclaiming that God "dwelleth not in temples made with hands" and accusing the priests of the temple of resisting the Holy Ghost and persecuting the prophets (Acts 7.48–60).

5. Resolve.
6. Would teach.
7. Acts 17.24 repeats the assertion of Acts 7 that God does not dwell in temples built by human hands.
8. Matthew 7.6. "Took": interpreted.
9. "The one . . . the other": i.e., the Bible . . . the mass.
1. Wicked.

such thing. But this was my saying: "That whatsoever he were which ministered unto me, his ill conditions could not hurt my faith, but in spirit I received nevertheless the body and blood of Christ." He asked me what I said concerning confession. I answered him my meaning, which was as Saint James sayeth, that every man ought to knowledge[2] his faults to other, and the one to pray for the other.

Sixthly, he asked me what I said to the king's book.[3] And I answered him that I could say nothing to it, because I never saw it.

Seventhly, he asked me if I had the spirit of God in me. I answered if I had not, I was but reprobate or cast away. Then he said he had sent for a priest to examine me, which was there at hand. The priest asked me what I said to the sacrament of the altar.[4] And required much to know therein my meaning. But I desired him again to hold me excused concerning that matter. None other answer would I make him, because I perceived him a papist.[5]

Eighthly, he asked me if I did not think that private masses did help souls departed.[6] And [I] said it was great idolatry to believe more in them than in the death which Christ died for us. Then they had me thence unto my lord mayor and he examined me, as they had before, and I answered him directly in all things as I answered the quest afore. Besides this my lord mayor laid one thing unto my charge which was never spoken of me but of them. And that was whether a mouse eating the host received God or no. This question did I never ask, but indeed they asked it of me, whereunto I made them no answer but smiled. Then the bishop's chancellor rebuked me and said that I was much to blame for uttering the Scriptures. For Saint Paul (he said) forbade women to speak or to talk of the word of God. I answered him that I knew Paul's meaning as well as he, which is, 1 Corinthians 14, that a woman ought not to speak in the congregation by the way of teaching. And then I asked him how many women he had seen go into the pulpit and preach? He said he never saw none. Then I said, he ought to find no fault in poor women, except they had offended the law. Then my lord mayor commanded me to ward. I asked him if sureties[7] would not serve me, and he made me short answer, that he would take none.

Then was I had to the Counter,[8] and there remained eleven days, no friend admitted to speak with me. But in the meantime there was a priest sent to me which said that he was commanded of the bishop to examine me, and to give me good counsel, which he did not. But first he asked me for what cause I was put in the Counter. And I told him I could not tell. Then he said it was great pity that I should be there without cause, and concluded that he was very sorry for me.

Secondly, he said it was told him that I should deny the sacrament of the altar. And I answered him again that, that I had said, I had said. Thirdly, he asked me if I were shriven.[9] I told him so that I might have one of these three, that is to say, Doctor Crome, Sir William, or Huntingdon,[1] I was

---

2. Acknowledge.
3. *A Necessary Doctrine and Erudition for Any Christian Man* (1543) sought to put a brake on reformers' "sinister understanding of Scripture, presumption, arrogancy, carnal liberty, and contention," by affirming a number of basically Catholic positions.
4. The Eucharist.

5. Follower of the pope—i.e., Roman Catholic.
6. By shortening their time in purgatory.
7. Guarantors of good behavior. "Ward": imprisonment.
8. A London prison.
9. Absolved after confessing to a priest.
1. Reformist preachers.

contented, because I knew them to be men of wisdom. "As for you or any other I will not dispraise, because I know ye not."

Then he said, "I would not have you think but that I or another that shall be brought you shall be as honest as they. For if we were not, ye may be sure, the king would not suffer us to preach."

Then I answered by the saying of Solomon, "By communing with the wise, I may learn wisdom: But by talking with a fool, I shall take scathe"[2] (Proverbs 1).

Fourthly, he asked me if the host should fall, and a beast did eat it, whether the beast did receive God or no. I answered, "Seeing ye have taken the pains to ask this question I desire you also to assoil it yourself. For I will not do it, because I perceive ye come to tempt me." And he said it was against the order of schools that he which asked the question should answer it. I told him I was but a woman and knew not the course of schools.[3] Fifthly, he asked me if I intended to receive the sacrament at Easter or no. I answered that else I were no Christian woman, and there I did rejoice, that the time was so near at hand. And then he departed thence with many fair words.

※　※　※

In the meanwhile he commanded his archdeacon to common[4] with me, who said unto me, "Mistress, wherefore are ye accused and thus troubled here before the bishop?"

To whom I answered again and said, "Sir, ask, I pray you, my accusers, for I know not as yet."

Then took he my book out of my hand and said, "Such books as this hath brought you to the trouble you are in. Beware," sayeth he, "beware, for he that made this book and was the author thereof was an heretic, I warrant you, and burnt in Smithfield."

Then I asked him if he were certain and sure that it was true that[5] he had spoken. And he said he knew well the book was of John Frith's making.[6] Then I asked him if he were not ashamed for to judge of the book before he saw it within or yet knew the truth thereof. I said also that such unadvised and hasty judgment is token apparent of a very slender wit.[7] Then I opened the book and showed it to him. He said he thought it had been another, for he could find no fault therein. Then I desired him no more to be so unadvisedly rash and swift in judgment, till he thoroughly knew the truth; and so he departed from me. ※ ※ ※

1546–47, 1563

---

2. Injury.
3. Rules governing Catholic theological debates; scholastic procedures.
4. Converse.
5. What.
6. The reformer John Frith was executed in 1533. *A Book Made by John Frith, Prisoner in the Tower*

of London, Answering unto Master More's Letter . . . Concerning the Sacrament of the Body and Blood of Christ, published in that year, was reissued in revised form in 1546, a few weeks before Askew was executed.
7. Shallow mind.

JOHN FOXE

John Foxe's career at Oxford University, where he had become a fellow of Magdalen College, was interrupted when his Puritan convictions led him to protest energetically against some college rules and practices. Foxe (1516–1587) then served as tutor to the children of various noble families, but when Mary became queen in 1553 and Protestants were once again persecuted, he fled to the Continent. His great book was already under way: the first version (Strasbourg, 1554) was in Latin and dealt with the persecutions suffered by the early reformers, particularly Wycliffe and John Hus. But the book grew and grew as Foxe received from England accounts of the hideous tortures and persecutions being inflicted on the Protestants there. When Elizabeth came to the throne in 1558, Foxe returned at once to England, and there he translated his Latin volume, adding to it hundreds of stories of the Marian martyrs (many based on eyewitness testimony, some on hearsay and rumor). The English edition was first published in 1563; often called "Foxe's Book of Martyrs," its title was *Acts and Monuments of these latter and perilous days, touching matters of the church, wherein are comprehended and described the great persecution and horrible troubles that have been wrought and practiced by the Romish prelates from the year of Our Lord a thousand to the time now present.*

It was immediately and enormously popular. Foxe saw life as an apocalyptic struggle between good and evil, Christ and Antichrist; his book is a compendium of memoirs, stories, personal letters, court records, and the like, rendering the words, acts, and sufferings of some hundreds of martyrs in graphic—if often fictionalized—detail. The final version of the book (1583) is massive—more than six thousand folio pages, containing four million words. Apart from fanning the flames of anti-Catholic feeling, Foxe had an immense influence on English nationalism. His stories, from the medieval crypto-Protestants burned for heresy to the Protestant martyrs who passed through the fiery trials of the Marian persecutions, portrayed England as the land of a new chosen people, destined to lead the way toward the kingdom of God on earth. Foxe's second edition (1570) was placed, by government order, in churches throughout England.

From Acts and Monuments

[THE DEATH OF ANNE ASKEW]

Hitherto we have entreated of this good woman; now it remaineth that we touch somewhat as touching her end and martyrdom. She being born of such stock and kindred that she might have lived in great wealth and prosperity, if she would rather have followed the world than Christ, but now she was so tormented, that she could neither live long in so great distress, neither yet by the adversaries be suffered to die in secret. Wherefore the day of her execution was appointed, and she brought into Smithfield in a chair, because she could not go on her feet, by means[1] of her great torments. When she was brought unto the stake she was tied by the middle with a chain that held up her body. When all things were thus prepared to the fire, the king's letters of pardon were brought, whereby to offer her safeguard of her life if she would recant, which she would neither receive, neither yet vouchsafe once to look upon. Shaxton[2] also was there present, who, openly that day recanting his opinions, went about with a long oration to cause her also to turn, against

---

1. Because.   2. Nicholas Shaxton, formerly bishop of Salisbury.

whom she stoutly resisted. Thus she being troubled so many manner of ways, and having passed through so many torments, having now ended the long course of her agonies, being compassed in with flames of fire, as a blessed sacrifice unto God, she slept in the Lord, in anno[3] 1546, leaving behind her a singular example of Christian constancy for all men to follow.

The Words and Behavior of the Lady Jane [Grey][4] upon the Scaffold

These are the words that the Lady Jane spake upon the scaffold, at the hour of her death. First, when she mounted upon the scaffold, she said to the people standing thereabout, "Good people, I am come hither to die, and by a law I am condemned to the same. The fact[5] against the queen's highness was unlawful, and the consenting thereunto by me; but, touching the procurement and desire thereof by me, or on my behalf, I do wash my hands thereof in innocency before God and the face of you, good Christian people, this day." And therewith she wrung her hands, wherein she had her book.[6] Then said she, "I pray you all, good Christian people, to bear me witness that I die a true Christian woman, and that I do look to be saved by no other mean but only by the mercy of God, in the blood of his only Son Jesus Christ; and I confess that when I did know the word of God I neglected the same, loved myself and the world; and therefore this plague and punishment is happily and worthily happened unto me for my sins; and yet I thank God of his goodness that he hath thus given me a time and respite to repent. And now, good people, while I am alive, I pray you assist me with your prayers." And then, kneeling down, she turned her to Fecknam,[7] saying, "Shall I say this psalm?" And he said, "Yea." Then said she the psalm of *Miserere mei Deus*[8] in English, in the most devout manner, throughout to the end; and then she stood up, and gave her maiden, Mistress Ellen, her gloves and handkerchief, and her book to Master Bruges.[9] And then she untied her gown, and the hangman pressed upon her to help her off with it; but she, desiring him to let her alone, turned towards her two gentlewomen, who helped her off therewith, and also with her frows paste[1] and neckerchief, giving her a fair handkerchief to knit about her eyes.

Then the hangman kneeled down and asked her forgiveness, whom she forgave most willingly. Then he willed her to stand upon the straw; which doing, she saw the block. Then she said, "I pray you, dispatch me quickly." Then she kneeled down, saying, "Will you take it off before I lay me down?" And the hangman said, "No, madam." Then tied she the kerchief about her eyes, and feeling for the block she said, "What shall I do? Where is it? Where is it?" One of the standers-by guiding her thereunto she laid her head down upon the block, and then stretched forth her body and said, "Lord, into thy

3. The year.
4. Daughter of the duke of Suffolk. On the death of King Edward VI she was proclaimed queen by the Protestant faction, but was overthrown by the Catholic Mary. For an account of her educational accomplishments, see Ascham's *The Schoolmaster* (p. 565).
5. Deed.
6. Bible.

7. John de Feckenham, last abbot of Westminster, employed by Queen Mary to convert obdurate heretics. He had tried in vain to convert Lady Jane to Catholicism.
8. Psalm 51.
9. Thomas Bridges, vice-lieutenant of the Tower of London.
1. Elaborate headdress.

hands I commend my spirit"; and so finished her life, in the year of our Lord God 1553, the twelfth day of February.

1563

BOOK OF COMMON PRAYER

The Protestant attack on Catholic rituals and the demand for worship in the vernacular led during the reign of Edward VI to the preparation of an English liturgical book, authorized to be the official and only text for public worship in England. Initiated by the Act of Uniformity in 1549, the work's principal architect was Thomas Cranmer (1489–1556). Cranmer, the archbishop of Canterbury, was at first careful to translate and shape the old Latin liturgy into a moderate, occasionally ambiguous compromise between Catholic and Protestant positions. His thorough revision in 1552 put the *Book of Common Prayer* much more decisively into the Protestant camp. Banned by the Catholic Mary Tudor, during whose reign Cranmer was executed, the *Book of Common Prayer* was restored, with small revisions, by Elizabeth, and has remained the basis of Anglican worship ever since. Cranmer was, among his other accomplishments, a brilliant prose stylist, and the cadences of the *Book of Common Prayer* have had a profound influence on the English language. The selection, part of the marriage service, is from the version used during the reign of Elizabeth.

From The Book of Common Prayer and Administration of the Sacraments and Other Rites and Ceremonies in the Church of England

From *The Form of Solemnization of Matrimony*

* * * At the day appointed for solemnization of matrimony, the persons to be married shall come into the body of the church with their friends and neighbors. And there the priest shall thus say:

Dearly beloved friends, we are gathered together here in the sight of God, and in the face of his congregation, to join together this man and this woman in holy matrimony, which is an honorable estate,[1] instituted of God in paradise, in the time of man's innocency, signifying unto us the mystical union that is betwixt Christ and his church: which holy estate Christ adorned and beautified with his presence and first miracle that he wrought in Cana of Galilee,[2] and is commended of Saint Paul to be honorable among all men,[3] and therefore is not to be enterprised[4] nor taken in hand unadvisedly, lightly, or wantonly, to satisfy men's carnal lusts and appetites, like brute beasts that have no understanding; but reverently, discreetly, advisedly, soberly, and in

---

1. State, condition.
2. He changed water into wine (John 2.1–11).
3. "Marriage is honorable in all, and the bed unde-

filed: but whoremongers and adulterers God will judge" (Hebrews 13.4).
4. Undertaken.

the fear of God, duly considering the causes for the which matrimony was ordained. One was, the procreation of children, to be brought up in the fear and nurture of the Lord, and praise of God. Secondly, it was ordained for a remedy against sin, and to avoid fornication, that such persons as have not the gift of continency might marry, and keep themselves undefiled members of Christ's body.[5] Thirdly, for the mutual society, help, and comfort that the one ought to have of the other, both in prosperity and adversity: into the which holy estate these two persons present come now to be joined. Therefore if any man can show any just cause why they may not lawfully be joined together, let him now speak, or else hereafter forever hold his peace.

And also speaking to the persons that shall be married, he shall say:

I require and charge you (as you will answer at the dreadful day of judgment, when the secrets of all hearts shall be disclosed) that if either of you do know any impediment why ye may not be lawfully joined together in matrimony, that ye confess it. For be ye well assured, that so many as be coupled together otherwise than God's word doth allow are not joined together by God, neither is their matrimony lawful.

At which day of marriage, if any man do allege and declare any impediment why they may not be coupled together in matrimony by God's law or the laws of this realm; and will be bound, and sufficient sureties with him, to the parties, or else put in a caution,[6] to the full value of such charges as the persons to be married doth sustain, to prove his allegation: then the solemnization must be deferred unto such time as the truth be tried. If no impediment be alleged, then shall the curate[7] say unto the man,

N.[8] Wilt thou have this woman to thy wedded wife, to live together after God's ordinance in the holy estate of matrimony? Wilt thou love her, comfort her, honor and keep her, in sickness and in health? And forsaking all other, keep thee only to her, so long as you both shall live?

The man shall answer,
I will.
Then shall the priest say to the woman,

N. Wilt thou have this man to thy wedded husband, to live together after God's ordinance in the holy estate of matrimony? Wilt thou obey him and serve him, love, honor, and keep him, in sickness and in health, and forsaking all other, keep thee only unto him, so long as you both shall live?

The woman shall answer,
I will.
Then shall the minister say,

Who giveth this woman to be married unto this man?

And the minister receiving the woman at her father or friend's hands, shall cause the man to take the woman by the right hand, and so either to give their troth[9] to other. The man first saying:

---

5. The church.
6. Surety.
7. A clergyman who has charge of a parish.

8. Name—i.e., the minister inserts the man's given name here.
9. Truth—i.e., pledge.

I N. take thee N. to my wedded wife, to have and to hold from this day forward, for better, for worse, for richer, for poorer, in sickness and in health, to love and to cherish, till death us depart,[1] according to God's holy ordinance: and thereto I plight thee my troth.

Then shall they loose their hands, and the woman taking again the man by the right hand shall say:

I N. take thee N. to my wedded husband, to have and to hold from this day forward, for better, for worse, for richer, for poorer, in sickness and in health, to love, cherish, and to obey, till death us depart, according to God's holy ordinance: and thereto I give thee my troth.

Then shall they again loose their hands, and the man shall give unto the woman a ring, laying the same upon the book with the accustomed duty[2] to the priest and clerk. And the priest taking the ring, shall deliver it unto the man, to put it upon the fourth finger of the woman's left hand. And the man taught by the priest shall say:

With this ring I thee wed: with my body I thee worship: and with all my worldly goods I thee endow. In the name of the Father, and of the Son, and of the Holy Ghost. Amen.

Then the man leaving the ring upon the fourth finger of the woman's left hand, the minister shall say:

O eternal God, creator and preserver of all mankind, giver of all spiritual grace, the author of everlasting life: send thy blessing upon these thy servants, this man and this woman, whom we bless in thy name; that as Isaac and Rebecca lived faithfully together,[3] so these persons may surely perform and keep the vow and covenant betwixt them made, whereof this ring given and received is a token and pledge, and may ever remain in perfect love and peace together, and live according unto thy laws: through Jesus Christ our Lord. Amen.

Then shall the priest join their right hands together, and say:

Those whom God hath joined together, let no man put asunder.

Then shall the minister speak unto the people:

Forasmuch as N. and N. have consented together in holy wedlock, and have witnessed the same before God and this company, and thereto have given and pledged their troth, either to other, and have declared the same by giving and receiving of a ring, and by joining of hands: I pronounce that they be man and wife together. In the name of the Father, and of the Son, and of the Holy Ghost. Amen.

And the minister shall add this blessing:

God the Father, God the Son, God the Holy Ghost, bless, preserve, and keep you: the Lord mercifully with his favor look upon you, and so fill you

---

1. Part.
2. Payment. "Book": Bible.

3. In Genesis 24–27.

with all spiritual benediction and grace that you may so live together in this life that in the world to come you may have life everlasting. Amen.

1559

BOOK OF HOMILIES

The Protestant archbishop of Canterbury, Thomas Cranmer, was responsible in 1547 for the publication of the *Book of Homilies*. Hoping to curb the influence of "ignorant preachers" and fearing the spread of unauthorized beliefs, Cranmer brought together twelve sermons that were, by royal and ecclesiastical decree, to be read over and over, in the order in which they were set forth, in parish churches throughout the realm. The *Homilies*, revised and reissued during the reign of Elizabeth, are political as well as religious documents. As the *Homily Against Disobedience* (added in 1570 in the aftermath of a Catholic uprising the preceding year) amply demonstrates, the intention was to teach the English people "to honor God and to serve their king with all humility and subjection, and godly and honestly to behave themselves toward all men." Artfully crafted and tirelessly reiterated, these sermons would have been familiar to almost everyone in the latter half of the sixteenth century.

From An Homily Against Disobedience and Willful Rebellion

* * * How horrible a sin against God and man rebellion is cannot possibly be expressed according unto the greatness thereof. For he that nameth rebellion, nameth not a singular, or one only sin, as is theft, robbery, murder, and suchlike, but he nameth the whole puddle and sink of all sins against God and man, against his prince, his country, his countrymen, his parents, his children, his kinfolks, his friends, and against all men universally: all sins, I say, against God and all men heaped together nameth he that nameth rebellion. For concerning the offense of God's majesty, who seeth not that rebellion riseth first by contempt of God and of his holy ordinances and laws, wherein he so straitly[1] commandeth obedience, forbiddeth disobedience and rebellion?[2] And besides the dishonor done by rebels unto God's holy name by their breaking of the oath made to their prince with the attestation of God's name and calling of his majesty to witness, who heareth not the horrible oaths and blasphemies of God's holy name that are used daily amongst rebels, that is[3] either amongst them or heareth the truth of their behavior? Who knoweth not that rebels do not only themselves leave all works necessary to be done upon workdays undone, whiles they accomplish their abominable work of rebellion, and do compel others that would gladly be well

---

1. Strictly.
2. Romans 13.1–2: "Let every soul be subject unto the higher powers. For there is no power but of God: the powers that be are ordained of God. Who- soever therefore resisteth the power, resisteth the ordinance of God: and they that resist shall receive to themselves damnation."
3. Who that is.

occupied to do the same, but also how rebels do not only leave the sabbath day of the Lord unsanctified, the temple and church of the Lord unresorted unto, but also do by their works of wickedness most horribly profane and pollute the sabbath day, serving Satan, and by doing of his work making it the devil's day instead of the Lord's day? Besides that, they compel good men that would gladly serve the Lord assembling in his temple and church upon his day, as becometh the Lord's servants, to assemble and meet armed in the field to resist the fury of such rebels. Yea, and many rebels, lest they should leave any part of God's commandments in the first table of his law[4] unbroken or any sin against God undone, do make rebellion for the maintenance of their images and idols, and of their idolatry committed or to be committed by them, and, in despite of God, cut and tear in sunder his Holy Word, and tread it under their feet, as of late ye know was done.[5]

As concerning the second table of God's law, and all sins that may be committed against man, who seeth not that they be all contained in rebellion? For first, the rebels do not only dishonor their prince, the parent of their country, but also do dishonor and shame their natural parents, if they have any, do shame their kindred and friends, disherit and undo forever their children and heirs. Thefts, robberies, and murders, which of all sins are most loathed of most men, are in no men so much, nor so perniciously and mischievously, as in rebels. For the most arrant thieves and cruelest murderers that ever were, so long as they refrain from rebellion, as they are not many in number, so spreadeth their wickedness and damnation unto a few: they spoil[6] but a few, they shed the blood but of few in comparison. But rebels are the cause of infinite robberies and murders of great multitudes, and of those also whom they should defend from the spoil and violence of other; and, as rebels are many in number, so doth their wickedness and damnation spread itself unto many. And if whoredom and adultery amongst such persons as are agreeable to such wickedness are (as they indeed be) most damnable, what are the forcible oppressions[7] of matrons and men's wives, and the violating and deflowering of virgins and maids, which are most rife with rebels; how horrible and damnable, think you, are they? Now, besides that rebels, by breach of their faith given and oath made to their prince, be guilty of most damnable perjury, it is wondrous to see what false colors and fained causes, by slanderous lies made upon their prince and the counselers, rebels will devise to cloak their rebellion withal, which is the worst and most damnable of all false-witness-bearing that may be possible. For what should I speak of coveting or desiring of other men's wives, houses, lands, goods, and servants in rebels, who by their wills would leave unto no man anything of his own?

Thus you see that all God's laws are by rebels violated and broken, and that all sins possible to be committed against God or man be contained in rebellion: which sins, if a man list[8] to name by the accustomed names of the seven capital or deadly sins, as pride, envy, wrath, covetousness, sloth, glut-

---

4. The first of the two "tables" (tablets) of stone on which God wrote the Ten Commandments (Deuteronomy 5.22): those on the first table specify our obligations to God, those on the second (below) our obligations to one another.
5. These enormities were purportedly perpetrated by the Catholic rebels who, in the winter of 1569, rose in the north of England against Queen Elizabeth and in support of her Catholic cousin, Mary, Queen of Scots (who had been imprisoned in England since 1568).
6. Despoil, plunder.
7. Rapes.
8. Wants.

tony, and lechery, he shall find them all in rebellion, and amongst rebels. For first, as ambition and desire to be aloft, which is the property of pride, stirreth up many men's minds to rebellion, so cometh it of a luciferian pride and presumption that a few rebellious subjects should set themselves up against the majesty of their prince, against the wisdom of the counselors, against the power and force of all nobility, and the faithful subjects and people of the whole realm. As for envy, wrath, murder, and desire of blood, and covetousness of other men's goods, lands, and livings, they are the inseparable accidents of all rebels, and peculiar properties[9] that do usually stir up wicked men unto rebellion. Now such as by riotousness, gluttony, drunkenness, excess of apparel, and unthrifty[1] games have wasted their own goods unthriftily, the same are most apt unto and most desirous of rebellion, whereby they trust to come by other men's goods unlawfully and violently. And where other gluttons and drunkards take too much of such meats and drinks as are served to tables, rebels waste and consume in short space all corn in barns, fields, or elsewhere, whole graners,[2] whole storehouses, whole cellars, devour whole flocks of sheep, whole droves of oxen and kine.[3] And as rebels that are married, leaving their own wives at home, do most ungraciously, so much more do unmarried men than any stallions or horses, being now by rebellion set at liberty from correction of laws which bridled them before, which abuse by force other men's wives and daughters, and ravish virgins and maidens most shamefully, abominably, and damnably. Thus all sins, by all names that sins may be named, and by all means that all sins may be committed and wrought, do all wholly upon heaps follow rebellion, and are to be found all together amongst rebels.

1570

9. Distinctive characteristics. "Inseparable accidents": unavoidable accompaniments.
1. Dissolute.

2. Granaries. "Corn": grain.
3. Cattle.

RICHARD HOOKER

Out of the long and bitter controversy over the government of the church in sixteenth-century England emerged one literary masterpiece. It is a work in eight books called *Of the Laws of Ecclesiastical Polity* (that is, the governmental system of the church). The author was the Oxford-educated Richard Hooker (1554–1600), a scholar and minister. In 1585 Hooker was master of the Temple (in modern terms, dean of a law school); one of his subordinates was a Puritan intellectual named Walter Travers. Between them a contentious debate developed on the burning question of how the church should be governed. The Puritan view was that no organization or authority in the church was valid unless it was based clearly and specifically on the Bible; the whole hierarchical system of the English church, with its deacons, priests, bishops, and archbishops, was accordingly wrong, along with its liturgy and most of its rituals. The position Hooker undertook to defend was that the Scriptures, or divine revelation, are not the only guide given to Christians for organizing and administering the church. Another guide is the law of nature, also divinely given, which can be discerned by the use of human reason.

In the book that grew out of his controversy with Travers, Hooker explained how the law of nature affords principles that justify the existing organization and practices of the English church. Book 1 of *Ecclesiastical Polity* deals with law in general and the several kinds of law; it pictures the entire universe, and also human society, as founded on reason and operating under various natural and divine laws. Book 2 deals with the nature, authority, and adequacy of Scripture. Books 3 to 5 explain and defend the rites, ceremonies, worship, and government of the English church. Books 6, 7, and 8 deal with various embodiments of authority, legitimate and illegitimate—elders, bishops, kings, and popes.

Hooker was a close and effective reasoner; avoiding the fiery invective or impassioned rhetoric that characterized most disputants of his time, he wrote in a calm, reasonable, and tolerant manner. His defense of existing ecclesiastical practices went back to fundamental principles, to a philosophy of nature and our place in it, to the subordination of the individual to a larger community and to God. It is this worldview, set forth in what is perhaps the period's most sonorous and quietly elegant prose, that makes *Ecclesiastical Polity* of enduring interest.

From Of the Laws of Ecclesiastical Polity

From *Book 1, Chapter* 3

[ON THE SEVERAL KINDS OF LAW, AND ON THE NATURAL LAW]

I am not ignorant that by law eternal the learned for the most part do understand the order, not which God hath eternally purposed himself in all his works to observe, but rather that which with himself he hath set down as expedient to be kept by all his creatures, according to the several[1] condition wherewith he hath indued them. They who thus are accustomed to speak apply the name of *Law* unto that only rule of working which superior authority imposeth; whereas we, somewhat more enlarging the sense thereof, term any kind of rule or canon whereby actions are framed a law. Now that law, which as it is laid up in the bosom of God they call *eternal*, receiveth according unto the different kinds of things which are subject unto it different and sundry kinds of names. That part of it which ordereth natural agents, we call usually *nature's* law; that which angels do clearly behold, and without any swerving observe, is a law *celestial* and heavenly; the law of *reason* that which bindeth creatures reasonable in this world, and with which by reason they may most plainly perceive themselves bound; that which bindeth them, and is not known but by special revelation from God, *divine* law; *human* law, that which out of the law either of reason or of God, men probably gathering to be expedient, they make it a law. All things, therefore, which are as they ought to be, are conformed unto *this second law eternal,* and even those things which to this *eternal* law are not conformable are notwithstanding in some sort ordered by *the first eternal law.* For what good or evil is there under the sun, what action correspondent to or repugnant unto the law which God hath imposed upon his creatures, but in or upon it God doth work according to the law which himself hath eternally purposed to keep, that is to say, the *first law eternal?* So that a twofold law eternal being thus made, it is not hard to conceive how they both take place in all things. Wherefore to come to the law of nature, albeit thereby we sometimes mean that manner of working

1. Different.

which God hath set for each created thing to keep, yet forasmuch as those things are termed most properly natural agents, which keep the law of their kind unwittingly, as the heavens and elements of the world, which can do no otherwise than they do, and forasmuch as we give unto intellectual natures the name of voluntary agents, that so we may distinguish them from the other, expedient it will be that we sever the law of nature observed by the one from that which the other is tied unto. Touching the former, their strict keeping of one tenure statute[2] and law is spoken of by all, but hath in it more than men have as yet attained to know, or perhaps ever shall attain, seeing the travail of wading herein is given of God to the sons of men, that perceiving how much the least thing in the world hath in it more than the wisest are able to reach unto, they may by this means learn humility. Moses in describing the work of creation, attributeth speech unto God: "God said, Let there be light, Let there be a firmament; Let the waters under the heaven be gathered together into one place; Let the earth bring forth; Let there be lights in the firmament of heaven."[3] Was this only the intent of Moses, to signify the greatness of God's power by the easiness of his accomplishing such effects without travail, pain, or labor? Surely it seemeth that Moses had herein besides this a further purpose: namely, first to teach that God did not work as a necessary, but a voluntary, agent, intending beforehand and decreeing with himself that which did outwardly proceed from him; secondly, to show that God did then institute a law natural to be observed by creatures, and therefore according to the manner of laws, the institution thereof is described as being established by solemn injunction. His commanding those things to be which are, and to be in such sort as they are, to keep that tenure and course which they do, importeth[4] the establishment of nature's law. This world's first creation, and the preservation since of things created, what is it but only so far forth a manifestation by execution, what the eternal law of God is concerning things natural? And as it cometh to pass in a kingdom rightly ordered, that after a law is once published, it presently takes effect far and wide, all states[5] framing themselves thereunto; even so let us think it fareth in the natural course of the world: since the time that God did first proclaim the edicts of his law upon it, heaven and earth have hearkened unto his voice, and their labor hath been to do his will. He made a law for the rain. He gave his decree unto the sea, that the waters should not pass his commandment.

Now if Nature should intermit her course and leave altogether, though it were but for a while, the observation of her own laws; if those principal and mother elements of the world, whereof all things in this lower world are made, should lose the qualities which now they have; if the frame of that heavenly arch erected over our heads should loosen and dissolve itself; if celestial spheres should forget their wonted motions and by irregular volubility[6] turn themselves any way as it might happen; if the prince of the lights of heaven, which now as a giant doth run his unwearied course, should as it were through a languishing faintness begin to stand and to rest himself; if

2. Decree establishing the domains of the various creatures and the conditions of service by which they hold these domains.
3. Genesis 1.3, 6, 9, 11, 14. In this period, Moses was generally assumed to be the author of the Book of Genesis.
4. Signifies, implies.
5. Conditions. "Presently": immediately.
6. Revolution, rotation.

the moon should wander from her beaten way, the times and seasons of the year blend themselves by disordered and confused mixture, the winds breathe out their last gasp, the clouds yield no rain, the earth be defeated of heavenly influence, the fruits of the earth pine away as children at the withered breasts of their mother no longer able to yield them relief, what would become of man himself, whom these things now do all serve? See we not plainly that obedience of creatures unto the law of Nature is the stay[7] of the whole world? Notwithstanding with Nature it cometh sometimes to pass as with art. Let Phidias[8] have rude and obstinate stuff to carve, though his art do that[9] it should, his work will lack that beauty which otherwise in fitter matter it might have had. He that striketh an instrument with skill may cause notwithstanding a very unpleasant sound, if the string whereon he striketh chance to be uncapable of harmony. In the matter whereof natural things consist, that of Theophrastus taketh place:[1] "much of it is oftentimes such as will by no means yield to receive that impression which were best and most perfect." Which defect in the matter of things natural, they who gave themselves unto the contemplation of Nature among the heathen observed often; but the true original cause thereof divine malediction,[2] laid for the sin of man upon those creatures which God had made for the use of man. This, being an article of that saving truth which God hath revealed unto his church, was above the reach of their[3] merely natural capacity and understanding. But howsoever these swervings are now and then incident into the course of Nature, nevertheless so constantly the laws of Nature are by natural agents observed that no man denieth but those things which Nature worketh are wrought either always or for the most part after one and the same manner. * * *

From *Book 1, Chapter 10*

[THE FOUNDATIONS OF SOCIETY]

That which hitherto we have set down is, I hope, sufficient to show their brutishness which imagine that religion and virtue are only as men will accompt of[4] them, that we might make as much accompt, if we would, of the contrary, without any harm unto ourselves, and that in Nature they are as indifferent one as the other. We see then how Nature itself teacheth laws and statutes to live by. The laws which have been hitherto mentioned do bind men absolutely, even as they are men, although they have never any settled fellowship, never any solemn agreement amongst themselves what to do or not to do. But forasmuch as we are not by ourselves sufficient to furnish ourselves with competent store[5] of things needful for such a life as our nature doth desire, a life fit for the dignity of man, therefore to supply those defects and imperfections which are in us living single and solely, by ourselves, we are naturally induced to seek communion and fellowship with others. This

7. Mainstay, support.
8. The greatest of ancient Greek sculptors (5th century B.C.E.).
9. What.
1. I.e., "that remark of Theophrastus carries weight." Theophrastus was a Greek writer of the 3rd century B.C.E., a follower of Aristotle and

inventor of the type of essay called the "character," which portrayed a type of person in concise form.
2. God's curse in Eden, which fell not only on sinful humankind but on the earth as well.
3. I.e., the ancient pagans'.
4. Esteem of, value.
5. Sufficient quantity.

was the cause of men's uniting themselves at the first in politic societies, which societies could not be without government, nor government without a distinct kind of law from that which hath been already declared. Two foundations there are which bear up public societies, the one a natural inclination whereby all men desire a sociable life and fellowship, the other an order expressly or secretly agreed upon, touching the manner of their union in living together. The latter is that which we call the law of a commonweal,[6] the very soul of a politic body, the parts whereof are by law animated, held together and set on work in such actions as the common good requireth. Laws politic, ordained for external order and regiment amongst men, are never framed as they should be, unless presuming the will of man to be inwardly obstinate, rebellious, and averse from all obedience unto the sacred laws of his nature—in a word, unless presuming man to be in regard of his depraved mind little better than a wild beast—they do accordingly provide notwithstanding so to frame his outward actions that they be no hindrance unto the common good for which societies are instituted; unless they do this, they are not perfect. It resteth therefore that we consider how Nature findeth out such laws of government as serve to direct even nature depraved to a right end.

All men desire to lead in this world an happy life. That life is led most happily, wherein all virtue is exercised without impediment or let. The Apostle[7] in exhorting men to contentment although they have in this world no more than very bare food and raiment, giveth us thereby to understand that those are even the lowest of things necessary; that if we should be stripped of all those things without which we might possibly be, yet these must be left, that destitution in these is such an impediment as, till it be removed, suffereth not the mind of man to admit any other care. For this cause first God assigned Adam maintenance of life, and then appointed him a law to observe. For this cause after men began to grow to a number, the first thing we read they gave themselves unto was the tilling of the earth and the feeding of cattle. Having by this mean whereon to live, the principal actions of their life afterward are noted by the exercise of their religion. True it is that the Kingdom of God must be the first thing in our purposes and desires. But inasmuch as righteous life presupposeth life, inasmuch as to live virtuously it is impossible except we live, therefore the first impediment which naturally we endeavor to remove is penury and want of things without which we cannot live. Unto life many implements are necessary; moe,[8] if we seek, as all men naturally do, such a life as hath in it joy, comfort, delight, and pleasure. To this end we see how quickly sundry arts mechanical were found out in the very prime of the world. As things of greatest necessity are always first provided for, so things of greatest dignity are most accompted of by all such as judge rightly. Although therefore riches be a thing which every man wisheth, yet no man of judgment can esteem it better to be rich than wise, virtuous, and religious. If we be both or either of these, it is not because we are so born. For into the world we come as empty of the one as of the other, as naked in mind as we are in body. Both which necessities of man had at the

6. Commonwealth, originally the "common good."
7. Paul, in 1 Timothy 6.8. "Let": hindrance.

8. More.

first no other helps and supplies than only domestical, such as that which the prophet[9] implieth, saying, "Can a mother forget her child?"; such as that which the Apostle[1] mentioneth, saying, "He that careth not for his own is worse than an infidel"; such as that concerning Abraham, "Abraham will command his sons and his household after him that they keep the way of the Lord."[2] But neither that which we learn of ourselves, nor that which others teach us, can prevail where wickedness and malice have taken deep root. If therefore when there was but as yet one only family in the world no means of instruction human or divine could prevent effusion of blood, how could it be chosen but[3] that when families were multiplied and increased upon earth, after separation each providing for itself, envy, strife, contention, and violence must grow amongst them? For hath not Nature furnished man with wit[4] and valor, as it were with armor, which may be used as well unto extreme evil as good? Yea, were they not used by the rest of the world unto evil, unto the contrary only by Seth, Enoch, and those few the rest in that line?[5] We all make complaint of the iniquity of our times; not unjustly, for the days are evil. But compare them with those times wherein there were no civil societies, with those times wherein there was as yet no manner of public regiment established, with those times wherein there were not above eight persons righteous living upon the face of the earth, and we have surely good cause to think that God hath blessed us exceedingly and hath made us behold most happy days. To take away all such mutual grievances, injuries, and wrongs, there was no way but only by growing into composition and agreement amongst themselves by ordaining some kind of government public and by yielding themselves subject thereunto, that unto whom they granted authority to rule and govern, by them the peace, tranquility, and happy estate of the rest might be procured. * * *

1593

9. Isaiah (49.17).
1. Paul, in 1 Timothy 5.8.
2. Genesis 18.19.
3. How could it be otherwise than.
4. Intelligence.

5. The virtuous line of Seth is described in Genesis 4.25–26. It was in the time of Seth and his son Enos that "men began to call upon the name of the Lord."

ROGER ASCHAM
1515–1568

When she heard of the death of her former tutor and Latin secretary, Queen Elizabeth is said to have exclaimed, "I would rather have cast ten thousand pounds in the sea than parted from my Ascham." Educated at St. John's College, Cambridge, one of the great centers of humanism in England, Ascham passionately believed in the study of the Greek and Latin classics, not merely for erudition and aesthetic pleasure but for guidance in moral values and in political activity. He corresponded widely in Latin with learned men on the Continent, but eager to influence his countrymen, whether they read Latin or not, he wrote several important books in English, including *Tox-*

ophilus, a dialogue in praise of archery with the traditional English longbow, and *A Report and Discourse of the State of Germany*, based on his experience as secretary to the English ambassador there in 1550–53. His most famous work in English was *The Schoolmaster*, published two years after his death.

The Schoolmaster eloquently opposes the widespread use of corporal punishment in schools. Instilling a love of learning, rather than a fear of physical pain, inspires young children to excel in their studies. Ascham advocates "double translation" as the most effective way of acquiring a sound Latin style: students would translate a passage from Latin to English and then, without making use of the Latin original, translate the English back into Latin. The approach thus downplays rote learning of the rules of grammar and emphasizes instead a sense of style.

In the hands of a pedant, Ascham's method (which included discouraging students from speaking Latin, for fear that everyday life would corrupt the linguistic purity of classical antiquity) could, like so many other educational reforms, harden into a rigid form into which individuals are hammered. But his ultimate goal is not a sterile miming but an ethical and aesthetic fashioning of the self. Deeply fearing what he called the "divorce between the tongue and the heart," he believed that education should teach a person to conjoin language and values in the achievement of what *The Schoolmaster* calls "decorum." Ascham's most despairing vision of a society without this moral decorum comes in his account of a brief trip to Italy. His finest tribute to the skill, alertness, and balance he admired, not only in the learning of Latin but in every human pursuit, comes in *Toxophilus* in a surprisingly lyrical praise of "comeliness."

From Toxophilus

From *The Second Book of the School of Shooting*

[COMELINESS]

* * * For this I am sure, in learning all other matters, nothing is brought to the most profitable use, which is not handled after the most comely fashion. As masters of fence[1] have no stroke fit either to hit another, or else to defend himself, which is not joined with a wonderful comeliness. A cook cannot chop his herbs neither quickly nor handsomely, except he keep such a measure with his chopping-knives as would delight a man both to see him and hear him. Every handcraftman that works best for his own profit, works most seemly to other men's sight. Again, in building a house, in making a ship, every part, the more handsomely they be joined for profit and last,[2] the more comely they be fashioned to every man's sight and eye.

Nature itself taught men to join always well-favoredness with profitableness. As in man, that joint or piece which is by any chance deprived of his comeliness, the same is also debarred of his use and profitableness. As he that is goggle-eyed, and looks asquint, hath both his countenance clean marred and his sight sore blemished; and so in all other members like.[3] Moreover, what time of the year bringeth most profit with it for man's use, the same also covereth and decketh both earth and trees with most comeliness for man's pleasure. And that time which taketh away the pleasure of

---

1. Fencing.
2. Usefulness and lastingness.

3. Likewise.

the ground carrieth with him also the profit of the ground, as every man by experience knoweth in hard and rough winters. Some things there be which have no other end but only comeliness, as painting and dancing. And virtue itself is nothing else but comeliness, as all philosophers do agree in opinion;[4] therefore, seeing that which is best done in any matters is always most comely done, as both Plato and Cicero in many places do prove, and daily experience doth teach in other things, I pray you, as I said before, teach me to shoot as fair and well-favoredly as you can imagine. * * *

1545

From The Schoolmaster

From *The First Book for the Youth*

[TEACHING LATIN]

There is a way, touched in the first book of Cicero *De oratore*,[1] which, wisely brought into schools, truly taught, and constantly used, would not only take wholly away this butcherly fear in making of Latins[2] but would also, with ease and pleasure and in short time, as I know by good experience, work a true choice and placing of words, a right ordering of sentences, an easy understanding of the tongue, a readiness to speak, a facility to write, a true judgment both of his own and other men's doings, what tongue soever he doth use.

The way is this. After the three concordances[3] learned, as I touched before, let the master read unto him the epistles of Cicero gathered together and chosen out by Sturmius[4] for the capacity of children.

First let him teach the child, cheerfully and plainly, the cause and matter of the letter; then, let him construe it into English so oft as the child may easily carry away the understanding of it; lastly, parse[5] it over perfectly. This done thus, let the child, by and by, both construe and parse it over again so that it may appear that the child doubteth in nothing that his master taught him before. After this, the child must take a paper book and, sitting in some place where no man shall prompt him, by himself, let him translate into English his former lesson. Then, showing it to his master, let the master take from him his Latin book, and, pausing an hour at the least, then let the child translate his own English into Latin again in another paper book. When the child bringeth it turned into Latin, the master must compare it with Tully's[6] book and lay them both together, and where the child doth well, either in choosing or true placing of Tully's words, let the master praise him and say, "Here ye do well." For I assure you, there is no such whetstone to sharpen a good wit and encourage a will to learning as is praise.

4. The reference is to the idea, originally and especially associated with Plato, that Goodness and Beauty (as well as Truth) are ultimately the same thing.
1. Cicero wrote three books *On the Orator*.
2. In Latin composition.
3. Agreement of noun and adjective, verb and noun, relative with antecedent.
4. Johannes Sturm (1507–1589), German scholar and educator.
5. Give a grammatical analysis.
6. Common English name for Marcus Tullius Cicero.

But if the child miss, either in forgetting a word, or in changing a good with a worse, or misordering the sentence, I would not have the master either frown or chide with him, if the child have done his diligence and used no truantship therein. For I know by good experience that a child shall take more profit of two faults gently warned of than of four things rightly hit. For then the master shall have good occasion to say unto him:

> N[omen],[7] Tully would have used such a word, not this; Tully would have placed this word here, not there; would have used this case, this number, this person, this degree, this gender; he would have used this mood, this tense, this simple rather than this compound; this adverb here, not there; he would have ended the sentence with this verb, not with that noun or participle, etc.

In these few lines I have wrapped up the most tedious part of grammar and also the ground of almost all the rules that are so busily taught by the master, and so hardly learned by the scholar, in all common schools, which after this sort,[8] the master shall teach without all error, and the scholar shall learn without great pain, the master being led by so sure a guide, and the scholar being brought into so plain and easy a way. And therefore we do not contemn rules, but we gladly teach rules, and teach them more plainly, sensibly, and orderly than they be commonly taught in common schools. For when the master shall compare Tully's book with his scholar's translation, let the master at the first lead and teach his scholar to join the rules of his grammar book with the examples of his present lesson, until the scholar by himself be able to fetch out of his grammar every rule for every example, so as the grammar book be ever in the scholar's hand and also used of him, as a dictionary, for every present use. This is a lively and perfect way of teaching of rules, where the common way, used in common schools, to read the grammar alone by itself, is tedious for the master, hard for the scholar, cold and uncomfortable to them both.

Let your scholar be never afraid to ask you any doubt,[9] but use discreetly the best allurements ye can to encourage him to the same, lest his overmuch fearing of you drive him to seek some misorderly shift,[1] as to seek to be helped by some other book, or to be prompted by some other scholar, and so go about to beguile you much and himself more.

[A TALK WITH LADY JANE GREY]

Therefore, to love or to hate, to like or contemn, to ply[2] this way or that way to good or to bad, ye shall have as ye use a child in his youth.

And one example, whether love or fear doth work more in a child for virtue and learning, I will gladly report; which may be heard with some pleasure and followed with more profit. Before I went into Germany,[3] I came to Broadgate in Leicestershire to take my leave of that noble Lady Jane Grey,[4] to

---

7. Substituting the child's name.
8. Method. "So hardly": with such difficulty.
9. Question.
1. Subterfuge.
2. Bend, mold.
3. In 1550, as secretary to the English ambassador to the emperor Charles V.

4. Lady Jane Grey (1537–1554) was the daughter of the duke of Suffolk. On the death of King Edward VI she was proclaimed queen by the Protestant faction but was overthrown by the Catholic Mary and executed. For an account of her death, see Foxe's Acts and Monuments (p. 551).

whom I was exceeding much beholding. Her parents, the duke and the duchess, with all the household, gentlemen and gentlewomen, were hunting in the park. I found her in her chamber reading *Phaedon Platonis*[5] in Greek, and that with as much delight as some gentleman would read a merry tale in Boccaccio.[6] After salutation and duty done, with some other talk, I asked her why she would lose[7] such pastime in the park. Smiling she answered me, "Iwis,[8] all their sport in the park is but a shadow to that pleasure that I find in Plato. Alas, good folk, they never felt what true pleasure meant." "And how came you, madam," quoth I, "to this deep knowledge of pleasure, and what did chiefly allure you unto it, seeing not many women, but very few men, have attained thereunto?" "I will tell you," quoth she, "and tell you a truth which perchance ye will marvel at. One of the greatest benefits that ever God gave me is that he sent me so sharp and severe parents and so gentle a schoolmaster. For when I am in presence either of father or mother, whether I speak, keep silence, sit, stand, or go, eat, drink, be merry or sad, be sewing, playing, dancing, or doing anything else, I must do it, as it were, in such weight, measure, and number, even so perfectly as God made the world, or else I am so sharply taunted, so cruelly threatened, yea, presently sometimes, with pinches, nips, and bobs,[9] and other ways which I will not name for the honor I bear them,[1] so without measure misordered, that I think myself in hell till time come that I must go to Master Aylmer,[2] who teacheth me so gently, so pleasantly, with such fair allurements to learning, that I think all the time nothing whilst I am with him. And when I am called from him, I fall on weeping, because whatsoever I do else but learning is full of grief, trouble, fear, and whole misliking unto me. And thus my book hath been so much my pleasure, and bringeth daily to me more pleasure and more, that in respect of it all other pleasures in very deed be but trifles and troubles unto me." I remember this talk gladly, both because it is so worthy of memory and because also it was the last talk that ever I had, and the last time that ever I saw, that noble and worthy lady.

[THE ITALIANATE ENGLISHMAN]

* * * But I am afraid that overmany of our travelers into Italy do not eschew the way to Circe's[3] court but go and ride and run and fly thither; they make great haste to come to her; they make great suit to serve her; yea, I could point out some with my finger that never had gone out of England but only to serve Circe in Italy. Vanity and vice and any license to ill-living in England was counted stale and rude unto them. And so, being mules and horses before they went, returned very swine and asses home again; yet everywhere very[4] foxes with subtle and busy heads and, where they may, very wolves with cruel malicious hearts. A marvelous monster which for filthiness of living, for dullness to learning himself, for wiliness in dealing with others, for malice

5. Plato's dialogue *Phaedo*.
6. Boccaccio's *Decameron* (1348–53), a collection of one hundred "merry," sometimes licentious, tales, not translated into English in Ascham's time.
7. Miss, forgo.
8. Truly.
9. Raps, blows. "Presently": on the spot.
1. Her parents.
2. John Aylmer (1521–1594). As a schoolboy he

attracted the notice of Henry Grey, marquis of Dorset, later duke of Suffolk, who provided for his education. After graduating from Cambridge in 1541 he became chaplain to Dorset and tutor to his children. Queen Elizabeth made him bishop of London in 1577.
3. An enchantress in Homer's *Odyssey* who changes men into swine and other animals.
4. True.

in hurting without cause, should carry at once in one body the belly of a swine, the head of an ass, the brain of a fox, the womb of a wolf. If you think we judge amiss and write too sore against you, hear what the Italian saith of the Englishman, what the master reporteth of the scholar, who uttereth plainly what is taught by him and what is learned by you, saying, *Inglese italianato è un diavolo incarnato*; that is to say, "You remain men in shape and fashion but become devils in life and condition." This is not the opinion of one, for some private spite, but the judgment of all in a common proverb which riseth of that learning and those manners which you gather in Italy, a good schoolhouse of wholesome doctrine, and worthy masters of commendable scholars, where the master had rather defame himself for his teaching than not shame his scholar for his learning. A good nature of the master and fair conditions of the scholars. And now choose you, you Italian Englishmen, whether you will be angry with us for calling you monsters, or with the Italians for calling you devils, or else with your own selves, that take so much pains and go so far to make yourselves both. If some yet do not well understand what is an Englishman Italianated, I will plainly tell him: he that by living and traveling in Italy bringeth home into England out of Italy the religion, the learning, the policy,[5] the experience, the manners of Italy. That is to say, for religion, papistry or worse; for learning, less, commonly, than they carried out with them; for policy, a factious heart, a discoursing head, a mind to meddle in all men's matters; for experience, plenty of new mischiefs never known in England before; for manners, variety of vanities and change of filthy living. These be the enchantments of Circe brought out of Italy to mar men's manners in England: much by example of ill life but more by precepts of fond[6] books, of late translated out of Italian into English, sold in every shop in London, commended by honest titles the sooner to corrupt honest manners, dedicated overboldly to virtuous and honorable personages, the easier to beguile simple and innocent wits. It is pity that those which have authority and charge to allow and disallow books to be printed be no more circumspect herein than they are. Ten sermons at Paul's Cross[7] do not so much good for moving men to true doctrine as one of those books do harm with enticing men to ill-living. Yea, I say farther, those books tend not so much to corrupt honest living as they do to subvert true religion. More papists be made by your merry books of Italy than by your earnest books of Louvain.[8] And because our great physicians do wink at the matter and make no count of this sore, I, though not admitted one of their fellowship, yet having been many years a prentice to God's true religion, and trust to continue a poor journeyman therein all days of my life, for the duty I owe and love I bear both to true doctrine and honest living, though I have no authority to amend the sore myself, yet I will declare my good will to discover the sore to others.

St. Paul saith that sects and ill opinions be the works of the flesh and fruits of sin.[9] This is spoken no more truly for the doctrine than sensibly for the reason. And why? For ill-doings breed ill-thinkings, and of corrupted manners spring perverted judgments. And how? There be in man

---

5. Trickery, deceit.
6. Foolish.
7. An outdoor pulpit near St. Paul's Cathedral where important and eloquent ministers preached.

8. Town in Belgium noted in the 16th century for its Catholic university, especially its theological faculty.
9. In Galatians 5.19–21.

two special things: man's will, man's mind. Where will inclineth to goodness the mind is bent to truth; where will is carried from goodness to vanity the mind is soon drawn from truth to false opinion. And so the readiest way to entangle the mind with false doctrine is first to entice the will to wanton living. Therefore, when the busy and open papists abroad could not by their contentious books turn men in England fast enough from truth and right judgment in doctrine, then the subtle and secret papists at home procured bawdy books to be translated out of the Italian tongue, whereby overmany young wills and wits, allured to wantonness, do now boldly contemn all severe[1] books that sound to honesty and godliness. In our forefathers' time, when papistry as a standing pool covered and overflowed all England, few books were read in our tongue, saving certain books of chivalry, as they said, for pastime and pleasure, which, as some say, were made in monasteries by idle monks or wanton canons; as one for example, *Morte Darthur*,[2] the whole pleasure of which book standeth in two special points—in open manslaughter and bold bawdry; in which book those be counted the noblest knights that do kill most men without any quarrel and commit foulest adulteries by subtlest shifts:[3] as Sir Lancelot with the wife of King Arthur his master, Sir Tristram with the wife of King Mark his uncle, Sir Lamorak with the wife of King Lot that was his own aunt. This is good stuff for wise men to laugh at or honest men to take pleasure at. Yet I know when God's Bible was banished the court and *Morte Darthur* received into the prince's chamber. * * *

1570

1. Serious.
2. Sir Thomas Malory's Arthurian romance.
3. Stratagems.

HENRY HOWARD, EARL OF SURREY
1517–1547

The axe that beheaded Surrey at the age of thirty had been hanging over his head for much of his life. In the court of Henry VIII, it was dangerous to be a potential claimant to the throne, and Surrey was descended from kings on both sides of his family. He was brought up at Windsor Castle as the close companion of Henry VIII's illegitimate son, the duke of Richmond, who married Surrey's sister. As the eldest son of the duke of Norfolk, the chief bulwark of the old Catholic aristocracy against the rising tide of "new men" and the reformed religion, Surrey was the heir not only to the Howard family's great wealth but also to their immense pride, their sense at once of noble privilege and of obligation. Like his father and grandfather, he was a brave and able soldier, serving in Henry VIII's French wars as "Lieutenant General of the King on Sea and Land." He was also repeatedly imprisoned for rash behavior, on one occasion for striking a courtier, on another for wandering through the streets of London breaking the windows of sleeping townspeople. In 1541 Surrey used his family connections—his first cousin, Catherine Howard, was queen—to secure the release from the Tower of his close friend, the poet Thomas Wyatt, who had been accused of treason. But a year later, Catherine Howard was executed for adultery. Power returned to the rival family of the former queen Jane Seymour, who had died in childbirth giving a son and heir to the aging Henry VIII. Surrey's situation was already precarious, and his vocal opposition to the Seymours, with their strong Protestant leanings, sealed his fate. Convicted of treason, he had the grim distinction of being Henry's last victim.

Poets and critics of the later sixteenth century, fascinated by Surrey's noble rank and his tragic fate, routinely praised him as one of the very greatest English poets. The full title of Tottel's influential miscellany, published in 1557 (ten years after Surrey's death), is *Songs and Sonnets written by the Right Honorable Lord Henry Howard Late Earl of Surrey and Other*. The principal "other" here is his older friend Wyatt, with whose poetry Surrey's is closely linked. Poets who circulated their verse in manuscript in a courtly milieu, both shared a passion for French and Italian poetry, especially for Petrarch's sonnets. Surrey established a form for these that was used by Shakespeare and that has become known as the English sonnet: three quatrains and a couplet, all in iambic pentameter and rhyming *abab cdcd efef gg*. Even more significant, he was the first English poet to publish in blank verse—unrhymed iambic pentameter—a verse form so popular in the succeeding centuries that it has come to seem almost indigenous to the language. The work in which he used his "strange meter," as the publisher called it, was a translation of part of Virgil's *Aeneid*. (Book 4 was published in 1554 and Book 2 in 1557.) Whether in blank verse or in rhyming forms, Surrey managed with exceptional skill the rhythmic fluency of the five-stress line, initiating the ease and grace that distinguish so many Elizabethan lyrics.

Though his historical importance continues to be acknowledged, Surrey's poetry, harmonious, musical, and metrically regular, is now often compared unfavorably to Wyatt's more vigorous, knotty, and idiosyncratic verse. But as the moving epitaph he published on Wyatt (*Wyatt resteth here, that quick could never rest*) amply demonstrates, Surrey could write with considerable power as well as grace. As a conventional love poet he is not very convincing—in 1593 Thomas Nashe wrote sardonically that Surrey "was more in love with his own curious forming fancy" than with his mistress's face—but his verse comes alive when he writes about his deep male friendships (*So cruel prison*) or imagines himself in a chorus of women longing for their men (*O happy dames*) or savagely attacks the "womanish delight" of an unmanly king (*Th'Assyrians' king*).

Our selections from Surrey are divided into three groups: sonnets; lyric and reflective poems; classical translations.

The soote season[1]

> The soote° season, that bud and bloom forth brings,   *sweet, fragrant*
> With green hath clad the hill and eke the vale.
> The nightingale with feathers new she sings;
> The turtle to her make° hath told her tale.   *turtledove to her mate*
> 5 Summer is come, for every spray now springs.
> The hart hath hung his old head on the pale;
> The buck in brake his winter coat he flings;
> The fishes float with new repairèd scale;
> The adder all her slough away she slings;
> 10 The swift swallow pursueth the flies small;
> The busy bee her honey now she mings.°   *mingles*

1. In this adaptation of Petrarch's *Rima* 310, Surrey has changed the details of nature from Italian to English. Note that the sonnet has only two rhymes.

Winter is worn, that was the flowers' bale.°   *harm*
And thus I see among these pleasant things,
Each care decays, and yet my sorrow springs.

1557

Love, that doth reign and live within my thought[1]

Love, that doth reign and live within my thought,
And built his seat within my captive breast,
Clad in the arms wherein with me he fought,
Oft in my face he doth his banner rest.
5 But she that taught me love and suffer pain,
My doubtful hope and eke° my hot desire   *also*
With shamefast° look to shadow and refrain,   *modest*
Her smiling grace converteth straight to ire.
And coward Love, then, to the heart apace
10 Taketh his flight, where he doth lurk and plain,°   *complain*
His purpose lost, and dare not show his face.
For my lord's guilt thus faultless bide I pain,
Yet from my lord shall not my foot remove:
Sweet is the death that taketh end by love.

1557

Alas! so all things now do hold their peace[1]

Alas! so all things now do hold their peace,
Heaven and earth disturbèd in no thing.
The beasts, the air, the birds their song do cease;
The nightès chare[2] the stars about doth bring;
5 Calm is the sea, the waves work less and less.
So am not I, whom love, alas, doth wring,
Bringing before my face the great increase
Of my desires, whereat I weep and sing,
In joy and woe, as in a doubtful ease.
10 For my sweet thoughts sometime do pleasure bring,
But by and by the cause of my disease[3]
Gives me a pang that inwardly doth sting,
When that I think what grief it is again
To live and lack the thing should rid my pain.

1557

---

1. Cf. Surrey's version of Petrarch's *Rima* 140
with Wyatt's adaptation of the same original
(p. 527).

1. Adapted from Petrarch's *Rima* 164.
2. From Italian *carro* (the Great Bear).
3. Dis-ease, i.e., discomfort.

Th'Assyrians' king,[1] in peace with foul desire

Th'Assyrians' king, in peace with foul desire
And filthy lust that stained his regal heart,
In war, that should set princely hearts afire,
Vanquished did yield for want° of martial art.   *lack*
5   The dint of swords from° kisses seemèd strange,   *after*
And harder than his lady's side, his targe;°   *shield*
From glutton feasts to soldier's fare, a change,
His helmet, far above a garland's charge.[2]
Who scace° the name of manhood did retain,   *scarcely*
10   Drenchèd in sloth and womanish delight,
Feeble of sprite,° unpatient° of pain,   *spirit / impatient*
When he had lost his honor and his right
(Proud, time of wealth; in storms, appall'd with dread),
Murdered himself, to show some manful deed.[3]

1557

So cruel prison how could betide[1]

So cruel prison how could betide,[2] alas,
As proud Windsor, where I in lust° and joy   *pleasure*
With a king's son my childish° years did pass   *youthful*
In greater feast than Priam's sons of Troy?[3]

5   Where each sweet place returns a taste full sour:
The large green courts, where we were wont to hove,°   *linger*
With eyes cast up unto the Maidens' Tower,
And easy sighs, such as folk draw in love.

The stately sales,° the ladies bright of hue,   *halls*
10   The dances short, long tales of great delight,
With words and looks that tigers could but rue,[4]
Where each of us did plead the other's right.

The palm play° where, dispoilèd° for the game,   *handball / stripped*
With dazed eyes oft we by gleams of love
15   Have missed the ball and got sight of our dame,
To bait° her eyes, which kept the leads[5] above.   *attract, as in fishing*

The graveled ground, with sleeves° tied on the helm,   *ladies' favors*
On foaming horse, with swords and friendly hearts,

1. Sardanapalus, who was often cited as an example of degenerate kingship. Surrey's poem may allude to Henry VIII.
2. I.e., a far heavier burden than a garland.
3. I.e., he was arrogant in good times but overcome with dread in times of trouble. He committed suicide by casting himself into a fire in which he had first burned up his treasure.
1. In the summer of 1537 Surrey was imprisoned at Windsor Castle for striking a courtier. The poem recalls his boyhood stay there (1530–32) with Henry Fitzroy, illegitimate son of Henry VIII.
2. I.e., how could there happen to be.
3. Priam, king of Troy in the *Iliad*, had fifty sons.
4. Sympathize with, despite tigers' legendary fierceness.
5. Lead-covered balustrades.

With cheer° as though one should overwhelm,   *countenance*
20   Where we have fought and chasèd oft with darts.°   *spears*

With silver drops the meads yet spread[6] for ruth,
In active games of nimbleness and strength,
Where we did strain, trailed by swarms of youth,
Our tender limbs that yet shot up in length.

25   The secret groves which oft we made resound
Of pleasant plaint and of our ladies' praise,
Recording soft what grace each one had found,
What hope of speed, what dread of long delays.

The wild forest, the clothèd holts[7] with green,
30   With reins availed° and swift ybreathèd horse,   *slackened*
With cry of hounds and merry blasts between,
Where we did chase the fearful hart a force.[8]

The void° walls eke that harbored us each night,   *empty*
Wherewith, alas, revive within my breast
35   The sweet accord, such sleeps as yet delight,
The pleasant dreams, the quiet bed of rest,

The secret thoughts imparted with such trust,
The wanton talk, the divers change of play,
The friendship sworn, each promise kept so just,
40   Wherewith we passed the winter nights away.

And with this thought, the blood forsakes my face,
The tears berain my cheeks of deadly hue,
The which as soon as sobbing sighs, alas,
Upsuppèd have, thus I my plaint renew:

45   "Oh place of bliss, renewer of my woes,
Give me accompt,° where is my noble fere,[9]   *account*
Whom in thy walls thou didst each night enclose,
To other lief,° but unto me most dear."   *dear*

Each stone, alas, that doth my sorrow rue,
50   Returns thereto a hollow sound of plaint.
Thus I alone, where all my freedom grew,
In prison pine with bondage and restraint.

And with remembrance of the greater grief
To banish the less, I find my chief relief.

1557

---

6. I.e., when the dew was still on the meadows.
7. I.e., wooded hills.
8. I.e., to run it down.

9. Companion. The reference is to Henry Fitzroy, who had died the year before, aged seventeen; he was married to Surrey's sister.

Wyatt resteth here, that quick could never rest

Wyatt resteth here, that quick° could never rest,   *alive*
Whose heavenly gifts, increasèd by disdain[1]
And virtue, sank the deeper in his breast:
Such profit he by envy could obtain.

5   A head where wisdom mysteries° did frame,   *subtle meanings*
Whose hammers beat still in that lively brain
As on a stith,° where that some work of fame   *anvil*
Was daily wrought to turn to Britain's gain.

A visage stern and mild, where both did grow
10 Vice to contemn, in virtue to rejoice;
Amid great storms whom grace assurèd so
To live upright and smile at fortune's choice.

A hand that taught what might be said in rhyme,
That reft° Chaucer the glory of his wit—   *bereft, robbed*
15 A mark the which, unperfited° for time,   *unperfected*
Some may approach but never none shall hit.

A tongue that served in foreign realms his king;
Whose courteous talk to virtue did inflame
Each noble heart: a worthy guide to bring
20 Our English youth by travail unto fame.

An eye whose judgment none affect° could blind, *passion, prejudice*
Friends to allure and foes to reconcile,
Whose piercing look did represent a mind
With virtue fraught, reposèd, void of guile.

25 A heart where dread yet never so impressed
To hide the thought that might the truth advance;
In neither fortune loft° nor yet repressed   *elevated*
To swell in wealth or yield unto mischance.

A valiant corpse[2] where force and beauty met,
30 Happy—alas, too happy, but for foes;
Lived and ran the race that Nature set,
Of manhood's shape, where she the mold did lose.[3]

But to the heavens that simple° soul is fled,   *innocent*
Which left with such as covet Christ to know
35 Witness of faith[4] that never shall be dead,
Sent for our health, but not receivèd so.

---

1. Hostility (equivalent to "envy" in line 4). I.e., he could turn hostility toward him to his advantage.
2. Body (not, as now, a dead one).
3. A conventional praise—that Nature, in creating someone, made a masterpiece and lost the pattern.
4. I.e., which left with Christians ("such as covet Christ to know") a testimony.

Thus for our guilt, this jewel have we lost;
The earth his bones, the heavens possess his ghost.°   *spirit*

1542

O happy dames, that may embrace[1]

O happy dames, that may embrace
The fruit of your delight,
Help to bewail the woeful case
And eke° the heavy plight   *also*
5   Of me, that wonted° to rejoice   *was accustomed*
The fortune of my pleasant choice:
Good ladies, help to fill my mourning voice.

In ship, freight° with rememberance   *loaded*
Of thoughts and pleasures past,
10   He sails, that hath in governance
My life, while it will last;
With scalding sighs, for lack of gale,
Furdering° his hope, that is his sail,   *pushing forward*
Toward me, the sweet port of his avail.°   *destination*

15   Alas, how oft in dreams I see
Those eyes, that were my food,
Which sometime so delighted me,
That yet they do me good;
Wherewith I wake with his return,
20   Whose absent flame did make me burn:
But when I find the lack, Lord how I mourn!

When other lovers in arms across°   *embracing*
Rejoice their chief delight,
Drowned in tears to mourn my loss
25   I stand the bitter night
In my window, where I may see
Before the winds how the clouds flee.
Lo, what a mariner love hath made me!

And in green waves when the salt flood
30   Doth rise by rage of wind,
A thousand fancies in that mood
Assail my restless mind.
Alas, now drencheth° my sweet foe,[2]   *drowns*
That with the spoil of my heart did go
35   And left me; but, alas, why did he so?

And when the seas wax calm again,
To chase from me annoy,

1. The speaker is a woman. The poem was probably written for Surrey's wife, from whom he was
separated while on military duty in France in the
1540s.
2. A conventional expression for a loved one, going
back as far as Chaucer.

My doubtful hope doth cause me plain,°   *to complain*
So dread cuts off my joy.
40 Thus is my wealth° mingled with woe,   *happiness*
And of each thought a doubt doth grow;
Now he comes! Will he come? Alas, no, no!

1557

Martial, the things that do attain[1]

Martial, the things for to attain
The happy life be these, I find:
The riches left, not got with pain;
The fruitful ground, the quiet mind;

5 The equal friend; no grudge nor strife;
No charge° of rule, nor governance;   *burden*
Without disease the healthy life;
The household of continuance;°   *long duration*

The mean diet, no delicate fare;
10 Wisdom joined with simplicity;
The night dischargèd of all care,
Where wine may bear no sovereignty;

The chaste wife, wise, without debate;°   *strife*
Such sleeps as may beguile the night;
15 Contented with thine own estate,
Neither wish death nor fear his might.

1547

From The Fourth Book of Virgil[1]

[THE JILTED QUEEN]

Unhappy Dido burns, and in her rage
Throughout the town she wand'reth up and down,
Like to the stricken hind with shaft[2] in Crete
Throughout the woods which chasing with his darts
90 Aloof, the shepherd smiteth at unwares
And leaves unwist° in her the thirling° head,   *unknown/piercing*
That through the groves and launds° glides in her flight;   *glades*
Amid whose side the mortal arrow sticks.
    Aeneas now about the walls she leads,
95 The town prepared and Carthage wealth to show.
Off'ring to speak, amid her voice, she whists.°   *falls silent*

---

1. A translation of an epigram by the Roman poet Martial (10.47). The theme, a glorification of "the mean estate," is very common in Elizabethan literature.
1. Surrey translated Books 2 and 4 of Virgil's

Aeneid. In this excerpt, Aeneas's lover Dido, queen of Carthage, rages and grieves at his impending departure.
2. I.e., like a deer shot with an arrow.

And when the day gan fail, new feasts she makes;
The Troys'° travails to hear anew she lists,°   *Trojans'/wants*
Enragèd all, and stareth in his face
100   That tells the tale. And when they were all gone,
And the dim moon doth eft° withhold the light,   *again*
And sliding stars provokèd unto sleep,
Alone she mourns within her palace void,
And sets her down on her forsaken bed;
105   And absent him she hears, when he is gone,
And seeth eke.° Oft in her lap she holds   *also*
Ascanius,[3] trapped by his father's form,
So to beguile the love° cannot be told.   *the love that*

1554

3. Aeneas's son.

SIR THOMAS HOBY
1530–1566

One of the great and influential books of the Renaissance was *Il Cortegiano* (The Courtier), published in 1528 in Italian by Count Baldassare Castiglione (1478–1529) and soon translated into all the major European languages. The English translation, by the humanist and diplomat Sir Thomas Hoby, was not published until 1561 but had been written earlier, probably during the reign of Queen Mary (1553–58), when Hoby lived abroad as a Protestant exile.

Castiglione's book describes, by means of dialogues between actual men and women living at the court of the duke of Urbino in the years 1504–1508, the qualities of the ideal courtier. Supreme among these qualities is grace, the mysterious attribute which renders a person's speech and actions not merely impressive or accomplished but persuasive, touching, and beautiful. Though a few people are born with grace, most actually learn to have it by the mastery of certain techniques. In a famous passage, one of *The Courtier*'s speakers, Count Lodovico Canossa, defines the most important of these techniques as *sprezzatura* or, as Hoby translates it, "recklessness." *Sprezzatura* is in fact close to the opposite of recklessness, as we ordinarily understand the term; it is a device for manipulating appearances and masking all the tedious memorizing of lines and secret rehearsals that underlie successful social performances.

The most famous passage in *The Courtier* is Peter Bembo's classic statement of the neoplatonic ideal of love. Bembo declares that love is not the mere gratification of the senses but is the yearning of the soul after beauty, which is finally identical with the good. Love properly understood is, therefore, a kind of ladder by which the soul progresses from lower to higher things. As he pursues his theme, Bembo becomes more and more enraptured and ends with a vision of the soul ravished by heavenly beauty, purged of the flesh, and admitted to the feast of the angels. One of the spirited ladies in the court, Emilia Pia, plucks his garment and gently reminds him that he has a body.

From Castiglione's *The Courtier*

From *Book 1*

[GRACE]

"* * * Perhaps I am able to tell you what a perfect Courtier ought to be, but not to teach you how ye should do to be one. Notwithstanding, to fulfill your request in what I am able, although it be (in manner) in a proverb that *Grace*[1] *is not to be learned*, I say unto you, whoso mindeth to be gracious or to have a good grace in the exercises of the body (presupposing first that he be not of nature unapt) ought to begin betimes, and to learn his principles of cunning[2] men. The which thing how necessary a matter Philip, king of Macedonia, thought it, a man may gather in that his will was that Aristotle, so famous a philosopher, and perhaps the greatest that ever hath been in the world, should be the man that should instruct Alexander, his son, in the first principles of letters. And of men whom we know nowadays, mark how well and with what a good grace Sir Galeazzo Sanseverino, master of the horse to the French king, doth all exercises of the body; and that because, besides the natural disposition of person that is in him, he hath applied all his study to learn of cunning men, and to have continually excellent men about him, and, of every one, to choose the best of that they have skill in. For as in wrestling, in vaulting, and in learning to handle sundry kind of weapons he hath taken for his guide our Master Peter Mount, who (as you know) is the true and only master of all artificial[3] force and sleight, so in riding, in jousting, and in every other feat, he hath always had before his eyes the most perfectest that hath been known to be in those professions.

"He therefore that will be a good scholar, beside the practicing of good things, must evermore set all his diligence to be like his master, and, if it were possible, change himself into him. And when he hath had some entry,[4] it profiteth him much to behold sundry men of that profession; and, governing himself with that good judgment that must always be his guide, go about to pick out, sometime of one and sometime of another, sundry matters. And even as the bee in the green meadows flieth always about the grass choosing out flowers, so shall our Courtier steal this grace from them that to his seeming[5] have it, and from each one that parcel that shall be most worthy praise. And not do as a friend of ours whom you all know, that thought he resembled much King Ferdinand the younger, of Aragon, and regarded not to resemble him in any other point but in the often lifting up his head, wrying[6] therewithal a part of his mouth, the which custom the king had gotten by infirmity. And many such there are that think they do much, so they resemble a great man in somewhat, and take many times the thing in him that worst becometh him.

"But I, imagining with myself often times how this grace cometh, leaving apart such as have it from above, find one rule that is most general which in this part (methink) taketh place in all things belonging to a man in word or

---

1. *Grace* had a wide range of meanings for Elizabethans, and many puns were made on the word. It refers especially to a natural, easy manner, and also to that favor of God that can be neither earned nor deserved.

2. Knowing. "Betimes": early.
3. Artful, skillful.
4. Introduction.
5. In his opinion.
6. Twisting awry.

deed above all other. And that is to eschew as much as a man may, and as a sharp and dangerous rock, *Affectation* or curiosity,[7] and, to speak a new word, to use in everything a certain Recklessness, to cover art[8] withal, and seem whatsoever he doth and sayeth to do it without pain, and, as it were, not minding it. And of this do I believe grace is much derived, for in rare matters and well brought to pass every man knoweth the hardness of them, so that a readiness therein maketh great wonder. And contrariwise to use force, and, as they say, to hale by the hair, giveth a great disgrace and maketh everything, how great soever it be, to be little esteemed. Therefore that may be said to be a very[9] art that appeareth not to be art; neither ought a man to put more diligence in anything than in covering it, for in case it be open, it loseth credit clean, and maketh a man little set by.[1] And I remember that I have read in my days that there were some most excellent orators which among other their cares enforced themselves to make every man believe that they had no sight[2] in letters, and dissembling their cunning, made semblant[3] their orations to be made very simply, and rather as nature and truth made them, than study and art, the which if it had been openly known would have put a doubt in the people's mind, for fear lest he beguiled them. You may see then how to show art and such bent study taketh away the grace of everything. * * *"

From *Book 4*

[THE LADDER OF LOVE]

Then the Lord Gaspar:[4] "I remember," quoth he, "that these lords yesternight, reasoning of the Courtier's qualities, did allow him to be a lover; and in making rehearsal[5] of as much as hitherto hath been spoken, a man may pick out a conclusion that the Courtier which with his worthiness and credit must incline his prince to virtue[6] must in manner of necessity be aged, for knowledge cometh very seldom-time before years, and specially in matters that be learned with experience. I cannot see, when he is well drawn[7] in years, how it will stand well with him to be a lover, considering, as it hath been said the other night, love frameth[8] not with old men, and the tricks that in young men be gallantness, courtesy, and preciseness[9] so acceptable to women, in them are mere follies and fondness[1] to be laughed at, and purchase him that useth them hatred of women and mocks of others. Therefore, in case this your Aristotle, an old Courtier, were a lover and practiced the feats that young lovers do, as some that we have seen in our days, I fear me he would forget to teach his prince; and peradventure boys would mock him behind his back, and women would have none other delight in him but to make him a jesting-stock."

Then said the Lord Octavian:[2] "Since all the other qualities appointed to

---

7. Overfastidiousness.
8. Artifice. "Recklessness": i.e., nonchalance. The Italian word—whose sense Hoby's translation does not clearly convey—is *sprezzatura*: a natural, easy grace.
9. True.
1. Lightly regarded.
2. Skill, insight.
3. Pretended.
4. Gasparo Pallavicino, whose attitude in the dia-

logue is usually that of the woman hater.
5. Reviewing.
6. The courtier's role in counseling his prince had been discussed in the preceding part of Book 4.
7. Advanced.
8. Suits.
9. Excessive neatness.
1. Foolishness.
2. Ottaviano Fregoso, a soldier, later doge of Genoa.

the Courtier are meet for him, although he be old, methink we should not then bar him from this happiness to love."

"Nay rather," quoth the Lord Gaspar, "to take this love from him is a perfection over and above, and a making him to live happily out of misery and wretchedness."

* * *

Then M. Peter[3] after a while's silence, somewhat settling himself as though he should entreat upon a weighty matter, said thus: "My Lords, to show that old men may love not only without slander, but otherwhile[4] more happily than young men, I must be enforced to make a little discourse to declare what love is, and wherein consisteth the happiness that lovers may have. Therefore I beseech you give the hearing with heedfulness, for I hope to make you understand that it were not unfitting for any man here to be a lover, in case he were fifteen or twenty years elder than M. Morello."[5]

And here, after they had laughed awhile, M. Peter proceeded: "I say, therefore, that according as it is defined of the wise men of old time, love is nothing else but a certain coveting to enjoy beauty; and forsomuch as coveting longeth for nothing but for things known, it is requisite that knowledge go evermore before coveting, which of his own nature willeth the good, but of himself is blind and knoweth it not. Therefore hath nature so ordained that to every virtue[6] of knowledge there is annexed a virtue of longing. And because in our soul there be three manner[7] ways to know, namely, by sense, reason, and understanding: of sense ariseth appetite or longing, which is common to us with brute beasts; of reason ariseth election or choice, which is proper to man; of understanding, by the which man may be partner with angels, ariseth will. Even as therefore the sense knoweth not but sensible matters and that which may be felt, so the appetite or coveting only desireth the same; and even as the understanding is bent but to behold things that may be understood, so is that will only fed with spiritual goods. Man of nature endowed with reason, placed, as it were, in the middle between these two extremities, may, through his choice inclining to sense or reaching to understanding, come nigh to the coveting, sometime of the one, sometime of the other part. In these sorts therefore may beauty be coveted, the general name whereof may be applied to all things, either natural or artificial, that are framed in good proportion and due temper,[8] as their nature beareth. But speaking of the beauty that we mean, which is only it that appeareth in bodies, and especially in the face of man, and moveth this fervent coveting which we call love, we will term it an influence of the heavenly bountifulness, the which for all it stretcheth over all things that be created (like the light of the sun), yet when it findeth out a face well proportioned, and framed with a certain lively agreement of several colors, and set forth with lights and shadows, and with an orderly distance and limits of lines, thereinto it distilleth itself and appeareth most well favored, and decketh out and lighteneth the subject where it shineth with a marvelous grace and glistering, like the

3. Peter Bembo (1470–1547), poet, Platonist, grammarian, and historian, later a cardinal. He undertakes to prove that it is suitable for an older courtier to be (in a special sense) a lover.
4. Sometimes.

5. Morello da Ortona, a courtier and musician.
6. Power.
7. Kinds of.
8. The right mixture or combination of elements.

sunbeams that strike against beautiful plate of fine gold wrought and set with precious jewels, so that it draweth unto it men's eyes with pleasure, and piercing through them imprinteth himself in the soul, and with an unwonted sweetness all to-stirreth[9] her and delighteth, and setting her on fire maketh her to covet him.

* * *

"Do you believe, M. Morello," quoth then Count Lewis,[1] "that beauty is always so good a thing as M. Peter Bembo speaketh of?"

"Not I, in good sooth," answered M. Morello. "But I remember rather that I have seen many beautiful women of a most ill inclination, cruel and spiteful, and it seemeth that, in a manner, it happeneth always so, for beauty maketh them proud, and pride, cruel."

Count Lewis said, smiling: "To you perhaps they seem cruel, because they content you not with it that you would have. But cause M. Peter Bembo to teach you in what sort old men ought to covet beauty, and what to seek at their ladies' hands, and what to content themselves withal; and in not passing out of these bounds ye shall see that they shall be neither proud nor cruel, and will satisfy you with what you shall require."

M. Morello seemed then somewhat out of patience, and said: "I will not know the thing that toucheth[2] me not. But cause you to be taught how the young men ought to covet this beauty that are not so fresh and lusty as old men be."

Here Sir Frederick,[3] to pacify M. Morello and to break their talk, would not suffer Count Lewis to make answer, but interrupting him said: "Perhaps M. Morello is not altogether out of the way in saying that beauty is not always good, for the beauty of women is many times cause of infinite evils in the world—hatred, war, mortality, and destruction, whereof the razing of Troy[4] can be a good witness; and beautiful women for the most part be either proud and cruel, as is said, or unchaste; but M. Morello would find no fault with that. There be also many wicked men that have the comeliness of a beautiful countenance, and it seemeth that nature hath so shaped them because they may be the readier to deceive, and that this amiable look were like a bait that covereth the hook."

Then M. Peter Bembo: "Believe not," quoth he, "but[5] beauty is always good."

Here Count Lewis, because he would return again to his former purpose, interrupted him and said: "Since M. Morello passeth[6] not to understand that which is so necessary for him, teach it me, and show me how old men may come by this happiness of love, for I will not care to be counted old, so it may profit me."

M. Peter Bembo laughed, and said: "First will I take the error out of these gentlemen's mind, and afterward will I satisfy you also." So beginning afresh: "My Lords," quoth he, "I would not that with speaking ill of beauty, which is a holy thing, any of us as profane and wicked should purchase him the

9. Moves violently. In this passage, "it" and "him" refer to beauty, "her" to the soul.
1. Lodovico Canossa, who had earlier discoursed on grace.
2. Concerns.
3. Federico Fregoso, later archbishop of Salerno.

4. The destruction of Troy by the Greeks, celebrated in Homer's *Iliad*, was caused by the Trojan Paris's abduction of Helen, the most beautiful woman in the world.
5. I.e., anything but that.
6. Cares.

wrath of God. Therefore, to give M. Morello and Sir Frederick warning, that they lose not their sight, as Stesichorus[7] did—a pain most meet for whoso dispraiseth beauty—I say that beauty cometh of God and is like a circle, the goodness whereof is the center. And therefore, as there can be no circle without a center, no more can beauty be without goodness. Whereupon doth very seldom an ill[8] soul dwell in a beautiful body. And therefore is the outward beauty a true sign of the inward goodness, and in bodies this comeliness is imprinted, more and less, as it were, for a mark of the soul, whereby she is outwardly known; as in trees, in which the beauty of the buds giveth a testimony of the goodness of the fruit. And the very same happeneth in bodies, as it is seen that palmisters[9] by the visage know many times the conditions and otherwhile the thoughts of men. And, which is more, in beasts also a man may discern by the face the quality of the courage, which in the body declareth itself as much as it can. Judge you how plainly in the face of a lion, a horse, and an eagle, a man shall discern anger, fierceness, and stoutness; in lambs and doves, simpleness and very innocency; the crafty subtlety in foxes and wolves; and the like, in a manner, in all other living creatures. The foul,[1] therefore, for the most part be also evil, and the beautiful good. Therefore it may be said that beauty is a face pleasant, merry, comely, and to be desired for goodness; and foulness a face dark, uglesome,[2] unpleasant, and to be shunned for ill. And in case you will consider all things, you shall find that whatsoever is good and profitable hath also evermore the comeliness of beauty. Behold the state of this great engine of the world, which God created for the health and preservation of everything that was made: the heaven round beset with so many heavenly lights; and in the middle the earth environed with the elements and upheld with the very weight of itself; the sun, that compassing about giveth light to the whole, and in winter season draweth to the lowermost sign, afterward by little and little climbeth again to the other part; the moon, that of him taketh her light, according as she draweth nigh or goeth farther from him; and the other five stars[3] that diversely keep the very same course. These things among themselves have such force by the knitting together of an order so necessarily framed that, with altering them any one jot, they should all be loosed and the world would decay. They have also such beauty and comeliness that all the wits men have cannot imagine a more beautiful matter.

"Think now of the shape of man, which may be called a little world, in whom every parcel of his body is seen to be necessarily framed by art and not by hap,[4] and then the form altogether most beautiful, so that it were a hard matter to judge whether the members (as the eyes, the nose, the mouth, the ears, the arms, the breast, and in like manner the other parts) give either more profit to the countenance and the rest of the body, or comeliness. The like may be said of all other living creatures. Behold the feathers of fowls, the leaves and boughs of trees, which be given them of nature to keep them in their being, and yet have they withal a very great sightliness. Leave nature, and come to art. What thing is so necessary in sailing vessels as the forepart, the sides, the main yards, the mast, the sails, the stern, oars, anchors, and

---

7. A notable poet which lost his sight for writing against Helena, and recanting, had his sight restored him again [Hoby's note].
8. Evil.
9. Fortune-tellers.

1. Ugly.
2. Horribly ugly (apparently first used by Hoby).
3. I.e., the five other planets then known: Mercury, Venus, Mars, Jupiter, and Saturn.
4. Chance.

tacklings? All these things notwithstanding are so wellfavored in the eye that unto whoso beholdeth them they seem to have been found out as well for pleasure as for profit. Pillars and great beams uphold high buildings and palaces, and yet are they no less pleasureful unto the eyes of the beholders than profitable to the buildings. When men began first to build, in the middle of temples and houses they reared the ridge of the roof, not to make the works to have a better show, but because the water might the more commodiously avoid[5] on both sides; yet unto profit there was forthwith adjoined a fair sightliness, so that if, under the sky where there falleth neither hail nor rain, a man should build a temple without a reared ridge, it is to be thought that it could have neither a sightly show nor any beauty. Besides other things, therefore, it giveth a great praise to the world in saying that it is beautiful. It is praised in saying the beautiful heaven, beautiful earth, beautiful sea, beautiful rivers, beautiful woods, trees, gardens, beautiful cities, beautiful churches, houses, armies. In conclusion, this comely and holy beauty is a wondrous setting out of everything. And it may be said that good and beautiful be after a sort one self thing, especially in the bodies of men; of the beauty whereof the nighest cause, I suppose, is the beauty of the soul; the which, as a partner of the right and heavenly beauty, maketh sightly and beautiful whatever she toucheth, and most of all, if the body, where she dwelleth, be not of so vile a matter that she cannot imprint in it her property. Therefore beauty is the true monument and spoil[6] of the victory of the soul, when she with heavenly influence beareth rule over material and gross nature, and with her light overcometh the darkness of the body. It is not, then, to be spoken that beauty maketh women proud or cruel, although it seem so to M. Morello. Neither yet ought beautiful women to bear the blame of that hatred, mortality, and destruction which the unbridled appetites of men are the cause of. I will not now deny but it is possible also to find in the world beautiful women unchaste; yet not because beauty inclineth them to unchaste living, for it rather plucketh them from it, and leadeth them into the way of virtuous conditions, through the affinity that beauty hath with goodness; but otherwhile ill bringing up, the continual provocations of lovers' tokens, poverty, hope, deceits, fear, and a thousand other matters, overcome the steadfastness, yea, of beautiful and good women; and for these and like causes may also beautiful men become wicked."

Then said the Lord Cesar:[7] "In case the Lord Gaspar's saying be true of yesternight, there is no doubt but the fair women be more chaste than the foul."

"And what was my saying?" quoth the Lord Gaspar.

The Lord Cesar answered: "If I do well bear in mind, your saying was that the women that are sued to always refuse to satisfy him that sueth to them, but those that are not sued to, sue to others. There is no doubt but the beautiful women have always more suitors, and be more instantly laid at[8] in love, than the foul. Therefore the beautiful always deny, and consequently be more chaste than the foul, which, not being sued to, sue unto others."

M. Peter Bembo laughed, and said: "This argument cannot be answered to."

Afterward he proceeded: "It chanceth also, oftentimes, that as the other

---

5. Escape.
6. Reward, trophy. "Property": attribute, quality.

7. Cesar Gonzaga, cousin of Castiglione.
8. Persistently urged.

senses, so the sight is deceived and judgeth a face beautiful which indeed is not beautiful. And because in the eyes and in the whole countenance of some woman a man beholdeth otherwhile a certain lavish wantonness painted, with dishonest flickerings, many, whom that manner delighteth because it promiseth them an easiness to come by the thing that they covet, call it beauty; but indeed it is a cloaked un-shamefastness,[9] unworthy of so honorable and holy a name."

M. Peter Bembo held his peace, but those lords still were earnest upon him to speak somewhat more of this love and of the way to enjoy beauty aright, and at the last: "Methink," quoth he, "I have showed plainly enough that old men may love more happily than young, which was my drift;[1] therefore it belongeth not to me to enter any farther."

Count Lewis answered: "You have better declared the unluckiness of young men than the happiness of old men, whom you have not as yet taught what way they must follow in this love of theirs; only you have said that they must suffer themselves to be guided by reason, and the opinion of many is that it is unpossible for love to stand with reason."

Bembo notwithstanding sought to make an end of reasoning, but the Duchess[2] desired him to say on, and he began thus afresh: "Too unlucky were the nature of man, if our soul, in which this so fervent coveting may lightly arise, should be driven to nourish it with that only which is common to her with beasts, and could not turn it to the other noble part,[3] which is proper to her. Therefore, since it is so your pleasure, I will not refuse to reason upon this noble matter. And because I know myself unworthy to talk of the most holy mysteries of Love, I beseech him to lead my thought and my tongue so that I may show this excellent Courtier how to love contrary to the wonted[4] manner of the common ignorant sort; and even as from my childhood I have dedicated all my whole life unto him, so also now that my words may be answerable to the same intent, and to the praise of him. I say, therefore, that since the nature of man in youthful age is so much inclined to sense, it may be granted the Courtier, while he is young, to love sensually; but in case afterward also, in his riper years, he chance to be set on fire with this coveting of love, he ought to be good and circumspect, and heedful that he beguile not himself to be led willfully into the wretchedness that in young men deserveth more to be pitied than blamed, and contrariwise in old men more to be blamed than pitied. Therefore when an amiable countenance of a beautiful woman cometh in his sight, that is accompanied with noble conditions and honest behaviors, so that, as one practiced in love, he wotteth[5] well that his hue hath an agreement with hers, as soon as he is aware that his eyes snatch that image and carry it to the heart, and that the soul beginneth to behold it with pleasure, and feeleth within herself the influence that stirreth her and by little and little setteth her in heat, and that those lively spirits[6] that twinkle out through the eyes put continually fresh nourishment to the fire, he ought in this beginning to seek a speedy remedy and to raise

---

9. Immodesty.
1. Purpose. In a passage omitted above, Bembo had argued that old men, whose senses have cooled, find it easier than young men to be guided in love by reason and can therefore more easily avoid the miseries that, he argues, inevitably follow from sensual love.

2. Elisabetta Gonzaga, duchess of Urbino, the presiding figure in the life of the court and in these dialogues.
3. I.e., reason.
4. Accustomed.
5. Knows.
6. Vital, animating powers.

up reason, and with her to fence the fortress of his heart, and to shut in such wise the passages against sense and appetites that they may enter neither with force nor subtle practice. Thus, if the flame be quenched, the jeopardy is also quenched. But in case it continue or increase, then must the Courtier determine, when he perceiveth he is taken, to shun throughly[7] all filthiness of common love, and so enter into the holy way of love with the guide of reason, and first consider that the body where that beauty shineth is not the fountain from whence beauty springeth, but rather because beauty is bodiless and, as we have said, an heavenly shining beam, she loseth much of her honor when she is coupled with that vile subject[8] and full of corruption, because the less she is partner thereof, the more perfect she is, and, clean sundered from it, is most perfect. And as a man heareth not with his mouth, nor smelleth with his ears, no more can he also in any manner wise enjoy beauty, nor satisfy the desire that she stirreth up in our minds, with feeling, but with the sense unto whom beauty is the very butt to level at,[9] namely, the virtue[1] of seeing. Let him lay aside, therefore, the blind judgment of the sense, and enjoy with his eyes the brightness, the comeliness, the loving sparkles, laughters, gestures, and all the other pleasant furnitures of beauty, especially with hearing the sweetness of her voice, the tunableness[2] of her words, the melody of her singing and playing on instruments (in case the woman beloved be a musician), and so shall he with most dainty food feed the soul through the means of these two senses which have little bodily substance in them and be the ministers of reason, without entering farther toward the body with coveting unto any longing otherwise than honest. Afterward let him obey, please, and honor with all reverence his woman, and reckon her more dear to him than his own life, and prefer all her commodities[3] and pleasures before his own, and love no less in her the beauty of the mind than of the body. Therefore let him have a care not to suffer her to run into any error, but with lessons and good exhortations seek always to frame her to modesty, to temperance, to true honesty, and so to work that there may never take place in her other than pure thoughts and far wide from all filthiness of vices. And thus in sowing of virtue in the garden of that mind, he shall also gather the fruits of most beautiful conditions, and savor them with a marvelous good relish. And this shall be the right engendering and imprinting of beauty in beauty, the which some hold opinion to be the end of love. In this manner shall our Courtier be most acceptable to his lady, and she will always show herself toward him tractable, lowly,[4] and sweet in language, and as willing to please him as to be beloved of him; and the wills of them both shall be most honest and agreeable, and they consequently shall be most happy."

Here M. Morello: "The engendering," quoth he, "of beauty in beauty aright were the engendering of a beautiful child in a beautiful woman; and I would think it a more manifest token a great deal that she loved her lover, if she pleased him with this than with the sweetness of language that you speak of."

M. Peter Bembo laughed, and said: "You must not, M. Morello, pass your

7. Thoroughly.
8. The body.
9. Target to aim at.
1. Power.

2. Musical quality.
3. Conveniences.
4. Modest.

bounds. I may tell you it is not a small token that a woman loveth when she giveth unto her lover her beauty, which is so precious a matter; and by the ways that be a passage to the soul (that is to say, the sight and the hearing) sendeth the looks of her eyes, the image of her countenance, and the voice of her words, that pierce into the lover's heart and give a witness of her love."

M. Morello said: "Looks and words may be, and oftentimes are, false witnesses. Therefore whoso hath not a better pledge of love, in my judgment he is in an ill assurance. And surely I looked still that you would have made this woman of yours somewhat more courteous and free toward the Courtier than my Lord Julian hath made his; but meseemeth ye be both of the property[5] of those judges that, to appear wise, give sentence against their own."

Bembo said: "I am well pleased to have this woman much more courteous toward my Courtier not young than the Lord Julian's is to the young; and that with good reason, because mine coveteth but honest matters, and therefore may the woman grant him them all without blame. But my Lord Julian's woman, that is not so assured of the modesty of the young man, ought to grant him the honest matters only, and deny him the dishonest. Therefore more happy is mine, that hath granted him whatsoever he requireth, than the other, that hath part granted and part denied. And because you may moreover the better understand that reasonable love is more happy than sensual, I say unto you that selfsame things in sensual ought to be denied otherwhile, and in reasonable granted; because in the one they be honest, and in the other dishonest. Therefore the woman, to please her good lover, besides the granting him merry countenances, familiar and secret talk, jesting, dallying, hand-in-hand, may also lawfully and without blame come to kissing, which in sensual love, according to the Lord Julian's rules, is not lawful. For since a kiss is a knitting together both of body and soul, it is to be feared lest the sensual lover will be more inclined to the part of the body than of the soul; but the reasonable lover wotteth well that although the mouth be a parcel[6] of the body, yet is it an issue for the words that be the interpreters of the soul, and for the inward breath, which is also called the soul; and therefore hath a delight to join his mouth with the woman's beloved with a kiss—not to stir him to any unhonest desire, but because he feeleth that that bond is the opening of an entry to the souls, which, drawn with a coveting the one of the other, pour themselves by turn the one into the other's body, and be so mingled together that each of them hath two souls, and one alone, so framed of them both, ruleth, in a manner, two bodies. Whereupon a kiss may be said to be rather a coupling together of the soul than of the body, because it hath such force in her that it draweth her unto it, and, as it were, separateth her from the body. For this do all chaste lovers covet a kiss as a coupling of souls together. And therefore Plato,[7] the divine lover, saith that in kissing his soul came as far as his lips to depart out of the body. And because the separating of the soul from the matters of the sense, and the thorough coupling of her with matters of understanding, may be betokened by a kiss, Solomon saith[8] in his heavenly book of ballads, 'Oh that he would kiss me with a kiss of his mouth,' to express the desire he had that

---

5. Nature. "Lord Julian": Giuliano de' Medici, younger son of Lorenzo the Magnificent. In Book 3, discussing the ideal courtier's female counterpart, he expresses the opinions alluded to here.

6. Part.
7. Plato's discussion of love in *The Symposium*.
8. Song of Solomon 1.2.

his soul might be ravished through heavenly love to the beholding of heavenly beauty in such manner that, coupling herself inwardly with it, she might forsake the body."

They stood all hearkening heedfully to Bembo's reasoning, and after he had stayed a while and saw that none spake, he said: "Since you have made me to begin to show our not young Courtier this happy love, I will lead him yet somewhat farther forwards, because to stand still at this stay were somewhat perilous for him, considering, as we have oftentimes said, the soul is most inclined to the senses, and for all reason with discourse chooseth well, and knoweth that beauty not to spring of the body, and therefore setteth a bridle to the unhonest desires, yet to behold it always in that body doth oftentimes corrupt the right judgment. And where no other inconvenience ensueth upon it, one's absence from the wight beloved carrieth a great passion with it; because the influence of that beauty when it is present giveth a wondrous delight to the lover, and, setting his heart on fire, quickeneth and melteth certain virtues in a trance and congealed in the soul, the which, nourished with the heat of love, flow about and go bubbling nigh the heart, and thrust out through the eyes those spirits which be most fine vapors made of the purest and clearest part of the blood, which receive the image of beauty and deck it with a thousand sundry furnitures.[9] Whereupon the soul taketh a delight, and with a certain wonder is aghast, and yet enjoyeth she it, and, as it were, astonied[1] together with the pleasure, feeleth the fear and reverence that men accustomably have toward holy matters, and thinketh herself to be in paradise. The lover, therefore, that considereth only the beauty in the body loseth this treasure and happiness as soon as the woman beloved with her departure leaveth the eyes without their brightness, and consequently the soul as a widow without her joy. For since beauty is far off, that influence of love setteth not the heart on fire, as it did in presence. Whereupon the pores be dried up and withered, and yet doth the remembrance of beauty somewhat stir those virtues of the soul in such wise that they seek to scatter abroad the spirits, and they, finding the ways closed up, have no issue, and still they seek to get out, and so with those shootings enclosed prick the soul and torment her bitterly, as young children when in their tender gums they begin to breed teeth. And hence come the tears, sighs, vexations, and torments of lovers; because the soul is always in affliction and travail and, in a manner, waxeth wood,[2] until the beloved beauty cometh before her once again, and then she is immediately pacified and taketh breath, and, throughly bent to it, is nourished with most dainty food, and by her will would never depart from so sweet a sight. To avoid, therefore, the torment of this absence, and to enjoy beauty without passion, the Courtier by the help of reason must full and wholly call back again the coveting of the body to beauty alone, and, in what he can, behold it in itself simple and pure, and frame it within his imagination sundered from all matter, and so make it friendly and loving to his soul, and there enjoy it, and have it with him day and night, in every time and place, without mistrust ever to lose it; keeping always fast in mind that the body is a most diverse[3] thing from

9. Love "melts" certain elements ("virtues") that were before "congealed," releasing the vital blood "spirits" that take in the image of beauty through the eyes.

1. Stunned.
2. Mad, crazy.
3. Very different.

beauty, and not only not increaseth but diminisheth the perfection of it. In this wise shall our not young Courtier be out of all bitterness and wretchedness that young men feel, in a manner continually, as jealousies, suspicions, disdains, angers, desperations, and certain rages full of madness, whereby many times they be led into so great error that some do not only beat the women whom they love, but rid themselves out of their life. He shall do no wrong to the husband, father, brethren, or kinsfolk of the woman beloved. He shall not bring her in slander. He shall not be in case with[4] much ado otherwhile to refrain his eyes and tongue from discovering his desires to others. He shall not take thought at departure or in absence, because he shall evermore carry his precious treasure about with him shut fast within his heart. And besides, through the virtue of imagination, he shall fashion within himself that beauty much more fair than it is indeed. But among these commodities the lover shall find another yet far greater, in case he will take this love for a stair, as it were, to climb up to another far higher than it. The which he shall bring to pass, if he will go and consider with himself what a strait bond it is to be always in the trouble to behold the beauty of one body alone. And therefore, to come out of this so narrow a room, he shall gather in his thought by little and little so many ornaments that meddling[5] all beauties together he shall make a universal concept, and bring the multitude of them to the unity of one alone, that is generally spread over all the nature of man. And thus shall he behold no more the particular beauty of one woman, but an universal, that decketh out all bodies. Whereupon, being made dim with this greater light, he shall not pass upon[6] the lesser, and, burning in a more excellent flame, he shall little esteem it that he set great store by at the first. This stair of love, though it be very noble and such as few arrive at it, yet is it not in this sort to be called perfect, forsomuch as where the imagination is of force to make conveyance and hath no knowledge but through those beginnings that the senses help her withal, she is not clean purged from gross darkness; and therefore, though she do consider that universal beauty in sunder and in itself alone, yet doth she not well and clearly discern it, nor without some doubtfulness, by reason of the agreement that the fancies have with the body. Wherefore such as come to this love are like young birds almost flush,[7] which for all they flutter a little their tender wings, yet dare they not stray far from the nest, nor commit themselves to the wind and open weather. When our Courtier, therefore, shall be come to this point, although he may be called a good and happy lover, in respect of them that be drowned in the misery of sensual love, yet will I not have him to set his heart at rest, but boldly proceed farther, following the highway after his guide, that leadeth him to the point of true happiness. And thus, instead of going out of his wit with thought, as he must do that will consider the bodily beauty, he may come into his wit[8] to behold the beauty that is seen with the eyes of the mind, which then begin to be sharp and through-seeing, when the eyes of the body lose the flower of their sightliness.

"Therefore the soul, rid of vices, purged with the studies of true philosophy, occupied in spiritual, and exercised in matters of understanding, turning

---

4. In the situation of having.
5. Mingling.
6. Make his destination.

7. Fledged, fit to fly.
8. Intellect.

her to the beholding of her own substance, as it were raised out of a most deep sleep, openeth the eyes that all men have and few occupy,[9] and seeth in herself a shining beam of that light which is the true image of the angel-like beauty partened[1] with her, whereof she also partneth with the body a feeble shadow; therefore, waxed blind about earthly matters, is made most quick of sight about heavenly. And otherwhile when the stirring virtues of the body are withdrawn alone through earnest beholding, either fast bound through sleep, when she is not hindered by them, she feeleth a certain privy[2] smell of the right angel-like beauty, and, ravished with the shining of that light, beginneth to be inflamed, and so greedily followeth after, that in a manner she waxeth drunken and beside herself, for coveting to couple herself with it, having found, to her weening,[3] the footsteps of God, in the beholding of whom, as in her happy end, she seeketh to settle herself. And therefore, burning in this most happy flame, she ariseth to the noblest part of her, which is the understanding, and there, no more shadowed with the dark night of earthly matters, seeth the heavenly beauty; but yet doth she not for all that enjoy it altogether perfectly, because she beholdeth it only in her particular understanding, which cannot conceive the passing[4] great universal beauty; whereupon, not throughly satisfied with this benefit, love giveth unto the soul a greater happiness. For like as through the particular beauty of one body he guideth her to the universal beauty of all bodies, even so in the last degree of perfection through particular understanding he guideth her to the universal understanding. Thus the soul kindled in the most holy fire of heavenly love fleeth to couple herself with the nature of angels, and not only clean forsaketh sense, but hath no more need of the discourse of reason, for, being changed into an angel, she understandeth all things that may be understood; and without any veil or cloud she seeth the main sea of the pure heavenly beauty, and receiveth it into her, and enjoyeth that sovereign happiness that cannot be comprehended of the senses. Since, therefore, the beauties which we daily see with these our dim eyes in bodies subject to corruption, that nevertheless be nothing else but dreams and most thin shadows of beauty, seem unto us so well favored and comely that oftentimes they kindle in us a most burning fire, and with such delight that we reckon no happiness may be compared to it that we feel otherwhile through the only look which the beloved countenance of a woman casteth at us; what happy wonder, what blessed abashment, may we reckon that to be that taketh the souls which come to have a sight of the heavenly beauty? What sweet flame, what sweet incense, may a man believe that to be which ariseth of the fountain of the sovereign and right beauty? Which is the origin of all other beauty, which never increaseth nor diminisheth, always beautiful, and of itself, as well on the one part as on the other, most simple, only like itself, and partner of none other, but in such wise beautiful that all other beautiful things be beautiful because they be partners of the beauty of it.

"This is the beauty unseparable from the high bounty which with her voice calleth and draweth to her all things; and not only to the endowed with understanding giveth understanding, to the reasonable reason, to the sensual sense and appetite to live, but also partaketh with plants and stones, as a

---

9. Use.
1. Shared.
2. Intimate.

3. Opinion, thought.
4. Surpassing. "Particular": individual.

print of herself, stirring, and the natural provocation of their properties. So much, therefore, is this love greater and happier than others as the cause that stirreth it is more excellent. And therefore, as common fire trieth gold and maketh it fine, so this most holy fire in souls destroyeth and consumeth whatsoever is mortal in them, and relieveth and maketh beautiful the heavenly part, which at the first by reason of the sense was dead and buried in them. This is the great fire in the which, the poets write, that Hercules was burned on the top of the mountain Oeta,[5] and, through that consuming with fire, after his death was holy and immortal. This is the fiery bush of Moses;[6] the divided tongues of fire;[7] the inflamed chariot of Elias;[8] which doubleth grace and happiness in their souls that be worthy to see it, when they forsake this earthly baseness and flee up into heaven. Let us, therefore, bend all our force and thoughts of soul to this most holy light, which showeth us the way which leadeth to heaven; and after it, putting off the affections we were clad withal at our coming down, let us climb up the stairs which at the lowermost step have the shadow of sensual beauty, to the high mansion place where the heavenly, amiable, and right beauty dwelleth, which lieth hid in the innermost secrets of God, lest unhallowed eyes should come to the sight of it; and there shall we find a most happy end for our desires, true rest for our travails, certain remedy for miseries, a most healthful medicine for sickness, a most sure haven in the troublesome storms of the tempestuous sea of this life.

"What tongue mortal is there then, Oh most holy love, that can sufficiently praise thy worthiness? Thou most beautiful, most good, most wise, art derived of the unity of heavenly beauty, goodness, and wisdom, and therein dost thou abide, and unto it through it, as in a circle, turnest about. Thou the most sweet bond of the world, a mean betwixt heavenly and earthly things, with a bountiful temper bendest the high virtues to the government of the lower, and turning back the minds of mortal men to their beginning, couplest them with it. Thou with agreement bringest the elements in one, and stirrest nature to bring forth that which ariseth and is born for the succession of the life. Thou bringest severed matters into one, to the unperfect givest perfection, to the unlike likeness, to enmity amity, to the earth fruits, to the sea calmness, to the heaven lively light. Thou art the father of true pleasures, of grace, peace, lowliness, and goodwill, enemy to rude wildness and sluggishness—to be short, the beginning and end of all goodness. And forsomuch as thou delightest to dwell in the flower of beautiful bodies and beautiful souls, I suppose that thy abiding-place is now here among us, and from above otherwhile showest thyself a little to the eyes and minds of them that be worthy to see thee. Therefore vouchsafe, Lord, to hearken to our prayers, pour thyself into our hearts, and with the brightness of thy most holy fire lighten our darkness, and, like a trusty guide in this blind maze, show us the right way; reform the falsehood of the senses, and after long

---

5. A mountain between Thessalia and Macedonia where is the sepulchre of Hercules [Hoby's note].
6. "And the angel of the Lord appeared unto [Moses] in a flame of fire out of the midst of a bush; and he looked, and, behold, the bush burned with fire, and the bush was not consumed" (Exodus 3.2).
7. "And there appeared unto [the Apostles] cloven tongues like as to fire, and it sat upon each of them.

And they were all filled with the Holy Ghost, and began to speak with other tongues, as the Spirit gave them utterance" (Acts 2.3–4).
8. "And it came to pass, as they still went on, and talked, that, behold, there appeared a chariot of fire, and horses of fire, and parted them both asunder: and Elijah went up by a whirlwind into heaven" (2 Kings 2.11).

wandering in vanity give us the right and sound joy. Make us to smell those spiritual savors that relieve the virtues of the understanding, and to hear the heavenly harmony so tunable that no discord of passion take place any more in us. Make us drunken with the bottomless fountain of contentation that always doth delight and never giveth fill, and that giveth a smack[9] of the right bliss unto whoso drinketh of the running and clear water thereof. Purge with the shining beams of thy light our eyes from misty ignorance, that they may no more set by[1] mortal beauty, and well perceive that the things which at the first they thought themselves to see be not indeed, and those that they saw not to be in effect. Accept our souls that be offered unto thee for a sacrifice. Burn them in the lively flame that wasteth all gross filthiness, that after they be clean sundered from the body they may be coupled with an everlasting and most sweet bond to the heavenly beauty. And we, severed from ourselves, may be changed like right lovers into the beloved, and, after we be drawn from the earth, admitted to the feast of the angels, where, fed with immortal ambrosia and nectar,[2] in the end we may die a most happy and lively death, as in times past died the fathers of old time, whose souls with most fervent zeal of beholding thou didst hale from the body and coupledst them with God."

When Bembo had hitherto spoken with such vehemency that a man would have thought him, as it were, ravished and beside himself, he stood still without once moving, holding his eyes toward heaven as astonied, when the Lady Emilia,[3] which together with the rest gave most diligent ear to this talk, took him by the plait of his garment and plucking him a little, said: "Take heed, M. Peter, that these thoughts make not your soul also to forsake the body."

"Madam," answered M. Peter, "it should not be the first miracle that love hath wrought in me."

Then the Duchess and all the rest began afresh to be instant[4] upon M. Bembo that he would proceed once more in his talk, and everyone thought he felt in his mind, as it were, a certain sparkle of that godly love that pricked him, and they all coveted to hear farther; but M. Bembo: "My Lords," quoth he, "I have spoken what the holy fury of love hath, unsought for, indited[5] to me; now that, it seemeth, he inspireth me no more, I wot not what to say. And I think verily that love will not have his secrets discovered any farther, nor that the Courtier should pass the degree that his pleasure is I should show him, and therefore it is not perhaps lawful to speak any more in this matter."

"Surely," quoth the Duchess, "if the not young Courtier be such a one that he can follow this way which you have showed him, of right he ought to be satisfied with so great a happiness, and not to envy the younger."

Then the Lord Cesar Gonzaga: "The way," quoth he, "that leadeth to this happiness is so steep, in my mind, that I believe it will be much ado to get to it."

The Lord Gaspar said: "I believe it be hard to get up for men, but unpossible for women."

The Lady Emilia laughed, and said: "If you fall so often to offend us, I promise you you shall be no more forgiven."

The Lord Gaspar answered: "It is no offense to you in saying that women's souls be not so purged from passions as men's be, nor accustomed in beholdings, as M. Peter hath said is necessary for them to be that will taste of the heavenly love. Therefore it is not read that ever woman hath had this grace; but many men have had it, as Plato, Socrates, Plotinus,[6] and many other, and a number of our holy fathers, as Saint Francis, in whom a fervent spirit of love imprinted the most holy seal of the five wounds.[7] And nothing but the virtue[8] of love could hale up Saint Paul the Apostle to the sight of those secrets which is not lawful for man to speak of; nor show Saint Stephen the heavens open."[9]

Here answered the Lord Julian: "In this point men shall nothing pass women, for Socrates himself doth confess that all the mysteries of love which he knew were oped unto him by a woman, which was Diotima.[1] And the angel that with the fire of love imprinted the five wounds in Saint Francis hath also made some women worthy of the same print in our age. You must remember, moreover, that Saint Mary Magdalen[2] had many faults forgiven her, because she loved much; and perhaps with no less grace than Saint Paul was she many times through angelic love haled up to the third heaven. And many other, as I showed you yesterday more at large, that for love of the name of Christ have not passed upon[3] life, nor feared torments, nor any other kind of death how terrible and cruel ever it were. And they were not, as M. Peter will have his Courtier to be, aged, but soft and tender maidens, and in the age when he saith that sensual love ought to be borne withal in men."

The Lord Gaspar began to prepare himself to speak, but the Duchess: "Of this," quoth she, "let M. Peter be judge, and the matter shall stand to his verdict, whether women be not as meet for heavenly love as men. But because the plead[4] between you may happen be too long, it shall not be amiss to defer it until tomorrow."

"Nay, tonight," quoth the Lord Cesar Gonzaga.

And how can it be tonight?" quoth the Duchess.

The Lord Cesar answered: "Because it is day already," and showed her the light that began to enter in at the clefts of the windows. Then every man arose upon his feet with much wonder, because they had not thought that the reasonings had lasted longer than the accustomed wont, saving only that they were begun much later, and with their pleasantness had deceived so the lords' minds that they wist[5] not of the going away of the hours. And not one of them felt any heaviness of sleep in his eyes, the which often happeneth when a man is up after his accustomed hour to go to bed. When the windows then were opened on the side of the palace that hath his prospect toward

6. Famous ancient philosophers, especially on the subject of love.
7. St. Francis of Assisi (1182–1226) is supposed to have received the stigmata, marking on his body the five wounds of Jesus on the Cross.
8. Power.
9. The first Christian martyr, who before he was stoned to death said, "Behold, I see the heavens opened, and the Son of man standing on the right hand of God" (Acts 7.56). St. Paul's praise of love is in 1 Corinthians 13.
1. In Plato's Symposium, Socrates claims that a wise woman, Diotima, taught him his philosophy of love.
2. The converted harlot who became one of Jesus' most faithful followers.
3. Cared for.
4. Controversy.
5. Knew.

the high top of Mount Catri, they saw already risen in the east a fair morning like unto the color of roses, and all stars voided, saving only the sweet governess of the heaven, Venus, which keepeth the bounds of the night and the day, from which appeared to blow a sweet blast that, filling the air with a biting cold, began to quicken the tunable notes of the pretty birds among the hushing woods of the hills at hand. Whereupon they all, taking their leave with reverence of the Duchess, departed toward their lodgings without torch, the light of the day sufficing.

And as they were now passing out at the great chamber door, the Lord General[6] turned him to the Duchess and said: "Madam, to take up the variance between the Lord Gaspar and the Lord Julian, we will assemble this night with the judge sooner than we did yesterday."

The Lady Emilia answered: "Upon condition that in case my Lord Gaspar will accuse women, and give them, as his wont is, some false report, he will also put us in surety to stand to trial,[7] for I reckon him a wavering starter."[8]

1561

6. Francesco Maria della Rovere, nephew and adopted heir of the duke.
7. I.e., he must give us some pawn ("surety") to guarantee that he will answer the charge of falsely accusing women.
8. One who starts well but doesn't follow through to the end.

QUEEN ELIZABETH
1533–1603

Elizabeth I, queen of England from 1558 to 1603, set her mark indelibly on the age that has come to bear her name. Endowed with intelligence, courage, cunning, and a talent for self-display, she managed to survive and flourish in a world that would have easily crushed a weaker person. Her birth was a disappointment to her father, Henry VIII, who had hoped for a male heir to the throne, and her prospects were further dimmed when her mother, Anne Boleyn, was executed three years later on charges of adultery and treason. At six years old, observers noted, Elizabeth had as much gravity as if she had been forty.

Under distinguished tutors, including the Protestant humanist Roger Ascham, the young princess received a rigorous education, with training in classical and modern languages, history, rhetoric, theology, and moral philosophy. Her religious orientation was Protestant, which put her in great danger during the reign of her Catholic older half-sister, Mary. Imprisoned in the Tower, interrogated and constantly spied upon, Elizabeth steadfastly professed innocence, loyalty, and a pious abhorrence of heresy. Upon Mary's death, she ascended the throne and quickly made clear that the official religion of the land would be Protestantism.

Elizabeth also made it clear that she would not be a figurehead. She gathered around her an able group of advisers, but she held firmly to the reins of power, playing one faction against another, conducting diplomatic affairs in her fluent French and Latin, and negotiating with an often contentious Parliament. Under great pressure to marry, she entered into protracted courtships with princely suitors, including the French duke of Anjou, but she ultimately refused all offers and declared repeatedly that she was wedded to her country.

In the face of deep skepticism about the ability of any woman to rule, Elizabeth strategically blended imperiousness with an elaborate cult of love. Her courtiers and advisers, on their knees, approached the queen, glittering in jewels and gorgeous gowns, and addressed her in extravagant terms that conjoined romantic passion and religious veneration. Artists and poets celebrated her in mythological dress—as Diana, the chaste goddess of the moon; Astraea, the goddess of justice; Gloriana, the queen of the fairies. Though she could suddenly veer whenever she chose toward bluntness and anger, Elizabeth herself often contrived to transform the language of politics into the language of love. "We all loved her," her godson John Harington wrote with a touch of irony, "for she said she loved us."

Throughout her life Elizabeth took pride in her command of languages and her felicity of expression. Her own writing includes carefully crafted letters and speeches on several state occasions; verse translations of selections from the Psalms, Petrarch, Seneca, and Horace; prose translations from Boethius, Plutarch, and the French Protestant Queen Margaret of Navarre; and a few original poems. The original poems known to be hers deal with actual events in her life. They are chiefly in octosyllabics or poulter's measure (rhyming couplets in which the first line has twelve and the second line fourteen syllables) and are rough-hewn, vigorous, and moralistic.

The doubt of future foes[1]

The doubt° of future foes exiles my present joy,   *fear*
And wit° me warns to shun such snares as threaten mine   *intelligence*
     annoy.[2]
For falsehood now doth flow, and subjects' faith doth ebb,[3]
Which would not be, if reason ruled or wisdom weaved the web.
5   But clouds of toys untried do cloak aspiring minds,
Which turn to rain of late repent, by course of changèd winds.[4]
The top of hope supposed, the root of ruth° will be,   *sorrow*
And fruitless all their graffèd guiles, as shortly ye shall see.[5]
The dazzled eyes with pride, which great ambition blinds,
10   Shall be unsealed by worthy wights° whose foresight falsehood   *men*
     finds.
The daughter of debate,[6] that eke° discord doth sow   *also*
Shall reap no gain where former rule[7] hath taught still° peace to   *stable*
     grow.
No foreign banished wight shall anchor in this port;
Our realm it brooks no stranger's force, let them elsewhere resort.
15   Our rusty sword with rest,[8] shall first his edge employ
To poll their tops[9] that seek such change and gape for future joy.

ca. 1568   1589

1. The poem concerns Elizabeth's Roman Catholic cousin Mary Stuart, queen of Scotland, who in 1567 sought refuge in England from her rebellious subjects. Mary was the focus of several Catholic conspiracies to place her on the English throne in place of Elizabeth.
2. I.e., threaten to harm ("annoy") me.
3. I.e., the tide of faith (loyalty) is ebbing, yielding to the rising tide of falsehood.
4. Clouds of tricks ("toys") not yet tested and detected ("untried") hide the "aspiring minds" of ambitious foes, but those clouds will turn at last

into rains of repentance.
5. The deceptions ("guiles") grafted ("graffèd") into them will not bear fruit.
6. Mary Stuart also was sometimes called "Mother of Debate," because she was constantly the focus of conspiracies and plots.
7. "Former rule": either the reign of Henry VIII or that of Edward VI, which established the Reformation in England.
8. Sword rusty from disuse.
9. Strike off their heads.

On Monsieur's Departure[1]

I grieve and dare not show my discontent,
I love and yet am forced to seem to hate,
I do, yet dare not say I ever meant,
I seem stark mute but inwardly do prate.°   chatter
5   I am and not, I freeze and yet am burned,
Since from myself another self I turned.

My care is like my shadow in the sun,
Follows me flying, flies when I pursue it,
Stands and lies by me, doth what I have done.[2]
10   His too familiar care[3] doth make me rue° it.   regret
No means I find to rid him from my breast,
Till by the end of things it be suppressed.

Some gentler passion slide into my mind,
For I am soft and made of melting snow;
15   Or be more cruel, love, and so be kind.
Let me or° float or sink, be high or low.   either
Or let me live with some more sweet content,
Or die and so forget what love ere meant.

ca. 1582   1823

Letters

To Sir Amyas Paulet[1]

[ca. September 1586]

Amyas, my most faithful and careful servant, God reward thee treblefold in the double for thy most troublesome charge[2] so well discharged. If you knew, my Amyas, how kindly, besides most dutifully, my grateful heart accepts and prizes your spotless endeavors and faultless actions, your wise orders and safe regard, performed in so dangerous and crafty a charge, it would ease your travails and rejoice your heart, in which I charge you place this most just thought, that I cannot balance in any weight of my judgment the value that I prize you at, and suppose no treasures to countervail such a faith. If I reward not such deserts, let me lack when I have most need of you, if I acknowledge not such merit, *non omnibus dictum*.[3]

---

1. The heading, present in two manuscripts, identifies the occasion of this poem as the breaking off of marriage negotiations between Queen Elizabeth and the French duke of Anjou in 1582. A third manuscript implies instead an association with Elizabeth's favorite, the earl of Essex, who led an abortive rebellion and was executed for treason in 1601.
2. Does everything I do.
3. I.e., my own care (i.e., sorrow) that he caused.
1. Paulet was the keeper of Mary, Queen of Scots, who had been imprisoned in England since 1567.

In 1586 a number of her supporters, led by Anthony Babington, plotted to murder Elizabeth and place Mary on the throne. The plot was discovered, and the plotters were executed in September. Mary, who had been complicit with them, was placed under stricter confinement.
2. Duty, responsibility.
3. In context, the phrase (which means "not said to [or by] all") is obscure. Perhaps Elizabeth's meaning is "if indeed I do not proclaim such merit to all."

Let your wicked murderess know how, with hearty sorrow, her vile deserts compel these orders; and bid her from me, ask God forgiveness for her treacherous dealings towards the savior of her life many a year, to the intolerable peril of my own, and yet, not contented with so many forgivenesses, must fault again so horribly, far passing woman's thought, much less a princess; instead of excusing whereof, not one can sorrow, it being so plainly confessed by the authors[4] of my guiltless death. Let repentance take place, and let not the fiend possess her, so as her better part may not be lost, for which I pray with hands lifted up to Him that may both save and spill.[5]

With my most loving adieu and prayer for thy long life, your most assured and loving sovereign, as thereby by good deserts induced.

1854

To Henry III, king of France[1]

January 1587

Sir, my Good Brother,

The old ground, on which I have often based my letters, appears to me so changed at present, that I am compelled to alter the style, and instead of returning thanks, to use complaints. My God! How could you be so unreasonable as to reproach the injured party, and to compass the death of an innocent one by allowing her to become the prey of a murderess? But, without reference to my rank, which is nowise inferior to your own, nor to my friendship to you, most sincere, for I have wellnigh forfeited all reputation among the princes of my own religion,[2] by neglecting them in order to prevent disturbances in your dominions; exposed to dangers such as scarcely any prince ever was before; expecting, at least, some ostensible reasons and offers for security against the daily danger, for the epilogue of this whole negotiation: you are, in spite of all this, so blinded by the words of those who I pray may not ruin you, that instead of a thousand thanks, which I had merited for such singular services, Monsieur de Bellievre has addressed language to my ears, which, in truth, I know not well how to interpret. For that you should be angry at my saving my own life seems to me the threat of an enemy, which, I assure you, will never put me in fear, but is the shortest way to make me dispatch the cause of so much mischief. Let me, I pray you, understand in what sense I am to take these words; for I will not live an hour to endure that any prince whatsoever should boast that he had humbled me into drinking such a cup as that. Monsieur de Bellievre has, indeed, somewhat softened his language, by adding that you in nowise wish any danger to accrue to me, and still less to cause me any. I therefore write you these few words, and if it please you to act accordingly, you shall never find a truer

4. I.e., the conspirators.
5. Destroy.
1. Translated from the original French by Agnes Strickland. In the aftermath of the conspiracy to set her on the throne, Mary was tried, convicted, and sentenced to death. On January 6, 1587, Monsieur de Bellievre, a special ambassador from the king of France, Henry III (to whose predecessor,

Henry II, Mary had briefly enjoyed a dynastic marriage, ended by the young king's death in 1560), pleaded Mary's cause before Elizabeth. The threats included in his remarks prompted her to write this strong letter to his master. On February 8 Mary was beheaded.
2. I.e., other Protestant monarchs.

friend; but if otherwise, I neither am in so low a place, nor govern realms so inconsiderable, that I should in right and honor yield to any living prince who would injure me; and I doubt not, by the grace of God, to make my cause good for my own security.

I beseech you to think rather of the means of maintaining than of diminishing my friendship. Your realm, my good brother, cannot abide many enemies. Give not the rein, in God's name, to wild horses, lest they should shake you from your saddle. I say this to you out of a true and upright heart, and implore the Creator to grant you long and happy life.

Elizabeth

1854

Speech to the Troops at Tilbury[1]

My loving people: We have been persuaded by some that are careful of[2] our safety, to take heed how we commit ourselves to armed multitudes, for fear of treachery. But I assure you I do not desire to live to distrust my faithful and loving people. Let tyrants fear! I have always so behaved myself that, under God, I have placed my chief strength and safeguard in the loyal hearts and goodwill of my subjects; and therefore I am come amongst you, as you see, at this time, not for my recreation and disport, but being resolved, in the midst of the heat of the battle, to live or die amongst you all; to lay down for my God, and for my kingdom, and for my people, my honor and my blood, even in the dust. I know I have the body but of a weak and feeble woman; but I have the heart and stomach of a king, and of a king of England too,[3] and think foul scorn that Parma[4] or Spain, or any prince of Europe, should dare to invade the borders of my realm; to which, rather than any dishonor should grow by me, I myself will take up arms, I myself will be your general, judge, and rewarder of every one of your virtues in the field. I know already, for your forwardness you have deserved rewards and crowns;[5] and we do assure you on the word of a prince, they shall be duly paid you. In the meantime, my lieutenant-general[6] shall be in my stead, than whom never prince commanded a more noble or worthy subject; not doubting but by your obedience to my general, by your concord in the camp, and your valor in the field, we shall shortly have a famous victory over those enemies of my God, of my kingdoms, and of my people.

1588   1752

1. Delivered by Elizabeth to the land forces assembled at Tilbury (Essex) to repel the anticipated invasion of the Spanish Armada, a fleet of warships sent by Philip II. The Armada was defeated at sea and never reached England, a miraculous deliverance and sign of God's special favor to Elizabeth and to England, in the general view.
2. Anxious about.
3. An allusion to the concept of the king's (or queen's) two bodies, the one natural and mortal,

the other an ideal and enduring political construct. "Stomach": valor.
4. Alexander Farnese, duke of Parma, allied with (the king of) Spain and expected to join with him in the invasion of England.
5. An English monetary unit.
6. Robert Dudley, earl of Leicester, led her armies; he was the queen's favorite courtier and at one time rumored to be her lover and a prospective husband.

The "Golden Speech"[1]

Mr. Speaker: We have heard your declaration and perceive your care of our state,[2] by falling into the consideration of a grateful acknowledgment of such benefits as you have received; and that your coming is to present thanks unto us, which I accept with no less joy than your loves can have desire to offer such a present.

I do assure you that there is no prince that loveth his subjects better, or whose love can countervail our love. There is no jewel, be it of never so rich a price, which I prefer before this jewel, I mean your love, for I do more esteem it than any treasure or riches: for that we know how to prize, but love and thanks I count inestimable. And though God has raised me high, yet this I count the glory of my crown, that I have reigned with your loves. This makes me that I do not so much rejoice that God hath made me to be a queen as to be a queen over so thankful a people. Therefore I have cause to wish nothing more than to content the subject, and that is a duty which I owe. Neither do I desire to live longer days than that I may see your prosperity, and that is my only desire. And as I am that person that still, yet under God, hath delivered you, so I trust, by the almighty power of God, that I still shall be His instrument to preserve you from envy, peril, dishonor, shame, tyranny, and oppression, partly by means of your intended helps, which we take very acceptably, because it manifests the largeness of your loves and loyalties unto your sovereign.

Of myself I must say this: I never was any greedy, scraping grasper, nor a strait fast-holding prince, nor yet a waster; my heart was never set on worldly goods, but only for my subjects' good. What you do bestow on me I will not hoard up, but receive it to bestow on you again. Yea, mine own properties I count yours, to be expended for your good. Therefore render unto them, I beseech you, Mr. Speaker, such thanks as you imagine my heart yieldeth, but my tongue cannot express.

Mr. Speaker, I would wish you and the rest to stand up, for I shall yet trouble you with longer speech.[3]

Mr. Speaker, you give me thanks, but I doubt me I have more cause to thank you all than you me: and I charge you to thank them of the House of

---

1. Elizabeth's speech to her last Parliament, 1601. The designation "Golden Speech" stems from the headnote to a version of it printed near the end of the Puritan interregnum (1659?): "This speech ought to be set in letters of gold, that as well the majesty, prudence, and virtue of this royal queen might in general most exquisitely appear, as also that her religious love and tender respect which she particularly and constantly did bear to her Parliament in unfeigned sincerity might (to the shame and perpetual disgrace and infamy of some of her successors) be nobly and truly vindicated."

The royal prerogatives included the right to grant or sell "letters patent," which gave the recipient monopoly control of some branch of commerce. (Sir Walter Ralegh, for example, was given the exclusive right, for a period of thirty years, to license all taverns.) Discontent with the monopolies—which had resulted in higher prices for a wide range of commodities, including such basic

ones as salt and starch—came to a head in the Parliament of 1601. Under parliamentary pressure (and in return for a subsidy granted to her treasury), Elizabeth agreed to revoke some of the most obnoxious patents and to allow the courts to rule freely on charges brought against the holders of others. She invited members of Parliament who wished to offer thanks for this largess to come to her in a body, and on November 30 received about 150 of them at Whitehall palace. After effusive remarks by the speaker of the House of Commons (John Croke), the queen responded more or less as recorded here. (Elizabeth revised the speech for publication; and none of the surviving versions of it—which differ considerably—was printed earlier than about 1628.)
2. Rank, position.
3. Up to this point, the assemblage had evidently been kneeling.

Commons from me, for had I not received a knowledge from you, I might have fallen into the lap of an error only for lack of true information.

Since I was queen, yet never did I put my pen to any grant but that upon pretext and semblance made unto me that it was both good and beneficial to the subjects in general, though a private profit to some of my ancient servants who had deserved well. But the contrary being found by experience, I am exceedingly beholding to such subjects as would move the same at first. And I am not so simple to suppose but that there be some of the Lower House[4] whom these grievances never touched, and for them I think they speak out of zeal to their countries[5] and not out of spleen or malevolent affection, as being parties grieved. And I take it exceeding grateful from them, because it gives us to know that no respects or interests had moved them other than the minds[6] they bear to suffer no diminution of our honor and our subjects' love unto us. The zeal of which affection, tending to ease my people and knit their hearts unto me, I embrace with a princely care.

Far above all earthly treasure I esteem my people's love, more than which I desire not to merit. That my grants should be grievous to my people and oppressions to be privileged under color of our patents, our kingly dignity shall not suffer[7] it. Yea, when I heard it, I could give no rest to my thoughts until I had reformed it.[8] Shall they think to escape unpunished that have thus oppressed you and have been respectless of their duty and regardless of our honor? No, Mr. Speaker, I assure you, were it more for conscience' sake than for any glory or increase of love that I desire these errors, troubles, vexations, and oppressions done by these varlets and lewd[9] persons, not worthy the name of subjects, should not escape without condign punishment. But I perceive they dealt with me like physicians who, ministering a drug, make it more acceptable by giving it a good aromatical savor, or, when they give pills, do gild them all over.

I have ever used to set the last judgment day before mine eyes and so to rule as I shall be judged to answer before a higher Judge. To Whose judgment seat I do appeal that never thought was cherished in my heart that tended not to my people's good. And if my kingly bounty have been abused and my grants turned to the hurt of my people, contrary to my will and meaning, or if any in authority under me have neglected or perverted what I have committed to them, I hope God will not lay their culps[1] and offenses to my charge. And though there were danger in repealing our grants, yet what danger would not I rather incur for your own good, than I would suffer them still to continue?

I know the title of a king is a glorious title, but assure yourself that the shining glory of princely authority hath not so dazzled the eyes of our understanding but that we well know and remember that we also are to yield an account of our actions before the Great Judge. To be a king and wear a crown is more glorious to them that see it than it is pleasure to them that bear it. For myself, I was never so much enticed with the glorious name of a king or royal authority of a queen as delighted that God hath made me this instru-

4. The House of Commons.
5. Their constituents.
6. Intentions.
7. Allow. "Color": pretext.
8. In fact, Elizabeth was extremely slow to respond

to the grievances, which had, for example, previously been raised in the Parliament of 1597.
9. Base.
1. Sins.

ment to maintain His truth and glory, and to defend this kingdom, as I said, from peril, dishonor, tyranny, and oppression.

There will never queen sit in my seat with more zeal to my country or care to my subjects, and that will sooner with willingness yield and venture her life for your good and safety than myself. And though you have had and may have many princes more mighty and wise sitting in this seat, yet you never had or shall have any that will be more careful and loving.

Should I ascribe anything to myself and my sexly weakness, I were not worthy to live then, and of all most unworthy of the mercies I have had from God, Who hath ever yet given me a heart which never yet feared foreign or home enemies. I speak it to give God the praise as a testimony before you, and not to attribute anything unto myself. For I, O Lord, what am I, whom practices and perils past should not fear?[2] O what can I do? That I should speak for any glory, God forbid!

This, Mr. Speaker, I pray you deliver unto the House, to whom heartily recommend me. And so I commit you all to your best fortunes and further counsels. And I pray you, Mr. Comptroller, Mr. Secretary,[3] and you of my council, that before these gentlemen depart into their countries,[4] you bring them all to kiss my hand.

1601   ca. 1628

2. Frighten. "Practices": treacherous schemes.   Cecil, earl of Salisbury.
3. William Knollys, earl of Banbury, and Robert   4. Districts.

ARTHUR GOLDING
1536–1605

A prolific translator, especially from Latin and French, Arthur Golding belonged to a wealthy, well-connected family in Essex and was educated at Jesus College, Cambridge. Golding was an ardent Puritan; he translated seven works of Calvin into English. His most celebrated rendering, however, was of Ovid's *Metamorphoses.* Golding's Ovid, the first complete English version to be published (four books in 1565, the full work in 1567), is in rhyming couplets of "fourteeners" (lines of fourteen syllables).

Ovid's vast poem, with its flood of erotic narratives about pagan gods and mortals caught up in ceaseless transformations (metamorphoses), is not an obvious subject for the sustained attention of a Puritan country gentleman soberly engaged for many years in the translation of Calvin's sermons. But in addition to powerful humanist interests that coexisted uneasily with religious commitments in many educated Elizabethans, there was a long medieval tradition of allegorical interpretation of the *Metamorphoses,* a tradition amply reflected in the six hundred lines of heavily moralizing commentary that Golding wrote and dedicated to the earl of Leicester.

Golding's Ovid was one of Shakespeare's favorite books; although the playwright was able to read the Latin original, his references to the classic myths related by Ovid often reflect Golding's English version. Most Elizabethans would have been familiar with Ovid's description of the Golden Age, from whose ideal state humankind has declined to the evil Iron Age of the present.

From Ovid's *Metamorphoses*[1]

[THE GOLDEN AGE]

Then sprang up first the golden age, which of itself maintained
The truth and right of everything unforced and unconstrained.
105 There was no fear of punishment, there was no threatening law
In brazen tables nailèd up, to keep the folk in awe.
There was no man would crouch or creep to judge with cap in hand,
They livèd safe without a judge, in every realm and land.
The lofty pinetree was not hewn from mountains where it stood,
110 In seeking strange and foreign lands, to rove upon the flood.
Men knew none other countries yet than where themselves did keep;
There was no town enclosèd yet, with walls and ditches deep.
No horn nor trumpet was in use, no sword nor helmet worn;
The world was such that soldiers' help might eas'ly be forborne.
115 The fertile earth as yet was free, untouched of spade or plow,
And yet it yielded of itself of every things enow.°   enough
And men themselves contented well with plain and simple food
That on the earth of nature's gift without their travail stood,
Did live by raspès, hips, and haws, by cornels,[2] plums, and cherries,
120 By sloes[3] and apples, nuts and pears, and loathsome bramble berries,
And by the acorns dropped on ground from Jove's broad tree[4] in field.
The springtime lasted all the year, and Zephyr[5] with his mild
And gentle blast did cherish things that grew of own accord;
The ground untilled all kinds of fruits did plenteously afford.
125 No muck nor tillage was bestowed on lean and barren land,
To make the corn[6] of better head and ranker for to stand.
Then streams ran milk, then streams ran wine, and yellow honey flowed
From each green tree whereon the rays of fiery Phoebus glowed.

1567

1. Our selection is drawn from Book 1.
2. Raspberries, hips of wild roses, hawthorn buds, fruit of cornelian cherry.
3. Fruit of the blackthorn bush.

4. Oak (called *Arbor Jovis* in Latin).
5. God of the west wind.
6. Grain.

GEORGE GASCOIGNE
1539–1578

George Gascoigne was the most important poet of the early Elizabethan period, forming the bridge between the Wyatt-Surrey tradition and that of Sidney and Spenser.
Though he was highly gifted and educated at Cambridge and the Inns of Court,
Gascoigne's life was filled with more setbacks than successes: he failed as a courtier
and was imprisoned for debt in 1570, in large part due to the expenses he incurred
trying to legitimate his wife's prior divorce. Accused of being a spy and an atheist, he
was barred in 1572 from taking the seat in Parliament he had already held twice.
Seeking success on the battlefield, he went off to fight in the Low Country wars,

where he discovered instead both inept leadership and his own lack of martial aptitude. After four months as a prisoner of the Spanish, to whom he had ingloriously surrendered, he returned to England, only to find that a book of erotic poetry he had published the year before, *A Hundreth Sundrie Flowers* (1573), had been attacked and censored. He revised the collection slightly, retitled it *The Posies* (1575), and released it again, in the hope of beginning a successful literary career. Instead, the book was once more banned.

Gascoigne's wry sense of his ineptitude and misfortune is brilliantly captured in *Woodmanship*, a poem characterized by vigorous, spare diction and a tone that mingles didacticism and rueful humor. Many of Gascoigne's satires, complaints, and autobiographical pieces are written in this "plain style," as it has been called, but in his restless career as a writer he also wrote songs and sonnets that display a more lyrical grace. He was a tireless experimenter and innovator, employing a considerable metrical range that includes poulter's measure, fourteeners, decasyllabic stanzas, and couplets. His play *The Supposes* (from Ariosto) was England's first translation of an Italian prose comedy and his translation of *Jocasta* the first version of a Greek tragedy performed in English, while his *Glass of Government* was the first English original blank-verse drama and his biting satire *The Steel Glass* the first original English poem in blank verse. Gascoigne's *Certain Notes of Instruction* is the first important treatise on English prosody, and his *Adventures of Master F. J.*, a surprisingly daring account of courtly sexual intrigue, is one of the first novel-like prose narratives in English.

Woodmanship

Gascoigne's woodmanship written to the Lord Grey of Wilton[1] upon this occasion, the said Lord Grey delighting (amongst many other good qualities) in choosing of his winter deer, and killing the same with his bow, did furnish the author with a crossbow *cum pertinenciis*[2] and vouchsafed to use his company in the said exercise, calling him one of his woodmen. Now the author shooting very often, could never hit any deer, yea and oftentimes he let the herd pass by as though he had not seen them. Whereat when this noble lord took some pastime, and had often put him in remembrance of his good skill in choosing, and readiness in killing, of a winter deer, he thought good thus to excuse it in verse.

> My worthy Lord, I pray you wonder not
> To see your woodman shoot so oft awry,
> Nor that he stands amazèd° like a sot,°   confused/fool
> And lets the harmless deer unhurt go by.
> 5 Or if he strike a doe which is but carren,[3]
> Laugh not good Lord, but favor such a fault,
> Take will in worth,[4] he would fain hit the barren,
> But though his heart be good, his hap° is naught.   luck
> And therefore now I crave your Lordship's leave,
> 10 To tell you plain what is the cause of this.
> First, if it please your honor to perceive
> What makes your woodman shoot so oft amiss,

1. Elizabeth's lord deputy for Ireland; Edmund Spenser served as his secretary there. But the hunting party that inspired Gascoigne's poem took place on one of Grey's estates in England.
2. With appurtenances.
3. Carrion—i.e., pregnant and therefore unfit for eating.
4. Accept the good intention.

Believe me, Lord, the case is nothing strange:
He shoots awry almost at every mark,
15 His eyes have been so usèd for to range,
That now God knows they be both dim and dark.
For proof he bears the note° of folly now,   *mark*
Who shot sometimes to hit Philosophy,[5]
And ask you why? forsooth I make avow,
20 Because his wanton wits went all awry.
Next that, he shot to be a man of law,
And spent some time with learnèd Littleton,[6]
Yet in the end he provèd but a daw,°   *jackdaw, i.e., fool*
For law was dark° and he had quickly done.   *obscure*
25 Then could he wish Fitzherbert such a brain
As Tully[7] had, to write the law by art,
So that with pleasure, or with little pain,
He might perhaps have caught a truant's part.°   *been able to play truant*
But all too late, he most misliked the thing
30 Which most might help to guide his arrow straight;
He winkèd[8] wrong, and so let slip the string,
Which cast him wide, for all his quaint conceit.°   *clever thought*
From thence he shot to catch a courtly grace,[9]
And thought even there to wield the world at will,
35 But, out alas, he much mistook the place,
And shot awry at every rover° still.   *random mark*
The blazing baits which draw the gazing eye
Unfeathered there his first affectiön;°   *inclination*
No wonder then although° he shot awry,   *that*
40 Wanting° the feathers of discretiön.   *not having*
Yet more than them, the marks of dignity
He much mistook, and shot the wronger way,
Thinking the purse of prodigality
Had been best mean to purchase such a prey.
45 He thought the flattering face which fleereth still,°   *always smiles*
Had been full fraught with all fidelity,
And that such words as courtiers use at will
Could not have varied from the verity.
But when his bonnet buttonèd with gold,
50 His comely cap beguarded° all with gay,   *ornamented*
His bombast° hose, with linings manifold,   *stuffed*
His knit silk stocks° and all his quaint array,   *stockings*
Had picked his purse of all the Peter-pence,[1]
Which might have paid for his promotiön,
55 Then (all too late) he found that light° expense   *careless*
Had quite quenched out the court's devotiön.
So that since then the taste of misery
Hath been always full bitter in his bit,°   *i.e., in his mouth*
And why? forsooth because he shot awry,

5. I.e., he formerly studied philosophy and then (lines 21 ff.) law.
6. Author (like Fitzherbert, below) of a standard law text.
7. Marcus Tullius Cicero (whose exemplary prose style Gascoigne wishes Fitzherbert had had the wherewithal to emulate).
8. Aimed (with one eye closed).
9. I.e., he next attempted to become a courtier.
1. I.e., money—from "Peter's pence," a tax formerly levied by the Roman church.

60　Mistaking still the marks which others hit.
　　But now behold what mark the man doth find:
　　He shoots to be a soldier in his age;
　　Mistrusting all the virtues of the mind,
　　He trusts the power of his personage.
65　As though long limbs led by a lusty heart
　　Might yet suffice to make him rich again;
　　But Flushing frays[2] have taught him such a part
　　That now he thinks the wars yield no such gain.
　　And sure I fear, unless your lordship deign
70　To train him yet into some better trade,
　　It will be long before he hit the vein
　　Whereby he may a richer man be made.
　　He cannot climb as other catchers° can,　　　　　*huntsmen*
　　To lead a charge before himself be led.
75　He cannot spoil° the simple sakeless° man,　　*despoil/poor innocent*
　　Which is content to feed him with his bread.
　　He cannot pinch° the painful soldier's pay,　　　　*stint*
　　And shear° him out his share in ragged sheets,　　*dole*
　　He cannot stoop to take a greedy prey
80　Upon his fellows groveling in the streets.
　　He cannot pull the spoil from such as pill,°　　　*pillage*
　　And seem full angry at such foul offense,
　　Although the gain content his greedy will,
　　Under the cloak of contrary pretense:
85　And nowadays, the man that shoots not so,
　　May shoot amiss, even as your woodman doth:
　　But then you marvel why I let them go,
　　And never shoot, but say farewell forsooth:
　　Alas, my Lord, while I do muse hereon,
90　And call to mind my youthful years misspent,
　　They give me such a bone to gnaw upon,
　　That all my senses are in silence pent.
　　My mind is rapt in contemplatiön,
　　Wherein my dazzled eyes only behold
95　The black hour of my constellatiön[3]
　　Which framèd me so luckless on the mold.°　　　*on earth*
　　Yet therewithal I cannot but confess,
　　That vain presumption makes my heart to swell,
　　For thus I think, not all the world (I guess)
100　Shoots bet than I, nay some shoots not so well.
　　In Aristotle somewhat did I learn,
　　To guide my manners° all by comeliness,°　　*behavior/decency*
　　And Tully taught me somewhat to discern
　　Between sweet speech and barbarous rudeness.
105　Old Parkins, Rastell, and Dan Bracton's° books　*authors of law books*
　　Did lend me somewhat of the lawless law;
　　The crafty courtiers with their guileful looks
　　Must needs put some experience in my maw:°　　*stomach*
　　Yet cannot these with many mast'ries moe°　　*many more skills*

2. I.e., fighting in the Low Countries.　　3. The unlucky alignment of planets at my birth.

110 Make me shoot straight at any gainful prick,°   *bull's-eye*
    Where some that never handled such a bow
    Can hit the white or touch it near the quick,
    Who can nor speak nor write in pleasant wise,
    Nor lead their life by Aristotle's rule,[4]
115 Nor argue well on questions that arise,
    Nor plead a case more than my lord mayor's mule,
    Yet can they hit the marks that I do miss,
    And win the mean° which may the man maintain.   *means*
    Now when my mind doth mumble upon this,
120 No wonder then although I pine for pain:
    And whiles mine eyes behold this mirror thus,
    The herd goeth by, and farewell gentle does:
    So that your lordship quickly may discuss°   *declare*
    What blinds mine eyes so oft (as I suppose).
125 But since my Muse can to my Lord rehearse°   *relate*
    What makes me miss, and why I do not shoot,
    Let me imagine in this worthless verse,
    If right before me, at my standing's° foot   *hunter's station*
    There stood a doe, and I should strike her dead,
130 And then she prove a carrion carcass too,
    What figure might I find within my head,
    To scuse the rage which ruled me so to do?
    Some might interpret with plain paraphrase,
    That lack of skill or fortune led the chance,
135 But I must otherwise expound the case;
    I say Jehovah did this doe advance,
    And made her bold to stand before me so,
    Till I had thrust mine arrow to her heart,
    That by the sudden° of her overthrow   *suddenness*
140 I might endeavor to amend my part
    And turn mine eyes that they no more behold
    Such guileful marks as seem more than they be:
    And though they glister° outwardly like gold,   *glisten*
    Are inwardly like brass, as men may see:
145 And when I see the milk hang in her teat,
    Methinks it saith, old babe, now learn to suck,
    Who in thy youth couldst never learn the feat
    To hit the whites which live with all good luck.
    Thus have I told my Lord (God grant in season)
150 A tedious tale in rhyme, but little reason.
        Haud ictus sapio.[5]

                                                                                     1573

---

4. I.e., the rule of moderation. Aristotle regarded   5. "Even though struck down, I have not learned
each virtue as the mean between two extremes.   wisdom."

ISABELLA WHITNEY
fl. 1567–1573

Isabella Whitney's name is nowhere mentioned in C. S. Lewis's encyclopedic survey of *English Literature in the Sixteenth Century* (1954), and until very recently it was absent from most other accounts of the period's literature. The significance of her writing is the discovery of contemporary scholars fascinated by the relatively small number of women in Early Modern England who were able to break through the formidable social barriers that inhibited female appearance in print. Little is known about how Isabella Whitney succeeded in doing so. The sister of a well-known writer of emblems, Geoffrey Whitney, she was perhaps the first woman writer in England to publish secular verses, having persuaded the London printer Richard Jones to print a set of verse epistles on love and inconstancy (*The Copy of a Letter*, 1567). She followed this initial effort with *A Sweet Nosegay or Pleasant Posy: Containing a Hundred and Ten Philosophical Flowers*, in 1573. This work begins with a series of moral adages, adapted from Sir Hugh Plat's *Flowers of Philosophy*. A second section returns to the genre of the epistle, with a collection of letters between family and friends that serves as the occasion for commentary on social and economic problems. The work's third and concluding section is the author's satirical *Will and Testament*.

An Act of Parliament in 1544 reaffirmed the long-standing legal prohibition upon the writing of wills by certain groups or classes of people: those groups included persons under the age of twenty-one, idiots, madmen—and wives. Thus for a woman to write her own will, let alone to publish it, was to lay claim to a certain legal, social, and economic independence. Whitney adopts this stance in order to survey the institutions, occupations, and commodities of London and, in leaving her mock bequests, to articulate a series of sharp criticisms. She writes in the voice of an impoverished gentlewoman who is compelled by her circumstances to leave the city and does so in a mood that mingles regret, complaint, irony, and aggression.

Will and Testament

The author (though loath to leave the city) upon her friend's procurement is constrained to depart, wherefore she feigneth as she would die and maketh her will and testament, as followeth, with large legacies of such goods and riches which she most abundantly hath left behind her, and thereof maketh London sole executor to see her legacies performed.

A communication which the author had to London, before she made her will

> The time is come I must depart
>   from thee, ah famous city.
> I never yet, to rue my smart,°   *pain*
>   did find that thou hadst pity.
> 5 Wherefore small cause there is that I
>   should grieve from thee [to] go.
> But many women foolishly,
>   like me, and other mo'e,°   *more*
> Do such a fixèd fancy set
> 10   on those which least deserve,
> That long it is ere° wit we get,   *before*
>   away from them to swerve.°   *turn*

But time with pity oft will tell
    to those that will her try,
15   Whether it best be more to mell,°   *associate with*
    or utterly defy.
And now hath time me put in mind
    of thy great cruelness,
That never once a help would find
20   to ease me in distress.
Thou never yet wouldst credit give
    to board me for a year,
Nor with apparel me relieve
    except thou payèd were.
25   No, no, thou never didst me good,
    nor ever wilt, I know;
Yet I am in no angry mood,
    but will, or ere I go,
In perfect love and charity
30   my testament here write,
And leave to thee such treasury
    as I in it recite.
Now stand aside and give me leave
    to write my latest will:
35   And see that none you do deceive
    of that I leave them till.°   *to them*

The manner of her will, and what she left to London and to all those in it at her departing

I whole in body and in mind,
    but very weak in purse,
Do make and write my testament
40   for fear it will be worse.
And first I wholly do commend
    my soul and body eke°   *also*
To God the Father and the Son,
    so long as I can speak.
45   And after speech, my soul to him,
    and body to the grave,
Till time that all shall rise again,
    their judgment for to have.
And then I hope they both shall meet
50   to dwell for aye° in joy   *ever*
Whereas° I trust to see my friends   *where*
    released from all annoy.
Thus have you heard touching my soul
    and body what I mean;
55   I trust you all will witness bear,
    I have a steadfast brain.
And now let me dispose such things
    as I shall leave behind,
That those which shall receive the same
60   may know my willing mind.

I first of all to London leave,
    because I there was bred,
Brave° buildings rare, of churches store,°   *splendid / abundance*
    and Paul's to the head.[1]
65 Between the same, fair streets there be
    and people goodly store;
Because their keeping craveth° cost,   *requires*
    I yet will leave hem° more.   *them*
First for their food, I butchers leave,
70   that every day shall kill;
By Thames you shall have brewers store,
    and bakers at your will.
And such as orders do observe,
    and eat fish thrice a week,[2]
75 I leave two streets full fraught therewith;
    they need not far to seek.
Watling Street and Canwick Street
    I full of woolen leave,
And linen store in Friday Street,
80   if they me not deceive.
And those which are of calling such
    that costlier they require,
I mercers[3] leave, with silk so rich
    as any would desire.
85 In Cheap,[4] of them they store shall find,
    and likewise in that street
I goldsmiths leave, with jewels such
    as are for ladies meet.°   *suitable*
And plate° to furnish cupboards with   *silver-plated dishes*
90   full brave there shall you find,
With purl° of silver and of gold   *thread or cord*
    to satisfy your mind.
With hoods, bongraces,° hats, or caps,   *sunshades*
    such store are in that street,
95 As if on tone side you should miss,
    the tother[5] serves you feat.°   *nicely*
For nets° of every kind of sort,   *hairnets*
    I leave within the pawn,[6]
French ruffs, high purls,° gorgets,° and sleeves   *ruff pleats / wimples*
100   of any kind of lawn.°   *fine linen*
For purse or knives, for comb or glass,
    or any needful knack,
I by the Stocks[7] have left a boy
    will ask you what you lack.
105 I hose do leave in Birchin Lane,
    of any kind of size,
For women stitched, for men both trunks

1. "And St. Paul's Cathedral foremost among them."
2. To encourage the fishing industry, an Act of 1563 ordered that fish was to be eaten three days a week.
3. Dealers in silk and other costly materials.
4. Cheapside Market, near St. Paul's.
5. "Tone . . . tother": the one . . . the other.
6. The upper walk or gallery of the Royal Exchange.
7. A market in the center of London.

and those of Gascon guise,[8]
Boots, shoes, or pantables° good store,   *overshoes*
110   Saint Martin's hath for you;
In Cornwall,[9] there I leave you beds,
   and all that 'longs° thereto.   *belongs*
For women, shall you tailors have:
   by Bow,[1] the chiefest dwell;
115 In every lane you some shall find
   can do indifferent well.
And for the men, few streets or lanes,
   but body-makers° be,   *tailors*
And such as make the sweeping cloaks
120   with guards° beneath the knee.   *ornamental borders*
Artillery° at Temple Bar   *weapons*
   and dagges° at Tower Hill;   *pistols*
Swords and bucklers of the best
   are nigh the Fleet until.°   *near to Fleet Street*
125 Now when thy folk are fed and clad
   with such as I have named,
For dainty mouths and stomachs weak
   some junkets° must be framed.   *milk puddings*
Wherefore I 'pothecaries[2] leave,
130   with banquets in their shop;
Physicians also for the sick,
   diseases for to stop.
Some roisters° still must bide in thee   *roisterers, bullies*
   and such as cut it out,°   *make a show*
135 That with the guiltless quarrel will,
   to let their blood about.
For them I cunning surgeons leave,
   some plasters° to apply,   *poultices*
That ruffians may not still be hanged,
140   nor quiet persons die.
For salt, oatmeal, candles, soap,
   or what you else do want,
In many places shops are full,
   I left you nothing scant.°   *scarce*
145 If they that keep what I you leave
   ask money, when they sell it,
At Mint there is such store it is
   unpossible to tell it.
At Steelyard[3] store of wines there be,
150   your dullèd minds to glad,
And handsome men that must not wed
   except they leave their trade.[4]
They oft shall seek for proper girls,
   and some perhaps shall find

8. Two kinds of breeches: trunk-hose (full and baglike) and gaskins (wide breeches).
9. "Cornwallish ground" in Vintry Ward.
1. The Church of St. Mary Bow.
2. Apothecaries sold various dainty dishes ("ban-

quets").
3. The place of business of the Hanseatic merchants, known for their Rhenish wines.
4. That is, the men are apprentices, who were not allowed to marry.

155   That need compels or lucre lures
     to satisfy their mind.
  And near the same I houses leave
     for people to repair,°   *resort*
  To bathe themselves, so to prevent
160   infection of the air.
  On Saturdays I wish that those
     which all the week do drug°   *drudge*
  Shall thither trudge to trim them up
     on Sundays to look smug.°   *neat, trim*
165   If any other thing be lacked
     in thee, I wish them look;
  For there it is: I little brought,
     but nothing from thee took.
  Now for the people in thee left,
170   I have done as I may,
  And that the poor, when I am gone,
     have cause for me to pray,
  I will to prisons portions leave,
     what though but very small,
175   Yet that they may remember me
     occasion be it shall.
  And first the Counter° they shall have,   *a debtors' prison*
     lest they should go to wrack,°   *ruin*
  Some coggers° and some honest men   *cheats*
180   that sergeants° draw aback.   *police officers*
  And such as friends will not them bail,
     whose coin is very thin,
  For them I leave a certain hole,
     and little ease within.
185   The Newgate° once a month shall have   *a prison for felons*
     a sessions° for his share,   *court*
  Lest being heaped,° infection might   *overcrowded*
     procure a further care.
  And at those sessions some shall 'scape
190   with burning near the thumb,°   *branding*
  And afterward to beg their fees[5]
     till they have got the sum.
  And such whose deeds deserveth death,
     and twelve° have found the same,   *a jury*
195   They shall be drawn up Holborn Hill
     to come to further shame.[6]
  Well, yet to such I leave a nag
     shall soon their sorrows cease,
  For he shall either break their necks
200   or gallop from the preace.°   *press, crowd*
  The Fleet° not in their circuit is,   *another prison*
     yet if I give him nought,
  It might procure his curse, ere I

5. I.e., the discharge fees that prisoners were required to pay.

6. The road to Tyburn—the place of execution—ran by Holborn Hill.

unto the ground be brought.
205 Wherefore I leave some papist old
    to underprop his roof,
And to the poor within the same,
    a box° for their behoof.°   *money box / benefit*
What makes you standers-by to smile,
210   and laugh so in your sleeve,
I think it is because that I
    to Ludgate° nothing give.   *debtors' prison*
I am not now in case to° lie,   *in a position to*
    here is no place of jest:
215 I did reserve that for myself,
    if I my health possessed°   *retained*
And ever came in credit so
    a debtor for to be,
When days of payment did approach,
220   I thither meant to flee,
To shroud myself amongst the rest
    that choose to die in debt
Rather than any creditor
    should money from them get.
225 Yet 'cause I feel myself so weak
    that none me credit dare,
I here revoke, and do it leave
    some bankrupts to his share.°   *to Ludgate's share*
To all the bookbinders by Paul's,°   *St. Paul's*
230   because I like their art,
They every week shall money have
    when they from books depart.°   *sell their books*
Amongst them all my printer must
    have somewhat to his share;
235 I will my friends these books to buy
    of him, with other ware.
For maidens poor, I widowers rich
    do leave, that oft shall dote
And by that means shall marry them,
240   to set the girls afloat.
And wealthy widows will I leave
    to help young gentlemen,
Which when you° have, in any case   *i.e., the young gentlemen*
    be courteous to them then.
245 And see their plate and jewels eke
    may not be marred with rust,
Nor let their bags too long be full,
    for fear that they do burst.
To every gate under the walls
250   that compass thee about,
I fruitwives° leave to entertain   *fruit sellers*
    such as come in and out.
To Smithfield⁷ I must something leave,

---

7. West Smithfield, known for its horse market.

my parents there did dwell:
255   So careless for to be of it,
     none would accompt° it well.   *account*
   Wherefore it thrice a week shall have
     of horse and neat° good store;   *oxen*
   And in his spittle° blind and lame   *hospital*
260   to dwell for evermore.
   And Bedlam° must not be forgot,   *the lunatic asylum*
     for that was oft my walk:
   I people there too many leave
     that out of tune do talk.
265   At Bridewell° there shall beadles be,   *a workhouse for the poor*
     and matrons that shall still
   See chalk well-chopped and spinning plied,
     and turning of the mill.
   For such as cannot quiet be,
270   but strive for house or land,
   At th'Inns of Court[8] I lawyers leave
     to take their cause in hand.
   And also leave I at each Inn
     of Court or Chancery,
275   Of gentlemen a youthful rout°   *crowd*
     full of activity:
   For whom I store of books have left
     at each bookbinder's stall,
   And part of all that London hath
280   to furnish them withal.°   *with*
   And when they are with study cloyed,
     to recreate their mind,
   Of tennis courts, of dancing schools,
     and fence° they store shall find.   *fencing*
285   And every Sunday at the least
     I leave, to make them sport,
   In divers places players° that   *actors*
     of wonders shall report.
   Now, London, have I (for thy sake),
290   within thee and without,
   As comes into my memory
     dispersèd round about
   Such needful things as they should have
     here left now unto thee:
295   When I am gone, with conscience
     let them dispersèd be.
   And though I nothing namèd have
     to bury me withal,
   Consider that above the ground
300   annoyance be I shall°   *I shall be*
   And let me have a shrouding sheet
     to cover me from shame,
   And in oblivion bury me

---

8. The Inns of Court and Inns of Chancery trained and housed lawyers.

and never more me name.

305 Ringings° nor other ceremonies   *of church bells*
    use you not for cost,°   *because of the expense*
Nor at my burial make no feast,
    your money were but lost.
Rejoice in God that I am gone

310   out of this vale so vile,
And that of each thing left such store
    as may your wants exile.[9]
I make thee sole executor, because
    I loved thee best.

315 And thee I put in trust to give
    the goods unto the rest.
Because thou shalt a helper need
    in this so great a charge,°   *task*
I wish Good Fortune be thy guide, lest

320   thou shouldst run at large.
The happy days and quiet times
    they both her servants be,
Which well will serve to fetch and bring
    such things as need° to thee.   *are needed*

325 Wherefore (good London) not refuse
    for helper her to take:
Thus being weak and weary both,
    an end here will I make.
To all that ask what end I made,

330   and how I went away,
Thou answer mayst: "like those which here
    no longer tarry may."
And unto all that wish me well
    or rue that I am gone,

335 Do me commend, and bid them cease
    my absence for to moan.
And tell them further, if they would
    my presence still have had,
They should have sought to mend my luck,

340   which ever was too bad.
So fare thou well a thousand times,
    God shield thee from thy foe,
And still make thee victorious
    of those that seek thy woe.

345 And though I am persuade that I
    shall never more thee see,
Yet to the last I shall not cease
    to wish much good to thee.
This twenty of October, I,

350   in Anno Domini
A thousand five hundred seventy-three,
    as almanacs descry,°   *declare*
Did write this will with mine own hand

9. I.e., rejoice that I've left you such abundance of everything that you will have no further needs.

and it to London gave,
355 In witness of the standers-by,
  whose names if you will have,
Paper, Pen, and Standish° were   inkstand
  at that same present by,
With Time, who promised to reveal,
360 so fast as she could hie,
The same, lest of my nearer kin
  for any thing should vary:[1]
So finally I make an end,
  no longer can I tarry.

1573

1. Time will hasten ("hie") to reveal the will, lest kinsfolk begin to quarrel over her property.

EDMUND SPENSER
1552–1599

Edmund Spenser set out, consciously and deliberately, to become the great English poet of his age. In a culture in which most accomplished poetry was written by those who were, or at least professed to be, principally interested in something else—advancement at court, diplomacy, statecraft, or the church—Spenser's ambition was altogether remarkable, and it is still more remarkable that he succeeded in reaching his goal. Unlike such poets as Wyatt, Surrey, and Sidney, born to privilege and social distinction, Spenser was born to parents of modest means and station, in London, probably in 1552. He nonetheless received an impressive education, first at the Merchant Taylors' School, under its demanding humanist headmaster, Richard Mulcaster, then at Pembroke College, Cambridge, where he was enrolled as a "sizar" or poor (meaning impoverished) scholar. In the Puritan environment of Cambridge, where the popular preacher Thomas Cartwright was beginning to make the authorities uneasy, Spenser started as a poet by translating some poems for a volume of anti-Catholic propaganda. He also began his friendship with Gabriel Harvey, an eccentric Cambridge don, humanist, and pamphleteer. Their correspondence shows that both men were passionately interested in theories of poetry and in experiments in quantitative versification in English.

After receiving the B.A. degree in 1573 and the M.A. in 1576, Spenser served as personal secretary and aide to several prominent men, including Dr. John Young, bishop of Rochester; and the earl of Leicester, the queen's principal favorite. During his employment in Leicester's household he came to know Sir Philip Sidney and his friend Sir Edward Dyer, courtiers who sought to promote a new English poetry. Spenser's contribution to the movement was *The Shepheardes Calender*, published in 1579 and dedicated to Sidney.

In *The Shepheardes Calender* Spenser used a deliberately archaic language, partly in homage to Chaucer, whose work he praised as a "well of English undefiled," and partly to achieve a rustic effect, in keeping with the feigned simplicity of pastoral poetry's shepherd singers. Sidney did not approve; in his *Defense of Poesy* he wrote, "*The Shepheardes Calender* hath much poetry in his eclogues, indeed worthy the reading, if I be not deceived. (That same framing of his style to an old rustic language

I dare not allow, since neither Theocritus in Greek, Virgil in Latin, nor Sannazzaro in Italian did affect it.)" Another classical purist, Ben Jonson, growled that Spenser "writ no language," and, in the eighteenth century, Samuel Johnson described the language of *The Shepheardes Calender* as "studied barbarity." Johnson's characterization is, in a way, quite accurate, for Spenser was attempting to conjure up a native English style to which he could wed the classical mode of the pastoral. Moreover, since pastoral was traditionally viewed as the prelude in a great national poet's career to more ambitious undertakings, Spenser was also in effect announcing his extravagant ambition.

There are thirteen different meters in *The Shepheardes Calender*. Some of these Spenser invented, some he adapted, but most of them were novel; only three or four were at all common in 1579. Spenser was a prolific experimenter who went on to make further innovations in his later poems: the special rhyme scheme of the Spenserian sonnet; the remarkably beautiful adaptation of the Italian *canzone* forms for the *Epithalamion* and *Prothalamion*; and the nine-line stanza of *The Faerie Queene*, with its hexameter (six-stress) line at the end, are the best known. Spenser is sometimes called the "poet's poet" because so many later English poets learned the art of versification from him. In the nineteenth century alone his influence may be seen in Shelley's *Revolt of Islam*, Byron's *Childe Harold's Pilgrimage*, Keats's *Eve of St. Agnes*, and Tennyson's *The Lotus-Eaters*.

The year after the publication of *The Shepheardes Calender*, Spenser went to Ireland as secretary and aide to Lord Grey of Wilton, lord deputy of Ireland. Although he tried continually to obtain appointments in England and to secure the patronage of the queen, he spent the rest of his career in Ireland, holding various minor government posts and hence participating actively in the English struggle against those who resisted their colonial authority. The grim realities of that struggle—massacre, the burning of miserable hovels and of crops with the deliberate intention of starving the inhabitants, the forced relocation of whole communities, the manipulation of treason charges so as to facilitate the seizure of lands, the endless repetition of acts of military "justice" calculated to intimidate and break the spirit—may be glimpsed in distorted and on occasion direct form throughout Spenser's writings, along with dreamlike depictions of the beauty of the Irish landscape. Those writings probably include *A View of the Present State of Ireland*, an anonymously published apology for the repressive English regime.

Spenser was rewarded for his efforts in Ireland with a castle and 3,028 acres of expropriated land at Kilcolman in the province of Munster. There he was visited by another colonist and poet, the powerful and well-connected Sir Walter Ralegh, to whom Spenser showed the great chivalric epic on which he was at work. With Ralegh's influential backing, Spenser traveled to England and published, in 1590, the first three books of *The Faerie Queene*, which made a strong bid for the queen's favor and patronage. He was rewarded with a handsome pension of fifty pounds a year for life, though the queen's principal councilor, Lord Burghley, is said to have complained that it was a lot for a song. Soon after, Spenser published a volume of poems called *Complaints;* a pastoral called *Colin Clouts Come Home Againe* (1595), commenting on the courtiers and ladies at the center of English court life at the time of his 1590 visit; his sonnet cycle, *Amoretti;* and two wedding poems, *Epithalamion* and *Prothalamion*. The six-book *Faerie Queene* was published in 1596, with some revisions in the first part and a changed ending to Book 3 to provide a bridge to the added books; the two so-called Mutability cantos and two stanzas of a third—perhaps part of an intended seventh book—appeared posthumously in the edition of 1609.

In 1598 there was an uprising in Munster, and rebels burned down the house in which Spenser lived. The poet fled with his wife; their newborn baby is said to have died in the flames. Spenser was sent to England with messages from the besieged English garrison. He died in Westminster on January 13, 1599, and was buried near his beloved Chaucer in what is now called the Poets' Corner of Westminster Abbey.

Spenser cannot be put into neatly labeled categories. His work is steeped in Renaissance Neoplatonism but is also earthy and practical. He is a lover and celebrator of physical beauty yet also a profound analyst of good and evil in all their perplexing shapes and complexities. In his early days he was strongly influenced by Puritanism, remained a thoroughgoing Protestant all his life, and portrayed the Roman Catholic church as a demonic villain in *The Faerie Queene*; yet his understanding of faith and of sin owes much to Catholic thinkers. He is a poet of sensuous images yet also something of an iconoclast, deeply suspicious of the power of images (material and verbal) to turn into idols. He is an idealist, drawn to courtesy, gentleness, and exquisite moral refinement, yet also a celebrant of English nationalism, empire, and martial power. He is in some ways a backward-looking poet who paid homage to Chaucer, used archaic language, and compared his own age unfavorably with the feudal past. Yet as a British epic poet and poet-prophet, he points forward to the poetry of the Romantics and especially Milton—who himself paid homage to the "sage and serious" Spenser as "a better teacher than Scotus or Aquinas."

Because it was a deliberate choice on Spenser's part that his language should seem antique, his poetry is always printed in the original spelling and punctuation; a few of the most confusing punctuation marks have, however, been altered in the present text. Spenser also spells words variably in such a way as to suggest rhymes to the eye or to suggest etymologies (often incorrect ones). This inconsistency in his spelling is typical of his time; in the sixteenth century people varied even the spelling of their own names.

The Shepheardes Calender

Pastoral poetry—with its odd idea of shepherds among their flocks piping on their flutes and singing beautiful songs of love, sadness, and complaint—was an influential classical form whose most famous practitioners were the Alexandrian poet Theocritus (the third century B.C.E.) and the Roman poet Virgil (the first century B.C.E.). The singers of the pastoral, or eclogue, were depicted as simple rustics who inhabited a world in which man and nature lived in harmony, but the form was always essentially urban, and Spenser, a Londoner, was self-consciously assuming a highly conventional literary role. That role enabled him at once to lay claim to the prestige of classical poetry and to insist upon his native Englishness, an insistence that is signaled by the deliberately archaic, pseudo-Chaucerian language. The rustic mask also allowed Spenser, in certain of the eclogues, to make sharply satirical comments on controversial religious and political issues of his day and to reflect on his own marginal position.

The twelves eclogues of *The Shepheardes Calender* are titled for the months of the year. Each is prefaced by an illustrative woodcut representing the characters or theme of the poem and picturing the appropriate sign of the zodiac for that month in the clouds above, and each is accompanied by a commentary ascribed to "E. K.," who also wrote an introductory epistle to the work as a whole. "E. K.," who has not been identified but must have been someone close to Spenser (or, in the opinion of some, Spenser himself), trumpets the arrival of a "new poet" whose skills are conspicuously displayed in the sequence of poems. *October* deals with the place of poetry and the responsibility of the poet in the world, an important theme throughout the *Calender* and in much of Spenser's work.

From The Shepheardes Calender

To His Booke

Goe little booke:[1] thy selfe present,
As child whose parent is unkent:°   *unknown*
To him that is the president°   *pattern*
Of noblesse and of chevalree,
5 And if that Envie barke at thee,
As sure it will, for succoure flee
  Under the shadow of his wing,[2]
And askèd, who thee forth did bring,
A shepheards swaine saye did thee sing,
10 All as his straying flocke he fedde:
And when his honor has thee redde,°   *seen*
Crave pardon for my hardyhedde.°   *boldness*
  But if that any aske thy name,
Say thou wert base° begot with blame: *lowly*
15 For thy° thereof thou takest shame.   *therefore*
And when thou art past jeopardee,
Come tell me, what was sayd of mee:
And I will send more after thee.
       IMMERITO.°   *unworthy*

October[3]

1. A deliberate echo of Chaucer's line, "Go, litel bok, go litel myn tragedye" (*Troilus and Criseyde* 5.1786).
2. I.e., the protective sponsorship of Sir Philip Sidney.
3. When *The Shepheardes Calender* was published in 1579, each of the twelve eclogues was followed by a "Glosse," which contained explications of dif-ficult or archaic words, together with learned dis-cussions of—and disagreements with—Spenser's ideas, imagery, and poetics. The glosses by "E. K." are made to look authoritative, but in fact serve to complicate the process of interpretation. We have included several of these glosses, to give the reader some sense of them. The original spelling is retained.

Aegloga decima[4]

ARGUMENT

In Cuddie[5] is set out the perfecte paterne of a Poete, which finding no maintenaunce of his state and studies, complayneth of the comtempte of Poetrie, and the causes thereof: Specially having bene in all ages, and even amongst the most barbarous alwayes of singular accounpt[6] and honor, and being indede so worthy and commendable an arte: or rather no arte, but a divine gift and heavenly instinct not to bee gotten by laboure and learning, but adorned with both: and poured into the witte by a certaine *enthousiasmos* and celestiall inspiration, as the Author hereof els where at large discourseth, in his booke called the English Poete,[7] which booke being lately come to my hands, I mynde[8] also by Gods grace upon further advisement to publish.

PIERCE   CUDDIE

Cuddie, for shame hold up thy heavye head,
And let us cast with what delight to chace,
And weary thys long lingring Phoebus race.[9]
Whilome° thou wont the shepheards laddes to leade, *once*
5 In rymes, in ridles, and in bydding base:[1]
Now they in thee, and thou in sleepe art dead.

CUDDIE

Piers, I have pypèd erst° so long with payne,° *up to now / care*
That all mine Oten reedes[2] bene rent and wore:
And my poore Muse hath spent her sparèd° store, *saved up*
10 Yet little good hath got, and much lesse gayne.
Such pleasaunce makes the Grashopper so poore,
And ligge so layd,[3] when Winter doth her straine.° *constrain*

The dapper° ditties, that I wont devise, *pretty*
To feede youthes fancie, and the flocking fry,[4]
15 Delighten much: what I the bett for thy?[5]
They han° the pleasure, I a sclender prise. *have*
I beate the bush, the byrds to them doe flye:
What good thereof to Cuddie can arise?

4. Tenth Eclogue. An eclogue ("aeglogue") is a short pastoral poem in the form of a dialogue or soliloquy. Spenser's spelling is based on a false etymology (aix, "goat" + logos, "speech"), signifying, according to E. K., "Goteheards tales." For this eclogue, E. K. identifies as sources Theocritus's *Idyl* 16, which reproves the tyrant Hiero of Syracuse for his neglect of poets, and also Baptista Spagnuoli (1448–1516), called Mantuan (the fifth eclogue). The illustration portrays Cuddie (left) holding a pipe and crowned with a laurel wreath (emblems of a poet). He talks with his fellow shepherd, Piers, in a pastoral landscape, with the court in the background. The astrological sign for October, Scorpio, is at the top of the picture.
5. E. K. queries "whether by Cuddie be specified the authour selfe, or some other," noting that in *August* he was introduced as singing a song "of Col-

ins making. So that some doubt, that the persons be different." It may be that Cuddie and Piers present different aspects of Spenser the poet.
6. Esteem.
7. The *English Poete* is evidently a lost work by Spenser. "*Enthousiasmos*": inspiration. The Greek word originally meant "possessed by a god."
8. Intend.
9. I.e., let us see how we may pass this long day pleasantly.
1. A popular game; here, perhaps a poetry contest.
2. The shepherd's pipe, symbol of pastoral poetry.
3. I.e., lie so subdued. The reference is to the fable of the industrious ant who laid up supplies for winter, and the carefree grasshopper who did not.
4. A bold Metaphore forced from the multitude of young fish he called the frye [E. K.].
5. I.e., how am I the better for that?

PIERS

Cuddie, the prayse is better, then° the price,   *than*
20 The glory eke° much greater then the gayne: *also*
O what an honor is it, to restraine
The lust of lawlesse youth with good advice:[6]
Or pricke° them forth with pleasaunce of   *spur*
  thy vaine,°   *poetic vein*
Whereto thou list° their traynèd° willes entice. *desire / ensnared*

25 Soone as thou gynst to sette thy notes in frame,
O how the rurall routes° to thee doe cleave: *crowds*
Seemeth thou dost their soule of sence bereave,[7]
All as the shepheard, that did fetch his dame
From Plutoes balefull bowre withouten leave:
30 His musicks might the hellish hound did tame.[8]

CUDDIE

So praysen babes the Peacoks spotted traine,
And wondren at bright Argus blazing eye:[9]
But who rewards him ere the more for thy?°   *therefore*
Or feedes him once the fuller by a graine?
35 Sike° prayse is smoke, that sheddeth° in the skye, *such / is dispersed*
Sike words bene wynd, and wasten soone in vayne.

PIERS

Abandon then the base and viler clowne,°   *rustic*
Lyft up thy selfe out of the lowly dust:
And sing of bloody Mars, of wars, of giusts.°   *jousts*
40 Turne thee to those, that weld° the awful crowne, *bear*
To doubted° Knights, whose woundlesse[1] armour rusts, *dreaded*
And helmes unbruzèd wexen dayly browne.

There may thy Muse display her fluttryng wing,
And stretch her selfe at large from East to West:[2]
45 Whither thou list in fayre Elisa rest,
Or if thee please in bigger notes to sing,
Advaunce° the worthy whome shee loveth best, *extol*
That first the white beare to the stake did bring.[3]

6. E. K. compares these lines with *The Laws* 1, in which Plato declares "that the first invention of Poetry, was of very vertuous intent."
7. I.e., hypnotize them. E. K. cites Plato and Pythagoras for the theory that the mind is made of "a certaine harmonie and musicall nombers" and gives several examples of music's irresistible power over the emotions.
8. Orpheus: of whom is sayd, that by his excellent skil in Musick and Poetry, he recovered his wife Eurydice from hell [E. K.]; that is, from "Plutoes balefull bowre."
9. E. K. recounts the myth of Argus of the hundred eyes, who, set by Juno to guard Io, Jupiter's paramour, was lulled asleep by Mercury's music and then killed. Juno placed his eyes in the tail of

her bird, the peacock, whose splendor elicits the praises even of "babes."
1. Unwounded in warre, doe rust through long peace [E. K.].
2. E. K. explains this "poeticall metaphore" as indicating the heroic subjects available to Cuddie if he wishes to "showe his skill in matter of more dignitie, then is the homely Aeglogue." These include "our most gratious soveraign whom (as before) he calleth Elisa" and also the "noble and valiaunt men" who deserve his praise and have been his patrons.
3. He meaneth (as I guesse) the most honorable and renowned the Erle of Leycester [E. K.]. Leicester's device was the bear and ragged staff.

And when the stubborne stroke of stronger stounds,°   *efforts*
50 Has somewhat slackt[4] the tenor of thy string:
Of love and lustihead tho° mayst thou sing,   *pleasure then*
And carrol lowde, and leade the Myllers rownde,[5]
All° were Elisa one of thilke same ring.[6]   *although*
So mought our Cuddies name to Heaven sownde.

CUDDIE

55 Indeede the Romish Tityrus,[7] I heare,
Through his Mecaenas left his Oaten reede,
Whereon he earst° had taught his flocks to feede,   *formerly*
And laboured lands to yield the timely eare,
And eft° did sing of warres and deadly drede,°   *afterward / danger*
60 So as the Heavens did quake his verse to here.[8]

But ah Mecaenas is yclad in claye,
And great Augustus long ygoe is dead:
And all the worthies liggen° wrapt in leade,   *lie*
That matter made for Poets on to play:
65 For ever, who in derring doe were dreade,°   *held in awe*
The loftie verse of hem was lovèd aye.[9]

But after vertue gan for age to stoupe,
And mighty manhode brought a bedde of ease:[1]
The vaunting Poets found nought worth a pease,°   *pea*
70 To put in preace among the learnèd troupe.
Tho gan the streames of flowing wittes to cease,
And sonnebright honour pend in shamefull coupe.[2]

And if that any buddes of Poesie,
Yet of the old stocke gan to shoote agayne:
75 Or° it mens follies mote° be forst to fayne,   *either / must*
And rolle with rest in rymes of rybaudrye:°   *ribaldry*
Or as it sprong, it wither must agayne:
Tom Piper makes us better melodie.[3]

PIERS

O pierlesse Poesye, where is then thy place?
80 If nor in Princes pallace thou doe sitt:

4. That is when thou chaungest thy verse from stately discourse, to matter of more pleasaunce and delight [E. K.].
5. A kind of daunce [E. K.].
6. A company of dauncers [E. K.].
7. Well knowen to be Virgile, who by Mecaenas means was brought into the favour of the Emperor Augustus, and by him moved to write in loftier kinde, then he erst had doen [E. K.]. Maecenas ("Mecaenas") was Virgil's patron.
8. In these three verses are the three severall workes of Virgile intended. For in teaching his flocks to feede, is meant his Aeglogues. In labouring of lands, is hys Georgiques. In singing of wars and deadly dreade, is his divine Aeneis figured [E. K.] The *Georgics* ("Georgiques") is Virgil's idealizing poem about farm life.
9. He sheweth the cause, why Poetes were wont be had in such honor of noble men; that is, that by them their worthines and valor shold through theyr famous Posies be commended to al posterities [E. K.]. "Derring doe": In manhoode and chevalrie [E. K.].
1. He sheweth the cause of contempt of Poetry to be idlenesse and basenesse of mynd [E. K.].
2. Cage. I.e., poets found nothing worthy to write of, and the spirit of heroic achievement (sun-bright honor) found expression neither in deeds nor in song. "To put in preace": put in practice, exercise.
3. An Ironicall Sarcasmus, spoken in derision of these rude wits, whych make more account of a ryming rybaud, then of skill grounded upon learning and judgment [E. K.].

(And yet is Princes pallace the most fitt)
Ne brest of baser birth[4] doth thee embrace.
Then make thee winges of thine aspyring wit,
And, whence thou camst, flye backe to heaven apace.

CUDDIE

85 Ah Percy it is all to° weake and wanne,   *too*
So high to sore,° and make so large a flight: *soar*
Her peecèd pyneons bene not so in plight,
For Colin fittes such famous flight to scanne:[5]
He, were he not with love so ill bedight,°   *afflicted*
90 Would mount as high, and sing as socte° as Swanne.[6]   *sweet*

PIERS

Ah fon,° for love does teach him climbe so hie,   *fool*
And lyftes him up out of the loathsome myre:
Such immortall mirrhor,[7] as he doth admire,
Would rayse ones mynd above the starry skie.
95 And cause a caytive corage[8] to aspire,
For lofty love doth loath a lowly eye.

CUDDIE

All otherwise the state of Poet stands,
For lordly love is such a Tyranne fell:°   *fierce*
That where he rules, all power he doth expell.
100 The vaunted verse a vacant head demaundes,
Ne wont with crabbèd care the Muses dwell:
Unwisely weaves, that takes two webbes in hand.[9]

Who ever casts° to compasse° weightye prise,   *tries / attain*
And thinks to throwe out thondring words of threate:
105 Let powre in lavish cups and thriftie bitts of meate,
For Bacchus fruite is frend to Phoebus wise.[1]
And when with Wine the braine begins to sweate,
The nombers flowe as fast as spring doth ryse.

Thou kenst° not Percie howe the ryme should rage.   *knowest*
110 O if my temples were distaind° with wine,   *stained*
And girt in girlonds of wild Yvie[2] twine,
How I could reare the Muse on stately stage,
And teache her tread aloft in buskin fine,
With queint Bellona[3] in her equipage.°   *retinue*

---

4. The meaner sort of men [E. K.].
5. Cuddie explains that the imperfect, patched wings ("peecèd pyneons") of his own poetic powers are not in condition, but that it is proper for ("fittes") Colin to attempt ("scanne") such a high poetic flight.
6. It is sayd of the learned that the swan a little before hir death, singeth most pleasantly [E. K.].
7. Beauty, which is an excellent object of Poeticall spirites [E. K.].
8. A base and abject minde [E. K.].
9. I.e., the Muses are not accustomed ("wont") to dwell with those afflicted by love ("crabbèd care"); he is an unwise weaver who takes two pieces of cloth ("webbes") in hand at once.
1. I.e., let him pour lavish drink but take only a little food, for wine ("Bacchus fruite") promotes poetry ("Phoebus"—Apollo— is god of poetry).
2. Worn by followers of Bacchus. "He seemeth here to be ravished with a Poetical furie. For (if one rightly mark) the numbers rise so ful, and the verse groweth so big, that it seemeth he hath forgot the meanenesse of shepheards state and stile" [E. K.].
3. Strange Bellona; the goddesse of battaile, that is Pallas [E. K.]. "Buskin": a boot worn by the actors in tragedies—hence, a symbol for tragedy.

115　But ah my corage cooles ere it be warme,
　　　For thy,° content us in thys humble shade:　　　　　　　*therefore*
　　　Where no such troublous tydes° han us assayde,°　　*times / assaulted*
　　　Here we our slender pipes may safely charme.[4]

PIERS

　　　And when my Gates shall han their bellies layd:[5]
120　*Cuddie* shall have a Kidde to store his farme.

Cuddies Embleme

Agitante calescimus illo &c.[6]

4. Temper and order [E. K.].
5. I.e., when my goats bear their young.
6. The Latin line, of which Spenser gives the first three words here, is from Ovid's *Fasti* 6.5: "There is a god within us; it is from his stirring that we feel warm." E. K. comments, "Hereby is meant, as also in the whole course of this Aeglogue, that Poetry is a divine instinct and unnatural rage passing the reache of comen reason."

The Faerie Queene

In a letter to Sir Walter Ralegh, appended to the first, 1590, edition of *The Faerie Queene*, Spenser describes his exuberant, multifaceted poem as an allegory—an extended metaphor or "dark conceit"—and invites us to interpret the characters and adventures in the several books in terms of the particular virtues and vices they enact or come to embody. Thus the Redcrosse Knight in Book 1 is the knight of Holiness (and also St. George, the patron saint of England); Sir Guyon in Book 2 is the knight of Temperance; the female knight Britomart in Book 3 is the knight of Chastity (chastity here meaning chaste love leading to marriage). The heroes of Books 4, 5, and 6 represent Friendship, Justice, and Courtesy. The poem's general end, Spenser writes, is "to fashion a gentleman or noble person in vertuous and gentle discipline," and the individual moral qualities, taken together, constitute the ideal human being.

However, Spenser's allegory is not as simple as the letter to Ralegh might suggest, and the fashioning of identity proves to be anything but straightforward. Far from being the static embodiments of abstract moral precepts, the knights have a surprisingly complex, altogether human relation to their allegorical identities, identities into which they grow only through painful trial and error in the course of their adventures. These adventures repeatedly take the form of mortal combat with sworn enemies—hence the Redcrosse Knight of Holiness smites the "Saracen" (that is, Muslim) Sansfoy (literally, "without faith")—but the enemies are revealed more often than not to be weirdly dissociated aspects of the knights themselves: when he encounters Sansfoy, Redcrosse has just been faithless to his lady Una, and his most dangerous enemy ultimately proves to be his own despair. Accordingly, the meaning of the various characters, episodes, and places is richly complex, revealed to us (and to the characters themselves) only by degrees.

The complexity is heightened by the inclusion, in addition to the moral allegory, of an historical allegory to which Spenser calls attention, in the letter to Ralegh, by observing that both the Faerie Queene and Britomart are personifications of Queen Elizabeth. Throughout the poem there is a dense network of allusions to events, issues, and particular persons in England and Ireland—for example, the queen, her rival Mary, Queen of Scots, the Spanish Armada, the English Reformation, the controversies over religious images, and the bitter colonial struggles against Irish rebellion. Some of Spenser's characters are identified by conventional symbols and attributes that would have been obvious to every reader of his time. For example, such a reader would know immediately that a woman who wears a miter and scarlet clothes and who dwells near the river Tiber represents (in one sense at least) the Roman Catholic Church, which had often been identified by Protestant preachers with the Whore of Babylon in the Book of Revelation. Marginal notes jotted in early copies of *The Faerie Queene* suggest, however, that there was no consensus among Spenser's contemporaries about the precise historical referents of others of the poem's myriad figures. (Sir Walter Ralegh's wife Bess, for example, seems to have identified many of the virtuous female characters as allegorical representations of herself.) Spenser's poem may be enjoyed as a fascinating story with multiple meanings, a story that works on several levels at once and continually eludes the full and definitive allegorical explanation it constantly promises to deliver.

The poem is also an epic. In moving from *The Shepheardes Calender* to *The Faerie Queene* Spenser deliberately fashioned himself after the great Roman poet Virgil, who began his poetic career with pastoral poetry and moved on to his epic poem, the *Aeneid*. The organization of each book into twelve cantos also imitates the twelve books of the *Aeneid*, and like Virgil, Spenser is deeply concerned with the dangerous struggles and painful renunciations required to achieve the highest values of human civilization. The heroic deeds of Spenser's brave knights are the achievements of individual aristocratic men and women, not the triumphs of armies or communities united in serving a common purpose, not even the triumph of the virtually invisible royal court of Gloriana, the Faerie Queene. Yet, taken together, the disjointed adventures of these solitary warriors constitute in Spenser's fervent vision the glory of Britain, the collective memory of its heroic past and the promise of a still more glorious future. And if the Faerie Queene herself is consigned to the margins of the poem that bears her name, she nonetheless is the symbolic embodiment of a shared national destiny, a destiny that reaches beyond mere political success to participate in the ultimate, millennial triumph of good over evil.

If *The Faerie Queene* is thus an epic celebration of Queen Elizabeth, the Protestant faith, and the English nation, it is also a chivalric romance, full of jousting knights and damsels in distress, dragons, witches, enchanted trees, wicked magicians, giants, dark caves, shining castles, and "paynims" (with French names). A clear, pleasant stream may be dangerous to drink from because to do so produces loss of strength. A pious hermit may prove to be a cunningly disguised villain. Houses, castles, and gardens are often places of education and challenge or of especially dense allegorical significance, as if they possess special, half-hidden keys to the meaning of the books in which they appear. As a romance, Spenser's poem is designed to produce wonder, to enthrall its readers with sprawling plots, marvelous adventures, heroic characters, ravishing descriptions, and esoteric mysteries.

The Faerie Queene constantly intertwines diverse literary and pictorial traditions. Entire episodes are adapted from two great Italian romantic epics, *Orlando furioso* (Orlando Mad, 1516), by Ariosto, and *Gerusalemme liberata* (Jerusalem Delivered, 1575), by Tasso. Ariosto and Tasso in turn were closely following Homer, Virgil, and Ovid, as well as other ancient poets. (For a Renaissance poet, borrowing from and reworking older materials was thought praiseworthy.) Places such as Lucifera's castle or the garden of Adonis, individual attributes such as Una's lamb or Speranza's anchor or Britomart's spear, and certain stock characters, with their names, physiognomies, and costumes, came to Spenser from the classics and the Bible, from theologians, from folk tales and medieval pageants, from tapestries, paintings, and collections of emblems.

The whole of *The Faerie Queene* is written in a remarkable nine-line stanza of closely interlocking rhymes (*ababbcbcc*), the first eight lines with five stresses each (iambic pentameter) and the final line with six stresses (iambic hexameter or alexandrine). The stanza gives the work a certain formal regularity, but the various books are composed on quite different structural principles. Book 1 is almost entirely self-contained; it has been called a miniature epic in itself, centering on the adventures of one principal hero, Redcrosse, who at length achieves the quest he undertakes at Una's behest: killing the dragon who has imprisoned her parents and thereby winning her as his bride. The spiritual allegory is similarly self-contained; it presents the Christian struggling heroically against many evils and temptations—doctrinal error, hypocrisy, the Seven Deadly Sins, and despair—to some of which he succumbs before finally emerging triumphant. It shows him separated from the one true faith and, aided by many interventions of divine grace, at length reunited with it once more. Then it treats his purgation from sin, his education in the House of Holiness, and his final salvation. By contrast the structure of Book 3 is more romancelike, with its multiplicity of principal characters (who present, allegorically, several varieties of chaste and unchaste love), its interwoven stories (Amoret and Scudamore, Belphoebe and Timias, Florimell and Marinell, Britomart and Artegall), and its conspicuous lack of closure.

To some degree a lack of closure characterizes all of *The Faerie Queene*, including the more self-contained of the six finished books, and it is fitting that there survives the fragment of another book, the cantos of Mutability, in which Spenser broods on the tension in nature between systematic order and ceaseless change. The poem as a whole is built around principles that pull tautly against one another: a commitment to a life of constant struggle and a profound longing for rest; a celebration of human heroism and a perception of ineradicable human sinfulness; a vision of evil as a terrifyingly potent force and a vision of evil as mere emptiness and filth; a faith in the supreme value of visionary art and a recurrent suspicion that art is dangerously allied to graven images and deception. That Spenser's knights never quite reach the havens they seek may reflect irresolvable tensions to which we owe much of the power and beauty of this great, unfinished work.

FROM THE FAERIE QUEENE

A Letter of the Authors[1]

EXPOUNDING HIS WHOLE INTENTION IN THE COURSE OF THIS WORKE: WHICH FOR THAT IT GIVETH GREAT LIGHT TO THE READER, FOR THE BETTER UNDERSTANDING IS HEREUNTO ANNEXED

To the Right noble, and Valorous, Sir Walter Raleigh knight, Lo. Wardein of the Stanneryes,[2] and her Majesties liefetenaunt of the County of Cornewayll

Sir knowing how doubtfully all Allegories may be construed, and this booke of mine, which I have entituled the **Faery Queene,** being a continued Allegory, or darke conceit,[3] I have thought good as well for avoyding of gealous opinions and misconstructions, as also for your better light in reading thereof, (being so by you commanded,) to discover unto you the general intention and meaning, which in the whole course thereof I have fashioned, without expressing of any particular purposes or by-accidents[4] therein occa-

---

1. The Letter was appended—not prefixed—to the 1590 edition of the poem. (It was omitted from the 1596 edition.) We follow the common practice of printing it as a "preface" to the work.

2. I.e., the mining districts of Cornwall and Devon. "Lo.": Lord.
3. Obscure or difficult poetic figure.
4. Secondary matters.

sioned. The generall end therefore of all the booke is to fashion a gentleman or noble person in vertuous and gentle[5] discipline: Which for that I conceived shoulde be most plausible and pleasing, being coloured with an historicall fiction, the which the most part of men delight to read, rather for variety of matter, then for profite of the ensample:[6] I chose the historye of King Arthure, as most fitte for the excellency of his person, being made famous by many mens former workes, and also furthest from the daunger of envy, and suspition of present time.[7] In which I have followed all the antique Poets historicall,[8] first Homere, who in the Persons of Agamemnon and Ulysses hath ensampled a good governour and a vertuous man, the one in his *Ilias*, the other in his *Odysseis:* then Virgil, whose like intention was to doe in the person of Aeneas: after him Ariosto comprised them both in his Orlando: and lately Tasso dissevered them againe, and formed both parts in two persons, namely that part which they in Philosophy call Ethice, or vertues of a private man, coloured in his Rinaldo: The other named Politice in his Godfredo.[9] By ensample of which excellente Poets, I labour to pourtraict in Arthure, before he was king, the image of a brave knight, perfected in the twelve private morall vertues, as Aristotle hath devised,[1] the which is the purpose of these first twelve bookes: which if I finde to be well accepted, I may be perhaps encouraged, to frame the other part of pollitice vertues in his person, after that hee came to be king. To some I know this Methode will seeme displeasaunt, which had rather have good discipline delivered plainly in way of precepts, or sermoned at large, as they use, then thus clowdily enwrapped in Allegoricall devises. But such, me seeme, should be satisfide with the use of these dayes, seeing all things accounted by their showes, and nothing esteemed of, that is not delightfull and pleasing to commune sence.[2] For this cause is Xenophon preferred before Plato, for that the one in the exquisite depth of his judgment, formed a Commune welth such as it should be, but the other in the person of Cyrus and the Persians fashioned a governement such as might best be:[3] So much more profitable and gratious is doctrine by ensample, then by rule. So have I laboured to doe in the person of Arthure: whome I conceive after his long education by Timon, to whom he was by Merlin delivered to be brought up, so soone as he was borne of the Lady Igrayne, to have seene in a dream or vision the Faery Queen, with whose excellent beauty ravished, he awaking resolved to seeke her out, and so being by Merlin armed, and by Timon throughly instructed, he went to seeke her forth in Faerye land. In that Faery Queene I meane glory in my generall intention, but in my particular I conceive the most excellent and glorious person of our soveraine the Queene, and her kingdome in Faery land. And yet in some places els, I doe otherwise shadow[4] her. For considering she beareth two persons, the one of a most royall Queene or Empresse,

5. Pertaining to a gentleman. "Fashion": (1) to represent; (2) to educate.
6. Example. "Then": than.
7. I.e., free from current political controversy.
8. I.e., epic.
9. Torquato Tasso (1544–1595) published his chivalric romance *Rinaldo* in 1562 and the epic *Gerusalemme liberata* (centered on the heroic figure of Count Godfredo) in 1581. Lodowick Ariosto (1474–1533) was author of the epic romance *Orlando furioso*, first published in complete form in 1532.

1. Aristotle did not devise twelve private moral virtues: Spenser was in fact relying on more modern philosophers—his friend Lodowick Bryskett and the Italian Piccolomini. That Spenser contemplated a poem four times as long as the six books we now have rather staggers the imagination.
2. The notions of the many. "Showes": appearances.
3. The allusion is to Plato's *Republic* and Xenophon's *Cyropaedia*.
4. Picture, portray.

the other of a most vertuous and beautifull Lady, this latter part in some places I doe express in Belphoebe, fashioning her name according to your owne excellent conceipt of Cynthia,[5] (Phoebe and Cynthia being both names of Diana.) So in the person of Prince Arthure I sette forth magnificence in particular, which vertue for that (according to Aristotle and the rest) it is the perfection of all the rest,[6] and conteineth in it them all, therefore in the whole course I mention the deedes of Arthure applyable to that vertue, which I write of in that booke. But of the xii. other vertues, I make xii. other knights the patrones, for the more variety of the history. Of which these three bookes contayn three, The first of the knight of the Redcrosse, in whome I expresse Holynes: The seconde of Sir Guyon, in whome I sette forth Temperaunce: The third of Britomartis a Lady knight, in whome I picture Chastity. But because the beginning of the whole worke seemeth abrupte and as depending upon other antecedents, it needs that ye know the occasion of these three knights severall adventures. For the Methode of a Poet historical is not such, as of an Historiographer.[7] For an Historiographer discourseth of affayres orderly as they were donne, accounting as well the times as the actions, but a Poet thrusteth into the middest, even where it most concerneth him, and there recoursing to the thinges forepaste,[8] and divining of thinges to come, maketh a pleasing Analysis of all. The beginning therefore of my history, if it were to be told by an Historiographer, should be the twelfth booke, which is the last, where I devise that the Faery Queene kept her Annuall feaste xii. dayes, uppon which xii. severall dayes, the occasions of the xii. severall adventures hapned, which being undertaken by xii. severall knights, are in these xii books severally handled and discoursed. The first was this. In the beginning of the feaste, there presented him selfe a tall clownishe[9] younge man, who falling before the Queen of Faeries desired a boone (as the manner then was) which during that feast she might not refuse: which was that hee might have the atchievement of any adventure, which during that feaste should happen, that being graunted, he rested him on the floore, unfitte through his rusticity for a better place. Soone after entred a faire Ladye in mourning weedes, riding on a white Asse, with a dwarfe behind her leading a warlike steed, that bore the Armes of a knight, and his speare in the dwarfes hand. Shee falling before the Queene of Faeries, complayned that her father and mother an ancient King and Queene, had bene by an huge dragon many years shut up in a brasen Castle, who thence suffred them not to yssew:[1] and therefore besought the Faery Queene to assygne her some one of her knights to take on him that exployt. Presently that clownish person upstarting, desired that adventure: whereat the Queene much wondering, and the Lady much gainesaying, yet he earnestly importuned his desire. In the end the Lady told him that unlesse that armour which she brought, would serve him (that is the armour of a Christian man specified by Saint Paul v. Ephes.[2])

5. Ralegh's poem *Cynthia* praised Queen Elizabeth.
6. For Aristotle, magnanimity ("magnificence" in Spenser)—greatness of soul—is the ultimate virtue.
7. Historian.
8. Past. "Thrusteth into the middest": referring to the critical dictum that epic should begin, as the Roman poet Horace said, *in medias res*—"in the

middle of things."
9. Rustic-looking.
1. Come forth.
2. Ephesians 6.11, "Put on the whole armor of God, that ye may be able to stand against the wiles of the devil." The parts (verses 14 to 17) are loins girt about with truth, breastplate of righteousness, feet shod with the gospel of peace, shield of faith "wherewith ye shall be able to quench all the fiery

that he could not succeed in that enterprise, which being forthwith put upon him with dewe furnitures[3] thereunto, he seemed the goodliest man in al that company, and was well liked of the Lady. And eftesoones[4] taking on him knighthood, and mounting on that straunge Courser, he went forth with her on that adventure: where beginneth the first booke, vz.

A gentle knight was pricking on the playne. &c.

The second day ther came in a Palmer[5] bearing an Infant with bloody hands, whose Parents he complained to have bene slayn by an Enchaunteresse called Acrasia: and therfore craved of the Faery Queene, to appoint him some knight, to performe that adventure, which being assigned to Sir Guyon, he presently went forth with that same Palmer: which is the beginning of the second booke and the whole subject thereof. The third day there came in, a Groome who complained before the Faery Queene, that a vile Enchaunter called Busirane had in hand a most faire Lady called Amoretta, whom he kept in most grievous torment, because she would not yield him the pleasure of her body. Whereupon Sir Scudamour the lover of that Lady presently tooke on him that adventure. But being unable to performe it by reason of the hard Enchauntments, after long sorrow, in the end met with Britomartis, who succoured him, and reskewed his love.

But by occasion hereof, many other adventures are intermedled, but rather as Accidents, then intendments.[6] As the love of Britomart, the overthrow of Marinell, the misery of Florimell, the vertuousnes of Belphoebe, the lasciviousnes of Hellenora, and many the like.

Thus much Sir, I have briefly overronne to direct your understanding to the wel-head of the History, that from thence gathering the whole intention of the conceit,[7] ye may as in a handfull gripe al the discourse, which otherwise may happily[8] seeme tedious and confused. So humbly craving the continuaunce of your honorable favour towards me, and th' eternall establishment of your happines, I humbly take leave.

23. January, 1589[9]
Yours most humbly affectionate.
ED. SPENSER.

---

darts of the wicked," helmet of salvation, and "sword of the Spirit, which is the word of God."
3. Suitable equipment.
4. Forthwith.
5. Pilgrim.
6. I.e., there are episodes that are not part of these

principal stores.
7. Conception.
8. Perhaps.
9. The date is actually 1590, because until England adopted the Gregorian calendar in 1752, the new year began on March 25.

The First Booke of The Faerie Queene

Contayning
The Legende of the
Knight of the Red Crosse,
or
Of Holinesse

1

Lo I the man, whose Muse whilome did maske,
    As time her taught, in lowly Shepheards weeds,[1]
Am now enforst a far unfitter taske,
    For trumpets sterne to chaunge mine Oaten reeds,[2]
5   And sing of Knights and Ladies gentle° deeds;   *noble*
    Whose prayses having slept in silence long,[3]
    Me, all too meane,° the sacred Muse areeds°   *low / counsels*
    To blazon° broad emongst her learned throng: *proclaim*
Fierce warres and faithfull loves shall moralize my song.

2

10 Helpe then, O holy Virgin chiefe of nine,[4]
    Thy weaker° Novice to performe thy will,   *too weak*
    Lay forth out of thine everlasting scryne°   *a chest for papers*
    The antique rolles, which there lye hidden still,
    Of Faerie knights and fairest Tanaquill,°   *i.e., Gloriana*
15 Whom that most noble Briton Prince[5] so long
    Sought through the world, and suffered so much ill,
    That I must rue his undeservèd wrong:
O helpe thou my weake wit, and sharpen my dull tong.

3

And thou most dreaded impe° of highest Jove,   *child, i.e., Cupid*
20 Faire Venus sonne, that with thy cruell dart
    At that good knight so cunningly didst rove,°   *shoot*
    That glorious fire it kindled in his hart,
    Lay now thy deadly Heben° bow apart,   *ebony*
    And with thy mother milde come to mine ayde:
25 Come both, and with you bring triumphant Mart,[6]
    In loves and gentle jollities arrayd,
After his murdrous spoiles and bloudy rage allayd.

4

And with them eke,° O Goddesse heavenly bright,   *also*
    Mirrour of grace and Majestie divine,

---

1. Garb. The poet appeared before ("whilome") as a writer of humble pastoral (i.e., *The Shepheardes Calender*). These lines are imitated from the verses prefixed to Renaissance editions of Virgil's *Aeneid.*
2. To write heroic poetry, of which the trumpet is a symbol, instead of pastoral poetry symbolized by the humble shepherd's pipe ("Oaten reeds").

3. Lines 5 and 6 are imitated from the opening lines of Ariosto's *Orlando furioso.*
4. Scholars have debated whether the reference is to Clio, the Muse of history, or to Calliope, the Muse of epic.
5. I.e., Arthur, named in 1.9.50.
6. Mars, god of war and lover of Venus.

30   Great Lady of the greatest Isle, whose light
      Like Phoebus lampe throughout the world doth shine,
      Shed thy faire beames into my feeble eyne,°   *eyes*
      And raise my thoughts too humble and too vile,°   *lowly*
      To thinke of that true glorious type[7] of thine,
35   The argument° of mine afflicted stile:°   *subject / humble work*
      The which to heare, vouchsafe, O dearest dred° a-while.   *object of awe*

Canto 1

The Patron of true Holinesse,
Foule Errour doth defeate:
Hypocrisie him to entrappe,
Doth to his home entreate.

1

    A Gentle Knight was pricking° on the plaine,   *spurring*
      Ycladd in mightie armes and silver shielde,
      Wherein old dints of deepe wounds did remaine,
      The cruell markes of many a bloudy fielde;
5   Yet armes till that time did he never wield:[8]
      His angry steede did chide his foming bitt,
      As much disdayning to the curbe to yield:
      Full jolly° knight he seemd, and faire did sitt,   *gallant*
    As one for knightly giusts° and fierce encounters   *tourneys, jousts*
        fitt.

2

10   But on his brest a bloudie Crosse he bore,
      The deare remembrance of his dying Lord,
      For whose sweete sake that glorious badge he wore,
      And dead as living ever him adored:
      Upon his shield the like was also scored,
15   For soveraine[9] hope, which in his helpe he had:
      Right faithfull true[1] he was in deede and word,
      But of his cheere[2] did seeme too solemne sad;°   *grave*
    Yet nothing did he dread, but ever was ydrad.°   *dreaded, feared*

3

    Upon a great adventure he was bond,
20   That greatest Gloriana to him gave,
      That greatest Glorious Queene of Faerie Lond,
      To winne him worship,° and her grace to have,   *honor*
      Which of all earthly things he most did crave;
      And ever as he rode, his hart did earne°   *yearn*
25   To prove his puissance in battell brave

7. I.e., Gloriana is the "type" (foreshadowing) of Queen Elizabeth.
8. Redcrosse wears the armor of the Christian man, as Spenser explained in the letter to Ralegh. It bears the dents of every Christian's fight against evil.

9. Having greatest power (often applied to medical remedies).
1. An echo of Revelation 19.11: "And I saw heaven opened; and behold a white horse; and he that sat upon him was called Faithful and True."
2. Facial expression, mood.

Upon his foe, and his new force to learne;
Upon his foe, a Dragon horrible and stearne.

4

A lovely Ladie rode him faire beside,
   Upon a lowly Asse more white then snow,
30   Yet she much whiter, but the same did hide
   Under a vele, that wimpled° was full low,   *lying in folds*
   And over all a blacke stole she did throw,
   As one that inly mournd: so was she sad,
35   Seemèd in heart some hidden care she had,
And by her in a line a milke white lambe she lad.

5

So pure an innocent, as that same lambe,
   She was in life and every vertuous lore,
   And by descent from Royall lynage came
40   Of ancient Kings and Queenes, that had of yore
   Their scepters stretcht from East to Westerne shore,
   And all the world in their subjection held;
   Till that infernall feend with foule uprore
   Forwasted° all their land, and them expeld: *laid waste*
45 Whom to avenge, she had this Knight from far compeld.°   *summoned*

6

Behind her farre away a Dwarfe did lag,
   That lasie seemd in being ever last,
   Or wearied with bearing of her bag
   Of needments at his backe. Thus as they past,
50   The day with cloudes was suddeine overcast,
   And angry Jove an hideous storme of raine
   Did poure into his Lemans[3] lap so fast,
   That every wight° to shrowd° it did constrain,   *creature / cover*
And this faire couple eke° to shroud themselves were fain.°   *also / eager*

7

55 Enforst to seeke some covert nigh at hand,
   A shadie grove not far away they spide,
   That promist ayde the tempest to withstand:
   Whose loftie trees yclad with sommers pride,
   Did spred so broad, that heavens light did hide,
60   Not perceable° with power of any starre: *penetrable*
   And all within were pathes and alleies wide,
   With footing worne, and leading inward farre:
Faire harbour that them seemes; so in they entred arre.

8

And foorth they passe, with pleasure forward led,
65   Joying to heare the birdes sweete harmony,

─────────────────
3. His lover's, i.e., the earth's.

Which therein shrouded from the tempest dred,°   *fearful*
Seemd in their song to scorne the cruell sky.
Much can° they prayse the trees, so straight and hy,   *did*
The sayling Pine, the Cedar proud and tall,
70   The vine-prop Elme, the Poplar never dry,
The builder Oake, sole king of forrests all,
The Aspine good for staves, the Cypresse funerall.

9

The Laurell, meed° of mightie Conquerours   *reward*
And Poets sage, the Firre that weepeth still,[4]
75   The Willow worne of forlorne Paramours,
The Eugh° obedient to the benders will,   *yew*
The Birch for shaftes, the Sallow° for the mill,   *willow*
The Mirrhe sweete bleeding in the bitter wound,
The warlike Beech, the Ash for nothing ill,
80   The fruitfull Olive, and the Platane° round,   *plane-tree*
The carver Holme,[5] the Maple seeldom inward sound.

10

Led with delight, they thus beguile the way,
Untill the blustring storme is overblowne;
When weening° to returne, whence they did stray,   *thinking*
85   They cannot finde that path, which first was showne,
But wander too and fro in wayes unknowne,
Furthest from end then, when they neerest weene,
That makes them doubt, their wits be not their owne:
So many pathes, so many turnings seene,
90   That which of them to take, in diverse doubt they been.

11

At last resolving forward still to fare,
Till that some end they finde or° in or out,   *either*
That path they take, that beaten seemed most bare,
And like to lead the labyrinth about°   *out of*
95   Which when by tract they hunted had throughout,
At length it brought them to a hollow cave,
Amid the thickest woods. The Champion stout
Eftsoones° dismounted from his courser brave,   *forthwith*
And to the Dwarfe a while his needlesse spere[6] he gave.

12

100   "Be well aware,"° quoth then that Ladie milde,   *watchful*
"Least suddaine mischiefe° ye too rash provoke: *misfortune*
The danger hid, the place unknowne and wilde,
Breedes dreadfull doubts: Oft fire is without smoke,
And perill without show: therefore your stroke
105   Sir knight with-hold, till further triall made."

---

4. I.e., exudes resin continuously. Spenser in these stanzas imitates Chaucer's catalog of trees in the *Parliament of Fowls*; the convention goes back to Ovid.

5. Holly or holm-oak, both suitable for carving.
6. "Needlesse" because the spear is used only on horseback. 'By tract' (line 95): by following the track.

"Ah Ladie," said he, "shame were to revoke°   *draw back*
The forward footing for° an hidden shade: *because of*
Vertue gives her selfe light, through darkenesse for to wade."

13

"Yea but," quoth she, "the perill of this place
110 I better wot then° you, though now too late   *know than*
To wish you backe returne with foule disgrace,
Yet wisedome warnes, whilest foot is in the gate,
To stay the stepe, ere forcèd to retrate.
This is the wandring wood, this Errours den,
115 A monster vile, whom God and man does hate:
Therefore I read° beware." "Fly fly," quoth then   *advise*
The fearefull Dwarfe: "this is no place for living men."

14

But full of fire and greedy hardiment,°   *boldness*
The youthfull knight could not for ought° be staide,   *anything*
120 But forth unto the darksome hole he went,
And lookèd in: his glistring° armor made   *shining*
A litle glooming light, much like a shade,
By which he saw the ugly monster plaine,
Halfe like a serpent horribly displaide,[7]
125 But th' other halfe did womans shape retaine,
Most lothsom, filthie, foule, and full of vile disdaine.° *loathsomeness*

15

And as she lay upon the durtie ground,
Her huge long taile her den all overspred,
Yet was in knots and many boughtes° upwound,   *coils*
130 Pointed with mortall sting. Of her there bred
A thousand yong ones, which she dayly fed,
Sucking upon her poisonous dugs, eachone
Of sundry shapes, yet all ill favorèd:
Soone as that uncouth° light upon them shone,   *unfamiliar*
135 Into her mouth they crept, and suddain all were gone.

16

Their dam upstart, out of her den effraide,°   *alarmed*
And rushèd forth, hurling her hideous taile
About her cursèd head, whose folds displaid°   *extended*
Were stretcht now forth at length without entraile.° *coiling*
140 She lookt about, and seeing one in mayle
Armèd to point,° sought backe to turne againe;   *i.e., completely*
For light she hated as the deadly bale,°   *injury*
Ay wont° in desert darknesse to remain,   *ever accustomed*
Where plaine none might her see, nor she see any plaine.

---

7. That Errour is half serpent reminds us of the primal error in Eden, which the serpent instigated. The description echoes both classical and biblical monsters (cf. Revelation 9.7–10).

17

145 Which when the valiant Elfe[8] perceived, he lept
As Lyon fierce upon the flying pray,
And with his trenchand° blade her boldly kept   *cutting*
From turning backe, and forcèd her to stay:
Therewith enraged she loudly gan to bray,
150 And turning fierce, her speckled taile advaunst,
Threatning her angry sting, him to dismay:°   *defeat*
Who nought aghast, his mightie hand enhaunst:°   *lifted up*
The stroke down from her head unto her shoulder glaunst.

18

Much daunted with that dint,° her sence was dazd,   *blow*
155 Yet kindling rage, her selfe she gathered round,
And all attonce her beastly body raizd
With doubled forces high above the ground:
Tho° wrapping up her wrethèd sterne arownd,   *then*
Lept fierce upon his shield, and her huge traine°   *tail*
160 All suddenly about his body wound,
That hand or foot to stirre he strove in vaine:
God helpe the man so wrapt in Errours endlesse traine.

19

His Lady sad to see his sore constraint,°   *fettered state*
Cride out, "Now now Sir knight, shew what ye bee,
165 Add faith unto your force, and be not faint:
Strangle her, else she sure will strangle thee."
That when he heard, in great perplexitie,⁵
His gall did grate for griefe° and high disdaine,   *wrath*
And knitting all his force got one hand free,
170 Wherewith he grypt her gorge⁶ with so great paine,   *throat*
That soone to loose her wicked bands did her constraine.

20

Therewith she spewd out of her filthy maw
A floud of poyson horrible and blacke,
Full of great lumpes of flesh and gobbets raw,
175 Which stunck so vildly, that it forst him slacke
His grasping hold, and from her turne him backe:
Her vomit full of bookes and papers was,[1]
With loathly frogs and toades, which eyes did lacke,
And creeping sought way in the weedy gras:
180 Her filthy parbreake° all the place defilèd has.[2]   *vomit*

21

As when old father Nilus gins to swell
With timely° pride above the Aegyptian vale,   *in season*

8. I.e., knight of Faerie Land.
9. In both the usual sense and the sense of "entangled condition."
1. Alluding (at one level) to books and pamphlets
of Catholic propaganda, notably attacks on Queen

Elizabeth.
2. Revelation 16.13: "And I saw three unclean
spirits like frogs come out of the mouth of the
dragon, and out of the mouth of the beast, and out
of the mouth of the false prophet."

His fattie° waves do fertile slime outwell,   *rich*
And overflow each plaine and lowly dale:
185 But when his later spring gins to avale,°   *subside*
Huge heapes of mudd he leaves, wherein there breed
Ten thousand kindes of creatures, partly male
And partly female of his fruitfull seed;
Such ugly monstrous shapes elswhere may no man reed.° *see*

22

190 The same so sore annoyèd has the knight,
That welnigh chokèd with the deadly stinke,
His forces faile, ne can no longer fight.
Whose corage when the feend perceived to shrinke,
She pourèd forth out of her hellish sinke
195 Her fruitfull cursèd spawne of serpents small,
Deformèd monsters, fowle, and blacke as inke,
Which swarming all about his legs did crall,
And him encombred sore, but could not hurt at all.

23

As gentle Shepheard in sweete even-tide,
200 When ruddy Phoebus gins to welke° in west,   *sink*
High on an hill, his flocke to vewen wide,
Markes° which do byte their hasty supper best; *observes*
A cloud of combrous° gnattes do him molest, *encumbering*
All striving to infixe their feeble stings,
205 That from their noyance he no where can rest,
But with his clownish° hands their tender wings *rustic*
He brusheth oft, and oft doth mar their murmurings.

24

Thus ill bestedd,° and fearful more of shame, *situated*
Then of the certaine perill he stood in,
210 Halfe furious unto his foe he came,
Resolved in minde all suddenly to win,
Or soone to lose, before he once would lin;°   *cease*
And strooke at her with more then manly force,
That from her body full of filthie sin
215 He raft° her hatefull head without remorse; *cut away*
A streame of cole black bloud forth gushèd from her corse.

25

Her scattred brood, soone as their Parent deare
They saw so rudely° falling to the ground, *with great force*
Groning full deadly, all with troublous feare,
220 Gathred themselves about her body round,
Weening° their wonted entrance to have found *thinking*
At her wide mouth: but being there withstood
They flockèd all about her bleeding wound,
And suckèd up their dying mothers blood,
225 Making her death their life, and eke° her hurt their good. *also*

26

That detestable sight him much amazde,° *stunned*
   To see th' unkindly Impes° of heaven accurst, *unnatural offspring*
   Devoure their dam; on whom while so he gazd,
   Having all satisfide their bloudy thurst,
230 Their bellies swolne he saw with fulnesse burst,
   And bowels gushing forth: well worthy end
   Of such as drunke her life, the which them nurst;
   Now needeth him no lenger labour spend,
His foes have slaine themselves, with whom he should contend.

27

235 His Ladie seeing all, that chaunst, from farre
   Approcht in hast to greet° his victorie, *congratulate*
   And said, "Faire knight, borne under happy starre,
   Who see your vanquisht foes before you lye;
   Well worthy be you of that Armorie,° *armor*
240 Wherein ye have great glory wonne this day,
   And prooved your strength on a strong enimie,
   Your first adventure: many such I pray,
And henceforth ever wish, that like succeed it may."

28

Then mounted he upon his Steede againe,
245 And with the Lady backward sought to wend;° *go*
   That path he kept, which beaten was most plaine,
   Ne ever would to any by-way bend,
   But still did follow one unto the end,
   The which at last out of the wood them brought.
250 So forward on his way (with God to frend)° *with God as friend*
   He passèd forth, and new adventure sought;
Long way he travelèd, before he heard of ought.

29

At length they chaunst to meet upon the way
   An aged Sire, in long blacke weedes yclad.³
255 His feete all bare, his beard all hoarie gray,
   And by his belt his booke he hanging had;
   Sober he seemde, and very sagely sad,° *grave*
   And to the ground his eyes were lowly bent,
   Simple in shew, and voyde of malice bad,
260 And all the way he prayèd, as he went,
And often knockt his brest, as one that did repent.

30

He faire the knight saluted, louting° low, *bowing*
   Who faire him quited,° as that courteous was: *answered*
   And after askèd him, if he did know
265 Of straunge adventures, which abroad did pas.

3. Dressed in long black garments.

"Ah my deare Sonne," quoth he, "how should, alas,
   Silly° old man, that lives in hidden cell,   *simple*
   Bidding his beades° all day for his trespas,   *saying his prayers*
   Tydings of warre and worldly trouble tell?
270 With holy father sits not with such things to mell.[4]

31

"But if of daunger which hereby doth dwell,
   And homebred evill ye desire to heare,
   Of a straunge man I can you tidings tell,
   That wasteth all this countrey farre and neare."
275 "Of such," said he, "I chiefly do inquere,
   And shall you well reward to shew the place,
   In which that wicked wight his dayes doth weare.°   *spend*
   For to all knighthood it is foule disgrace,
That such a cursed creature lives so long a space."

32

280 "Far hence," quoth he, "in wastfull° wildernesse   *desolate*
   His dwelling is, by which no living wight
   May ever passe, but thorough great distresse."
   "Now," sayd the Lady, "draweth toward night,
   And well I wote, that of your later° fight   *recent*
285 Ye all forwearied be: for what so strong,
   But wanting rest will also want of might?
   The Sunne that measures heaven all day long,
At night doth baite° his steedes the Ocean waves emong.   *feed, refresh*

33

"Then with the Sunne take Sir, your timely rest,
290 And with new day new worke at once begin:
   Untroubled night they say gives counsell best."
   "Right well Sir knight ye have advisèd bin,"
   Quoth then that agèd man; "the way to win
   Is wisely to advise:° now day is spent;   *take thought*
295 Therefore with me ye may take up your In°   *lodging*
   For this same night." The knight was well content.
So with that godly father to his home they went.

34

A little lowly Hermitage it was,
   Downe in a dale, hard by a forests side,
300 Far from resort of people, that did pas
   In travell to and froe: a little wyde°   *apart*
   There was an holy Chappell edifyde,°   *built*
   Wherein the Hermite dewly wont° to say   *was accustomed*
   His holy things° each morne and eventyde: *prayers*
305 Thereby a Christall streame did gently play,
Which from a sacred fountaine wellèd forth alway.

---

4. I.e., it is not fitting for a holy hermit to meddle ("mell") with such things.

35

Arrivèd there, the little house they fill,
   Ne looke for entertainement, where none was:
   Rest is their feast, and all things at their will;
310   The noblest mind the best contentment has.
   With faire discourse the evening so they pas:
   For that old man of pleasing wordes had store,
   And well could file° his tongue as smooth as glas;   *polish*
   He told of Saintes and Popes, and evermore
315 He strowd an *Ave-Mary*[5] after and before.

36

The drouping Night thus creepeth on them fast,
   And the sad humour;° loading their eye liddes,   *heavy moisture*
   As messenger of Morpheus° on them cast   *god of dreams*
   Sweet slombring deaw, the which to sleepe them biddes.
320 Unto their lodgings then his guestes he riddes:°   *leads*
   Where when all drownd in deadly sleepe;° he findes,   *sleep like death*
   He to his study goes, and there amiddes
   His Magick bookes and artes of sundry kindes,
He seekes out mighty charmes, to trouble sleepy mindes.

37

325 Then choosing out few wordes most horrible
   (Let none them read), thereof did verses frame,
   With which and other spelles like terrible,
   He bade awake blacke Plutoes griesly Dame,[6]
   And cursèd heaven, and spake reprochfull shame
330 Of highest God, the Lord of life and light.
   A bold bad man, that dared to call by name
   Great Gorgon,[7] Prince of darknesse and dead night,
At which Cocytus quakes, and Styx is put to flight.

38

And forth he cald out of deepe darknesse dred
335 Legions of Sprights, the which like little flyes;[8]
   Fluttring about his ever damnèd hed,
   A-waite whereto their service he applyes,
   To aide his friends, or fray° his enimies: *frighten*
   Of those he chose out two, the falsest twoo,
340 And fittest for to forge true-seeming lyes;
   The one of them he gave a message too,
The other by him selfe staide other worke to doo.

39

He making speedy way through spersèd° ayre,   *dispersed*
   And through the world of waters wide and deepe,

---

5. "Hail Mary"—that is, a Catholic prayer.
6. Proserpine, as patron of witchcraft.
7. Demogorgon, in some myths the progenitor of all the gods, so powerful that the mention of his

name causes hell's rivers (Styx and Cocytus) to tremble.
8. The simile associates him with Beelzebub (Lord of Flies).

345 To Morpheus house doth hastily repaire.
    Amid the bowels of the earth full steepe,
    And low, where dawning day doth never peepe,
    His dwelling is; there Tethys° his wet bed   *the wife of Ocean*
    Doth ever wash, and Cynthia[9] still° doth steepe   *continually*
350 In silver deaw his ever-drouping hed,
    Whiles sad° Night over him her mantle black doth spred.   *sober*

40

    Whose double gates he findeth lockèd fast,
    The one faire framed of burnisht Yvory,
    The other all with silver overcast;
355 And wakefull dogges before them farre do lye,
    Watching to banish Care their enimy,
    Who oft is wont° to trouble gentle Sleepe.   *accustomed to*
    By them the Sprite doth passe in quietly,
    And unto Morpheus comes, whom drownèd deepe
360 In drowsie fit he findes: of nothing he takes keepe.°   *notice*

41

And more, to lulle him in his slumber soft,
    A trickling streame from high rocke tumbling downe
    And ever-drizling raine upon the loft,
    Mixt with a murmuring winde, much like the sowne°   *sound*
365 Of swarming Bees, did cast him in a swowne:°   *swoon*
    No other noyse, nor peoples troublous cryes,
    As still° are wont t'annoy the wallèd towne,   *always*
    Might there be heard: but carelesse° Quiet lyes,   *free from care*
    Wrapt in eternall silence farre from enemyes.[1]

42

370 The messenger approching to him spake,
    But his wast° wordes returnd to him in vaine: *wasted*
    So sound he slept, that nought mought° him awake.   *might*
    Then rudely he him thrust, and pusht with paine,°   *effort*
    Whereat he gan to stretch: but he againe
375 Shooke him so hard, that forcèd him to speake.
    As one then in a dreame, whose dryer braine[2]
    Is tost with troubled sights and fancies° weake,   *fantasies*
He mumbled soft, but would not all his silence breake.

43

    The Sprite then gan more boldly him to wake,
380 And threatned unto him the dreaded name
    Of Hecate:° whereat he gan to quake,   *queen of Hades*
    And lifting up his lumpish head, with blame
    Halfe angry askèd him, for what° he came.   *why*

---

9. Diana, the goddess of the moon.
1. Spenser is imitating descriptions of the house of Morpheus in Chaucer and Ovid.

2. According to the old physiology, elderly people and other light sleepers had too little moisture in the brain.

"Hither," quoth he, "me Archimago[3] sent,
385   He that the stubborne Sprites can wisely tame,
    He bids thee to him send for his intent
    A fit false dreame, that can delude the sleepers sent."°   *senses*

44

The God obayde, and calling forth straight way
    A diverse° dreame out of his prison darke,   *distracting*
390   Delivered it to him, and downe did lay
    His heavie head, devoide of carefull carke,°   *anxious concerns*
    Whose sences all were straight benumbd and starke.
    He backe returning by the Yvorie dore,[4]
    Remounted up as light as chearefull Larke,
395   And on his litle winges the dreame he bore
In hast unto his Lord, where he him left afore.

45

Who all this while with charmes and hidden artes,
    Had made a Lady of that other Spright,
    And framed of liquid ayre her tender partes
400   So lively,° and so like in all mens sight,   *lifelike*
    That weaker° sence it could have ravisht quight: *too weak*
    The maker selfe for all his wondrous witt,
    Was nigh beguilèd with so goodly sight:
    Her all in white he clad, and over it
405 Cast a blacke stole, most like to seeme for Una[5] fit.°   *fitting*

46

Now when that ydle dreame was to him brought
    Unto that Elfin knight he bad him fly,
    Where he slept soundly void of evill thought
    And with false shewes abuse his fantasy,°   *imagination*
410   In sort as° he him schoolèd privily: *in the way that*
    And that new creature borne without her dew°   *unnaturally*
    Full of the makers guile, with usage sly
    He taught to imitate that Lady trew,
Whose semblance she did carrie under feignèd hew.°   *form*

47

415 Thus well instructed, to their worke they hast
    And comming where the knight in slomber lay
    The one upon his hardy head him plast,°   *placed*
    And made him dreame of loves and lustfull play
    That nigh his manly hart did melt away,
420   Bathèd in wanton blis and wicked joy:
    Then seemèd him his Lady by him lay,

3. The name can be construed as meaning both "archmagician" and "architect of images."
4. According to Homer (*Odyssey* 19.562–67) and Virgil (*Aeneid* 6.893–96), false dreams come through Sleep's ivory gate, true dreams through his gate of horn.
5. Her name means "one, unity." Elizabethan readers would know the Latin phrase *Una Vera Fides* ("one true faith") and also the proverb "Truth is one."

And to him playnd,° how that false wingèd boy;°   *complained / Cupid*
Her chast hart had subdewd, to learne Dame pleasures toy.°   *lustful play*

48

And she her selfe of beautie soveraigne Queene
425   Faire Venus seemde unto his bed to bring
    Her, whom he waking evermore did weene°   *think*
    To be the chastest flowre, that ay° did spring   *ever*
    On earthly braunch, the daughter of a king,
    Now a loose Leman° to vile service bound: *paramour*
430   And eke° the Graces seemèd all to sing,   *also*
    Hymen iô Hymen, dauncing all around,
Whilst freshest Flora her with Yvie girlond crownd.[6]

49

In this great passion of unwonted° lust,   *unaccustomed*
    Or wonted feare of doing ought amis,
435   He started up, as seeming to mistrust°   *suspect*
    Some secret ill, or hidden foe of his:
    Lo there before his face his Lady is,
    Under blake stole hyding her bayted hooke,
    And as halfe blushing offred him to kis,
440   With gentle blandishment and lovely° looke,   *loving*
Most like that virgin true, which for her knight him took.

50

All cleane dismayd to see so uncouth° sight,   *unseemly*
    And halfe enragèd at her shamelesse guise,
    He thought have slaine her in his fierce despight:°   *indignation*
445   But hasty heat tempring with sufferance wise,
    He stayde his hand, and gan himselfe advise
    To prove his sense, and tempt° her faignèd truth.   *test*
    Wringing her hands in wemens pitteous wise,
    Tho can° she weepe, to stirre up gentle ruth,°   *then did / pity*
450 Both for her noble bloud, and for her tender youth.

51

And said, "Ah Sir, my liege Lord and my love,
    Shall I accuse the hidden cruell fate,
    And mightie causes wrought in heaven above,
    Or the blind God, that doth me thus amate,°   *dismay*
455   For° hopèd love to winne me certaine hate?   *instead of*
    Yet thus perforce° he bids me do, or die.   *forcibly*
    Die is my dew:[7] yet rew° my wretched state   *pity*
    You, whom my hard avenging destinie
Hath made judge of my life or death indifferently.

---

6. The three graces of classical mythology were personifications of grace and beauty; here they sing a call to the pleasures of the marriage bed (Hymen was god of marriage). In the March eclogue of *The*

Shepheardes Calender, E. K. glossed Flora as "the Goddesse of flowres, but indede (as saith Tacitus) a famous harlot."
7. I.e., I deserve to die.

52

460 "Your owne deare sake forst me at first to leave
My Fathers kingdome," There she stopt with teares;
Her swollen hart her speach seemd to bereave,
And then againe begun, "My weaker yeares
Captived to fortune and frayle worldly feares,
465 Fly to your faith for succour and sure ayde:
Let me not dye in languor° and long teares.   sorrow
"Why Dame," quoth he, "what hath ye thus dismayd?
What frayes° ye, that were wont to comfort me affrayd?"   frightens

53

"Love of your selfe," she said, "and deare° constraint   dire
470 Lets me not sleepe, but wast the wearie night
In secret anguish and unpittied plaint,
Whiles you in carelesse sleepe are drownèd quight."
Her doubtfull words made that redoubted[8] knight
Suspect her truth: yet since no untruth he knew,
475 Her fawning love with foule disdainefull spight
He would not shend,° but said, "Deare dame I rew,   reject
That for my sake unknowne such griefe unto you grew.

54

"Assure your selfe, it fell not all to ground;
For all so deare as life is to my hart,
480 I deeme your love, and hold me to you bound;
Ne let vaine feares procure your needlesse smart,°   pain
Where cause is none, but to your rest depart."
Not all content, yet seemd she to appease°   cease
Her mournefull plaintes, beguilèd° of her art,   foiled
485 And fed with words, that could not chuse but please,
So slyding softly forth, she turnd° as to her ease.   returned

55

Long after lay he musing at her mood,
Much grieved to thinke that gentle Dame so light,°   frivolous
For whose defence he was to shed his blood.
490 At last dull wearinesse of former fight
Having yrockt a sleepe his irkesome spright,°   weary mind
That troublous dreame gan freshly tosse his braine,
With bowres and beds, and Ladies deare delight:
But when he saw his labour all was vaine,
495 With that misformèd spright[9] he backe returnd againe.

---

8. Dreaded, also doubting again. "Doubtfull":   9. I.e., with the spirit impersonating Una.
fearful, also questionable.

Canto 2

The guilefull great Enchaunter parts
The Redcrosse Knight from Truth:
Into whose stead faire falshood steps,
And workes him wofull ruth.

1

    By this the Northerne wagoner had set
      His seven fold teame behind the stedfast starre,[1]
      That was in Ocean waves yet never wet,
      But firme is fixt, and sendeth light from farre
5   To all, that in the wide deepe wandring arre:
      And chearefull Chaunticlere with his note shrill
      Had warnèd once, that Phoebus fiery carre[2]
      In hast was climbing up the Easterne hill,
    Full envious that night so long his roome did fill.

2

10   When those accursèd messengers of hell,
      That feigning dreame, and that faire-forgèd Spright
      Came to their wicked maister, and gan tell
      Their bootelesse° paines, and ill succeeding night: *useless*
      Who all in rage to see his skilfull might
15   Deluded so, gan threaten hellish paine
      And sad Proserpines wrath, them to affright.
      But when he saw his threatning was but vaine,
    He cast about, and searcht his balefull° bookes againe.   *deadly*

3

    Eftsoones° he tooke that miscreated faire,   *forthwith*
20   And that false other Spright, on whom he spred
      A seeming body of the subtile° aire,   *rarefied*
      Like a young Squire, in loves and lusty-hed
      His wanton dayes that ever loosely led,
      Without regard of armes and dreaded fight:
25   Those two he tooke, and in a secret bed,
      Covered with darknesse and misdeeming° night,   *misleading*
    Them both together laid, to joy in vaine delight.

4

    Forthwith he runnes with feignèd faithfull hast
      Unto his guest, who after troublous sights
30   And dreames, gan now to take more sound repast,°   *rest*
      Whom suddenly he wakes with fearefull frights,
      As one aghast with feends or damnèd sprights,
      And to him cals, "Rise rise unhappy Swaine,
      That here wex° old in sleepe, whiles wicked wights   *grow*

---

1. I.e., by this time the Big Dipper had set behind the North Star.

2. The chariot of the sun. "Chaunticlere": Chanticleer is the generic name for a rooster.

35 Have knit themselves in Venus shamefull chaine;
  Come see, where your false Lady doth her honour staine."

5

 All in amaze he suddenly up start
  With sword in hand, and with the old man went;
  Who soone him brought into a secret part,
40 Where that false couple were full closely ment°   *mingled*
  In wanton lust and lewd embracèment:
  Which when he saw, he burnt with gealous fire,
  The eye of reason was with rage yblent,°   *blinded*
  And would have slaine them in his furious ire,
45 But hardly° was restreinèd of° that aged sire. *with difficulty / by*

6

 Returning to his bed in torment great,
  And bitter anguish of his guiltie sight,
  He could not rest, but did his stout heart eat,
  And wast his inward gall with deepe despight,°   *malice*
50 Yrkesome° of life, and too long lingring night.   *tired*
  At last faire Hesperus[3] in highest skie
  Had spent his lampe, and brought forth dawning light,
  Then up he rose, and clad him hastily;
 The Dwarfe him brought his steed: so both away do fly.

7

55 Now when the rosy-fingred Morning faire.
  Weary of aged Tithones[4] saffron bed,
  Had spred her purple robe through deawy aire,
  And the high hils Titan° discoverèd,°   *the sun / revealed*
  The royall virgin shooke off drowsy-hed.
60 And rising forth out of her baser° bowre,   *too lowly*
  Lookt for her knight, who far away was fled,
  And for her Dwarfe, that wont to wait each houre:
 Then gan she waile and weepe, to see that woefull stowre.° *affliction*

8

 And after him she rode with so much speede
65 As her slow beast could make; but all in vaine:
  For him so far had borne his light-foot steede,
  Prickèd with wrath and fiery fierce disdaine,°   *indignation*
  That him to follow was but fruitlesse paine;
  Yet she her weary limbes would never rest,
70 But every hill and dale, each wood and plaine
  Did search, sore grievèd in her gentle brest,
 He so ungently left her, whom she lovèd best.

9

 But subtill° Archimago, when his guests   *cunning*
  He saw divided into double parts,

3. The morning star.
4. Tithonus is the husband of Aurora, goddess of the dawn.

75 And Una wandring in woods and forrests,
    Th' end of his drift,° he praisd his divelish arts   plot
    That had such might over true meaning harts;
    Yet rests not so, but other meanes doth make,
    How he may worke unto her further smarts:
80 For her he hated as the hissing snake,
    And in her many troubles did most pleasure take.

                        10

    He then devisde himselfe how to disguise;
        For by his mightie science° he could take   knowledge
        As many formes and shapes in seeming wise,°   in appearance
85 As ever Proteus⁵ to himselfe could make:
    Sometime a fowle, sometime a fish in lake,
    Now like a foxe, now like a dragon fell,°   fierce
    That of himselfe he oft for feare would quake,
    And oft would flie away. O who can tell
90 The hidden power of herbes, and might of Magicke spell?

                        11

    But now seemde best, the person to put on
        Of that good knight, his late beguilèd guest:
        In mighty armes he was yclad anon,
        And silver shield: upon his coward brest
95 A bloudy crosse, and on his craven crest
    A bounch of haires discolourd diversly:°   variously colored
    Full jolly° knight he seemde, and well addrest,°   gallant / armed
    And when he sate upon his courser free,
    Saint George himself ye would have deemèd him to be.

                        12

100 But he the knight, whose semblaunt° he did beare,   likeness
        The true Saint George was wandred far away,
        Still flying from° his thoughts and gealous feare;   because of
        Will was his guide,⁶ and griefe led him astray.
        At last him chaunst to meete upon the way
105 A faithlesse Sarazin° all armed to point,   Saracen
    In whose great shield was writ with letters gay
    Sans foy:⁷ full large of limbe and every joint
    He was, and carèd not for God or man a point.°   at all

                        13

    He had a faire companion of his way,
110   A goodly Lady clad in scarlet red,
        Purfled° with gold and pearle of rich assay,⁸   decorated
        And like a Persian mitre on her hed

5. A sea god who could change his shape at will   son or truth.
(*Odyssey* 4.398–424).   7. Literally, without faith, faithless.
6. Will should itself be under the guidance of rea- 8. Proven valuable by analysis.

She wore, with crownes and owches° garnishèd,   *brooches*
The which her lavish lovers to her gave;[9]
115 Her wanton° palfrey all was overspred   *unruly*
With tinsell trappings, woven like a wave,
Whose bridle rung with golden bels and bosses brave.°   *handsome studs*

14

With faire disport° and courting dalliaunce   *diversion*
She intertainde her lover all the way:
120 But when she saw the knight his speare advaunce,
She soone left off her mirth and wanton play,
And bad her knight addresse him to the fray:
His foe was nigh at hand. He prickt with pride
And hope to winne his Ladies heart that day,
125 Forth spurrèd fast: adowne his coursers side
The red bloud trickling staind the way, as he did ride.

15

The knight of the Redcrosse when him he spide,
Spurring so hote with rage dispiteous,°   *cruel*
Gan fairely couch° his speare, and towards ride: *lower*
130 Soone meete they both, both fell and furious,
That daunted with their forces hideous,
Their steeds do stagger, and amazèd stand,
And eke° themselves too rudely rigorous,°   *also / violent*
Astonied° with the stroke of their owne hand,   *stunned*
135 Do backe rebut,° and each to other yeeldeth land.   *recoil*

16

As when two rams stird with ambitious pride,
Fight for the rule of the rich fleecèd flocke,
Their hornèd fronts so fierce on either side
Do meete, that with the terrour of the shocke
140 Astonied both, stand sencelesse as a blocke,
Forgetfull of the hanging° victory: *in the balance*
So stood these twaine, unmovèd as a rocke,
Both staring fierce, and holding idely
The broken reliques of their former cruelty.

17

145 The Sarazin sore daunted with the buffe
Snatcheth his sword, and fiercely to him flies;
Who well it wards, and quyteth° cuff with cuff: *requites*
Each others equall puissaunce envies,
And through their iron sides with cruell spies°   *looks*

9. The lady's garb associates her with the Whore of Babylon (Revelation 17.3–4): "And I saw a woman sit upon a scarlet colored beast, full of names of blasphemy, having seven heads and ten horns. And the woman was arrayed in purple and scarlet color, and decked with gold and precious stones and pearls, having a golden cup in her hand full of abominations and filthiness of her fornication."

150 Does seeke to perce: repining courage yields
No foote to foe. The flashing fier flies
As from a forge out of their burning shields,
And streames of purple bloud new dies the verdant fields.

18

"Curse on that Crosse," quoth then the Sarazin,
155 "That keepes thy body from the bitter fit;°   *death pangs*
Dead long ygoe I wote° thou haddest bin,   *thought*
Had not that charme from thee forwarnèd° it: *prevented*
But yet I warne thee now assurèd° sitt,   *securely*
And hide thy head." Therewith upon his crest
160 With rigour° so outrageous he smitt,   *violence*
That a large share it hewd out of the rest,
And glauncing downe his shield, from blame him fairely blest.[1]

19

Who thereat wondrous wroth, the sleeping spark
Of native vertue° gan eftsoones revive,   *strength*
165 And at his haughtie helmet making mark,
So hugely° stroke, that it the steele did rive,   *mightily*
And cleft his head. He tumbling downe alive,
With bloudy mouth his mother earth did kis
Greeting his grave: his grudging° ghost did strive   *complaining*
170 With the fraile flesh; at last it flitted is,
Whither the soules do fly of men, that live amis.

20

The Lady when she saw her champion fall,
Like the old ruines of a broken towre,
Staid not to waile his woefull funerall,°   *death*
175 But from him fled away with all her powre;
Who after her as hastily gan scowre,°   *scurry*
Bidding the Dwarfe with him to bring away
The Sarazins shield, signe of the conqueroure.
Her soone he overtooke, and bad to stay,
180 For present cause was none of dread her to dismay.

21

She turning backe with ruefull countenaunce,
Cride, "Mercy mercy Sir vouchsafe to show
On silly° Dame, subject to hard mischaunce,   *helpless*
And to your mighty will." Her humblesse low
185 In so ritch weedes° and seeming glorious show,   *clothes*
Did much emmove his stout heroicke heart,
And said, "Deare dame, your suddein overthrow
Much rueth° me; but now put feare apart,   *grieves*
And tell, both who ye be, and who that tooke your part."

1. Preserved him from harm.

22

190 Melting in teares, then gan she thus lament;
"The wretched woman, whom unhappy howre
Hath now made thrall° to your commandèment,   slave
Before that angry heavens list to lowre,°   frown
And fortune false betraide me to your powre
195 Was (O what now availeth that I was!)
Borne the sole daughter of an Emperour,
He that the wide West under his rule has,
And high hath set his throne, where Tiberis doth pas.²

23

"He in the first flowre of my freshest age,
200 Betrothèd me unto the onely haire°   heir
Of a most mighty king, most rich and sage;
Was never Prince so faithfull and so faire,
Was never Prince so meeke and debonaire;°   gracious
But ere my hopèd day of spousall shone,
205 My dearest Lord fell from high honours staire,
Into the hands of his accursèd fone,°   foes
And cruelly was slaine, that shall I ever mone.³

24

"His blessed body spoild of lively breath,
Was afterward, I know not how, convaid°   carried away
210 And fro me hid: of whose most innocent death
When tidings came to me unhappy maid,
O how great sorrow my sad soule assaid.°   afflicted
Then forth I went his woefull corse to find,
And many yeares throughout the world I straid,
215 A virgin widow, whose deepe wounded mind
With love, long time did languish as the striken hind.°   deer

25

"At last it chauncèd this proud Sarazin
To meete me wandring, who perforce° me led   by violence
With him away, but yet could never win
220 The fort, that Ladies hold in soveraigne dread.
There lies he now with foule dishonour dead,
Who whiles he livde, was callèd proud Sans foy,
The eldest of three brethren, all three bred
Of one bad sire, whose youngest is Sans joy,
225 And twixt them both was borne the bloudy bold Sans loy.⁴

26

"In this sad plight, friendlesse, unfortunate,
Now miserable I Fidessa° dwell,   Faith

2. The Tiber River runs through Rome. The lady
is hence associated with the Catholic church. Her
father, she says, is ruler of the west—but Una's
father had the rule of both east *and* west (1.1.41);
historically, the true church once embraced east
and west.
3. The lady claims to have been betrothed to
Christ, bridegroom of the church.
4. Literally, without law. *Sans joy* means "without
joy, darkness of spirit."

Craving of you in pitty of my state,
To do none° ill, if please ye not do well."   no
230 He in great passion all this while did dwell,°   continue
More busying his quicke eyes, her face to view,
Then his dull eares, to heare what she did tell;
And said, "Faire Lady hart of flint would rew
The undeservèd woes and sorrowes, which ye shew.

27

235 "Henceforth in safe assuraunce may ye rest,
Having both found a new friend you to aid,
And lost an old foe, that did you molest:
Better new friend than an old foe is° said."   it is
With chaunge of cheare the seeming simple maid
240 Let fall her eyen, as shamefast° to the earth,   as if modestly
And yeelding soft, in that she nought gain-said,
So forth they rode, he feining° seemely merth,   simulating
And she coy lookes: so dainty they say maketh derth.[5]

28

Long time they thus together traveilèd,
245 Till weary of their way, they came at last,
Where grew two goodly trees, that faire did spred
Their armes abroad, with gray mosse overcast,
And their greene leaves trembling with every blast,°   breeze
Made a calme shadow far in compasse round:
250 The fearefull Shepheard often there aghast
Under them never sat, ne wont° there sound   nor was accustomed to
His mery oaten pipe, but shund th' unlucky ground.

29

But this good knight soone as he them can° spie,   did
For the coole shade him thither hastly got:
255 For golden Phoebus now ymounted hie,
From fiery wheeles of his faire chariot
Hurlèd his beame so scorching cruell hot,
That living creature mote° it not abide;   might
And his new Lady it endurèd not.
260 There they alight, in hope themselves to hide
From the fierce heat, and rest their weary limbs a tide.°   time

30

Faire seemely pleasaunce° each to other makes,   courtesy
With goodly purposes there as they sit:
And in his falsèd° fancy he her takes   deceived
265 To be the fairest wight° that livèd yit;   creature
Which to expresse, he bends his gentle wit,
And thinking of those braunches greene to frame
A girlond for her dainty forehead fit,
He pluckt a bough; out of whose rift there came
270 Small drops of gory bloud, that trickled downe the same.

5. Proverbial: what's dear is rare; here, coyness creates unsatisfied desire.

31

Therewith a piteous yelling voyce was heard,
  Crying, "O spare with guilty hands to teare
  My tender sides in this rough rynd embard,°   *imprisoned*
  But fly, ah fly far hence away, for feare
275 Least° to you hap, that happened to me heare,   *lest*
  And to this wretched Lady, my deare love,
  O too deare love, love bought with death too deare."
Astond he stood, and up his haire did hove°   *heave, raise*
And with that suddein horror could no member move.

32

280 At last whenas the dreadfull passiön
  Was overpast, and manhood well awake,
  Yet musing at the straunge occasiön
  And doubting much his sence, he thus bespake;
  "What voyce of damnèd Ghost from Limbo[6] lake,
285 Or guilefull spright wandring in empty aire,
  Both which fraile men do oftentimes mistake,°   *mislead*
  Sends to my doubtfull eares these speaches rare,
And ruefull plaints, me bidding guiltlesse bloud to spare?"

33

Then groning deepe, "Nor damned Ghost," quoth he,
290 "Nor guilefull sprite to thee these wordes doth speake,
  But once a man Fradubio,[7] now a tree,
  Wretched man, wretched tree; whose nature weake,
  A cruell witch her cursèd will to wreake,
  Hath thus transformed, and plast in open plaines,
295 Where Boreas° doth blow full bitter bleake,   *the north wind*
  And scorching Sunne does dry my secret vaines:
For though a tree I seeme, yet cold and heat me paines."

34

"Say on Fradubio then, or° man, or tree,"   *whether*
  Quoth then the knight, "by whose mischievous arts
300 Art thou misshapèd thus, as now I see?
  He oft finds med'cine, who his griefe imparts:
  But double griefs afflict concealing harts,
  As raging flames who striveth to suppresse."
  "The author then," said he, "of all my smarts,
305 Is one Duessa[8] a false sorceresse,
That many errant° knights hath brought to wretchednesse. *wandering*

35

"In prime of youthly yeares, when corage hot
  The fire of love and joy of chevalree
  First kindled in my brest, it was my lot

6. A region of hell, traditionally the abode of the unbaptized.
7. *Fra* (Italian "in" or "brother") + *dubbio* ("doubt"). The motif of a man imprisoned in a tree

derives from Virgil (*Aeneid* 3.27–42) and is used by Ariosto (*Orlando furioso* 6.26–53).
8. *Duessa* means "double being." *Due* (Italian "two") + *esse* (Latin "being").

310   To love this gentle Lady, whom ye see,
       Now not a Lady, but a seeming tree;
       With whom as once I rode accompanyde,
       Me chauncèd of a knight encountred bee,
       That had a like faire Lady by his syde,
315   Like a faire Lady, but did fowle Duessa hyde.

36

       "Whose forgèd beauty he did take in hand,°   *he maintained*
       All other Dames to have exceeded farre,
       I in defence of mine did likewise stand,
       Mine, that did then shine as the Morning starre:
320   So both to battell fierce arraungèd arre,
       In which his harder fortune was to fall
       Under my speare: such is the dye° of warre: *hazard*
       His Lady left as a prise martiall,°   *spoil of battle*
       Did yield her comely person, to be at my call.

37

325   "So doubly loved of Ladies unlike° faire,   *diversely*
       Th' one seeming such, the other such indeede,
       One day in doubt I cast° for to compare,   *determined*
       Whether° in beauties glorie did exceede;   *which one (of two)*
       A Rosy girlond was the victors meede:°   *reward*
330   Both seemde to win, and both seemde won to bee,
       So hard the discord was to be agreede.
       Fraelissa⁹ was as faire, as faire mote bee,
       And ever false Duessa seemde as faire as shee.

38

       "The wicked witch now seeing all this while
335   The doubtfull ballaunce equally to sway,
       What not by right, she cast to win by guile,
       And by her hellish science° raisd streight way   *magic*
       A foggy mist, that overcast the day,
       And a dull blast, that breathing on her face,
340   Dimmed her former beauties shining ray,
       And with foule ugly forme did her disgrace:
       Then was she faire alone, when none was faire in place.¹

39

       "Then cride she out, 'Fye, fye, deformèd wight,
       Whose borrowed beautie now appeareth plaine
345   To have before bewitchèd all mens sight;
       O leave her soone, or let her soone be slaine.'
       Her lothly visage viewing with disdaine,
       Eftsoones I thought her such, as she me told,
       And would have kild her; but with faignèd paine,
350   The false witch did my wrathfull hand withhold;
       So left her, where she now is turnd to treën mould.°   *the form of a tree*

9. Frailty (Italian *Fralezza*).   1. When nobody else was fair. "She": Duessa.

40

"Thens forth I tooke Duessa for my Dame,
  And in the witch unweeting° joyd long time,   *unknowingly*
  Ne ever wist, but that she was the same,
355 Till on a day (that day is every Prime,²
  When Witches wont do penance for their crime)
  I chaunst to see her in her proper hew.°   *in her own shape*
  Bathing her selfe in origane and thyme:³
  A filthy foule old woman I did vew,
360 That ever to have toucht her, I did deadly rew.°   *regret*

41

"Her neather partes misshapen, monstruous,
  Were hidd in water, that I could not see,
  But they did seeme more foule and hideous,
  Then womans shape man would beleeve to bee.
365 Thens forth from her most beastly companie
  I gan refraine, in minde to slip away,
  Soone as appeard safe opportunitie:
  For danger great, if not assured decay°   *destruction*
  I saw before mine eyes, if I were knowne to stray.

42

370 "The divelish hag by chaunges of my cheare°   *countenance*
  Perceived my thought, and drownd in sleepie night,
  With wicked herbes and ointments did besmeare
  My bodie all, through charmes and magicke might,
  That all my senses were bereavèd quight:°   *quite*
375 Then brought she me into this desert waste,
  And by my wretched lovers side me pight,°   *planted*
  Where now enclosd in wooden wals full faste,⁴
  Banisht from living wights, our wearie dayes we waste."

43

"But how long time," said then the Elfin knight,
380 "Are you in this misformèd house to dwell?"
  "We may not chaunge," quoth he, "this evil plight,
  Till we be bathèd in a living well;⁵
  That is the terme prescribèd by the spell."
  "O how," said he, "mote° I that well out find,   *might*
385 That may restore you to your wonted well?"°   *well-being*
  "Time and suffisèd fates to former kynd
  Shall us restore,⁶ none else from hence may us unbynd."

44

The false Duessa, now Fidessa hight,°   *called*
  Heard how in vaine Fradubio did lament,

---

2. Spring; or the first appearance of the new moon.
3. Oregano and thyme were used to cure scabs and itching.
4. I.e., imprisoned within the trees.

5. With allusion to 1 John 4.14, the "well of water, springing up into eternal life."
6. I.e., time and the satisfaction of the fates alone can restore us to our former human nature.

390   And knew well all was true. But the good knight
       Full of sad feare and ghastly dreriment,°   *gloom*
       When all this speech the living tree had spent,
       The bleeding bough did thrust into the ground,
       That from the bloud he might be innocent,
395   And with fresh clay did close the wooden wound:
    Then turning to his Lady, dead with feare her found.

45

    Her seeming dead he found with feignèd feare,
      As all unweeting of that well she knew,[7]
      And paynd himselfe with busie care to reare
400   Her out of carelesse° swowne. Her eylids blew   *unconscious*
      And dimmèd sight with pale and deadly hew°   *deathlike appearance*
      At last she up gan lift: with trembling cheare°   *demeanor*
      Her up he tooke, too simple and too trew,
      And oft her kist. At length all passèd feare,[8]
405   He set her on her steede, and forward forth did beare.

Canto 3

    Forsaken Truth long seekes her love,
      And makes the Lyon mylde,
    Marres° blind Devotions mart,° and fals   *spoils / trade*
      In hand of leachour° vylde.   *lecher*

1

    Nought is there under heav'ns wide hollownesse,°   *concavity*
      That moves more deare compassiön of mind,
      Then beautie brought t' unworthy° wretchednesse   *undeserved*
      Through envies snares or fortunes freakes° unkind: *sudden changes*
5   I, whether lately through her brightnesse blind,
      Or through alleageance and fast fealtie,
      Which I do owe unto all woman kind,
      Feele my heart perst° with so great agonie,   *pierced*
    When such I see, that all for pittie I could die.

2

10   And now it is empassionèd° so deepe,   *moved*
      For fairest Unas sake, of whom I sing,
      That my fraile eyes these lines with teares do steepe,
      To thinke how she through guilefull handeling,°   *treatment*
      Though true as touch,° though daughter of a king, *touchstone*
15   Though faire as ever living wight was faire,
      Though nor in word nor deede ill meriting,
      Is from her knight divorcèd° in despaire   *separated*
    And her due loves derived° to that vile witches share. *diverted*

---

7. I.e., pretending ignorance of what she knew   8. I.e., having overcome all fear.
well.

3

Yet she most faithfull Ladie all this while

20   Forsaken, wofull, solitarie mayd

Farre from all peoples prease,° as in exile,   *press, crowd*

In wildernesse and wastfull° deserts strayd,   *desolate*

To seeke her knight; who subtilly betrayd

Through that late vision, which th' Enchaunter wrought,

25   Had her abandond. She of nought affrayd,

Through woods and wastnesse° wide him daily sought;   *wilderness*

Yet wishèd tydings none of him unto her brought.

4

One day nigh wearie of the yrkesome way,

From her unhastie° beast she did alight,   *slow*

30   And on the grasse her daintie limbes did lay

In secret shadow,° farre from all mens sight: *shade*

From her faire head her fillet she undight,[9]

And laid her stole aside. Her angels face

As the great eye of heaven shynèd bright,

35   And made a sunshine in the shadie place;

Did never mortall eye behold such heavenly grace.

5

It fortunèd° out of the thickest wood   *chanced*

A ramping° Lyon rushèd suddainly,   *raging*

Hunting full greedie after salvage blood;°   *wild game*

40   Soone as the royall virgin he did spy,

With gaping mouth at her ran greedily,

To have attonce° devoured her tender corse;°   *at once / body*

But to the pray when as he drew more ny,

His bloudie rage asswagèd with remorse,

45   And with the sight amazd, forgat his furious forse.

6

In stead thereof he kist her wearie feet,

And lickt her lilly hands with fawning tong,

As he her wrongèd innocence did weet.°   *understand*

O how can beautie maister the most strong,

50   And simple truth subdue avenging wrong?

Whose yeelded pride and proud submissiön,

Still dreading death, when she had markèd long,

Her hart gan melt in great compassiön,

And drizling teares did shed for pure affectiön.

7

55   "The Lyon Lord of everie beast in field,"

Quoth she, "his princely puissance° doth abate   *power*

And mightie proud to humble weake does yield,

Forgetfull of the hungry rage, which late

9. She took off her headband.

    Him prickt, in pittie of my sad estate:°   *condition*
60   But he my Lyon, and my noble Lord,
    How does he find in cruell hart to hate
    Her that him loved, and ever most adord,
As the God of my life? why hath he me abhord?"

8

    Redounding° teares did choke th' end of her plaint,   *overflowing*
65   Which softly ecchoed from the neighbour wood;
    And sad to see her sorrowfull constraint°   *affliction*
    The kingly beast upon her gazing stood;
    With pittie calmd, downe fell his angry mood.
    At last in close hart shutting up her paine,
70   Arose the virgin borne of heavenly brood,°   *parentage*
    And to her snowy Palfrey got againe,
To seeke her strayèd Champion, if she might attaine.°   *overtake*

9

    The Lyon would not leave her desolate,
    But with her went along, as a strong gard
75   Of her chast person, and a faithfull mate
    Of her sad troubles and misfortunes hard:
    Still° when she slept, he kept both watch and ward,   *always*
    And when she wakt, he waited diligent,
    With humble service to her will prepard:
80   From her faire eyes he tooke commaundèment,
And ever by her lookes conceivèd her intent.

10

Long she thus traveilèd through deserts wyde,
    By which she thought her wandring knight shold pas,
    Yet never shew of living wight espyde;
85   Till that at length she found the troden gras,
    In which the tract° of peoples footing was,   *track*
    Under the steepe foot of a mountaine hore;°   *gray*
    The same she followes, till at last she has
    A damzell spyde slow footing her before,[1]
90   That on her shoulders sad° a pot of water bore.   *heavy*

11

To whom approching she to her gan call,
    To weet, if dwelling place were nigh at hand;
    But the rude° wench her answered nought at all,   *ignorant*
    She could not heare, nor speake, nor understand;[2]
95   Till seeing by her side the Lyon stand,
    With suddaine feare her pitcher downe she threw,
    And fled away: for never in that land
    Face of faire Ladie she before did vew,
And that dread Lyons looke her cast in deadly° hew.   *deathlike*

---

1. I.e., walking slowly in front of her.
2. Cf. Mark 4.11–12: "unto them that are without, all these things are done in parables: That seeing they may see, and not perceive; and hearing they may hear, and not understand."

12

100 Full fast she fled, ne ever lookt behynd,
　　　As if her life upon the wager lay,°　　　　　　　　*were at stake*
　　　And home she came, whereas her mother blynd
　　　Sate in eternall night: nought could she say,
　　　But suddaine catching hold, did her dismay
105　　With quaking hands, and other signes of feare:
　　　Who full of ghastly fright and cold affray,°　　　　*terror*
　　　Gan shut the dore. By this arrivèd there
　　　Dame Una, wearie Dame, and entrance did requere.°　　*request*

13

　　　Which when none yeelded, her unruly Page
110　　With his rude° clawes the wicket° open rent,　　　*rough / door*
　　　And let her in; where of his cruell rage
　　　Nigh dead with feare, and faint astonishment,[3]
　　　She found them both in darkesome corner pent;°　　*huddled*
　　　Where that old woman day and night did pray
115　　Upon her beades° devoutly penitent;　　　　　　*rosary*
　　　Nine hundred *Pater nosters* every day,
　　And thrise nine hundred *Aves* she was wont to say.[4]

14

　　And to augment her painefull pennance more,
　　　Thrise every weeke in ashes she did sit,
120　　And next her wrinkled skin rough sackcloth wore,[5]
　　　And thrise three times did fast from any bit:°　　　*food*
　　　But now for feare her beads she did forget.
　　　Whose needlesse dread for to remove away,
　　　Faire Una framèd words and count'nance fit:
125　　Which hardly° doen, at length she gan them pray,　*with difficulty*
　　That in their cotage small, that night she rest her may.[6]

15

　　The day is spent, and commeth drowsie night,
　　　When every creature shrowded is in sleepe;
　　　Sad Una downe her laies in wearie plight,
130　　And at her feet the Lyon watch doth keepe:
　　　In stead of rest, she does lament, and weepe
　　　For the late° losse of her deare lovèd knight,　　　*recent*
　　　And sighes, and grones, and evermore does steepe
　　　Her tender brest in bitter teares all night,
135　All night she thinks too long, and often lookes for light.

16

　　Now when Aldeboran was mounted hie
　　　Above the shynie Cassiopeias chaire,[7]
　　　And all in deadly sleepe did drownèd lie,

---

3. I.e., fainting with amazement.
4. Her prayers are the Lord's Prayer ("Our Father") and the Hail Mary.
5. Sackcloth and ashes are symbols of penitence.

6. I.e., that she might rest herself.
7. The star Aldebaran, in the constellation Taurus, mounts over the constellation Cassiopeia.

One knockèd at the dore, and in would fare;°   *come*
140 He knockèd fast,° and often curst, and sware,   *insistently*
That readie entrance was not at his call:
For on his backe a heavy load he bare
Of nightly stelths and pillage severall,[8]
Which he had got abroad by purchase° criminall.   *acquisition*

17

145 He was to weete° a stout and sturdie thiefe,   *in fact*
Wont to robbe Churches of their ornaments,
And poore mens boxes[9] of their due reliefe,
Which given was to them for good intents;
The holy Saints of their rich vestiments
150 He did disrobe, when all men carelesse slept,
And spoild the Priests of their habiliments,°   *vestments*
Whiles none the holy things in safety kept;
Then he by cunning sleights in at the window crept.

18

And all that he by right or wrong could find,
155 Unto this house he brought, and did bestow
Upon the daughter of this woman blind,
Abessa daughter of Corceca[1] slow,
With whom he whoredome usd, that few did know,
And fed her fat with feast of offerings,
160 And plentie, which in all the land did grow;
Ne sparèd he to give her gold and rings:
And now he to her brought part of his stolen things.

19

Thus long the dore with rage and threats he bet,°   *beat*
Yet of those fearefull women none durst rize,
165 The Lyon frayèd them, him in to let:[2]
He would no longer stay him to advize,°   *consider*
But open breakes the dore in furious wize,
And entring is; when that disdainfull° beast   *indignant*
Encountring fierce, him suddaine doth surprize,
170 And seizing° cruell clawes on trembling brest,   *fastening*
Under his Lordly foot him proudly hath supprest.

20

Him booteth not resist,[3] nor succour call,
His bleeding hart is in the vengers hand,
Who streight him rent in thousand peeces small,
175 And quite dismembred hath: the thirstie land
Drunke up his life; his corse left on the strand.°   *ground*

---

8. I.e., he carried the booty gained from nightly
thefts and various kinds of pillage.
9. A box for alms for the poor.
1. *Corceca* means "blind heart." Abessa's name
comes from "abbess," also *ab* + *esse* (Latin): "from

being," i.e., without substance.
2. I.e., neither of the women dared rise to let him
in because the lion terrified ("frayed") them.
3. It does him no good to resist.

His fearefull friends weare out the wofull night,
Ne dare to weepe, nor seeme to understand
The heavie hap,° which on them is alight,°   *lot / fallen*
180 Affraid, least to themselves the like mishappen might.[4]

21

Now when broad day the world discovered° has,   *revealed*
Up Una rose, up rose the Lyon eke,
And on their former journey forward pas,
In wayes unknowne, her wandring knight to seeke,
185 With paines farre passing that long wandring Greeke,
That for his love refusèd deitie;[5]
Such were the labours of this Lady meeke,
Still seeking him, that from her still did flie,
Then furthest from her hope, when most she weenèd nie.°   *believed near*

22

190 Soone as she parted thence, the fearefull twaine,
That blind old woman and her daughter deare
Came forth, and finding Kirkrapine° there slaine,   *church robber*
For anguish great they gan to rend their heare,
And beat their brests, and naked flesh to teare.
195 And when they both had wept and wayld their fill,
Then forth they ranne like two amazèd deare,
Halfe mad through malice, and revenging will,°   *desire of revenge*
To follow her, that was the causer of their ill.

23

Whom overtaking, they gan loudly bray,
200 With hollow howling, and lamenting cry,
Shamefully at her rayling all the way,
And her accusing of dishonesty,°   *unchastity*
That was the flowre of faith and chastity;
And still amidst her rayling, she[6] did pray,
205 That plagues, and mischiefs, and long misery
Might fall on her, and follow all the way,
And that in endlesse error° she might ever stray.   *wandering*

24

But when she saw her prayers nought prevaile,
She backe returnèd with some labour lost.
210 And in the way as she did weepe and waile
A knight her met in mighty armes embost,°   *encased*
Yet knight was not for all his bragging bost,°   *boast*
But subtill Archimag, that Una sought
By traynes° into new troubles to have tost: *tricks*
215 Of that old woman tydings he besought,
If that of such a Ladie she could tellen ought.[7]

---

4. I.e., lest the same thing might happen amiss ("mishappen") to them.
5. Odysseus, who rejected immortality and the love of the nymph Calypso for his wife, Penelope.
6. Corceca. (Abessa cannot speak.)
7. I.e., if she could tell anything ("ought") about such a lady.

25

Therewith she gan her passion to renew,
    And cry, and curse, and raile, and rend her heare,°   *hair*
    Saying, that harlot she too lately knew,
220   That causd her shed so many a bitter teare,
    And so forth told the story of her feare:
    Much seeměd he to mone her haplesse chaunce,
    And after for that Ladie did inquere;
    Which being taught, he forward gan advaunce
225 His fair enchaunted steed, and eke° his charměd launce.   *also*

26

Ere long he came, where Una traveild slow,
    And that wilde Champion wayting° her besyde: *attending*
    Whom seeing such, for dread he durst not show
    Himselfe too nigh at hand, but turněd wyde
230   Unto an hill; from whence when she him spyde,
    By his like seeming shield, her knight by name
    She weend it was, and towards him gan ryde:
    Approching nigh, she wist° it was the same,   *believed*
And with faire fearefull humblesse° towards him shee came.   *humility*

27

235 And weeping said, "Ah my long lackěd Lord,
    Where have ye bene thus long out of my sight?
    Much fearěd I to have bene quite abhord,
    Or ought° have done, that ye displeasen might,   *aught*
    That should as death unto my deare hart light:[8]
240   For since mine eye your joyous sight did mis,
    My chearefull day is turnd to chearelesse night,
    And eke my night of death the shadow is;
But welcome now my light, and shining lampe of blis."

28

He thereto meeting[9] said, "My dearest Dame,
245   Farre be it from your thought, and fro my will,
    To thinke that knighthood I so much should shame,
    As you to leave, that have me lověd still.
    And chose in Faery court of meere° goodwill,   *pure*
    Where noblest knights were to be found on earth:
250   The earth shall sooner leave her kindly° skill   *natural*
    To bring forth fruit, and make eternall derth,°   *desert*
Then I leave you, my liefe,° yborne of heavenly berth.   *beloved*

29

"And sooth to say, why I left you so long,
    Was for to seeke adventure in strange place,
255   Where Archimago said a felon strong

8. I.e., be as a death blow to my loving heart.   9. Answering in like manner.
("Deare" can also mean *heavy, sore*.)

To many knights did daily worke disgrace;
But knight he now shall never more deface:°   *discredit*
Good cause of mine excuse; that mote° ye please   *may*
Well to accept, and evermore embrace
260   My faithfull service, that by land and seas
Have vowd you to defend, now then your plaint appease."°   *cease*

30

His lovely° words her seemd due recompence   *loving*
Of all her passèd paines: one loving howre
For many yeares of sorrow can dispence:°   *make amends*
265   A dram of sweet is worth a pound of sowre:
She has forgot, how many a wofull stowre°   *trouble*
For him she late endured; she speakes no more
Of past: true is, that true love hath no powre
To looken backe; his eyes be fixt before.
270   Before her stands her knight, for whom she toyld so sore.

31

Much like, as when the beaten marinere,
That long hath wandred in the Ocean wide,
Oft soust° in swelling Tethys[1] saltish teare,   *soaked*
And long time having tand his tawney hide
275   With blustring breath of heaven, that none can bide,
And scorching flames of fierce Orions hound,[2]
Soone as the port from farre he has espide,
His chearefull whistle merrily doth sound,
And Nereus crownes with cups;[3] his mates him pledg° around.   *toast*

32

280 Such joy made Una, when her knight she found;
And eke th' enchaunter joyous seemd no lesse,
Then the glad marchant, that does vew from ground
His ship farre come from watrie wildernesse,
He hurles out vowes, and Neptune oft doth blesse:
285   So forth they past, and all the way they spent
Discoursing of her dreadfull late distresse,
In which he askt her, what the Lyon ment:
Who told her all that fell in journey as she went.[4]

33

They had not ridden farre, when they might see
290   One pricking° towards them with hastie heat,   *spurring*
Full strongly armd, and on a courser free,°   *eager to charge*
That through his fiercenesse fomed all with sweat,
And the sharpe yron° did for anger eat,   *bit*
When his hot ryder spurd his chauffèd° side;   *chafed, heated*

---

1. The wife of Ocean; here, the Ocean.
2. Sirius, the dog star, symbolizing hot weather (the dog days).
3. Nereus, a benevolent sea god, to whom the mariner in gratitude makes libations.
4. I.e., she told all that had befallen her on her journey.

295 His looke was sterne, and seemèd still to threat
      Cruell revenge, which he in hart did hyde,
And on his shield Sans loy in bloudie lines was dyde.

34

      When nigh he drew unto this gentle payre
      And saw the Red-crosse, which the knight did beare,
300   He burnt in fire, and gan eftsoones prepare
      Himselfe to battell with his couchèd speare.
      Loth was that other, and did faint through feare,
      To taste th' untryed dint° of deadly steele;   *blow*
      But yet his Lady did so well him cheare,
305   That hope of new good hap he gan to feele;
So bent° his speare, and spurnd his horse with yron heele.   *lowered*

35

      But that proud Paynim° forward came so fierce,   *pagan*
      And full of wrath, that with his sharp-head speare
      Through vainely crossèd shield[5] he quite did pierce,
310   And had his staggering steede not shrunke for feare,
      Through shield and bodie eke he should him beare:°   *thrust*
      Yet so great was the puissance of his push,
      That from his saddle quite he did him beare:
      He tombling rudely° downe to ground did rush,   *violently*
315 And from his gorèd wound a well of bloud did gush.

36

      Dismounting lightly from his loftie steed,
      He to him lept, in mind to reave° his life,   *take*
      And proudly said, "Lo there the worthie meed°   *recompense*
      Of him, that slew Sans foy with bloudie knife;
320   Henceforth his ghost freed from repining strife,
      In peace may passen over Lethe[6] lake,
      When mourning altars purgd° with enemies life,   *cleansed*
      The blacke infernall Furies[7] doen aslake:°   *appease*
Life from Sans foy thou tookst, Sans loy shall from thee take."

37

325 Therewith in haste his helmet gan unlace,
      Till Una cride, "O hold that heavie hand,
      Deare Sir, what ever that thou be in place:°   *whoever you are*
      Enough is, that thy foe doth vanquisht stand
      Now at thy mercy: Mercie not withstand:
330   For he is one the truest knight alive,[8]

---

5. The cross on Archimago's shield was false and did not give him the protection the Redcrosse knight received in his fight with Sansfoy (see canto 2, stanza 18).

6. The river of forgetfulness in Hades.
7. Spirits of discord and revenge.
8. I.e., do not withhold mercy, for he is the one truest knight.

Though conquered now he lie on lowly land,°   *i.e., low on the ground*
And whilest him fortune favour, faire did thrive
In bloudie field: therefore of life him not deprive."

38

Her piteous words might not abate his rage,
335   But rudely rending up his helmet, would
Have slaine him straight: but when he sees his age,
And hoarie head of Archimago old,
His hastie hand he doth amazèd hold,
And halfe ashamèd, wondred at the sight:
340   For the old man well knew he, though untold,[9]
In charmes and magicke to have wondrous might,
Ne ever wont in field, ne in round lists[1] to fight.

39

And said, "Why Archimago, lucklesse syre,
What doe I see? what hard mishap is this,
345   That hath thee hither brought to taste mine yre?
Or thine the fault, or mine the error is,
In stead of foe to wound my friend amis?"
He answered nought, but in a traunce still lay,
And on those guilefull dazèd eyes of his
350   The cloud of death did sit. Which doen away,°   *when the swoon passed*
He left him lying so, ne would no lenger stay.

40

But to the virgin comes, who all this while
Amasèd stands, her selfe so mockt° to see   *deceived*
By him, who has the guerdon° of his guile,   *reward*
355   For so misfeigning her true knight to bee:
Yet is she now in more perplexitie,°   *trouble*
Left in the hand of that same Paynim bold,
From whom her booteth not° at all to flie;   *is of no use*
Who by her cleanly° garment catching hold,   *pure*
360 Her from her Palfrey pluckt, her visage to behold.

41

But her fierce servant full of kingly awe
And high disdaine,° whenas his soveraine Dame   *indignation*
So rudely handled by her foe he sawe,
With gaping jawes full greedy at him came,
365   And ramping on his shield, did weene° the same   *intend*
Have reft away with his sharpe rending clawes:
But he was stout, and lust did now inflame
His corage more, that from his griping pawes
He hath his shield redeemed,° and foorth his swerd he   *recovered*
   drawes.

9. I.e., without needing to be told.   1. Enclosures for fighting tournaments.

42

370 O then too weake and feeble was the forse
   Of salvage beast, his puissance to withstand:
   For he was strong, and of so mightie corse,°   *body*
   As ever wielded speare in warlike hand,
   And feates of armes did wisely° understand.   *skillfully*
375 Eftsoones he percèd through his chaufèd chest
   With thrilling point of deadly yron brand,[2]
   And launcht° his Lordly hart: with death opprest   *pierced*
He roared aloud, whiles life forsooke his stubborne brest.

43

Who now is left to keepe the forlorne maid
380   From raging spoile of lawlesse victors will?
   Her faithfull gard removed, her hope dismaid,
   Her selfe a yeelded pray to save or spill.°   *destroy*
   He now Lord of the field, his pride to fill,
   With foule reproches, and disdainfull spight
385   Her vildly entertaines, and will or nill,
   Beares her away upon his courser light:[3]
Her prayers nought prevaile; his rage is more of might.

44

And all the way, with great lamenting paine,
   And piteous plaints she filleth his dull° eares,   *deaf*
390   That stony hart could riven have in twaine,
   And all the way she wets with flowing teares:
   But he enraged with rancor, nothing heares.
   Her servile beast° yet would not leave her so,   *the palfrey*
   But followes her farre off, ne ought he feares,
395   To be partaker of her wandring woe,
More mild in beastly kind,° then that her beastly foe.   *nature*

Canto 4

To sinfull house of Pride, Duessa
guides the faithfull knight,
Where brothers death to wreak° Sansjoy   *avenge*
doth chalenge him to fight.

1

Young knight, what ever that dost armes professe,
   And through long labours huntest after fame,
   Beware of fraud, beware of ficklenesse,
   In choice, and change of thy deare lovèd Dame,
5   Least thou of her beleeve too lightly blame,
   And rash misweening° doe thy hart remove: *misjudgment*
   For unto knight there is no greater shame,

---

2. I.e., he pierced through the lion's angry
("chaufèd") chest with the penetrating ("thrilling")
point of his sword.

3. I.e., he treats her basely ("vildly") and willingly
or not bears her away quickly ("light") on his horse.

Then lightnesse and inconstancie in love;
That doth this Redcrosse knights ensample° plainly prove.   *example*

2

10　Who after that he had faire Una lorne,°   *forsaken*
　　Through light misdeeming° of her loialtie,   *misjudging*
　　And false Duessa in her sted had borne,³   *taken as companion*
　　Called Fidess', and so supposd to bee;
　　Long with her traveild, till at last they see
15　A goodly building, bravely garnishèd,°   *adorned*
　　The house of mightie Prince it seemd to bee:
　　And towards it a broad high way⁴ that led,
All bare through peoples feet, which thither traveilèd.

3

　　Great troupes of people traveild thitherward
20　Both day and night, of each degree and place,°   *rank*
　　But few returnèd, having scapèd hard,°   *with difficulty*
　　With balefull° beggerie, or foule disgrace,   *wretched*
　　Which ever after in most wretched case,
　　Like loathsome lazars,° by the hedges lay.   *lepers*
25　Thither Duessa bad him bend his pace:°   *direct his steps*
　　For she is wearie of the toilesome way,
And also nigh consumèd is the lingring day.

4

　　A stately Pallace built of squarèd bricke,
　　Which cunningly was without morter laid,
30　Whose wals were high, but nothing strong, nor thick,
　　And golden foile° all over them displaid,   *thin layer of gold*
　　That purest skye with brightnesse they dismaid:°   *outdid*
　　High lifted up were many loftie towres,
　　And goodly galleries farre over laid,°   *placed above*
35　Full of faire windowes, and delightfull bowres;
And on the top a Diall told the timely howres.⁵

5

　　It was a goodly heape° for to behould,   *building*
　　And spake the praises of the workmans wit;°   *skill*
　　But full great pittie, that so faire a mould°   *structure*
40　Did on so weake foundation ever sit:
　　For on a sandie hill,⁶ that still did flit,°   *shift*
　　And fall away, it mounted was full hie,
　　That every breath of heaven shakèd it:
　　And all the hinder parts, that few could spie,
45　Were ruinous and old, but painted cunningly.

---

4. "Broad is the way that leadeth to destruction" (Matthew 7.13).
5. A sundial measured the hours of the day.
6. Matthew 7.26–27: "A foolish man . . . built his house upon the sand: And the rain descended, and the floods came, and the winds blew, and beat upon that house: and it fell; and great was the fall of it."

6

Arrivèd there they passèd in forth right;
  For still to all the gates stood open wide,
  Yet charge of them was to a Porter hight°   *committed*
  Cald Malvenù,[7] who entrance none denide:
50 Thence to the hall, which was on every side
  With rich array and costly arras dight:[8]
  Infinite sorts of people did abide
  There waiting long, to win the wishèd sight
Of her, that was the Lady of that Pallace bright.

7

55 By them they passe, all gazing on them round,
  And to the Presence[9] mount; whose glorious vew
  Their frayle amazèd senses did confound:
  In living Princes court none ever knew
  Such endlesse richesse, and so sumptuous shew;
60 Ne Persia selfe, the nourse of pompous pride
  Like ever saw. And there a noble crew
  Of Lordes and Ladies stood on every side,
Which with their presence faire, the place much beautifide.

8

High above all a cloth of State° was spred,   *canopy*
65 And a rich throne, as bright as sunny day,
  On which there sate most brave embellishèd°   *handsomely clad*
  With royall robes and gorgeous array,
  A mayden Queene, that shone as Titans° ray,   *the sun's*
  In glistring gold, and peerelesse pretious stone:
70 Yet her bright blazing beautie did assay°   *attempt*
  To dim the brightnesse of her glorious throne,
As envying her selfe, that too exceeding shone.

9

Exceeding shone, like Phoebus fairest childe,
  That did presume his fathers firie wayne,°   *chariot*
75 And flaming mouthes of steedes unwonted° wilde *unusually*
  Through highest heaven with weaker° hand to rayne; *too weak*
  Proud of such glory and advancement vaine,
  While flashing beames do daze his feeble eyen,
  He leaves the welkin° way most beaten plaine,   *heavenly*
80 And rapt° with whirling wheeles, inflames the skyen, *carried away*
With fire not made to burne, but fairely for to shyne.[1]

10

So proud she shynèd in her Princely state,
  Looking to heaven; for earth she did disdayne,

---

7. The name means unwelcome. In courtly love allegories, the porter is often called Bienvenu or Bel-accueil ("welcome").
8. Decorated with costly wall hangings.

9. Presence chamber, where a sovereign receives guests.
1. Phaëthon tried to drive the chariot of Phoebus, his father, but set the skies on fire and fell.

And sitting high; for lowly° she did hate: *lowliness*
85   Lo underneath her scornefull feete, was layne
A dreadfull Dragon with an hideous trayne,°   *tail*
And in her hand she held a mirrhour bright,[2]
Wherein her face she often vewèd fayne,°   *with pleasure*
And in her selfe-loved semblance tooke delight;
90   For she was wondrous faire, as any living wight.

11

Of griesly° Pluto she the daughter was,   *horrid*
And sad Proserpina the Queene of hell;
Yet did she thinke her pearelesse worth to pas°   *surpass*
That parentage, with pride so did she swell,
95   And thundring Jove, that high in heaven doth dwell,
And wield° the world, she claymèd for her syre,   *govern*
Or if that any else did Jove excell:
For to the highest she did still aspyre,
Or if ought° higher were then that, did it desyre.   *anything*

12

100 And proud Lucifera men did her call,
That made her selfe a Queene, and crownd to be,
Yet rightfull kingdome she had none at all,
Ne heritage of native soveraintie,
But did usurpe with wrong and tyrannie
105 Upon the scepter, which she now did hold:
Ne ruld her Realmes with lawes, but pollicie,°   *political cunning*
And strong advizement of six wisards old,
That with their counsels bad her kingdome did uphold.

13

Soone as the Elfin knight in presence came,
110 And false Duessa seeming Lady faire,
A gentle Husher,° Vanitie by name   *usher*
Made rowme, and passage for them did prepaire:
So goodly° brought them to the lowest staire   *graciously*
Of her high throne, where they on humble knee
115 Making obeyssance,° did the cause declare,   *submission*
Why they were come, her royall state to see,
To prove° the wide report of her great Majestee.   *verify*

14

With loftie eyes, halfe loth to looke so low,
She thankèd them in her disdainefull wise,°   *manner*
120 Ne other grace vouchsafèd them to show
Of Princesse worthy, scarse them bad arise.
Her Lordes and Ladies all this while devise°   *make ready*
Themselves to setten forth to straungers sight:
Some frounce° their curlèd haire in courtly guise,   *frizzle*

---

2. Pride and figures associated with her in Renaissance literature and art often hold a mirror, emblematic of self-love.

125 Some prancke° their ruffes, and others trimly dight° *pleat / arrange*
  Their gay attire: each others greater pride does spight.³

15

  Goodly they all that knight do entertaine,
   Right glad with him to have increast their crew:
   But to Duess' each one himselfe did paine
130 All kindnesse and faire courtesie to shew;
   For in that court whylome° her well they knew: *formerly*
   Yet the stout Faerie mongst the middest° crowd *thickest*
   Thought all their glorie vaine in knightly vew,
   And that great Princesse too exceeding prowd,
135 That to strange° knight no better countenance° allowd. *stranger / favor*

16

  Suddein upriseth from her stately place
   The royall Dame, and for her coche doth call:
   All hurtlen° forth and she with Princely pace, *rush*
   As faire Aurora in her purple pall,⁴
140 Out of the East the dawning day doth call:
   So forth she comes: her brightnesse brode° doth blaze; *abroad*
   The heapes of people thronging in the hall,
   Do ride° each other, upon her to gaze: *climb up*
  Her glorious glitterand° light doth all mens eyes amaze. *glittering*

17

145 So forth she comes, and to her coche does clyme,
   Adornèd all with gold, and girlonds gay,
   That seemd as fresh as Flora in her prime,
   And strove to match, in royall rich array,
   Great Junos golden chaire,° the which they say *chariot*
150 The Gods stand gazing on, when she does ride
   To Joves high house through heavens bras-pavèd way
   Drawne of faire Pecocks, that excell in pride,
  And full of Argus eyes their tailes dispredden wide.⁵

18

  But this was drawne of six unequall beasts,
155 On which her six sage Counsellours did ryde,
   Taught to obay their bestiall beheasts,
   With like conditions to their kinds applyde:⁶
   Of which the first, that all the rest did guyde,
   Was sluggish Idlenesse the nourse of sin;
160 Upon a slouthfull Asse he chose to ryde,
   Arayd in habit blacke, and amis thin,⁷
  Like to an holy Monck, the service to begin.

3. Each begrudges the others' greater pride.
4. Goddess of dawn, in her crimson robe ("purple pall").
5. Peacocks, with their tails outspread ("dispredden wide"), are a symbol of pride. The hundred-eyed monster Argus was set by Juno to watch Io, Jupiter's love. When Mercury killed Argus, his eyes were put in the peacock's tail feathers.
6. Because riders and their mounts are alike bestial, the same conditions pertain (are "applyde") to both natures ("kinds"). This procession of the Seven Deadly Sins—of which Pride is queen—had a long tradition in medieval art and literature (see also Marlowe, *Dr. Faustus* 5.280–330, pp. 1007–08).
7. Idleness wears the gown ("habit") and hood or amice ("amis") of a monk. Traditionally, Idleness led the procession of the deadly sins.

19

And in his hand his Portesse° still he bare,   *breviary*
   That much was worne, but therein little red,
165 For of devotion he had little care,
   Still drownd in sleepe, and most of his dayes ded;
   Scarse could he once uphold his heavie hed,
   To looken, whether it were night or day:
   May seeme the wayne° was very evill led,   *chariot*
170 When such an one had guiding of the way,
That knew not, whether right he went, or else astray.

20

From worldly cares himselfe he did esloyne,°   *withdraw*
   And greatly shunnèd manly exercise,
   From every worke he chalengèd essoyne,°   *claimed exemption*
175 For contemplation sake: yet otherwise,
   His life he led in lawlesse riotise;°   *riotous conduct*
   By which he grew to grievous malady;
   For in his lustlesse° limbs through evill guise°   *feeble / living*
   A shaking fever raignd continually:
180 Such one was Idlenesse, first of this company.

21

And by his side rode loathsome Gluttony,
   Deformèd creature, on a filthie swyne,
   His belly was up-blowne with luxury.°   *indulgence*
   And eke with fatnesse swollen were his eyne,
185 And like a Crane his necke was long and fyne,[8]
   With which he swallowd up excessive feast,
   For want whereof poore people oft did pyne;°   *starve*
   And all the way, most like a brutish beast,
He spuèd up his gorge,[9] that° all did him deteast.   *so that*

22

190 In greene vine leaves he was right fitly clad;
   For other clothes he could not weare for heat,
   And on his head an yvie girland had,[1]
   From under which fast trickled downe the sweat:
   Still as he rode, he somewhat° still did eat,   *something*
195 And in his hand did beare a bouzing° can,   *drinking*
   Of which he supt so oft, that on his seat
   His dronken corse° he scarse upholden can,   *body*
In shape and life more like a monster, then° a man.   *than*

23

Unfit he was for any worldly thing,
200 And eke unhable once° to stirre or go,°   *at all / walk*
   Not meet° to be of counsell to a king,   *fit*

---

8. The crane is a common symbol of gluttony because its long and thin ("fyne") neck allows extended pleasure in swallowing.
9. Vomited up what he had swallowed.

1. He resembles the drunken satyr Silenus, foster father of Bacchus, god of wine; ivy is sacred to Bacchus.

Whose mind in meat and drinke was drownèd so,
That from his friend he seldome knew his fo:
Full of diseases was his carcas blew,
205 And a dry dropsie through his flesh did flow:
Which by misdiet daily greater grew:
Such one was Gluttony, the second of that crew.

24

And next° to him rode lustfull Lechery,   *just after*
  Upon a bearded Goat,[2] whose rugged haire,
210 And whally° eyes (the signe of gelosy,°)   *glaring / jealousy*
  Was like the person selfe, whom he did beare:
  Who rough, and blacke, and filthy did appeare,
  Unseemely man to please faire Ladies eye;
  Yet he of Ladies oft was lovèd deare,
215 When fairer faces were bid standen by:°   *away*
O who does know the bent of womens fantasy?

25

In a greene gowne he clothèd was full faire,
  Which underneath did hide his filthinesse,
  And in his hand a burning hart he bare,
220 Full of vaine follies, and new fangleness:°   *fickleness*
  For he was false, and fraught with ficklenesse,
  And learnèd had to love with secret lookes,
  And well could daunce, and sing with ruefulnesse,°   *pathos*
  And fortunes tell, and read in loving bookes,[3]
225 And thousand other wayes, to bait his fleshly hookes.

26

Inconstant man, that lovèd all he saw,
  And lusted after all, that he did love,
  Ne would his looser life be tide to law,
  But joyd weake wemens hearts to tempt and prove°   *try*
230 If from their loyall loves he might them move;
  Which lewdnesse fild him with reprochfull paine
  Of that fowle evill, which all men reprove,
  That rots the marrow, and consumes the braine:°   *i.e., syphilis*
Such one was Lecherie, the third of all this traine.

27

235 And greedy Avarice by him did ride,
  Upon a Camell loaden all with gold;[4]
  Two iron coffers hong on either side,
  With precious mettall full, as they might hold,
  And in his lap an heape of coine he told;°   *counted*
240 For of his wicked pelfe° his God he made,   *money*

2. Traditional symbol of Lust.
3. Either manuals on the art of love (e.g., Ovid's *Ars Amatoria*) or erotic books.
4. The camel as a symbol of avarice is based on

Matthew 19.24: "It is easier for a camel to go through the eye of a needle, than for a rich man to enter into the kingdom of God."

And unto hell him selfe for money sold;
Accursèd usurie was all his trade,
And right and wrong ylike in equall ballaunce waide.[5]

28

His life was nigh unto deaths doore yplast,
245   And thread-bare cote, and cobled shoes he ware,
    Ne scarse good morsell all his life did tast,
    But both from backe and belly still did spare,
    To fill his bags, and richesse to compare;°   *acquire*
    Yet chylde ne kinsman living had he none
250   To leave them to; but thorough daily care
    To get, and nightly feare to lose his owne,
He led a wretched life unto him selfe unknowne.

29

Most wretched wight, whom nothing might suffise,
    Whose greedy lust did lacke in greatest store,°   *plenty*
255   Whose need had end, but no end covetise,
    Whose wealth was want, whose plenty made him pore,
    Who had enough, yet wishèd ever more;
    A vile disease, and eke in foote and hand
    A grievous gout tormented him full sore,
260   That well he could not touch, not go,° nor stand: *walk*
Such one was Avarice, the fourth of this faire band.

30

And next to him malicious Envie rode,
    Upon a ravenous wolfe, and still° did chaw   *continually*
    Betweene his cankred° teeth a venemous tode,   *infected*
265   That all the poison ran about his chaw;°   *jaw*
    But inwardly he chawèd his owne maw°   *entrails*
    At neighbours wealth, that made him ever sad;
    For death it was, when any good he saw,
    And wept, that cause of weeping none he had,
270 But when he heard of harme, he wexèd wondrous glad.

31

All in a kirtle of discolourd say[6]
    He clothèd was, ypainted full of eyes;
    And in his bosome secretly there lay
    An hatefull Snake,[7] the which his taile uptyes
275   In many folds, and mortall sting implyes.°   *enfolds*
    Still as he rode, he gnasht his teeth, to see
    Those heapes of gold with griple Covetyse,°   *grasping Avarice*
    And grudgèd at the great felicitie
Of proud Lucifera, and his owne companie.

---

5. I.e., he made no distinction between right and wrong.

6. Jacket of many-colored wool.
7. Traditional attribute of Envy.

32

280 He hated all good workes and vertuous deeds,
And him no lesse, that any like did use,°   *perform*
And who with gracious bread the hungry feeds,
His almes for want of faith he doth accuse;[8]
So every good to bad he doth abuse:°   *twist*
285 And eke° the verse of famous Poets witt   *also*
He does backebite, and spightfull poison spues
From leprous mouth on all, that ever writt:
Such one vile Envie was, that fifte in row did sitt.

33

And him beside rides fierce revenging Wrath,
290 Upon a Lion, loth for to be led;
And in his hand a burning brond° he hath,   *sword*
The which he brandisheth about his hed;
His eyes did hurle forth sparkles fiery red,
And starèd sterne on all, that him beheld,
295 As ashes pale of hew and seeming ded;
And on his dagger still his hand he held,
Trembling through hasty rage, when choler° in him sweld.   *anger*

34

His ruffin° raiment all was staind with blood,   *disorderly*
Which he had spilt, and all to rags yrent,°   *torn*
300 Through unadvisèd rashnesse woxen wood,[9]
For of his hands he had no governement,°   *control*
Ne cared for bloud in his avengement:
But when the furious fit was overpast,
His cruell facts° he often would repent;   *actions*
305 Yet wilfull man he never would forecast,
How many mischieves should ensue his heedlesse hast.[1]

35

Full many mischiefes follow cruell Wrath;
Abhorrèd bloudshed, and tumultuous strife,
Unmanly murder, and unthrifty scath,[2]
310 Bitter despight,° with rancours rusty knife,   *malice*
And fretting griefe the enemy of life;
All these, and many evils moe° haunt ire,°   *more / anger*
The swelling Splene,[3] and Frenzy raging rife,
The shaking Palsey, and Saint Fraunces fire:[4]
315 Such one was Wrath, the last of this ungoldly tire.°   *train*

36

And after all, upon the wagon beame
Rode Sathan, with a smarting whip in hand,

8. Envy perversely discounts others' good works by attributing them to a selfish motive: the desire to compensate (in God's eyes) for lack of faith.
9. Grown insane.
1. I.e., he never would foresee ("forecast") the calamities his "heedless haste" caused.

2. I.e., inhuman murder and destructive harm.
3. Organ associated with anger in Renaissance physiology.
4. St. Anthony's fire, erysipelas, or the flaming itch; appropriate to Wrath.

With which he forward lasht the laesie teme,
So oft as Slowth° still in the mire did stand.   *Idleness*
320   Huge routs° of people did about them band,   *crowds*
Showting for joy, and still before their way
A foggy mist had covered all the land;
And underneath their feet, all scattered lay
Dead sculs and bones of men, whose life had gone astray.

37

325   So forth they marchen in this goodly sort,
To take the solace° of the open aire,   *pleasure*
And in fresh flowring fields themselves to sport;
Emongst the rest rode that false Lady faire,
The fowle Duessa, next unto the chaire
330   Of proud Lucifera, as one of the traine:
But that good knight would not so nigh repaire,°   *approach*
Him selfe estraunging from their joyaunce° vaine,   *festivity*
Whose fellowship seemd far unfit for warlike swaine.

38

So having solacèd themselves a space
335   With pleasaunce of the breathing° fields yfed,   *emitting fragrance*
They backe returnèd to the Princely Place;
Whereas an errant knight in armes ycled,°   *clad*
And heathnish shield, wherein with letters red
Was writ Sans joy, they new arrivèd find:
340   Enflamed with fury and fiers hardy-hed,°   *hardihood, boldness*
He seemd in hart to harbour thoughts unkind,
And nourish bloudy vengeaunce in his bitter mind.

39

Who when the shamèd shield⁵ of slaine Sans foy
He spied with that same Faery champions page,
345   Bewraying° him, that did of late destroy   *revealing*
His eldest brother, burning all with rage
He to him leapt, and that same envious gage°   *envied prize*
Of victors glory from him snatcht away:
But th 'Elfin knight, which ought that warlike wage,⁶
350   Disdaind to loose the meed he wonne in fray,°   *battle*
And him rencountring fierce, reskewd the noble pray.

40

Therewith they gan to hurtlen° greedily,   *rush together*
Redoubted battaile ready to darrayne,°   *contest*
And clash their shields, and shake their swords on hy,
355   That with their sturre° they troubled all the traine;   *tumult*
Till that great Queene upon eternall paine
Of high displeasure, that ensewen° might,   *ensue*
Commaunded them their fury to refraine,

---

5. Carrying a shield upside down, with the heraldic arms reversed, was a great insult (see line 369).

6. The knight (Redcrosse) who owned ("ought") that spoil of war ("warlike wage").

And if that either to that shield had right,
360　In equall lists[7] they should the morrow next it fight.

41

"Ah dearest Dame," quoth then the Paynim bold,
　"Pardon the errour of enragèd wight,
　Whom great griefe made forget the raines to hold
　Of reasons rule, to see this recreant° knight,　　　　　　　*cowardly*
365　No knight, but treachour° full of false despight°　　*traitor / disdain*
　And shamefull treason, who through guile hath slayn
　The prowest° knight, that ever field did fight,　　　　　*bravest*
　Even stout Sans foy (O who can then refrayn?)
Whose shield he beares renverst, the more to heape disdayn.

42

370　"And to augment the glorie of his guile,
　His° dearest love the faire Fidessa loe　　　　　*i.e., Sansfoy's*
　Is there possessèd of[8] the traytour vile,
　Who reapes the harvest sowen by his foe,
　Sowen in bloudy field, and bought with woe:
375　That° brothers hand shall dearely well requight　　　*that act*
　So be, O Queene, you equall favour showe."[9]
　Him litle answerd th'angry Elfin knight:
He never meant with words, but swords to plead his right.

43

But threw his gauntlet as a sacred pledge,
380　His cause in combat the next day to try:
　So been they parted both, with harts on edge,
　To be avenged each on his enimy.
　That night they pas in joy and jollity,
　Feasting and courting both in bowre and hall;
385　For Steward was excessive Gluttonie,
　That of his plenty pourèd forth to all;
Which doen,° the Chamberlain[1] Slowth did to rest them call.　　*done*

44

Now whenas darkesome night had all displayd
　Her coleblacke curtein over brightest skye,
390　The warlike youthes on dayntie° couches layd,　　　　*fine*
　Did chace away sweet sleepe from sluggish eye,
　To muse on meanes of hopèd victory.
　But whenas Morpheus° had with leaden mace　　*the god of sleep*
　Arrested all that courtly company,
395　Up-rose Duessa from her resting place,
And to the Paynims° lodging comes with silent pace.　　*pagan's*

---

7. I.e., in impartial formal combat.
8. Possessed by (i.e., sexually).
9. I.e., if, O Queen, you show impartiality ("equall

favour").
1. The court attendant in charge of the bedchambers.

45

Whom broad awake she finds, in troublous fit,°   *troubled mood*
  Forecasting, how his foe he might annoy,°   *injure*
  And him amoves° with speaches seeming fit: *arouses*
400 "Ah deare Sans joy, next dearest to Sans foy,
  Cause of my new griefe, cause of my new joy,
  Joyous, to see his ymage in mine eye,
  And greeved, to thinke how foe did him destroy,
  That was the flowre of grace and chevalrye;
405 Lo his Fidessa to thy secret faith I flye."

46

With gentle wordes he can° her fairely° greet,   *did / courteously*
  And bad say on the secret of her hart.
  Then sighing soft, "I learne that litle sweet
  Oft tempred is," quoth she, "with muchell° smart: *much*
410 For since my brest was launcht with lovely dart[2]
  Of deare Sans foy, I never joyèd howre,
  But in eternall woes my weaker hart
  Have wasted, loving him with all my powre,
And for his sake have felt full many an heavie stowre.°   *grief*

47

415 "At last when perils all I weenèd past,
  And hoped to reape the crop of all my care,
  Into new woes unweeting° I was cast,   *unknowing*
  By this false faytor,° who unworthy ware°   *imposter / wore*
  His worthy shield, whom he with guilefull snare
420 Entrappèd slew, and brought to shamefull grave.
  Me silly° maid away with him he bare,   *helpless*
  And ever since hath kept in darksome cave,
For that I would not yeeld, that° to Sans foy I gave.   *what*

48

"But since faire Sunne hath sperst° that lowring clowd,   *dispersed*
425 And to my loathèd life now shewes some light,
  Under your beames I will me safely shrowd,°   *take shelter*
  From dreaded storme of his disdainfull spight:
  To you th' inheritance belongs by right
  Of brothers prayse, to you eke longs° his love.   *belongs*
430 Let not his love, let not his restlesse spright°   *ghost*
  Be unrevenged, that calles to you above
From wandring Stygian[3] shores, where it doth endlesse move."

49

Thereto said he, "Faire Dame be nought dismaid
  For sorrowes past; their griefe is with them gone:
435 Ne yet of present perill be affraid;

---

2. I.e., since my breast was pierced with the dart
of love.

3. I.e., from wandering on the banks of the river
Styx, in Hades.

    For needlesse feare did never vantage° none,   *aid*
    And helplesse hap it booteth not to mone.[4]
    Dead is Sans-foy, his vitall° paines are past,   *living*
    Though greevèd ghost for vengeance deepe do grone:
440   He lives, that shall him pay his dewties° last,   *rites*
And guiltie Elfin bloud shall sacrifice in hast."

50

    "O but I feare the fickle freakes,"° quoth shee,   *unpredictable tricks*
    "Of fortune false, and oddes of armes[5] in field."
    "Why dame," quoth he, "what oddes can ever bee,
445   Where both do fight alike, to win or yield?"
    "Yea but," quoth she, "he beares a charmèd shield,
    And eke enchaunted armes, that none can perce,
    Ne none can wound the man, that does them wield."
    "Charmd or enchaunted," answerd he then ferce,°   *fiercely*
450 "I no whit reck,[6] ne you the like need to reherce.°   *recount*

51

    "But faire Fidessa, sithens° fortunes guile,   *since*
    Or enimies powre hath now captivèd you,
    Returne from whence ye came, and rest a while
    Till morrow next, that I the Elfe subdew,
455   And with Sans foyes dead dowry you endew."[7]
    "Ay me, that is a double death," she said,
    "With proud foes sight my sorrow to renew:
    Where ever yet I be, my secrete aid
Shall follow you." So passing forth she him obaid.

Canto 5

The faithfull knight in equall field
subdewes his faithlesse foe,
Whom false Duessa saves, and for
his cure to hell does goe.

1

The noble hart, that harbours vertuous thought,
    And is with child of glorious great intent,
    Can never rest, untill it forth have brought
    Th 'eternall brood of glorie excellent:[8]
5   Such restlesse passion did all night torment
    The flaming corage of that Faery knight,
    Devizing, how that doughtie° turnament   *worthy*
    With greatest honour he atchieven might;
Still did he wake, and still did watch for dawning light.

4. I.e., it does not help to moan over that which is beyond help ("helplesse hap").
5. Advantage of superior arms.
6. I do not care at all.
7. I.e., endow you with the legacy of the dead Sansfoy.
8. That good is manifested only in action, not in mere intent, is an important Renaissance commonplace.

2

10 At last the golden Orientall gate
    Of greatest heaven gan to open faire,
    And Phoebus[9] fresh, as bridegrome to his mate,
    Came dauncing forth, shaking his deawie haire:
    And hurld his glistring beames through gloomy aire.
15 Which when the wakeful Elfe perceived, streight way
    He started up, and did him selfe prepaire,
    In sun-bright armes, and battailous° array: *warlike*
For with that Pagan proud he combat will that day.

3

And forth he comes into the commune hall,
20 Where earely waite him many a gazing eye,
    To weet what end to straunger knights may fall.
    There many Minstrales maken melody,
    To drive away the dull melancholy,
    And many Bardes, that to the trembling chord
25 Can tune their timely° voyces cunningly,   *measured*
    And many Chroniclers, that can record
Old loves, and warres for ladies doen° by many a Lord.[1]   *done*

4

Soone after comes the cruell Sarazin,
    In woven maile all armèd warily,
30 And sternly lookes at him, who not a pin
    Does care for looke of living creatures eye.
    They bring them wines of Greece and Araby,
    And daintie spices fetcht from furthest Ynd,°   *India*
    To kindle heat of courage privily:°   *within*
35 And in the wine a solemne oth they bynd
T'observe the sacred lawes of armes, that are assynd.

5

At last forth comes that far renowmèd Queene,
    With royall pomp and Princely majestie;
    She is ybrought unto a palèd° greene,   *fenced*
40 And placèd under stately canapee,°   *canopy*
    The warlike feates of both those knights to see.
    On th' other side in all mens open vew
    Duessa placèd is, and on a tree
    Sans-foy his shield is hangd with bloudy hew:
45 Both those the lawrell girlonds[2] to the victor dew.

6

A shrilling trompet sownded from on hye,
    And unto battaill bad them selves addresse:

9. The sun. Cf. Psalm 19.4–5: "In them hath he sat a Tabernacle for the sun, Which is as a bridegroom coming out of his chamber."
1. Minstrels play the music on their instruments, Bards sing the words, Chroniclers—historians, epic poets—write of love and war.
2. Laurel wreaths were awarded to the victor of a joust.

Their shining shieldes about their wrestes° they tye,   *wrists*
And burning blades about their heads do blesse,°   *brandish*
50 The instruments of wrath and heavinesse:°   *rage*
With greedy force each other doth assayle,
And strike so fiercely, that they do impresse
Deepe dinted furrowes in the battred mayle;
The yron walles to ward their blowes are weake and fraile.[3]

7

55 The Sarazin was stout,° and wondrous strong,   *bold*
And heapèd blowes like yron hammers great:
For after bloud and vengeance he did long.
The knight was fiers,° and full of youthly heat: *high spirited*
And doubled strokes, like dreaded thunders threat:
60 For all for prayse and honour he did fight.
Both stricken strike, and beaten both do beat,
That from their shields forth flyeth firie light,
And helmets hewen deepe, shew marks of eithers might.

8

So th' one for wrong, the other strives for right:
65 As when a Gryfon[4] seizèd° of his pray,   *in possession*
A Dragon fiers encountreth in his flight,
Through widest ayre making his ydle° way,   *casual*
That would his rightfull ravine° rend away;   *plunder*
With hideous horrour both together smight,
70 And souce° so sore, that they the heavens affray: *strike*
The wise Southsayer° seeing so sad sight,   *soothsayer*
Th' amazèd vulgar tels of warres and mortall fight.

9

So th' one for wrong, the other strives for right,
And each to deadly shame would drive his foe:
75 The cruell steele so greedily doth bight
In tender flesh, that streames of bloud down flow,
With which the armes, that earst° so bright did show,   *at first*
Into a pure vermillion now are dyde:
Great ruth° in all the gazers harts did grow,   *pity*
80 Seeing the gorèd woundes to gape so wyde,
That victory they dare not wish to either side.

10

At last the Paynim chaunst to cast his eye,
His suddein° eye, flaming with wrathfull fyre,   *darting*
Upon his brothers shield, which hong thereby:
85 Therewith redoubled was his raging yre,°   *anger*
And said, "Ah wretched sonne of wofull syre,
Doest thou sit wayling by black Stygian lake

---

3. I.e., their armor is too frail to withstand such 4. A legendary monster, half-eagle, half-lion.
blows.

    Whilest here thy shield is hangd for victors hyre,°   *reward*
    And sluggish german⁵ doest thy forces slake,°   *slacken*
90 To after-send his foe, that him may overtake?

11

    "Goe caytive° Elfe, him quickly overtake,   *servile*
    And soone redeeme from his long wandring woe;
    Goe guiltie ghost, to him my message make,
    That I his shield have quit° from dying foe."   *rescued*
95 Therewith upon his crest he stroke him so,
    That twise he reelèd, readie twise to fall;
    End of the doubtfull battell deemèd tho
    The lookers on,⁶ and lowd to him gan call
The false Duessa, "Thine the shield, and I, and all."

12

100 Soone as the Faerie heard his Ladie speake,
    Out of his swowning dreame he gan awake,
    And quickning° faith, that earst was woxen weake,   *life-restoring*
    The creeping deadly cold away did shake:
    Tho moved with wrath, and shame, and Ladies sake,°   *cause*
105 Of all attonce he cast° avengd to bee,   *determined*
    And with so'exceeding furie at him strake,
    That forcèd him to stoupe upon his knee;
Had he not stoupèd so, he should have cloven bee.

13

    And to him said, "Goe now proud Miscreant,°   *misbeliever*
110 Thy selfe thy message doe° to german deare,   *give*
    Alone he wandring thee too long doth want:
    Goe say, his foe thy shield with his doth beare."
    Therewith his heavie hand he high gan reare,
    Him to have slaine; when loe a darkesome clowd
115 Upon him fell: he no where doth appeare,
    But vanisht is. The Elfe him cals alowd,
But answer none receives: the darknes him does shrowd.⁷

14

    In haste Duessa from her place arose,
    And to him running said, "O prowest° knight,   *bravest*
120 That ever Ladie to her love did chose,
    Let now abate the terror of your might,
    And quench the flame of furious despight,°   *anger*
    And bloudie vengeance; lo th' infernall powres
    Covering your foe with cloud of deadly night,

---

5. Kinsman; here, brother.
6. I.e., the onlookers then ("tho") thought this would end the battle, heretofore in doubt ("doubtfull").

7. The device of a god rescuing a hero in danger by hiding him in a cloud has parallels in *Iliad* 3.380, *Aeneid* 5.810–12, and *Gerusalemme liberata* 7.44–45

125   Have borne him hence to Plutoes balefull bowres.°   *Hades*
    The conquest yours, I yours, the shield, and glory yours."

15

    Not all so satisfide, with greedie eye
        He sought all round about, his thirstie blade
        To bath in bloud of faithlesse enemy;
130   Who all that while lay hid in secret shade:
        He standes amazèd, how he thence should fade.
        At last the trumpets Triumph sound on hie,
        And running Heralds humble homage made,
        Greeting him goodly with new victorie,
135   And to him brought the shield, the cause of enmitie.

16

    Wherewith he goeth to that soveraine Queene,
        And falling her before on lowly knee,
        To her makes present of his service seene;°   *proved*
        Which she accepts, with thankes, and goodly gree,°   *favor*
140   Greatly advauncing° his gay chevalree.   *extolling*
        So marcheth home, and by her takes the knight,
        Whom all the people follow with great glee,
        Shouting, and clapping all their hands on hight,°   *aloud*
    That all the aire it fils, and flyes to heaven bright.

17

145   Home is he brought, and laid in sumptuous bed:
        Where many skilfull leaches° him abide,°   *doctors / attend*
        To salve° his hurts, that yet still freshly bled.   *anoint*
        In wine and oyle they wash his woundes wide,
        And softly can embalme° on every side.   *carefully did anoint*
150   And all the while, most heavenly melody
        About the bed sweet musicke did divide,°   *descanted*
        Him to beguile of griefe and agony:
    And all the while Duessa wept full bitterly.

18

    As when a wearie traveller that strayes
155   By muddy shore of broad seven-mouthèd Nile,
        Unweeting of the perillous wandring wayes,
        Doth meet a cruell craftie Crocodile,
        Which in false griefe hyding his harmefull guile,
        Doth weepe full sore, and sheddeth tender teares:
160   The foolish man, that pitties all this while
        His mournefull plight, is swallowed up unwares,°   *unexpectedly*
    Forgetfull of his owne, that mindes anothers cares.

19

    So wept Duessa untill eventide,
        That shyning lampes in Joves high house were light:[8]

---

8. I.e., when ("that") the stars came out.

165   Then forth she rose, ne lenger would abide.
        But comes unto the place, where th' Hethen knight
        In slombring swownd nigh voyd of vitall spright,[9]
        Lay covered with inchaunted cloud all day:
        Whom when she found, as she him left in plight,[1]
170   To wayle his woefull case she would not stay,
        But to the easterne coast of heaven makes speedy way.

20

        Where griesly° Night, with visage deadly sad,   *grim, horrible*
        That Phoebus chearefull face durst never vew,
        And in a foule blacke pitchie mantle clad,
175   She findes forth comming from her darkesome mew,°   *den*
        Where she all day did hide her hated hew.°   *shape, color*
        Before the dore her yron charet stood,
        Alreadie harnessèd for journey new;
        And cole blacke steedes yborne of hellish brood,
180   That on their rustie bits did champ, as they were wood.°   *mad*

21

        Who when she saw Duessa sunny bright,
        Adorned with gold and jewels shining cleare.°   *brightly*
        She greatly grew amazèd at the sight,
        And th' unacquainted° light began to feare: *unfamiliar*
185   For never did such brightnesse there appeare,
        And would have backe retyred to her cave,
        Untill the witches speech she gan to heare,
        Saying, "Yet O thou dreaded Dame, I crave
        Abide,° till I have told the message, which I have."   *stay*

22

190   She stayd, and foorth Duessa gan proceede,
        "O thou most auncient Grandmother of all,[2]
        More old then Jove, whom thou at first didst breede,
        Or that great house of Gods caelestiall,
        Which wast begot in Daemogorgons hall,
195   And sawst the secrets of the world unmade,°   *before it was made*
        Why suffredst thou thy Nephewes° deare to fall   *grandsons*
        With Elfin sword, most shamefully betrade?
        Lo where the stout Sans joy doth sleepe in deadly shade.

23

        "And him before, I saw with bitter eyes
200   The bold Sans foy shrinke underneath his speare;
        And now the pray of fowles in field he lyes,
        Nor wayld of friends, nor laid on groning beare,[3]
        That whylome was to me too dearely deare.

9. Nearly ("nigh") devoid of life.
1. I.e., in the same desperate state she left him.
2. By tradition Night was eldest of the gods, existing before the world was formed and the Olympian gods were begotten in the hall of Demogorgon (Chaos).
3. Bier attended by mourners ("groning").

O what of Gods then boots it° to be borne,   *is it worth*
205 If old Aveugles sonnes so evill heare?[4]
  Or who shall not great Nightès children scorne,
  When two of three her Nephews are so fowle forlorne.° *wretchedly lost*

24

 "Up then, up dreary Dame, of darknesse Queene,
  Go gather up the reliques of thy race,
210 Or else goe them avenge, and let be seene,
  That dreaded Night in brightest day hath place,
  And can the children of faire light deface."°   *destroy*
  Her feeling speeches some compassion moved
  In hart, and chaunge in that great mothers face:
215 Yet pittie in her hart was never proved°   *known*
 Till then: for evermore she hated, never loved.

25

 And said, "Deare daughter rightly may I rew
  The fall of famous children borne of mee,
  And good successes, which their foes ensew:° *attend*
220 But who can turne the streame of destinee,
  Or breake the chayne of strong necessitee,
  Which fast is tyde to Joves eternall seat?[5]
  The sonnes of Day he favoureth, I see,
  And by my ruines thinkes to make them great:
225 To make one great by others losse, is bad excheat.° *exchange*

26

 "Yet shall they not escape so freely all;
  For some shall pay the price of others guilt:
  And he the man that made Sans foy to fall,
  Shall with his owne bloud price° that he hath spilt. *pay for*
230 But what art thou, that telst of Nephews kilt?"
  "I that do seeme not I, Duessa am,"
  Quoth she, "how ever now in garments gilt,
  And gorgeous gold arayd I to thee came:
 Duessa I, the daughter of Deceipt and Shame."

27

235 Then bowing downe her agèd backe, she kist
  The wicked witch, saying; "In that faire face
  The false resemblance of Deceipt, I wist°   *knew*
  Did closely° lurke; yet so true-seeming grace *secretly*
  It carried, that I scarse in darkesome place
240 Could it discerne, though I the mother bee
  Of falshood, and root of Duessaes race.
  O welcome child, whom I have longd to see,
 And now have seene unwares.° Lo now I go with thee." *unexpectedly*

---

4. I.e., are so badly thought of. "Aveugle": "blind." He is the son of Night and father of Sansfoy, Sansjoy, and Sansloy.

5. The golden chain that binds the entire universe; the image goes back as far as Homer (*Iliad* 8.18–27).

28

Then to her yron wagon she betakes,
245   And with her beares the fowle welfavourd witch:
    Through mirkesome° aire her readie way she makes.   *murky, dense*
    Her twyfold° Teme, of which two blacke as pitch,   *twofold*
    And two were browne, yet each to each unlich,°   *unlike*
    Did softly swim away, ne ever stampe,
250   Unlesse she chaunst their stubborne mouths to twitch;
    Then foming tarre,° their bridles they would champe,   *black froth*
And trampling the fine element,° would fiercely rampe.° *the air / rear up*

29

So well they sped, that they be come at length
    Unto the place, whereas the Paynim lay,
255   Devoid of outward sense, and native strength,
    Coverd with charmèd cloud from vew of day,
    And sight of men, since his late luckelesse fray.
    His cruell wounds with cruddy° bloud congealed,   *clotted*
    They binden up so wisely,° as they may,   *skillfully*
260   And handle softly, till they can be healed:
So lay him in her charet, close in night concealed.

30

And all the while she stood upon the ground,
    The wakefull dogs did never cease to bay,
    As giving warning of th' unwonted° sound,   *unusual*
265   With which her yron wheeles did them affray,
    And her darke griesly° looke them much dismay;   *horrid*
    The messenger of death, the ghastly Owle
    With drearie shriekes did also her bewray;°   *reveal*
    And hungry Wolves continually did howle,
270 At her abhorrèd face, so filthy and so fowle.

31

Thence turning backe in silence soft they stole,
    And brought the heavie corse with easie pace
    To yawning gulfe of deepe Avernus hole.[6]
    By that same hole an entrance darke and bace
275   With smoake and sulphure hiding all the place,
    Descends to hell: there creature never past,
    That backe returnèd without heavenly grace;
    But dreadfull Furies, which their chaines have brast,°   *burst*
And damnèd sprights sent forth to make ill° men aghast.   *evil*

32

280 By that same way the direfull dames doe drive
    Their mournefull charet, fild° with rusty blood,   *defiled*
    And downe to Plutoes house are come bilive:°   *quickly, alive*
    Which passing through, on every side them stood

6. In classical mythology Avernus is hell, where Pluto (line 282) reigns.

The trembling ghosts with sad amazèd mood,
285   Chattring their yron teeth, and staring wide
With stonie eyes; and all the hellish brood
Of feends infernall flockt on every side,
To gaze on earthly wight, that with the Night durst ride.

33

They pas the bitter waves of Acheron,
290   Where many soules sit wailing woefully,
And come to fiery flood of Phlegeton,[7]
Whereas the damnèd ghosts in torments fry,
And with sharpe shrilling shriekes doe bootlesse° cry,   *without avail*
Cursing high Jove, the which them thither sent.
295   The house of endlesse paine is built thereby,
In which ten thousand sorts of punishment
The cursèd creatures doe eternally torment.

34

Before the threshold dreadfull Cerberus[8]
His three deformèd heads did lay along,°   *at full length*
300   Curled with thousand adders venemous,
And lillèd° forth his bloudie flaming tong: *lolled*
At them he gan to reare his bristles strong,
And felly gnarre,° untill dayes enemy   *savagely snarl*
Did him appease; then downe his taile he hong
305   And suffered them to passen quietly:
For she in hell and heaven had power equally.

35

There was Ixion turnèd on a wheele,
For daring tempt the Queene of heaven to sin;
And Sisyphus an huge round stone did reele°   *roll*
310   Against an hill, ne° might from labour lin;°   *nor / cease*
There thirstie Tantalus hong by the chin;
And Tityus fed a vulture on his maw;°   *liver*
Typhoeus joynts were stretchèd on a gin,°   *rack*
Theseus condemned to endlesse slouth° by law,   *sloth*
315   And fifty sisters water in leake vessels draw.[9]

36

They all beholding worldly° wights in place,°   *mortal / there*
Leave off their worke, unmindfull of their smart,
To gaze on them; who forth by them doe pace,
Till they be come unto the furthest part:

---

7. Acheron and Phlegeton are rivers in hell.
8. The three-headed dog that guards hell. Stanzas 31–35 recall Aeneas's descent into hell (Virgil, *Aeneid* 6.200, 239–40).
9. Ixion was being punished for attempting to seduce Juno; Sisyphus, for refusing to pray to the gods; Tantalus, for stealing the gods' nectar; Tityus, for having tried to seduce Apollo's mother;

the monster Typhoeus, for creating destructive winds; Theseus, for stealing Persephone from Hades; and the daughters of King Danaus, for having killed their husbands on their wedding night. Tantalus stood chin-deep in water that receded whenever he tried to drink—hence he is "thirstie." Ovid, Virgil, and Homer are Spenser's sources here.

320　　Where was a Cave ywrought by wondrous art,
　　　　　Deepe, darke, uneasie,° dolefull, comfortlesse,　　　　*lacking ease*
　　　　　In which sad Aesculapius° farre a part　　　　*the god of medicine*
　　　　　Emprisond was in chaines remedilesse,°　　　　*beyond any remedy*
　　　　　For that Hippolytus rent corse he did redresse.°　　　　*cure*

37

325　　Hippolytus a jolly° huntsman was,　　　　*gallant*
　　　　　That wont° in charet chace the foming Bore;　　　　*used to*
　　　　　He all his Peeres in beautie did surpas,
　　　　　But Ladies love as losse of time forbore:
　　　　　His wanton stepdame[1] lovèd him the more,
330　　But when she saw her offred sweets refused
　　　　　Her love she turnd to hate, and him before
　　　　　His father fierce of treason false accused,
　　　　And with her gealous° termes his open eares abused.　　　*arousing jealousy*

38

　　　　Who all in rage his Sea-god syre° besought,　　　　*Poseidon (Neptune)*
335　　Some cursèd vengeance on his sonne to cast:
　　　　　From surging gulf two monsters straight were brought,
　　　　　With dread whereof his chasing steedes aghast,
　　　　　Both charet swift and huntsman overcast.
　　　　　His goodly corps on ragged cliffs yrent,°　　　　*torn*
340　　Was quite dismembred, and his members chast
　　　　　Scattered on every mountaine, as he went,
　　　　That of Hippolytus was left no moniment.[2]

39

　　　　His cruell stepdame seeing what was donne,
　　　　　Her wicked dayes with wretched knife did end,
345　　In death avowing th' innocence of her sonne.
　　　　　Which hearing his rash Syre, began to rend
　　　　　His haire, and hastie tongue, that did offend:
　　　　　Tho° gathering up the relicks of his smart[3]　　　　*then*
　　　　　By Dianes meanes, who was Hippolyts frend,
350　　Them brought to Aesculape, that by his art
　　　　Did heale them all againe, and joynèd every part.

40

　　　　Such wondrous science in mans wit to raine
　　　　　When Jove avizd,° that could the dead revive,　　　　*discovered*
　　　　　And fates expirèd[4] could renew againe,
355　　Of endlesse life he might him not deprive,
　　　　　But unto hell did thrust him downe alive,
　　　　　With flashing thunderbolt ywounded sore:
　　　　　Where long remaining, he did alwaies strive
　　　　　Himselfe with salves to health for to restore,
360　　And slake the heavenly fire, that raged evermore.

---

1. Phaedra, the wife of his father, Theseus.　　　　3. I.e., his son's remains, that caused his grief.
2. I.e., no trace of identity.　　　　4. The completed term of life as fixed by the Fates.

41

There auncient Night arriving, did alight
   From her nigh wearie waine,[5] and in her armes
   To Aesculapius brought the wounded knight:
   Whom having softly disarayd of armes,
365   Tho gan to him discover all his harmes,
   Beseeching him with prayer, and with praise,
   If either salves, or oyles, or herbes, or charmes
   A fordonne° wight from dore of death mote raise,   *undone*
He would at her request prolong her nephews daies.

42

370 "Ah Dame," quoth he, "thou temptest me in vaine,
   To dare the thing, which daily yet I rew,
   And the old cause of my continued paine
   With like attempt to like end to renew.
   Is not enough, that thrust from heaven dew[6]
375   Here endlesse penance for one fault I pay,
   But that redoubled crime with vengeance new
   Thou biddest me to eeke?° Can Night defray°   *increase/appease*
The wrath of thundring Jove, that rules both night and day?"

43

"Not so," quoth she; "but sith that heavens king
380   From hope of heaven hath thee excluded quight,
   Why fearest thou, that canst not hope for thing,°   *anything*
   And fearest not, that more thee hurten might,
   Now in the powre of everlasting Night?
   Goe to then, O thou farre renowmèd sonne
385   Of great Apollo, shew thy famous might
   In medicine, that else° hath to thee wonne   *already*
Great paines, and greater praise, both never to be donne."°   *ended*

44

Her words prevaild: And then the learnèd leach°   *doctor*
   His cunning hand gan to his wounds to lay,
390   And all things else, the which his art did teach:
   Which having seene, from thence arose away
   The mother of dread darknesse, and let stay
   Aveugles sonne there in the leaches cure,°   *care*
   And backe returning tooke her wonted way,
395   To runne her timely race,° whilst Phoebus pure   *her nightly journey*
In westerne waves his wearie wagon did recure.°   *refresh*

45

The false Duessa leaving noyous° Night,   *harmful*
   Returnd to stately pallace of dame Pride;
   Where when she came, she found the Faery knight

---

5. I.e., the horses of Night's chariot are nearly exhausted.   6. The proper ("dew") place for a god.

400   Departed thence, albe° his woundès wide   *although*
        Not throughly heald, unreadie were to ride.
        Good cause he had to hasten thence away;
        For on a day his wary Dwarfe had spide,
        Where in a dongeon deepe huge numbers lay
405   Of caytive° wretched thrals,° that waylèd night and day   *captive / slaves*

46

A ruefull sight, as could be seene with eie;
        Of whom he learnèd had in secret wise
        The hidden cause of their captivitie,
        How mortgaging their lives to Covetise,
410   Through wastfull° Pride, and wanton Riotise,   *causing desolation*
        They were by law of that proud Tyrannesse[7]
        Provokt with Wrath, and Envies false surmise,
        Condemnèd to that Dongeon mercilesse,
Where they should live in woe, and die in wretchednesse.

47

415 There was that great proud king of Babylon[8]
        That would compell all nations to adore,
        And him as onely God to call upon,
        Till through celestiall doome° throwne out of dore,   *judgment*
        Into an Oxe he was transformed of yore:
420   There also was king Croesus,[9] that enhaunst°   *exalted*
        His heart too high through his great riches store;
        And proud Antiochus,[1] the which advaunst
His cursèd hand gainst God, and on his altars daunst.°   *danced*

48

And them long time before, great Nimrod[2] was,
425   That first the world with sword and fire warrayd;°   *ravaged*
        And after him old Ninus farre did pas°   *surpass*
        In princely pompe, of all the world obayd;
        There also was that mightie Monarch layd
        Low under all, yet above all in pride,
430   That name of native° syre did fowle upbrayd,   *natural*
        And would as Ammons sonne[3] be magnifide,
Till scornd of God and man a shamefull death he dide.

49

All these together in one heape were throwne,
        Like carkases of beasts in butchers stall.
435   And in another corner wide were strowne

7. Lucifera. The noble sinners named in stanzas 47–50 exemplify a theme common in Renaissance morality, the fall of princes.
8. Nebuchadnezzar (Daniel 3–4).
9. King of Lydia, famous for his riches.
1. King of Syria, who desecrated the Jewish temple of Jerusalem (1 Maccabees 1.20–24).

2. Nimrod, identified as the first tyrant, caused the Tower of Babel to be built in defiance of God (Genesis 10.9). Ninus was founder of Nineveh, archetype of the wicked city (see the Book of Jonah).
3. Alexander the Great was occasionally worshiped as the son of Jupiter Ammon.

The antique ruines of the Romaines fall:
Great Romulus the Grandsyre of them all,
Proud Tarquin, and too lordly Lentulus,
Stout Scipio, and stubborne Hanniball,
440 Ambitious Sylla, and sterne Marius,
High Caesar, great Pompey, and fierce Antonius.[4]

50

Amongst these mighty men were wemen mixt,
Proud wemen, vaine, forgetfull of their yoke:°   *duty*
The bold Semiramis,° whose sides transfixt   *wife of Ninus*
445 With sonnes owne blade, her fowle reproches spoke;
Faire Sthenoboea,[5] that her selfe did choke
With wilfull cord, for wanting° of her will;   *lacking*
High minded Cleopatra, that with stroke
Of Aspes sting her selfe did stoutly kill:
450 And thousands moe the like, that did that dongeon fill.

51

Besides the endlesse routs° of wretched thralles,   *crowds*
Which thither were assembled day by day,
From all the world after their wofull falles,
Through wicked pride, and wasted wealthes decay.
455 But most of all, which in that Dongeon lay
Fell from high Princes courts, or Ladies bowres,
Where they in idle pompe, or wanton play,
Consumèd had their goods, and thriftlesse howres,
And lastly throwne themselves into these heavy stowres.°   *disasters*

52

460 Whose case wheneas the carefull° Dwarfe had tould,   *anxious*
And made ensample of their mournefull sight
Unto his maister, he no lenger would
There dwell in perill of like painefull plight,
But early rose, and ere that dawning light
465 Discovered had the world to heaven wyde,
He by a privie Posterne° tooke his flight,   *secret back door*
That of no envious eyes he mote be spyde:
For doubtlesse death ensewd, if any him descryde.

53

Scarse could he footing find in that fowle way,
470 For many corses, like a great Lay-stall°   *burial place, rubbish heap*
Of murdred men which therein strowèd lay,
Without remorse, or decent funerall:
Which all through that great Princesse pride did fall

---

4. Romulus was the founder of Rome; Tarquin, a
Roman tyrant; Lentulus, a conspirator with Catiline; Scipio, a Roman general, conqueror of Carthage; Hannibal, a Carthaginian general; Sulla, a
Roman civil war general; Marius, Sulla's rival. The

figures in the final line are Julius Caesar, Pompey
the Great, and Mark Antony. All are memorialized
in Plutarch's *Lives*.
5. Queen of King Proteus of Argos; she lusted
after her brother-in-law Bellerophon.

And came to shamefull end. And them beside
475 Forth ryding underneath the castell wall,
A donghill of dead carkases he spide,
The dreadfull spectacle° of that sad house of Pride.[6]   *sign, example*

Canto 6

From lawlesse lust by wondrous grace
fayre Una is releast:
Whom salvage° nation does adore,   *wild, of the woods*
and learnes her wise beheast.°   *bidding*

1

As when a ship, that flyes faire under saile,
An hidden rocke escapèd hath unwares,°   *unexpectedly*
That lay in waite her wrack for to bewaile,[7]
The Marriner yet halfe amazèd stares
5   At perill past, and yet in doubt ne dares
To joy at his foole-happie oversight:°   *lucky ignorance*
So doubly is distrest twixt joy and cares
The dreadlesse° courage of this Elfin knight,   *fearless*
Having escapt so sad ensamples in his sight.

2

10   Yet sad he was that his too hastie speed
The faire Duess' had forst him leave behind;
And yet more sad, that Una his deare dreed°   *object of reverence*
Her truth had staind with treason so unkind;
Yet crime in her could never creature find,
15   But for his love, and for her owne selfe sake,
She wandred had from one to other Ynd,[8]
Him for to seeke, ne ever would forsake,
Till her unwares the fierce Sansloy did overtake.

3

Who after Archimagoes fowle defeat,
20   Led her away into a forrest wilde,
And turning wrathfull fire to lustfull heat,
With beastly sin thought her to have defilde,
And made the vassall of his pleasures vilde.°   *vile*
Yet first he cast by treatie,° and by traynes,°   *persuasion / tricks*
25   Her to perswade, that stubborne fort to yilde:
For greater conquest of hard love he gaynes,
That workes it to his will, then he that it constraines.°   *forces*

4

With fawning wordes he courted her a while,
And looking lovely,° and oft sighing sore,   *lovingly*

6. Named now, after we have been shown what
the name means.
7. I.e., cause the shipwreck and thereby cause it
to be bewailed.
8. I.e., she would have wandered from the East to
the West Indies.

30   Her constant hart did tempt with diverse guile:
        But wordes, and lookes, and sighes she did abhore,
        As rocke of Diamond stedfast evermore.[9]
        Yet for to feed his fyrie lustfull eye,
        He snatcht the vele, that hong her face before;
35   Then gan her beautie shine, as brightest skye,
   And burnt his beastly hart t' efforce° her chastitye.   violate

                                5

   So when he saw his flatt'ring arts to fayle,
        And subtile engines bet from batteree,[1]
        With greedy force he gan the fort assayle,
40   Whereof he weend° possessèd soone to bee,   thought
        And win rich spoile of ransackt chastetee.
        Ah heavens, that do this hideous act behold,
        And heavenly virgin thus outragèd see,
        How can ye vengeance just so long withhold,
45   And hurle not flashing flames upon that Paynim bold?

                                6

   The pitteous maden carefull° comfortlesse,   full of cares
        Does throw out thrilling° shriekes, and shrieking cryes,   piercing
        The last vaine helpe of womens great distresse,
        And with loud plaints importuneth the skyes,
50   That molten starres do drop like weeping eyes;
        And Phoebus flying so most shamefull sight,
        His blushing face in foggy cloud[2] implyes,°   buries
        And hides for shame. What wit of mortall wight
   Can now devise to quit a thrall° from such a plight?   release a victim

                                7

55   Eternall providence exceeding° thought,   transcending
        Where none appeares can make her selfe a way:
        A wondrous way it for this Lady wrought,
        From Lyons clawes to pluck the gripèd° pray.   grasped
        Her shrill outcryes and shriekes so loud did bray,
60   That all the woodes and forestes did resownd;
        A troupe of Faunes and Satyres[3] far away
        Within the wood were dauncing in a rownd,
   Whiles old Sylvanus slept in shady arber sownd.

                                8

   Who when they heard that pitteous strainèd voice,
65   In hast forsooke their rurall meriment,
        And ran towards the far rebownded° noyce,   re-echoed
        To weet, what wight so loudly did lament.

9. The diamond, because of its hardness, was an emblem of fidelity.
1. I.e., beaten ("bet") from their fruitless assault ("batteree") on her unmovable virtue.
2. The sun is overcast by clouds.

3. Woodland deities with men's bodies above the waist and goats' bodies below, noted for their sensuality. Sylvanus, Roman god of the woods, is traditionally associated with fauns.

Unto the place they come incontinent:°   *immediately*
Whom when the raging Sarazin espide,
70   A rude, misshapen, monstrous rablement,
Whose like he never saw, he durst not bide,
But got his ready steed, and fast away gan ride.

9

The wyld woodgods arrivèd in the place,
There find the virgin dolefull desolate,
75   With ruffled rayments, and faire blubbred° face,   *flooded with tears*
As her outrageous foe had left her late,
And trembling yet through feare of former hate;
All stand amazèd at so uncouth° sight,   *strange*
And gin to pittie her unhappie state,
80   All stand astonied° at her beautie bright,   *stupified*
In their rude° eyes unworthie° of so wofull plight.   *rustic / undeserving*

10

She more amazed, in double dread doth dwell;
And every tender part for feare does shake:
As when a greedie Wolfe through hunger fell
85   A seely° Lambe farre from the flocke does take,   *innocent*
Of whom he meanes his bloudie feast to make,
A Lyon spyes fast running towards him,
The innocent pray in hast he does forsake,
Which quit from death yet quakes in every lim
90   With chaunge of feare, to see the Lyon looke so grim.°   *savage*

11

Such fearefull fit assaid° her trembling hart,   *assailed*
Ne word to speake, ne joynt to move she had:
The salvage nation feele her secret smart,
And read her sorrow in her count'nance sad;
95   Their frowning forheads with rough hornes yclad,
And rusticke horror° all a side doe lay,   *roughness*
And gently grenning, shew a semblance glad
To comfort her, and feare to put away,
Their backward bent knees teach her humbly to obay.[4]

12

100   The doubtfull Damzell dare not yet commit
Her single person to their barbarous truth,[5]
But still twixt feare and hope amazd does sit,
Late learnd° what harme to hastie trust ensu'th,   *taught*
They in compassion of her tender youth,
105   And wonder of her beautie soveraine,
Are wonne with pitty and unwonted ruth,°   *pity*
And all prostrate upon the lowly plaine,
Do kisse her feete, and fawne on her with count'nance faine.°   *glad*

---

4. I.e., teach their knees, bent backward like a goat's, to obey her.

5. I.e., her solitary self to their wild allegiance ("barbarous truth").

13

Their harts she ghesseth by their humble guise,°   *appearance*
110   And yieldes her to extremitie of time;[6]
    So from the ground she fearelesse doth arise,
    And walketh forth without suspect° of crime: *suspicion*
    They all as glad, as birdes of joyous Prime,°   *springtime*
    Thence lead her forth, about her dauncing round,
115   Shouting, and singing all a shepheards ryme,
    And with greene braunches strowing all the ground,
Do worship her, as Queene, with olive girlond cround.

14

And all the way their merry pipes they sound,
    That all the woods with doubled Eccho ring,
120   And with their hornèd feet do weare the ground,
    Leaping like wanton kids in pleasant Spring.
    So towards old Sylvanus they her bring;
    Who with the noyse awakèd, commeth out,
    To weet° the cause, his weake steps governing   *learn*
125   And agèd limbs on Cypresse stadle° stout,   *staff*
And with an yvie twyne his wast is girt about.

15

Far off he wonders, what them makes so glad,
    Or Bacchus merry fruit they did invent,[7]
    Or Cybeles franticke rites[8] have made them mad;
130   They drawing nigh, unto their God present
    That flowre of faith and beautie excellent.
    The God himselfe vewing that mirrhour rare,
    Stood long amazd, and burnt in his intent;[9]
    His owne faire Dryope now he thinkes not faire,
135   And Pholoe fowle, when her to this he doth compaire.[1]

16

The woodborne people fall before her flat,
    And worship her as Goddesse of the wood;
    And old Sylvanus selfe bethinkès not,° what   *cannot decide*
    To thinke of wight so faire, but gazing stood,
140   In doubt to deeme her borne of earthly brood;
    Sometimes Dame Venus selfe he seemes to see,
    But Venus never had so sober mood;
    Sometimes Diana he her takes to bee,
But misseth bow, and shaftes, and buskins° to her knee.   *soft boots*

17

145   By vew of her he ginneth to revive
    His ancient love, and dearest Cyparisse,[2]

---

6. I.e., necessity of the time.
7. I.e., whether ("or") they did find ("invent") wine grapes.
8. Orgiastic dances in worship of Cybele, goddess of the powers of Nature.
9. Glowed with intense concentration. Una is a "mirrhour rare" in that she reflects heavenly

beauty.
1. Dryope and Pholoe were nymphs loved by Faunus and Pan; for Spenser, the names *Faunus, Pan,* and *Sylvanus* were apparently interchangeable.
2. A fair youth, beloved of Sylvanus, turned into a cypress tree.

And calles to mind his pourtraiture alive,[3]
How faire he was, and yet not faire to° this,   *compared to*
And how he slew with glauncing dart amisse
150 A gentle Hynd, the which the lovely boy
Did love as life, above all worldly blisse;
For griefe whereof the lad n'ould° after joy,   *would not*
But pynd away in anguish and selfe-wild annoy.°   *suffering*

18
The wooddy Nymphes, faire Hamadryades[4]
155 Her to behold do thither runne apace,
And all the troupe of light-foot Naiades,°   *water nymphs*
Flocke all about to see her lovely face:
But when they vewèd have her heavenly grace,
They envie her in their malitious mind,
160 And fly away for feare of fowle disgrace:
But all the Satyres scorne their woody kind,°   *woodborn race*
And henceforth nothing faire, but her on earth they find.

19
Glad of such lucke, the luckelesse lucky maid,
Did her content to please their feeble eyes,
165 And long time with that salvage people staid,
To gather breath in many miseries.
During which time her gentle wit she plyes,
To teach them truth, which worshipt her in vaine,
And made her th' Image of Idolatryes;[5]
170 But when their bootlesse° zeale she did restraine   *useless*
From her own worship, they her Asse would worship fayn.° *willingly*

20
It fortunèd a noble warlike knight
By just occasion to that forrest came,
To seeke his kindred, and the lignage right,°   *true*
175 From whence he tooke his well deservèd name:
He had in armes abroad wonne muchell° fame,   *great*
And fild far landes with glorie of his might,
Plaine, faithfull, true, and enimy of shame,
And ever loved to fight for Ladies right,
180 But in vaine glorious frayes he litle did delight.

21
A Satyres sonne yborne in forrest wyld,
By straunge adventure as it did betyde,°   *happen*
And there begotten of a Lady myld,
Faire Thyamis the daughter of Labryde,
185 That was in sacred bands of wedlocke tyde
To Therion,[6] a loose unruly swayne;
Who had more joy to raunge the forrest wyde,

---

3. I.e., his appearance when alive.
4. Spirits of trees whose lives ended when the tree they inhabited died.

5. The idol of their idolatries.
6. Wild beast. "Thyamis": passion. "Labryde": turbulence.

And chase the salvage beast with busie payne,°   *painstaking care*
Then serve his Ladies love, and wast° in pleasures vayne.   *live idly*

22

190 The forlorne mayd did with loves longing burne,
    And could not lacke° her lovers company,   *be without*
    But to the wood she goes, to serve her turne,
    And seeke her spouse, that from her still does fly,
    And followes other game and venery:[7]
195 A Satyre chaunst her wandring for to find,
    And kindling coles of lust in brutish eye,
    The loyall links of wedlocke did unbind,
And made her person thrall unto his beastly kind.

23

So long in secret cabin there he held
200   Her captive to his sensuall desire,
    Till that with timely fruit her belly sweld,
    And bore a boy unto that salvage sire:
    Then home he suffred her for to retire,°   *return*
    For ransome leaving him the late borne childe;
205 Whom till to ryper yeares he gan aspire,°   *grow up*
    He noursled° up in life and manners wilde,   *reared*
Emongst wild beasts and woods, from lawes of men exilde.

24

For all he taught the tender ymp,° was but   *child*
    To banish cowardize and bastard° feare;   *base*
210 His trembling hand he would him force to put
    Upon the Lyon and the rugged Beare,
    And from the she Beares teats her whelps to teare;
    And eke wyld roring Buls he would him make
    To tame, and ryde their backes not made to beare;
215 And the Robuckes[8] in flight to overtake,
That every beast for feare of him did fly and quake.

25

Thereby so fearelesse, and so fell° he grew,   *fierce*
    That his owne sire and maister of his guise°   *teacher of his behavior*
    Did often tremble at his horrid vew,°   *rough appearance*
220 And oft for dread of hurt would him advise,
    The angry beasts not rashly to despise,
    Nor too much to provoke; for he would learne°   *teach*
    The Lyon stoup to him in lowly wise,
    (A lesson hard) and make the Libbard° sterne   *leopard*
225 Leave roaring, when in rage he for revenge did earne.°   *yearn*

26

And for to make his powre approvèd° more,   *demonstrated*
    Wyld beasts in yron yokes he would compell;

---

7. The word means both hunting and sexual play.   8. Deer, especially noted for their speed.

The spotted Panther, and the tuskèd Bore,
The Pardale° swift, and the Tigre cruell: *female leopard*
230   The Antelope, and Wolfe both fierce and fell;°   *savage*
And them constraine in equall teme⁹ to draw.
Such joy he had, their stubborne harts to quell,
And sturdie courage tame with dreadfull aw,
That his beheast they fearèd, as a tyrans law.

27

235   His loving mother came upon a day
Unto the woods, to see her little sonne;
And chaunst unwares° to meet him in the way,   *unexpectedly*
After his sportes, and cruell pastime donne,
When after him a Lyonesse did runne,
240   That roaring all with rage, did lowd requere°   *demand*
Her children deare, whom he away had wonne:°   *seized*
The Lyon whelpes she saw how he did beare,
And lull in rugged armes, withouten childish feare.

28

The fearefull Dame all quakèd at the sight,
245   And turning backe, gan fast to fly away,
Untill with love revokt° from vaine affright,   *recalled*
She hardly° yet perswaded was to stay,   *with difficulty*
And then to him these womanish words gan say;
"Ah Satyrane, my dearling, and my joy,
250   For love of me leave off this dreadfull play;
To dally thus with death, is no fit toy,
Go find some other play-fellowes, mine own sweet boy."

29

In these and like delights of bloudy game
He traynèd was, till ryper yeares he raught,°   *reached*
255   And there abode, whilst any beast of name
Walkt in that forest, whom he had not taught
To feare his force: and then his courage haught°   *high*
Desird of forreine foemen to be knowne;
And far abroad for straunge adventures sought:
260   In which his might was never overthrowne,
But through all Faery lond his famous worth was blown.°   *spread*

30

Yet evermore it was his manner faire,
After long labours and adventures spent,
Unto those native woods for to repaire,°   *return*
265   To see his sire and ofspring° auncient.   *origin*
And now he thither came for like intent;
Where he unwares the fairest Una found,
Straunge Lady, in so straunge habiliment,°   *attire*

9. Side by side, yoked together in a team.

Teaching the Satyres, which her sat around,
270 Trew sacred lore, which from her sweet lips did redound.°   *flow*

31

He wondred at her wisedome heavenly rare,
   Whose like in womens wit he never knew;
And when her curteous deeds he did compare,
   Gan her admire, and her sad sorrowes rew,°   *pity*
275 Blaming of Fortune, which such troubles threw,
   And joyd to make proofe of her crueltie
On gentle Dame, so hurtlesse,° and so trew: *harmless*
   Thenceforth he kept her goodly company,
And learnd her discipline° of faith and veritie.   *teachings*

32

280 But she all vowd° unto the Redcrosse knight,   *entirely promised*
   His wandring perill closely° did lament,   *secretly*
Ne in this new acquaintaunce could delight,
   But her deare° heart with anguish did torment,   *loving*
And all her wit in secret counsels spent,
285 How to escape. At last in privie wise°   *privately*
   To Satyrane she shewèd her intent;
Who glad to gain such favour, gan devise,
   How with that pensive Maid he best might thence arise.°   *depart*

33

So on a day when Satyres all were gone,
290   To do their service to Sylvanus old,
The gentle virgin left behind alone
   He led away with courage stout and bold.
Too late it was, to Satyres to be told,
   Or ever hope recover her againe:
295 In vaine he seekes that having cannot hold.
   So fast he carried her with carefull paine,°   *painstaking care*
That they the woods are past, and come now to the plaine.

34

The better part now of the lingring day,
   They traveild had, when as they farre espide
300 A wearie wight forwandring° by the way,   *wandering far and wide*
   And towards him they gan in hast to ride,
To weet of newes, that did abroad betide,
   Or tydings of her knight of the Redcrosse.
But he them spying, gan to turne aside,
305   For feare as seemid, or for some feignèd losse;°   *pretended harm*
More greedy they of newes, fast towards him do crosse.

35

A silly° man, in simple weedes forworne,°   *simple/worn out*
   And soild with dust of the long drièd way;

His sandales were with toilesome travell torne,
310 And face all tand with scorching sunny ray,
As he had traveild many a sommers day,
Through boyling sands of Arabie and Ynde;°   *India*
And in his hand a Jacobs staffe,° to stay   *pilgrim's staff*
His wearie limbes upon: and eke behind,
315 His scrip° did hang, in which his needments he did bind.   *bag*

36

The knight approching nigh, of him inquerd
Tydings of warre, and of adventures new;
But warres, nor new adventures none he herd.
Then Una gan to aske, if ought he knew,
320 Or heard abroad of that her champion trew,
That in his armour bare a croslet° red.   *small cross*
"Aye me, Deare dame," quoth he, "well may I rew
To tell the sad sight, which mine eies have red:°   *beheld*
These eyes did see that knight both living and eke ded."

37

325 That cruell word her tender hart so thrild,°   *pierced*
That suddein cold did runne through every vaine,
And stony horrour all her sences fild
With dying fit,° that downe she fell for paine.   *deathlike swoon*
The knight her lightly° rearèd up againe,   *quickly*
330 And comforted with curteous kind reliefe:
Then wonne from death, she bad him tellen plaine
The further processe° of her hidden griefe;   *account*
The lesser pangs can beare, who hath endured the chiefe.

38

Then gan the Pilgrim thus, "I chaunst this day,
335 This fatall day, that shall I ever rew,
To see two knights in travell on my way
(A sory° sight) arraunged in battell new,   *grievous*
Both breathing vengeaunce, both of wrathfull hew:
My fearefull flesh did tremble at their strife,
340 To see their blades so greedily imbrew,[1]
That drunke with bloud, yet thristed after life:
What more? the Redcrosse knight was slaine with Paynim knife."

39

"Ah dearest Lord," quoth she, "how might that bee,
And he the stoutest knight, that ever wonne?"°   *lived*
345 "Ah dearest dame," quoth he, "how might I see
The thing, that might not be, and yet was donne?"
"Where is," said Satyrane, "that Paynims sonne,
That him of life, and us of joy hath reft?"
"Not far away," quoth he, "he hence doth wonne°   *stay*

---

1. Soak themselves in blood.

350   Foreby° a fountaine, where I late him left   *close by*
        Washing his bloudy wounds, that through° the steele were cleft."   *by*

40

    Therewith the knight thence marchèd forth in hast,
        Whiles Una with huge heavinesse° opprest,   *grief*
        Could not for sorrow follow him so fast;
355   And soone he came, as he the place had ghest,
        Whereas that Pagan proud him selfe did rest,
        In secret shadow by a fountaine side:
        Even he it was, that earst would have supprest°   *violated*
        Faire Una: whom when Satyrane espide,
360   With fowle reprochfull words he boldly him defide.

41

    And said, "Arise thou cursèd Miscreaunt,°   *infidel*
        That hast with knightlesse° guile and trecherous   *unknightly*
           train°   *deceit*
        Faire knighthood fowly shamed, and doest vaunt
        That good knight of the Redcrosse to have slain:
365   Arise, and with like treason now maintain°   *defend*
        Thy guilty wrong, or else thee guilty yield."
        The Sarazin this hearing, rose amain,°   *at once*
        And catching up in hast his three square° shield,   *triangular*
    And shining helmet, soone him buckled to the field.

42

370   And drawing nigh him said, "Ah misborne Elfe,[2]
        In evill houre thy foes thee hither sent,
        Anothers wrongs to wreake upon thy selfe:
        Yet ill thou blamest me, for having blent°   *stained*
        My name with guile and traiterous intent;
375   That Redcrosse knight, perdie, I never slew,
        But had he beene, where earst° his armes were lent,   *before*
        Th' enchaunter vaine his errour should not rew:
    But thou his errour shalt, I hope now proven trew."[3]

43

    Therewith they gan, both furious and fell,°   *fierce*
380   To thunder blowes, and fiersly to assaile
        Each other bent° his enimy to quell,°   *determined/kill*
        That with their force they perst° both plate and maile,   *pierced*
        And made wide furrowes in their fleshes fraile,
        That it would pitty° any living eie.   *bring pity to*
385   Large floods of bloud adowne their sides did raile:°   *flow*
        But floods of bloud could not them satisfie:
    Both hungred after death: both chose to win, or die.

---

2. Base-born knight of Faerie Land ("Elfe").
3. I.e., had Redcrosse been wearing his arms the
enchanter Archimago would not have to regret his
error in fighting me. But you will now repeat that
error and that regret.

44

So long they fight, and fell revenge pursue,
  That fainting each, themselves to breathen let,
390   And oft refreshèd, battell oft renue:
  As when two Bores with rancling malice met,
  Their gory sides fresh bleeding fiercely fret,°   *tear*
  Til breathlesse both them selves aside retire,
  Where foming wrath, their cruell tuskes they whet,
395   And trample th' earth, the whiles they may respire
  Then backe to fight againe, new breathèd and entire.°   *fresh*

45

So fiersly, when these knights had breathèd once,
  They gan to fight returne, increasing more
  Their puissant force, and cruell rage attonce,
400   With heapèd strokes more hugely, then before,
  That with their drerie° wounds and bloudy gore   *gory*
  They both deformèd,° scarsely could be known.   *disfigured*
  By this sad Una fraught with anguish sore,
  Led with their noise, which through the aire was thrown,
405   Arrived, where they in erth their fruitles bloud had sown.

46

Whom all so soone as that proud Sarazin
  Espide, he gan revive the memory
  Of his lewd lusts, and late attempted sin,
  And left the doubtfull° battell hastily,   *undecided*
410   To catch her, newly offred to his eie:
  But Satyrane with strokes him turning, staid,
  And sternely bad him other businesse plie,
  Then hunt the steps of pure unspotted Maid:
  Wherewith he all enraged, these bitter speaches said.

47

415   "O foolish faeries sonne, what furie mad
  Hath thee incenst, to hast thy dolefull fate?
  Were it not better, I that Lady had,
  Then that thou hadst repented it too late?
  Most sencelesse man he, that himselfe doth hate,
420   To love another. Lo then for thine ayd
  Here take thy lovers token on thy pate."
  So they to fight; the whiles the royall Mayd
  Fled farre away, of that proud Paynim sore afrayd.

48

But that false Pilgrim, which that leasing° told,   *lie*
425   Being in deed old Archimage, did stay
  In secret shadow, all this to behold,
  And much rejoycèd in their bloudy fray:
  But when he saw the Damsell passe away

He left his stond,° and her pursewd apace,   *place*
430 In hope to bring her to her last decay.°   *death*
But for to tell her lamentable cace,
And eke° this battels end, will need another place.   *also*

Canto 7

The Redcrosse knight is captive made
By Gyaunt proud opprest,°   *overwhelmed*
Prince Arthur meets with Una greatly
with those newes distrest.

1

What man so wise, what earthly wit so ware,°   *wary*
As to descry° the crafty cunning traine,°   *perceive / guile*
By which deceipt doth maske in visour° faire,   *a mask*
And cast her colours dyèd deepe in graine,[4]
5   To seeme like Truth, whose shape she well can faine,
And fitting gestures to her purpose frame,
The guiltlesse man with guile to entertaine?°   *receive*
Great maistresse of her art was that false Dame,
The false Duessa, clokèd with Fidessaes name.

2

10   Who when returning from the drery Night,
She fownd not in that perilous house of Pryde,
Where she had left, the noble Redcrosse knight,
Her hopèd pray, she would no lenger bide,
But forth she went, to seeke him far and wide.
15   Ere long she fownd, whereas° he wearie sate,   *where*
To rest him selfe, foreby° a fountaine side,   *beside*
Disarmèd all of yron-coted Plate,
And by his side his steed the grassy forage ate.

3

He feedes upon the cooling shade, and bayes°   *bathes*
20   His sweatie forehead in the breathing wind,
Which through the trembling leaves full gently playes
Wherein the cherefull birds of sundry kind
Do chaunt sweet musick, to delight his mind:
The Witch approaching gan him fairely° greet,   *courteously*
25   And with reproch of carelesnesse° unkind   *indifference*
Upbrayd, for leaving her in place unmeet,°   *unfitting*
With fowle words tempring faire, soure gall with hony sweet.

4

Unkindnesse past, they gan of solace treat,°   *speak*
And bathe in pleasaunce of the joyous shade,
30   Which shielded them against the boyling heat,

4. I.e., Deceit disposes her colors, thoroughly dyed, so as to seem like Truth.

And with greene boughes decking a gloomy glade,
About the fountaine like a girlond made;
Whose bubbling wave did ever freshly well,
Ne ever would through fervent° sommer fade:°   *hot/dry up*
35   The sacred Nymph, which therein wont to dwell,
Was out of Dianes favour, as it then befell.

5

The cause was this: one day when Phoebe[5] fayre
With all her band was following the chace,°   *hunt*
This Nymph, quite tyred with heat of scorching ayre
40   Sat downe to rest in middest of the race:
The goddesse wroth gan fowly her disgrace,
And bad the waters, which from her did flow,
Be such as she her selfe was then in place.°   *there*
Thenceforth her waters waxèd dull and slow,
45 And all that drunke thereof, did faint and feeble grow.

6

Hereof this gentle knight unweeting° was,   *ignorant*
And lying downe upon the sandie graile,°   *gravel*
Drunke of the streame, as cleare as cristall glas;
Eftsoones his manly forces gan to faile,
50   And mightie strong was turnd to feeble fraile.
His chaunged powres at first themselves not felt,
Till crudled° cold his corage° gan assaile,   *congealing/vigor*
And chearefull° bloud in faintnesse chill did melt,   *lively*
Which like a fever fit through all his body swelt.°   *raged*

7

55 Yet goodly court he made still to his Dame,
Pourd out in loosnesse[6] on the grassy grownd,
Both carelesse of his health, and of his fame:
Till at the last he heard a dreadfull sownd,
Which through the wood loud bellowing, did rebownd,
60   That all the earth for terrour seemed to shake,
And trees did tremble. Th' Elfe therewith astownd,°   *amazed*
Upstarted lightly° from his looser make,[7]   *quickly*
And his unready weapons gan in hand to take.

8

But ere he could his armour on him dight,
65   Or get his shield, his monstrous enimy
With sturdie steps came stalking in his sight,
An hideous Geant horrible and hye,
That with his talnesse seemd to threat the skye,
The ground eke° groned under him for dreed;   *also*
70   His living like saw never living eye,

5. I.e., Diana, goddess of the moon and of chastity.
6. Stretched out and indulging in amorous play ("loosnesse").
7. More licentious ("looser") companion.

Ne durst behold: his stature did exceed
The hight of three the tallest sonnes of mortall seed.

9

The greatest Earth his uncouth mother was,
   And blustring Aeolus his boasted sire,[8]
75   Who with his breath, which through the world doth pas,
   Her hollow womb did secretly inspire,°   *breathe into*
   And fild her hidden caves with stormie yre,
   That she conceived; and trebling the dew time,
   In which the wombes of women do expire,°   *bring forth*
80   Brought forth this monstrous masse of earthly slime,
Puft up with emptie wind, and fild with sinfull crime.

10

So growen great through arrogant delight
   Of th' high descent, whereof he was yborne,
   And through presumption of his matchlesse might,
85   All other powres and knighthood he did scorne.
   Such now he marcheth to this man forlorne,°   *abandoned*
   And left to losse:° his stalking steps are stayde   *destruction*
   Upon a snaggy Oke,[9] which he had torne
   Out of his mothers bowelles, and it made
90   His mortall° mace, wherewith his foemen he dismayde.[1]   *death-dealing*

11

That when the knight he spide, he gan advance
   With huge force and insupportable mayne,°   *irresistible power*
   And towardes him with dreadfull fury praunce;
   Who haplesse, and eke hopelesse, all in vaine
95   Did to him pace, sad battaile to darrayne,°   *engage*
   Disarmd, disgrast, and inwardly dismayde,
   And eke so faint in every joynt and vaine,
   Through that fraile° fountaine, which him feeble made,   *enfeebling*
That scarsely could he weeld his bootlesse° single blade.   *useless*

12

100 The Geaunt strooke so maynly° mercilesse,   *mightily*
   That could have overthrowne a stony towre,
   And were not heavenly grace, that him did blesse,
   He had beene pouldred° all, as thin as flowre: *powdered*
   But he was wary of that deadly stowre,°   *peril*
105   And lightly° lept from underneath the blow: *quickly*
   Yet so exceeding was the villeins powre,
   That with the wind it did him overthrow,
And all his sences stound,° that still he lay full low.   *stunned*

---

8. Aeolus was keeper of the winds. The giant's descent from Earth and Wind links him to earthquakes.
9. I.e., he uses as walking stick a knotty ("snaggy")

oak tree.
1. In its usual sense, but also "dis-made, dissolved."

13

As when that divelish yron Engin° wrought   *i.e., cannon*
110   In deepest Hell, and framd by Furies skill,
With windy Nitre and quick Sulphur fraught,[2]
And ramd with bullet round, ordaind to kill,
Conceiveth fire, the heavens it doth fill
With thundring noyse, and all the ayre doth choke,
115   That none can breath, nor see, nor heare at will,
Through smouldry cloud of duskish stincking smoke,
That th' onely breath him daunts,[3] who hath escapt the stroke.

14

So daunted when the Geaunt saw the knight,
His heavie hand he heavèd up on hye,
120   And him to dust thought to have battred quight,
Untill Duessa loud to him gan crye;
"O great Orgoglio,[4] greatest under skye,
O hold thy mortall hand for Ladies sake,
Hold for my sake, and do him not to dye,°   *do not cause him to die*
125   But vanquisht thine eternall bondslave make,
And me thy worthy meed unto thy Leman take."[5]

15

He hearkned, and did stay° from further harmes,   *refrain*
To gayne so goodly guerdon,° as she spake: *reward*
So willingly she came into his armes,
130   Who her as willingly to grace° did take,   *favor*
And was possessèd of his new found make.°   *mate*
Then up he tooke the slombred° sencelesse corse,   *unconscious*
And ere he could out of his swowne awake,
Him to his castle brought with hastie forse,
135   And in a Dongeon deepe him threw without remorse.

16

From that day forth Duessa was his deare,
And highly honourd in his haughtie eye,
He gave her gold and purple pall° to weare,   *crimson robe of royalty*
And triple crowne set on her head full hye,[6]
140   And her endowd with royall majestye:
Then for to make her dreaded more of men,
And peoples harts with awfull terrour tye,°   *enthrall*
A monstrous beast ybred in filthy fen
He chose, which he had kept long time in darksome den.

17

145   Such one it was, as that renowmèd Snake
Which great Alcides in Stremona slew,

2. Filled ("fraught") with gunpowder ("Nitre" and "Sulphur").
3. I.e., the blast or smell alone ("onely") overcomes him.
4. Italian for "pride, haughtiness, disdain."

5. I.e., take me, your worthy reward, as your mistress.
6. Duessa is attired like the Whore of Babylon in Revelation 17.3–4; the triple crown is that of the papacy (see canto 2, stanzas 13 and 22).

Long fostred in the filth of Lerna lake,[7]
Whose many heads out budding ever new,
Did breed° him endlesse labour to subdew: *cause*
150 But this same Monster much more ugly was;
For seven great heads out of his body grew,
An yron brest, and backe of scaly bras,
And all embrewd° in bloud, his eyes did shine as glas.   *stained*

18

His tayle was stretchèd out in wondrous length,
155 That to the house of heavenly gods it raught,°   *reached*
And with extorted powre, and borrowed strength,
The ever-burning lamps° from thence it brought,   *stars*
And prowdly threw to ground, as things of nought;
And underneath his filthy feet did tread
160 The sacred things, and holy heasts foretaught.[8]
Upon this dreadfull Beast with sevenfold head
He set the false Duessa, for more aw and dread.

19

The wofull Dwarfe, which saw his maisters fall,
Whiles he had keeping of his grasing steed,
165 And valiant knight become a caytive° thrall,   *captive*
When all was past, tooke up his forlorne weed,°   *abandoned garment*
His mightie armour, missing most at need;
His silver shield, now idle maisterlesse;
His poynant° speare, that many made to bleed,   *sharp*
170 The ruefull moniments° of heavinesse,°   *memorials/grief*
And with them all departes, to tell his great distresse.

20

He had not travaild long, when on the way
He wofull Ladie, wofull Una met,
Fast flying from the Paynims greedy pray,°   *clutch*
175 Whilest Satyrane him from pursuit did let:°   *prevent*
Who when her eyes she on the Dwarfe had set,
And saw the signes, that deadly tydings spake,
She fell to ground for sorrowfull regret,°   *grief*
And lively breath her sad brest did forsake,
180 Yet might her pitteous hart be seene to pant and quake.

21

The messenger of so unhappie newes
Would faine have dyde: dead was his hart within,
Yet outwardly some little comfort shewes:
At last recovering hart, he does begin

---

7. The nine-headed Lernean hydra slain by Hercules (Alcides). The seven-headed monster recalls the red dragon of Revelation: "behold a great red dragon, having seven heads and ten horns, and seven crowns upon his heads . . . [whose] tail drew the third part of the stars of heaven, and did cast

them to the earth . . . [he is] that old serpent, called the Devil, and Satan, which deceiveth the whole world" (12.3–14.9). Many Protestants associated the Beast with the Roman church.
8. Doctrines ("holy heasts") previously taught.

185   To rub her temples, and to chaufe her chin,
       And every tender part does tosse and turne:
       So hardly he the flitted life does win,
       Unto her native prison to retourne:[9]
    Then gins her grievèd ghost° thus to lament and mourne.   *spirit*

22

190   "Ye dreary instruments of dolefull sight,
       That doe this deadly spectacle behold,
       Why do ye lenger feed on loathèd light,
       Or liking find to gaze on earthly mould,[1]
       Sith cruell fates the carefull° threeds unfould,   *intricate*
195   The which my life and love together tyde?
       Now let the stony dart of senselesse cold°   *i.e., death*
       Perce to my hart, and pas through every side,
    And let eternall night so sad sight fro me hide.

23

    "O lightsome day, the lampe of highest Jove,
200   First made by him,[2] mens wandring wayes to guyde,
       When darknesse he in deepest dongeon drove,
       Henceforth thy hated face for ever hyde,
       And shut up heavens windowes shyning wyde:
       For earthly sight can nought but sorrow breed,
205   And late° repentance, which shall long abyde.   *too late*
       Mine eyes no more on vanitie shall feed,
    But seelèd up with death, shall have their deadly meed."°   *reward of death*

24

    Then downe againe she fell unto the ground;
       But he her quickly rearèd up againe:
210   Thrise did she sinke adowne in deadly swownd,
       And thrise he her revived with busie paine:°   *care*
       At last when life recovered had the raine,°   *rein*
       And over-wrestled his strong enemie,
       With foltring° tong, and trembling every vaine,   *faltering*
215   "Tell on," quoth she, "the wofull Tragedie,
    The which these reliques sad present unto mine eie.

25

    "Tempestuous fortune hath spent all her spight,
       And thrilling° sorrow throwne his utmost dart;   *piercing*
       Thy sad tongue cannot tell more heavy plight,
220   Then that I feele, and harbour in mine hart:
       Who hath endured the whole, can beare each part.
       If death it be, it is not the first wound,
       That launchèd° hath my brest with bleeding smart.   *pierced*

---

9. I.e., with such difficulty ("so hardly") he persuades ("does win") the life back to her body ("native prison").
1. I.e., or find it pleasure to gaze on earthly forms ("mould").
2. An allusion to Genesis 1.3: "And God said, Let there be light: and there was light."

Begin, and end the bitter balefull stound;°   time (of sorrow)
225   If lesse, then that I feare, more favour I have found."

26

Then gan the Dwarfe the whole discourse° declare,   story
      The subtill traines° of Archimago old;   wiles
      The wanton loves of false Fidessa faire,
      Bought with the bloud of vanquisht Paynim bold:
230   The wretched payre transformed to treen mould;°   shape of a tree
      The house of Pride, and perils round about;
      The combat, which he with Sans joy did hould;
      The lucklesse conflict with the Gyant stout,
Wherein captived, of life or death he stood in doubt.

27

235   She heard with patience all unto the end,
      And strove to maister sorrowfull assay,°   affliction
      Which greater grew, the more she did contend,
      And almost rent her tender hart in tway°   two
      And love fresh coles unto her fire did lay:
240   For greater love, the greater is the losse.
      Was never Ladie lovèd dearer day,[3]
      Then she did love the knight of the Redcrosse;
For whose deare sake so many troubles her did tosse.

28

At last when fervent sorrow slakèd was,
245   She up arose, resolving him to find
      Alive or dead: and forward forth doth pas,
      All° as the Dwarfe the way to her assynd:°   just/showed
      And evermore in constant carefull mind
      She fed her wound with fresh renewèd bale;°   anguish
250   Long tost with stormes, and bet° with bitter wind,   beaten
      High over hils, and low adowne the dale,
She wandred many a wood, and measurd many a vale.

29

At last she chauncèd by good hap to meet
      A goodly knight, faire marching by the way
255   Together with his Squire, arayèd meet:°   properly
      His glitterand° armour shinèd farre away,   glittering
      Like glauncing° light of Phoebus brightest ray;   flashing
      From top to toe no place appearèd bare,
      That deadly dint° of steele endanger may: stroke
260   Athwart his brest a bauldrick[4] brave he ware,
That shynd, like twinkling stars, with stons most pretious rare.

30

And in the midst thereof one pretious stone
      Of wondrous worth, and eke° of wondrous mights,°   also/powers

---

3. I.e., there was never a lady who loved life
("day") more dearly than she loved Redcrosse.

4. Sash worn over the shoulder to support the
sword.

Shapt like a Ladies head, exceeding shone,
265 Like Hesperus° emongst the lesser lights,°   *evening star/stars*
And strove for to amaze the weaker sights;
Thereby his mortall blade full comely hong
In yvory sheath, ycarved with curious slights;°   *designs*
Whose hilts were burnisht gold, and handle strong
270 Of mother pearle, and buckled with a golden tong.°   *pin*

31

His haughtie helmet, horrid° all with gold,   *bristling*
Both glorious brightnesse, and great terrour bred;
For all the crest a Dragon did enfold
With greedie pawes, and over all did spred
275 His golden wings: his dreadfull hideous hed
Close couchèd on the bever,° seemed to throw   *visor*
From flaming mouth bright sparkles fierie red,
That suddeine horror to faint harts did show;
And scaly tayle was stretcht adowne his backe full low.

32

280 Upon the top of all his loftie crest,°   *top of helmet*
A bunch of haires discolourd° diversly,   *dyed*
With sprincled pearle, and gold full richly drest,
Did shake, and seemed to daunce for jollity,
Like to an Almond tree ymounted hye
285 On top of greene Selinis⁵ all alone,
With blossomes brave bedeckèd daintily;
Whose tender locks do tremble every one
At every little breath, that under heaven is blowne.

33

His warlike shield all closely covered was,
290 Ne might of mortall eye be ever seene;
Not made of steele, nor of enduring bras,
Such earthly mettals soone consumèd bene:
But all of Diamond perfect pure and cleene°   *clear*
It framèd was, one massie entire mould,⁶
295 Hewen out of Adamant rocke with engines keene,
That point of speare it never percen could,
Ne dint of direfull sword divide the substance would.

34

The same to wight° he never wont disclose,   *creature*
But° when as monsters huge he would dismay,   *except*
300 Or daunt unequall armies of his foes,
Or when the flying heavens he would affray;⁷
For so exceeding shone his glistring ray,
That Phoebus golden face it did attaint,°   *make dim*

5. Town associated with the palm awarded to victors (Virgil, *Aeneid* 3.705).
6. The shield was made of one solid piece of diamond, whose qualities—unflawed, unpierceable, translucent—point to this knight's significance and role.
7. I.e., when he would frighten ("affray") the revolving constellations.

As when a cloud his beames doth over-lay;
305   And silver Cynthia° wexèd pale and faint,   *the moon*
As when her face is staynd with magicke arts constraint.[8]

35

No magicke arts hereof had any might,
    Nor bloudie wordes of bold Enchaunters call,
    But all that was not such, as seemd in sight,
310   Before that shield did fade, and suddeine fall:
    And when him list the raskall routes° appall,   *unruly mobs*
    Men into stones therewith he could transmew,°   *change*
    And stones to dust, and dust to nought at all;
    And when him list the prouder lookes subdew,
315 He would them gazing blind, or turne to other hew.°   *form*

36

Ne let it seeme, that credence this exceedes,
    For he that made the same, was knowne right well
    To have done much more admirable° deedes.   *marvelous*
    It Merlin was, which whylome° did excell   *formerly*
320   All living wightes in might of magicke spell:
    Both shield, and sword, and armour all he wrought
    For this young Prince, when first to armes he fell;°   *came*
    But when he dyde, the Faerie Queene it brought
To Faerie lond, where yet it may be seene, if sought.[9]

37

325 A gentle youth, his dearely lovèd Squire
    His speare of heben° wood behind him bare,   *ebony*
    Whose harmefull head, thrice heated in the fire,
    Had riven many a brest with pikehead square;
    A goodly person, and could menage° faire   *control*
330   His stubborne steed with curbèd canon bit,[1]
    Who under him did trample as the aire,
    And chauft,° that any on his backe should sit;   *fretted*
The yron rowels° into frothy fome he bit.   *ends of the bit*

38

When as this knight nigh to the Ladie drew,
335   With lovely° court he gan her entertaine;   *kind*
    But when he heard her answers loth, he knew
    Some secret sorrow did her heart distraine:°   *afflict*
    Which to allay, and calme her storming paine,
    Faire feeling words he wisely gan display,°   *pour forth*
340   And for her humour fitting purpose faine,[2]
    To tempt the cause it selfe for to bewray;°   *reveal*
Wherewith emmoved, these bleeding words she gan to say.

8. Magicians were believed to be able to cause an eclipse of the moon.
9. I.e., Arthur's virtues may be seen still in Queen Elizabeth's England. By the references to Merlin and the Faerie Queene, we now know that this knight is Arthur, identified in the *Letter to Ralegh* with "magnificence," understood as the perfection of all the virtues and containing them all.
1. "Cannon bit": a smooth, round bit.
2. I.e., suited his manner to her mood.

39

"What worlds delight, or joy of living speach
  Can heart, so plunged in sea of sorrowes deepe,
345 And heapèd with so huge misfortunes, reach?
  The carefull° cold beginneth for to creepe,   *afflicting*
  And in my heart his yron arrow steepe,
  Soone as I thinke upon my bitter bale:°   *grief*
  Such helplesse harmes yts better hidden keepe,
350 Then° rip up griefe, where it may not availe,   *than*
My last left comfort is, my woes to weepe and waile."

40

"Ah Ladie deare," quoth then the gentle knight,
  "Well may I weene, your griefe is wondrous great;
  For wondrous great griefe groneth in my spright,°   *spirit*
355 Whiles thus I heare you of your sorrowes treat.
  But wofull Ladie let me you intrete,
  For to unfold the anguish of your hart:
  Mishaps are maistred by advice discrete,
  And counsell mittigates the greatest smart;
360 Found never helpe, who never would his hurts impart."[3]

41

"O but," quoth she, "great griefe will not be tould,
  And can more easily be thought, then said."
  "Right so"; quoth he, "but he, that never would,
  Could never: will to might gives greatest aid."[4]
365 "But grief," quoth she, "does greater grow displaid,
  If then it find not helpe, and breedes despaire."
  "Despaire breedes not," quoth he, "where faith is staid."°   *firm*
  "No faith so fast," quoth she, "but flesh does paire."°   *impair*
"Flesh may empaire," quoth he, "but reason can repaire."

42

370 His goodly reason, and well guided speach
  So deepe did settle in her gratious thought,
  That her perswaded to disclose the breach,
  Which love and fortune in her heart had wrought,
  And said; "Faire Sir, I hope good hap hath brought
375 You to inquire the secrets of my griefe,
  Or° that your wisedome will direct my thought,   *either*
  Or that your prowesse can me yield reliefe:
Then heare the storie sad, which I shall tell you briefe.

43

"The forlorne° Maiden, whom your eyes have seene   *forsaken*
380 The laughing stocke of fortunes mockeries,
  Am th' only daughter of a King and Queene,

---

3. I.e., he never found help who would not tell his sorrows.
4. I.e., he that fails to will something cannot do it: willing gives the greatest help to one's power ("might").

Whose parents deare, whilest equall destinies
Did runne about,[5] and their felicities
The favourable heavens did not envy,
385   Did spread their rule through all the territories,
Which Phison and Euphrates floweth by,
And Gehons golden waves doe wash continually.[6]

44

"Till that their cruell cursèd enemy,
An huge great Dragon horrible in sight,
390   Bred in the loathly lakes of Tartary,°   Tartarus (hell)
With murdrous ravine,° and devouring might   destruction
Their kingdome spoild, and countrey wasted quight:
Themselves, for feare into his jawes to fall,
He forst to castle strong to take their flight,
395   Where fast embard° in mightie brasen wall,   imprisoned
He has them now foure yeres besiegd to make them thrall.

45

"Full many knights adventurous and stout
Have enterprizd that Monster to subdew;
From every coast° that heaven walks about,   land
400   Have thither come the noble Martiall crew,
That famous hard atchievements still pursew,
Yet never any could that girlond win,
But all still shronke,° and still he greater grew: quailed
All they for want of faith, or guilt of sin,
405   The pitteous pray of his fierce crueltie have bin.

46

"At last yledd° with farre reported praise,   led
Which flying fame throughout the world had spread,
Of doughtie° knights, whom Faery land did raise,   brave
That noble order hight° of Maidenhed,[7]   called
410   Forthwith to court of Gloriane I sped,
Of Gloriane great Queene of glory bright,
Whose kingdomes seat Cleopolis[8] is red,°   named
There to obtaine some such redoubted knight,
That Parents deare from tyrants powre deliver might.

47

415   "It was my chance (my chance was faire and good)
There for to find a fresh unprovèd° knight,   untried
Whose manly hands imbrewed in guiltie blood
Had never bene,[9] ne ever by his might
Had throwne to ground the unregarded° right: unrespected

5. I.e., while the impartial fates ran their course.
6. Because these three rivers flow in the Garden of Eden (Genesis 2.11–14), we know that Eden is the country of Una's parents.
7. The type or analogue of the Order of the Garter.

Its emblem shows St. George killing the dragon and its star is the Red Cross.
8. Cleopolis means "famous city."
9. I.e., his strong hands had never been guiltily stained ("imbrewed") with blood.

420   Yet of his prowesse proofe he since hath made
        (I witnesse am) in many a cruell fight;
        The groning ghosts of many one dismaide°   *defeated*
    Have felt the bitter dint of his avenging blade.

48

    "And ye the forlorne reliques of his powre,
425   His byting sword, and his devouring speare,
        Which have endurèd many a dreadfull stowre,°   *conflict*
        Can speake his prowesse, that did earst° you beare,   *before*
        And well could rule: now he hath left you heare,
        To be the record of his ruefull losse,
430   And of my dolefull disaventurous deare:°   *sad unfortunate dear one*
        O heavie record of the good Redcrosse,
    Where have you left your Lord, that could so well you tosse?°   *handle*

49

    "Well hopèd I, and faire beginnings had,
        That he my captive langour should redeeme,[1]
435   Till all unweeting,° an Enchaunter bad   *unknowing*
        His sence abusd, and made him to misdeeme°   *misjudge*
        My loyalty, not such as it did seeme;
        That rather death desire, then such despight.[2]
        Be judge ye heavens, that all things right esteeme,°   *judge rightly*
440   How I him loved, and love with all my might,
    So thought I eke of him, and thinke I thought aright.

50

    "Thenceforth me desolate he quite forsooke,
        To wander, where wilde fortune would me lead,
        And other bywaies he himselfe betooke,
445   Where never foot of living wight did tread,
        That brought not backe the balefull body dead;°   *i.e., who returned alive*
        In which him chauncèd false Duessa meete,
        Mine onely foe, mine onely deadly dread,[3]
        Who with her witchcraft and misseeming° sweete,   *false appearance*
450   Inveigled him to follow her desires unmeete.°   *improper*

51

    "At last by subtill sleights she him betraid
        Unto his foe, a Gyant huge and tall,
        Who him disarmèd, dissolute,° dismaid,   *enfeebled*
        Unwares surprisèd and with mightie mall°   *club*
455   The monster mercilesse him made to fall,
        Whose fall did never foe before behold;
        And now in darkesome dungeon, wretched thrall,
        Remedilesse, for aie[4] he doth him hold;
    This is my cause of griefe, more great, then may be told."

---

1. I.e., relieve my state, captive to sadness.
2. I.e., I, who prefer death to such treachery ("despight").
3. I.e., the only object of my mortal fear.
4. I.e., forever ("for aie") without hope of rescue ("remedilesse").

52

460 Ere she had ended all, she gan to faint:
But he her comforted and faire bespake,
"Certes, Madame, ye have great cause of plaint,
That stoutest heart, I weene, could cause to quake.
But be of cheare, and comfort to you take:
465 For till I have acquit° your captive knight,   *freed*
Assure your selfe, I will you not forsake."
His chearefull words revived her chearelesse spright,
So forth they went, the Dwarfe them guiding ever right.

Canto 8

*Faire virgin to redeeme her deare
brings Arthur to the fight:
Who slayes the Gyant, wounds the beast,
and strips Duessa quight.*

1

Ay me, how many perils doe enfold
The righteous man, to make him daily fall?
Were not, that heavenly grace doth him uphold,
And stedfast truth acquite° him out of all.   *deliver*
5 Her love is firme, her care continuall,
So oft as he through his owne foolish pride,
Or weaknesse is to sinfull bands° made thrall: *bonds*
Else should this Redcrosse knight in bands have dyde,
For whose deliverance she this Prince doth thither guide.

2

10 They sadly traveild thus, untill they came
Nigh to a castle builded strong and hie:
Then cryde the Dwarfe, "lo yonder is the same;
In which my Lord my liege doth lucklesse lie,
Thrall to that Gyants hatefull tyrannie:
15 Therefore, deare Sir, your mightie powres assay."°   *put to trial*
The noble knight alighted by and by°   *immediately*
From loftie steede, and bad the Ladie stay,
To see what end of fight should him befall that day.

3

So with the Squire, th' admirer of his might,
20 He marchèd forth towards that castle wall;
Whose gates he found fast shut, ne living wight
To ward° the same, nor answere commers call.   *guard*
Then tooke that Squire an horne of bugle° small,   *wild ox*
Which hong adowne his side in twisted gold,
25 And tassels gay. Wyde wonders over all°   *everywhere*
Of that same hornes great vertues weren told,[5]
Which had approvèd° bene in uses manifold.   *demonstrated*

---

5. "Wide wonders": (marvelous tales) told of the horn connect it with the horn of the legendary French hero Roland and the ram's horn of Joshua, with which he razed the walls of Jericho (Joshua 6.5); see also Romans 10.18, referring to the word of God as the horn of salvation.

4

Was never wight, that heard that shrilling sound,
  But trembling feare did feele in every vaine;
30 Three miles it might be easie heard around,
  And Ecchoes three answered it selfe againe:
  No false enchauntment, nor deceiptfull traine°   *snare*
  Might once abide the terror of that blast,
  But presently° was voide and wholly vaine: *at once*
35 No gate so strong, no locke so firme and fast,
  But with that percing noise flew open quite, or brast.°   *burst*

5

The same before the Geants gate he blew,
  That all the castle quakèd from the ground,
  And every dore of freewill open flew.
40 The Gyant selfe dismaièd with that sownd,
  Where he with his Duessa dalliance° fownd,   *amorous play*
  In hast came rushing forth from inner bowre,
  With staring° countenance sterne, as one astownd,   *glaring*
  And staggering steps, to weet, what suddein stowre°   *disturbance*
45 Had wrought that horror strange, and dared his dreaded powre.

6

And after him the proud Duessa came,
  High mounted on her manyheaded beast,
  And every head with fyrie tongue did flame,
  And every head was crownèd on his creast,
50 And bloudie mouthèd with late cruell feast.
  That when the knight beheld, his mightie shild
  Upon his manly arme he soone addrest,ᶜ   *made ready*
  And at him fiercely flew, with courage fild,
  And eger greedinesse° through every member thrild.   *eagerness for battle*

7

55 Therewith the Gyant buckled him to fight,
  Inflamed with scornefull wrath and high disdaine,°   *indignation*
  And lifting up his dreadfull club on hight,
  All armed with ragged snubbes° and knottie graine,   *snags*
  Him thought at first encounter to have slaine.
60 But wise and warie was that noble Pere,°   *peer*
  And lightly leaping from so monstrous maine,°   *force*
  Did faire° avoide the violence him nere;   *quite*
  It booted nought, to thinke, such thunderbolts to beare.⁶

8

Ne shame he thought to shunne so hideous might:
65 The idleᶜ stroke, enforcing furious way,   *useless*
  Missing the marke of his misaymèd sight
  Did fall to ground, and with his° heavie sway°   *its/force*

6. I.e., it was useless to think of withstanding such blows.

So deepely dinted in the driven clay,
That three yardes deepe a furrow up did throw:
70 The sad earth wounded with so sore assay,°   assault
Did grone full grievous underneath the blow,
And trembling with strange feare, did like an earthquake show.

9

As when almightie Jove in wrathfull mood,
To wreake° the guilt of mortall sins is bent,   punish
75 Hurles forth his thundring dart with deadly food,°   hatred (feud)
Enrold in flames, and smouldring dreriment,°   smothering darkness
Through riven cloudes and molten firmament;
The fierce threeforkèd engin° making way,   weapon
Both loftie towres and highest trees hath rent,
80 And all that might his angrie passage stay,
And shooting in the earth, casts up a mount of clay.

10

His boystrous° club, so buried in the ground,   massive
He could not rearen up againe so light,°   easily
But that the knight him at avantage found,
And whiles he strove his combred° clubbe to   encumbered
85 quight°   release
Out of the earth, with blade all burning bright
He smote off his left arme, which like a blocke
Did fall to ground, deprived of native might;
Large streames of bloud out of the trunckèd stocke° truncated stump
90 Forth gushèd, like fresh water streame from riven rocke.[7]

11

Dismaièd with so desperate deadly wound,
And eke° impatient of unwonted paine,[8]   also
He loudly brayd with beastly yelling sound,
That all the fields rebellowèd againe;
95 As great a noyse, as when in Cymbrian[9] plaine
An heard of Bulles, whom kindly° rage doth sting,   natural
Do for the milkie mothers want complaine,[1]
And fill the fields with troublous bellowing,
The neighbour woods around with hollow murmur ring.

12

100 That when his deare Duessa heard, and saw
The evill stownd, that daungerd her estate,[2]
Unto his aide she hastily did draw
Her dreadfull beast, who swolne with bloud of late
Came ramping° forth with proud presumpteous gate,° rearing/gait

---

7. Cf. Exodus 17.6, where Moses smites the rock
and water flows forth.
8. I.e., unable to bear ("impatient of") this unfamiliar ("unwonted") pain.

9. Jutland, once called the Cimbric peninsula.
1. I.e., mourn the cows' absence.
2. I.e., the peril ("stownd") that endangered her
state.

105   And threatned all his heads like flaming brands.°   *torches*
        But him the Squire made quickly to retrate,
        Encountring fierce with single° sword in hand,   *only*
  And twixt him and his Lord did like a bulwarke stand.

13

  The proud Duessa full of wrathfull spight,
110   And fierce disdaine, to be affronted so,
        Enforst her purple beast with all her might
        That stop° out of the way to overthroe,   *obstacle*
        Scorning the let° of so unequall foe: *hindrance*
        But nathemore° would that courageous swayne   *never the more*
115   To her yeeld passage, gainst his Lord to goe,
        But with outrageous° strokes did him restraine,   *exceedingly fierce*
  And with his bodie bard the way atwixt them twaine.

14

  Then tooke the angrie witch her golden cup,
        Which still she bore, replete with magick artes;[3]
120   Death and despeyre did many thereof sup,
        And secret poyson through their inner parts,
        Th' eternall bale° of heavie wounded harts;   *woe*
        Which after charmes and some enchauntments said,
        She lightly sprinkled on his weaker° parts;   *too weak*
125   Therewith his sturdie courage soone was quayd,°   *quelled*
  And all his senses were with suddeine dread dismayd.

15

  So downe he fell before the cruell beast,
        Who on his necke his bloudie clawes did seize,
        That life nigh crusht out of his panting brest:
130   No powre he had to stirre, nor will to rize.
        That when the carefull° knight gan well avise,°   *watchful / observe*
        He lightly° left the foe, with whom he fought,   *quickly*
        And to the beast gan turne his enterprise;
        For wondrous anguish in his hart it wrought,
135   To see his lovèd Squire into such thraldome° brought.   *slavery*

16

  And high advauncing° his bloud-thirstie blade,   *lifting up*
        Stroke one of those deformèd heads so sore,[4]
        That of his puissance proud ensample made;
        His monstrous scalpe° downe to his teeth it tore   *skull*
140   And that misformèd shape mis-shapèd more:
        A sea of bloud gusht from the gaping wound,
        That her gay garments staynd with filthy gore,

3. Alludes to the golden cup of the woman in Revelation, which is "full of abominations and filthiness of her fornications" (17.4); the chalice of the Roman church; and the cup of Circe, the sorceress who turned men into beasts (in *Odyssey* 10).
4. "I saw one of [the beast's] heads as it were wounded to death" (Revelation 13.3).

And overflowèd all the field around;
That over shoes in bloud he waded on the ground.

17

145 Thereat he roarèd for exceeding paine,
    That to have heard, great horror would have bred,°   *produced*
    And scourging th' emptie ayre with his long traine,°   *tail*
    Through great impatience of his grievèd hed[5]
    His gorgeous ryder from her loftie sted°   *place*
150 Would have cast downe, and trod in durtie myre,
    Had not the Gyant soone her succourèd;
    Who all enraged with smart° and franticke yre,°   *pain/anger*
Came hurtling in full fierce, and forst the knight retyre.

18

The force, which wont in two to be disperst,
155   In one alone left hand[6] he now unites,
    Which is through rage more strong then both were erst;°   *before*
    With which his hideous club aloft he dites,°   *raises*
    And at his foe with furious rigour° smites,   *violence*
    That strongest Oake might seeme to overthrow:
160 The stroke upon his shield so heavie lites,
    That to the ground it doubleth him full low:
What mortall wight could ever beare so monstrous blow?

19

And in his fall his shield, that covered was,
    Did loose his vele° by chaunce, and open flew: *its covering*
165 The light whereof, that heavens light did pas,°   *surpass*
    Such blazing brightnesse through the aier threw,
    That eye mote not the same endure to vew.
    Which when the Gyaunt spyde with staring eye,
    He downe let fall his arme, and soft withdrew
170 His weapon huge, that heavèd was on hye
For to have slaine the man, that on the ground did lye.

20

And eke the fruitfull-headed° beast, amazed   *many-headed*
    At flashing beames of that sunshiny shield,
    Became starke blind, and all his senses dazed,
175 That downe he tumbled on the durtie field,
    And seemed himselfe as conquerèd to yield.
    Whom when his maistresse proud perceived to fall,
    Whiles yet his feeble feet for faintnesse reeld,
    Unto the Gyant loudly she gan call,
180 "O helpe Orgoglio, helpe, or else we perish all."

21

At her so pitteous cry was much amooved
    Her champion stout, and for to ayde his frend,°   *lover*

---

5. I.e., through inability to endure ("impatience")   6. I.e., in the one hand left to him.
his afflicted ("grievèd") head.

Againe his wonted angry weapon prooved:°   *tried*
But all in vaine: for he has read his end
185   In that bright shield, and all their forces spend
Themselves in vaine: for since that glauncing° sight,   *flashing*
He hath no powre to hurt, nor to defend;
As where th' Almighties lightning brond does light,
It dimmes the dazèd eyen, and daunts the senses quight.

22

190   Whom when the Prince, to battell new addrest,
And threatning high his dreadfull stroke did see,
His sparkling blade about his head he blest,°   *brandished*
And smote off quite his right leg by the knee,
That downe he tombled; as an aged tree,
195   High growing on the top of rocky clift,
Whose hartstrings with keene steele nigh hewen be,
The mightie trunck halfe rent, with ragged rift°   *split*
Doth roll adowne the rocks, and fall with fearefull drift.°   *impact*

23

Or as a Castle rearèd high and round,
200   By subtile engins and malitious slight[7]
Is underminèd from the lowest ground,
And her foundation forst,° and feebled quight,   *shattered*
At last downe falles, and with her heapèd hight
Her hastie ruine does more heavie make,
205   And yields it selfe unto the victours might;
Such was this Gyaunts fall, that seemed to shake
The stedfast globe of earth, as it for feare did quake.

24

The knight then lightly° leaping to the pray,   *quickly*
With mortall steele him smot againe so sore,
210   That headlesse his unweldy bodie lay,
All wallowd in his owne fowle bloudy gore,
Which flowèd from his wounds in wondrous store.°   *abundance*
But soone as breath out of his breast did pas,
That huge great body, which the Gyaunt bore,
215   Was vanisht quite, and of that monstrous mas
Was nothing left, but like an emptie bladder was.

25

Whose grievous fall, when false Duessa spide,
Her golden cup she cast unto the ground,
And crownèd mitre[8] rudely° threw aside.   *violently*
220   Such percing griefe her stubborne hart did wound,
That she could not endure that dolefull stound,°   *sorrow*
But leaving all behind her, fled away:
The light-foot Squire her quickly turned around,

---

7. Clever machines of war ("engins") and evil   8. An allusion to the pope's triple tiara.
strategy.

And by hard meanes enforcing her to stay,
225 So brought unto his Lord, as his deservèd pray.

26

The royall Virgin, which beheld from farre,
  In pensive° plight, and sad perplexitie,   *anxious*
  The whole atchievement of this doubtfull warre,[9]
  Came running fast to greet his victorie,
230   With sober gladnesse, and myld modestie,
  And with sweet joyous cheare him thus bespake;
  "Faire braunch of noblesse, flowre of chevalrie,
  That with your worth the world amazèd make,
How shall I quite° the paines, ye suffer for my sake?   *requite*

27

235 "And you° fresh bud of vertue springing fast,   *i.e., the Squire*
  Whom these sad eyes saw nigh unto deaths dore,
  What hath poore Virgin for such perill past,
  Wherewith you to reward? Accept therefore
  My simple selfe, and service evermore;
240   And he that high does sit, and all things see
  With equall° eyes, their merites to restore,°   *impartial / reward*
  Behold what ye this day have done for mee,
And what I cannot quite, requite with usuree.°   *interest*

28

"But sith the heavens, and your faire handeling°   *conduct*
245   Have made you maister of the field this day,
  Your fortune maister eke with governing,[1]
  And well begun end all so well, I pray,
  Ne let that wicked woman scape away;
  For she it is, that did my Lord bethrall,
250   My dearest Lord, and deepe in dongeon lay,
  Where he his better dayes hath wasted all.[2]
O heare, how piteous he to you for ayd does call."

29

Forthwith he gave in charge unto his Squire,
  That scarlot whore to keepen carefully;
255   Whiles he himselfe with greedie° great desire   *eager*
  Into the Castle entred forcibly,
  Where living creature none he did espye;
  Then gan he lowdly through the house to call:
  But no man cared to answere to his crye.
260   There raignd a solemne silence over all,
Nor voice was heard, nor wight was seene in bowre or hall.

30

At last with creeping crooked pace forth came
  An old old man, with beard as white as snow,

9. I.e., the final outcome, long in doubt ("doubt-full") of this battle.
1. Secure your good fortune also by prudent man-agement.
2. I.e., he has consumed ("wasted") here his best days.

That on a staffe his feeble steps did frame,°   *support*
265 And guide his wearie gate° both too and fro: *gait*
For his eye sight him failèd long ygo,
And on his arme a bounch of keyes he bore,
The which unusèd rust did overgrow:
Those were the keyes of every inner dore,
270 But he could not them use, but kept them still in store.

31

But very uncouth° sight was to behold,   *strange*
How he did fashion his untoward° pace,   *awkward*
For as he forward mooved his footing old,
So backward still was turned his wrincled face,
275 Unlike to men, who ever as they trace,°   *walk*
Both feet and face one way are wont to lead.
This was the auncient keeper of that place,
And foster father of the Gyant dead;
His name Ignaro did his nature right aread.[3]

32

280 His reverend haires and holy gravitie
The knight much honord, as beseemèd well,°   *seemed proper*
And gently° askt, where all the people bee,   *courteously*
Which in that stately building wont to dwell.
Who answerd him full soft, he could not tell.
285 Againe he askt, where that same knight was layd,
Whom great Orgoglio with his puissaunce fell
Had made his caytive° thrall; againe he sayde,   *captive*
He could not tell: ne ever other answere made.

33

Then askèd he, which way he in might pas:
290 He could not tell, againe he answerèd.
Thereat the curteous knight displeasèd was,
And said, "Old sire, it seemes thou hast not red°   *recognized*
How ill it sits with° that same silver hed   *suits*
In vaine to mocke, or mockt in vaine to bee:
295 But if thou be, as thou art pourtrahèd
With natures pen, in ages grave degree,°   *i.e., dignity*
Aread° in graver wise, what I demaund° of thee."   *answer/ask*

34

His answere likewise was, he could not tell.
Whose sencelesse speach, and doted° ignorance   *foolish*
300 When as the noble Prince had markèd well,
He ghest his nature by his countenance,
And calmd his wrath with goodly temperance.
Then to him stepping, from his arme did reach
Those keyes, and made himselfe free enterance.

3. His name Ignaro made clear ("did aread") that his nature was Ignorance.

305   Each dore he opened without any breach;°   *forcing*
        There was no barre to stop, nor foe him to empeach.°   *hinder*

35

    There all within full rich arayd he found,
        With royal arras° and resplendent gold.   *tapestry*
        And did with store of every thing abound,
310   That greatest Princes presence° might behold.   *person*
        But all the floore (too filthy to be told)
        With bloud of guiltlesse babes, and innocents trew,[4]
        Which there were slaine, as sheepe out of the fold,
        Defilèd was, that dreadfull was to vew,
315   And sacred ashes over it was strowèd new.

36

    And there beside of marble stone was built
        An Altare, carved with cunning imagery,°   *images*
        On which true Christians bloud was often spilt,
        And holy Martyrs often doen to dye,°   *put to death*
320   With cruell malice and strong tyranny:
        Whose blessed sprites from underneath the stone
        To God for vengeance cryde continually,[5]
        And with great griefe were often heard to grone,
    That hardest heart would bleede, to heare their piteous mone.

37

325   Through every rowme he sought, and every bowr,
        But no where could he find that wofull thrall:
        At last he came unto an yron doore,
        That fast was lockt, but key found not at all
        Emongst that bounch, to open it withall;
330   But in the same a little grate was pight,°   *placed*
        Through which he sent his voyce, and lowd did call
        With all his powre, to weet,° if living wight   *learn*
    Were housèd therewithin, whom he enlargen° might.   *set free*

38

    Therewith an hollow, dreary, murmuring voyce
335   These piteous plaints and dolours° did resound;   *laments*
        "O who is that, which brings me happy choyce°   *chance*
        Of death, that here lye dying every stound,°   *moment*
        Yet live perforce in balefull° darkenesse bound?   *evil*
        For now three Moones have changèd thrice their hew,°   *shape*
340   And have beene thrice hid underneath the ground,
        Since I the heavens chearefull face did vew,
    O welcome thou, that doest of death bring tydings trew."

4. Probably a reference to Herod's massacre of the Innocents (Matthew 2.16), traditionally viewed as the first martyrs for Christ.
5. "And when he had opened the fifth seal, I saw under the altar the souls of them that were slain for the word of God, and for the testimony which they held: And they cried with a loud voice, saying, How long, O Lord, holy and true, dost thou not judge and avenge our blood on them that dwell on the earth?" (Revelation 6.9–10).

39

Which when that Champion heard, with percing point
  Of pitty deare° his hart was thrillèd sore,   *extreme*
345 And trembling horrour ran through every joynt,
  For ruth of gentle knight so fowle forlore:°   *foully forsaken*
  Which shaking off, he rent that yron dore,
  With furious force, and indignation fell;°   *fierce*
  Where entred in, his foot could find no flore,
350 But all a deepe descent, as darke as hell,
That breathèd ever forth a filthie banefull smell.

40

But neither darkenesse fowle, nor filthy bands,°   *bonds*
  Nor noyous° smell his purpose could withhold,   *noxious*
  (Entire affection hateth nicer° hands)   *too fastidious*
355 But that with constant zeale, and courage bold,
  After long paines and labours manifold,
  He found the meanes that Prisoner up to reare;
  Whose feeble thighes, unhable to uphold
  His pinèd° corse, him scarse to light could beare,   *wasted*
360 A ruefull spectacle of deathe and ghastly drere.° *sorrow, wretchedness*

41

His sad dull eyes deepe sunck in hollow pits,
  Could not endure th' unwonted sunne to view;
  His bare thin cheekes for want of better bits,°   *food*
  And empty sides deceivèd° of their dew,   *cheated*
365 Could make a stony hart his hap to rew;
  His rawbone armes, whose mighty brawnèd bowrs° *brawny muscles*
  Were wont to rive steele plates, and helmets hew,
  Were cleane consumed, and all his vitall powres
Decayd, and all his flesh shronk up like withered flowres.

42

370 Whom when his Lady saw, to him she ran
  With hasty joy: to see him made her glad,
  And sad to view his visage pale and wan,
  Who earst in flowres of freshest youth was clad.
  Tho° when her well of teares she wasted had,   *then*
375 She said, "Ah dearest Lord, what evill starre
  On you hath frownd, and pourd his influence bad,
  That of your selfe ye thus berobbèd arre,
And this misseeming hew° your manly looks doth *unseemly appearance*
    marre?

43

"But welcome now my Lord, in wele or woe,
380 Whose presence I have lackt to long a day;
  And fie on Fortune mine avowèd foe,
  Whose wrathfull wreakes° them selves do now alay. *punishments*
  And for these wrongs shall treble penaunce pay

Of treble good: good growes of evils priefe."[6]
385   The chearelesse man, whom sorrow did dismay,°   *unnerve*
  Had no delight to treaten° of his griefe;   *speak*
His long endurèd famine needed more reliefe.

44

"Faire Lady," then said that victorious knight,°   *i.e., Arthur*
  "The things, that grievous were to do, or beare,
390   Them to renew,° I wote,° breeds no delight;   *recall / know*
  Best musicke breeds delight in loathing eare:
  But th' onely good, that growes of passèd feare,
  Is to be wise, and ware° of like agein.   *wary*
  This dayes ensample hath this lesson deare
395   Deepe written in my heart with yron pen,
That blisse may not abide in state of mortall men.

45

"Henceforth sir knight, take to you wonted strength,
  And maister these mishaps with patient might;
  Loe where your foe lyes stretcht in monstrous length,
400   And loe that wicked woman in your sight,
  The roote of all your care, and wretched plight,
  Now in your powre, to let her live, or dye."
  "To do her dye," quoth Una, "were despight,[7]
  And shame t' avenge so weake an enimy;
405 But spoile° her of her scarlot robe, and let her fly."   *despoil*

46

So as she bad, that witch they disaraid,
  And robd of royall robes, and purple pall,°   *cloak*
  And ornaments that richly were displaid;
  Ne sparèd they to strip her naked all.
410   Then when they had despoild her tire° and call,° *robe / headdress*
  Such as she was, their eyes might her behold,
  That her misshapèd parts did them appall,
  A loathly, wrinckled hag, ill favoured, old,
Whose secret filth good manners biddeth not be told.

47

415 Her craftie head was altogether bald,
  And as in hate of honorable eld,°   *age*
  Was overgrowne with scurfe° and filthy scald;[8]   *scabs*
  Her teeth out of her rotten gummes were feld,°   *fallen*
  And her sowre breath abhominably smeld;
420   Her drièd dugs, like bladders lacking wind,
  Hong downe, and filthy matter from them weld;°   *welled*
  Her wrizled° skin as rough, as maple rind,   *wrinkled*
So scabby was, that would have loathd all womankind.

---

6. I.e., Fortune will now make amends for his wrongs with triple benefits, as good comes from evils endured ("priefe").

7. I.e., to cause her to die would be spiteful.

8. A scabby disease of the scalp.

48

Her neather parts, the shame of all her kind,°　　　　*i.e., womankind*
My chaster Muse for shame doth blush to write;
But at her rompe she growing had behind
A foxes taile, with dong all fowly dight;°　　　　*covered*
And eke her feete most monstrous were in sight;
For one of them was like an Eagles claw,
With griping talaunts armd to greedy fight,
The other like a Beares uneven° paw:　　　　*rough*
More ugly shape yet never living creature saw.⁹

49

Which when the knights beheld, amazd they were,
And wondred at so fowle deformèd wight.
"Such then," said Una, "as she seemeth here,
Such is the face of falshood, such the sight
Of fowle Duessa, when her borrowed light
Is laid away, and counterfesaunce° knowne."　　　　*deceit*
Thus when they had the witch disrobèd quight,
And all her filthy feature° open showne,　　　　*form*
They let her goe at will, and wander wayes unknowne.

50

She flying fast from heavens hated face,
And from the world that her discovered wide,°　　　　*widely*
Fled to the wastfull° wildernesse apace,　　　　*desolate*
From living eyes her open shame to hide,
And lurkt in rocks and caves long unespide.
But that faire crew° of knights, and Una faire　　　　*company*
Did in that castle afterwards abide,
To rest them selves, and weary powres repaire,
Where store they found of all, that dainty° was and rare.　　　　*precious*

Canto 9

His loves and lignage Arthur tells:
The knights knit friendly bands:°　　　　*bonds*
Sir Trevisan flies from Despayre,
Whom Redcrosse knight withstands.

1

O goodly golden chaine,¹ wherewith yfere°　　　　*together*
The vertues linkèd are in lovely wize:°　　　　*manner*
And noble minds of yore allyèd were,
In brave poursuit of chevalrous emprize,°　　　　*adventure*
That none did others safety despize,°　　　　*disregard*
Nor aid envy° to him, in need that stands,　　　　*begrudge*

---

9. The passage alludes to Revelation 17.16: "these shall hate the whore, and shall make her desolate and naked." Foxes were emblems of cunning; eagles and bears, of rapacity, cruelty, and brutality.

1. The golden chain of love or concord that binds the world and the human race together (cf. 1.5.25 and n. 5).

But friendly each did others prayse devize
How to advaunce with favourable hands,
As this good Prince redeemd the Redcrosse knight from bands.

2

10 Who when their powres, empaird through labour long,
    With dew repast they had recurèd° well,   *restored*
    And that weake captive wight now wexèd strong,
    Them list no lenger there at leasure dwell,
    But forward fare, as their adventures fell,
15   But ere they parted, Una faire besought
    That straunger knight his name and nation tell;
    Least so great good, as he for her had wrought,
Should die unknown, and buried be in thanklesse thought.

3

    "Faire virgin," said the Prince, "ye me require
20   A thing without the compas of° my wit: *beyond the reach of*
    For both the lignage and the certain Sire,
    From which I sprong, from me are hidden yit.
    For all so soone as life did me admit
    Into this world, and shewèd heavens light,
25   From mothers pap I taken was unfit:°   *not yet weaned*
    And streight delivered to a Faery knight,
To be upbrought in gentle thewes° and martiall might.   *manners*

4

    "Unto old Timon[2] he me brought bylive,°   *immediately*
    Old Timon, who in youthly yeares hath beene
30   In warlike feates th' expertest man alive,
    And is the wisest now on earth I weene;
    His dwelling is low in a valley greene,
    Under the foot of Rauran mossy hore,°   *gray*
    From whence the river Dee as silver cleene°   *pure*
35   His tombling billowes rolls with gentle rore:[3]
There all my dayes he traind me up in vertuous lore.

5

    "Thither the great Magicien Merlin came,
    As was his use,° ofttimes to visit me: *custom*
    For he had charge my discipline° to frame,   *education*
40   And Tutours nouriture° to oversee.   *upbringing*
    Him oft and oft I askt in privitie,
    Of what loines and what lignage I did spring:
    Whose aunswere bad me still assurèd bee,
    That I was sonne and heire unto a king,
45 As time in her just terme° the truth to light should bring."   *due course*

---

2. The name means "honor."
3. The hill Rauran is in Wales; the river Dee also flows in, and forms part of the boundary of, Wales.

The Tudors (Queen Elizabeth's family) were originally Welsh, and the legends of Arthur had their beginnings in the Celtic mythology of early Wales.

6

"Well worthy impe,"° said then the Lady gent,°   *offspring/gentle*
    "And Pupill fit for such a Tutours hand.
    But what adventure, or what high intent
    Hath brought you hither into Faery land,
50 Aread° Prince Arthur,[4] crowne of Martiall band?"   *declare*
    "Full hard it is," quoth he, "to read° aright   *discern*
    The course of heavenly cause, or understand
    The secret meaning of th' eternall might,
That rules mens wayes, and rules the thoughts of living wight.

7

55 "For whither he through fatall deepe foresight[5]
    Me hither sent, for cause to me unghest,
    Or that fresh bleeding wound, which day and night
    Whilome° doth rancle in my riven brest,   *all the while*
    With forcèd fury following his° behest,   *its*
60 Me hither brought by wayes yet never found,
    You to have helpt I hold my selfe yet blest."
    "Ah curteous knight," quoth she, "what secret wound
Could ever find,° to grieve the gentlest hart on ground?"   *succeed*

8

    "Deare Dame," quoth he, "you sleeping sparkes awake,
65 Which troubled once, into huge flames will grow,
    Ne ever will their fervent fury slake
    Till living moysture into smoke do flow,
    And wasted° life do lye in ashes low.   *consumed*
    Yet sithens° silence lesseneth not my fire,   *since*
70 But told it flames, and hidden it does glow,
    I will revele, what ye so much desire:
Ah Love, lay downe thy bow, the whiles I may respire.°   *take breath*

9

    "It was in freshest flowre of youthly yeares,
    When courage first does creepe in manly chest,
75 Then first the coale of kindly° heat appeares   *natural*
    To kindle love in every living brest;
    But me had warnd old Timons wise behest,
    Those creeping flames by reason to subdew,
    Before their rage grew to so great unrest,
80 As miserable lovers use° to rew,   *are accustomed*
Which still wex° old in woe, whiles woe still wexeth new.   *grow*

10

    "That idle name of love, and lovers life,
    As losse of time, and vertues enimy

4. Arthur had been named in the quatrains that precede cantos 7 and 8, but not previously in the body of the text.

5. I.e., whether he (God, "eternal might") sent me here through foresight ordained by fate ("fatall").

I ever scornd, and joyd to stirre up strife,
85 In middest of their mournfull Tragedy,
Ay wont to laugh, when them I heard to cry,
And blow the fire, which them to ashes brent:°   burned
Their God himselfe, grieved at my libertie,
Shot many a dart at me with fiers intent,
90 But I them warded all with wary government.[6]

11
"But all in vaine: no fort can be so strong,
Ne fleshly brest can armèd be so sound,
But will at last be wonne with battrie° long,   siege
Or unawares at disavantage found;
95 Nothing is sure, that growes on earthly ground:
And who most trustes in arme of fleshly might,
And boasts, in beauties chaine not to be bound,
Doth soonest fall in disaventrous° fight.   disastrous
And yeeldes his caytive neck to victours most° despight. greatest

12
100 "Ensample make of him your haplesse joy,°   i.e., Redcrosse
And of my selfe now mated,° as ye see;   overcome
Whose prouder° vaunt that proud avenging boy   too proud
Did soone pluck downe, and curbd my libertie.
For on a day prickt° forth with jollitie   spurred
105 Of looser life, and heat of hardiment,°   boldness
Raunging the forest wide on courser free,
The fields, the floods, the heavens with one consent
Did seeme to laugh on me, and favour mine intent.

13
"For-wearied° with my sports, I did alight   utterly wearied
110 From loftie steed, and downe to sleepe me layd;
The verdant° gras my couch did goodly dight,°   green/make
And pillow was my helmet faire displayd:
Whiles every sence the humour sweet embayd,[7]
And slombring soft my hart did steale away,
115 Me seemèd, by my side a royall Mayd
Her daintie limbes full softly down did lay:
So faire a creature yet saw never sunny day.

14
"Most goodly glee° and lovely blandishment°   entertainment/compliment
She to me made, and bad me love her deare,
120 For dearely sure her love was to me bent,
As when just time expirèd[8] should appeare.
But whether dreames delude, or true it were,

---

6. I.e., self-control. The descriptions here of Cupid's archery and of the siege of the castle of chastity (in the next stanza) have many echoes from the courtly love tradition.

7. I.e., while the dew of sleep ("humour") pervaded ("embayd") every sense.
8. A fitting length of time having passed.

Was never hart so ravisht with delight,
Ne living man like words did ever heare,
125 As she to me delivered all that night;
And at her parting said, She Queene of Faeries hight.[9]

15

"When I awoke, and found her place devoyd,°   *empty*
And nought but pressèd gras, where she had lyen,
I sorrowed all so much, as earst I joyd,
130 And washèd all her place with watry eyen.
From that day forth I loved that face divine;
From that day forth I cast in carefull° mind,   *care-filled*
To seeke her out with labour, and long tyne,°   *hardship*
And never vow to rest, till her I find,
135 Nine monethes I seeke in vaine yet ni'll° that vow unbind." *will not*

16

Thus as he spake, his visage wexèd pale,
And chaunge of hew great passion did bewray;°   *reveal*
Yet still he strove to cloke his inward bale,°   *grief*
And hide the smoke, that did his fire display,
140 Till gentle Una thus to him gan say;
"Oh happy Queene of Faeries, that hast found
Mongst many, one that with his prowesse may
Defend thine honour, and thy foes confound:
True Loves are often sown, but seldom grow on ground."

17

145 "Thine, O then," said the gentle Redcrosse knight,
"Next to that Ladies love, shalbe the place,
O fairest virgin, full of heavenly light,
Whose wondrous faith, exceeding earthly race,
Was firmest fixt in mine extremest case.°   *plight*
150 And you, my Lord, the Patrone° of my life,   *protector*
Of that great Queene may well gaine worthy grace:
For onely worthy you through prowes priefe° *demonstration of prowess*
Yf living man mote° worthy be, to be her liefe."° *may/love*

18

So diversly discoursing of their loves,
155 The golden Sunne his glistring head gan shew,
And sad remembraunce now the Prince amoves,
With fresh desire his voyage to pursew:
Als° Una earnd° her traveill to renew.   *also/yearned*
Then those two knights, fast friendship for to bynd,
160 And love establish each to other trew,
Gave goodly gifts, the signes of gratefull mynd,
And eke as pledges firme, right hands together joynd.

---

9. Was called. In the background are many folktales and ballads of a hero bewitched by a fairy. Spenser's *Letter to Ralegh* identifies Gloriana allegorically with glory and with Queen Elizabeth.

19

Prince Arthur gave a boxe of Diamond sure,°   *true*
    Embowd° with gold and gorgeous ornament,   *bound*
165 Wherein were closd few drops of liquor pure,
    Of wondrous worth, and vertue° excellent,   *power*
    That any wound could heale incontinent:°   *immediately*
    Which to requite, the Redcrosse knight him gave
    A booke, wherein his Saveours testament
170 Was writ with golden letters rich and brave;°   *splendid*
    A worke of wondrous grace, and able soules to save.[1]

20

Thus beene they parted, Arthur on his way
    To seeke his love, and th' other for to fight
    With Unas foe, that all her realme did pray.°   *prey on*
175 But she now weighing the decayèd plight,
    And shrunken synewes of her chosen knight,
    Would not a while her forward course pursew,
    Ne bring him forth in face of dreadfull fight,
    Till he recovered had his former hew:°   *appearance*
180 For him to be yet weake and wearie well she knew.

21

So as they traveild, lo they gan espy
    An armèd knight towards them gallop fast,
    That seemèd from some fearèd foe to fly,
    Or other griesly thing, that him agast.°   *terrified*
185 Still as he fled, his eye was backward cast,
    As if his feare still followed him behind;
    Als flew his steed, as he his bands had brast,°   *broken*
    And with his wingèd heeles did tread the wind,
    As he had beene a fole of Pegasus his kind.[2]

22

190 Nigh as he drew, they might perceive his head
    To be unarmd, and curld uncombèd heares
    Upstaring° stiffe, dismayd with uncouth° dread;   *bristling/unknown*
    Nor drop of bloud in all his face appeares
    Nor life in limbe: and to increase his feares,
195 In fowle reproch° of knighthoods faire degree,°   *disgrace/condition*
    About his neck an hempen rope he weares,
    That with his glistring armes does ill agree;
    But he of rope or armes has now no memoree.

23

The Redcrosse knight toward him crossèd fast,
200 To weet, what mister° wight was so dismayd: *kind of*

1. Medieval romances mention such healing
balms, but here the "drops of liquor pure" represent grace, perhaps in the Eucharist; Redcrosse
gives Arthur the New Testament.
2. I.e., as if he had been a foal of a horse like Pegasus (a flying horse).

There him he finds all sencelesse and aghast,
That of him selfe he seemd to be afrayd;
Whom hardly he from flying forward stayd,
Till he these wordes to him deliver might;
205 "Sir knight, aread° who hath ye thus arayd,   *declare*
And eke from whom make ye this hasty flight:
For never knight I saw in such misseeming° plight."   *unseemly*

24

He answerd nought at all, but adding new
Feare to his first amazment, staring wide
210 With stony eyes, and hartlesse hollow hew,[3]
Astonisht stood, as one that had aspide
Infernall furies, with their chaines untide.
Him yet againe, and yet againe bespake
The gentle knight; who nought to him replide,
215 But trembling every joynt did inly quake,
And foltring tongue at last these words seemd forth to shake.

25

"For Gods deare love, Sir knight, do me not stay;
For loe he comes, he comes fast after mee."
Eft° looking backe would faine have runne away;   *again*
220 But he him forst to stay, and tellen free
The secret cause of his perplexitie:°   *distress*
Yet nathemore° by his bold hartie speach,   *not at all*
Could his bloud-frosen hart emboldned bee,
But through his boldnesse rather feare did reach,
225 Yet forst, at last he made through silence suddein breach.

26

"And am I now in safetie sure," quoth he,
"From him, that would have forcèd me to dye?
And is the point of death now turnd fro mee,
That I may tell this haplesse history?"
230 "Feare nought:" quoth he, "no daunger now is nye."
"Then shall I you recount a ruefull cace,"°   *event*
Said he, "the which with this unlucky eye
I late beheld, and had not greater grace
Me reft° from it, had bene partaker of the place.[4]   *carried*

27

235 "I lately chaunst (Would I had never chaunst)
With a faire knight to keepen companee,
Sir Terwin[5] hight,° that well himselfe advaunst   *named*
In all affaires, and was both bold and free,
But not so happie as mote happie bee:
240 He loved, as was his lot, a Ladie gent,°   *gentle*

---

3. I.e., with blanched, bloodless countenance.   5. His name may connote weariness or fatigue
4. I.e., shared the same fate.   ("terwyn").

That him againe° loved in the least degree: *in return*
For she was proud, and of too high intent,°   *mind*
And joyd to see her lover languish and lament.

28

"From whom returning sad and comfortlesse,°   *desolate*
245   As on the way together we did fare,
We met that villen (God from him me blesse°)   *defend*
That cursèd wight, from whom I scapt whyleare,°   *a while before*
A man of hell, that cals himselfe Despaire;[6]
Who first us greets, and after faire areedes°   *tells*
250   Of tydings strange, and of adventures rare:
So creeping close, as Snake in hidden weedes,
Inquireth of our states, and of our knightly deedes.

29

"Which when he knew, and felt our feeble harts
Embost° with bale,° and bitter byting griefe,   *exhausted / sorrow*
255   Which love had launchèd° with his deadly darts,   *pierced*
With wounding words and termes of foule repriefe°   *insult*
He pluckt from us all hope of due reliefe,
That earst us held in love of lingring life;
Then hopelesse hartlesse, gan the cunning thiefe
260   Perswade us die, to stint° all further strife: *end*
To me he lent this rope, to him a rustie knife.

30

"With which sad instrument of hastie death,
That wofull lover, loathing lenger° light,   *longer*
A wide way made to let forth living breath.
265   But I more fearefull, or more luckie wight,
Dismayd with that deformèd dismall sight,
Fled fast away, halfe dead with dying feare:°   *fear of death*
Ne yet assur'd of life by you, Sir knight,
Whose like infirmitie like chaunce may beare:
270 But God you never let his charmèd speeches heare."[7]

31

"How may a man," said he, "with idle speach
Be wonne, to spoyle° the Castle of his health?"   *destroy*
"I wote," quoth he, "whom triall° late did teach,   *experience*
That like would not[8] for all this worldes wealth:
275   His subtill tongue, like dropping honny, mealt'th°   *melts*
Into the hart, and searcheth every vaine,
That ere one be aware, by secret stealth
His powre is reft, and weakenesse doth remaine.
O never Sir desire to try° his guilefull traine."°   *test / treachery*

---

6. Despair is the ultimate Christian sin, denying the possibility of Divine mercy and grace.
7. I.e., may God never let you hear his mesmer-izing ("charmed") speeches.
8. I.e., would not do the like again.

32

280 "Certes,"° said he, "hence shall I never rest,   *surely*
        Till I that treachours art have heard and tride;
        And you Sir knight, whose name mote° I request,   *might*
        Of grace° do me unto his cabin° guide."   *favor / cave*
        "I that hight° Trevisan," quoth he, "will ride   *am called*
285   Against my liking backe, to doe you grace:°   *a favor*
        But nor for gold nor glee⁹ will I abide
        By you. when ye arrive in that same place;
    For lever° had I die, then° see his deadly face."   *rather / than*

33

    Ere long they come, where that same wicked wight
290   His dwelling has, low in an hollow cave,
        Farre underneath a craggie clift ypight,°   *placed*
        Darke, dolefull, drearie, like a greedie grave,
        That still for carrion carcases doth crave:
        On top whereof aye dwelt the ghastly Owle,¹
295   Shrieking his balefull note, which ever drave
        Farre from that haunt all other chearefull fowle;
    And all about it wandring ghostes did waile and howle.

34

    And all about old stockes° and stubs of trees,   *stumps*
        Whereon nor fruit, nor leafe was ever seene,
300   Did hang upon the ragged rocky knees;°   *crags*
        On which had many wretches hangèd beene,
        Whose carcases were scattered on the greene,
        And throwne about the cliffs. Arrivèd there,
        That bare-head knight for dread and dolefull teene,°   *grief*
305   Would faine° have fled, ne durst approachen neare,   *gladly*
    But th' other forst him stay, and comforted in feare.

35

    That darkesome cave they enter, where they find
        That cursèd man, low sitting on the ground,
        Musing full sadly in his sullein° mind;   *morose*
310   His griesie° lockes, long growen, and unbound,   *gray*
        Disordred hong about his shoulders round,
        And hid his face; through which his hollow eyne
        Lookt deadly dull, and starèd as astound;
        His raw-bone cheekes through penurie and pine,°   *starvation*
315 Were shronke into his jawes, as° he did never dine.   *as if*

36

    His garment nought but many ragged clouts,°   *rags*
        With thornes together pind and patchèd was,
        The which his naked sides he wrapt abouts;
        And him beside there lay upon the gras

9. Song; i.e., anything you can say to me.   1. Traditionally a messenger of death.

320   A drearie° corse, whose life away did pas,   *bloody*
         All wallowd in his owne yet luke-warme blood,
         That from his wound yet wellèd fresh alas;
         In which a rustie° knife fast fixèd stood,   *bloodstained*
         And made an open passage for the gushing flood.

37

325   Which piteous spectacle, approving° trew   *confirming*
         The wofull tale that Trevisan had told,
         When as the gentle Redcrosse knight did vew,
         With firie zeale he burnt in courage bold,
         Him to avenge, before his bloud were cold,
330   And to the villein said, "Thou agèd damnèd wight,
         The author of this fact,° we here behold,   *deed*
         What justice can but judge against thee right,
    With thine owne bloud to price° his bloud, here shed in sight?" *pay for*

38

    "What franticke fit," quoth he,° "hath thus distraught   *i.e., Despaire*
335   Thee, foolish man, so rash a doome° to give?   *judgment*
         What justice ever other judgement taught,
         But he should die, who merites not to live?
         None else to death this man despayring drive,°   *drove*
         But his owne guiltie mind deserving death.
340   Is then unjust to each his due to give?
         Or let him die, that loatheth living breath?
    Or let him die at ease, that liveth here uneath?°   *in unease*

39

    "Who travels by the wearie wandring way,
         To come unto his wishèd home in haste,
345   And meetes a flood, that doth his passage stay,
         Is not great grace to helpe him over past,
         Or free his feet, that in the myre sticke fast?
         Most envious man, that grieves at neighbours good,
         And fond,° that joyest in the woe thou hast,   *foolish*
350   Why wilt not let him passe, that long hath stood
    Upon the banke, yet wilt thy selfe not passe the flood?

40

    "He there does now enjoy eternall rest
         And happie ease, which thou doest want and crave,
         And further from it daily wanderest:
355   What if some litle paine the passage have,
         That makes fraile flesh to feare the bitter wave?
         Is not short paine well borne, that brings long ease,
         And layes the soule to sleepe in quiet grave?
         Sleepe after toyle, port after stormie seas,
360   Ease after warre, death after life does greatly please."[2]

---

2. Despaire's arguments on behalf of suicide as against a painful life are derived, like those of Hamlet in his third soliloquy (*Hamlet* 3.1.58–90), principally from Seneca, Marcus Aurelius, other ancient Stoics, and Old Testament statements on divine justice.

41

The knight much wondred at his suddeine wit,°   *quick intelligence*
    And said, "The terme of life is limited,
    Ne may a man prolong, nor shorten it;
    The souldier may not move from watchfull sted,[3]
365   Nor leave his stand, untill his Captaine bed."°   *commands*
    "Who life did limit by almightie doome,"
    Quoth he,° "knowes best the termes establishèd;   *Despaire*
    And he, that points the Centonell his roome,°   *station*
Doth license him depart at sound of morning droome.[4]

42

370 "Is not his deed, what ever thing is donne,
    In heaven and earth? did not he all create
    To die againe? all ends that was begonne.
    Their times in his eternall booke of fate
    Are written sure, and have their certaine° date.   *fixed*
375   Who then can strive with strong necessitie,
    That holds the world in his still chaunging state,
    Or shunne the death ordaynd by destinie?
When houre of death is come, let none aske whence, nor why.

43

 "The lenger° life, I wote° the greater sin,   *longer/know*
380   The greater sin, the greater punishment:
    All those great battels, which thou boasts to win,
    Through strife, and bloud-shed, and avengement,
    Now praysd, hereafter deare° thou shalt repent: *bitterly*
    For life must life, and bloud must bloud repay.[5]
385   Is not enough thy evill life forespent?
    For he, that once hath missèd the right way,
The further he doth goe, the further he doth stray.

44

 "Then do no further goe, no further stray,
    But here lie downe, and to thy rest betake,
390   Th' ill to prevent, that life ensewen may.[6]
    For what hath life, that may it lovèd make,
    And gives not rather cause it to forsake?
    Feare, sicknesse, age, losse, labour, sorrow, strife,
    Paine, hunger, cold, that makes the hart to quake;
395   And ever fickle fortune rageth rife,
All which, and thousands mo° do make a loathsome life.   *more*

45

 "Thou wretched man, of death hast greatest need,
    If in true ballance thou wilt weigh thy state:
    For never knight, that darèd warlike deede,
400   More lucklesse disaventures° did amate:°   *mishaps/daunt*

3. The sentry post assigned him.
4. Drum, with a pun on *doom.*
5. An echo of Genesis 9.6: "Whoso sheddeth

man's blood, by man shall his blood be shed."
6. I.e., to prevent the evil that will ensue in the rest of your life.

Witnesse the dungeon deepe, wherein of late
  Thy life shut up, for death so oft did call;
    And though good lucke prolongèd hath thy date,°   *span of life*
  Yet death then, would the like mishaps forestall,
405 Into the which hereafter thou maiest happen fall.°   *happen to fall*

46

"Why then doest thou, O man of sin, desire
  To draw thy dayes forth to their last degree?
    Is not the measure of thy sinfull hire°   *service to sin*
  High heapèd up with huge iniquitie,
410 Against the day of wrath,° to burden thee?   *Judgment Day*
  Is not enough that to this Ladie milde
    Thou falsèd° hast thy faith with perjurie,   *betrayed*
    And sold thy selfe to serve Duessa vilde,°   *vile*
With whom in all abuse thou hast thy selfe defilde?

47

415 "Is not he just, that all this doth behold
  From highest heaven, and beares an equall° eye?   *impartial*
    Shall he thy sins up in his knowledge fold,
  And guiltie be of thine impietie?
  Is not his law, Let every sinner die:[7]
420 Die shall all flesh? what then must needs be donne,
  Is it not better to doe willinglie,
    Then linger, till the glasse° be all out ronne?   *hourglass*
Death is the end of woes: die soone, O faeries sonne."

48

The knight was much enmovèd with his speach,
425 That as a swords point through his hart did perse,
  And in his conscience made a secret breach,
  Well knowing true all, that he did reherse°   *recount*
    And to his fresh remembrance did reverse°   *bring back*
  The ugly vew of his deformèd crimes,
430 That all his manly powres it did disperse,
  As he were charmèd with inchaunted rimes,
That oftentimes he quakt, and fainted oftentimes.

49

In which amazement, when the Miscreant°   *misbeliever*
  Perceivèd him to waver weake and fraile,
435 Whiles trembling horror did his conscience dant,°   *daunt*
  And hellish anguish° did his soule assaile,   *i.e., fear of hell*
    To drive him to despaire, and quite to quaile,°   *be dismayed*
  He shewed him painted in a table° plaine,   *picture*
  The damnèd ghosts, that doe in torments waile,
440 And thousand feends that doe them endlesse paine
With fire and brimstone, which for ever shall remaine.

---

7. Despaire cites only half of the Scripture verse: "The wages of sin is death; but the gift of God is eternal life through Jesus Christ our Lord" (Romans 6.23).

50

The sight whereof so throughly him dismaid,
  That nought but death before his eyes he saw,
  And ever burning wrath before him laid,
445 By righteous sentence of th' Almighties law:
  Then gan the villein him to overcraw,°   *exult over*
  And brought unto him swords, ropes, poison, fire,
  And all that might him to perdition draw;
  And bad him choose, what death he would desire:
450 For death was due to him, that had provokt Gods ire.

51

But when as none of them he saw him take,
  He to him raught° a dagger sharpe and keene,   *reached*
  And gave it him in hand: his hand did quake,
  And tremble like a leafe of Aspin greene,
455 And troubled bloud through his pale face was seene
  To come, and goe with tydings from the hart,
  As it a running messenger had beene.
  At last resolved to worke his finall smart,
He lifted up his hand, that backe againe did start.

52

460 Which when as Una saw, through every vaine
  The crudled° cold ran to her well of life,°   *congealing/heart*
  As in a swowne: but soone relived° againe,   *revived*
  Out of his hand she snatcht the cursèd knife,
  And threw it to the ground, enragèd rife,°   *deeply*
465 And to him said, "Fie, fie, faint harted knight,
  What meanest thou by this reprochfull° strife?   *deserving reproach*
  Is this the battell, which thou vauntst to fight
With the fire-mouthèd Dragon, horrible and bright?

53

"Come, come away, fraile, feeble, fleshly wight,
470 Ne let vaine words bewitch thy manly hart,
  Ne divelish thoughts dismay thy constant spright.
  In heavenly mercies hast thou not a part?
  Why shouldst thou then despeire, that chosen[8] art?
  Where justice growes, there grows eke° greater grace,   *also*
475 The which doth quench the brond of hellish smart,
  And that accurst hand-writing[9] doth deface.°   *blot out*
Arise, Sir knight arise, and leave this cursèd place."

54

So up he rose, and thence amounted° streight.   *mounted his horse*
  Which when the carle° beheld, and saw his guest   *churl*

8. Cf. 2 Thessalonians 2.13: "God hath from the beginning chosen you to salvation through sanctification of the Spirit and belief of the truth."
9. An echo of Colossians 2.14: "Blotting out the handwriting of ordinances [i.e., the Old Testament Law] that was against us, which was contrary to us, and took it out of the way, nailing it to his cross."

480 Would safe depart, for° all his subtill sleight,   *in spite of*
He chose an halter from among the rest,
And with it hung himselfe, unbid° unblest.   *unprayed for*
But death he could not worke himselfe thereby;
For thousand times he so himselfe had drest,°   *made ready*
485 Yet nathelesse it could not doe° him die,   *make*
Till he should die his last, that is eternally.

Canto 10

Her faithfull knight faire Una brings
to house of Holinesse,
Where he is taught repentance, and
the way to heavenly blesse.°   *bliss*

1

What man is he, that boasts of fleshly might,
And vaine assurance of mortality,°   *mortal life*
Which all so soone, as it doth come to fight,
Against spirituall foes, yeelds by and by,°   *immediately*
5 Or from the field most cowardly doth fly?
Ne let the man ascribe it to his skill,
That thorough grace hath gainèd victory.
If any strength we have, it is to ill,
But all the good is Gods, both power and eke° will.[1]   *also*

2

10 By that, which lately hapned, Una saw,
That this her knight was feeble, and too faint;
And all his sinews woxen weake and raw,°   *unready*
Through long enprisonment, and hard constraint,°   *affliction*
Which he endurèd in his late restraint,
15 That yet he was unfit for bloudie fight:
Therefore to cherish him with diets daint,°   *choice*
She cast to bring him, where he chearen° might,   *be cheered*
Till he recovered had his° late decayèd plight.   *i.e., from his*

3

There was an auntient house not farre away,
20 Renowmd throughout the world for sacred lore,
And pure unspotted life: so well they say
It governd was, and guided evermore,
Through wisedome of a matrone grave and hore;°   *venerable*
Whose onely joy was to relieve the needes
25 Of wretched soules, and helpe the helpelesse pore:
All night she spent in bidding of her bedes,°   *saying prayers*
And all the day in doing good and godly deedes.

1. "For by grace are ye saved through faith; and that not of yourselves: it is the gift of God: Not of works, lest any man should boast" (Ephesians 2.8–9).

4

Dame Caelia[2] men did her call, as thought
   From heaven to come, or thither to arise,
30   The mother of three daughters, well upbrought
   In goodly thewes,° and godly exercise: *habits*
   The eldest two most sober, chast, and wise,
   Fidelia and Speranza virgins were,
   Though spousd, yet wanting wedlocks solemnize;
35   But faire Charissa to a lovely fere°   *loving mate*
Was linckèd, and by him had many pledges dere.[3]

5

Arrivèd there, the dore they find fast lockt;
   For it was warely watchèd night and day,
   For feare of many foes: but when they knockt,
40   The Porter opened unto them streight way:
   He was an agèd syre, all hory gray,
   With lookes full lowly cast, and gate° full slow,   *gait*
   Wont on a staffe his feeble steps to stay,
   Hight Humilta.° They passe in stouping low;   *called Humility*
45 For streight and narrow was the way, which he did show.[4]

6

Each goodly thing is hardest to begin,
   But entred in a spacious court they see,
   Both plaine, and pleasant to be walkèd in,
   Where them does meete a francklin[5] faire and free,
50   And entertaines with comely courteous glee,
   His name was Zele,° that him right well became,   *zeal*
   For in his speeches and behaviour hee
   Did labour lively to expresse the same,
And gladly did them guide, till to the Hall they came.

7

55 There fairely them receives a gentle Squire,
   Of milde demeanure, and rare courtesie,
   Right cleanly clad in comely sad° attire;   *sober*
   In word and deede that shewed great modestie,
   And knew his good° to all of each degree,   *proper respect*
60   Hight Reverence. He them with speeches meet
   Does faire entreat; no courting nicetie;[6]
   But simple true, and eke unfainèd sweet,
As might become a Squire so great persons to greet.

2. The name means "heavenly."
3. I.e., many children. The daughters' names mean "faith," "hope," and "charity"; cf. the three Saracens: Sansfoy, Sansjoy, and Sansloy. This canto draws heavily on scriptural references, especially 1 Corinthians 13.13: "And now abideth faith, hope, charity, these three; but the greatest of these is charity." Many aspects of the House of Holiness

oppose their counterparts in the House of Pride (1.4). "Spousd": betrothed. "Solemnize": solemnization.
4. See the note to stanza 10 below.
5. Freeholder, landowner.
6. He treats them courteously ("faire"); no courtly affectation ("nicetie").

8

And afterwards them to his Dame he leades,
65   That agèd Dame, the Ladie of the place:
    Who all this while was busie at her beades:
    Which doen, she up arose with seemely grace,
    And toward them full matronely⁷ did pace.
    Where when that fairest Una she beheld,
70   Whom well she knew to spring from heavenly race,
    Her hart with joy unwonted inly sweld,°   *swelled*
    As feeling wondrous comfort in her weaker eld.°   *older age*

9

And her embracing said, "O happie earth,
    Whereon thy innocent feet doe ever tread,
75   Most vertuous virgin borne of heavenly berth,
    That to redeeme thy woefull parents head,
    From tyrans rage, and ever-dying dread,°   *constant fear of death*
    Hast wandred through the world now long a day°   *many a long day*
    Yet ceasest not thy wearie soles to lead,
80   What grace hath thee now hither brought this way?
    Or doen thy feeble feet unweeting° hither stray?   *unwittingly*

10

"Strange thing it is an errant° knight to see   *wandering*
    Here in this place, or any other wight,
    That hither turnes his steps. So few there bee,
85   That chose the narrow path, or seeke the right:
    All keepe the broad high way, and take delight
    With many rather for to go astray,
    And be partakers of their evill plight,
    Then with a few to walke the rightest way;⁸
90   O foolish men, why haste ye to your owne decay?"

11

"Thy selfe to see, and tyred limbs to rest,
    O matrone sage," quoth she, "I hither came,
    And this good knight his way with me addrest,°   *directed*
    Led with thy prayses and broad-blazèd fame,
95   That up to heaven is blowne."⁹ The auncient Dame
    Him goodly greeted in her modest guise,
    And entertaynd them both, as best became,
    With all the court'sies,° that she could devise,   *courtesies*
Ne wanted ought, to shew her bounteous or wise.

12

100 Thus as they gan of sundry things devise,°   *talk*
    Loe two most goodly virgins came in place,

---

7. Like a matron, i.e., a woman in charge of an establishment.
8. An echo of Matthew 7.13–14: "Broad is the way that leadeth to destruction, and many there be which go in thereat: . . . strait is the gate and narrow is the way, which leadeth unto life, and few there be that find it."
9. I.e., your praises and fame are widely celebrated ("blazed"), reaching ("blowne") up to heaven.

Ylinkèd arme in arme in lovely wise,°   *loving fashion*
With countenance demure, and modest grace,
They numbred even steps and equall pace:
105   Of which the eldest, that Fidelia hight,
Like sunny beames threw from her Christall face,
That could have dazd° the rash beholders sight,   *dazzled*
And round about her head did shine like heavens light.

13

She was araièd° all in lilly white,   *arrayed*
110   And in her right hand bore a cup of gold,
With wine and water fild up to the hight,
In which a Serpent[1] did himselfe enfold,
That horrour made to all, that did behold;
But she no whit did chaunge her constant mood:°   *expression*
115   And in her other hand she fast did hold
A booke, that was both signd and seald with blood,
Wherein darke things were writ, hard to be understood.[2]

14

Her younger sister, that Speranza hight,
Was clad in blew, that her beseemèd well;
120   Not all so chearefull seemèd she of sight,°   *in appearance*
As was her sister; whether dread° did dwell,   *fear*
Or anguish in her hart, is hard to tell:
Upon her arme a silver anchor[3] lay,
Whereon she leanèd ever, as befell:°   *as was fitting*
125   And ever up to heaven, as she did pray,
Her stedfast eyes were bent, ne swarvèd other way.

15

They seeing Una, towards her gan wend,°   *walk*
Who them encounters° with like courtesie;   *meets*
Many kind speeches they betwene them spend,
130   And greatly joy each other well to see:
Then to the knight with shamefast° modestie   *humble*
They turne themselves, at Unas meeke request,
And him salute with well beseeming glee;°   *appropriate joy*
Who faire them quites,° as him beseemèd best,   *requites*
135   And goodly gan discourse of many a noble gest.°   *deed*

16

Then Una thus; "But she your sister deare,
The deare Charissa where is she become?°   *gone to*
Or wants she health, or busie is elsewhere?"

1. The cup of wine and water signifies the sacrament of Communion; the serpent is a symbol of
the crucified Christ (of whom the serpent lifted up
by Moses, Numbers 21.9, is a recognized type).

2. The New Testament. See 2 Peter 3.16: "in
which are some things hard to be understood."
3. The iconographic symbol of hope.

"Ah no," said they, "but forth she may not come:
140   For she of late is lightned of her wombe,
And hath encreast the world with one sonne more,[4]
That her to see should be but troublesome."
"Indeede," quoth she, "that should her trouble sore,
But thankt be God, that her encrease so evermore."[5]

17

145   Then said the aged Caelia, "Deare dame,
And you good Sir, I wote that of your toyle,
And labours long, through which ye hither came,
Ye both forwearied° be: therefore a whyle   *utterly weary*
I read° you rest, and to your bowres recoyle."[6]   *counsel*
150   Then callèd she a Groome, that forth him led
Into a goodly lodge, and gan despoile°   *disrobe*
Of puissant armes, and laid in easie bed;
His name was meeke Obedience rightfully aréd.°   *understood*

18

Now when their wearie limbes with kindly° rest,   *natural*
155   And bodies were refresht with due repast,
Faire Una gan Fidelia faire request,
To have her knight into her schoolehouse plaste,
That of her heavenly learning he might taste,
And heare the wisedome of her words divine.
160   She graunted, and that knight so much agraste,°   *favored*
That she him taught celestiall discipline,
And opened his dull eyes, that light mote in them shine.

19

And that her sacred Booke, with bloud° ywrit,   *i.e., the blood of Christ*
That none could read, except she did them teach,
165   She unto him disclosèd every whit,
And heavenly documents° thereout did preach,   *doctrines*
That weaker wit of man could never reach,
Of God, of grace, of justice, of free will,
That wonder was to heare her goodly speach:
170   For she was able, with her words to kill,
And raise againe to life the hart, that she did thrill.°   *pierce*

20

And when she list° poure out her larger spright,°   *chose to/greater power*
She would commaund the hastie Sunne to stay,
Or backward turne his course from heavens hight;
175   Sometimes great hostes of men she could dismay,
Dry-shod to passe, she parts the flouds in tway;
And eke huge mountaines from their native seat
She would commaund, themselves to beare away,

---

4. Charity, the fruitful virtue, is often depicted as a mother with many children.
5. I.e., God be thanked, who continually increases her thus.
6. Retire to your rooms.

And throw in raging sea with roaring threat.
180   Almightie God her gave such powre, and puissance great.[7]

21

The faithfull knight now grew in litle space,°   *time*
  By hearing her, and by her sisters lore,
  To such perfection of all heavenly grace,
  That wretched world he gan for to abhore,[8]
185   And mortall life gan loath, as thing forelore,°   *doomed*
  Greeved with remembrance of his wicked wayes,
  And prickt with anguish of his sinnes so sore,
  That he desirde to end his wretched dayes:
So much the dart of sinfull guilt the soule dismayes.

22

190   But wise Speranza gave him comfort sweet,
  And taught him how to take assurèd hold
  Upon her silver anchor, as was meet;
  Else had his sinnes so great, and manifold
  Made him forget all that Fidelia told.
195   In this distressèd doubtfull° agonie,   *fearful*
  When him his dearest Una did behold,
  Disdeining life, desiring leave to die,
She found her selfe assayld with great perplexitie.°   *distress*

23

And came to Caelia to declare her smart,
200   Who well acquainted with that commune° plight,   *common*
  Which sinfull horror° workes in wounded hart,   *horror of sin*
  Her wisely comforted all that she might,
  With goodly counsell and advisement right;
  And streightway sent with carefull diligence,
205   To fetch a Leach,° the which had great insight   *doctor*
  In that disease of grievèd° conscience,   *distressed*
And well could cure the same; His name was Patience.

24

Who comming to that soule-diseasèd knight,
  Could hardly° him intreat, to tell his griefe: *with difficulty*
210   Which knowne, and all that noyd° his heavie spright   *troubled*
  Well searcht,° eftsoones° he gan apply reliefe   *probed/forthwith*
  Of salves and med'cines, which had passing priefe,[9]
  And thereto added words of wondrous might:
  By which to ease he him recurèd briefe,[1]
215   And much asswaged the passion° of his plight,   *suffering*
That he his paine endured, as seeming now more light.

---

7. Joshua made the sun stand still (Joshua 10.12); Hezekiah made it turn backward (2 Kings 20.10); Gideon was victorious over the Midianite hosts (Judges 7.7); Moses led the Israelites through the parted waters of the Red Sea (Exodus 14.21–31); faith, said Christ, can move mountains (Matthew 21.21). All these are miracles of faith.
8. I.e., he began to abhor the world.
9. Which had extraordinary power.
1. I.e., he spoke words of spiritual consolation to ease the knight he had quickly cured of sin.

25

But yet the cause and root of all his ill,
   Inward corruption, and infected sin,[2]
   Not purged nor heald, behind remainèd still,
220   And festring sore did rankle yet within,
   Close° creeping twixt the marrow and the skin.   *secretly*
   Which to extirpe,° he laid him privily   *extirpate*
   Downe in a darkesome lowly place farre in,
   Whereas he meant his corrosives to apply,
225 And with streight° diet tame his stubborne malady.   *strict*

26

In ashes and sackcloth he did array
   His daintie corse, proud humors[3] to abate,
   And dieted with fasting every day,
   The swelling of his wounds to mitigate,
230   And made him pray both earely and eke late:
   And ever as superfluous flesh did rot
   Amendment readie still at hand did wayt,
   To pluck it out with pincers firie whot,°   *hot*
That soone in him was left no one corrupted jot.

27

235 And bitter Penance with an yron whip,
   Was wont him once to disple° every day: *discipline*
   And sharpe Remorse his hart did pricke and nip,
   That drops of bloud thence like a well did play;
   And sad Repentance usèd to embay°   *bathe*
240   His bodie in salt water smarting sore,
   The filthy blots of sinne to wash away.[4]
So in short space they did to health restore
The man that would not live, but earst° lay at deathes dore.   *formerly*

28

In which his torment often was so great,
245   That like a Lyon he would cry and rore,
   And rend his flesh, and his owne synewes eat.
   His own deare Una hearing evermore
   His ruefull shriekes and gronings, often tore
   Her guiltlesse garments, and her golden heare,
250   For pitty of his paine and anguish sore;
   Yet all with patience wisely she did beare;
For well she wist, his crime could else be never cleare.°   *cleansed*

29

Whom thus recovered by wise Patience,
   And trew Repentance they to Una brought:
255   Who joyous of his curèd conscience,

---

2. I.e., the effects of original sin.
3. Whatever is conducive to pride.

4. "Wash me throughly from mine iniquity, and cleanse me from my sin" (Psalms 51.2).

Him dearely kist, and fairely° eke besought   *courteously*
Himselfe to chearish,° and consuming thought   *cheer, cherish*
To put away out of his carefull° brest.   *care-full*
By this° Charissa, late in child-bed brought,   *by this time*
260   Was woxen strong, and left her fruitfull nest;
To her faire Una brought this unacquainted guest.

30

She was a woman in her freshest age,
  Of wondrous beauty, and of bountie° rare,   *goodness*
  With goodly grace and comely personage,°   *appearance*
265   That was on earth not easie to compare;°   *rival*
  Full of great love, but Cupids wanton snare
  As hell she hated, chast in worke and will;
  Her necke and breasts were ever open bare,
  That ay thereof her babes might sucke their fill;
270 The rest was all in yellow robes arayèd still.[5]

31

A multitude of babes about her hong,
  Playing their sports, that joyd her to behold,
  Whom still she fed, whiles they were weake and young,
  But thrust them forth still, as they wexèd old:
275   And on her head she wore a tyre° of gold,   *headdress*
  Adornd with gemmes and owches° wondrous faire,   *jewels*
  Whose passing° price uneath° was to be told; *surpassing/scarcely*
  And by her side there sate a gentle paire
Of turtle doves,[6] she sitting in an yvorie chaire.

32

280 The knight and Una entring, faire her greet,
  And bid her joy of that her happie brood;
  Who them requites with court'sies seeming meet,°   *appropriate*
  And entertaines with friendly chearefull mood.
  Then Una her besought, to be so good,
285   As in her vertuous rules to schoole her knight,
  Now after all his torment well withstood,
  In that sad° house of Penaunce, where his spright   *solemn*
Had past° the paines of hell, and long enduring night. *passed through*

33

She was right joyous of her just request,
290   And taking by the hand that Faeries sonne,
  Gan him instruct in every good behest,°   *command*
  Of love, and righteousness, and well to donne,° *i.e., right action*
  And wrath, and hatred warely° to shonne,   *warily*
  That drew on men Gods hatred, and his wrath,
295   And many soules in dolours° had fordonne:° *misery/destroyed*

5. Her yellow (saffron) robe is the color of marriage, fertility, and maternity. Her chaste, fruitful love (Christian *agape*) is opposed to "Cupid's wanton snare" (*eros*).

6. Emblem of true love and faithful marriage.

In which when him she well instructed hath,
From thence to heaven she teacheth him the ready° path.   *direct*

34

Wherein his weaker° wandring steps to guide,   *too weak*
   An auncient matrone she to her does call,
300   Whose sober lookes her wisedome well describe:°   *made known*
   Her name was Mercie, well knowne over all,
   To be both gratious, and eke liberall:
   To whom the carefull charge of him she gave,
   To lead aright, that he should never fall
305   In all his wayes through this wide worldès wave,°   *expanse*
That Mercy in the end his righteous soule might save.

35

The godly Matrone by the hand him beares°   *leads*
   Forth from her° presence, by a narrow way,   *i.e., Charissa's*
   Scattred with bushy thornes, and ragged breares,°   *briers*
310   Which still before him she removed away,
   That nothing might his ready passage stay:
   And ever when his feet encombred were,
   Or gan to shrinke, or from the right to stray,
   She held him fast, and firmely did upbeare,
315 As carefull Nourse her child from falling oft does reare.

36

Eftsoones unto an holy Hospitall,[7]
   That was fore° by the way, she did him bring,   *close*
   In which seven Bead-men° that had vowèd all   *men of prayer*
   Their life to service of high heavens king
320   Did spend their dayes in doing godly thing:
   Their gates to all were open evermore,
   That by the wearie way were traveiling,
   And one sate wayting ever them before,
To call in commers-by, that needy were and pore.[8]

37

325 The first of them that eldest was, and best,°   *chiefest*
   Of all the house had charge and governement,
   As Guardian and Steward of the rest:
   His office° was to give entertainement   *duty*
   And lodging, unto all that came, and went:
330   Not unto such, as could him feast againe,°   *in return*
   And double quite,° for that he on them spent,   *repay*
   But such, as want of harbour° did constraine:°   *shelter/afflict*
Those for Gods sake his dewty was to entertaine.

38

The second was as Almner[9] of the place,
335   His office was, the hungry for to feed,

7. House of rest for pilgrims and travelers.
8. I.e., one beadsman sat in front of the gates, to call in needy wayfarers.

9. An almoner distributed charity (*alms*) to the poor.

And thristy give to drinke, a worke of grace:
He feard not once him selfe to be in need,
Ne cared to hoord for those, whom he did breede:°   *i.e., his children*
The grace of God he layd up still in store,
340 Which as a stocke° he left unto his seede;°   *resource/children*
He had enough, what need him care for more?
And had he lesse, yet some he would give to the pore.

39

The third had of their wardrobe custodie,
In which were not rich tyres,° nor garments gay,   *attire*
345 The plumes of pride, and wings of vanitie,
But clothes meet to keepe keene could° away,   *cold*
And naked nature seemely° to aray;   *decently*
With which bare wretched wights he dayly clad,
The images of God in earthly clay;
350 And if that no spare clothes to give he had,
His owne coate he would cut, and it distribute glad.

40

The fourth appointed by his office was,
Poore prisoners to relieve with gratious ayd,
And captives to redeeme with price of bras,°   *payment of money*
355 From Turkes and Sarazins, which them had stayd;°   *held captive*
And though they faultie were, yet well he wayd,
That God to us forgiveth every howre
Much more then that, why° they in bands° were layd,   *for which/bonds*
And he that harrowd hell[1] with heavie stowre,°   *assault*
360 The faultie° soules from thence brought to his heavenly bowre.   *sinful*

41

The fift had charge sicke persons to attend,
And comfort those, in point of death which lay;
For them most needeth comfort in the end,
When sin, and hell, and death do most dismay
365 The feeble soule departing hence away.
All is but lost, that living we bestow,°   *store up*
If not well ended at our dying day.
O man have mind of that last bitter throw;°   *throes of death*
For as the tree does fall, so lyes it ever low.[2]

42

370 The sixt had charge of them now being dead,
In seemely sort their corses to engrave,°   *bodies to bury*
And deck with dainty flowres their bridall bed,
That to their heavenly spouse both sweet and brave°   *fair*
They might appeare, when he their soules shall save.

1. Christ, who journeyed to hell to deliver those
good people who lived before his time, according
to a popular story in the Middle Ages. It originated
in the apocryphal gospel of Nicodemus (cf. *Piers*
Plowman, Passus 18).
2. "In the place where the tree falleth, there it
shall be" (Ecclesiastes 11.3).

375   The wondrous workemanship of Gods owne mould,[3]
      Whose face he made, all beasts to feare, and gave
      All in his hand, even dead we honour should.
      Ah dearest God me graunt, I dead be not defould.°   *defiled*

43

   The seventh now after death and buriall done,
380   Had charge the tender Orphans of the dead
      And widowes ayd, least° they should be undone: *lest*
      In face of judgement° he their right would plead,   *i.e., in court*
      Ne ought° the powre of mighty men did dread   *nor at all*
      In their defence, nor would for gold or fee°   *bribe*
385   Be wonne their rightfull causes downe to tread:
      And when they stood in most necessitee,
      He did supply their want, and gave them ever free.[4]

44

   There when the Elfin knight arrivèd was,
      The first and chiefest of the seven, whose care
390   Was guests to welcome, towardes him did pas:
      Where seeing Mercie, that his steps up bare,°   *supported*
      And always led, to her with reverence rare
      He humbly louted° in meeke lowlinesse,   *bowed*
      And seemely welcome for her did prepare:
395   For of their order she was Patronesse,
      Albe° Charissa were their chiefest founderesse.   *although*

45

   There she awhile him stayes, him selfe to rest,
      That to the rest more able he might bee:
      During which time, in every good behest°   *command*
400   And godly worke of Almes and charitee
      She him instructed with great industree;
      Shortly therein so perfect he became,
      That from the first unto the last degree,
      His mortall life he learnèd had to frame
405 In holy righteousnesse, without rebuke or blame.

46

   Thence forward by that painfull way they pas,
      Forth to an hill, that was both steepe and hy;
      On top whereof a sacred chappell was,
      And eke a litle Hermitage thereby,
410   Wherein an agèd holy man did lye,°   *live*
      That day and night said his devotion,
      Ne other worldly busines did apply;[5]
      His name was heavenly Contemplation;
      Of God and goodnesse was his meditation.

3. The human body is God's own image ("mould") and a "mould" of God's making (see Genesis 1.26–30, 2.7).
4. Always freely. The seven beadsmen here correspond to, and perform, the seven works of charity, or corporal mercy: lodging the homeless, feeding the hungry, clothing the naked, redeeming the captive, comforting the sick, burying the dead, and succoring the orphan.
5. I.e., he did not attend to any worldly activities.

47

415   Great grace that old man to him given had;
     For God he often saw from heavens hight,
     All° were his earthly eyen both blunt° and bad,   *although / dim*
     And through great age had lost their kindly° sight,   *natural*
     Yet wondrous quick and persant° was his spright,°   *piercing / spirit*
420   As Eagles eye, that can behold the Sunne:
     That hill they scale with all their powre and might,
     That his frayle thighes nigh wearie and fordonne°   *exhausted*
  Gan faile, but by her helpe the top at last he wonne.

48

  There they do finde that godly agèd Sire,
425   With snowy lockes adowne his shoulders shed,
     As hoarie frost with spangles doth attire
     The mossy braunches of an Oke halfe ded.
     Each bone might through his body well be red,°   *seen*
     And every sinew seene through° his long fast: *because of*
430   For nought he cared his carcas long unfed;
     His mind was full of spirituall repast,
  And pyned° his flesh, to keepe his body low° and chast.   *starved / thin*

49

  Who when these two approching he aspide,
     At their first presence grew agrievèd sore,[6]
435   That forst him lay his heavenly thoughts aside;
     And had he not that Dame respected more,°   *greatly*
     Whom highly he did reverence and adore,
     He would not once have movèd for the knight.
     They him saluted standing far afore;°   *away*
440   Who well them greeting, humbly did requight,°   *respond*
  And askèd, to what end they clomb° that tedious height.   *had climbed*

50

  "What end," quoth she, "should cause us take such paine,
     But that same end, which every living wight
     Should make his marke,° high heaven to attaine?   *goal*
445   Is not from hence the way, that leadeth right
     To that most glorious house, that glistreth bright
     With burning starres, and everliving fire,
     Whereof the keyes are to thy hand behight°   *entrusted*
     By wise Fidelia? she doth thee require,
450   To shew it to this knight, according° his desire."   *granting*

51

  "Thrise happy man," said then the father grave,
     "Whose staggering steps thy° steady hand doth lead,   *i.e., Mercy's*
     And shewes the way, his sinfull soule to save.
     Who better can the way to heaven aread°   *direct*
455   Then thou thy selfe, that was both borne and bred

6. I.e., he was at first sorely grieved at their arrival.

In heavenly throne, where thousand Angels shine?
Thou doest the prayers of the righteous sead°   seed
Present before the majestie divine,
And his avenging wrath to clemencie incline.

52

460 "Yet since thou bidst, thy pleasure shalbe donne.
Then come thou man of earth,[7] and see the way,
That never yet was seene of Faeries sonne,
That never leads the traveiler astray,
But after labours long, and sad delay,
465 Brings them to joyous rest and endlesse blis.
But first thou must a season fast and pray,
Till from her bands the spright assoilèd° is,   spirit released
And have her strength recured° from fraile infirmitis."   recovered

53

That done, he leads him to the highest Mount;
470 Such one, as that same mighty man of God,
That bloud-red billowes like a wallèd front
On either side disparted° with his rod,   parted asunder
Till that his army dry-foot through them yod,°   went
Dwelt fortie dayes upon; where writ in stone
475 With bloudy letters by the hand of God,
The bitter doome of death and balefull mone[8]
He did receive, whiles flashing fire about him shone.

54

Or like that sacred hill, whose head full hie,
Adornd with fruitfull Olives all arownd,
480 Is, as it were for endlesse memory
Of that deare Lord, who oft thereon was fownd,
For ever with a flowring girlond crownd:
Or like that pleasaunt Mount, that is for ay
Through famous Poets verse each where° renownd,   everywhere
485 On which the thrise three learned Ladies play
Their heavenly notes, and make full many a lovely lay.[9]

55

From thence, far off he unto him did shew
A litle path, that was both steepe and long,
Which to a goodly Citie led his vew;
490 Whose wals and towres were builded high and strong
Of perle and precious stone, that earthly tong
Cannot describe, nor wit of man can tell;

7. An allusion to humankind's formation from the dust of the earth (Genesis 2.7) and also to the knight's name (see below, stanza 66 and note 8).
8. I.e., the Ten Commandments ("bloudy letters") carried with them the judgment ("doome") of death and pain (causing sorrowful moans—"balefull mone").

9. Song. The mountain is successively compared with Mount Sinai, where Moses, after parting the "bloud-red billowes" of the Red Sea, received the tablets of the Ten Commandments; to the Mount of Olives, associated with Christ; and to Mount Parnassus, where the Nine Muses of art and poetry dwelt.

Too high a ditty° for my simple song;   *subject*
The Citie of the great king hight it well,
495 Wherein eternall peace and happinesse doth dwell.

56

As he thereon stood gazing, he might see
The blessed Angels to and fro descend
From highest heaven, in gladsome companee,
And with great joy into that Citie wend,
500 As commonly° as friend does with his frend.[1]   *familiarly*
Whereat he wondred much, and gan enquere,
What stately building durst so high extend
Her loftie towres unto the starry sphere,
And what unknowen nation there empeopled were.

57

505 "Faire knight," quoth he, "Hierusalem that is,
The new Hierusalem, that God has built
For those to dwell in, that are chosen his,
His chosen people purged from sinfull guilt,
With pretious bloud, which cruelly was spilt
510 On cursèd tree, of that unspotted lam,[2]
That for the sinnes of all the world was kilt:
Now are they Saints all in that Citie sam,°   *together*
More deare unto their God, then younglings to their dam."[3]

58

"Till now," said then the knight, "I weenèd well,
515 That great Cleopolis,[4] where I have beene,
In which that fairest Faerie Queene doth dwell,
The fairest Citie was, that might be seene;
And that bright towre all built of christall cleene,°   *clear*
Panthea,[5] seemd the brightest thing, that was:
520 But now by proofe all otherwise I weene;
For this great Citie that[6] does far surpas,
And this bright Angels towre quite dims that towre of glas."

59

"Most trew," then said the holy agèd man;
"Yet is Cleopolis for earthly frame,°   *structure*
525 The fairest peece,° that eye beholden can: *masterpiece*
And well beseemes° all knights of noble name,   *becomes*
That covet in th' immortall booke of fame
To be eternizèd, that same to haunt,°   *frequent*

---

1. Cf. Jacob's ladder, which "reached to heaven; and behold the angels of God ascending and descending on it" (Genesis 28.12).
2. Lamb; a reference to Christ (the lamb of God), whose death on the cross ("cursèd tree") purged the guilt of sin from those "chosen his."
3. The New Jerusalem is described in Revelation 21–22; "the nations of them which are saved shall

walk in the light of it" (21.24).
4. London. Camelot—the earthly counterpart of the Heavenly Kingdom.
5. Reminiscent of the temple of glass in Chaucer's *House of Fame*; perhaps intended to allude to Richmond Palace or Westminster Abbey.
6. I.e., The New Jerusalem far surpasses Cleopolis ("that").

And doen their service to that soveraigne Dame,
530   That glorie does to them for guerdon° graunt: *reward*
    For she is heavenly borne, and heaven may justly vaunt.°   *claim*

60

"And thou faire ymp,° sprong out from English race,   *youth*
    How ever now accompted° Elfins sonne,   *accounted*
    Well worthy doest thy service for her grace,°   *favor*
535   To aide a virgin desolate foredonne.°   *undone*
    But when thou famous victorie hast wonne,
    And high emongst all knights hast hong thy shield,
    Thenceforth the suit° of earthly conquest shonne,   *pursuit*
    And wash thy hands from guilt of bloudy field:
540 For bloud can nought but sin, and wars but sorrowes yield.

61

"Then seeke this path, that I to thee presage,°   *show prophetically*
    Which after all to heaven shall thee send;
    Then peaceably thy painefull° pilgrimage   *laborious*
    To yonder same Hierusalem do bend,
545   Where is for thee ordaind a blessèd end:
    For thou emongst those Saints, whom thou doest see,
    Shalt be a Saint, and thine owne nations frend
    And Patrone: thou Saint George shalt callèd bee,
Saint George of mery England, the signe of victoree."[7]

62

550 "Unworthy wretch," quoth he, "of so great grace,
    How dare I thinke such glory to attaine?"
    "These that have it attaind, were in like cace,"
    Quoth he, "as wretched, and lived in like paine."
    "But deeds of armes must I at last be faine,°   *content (to leave)*
555   And Ladies love to leave so dearely bought?"
    "What need of armes, where peace doth ay remaine,"
    Said he, "and battailes none are to be fought?
As for loose loves are° vaine, and vanish into nought."   *i.e., they are*

63

"O let me not," quoth he, "then turne againe
560   Backe to the world, whose joyes so fruitlesse are;
    But let me here for aye in peace remaine,
    Or streight way on that last long voyage fare,
    That nothing may my present hope empare."°   *impair*
    "That may not be," said he, "ne maist thou yit
565   Forgo that royall maides bequeathèd care,°   *charge*
    Who did her cause into thy hand commit,
Till from her cursèd foe thou have her freely quit."°   *released*

7. Spenser's conception of St. George, patron saint of England, draws on the *Legenda Aurea* (*The Golden Legend*—a medieval manual of ecclesiastical lore, translated into English by William Caxton in 1487) and on pictures, tapestries, pageants, and folklore.

64

"Then shall I soone," quoth he, "so God me grace,
 Abet° that virgins cause disconsolate,   *maintain*
570 And shortly backe returne unto this place
 To walke this way in Pilgrims poore estate.
 But now aread,° old father, why of late   *declare*
 Didst thou behight° me borne of English blood,   *call*
 Whom all a Faeries sonne doen nominate?"°   *name*
575 "That word shall I," said he, "avouchen° good,   *prove*
Sith° to thee is unknowne the cradle of thy brood.   *since*

65

"For well I wote,° thou springst from ancient race   *know*
 Of Saxon kings, that have with mightie hand
 And many bloudie battailes fought in place°   *there*
580 High reard their royall throne in Britane land,
 And vanquisht them, unable to withstand:
 From thence a Faerie thee unweeting reft,°   *secretly stole*
 There as thou slepst in tender swadling band,
 And her base Elfin brood there for thee left.
585 Such men do Chaungelings call, so chaungd by Faeries theft.

66

"Thence she thee brought into this Faerie lond,
 And in an heapèd furrow did thee hyde,
 Where thee a Ploughman all unweeting° fond,   *unknowing*
 As he his toylesome teme° that way did guyde,   *team of oxen*
590 And brought thee up in ploughmans state to byde,
 Whereof Georgos he thee gave to name;[8]
 Till prickt° with courage, and thy forces pryde,   *spurred*
 To Faery court thou cam'st to seeke for fame,
And prove thy puissaunt armes, as seemes thee best
  became."°   *as best suited you*

67

595 "O holy Sire," quoth he, "how shall I quight°   *repay*
 The many favours I with thee have found,
 That hast my name and nation red aright,
 And taught the way that does to heaven bound?"°   *go*
 This said, adowne he lookèd to the ground,
600 To have returnd, but dazèd° were his eyne,   *dazzled*
 Through passing° brightnesse, which did quite confound *surpassing*
 His feeble sence, and too exceeding shyne.
So darke are earthly things compard to things divine.

68

 At last whenas himselfe he gan to find,°   *recover*
605 To Una back he cast him to retire;

8. I.e., as a name. *Georgos* is Greek for "farmer" (cf. Virgil's *Georgics*, on farming).

Who him awaited still with pensive° mind.   *anxious*
Great thankes and goodly meed° to that good syre, *gift*
He thence departing gave for his paines hyre.° *reward*
So came to Una, who him joyd to see,
610 And after litle rest, gan him desire,
Of her adventure mindfull for to bee.
So leave they take of Caelia, and her daughters three.

Canto 11

*The knight with that old Dragon fights
 two dayes incessantly:
The third him overthrowes, and gayns
 most glorious victory.*

1

High time now gan it wex° for Una faire, *grow*
 To thinke of those her captive Parents deare,
 And their forwasted kingdome to repaire:⁹
 Whereto whenas they now approachèd neare,
5 With hartie° words her knight she gan to cheare, *bold*
 And in her modest manner thus bespake;
 "Deare knight, as deare, as ever knight was deare,
 That all these sorrowes suffer for my sake,
High heaven behold the tedious toyle, ye for me take.

2

10 "Now are we come unto my native soyle,
 And to the place, where all our perils dwell;
 Here haunts that feend, and does his dayly spoyle,
 Therefore henceforth be at your keeping well,° *be well on your guard*
 And ever ready for your foeman fell.
15 The sparke of noble courage now awake,
 And strive your excellent selfe to excell;
 That shall ye evermore renowmèd make,
Above all knights on earth, that batteill undertake."

3

And pointing forth, "lo yonder is," said she,
20 "The brasen towre in which my parents deare
 For dread of that huge feend emprisond be,
 Whom I from far see on the walles appeare,
 Whose sight my feeble soule doth greatly cheare:
 And on the top of all I do espye
25 The watchman wayting tydings glad to heare,
 That O my parents might I happily
Unto you bring, to ease you of your misery."

---

9. I.e., to restore their kingdom, laid waste (by the dragon).

4

With that they heard a roaring hideous sound,
  That all the ayre with terrour fillèd wide,
30 And seemd uneath° to shake the stedfast ground.   *almost*
  Eftsoones that dreadfull Dragon they espide,
  Where stretcht he lay upon the sunny side
  Of a great hill, himselfe like a great hill.
  But all so soone, as he from far descride
35 Those glistring armes, that heaven with light did fill,
He rousd himselfe full blith,° and hastned them untill.°   *joyfully/toward*

5

Then bad the knight his Lady yede° aloofe,   *go*
  And to an hill her selfe withdraw aside,
  From whence she might behold that battailles proof°   *outcome*
40 And eke° be safe from daunger far descryde: *also*
  She him obayd, and turnd a little wyde.°   *aside*
  Now O thou sacred Muse, most learnèd Dame,
  Faire ympe° of Phoebus, and his aged bride,[1]   *child*
  The Nourse of time, and everlasting fame,
45 That warlike hands ennoblest with immortall name;

6

O gently come into my feeble brest,
  Come gently, but not with that mighty rage,
  Wherewith the martiall troupes thou doest infest,°   *arouse*
  And harts of great Heroës doest enrage,
50 That nought their kindled courage may aswage,
  Soone as thy dreadfull trompe° begins to sownd;   *trumpet*
  The God of warre with his fiers equipage
  Thou doest awake, sleepe never he so sownd,°   *sound*
And scarèd nations doest with horrour sterne astown.°   *appall*

7

55 Faire Goddesse lay that furious fit° aside,   *strain*
  Till I of warres and bloudy Mars do sing[2]
  And Briton fields with Sarazin bloud bedyde,
  Twixt that great faery Queene and Paynim king,
  That with their horrour heaven and earth did ring,
60 A worke of labour long, and endlesse prayse:
  But now a while let downe that haughtie string,
  And to my tunes thy second tenor rayse,[3]
That I this man of God his godly armes may blaze.°   *proclaim*

8

By this the dreadfull Beast drew nigh to hand,
65 Halfe flying, and halfe footing° in his hast,   *walking*

1. I.e., Mnemosyne (memory), mother of the Muses.
2. Perhaps a reference to a projected but unwritten book of *The Faerie Queene*.
3. The "haughtie" (high-pitched) mode would be appropriate to a large-scale epic war; the "second tenor" (lower in pitch) to this present battle.

That with his largenesse measurèd much land,
And made wide shadow under his huge wast;°   girth
As mountaine doth the valley overcast.
Approching nigh, he rearèd high afore
His body monstrous, horrible, and vast,
Which to increase his wondrous greatnesse more,
Was swolne with wrath, and poyson, and with bloudy gore.

9

And over, all with brasen scales was armd,
Like plated coate of steele, so couchèd neare,°   placed so closely
That nought mote perce,[4] ne might his corse° be harmd   body
With dint of sword, nor push of pointed speare;
Which as an Eagle, seeing pray appeare,
His aery Plumes doth rouze,° full rudely dight,°   shake / ruggedly arrayed
So shakèd he, that horrour was to heare,
For as the clashing of an Armour bright,
Such noyse his rouzèd scales did send unto the knight.

10

His flaggy° wings when forth he did display,   drooping
Were like two sayles, in which the hollow wynd
Is gathered full, and worketh speedy way:
And eke the pennes,° that did his pineons bynd,   quills
Were like mayne-yards, with flying canvas lynd,
With which whenas him list the ayre to beat,
And there by force unwonted° passage find,   unaccustomed
The cloudes before him fled for terrour great,
And all the heavens stood still amazèd with his threat.

11

His huge long tayle wound up in hundred foldes,
Does overspred his long bras-scaly backe,
Whose wreathèd boughts° when ever he unfoldes,   coils
And thicke entangled knots adown does slacke,
Bespotted as with shields° of red and blacke,   scales
It sweepeth all the land behind him farre,
And of three furlongs does but litle lacke;
And at the point two stings in-fixèd arre,
Both deadly sharpe, that sharpest steele exceeden farre.

12

But stings and sharpest steele did far exceed°   i.e., were far exceeded by
The sharpnesse of his cruell rending clawes;
Dead was it sure, as sure as death in deed,°   in its effect
What ever thing does touch his ravenous pawes,
Or what within his reach he ever drawes.
But his most hideous head my toung to tell
Does tremble: for his deepe devouring jawes

4. Nothing might pierce.

Wide gapèd, like the griesly° mouth of hell,   *horrid*
Through which into his darke abisse all ravin° fell.   *prey, booty*

13

And that° more wondrous was, in either jaw   *what*
110   Three ranckes of yron teeth enraungèd were,
    In which yet trickling bloud and gobbets raw°   *chunks of undigested food*
    Of late° devourèd bodies did appeare,   *recently*
    That sight thereof bred cold congealèd feare:
    Which to increase, and all at once to kill,
115   A cloud of smoothering smoke and sulphur seare°   *burning*
    Out of his stinking gorge° forth steemèd still,   *maw*
That all the ayre about with smoke and stench did fill.

14

His blazing eyes, like two bright shining shields,
    Did burne with wrath, and sparkled living fyre;
120   As two broad Beacons, set in open fields,
    Send forth their flames farre off to every shyre,°   *shire*
    And warning give, that enemies conspyre,
    With fire and sword the region to invade;
    So flamed his eyne° with rage and rancorous yre:°   *eyes/ire*
125   But farre within, as in a hollow glade,
Those glaring lampes were set, that made a dreadfull shade.

15

So dreadfully he towards him did pas,
    Forelifting up aloft his speckled brest,
    And often bounding on the brusèd gras,
130   As for great joyance of his newcome guest.
    Eftsoones he gan advance his haughtie crest,
    As chauffèd° Bore his bristles doth upreare,   *angry*
    And shoke his scales to battell readie drest;°   *prepared*
    That made the Redcrosse knight nigh quake for feare,
135 As bidding bold defiance to his foeman neare.

16

The knight gan fairely couch° his steadie speare,   *rest, aim*
    And fiercely ran at him with rigorous° might: *violent*
    The pointed steele arriving rudely° theare,   *roughly*
    His harder hide would neither perce, nor bight,
140   But glauncing by forth passèd forward right;
    Yet sore amovèd with so puissant push,
    The wrathfull beast about him turnèd light,°   *quickly*
    And him so rudely passing by, did brush
With his long tayle, that horse and man to ground did rush.

17

145 Both horse and man up lightly rose againe,
    And fresh encounter towards him addrest:
    But th' idle stroke yet backe recoyld in vaine,

And found no place his° deadly point to rest.   *its*
Exceeding rage enflamed the furious beast,
150   To be avengèd of so great despight;°   *outrage*
For never felt his imperceable brest
So wondrous force, from hand of living wight;
Yet had he proved° the powre of many a puissant knight.   *tested*

18

Then with his waving wings displayèd wyde,
155   Himselfe up high he lifted from the ground,
And with strong flight did forcibly divide
The yielding aire, which nigh too feeble found
Her flitting° partes, and element unsound,°   *moving/weak*
To beare so great a weight: he cutting way
160   With his broad sayles, about him soarèd round:
At last low stouping with unweldie sway,°   *ponderous force*
Snatcht up both horse and man, to beare them quite away.

19

Long he them bore above the subject plaine,°   *i.e., the ground below*
So farre as Ewghen° bow a shaft may send,   *yewen, of yew*
165   Till struggling strong did him at last constraine,
To let them downe before his flightès end:
As hagard° hauke presuming to contend   *untamed*
With hardie fowle, above his hable might,°   *able power*
His wearie pounces° all in vaine doth spend,   *claws*
170   To trusse° the pray too heavie for his flight;   *seize*
Which comming downe to ground, does free it selfe by fight.

20

He so disseizèd of his gryping grosse,[5]
The knight his thrilant° speare againe assayd   *piercing*
In his bras-plated body to embosse,°   *plunge*
175   And three mens strength unto the stroke he layd;
Wherewith the stiffe beame quakèd, as affrayd,
And glauncing from his scaly necke, did glyde
Close under his left wing, then broad displayd.
The percing steele there wrought a wound full wyde,
180   That with the uncouth° smart the Monster lowdly cryde.   *unfamiliar*

21

He cryde, as raging seas are wont to rore,
When wintry storme his wrathfull wreck does threat,
The rolling billowes beat the ragged shore,
As they the earth would shoulder from her seat,
185   And greedie gulfe° does gape, as he would eat   *i.e., the sea*
His neighbour element° in his revenge: *earth*
Then gin the blustring brethren° boldly threat,   *the winds*
To move the world from off his stedfast henge,°   *axis*
And boystrous battell make, each other to avenge.

5. Freed from his formidable grip.

22

190   The steely head stucke fast still in his flesh,
        Till with his cruell clawes he snatcht the wood,
        And quite a sunder broke. Forth flowèd fresh
        A gushing river of blacke goarie° blood,   *clotted*
        That drownèd all the land, whereon he stood;
195   The stream thereof would drive a water-mill.
        Trebly augmented was his furious mood
        With bitter sense of his deepe rooted ill,°   *injury*
    That flames of fire he threw forth from his large nosethrill.

23

    His hideous tayle then hurlèd he about,
200   And therewith all enwrapt the nimble thyes°   *thighs*
        Of his froth-fomy steed, whose courage stout
        Striving to loose the knot, that fast him tyes,
        Himselfe in streighter° bandes too rash implyes,⁶   *tighter*
        That to the ground he is perforce constraynd
205   To throw his rider: who can° quickly ryse   *did*
        From off the earth, with durty bloud distaynd,°   *defiled*
    For that reprochfull fall right fowly he disdaynd.

24

    And fiercely tooke his trenchand° blade in hand,   *sharp*
        With which he stroke so furious and so fell,
210   That nothing seemd the puissance could withstand:
        Upon his crest the hardned yron fell,
        But his more hardned crest was armd so well,
        That deeper dint therein it would not make;⁷
        Yet so extremely did the buffe° him quell,°   *blow/dismay*
215   That from thenceforth he shund the like to take,
    But when he saw them come, he did them still forsake.°   *avoid*

25

    The knight was wrath to see his stroke beguyld,°   *foiled*
        And smote againe with more outrageous might;
        But backe againe the sparckling steele recoyld,
220   And left not any marke, where it did light;
        As if in Adamant rocke it had bene pight.°   *struck against*
        The beast impatient of his smarting wound,
        And of so fierce and forcible despight,°   *powerful injury*
        Thought with his wings to stye° above the ground;   *mount*
225   But his late wounded wing unserviceable found.

26

    Then full of griefe and anguish vehement,
        He lowdly brayd, that like was never heard,
        And from his wide devouring oven sent
        A flake° of fire, that flashing in his beard,   *flash*

6. I.e., too quickly entangles.   7. I.e., it could not make a deep gash there.

230   Him all amazd, and almost made affeard;
      The scorching flame sore swingèd° all his face,   *singed*
      And through his armour all his bodie seard,
      That he could not endure so cruell cace,°   *plight*
      But thought his armes to leave, and helmet to unlace.

27

235   Not that great Champion of the antique world,
      Whom famous Poetes verse so much doth vaunt,
      And hath for twelve huge labours high extold,
      So many furies and sharpe fits did haunt,
      When him the poysoned garment did enchaunt
240   With Centaures bloud, and bloudie verses charmed,
      As did this knight twelve thousand dolours° daunt,   *pains*
      Whom fyrie steele now burnt, that earst° him armed,   *formerly*
      That erst him goodly armed, now most of all him harmed.[8]

28

      Faint, wearie, sore, emboylèd, grievèd, brent°   *burned*
245   With heat, toyle, wounds, armes, smart, and inward fire
      That never man such mischiefes° did torment;   *misfortunes*
      Death better were, death did he oft desire,
      But death will never come, when needes require.
      Whom so dismayd when that his foe beheld,
250   He cast to suffer him no more respire,°   *live*
      But gan his sturdie sterne° about to weld,°   *tail/lash*
      And him so strongly stroke, that to the ground him feld.

29

      It fortunèd (as faire it then befell)
      Behind his backe unweeting,° where he stood,   *unnoticed*
255   Of auncient time there was a springing well,
      From which fast trickled forth a silver flood,
      Full of great vertues, and for med'cine good.
      Whylome,° before that cursèd Dragon got   *formerly*
      That happie land, and all with innocent blood
260   Defyld those sacred waves, it rightly hot°   *was called*
      The Well of Life,[9] ne yet his vertues° had forgot.   *powers*

30

      For unto life the dead it could restore,
      And guilt of sinfull crimes cleane wash away,
      Those that with sicknesse were infected sore,
265   It could recure, and agèd long decay
      Renew, as one were borne that very day.

---

8. Redcrosse's fire baptism is compared with the
burning shirt of Nessus, which killed Hercules,
"that great Champion of the antique world" (line
235). His "twelve huge labours" are paralleled to
the knight's "twelve thousand dolours."
9. An allusion to Revelation 22.1–2: "And he
showed me a pure river of water of life, clear as
crystal, proceeding out of the throne of God, and
of the Lamb. In the midst of the street of it, and
on either side of the river, was the tree of life which
bare twelve manner of fruits and yielded her fruit
every month: and the leaves of the tree were for
the healing of the nations."

Both Silo this, and Jordan did excell,
And th' English Bath, and eke the german Spau,
Ne can Cephise, nor Hebrus match this well:
270 Into the same the knight backe overthrowen, fell.[1]

31

Now gan the golden Phoebus for to steepe
His fierie face in billowes of the west,
And his faint steedes watred in Ocean deepe,
Whiles from their journall° labours they did rest,   *daily*
275 When that infernall Monster, having kest°   *cast*
His wearie foe into that living well,
Can° high advaunce his broad discoloured brest,   *did*
Above his wonted pitch,° with countenance fell,°   *height/sinister*
And clapt his yron wings, as victor he did dwell.°   *remain*

32

280 Which when his pensive Ladie saw from farre,
Great woe and sorrow did her soule assay,°   *assail*
As weening that the sad end of the warre,
And gan to highest God entirely° pray,   *earnestly*
That feared chaunce° from her to turne away;   *fate*
285 With folded hands and knees full lowly bent
All night she watcht, ne once adowne would lay
Her daintie limbs in her sad dreriment,°   *dismal condition*
But praying still did wake, and waking did lament.

33

The morrow next gan early to appeare,
290 That° Titan° rose to runne his daily race;   *when/the sun god*
But early ere the morrow next gan reare
Out of the sea faire Titans deawy face,
Up rose the gentle virgin from her place,
And lookèd all about, if she might spy
295 Her lovèd knight to move his manly pace:
For she had great doubt of his safety,
Since late she saw him fall before his enemy.

34

At last she saw, where he upstarted brave
Out of the well, wherein he drenchèd lay;
300 As Eagle fresh out of the Ocean wave,
Where he hath left his plumes all hoary gray,
And deckt himselfe with feathers youthly gay,
Like Eyas° hauke up mounts unto the skies,   *young*
His newly budded pineons to assay,

1. The Well of Life, with its powers of renewal, is successively compared with waters of the Bible, of England and Europe, and of classical antiquity. In Siloam ("Silo") a blind man was cured by Christ (John 9.7); the crossing of the river Jordan saved the Jews (Deuteronomy 27.2–9), and Christ was baptized therein (Matthew 3.16). "Bath" and "Spau" (Spa) were famed for their medicinal waters. "Cephise" and "Hebrus" in Greece were noted for purifying and healing powers.

305 And marveiles at himselfe, still as he flies:
   So new this new-borne knight to battell new did rise.[2]

35

Whom when the damnèd feend so fresh did spy,
   No wonder if he wondred at the sight,
   And doubted, whether his late enemy
310   It were, or other new supplièd knight.
   He, now to prove his late renewèd might,
   High brandishing his bright deaw-burning blade,
   Upon his crested scalpe so sore did smite,
   That to the scull a yawning wound it made:
315 The deadly dint° his dullèd senses all dismaid.   blow

36

I wote° not, whether the revenging steele   know
   Were hardnèd with that holy water dew,
   Wherein he fell, or sharper edge did feele,
   Or his baptizèd hands now greater° grew;   stronger
320   Or other secret vertue° did ensew;   power
   Else never could the force of fleshly arme,
   Ne molten mettall in his bloud embrew:°   plunge
   For till that stownd° could never wight him harme,   moment
   By subtilty, nor slight,° nor might, nor mighty charme.   trickery

37

325 The cruell wound enragèd him so sore,
   That loud he yellèd for exceeding paine;
   As hundred ramping Lyons seemed to rore,
   Whom ravenous hunger did thereto constraine:
   Then gan he tosse aloft his stretchèd traine,°   tail
330   And therewith scourge the buxome° aire so sore,   yielding
   That to his force to yeelden it was faine;°   obliged
   Ne ought his sturdie strokes might stand afore,[3]
   That high trees overthrew, and rocks in peeces tore.

38

The same advauncing high above his head,
335   With sharpe intended° sting so rude° him smot,   extended / roughly
   That to the earth him drove, as stricken dead,
   Ne living wight would have him life behot:[4]
   The mortall sting his angry needle shot
   Quite through his shield, and in his shoulder seasd,
340   Where fast it stucke, ne would there out be got:
   The griefe° thereof him wondrous sore diseasd,°   pain / afflicted
   Ne might his ranckling paine with patience be appeasd.

39

But yet more mindfull of his honour deare,
   Then of the grievous smart, which him did wring,°   torment

2. Legend had it that the eagle could renew its
youth by bathing in a spring.
3. I.e., neither could anything ("ought") stand

before his violent ("sturdie") strokes.
4. Promised. I.e., no one would have thought he
could survive the blow.

345 From loathèd soile he can° him lightly reare,   *did*
    And strove to loose the farre infixèd sting:
    Which when in vaine he tryde with struggeling,
    Inflamed with wrath, his raging blade he heft,°   *heaved*
    And strooke so strongly, that the knotty string
350 Of his huge taile he quite a sunder cleft,
    Five joynts thereof he hewd, and but the stump him left.

40

Hart cannot thinke, what outrage,° and what cryes,   *violent clamor*
    With foule enfouldred⁵ smoake and flashing fire,
    The hell-bred beast threw forth unto the skyes,
355 That all was coverèd with darknesse dire:
    Then fraught° with rancour, and engorgèd° ire,   *filled/swollen*
    He cast at once him to avenge for all,
    And gathering up himselfe out of the mire,
    With his uneven wings did fiercely fall
360 Upon his sunne-bright shield, and gript it fast withall.

41

Much was the man encombred with his hold,
    In feare to lose his weapon in his paw,
    Ne wist yet, how his talents° to unfold;   *talons*
    Nor harder was from Cerberus⁶ greedie jaw
365 To plucke a bone, then° from his cruell claw   *than*
    To reave° by strength the gripèd gage° away: *seize/prize*
    Thrise he assayd it from his foot to draw,
    And thrise in vaine to draw it did assay,
    It booted nought to thinke, to robbe him of his pray.

42

370 Tho° when he saw no power might prevaile,   *then*
    His trustie sword he cald to his last aid,
    Wherewith he fiercely did his foe assaile,
    And double blowes about him stoutly laid,
    That glauncing fire out of the yron plaid:
375 As sparckles from the Andvile° use to fly,   *anvil*
    When heavie hammers on the wedge are swaid;°   *struck*
    Therewith at last he forst him to unty°   *loosen*
    One of his grasping feete, him to defend thereby.

43

The other foot, fast fixèd on his shield,
380 Whenas no strength, nor stroks mote° him constraine   *might*
    To loose, ne yet the warlike pledge to yield,
    He smot thereat with all his might and maine,
    That nought so wondrous puissance might sustaine;
    Upon the joynt the lucky steele did light,
385 And made such way, that hewd it quite in twaine;

---

5. Black as a thundercloud.   6. The dog that guards the mouth of hell.

The paw yet missèd not his minisht° might,   *lessened*
But hong still on the shield, as it at first was pight.°   *placed*

44

For griefe thereof, and divelish despight,
  From his infernall fournace forth he threw
390 Huge flames, that dimmèd all the heavens light,
  Enrold in duskish smoke and brimstone blew;
  As burning Aetna from his boyling stew°   *cauldron*
  Doth belch out flames, and rockes in peeces broke,
  And ragged ribs of mountaines molten new
395 Enwrapt in coleblacke clouds and filthy smoke,
That all the land with stench, and heaven with horror choke.

45

The heate whereof, and harmefull pestilence
  So sore him noyd,° that forst him to retire   *troubled*
  A little backward for his best defence,
400 To save his bodie from the scorching fire,
  Which he from hellish entrailes did expire.°   *breathe out*
  It chaunst (eternall God that chaunce did guide)
  As he recoylèd backward, in the mire
  His nigh forwearied feeble feet did slide,
405 And downe he fell, with dread of shame sore terrifide.

46

There grew a goodly tree him faire beside,
  Loaden with fruit and apples rosie red,
  As they in pure vermilion had beene dide,
  Whereof great vertues over all were red:°   *everywhere were told*
410 For happie life to all, which thereon fed,
  And life eke everlasting did befall:
  Great God it planted in that blessed sted°   *place*
  With his almightie hand, and did it call
The Tree of Life, the crime of our first fathers fall.[7]

47

415 In all the world like was not to be found,
  Save in that soile, where all good things did grow,
  And freely sprong out of the fruitfull ground,
  As incorrupted Nature did them sow,
  Till that dread Dragon all did overthrow.
420 Another like faire tree eke grew thereby,
  Whereof who so did eat, eftsoones did know

---

7. Genesis 2.9 describes the Tree of Life and also
the Tree of Knowledge of Good and Evil, both of
which God planted in the Garden of Eden. The
"crime of our first fathers fall" is that Adam, in
eating of the second and being banished from
Eden, separated himself—and (according to Christian doctrine) us—from the first. The Tree of Life
appears again in the New Jerusalem (Revelation
22.2).

Both good and ill: O mornefull memory:
That tree through one mans fault hath doen us all to dy.°   *i.e., killed us*

48

From that first tree forth flowd, as from a well,
425   A trickling streame of Balme, most soveraine°   *powerful for cures*
   And daintie deare,° which on the ground still fell,   *precious*
   And overflowèd all the fertill plaine,
   As it had deawèd bene with timely° raine: *seasonable*
   Life and long health that gratious° ointment gave,   *full of grace*
430   And deadly woundes could heale, and reare° againe   *raise*
   The senselesse corse appointed° for the grave.   *made ready*
Into that same he fell: which did from death him save.[8]

49

For nigh thereto the ever damnèd beast
   Durst not approch, for he was deadly made,°   *i.e., a child of death*
435   And all that life preservèd, did detest:
   Yet he it oft adventured° to invade.   *attempted*
   By this the drouping day-light gan to fade,
   And yeeld his roome to sad succeeding night,
   Who with her sable mantle gan to shade
440   The face of earth, and wayes of living wight,
And high her burning torch set up in heaven bright.

50

When gentle Una saw the second fall
   Of her deare knight, who wearie of long fight,
   And faint through losse of bloud, moved not at all,
445   But lay as in a dreame of deepe delight,
   Besmeard with pretious Balme, whose vertuous might
   Did heale his wounds, and scorching heat alay,[9]
   Againe she stricken was with sore affright,
   And for his safetie gan devoutly pray;
450   And watch the noyous° night, and wait for joyous day.   *noxious*

51

The joyous day gan early to appeare,
   And faire Aurora from the deawy bed
   Of aged Tithone gan her selfe to reare,[1]
   With rosie cheekes, for shame as blushing red;
455   Her golden lockes for haste were loosely shed
   About her eares, when Una her did marke
   Clymbe to her charet, all with flowers spred,
   From heaven high to chase the chearelesse darke;
With merry note her loud salutes the mounting larke.

8. The healing balm flowing from the Tree of Life is understood to be Christ's blood, shed to redeem humankind from eternal damnation.
9. Cf. Revelation 2.7, 11: "To him that over-cometh will I give to eat of the tree of life" and "He that overcometh shall not be hurt of the second death."
1. Aurora is goddess of the dawn, Tithonus her husband ("aged" because he was granted everlast-ing life without everlasting youth).

52

460 Then freshly up arose the doughtie knight,
　　All healèd of his hurts and woundès wide,
　　And did himselfe to battell readie dight;°   *prepare*
　　Whose early foe awaiting him beside
　　To have devourd, so soone as day he spyde,
465 　　When now he saw himselfe so freshly reare,
　　As if late fight had nought him damnifyde,°   *injured*
　　He woxe° dismayd, and gan his fate to feare;   *grew*
　　Nathlesse° with wonted rage he him advauncèd neare.   *nevertheless*

53

　　And in his first encounter, gaping wide,
470 　　He thought attonce him to have swallowed quight,
　　And rusht upon him with outragious pride;
　　Who him r'encountring fierce, as hauke in flight,
　　Perforce rebutted° backe. The weapon bright   *drove*
　　Taking advantage of his open jaw,
475 　　Ran through his mouth with so importune° might,   *violent*
　　That deepe emperst his darksome hollow maw,
　　And back retyrd,[2] his life bloud forth with all did draw.

54

　　So downe he fell, and forth his life did breath,
　　That vanisht into smoke and cloudès swift;
480 　　So downe he fell, that th' earth him underneath
　　Did grone, as feeble so great load to lift;
　　So downe he fell, as an huge rockie clift,
　　Whose false° foundation waves have washt away,   *insecure*
　　With dreadfull poyse° is from the mayneland rift,°   *falling weight/split*
485 　　And rolling downe, great Neptune doth dismay;
　　So downe he fell, and like an heapèd mountaine lay.

55

　　The knight himselfe even trembled at his fall,
　　So huge and horrible a masse it seemed;
　　And his deare Ladie, that beheld it all,
490 　　Durst not approch for dread, which she misdeemed,°   *misjudged*
　　But yet at last, when as the direfull feend
　　She saw not stirre, off-shaking vaine affright,
　　She nigher drew, and saw that joyous end:
　　Then God she praysd, and thankt her faithfull knight,
495 That had atchiev'd so great a conquest by his might.

---

2. I.e., on being drawn back.

Canto 12

Faire Una to the Redcrosse knight
betrouthèd is with joy:
Though false Duessa it to barre
her false sleights doe imploy.

I

Behold I see the haven nigh at hand,
  To which I meane my wearie course to bend;
  Vere the maine shete, and beare up with the land,[3]
  The which afore is fairely to be kend,°   *recognized*
5 And seemeth safe from stormes, that may offend;
  There this faire virgin wearie of her way
  Must landed be, now at her journeyes end:
  There eke my feeble barke° a while may stay,   *ship*
Till merry° wind and weather call her thence away.   *favorable*

2

10 Scarsely had Phoebus in the glooming East°   *i.e., dawn*
  Yet harnessèd his firie-footed teeme,
  Ne reard above the earth his flaming creast,°   *crest*
  When the last deadly smoke aloft did steeme,
  That signe of last outbreathèd life did seeme
15 Unto the watchman on the castle wall;
  Who thereby dead that balefull° Beast did deeme,   *evil*
  And to his Lord and Ladie lowd gan call,
To tell, how he had seene the Dragons fatall fall.

3

Uprose with hastie joy, and feeble speed
20 That agèd Sire, the Lord of all that land,
  And lookèd forth, to weet, if true indeede
  Those tydings were, as he did understand,
  Which whenas true by tryall he out fond,
  He bad to open wyde his brazen gate,
25 Which long time had bene shut, and out of hond°   *straightway*
  Proclaymèd joy and peace through all his state;
For dead now was their foe, which them forrayèd late.[4]

4

Then gan triumphant Trompets sound on hie,
  That sent to heaven the ecchoèd report
30 Of their new joy, and happie victorie
  Gainst him, that had them long opprest with tort,°   *wrong*
  And fast imprisonèd in siegèd fort.
  Then all the people, as in solemne feast,
  To him assembled with one full consort,°   *all together*

3. Release the mainsail line and sail toward the
land. The nautical metaphor echoes many classical
authors and Chaucer's *Troilus and Criseyde*
(2.1–7).
4. Had recently ravaged.

35   Rejoycing at the fall of that great beast,
        From whose eternall bondage now they were releast.

                                5

        Forth came that auncient Lord and aged Queene,
            Arayd in antique robes downe to the ground,
            And sad habiliments right well beseene;⁵
40   A noble crew about them waited round
            Of sage and sober Peres,° all gravely gownd;   peers
            Whom farre before did march a goodly band
            Of tall young men, all hable armes to sownd,⁶
            But now they laurell braunches bore in hand;
45   Glad signe of victorie and peace in all their land.

                                6

        Unto that doughtie Conquerour they came,
            And him before themselves prostrating low,
            Their Lord and Patrone° loud did him proclame,   defender
            And at his feet their laurell boughes did throw.
50   Soone after them all dauncing on a row
            The comely virgins came, with girlands dight,°   adorned
            As fresh as flowres in medow greene do grow,
            When morning deaw upon their leaves doth light:
        And in their hands sweet Timbrels° all upheld on hight. tambourines

                                7

55   And them before, the fry° of children young   crowd
            Their wanton° sports and childish mirth did play,   playful
            And to the Maydens sounding tymbrels sung
            In well attunèd notes, a joyous lay,
            And made delightfull musicke all the way,
60   Untill they came, where that faire virgin stood;
            As faire Diana° in fresh sommers day   goddess of the hunt
            Beholds her Nymphes, enraunged° in shadie wood,   ranged
        Some wrestle, some do run, some bathe in christall flood.

                                8

        So she beheld those maydens meriment
65   With chearefull vew; who when to her they came,
            Themselves to ground with gratious humblesse° bent, humility
            And her adored by honorable name,°   with titles of honor
            Lifting to heaven her everlasting fame:
            Then on her head they set a girland greene,
70   And crownèd her twixt earnest and twixt game:°   i.e., half in fun
            Who in her selfe-resemblance well beseene,⁷
        Did seeme such, as she was, a goodly maiden Queene.

---

5. I.e., their sober, appropriate ("right well   6. Able to fight with weapons.
beseene") attire.   7. I.e., looking appropriately like herself.

9

And after all, the raskall many° ran,   *rabble throng*
Heapèd together in rude rablement,°   *confusion*
75   To see the face of that victorious man:
Whom all admirèd,° as from heaven sent,   *wondered at*
And gazd upon with gaping wonderment.
But when they came, where that dead Dragon lay,
Stretcht on the ground in monstrous large extent,
80   The sight with idle° feare did them dismay,   *baseless*
Ne durst approch him nigh, to touch, or once assay.

10

Some feard, and fled; some feard and well it faynd;°   *concealed*
One that would wiser seeme, then all the rest,
Warnd him not touch, for yet perhaps remaynd
85   Some lingring life within his hollow brest,
Or in his wombe might lurke some hidden nest
Of many Dragonets,° his fruitfull seed;   *young dragons*
Another said, that in his eyes did rest
Yet sparckling fire, and bad thereof take heed;
90   Another said, he saw him move his eyes indeed.

11

One mother, when as her foolehardie chyld
Did come too neare, and with his talants° play,   *talons*
Halfe dead through feare, her litle babe revyld,°   *scolded*
And to her gossips° gan in counsell° say;   *women friends / private*
95   "How can I tell, but that his talants may
Yet scratch my sonne, or rend his tender hand?"
So diversly themselves in vaine they fray;°   *scare*
Whiles some more bold, to measure him nigh stand,
To prove° how many acres he did spread of land.   *determine*

12

100 Thus flockèd all the folke him round about,
The whiles that hoarie° king, with all his traine,   *gray-haired*
Being arrivèd, where that champion stout
After his foes defeasance° did remaine,   *defeat*
Him goodly greetes, and faire does entertaine,
105 With princely gifts of yvorie and gold,
And thousand thankes him yeelds for all his paine.
Then when his daughter deare he does behold,
Her dearely doth imbrace, and kisseth manifold.°   *many times*

13

And after to his Pallace he them brings,
110 With shaumes,[8] and trompets, and with Clarions sweet;
And all the way the joyous people sings,
And with their garments strowes the pavèd street:
Whence mounting up, they find purveyance° meet   *provisions*
Of all, that royall Princes court became,°   *suited*

8. Medieval and Renaissance predecessor of the oboe.

115   And all the floore was underneath their feet
       Bespred with costly scarlot of great name,°   *i.e., famous scarlet cloth*
On which they lowly sit, and fitting purpose frame.[9]

14

    What needs me tell their feast and goodly guize,°   *behavior*
       In which was nothing riotous nor vaine?
120   What needs of daintie dishes to devize,°   *talk*
       Of comely services, or courtly trayne?°   *assembly*
       My narrow leaves cannot in them containe
       The large discourse° of royall Princes state.   *i.e., full description*
       Yet was their manner then but bare and plaine:
125   For th' antique world excesse and pride did hate,
Such proud luxurious pompe is swollen up but late.°   *just recently*

15

    Then when with meates and drinkes of every kinde
       Their fervent appetites they quenchèd had,
       That auncient Lord gan fit occasion finde,
130   Of straunge adventures, and of perils sad,°   *grave*
       Which in his travell him befallen had,
       For to demaund of his renowmèd guest:
       Who then with utt'rance grave, and count'nance sad,
       From point to point, as is before exprest,
135   Discourst his voyage long, according° his request.   *granting*

16

    Great pleasure mixt with pittifull° regard,   *sympathetic*
       That godly King and Queene did passionate,°   *i.e., feel and express*
       Whiles they his pittifull° adventures heard,   *deserving pity*
       That oft they did lament his lucklesse state,
140   And often blame the too importune° fate,   *severe*
       That heapd on him so many wrathfull wreakes:°   *vengeful injuries*
       For never gentle knight, as he of late,
       So tossèd was in fortunes cruell freakes,°   *whims*
And all the while salt teares bedeawd the hearers cheaks.

17

145   Then said that royall Pere in sober wise:
       "Deare Sonne, great beene the evils, which ye bore
       From first to last in your late enterprise,
       That I note,° whether prayse, or pitty more: *know not*
       For never living man, I weene, so sore
150   In sea of deadly daungers was distrest;
       But since now safe ye seisèd° have the shore,   *reached*
       And well arrivèd are (high God be blest),
Let us devize° of ease and everlasting rest."   *think*

18

    "Ah dearest Lord," said then that doughty knight,
155   "Of ease or rest I may not yet devize;

9. Make seemly conversation.

For by the faith, which I to armes have plight,°   *pledged*
I bounden am streight after this emprize,°   *enterprise*
As that your daughter can ye well advize,
  Backe to returne to that great Faerie Queene,
160   And her to serve six yeares in warlike wize,
  Gainst that proud Paynim king, that workes her teene:°   *sorrow*
Therefore I ought° crave pardon, till I there have beene."[1]   *must*

19

"Unhappie falles that hard necessitie,"
  Quoth he, "the troubler of my happie peace,
165   And vowèd foe of my felicitie;
  Ne° I against the same can justly preace:°   *nor / press, contend*
  But since that band° ye cannot now release,   *obligation*
Nor doen undo (for vowes may not be vaine),[2]
  Soone as the terme of those six yeares shall cease,
170   Ye then shall hither backe returne againe,
The marriage to accomplish vowd betwixt you twain.

20

"Which for my part I covet to performe,
  In sort as° through the world I did proclame,   *even as*
  That who so kild that monster most deforme,
175   And him in hardy battaile overcame,
  Should have mine onely daughter to his Dame,°   *wife*
  And of my kingdome heire apparaunt bee:
  Therefore since now to thee perteines° the same,   *belongs*
  By dew desert of noble chevalree,
180 Both daughter and eke° kingdome, lo I yield to thee."   *also*

21

Then forth he callèd that his daughter faire,
  The fairest Un' his onely daughter deare,
  His onely daughter, and his onely heyre;
  Who forth proceeding with sad° sober cheare,°   *grave / countenance*
185   As bright as doth the morning starre appeare
  Out of the East, with flaming lockes bedight,°   *bedecked*
  To tell that dawning day is drawing neare,
  And to the world does bring long wishèd light:
So faire and fresh that Lady shewd her selfe in sight.

22

190 So faire and fresh, as freshest flowre in May;
  For she had layd her mournefull stole aside,
  And widow-like sad wimple° throwne away,   *veil*
  Wherewith her heavenly beautie she did hide,
  Whiles on her wearie journey she did ride;
195   And on her now a garment she did weare,
  All lilly white, withoutten spot, or pride,°   *ornament*

---

1. The final Christian triumph, the marriage of Christ and the true church, will be achieved only at the end of time. Meanwhile, the struggle against evil (and the Roman church) continues.
2. I.e., you cannot undo what is done ("doen"), for vows may not be (made) vain.

That seemed like silke and silver woven neare,°   *tightly*
But neither silke nor silver therein did appeare.[3]

23

The blazing brightnesse of her beauties beame,
200   And glorious light of her sunshyny face[4]
To tell, were as to strive against the streame.
My ragged rimes are all too rude and bace,
Her heavenly lineaments for to enchace.°   *adorn*
Ne wonder; for her owne deare lovèd knight,
205   All° were she dayly with himselfe in place,   *although*
Did wonder much at her celestiall sight:
Oft had he seene her faire, but never so faire dight.

24

So fairely dight, when she in presence came,
She to her Sire made humble reverence,
210   And bowèd low, that her right well became,
And added grace unto her excellence:
Who with great wisdome, and grave eloquence
Thus gan to say. But eare° he thus had said,   *ere*
With flying speede, and seeming great pretence,°   *purpose*
215   Came running in, much like a man dismaid,
A Messenger with letters, which his message said.

25

All in the open hall amazèd stood,
At suddeinnesse of that unwarie° sight,   *unexpected*
And wondred at his breathlesse hastie mood.
220   But he for nought would stay his passage right°   *direct*
Till fast° before the king he did alight;   *close*
Where falling flat, great humblesse he did make,
And kist the ground, whereon his foot was pight;°   *placed*
Then to his hands that writ° he did betake,°   *document / deliver*
225   Which he disclosing, red thus, as the paper spake.

26

"To thee, most mighty king of Eden faire,
Her greeting sends in these sad lines addrest,
The wofull daughter, and forsaken heire
Of that great Emperour of all the West;
230   And bids thee be advizèd for the best,
Ere thou thy daughter linck in holy band
Of wedlocke to that new unknowen guest:
For he already plighted his right hand
Unto another love, and to another land.

---

3. "The marriage of the Lamb is come, and his wife hath made herself ready. And to her was granted that she should be arrayed in fine linen, clean and white: for the fine linen is the right-   eousness of saints" (Revelation 19.7–8).
4. Revelation 21.9, 11 describes the New Jerusalem as "the bride, the Lamb's wife . . . her light was like unto a stone most precious."

27

235 "To me sad mayd, or rather widow sad,
    He was affiauncèd long time before,
    And sacred pledges he both gave, and had,
    False erraunt knight, infamous, and forswore:
    Witnesse the burning Altars, which° he swore,   *by which*
240 And guiltie heavens of⁵ his bold perjury,
    Which though he hath polluted oft of yore,
    Yet I to them for judgement just do fly,
And them conjure° t' avenge this shamefull injury.   *implore*

28

"Therefore since mine he is, or° free or bond,°   *whether/bound*
245 Or false or trew, or living or else dead,
    Withhold, O soveraine Prince, your hasty hond
    From knitting league with him, I you aread;°   *advise*
    Ne wene° my right with strength adowne to tread,   *think*
    Through weakenesse of my widowhed, or woe:
250 For truth is strong, her rightfull cause to plead,
    And shall find friends, if need requireth soe,
So bids thee well to fare, Thy neither friend, nor foe, Fidessa."

29

When he these bitter byting words had red,
    The tydings straunge did him abashèd make,
255 That still he sate long time astonishèd
    As in great muse,° ne word to creature spake.   *amazement*
    At last his solemne silence thus he brake,
    With doubtfull eyes fast fixèd on his guest:
    "Redoubted° knight, that for mine onely sake⁶   *honored*
260 Thy life and honour late adventurest,
Let nought be hid from me, that ought to be exprest.

30

"What meane these bloudy vowes, and idle threats,
    Throwne out from womanish impatient mind?
    What heavens? what altars? what enragèd heates
265 Here heapèd up with termes of love unkind,°   *unnatural*
    My conscience cleare with guilty bands° would bind?   *bonds of guilt*
    High God be witnesse, that I guiltlesse ame.
    But if your selfe, Sir knight, ye faultie° find,   *guilty*
    Or wrappèd be in loves of former Dame,
270 With crime do not it cover, but disclose the same."

31

To whom the Redcrosse knight this answere sent,
    "My Lord, my King, be nought hereat dismayd,
    Till well ye wote by grave intendiment,°   *serious investigation*
    What woman, and wherefore doth me upbrayd

5. I.e., and heavens polluted by.   6. For my sake alone.

275　　With breach of love, and loyalty betrayd.
　　　　It was in my mishaps, as hitherward
　　　　I lately traveild, that unwares I strayd
　　　　Out of my way, through perils straunge and hard;
　　　That day should faile me, ere I had them all declard.

32

280　"There did I find, or rather I was found
　　　　Of this false woman, that Fidessa hight,
　　　　Fidessa hight the falsest Dame on ground,
　　　　Most false Duessa, royall richly dight,
　　　　That easie was t' invegle° weaker sight:　　　　　　　*deceive*
285　　Who by her wicked arts, and wylie skill,
　　　　Too false and strong for earthly skill or might,
　　　　Unwares me wrought unto her wicked will,
　　　And to my foe betrayd, when least I fearèd ill."

33

Then steppèd forth the goodly royall Mayd,
290　　And on the ground her selfe prostrating low,
　　　　With sober countenaunce thus to him sayd:
　　　　"O pardon me, my soveraigne Lord, to show
　　　　The secret treasons, which of late I know
　　　　To have bene wroght by that false sorceresse.
295　　She onely she it is, that earst did throw
　　　　This gentle knight into so great distresse,
　　　That death him did awaite in dayly wretchednesse.

34

"And now it seemes, that she subornèd hath
　　　　This craftie messenger with letters vaine,
300　　To worke new woe and improvided scath,°　　　　*unexpected harm*
　　　　By breaking of the band betwixt us twaine;
　　　　Wherein she usèd hath the practicke paine°　　　*treacherous skill*
　　　　Of this false footman, clokt with simplenesse,
　　　　Whom if ye please for to discover plaine,
305　　Ye shall him Archimago find, I ghesse,
　　　The falsest man alive; who tries shall find no lesse."

35

The king was greatly movèd at her speach,
　　　　And all with suddein indignation fraight,°　　　　*filled*
　　　　Bad° on that Messenger rude hands to reach.　　　*bade*
310　　Eftsoones° the Gard, which on his state did wait,　*forthwith*
　　　　Attacht that faitor° false, and bound him strait:　*impostor*
　　　　Who seeming sorely chauffèd° at his band,　　　　*angered*
　　　　As chainèd Beare, whom cruell dogs do bait,
　　　　With idle force did faine them to withstand,
315　And often semblaunce made to scape out of their hand.

36

But they him layd full low in dungeon deepe,
　　　　And bound him hand and foote with yron chains.

And with continuall watch did warely° keepe;   *vigilantly*
Who then would thinke, that by his subtile trains
320   He could escape fowle death or deadly paines?[7]
Thus when that Princes wrath was pacifide,
He gan renew the late forbidden banes,[8]
And to the knight his daughter deare he tyde,
With sacred rites and vowes for ever to abyde.

37

325   His owne two hands the holy knots did knit,
That none but death for ever can devide;
His owne two hands, for such a turne° most fit,   *act*
The housling° fire did kindle and provide,   *sacramental*
And holy water thereon sprinckled wide;[9]
330   At which the bushy Teade° a groome did light,   *marriage torch*
And sacred lampe in secret chamber hide,
Where it should not be quenchèd day nor night,
For feare of evill fates, but burnen ever bright.

38

Then gan they sprinckle all the posts with wine,
335   And made great feast to solemnize that day;
They all perfumde with frankencense divine,
And precious odours fetcht from far away,
That all the house did sweat with great aray:
And all the while sweete Musicke did apply
340   Her curious° skill, the warbling notes to play,   *intricate*
To drive away the dull Melancholy;
The whiles one sung a song of love and jollity.

39

During the which there was an heavenly noise
Heard sound through all the Pallace pleasantly,
345   Like as it had bene many an Angels voice.
Singing before th' eternall majesty,
In their trinall triplicities[1] on hye;
Yet wist no creature, whence that heavenly sweet°   *delight*
Proceeded, yet each one felt secretly°   *inwardly*
350   Himselfe thereby reft of his sences meet,°   *proper*
And ravishèd with rare impression in his sprite.[2]

40

Great joy was made that day of young and old,
And solemne feast proclaimd throughout the land,

7. "And he laid hold on the dragon, that old serpent, which is the Devil, and Satan, and bound him a thousand years, And cast him into the bottomless pit, and shut him up, and set a seal upon him, that he should deceive the nations no more, till the thousand years should be fulfilled: and after that he must be loosed a little season" (Revelation 20.2–3).
8. Banns, i.e., announcements of marriage.
9. Marriages in ancient times were solemnized with sacramental fire and water.

1. The "trinall triplicities" are the nine angelic orders, divided into three groups of three, the whole hierarchy corresponding to the nine spheres of the universe. The music heard in this stanza is the music of the spheres, not audible on earth since the Fall.
2. Spirit. "Let us be glad and rejoice, and give honor to him: for the marriage of the Lamb is come" (Revelation 9.6). In Revelation, the marriage of Christ and the New Jerusalem signals the general redemption.

That their exceeding merth may not be told:
355   Suffice it heare by signes to understand
The usuall joyes at knitting of loves band.
Thrise happy man the knight himselfe did hold,
Possessèd of his Ladies hart and hand,
And ever, when his eye did her behold,
360 His heart did seeme to melt in pleasures manifold.

41

Her joyous presence and sweet company
In full content he there did long enjoy,
Ne wicked envie, ne vile gealosy
His deare delights were able to annoy:
365   Yet swimming in that sea of blisfull joy,
He nought forgot, how he whilome had sworne,
In case he could that monstrous beast destroy,
Unto his Faerie Queene backe to returne:
The which he shortly did, and Una left to mourne.

42

370 Now strike your sailes ye jolly Mariners,
   For we be come unto a quiet rode,°   *harbor*
Where we must land some of our passengers,
And light this wearie vessell of her lode.
Here she a while may make her safe abode,
375   Till she repairèd have her tackles spent,°   *worn out*
And wants supplide. And then againe abroad
On the long voyage whereto she is bent:
Well may she speede and fairely finish her intent.

From The Second Booke of The Faerie Queene

Contayning
The Legend of Sir Guyon,
or
Of Temperaunce

Summary   In Book Two, Sir Guyon represents and becomes the virtue of Temperance, which requires moderation, self-control, and sometimes abstinence in regard to anger, sex, greed, ambition, and the whole spectrum of passions, desires, pleasures, and material goods. In his climactic adventure, he visits and destroys the Bower of Bliss of the witch Acrasia.

From *Canto 12*

[THE BOWER OF BLISS]¹

42

370　Thence passing forth, they² shortly do arrive,
　　　Whereas the Bowre of Blisse was situate;
　　　A place pickt out by choice of best alive,°　　　　　　　*the best living artisans*
　　　That natures worke by art can imitate:
　　　In which what ever in this worldly state
375　Is sweet, and pleasing unto living sense,
　　　Or that may dayntiest fantasie aggrate,°　　　　　　　　*please, satisfy*
　　　Was pourèd forth with plentifull dispence,°　　　　　　*liberality*
　　And made there to abound with lavish affluence.

43

　　　Goodly it was enclosèd round about,
380　Aswell their entred guests to keepe within,
　　　As those unruly beasts to hold without;
　　　Yet was the fence thereof but weake and thin;
　　　Nought feard their force, that fortilage° to win,　　　*fortress*
　　　But wisedomes powre, and temperaunces might,
385　By which the mightiest things efforcèd bin:°　　　　　*are compelled*
　　　And eke° the gate was wrought of substaunce light,　*also*
　　Rather for pleasure, then° for battery or fight.　　　　*than*

44

　　　Yt framèd was of precious yvory,
　　　That seemd a worke of admirable wit;°　　　　　　　*marvelous skill*
390　And therein all the famous history
　　　Of Jason and Medaea was ywrit;
　　　Her mighty charmes, her furious loving fit,
　　　His goodly conquest of the golden fleece,
　　　His falsèd° faith, and love too lightly flit,°　　　*violated/altering*
395　The wondred° Argo, which in venturous peece³　　　*admired*
　　First through the Euxine seas bore all the flowr of Greece.⁴

45

　　　Ye might have seene the frothy billowes fry°　　　*foam*
　　　Under the ship, as thorough them she went,
　　　That seemd the waves were into yvory,
400　Or yvory into the waves were sent;

1. The Bower of Bliss, perhaps the most famous of Spenser's symbolic places, has been variously interpreted. Some critics emphasize its aspects of sterility and artifice; others, its seductive and threatening eroticism and idolatry akin to that associated with the New World and Ireland.
2. I.e., Guyon and a character called the Palmer, who is his guide throughout Book 2 (and who is usually thought to represent reason). Pilgrims to the Holy Land were called palmers in token of the palm leaves they often brought back.
3. I.e., adventurous vessel.
4. Jason, in his ship the *Argo*, sought the Golden Fleece of the king of Colchis; the witch Medea, the king's daughter, fell in love with him and used "her mighty charmes" to help him obtain it.

And other where the snowy substaunce sprent°   *sprinkled*
With vermell,° like the boyes bloud⁵ therein shed, *vermilion*
A piteous spectacle did represent,
And otherwhiles° with gold besprinkelèd;   *elsewhere*
405 Yt seemd th' enchaunted flame, which did Creüsa wed.⁶

46

All this, and more might in that goodly gate
 Be red; that ever open stood to all,
 Which thither came: but in the Porch there sate
 A comely personage of stature tall,
410 And semblaunce° pleasing, more then naturall, *appearance*
 That travellers to him seemd to entize;
 His looser° garment to the ground did fall, *too loose*
 And flew about his heeles in wanton wize,
Not fit for speedy pace, or manly exercize.

47

415 They in that place him Genius° did call: *presiding spirit*
 Not that celestiall powre,⁷ to whom the care
 Of life, and generatiön of all
 That lives, pertaines in charge particulare,
 Who wondrous things concerning our welfare,
420 And strange phantomes doth let us oft forsee,
 And oft of secret ill bids us beware:
 That is our Selfe, whom though we do not see,
Yet each doth in him selfe it well perceive to bee.

48

Therefore a God him sage Antiquity
425 Did wisely make, and good Agdistes call:
 But this same was to that quite contrary,
 The foe of life, that good envyes° to all, *grudges*
 That secretly doth us procure° to fall, *cause*
 Through guilefull semblaunts,° which he makes us see. *illusions*
430 He of this Gardin had the governall,° *management*
 And Pleasures porter was devizd° to bee, *appointed*
Holding a staffe in hand for more formalitee.

49

With diverse flowres he daintily was deckt,
 And strowèd round about, and by his side
435 A mighty Mazer bowle⁸ of wine was set,
 As if it had to him bene sacrifide;° *consecrated*
 Wherewith all new-come guests he gratifide:
 So did he eke Sir Guyon passing by:

5. Refers to Absyrtus, Medea's younger brother, whose body she cut into pieces and scattered to delay her father's pursuit.
6. Jason later deserted Medea for Creüsa. In revenge, Medea gave the girl a dress that burst into flame when she put it on; the flame consumed and thus "wed" her.
7. I.e., not Agdistes (see next stanza), the god of generation. The true Agdistes appears in the Garden of Adonis canto (3.6, stanzas 31–33).
8. A drinking cup of maple.

But he his idle curtesie defide,
440   And overthrew his bowle disdainfully;
And broke his staffe, with which he charmèd semblants sly.[9]

50

Thus being entred, they behold around
    A large and spacious plaine, on every side
    Strowed with pleasauns,° whose faire grassy ground   *gardens*
445   Mantled with greene, and goodly beautifide
    With all the ornaments of Floraes° pride,   *goddess of flowers*
    Wherewith her mother Art, as halfe in scorne
    Of niggard Nature, like a pompous bride
    Did decke her, and too lavishly adorne,
450 When forth from virgin bowre she comes in th' early morne.

51

Thereto the Heavens alwayes Joviall,[1]
    Lookt on them lovely,° still in stedfast state,   *lovingly*
    Ne° suffred storme nor frost on them to fall,   *nor*
    Their tender buds or leaves to violate,
455   Nor scorching heat, nor cold intemperate
    T' afflict the creatures, which therein did dwell,
    But the milde aire with season moderate
    Gently attempred, and disposd so well,
That still it breathèd forth sweet spirit° and holesome smell.   *breath*

52

460 More sweet and holesome, then the pleasaunt hill
    Of Rhodope, on which the Nimphe, that bore
    A gyaunt babe, her selfe for griefe did kill;
    Or the Thessalian Tempe, where of yore
    Faire Daphne Phoebus hart with love did gore;
465   Or Ida, where the Gods lov'd to repaire,°   *resort*
    When ever they their heavenly bowres forlore;°   *deserted*
    Or sweet Parnasse, the haunt of Muses faire;[2]
Or Eden selfe, if ought with Eden mote compaire.

53

Much wondred Guyon at the faire aspect
470   Of that sweet place, yet suffred no delight
    To sincke into his sence, nor mind affect,
    But passèd forth, and lookt still forward right,°   *straight ahead*
    Bridling his will, and maistering his might:
    Till that he came unto another gate;
475   No gate, but like one, being goodly dight°   *arrayed*

9. Raised deceitful apparitions. The rod and bowl are traditional emblems of enchantment (cf. Duessa's cup, 1.8, stanza 14).
1. Serene and beneficent, as influenced by the planet Jupiter.
2. The nymph Rhodope, who had a "gyaunt babe," Athos, by Neptune, was turned into a mountain.

Daphne, another nymph, charmed Apollo so that he pursued her until she prayed for aid and was turned into a laurel tree. Mount Ida was the scene of the rape of Ganymede by Jupiter, the judgment of Paris, and the gods' vantage point for viewing the Trojan War. Mount Parnassus is the home of the Muses.

With boughes and braunches, which did broad dilate°   *spread out*
Their clasping armes, in wanton wreathings intricate.

54

So fashionèd a Porch with rare device,°   *design*
  Archt over head with an embracing vine,
480 Whose bounches hanging downe, seemed to entice
  All passers by, to tast their lushious wine,
  And did themselves into their hands incline,
  As freely offering to be gatherèd:
  Some deepe empurpled as the Hyacint,[3]
485 Some as the Rubine,° laughing sweetly red,   *ruby*
Some like faire Emeraudes, not yet well ripenèd.

55

And them amongst, some were of burnisht gold,
  So made by art, to beautifie the rest,
  Which did themselves emongst the leaves enfold,
490 As lurking from the vew of covetous guest,
  That the weake bowes,° with so rich load opprest,   *boughs*
  Did bowe adowne, as over-burdenèd.
  Under that Porch a comely dame did rest,
  Clad in faire weedes,° but fowle disorderèd,   *garments*
495 And garments loose, that seemd unmeet for womanhed.°   *womanhood*

56

In her left hand a Cup of gold she held,
  And with her right the riper° fruit did reach,   *overripe*
  Whose sappy liquor, that with fulnesse sweld,
  Into her cup she scruzd,° with daintie breach°   *squeezed/crushing*
500 Of her fine fingers, without fowle empeach,°   *injury*
  That so faire wine-presse made the wine more sweet:
  Thereof she usd to give to drinke to each,
  Whom passing by she happenèd to meet:
It was her guise,° all Straungers goodly so to greet.   *custom*

57

505 So she to Guyon offred it to tast;
  Who taking it out of her tender hond,
  The cup to ground did violently cast,
  That all in peeces it was broken fond,°   *found*
  And with the liquor stainèd all the lond:°   *land*
510 Whereat Excesse exceedingly was wroth,
  Yet no'te° the same amend, ne yet withstond,   *knew not how to*
  But suffered him to passe, all° were she loth;   *although*
Who nought regarding her displeasure forward goth.

58

There the most daintie Paradise on ground,
515 It selfe doth offer to his sober eye,

---

3. The hyacinth or jacinth, a sapphire-colored stone.

In which all pleasures plenteously abound,
And none does others happinesse envye:
The painted° flowres, the trees upshooting hye,   *brightly colored*
The dales for shade, the hilles for breathing space,
520   The trembling groves, the Christall° running by;   *clear stream*
And that, which all faire workes doth most aggrace,°   *add grace to*
The art, which all that wrought, appearèd in no place.

59

One would have thought (so cunningly, the rude,
And scornèd parts were mingled with the fine)
525   That nature had for wantonesse ensude°   *imitated*
Art, and that Art at nature did repine;°   *complain*
So striving each th' other to undermine,
Each did the others worke more beautifie;
So diff'ring both in willes, agreed in fine:°   *in the end*
530   So all agreed through sweete diversitie,
This Gardin to adorne with all varietie.

60

And in the midst of all, a fountaine stood,
Of richest substaunce, that on earth might bee,
So pure and shiny, that the silver flood
535   Through every channell running one might see;
Most goodly it with curious imageree
Was over-wrought, and shapes of naked boyes,
Of which some seemd with lively jollitee,
To fly about, playing their wanton toyes,°   *sports*
540   Whilest others did them selves embay° in liquid joyes.   *bathe*

61

And over all, of purest gold was spred,
A trayle of yvie in his native hew:
For the rich mettall was so colourèd,
That wight, who did not well avis'd° it vew,   *carefully*
545   Would surely deeme it to be yvie trew:
Low his lascivious armes adown did creepe,
That themselves dipping in the silver dew,
Their fleecy flowres they tenderly did steepe,
Which° drops of Christall seemd for wantones°   *on which / wantonness*
    to weepe.

62

550 Infinit streames continually did well
Out of this fountaine, sweet and faire to see,
The which into an ample laver° fell,   *basin*
And shortly grew to so great quantitie,
That like a little lake it seemd to bee;
555 Whose depth exceeded not three cubits⁴ hight,
That through the waves one might the bottom see,

4. A cubit is about twenty inches (thus the depth is less than five feet).

All pav'd beneath with Jaspar shining bright,
That seemd the fountaine in that sea did sayle upright.

63

And all the margent° round about was set,   *border*
560 With shady Laurell trees, thence to defend°   *ward off*
The sunny beames, which on the billowes bet,°   *beat*
And those which therein bathèd, mote offend.°   *harm*
As Guyon hapned by the same to wend,
Two naked Damzelles he therein espyde,
565 Which therein bathing, seemèd to contend,
And wrestle wantonly, ne car'd to hyde,
Their dainty parts from vew of any, which them eyde.

64

Sometimes the one would lift the other quight
Above the waters, and then downe againe
570 Her plong,° as over maisterèd by might,   *plunge*
Where both awhile would coverèd remaine,
And each the other from to rise° restraine;   *rising*
The whiles their snowy limbes, as through a vele,
So through the Christall waves appearèd plaine:
575 Then suddeinly both would themselves unhele,° *uncover*
And th' amarous sweet spoiles to greedy eyes revele.

65

As that faire Starre, the messenger of morne,[5]
His deawy face out of the sea doth reare:
Or as the Cyprian goddess,[6] newly borne
580 Of th' Oceans fruitfull froth,° did first appeare: *foam*
Such seemèd they, and so their yellow heare
Christalline humour° droppèd downe apace.   *clear water*
Whom such when Guyon saw, he drew him neare,
And somewhat gan relent his earnest pace,
585 His stubborne brest gan secret pleasaunce to embrace.

66

The wanton Maidens him espying, stood
Gazing a while at his unwonted guise;°   *manner*
Then th' one her selfe low duckèd in the flood,
Abasht, that her a straunger did avise:°   *see*
590 But th' other rather higher did arise,
And her two lilly paps aloft displayd,
And all, that might his melting hart entise
To her delights, she unto him bewrayed:°   *revealed*
The rest hid underneath, him more desirous made.

67

595 With that, the other likewise up arose,
And her faire lockes, which formerly were bownd

---

5. "His" in the next line implies that the reference is not to Venus but to Phosphorus (or Heophorus), the minor male divinity sometimes identified with the morning star.
6. Venus, one of whose principal shrines was on the island of Cyprus.

Up in one knot, she low adowne did lose:°   *loosen*
  Which flowing long and thick, her cloth'd arownd,
  And th' yvorie in golden mantle gownd:
600 So that faire spectacle from him was reft,°   *taken*
  Yet that, which reft it, no lesse faire was fownd:
  So hid in lockes and waves from lookers theft,
Nought but her lovely face she for his looking left.

68

Withall she laughèd, and she blusht withall,
605 That blushing to her laughter gave more grace,
  And laughter to her blushing, as did fall:
  Now when they spide the knight to slacke his pace,
  Them to behold, and in his sparkling face
  The secret signes of kindled lust appeare,
610 Their wanton meriments they did encreace,
  And to him beckned, to approch more neare,
And shewd him many sights, that courage cold could reare.[7]

69

On which when gazing him the Palmer saw,
  He much rebukt those wandring eyes of his,
615 And counseld well, him forward thence did draw.
  Now are they come nigh to the Bowre of blis
  Of her fond favorites so named amis:
  When thus the Palmer; "Now Sir, well avise;°   *take care*
  For here the end of all our travell is:
620 Here wonnes° Acrasia, whom we must surprise,   *dwells*
Else she will slip away, and all our drift° despise."   *plan, effort*

70

Eftsoones they heard a most melodious sound,
  Of all that mote delight a daintie eare,
  Such as attonce might not on living ground,
625 Save in this Paradise, be heard elswhere:
  Right hard it was, for wight, which did it heare,
  To read,° what manner musicke that mote bee: *discern*
  For all that pleasing is to living eare,
  Was there consorted in one harmonee,
630 Birdes, voyces, instruments, windes, waters, all agree.

71

The joyous birdes shrouded in chearefull shade,
  Their notes unto the voyce attempred° sweet;   *attuned*
  Th' Angelicall soft trembling voyces made
  To th' instruments divine respondence meet:°   *fitting*
635 The silver sounding instruments did meet°   *join*
  With the base murmure of the waters fall:
  The waters fall with difference discreet,°   *distinct variations*
  Now soft, now loud, unto the wind did call:
The gentle warbling wind low answerèd to all.

7. That could arouse sexual desire ("courage") when cold.

72

640 There, whence that Musick seeméd heard to bee,
    Was the faire Witch her selfe⁸ now solacing,
    With a new Lover, whom through sorceree
    And witchcraft, she from farre did thither bring:
    There she had him now layd a slombering,
645 In secret shade, after long wanton joyes:
    Whilst round about them pleasauntly did sing
    Many faire Ladies, and lascivious boyes,
    That ever mixt their song with light licentious toyes.°   *amorous play*

73

    And all that while, right over him she hong,
650 With her false° eyes fast fixéd in his sight,   *deceitful*
    As seeking medicine, whence she was stong,
    Or greedily depasturing° delight: *feeding on*
    And oft inclining downe with kisses light,
    For feare of waking him, his lips bedewd,
655 And through his humid eyes did sucke his spright,
    Quite molten into lust and pleasure lewd;
    Wherewith she sighéd soft, as if his case she rewd.°   *pitied*

74

    The whiles some one did chaunt this lovely lay:⁹
    "Ah see, who so faire thing doest faine° to see,   *delight*
660 In springing flowre the image of thy day;
    Ah see the Virgin Rose, how sweetly shee
    Doth first peepe forth with bashfull modestee,
    That fairer seemes, the lesse ye see her may;
    Lo see soone after, how more bold and free
665 Her baréd bosome she doth broad display;
    Loe see soone after, how she fades, and falles away.

75

    "So passeth, in the passing of a day,
    Of mortall life the leafe, the bud, the flowre,
    Ne more doth flourish after first decay,
670 That earst° was sought to decke both bed and bowre,   *formerly*
    Of many a Ladie, and many a Paramowre:°   *lover*
    Gather therefore the Rose, whilest yet is prime,°   *(its) springtime*
    For soone comes age, that will her pride deflowre:
    Gather the Rose of love, whilest yet is time,
675 Whilest loving thou mayst lovéd be with equal crime."

76

    He ceast, and then gan all the quire of birdes
    Their diverse notes t' attune unto his lay,

8. Acrasia—whose name means both "excess" and "impotence"—bears many resemblances to Circe (in *Odyssey* 10 as well as the more witchlike and seductive figure in Ovid's *Metamorphoses* 14) and also to the enchantresses of Italian romance who derive from Circe: Acratia in Trissino's *L'Italia liberata* and Armida in Tasso's *Gerusalemme liberata*.

Much of the description in this scene is imitated from Armida's garden.
9. The song ("lay") of stanzas 74 and 75 imitates that in *Gerusalemme liberata* 16.14–15; this is a classic statement of the *carpe florem* theme—pick the flower of youth before it fades.

As in approvance of his pleasing words.
The constant paire[1] heard all, that he did say,
680 Yet swarvèd not, but kept their forward way,
Through many covert groves, and thickets close,
In which they creeping did at last display°   discover
That wanton Ladie, with her lover lose,°   loose, wanton
Whose sleepie head she in her lap did soft dispose.

77

685 Upon a bed of Roses she was layd,
As faint through heat, or dight to° pleasant sin,   ready for
And was arayd, or rather disarayd,
All in a vele of silke and silver thin,
That hid no whit her alablaster skin,
690 But rather shewd more white, if more might bee:
More subtile web Arachne° cannot spin,   the spider
Nor the fine nets, which oft we woven see
Of scorchèd deaw, do not in th' aire more lightly flee.°   float

78

Her snowy brest was bare to readie spoyle
695 Of hungry eies, which n'ote° therewith be fild,   could not
And yet through languor of her late sweet toyle,
Few drops, more cleare then Nectar, forth distild,
That like pure Orient perles[2] adowne it trild,°   trickled
And her faire eyes sweet smyling in delight,
700 Moystened their fierie beames, with which she thrild°   pierced
Fraile harts, yet quenchèd° not; like starry light   killed
Which sparckling on the silent waves, does seeme more bright.

79

The young man sleeping by her, seemd to bee
Some goodly swayne of honorable place,°   rank
705 That certès it great pittie was to see
Him his nobilitie so foule deface;°   disgrace
A sweet regard,° and amiable grace,   demeanor
Mixèd with manly sternnesse did appeare
Yet sleeping, in his well proportioned face,
710 And on his tender lips the downy heare
Did now but freshly spring, and silken blossomes beare.

80

His warlike armes, the idle instruments
Of sleeping praise,° were hong upon a tree,   worthiness
And his brave shield, full of old moniments,°   marks of honor
715 Was fowly ra'st,° that none the signes might see;   erased
Ne for them, ne for honour carèd hee,
Ne ought, that did to his advauncement tend,
But in lewd loves, and wastfull luxuree,°   licentiousness
His dayes, his goods, his bodie he did spend:
720 O horrible enchantment, that him so did blend.°   blind

---

1. I.e., Guyon and the Palmer.   2. Lustrous pearls of the East.

81

The noble Elfe,[3] and carefull Palmer drew
  So nigh them, minding nought, but lustfull game,
  That suddein forth they on them rusht, and threw
  A subtile net, which onely for the same
725 The skilfull Palmer formally° did frame.   *expressly*
  So held them under fast, the whiles the rest
  Fled all away from feare of fowler shame.
  The faire Enchauntresse, so unwares opprest,°   *surprised*
Tryde all her arts, and all her sleights, thence out to wrest.

82

730 And eke° her lover strove: but all in vaine;   *also*
  For that same net so cunningly was wound,
  That neither guile, nor force might it distraine.°   *tear*
  They tooke them both, and both them strongly bound
  In captive bandes,° which there they readie found: *bonds*
735 But her in chaines of adamant[4] he tyde;
  For nothing else might keepe her safe and sound;
  But Verdant[5] (so he hight°) he soone untyde,   *was called*
And counsell sage in steed° thereof to him applyde.   *instead*

83

But all those pleasant bowres and Pallace brave,°   *splendid*
740 Guyon broke downe, with rigour pittilesse;
  Ne ought their goodly workmanship might save
  Them from the tempest of his wrathfulnesse,
  But that their blisse he turn'd to balefulnesse:°   *distress*
  Their groves he feld, their gardins did deface,
745 Their arbers spoyle, their Cabinets° suppresse,   *bowers*
  Their banket° houses burne, their buildings race,°   *banquet/raze*
And of the fairest late, now made the fowlest place.

84

Then led they her away, and eke that knight
  They with them led, both sorrowfull and sad:
750 The way they came, the same retourn'd they right,
  Till they arrivèd, where they lately had
  Charm'd those wild-beasts, that rag'd with furie mad.
  Which now awaking, fierce at them gan fly,
  As in their mistresse reskew, whom they lad;°   *led*
755 But them the Palmer soone did pacify.
Then Guyon askt, what meant those beastes, which there did ly.

85

Said he, "These seeming beasts are men indeed,
  Whom this Enchauntresse hath transformèd thus,
  Whylome° her lovers, which her lusts did feed,   *formerly*

3. Knight of Faerie Land, here, Guyon.
4. Steel or some other extremely hard substance.

5. His name, meaning "green," points to aspects
of his nature.

760 Now turnèd into figures hideous,
According to their mindes like monstruous."[6]
"Sad end," quoth he, "of life intemperate,
And mournefull meed° of joyes delicious: reward
But Palmer, if it mote thee so aggrate,°   please
765 Let them returnèd be unto their former state."

86

Streight way he with his vertuous° staffe them strooke,   powerful
And streight of beasts they comely men became;
Yet being men they did unmanly looke,
And starèd ghastly, some for inward shame,
770 And some for wrath, to see their captive Dame:
But one above the rest in speciall,
That had an hog beene late, hight° Grille[7] by name,   called
Repinèd greatly, and did him miscall,°   revile
That had from hoggish forme him brought to naturall.

87

775 Said Guyon, "See the mind of beastly man,
That hath so soone forgot the excellence
Of his creation, when he life began,
That now he chooseth, with vile difference,°   preference
To be a beast, and lacke intelligence."
780 To whom the Palmer thus, "The donghill kind
Delights in filth and foule incontinence:
Let Grill be Grill, and have his hoggish mind,
But let us hence depart, whilest wether serves and wind."

From The Third Booke of The Faerie Queene

Contayning
The Legend of Britomartis,[1]
or
Of Chastitie

I

It falles° me here to write of Chastity,   falls to
That fairest vertue, farre above the rest;
For which what needs me fetch from Faery
Forreine ensamples, it to have exprest?
5 Sith° it is shrinèd in my Soveraines[2] brest,   since
And form'd so lively° in each perfect part,   lifelike
That to all Ladies, which have it profest,

6. Even as their own minds were similarly monstrous. Circe changed Odysseus's companions into animals, but Odysseus had a charm to release them.
7. According to one of Plutarch's dialogues, a man named Gryllus ("fierce," "cruel"), having been changed into a hog by Circe, refused to be restored to human form by Odysseus.
1. The heroine's name is taken from Virgil's Britomartis (*Ciris* 295–305), a goddess associated with Diana, chaste goddess of the moon. Spenser intends the etymology *Brito* ("Britain") + *Mart* ("Mars," god of war).
2. Elizabeth, the Virgin Queen.

Need but behold the pourtraict° of her hart,   *picture*
If pourtrayd it might be by any living art.

2

10   But living art may not least part expresse,°   *portray*
      Nor life-resembling pencill° it can paint,[3]   *brush*
      All were it Zeuxis or Praxiteles:
      His daedale[4] hand would faile, and greatly faint,
      And her perfections with his error taint:
15   Ne Poets wit, that passeth Painter farre
      In picturing the parts of beautie daint,°   *choice*
      So hard a workmanship adventure darre,[5]
For fear through want of words her excellence to marre.

3

How then shall I, Apprentice of the skill,
20   That whylome° in divinest wits did raine,°   *formerly/reign*
      Presume so high to stretch mine humble quill?
      Yet now my lucklesse lot doth me constraine
      Hereto perforce. But O dred° Soveraine   *revered*
      Thus farre forth pardon, sith that choicest wit
25   Cannot your glorious pourtraict figure plaine
      That I in colourd showes may shadow it,[6]
And antique° praises unto present persons fit.   *ancient*

4

But if in living colours, and right hew,
      Your selfe you covet to see picturèd,
30   Who can it doe more lively, or more trew,
      Then° that sweet verse, with Nectar sprinckelèd,   *than*
      In which a gracious servant picturèd
      His Cynthia, his heavens fairest light?[7]
      That with his melting sweetnesse ravishèd,
35   And with the wonder of her beamès bright,
My senses lullèd are in slomber of delight.

5

But let that same delitious° Poet lend   *sweet*
      A little leave unto a rusticke Muse[8]
      To sing his mistresse prayse, and let him mend,
40   If ought° amis her liking may abuse: *anything*
      Ne let his fairest Cynthia refuse,
      In mirrours more then one her selfe to see,
      But either Gloriana let her chuse,

---

3. I.e., nor can any artist, however lifelike the representation, paint her heart.
4. Skillful, like the hand of Daedalus, the Greek artificer who devised wings for himself and his son Icarus, to escape from a labyrinth. Zeuxis and Praxiteles were a Greek painter and sculptor, respectively, famed for lifelike representations.
5. I.e., nor can a poet's ingenuity, which far surpasses ("passeth") that of a painter, dare to undertake such a difficult task.

6. I.e., because none can portray you as you truly are ("plaine"), may I do so by artful but imperfect images ("colourd showes"). In Platonic terms, everything in the material world is but a shadow of the true reality in the world of ideas. Britomart also foreshadows her descendant, Queen Elizabeth.
7. The reference is to Sir Walter Ralegh's poem in praise of Elizabeth, *Cynthia*.
8. Spenser, in his shepherd persona, Colin Clout.

Or in Belphoebe fashionèd to bee:
45   In th' one her rule, in th' other her rare chastitee.⁹

Canto 1

Guyon encountreth Britomart,
  faire Florimell is chaced:
Duessaes traines° and Malecastaes   *schemes*
  champions are defaced.°   *defeated*

1

The famous Briton Prince and Faerie knight,¹
  After long wayes and perilous paines endured,
  Having their wearie limbes to perfect plight°   *condition*
  Restord. and sory° wounds right well recured,°   *painful/healed*
5   Of the faire Alma² greatly were procured,°   *urged*
  To make there lenger sojourne and abode;
  But when thereto they might not be allured,
  From seeking praise, and deeds of armes abrode,
They courteous congè° tooke, and forth together yode.°   *farewell/went*

2

10   But the captived Acrasia he³ sent,
  Because of travell long, a nigher° way,   *nearer*
  With a strong gard, all reskew to prevent,
  And her to Faerie court safe to convay,
  That her for witnesse of his hard assay,°   *trial*
15   Unto his Faerie Queene he might present:
  But he himselfe betooke another way,
  To make more triall of his hardiment,°   *daring*
And seeke adventures, as he with Prince Arthur went.

3

Long so they travellèd through wastefull° wayes,   *desolate*
20   Where daungers dwelt, and perils most did wonne,°   *inhabit*
  To hunt for glorie and renowmèd praise;
  Full many Countries they did overronne,°   *pass through*
  From the uprising to the setting Sunne,
  And many hard adventures did atchieve;
25   Of all the which they honour ever wonne,
  Seeking the weake oppressèd to relieve,
And to recover right for such, as wrong did grieve.⁴

4

At last as through an open plaine they yode,°   *went*
  They spide a knight, that towards prickèd faire,⁵
30   And him beside an agèd Squire there rode,
  That seemed to couch° under his shield three-square,⁶   *stoop*

9. Diana, Phoebe, and Cynthia are all names for the goddess of the moon and of chastity. Hence Spenser's name, *Bel* ("beautiful") + *Phoebe*.
1. Guyon, the hero of Book 2, here rides with the "Briton Prince" Arthur.
2. Alma is a character in Book 2.

3. Guyon, who took the witch Acrasia prisoner in the final canto of Book 2 (above).
4. I.e., to restore their rights to those grieved by wrongs.
5. Rode in their direction.
6. With three equal sides.

As if that age bad him that burden spare,
And yield it those, that stouter could it wield:
He them espying, gan himselfe prepare,[7]
35 And on his arme addresse° his goodly shield   *make ready*
That bore a Lion passant in a golden field.[8]

5

Which seeing good Sir Guyon, deare besought
The Prince of grace,[9] to let him runne that turne.
He graunted: then the Faery quickly raught°   *seized*
40 His poinant° speare, and sharpely gan to spurne°   *sharp/spur*
His fomy° steed, whose fierie feete did burne   *covered with foam*
The verdant° grasse, as he thereon did tread;   *green*
Ne did the other backe his foot returne,
But fiercely forward came withouten dread,
45 And bent° his dreadfull speare against the others head.   *aimed*

6

They bene ymet, and both their points arrived,[1]
But Guyon drove so furious and fell,°   *fierce*
That seemed both shield and plate° it would have rived;   *armor*
Nathelesse it bore his foe not from his sell,°   *seat*
50 But made him stagger, as he were not well:
But Guyon selfe, ere well he was aware,
Nigh a speares length behind his crouper[2] fell,
Yet in his fall so well him selfe he bare,°   *bore*
That mischievous mischance his life and limbes did spare.

7

55 Great shame and sorrow of that fall he tooke;
For never yet, sith warlike armes he bore,
And shivering[3] speare in bloudie field first shooke,°   *wielded*
He found himselfe dishonorèd so sore.
Ah gentlest knight, that ever armour bore,
60 Let not thee grieve dismounted to have beene,
And brought to ground, that never wast before;
For not thy fault, but secret powre unseene,
That speare enchaunted was, which layd thee on the greene.

8

But weenedst thou what wight thee overthrew,[4]
65 Much greater griefe and shamefuller regret
For thy hard fortune then thou wouldst renew,
That of a single damzell thou wert met
On equall plaine, and there so hard beset;

---

7. Began to prepare himself.
8. Heraldic description of a walking lion, against a golden background—the arms of Brute (ancestor of Britomart), who, according to legend, founded Britain.
9. Guyon, seeing this, asked Arthur as a matter of favor (perhaps with a pun on Arthur's symbolic sig-

nificance as God's grace).
1. I.e., they came together, with each spear hitting on the other's shield.
2. The back of the saddle; i.e., he fell behind the horse a spear's length. "Rived" (line 48): torn.
3. Capable of splitting, or quivering at the ready.
4. I.e., if you knew what person overthrew you.

Even the famous Britomart it was,
Whom straunge adventure° did from Britaine fet,°   *chance/fetch*
To seeke her lover (love farre sought alas)
Whose image she had seene in Venus looking glas.

9

Full of disdainefull° wrath, he fierce uprose,   *indignant*
For to revenge that foule reprochfull shame,
And snatching his bright sword began to close
With her on foot, and stoutly forward came;
Die rather would he, then endure that same.
Which when his Palmer⁵ saw, he gan to feare
His toward° perill and untoward blame,°   *approaching/injury, shame*
Which by that new rencounter he should reare:°   *bring about*
For death sate on the point of that enchaunted speare.

10

And hasting towards him gan faire perswade,
Not to provoke misfortune, nor to weene°   *think*
His speares default to mend with cruell blade;
For by his mightie Science° he had seene   *knowledge*
The secret vertue of that weapon keene,⁶
That mortall puissance mote° not withstond: *might*
Nothing on earth mote alwaies happie° beene.   *fortunate*
Great hazard were it, and adventure fond,°   *foolish*
To loose long gotten honour with one evill hond.°   *action*

11

By such good meanes he him discounselled,°   *dissuaded*
From prosecuting his revenging rage;
And eke° the Prince like treaty° handelèd,   *also/entreaty*
His wrathfull will with reason to asswage.
And laid the blame, not to his carriage,°   *conduct*
But to his starting steed, that swarved asyde,
And to the ill purveyance° of his page,   *preparation*
That had his furnitures° not firmely tyde: *harness*
So is his angry courage° fairely° pacifyde.   *spirit/entirely*

12

Thus reconcilement was betweene them knit,
Through goodly temperance, and affection chaste,⁷
And either vowd with all their power and wit,°   *skill*
To let not others honour be defaste,
Of friend or foe, who ever it embaste,⁸
Ne armes to beare against the others syde:
In which accord the Prince was also plaste,°   *placed*

5. The Palmer (often identified as reason) was Guyon's guide in Book 2.
6. The Palmer has seen the secret power ("vertue") of Britomart's spear, which symbolizes the power of the virtue asscciated with her, chastity.

7. The special moral qualities of the two knights signify the ground of their accord.
8. I.e., neither would let the other's honor be defaced by friend or foe who might seek to degrade it.

And with that golden chaine of concord tyde.
So goodly all agreed, they forth yfere° did ryde.   *together*

13

O goodly usage of those antique times,
110   In which the sword was servant unto right;
        When not for malice and contentious crimes,
        But all for praise, and proofe of manly might,
        The martiall brood accustomèd to fight:
        Then honour was the meed° of victorie,   *reward*
115   And yet the vanquishèd had no despight:
        Let later age that noble use envie,°   *emulate*
Vile rancour to avoid, and cruell surquedrie.⁹

14

Long they thus travellèd in friendly wise,
        Through countries waste, and eke well edifyde,°   *built up*
120   Seeking adventures hard, to exercise
        Their puissance, whylome full dernely tryde:¹
        At length they came into a forrest wyde,
        Whose hideous horror and sad trembling sound
        Full griesly° seem'd: Therein they long did ryde,   *horrible*
125   Yet tract° of living creatures none they found,   *trace*
Save Beares, Lions, and Buls, which romèd them around.

15

All suddenly out of the thickest brush,
        Upon a milk-white Palfrey° all alone,   *saddle horse*
        A goodly Ladie² did foreby° them rush,   *close by*
130   Whose face did seeme as cleare° as Christall stone,   *shining*
        And eke through feare as white as whalès bone:
        Her garments all were wrought of beaten gold,
        And all her steed with tinsell° trappings shone,   *glittering*
        Which fled so fast, that nothing mote° him hold,   *might*
135   And scarse them leasure gave, her passing to behold.

16

Still as she fled, her eye she backward threw,
        As fearing evill, that pursewd her fast;
        And her faire yellow locks behind her flew,
        Loosely disperst with puffe of every blast:
140   All as a blazing starre° doth farre outcast   *i.e., comet*
        His hearie° beames, and flaming lockes dispred,   *hairy*
        At sight whereof the people stand aghast:
        But the sage wisard telles, as he has red,°   *interpreted*
That it importunes death and dolefull drerihed.°   *disaster*

---

9. The arrogance of the victor. "Rancour": the
enmity felt by the vanquished.
1. I.e., their power ("puissance") at times ("whylome") sorely ("dernely") tried.
2. Identified in the preliminary quatrain as Florimell; her name combines *flower* and *honey*.

17

145 So as they gazèd after her a while,
    Lo where a griesly Foster° forth did rush,   *horrible forester*
    Breathing out beastly lust her to defile:
    His tyreling jade° he fiercely forth did push,   *tired nag*
    Through thicke and thin, both over banke and bush
150 In hope her to attaine by hooke or crooke,
    That from his gorie sides the bloud did gush:
    Large were his limbes, and terrible his looke,
And in his clownish° hand a sharp bore speare he shooke.   *rustic*

18

Which outrage when those gentle knights did see,
155   Full of great envie and fell gealosy,
    They stayd not to avise,° who first should bee,   *consider*
    But all spurd after fast, as they mote° fly,   *might*
    To reskew her from shamefull villany.
    The Prince and Guyon equally bylive°   *with equal speed*
160   Her selfe pursewd, in hope to win thereby
    Most goodly meede,° the fairest Dame alive: *reward*
But after the foule foster Timias[3] did strive.

19

The whiles faire Britomart, whose constant mind,
    Would not so lightly follow beauties chace,[4]
165   Ne reckt of Ladies Love, did stay behind,
    And them awayted there a certaine space,
    To weet° if they would turne backe to that place: *know*
    But when she saw them gone, she forward went,
    As lay her journey, through that perlous Pace,°   *perilous passage*
170   With stedfast courage and stout hardiment;
Ne evill thing she fear'd, ne evill thing she ment.°   *intended*

20

At last as nigh out of the wood she came,
    A stately Castle farre away she spyde,
    To which her steps directly she did frame.°   *direct*
175   That Castle was most goodly edifyde,°   *built*
    And plaste for pleasure nigh that forrest syde:
    But faire before the gate a spatious plaine,
    Mantled with greene, it selfe did spredden wyde,
    On which she saw six knights, that did darraine°   *wage*
180 Fierce battell against one, with cruell might and maine.

21

Mainly° they all attonce upon him laid,   *mightily*
    And sore beset on every side around,

---

3. Arthur's squire, who also appears in Books 1 and 2. His name means "honored."

4. Florimell is here identified with Beauty; the pun chased/chaste is probably intended.

That nigh he breathlesse grew, yet nought dismaid,
Ne ever to them yielded foot of ground
185   All° had he lost much bloud through many a wound,   *although*
But stoutly dealt his blowes, and every way
To which he turnèd in his wrathfull stound,°   *his violent wrath*
Made them recoile, and fly from dred decay,°   *death*
That none of all the sixe before, him durst assay.[5]

22

190   Like dastard Curres, that having at a bay[6]
The salvage beast embost° in wearie chace,   *exhausted*
Dare not adventure on the stubborne pray,
Ne byte before, but rome from place to place,
To get a snatch, when turnèd is his face.
195   In such distresse and doubtfull° jeopardy,   *fearful*
When Britomart him saw, she ran a pace°   *apace, quickly*
Unto his reskew, and with earnest cry,
Bad those same sixe forbeare that single enimy.

23

But to her cry they list not lenden eare,
200   Ne ought the more their mightie strokes surceasse,[7]
But gathering him round about more neare,
Their direfull rancour rather did encrease;
Till that she rushing through the thickest preasse,°   *crush*
Perforce disparted their compacted gyre,[8]
205   And soone compeld to hearken unto peace:
Tho° gan she myldly of them to inquyre   *then*
The cause of their dissention and outrageous yre.°   *ire*

24

Whereto that single knight did answere frame;°   *make*
These sixe would me enforce by oddes of might,
210   To chaunge my liefe,° and love another Dame,   *dear*
That death me liefer were, then° such despight,   *than*
So unto wrong to yield my wrested right:[9]
For I love one, the truest one on ground,
Ne list me chaunge; she th' Errant Damzell[1] hight,°   *called*
215   For whose deare sake full many a bitter stownd,°   *peril*
I have endur'd, and tasted many a bloudy wound.

25

"Certès," said she, "then bene° ye sixe to blame,   *are*
To weene° your wrong by force to justifie: *think*

5. I.e., none of the six knights dared to assail him
from the front.
6. At close quarters, when a hunted animal turns
to confront its pursuers.
7. They did not wish to lend an ear, nor did they
at all stop their mighty blows.
8. Forcibly broke up their circling about the
knight.

9. I.e., death is preferable to such dishonor as to
yield my own right love of my lady under duress to
(their) wrong.
1. This epithet indicates that the lady is Una
(Truth), the heroine of Book 1: in Book 2 that epithet is specifically assigned to her. By this identification we also know the knight to be Una's
betrothed, Redcrosse, the hero of Book 1.

For knight to leave his Ladie were great shame,
220   That faithfull is, and better were to die.
All losse is lesse,² and lesse the infamie,
Then losse of love to him, that loves but one;
Ne may love be compeld by maisterie;°   *superior force*
For soone as maisterie comes, sweet love anone°   *immediately*
225   Taketh his nimble wings, and soone away is gone."

26

Then spake one of those sixe, "There dwelleth here
   Within this castle wall a Ladie faire,
Whose soveraine beautie hath no living pere,
Thereto° so bounteous and so debonaire,°   *in addition / gracious*
230   That never any mote° with her compaire.   *might*
She hath ordaind this law, which we approve,°   *uphold*
   That every knight, which doth this way repaire,°   *travel*
In case he have no Ladie, nor no love,
Shall doe unto her service never to remove.°   *leave*

27

235   "But if he have a Ladie or a Love,
   Then must he her forgoe with foule defame,°   *dishonor*
Or else with us by dint of sword approve,°   *prove*
   That she is fairer, then our fairest Dame.
As did this knight, before ye hither came."
240   "Perdie,"° said Britomart, "the choise is hard: *truly (by God)*
   But what reward had he, that overcame?"
"He should advauncèd be to high regard,"
Said they, "and have our Ladies love for his reward."

28

   "Therefore aread° Sir, if thou have a love."   *tell*
245   "Love have I sure," quoth she, "but Lady none;
Yet will I not fro mine owne love remove,
Ne to your Lady will I service done,°   *do*
   But wreake your wrongs wrought to this knight alone,³
And prove his cause." With that her mortall speare
250   She mightily aventred° towards one,   *cast*
And downe him smot, ere well aware° he weare,   *on guard*
Then to the next she rode, and downe the next did beare.

29

Ne did she stay, till three on ground she layd,
   That none of them himselfe could reare° againe;   *rise*
255   The fourth was by that other knight dismayd,°   *defeated*
All were he wearie of his former paine,
   That now there do but two of six remaine;
Which two did yield, before she did them smight.
"Ah," said she then, "now may ye all see plaine,

2. I.e., any loss (even death) is less than such a   3. I.e., visit on you the wrongs you visited on this
loss of a faithful lover.   single knight.

260   That truth is strong, and trew love most of might,
      That for his trusty servaunts doth so strongly fight."

30

"Too well we see," said they, "and prove too well
    Our faulty weaknesse,[4] and your matchlesse might:
    For thy,° faire Sir, yours be the Damozell,   *therefore*
265   Which by her owne law to your lot doth light,
    And we your liege men faith unto you plight."
    So underneath her feet their swords they mard,°   *debased*
    And after her besought, well as they might,
    To enter in, and reape the dew reward:
270 She graunted, and then in they all together far'd.°   *fared, went*

31

Long were it to describe the goodly frame,°   *structure*
    And stately port° of Castle Joyeous,   *appearance*
    (For so that Castle hight° by commune name)   *was called*
    Where they were entertaind with curteous
275   And comely glee° of many gracious   *entertainment*
    Faire Ladies, and of many a gentle knight,
    Who through a Chamber long and spacious,
    Eftsoones° them brought unto their Ladies sight,   *soon after*
That of them cleepèd° was the Lady of delight.   *named*

32

280 But for to tell the sumptuous aray
    Of that great chamber, should be labour lost:
    For living wit, I weene,° cannot display   *think*
    The royall riches and exceeding cost,
    Of every pillour and of every post;
285   Which all of purest bullion° framèd were,   *gold*
    And with great pearles and pretious stones embost,
    That the bright glister of their beamès cleare
Did sparckle forth great light, and glorious did appeare.

33

These straunger knights through passing, forth were led
290   Into an inner rowme,° whose royaltee   *room*
    And rich purveyance might uneath be red;
    Mote Princes place beseeme so deckt to bee.[5]
    Which stately manner when as they did see,
    The image of superfluous riotize,°   *immoderate extravagance*
295   Exceeding much the state of meane° degree,   *moderate*
    They greatly wondred, whence so sumptuous guize°   *fashion*
Might be maintaynd, and each gan° diversely devize.°   *began / guess*

34

The wals were round about apparellèd
    With costly clothes of Arras and of Toure,[6]

---

4. I.e., weakness because they are at fault.
5. I.e., whose rich furnishings can hardly be told; it would become a prince's palace to be so ornamented.
6. Arras and Tours (France) were famous for their tapestries.

300   In which with cunning hand was pourtrahèd°   *portrayed*
        The love of Venus and her Paramoure
        The faire Adonis, turnèd to a flowre,[7]
        A worke of rare device,° and wondrous wit.°   *design/skill*
        First did it shew the bitter balefull stowre,°   *turmoil*
305   Which her assayd with many a fervent fit,
        When first her tender hart was with his beautie smit.

35

        Then with what sleights and sweet allurements she
        Entyst the Boy, as well that art she knew,
        And wooèd him her Paramoure to be;
310   Now making girlonds of each flowre that grew,
        To crowne his golden lockes with honour dew;
        Now leading him into a secret shade
        From his Beauperes,° and from bright heavens vew,   *companions*
        Where him to sleepe she gently would perswade,
315   Or bathe him in a fountaine by some covert glade.

36

        And whilst he slept, she over him would spred
        Her mantle, coloured like the starry skyes,
        And her soft arme lay underneath his hed,
        And with ambrosiall kisses bathe his eyes;
320   And whilest he bathed, with her two crafty spyes,
        She secretly would search each daintie lim,
        And throw into the well sweet Rosemaryes,
        And fragrant violets, and Pances trim,[8]
        And ever with sweet Nectar she did sprinkle him.

37

325   So did she steale his heedelesse hart away,
        And joyed his love in secret unespyde.
        But for° she saw him bent to cruell play,   *because*
        To hunt the salvage beast in forrest wyde,
        Dreadfull° of daunger, that mote him betyde,   *fearful*
330   She oft and oft adviz'd him to refraine
        From chase of greater beasts, whose brutish pryde
        Mote breede him scath unwares:[9] but all in vaine;
        For who can shun the chaunce, that dest'ny doth ordaine?

38

        Lo, where beyond he lyeth languishing,°   *growing weak*
335   Deadly° engorèd of a great wild Bore,   *fatally*
        And by his side the Goddesse groveling°   *lying prostrate*
        Makes for him endlesse mone, and evermore
        With her soft garment wipes away the gore,

---

7. The tapestries depict the myth of Venus and Adonis—Venus's first love passion, her wooing of Adonis, their lovemaking, his wounding and death from the boar (signifying lust), and his metamorphosis to a flower (the anemone). The myth provides a reference point for the love stories that follow in Book 3.

8. Violets and pansies ("pances") have erotic associations. Rosemary ("rosemaryes") is associated with remembrance.

9. I.e., might cause him harm when he was unwary.

Which staines his snowy skin with hatefull hew:
But when she saw no helpe might him restore,
Him to a daintie flowre she did transmew,°   *transmute*
Which in that cloth was wrought, as if it lively° grew.   *living*

39

So was that chamber clad in goodly wize,
And round about it many beds° were dight,°   *couches / arranged*
As whilome° was the antique worldès guize,°   *formerly / custom*
Some for untimely ease, some for delight,
As pleasèd them to use, that use it might:
And all was full of Damzels, and of Squires,
Dauncing and reveling both day and night,
And swimming deepe in sensuall desires,
And Cupid still emongst them kindled lustfull fires.

40

And all the while sweet Musicke did divide
Her looser notes with Lydian[1] harmony;
And all the while sweet birdes thereto applide
Their daintie layes and dulcet melody,
Ay° caroling of love and jollity,   *always*
That wonder was to heare their trim consort.[2]
Which when those knights beheld, with scornefull eye,
They sdeignèd° such lascivious disport,   *disdained*
And loathed the loose demeanure of that wanton sort.°   *company*

41

Thence they were brought to that great Ladies vew,
Whom they found sitting on a sumptuous bed,
That glistred all with gold and glorious shew,°   *show*
As the proud Persian Queenes accustomèd:
She seemd a woman of great bountihed,°   *generosity*
And of rare beautie, saving that askaunce°   *sidelong*
Her wanton eyes, ill signes of womanhed,
Did roll too lightly, and too often glaunce,
Without regard of grace,[3] or comely amenaunce.°   *conduct*

42

Long worke it were, and needlesse to devize°   *describe*
Their goodly entertainement and great glee:
She causèd them be led in curteous wize
Into a bowre, disarmèd for to bee,
And chearèd well with wine and spiceree:°   *spiced wine*
The Redcrosse Knight was soone disarmèd there,
But the brave Mayd would not disarmèd bee,
But onely vented up her umbriere,[4]
And so did let her goodly visage to appere.

---

1. The mode of Greek music associated with soft, sensuous qualities and emotions.
2. Well-balanced ensemble, pleasing harmony.
3. Echoing 2 Peter 2.14: "Having eyes full of adul-tery, and that cannot cease from sin, beguiling unstable souls."
4. Raised the face guard of her helmet.

43

As when faire Cynthia, in darkesome night,
380   Is in a noyous° cloud envelopèd,   *troublesome*
      Where she may find the substaunce thin and light,
      Breakes forth her silver beames, and her bright hed
      Discovers to the world discomfited;[5]
      Of the poore traveller, that went astray,
385   With thousand blessings she is herièd;°   *praised*
      Such was the beautie and the shining ray,
With which faire Britomart gave light unto the day.

44

And eke° those six, which lately with her fought,   *also*
      Now were disarmd, and did them selves present
390   Unto her vew, and company unsoght;
      For they all seemèd curteous and gent,°   *noble*
      And all sixe brethren, borne of one parent,
      Which had them traynd in all civilitee,°   *courtly graces*
      And goodly taught to tilt and turnament;[6]
395   Now were they liegemen to this Lady free,
And her knights service ought, to hold of her in fee.[7]

45

The first of them by name Gardante hight,
      A jolly person, and of comely vew;
      The second was Parlante, a bold knight,
400   And next to him Jocante did ensew;
      Basciante did him selfe most curteous shew;
      But fierce Bacchante seemd too fell° and keene;   *fierce*
      And yet in armes Noctante[8] greater grew:
      All were faire knights, and goodly well beseene,°   *of good appearance*
405   But to faire Britomart they all but shadowes beene.

46

For she was full of amiable grace,
      And manly terrour mixèd therewithall,
      That as the one stird up affections bace,
      So th' other did mens rash desires apall,
410   And hold them backe, that would in errour fall;
      As he, that hath espide a vermeill° Rose,   *vermilion*
      To which sharpe thornes and breres° the way forstall,   *briars*
      Dare not for dread his hardy hand expose,
But wishing it far off, his idle wish doth lose.

5. I.e., as when the moon, after being hidden by a cloud, breaks forth in splendor on a world troubled by the loss of her light.
6. A tilt is an encounter between two mounted knights armed with spears; a tournament involves many knights armed with spears and swords.
7. They were feudal vassals ("liegemen") of the lady, holding all their goods and privileges from her grant and owing all knightly service to her.
8. The names of these knights denote the rungs of the ladder of lechery: gazing ("Gardante"), conversing ("Parlante"), joking ("Jocante"), kissing ("Basciante"), drunken reveling ("Bacchante," from Bacchus, god of wine), and consummation of love at night ("Noctante").

47

415　Whom when the Lady saw so faire a wight,
　　　All ignoraunt of her contrary sex,
　　　(For she her weend a fresh and lusty knight)
　　　She greatly gan enamourèd to wex,[9]
　　　And with vaine thoughts her falsèd° fancy vex:　　　　*deceived*
420　Her fickle hart conceivèd hasty fire,
　　　Like sparkes of fire, which fall in sclender flex,°　　　*flakes*
　　　That shortly brent° into extreme desire,　　　　　　*burned*
And ransackt all her veines with passiön entire.

48

Eftsoones° she grew to great impatience　　　　　　*forthwith*
425　And into terms of open outrage brust,
　　　That plaine discovered her incontinence,[1]
　　　Ne reckt° she, who her meaning did mistrust;°　　*cared/suspect*
　　　For she was given all to fleshly lust,
　　　And pourèd forth in sensuall delight,
430　That all regard of shame she had discust,°　　　　　*discarded*
　　　And meet respect of honour put to flight:
So shamelesse beauty soone becomes a loathly° sight.　　*loathsome*

49

Faire Ladies, that to love captivèd arre,
　　　And chaste desires to nourish in your mind,
435　Let not her fault your sweet affections marre,
　　　Ne° blot the bounty° of all womankind;　　　　　*nor/goodness*
　　　'Mongst thousands good one wanton Dame to find:
　　　Emongst the Roses grow some wicked weeds;
　　　For this was not to love, but lust inclind;
440　For love does alwayes bring forth bounteous deeds,
And in each gentle hart desire of honour breeds.

50

Nought so of love this looser Dame did skill,[2]
　　　But as a coale to kindle fleshly flame,
　　　Giving the bridle to her wanton will,
445　And treading under foote her honest name:
　　　Such love is hate, and such desire is shame.
　　　Still did she rove[3] at her with crafty glaunce
　　　Of her false eyes, that at her hart did ayme,
　　　And told her meaning in her countenaunce;
450　But Britomart dissembled it with ignoraunce.[4]

51

Supper was shortly dight° and downe they sat,　　　*prepared*
　　　Where they were servèd with all sumptuous fare,

---

9. I.e., she began to grow greatly enamored.
1. I.e., she soon burst forth in language so sexually explicit as to make very clear her intemperance.
2. I.e., this too-loose lady did not understand love

in that way.
3. Shoot an arrow at a mark chosen at will.
4. I.e., pretended not to know her meaning.

Whiles fruitfull Ceres, and Lyaeus fat[5]
Pourd out their plenty, without spight° or spare: grudging
455 Nought wanted there, that dainty° was and rare;   precious
And aye° the cups their bancks did overflow,   ever
And aye betweene the cups, she did prepare
Way to her love, and secret darts did throw;
But Britomart would not such guilfull message know.

52

460 So when they slakèd had the fervent heat
Of appetite with meates° of every sort,   food
The Lady did faire Britomart entreat,
Her to disarme, and with delightfull sport
To loose her warlike limbs and strong effort,[6]
465 But when she mote not thereunto be wonne,
(For she her sexe under that straunge purport
Did use to hide, and plaine apparaunce shonne:)[7]
In plainer wise to tell her grievaunce she begonne.

53

And all attonce discovered° her desire   revealed
470 With sighes, and sobs, and plaints, and piteous griefe,
The outward sparkes of her in° burning fire;   inner
Which spent in vaine, at last she told her briefe,
That but if° she did lend her short° reliefe,   unless / immediate
And do her comfort, she mote algates° dye.   must otherwise
475 But the chaste damzell, that had never priefe°   experience
Of such malengine° and fine forgerie,   deceit
Did easily beleeve her strong extremitie.

54

Full easie was for her to have beliefe,
Who by self-feeling of her feeble sexe,
480 And by long triall of the inward griefe,
Wherewith imperious love her hart did vexe,
Could judge what paines do loving harts perplexe.°   torment
Who meanes no guile, beguilèd soonest shall,
And to faire semblaunce doth light faith annexe;[8]
485 The bird, that knowes not the false fowlers call,
Into his hidden net full easily doth fall.

55

For thy° she would not in discourteise wise,°   therefore / manner
Scorne the faire offer of good will profest;
For great rebuke° it is, love to despise,   shame
490 Or rudely sdeigne° a gentle harts request;   disdain

5. Ceres is goddess of crops, Lyaeus (Bacchus) god of wine.
6. I.e., the lady entreated Britomart to unloose her "warlike limbs" from their armor and relax her martial force in delightful sport.
7. I.e., Britomart refused to disarm because she used that disguise ("strange purport") to hide her female sex.
8. I.e., one who means no guile is easily beguiled, and gives ready ("light") faith to false appearances.

But with faire countenaunce, as beseemèd best,
Her entertaynd; nath'lesse she inly deemd
Her love too light, to wooe a wandring guest:
Which she° misconstruing, thereby esteemd   *i.e., the lady*
495   That from like inward fire that outward smoke had steemd.

56

Therewith a while she her flit° fancy fed,   *flitting*
    Till she mote winne fit time for her desire,
But yet her wound still inward freshly bled,
And through her bones the false instillèd fire
500   Did spred it selfe, and venime close° inspire.   *secret*
Tho° were the tables taken all away,   *then*
And every knight, and every gentle Squire
Gan choose his dame with *Basciomani*⁹ gay,
With whom he meant to make his sport and courtly play.

57

505   Some fell to daunce, some fell to hazardry,°   *gambling*
    Some to make love,° some to make meriment,   *court, woo*
As diverse wits to divers things apply;
And all the while faire Malecasta¹ bent
Her crafty engins° to her close intent.   *wiles*
510   By this th' eternall lampes, wherewith high Jove
Doth light the lower world, were halfe yspent,
And the moist daughters of huge Atlas² strove
Into the *Ocean* deepe to drive their weary drove.°   *flock*

58

High time it seemèd then for every wight
515   Them to betake unto their kindly° rest;   *natural*
Eftsoones long waxen torches weren light,
Unto their bowres to guiden every guest:
Tho when the Britonesse saw all the rest
Avoided° quite, she gan her selfe despoile,°   *retired/undress*
520   And safe commit to her soft fethered nest,
Where through long watch, and late dayes weary toile,
She soundly slept, and carefull thoughts did quite assoile.° *dispel*

59

Now whenas all the world in silence deepe
Yshrowded was, and every mortall wight
525   Was drownèd in the depth of deadly° sleepe,   *deathlike*
Faire Malecasta, whose engrievèd spright°   *spirit*
Could find no rest in such perplexèd plight,
Lightly arose out of her wearie bed,
And under the blacke vele of guilty Night,

---

9. Italian, "I kiss your hand."
1. Now that her nature has been fully revealed by her actions, she is named: Malecasta, unchaste (*malus,* "bad" + *castus,* "chaste").

2. The seven stars in the constellation Taurus, called the daughters of Atlas. Their setting locates this episode at midnight.

530 Her with a scarlot mantle coverèd,
  That was with gold and Ermines faire envelopèd.

60

  Then panting soft, and trembling everie joynt,
   Her fearfull feete towards the bowre she moved;
   Where she for secret purpose did appoynt
535   To lodge the warlike mayd unwisely loved,
   And to her bed approching, first she prooved,°   *tested*
   Whether she slept or wakt, with her soft hand
   She softly felt, if any member mooved,
   And lent her wary eare to understand,
540 If any puffe of breath, or signe of sence she fond.

61

  Which whenas none she fond, with easie shift,°   *movement*
   For feare least her unwares she should abrayd,°   *startle*
   Th' embroderd quilt she lightly up did lift,
   And by her side her selfe she softly layd.
545   Of every finest fingers touch affrayd;
   Ne any noise she made, ne word she spake,
   But inly sigh'd. At last the royall Mayd
   Out of her quiet slomber did awake,
  And chaungd her weary side, the better ease to take.

62

550 Where feeling one close couchèd by her side,
   She lightly° lept out of her filèd° bed,   *quickly/defiled*
   And to her weapon ran, in minde to gride°   *pierce*
   The loathèd leachour. But the Dame halfe ded
   Through suddein feare and ghastly drerihed,°   *terror*
555   Did shrieke alowd, that through the house it rong,
   And the whole family therewith adred,
   Rashly° out of their rouzèd couches sprong,   *hastily*
  And to the troubled chamber all in armes did throng.

63

  And those six Knights that Ladies Champions,
560   And eke the Redcrosse knight ran to the stownd,°   *uproar*
   Halfe armd and halfe unarmd, with them attons:°   *together*
   Where when confusedly they came, they fownd
   Their Lady lying on the sencelesse grownd;
   On th' other side, they saw the warlike Mayd
565   All in her snow-white smocke, with locks unbownd,
   Threatning the point of her avenging blade,
  That with so troublous terrour they were all dismayde.

64

  About their Lady first they flockt arownd,
   Whom having laid in comfortable couch,
570   Shortly they reard out of her frosen swownd;°   *cold faint, swoon*

And afterwards they gan with fowle reproch
To stirre up strife, and troublous contecke° broch: *discord*
But by ensample of the last dayes losse,
None of them rashly durst to her approch,
575   Ne in so glorious spoile themselves embosse;[3]
Her succourd eke the Champion of the bloudy Crosse.

65

But one of those sixe knights, Gardante hight,°   *named*
Drew out a deadly bow and arrow keene,
Which forth he sent with felonous despight,°   *fierce spite*
580   And fell intent against the virgin sheene:°   *shining*
The mortall steele stayd not, till it was seene
To gore her side, yet was the wound not deepe,
But lightly rasèd° her soft silken skin,   *grazed*
That drops of purple bloud thereout did weepe,
585   Which did her lilly smock with staines of vermeil° steepe.   *vermilion*

66

Wherewith enrag'd she fiercely at them flew,
And with her flaming sword about her layd,
That none of them foule mischiefe° could eschew,°   *harm/escape*
But with her dreadfull strokes were all dismayd:
590   Here, there, and every where about her swayd
Her wrathfull steele, that none mote it abide;
And eke the Redcrosse knight gave her good aid,
Ay joyning foot to foot, and side to side,
That in short space their foes they have quite terrifide.

67

595   Tho whenas all were put to shamefull flight,
The noble Britomartis her arayd,
And her bright armes about her body dight:°   *drew*
For nothing would she lenger° there be stayd,   *longer*
Where so loose life, and so ungentle trade
600   Was usd of Knights and Ladies seeming gent:[4]
So earely ere the grosse Earthes gryesy° shade   *gray*
Was all disperst out of the firmament,
They tooke their steeds, and forth upon their journey went.

Canto 2

*The Redcrosse knight to Britomart
        describeth Artegall:
The wondrous myrrhour, by which she
        in love with him did fall.*

1

Here have I cause, in men just blame to find,
That in their proper° prayse too partiall bee,   *own*

---

3. I.e., none tries to cover himself with glory by
taking her as his spoil or booty.
4. I.e., she would not stay where such discourte-

ous and ignoble conduct ("ungentle trade") was
used by knights and ladies seemingly of gentle
birth.

And not indifferent° to woman kind,   *just*
　　To whom no share in armes and chevalrie
5　　They do impart, ne maken memorie
　　Of their brave gestes° and prowesse martiall;   *deeds*
　　Scarse do they spare to one or two or three,
　　Rowme in their writs; yet the same writing small
Does all their deeds deface, and dims their glories all.⁵

2

10　But by record of antique° times I find,   *ancient*
　　That women wont° in warres to beare most sway,   *were accustomed*
　　And to all great exploits them selves inclind:
　　Of which they still the girlond bore away,⁶
　　Till envious Men fearing their rules decay,
15　Gan coyne streight° lawes to curb their liberty;   *strict*
　　Yet sith they warlike armes have layd away,
　　They have exceld in artes and pollicy,
That now we foolish men that prayse gin eke° enuy.⁷   *also*

3

Of warlike puissaunce in ages spent,
20　Be thou faire Britomart, whose prayse I write,
　　But of all wisedome be thou precedent,°   *pattern*
　　O soveraigne Queene, whose prayse I would endite,°   *write*
　　Endite I would as dewtie doth excite;
　　But ah my rimes too rude and rugged arre,
25　When in so high an object they do lite,
　　And striving, fit to make,⁸ I feare do marre:
Thy selfe thy prayses tell, and make them knowen farre.

4

She travelling with Guyon⁹ by the way,
　　Of sundry things faire purpose° gan to find,   *conversation*
30　T' abridg their journey long, and lingring day;
　　Mongst which it fell into that Faeries mind,
　　To aske this Briton Mayd, what uncouth° wind,   *strange*
　　Brought her into those parts, and what inquest°   *quest*
　　Made her dissemble her disguisèd kind:°   *nature*
35　Faire Lady she him seemd, like Lady drest,
But fairest knight alive, when armèd was her brest.

5

Thereat she sighing softly, had no powre
　　To speake a while, ne ready answere make,
　　But with hart-thrilling throbs and bitter stowre,°   *turmoil*
40　As if she had a fever fit, did quake,
　　And every daintie limbe with horrour shake;

5. I.e., men scarcely spare room in their writings to one or two or three women, yet those brief accounts outshine all the mens' deeds and glory.
6. I.e., they always won the greatest praise ("bore the garland away") in these exploits.
7. I.e., now we foolish men begin also to envy women that praise (of excelling in arts and statesmanship).
8. I.e., to compose fitting verse.
9. A mistake for Redcrosse; see introductory lines to this canto and below, stanza 16.

And ever and anone the rosy red,
Flasht through her face, as it had been a flake°   *flash*
Of lightning, through bright heaven fulminèd;°   *thundered*
45 At last the passion past she thus him answerèd.

6

"Faire Sir, I let you weete,° that from the howre   *know*
I taken was from nourses tender pap,°   *breast*
I have beene trainèd up in warlike stowre,
To tossen speare and shield, and to affrap°   *hit*
50 The warlike ryder to his most mishap;
Sithence° I loathèd have my life to lead,   *ever since*
As Ladies wont, in pleasures wanton lap,
To finger the fine needle and nyce° thread;   *slender*
Me lever were° with point of foemans speare be dead.   *I had rather*

7

55 "All my delight on deedes of armes is set,
To hunt out perils and adventures hard,
By sea, by land, where so they may be met,
Onely for honour and for high regard,
Without respect of richesse or reward.
60 For such intent into these parts I came,
Withouten compasse, or withouten card,°   *map*
Far fro my native soyle, that is by name
The greater Britaine,[1] here to seeke for prayse and fame.

8

"Fame blazèd hath, that here in Faery lond
65 Do many famous Knightes and Ladies wonne,°   *dwell*
And many straunge adventures to be fond,
Of which great worth and worship° may be wonne;   *renown*
Which I to prove, this voyage have begonne.
But mote° I weet° of you, right curteous knight,   *might/know*
70 Tydings of one, that hath unto me donne
Late foule dishonour and reprochfull spight,
The which I seeke to wreake,° and Arthegall[2] he hight."°   *avenge/is called*

9

The word gone out, she backe againe would call,
As her repenting so to have missayd,
75 But that he it up-taking ere the fall,[3]
Her shortly answered; "Faire martiall Mayd
Certès ye misavisèd° beene, t' upbrayd   *misinformed*
A gentle knight with so unknightly blame:
For weet° ye well of all, that ever playd   *know*
80 At tilt or tourney, or like warlike game,
The noble Arthegall hath ever borne the name.°   *won the title*

---

1. Great Britain, not Brittany in France.
2. The name suggests "equal to Arthur" (Arthegall).
3. I.e., before she finished speaking.

10

"For thy° great wonder were it, if such shame   *therefore*
    Should ever enter in his bounteous thought,
    Or ever do, that mote deserven blame:⁴
85   The noble courage° never weeneth° ought,   *nature/thinks*
    That may unworthy of it selfe be thought.
    Therefore, faire Damzell, be ye well aware,
    Least° that too farre ye have your sorrow sought: *lest*
    You and your countrey both I wish welfare,°   *to fare well*
90 And honour both; for each of other worthy are."

11

The royall Mayd woxe° inly wondrous glad,   *grew*
    To heare her Love so highly magnifide,°   *extolled*
    And joyd that ever she affixèd had,
    Her hart on knight so goodly glorifide,
95   How ever finely° she it faind° to hide: *cunningly/pretended*
    The loving mother, that nine monethes did beare,
    In the deare closet of her painefull side,
    Her tender babe, it seeing safe appeare,
Doth not so much rejoyce, as she rejoycèd theare.

12

100 But to occasion him to further talke,
    To feed her humour with his pleasing stile,
    Her list in strifull termes with him to balke,⁵
    And thus replide, "How ever, Sir, ye file
    Your curteous tongue, his prayses to compile,⁶
105   It ill beseemes a knight of gentle sort,
    Such as ye have him boasted, to beguile
    A simple mayd, and worke so haynous tort,°   *wrong*
In shame of knighthood, as I largely° can report.   *at length*

13

"Let be° therefore my vengeaunce to disswade,   *cease*
110 And read,° where I that faytour° false may find."   *tell/deceiver*
    "Ah, but if reason faire might you perswade,
    To slake your wrath, and mollifie your mind,"
    Said he, "perhaps ye should it better find:
    For hardy° thing it is, to weene° by might,   *bold/think*
115   That man to hard conditions to bind,
    Or ever hope to match in equall fight,
Whose prowesse paragon saw never living wight.⁷

14

"Ne soothlich° is it easie for to read,   *truly*
    Where now on earth, or how he may be found;

4. I.e., it would be a great wonder if he would
think or do anything shameful or blameworthy.
5. It pleased her ("her list") to oppose him with
hostile words.

6. I.e., speak falsely in praise of his virtues.
7. I.e., no living person ever saw the equal of his
prowess.

120   For he ne wonneth° in one certaine stead,°   *dwells/place*
       But restlesse walketh all the world around,
       Ay doing things, that to his fame redound,
       Defending Ladies cause, and Orphans right,
       Where so he heares, that any doth confound°   *overthrow*
125   Them comfortlesse, through tyranny or might;
    So is his soveraine honour raisde to heavens hight."

15

    His feeling words her feeble sence much pleased,
       And softly sunck into her molten hart;
       Hart that is inly hurt, is greatly eased
130   With hope of thing, that may allegge° his smart;   *allay*
       For pleasing words are like to Magick art,
       That doth the charmèd Snake in slomber lay:
       Such secret ease felt gentle Britomart,
       Yet list the same efforce with faind gainesay;[8]
135   So dischord oft in Musick makes the sweeter lay.°   *song*

16

    And said, "Sir knight, these idle termes forbeare,
       And sith it is uneath° to find his haunt,°   *difficult/abode*
       Tell me some markes, by which he may appeare,
       If chaunce I him encounter paravaunt;°   *by chance*
140   For perdie° one shall other slay, or daunt:°   *surely/subdue*
       What shape, what shield, what armes, what steed, what sted,°   *mark*
       And what so else his person most may vaunt?"°   *display*
       All which the Redcrosse knight to point ared,°   *exactly declared*
       And him in every part before her fashionèd.

17

145   Yet him in every part before she knew,
       How ever list her now her knowledge faine,°   *disguise*
       Sith him whilome° in Britaine she did vew,   *formerly*
       To her revealèd in a mirrhour plaine,
       Whereof did grow her first engraffèd° paine;   *engrafted*
150   Whose root and stalke so bitter yet did tast,
       That but the fruit more sweetnesse did containe,
       Her wretched dayes in dolour she mote° wast,   *must*
       And yield the pray of love[9] to lothsome death at last.

18

    By strange occasion she did him behold,
155   And much more strangely gan to love his sight,
       As it in bookes hath written bene of old.
       In Deheubarth that now South-wales is hight,
       What time king Ryence[1] raigned, and dealèd right,

---

8. I.e., she chose to reinforce the pleasure by pretending to disagree with him.
9. I.e., yield (herself) the prey of love.

1. In Sir Thomas Malory's medieval romance, *Morte Darthur*, Reyence is a king of North Wales and enemy of Arthur.

The great Magitian Merlin had deviz'd,
160 By his deepe science,° and hell-dreadèd might,   *wizardry*
    A looking glasse,[2] right wondrously aguiz'd,°   *fashioned*
    Whose vertues through the wyde world soone were
      solemniz'd.°   *celebrated*

19

It vertue° had, to shew in perfect sight,   *power*
    What ever thing was in the world contaynd,
165 Betwixt the lowest earth and heavens hight,
    So that it to the looker appertaynd;[3]
    What ever foe had wrought,° or frend had faynd,°   *done/pretended*
    Therein discovered was, ne ought° mote pas,   *anything*
    Ne ought in secret from the same remaynd;
170 For thy° it round and hollow shapèd was,   *therefore*
Like to the world it selfe, and seem'd a world of glas.

20

Who wonders not, that reades° so wonderous worke?   *sees*
    But who does wonder, that has red the Towre,
    Wherein th' Aegyptian Phao[4] long did lurke
175 From all mens vew, that none might her discoure,°   *discover*
    Yet she might all men vew out of her bowre?
    Great Ptolomaee[5] it for his lemans° sake   *lover's*
    Ybuilded all of glasse, by Magicke powre,
    And also it impregnable did make;
180 Yet when his love was false, he with a peaze° it brake.   *blow*

21

Such was the glassie globe that Merlin made,
    And gave unto king Ryence for his gard,°   *to protect him*
    That never foes his kingdome might invade,
    But he it knew at home before he hard°   *heard*
185 Tydings thereof, and so them still debar'd.
    It was a famous Present for a Prince,
    And worthy worke of infinite reward,
    That treasons could bewray,° and foes convince;°   *reveal/vanquish*
Happie this Realme, had it remainèd ever since.

22

190 One day it fortunèd, faire Britomart
    Into her fathers closet° to repayre;°   *chamber/go*
    For nothing he from her reserv'd apart,
    Being his onely daughter and his hayre:°   *heir*
    Where when she had espyde that mirrhour fayre,
195 Her selfe a while therein she vewd in vaine;°   *to no purpose*

2. A glass globe (like that of a fortune-teller).
3. I.e., provided that it pertained to the viewer.
4. Spenser's source for this myth has not been found.
5. Ptolemy II, confused with the astronomer Ptolemy who built the lighthouse and library at Alexandria and who was considered in the Renaissance to be a magician and esoteric philosopher.

Tho° her avizing° of the vertues rare,   *then/remembering*
Which thereof spoken were, she gan againe
Her to bethinke of, that mote to her selfe pertaine.[6]

23

But as it falleth, in the gentlest harts
200   Imperious Love hath highest set his throne,
And tyrannizeth in the bitter smarts
Of them, that to him buxome° are and prone:°   *yielding/submissive*
So thought this Mayd (as maydens use° to done)   *are accustomed*
Whom fortune for her husband would allot,
205   Not that she lusted after any one;
For she was pure from blame of sinfull blot,
Yet wist° her life at last must lincke in that same knot.   *knew*

24

Eftsoones° there was presented to her eye   *soon after*
A comely knight, all arm'd in complete wize,
210   Through whose bright ventayle[7] lifted up on hye
His manly face, that did his foes agrize,°   *terrify*
And friends to termes of gentle truce entize,
Lookt foorth, as Phoebus face° out of the east,   *the sun*
Betwixt two shadie mountaines doth arize;
215   Portly° his person was, and much increast   *dignified*
Through his Heroicke grace, and honorable gest.°   *bearing*

25

His crest was coverd with a couchant Hound,[8]
And all his armour seem'd of antique mould,
But wondrous massie° and assurèd sound,   *heavy*
220   And round about yfretted° all with gold,   *decorated*
In which there written was with cyphers° old,   *letters*
Achilles armes, which Arthegall did win.[9]
And on his shield enveloped sevenfold
He bore a crownèd litle Ermilin,[1]
225   That deckt the azure field with her faire pouldred° skin.   *spotted*

26

The Damzell well did vew his personage,
And likèd well, ne further fastned not,[2]
But went her way; ne her unguilty age
Did weene, unwares, that her unlucky lot
230   Lay hidden in the bottome of the pot;[3]
Of hurt unwist° most daunger doth redound: *unknown*

6. I.e., she began to think of those things that might pertain to herself.
7. Lower moveable part of a helmet.
8. The emblem of a hound lying in crouched position, ready to spring.
9. It is traditional for heroes of romance to inherit the arms (and thereby the qualities) of Homeric and Virgilian heroes. Achilles was the greatest of the Greeks in martial prowess.

1. Achilles' shield was made of seven layers of skins. Arthegall's heraldic arms are a crowned ermine (associated with Elizabeth, the Virgin Queen) on a blue field.
2. I.e., gave no further thought to him.
3. I.e., she did not suppose that her lot would remain hidden (until revealed by Merlin).

But the false Archer, which that arrow shot
So slyly, that she did not feele the wound,
Did smyle full smoothly at her weetlesse wofull stound.[4]

27

235 Thenceforth the feather in her loftie crest,
Ruffèd of love, gan lowly to availe,[5]
And her proud portance,° and her princely gest,°   *bearing/mien*
With which she earst° tryumphèd, now did quaile:°   *formerly/decline*
Sad, solemne, sowre, and full of fancies fraile
240 She woxe,° yet wist° she neither how, nor why,   *grew/knew*
She wist not, silly° Mayd, what she did aile,   *innocent*
Yet wist, she was not well at ease perdy,°   *certainly*
Yet thought it was not love, but some melancholy.

28

So soone as Night had with her pallid° hew   *pale*
245 Defast° the beautie of the shining sky,   *defaced*
And reft from men the worlds desirèd vew,
She with her Nourse adowne to sleepe did lye;
But sleepe full farre away from her did fly:
In stead thereof sad sighes, and sorrowes deepe
250 Kept watch and ward about her warily,
That nought she did but wayle, and often steepe
Her daintie couch with teares, which closely° she did weepe.   *secretly*

29

And if that any drop of slombring rest
Did chaunce to still° into her wearie spright,   *distill*
255 When feeble nature felt her selfe opprest,
Streight way with dreames, and with fantasticke sight
Of dreadfull things the same[c] was put to flight,   *i.e., the drop of sleep*
That oft out of her bed she did astart,°   *start up*
As one with vew of ghastly feends affright:°   *terrified*
260 Tho gan she to renew her former smart,°   *pain*
And thinke of that faire visage, written in her hart.

30

One night, when she was tost with such unrest,
Her agèd Nurse, whose name was Glauce[6] hight,
Feeling her leape out of her loathèd nest,
265 Betwixt her feeble armes her quickly keight,°   *caught*
And downe againe in her warme bed her dight;°   *placed*
"Ah my deare daughter, ah my dearest dread,°   *object of anxiety*
What uncouth° fit," said she, "what evill plight   *strange*
Hath thee opprest, and with sad drearyhead°   *sorrow*
270 Chaungèd thy lively cheare,° and living made thee dead?   *expression*

---

4. I.e., Cupid wounded her (all unawares) with his arrow of love and smiled at what was to her inexplicable pain.
5. I.e., the feather in her helmet's crest, ruffled by

love, began to droop.
6. Her name associates her with the mother of the goddess Diana and, in its Greek etymology, with the owl, companion of Minerva.

31

"For not of nought these suddeine ghastly feares
All night afflict thy naturall repose,
And all the day, when as thine equall peares°   *peers*
Their fit° disports with faire delight doe chose,   *appropriate*
275   Thou in dull corners doest thy selfe inclose,
Ne tastest Princes pleasures, ne doest spred
Abroad thy fresh youthes fairest flowre, but lose
Both leafe and fruit, both too untimely shed,
As one in wilfull bale° for ever burièd.   *misery*

32

280   "The time, that mortall men their weary cares
Do lay away, and all wilde beastes do rest,
And every river eke° his course forbeares,   *also*
Then doth this wicked evill thee infest,°   *infect*
And rive° with thousand throbs thy thrillèd° brest;   *tear/pierced*
285   Like an huge Aetn°[7] of deepe engulfèd griefe,
Sorrow is heapèd in thy hollow chest,
Whence forth it breakes in sighes and anguish rife,
As smoke and sulphure mingled with confusèd strife.

33

"Aye me, how much I feare, least° love it bee;   *lest*
290   But if that love it be, as sure I read°   *discern*
By knowen signes and passions, which I see,
Be it worthy of thy race and royall sead,
Then I avow by this most sacred head
Of my deare foster child, to ease thy griefe,
295   And win thy will: Therefore away doe dread;[8]
For death nor daunger from thy dew reliefe
Shall me debarre, tell me therefore my liefest liefe."°   *dearest love*

34

So having said, her twixt her armès twaine
She straightly straynd, and collèd tenderly,[9]
300   And every trembling joynt, and every vaine°   *vein*
She softly felt, and rubbèd busily,
To doe° the frosen cold away to fly;   *make*
And her faire deawy eies with kisses deare
She oft did bath, and oft againe did dry;
305   And ever her importund, not to feare
To let the secret of her hart to her appeare.

35

The Damzell pauzd, and then thus fearefully;
"Ah Nurse, what needeth thee to eke° my paine?   *increase*
Is not enough, that I alone doe dye,

---

7. Aetna, a volcanic mountain in Sicily.
8. I.e., to gain your wish. Therefore, do away with
fear.
9. I.e., she tightly clasped and embraced tenderly.

310   But it must doubled be with death of twaine?
       For nought for me but death there doth remaine."
       "O daughter deare," said she, "despaire no whit;
       For never sore, but might a salve obtaine:
       That blinded God, which hath ye blindly smit,
315 Another arrow hath your lovers hart to hit."[1]

36

       "But mine is not," quoth she, "like others wound;
       For which° no reason can find remedy."   *i.e., my wound*
       "Was never such, but mote° the like be found,"   *may*
       Said she, "and though no reason may apply
320   Salve to your sore, yet love can higher stye,°   *fly*
       Then reasons reach, and oft hath wonders donne."
       "But neither God of love, nor God of sky
       Can doe," said she, "that, which cannot be donne."
       "Things oft impossible," quoth she, "seeme, ere begonne."

37

325 "These idle words," said she, "doe nought asswage
       My stubborne smart, but more annoyance breed,
       For no no usuall fire, no usuall rage
       It is, O Nurse, which on my life doth feed,
       And suckes the bloud, which from my hart doth bleed.
330   But since thy faithfull zeale lets me not hyde
       My crime, (if crime it be) I will it reed.°   *tell*
       Nor Prince, nor pere[2] it is, whose love hath gryde°   *pierced*
       My feeble brest of late, and launchèd° this wound wyde.   *cut*

38

       "Nor man it is, nor other living wight;
335   For then some hope I might unto me draw,
       But th' only shade and semblant of a knight,[3]
       Whose shape or person yet I never saw,
       Hath me subjected to loves cruell law:
       The same one day, as me misfortune led,
340   I in my fathers wondrous mirrhour saw,
       And pleasèd with that seeming goodly-hed,°   *goodly appearance*
       Unwares the hidden hooke with baite I swallowèd.

39

       "Sithens° it hath infixèd faster hold   *since then*
       Within my bleeding bowels,[4] and so sore
345   Now ranckleth in this same fraile fleshly mould,°   *body*
       That all mine entrailes flow with poysnous gore,
       And th' ulcer groweth daily more and more;
       Ne can my running sore find remedie,
       Other then my hard fortune to deplore,

---

1. I.e., blind Cupid, who has blindly smitten you,
has another arrow to smite your beloved's heart
with love.

2. Peer, nobleman.
3. I.e., but only the illusion and image of a knight.
4. Internal organs, seat of the tender passions.

350 And languish as the leafe falne from the tree,
Till death make one end of my dayes and miserie."

40

"Daughter," said she, "what need ye be dismayd,
Or why make ye such Monster of your mind?
Of much more uncouth° thing I was affrayd;   stranger
355 Of filthy lust, contrarie unto kind:°   nature
But this affection nothing straunge I find;
For who with reason can you aye° reprove,   ever
To love the semblant° pleasing most your mind,   image
And yield your heart, whence ye cannot remove?
360 No guilt in you, but in the tyranny of love.

41

"Not so th' Arabian Myrrhe did set her mind;
Nor so did Biblis spend her pining hart,
But loved their native flesh against all kind,
And to their purpose usèd wicked art:[5]
365 Yet playd Pasiphaë a more monstrous part,
That loved a Bull, and learnd a beast to bee;[6]
Such shamefull lusts who loaths not, which depart
From course of nature and of modestie?
Sweet love such lewdnes bands° from his faire companie.   bans

42

370 "But thine my Deare (welfare thy heart my deare)[7]
Though strange beginning had, yet fixèd is
On one, that worthy may perhaps appeare;
And certès seemes bestowèd not amis:
Joy thereof have thou and eternall blis."
375 With that upleaning on her elbow weake,
Her alablaster brest she soft did kis,
Which all that while she felt to pant and quake,
As it an Earth-quake were; at last she thus bespake.

43

"Beldame,° your words doe worke me litle ease;   good mother
380 For though my love be not so lewdly bent,
As those ye blame, yet may it nought appease
My raging smart, ne ought my flame relent,°   abate
But rather doth my helpelesse griefe augment.
For they, how ever shamefull and unkind,°   unnatural
385 Yet did possesse their horrible intent:
Short end of sorrowes they thereby did find;
So was their fortune good, though wicked were their mind.

5. Myrrha tricked her father into committing incest with her; Biblis lusted after her brother.
6. Pasiphae placed herself inside the statue of a cow to enjoy the love of a bull, to whom she bore the Minotaur.
7. I.e., may thy heart fare well (in this love adventure).

44

"But wicked fortune mine, though mind be good,
    Can have no end, nor hope of my desire,
390   But feed on shadowes, whiles I die for food,
    And like a shadow wexe,° whiles with entire   *grow*
    Affection, I doe languish and expire.
    I fonder, then° Cephisus foolish child,   *than*
    Who having vewèd in a fountaine shere°   *clear*
395   His face, was with the love thereof beguild;[8]
I fonder° love a shade, the bodie farre exild."   *more foolish*

45

"Nought like," quoth she, "for that same wretched boy
    Was of himselfe the idle Paramoure;
    Both love and lover, without hope of joy,
400   For which he faded to a watry flowre.
    But better fortune thine, and better howre,°   *occasion*
    Which lov'st the shadow of a warlike knight;
    No shadow, but a bodie hath in powre:[9]
    That bodie, wheresoever that it light,°   *lodges*
405 May learnèd be by cyphers,° or by Magicke might. *signs*

46

"But if thou may with reason yet represse
    The growing evill, ere it strength have got,
    And thee abandond wholly doe possesse,
    Against it strongly strive, and yield thee not,
410   Till thou in open field adowne be smot.[1]
    But if the passion mayster thy fraile might,
    So that needs love or death must be thy lot,
    Then I avow to thee, by wrong or right
To compasse thy desire, and find that lovèd knight."

47

415 Her chearefull words much cheard the feeble spright° *spirit*
    Of the sicke virgin, that her downe she layd
    In her warme bed to sleepe, if that she might;
    And the old-woman carefully displayd
    The clothes about her round with busie ayd;
420 So that at last a little creeping sleepe
    Surprisd her sense: She therewith well apayd,° *satisfied*
    The drunken lampe downe in the oyle did steepe,[2]
And set her by to watch, and set her by to weepe.

48

Earely the morrow next, before that day
425   His joyous face did to the world reveale,

8. Narcissus, who drowned in a pool trying to kiss his own reflection; he was then transformed into the flower that bears his name.
9. I.e., this is not really a shadow, but has a body producing it.
1. I.e., till you be struck down in battle.
2. I.e., drowned the lamplight in its own oil.

They both uprose and tooke their readie° way   *direct*
Unto the Church, their prayers to appeale,°   *offer*
With great devotion, and with litle zeale:
For the faire Damzell from the holy herse°   *ceremony*
430 Her love-sicke hart to other thoughts did steale;
And that old Dame said many an idle verse,°   *i.e., charm, incantation*
Out of her daughters hart fond fancies to reverse.°   *turn away*

49

Returnèd home, the royall Infant° fell   *princess*
Into her former fit; for why,° no powre   *because*
435 Nor guidance of her selfe in her did dwell.
But th' agèd Nurse her calling to her bowre,
Had gathered Rew, and Savine, and the flowre
Of Camphora, and Calamint, and Dill,[3]
All which she in a earthen Pot did poure,
440 And to the brim with Colt wood° did it fill,   *coltsfoot*
And many drops of milke and bloud through it did spill.

50

Then taking thrise three haires from off her head,
Them trebly breaded° in a threefold lace,   *braided*
And round about the pots mouth, bound the thread,
445 And after having whisperèd a space
Certaine sad° words, with hollow voice and bace,° *solemn / low, bass*
She to the virgin said, thrise said she it;
"Come daughter come, come; spit upon my face,
Spit thrise upon me, thrise upon me spit;
450 Th' uneven number for this businesse is most fit."

51

That sayd, her round about she from her turnd,
She turnèd her contrarie to the Sunne,
Thrise she her turnd contrary, and returnd,
All contrary, for she the right did shunne,
455 And ever what she did, was streight undonne.
So thought she to undoe her daughters love:
But love, that is in gentle brest begonne,
No idle charmes so lightly may remove,
That well can witnesse, who by triall° it does prove. *experience*

52

460 Ne ought it mote the noble Mayd avayle,[4]
Ne slake the furie of her cruell flame,
But that she still did waste, and still did wayle,
That through long languour,° and hart-burning brame° *affliction / desire*
She shortly like a pynèd ghost became,
465 Which long hath waited by the Stygian strond.[5]

3. All these medicinal herbs were thought to damp the fires of love. Glauce here attempts to cast a spell or charm to undo Britomart's love melancholy.

4. I.e., neither could it help the noble maid.
5. I.e., like one of the dead, who had to wait by the river Styx in hell until ferried to the underworld by Charon.

That when old Glauce saw, for feare least° blame   *lest*
  Of her miscarriage° should in her be fond,   *overthrow*
  She wist not how t' amend, nor how it to withstond.

From *Canto* 3

[THE VISIT TO MERLIN]

    Merlin bewrayes° to Britomart,   *reveals*
      the state of Artegall.
    And shewes the famous° Progeny   *fated*
      which from them springen shall.

1

Most sacred fire, that burnest mightily
  In living brests, ykindled first above,
  Emongst th' eternall spheres and lamping° sky,   *star-lit*
  And thence pourd into men, which men call Love;
5   Not that same, which doth base affections° move   *passions*
  In brutish minds, and filthy lust inflame,
  But that sweet fit, that doth true beautie love,
  And choseth vertue for his dearest Dame,⁶
Whence spring all noble deeds and never dying fame:

2

10 Well did Antiquitie a God thee deeme,
  That over mortall minds hast so great might,
  To order them, as best to thee doth seeme,
  And all their actions to direct aright;
  The fatall° purpose of divine foresight,   *fated*
15 Thou doest effect in destinèd descents,°   *lineages*
  Through deepe impression of thy secret might,
  And stirrèdst up th' Heroes high intents,
Which the late world admyres for wondrous moniments.°   *memorials*

3

But thy dread darts in none doe triumph more,
20 Ne braver proofe in any, of thy powre
  Shewedst thou, then in this royall Maid of yore,
  Making her seeke an unknowne Paramoure,°   *lover*
  From the worlds end, through many a bitter stowre:°   *trial*
  From whose two loynes thou afterwards did rayse
25 Most famous fruits of matrimoniall bowre,
  Which through the earth have spred their living prayse,
That fame in trompe of gold⁷ eternally displayes.

4

Begin then, O my dearest sacred Dame,
  Daughter of Phoebus and of Memorie,
30 That doest ennoble with immortall name

---

6. Spenser invokes the Neoplatonic doctrines that love is the desire for beauty, and that virtue is true beauty (see *The Courtier*, pp. 578–93).
7. I.e., the golden trumpet, emblem of good fame.

The warlike Worthies, from antiquitie,
In thy great volume of Eternitie:
Begin, O Clio,[8] and recount from hence
My glorious Soveraines goodly auncestrie,
35 Till that by dew degrees and long protense,°   duration
Thou have it lastly° brought unto her Excellence.[9]   at last

5

Full many wayes within her troubled mind,
Old Glauce cast,° to cure this Ladies griefe: considered
Full many waies she sought, but none could find,
40 Nor herbes, nor charmes, nor counsell that is chiefe
And choisest med'cine for sicke harts reliefe:
For thy° great care she tooke, and greater feare,   therefore
Least that it should her turne to foule repriefe,°   reproof
And sore reproch, when so her father deare
45 Should of his dearest daughters hard misfortune heare.

6

At last she her avisd,° that he, which made   recalled
That mirrhour, wherein the sicke Damosell
So straungely vewèd her straunge lovers shade,
To weet, the learnèd Merlin, well could tell,
50 Under what coast° of heaven the man did dwell,   region
And by what meanes his love might best be wrought:°   gained
For though beyond the Africk Ismaell,[1]
Or th' Indian Peru he were, she thought
Him forth through infinite endevour to have sought.

7

55 Forthwith themselves disguising both in straunge
And base attyre, that none might them bewray,°   discover
To Maridunum, that is now by chaunge
Of name Cayr-Merdin[2] cald, they tooke their way:
There the wise Merlin whylome wont (they say)
60 To make his wonne,[3] low underneath the ground,
In a deepe delve,° farre from the vew of day,   cave
That of no living wight he mote° be found,   might
When so he counseld with his sprights encompast round.[4]

8

And if thou ever happen that same way
65 To travell, goe to see that dreadfull place:
It is an hideous hollow cave (they say)
Under a rocke that lyes a litle space
From the swift Barry, tombling downe apace,
Emongst the woodie hilles of Dynevowre:[5]

---

8. Clio, muse of history, is invoked (instead of Calliope, muse of epic poetry) because this book incorporates a chronicle history of Britain.
9. I.e., Queen Elizabeth.
1. Africa was supposedly inhabited by the descendants of the biblical Ishmael.
2. Carmethen, in Wales.

3. I.e., Merlin was formerly accustomed ("whylome wont") to make his dwelling place ("wonne") there.
4. I.e., when he conjured with his spirits gathered around him.
5. Dynevor Castle, seat of the princes of South Wales. "Barry": the river Cadoxton in Wales.

70   But dare thou not, I charge, in any cace,
     To enter into that same balefull Bowre,
     For feare the cruell Feends should thee unwares devowre.

9

     But standing high aloft, low lay thine eare,
     And there such ghastly noise of yron chaines,
75   And brasen Caudrons thou shalt rombling heare,
     Which thousand sprights with long enduring paines
     Doe tosse,° that it will stonne° thy feeble braines,   *stir / stun*
     And oftentimes great grones, and grievous stounds,°   *roars*
     When too huge toile and labour them constraines:°   *afflicts*
80   And oftentimes loud strokes, and ringing sounds
     From under that deepe Rocke most horribly rebounds.

10

     The cause some say is this: A litle while
     Before that Merlin dyde, he did intend,
     A brasen wall in compas to compile
85   About Cairmardin,[6] and did it commend
     Unto these Sprights, to bring to perfect end.
     During which worke the Ladie of the Lake,
     Whom long he loved, for him in hast did send,
     Who thereby forst his workemen to forsake,
90   Them bound till his returne, their labour not to slake.°   *slacken*

11

     In the meane time through that false Ladies traine,°   *treachery*
     He was surprisd, and buried under beare,°   *bier*
     Ne ever to his worke returnd againe:
     Nath'lesse those feends may not their worke forbeare,
95   So greatly his commaundèment they feare,
     But there doe toyle and travell° day and night,   *travail*
     Untill that brasen wall they up doe reare:
     For Merlin had in Magicke more insight,
     Then ever him before or after living wight.[7]

12

100   For he by words could call out of the sky
     Both Sunne and Moone, and make them him obay:
     The land to sea, and sea to maineland dry,
     And darkesome night he eke° could turne to day: *also*
     Huge hostes of men he could alone dismay,°   *defeat*
105   And hostes of men of° meanest things could frame,°   *out of / create*
     When so him list° his enimies to fray:°   *he wished / terrify*
     That to this day for terror of his fame,
     The feends do quake, when any him to them does name.

---

6. I.e., Merlin intended to build ("compile") a wall of brass to encompass ("in compas") Cairmardin.

7. I.e., Merlin had more understanding of magic than any person before or after him.

13

And sooth, men say that he was not the sonne
110   Of mortall Syre, or other living wight,
But wondrously begotten, and begonne
By false illusion of a guilefull Spright,
On a faire Ladie Nonne, that whilome hight°   *was formerly called*
Matilda, daughter to Pubidius,
115   Who was the Lord of Mathravall by right,
And coosen° unto king Ambrosius:[8]   *kinsman*
Whence he induèd° was with skill so marvellous.   *endowed*

14

They here ariving, staid a while without,
    Ne durst adventure rashly in to wend,°   *go*
120   But of their first intent gan make new dout°   *scruple*
For dread of daunger, which it might portend:
Untill the hardie° Mayd (with love to frend)[9]   *bold*
First entering, the dreadfull Mage° there found   *awesome magician*
Deepe busièd bout worke of wondrous end,
125   And writing strange characters in the ground,
With which the stubborn feends he to his service bound.

15

He nought was movèd° at their entrance bold: *surprised*
For of their comming well he wist° afore,   *knew*
Yet list them bid their businesse to unfold,
130   As if ought in this world in secret store
Were from him hidden, or unknowne of yore.
Then Glauce thus, "Let not it thee offend,
That we thus rashly through thy darkesome dore,
Unwares have prest: for either fatall end,°   *fated purpose*
135   Or other mightie cause us two did hither send."

16

He bad tell on; And then she thus began.
    "Now have three Moones with borrowed brothers light,
Thrice shinèd faire, and thrice seemed dim and wan,[1]
Sith° a sore evill, which this virgin bright   *since*
140   Tormenteth, and doth plonge in dolefull plight,
First rooting tooke; but what thing it mote° bee,   *might*
Or whence it sprong, I cannot read aright:
But this I read,° that but if° remedee   *know / unless*
Thou her afford, full shortly I her dead shall see."

---

8. Spenser here elaborates on the account in Geoffrey of Monmouth's *History of the Kings of Britain* (12th century). Mathravall was one of the three divisions of Wales; Ambrosius was king just before his brother, Uther Pendragon (father of King Arthur).

9. I.e., with her love acting as a friend, encouraging her.
1. The moon, borrowing its light from the sun (Apollo, god of the sun, is brother of Diana, goddess of the moon), has gone through three cycles of waxing and waning.

17

145 Therewith th' Enchaunter softly gan to smyle
  At her smooth speeches, weeting° inly well,   *knowing*
  That she to him dissembled womanish guyle,[2]
  And to her said, "Beldame,° by that ye tell,   *good mother*
  More need of leach-craft° hath your Damozell,   *doctor's skill*
150 Then of my skill: who helpe may have elsewhere,
  In vaine seekes wonders out of Magicke spell."
  Th' old woman wox half blanck,° those words to heare;   *bewildered*
And yet was loth to let her purpose plaine appeare.

18

  And to him said, "If any leaches skill,
155 Or other learnèd meanes could have redrest°   *healed*
  This my deare daughters deepe engraffèd° ill,   *engrafted*
  Certès I should be loth thee to molest:
  But this sad evill, which doth her infest,°   *infect*
  Doth course of naturall cause farre exceed,
160 And housèd is within her hollow brest,
  That either seemes some cursèd witches deed,
Or evill spright, that in her doth such torment breed."

19

  The wisard could no lenger beare her bord,°   *idle talk*
  But brusting forth in laughter, to her sayd;
165 "Glauce, what needs this colourable° word,   *deceiving*
  To cloke the cause, that hath it selfe bewrayd?°   *revealed*
  Ne ye faire Britomartis, thus arayd,
  More hidden are, then Sunne in cloudy vele;
  Whom thy good fortune, having fate obayd,
170 Hath hither brought, for succour to appele:
The which the powres to thee are pleasèd to revele."

20

  The doubtfull° Mayd, seeing her selfe descryde,°   *apprehensive/discovered*
  Was all abasht, and her pure yvory
  Into a cleare Carnation suddeine dyde;
175 As faire Aurora rising hastily,
  Doth by her blushing tell, that she did lye
  All night in old Tithonus frosen bed,[3]
  Whereof she seemes ashamèd inwardly.
  But her old Nourse was nought dishartenèd,
180 But vauntage° made of that, which Merlin had ared.°   *opportunity/disclosed*

21

  And sayd, "Sith then thou knowest all our griefe,
  (For what doest not thou know?) of grace° I pray,   *by your favor*
  Pitty our plaint, and yield us meet° reliefe."   *fitting*

2. He knows that Glauce does understand what
ails Britomart.
3. Aurora, goddess of dawn, won for her mortal
husband, Tithonus, the boon of immortality, but
because he grows ever older she rises "hastily" from
his "frosen bed."

With that the Prophet still awhile did stay,
185   And then his spirite thus gan forth display;°   *declare*
       "Most noble Virgin, that by fatall lore°   *the teaching of fate*
       Hast learned to love, let no whit thee dismay
       The hard begin,° that meets thee in the dore,   *beginning*
       And with sharpe fits° thy tender hart oppresseth sore.   *pains*

22

190   "For so must all things excellent begin,
       And eke° enrooted deepe must be that Tree,   *also*
       Whose big embodied braunches shall not lin,°   *cease*
       Till they to heavens hight forth stretchèd bee.
       For from thy wombe a famous Progenie
195   Shall spring, out of the auncient Trojan blood,
       Which shall revive the sleeping memorie
       Of those same antique Peres, the heavens brood,
       Which Greeke and Asian rivers stainèd with their blood.[4]

23

       "Renowmèd kings, and sacred Emperours,
200   Thy fruitfull Ofspring, shall from thee descend,
       Brave Captaines, and most mighty warriours,
       That shall their conquests through all lands extend,
       And their decayèd kingdomes shall amend:°   *restore*
       The feeble Britons, broken with long warre,
205   They shall upreare,° and mightily defend   *raise up*
       Against their forrein foe, that comes from farre,
       Till universall peace compound° all civill iarre.[5]   *settle*

24

       "It was not, Britomart, thy wandring eye,
       Glauncing unwares° in charmèd looking glas,   *by chance*
210   But the streight° course of heavenly destiny,   *strict*
       Led with eternall providence, that has
       Guided thy glaunce, to bring his will to pas:
       Ne° is thy fate, ne is thy fortune ill,   *nor*
       To love the prowest° knight, that ever was.   *strongest*
215   Therefore submit thy wayes unto his will,
       And do by all dew meanes thy destiny fulfill."

25

       "But read,"° said Glauce, "thou Magitian   *tell*
       What meanes shall she out seeke, or what wayes take?
       How shall she know, how shall she find the man?
220   Or what needs her to toyle, sith fates can make
       Way for themselves, their purpose to partake?"°   *fulfill*
       Then Merlin thus; "Indeed the fates are firme,

---

4. The chroniclers usually traced the origins of the British people to Brute, great-grandson of Aeneas; the Britons are thereby descendants of the Trojan heroes ("those same antique Peres"), who were descended from the gods.
5. A brief forecasting of the long history of Britomart's descendants, concluding with the universal peace of Elizabeth's reign.

And may not shrinck, though all the world do shake:
Yet ought mens good endevours them confirme,
225 And guide the heavenly causes to their constant terme.°   *fixed ends*

26

"The man whom heavens have ordaynd to bee
The spouse of Britomart, is Arthegall:
He wonneth° in the land of Fayeree,   *dwells*
Yet is no Fary borne, ne sib° at all   *kin*
230 To Elfes, but sprong of seed terrestriall,
And whilome° by false Faries stolne away,   *formerly*
Whiles yet in infant cradle he did crall;
Ne other to himselfe is knowne this day,
But that he by an Elfe was gotten of a Fay."[6]

Summary   In the remainder of the canto, Merlin recounts a chronicle history of Britain, deriving the British kings from the union of Britomart and Arthegall (half-brother to Arthur). He narrates the struggles of Britons and Saxons, the succession of Saxon and then Norman kings, and the return of Briton rule with the Tudor monarchs; he concludes with a prophecy of Elizabeth's glorious reign. Inspired to fulfill the prophecy, Britomart takes on the role and arms of a knight, with her nurse, Glauce, as her squire.

Canto 4 *Summary*   This canto treats the story of Marinell, a figure of the sea and its riches, and Florimell, whose name suggests the rich products of the land, flowers and honey. Florimell also represents Beauty itself, which attracts all men and makes female chastity vulnerable to all. Florimell loves Marinell, but he, warned that a woman will do him deadly harm, has repudiated all women. However, the prophecy is fulfilled when he accosts Britomart (not knowing she is a woman) and she wounds him almost to the death—suggesting the opposition between Britomart's chaste love and the fear-inspired renunciations of Marinell. Seeing Florimell in flight from a lecherous forester, Arthur pursues them, but is forced to abandon his quest at nightfall.

From *Canto 5*

Summary   In stanzas 1 to 26, Arthur learns from Florimell's dwarf about her love of Marinell, Marinell's repudiation of her and its cause, and Florimell's flight from the court at the report of Marinell's supposed death. Meanwhile, Arthur's squire, Timias, fights and kills the forester and his two brothers, but the desperate fight leaves him near death himself.

[BELPHOEBE AND TIMIAS]

27

Providence heavenly passeth° living thought,   *surpasses*
And doth for wretchèd mens reliefe make way;

---

6. He is a Briton knight kidnapped in his cradle by fairies, and so he thinks himself a fairy knight. "Elf" and "Fay" refer to male and female inhabitants of Faerie Land, without connotations of the supernatural or the diminutive.

230   For loe great grace or fortune thither brought
      Comfort° to him, that comfortlesse now lay.   *help*
    In those same woods, ye well remember may,
    How that a noble hunteresse did wonne,°   *dwell*
    She, that base Braggadochio did affray,°   *frighten*
235   And made him fast out of the forrest runne;[7]
  Belphoebe was her name, as faire as Phoebus sunne.[8]

28

  She on a day, as she pursewd the chace
    Of some wild beast, which with her arrowes keene
    She wounded had, the same along did trace
240   By tract° of bloud, which she had freshly seene,   *track*
    To have besprinckled all the grassy greene;
    By the great persue,° which she there perceaved,   *track of blood*
    Well hopèd she the beast engored had beene,
    And made more hast, the life to have bereaved:[9]
245   But ah, her expectation greatly was deceaved.

29

  Shortly she came, whereas that woefull Squire
    With bloud deformèd,° lay in deadly swownd:[1]   *disfigured*
    In whose faire eyes, like lamps of quenchèd fire,
    The Christall humour° stood congealèd rownd;   *fluid*
250   His locks, like faded leaves fallen to grownd,
    Knotted with bloud, in bounches rudely° ran,   *coarsely*
    And his sweete lips, on which before that stownd° *violent attack*
    The bud of youth to blossome faire began,
  Spoild of their rosie red, were woxen° pale and wan.   *grown*

30

255   Saw never living eye more heavy sight,
    That could have made a rocke of stone to rew,°   *pity*
    Or rive° in twaine: which when that Lady bright   *split*
    Besides all hope with melting eyes did vew,
    All suddeinly abasht she chaungèd hew,
260   And with sterne horrour backward gan to start:
    But when she better him beheld, she grew
    Full of soft passion and unwonted smart:°   *unfamiliar pain*
  The point of pitty percèd through her tender hart.[2]

31

  Meekely she bowèd downe, to weete° if life   *know*
265   Yet in his frosen members did remaine,

7. In 2.3, the braggart but cowardly knight fitly named Braggadochio sought to force his love on Belphoebe and was put to ignominious flight.
8. Her name relates her to Phoebe (Diana), goddess of the moon, of the hunt, and of chastity, but also to the sun god Phoebus for her bright beauty.
9. She hoped the beast had been wounded and

hastened to finish the kill.
1. Arthur's squire, Timias, sorely wounded from his battle with the forester pursuing Florimell and the forester's two brothers.
2. An echo of Chaucer's *Knight's Tale* (line 1761): "For pitee renneth soone in gentil herte."

And feeling by his pulses beating rife,°   *strongly*
That the weake soule her seat did yet retaine,
She cast to comfort him with busie paine:°   *care*
His double folded necke she reard upright,
270   And rubd his temples, and each trembling vaine;
His maylèd haberjeon° she did undight,°   *coat of mail/undo*
And from his head his heavy burganet° did light.°   *helmet/remove*

32

Into the woods thenceforth in hast she went,
To seeke for hearbes, that mote° him remedy;   *might*
275   For she of hearbes had great intendiment,°   *understanding*
Taught of the Nymphe, which from her infancy
Her nourcèd had in trew Nobility:
There, whether it divine Tobacco were,
Or Panachaea, or Polygony.[3]
280   She found, and brought it to her patient deare
Who al this while lay bleeding out his hart-bloud neare.

33

The soveraigne weede betwixt two marbles plaine[4]
She pownded small, and did in peeces bruze,°   *crush*
And then atweene her lilly handès twaine,
285   Into his wound the juyce thereof did scruze,°   *squeeze*
And round about, as she could well it uze,
The flesh therewith she suppled° and did steepe,   *massaged*
T' abate all spasme, and soke the swelling bruze,
And after having searcht° the intuse° deepe,   *probed/wound*
290   She with her scarfe did bind the wound from cold to keepe.

34

By this he had sweete life recured° againe,   *recovered*
And groning inly deepe, at last his eyes,
His watry eyes, drizling like deawy raine,
He up gan lift toward the azure skies,
295   From whence descend all hopelesse° remedies: *unhoped for*
Therewith he sighed, and turning him aside,
The goodly Mayd full of divinities,°   *divine qualities*
And gifts of heavenly grace he by him spide,
Her bow and gilden° quiver lying him beside.   *golden*

35

300   "Mercy deare Lord," said he, "what grace is this,
That thou hast shewèd to me sinfull wight,
To send thine Angell from her bowre of blis,
To comfort me in my distressèd plight?
Angell, or Goddesse do I call thee right?

---

3. All these herbs were thought to have curative properties. This is the first reference in English literature to tobacco, introduced to England in 1584.

4. Flat pieces of marble. "Soveraigne": supremely effective for cures.

305   What service may I do unto thee meete,°   *fitting*
        That hast from darkenesse me returnd to light,[5]
        And with thy heavenly salves and med'cines sweete,
    Hast drest my sinfull wounds? I kisse thy blessèd feete."

36

    Thereat she blushing said, "Ah gentle Squire,
310   Nor Goddesse I, nor Angell, but the Mayd,
        And daughter of a woody Nymphe,[6] desire
        No service, but thy safety and ayd;
        Which if thou gaine, I shalbe well apayd.°   *repayed*
        We mortall wights, whose lives and fortunes bee
315   To commun accidents still open layd,
    Are bound with commun bond of frailtee,
To succour wretched wights, whom we captivèd see."

37

    By this her Damzels, which the former chace
        Had undertaken after her, arriv'd,
320   As did Belphoebe, in the bloudy place,
        And thereby deemd the beast had bene depriv'd
        Of life, whom late their Ladies arrow ryv'd:°   *pierced*
        For thy° the bloudy tract° they followd fast,   *therefore / track*
        And every one to runne the swiftest stryv'd;
325   But two of them the rest far overpast,
And where their Lady was, arrivèd at the last.

38

    Where when they saw that goodly boy, with blood
        Defowlèd, and their Lady dresse his wownd,
        They wondred much, and shortly understood,
330   How him in deadly case their Lady fownd,
        And reskewed out of the heavy stownd.°   *trouble*
        Eftsoones° his warlike courser, which was strayd   *soon after*
        Farre in the woods, whiles that he lay in swownd,°   *swoon*
        She made those Damzels search, which being stayd,
335 They did him set thereon, and forth with them convayd.

39

    Into that forest farre they thence him led,
        Where was their dwelling, in a pleasant glade,
        With mountaines round about environèd,
        And mighty woods, which did the valley shade,
340   And like a stately Theatre[7] it made,
        Spreading it selfe into a spatious plaine.
        And in the midst a little river plaide°   *played*
        Emongst the pumy° stones, which seemd to plaine° *pumice / complain*
    With gentle murmure, that his course they did restraine.

---

5. A biblical echo: "who hath called you out of darkness into his marvelous light" (1 Peter 2.9).
6. I.e., the woodland nymph who raised her.

7. I.e., an amphitheater formed by elements of nature.

40

345 Beside the same a dainty place there lay,
Planted with mirtle trees[8] and laurels greene,
In which the birds song many a lovely lay
Of gods high prayse, and of their loves sweet teene,°   *sorrow*
As it an earthly Paradize had beene:
350 In whose enclosèd shadow there was pight°   *placed*
A faire Pavilion, scarcely to be seene,
The which was all within most richly dight,°   *ornamented*
That greatest Princes living it mote° well delight.   *might*

41

Thither they brought that wounded Squire, and layd
355 In easie couch his feeble limbes to rest.
He rested him a while, and then the Mayd
His ready° wound with better salves new drest;   *prepared*
Dayly she dressèd him, and did the best
His grievous hurt to garish,° that she might,   *cure*
360 That shortly she his dolour° hath redrest,°   *pain/relieved*
And his foule sore reducèd to faire plight:°   *condition*
It she reducèd, but himselfe destroyed quight.

42

O foolish Physick, and unfruitfull paine,°   *labor*
That heales up one and makes another wound:
365 She his hurt thigh to him recured againe,
But hurt his hart, the which before was sound,
Through an unwary° dart, which did rebound   *unexpected*
From her faire eyes and gracious countenaunce.
What bootes it him from death to be unbound,
370 To be captivèd in endlesse duraunce°   *prison*
Of sorrow and despaire without aleggeaunce?°   *relief*

43

Still as his wound did gather,[9] and grow hole,
So still his hart woxe° sore, and health decayd: *grew*
Madnesse to save a part, and lose the whole.
375 Still whenas he beheld the heavenly Mayd,
Whiles dayly plaisters to his wound she layd,
So still his Malady the more increast,
The whiles her matchlesse beautie him dismayd.°   *conquered*
Ah God, what other could he do at least,
380 But love so faire a Lady, that his life releast?°   *saved*

44

Long while he strove in his courageous brest,
With reason dew° the passion to subdew,   *proper*
And love for to dislodge out of his nest:
Still when her excellencies he did vew,

8. Myrtles are sacred to Venus.   9. I.e., permitting the infection to be drawn out.

385 Her soveraigne bounty, and celestiall hew,
   The same to love he strongly was constraind:
   But when his meane estate° he did revew,   *humble condition*
   He from such hardy boldnesse was restraind,
  And of his lucklesse lot and cruell love thus plaind.

45

390 "Unthankfull wretch," said he, "is this the meed,°   *recompense*
   With which her soveraigne mercy thou doest quight?° *requite*
   Thy life she savèd by her gracious deed,
   But thou doest weene° with villeinous despight,° *think/wickedness*
   To blot her honour, and her heavenly light.
395 Dye rather, dye, then so disloyally
   Deeme of her high desert, or seeme so light:
   Faire death it is to shonne more shame, to dye:[1]
  Dye rather, dye, then ever love disloyally.

46

   "But if to love disloyalty it bee,
400 Shall I then hate her, that from deathès dore
   Me brought? ah farre be such reproch fro mee.
   What can I lesse do, then her love therefore,
   Sith I her dew reward cannot restore:
   Dye rather, dye, and dying do her serve,
405 Dying her serve, and living her adore;
   Thy life she gave, thy life she doth deserve:
  Dye rather, dye, then ever from her service swerve.

47

   "But foolish boy, what bootes thy service bace
   To her, to whom the heavens do serve and sew?° *pay homage*
410 Thou a meane Squire, of meeke and lowly place,
   She heavenly borne, and of celestiall hew.
   How then? of all° love taketh equall vew: *i.e., of all people*
   And doth not highest God vouchsafe to take
   The love and service of the basest crew?
415 If she will not, dye meekly for her sake;
  Dye rather, dye, then ever so faire love forsake."

48

  Thus warreid° he long time against his will,   *waged war*
   Till that through weaknesse he was forst at last,
   To yield himselfe unto the mighty ill:
420 Which as a victour proud, gan ransack fast
   His inward parts, and all his entrayles wast,
   That neither bloud in face, nor life in hart
   It left, but both did quite drye up, and blast;° *wither*
   As percing levin, which the inner part
425 Of every thing consumes, and calcineth by art.[2]

---

1. I.e., it is a worthy death to die to avoid more shame.
2. I.e., piercing lightning ("levin") disintegrates the body's inward parts, and by its action ("art") reduces everything to dust ("calcineth").

49

Which seeing faire Belphoebe, gan to feare,
    Least that his wound were inly well not healed,
    Or that the wicked steele empoysned were:
    Litle she weend,° that love he close concealed;   *thought*
430 Yet still he wasted, as the snow congealed,
    When the bright sunne his beams thereon doth beat;
    Yet never he his hart to her revealed,
    But rather chose to dye for sorrow great,
Then with dishonorable termes her to entreat.

50

435 She gracious Lady, yet no paines did spare,
    To do him ease, or do him remedy:
    Many Restoratives of vertues rare,
    And costly Cordialles° she did apply,   *medicines*
    To mitigate his stubborne mallady:
440 But that sweet Cordiall, which can restore
    A love-sick hart, she did to him envy;°   *refuse*
    To him, and to all th' unworthy world forlore°   *forsaken*
She did envy that soveraigne salve, in secret store.

51

That dainty Rose, the daughter of her Morne,
445 More deare then life she tenderèd,° whose flowre   *cherished*
    The girlond of her honour did adorne:[3]
    Ne suffred she the Middayes scorching powre,
    Ne the sharp Northerne wind thereon to showre,
    But lappèd up her silken leaves most chaire,
450 When so the froward skye began to lowre:[4]
    But soone as calmèd was the Christall aire,
She did it faire dispred, and let to florish faire.

52

Eternall God in his almighty powre,
    To make ensample of his heavenly grace,
455 In Paradize whilome° did plant this flowre;   *formerly*
    Whence he it fetcht out of her native place,
    And did in stocke of earthly flesh enrace,°   *implant*
    That mortall men her glory should admire:
    In gentle Ladies brest, and bounteous race
460 Of woman kind it fairest flowre doth spire,°   *put forth*
And beareth fruit of honour and all chast desire.

53

Faire ympes° of beautie, whose bright shining beames   *offspring*
    Adorne the world with like to heavenly light,
    And to your willes both royalties and Realmes
465 Subdew, through conquest of your wondrous might,

3. The rose is a long-enduring symbol of female virginity.
4. I.e., she folded up ("lapped") the rose's leaves most carefully ("chaire"), when the angry sky began to threaten.

With this faire flowre your goodly girlonds dight,°   *adorn*
    Of chastity and vertue virginall,
    That shall embellish more your beautie bright,
    And crowne your heades with heavenly coronall,
470   Such as the Angels weare before Gods tribunall.

54

To youre faire selves a faire ensample frame,
    Of this faire virgin, this Belphoebe faire,
    To whom in perfect love, and spotlesse fame
    Of chastitie, none living may compaire:
475   Ne poysnous Envy justly can empaire
    The prayse of her fresh flowring Maidenhead;
    For thy° she standeth on the highest staire   *therefore*
    Of th' honorable stage of womanhead,
That Ladies all may follow her ensample dead.°   *i.e., when she is dead*

55

480   In so great prayse° of stedfast chastity,   *worth*
    Nathlesse she was so curteous and kind,
    Tempred° with grace, and goodly modesty,   *mixed, balanced*
    That seemèd those two vertues strove to find
    The higher place in her Heroick mind:
485   So striving each did other more augment,
    And both encreast the prayse of woman kind,
    And both encreast her beautie excellent;
So all did make in her a perfect complement.°   *completeness*

Canto 6

The birth of faire Belphoebe and
Of Amoret is told.
The Gardins of Adonis fraught
With pleasures manifold.

1

Well may I weene, faire Ladies, all this while
    Ye wonder, how this noble Damozell
    So great perfections did in her compile,°   *gather together*
    Sith that in salvage° forests she did dwell,   *wild*
5   So farre from court and royall Citadell,
    The great schoolmistresse of all curtesy:
    Seemeth that such wild woods should far expell
    All civill° usage and gentility,   *polite*
And gentle sprite deforme with rude rusticity.

2

10   But to this faire Belphoebe in her berth
    The heavens so favourable were and free,°   *generous*
    Looking with myld aspect upon the earth,
    In th' Horoscope of her nativitee,
    That all the gifts of grace and chastitee

15   On her they pourèd forth of plenteous horne;[5]
       Jove laught on Venus from his soveraigne see,°   *throne*
       And Phoebus with faire beames did her adorne,
       And all the Graces rockt her cradle being borne.

3

       Her berth was of the wombe of Morning dew,[6]
20   And her conception of the joyous Prime,°   *springtime*
       And all her whole creation did her shew
       Pure and unspotted from all loathly crime,
       That is ingenerate in fleshly slime.[7]
       So was this virgin borne, so was she bred,[8]
25   So was she traynèd up from time to time,°   *at all times*
       In all chast vertue, and true bounti-hed°   *goodness*
       Till to her dew perfection she was ripenèd.

4

       Her mother was the faire Chrysogonee,
       The daughter of Amphisa,[9] who by race
30   A Faerie was, yborne of high degree,
       She bore Belphoebe, she bore in like cace
       Faire Amoretta in the second place:
       These two were twinnes, and twixt them two did share
       The heritage of all celestiall grace.
35   That all the rest it seem'd they robbèd bare
       Of bountie,° and of beautie, and all vertues rare.   *goodness*

5

       It were a goodly storie, to declare,
       By what straunge accident° faire Chrysogone   *happening*
       Conceivèd these infants, and how them she bare,
40   In this wild forrest wandring all alone,
       After she had nine moneths fulfild and gone:
       For not as other wemens commune brood,
       They were enwombèd in the sacred throne
       Of her chaste bodie, nor with commune food,
45   As other wemens babes, they suckèd vitall blood.

6

       But wondrously they were begot, and bred
       Through influence of th' heavens fruitfull ray,[1]
       As it in antique bookes is mentionèd.
       It was upon a Sommers shynie day,
50   When Titan[2] faire his beamès did display,

---

5. Horn of plenty, cornucopia. The planets were in favorable relationship ("myld aspect") at her birth; the combination of Jupiter ("Jove") and Venus was thought to be especially fortunate.
6. An echo of Psalm 110.3 (Book of Common Prayer): "The dew of thy birth is of the womb of the morning," taken to refer to the conception and birth of Christ.
7. Like Christ or the Virgin, she is said to be free of original sin, which is innate ("ingenerate") in

human flesh.
8. I.e., nourished in the womb.
9. Of double nature (Greek). "Chrysogonee": golden-born (Greek), alluding to Danaë, who conceived when Jove visited her as a golden shower.
1. I.e., an emanation from the heavens—continuing the analogue to the Virgin's miraculous conception of Christ.
2. The sun; the first Greek sun god, Helios, was descended from the Titans.

In a fresh fountaine, farre from all mens vew,
She bathed her brest, the boyling heat t' allay;
She bathed with roses red, and violets blew,
And all the sweetest flowres, that in the forrest grew.

7

55 Till faint through irkesome° wearinesse, adowne   *burdensome*
    Upon the grassie ground her selfe she layd
    To sleepe, the whiles a gentle slombring swowne°   *deep sleep*
    Upon her fell all naked bare displayd;
    The sunne-beames bright upon her body playd,
60   Being through former bathing mollifide,°   *softened*
    And pierst into her wombe, where they embayd°   *steeped*
    With so sweet sence° and secret power unspide,   *sensation*
That in her pregnant flesh they shortly fructifide.

8

    Miraculous may seeme to him, that reades
65   So straunge ensample of conception;
    But reason teacheth that the fruitfull seades
    Of all things living, through impression
    Of the sunbeames in moyst complexion,
    Doe life conceive and quickned are by kynd:°   *nature*
70   So after Nilus° inundation,   *the Nile*
    Infinite shapes of creatures men do fynd,
Informèd in° the mud, on which the Sunne hath shynd.[3]   *formed within*

9

    Great father he of generation
    Is rightly cald, th' author of life and light;[4]
75   And his faire sister for creation
    Ministreth matter fit, which tempred right
    With heate and humour, breedes the living wight.
    So sprong these twinnes in wombe of Chrysogone,
    Yet wist° she nought thereof, but sore affright,   *knew*
80   Wondred to see her belly so upblone,
Which still increast, till she her terme had full outgone.

10

    Whereof conceiving shame and foule disgrace,
    Albe° her guiltlesse conscience her cleard,   *albeit*
    She fled into the wildernesse a space,
85   Till that unweeldy burden she had reard,°   *brought forth*
    And shund dishonor, which as death she feard:
    Where wearie of long travell, downe to rest
    Her selfe she set, and comfortably cheard;[5]
    There a sad° cloud of sleepe her overkest,°   *heavy/overcast*
90   And seizèd every sense with sorrow sore opprest.

---

3. The theory that life was spontaneously generated by the sun's influence on the moist earth is drawn from Ovid and Lucretius.
4. The sun. His sister (the moon) is said to be propitious to generation in that it stimulates the moist fluids ("humour") of the body.
5. I.e., weary of her long travels she sat down to rest and was cheered by that comfort.

11

It fortunèd,° faire Venus having lost   *chanced*
    Her little sonne, the wingèd god of love,
    Who for some light displeasure, which him crost,
    Was from her fled, as flit as ayerie Dove,[6]
95   And left her blisfull bowre of joy above.
    (So from her often he had fled away,
    When she for ought him sharpely did reprove,
    And wandred in the world in strange aray,
Disguiz'd in thousand shapes, that none might him bewray.°)   *reveal*

12

100 Him for to seeke, she left her heavenly hous,
    The house of goodly formes and faire aspects,[7]
    Whence all the world derives the glorious
    Features of beautie, and all shapes select,°   *choice*
    With which high God his workmanship hath deckt;°   *adorned*
105 And searchèd every way, through which his wings
    Had borne him, or his tract° she mote° detect: *track/might*
    She promist kisses sweet, and sweeter things
Unto the man, that of him tydings to her brings.

13

First she him sought in Court, where most he used
110   Whylome° to haunt, but there she found him not;   *formerly*
    But many there she found, which sore accused
    His falsehood, and with foule infamous blot
    His cruell deedes and wicked wyles did spot:°   *vilify*
    Ladies and Lords she every where mote heare
115 Complayning, how with his empoysned shot
    Their wofull harts he wounded had whyleare,°   *a while before*
And so had left them languishing twixt hope and feare.

14

She then the Citties sought from gate to gate,
    And every one did aske, did he him see;
120 And every one her answerd, that too late
    He had him seene, and felt the crueltie
    Of his sharpe darts and whot artillerie;°   *hot weapons*
    And every one threw forth reproches rife
    Of his mischievous deedes, and said, That hee
125 Was the disturber of all civill life,
The enimy of peace, and author of all strife.

15

Then in the countrey she abroad him sought,
    And in the rurall cottages inquired,
    Where also many plaints to her were brought,
130 How he their heedlesse harts with love had fyred,

6. Venus's bird. Venus's search for the lost Cupid is based on a Greek poem by Moschus (2nd cen- tury B.C.E.), often imitated in the Renaissance.
7. Astrological aspects of the planet Venus.

And his false venim through their veines inspyred;
And eke° the gentle shepheard swaynes,° which sat   *also/lovers*
Keeping their fleecie flockes, as they were hyred,
She sweetly heard complaine, both how and what
135 Her sonne had to them doen; yet she did smile thereat.

16

But when in none of all these she him got,
 She gan avize,° where else he mote him hyde: *consider*
At last she her bethought, that she had not
Yet sought the salvage° woods and forrests wyde,   *wild*
140 In which full many lovely Nymphes abyde,
Mongst whom might be, that he did closely lye,
Or that the love of some of them him tyde:[8]
 For thy° she thither cast° her course t' apply,   *therefore/resolved*
To search the secret haunts of Dianes company.

17

145 Shortly unto the wastefull° woods she came,   *desolate*
 Whereas she found the Goddesse with her crew,
After late chace of their embrewèd° game,   *bloodstained*
Sitting beside a fountaine in a rew,°   *row*
Some of them washing with the liquid dew
150 From off their dainty limbes the dustie sweat,
And soyle which did deforme their lively hew;
 Others lay shaded from the scorching heat;
The rest upon her person gave attendance great.[9]

18

She having hong upon a bough on high
155 Her bow and painted quiver, had unlaste°   *unlaced*
 Her silver buskins° from her nimble thigh,   *boots*
And her lancke loynes° ungirt, and brests unbraste,   *slender hips*
After her heat the breathing cold to taste;
Her golden lockes, that late in tresses bright
160 Embreaded were for hindring of her haste,[1]
 Now loose about her shoulders hong undight,°   *unbound*
And were with sweet Ambrosia° all besprinckled light.   *perfume*

19

Soone as she Venus saw behind her backe,
 She was ashamed to be so loose surprized,
165 And woxe halfe wroth against her damzels slacke,
That had not her thereof before avized,[2]
 But suffred her so carelesly disguized°   *undressed*
Be overtaken. Soone her garments loose

---

8. I.e., bound him to them.
9. This episode alludes to the myth of Actaeon, who angered Diana by surprising her in her bath; she transformed him into a stag and he was torn apart by his own hounds.

1. I.e., her golden locks were braided ("embreaded"), lest they should hinder her swiftness.
2. I.e., she was half-angered at her nymphs, who were remiss in not warning her (of Venus's presence).

Upgath'ring, in her bosome she comprized,°   *drew together*
170   Well as she might, and to the Goddesse rose,
    Whiles all her Nymphes did like a girlond her enclose.

20

    Goodly° she gan faire Cytherea³ greet,   *courteously*
    And shortly askèd her, what cause her brought
    Into that wildernesse for her unmeet,°   *unsuitable*
175   From her sweete bowres, and beds with pleasures fraught:
    That suddein change she strange adventure° thought.   *chance*
    To whom halfe weeping, she thus answerèd,
    That she her dearest sonne Cupido sought,
    Who in his frowardnesse° from her was fled;   *stubbornness*
180 That she repented sore, to have him angerèd.

21

    Thereat Diana gan to smile, in scorne
    Of her vaine plaint, and to her scoffing sayd;
    "Great pittie sure, that ye be so forlorne°   *bereft*
    Of your gay sonne, that gives ye so good ayd
185   To your disports: ill mote ye bene apayd."⁴
    But she was more engrievèd, and replide;
    "Faire sister, ill beseemes it to upbrayd
    A dolefull heart with so disdainfull pride;
    The like that mine, may be your paine another tide.°   *time*

22

190 "As you in woods and wanton wildernesse
    Your glory set, to chace the salvage beasts,
    So my delight is all in joyfulnesse,
    In beds, in bowres, in banckets,° and in feasts: *banquets*
    And ill becomes you with your loftie creasts,°   *helmets*
195   To scorne the joy, that Jove is glad to seeke;
    We both are bound to follow heavens beheasts,
    And tend our charges with obeisance meeke:
    Spare, gentle sister, with reproch my paine to eeke.°   *augment*

23

    "And tell me, if that ye my sonne have heard,
200   To lurk emongst your Nymphes in secret wize;
    Or keepe their cabins:° much I am affeard,   *caves*
    Least° he like one of them him selfe disguize,   *lest*
    And turne his arrowes to their exercize:⁵
    So may he long himselfe full easie hide:
205   For he is faire and fresh in face and guize,
    As any Nymph (let not it be envyde.°)"   *begrudged*
    So saying every Nymph full narrowly she eyde.

3. Venus, so named in allusion to her emergence
from the sea on the island of Cythera.
4. I.e., your son aids you in your bad sports; may
you be repaid in kind by this ill trick he plays on
you.
5. I.e., he may shoot his arrows disguised as one
of Diana's hunting nymphs (also, he may shoot at
them, causing them to fall in love).

24

But Phoebe° therewith sore was angerèd,   *another name for Diana*
And sharply said; "Goe Dame, goe seeke your boy,
210 Where you him lately left, in Mars his bed;[6]
He comes not here, we scorne his foolish joy,
Ne lend we leisure to his idle toy:°   *game*
But if I catch him in this company,
By Stygian lake I vow, whose sad annoy°   *grievous affliction*
215 The Gods doe dread,[7] he dearely shall abye:°   *suffer*
Ile clip his wanton wings, that he no more shall fly."

25

Whom when as Venus saw so sore displeased,
She inly sory was, and gan relent,°   *soften*
What she had said: so her she soone appeased,
220 With sugred words and gentle blandishment,[8]
Which as a fountaine from her sweet lips went,
And wellèd goodly forth, that in short space
She was well pleasd, and forth her damzels sent,
Through all the woods, to search from place to place,
225 If any tract° of him or tydings they mote trace.   *track*

26

To search the God of love, her Nymphes she sent
Throughout the wandring forrest every where:
And after them her selfe eke° with her went   *also*
To seeke the fugitive, both farre and nere.
230 So long they sought, till they arrivèd were
In that same shadie covert, whereas lay
Faire Crysogone in slombry traunce whilere:°   *a while before*
Who in her sleepe (a wondrous thing to say)
Unwares had borne two babes, as faire as springing° day.   *dawning*

27

235 Unwares she them conceived, unwares she bore,
She bore withouten paine, that she conceived
Withouten pleasure: ne her need° implore   *nor did she need to*
Lucinaes[9] aide: which when they both perceived,
They were through wonder nigh of sense bereaved,
240 And gazing each on other, nought bespake:
At last they both agreed, her seeming grieved°   *oppressed (with sleep)*
Out of her heavy swowne not to awake,
But from her loving side the tender babes to take.

28

Up they them tooke, each one a babe uptooke,
245 And with them carried, to be fosterèd;
Dame Phoebe to a Nymph her babe betooke,°   *gave in charge*

6. Referring to Venus's love affair with Mars.
7. An oath sworn on the river Styx even the gods
feared to break.

8. In making peace with her opposite, Venus here
enacts one of her traditional roles, Concord.
9. Another name for Juno as goddess of childbirth.

To be upbrought in perfect Maydenhed,°   *virginity*
And of her selfe her name Belphoebe red:°   *called*
But Venus hers thence farre away convayd,
250   To be upbrought in goodly womanhed,
And in her litle loves stead, which was strayd,
Her Amoretta[1] cald, to comfort her dismayd.

29

She brought her to her joyous Paradize,
Where most she wonnes,° when she on earth does dwel.   *dwells*
255   So faire a place, as Nature can devize:
Whether in Paphos, or Cytheron hill,
Or it in Gnidus be, I wote not well;[2]
But well I wote° by tryall,° that this same   *know/experience*
All other pleasant places doth excell,
260   And callèd is by her lost lovers name,
The Gardin of Adonis, farre renowmd by fame.

30

In that same Gardin all the goodly flowres,
Wherewith dame Nature doth her beautifie,
And decks the girlonds° of her paramoures,   *garlands*
265   Are fetcht: there is the first seminarie°   *seedbed*
Of all things, that are borne to live and die,
According to their kindes. Long worke it were,
Here to account° the endlesse progenie   *recount*
Of all the weedes,° that bud and blossome there;   *plants*
270   But so much as doth need, must needs be counted° here.   *recounted*

31

It sited° was in fruitfull soyle of old,   *placed*
And girt in with two walles on either side;
The one of yron, the other of bright gold,
That none might thorough breake, nor over-stride:
275   And double gates it had, which opened wide,
By which both in and out men moten pas;
Th' one faire and fresh, the other old and dride:
Old Genius[3] the porter of them was,
Old Genius, the which a double nature has.

32

280   He letteth in, he letteth out to wend,
All that to come into the world desire;
A thousand thousand naked babes attend
About him day and night, which doe require,
That he with fleshly weedes would them attire:[4]

1. Because she takes the place of Cupid (Amor), she is named Amoretta, "a little love."
2. These are all shrines of Venus.
3. God of generation and so of the natural processes, birth and death. The Gardin of Adonis is a myth of Spenser's devising. See 3.1, stanzas 34–38, for the account of the traditional myth of Venus and Adonis, as portrayed in Malecasta's tapestries.
4. I.e., the souls in their preexistent state ("naked babes") request to be clothed with flesh.

285   Such as him list,° such as eternall fate   *as he chooses*
    Ordainèd hath, he clothes with sinfull mire,°   *earth*
    And sendeth forth to live in mortall state,
    Till they againe returne backe by the hinder gate.

33

    After that they againe returnèd beene,
290   They in that Gardin planted be againe;
    And grow afresh, as they had never seene
    Fleshly corruption, nor mortall paine.
    Some thousand yeares so doen they there remaine;
    And then of him are clad with other hew,°   *form*
295   Or sent into the chaungefull world againe,
    Till thither they returne, where first they grew:
    So like a wheele around they runne from old to new.[5]

34

    Ne° needs there Gardiner to set, or sow,   *neither*
    To plant or prune: for of their owne accord
300   All things, as they created were, doe grow,
    And yet remember well the mightie word,
    Which first was spoken by th' Almightie lord,
    That bad them to increase and multiply:[6]
    Ne° doe they need with water of the ford,°   *nor/stream*
305   Or of the clouds to moysten their roots dry;
    For in themselves eternall moisture they imply.°   *contain*

35

    Infinite shapes of creatures there are bred,
    And uncouth° formes, which none yet ever knew,   *strange*
    And every sort is in a sundry° bed   *separate*
310   Set by it selfe, andranckt in comely rew:°   *row*
    Some fit for reasonable soules t' indew,[7]
    Some made for beasts, some made for birds to weare,
    And all the fruitfull spawne of fishes hew°   *shape*
    In endlesse rancks along enraungèd were,
315   That seem'd the Ocean could not containe them there.

36

    Daily they grow, and daily forth are sent
    Into the world, it to replenish more;
    Yet is the stocke° not lessenèd, nor spent,   *matter*
    But still remaines in everlasting store,
320   As it at first created was of yore.
    For in the wide wombe of the world there lyes,
    In hatefull darkenesse and in deepe horrore,

---

5. The original source for Spenser's myth of cyclic generation and reincarnation is Plato's *Republic* 10 (the myth of Er).
6. "And God said unto them, Be fruitful, and multiply, and replenish the earth" (Genesis 1.28).

7. I.e., some of these shapes are fit for humans to assume. An echo of 1 Corinthians 15.39: "All flesh is not the same flesh: but there is one kind of flesh of men, another flesh of beasts, another of fishes, and another of birds."

An huge eternall Chaos, which supplyes
The substances of natures fruitfull progenyes.

37

325 All things from thence doe their first being fetch,
And borrow matter, whereof they are made,
Which when as forme and feature it does ketch,°   *take*
Becomes a bodie, and doth then invade°   *enter*
The state of life, out of the griesly° shade.   *ghastly*
330 That substance° is eterne, and bideth so,   *matter*
Ne when the life decayes, and forme does fade,
Doth it consume,° and into nothing go,   *is it destroyed*
But chaungèd is, and often altred to and fro.

38

The substance is not chaunged, nor alterèd,
335 But th' only forme° and outward fashion;   *except only the form*
For every substance is conditionèd
To change her hew, and sundry formes to don,
Meet° for her temper and complexion: *suited*
For formes are variable and decay,
340 By course of kind,° and by occasion;   *nature*
And that faire flowre of beautie fades away,
As doth the lilly fresh before the sunny ray.

39

Great enimy to it, and to all the rest,
That in the Gardin of Adonis springs,
345 Is wicked Time, who with his scyth addrest,°   *armed*
Does mow the flowring herbes and goodly things,
And all their glory to the ground downe flings,
Where they doe wither, and are fowly mard:°   *marred*
He flyes about, and with his flaggy° wings   *drooping*
350 Beates downe both leaves and buds without regard,
Ne ever pittie may relent° his malice hard.   *soften*

40

Yet pittie often did the gods relent,
To see so faire things mard, and spoylèd quight:°   *quite*
And their great mother Venus did lament
355 The losse of her deare brood, her deare delight;
Her hart was pierst with pittie at the sight,
When walking through the Gardin, them she spyde,
Yet no'te° she find redresse for such despight.°   *could not/wrong*
For all that lives, is subject to that law:
360 All things decay in time, and to their end do draw.

41

But were it not, that Time their troubler is,
All that in this delightfull Gardin growes,
Should happie be, and have immortall blis:

For here all plentie, and all pleasure flowes,
365   And sweet love gentle fits° emongst them throwes,   *i.e., fits of passion*
  Without fell rancor, or fond° gealosie;   *foolish*
  Franckly each paramour his leman knowes,[8]
  Each bird his mate, ne any does envie
Their goodly meriment, and gay felicitie.

42

370 There is continuall spring, and harvest there[9]
  Continuall, both meeting at one time:
  For both the boughes doe laughing blossomes beare,
  And with fresh colours decke the wanton Prime,°   *spring*
  And eke attonce the heavy trees they clime,
375   Which seeme to labour under their fruits lode:
  The whiles the joyous birdes make their pastime
  Emongst the shadie leaves, their sweet abode,
And their true loves without suspition tell abrode.

43

Right in the middest of that Paradise,
380   There stood a stately Mount, on whose round top
  A gloomy grove of mirtle trees[1] did rise,
  Whose shadie boughes sharpe steele did never lop,
  Nor wicked beasts their tender buds did crop,
  But like a girlond compassèd the hight,
385   And from their fruitfull sides sweet gum did drop,
  That all the ground with precious deaw bedight,
Threw forth most dainty odours, and most sweet delight.

44

And in the thickest covert of that shade,
  There was a pleasant arbour, not by art,
390   But of the trees owne inclination° made,   *inclining*
  Which knitting their rancke° braunches part to part,   *dense*
  With wanton yvie twyne entrayld athwart,[2]
  And Eglantine, and Caprifole° emong,   *honeysuckle*
  Fashiond above within their inmost part,
395   That nether Phoebus beams could through them throng,°   *press*
Nor Aeolus° sharp blast could worke them any wrong.   *god of winds*

45

And all about grew every sort° of flowre,   *species*
  To which sad lovers were transformd of yore;
  Fresh Hyacinthus, Phoebus paramoure,
400   And dearest love,[3]
  Foolish Narcisse, that likes the watry shore,

---

8. Openly each lover has intercourse with ("knowes") his mistress.
9. The coincidence of spring and autumn is characteristic of unfallen nature in Eden; other features of this description are drawn from a common literary topic, the *locus amoenus* (pleasant place).

1. Myrtle ("mirtle") trees were sacred to Venus. "Mount": with allusion to the *mons veneris*.
2. I.e., with luxuriant ivy entwined among them.
3. This quatrain is damaged—in rhyme pattern as well as in the truncated fourth line.

Sad Amaranthus, made a flowre but late,°   *only recently*
Sad Amaranthus, in whose purple gore
Me seemes I see Amintas wretched fate,
405   To whom sweet Poets verse hath given endlesse date.[4]

46

There wont° faire Venus often to enjoy   *was accustomed*
Her deare Adonis joyous company,
And reape sweet pleasure of the wanton boy;
There yet, some say, in secret he does ly,
410   Lappèd in flowres and pretious spycery,°   *spices*
By her hid from the world, and from the skill°   *knowledge*
Of Stygian Gods,[5] which doe her love envy;
But she her selfe, when ever that she will,
Possesseth° him, and of his sweetnesse takes her fill.   *i.e., sexually*

47

415   And sooth° it seemes they say: for he may not   *truth*
For ever die, and ever buried bee
In balefull night, where all things are forgot;
All° be he subject to mortalitie,   *although*
Yet is eterne in mutabilitie,
420   And by succession made perpetuall,
Transformèd oft, and chaungèd diverslie:
For him the Father of all formes they call;[6]
Therefore needs mote° he live, that living gives to all.   *must*

48

There now he liveth in eternall blis,
425   Joying° his goddesse, and of her enjoyd: *enjoying*
Ne feareth he henceforth that foe of his,
Which with his cruell tuske him deadly cloyd:°   *gored*
For that wilde Bore, the which him once annoyd,°   *injured*
She firmely hath emprisonèd for ay,
430   That her sweet love his malice mote° avoyd,   *might*
In a strong rocky Cave, which is they say,
Hewen underneath that Mount, that none him losen°   *loosen, set free*
     may.

49

There now he lives in everlasting joy,
With many of the Gods in company,
435   Which thither haunt,° and with the wingèd boy   *frequent*
Sporting himselfe in safe felicity:
Who when he[7] hath with spoiles and cruelty

4. The purple Amaranthus is a symbol of immortality; the Greek name means "unfading." By one poetic account, Amintas died for the love of Phillis and was transformed into the Amaranthus. Hyacinth and Narcissus were also transformed into flowers and thereby eternized.
5. Gods of the underworld (e.g., Pluto, Hecate, the Furies, Charon) who have a claim on Adonis in that in the usual formulation of the myth he was killed by the boar (see 3.1, stanzas 34–38).
6. Adonis imposes successive forms on enduring substance and thereby brings living creatures into being.
7. Cupid, now restored to Venus.

Ransackt the world, and in the wofull harts
Of many wretches set his triumphes hye,
440   Thither resorts, and laying his sad darts
Aside, with faire Adonis playes his wanton parts.

50

And his true love faire Psyche with him playes,[8]
    Faire Psyche to him lately reconcyld,
    After long troubles and unmeet upbrayes,°   *upbraidings*
445   With which his mother Venus her revyld,°   *reviled*
    And eke himselfe her cruelly exyld:
    But now in stedfast love and happy state
    She with him lives, and hath him borne a chyld,
    Pleasure, that doth both gods and men aggrate,°   *gratify*
450 Pleasure, the daughter of Cupid and Psyche late.°   *recently born*

51

Hither great Venus brought this infant faire,
    The younger daughter of Chrysogonee,
    And unto Psyche with great trust and care
    Committed her, yfosterèd to bee,
455   And trainèd up in true feminitee:°   *womanliness*
    Who no lesse carefully her tenderèd,°   *cared for*
    Then her owne daughter Pleasure, to whom shee
    Made her companion, and her lessonèd
In all the lore of love, and goodly womanhead.

52

460 In which when she to perfect ripenesse grew,
    Of grace and beautie noble Paragone,
    She brought her forth into the worldès vew,
    To be th' ensample of true love alone,
    And Lodestarre° of all chaste affectione,   *guiding star*
465   To all faire Ladies, that doe live on ground.
    To Faery court she came, where many one
    Admyrd her goodly haveour,° and found   *demeanor*
His feeble hart wide launchèd° with loves cruell wound. *pierced*

53

But she to none of them her love did cast,
470   Save to the noble knight Sir Scudamore,
    To whom her loving hart she linkèd fast
    In faithfull love, t' abide for evermore,
    And for his dearest sake endurèd sore,
    Sore trouble of an hainous enimy;

---

8. "Playes" suggests, as well, sexual play. Cupid abandoned Psyche when she disobeyed his command not to look on his face; she became his bride, and immortal, after enduring many severe trials imposed by Venus. The myth was often read as an allegory of the soul's trials in this life before it gains heaven.

475   Who her would forcèd have to have forlore°   *forsaken*
          Her former love, and stedfast loyalty,
          As ye may elsewhere read that ruefull history.

54

          But well I weene, ye first desire to learne,
          What end unto that fearefull Damozell,
480   Which fled so fast from that same foster stearne,[9]
          Whom with his brethren Timias slew, befell:
          That was to weet, the goodly Florimell;
          Who wandring for to seeke her lover deare,
          Her lover deare, her dearest Marinell,
485   Into misfortune fell, as ye did heare,
          And from Prince Arthur fled with wings of idle feare.

Cantos 7 and 8 *Summary*   These cantos treat the adventures of the true and false Florimells. Always in flight, Florimell narrowly escapes a series of disasters. The son of a witch in whose cottage she takes refuge is smitten with passion for her; when she escapes in the night the witch sends a hyena "that feeds on womens flesh" to capture or kill her. To escape him she leaps into the boat of an aged fisherman who promptly tries to rape her; she is saved by the god Proteus, who carries her off to his bower in the sea and presses his suit to her continually, in every shape and guise. Meantime, to save her pining son from death, the witch creates for him a false Florimell made of snow, but he loses her quickly to the braggart knight Braggadochio, who himself loses her to a stranger knight. Meanwhile, Sir Satyrane (1.6) tames the hyena and rescues the Squire of Dames (a knight whose name reflects his promiscuity) from the giantess Argante, a figure of unnatural lust in female form. These two knights meet up with a third, Paridell, and all seek shelter from a sudden thunderstorm in Malbecco's castle.

Cantos 9 and 10 *Summary*   These cantos tell the story of Paridell, Hellenore, and Malbecco. Malbecco, miser and aged husband of a young wife, Hellenore, at first refuses entrance to the three knights and to Britomart, who also seeks shelter from the storm. But at length he gives way before their show of force. At dinner Paridell woos Hellenore with all manner of courtly address. He also tells the story of Troy, identifying himself as the descendant of Paris; at Britomart's behest he carries the tale forward to the founding of Troynovant (Britain) by Aeneas's descendant, Brute. Soon after, Paridell enacts a version of Paris's rape of Helen from Menelaus: he entices Hellenore to flee with him, setting fire to the castle. The miser saves his money first and then goes after his wife (whom Paridell quickly abandons); he finds her serving as sexual partner to a band of satyrs, but she flatly refuses to leave them to return to him. He is also tricked out of his money by Braggadochio. Desperate, he wastes away and is transformed into the very allegorical essence of jealousy: "he has quight/Forgot he was a man, and *Gealosie* is hight."

9. I.e., the cruel forester pursuing Florimell (3.1).

Canto 11

Britomart chaceth Ollyphant,
findes Scudamour distrest:
Assayes° *the house of Busyrane,*   *assails*
where Loves spoyles are exprest.°   *displayed*

1

O Hatefull hellish Snake, what furie furst
    Brought thee from balefull house of Proserpine,[1]
    Where in her bosome she thee long had nurst,
    And fostred up with bitter milke of tine,°   *anguish*
5   Fowle Gealosie,[2] that turnest love divine
    To joylesse dread, and mak'st the loving hart
    With hatefull thoughts to languish and to pine,
    And feed it selfe with selfe-consuming smart?
Of all the passions in the mind thou vilest art.

2

10 O let him far be banishèd away,
    And in his stead let Love for ever dwell,
    Sweet Love, that doth his golden wings embay°   *steep*
    In blessèd Nectar,° and pure Pleasures well,   *the drink of the gods*
    Untroubled of vile feare, or bitter fell.°   *gall, rancor*
15   And ye faire Ladies, that your kingdomes make
    In th' harts of men, them governe wisely well,
    And of faire Britomart ensample take,
That was as trew in love, as Turtle to her make.[3]

3

Who with Sir Satyrane, as earst ye red,[4]
20   Forth ryding from Malbeccoes hostlesse° hous,   *inhospitable*
    Far off aspyde a young man, the which fled
    From an huge Geaunt, that with hideous
    And hatefull outrage long him chacèd thus;
    It was that Ollyphant, the brother deare
25   Of that Argante vile and vitious,
    From whom the Squire of Dames was reft whylere;° *formerly*
This all as bad as she, and worse, if worse ought° were.[5] *anything*

4

For as the sister did in feminine
    And filthy lust exceed all woman kind,
30   So he surpassèd his sex masculine,
    In beastly use that I did ever find;
    Whom when as Britomart beheld behind

1. Queen of Hades and consort of Pluto.
2. The snake is an attribute of Envy, to which Jealousy is related; also the hair of the vengeful deities, the Furies, is made up of snakes.
3. The turtledove was a common symbol of mat-rimonial love and fidelity.
4. As you saw before (in 3.10, stanza 1).
5. Ollyphant and Argante, brother and sister giants, lived in incest and practiced many other sexual evils.

The fearefull boy so greedily pursew,
    She was emmovèd in her noble mind,
35   T' employ her puissaunce° to his reskew,   *power*
    And prickèd° fiercely forward, where she him did vew.   *spurred*

5

Ne was Sir Satyrane her far behinde,
    But with like fiercenesse did ensew° the chace: *follow*
    Whom when the Gyaunt saw, he soone resinde°   *resigned*
40   His former suit, and from them fled apace;
    They after both, and boldly bad him bace,°   *challenged him*
    And each did strive the other to out-goe,
    But he them both outran a wondrous space,
    For he was long, and swift as any Roe,°   *female deer*
45 And now made better speed, t' escape his fearèd foe.

6

It was not Satyrane, whom he did feare,
    But Britomart the flowre of chastity;
    For he the powre of chast hands might not beare,
    But alwayes did their dread encounter fly:
50   And now so fast his feet he did apply,°   *direct*
    That he has gotten to a forrest neare,
    Where he is shrowded in security.
    The wood they enter, and search every where,
    They searched diversely,° so both divided were.   *in different directions*

7

55 Faire Britomart so long him followèd,
    That she at last came to a fountaine sheare,°   *clear*
    By which there lay a knight all wallowèd°   *lying prostrate*
    Upon the grassy ground, and by him neare
    His haberjeon,° his helmet, and his speare;   *coat of mail*
60   A little off, his shield was rudely throwne,
    On which the wingèd boy in colours cleare
    Depeincted° was, full easie to be knowne,   *depicted*
    And he thereby, where ever it in field was showne.[6]

8

His face upon the ground did groveling° ly,   *prone*
65   As if he had bene slombring in the shade,
    That the brave Mayd would not for courtesy,
    Out of his quiet slomber him abrade,°   *arouse*
    Nor seeme too suddeinly him to invade:°   *intrude on*
    Still as she stood, she heard with grievous throb
70   Him grone, as if his hart were peeces made,
    And with most painefull pangs to sigh and sob,
    That pitty did the Virgins hart of patience rob.

6. The knight, soon identified as Scudamore (Italian *scudo* + *amore*), takes his name from his shield on which the figure of Cupid is painted. That shield indicates both his identity and his nature.

9

At last forth breaking into bitter plaintes
   He said, "O soveraigne Lord that sit'st on hye,
75 And raignst in blis emongst thy blessèd Saintes,
   How suffrest thou such shamefull cruelty,
   So long unwreakèd° of thine enimy?   *unrevenged*
   Or hast thou, Lord, of good mens cause no heed?
   Or doth thy justice sleepe, and silent ly?
80 What booteth then° the good and righteous deed,   *what is the use of*
   If goodnesse find no grace, nor righteousnesse no meed?°   *reward*

10

"If good find grace, and righteousnesse reward,
   Why then is Amoret in caytive° band,   *captive*
   Sith° that more bounteous° creature never fared   *since/virtuous*
85 On foot, upon the face of living land?
   Or if that heavenly justice may withstand
   The wrongfull outrage of unrighteous men,
   Why then is Busirane[7] with wickèd hand
   Suffred, these seven monethes day in secret den
90 My Lady and my love so cruelly to pen?

11

"My Lady and my love is cruelly pend
   In dolefull darkenesse from the vew of day,
   Whilest deadly torments do her chast brest rend,
   And the sharpe steele doth rive° her hart in tway,°   *cut/two*
95 All for° she Scudamore will not denay.°   *because/deny*
   Yet thou vile man, vile Scudamore art sound,
   Ne° canst her ayde, ne° canst her foe dismay;°   *neither/nor/defeat*
   Unworthy wretch to tread upon the ground,
For whom so faire a Lady feeles so sore a wound."

12

100 There an huge heape of singulfes° did oppresse   *sobs*
   His strugling soule, and swelling throbs empeach°   *hinder*
   His foltring toung with pangs of drerinesse,°   *anguish*
   Choking the remnant of his plaintife speach,
   As if his dayes were come to their last reach.
105 Which when she heard, and saw the ghastly fit,
   Threatning into his life to make a breach,
   Both with great ruth° and terrour she was smit,   *pity*
Fearing least from her cage the wearie soule would flit.

13

Tho° stooping downe she him amovèd° light;   *then/touched*
110 Who therewith somewhat starting, up gan looke,

7. His name associates him with Busiris, an Egyptian king famous for his cruelty and identified with the Pharaoh of Exodus; hence, he is a symbol of tyranny.

And seeing him behind a straunger knight,
Whereas no living creature he mistooke,°   *thought to be*
With great indignaunce he that sight forsooke,
And downe againe himselfe disdainefully
115   Abjecting, th' earth with his faire forhead strooke:
Which the bold Virgin seeing, gan apply
Fit medcine to his griefe, and spake thus courtesly.

14

"Ah gentle knight, whose deepe conceivèd griefe
Well seemes t' exceede the powre of patience,
120   Yet if that heavenly grace some good reliefe
You send, submit you to high providence,
And ever in your noble hart prepense,°   *consider before*
That all the sorrow in the world is lesse,
Then vertues might, and values° confidence,   *valor's*
125   For who nill° bide the burden of distresse,   *will not*
Must not here thinke to live: for life is wretchednesse.

15

"Therefore, faire Sir, do comfort to you take,
And freely read,° what wicked felon so   *tell*
Hath outraged you, and thrald° your gentle make.°   *enslaved/lover*
130   Perhaps this hand may helpe to ease your woe,
And wreake° your sorrow on your cruell foe,   *revenge*
At least it faire endevour will apply."
Those feeling wordes so neare the quicke° did goe,   *heart*
That up his head he rearèd easily,
135   And leaning on his elbow, these few wordes let fly.

16

"What boots it plaine, that cannot be redrest,[8]
And sow vaine sorrow in a fruitlesse eare,
Sith powre of hand, nor skill of learnèd brest,
Ne worldly price cannot redeeme my deare,
140   Out of her thraldome° and continuall feare?   *slavery*
For he the tyrant, which her hath in ward°   *in his power*
By strong enchauntments and blacke Magicke leare,°   *lore*
Hath in a dungeon deepe her close embard,
And many dreadfull feends hath pointed° to her gard.   *appointed*

17

145   "There he tormenteth her most terribly,
And day and night afflicts with mortall paine.
Because to yield him love she doth deny.
Once to me yold,° not to be yold againe:[9]   *yielded*
But yet by torture he would her constraine
150   Love to conceive in her disdainfull brest:

8. What is the use of complaining for what cannot be helped.

9. Scudamore's courtship and winning of Amoret as his love is described in 4.10.

Till so she do, she must in doole° remaine,   *pain*
Ne may by living meanes be thence relest:
What boots it then to plaine, that cannot be redrest?"

18

With this sad hersall° of his heavy stresse,°   *tale/affliction*
155   The warlike Damzell was empassiond sore,
And said, "Sir knight, your cause is nothing lesse,
Then is your sorrow, certès if not more;[1]
For nothing so much pitty doth implore,
As gentle Ladies helplesse misery.
160   But yet, if please ye listen to my lore,°   *teaching*
I will with proofe of last extremity,[2]
Deliver her fro thence, or with her for you dy."

19

"Ah gentlest° knight alive," said Scudamore,   *noblest*
"What huge heroicke magnanimity[3]
165   Dwels in thy bounteous brest? what couldst thou more,
If she were thine, and thou as now am I?
O spare thy happy dayes, and them apply
To better boot,° but let me dye, that ought;   *use*
More is more losse: one is enough to dy."
170   "Life is not lost," said she, "for which is bought
Endlesse renowm, that more then death is to be sought."

20

Thus she at length perswaded him to rise,
And with her wend,° to see what new successe   *go*
Mote° him befall upon new enterprise;   *might*
175   His armes, which he had vowed to disprofesse,°   *renounce*
She gathered up and did about him dresse,
And his forwandred° steed unto him got: *wandered away*
So forth they both yfere° make their progresse,   *together*
And march not past the mountenaunce of a shot,
180   Till they arrived, whereas their purpose they did plot.[4]

21

There they dismounting, drew their weapons bold
And stoutly° came unto the Castle gate;   *bravely*
Whereas no gate they found, them to withhold,
Nor ward° to wait at morne and evening late,   *guard*
185   But in the Porch, that did them sore amate,°   *dismay*
A flaming fire, ymixt with smouldry smoke,
And stinking Sulphure, that with griesly° hate   *horrid*
And dreadfull horrour did all entraunce choke,
Enforcèd them their forward footing to revoke.°   *draw back*

---

1. I.e., your cause is worthy of your great sorrow, or even more.
2. I.e., at the extreme peril of my life.
3. Nobility of mind, which produces the highest virtues and the greatest deeds.
4. I.e., they went no further than the distance of a bow shot before they arrived at the place they purposed to go.

22

190   Greatly thereat was Britomart dismayd,
          Ne in that stownd wist,[5] how her selfe to beare;
          For daunger vaine it were, to have assayd°   *attempted*
          That cruell element, which all things feare,
          Ne none can suffer to approchen neare:
195   And turning backe to Scudamour, thus sayd;
          "What monstrous enmity provoke° we heare,   *challenge*
          Foolhardy as th' Earthes children, the which made
      Battell against the Gods?[6] so we a God invade.

23

      "Daunger without discretion to attempt,
200   Inglorious and beastlike is: therefore Sir knight,
          Aread° what course of you is safest dempt,°   *declare / deemed*
          And how we with our foe may come to fight."
          "This is." quoth he, "the dolorous despight,°   *evil*
          Which earst° to you I playnd:° for neither may   *earlier / complained of*
205   This fire be quencht by any wit or might,
          Ne yet by any meanes remov'd away,
      So mighty be th' enchauntments, which the same do stay.°   *maintain*

24

      "What is there else, but cease these fruitlesse paines,
          And leave me to my former languishing?
210   Faire Amoret must dwell in wicked chaines,
          And Scudamore here dye with sorrowing."
          "Perdy° not so," said she, "for shamefull thing   *truly*
          It were t' abandon noble chevisaunce,°   *chivalric enterprise*
          For shew of perill, without venturing:
215   Rather let try extremities of chaunce,
      Then enterprisèd prayse for dread to disavaunce."[7]

25

      Therewith resolv'd to prove her utmost might,
          Her ample shield she threw before her face,
          And her swords point directing forward right,
220   Assayld° the flame, the which eftsoones° gave place,   *assaulted / forthwith*
          And did it selfe divide with equall space,°   *equally on both sides*
          That through she passèd; as a thunder bolt
          Perceth the yielding ayre, and doth displace
          The soring clouds into sad showres ymolt;°   *melted*
225   So to her yold the flames, and did their force revolt.°   *turn back*

26

      Whom whenas Scudamour saw past the fire,
          Safe and untoucht, he likewise gan assay,

5. I.e., nor in that trouble ("stownd") did she know
("wist") what to do.
6. I.e., we are like the Titans who dared to do battle against the Olympian gods.

7. I.e., it is better to chance extreme danger than
retreat from praiseworthy enterprises because of
fear.

With greedy will, and envious desire,
And bad the stubborne flames to yield him way:
230 But cruell Mulciber[8] would not obay
His threatfull pride, but did the more augment
His mighty rage, and with imperious sway
Him forst (maulgre)° his fiercenesse to relent,°   *despite / give way*
And backe retire, all scorcht and pitifully brent.

27

235 With huge impatience he inly swelt,°   *burned*
More for great sorrow, that he could not pas,
Then for the burning torment, which he felt,
That with fell woodnesse he effiercèd was,[9]
And wilfully him throwing on the gras,
240 Did beat and bounse° his head and brest full sore;   *thump*
The whiles the Championesse now entred has
The utmost rowme,° and past the formest° dore   *outermost room / foremost*
The utmost rowme, abounding with all precious store.

28

For round about, the wals yclothed were
245 With goodly arras° of great majesty,   *tapestries*
Woven with gold and silke so close and nere,°   *tight*
That the rich metall lurkèd privily,°   *secretly*
As faining to be hid from envious eye;
Yet here, and there, and every where unwares°   *unexpectedly*
250 It shewd it selfe, and shone unwillingly;
Like a discolourd° Snake, whose hidden snares   *multicolored*
Through the greene gras his long bright burnisht backe declares.

29

And in those Tapets° weren fashionèd   *tapestries*
Many faire pourtraicts, and many a faire feate,
255 And all of love, and all of lusty-hed,
As seemèd by their semblaunt did entreat;[1]
And eke° all Cupids warres they did repeate,°   *also / recount*
And cruell battels, which he whilome° fought   *formerly*
Gainst all the Gods, to make his empire great;
260 Besides the huge massacres, which he wrought
On mighty kings and kesars,° into thraldome brought.   *caesars*

30

Therein was writ,° how often thundring Jove   *woven*
Had felt the point of his hart-percing dart,
And leaving heavens kingdome, here did rove
265 In straunge disguize, to slake his scalding smart;
Now like a Ram, faire Helle to pervart,

---

8. God of fire. The manner of Scudamore's assault
on the flames suggests why he is unsuccessful.
9. I.e., he was maddened with fierce fury.

1. I.e., the pictures ("semblaunt") seemed
to treat entirely of deeds of love and merriment
("lusty-hed").

Now like a Bull, Europa to withdraw:[2]
Ah, how the fearefull Ladies tender hart
Did lively° seeme to tremble, when she saw   *lifelike*
270 The huge seas under her t' obay her servaunts° law.   *lover's*

31

Soone after that into a golden showre
     Him selfe he chaunged faire Danaë to vew,
     And through the roofe of her strong brasen towre
     Did raine into her lap an hony dew,[3]
275   The whiles her foolish garde, that little knew
     Of such deceipt, kept th' yron dore fast bard,
     And watcht, that none should enter nor issew;°   *go out*
     Vaine was the watch, and bootlesse° all the ward,   *useless*
Whenas the God to golden hew° him selfe transfard.°   *shape / transformed*

32

280 Then was he turnd into a snowy Swan,
     To win faire Leda to his lovely° trade:[4]   *loving*
     O wondrous skill, and sweet wit° of the man,   *ingenuity*
     That her in daffadillies sleeping made,
     From scorching heat her daintie limbes to shade:
285   Whiles the proud Bird ruffing° his fethers wyde,   *ruffling*
     And brushing° his faire brest, did her invade;   *preening*
     She slept, yet twixt her eyelids closely spyde,
How towards her he rusht, and smilèd at his pryde.

33

Then shewd it, how the Thebane Semelee
290   Deceived of gealous Juno, did require
     To see him in his soveraigne majestee,
     Armd with his thunderbolts and lightning fire,
     Whence dearely she with death bought her desire.[5]
     But faire Alcmena better match did make,
295   Joying his love in likenesse more entire;
     Three nights in one, they say, that for her sake
He then did put, her pleasures lenger° to partake.[6]   *longer*

34

Twise was he seene in soaring Eagles shape,
     And with wide wings to beat the buxome° ayre,   *yielding*
300   Once, when he with Asterie did scape,
     Againe, when as the Trojane boy so faire
     He snatcht from Ida hill, and with him bare:[7]

2. A golden ram (not specifically identified in legend as Jove) came to carry away ("pervert") Helle from the fury of her stepmother Ino; Jove assumed the shape of a bull to seduce Europa and carried her over the seas.
3. In another part of the tapestry ("soone after") Jove is shown as a shower of gold, impregnating Danaë.
4. Jove became a swan to seduce Leda.
5. Juno tricked Semele into having Jove visit her in all his power; she was burned to death by lightning and thunderbolts.
6. Jove visited Alcmena in the likeness of her husband Amphitryon and made that one night the length of three.
7. Asterie changed herself into a quail to avoid Jove's advances, but he captured her as an eagle; in that form he also snatched Ganymede, who became cupbearer to the gods.

Wondrous delight it was, there to behould,
How the rude Shepheards after him did stare,
305 Trembling through feare, least° down he fallen should,   *lest*
And often to him calling, to take surer hould.

35

In Satyres shape Antiopa he snatcht:
And like a fire, when he Aegin' assayd:
A shepheard, when Mnemosyne he catcht:
310 And like a Serpent to the Thracian mayd.[8]
Whiles thus on earth great Jove these pageaunts playd,
The wingèd boy did thrust into his throne,
And scoffing, thus unto his mother sayd,
"Lo now the heavens obey to me alone,
315 And take me for their Jove, while Jove to earth is gone."

36

And thou, faire Phoebus, in thy colours bright
Wast there enwoven, and the sad distresse,
In which that boy thee plongèd, for despight,
That thou bewrayedst his mothers wantonnesse,
320 When she with Mars was meynt° in joyfulnesse: *mingled, joined*
For thy° he thrild° thee with a leaden dart,   *therefore / pierced*
To love faire Daphne, which thee lovèd lesse:[9]
Lesse she thee loved, then was thy just desart,
Yet was thy love her death, and her death was thy smart.°   *pain*

37

325 So lovedst thou the lusty° Hyacinct,   *handsome*
So lovedst thou the faire Coronis deare:
Yet both are of thy haplesse hand extinct,
Yet both in flowres do live, and love thee beare,
The one a Paunce, the other a sweet breare:[1]
330 For griefe whereof, ye mote have lively° seene   *lifelike*
The God himselfe rending his golden heare,
And breaking quite his gyrlond° ever greene,   *garland*
With other signes of sorrow and impatient teene.°   *grief*

38

Both for those two, and for his owne deare sonne,
335 The sonne of Climene he did repent,
Who bold to guide the charet of the Sunne,
Himselfe in thousand peeces fondly rent,[2]

8. Jove came as a satyr to Antiope; in fire to Aegina; as a shepherd to Mnemosyne, goddess of memory (who bore the Nine Muses); and as a serpent to Proserpina, "the Thracian maid."
9. Two stories are combined: Apollo's punishment for revealing Venus's adultery with Mars was "the sad distresse" of doting on Leucothoe; later he chased Daphne, who escaped by metamorphosis into a laurel tree. Cupid's lead-tipped arrows produce unhappiness in love.

1. Apollo accidentally killed his lover Hyacinth at a game of quoits, and transformed him into a flower ("paunce," pansy); he killed Coronis out of jealousy, but her transformation to a sweetbriar seems to be Spenser's invention.
2. Foolishly tore apart. Phaëthon, son of Apollo and Climene, extracted permission to drive the chariot of the Sun through the heavens; unable to control the horses, he killed himself and almost destroyed the world.

And all the world with flashing fier brent:
So like, that all the walles did seeme to flame.
340   Yet cruell Cupid, not herewith content,
Forst him eftsoones° to follow other game,   *soon after*
And love a Shepheards daughter for his dearest Dame.

39

He lovèd Isse for his dearest Dame,
And for her sake her cattell fed a while,
345   And for her sake a cowheard vile became.
The servant of Admetus cowheard vile,
Whiles that from heaven he suffered exile.[3]
Long were to tell each other lovely fit,°   *amorous passion*
Now like a Lyon, hunting after spoile,
350   Now like a Stag, now like a faulcon flit:°   *fleet*
All which in that faire arras was most lively writ.

40

Next unto him was Neptune[4] picturèd,
In his divine resemblance wondrous lyke:
His face was rugged, and his hoarie hed
355   Droppèd with brackish° deaw; his three-forkt Pyke   *salty*
He stearnly shooke, and therewith fierce did stryke
The raging billowes, that on every syde
They trembling stood, and made a long broad dyke,
That his swift charet might have passage wyde,
360   Which foure great Hippodames did draw in temewise tyde.

41

His sea-horses did seeme to snort amayne,°   *violently*
And from their nosethrilles° blow the brynie streame,   *nostrils*
That made the sparckling waves to smoke agayne,
And flame with gold, but the white fomy creame,
365   Did shine with silver, and shoot forth his beame.
The God himselfe did pensive seeme and sad,
And hong adowne his head, as he did dreame:
For privy° love his brest empiercèd had,   *secret*
Ne ought but deare Bisaltis[5] ay could make him glad.

42

370   He loved eke° Iphimedia deare,   *also*
And Aeolus faire daughter Arne hight,°   *called*
For whom he turnd him selfe into a Steare,°   *steer*
And fed on fodder, to beguile her sight.
Also to win Deucalions daughter bright,
375   He turnd him selfe into a Dolphin fayre;[6]

---

3. Two stories are combined: Apollo disguising himself as a shepherd to gain Isse, and serving Admetus as a cowherd.
4. Neptune, god of the sea, is here portrayed with his trident ("three-forkt Pyke") and riding in a chariot ("charet") drawn by a team of four sea horses ("Hippodames").

5. In Greek myth it was Bisaltes's daughter Theophane who made Neptune happy: he made love to her in the form of a ram.
6. Neptune came to Iphimedia as a flowing river, to Arne as a steer, and to Deucalion's daughter Melantho as a dolphin.

And like a wingèd horse he tooke his flight,
To snaky-locke Medusa to repayre,
On whom he got faire Pegasus, that flitteth in the ayre.[7]

43

Next Saturne was, (but who would ever weene,°   *think*
380   That sullein Saturne ever weend° to love?   *was minded*
Yet love is sullein,° and Saturnlike seene,   *melancholy*
As he did for Erigone it prove,)
That to a Centaure did him selfe transmove.
So prooved it eke that gracious° God of wine,   *graceful*
385   When for to compasse Philliras hard love,
He turnd himselfe into a fruitfull vine,
And into her faire bosome made his grapes decline.[8]

44

Long were to tell the amorous assayes,°   *assaults*
And gentle pangues, with which he° makèd meeke   *i.e., Cupid*
390   The mighty Mars, to learne his wanton playes:
How oft for Venus, and how often eek
For many other Nymphes he sore did shreek,
With womanish teares, and with unwarlike smarts,° *pains*
Privily° moystening his horrid° cheek.   *secretly/bristly*
395   There was he painted full of burning darts,
And many wide woundes launchèd° through his inner parts. *torn*

45

Ne did he spare (so cruell was the Elfe)
His owne deare mother, (ah why should he so?)
Ne did he spare sometime to pricke himselfe,
400   That he might tast the sweet consuming woe,
Which he had wrought to many others moe.°   *more*
But to declare the mournfull Tragedyes,
And spoiles, wherewith he all the ground did strow,
More eath° to number, with how many eyes   *easy*
405 High heaven beholds sad lovers nightly theeveryes.[9]

46

Kings Queenes, Lords Ladies, Knights and Damzels gent° *gentle*
Were heaped together with the vulgar sort,
And mingled with the raskall rablement,°   *rabble, masses*
Without respect of person or of port,°   *position*
410   To shew Dan° Cupids powre and great effort:° *master/strength*
And round about a border was entrayld,°   *woven*
Of broken bowes and arrowes shivered short,

---

7. Neptune ravished Medusa in Minerva's temple, for which cause her hair was turned to snakes; she gave birth to the winged horse, Pegasus.
8. Hang down. Saturn, associated with melancholy, is not usually portrayed as a lover. Spenser here transposes two myths: Saturn loved Philyra

("Philliras") not Erigone, from which union came the Centaur; Bacchus ("God of wine") tricked Erigone with a false bunch of grapes.
9. I.e., it would be easier to number the stars ("eyes") that watch lovers' nightly exploits (thieveries) than the tragedies caused by love.

And a long bloudy river through them rayld,°   *flowed*
So lively and so like, that living sence it fayld.[1]

47

415 And at the upper end of that faire rowme,
    There was an Altar built of pretious stone,
    Of passing° valew, and of great renowme,   *surpassing*
    On which there stood an Image all alone,
    Of massy° gold, which with his owne light shone;   *solid*
420   And wings it had with sundry colours dight,°   *adorned*
    More sundry colours, then the proud Pavone°   *peacock*
    Beares in his boasted fan, or Iris° bright,   *goddess of the rainbow*
When her discolourd[2] bow she spreds through heaven bright.

48

Blindfold he was, and in his cruell fist
425   A mortall° bow and arrowes keene did hold,   *deadly*
    With which he shot at randon, when him list,°   *when it pleased him*
    Some headed with sad lead, some with pure gold;[3]
    (Ah man beware, how thou those darts behold)
    A wounded Dragon[4] under him did ly,
430   Whose hideous tayle his left foot did enfold,
    And with a shaft was shot through either eye,
That no man forth might draw, ne no man remedye.

49

And underneath his feet was written thus,
    Unto the Victor of the Gods this bee:
435   And all the people in that ample hous
    Did to that image bow their humble knee,
    And oft committed fowle Idolatree.
    That wondrous sight faire Britomart amazed,
    Ne seeing could her wonder satisfie,
440   But ever more and more upon it gazed,
The whiles the passing brightnes her fraile sences dazed.

50

Tho° as she backward[5] cast her busie eye,   *then*
    To search each secret of that goodly sted,°   *place*
    Over the dore thus written she did spye
445   *Be bold:* she oft and oft it over-red,
    Yet could not find what sence it figurèd:
    But what so were therein or° writ or ment,   *either*
    She was no whit thereby discouragèd
    From prosecuting of her first intent,
450 But forward with bold steps into the next roome went.

1. I.e., so animated and so lifelike that it deceived ("fayled") the senses of those looking on.
2. Multicolored.
3. Cupid, by tradition blindfolded, shoots at random ("randon"). His leaden arrows cause unhap-piness in love; his golden arrows, happiness.
4. The dragon is traditionally a guard, symbolic of vigilance.
5. I.e., behind the statue.

51

Much fairer, then° the former, was that roome,   *than*
 And richlier by many partes arayd:[6]
For not with arras made in painefull° loome,   *painstaking*
 But with pure gold it all was overlayd,
455 Wrought with wilde Antickes,[7] which their follies playd,
 In the rich metall, as° they living were: *as if*
A thousand monstrous formes therein were made,
 Such as false love doth oft upon him weare,
For love in thousand monstrous formes doth oft appeare.

52

460 And all about, the glistring walles were hong
 With warlike spoiles, and with victorious prayes,° *prizes*
Of mighty Conquerours and Captaines strong,
 Which were whilome° captivèd in their dayes *formerly*
To cruell love, and wrought their owne decayes:
465 Their swerds° and speres were broke, and *swords*
  hauberques° rent;   *coats of mail*
And their proud girlonds of tryumphant bayes[8]
 Troden in dust with fury insolent,
To shew the victors might and mercilesse intent.

53

The warlike Mayde beholding earnestly
470 The goodly ordinance° of this rich place,   *ordnance*
Did greatly wonder, ne could satisfie
 Her greedy eyes with gazing a long space,
But more she mervaild that no footings trace,° *trace of footprints*
 Nor wight appear'd, but wastefull° emptinesse, *uninhabited*
475 And solemne silence over all that place:
 Straunge thing it seem'd, that none was to possesse
So rich purveyance,° ne them keepe with carefulnesse. *furnishings*

54

And as she lookt about, she did behold,
 How over that same dore was likewise writ,
480 *Be bold, be bold*, and every where *Be bold*,
 That much she muz'd, yet could not construe it
By any ridling skill, or commune wit.°   *common sense*
 At last she spyde at that roomes upper end,
Another yron dore, on which was writ,
485 *Be not too bold*; whereto though she did bend
Her earnest mind, yet wist not what it might intend.° *mean*

55

Thus she there waited untill eventyde,
 Yet living creature none she saw appeare:

---

6. I.e., much ("by many parts") more richly decorated ("arayd").
7. Grotesque statues.

8. Wreaths of laurel ("bays") were traditionally
awarded to great military conquerors.

And now sad° shadowes gan the world to hyde,   *somber*
490   From mortall vew, and wrap in darkenesse dreare;
       Yet nould° she d' off her weary armes, for feare   *would not*
       Of secret daunger, ne let sleepe oppresse
       Her heavy eyes with natures burdein deare,
       But drew her selfe aside in sickernesse,°   *safety*
495 And her welpointed weapons did about her dresse.⁹

Canto 12

The maske¹ of Cupid, and th' enchaunted
Chamber are displayd,
Whence Britomart redeemes faire
Amoret, through charmes decayd.°   *wasted away*

1

Tho° when as chearelesse Night ycovered had   *then*
     Faire heaven with an universall cloud,
     That every wight dismayd with darknesse sad,°   *sober*
     In silence and in sleepe themselves did shroud,
5   She heard a shrilling Trompet sound aloud,
     Signe of nigh° battell, or got° victory;   *approaching/achieved*
     Nought therewith daunted was her courage proud,
     But rather stird to cruell° enmity,   *fierce*
Expecting° ever, when some foe she might descry.   *waiting*

2

10 With that, an hideous storme of winde arose,
     With dreadfull thunder and lightning atwixt,
     And an earth-quake, as if it streight would lose°   *loosen*
     The worlds foundations from his centre fixt;
     A direfull stench of smoke and sulphure mixt
15   Ensewd, whose noyance° fild the fearefull sted,°   *annoyance/place*
     From the fourth houre of night untill the sixt;²
     Yet the bold Britonesse was nought ydred,
Though much emmoved, but stedfast still perseverèd.

3

All suddenly a stormy whirlwind blew
20   Throughout the house, that clappèd° every dore,   *slammed*
     With which that yron wicket° open flew,   *door*
     As it with mightie levers had bene tore:
     And forth issewd, as on the ready flore
     Of some Theatre, a grave personage,
25   That in his hand a branch of laurell bore,

9. Her well-appointed (and/or sharp) weapons she drew ("did dresse") about her.
1. This episode resembles a court masque with allegorical personages and emblematic clothing and properties—possibly the masque for the wedding of Amoret and Scudamore. It is also a "Triumph" of Cupid, who is preceded and followed by the allegorical qualities that attend on his reign and who displays Amoret as the spoils of his victory, the victim of the attitudes toward love which he promotes.
2. Night begins at 6 P.M., so these effects take place from 10 P.M. to midnight, when the masque begins.

With comely haveour° and count'nance sage,   *bearing*
Yclad in costly garments, fit for tragicke Stage.

4

Proceeding to the midst, he still did stand,
     As if in mind he somewhat had to say,
30   And to the vulgar° beckning with his hand,   *groundlings*
     In signe of silence, as to heare a play,
     By lively actions he gan bewray°   *reveal*
     Some argument of matter passionèd;
     Which doen, he backe retyrèd soft away,
35   And passing by, his name discoverèd,
Ease, on his robe in golden letters cypherèd.[3]

5

The noble Mayd, still standing all this vewd,
     And merveild at his strange intendiment;°   *purpose*
     With that a joyous fellowship issewd
40   Of Minstrals, making goodly meriment,
     With wanton Bardes, and Rymers impudent,
     All which together sung full chearefully
     A lay° of loves delight, with sweet concent:°   *song/harmony*
     After whom marcht a jolly company,
45   In manner of a maske, enrangèd orderly.[4]

6

The whiles a most delitious harmony,
     In full straunge notes was sweetly heard to sound,
     That the rare sweetnesse of the melody
     The feeble senses wholly did confound,
50   And the fraile soule in deepe delight nigh dround:
     And when it ceast, shrill trompets loud did bray,
     That their report° did farre away rebound,   *echo*
     And when they ceast, it gan againe to play,
The whiles the maskers marchèd forth in trim aray.

7

55   The first was Fancy,[5] like a lovely boy,
     Of rare aspect, and beautie without peare;
     Matchable either to that ympe of Troy,[6]
     Whom Jove did love, and chose his cup to beare,
     Or that same daintie lad, which was so deare
60   To great Alcides,[7] that when as he dyde,
     He wailèd womanlike with many a teare,

---

3. I.e., by pantomime he indicates that the subject ("argument") of the masque concerns passion. The part of presenter is taken by Ease, suggesting that it predisposes to lechery. Similarly, Idleness leads the procession of the Seven Deadly Sins (1.4, stanzas 18–20).
4. As here, most masques had twelve masquers,

forming six couples. The love song at the processional is performed by musicians ("Minstrals") and poets of varying quality ("Bardes" and "Rymers").
5. The mind's power to produce images that are often misleading or false.
6. Ganymede, as in 3.11.301–06.
7. Hercules, whose beloved Hylas was drowned.

And every wood, and every valley wyde
He fild with Hylas name; the Nymphes eke° Hylas cryde.　　　　*also*

8

His garment neither was of silke nor say,°　　　　　　　*fine wool*
65　　But painted plumes, in goodly order dight,
　　　Like as the sunburnt Indians° do aray　　　　*Native Americans*
　　　Their tawney bodies, in their proudest plight:°　　　*attire*
　　　As those same plumes, so seemd he vaine and light,
　　　That by his gate might easily appeare;
70　　For still he far'd as dauncing in delight,
　　　And in his hand a windy° fan did beare,　　　　*causing wind*
That in the idle aire he mov'd still here and there.

9

And him beside marcht amorous Desyre,
　　　Who seemd of riper yeares, then th' other Swaine,°　　*lover*
75　　Yet was that other swayne this elders syre,
　　　And gave him being, commune to them twaine:
　　　His garment was disguisèd very vaine,[3]
　　　And his embrodered Bonet sat awry;
　　　Twixt both his hands few sparkes he close did straine,°　*clasp*
80　　Which still he blew, and kindled busily,
That soone they life conceiv'd, and forth in flames did fly.

10

Next after him went Doubt, who was yclad
　　　In a discolour'd° cote, of straunge disguyse,　　　*multicolored*
　　　That at his backe a brode Capuccio had,
85　　And sleeves dependant Albanese-wyse:[9]
　　　He lookt askew with his mistrustfull eyes,
　　　And nicely trode, as thornes lay in his way,
　　　Or that the flore to shrinke he did avyse,
　　　And on a broken reed he still did stay
90　His feeble steps, which shrunke, when hard theron he lay.[1]

11

With him went Daunger, clothed in ragged weed,°　　　*garment*
　　　Made of Beares skin, that him more dreadfull made,
　　　Yet his owne face was dreadfull, ne did need
　　　Straunge horrour, to deforme his griesly shade;
95　　A net in th' one hand, and a rustie blade[2]
　　　In th' other was, this Mischiefe, that Mishap;
　　　With th' one his foes he threatned to invade,°　　　*attack*

8. I.e., Desire seems older than Fancy, but Fancy is in fact his father; he was dressed fantastically ("disguised very vaine").
9. Perhaps like those of an alb, a priest's long tunic. His hood ("Capucchio") resembles that of a Capuchin monk.
1. I.e., he trod with great precision and care ("nicely") as if thorns lay in his path or as if he perceived ("did avyse") the floor to give way ("shrinke"). His cane was a broken reed, which collapsed ("shrunke") when he leaned on it.
2. Danger's face was terrifying, needing nothing external ("strange") to further deform his horrid ("griesly") appearance. His net and bloodstained ("rustie") knife indicate the kinds of perils he signifies.

With th' other he his friends ment to enwrap:
For whom he could not kill, he practizd° to entrap.   *plotted*

12

100   Next him was Feare, all arm'd from top to toe,
    Yet thought himselfe not safe enough thereby,
    But feard each shadow moving to and fro,
    And his owne armes when glittering he did spy,
    Or clashing heard, he fast away did fly,
105   As ashes pale of hew, and wingyheeld;[3]
    And evermore on Daunger fixt his eye,
    Gainst whom he alwaies bent° a brasen shield,   *turned*
Which his right hand unarmèd fearefully did wield.

13

With him went Hope in rancke, a handsome Mayd,
110   Of chearefull looke and lovely to behold;
    In silken samite° she was light arayd,   *a rich silk*
    And her faire lockes were woven up in gold;
    She alway smyld, and in her hand did hold
    An holy water Sprinckle,[4] dipt in deowe,°   *water (dew)*
115   With which she sprinckled favours manifold,
    On whom she list, and did great liking sheowe,
Great liking unto many, but true love to feowe.°   *few*

14

And after them Dissemblance, and Suspect[5]
    Marcht in one rancke, yet an unequall paire:
120   For she was gentle, and of milde aspect,
    Courteous to all, and seeming debonaire,°   *gracious*
    Goodly adornèd, and exceeding faire:
    Yet was that all but painted, and purloynd,°   *stolen*
    And her bright browes were deckt with borrowed haire:
125   Her deedes were forgèd, and her words false coynd,
And alwaies in her hand two clewes° of silke she twynd.   *balls*

15

But he was foule, ill favourèd, and grim,
    Under his eyebrowes looking still askaunce;°   *sideways*
    And ever as Dissemblance laught on him,
130   He lowrd° on her with daungerous° eyeglaunce;   *scowled/threatening*
    Shewing his nature in his countenance;
    His rolling eyes did never rest in place,
    But walkt° each where, for feare of hid mischaunce,   *moved*
    Holding a lattice° still before his face,   *screen*
135 Through which he still did peepe, as forward he did pace.

---

3. I.e., he was pale as ashes and fled as if his heels had wings.
4. Aspergillum, a brush to sprinkle holy water.
5. Dissimulation and Suspicion.

16

Next him went Griefe, and Fury matcht yfere;°   *together*
  Griefe all in sable sorrowfully clad,
  Downe hanging his dull head, with heavy chere,° *countenance*
  Yet inly being more, then° seeming sad: *than*
140 A paire of Pincers in his hand he had,
  With which he pinchèd people to the hart,
  That from thenceforth a wretchèd life they lad,° *led*
  In wilfull languor° and consuming smart,° *pining / pain*
Dying each day with inward wounds of dolours dart.

17

145 But Fury was full ill appareilèd
  In rags, that naked nigh° she did appeare, *nearly*
  With ghastly lookes and dreadfull drerihed;° *wretchedness*
  For from her backe her garments she did teare,
  And from her head oft rent her snarled heare:
150 In her right hand a firebrand she did tosse° *brandish*
  About her head, still roming here and there;
  As a dismayèd° Deare in chace embost,° *panic-stricken / hard-pressed*
Forgetfull of his safety, hath his right way lost.

18

After them went Displeasure and Pleasance,
155 He looking lompish° and full sullein sad,° *dejected / morose*
  And hanging downe his heavy countenance;
  She chearefull fresh and full of joyance glad,
  As if no sorrow she ne felt ne drad;° *feared*
  That evill matchèd paire they seemd to bee:
160 An angry Waspe th' one in a viall had,
  Th' other in hers an hony-lady Bee;
Thus marchèd these sixe couples forth in faire degree.° *order*

19

After all these there marcht a most faire Dame,
  Led of two grysie° villeins, th' one Despight, *grim*
165 The other clepèd° Cruelty by name:⁶ *called*
  She dolefull Lady, like a dreary Spright,
  Cald by strong charmes out of eternall night,
  Had deathes owne image figurd in her face,
  Full of sad signes, fearefull to living sight;
170 Yet in that horror shewd a seemely grace,
And with her feeble feet did move a comely pace.

20

Her brest all naked, as net° ivory,   *pure*
  Without adorne° of gold or silver bright, *adornment*
  Wherewith the Craftesman wonts it beautify,⁷

6. Typical attributes of the lady in the world of courtly love and the love sonnets: her "cruelty" causes her to reject her lover with scorn ("despight").

7. I.e., without the jewels that usually beautify her breast.

175 Of her dew honour was despoylèd quight,
And a wide wound therein (O ruefull sight)
Entrenchèd deepe with knife accursèd keene,
Yet freshly bleeding forth her fainting spright,°   *spirit*
(The worke of cruell hand) was to be seene,
180 That dyde in sanguine° red her skin all snowy cleene.   *bloody*

21

At that wide orifice her trembling hart
Was drawne forth, and in silver basin layd,
Quite through transfixèd with a deadly dart,
And in her bloud yet steeming fresh embayd:°   *steeped*
185 And those two villeins, which her steps upstayd,
When her weake feete could scarcely her sustaine,
And fading vitall powers gan to fade,
Her forward still with torture did constraine,
And evermore encreasèd her consuming paine.

22

190 Next after her the wingèd God himselfe°   *Cupid*
Came riding on a Lion ravenous,
Taught to obay the menage° of that Elfe,   *horsemanship*
That man and beast with powre imperious
Subdeweth to his kingdome tyrannous:
195 His blindfold eyes he bad a while unbind,
That his proud spoyle of that same dolorous
Faire Dame he might behold in perfect kind;°   *clearly*
Which seene, he much rejoycèd in his cruell mind.

23

Of which full proud, himselfe up rearing hye,
200 He lookèd round about with sterne disdaine;
And did survay his goodly company:
And marshalling the evill ordered traine,
With that the darts which his right hand did straine,°   *clasp*
Full dreadfully he shooke that all did quake,
205 And clapt on hie his coulourd wingès twaine,
That all his many° it affraide did make: *company*
Tho blinding° him againe, his way he forth did take.   *then blindfolding*

24

Behinde him was Reproch, Repentance, Shame;
Reproch the first, Shame next, Repent behind:
210 Repentance feeble, sorrowfull, and lame:
Reproch despightfull, carelesse, and unkind;[8]
Shame most ill favourd, bestiall, and blind:
Shame lowrd,° Repentance sigh'd, Reproch did scould;   *scowled*
Reproch sharpe stings, Repentance whips entwind,

8. I.e., full of scorn, careless of where his attacks fall, unnatural.

215   Shame burning brond-yrons in her hand did hold:
All three to each unlike, yet all made in one mould.

25

And after them a rude confusèd rout
   Of persons flockt, whose names is hard to read:°   *interpret*
   Emongst them was sterne Strife, and Anger stout,°   *fierce*
220   Unquiet Care, and fond° Unthriftihead,   *foolish*
   Lewd° Losse of Time, and Sorrow seeming dead,   *base*
   Inconstant Chaunge, and false Disloyaltie,
   Consuming Riotise,° and guilty Dread   *debauchery*
   Of heavenly vengeance, faint Infirmitie,
225 Vile Povertie, and lastly Death with infamie.

26

There were full many moe° like maladies,   *more*
   Whose names and natures I note readen well;° *I cannot well interpret*
   So many moe, as there be phantasies
   In wavering wemens wit, that none can tell,°   *count*
230   Or paines in love, or punishments in hell;
   All which disguizèd marcht in masking wise,
   About the chamber with that Damozell,
   And then returnèd, having marchèd thrise,
Into the inner roome, from whence they first did rise.

27

235 So soone as they were in, the dore streight way
   Fast lockèd, driven with that stormy blast,
   Which first it opened; and bore all away.
   Then the brave Maid, which all this while was plast°   *placed*
   In secret shade, and saw both first and last,
240   Issewèd° forth, and went unto the dore,   *came*
   To enter in, but found it lockèd fast:
   It vaine she thought with rigorous uprore°   *violent force*
For to efforce, when charmes had closèd it afore.

28

Where force might not availe, there sleights and art
245   She cast° to use, both fit for hard emprize;° *resolved / enterprise*
   For thy° from that same roome not to depart   *therefore*
   Till morrow next, she did her selfe avize,°   *counsel*
   When that same Maske againe should forth arize.
   The morrow next appeard with joyous cheare,
250   Calling men to their daily exercize,
   Then she, as morrow fresh, her selfe did reare
Out of her secret stand,° that day for to out weare.   *standing place*

29

All that day she outwore in wandering,
   And gazing on that Chambers ornament,

255 Till that againe the second evening
     Her covered with her sable vestiment,
     Wherewith the worlds faire beautie she hath blent:°   obscured
     Then when the second watch[9] was almost past,
     That brasen dore flew open, and in went
260 Bold Britomart, as she had late forecast,°   planned
     Neither of idle shewes, nor of false charmes aghast.°   terrified

30

     So soone as she was entred, round about
       She cast her eies, to see what was become
       Of all those persons, which she saw without:
265 But lo, they streight° were vanisht all and some,   immediately
       Ne living wight she saw in all that roome,
       Save that same woefull Ladie, both whose hands
       Were bounden fast, that did her ill become,
       And her small wast girt round with yron bands,
270 Unto a brasen pillour, by the which she stands.

31

     And her before the vile Enchaunter sate,
       Figuring straunge characters of his art,
       With living bloud he those characters wrate,°   wrote
       Dreadfully dropping from her dying hart,
275 Seeming transfixèd with a cruell dart,
       And all perforce° to make her him to love.   by force
       Ah who can love the worker of her smart?
       A thousand charmes he formerly did prove;°   try
     Yet thousand charmes could not her stedfast heart remove.

32

280 Soone as that virgin knight he saw in place,
       His wicked bookes in hast he overthrew,
       Not caring his long labours to deface,[1]
       And fiercely ronning to that Lady trew,
       A murdrous knife out of his pocket drew,
285 The which he thought, for villeinous despight,°   cruelty
       In her tormented bodie to embrew:°   plunge
       But the stout° Damzell to him leaping light,   fierce
     His cursèd hand withheld, and maisterèd his might.

33

     From her, to whom his fury first he ment,°   directed
290 The wicked weapon rashly he did wrest,
       And turning to her selfe his fell intent,
       Unwares° it strooke into her snowie chest,   suddenly
       That little drops empurpled her faire brest.
       Exceeding wroth therewith the virgin grew,
295 Albe° the wound were nothing deepe imprest,   although

9. From 9 P.M. to midnight.
1. I.e., he did not care if he ruined the spells he had labored over.

And fiercely forth her mortall blade she drew,
To give him the reward for such vile outrage dew.

34

So mightily she smote him, that to ground
  He fell halfe dead; next stroke him should have slaine,
300 Had not the Lady, which by him stood bound,
  Dernely° unto her callèd to abstaine,   *dismally*
  From doing him to dy. For else her paine
  Should be remedilesse, sith none but hee,
  Which wrought it, could the same recure° againe.   *heal*
305 Therewith she stayd her hand, loth stayd to bee;
  For life she him envyde,° and long'd revenge to see.   *begrudged*

35

And to him said, "Thou wicked man, whose meed°   *reward*
  For so huge mischiefe, and vile villany
  Is death, or if that ought do death exceed,
310 Be sure, that nought may save thee from to dy,
  But if that thou this Dame doe presently
  Restore unto her health, and former state;[2]
  This doe and live, else die undoubtedly."
  He glad of life, that lookt for death but late,°   *just recently*
315 Did yield himselfe right willing to prolong his date.°   *term of life*

36

And rising up, gan streight to overlooke°   *look over*
  Those cursèd leaves, his charmes backe to reverse;
  Full dreadfull things out of that balefull booke
  He red, and measured many a sad verse,[3]
320 That horror gan the virgins hart to perse,°   *pierce*
  And her faire locks up starèd° stiffe on end,   *stood*
  Hearing him those same bloudy lines reherse;°   *say over again*
  And all the while he red, she did extend
  Her sword high over him if ought he did offend.

37

325 Anon she gan perceive the house to quake,
  And all the dores to rattel round about;
  Yet all that did not her dismaièd make,
  Nor slacke her threatfull hand for daungers dout,[4]
  But still with stedfast eye and courage stout
330 Abode,° to weet° what end would come of all.   *waited/learn*
  At last that mightie chaine, which round about
  Her tender waste was wound, adowne gan fall,
And that great brasen pillour broke in peeces small.

---

2. I.e., you deserve death or, if possible, something worse than death, and nothing will save you from death ("to dy") unless ("But if") you immediately ("presently") restore this lady.

3. I.e., he pronounced in proper meter many distressing verses (incantations).

4. I.e., nor relax her threatening hand for fear of dangers.

38

The cruell steele, which thrild° her dying hart,   *pierced*
335   Fell softly forth, as of his owne accord,
    And the wyde wound, which lately did dispart°   *divide*
    Her bleeding brest, and riven bowels° gor'd,   *intestines*
    Was closèd up, as it had not bene bor'd,
    And every part to safety full sound,
340   As she were never hurt, was soone° restor'd: *immediately*
    Tho° when she felt her selfe to be unbound,   *then*
And perfect hole, prostrate she fell unto the ground.

39

Before Faire Britomart, she fell prostrate,
    Saying, "Ah noble knight, what worthy meed
345   Can wretched Lady, quit from wofull state,
    Yield you in liew° of this your gratious deed?   *as reward*
    Your vertue selfe her owne reward shall breed,
    Even immortall praise, and glory wyde,
    Which I your vassall, by your prowesse freed,
350   Shall through the world make to be notifyde,
And goodly well advance, that goodly well was tryde."⁵

40

But *Britomart* uprearing her from ground,
    Said, "Gentle Dame, reward enough I weene°   *think*
    For many labours more, then I have found,
355   This, that in safety now I have you seene,
    And meane° of your deliverance have beene: *means*
    Henceforth faire Lady comfort to you take,
    And put away remembrance of late teene;°   *pain*
    In stead thereof know, that your loving Make,°   *mate*
360   Hath no lesse griefe endurèd for your gentle sake."

41

She much was cheard to heare him mentiònd,
    Whom of all living wights she lovèd best.
    Then laid the noble Championesse strong hond
    Upon th' enchaunter, which had her distrest
365   So sore, and with foule outrages opprest:
    With that great chaine, wherewith not long ygo
    He bound that pitteous Lady prisoner, now relest,°   *released*
    Himselfe she bound, more worthy to be so,
And captive with her led to wretchednesse and wo.

42

370 Returning backe, those goodly roomes, which erst°   *before*
    She saw so rich and royally arayd,
    Now vanisht utterly, and cleane subverst°   *overturned*

---

5. I.e., as your vassal I will make known ("notifyed") throughout the world and extol ("advaunce") your virtue, which was so fully tested ("tryde").

She found, and all their glory quite decayd,°   *destroyed*
That sight of such a chaunge her much dismayd.
375 Thence forth descending to that perlous° Porch,   *perilous*
Those dreadfull flames she also found delayd,°   *allayed*
And quenchèd quite, like a consumèd torch,
That erst all entrers wont so cruelly to scorch.

43

More easie issew now, then entrance late
380 She found: for now that fainèd° dreadfull flame,   *imagined*
Which chokt the porch of that enchaunted gate,
And passage bard to all, that thither came,
Was vanisht quite, as it were not the same,
And gave her leave at pleasure forth to passe.
385 Th' Enchaunter selfe, which all that fraud did frame,
To have efforst° the love of that faire lasse,   *enforced*
Seeing his worke now wasted deepe engrievèd was.

44

But when the victoresse arrivèd there,
Where late she left the pensife Scudamore,
390 With her owne trusty Squire,[6] both full of feare,
Neither of them she found where she them lore:°   *left*
Thereat her noble hart was stonisht sore;
But most faire Amoret, whose gentle spright
Now gan to feede on hope, which she before
395 Conceivèd had, to see her owne deare knight,
Being thereof beguyld was fild with new affright.

45

But he sad° man, when he had long in drede   *sorrowful*
Awayted there for Britomarts returne,
Yet saw her not nor signe of her good speed,°   *success*
400 His expectation to despaire did turne,
Misdeeming[7] sure that her those flames did burne;
And therefore gan advize° with her old Squire,   *consult*
Who her deare nourslings losse no lesse did mourne,
Thence to depart for further aide t' enquire:
405 Where let them wend at will, whilest here I doe respire.[8]

1590, 1596

Amoretti and Epithalamion   In the early 1590s the widowed Spenser wooed and won Elizabeth Boyle, who became his wife in 1594. The next year he published a small volume that included the sonnet sequence *Amoretti* ("little loves"

6. Her nurse, Glauce, was her squire.
7. Mistakenly thinking.
8. Take a breath, rest from my labors. In the 1590 edition, Book 3, and the poem, ended with the

happy reunion of Scudamour and Amoret. But in the 1596 edition Spenser made a bridge to his three added books by replacing the earlier ending with stanzas 43–45, as given here.

or "little cupids") and the *Epithalamion*. Several of the sonnets explicitly address an "Elizabeth," and the volume's subtitle, "Written not long since," suggest that these poems, taken together, are a portrait of Spenser's recent courtship and marriage. It was unusual to write sonnets about a happy and successful love; traditionally, the sonneteer's love was for someone painfully inaccessible. Spenser rehearses some of the conventional motifs of frustration and longing, but his cycle of polished, eloquent poems leads toward joyous possession. Thus, for example, in sonnet 67 ("Lyke as a huntman after weary chace"), he transforms a Petrarchan lament into a vision of unexpected fulfillment.

Spenser's great celebration of this fulfillment is the *Epithalamion*. A learned poet, he was acutely conscious that he was writing within a tradition: an epithalamion is a wedding song whose Greek name conveys that it was sung on the threshold of the bridal chamber. The genre, which goes back at least as far as Sappho (ca. 612 B.C.E.), was widely practiced by the Latin poets, particularly Catullus, and imitated in the Renaissance. Its elements typically include an invocation of the Muses, followed by a celebratory description of the procession of the bride, the religious rites, the singing and dancing at the wedding party, the preparations for the wedding night, and the sexual consummation of the marriage.

In long, flowing stanzas, Spenser follows these conventions closely, adapting them with exquisite delicacy to his small-town Irish setting and native folklore. But his first stanza announces a major innovation: "So I unto myselfe alone will sing." Traditionally, the poet of an epithalamion was an admiring observer, a kind of master of ceremonies; by combining the roles of poet and bridegroom, Spenser transforms a genial social performance into a passionate lyric utterance. Equally remarkable innovations are the complex stanza form, for which no direct model has been discovered, and the still more complex overall structure. That structure is a triumph of symbolic patterning; the more scholars have studied it, the more elaborate the order they have uncovered. For example, the poem has exactly 365 long lines (composed of five or more metrical feet) matching the number of days in the year. There are twenty-four stanzas, counting the closing "envoy," matching the hours of one full day. Of these stanzas, the first sixteen describe the course of the day, in which the woods echo the various sounds; the last eight describe the night, a time of silence in which the woods no longer echo. (At the summer solstice [cf. line 266 and note 2] in the latitude of Ireland, night falls after sixteen hours of daylight.)

This subtle and rich poetic structure conjures up not only a single day of celebration but also, beyond this particular event, an orderly, harmonious universe, with a hidden pattern of coherence and regularity. If the *Epithalamion* goes to remarkable lengths to affirm this pattern, it is perhaps because it also registers so insistently all that threatens the enduring happiness of wedded love and indeed of human life itself. The greatest threat is the force over which the poem exercises its greatest power: time.

From Amoretti

Sonnet 1

Happy ye leaves[1] when as those lilly hands,
   Which hold my life in their dead doing° might,   *killing*
   Shall handle you and hold in loves soft bands,°   *bonds*
   Lyke captives trembling at the victors sight.
5 And happy lines, on which with starry light,
   Those lamping° eyes will deigne sometimes to look   *flashing*
   And reade the sorrowes of my dying spright,°   *spirit*

1. I.e., of the book: pages.

Written with teares in harts close° bleeding book.   secret
And happy rymes bath'd in the sacred brooke
10   Of Helicon² whence she derivèd is,
When ye behold that Angels blessèd looke,
My soules long lackèd foode, my heavens blis.
Leaves, lines, and rymes, seeke her to please alone,
Whom if ye please, I care for other none.

Sonnet 34³

Lyke as a ship that through the Ocean wyde,
By conduct of some star doth make her way,
Whenas a storme hath dimd her trusty guyde,
Out of her course doth wander far astray:
5   So I whose star, that wont° with her bright ray   was accustomed
Me to direct, with cloudes is overcast,
Doe wander now in darknesse and dismay,
Through hidden perils round about me plast.°   placed
Yet hope I well, that when this storme is past
10   My Helice⁴ the lodestar of my lyfe
Will shine again, and looke on me at last,
With lovely light to cleare my cloudy grief.
Till then I wander carefull° comfortlesse,   full of cares
In secret sorow and sad pensivenesse.

Sonnet 37

What guyle is this, that those her golden tresses,
She doth attyre under a net of gold:
And with sly° skill so cunningly them dresses,   clever
That which is gold or heare,° may scarse be told?   hair
5   Is it that mens frayle eyes, which gaze too bold,
She may entangle in that golden snare:
And being caught may craftily enfold
Theyr weaker harts, which are not wel aware?
Take heed therefore, myne eyes, how ye doe stare
10   Henceforth too rashly on that guilefull net,
In which if ever ye entrappèd are,
Out of her bands ye by no means shall get.
Fondnesse° it were for any being free,   foolishness
To covet fetters, though they golden bee.

Sonnet 54

Of this worlds Theatre in which we stay,
My love like the Spectator ydly sits
Beholding me that all the pageants° play,   roles
Disguysing diversly my troubled wits.
5   Sometimes I joy when glad occasion fits,

---

2. The "sacred brooke" is Hippocrene, which flows from Mount Helicon, the mountain sacred to the Muses.

3. An adaptation of Petrarch's *Rima* 189 (translated by Sir Thomas Wyatt, p. 528).

4. The Big Dipper or North Star.

And mask in myrth lyke to a Comedy:
Soone after when my joy to sorrow flits,
I waile and make my woes a Tragedy.
Yet she beholding me with constant eye,
10   Delights not in my merth nor rues my smart:°   *pities my hurt*
But when I laugh she mocks, and when I cry
She laughes and hardens evermore her hart.
What then can move her? if nor merth nor mone,°   *moan*
She is no woman, but a sencelesse stone.

Sonnet 64[5]

Comming to kisse her lyps (such grace I found)
Me seemd I smelt a gardin of sweet flowres
That dainty odours from them threw around,
For damzels fit to decke their lovers bowres.
5   Her lips did smell lyke unto Gillyflowers,°   *carnations*
Her ruddy cheeks lyke unto Roses red;
Her snowy browes lyke budded Bellamoures,[6]
Her lovely eyes like Pincks but newly spred,
Her goodly bosome lyke a Strawberry bed,
10   Her neck lyke to a bounch of Cullambynes;
Her brest lyke lillyes, ere theyr leaves be shed,
Her nipples lyke yong blossomd Jessemynes.°   *jasmines*
Such fragrant flowres doe give most odorous smell,
But her sweet odour did them all excell.

Sonnet 65

The doubt which ye misdeeme,° fayre love, is vaine,   *misconceive*
That fondly° feare to loose your liberty,   *foolishly*
When loosing one, two liberties ye gayne,
And make him bond that bondage earst° dyd fly.   *formerly*
5   Sweet be the bands, the which true love doth tye,
Without constraynt or dread of any ill:
The gentle birde feels no captivity
Within her cage, but singes and feeds her fill.
There pride dare not approch, nor discord spill°   *destroy*
10   The league twixt them, that loyal love hath bound;
But simple truth and mutuall good will
Seekes with sweet peace to salve each others wound.
There fayth doth fearlesse dwell in brasen towre,
And spotlesse pleasure builds her sacred bowre.

Sonnet 67[7]

Lyke as a huntsman after weary chace,
Seeing the game from him escapt away,
Sits downe to rest him in some shady place,
With panting hounds beguilèd of their pray:

---

5. Much of the imagery of this sonnet is imitated from the Song of Solomon 4.10–16.
6. Unidentified flower, evidently white.

7. An imitation of Petrarch's *Rima* 190 but with a very different ending. Cf. Wyatt's *Whoso list to hunt*, p. 527.

5   So after long pursuit and vaine assay,°   *attempt*
     When I all weary had the chace forsooke,
     The gentle deare returnd the selfe-same way,
     Thinking to quench her thirst at the next° brooke.   *nearby*
   There she beholding me with mylder looke,
10   Sought not to fly, but fearelesse still did bide:
     Till I in hand her yet halfe trembling tooke,
     And with her owne goodwill hir fyrmely tyde.
   Strange thing me seemd to see a beast so wyld,
     So goodly wonne with her owne will beguyld.°   *entangled*

Sonnet 68

Most glorious Lord of lyfe, that on this day,°   *i.e., Easter*
   Didst make thy triumph over death and sin:
   And having harrowd hell,[8] didst bring away
   Captivity thence captive us to win:
5   This joyous day, deare Lord, with joy begin,
     And grant that we for whom thou diddest dye
     Being with thy deare blood clene washt from sin,
     May live for ever in felicity.
   And that thy love we weighing worthily,
10   May likewise love thee for the same againe:
     And for thy sake that all lyke deare didst buy,[9]
     With love may one another entertayne.
   So let us love, deare love, lyke as we ought,
     Love is the lesson which the Lord us taught.[1]

Sonnet 74

Most happy letters fram'd by skilfull trade,°   *practice*
   With which that happy name° was first desynd: *i.e., Elizabeth*
   The which three times thrise happy hath me made,
   With guifts of body, fortune and of mind.
5   The first my being to me gave by kind,°   *nature*
     From mothers womb deriv'd by dew descent,
     The second is my sovereigne Queene most kind,
     That honour and large richesse to me lent.
   The third my love, my lives last ornament,
10   By whom my spirit out of dust was raysed:
     To speake her prayse and glory excellent,
     Of all alive most worthy to be praysed.
   Ye three Elizabeths for ever live,
     That three such graces did unto me give.

Sonnet 75

One day I wrote her name upon the strand,°   *beach*
   But came the waves and washèd it away:

---

8. In the apocryphal gospels, Christ descended into hell and led out those who had lived before his time that deserved to be saved. "Captivity thence captive" is a biblical phrase, as in Judges 5.12 and Ephesians 4.8.

9. I.e., Christ bought all people at the same great cost.
1. Cf. John 15.12: "This is my commandment, That ye love one another, as I have loved you."

Agayne I wrote it with a second hand,
But came the tyde, and made my paynes his pray.°   *prey*
5 "Vayne man," sayd she, "that doest in vaine assay,°   *attempt*
A mortall thing so to immortalize,
For I my selve shall lyke to this decay,
And eek° my name bee wypèd out lykewize."   *also*
"Not so," quod° I, "let baser things devize°   *quoth/contrive*
10 To dy in dust, but you shall live by fame:
My verse your vertues rare shall eternize,
And in the heavens wryte your glorious name.
Where whenas death shall all the world subdew,
Our love shall live, and later life renew."

Sonnet 79

Men call you fayre, and you doe credit° it,   *believe*
For that your selfe ye dayly such doe see:
But the trew fayre,° that is the gentle wit,   *beauty*
And vertuous mind, is much more praysd of me.
5 For all the rest, how ever fayre it be,
Shall turne to nought and loose that glorious hew:°   *form*
But onely that is permanent and free
From frayle corruption, that doth flesh ensew.°   *outlast*
That is true beautie: that doth argue you
10 To be divine and borne of heavenly seed:
Deriv'd from that fayre Spirit,° from whom al true   *i.e., God*
And perfect beauty did at first proceed.
He onely fayre, and what he fayre hath made:
All other fayre, lyke flowres, untymely fade.

1595

Epithalamion

Ye learnèd sisters which have oftentimes
Beene to me ayding, others to adorne:[1]
Whom ye thought worthy of your gracefull rymes,
That even the greatest did not greatly scorne
5 To heare theyr names sung in your simple layes,
But joyèd in theyr prayse.
And when ye list° your owne mishaps to mourne,   *chose*
Which death, or love, or fortunes wreck did rayse,
Your string could soone to sadder tenor° turne,   *mood*
10 And teach the woods and waters to lament
Your dolefull dreriment.°   *sorrow*
Now lay those sorrowfull complaints aside,
And having all your heads with girland crownd,
Helpe me mine owne loves prayses to resound,
15 Ne let the same of° any be envide: *by*

---

1. To write poems in praise of others. The "learned sisters" are the Muses.

So Orpheus did for his owne bride,[2]
So I unto my selfe alone will sing,
The woods shall to me answer and my Eccho ring.

Early before the worlds light giving lampe,
His golden beame upon the hils doth spred,
Having disperst the nights unchearefull dampe,
Doe ye awake, and with fresh lustyhed°   vigor
Go to the bowre° of my belovèd love,   bedchamber
My truest turtle dove,
Bid her awake; for Hymen[3] is awake,
And long since ready forth his maske to move,
With his bright Tead[4] that flames with many a flake,°   spark
And many a bachelor to waite on him,
In theyr fresh garments trim.
Bid her awake therefore and soone her dight,°   dress
For lo the wishèd day is come at last,
That shall for al the paynes and sorrowes past,
Pay to her usury° of long delight: interest
And whylest she doth her dight,
Doe ye to her of joy and solace sing,
That all the woods may answer and your Eccho ring.

Bring with you all the Nymphes that you can
    heare°   that can hear you
Both of the rivers and the forrests greene:
And of the sea that neighbours to her neare,
Al with gay girlands goodly wel beseene.°   beautified
And let them also with them bring in hand,
Another gay girland
For my fayre love of lillyes and of roses,
Bound truelove wize° with a blew silke riband.   i.e., in a love knot
And let them make great store of bridale poses,°   posies
And let them eeke° bring store of other flowers   also
To deck the bridale bowers.
And let the ground whereas her foot shall tread,
For feare the stones her tender foot should wrong
Be strewed with fragrant flowers all along,
And diapred lyke the discolored mead.[5]
Which done, doe at her chamber dore awayt,
For she will waken strayt,°   straightway
The whiles doe ye this song unto her sing,
The woods shall to you answer and your Eccho ring.

Ye Nymphes of Mulla[6] which with careful heed,
The silver scaly trouts doe tend full well,
And greedy pikes which use therein to feed,

20

25

30

35

40

45

50

55

2. Orpheus, archetype of the poet in classical antiquity, was famous for his love for his wife, Eurydice.
3. The god of marriage, who leads a "maske" or procession at weddings.
4. A ceremonial torch, associated with marriages since classical times.
5. Ornamented like the many-colored meadow.
6. The vale of Mulla, near Spenser's home in Ireland.

(Those trouts and pikes all others doo excell)
60 And ye likewise, which keepe the rushy lake,
    Where none doo fishes take,
    Bynd up the locks the which hang scatterd light,
    And in his waters which your mirror make,
    Behold your faces as the christall bright,
65 That when you come whereas° my love doth lie,   *where*
    No blemish she may spie.
    And eke° ye lightfoot mayds which keepe the deere,   *also*
    That on the hoary mountayne use to towre,⁷
    And the wylde wolves which seeke them to devoure,
70 With your steele darts doo chace from comming neer
    Be also present heere,
    To helpe to decke her and to help to sing,
    That all the woods may answer and your Eccho ring.

    Wake, now my love, awake; for it is time,
75 The Rosy Morne long since left Tithones bed,⁸
    All ready to her silver coche° to clyme,   *coach*
    And Phoebus gins to shew his glorious hed.
    Hark how the cheerefull birds do chaunt theyr laies°   *songs*
    And carroll of loves praise.
80 The merry Larke hir mattins° sings aloft,   *morning prayers*
    The thrush replyes, the Mavis descant playes,
    The Ouzell shrills, the Ruddock warbles soft,⁹
    So goodly all agree with sweet consent,
    To this dayes merriment.
85 Ah my deere love why doe ye sleepe thus long,
    When meeter° were that ye should now awake,   *more fitting*
    T' awayt the comming of your joyous make,°   *mate*
    And hearken to the birds lovelearnèd song,
    The deawy leaves among.
90 For they of joy and pleasance to you sing,
    That all the woods them answer and theyr Eccho ring.

    My love is now awake out of her dreame,
    And her fayre eyes like stars that dimmèd were
    With darksome cloud, now shew theyr goodly beams
95 More bright then Hesperus° his head doth rere.   *evening star*
    Come now ye damzels, daughters of delight,
    Helpe quickly her to dight,°   *adorn*
    But first come ye fayre houres which were begot
    In Joves sweet paradice, of Day and Night,
100 Which doe the seasons of the yeare allot,

---

7. A falconry term meaning to occupy heights. "The deere": all wild animals, kept by the forest nymphs.
8. See Song of Solomon 2.10–13: "Rise up, my love, my fair one, and come away. For, lo, the winter is past, the rain is over and gone; the flowers appear on the earth; the time of the singing of birds is come." In classical myth, Tithonus is the aged husband of Aurora, the dawn.
9. "Descant": a melody or counterpoint written above a musical theme—a soprano obbligato. The "Mavis" is the song thrush; the "Ouzell," the blackbird (which sings in England); and the "Ruddock," the European robin. The birds' concert is a convention of medieval love poetry.

And al that ever in this world is fayre
Doe make and still° repayre.   *continuously*
And ye three handmayds of the Cyprian Queene,[1]
The which doe still adorne her beauties pride,
105 Helpe to addorne my beautifullest bride:
And as ye her array, still throw betweene°   *at intervals*
Some graces to be seene,
And as ye use° to Venus, to her sing,   *are accustomed*
The whiles the woods shal answer and your Eccho ring.

110 Now is my love all ready forth to come,
Let all the virgins therefore well awayt,
And ye fresh boyes that tend upon her groome
Prepare your selves; for he is comming strayt.°   *straightway*
Set all your things in seemly good aray°   *order*
115 Fit for so joyfull day,
The joyfulst day that ever sunne did see.
Faire Sun, shew forth thy favourable ray,
And let thy lifull° heat not fervent be   *life-giving*
For feare of burning her sunshyny face,
120 Her beauty to disgrace.
O fayrest Phoebus, father of the Muse,[2]
If ever I did honour thee aright,
Or sing the thing, that mote° thy mind delight,   *might*
Doe not thy servants simple boone° refuse,   *request*
125 But let this day let this one day be myne,
Let all the rest be thine.
Then I thy soverayne prayses loud wil sing,
That all the woods shal answer and theyr Eccho ring.

Harke how the Minstrels gin° to shrill aloud   *begin*
130 Their merry Musick that resounds from far,
The pipe, the tabor,° and the trembling Croud,[3]   *small drum*
That well agree withouten breach or jar.°   *discord*
But most of all the Damzels doe delite,
When they their tymbrels° smyte,   *tambourines*
135 And thereunto doe daunce and carrol sweet,
That all the sences they doe ravish quite,
The whyles the boyes run up and downe the street,
Crying aloud with strong confusèd noyce,
As if it were one voyce.
140 *Hymen iô Hymen, Hymen*[4] they do shout,
That even to the heavens theyr shouting shrill
Doth reach, and all the firmament doth fill,
To which the people standing all about,
As in approvance doe thereto applaud

1. The Graces attending on Venus ("Cyprian Queene"), representing brightness, joy, and bloom.
2. Phoebus (Apollo), god of the sun, was also god of music and poetry, but he was not normally regarded as the father of the Nine Muses (Zeus was).
3. Primitive fiddle. Spenser here designates Irish, not classical, instruments and music for the classical masque or ballet.
4. The name of the god of marriage, used as a conventional exclamation at weddings.

145 And loud advaunce her laud,°   *praise*
     And evermore they *Hymen Hymen* sing,
     That all the woods them answer and theyr Eccho ring.

     Loe where she comes along with portly° pace   *stately*
     Lyke Phoebe from her chamber of the East,
150 Arysing forth to run her mighty race,[5]
     Clad all in white, that seemes° a virgin best.   *beseems, suits*
     So well it her beseems that ye would weene°   *think*
     Some angell she had beene.
     Her long loose yellow locks lyke golden wyre,
155 Sprinckled with perle, and perling° flowres a tweene,   *winding*
     Doe lyke a golden mantle her attyre,
     And being crownèd with a girland greene,
     Seeme lyke some mayden Queene.
     Her modest eyes abashèd to behold
160 So many gazers, as on her do stare,
     Upon the lowly ground affixèd are.
     Ne dare lift up her countenance too bold,
     But blush to heare her prayses sung so loud,
     So farre from being proud.
165 Nathlesse doe ye still loud her prayses sing.
     That all the woods may answer and your Eccho ring.

     Tell me ye merchants daughters did ye see
     So fayre a creature in your towne before,
     So sweet, so lovely, and so mild as she,
170 Adornd with beautyes grace and vertues store,
     Her goodly eyes lyke Saphyres shining bright,
     Her forehead yvory white,
     Her cheekes lyke apples which the sun hath rudded,°   *made red*
     Her lips lyke cherryes charming men to byte,
175 Her brest like to a bowle of creame uncrudded,°   *uncurdled*
     Her paps lyke lyllies budded,
     Her snowie necke lyke to a marble towre,
     And all her body like a pallace fayre,
     Ascending uppe with many a stately stayre,
180 To honors seat and chastities sweet bowre.[6]
     Why stand ye still ye virgins in amaze,
     Upon her so to gaze,
     Whiles ye forget your former lay to sing,
     To which the woods did answer and your Eccho ring.

185 But if ye saw that which no eyes can see,
     The inward beauty of her lively spright,°   *living spirit, soul*
     Garnisht with heavenly guifts of high degree,
     Much more then would ye wonder at that sight,

---

5. Phoebe is the moon, a virgin like the bride; the reference to her anticipates the night.
6. The head, where the higher faculties are. The catalog of qualities is a convention in love poetry (cf. Song of Solomon 4–8).

And stand astonisht lyke to those which red°   *saw*
190 Medusaes mazeful hed.[7]
There dwels sweet love and constant chastity,
Unspotted fayth and comely womanhood,
Regard of honour and mild modesty,
There vertue raynes as Queene in royal throne,
195 And giveth lawes alone.
The which the base° affections doe obay,   *lower*
And yeeld theyr services unto her will.
Ne thought of thing uncomely ever may
Thereto approch to tempt her mind to ill.
200 Had ye once seene these her celestial threasures,
And unrevealèd pleasures,
Then would ye wonder and her prayses sing,
That all the woods should answer and your Eccho ring.

Open the temple gates unto my love,
205 Open them wide that she may enter in,[8]
And all the postes adorne as doth behove,[9]
And all the pillours deck with girlands trim,
For to recyve this Saynt with honour dew,
That commeth in to you.
210 With trembling steps and humble reverence,
She commeth in, before th' almighties vew,
Of her ye virgins learne obedience,
When so ye come into those holy places,
To humble your proud faces:
215 Bring her up to th' high altar, that she may
The sacred ceremonies there partake,
The which do endless matrimony make,
And let the roring Organs loudly play
The praises of the Lord in lively notes,
220 The whiles with hollow throates
The Choristers the joyous Antheme sing,
That all the woods may answere and theyr Eccho ring.

Behold whiles she before the altar stands
Hearing the holy priest that to her speakes
225 And blesseth her with his two happy hands,
How the red roses flush up in her cheekes,
And the pure snow with goodly vermill° stayne, *vermilion*
Like crimsin dyde in grayne,°   *fast color*
That even th' Angels which continually,
230 About the sacred Altare doe remaine,
Forget their service and about her fly,
Ofte peeping in her face that seemes more fayre,
The more they on it stare.

---

7. Medusa, one of the Gorgons, had serpents instead of hair (hence a "mazeful hed"): the effect on beholders was to turn them to stone.
8. Cf. Psalm 24.7: "Lift up your heads, O ye gates; and be ye lift up, ye everlasting doors; and the King of glory shall come in."
9. As is proper. The doorposts were trimmed for weddings in classical times, and the custom was often referred to in classical and later love poetry.

But her sad° eyes still fastened on the ground,   *serious*
235 Are governèd with goodly modesty,
That suffers not one looke to glaunce awry,
Which may let in a little thought unsownd.
Why blush ye love to give to me your hand,
The pledge of all our band?°   *bond, tie*
240 Sing ye sweet Angels, Alleluya sing,
That all the woods may answere and your Eccho ring.

Now al is done; bring home the bride againe,
Bring home the triumph of our victory,
Bring home with you the glory of her gaine,[1]
245 With joyance bring her and with jollity.
Never had man more joyfull day then this,
Whom heaven would heape with blis.
Make feast therefore now all this live long day,
This day for ever to me holy is,
250 Poure out the wine without restraint or stay,
Poure not by cups, but by the belly full,
Poure out to all that wull,°   *want it*
And sprinkle all the postes and wals with wine,
That they may sweat, and drunken be withall.
255 Crowne ye God Bacchus° with a coronall,°   *god of wine/garland*
And Hymen also crowne with wreathes of vine,
And let the Graces daunce unto the rest;
For they can doo it best:
The whiles the maydens doe theyr carroll sing,
260 To which the woods shall answer and theyr Eccho ring.

Ring ye the bels, ye young men of the towne,
And leave your wonted° labors for this day: *usual*
This day is holy; doe ye write it downe,
That ye for ever it remember may.
265 This day the sunne is in his chiefest hight,
With Barnaby the bright,[2]
From whence declining daily by degrees,
He somewhat loseth of his heat and light,
When once the Crab[3] behind his back he sees.
270 But for this time it ill ordainèd was,
To chose the longest day in all the yeare,
And shortest night, when longest fitter weare:
Yet never day so long, but late° would passe.   *at last*
Ring ye the bels, to make it weare away,
275 And bonefiers° make all day,   *bonfires*
And daunce about them, and about them sing:
That all the woods may answer, and your Eccho ring.

Ah when will this long weary day have end,
And lende me leave to come unto my love?

---

1. I.e., the glory of gaining her.
2. St. Barnabas's Day, at the time of the summer solstice.

3. The constellation Cancer between Gemini and Leo. The sun, passing through the zodiac, leaves the Crab behind toward the end of July.

280   How slowly do the houres theyr numbers spend?
      How slowly does sad Time his feathers move?
      Hast thee O fayrest Planet to thy home
      Within the Westerne fome:
      Thy tyred steedes long since have need of rest.[4]
285   Long though it be, at last I see it gloome,
      And the bright evening star° with golden creast°   *Hesperus/crest*
      Appeare out of the East.
      Fayre childe of beauty, glorious lampe of love
      That all the host of heaven in rankes doost lead,
290   And guydest lovers through the nightès dread,
      How chearefully thou lookest from above,
      And seemst to laugh atweene thy twinkling light
      As joving in the sight
      Of these glad many which for joy doe sing,
295   That all the woods them answer and theyr Eccho ring.

      Now ceasse ye damsels your delights forepast;
      Enough is it, that all the day was youres:
      Now day is doen, and night is nighing fast:
      Now bring the Bryde into the brydall boures.
300   Now night is come, now soone her disaray,
      And in her bed her lay;
      Lay her in lillies and in violets,
      And silken courteins over her display,°   *spread*
      And odourd° sheetes, and Arras° coverlets.   *perfumed/tapestry*
305   Behold how goodly my faire love does ly
      In proud humility;
      Like unto Maia,[5] when as Jove her tooke,
      In Tempe,[6] lying on the flowry gras,
      Twixt sleepe and wake, after she weary was,
310   With bathing in the Acidalian brooke.[7]
      Now it is night, ye damsels may be gon,
      And leave my love alone,
      And leave likewise your former lay to sing:
      The woods no more shall answere, nor your Eccho ring.

315   Now welcome night, thou night so long expected,
      That long daies labour doest at last defray,°   *pay for*
      And all my cares, which cruell love collected,
      Hast sumd in one, and cancellèd for aye:
      Spread thy broad wing over my love and me,
320   That no man may us see,
      And in thy sable mantle us enwrap,
      From feare of perrill and foule horror free.
      Let no false treason seeke us to entrap,
      Nor any dread disquiet once annoy

4. The sun's chariot completes its daily course in the western sea.
5. The eldest and most beautiful of the seven daughters of Atlas. (They were stellified as the Pleiades.) Jove fathered Mercury on her.
6. The Vale of Tempe in Thessaly (not, however, traditionally the site of Jove's encounter with Maia).
7. The Acidalian brook is associated with Venus.

325   The safety of our joy:
        But let the night be calme and quietsome,
        Without tempestuous storms or sad afray:°   *fear*
        Lyke as when Jove with fayre Alcmena[8] lay,
        When he begot the great Tirynthian groome:
330   Or lyke as when he with thy selfe[9] did lie,
        And begot Majesty.
        And let the mayds and yongmen cease to sing:
        Ne let the woods them answer, nor theyr Eccho ring.

        Let no lamenting cryes, nor dolefull teares,
335   Be heard all night within nor yet without:
        Ne let false whispers, breeding hidden feares,
        Breake gentle sleepe with misconceivèd dout.°   *fear*
        Let no deluding dreames, nor dreadful sights
        Make sudden sad affrights;
340   Ne let housefyres, nor lightnings helpelesse harmes,
        Ne let the Pouke,[1] nor other evill sprights,
        Ne let mischivous witches with theyr charmes,
        Ne let hob Goblins, names whose sence we see not,
        Fray° us with things that be not.   *terrify*
345   Let not the shriech Oule, nor the Storke be heard:
        Nor the night Raven that still° deadly yels,[2]   *continuously*
        Nor damnèd ghosts cald up with mighty spels,
        Nor griesly° vultures make us once affeard: *horrid*
        Ne let th' unpleasant Quyre of Frogs still croking
350   Make us to wish theyr choking.
        Let none of these theyr drery accents sing;
        Ne let the woods them answer, nor theyr Eccho ring.

        But let stil Silence trew night watches keepe,
        That sacred peace may in assurance rayne,
355   And tymely Sleep, when it is tyme to sleepe,
        May poure his limbs forth on your pleasant playne,
        The whiles an hundred little wingèd loves,°   *cupids (or amoretti)*
        Like divers fethered doves,
        Shall fly and flutter round about your bed,
360   And in the secret darke, that none reproves,
        Their prety stealthes shal worke, and snares shal spread
        To filch away sweet snatches of delight,
        Conceald through covert night.
        Ye sonnes of Venus, play your sports at will,
365   For greedy pleasure, carelesse of your toyes,°   *amorous dallying*
        Thinks more upon her paradise of joyes,
        Then° what ye do, albe it good or ill.   *than*
        All night therefore attend your merry play,
        For it will soone be day:

8. The mother of Hercules ("the great Tirynthian groome"). Jove made that first night last as long as three.
9. Night. This is Spenser's own myth.
1. Puck, Robin Goodfellow—here more powerful

and evil than Shakespeare made him.
2. The owl and the night raven were birds of ill omen; the stork, in Chaucer's *Parliament of Fowls,* is called an avenger of adultery.

370   Now none doth hinder you, that say or sing,
        Ne will the woods now answer, nor your Eccho ring.

        Who is the same, which at my window peepes?
        Or whose is that faire face, that shines so bright,
        Is it not Cinthia,[3] she that never sleepes,
375   But walkes about high heaven al the night?
        O fayrest goddesse, do thou not envy
        My love with me to spy:
        For thou likewise didst love, though now unthought,°   *not thought of*
        And for a fleece of woll,° which privily,   *wool*
380   The Latmian shephard[4] once unto thee brought,
        His pleasures with thee wrought,
        Therefore to us be favorable now;
        And sith° of wemens labours thou hast charge,[5]   *since*
        And generation goodly dost enlarge,
385   Encline thy will t' effect our wishfull vow,
        And the chast wombe informe° with timely seed,   *give life to*
        That may our comfort breed:
        Till which we cease our hopefull hap° to sing,   *fortune we hope for*
        Ne let the woods us answer, nor our Eccho ring.

390   And thou great Juno, which with awful might
        The lawes of wedlock still dost patronize,
        And the religion° of the faith first plight   *sanctity*
        With sacred rites hast taught to solemnize:
        And eeke° for comfort often callèd art   *also*
395   Of women in their smart,°   *labor*
        Eternally bind thou this lovely band,°   *bond*
        And all thy blessings unto us impart.
        And thou glad Genius,[6] in whose gentle hand,
        The bridale bowre and geniall bed remaine,
400   Without blemish or staine,
        And the sweet pleasures of theyr loves delight
        With secret ayde doest succour and supply,
        Till they bring forth the fruitfull progeny,
        Send us the timely fruit of this same night.
405   And thou fayre Hebe,[7] and thou Hymen free,
        Grant that it may so be.
        Til which we cease your further prayse to sing,
        Ne any woods shall answer, nor your Eccho ring.

        And ye high heavens, the temple of the gods,
410   In which a thousand torches flaming bright
        Doe burne, that to us wretched earthly clods,
        In dreadful darknesse lend desirèd light;
        And all ye powers which in the same remayne,
        More than we men can fayne,°   *imagine*

---

3. Cynthia (or Diana) is goddess of the moon.
4. Endymion, beloved by the moon. The "fleece of woll," however, comes from another story—that of Pan's enticement of the moon.

5. Diana is, as Lucina, patroness of births. The "labours" are of course, those of childbirth.
6. Patron of sex, pregnancy, and reproduction.
7. Patron of youth and freedom.

415 Poure out your blessing on us plentiously,
     And happy influence upon us raine,
     That we may raise a large posterity,
     Which from the earth, which they may long possesse,
     With lasting happinesse,
420 Up to your haughty pallaces may mount,
     And for the guerdon° of theyr glorious merit   *reward*
     May heavenly tabernacles there inherit,
     Of blessèd Saints for to increase the count.
     So let us rest, sweet love, in hope of this,
425 And cease till then our tymely joyes to sing,
     The woods no more us answer, nor our Eccho ring.

     Song made in lieu of many ornaments,
     With which my love should duly have bene dect,°   *adorned*
     Which cutting off through hasty accidents,
430 Ye would not stay your dew time to expect,°   *await*
     But promist both to recompens,
     Be unto her a goodly ornament,
     And for short time an endlesse moniment.[8]

                                                            1595

8. The envoy is traditionally apologetic in tone: the poem is offered as a substitute for wedding presents ("ornaments") that did not arrive in time for the wedding. But this elaborate poem is itself a "goodly ornament," for it stands as a timeless monument of art to the passing day that it celebrates.

SIR WALTER RALEGH
1552–1618

The brilliant and versatile Sir Walter Ralegh was a soldier, courtier, philosopher, explorer and colonist, student of science, historian, and poet. Born to West Country gentry of modest means, Ralegh amassed great wealth thanks to his position at court, leading him to be denounced by some as an upstart and hated by others as a rapacious monopolist. He fought ruthlessly in Ireland and Cádiz, directed the colonization of Virginia, introduced the potato to Ireland and tobacco to Europe, brought Spenser from Ireland to the English court, conducted scientific experiments, led expeditions to Guiana in an unsuccessful effort to find gold, and wrote several reports urging England to challenge Spanish dominance in the New World. He was known for his violent temper, his dramatic sense of life, his extravagant dress, his skepticism in religious matters, his bitter hatred of Spain, and his great favor with Queen Elizabeth, interrupted in 1592 when he seduced, and then married, one of her ladies-in-waiting. His long poem to the queen, *The Ocean to Cynthia*, remains in fragments of manuscript, one of more than five hundred lines. His best-known shorter poems include the reply to Marlowe's *Passionate Shepherd* and *The Lie*, an attack on social classes and institutions which itself provoked many replies. His active resistance to printing his poems—in one case he forced a printer to recall a volume and paste a slip of paper over his initials—makes it very difficult to put the copies that circulated in manuscript in any reliable chronological order.

King James suspected Ralegh of opposing his succession and threw him into the Tower of London in 1603 on trumped-up charges of treason; there he remained for the rest of his life save for an ill-fated last voyage to Guiana in 1617, which again failed to discover gold. In prison he wrote his long, unfinished *History of the World*, which begins with the Creation, emphasizes the providential punishment of evil princes, and projects a treatment of English history—although not of recent events because, he declared, he who follows truth too closely at the heels might get kicked in the teeth. The work was to have been dedicated to Henry, prince of Wales, Ralegh's most powerful friend and supporter, who declared, "Only my father would keep such a bird in a cage." But Henry died in 1612, and Ralegh broke off his narrative at 168 B.C.E. Six years later James, bowing to Spanish pressure, had Ralegh executed on the old treason charge.

he was a sinic.

The Nymph's Reply to the Shepherd

a response to Marlowe's Passionate shepherd...

If all the world and love were young,
And truth in every shepherd's tongue,
These pretty pleasures might me move
To live with thee and be thy love.

5   Time drives the flocks from field to fold
When rivers rage and rocks grow cold,
And Philomel° becometh dumb;   *the nightingale*
The rest complains of cares to come.

The flowers do fade, and wanton fields   *things change & grow old*
10 To wayward winter reckoning yields;
A honey tongue, a heart of gall, *sweet talking won't*
Is fancy's spring, but sorrow's fall. *last b/c she has a bitter heart.*

Thy gowns, thy shoes, thy beds of roses,
Thy cap, thy kirtle,° and thy posies   *skirt, outer petticoat*
15 Soon break, soon wither, soon forgotten—
In folly ripe, in reason rotten.

Thy belt of straw and ivy buds,   *these material*
Thy coral clasps and amber studs,   *things don't*
All these in me no means can move   *last forever,*
20 To come to thee and be thy love.   *give her endless love.*

But could youth last and love still breed,
Had joys no date° nor age no need,   *ending*
Then these delights my mind might move
To live with thee and be thy love.

1600

What is our life?

What is our life? a play of passion;
Our mirth the music of division;[1]

1. The rapid accompaniment to, or variation on, a musical theme.

Our mothers' wombs the tiring-houses[2] be
Where we are dressed for this short comedy.
5   Heaven the judicious sharp spectator is,
That sits and marks still who doth act amiss;
Our graves that hide us from the searching sun
Are like drawn curtains when the play is done.
Thus march we, playing, to our latest rest,
10   Only we die in earnest—that's no jest.

1612

[Sir Walter Ralegh to His Son][1]

Three things there be that prosper up apace
And flourish, whilst they grow asunder far,
But on a day, they meet all in one place,
And when they meet, they one another mar;
5   And they be these: the wood, the weed, the wag.
The wood is that which makes the gallow tree;
The weed is that which strings the hangman's bag;
The wag, my pretty knave, betokeneth thee.
Mark well, dear boy, whilst these assemble not,
10   Green springs the tree, hemp grows, the wag is wild,
But when they meet, it makes the timber rot,
It frets the halter, and it chokes the child.
Then bless thee, and beware, and let us pray
We part not with thee at this meeting day.

ca. 1600

The Lie

Go, soul, the body's guest,
   Upon a thankless errand;
Fear not to touch the best;
   The truth shall be thy warrant.
5   Go, since I needs must die,
   And give the world the lie.[1]

Say to the court, it glows
   And shines like rotten wood;
Say to the church, it shows
10   What's good, and doth no good.
If church and court reply,
   Then give them both the lie.

Tell potentates they live
   Acting by others' action;

2. Dressing rooms in an Elizabethan theater.
1. The poem has this title in one of the manuscripts in which it appears.
1. "Give the lie": accuse of lying.

15 Not loved unless they give,
    Not strong but by a faction.
  If potentates reply,
    Give potentates the lie.

  Tell men of high condition,
20   That manage the estate,°   *state*
  Their purpose is ambition,
    Their practice only hate.
  And if they once reply,
    Then give them all the lie.

25 Tell them that brave it² most,
    They beg for more by spending,
  Who, in their greatest cost,
    Seek nothing but commending.
  And if they make reply,
30   Then give them all the lie.

  Tell zeal it wants° devotion;   *lacks*
    Tell love it is but lust;
  Tell time it is but motion;
    Tell flesh it is but dust.
35 And wish them not reply,
    For thou must give the lie.

  Tell age it daily wasteth;
    Tell honor how it alters;
  Tell beauty how she blasteth;°   *withers away*
40   Tell favor how it falters.
  And as they shall reply,
    Give every one the lie.

  Tell wit how much it wrangles
    In tickle points of niceness;°   *in trivial distinctions*
45 Tell wisdom she entangles
    Herself in overwiseness.
  And when they do reply,
    Straight give them both the lie.

  Tell physic° of her boldness;   *medicine*
50   Tell skill it is pretension;
  Tell charity of coldness;
    Tell law it is contention.
  And as they do reply,
    So give them still the lie.

55 Tell fortune of her blindness;
    Tell nature of decay;
  Tell friendship of unkindness;

2. I.e., those who spend much on clothes.

Tell justice of delay.
And if they will reply,
60   Then give them all the lie.

Tell arts they have no soundness,
    But vary by esteeming;
Tell schools they want profoundness,
    And stand too much on seeming.
65   If arts and schools reply,
      Give arts and schools the lie.

Tell faith it's fled the city;
    Tell how the country erreth;
Tell manhood shakes off pity;
70   Tell virtue least preferreth.°   *advances, succeeds*
And if they do reply,
    Spare not to give the lie.

So when thou hast, as I
    Commanded thee, done blabbing—
75   Although to give the lie
    Deserves no less than stabbing—
Stab at thee he that will,
    No stab thy soul can kill.

ca. 1592   1608

Farewell, false love

Farewell, false love, the oracle of lies,
A mortal foe and enemy to rest;
An envious boy, from whom all cares arise,
A bastard vile, a beast with rage possessed;
5   A way of error, a temple full of treason,
In all effects contrary unto reason.

A poisoned serpent covered all with flowers,
Mother of sighs and murtherer of repose,
A sea of sorrows from whence are drawn such showers
10   As moisture lends to every grief that grows;
A school of guile, a net of deep deceit,
A gilded hook that holds a poisoned bait.

A fortress foiled° which reason did defend,   *overthrown*
A siren song, a fever of the mind,
15   A maze wherein affection finds no end,
A raging cloud that runs before the wind,
A substance like the shadow of the sun,
A goal of grief for which the wisest run.

A quenchless fire, a nurse of trembling fear,
20   A path that leads to peril and mishap;

A true retreat of sorrow and despair,
An idle boy that sleeps in pleasure's lap,
A deep distrust of that which certain seems,
A hope of that which reason doubtful deems.

25 Sith° then thy trains° my younger years betrayed,   *since/tricks*
And for my faith ingratitude I find,
And sith repentance hath my wrongs bewrayed°   *revealed*
Whose course was ever contrary to kind°—   *nature*
False love, desire, and beauty frail, adieu!
30 Dead is the root whence all these fancies grew.

1588

Methought I saw the grave where Laura lay[1]

Methought I saw the grave where Laura lay,
Within that temple where the vestal° flame   *celebrating virginity*
Was wont to burn; and passing by that way
To see that buried dust of living fame,
5 Whose tomb fair love and fairer virtue kept,
All suddenly I saw the Fairy Queen;
At whose approach the soul of Petrarch wept,
And from thenceforth those graces were not seen,
For they this Queen attended; in whose stead
10 Oblivion laid him down on Laura's hearse.
Hereat the hardest stones were seen to bleed,
And groans of buried ghosts the heavens did pierce;
    Where Homer's sprite[2] did tremble all for grief,
    And cursed th' access of that celestial thief.

1590

Nature, that washed her hands in milk

    Nature, that washed her hands in milk,
        And had forgot to dry them,
    Instead of earth took snow and silk,
        At Love's request to try them,
5   If she a mistress could compose
    To please Love's fancy out of those.

    Her eyes he would should be of light,
        A violet breath, and lips of jelly;
    Her hair not black, nor overbright,
10   And of the softest down her belly;

1. A commendatory sonnet to the first three books of *The Faerie Queene* by Ralegh's friend Spenser. Laura was the lady celebrated in the sonnets of Petrarch (1304–1374).

2. The spirit of Homer. Ralegh is giving extravagant praise to Spenser's poem as an epic, the type of poem Homer wrote.

As for her inside he'd have it
Only of wantonness and wit.

At Love's entreaty such a one
    Nature made, but with her beauty
15 She hath framed a heart of stone;
    So as Love, by ill destiny,
Must die for her whom Nature gave him,
Because her darling would not save him.

But Time (which Nature doth despise,
20   And rudely gives her love the lie,
Makes Hope a fool, and Sorrow wise)
    His hands do neither wash nor dry;
But being made of steel and rust,
Turns snow and silk and milk to dust.

25 The light, the belly, lips, and breath,
        He dims, discolors, and destroys;
With those he feeds but fills not death,
    Which sometimes were the food of joys.
Yea, Time doth dull each lively wit,
30 And dries all wantonness with it.

Oh, cruel Time! which takes in trust
    Our youth, our joys, and all we have,
And pays us but with age and dust;
    Who in the dark and silent grave
35 When we have wandered all our ways
Shuts up the story of our days.

                                                        1902

[The Author's Epitaph, Made by Himself][1]

Even such is time, which takes in trust
Our youth, our joys, and all we have,
And pays us but with age and dust;
Who in the dark and silent grave,
5   When we have wandered all our ways,
Shuts up the story of our days:
And from which earth, and grave, and dust
The Lord shall raise me up, I trust.

                                                        1628

1. In the 17th century it was thought that Ralegh composed this poem the night before his execution and wrote it in his Bible. It is actually a version of the last stanza of the preceding poem.

From The discovery of the large, rich, and beautiful Empire of Guiana, with a relation of the great and golden city of Manoa (which the Spaniards call El Dorado)[1]

* * * When we were come to the tops of the first hills of the plains adjoining to the river, we beheld that wonderful breach of waters which ran down Caroni:[2] and might from that mountain see the river how it ran in three parts, above twenty miles off, and there appeared some ten or twelve overfalls in sight, every one as high over the other as a church tower, which fell with that fury, that the rebound of water made it seem as if it had been all covered over with a great shower of rain: and in some places we took it at the first for a smoke that had risen over some great town. For mine own part, I was well persuaded from thence to have returned, being a very ill footman,[3] but the rest were all so desirous to go near the said strange thunder of waters as they drew me on by little and little till we came into the next valley, where we might better discern the same. I never saw a more beautiful country nor more lively prospects, hills so raised here and there over the valleys, the river winding into divers branches, the plains adjoining without bush or stubble, all fair green grass, the ground of hard sand easy to march on either for horse or foot, the deer crossing in every path, the birds towards the evening singing on every tree with a thousand several tunes, cranes and herons of white, crimson, and carnation perching in the river's side, the air fresh with a gentle easterly wind, and every stone that we stooped to take up promised either gold or silver by his complexion. * * *

* * *

* * * I will promise these things that follow, which I know to be true. Those that are desirous to discover and to see many nations may be satisfied within this river,[4] which bringeth forth so many arms and branches leading to several countries and provinces, above 2000 miles east and west, and 800 miles south and north, and of these, the most either rich in gold, or in other merchandises. The common soldier shall here fight for gold, and pay himself instead of pence, with plates of half a foot broad, whereas he breaketh his bones in other wars for provant[5] and penury. Those commanders and chieftains that shoot at honor and abundance, shall find there more rich and beautiful cities, more temples adorned with golden images, more sepulchers filled with treasure, than either Cortez found in Mexico, or Pizarro in Peru: and the shining glory of this conquest will eclipse all those so far extended beams of the Spanish nation. There is no country which yieldeth more pleasure to the inhabitants, either for those common delights of hunting, hawking, fishing, fowling, or the rest, than Guiana doth. * * *

1. Ralegh had reports from several Spaniards of the unexplored Indian kingdom of Guiana ("Land of Waters"; now a part of Venezuela). Lying between the Orinoco and Amazon rivers, the kingdom supposedly included the city the Spaniards called El Dorado—The Golden City. Ralegh led an expedition to Guiana in 1595 and the following year published an account of it, which was reprinted in 1598–1600 in Richard Hakluyt's mas-sive collection, *The Principal Navigations, Voyages, Traffics, and Discoveries of the English Nation*.
2. The Caroni River is a tributary of the Orinoco. Intrigued by reports of its waterfalls and the country above them, Ralegh led a small group to explore the region.
3. Poor walker.
4. The Orinoco.
5. Provender, rations.

* * * Both for health, good air, pleasure, and riches I am resolved it cannot be equalled by any region either in the east or west. Moreover the country is so healthful, as of an hundred persons and more (which lay without shift most sluttishly, and were every day almost melted with heat in rowing and marching, and suddenly wet again with great showers, and did eat of all sorts of corrupt fruits, and made meals of fresh fish without seasoning, of tortugas, of lagartos[6] or crocodiles, and of all sorts good and bad, without either order or measure, and besides lodged in the open air every night) we lost not any one, nor had one ill disposed to my knowledge, nor found any calentura, or other of those pestilent diseases which dwell in all hot regions, and so near the equinoctial line.

Where there is store of gold, it is in effect needless to remember other commodities for trade: but it hath towards the south part of the river, great quantities of brazil-wood, and diverse berries that dye a most perfect crimson and carnation. * * * All places yield abundance of cotton, of silk, of balsam, and of those kinds most excellent and never known in Europe, of all sorts of gums, of Indian pepper: and what else the countries may afford within the land we know not, neither had we time to abide the trial, and search. The soil besides is so excellent and so full of rivers, as it will carry sugar, ginger, and all those other commodities which the West Indies have.

The Navigation is short, for it may be sailed with an ordinary wind in six weeks, and in the like time back again. * * *

* * *

* * * Guiana is a country that hath yet her maidenhead, never sacked, turned, nor wrought,[7] the face of the earth hath not been torn, nor the virtue and salt of the soil spent by manurance, the graves have not been opened for gold, the mines not broken with sledges, nor their images pulled down out of their temples. It hath never been entered by any army of strength, and never conquered or possessed by any Christian prince. It is besides so defensible, that if two forts be builded in one of the provinces which I have seen, the flood[8] setteth in so near the bank, where the channel also lieth, that no ship can pass up but within a pike's length of the artillery, first of the one, and afterwards of the other. * * *

* * * Guiana hath but one entrance by the sea (if it hath that) for any vessels of burden: so as whosoever shall first possess it, it shall be found unaccessible for any enemy, except he come in wherries,[9] barges, or canoes, or else in flat-bottomed boats, and if he do offer to enter it in that manner, the woods are so thick two hundred miles together upon the rivers of such entrance, as a mouse cannot sit in a boat unhit from the bank. By land it is more impossible to approach, for it hath the strongest situation of any region under the sun, and is so environed with impassable mountains on every side, as it is impossible to victual any company in the passage: which hath been well proved by the Spanish nation, who since the conquest of Peru have never left five years free from attempting this empire, or discovering some way into it, and yet of three and twenty several gentlemen, knights, and noblemen, there was never any that knew which way to lead an army by land,

---

6. Alligators. "Tortugas": tortoises.
7. Quarried or mined. "Turned": tilled.

8. Tide.
9. Rowboats.

or to conduct ships by sea, anything near the said country. Orellana, of whom the river of Amazones taketh name, was the first, and Don Antonio de Berreo[1] (whom we displanted) the last: and I doubt much, whether he himself or any of his yet know the best way into the said empire. * * *

* * *

The West Indies were first offered Her Majesty's grandfather[2] by Columbus, a stranger, in whom there might be doubt[3] of deceit, and besides it was then thought incredible that there were such and so many lands and regions never written of before. This empire is made known to Her Majesty by her own vassal, and by him that oweth to her more duty than an ordinary subject, so that it shall ill sort with the many graces and benefits which I have received to abuse Her Highness, either with fables or imaginations. The country is already discovered, many nations won to Her Majesty's love and obedience, and those Spaniards which have latest and longest labored about the conquest, beaten out, discouraged and disgraced, which among these nations were thought invincible. Her Majesty may in this enterprise employ all those soldiers and gentlemen that are younger brethren, and all captains and chieftains that want employment, and the charge will be only the first setting out in victualing and arming them: for after the first or second year I doubt not but to see in London a contractation house[4] of more receipt for Guiana, than there is now in Seville for the West Indies.

And I am resolved that if there were but a small army afoot in Guiana, marching towards Manoa the chief city of Inca, he[5] would yield to Her Majesty by composition[6] so many hundred thousand pounds yearly, as should both defend all enemies abroad and defray all expenses at home, and that he would besides pay a garrison of three or four thousand soldiers very royally to defend him against other nations. * * * For whatsoever prince shall possess it, shall be greatest, and if the king of Spain enjoy it, he will become unresistible. Her Majesty hereby shall confirm and strengthen the opinions of all nations, as touching her great and princely actions. * * *

To speak more at this time, I fear would be but troublesome: I trust in God, this being true, will suffice, and that he which is King of all Kings and Lord of Lords, will put it into her heart which is Lady of Ladies to possess it; if not, I will judge those men worthy to be kings thereof, that by her grace and leave will undertake it of themselves.

1596, 1599

1. One of Ralegh's informants, a captured Spanish officer at Trinidad. Francisco de Orellana (ca. 1490–ca. 1546), a Spanish soldier, was the first explorer of the Amazon.
2. Henry VII. In 1488 Bartholomew Columbus petitioned Henry to sponsor his brother Christopher in an attempt to find a new route to the (East) Indies, by sailing west. The king declined, so Christopher sought the sponsorship of Queen Isabella of Spain.

3. Fear.
4. Place for receiving the goods contracted to be sent back to the investors who would finance the Guiana expedition. But in fact Ralegh's proposal for the conquest of Guiana failed to gain the queen's support.
5. The Inca, the supposed ruler of Guiana and its chief city, Manoa.
6. Treaty.

From The History of the World

[CONCLUSION: ON DEATH]

It is * * * Death alone that can suddenly make man to know himself. He tells the proud and insolent that they are but abjects,[1] and humbles them at the instant; makes them cry, complain, and repent, yea, even to hate their forepassed happiness. He takes the account of the rich, and proves him a beggar, a naked beggar, which hath interest in nothing but in the gravel that fills his mouth. He holds a glass before the eyes of the most beautiful, and makes them see therein their deformity and rottenness, and they acknowledge it.

O eloquent, just, and mighty Death! Whom none could advise, thou hast persuaded; what none hath dared, thou hast done; and whom all the world hath flattered, thou only hast cast out of the world and despised; thou hast drawn together all the far-stretched greatness, all the pride, cruelty, and ambition of man, and covered it all over with these two narrow words: *Hic jacet!*[2] * * *

1614

1. Castoffs.
2. Latin for "Here lies," often carved on tombstones

The Wider World

In 1496 a Venetian tradesman living in Bristol, John Cabot, was granted a license by Henry VII to sail on a voyage of exploration. In 1497, he reached Newfoundland. Other remarkable feats of seamanship and reconaissance followed, including what was the Elizabethan Age's supreme maritime achievement: on his ship *The Golden Hind*, Sir Francis Drake circumnavigated the globe in a three-year voyage from 1577 to 1580 and laid claim to California on behalf of the queen; a few years later (1586–88) a ship commanded by Thomas Cavendish also accomplished a circumnavigation. Though they failed to rival the Spanish and Portuguese in their astonishing national enterprises of exploration and conquest, the range of sixteenth-century English naval ventures, always difficult and dangerous, is extraordinary. Sir Martin Frobisher explored bleak Baffin Island in search of a northwest passage to the Orient; Sir John Davis explored the west coast of Greenland and discovered the Falkland Islands off the coast of Argentina; Sir John Hawkins made large profits by carrying shiploads of black slaves from West Africa for sale in the Caribbean; Sir Walter Ralegh ventured up the Orinoco delta, in what is now Venezuela, in search of the mythical land of El Dorado.

Accounts of these and many other exploits were collected by a clergyman, geographer, and tireless promoter of empire, Richard Hakluyt (1552?–1616), and published as *The Principal Navigations, Voyages, Traffics, and Discoveries of the English Nation* (1589; expanded three-volume edition 1598–1600). Hakluyt writes that he was incited to undertake his huge editorial labors during a stay in France, where he heard "other nations miraculously extolled for their discoveries and notable enterprises by sea, but the English of all others for their sluggish security and continual neglect of the like attempts, either ignominiously reported or exceedingly condemned." His response was to assemble the records of English voyages "to the most remote and farthest distant quarters of the earth, at any time within the compass of these 1500 years."

"To seek new worlds for gold, for praise, for glory," as Ralegh characterized such enterprises, was not for the faint of heart: Drake, Cavendish, Frobisher, and Hawkins all died at sea, as did huge numbers of those who sailed under their command. Elizabethans who were sensible enough to stay at home could have a few material glimpses of their fellow countrymen's far-reaching voyages. Expeditions brought back native plants (including, most famously, tobacco), animals, cultural artifacts, and, on occasion, some native people, most often seized against their will. There were exhibitions in London of a kidnapped Eskimo with his kayak and of Virginians with their canoes. Most of these miserable captives, violently uprooted and vulnerable to European diseases, quickly perished, but even in death they were evidently valuable property: while the English will not give one small coin "to relieve a lame beggar," one of the characters in *The Tempest* wryly remarks, "they will lay out ten to see a dead Indian" (2.2.32–33).

But the principal way in which stay-at-homes encountered the rapidly expanding world was through eyewitness accounts of the kind we present here. These accounts were not, on the whole, rhetorically ornate. Travelers' tales had an ancient and well-deserved reputation for exaggeration and outright mendacity; consequently Elizabethan writers strove for the effect of factual directness, simplicity, and trustworthiness. But the encounters they described were so remarkable, calling into question many of their culture's rooted assumptions about human behavior, that their writings often have the mingled wonder, fear, and longing that characterize the most extravagant literary romance. The greatest Elizabethan writer of romance, Edmund Spenser, acknowledged the affinity in defending his Faerie Land against anyone who might complain that it was unreal:

> But let that man with better sense advise,
>   That of the world least part to us is read:
>   And daily how through hardy enterprise
>   Many great regions are discovered,
>   Which to late age were never mentioned.
>   Who ever heard of th'Indian Peru?
>   Or who in venturous vessel measured
>   The Amazons' huge river, now found true?
> Or fruitfullest Virginia who did ever view?

FROBISHER'S VOYAGES TO THE ARCTIC, 1576–78

George Best, a navigator, was captain of a vessel in two of the three voyages led by Martin Frobisher (1535?–1594) to discover a northwest passage to China. On his return from the third voyage, Best published A true discourse of the late voyages of discovery, for the finding of a passage to Cathay. The expeditions, to a remote island dubbed Meta Incognita (the Unknown Boundary, now known as Baffin Island), were extremely arduous and ultimately proved disastrous. The northwest passage was not found, and five English sailors were seized by the Eskimos and never recovered. Frobisher kidnapped several Eskimos and brought them back to England, along with 1,296 tons of promising-looking ore. The captives caused a sensation in London, but they quickly died; and the ore proved to contain only fool's gold.

From A true discourse of the late voyages of discovery, for the finding of a passage to Cathay by the Northwest, under the conduct of Martin Frobisher

God having blessed us with so happy a landfall,[1] we bare into the straits which run in next hand, and somewhat further up to the northward, and came as near the shore as we might for the ice, and upon the eighteenth day of July our general taking the goldfiners[2] with him, attempted to go on shore with a small rowing pinnace, upon the small island where the ore was taken up, to prove whether there were any store[3] thereof to be found, but he could

1. At what is now called Frobisher Bay, a deep inlet in southeastern Baffin Island. Frobisher thought it was a strait—the entrance to the Northwest Passage.
2. Refiners of gold. The main purpose of Fro-

bisher's second and third voyages was to seek out gold mines.
3. Abundance. "Taken up": i.e., during the previous year's voyage.

not get in all that island a piece so big as a walnut, where the first was found. But our men which sought the other islands thereabouts found them all to have good store of the ore, whereupon our general with these good tidings returned aboard about ten of the clock at night, and was joyfully welcomed of the company with a volley of shot. He brought eggs, fowls, and a young seal aboard, which the company had killed ashore, and having found upon those islands gins[4] set to catch fowl, and sticks new cut, with other things, he well perceived that not long before some of the country people had resorted thither.

Having therefore found those tokens of the people's access in those parts, and being in his first voyage well acquainted with their subtle and cruel disposition, he provided well for his better safety, and on Friday the nineteenth of July in the morning early, with his best company of gentlemen and soldiers, to the number of forty persons, went on shore, as well to discover the inland and habitation of the people as also to find out some fit harbor for our ships. And passing towards the shore with no small difficulty by reason of the abundance of ice which lay alongst the coast so thick together that hardly any passage through them might be discovered, we arrived at length upon the main of Hall's greater island,[5] and found there also as well as in the other small islands good store of the ore. And leaving his boats here with sufficient guard, we passed up into the country about two English miles, and recovered the top of a high hill, on the top whereof our men made a column or cross of stones heaped up of a good height together in good sort, and solemnly sounded a trumpet, and said certain prayers kneeling about the ensign, and honored the place by the name of Mount Warwick, in remembrance of the Right Honorable the Lord Ambrose Dudley, earl of Warwick,[6] whose noble mind and good countenance in this, as in all other good actions, gave great encouragement and good furtherance. This done, we retired our companies, not seeing anything here worth further discovery, the country seeming barren and full of ragged mountains, and in most parts covered with snow.

And thus marching towards our boats, we espied certain of the country people on the top of Mount Warwick with a flag wafting us back again and making great noise, with cries like the mowing of bulls, seeming greatly desirous of conference with us: whereupon the general being therewith better acquainted, answered them again with the like cries, whereat and with the noise of our trumpets they seemed greatly to rejoice, skipping, laughing, and dancing for joy. And hereupon we made signs unto them, holding up two fingers, commanding two of our men to go apart from our companies, whereby they might do the like. So that forthwith two of our men and two of theirs met together a good space from company, neither party having their weapons about them. Our men gave them pins and points[7] and such trifles as they had. And they likewise bestowed on our men two bow cases and such things as they had. They earnestly desired our men to go up into their country, and our men offered them like kindness aboard our ships, but neither part (as it seemed) admitted or trusted the other's courtesy. Their manner of traffic is thus: they do use to lay down of their merchandise upon the

4. Snares.
5. Named, the preceding year, after the captain of one of Frobisher's ships.
6. Dudley (1528?–1590), a man distinguished in

public service both civil and martial, was the chief promoter of Frobisher's explorations.
7. Laces.

ground so much as they mean to part withal, and so looking that the other party with whom they make trade should do the like, they themselves do depart, and then if they do like of their mart they come again, and take in exchange the other's merchandise; otherwise if they like not, they take their own and depart. The day being thus well-near spent, in haste we retired our companies into our boats again, minding forthwith to search alongst the coast for some harbor fit for our ships: for the present necessity thereof was much, considering that all this while they lay off and on between the two lands, being continually subject as well to great danger of fleeting ice, which environed them, as to the sudden flaws[8] which the coast seemeth much subject unto. But when the people perceived our departure, with great tokens of affection they earnestly called us back again, following us almost to our boats: whereupon our general taking his master[9] with him, who was best acquainted with their manners, went apart unto two of them, meaning, if they could lay sure hold upon them, forcibly to bring them aboard, with intent to bestow certain toys[1] and apparel upon the one, and so to dismiss him with all arguments of courtesy, and retain the other for an interpreter. The general and his master being met with their two companions together, after they had exchanged certain things the one with the other, one of the savages for lack of better merchandise cut off the tail of his coat (which is a chief ornament among them) and gave it unto our general for a present. But he presently upon a watchword given with his master suddenly laid hold upon the two savages. But the ground underfoot being slippery with the snow on the side of the hill, their handfast failed, and their prey escaping ran away and lightly recovered their bow and arrows, which they had hid not far from them behind the rocks. And being only two savages in sight, they so fiercely, desperately, and with such fury assaulted and pursued our general and his master, being altogether unarmed, and not mistrusting their subtlety, that they chased them to their boats, and hurt the general in the buttock with an arrow, who the rather speedily fled back because they suspected a greater number behind the rocks. Our soldiers (which were commanded before to keep their boats) perceiving the danger, and hearing our men calling for shot, came speedily to rescue, thinking there had been a greater number. But when the savages heard the shot of one of our calivers[2] (and yet having first bestowed their arrows), they ran away, our men speedily following them. But a servant of my Lord of Warwick, called Nicholas Conger, a good footman, and uncumbered with any furniture,[3] having only a dagger at his back, over-took one of them, and being a Cornishman and a good wrestler, showed his companion such a Cornish trick that he made his sides ache against the ground for a month after. And so being stayed, he was taken alive and brought away, but the other escaped. Thus with their strange and new prey our men repaired to their boats, and passed from the main to a small island of a mile compass, where they resolved to tarry all night; for even now a sudden storm was grown so great at sea that by no means they could recover their ships. And here every man refreshed himself with a small portion of victuals which was laid into the boats for their dinners, having neither eat nor drunk all the day before. But because they knew not how long the storm

---

8. Squalls.
9. Ship's captain.
1. Trifles.

2. Light muskets.
3. Equipment.

might last, nor how far off the ships might be put to sea, nor whether they should ever recover them again or not, they made great spare of their victuals, as it greatly behooved them: for they knew full well that the best cheer the country could yield them was rocks and stones, a hard food to live withal, and the people more ready to eat them than to give them wherewithal to eat. And thus keeping very good watch and ward, they lay there all night upon hard cliffs of snow and ice, both wet, cold, and comfortless.

* * *

Upon the mainland over against the Countess's Island[4] we discovered and beheld to our great marvel the poor caves and houses of those country people, which serve them (as it should seem) for their winter dwellings, and are made two fathom[5] underground, in compass round like to an oven, being joined fast one by another, having holes like to a foxe or cony berry,[6] to keep and come together. They undertrenched these places with gutters, so that the water falling from the hills above them may slide away without their annoyance: and are seated commonly in the foot of a hill, to shield them better from the cold winds, having their door and entrance ever open towards the south. From the ground upward they build with whales' bones, for lack of timber, which bending one over another are handsomely compacted in the top together, and are covered over with sealskins, which, instead of tiles, fence them from the rain. In which house they have only one room, having the one half of the floor raised with broad stones a foot higher than the other, whereon strewing moss, they make their nests to sleep in. They defile these dens most filthily with their beastly feeding, and dwell so long in a place (as we think) until their sluttishness loathing them,[7] they are forced to seek a sweeter air and a new seat, and are (no doubt) a dispersed and wandering nation, as the Tartarians, and live in hordes and troops without any certain abode, as may appear by sundry circumstances of our experience.

Here our captive being ashore with us, to declare the use of such things as we saw, stayed himself alone behind the company, and did set up five small sticks round in a circle one by another, with one small bone placed just in the midst of all: which thing when one of our men perceived, he called us back to behold the matter, thinking that he had meant some charm or witchcraft therein. But the best conjecture we could make thereof was that he would thereby his countrymen should understand that for our five men which they betrayed[8] the last year (whom he signified by the five sticks) he was taken and kept prisoner, which he signified by the bone in the midst. For afterwards when we showed him the picture of his countryman which the last year was brought into England (whose counterfeit[9] we had drawn, with boat and other furniture, both as he was in his own, and also in English apparel), he was upon the sudden much amazed thereat, and beholding advisedly the same with silence a good while, as though he would strain courtesy whether[1] should begin the speech (for he thought him no doubt a lively[2] creature), at length began to question with him, as with his compan-

---

4. Named after the countess of Warwick.
5. Twelve feet.
6. Rabbit burrows.
7. Until their squalor becomes unbearable to them.

8. I.e., captured.
9. Likeness.
1. Which of them.
2. Living.

ion, and, finding him dumb and mute, seemed to suspect him, as one disdainful, and would with a little help have grown into choler at the matter, until at last, by feeling and handling, he found him but a deceiving picture. And then with great noise and cries ceased not wondering, thinking that we could make men live or die at our pleasure.

And thereupon calling the matter to his remembrance, he gave us plainly to understand by signs that he had knowledge of the taking of our five men the last year, and confessing the manner of each thing, numbered the five men upon his five fingers and pointed unto a boat in our ship which was like unto that wherein our men were betrayed: and when we made him signs that they were slain and eaten, he earnestly denied, and made signs to the contrary.

1578, 1598–1600

DRAKE'S CIRCUMNAVIGATION OF THE GLOBE, 1577–80

The Spanish and Portuguese had been exploring the Pacific long before the great Elizabethan admiral and sometime privateer Francis Drake (ca. 1540–1596) caught sight of its waters in 1573. Drake returned to the Pacific in the course of an epochal journey chronicled in a narrative entitled *The famous voyage of Sir Francis Drake into the South Sea, and therehence about the whole Globe of the Earth.* The narrative, assembled by Hakluyt from several eyewitness accounts, includes a description of the place Drake called *Nova Albion* (New England), better known by the name given to it by Spanish explorers, California. Somewhere in the vicinity of what is now San Francisco (perhaps Drake's Bay, on the Point Reyes peninsula), the English believed (or claimed to believe) that the native "king" gave to Drake title to the whole land. The brass plate mentioned in the account has never been found, though a forgery sat for some years in a display case at the University of California, Berkeley.

From The famous voyage of Sir Francis Drake into the South Sea, and therehence about the whole Globe of the Earth, begun in the year of our Lord 1577

The 5th day of June, being in 43 degrees towards the pole arctic,[1] we found the air so cold that our men, being grievously pinched with the same, complained of the extremity thereof, and the further we went, the more the cold increased upon us. Whereupon we thought it best for that time to seek the land, and did so, finding it not mountainous but low plain land, till we came within 38 degrees towards the line.[2] In which height it pleased God to send us into a fair and good bay, with a good wind to enter the same.

1. I.e., 43° north latitude. The year is 1579.
2. The equator. "38 degrees": a latitude a little north of present-day San Francisco.

In this bay we anchored, and the people of the country having their houses close by the water's side showed themselves unto us, and sent a present to our general.

When they came unto us, they greatly wondered at the things that we brought, but our general (according to his natural and accustomed humanity) courteously entreated them, and liberally bestowed on them necessary things to cover their nakedness, whereupon they supposed us to be gods, and would not be persuaded to the contrary. The presents which they sent to our general were feathers, and cauls of net-work.

Their houses are digged round about with earth, and have from the uttermost brims of the circle clefts of wood set upon them, joining close together at the top like a spire steeple, which by reason of that closeness are very warm.

Their beds is the ground with rushes strewed on it, and lying about the house, have the fire in the midst. The men go naked, the women take bulrushes and comb them after the manner of hemp, and thereof make their loose garments, which being knit about their middles, hang down about their hips, having also about their shoulders a skin of deer, with the hair upon it. These women are very obedient and serviceable to their husbands.

After they were departed from us, they came and visited us the second time and brought with them feathers and bags of tobacco for presents; and when they came to the top of the hill (at the bottom whereof we had pitched our tents), they stayed themselves: where one appointed for speaker wearied himself with making a long oration, which done, they left their bows upon the hill and came down with their presents.

In the meantime the women, remaining on the hill, tormented themselves lamentably, tearing their flesh from their cheeks, whereby we perceived that they were about[3] a sacrifice. In the meantime our general with his company went to prayer, and to reading of the Scriptures, at which exercise they were attentive, and seemed greatly to be affected with it: but when they were come unto us, they restored again unto us those things which before we bestowed upon them.

The news of our being there being spread through the country, the people that inhabited round about came down, and amongst them the king himself, a man of a goodly stature and comely personage, with many other tall and warlike men: before whose coming were sent two ambassadors to our general to signify that their king was coming, in doing of which message their speech was continued about half an hour. This ended, they by signs requested our general to send something by their hand to their king, as a token that his coming might be in peace: wherein our general having satisfied them, they returned with glad tidings to their king, who marched to us with a princely majesty, the people crying continually after their manner; and as they drew near unto us, so did they strive to behave themselves in their actions with comeliness.

In the forefront was a man of a goodly personage, who bare the scepter or mace before the king, whereupon hanged two crowns, a less and a bigger, with three chains of a marvelous length. The crowns were made of knit-work wrought artificially with feathers of divers colors; the chains were made of a

3. Were performing.

bonny substance, and few be the persons among them that are admitted to wear them—and of that number also the persons are stinted,[4] as some ten, some 12, etc. Next unto him which bare the scepter was the king himself, with his guard about his person, clad with cony[5] skins and other skins; after them followed the naked common sort of people, everyone having his face painted, some with white, some with black and other colors, and having in their hands one thing or another for a present, not so much as their children, but they also brought their presents.

In the meantime our general gathered his men together and marched within his fenced place, making against their approaching a very warlike show. They being trooped together in their order, and a general salutation being made, there was presently a general silence. Then he that bare the scepter before the king, being informed by another, whom they assigned to that office, with a manly and lofty voice proclaimed that which the other spake to him in secret, continuing half an hour: which ended, and a general Amen as it were given, the king with the whole number of men and women (the children excepted) came down without any weapon, who descending to the foot of the hill set themselves in order.

In coming towards our bulwarks and tents, the scepter-bearer began a song, observing his measures in a dance, and that with a stately countenance, whom the king with his guard, and every degree of persons following, did in like manner sing and dance, saving only the women, which danced and kept silence. The general permitted them to enter within our bulwark, where they continued their song and dance a reasonable[6] time. When they had satisfied themselves, they made signs to our general to sit down, to whom the king and divers others made several orations, or rather supplications, that he would take their province and kingdom into his hand and become their king, making signs that they would resign unto him their right and title of the whole land and become his subjects. In which to persuade us the better, the king and the rest, with one consent and with great reverence, joyfully singing a song, did set the crown upon his head, enriched his neck with all their chains, and offered unto him many other things, honoring him by the name of Hioh, adding thereunto, as it seemed, a sign of triumph: which thing our general thought not meet[7] to reject, because he knew not what honor and profit it might be to our country. Wherefore in the name and to the use of Her Majesty he took the scepter, crown, and dignity of the said country into his hands, wishing that the riches and treasure thereof might so conveniently be transported to the enriching of her kingdom at home, as it aboundeth in the same.

The common sort of people, leaving the king and his guard with our general, scattered themselves together with their sacrifices among our people, taking a diligent view of every person: and such as pleased their fancy (which were the youngest), they enclosing them about offered their sacrifices unto them with lamentable weeping, scratching, and tearing the flesh from their faces with their nails, whereof issued abundance of blood. But we used signs to them of disliking this, and stayed their hands from force, and directed them upwards to the living God, whom only they ought to worship. They

---

4. Limited, restricted.
5. Rabbit.

6. Considerable.
7. Not fitting.

showed unto us their wounds and craved help of them at our hands, whereupon we gave them lotions, plasters, and ointments agreeing to the state of their griefs, beseeching God to cure their diseases. Every third day they brought their sacrifices unto us, until they understood our meaning, that we had no pleasure in them: yet they could not be long absent from us, but daily frequented our company to the hour of our departure, which departure seemed so grievous unto them that their joy was turned into sorrow. They entreated us that being absent we would remember them, and by stealth provided a sacrifice, which we misliked.

Our necessary business being ended, our general with his company traveled up into the country to their villages, where we found herds of deer by 1000 in a company, being most large and fat of body.

We found the whole country to be a warren of a strange kind of conies, their bodies in bigness as be the Barbary conies, their heads as the heads of ours, the feet of a want,[8] and the tail of a rat, being of great length; under her chin is on either side a bag, into the which she gathereth her meat,[9] when she hath filled her belly abroad. The people eat their bodies and make great accompt[1] of their skins, for their king's coat was made of them.

Our general called this country Nova Albion,[2] and that for two causes: the one in respect of the white banks and cliffs which lie towards the sea; and the other, because[3] it might have some affinity with our country in name, which sometime was so called.

There is no part of earth here to be taken up wherein there is not some probable show of gold or silver.

At our departure hence our general set up a monument of our being there, as also of Her Majesty's right and title to the same, namely a plate nailed upon a fair great post, whereupon was engraven Her Majesty's name, the day and year of our arrival there, with the free giving up of the province and people into Her Majesty's hands, together with Her Highness' picture and arms[4] in a piece of sixpence of current English money under the plate, whereunder was also written the name of our general.

1589

---

8. Mole.
9. Food.
1. Account.
2. Albion is the Latin name for Britain. The word is thought to derive from either the Celtic word for "high" or the Latin word for "white," *albus*. Either

etymology fits with the White Cliffs of Dover, the dominant feature of the island when approached from ancient Gaul.
3. So that.
4. Coat of arms.

AMADAS AND BARLOWE'S VOYAGE TO VIRGINIA, 1584

The first English voyage to Virginia, in 1584, was commanded by Philip Amadas and Arthur Barlowe. The two captains had been sent forth by Sir Walter Ralegh to discover territories in North America suitable for colonization. In Barlowe's account, they encountered a people living very close to the blessed state of the inhabitants of the

Golden Age celebrated by classical poets like Ovid, a state of simplicity, honesty, generosity, and peace. All the same, when a group of Algonkian hunters suddenly return home, the English colonists immediately reach for their weapons.

From The first voyage made to Virginia

The second of July we found shoal water, which smelt so sweetly and was so strong a smell as if we had been in the midst of some delicate garden abounding with all kind of odoriferous flowers, by which we were assured that the land could not be far distant. And keeping good watch and bearing but slack sail, the fourth of the same month we arrived upon the coast, which we supposed to be a continent and firm land, and we sailed along the same 120 English miles before we could find any entrance, or river issuing into the sea. The first that appeared unto us we entered, though not without some difficulty, and cast anchor three arquebus-shot[1] within the haven's mouth, on the left hand of the same. And after thanks given to God for our safe arrival thither, we manned our boats, and went to view the land next adjoining and to take possession of the same in the right of the Queen's most excellent Majesty, as rightful Queen and Princess of the same, and after delivered the same over to your use, according to her Majesty's grant and letters patents,[2] under her Highness's Great Seal. Which being performed, according to the ceremonies used in such enterprises, we viewed the land about us, being whereas we first landed very sandy and low towards the waterside, but so full of grapes as the very beating and surge of the sea overflowed them. Of which we found such plenty, as well there as in all places else, both on the sand and on the green soil on the hills, as in the plains, as well on every little shrub, as also climbing towards the tops of high cedars, that I think in all the world the like abundance is not to be found. And myself having seen those parts of Europe that most abound, find such difference as were incredible to be written.

We passed from the seaside towards the tops of those hills next adjoining, being but of mean height, and from thence we beheld the sea on both sides, to the north and to the south, finding no end any of both ways. This land lay stretching itself to the west, which after we found to be but an island of twenty leagues long and not above six miles broad. Under the bank or hill whereon we stood, we beheld the valleys replenished with goodly cedar trees, and having discharged our arquebus-shot, such a flock of cranes (the most part white) arose under us, with such a cry redoubled by many echoes, as if an army of men had shouted all together.

This island had many goodly woods, and full of deer, conies,[3] hares, and fowl, even in the midst of summer, in incredible abundance. The woods are not such as you find in Bohemia, Moscovia, or Hyrcania,[4] barren and fruitless, but the highest and reddest cedars of the world, far bettering the cedars of the Azores, of the Indies, or of Lybanus,[5] pines, cypress, sassafras, the lentisk or the tree that beareth the mastic,[6] the tree that beareth the rind of

---

1. Harquebus, a heavy but portable firearm.
2. Documents issued by the sovereign granting certain rights to the bearer. "Your use": i.e., Ralegh's.
3. Rabbits.

4. A region near the Caspian Sea.
5. Lebanon.
6. Resin exuded from the bark of *Pistacio lentiscus* ("the lentisk"), supposed to have medicinal value.

black cinnamon, of which Master Winter brought from the Straits of Magellan, and many other of excellent smell and quality.[7]

We remained by the side of this island two whole days before we saw any people of the country. The third day we espied one small boat rowing towards us, having in it three persons. This boat came to the land's side, four arquebus-shot from our ships; and there two of the people remaining, the third came along the shore side towards us, and we being then all within board, he walked up and down upon the point of the land next unto us. Then the master and the pilot of the Admiral, Simon Ferdinando, and the captain, Philip Amadas, myself, and others, rowed to the land; whose coming this fellow attended, never making any show of fear or doubt. And after he had spoken of many things not understood by us, we brought him, with his own good liking, aboard the ships, and gave him a shirt, a hat, and some other things, and made him taste of our wine and our meat,[8] which he liked very well. And after having viewed both barks he departed and went to his own boat again, which he had left in a little cove or creek adjoining. As soon as he was two bow-shot into the water he fell to fishing, and in less than half an hour he had laden his boat as deep as it could swim, with which he came again to the point of the land, and there he divided his fish into two parts, pointing one part to the ship and the other to the pinnace.[9] Which, after he had (as much as he might) requited the former benefits received, he departed out of our sight.

The next day there came unto us divers boats, and in one of them the king's brother, accompanied with forty or fifty men, very handsome and goodly people, and in their behavior as mannerly and civil as any of Europe. His name was Granganimeo, and the king is called Wingina; the country, Wingandacoa (and now, by her Majesty, Virginia). The manner of his coming was in this sort: he left his boats all together, as the first man did, a little from the ships by the shore, and came along to the place over against the ships, followed with forty men. When he came to the place, his servants spread a long mat upon the ground, on which he sat down, and at the other end of the mat four others of his company did the like. The rest of his men stood round about him somewhat afar off. When we came to the shore to him, with our weapons, he never moved from his place, nor any of the other four, nor never mistrusted any harm to be offered from us; but, sitting still, he beckoned us to come and sit by him, which we performed. And, being set, he made all signs of joy and welcome, striking on his head and his breast and afterwards on ours, to show we were all one, smiling and making show the best he could of all love and familiarity. After he had made a long speech unto us we presented him with divers things, which he received very joyfully and thankfully. None of his company durst speak one word all the time; only the four which were at the other end spake one in the other's ear very softly.

The king is greatly obeyed, and his brothers and children reverenced. The king himself in person was at our being there sore wounded in a fight which he had with the king of the next country, called Wingiana, and was shot in two places through the body, and once clean through the thigh, but yet he recovered. By reason whereof, and for that he lay at the chief town of the country, being six days' journey off, we saw him not at all.

7. Michael Drayton drew on this passage for his *Ode. To the Virginian Voyage*, which praises "The cedar reaching high / To kiss the sky, / The cypress, pine, / And useful sassafras" (pp. 968–69).
8. Food in general (not necessarily flesh).
9. Light vessel attending on a larger ship.

After we had presented this his brother with such things as we thought he liked, we likewise gave somewhat to the other that sat with him on the mat. But presently he arose and took all from them and put it into his own basket, making signs and tokens that all things ought to be delivered unto him, and the rest were but his servants and followers. A day or two after this we fell to trading with them, exchanging some things that we had for chamois, buff, and deer skins. When we showed him all our packet of merchandise, of all things that he saw a bright tin dish most pleased him, which he presently took up and clapt it before his breast, and after made a hole in the brim thereof and hung it about his neck, making signs that it would defend him against his enemies' arrows. For those people maintain a deadly and terrible war with the people and king adjoining. We exchanged our tin dish for twenty skins, worth twenty crowns or twenty nobles; and a copper kettle for fifty skins, worth fifty crowns. They offered us good exchange for our hatchets and axes, and for knives, and would have given anything for swords; but we would not depart with any. * * *

* * * We found the people most gentle, loving, and faithful, void of guile and treason, and such as live after the manner of the golden age.[1] The people only care how to defend themselves from the cold in their short winter, and to feed themselves with such meat as the soil affordeth; their meat is very well sodden,[2] and they make broth very sweet and savory. Their vessels are earthen pots, very large, white, and sweet; their dishes are wooden platters of sweet timber. Within the place where they feed was their lodging, and within that their idol, which they worship, of which they speak incredible things. While we were at meat, there came in at the gates two or three men with their bows and arrows from hunting, whom when we espied we began to look one towards another, and offered to reach our weapons. But as soon as she[3] espied our mistrust, she was very much moved, and caused some of her men to run out, and take away their bows and arrows and break them, and withal beat the poor fellows out of the gate again. When we departed in the evening and would not tarry all night, she was very sorry, and gave us into our boat our supper half-dressed, pots and all, and brought us to our boat's side, in which we lay all night, removing the same a pretty[4] distance from the shore. She perceiving our jealousy[5] was much grieved, and sent divers men and thirty women to sit all night on the bank's side by us, and sent us into our boats fine mats to cover us from the rain, using very many words to entreat us to rest in their houses. But because we were few men, and if we had miscarried the voyage had been in very great danger, we durst not adventure anything, although there was no cause of doubt.[6] For a more kind and loving people there cannot be found in the world, as far as we have hitherto had trial.

* * *

1. Drayton's *Ode* (lines 37–42) picks up on this reference to the Golden Age. A different fantasy of a seemingly ideal society in the New World is found in Thomas More's *Utopia* (pp. 506–23).
2. Boiled.

3. The wife of Granganimeo, the king's brother.
4. Considerable.
5. Suspicion.
6. Fear.

We brought home also two of the savages, being lusty[7] men, whose names were Wanchese and Manteo.

1589

7. Vigorous.

HARIOT'S REPORT ON VIRGINIA, 1585

Thomas Hariot (1560–1621), mathematician, astronomer, and surveyor in the service of Sir Walter Ralegh, was observing sunspots and using a telescope at about the same time as Galileo; he also made important discoveries in algebra. He accompanied Sir Richard Grenville's expedition to Virginia in 1585 and wrote an account of it intended to promote colonization. He describes the geography, climate, vegetation, wildlife, and, especially, inhabitants of the New World, about whom the English were intensely curious. Reports had begun to circulate in England about tensions with the Algonkian Indians, upon whom the colonists were almost completely dependent for food, and Hariot's brief ethnographic observations sketch the grounds for reassurance that the natives "are not to be feared."

From A brief and true report of the new-found land of Virginia

Of the commodities there found and to be raised, as well merchantable as others

OF THE NATURE AND MANNERS OF THE PEOPLE

It resteth[1] I speak a word or two of the natural inhabitants, their natures and manners, leaving large discourse thereof until time more convenient hereafter: now only so far forth, as that you may know how that they in respect of troubling our inhabiting and planting are not to be feared, but that they shall have cause both to fear and love us that shall inhabit with them.

They are a people clothed with loose mantles made of deerskins, and aprons of the same round about their middles, all else naked, of such a difference of statures only as we in England,[2] having no edge tools or weapons of iron or steel to offend us withal, neither know they how to make any. Those weapons that they have, are only bows made of witch hazel and arrows of reeds, flat-edged truncheons also of wood about a yard long, neither have they anything to defend themselves but targets[3] made of barks, and some armors made of sticks wickered together with thread.

Their towns are but small, and near the seacoast but few, some containing but ten or twelve houses, some twenty; the greatest that we have seen hath been but of thirty houses. If they be walled, it is only done with barks of trees

1. Remains that.
2. I.e., the variability of height among them is similar to that among the English.
3. Shields.

made fast to stakes, or else with poles only fixed upright, and close one by another.

Their houses are made of small poles, made fast at the tops in round form after the manner as is used in many arbories in our gardens of England; in most towns covered with barks, and in some with artificial mats made of long rushes, from the tops of the houses down to the ground. The length of them is commonly double to the breadth; in some places they are but twelve and sixteen yards long, and in other some we have seen, of four-and-twenty.

In some places of the country, one only town belongeth to the government of a Wiroans or chief Lord, in other some two or three, in some six, eight, and more. The greatest Wiroans that yet we had dealing with had but eighteen towns in his government and able to make not above seven or eight hundred fighting men at the most. The language of every government is different from any other, and the further they are distant, the greater is the difference.

Their manner of wars amongst themselves is either by sudden surprising one another, most commonly about the dawning of the day, or moonlight, or else by ambushes or some subtle devices. Set battles are very rare, except it fall out where there are many trees, where either part may have some hope of defense, after the delivery of every arrow, in leaping behind some or other.

If there fall out any wars between us and them, what their fight is likely to be, we having advantages against them so many manner of ways, as by our discipline, our strange weapons and devices else, especially ordnance[4] great and small, it may easily be imagined: by the experience we have had in some places, the turning up of their heels against us in running away was their best defense.

In respect of us they are a people poor, and for want of skill and judgment in the knowledge and use of our things, do esteem our trifles before things of greater value. Notwithstanding, in their proper manner (considering the want of such means as we have), they seem very ingenious. For although they have no such tools, nor any such crafts, sciences, and arts as we, yet in those things they do, they show excellency of wit.[5] And by how much they upon due consideration shall find our manner of knowledges and crafts to exceed theirs in perfection, and speed for doing or execution, by so much the more is it probable that they should desire our friendship and love, and have the greater respect for pleasing and obeying us. Whereby may be hoped, if means of good government be used, that they may in short time be brought to civility and the embracing of true religion.

Some religion they have already, which although it be far from the truth, yet being as it is, there is hope it may be the easier and sooner reformed.

They believe that there are many gods, which they call Mantóac, but of different sorts and degrees, one only chief and great god, which hath been from all eternity. Who, as they affirm, when he purposed to make the world, made first other gods of a principal order to be as means and instruments to be used in the creation and government to follow, and after the sun, moon, and stars as petty gods, and the instruments of the other order more principal. First, they say, were made waters, out of which by the gods was made all diversity of creatures that are visible or invisible.

4. Artillery.   5. Intelligence.

For mankind, they say a woman was made first, which, by the working of one of the gods, conceived and brought forth children. And in such sort, they say, they had their beginning. But how many years or ages have passed since, they say they can make no relation, having no letters nor other such means as we to keep records of the particularities of times past, but only tradition from father to son.

They think that all the gods are of human shape, and therefore they represent them by images in the forms of men, which they call Kewasowok; one alone is called Kewas: them they place in houses appropriate, or temples, which they call Machicomuck, where they worship, pray, sing, and make many times offering unto them. In some Machicomuck we have seen but one Kewas, in some two, and in other some three. The common sort think them to be also gods.

They believe also the immortality of the soul, that after this life as soon as the soul is departed from the body, according to the works it hath done, it is either carried to heaven, the habitacle of gods, there to enjoy perpetual bliss and happiness, or else to a great pit or hole, which they think to be in the furthest parts of their part of the world toward the sunset, there to burn continually. The place they call Popogusso.

For the confirmation of this opinion, they told me two stories of two men that had been lately dead and revived again. The one happened, but few years before our coming into the country, of a wicked man, which having been dead and buried, the next day the earth of the grave being seen to move, was taken up again; who made declaration where his soul had been—that is to say, very near entering into Popogusso, had not one of the gods saved him and gave him leave to return again and teach his friends what they should do to avoid that terrible place of torment. The other happened in the same year we were there, but in a town that was sixty miles from us, and it was told me for strange news; that one being dead, buried, and taken up again as the first, showed that although his body had lain dead in the grave, yet his soul was alive and had traveled far in a long broad way, on both sides whereof grew most delicate and pleasant trees, bearing more rare and excellent fruits than ever he had seen before or was able to express, and at length came to most brave[6] and fair houses, near which he met his father that had been dead before, who gave him great charge to go back and show his friends what good they were to do to enjoy the pleasures of that place, which when he had done he should after come again.

What subtlety soever be in the Wiroances and priests, this opinion worketh so much in many of the common and simple sort of people that it maketh them have great respect to their governors, and also great care what they do, to avoid torment after death and to enjoy bliss; although notwithstanding there is punishment ordained for malefactors, as stealers, whoremongers, and other sorts of wicked-doers, some punished with death, some with forfeitures, some with beating, according to the greatness of the facts.[7]

And this is the sum of their religion, which I learned by having special familiarity with some of their priests. Wherein they were not so sure grounded, nor gave such credit to their traditions and stories, but through

6. Fine, splendid.   7. Deeds. "Forfeitures": fines.

conversing with us they were brought into great doubts of their own,[8] and no small admiration of ours, with earnest desire in many to learn more than we had means, for want of perfect utterance in their language, to express.

Most things they saw with us, as mathematical instruments, sea compasses, the virtue[9] of the lodestone in drawing iron, a perspective glass whereby was showed many strange sights, burning glasses, wildfire works,[1] guns, hooks, writing and reading, spring-clocks that seem to go of themselves, and many other things that we had, were so strange unto them, and so far exceeded their capacities to comprehend the reason and means how they should be made and done, that they thought they were rather the works of gods than of men, or at the leastwise they had been given and taught us of the gods. Which made many of them to have such opinion of us, as that if they knew not the truth of God and religion already, it was rather to be had from us whom God so specially loved, than from a people that were so simple as they found themselves to be in comparison of us. Whereupon greater credit was given unto that we spoke of concerning such matters.

Many times and in every town where I came, according as I was able, I made declaration of the contents of the Bible, that therein was set forth the true and only God and his mighty works, that therein was contained the true doctrine of salvation through Christ, with many particularities of miracles and chief points of religion, as I was able then to utter, and thought fit for the time. And although I told them the book materially and of itself was not of any such virtue as I thought they did conceive, but only the doctrine therein contained, yet would many be glad to touch it, to embrace it, to kiss it, to hold it to their breasts and heads, and stroke over all their body with it, to show their hungry desire of that knowledge which was spoken of.

* * *

There could at no time happen any strange sickness, losses, hurts, or any other cross[2] unto them, but that they would impute to us the cause or means thereof, for offending or not pleasing us. One other rare and strange accident, leaving others, will I mention before I end, which moved the whole country that either knew or heard of us to have us in wonderful admiration.

There was no town where we had any subtle device practiced against us, we leaving it unpunished or not revenged (because we sought by all means possible to win them by gentleness), but that within a few days after our departure from every such town the people began to die very fast, and many in short space, in some towns about twenty, in some forty, and in one six score, which in truth was very many in respect of their numbers. This happened in no place that we could learn, but where we had been, where they used some practice against us, and after such time. The disease also was so strange that they neither knew what it was nor how to cure it, the like by report of the oldest men in the country never happened before, time out of

8. I.e., their own religion.
9. Power.
1. "Wildfire" was a composition of highly flammable substances, easy to ignite and very difficult to extinguish, used in warfare. "Burning glasses"

were concave mirrors used to concentrate the sun's rays. The "perspective glass" was an early telescope Hariot had devised.
2. Affliction.

mind—a thing specially observed by us, as also by the natural inhabitants themselves. Insomuch that when some of the inhabitants which were our friends, and especially the Wiroans Wingina, had observed such effects in four or five towns to follow their wicked practices, they were persuaded that it was the work of our God through our means, and that we by him might kill and slay whom we would without weapons, and not come near them. And thereupon when it had happened that they had understanding that any of their enemies had abused us in our journeys, hearing that we had wrought no revenge with our weapons, and fearing upon some cause the matter should so rest, did come and entreat us that we would be a means to our God that they, as others that had dealt ill with us, might in like sort die, alleging how much it would be for our credit and profit, as also theirs, and hoping furthermore that we would do so much at their requests in respect of the friendship we professed them.

Whose entreaties although we showed that they were ungodly, affirming that our God would not subject himself to any such prayers and requests of men—that indeed all things have been and were to be done according to his good pleasure as he had ordained, and that we to show ourselves his true servants ought rather to make petition for the contrary, that they with them might live together with us, be made partakers of his truth, and serve him in righteousness, but notwithstanding in such sort that we refer that, as all other things, to be done according to his divine will and pleasure, and as by his wisdom he had ordained to be best—yet because the effect fell out so suddenly and shortly after according to their desires, they thought nevertheless it came to pass by our means, and that we in using such speeches unto them did but dissemble the matter, and therefore came unto us to give us thanks in their manner, that although we satisfied them not in promise, yet in deeds and effect we had fulfilled their desires.

This marvelous accident in all the country wrought so strange opinions of us that some people could not tell whether to think us gods or men, and the rather because that all the space of their sickness there was no man of ours known to die, or that was specially sick: they noted also that we had no women amongst us, neither that we did care for any of theirs.

Some therefore were of opinion that we were not born of women, and therefore not mortal, but that we were men of an old generation many years past, then risen again to immortality.

Some would likewise seem to prophesy that there were more of our generation yet to come, to kill theirs and take their places, as some thought the purpose was, by[3] that which was already done. Those that were immediately to come after us they imagined to be in the air, yet invisible and without bodies, and that they by our entreaty and for the love of us did make the people to die in that sort as they did, by shooting invisible bullets into them.

To confirm this opinion, their physicians (to excuse their ignorance in curing the disease) would not be ashamed to say, but earnestly make the simple people believe, that the strings of blood that they sucked out of the sick bodies were the strings wherewithal the invisible bullets were tied and cast. Some also thought that we shot them ourselves out of our pieces[4] from the place where we dwelt, and killed the people in any town that had

3. Judging by.   4. Firearms.

offended us as we listed,[5] how far distant from us soever it were. And other some said that it was the special work of God for our sakes (as we ourselves have cause in some sort to think no less, whatsoever some do or may imagine to the contrary), specially some astrologers, knowing of the eclipse of the sun which we saw the same year before in our voyage thitherward, which unto them appeared very terrible; and also of a comet which began to appear but a few days before the beginning of the said sickness. But to exclude them from being the special causes of so special an accident, there are further reasons than I think fit at this present to be alleged. These their opinions I have set down the more at large, that it may appear unto you that there is good hope they may be brought through discreet dealing and government to the embracing of the truth, and consequently to honor, obey, fear, and love us.

And although some of our company towards the end of the year showed themselves too fierce in slaying some of the people in some towns, upon causes that of our part might easily enough have been borne withal, yet notwithstanding, because it was on their part justly deserved, the alteration of their opinions generally and for the most part concerning us is the less to be doubted.[6] And whatsoever else they may be, by carefulness of ourselves need nothing at all to be feared.

1588, 1589, 1590

5. As we pleased.   6. Feared.

JOHN LYLY
1554–1606

John Lyly was the grandson of William Lily, the author of the standard Latin grammar that every English schoolboy studied. After receiving the M.A. degree at Oxford, Lyly went to London, where with the publication of *Euphues* (1578) he became instantly famous. He gained the patronage of Elizabeth's lord treasurer, William Cecil (Lord Burleigh), wrote several elegant and sophisticated plays acted at court by the Children's companies, took part in the Marprelate controversy supporting the bishops, and served several terms as a member of Parliament.

The title *Euphues*, taken from the name of that book's hero, is Greek for "of good natural parts, graceful, witty"; the subtitle, *Anatomy of Wit*, means something like "analysis of the mental faculties." The plot of the work involves a young man who leaves university for the carnal temptations of the city, falls in love, betrays his best friend, is in turn betrayed, repents, and thereafter ladles out great quantities of moral wisdom. But the story of the repentant prodigal is distinctly secondary to the prose style which has come to be known as Euphuism. It has two features: an elaborately patterned sentence structure based on syntactically parallel figures of comparison and antithesis, and a wealth of ornament including proverbs, incidents from history and poetry, and fanciful similes drawn from pseudoscience, from the Roman writer Pliny, from textbooks, or from the author's imagination. Euphuism became a rage for a while, especially at court, though it was criticized by Sidney, parodied by Shakespeare, and mocked by Nashe and Jonson. The style may have been particularly popular among court women; the publisher of Lyly's *Six Court Comedies* in 1632 informed his readers that "All our ladies were then his [Euphues's or Lyly's] scholars, and the beauty in court who could not parley Euphuism was as little regarded as she which now there speaks not French." Although it did not last, this highly self-conscious, overwrought style is an example of the Elizabethans' fascination with language and artifice.

From Euphues: The Anatomy of Wit

[EUPHUES INTRODUCED]

There dwelt in Athens a young gentleman of great patrimony, and of so comely a personage, that it was doubted[1] whether he were more bound to Nature for the lineaments of his person, or to Fortune for the increase of his possessions. But Nature impatient of comparisons, and as it were disdaining a companion or copartner in her working, added to this comeliness of his body such a sharp capacity of mind, that not only she proved Fortune counterfeit, but was half of that opinion that she herself was only current.[2] This young gallant, of more wit than wealth, and yet of more wealth than wisdom, seeing himself inferior to none in pleasant conceits,[3] thought himself superior to all in honest conditions, insomuch that he deemed himself so apt to all things, that he gave himself almost to nothing, but practicing of those things commonly which are incident to these sharp wits, fine phrases, smooth quipping, merry taunting, using jesting without mean,[4] and abusing mirth without measure. As therefore the sweetest rose hath his prickle, the finest velvet his brack,[5] the fairest flower his bran,[6] so the sharpest wit hath his wanton will, and the holiest head his wicked way. And true it is that some men write and most men believe, that in all perfect shapes, a blemish bringeth rather a liking every way to the eyes, than a loathing any way to the mind. Venus had her mole in her cheek which made her more amiable: Helen[7] her scar on her chin which Paris called *cos amoris*, the whetstone of love. Aristippus his wart, Lycurgus[8] his wen: So likewise in the disposition of the mind, either virtue is overshadowed with some vice, or vice overcast with some virtue. Alexander valiant in war, yet given to wine. Tully eloquent in his glozes, yet vainglorious: Solomon wise, yet too too wanton: David holy but yet an homicide:[9] none more witty than Euphues, yet at the first none more wicked. The freshest colors soonest fade, the teenest[1] razor soonest turneth his edge, the finest cloth is soonest eaten with moths, and the cambric sooner stained than the coarse canvas: which appeared well in this Euphues, whose wit being like wax apt to receive any impression, and having the bridle in his own hands, either to use the rein or the spur, disdaining counsel, leaving his

1. Wondered.
2. Genuine.
3. Witty expressions.
4. Moderation.
5. Break, flaw.
6. Husk.
7. The Greek queen whom Paris abducted to Troy; supposedly the most beautiful woman in the world.
8. Aristippus was a Greek philosopher and a dis-

ciple of Socrates who was known for his pursuit of pleasure. Lycurgus was a Spartan lawmaker.
9. Alexander the Great killed his friend Clitus in a drunken brawl. Tully (Marcus Tullius Cicero) was the great Roman orator, famous for his "glozes" (flattering speeches). Solomon was famous both for his wisdom and for his many wives. His father, David, loved Bathsheba and had her husband, Uriah, killed so he could marry her.
1. Keenest.

country, loathing his old acquaintance, thought either by wit to obtain some conquest, or by shame to abide some conflict, and leaving the rule of reason, rashly ran unto destruction. Who preferring fancy before friends, and his present humor[2] before honor to come, laid reason in water being too salt for his taste, and followed unbridled affection,[3] most pleasant for his tooth. When parents have more care how to leave their children wealthy than wise, and are more desirous to have them maintain the name than the nature of a gentleman; when they put gold into the hands of youth, where they should put a rod under their girdle,[4] when instead of awe they make them past grace, and leave them rich executors of goods, and poor executors of godliness, then is it no marvel that the son, being left rich by his father's will, become retchless by his own will.[5]

It hath been an old said saw,[6] and not of less truth than antiquity, that wit is the better if it be the dearer bought: as in the sequel of this history shall most manifestly appear. It happened this young imp[7] to arrive at Naples (a place of more pleasure than profit, and yet of more profit than piety), the very walls and windows whereof shewed it rather to be the Tabernacle of Venus than the Temple of Vesta.[8]

There was all things necessary and in readiness that might either allure the mind to lust or entice the heart to folly, a court more meet[9] for an atheist than for one of Athens, for Ovid than for Aristotle, for a graceless lover than for a godly liver: more fitter for Paris than Hector, and meeter for Flora than Diana.[1]

Here my youth (whether for weariness he could not, or for wantonness would not, go any further) determined to make his abode: whereby it is evidently seen that the fleetest fish swalloweth the delicatest bait, that the highest soaring hawk traineth[2] to the lure, and that the wittiest sconce[3] is inveigled with the sudden view of alluring vanities.

Here he wanted[4] no companions which courted him continually with sundry kinds of devices, whereby they might either soak his purse to reap commodity, or soothe his person to win credit, for he had guests and companions of all sorts.

There frequented to this lodging and mansion house as well the spider to suck poison of his fine wit as the bee to gather honey, as well the drone as the dove, the fox as the lamb, as well Damocles[5] to betray him as Damon[6] to be true to him: yet he behaved himself so warily, that he singled his game[7] wisely. He could easily discern Apollo's music from Pan his pipe,[8] and Venus's beauty from Juno's bravery,[9] and the faith of

2. Whimsy.
3. Passion.
4. I.e., whip them.
5. Appetite, the opposite of reason. "Retchless": reckless.
6. Saying, proverb.
7. Novice.
8. Symbolizing chastity, in contrast to Venus.
9. Fitting.
1. Ovid was famous for his love poems, Aristotle for his profound philosophical works. Paris was the lover of Helen, in contrast to his brother Hector, a great Trojan soldier. Flora was a fertility goddess whose annual celebrations were noted for lasciviousness. Diana was the goddess of chastity.

2. Is attracted to.
3. Head, brain.
4. Lacked.
5. Famous as a flatterer of Dionysius, who gave him a gorgeous banquet but made him sit with a sword suspended over his head by a single hair, to show how dangerous eminence is.
6. Famous in classical legend as the friend of Pythias, so loyal to him that he offered to be executed in his place.
7. Separated his target animal from the herd—that is, made distinctions.
8. In classical myth, Apollo's music was much superior to that which Pan produced on his pipes.
9. Splendid attire.

Laelius[1] from the flattery of Aristippus, he welcomed all but trusted none, he was merry but yet so wary that neither the flatterer could take advantage to entrap him in his talk nor the wisest any assurance of his friendship: who being demanded of one what countryman he was, he answered, "What countryman am I not? If I be in Crete, I can lie, if in Greece I can shift, if in Italy I can court it:[2] if thou ask whose son I am also, I ask thee whose son I am not. I can carouse with Alexander, abstain with Romulus, eat with the Epicure, fast with the Stoic, sleep with Endymion, watch with Chrysippus,"[3] using these speeches and other like. An old gentleman in Naples seeing his pregnant wit, his eloquent tongue somewhat taunting, yet with delight, his mirth without measure yet not without wit, his sayings vainglorious yet pithy, began to bewail his nurture and to muse at his nature, being incensed against the one as most pernicious, and enflamed with the other as most precious: for he well knew that so rare a wit would in time either breed an intolerable trouble or bring an incomparable treasure to the common weal: at the one he greatly pitied, at the other he rejoiced.

1578

1. Laelius was famous as the faithful friend of Scipio Africanus the younger; central figure in Cicero's treatise on friendship.
2. Inhabitants of the island of Crete early had a reputation as liars. Lyly is elaborating or inventing when he says that the Greeks "shift" (practice or live by deceit) and that the Italians "court it" (behave in a courtly manner).
3. Romulus was the legendary founder and first king of Rome. Exposed as an infant with his brother Remus, he was rescued and suckled by a she-wolf and became a symbol of abstinence. The followers of Epicurus (Epicureans) were thought to care for nothing but pleasure; the more austere Stoics venerated duty. Endymion was a youth in Greek legend renowned for his beauty and his eternal sleep on Mount Latmus, where the moon goddess fell in love with him. Chrysippus was a celebrated Stoic philosopher, so devoted to study that he would "watch" (stay up all night) with his books.

SIR PHILIP SIDNEY
1554–1586

Sir Philip Sidney's face was "spoiled with pimples," Ben Jonson remarked in 1619, wryly distancing himself from the virtual Sidney cult that had arisen in the years after his death. Knight, soldier, poet, friend, and patron, Sidney seemed to the Elizabethans to embody all the traits of character and personality they admired: he was Castiglione's perfect courtier come to life. When he was killed in battle in the Low Countries at the age of thirty-two, fighting for the Protestant cause against the hated Spanish, all England mourned. Stories, possibly apocryphal, began immediately to circulate about his gallantry on the battlefield—grievously wounded, he gave his water to a dying foot soldier with the words "Thy necessity is yet greater than mine"—and about his astonishing self-composure as he himself lay dying: suffering from his putrifying, gangrenous wound, Sidney composed a song and had it sung by his deathbed. When his corpse was brought back to England for burial, the spectacular funeral procession, one of the most elaborate ever staged, almost bankrupted his father-in-law, Francis Walsingham, the wealthy head of Queen Elizabeth's secret service.

Philip Sidney's father was Sir Henry Sidney, thrice lord deputy (governor) of Ireland, and his mother was a sister of Robert Dudley, earl of Leicester, the most spectacular and powerful of all the queen's favorites. He entered Shrewsbury School in 1564, at the age of ten, on the same day as Fulke Greville, who became his lifelong friend and his biographer. Greville wrote of Sidney, "though I lived with him and knew him from a child, yet I never knew him other than a man—with such staidness of mind, lovely and familiar gravity, as carried grace and reverence above greater years." He attended Oxford but left without taking a degree and completed his education by extended travels on the Continent. There he met many of the most important people of the time, from kings and queens to philosophers, theologians, and poets. In France he witnessed the Massacre of St. Bartholomew's Day, which began in Paris on August 24, 1572, and raged through France for more than a month, as Catholic mobs incited by Queen Catherine de Médicis slaughtered perhaps 50,000 Huguenots (French Protestants). This experience undoubtedly strengthened Sidney's ardent Protestantism, which had been inculcated by his family background and education. In an intense correspondence with his mentor, the Burgundian humanist Hubert Languet, he brooded on how he could help to save Europe from what he viewed as the Roman Catholic menace.

When he returned to England Sidney found the direct path to heroic action blocked by the caution and hard-nosed realism of Queen Elizabeth and her principal advisers. Though she sent him on some diplomatic missions, the queen clearly regarded the zealous young man with considerable skepticism. As a prominent, well-connected courtier with literary interests, Sidney actively encouraged authors such as Edward Dyer, Greville, and, most important, Edmund Spenser, who dedicated *The Shepheardes Calender* to him as "the president [chief exemplar] of noblesse and of chevalree." But he clearly longed to be something more than an influential patron of letters. In 1580 his Protestant convictions led him publicly to oppose Queen Elizabeth's projected marriage to the Catholic duke of Anjou. The queen, who hated interference with her diplomatic maneuvers, angrily dismissed Sidney from the court.

He retired to Wilton, the estate of his beloved and learned sister, Mary Herbert, countess of Pembroke, and there he wrote a long, elaborate epic romance in prose called *Arcadia*. Sidney's claim, made with studied nonchalance, that the work was casually tossed off for his sister's private entertainment is belied by its considerable literary, political, and moral ambitions, qualities that were reinforced and intensified in the extensive revisions he began to make to it in 1582. Our selection is from this revised version, termed by scholars the *New Arcadia*.

In addition to *Arcadia*, which inspired many imitations, including the *Urania* of Sidney's niece, Lady Mary Wroth, two other influential works by Sidney have had still more lasting importance. One of these was occasioned by a small book, *The School of Abuse*, published in 1579 and misguidedly dedicated to Sidney. Its author, the playwright turned moralist Stephen Gosson, attacked poets and actors from a narrowly Puritan perspective that called into question the morality of any fiction-making. Sidney did not specifically answer Gosson's polemic, but he must have had it in mind when he composed, perhaps in the same year, a major piece of critical prose that was published after his death under two titles, *The Defense of Poesy* and *An Apology for Poetry*. In this long essay Sidney eloquently defends poetry (his term for all imaginative literature) against its attackers and, in the process, greatly exalts the role of the poet, the freedom of the imagination, and the moral value of fiction. This is the major work of literary criticism produced in the English Renaissance.

Perhaps Sidney's finest literary achievement is *Astrophil and Stella* (*Starlover and Star*), the first of the great Elizabethan sonnet cycles. The 108 sonnets and eleven songs rely heavily, as do virtually all sonnets in the period, on the conventions established by Petrarch, but Sidney manages at once to play a series of games with these conventions and to freight them with personal significance. The sense of the poet's daring self-exposure, his hinting at intimate psychological and social secrets, has provoked much biographical speculation centered on Sidney's ambiguous relationship with Penelope Devereux, the supposed original of Stella. A marriage between the two had been proposed in 1576 and was talked about for some years, but in 1581 she married Lord Robert Rich, and two years later Sidney also married. (At their high social rank, marriages were negotiated in the interests of the powerful families involved, not of the individuals.) Some of the sonnets contain sly puns on the name *Rich*, and it seems likely that there are autobiographical elements in the shadowy narrative sketched by the work. But the principal focus of the sonnets is not a sequence of events or an unfolding relationship. Rather, *Astrophil and Stella* explores the lover's state of mind and soul, the contradictory impulses, intense desires, and frustrations that haunt him.

In 1585 Sidney tried to join Sir Francis Drake's West Indian expedition but was prevented by the queen; instead, she appointed him governor of Flushing in the Netherlands, where as a volunteer and knight-errant he engaged in several vicious skirmishes in the war against Spain. At Zutphen on September 13, 1586, leading a charge against great odds, Sidney was wounded in the thigh, shortly after he had thrown away his thigh armor in an ill-fated chivalric gesture. He died after lingering for twenty-six days.

Sidney called poetry his "unelected vocation," and in keeping with the norms of his class, he did not publish any of his major literary works himself. His ambition, continually thwarted, was to be a man of action whose deeds would affect his country's destiny. Yet he was the author of the most ambitious work of prose fiction, the most important piece of literary criticism, and the most influential sonnet cycle of the Elizabethan Age.

The Countess of Pembroke's Arcadia

Sidney's epic romance exists in two forms which scholars have dubbed the *Old Arcadia* and the *New Arcadia*. Shortly after the *Old Arcadia* was completed, Sidney began to recast and greatly expand it but broke off in mid-sentence and left the revision unfinished. This revised fragment, almost three books, is known as the *New Arcadia*; it was published posthumously in 1590. In 1593 Sidney's sister, the countess of Pembroke, herself a gifted writer, made some small changes to the *New Arcadia* and the last two books of the *Old*, stitched them together, and published them as a single text. (The complete *Old Arcadia*, as Sidney had left it in manuscript, was not rediscovered and published until the twentieth century.) Both versions are full of oracles, princes disguised as shepherd and amazon, mistaken identity, melodramatic incidents, and tangled love situations, but the *New Arcadia* has a much more labyrinthine, interwoven plot as well as a more consistently elevated tone of moral and heroic high seriousness. Some episodes are of political interest, and Sidney clearly put into the work more of his serious thought on statecraft (the responsibilities of a king or queen, the evils of rebellion, and the duties of ministers, judges, and advisers of state) than he pretends when he describes *Arcadia* as mere entertainment. Many poems—pastoral eclogues and songs—are interspersed throughout the narrative; they represent Sidney's experiments with diverse lyric kinds and verse forms.

Prior to the chapter reprinted below, Pyrocles, prince of Macedon, has fallen in love with Philoclea, daughter of Basilius and Gynecia, the king and queen of Arcadia. To gain entrance to the royal household, he has disguised himself as a woman, the amazon Zelmane. To his dismay, though, both Basilius and Gynecia (who sees through his disguise) have fallen in love with him.

From The Second Book of the Countess of Pembroke's Arcadia

Chapter 1

In these pastoral pastimes[1] a great number of days were sent to follow their flying predecessors, while the cup of poison[2] (which was deeply tasted of this noble company) had left no sinew of theirs without mortally searching into it; yet never manifesting his venomous work, till once that the night (parting away angry that she could distill no more sleep into the eyes of lovers) had no sooner given place to the breaking out of the morning light and the sun bestowed his beams upon the tops of the mountains, but that the woeful Gynecia (to whom rest was no ease) had left her loathed lodging and gotten herself into the solitary places those deserts[3] were full of, going up and down with such unquiet motions as a grieved and hopeless mind is wont to bring forth. There appeared unto the eyes of her judgment the evils she was like to run into, with ugly infamy waiting upon them: she felt the terrors of her own conscience; she was guilty of a long exercised virtue which made this vice the fuller of deformity. The uttermost of the good she could aspire unto was a mortal wound to her vexed spirits; and lastly, no small part of her evils was that she was wise to see her evils. Insomuch that, having a great while thrown her countenance ghastly about her (as if she had called all the powers of the world to be witness of her wretched estate), at length casting up her watery eyes to heaven:

"O sun," said she, "whose unspotted light directs the steps of mortal mankind, art thou not ashamed to impart the clearness of thy presence to such a dust-creeping worm as I am? O you heavens, which continually keep the course allotted unto you, can none of your influences prevail so much upon the miserable Gynecia as to make her preserve a course so long embraced by her? O deserts, deserts, how fit a guest am I for you, since my heart can people you with wild ravenous beasts, which in you are wanting! O virtue, where dost thou hide thyself? What hideous thing is this which doth eclipse thee? Or is it true that thou wert never but a vain name and no essential thing, which hast thus left thy professed servant when she had most need of thy lovely presence? O imperfect proportion of reason, which can too much foresee and too little prevent! Alas, alas," said she, "if there were but one hope for all my pains or but one excuse for all my faultiness! But wretch that I am, my torment is beyond all succor, and my evil deserving doth exceed my evil fortune. For nothing else did my husband take this strange resolution to live so solitarily, for nothing else have the winds delivered this strange guest to my country, for nothing else have the destinies reserved my life to this time, but that only I, most wretched I, should become a plague to myself and a shame to womankind. Yet if my desire, how unjust soever it be, might take effect, though a thousand deaths followed it and every death were followed with a thousand shames, yet should not my sepulcher receive me without some contentment. But alas, though sure I am that Zelmane is such

---

1. The reference is to the elaborate entertainment, featuring a series of pastoral songs, that concluded Book 1.
2. I.e., love.

3. In consequence of an oracle, Basilius has taken the royal family to live in "a certain forest which he calleth his desert."

as can answer my love, yet as sure I am that this disguising must needs come for some foretaken conceit.[4] And then, wretched Gynecia, where canst thou find any small ground-plot for hope to dwell upon? No, no, it is Philoclea his heart is set upon; it is my daughter I have borne to supplant me. But if it be so, the life I have given thee, ungrateful Philoclea, I will sooner with these hands bereave thee of than my birth[5] shall glory she hath bereaved me of my desires. In shame there is no comfort but to be beyond all bounds of shame."

Having spoken thus, she began to make a piteous war with her fair hair, when she might hear not far from her an extremely doleful voice, but so suppressed with a kind of whispering note that she could not conceive the words distinctly. But as a lamentable tune is the sweetest music to a woeful mind, she drew thither near-away[6] in hope to find some companion of her misery; and as she paced on she was stopped with a number of trees so thickly placed together that she was afraid she should, with rushing through, stop the speech of the lamentable party which she was so desirous to understand. And therefore sitting her down as softly as she could (for she was now in distance to hear) she might first perceive a lute excellently well played upon, and then the same doleful voice accompanying it with these verses:

> In vain, mine eyes, you labor to amend
> With flowing tears your fault of hasty sight;
> Since to my heart her shape you so did send,
> That her I see, though you did lose your light.
>
> In vain, my heart, now you with sight are burned,
> With sighs you seek to cool your hot desire;
> Since sighs, into mine inward furnace turned,
> For bellows serve to kindle more the fire.
>
> Reason in vain, now you have lost my heart,
> My head you seek, as to your strongest fort;
> Since there mine eyes have played so false a part,
> That to your strength your foes have sure resort.
> Then since in vain I find were all my strife,
> To this strange death I vainly yield my life.

The ending of the song served but for a beginning of new plaints, as if the mind, oppressed with too heavy a burden of cares, was fain to discharge itself of all sides and, as it were, paint out the hideousness of the pain in all sorts of colors. For the woeful person (as if the lute had evil joined with the voice) threw it to the ground with suchlike words:

"Alas, poor lute, how much art thou deceived to think that in my miseries thou could'st ease my woes, as in my careless times thou wast wont to please my fancies! The time is changed, my lute, the time is changed; and no more did my joyful mind then receive everything to a joyful consideration than my careful[7] mind now makes each thing taste like the bitter juice of care. The evil is inward, my lute, the evil is inward; which all thou dost doth serve but to make me think more freely of, and the more I think, the more cause I find

4. With some prior purpose.
5. Offspring.

6. Near to it.
7. Full of care.

of thinking, but less of hoping. And alas, what is then thy harmony but the sweetmeats of sorrow? The discord of my thoughts, my lute, doth ill agree to the concord of thy strings; therefore be not ashamed to leave thy master, since he is not afraid to forsake himself."

And thus much spoken, instead of a conclusion was closed up with so hearty a groaning that Gynecia could not refrain to show herself, thinking such griefs could serve fitly for nothing but her own fortune. But as she came into the little arbor of this sorrowful music, her eyes met with the eyes of Zelmane, which was the party that thus had indicted herself of misery, so that either of them remained confused with a sudden astonishment, Zelmane fearing lest she had heard some part of those complaints which she had risen up that morning early of purpose to breathe out in secret to herself. But Gynecia a great while stood still with a kind of dull amazement, looking steadfastly upon her. At length returning to some use of herself, she began to ask Zelmane what cause carried her so early abroad. But, as if the opening of her mouth to Zelmane had opened some great floodgate of sorrow whereof her heart could not abide the violent issue, she sank to the ground with her hands over her face, crying vehemently, "Zelmane, help me, O Zelmane have pity on me!"

Zelmane ran to her, marveling what sudden sickness had thus possessed her; and beginning to ask her the cause of her pain and offering her service to be employed by her, Gynecia opening her eyes wildly upon her, pricked with the flames of love and the torments of her own conscience, "O Zelmane, Zelmane," said she, "dost thou offer me physic, which art my only poison? Or wilt thou do me service which hast already brought me into eternal slavery?"

Zelmane then knowing well at what mark she shot, yet loth to enter into it, "Most excellent lady," said she, "you were best retire yourself into your lodging, that you the better may pass this sudden fit."

"Retire myself?" said Gynecia, "If I had retired myself into myself when thou (to me unfortunate guest) camest to draw me from myself, blessed had I been, and no need had I had of this counsel. But now alas, I am forced to fly to thee for succor whom I accuse of all my hurt, and make thee judge of my cause, who art the only author of my mischief."

Zelmane the more astonished, the more she understood her, "Madam," said she, "whereof do you accuse me that I will not clear myself? Or wherein may I stead[8] you that you may not command me?"

"Alas!" answered Gynecia, "What shall I say more? Take pity of me, O Zelmane, but not as Zelmane, and disguise not with me in words, as I know thou dost in apparel."

Zelmane was much troubled with that word, finding herself brought to this strait. But as she was thinking what to answer her, they might see old Basilius pass hard by them without ever seeing them, complaining likewise of love very freshly, and ending his complaint with this song, love having renewed both his invention and voice:

> Let not old age disgrace my high desire;
>   O heavenly soul in human shape contained:
> Old wood inflamed doth yield the bravest fire,
>   When younger doth in smoke his virtue spend,

8. Be of use to.

> Ne let white hairs which on my face do grow
>   Seem to your eyes of a disgraceful hue,
> Since whiteness doth present the sweetest show,
>   Which makes all eyes do homage unto you.
>
> Old age is wise and full of constant truth;
>   Old age well stayed from ranging humor[9] lives;
> Old age hath known whatever was in youth;
>   Old age o'ercome, the greater honor gives.
> And to old age since you yourself aspire,
> Let not old age disgrace my high desire.

Which being done, he looked very curiously upon himself, sometimes fetching a little skip as if he had said his strength had not yet forsaken him.

But Zelmane, having in this time gotten some leisure to think for an answer, looking upon Gynecia as if she thought she did her some wrong, "Madam," said she, "I am not acquainted with those words of disguising; neither is it the profession of an Amazon; neither are you a party with whom it is to be used. If my service may please you, employ it, so long as you do me no wrong in misjudging of me."

"Alas, Zelmane," said Gynecia, "I perceive you know full little how piercing the eyes are of a true lover. There is no one beam of those thoughts you have planted in me but is able to discern a greater cloud than you do go in. Seek not to conceal yourself further from me, nor force not the passion of love into violent extremities."

Now was Zelmane brought to an exigent,[1] when the king, turning his eyes that way through the trees, perceived his wife and mistress[2] together; so that framing the most lovely countenance he could, he came straightway towards them, and at the first word, thanking his wife for having entertained Zelmane, desired her she would now return into the lodge because he had certain matters of estate[3] to impart to the Lady Zelmane. The queen, being nothing troubled with jealousy in that point, obeyed the king's commandment, full of raging agonies, and determinately bent[4] that as she would seek all loving means to win Zelmane, so she would stir up terrible tragedies rather than fail of her intent. And so went she from them to the lodge-ward;[5] with such a battle in her thoughts and so deadly an overthrow given to her best resolutions that even her body (where the field was fought) was oppressed withal, making a languishing sickness wait upon the triumph of passion,[6] which the more it prevailed in her, the more it made her jealousy watchful both over her daughter and Zelmane, having ever one of them entrusted to her own eyes.[7]

But as soon as Basilius was rid of his wife's presence, falling down on his knees, "O lady," said he, "which hast only had the power to stir up again those flames which had so long lain dead in me, see in me the power of your beauty, which can make old age come to ask counsel of youth, and a prince unconquered to become a slave to a stranger. And when you see that power of yours, love that at least in me, since it is yours, although of me you see nothing to be loved."

9. Caprice. "Stayed": settled.
1. Crisis.
2. I.e., the woman who rules his heart.
3. State.

4. Resolutely determined.
5. Toward the lodge.
6. Attend upon passion's victory procession.
7. Always having one of them in her sight.

"Worthy prince," answered Zelmane, taking him up from his kneeling, "both your manner and your speech are so strange unto me as I know not how to answer it better than with silence."

"If silence please you," said the king, "it shall never displease me, since my heart is wholly pledged to obey you. Otherwise, if you would vouchsafe mine ears such happiness as to hear you, they shall convey your words to such a mind which is with the humblest degree of reverence to receive them."

"I disdain not to speak to you, mighty prince," said Zelmane, "but I disdain to speak to any matter which may bring my honor into question."

And therewith, with a brave counterfeited scorn she departed from the king, leaving him not so sorry for his short answer as proud in himself that he had broken[8] the matter. And thus did the king, feeding his mind with those thoughts, pass great time in writing verses and making more of himself than he was wont to do, that, with a little help, he would have grown into a pretty kind of dotage.

But Zelmane, being rid of this loving but little loved company, "Alas," said she, "poor Pyrocles, was there ever one but I that had received wrong and could blame nobody, that having more than I desire, am still in want of that I would?[9] Truly, love, I must needs say thus much on thy behalf; thou hast employed my love there where all love is deserved, and for recompense hast sent me more love than ever I desired. But what wilt thou do, Pyrocles? Which way canst thou find to rid thee of thy intricate troubles? To her whom I would be known to, I live in darkness; and to her am revealed from whom I would be most secret. What shift[1] shall I find against the diligent love of Basilius? What shield against the violent passions of Gynecia? And if that be done, yet how am I the nearer to quench the fire that consumes me? Well, well, sweet Philoclea, my whole confidence must be builded in thy divine spirit, which cannot be ignorant of the cruel wound I have received by you."

1578–83   1593

Astrophil and Stella

For its original coterie audience, Sidney's sonnet sequence must have been an elaborate game of literary masks, psychological risk-taking, and open secrets. The loosely linked succession of poems, with its dazzling display of technical virtuosity, provides tantalizing glimpses of identifiable characters and, still more, a sustained and remarkably intimate portrait of the poet's inner life. Sidney was hardly indifferent to his privacy: "I assure you before God," he had written once in an angry letter to his father's private secretary, Molyneux, "that if ever I know you do so much as read any letter I write to my father, without his commandment or my consent, I will thrust my dagger into you. And trust to it, for I speak it in earnest." Yet in *Astrophil and Stella* he seems to hold up a mirror to every nuance of his emotional being. That Sidney could do so safely depends in part upon his use of well-established conventions, borrowed from Petrarch and his many Italian, French, and Spanish imitators. These conventions bequeathed a loose framework of plot, marking the stages of a love relationship from its starting point in the lover's attraction to the lady's beauty through various trials, sufferings, conflicts, and occasional encour-

8. Broached.   1. Evasion, stratagem.
9. Of the thing I desire.

agements to a conclusion in which nothing is resolved. The poet undertook to produce an anatomy of love, displaying its shifting and often contradictory states: hope and despair, tenderness and bitterness, exultation and modesty, bodily desire and spiritual transcendence. Petrarch had deployed a series of ingenious metaphors to describe these states, but by Sidney's time the metaphors—love as a freezing fire, the beloved's glance as an arrow striking the lover's heart, and so forth—had through endless repetition become familiar and predictable, less a revelation than a role. Sidney, in the role of Astrophil, protests that he uses no standard conventional phrases, that his verse is original and comes from his heart. This protest is itself conventional, and yet Sidney manages to infuse his sonnets with an extraordinary vigor and freshness. Certain of the sonnets have, within their narrow fourteen-line bounds, the force of the drama: *Fly, fly, my friends, I have my death-wound, fly* or *What, have I thus betrayed my liberty?* Others, in their grappling with insistent desire, have the probing, psychological resonance of private confession: *With what sharp checks I in myself am shent* or *Who will in fairest book of Nature know*. Still others ask crucial questions about the whole project of self-representation: *Stella oft sees the very face of woe*. Virtually all of them manifest the exceptional *energia*—forcibleness—that Sidney, in *The Defense of Poesy*, says is the key ingredient of good poetry.

From Astrophil and Stella

1[1]

Loving in truth, and fain° in verse my love to show,	*desirous*
That the dear She might take some pleasure of my pain,	
Pleasure might cause her read, reading might make her know,	
Knowledge might pity win, and pity grace obtain,	
5 I sought fit words to paint the blackest face of woe,	
Studying inventions fine, her wits to entertain,	
Oft turning others' leaves, to see if thence would flow	
Some fresh and fruitful showers upon my sunburned brain.	
But words came halting forth, wanting Invention's stay;°	*prop*
10 Invention, Nature's child, fled step-dame Study's blows,	
And others' feet still seemed but strangers in my way.	
Thus great with child to speak, and helpless in my throes,	
Biting my trewand° pen, beating myself for spite,	*truant*
"Fool," said my Muse to me, "look in thy heart and write."	

2

Not at first sight, nor with a dribbèd[2] shot
    Love gave the wound, which while I breathe will bleed,
    But known worth did in mine[3] of time proceed,
Till by degrees it had full conquest got.
5   I saw and liked, I liked but lovèd not,
      I loved, but straight did not what *Love* decreed;
      At length to Love's decrees, I, forced, agreed,
Yet with repining at so partial° lot.   *unfair*
    Now even that footstep of lost liberty

---

1. One of six sonnets in the sequence written in hexameters.

2. Ineffectual or at random.
3. Tunnel dug to undermine a besieged fortress.

10   Is gone, and now like slave-borne Muscovite,[4]
    I call it praise to suffer tyranny;
    And now employ the remnant of my wit,°   *intelligence*
    To make myself believe that all is well,
    While with a feeling skill I paint my hell.

5

    It is most true that eyes are formed to serve
    The inward light,° and that the heavenly part   *reason, understanding*
    Ought to be king, from whose rules who do swerve,
    Rebels to Nature, strive for their own smart.
5   It is most true, what we call Cupid's dart
    An image is, which for ourselves we carve;
    And, fools, adore in temple of our heart,
    Till that good god make church and churchman starve.[5]
     True, that true beauty virtue is indeed,
10 Whereof this beauty can be but a shade,°   *shadow*
    Which elements with mortal mixture[6] breed;
    True, that on earth we are but pilgrims made,
     And should in soul up to our country move:
     True, and yet true that I must *Stella* love.

6

    Some lovers speak, when they their muses entertain,
    Of hopes begot by fear, of wot° not what desires,   *know*
    Of force of heavenly beams infusing hellish pain,
    Of living deaths, dear wounds, fair storms, and freezing fires;[7]
5   Some one his song in Jove, and Jove's strange tales attires,
    Broidered with bulls and swans, powdered with golden rain;[8]
    Another humbler wit to shepherd's pipe retires,
    Yet hiding royal blood full oft in rural vein.[9]
     To some a sweetest plaint a sweetest style affords,[1]
10 While tears pour out his ink, and sighs breathe out his words,
    His paper pale despair, and pain his pen doth move.
    I can speak what I feel, and feel as much as they,
    But think that all the map of my state I display,
    When trembling voice brings forth that I do Stella love.

7

    When Nature made her chief work, Stella's eyes,
    In color black why wrapped she beams so bright?

---

4. Inhabitant of Muscovy, an important Russian principality ruled from Moscow; 16th-century travel books describe Muscovites as contented slaves.
5. The concessions made in the argument are to Neoplatonic and Christian doctrines opposed to romantic love. Neoplatonic theory held that physical beauty is only a shadow of inner virtue, which is at one with the true, transcendent and immortal Idea of Beauty. For a highly influential exposition of this theory, see the excerpts from Castiglione's *The Courtier*, pp. 578–93.

6. Physical beauty is a mixture of the four elements (earth, air, water, and fire) and so is mortal.
7. Conventional Petrarchan oxymorons.
8. I.e., embroidered with mythological figures. Jove courted Europa in the shape of a bull; Leda, as a swan; and Danaë, as a golden shower.
9. Pastoral allegory. By convention, a pastoral poet pipes his songs on an oaten or reed pipe.
1. Overuse of the word *sweet* in love complaints, with allusion to the very musical *dolce stil nuovo* (sweet new style) associated with Dante and his Italian contemporaries.

Would she in beamy° black, like painter wise,   *radiant*
Frame daintiest luster, mixed of shades and light?
5   Or did she else that sober hue devise,
In object° best to knit and strength° our sight,   *with purpose / strengthen*
Lest if no veil those brave gleams did disguise,
They sun-like should more dazzle than delight?
    Or would she her miraculous power show,
10 That whereas black seems beauty's contrary,
She even in black doth make all beauties flow?
    Both so and thus: she, minding° Love should be   *remembering*
    Placed ever there, gave him this mourning weed,°   *funeral garb*
To honor all their deaths, who for her bleed.

9

Queen Virtue's court, which some call Stella's face,
    Prepared by Nature's chiefest furniture,[2]
    Hath his front° built of alablaster° pure;   *i.e., Stella's forehead / alabaster*
Gold is the covering of that stately place.
5   The door, by which sometimes comes forth her Grace,
    Red porphir[3] is, which lock of pearl makes sure;
    Whose porches rich (which name of cheeks endure),
Marble mixed red and white do interlace.
    The windows now through which this heavenly guest
10 Looks over the world, and can find nothing such,
Which dare claim from those lights the name of best,
    Of touch[4] they are that without touch doth touch,
    Which Cupid's self from Beauty's mine did draw:
Of touch they are, and poor I am their straw.

10

Reason, in faith thou art well served, that still
    Wouldst brabling° be with sense and love in me: *quarreling*
    I rather wished thee climb the Muses' hill,[5]
Or reach the fruit of Nature's choicest tree,[6]
5   Or seek heaven's course, or heaven's inside to see.
Why shouldst thou toil our thorny soil to till?
Leave sense, and those which sense's objects be:
Deal thou with powers of thoughts, leave love to will.
    But thou wouldst needs fight both with love and sense,
10 With sword of wit, giving wounds of dispraise,
Till downright blows did foil thy cunning fence:°   *swordplay*
    For soon as they strake° thee with Stella's rays,   *struck*
    Reason thou kneel'dst, and offeredst straight to prove
By reason good, good reason her to love.

---

2. The best materials Nature furnishes.
3. Porphyry, an ornamental red or purple stone.
4. Glossy black stone (lignite or jet) able to attract light bodies such as straw by static electricity.

5. Mount Helicon in Greece, sacred to the Nine Muses—a symbol of poetic inspiration.
6. The tree of knowledge.

15

You that do search for every purling° spring   *murmuring*
   Which from the ribs of old Parnassus[7] flows,
   And every flower,[8] not sweet perhaps, which grows
Near therabout, into your poesy[9] wring;
5 You that do dictionary's method bring
   Into your rhymes, running in rattling rows;
   You that poor Petrarch's long-deceasèd woes
With new-born sighs and denizened wit° do sing;   *naturalized ingenuity*
   You take wrong ways, those far-fet° helps be such,   *far-fetched*
10 As do bewray a want of inward touch,[1]
And sure at length stolen goods do come to light.
   But if (both for your love and skill) your name
   You seek to nurse at fullest breasts of Fame,
Stella behold, and then begin to endite.°   *write*

16

In nature apt to like when I did see
   Beauties, which were of many carats fine,
   My boiling sprites° did thither soon incline,   *spirits*
And, Love, I thought that I was full of thee:
5 But finding not those restless flames in me,
   Which others said did make their souls to pine,
   I thought those babes of some pin's hurt did whine,
By my love judging what love's pain might be.
   But while I thus with this young lion[2] played,
10 Mine eyes (shall I say cursed or blessed) beheld
Stella; now she is named, need more be said?
   In her sight I a lesson new have spelled,
   I now have learned love right, and learned even so,
   As who by being poisoned doth poison know.

18

With what sharp checks° I in myself am shent,°   *rebukes/shamed*
   When into Reason's audit I do go,
   And by just counts myself a bankrout° know   *bankrupt*
Of all those goods, which heaven to me hath lent;
5 Unable quite to pay even Nature's rent,
   Which unto it by birthright I do owe;
   And which is worse, no good excuse can show,
But that my wealth I have most idly spent.
   My youth doth waste, my knowledge brings forth toys,[3]
10 My wit° doth strive those passions to defend,   *intellect*
   Which for reward spoil it with vain annoys.
   I see my course to lose myself doth bend:

---

7. Mountain near Delphos in Greece, sacred to the Muses, who foster poetry and other arts.
8. Also, poetic figures (flowers of rhetoric).
9. Also, a nosegay (posy).
1. Reveal a lack of innate talent.

2. In a popular fable, a shepherd raised a lion cub that, while young, was a pet for his children but when grown destroyed all his flocks.
3. Trifles, i.e., these poems.

I see and yet no greater sorrow take,
Than that I lose no more for Stella's sake.

20

Fly, fly, my friends, I have my death-wound, fly;
See there that boy, that murth'ring° boy, I say,   *murdering*
Who, like a thief, hid in dark bush doth lie
Till bloody bullet get him wrongful prey.
5   So tyran° he no fitter place could spy,   *tyrant*
Nor so fair level° in so secret stay,°   *aim / stopping place*
As that sweet black° which veils the heav'nly eye;   *pupil*
There himself with his shot he close° doth lay.   *secretly*
     Poor passenger,° pass now thereby I did,   *passerby*
10 And stay'd, pleas'd with the prospect of the place,
While that black hue from me the bad guest hid;
But straight I saw motions of lightning grace,
     And then descried the glist'ring° of his dart;   *glittering*
     But ere I could fly thence, it pierc'd my heart.

21

Your words, my friend (right healthful caustics),⁴ blame
My young mind marred, whom Love doth windlass° so,   *ensnare*
That mine own writings like bad servants show
My wits, quick in vain thoughts, in virtue lame;
5   That Plato I read for nought, but if° he tame   *unless*
Such coltish gyres,⁵ that to my birth I owe
Nobler desires, least° else that friendly foe   *lest*
Great expectation, wear a train of shame.
     For since mad March great promise made of me,
10 If now the May of my years much decline,
What can be hoped my harvest time will be?
     Sure you say well; your wisdom's golden mine
     Dig deep with learning's spade; now tell me this,
     Hath this world ought so fair as Stella is?

28

You that with allegory's curious frame
Of others' children changelings use to make,
With me those pains, for God's sake, do not take;
I list not° dig so deep for brazen fame.   *I don't care to*
5   When I say Stella, I do mean the same
Princess of beauty for whose only sake
The reins of love I love, though never slake,°   *slack*
And joy therein, though nations count it shame.
     I beg no subject to use eloquence,⁶

---

4. Caustic substances for burning away diseased tissue.
5. Wild circles, like those of a young horse; there is a probable reference to Plato's story of the char-

ioteer Reason reining in the horses of Passion (*Phaedrus* 254).
6. I.e., I don't ask for a topic simply as an excuse to display my rhetorical skills.

10 Nor in hid ways do guide philosophy;
Look at my hands for no such quintessence,[7]
But know that I in pure simplicity
    Breathe out the flames which burn within my heart,
    Love only reading unto me this art.

31

With how sad steps, O Moon, thou climb'st the skies,
    How silently, and with how wan a face!
    What, may it be that even in heavenly place
That busy archer° his sharp arrows tries?   *Cupid*
5 Sure, if that long-with-love-acquainted eyes
    Can judge of love, thou feel'st a lover's case;
    I read it in thy looks: thy languished grace,
To me that feel the like, thy state descries.
    Then even of fellowship, O Moon, tell me,
10 Is constant love deemed there but want of wit?
Are beauties there as proud as here they be?
Do they above love to be loved, and yet
    Those lovers scorn whom that love doth possess?
    Do they call virtue there ungratefulness?[8]

37

My mouth doth water, and my breast doth swell,
    My tongue doth itch, my thoughts in labor be:
    Listen then, lordings, with good ear to me,
For of my life I must a riddle tell.
5 Towards Aurora's court a nymph doth dwell,[9]
    Rich in all beauties which man's eye can see,
    Beauties so far from reach of words, that we
Abase her praise, saying she doth excel:
    Rich in the treasure of deserved renown,
10 Rich in the riches of a royal heart,
Rich in those gifts which give th'eternal crown;
Who though most rich in these and every part,
    Which make the patents[1] of true worldly bliss,
    Hath no misfortune, but that Rich she is.

39

Come sleep! O sleep the certain knot of peace,
The baiting place[2] of wit, the balm of woe,
The poor man's wealth, the prisoner's release,
Th' indifferent° judge between the high and low;   *impartial*

---

7. The mysterious "fifth element" of matter (supplementary to earth, air, fire, and water), which alchemists labored to extract.
8. I.e., is the lady's ingratitude considered virtue in heaven (as here)? Also, is the lover's virtue (fidelity) considered distasteful in heaven (as here)?

9. Aurora (the dawn) has her court in the east; Penelope Devereux Rich, the original of Stella, dwells in Essex, one of the eastern counties. Sidney puns on her married name throughout this sonnet.
1. Grants, titles to possession.
2. Resting place on a journey.

5   With shield of proof shield me from out the prease°   *throng*
Of those fierce darts Despair at me doth throw:
O make in me those civil wars to cease;
I will good tribute pay if thou do so.
       Take thou of me smooth pillows, sweetest bed,
10   A chamber deaf to noise and blind to light,
A rosy garland, and a weary head:³
And if these things, as being thine by right,
       Move not thy heavy grace, thou shalt in me
       Livelier than elsewhere Stella's image see.

41

Having this day my horse, my hand, my lance
       Guided so well that I obtained the prize,
       Both by the judgment of the English eyes
And of some sent from that sweet enemy France;⁴
5   Horsemen my skill in horsemanship advance;
       Townfolks my strength; a daintier° judge applies   *more precise*
       His praise to sleight,° which from good use° doth rise; *art/experience*
Some lucky wits impute it but to chance;
       Others, because of both sides I do take
10   My blood from them who did excel in this,⁵
Think Nature me a man of arms did make.
How far they shoot awry! The true cause is,
       Stella looked on, and from her heavenly face
       Sent forth the beams which made so fair my race.

45

Stella oft sees the very face of woe
       Painted in my beclouded stormy face,
       But cannot skill° to pity my disgrace,⁶   *is unable to*
Not though thereof the cause herself she know.⁷
5   Yet hearing late a fable which did show,
       Of lovers never known, a grievous case,
       Pity thereof gate° in her breast such place   *got*
That, from that sea derived, tears' spring did flow.
       Alas, if fancy,° drawn by imaged things,   *fantasy*
10   Though false, yet with free scope more grace doth breed
Than servant's wrack, where new doubts honor brings,⁸
Then think, my dear, that you in me do read
       Of lover's ruin some sad tragedy:
       I am not I; pity the tale of me.

---

3. The offer of gifts to Morpheus, god of sleep, is a poetic convention. A likely source is Chaucer's *Book of the Duchess*, lines 240–69. "Proof" (line 5): proven strength.
4. Sidney took part in several tournaments between 1579 and 1585 with French spectators present, but the one in May 1581 was devised specifically to entertain French commissioners.
5. Sidney's father and grandfather and his mater-

nal uncles, the earls of Leicester and Warwick, were frequent participants in tournaments.
6. The state of being out of favor.
7. I.e., even though she knows she herself is the cause of it.
8. I.e., than the ruin of her lover ("servant"), caused by the new scruples ("doubts") her honor brings up.

47

What, have I thus betrayed my liberty?
   Can those black beams such burning marks° engrave   *brands of slavery*
   In my free side? or am I born a slave,
Whose neck becomes° such yoke of tyranny?   *is suited to*
5   Or want I sense to feel my misery?
   Or sprite,° disdain of such disdain to have?   *spirit*
   Who for long faith, though daily help I crave,
May get no alms but scorn of beggary.⁹
   Virtue awake! Beauty but beauty is;
10 I may, I must, I can, I will, I do
Leave following that which it is gain to miss.
   Let her go. Soft, but here she comes. Go to,
   Unkind, I love you not. O me, that eye
   Doth make my heart give to my tongue the lie.

49

I on my horse, and Love on me doth try
   Our horsemanships, while by strange work I prove
   A horseman to my horse, a horse to Love;
And now man's wrongs in me, poor beast, descry.°   *discover*
5   The reins wherewith my rider doth me tie
   Are humbled thoughts, which bit of reverence move,
   Curbed in with fear, but with gilt bosse° above   *gold studs*
Of hope, which makes it seem fair to the eye.
   The wand° is will; thou, fancy, saddle art,¹   *whip*
10 Girt fast by memory; and while I spur
My horse, he spurs with sharp desire my heart;
   He sits me fast, however I do stir,
   And now hath made me to his hand so right
   That in the manage² myself takes delight.

52

A strife is grown between Virtue and Love,
   While each pretends° that Stella must be his: *claims*
   Her eyes, her lips, her all, saith Love, do this,
Since they do wear his badge,³ most firmly prove.
5   But Virtue thus that title doth disprove:
   That Stella (O dear name) that Stella is
   That virtuous soul, sure heir of heavenly bliss;
Not this fair outside, which our hearts doth move.
   And therefore, though her beauty and her grace
10 Be Love's indeed, in Stella's self he may
By no pretence claim any manner° place.   *kind of*
   Well, Love, since this demur° our suit⁴ doth stay,°   *objection/stop*

---

9. I.e., scorn for [my] begging.
1. I.e., you, Fancy (imagination), are the saddle.
2. Training or handling of a horse.

3. Device or livery worn to identify someone's (here, Cupid's) servants.
4. "Courtship," in addition to the legal meaning.

Let Virtue have that Stella's self; yet thus,
That Virtue but° that body grant to us.   *only*

53

In martial sports I had my cunning tried,
  And yet to break more staves° did me address;   *lances*
  While with the people's shouts, I must confess,
Youth, luck, and praise even filled my veins with pride.
5 When Cupid, having me his slave descried°   *discerned*
  In Mars's livery,[5] prancing in the press,°   *throng*
  "What now, Sir Fool," said he, "I would no less;[6]
Look here, I say." I looked, and Stella spied,
  Who hard by° made a window send forth light.   *nearby*
10 My heart then quaked, then dazzled were mine eyes,
  One hand forgot to rule,° th' other to fight.   *govern the horse*
  Nor trumpets' sound I heard, nor friendly cries;
    My foe came on, and beat the air for me,[7]
    Till that her blush taught me my shame to see.

56

Fie, school of Patience, fie, your lesson is
  Far far too long to learn it without book:°   *by memory*
  What, a whole week without one piece of look,[8]
And think I should not your large precepts miss?°   *forget*
5 When I might read those letters fair of bliss,
  Which in her face teach virtue, I could brook°   *bear*
  Somewhat thy leaden counsels, which I took
As of a friend that meant not much amiss.
  But now that I, alas, do want° her sight,   *lack*
10 What, dost thou think that I can ever take
  In thy cold stuff a phlegmatic delight?
No, Patience, if thou wilt my good, then make
    Her come and hear with patience my desire,
    And then with patience bid me bear my fire.

61

Oft with true sighs, oft with uncallèd tears,
Now with slow words, now with dumb eloquence
I Stella's eyes assail, invade her ears;
But this at last is her sweet-breathed defence:
5   That who indeed infelt affection bears,
So captives to his saint both soul and sense
That, wholly hers, all selfness° he forbears;   *concern with self*
Thence his desires he learns, his life's course thence.
    Now since her chaste mind hates this love in me,

---

5. The uniform that identifies the servants belonging to a nobleman's household; here, to Mars, god of war.

6. I.e., I want no less [service from you].
7. Struck the empty air instead of me.
8. Without the briefest glimpse of her.

10   With chastened mind I straight must shew° that she   *show*
    Shall quickly me from what she hates remove.
       O Doctor[9] Cupid, thou for me reply,
       Driven else to grant by angel's sophistry,
    That I love not, without I leave to love.°   *unless I stop loving*

69

    O joy, too high for my low style to show,
       O bliss, fit for a nobler state than me!
       Envy, put out thine eyes, lest thou do see
    What oceans of delight in me do flow.
5   My friend, that oft saw through all masks my woe,
       Come, come, and let me pour myself on thee:
       Gone is the winter of my misery;
    My spring appears; O see what here doth grow.
    For Stella hath, with words where faith doth shine,
10   Of her high heart given me the monarchy:
    I, I, O I may say that she is mine.
       And though she give but thus conditionly
       This realm of bliss, while virtuous course I take,
       No kings be crowned but° they some covenants[1] make.   *unless*

71

    Who will in fairest book of Nature know
       How Virtue may best lodged in beauty be,
       Let him but learn of Love to read in thee,
    Stella, those fair lines, which true goodness show.
5   There shall he find all vices' overthrow,
       Not by rude force, but sweetest sovereignty
       Of reason, from whose light those night-birds[2] fly;
    That inward sun in thine eyes shineth so.
       And not content to be Perfection's heir
10   Thyself, dost strive all minds that way to move,
    Who mark° in thee what is in thee most fair.[3]   *perceive*
    So while thy beauty draws the heart to love,
       As fast° thy Virtue bends that love to good;   *at the same rate*
       "But, ah," Desire still cries, "give me some food."

72

    Desire, though thou my old companion art,
       And oft so clings to my pure Love that I
       One from the other scarcely can descry,°   *distinguish*
    While each doth blow the fire of my heart,

---

9. In the sense of eminently learned scholar.
1. Solemn coronation oaths taken by English monarchs, promising to protect the laws and the people.

2. The owl, for example, was an emblem of various vices.
3. I.e., her virtue, which is fairer even than her beauty.

5   Now from thy fellowship I needs must part:
        Venus is taught with Dian's wings to fly;[4]
        I must no more in thy sweet passions lie;
    Virtue's gold now must head my Cupid's dart.
        Service and honor, wonder with delight,
10 Fear to offend, will worthy to appear,[5]
    Care shining in mine eyes, faith in my sprite:°   spirit
    These things are left me by my only dear;
        But thou, Desire, because thou wouldst have all,
        Now banished art. But yet alas how shall?

74

    I never drank of Aganippe well,
    Nor ever did in shade of Tempe[6] sit;
    And Muses scorn with vulgar brains to dwell;
    Poor layman I, for sacred rites unfit.
5   Some do I hear of Poets' fury° tell,   inspiration
    But God wot,° wot not what they mean by it;   knows
    And this I swear by blackest brook of hell,[7]
    I am no pick-purse of another's wit.
        How falls it then that with so smooth an ease
10 My thoughts I speak, and what I speak doth flow
    In verse, and that my verse best wits doth please?
    Guess we the cause. "What, is it thus?" Fie no.
        "Or so?" Much less. "How then?" Sure thus it is:
        My lips are sweet, inspired with Stella's kiss.[8]

81

    O kiss, which dost those ruddy gems impart,
    Or° gems, or fruits of new-found Paradise,   either
    Breathing all bliss and sweet'ning to the heart,
    Teaching dumb lips a nobler exercise!
5   O kiss, which souls, even souls, together ties
    By links of love, and only nature's art,
    How fain° would I paint thee to all men's eyes,   gladly
    Or of thy gifts at least shade out° some part.   sketch
        But she forbids, with blushing words, she says
10   She builds her fame on higher-seated praise.
    But my heart burns, I cannot silent be.
        Then since (dear life) you fain would have me peace,[9]
        And I, mad with delight, want wit[1] to cease,
    Stop you my mouth with still still kissing me.

---

4. Diana, goddess of the moon and patron of chastity; Venus, goddess of beauty and love, mother of
Cupid.
5. The phrase can mean either "the wish to appear
worthy" or "desire that is worthy to appear [i.e., not
shameful]."
6. Valley beside Mount Olympus, sacred to
Apollo, the god of song. "Aganippe": fountain at

the foot of Mount Helicon in Greece, sacred to the
Muses.
7. The most binding of all oaths were those sworn
by the river Styx.
8. A kiss he stole from Stella when he caught her
napping (Song 2).
9. You want me to be silent.
1. Lack the mental faculties.

Fourth Song[2]

Only joy, now here you are,
Fit to hear and ease my care;
Let my whispering voice obtain
Sweet reward for sharpest pain:
5 Take me to thee, and thee to me.
"No, no, no, no, my dear, let be."

Night hath closed all in her cloak,
Twinkling stars love-thoughts provoke,
Danger hence good care doth keep,
10 Jealousy itself doth sleep:
Take me to thee, and thee to me.
"No, no, no, no, my dear, let be."

Better place no wit can find,
Cupid's yoke to loose or bind;
15 These sweet flowers on fine bed, too,
Us in their best language woo:
Take me to thee, and thee to me.
"No, no, no, no, my dear, let be."

This small light the moon bestows
20 Serves thy beams but to disclose,
So to raise my hap more high;
Fear not else, none can us spy:
Take me to thee, and thee to me.
"No, no, no, no, my dear, let be."

25 That you heard was but a mouse,
Dumb sleep holdeth all the house;
Yet asleep methinks they say,
"Young folks, take time while you may."
Take me to thee, and thee to me.
30 "No, no, no, no, my dear, let be."

Niggard Time threats, if we miss
This large offer of our bliss,
Long stay° ere he grant the same;   wait
Sweet, then, while each thing doth frame,°   serve
35 Take me to thee, and thee to me.
"No, no, no, no, my dear, let be."

Your fair mother is abed,
Candles out, and curtains spread;
She thinks you do letters write:
40 Write, but first let me indite:°   dictate

2. Like Petrarch, Sidney intersperses songs (eleven of them) in his sequence, thereby extending its emotional range. Some of them incorporate Stella's voice. This song appears between sonnets 85 and 86.

Take me to thee, and thee to me.
"No, no, no, no, my dear, let be."

Sweet, alas, why strive you thus?
Concord better fitteth us.
45   Leave to Mars the force of hands,
Your power in your beauty stands:
Take me to thee, and thee to me.
"No, no, no, no, my dear, let be."

Woe to me, and do you swear
50   Me to hate? But I forbear.
Cursèd be my destines° all,   *fates*
That brought me so high to fall:
Soon with my death I will please thee.
"No, no, no, no, my dear, let be."

87

When I was forced from Stella ever dear,
Stella, food of my thoughts, heart of my heart,
Stella, whose eyes make all my tempests clear,
By iron laws of duty to depart,
5   Alas, I found that she with me did smart;
I saw that tears did in her eyes appear;
I saw that sighs her sweetest lips did part,
And her sad words my sadded sense did hear.
      For me, I wept to see pearls scattered so,
10   I sighed her sighs, and wailèd for her woe,
Yet swam in joy, such love in her was seen.
      Thus while th' effect most bitter was to me,
      And nothing than the cause more sweet could be,
I had been° vexed, if vexed I had not been.   *i.e., would have been*

89³

Now that of absence the most irksome night
      With darkest shade doth overcome my day,
      Since Stella's eyes, wont° to give me my day,   *accustomed*
Leaving my hemisphere, leave me in night,
5   Each day seems long, and longs for long-stayed° night;   *long-delayed*
      The night, as tedious, woos th' approach of day.
      Tired with the dusty toils of busy day,
Languished with horrors of the silent night,
Suffering the evils both of the day and night,
10   While no night is more dark than is my day,
Nor no day hath less quiet than my night:
      With such bad mixture of my night and day
That, living thus in blackest winter night,
      I feel the flames of hottest summer day.

---

3. A sonnet with only two rhyme words, *night* and *day*.

91

Stella, while now by Honor's cruel might
  I am from° you, light of my life, mis-led,   *away from*
  And that fair you, my sun, thus overspread
With absence' veil, I live in Sorrow's night,
5 If this dark place yet shew, like candlelight,
  Some beauty's piece,⁴ as amber-colored head,
  Milk hands, rose cheeks, or lips more sweet, more red,
Or seeing jets,° black, but in blackness bright,   *eyes*
  They please I do confess, they please mine eyes;
10 But why? because of you they models be;
Models such be wood-globes of glist'ring° skies.⁵   *glittering*
Dear, therefore be not jealous over me,
  If you hear that they seem my heart to move:
  Not them, O no, but you in them I love.

Eleventh Song⁶

"Who is it that this dark night
Underneath my window plaineth?"⁷
It is one who from thy sight
Being (ah) exiled, disdaineth
5 Every other vulgar light.

"Why, alas, and are you he?
Be not yet those fancies changèd?"
Dear, when you find change in me,
Though from me you be estrangèd,
10 Let my change to ruin be.

"Well, in absence this will die;
Leave to see, and leave to wonder."
Absence sure will help, if I
Can learn how myself to sunder
15 From what in my heart doth lie.

"But time will these thoughts remove:
Time doth work what no man knoweth."
Time doth as the subject prove;⁸
With time still th' affection groweth
20 In the faithful turtledove.

"What if you new beauties see;
Will not they stir new affectiön?"
I will think they pictures be,
Image-like of saints' perfectiön,
25 Poorly counterfeiting thee.

4. Some beauties in other women.
5. Wooden globes of the heavens, with painted constellations and planets.
6. This last song, a dialogue between Astrophil and Stella, is located between sonnets 104 and 105.
7. Complains (in song) of his love woes.
8. Things change in time according to their natures.

"But your reason's purest light,
Bids you leave such minds to nourish."[9]
Dear, do reason no such spite:
Never doth thy beauty flourish
30 More than in my reason's sight.

"But the wrongs love bears will make
Love at length leave undertaking."
No, the more fools it do shake,
In a ground of so firm making,
35 Deeper still they drive the stake.

"Peace, I think that some give ear:
Come no more, lest I get anger."
Bliss, I will my bliss forbear,
Fearing, sweet, you to endanger,
40 But my soul shall harbor there.

"Well, begone, begone I say,
Lest that Argus'[1] eyes perceive you."
O unjustest fortune's sway,°   power
Which can make me thus to leave you,
45 And from louts to run away.

108[2]

When Sorrow (using mine own fire's might)
  Melts down his lead into my boiling breast,
  Through that dark furnace to my heart oppressed
There shines a joy from thee, my only light;
5 But soon as thought of thee breeds my delight,
  And my young soul flutters to thee, his nest,
  Most rude Despair, my daily unbidden guest,
Clips straight° my wings, straight wraps me in his night,   immediately
  And makes me then bow down my head and say,
10 "Ah, what doth Phoebus'° gold that wretch avail,   god of the sun
Whom iron doors do keep from use of day?"
So strangely (alas) thy works in me prevail,
  That in my woes for thee thou art my joy,
  And in my joys for thee my only annoy.

1582?   1591, 1598

---

9. Stop indulging such thoughts.
1. The hundred-eyed monster set by Juno to guard
Io, a mistress of Jupiter whom Juno had trans-

formed into a cow.
2. In many sonnet sequences, as here, the final
sonnet brings no resolution.

The nightingale[1]

The nightingale, as soon as April bringeth[2]
Unto her rested sense a perfect waking
(While late bare earth, proud of new clothing, springeth),
Sings out her woes, a thorn her song-book making,
5   And mournfully bewailing,
    Her throat in tunes expresseth
    What grief her breast oppresseth,
For Thereus' force on her chaste will prevailing.
    O Philomela fair, O take some gladness,
10   That here is juster cause of plaintful sadness:
    Thine earth now springs, mine fadeth;
    Thy thorn without, my thorn my heart invadeth.

Alas, she hath no other cause of anguish
But Thereus' love, on her by strong hand wroken,°   *inflicted*
15   Wherein she suffering, all her spirits languish;
Full womanlike complains her will was broken.
    But I who daily craving,
    Cannot have to content me,
    Have more cause to lament me,
20   Since wanting is more woe than too much having.
    O Philomela fair, O take some gladness,
    That here is juster cause of plaintful sadness:
    Thine earth now springs, mine fadeth;
    Thy thorn without, my thorn my heart invadeth.

ca. 1581   1598

Thou blind man's mark[1]

Thou blind man's mark,° thou fool's self-chosen snare,   *target*
Fond fancy's scum, and dregs of scattered thought,
Band° of all evils, cradle of causeless care,   *swaddling band*
Thou web of will, whose end is never wrought—

5   Desire, desire! I have too dearly bought,
With price of mangled mind, thy worthless ware;
Too long, too long asleep thou hast me brought,
Who should my mind to higher things prepare.

But yet in vain thou hast my ruin sought;
10   In vain thou madest me to vain things aspire;
In vain thou kindlest all thy smoky fire;

---

1. This and the following two poems are from *Certain Sonnets*, a miscellany of thirty-two poems (not all of them sonnets in the modern sense) apparently written before *Astrophil and Stella*.
2. In England, the nightingale's song is heard only in the spring. According to myth, the nightingale

was once Philomela, who was raped and had her tongue cut out by her brother-in-law, King Tereus; she presses her breast against a thorn while singing to remind herself of that pain.

1. This and the next sonnet close *Certain Sonnets*.

For virtue hath this better lesson taught—
Within myself to seek my only hire,°   reward
Desiring nought but how to kill desire.

ca. 1581   1598

Leave me, O Love

Leave me, O Love which reachest but to dust,
And thou my mind aspire to higher things;
Grow rich in that which never taketh rust:
Whatever fades but fading pleasure brings.

5   Draw in thy beams, and humble all thy might
To that sweet yoke where lasting freedoms be;
Which breaks the clouds and opens forth the light,
That doth both shine and give us sight to see.

     O take fast hold; let that light be thy guide
10   In this small course which birth draws out to death,
     And think how evil becometh him to slide,
     Who seeketh heav'n, and comes of heav'nly breath.[1]
     Then farewell world, thy uttermost I see;
     Eternal Love, maintain thy life in me.

ca. 1581   1598

The Defense of Poesy

The Defense of Poesy, probably written in 1579 though not published until 1595, is an eloquent argument for the dignity, social efficacy, and moral value of imaginative literature in verse or prose. Sidney responds to ancient charges against poetic fictions—charges of irresponsibility and unreality—that had been revived in his own time most strenuously by Puritan moralists. In a graceful, if strikingly paradoxical, rhetorical performance, the Defense argues both that the poet, liberated from the world, is free to range "within the zodiac of his own wit" and that poetry actively intervenes in the world and transforms it for the good. After a slyly self-deprecating introduction, Sidney points out the antiquity of poetry, its prestige in the biblical and classical worlds, and its universality; also, he cites the names given to poets—*vates*, or "prophet," by the Romans and *poietes*, or "maker," by the Greeks—as evidence of their ancient dignity. But he bases his defense essentially on the special status of the poetic imagination. While all arts, from astronomy to music to medicine, depend ultimately on nature as their object, poetry, he claims, is uniquely free: "Only the poet, disdaining to be tied to any such subjection, lifted up with the vigor of his own invention, doth grow in effect another nature."

This freedom, Sidney argues, enables the poet to present virtues and vices in a livelier and more affecting way than nature does, teaching, delighting, and moving the reader at the same time. The poet is superior to both the philosopher and the historian, because he is more concrete than the one and more universal than the other. The *Defense* also refutes Plato's charge that poets are liars by arguing that the

1. I.e., it ill becomes one who has a soul and seeks heaven to "slide" to earthly things.

poet "nothing affirms, and therefore never lieth," and it denies as well the Platonic claim that poetry arouses base desires. Tragedy, for example, "openeth the greatest wounds," in Sidney's account, "and showeth forth the ulcers that are covered with tissue," thereby making "kings fear to be tyrants." Surveying the English literary scene of his own century, Sidney finds little to praise except for Surrey's lyrics, the moralizing narratives of *A Mirror for Magistrates*, and Spenser's *Shepheardes Calender*; the drama he faults for "mingling kings and clowns" and for unrealistic distortions of time and space. (The great, sprawling plays of Marlowe and Shakespeare, plays that triumphantly violated many of Sidney's cherished principles, lay just ahead.) The *Defense* ends with a mock conjuration and a playful curse, reminders of the magical power of poetry, a power that lurks beneath both Sidney's idealism and his didacticism.

From The Defense of Poesy

[THE LESSONS OF HORSEMANSHIP]

When the right virtuous Edward Wotton and I were at the Emperor's court together,[1] we gave ourselves to learn horsemanship of John Pietro Pugliano, one that with great commendation had the place of an esquire[2] in his stable. And he, according to the fertileness of the Italian wit, did not only afford us the demonstration of his practice but sought to enrich our minds with the contemplations therein which he thought most precious. But with none I remember mine ears were at any time more loaden, than when (either angered with slow payment, or moved with our learner-like admiration) he exercised his speech in the praise of his faculty.[3] He said soldiers were the noblest estate of mankind, and horsemen the noblest of soldiers. He said they were the masters of war and ornaments of peace, speedy goers and strong abiders, triumphers both in camps and courts. Nay, to so unbelieved a point he proceeded, as that no earthly thing bred such wonder to a prince as to be a good horseman. Skill of government was but a *pedanteria*[4] in comparison. Then would he add certain praises by telling what a peerless beast the horse was, the only serviceable courtier without flattery, the beast of most beauty, faithfulness, courage, and such more, that if I had not been a piece of a logician[5] before I came to him I think he would have persuaded me to have wished myself a horse. But thus much at least with his no few words he drave into me, that self-love is better than any gilding[6] to make that seem gorgeous wherein ourselves be parties. Wherein, if Pugliano's strong affection and weak arguments will not satisfy you, I will give you a nearer example of myself, who (I know not by what mischance) in these my not old years and idlest times having slipped into the title of a poet, am provoked to say something unto you in the defense of that my unelected vocation, which if I handle with more good will than good reasons, bear with me, since the scholar is to be pardoned that followeth the steps of his master.[7] And yet I must say that, as I have just cause to make a pitiful defense of poor poetry,

---

1. Sidney and Edward Wotton (1548–1626), an English courtier and diplomat, became good friends at the court of Maximilian II (the Holy Roman Emperor) in Vienna in 1574–75.
2. Equerry, an officer in charge of the horses and stables of a noble house.

3. Field of learning.
4. Pedantry, narrow and overly detailed knowledge, of use only to schoolmasters.
5. I.e., if I had not had some skill in logic.
6. With a pun on *gelding*.
7. I.e., Pugliano.

which from almost the highest estimation of learning is fallen to be the laughingstock of children, so have I need to bring some more available[8] proofs; since the former is by no man barred of his deserved credit, the silly[9] latter hath had even the names of philosophers used to the defacing of it, with great danger of civil war among the Muses.

* * *

[THE POET, POETRY]

* * * Since the authors of most of our sciences[1] were the Romans, and before them the Greeks, let us a little stand upon their authorities, but even so far as to see what names they have given unto this now scorned skill.[2]

Among the Romans a poet was called *vates*, which is as much as a diviner, foreseer, or prophet, as by his conjoined words *vaticinium* and *vaticinari*[3] is manifest: so heavenly a title did that excellent people bestow upon this heart-ravishing knowledge. And so far were they carried into the admiration thereof, that they thought in the chanceable hitting upon any such verses great foretokens of their following fortunes were placed. Whereupon grew the word of *Sortes Virgilianae*,[4] when by sudden opening Virgil's book they lighted upon any verse of his making, whereof the histories of the emperors' lives are full: as of Albinus,[5] the governor of our island, who in his childhood met with this verse

Arma amens capio nec sat rationis in armis[6]

and in his age performed it. Which, although it were a very vain and godless superstition, as also it was to think spirits were commanded by such verses— whereupon this word charms, derived of *carmina*,[7] cometh—so yet serveth it to show the great reverence those wits were held in; and altogether not without ground, since both the oracles of Delphos and Sibylla's prophecies[8] were wholly delivered in verses. For that same exquisite observing of number and measure in the words, and that high flying liberty of conceit[9] proper to the poet, did seem to have some divine force in it.

And may not I presume a little further, to show the reasonableness of this word *vates*, and say that the holy David's[1] Psalms are a divine poem? If I do, I shall not do it without the testimony of great learned men, both ancient and modern. But even the name of Psalms will speak for me, which being interpreted, is nothing but songs; then that it is fully written in meter, as all learned hebricians agree, although the rules be not yet fully found;[2] lastly and principally, his handling his prophecy, which is merely[3] poetical: for

8. Effective.
9. Weak, poor.
1. Branches of knowledge.
2. I.e., poetry.
3. To prophesy. "Vates": poet-prophet. "Vaticinium": a prophecy.
4. Casting of lots out of Virgil, i.e., accepting as prophecy a line of Virgil chosen by random opening of the *Aeneid*.
5. Roman governor of Britain, declared emperor by his troops in 193 C.E. but defeated four years later.
6. Frantic, I take up arms, yet there is little purpose in arms (*Aeneid* 2.314).
7. Songs, poems.

8. The Pythia (priestesses) at Delphi in Greece proclaimed Apollo's oracles. The Sibyls were thought to be prophetesses from the east. The Cumaean Sibyl directed Aeneas to the underworld and brought the famous Sibylline Books to Rome.
9. Imaginative conception.
1. The biblical King David, commonly identified in the Renaissance as author of the Book of Psalms.
2. Many Renaissance scholars who knew some Hebrew ("hebricians") thought the psalms were written in verse forms approximating classical Greek and Latin meters.
3. Entirely.

what else is the awaking his musical instruments, the often and free changing of persons, his notable *prosopopoeias*,[4] when he maketh you, as it were, see God coming in His majesty, his telling of the beasts' joyfulness and hills leaping, but a heavenly poesy, wherein almost[5] he showeth himself a passionate lover of that unspeakable and everlasting beauty to be seen by the eyes of the mind, only cleared by faith? But truly now having named him, I fear me I seem to profane that holy name, applying it to poetry, which is among us thrown down to so ridiculous an estimation. But they that with quiet judgments will look a little deeper into it, shall find the end and working of it such as, being rightly applied, deserveth not to be scourged out of the Church of God.

But now let us see how the Greeks named it, and how they deemed of it. The Greeks called him a "poet," which name hath, as the most excellent, gone through other languages. It cometh of this word *poiein*, which is, to make: wherein, I know not whether by luck or wisdom, we Englishmen have met with the Greeks in calling him a maker:[6] which name, how high and incomparable a title it is, I had rather were known by marking the scope of other sciences than by any partial[7] allegation.

There is no art delivered to mankind that hath not the works of nature for his principal object, without which they[8] could not consist, and on which they so depend, as they become actors and players, as it were, of what nature will have set forth. So doth the astronomer look upon the stars, and, by that he seeth, set down what order nature hath taken therein. So doth the geometrician and arithmetician in their diverse sorts of quantities. So doth the musicians in time tell you which by nature agree,[9] which not. The natural philosopher thereon hath his name, and the moral philosopher standeth upon[1] the natural virtues, vices, or passions of man; and follow nature (saith he) therein, and thou shalt not err. The lawyer saith what men have determined; the historian what men have done. The grammarian speaketh only of the rules of speech; and the rhetorician and logician, considering what in nature will soonest prove and persuade, thereon give artificial rules, which still are compassed within the circle of a question according to the proposed matter.[2] The physician weigheth[3] the nature of man's body, and the nature of things helpful or hurtful unto it. And the metaphysic, though it be in the second and abstract notions, and therefore be counted supernatural, yet doth he indeed build upon the depth of nature. Only the poet, disdaining to be tied to any such subjection, lifted up with the vigor of his own invention, doth grow in effect another nature, in making things either better than nature bringeth forth, or, quite anew, forms such as never were in nature, as the Heroes, Demigods, Cyclops, Chimeras, Furies,[4] and such like: so as he goeth hand in hand with nature, not enclosed within the narrow warrant of her gifts, but freely ranging only within the zodiac of his own wit.[5] Nature

---

4. Personifications.
5. Indeed.
6. A common word for *poet* in 16th-century England. "Met with": agreed with.
7. Biased.
8. The several arts.
9. Which rhythms are naturally consonant.
1. Takes as subject matter. "Natural philosopher": scientist. "Thereon": i.e., from nature.
2. The rules of those arts ("artificial rules") are

always limited in their application to questions pertaining to the subject at hand.
3. Considers.
4. Avenging deities who punish crimes both in this world and after death. "Heroes": in the Greek sense, part human, part divine. "Cyclops": one-eyed giants in Homer's *Odyssey*. "Chimeras": fire-breathing monsters with lion's head, goat's body, and serpent's tail.
5. Intellect.

never set forth the earth in so rich tapestry as divers poets have done; neither with so pleasant rivers, fruitful trees, sweet-smelling flowers, nor whatsoever else may make the too much loved earth more lovely. Her world is brazen, the poets only deliver a golden.[6]

But let those things alone, and go to man—for whom as the other things are, so it seemeth in him her uttermost cunning is employed—and know whether she have brought forth so true a lover as Theagenes, so constant a friend as Pylades, so valiant a man as Orlando, so right a prince as Xenophon's Cyrus,[7] so excellent a man every way as Virgil's Aeneas. Neither let this be jestingly conceived, because the works of the one be essential, the other in imitation or fiction,[8] for any understanding knoweth the skill of each artificer standeth in that *idea* or fore-conceit[9] of the work, and not in the work itself. And that the poet hath that *idea* is manifest, by delivering them forth in such excellency as he had imagined them. Which delivering forth also is not wholly imaginative,[1] as we are wont to say by them that build castles in the air; but so far substantially it worketh, not only to make a Cyrus, which had been but a particular excellency as nature might have done, but to bestow a Cyrus upon the world to make many Cyruses, if they will learn aright why and how that maker made him.

Neither let it be deemed too saucy a comparison to balance the highest point of man's wit with the efficacy of nature; but rather give right honor to the heavenly Maker of that maker, who having made man to His own likeness, set him beyond and over all the works of that second nature:[2] which in nothing he showeth so much as in poetry, when with the force of a divine breath he bringeth things forth surpassing her doings—with no small arguments to the credulous of that first accursed fall of Adam, since our erected wit maketh us know what perfection is, and yet our infected will[3] keepeth us from reaching unto it. But these arguments will by few be understood, and by fewer granted. This much (I hope) will be given me, that the Greeks with some probability of reason gave him the name above all names of learning.

Now let us go to a more ordinary opening[4] of him, that the truth may be the more palpable: and so I hope, though we get not so unmatched a praise as the etymology of his names will grant, yet his very description, which no man will deny, shall not justly be barred from a principal commendation.

Poesy therefore is an art of imitation, for so Aristotle termeth it in the word *mimesis*[5]—that is to say, a representing, counterfeiting, or figuring forth—to speak metaphorically, a speaking picture—with this end, to teach and delight.

---

6. A reference to the classical tradition of "The Four Ages of Man," the idea that the world has declined from the first and perfect Golden Age, through the Silver, Bronze, and Iron ages. "Her": Nature's.
7. Cyrus the Great of Persia, exemplary hero of Xenophon's prose romance, the *Cyropaedia* (4th century B.C.E.); Theagenes, hero of Heliodorus's Greek romance, *Aethiopica* (3rd century C.E.); Pylades, friend of the Greek hero Orestes;

Orlando, hero of Ariosto's *Orlando furioso* (1516).
8. The works of nature are real ("essential"); those of the poet are fiction.
9. Imaginative plan, conception.
1. Fanciful.
2. Physical nature.
3. Will corrupted in the Fall by Original Sin.
4. Analysis or explanation.
5. *Poetics* 1.2.

[THREE KINDS OF POETS]

Of this have been three general kinds. The chief, both in antiquity and excellency, were they that did imitate the unconceivable excellencies of God. Such were David in his Psalms; Solomon in his Song of Songs, in his Ecclesiastes, and Proverbs; Moses and Deborah in their Hymns; and the writer of Job: which, beside other, the learned Emanuel Tremellius and Franciscus Junius[6] do entitle the poetical part of the Scripture. Against these none will speak that hath the Holy Ghost in due holy reverence. (In this kind, though in a full wrong divinity, were Orpheus, Amphion, Homer in his Hymns, and many other, both Greeks and Romans.) And this poesy must be used by whosoever will follow St. James's counsel in singing psalms when they are merry,[7] and I know is used with the fruit of comfort by some, when, in sorrowful pangs of their death-bringing sins, they find the consolation of the never-leaving goodness.

The second kind is of them that deal with matters philosophical, either moral, as Tyrtaeus, Phocylides, Cato,[8] or natural, as Lucretius and Virgil's *Georgics*; or astronomical, as Manilius and Pontanus; or historical, as Lucan:[9] which who mislike, the fault is in their judgment quite out of taste, and not in the sweet food of sweetly uttered knowledge.

But because this second sort is wrapped within the fold of the proposed subject, and takes not the course of his own invention, whether they properly be poets or no let grammarians dispute, and go to the third, indeed right poets, of whom chiefly this question ariseth: betwixt whom and these second is such a kind of difference as betwixt the meaner[1] sort of painters, who counterfeit only such faces as are set before them, and the more excellent, who having no law but wit, bestow that in colors upon you which is fittest for the eye to see: as the constant though lamenting look of Lucretia, when she punished in herself another's fault,[2] wherein he painteth not Lucretia whom he never saw, but painteth the outward beauty of such a virtue. For these third[3] be they which most properly do imitate to teach and delight, and to imitate borrow nothing of what is, hath been, or shall be; but range, only reined with learned discretion, into the divine consideration of what may be and should be. These be they that, as the first and most noble sort may justly be termed *vates*, so these are waited on in the excellentest languages and best understandings with the fore-described name of poets. For these indeed do merely[4] make to imitate, and imitate both to delight and teach; and delight, to move men to take that goodness in hand, which without delight they would fly as from a stranger; and teach, to make them know that goodness whereunto they are moved—which being the noblest scope to which ever any learning was directed, yet want there not idle tongues to bark at them.

6. Two scholars who published a Protestant Latin translation of the Bible in 1579.
7. "Is any merry? Let him sing psalms" (James 5.13).
8. Tyrtaeus and Phocylides were Greek poets; the Roman Marcus Cato was the author of *Disticha de moribus*, an immensely popular collection, in verse and prose, of moral maxims.
9. Lucan wrote *De bello civili* (*Pharsalia*), an epic poem on the struggle between Caesar and Pompey.

Lucretius wrote a philosophical poem *De rerum natura* (On the Nature of Things). Virgil's *Georgics* exalts the life and work of the farmer.
1. Lower.
2. A notable exemplar of chastity and honor, the Roman matron Lucretia committed suicide after being raped by the son of King Tarquinius Superbus.
3. I.e., the right poets.
4. Only.

These be subdivided into sundry more special denominations. The most notable be the heroic, lyric, tragic, comic, satiric, iambic, elegiac, pastoral, and certain others, some of these being termed according to the matter they deal with, some by the sorts of verses they liked best to write in; for indeed the greatest part of poets have apparelled their poetical inventions in that numbrous[5] kind of writing which is called verse—indeed but apparelled, verse being but an ornament and no cause to poetry, since there have been many most excellent poets that never versified, and now swarm many versifiers that need never answer to the name of poets. For Xenophon, who did imitate so excellently as to give us *effigiem iusti imperii*, the portraiture of a just empire, under the name of Cyrus (as Cicero saith of him), made therein an absolute heroical poem. So did Heliodorus in his sugared invention of that picture of love in Theagenes and Chariclea; and yet both these wrote in prose: which I speak to show that it is not rhyming and versing that maketh a poet—no more than a long gown maketh an advocate, who though he pleaded in armor should be an advocate and no soldier. But it is that feigning notable images of virtues, vices, or what else, with that delightful teaching, which must be the right describing note to know a poet by; although indeed the senate of poets hath chosen verse as their fittest raiment, meaning, as in matter they passed all in all,[6] so in manner to go beyond them: not speaking (table-talk fashion or like men in a dream) words as they chanceably fall from the mouth, but peising[7] each syllable of each word by just proportion according to the dignity of the subject.

[POETRY, PHILOSOPHY, HISTORY]

Now therefore it shall not be amiss first to weigh this latter sort of poetry by his works, and then by his parts; and if in neither of these anatomies he be condemnable, I hope we shall obtain a more favorable sentence.[8]

This purifying of wit—this enriching of memory, enabling of judgment, and enlarging of conceit[9]—which commonly we call learning, under what name soever it come forth, or to what immediate end soever it be directed, the final end is to lead and draw us to as high a perfection as our degenerate souls, made worse by their clayey lodgings, can be capable of.

This, according to the inclination of the man, bred many-formed[1] impressions. For some that thought this felicity principally to be gotten by knowledge, and no knowledge to be so high or heavenly as acquaintance with the stars, gave themselves to astronomy; others, persuading themselves to be demigods if they knew the causes of things, became natural and supernatural philosophers; some an admirable delight drew to music; and some the certainty of demonstration to the mathematics. But all, one and other, having this scope:[2] to know, and by knowledge to lift up the mind from the dungeon of the body to the enjoying his own divine essence.

But when by the balance of experience it was found that the astronomer, looking to the stars, might fall in a ditch, that the inquiring philosopher might be blind in himself, and the mathematician might draw forth a straight line

5. I.e., in numbers, poetic meters.
6. All others, in all respects.
7. Weighing.
8. Judgment. "Anatomies": analyses.

9. Conceptual power.
1. Manifold.
2. Aim.

with a crooked heart, then lo, did proof, the overruler of opinions, make manifest that all these are but serving sciences, which, as they have each a private end in themselves, so yet are they all directed to the highest end of the mistress-knowledge, by the Greeks called *architectonike*,[3] which stands (as I think) in the knowledge of a man's self, in the ethic and politic consideration, with the end of well-doing and not of well-knowing only—even as the saddler's next[4] end is to make a good saddle, but his further end to serve a nobler faculty, which is horsemanship, so the horseman's to soldiery, and the soldier not only to have the skill, but to perform the practice of a soldier. So that, the ending end of all earthly learning being virtuous action, those skills that most serve to bring forth that have a most just title to be princes over all the rest.

Wherein, if we can, show we the poet's nobleness, by setting him before his other competitors. Among whom as principal challengers step forth the moral philosophers, whom, methinketh, I see coming towards me with a sullen gravity, as though they could not abide vice by daylight, rudely clothed for to witness outwardly their contempt of outward things, with books in their hands against glory, whereto they set their names, sophistically[5] speaking against subtlety, and angry with any man in whom they see the foul fault of anger. These men casting largess as they go, of definitions, divisions, and distinctions,[6] with a scornful interrogative do soberly ask whether it be possible to find any path so ready to lead a man to virtue as that which teacheth what virtue is; and teach it not only by delivering forth his very being, his causes and effects, but also by making known his enemy, vice, which must be destroyed, and his cumbersome servant, passion, which must be mastered; by showing the generalities that containeth it, and the specialities that are derived from it; lastly, by plain setting down how it extendeth itself out of the limits of a man's own little world to the government of families and maintaining of public societies.

The historian scarcely giveth leisure to the moralist to say so much, but that he, laden with old mouse-eaten records, authorizing himself[7] (for the most part) upon other histories, whose greatest authorities are built upon the notable foundation of hearsay; having much ado to accord differing writers and to pick truth out of their partiality;[8] better acquainted with a thousand years ago than with the present age, and yet better knowing how this world goeth than how his own wit runneth; curious for antiquities and inquisitive of novelties; a wonder to young folks and a tyrant in table talk, denieth, in a great chafe,[9] that any man for teaching of virtue, and virtuous actions, is comparable to him. "I am *testis temporum, lux veritatis, vita memoriae, magistra vitae, nuntia vetustatis.*[1] The philosopher," saith he, "teacheth a disputative virtue, but I do an active. His virtue is excellent in the dangerless Academy of Plato, but mine showeth forth her honorable face in the battles of Marathon, Pharsalia, Poitiers, and Agincourt.[2] He teacheth virtue by certain abstract considerations, but I only bid you follow the footing of

3. The "chief art," to which all others are subordinate.
4. Nearest.
5. Subtly.
6. Bountiful gifts of scholastic terms and arguments.
7. Basing his authority.
8. Bias.

9. Temper.
1. I am the witness of times, the light of truth, the life of memory, the teacher of life, and the messenger of antiquity (Cicero, *De oratore* 2.9.36).
2. At Marathon, the Greeks defeated the Persians (490 B.C.E.); at Pharsalia, Caesar defeated Pompey (48 B.C.E.); and at Poitiers (1356) and Agincourt (1415), the English defeated the French.

them that have gone before you. Old-aged experience goeth beyond the fine-witted philosopher, but I give the experience of many ages. Lastly, if he make the songbook, I put the learner's hand to the lute; and if he be the guide, I am the light." Then would he allege you innumerable examples, confirming story by stories, how much the wisest senators and princes have been directed by the credit of history, as Brutus, Alphonsus of Aragon,[3] and who not, if need be? At length the long line of their disputation maketh a point in this, that the one giveth the precept, and the other[4] the example.

* * *

Now, to that which commonly is attributed to the praise of history, in respect of the notable learning is got by marking the success,[5] as though therein a man should see virtue exalted and vice punished—truly that commendation is particular to poetry, and far off from history. For indeed poetry ever sets virtue so out in her best colors, making Fortune her well-waiting handmaid, that one must needs be enamored of her. Well may you see Ulysses in a storm,[6] and in other hard plights; but they are but exercises of patience and magnanimity, to make them shine the more in the near-following prosperity. And of the contrary part, if evil men come to the stage, they ever go out (as the tragedy writer[7] answered to one that misliked the show of such persons) so manacled as they little animate folks to follow them. But the history, being captived to the truth of a foolish world, is many times a terror from well-doing, and an encouragement to unbridled wickedness. For see we not valiant Miltiades rot in his fetters? The just Phocion and the accomplished Socrates put to death like traitors? The cruel Severus live prosperously? The excellent Severus miserably murdered? Sulla and Marius dying in their beds? Pompey and Cicero[8] slain then when they would have thought exile a happiness? See we not virtuous Cato driven to kill himself,[9] and rebel Caesar so advanced that his name yet, after 1600 years, lasteth in the highest honor? And mark but even Caesar's own words of the aforenamed Sulla (who in that only did honestly, to put down his dishonest tyranny), *literas nescivit,* as if want of learning caused him to do well.[1] He meant it not by poetry, which, not content with earthly plagues, deviseth new punishments in hell for tyrants, nor yet by philosophy, which teacheth *occidendos esse;*[2] but no doubt by skill in history, for that indeed can afford you Cypselus, Periander, Phalaris, Dionysius,[3] and I know not how many more of the same kennel, that speed[4] well enough in their abominable injustice of usurpation.

I conclude, therefore, that he[5] excelleth history, not only in furnishing the

3. Marcus Brutus was inspired to rise up against Caesar by the history of his great republican ancestor, Junius Brutus, who expelled the Tarquin kings. Alphonsus V of Aragon (1396–1458) carried the histories of Livy and Caesar into battle with him.
4. History. "The one": philosophy.
5. The outcome.
6. In *Odyssey* 5.291ff.
7. Euripides (as reported by Plutarch).
8. Great statesman and orator killed at Mark Antony's command. Miltiades, Athenian general and victor at Marathon, later imprisoned by the Athenians. Phocion, Athenian general and statesman executed for treason because he opposed an unjust war. "Cruel Severus": Emperor Lucius Septimius Severus, a plunderer of cities. "Excellent Severus": Emperor Alexander Severus, a reformer

slain by his troops. Sulla and Marius, political rivals who brought unrest and destruction to Rome for more than twenty years. Pompey: Pompey the Great, defeated by Caesar at Pharsalia and slain in Egypt.
9. Cato the Younger committed suicide after his party failed to defeat Caesar.
1. When Sulla resigned his dictatorship, Caesar joked that he was illiterate (*litteras nescivit*), since he left the *dictatura* (which means both "dictatorship" and "dictation") to others.
2. They [tyrants] must be killed.
3. Four famous tyrants of the classical world: the first two were from Corinth; Phalaris, Agrigentum; Dionysus the Elder, Syracuse.
4. Succeed.
5. The poet.

mind with knowledge, but in setting it forward to that which deserveth to be called and accounted good: which setting forward, and moving to well-doing, indeed setteth the laurel crown upon the poets as victorious, not only of the historian, but over the philosopher, howsoever in teaching it may be questionable.[6]

For suppose it be granted (that which I suppose with great reason may be denied) that the philosopher, in respect of his methodical proceeding, doth teach more perfectly than the poet, yet do I think that no man is so much *philophilosophos*[7] as to compare the philosopher in moving with the poet. And that moving is of a higher degree than teaching, it may by this appear, that it is well nigh both the cause and effect of teaching. For who will be taught, if he be not moved with desire to be taught? And what so much good doth that teaching bring forth (I speak still of moral doctrine) as that it moveth one to do that which it doth teach? For, as Aristotle saith, it is not *gnosis* but *praxis*[8] must be the fruit. And how *praxis* can be, without being moved to practice, it is no hard matter to consider.

The philosopher showeth you the way, he informeth you of the particularities, as well of the tediousness of the way, as of the pleasant lodging you shall have when your journey is ended, as of the many by-turnings that may divert you from your way. But this is to no man but to him that will read him, and read him with attentive studious painfulness;[9] which constant desire whosoever hath in him, hath already passed half the hardness of the way, and therefore is beholding to the philosopher but for the other half. Nay truly, learned men have learnedly thought that where once reason hath so much overmastered passion as that the mind hath a free desire to do well, the inward light each mind hath in itself is as good as a philosopher's book; since in nature[1] we know it is well to do well, and what is well, and what is evil, although not in the words of art which philosophers bestow upon us; for out of natural conceit[2] the philosophers drew it. But to be moved to do that which we know, or to be moved with desire to know, *hoc opus, hic labor est.*[3]

Now therein of all sciences (I speak still of human,[4] and according to the human conceit) is our poet the monarch. For he doth not only show the way, but giveth so sweet a prospect into the way, as will entice any man to enter into it. Nay, he doth, as if your journey should lie through a fair vineyard, at the first give you a cluster of grapes, that full of that taste, you may long to pass further. He beginneth not with obscure definitions, which must blur the margin with interpretations, and load the memory with doubtfulness; but he cometh to you with words set in delightful proportion, either accompanied with, or prepared for, the well enchanting skill of music; and with a tale forsooth he cometh unto you, with a tale which holdeth children from play, and old men from the chimney corner. And, pretending no more, doth intend the winning of the mind from wickedness to virtue—even as the child is often brought to take most wholesome things by hiding them in such other as have a pleasant taste, which, if one should begin to tell them the nature

---

6. Arguable.
7. A lover of philosophers.
8. Not knowing but doing (*Ethics* 1.1).
9. Carefulness.
1. Considering that by nature.
2. Natural understanding, as opposed to the phi-

losophers' special vocabulary ("words of art").
3. This is the task, this is the work to be done (Virgil, *Aeneid* 6.129).
4. As opposed to divine. "Sciences": branches of learning.

of *aloes* or *rhabarbarum*[5] they should receive, would sooner take their physic at their ears than at their mouth.[6] So is it in men (most of which are childish in the best things, till they be cradled in their graves): glad will they be to hear the tales of Hercules, Achilles, Cyrus, Aeneas; and, hearing them, must needs hear the right description of wisdom, valor, and justice; which, if they had been barely, that is to say philosophically, set out, they would swear they be brought to school again.

* * *

[THE POETIC KINDS]

But I am content not only to decipher him[7] by his works (although works, in commendation or dispraise, must ever hold a high authority), but more narrowly will examine his parts; so that (as in a man) though all together may carry a presence full of majesty and beauty, perchance in some one defectous piece[8] we may find blemish.

Now in his parts, kinds, or species (as you list[9] to term them), it is to be noted that some poesies have coupled together two or three kinds, as the tragical and comical, whereupon is risen the tragi-comical. Some, in the manner, have mingled prose and verse, as Sannazzaro and Boethius.[1] Some have mingled matters heroical and pastoral. But that cometh all to one in this question, for, if severed they be good, the conjunction cannot be hurtful. Therefore, perchance forgetting some and leaving some as needless to be remembered, it shall not be amiss in a word to cite the special kinds, to see what faults may be found in the right use of them.

Is it then the Pastoral poem which is misliked? (For perchance where the hedge is lowest[2] they will soonest leap over.) Is the poor pipe[3] disdained, which sometime out of Meliboeus' mouth can show the misery of people under hard lords or ravening soldiers, and again, by Tityrus, what blessedness is derived to them that lie lowest from the goodness of them that sit highest;[4] sometimes, under the pretty tales of wolves and sheep, can include the whole considerations of wrong-doing and patience; sometimes show that contentions for trifles can get but a trifling victory: where perchance a man may see that even Alexander and Darius, when they strave who should be cock of this world's dunghill, the benefit they got was that the after-livers may say

> Haec memini et victum frustra contendere Thirsin:
> Ex illo Corydon, Corydon est tempore nobis.[5]

Or is it the lamenting Elegiac; which in a kind heart would move rather pity than blame; who bewails with the great philosopher Heraclitus[6] the weakness of mankind and the wretchedness of the world; who surely is to

---

5. Two bitter purgatives.
6. That is, would rather have a box on the ear than take the medicine.
7. I.e., poetry.
8. Defective part.
9. May choose.
1. Both Jacopo Sannazaro's pastoral romance *Arcadia* (1502), which greatly influenced Sidney's own *Arcadia*, and Boethius's *Consolation of Philosophy* (524 C.E.) mixed prose and verse.
2. Pastoral was considered the humblest kind of poetry, written in the lowest style.
3. The shepherd's oaten flute, symbol of pastoral

poetry.
4. In Virgil's first eclogue, Meliboeus laments the seizure of his land while Tityrus rejoices that his lands were protected by the emperor.
5. "This I remember, and how Thyrsis, vanquished, strove in vain. / From that day it is Corydon, Corydon with us" (Virgil, *Eclogue* 7.69–70). I.e., the great victory of Alexander the Great over Darius of Persia comes to the same thing as Corydon's victory over Thyrsis in a singing contest.
6. Ancient Greek philosopher who lamented that everything is subject to mutability.

be praised, either for compassionate accompanying just causes of lamentations, or for rightly painting out how weak be the passions of woefulness?[7] Is it the bitter but wholesome Iambic,[8] who rubs the galled mind, in making shame the trumpet of villainy, with bold and open crying out against naughtiness? Or the Satiric, who

Omne vafer vitium ridenti tangit amico;[9]

who sportingly never leaveth till he make a man laugh at folly, and at length ashamed, to laugh at himself, which he cannot avoid without avoiding the folly; who, while

circum praecordia ludit,[1]

giveth us to feel how many headaches a passionate life bringeth us to; how, when all is done,

Est Ulubris, animus si nos non deficit aequus?[2]

No, perchance it is the Comic, whom naughty play-makers and stage-keepers have justly made odious. To the arguments of abuse I will answer after. Only this much now is to be said, that the comedy is an imitation of the common errors of our life, which he representeth in the most ridiculous and scornful sort that may be, so as it is impossible that any beholder can be content to be such a one. Now, as in geometry the oblique must be known as well as the right, and in arithmetic the odd as well as the even, so in the actions of our life who seeth not the filthiness of evil wanteth a great foil to perceive the beauty of virtue. This doth the comedy handle so in our private and domestical matters as with hearing it we get as it were an experience what is to be looked for of a niggardly Demea, of a crafty Davus, of a flattering Gnatho, of a vainglorious Thraso;[3] and not only to know what effects are to be expected, but to know who be such, by the signifying badge given them by the comedian.[4] And little reason hath any man to say that men learn the evil by seeing it so set out, since, as I said before, there is no man living but, by the force truth hath in nature, no sooner seeth these men play their parts, but wisheth them *in pistrinum*;[5] although perchance the sack of his own faults lie so hidden behind his back that he seeth not himself dance the same measure;[6] whereto yet nothing can more open his eyes than to find his own actions contemptibly set forth.

So that the right use of comedy will (I think) by nobody be blamed; and much less of the high and excellent Tragedy, that openeth the greatest wounds, and showeth forth the ulcers that are covered with tissue; that maketh kings fear to be tyrants, and tyrants manifest their tyrannical humors; that, with stirring the affects[7] of admiration and commiseration, teacheth

---

7. Sidney restricts the elegaic to lamentations; classical poets used elegiac meter for this purpose but also in poems treating love and other topics.

8. Iambic trimeter was first used by Greek poets for direct attacks (as opposed to the wit and ironic indirection that mark satire).

9. Persius (*Satires* 1.116) on the satire of Horace, who "probes every fault while making his friends laugh."

1. "He plays with the very vitals [of his target]" (Persius, *Satires* 1.117).

2. "It is at Ulubrae, if a well-balanced mind does not fail us" (an adaptation of Horace, *Epistles* 1.11.30). Ulubrae was a proverbially uninspiring town surrounded by marshes.

3. Type characters in the Roman comedies of Terence (195–159 B.C.E.), respectively, the harsh father, clever servant, parasite, and braggart. Terence and Plautus (251–184 B.C.E.) were the chief classical models for comedy for the Renaissance.

4. Writer of comedies.

5. Mill used for punishment of Roman slaves.

6. In a fable of Aesop, a sack filled with one's own faults is carried (out of sight) on the back, while one filled with the faults of others is carried in front.

7. Feelings. "Humors": natures or dispositions, as influenced by the balance of four chief bodily fluids, or humors—blood, phlegm, choler, and bile.

the uncertainty of this world, and upon how weak foundations gilden roofs are builded; that maketh us know

> Qui sceptra saevus duro imperio regit
> Timet timentes; metus in auctorem redit.[8]

But how much it can move, Plutarch yieldeth a notable testimony of the abominable tyrant Alexander Pheraeus,[9] from whose eyes a tragedy, well made and represented, drew abundance of tears, who without all pity had murdered infinite numbers, and some of his own blood: so as he, that was not ashamed to make matters for tragedies, yet could not resist the sweet violence of a tragedy. And if it wrought no further good in him, it was that he, in despite of himself, withdrew himself from hearkening to that which might mollify his hardened heart. But it is not the tragedy they do mislike; for it were too absurd to cast out so excellent a representation of whatsoever is most worthy to be learned.

Is it the Lyric[1] that most displeaseth, who with his tuned lyre and well-accorded voice, giveth praise, the reward of virtue, to virtuous acts; who gives moral precepts, and natural problems; who sometimes raiseth up his voice to the height of the heavens, in singing the lauds of the immortal God? Certainly, I must confess my own barbarousness, I never heard the old song of Percy and Douglas[2] that I found not my heart moved more than with a trumpet; and yet is it sung but by some blind crowder,[3] with no rougher voice than rude style; which, being so evil appareled in the dust and cobwebs of that uncivil age, what would it work trimmed in the gorgeous eloquence of Pindar?[4] In Hungary I have seen it the manner at all feasts, and other such meetings, to have songs of their ancestors' valor, which that right soldierlike nation think one of the chiefest kindlers of brave courage. The incomparable Lacedemonians[5] did not only carry that kind of music ever with them to the field, but even at home, as such songs were made, so were they all content to be singers of them—when the lusty men were to tell what they did, the old men what they had done, and the young what they would do. And where a man may say that Pindar many times praiseth highly victories of small moment, matters rather of sport than virtue; as it may be answered, it was the fault of the poet, and not of the poetry, so indeed the chief fault was in the time and custom of the Greeks, who set those toys at so high a price that Philip of Macedon reckoned a horserace won at Olympus among his three fearful felicities.[6] But as the unimitable Pindar often did, so is that kind most capable and most fit to awake the thoughts from the sleep of idleness to embrace honorable enterprises.

There rests the Heroical[7]—whose very name (I think) should daunt all backbiters: for by what conceit[8] can a tongue be directed to speak evil of that

8. "He who rules his people with a harsh government/Fears those who fear him; the fear returns upon its author" (Seneca, *Oedipus*, 705–06).

9. Plutarch records that this cruel tyrant wept at the sufferings of Hecuba and Andromache in Euripides' *Troades*.

1. Here defined as poetry concerned chiefly with praise, and sung (originally) to musical accompaniment.

2. Ballad of Chevy Chase.

3. Fiddler.

4. Pindar's odes, the most exalted lyric poetry of Greece, celebrated victors in athletic games. "That uncivil age": the Middle Ages.

5. Spartans.

6. Plutarch records that Philip received three awesome tidings in one day: that his general was victorious in battle, that his wife had borne a son, and that his horse had won a race at Olympia.

7. I.e., epic. "Rests": remains.

8. Conception.

which draweth with him no less champions than Achilles, Cyrus, Aeneas, Turnus, Tydeus, and Rinaldo?[9]—who doth not only teach and move to a truth, but teacheth and moveth to the most high and excellent truth; who maketh magnanimity and justice shine through all misty fearfulness and foggy desires; who, if the saying of Plato and Tully[1] be true, that who could see virtue would be wonderfully ravished with the love of her beauty—this man sets her out to make her more lovely in her holiday apparel, to the eye of any that will deign not to disdain until they understand. But if anything be already said in the defense of sweet poetry, all concurreth to the maintaining the heroical, which is not only a kind, but the best and most accomplished kind of poetry. For, as the image of each action stirreth and instructeth the mind, so the lofty image of such worthies most inflameth the mind with desire to be worthy, and informs with counsel how to be worthy. Only let Aeneas be worn in the tablet of your memory, how he governeth himself in the ruin of his country; in the preserving his old father, and carrying away his religious ceremonies;[2] in obeying God's commandment to leave Dido, though not only all passionate kindness, but even the human consideration of virtuous gratefulness, would have craved other of him; how in storms, how in sports, how in war, how in peace, how a fugitive, how victorious, how besieged, how besieging, how to strangers, how to allies, how to enemies, how to his own; lastly, how in his inward self, and how in his outward government—and I think, in a mind not prejudiced with a prejudicating humor, he will be found in excellency fruitful, yea, even as Horace saith,

> melius Chrysippo et Crantore.[3]

But truly I imagine it falleth out with these poet-whippers, as with some good women, who often are sick, but in faith they cannot tell where; so the name of poetry is odious to them, but neither his cause nor effects, neither the sum that contains him, nor the particularities descending from him, give any fast[4] handle to their carping dispraise.

Since then poetry is of all human learning the most ancient and of most fatherly antiquity, as from whence other learnings have taken their beginnings; since it is so universal that no learned nation doth despise it, nor barbarous nation is without it; since both Roman and Greek gave such divine names unto it, the one of prophesying, the other of making, and that indeed that name of making is fit for him, considering that where all other arts retain themselves within their subject, and receive, as it were, their being from it, the poet only bringeth his own stuff, and doth not learn a conceit out of a matter, but maketh matter for a conceit; since neither his description nor end containing any evil, the thing described cannot be evil; since his effects be so good as to teach goodness and to delight the learners; since therein (namely in moral doctrine, the chief of all knowledges) he doth not only far

---

9. In Ariosto's *Orlando furioso* and Tasso's *Gerusalemme liberata*. "Tydeus": in Statius's epic, *Thebaid*. Turnus is Aeneas's great antagonist.
1. Marcus Tullius Cicero.
2. Sacred objects, household gods. After fleeing Troy, Aeneas and his men stayed for a time in Carthage, whose queen, Dido, became Aeneas's lover. She killed herself when Aeneas (at the gods' command) sailed away to accomplish his fate, the founding of the Roman empire.
3. In *Epistles* 1.2.4, Horace praises Homer as a "better [teacher] than Chrysippus [a great Stoic philosopher] and Crantor" (a commentator on Plato).
4. Firm.

pass the historian, but, for instructing, is well nigh comparable to the philosopher, for moving leaves him behind him; since the Holy Scripture (wherein there is no uncleanness) hath whole parts in it poetical, and that even our Savior Christ vouchsafed to use the flowers of it; since all his kinds are not only in their united forms but in their severed dissections fully commendable; I think (and think I think rightly) the laurel crown appointed for triumphant captains doth worthily (of all other learnings) honor the poet's triumph.

* * *

[ANSWERS TO CHARGES AGAINST POETRY]

Now then go we to the most important imputations laid to the poor poets. For aught I can yet learn, they are these. First, that there being many other more fruitful knowledges, a man might better spend his time in them than in this. Secondly, that it is the mother of lies. Thirdly, that it is the nurse of abuse, infecting us with many pestilent desires; with a siren's sweetness drawing the mind to the serpent's tail of sinful fancies (and herein, especially, comedies give the largest field to ear,[5] as Chaucer saith); how, both in other nations and in ours, before poets did soften us, we were full of courage, given to martial exercises, the pillars of manlike liberty, and not lulled asleep in shady idleness with poets' pastimes. And lastly, and chiefly, they cry out with open mouth as if they had overshot Robin Hood, that Plato banished them out of his commonwealth.[6] Truly, this is much, if there be much truth in it.

First, to the first.[7] That a man might better spend his time, is a reason indeed; but it doth (as they say) but *petere principium*.[8] For if it be as I affirm, that no learning is so good as that which teacheth and moveth to virtue; and that none can both teach and move thereto so much as poetry: then is the conclusion manifest that ink and paper cannot be to a more profitable purpose employed. And certainly, though a man should grant their first assumption, it should follow (methinks) very unwillingly, that good is not good because better is better. But I still and utterly deny that there is sprung out of earth a more fruitful knowledge.

To the second, therefore, that they should be the principal liars, I will answer paradoxically, but truly, I think truly, that of all writers under the sun the poet is the least liar, and, though he would, as a poet can scarcely be a liar. The astronomer, with his cousin the geometrician, can hardly escape,[9] when they take upon them to measure the height of the stars. How often, think you, do the physicians lie, when they aver things good for sicknesses, which afterwards send Charon[1] a great number of souls drowned in a potion before they come to his ferry? And no less of the rest, which take upon them to affirm. Now, for the poet, he nothing affirms, and therefore never lieth. For, as I take it, to lie is to affirm that to be true which is false. So as the other artists,[2] and especially the historian, affirming many things, can, in the cloudy knowledge of mankind, hardly escape from many lies. But

---

5. To plow (*Knight's Tale*, 28).
6. Plato argued that most sorts of poets would be banished from an ideal commonwealth, because they stir up unworthy emotions and because their imitations are far removed from truth (*Republic* 10.595–608).
7. First objection.
8. Beg the question.
9. I.e., can hardly avoid lying.
1. In classical myth, the ferryman who takes the souls of the dead over the river Styx.
2. Practitioners of the liberal arts.

the poet (as I said before) never affirmeth. The poet never maketh any circles[3] about your imagination, to conjure you to believe for true what he writes. He citeth not authorities of other histories, but even for his entry[4] calleth the sweet Muses to inspire into him a good invention; in truth, not laboring to tell you what is or is not, but what should or should not be. And therefore, though he recount things not true, yet because he telleth them not for true, he lieth not—without we will say that Nathan lied in his speech before-alleged to David;[5] which as a wicked man durst scarce say, so think I none so simple would say that Aesop lied in the tales of his beasts; for who thinks that Aesop wrote it for actually true were well worthy to have his name chronicled among the beasts he writeth of. What child is there, that, coming to a play, and seeing *Thebes* written in great letters upon an old door, doth believe that it is Thebes? If then a man can arrive to that child's age to know that the poets' persons and doings are but pictures what should be, and not stories what have been, they will never give the lie to[6] things not affirmatively but allegorically and figuratively written.

* * *

So that, since the excellencies of it may be so easily and so justly confirmed, and the low-creeping objections so soon trodden down: it not being an art of lies, but of true doctrine; not of effeminateness, but of notable stirring of courage; not of abusing man's wit, but of strengthening man's wit; not banished, but honored by Plato:[7] let us rather plant more laurels for to engarland the poets' heads (which honor of being laureate, whereas besides them only triumphant captains were, is a sufficient authority to show the price they ought to be held in) than suffer the ill-favored breath of such wrong-speakers once to blow upon the clear springs of poesy.

[POETRY IN ENGLAND]

But since I have run so long a career[8] in this matter, methinks, before I give my pen a full stop, it shall be but a little more lost time to inquire why England, the mother of excellent minds, should be grown so hard a step-mother to poets, who certainly in wit ought to pass all other, since all only proceedeth from their wit, being indeed makers of themselves, not takers of others.

* * *

* * * But I that, before ever I durst aspire unto the dignity, am admitted into the company of the paper-blurrers, do find the very true cause of our wanting estimation is want of desert—taking upon us to be poets in despite of Pallas.[9]

Now, wherein we want desert were a thankworthy labor to express; but if I knew, I should have mended myself. But I, as I never desired the title, so have I neglected the means to come by it. Only, overmastered by some

---

3. As a magician does in conjuring.
4. In his opening lines.
5. Nathan's parable (2 Samuel 12.1–15) of a man robbed of his one ewe lamb by a rich man. "Without": unless.
6. Accuse of lying.

7. Plato did no such thing—though Sidney had sophistically argued (in a passage omitted here) that he did.
8. Course.
9. I.e., scorning the dictates of Wisdom.

thoughts, I yielded an inky tribute unto them. Marry, they that delight in poesy itself should seek to know what they do, and how they do; and especially look themselves in an unflattering glass of reason, if they be inclinable unto it. For poesy must not be drawn by the ears; it must be gently led, or rather it must lead—which was partly the cause that made the ancient-learned affirm it was a divine gift, and no human skill: since all other knowledges lie ready for any that hath strength of wit. A poet no industry can make, if his own genius be not carried into it; and therefore it is an old proverb, *orator fit, poeta nascitur.*[1]

Yet confess I always that as the fertilest ground must be manured, so must the highest-flying wit have a Daedalus[2] to guide him. That Daedalus, they say, both in this and in other, hath three wings to bear itself up into the air of due commendation: that is, art, imitation, and exercise. But these, neither artificial rules nor imitative patterns, we much cumber ourselves withal. Exercise indeed we do, but that very forebackwardly: for where we should exercise to know, we exercise as having known; and so is our brain delivered of much matter which never was begotten by knowledge. For there being two principal parts, matter to be expressed by words and words to express the matter, in neither we use art or imitation rightly. Our matter is *quodlibet* indeed, though wrongly performing Ovid's verse,

Quicquid conabor dicere, versus erit;[3]

never marshaling it into any assured rank, that almost the readers cannot tell where to find themselves.

Chaucer, undoubtedly, did excellently in his *Troilus and Criseyde;* of whom, truly, I know not whether to marvel more, either that he in that misty time could see so clearly, or that we in this clear age go so stumblingly after him. Yet had he great wants, fit to be forgiven in so reverent an antiquity. I account the *Mirror of Magistrates*[4] meetly furnished of beautiful parts, and in the Earl of Surrey's lyrics many things tasting of a noble birth, and worthy of a noble mind. The *Shepherds' Calendar*[5] hath much poetry in his eclogues, indeed worthy the reading, if I be not deceived. (That same framing of his style to an old rustic language I dare not allow, since neither Theocritus in Greek, Virgil in Latin, nor Sannazzaro in Italian did affect it.[6]) Besides these I do not remember to have seen but few (to speak boldly) printed that have poetical sinews in them; for proof whereof, let but most of the verses be put in prose, and then ask the meaning, and it will be found that one verse did but beget another, without ordering at the first what should be at the last; which becomes a confused mass of words, with a tingling sound of rhyme, barely accompanied with reason.

Our tragedies and comedies (not without cause cried out against), observing rules neither of honest civility nor skillful poetry—excepting *Gorboduc*[7]

---

1. An orator is made; a poet is born.
2. The legendary craftsman who invented wings of wax for himself and his son, Icarus. Ignoring his father's instructions, Icarus flew too close to the sun, melted his wings, and fell into the sea.
3. "Whatever I try to say will turn to verse" (Ovid, *Tristia* 4.10.26). "*Quodlibet*": what you will.
4. A large collection of Elizabethan poems on the downfall of princes and other notables.
5. Spenser's first major work (1579), dedicated to Sidney.
6. That is, none of the great models for pastoral poetry offered a precedent for Spenser's archaic diction.
7. Senecan tragedy by Thomas Sackville and Thomas Norton (1561): the earliest English tragedy written in blank verse. The highly rhetorical and declamatory Roman tragedies of Seneca (5 B.C.E.–65 C.E.) were models of the grand tragic style in the Renaissance.

(again, I say, of those that I have seen), which notwithstanding as it is full of stately speeches and well-sounding phrases, climbing to the height of Seneca's style, and as full of notable morality, which it doth most delightfully teach, and so obtain the very end of poesy, yet in truth it is very defectuous in the circumstances, which grieveth me, because it might not remain as an exact model of all tragedies. For it is faulty both in place and time, the two necessary companions of all corporal actions. For where the stage should always represent but one place, and the uttermost time presupposed in it should be, both by Aristotle's precept and common reason, but one day, there is both many days, and many places, inartificially[8] imagined.

But if it be so in *Gorboduc*, how much more in all the rest, where you shall have Asia of the one side, and Afric of the other, and so many other under-kingdoms, that the player, when he cometh in, must ever begin with telling where he is, or else the tale will not be conceived? Now you shall have three ladies walk to gather flowers: and then we must believe the stage to be a garden. By and by we hear news of shipwreck in the same place: and then we are to blame if we accept it not for a rock. Upon the back of that comes out a hideous monster with fire and smoke: and then the miserable beholders are bound to take it for a cave. While in the meantime two armies fly in, represented with four swords and bucklers:[9] and then what hard heart will not receive it for a pitched field?

Now, of time they are much more liberal: for ordinary it is that two young princes fall in love; after many traverses,[1] she is got with child, delivered of a fair boy; he is lost, groweth a man, falls in love, and is ready to get another child; and all this in two hours' space: which, how absurd it is in sense, even sense may imagine, and art hath taught, and all ancient examples justified— and at this day, the ordinary players in Italy will not err in. Yet will some bring in an example of *Eunuchus* in Terence, that containeth matter of two days,[2] yet far short of twenty years. True it is, and so was it to be played in two days, and so fitted to the time it set forth. And though Plautus have in one place done amiss,[3] let us hit with him, and not miss with him.

But they will say: How then shall we set forth a story which containeth both many places and many times? And do they not know that a tragedy is tied to the laws of poesy, and not of history; not bound to follow the story, but having liberty either to feign a quite new matter or to frame the history to the most tragical conveniency? Again, many things may be told which cannot be showed, if they know the difference betwixt reporting and representing. As, for example, I may speak (though I am here) of Peru, and in speech digress from that to the description of Calicut; but in action I cannot represent it without Pacolet's horse;[4] and so was the manner the ancients took, by some *Nuntius*[5] to recount things done in former time or other place. Lastly, if they will represent a history, they must not (as Horace saith) begin

---

8. Unskillfully. Sidney here voices the Renaissance commonplace (erroneously derived from Aristotle's *Poetics*) that tragedies should observe the "three unities": of time (one day), place (one locale), and action (one plot). Aristotle insisted only on unity of action.
9. Shields.
1. Difficulties, mishaps.

2. In point of fact, the action of Terence's *Eunuch* takes place in a single day.
3. Plautus's *Captives* does violate the unity of time.
4. A flying horse in the French romance *Valentine and Orson* (1489). "Calicut": Calcutta.
5. Messenger.

ab ovo;[6] but they must come to the principal point of that one action which they will represent.

By example this will be best expressed. I have a story of young Polydorus,[7] delivered for safety's sake, with great riches, by his father Priam to Polymnestor, king of Thrace, in the Trojan war time; he, after some years, hearing the overthrow of Priam, for to make the treasure his own, murdereth the child; the body of the child is taken up by Hecuba; she, the same day, findeth a sleight[8] to be revenged most cruelly of the tyrant. Where now would one of our tragedy writers begin, but with the delivery of the child? Then should he sail over into Thrace, and so spend I know not how many years, and travel numbers of places. But where doth Euripides? Even with the finding of the body, leaving the rest to be told by the spirit of Polydorus. This need no further to be enlarged; the dullest wit may conceive it.

But besides these gross absurdities, how all their plays be neither right tragedies, nor right comedies, mingling kings and clowns, not because the matter so carrieth it, but thrust in the clown by head and shoulders to play a part in majestical matters with neither decency nor discretion,[9] so as neither the admiration and commiseration, nor the right sportfulness,[1] is by their mongrel tragi-comedy obtained. I know Apuleius[2] did somewhat so, but that is a thing recounted with space of time, not represented in one moment; and I know the ancients have one or two examples of tragi-comedies, as Plautus hath *Amphitruo;*[3] but, if we mark them well, we shall find that they never, or very daintily, match hornpipes[4] and funerals. So falleth it out that, having indeed no right comedy, in that comical part of our tragedy, we have nothing but scurrility, unworthy of any chaste ears, or some extreme show of doltishness, indeed fit to lift up a loud laughter, and nothing else: where the whole tract of a comedy should be full of delight, as the tragedy should be still maintained in a well-raised admiration.

But our comedians think there is no delight without laughter; which is very wrong, for though laughter may come with delight, yet cometh it not of delight, as though delight should be the cause of laughter; but well may one thing breed both together. Nay, rather in themselves they have, as it were, a kind of contrariety: for delight we scarcely do but in things that have a conveniency to ourselves or to the general nature; laughter almost ever cometh of things most disproportioned to ourselves and nature. Delight hath a joy in it, either permanent or present. Laughter hath only a scornful tickling.

For example, we are ravished with delight to see a fair woman, and yet are far from being moved to laughter; we laugh at deformed creatures, wherein certainly we cannot delight. We delight in good chances, we laugh at mischances: we delight to hear the happiness of our friends, or country, at which he were worthy to be laughed at that would laugh; we shall, contrarily, laugh sometimes to find a matter quite mistaken and go down the hill against the bias[5] in the mouth of some such men—as for the respect of them one shall

6. From the beginning. literally, from the egg (*Ars Poetica,* 147).
7. In Euripides' *Hecuba.*
8. Trick, contrivance.
9. Sidney regards tragicomedy as violating the unity of action and offending decorum.
1. Effect proper to comedy, as "admiration and commiseration" are proper to tragedy.
2. Roman author of *The Golden Ass,* a satirical romance (2nd century C.E.).
3. *Amphitruo* is tragicomic only in that it contains gods and heroes; otherwise it is pure comedy.
4. Merry tunes for country dances. "Mark them well": inspect them carefully.
5. End in unexpected disaster, as when in the game of bowls a hill deflects the ball from its course or "bias."

be heartily sorry, he cannot choose but laugh, and so is rather pained than delighted with laughter.

Yet deny I not but that they may go well together. For as in Alexander's picture well set out we delight without laughter, and in twenty mad antics we laugh without delight; so in Hercules, painted with his great beard and furious countenance, in a woman's attire, spinning at Omphale's commandment,[6] it breedeth both delight and laughter: for the representing of so strange a power in love procureth delight, and the scornfulness of the action stirreth laughter. But I speak to this purpose, that all the end of the comical part be not upon such scornful matters as stir laughter only, but, mixed with it, that delightful teaching which is the end of poesy. And the great fault even in that point of laughter, and forbidden plainly by Aristotle, is that they stir laughter in sinful things, which are rather execrable than ridiculous, or in miserable, which are rather to be pitied than scorned. For what is it to make folks gape at a wretched beggar and a beggarly clown; or, against law of hospitality, to jest at strangers, because they speak not English so well as we do? What do we learn, since it is certain

> Nil habet infelix paupertas durius in se,
> Quam quod ridiculos homines facit?[7]

But rather, a busy loving courtier and a heartless threatening Thraso; a self-wise-seeming schoolmaster; an awry-transformed traveler. These, if we saw walk in stage names, which we play naturally, therein were delightful laughter, and teaching delightfulness—as in the other, the tragedies of Buchanan[8] do justly bring forth a divine admiration.

But I have lavished out too many words of this play matter. I do it because, as they are excelling parts of poesy, so is there none so much used in England, and none can be more pitifully abused; which, like an unmannerly daughter showing a bad education, causeth her mother Poesy's honesty to be called in question.

Other sort of poetry almost have we none, but that lyrical kind of songs and sonnets: which, Lord, if He gave us so good minds, how well it might be employed, and with how heavenly fruit, both private and public, in singing the praises of the immortal beauty: the immortal goodness of that God who giveth us hands to write and wits to conceive; of which we might well want words, but never matter; of which we could turn our eyes to nothing, but we should ever have new-budding occasions. But truly many of such writings as come under the banner of unresistible love, if I were a mistress, would never persuade me they were in love: so coldly they apply fiery speeches, as men that had rather read lovers' writings—and so caught up certain swelling phrases which hang together like a man that once told my father that the wind was at northwest and by south, because he would be sure to name winds enough—than that in truth they feel those passions, which easily (as I think) may be bewrayed by that same forcibleness or *energia* (as the Greeks call it) of the writer. But let this be a sufficient though short note, that we miss the right use of the material point of poesy.

---

6. Hercules, infatuated with Omphale, queen of Lydia, submitted to be dressed as her female slave and to spin wool.
7. "Unfortunate poverty has in itself nothing harder to bear than that it makes men ridiculous" (Juvenal, *Satires* 3.152–53).
8. George Buchanan (1506–1582), influential Scottish humanist and poet.

* * *

Now of versifying there are two sorts, the one ancient, the other modern: the ancient marked the quantity of each syllable, and according to that framed his verse; the modern, observing only number[9] (with some regard of the accent), the chief life of it standeth in that like sounding of the words, which we call rhyme. Whether of these be the more excellent, would bear many speeches: the ancient (no doubt) more fit for music, both words and time observing quantity, and more fit lively to express diverse passions, by the low or lofty sound of the well-weighed syllable; the latter likewise, with his rhyme, striketh a certain music to the ear, and, in fine, since it doth delight, though by another way, it obtains the same purpose: there being in either sweetness, and wanting[1] in neither majesty. Truly the English, before any vulgar[2] language I know, is fit for both sorts. For, for the ancient, the Italian is so full of vowels that it must ever be cumbered with elisions; the Dutch[3] so, of the other side, with consonants, that they cannot yield the sweet sliding, fit for a verse; the French in his whole language hath not one word that hath his accent in the last syllable saving two, called *antepenultima*; and little more hath the Spanish, and therefore very gracelessly may they use dactyls.[4] The English is subject to none of these defects. Now for the rhyme, though we do not observe quantity, yet we observe the accent very precisely, which other languages either cannot do, or will not do so absolutely. That *caesura*,[5] or breathing place in the midst of the verse, neither Italian nor Spanish have, the French and we never almost fail of. Lastly, even the very rhyme itself, the Italian cannot put it in the last syllable, by the French named the masculine rhyme, but still in the next to the last, which the French call the female, or the next before that, which the Italians term *sdrucciola*. The example of the former is *buono: suono,* of the *sdrucciola* is *femina: semina.* The French, of the other side, hath both the male, as *bon: son,* and the female, as *plaise: taise,* but the *sdrucciola* he hath not: where the English hath all three, as due: true, father: rather, motion: potion[6]—with much more which might be said, but that already I find the triflingness of this discourse is much too much enlarged.

[CONCLUSION]

So that since the ever-praiseworthy Poesy is full of virtue-breeding delightfulness, and void of no gift that ought to be in the noble name of learning; since the blames laid against it are either false or feeble; since the cause why it is not esteemed in England is the fault of poet-apes, not poets; since, lastly, our tongue is most fit to honor poesy, and to be honored by poesy; I conjure you all that have had the evil luck to read this ink-wasting toy of mine, even

9. Classical "quantity" meant the length or duration of syllables. Moderns simply count the "number" of syllables.
1. Lacking.
2. The common or "vulgar" people spoke the vernacular languages, whereas the learned could speak and write in Latin.
3. German.
4. "Dactyls": see "Rhythm and Meter" in the appendices to this volume. Because of the accent

patterns in French and Spanish, those languages cannot make good use of this poetic foot.
5. In its use of "caesuras" (see "Rhythm and Meter," in the appendices to this volume) as well as the several kinds of metrical feet, Sidney claims, English poetry achieves greater variety and flexibility than poetry in the other vernacular languages.
6. Pronounced with three syllables, accented on the first.

in the name of the nine Muses, no more to scorn the sacred mysteries of poesy; no more to laugh at the name of poets, as though they were next inheritors to fools; no more to jest at the reverent title of a rhymer; but to believe, with Aristotle, that they were the ancient treasurers of the Grecians' divinity; to believe, with Bembus, that they were first bringers-in of all civility; to believe, with Scaliger, that no philosopher's precepts can sooner make you an honest man than the reading of Virgil; to believe, with Clauserus, the translator of Cornutus, that it pleased the heavenly Deity, by Hesiod[7] and Homer, under the veil of fables, to give us all knowledge, logic, rhetoric, philosophy natural and moral, and *quid non?*;[8] to believe, with me, that there are many mysteries contained in poetry, which of purpose were written darkly, lest by profane wits it should be abused; to believe, with Landino,[9] that they are so beloved of the gods that whatsoever they write proceeds of a divine fury; lastly, to believe themselves, when they tell you they will make you immortal by their verses. Thus doing, your name shall flourish in the printers' shops; thus doing, you shall be of kin to many a poetical preface; thus doing, you shall be most fair, most rich, most wise, most all, you shall dwell upon superlatives; thus doing, though you be *libertino patre natus*, you shall suddenly grow *Herculea proles*,[1]

> Si quid mea carmina possunt;[2]

thus doing, your soul shall be placed with Dante's Beatrice, or Virgil's Anchises.[3] But if (fie of such a but) you be born so near the dull-making cataract of Nilus that you cannot hear the planet-like[4] music of poetry; if you have so earth-creeping a mind that it cannot lift itself up to look to the sky of poetry, or rather, by a certain rustical disdain, will become such a mome as to be a Momus[5] of poetry; then, though I will not wish unto you the ass's ears of Midas,[6] nor to be driven by a poet's verses, as Bubonax[7] was, to hang himself, nor to be rhymed to death, as is said to be done in Ireland;[8] yet thus much curse I must send you, in the behalf of all poets, that while you live, you live in love, and never get favor for lacking skill of a sonnet;[9] and, when you die, your memory die from the earth for want of an epitaph.

ca. 1579   1595

---

7. "Hesiod": early Greek poet whose *Theogony* recounts myths of the birth and warfare of the Gods and the origin of the world. "Bembus": Cardinal Pietro Bembo, Italian poet, Platonist philosopher, and character in Castiglione's *Courtier*. "Scaliger": Julius Caesar Scaliger, Italian scholar and author of a highly influential treatise on poetry (*Poetices*, 1561). "Clauserus": Conrad Clauser, a German scholar who translated a Greek treatise by Cornutus, a Stoic pedagogue of Nero's time.
8. What not?
9. Christoforo Landino, Florentine humanist who developed this argument in his edition of Dante's *Divine Comedy* (1481).
1. "Offspring of Hercules." "*Libertino patre natus*": "born of a freed-slave father" (Horace, *Satires* 1.6.45).
2. "If my songs are of any avail" (*Aeneid* 9.446).

3. I.e., in Paradise with Dante's beloved or in the Elysian fields with Aeneas's honored father.
4. Resembling the music of the spheres, most beautiful of all music. According to Cicero, the noise of the Nile's cataracts deafened those who lived nearby.
5. God of ridicule, son of Night and Sleep, hence, a critic. "Mome": a stupid person.
6. He was given ass's ears because he preferred Pan's music to Apollo's (Ovid, *Metamorphoses* 11.146–79).
7. Bupalus, a sculptor who hanged himself when his works were satirized by the poet Hipponax. Sidney fuses the two names.
8. Irish bards were thought to be able to cause death with their rhymed charms.
9. Because you are unable to write a sonnet.

FULKE GREVILLE, LORD BROOKE
1554–1628

Fulke Greville came from a wealthy family, was educated at Shrewsbury and Cambridge, and was a successful courtier under three sovereigns, Elizabeth I, James I, and Charles I. Greville, who never married, wrote some conventional heterosexual verse, but his most passionate expressions of love were for his friend Sir Philip Sidney, whose death in 1586 he never ceased to mourn. Greville refused to publish any of his own work, but he brought out the 1590 version of Sidney's *Arcadia* and wrote his friend's biography. Greville began a sonnet cycle, *Caelica*, in the manner of Sidney's *Astrophil and Stella*, but the later poems in the sequence are in a very different style, somber, brooding, and philosophical. He also wrote long philosophical verse treatises and several politically charged closet dramas (plays meant to be read, not acted on stage). His most famous poem is a bleak chorus from one of these dramas, *Mustapha*. The end of Greville's life was grimly in keeping with his pessimistic vision of human fate: he was stabbed to death by a long-time servant.

From Caelica

100

In night when colors all to black are cast,
Distinction lost, or gone down with the light,
The eye a watch to inward senses placed,
Not seeing, yet still having power of sight,

5 Gives vain alarums to the inward sense,
Where fear stirred up with witty tyranny[1]
Confounds all powers and thorough self-offense°   *through self-injury*
Doth forge and raise impossibility:

Such as in thick depriving darknesses
10 Proper reflections of the error be,
And images of self-confusednesses,
Which hurt imaginations only see;
    And from this nothing seen tells news of devils,
    Which but expressions be of inward evils.

ca. 1580–1600   1633

Chorus Sacerdotum[1]

O wearisome condition of humanity!
Born under one law, to another bound;
Vainly begot and yet forbidden vanity;
Created sick, commanded to be sound.
5 What meaneth nature by these diverse laws?

1. The tyranny of imaginings.
1. Chorus of priests, from *Mustapha*, one of Greville's two surviving closet tragedies. He may have composed a version of the play as early as 1600, but whether the chorus was in that version or written about 1609 is uncertain.

Passion and reason, self-division cause.
Is it the mark or majesty of power
To make offenses that it may forgive?
Nature herself doth her own self deflower
10 To hate those errors she herself doth give.
For how should man think that he may not do,
If nature did not fail and punish, too?
Tyrant to others, to herself unjust,
Only commands things difficult and hard,
15 Forbids us all things which it knows is lust,°   *pleasure*
Makes easy pains, unpossible reward.
If nature did not take delight in blood,
She would have made more easy ways to good.
We that are bound by vows and by promotion,[2]
20 With pomp of holy sacrifice and rites,
To teach belief in good and still° devotion,   *instill*
To preach of heaven's wonders and delights;
Yet when each of us in his own heart looks
He finds the God there, far unlike his books.

1609

2. Motion or stirring of the mind.

ROBERT SOUTHWELL
1561–1595

Robert Southwell, the younger son of a prominent Roman Catholic family, went to
the English seminary for Catholics at Douai, France, in his youth, then to Rome
where he entered the Society of Jesus (the Jesuits). In 1586 he returned to England
to minister to English Catholics. His mission was a dangerous one because of laws
that proscribed Roman Catholic worship and banished priests; in 1592 he was apprehended, imprisoned, tortured, and, three years later, executed as a traitor in the usual
grisly manner—by being hanged, disemboweled, and then beheaded. Southwell wrote
a good deal of religious prose and verse; the most famous of his lyrics is *The Burning
Babe*. Ben Jonson told his friend William Drummond of Hawthornden that if he had
written *The Burning Babe* he would have been content to destroy many of his own
poems.

The Burning Babe

As I in hoary winter's night stood shivering in the snow,
Surprised I was with sudden heat which made my heart to glow;
And lifting up a fearful eye to view what fire was near,
A pretty babe all burning bright did in the air appear;
5   Who, scorchèd with excessive heat, such floods of tears did shed

As though his floods should quench his flames which with his tears
    were fed.
"Alas," quoth he, "but newly born in fiery heats I fry,[1]
Yet none approach to warm their hearts or feel my fire but I!
My faultless breast the furnace is, the fuel wounding thorns,
10 Love is the fire, and sighs the smoke, the ashes shame and scorns;
The fuel justice layeth on, and mercy blows the coals,
The metal in this furnace wrought are men's defilèd souls,
For which, as now on fire I am to work them to their good,
So will I melt into a bath to wash them in my blood."
15 With this he vanished out of sight and swiftly shrunk away,
And straight[2] I callèd unto mind that it was Christmas day.

1602

1. Burn.   2. Straightway, immediately.

MARY (SIDNEY) HERBERT, COUNTESS OF PEMBROKE
1562–1621

When her brother, the celebrated courtier and author Philip Sidney, died in 1586, Mary Sidney, the countess of Pembroke, became the custodian not only of his writings but also of his last name. Though her marriage in 1577 to Henry Herbert, the second earl of Pembroke, represented a great social advance for her family—her offspring would no longer be members of the gentry but rather would be among the nation's tiny number of landed aristocrats—yet throughout her life the countess of Pembroke held onto her identity as a Sidney.

She had good reason to do so. The Sidneys were celebrated for their generous support of poets, clergy, alchemists, naturalists, scientists, and musicians. The Pembroke country estate, Wilton, quickly became a gathering place for thinkers who enjoyed the countess's patronage and shared her staunch Protestant convictions and her literary interests. Books, pamphlets, and scores of poems were dedicated in the 1590s and thereafter to her, as well as to her brother Robert (his country house, Penshurst, is praised in a well-known poem by Ben Jonson). Nicholas Breton and Samuel Daniel in particular benefited from her support, as did her niece, goddaughter, and frequent companion, Mary Wroth.

In one of the dedicatory poems to *Salve Deus Rex Judaeorum*, Aemilia Lanyer praises Mary Sidney not only for her generosity toward poets but also for those "works that are more deep and more profound." These include her translation of Robert Garnier's neoclassical French tragedy *Antonius* and a prose translation of the religious tract *A Discourse of Life and Death* by the French Protestant Philippe de Mornay. Her translation of Petrarch's *Triumph of Death* was the first in English to maintain the original *terza rima* (a particularly challenging rhyme scheme for an English versifier). Although translation was considered an especially appropriate genre for women to work in, it is a mistake to assume that Mary Sidney's efforts as a poet are merely derivative: Elizabethans understood that translation offered the opportunity not only for the display of linguistic and technical skills but also for the indirect expression of personal and political concerns. Mary Sidney also expressed these concerns directly: among her original poems was a powerful elegy for her brother Philip and a short pastoral entertainment for Queen Elizabeth.

Mary Sidney was best known for having prepared a composite edition of Philip Sidney's *Arcadia* and for contributing the larger number (107) of the series of 150 poetic translations of the psalms begun by her brother. Her very free renderings recreate the psalms as English poems, using an amazing variety of stanzaic and metrical patterns and some strikingly effective images. This widely circulated and influential volume was an important bridge between the many metrical paraphrases of psalms in this period and the works of the great religious lyric poets of the seventeenth century, especially George Herbert. Donne's poem *Upon the Translation of the Psalms by Sir Philip Sidney and the Countess of Pembroke His Sister* testifies to that importance: "They tell us *why*, and teach us *how* to sing."

To the Angel Spirit of the Most Excellent Sir Philip Sidney[1]

To thee, pure sprite,° to thee alone's addressed   *spirit*
   This coupled work, by double int'rest thine:
   First raised by thy blessed hand, and what is mine
Inspired by thee, thy secret power impressed.°   *i.e., investing her*
5   So dared my Muse with thine itself combine,
    As mortal stuff with that which is divine.
Thy light'ning beams give luster to the rest,

That heaven's king may deign his own transformed
   In substance no, but superficial tire°   *attire*
10   By thee put on; to praise, not to aspire
To those high tones, so in themselves adorned,
    Which angels sing in their celestial choir,
    And all of tongues with soul and voice admire
These sacred hymns thy kingly prophet[2] formed.

15   Oh, had that soul which honor brought to rest
   Too soon not left, and reft° the world of all   *deprived*
   What man could show, which we perfection call,
This half-maimed piece had sorted° with the best.   *consorted, equaled*
    Deep wounds enlarged, long festered in their gall,
20   Fresh bleeding smart;° not eye- but heart-tears fall.   *pain, grief*
Ah memory, what needs this new arrest?°   *delay*

Yet here behold (oh, wert thou to behold!)
   This° finished now, thy matchless Muse begun,   *the translation*
   The rest but pieced, as left by thee undone.

---

1. This is the dedicatory poem to the translation of the Psalms begun by Philip Sidney and completed, after his death, by Mary.
2. The Old Testament King David, supposed author of the Psalms. Herbert says that in trans-

lating the Psalms her brother intended not to rival the originals—which angels sing and which all those learned in ancient languages ("all of tongues") admire—but simply to praise God.

25   Pardon (oh, blessed soul) presumption too too bold,[3]
        If love and zeal such error ill become,[3]
        'Tis zealous love, love which hath never done,
     Nor can enough in world of words unfold.

     And sith° it hath no further scope to go,   *since*
30   Nor other purpose but to honor thee,
        Thee in thy works, where all the Graces[4] be,
     As little streams with all their all do flow
        To their great sea, due tribute's grateful fee;
        So press my thoughts, my burdened thoughts, in me,
35   To pay the debt of infinites I owe

     To thy great worth. Exceeding Nature's store,°   *abundance*
        Wonder of men, sole° born perfection's kind,   *alone*
        Phoenix[5] thou wert. So rare thy fairest mind,
     Heav'nly adorned, Earth justly might adore,
40   Where truthful praise in highest glory shined,
        For there alone° was praise to truth confined;   *i.e., in heaven*
     And where but there to live forevermore?

     Oh! When to this accompt,° this cast-up° sum,   *account/totaled*
        This reckoning made, this audit of my woe,
45   I call my thoughts, whence so strange passions flow,
     How works my heart, my senses stricken dumb?
        That would thee[6] more than ever heart could show,
        And all too short:° who knew thee best doth know   *inadequate*
     There lives no wit° that may thy praise become.°   *mind/express*

50   Truth I invoke (who scorn elsewhere to move,
        Or here in aught my blood should partialize),[7]
        Truth, sacred Truth, thee sole to solemnize.
     Those precious rights well known best minds approve;
        And who but doth, hath wisdom's open eyes,
55   Not owly blind the fairest light still flies,
     Confirm no less?[8] At least 'tis sealed above.°   *acknowledged in heaven*

     Where thou art fixed among thy fellow lights:
        My day put out, my life in darkness cast,
        Thy angel's soul with highest angels placed
60   There blessèd sings enjoying heav'n-delights,
        Thy maker's praise, as far from earthly taste
        As here thy works so worthily embraced
     By all of worth, where never envy bites.

3. I.e., if it's unbecoming for (her) love and zeal to
have presumed to complete the translation.
4. The three Graces of classical mythology, goddesses who presided over all social pleasures and
polite accomplishments.
5. The phoenix was a mythical Arabian bird, only
one of which existed at any one time. Often associated with Christ, it symbolizes unique perfection.

6. I.e., my thoughts would (if they could) praise
you.
7. I scorn demonstrating partiality to my kinsman.
8. I.e., those who have the open eyes of wisdom—
are not blind like an owl always fleeing the fairest
light—will confirm what I've said about Sidney's
worth.

As goodly buildings to some glorious end
65   Cut off by Fate, before the Graces had
        Each wond'rous part in all their beauties clad,
Yet so much done, as art could not amend;[9]
        So thy rare works to which no wit can add,
        In all men's eyes, which are not blindly mad,
70 Beyond compare, above all praise extend.

Immortal monuments of thy fair fame,
        Though not complete, nor in the reach of thought,
        How on that passing peacetime would have wrought,
Had Heav'n so spared the life of life to frame
75   The rest?[1] But ah, such loss! Hath this world aught
        Can equal it? Or which like grievance brought?
Yet there will live thy ever-praisèd name.

To which these dearest off'rings of my heart,
        Dissolved to ink, while pen's impressions move
80   The bleeding veins of never-dying love,
I render here: these wounding lines of smart,
        Sad characters indeed of simple love,
        Not art nor skill, which abler wits do prove,°   experience
Of my full soul receive the meanest part.[2]

85 Receive these hymns,° these obsequies° receive: the psalms/funeral rites
        If any mark of thy sweet sprite appear,
        Well are they born; no title else shall bear.
I can no more. Dear soul, I take my leave;
        Sorrow still strives, would mount thy highest sphere,
90   Presuming so just cause might meet thee there.[3]
Oh happy change, could so I take my leave!

ca. 1595   1623

Psalm 52

        Tyrant, why swell'st thou thus,
            Of mischief vaunting?
        Since help from God to us
            Is never wanting.

5   Lewd lies thy tongue contrives,
            Loud lies it soundeth;
        Sharper than sharpest knives
            With lies it woundeth.

---

9. I.e., the part that was completed could not be improved upon; the same is true of Sidney's unfinished literary works.
1. If heaven had spared your life so that you could have completed your representation of human life.
2. The least part—all that she, with her limitations

as a writer, is able to express. Professions of a writer's inadequacy are conventional.
3. My sorrow would mount to heaven to meet you, presuming that the justness of my cause would allow me (however personally unworthy) entrance there.

Falsehood thy wit° approves,   *mind*
10   All truth rejected:
Thy will all vices loves,
        Virtue neglected.

Not words from cursèd thee,
        But gulfs° are pourèd;   *abysses, yawning chasms*
15 Gulfs wherein daily be
        Good men devourèd.

Think'st thou to bear it° so?   *bear it off, triumph*
        God shall displace thee;
God shall thee overthrow,
20   Crush thee, deface thee.

The just shall fearing see
        These fearful chances,
And laughing shoot at thee
        With scornful glances.

25 Lo, lo, the wretched wight,
        Who, God disdaining,
His mischief made his might,
        His guard his gaining.°   *riches*

I as an olive tree
30   Still green shall flourish:
God's house the soil shall be
        My roots to nourish.

My trust on his true love
        Truly attending,
35 Shall never thence remove,
        Never see ending.

Thee will I honor still,
        Lord, for this justice;
There fix my hopes I will
40   Where thy saints' trust is.

Thy saints trust in thy name,
        Therein they joy them:
Protected by the same,
        Nought° can annoy° them.   *nothing / harm*

ca. 1595   1823

Psalm 139

O Lord, in me there lieth nought
But to thy search revealèd lies:

          For when I sit
          Thou markest it;°   *you note it*
5   No less thou notest when I rise;
       Yea, closest closet of my thought
          Hath open windows to thine eyes.

       Thou walkest with me when I walk;
          When to my bed for rest I go,
10   I find thee there,
             And everywhere:
       Not youngest thought in me doth grow,
       No, not one word I cast° to talk   *resolve*
          But yet unuttered thou dost know.

15   If forth I march, thou goest before,
          If back I turn, thou com'st behind:
             So forth nor back
             Thy guard I lack,
       Nay on me too thy hand I find.
20   Well I thy wisdom may adore,
          But never reach with earthy mind.

       To shun thy notice, leave thine eye,
          O whither might I take my way?
             To starry sphere?
25   Thy throne is there.
       To dead men's undelightsome stay?
       There is thy walk, and there to lie
          Unknown in vain I should assay.°   *attempt*

       O sun, whom light nor flight can match,
30   Suppose thy lightful flightful wings
             Thou lend to me,
             And I could flee
       As far as thee the ev'ning brings:
       Even led to west he would me catch,
35   Nor should I lurk with western things.

       Do thou thy best, O secret night,
          In sable veil to cover me:
             Thy sable veil
             Shall vainly fail;
40   With day unmasked my night shall be,
       For night is day and darkness light,
          O father of all lights, to thee.

       Each inmost piece in me is thine:
          While yet I in my mother dwelt,
45   All that me clad
             From thee I had.

  Thou in my frame° hast strangely dealt: *form*
   Needs in my praise thy works must shine,
    So inly them my thoughts have felt.

50 Thou, how my back was beam-wise laid,
   And raft'ring of my ribs, dost know;
     Know'st every point
     Of bone and joint,
   How to this whole these parts did grow,
55 In brave embroid'ry fair arrayed,
    Though wrought in shop both dark and low.

   Nay fashionless, ere form I took,
    Thy all and more beholding eye
     My shapeless shape
60   Could not escape:
   All these, with times appointed by,[1]
   Ere one had being, in the book
    Of thy foresight enrolled did lie.

   My God, how I these studies prize,
65   That do thy hidden workings show!
     Whose sum is such
     No sum so much:
   Nay, summed as° sand they sumless grow: *like*
   I lie to sleep, from sleep I rise,
70   Yet still in thought with thee I go.

   My God, if thou but one° wouldst kill, *only one (wicked man)*
    Then straight would leave my further chase[2]
     This cursèd brood
     Inured to blood,
75   Whose graceless taunts at thy disgrace
   Have aimèd oft, and hating still
    Would with proud lies thy truth outface.

   Hate not I them, who thee do hate?
    Thine, Lord, I will the censure be.[3]
80   Detest I not
     The cankered knot
   Whom I against thee banded see?
   O Lord, thou know'st in highest rate
    I hate them all as foes to me.

85 Search me, my God, and prove my heart,
   Examine me, and try° my thought;   *test*
     And mark in me
     If ought there be

1. With appropriate times indicated (for each step of the work of creation).
2. Then immediately [the wicked] would stop pursuing me.
3. I.e., I leave it to you to censure them.

That hath with cause their anger wrought.
90 If not (as not) my life's each part,
Lord, safely guide from danger brought.

ca. 1595   1823

SAMUEL DANIEL
1562–1619

Samuel Daniel was a gifted, learned, and deeply thoughtful poet, playwright, historian, and translator. He was a member of the circle of Mary Sidney, countess of Pembroke, whose son he tutored, and later held various offices in the household of James I's queen, Anne of Denmark. He wrote tragedies, court masques, a historical epic called *The Civil Wars Between the Two Houses of Lancaster and York* (1595), a prose *History of England*, several fine verse epistles, one of the better Elizabethan sonnet sequences, *Delia* (1592), and a remarkable verse colloquy on the purpose of writing poetry, *Musophilus*. Daniel's lyrics are marked by clarity, restraint, and quiet eloquence. His *Defense of Rhyme* (1603), an answer to Thomas Campion's classicizing strictures on the use of rhyme, defends native English traditions in poetry. His Jacobean writings often implicitly criticize James's reign. Accused of sedition in his tragedy *Philotas* (1604), he successfully defended himself by citing his classical sources.

From Delia

33

When men shall find thy flower, thy glory pass,
And thou, with careful° brow sitting alone,   *full of care*
Receivèd hast this message from thy glass,°   *looking glass*
That tells thee truth, and says that all is gone,
5 Fresh shalt thou see in me the wounds thou madest,
Though spent thy flame, in me the heat remaining:
I that have loved thee thus before thou fadest,
My faith shall wax, when thou art in thy waning.
The world shall find this miracle in me,
10 That fire can burn when all the matter's spent;
Then what my faith hath been thyself shall see,
And that thou wast unkind thou mayst repent.
Thou mayst repent that thou hast scorned my tears,
When winter snows upon thy golden hairs.

45

Care-charmer Sleep, son of the sable Night,
Brother to Death, in silent darkness born,
Relieve my languish and restore the light;

With dark forgetting of my cares, return.
5   And let the day be time enough to mourn
The shipwreck of my ill-adventured youth;
Let waking eyes suffice to wail their scorn
Without the torment of the night's untruth.
Cease, dreams, th' imagery of our day desires,
10   To model forth the passions of the morrow;
Never let rising sun approve° you liars,   *prove*
To add more grief to aggravate my sorrow.
Still let me sleep, embracing clouds in vain,
And never wake to feel the day's disdain.

46

Let others sing of knights and paladins[1]
In agèd accents and untimely° words,   *obsolete*
Paint shadows in imaginary lines
Which well the reach of their high wits records;
5   But I must sing of thee, and those fair eyes
Authentic° shall my verse in time to come,   *authenticate*
When yet th' unborn shall say, "Lo where she lies,
Whose beauty made him speak that else was dumb."
These are the arks,[2] the trophies I erect,
10   That fortify thy name against old age;
And these thy sacred virtues must protect
Against the dark and time's consuming rage.
Though th' error of my youth they shall discover,
Suffice they show I lived and was thy lover.

                                           1592

From Musophilus[1]

[IMPERIAL ELOQUENCE]

Power above powers, O heavenly Eloquence,
940   That with the strong rein of commanding words
Dost manage, guide, and master th' eminence
Of men's affections, more than all their swords:
Shall we° not offer to thy excellence   *i.e., the English nation*
The richest treasure that our wit° affords?   *intellect*
945 Thou that canst do much more with one poor pen
Than all the powers of princes can effect,
And draw, divert, dispose, and fashion men
Better than force or rigor can direct:
Should we this ornament of glory then,
950   As th' unmaterial fruits of shades,° neglect?   *the dead*

1. Renowned champions, especially those associated with the court of Charlemagne.
2. Precious boxes, with allusion to the Ark of the Covenant, the sacred wooden coffer containing the Tables of the Law given to Moses.

1. *Musophilus*, a poem of 1012 lines that constitutes "a general defense of all learning," is a dialogue between Philocosmus ("Lover of the World") and Musophilus ("Lover of the Muses"). The latter clearly speaks for Daniel himself.

Or should we careless come behind the rest
   In power of words, that go before in worth,
   Whenas our accents° equal to the best   *speech, language*
   Is able greater wonders to bring forth;
955   When all that ever hotter spirits expressed
   Comes bettered by the patience of the North?
And who, in time, knows whither we may vent°   *vend*
   The treasure of our tongue, to what strange shores
   This gain of our best glory shall be sent,
960   T' enrich unknowing nations with our stores?°   *abundance*
   What worlds in th' yet unformèd Occident°   *i.e., the Americas*
   May come° refined with th' accents that are ours?   *become*
Or who can tell for what great work in hand
   The greatness of our style is now ordained?
965   What powers it shall bring in, what spirits command,
   What thoughts let out, what humors° keep restrained,   *caprices*
   What mischief it may pow'rfully withstand,
   And what fair ends may thereby be attained?
And as for Poesy, mother of this force,
970   That breeds, brings forth, and nourishes this might,
   Teaching it in a loose, yet measured course,
   With comely motions how to go upright,
   And fost'ring it with bountiful discourse
   Adorns it thus in fashions of delight,
975 What should I say? since it is well approved
   The speech of heaven, with whom they have commerce
   That only seem out of themselves removed
   And do with more than human skills converse.
   Those numbers° wherewith heaven and earth are moved,   *verses*
980   Show weakness speaks in prose, but power in verse.

1599

MICHAEL DRAYTON
1563–1631

Michael Drayton was born about a year before Shakespeare and in the same county, Warwickshire. He had a long career as poet, extending from the early 1590s until well into the seventeenth century. He collaborated on plays, wrote scriptural paraphrases, pastorals, odes, poetic epistles, verse legends, and a historical epic called *The Barons' Wars*. His self-styled masterpiece is *Poly-Olbion*, a thirty-thousand-line historical-geographical poem celebrating all the counties of England and Wales. He made a significant contribution as well to the period's vogue for sonnets, publishing a sequence called *Idea's Mirror* (1594) that, following substantial revision, he republished as *Idea*. It was in fact Drayton's standard practice to revise and add to his poems in each new edition, so that one can trace his response to shifting fashions, his rethinking of his antiquarian fascinations, and his development from an Elizabethan to a seventeenth-century poet.

From Idea

To the Reader of These Sonnets

Into these loves who but for passion looks,
At this first sight here let him lay them by,
And seek elsewhere, in turning other books
Which better may his labor satisfy.
5   No farfetched sigh shall ever wound my breast,
Love from mine eye a tear shall never wring,
Nor in *Ah me's* my whining sonnets dressed;
A libertine, fantastically[1] I sing.
My verse is the true image of my mind,
10   Ever in motion, still° desiring change;   ever
And as thus to variety inclined,
So in all humors° sportively I range;   caprices
My muse is rightly of the English strain,
That cannot long one fashion entertain.

1599

6

How many paltry, foolish, painted things,
That now in coaches trouble every street,
Shall be forgotten, whom no poet sings,
Ere they be well wrapped in their winding sheet?°   shroud
5   Where° I to thee eternity shall give,   whereas
When nothing else remaineth of these days,
And queens hereafter shall be glad to live
Upon the alms of thy superfluous praise.
Virgins and matrons, reading these my rhymes,
10   Shall be so much delighted with thy story
That they shall grieve they lived not in these times
To have seen thee, their sex's only glory;
So shalt thou fly above the vulgar throng,
Still to survive in my immortal song.

1619

61

Since there's no help, come, let us kiss and part;
Nay, I have done, you get no more of me,
And I am glad, yea glad with all my heart
That thus so cleanly I myself can free.
5   Shake hands forever, cancel all our vows,
And when we meet at any time again,
Be it not seen in either of our brows
That we one jot of former love retain.
Now at the last gasp of love's latest breath,

---

1. Capriciously. "Libertine": one who follows his own inclinations.

10 When, his pulse failing, passion speechless lies,
When faith is kneeling by his bed of death,
And innocence is closing up his eyes;
Now if thou wouldst, when all have given him over,
From death to life thou mightst him yet recover.

1619

Ode. To the Virginian Voyage[1]

You brave heroic minds,
Worthy your country's name,
    That honor still pursue,
    Go, and subdue,
5   Whilst loit'ring hinds°   rustics
Lurk here at home, with shame.

Britons, you stay too long;
Quickly aboard bestow you,
    And with a merry gale
10   Swell your stretched sail,
With vows as strong
As the winds that blow you.

Your course securely steer,
West and by south forth keep,
15   Rocks, lee shores, nor shoals,
    When Aeolus[2] scowls,
You need not fear,
So absolute the deep.

And cheerfully at sea,
20 Success you still entice,
    To get the pearl and gold,
    And ours to hold,
Virginia,
Earth's only paradise,

25 Where nature hath in store
Fowl, venison, and fish,
    And the fruitful'st soil
    Without your toil
Three harvests more,
30 All greater than your wish.

And the ambitious vine
Crowns with his purple mass,
    The cedar reaching high

1. The expedition was ordered in April 1606. Three ships set out in December, after Drayton's poem was published.

2. In Greek mythology, the controller of the winds.

> To kiss the sky,
35 The cypress, pine,
> And useful sassafras.[3]

> To whose the golden age
> Still nature's laws doth give,
>   No other cares that tend,
40   But them to defend
> From winter's age,
> That long there doth not live.

> Whenas the luscious smell
> Of that delicious land,
45   Above the seas that flows,
>   The clear wind throws,
> Your hearts to swell
> Approaching the dear strand,°   shore

> In kenning° of the shore,   sighting
50 Thanks to God first given,
>   O you, the happi'st men,
>   Be frolic then,
> Let cannons roar,
> Frighting the wide heaven.

55 And in regions far
> Such heroes bring ye forth
>   As those from whom we came,
>   And plant our name
> Under that star
60 Not known unto our north.

> And as there plenty grows
> Of laurel everywhere,
>   Apollo's sacred tree,
>   You it may see
65 A poet's brows
> To crown, that may sing there.

> Thy voyages attend,
> Industrious Hakluyt,[4]
>   Whose reading shall inflame
70   Men to seek fame,
> And much commend
> To after times thy wit.°   intellect

1606

3. The sassafras tree (native to North America), its bark useful both as a flavoring and as a source of oil.
4. Richard Hakluyt (1553–1616), geographer and author of *The Principal Navigations, Voyages, Traffics, and Discoveries of the English Nation* (1589; 1598–1600). Drayton evidently pronounced his name with three syllables: *Hack-loo-it.*

CHRISTOPHER MARLOWE
1564–1593

The son of a Canterbury shoemaker, Christopher Marlowe was born two months before William Shakespeare. In 1580 he went to Corpus Christi College, Cambridge, on a scholarship that was ordinarily awarded to students preparing for the ministry. He held the scholarship for the maximum time, six years, but did not take holy orders. Instead, he began to write plays. When he applied for his Master of Arts degree in 1587, the university was about to deny it to him on the ground that he intended to go abroad to Rheims, the center of Catholic intrigue and propaganda against Elizabeth, and remain there. But the Privy Council intervened and requested that because Marlowe had done the queen "good service"—evidently as some kind of secret agent—he be granted his degree at the next commencement. "It is not Her Majesty's pleasure," the government officials added, "that anyone employed as he had been in matters touching the benefit of his country should be defamed by those that are ignorant in the affairs he went about." Although much sensational information about Marlowe has been discovered in modern times, we are still largely "ignorant in the affairs he went about." The likeliest possibility is that he served as a spy or *agent provocateur* against English Catholics who were conspiring to overthrow the Protestant regime.

Before he left Cambridge, Marlowe had certainly written his tremendously successful play *Tamburlaine* and perhaps also, in collaboration with his younger Cambridge contemporary, Thomas Nashe, the tragedy of *Dido, Queen of Carthage*. *Tamburlaine* dramatizes the exploits of a fourteenth-century Mongol warrior who rose from humble origins to conquer a huge territory that extended from the Black Sea to Delhi. In some sixteenth-century chronicles, Tamburlaine is represented as God's scourge, the instrument of divine wrath. In Marlowe's play there are few if any glimpses of a transcendent design. His hero is the vehicle for the expression of boundless energy and ambition, the impulse to strive ceaselessly for absolute power. When one of his victims accuses him of bloody cruelty, Tamburlaine answers that strife, restlessness, and unfettered ambition are embedded in the laws of nature and in basic human psychology:

> Nature that framed us of four elements
> Warring within our breasts for regiment,
> Doth teach us all to have aspiring minds;
> Our souls, whose faculties can comprehend
> The wondrous architecture of the world
> And measure every wandering planet's course,
> Still climbing after knowledge infinite,
> And always moving as the restless spheres,
> Wills us to wear ourselves and never rest
> Until we reach the ripest fruit of all,
> That perfect bliss and sole felicity,
> The sweet fruition of an earthly crown.

The English theater audience had never before heard such resonant, immensely energetic blank verse. The great period of Elizabethan drama was launched by what Marlowe called his "high astounding terms."

From the time of his first theatrical success, when he was twenty-three, Marlowe had only six years to live. They were not calm years. In 1589 he was involved in a brawl with one William Bradley, in which the poet Thomas Watson intervened and killed Bradley. Both poets were jailed, but Watson got off on a plea of self-defense, and Marlowe was released. In 1591 Marlowe was living in London with the playwright

Thomas Kyd, who later, under torture, gave information to the Privy Council accusing him of atheism and treason. On May 30, 1593, at an inn in the London suburb of Deptford, Marlowe was killed by a dagger thrust, purportedly in an argument over the bill. Modern scholars have discovered that the murderer and the others present in the room at the inn had connections to the world of spies, double agents, and swindlers to which Marlowe himself was in some way linked. Those who were arrested in connection with the murder were briefly held and then quietly released.

In the turbulent years before his death at the age of twenty-nine, Marlowe composed five more plays: a sequel to *Tamburlaine; The Massacre at Paris;* two major tragedies, *The Jew of Malta* and *Doctor Faustus;* and a chronicle history play about the tragic fate of a homosexual king, *Edward II.*

Hero and Leander   Marlowe's mythological erotic poem is a free and original treatment of a classic tale about two ill-fated lovers. The story derives from a version by the Alexandrian poet Musaeus (fifth century C.E.), but in its blend of poignancy and irony *Hero and Leander* is closer to that of the Roman poet Ovid, who briefly recounts the story in two epistles of his *Heroides* and who refers to it in one of his *Elegies*, which Marlowe translated.

Hero and Leander is a rich and elusive poem: it is comic, erotic, decorative, cruel; now swiftly narrative, now digressive, playful and yet, in a light way, philosophical. The characters are evidently not intended to be consistent or psychologically credible; they inhabit a world of fancy, of strange contrasts between innocence and the wild riot of amorous intrigues among the gods that is Ovid's subject matter. Hero is paradoxically a nun vowed to chastity and a devotee of Venus, the love goddess; Leander is both a sharp, sophisticated seducer and an incredibly innocent novice in sex. The deadpan asides, with their irony, hyperbole, and cynicism mingling with exuberant delight in the body's instinctual freedom, heighten the poem's elusiveness, its cunning evasion of all fixed categories.

Hero and Leander cannot be precisely dated. Marlowe's translations of Ovid, to which *Hero and Leander* is closely related in spirit, are generally thought to be work of the later 1580s. But Marlowe may alternatively have been participating in a vogue for brief erotic epics (epyllia, as they are sometimes called) that dates from the early 1590s when Shakespeare composed his contribution to the genre, *Venus and Adonis.* *Hero and Leander* was entered in the Stationers' Register (a list of forthcoming titles) on September 28, 1593, four months after the poet's death, but the earliest known edition was not published until 1598.

Marlowe left his poem unfinished; George Chapman, the playwright and translator of Homer, undertook to complete it. Chapman's moralizing, weightily philosophical continuation, which divides the poem into "sestiads" (named after Sestos, where Hero lived), was published shortly after Marlowe's fragment. The work is printed here without Chapman's additions.

Hero and Leander

On Hellespont, guilty of true-loves'° blood,   *sweethearts'*
In view and opposite, two cities stood,
Sea-borderers, disjoined by Neptune's might;
The one Abydos, the other Sestos hight.°   *called*
5   At Sestos Hero dwelt; Hero the fair,

Whom young Apollo courted for her hair,
And offered as a dower his burning throne,
Where she should sit for men to gaze upon.
The outside of her garments were of lawn,[1]
10   The lining purple silk, with gilt stars drawn;
Her wide sleeves green, and bordered with a grove
Where Venus in her naked glory strove
To please the careless and disdainful eyes
Of proud Adonis, that before her lies;[2]
15   Her kirtle° blue, whereon was many a stain,   skirt
Made with the blood of wretched lovers slain.[3]
Upon her head she ware a myrtle wreath,
From whence her veil reached to the ground beneath.
Her veil was artificial flowers and leaves,
20   Whose workmanship both man and beast deceives;
Many would praise the sweet smell as she passed,
When 'twas the odor which her breath forth cast;
And there for honey, bees have sought in vain,
And, beat from thence, have lighted there again.
25   About her neck hung chains of pebble-stone,
Which, lightened° by her neck, like diamonds shone.   illuminated
She ware no gloves, for neither sun nor wind
Would burn or parch her hands, but to her mind°   as she wished
Or° warm or cool them, for they took delight   either
30   To play upon those hands, they were so white.
Buskins° of shells all silvered usèd she,   high shoes, boots
And branched with blushing coral to the knee,
Where sparrows perched, of hollow pearl and gold,
Such as the world would wonder to behold;
35   Those with sweet water oft her handmaid fills,
Which, as she went,° would chirrup through the bills.   walked
Some say, for her the fairest Cupid pined,
And looking in her face, was strooken blind.
But this is true: so like was one the other,
40   As he imagined Hero was his mother;°   i.e., Venus
And oftentimes into her bosom flew,
About her naked neck his bare arms threw,
And laid his childish head upon her breast,
And with still° panting rocked, there took his rest.   continual
45   So lovely fair was Hero, Venus' nun,[4]
As Nature wept, thinking she was undone,
Because she took more from her than she left
And of such wondrous beauty her bereft;
Therefore, in sign her treasure° suffered wrack,   i.e., Nature's
50   Since Hero's time hath half the world been black.
Amorous Leander, beautiful and young,

---

1. A kind of fine linen or thin cambric.
2. Venus's love for the young hunter Adonis and his death in a boar hunt are told by Ovid and by Shakespeare in *Venus and Adonis*.
3. The extravagant claim is made that many "wretched lovers" had committed suicide at her

feet because Hero would not have them.
4. The connotations of these two words are contradictory. Hero is a maiden in attendance at the temple of Venus, who is, of course, the goddess of love.

(Whose tragedy divine Musaeus[5] sung)
Dwelt at Abydos; since him dwelt there none
For whom succeeding times make greater moan.
55 His dangling tresses that were never shorn,
Had they been cut and unto Colchos borne,
Would have allured the vent'rous youth of Greece[6]
To hazard more than for the Golden Fleece.
Fair Cynthia° wished his arms might be her sphere;°   the moon/orbit
60 Grief makes her pale, because she moves not there.
His body was as straight as Circe's wand;[7]
Jove might have sipped out nectar from his hand.
Even as delicious meat is to the taste,
So was his neck in touching, and surpassed
65 The white of Pelops' shoulder.[8] I could tell ye
How smooth his breast was, and how white his belly,
And whose immortal fingers did imprint
That heavenly path, with many a curious° dint,   exquisite
That runs along his back; but my rude° pen   crude
70 Can hardly blazon forth the loves of men,
Much less of powerful gods; let it suffice
That my slack° muse sings of Leander's eyes,   dull
Those orient° cheeks and lips, exceeding his   shining
That leapt into the water for a kiss
75 Of his own shadow, and despising many,
Died ere he could enjoy the love of any.[9]
Had wild Hippolytus[1] Leander seen,
Enamored of his beauty had he been;
His presence made the rudest peasant melt,
80 That in the vast uplandish country dwelt;
The barbarous Thracian soldier, moved with naught,
Was moved with him, and for his favor sought.
Some swore he was a maid in man's attire,
For in his looks were all that men desire:
85 A pleasant smiling cheek, a speaking° eye,   expressive
A brow for love to banquet royally;
And such as knew he was a man, would say,
"Leander, thou art made for amorous play;
Why art thou not in love, and loved of all?
90 Though thou be fair, yet be not thine own thrall."
    The men of wealthy Sestos every year,
For his sake whom their goddess held so dear,
Rose-cheeked Adonis, kept a solemn feast.
Thither resorted many a wandering guest
95 To meet their loves; such as had none at all
Came lovers home from this great festival;
For every street, like to a firmament,

---

5. The author of the Greek poem on which *Hero and Leander* is remotely based. He was sometimes confused with a legendary early Musaeus, supposed son of Orpheus—hence Marlowe calls him "divine."
6. "Colchos": a country in Asia where the Argonauts ("the ven'trous youth of Greece") found the Golden Fleece.
7. The wand with which Circe, in the *Odyssey*, turned men into beasts.
8. Pelops, according to Ovid, had a shoulder of ivory.
9. An allusion to Narcissus.
1. Like Adonis, he preferred hunting to love.

Glistered with breathing stars, who, where they went,
Frighted the melancholy earth, which deemed
100 Eternal heaven to burn, for so it seemed
As if another Phaëton[2] had got
The guidance of the sun's rich chariot.
But, far above the loveliest, Hero shined,
And stole away th' enchanted gazer's mind;
105 For like sea nymphs' inveigling harmony,
So was her beauty to the standers by.
Nor that night-wandering pale and watery star°   *the moon*
(When yawning dragons draw her thirling[3] car
From Latmos' mount up to the gloomy sky,
110 Where, crowned with blazing light and majesty,
She proudly sits) more over-rules° the flood   *rules over*
Than she the hearts of those that near her stood.
Even as when gaudy nymphs pursue the chase,°   *hunt*
Wretched Ixion's shaggy-footed race,[4]
115 Incensed with savage heat, gallop amain
From steep pine-bearing mountains to the plain,
So ran the people forth to gaze upon her,
And all that viewed her were enamored on her.
And as in fury of a dreadful fight,
120 Their fellows being slain or put to flight,
Poor soldiers stand with fear of death dead-strooken,
So at her presence all, surprised and tooken,
Await the sentence of her scornful eyes;
He whom she favors lives, the other dies.
125 There might you see one sigh, another rage,
And some, their violent passions to assuage,
Compile sharp satires; but alas, too late,
For faithful love will never turn to hate.
And many, seeing great princes were denied,
130 Pined as they went, and thinking on her, died.
On this feast day, oh, cursèd day and hour!
Went Hero thorough° Sestos, from her tower   *through*
To Venus' temple, where unhappily,
As after chanced, they did each other spy.
135 So fair a church as this had Venus none;
The walls were of discolored° jasper stone,   *many-colored*
Wherein was Proteus[5] carvèd, and o'erhead
A lively° vine of green sea-agate spread,   *lifelike*
Where, by one hand, light-headed Bacchus[6] hung,
140 And with the other, wine from grapes out-wrung.
Of crystal shining fair the pavement was;
The town of Sestos called it Venus' glass;°   *looking glass*
There might you see the gods in sundry shapes,

---

2. A son of the sun god, he drove his father's chariot across the sky and almost burned up the world.
3. Flying like a spear. Latmos was the mountain
where the moon visited her lover, Endymion.
4. The centaurs, fathered by Ixion on a cloud. For
his presumption in loving Juno, Ixion was chained
to a wheel, hence "wretched."
5. A sea god, who could change his shape at will.
6. God of wine and revelry.

Committing heady° riots, incest, rapes: *passionate, violent*
145 For know that underneath this radiant floor
Was Danaë's statue in a brazen tower,
Jove slyly stealing from his sister's[7] bed
To dally with Idalian Ganymed,
And for his love Europa bellowing loud,[8]
150 And tumbling with the rainbow in a cloud;[9]
Blood-quaffing Mars heaving the iron net
Which limping Vulcan and his Cyclops set;[1]
Love kindling fire to burn such towns as Troy;
Silvanus weeping for the lovely boy[2]
155 That now is turned into a cypress tree,
Under whose shade the wood-gods love to be.
And in the midst a silver altar stood;
There Hero sacrificing turtles'[3] blood,
Vailed° to the ground, veiling her eyelids close,   *bowed, bent*
160 And modestly they opened as she rose;
Thence flew love's arrow with the golden head,[4]
And thus Leander was enamorèd.
Stone still he stood, and evermore he gazed,
Till with the fire that from his countenance blazed,
165 Relenting Hero's gentle heart was strook;
Such force and virtue° hath an amorous look.   *power, efficacy*
    It lies not in our power to love or hate,
For will in us is overruled by fate.
When two are stripped, long ere the course° begin   *race*
170 We wish that one should lose, the other win;
And one especially do we affect°   *fancy*
Of two gold ingots, like in each respect.
The reason no man knows, let it suffice,
What we behold is censured° by our eyes.   *judged*
175 Where both deliberate, the love is slight;
Who ever loved, that loved not at first sight?[5]
    He kneeled, but unto her devoutly prayed.
Chaste Hero to herself thus softly said,
"Were I the saint he worships, I would hear him,"
180 And as she spake those words, came somewhat near him.
He started up; she blushed as one ashamed,
Wherewith Leander much more was inflamed.
He touched her hand; in touching it she trembled:
Love deeply grounded hardly° is dissembled.   *with difficulty*
185 These lovers parlèd° by the touch of hands;   *spoke*
True love is mute, and oft amazèd stands.

7. Juno's; she was Jove's wife. Danaë, imprisoned in a tower, was visited by Jove in the form of a shower of gold.
8. To seduce Europa, Jove took the form of a "bellowing" bull. "Ganymed": a beautiful youth whom Jove kidnapped from Mount Ida, hence "Idalian."
9. Jove as Jupiter Pluvius, god of rain, frolicking with Iris, goddess of the rainbow. But no such tryst is found in classical mythology.

1. Vulcan used a net to trap Venus (his wife) and Mars, "blood-quaffing" god of war, in the act of love.
2. Cyparissus, beloved of the wood god Sylvanus.
3. Turtledoves, symbolic of constancy in love.
4. The "golden head" of some of Cupid's arrows produced love; he had others, of lead, that produced dislike
5. Shakespeare quotes this line in *As You Like It* (3.5.83).

Thus, while dumb signs their yielding hearts entangled,
The air with sparks of living fire was spangled,
And Night, deep drenched in misty Acheron,[6]
190   Heaved up her head, and half the world upon
Breathed darkness forth. (Dark night is Cupid's day.)
And now begins Leander to display
Love's holy fire, with words, with sighs and tears,
Which like sweet music entered Hero's ears,
195   And yet at every word she turned aside
And always cut him off as he replied.
At last, like to a bold sharp sophister,[7]
With cheerful hope thus he accosted° her: *wooed*
"Fair creature, let me speak without offense;
200   I would my rude° words had the influence   *rough, inexperienced*
To lead thy thoughts as thy fair looks do mine;
Then shouldst thou be his prisoner, who is thine.
Be not unkind and fair—misshapen stuff°   *persons*
Are of behavior boisterous and rough.
205   O shun me not, but hear me ere you go;
God knows I cannot force° love, as you do.   *compel*
My words shall be as spotless as my youth,
Full of simplicity and naked truth.
This sacrifice, whose sweet perfume descending
210   From Venus' altar to your footsteps bending,°   *turning*
Doth testify that you exceed her far
To whom you offer and whose nun you are.
Why should you worship her? Her you surpass
As much as sparkling diamonds flaring° glass.   *glaring, gaudy*
215   A diamond set in lead his worth retains;
A heavenly nymph, beloved of human swains,
Receives no blemish but ofttimes more grace;
Which makes me hope, although I am but base—
Base in respect of° thee, divine and pure—   *in comparison with*
220   Dutiful service may thy love procure;
And I in duty will excel all other,
As thou in beauty dost exceed Love's mother.
Nor heaven, nor thou, were made to gaze upon;
As heaven preserves all things, so save thou one.
225   A stately builded ship, well rigged and tall,
The ocean maketh more majestical:
Why vowest thou then to live in Sestos here,
Who on Love's seas more glorious wouldst appear?
Like untuned golden strings all women are,
230   Which, long time lie untouched, will harshly jar.[8]
Vessels of brass, oft handled, brightly shine;
What difference betwixt the richest mine°   *ore*
And basest mold,° but use? for both not used   *earth*
Are of like worth. Then treasure is abused

---

6. One of the rivers of Hades.
7. Sophist, person skilled in arguments, especially specious ones.

8. I.e., instruments not played will be out of tune and harsh.

235   When misers keep it; being put to loan,
       In time it will return us two for one.
       Rich robes themselves and others do adorn;
       Neither themselves nor others, if not worn.
       Who builds a palace and rams up the gate
240   Shall see it ruinous and desolate.
       Ah, simple Hero, learn thyself to cherish;
       Lone women, like to empty houses, perish.
       Less sins the poor rich man that starves himself
       In heaping up a mass of drossy pelf,
245   Than such as you: his golden earth remains,
       Which after his decease some other gains.
       But this fair gem, sweet in the loss alone,
       When you fleet hence can be bequeathed to none.
       Or if it could, down from th' enameled° sky   *many-colored*
250   All heaven would come to claim this legacy,
       And with intestine° broils the world destroy   *internal, civil*
       And quite confound Nature's sweet harmony.
       Well therefore by the gods decreed it is,
       We human creatures should enjoy that bliss.
255   One is no number;[9] maids are nothing then
       Without the sweet society of men.
       Wilt thou live single still? One shalt thou be,
       Though never-singling Hymen[1] couple thee.
       Wild savages, that drink of running springs,
260   Think water far excels all earthly things;
       But they that daily taste neat° wine despise it.   *undiluted*
       Virginity, albeit some highly prize it,
       Compared with marriage, had you tried them both,
       Differs as much as wine and water doth.
265   Base bullion for the stamp's sake[2] we allow:
       Even so for men's impression do we you;
       By which alone, our reverend fathers[3] say,
       Women receive perfection every way.
       This idol which you term Virginity,
270   Is neither essence,° subject to the eye—   *real, substantial*
       No, nor to any one exterior sense;
       Nor hath it any place of residence,
       Nor is 't of earth or mold° celestial,   *form*
       Or capable of any form at all.
275   Of that which hath no being do not boast:
       Things that are not at all are never lost.
       Men foolishly do call it virtuous:
       What virtue is it that is born with us?[4]
       Much less can honor be ascribed thereto:
280   Honor is purchased by the deeds we do.
       Believe me, Hero, honor is not won

---

9. A traditional concept, going back to Aristotle.
1. God of marriage. "Never-singling": i.e., one who never separates, but always joins.
2. For the impression that makes metal ("bullion")
into a coin.
3. Ancient philosophers, like Aristotle.
4. I.e., a virtue is not a virtue unless it is acquired.

Until some honorable deed be done.
Seek you for chastity, immortal fame,
And know that some have wronged Diana's name?[5]
285 Whose name is it, if she be false or not,
So she be fair, but some vile tongues will blot?
But you are fair, aye me! so wondrous fair,
So young, so gentle, and so debonair,°   *affable, agreeable*
As Greece will think, if thus you live alone,
290 Some one or other keeps you as his own.
Then, Hero, hate me not, nor from me fly
To follow swiftly-blasting infamy.
Perhaps thy sacred priesthood makes thee loath.
Tell me, to whom madest thou that heedless oath?"
295   "To Venus," answered she, and as she spake,
Forth from those two tralucent cisterns° brake   *i.e., translucent eyes*
A stream of liquid pearl, which down her face
Made milk-white paths whereon the gods might trace°   *go*
To Jove's high court. He thus replied: "The rites
300 In which Love's beauteous empress most delights
Are banquets, Doric music,[6] midnight revel,
Plays, masques, and all that stern age counteth evil.
Thee as a holy idiot doth she scorn;
For thou, in vowing chastity, hast sworn
305 To rob her name and honor, and thereby
Commit'st a sin far worse than perjury—
Even sacrilege against her Deity,
Through regular and formal purity.
To expiate which sin, kiss and shake hands;
310 Such sacrifice as this Venus demands."
    Thereat she smiled and did deny him so
As, put° thereby, yet might he hope for mo.°   *put off/more*
Which makes him quickly reinforce his speech
And her in humble manner thus beseech:
315   "Though neither gods nor men may thee deserve,
Yet for her sake whom you have vowed to serve,
Abandon fruitless, cold Virginity,
The gentle Queen of Love's sole enemy.
Then shall you most resemble Venus' nun,
320 When Venus' sweet rites are performed and done.
Flint-breasted Pallas[7] joys in single life,
But Pallas and your mistress are at strife.
Love, Hero, then, and be not tyrannous,
But heal the heart that thou hast wounded thus,
325 Nor stain thy youthful years with avarice;[8]
Fair fools delight to be accounted nice.°   *shy, reluctant*
The richest corn° dies, if it be not reaped;   *grain*
Beauty alone is lost, too warily kept."

---

5. I.e., no fame for chastity is secure. Even Diana, goddess of chastity, has been slandered.
6. A solemn, military mode. Leander would more appropriately have said "Lydian" (as in Milton's *L'Allegro*, line 136); Lydian music was soft and sensual.
7. Athena, a rival goddess, usually portrayed in armor.
8. I.e., by hoarding the treasure of her beauty.

These arguments he used, and many more,
330 Wherewith she yielded, that was won before.
Hero's looks yielded, but her words made war:
Women are won when they begin to jar.°   *dispute*
Thus, having swallowed Cupid's golden hook,
The more she strived, the deeper was she strook.
335 Yet, evilly feigning anger, strove she still
And would be thought to grant against her will.
So having paused a while, at last she said:
"Who taught thee rhetoric to deceive a maid?
Aye me, such words as these should I abhor,
340 And yet I like them for the orator."
    With that, Leander stooped to have embraced her,
But from his spreading arms away she cast her,°   *i.e., she withdrew*
And thus bespake him: "Gentle youth, forbear
To touch the sacred garments which I wear.
345   "Upon a rock, and underneath a hill,
Far from the town, where all is whist° and still,   *silent*
Save that the sea, playing on yellow sand,
Sends forth a rattling murmur to the land,
Whose sound allures the golden Morpheus⁹
350 In silence of the night to visit us,
My turret stands, and there, God knows, I play
With Venus' swans and sparrows¹ all the day.
A dwarfish beldame° bears me company,   *old hag*
That hops about the chamber where I lie
355 And spends the night, that might be better spent,
In vain discourse and apish° merriment.   *silly*
Come thither." As she spake this, her tongue tripped,
For unawares "Come thither" from her slipped;
And suddenly her former color changed
360 And here and there her eyes through anger ranged.
And like a planet, moving several° ways,²   *different*
At one self° instant, she, poor soul, assays°   *one and the same / tries*
Loving, not to love at all, and every part
Strove to resist the motions of her heart;
365 And hands so pure, so innocent, nay, such
As might have made heaven stoop to have a touch,
Did she uphold to Venus, and again
Vowed spotless chastity, but all in vain.
Cupid beat down her prayers with his wings;
370 Her vows above the empty air he flings.
All deep enraged, his sinewy° bow he bent,   *strong*
And shot a shaft that burning from him went,
Wherewith she, strooken, looked so dolefully
As made Love sigh to see his tyranny.
375 And as she wept, her tears to pearl he turned,
And wound them on his arm, and for her mourned.

---

9. God of sleep. "Golden slumbers" was a common
expression.
1. Venus was often portrayed in a chariot drawn
by swans, and sparrows were associated with her

because of their traditional lechery.
2. In Ptolemaic astronomy each planet moved in
its own orbit or sphere but was also carried along
in the motion of surrounding spheres.

Then towards the palace of the Destinies,°   *the Fates*
Laden with languishment and grief, he flies,
And to those stern nymphs humbly made request
380 Both might enjoy each other and be blessed.
But with a ghastly dreadful countenance,
Threatening a thousand deaths at every glance,
They answered Love, nor would vouchsafe so much
As one poor word, their hate to him was such.
385 Harken a while, and I will tell you why:
Heaven's wingèd herald, Jove-born Mercury,
The selfsame day that he asleep had laid
Enchanted Argus,[3] spied a country maid
Whose careless hair, instead of pearl t' adorn it,
390 Glistered with dew, as one that seemed to scorn it;[4]
Her breath as fragrant as the morning rose,
Her mind pure, and her tongue untaught to glose.°   *speak insincerely*
Yet proud she was, for lofty pride that dwells
In towered courts is oft in shepherds' cells,°   *huts*
395 And too-too well the fair vermilion knew,
And silver tincture of her cheeks, that drew
The love of every swain. On her, this god
Enamored was, and with his snaky rod[5]
Did charm her nimble feet and made her stay;
400 The while upon a hillock down he lay,
And sweetly on his pipe began to play,
And with smooth speech, her fancy to assay,
Till in his twining arms he locked her fast,
And then he wooed with kisses, and at last,
405 As shepherds do, her on the ground he laid,
And tumbling in the grass, he often strayed
Beyond the bounds of shame, in being bold
To eye those parts which no eye should behold;
And, like an insolent commanding lover,
410 Boasting his parentage, would needs discover
The way to new Elysium; but she,
Whose only dower was her chastity,
Having striven in vain, was now about to cry
And crave the help of shepherds that were nigh.
415 Herewith he stayed his fury,° and began   *passion*
To give her leave to rise. Away she ran;
After went Mercury, who used such cunning
As she, to hear his tale, left off her running.
Maids are not won by brutish force and might,
420 But speeches full of pleasure and delight.
And knowing Hermes courted her, was glad
That she such loveliness and beauty had
As could provoke his liking, yet was mute,
And neither would deny nor grant his suit.
425 Still vowed he love; she, wanting no excuse

3. Mercury (or Hermes), the messenger god with winged feet, put to sleep Argus, the hundred-eyed monster whom Juno had placed as a guard over Io, with whom her husband, Jupiter, was in love.
4. I.e., pearl or other jewelry.
5. The caduceus (now the symbol of medicine).

To feed him with delays, as women use,°   *as women usually do*
Or thirsting after immortality
(All women are ambitious naturally),
Imposed upon her lover such a task
430   As he ought not perform, nor yet she ask.
A draft of flowing nectar she requested,
Wherewith the king of gods and men is feasted.
He, ready to accomplish what she willed,
Stole some from Hebe (Hebe Jove's cup filled)
435   And gave it to his simple rustic love,
Which being known (as what is hid from Jove?)
He inly stormed and waxed more furious
Than for the fire filched by Prometheus,
And thrusts him down from heaven. He, wandering here,
440   In mournful terms,° with sad and heavy cheer,°   *condition/countenance*
Complained to Cupid. Cupid, for his sake,
To be revenged on Jove did undertake;
And those on whom heaven, earth, and hell relies
(I mean the adamantine⁶ Destinies)
445   He wounds with love and forced them equally
To dote upon deceitful Mercury.
They offered him the deadly fatal knife
That shears the slender threads of human life;⁷
At his fair feathered feet the engines laid
450   Which th' earth from ugly Chaos' den upweighed.⁸
These he regarded not, but did entreat
That Jove, usurper of his father's seat,
Might presently be banished into hell
And agèd Saturn in Olympus dwell.
455   They granted what he craved, and once again
Saturn and Ops began their golden reign.
Murder, rape, war, lust, and treachery
Were with Jove closed in Stygian empery.°   *dominion, realm*
But long this blessèd time continued not;
460   As soon as he his wishèd purpose got,
He, reckless of his promise, did despise
The love of th' everlasting Destinies.
They seeing it, both Love and him abhorred,
And Jupiter unto his place restored.⁹
465   And but that Learning, in despite of Fate,
Will mount aloft and enter heaven gate,
And to the seat of Jove itself advance,

---

6. Of extreme hardness (so called because the Destinies' decrees were irrevocable).

7. According to classical mythology, the Fates spun and cut the threads that measure each human life.

8. The Fates also controlled the supports that had held up ("upweighed") the earth since it arose out of Chaos, the yawning abyss from which all things came.

9. The story in lines 451–64 may be summarized as follows: Mercury scorns the gifts offered by the Fates but asks instead that Jove be dethroned (Jove had overthrown his father, Saturn, who ruled heaven during the Golden Age). Mercury persuades the Fates to reverse this revolution, so Saturn and his wife, Ops, return to Olympus and Jove is thrust down into "Stygian empery" (line 458), or Hades. During the Golden Age there was no murder, rape, war, lust, or treachery; these came in with Jove, so when he is sent to Hades these crimes go with him. But this second Golden Age did not last long, because once he got what he wanted, Mercury forgot the Destinies and they restored Jove.

Hermes had slept in hell with Ignorance.
Yet as a punishment they added this,
470 That he and Poverty should always kiss.[1]
And to this day is every scholar poor;
Gross gold from them runs headlong to the boor.
Likewise the angry sisters, thus deluded,
To venge themselves on Hermes, have concluded
475 That Midas' brood[2] shall sit in Honor's chair,
To which the Muses' sons are only heir.
And fruitful wits that inaspiring[3] are
Shall discontent run into regions far;
And few great lords in virtuous deeds shall joy,
480 But be surprised with every garish toy,
And still enrich the lofty servile clown°   *ignorant person*
Who, with encroaching guile, keeps learning down.
Then muse not° Cupid's suit no better sped,   *i.e., don't be surprised*
Seeing in their loves the Fates were injurèd.
485   By this, sad Hero, with love unacquainted,
Viewing Leander's face, fell down and fainted.
He kissed her and breathed life into her lips,
Wherewith, as one displeased, away she trips.
Yet as she went, full often looked behind,
490 And many poor excuses did she find
To linger by the way, and once she stayed
And would have turned again, but was afraid
In offering parley to be counted light.°   *easy, immodest*
So on she goes, and in her idle flight
495 Her painted fan of curlèd plumes let fall,
Thinking to train° Leander therewithal.   *entice*
He, being a novice, knew not what she meant,
But stayed, and after her a letter sent,
Which joyful Hero answered in such sort
500 As he had hope to scale the beauteous fort
Wherein the liberal Graces[4] locked their wealth,
And therefore to her tower he got by stealth.
Wide open stood the door; he need not climb,
And she herself before the pointed° time   *appointed*
505 Had spread the board,° with roses strewed the room, *set the table*
And oft looked out, and mused he did not come.
At last he came; O who can tell the greeting
These greedy lovers had at their first meeting?
He asked, she gave, and nothing was denied;
510 Both to each other quickly were affied.°   *engaged*
Look how° their hands, so were their hearts united, *just as*
And what he did, she willingly requited.
(Sweet are the kisses, the embracements sweet,

---

1. Marlowe invents the myth that Mercury, the god of learning, would have slept in hell with Ignorance were it not that Learning is so divine that it always mounts up, even to heaven, the "seat of Jove." But it was not beyond the Fates' power to make Learning and Poverty go together, which they decreed in revenge for Mercury's neglect.

2. The rich, because everything Midas touched turned to gold; also the stupid, because Midas, judging a musical contest between Apollo and Pan, preferred the latter, against all sensible opinion.
3. Not ambitious for riches or power.
4. Three goddesses, embodying aspects of beauty.

When like desires and affections meet,
515   For from the earth to heaven is Cupid raised
Where fancy is in equal balance peised.°)   *weighed*
Yet she this rashness suddenly repented
And turned aside and to herself lamented,
As if her name and honor had been wronged
520   By being possessed of him for whom she longed.
Ay, and she wished, albeit not from her heart,
That he would leave her turret and depart.
The mirthful god of amorous pleasure smiled
To see how he this captive nymph beguiled,
525   For hitherto he did but fan the fire
And kept it down that it might mount the higher.
Now waxed she jealous° lest his love abated,   *fearful*
Fearing her own thoughts made her to be hated.
Therefore unto him hastily she goes
530   And, like light Salmacis,[5] her body throws
Upon his bosom where, with yielding eyes,
She offers up herself a sacrifice
To slake his anger; if he were displeased,
O what god would not therewith be appeased?
535   Like Aesop's cock,[6] this jewel he enjoyed,
And as a brother with his sister toyed,
Supposing nothing else was to be done,
Now he her favor and good will had won.
But know you not that creatures wanting sense°   *intelligence*
540   By nature have a mutual appetence,[7]
And wanting organs to advance a step,
Moved by love's force, unto each other leap?
Much more in subjects having intellect
Some hidden influence breeds like effect.
545   Albeit Leander, rude° in love and raw,   *untutored*
Long dallying with Hero, nothing saw
That might delight him more, yet he suspected
Some amorous rites or other were neglected.
Therefore unto his body, hers he clung;
550   She, fearing on the rushes[8] to be flung,
Strived with redoubled strength; the more she strived,
The more a gentle, pleasing heat revived,
Which taught him all that elder lovers know.
And now the same gan so to scorch and glow,
555   As, in plain terms, yet cunningly,° he craved it.   *skillfully*
(Love always makes those eloquent that have it.)
She, with a kind of granting, put him by it,
And, ever as he thought himself most nigh it,
Like to the tree of Tantalus,[9] she fled,
560   And, seeming lavish, saved her maidenhead.

---

5. An amorous nymph in Ovid's *Metamorphoses*.
6. In Aesop's fable, a cock, scratching in the barnyard, uncovers a jewel but prefers a barley corn to it.
7. Attraction, as iron to a magnet.

8. Reeds used as carpeting in Elizabethan homes.
9. Tantalus was punished in Hades by constantly reaching for fruit from a tree that eluded him and by trying to drink water that also escaped him.

Ne'er king more sought to keep his diadem
Than Hero this inestimable gem.
Above our life we love a steadfast friend;
Yet, when a token of great worth we send,
565 We often kiss it, often look thereon,
And stay the messenger that would be gone.
No marvel then, though Hero would not yield
So soon to part from that she dearly held.
Jewels being lost are found again, this never;
570 'Tis lost but once, and once lost, lost forever.
    Now had the Morn espied her lover's steeds,[1]
Whereat she starts, puts on her purple weeds,°   *clothes*
And, red for anger that he stayed so long,
All headlong throws herself the clouds among.
575 And now Leander, fearing to be missed,
Embraced her suddenly, took leave, and kissed;
Long was he taking leave, and loath to go,
And kissed again, as lovers use to do.
Sad Hero wrung him by the hand and wept,
580 Saying, "Let your vows and promises be kept."
Then, standing at the door, she turned about,
As loath to see Leander going out.
And now the sun that through th' horizon peeps,
As pitying these lovers, downward creeps,
585 So that in silence of the cloudy night,
Though it was morning, did he take his flight.
But what the secret trusty night concealed,
Leander's amorous habit° soon revealed.   *dress*
With Cupid's myrtle[2] was his bonnet° crowned;   *hat*
590 About his arms the purple riband° wound   *ribbon*
Wherewith she wreathed her largely spreading hair;
Nor could the youth abstain but he must wear
The sacred ring wherewith she was endowed
When first religious chastity she vowed;
595 Which made his love through Sestos to be known,
And thence unto Abydos sooner blown
Than he could sail, for incorporeal Fame,
Whose weight consists in nothing but her name,
Is swifter than the wind, whose tardy plumes
600 Are reeking water and dull earthly fumes.[3]
Home when he came, he seemed not to be there,
But like exilèd air thrust from his sphere,
Set in a foreign place, and straight from thence,
Alcides-like,[4] by mighty violence
605 He would have chased away the swelling main
That him from her unjustly did detain.
Like as the sun in a diameter[5]
Fires and inflames objects removèd far,
And heateth kindly, shining lat'rally,

1. The horses that pull the chariot of the sun.
2. A plant sacred to Venus or Cupid, symbolic of love.
3. I.e., fame is as incorporeal as mist or smoke.
4. Like Hercules, with brute force.
5. I.e., shining straight down.

610 So beauty sweetly quickens when 'tis nigh,
But being separated and removed,
Burns where it cherished, murders where it loved.[6]
Therefore, even as an index to a book,
So to his mind was young Leander's look.

615 O none but gods have power their love to hide:
Affection by the count'nance is descried.°   *revealed*
The light of hidden fire itself discovers,
And love that is concealed betrays° poor lovers.   *gives away*
His secret flame apparently° was seen;   *openly*

620 Leander's father knew where he had been,
And for the same mildly rebuked his son,
Thinking to quench the sparkles new begun.
But love, resisted once, grows passionate,
And nothing more than counsel lovers hate.

625 For as a hot, proud horse highly disdains
To have his head controlled, but breaks the reins,
Spits forth the ringled° bit, and with his hooves   *with rings at the ends*
Checks° the submissive ground; so he that loves,   *stamps*
The more he is restrained, the worse he fares.

630 What is it now but mad Leander dares?[7]
"O Hero, Hero!" thus he cried full oft,
And then he got him to a rock aloft,
Where, having spied her tower, long stared he on 't
And prayed the narrow toiling Hellespont

635 To part in twain, that he might come and go;
But still the rising billows answered "No!"
With that he stripped him to the ivory skin,
And crying, "Love, I come!" leapt lively in.
Whereat the sapphire-visaged god° grew proud,   *Neptune, god of the sea*

640 And made his capering Triton[8] sound aloud;
Imagining that Ganimed,[9] displeased,
Had left the heavens, therefore on him seized.
Leander strived; the waves about him wound
And pulled him to the bottom, where the ground

645 Was strewed with pearl, and in low coral groves
Sweet singing mermaids sported with their loves
On heaps of heavy gold and took great pleasure
To spurn in careless sort° the shipwrack treasure;   *manner*
For here the stately azure palace stood

650 Where kingly Neptune and his train abode.
The lusty god embraced him, called him love,
And swore he never should return to Jove.
But when he knew it was not Ganimed,
For under water he was almost dead,

655 He heaved him up, and looking on his face,
Beat down the bold waves with his triple mace,[1]
Which mounted up, intending to have kissed him,

6. I.e., inaccessible beauty can burn and murder.
7. I.e., what is there now Leander dares not do?
8. A subordinate sea god who blew on a conch shell.
9. Ganymede, a beautiful boy taken by Jove to be his cup bearer.
1. The three-pronged fork carried by Neptune.

And fell in drops like tears because they missed him.
Leander being up, began to swim,
660 And, looking back, saw Neptune follow him;
Whereat aghast, the poor soul gan to cry,
"O let me visit Hero ere I die!"
The god put Helle's bracelet[2] on his arm,
And swore the sea should never do him harm.
665 He clapped his plump cheeks, with his tresses played,
And, smiling wantonly, his love bewrayed.°   revealed
He watched his arms, and as they opened wide,
At every stroke betwixt them he would slide
And steal a kiss, and then run out and dance
670 And, as he turned, cast many a lustful glance
And throw him gaudy toys to please his eye,
And dive into the water and there pry
Upon his breast, his thighs, and every limb,
And up again and close beside him swim,
675 And talk of love. Leander made reply,
"You are deceived; I am no woman, I."
Thereat smiled Neptune, and then told a tale
How that a shepherd, sitting in a vale,
Played with a boy so lovely fair and kind,
680 As for his love both earth and heaven pined;
That of the cooling river durst not drink,
Lest water nymphs should pull him from the brink.
And when he sported in the fragrant lawns,
Goat-footed satyrs and up-staring fawns[3]
685 Would steal him thence. Ere half this tale was done
"Ay me!" Leander cried, "th' enamored sun
That now should shine on Thetis' glassy bower[4]
Descends upon my radiant Hero's tower.
O that these tardy arms of mine were wings!"
690 And as he spake, upon the waves he springs.
Neptune was angry that he gave no ear,
And in his heart revenging malice bare.
He flung at him his mace, but as it went
He called it in, for love made him repent.
695 The mace returning back, his own hand hit,
As meaning to be venged for darting it.
When this fresh bleeding wound Leander viewed,
His color went and came, as if he rued
The grief° which Neptune felt. In gentle breasts   pain
700 Relenting thoughts, remorse, and pity rests;
And who have hard hearts and obdurate minds
But vicious, harebrained, and illit'rate hinds?°   rustics, boors
The god, seeing him with pity to be moved,
Thereon concluded that he was beloved.

---

2. Helle was the daughter of King Athamas of Thebes. To escape a cruel stepmother, she fled on a winged, golden-fleeced ram but fell off into the Hellespont, which was named for her. Marlowe apparently invented the detail of the bracelet.

3. Woodland spirits, who prophesied by looking up to the heavens.
4. I.e., the sea; Thetis was a sea nymph, mother of the hero Achilles.

705 (Love is too full of faith, too credulous,
With folly and false hope deluding us.)
Wherefore Leander's fancy to surprise,°   *i.e., to capture his love*
To the rich ocean for gifts he flies.
'Tis wisdom to give much; a gift prevails
710 When deep persuading oratory fails.
By this° Leander, being near the land,   *by this time*
Cast down his weary feet and felt the sand.
Breathless albeit he were, he rested not
Till to the solitary tower he got,
715 And knocked and called; at which celestial noise
The longing heart of Hero much more joys
Than nymphs and shepherds when the timbrel° rings,   *tambourine*
Or crooked⁵ dolphin when the sailor sings.
She stayed not for her robes, but straight arose
720 And, drunk with gladness, to the door she goes;
Where, seeing a naked man, she screeched for fear
(Such sights as this to tender maids are rare)
And ran into the dark herself to hide.
Rich jewels in the dark are soonest spied.
725 Unto her was he led, or rather drawn
By those white limbs which sparkled through the lawn.°   *fine linen*
The nearer that he came, the more she fled,
And, seeking refuge, slipped into her bed.
Whereon Leander sitting, thus began,
730 Through numbing cold, all feeble, faint, and wan:
    "If not for love, yet, love, for pity's sake
Me in thy bed and maiden bosom take;
At least vouchsafe these arms some little room,
Who, hoping to embrace thee, cheerly° swum.   *gladly*
735 This head was beat with many a churlish billow,
And therefore let it rest upon thy pillow."
Herewith affrighted Hero shrunk away
And in her lukewarm place Leander lay;
Whose lively heat, like fire from heaven fet,°   *fetched*
740 Would animate gross clay, and higher set
The drooping thoughts of base declining souls
Than dreary° Mars° carousing nectar bowls.   *bloody/god of war*
His hands he cast upon her like a snare:
She, overcome with shame and sallow fear,
745 Like chaste Diana when Actaeon⁶ spied her,
Being suddenly betrayed, dived down to hide her,
And as her silver body downward went,
With both her hands she made the bed a tent,
And in her own mind thought herself secure,
750 O'ercast with dim and darksome coverture.
And now she lets him whisper in her ear,
Flatter, entreat, promise, protest, and swear;

---

5. "Crooked" because of the undulating path of the dolphin in the water. The musician Arion was saved from drowning by a dolphin charmed by his music.

6. A hunter who happened on Diana bathing. She turned him into a stag, and he was killed by his own hounds.

Yet ever as he greedily assayed
To touch those dainties, she the Harpy[7] played,
755 And every limb did, as a soldier stout,
Defend the fort and keep the foeman out.
For though the rising ivory mount he scaled,
Which is with azure circling lines empaled,°   surrounded
Much like a globe (a globe may I term this,
760 By which love sails to regions full of bliss),
Yet there with Sisyphus[8] he toiled in vain,
Till gentle parley did the truce obtain.[9]
Wherein Leander on her quivering breast,
Breathless spoke something, and sighed out the rest;
765 Which so prevailed, as he, with small ado,
Enclosed her in his arms and kissed her, too.
And every kiss to her was as a charm,
And to Leander as a fresh alarm,°   call to battle
So that the truce was broke, and she, alas,
770 Poor silly° maiden, at his mercy was.   innocent
Love is not full of pity, as men say,
But deaf and cruel, where he means to prey.
Even as a bird which in our hands we wring
Forth plungeth and oft flutters with her wing,
775 She trembling strove; this strife of hers, like that
Which made the world,[1] another world begat
Of unknown joy. Treason was in her thought,
And cunningly to yield herself she sought.
Seeming not won, yet won she was, at length.
780 (In such wars women use but half their strength.)
Leander now, like Theban Hercules,
Entered the orchard of th' Hesperides,
Whose fruit none rightly can describe but he
That pulls or shakes it from the golden tree.[2]
785 And now she wished this night were never done,
And sighed to think upon th' approaching sun,
For much it grieved her that the bright daylight
Should know the pleasure of this blessèd night,
And them like Mars and Erycine[3] displayed,
790 Both in each other's arms chained as they laid.
Again she knew not how to frame her look
Or speak to him who in a moment took

---

7. A monster, half-bird, half-woman, who snatches away banquets in Virgil's *Aeneid* and Shakespeare's *Tempest*.
8. Condemned in Hades endlessly to roll a stone uphill.
9. In both the authoritative early printings of the poem (1598), the lines here numbered 775–84 follow at this point (that is, they precede the lines here numbered 763–74). Like almost all modern editors, though, we have adopted the rearrangement first made in 1910 by Tucker Brooke, in his edition of Marlowe's *Works*. The original order, Brooke thought, did not make good sense; he hypothesized that two sheets of Marlowe's manuscript had been accidentally reversed by the time

(five years after his death) the poem was printed. Students may, though, want to read the passage both ways and make up their own minds as to which order is preferable.
1. The Greek philosopher Empedocles held that creation was the result of love and strife acting in opposition to each other and alternately ruling the universe.
2. One of Hercules' labors was to get the golden apples of the Hesperides, guarded by a dragon. Hercules was born in Thebes.
3. A name for Venus, who was caught in bed with Mars by her husband, Vulcan, who cast a fine chain net over them.

That which so long so charily she kept;
And fain by stealth away she would have crept
795 And to some corner secretly have gone,
Leaving Leander in the bed alone.
But as her naked feet were whipping out,
He on the sudden clinged her so about
That mermaid-like unto the floor she slid:
800 One half appeared, the other half was hid.
Thus near the bed she blushing stood upright;
And from her countenance behold ye might
A kind of twilight break, which through the hair,
As from an orient° cloud, glims° here and there,   *bright/gleams*
805 And round about the chamber this false morn
Brought forth the day before the day was born.
So Hero's ruddy cheek Hero betrayed,
And her all naked to his sight displayed,
Whence his admiring eyes more pleasure took
810 Than Dis[4] on heaps of gold fixing his look.
By this Apollo's golden harp began
To sound forth music to the Ocean,
Which watchful Hesperus[5] no sooner heard
But he the day's bright-bearing car prepared,
815 And ran before, as harbinger of light,
And with his flaring beams mocked ugly Night
Till she, o'ercome with anguish, shame, and rage,
Danged° down to hell her loathsome carriage.   *hurled*
          Desunt nonnulla.°   *something is lacking*

[handwritten:] Marlowe was a spy for Queen E. he was stabbed to death by other fellow spys bc he might tell her secrets.   *[handwritten:] 1598*

The Passionate Shepherd to His Love[1]

Come live with me and be my love,
And we will all the pleasures prove°   *test, experience*
That valleys, groves, hills, and fields,
Woods, or steepy mountain yields.

[handwritten:] this is an argument.

5 And we will sit upon the rocks,
Seeing the shepherds feed their flocks,
By shallow rivers to whose falls
Melodious birds sing madrigals.

And I will make thee beds of roses
10 And a thousand fragrant posies,
A cap of flowers, and a kirtle°   *skirt*
Embroidered all with leaves of myrtle;

[handwritten:] all very material + optimistic

---

4. Pluto, god of the underworld and of wealth.
5. The evening star; one would expect Lucifer, the morning star.
1. This pastoral lyric of invitation is one of the most famous of Elizabethan songs, and a few lines

from it are sung in Shakespeare's *Merry Wives of Windsor.* Many poets have written replies to it, the best known of which is by Sir Walter Ralegh (p. 879).

they are self-suficient

A gown made of the finest wool
Which from our pretty lambs we pull;
Fair linèd slippers for the cold,   15
With buckles of the purest gold;

A belt of straw and ivy buds,
With coral clasps and amber studs: *for love*
And if these pleasures may thee move,
Come live with me, and be my love.   20

The shepherd swains shall dance and sing
For thy delight each May morning:
If these delights thy mind may move,
Then live with me and be my love.

1599, 1600

Doctor Faustus

Marlowe's major dramas, *Tamburlaine*, *The Jew of Malta*, and *Doctor Faustus*, all portray heroes who passionately seek power—the power of rule, the power of money, and the power of knowledge, respectively. Each of the heroes is an overreacher, striving to get beyond the conventional boundaries established to contain the human will.

Unlike Tamburlaine, whose aim and goal is "the sweet fruition of an earthly crown," and Barabas, the Jew of Malta, who lusts for "infinite riches in a little room," Faustus seeks the power and voluptuous pleasure that come from forbidden knowledge. To get this power Faustus must make—or chooses to make—a bargain with Lucifer. This is an old folklore motif, but it would have been taken seriously in a time when belief in the reality of devils was almost universal. The story's power over its original audience is vividly suggested by the numerous accounts of uncanny events at performances of the play: strange noises in the theater or extra devils who suddenly appeared among the actors on stage, causing panic.

In the opening soliloquy, Marlowe's Faustus bids farewell to each of his studies—logic, medicine, law, and divinity—as something he has used up. He turns instead to black magic, but the devil exacts a fearful price in exchange: the eternal damnation of Faustus's soul. This fate would also have been taken literally by an Elizabethan audience. Faustus aspires to be more than a man: "A sound magician is a mighty god," he declares. His fall is caused by the same pride and ambition that caused the fall of the angels in heaven and of humankind in the Garden of Eden. But it is characteristic of Marlowe that he makes those aspirations nonetheless magnificent.

The immediate source of the play is a German narrative called, in its English translation, *The History of the Damnable Life and Deserved Death of Doctor John Faustus*. That source supplies Marlowe's drama with the scenes of horseplay and low practical joking that contrast so markedly with the passages of huge ambition. It is quite possible that these comic scenes are the work of a collaborator; but no other Elizabethan could have written the first scene (with its brilliant representation of the insatiable aspiring mind of the hero), the ecstatic address to Helen of Troy, or the searing scene of Faustus's last hour. And though compared with these celebrated passages, the comic scenes often seem crude, they too contribute to the overarching vision of Faustus's fate: the half-trivial, half-daring exploits, the alternating states of bliss and despair, the questions that are not answered and the answers that bring no real satisfaction, the heroic wanderings that lead nowhere.

Marlowe's play exists in two very different forms: the A text (1604) and the much longer B text (1616), which, according to theatrical records, contains yet more scenes by other hands and which has also been revised to conform to the severe censorship statutes of 1606. We use Roma Gill's edition, based on the A text. In the selection of contextual material that follows the play, there are parallel versions of a key scene that will enable the reader to compare the two texts.

The Tragical History of Doctor Faustus

DRAMATIS PERSONAE[1]

CHORUS
DR. JOHN FAUSTUS
WAGNER, *his servant, a student*
VALDES
CORNELIUS ⎱ *his friends, magicians*
THREE SCHOLARS
GOOD ANGEL
EVIL ANGEL
MEPHASTOPHILIS
LUCIFER
BELZEBUB
OLD MAN
CLOWN
ROBIN ⎱ *ostlers at an inn*
RAFE ⎰
VINTNER
HORSE-COURSER
THE POPE
THE CARDINAL OF LORRAINE
CHARLES V, EMPEROR OF GERMANY
A KNIGHT *at the* EMPEROR'S *court*
DUKE OF VANHOLT
DUCHESS OF VANHOLT

Spirits presenting
THE SEVEN DEADLY SINS
   PRIDE
   COVETOUSNESS
   WRATH
   ENVY
   GLUTTONY
   SLOTH
   LECHERY
ALEXANDER THE GREAT *and his* PARAMOUR
HELEN OF TROY

ATTENDANTS, FRIARS, *and* DEVILS

---

1. There is no list of characters in the A text. The one here is an editorial construction.

Prologue

[*Enter* CHORUS.][2]

CHORUS   Not marching now in fields of Thrasimene,
    Where Mars[3] did mate° the Carthaginians,   *join with*
    Nor sporting in the dalliance of love,
    In courts of kings where state° is overturned,   *political power*
5   Nor in the pomp of proud audacious deeds,
    Intends our Muse to vaunt his heavenly verse:
    Only this (Gentlemen) we must perform,
    The form of Faustus' fortunes good or bad.
    To patient judgments we appeal our plaud,°   *applause*
10   And speak for Faustus in his infancy:
    Now is he born, his parents base of stock,
    In Germany, within a town called Rhodes;
    Of riper years to Wittenberg[4] he went,
    Whereas° his kinsmen chiefly brought him up.   *where*
15   So soon he profits in divinity,
    The fruitfull plot of scholarism graced,
    That shortly he was graced with doctor's name,[5]
    Excelling all, whose sweet delight disputes[6]
    In heavenly matters of theology.
20   Till, swollen with cunning,° of a self-conceit,   *knowledge*
    His waxen wings did mount above his reach,
    And melting heavens conspired his overthrow.[7]
    For falling to a devilish exercise,
    And glutted more with learning's golden gifts,
25   He surfeits upon cursed necromancy:°   *black magic*
    Nothing so sweet as magic is to him,
    Which he prefers before his chiefest bliss.[8]
    And this the man[9] that in his study sits.   [*Exit.*]

SCENE 1

[*Enter* FAUSTUS *in his study.*]

FAUSTUS   Settle thy studies, Faustus, and begin
    To sound the depth of that thou wilt profess:
    Having commenced, be a divine in show,[1]
    Yet level° at the end of every art,   *aim*
5   And live and die in Aristotle's works.
    Sweet *Analytics*, 'tis thou hast ravished me:
    Bene disserere est finis logices.[2]

2. A single actor who recited a prologue to an act or a whole play, and occasionally delivered an epilogue.
3. God of war. The battle of Lake Trasimene (217 B.C.E.) was one of the Carthaginian leader Hannibal's great victories.
4. The famous university where Martin Luther studied, as did Shakespeare's Hamlet and Horatio. "Rhodes": Roda, or Stadtroda, in Germany.
5. The lines play on two senses of *graced*: he so (1) adorned the place ("plot") of scholarship—i.e., the university—that shortly he was (2) honored with a doctor's degree.
6. Referring to formal disputations, academic

exercises that took the place of examinations.
7. In Greek myth, Icarus flew too near the sun on wings of feathers and wax made by his father, Daedalus; the wax melted, and he fell into the sea and drowned.
8. The salvation of his soul.
9. Apparently a cue for the Chorus to draw aside the curtain to the enclosed space at the rear of the stage.
1. In external appearance. "Commenced": graduated, i.e., received the doctor's degree.
2. To carry on a disputation well is the end or purpose of logic. "*Analytics*": the title of two treatises on logic by Aristotle.

Is, to dispute well, logic's chiefest end?
Affords this art no greater miracle?
10   Then read no more, thou hast attained the end;
A greater subject fitteth Faustus' wit.°   intellect
Bid *on kai me on* farewell; Galen[3] come:
Seeing, *ubi desinit philosophus, ibi incipit medicus.*[4]
Be a physician, Faustus, heap up gold,
15   And be eternized for some wondrous cure.
Summum bonum medicinae sanitas:[5]
The end of physic° is our body's health.   medicine
Why Faustus, hast thou not attained that end?
Is not thy common talk found aphorisms?[6]
20   Are not thy bills° hung up as monuments,   prescriptions
Whereby whole cities have escaped the plague,
And thousand desperate maladies been eased?
Yet art thou still but Faustus, and a man.
Couldst thou make men to live eternally,
25   Or, being dead, raise them to life again,
Then this profession were to be esteemed.
Physic farewell! Where is Justinian?[7]
Si una eademque res legatur duobus,
Alter rem alter valorem rei, etc.[8]
30   A pretty case of paltry legacies:
Exhereditare filium non potest pater nisi . . . [9]
Such is the subject of the Institute,
And universal body of the law:
This study fits a mercenary drudge
35   Who aims at nothing but external trash!
Too servile and illiberal for me.
When all is done, divinity is best:
Jerome's Bible,[1] Faustus, view it well:
Stipendium peccati mors est: ha! *Stipendium, etc.*[2]
40   The reward of sin is death? That's hard.
Si pecasse negamus, fallimur, et nulla est in nobis veritas.[3]
If we say that we have no sin,
We deceive ourselves, and there's no truth in us.
Why then belike we must sin,
45   And so consequently die.
Ay, we must die an everlasting death.
What doctrine call you this? *Che sarà, sarà:*[4]
What will be, shall be! Divinity, adieu!
These metaphysics° of magicians,   basic principles
50   And necromantic books are heavenly!
Lines, circles, schemes, letters, and characters!
Ay, these are those that Faustus most desires.
O what a world of profit and delight,

---

3. The ancient authority on medicine (2nd century C.E.). The Greek means, "Being and not being," i.e., philosophy.
4. Where the philosopher leaves off the physician begins.
5. The Latin is translated in the line below.
6. I.e., generally accepted wisdom.
7. Roman emperor and authority on law (483–565 C.E.), author of the *Institutes*.

8. If something is bequeathed to two persons, one shall have the thing itself, the other something of equal value.
9. A father cannot disinherit his son unless . . .
1. The Latin translation, or "Vulgate," of St. Jerome (ca. 340–420 C.E.).
2. Romans 5.23, translated in the line below.
3. 1 John 1.8, translated in the next two lines.
4. Translated in the first half of the next line.

Of power, of honor, of omnipotence
55 Is promised to the studious artisan![5]
All things that move between the quiet° poles   *unmoving*
Shall be at my command: emperors and kings
Are but obeyed in their several provinces,
Nor can they raise the wind, or rend the clouds;
60 But his dominion that exceeds in this
Stretcheth as far as doth the mind of man:
A sound magician is a mighty god.
Here Faustus, try thy brains to gain a deity.
        [*Enter* WAGNER.]
Wagner, commend me to my dearest friends,
65   The German Valdes, and Cornelius,
Request them earnestly to visit me.
    WAGNER   I will sir.   [*Exit.*]
    FAUSTUS   Their conference will be a greater help to me
Than all my labors, plod I ne'er so fast.
        [*Enter the* GOOD ANGEL *and the* EVIL ANGEL.]
70 GOOD ANGEL   O Faustus, lay that damnèd book aside,
And gaze not on it, lest it tempt thy soul,
And heap God's heavy wrath upon thy head:
Read, read the Scriptures; that is blasphemy.
    EVIL ANGEL   Go forward, Faustus, in that famous art,
75   Wherein all nature's treasury is contained:
Be thou on earth as Jove[6] is in the sky,
Lord and commander of these elements.   [*Exeunt.*]
    FAUSTUS   How am I glutted with conceit° of this!   *filled with the idea*
Shall I make spirits fetch me what I please,
80   Resolve me of all ambiguities,
Perform what desperate enterprise I will?
I'll have them fly to India[7] for gold,
Ransack the ocean for orient pearl,
And search all corners of the new-found world
85   For pleasant fruits and princely delicates.
I'll have them read me strange philosophy,
And tell the secrets of all foreign kings;
I'll have them wall all Germany with brass,
And make swift Rhine circle fair Wittenberg;[8]
90   I'll have them fill the public schools[9] with silk,
Wherewith the students shall be bravely° clad.   *splendidly*
I'll levy soldiers with the coin they bring,
And chase the Prince of Parma[1] from our land,
And reign sole king of all our provinces.
95   Yea, stranger engines for the brunt of war
Than was the fiery keel at Antwerp's bridge,[2]
I'll make my servile spirits to invent.
Come German Valdes and Cornelius,

---

5. A master of the occult arts, such as necromancy.
6. God, a common substitution in Elizabethan drama.
7. "India" could refer to the West Indies, America, or Ophir (in the east).
8. Wittenberg is in fact on the Elbe River.

9. The university lecture rooms.
1. The duke of Parma was the Spanish governor-general of the Low Countries, 1579–92.
2. A reference to the burning ship sent by the Netherlanders in 1585 against the barrier on the river Scheldt that Parma had built as a part of the blockade of Antwerp.

And make me blest with your sage conference.
    [*Enter* VALDES *and* CORNELIUS.]
100   Valdes, sweet Valdes, and Cornelius,
     Know that your words have won me at the last
     To practise magic and concealed arts;
     Yet not your words only, but mine own fantasy,
     That will receive no object[3] for my head,
105   But ruminates on necromantic skill.
     Philosophy is odious and obscure,
     Both law and physic are for petty wits;
     Divinity is basest of the three,
     Unpleasant, harsh, contemptible, and vile.
110   'Tis magic, magic that hath ravished me.
     Then, gentle friends, aid me in this attempt,
     And I, that have with concise syllogisms
     Graveled° the pastors of the German church,   *confounded*
     And made the flowering pride of Wittenberg
115   Swarm to my problems,[4] as the infernal spirits
     On sweet Musaeus when he came to hell,
     Will be as cunning as Agrippa was,
     Whose shadows made all Europe honor him.[5]
   VALDES   Faustus, these books, thy wit, and our experience
120   Shall make all nations to canonize us.
     As Indian Moors[6] obey their Spanish lords,
     So shall the spirits of every element
     Be always serviceable to us three.
     Like lions shall they guard us when we please,
125   Like Almaine rutters° with their horsemen's staves,   *German horsemen*
     Or Lapland giants trotting by our sides;
     Sometimes like women, or unwedded maids,
     Shadowing° more beauty in their airy brows   *harboring*
     Than in the white breasts of the Queen of Love.
130   From Venice shall they drag huge argosies,
     And from America the golden fleece
     That yearly stuffs old Philip's° treasury,   *Philip II, king of Spain*
     If learnèd Faustus will be resolute.
   FAUSTUS   Valdes, as resolute am I in this
135   As thou to live, therefore object it not.[7]
   CORNELIUS   The miracles that magic will perform
     Will make thee vow to study nothing else.
     He that is grounded in astrology,
     Enriched with tongues,° well seen° in minerals,   *languages/expert*
140   Hath all the principles magic doth require:
     Then doubt not, Faustus, but to be renowned
     And more frequented for this mystery°   *craft*
     Than heretofore the Delphian oracle.[8]
     The spirits tell me they can dry the sea,
145   And fetch the treasure of all foreign wrecks,

---

3. That will pay no attention to physical reality.
4. Lectures in logic and mathematics.
5. Musaeus was a mythical singer, son of Orpheus; it was, however, Orpheus who charmed the denizens of hell with his music. Cornelius Agrippa, German author of *The Vanity and Uncer-*

tainty of Arts and Sciences (1530), was popularly supposed to have had the power of calling up the "shadows" or shades of the dead.
6. Dark-skinned native Americans.
7. Do not make it a condition.
8. The oracle of Apollo at Delphi in Greece.

Ay, all the wealth that our forefathers hid
Within the massy° entrails of the earth.   massive
Then tell me, Faustus, what shall we three want?
FAUSTUS   Nothing, Cornelius. O this cheers my soul!
150   Come, show me some demonstrations magical,
That I may conjure in some lusty° grove,   flourishing, beautiful
And have these joys in full possessiön.
VALDES   Then haste thee to some solitary grove,
And bear wise Bacon's and Abanus'⁹ works,
155   The Hebrew Psalter, and New Testament;
And whatsoever else is requisite
We will inform thee ere our conference cease.
CORNELIUS   Valdes, first let him know the words of art,
And then, all other ceremonies learned,
160   Faustus may try his cunning by himself.
VALDES   First, I'll instruct thee in the rudiments,
And then wilt thou be perfecter than I.
FAUSTUS   Then come and dine with me, and after meat
We'll canvass every quiddity° thereof: essential feature
165   For ere I sleep, I'll try what I can do.
This night I'll conjure,° though I die therefore.   call up spirits
                                                    [Exeunt.]

SCENE 2

[Enter two SCHOLARS.]
1 SCHOLAR   I wonder what's become of Faustus, that was wont to
make our schools ring with *sic probo*.¹
2 SCHOLAR   That shall we know; for see, here comes his boy.²
        [Enter WAGNER.]
SCHOLAR   How now sirra, where's thy master?
5   WAGNER   God in heaven knows.
2 SCHOLAR   Why, dost not thou know?
WAGNER   Yes I know, but that follows not.
1 SCHOLAR   Go to sirra, leave your jesting, and tell us where he is.
WAGNER   That follows not necessary by force of argument, that you,
10   being licentiates,³ should stand upon't; therefore acknowledge your
error, and be attentive.
2 SCHOLAR   Why, didst thou not say thou knew'st?
WAGNER   Have you any witness on't?
1 SCHOLAR   Yes sirra, I heard you.
15   WAGNER   Ask my fellow if I be a thief.
2 SCHOLAR   Well, you will not tell us.
WAGNER   Yes sir, I will tell you; yet if you were not dunces you would
never ask me such a question. For is not he *corpus naturale*? And
is not that *mobile*?⁴ Then wherefore should you ask me such a ques-
20   tion? But that I am by nature phlegmatic,⁵ slow to wrath, and prone
to lechery—to love I would say—it were not for you to come within
forty foot of the place of execution,⁶ although I do not doubt to see

---

9. Roger Bacon, the medieval friar and scientist
popularly thought to be a magician, and Pietro
d'Abano, 13th-century alchemist.
1. Thus I prove; a phrase in scholastic disputation.
2. Poor student acting as servant to earn his living.
3. Graduate students.
4. *Corpus naturale et mobile* ("matter natural and

movable") was a scholastic definition of the subject
matter of physics. Wagner is here parodying the
language of learning at the university.
5. Dominated by the phlegm, one of the four
humors of medieval medicine and psychology.
6. The dining room.

you both hanged the next sessions. Thus having triumphed over
you, I will set my countenance like a precisian,[7] and begin to speak
25   thus: Truly my dear brethren, my master is within at dinner with
Valdes and Cornelius, as this wine, if it could speak, it would inform
your worships. And so the Lord bless you, preserve you, and keep
you, my dear brethren, my dear brethren.   [*Exit.*]
1 SCHOLAR   Nay then, I fear he is fallen into that damned art, for
30   which they two are infamous through the world.
2 SCHOLAR   Were he a stranger, and not allied to me, yet should I
grieve for him. But come, let us go and inform the Rector,[8] and see
if he by his grave counsel can reclaim him.
1 SCHOLAR   Ay, but I fear me nothing can reclaim him.
35   2 SCHOLAR   Yet let us try what we can do.   [*Exeunt.*]

SCENE 3

[*Enter* FAUSTUS *to conjure.*]
FAUSTUS   Now that the gloomy shadow of the earth,
Longing to view Orion's drizzling look,[9]
Leaps from th'antarctic world unto the sky,
And dims the welkin° with her pitchy breath,   *sky*
5   Faustus, begin thine incantations,
And try if devils will obey thy hest,
Seeing thou hast prayed and sacrificed to them.
Within this circle[1] is Jehovah's name,
Forward and backward anagrammatized;
10   Th'abbreviated names of holy saints,
Figures of every adjunct to the heavens,
And characters of signs and erring stars,[2]
By which the spirits are enforced to rise.
Then fear not Faustus, but be resolute,
15   And try the uttermost magic can perform.
Sint mihi dei Acherontis propitii! Valeat numen triplex Jehovae!
Ignei, aerii, aquatici, terreni spiritus salvete! Orientis princeps, Bel-
zebub inferni ardentis monarcha, et Demogorgon, propitiamus vos ut
appareat et surgat Mephastophilis. Quid tu moraris? Per Jehovam,
20   *Gehennam, et consecratam aquam quam nunc spargo, signumque*
crucis quod nunc facio, et per vota nostra, ipse nunc surgat nobis
dicatus Mephastophilis.[3]
[*Enter a* DEVIL.]
I charge thee to return and change thy shape,
Thou art too ugly to attend on me;
25   Go and return an old Franciscan friar,
That holy shape becomes a devil best.   [*Exit* DEVIL.]
I see there's virtue° in my heavenly words!   *power*

---

7. Puritan. The rest of his speech is in the style of
the Puritans.
8. The head of a German university.
9. The constellation Orion appears at the beginning of winter. The phrase is a reminiscence of
Virgil.
1. The magic circle drawn on the ground, within
which the magician would be safe from the spirits
he conjured.
2. The moving planets. "Adjunct": heavenly body,
thought to be joined to the solid firmament of the
sky. "Characters of signs": signs of the zodiac and

the planets.
3. May the gods of the lower regions favor me!
Farewell to the Trinity! Hail, spirits of fire, air,
water, and earth! Prince of the East, Belzebub,
monarch of burning hell, and Demogorgon, we
pray to you that Mephastophilis may appear and
rise. What are you waiting for? By Jehovah,
Gehenna, and the holy water that I now sprinkle,
and the sign of the cross that I now make, and by
our vows, may Mephastophilis himself now rise to
serve us.

Who would not be proficient in this art?
How pliant is this Mephastophilis,
30 Full of obedience and humility,
Such is the force of magic and my spells.
Now Faustus, thou art conjurer laureate
That canst command great Mephastophilis.
Quin redis, Mephastophilis, fratris imagine![4]
[*Enter* MEPHASTOPHILIS.]
35 MEPHASTOPHILIS   Now Faustus, what would'st thou have me do?
FAUSTUS   I charge thee wait upon me whilst I live,
To do whatever Faustus shall command,
Be it to make the moon drop from her sphere,
Or the ocean to overwhelm the world.
40 MEPHASTOPHILIS   I am a servant to great Lucifer,
And may not follow thee without his leave;
No more than he commands must we perform.
FAUSTUS   Did not he charge thee to appear to me?
MEPHASTOPHILIS   No, I came now hither of mine own accord.
45 FAUSTUS   Did not my conjuring speeches raise thee? Speak!
MEPHASTOPHILIS   That was the cause, but yet *per accidens*,[5]
For when we hear one rack[6] the name of God,
Abjure the Scriptures, and his savior Christ,
We fly in hope to get his glorious soul;
50 Nor will we come unless he use such means
Whereby he is in danger to be damned:
Therefore the shortest cut for conjuring
Is stoutly to abjure the Trinity,
And pray devoutly to the prince of hell.
55 FAUSTUS   So Faustus hath already done, and holds this principle:
There is no chief but only Belzebub,
To whom Faustus doth dedicate himself.
This word damnation terrifies not him,
For he confounds hell in Elysium:
60 His ghost be with the old philosophers.[7]
But leaving these vain trifles of men's souls,
Tell me, what is that Lucifer thy lord?
MEPHASTOPHILIS   Arch-regent and commander of all spirits.
FAUSTUS   Was not that Lucifer an angel once?
65 MEPHASTOPHILIS   Yes Faustus, and most dearly loved of God.
FAUSTUS   How comes it then that he is prince of devils?
MEPHASTOPHILIS   O, by aspiring pride and insolence,
For which God threw him from the face of heaven.
FAUSTUS   And what are you that live with Lucifer?
70 MEPHASTOPHILIS   Unhappy spirits that fell with Lucifer,
Conspired against our God with Lucifer,
And are forever damned with Lucifer.
FAUSTUS   Where are you damned?
MEPHASTOPHILIS   In hell.
75 FAUSTUS   How comes it then that thou art out of hell?
MEPHASTOPHILIS   Why this is hell, nor am I out of it.
Think'st thou that I, who saw the face of God,

4. Return, Mephastophilis, in the shape of a friar.
5. The immediate, not ultimate, cause.
6. Torture (by anagrammatizing).

7. Faustus considers hell to be the Elysium of the
classical philosophers, not the Christian hell of torment.

And tasted the eternal joys of heaven,
Am not tormented with ten thousand hells
80 In being deprived of everlasting bliss?[8]
O Faustus, leave these frivolous demands,
Which strike a terror to my fainting soul.
FAUSTUS What, is great Mephastophilis so passionate
For being deprivèd of the joys of heaven?
85 Learn thou of Faustus manly fortitude,
And scorn those joys thou never shalt possess.
Go bear these tidings to great Lucifer,
Seeing Faustus hath incurred eternal death
By desperate thoughts against Jove's deity:
90 Say, he surrenders up to him his soul
So he will spare him four and twenty years,
Letting him live in all voluptuousness,
Having thee ever to attend on me,
To give me whatsoever I shall ask,
95 To tell me whatsoever I demand,
To slay mine enemies, and aid my friends,
And always be obedient to my will.
Go, and return to mighty Lucifer,
And meet me in my study at midnight
100 And then resolve me of thy master's mind.[9]
MEPHASTOPHILIS I will, Faustus.   [*Exit.*]
FAUSTUS Had I as many souls as there be stars,
I'd give them all for Mephastophilis.
By him I'll be great emperor of the world,
105 And make a bridge through the moving air
To pass the ocean with a band of men;
I'll join the hills that bind the Afric shore,
And make that land continent to Spain,
And both contributory to my crown.
110 The emperor[1] shall not live but by my leave,
Nor any potentate of Germany.
Now that I have obtained what I desire,
I'll live in speculation° of this art   contemplation
Till Mephastophilis return again.   [*Exit.*]

SCENE 4

[*Enter* WAGNER *and the* CLOWN.[2]]
WAGNER Sirra boy, come hither.
CLOWN How, boy? Zounds, boy! I hope you have seen many boys
with such pickadevants as I have. Boy, quotha![3]
WAGNER Tell me sirra, hast thou any comings in?[4]
5 CLOWN Ay, and goings out too; you may see else.[5]
WAGNER Alas poor slave, see how poverty jesteth in his nakedness!
The villain is bare, and out of service,[6] and so hungry that I know

8. This is the punishment of loss of God's presence, which is supposed to be the greatest torment of hell.
9. I.e., give me his decision.
1. The Holy Roman Emperor.
2. Not a court jester (as in some of Shakespeare's plays) but an older stock character, a rustic buffoon.

3. Says he. The point of the clown's retort is that he is a man and wears a beard. "Zounds": an oath, meaning "God's wounds." "Pickadevants": small, pointed beards.
4. Income, but the clown then puns on the literal meaning.
5. I.e., if you don't believe me.
6. Out of a job.

he would give his soul to the devil for a shoulder of mutton, though
it were blood raw.

10 CLOWN   How, my soul to the devil for a shoulder of mutton though
'twere blood raw? Not so good friend; by'rlady,[7] I had need have it
well roasted, and good sauce to it, if I pay so dear.

WAGNER   Well, wilt thou serve me, and I'll make thee go like *qui
mihi discipulus?*[8]

15 CLOWN   How, in verse?

WAGNER   No sirra; in beaten silk and stavesacre.[9]

CLOWN   How, how, knavesacre?[1] Ay I thought that was all the land
his father left him! Do ye hear, I would be sorry to rob you of your
living.

20 WAGNER   Sirra, I say in stavesacre.

CLOWN   Oho, oho, stavesacre! Why then belike, if I were your man,
I should be full of vermin.

WAGNER   So thou shalt, whether thou be'st with me or no. But sirra,
leave your jesting, and bind your self presently unto me for seven
25 years, or I'll turn all the lice about thee into familiars,[2] and they
shall tear thee in pieces.

CLOWN   Do you hear, sir? You may save that labor: they are too familiar with me already—zounds, they are as bold with my flesh as if
they had paid for my meat and drink.

30 WAGNER   Well, do you hear, sirra? Hold, take these guilders.[3]

CLOWN   Gridirons; what be they?

WAGNER   Why, French crowns.[4]

CLOWN   'Mass, but for the name of French crowns a man were as
good have as many English counters![5] And what should I do with
35 these?

WAGNER   Why, now, sirra, thou art at an hour's warning whensoever
or wheresoever the devil shall fetch thee.

CLOWN   No, no, here take your gridirons again.

WAGNER   Truly I'll none of them.

40 CLOWN   Truly but you shall.

WAGNER   Bear witness I gave them him.

CLOWN   Bear witness I give them you again.

WAGNER   Well, I will cause two devils presently to fetch thee away.
Baliol[6] and Belcher!

45 CLOWN   Let your Baliol and your Belcher come here, and I'll knock[7]
them, they were never so knocked since they were devils! Say I
should kill one of them, what would folks say? Do ye see yonder tall
fellow in the round slop?[8] He has killed the devil! So I should be
called "Killdevil" all the parish over.

[*Enter two* DEVILS, *and the* CLOWN *runs up and down crying.*]

50 WAGNER   Baliol and Belcher, spirits, away!   [*Exeunt* DEVILS.]

CLOWN   What, are they gone? A vengeance on them! They have vile
long nails. There was a he devil and a she devil. I'll tell you how
you shall know them: all he devils has horns, and all she devils has
clefts and cloven feet.

---

7. An oath: "by Our Lady."
8. You who are my pupil (the opening phrase of a
poem on how students should behave, from Lily's
Latin Grammar, ca. 1509). Wagner means "like a
proper servant of a learned man."
9. A kind of delphinium used for killing vermin.
1. Wordplay, here and below.
2. Familiar spirits, demons.

3. Coins.
4. French crowns, legal tender in England at this
period, were easily counterfeited.
5. Worthless tokens.
6. Probably a corruption of Belial.
7. Beat.
8. Baggy pants. "Tall": fine.

55 WAGNER   Well sirra, follow me.
CLOWN   But do you hear? If I should serve you, would you teach me
to raise up Banios and Belcheos?
WAGNER   I will teach thee to turn thyself to anything, to a dog, or a
cat, or a mouse, or a rat, or anything.
60 CLOWN   How! A Christian fellow to a dog. or a cat, a mouse, or a
rat? No, no sir, if you turn me into anything, let it be in the likeness
of a little pretty frisking flea, that I may be here, and there, and
everywhere. O I'll tickle the pretty wenches' plackets! I'll be
amongst them, i'faith.⁹
65 WAGNER   Well sirra, come.
CLOWN   But, do you hear, Wagner . . . ?
WAGNER   How? Baliol and Belcher!
CLOWN   O Lord I pray, sir, let Banio and Belcher go sleep.
WAGNER   Villain, call me Master Wagner; and let thy left eye be dia-
70 metarily fixed upon my right heel, with *quasi vestigias nostras insis-
tere.*¹   [*Exit.*]
CLOWN   God forgive me, he speaks Dutch fustian!² Well, I'll follow
him, I'll serve him; that's flat.   [*Exit.*]

SCENE 5

[*Enter* FAUSTUS *in his study.*]
FAUSTUS   Now Faustus, must thou needs be damned,
And canst thou not be saved.
What boots° it then to think of God or heaven?   avails
Away with such vain fancies, and despair,
5 Despair in God, and trust in Belzebub.
Now go not backward: no, Faustus, be resolute;
Why waverest thou? O, something soundeth in mine ears:
"Abjure this magic, turn to God again."
Ay, and Faustus will turn to God again.
10 To God? He loves thee not:
The god thou servest is thine own appetite
Wherein is fixed the love of Belzebub.
To him I'll build an altar and a church,
And offer lukewarm blood of newborn babes.
[*Enter* GOOD ANGEL *and* EVIL.]
15 GOOD ANGEL   Sweet Faustus, leave that execrable art.
FAUSTUS   Contrition, prayer, repentance: what of them?
GOOD ANGEL   O they are means to bring thee unto heaven.
EVIL ANGEL   Rather illusions, fruits of lunacy,
That makes men foolish that do trust them most.
20 GOOD ANGEL   Sweet Faustus, think of heaven, and heavenly things.
EVIL ANGEL   No Faustus, think of honor and of wealth.
[*Exeunt.*]
FAUSTUS   Of wealth!
Why, the signory of Emden³ shall be mine.
When Mephastophilis shall stand by me.
25 What god can hurt thee, Faustus? Thou art safe,
Cast no more doubts. Come, Mephastophilis,

9. In faith. "Plackets" slits in garments—but with
an obvious sexual allusion.
1. A pedantic way of saying "Follow my footsteps."
"Diametarily": diametrically.
2. Gibberish.
3. A wealthy German trade center.

And bring glad tidings from great Lucifer.
Is't not midnight? Come, Mephastophilis:
Veni, veni, Mephastophile![4]
[*Enter* MEPHASTOPHILIS.]
30 Now tell, what says Lucifer thy lord?
MEPHASTOPHILIS   That I shall wait on Faustus whilst he lives,
So he will buy my service with his soul.
FAUSTUS   Already Faustus hath hazarded that for thee.
MEPHASTOPHILIS   But Faustus, thou must bequeath it solemnly,
35 And write a deed of gift with thine own blood,
For that security craves great Lucifer.
If thou deny it, I will back to hell.
FAUSTUS   Stay, Mephastophilis, and tell me,
What good will my soul do thy lord?
40 MEPHASTOPHILIS   Enlarge his kingdom.
FAUSTUS   Is that the reason he tempts us thus?
MEPHASTOPHILIS   *Solamen miseris socios habuisse doloris.*[5]
FAUSTUS   Have you any pain that tortures others?
MEPHASTOPHILIS   As great as have the human souls of men.
45 But tell me Faustus, shall I have thy soul?
And I will be thy slave and wait on thee,
And give thee more than thou hast wit to ask.
FAUSTUS   Ay Mephastophilis, I give it thee.
MEPHASTOPHILIS   Then stab thine arm courageously,
50 And bind thy soul, that at some certain day
Great Lucifer may claim it as his own,
And then be thou as great as Lucifer.
FAUSTUS   Lo Mephastophilis, for love of thee,
I cut my arm, and with my proper° blood   *own*
55 Assure my soul to be great Lucifer's,
Chief lord and regent of perpetual night.
View here the blood that trickles from mine arm,
And let it be propitious for my wish.
MEPHASTOPHILIS   But Faustus, thou must write it
60 In manner of a deed of gift.
FAUSTUS   Ay, so I will; but, Mephastophilis,
My blood congeals and I can write no more.
MEPHASTOPHILIS   I'll fetch thee fire to dissolve it straight.   [*Exit.*]
FAUSTUS   What might the staying of my blood portend?
65 Is it unwilling I should write this bill?°   *contract*
Why streams it not, that I may write afresh:
"Faustus gives to thee his soul"? Ah, there it stayed!
Why should'st thou not? Is not thy soul thine own?
Then write again: "Faustus gives to thee his soul."
[*Enter* MEPHASTOPHILIS *with a chafer*° *of coals.*]   *a portable grate*
70 MEPHASTOPHILIS   Here's fire, come Faustus, set it on.
FAUSTUS   So, now the blood begins to clear again.
Now will I make an end immediately.
MEPHASTOPHILIS   Oh what will not I do to obtain his soul!
FAUSTUS   *Consummatum est,*[6] this bill is ended,
75 And Faustus hath bequeathed his soul to Lucifer.

4. Come, come, Mephastophilis!
5. Misery loves company.

6. It is finished; a blasphemy, because these are
the words of Christ on the Cross (John 19.30).

But what is this inscription on mine arm?
Homo fuge.° Whither should I fly?   *O man, fly*
If unto God, he'll throw me down to hell;
My senses are deceived, here's nothing writ;
80   I see it plain, here in this place is writ,
Homo fuge! Yet shall not Faustus fly.
MEPHASTOPHILIS   I'll fetch him somewhat to delight his mind.   [*Exit.*]
    [*Enter with* DEVILS, *giving crowns and rich apparel to* FAUS-
    TUS, *and dance, and then depart.*]
FAUSTUS   Speak, Mephastophilis, what means this show?
MEPHASTOPHILIS   Nothing, Faustus, but to delight thy mind withal,
85   And to show thee what magic can perform.
FAUSTUS   But may I raise up spirits when I please?
MEPHASTOPHILIS   Ay, Faustus, and do greater things than these.
FAUSTUS   Then there's enough for a thousand souls!
    Here, Mephastophilis, receive this scroll,
90   A deed of gift of body and of soul:
    But yet conditionally, that thou perform
    All articles prescribed between us both.
MEPHASTOPHILIS   Faustus, I swear by hell and Lucifer
    To effect all promises between us made.
95   FAUSTUS   Then hear me read them. On these conditions following:
    First, that Faustus may be a spirit[7] *in form and substance.*
    Secondly, that Mephastophilis shall be his servant, and at his com-
    mand.
    Thirdly, that Mephastophilis shall do for him, and bring him whatso-
100   *ever.*
    Fourthly, that he shall be in his chamber or house invisible.
    Lastly, that he shall appear to the said John Faustus at all times, in
    what form or shape soever he please.
    I, John Faustus of Wittenberg, doctor, by these presents,[8] *do give both*
105   *body and soul to Lucifer, Prince of the East, and his minister Mephas-*
    tophilis; and furthermore grant unto them that, four and twenty years
    being expired, the articles above-written inviolate, full power to fetch
    or carry the said John Faustus, body and soul, flesh, blood, or goods,
    into their habitation wheresoever.
110   *By me John Faustus.*
MEPHASTOPHILIS   Speak, Faustus: do you deliver this as your deed?
FAUSTUS   Ay, take it; and the devil give thee good on't.
MEPHASTOPHILIS   Now, Faustus, ask what thou wilt.
FAUSTUS   First will I question with thee about hell:
115   Tell me, where is the place that men call hell?
MEPHASTOPHILIS   Under the heavens.
FAUSTUS   Ay, but whereabouts?
MEPHASTOPHILIS   Within the bowels of these elements,
    Where we are tortured and remain for ever.
120   Hell hath no limits, nor is circumscribed
    In one self place; for where we are is hell,
    And where hell is, there must we ever be.
    And to conclude, when all the world dissolves,
    And every creature shall be purified,
125   All places shall be hell that is not heaven.

7. I.e., have the supernatural powers of a spirit.   8. Legal articles.

FAUSTUS   Come, I think hell's a fable.

MEPHASTOPHILIS   Ay, think so still, till experience change thy
mind.

FAUSTUS   Why? think'st thou then that Faustus shall be damned?

130   MEPHASTOPHILIS   Ay, of necessity, for here's the scroll
Wherein thou hast given thy soul to Lucifer.

FAUSTUS   Ay, and body too; but what of that?
Think'st thou that Faustus is so fond° to imagine   *foolish*
That after this life there is any pain?

135   Tush, these are trifles and mere old wives' tales.

MEPHASTOPHILIS   But Faustus, I am an instance to prove the contrary;
For I am damned, and am now in hell.

FAUSTUS   How, now in hell? Nay, and this be hell, I'll willingly be
damned here! What? walking, disputing, etc. . . . . But leaving off

140   this, let me have a wife, the fairest maid in Germany, for I am
wanton and lascivious, and cannot live without a wife.

MEPHASTOPHILIS   How, a wife? I prithee Faustus, talk not of a wife.⁹

FAUSTUS   Nay sweet Mephastophilis, fetch me one, for I will have
one.

145   MEPHASTOPHILIS   Well, thou wilt have one; sit there till I come.
I'll fetch thee a wife in the devil's name.   [*Exit.*]
[*Enter with a* DEVIL *dressed like a woman, with fireworks.*]

MEPHASTOPHILIS   Tell, Faustus, how dost thou like thy wife?

FAUSTUS   A plague on her for a hot whore!

MEPHASTOPHILIS   Tut, Faustus, marriage is but a ceremonial toy;

150   If thou lovest me, think no more of it.
I'll cull thee out the fairest courtesans
And bring them every morning to thy bed:
She whom thine eye shall like, thy heart shall have,
Be she as chaste as was Penelope,

155   As wise as Saba,¹ or as beautiful
As was bright Lucifer before his fall.
Hold, take this book, peruse it thoroughly:
The iterating° of these lines brings gold;   *repeating*
The framing° of this circle on the ground   *drawing*

160   Brings whirlwinds, tempests, thunder and lightning.
Pronounce this thrice devoutly to thyself,
And men in armor shall appear to thee,
Ready to execute what thou desirest.

FAUSTUS   Thanks, Mephastophilis, yet fain would I have a book

165   wherein I might behold all spells and incantations, that I might raise
up spirits when I please.

MEPHASTOPHILIS   Here they are in this book.   [*There turn to them.*]

FAUSTUS   Now would I have a book where I might see all characters
and planets of the heavens, that I might know their motions and

170   dispositions.

MEPHASTOPHILIS   Here they are too.   [*Turn to them.*]

FAUSTUS   Nay, let me have one book more, and then I have done,
wherein I might see all plants, herbs, and trees that grow upon the
earth.

9. Mephastophilis cannot produce a wife for
Faustus because marriage is a sacrament.

1. The queen of Sheba. "Penelope": the wife of
Ulysses, famed for chastity and fidelity.

175　MEPHASTOPHILIS　Here they be.

FAUSTUS　O thou art deceived!

MEPHASTOPHILIS　Tut, I warrant thee.　　　　　　　　[*Turn to them.*]

FAUSTUS　When I behold the heavens, then I repent,
　　And curse thee, wicked Mephastophilis,

180　Because thou hast deprived me of those joys.

MEPHASTOPHILIS　Why Faustus,
　　Think'st thou that heaven is such a glorious thing?
　　I tell thee 'tis not half so fair as thou,
　　Or any man that breathes on earth.

185　FAUSTUS　How prov'st thou that?

MEPHASTOPHILIS　It was made for man, therefore is man more excel-
　　lent.

FAUSTUS　If it were made for man, 'twas made for me:
　　I will renounce this magic, and repent.
　　　　　[*Enter* GOOD ANGEL *and* EVIL ANGEL.]

190　GOOD ANGEL　Faustus, repent, yet° God will pity thee.　　　　　*still*

EVIL ANGEL　Thou art a spirit,° God cannot pity thee.　　*evil spirit, devil*

FAUSTUS　Who buzzeth in mine ears I am a spirit?
　　Be I a devil, yet God may pity me.
　　Ay, God will pity me if I repent.

195　EVIL ANGEL　Ay, but Faustus never shall repent.　　　　[*Exeunt.*]

FAUSTUS　My heart's so hardened[2] I cannot repent!
　　Scarce can I name salvation, faith, or heaven,
　　But fearful echoes thunders in mine ears,
　　"Faustus, thou are damned"; then swords and knives,

200　Poison, guns, halters,° and envenomed steel　　　　*ropes for hanging*
　　Are laid before me to dispatch myself:
　　And long ere this I should have slain myself,
　　Had not sweet pleasure conquered deep despair.
　　Have I not made blind Homer sing to me

205　Of Alexander's[3] love, and Oenon's death?
　　And hath not he that built the walls of Thebes
　　With ravishing sound of his melodious harp,[4]
　　Made music with my Mephastophilis?
　　Why should I die then, or basely despair?

210　I am resolved! Faustus shall ne'er repent.
　　Come, Mephastophilis, let us dispute again,
　　And argue of divine astrology.
　　Tell me, are there many heavens above the moon?
　　Are all celestial bodies but one globe,

215　As is the substance of this centric earth?[5]

MEPHASTOPHILIS　As are the elements, such are the spheres,
　　Mutually folded in each other's orb.
　　And, Faustus, all jointly move upon one axletree
　　Whose termine° is termed the world's wide pole,　　　　*end*

2. Hardness of heart is the desperate spiritual state of the reprobate who will suffer eternal damnation.
3. Alexander is another name for Paris, the lover of Oenone; later he deserted her and abducted Helen, causing the Trojan War. Oenone refused to heal the wounds Paris received in battle, and when he died of them, she killed herself in remorse.
4. The legendary musician Amphion, whose harp caused stones, of themselves, to form the walls of Thebes.
5. Faustus asks whether all the apparently different heavenly bodies form really "one globe" like the earth. Mephastophilis answers that like the elements, which are separate but combined, the heavenly bodies are separate but their spheres are enfolded and they move on one axletree.

220   Nor are the names of Saturn, Mars, or Jupiter
       Feigned, but are erring stars.[6]
       FAUSTUS   But tell me, have they all one motion, both *situ et tempore*?[7]
       MEPHASTOPHILIS   All jointly move from east to west in four-and-
       twenty hours upon the poles of the world, but differ in their motion
225   upon the poles of the zodiac.[8]
       FAUSTUS   Tush, these slender trifles Wagner can decide!
       Hath Mephastophilis no greater skill?
       Who knows not the double motion of the planets?
       The first is finished in a natural day, the second thus: as Saturn in
230   thirty years; Jupiter in twelve; Mars in four; the Sun, Venus, and
       Mercury in a year; the Moon in twenty-eight days. Tush, these are
       freshmen's suppositions. But tell me, hath every sphere a dominion
       or *intelligentia*?[9]
       MEPHASTOPHILIS   Ay.
235   FAUSTUS   How many heavens or spheres are there?
       MEPHASTOPHILIS   Nine: the seven planets, the firmament, and the
       empyreal heaven.[1]
       FAUSTUS   Well, resolve me then in this question: why have we not
       conjunctions, oppositions,[2] aspects, eclipses, all at one time, but in
240   some years we have more, in some less?
       MEPHASTOPHILIS   *Per inaequalem motum respectu totius.*[3]
       FAUSTUS   Well, I am answered. Tell me who made the world?
       MEPHASTOPHILIS   I will not.
       FAUSTUS   Sweet Mephastophilis, tell me.
245   MEPHASTOPHILIS   Move° me not, for I will not tell thee.   *anger*
       FAUSTUS   Villain, have I not bound thee to tell me anything?
       MEPHASTOPHILIS   Ay, that is not against our kingdom; but this is.
       Think thou on hell, Faustus, for thou art damned.
       FAUSTUS   Think, Faustus, upon God, that made the world.
250   MEPHASTOPHILIS   Remember this.   [*Exit.*]
       FAUSTUS   Ay, go accursèd spirit, to ugly hell,
       'Tis thou hast damned distressèd Faustus' soul:
       Is't not too late?
             [*Enter* GOOD ANGEL *and* EVIL.]
       EVIL ANGEL   Too late.
255   GOOD ANGEL   Never too late, if Faustus will repent.
       EVIL ANGEL   If thou repent, devils shall tear thee in pieces.
       GOOD ANGEL   Repent, and they shall never raze° thy skin.   *tear*
             [*Exeunt.*]
       FAUSTUS   Ah Christ my Savior! seek to save
       Distressèd Faustus' soul!
             [*Enter* LUCIFER, BELZEBUB, *and* MEPHASTOPHILIS.]
260   LUCIFER   Christ cannot save thy soul, for he is just.
       There's none but I have interest in the same.

---

6. It is appropriate to give individual names to Saturn, Mars, Jupiter, and the other planets—which are called wandering, or "erring" stars. The fixed stars were in the eighth sphere (the firmament, or crystalline sphere).
7. In position and time.
8. The common axletree on which all the spheres revolve.
9. An angel, or intelligence, thought to be the source of motion in each sphere.
1. The ninth sphere was the immovable empyrean.
2. "Conjunctions": the apparent joinings of two planets. "Oppositions": when two planets are most remote.
3. Because of their unequal velocities within the system.

FAUSTUS   O who art thou that look'st so terrible?

LUCIFER   I am Lucifer, and this is my companion prince in hell.

FAUSTUS   O Faustus, they are come to fetch away thy soul!

265   LUCIFER   We come to tell thee thou dost injure us.
    Thou talk'st of Christ, contrary to thy promise.
    Thou should'st not think of God; think of the devil,
    And his dam[4] too.

FAUSTUS   Nor will I henceforth: pardon me in this,

270   And Faustus vows never to look to heaven,
    Never to name God, or to pray to him,
    To burn his Scriptures, slay his ministers,
    And make my spirits pull his churches down.

LUCIFER   Do so, and we will highly gratify thee. Faustus, we are

275   come from hell to show thee some pastime; sit down, and thou shalt
    see all the Seven Deadly Sins[5] appear in their proper shapes.

FAUSTUS   That sight will be as pleasing unto me as Paradise was to
    Adam, the first day of his creation.

LUCIFER   Talk not of Paradise, nor creation, but mark this show; talk

280   of the devil and nothing else. Come away.
    [*Enter the* SEVEN DEADLY SINS.]
    Now Faustus, examine them of their several names and disposi-
    tions.

FAUSTUS   What art thou, the first?

PRIDE   I am Pride: I disdain to have any parents. I am like to Ovid's

285   flea,[6] I can creep into every corner of a wench: sometimes like a
    periwig, I sit upon her brow; or like a fan of feathers, I kiss her lips.
    Indeed I do—what do I not! But fie, what a scent is here? I'll not
    speak another word, except the ground were perfumed and covered
    with cloth of arras.[7]

290   FAUSTUS   What art thou, the second?

COVETOUSNESS   I am Covetousness, begotten of an old churl in an
    old leathern bag; and might I have my wish, I would desire that this
    house, and all the people in it, were turned to gold, that I might
    lock you up in my good chest. O my sweet gold!

295   FAUSTUS   What art thou, the third?

WRATH   I am Wrath. I had neither father nor mother: I leaped out
    of a lion's mouth when I was scarce half an hour old, and ever since
    I have run up and down the world, with this case of rapiers, wound-
    ing myself when I had nobody to fight withal. I was born in hell—

300   and look to it, for some of you shall be my father.

FAUSTUS   What art thou, the fourth?

ENVY   I am Envy, begotten of a chimney-sweeper and an oyster-wife.
    I cannot read, and therefore wish all books were burnt; I am lean
    with seeing others eat—O that there would come a famine through

305   all the world, that all might die, and I live alone; then thou should'st
    see how fat I would be! But must thou sit and I stand? Come down,
    with a vengeance!

---

4. Mother. "The devil and his dam" was a common colloquial expression.
5. Pride, avarice, lust, anger, gluttony, envy, and sloth, called deadly because they lead to spirtual death. All other sins are said to grow out of them (cf. the procession of the Seven Deadly Sins in

Spenser's *The Faerie Queene* 1.4, stanzas 16–37, pp. 666–71).
6. A salacious medieval poem *Carmen de Pulice* (Song of the Flea) was attributed to Ovid.
7. Arras in Flanders exported fine cloth used for tapestry hangings. "Except": unless.

FAUSTUS   Away, envious rascal! What art thou, the fifth?

GLUTTONY   Who, I sir? I am Gluttony. My parents are all dead, and
310   the devil a penny they have left me but a bare pension, and that is
thirty meals a day and ten bevers[8]—a small trifle to suffice nature.
O, I come of a royal parentage: my grandfather was a gammon[9] of
bacon, my grandmother a hogshead of claret wine; my godfathers
were these: Peter Pickled-Herring, and Martin Martlemas-Beef.[1] O,
315   but my godmother! She was a jolly gentlewoman, and well-beloved
in every good town and city; her name was Mistress Margery March-
Beer.[2] Now, Faustus, thou hast heard all my progeny;[3] wilt thou bid
me to supper?

FAUSTUS   No, I'll see thee hanged; thou wilt eat up all my victuals.

320   GLUTTONY   Then the devil choke thee!

FAUSTUS   Choke thyself, Glutton. What art thou, the sixth?

SLOTH   I am Sloth; I was begotten on a sunny bank, where I have
lain ever since—and you have done me great injury to bring me
from thence. Let me be carried thither again by Gluttony and Lech-
325   ery. I'll not speak another word for a king's ransom.

FAUSTUS   What are you, Mistress Minx, the seventh and last?

LECHERY   Who, I sir? I am one that loves an inch of raw mutton
better than an ell of fried stockfish;[4] and the first letter of my name
begins with Lechery.

330   LUCIFER   Away! To hell, to hell!   [Exeunt the SINS.]
Now Faustus, how dost thou like this?

FAUSTUS   O this feeds my soul!

LUCIFER   Tut, Faustus, in hell is all manner of delight.

FAUSTUS   O might I see hell, and return again, how happy were I
335   then!

LUCIFER   Thou shalt; I will send for thee at midnight. In meantime,
take this book, peruse it thoroughly, and thou shalt turn thyself into
what shape thou wilt.

FAUSTUS   Great thanks, mighty Lucifer; this will I keep as chary[5] as
340   my life.

LUCIFER   Farewell, Faustus; and think on the devil.

FAUSTUS   Farewell, great Lucifer; come, Mephastophilis.
                                                                    [Exeunt OMNES.]

SCENE 6
[Enter ROBIN the ostler[6] with a book in his hand.]

ROBIN   O this is admirable! here I ha' stolen one of Doctor Faustus'
conjuring books, and i'faith I mean to search some circles[7] for my
own use: now will I make all the maidens in our parish dance at my
pleasure stark naked before me, and so by that means I shall see
5   more than ere I felt or saw yet.
                        [Enter RAFE calling ROBIN.]

RAFE   Robin, prithee come away, there's a gentleman tarries to have
his horse, and he would have his things rubbed and made clean.

---

8. Snacks.
9. The lower side of pork, including the leg.
1. Meat, salted to preserve it during the winter,
was prepared around Martinmas (November 11).
2. A rich ale, made in March.
3. Ancestry, lineage.

4. Dried cod. "Mutton": frequently a bawdy term
in Elizabethan English; here, the penis. "Ell": forty-
five inches.
5. Carefully.
6. Hostler, stablehand.
7. Magicians' circles, but with a sexual innuendo.

He keeps such a chafing[8] with my mistress about it, and she has
sent me to look thee out. Prithee, come away.

10 ROBIN Keep out, keep out; or else you are blown up, you are dismembered, Rafe. Keep out, for I am about a roaring[9] piece of work.

RAFE Come, what dost thou with that same book? Thou canst not
read!

ROBIN Yes, my master and mistress shall find that I can read—he
15 for his forehead,[1] she for her private study. She's born to bear with
me,[2] or else my art fails.

RAFE Why Robin, what book is that?

ROBIN What book? Why the most intolerable[3] book for conjuring
that ere was invented by any brimstone devil.

20 RAFE Canst thou conjure with it?

ROBIN I can do all these things easily with it: first, I can make thee
drunk with 'ipocrase[4] at any tavern in Europe for nothing, that's
one of my conjuring works.

RAFE Our master parson says that's nothing.

25 ROBIN True, Rafe! And more, Rafe, if thou hast any mind to Nan
Spit, our kitchen maid, then turn her and wind her to thy own use,
as often as thou wilt, and at midnight.

RAFE O brave Robin! Shall I have Nan Spit, and to mine own use?
On that condition I'll feed thy devil with horsebread as long as he
30 lives, of free cost.[5]

ROBIN No more, sweet Rafe; let's go and make clean our boots which
lie foul upon our hands, and then to our conjuring in the devil's
name. [Exeunt.]

CHORUS 2

[Enter WAGNER solus.]

WAGNER Learned Faustus,
To know the secrets of astronomy
Graven in the book of Jove's high firmament,
Did mount himself to scale Olympus'[6] top.
5 Being seated in a chariot burning bright,
Drawn by the strength of yokèd dragons' necks.
He now is gone to prove cosmography,[7]
And, as I guess, will first arrive at Rome
To see the pope, and manner of his court,
10 And take some part of holy Peter's feast,[8]
That to this day is highly solemnized. [Exit WAGNER.]

SCENE 7

[Enter FAUSTUS and MEPHASTOPHILIS.]

FAUSTUS Having now, my good Mephastophilis,
Passed with delight the stately town of Trier,[9]
Environed round with airy mountain tops,

8. Scolding.
9. Dangerous.
1. That is, Robin intends to give his master
horns—cuckold him.
2. I.e., bear his weight, or bear him a child.
3. Irresistible.
4. Robin's pronunciation of *hippocras,* a spiced

wine.
5. Free of charge. "Horsebread": fodder.
6. The home of the gods in Greek mythology.
7. To test the accuracy of maps.
8. St. Peter's feast is June 29.
9. Treves (in Prussia).

With walls of flint, and deep entrenchèd lakes,°   *moats*
5   Not to be won by any conquering prince;
From Paris next, coasting° the realm of France,   *traversing*
We saw the river Main fall into Rhine,
Whose banks are set with groves of fruitful vines;
Then up to Naples, rich Campania,
10 With buildings fair and gorgeous to the eye,
The streets straight forth, and paved with finest brick,
Quarters the town in four equivalents;
There saw we learned Maro's[1] golden tomb,
The way° he cut, an English mile in length,   *tunnel*
15 Thorough a rock of stone in one night's space.
From thence to Venice, Padua, and the rest,
In midst of which a sumptuous temple° stands   *St. Mark's in Venice*
That threats the stars with her aspiring top.
Thus hitherto hath Faustus spent his time.
20 But tell me now, what resting place is this?
Hast thou, as erst° I did command,   *earlier*
Conducted me within the walls of Rome?
MEPHASTOPHILIS Faustus, I have; and because we will not be unpro-
vided, I have taken up his holiness' privy chamber for our use.
25 FAUSTUS I hope his holiness will bid us welcome.
MEPHASTOPHILIS Tut, 'tis no matter, man, we'll be bold with his
good cheer.
And now, my Faustus, that thou may'st perceive
What Rome containeth to delight thee with,
30 Know that this city stands upon seven hills
That underprop the groundwork of the same;
Just through the midst runs flowing Tiber's stream,
With winding banks, that cut it in two parts;
Over the which four stately bridges lean,
35 That makes safe passage to each part of Rome.
Upon the bridge called Ponte Angelo
Erected is a castle passing strong,[2]
Within whose walls such store of ordinance are
And double cannons, framed of carvèd brass,
40 As match the days within one complete year—
Besides the gates and high pyramides°   *obelisks*
Which Julius Caesar brought from Africa.
FAUSTUS Now by the kingdoms of infernal rule,
Of Styx, Acheron, and the fiery lake
45 Of ever-burning Phlegethon,[3] I swear
That I do long to see the monuments
And situation of bright-splendent Rome.
Come therefore, let's away.
MEPHASTOPHILIS Nay, Faustus, stay. I know you'd fain see the pope,
50 And take some part of holy Peter's feast,
Where thou shalt see a troup of bald-pate friars,
Whose *summum bonum*[4] is in belly-cheer.
FAUSTUS Well, I am content to compass[5] then some sport,

---

1. Virgil's. In medieval legend the Roman poet Virgil was considered a magician whose powers produced a tunnel on the promontory of Posilippo at Naples, near his tomb.
2. Actually the castle is on the bank, not the bridge. "Passing": surpassingly.
3. Classical names for rivers of the underworld.
4. The greatest good; often refers to God.
5. Take part in.

And by their folly make us merriment.
55   Then charm me that I may be invisible, to do what I please unseen
    of any whilst I stay in Rome.
    MEPHASTOPHILIS [*casts a spell on him*].   So Faustus, now do what
    thou wilt, thou shalt not be discerned.
          [*Sound a sennet;*[6] *enter the* POPE *and the* CARDINAL OF LOR-
          RAINE *to the banquet, with* FRIARS *attending.*]
    POPE   My lord of Lorraine, will't please you draw near.
60   FAUSTUS   Fall to; and the devil choke you and[7] you spare.
    POPE   How now, who's that which spake? Friars, look about.
    1 FRIAR   Here's nobody, if it like[8] your holiness.
    POPE   My lord, here is a dainty dish was sent to me from the bishop
    of Milan.
65   FAUSTUS   I thank you, sir.   [*Snatch it.*]
    POPE   How now, who's that which snatched the meat from me? Will
    no man look? My lord, this dish was sent me from the cardinal of
    Florence.
    FAUSTUS   You say true? I'll have't.   [*Snatch it.*]
70   POPE   What, again! My lord, I'll drink to your grace.
    FAUSTUS   I'll pledge your grace.   [*Snatch the cup.*]
    LORRAINE   My lord, it may be some ghost newly crept out of purga-
    tory come to beg a pardon of your holiness.
    POPE   It may be so; friars; prepare a dirge[9] to lay the fury of this ghost.
75   Once again my lord, fall to.   [*The* POPE *crosseth himself.*]
    FAUSTUS   What, are you crossing of your self? Well, use that trick no
    more, I would advise you.
        [*Cross again.*]
    FAUSTUS   Well, there's the second time; aware the third! I give you
    fair warning.
        [*Cross again, and* FAUSTUS *hits him a box of the ear, and they
        all run away.*]
80   FAUSTUS   Come on, Mephastophilis, what shall we do?
    MEPHASTOPHILIS   Nay, I know not; we shall be cursed with bell,
    book, and candle.[1]
    FAUSTUS   How! Bell, book, and candle; candle, book, and bell,
    Forward and backward, to curse Faustus to hell.
85   Anon you shall hear a hog grunt, a calf bleat, and an ass bray,
    Because it is St. Peter's holy day.
        [*Enter all the* FRIARS *to sing the Dirge.*]
    1 FRIAR   Come brethren, let's about our business with good devo-
    tion.
        [*Sing this.*]
    Cursed be he that stole away his holiness' meat from the table.
90   Maledicat Dominus.[2]
    Cursed be he that struck his holiness a blow on the face.
      Maledicat Dominus.
    Cursed be he that took Friar Sandelo a blow on the pate.
      Maledicat Dominus.
95   Cursed be he that disturbeth our holy dirge.
      Maledicat Dominus.

---

6. A set of notes on the trumpet or cornet.
7. If. "Fall to": get on with it.
8. Please.
9. A requiem mass. But what actually follows is a

litany of curses. "Pledge": toast.
1. The traditional paraphernalia for cursing and excommunication.
2. May the Lord curse him.

Cursed be he that took away his holiness' wine.
    Maledicat dominus.
            Et omnes sancti.[3] Amen.
[*Beat the* FRIARS, *and fling fireworks among them, and so Exeunt.*]

SCENE 8

[*Enter* ROBIN *and* RAFE *with a silver goblet.*]

ROBIN   Come, Rafe, did not I tell thee we were forever made by this Doctor Faustus' book? *Ecce signum!*[4] Here's a simple purchase for horsekeepers: our horses shall eat no hay as long as this lasts.
    [*Enter the* VINTNER.]

RAFE   But Robin, here comes the vintner.

5   ROBIN   Hush, I'll gull him supernaturally! Drawer,[5] I hope all is paid; God be with you. Come, Rafe.

VINTNER   Soft, sir, a word with you. I must yet have a goblet paid from you ere you go.

ROBIN   I, a goblet, Rafe? I, a goblet? I scorn you: and you are but a
10   &c.[6] . . . I, a goblet? Search me.

VINTNER   I mean so, sir, with your favor.   [*Searches* ROBIN.]

ROBIN   How say you now?

VINTNER   I must say somewhat to your fellow; you, sir!

RAFE   Me, sir? Me, sir? Search your fill. Now sir, you may be ashamed
15   to burden honest men with a matter of truth.

VINTNER [*searches* RAFE]   Well, t'one of you hath this goblet about you.

ROBIN   You lie, drawer; 'tis afore me. Sirra you, I'll teach ye to impeach honest men: [*to* RAFE] stand by. [*to the* VINTNER] I'll scour
20   you for a goblet—stand aside, you were best—I charge you in the name of Belzebub—look to the goblet, Rafe!

VINTNER   What mean you, sirra?

ROBIN   I'll tell you what I mean: [*he reads*] Sanctobulorum Periphrasticon—nay, I'll tickle you, vintner—look to the goblet, Rafe—*Poly-*
25   *pragmos Belseborams framanto pacostiphos tostis Mephastophilis,*
    &c. . . . [7]
        [*Enter* MEPHASTOPHILIS: *sets squibs*[8] *at their backs: they run about.*]

VINTNER   O nomine Domine![9] What mean'st thou, Robin? Thou hast no goblet.

RAFE   Peccatum peccatorum![1] Here's thy goblet, good vintner.

30   ROBIN   Misericordia pro nobis![2] What shall I do? Good devil, forgive me now, and I'll never rob thy library more.
        [*Enter to them* MEPHASTOPHILIS.]

MEPHASTOPHILIS   Vanish, villains, th'one like an ape, another like a bear, the third an ass, for doing this enterprise.   [*Exit* VINTNER.]
    Monarch of hell, under whose black survey

---

3. And all the saints (also curse him).
4. Behold the proof.
5. Wine-drawer. "Gull": trick.
6. The actor might ad lib abuse at this point.
7. Dog-Latin, as Robin attempts to conjure from Faustus's book.
8. Firecrackers. Evidently Mephastophilis is on

stage only long enough to set off the firecrackers and is not seen by Robin, Rafe, or the Vintner. He then reenters at line 32.
9. In the name of the Lord; the Latin invocations are used in swearing.
1. Sin of sins!
2. Have mercy on us!

35   Great potentates do kneel with awful fear;
     Upon whose altars thousand souls do lie;
     How am I vexèd with these villains' charms!
     From Constantinople am I hither come,
     Only for pleasure of these damnèd slaves.
40 ROBIN   How, from Constantinople? You have had a great journey!
     Will you take sixpence in your purse to pay for your supper, and be
     gone?
     MEPHASTOPHILIS   Well, villains, for your presumption, I transform
     thee into an ape, and thee into a dog; and so begone!   [Exit.]
45 ROBIN   How, into an ape? That's brave: I'll have fine sport with the
     boys; I'll get nuts and apples enow.[3]
     RAFE   And I must be a dog.
     ROBIN   I'faith, thy head will never be out of the potage[4] pot.

                                   [Exeunt.]

CHORUS 3

     [Enter CHORUS.[5]]
    CHORUS   When Faustus had with pleasure ta'en the view
     Of rarest things, and royal courts of kings,
     He stayed his course, and so returnèd home;
     Where such as bare his absence but with grief—
5   I mean his friends and nearest companions—
     Did gratulate his safety with kind words.
     And in their conference of what befell,
     Touching his journey through the world and air,
     They put forth questions of astrology,
10   Which Faustus answered with such learnèd skill,
     As they admired and wondered at his wit.
     Now is his fame spread forth in every land:
     Amongst the rest the emperor is one,
     Carolus the Fifth,[6] at whose palace now
15   Faustus is feasted 'mongst his noblemen.
     What there he did in trial of his art
     I leave untold: your eyes shall see performed.   [Exit.]

SCENE 9

     [Enter EMPEROR, FAUSTUS, and a KNIGHT, with Attendants.]
    EMPEROR   Master Doctor Faustus, I have heard strange report of thy
     knowledge in the black art, how that none in my empire, nor in the
     whole world, can compare with thee for the rare effects of magic.
     They say thou hast a familiar spirit, by whom thou canst accomplish
5   what thou list! This therefore is my request: that thou let me see
     some proof of thy skill, that mine eyes may be witnesses to confirm
     what mine ears have heard reported. And here I swear to thee, by
     the honor of mine imperial crown, that whatever thou dost, thou
     shalt be in no ways prejudiced or endamaged.
10 KNIGHT [aside]   I'faith, he looks much like a conjuror.
    FAUSTUS   My gracious sovereign, though I must confess myself far

---

3. Enough. "Brave": splendid.
4. Porridge.
5. I.e., Wagner.

6. The Holy Roman Emperor Charles V (reigned
1519–1556)

inferior to the report men have published, and nothing answerable
to the honor of your imperial majesty, yet for that love and duty
binds me thereunto, I am content to do whatsoever your majesty
15   shall command me.
EMPEROR   Then Doctor Faustus, mark what I shall say. As I was
sometime solitary set within my closet,[7] sundry thoughts arose
about the honor of mine ancestors—how they had won by prowess
such exploits, got such riches, subdued so many kingdoms, as we
20   that do succeed, or they that shall hereafter possess our throne,
shall (I fear me) never attain to that degree of high renown and
great authority. Amongst which kings is Alexander the Great,[8] chief
spectacle of the world's pre-eminence:
The bright shining of whose glorious acts
25   Lightens the world with his reflecting beams;
As when I hear but motion° made of him,   mention
It grieves my soul I never saw the man.
If therefore thou, by cunning of thine art,
Canst raise this man from hollow vaults below,
30   Where lies entombed this famous conqueror,
And bring with him his beauteous paramour,[9]
Both in their right shapes, gesture, and attire
They used to wear during their time of life,
Thou shalt both satisfy my just desire,
35   And give me cause to praise thee whilst I live.
FAUSTUS   My gracious lord, I am ready to accomplish your request,
so far forth as by art and power of my spirit I am able to perform.
KNIGHT [aside]   I'faith, that's just nothing at all.
FAUSTUS   But, if it like your grace, it is not in my ability to present
40   before your eyes the true substantial bodies of those two deceased
princes, which long since are consumed to dust.
KNIGHT [aside]   Ay, marry,[1] master doctor, now there's a sign of grace
in you, when you will confess the truth.
FAUSTUS   But such spirits as can lively resemble Alexander and his
45   paramour shall appear before your grace, in that manner that they
best lived in, in their most flourishing estate: which I doubt not
shall sufficiently content your imperial majesty.
EMPEROR   Go to, master doctor, let me see them presently.[2]
KNIGHT   Do you hear, master doctor? You bring Alexander and his
50   paramour before the emperor!
FAUSTUS   How then, sir?
KNIGHT   I'faith, that's as true as Diana turned me to a stag.
FAUSTUS   No sir; but when Actaeon died, he left the horns[3] for you!
Mephastophilis, begone!   [Exit MEPHASTOPHILIS.]
55   KNIGHT   Nay, and[4] you go to conjuring I'll be gone. [Exit KNIGHT.]
FAUSTUS   I'll meet with you anon for interrupting me so. Here they
are, my gracious lord.
[Enter MEPHASTOPHILIS with ALEXANDER and his PARAMOUR.]

---

7. Private chamber.
8. The emperor traces his ancestry to the great
world conqueror (356–323 B.C.E.).
9. Probably Roxana, Alexander's wife.
1. To be sure.
2. Immediately.
3. Horns were traditionally a sign of the cuckolded

husband (cf. Scene 6, lines 14–15). "Actaeon": the
hunter of classical legend who happened to see the
goddess Diana bathing. For punishment he was
changed into a stag; he was then chased and killed
by his own hounds.
4. If.

EMPEROR Master doctor, I heard this lady, while she lived, had a
    wart or mole in her neck; how shall I know whether it be so or no?
60 FAUSTUS Your highness may boldly go and see.
        [*The* EMPEROR *examines the lady's neck.*]
    EMPEROR Sure, these are no spirits, but the true substantial bodies
    of those two deceased princes.
        [*Exit* ALEXANDER (*and his* PARAMOUR).]
    FAUSTUS Will't please your highness now to send for the knight that
    was so pleasant with me here of late?
65 EMPEROR One of you call him forth.
        [*Enter the* KNIGHT *with a pair of horns on his head.*]
    EMPEROR How now, sir knight? Why, I had thought thou hadst
    been a bachelor, but now I see thou hast a wife that not only gives
    thee horns but makes thee wear them! Feel on thy head.
    KNIGHT Thou damnèd wretch and execrable dog,
70   Bred in the concave of some monstrous rock,
        How dar'st thou thus abuse a gentleman?
        Villain, I say, undo what thou hast done.
    FAUSTUS O not so fast, sir, there's no haste but good. Are you
    remembered[5] how you crossed me in my conference with the
75 emperor? I think I have met with[6] you for it.
    EMPEROR Good master doctor, at my entreaty release him; he hath
    done penance sufficient.
    FAUSTUS My gracious lord, not so much for the injury he offered me
    here in your presence as to delight you with some mirth, hath Faus-
80 tus worthily requited this injurious knight; which being all I desire,
    I am content to release him of his horns. And, sir knight, hereafter
    speak well of scholars: Mephastophilis, transform him straight.[7]
    Now, my good lord, having done my duty, I humbly take my leave.
    EMPEROR Farewell, master doctor; yet ere you go, expect from me a
85 bounteous reward.
        [*Exit* EMPEROR (*and his* ATTENDANTS).]
    FAUSTUS Now, Mephastophilis, the restless course
        That time doth run with calm and silent foot,
        Shortening my days and thread of vital life,
        Calls for the payment of my latest years;
90   Therefore, sweet Mephastophilis, let us make haste to Wittenberg.
    MEPHASTOPHILIS What, will you go on horseback or on foot?
    FAUSTUS Nay, till I am past this fair and pleasant green, I'll walk on
    foot.

SCENE 10

[*Enter a* HORSE-COURSER.[8]]

HORSE-COURSER I have been all this day seeking one Master Fus-
    tian: 'mass,[9] see where he is! God save you, master doctor.
FAUSTUS What, horse-courser: you are well met.

---

5. Have you forgotten. "No haste but good": a
proverb: no point hurrying, unless it's to good
effect.
6. Been revenged upon.
7. Immediately.

8. Horse trader, traditionally a sharp bargainer or
cheat.
9. By the Mass. "Fustian": the horse-courser's
mispronunciation of Faustus's name.

HORSE-COURSER   Do you hear, sir; I have brought you forty dollars[1]
5   for your horse.
FAUSTUS   I cannot sell him so: if thou lik'st him for fifty, take him.
HORSE-COURSER   Alas sir, I have no more. I pray you speak for me.
MEPHASTOPHILIS   I pray you let him have him; he is an honest fellow,
   and he has a great charge[2]—neither wife nor child.
10   FAUSTUS   Well, come, give me your money; my boy will deliver him
   to you. But I must tell you one thing before you have him: ride him
   not into the water at any hand.
HORSE-COURSER   Why sir, will he not drink of all waters?
FAUSTUS   O yes, he will drink of all waters, but ride him not into the
15   water. Ride him over hedge or ditch, or where thou wilt, but not
   into the water.
HORSE-COURSER   Well sir. Now am I made man forever: I'll not leave
   my horse for forty! If he had but the quality of hey ding ding, hey
   ding ding,[3] I'd make a brave living on him! He has a buttock as slick
20   as an eel. Well, God b'y,[4] sir; your boy will deliver him me. But hark
   ye sir, if my horse be sick, or ill at ease, if I bring his water[5] to you,
   you'll tell me what it is?
      [*Exit* HORSE-COURSER.]
FAUSTUS   Away, you villain! What, dost think I am a horse-doctor?
   What art thou, Faustus, but a man condemned to die?
25   Thy fatal time doth draw to final end.
   Despair doth drive distrust unto my thoughts:
   Confound these passions with a quiet sleep.
   Tush, Christ did call the thief upon the cross;[6]
   Then rest thee, Faustus, quiet in conceit.°   *in mind*
                                          [*Sleep in his chair.*]
      [*Enter* HORSE-COURSER *all wet, crying.*]
30   HORSE-COURSER   Alas, alas, Doctor Fustian, quoth 'a: 'mass, Doctor
   Lopus[7] was never such a doctor! H'as given me a purgation, h'as
   purged me of forty dollars! I shall never see them more. But yet,
   like an ass as I was, I would not be ruled by him; for he bade me I
   should ride him into no water. Now I, thinking my horse had had
35   some rare quality that he would not have had me known of, I, like
   a vent'rous youth, rid him into the deep pond at the town's end. I
   was no sooner in the middle of the pond, but my horse vanished
   away, and I sat upon a bottle[8] of hay, never so near drowning in my
   life! But I'll seek out my doctor, and have my forty dollars again, or
40   I'll make it the dearest[9] horse. O, yonder is his snipper-snapper! Do
   you hear, you hey-pass,[1] where's your master?
MEPHASTOPHILIS   Why, sir, what would you? You cannot speak with
   him.
HORSE-COURSER   But I will speak with him.
45   MEPHASTOPHILIS   Why, he's fast asleep; come some other time.

---

1. Common German coins.
2. Burden.
3. I.e., he wishes his horse were a stallion, not a gelding, so he could put him to stud.
4. Good-bye (contracted from "God be with you").
5. Urine.
6. In Luke 23.39–43 one of the two thieves crucified with Jesus is promised paradise.

7. In February 1594 Roderigo Lopez, the queen's personal physician, was executed for plotting to poison her. Obviously Marlowe, who died in 1593, did not write the line.
8. Bundle.
9. Most expensive.
1. A conjurer's phrase. "Snipper-snapper": insignificant youth, whipper-snapper.

HORSE-COURSER   I'll speak with him now, or I'll break his glass-
windows² about his ears.
MEPHASTOPHILIS   I tell thee, he has not slept this eight nights.
HORSE-COURSER   And he have not slept this eight weeks I'll speak
50   with him.
MEPHASTOPHILIS   See where he is, fast asleep.
HORSE-COURSER   Ay, this is he; God save ye master doctor, master
doctor, master Doctor Fustian, forty dollars, forty dollars for a bottle
of hay.
55   MEPHASTOPHILIS   Why, thou seest he hears thee not.
HORSE-COURSER   So ho ho; so ho ho.³ [halloo in his ear] No, will you
not wake? I'll make you wake ere I go. [pull him by the leg, and pull
it away] Alas, I am undone! What shall I do?
FAUSTUS   O my leg, my leg! Help, Mephastophilis! Call the officers!
60   My leg, my leg!
MEPHASTOPHILIS   Come villain, to the constable.
HORSE-COURSER   O Lord, sir! Let me go, and I'll give you forty dollars
more.
MEPHASTOPHILIS   Where be they?
65   HORSE-COURSER   I have none about me: come to my ostry⁴ and I'll
give them you.
MEPHASTOPHILIS   Begone quickly!
    [HORSE-COURSER runs away.]
FAUSTUS   What, is he gone? Farewell he: Faustus has his leg again,
and the horse-courser—I take it—a bottle of hay for his labor! Well,
70   this trick shall cost him forty dollars more.
    [Enter WAGNER.]
How now, Wagner, what's the news with thee?
WAGNER   Sir, the Duke of Vanholt doth earnestly entreat your company.
FAUSTUS   The Duke of Vanholt! An honorable gentleman, to whom
75   I must be no niggard of my cunning. Come, Mephastophilis, let's
away to him.   [Exeunt.]

SCENE 11

    [FAUSTUS and MEPHASTOPHILIS return to the stage. Enter to
    them the DUKE and the DUCHESS; the DUKE speaks.]
DUKE   Believe me, master doctor, this merriment hath much pleased
me.
FAUSTUS   My gracious Lord, I am glad it contents you so well: but it
may be, madam, you take no delight in this; I have heard that great-
5   bellied women do long for some dainties or other—what is it,
madam? Tell me, and you shall have it.
DUCHESS   Thanks, good master doctor; and for I see your courteous
intent to pleasure me, I will not hide from you the thing my heart
desires. And were it now summer, as it is January and the dead of
10   winter, I would desire no better meat than a dish of ripe grapes.
FAUSTUS   Alas madam, that's nothing! Mephastophilis, begone! [Exit
MEPHASTOPHILIS.] Were it a greater thing than this, so it would

2. Spectacles.   4. Hostelry, inn.
3. The huntsman's cry, when he sights the quarry.

content you, you should have it. [*Enter* MEPHASTOPHILIS *with the grapes.*] Here they be, madam; will't please you taste on them?

15 DUKE Believe me, master doctor, this makes me wonder above the rest: that being in the dead time of winter, and in the month of January, how you should come by these grapes?

FAUSTUS If it like your grace, the year is divided into two circles over the whole world, that when it is here winter with us, in the contrary
20 circle it is summer with them, as in India, Saba,[5] and farther countries in the east; and by means of a swift spirit that I have, I had them brought hither, as ye see. How do you like them, madam; be they good?

DUCHESS Believe me, master doctor, they be the best grapes that ere
25 I tasted in my life before.

FAUSTUS I am glad they content you so, madam.

DUKE Come madam, let us in, where you must well reward this learned man for the great kindness he hath showed to you.

DUCHESS And so I will, my lord; and whilst I live, rest beholding for
30 this courtesy.

FAUSTUS I humbly thank your grace.

DUKE Come, master doctor, follow us, and receive your reward.

[*Exeunt.*]

CHORUS 4

[*Enter* WAGNER *solus.*]
WAGNER I think my master means to die shortly,
For he hath given to me all his goods!
And yet methinks, if that death were near,
He would not banquet, and carouse, and swill
5 Amongst the students, as even now he doth,
Who are at supper with such belly-cheer
As Wagner ne'er beheld in all his life.
See where they come: belike the feast is ended.

[*Exit.*]

SCENE 12

[*Enter* FAUSTUS (*and* MEPHASTOPHILIS), *with two or three* SCHOLARS.]

1 SCHOLAR Master Doctor Faustus, since our conference about fair ladies, which was the beautifulest in all the world, we have determined with ourselves that Helen of Greece was the admirablest lady that ever lived. Therefore, master doctor, if you will do us that favor
5 as to let us see that peerless dame of Greece, whom all the world admires for majesty, we should think ourselves much beholding unto you.

FAUSTUS Gentlemen, for that I know your friendship is unfeigned,
And Faustus' custom is not to deny
10 The just requests of those that wish him well,
You shall behold that peerless dame of Greece,

5. Sheba, Yemen.

No otherways for pomp and majesty
Than when Sir Paris crossed the seas with her
And brought the spoils to rich Dardania.°   *Troy*
15   Be silent then, for danger is in words.
          [*Music sounds, and* HELEN *passeth over the stage.*]
      2 SCHOLAR   Too simple is my wit to tell her praise,
      Whom all the world admires for majesty.
      3 SCHOLAR   No marvel though the angry Greeks pursued
      With ten years' war the rape of such a queen,
20   Whose heavenly beauty passeth all compare.
      1 SCHOLAR   Since we have seen the pride of Nature's works
      And only paragon of excellence,
      Let us depart; and for this glorious deed
      Happy and blest be Faustus evermore.
25 FAUSTUS   Gentlemen farewell; the same I wish to you.
                                              [*Exeunt* SCHOLARS.]
          [*Enter an* OLD MAN.]
      OLD MAN   Ah Doctor Faustus, that I might prevail
      To guide thy steps unto the way of life,
      By which sweet path thou may'st attain the goal
      That shall conduct thee to celestial rest.
30   Break heart, drop blood, and mingle it with tears,
      Tears falling from repentant heaviness
      Of thy most vile and loathsome filthiness,
      The stench whereof corrupts the inward soul
      With such flagitious° crimes of heinous sins,   *villainous*
35   As no commiseration may expel
      But mercy, Faustus, of thy savior sweet,
      Whose blood alone must wash away thy guilt.
      FAUSTUS   Where art thou, Faustus? Wretch, what hast thou done!
      Damned art thou, Faustus, damned; despair and die!
40   Hell calls for right, and with a roaring voice
      Says, "Faustus, come: thine hour is come!"
          [MEPHASTOPHILIS *gives him a dagger.*]
      And Faustus will come to do thee right.
      OLD MAN   Ah stay, good Faustus, stay thy desperate steps!
      I see an angel hovers o'er thy head
45   And with a vial full of precious grace
      Offers to pour the same into thy soul!
      Then call for mercy, and avoid despair.
      FAUSTUS   Ah my sweet friend, I feel thy words
      To comfort my distressed soul;
50   Leave me awhile to ponder on my sins.
      OLD MAN   I go, sweet Faustus; but with heavy cheer,°   *i.e., heavy heart*
      Fearing the ruin of thy hopeless soul.   [*Exit.*]
      FAUSTUS   Accursèd Faustus, where is mercy now?
      I do repent, and yet I do despair:
55   Hell strives with grace for conquest in my breast!
      What shall I do to shun the snares of death?
      MEPHASTOPHILIS   Thou traitor, Faustus: I arrest thy soul
      For disobedience to my sovereign lord.
      Revolt,⁶ or I'll in piecemeal tear thy flesh.

6. Turn back (to your allegiance to Lucifer).

60 FAUSTUS   Sweet Mephastophilis, entreat thy lord
    To pardon my unjust presumptiön;
    And with my blood again I will confirm
    My former vow I made to Lucifer.
    MEPHASTOPHILIS   Do it then quickly, with unfeignèd heart,
65   Lest greater danger do attend thy drift.°   *intent*
    FAUSTUS   Torment, sweet friend, that base and crooked age
    That durst dissuade me from thy Lucifer,
    With greatest torments that our hell affords.
    MEPHASTOPHILIS   His faith is great, I cannot touch his soul,
70   But what I may afflict his body with
    I will attempt—which is but little worth.
    FAUSTUS   One thing, good servant, let me crave of thee,
    To glut the longing of my heart's desire:
    That I might have unto my paramour
75   That heavenly Helen which I saw of late,
    Whose sweet embracings may extinguish clean
    These thoughts that do dissuade me from my vow:
    And keep mine oath I made to Lucifer.
    MEPHASTOPHILIS   Faustus, this, or what else thou shalt desire,
80   Shall be performed in twinkling of an eye.
          [*Enter* HELEN.]
    FAUSTUS   Was this the face that launched a thousand ships,
    And burnt the topless[7] towers of Ilium?°   *Troy*
    Sweet Helen, make me immortal with a kiss:
    Her lips sucks forth my soul, see where it flies!
85   Come Helen, come, give me my soul again.
    Here will I dwell, for heaven be in these lips,
    And all is dross that is not Helena!
          [*Enter* OLD MAN.]
    I will be Paris, and for love of thee,
    Instead of Troy shall Wittenberg be sacked;
90   And I will combat with weak Menelaus,°   *Helen's husband*
    And wear thy colors on my plumèd crest:
    Yea, I will wound Achilles in the heel,[8]
    And then return to Helen for a kiss.
    O thou art fairer than the evening air,
95   Clad in the beauty of a thousand stars,
    Brighter art thou than flaming Jupiter
    When he appeared to hapless Semele;[9]
    More lovely than the monarch of the sky
    In wanton Arethusa's azured arms;[1]
100   And none but thou shalt be my paramour.
          [*Exeunt* (FAUSTUS *and* HELEN).]
    OLD MAN   Accursèd Faustus, miserable man,
    That from thy soul exclud'st the grace of heaven
    And fliest the throne of His tribunal seat!
          [*Enter the* DEVILS.]
    Satan begins to sift me with his pride,[2]

---

7. So high they seemed to have no tops.
8. Achilles could only be wounded in his heel—
where he was shot by Paris.
9. A Theban girl, loved by Jupiter and destroyed
by the fire of his lightning when he appeared to her
in his full splendor.

1. Arethusa was the nymph of a fountain, as well
as the fountain itself; she excited the passion of
the river god Alpheus, who was by some accounts
related to the sun.
2. To test me with his strength.

105 As in this furnace God shall try my faith.
My faith, vile hell, shall triumph over thee!
Ambitious fiends, see how the heavens smiles
At your repulse, and laughs your state° to scorn.   royal power
Hence hell, for hence I fly unto my God.   [Exeunt.]

SCENE 13

[Enter FAUSTUS with the SCHOLARS.]

FAUSTUS   Ah, gentlemen!

1 SCHOLAR   What ails Faustus?

FAUSTUS   Ah, my sweet chamber-fellow, had I lived with thee, then
had I lived still; but now I die eternally. Look, comes he not, comes
5   he not?

2 SCHOLAR   What means Faustus?

3 SCHOLAR   Belike he is grown into some sickness by being over-
solitary.

1 SCHOLAR   If it be so, we'll have physicians to cure him; 'tis but a
10   surfeit:[3] never fear, man.

FAUSTUS   A surfeit of deadly sin, that hath damned both body and
soul.

2 SCHOLAR   Yet Faustus, look up to heaven; remember God's mercies
are infinite.

15   FAUSTUS   But Faustus' offense can ne'er be pardoned! The serpent
that tempted Eve may be saved, but not Faustus. Ah gentlemen,
hear me with patience, and tremble not at my speeches, though my
heart pants and quivers to remember that I have been a student
here these thirty years—O would I had never seen Wittenberg,
20   never read book—and what wonders I have done, all Wittenberg
can witness—yea, all the world; for which Faustus hath lost both
Germany and the world—yea, heaven itself—heaven, the seat of
God, the throne of the blessed, the kingdom of joy; and must remain
in hell forever—hell, ah, hell forever! Sweet friends, what shall
25   become of Faustus, being in hell forever?

3 SCHOLAR   Yet Faustus, call on God.

FAUSTUS   On God, whom Faustus hath abjured? On God, whom
Faustus hath blasphemed? Ah my God—I would weep, but the devil
draws in my tears! gush forth blood, instead of tears—yea, life and
30   soul! O, he stays my tongue! I would lift up my hands, but see, they
hold them, they hold them!

ALL   Who, Faustus?

FAUSTUS   Lucifer and Mephastophilis! Ah gentlemen, I gave them
my soul for my cunning.

35   ALL   God forbid!

FAUSTUS   God forbade it indeed, but Faustus hath done it: for the
vain pleasure of four-and-twenty years hath Faustus lost eternal joy
and felicity. I writ them a bill with mine own blood, the date is
expired, the time will come, and he will fetch me.

40   1 SCHOLAR   Why did not Faustus tell us of this before, that divines
might have prayed for thee?

FAUSTUS   Oft have I thought to have done so, but the devil threatened to tear me in pieces if I named God, to fetch both body and

---

3. Indigestion caused by overeating.

soul, if I once gave ear to divinity; and now 'tis too late. Gentlemen
45   away, lest you perish with me!

    2 SCHOLAR   O what shall we do to save Faustus?

    3 SCHOLAR   God will strengthen me. I will stay with Faustus.

    1 SCHOLAR   Tempt not God, sweet friend, but let us into the next
    room, and there pray for him.

50   FAUSTUS   Ay, pray for me, pray for me; and what noise soever ye hear,
    come not unto me, for nothing can rescue me.

    2 SCHOLAR   Pray thou, and we will pray, that God may have mercy
    upon thee.

    FAUSTUS   Gentlemen, farewell. If I live till morning, I'll visit you; if
55   not, Faustus is gone to hell.

    ALL   Faustus, farewell.   [*Exeunt* SCHOLARS.]

        [*The clock strikes eleven.*]

    FAUSTUS   Ah Faustus,
    Now hast thou but one bare hour to live,
    And then thou must be damned perpetually.
60   Stand still, you ever-moving spheres of heaven,
    That time may cease, and midnight never come.
    Fair Nature's eye, rise, rise again, and make
    Perpetual day, or let this hour be but
    A year, a month, a week, a natural day,
65   That Faustus may repent and save his soul.
    O lente, lente currite noctis equi![4]
    The stars move still, time runs, the clock will strike,
    The devil will come, and Faustus must be damned.
    O I'll leap up to my God! Who pulls me down?
70   See, see where Christ's blood streams in the firmament!
    One drop would save my soul, half a drop: ah my Christ—
    Ah, rend not my heart for naming of my Christ;
    Yet will I call on him—O spare me, Lucifer!
    Where is it now? 'Tis gone: and see where God
75   Stretcheth out his arm, and bends his ireful brows!
    Mountains and hills, come, come and fall on me,
    And hide me from the heavy wrath of God.
    No, no?
    Then will I headlong run into the earth:
80   Earth, gape! O no, it will not harbor me.
    You stars that reigned at my nativity,
    Whose influence hath allotted death and hell,
    Now draw up Faustus like a foggy mist
    Into the entrails of yon laboring cloud,
85   That when you vomit forth into the air
    My limbs may issue from your smoky mouths,
    So that my soul may but ascend to heaven.[5]
        [*The watch strikes.*]
    Ah, half the hour is past: 'twill all be past anon.
    O God, if thou wilt not have mercy on my soul,
90   Yet for Christ's sake, whose blood hath ransomed me,
    Impose some end to my incessant pain:

---

4. Slowly, slowly run, O horses of the night; adapted from a line in Ovid's *Amores*.
5. Faustus wants to be drawn up into a cloud, which would compact his body into a thunderstone so that his soul, thus purified, might ascend to heaven.

Let Faustus live in hell a thousand years,
A hundred thousand, and at last be saved.
O no end is limited to damnèd souls!
95 Why wert thou not a creature wanting soul?
Or why is this immortal that thou hast?
Ah, Pythagoras' *metempsychosis*[6]—were that true,
This soul should fly from me, and I be changed
Unto some brutish beast:
100 All beasts are happy, for when they die,
Their souls are soon dissolved in elements;
But mine must live still° to be plagued in hell.   *always*
Cursed be the parents that engendered me:
No, Faustus, curse thy self, curse Lucifer,
105 That hath deprived thee of the joys of heaven.
                        [*The clock striketh twelve.*]
O it strikes, it strikes! Now body, turn to air,
Or Lucifer will bear thee quick° to hell.   *alive*
                        [*Thunder and lightning.*]
O soul, be changed into little water drops,
And fall into the ocean, ne'er be found.
110 My God, my God, look not so fierce on me!
                        [*Enter* DEVILS.]
Adders and serpents, let me breathe awhile!
Ugly hell gape not! Come not, Lucifer!
I'll burn my books—ah, Mephastophilis!
                        [*Exeunt with him.*]

Epilogue

        [*Enter* CHORUS.]
Cut is the branch that might have grown full straight,
And burnèd is Apollo's laurel bough,[7]
That sometime grew within this learnèd man.
Faustus is gone! Regard his hellish fall,
5 Whose fiendful fortune° may exhort the wise   *devilish fate*
Only to wonder at[8] unlawful things:
Whose deepness doth entice such forward wits
To practice more than heavenly power permits.   [*Exit.*]

        Terminat hora diem, terminat author opus.[9]

                                        1604, 1616

The Two Texts of *Doctor Faustus*

The following excerpts enable readers to compare a sample passage (from Scene 12) of the A text (1604) with the corresponding passage of the B text (1616). (On the two texts, see above, p. 991.) Here the differences in tone and content in the two versions of the Old Man's speech may signal different attitudes toward the finality of Faustus's damnation.

6. Pythagoras's doctrine of the transmigration of souls.
7. The laurel crown of Apollo symbolizes (among other things) learning and wisdom.

8. Be content simply to observe with awe.
9. The hour ends the day, the author ends his work; this motto was probably added by the printer.

Doctor Faustus, A Text

[*Enter an* OLD MAN.]

OLD MAN   Ah Doctor Faustus, that I might prevail
    To guide thy steps unto the way of life,
    By which sweet path thou may'st attain the goal
    That shall conduct thee to celestial rest.
5   Break heart, drop blood, and mingle it with tears,
    Tears falling from repentant heaviness
    Of thy most vile and loathsome filthiness,
    The stench whereof corrupts the inward soul
    With such flagitious° crimes of heinous sins   *villainous*
10   As no commiseration may expel
    But mercy, Faustus, of thy savior sweet,
    Whose blood alone must wash away thy guilt.
FAUSTUS   Where art thou, Faustus? Wretch, what hast thou done!
    Damned art thou, Faustus, damned; despair and die!
15   Hell calls for right, and with a roaring voice
    Says, "Faustus, come: thine hour is come!"
    [MEPHASTOPHILIS *gives him a dagger.*]
    And Faustus will come to do thee right.
OLD MAN   Ah stay, good Faustus, stay thy desperate steps!
    I see an angel hovers o'er thy head
20   And with a vial full of precious grace
    Offers to pour the same into thy soul!
    Then call for mercy, and avoid despair.
FAUSTUS   Ah my sweet friend, I feel thy words
    To comfort my distressed soul;
25   Leave me awhile to ponder on my sins.
OLD MAN   I go, sweet Faustus; but with heavy cheer,°   *i.e., heavy heart*
    Fearing the ruin of thy hopeless soul.   [*Exit.*]
FAUSTUS   Accursèd Faustus, where is mercy now?
    I do repent, and yet I do despair:
30   Hell strives with grace for conquest in my breast!
    What shall I do to shun the snares of death?
MEPHASTOPHILIS   Thou traitor, Faustus: I arrest thy soul
    For disobedience to my sovereign lord.
    Revolt,[1] or I'll in piecemeal tear thy flesh.

---

1. Turn back (to your allegiance to Lucifer).

Doctor Faustus, B Text

[*Enter an* OLD MAN.]

OLD MAN   O gentle Faustus, leave this damnèd art,
This magic that will charm thy soul to hell
And quite bereave thee of salvation.
Though thou hast now offended like a man,
5   Do not persèver° in it like a devil.   *persevere*
Yet, yet, thou hast an amiable° soul,   *worthy of (divine) love*
If sin by custom grow not into nature.
Then, Faustus, will repentance come too late;
Then thou art banished from the sight of heaven.
10   No mortal can express the pains of hell.
It may be this my exhortation
Seems harsh and all unpleasant; let it not,
For, gentle son, I speak it not in wrath
Or envy of° thee, but in tender love   *ill will toward*
15   And pity of thy future misery.
And so have hope that this my kind rebuke,
Checking° thy body, may amend thy soul.   *rebuking*
FAUSTUS   Where art thou, Faustus? Wretch, what hast thou done?
Hell claims his right, and with a roaring voice
20   Says, "Faustus, come; thine hour is almost come";
And Faustus now will come to do thee right.
[MEPHOSTOPHILIS *gives him a dagger.*]
OLD MAN   O stay, good Faustus, stay thy desperate steps.
I see an angel hover o'er thy head,
And with a vial full of precious grace
25   Offers to pour the same into thy soul.
Then call for mercy and avoid despair.
FAUSTUS   O friend, I feel thy words
To comfort my distressèd soul.
Leave me a while to ponder on my sins.
30   OLD MAN   Faustus, I leave thee, but with grief of heart,
Fearing the enemy of thy hapless soul.   [*Exit.*]
FAUSTUS   Accursèd Faustus, wretch, what hast thou done?
I do repent, and yet I do despair.
Hell strives with grace for conquest in my breast.
35   What shall I do to shun the snares of death?
MEPHOSTOPHILIS   Thou traitor, Faustus, I arrest thy soul
For disobedience to my sovereign lord.
Revolt,[1] or I'll in piecemeal tear they flesh.

---

1. Turn back (to your allegiance to Lucifer).

WILLIAM SHAKESPEARE
1564–1616

William Shakespeare was born in the small market town of Stratford-on-Avon in April (probably April 23) 1564. His father, a successful glovemaker, landowner, money-lender, and dealer in agricultural commodities, was elected to several important posts in local government but later suffered financial and social reverses, possibly as a result of adherence to the Catholic faith. Shakespeare almost certainly attended the free Stratford grammar school, where he could have acquired a reasonably impressive education, including a respectable knowledge of Latin, but he did not proceed to Oxford or Cambridge. There are legends about Shakespeare's youth but no docu-mented facts. The first record we have of his life after his christening is that of his marriage in 1582, at age eighteen, to Anne Hathaway, eight years his senior. A daugh-ter, Susanna, was born six months later, in 1583, and twins, Hamnet and Judith, in 1585. We possess no information about his activities for the next seven years, but by 1592 he was in London as an actor and apparently already well known as a playwright, for a rival dramatist, Robert Greene, refers to him resentfully in *A Groatsworth of Wit* as "an upstart crow, beautified with our feathers."

At this time, there were several companies of professional actors in London and in the provinces. What connection Shakespeare had with one or more of them before 1592 is conjectural, but we do know of his long and fruitful connection with the most successful troupe, the Lord Chamberlain's Men, who later, when James I came to the throne, became the King's Men. Shakespeare not only acted with this company but eventually became a leading shareholder and the principal playwright. Then as now, making a living in the professional theater was not easy: competition among the repertoire companies was stiff, civic officials and religious moralists regarded play-acting as a sinful, time-wasting nuisance and tried to ban it altogether, government officials exercised censorship over the contents of the plays, and periodic outbreaks of bubonic plague led to temporary closing of the London theaters. But Shakespeare's company, which included some of the most famous actors of the day, nonetheless thrived and in 1599 began to perform in the Globe, a fine, open-air theater that the company built for itself on the south bank of the Thames. The company also per-formed frequently at court and, after 1608, at Blackfriars, an indoor London theater. Already by 1597 Shakespeare had so prospered that he was able to purchase New Place, a handsome house in Stratford; he could now call himself a gentleman, as his father had (probably with the financial assistance of his successful playwright son) been granted a coat of arms the previous year.

Shakespeare himself evidently had no interest in preserving for posterity the sum of his writings, let alone in clarifying the chronology of his works or in specifying which plays he wrote alone and which with collaborators. He wrote plays for perfor-mance by his company, and his scripts existed in his own handwritten manuscripts or in scribal copies, in playhouse prompt books, and probably in pirated texts based on shorthand reports of a performance or on reconstructions from memory by an actor or spectator. None of these manuscript versions has survived. Eighteen of his plays were published during his lifetime in the small-format, inexpensive books called quartos; to these were added eighteen other plays, never before printed, in the large, expensive folio volume of *Mr. William Shakespeares Comedies, Histories, & Tragedies* (1623), published seven years after his death. This First Folio, edited by two of his friends and fellow actors, John Heminges and Henry Condell, is organized by genre and makes no attempt to establish a chronology. We do not know how long a time would normally have elapsed between the writing of a play and its first per-formance, nor, with a very few exceptions, do we know with any certainty the month or even the year of the first performance of Shakespeare's plays. But scholars have gradually assembled a considerable archive of evidence, both external and internal, for dating the composition of the plays.

Shakespeare began his career, probably in the early 1590s, by writing both comedies and history plays. The earliest of these histories, generally based on the accounts of English kings written by Raphael Holinshed and other sixteenth-century chroniclers, seem theatrically vital but crude, as does an early attempt at tragedy, *Titus Andronicus*. But Shakespeare very quickly moved on to create, in *Richard III* (ca. 1592), a brilliantly conceived central character and to display a dazzling command of histrionic rhetoric and an overarching moral vision of English history. In the later 1590s he wrote a sequence of profoundly searching and ambitious history plays— *Richard II*, the first and second parts of *Henry IV*, and *Henry V*—which together explore the death throes of feudal England and the birth of the modern nation-state ruled by a charismatic monarch.

Shakespeare's first comedies show even fewer signs of an apprenticeship. *The Comedy of Errors*, one of his early efforts in this genre, already displays a rare command of the resources of comedy—mistaken identity, madcap confusion, and the threat of disaster, giving way in the end to reconciliation, recovery, and love. Successful as are these early histories and comedies, and indicative of an extraordinary theatrical talent, Shakespeare's achievement only a few years later would still have been all but impossible to foresee. Starting with *A Midsummer Night's Dream* (ca. 1595), he wrote an unprecedented succession of romantic comedies—*The Merchant of Venice, The Merry Wives of Windsor, Much Ado About Nothing, As You Like It*, and *Twelfth Night* (ca. 1601)—whose poetic richness and emotional complexity remain unmatched.

In the same year that Shakespeare wrote *Twelfth Night*, often regarded as the greatest of his comedies, he also probably wrote *Hamlet*, initiating an outpouring of great tragic dramas: *Othello, King Lear, Macbeth, Antony and Cleopatra*, and *Coriolanus*. These plays, written from 1601 to 1607, seem to mark a major shift in sensibility, an existential and metaphysical darkening that many readers think must have originated in a deep personal anguish, perhaps caused by the death of his father, John, in 1601.

Whatever the truth of these speculations—and we have no direct testimony either to support or to undermine them—there appears to have occurred in the same period a shift as well in Shakespeare's comic sensibility. The comedies written between 1601 and 1604, *Troilus and Cressida, All's Well That Ends Well*, and *Measure for Measure*, are sufficiently different from the earlier comedies—more biting in tone, more uneasy with comic conventions, more ruthlessly questioning of the values of the characters and the resolutions of the plots—to have led some modern scholars to classify them as "problem plays" or "dark comedies." Another group of plays, among the last that Shakespeare wrote, similarly constitutes a distinct category not recognized by the editors of the First Folio. *Pericles, Cymbeline, The Winter's Tale*, and *The Tempest*, written between 1608 and 1611, when Shakespeare had developed a remarkably fluid, dreamlike sense of plot and a poetic style that could veer, apparently effortlessly, from the tortured to the ineffably sweet, are now commonly known as the "romances." These plays share an interest in the moral and emotional life less of the adolescents who dominate the earlier comedies than of their parents. The "romances" are deeply concerned with patterns of loss and recovery, suffering and redemption, despair and renewal. They have seemed to many critics to constitute a self-conscious conclusion to a career that opened with histories and comedies and passed through the dark and tormented tragedies. Shakespeare evidently wrote the last of his plays in Stratford, where he retired about 1610. He died in 1616, shortly after the marriage festivities for his daughter Judith. His best epitaph is a famous line from a poem that his friend and rival Ben Jonson wrote in the First Folio: "He was not of an age, but for all time!"

Sonnets   In Elizabethan England aristocratic patronage, with the money, protection and prestige it alone could provide, was probably a professional writer's most important asset. This patronage, or at least Shakespeare's quest for it, is most visible in his dedication in 1593 and 1594 of his narrative poems, *Venus and Adonis* and *The Rape of Lucrece*, to the young nobleman Henry Wriothesley, earl of Southampton. What return the poet got for his exquisite offerings is unknown. We do know that among wits and gallants the narrative poems won Shakespeare a fine reputation as an immensely stylish and accomplished poet. This reputation was enhanced as well by manuscript circulation of his sonnets, which were mentioned admiringly in print more than ten years before they were published in 1609 (apparently without his personal supervision and perhaps without his consent).

Shakespeare's sonnets are quite unlike the other sonnet sequences of his day, notably in his almost unprecedented choice of a beautiful young man (rather than a lady) as the principal object of praise, love, and idealizing devotion and in his portrait of a dark, sensuous, and sexually promiscuous mistress (rather than the usual chaste and aloof blond beauty). Nor are the moods confined to what the Renaissance thought were those of the despairing Petrarchan lover: they include delight, pride, melancholy, shame, disgust, and fear. Shakespeare's sequence suggests a story, although the details are vague, and there is even doubt whether the sonnets as published are in an order established by the poet himself. Certain motifs are evident: an introductory series (1 to 17) celebrates the beauty of a young man and urges him to marry and beget children who will bear his image. The subsequent long sequence (18 to 126), passionately focused on the same beloved young man, develops as a dominant motif the transience and destructive power of time, countered only by the force of love and the permanence of poetry. The remaining sonnets focus chiefly on the so-called Dark Lady as an alluring but degrading object of desire. Some sonnets (like 144) intimate a love triangle involving the speaker, the male friend, and the woman; others take note of a rival poet (sometimes identified as George Chapman or Christopher Marlowe). The biographical background of the sonnets has inspired a mountain of speculation, but very little of it has any factual support.

Though there are many variations, Shakespeare's most frequent rhyme scheme in the sonnets is *abab cdcd efef gg*. This so-called Shakespearean pattern often (though not always) calls attention to three distinct quatrains (each of which may develop a separate metaphor), followed by a closing couplet that may either confirm or pull sharply against what has gone before. Startling shifts in direction may occur in lines other than the closing ones; consider, for example, the twists and turns in the opening lines of sonnet 138: "When my love swears that she is made of truth, / I do believe her, though I know she lies." Shakespeare's sonnets as a whole are strikingly intense, conveying a sense of high psychological and moral stakes. They are also remarkably dense, written with a daunting energy, concentration, and compression. Often the main idea of the poem may be grasped quickly, but the precise movement of thought and feeling, the links among the shifting images, the syntax, tone, and rhetorical structure prove immensely challenging. These are poems that famously reward rereading.

SONNETS

To the Only Begetter of
These Ensuing Sonnets
Mr. W. H. All Happiness
and That Eternity
Promised
By
Our Ever-Living Poet
Wisheth
the Well-Wishing
Adventurer in
Setting Forth
T. T.[1]

1

From fairest creatures we desire increase,
That thereby beauty's rose might never die,
But as the riper should by time decease,
His tender heir might bear his memory;
5 But thou, contracted[2] to thine own bright eyes,
Feed'st thy light's flame with self-substantial[3] fuel
Making a famine where abundance lies,
Thyself thy foe, to thy sweet self too cruel.
Thou that art now the world's fresh ornament
10 And only[4] herald to the gaudy spring,
Within thine own bud buriest thy content[5]
And, tender churl,[6] mak'st waste in niggarding.°   hoarding
    Pity the world, or else this glutton be,
    To eat the world's due,[7] by the grave and thee.

3

Look in thy glass° and tell the face thou viewest   mirror
Now is the time that face should form another,
Whose fresh repair if now thou not renewest,
Thou dost beguile the world, unbless some mother.

1. This odd dedication bears the initials of the publisher, Thomas Thorpe. The W. H. addressed here may or may not be the male friend addressed in sonnets 1 to 126. Leading candidates for that role are Henry Wriothesley, earl of Southampton, the dedicatee of *Venus and Adonis* (1593) and *The Rape of Lucrece* (1594), and William Herbert, earl of Pembroke, a dedicatee of the First Folio. But there is no hard evidence to support these or other suggested identifications of the male friend or of the so-called Dark Lady; these sonnet personages may or may not have had real-life counterparts.
Since all the sonnets save two were first pub-

lished in 1609, we do not repeat the date after each one. Numbers 138 and 144 were first published in 1599, in a verse miscellany called *The Passionate Pilgrim.*
2. Betrothed, also withdrawn into.
3. Of your own substance.
4. Principal, with overtones of single, solitary.
5. What you contain (potential for fatherhood), also what would content you (marriage and fatherhood).
6. Gentle boor (an oxymoron).
7. I.e., by willfully dying without issue.

5 For where is she so fair whose uneared° womb   *unplowed*
Disdains the tillage of thy husbandry?
Or who is he so fond° will be the tomb   *foolish*
Of his self-love, to stop posterity?
Thou art thy mother's glass, and she in thee
10 Calls back the lovely April of her prime;
So thou through windows of thine age shalt see,
Despite of wrinkles, this thy golden time.
    But if thou live rememb'red not to be,
    Die single, and thine image dies with thee.

12

When I do count the clock that tells the time
And see the brave° day sunk in hideous night,   *splendid*
When I behold the violet past prime
And sable curls all silvered o'er with white,
5 When lofty trees I see barren of leaves,
Which erst° from heat did canopy the herd   *formerly*
And summer's green all girded up in sheaves
Borne on the bier with white and bristly beard:
Then of thy beauty do I question make°   *speculate*
10 That thou among the wastes of time must go,
Since sweets and beauties do themselves forsake,
And die as fast as they see others grow,
    And nothing 'gainst Time's scythe can make defense
    Save breed, to brave[8] him when he takes thee hence.

15

When I consider every thing that grows
Holds° in perfection but a little moment;   *remains*
That this huge stage presenteth naught but shows
Whereon the stars in secret influence comment;[9]
5 When I perceive that men as plants increase,
Cheerèd and checked[1] even by the selfsame sky,
Vaunt[2] in their youthful sap, at height decrease,
And wear their brave state out of memory;[3]
Then the conceit° of this inconstant stay   *conception*
10 Sets you most rich in youth before my sight,
Where wasteful Time debateth[4] with Decay
To change your day of youth to sullied° night,   *soiled, blackened*
    And all in war with Time for love of you,
    As he takes from you, I ingraft[5] you new.

8. Defy. "Breed": offspring.
9. The stars secretly affect human actions. "Shows": (1) appearances, (2) performances.
1. Encouraged and reproached or stopped.
2. Exult, display themselves.

3. Wear their showy splendor out and are forgotten.
4. (1)Fights, (2) joins forces.
5. Renew by grafting, implant beauty again (by my verse).

18

Shall I compare thee to a summer's day?
Thou art more lovely and more temperate:
Rough winds do shake the darling buds of May,
And summer's lease hath all too short a date;
5 Sometime too hot the eye of heaven shines,
And often is his gold complexion dimmed;
And every fair from fair sometime declines,
By chance or nature's changing course untrimmed.[6]
But thy eternal summer shall not fade,
10 Nor lose possession of that fair thou ow'st;°   *ownest*
Nor shall death brag thou wander'st in his shade,
When in eternal lines to time thou grow'st:°   *are grafted*
    So long as men can breathe or eyes can see,
    So long lives this, and this gives life to thee.[7]

19

Devouring Time, blunt thou the lion's paws,
And make the earth devour her own sweet brood;
Pluck the keen teeth from the fierce tiger's jaws,
And burn the long-lived phoenix in her blood;[8]
5 Make glad and sorry seasons as thou fleet'st,
And do whate'er thou wilt, swift-footed Time,
To the wide world and all her fading sweets,
But I forbid thee one most heinous crime:
O carve not with thy hours my love's fair brow,
10 Nor draw no lines there with thine antique[9] pen;
Him in thy course untainted[1] do allow,
For beauty's pattern to succeeding men.
    Yet do thy worst, old Time: despite thy wrong,
    My love shall in my verse ever live young.

[handwritten: Iambic pentameter]
[handwritten: (like a woman)]
[handwritten: his heart is gentel & unchanging (like a man)]
[handwritten: 14 lines]
[handwritten: 4/4/6]

20

[handwritten: a woman stole a good looking mans from him]
A woman's face with Nature's own hand painted[2] *[A]* *[handwritten: quatrains]*
Hast thou, the master mistress of my passion;[3] *[B]* *[handwritten: 8/6 — sestet]*
A woman's gentle heart but not acquainted *[A]* *[handwritten: octave]*
With shifting change as is false women's fashion;[B]
5 An eye more bright than theirs, less false in rolling,°   *roving*

[handwritten: man: good looking in charge of his feelings, w/ a womans heart (shifting quickly)]
[handwritten: women are fickle]

6. Stripped of gay apparel.
7. The boast of immortality for one's verse was a convention going back to the classics. It may be thought to imply not egotism on the part of the poet but faith in the permanence of poetry.
8. In full vigor of life (a hunting term). The phoenix was a mythical bird that lived five hundred years, then died in flames to rise again from its ashes.
9. (1) Old, (2) fantastic.
1. (1) Undefiled, (2) untouched by a weapon (a term from jousting).
2. I.e., not made up with cosmetics.
3. (1) Strong feeling, (2) poem.

women make things more precious.

Gilding the object whereupon it gazeth; D
A man in hue all hues[4] in his controlling, *C he looks like a man he is the ultimate man*
Which steals men's eyes and women's souls amazeth. D
And for a woman wert thou first created, E

10 Till Nature as she wrought thee fell a-doting,[5] F
And by addition me of thee defeated, E *nature makes him a woman, but turns him into a man.*
By adding one thing to my purpose nothing. F *is enfatuated &*
    But since she pricked° thee out for women's pleasure, G *into a man.*
    Mine be thy love, and thy love's use their treasure.[7] G

now that he is a man he isn't in love w/ shakespeare

29

he wants to be someone else to win his lovers affections

When, in disgrace° with Fortune and men's eyes,   *disfavor*
I all alone beweep my outcast state,
And trouble deaf heaven with my bootless° cries,   *futile*
And look upon myself and curse my fate, *he doesn't think there is anything to hope for.*

5 Wishing me like to one more rich in hope,
Featured like him, like him with friends possessed,[8]
Desiring this man's art° and that man's scope,°   *skill / ability*
With what I most enjoy contented least;
Yet in these thoughts myself almost despising,

10 Haply I think on thee, and then my state[9] *you can be happy w/ what you have, but seeing others with more makes you feel shitty if i gave.*
(Like to the lark at break of day arising
From sullen earth) sings hymns at heaven's gate;
    For thy sweet love remembered such wealth brings
he likes who he is & he wouldn't trade places with a king. That then I scorn to change my state with kings.

30

it isn't positions that matter, but the love people share.

When to the sessions[1] of sweet silent thought
I summon up remembrance of things past,
I sigh the lack of many a thing I sought,
And with old woes new wail° my dear time's waste: *bewail anew*

5 Then can I drown an eye (unused to flow)
For precious friends hid in death's dateless° night,   *endless*
And weep afresh love's long since canceled woe,
And moan th' expense° of many a vanished sight: *loss*
Then can I grieve at grievances foregone,°   *former*

10 And heavily from woe to woe tell° o'er   *count*
The sad account of fore-bemoanèd moan,
Which I new pay as if not paid before.
    But if the while I think on thee, dear friend,
    All losses are restored and sorrows end.

---

4. "Hue" probably means appearance or form. In the first edition, "hues" is spelled "Hews," which some have taken as indicating a pun on a proper name. It has also been suggested that "man in" is a copyist's or compositor's misreading of "maiden."
5. (1) Crazy, (2) infatuated.
6. Marked, with obvious sexual pun.

7. (1) Sexual enjoyment, (2) interest (as in usury).
8. I.e., I wish I had one man's looks, another man's friends.
9. Condition, state of mind; but in line 14 there is a pun on *state* meaning chair of state, throne.
1. Sittings of court. "Summon up" (next line) continues the metaphor.

33

Full many a glorious morning have I seen
Flatter the mountain tops with sovereign eye,°   *sunlight*
Kissing with golden face the meadows green,
Gilding pale streams with heavenly alchemy;
5   Anon° permit the basest° clouds to ride   *(but) soon / darkest*
With ugly rack° on his celestial face,   *cloudy mask*
And from the forlorn world his visage hide,
Stealing unseen to west with this disgrace.
Even so my sun one early morn did shine
10 With all triumphant splendor on my brow;
But out, alack,° he was but one hour mine;   *alas*
The region° cloud hath masked him from me now.   *high*
    Yet him for this my love no whit disdaineth:
    Suns of the world may stain° when heaven's sun staineth.   *darken*

35

No more be grieved at that which thou hast done:
Roses have thorns, and silver fountains mud.
Clouds and eclipses stain° both moon and sun,   *dim*
And loathsome canker° lives in sweetest bud.   *rose worm*
5   All men make faults, and even I in this,
Authorizing thy trespass with compare,
Myself corrupting, salving thy amiss,°   *palliating your offense*
Excusing thy sins more than thy sins are;
For to thy sensual fault I bring in sense°—   *reason*
10 Thy adverse party is thy advocate—
And 'gainst myself a lawful plea commence.
Such civil war is in my love and hate,
    That I an accessary needs must be
    To that sweet thief which sourly robs from me.

55

Not marble, nor the gilded monuments
Of princes, shall outlive this powerful rhyme;
But you shall shine more bright in these contents
Than unswept stone, besmeared with sluttish time.²
5   When wasteful war shall statues overturn,
And broils root out the work of masonry,
Nor Mars his° sword nor war's quick fire shall burn   *neither Mars's*
The living record of your memory.
'Gainst death and all-oblivious enmity³

2. I.e., than in a stone tomb or effigy that time   3. The enmity of oblivion, of being forgotten.
wears away and covers with dust.

10   Shall you pace forth; your praise shall still find room
     Even in the eyes of all posterity
     That wear this world out to the ending doom.°   *Judgment Day*
        So, till the judgment that yourself arise,[4]
        You live in this, and dwell in lovers' eyes.

60

     Like as the waves make towards the pebbled shore,
     So do our minutes hasten to their end;
     Each changing place with that which goes before,
     In sequent toil all forwards do contend.[5]
5   Nativity, once in the main° of light,   *broad expanse*
     Crawls to maturity, wherewith being crowned,
     Crooked eclipses 'gainst his glory fight,
     And Time that gave doth now his gift confound.
     Time doth transfix the flourish set on youth
10   And delves the parallels[6] in beauty's brow,
     Feeds on the rarities of nature's truth,
     And nothing stands but for his scythe to mow.
        And yet to times in hope° my verse shall stand,   *future times*
        Praising thy worth, despite his cruel hand.

65

     Since[7] brass, nor stone, nor earth, nor boundless sea,
     But sad mortality o'ersways their power,
     How with this rage° shall beauty hold a plea,   *destructive power*
     Whose action is no stronger than a flower?
5   O how shall summer's honey breath hold out
     Against the wrackful° siege of batt'ring days,   *destructive*
     When rocks impregnable are not so stout,
     Nor gates of steel so strong, but Time decays?
     O fearful meditation! where, alack,
10   Shall Time's best jewel from Time's chest[8] lie hid?
     Or what strong hand can hold his swift foot back?
     Or who his spoil° of beauty can forbid?   *ravaging*
        O none, unless this miracle have might,
        That in black ink my love may still shine bright.

71

     No longer mourn for me when I am dead
     Than you shall hear the surly sullen bell[9]

---

4. Until you rise from the dead on Judgment Day.
5. Toiling and following each other, the waves struggle to press forward.
6. Digs the parallel furrows (wrinkles). "Transfix the flourish": remove the embellishment. To "flourish" is also to blossom.

7. I.e., because there is neither.
8. I.e., from being coffered up by Time.
9. The bell was tolled to announce the death of a member of the parish—one stroke for each year of his or her life.

Give warning to the world that I am fled
From this vile world, with vilest worms to dwell:
5   Nay, if you read this line, remember not
The hand that writ it; for I love you so,
That I in your sweet thoughts would be forgot,
If thinking on me then should make you woe.
Oh, if, I say, you look upon this verse
10   When I perhaps compounded am with clay,
Do not so much as my poor name rehearse,
But let your love even with my life decay;
    Lest the wise world should look into your moan,
    And mock you with me after I am gone.

73 *he is dying*

That time of year thou mayst in me behold
When yellow leaves, or none, or few, do hang   *november: fall/winter*
Upon those boughs which shake against the cold,   *he will die on*
Bare ruined choirs,[1] where late the sweet birds sang.   *so Dec. 31*
5   In me thou seest the twilight of such day   *the birds sing in*
As after sunset fadeth in the west;   *the bare, dangeras*
Which by and by black night doth take away,   *trees*
Death's second self that seals up all in rest.   *sleep is like death.*
In me thou seest the glowing of such fire
10   That on the ashes of his youth doth lie,   *Fire dying down*
As the deathbed whereon it must expire,
Consumed with that which it was nourished by.[2]
    This thou perceiv'st, which makes thy love more strong,
    To love that well, which thou must leave ere long.   *he is going to die & leave the person he loves.*

that he is so close to death, love him more.

74

But be contented; when that fell[3] arrest
Without all bail shall carry me away,
My life hath in this line some interest,[4]
Which for memorial still° with thee shall stay.   *always*
5   When thou reviewest this, thou dost review
The very part was° consecrate to thee.   *i.e., which was*
The earth can have but earth, which is his due;
My spirit is thine, the better part of me.
So then thou hast but lost the dregs of life,
10   The prey of worms, my body being dead,
The coward conquest of a wretch's knife,[5]
Too base of thee to be rememberèd.
    The worth of that is that which it contains,[6]
    And that is this, and this with thee remains.

1. The part of a church where divine service was sung.
2. Choked by the ashes of that which once nourished its flame.
3. Cruel. Hamlet says "this fell sergeant / Death

is strict in his arrest" (5.2.278–79).
4. Share, participation. "In this line": i.e., poetry.
5. Death's weapon (like Time's scythe).
6. I.e., the only value of the body is that it contains the spirit.

87

Farewell: thou art too dear[7] for my possessing,
And like enough thou know'st thy estimate.°   *value*
The charter° of thy worth gives thee releasing;   *deed, contract for property*
My bonds in thee are all determinate.°   *expired*
5 For how do I hold thee but by thy granting,
And for that riches where is my deserving?
The cause of this fair gift in me is wanting,
And so my patent° back again is swerving.   *title*
Thy self thou gav'st, thy own worth then not knowing,
10 Or me, to whom thou gav'st it, else mistaking;
So thy great gift, upon misprision° growing,   *mistake, oversight*
Comes home again, on better judgment making.
    Thus have I had thee as a dream doth flatter,
    In sleep a king, but waking no such matter.

94

They that have power to hurt and will do none,
That do not do the thing they most do show,°   *seem to do*
Who, moving others, are themselves as stone,
Unmovèd, cold, and to temptation slow;
5 They rightly do inherit heaven's graces
And husband nature's riches from expense;[8]
They are the lords and owners of their faces,
Others but stewards of their excellence.
The summer's flower is to the summer sweet,
10 Though to itself it only live and die,
But if that flower with base infection meet,
The basest weed outbraves° his dignity: *surpasses*
    For sweetest things turn sourest by their deeds;
    Lilies that fester smell far worse than weeds.[9]

97

How like a winter hath my absence been
From thee, the pleasure of the fleeting year!
What freezings have I felt, what dark days seen!
What old December's bareness everywhere!
5 And yet this time removed[1] was summer's time,
The teeming autumn, big with rich increase,
Bearing the wanton burthen of the prime,[2]
Like widowed wombs after their lords' decease;

---

7. (1) Expensive, (2) beloved.
8. I.e., they do not squander nature's gifts.
9. This line also appears in *Edward III* (2.1.451), an apocryphal Shakespearean play licensed December 1, 1595.

1. I.e., when I was absent.
2. Spring, which has engendered the lavish crop ("wanton burthen") that autumn is now left to bear.

Yet this abundant issue seemed to me
10 But hope of orphans and unfathered fruit;
For summer and his pleasures wait on thee,
And, thou away, the very birds are mute;
    Or, if they sing, 'tis with so dull a cheer°   *disposition*
    That leaves look pale, dreading the winter's near.

98

From you have I been absent in the spring,
When proud-pied³ April, dressed in all his trim,
Hath put a spirit of youth in everything,
That heavy Saturn° laughed and leapt with him.   *god of melancholy*
5 Yet nor° the lays° of birds, nor the sweet smell   *neither / songs*
Of different flowers in odor and in hue,
Could make me any summer's story tell,
Or from their proud lap pluck them where they grew;
Nor did I wonder at° the lily's white,   *admire*
10 Nor praise the deep vermilion in the rose;
They were but sweet, but figures of delight,
Drawn after you, you pattern of all those.
    Yet seemed it winter still, and, you away,
    As with your shadow I with these did play.

106

When in the chronicle of wasted° time   *past*
I see descriptions of the fairest wights,°   *persons*
And beauty making beautiful old rhyme
In praise of ladies dead and lovely knights,
5 Then, in the blazon⁴ of sweet beauty's best,
Of hand, of foot, of lip, of eye, of brow,
I see their antique pen would have expressed
Even such a beauty as you master now.
So all their praises are but prophecies
10 Of this our time, all you prefiguring;
And, for they looked but with divining eyes,⁵
They had not skill enough your worth to sing:
    For we, which now behold these present days,
    Have eyes to wonder, but lack tongues to praise.

107

Not mine own fears, nor the prophetic soul
Of the wide world dreaming on things to come,⁶

3. Magnificent in many colors.
4. Catalog of excellencies.
5. Because ("for") they were able only ("but") to
foresee prophetically.

6. This sonnet refers to contemporary events and
the prophecies, common in Elizabethan almanacs,
of disaster.

Can yet the lease of my true love control,
Supposed as forfeit to a confinèd doom.[7]
5 The mortal moon hath her eclipse endured,
And the sad augurs mock their own presage;[8]
Incertainties now crown themselves assured,
And peace[9] proclaims olives of endless age.
Now with the drops of this most balmy time
10 My love looks fresh, and death to me subscribes,°   *submits*
Since, spite of him, I'll live in this poor rhyme,
While he insults o'er dull and speechless tribes:
    And thou in this shalt find thy monument,
    When tyrants' crests and tombs of brass are spent.°   *wasted away*

110

Alas, 'tis true I have gone here and there
And made myself a motley° to the view,   *fool, jester*
Gored mine own thoughts, sold cheap what is most dear,
Made old offenses of affections° new.   *passions*
5 Most true it is that I have looked on truth
Askance and strangely;[1] but, by all above,
These blenches° gave my heart another youth,   *turnings aside*
And worse essays[2] proved thee my best of love.
Now all is done, have what shall have no end:
10 Mine appetite I never more will grind°   *whet*
On newer proof,° to try an older friend,   *experiences*
A god in love, to whom I am confined.
    Then give me welcome, next my heaven the best,[3]
    Even to thy pure and most most loving breast.

116

[handwritten margin note: you love someone & except their faults & not try to change them.]

Let me not to the marriage of true minds
Admit impediments;[4] love is not love
Which alters when it alteration finds,
Or bends with the remover to remove:
5 O, no, it is an ever-fixèd mark,[5]   *[handwritten: love doesn't change]*
That looks on tempests and is never shaken;   *[handwritten: love is like the]*
It is the star to every wand'ring bark(ship),   *[handwritten: north star.]*
Whose worth's unknown, although his highth[6] be taken.   *[handwritten: incalculable]*

---

7. I.e., can yet put an end to my love, which I thought doomed to early forfeiture.
8. The "mortal moon" is Queen Elizabeth; her "eclipse" is probably her climacteric year, her sixty-third (thought meaningful because the product of two "significant" numbers, 7 and 9), which ended in September 1596. The sober astrologers ("sad augurs") now ridicule their own predictions ("presage") of catastrophe, because they turned out to be false.
9. Probably the agreement between Henry IV of France and Elizabeth.

1. Obliquely or asquint, and coldly (like a stranger). "Gored" (line 3): wounded, pierced.
2. Trials of worse relationships.
3. I.e., the next best thing to the Christian heaven.
4. From the marriage service: "If any of you know cause or just impediment why these persons should not be joined together . . ."
5. Seamark (cf. *landmark*).
6. The star's value is incalculable, although its "highth" (altitude) may be known and used for practical purposes.

[handwritten: time doesn't matter in love.]

Love's not Time's fool,° though rosy lips and cheeks   *plaything, victim*
10   Within his[7] bending sickle's compass come; *[handwritten: everyone dies.]*
Love alters not with his brief hours and weeks,
But bears it out even to the edge of doom.°   *brink of Judgment Day*
     [handwritten: forever]
   If this be error and upon me proved,
   I never writ, nor no man ever loved.   *[handwritten: If his sonnet isn't true, then he never wrote...]*

126

O thou, my lovely boy, who in thy power
Dost hold Time's fickle glass,[8] his sickle, hour;°   *hourglass*
Who hast by waning grown and therein show'st°   *i.e., in contrast*
Thy lovers withering as thy sweet self grow'st;
5   If Nature (sovereign mistress over wrack°)   *destruction, ruin*
As thou goest onwards still will pluck thee back,
She keeps thee to this purpose, that her skill
May Time disgrace and wretched minutes kill.
Yet fear her, O thou minion° of her pleasure,   *darling, plaything*
10   She may detain, but not still° keep, her treasure!   *always, forever*
Her audit° (though delayed) answered must be,   *accounting*
And her quietus° to render° thee.   *settlement / surrender*

127

In the old age black was not counted fair,[9]
Or, if it were, it bore not beauty's name;
But now is black beauty's successive heir,[1]
And beauty slandered with a bastard shame;°   *declared illegitimate*
5   For since each hand hath put on nature's power,
Fairing the foul with art's false borrowed face,°   *i.e., with cosmetics*
Sweet beauty hath no name, no holy bower,[2]
But is profaned, if not lives in disgrace.
Therefore my mistress' brows are raven black,
10   Her eyes so suited,° and they mourners seem   *i.e., also black*
At° such who, not born fair, no beauty lack,[3]   *for*
Sland'ring creation with a false esteem:
   Yet so they mourn, becoming of° their woe,   *gracing*
   That every tongue says beauty should look so.

128

How oft when thou, my music, music play'st
Upon that blessèd wood[4] whose motion sounds

---

7. Time's (as also in line 11).
8. Mirror, fickle because as the subject ages the mirror reflects a changed image
9. Beautiful, equated with blond hair and coloring. "Old": former. "Black": dark hair and coloring, equated with ugliness.

1. Heir in line of succession.
2. Shrine. The next line suggests that natural (unpainted) beauty is now discredited.
3. I.e., nevertheless possess the appearance of beauty.
4. Keys of the spinet or virginal.

With thy sweet fingers when thou gently sway'st°   *governest*
The wiry concord that mine ear confounds,[5]
5 Do I envy those jacks[6] that nimble leap
To kiss the tender inward of thy hand,
Whilst my poor lips, which should that harvest reap,
At the wood's boldness by thee blushing stand.
To be so tickled they would change their state
10 And situation[7] with those dancing chips,
O'er whom thy fingers walk with gentle gait,
Making dead wood more blessed than living lips.
    Since saucy jacks[8] so happy are in this,
    Give them thy fingers, me thy lips to kiss.

129

Th' expense of spirit in a waste of shame
Is lust in action;[9] and till action, lust
Is perjured, murd'rous, bloody, full of blame,
Savage, extreme, rude,° cruel, not to trust;   *brutal*
5 Enjoyed no sooner but despisèd straight:
Past reason hunted; and no sooner had,
Past reason hated, as a swallowed bait,
On purpose laid to make the taker mad:
Mad in pursuit, and in possession so;
10 Had, having, and in quest to have, extreme;
A bliss in proof[1] and proved, a very° woe;   *true*
Before, a joy proposed; behind, a dream.
    All this the world well knows; yet none knows well
    To shun the heaven that leads men to this hell.

[handwritten annotation: antisonnet (against sonnet convention golden hair, red lips...)]

130

[handwritten annotation: She isn't typically beautiful, which is why his love is great. he loves her for who she is]

My mistress' eyes are nothing like the sun;[2]
Coral is far more red than her lips' red;
If snow be white, why then her breasts are dun;
If hairs be wires, black wires grow on her head.
5 I have seen roses damasked,° red and white,   *variegated*
But no such roses see I in her cheeks;
And in some perfumes is there more delight
Than in the breath that from my mistress reeks.[3]
I love to hear her speak, yet well I know
10 That music hath a far more pleasing sound;

---

5. The harmony from the strings that overcomes my ear with delight.
6. The keys (actually, "jacks" are the plectra that pluck the strings when activated by the keys).
7. Physical location. "State": place in the order of things.
8. With a quibble on the sense "impertinent fellows."
9. The word order here is inverted and slightly obscures the meaning. Lust, when put into action,

expends "spirit" (life, vitality; also semen) in a "waste" (desert; also with a pun on *waist*) of shame.
1. A bliss during the experience.
2. An anti-Petrarchan sonnet. All of the details commonly attributed by other Elizabethan sonneteers to their ladies are here denied to the poet's mistress.
3. Not with our pejorative sense, but simply "emanates."

I grant I never saw a goddess go;°   *walk*
My mistress, when she walks, treads on the ground.
   And yet, by heaven, I think my love as rare°   *admirable, extraordinary*
   As any she belied° with false compare.   *misrepresented*

135

Whoever hath her wish, thou hast thy *Will*,[4]
And *Will* to boot, and *Will* in overplus;
More than enough am I that vex thee still,°   *always*
To thy sweet will making addition thus.
5 Wilt thou, whose will is large and spacious,
Not once vouchsafe° to hide my will in thine?   *consent*
Shall will in others seem right gracious,
And in° my will no fair acceptance shine?   *in the case of*
The sea, all water, yet receives rain still,
10 And in abundance addeth to his store,°   *plenty*
So thou being rich in *Will* add to thy *Will*
One will of mine to make thy large *Will* more.
   Let no unkind, no fair beseechers kill;[5]
   Think all but one, and me in that one *Will*.

138

When my love swears that she is made of truth,
I do believe her, though I know she lies,[6]
That she might think me some untutored youth,
Unlearnèd in the world's false subtleties.
5 Thus vainly thinking that she thinks me young,
Although she knows my days are past the best,[7]
Simply° I credit her false-speaking tongue: *like a simpleton*
On both sides thus is simple truth suppressed.
But wherefore says she not she is unjust?°   *unfaithful*
10 And wherefore say not I that I am old?
Oh, love's best habit[8] is in seeming trust,
And age in love loves not to have years told.°   *counted*
   Therefore I lie with her and she with me,
   And in our faults by lies we flattered be.

144

Two loves I have of comfort and despair,[9]
Which like two spirits do suggest me still:°   *tempt me constantly*

---

4. (1) Wishes, (2) carnal desire, (3) the male and female sexual organs, (4) a lover—Shakespeare?—named Will. This is one of three, possibly four, sonnets punning on the word.
5. I.e., do not kill with unkindness any of your wooers.
6. With the obvious sexual pun (as also in lines 13–14). "Made of truth": (1) is utterly honest, (2)

is faithful.
7. Shakespeare was thirty-five or younger when he wrote this sonnet (it first appeared in *The Passionate Pilgrim*, 1599).
8. Appearance, deportment.
9. I have two beloveds, one bringing me comfort and the other despair.

The better angel is a man right fair,
The worser spirit a woman colored ill.°   *dark*
5   To win me soon to hell, my female evil
Tempteth my better angel from my side,
And would corrupt my saint to be a devil,
Wooing his purity with her foul pride.[1]
And whether that my angel be turned fiend
10 Suspect I may, yet not directly tell;
But being both from me, both to each[2] friend,
I guess one angel in another's hell.[3]
     Yet this shall I ne'er know, but live in doubt,
     Till my bad angel fire my good one out.[4]

146

Poor soul, the center of my sinful earth,
Lord of[5] these rebel powers that thee array,[6]
Why dost thou pine within and suffer dearth,
Painting thy outward walls so costly gay?
5   Why so large cost, having so short a lease,
Dost thou upon thy fading mansion spend?
Shall worms, inheritors of this excess,
Eat up thy charge?[7] Is this thy body's end?
Then, soul, live thou upon thy servant's loss,
10 And let that pine to aggravate thy store;[8]
Buy terms divine in selling hours of dross;[9]
Within be fed, without be rich no more.
     So shalt thou feed on death, that feeds on men,
     And death once dead, there's no more dying then.

147

My love is as a fever, longing still°   *continually*
For that which longer nurseth[1] the disease,
Feeding on that which doth preserve the ill,°   *maintain the illness*
Th' uncertain sickly appetite[2] to please.
5   My reason, the physician to my love,
Angry that his prescriptions are not kept,
Hath left me, and I desperate now approve
Desire is death, which physic did except.[3]
Past cure I am, now reason is past care,[4]

---

1. (1) Vanity, (2) sexuality.
2. Each other. "From": away from.
3. A double entendre.
4. I.e., until she infects him with venereal disease.
5. An emendation. The 1609 edition repeats the last three words of line 1. Other suggestions are "Thrall to," "Starved by," "Pressed by," and leaving the repetition but dropping "that thee" in line 2.
6. Dress out, often used in a military sense.
7. What you have spent so much on.

8. Let "that" (i.e., the body) deteriorate to increase ("aggravate") the soul's riches ("thy store").
9. Refuse, rubbish. "Terms": long periods.
1. (1) Nourishes, (2) takes care of.
2. (1) Desire for food, (2) lust.
3. I.e., I learn by experience that desire, which rejected reason's medicine, is death.
4. I.e., medical care (of me). The line is a version of the proverb "past cure, past care."

10   And frantic mad with evermore unrest;
    My thoughts and my discourse as madmen's are,
    At random from the truth, vainly expressed;[5]
      For I have sworn thee fair, and thought thee bright,
    Who art as black as hell, as dark as night.

Twelfth Night Women did not perform on the English public stage during Shakespeare's lifetime; all the great women's roles in Elizabethan and Jacobean plays, from Juliet and Lady Macbeth to the duchess of Malfi, were written to be performed by trained adolescent boys. These boy actors were evidently extraordinarily skillful, and the audiences were sufficiently immersed in the conventions both of theater and of social life in general to accept gesture, makeup, and above all dress as a convincing representation of femininity. *Twelfth Night, or What You Will*, written for Shakespeare's all-male company, plays brilliantly with these conventions. The comedy depends upon an actor's ability to transform himself, through costume, voice, and gesture, into a young noblewoman, Viola, who transforms herself, through costume, voice, and gesture, into a young man, Cesario. The play's delicious complications follow from the emotional tangles that these transformations engender, unsettling fixed categories of sexual identity and social class and allowing characters to explore emotional territory that a culture officially hostile to same-sex desire and cross-class marriage would ordinarily have ruled out of bounds. In *Twelfth Night* conventional expectations repeatedly give way to a different mode of perceiving the world.

    Shakespeare wrote *Twelfth Night* around 1601. He had already written such comedies as *A Midsummer Night's Dream, Much Ado About Nothing*, and *As You Like It*, with their playful, subtly ironic investigations of the ways in which heterosexual couples are produced out of the murkier crosscurrents of male and female friendships; as interesting, perhaps, he had probably just recently completed *Hamlet*, with its unprecedented exploration of mourning, betrayal, antic humor, and tragic isolation. *Twelfth Night* would prove to be, in the view of many critics, both the most nearly perfect and in some sense the last of the great festive comedies. Shakespeare returned to comedy later in his career but always with more insistent overtones of bitterness, loss, and grief. There are dark notes in *Twelfth Night* as well—the countess Olivia is in mourning for her brother, Viola thinks that her brother too is dead, Antonio believes that he has been betrayed by the man he loves, Duke Orsino threatens to kills Cesario—but these notes are swept up in a giddy, carnivalesque dance of illusion, disguise, folly, and clowning.

    The play's subtitle, *What You Will*, underscores the celebratory spirit associated with Twelfth Night, the Feast of the Epiphany (January 6), that in Elizabethan England marked the culminating night of the traditional Christmas revels. In the time-honored festivities associated with the midwinter season, a rigidly hierarchical social order that ordinarily demanded deference, sobriety, and strict obedience to authority temporarily gave way to raucous rituals of inversion: young boys were crowned for a day as bishops and carried through the streets in mock religious processions, abstemiousness was toppled by bouts of heavy drinking and feasting, and the spirit of parody, folly, and misrule reigned briefly in places normally reserved for stern-faced moralists and sober judges. The fact that these festivities were associated with Christian holidays—the Epiphany marked the visit of the Three Kings to Bethlehem to worship the Christ child—did not altogether obscure the continuities with pagan winter rituals such as the Roman Saturnalia, with its comparably explosive

5. Wide of the mark and senselessly uttered.

release from everyday discipline into a disorderly realm of belly laughter and belly cheer. Puritans emphasized these continuities in launching a fierce attack on the Elizabethan festive calendar and its whole ethos, just as they attacked the theater for what they saw as its links with paganism, idleness, and sexual license. Elizabethan and Jacobean authorities in the church and the state had their own concerns about idleness and subversion, but they generally protected and patronized both festive ritual and theater on the ground that these provided a valuable release from tensions that might otherwise prove dangerous. Sobriety, piety, and discipline were no doubt admirable virtues, but most human beings were not saints. "Dost thou think because thou art virtuous," the drunken Sir Toby asks the censorious steward Malvolio, "there shall be no more cakes and ale?" (2.3.107–08).

Fittingly, the earliest firm record of a performance of *Twelfth Night*, as noted in the diary of John Manningham, was "at our feast" in the Middle Temple (one of London's law schools) in February 1602. Manningham noted cannily the comedy's resemblance to Shakespeare's earlier play on twins, *The Comedy of Errors*, as well as to the Roman playwright Plautus's *Menaechmi* and to an early sixteenth-century Italian comedy, *Gl'Ingannati* (The Deceived). Shakespeare also drew upon an English story, Barnabe Riche's tale of *Apollonius and Silla* in *Riche His Farewell to the Military Profession* (1581), which was in turn based on French and Italian sources. There is, however, little precedent, in Riche or in any of the known sources, for the aspect of *Twelfth Night* that Manningham found particularly memorable and that has continued to delight audiences: the cruel gulling of Malvolio.

Malvolio (in Italian, "ill will") is explicitly linked to those among Shakespeare's contemporaries most hostile to the theater and to such holidays as Twelfth Night: "Sometimes," says the Lady Olivia's gentlewoman Maria, "he is a kind of puritan" (2.3.131). Shakespeare does not hide the cruelty of the treatment to which Malvolio is subjected—"He hath been most notoriously abused" (5.1.374), says Olivia—nor does he shrink from showing the audience other disagreeable qualities in Olivia's kinsman Sir Toby Belch and his companions. But while the close of the comedy seems to embrace these failings in a tolerant, bemused, aristocratic recognition of human folly, it can find no place for Malvolio's blend of puritanism and social-climbing.

Malvolio is scapegoated for indulging in a fantasy that colors several of the key relationships in *Twelfth Night*: the fantasy of winning the favor, and ultimately the hand, of the noble and wealthy aristocrats who reign over the social world of the play. The beautiful heiress Olivia, mistress of a great house, is a glittering prize that lures not only Malvolio but also the foolish Sir Andrew and the elegant, imperious Duke Orsino. In falling in love with the duke's graceful messenger (and, as she thinks she has done, in marrying him), Olivia seems to have made precisely the kind of match that had fueled Malvolio's social-climbing imagination. As it turns out, the match is not between unequals: "Be not amazed," the duke tells her when she realizes that she has married someone she scarcely knows. "Right noble is his blood" (5.1.262). The social order then has not been overturned: as in a carnival, when the disguises are removed, the revelers resume their "proper," socially and sexually approved positions.

Yet there is something irreducibly strange about the marriages with which *Twelfth Night* ends. Sir Toby has married the lady's maid Maria as a reward for devising the plot against Malvolio. Olivia has entered into a "contract of eternal bond of love" (5.1.153) with someone whose actual identity is only revealed to her after the marriage is consummated. The strangeness of the bond between virtual strangers is matched by the strangeness of Orsino's instantaneous decision to marry Cesario—as soon as "he" can become Viola by changing into women's clothes.

Part of the quirky delight of the play's conclusion depends upon the resilient hopefulness of its central character, Viola, a hopefulness that is linked to her improvisational boldness, eloquent tongue, and keen wit. These qualities link her to the fool Feste, who does not have a major part in the comedy's plot, but who occupies a place at its imaginative center. Viola seems to acknowledge this place in paying handsome tribute to Feste's intelligence: "This fellow is wise enough to play the fool, / And to do that well craves a kind of wit" (3.1.59–60). His wit often takes the form of a perverse literalism that slyly calls attention to the play's repeated confounding of such simple binaries as male and female, outside and inside, role and reality. Feste is irresponsible, vulnerable, and dependent, but he also understands, as he teasingly shows Olivia, that it is foolish to bewail forever a loss that cannot be recovered. And he understands that it is important to take such pleasures as life offers and not to wait: "In delay there lies no plenty," he sings, "Then come kiss me, sweet and twenty. / Youth's a stuff will not endure" (2.3.48–50). There is in this wonderful song, as in all of his jests, a current of sadness. Feste knows, as the refrain of the last of his songs puts it, that "the rain it raineth every day" (5.1.387). His counsel is for "present mirth" and "present laughter" (2.3.46). This is, of course, the advice of a fool. But do the Malvolios of the world have anything wiser to suggest?

Twelfth Night, or What You Will

THE PERSONS OF THE PLAY

ORSINO, duke of Illyria
VALENTINE ⎱ attending on Orsino
CURIO ⎰
FIRST OFFICER
SECOND OFFICER
VIOLA, a lady, later disguised as Cesario
A CAPTAIN
SEBASTIAN, her twin brother
ANTONIO, another sea-captain
OLIVIA, a countess
MARIA, her waiting-gentlewoman
SIR TOBY Belch, Olivia's kinsman
SIR ANDREW Aguecheek, companion of Sir Toby
MALVOLIO, Olivia's steward
FABIAN, a member of Olivia's household
FESTE the clown, her jester
A PRIEST
A SERVANT of Olivia
Musicians, sailors, lords, attendants

1.1

Music. Enter ORSINO *Duke of Illyria,* CURIO, *and other lords*

ORSINO   If music be the food of love, play on,
    Give me excess of it that, surfeiting,
    The appetite may sicken and so die.
    That strain again, it had a dying fall.°   *cadence*
5   O, it came o'er my ear like the sweet sound
    That breathes upon a bank of violets,
    Stealing and giving odor. Enough, no more,
    'Tis not so sweet now as it was before.
    [*Music ceases*]

1.1 Location: Illyria, Greek and Roman name for the eastern Adriatic coast; probably not suggesting a real country to Shakespeare's audience.

O spirit of love, how quick and fresh° art thou   *lively and eager*
10 That, notwithstanding thy capacity
Receiveth as the sea,° naught enters there,   *receives without limit*
Of what validity° and pitch° so e'er,   *value/height, excellence*
But falls into abatement° and low price   *lesser value*
Even in a minute! So full of shapes is fancy
15 That it alone is high fantastical.°   *uniquely imaginative*
CURIO   Will you go hunt, my lord?
ORSINO   What, Curio?
CURIO   The hart.
ORSINO   Why so I do, the noblest that I have.[1]
O, when mine eyes did see Olivia first
Methought she purged the air of pestilence;[2]
20 That instant was I turned into a hart,
And my desires, like fell° and cruel hounds,   *savage*
E'er since pursue me.[3]
              Enter VALENTINE
                        How now, what news from her?
VALENTINE   So please my lord, I might not be admitted,
But from her handmaid do return this answer:
25 The element itself till seven years' heat[4]
Shall not behold her face at ample° view,   *full*
But like a cloistress° she will veilèd walk   *nun*
And water once a day her chamber round
With eye-offending brine°—all this to season   *stinging tears*
30 A brother's dead love,[5] which she would keep fresh
And lasting in her sad remembrance.
ORSINO   O, she that hath a heart of that fine° frame   *exquisitely made*
To pay this debt of love but to a brother,
How will she love when the rich golden shaft[6]
35 Hath killed the flock of all affections else°   *other emotions*
That live in her—when liver, brain, and heart,[7]
These sovereign thrones, are all supplied, and filled
Her sweet perfections[8] with one self° king!   *one and the same*
Away before me to sweet beds of flowers.
40 Love-thoughts lie rich when canopied with bowers.
                              Exeunt

1.2

Enter VIOLA, A CAPTAIN, *and sailors*
VIOLA[1]   What country, friends, is this?
CAPTAIN   This is Illyria, lady.
VIOLA   And what should I do in Illyria?
My brother, he is in Elysium.[2]

---

1. Orsino plays on "hart/heart."
2. Plague and other illnesses were thought to be caused by bad air.
3. Alluding to the classical legend of Actaeon, who was turned into a stag and hunted by his own hounds for having seen Diana naked.
4. The sky itself for seven hot summers.
5. I.e., all this to preserve (by the salt of the tears) the love of a dead brother.

6. Of Cupid's golden-tipped arrow, which caused desire.
7. In Elizabethan psychology, the seats of passion, intellect, and feeling.
8. And her sweet perfections have been filled.
1.2 Location: The coast of Illyria.
1. Viola is not named in the dialogue until 5.1.242.
2. The heaven of classical mythology.

Perchance° he is not drowned. What think you sailors?   *perhaps*
5 CAPTAIN It is perchance° that you yourself were saved.   *by chance*
VIOLA O my poor brother!—and so perchance may he be.
CAPTAIN True, madam, and to comfort you with chance,³
     Assure yourself, after our ship did split,
     When you and those poor number saved with you
10   Hung on our driving boat,⁴ I saw your brother,
     Most provident in peril, bind himself—
     Courage and hope both teaching him the practice—
     To a strong mast that lived° upon the sea,   *remained afloat*
     Where, like Arion⁵ on the dolphin's back,
15   I saw him hold acquaintance with the waves
     So long as I could see.
VIOLA [*giving money*] For saying so, there's gold.
     Mine own escape unfoldeth to° my hope,   *encourages*
     Whereto thy speech serves for authority,°   *support*
     The like of him.⁶ Know'st thou this country?
20 CAPTAIN Ay, madam, well, for I was bred and born
     Not three hours' travel from this very place.
VIOLA Who governs here?
CAPTAIN   A noble duke, in nature
     As in name.
VIOLA   What is his name?
CAPTAIN   Orsino.
VIOLA Orsino. I have heard my father name him.
25   He was a bachelor then.
CAPTAIN And so is now, or was so very late,°   *lately*
     For but a month ago I went from hence,
     And then 'twas fresh in murmur°—as, you know,   *newly rumored*
     What great ones do the less will prattle of—
30   That he did seek the love of fair Olivia.
VIOLA What's she?
CAPTAIN A virtuous maid, the daughter of a count
     That died some twelvemonth since, then leaving her
     In the protection of his son, her brother,
35   Who shortly also died, for whose dear love,
     They say, she hath abjured the sight
     And company of men.
VIOLA   O that I served that lady,
     And might not be delivered° to the world   *revealed*
     Till I had made mine own occasion mellow,°   *ripe (to be revealed)*
     What my estate° is.   *social rank*
40 CAPTAIN   That were hard to compass,°   *achieve*
     Because she will admit no kind of suit,°   *petition*
     No, not the Duke's.
VIOLA There is a fair behavior⁷ in thee, captain,
     And though that nature with a beauteous wall

---

3. With what may have happened.
4. The ship's boat. "Driving": being driven by the wind.
5. A legendary Greek musician who, in order to save
himself from being murdered on a voyage, jumped over-

board and was carried to land by a dolphin.
6. I.e., that he too has survived.
7. Outward appearance, conduct.

45   Doth oft close in pollution, yet of thee
        I will believe thou hast a mind that suits
        With this thy fair and outward character.[8]
        I pray thee—and I'll pay thee bounteously—
        Conceal me what I am, and be my aid
50   For such disguise as haply shall become
        The form of my intent.[9] I'll serve this duke.
        Thou shalt present me as an eunuch[1] to him.
        It may be worth thy pains, for I can sing,
        And speak to him in many sorts of music
55   That will allow° me very worth his service.   prove
        What else may hap, to time I will commit.
        Only shape thou thy silence to my wit.°   imagination, plan
CAPTAIN   Be you his eunuch, and your mute[2] I'll be.
        When my tongue blabs, then let mine eyes not see.
60 VIOLA   I thank thee. Lead me on.   *Exeunt*

1.3

Enter SIR TOBY [*Belch*] *and* MARIA

SIR TOBY   What a plague means my niece to take the death
        of her brother thus? I am sure care's an enemy to life.
MARIA   By my troth, Sir Toby, you must come in earlier o'
        nights. Your cousin,[1] my lady, takes great exceptions to
5   your ill hours.
SIR TOBY   Why, let her except, before excepted.[2]
MARIA   Ay, but you must confine yourself within the mod-
        est° limits of order.   moderate
SIR TOBY   Confine? I'll confine myself no finer[3] than I am.
10   These clothes are good enough to drink in, and so be
        these boots too; an° they be not, let them hang themselves   if
        in their own straps.
MARIA   That quaffing and drinking will undo you. I heard
        my lady talk of it yesterday, and of a foolish knight that
15   you brought in one night here to be her wooer.
SIR TOBY   Who, Sir Andrew Aguecheek?
MARIA   Ay, he.
SIR TOBY   He's as tall a man as any's[4] in Illyria.
MARIA   What's that to th' purpose?
20 SIR TOBY   Why, he has three thousand ducats a year.
MARIA   Ay, but he'll have but a year in all these ducats.[5]
        He's a very° fool, and a prodigal.   an absolute

---

8. Appearance (suggesting moral qualities).
9. That perhaps may be fitting to my purpose. "Form": shape.
1. Castrati (hence, "eunuchs") were prized as male sopranos; the disguise would have explained Viola's feminine voice. Viola (or perhaps Shakespeare) seems to have changed plans: she presents herself instead as a young page.
2. In Turkish harems, eunuchs served as guards and were assisted by "mutes" (usually servants whose tongues had been cut out).

1.3 Location: The Countess Olivia's house.
1. Term used generally of kinsfolk.
2. Playing on the legal jargon *exceptis excipiendis*, "with the previous stated exceptions." Sir Toby refuses to take Olivia's displeasure seriously.
3. Suggesting both "a refined manner of dress" and "narrowly" (referring to his girth).
4. Any (man who) is. "Tall": brave; worthy. (Maria takes it in the modern sense of height.)
5. I.e., he'll spend his fortune in a year.

SIR TOBY Fie that you'll say so! He plays o'th' viol-de-
gamboys,[6] and speaks three or four languages word for
25 word without book,° and hath all the good gifts of nature. *from memory*
MARIA He hath indeed, almost natural,[7] for besides that
he's a fool, he's a great quarreller, and but that he hath
the gift° of a coward to allay the gust° he hath in quar- *talent; present/gusto*
relling, 'tis thought among the prudent he would quickly
30 have the gift of a grave.
SIR TOBY By this hand, they are scoundrels and substrac-
tors[8] that say so of him. Who are they?
MARIA They that add, moreover, he's drunk nightly in your
company.
35 SIR TOBY With drinking healths to my niece. I'll drink to
her as long as there is a passage in my throat and drink
in Illyria. He's a coward and a coistrel° that will not drink *horse groom, lout*
to my niece till his brains turn o'th' toe, like a parish top.
What wench, *Castiliano, vulgo,*[9] for here comes Sir
40 Andrew Agueface.
     Enter SIR ANDREW [*Aguecheek*]
SIR ANDREW Sir Toby Belch! How now, Sir Toby Belch?
SIR TOBY Sweet Sir Andrew.
SIR ANDREW [*to* MARIA] Bless you, fair shrew.[1]
MARIA And you too, sir.
45 SIR TOBY Accost, Sir Andrew, accost.[2]
SIR ANDREW What's that?
SIR TOBY My niece's chambermaid.[3]
SIR ANDREW Good Mistress Accost, I desire better
acquaintance.
50 MARIA My name is Mary, sir.
SIR ANDREW Good Mistress Mary Accost.
SIR TOBY You mistake, knight. "Accost" is front° her, board *confront*
her, woo her, assail[4] her.
SIR ANDREW By my troth, I would not undertake[5] her in
55 this company.° Is that the meaning of "accost"? *i.e., the audience*
MARIA Fare you well, gentlemen.
SIR TOBY An thou let part so,[6] Sir Andrew, would thou
mightst never draw sword again.
SIR ANDREW An you part so, mistress, I would I might
60 never draw sword again. Fair lady, do you think you have
fools in hand?° *to deal with*
MARIA Sir, I have not you by th' hand.

SIR ANDREW Marry, but you shall have, and here's my
hand.

65 MARIA [*taking his hand*] Now sir, thought is free.[7] I pray
you, bring your hand to th' buttery-bar,[8] and let it drink.

SIR ANDREW Wherefore, sweetheart? What's your metaphor?

MARIA It's dry,[9] sir.

70 SIR ANDREW Why, I think so. I am not such an ass but I
can keep my hand dry.[1] But what's your jest?

MARIA A dry jest,[2] sir.

SIR ANDREW Are you full of them?

MARIA Ay, sir, I have them at my fingers' ends.[3] Marry,
75 now I let go your hand I am barren.°   Exit   empty of jokes

SIR TOBY O knight, thou lackest a cup of canary.[4] When
did I see thee so put down?[5]

SIR ANDREW Never in your life, I think, unless you see
canary put me down. Methinks sometimes I have no
80 more wit than a Christian° or an ordinary man has; but I   an average man
am a great eater of beef,[6] and I believe that does harm to
my wit.

SIR TOBY No question.

SIR ANDREW An I thought that, I'd forswear it. I'll ride
85 home tomorrow, Sir Toby.

SIR TOBY *Pourquoi*,° my dear knight?   why

SIR ANDREW What is "Pourquoi"? Do, or not do? I would
I had bestowed that time in the tongues[7] that I have in
fencing, dancing, and bear-baiting. O, had I but followed
90 the arts!

SIR TOBY Then hadst thou had an excellent head of hair.

SIR ANDREW Why, would that have mended° my hair?   improved

SIR TOBY Past question, for thou seest it will not curl by
nature.[8]

95 SIR ANDREW But it becomes me well enough, does't not?

SIR TOBY Excellent, it hangs like flax on a distaff,[9] and I
hope to see a housewife[1] take thee between her legs and
spin it off.[2]

SIR ANDREW Faith, I'll home tomorrow, Sir Toby. Your
100 niece will not be seen, or if she be, it's four to one she'll
none of me. The Count himself here hard by woos her.

SIR TOBY She'll none o'th' Count. She'll not match above

7. The customary retort to "Do you think I am a fool?"
8. Ledge on the half-door to a buttery or a wine cellar,
on which drinks were served.
9. Thirsty; but a dry hand was also thought to be a sign
of impotence.
1. Alluding to the proverb "Even fools have enough wit
to come in out of the rain."
2. A stupid joke (referring to Andrew's stupidity); an
ironic quip; a joke about dryness.
3. Always ready; or "by th'hand" (line 62).
4. A sweet wine, like sherry, originally from the Canary
Islands.

5. Defeated in repartee; "put down" with drink.
6. Contemporary medicine held that beef dulled the
intellect.
7. Foreign languages; Toby takes him to mean "curling
tongs."
8. To contrast with Andrew's "arts" (line 90).
9. In spinning, flax would hang in long, thin, yellowish
strings on the "distaff," a pole held between the knees.
1. Housewives spun flax; the pronunciation, "huswife,"
also suggests the meaning "prostitute."
2. Make him bald (as a result of venereal disease).

her degree,° neither in estate,[3] years, nor wit, I have heard   *social rank*
her swear't. Tut, there's life in't,[4] man.

105 SIR ANDREW I'll stay a month longer. I am a fellow o'th'
strangest mind o'th' world. I delight in masques and revels sometimes altogether.

SIR TOBY Art thou good at these kickshawses,[5] knight?

SIR ANDREW As any man in Illyria, whatsoever he be,
110 under the degree of my betters; and yet I will not compare
with an old man.[6]

SIR TOBY What is thy excellence in a galliard,[7] knight?

SIR ANDREW Faith, I can cut a caper.[8]

SIR TOBY And I can cut the mutton to't.

115 SIR ANDREW And I think I have the back-trick[9] simply as
strong as any man in Illyria.

SIR TOBY Wherefore are these things hid? Wherefore have
these gifts a curtain[1] before 'em? Are they like to take
dust, like Mistress Mall's[2] picture? Why dost thou not go
120 to church in a galliard, and come home in a coranto?[3]
My very walk should be a jig. I would not so much as
make water but in a cinquepace.[4] What dost thou mean?
Is it a world to hide virtues in? I did think by the excellent
constitution of thy leg it was formed under the star of a
125 galliard.[5]

SIR ANDREW Ay, 'tis strong, and it does indifferent° well   *moderately*
in a divers-colored stock.° Shall we set about some revels?   *stocking*

SIR TOBY What shall we do else—were we not born under
Taurus?[6]

130 SIR ANDREW Taurus? That's sides and heart.

SIR TOBY No, sir, it is legs and thighs: let me see thee
caper.
[SIR ANDREW *capers*]
Ha, higher! Ha ha, excellent.   *Exeunt*

1.4

Enter VALENTINE, *and* VIOLA [*as Cesario*] *in man's
attire*

VALENTINE If the Duke continue these favors towards you,
Cesario, you are like to be much advanced. He hath
known you but three days, and already you are no
stranger.

5 VIOLA You either fear his humor° or my negligence, that   *moodiness*

---

3. Status, possession.
4. Proverbial: "While there's life, there's hope."
5. Trifles, trivialities (from the French *quelque chose*).
6. Expert (perhaps a backhanded compliment).
7. A lively, complex dance, including the caper.
8. Leap. (Toby puns on the pickled flower buds used in a sauce of mutton.)
9. Probably a dance movement, a kick of the foot behind the body (also suggesting sexual prowess, with later reference to "mutton" as "prostitute").

1. Used to protect paintings from dust.
2. Like 'Moll[y]," "Mall" was a nickname for "Mary."
3. An even more rapid dance than the galliard.
4. Galliard, or, more properly, the steps joining the figures of the dance; punning on "sink," as in "sewer."
5. Astrological influences favorable to dancing.
6. The astrological sign of the bull was usually thought to govern the neck and throat (appropriate to heavy drinkers).
1.4 Location: Orsino's palace.

you call in question the continuance of his love. Is he
inconstant, sir, in his favors?
VALENTINE   No, believe me.
        Enter DUKE, CURIO, *and attendants*
VIOLA   I thank you. Here comes the Count.
10 ORSINO   Who saw Cesario, ho?
VIOLA   On your attendance,° my lord, here.   *waiting at your service*
ORSINO [*to* CURIO *and attendants*]   Stand you a while
        aloof.° [*To* VIOLA] Cesario,   *aside*
Thou know'st no less but all.° I have unclasped   *than everything*
To thee the book even of my secret soul.
15 Therefore, good youth, address thy gait° unto her,   *go*
Be not denied access, stand at her doors,
And tell them there thy fixèd foot shall grow°   *take root*
Till thou have audience.
VIOLA   Sure, my noble lord,
If she be so abandoned to her sorrow
20 As it is spoke, she never will admit me.
ORSINO   Be clamorous, and leap all civil bounds,[1]
Rather than make unprofited° return.   *unsuccessful*
VIOLA   Say I do speak with her, my lord, what then?
ORSINO   O then unfold the passion of my love,
25 Surprise[2] her with discourse of my dear° faith.   *heartfelt*
It shall become thee well to act my woes—
She will attend it better in thy youth
Than in a nuncio's° of more grave aspect.°   *messenger's/appearance*
VIOLA   I think not so, my lord.
ORSINO   Dear lad, believe it;
30 For they shall yet belie thy happy years
That say thou art a man. Diana's lip
Is not more smooth and rubious;° thy small pipe°   *ruby red/voice*
Is as the maiden's organ, shrill and sound,[3]
And all is semblative° a woman's part.   *like*
35 I know thy constellation[4] is right apt
For this affair. [*To* CURIO *and attendants*] Some four or
        five attend him.
All if you will, for I myself am best
When least in company. [*To* VIOLA] Prosper well in this
And thou shalt live as freely as thy lord,
To call his fortunes thine.
40 VIOLA   I'll do my best
To woo your lady—[*aside*] yet a barful strife[5]—
Whoe'er I woo, myself would be his wife.   *Exeunt*

1. All constraints of polite behavior.
2. Capture by unexpected attack.
3. High-pitched and uncracked.

4. Nature and abilities (as supposedly determined by
the stars).
5. An undertaking full of impediments.

1.5

Enter MARIA, *and* [FESTE,[1] *the*] *clown*

MARIA Nay, either tell me where thou hast been or I will
not open my lips so wide as a bristle may enter in° way   by
of thy excuse. My lady will hang thee for thy absence.

FESTE Let her hang me. He that is well hanged in this
5   world needs to fear no colors.[2]

MARIA Make that good.°   explain that

FESTE He shall see none to fear.

MARIA A good lenten[3] answer. I can tell thee where that
saying was born, of "I fear no colors."

10 FESTE Where, good Mistress Mary?

MARIA In the wars,[4] and that may you be bold to say in
your foolery.

FESTE Well, God give them wisdom that have it; and those
that are fools, let them use their talents.[5]

15 MARIA Yet you will be hanged for being so long absent, or
to be turned away[6]—is not that as good as a hanging to
you?

FESTE Many a good hanging prevents a bad marriage;[7] and
for turning away, let summer bear it out.°   make it endurable

20 MARIA You are resolute then?

FESTE Not so neither, but I am resolved on two points.°   matters; laces

MARIA That if one break, the other will hold; or if both
break, your gaskins° fall.   wide breeches

FESTE Apt, in good faith, very apt. Well, go thy way. If Sir
25   Toby would leave drinking thou wert as witty a piece of
Eve's flesh[8] as any in Illyria.

MARIA Peace, you rogue, no more o' that. Here comes my
lady. Make your excuse wisely, you were best.°   [Exit]   you had better

Enter Lady OLIVIA, *with* MALVOLIO [*and attendants*]

FESTE [*aside*] Wit,[9] an't° be thy will, put me into good fool-   if it
30   ing! Those wits that think they have thee do very oft prove
fools, and I that am sure I lack thee may pass for a wise
man. For what says Quinapalus?[1]—"Better a witty fool
than a foolish wit." [*To* OLIVIA] God bless thee, lady.

OLIVIA [*to attendants*] Take the fool away.

35 FESTE Do you not hear, fellows? Take away the lady.

OLIVIA Go to, you're a dry[2] fool. I'll no more of you. Besides, you grow dishonest.°   unreliable

FESTE Two faults, madonna,° that drink and good counsel   my lady

---

1.5 Location: Olivia's house.
1. The name is used only once, at 2.4.11.
2. Proverbial for "fear nothing." "Colors": worldly
deceptions, with a pun on "collars" as "hangman's
noose."
3. Thin or meager (like Lenten fare).
4. "Colors" in line 9 refers to military flags.
5. Alluding to the parable of the talents, Matthew 25.
The comic implication is that a fool should strive to
increase his measure of folly. Since "fool" and "fowl"
had similar pronunciations, there may also be a play on

"talents/talons."
6. Dismissed; also, perhaps, turned off or hanged.
7. Proverbial. "Hanging": execution; sexual prowess.
8. Woman. Feste may imply both that Maria and Toby
would make a good match and that Maria is as witty as
Toby is sober.
9. Intelligence, which is often contrasted with will.
1. Feste frequently invents his own authorities.
2. Dull, but Feste interprets as "thirsty." "Go to": an
expression of impatience.

will amend, for give the dry fool drink, then is the fool
40 not dry; bid the dishonest man mend° himself: if he   *reform*
mend, he is no longer dishonest; if he cannot, let the
botcher° mend him. Anything that's mended is but   *tailor, cobbler*
patched. Virtue that transgresses is but patched with sin,
and sin that amends is but patched with virtue. If that
45 this simple syllogism will serve, so. If it will not, what
remedy? As there is no true cuckold but calamity, so
beauty's a flower.[3] The lady bade take away the fool,
therefore I say again, take her away.

OLIVIA   Sir, I bade them take away you.

50 FESTE   Misprision[4] in the highest degree! Lady, "*Cucullus
non facit monachum*"[5]—that's as much to say as I wear
not motley[6] in my brain. Good madonna, give me leave
to prove you a fool.

OLIVIA   Can you do it?

55 FESTE   Dexteriously,° good madonna.   *dexterously*

OLIVIA   Make your proof.

FESTE   I must catechize[7] you for it, madonna. Good my
mouse of virtue,° answer me.   *my good virtuous mouse*

OLIVIA   Well, sir, for want of other idleness° I'll bide° your   *pastime / await*
60 proof.

FESTE   Good madonna, why mournest thou?

OLIVIA   Good fool, for my brother's death.

FESTE   I think his soul is in hell, madonna.

OLIVIA   I know his soul is in heaven, fool.

65 FESTE   The more fool, madonna, to mourn for your
brother's soul, being in heaven. Take away the fool, gentlemen.

OLIVIA   What think you of this fool, Malvolio? Doth he not
mend?[8]

70 MALVOLIO   Yes, and shall do till the pangs of death shake
him. Infirmity,° that decays the wise, doth ever make the   *(old) age*
better fool.[9]

FESTE   God send you, sir, a speedy infirmity for the better
increasing your folly. Sir Toby will be sworn that I am no
75 fox, but he will not pass his word for twopence that you
are no fool.

OLIVIA   How say you to that, Malvolio?

MALVOLIO   I marvel your ladyship takes delight in such a
barren rascal. I saw him put down° the other day with an   *defeated in repartee*
80 ordinary fool that has no more brain than a stone. Look
you now, he's out of his guard° already. Unless you laugh   *defenseless*
and minister occasion[1] to him, he is gagged. I protest I

---

3. In taking her vow (1.2.36–37), Olivia has wedded
herself to calamity but must be unfaithful, or let pass
her moment of beauty.
4. Misapprehension; wrongful arrest.
5. The cowl does not make the monk (a Latin proverb).
6. The multicolored costume of a fool.

7. Question (as in catechism, which tests the orthodoxy of belief).
8. Improve, but Malvolio takes "mend" to mean "grow
more foolish."
9. Make the fool more foolish.
1. And give opportunity.

take these wise men that crow so at these set° kind of *artificial*
fools no better than the fools' zanies.° *"straight men"*
85   OLIVIA   O, you are sick of self-love, Malvolio, and taste
with a distempered² appetite. To be generous, guiltless,
and of free° disposition is to take those things for bird- *magnanimous*
bolts³ that you deem cannon bullets. There is no slander
in an allowed fool, though he do nothing but rail; nor no
90   railing in a known discreet man, though he do nothing
but reprove.
FESTE   Now Mercury indue thee with leasing,⁴ for thou
speakest well of fools.
        Enter MARIA
MARIA   Madam, there is at the gate a young gentleman
95   much desires to speak with you.
OLIVIA   From the Count Orsino, is it?
MARIA   I know not, madam. 'Tis a fair young man, and well
attended.
OLIVIA   Who of my people hold him in delay?
100 MARIA   Sir Toby, madam, your kinsman.
OLIVIA   Fetch him off, I pray you, he speaks nothing but
madman.° Fie on him. Go you, Malvolio. If it be a suit *madman's talk*
from the Count, I am sick, or not at home—what you
will to dismiss it.   *Exit* MALVOLIO
105 Now you see, sir, how your fooling grows old,° and people *stale*
dislike it.
FESTE   Thou hast spoke for us, madonna, as if thy eldest
son should be a fool, whose skull Jove cram with brains,
for—here he comes—
        Enter SIR TOBY
110 one of thy kin has a most weak *pia mater.*⁵
OLIVIA   By mine honor, half-drunk. What is he at the gate,
cousin?° *kinsman*
SIR TOBY   A gentleman.
OLIVIA   A gentleman? What gentleman?
115 SIR TOBY   'Tis a gentleman here. [*He belches*] A plague o'
these pickle herring! [*To* FESTE] How now, sot?° *fool, drunkard*
FESTE   Good Sir Toby.
OLIVIA   Cousin, cousin, how have you come so early by this
lethargy?
120 SIR TOBY   Lechery? I defy lechery. There's one° at the gate. *someone*
OLIVIA   Ay, marry, what is he?
SIR TOBY   Let him be the devil an° he will, I care not. Give *if*
me faith,⁶ say I. Well, it's all one.° *Exit* *it doesn't matter*
OLIVIA   What's a drunken man like, fool?
125 FESTE   Like a drowned man, a fool, and a madman—one

2. Unbalanced, sick.   the talent of tactful lying.
3. Blunt arrows for shooting birds.   5. Brain; or literally, the membrane enclosing it.
4. May Mercury, the god of deception, endow you with   6. To defy the devil by faith alone.

draught above heat[7] makes him a fool, the second mads
him, and a third drowns him.

OLIVIA   Go thou and seek the coroner, and let him sit o'°   *hold an inquest for*
my coz,° for he's in the third degree of drink, he's   *cousin, uncle*
130 drowned. Go look after him.

FESTE   He is but mad yet, madonna, and the fool shall look
to the madman.   *[Exit]*
      Enter MALVOLIO

MALVOLIO   Madam, yon young fellow swears he will speak
with you. I told him you were sick—he takes on him to
135 understand so much, and therefore° comes to speak with   *for that very reason*
you. I told him you were asleep—he seems to have a
foreknowledge of that too, and therefore comes to speak
with you. What is to be said to him, lady? He's fortified
against any denial.

140 OLIVIA   Tell him he shall not speak with me.

MALVOLIO   He's been told so, and he says he'll stand at
your door like a sheriff's post,[8] and be the supporter to a
bench, but he'll speak with you.

OLIVIA   What kind o' man is he?

145 MALVOLIO   Why, of mankind.°   *like any other*

OLIVIA   What manner of man?

MALVOLIO   Of very ill manner: he'll speak with you, will
you or no.

OLIVIA   Of what personage° and years is he?   *appearance*

150 MALVOLIO   Not yet old enough for a man, nor young
enough for a boy; as a squash[9] is before 'tis a peascod, or
a codling° when 'tis almost an apple. 'Tis with him in   *an unripe apple*
standing water° between boy and man. He is very well-   *at the turn of the tide*
favored,° and he speaks very shrewishly.° One would   *handsome/sharply*
155 think his mother's milk were scarce out of him.

OLIVIA   Let him approach. Call in my gentlewoman.

MALVOLIO   Gentlewoman, my lady calls.   *Exit*
      Enter MARIA

OLIVIA   Give me my veil. Come, throw it o'er my face.
We'll once more hear Orsino's embassy.
      Enter VIOLA *[as Cesario]*

160 VIOLA   The honorable lady of the house, which is she?

OLIVIA   Speak to me, I shall answer for her. Your will.

VIOLA   Most radiant, exquisite, and unmatchable beauty.—
I pray you, tell me if this be the lady of the house, for
I never saw her. I would be loath to cast away° my   *waste*
165 speech, for besides that it is excellently well penned, I
have taken great pains to con° it. Good beauties, let me   *memorize*
sustain° no scorn; I am very 'countable,° even to the least   *suffer/sensitive*
sinister usage.[1]

---

7. One drink ("draught") beyond the quantity necessary to warm him.
8. A decorative post set before a sheriff's door, as a sign

of authority.
9. An undeveloped pea pod.
1. To the slightest discourteous treatment.

OLIVIA   Whence came you, sir?

170 VIOLA   I can say little more than I have studied,[2] and that
question's out of my part. Good gentle one, give me mod-
est° assurance if you be the lady of the house, that I may   *adequate*
proceed in my speech.

OLIVIA   Are you a comedian?°   *an actor*

175 VIOLA   No, my profound heart;[3] and yet—by the very fangs
of malice I swear—I am not that° I play. Are you the lady   *what*
of the house?

OLIVIA   If I do not usurp[4] myself, I am.

VIOLA   Most certain if you are she you do usurp yourself,
180 for what is yours to bestow is not yours to reserve. But
this is from my commission.° I will on with my speech in   *beyond my instructions*
your praise, and then show you the heart of my message.

OLIVIA   Come to what is important in't, I forgive you° the   *excuse you from*
praise.

185 VIOLA   Alas, I took great pains to study it, and 'tis poetical.

OLIVIA   It is the more like to be feigned, I pray you keep it
in. I heard you were saucy° at my gates, and allowed your   *impertinent*
approach rather to wonder at you than to hear you. If you
be not mad, be gone. If you have reason,° be brief. 'Tis   *any sanity*
190 not that time of moon with me to make one in so skipping
a dialogue.[5]

MARIA   Will you hoist sail, sir? Here lies your way.

VIOLA   No, good swabber, I am to hull[6] here a little longer.
[*To* OLIVIA] Some mollification for your giant,[7] sweet
195 lady. Tell me your mind, I am a messenger.[8]

OLIVIA   Sure, you have some hideous matter to deliver
when the courtesy° of it is so fearful. Speak your office.°   *introduction/business*

VIOLA   It alone concerns your ear. I bring no overture° of   *declaration*
war, no taxation of homage.[9] I hold the olive[1] in my hand.
200 My words are as full of peace as matter.°   *meaning*

OLIVIA   Yet you began rudely. What are you? What would
you?

VIOLA   The rudeness that hath appeared in me have I
learned from my entertainment.° What I am and what I   *reception*
205 would are as secret as maidenhead;° to your ears, divinity;   *virginity*
to any others', profanation.

OLIVIA [*to* MARIA *and attendants*]   Give us the place alone,
we will hear this divinity.°   *religious discourse*

[*Exeunt* MARIA *and attendants*]

Now sir, what is your text?[2]

2. Learned by heart (a theatrical term).
3. My most wise lady; upon my soul.
4. Counterfeit; misappropriate.
5. I am not lunatic enough to take part in so flighty a
conversation. (Lunacy was thought to be influenced by
the phases of the moon.)
6. To lie unanchored with lowered sails.
7. Mythical giants guarded ladies; here, also mocking

Maria's diminutive size. "Some . . . for": please pacify.
8. From Orsino; Olivia pretends she understands her
to mean a king's messenger, or a messenger-at-arms,
employed on important state affairs.
9. Demand for dues paid to a superior.
1. Olive branch (as a symbol of peace).
2. Quotation (as a theme of a sermon, in keeping with
"divinity," "doctrine," "heresy," etc.).

210 VIOLA Most sweet lady—

OLIVIA A comfortable° doctrine, and much may be said of °*comforting*
it. Where lies your text?

VIOLA In Orsino's bosom.

OLIVIA In his bosom? In what chapter of his bosom?

215 VIOLA To answer by the method,° in the first of his heart. °*in the same style*

OLIVIA O, I have read it. It is heresy. Have you no more
to say?

VIOLA Good madam, let me see your face.

OLIVIA Have you any commission from your lord to nego-
220 tiate with my face? You are now out of° your text. But we °*straying from*
will draw the curtain and show you the picture.
    [*She unveils*] ·
Look you, sir, such a one I was this present.³ Is't not well
done?

VIOLA Excellently done, if God did all.⁴

225 OLIVIA 'Tis in grain,° sir, 'twill endure wind and weather. °*the dye is fast*

VIOLA 'Tis beauty truly blent,⁵ whose red and white
Nature's own sweet and cunning° hand laid on. °*skillful*
Lady, you are the cruell'st she° alive °*woman*
If you will lead these graces to the grave
230 And leave the world no copy.⁶

OLIVIA O sir, I will not be so hardhearted. I will give out
divers schedules° of my beauty. It shall be inventoried °*various inventories*
and every particle and utensil labelled⁷ to my will, as,
item, two lips, indifferent° red; *item,* two grey eyes, with °*moderate*
235 lids⁸ to them; *item,* one neck, one chin, and so forth.
Were you sent hither to praise° me? °*appraise; flatter*

VIOLA I see you what you are, you are too proud,
But if° you were the devil, you are fair. °*even if*
My lord and master loves you. O, such love
240 Could be but recompensed though⁹ you were crowned
The nonpareil of beauty.° °*an unequaled beauty*

OLIVIA   How does he love me?

VIOLA With adorations, fertile° tears, °*ever-flowing*
With groans that thunder love, with sighs of fire.

OLIVIA Your lord does know my mind, I cannot love him.
245 Yet I suppose him virtuous, know him noble,
Of great estate, of fresh and stainless youth,
In voices well divulged,° free,° learned, and valiant, °*spoken of/generous*
And in dimension and the shape of nature¹
A gracious person; but yet I cannot love him.
250 He might have took his answer long ago.

3. Portraits usually gave the year of painting. "This present" was a term used to date letters.
4. If it is natural (without the use of cosmetics).
5. Blended, or mixed (of paints). Shakespeare uses the same metaphor in sonnet 20, lines 1–2, and Viola's next lines recall sonnet 11, lines 13–14. As Cesario, Viola is playing with established conventions of poetic courtship.
6. Viola means "child"; Olivia takes her to mean "list"

or "inventory."
7. Every single part and article added as a codicil (parodying the legal language of a last will and testament).
8. Eyelids, but also punning on "pot lids" (punning on "utensil" as a household implement).
9. Would have to be requited even if.
1. "Dimension" and "shape of nature" are synonymous, meaning "bodily form."

VIOLA   If I did love you in° my master's flame,°   *with / passion*
    With such a suff'ring, such a deadly° life,   *deathlike*
    In your denial I would find no sense,
    I would not understand it.
OLIVIA   Why, what would you?
255 VIOLA   Make me a willow² cabin at your gate
    And call upon my soul° within the house,   *i.e., Olivia*
    Write loyal cantons of contemnèd° love,   *songs of rejected*
    And sing them loud even in the dead of night;
    Halloo³ your name to the reverberate° hills,   *echoing*
260 And make the babbling gossip of the air⁴
    Cry out "Olivia!" O, you should not rest
    Between the elements of air and earth
    But you should pity me.
OLIVIA   You might do much.
265 What is your parentage?
VIOLA   Above my fortunes, yet my state° is well.   *social status*
    I am a gentleman.
OLIVIA   Get you to your lord.
    I cannot love him. Let him send no more,
    Unless, perchance, you come to me again
270 To tell me how he takes it. Fare you well.
    I thank you for your pains. [*Offering a purse*] Spend this for me.
VIOLA   I am no fee'd post,° lady. Keep your purse.   *hired messenger*
    My master, not myself, lacks recompense.
    Love make his heart of flint that you shall love,⁵
275 And let your fervor, like my master's, be
    Placed in contempt. Farewell, fair cruelty.   *Exit*
OLIVIA   "What is your parentage?"
    "Above my fortunes, yet my state is well.
    I am a gentleman." I'll be sworn thou art.
280 Thy tongue, thy face, thy limbs, actions, and spirit
    Do give thee five-fold blazon.⁶ Not too fast. Soft,° soft—   *wait*
    Unless the master were the man.⁷ How now?
    Even so quickly may one catch the plague?
    Methinks I feel this youth's perfections
285 With an invisible and subtle stealth
    To creep in at mine eyes. Well, let it be.
    What ho, Malvolio.
        Enter MALVOLIO
MALVOLIO   Here, madam, at your service.
OLIVIA   Run after that same peevish messenger
    The County's° man. He left this ring behind him,   *Count's*
290 Would I° or not. Tell him I'll none of it.   *whether I wished it*
    Desire him not to flatter with° his lord,   *encourage*

2. Traditional symbol of rejected love.
3. Shout; or perhaps "hallow," as in "bless."
4. For the love of Narcissus, the nymph Echo wasted away to a mere voice, only able to repeat whatever she heard spoken.
5. May love make the heart of the man you love as hard as flint.
6. Formal description of a gentleman's coat of arms.
7. If Orsino were Cesario ("man": servant).

Nor hold him up with hopes. I am not for him.
If that the youth will come this way tomorrow,
I'll give him reasons for't. Hie thee,° Malvolio.   *hurry*
295   MALVOLIO   Madam, I will.   *Exit [at one door]*
OLIVIA   I do I know not what, and fear to find
Mine eye too great a flatterer for my mind.[8]
Fate, show thy force. Ourselves we do not owe.°   *own*
What is decreed must be; and be this so.
[Exit at another door]

2.1

Enter ANTONIO *and* SEBASTIAN

ANTONIO   Will you stay no longer, nor will° you not that I   *wish*
go with you?
SEBASTIAN   By your patience, no. My stars shine darkly[1]
over me. The malignancy of my fate[2] might perhaps dis-
5   temper° yours, therefore I shall crave of you your leave   *infect*
that I may bear my evils alone. It were a bad recompense
for your love to lay any of them on you.
ANTONIO   Let me yet know of you whither you are bound.
SEBASTIAN   No, sooth,° sir. My determinate° voyage is   *truly/destined*
10   mere extravagancy.° But I perceive in you so excellent a   *idle wandering*
touch of modesty° that you will not extort from me what   *politeness*
I am willing to keep in. Therefore it charges me in man-
ners[3] the rather to express° myself. You must know of me   *reveal*
then, Antonio, my name is Sebastian, which I called Rod-
15   erigo. My father was that Sebastian of Messaline[4] whom
I know you have heard of. He left behind him myself and
a sister, both born in an° hour. If the heavens had been   *within the same*
pleased, would we had so ended. But you, sir, altered
that, for some hour before you took me from the breach°   *surf*
20   of the sea was my sister drowned.
ANTONIO   Alas the day!
SEBASTIAN   A lady, sir, though it was said she much resembled me, was yet of many accounted beautiful. But
though I could not with such estimable° wonder over-far   *appreciative*
25   believe that, yet thus far I will boldly publish° her: she   *proclaim*
bore a mind that envy° could not but call fair. She is   *malice*
drowned already, sir, with salt water, though I seem to
drown her remembrance again with more.
ANTONIO   Pardon me, sir, your bad entertainment.[5]
30   SEBASTIAN   O good Antonio, forgive me your trouble.
ANTONIO   If you will not murder me[6] for my love, let me
be your servant.
SEBASTIAN   If you will not undo what you have done—that

---

8. I.e., my eye (through which love has entered my
heart) has seduced my reason.
2.1 Location: Near the coast of Illyria.
1. Forebodingly, unfavorably.
2. Evil influence of the stars; "malignancy" also signi-

fies a deadly disease.
3. Therefore courtesy requires.
4. Possibly Messina, Sicily.
5. Your poor reception; your inhospitality.
6. I.e., murder him by insisting that they part.

is, kill him whom you have recovered°—desire it not. Fare   *rescued*
35   ye well at once. My bosom is full of kindness,° and I am   *tender emotion*
yet° so near the manners of my mother⁷ that upon the   *still*
least occasion more mine eyes will tell tales of me.° I am   *betray my feelings*
bound to the Count Orsino's court. Farewell.   *Exit*
ANTONIO   The gentleness° of all the gods go with thee!   *favor*
40   I have many enemies in Orsino's court,
Else would I very shortly see thee there.
But come what may, I do adore thee so
That danger shall seem sport, and I will go.   *Exit*

2.2

Enter VIOLA *as Cesario, and* MALVOLIO, *at several*°   *separate*
doors

MALVOLIO   Were not you ev'n° now with the Countess Olivia?   *just*
VIOLA   Even now, sir, on° a moderate pace, I have since   *at*
arrived but hither.°   *come only this far*
MALVOLIO [*offering a ring*]   She returns this ring to you,
5   sir. You might have saved me my pains to have taken° it   *by taking*
away yourself. She adds, moreover, that you should put
your lord into a desperate assurance° she will none of   *hopeless certainty*
him. And one thing more: that you be never so hardy° to   *bold*
come again in his affairs, unless it be to report your lord's
10   taking of this.¹ Receive it so.
VIOLA   She took the ring of me.² I'll none of it.
MALVOLIO   Come, sir, you peevishly threw it to her, and
her will is it should be so returned.
    [*He throws the ring down*]
If it be worth stooping for, there it lies, in your eye;° if   *sight*
15   not, be it his that finds it.   *Exit*
VIOLA [*picking up the ring*]   I left no ring with her. What
    means this lady?
Fortune forbid my outside° have not charmed her.   *appearance*
She made good view of° me, indeed so much   *looked carefully at*
That straight methought her eyes had lost° her tongue,   *made her lose*
20   For she did speak in starts, distractedly.
She loves me, sure. The cunning of her passion
Invites me in° this churlish messenger.   *by means of*
None of my lord's ring! Why, he sent her none.
I am the man.³ If it be so—as 'tis—
25   Poor lady, she were better love a dream!
Disguise, I see thou art a wickedness
Wherein the pregnant enemy⁴ does much.
How easy is it for the proper false⁵
In women's waxen hearts to set their forms!⁶

---

7. I.e., so near woman's readiness to weep.
2.2 Location: Between Olivia's house and Orsino's palace.
1. Reception of this (rejection).
2. Viola pretends to believe Olivia's story. "Of": from.

3. I.e., the man with whom she has fallen in love.
4. The devil. "Pregnant": teeming with ideas.
5. Handsome, but deceitful (men).
6. To impress their images on women's affections (as a seal stamps its image in wax).

30 Alas, our frailty is the cause, not we,
For such as we are made of, such we be.[7]
How will this fadge?° My master loves her dearly,   *turn out*
And I, poor monster,[8] fond° as much on him,   *dote*
And she, mistaken, seems to dote on me.
35 What will become of this? As I am man,
My state is desperate° for my master's love.   *hopeless*
As I am woman, now, alas the day,
What thriftless° sighs shall poor Olivia breathe!   *unprofitable*
O time, thou must untangle this, not I.
40 It is too hard a knot for me t'untie.   [*Exit*]

2.3

Enter SIR TOBY *and* SIR ANDREW

SIR TOBY   Approach, Sir Andrew. Not to be abed after midnight is to be up betimes,° and *diliculo surgere,*[1] thou   *early*
knowest.

SIR ANDREW   Nay, by my troth,° I know not; but I know to   *faith*
5   be up late is to be up late.

SIR TOBY   A false conclusion. I hate it as an unfilled can.°   *tankard*
To be up after midnight and to go to bed then is early; so
that to go to bed after midnight is to go to bed betimes.
Does not our lives consist of the four elements?[2]

10 SIR ANDREW   Faith, so they say, but I think it rather
consists of eating and drinking.

SIR TOBY   Thou'rt a scholar; let us therefore eat and drink.
Marian, I say, a stoup° of wine.   *two-pint tankard*

Enter [FESTE, *the*] *clown*

SIR ANDREW   Here comes the fool, i'faith.

15 FESTE   How now, my hearts. Did you never see the picture
of "we three"?[3]

SIR TOBY   Welcome, ass. Now let's have a catch.[4]

SIR ANDREW   By my troth, the fool has an excellent breast.°   *singing voice*
I had rather than forty shillings I had such a leg,° and so   *(for dancing)*
20 sweet a breath to sing, as the fool has. In sooth, thou
wast in very gracious fooling last night, when thou spokest of Pigrogromitus, of the Vapians passing the equinoctial of Queubus.[5] 'Twas very good, i'faith. I sent thee
sixpence for thy leman.° Hadst it?   *sweetheart*

25 FESTE   I did impeticos thy gratility;[6] for Malvolio's nose is
no whipstock. My lady has a white hand, and the Myr-
midons are no bottle-ale houses.[7]

---

7. For being made of frail flesh, we are frail.
8. Since she is both man and woman.
2.3 Location: Olivia's house.
1. Part of a Latin proverb, meaning "to rise at dawn (is
most healthy)."
2. The four elements, thought to make up all matter,
were earth, air, fire, and water.
3. A trick picture portraying two fools' or asses' heads,
the third being the viewer.
4. Round: a simple song for several voices.

5. "Pigrogromitus . . . Queubus": Feste's mock learning. "Equinoctial": equator of the astronomical heavens.
6. Comic jargon for "impocket (or impetticoat) your
gratuity."
7. Perhaps it is the sheer inscrutability of Feste's foolery that so impresses Sir Andrew (line 28). "Whipstock": handle of a whip. "Bottle-ale houses": cheap
taverns.

SIR ANDREW Excellent! Why, this is the best fooling, when
    all is done. Now a song.
30 SIR TOBY [*to* FESTE] Come on, there is sixpence for you.
    Let's have a song.
SIR ANDREW [*to* FESTE] There's a testril⁸ of me, too. If one
    knight give a—⁹
FESTE Would you have a love-song, or a song of good life?
35 SIR TOBY A love-song, a love-song.
SIR ANDREW Ay, ay. I care not for good life.
FESTE (*sings*)
    O mistress mine, where are you roaming?
    O stay and hear, your true love's coming,
      That can sing both high and low.
40   Trip° no further, pretty sweeting.   *go*
    Journeys end in lovers meeting,
      Every wise man's son doth know.¹
SIR ANDREW Excellent good, i'faith.
SIR TOBY Good, good.
45 FESTE What is love? 'Tis not hereafter,
    Present mirth hath present laughter.
      What's to come is still° unsure.   *always*
    In delay there lies no plenty,
    Then come kiss me, sweet and twenty.°   *twenty-times sweet*
50   Youth's a stuff will not endure.
SIR ANDREW A mellifluous voice, as I am true knight.
SIR TOBY A contagious breath.²
SIR ANDREW Very sweet and contagious, i'faith.
SIR TOBY To hear by the nose, it is dulcet in contagion.³
55   But shall we make the welkin° dance indeed? Shall we   *sky*
    rouse the night-owl in a catch that will draw three souls
    out of one weaver?⁴ Shall we do that?
SIR ANDREW An° you love me, let's do't. I am dog° at a   *if/clever*
    catch.
60 FESTE By'r Lady, sir, and some dogs will catch well.
SIR ANDREW Most certain. Let our catch be "Thou knave."
FESTE "Hold thy peace, thou knave,"⁵ knight. I shall be
    constrained in't to call thee knave, knight.
SIR ANDREW 'Tis not the first time I have constrained one
65   to call me knave. Begin, fool. It begins "Hold thy peace."
FESTE I shall never begin if I hold my peace.
AIR ANDREW Good, i'faith. Come, begin.
      [*They sing the*] *catch.*

8. Sir Andrew's version of "tester" (sixpence).
9. In the First Folio, "give a" appears at the end of a
justified line; an omission is possible.
1. The words of the song are not certainly Shakespeare's; they fit the tune of an instrumental piece
printed in Thomas Morley's *First Book of Consort Lessons* (1599). "Wise man's son": wise men were thought
to have foolish sons.
2. Catchy voice; with a play on "disease-causing air."
3. If one could hear through the nose, the sound would

be sweetly ("dulcet") infectious.
4. Weavers were traditionally addicted to psalm singing, so to move them with popular catches would be a
great triumph. Music was said to be able to draw the
soul from the body.
5. The words of the catch are "Hold thy peace, I
prithee hold thy peace, thou knave." Each singer
repeatedly calls the others knaves and tells them to stop
singing.

Enter MARIA

MARIA   What a caterwauling do you keep here! If my lady
have not called up her steward Malvolio and bid him turn
70   you out of doors, never trust me.

SIR TOBY   My lady's a Cathayan,[6] we are politicians,° Mal-   *schemers*
volio's a Peg-o'-Ramsey,[7] and "Three merry men be we."
Am not I consanguineous?[8] Am I not of her blood? Tilly-
vally°—"lady"! "There dwelt a man in Babylon, lady,   *fiddlesticks*
75   lady."[9]

FESTE   Beshrew° me, the knight's in admirable fooling.   *curse*

SIR ANDREW   Ay, he does well enough if he be disposed,
and so do I, too. He does it with a better grace, but I do
it more natural.[1]

80   SIR TOBY   "O' the twelfth day of December"[2]—

MARIA   For the love o' God, peace.

Enter MALVOLIO

MALVOLIO   My masters, are you mad? Or what are you?
Have you no wit,° manners, nor honesty,° but to gabble   *sense / decency*
like tinkers at this time of night? Do ye make an alehouse
85   of my lady's house, that ye squeak out your coziers'°   *cobblers'*
catches without any mitigation or remorse[3] of voice? Is
there no respect of place, persons, nor time in you?

SIR TOBY   We did keep time, sir, in our catches. Sneck up!°   *go hang yourself*

MALVOLIO   Sir Toby, I must be round° with you. My lady   *plainspoken*
90   bade me tell you that though she harbors you as her kins-
man she's nothing allied to your disorders. If you can
separate yourself and your misdemeanors you are welcome to the house. If not, an it would please you to take
leave of her she is very willing to bid you farewell.

95   SIR TOBY   "Farewell, dear heart, since I must needs be gone."[4]

MARIA   Nay, good Sir Toby.

FESTE   "His eyes do show his days are almost done."

MALVOLIO   Is't even so?

SIR TOBY   "But I will never die."

100   FESTE   "Sir Toby, there you lie."

MALVOLIO   This is much credit to you.

SIR TOBY   "Shall I bid him go?"

FESTE   "What an if° you do?"   *an if = if*

SIR TOBY   "Shall I bid him go, and spare not?"

105   FESTE   "O no, no, no, no, you dare not."

SIR TOBY   Out o' tune, sir, ye lie. [*To* MALVOLIO] Art any
more than a steward? Dost thou think because thou art
virtuous there shall be no more cakes and ale?[5]

---

6. Chinese; but also ethnocentric slang for "trickster"
or "cheat."
7. Name of a dance and popular song; here, used contemptuously.
8. A blood relative (of Olivia's). "Three . . . we": a
refrain from a popular song.
9. The opening and refrain of a popular song.
1. Effortlessly; but unconsciously playing on the sense

of *natural* as "fool" or "idiot."
2. Snatch of a ballad; or possibly a drunken version of
"twelfth day of Christmas," that is, Twelfth Night.
3. Without any abating or softening.
4. Part of another song that Sir Toby and Feste adapt
for the occasion.
5. Traditionally associated with church festivals and
therefore disliked by Puritans.

FESTE   Yes, by Saint Anne, and ginger[6] shall be hot i'th'
110   mouth, too.

SIR TOBY   Thou'rt i'th' right. [*To* MALVOLIO] Go, sir, rub
your chain with crumbs.[7] [*To* MARIA] A stoup of wine,
Maria.

MALVOLIO   Mistress Mary, if you prized my lady's favour
115   at any thing more than contempt you would not give
means° for this uncivil rule.° She shall know of it, by this   *drink/behavior*
hand.   *Exit*[8]

MARIA   Go shake your ears.°   *(like an ass)*

SIR ANDREW   'Twere as good a deed as to drink when a
120   man's a-hungry to challenge him the field° and then to   *to a duel*
break promise with him, and make a fool of him.

SIR TOBY   Do't, knight. I'll write thee a challenge, or I'll
deliver thy indignation to him by word of mouth.

MARIA   Sweet Sir Toby, be patient for tonight. Since the
125   youth of the Count's was today with my lady she is much
out of quiet. For Monsieur Malvolio, let me alone with
him. If I do not gull him into a nayword[9] and make him
a common recreation,° do not think I have wit enough to   *sport, jest*
lie straight in my bed. I know I can do it.

130   SIR TOBY   Possess° us, possess us, tell us something of him.   *inform*

MARIA   Marry, sir, sometimes he is a kind of puritan.[1]

SIR ANDREW   O, if I thought that I'd beat him like a dog.

SIR TOBY   What, for being a puritan? Thy exquisite° reason,   *ingenious*
dear knight.

135   SIR ANDREW   I have no exquisite reason for't, but I have
reason good enough.

MARIA   The dev'l a puritan that he is, or anything con-
stantly but a time-pleaser,° an affectioned° ass that cons   *boot licker/affected*
state without book and utters it by great swathes;[2] the
140   best persuaded of himself,[3] so crammed, as he thinks,
with excellencies, that it is his grounds of faith° that all   *his creed*
that look on him love him; and on that vice in him will
my revenge find notable cause to work.

SIR TOBY   What wilt thou do?

145   MARIA   I will drop in his way some obscure epistles of love,
wherein by the color of his beard, the shape of his leg,
the manner of his gait, the expressure° of his eye, fore-   *expression*
head, and complexion, he shall find himself most feel-
ingly personated.° I can write very like my lady your niece;   *represented*
150   on a forgotten matter we can hardly make distinction of
our hands.°   *handwriting*

---

6. Used to spice ale. Saint Anne was the mother of the
Virgin; the oath would be offensive to Puritans, who
attacked her cult.
7. Clean your steward's chain; mind your own business.
8. Feste plays no further part in this scene. This is the
suggested exit for him.
9. If I do not trick ("gull") him into a byword (for

"dupe")
1. Could mean "morally strict and censorious," as well
as "a follower of the Puritan religious faith."
2. Memorizes dignified and high-flown language and
utters it in great sweeps (like hay falling under a
scythe).
3. Having the highest opinion of himself.

SIR TOBY   Excellent, I smell a device.

SIR ANDREW   I have't in my nose too.

SIR TOBY   He shall think by the letters that thou wilt drop
155   that they come from my niece, and that she's in love with
him.

MARIA   My purpose is indeed a horse of that color.

SIR ANDREW   And your horse now would make him an ass.

MARIA   Ass° I doubt not.   *(punning on "as")*

160   SIR ANDREW   O, 'twill be admirable.

MARIA   Sport royal, I warrant you. I know my physic° will   *medicine*
work with him. I will plant you two—and let the fool
make a third—where he shall find the letter. Observe his
construction° of it. For this night, to bed, and dream on   *interpretation*
165   the event.° Farewell.   *Exit*   *outcome*

SIR TOBY   Good night, Penthesilea.[4]

SIR ANDREW   Before me,[5] she's a good wench.

SIR TOBY   She's a beagle true bred, and one that adores
me. What o' that?

170   SIR ANDREW   I was adored once, too.

SIR TOBY   Let's to bed, knight. Thou hadst need send for
more money.

SIR ANDREW   If I cannot recover° your niece, I am a foul   *win*
way out.°   *out of money*

175   SIR TOBY   Send for money, knight. If thou hast her not i'th'
end, call me cut.[6]

SIR ANDREW   If I do not, never trust me, take it how you
will.

SIR TOBY   Come, come, I'll go burn some sack,[7] 'tis too late
180   to go to bed now. Come knight, come knight.   *Exeunt*

2.4

Enter Duke, VIOLA *[as Cesario],* CURIO, *and others*

ORSINO   Give me some music. Now good morrow,°   *morning*
friends.
Now good Cesario, but° that piece of song,   *just*
That old and antic° song we heard last night.   *quaint*
Methought it did relieve my passion° much,   *suffering*
5   More than light airs and recollected° terms   *studied, artificial*
Of these most brisk and giddy-pacèd times.
Come, but one verse.

CURIO   He is not here, so please your lordship, that should
sing it.

10   ORSINO   Who was it?

CURIO   Feste the jester, my lord, a fool that the lady Olivia's father took much delight in. He is about the house.

ORSINO   Seek him out, and play the tune the while.

[Exit CURIO*]*

---

4. Queen of the Amazons (a joke about Maria's small
size).
5. On my soul (a mild oath).
6. A dock-tailed horse; also, slang for "gelding" or for

"female genitals."
7. I'll go warm and spice some Spanish wine.
2.4 Location: Orsino's palace.

Music plays
[*To* VIOLA] Come hither, boy. If ever thou shalt love,
15   In the sweet pangs of it remember me;
     For such as I am, all true lovers are,
     Unstaid° and skittish in all motions° else   *unstable / emotions*
     Save in the constant image of the creature
     That is beloved. How dost thou like this tune?
20   VIOLA   It gives a very echo to the seat
     Where love is throned.[1]
     ORSINO   Thou dost speak masterly.°   *expertly*
     My life upon't, young though thou art thine eye
     Hath stayed upon some favor° that it loves.   *face*
     Hath it not, boy?
     VIOLA   A little, by your favor.°   *leave; face*
     ORSINO   What kind of woman is't?
25   VIOLA   Of your complexion.
     ORSINO   She is not worth thee then. What years, i'faith?
     VIOLA   About your years, my lord.
     ORSINO   Too old, by heaven. Let still° the woman take   *always*
     An elder than herself. So wears° she to him;   *adapts*
30   So sways she level[2] in her husband's heart.
     For, boy, however we do praise ourselves,
     Our fancies° are more giddy and unfirm,   *affections*
     More longing, wavering, sooner lost and worn,°   *exhausted*
     Than women's are.
     VIOLA   I think° it well, my lord.   *believe*
35   ORSINO   Then let thy love be younger than thyself,
     Or thy affection cannot hold the bent;[3]
     For women are as roses, whose fair flower
     Being once displayed,° doth fall that very hour.   *opened*
     VIOLA   And so they are. Alas that they are so:
40   To die even° when they to perfection grow.   *just*
           Enter CURIO *and* [FESTE, *the*] *clown*
     ORSINO [*to* FESTE]   O fellow, come, the song we had last night.
     Mark it, Cesario, it is old and plain.
     The spinsters,° and the knitters in the sun,   *spinners*
     And the free° maids that weave their thread with bones,[4]   *carefree*
45   Do use to chant it. It is silly sooth,
     And dallies with° the innocence of love,   *lingers lovingly on*
     Like the old° age.   *golden*
     FESTE   Are you ready, sir?
     ORSINO   I prithee, sing.
           Music
50   FESTE [*sings*]   Come away,° come away death,   *come hither*
                    And in sad cypress[5] let me be laid.

---

1. I.e., it reflects back to the heart.
2. So does she balance (influence and affection).
3. Cannot remain at full stretch (like the tautness of a bowstring).
4. Spools made from bone on which lace (called "bone lace") was woven.
5. Cypress-wood coffin. Like yews, cypresses were emblematic of mourning.

Fie away, fie away breath,
    I am slain by a fair cruel maid.
My shroud of white, stuck all with yew,°   *yew sprigs*
55   O prepare it.
My part of death no one so true
    Did share it.[6]

Not a flower, not a flower sweet
    On my black coffin let there be strewn.
60 Not a friend, not a friend greet
      My poor corpse, where my bones shall be thrown.
A thousand thousand sighs to save,
      Lay me O where
Sad true lover never find my grave,
65   To weep there.

ORSINO [*giving money*]   There's for thy pains.
FESTE   No pains, sir. I take pleasure in singing, sir.
ORSINO   I'll pay thy pleasure then.
FESTE   Truly, sir, and pleasure will be paid,° one time or   *paid for*
70   another.
ORSINO   Give me now leave° to leave° thee.   *permission / dismiss*
FESTE   Now the melancholy god[7] protect thee, and the tai-
lor make thy doublet° of changeable taffeta,[8] for thy mind   *close-fitting jacket*
is a very opal.[9] I would have men of such constancy put
75   to sea, that their business might be everything, and their
intent° everywhere, for that's it that always makes a good   *destination*
voyage of nothing.[1] Farewell.   *Exit*
ORSINO   Let all the rest give place:°   *withdraw*
[*Exeunt* CURIO *and others*]
               Once more, Cesario,
Get thee to yon same sovereign cruelty.
80 Tell her my love, more noble than the world,
Prizes not quantity of dirty lands.
The parts° that fortune hath bestowed upon her   *possessions*
Tell her I hold as giddily[2] as fortune;
But 'tis that miracle and queen of gems
85 That nature pranks° her in attracts my soul.   *adorns*
VIOLA   But if she cannot love you, sir?
ORSINO   I cannot be so answered.
VIOLA   Sooth,° but you must.   *in truth*
Say that some lady, as perhaps there is,
Hath for your love as great a pang of heart
90 As you have for Olivia. You cannot love her.
You tell her so. Must she not then be answered?
ORSINO   There is no woman's sides

---

6. I.e., no one has died so true to love as I.
7. Saturn (thought to control the melancholic).
8. Shot silk, whose color changes with the angle of vision.
9. An iridescent gemstone that changes color depend-

ing on the angle from which it is seen.
1. I.e., this fickle lack of direction can make a voyage in the notoriously changeful sea carefree and conso-nant with one's desires.
2. Lightly (fortune being fickle).

Can bide° the beating of so strong a passion   *withstand*
As love doth give my heart; no woman's heart
95   So big, to hold so much. They lack retention.°   *constancy*
Alas, their love may be called appetite,
No motion° of the liver, but the palate,[3]   *impulse*
That suffer surfeit, cloyment,° and revolt.°   *satiety/revulsion*
But mine is all as hungry as the sea,
100   And can digest as much. Make no compare
Between that love a woman can bear me
And that I owe° Olivia.   *have for*
VIOLA   Ay, but I know—
ORSINO   What dost thou know?
105 VIOLA   Too well what love women to men may owe.
In faith, they are as true of heart as we.
My father had a daughter loved a man
As it might be, perhaps, were I a woman
I should your lordship.
ORSINO   And what's her history?
110 VIOLA   A blank, my lord. She never told her love,
But let concealment, like a worm i'th' bud,
Feed on her damask[4] cheek. She pined in thought,
And with a green and yellow° melancholy   *pale and sallow*
She sat like patience on a monument,[5]
115   Smiling at grief. Was not this love indeed?
We men may say more, swear more, but indeed
Our shows are more than will;[6] for still° we prove   *always*
Much in our vows, but little in our love.
ORSINO   But died thy sister of her love, my boy?
120 VIOLA   I am all the daughters of my father's house,
And all the brothers too; and yet I know not.
Sir, shall I to this lady?
ORSINO   Ay, that's the theme,
To her in haste. Give her this jewel. Say
My love can give no place, bide no denay.[7]

                        Exeunt [severally]

2.5

Enter SIR TOBY, SIR ANDREW, *and* FABIAN

SIR TOBY   Come thy ways,° Signor Fabian.   *come along*
FABIAN   Nay, I'll come. If I lose a scruple° of this sport let   *miss a scrap*
    me be boiled to death with melancholy.[1]
SIR TOBY   Wouldst thou not be glad to have the niggardly
5   rascally sheep-biter[2] come by some notable shame?

---

3. Appetite, like the palate, is easily sated and thus lacks the emotional depth and complexity of real love, whose seat is the liver.
4. Pink and white, like a damask rose.
5. A memorial statue symbolizing patience.
6. Our displays of love are greater than our actual feelings.

7. My love cannot be bated, nor tolerate refusal.
2.5 Location: Olivia's garden.
1. Melancholy was a cold humor; "boiled" puns on "bile," the surplus of which produced melancholy.
2. Literally, a dog that attacks sheep; here, a malicious sneak.

FABIAN   I would exult, man. You know he brought me out
o' favour with my lady about a bear-baiting[3] here.

SIR TOBY   To anger him we'll have the bear again, and we
will fool° him black and blue, shall we not, Sir Andrew?   *mock*

10   SIR ANDREW   An° we do not, it is pity of our lives.   *if*

Enter MARIA [*with a letter*]

SIR TOBY   Here comes the little villain. How now, my metal
of India?[4]

MARIA   Get ye all three into the box-tree.° Malvolio's com-   *hedge of boxwood*
ing down this walk. He has been yonder i' the sun prac-
15   tising behavior to his own shadow this half-hour. Observe
him, for the love of mockery, for I know this letter will
make a contemplative° idiot of him. Close,° in the name   *vacuous / hide*
of jesting!

[*The men hide.* MARIA *places the letter*]

Lie thou there, for here comes the trout that must be
20   caught with tickling.[5]   *Exit*

Enter MALVOLIO

MALVOLIO   'Tis but fortune, all is fortune. Maria once told
me she° did affect° me, and I have heard herself come   *i.e., Olivia / care for*
thus near, that should she fancy° it should be one of my   *fall in love*
complexion. Besides, she uses me with a more exalted
25   respect than anyone else that follows her. What should I
think on't?

SIR TOBY   Here's an overweening rogue.

FABIAN   O, peace! Contemplation makes a rare turkey-
cock[6] of him—how he jets° under his advanced° plumes!   *struts / raised*

30   SIR ANDREW   'Slight,[7] I could so beat the rogue.

SIR TOBY   Peace, I say.

MALVOLIO   To be Count Malvolio!

SIR TOBY   Ah, rogue.

SIR ANDREW   Pistol him, pistol him.

35   SIR TOBY   Peace, peace.

MALVOLIO   There is example° for't: the Lady of the Stra-   *precedent*
chey married the yeoman of the wardrobe.[8]

SIR ANDREW   Fie on him, Jezebel.[9]

FABIAN   O peace, now he's deeply in. Look how imagina-
40   tion blows him.°   *puffs him up*

MALVOLIO   Having been three months married to her, sit-
ting in my state°—   *chair of state*

SIR TOBY   O for a stone-bow[1] to hit him in the eye!

MALVOLIO   Calling my officers° about me, in my branched[2]   *household attendants*

---

3. Puritans disapproved of blood sports like bearbaiting.
4. A woman worth her weight in gold.
5. Flattery; trout can supposedly be caught by stroking
them under the gills.
6. Proverbially proud; they display their feathers like
peacocks.
7. By God's light (an oath).

8. Perhaps an allusion to a noblewoman who had married her manservant, but there is no certain identification. "Yeoman of the wardrobe": keeper of clothes
and linen.
9. Biblical allusion to the proud wife of Ahab, king of
Israel.
1. Catapult, or crossbow for stones.
2. Embroidered with branch patterns.

45   velvet gown, having come from a day-bed° where I have   *couch*
        left Olivia sleeping—

    SIR TOBY   Fire and brimstone!

    FABIAN   O peace, peace.

    MALVOLIO   And then to have the humor of state[3] and—
50   after a demure travel of regard,[4] telling them I know my
        place, as I would they should do theirs—to ask for my
        kinsman Toby.

    SIR TOBY   Bolts and shackles!

    FABIAN   O peace, peace, peace, now, now.

55   MALVOLIO   Seven of my people with an obedient start
        make° out for him. I frown the while, and perchance wind   *go*
        up my watch, or play with my—[*touching his chain*][5]
        some rich jewel. Toby approaches; curtsies° there to me.   *bows*

    SIR TOBY   Shall this fellow live?

60   FABIAN   Though our silence be drawn from us with cars,[6]
        yet peace.

    MALVOLIO   I extend my hand to him thus, quenching my
        familiar smile with an austere regard of control—

    SIR TOBY   And does not Toby take° you a blow o' the lips,   *give*
65   then?

    MALVOLIO   Saying "Cousin Toby, my fortunes, having cast
        me on your niece, give me this prerogative of speech"—

    SIR TOBY   What, what!

    MALVOLIO   "You must amend your drunkenness."

70   SIR TOBY   Out, scab.

    FABIAN   Nay, patience, or we break the sinews of our plot.

    MALVOLIO   "Besides, you waste the treasure of your time
        with a foolish knight"—

    SIR ANDREW   That's me, I warrant you.

75   MALVOLIO   "One Sir Andrew."

    SIR ANDREW   I knew 'twas I, for many do call me fool.

    MALVOLIO [*seeing the letter*]   What employment° have we   *business*
        here?

    FABIAN   Now is the woodcock near the gin.[7]

80   SIR TOBY   O peace, and the spirit of humors intimate[8] read-
        ing aloud to him.

    MALVOLIO [*taking up the letter*]   By my life, this is my lady's
        hand. These be her very c's, her u's, and her t's,[9] and thus
        makes she her great P's. It is in contempt of° question   *beyond*
85   her hand.

    SIR ANDREW   Her c's, her u's, and her t's? Why that?

    MALVOLIO [*reads*]   "To the unknown beloved, this, and my

---

3. To adopt the grand air of exalted greatness.
4. After casting my eyes gravely about the room.
5. Malvolio momentarily forgets that he will have abandoned his steward's chain; watches were an expensive luxury at this time.
6. A prisoner might be tied to two carts or chariots ("cars") and pulled by horses in opposite directions to

extort information.
7. Snare. The woodcock is a proverbially foolish bird.
8. And may a capricious impulse suggest.
9. Malvolio unwittingly spells out "cut," slang for "female genitals"; the meaning is compounded by "great P's." In fact, these letters do not appear on the outside of the letter.

good wishes." Her very phrases! [*Opening the letter*] By
your leave, wax[1]—soft,° and the impressure her Lucrece,[2]   *wait*
90 with which she uses to seal°—'tis my lady. To whom   *habitually seals*
should this be?

FABIAN This wins him, liver and all.

MALVOLIO   "Jove knows I love,
            But who?
95   Lips do not move,
            No man must know."
"No man must know." What follows? The numbers
altered.° "No man must know." If this should be thee,   *meter changed*
Malvolio?

100 SIR TOBY Marry, hang thee, brock.[3]

MALVOLIO "I may command where I adore,
            But silence like a Lucrece knife
            With bloodless stroke my heart doth gore.
            M.O.A.I. doth sway my life."

105 FABIAN A fustian° riddle.   *bombastic*

SIR TOBY Excellent wench, say I.

MALVOLIO "M.O.A.I. doth sway my life." Nay, but first let
me see, let me see, let me see.

FABIAN What dish o' poison has she dressed° him!   *prepared*

110 SIR TOBY And with what wing the staniel checks at it![4]

MALVOLIO "I may command where I adore." Why, she may
command me. I serve her, she is my lady. Why, this is
evident to any formal capacity.° There is no obstruction   *normal intelligence*
in this. And the end—what should that alphabetical posi-
115 tion° portend? If I could make that resemble something   *arrangements*
in me. Softly—'M.O.A.I.'

SIR TOBY O ay,[5] make up that, he is now at a cold scent.

FABIAN Sowter will cry upon't for all this, though° it be as   *as though*
rank as a fox.[6]

120 MALVOLIO "M." Malvolio—'M'—why, that begins my name.

FABIAN Did not I say he would work it out? The cur is
excellent at faults.[7]

MALVOLIO "M." But then there is no consonancy in the
sequel.[8] That suffers under probation.[9] "A" should follow,
125 but "O" does.

FABIAN And "O"[1] shall end, I hope.

SIR TOBY Ay, or I'll cudgel him, and make him cry "O!"

MALVOLIO And then "I" comes behind.

FABIAN Ay, an you had any eye behind you you might see
130 more detraction° at your heels than fortunes before you.   *defamation*

1. He addresses himself to the sealing wax.
2. The figure of Lucrece, Roman model of chastity, is
the device ("impressure") imprinted on the seal.
3. Badger (proverbially stinking).
4. And with what alacrity the sparrow hawk goes after
it.
5. Playing on "O.I."
6. "Sowter" (the name of a hound), having lost the

scent, will start to bay loudly as he picks up the new,
rank (stinking) smell of the fox.
7. At picking up a scent after it is momentarily lost. A
"fault" is a "cold scent" (line 117).
8. There is no consistency in what follows.
9. That weakens upon being put to the test.
1. As in the hangman's noose; the last letter of Malvolio's name; or "O" as a lamentation.

MALVOLIO "M.O.A.I." This simulation° is not as the for-   *disguise; riddle*
  mer; and yet to crush° this a little, it would bow° to me,   *force/yield; point*
  for every one of these letters are in my name. Soft, here
  follows prose: "If this fall into thy hand, revolve.° In my   *consider*
135 stars° I am above thee, but be not afraid of greatness.   *fortunes*
  Some are born great, some achieve greatness, and some
  have greatness thrust upon 'em. Thy fates open their
  hands,° let thy blood and spirit embrace them, and to   *bestow gifts*
  inure° thyself to what thou art like° to be, cast thy humble   *accustom/likely*
140 slough,[2] and appear fresh. Be opposite° with a kinsman,   *contrary*
  surly with servants. Let thy tongue tang arguments of
  state;[3] put thyself into the trick of singularity.° She thus   *cultivate eccentricity*
  advises thee that sighs for thee. Remember who com-
  mended thy yellow stockings, and wished to see thee ever
145 cross-gartered.[4] I say remember, go to,[5] thou art made if
  thou desirest to be so; if not, let me see thee a steward
  still, the fellow of servants, and not worthy to touch Fortune's fingers. Farewell. She that would alter services[6]
  with thee,
150   The Fortunate-Unhappy."
  Daylight and champaign discovers[7] not more. This is
  open.° I will be proud, I will read politic° authors, I will   *clear/political*
  baffle[8] Sir Toby, I will wash off gross acquaintance, I will
  be point-device the very man.[9] I do not now fool myself,
155 to let imagination jade° me; for every reason excites to   *trick*
  this, that my lady loves me. She did commend my yellow
  stockings of late, she did praise my leg, being cross-
  gartered, and in this she manifests herself to my love, and
  with a kind of injunction drives me to these habits° of her   *clothes*
160 liking. I thank my stars, I am happy. I will be strange,°   *aloof*
  stout,° in yellow stockings, and cross-gartered, even with   *proud*
  the swiftness of putting on. Jove and my stars be praised.
  Here is yet a postscript. "Thou canst not choose but know
  who I am. If thou entertainest° my love, let it appear in   *accept*
165 thy smiling, thy smiles become thee well. Therefore in
  my presence still° smile, dear my sweet, I prithee." Jove,   *constantly*
  I thank thee. I will smile, I will do everything that thou
  wilt have me.   *Exit*
      [SIR TOBY, SIR ANDREW, *and* FABIAN *come from hiding*]
FABIAN I will not give my part of this sport for a pension
170 of thousands to be paid from the Sophy.°   *shah of Persia*
SIR TOBY I could marry this wench for this device.
SIR ANDREW So could I, too.

---

2. A snake's old skin, which peels away.
3. Let your tongue ring out arguments of statecraft or
politics.
4. An antiquated way of adjusting a garter—going once
below the knee, crossing behind it, and knotting above
the knee at the side.
5. An emphatic expression, like "I tell you."

6. Change places (of servant and mistress or master).
7. Open countryside reveals.
8. Term used to describe the formal unmaking of a
knight; hence, "disgrace."
9. I will be in every detail the identical man (described
in the letter).

SIR TOBY   And ask no other dowry with her but such
another jest.

Enter MARIA

175   SIR ANDREW   Nor I neither.

FABIAN   Here comes my noble gull-catcher.°   *trickster*

SIR TOBY [*to* MARIA]   Wilt thou set thy foot o' my neck?

SIR ANDREW [*to* MARIA]   Or o' mine either?

SIR TOBY [*to* MARIA]   Shall I play° my freedom at tray-trip,[1]   *wager*
180   and become thy bondslave?

SIR ANDREW [*to* MARIA]   I'faith, or I either?

SIR TOBY [*to* MARIA]   Why, thou hast put him in such a
dream that when the image of it leaves him, he must run
mad.

185   MARIA   Nay, but say true, does it work upon him?

SIR TOBY   Like aqua vitae° with a midwife.   *spirits, liquor*

MARIA   If you will then see the fruits of the sport, mark his
first approach before my lady. He will come to her in
yellow stockings, and 'tis a color she abhors, and cross-
190   gartered, a fashion she detests; and he will smile upon
her, which will now be so unsuitable to her disposition,
being addicted to a melancholy as she is, that it cannot
but turn him into a notable contempt.[2] If you will see it,
follow me.

195   SIR TOBY   To the gates of Tartar,° thou most excellent devil   *hell*
of wit.

SIR ANDREW   I'll make one,° too.   *Exeunt*   *go along*

3.1

Enter VIOLA [*as Cesario*] *and* [FESTE, *the*] *clown* [*with
pipe and tabor*][1]

VIOLA   Save° thee, friend, and thy music. Dost thou live by   *God save*
thy tabor?

FESTE   No, sir, I live by° the church.   *near*

VIOLA   Art thou a churchman?

5   FESTE   No such matter, sir. I do live by[2] the church for I
do live at my house, and my house doth stand by the
church.

VIOLA   So thou mayst say the king lies by[3] a beggar if a
beggar dwell near him, or the church stands° by thy tabor   *is maintained*
10   if thy tabor stand by the church.

FESTE   You have said, sir. To see this age!—A sentence° is   *saying*
but a cheverel° glove to a good wit, how quickly the wrong   *kidskin*
side may be turned outward.

VIOLA   Nay, that's certain. They that dally nicely° with   *play subtly*
15   words may quickly make them wanton.[4]

---

1. A game of dice in which the winner throws a three
("tray" is from the Spanish *tres*).
2. A notorious object of contempt.
3.1 Location: Olivia's garden.
1. The dialogue demands only a tabor, but jesters commonly played a pipe with one hand while tapping a

tabor (small drum, hanging from the neck) with the
other.
2. I do earn my keep with.
3. Lives near; punning on "goes to bed with."
4. Equivocal; Viola puns on the sense "unchaste."

FESTE I would therefore my sister had had no name, sir.

VIOLA Why, man?

FESTE Why, sir, her name's a word, and to dally with that
word might make my sister wanton. But indeed, words
20 are very rascals since bonds disgraced them.[5]

VIOLA Thy reason, man?

FESTE Troth, sir, I can yield you none without words, and
words are grown so false I am loath to prove reason with
them.

25 VIOLA I warrant thou art a merry fellow, and carest for
nothing.

FESTE Not so, sir, I do care for something; but in my conscience, sir, I do not care for you. If that be to care for
nothing, sir, I would it would make you invisible.

30 VIOLA Art not thou the Lady Olivia's fool?

FESTE No indeed, sir, the Lady Olivia has no folly, she will
keep no fool, sir, till she be married, and fools are as like
husbands as pilchards[5] are to herrings—the husband's
the bigger. I am indeed not her fool, but her corrupter of
35 words.

VIOLA I saw thee late° at the Count Orsino's.   *lately*

FESTE Foolery, sir, does walk about the orb[7] like the sun,
it shines everywhere. I would be sorry, sir, but the fool
should be as oft with your master as with my mistress.[8] I
40 think I saw your wisdom[9] there.

VIOLA Nay, an thou pass upon[1] me, I'll no more with thee.
[*giving money*] Hold, there's expenses for thee.

FESTE Now Jove in his next commodity° of hair send thee   *shipment*
a beard.

45 VIOLA By my troth I'll tell thee, I am almost sick for one,[2]
though I would not have it grow on *my* chin. Is thy lady
within?

FESTE Would not a pair of these have bred,[3] sir?

VIOLA Yes, being kept together and put to use.[4]

50 FESTE I would play Lord Pandarus[5] of Phrygia, sir, to bring
a Cressida to this Troilus.

VIOLA [*giving money*] I understand you, sir, 'tis well
begged.

FESTE The matter I hope is not great, sir; begging but a
55 beggar—Cressida was a beggar.[6] My lady is within, sir. I
will conster° to them whence you come. Who you are and   *explain*

---

5. Since legal contracts replaced a man's word of
honor. ("Bonds" plays on "sworn statements" and "fetters," betokening criminality.)
6. Small fish similar to herring.
7. World; the sun was still believed to circle the earth.
8. Unless ("but") Feste should visit his foolery upon
others but also unless Orsino should be called "fool" as
often as Olivia.
9. A mocking title for Cesario.
1. If you express an opinion of; if you joke about.

2. Almost eager for a beard; almost pining for a man
(Orsino).
3. Would not a pair of coins such as these have multiplied (with possible pun on "be enough to buy bread").
4. Invested to produce interest.
5. Go-between or "pander," since Feste needs a "mate"
for his coin(s). Shakespeare dramatizes the story in
Troilus and Cressida.
6. In asking for the "mate" to his Troilus coin, Feste
draws on a version of the story of Troilus and Cressida

what you would are out of my welkin—I might say "element," but the word is over-worn.[7]   *Exit*

VIOLA   This fellow is wise enough to play the fool,
60   And to do that well craves a kind of wit.°   *intelligence*
        He must observe their mood on whom he jests,
        The quality of persons, and the time,
        And, like the haggard, check at every feather
        That comes before his eye.[8] This is a practice°   *skill*
65   As full of labor as a wise man's art,
        For folly that he wisely shows is fit,[9]
        But wise men, folly-fall'n,° quite taint[1] their wit.   *fallen into folly*
            Enter SIR TOBY *and* [SIR] ANDREW
SIR TOBY   Save you, gentleman.
VIOLA   And you, sir.
70 SIR ANDREW   *Dieu vous garde,*[2] monsieur.
VIOLA   *Et vous aussi, votre serviteur.*[3]
SIR ANDREW   I hope, sir, you are, and I am yours.
SIR TOBY   Will you encounter[4] the house? My niece is
        desirous you should enter if your trade be to her.
75 VIOLA   I am bound to° your niece, sir: I mean she is the   *for*
        list° of my voyage.   *destination*
SIR TOBY   Taste° your legs, sir, put them to motion.   *try*
VIOLA   My legs do better understand° me, sir, than I under-   *stand under*
        stand what you mean by bidding me taste my legs.
80 SIR TOBY   I mean to go, sir, to enter.
VIOLA   I will answer you with gait and entrance.
            Enter OLIVIA, *and* [MARIA, *her*] *gentlewoman*
        But we are prevented.° [*To* OLIVIA] Most excellent accom-   *anticipated*
        plished lady, the heavens rain odors on you.
SIR ANDREW [*to* SIR TOBY]   That youth's a rare° courtier;   *well put*
85   "rain odors"—well.°
VIOLA   My matter hath no voice,° lady, but to your own   *must not be spoken*
        most pregnant° and vouchsafed° ear.   *receptive/proffered*
SIR ANDREW [*to* SIR TOBY]   "Odors," "pregnant," and
        "vouchsafed"—I'll get 'em all three all ready.[5]
90 OLIVIA   Let the garden door be shut, and leave me to my
        hearing.   [*Exeunt* SIR TOBY, SIR ANDREW, *and* MARIA]
        Give me your hand, sir.
VIOLA   My duty, madam, and most humble service.
OLIVIA   What is your name?
95 VIOLA   Cesario is your servant's name, fair princess.
OLIVIA   My servant, sir? 'Twas never merry world[6]

---

in which Cressida became a leprous beggar.
7. "Welkin" (sky or air) is synonymous with one meaning of "element," used in what Feste regards as the over-
worn phrase "out of my element."
8. I.e., as a wild hawk ("haggard") must be sensitive to
its prey's disposition.
9. For folly that he skillfully displays is proper.
1. Discredit; spoil.

2. God protect you (French).
3. And you also, (I am) your servant. (Sir Andrew's
awkward reply demonstrates that his French is limited.)
4. Pedantry for "enter" (Toby mocks Viola's courtly
language).
5. I.e., to commit to memory for later use.
6. The proverbial "Things have never been the same."

Since lowly feigning° was called compliment.　　　　　　　　　*pretended humility*
You're servant to the Count Orsino, youth.
VIOLA　And he is yours, and his must needs be yours.
100　Your servant's servant is *your* servant, madam.
OLIVIA　For° him, I think not on him. For his thoughts,　　　　　　　*as for*
Would they were blanks rather than filled with me.
VIOLA　Madam, I come to whet your gentle thoughts
On his behalf.
OLIVIA　　　　　O by your leave,[7] I pray you.
105　I bade you never speak again of him;
But would you undertake another suit,
I had rather hear you to solicit that
Than music from the spheres.[8]
VIOLA　　　　　　　　　　　Dear lady—
OLIVIA　Give me leave, beseech you. I did send,
110　After the last enchantment you did here,
A ring in chase of you. So did I abuse°　　　　　　　*deceive; dishonor*
Myself, my servant, and I fear me you.°　　　　　　　*and, as I fear, you*
Under your hard construction[9] must I sit,
To force° that on you in a shameful cunning　　　　　　　*for forcing*
115　Which you knew none of yours. What might you think?
Have you not set mine honor at the stake
And baited it with all th'unmuzzled thoughts[1]
That tyrannous heart can think? To one of your receiving°　　　*perception*
Enough is shown. A cypress,[2] not a bosom,
120　Hides my heart. So let me hear you speak.
VIOLA　I pity you.
OLIVIA　　　　　That's a degree to° love.　　　　　　　　　*toward*
VIOLA　No, not a grece,° for 'tis a vulgar proof°　　　*step/common experience*
That very oft we pity enemies.
OLIVIA　Why then, methinks 'tis time to smile again.[3]
125　O world, how apt° the poor are to be proud!　　　　　　　*ready*
If one should be a prey, how much the better
To fall before the lion than the wolf![4]
　　　　Clock strikes
The clock upbraids me with the waste of time.
Be not afraid, good youth, I will not have you;
130　And yet when wit and youth is come to harvest
Your wife is like to reap a proper° man.　　　　　　　*handsome, worthy*
There lies your way, due west.
VIOLA　　　　　　　　　　Then westward ho![5]
Grace and good disposition° attend your ladyship.　　　　　*peace of mind*
You'll nothing, madam, to my lord by me?

---

7. Permit me to interrupt (polite expression).
8. Exquisite music thought to be made by the planets as they moved, but inaudible to mortal ears.
9. Your unfavorable interpretation (of my behavior).
1. As bears that were tied up at the stake and baited with dogs.
2. Veil of transparent silken gauze; the cypress tree was also emblematic of mourning.
3. Time to discard love's melancholy.
4. I.e., if I had to fall prey to love, it would have been better to succumb to the noble Orsino than to the hard-hearted Cesario.
5. Thames watermen's cry to attract passengers for the court at Westminster from London.

135   OLIVIA   Stay. I prithee tell me what thou[6] think'st of me.
        VIOLA   That you do think you are not what you are.[7]
        OLIVIA   If I think so, I think the same of you.[8]
        VIOLA   Then think you right, I am not what I am.
        OLIVIA   I would you were as I would have you be.
140   VIOLA   Would it be better, madam, than I am?
        I wish it might, for now I am your fool.[9]
        OLIVIA [*aside*]   O, what a deal of scorn looks beautiful
        In the contempt and anger of his lip!
        A murd'rous guilt shows not itself more soon
145   Than love that would seem hid. Love's night is noon.[1]
        [*To* VIOLA] Cesario, by the roses of the spring,
        By maidhood, honor, truth, and everything,
        I love thee so that, maugre° all thy pride,   *despite*
        Nor° wit nor reason can my passion hide.   *neither*
150   Do not extort thy reasons from this clause,[2]
        For that° I woo, thou therefore hast no cause.   *that because*
        But rather reason thus with reason fetter:[3]
        Love sought is good, but given unsought, is better.
        VIOLA   By innocence I swear, and by my youth,
155   I have one heart, one bosom, and one truth,
        And that no woman has, nor never none
        Shall mistress be of it save I alone.
        And so adieu, good madam. Never more
        Will I my master's tears to you deplore.°   *lament*
160   OLIVIA   Yet come again, for thou perhaps mayst move
        That heart which now abhors, to like his love.

                                Exeunt [*severally*]

3.2
Enter SIR TOBY, SIR ANDREW, *and* FABIAN

  SIR ANDREW   No, faith, I'll not stay a jot longer.
  SIR TOBY   Thy reason, dear venom,° give thy reason.   *venomous one*
  FABIAN   You must needs yield your reason, Sir Andrew.
  SIR ANDREW   Marry, I saw your niece do more favors to
5   the Count's servingman than ever she bestowed upon me.
        I saw't i'th' orchard.°   *garden*
  SIR TOBY   Did she see thee the while, old boy? Tell me that.
  SIR ANDREW   As plain as I see you now.
  FABIAN   This was a great argument° of love in her toward   *proof*
10   you.
  SIR ANDREW   'Slight,° will you make an ass o' me?   *by God's light*

---

6. Olivia changes from "you" to the familiar "thou."
7. That you think you are in love with a man, but you are mistaken.
8. Olivia may think that Cesario has suggested that she is mad; or she may imply that she thinks that Cesario, despite his subordinate position, is noble.
9. You have made a fool of me.

1. Love, though attempting secrecy, still shines out as bright as day.
2. Do not take the position that just because I woo you, you are under no obligation to reciprocate.
3. But instead constrain your reasoning with this argument.
3.2 Location: Olivia's house.

FABIAN   I will prove it legitimate, sir, upon the oaths of
judgment and reason.

SIR TOBY   And they have been grand-jurymen[1] since before
15   Noah was a sailor.

FABIAN   She did show favor to the youth in your sight only
to exasperate you, to awake your dormouse° valor, to put   *meek, timid*
fire in your heart and brimstone in your liver. You should
then have accosted her, and with some excellent jests,
20   fire-new from the mint,° you should have banged the   *newly minted*
youth into dumbness. This was looked for at your hand,
and this was balked.° The double gilt[2] of this opportunity   *neglected*
you let time wash off, and you are now sailed into the
north of my lady's opinion,[3] where you will hang like an
25   icicle on a Dutchman's[4] beard unless you do redeem it
by some laudable attempt either of valor or policy.°   *cunning*

SIR ANDREW   An't° be any way, it must be with valour, for   *if it*
policy I hate. I had as lief° be a Brownist as a politician.[5]   *as soon*

SIR TOBY   Why then, build me thy fortunes upon the basis
30   of valor. Challenge me° the Count's youth to fight with   *for me*
him, hurt him in eleven places. My niece shall take note
of it; and assure thyself, there is no love-broker in the
world can more prevail in man's commendation with
woman than report of valor.

35   FABIAN   There is no way but this, Sir Andrew.

SIR ANDREW   Will either of you bear me a challenge to
him?

SIR TOBY   Go, write it in a martial hand, be curst° and brief.   *sharp*
It is no matter how witty so it be eloquent and full of
40   invention.° Taunt him with the license of ink.[6] If thou   *imagination; untruth*
"thou'st"[7] him some thrice, it shall not be amiss, and as
many lies° as will lie in thy sheet of paper, although the   *accusations of lying*
sheet were big enough for the bed of Ware,[8] in England,
set 'em down, go about it. Let there be gall[9] enough in
45   thy ink; though thou write with a goose-pen,[1] no matter.
About it.

SIR ANDREW   Where shall I find you?

SIR TOBY   We'll call thee at the cubiculo.° Go.   *little chamber*

Exit SIR ANDREW

FABIAN   This is a dear manikin° to you, Sir Toby.   *puppet*

50   SIR TOBY   I have been dear° to him, lad, some two thousand   *costly*
strong or so.

---

1. Grand jurymen were supposed to be good judges of
evidence.
2. Twice glided, and as such, Sir Andrew's "golden
opportunity" to prove both love and valor.
3. Into Olivia's cold disfavor.
4. Perhaps an allusion to William Barentz, who led an
expedition to the Arctic in 1596–97.
5. Schemer. A Brownist was a member of the Puritan
sect founded in 1581 by Robert Browne.
6. I.e., with the freedom taken in writing but not risked

in conversation.
7. Call him "thou" (an insult to a stranger).
8. Famous Elizabethan bedstead, nearly eleven feet
square, now in the Victoria and Albert Museum, London.
9. (1) Oak gall, an ingredient in ink; (2) bitterness or
rancor.
1. Quill made of a goose feather. (The goose was proverbially cowardly and foolish.)

FABIAN   We shall have a rare letter from him; but you'll not
deliver't.

SIR TOBY   Never trust me then; and by all means stir on
the youth to an answer. I think oxen and wain-ropes[2]
cannot hale° them together. For Andrew, if he were   *drag*
opened and you find so much blood in his liver[3] as will
clog° the foot of a flea, I'll eat the rest of th'anatomy.°   *weigh down/cadaver*

FABIAN   And his opposite,° the youth, bears in his visage   *adversary*
no great presage of cruelty.

   Enter MARIA

SIR TOBY   Look where the youngest wren of nine[4] comes.

MARIA   If you desire the spleen,° and will laugh yourselves   *a laughing fit*
into stitches, follow me. Yon gull° Malvolio is turned hea-   *fool*
then, a very renegado,[5] for there is no Christian that
means to be saved by believing rightly can ever believe
such impossible passages of grossness.[6] He's in yellow
stockings.

SIR TOBY   And cross-gartered?

MARIA   Most villainously,° like a pedant° that keeps a   *abominably/teacher*
school i'th' church.[7] I have dogged him like his murderer.
He does obey every point of the letter that I dropped to
betray him. He does smile his face into more lines than
is in the new map with the augmentation of the Indies.[8]
You have not seen such a thing as 'tis. I can hardly forbear
hurling things at him. I know my lady will strike him. If
she do, he'll smile, and take't for a great favor.

SIR TOBY   Come bring us, bring us where he is.   *Exeunt*

3.3

Enter SEBASTIAN *and* ANTONIO

SEBASTIAN   I would not by my will have troubled you,
But since you make your pleasure of your pains
I will no further chide you.

ANTONIO   I could not stay behind you. My desire,
More sharp than filèd steel, did spur me forth,
And not all° love to see you—though so much   *only*
As might have drawn one to a longer voyage—
But jealousy° what might befall your travel,   *apprehension*
Being skilless in° these parts, which to a stranger,   *unfamiliar to*
Unguided and unfriended, often prove
Rough and unhospitable. My willing love
The rather° by these arguments of fear   *more willingly*
Set forth in your pursuit.

SEBASTIAN   My kind Antonio,

---

2. Wagon ropes pulled by oxen.
3. Supposed to be the source of blood, which engendered courage.
4. The smallest of small birds; the smallest wren in a
family of nine.
5. Renegade (Spanish); a Christian converted to Islam.
6. Such patent absurdities (in the letter).

7. Because no schoolroom is available in a small rustic
community.
8. Possibly refers to a map published in 1599 showing
the East Indies more fully than in earlier maps and
crisscrossed by many rhumb lines.
3.3 Location: A street scene.

I can no other answer make but thanks,
15 And thanks; and ever oft° good turns   *very often*
Are shuffled off° with such uncurrent[1] pay.   *shrugged off*
But were my worth as is my conscience° firm,   *sense of indebtedness*
You should find better dealing. What's to do?
Shall we go see the relics° of this town?   *sights*
20 ANTONIO   Tomorrow, sir. Best first go see your lodging.
SEBASTIAN   I am not weary, and 'tis long to night.
I pray you let us satisfy our eyes
With the memorials and the things of fame
That do renown this city.
ANTONIO   Would you'd pardon me.
25 I do not without danger walk these streets.
Once in a sea-fight 'gainst the Count his° galleys   *i.e., the Count's*
I did some service, of such note indeed
That were I ta'en° here it would scarce be answered.[2]   *captured*
SEBASTIAN   Belike° you slew great number of his people.   *perhaps*
30 ANTONIO   Th'offense is not of such a bloody nature,
Albeit the quality° of the time and quarrel   *circumstances*
Might well have given us bloody argument.°   *cause for bloodshed*
It might have since been answered in repaying
What we took from them, which for traffic's° sake   *trade's*
35 Most of our city did. Only myself stood out,
For which if I be latchèd° in this place   *caught*
I shall pay dear.
SEBASTIAN   Do not then walk too open.
ANTONIO   It doth not fit me. Hold, sir, here's my purse.
In the south suburbs at the Elephant°   *name of an inn*
40 Is best to lodge. I will bespeak our diet°   *order our meals*
Whiles you beguile° the time and feed your knowledge   *pass*
With viewing of the town. There shall you have me.
SEBASTIAN   Why I your purse?
ANTONIO   Haply° your eye shall light upon some toy°   *perhaps/trifle*
45 You have desire to purchase; and your store°   *resources*
I think is not for idle markets,[3] sir.
SEBASTIAN   I'll be your purse-bearer, and leave you
For an hour.
ANTONIO   To th' Elephant.
SEBASTIAN   I do remember.
Exeunt [severally]

3.4

Enter OLIVIA *and* MARIA
OLIVIA [*aside*]   I have sent after him, he says he'll come.
How shall I feast him? What bestow of° him?   *on*
For youth is bought more oft than begged or borrowed.[1]
I speak too loud.

---

1. Out of currency; worthless.
2. It would be difficult for me to make reparation (and thus my life would be in danger).

3. Not large enough to spend on luxuries.
3.4 Location: The garden of Olivia's house.
1. "Better to buy than to beg or borrow" was proverbial.

5 [*To* MARIA] Where's Malvolio? He is sad° and civil,°   *sober/respectful*
And suits well for a servant with my fortunes.
Where is Malvolio?

MARIA   He's coming, madam, but in very strange manner.
He is sure possessed,° madam.   *(by the devil); insane*

10 OLIVIA   Why, what's the matter? Does he rave?

MARIA   No, madam, he does nothing but smile. Your ladyship were best to have some guard about you if he come,
for sure the man is tainted in's wits.

OLIVIA   Go call him hither.   [*Exit* MARIA]
I am as mad as he,

15 If sad and merry madness equal be.
    Enter MALVOLIO [*cross-gartered and wearing yellow
    stockings, with* MARIA]
How now, Malvolio?

MALVOLIO   Sweet lady, ho, ho!

OLIVIA   Smil'st thou? I sent for thee upon a sad occasion.°   *about a serious matter*

MALVOLIO   Sad, lady? I could be sad. This does make some
20   obstruction in the blood, this cross-gartering, but what of
that? If it please the eye of one, it is with me as the very
true sonnet° is, "Please one, and please all."[2]   *song*

OLIVIA   Why, how dost thou, man? What is the matter with
thee?

25 MALVOLIO   Not black in my mind, though yellow[3] in my
legs. It did come to his hands, and commands shall be
executed. I think we do know the sweet roman hand.°   *italic calligraphy*

OLIVIA   Wilt thou go to bed,[4] Malvolio?

MALVOLIO [*kissing his hand*]   To bed? "Ay, sweetheart, and
30   I'll come to thee."[5]

OLIVIA   God comfort thee. Why dost thou smile so, and
kiss thy hand so oft?

MARIA   How do you, Malvolio?

MALVOLIO   At your request?—yes, nightingales answer
35   daws.[6]

MARIA   Why appear you with this ridiculous boldness
before my lady?

MALVOLIO   "Be not afraid of greatness"—'twas well writ.

OLIVIA   What meanest thou by that, Malvolio?

40 MALVOLIO   "Some are born great"—

OLIVIA   Ha?

MALVOLIO   "Some achieve greatness"—

OLIVIA   What sayst thou?

MALVOLIO   "And some have greatness thrust upon them."

45 OLIVIA   Heaven restore thee.

MALVOLIO   "Remember who commended thy yellow
stockings"—

---

2. If I please one, I please all I care to please (words
of a popular bawdy ballad).
3. Black and yellow biles indicated choleric and melancholic dispositions, respectively. "Black and yellow"
was the name of a popular song; to "wear yellow hose"
was to be jealous.

4. In order to cure his madness with sleep.
5. A line from a popular song.
6. Shall I deign to reply to you? Yes, since even the
nightingale sings in response to the crowing of the jackdaw.

OLIVIA "Thy yellow stockings"?

MALVOLIO "And wished to see thee cross-gartered."

50   OLIVIA "Cross-gartered"?

MALVOLIO "Go to, thou art made, if thou desirest to be so."

OLIVIA Am I made?

MALVOLIO "If not, let me see thee a servant still."

55   OLIVIA Why, this is very midsummer madness.

Enter a SERVANT

SERVANT Madam, the young gentleman of the Count Orsino's is returned. I could hardly entreat him back. He attends your ladyship's pleasure.

OLIVIA I'll come to him.   [*Exit* SERVANT]

60   Good Maria, let this fellow be looked to. Where's my cousin Toby? Let some of my people have a special care of him, I would not have him miscarry° for the half of my   come to harm
dowry.   *Exeunt* [OLIVIA *and* MARIA, *severally*]

MALVOLIO O ho, do you come near° me now? No worse   appreciate

65   man than Sir Toby to look to me. This concurs directly with the letter, she sends him on purpose, that I may appear stubborn to him, for she incites me to that in the letter. "Cast thy humble slough," says she, "be opposite with a kinsman, surly with servants, let thy tongue tang

70   arguments of state, put thyself into the trick of singularity," and consequently° sets down the manner how, as a   subsequently
sad face, a reverend carriage, a slow tongue, in the habit of some sir of note,° and so forth. I have limed[7] her, but   gentleman
it is Jove's doing, and Jove make me thankful. And when

75   she went away now, "let this fellow be looked to." Fellow![8]—not "Malvolio," nor after my degree, but "fellow." Why, everything adheres together that no dram of a scruple, no scruple of a scruple,[9] no obstacle, no incredulous or unsafe circumstance—what can be said?—nothing

80   that can be can come between me and the full prospect of my hopes. Well, Jove, not I, is the doer of this, and he is to be thanked.

Enter [SIR] TOBY, FABIAN, *and* MARIA

SIR TOBY Which way is he, in the name of sanctity? If all the devils of hell be drawn in little,[1] and Legion[2] himself

85   possessed him, yet I'll speak to him.

FABIAN Here he is, here he is. [*To* MALVOLIO] How is't with you, sir? How is't with you, man?

MALVOLIO Go off, I discard you. Let me enjoy my private.°   privacy
Go off.

90   MARIA Lo, how hollow° the fiend speaks within him. Did   resonantly

---

7. Birds were caught by smearing sticky birdlime on branches.
8. Malvolio takes the word to mean "companion."
9. Both phrases mean "no scrap of a doubt." "Dram": one-eighth of a fluid ounce. "Scruple": one-third of a dram.
1. Be contracted into a small space (punning on

"painted in miniature").
2. Alluding to a scene of exorcism in Mark 5.8–9: "For he [Jesus] said unto him, Come out of the man, thou unclean spirit. And he asked him, What is thy name? And he answered saying, My name is Legion: for we are many."

not I tell you? Sir Toby, my lady prays you to have a care
of him.

MALVOLIO Aha, does she so?

SIR TOBY Go to, go to. Peace, peace, we must deal gently
95 with him. Let me alone.° How do you, Malvolio? How is't   *leave him to me*
with you? What, man, defy the devil. Consider, he's an
enemy to mankind.

MALVOLIO Do you know what you say?

MARIA La° you, an you speak ill of the devil, how he takes   *look*
100 it at heart. Pray God he be not bewitched.

FABIAN Carry his water to th' wise woman.[3]

MARIA Marry, and it shall be done tomorrow morning, if
I live. My lady would not lose him for more than I'll say.

MALVOLIO How now, mistress?

105 MARIA O Lord!

SIR TOBY Prithee hold thy peace, this is not the way. Do
you not see you move° him? Let me alone with him.   *anger*

FABIAN No way but gentleness, gently, gently. The fiend
is rough,° and will not be roughly used.   *violent*

110 SIR TOBY Why how now, my bawcock?[4] How dost thou,
chuck?

MALVOLIO Sir!

SIR TOBY Ay, biddy,° come with me. What, man, 'tis not   *hen*
for gravity° to play at cherry-pit[5] with Satan. Hang him,   *for a man of dignity*
115 foul collier.[6]

MARIA Get him to say his prayers. Good Sir Toby, get him
to pray.

MALVOLIO My prayers, minx?°   *impertinent girl*

MARIA No, I warrant you, he will not hear of godliness.

120 MALVOLIO Go hang yourselves, all. You are idle° shallow   *foolish*
things, I am not of your element.° You shall know more   *social sphere*
hereafter.   *Exit*

SIR TOBY Is't possible?

FABIAN If this were played upon a stage, now, I could con-
125 demn it as an improbable fiction.

SIR TOBY His very genius° hath taken the infection of the   *spirit*
device,° man.   *trick*

MARIA Nay, pursue him now, lest the device take air and
taint.[7]

130 FABIAN Why, we shall make him mad indeed.

MARIA The house will be the quieter.

SIR TOBY Come, we'll have him in a dark room and bound.[8]
My niece is already in the belief that he's mad. We may
carry it thus° for our pleasure and his penance till our   *continue the pretense*
135 very pastime, tired out of breath, prompt us to have mercy

---

3. Local healer, "good witch." "Water": urine (for medical diagnosis).
4. Fine fellow (from the French *beau coq*, "fine bird").
5. A children's game in which cherry stones were
thrown into a hole.

6. Dirty coalman (the devil was supposed to be black).
7. Spoil (like leftover food) by exposure to air; become
known (and thus ruined).
8. Customary treatments for madness.

on him, at which time we will bring the device to the bar⁹
and crown thee for a finder of madmen.¹ But see, but see.

Enter SIR ANDREW [*with a paper*]

FABIAN More matter for a May morning.²

SIR ANDREW Here's the challenge, read it. I warrant
140   there's vinegar and pepper in't.

FABIAN Is't so saucy?

SIR ANDREW Ay—is't? I warrant him. Do but read.

SIR TOBY Give me.
    [*Reads*] "Youth, whatsoever thou art, thou art but a scurvy
145   fellow."

FABIAN Good, and valiant.

SIR TOBY "Wonder not, nor admire° not in thy mind why   marvel
    I do call thee so, for I will show thee no reason for't."

FABIAN A good note, that keeps you from the blow of the
150   law.³

SIR TOBY "Thou comest to the Lady Olivia, and in my sight
    she uses thee kindly; but thou liest in thy throat,° that is   deeply
    not the matter I challenge thee for."

FABIAN Very brief, and to exceeding good sense [*aside*]
155   -less.⁴

SIR TOBY "I will waylay thee going home, where if it be thy
    chance to kill me"—

FABIAN Good.

SIR TOBY "Thou killest me like a rogue and a villain."

160 FABIAN Still you keep o'th' windy side⁵ of the law—good.

SIR TOBY "Fare thee well, and God have mercy upon one
    of our souls. He may have mercy upon mine, but my hope
    is better,⁶ and so look to thyself.
    Thy friend as thou usest him, and thy sworn enemy,
165   Andrew Aguecheek."
    If this letter move° him not, his legs cannot. I'll give't him.   provoke

MARIA You may have very fit occasion for't. He is now in
    some commerce° with my lady, and will by and by depart.   conversation

SIR TOBY Go, Sir Andrew. Scout me° for him at the corner   look out
170   of the orchard like a bum-baily.⁷ So soon as ever thou
    seest him, draw, and as thou drawest, swear horrible, for
    it comes to pass oft that a terrible oath, with a swaggering
    accent sharply twanged off, gives manhood more appro-
    bation° than ever proof° itself would have earned him.   credit/trial
175   Away.

SIR ANDREW Nay, let me alone for swearing.⁸   *Exit*

SIR TOBY Now will not I deliver his letter, for the behavior
    of the young gentleman gives him out to be of good

9. Into the open court (to be judged).
1. I.e., one of a jury "finding," or declaring, a man to
be mad.
2. More pastime fit for a holiday.
3. That protects you from a charge of a breach of
peace.
4. The Folio's "sence-lesse" appears to use the hyphen

to signal an aside.
5. To windward (and therefore safe, not exposed to the
law's blasts).
6. Andrew means he expects to survive, but he ineptly
implies that he expects to be damned.
7. Petty sheriff's officer employed to arrest debtors.
8. Have no doubts as to my swearing ability.

capacity° and breeding. His employment between his lord   *ability*
180 and my niece confirms no less. Therefore this letter,
being so excellently ignorant, will breed no terror in the
youth. He will find it comes from a clodpoll.° But, sir, I   *blockhead*
will deliver his challenge by word of mouth, set upon
Aguecheek a notable report of valor, and drive the gen-
185 tleman—as I know his youth will aptly receive it⁹—into
a most hideous opinion of his rage, skill, fury, and impet-
uosity. This will so fright them both that they will kill one
another by the look, like cockatrices.¹

    Enter OLIVIA, *and* VIOLA [*as Cesario*]

FABIAN   Here he comes with your niece. Give them way°   *stand aside*
190 till he take leave, and presently after him.
SIR TOBY   I will meditate the while upon some horrid message for a challenge.

    [*Exeunt* SIR TOBY, FABIAN, *and* MARIA]

OLIVIA   I have said too much unto a heart of stone,
And laid mine honor too unchary° out.   *carelessly*
195 There's something in me that reproves my fault,
But such a headstrong potent fault it is
That it but mocks reproof.
VIOLA   With the same 'havior
That your passion bears² goes on my master's griefs.
OLIVIA [*giving a jewel*]   Here, wear this jewel³ for me, 'tis
    my picture—
200 Refuse it not, it hath no tongue to vex you—
And I beseech you come again tomorrow.
What shall you ask of me that I'll deny,
That honor, saved, may upon asking give?⁴
VIOLA   Nothing but this: your true love for my master.
205 OLIVIA   How with mine honor may I give him that
Which I have given to you?
VIOLA   I will acquit you.⁵
OLIVIA   Well, come again tomorrow. Fare thee well.
A fiend like thee might bear my soul to hell.   *Exit*

    Enter [SIR] TOBY *and* FABIAN

SIR TOBY   Gentleman, God save thee.
210 VIOLA   And you, sir.
SIR TOBY   That defense thou hast, betake thee to't. Of what
nature the wrongs are thou hast done him, I know not,
but thy intercepter, full of despite,° bloody as the hunter,   *defiance*
attends° thee at the orchard end. Dismount thy tuck,⁶ be   *awaits*
215 yare° in thy preparation, for thy assailant is quick, skillful,   *prompt*
and deadly.

---

9. As I know his inexperience will readily believe the
report.
1. Basilisks; mythical creatures supposed to kill at a
glance.
2. Behavior that characterizes your lovesickness.

3. Jeweled ornament, here a brooch or a locket with
Olivia's picture.
4. That honor may grant without compromising itself.
5. I will release you from your promise.
6. Draw your rapier.

VIOLA You mistake, sir, I am sure no man hath any quarrel
to me. My remembrance° is very free and clear from any   *memory*
image of offense done to any man.

220 SIR TOBY You'll find it otherwise, I assure you. Therefore,
if you hold your life at any price, betake you to your guard,
for your opposite° hath in him what youth, strength, skill,   *opponent*
and wrath can furnish man withal.

VIOLA I pray you, sir, what is he?

225 SIR TOBY He is knight dubbed with unhatched[7] rapier and
on carpet consideration,[8] but he is a devil in private
brawl. Souls and bodies hath he divorced three, and his
incensement at this moment is so implacable that satisfaction can be none but by pangs of death and sepulchre.

230 Hob nob[9] is his word,° give't or take't.   *motto*

VIOLA I will return again into the house and desire some
conduct° of the lady. I am no fighter. I have heard of some   *escort*
kind of men that put quarrels purposely on others, to
taste° their valor. Belike this is a man of that quirk.   *test*

235 SIR TOBY Sir, no. His indignation derives itself out of a
very competent° injury, therefore get you on, and give him   *sufficient*
his desire. Back you shall not to the house unless you
undertake that° with me which with as much safety you   *i.e., a duel*
might answer him. Therefore on, or strip your sword stark

240 naked, for meddle° you must, that's certain, or forswear   *engage in a duel*
to wear iron about you.[1]

VIOLA This is as uncivil as strange. I beseech you do me
this courteous office, as to know of° the knight what my   *ascertain from*
offense to him is. It is something of my negligence, noth-

245 ing of my purpose.

SIR TOBY I will do so. Signor Fabian, stay you by this gentleman till my return.   *Exit*

VIOLA Pray you, sir, do you know of this matter?

FABIAN I know the knight is incensed against you even to

250 a mortal arbitrement,° but nothing of the circumstance   *deadly duel*
more.

VIOLA I beseech you, what manner of man is he?

FABIAN Nothing of that wonderful promise to read him by
his form[2] as you are like to find him in the proof of his

255 valor. He is indeed, sir, the most skillful, bloody, and fatal
opposite that you could possibly have found in any part
of Illyria. Will you° walk towards him, I will make your   *if you will*
peace with him if I can.

VIOLA I shall be much bound to you for't. I am one that

260 had rather go with Sir Priest[3] than Sir Knight—I care not
who knows so much of my mettle.°   *Exeunt*   *disposition*

---

7. Unhacked, or undented, never used in battle.
8. A "carpet knight" obtained his title through connections at court rather than valor on the battlefield.
9. Have or have not ("all or nothing").

1. Or forfeit your right to wear a sword.
2. I.e., from his outward appearance, you cannot perceive him to be as remarkable.
3. Priests were often addressed as "sir."

Enter [SIR] TOBY *and* [SIR] ANDREW

SIR TOBY   Why, man, he's a very devil, I have not seen such
a virago.[4] I had a pass° with him, rapier, scabbard, and   *fencing bout*
all, and he gives me the stuck-in[5] with such a mortal
265   motion that it is inevitable, and on the answer,° he pays   *return hit*
you as surely as your feet hits the ground they step on.
They say he has been fencer to the Sophy.°   *shah of Persia*

SIR ANDREW   Pox on't, I'll not meddle with him.

SIR TOBY   Ay, but he will not now be pacified, Fabian can
270   scarce hold him yonder.

SIR ANDREW   Plague on't, an° I thought he had been val-   *if*
iant and so cunning in fence I'd have seen him damned
ere I'd have challenged him. Let him let the matter slip
and I'll give him my horse, grey Capulet.

275   SIR TOBY   I'll make the motion.° Stand here, make a good   *offer*
show on't—this shall end without the perdition of souls.°   *loss of lives*
[*Aside*] Marry, I'll ride your horse as well as I ride you.

Enter FABIAN, *and* VIOLA [*as Cesario*]

[*Aside to* FABIAN] I have his horse to take up° the quarrel,   *settle*
I have persuaded him the youth's a devil.

280   FABIAN [*aside to* SIR TOBY]   He is as horribly conceited[6] of
him, and pants and looks pale as if a bear were at his
heels.

SIR TOBY [*to* VIOLA]   There's no remedy, sir, he will fight
with you for's oath' sake. Marry, he hath better bethought
285   him of his quarrel, and he finds that now scarce to be
worth talking of. Therefore draw for the supportance of
his vow, he protests he will not hurt you.

VIOLA [*aside*]   Pray God defend me. A little thing would
make me tell them how much I lack of a man.

FABIAN [*to* SIR ANDREW]   Give ground if you see him furi-
290   ous.

SIR TOBY   Come, Sir Andrew, there's no remedy, the gentleman will for his honor's sake have one bout with you,
he cannot by the duello° avoid it, but he has promised   *code of dueling*
me, as he is a gentleman and a soldier, he will not hurt
295   you. Come on, to't.

SIR ANDREW   Pray God he keep his oath.

Enter ANTONIO

VIOLA   I do assure you 'tis against my will.

[SIR ANDREW *and* VIOLA *draw their swords*]

ANTONIO [*drawing his sword, to* SIR ANDREW]   Put up your
sword. If this young gentleman
Have done offense, I take the fault on me.
300   If you offend him, I for him defy you.

SIR TOBY   You, sir? Why, what are you?

ANTONIO   One, sir, that for his love dares yet do more

---

4. Woman warrior (suggesting great ferocity with a
feminine appearance).

5. Thrust (from the Italian *stoccata*).
6. He has as terrifying an idea.

Than you have heard him brag to you he will.

SIR TOBY [*drawing his sword*]   Nay, if you be an under-
305   taker,[7] I am for you.
              Enter OFFICERS

FABIAN   O, good Sir Toby, hold. Here come the officers.

SIR TOBY [*to* ANTONIO]   I'll be with you anon.

VIOLA [*to* SIR ANDREW]   Pray, sir, put your sword up if you
   please.

310 SIR ANDREW   Marry will I, sir, and for that° I promised you   *as for that*
   I'll be as good as my word. He will bear you easily, and
   reins well.
      [SIR ANDREW *and* VIOLA *put up their swords*]

FIRST OFFICER   This is the man, do thy office.

SECOND OFFICER   Antonio, I arrest thee at the suit of
315   Count Orsino.

ANTONIO   You do mistake me, sir.

FIRST OFFICER   No, sir, no jot. I know your favor° well,   *face*
   Though now you have no seacap on your head.
   [*To* SECOND OFFICER] Take him away, he knows I know him well.

320 ANTONIO   I must obey. [*To* VIOLA] This comes with seeking you.
   But there's no remedy, I shall answer° it.   *answer for*
   What will you do now my necessity
   Makes me to ask you for my purse? It grieves me
   Much more for what I cannot do for you
325   Than what befalls myself. You stand amazed,
   But be of comfort.

SECOND OFFICER   Come, sir, away.

ANTONIO [*to* VIOLA]   I must entreat of you some of that money.

VIOLA   What money, sir?
   For the fair kindness you have showed me here,
330   And part° being prompted by your present trouble,   *in part*
   Out of my lean and low ability
   I'll lend you something. My having is not much.
   I'll make division of my present° with you.   *ready money*
   Hold, [*offering money*] there's half my coffer.

ANTONIO   Will you deny me now?
335   Is't possible that my deserts to you
   Can lack persuasion?[8] Do not tempt my misery,
   Lest that it make me so unsound° a man   *morally weak*
   As to upbraid you with those kindnesses
   That I have done for you.

VIOLA   I know of none,
340   Nor know I you by voice, or any feature.
   I hate ingratitude more in a man
   Than lying, vainness, babbling drunkenness,
   Or any taint of vice whose strong corruption
   Inhabits our frail blood.

---

7. One who would take upon himself a task (here, a
challenge).

8. Is it possible my past kindness can fail to persuade
you?

ANTONIO   O heavens themselves!

345   SECOND OFFICER   Come, sir, I pray you go.

ANTONIO   Let me speak a little. This youth that you see here
    I snatched one half out of the jaws of death,
    Relieved him with such sanctity° of love,   *great devotion*
    And to his image,⁹ which methought did promise

350   Most venerable worth,¹ did I devotion.

FIRST OFFICER   What's that to us? The time goes by, away.

ANTONIO   But O, how vile an idol proves this god!
    Thou hast, Sebastian, done good feature° shame.   *physical beauty*
    In nature there's no blemish but the mind.

355   None can be called deformed but the unkind.
    Virtue is beauty, but the beauteous evil
    Are empty trunks o'er-flourished² by the devil.

FIRST OFFICER   The man grows mad, away with him.
    Come, come, sir.

ANTONIO   Lead me on.   *Exit* [*with* OFFICERS]

360   VIOLA [*aside*]   Methinks his words do from such passion fly
    That he believes himself. So do not I.³
    Prove true, imagination, O prove true,
    That I, dear brother, be now ta'en for you!

SIR TOBY   Come hither, knight. Come hither, Fabian. We'll

365   whisper o'er a couplet or two of most sage saws.°   *sayings, maxims*
       [*They stand aside*]

VIOLA   He named Sebastian. I my brother know
    Yet living in my glass.° Even such and so   *mirror*
    In favor° was my brother, and he went   *appearance*
    Still° in this fashion, color, ornament,   *always*

370   For him I imitate. O, if it prove,
    Tempests are kind, and salt waves fresh in love!   *Exit*

SIR TOBY [*to* SIR ANDREW]   A very dishonest,° paltry boy,   *dishonorable*
    and more a coward than a hare. His dishonesty appears
    in leaving his friend here in necessity, and denying him;

375   and for his cowardship, ask Fabian.

FABIAN   A coward, a most devout coward, religious in it.

SIR ANDREW   'Slid,° I'll after him again, and beat him.   *by God's eyelid*

SIR TOBY   Do, cuff him soundly, but never draw thy sword.

SIR ANDREW   An I do not—   [*Exit*]

380   FABIAN   Come, let's see the event.°   *outcome*

SIR TOBY   I dare lay any money 'twill be nothing yet.°   *after all*

                                            Exeunt

4.1

Enter SEBASTIAN *and* [FESTE, *the*] *clown*

FESTE   Will you° make me believe that I am not sent for   *are you trying to*
    you?

---

9. Appearance (with a play on "religious icon").
1. Was worthy of veneration.
2. Chests decorated with carving or painting; beautified bodies.

3. I.e., I do not entirely believe the passionate hope (for my brother's rescue) that is arising in me.
4.1 Location: Near Olivia's house.

SEBASTIAN   Go to, go to, thou art a foolish fellow,
   Let me be clear° of thee.   *rid*

5 FESTE   Well held out,° i'faith! No, I do not know you, nor   *kept up*
   I am not sent to you by my lady to bid you come speak
   with her, nor your name is not Master Cesario, nor this
   is not my nose, neither. Nothing that is so, is so.

SEBASTIAN   I prithee vent° thy folly somewhere else,   *utter, excrete*
10 Thou know'st not me.

FESTE   Vent my folly! He has heard that word of some great
   man, and now applies it to a fool. Vent my folly—I am
   afraid this great lubber° the world will prove a cockney.°   *lout!pampered child*
   I prithee now ungird thy strangeness,[1] and tell me what
15 I shall "vent" to my lady? Shall I "vent" to her that thou
   art coming?

SEBASTIAN   I prithee, foolish Greek,° depart from me   *buffoon*
   There's money for thee. If you tarry longer
   I shall give worse payment.

20 FESTE   By my troth, thou hast an open hand. These wise
   men that give fools money get themselves a good report,°   *reputation*
   after fourteen years' purchase.[2]
       Enter [SIR] ANDREW, [SIR] TOBY, *and* FABIAN

SIR ANDREW [*to* SEBASTIAN]   Now, sir, have I met you
   again? [*Striking him*] There's for you.

SEBASTIAN [*striking* SIR ANDREW *with his dagger*]   Why,
     there's for thee, and there, and there.
25   Are all the people mad?

SIR TOBY [*to* SEBASTIAN, *holding him back*]   Hold, sir, or
   I'll throw your dagger o'er the house.

FESTE   This will I tell my lady straight,° I would not be in   *straightway*
30 some of your coats for twopence.   [*Exit*]

SIR TOBY   Come on, sir, hold.

SIR ANDREW   Nay, let him alone, I'll go another way to
   work with him. I'll have an action of battery° against him   *a lawsuit for assault*
   if there be any law in Illyria. Though I struck him first,
35 yet it's no matter for that.

SEBASTIAN   Let go thy hand.

SIR TOBY   Come, sir, I will not let you go. Come, my young
   soldier, put up your iron. You are well fleshed.[3] Come on.

SEBASTIAN [*freeing himself*]   I will be free from thee.
   What wouldst thou now?
40 If thou dar'st tempt me further, draw thy sword.

SIR TOBY   What, what? Nay then, I must have an ounce
   or two of this malapert° blood from you.   *impudent*
       [SIR TOBY *and* SEBASTIAN *draw their swords.*]
       Enter OLIVIA

OLIVIA   Hold, Toby, on thy life I charge thee hold.

SIR TOBY   Madam.

---

1. I.e., stop pretending not to know me. (Feste mocks Sebastian's affected language.)
2. I.e., at a high price. The purchase price of land was normally twelve times its annual rent.
3. Experienced in combat. Hunting hounds were said to be "fleshed" after being fed part of their first kill.

45   OLIVIA   Will it be ever thus? Ungracious wretch,
        Fit for the mountains and the barbarous caves,
        Where manners ne'er were preached—out of my sight!
        Be not offended, dear Cesario.
        [*To* SIR TOBY] Rudesby,° be gone.   *ruffian*
                    [*Exeunt* SIR TOBY, SIR ANDREW, *and* FABIAN]
                                        I prithee, gentle friend,
50   Let thy fair wisdom, not thy passion sway
        In this uncivil and unjust extent°   *assault*
        Against thy peace. Go with me to my house,
        And hear thou there how many fruitless pranks
        This ruffian hath botched up,° that thou thereby   *clumsily contrived*
55   Mayst smile at this. Thou shalt not choose but go.
        Do not deny. Beshrew° his soul for me,   *curse*
        He started one poor heart of mine in thee.[4]
    SEBASTIAN   What relish° is in this? How runs the stream?   *task; meaning*
        Or° I am mad, or else this is a dream.   *either*
60   Let fancy° still my sense in Lethe[5] steep.   *imagination*
        If it be thus to dream, still let me sleep.
    OLIVIA   Nay, come, I prithee, would thou'dst be ruled by me.
    SEBASTIAN   Madam, I will.
    OLIVIA   O, say so, and so be.   *Exeunt*

                            4.2
            Enter MARIA [*carrying a gown and false beard, and*
            FESTE, *the*] *clown*
    MARIA   Nay, I prithee put on this gown and this beard,
        make him believe thou art Sir Topas[1] the curate. Do it
        quickly. I'll call Sir Toby the whilst.°   *in the meantime   Exit*
    FESTE   Well, I'll put it on, and I will dissemble[2] myself in't,
5   and I would I were the first that ever dissembled in such
        a gown.
            [*He disguises himself*]
        I am not tall enough to become the function well,[3] nor
        lean enough to be thought a good student,° but to be said°   *(of divinity)/reputed*
        "an honest man and a good housekeeper"° goes as fairly   *host*
10   as[4] to say "a careful man and a great scholar." The com-
        petitors° enter.   *associates*
            Enter [SIR] TOBY [*and* MARIA]
    SIR TOBY   Jove bless thee, Master Parson.
    FESTE   Bonos dies,[5] Sir Toby, for, as the old hermit of
        Prague,[6] that never saw pen and ink, very wittily° said to   *intelligently*
15   a niece of King Gorboduc,° "That that is, is." So I, being   *legendary British king*
        Master Parson, am Master Parson; for what is "that" but
        "that," and "is" but "is"?

---

4. By attacking Sebastian, Sir Toby frightened Olivia,
who has exchanged hearts with Sebastian. "Started": an
allusion to hunting, creating a pun on "hart/heart."
5. The mythical river of oblivion.
4.2 Location: Olivia's house, where Malvolio will be
found (offstage) "in a dark room and bound" (3.4.132).
1. The comical hero of Chaucer's *Tale of Sir Thopas.*
Also alluding to the topaz stone, which was thought to

have special curative qualities for insanity.
2. Disguise; with subsequent play on "lie."
3. Grace the priestly office. "Tall": stout, rather than
of great height.
4. Sounds as well as.
5. Good day (false Latin).
6. Probably an invented authority.

SIR TOBY   To him, Sir Topas.

FESTE   What ho, I say, peace in this prison.

20   SIR TOBY   The knave counterfeits well—a good knave.

          MALVOLIO *within*

MALVOLIO   Who calls there?

FESTE   Sir Topas the curate, who comes to visit Malvolio
     the lunatic.

MALVOLIO   Sir Topas, Sir Topas, good Sir Topas, go to my
25   lady.

FESTE   Out, hyperbolical fiend,[7] how vexest thou this man!
     Talkest thou nothing but of ladies?

SIR TOBY   Well said, Master Parson.

MALVOLIO   Sir Topas, never was man thus wronged. Good
30   Sir Topas, do not think I am mad. They have laid me here
     in hideous darkness.

FESTE   Fie, thou dishonest Satan—I call thee by the most
     modest° terms, for I am one of those gentle ones that will   *mildest*
     use the devil himself with courtesy. Sayst thou that
35   house° is dark?   *room*

MALVOLIO   As hell, Sir Topas.

FESTE   Why, it hath bay windows transparent as barrica-
     does, and the clerestories[8] toward the south-north are as
     lustrous as ebony,[9] and yet complainest thou of obstruc-
40   tion?

MALVOLIO   I am not mad, Sir Topas; I say to you this house
     is dark.

FESTE   Madman, thou errest. I say there is no darkness but
     ignorance, in which thou art more puzzled than the Egyp-
45   tians in their fog.[1]

MALVOLIO   I say this house is as dark as ignorance, though
     ignorance were as dark as hell; and I say there was never
     man thus abused. I am no more mad than you are. Make
     the trial of it in any constant question.°   *logical discussion*

50   FESTE   What is the opinion of Pythagoras[2] concerning
     wildfowl?

MALVOLIO   That the soul of our grandam might haply°   *perhaps*
     inhabit a bird.

FESTE   What thinkest thou of his opinion?

55   MALVOLIO   I think nobly of the soul, and no way approve
     his opinion.

FESTE   Fare thee well. Remain thou still in darkness. Thou
     shalt hold th'opinion of Pythagoras ere I will allow of thy
     wits,° and fear to kill a woodcock[3] lest thou dispossess   *certify your sanity*
60   the soul of thy grandam. Fare thee well.

MALVOLIO   Sir Topas, Sir Topas!

---

7. Feste treats Malvolio as a man possessed by vehement ("hyperbolical") evil spirits.
8. Upper windows, usually in a church or great hall.
"Barricadoes": barricades (subsequent paradoxes are
equivalent to "as clear as mud").
9. A dense and naturally dull black wood.

1. One of the plagues of Egypt was a "black darkness"
lasting for three days (Exodus 10.21–23).
2. An ancient Greek philosopher who held that the
same soul could successively inhabit different creatures.
3. A traditionally stupid bird.

SIR TOBY   My most exquisite Sir Topas.

FESTE   Nay, I am for all waters.[4]

MARIA   Thou mightst have done this without thy beard and
65   gown, he sees thee not.

SIR TOBY [*to* FESTE]   To him in thine own voice, and bring
me word how thou findest him. I would we were well rid
of this knavery. If he may be conveniently delivered, I
would he were, for I am now so far in offence with my
70   niece that I cannot pursue with any safety this sport to
the upshot. [*To* MARIA] Come by and by to my
chamber.   *Exit* [*with* MARIA]

FESTE [*sings*][5]   "Hey Robin, jolly Robin,
Tell me how thy lady does."

75   MALVOLIO   Fool!

FESTE   "My lady is unkind, pardie."[6]

MALVOLIO   Fool!

FESTE   "Alas, why is she so?"

MALVOLIO   Fool, I say!

80   FESTE   "She loves another."
Who calls, ha?

MALVOLIO   Good fool, as ever thou wilt deserve well at my
hand, help me to a candle and pen, ink, and paper. As I
am a gentleman, I will live to be thankful to thee for't.

85   FESTE   Master Malvolio?

MALVOLIO   Ay, good fool.

FESTE   Alas, sir, how fell you besides° your five wits?[7]   *out of*

MALVOLIO   Fool, there was never man so notoriously°   *outrageously*
abused. I am as well in my wits, fool, as thou art.

90   FESTE   But as well? Then you are mad indeed, if you be no
better in your wits than a fool.

MALVOLIO   They have here propertied me,[8] keep me in
darkness, send ministers to me, asses, and do all they can
to face me[9] out of my wits.

95   FESTE   Advise you° what you say, the minister is here.   *be careful*
[*As Sir Topas*] Malvolio, Malvolio, thy wits the heavens
restore. Endeavor thyself to sleep, and leave thy vain
bibble-babble.

MALVOLIO   Sir Topas.

100   FESTE [*as Sir Topas*]   Maintain no words with him, good
fellow. [*As himself*] Who I, sir? Not I, sir. God b'wi' you,°   *God be with you*
good Sir Topas. [*As Sir Topas*] Marry, amen. [*As himself*]
I will, sir, I will.

MALVOLIO   Fool, fool, fool, I say.

105   FESTE   Alas, sir, be patient. What say you, sir? I am shent°   *scolded*
for speaking to you.

MALVOLIO   Good fool, help me to some light and some

---

4. I am able to turn my hand to anything.
5. Feste's song, which makes Malvolio aware of his
presence, is traditional. There is a version by Sir Thomas Wyatt.
6. A corruption of the French *pardieu*, "by God."

7. Usually regarded as common sense, fantasy, memory, judgment, and imagination.
8. Treated me as a piece of property.
9. Brazenly construe me as.

paper. I tell thee I am as well in my wits as any man in
Illyria.

110 FESTE Well-a-day° that you were, sir.   *alas*

MALVOLIO By this hand, I am. Good fool, some ink, paper,
and light, and convey what I will set down to my lady. It
shall advantage thee more than ever the bearing of letter
did.

115 FESTE I will help you to't. But tell me true, are you not
mad indeed, or do you but counterfeit?

MALVOLIO Believe me, I am not, I tell thee true.

FESTE Nay, I'll ne'er believe a madman till I see his brains.
I will fetch you light, and paper, and ink.

120 MALVOLIO Fool, I'll requite it in the highest degree. I
prithee, be gone.

FESTE   I am gone, sir,
                     And anon, sir,
                        I'll be with you again,
125   In a trice,
                     Like to the old Vice,[1]
                        Your need to sustain,
                     Who with dagger of lath
                     In his rage and his wrath
130   Cries "Aha," to the devil,
                     Like a mad lad,
                     "Pare thy nails, dad,
                        Adieu, goodman[2] devil."   *Exit*

4.3

Enter SEBASTIAN

SEBASTIAN This is the air, that is the glorious sun.
This pearl she gave me, I do feel't and see't,
And though 'tis wonder that enwraps me thus,
Yet 'tis not madness. Where's Antonio then?

5 I could not find him at the Elephant,
Yet there he was,° and there I found this credit,°   *had been / report*
That he did range the town to seek me out.
His counsel now might do me golden service,
For though my soul disputes well with my sense[1]

10 That this may be some error but no madness,
Yet doth this accident and flood of fortune
So far exceed all instance,° all discourse,°   *precedent / reasoning*
That I am ready to distrust mine eyes
And wrangle with my reason that persuades me

15 To any other trust° but that I am mad,   *belief*
Or else the lady's mad. Yet if 'twere so
She could not sway° her house, command her followers,   *rule*
Take and give back affairs and their dispatch[2]

---

1. A stock comic figure in the old morality plays; the
Vice often carried a wooden dagger.
2. Yeoman; a title given to one not of gentle birth,
hence a parting insult to Malvolio.

4.3 Location: Near Olivia's house.
1. For though my reason and my sense both concur.
2. Undertake business, and ensure that it is carried
out.

With such a smooth, discreet, and stable bearing
20   As I perceive she does. There's something in't
That is deceivable.° But here the lady comes.   *deceptive*

Enter OLIVIA *and* PRIEST

OLIVIA   Blame not this haste of mine. If you mean well
Now go with me, and with this holy man,
Into the chantry by.° There before him,   *nearby chapel*
25   And underneath that consecrated roof,
Plight me the full assurance of your faith,[3]
That my most jealous° and too doubtful soul   *anxious*
May live at peace. He shall conceal it
Whiles° you are willing it shall come to note,   *until*
30   What° time we will our celebration keep   *at which*
According to my birth.° What do you say?   *rank*
SEBASTIAN   I'll follow this good man, and go with you,
And having sworn truth, ever will be true.
OLIVIA   Then lead the way, good father, and heavens so
     shine
35   That they may fairly note° this act of mine.   *Exeunt*   *look favorably upon*

5.1
Enter [FESTE, *the*] *clown and* FABIAN
FABIAN   Now, as thou lovest me, let me see his letter.
FESTE   Good Master Fabian, grant me another request.
FABIAN   Anything.
FESTE   Do not desire to see this letter.
5   FABIAN   This is to give a dog, and in recompense desire my
     dog again.[1]

Enter Duke, VIOLA [*as Cesario*], CURIO, *and lords*

ORSINO   Belong you to the Lady Olivia, friends?
FESTE   Ay, sir, we are some of her trappings.°   *ornaments*
ORSINO   I know thee well. How dost thou, my good fellow?
10   FESTE   Truly, sir, the better for my foes and the worse for
     my friends.
ORSINO   Just the contrary—the better for thy friends.
FESTE   No, sir, the worse.
ORSINO   How can that be?
15   FESTE   Marry, sir, they praise me, and make an ass of me.
     Now my foes tell me plainly I am an ass, so that by my
     foes, sir, I profit in the knowledge of myself, and by my
     friends I am abused;° so that, conclusions to be as kisses,   *deceived*
     if your four negatives make your two affirmatives,[2] why
20   then the worse for my friends and the better for my foes.
ORSINO   Why, this is excellent.
FESTE   By my troth, sir, no, though it please you to be one
     of my friends.

---

3. Enter into the solemn contract of betrothal.
5.1 Location: Before Olivia's house.
1. Perhaps a reference to an anecdote, recorded in John Manningham's diary, in which Queen Elizabeth requested a dog, and the donor, when granted a wish in return, asked for the dog back.
2. As in grammar a double negative can make an affirmative (and therefore four negatives can make two affirmatives), so when a coy girl is asked for a kiss, her four refusals can be construed as "yes, yes."

ORSINO [*giving money*] Thou shalt not be the worse for
25   me. There's gold.

FESTE But° that it would be double-dealing,³ sir, I would   *except for the fact*
       you could make it another.

ORSINO O, you give me ill counsel.

FESTE Put your grace in your pocket,⁴ sir, for this once,
30   and let your flesh and blood obey it.⁵

ORSINO Well, I will be so much a sinner to° be a double-   *as to*
       dealer. [*Giving money*] There's another.

FESTE *Primo, secundo, tertio*⁶ is a good play,° and the old   *game*
       saying is "The third pays for all."⁷ The triplex,° sir, is a   *triple time in music*
35   good tripping measure, or the bells of Saint Bennet,⁸ sir,
       may put you in mind—"one, two, three".

ORSINO You can fool no more money out of me at this
       throw.° If you will let your lady know I am here to speak   *throw of the dice*
       with her, and bring her along with you, it may awake my
40   bounty° further.   *generosity*

FESTE Marry, sir, lullaby to your bounty till I come again.
       I go, sir, but I would not have you to think that my desire
       of having is the sin of covetousness. But as you say, sir,
       let your bounty take a nap, I will awake it anon.   *Exit*
           Enter ANTONIO *and* OFFICERS

45 VIOLA Here comes the man, sir, that did rescue me.

ORSINO That face of his I do remember well,
       Yet when I saw it last it was besmeared
       As black as Vulcan⁹ in the smoke of war.
       A baubling° vessel was he captain of,   *trifling*
50   For shallow draught and bulk unprizable,¹
       With which such scatheful° grapple did he make   *destructive*
       With the most noble bottom° of our fleet   *ship*
       That very envy° and the tongue of loss°   *even enmity/the losers*
       Cried fame and honor on him. What's the matter?

55 FIRST OFFICER Orsino, this is that Antonio
       That took the *Phoenix* and her freight from Candy,²
       And this is he that did the *Tiger* board
       When your young nephew Titus lost his leg.
       Here in the streets, desperate of shame and state,³
60   In private brabble° did we apprehend him.   *brawl*

VIOLA He did me kindness, sir, drew on my side,⁴
       But in conclusion put strange speech upon° me.   *spoke strangely to*
       I know not what 'twas but distraction.°   *if not insanity*

ORSINO [*to* ANTONIO] Notable° pirate, thou salt-water thief,   *notorious*

---

3. (1) A duplicity; (2) a double donation.
4. Set aside (pocket up) your virtue; also (with a play
on the customary form of address for a duke, "your
grace"), reach into your pocket and grace me with
another coin.
5. Let your normal human instincts (as opposed to
grace) follow the "ill counsel" (line 28).
6. First, second, third (Latin): perhaps an allusion to a
dice throw or a child's game.
7. Third time lucky (proverbial).

8. A London church, across the Thames from the
Globe, was known as St. Bennet Hithe.
9. Blacksmith of the Roman gods.
1. Of no value because of its small size. "Draught":
water displaced by a vessel.
2. Candia, capital of Crete.
3. Recklessly oblivious of the danger to his honor and
his position (as a free man and public enemy).
4. Drew his sword in my defense.

65   What foolish boldness brought thee to their mercies
      Whom thou in terms so bloody and so dear°   *dire*
      Hast made thine enemies?
      ANTONIO   Orsino, noble sir,
      Be pleased that I shake off these names you give me.
      Antonio never yet was thief or pirate,
70   Though, I confess, on base° and ground enough   *foundation*
      Orsino's enemy. A witchcraft drew me hither.
      That most ingrateful boy there by your side
      From the rude sea's enraged and foamy mouth
      Did I redeem. A wreck past hope he was.
75   His life I gave him, and did thereto add
      My love without retention° or restraint,   *reservation*
      All his in dedication. For his sake
      Did I expose myself, pure° for his love,   *only*
      Into the danger of this adverse° town,   *hostile*
80   Drew to defend him when he was beset,
      Where being apprehended, his false cunning—
      Not meaning to partake with me in danger—
      Taught him to face me out of his acquaintance,[5]
      And grew a twenty years' removèd thing
85   While one would wink,[6] denied me mine own purse,
      Which I had recommended° to his use   *consigned*
      Not half an hour before.
      VIOLA   How can this be?
      ORSINO   When came he to this town?
90   ANTONIO   Today, my lord, and for three months before,
      No int'rim, not a minute's vacancy,°   *interval*
      Both day and night did we keep company.
                Enter OLIVIA *and attendants*
      ORSINO   Here comes the Countess. Now heaven walks on earth.
      But for thee, fellow—fellow, thy words are madness.
95   Three months this youth hath tended upon me.
      But more of that anon. Take him aside.
      OLIVIA   What would my lord, but that he may not have,[7]
      Wherein Olivia may seem serviceable?
      Cesario, you do not keep promise with me.
100   VIOLA   Madam—
      ORSINO   Gracious Olivia—
      OLIVIA   What do you say, Cesario? Good my lord—
      VIOLA   My lord would speak, my duty hushes me.
      OLIVIA   If it be aught° to the old tune, my lord,   *anything*
105   It is as fat and fulsome° to mine ear   *gross and offensive*
          As howling after music.
      ORSINO   Still so cruel?
      OLIVIA   Still so constant, lord.
      ORSINO   What, to perverseness? You uncivil lady,

---

5. To brazenly deny my acquaintance.
6. I.e., in the wink of an eye, pretended we had been
estranged for twenty years.
7. Except that which he may not have (my love).

110 To whose ingrate and unauspicious° altars   *unfavorable*
    My soul the faithfull'st off'rings hath breathed out
    That e'er devotion tendered—what shall I do?
    OLIVIA   Even what it please my lord that shall become° him.   *be fitting for*
    ORSINO   Why should I not, had I the heart to do it,
115 Like to th' Egyptian thief, at point of death
    Kill what I love[8]—a savage jealousy
    That sometime savors nobly.° But hear me this: *of nobility*
    Since you to non-regardance° cast my faith,   *oblivion*
    And that I partly know the instrument
120 That screws° me from my true place in your favour,   *wrenches*
    Live you the marble-breasted tyrant still.
    But this your minion,° whom I know you love,   *darling*
    And whom, by heaven I swear, I tender° dearly,   *regard*
    Him will I tear out of that cruel eye
125 Where he sits crownèd in his master's spite.[9]
    [*To* VIOLA] Come, boy, with me. My thoughts are ripe in mischief.
    I'll sacrifice the lamb that I do love
    To spite a raven's heart within a dove.
    VIOLA   And I most jocund,° apt,° and willingly   *cheerfully/ready*
130 To do you rest a thousand deaths would die.
    OLIVIA   Where goes Cesario?
    VIOLA   After him I love
    More than I love these eyes, more than my life,
    More by all mores[1] than e'er I shall love wife.
    If I do feign, you witnesses above,
135 Punish my life for tainting of my love.
    OLIVIA   Ay me detested, how am I beguiled!
    VIOLA   Who does beguile you? Who does do you wrong?
    OLIVIA   Hast thou forgot thyself? Is it so long?
    Call forth the holy father.   [*Exit an attendant*]
    ORSINO [*to* VIOLA]   Come, away.
140 OLIVIA   Whither, my lord? Cesario, husband, stay.
    ORSINO   Husband?
    OLIVIA   Ay, husband. Can he that deny?
    ORSINO [*to* VIOLA]   Her husband, sirrah?[2]
    VIOLA   No, my lord, not I.
    OLIVIA   Alas, it is the baseness of thy fear
    That makes thee strangle thy propriety.[3]
145 Fear not, Cesario, take thy fortunes up,
    Be that thou know'st thou art, and then thou art
    As great as that° thou fear'st.   *him whom*
              Enter PRIEST
                                O welcome, father.

---

8. In Heliodorus's *Ethiopica*, a Greek prose romance
translated into English in 1569 and popular in Shakespeare's day, the Egyptian robber chief Thyamis tries to
kill his captive Chariclea, whom he loves, when he is
in danger from a rival band.

9. To the mortification of his master.
1. More beyond all comparison.
2. Contemptuous form of address to an inferior.
3. That makes you deny your identity (as my husband).

Father, I charge thee by thy reverence
Here to unfold—though lately we intended
150 To keep in darkness what occasion° now   *necessity*
Reveals before 'tis ripe—what thou dost know
Hath newly passed between this youth and me.
PRIEST   A contract of eternal bond of love,
Confirmed by mutual joinder° of your hands,   *joining*
155 Attested by the holy close° of lips,   *meeting*
Strengthened by interchangement of your rings,
And all the ceremony of this compact
Sealed in my function,[4] by my testimony;
Since when, my watch hath told me, toward my grave
160 I have traveled but two hours.
ORSINO [*to* VIOLA]   O thou dissembling cub, what wilt thou be
When time hath sowed a grizzle on thy case?[5]
Or will not else thy craft° so quickly grow   *craftiness*
That thine own trip shall be thine overthrow?[6]
165 Farewell, and take her, but direct thy feet
Where thou and I henceforth may never meet.
VIOLA   My lord, I do protest.
OLIVIA   O, do not swear!
Hold little° faith, though thou hast too much fear.   *preserve some*
        Enter SIR ANDREW
SIR ANDREW   For the love of God, a surgeon—send one
170 presently° to Sir Toby.   *immediately*
OLIVIA   What's the matter?
SIR ANDREW   He's broke° my head across, and has given   *cut*
Sir Toby a bloody coxcomb,[7] too. For the love of God,
your help! I had rather than forty pound I were at home.
175 OLIVIA   Who has done this, Sir Andrew?
SIR ANDREW   The Count's gentleman, one Cesario. We
took him for a coward, but he's the very devil incardi-
nate.[8]
ORSINO   My gentleman, Cesario?
180 SIR ANDREW   'Od's lifelings,° here he is. [*To* VIOLA] You   *by God's little lives*
broke my head for nothing, and that that I did I was set
on to do't by Sir Toby.
VIOLA   Why do you speak to me? I never hurt you.
You drew your sword upon me without cause,
185 But I bespake you fair,[9] and hurt you not.
        Enter [SIR] TOBY *and* [FESTE, *the*] *clown*
SIR ANDREW   If a bloody coxcomb be a hurt you have hurt
me. I think you set nothing by° a bloody coxcomb. Here   *think nothing of*
comes Sir Toby, halting.° You shall hear more; but if° he   *limping/if only*
had not been in drink he would have tickled° you other-   *chastised*
190 gates° than he did.   *in other ways*

---

4. Ratified by priestly authority.
5. A gray hair ("grizzle") on your hide (sustaining the metaphor of "cub").
6. That your attempt to trip someone else will be the cause of your downfall.

7. Head; also, a fool's cap, which resembles the crest of a cock.
8. Sir Andrew's blunder for "incarnate" (in the flesh).
9. But I spoke courteously to you.

ORSINO [*to* SIR TOBY] How now, gentleman? How is't with
  you?

SIR TOBY That's all one,° he's hurt me, and there's th'end   *no matter*
  on't.

195 [*To* FESTE] Sot,° didst see Dick Surgeon, sot?   *fool, drunkard*

FESTE O, he's drunk, Sir Toby, an hour agone. His eyes
  were set[1] at eight i'th' morning.

SIR TOBY Then he's a rogue, and a passy-measures pavan.[2]
  I hate a drunken rogue.

OLIVIA Away with him! Who hath made this havoc with
200 them?

SIR ANDREW I'll help you, Sir Toby, because we'll be
  dressed[3] together.

SIR TOBY Will *you* help—an ass-head, and a coxcomb,°   *fool*
  and a knave, a thin-faced knave, a gull?°   *dupe*

205 OLIVIA Get him to bed, and let his hurt be looked to.
          [*Exeunt* SIR TOBY, SIR ANDREW, FESTE, *and* FABIAN]
          Enter SEBASTIAN

SEBASTIAN [*to* OLIVIA] I am sorry, madam, I have hurt your
  kinsman,
  But had it been the brother of my blood
  I must have done no less with wit and safety.[4]
  You throw a strange regard upon me,° and by that   *regard me strangely*
210 I do perceive it hath offended you.
  Pardon me, sweet one, even for the vows
  We made each other but so late ago.

ORSINO One face, one voice, one habit, and two persons,
  A natural perspective,[5] that is and is not.

215 SEBASTIAN Antonio! O, my dear Antonio,
  How have the hours racked and tortured me
  Since I have lost thee!

ANTONIO Sebastian are you?

SEBASTIAN Fear'st thou° that, Antonio?   *do you doubt*

220 ANTONIO How have you made division of yourself?
  An apple cleft in two is not more twin
  Than these two creatures. Which is Sebastian?

OLIVIA Most wonderful!°   *full of wonder*

SEBASTIAN [*seeing* VIOLA] Do I stand there? I never had a brother,
225 Nor can there be that deity° in my nature   *divine power*
  Of here and everywhere.° I had a sister,   *of omnipresence*
  Whom the blind waves and surges have devoured.
  Of charity,° what kin are you to me?   *please*
  What countryman? What name? What parentage?

230 VIOLA Of Messaline. Sebastian was my father.
  Such a Sebastian was my brother, too.
  So went he suited° to his watery tomb.   *in appearance; clad*
  If spirits can assume both form and suit

1. Closed (as the sun sets).
2. A variety of the slow dance known as "pavane" (from
the Italian *passemezzo pavana*). Sir Toby may think its
swaying movements suggest drunkenness.
3. We'll have our wounds dressed.
4. With any sense of my welfare.
5. An optical illusion produced by nature (rather than
by a mirror).

You come to fright us.

SEBASTIAN   A spirit I am indeed,
235   But am in that dimension grossly clad
Which from the womb I did participate.[6]
Were you a woman, as the rest goes even,°   *the rest suggests*
I should my tears let fall upon your cheek
And say "Thrice welcome, drownèd Viola."
240   VIOLA   My father had a mole upon his brow.

SEBASTIAN   And so had mine.

VIOLA   And died that day when Viola from her birth
Had numbered thirteen years.

SEBASTIAN   O, that record is lively[7] in my soul.
245   He finishèd indeed his mortal act
That day that made my sister thirteen years.

VIOLA   If nothing lets° to make us happy both   *hinders*
But this my masculine usurped attire,
Do not embrace me till each circumstance
250   Of place, time, fortune do cohere and jump°   *agree*
That I am Viola, which to confirm
I'll bring you to a captain in this town
Where lie my maiden weeds,° by whose gentle help   *clothes*
I was preserved to serve this noble count.
255   All the occurrence of my fortune since
Hath been between this lady and this lord.

SEBASTIAN [*to* OLIVIA]   So comes it, lady, you have been mistook.
But nature to her bias drew in that.[8]
You would have been contracted° to a maid,   *betrothed*
260   Nor are you therein, by my life, deceived.
You are betrothed both to a maid and man.[9]

ORSINO [*to* OLIVIA]   Be not amazed. Right noble is his blood.
If this be so, as yet the glass seems true,[1]
I shall have share in this most happy wreck.
265   [*To* VIOLA] Boy, thou hast said to me a thousand times
Thou never shouldst love woman like to me.

VIOLA   And all those sayings will I overswear,°   *swear again*
And all those swearings keep as true in soul
As doth that orbèd continent[2] the fire
That severs day from night.
270   ORSINO   Give me thy hand,
And let me see thee in thy woman's weeds.

VIOLA   The captain that did bring me first on shore
Hath my maid's garments. He upon some action°   *legal charge*
Is now in durance,° at Malvolio's suit,   *prison*
275   A gentleman and follower of my lady's.

OLIVIA   He shall enlarge° him. Fetch Malvolio hither—   *release*

---

6. I.e., I am clad, like all mortals, in the flesh in which
I was born.
7. The memory of that is vivid.
8. But nature followed her inclination. (The image is
from the game of bowls, which uses a ball with an off-
center weight that causes it to curve away from a

straight course.)
9. I.e., a man who is a virgin.
1. The "natural perspective" (line 214) continues to
seem real.
2. Referring to either the sun or the sphere within
which the sun was thought to be fixed.

And yet, alas, now I remember me,
They say, poor gentleman, he's much distraught.
    Enter [FESTE, *the*] *clown with a letter, and* FABIAN
A most extracting° frenzy of mine own   *distracting*
280 From my remembrance clearly banished his.
How does he, sirrah?
FESTE   Truly, madam, he holds Beelzebub at the stave's
    end[3] as well as a man in his case may do. He's here writ
    a letter to you. I should have given't you today morning.
285   But as a madman's epistles are no gospels,[4] so it skills°   *matters*
    not much when they are delivered.
OLIVIA   Open't and read it.
FESTE   Look then to be well edified when the fool delivers°   *speaks the words of*
    the madman. [*Reads*] "By the Lord, madam"—
290 OLIVIA   How now, art thou mad?
FESTE   No, madam, I do but read madness. An your lady-
    ship will have it as it ought to be you must allow *vox*.[5]
OLIVIA   Prithee, read i'thy right wits.
FESTE   So I do, madonna, but to read his right wits[6] is
295   to read thus. Therefore perpend,° my princess, and give   *pay attention*
    ear.
OLIVIA [*to* FABIAN]   Read it you, sirrah.
        [FESTE *gives the letter to* FABIAN]
FABIAN (*reads*)   "By the Lord, madam, you wrong me, and
    the world shall know it. Though you have put me into
300   darkness and given your drunken cousin rule over me, yet
    have I the benefit of my senses as well as your ladyship.
    I have your own letter that induced me to the semblance
    I put on, with the which I doubt not but to do myself
    much right or you much shame. Think of me as you
305   please. I leave my duty a little unthought of, and speak
    out of my injury.[7]
                    The madly-used Malvolio."
OLIVIA   Did he write this?
FESTE   Ay, madam.
310 ORSINO   This savors not much of distraction.°   *insanity*
OLIVIA   See him delivered,° Fabian, bring him hither.   *released*
    My lord, so please you—these things further thought on—
    To think me as well a sister as a wife,[8]
    One day shall crown th'alliance[9] on't, so please you,
315   Here at my house and at my proper cost.°   *own expense*
ORSINO   Madam, I am most apt° t'embrace your offer.   *ready*
    [*To* VIOLA] Your master quits° you, and for your service done him   *releases*
    So much against the mettle° of your sex,   *disposition*
    So far beneath your soft and tender breeding,

---

3. He holds the devil (who threatens to possess him)
at a distance (proverbial).
4. Gospel truths. "Epistles": letters (playing on the
sense of apostolic accounts of Christ in the New Testament).
5. The appropriate voice (Latin).

6. To accurately represent his mental state.
7. I neglect the formality I owe you as your servant and
speak as an injured person.
8. To think as well of me as a sister-in-law as you would
have thought of me as a wife.
9. The impending double-marriage ceremony.

320 And since you called me master for so long,
Here is my hand. You shall from this time be
Your master's mistress.
OLIVIA [*to* VIOLA]   A sister, you are she.
          Enter MALVOLIO
ORSINO   Is this the madman?
OLIVIA   Ay, my lord, this same.
How now, Malvolio?
MALVOLIO   Madam, you have done me wrong,
Notorious wrong.
325 OLIVIA   Have I, Malvolio? No.
MALVOLIO [*showing a letter*]   Lady, you have. Pray you
peruse that letter.
You must not now deny it is your hand.°   handwriting
Write from° it if you can, in hand or phrase,   differently from
Or say 'tis not your seal, not your invention.°   composition
330 You can say none of this. Well, grant it then,
And tell me in the modesty of honor[1]
Why you have given me such clear lights° of favor,   signs
Bade me come smiling and cross-gartered to you,
To put on yellow stockings, and to frown
335 Upon Sir Toby and the lighter° people,   lesser
And acting° this in an obedient hope,   upon doing
Why have you suffered me to be imprisoned,
Kept in a dark house, visited by the priest,
And made the most notorious geck° and gull   fool
340 That e'er invention° played on? Tell me why?   trickery
OLIVIA   Alas, Malvolio, this is not my writing,
Though I confess much like the character,°   handwriting
But out of question, 'tis Maria's hand.
And now I do bethink me, it was she
345 First told me thou wast mad; then cam'st° in smiling,   you came
And in such forms which here were presupposed°   previously suggested
Upon thee in the letter. Prithee be content;
This practice hath most shrewdly passed[2] upon thee,
But when we know the grounds and authors of it
350 Thou shalt be both the plaintiff and the judge
Of thine own cause.
FABIAN   Good madam, hear me speak,
And let no quarrel nor no brawl to come
Taint the condition of this present hour,
Which I have wondered at. In hope it shall not,
355 Most freely I confess myself and Toby
Set this device against Malvolio here
Upon° some stubborn and uncourteous parts°   because / behavior
We had conceived against him.[3] Maria writ   importunity
The letter, at Sir Toby's great importance,°
360 In recompense whereof he hath married her.

1. Tell me with the propriety that becomes a noble-   2. This trick has most mischievously played.
woman.   3. To which we took exception.

How with a sportful malice it was followed°   *followed through*
May rather pluck on° laughter than revenge   *incite*
If that the injuries be justly weighed
That have on both sides passed.

OLIVIA [*to* MALVOLIO]   Alas, poor fool, how have they baf-
365   fled° thee!   *disgraced*

FESTE   Why. "Some are born great, some achieve grea-
ness, and some have greatness thrown upon them." I was
one, sir, in this interlude,° one Sir Topas, sir; but that's   *comedy*
all one. "By the Lord, fool, I am not mad"—but do you
370   remember, "Madam, why laugh you at such a barren rascal, an you smile not, he's gagged"—and thus the whirl-
igig° of time brings in his revenges.   *spinning top*

MALVOLIO   I'll be revenged on the whole pack of you.
                                                        [*Exit*]
OLIVIA   He hath been most notoriously abused.
375 ORSINO   Pursue him, and entreat him to a peace.
He hath not told us of the captain yet.
                                            [*Exit one or more*]
When that is known, and golden time convents,°   *summons; is convenient*
A solemn combination shall be made
Of our dear souls. Meantime, sweet sister,
380   We will not part from hence.° Cesario, come—   *(Olivia's house)*
For so you shall be while you are a man;
But when in other habits you are seen,
Orsino's mistress, and his fancy's° queen.   *love's; imagination's*
                                            Exeunt [*all but* FESTE]

FESTE   (*sings*)   When that I was and a little tiny boy,
385   With hey, ho, the wind and the rain,
                        A foolish thing was but a toy,
                            For the rain it raineth every day.

                        But when I came to man's estate,
                            With hey, ho, the wind and the rain,
390   'Gainst knaves and thieves men shut their gate,
                            For the rain it raineth every day.

                        But when I came, alas, to wive,
                            With hey, ho, the wind and the rain,
                        By swaggering° could I never thrive,   *bullying*
395   For the rain it raineth every day.

                        But when I came unto my beds,
                            With hey, ho, the wind and the rain,
                        With tosspots° still had drunken heads,   *drunkards*
                            For the rain it raineth every day.

400   A great while ago the world begun,
                            With hey, ho, the wind and the rain,
                        But that's all one, our play is done,
                            And we'll strive to please you every day.
                                                        Exit

King Lear The story of King Lear and his three daughters had often been told, in chronicles, poems, and sermons as well as on stage, when Shakespeare undertook to make it the subject of a tragedy. The play, performed at court in December 1605, was probably written and first performed somewhat earlier, though not before 1603, since it contains allusions to a florid piece of anti-Catholic propaganda published that year, Samuel Harsnett's *Declaration of Egregious Popish Impostures*. Thus scholars generally assign Shakespeare's composition of *King Lear* to 1604–05, shortly after *Othello* (ca. 1603–04) and before *Macbeth* (ca. 1606): an astounding succession of tragic masterpieces.

When *King Lear* was first performed it may have struck contemporaries as strangely timely in the wake of a lawsuit that had occurred in late 1603. The two elder daughters of a doddering gentleman named Sir Brian Annesley attempted to get him legally certified as insane, thereby enabling themselves to take over his estate, while his youngest daughter vehemently protested on her father's behalf. The youngest daughter's name happened to be Cordell, a name uncannily close to that of Lear's youngest daughter, Cordelia, who tries to save her father from the malevolent designs of her older sisters.

The Annesley case directs our own attention to the ordinary family tensions and fears around which *King Lear*, for all its wildness, violence, and strangeness, is constructed. Though the Lear story has the mythic quality of a folktale (specifically, it resembles both the tale of Cinderella and the tale of a daughter who falls into disfavor for telling her father she loves him as much as salt), it was rehearsed in Shakespeare's time both as a piece of authentic British history from the very ancient past (ca. 800 B.C.E.) and as a warning to contemporary fathers not to put too much trust in the flattery of their children. In some versions of the story, including Shakespeare's, the warning centers on a decision to retire.

Retirement has come to seem a routine event, but in the patriarchal culture of Tudor and Stuart England, where the old demanded the public deference of the young, it was generally shunned. When through illness or extreme old age, it became unavoidable, retirement put a severe strain on the politics and psychology of deference by driving a wedge between status—what Lear at society's pinnacle calls "The name, and all the additions to a king" (1.1.137)—and power. In both the state and the family, the strain could be somewhat eased by transferring power to the eldest legitimate male successor, but as the families of both the legendary Lear and the real Brian Annesley show, such a successor did not always exist. In the absence of a male heir, the aged Lear, determined to "shake all cares and business" from himself and confer them on "younger strengths," attempts to divide his kingdom among his daughters so that, as he puts it, "future strife / May be prevented now" (1.1.38–44). But this attempt, centered on a public love test, is a disastrous failure, since it leads him to banish the one child who truly loves him.

Shakespeare contrives to show that the problem with which his characters are grappling does not simply result from the absence of a son and heir. In his most brilliant and complex use of a double plot, he intertwines the story of Lear and his three daughters with the story of Gloucester and his two sons, a story he adapted from an episode in Philip Sidney's prose romance, *Arcadia*. Gloucester has a legitimate heir, his elder son, Edgar, as well as an illegitimate son, Edmund, and in this family the tragic conflict originates not in an unusual manner of transferring property from one generation to another but rather in the reverse: Edmund seethes with murderous resentment at the disadvantage entirely customary for someone in his position, both as a younger son and as what was called a "base" or "natural" child.

But why does Lear, who has, as the play begins, already drawn up the map equitably dividing the kingdom, stage the love test? In Shakespeare's principal source, an anonymous play called *The True Chronicle History of King Leir* (published in 1605 but dating from 1594 or earlier), there is a gratifyingly clear answer. Leir's strong-willed daughter Cordella has vowed that she will marry only a man whom she herself loves; Leir wishes her to marry the man he chooses for his own dynastic purposes. He stages the love test, anticipating that in competing with her sisters, Cordella will declare that she loves her father best, at which point Leir will demand that she prove her love by marrying the suitor of his choice. The stratagem backfires, but its purpose is clear.

By stripping his character of a comparable motive, Shakespeare makes Lear's act seem stranger, at once more arbitrary and more rooted in deep psychological needs. His Lear is a man who has determined to retire from power but who cannot endure dependence. Unwilling to lose his identity as an absolute authority both in the state and in the family, he arranges a public ritual—"Which of you shall we say doth love us most?" (1.1.50)—whose aim seems to be to allay his own anxiety by arousing it in his children. But Cordelia refuses to perform: "What shall Cordelia speak? Love and be silent" (1.1.61). When she says "Nothing," a word that echoes darkly throughout the play, Lear hears what he most dreads: emptiness, loss of respect, the extinction of identity. And when, under further interrogation, she declares that she loves her father "according to my bond" (1.1.93), Lear understands these words too to be the equivalent of "nothing."

As Cordelia's subsequent actions demonstrate, his youngest daughter's bond is in reality a sustaining, generous love, but it is a love that ultimately leads to her death. Here Shakespeare makes an even more startling departure not only from *The True Chronicle History of King Leir* but from all his known sources. The earliest of these, the account in Geoffrey of Monmouth's twelfth-century *Historia Regum Britanniae*, sets the pattern repeated in John Higgins's *A Mirror for Magistrates* (1574 ed.), William Warner's *Albion's England* (1586), Raphael Holinshed's *Chronicles* (1587), and Edmund Spenser's *Faerie Queene* (1590: 2.10.27–32): the aged Lear is overthrown by his wicked daughters and their husbands, but he is restored to the throne by the army of his good daughter's husband, the king of France. The story then is one of loss and restoration: Lear resumes his reign, and then "made ripe for death" by old age, as Spenser puts it, he dies and is succeeded by Cordelia. The conclusion is not unequivocally happy: in all of the known chronicles, Cordelia rules worthily for several years and then, after being deposed and imprisoned by her nephews, in despair commits suicide. But Shakespeare's ending is unprecedented in its tragic devastation. When in Act 5 Lear suddenly enters with the lifeless body of Cordelia in his arms, the original audience, secure in the expectation of a very different resolution, must have been doubly shocked, a shock cruelly reinforced when the signs that she might be reviving—"This feather stirs; she lives!" (5.3.265)—all prove false. Lear apparently dies in the grip of the illusion that he detects some breath on his daughter's lips, but we know that Cordelia will, as he says a moment earlier, "come no more,/ Never, never, never, never, never!" (5.3.307–08).

Those five reiterated words, the bleakest pentameter line Shakespeare ever wrote, are the climax of an extraordinary poetics of despair that is set in motion when Lear disinherits Cordelia and when Gloucester credits Edmund's lies about Edgar. *King Lear* has seemed to many modern readers and audiences the greatest of Shakespeare's tragedies precisely because of its anguished look into the heart of darkness, but its vision of suffering and evil has not always commanded unequivocal admiration. In the eighteenth century Samuel Johnson wrote that "I was many years ago so shocked by Cordelia's death that I know not whether I ever endured to read again the last scenes of the play till I undertook to revise them as an editor." Johnson's contemporaries preferred a revision of Shakespeare's tragedy undertaken in 1681 by Nahum Tate. Finding the play, he writes, "a Heap of Jewels, unstrung, and unpolished," Tate proceeded to restring them in order to save Cordelia's life and to produce the unambiguous and happy triumph of the forces of good.

Only in the nineteenth century was Shakespeare's deeply pessimistic ending—the old generation dead or dying, the survivors shaken to the core, the ruling families all broken with no impending marriage to promise renewal—generally restored to theatrical performance and the tragedy's immense power fully acknowledged. Even passionate admirers of *King Lear*, however, continued to express deep uneasiness, questioning whether the tragedy was suitable for the stage. Charles Lamb, for example, concluded flatly that "Lear is essentially impossible to be represented on stage." "To see Lear acted," Lamb wrote, "to see an old man tottering about the stage with a walking stick, turned out of doors by his daughters in a rainy night, has nothing in it but what is painful and disgusting." In such a view, *King Lear* could only be staged successfully in the imagination, where, freed from the limits of the human body, it could assume its true, stupendous proportions and enable the reader to grasp its ultimate spiritual meaning.

A succession of brilliant stage performances and, more recently, films has not only belied the view that *King Lear* is unactable but also underscored the crucial importance in the play of the body. If Shakespeare explores the extremes of the mind's anguish and the soul's devotion, he never forgets that his characters have bodies as well, bodies that have needs, cravings, and terrible vulnerabilities. When in this tragedy characters fall from high station, they plunge unprotected into a world of violent storms, murderous cruelty, and physical horror. The old king wanders raging on the heath, through a wild night of thunder and rain. Disguised as Poor Tom, a mad beggar possessed by demons, Gloucester's son Edgar enacts a life of utmost degradation. Gloucester's fate is even more terrible: betrayed by his son Edmund, he is seized in his own house by Lear's reptilian daughter Regan and her husband Cornwall, tied to a chair, brutally interrogated, blinded, and then thrust bleeding out of doors.

The body in *King Lear* is a site not only of abject misery, nausea, and pain but also of care and a nascent moral awareness. In the midst of his mad ravings, Lear turns to the shivering Fool and asks, "Art cold?" (3.2.68). The question anticipates his recognition a few moments later that there is more suffering in the world than his own. Such signs of goodness and empathy, as simple as offering one's hand to someone who is frightened, do not outweigh the harshness of the physical world of the play, let alone cancel out the vicious cruelty of certain of its inhabitants, but they do qualify its moral bleakness. For a time evil seems to flourish unchecked in the world of the play, but the wicked do not ultimately triumph, and, in the midst of their anguish, humiliation, and pain, Lear and Gloucester achieve flashes of insight.

The tragedy is not only that the intervals of moral resolution, mental lucidity, and spiritual calm are so brief, continually giving way to feverish grief and rage, but also that the modest human understandings, moving in their simplicity, cost such an enormous amount of pain. Edgar saves his father from despair but also in some sense breaks his father's heart. Cordelia's steadfast honesty, her refusal to flatter the father she loves, is admirable but has disastrous consequences, and her attempt to save Lear leads only to her own death. For a sublime moment, Lear actually *sees* his daughter, understands her separateness, acknowledges her existence:

> Do not laugh at me;
> For, as I am a man, I think this lady
> To be my child Cordelia. (4.7.69–71)

But it has taken the destruction of virtually his whole world to reach this recognition.

An apocalyptic dream of last judgment and redemption hovers over the entire tragedy, but it is a dream forever deferred. At the sight of the howling Lear with the dead Cordelia in his arms, the bystanders can only ask a succession of stunned questions. Lear's own question seems the most terrible and the most important:

> Why should a dog, a horse, a rat, have life,
> And thou no breath at all? (5.3.306–07)

It is a sign of *King Lear*'s astonishing freedom from orthodoxy that it refuses to offer any of the conventional answers to this question, answers that serve largely to conceal or deflect the mourner's anguish.

King Lear first appeared in print in a quarto published in 1608 entitled *The History of King Lear*; a substantially different text, entitled *The Tragedy of King Lear* and grouped with the other tragedies, was printed in the 1623 Folio. From the eighteenth century, when the difference between the two texts was first noted, editors, assuming that they were imperfect versions of the identical play, customarily conflated them, blending together the approximately one hundred folio lines not printed in the quarto with the approximately three hundred quarto lines not printed in the folio and selecting as best they could among the hundreds of particular alternative readings. But there is a growing scholarly consensus that the 1608 text of *Lear* represents the play as Shakespeare first wrote it and that the 1623 text represents a substantial revision. In order to make available as much of both texts as possible within the space constraints of this anthology, we here present a conflated version. We add, on facing pages, a sample in which readers can compare in detail *The History of King Lear* and *The Tragedy of King Lear*. Readers who wish to pursue this comparison further may consult the *Norton Shakespeare*, where the two texts are printed in their entirety on facing pages.

King Lear

THE PERSONS OF THE PLAY

LEAR, king of Britain
GONERIL, Lear's eldest daughter
Duke of ALBANY, her husband
REGAN, Lear's second daughter
Duke of CORNWALL, her husband
CORDELIA, Lear's youngest daughter
King of FRANCE }
Duke of BURGUNDY } suitors of Cordelia
Earl of KENT, later disguised as Caius
Earl of GLOUCESTER
EDGAR, elder son of Gloucester, later disguised as Tom o' Bedlam
EDMUND, bastard son of Gloucester
OLD MAN, Gloucester's tenant
CURAN, Gloucester's retainer
Lear's FOOL
OSWALD, Goneril's steward
A DOCTOR
A CAPTAIN
A GENTLEMAN
A HERALD
SERVANTS to Cornwall
Knights, officers, messengers, soldiers, attendants

1.1

Enter KENT, GLOUCESTER,[1] *and* EDMUND

KENT   I thought the king had more affected° the Duke of   *favored*
    Albany° than Cornwall.   *Scotland*
GLOUCESTER   It did always seem so to us; but now, in the

1.1 Location: King Lear's court.

1. Pronounced "Gloster."

division of the kingdom, it appears not° which of the   *is not clear*

5   dukes he values most; for equalities° are so weighed,° that   *shares/equal*

curiosity in neither can make choice of either's moiety.[2]

KENT   Is not this your son, my lord?

GLOUCESTER   His breeding,° sir, hath been at my charge.[3]   *upbringing*

I have so often blushed to acknowledge him, that now I

10   am brazed° to it.   *hardened*

KENT   I cannot conceive° you.   *comprehend*

GLOUCESTER   Sir, this young fellow's mother could;[4]

whereupon she grew round-wombed, and had, indeed,

sir, a son for her cradle ere she had a husband for her

15   bed. Do you smell a fault?[5]

KENT   I cannot wish the fault undone, the issue° of it being   *offspring; result*

so proper.°   *handsome; right*

GLOUCESTER   But I have, sir, a son by order of law,° some   *legitimate*

year elder than this, who yet is no dearer in my account.°   *estimation*

20   Though this knave° came something saucily[6] into the   *scamp, fellow*

world before he was sent for, yet was his mother fair;

there was good sport at his making, and the whoreson°   *rogue; bastard*

must be acknowledged. Do you know this noble gentle-

man, Edmund?

25 EDMUND   No, my lord.

GLOUCESTER   My lord of Kent. Remember him hereafter

as my honorable friend.

EDMUND   My services to your lordship.

KENT   I must love you, and sue° to know you better.   *ask*

30 EDMUND   Sir, I shall study deserving.°   *shall learn to deserve*

GLOUCESTER   He hath been out° nine years, and away he   *away, abroad*

shall again. (*Sound a sennet*°) The king is coming.   *fanfare of trumpets*

    Enter one bearing a coronet, then King LEAR, CORN-

    WALL, ALBANY, GONERIL, REGAN, CORDELIA, *and*

    attendants

LEAR   Attend the lords of France and Burgundy, Gloucester.

GLOUCESTER   I shall, my liege.°   *feudal superior*

    Exeunt GLOUCESTER *and* EDMUND

35 LEAR   Meantime we° shall express our darker° purpose.   *("royal" we)/more secret*

Give me the map there. Know that we have divided

In three our kingdom; and 'tis our fast° intent   *steadfast*

To shake all cares and business from our age,

Conferring them on younger strengths, while we

40 Unburthened crawl toward death. Our son° of Cornwall,   *son-in-law*

And you, our no less loving son of Albany,

We have this hour a constant will to publish[7]

Our daughters' several dowers,° that future strife   *individual dowries*

May be prevented now. The princes, France and Bur-

gundy,

45 Great rivals in our youngest daughter's love,

---

2. I.e., that careful scrutiny ("curiosity") of both parts cannot determine which portion ("moiety") is preferable.
3. My responsibility; at my cost.
4. Could conceive; punning on biological conception.
5. (1) Sin, wrongdoing; (2) female genitals.
6. Somewhat rudely; somewhat shamefully.
7. A fixed determination to announce publicly.

Long in our court have made their amorous sojourn,
And here are to be answered. Tell me, my daughters—
Since now we will divest us, both of rule,
Interest° of territory, cares of state—   *legal title*
50   Which of you shall we say doth love us most?
That° we our largest bounty° may extend   *so that / generosity*
Where nature doth with merit challenge.[8] Goneril,
Our eldest-born, speak first.
    GONERIL   Sir, I love you more than words can wield° the   *convey*
      matter;
55   Dearer than eye-sight, space,° and liberty;   *freedom of movement*
Beyond what can be valued, rich or rare;
No less than life, with grace, health, beauty, honor;
As much as child e'er loved, or father found;
A love that makes breath° poor, and speech unable;   *language*
60   Beyond all manner of so much° I love you.   *beyond all comparison*
    CORDELIA (*aside*)   What shall Cordelia speak? Love, and be silent.
    LEAR   Of all these bounds, even from this line to this,
With shadowy forests and with champains riched,°   *plains enriched*
With plenteous rivers and wide-skirted meads,°   *broad meadows*
65   We make thee lady: to thine and Albany's issue°   *children, heirs*
Be this perpetual. What says our second daughter,
Our dearest Regan, wife to Cornwall? Speak.
    REGAN   Sir, I am made
Of the self-same metal° that my sister is,   *spirit, substance*
70   And prize me at her worth.° In my true heart   *believe myself her equal*
I find she names my very deed of love;
Only she comes too short, that° I profess   *in that*
Myself an enemy to all other joys,
Which the most precious square of sense possesses,[9]
75   And find I am alone felicitate°   *am only made happy*
In your dear highness' love.
    CORDELIA (*aside*)   Then poor Cordelia!
And yet not so; since, I am sure, my love's
More ponderous° than my tongue.   *weighty*
    LEAR   To thee and thine hereditary ever
80   Remain this ample third of our fair kingdom;
No less in space, validity,° and pleasure,   *value*
Than that conferred on Goneril. Now, our joy,
Although our last and least;° to whose young love   *youngest, smallest*
The vines of France and milk of Burgundy
85   Strive to be interessed,° what can you say to draw   *given access to*
A third more opulent than your sisters? Speak.
    CORDELIA   Nothing, my lord.
    LEAR   Nothing?
    CORDELIA   Nothing.
90   LEAR   Nothing will come of nothing,[1] speak again.
    CORDELIA   Unhappy that I am, I cannot heave

---

8. I.e., to the one whose natural love and good deeds
mutually enhance each other.

9. That the body can enjoy.
1. An Aristotelian maxim.

My heart into my mouth. I love your majesty
According to my bond;° nor more nor less. *filial duty*

LEAR   How, how, Cordelia! mend your speech a little,
Lest it may mar your fortunes.

95   CORDELIA   Good my lord,
You have begot me, bred me, loved me; I
Return those duties back as are right fit,
Obey you, love you, and most honor you.
Why have my sisters husbands, if they say

100   They love you all? Haply,° when I shall wed, *perhaps*
That lord whose hand must take my plight° shall carry   *marriage vow; condition*
Half my love with him, half my care and duty.
Sure, I shall never marry like my sisters,
To love my father all.° *completely*

105   LEAR   But goes thy heart with this?

CORDELIA   Ay, good my lord.

LEAR   So young, and so untender?

CORDELIA   So young, my lord, and true.° *honest, faithful*

LEAR   Let it be so! Thy truth, then, be thy dower!

110   For, by the sacred radiance of the sun,
The mysteries of Hecate,[2] and the night;
By all the operation of the orbs
From whom we do exist and cease to be;[3]
Here I disclaim all my paternal care,

115   Propinquity° and property of blood,° *closeness / kinship*
And as a stranger to my heart and me
Hold thee, from this,° for ever. The barbarous Scythian,[4]   *this time*
Or he that makes his generation messes[5]
To gorge his appetite, shall to my bosom

120   Be as well neighbored, pitied, and relieved,
As thou my sometime° daughter. *former*

KENT   Good my liege—

LEAR   Peace, Kent!
Come not between the dragon and his wrath.
I loved her most, and thought to set my rest[6]

125   On her kind nursery.° Hence, and avoid my sight! *care*
So be my grave my peace,[7] as here I give
Her father's heart from her! Call France; who stirs?[8]
Call Burgundy, Cornwall and Albany,
With my two daughters' dowers digest° this third: *incorporate*

130   Let pride, which she calls plainness,° marry her. *directness*
I do invest you jointly with my power,
Pre-eminence, and all the large effects° *outward shows, trappings*

---

2. Classical goddess of the moon and patron of witchcraft.
3. Referring to the belief that the movements of stars and planets ("orbs") corresponded to physical and spiritual motions in a person and thus controlled his or her fate.
4. Notoriously savage Crimean nomads of classical antiquity.

5. I.e., he who makes meals of his parents or his children.
6. To secure my repose; to stake my all, as in the card game known as primero.
7. So may I rest in peace.
8. Does nobody stir? An order, with the force of "Get moving."

That troop with° majesty. Ourself, by monthly course,   *accompany*
With reservation° of an hundred knights,   *legal right to retain*
135 By you to be sustained, shall our abode
Make with you by due turns. Only we still retain
The name, and all the additions° to a king;   *prerogatives*
The sway,° revenue, execution of the rest,   *power*
Beloved sons, be yours; which to confirm,
This coronet⁹ part betwixt you.

140 KENT   Royal Lear,
Whom I have ever honored as my king,
Loved as my father, as my master followed,
As my great patron thought on in my prayers—
LEAR   The bow is bent and drawn, make from° the shaft.   *get clear of*
145 KENT   Let it fall° rather, though the fork° invade   *strike home / arrowhead*
The region of my heart: be Kent unmannerly,
When Lear is mad. What wilt thou do, old man?
Think'st thou that duty shall have dread to speak,
When power to flattery bows? To plainness° honor's   *plain speaking*
bound,
150 When majesty stoops to folly. Reverse thy doom,°   *revoke your sentence*
And, in thy best consideration, check°   *halt*
This hideous rashness. Answer my life my judgment,¹
Thy youngest daughter does not love thee least;
Nor are those empty-hearted whose low sounds
Reverb no hollowness.°   *echo no insincerity*
155 LEAR   Kent, on thy life, no more.
KENT   My life I never held but as a pawn°   *chess piece; stake*
To wage° against thy enemies; nor fear to lose it,   *wager*
Thy safety being the motive.
LEAR   Out of my sight!
KENT   See better, Lear; and let me still° remain   *always*
160 The true blank° of thine eye.   *precise bull's-eye*
LEAR   Now, by Apollo—
KENT   Now, by Apollo, king,
Thou swear'st thy gods in vain²
LEAR   O, vassal! miscreant!°   *villain; unbeliever*
Laying his hand on his sword
ALBANY   } Dear sir, forbear.
CORNWALL
KENT   Do;
165 Kill thy physician, and the fee bestow
Upon thy foul disease.³ Revoke thy doom;
Or, whilst I can vent clamor from my throat,
I'll tell thee thou dost evil.
LEAR   Hear me, recreant!°   *traitor*
On thine allegiance, hear me!

9. Cordelia's crown, symbol of the endowment she has lost.
1. I'll stake my life on my opinion.
2. You invoke your gods falsely and without effect.

Lear's blindness and misdirected imprecations are particularly inapt for Apollo, god of the sun and of archery.
3. You would not only kill the doctor but hand his fee over to the disease.

170 Since thou hast sought to make us break our vow,
    Which we durst never yet, and with strained° pride   *overblown*
    To come between our sentence and our power,
    Which nor our nature nor our place⁴ can bear,
    Our potency made good,° take thy reward.   *demonstrated*
175 Five days we do allot thee, for provision
    To shield thee from diseases of the world;
    And on the sixth to turn thy hated back
    Upon our kingdom: if, on the tenth day following,
    Thy banished trunk° be found in our dominions,   *body*
180 The moment is thy death. Away! by Jupiter,
    This shall not be revoked.
    KENT   Fare thee well, king. Sith° thus thou wilt appear,   *since*
    Freedom lives hence, and banishment is here.
    (*To* CORDELIA) The gods to their dear shelter take thee, maid,
185 That justly think'st, and hast most rightly said!
    (*To* REGAN *and* GONERIL) And your large speeches may your deeds
      approve,⁵
    That good effects may spring from words of love.
    Thus Kent, O princes, bids you all adieu;
    He'll shape his old course in a country new.   *Exit*
      Flourish.° Re-enter GLOUCESTER, *with* FRANCE, BUR-   *fanfare of trumpets*
      GUNDY, *and attendants*
190 GLOUCESTER   Here's France and Burgundy, my noble lord.
    LEAR   My lord of Burgundy,
    We first address towards you, who with this king
    Hath rivaled for our daughter. What, in the least,
    Will you require in present dower with her,
    Or cease your quest of love?
195 BURGUNDY   Most royal majesty,
    I crave no more than what your highness offered,
    Nor will you tender° less.   *offer*
    LEAR   Right noble Burgundy,
    When she was dear to us, we did hold her so;
    But now her price is fallen. Sir, there she stands;
200 If aught within that little seeming substance,⁶
    Or all of it, with our displeasure pieced,°   *joined*
    And nothing more, may fitly like° your grace,   *please*
    She's there, and she is yours.
    BURGUNDY   I know no answer.
    LEAR   Will you, with those infirmities she owes,°   *owns*
205 Unfriended, new-adopted to our hate,
    Dowered with our curse, and strangered° with our oath,   *estranged*
    Take her, or leave her?
    BURGUNDY   Pardon me, royal sir;
    Election makes not up on such conditions.⁷
    LEAR   Then leave her, sir; for, by the power that made me,

---

4. Which neither my temperament nor my royal position.
5. And let your actions live up to your fine words.

6. I.e., one who appears more substantial than she is;
one who will not pretend.
7. A choice cannot be made under those terms.

210	I tell you° all her wealth. (*To* FRANCE) For° you, great king,	*inform you of/as for*
	I would not from your love make such a stray°	*stray so far*
	To° match you where I hate; therefore beseech you	*as to*
	To avert your liking° a more worthier way	*to turn your affections*
	Than on a wretch whom nature is ashamed	
	Almost to acknowledge hers.	
215	FRANCE This is most strange,	
	That she, whom even but now was your best object,	
	The argument° of your praise, balm of your age,	*theme*
	Most best, most dearest, should in this trice° of time	*moment*
	Commit a thing so monstrous, to dismantle°	*as to strip off, disrobe*
220	So many folds of favor. Sure, her offense	
	Must be of such unnatural degree,	
	That monsters it,° or your fore-vouched affection	*makes it monstrous*
	Fall'n into taint;[8] which to believe of her,	
	Must be a faith that reason without miracle	
	Could never plant in me.	
225	CORDELIA I yet beseech your majesty—	
	If for I want° that glib and oily art,	*because I lack*
	To speak and purpose not°—since what I well intend,	*and not intend*
	I'll do't before I speak—that you make known	
	It is no vicious blot, murder, or foulness,	
230	No unchaste action, or dishonored step,	
	That hath deprived me of your grace and favor;	
	But even for want of that for which I am richer,	
	A still-soliciting° eye, and such a tongue	*an always-begging*
	As I am glad I have not, though not to have it	
	Hath lost me in your liking.	
235	LEAR Better thou	
	Hadst not been born than not to have pleased me better.	
	FRANCE Is it but this—a tardiness in nature	
	Which often leaves the history unspoke	
	That it intends to do?[9] My lord of Burgundy,	
240	What say you to the lady? Love's not love	
	When it is mingled with regards° that stands	*considerations*
	Aloof from th' entire point. Will you have her?	
	She is herself a dowry.	
	BURGUNDY Royal Lear,	
	Give but that portion which yourself proposed,	
245	And here I take Cordelia by the hand,	
	Duchess of Burgundy.	
	LEAR Nothing! I have sworn; I am firm.	
	BURGUNDY I am sorry, then, you have so lost a father	
	That you must lose a husband.	
	CORDELIA Peace be with Burgundy!	
250	Since that respects of fortune are his love,	

8. I.e., or else the love you earlier swore for Cordelia must be regarded with suspicion. "Or" may also mean "before," in which case the phrase would mean "before the love you once proclaimed could have decayed."
9. A natural reserve that inhibits voicing one's intentions.

I shall not be his wife.

FRANCE   Fairest Cordelia, that art most rich, being poor;
Most choice, forsaken; and most loved, despised!
Thee and thy virtues here I seize upon:

255   Be it lawful I take up what's cast away.
Gods, gods! 't is strange that from their cold'st neglect
My love should kindle to inflamed respect.°   *ardent regard*
Thy dowerless daughter, king, thrown to my chance,
Is queen of us, of ours, and our fair France.

260   Not all the dukes of waterish° Burgundy   *irrigated, watery; weak*
Can buy this unprized° precious maid of me.   *unappreciated*
Bid them farewell, Cordelia, though unkind;°   *though they are unkind*
Thou losest here,° a better where° to find.   *this place/place*

LEAR   Thou hast her, France; let her be thine; for we

265   Have no such daughter, nor shall ever see
That face of hers again. Therefore be gone
Without our grace, our love, our benison.°   *blessing*
Come, noble Burgundy.

     Flourish. Exeunt all but FRANCE, GONERIL, REGAN,
     and CORDELIA

FRANCE   Bid farewell to your sisters.

270 CORDELIA   The jewels of our father, with washed eyes
Cordelia leaves you. I know you what you are,
And like a sister am most loath to call
Your faults as they are named.° Love well our father.   *are properly called*
To your professed bosoms° I commit him;   *publicly proclaimed love*

275   But yet, alas, stood I within his grace,
I would prefer° him to a better place.   *promote, recommend*
So, farewell to you both.

REGAN   Prescribe not us our duties.

GONERIL   Let your study
Be to content your lord, who hath received you

280   At fortune's alms.[1] You have obedience scanted,°   *stinted on*
And well are worth the want that you have wanted.[2]

CORDELIA   Time shall unfold what pleated cunning hides:
Who cover faults, at last shame them derides.[3]
Well may you prosper!

FRANCE   Come, my fair Cordelia.

     Exeunt FRANCE *and* CORDELIA

285 GONERIL   Sister, it is not a little I have to save of what most
nearly appertains to us both. I think our father will hence
to-night.

REGAN   That's most certain, and with you; next month with
us.

290 GONERIL   You see how full of changes° his age is; the   *fickleness*
observation we have made of it hath not been little:[4] he

---

1. As a charitable gift from Dame Fortune.
2. And you deserve to get no more love (from your husband) than you have given (to your father). "Want" plays on its alternative meanings of "lack" and "desire."
3. Those who hide their faults will in the end be put to shame.
4. We have observed it more than a little.

always loved our sister most; and with what poor judgment he hath now cast her off appears too grossly.° *blatantly*
REGAN   'Tis the infirmity of his age; yet he hath ever but
295 slenderly known himself.
GONERIL   The best and soundest of his time hath been but
rash;⁵ then° must we look to receive from his age, not   *therefore*
alone the imperfections of long-engraffed condition,° but   *deep-rooted habit*
therewithal the unruly waywardness that infirm and chol-
300 eric years bring with them.
REGAN   Such unconstant starts⁶ are we like° to have from   *likely*
him as this of Kent's banishment.
GONERIL   There is further compliment° of leave-taking   *ceremony*
between France and him. Pray you, let's hit° together: if   *join; strike*
305 our father carry authority with such dispositions⁷ as he
bears, this last surrender° of his will but offend° us.   *abdication / harm*
REGAN   We shall further think on 't.
GONERIL   We must do something, and i' the heat.° *Exeunt*   *while the iron is hot*

1.2

Enter EDMUND, *with a letter*

EDMUND   Thou, nature, art my goddess; to thy law
My services are bound.¹ Wherefore° should I   *why*
Stand in the plague of custom,² and permit
The curiosity° of nations to deprive me,   *legal niceties*
5   For that° I am some twelve or fourteen moonshines°   *because / months*
Lag of° a brother? Why bastard? wherefore base?   *younger than*
When my dimensions are as well compact,°   *composed*
My mind as generous° and my shape as true,   *noble*
As honest° madam's issue? Why brand they us   *married; chaste*
10 With base? with baseness? bastardy? base, base?
Who, in the lusty stealth of nature, take
More composition and fierce quality³
Than doth, within a dull, stale, tired bed,
Go to creating a whole tribe of fops,°   *fools*
15 Got° 'tween asleep and wake? Well, then,   *begotten*
Legitimate Edgar, I must have your land.
Our father's love is to° the bastard Edmund   *as much to*
As to the legitimate. Fine word—"legitimate"!
Well, my legitimate, if this letter speed,°   *succeed*
20 And my invention° thrive, Edmund the base   *plot*
Shall top° the legitimate. I grow; I prosper.   *overcome, usurp*
Now, gods, stand up for bastards!

5. Even in the prime of his life he was impetuous.
6. Such impulsive outbursts.
7. Frame of mind.
1.2 Location: The earl of Gloucester's house.
1. Edmund declares the raw force of unsocialized and
unregulated existence, as opposed to human law, to be
his ruler; ironically, "nature" also means "natural filial
affection." A "natural" was another word for "bastard"
(illegitimate child).
2. Submit to the imposition of inheritance law.

3. Whose begetting, by reason of its furtiveness and
heightened excitement, requires better execution and
more vigor. Alternatively (with "take" having the meaning "give"), whose begetting produces (a person of)
more mixture and vigor. "Composition," or mixture,
may refer to the belief that the perfect offspring was
conceived from an equal quantity of male and female
essence and that physical and mental abnormalities
were caused by a predominance of one or the other.

Enter GLOUCESTER

GLOUCESTER   Kent banished thus? and France in choler
   parted?°   *in anger departed*
   And the king gone tonight?° subscribed° his power?   *last night / limited*
25   Confirmed to exhibition?⁴ All this done
   Upon the gad?° Edmund, how now! what news?   *spur of the moment*

EDMUND   So please your lordship, none.

                                 Putting up the letter

GLOUCESTER   Why so earnestly seek you to put up that
   letter?
30   EDMUND   I know no news, my lord.

GLOUCESTER   What paper were you reading?

EDMUND   Nothing, my lord.

GLOUCESTER   No? What needed, then, that terrible dis-
   patch° of it into your pocket? The quality of nothing hath   *frightened haste*
35   not such need to hide itself. Let's see. Come, if it be
   nothing, I shall not need spectacles.

EDMUND   I beseech you, sir, pardon me. It is a letter from
   my brother, that I have not all o'er-read; and for so much
   as I have perused, I find it not fit for your o'er-looking.

40   GLOUCESTER   Give me the letter, sir.

EDMUND   I shall offend, either to detain or give it. The
   contents, as in part I understand them, are to blame.

GLOUCESTER   Let's see, let's see.

EDMUND   I hope, for my brother's justification, he wrote
45   this but as an essay or taste⁵ of my virtue.

GLOUCESTER   (*reads*)   "This policy and reverence of age
   makes the world bitter to the best of our times;⁶ keeps
   our fortunes from us till our oldness cannot relish them.
   I begin to find an idle and fond° bondage in the oppres-   *a useless and foolish*
50   sion of aged tyranny; who sways, not as it hath power,
   but as it is suffered.⁷ Come to me, that of this I may speak
   more. If our father would sleep till I waked him, you
   should enjoy half his revenue for ever, and live the
   beloved of your brother, Edgar."
55   Hum—conspiracy!—"Sleep till I waked him—you
   should enjoy half his revenue"—My son Edgar! Had he
   a hand to write this? a heart and brain to breed it in?—
   When came this to you? who brought it?

EDMUND   It was not brought me, my lord; there's the cun-
60   ning of it; I found it thrown in at the casement° of my   *window*
   closet.°   *private room*

GLOUCESTER   You know the character° to be your   *handwriting*
   brother's?

4. Established as mere show; relegated to pension.
5. I.e., simply as a proof or test. Both terms derive from
metallurgy.
6. The established primacy of the elderly embitters us

at the prime of our lives. "Policy": statecraft; craftiness;
established order.
7. I.e., which rules not because it is powerful but
because it is permitted to ("suffered").

EDMUND If the matter° were good, my lord, I durst swear   *content*
65   it were his; but, in respect of that, I would fain° think it   *gladly*
        were not.
GLOUCESTER It is his.
EDMUND It is his hand, my lord; but I hope his heart is
        not in the contents.
70 GLOUCESTER Hath he never heretofore sounded you° in   *sounded you out*
        this business?
EDMUND Never, my lord. But I have heard him oft main-
        tain it to be fit, that, sons at perfect age,° and fathers   *at maturity*
        declining, the father should be as ward[8] to the son, and
75   the son manage his revenue.
GLOUCESTER O villain, villain! His very opinion in the let-
        ter! Abhorred villain! Unnatural, detested, brutish villain!
        worse than brutish! Go, sirrah,[9] seek him. I'll apprehend
        him. Abominable villain! Where is he?
80 EDMUND I do not well know, my lord. If it shall please you
        to suspend your indignation against my brother till you
        can derive from him better testimony of his intent, you
        shall run a certain° course; where,° if you violently pro-   *safe, reliable / whereas*
        ceed against him, mistaking his purpose, it would make
85   a great gap in your own honor and shake in pieces the
        heart of his obedience. I dare pawn down° my life for him   *I dare stake*
        that he hath wrote this to feel° my affection to your   *feel out*
        honor, and to no further pretense of danger.[1]
GLOUCESTER Think you so?
90 EDMUND If your honor judge it meet,° I will place you   *appropriate*
        where you shall hear us confer of this, and by an auricular
        assurance have your satisfaction; and that without any
        further delay than this very evening.
GLOUCESTER He cannot be such a monster—
95 EDMUND Nor is not, sure.
GLOUCESTER To his father, that so tenderly and entirely
        loves him. Heaven and earth! Edmund, seek him out;
        wind me into him,[2] I pray you; frame° the business after   *arrange*
        your own wisdom. I would unstate myself, to be in a due
100   resolution.[3]
EDMUND I will seek him, sir, presently;° convey° the busi-   *immediately / carry out*
        ness as I shall find means, and acquaint you withal.°   *therewith*
GLOUCESTER These late° eclipses in the sun and moon   *recent*
        portend no good to us.[4] Though the wisdom of nature
105   can reason it thus and thus, yet nature finds itself
        scourged by the sequent effects.[5] Love cools, friendship

8. A child under eighteen years who was legally
dependent, often orphaned.
9. A form of address used with children or social inferiors.
1. No further intention to do harm.
2. Worm your way into his confidence (with "me" as
an intensifier); worm your way into his confidence for
me ("me" as a term of respect).
3. I would give up everything to have my doubts

resolved.
4. Lunar and solar eclipses that were seen in London
about a year before the play's first recorded performance would have added spice to this superstitious
belief in the role of heavenly bodies as augurs of misfortune.
5. Though natural science may explain the eclipses
this way or that, nature (and family bonds) suffers in
the effects that follow.

falls off, brothers divide; in cities, mutinies; in countries,
discord; in palaces, treason; and the bond cracked 'twixt
son and father. This villain of mine comes under the pre-
110   diction; there's son against father. The king falls from
bias of nature;[6] there's father against child. We have seen
the best of our time. Machinations, hollowness,° treach-   *insincerity*
ery, and all ruinous disorders, follow us disquietly to our
graves. Find out this villain, Edmund; it shall lose thee
115   nothing; do it carefully. And the noble and true-hearted
Kent banished! his offense, honesty! 'Tis strange. *Exit*

EDMUND   This is the excellent foppery° of the world, that,   *foolishness*
when we are sick in fortune, often the surfeit° of our own   *excesses*
behavior, we make guilty of° our disasters the sun, the   *we hold responsible for*
120   moon, and the stars; as if we were villains by necessity;
fools by heavenly compulsion; knaves, thieves, and
treachers, by spherical predominance;[7] drunkards, liars,
and adulterers, by an enforced obedience of planetary
influence; and all that we are evil in, by a divine thrusting
125   on.° An admirable° evasion of whore-master man, to lay   *imposition / amazing*
his goatish disposition to the charge of a star![8] My father
compounded° with my mother under the dragon's tail,   *coupled*
and my nativity was under Ursa Major,[9] so that it follows,
I am rough and lecherous. Fut!° I should have been that°   *by Christ's foot / what*
130   I am, had the maidenliest star in the firmament twinkled
on my bastardizing. Edgar—
          Enter EDGAR
and pat° he comes like the catastrophe° of the old com-   *on cue / resolution*
edy. My cue is villainous melancholy, with a sigh like Tom
o' Bedlam.[1] O, these eclipses do portend these divisions!
135   Fa, sol, la, mi.[2]

EDGAR   How now, brother Edmund? What serious contemplation are you in?

EDMUND   I am thinking, brother, of a prediction I read this
other day, what should follow these eclipses.

140   EDGAR   Do you busy yourself about that?

EDMUND   I promise you, the effects he writes of succeed°   *follow*
unhappily; as of unnaturalness between the child and the
parent; death, dearth, dissolutions of ancient amities;
divisions in state, menaces and maledictions against king
145   and nobles; needless diffidences,° banishment of friends,   *baseless suspicions*
dissipation of cohorts,[3] nuptial breaches, and I know not
what.

---

6. The king deviates from his natural inclination. In
the game of bowls, the "bias" ("course") is the eccentric
path taken by the weighted ball when thrown.
7. By the ascendancy of a particular planet. In the universe as conceived by Ptolemy, the planets revolved
about the earth on crystalline spheres.
8. I.e., to hold a star responsible for his lustful desires.
9. Constellations: "Dragon's tail" = Draco; and "Ursa
Major" = Great Bear.
1. The usual name for lunatic beggars; "Bethlehem,"

shortened to "Bedlam," was the name of the oldest and
best-known London madhouse.
2. In the musical notation of Shakespeare's time,
Edmund's sequence of tones spans an augmented
fourth (F to B), an interval regarded then as now as
especially dissonant; it was sometimes referred to as
"the devil in music." "Divisions": social fractures;
melodic embellishments.
3. Scattering of forces.

EDGAR How long have you been a sectary astronomical?°   *a devotee of astrology*
EDMUND Come, come! When saw you my father last?
150 EDGAR Why, the night gone by.
EDMUND Spake you with him?
EDGAR Ay, two hours together.
EDMUND Parted you in good terms? Found you no displeasure in him by word or countenance?°   *appearance, demeanor*
155 EDGAR None at all.
EDMUND Bethink yourself wherein you may have
offended him; and at my entreaty forbear° his presence   *avoid*
till some little time hath qualified° the heat of his dis-   *mollified*
pleasure; which at this instant so rageth in him, that with
160 the mischief of your person it would scarcely allay.[4]
EDGAR Some villain hath done me wrong.
EDMUND That's my fear. I pray you, have a continent for-
bearance° till the speed of his rage goes slower; and, as I   *restrained absence*
say, retire with me to my lodging, from whence I will fitly°   *when suitable*
165 bring you to hear my lord speak. Pray ye, go! There's my
key. If you do stir abroad, go armed.
EDGAR Armed, brother?
EDMUND Brother, I advise you to the best. Go armed. I
am no honest man if there be any good meaning towards
170 you. I have told you what I have seen and heard; but
faintly, nothing like the image and horror of it. Pray you,
away!
EDGAR Shall I hear from you anon?
EDMUND I do serve you in this business.   *Exit* EDGAR
175 A credulous father, and a brother noble,
Whose nature is so far from doing harms,
That he suspects none; on whose foolish honesty
My practices° ride easy! I see the business.[5]   *plots*
Let me, if not by birth, have lands by wit:°   *intelligence*
180 All with me's meet that I can fashion fit.[6]   *Exit*

1.3

Enter GONERIL, *and* OSWALD, *her steward*

GONERIL Did my father strike my gentleman for chiding of his fool?
OSWALD Yes, madam.
GONERIL By day and night he wrongs me; every hour
He flashes into one gross crime° or other,   *offense*
5 That sets us all at odds. I'll not endure it.
His knights grow riotous, and himself upbraids us
On every trifle. When he returns from hunting,
I will not speak with him. Say I am sick.
If you come slack of former services,[1]

---

4. Even harming you bodily would hardly relieve his
anger; alternatively, with the irritant of your presence,
it (Gloucester's anger) would not be abated.
5. It is now clear to me what needs to be done.
6. Anything is fine by me as long as I can make it serve

my purpose. "Meet": justifiable; appropriate.
1.3 Location: The duke of Albany's castle.
1. If you offer him less service (and respect) than
before.

10 You shall do well; the fault of it I'll answer.°   *answer for*
OSWALD   He's coming, madam; I hear him.
    Horns within°   *hunting horns offstage*
GONERIL   Put on what weary negligence you please,
  You and your fellows.° I'd have it come to question.   *servants*
  If he dislike it, let him to our sister,
15   Whose mind and mine, I know, in that are one,
  Not to be overruled. Idle° old man,   *foolish*
  That still would manage those authorities
  That he hath given away! Now, by my life,
  Old fools are babes again, and must be used
20   With checks as flatteries, when they are seen abused.[2]
  Remember what I tell you.
OSWALD   Well, madam.
GONERIL   And let his knights have colder looks among you.
  What grows of it, no matter; advise your fellows so.
  I would breed from hence occasions, and I shall,
25   That I may speak.[3] I'll write straight° to my sister,   *straightaway*
  To hold my very° course. Prepare for dinner.   *Exeunt*   *exact*

1.4

Enter KENT, *disguised*
KENT   If but as well[1] I other accents borrow,
  That can my speech defuse,° my good intent   *disguise*
  May carry through itself to that full issue°   *result*
  For which I razed my likeness.[2] Now, banished Kent,
5   If thou canst serve where thou dost stand condemned,
  So may it come,° thy master, whom thou lovest,   *come to pass*
  Shall find thee full of labors.°   *helpful, keen*
    Horns within. Enter LEAR, *knights, and attendants*
LEAR   Let me not stay° a jot for dinner; go get it ready.   *wait*
    Exit an attendant
  How now! What° art thou?   *who*
10 KENT   A man, sir.
LEAR   What dost thou profess?[3] What wouldst thou with
  us?
KENT   I do profess to be no less than I seem; to serve him
  truly that will put me in trust; to love him that is honest;
15   to converse° with him that is wise and says little; to fear   *associate*
  judgment; to fight when I cannot choose;° and to eat no   *when I must*
  fish.[4]
LEAR   What art thou?
KENT   A very honest-hearted fellow, and as poor as the
20   king.

---

2. When foolish old men act like children, rebukes are the kindest treatment when kind treatment is abused.
3. I wish to foster situations, and I shall, in which to speak my mind.
1.4 Location: As before.
1. As well as disguising my appearance.
2. Disguised my appearance; shaved off my beard (with a pun on "razor").
3. What is your job (profession)? Kent, in reply, uses "profess" punningly to mean "claim."
4. And not to be a Catholic or penitent (Catholics were obliged to eat fish on specified occasions and as penance); alternatively, to be a manly man, a meat eater.

LEAR   If thou be as poor for a subject as he is for a king,
    thou art poor enough. What wouldst thou?
KENT   Service.
LEAR   Who wouldst thou serve?
25 KENT   You.
LEAR   Dost thou know me, fellow?
KENT   No, sir; but you have that in your countenance
    which I would fain° call master.   *gladly*
LEAR   What's that?
30 KENT   Authority.
LEAR   What services canst thou do?
KENT   I can keep honest counsel,° ride, run, mar a curious   *keep secrets*
    tale in telling it, and deliver a plain message bluntly. That
    which ordinary men are fit for, I am qualified in; and the
35   best of me is diligence.
LEAR   How old art thou?
KENT   Not so young, sir, to love a woman for singing, nor
    so old to dote on her for anything. I have years on my
    back forty-eight.
40 LEAR   Follow me; thou shalt serve me. If I like thee no
    worse after dinner, I will not part from thee yet. Dinner,
    ho dinner! Where's my knave? my fool? Go you, and call
    my fool hither.   *Exit an attendant*
        Enter OSWALD
    You, you, sirrah, where's my daughter?
45 OSWALD   So please you—   *Exit*
LEAR   What says the fellow there? Call the clotpoll° back.   *blockhead*
    (*Exit a* KNIGHT) Where's my fool, ho? I think the world's
    asleep.
        Re-enter KNIGHT
    How now! where's that mongrel?
50 KNIGHT   He says, my lord, your daughter is not well.
LEAR   Why came not the slave back to me when I called
    him?
KNIGHT   Sir, he answered me in the roundest° manner, he   *bluntest, rudest*
    would not.
55 LEAR   He would not!
KNIGHT   My lord, I know not what the matter is; but, to
    my judgment, your highness is not entertained with that
    ceremonious affection as you were wont,° there's a great   *accustomed to*
    abatement of kindness appears as well in the general
60   dependants° as in the duke himself also and your daugh-   *servants*
    ter.
LEAR   Ha! sayest thou so?
KNIGHT   I beseech you pardon me, my lord, if I be mis-
    taken; for my duty cannot be silent when I think your
65   highness wronged.
LEAR   Thou but rememberest° me of mine own con-   *remind*
    ception.° I have perceived a most faint neglect of late;   *perception*
    which I have rather blamed as mine own jealous curios-

ity[5] than as a very pretense° and purpose of unkindness.   *a true intention*

70   I will look further into 't. But where's my fool? I have not
seen him this two days.

KNIGHT   Since my young lady's going into France, sir, the
fool hath much pined away.

LEAR   No more of that; I have noted it well. Go you and

75   tell my daughter I would speak with her.   *Exit* KNIGHT
Go you, call hither my fool.   *Exit an attendant*
      Re-enter OSWALD
O, you sir, you! Come you hither, sir. Who am I, sir?

OSWALD   My lady's father.

LEAR   "My lady's father"! My lord's knave! You whoreson

80   dog! you slave! you cur!

OSWALD   I am none of these, my lord; I beseech your pardon.

LEAR   Do you bandy looks with me, you rascal? (*Striking
him*)

OSWALD   I'll not be struck, my lord.

85   KENT   Nor tripped neither, you base foot-ball player.[6]
      Tripping up his heels

LEAR   I thank thee, fellow; thou servest me, and I'll love
thee.

KENT   Come, sir, arise, away! I'll teach you differences.°   *(of rank)*
Away, away! If you will measure your lubber's length

90   again,[7] tarry; but away! Go to! Have you wisdom? so.
      Pushes OSWALD *out*

LEAR   Now, my friendly knave, I thank thee: there's earnest
of° thy service. (*Giving* KENT *money*)   *downpayment for*
      Enter FOOL

FOOL   Let me hire him too. Here's my coxcomb.°   *fool's cap*
      Offering KENT *his cap*

LEAR   How now, my pretty knave! How dost thou?

95   FOOL   Sirrah, you were best take my coxcomb.

KENT   Why, fool?

FOOL   Why, for taking one's part that's out of favor. Nay,
an thou canst not smile as the wind sits, thou'lt catch
cold shortly.[8] There, take my coxcomb! Why, this fellow

100   has banished two on's daughters,[9] and did the third a
blessing against his will. If thou follow him, thou must
needs wear my coxcomb. How now, nuncle!° Would I had   *(mine) uncle*
two coxcombs and two daughters!

LEAR   Why, my boy?

105   FOOL   If I gave them all my living,° I'd keep my coxcombs   *goods*
myself.[1] There's mine; beg another of thy daughters.

LEAR   Take heed, sirrah; the whip.

---

5. Paranoid concern with niceties.
6. Football was a rough street game played by the poor.
7. If you will be stretched out by me again. "Lubber":
clumsy oaf.
8. If you can't keep in with those in power, you will

soon find yourself left out in the cold.
9. By abdicating, Lear has in effect prevented his
daughters from any longer being his subjects, just as if
he had banished them.
1. I.e., I'd be twice as much a fool.

FOOL   Truth's a dog must to° kennel; he must be whipped   *go to*
       out, when Lady the brach² may stand by the fire and
110   stink.

LEAR   A pestilent gall° to me!   *annoyance, bitterness*

FOOL   Sirrah, I'll teach thee a speech.

LEAR   Do.

FOOL   Mark it, nuncle:
115   Have more than thou showest,
               Speak less than thou knowest,
               Lend less than thou owest,°   *own*
               Ride more than thou goest,°   *walk*
               Learn° more than thou trowest,°   *hear/believe*
120   Set less than thou throwest,³
               Leave thy drink and thy whore,
               And keep in-a-door,
               And thou shalt have more
               Than two tens to a score.⁴
125 KENT   This is nothing, fool.

FOOL   Then 'tis like the breath° of an unfeed° lawyer; you   *speech/unpaid*
       gave me nothing for 't. Can you make no use of nothing,
       nuncle?

LEAR   Why, no, boy; nothing can be made out of nothing.

130 FOOL (*to* KENT)   Prithee, tell him, so much the rent of his
       land comes to.⁵ He will not believe a fool.

LEAR   A bitter fool!

FOOL   Dost thou know the difference, my boy, between a
       bitter fool and a sweet fool?

135 LEAR   No, lad; teach me.

FOOL   That lord that counseled thee
                 To give away thy land,
                 Come place him here by me,
                 Do thou for him stand:°   *represent him*
140   The sweet and bitter fool
                 Will presently appear;
                 The one in motley⁶ here,
                 The other found out there.

LEAR   Dost thou call me fool, boy?

145 FOOL   All thy other titles thou hast given away; that thou
       wast born with.

KENT   This is not altogether fool,° my lord.   *foolish, folly*

FOOL   No, faith, lords and great men will not let me; if I
       had a monopoly out, they would have part on 't: and ladies
150   too, they will not let me have all fool to myself; they'll be
       snatching. Give me an egg, nuncle, and I'll give thee two
       crowns.

---

2. Lady the bitch. Pet dogs were often called "Lady"
such-and-such. The allusion is to Regan and Goneril,
who are now being preferred to truthful Cordelia.
3. Don't gamble everything on a single cast of the dice.
4. And there will be more than two tens in your twenty;

that is, you will become richer.
5. Remind him that no land means no rent; with a pun
on "rent" meaning "torn, divided."
6. Multicolored dress of a court jester.

LEAR   What two crowns shall they be?

FOOL   Why, after I have cut the egg i' the middle, and eat
155   up the meat,° the two crowns of the egg. When thou clov-   *edible part*
est° thy crown i' the middle, and gavest away both parts,   *cleaved*
thou borest° thy ass on thy back o'er the dirt.[7] Thou hadst   *you carried*
little wit° in thy bald crown, when thou gavest thy golden   *sense*
one away. If I speak like myself° in this, let him be   *(like a fool)*
160   whipped that first finds it so.[8]
        Singing
            Fools had ne'er less wit in a year;
                For wise men are grown foppish,[9]
            They know not how their wits to wear,
                Their manners are so apish.°   *stupid; imitative*
165   LEAR   When were you wont° to be so full of songs, sirrah?   *accustomed*

FOOL   I have used° it, nuncle, ever since thou madest thy   *practiced*
daughters thy mother; for when thou gavest them the rod,
and put'st down thine own breeches,
        Singing
            Then they for sudden joy did weep,
170   And I for sorrow sung,
            That such a king should play bo-peep,°   *a child's game*
                And go the fools among.
Prithee, nuncle, keep a schoolmaster that can teach thy
fool to lie. I would fain learn to lie.

175   LEAR   An° you lie, sirrah, we'll have you whipped.   *if*

FOOL   I marvel what kin° thou and thy daughters are.   *how alike*
They'll have me whipped for speaking true, thou'lt have
me whipped for lying; and sometimes I am whipped for
holding my peace. I had rather be any kind o' thing than
180   a fool; and yet I would not be thee, nuncle; thou hast
pared thy wit o' both sides, and left nothing i' the middle.
Here comes one o' the parings.
        Enter GONERIL

LEAR   How now, daughter! What makes that frontlet[1] on?
Methinks you are too much of late i' the frown.

185   FOOL   Thou wast a pretty fellow when thou hadst no need
to care for her frowning; now thou art an O without a
figure.[2] I am better than thou art now; I am a fool, thou
art nothing. [*To* GONERIL] Yes, forsooth, I will hold my
tongue; so your face bids me, though you say nothing.
190   Mum, mum,
            He that keeps nor crust nor crum,
                Weary of all, shall want° some.   *lack, be in need of*
        (*Pointing to* LEAR) That's a shealed peascod.°   *empty pea pod*

GONERIL   Not only, sir, this your all-licensed° fool,   *unrestrained*
195   But other of your insolent retinue

---

7. In a fable of Aesop, a man carried his ass instead of
riding it, thereby reversing the order of nature.
8. I.e., who first discovers for himself that this is true;
colloquially, who deserves to be whipped as a fool.
9. Professional fools have gone out of favor ("grace")

since wise men have lately outdone them in idiocy.
1. Band worn on the forehead; here, a metaphor for
"frown."
2. A zero without a preceding digit; nothing.

Do hourly carp and quarrel, breaking forth
In rank° and not-to-be-endured riots. Sir,   *foul; spreading*
I had thought, by making this well known unto you,
To have found a safe° redress; but now grow fearful,   *sure*
200   By what yourself too late° have spoke and done,   *recently*
That you protect this course, and put it on°   *encourage it*
By your allowance; which if you should, the fault
Would not 'scape censure, nor the redresses sleep,
Which, in the tender of a wholesome weal,
205   Might in their working do you that offense,
Which else were shame, that then necessity
Will call discreet proceeding.[3]
FOOL   For, you know, nuncle,
         The hedge-sparrow fed the cuckoo[4] so long,
210   That it had it° head bit off by it young.°   *its/(the young cuckoo)*
So, out went the candle, and we were left darkling.°   *in the dark*
LEAR   Are you our daughter?
GONERIL   Come, sir.
I would you would make use of that good wisdom,
215   Whereof I know you are fraught,° and put away   *full*
These dispositions,° that of late transform you   *moods, attitudes*
From what you rightly are.
FOOL   May not an ass know when the cart draws the horse?
Whoop, Jug![5] I love thee.
220   LEAR   Doth any here know me? This is not Lear.
Doth Lear walk thus? speak thus? Where are his eyes?
Either his notion° weakens, his discernings   *intellect*
Are lethargied—Ha! waking?° 'Tis not so.   *am I awake*
Who is it that can tell me who I am?
225   FOOL   Lear's shadow.
LEAR   I would° learn that; for, by the marks° of sovereignty,   *wish to/evidence*
    knowledge, and reason, I should be false persuaded I had
    daughters.
FOOL   Which° they will make an obedient father.   *whom*
230   LEAR   Your name, fair gentlewoman?
GONERIL   This admiration,° sir, is much o' the savor   *excessive amazement*
Of other your new pranks. I do beseech you
To understand my purposes aright.
As you are old and reverend, you should be wise.
235   Here do you keep a hundred knights and squires;
Men so disordered,° so deboshed° and bold,   *disorderly/debauched*
That this our court, infected with their manners,
Shows° like a riotous inn. Epicurism° and lust   *appears/gluttony*
Make it more like a tavern or a brothel
240   Than a graced° palace. The shame itself doth speak   *an honored*

---

3. I.e., if you do approve (of your attendants' behavior), you will not escape criticism, nor will it be without retribution, which for the common good will cause you pain. While this would otherwise be improper, it will be seen as a prudent ("discreet") action under the cir-cumstances. "Tender of": concern for. "Weal": state, commonwealth. "Then necessity": the demands of the time.
4. The cuckoo lays its eggs in other birds' nests.
5. Nickname for "Joan"; sobriquet for a whore.

For instant remedy; be then desired
By her, that else will take the thing she begs,
A little to disquantity your train;°   *to reduce your retinue*
And the remainder that shall still depend,°   *be retained*
245 To be such men as may besort° your age,   *befit*
And know themselves° and you.   *know their place*

LEAR   Darkness and devils!
Saddle my horses! call my train together!
Degenerate bastard! I'll not trouble thee.
Yet° have I left a daughter.   *still*

250 GONERIL   You strike my people, and your disordered rabble
Make servants of their betters.
        Enter ALBANY

LEAR   Woe that° too late repents!—(*To* ALBANY)   *woe to him who*
O, sir, are you come?
Is it your will? Speak, sir. Prepare my horses!
255 Ingratitude, thou marble-hearted fiend,
More hideous when thou show'st thee in a child
Than the sea-monster!

ALBANY   Pray, sir, be patient.

LEAR (*to* GONERIL)   Detested kite!° thou liest: *carrion-eating hawk*
My train are men of choice and rarest parts,°   *qualities*
260 That all particulars of duty know,
And in the most exact regard support
The worships of° their name. O most small fault,   *honors accorded*
How ugly didst thou in Cordelia show!
That, like an engine, wrench'd my frame of nature
265 From the fixed place;[6] drew from my heart all love,
And added to the gall. O Lear, Lear, Lear!
Beat at this gate, that let thy folly in, (*striking his head*)
And thy dear° judgment out! Go, go, my people.   *precious*

ALBANY   My lord, I am guiltless, as I am ignorant
Of what hath moved you.

270 LEAR   It may be so, my lord.
Hear, Nature, hear! dear goddess, hear!
Suspend thy purpose, if thou didst intend
To make this creature fruitful!
Into her womb convey sterility!
275 Dry up in her the organs of increase;
And from her derogate° body never spring   *debased*
A babe to honor her! If she must teem,°   *breed*
Create her child of spleen,° that it may live   *malice*
And be a thwart, disnatured° torment to her!   *a perverse unnatural*
280 Let it stamp wrinkles in her brow of youth;
With cadent° tears fret° channels in her cheeks;   *flowing/carve*
Turn all her mother's pains and benefits°   *cares and kind actions*
To laughter and contempt, that she may feel
How sharper than a serpent's tooth it is

---

6. I.e., as a machine (or lever) dislocated my natural affections from their proper foundations.

285   To have a thankless child! Away, away!   *Exit*
    ALBANY   Now, gods that we adore, whereof comes this?
    GONERIL   Never afflict yourself to know the cause;
    But let his disposition have that scope
    That dotage gives it.
              Re-enter LEAR
290   LEAR   What, fifty of my followers at a clap?
    Within a fortnight?
    ALBANY   What's the matter, sir?
    LEAR   I'll tell thee. (*To* GONERIL) Life and death! I am ashamed
    That thou hast power to shake my manhood thus;
    That these hot tears, which break from me perforce,°   *against my will*
295   Should make thee worth them. Blasts and fogs upon thee!
    The untented woundings° of a father's curse   *the undressed wounds*
    Pierce every sense about thee! Old fond° eyes,   *foolish*
    Beweep° this cause again, I'll pluck ye out,   *if you weep over*
    And cast you, with the waters that you lose,
300   To temper° clay. Yea, is it come to this?   *soften*
    Let it be so. Yet have I left a daughter,
    Who, I am sure, is kind and comfortable.°   *comforting*
    When she shall hear this of thee, with her nails
    She'll flay thy wolvish visage. Thou shalt find
305   That I'll resume the shape which thou dost think
    I have cast off for ever; thou shalt, I warrant thee.
             Exeunt LEAR, KENT, *and attendants*
    GONERIL. Do you mark that, my lord?
    ALBANY   I cannot be so partial,° Goneril,   *biased*
    To° the great love I bear you—   *because of*
310   GONERIL   Pray you, content.° What, Oswald, ho! (*To the*   *be quiet*
    FOOL) You sir, more knave than fool, after your master!
    FOOL   Nuncle Lear, nuncle Lear, tarry and take the fool
    with thee.
           A fox, when one has caught her,
315   And such a daughter,
           Should sure° to the slaughter,   *surely be sent*
           If my cap would buy a halter:°   *collar; noose*
           So the fool follows after.   *Exit*
    GONERIL   This man hath had good counsel!—a hundred
    knights?
320   'Tis politic° and safe to let him keep   *prudent*
    At point° a hundred knights? Yes, that on every dream,   *armed*
    Each buzz,° each fancy, each complaint, dislike,   *rumor*
    He may enguard° his dotage with their powers,   *protect*
    And hold our lives in mercy. Oswald, I say!
    ALBANY   Well, you may fear too far.
325   GONERIL   Safer than trust too far:
    Let me still° take away the harms I fear,   *always*
    Not° fear still to be taken. I know his heart.   *rather than*
    What he hath uttered I have writ my sister.
    If she sustain him and his hundred knights,

When I have showed the unfitness—

Re-enter OSWALD

330 How now, Oswald!
What, have you writ that letter to my sister?

OSWALD Yes, madam.

GONERIL Take you some company, and away to horse!
Inform her full of my particular fear,

335 And thereto add such reasons of your own
As may compact° it more. Get you gone,   *compound*
And hasten your return.   *Exit* OSWALD
No, no, my lord,
This milky gentleness and course of yours

340 Though I condemn not, yet, under pardon,°   *begging your pardon*
You are much more attaxed° for want of wisdom   *taken to task, censured*
Than praised for harmful mildness.

ALBANY How far your eyes may pierce° I cannot tell: *foresee*
Striving to better, oft we mar what's well.

345 GONERIL Nay, then—

ALBANY Well, well; the event.°   *Exeunt*   *time will tell*

1.5

Enter LEAR, KENT, *and* FOOL

LEAR Go you before° to Gloucester[1] with these letters.   *on ahead*
Acquaint my daughter no further with any thing you
know than comes from her demand out of the letter.[2] If
your diligence be not speedy, I shall be there afore you.

5 KENT I will not sleep, my lord, till I have delivered your
letter.   *Exit*

FOOL If a man's brains were in 's heels, were't not in danger of kibes?°   *chilblains*

LEAR Ay, boy.

10 FOOL Then, I prithee, be merry; thy wit shall ne'er go slip-
shod.[3]

LEAR Ha, ha, ha!

FOOL Shalt° see thy other daughter will use thee kindly;   *thou shalt*
for though she's as like this as a crab's° like an apple, yet   *crab apple, sour apple*

15 I can tell what I can tell.

LEAR Why, what canst thou tell, my boy?

FOOL She will taste as like this as a crab does to a crab.
Thou canst tell why one's nose stands i' the middle on's°   *of one's*
face?

20 LEAR No.

FOOL Why, to keep one's eyes of either side's nose, that
what a man cannot smell out, 'a° may spy into.   *he*

LEAR I did her° wrong—   *(Cordelia)*

FOOL Canst tell how an oyster makes his shell?

25 LEAR No.

1.5 Location: Before Albany's castle.
1. To the city of Gloucester.
2. Other than such questions as are prompted by the letter.

3. Literally, your brains will not wear slippers (to warm feet that are afflicted with chilblains); feet of any intelligence would not walk toward Regan.

FOOL Nor I neither; but I can tell why a snail has a house.

LEAR Why?

FOOL Why, to put his head in; not to give it away to his
daughters, and leave his horns without a case.[4]

30 LEAR I will forget my nature.° So kind a father! Be my   *lose my fatherly feelings*
horses ready?

FOOL Thy asses° are gone about 'em. The reason why the   *(servants)*
seven stars° are no more than seven is a pretty reason.   *the Pleiades*

LEAR Because they are not eight?

35 FOOL Yes, indeed. Thou wouldst make a good fool.

LEAR To take 't again perforce![5] Monster ingratitude!

FOOL If thou wert my fool, nuncle, I'd have thee beaten
for being old before thy time.

LEAR How's that?

40 FOOL Thou shouldst not have been old till thou hadst been wise.

LEAR O, let me not be mad, not mad, sweet heaven!
Keep me in temper;° I would not be mad!   *sane*
    Enter GENTLEMEN
How now! Are the horses ready?

GENTLEMEN Ready, my lord.

45 LEAR Come, boy.

FOOL She that's a maid now, and laughs at my departure,
Shall not be a maid long, unless things be cut shorter.[6]
                              Exeunt

2.1
    Enter EDMUND *and* CURAN *meeting*

EDMUND Save° thee, Curan.   *God save*

CURAN And you, sir. I have been with your father, and
given him notice that the Duke of Cornwall and Regan
his duchess will be here with him this night.

5 EDMUND How comes that?

CURAN Nay, I know not. You have heard of the news
abroad—I mean the whispered ones, for they are yet but
ear-bussing arguments?[1]

EDMUND Not I. Pray you, what are they?

10 CURAN Have you heard of no likely wars toward,° 'twixt   *impending*
the Dukes of Cornwall and Albany?

EDMUND Not a word.

CURAN You may do, then, in time. Fare you well, sir. *Exit*

EDMUND The duke be here tonight? The better! best!

15 This weaves itself perforce into my business.
My father hath set guard to take my brother;
And I have one thing, of a queasy question,[2]
Which I must act. Briefness and fortune, work!°   *be with me*

---

4. Protective covering for his head or concealment for
his horns (horns were the conventional sign of a cuckold). The Fool reflects the cynical view, common in the
period, that all married men are inevitably cuckolded.
5. To take it back by force. Lear may refer to Goneril's
treachery, or he may be contemplating resuming his
authority.

6. A girl who would laugh at my leaving would be so
foolish that she could not remain a virgin for long;
"things" refers both to the unfolding event and to
penises.
2.1 Location: Gloucester's castle.
1. Barely whispered affairs. "Bussing": kissing.
2. And I have a hazardous and delicate problem.

Brother, a word! Descend! Brother, I say!

Enter EDGAR

20 My father watches. O sir, fly this place!
Intelligence is given where you are hid.
You have now the good advantage of the night.
Have you not spoken 'gainst the Duke of Cornwall?
He's coming hither; now, i' the night, i' the haste,
25 And Regan with him: have you nothing said
Upon his party° 'gainst the Duke of Albany?   *on his (Cornwall's) side*
Advise yourself.°   *consider carefully*

EDGAR   I am sure on't,° not a word.   *of it*

EDMUND   I hear my father coming. Pardon me!
In cunning I must draw my sword upon you:
30 Draw; seem to defend yourself; now quit you° well.   *acquit yourself*
Yield! Come before my father. Light, ho, here!
Fly, brother. Torches, torches! So farewell.   *Exit* EDGAR
Some blood drawn on me would beget opinion°   *produce the impression*
     (*wounds his arm*)
Of my more fierce endeavor. I have seen drunkards
35 Do more than this in sport. Father, father!
Stop, stop! No help?

Enter GLOUCESTER, *and servants with torches*

GLOUCESTER   Now, Edmund, where's the villain?

EDMUND   Here stood he in the dark, his sharp sword out,
Mumbling of wicked charms, conjuring the moon
To stand° auspicious mistress,—   *to act as his*

40 GLOUCESTER   But where is he?

EDMUND   Look, sir, I bleed.

GLOUCESTER   Where is the villain, Edmund?

EDMUND   Fled this way, sir. When by no means he could—

GLOUCESTER   Pursue him, ho! Go after.

                     Exeunt some servants

By no means what?

45 EDMUND   Persuade me to the murder of your lordship;
But that° I told him, the revenging gods   *in response to that*
'Gainst parricides did all their thunders bend;
Spoke, with how manifold and strong a bond
The child was bound to the father; sir, in fine,°   *finally*
50 Seeing how loathly opposite° I stood   *opposed*
To his unnatural purpose, in fell° motion,   *deadly*
With his prepared sword, he charges home°   *strikes to the heart of*
My unprovided° body, lanched° mine arm: *unprotected / wounded*
But when he saw my best alarumed spirits,
55 Bold in the quarrel's right,[3] roused to the encounter,
Or whether gasted° by the noise I made,   *frightened*
Full suddenly he fled.

GLOUCESTER   Let him fly far.
Not in this land shall he remain uncaught;
And found—dispatch.° The noble duke my master,   *and once found—killed*

---

3. I.e., that I was fully roused to action, made brave by righteousness.

60 My worthy arch° and patron, comes to-night: *lord*
    By his authority I will proclaim it,
    That he which finds him shall deserve our thanks,
    Bringing the murderous caitiff° to the stake;[4]   *wretch*
    He that conceals him, death.

65 EDMUND   When I dissuaded him from his intent,
    And found him pight° to do it, with curst° speech   *resolved / bitter*
    I threatened to discover° him. He replied,   *expose*
    "Thou unpossessing bastard! dost thou think
    If I would stand against thee, would the reposal°   *placing*
70 Of any trust, virtue, or worth in thee
    Make thy words faithed?° No. What I should deny—   *credible*
    As this I would; ay, though thou didst produce
    My very character[5]—I'd turn it all
    To[6] thy suggestion, plot, and damned practice:°   *scheming*
75 And thou must make a dullard of the world,
    If they not thought the profits of my death
    Were very pregnant° and potential spurs°   *full / powerful temptations*
    To make thee seek it."[7]

GLOUCESTER   Strong° and fast'ned° villain!   *flagrant / incorrigible*
    Would he deny his letter? I never got° him.   *begot*
       Tucket° within   *flourish of trumpets*
80 Hark, the Duke's trumpets! I know not why he comes.
    All ports° I'll bar; the villain shall not 'scape;   *seaports; exits*
    The duke must grant me that. Besides, his picture[8]
    I will send far and near, that all the kingdom
    May have due note of him; and of my land,
85 Loyal and natural° boy, I'll work the means   *loving; illegitimate*
    To make thee capable.°   *legally able to inherit*
       Enter CORNWALL, REGAN, *and attendants*

CORNWALL   How now, my noble friend! Since I came
    hither,
    (Which I can call but now) I have heard strange news.

REGAN   If it be true, all vengeance comes too short
90 Which can pursue the offender. How dost, my lord?

GLOUCESTER   O, madam, my old heart is cracked, is
    cracked!

REGAN   What, did my father's godson seek your life?
    He whom my father named? Your Edgar?

GLOUCESTER   O, lady, lady, shame would have it hid!

95 REGAN   Was he not companion with the riotous knights
    That tend° upon my father?   *attend*

GLOUCESTER   I know not, madam. 'Tis too bad, too bad!

EDMUND   Yes, madam, he was of that consort.°   *company*

REGAN   No marvel, then, though° he were ill affected.°   *that / ill disposed*
100 'Tis they have put him on° the old man's death,   *have urged him to seek*

---

4. Treachery and rebellion were crimes for which one could be burned.
5. Handwriting; but also, a true summary of my character.
6. I'd blame it all on.
7. And do you think the world so stupid that it could

not see the benefit you would get from my death (and thus a motive for plotting to kill me)?
8. Likenesses of outlaws were drawn up, printed, and publicly displayed, sometimes with an offer of reward as in "Wanted" posters.

To have th' expense° and waste of his revenues.   use
I have this present evening from my sister
Been well informed of them; and with such cautions
That if they come to sojourn at my house,
I'll not be there.
105 CORNWALL   Nor I, assure thee, Regan.
Edmund, I hear that you have shown your father
A child-like office.°   filial service
EDMUND   'Twas my duty, sir.
GLOUCESTER   He did bewray his practice,° and received   reveal his (Edgar's) plot
This hurt you see, striving to apprehend him.
CORNWALL   Is he pursued?
110 GLOUCESTER   Ay, my good lord.
CORNWALL   If he be taken, he shall never more
Be feared of doing harm. Make your own purpose,
How in my strength you please.⁹ For you, Edmund,
Whose virtue and obedience doth this instant
115 So much commend itself, you shall be ours.
Natures of such deep trust we shall much need;
You we first seize on.
EDMUND   I shall serve you, sir,
Truly, however else.°   if nothing else
GLOUCESTER   For him I thank your grace.
CORNWALL   You know not why we came to visit you—
120 REGAN   Thus out of season, threading dark-eyed night.
Occasions, noble Gloucester, of some poise,°   weight
Wherein we must have use of your advice:
Our father he hath writ, so hath our sister,
Of differences,° which I least thought of fit   quarrels
125 To answer from our home. The several° messengers   various
From hence attend° dispatch. Our good old friend,   await
Lay comforts to your bosom, and bestow
Your needful° counsel to our business,   badly needed
Which craves the instant use.¹
GLOUCESTER   I serve you, madam.
130 Your graces are right welcome.   *Exeunt*

2.2

Enter KENT *and* OSWALD, *severally°*   separately
OSWALD   Good dawning to thee, friend. Art° of this house?   are you a servant
KENT   Ay.
OSWALD   Where may we set our horses?
KENT   I' the mire.
5 OSWALD   Prithee, if thou lovest me,° tell me.   if you will be so kind
KENT   I love thee not.
OSWALD   Why, then, I care not for thee.

---

9. Devise your plots making use of my forces and   1. Which requires immediate attention.
authority as you see fit.   2.2 Location: Before Gloucester's house.

KENT   If I had thee in Lipsbury pinfold,[1] I would make thee
10   care for me.

OSWALD   Why dost thou use° me thus? I know thee not.   *treat*

KENT   Fellow, I know thee.

OSWALD   What dost thou know me for?

KENT   A knave; a rascal; an eater of broken meats;° a base,   *scraps*
      proud, shallow, beggarly, three-suited, hundred-pound,
15   filthy, worsted-stocking knave;[2] a lily-livered,° action-   *cowardly*
      taking knave; a whoreson, glass-gazing,° superservice-   *mirror-gazing*
      able, finical° rogue; one-trunk-inheriting slave;[3] one that   *finicky, fastidious*
      wouldst be a bawd in way of good service,[4] and art noth-
      ing but the composition° of a knave, beggar, coward, pan-   *combination*
20   dar, and the son and heir of a mongrel bitch; one whom
      I will beat into clamorous whining, if thou deniest the
      least syllable of thy addition.[5]

OSWALD   Why, what a monstrous fellow art thou, thus to
      rail on one that is neither known of° thee nor knows thee!   *by*
25 KENT   What a brazen-faced varlet° art thou, to deny thou   *rascal*
      knowest me! Is it two days ago since I tripped up thy
      heels, and beat thee before the king? Draw, you rogue!
      For, though it be night, yet the moon shines. I'll make a
      sop of the moonshine[6] of you. Draw, you whoreson cul-
30   lionly barber-monger,[7] draw!
          Drawing his sword

OSWALD   Away! I have nothing to do with thee.

KENT   Draw, you rascal! You come with letters against the
      king, and take Vanity the puppet's part against the royalty
      of her father.[8] Draw, you rogue, or I'll so carbonado[9] your
35   shanks! Draw, you rascal! Come your ways!°   *come forward*

OSWALD   Help, ho! murther! help!

KENT   Strike, you slave! Stand, rogue! Stand, you neat°   *elegant; foppish*
      slave! Strike! [*Beating him*]

OSWALD   Help, ho! murther! murther!
          Enter EDMUND *with his rapier drawn,* CORNWALL,
          REGAN, GLOUCESTER, *and servants*
40 EDMUND   How now! What's the matter?
          Parts them

KENT   With you, goodman boy, an° you please! Come, I'll   *if*
      flesh ye![1] Come, on, young master!

---

1. If I had you in the enclosure of my mouth (gripped
in my teeth). Lipsbury is probably an invented place-
name. "Pinfold": pen, animal enclosure.
2. Oswald is being called a poor imitation of a gentleman. Servants were permitted three suits a year; one
hundred pounds was the minimum qualification for the
purchase of one of King James's knighthoods; a gentleman would wear silk, not "worsted" (of thick woolen
material), stockings.
3. "One-trunk-inheriting": owning only what would fill
one trunk. "Superserviceable": overly officious, or too
ready to serve. "Action-taking": litigious, one who
would rather use the law than his fists.
4. One who would be a pimp if called upon.

5. Of the descriptions Kent has just applied to him.
"Addition": title (used ironically).
6. Kent proposes so to skewer and pierce Oswald that
his body might soak up moonlight. "Sop": piece of bread
to be steeped or dunked in soup.
7. Despicable frequenter of hairdressers. A "cullion" is
a testicle.
8. And support Goneril, here depicted as a dressed-up
doll whose pride is contrasted with Lear's kingliness.
9. Slash or score as one would the surface of meat in
preparation for broiling.
1. I'll blood you (as a hunting dog); I'll initiate you into
fighting.

GLOUCESTER Weapons! arms! What's the matter here?

CORNWALL Keep peace, upon your lives!

He dies that strikes again. What is the matter?

REGAN The messengers from our sister and the king.

CORNWALL What is your difference? Speak.

OSWALD I am scarce in breath, my lord.

KENT No marvel, you have so bestirred your valor. You
cowardly rascal, nature disclaims° in thee; a tailor made   disowns her part
thee.

CORNWALL Thou art a strange fellow. A tailor² make a
man?

KENT Ay, a tailor, sir. A stone-cutter or a painter could not
have made him so ill,° though he had been but two hours   so badly
at the trade.

CORNWALL Speak yet, how grew your quarrel?

OSWALD This ancient ruffian, sir, whose life I have spared
at suit of° his gray beard—   on account of

KENT Thou whoreson zed!³ thou unnecessary letter! My
lord, if you will give me leave, I will tread this unbolted°   unsifted, coarse
villain into mortar, and daub the walls of a jakes° with   privy, toilet
him. Spare my gray beard, you wagtail?⁴

CORNWALL Peace, sirrah!

You beastly knave, know you no reverence?°   respect

KENT Yes, sir, but anger hath a privilege.

CORNWALL Why art thou angry?

KENT That such a slave as this should wear a sword,
Who wears no honesty. Such smiling rogues as these,
Like rats, oft bite the holy cords⁵ a-twain
Which are too intrinse° t' unloose; smooth° every passion   intricate / flatter
That in natures of their lords rebel;
Bring oil to fire, snow to their colder moods;
Renege,° affirm, and turn their halcyon beaks⁶   deny
With every gale and vary° of their masters,   mood
Knowing nought, like dogs, but following.
A plague upon your epileptic° visage!   distorted, grimacing
Smile you° my speeches, as° I were a fool?   do you smile at / as if
Goose, if I had you upon Sarum plain
I'ld drive ye cackling home to Camelot.⁷

CORNWALL What, art thou mad, old fellow?

GLOUCESTER How fell you out? say that.

KENT No contraries° hold more antipathy   opposites
Than I and such a knave.

---

2. Tailors, considered effeminate, were stock objects of mockery.

3. The letter Z (zed) was considered superfluous and omitted from many dictionaries.

4. A common English bird that takes its name from the up-and-down flicking of its tail; this, and its characteristic hopping from foot to foot, causes it to appear nervous.

5. Bonds of kinship, affection, marriage, or rank.

6. It was believed that the kingfisher (in Greek, *halcyon*) could be used as a weather vane when dead: suspended by a fine thread, its beak would turn whatever way the wind blew.

7. Comparing him to a cackling goose, Kent tells Oswald that if he had him on Salisbury Plain, he would drive him all the way to Camelot, legendary home of King Arthur.

85 CORNWALL Why dost thou call him knave? What's his
              offense?
   KENT His countenance likes° me not.   *pleases*
   CORNWALL No more, perchance, does mine, nor his, nor
              hers.
   KENT Sir, 'tis my occupation to be plain.
         I have seen better faces in my time
90   Than stands on any shoulder that I see
         Before me at this instant.
   CORNWALL   This is some fellow,
         Who, having been praised for bluntness, doth affect
         A saucy roughness, and constrains the garb
         Quite from his nature.[8] He cannot flatter, he,
95   An honest mind and plain, he must speak truth!
         An they will take it, so; if not, he's plain.[9]
         These kind of knaves I know, which in this plainness
         Harbor more craft and more corrupter ends
         Than twenty silly ducking observants
100   That stretch their duties nicely.[1]
   KENT Sir, in good sooth, in sincere verity,
         Under the allowance of your great aspect,[2]
         Whose influence, like the wreath of radiant fire
         On flickering Phoebus' front,°   *the sun god's forehead*
   CORNWALL   What mean'st by this?
105 KENT To go out of my dialect,° which you discommend   *normal mode of speech*
         so much. I know, sir, I am no flatterer. He that beguiled
         you in a plain accent was a plain knave; which for my
         part I will not be, though I should win your displeasure
         to entreat me to 't.[3]
110 CORNWALL What was the offense you gave him?
   OSWALD I never gave him any:
         It pleased the king his master very late°   *lately*
         To strike at me, upon his misconstruction,°   *misunderstanding (me)*
         When he, conjunct,° and flattering his displeasure,   *in league with*
115   Tripped me behind; being down, insulted,° railed,   *I being down, he insulted*
         And put upon him such a deal of man,
         That worthied him,[4] got praises of the king
         For him attempting who was self-subdued;[5]
         And, in the fleshment° of this dread exploit,   *excitement; flush*
         Drew on me here again.
120 KENT   None of these rogues and cowards

---

8. I.e., and assumes the appearance though it is untrue
to his real self. Alternatively (with "his" meaning "its"),
and distorts the true shape of plainness from what it
naturally is (by turning it into disrespect).
9. If they will accept (Kent's attitude), well and good;
if not, he is a plainspoken man (and does not care).
1. Than twenty obsequious attendants who constantly
bow idiotically and who perform their functions with
excessive diligence ("nicely").
2. With the permission of your great countenance.

"Aspect' also refers to the astrological position of a
planet; Kent's bombastic language here raises Cornwall
to the mock-heroic proportions of a heavenly body.
3. The person who tried to hoodwink you with plain
speaking was, indeed, a pure knave—something I won't
be, even if you were to beg me to be one (a plain knave,
or flatterer).
4. And put on such a show of manliness that he was
thought a worthy fellow.
5. For attacking a man who had already surrendered.

But Ajax is their fool.[6]

CORNWALL   Fetch forth the stocks!
You stubborn miscreant knave, you reverent° braggart,   old; revered
We'll teach you—
KENT   Sir, I am too old to learn.
Call not your stocks for me. I serve the king;
125   On whose employment I was sent to you:
You shall do small respect, show too bold malice
Against the grace° and person° of my master,   majesty / personal honor
Stocking° his messenger.   by stocking
CORNWALL   Fetch forth the stocks! As I have life and
honor,
130   There shall he sit till noon.
REGAN   Till noon? Till night, my lord, and all night too!
KENT   Why, madam, if I were your father's dog,
You should not use me so.
REGAN   Sir, being° his knave, I will.   since you are
CORNWALL   This is a fellow of the self-same color°   character
135   Our sister° speaks of. Come, bring away the stocks!   sister-in-law
         Stocks brought out
GLOUCESTER   Let me beseech your grace not to do so.
His fault is much, and the good king his master
Will check° him for't. Your purposed° low correction   reprimand / intended
Is such as basest and contemned'st wretches
140   For pilferings and most common trespasses
Are punished with: the king must take it ill,
That he, so slightly valued in his messenger,
Should have him thus restrained.
CORNWALL   I'll answer° that.   be responsible for
REGAN   My sister may receive it much more worse,
145   To have her gentleman abused, assaulted,
For following° her affairs. Put in his legs.   carrying out
         KENT is put in the stocks
Come, my good lord, away.
              Exeunt all but GLOUCESTER and KENT
GLOUCESTER   I am sorry for thee, friend: 'tis the duke's pleasure,
Whose disposition, all the world well knows,
150   Will not be rubbed° nor stopped: I'll entreat for thee.   obstructed
KENT   Pray, do not sir. I have watched° and traveled hard;   gone without sleep
Some time I shall sleep out, the rest I'll whistle.
A good man's fortune may grow out at heels:[7]
Give° you good morrow!   God give
155   GLOUCESTER   The duke's to blame in this; 't will be ill-
taken.   Exit
KENT   Good king, that must approve° the common saw,°   prove / saying
Thou out of heaven's benediction comest

---

6. Such rogues and cowards as these talk as if they were greater warriors (and blusterers) than Ajax; such rogues always make even mighty Ajax out to be a fool.

7. The fortunes of even good men sometimes wear thin.

To the warm sun!⁸
Approach, thou beacon⁹ to this under globe,
160　That by thy comfortable beams I may
Peruse this letter! Nothing almost sees miracles
But misery.¹ I know 'tis from Cordelia,
Who hath most fortunately been informed
Of my obscurèd° course; (*reads*) "and shall find time　　　*hidden, disguised*
165　From this enormous state,° seeking to give　　　*awful state of affairs*
Losses their remedies." All weary and o'er-watched,°　　　*too long awake*
Take vantage,° heavy eyes, not to behold　　　*the opportunity*
This shameful lodging.
Fortune, good night; smile once more; turn thy wheel!²
　　　　　　　　　　　　　　　　　　　　　　　Sleeps

2.3

Enter EDGAR

EDGAR　I heard myself proclaimed;°　　　*declared an outlaw*
And by the happy° hollow of a tree　　　*opportune*
Escaped the hunt. No port° is free; no place,　　　*seaport; exit*
That guard, and most unusual vigilance,
5　Does not attend my taking.° Whiles° I may 'scape,　　*await my capture / until*
I will preserve myself; and am bethought°　　　*resolved*
To take the basest and most poorest shape
That ever penury, in contempt of° man,　　　*for*
Brought near to beast. My face I'll grime with filth,
10　Blanket my loins, elf¹ all my hair in knots,
And with presented° nakedness out-face　　　*exposed*
The winds and persecutions of the sky.
The country gives me proof and precedent
Of Bedlam beggars, who, with roaring voices,
15　Strike° in their numbed and mortified° bare arms　　*stick / deadened*
Pins, wooden pricks, nails, sprigs of rosemary;
And with this horrible object,° from low farms,　　　*spectacle*
Poor pelting° villages, sheep-cotes, and mills,　　*paltry, contemptible*
Sometime with lunatic bans,° sometime with prayers,　　　*curses*
20　Enforce their charity. Poor Turlygod!² poor Tom!
That's something yet! Edgar I nothing am.³　　　*Exit*

2.4

Enter LEAR, FOOL, *and* GENTLEMAN¹

LEAR　'Tis strange that they should so depart from home,
And not send back my messenger.

---

8. You come from the blessing of heaven into the heat of the sun (go from good to bad).
9. It is arguable whether Kent here refers to the sun or the moon.
1. Only those suffering misery are granted miracles; any comfort seems miraculous to those who are miserable.
2. The goddess Fortune was traditionally depicted with a wheel to signify her mutability and caprice. She was believed to take pleasure in arbitrarily lowering those

at the top of her wheel and raising those at the bottom.
2.3 Location: As before.
1. Tangle the hair into "elf locks," supposed to be a favorite trick of malicious elves.
2. A word of unknown origin.
3. Edgar, I am nothing; I am no longer Edgar.
2.4 Location: As before.
1. The Folio seems to reserve "a Gentleman" for this particular character, who returns in 5.3.

GENTLEMAN   As I learned,
   The night before there was no purpose in them°   *they had no intention*
   Of this remove.°   *change of residence*
KENT   Hail to thee, noble master!
5 LEAR   Ha!
   Makest thou this shame thy pastime?
KENT   No, my lord.
FOOL   Ha, ha! he wears cruel garters.[2] Horses are tied by
   the heads, dogs and bears by the neck, monkeys by the
   loins, and men by the legs. When a man's over-lusty at
10 legs,[3] then he wears wooden nether-stocks.°   *knee socks*
LEAR   What's° he that hath so much thy place° mistook   *who's / position*
   To set thee here?
KENT   It is both he and she;
   Your son° and daughter.   *son-in-law*
LEAR   No.
15 KENT   Yes.
LEAR   No, I say.
KENT   I say, yea.
LEAR   No, no, they would not!
KENT   Yes, yes, they have!
20 LEAR   By Jupiter, I swear, no!
KENT   By Juno,[4] I swear, aye!
LEAR   They durst not do 't;
   They would not, could not do 't. 'Tis worse than murder,
   To do upon respect[5] such violent outrage.
   Resolve° me, with all modest° haste, which way   *inform / reasonable*
25 Thou mightst deserve, or they impose, this usage,
   Coming from us.
KENT   My lord, when at their home
   I did commend° your highness' letters to them,   *deliver*
   Ere I was risen from the place that showed
   My duty kneeling, came there a reeking° post,   *steaming*
30 Stewed in his haste, half breathless, panting forth
   From Goneril his mistress, salutations;
   Delivered letters, spite of intermission,[6]
   Which presently° they read; on whose contènts,   *immediately*
   They summoned up their meiny,° straight° took horse;   *retinue / straightaway*
35 Commanded me to follow, and attend
   The leisure of their answer, gave me cold looks,
   And meeting here the other messenger,
   Whose welcome, I perceived, had poisoned mine—
   Being the very° fellow that of late   *same*
40 Displayed so saucily° against your highness—   *acted so insolently*
   Having more man° than wit° about me, drew.   *courage / sense*

2. Worsted garters, punning on "crewel," a thin yarn.   whom she constantly quarreled.
The Fool is actually referring to the stocks in which   5. To do to one who deserves respect.
Kent's feet are held.   6. Regardless of interrupting me; despite the interrup-
3. When a man's liable to run away.   tions in his account (as he gasped for breath).
4. Queen of the Roman gods and wife of Jupiter, with

He raised the house with loud and coward cries.
Your son and daughter found this trespass worth°   *deserving of*
The shame which here it suffers.

45   FOOL   Winter's not gone yet, if the wild-geese fly that way.[7]
        Fathers that wear rags
          Do make their children blind;[8]
        But fathers that bear bags
          Shall see their children kind.
50   Fortune, that arrant whore,
          Ne'er turns the key° to the poor.   *opens the door*
But, for all this, thou shalt have as many dolors[9] for thy
daughters as thou canst tell° in a year.   *count*
  LEAR   O, how this mother° swells up toward my heart!   *hysteria*
55   *Hysterica passio*, down, thou climbing sorrow,[1]
Thy element's° below! Where is this daughter?   *natural place is*
  KENT   With the earl, sir, here within.
  LEAR   Follow me not; stay
  here.   *Exit*
  GENTLEMAN   Made you no more offenses but what you
  speak of?
60   KENT   None. How chance the king comes with so small a
  train?
  FOOL   An° thou hadst been set i' the stocks for that ques-   *if*
  tion, thou hadst well deserved it.
  KENT   Why, fool?
65   FOOL   We'll set thee to school to an ant, to teach thee
  there's no laboring i' the winter.[2] All that follow their
  noses are led by their eyes but blind men, and there's not
  a nose among twenty but can smell him that's stinking.°   *(as his fortunes decay)*
  Let go thy hold when a great wheel runs down a hill,[3] lest
70   it break thy neck with following it; but the great one that
  goes up the hill, let him draw thee after. When a wise
  man gives thee better counsel, give me mine again. I
  would have none but knaves follow it, since a fool gives
  it.
75   That sir which serves and seeks for gain,
          And follows but for form,
        Will pack° when it begins to rain,   *pack up and go*
          And leave thee in the storm.
        But I will tarry; the fool will stay,
80   And let the wise man fly.
        The knave turns fool that runs away;[4]
          The fool no knave, perdy.°   *by God* (pardieu)

---

7. That is, things will get worse before they get better.
8. Blind to their father's needs.
9. Pains, sorrows; punning on "dollar," the English term for the German 'thaler," a large silver coin.
1. *Hysterica passio* (a Latin expression originating in the Greek *steiros*, "suffering in the womb") was an inflammation of the senses. In Renaissance medicine, vapors from the abdomen were thought to rise up through the body, and in women, the uterus itself to

wander around.
2. Ants, proverbially prudent, do not work in winter. Implicitly, a wise person should know better than to look for sustenance to an old man who has fallen on wintry times.
3. A great wheel is a figure for Lear and of Fortune's wheel itself, which has swung downward.
4. The scoundrel who runs away is the real fool.

KENT   Where learned you this, fool?

FOOL   Not i' the stocks, fool.

     Re-enter LEAR, *with* GLOUCESTER

85   LEAR   Deny to speak with me? They are sick? They are weary?

    They have traveled all the night? Mere fetches;°   *ruses, pretexts*

    The images of revolt and flying off.[5]

    Fetch me a better answer.

GLOUCESTER   My dear lord,

    You know the fiery quality° of the duke;   *disposition*

90   How unremoveable and fixed he is

    In his own course.

    LEAR   Vengeance! plague! death! confusion!°   *destruction*

    Fiery? what quality? Why, Gloucester, Gloucester,

    I'd speak with the Duke of Cornwall and his wife.

95   GLOUCESTER   Well, my good lord, I have informed them so.

    LEAR   Informed them! Dost thou understand me, man?

    GLOUCESTER   Ay, my good lord.

    LEAR   The king would speak with Cornwall; the dear father

    Would with his daughter speak, commands her service.

100   Are they informed of this? My breath and blood!

    Fiery? the fiery duke? Tell the hot duke that—

    No, but not yet. May be he is not well.

    Infirmity doth still° neglect all office°   *always/obligation*

    Whereto our health is bound; we are not ourselves

105   When nature, being oppressed, commands the mind

    To suffer with the body. I'll forbear;

    And am fallen out with my more headier will,[6]

    To take° the indisposed and sickly fit   *mistake*

    For the sound man. Death on my state![7] Wherefore°   *why*

     looking on KENT

110   Should he sit here? This act persuades me

    That this remotion° of the duke and her   *remoteness, aloofness*

    Is practice° only. Give me my servant forth.   *trickery*

    Go tell the duke and 's wife I'd speak with them,

    Now, presently!° Bid them come forth and hear me,   *at once*

115   Or at their chamber-door I'll beat the drum

    Till it cry sleep to death.[8]

    GLOUCESTER   I would have all well betwixt you.   *Exit*

    LEAR   O me, my heart, my rising heart! but, down!

    FOOL   Cry to it, nuncle, as the cockney° did to the eels   *Londoner (city woman)*

120   when she put 'em i' the paste° alive; she knapped 'em o'   *pie, pastry*

    the coxcombs° with a stick, and cried "Down, wantons,°   *heads/rogues*

    down!" 'Twas her brother that, in pure kindness to his

    horse, buttered his hay.[9]

     Enter CORNWALL, REGAN, GLOUCESTER, *and servants*

---

5. Signs of revolt and of desertion or insurrection.
6. And disagree with my (earlier) more rash intention.
7. May my royal authority end (an oath). Ironically, this has already happened.
8. Till the noise kills sleep.

9. Like that of his sister (who wanted to make eel pie without killing the eels), his kindness was misplaced: horses will not eat buttered hay. Lear's earlier kindness to his daughters was equally foolish.

LEAR   Good morrow to you both.

CORNWALL   Hail to your grace!

       KENT *is set at liberty*

125 REGAN   I am glad to see your highness.

LEAR   Regan, I think you are; I know what reason
  I have to think so. If thou shouldst not be glad,
  I would divorce me from thy mother's tomb,
  Sepulchring° an adultress. (*To* KENT) O, are you free?   *because it entombed*
130   Some other time for that. Belovèd Regan,
  Thy sister's naught.° O Regan, she hath tied   *wicked; nothing*
  Sharp-toothed unkindness, like a vulture, here!

      Points to his heart

  I can scarce speak to thee; thou'lt not believe
  With how depraved a quality—O Regan!
135 REGAN   I pray you, sir, take patience. I have hope
  You less know how to value her desert
  Than she to scant her duty.[1]

LEAR   Say, how is that?

REGAN   I cannot think my sister in the least
  Would fail her obligation. If, sir, perchance
140   She have restrained the riots of your followers,
  'Tis on such ground, and to such wholesome end,
  As clears her from all blame.

LEAR   My curses on her!

REGAN   O, sir, you are old;
  Nature° in you stands on the very verge   *life*
145   Of her confine.° You should be ruled and led   *of its limit*
  By some discretion,° that discerns your state   *discreet person*
  Better than you yourself. Therefore, I pray you,
  That to our sister you do make return;
  Say you have wronged her, sir.

LEAR   Ask her forgiveness?
150   Do you but mark how this becomes the house:[2]
  "Dear daughter, I confess that I am old; (*kneeling*)
  Age° is unnecessary. On my knees I beg   *an old man*
  That you'll vouchsafe me raiment,° bed, and food."   *grant me clothing*

REGAN   Good sir, no more! These are unsightly tricks.
  Return you to my sister.

155 LEAR (*rising*)   Never, Regan!
  She hath abated° me of half my train;   *deprived*
  Looked black upon me; struck me with her tongue
  Most serpent-like, upon the very heart.
  All° the stored vengeances of heaven fall   *let all*
160   On her ingrateful top!° Strike her young bones,   *head*
  You taking° airs, with lameness!   *infectious, malignant*

CORNWALL   Fie, sir, fie!

LEAR   You nimble lightnings, dart your blinding flames

---

1. I expect that you are worse at valuing her deservings than she is at neglecting her duty. The double negative here ("less," "scant") is acceptable Jacobean usage.

2. Do you see how appropriate this is among members of a family (spoken ironically)?

Into her scornful eyes! Infect her beauty,
You fen-sucked fogs, drawn by the powerful sun,[3]
165   To fall and blast her pride!
REGAN   O the blest gods! so will you wish on me,
When the rash mood is on.
LEAR   No, Regan, thou shalt never have my curse.
Thy tender-hafted[4] nature shall not give
170   Thee o'er to harshness. Her eyes are fierce; but thine
Do comfort and not burn. 'Tis not in thee
To grudge my pleasures, to cut off my train,
To bandy hasty words, to scant my sizes,°   *reduce my allowances*
And in conclusion to oppose the bolt°   *to lock the door*
175   Against my coming in. Thou better know'st
The offices° of nature, bond of childhood,   *duties*
Effects° of courtesy, dues of gratitude;   *actions*
Thy half o' the kingdom hast thou not forgot,
Wherein I thee endowed.
REGAN   Good sir, to the purpose.°   *get to the point*
LEAR   Who put my man i' the stocks?
      Tucket within
180 CORNWALL   What trumpet's that?
REGAN   I know't, my sister's. This approves° her letter,   *confirms*
That she would soon be here.
      Enter OSWALD
                         Is your lady come?
LEAR   This is a slave, whose easy-borrowed pride[5]
Dwells in the fickle grace of her he follows.
Out varlet,° from my sight!   *wretch*
185 CORNWALL   What means your grace?
LEAR   Who stocked my servant? Regan, I have good hope
Thou didst not know on 't.°   *of it*
      Enter GONERIL
                    Who comes here? O heavens,
If you do love old men, if your sweet sway
Allow obedience, if yourselves are old,
190   Make it your cause! Send down, and take my part!
(*To* GONERIL) Art not ashamed to look upon this beard?
O Regan, wilt thou take her by the hand?
GONERIL   Why not by the hand, sir? How have I offended?
All's not offense that indiscretion finds
And dotage terms so.
195 LEAR   O sides,[6] you are too tough!
Will you yet hold? How came my man i' the stocks?
CORNWALL   I set him there, sir; but his own disorders°   *disorderly behavior*
Deserved much less advancement.[7]

---

3. The sun was thought to suck poisonous vapors from marshy ground.
4. Tenderly placed; firmly set in a tender disposition (as a knife blade into its haft).
5. Unmerited and unpaid-for arrogance; "pride" may

also refer to Oswald's fine clothing received for his services to Goneril.
6. Chest, where Lear's heart is swelling with emotion.
7. Deserved far worse treatment.

LEAR   You! did you?

REGAN   I pray you, father, being weak, seem so.°   *behave so*

200   If, till the expiration of your month,
You will return and sojourn with my sister,
Dismissing half your train, come then to me.
I am now from home, and out of that provision
Which shall be needful for your entertainment.

205   LEAR   Return to her, and fifty men dismissed?
No, rather I abjure all roofs, and choose
To wage against the enmity o' the air;
To be a comrade with the wolf and owl—
Necessity's sharp pinch!⁸ Return with her?

210   Why, the hot-blooded France, that dowerless took
Our youngest born, I could as well be brought
To knee° his throne, and, squire-like, pension beg   *kneel to*
To keep base life afoot. Return with her?
Persuade me rather to be slave and sumpter°   *pack horse*
To this detested groom. (*Pointing at* OSWALD)

215   GONERIL   At your choice, sir.

LEAR   I prithee, daughter, do not make me mad.
I will not trouble thee, my child; farewell.
We'll no more meet, no more see one another.
But yet thou art my flesh, my blood, my daughter;

220   Or rather a disease that's in my flesh,
Which I must needs call mine. Thou art a boil,
A plague-sore, an embossed carbuncle,°   *a swollen tumor*
In my corrupted blood. But I'll not chide thee;
Let shame come when it will, I do not call° it.   *call upon*

225   I do not bid the Thunder-bearer° shoot,   *i.e., Jove*
Nor tell tales of thee to high-judging Jove.
Mend when thou canst; be better at thy leisure.
I can be patient, I can stay with Regan,
I and my hundred knights.

REGAN   Not altogether so.

230   I looked not for° you yet, nor am provided   *I did not expect*
For your fit welcome. Give ear, sir, to my sister;
For those that mingle reason with your passion⁹
Must be content to think you old, and so—
But she knows what she does.

LEAR   Is this well° spoken?   *earnestly*

235   REGAN   I dare avouch° it, sir. What, fifty followers?   *vouch for*
Is it not well? What should you need of more?
Yea, or so many, sith° that both charge° and danger   *since/expense*
Speak 'gainst so great a number? How, in one house,
Should many people, under two commands,

240   Hold amity? 'Tis hard; almost impossible.

GONERIL   Why might not you, my lord, receive attendance

---

8. To counter, like predators, the harshness of the elements with the hardness brought on by the stress or pressure of necessity.

9. For those who temper your passionate argument with their own calm reasoning.

From those that she calls servants, or from mine?
REGAN Why not, my lord? If then they chanced to slack°   *neglect*
  you,
We could control them. If you will come to me—
245   For now I spy a danger—I entreat you
To bring but five-and-twenty. To no more
Will I give place or notice.°   *acknowledgment*
LEAR I gave you all—
REGAN   And in good time° you gave it.   *it was about time*
LEAR Made you my guardians, my depositaries;°   *trustees*
250   But kept a reservation° to be followed   *reserved a right*
With such a number. What, must I come to you
With five-and-twenty, Regan? Said you so?
REGAN And speak't again, my lord; no more with me.
LEAR Those wicked creatures yet do look well-favored,°   *attractive*
255   When others are more wicked; not being the worst
Stands in some rank of praise.[1] (*To* GONERIL) I'll go with thee:
Thy fifty yet doth double five-and-twenty,
And thou art twice her love.
GONERIL   Hear me, my lord.
What need you five-and-twenty, ten, or five,
260   To follow in a house where twice so many
Have a command to tend you?
REGAN   What need one?
LEAR O, reason not the need! Our basest beggars
Are in the poorest thing superfluous.[2]
Allow not° nature more than nature needs,   *if you don't allow*
265   Man's life's as cheap as beast's. Thou art a lady;
If only to go warm were gorgeous,
Why, nature needs not what thou gorgeous wear'st,
Which scarcely keeps thee warm.[3] But, for true need—
You heavens, give me that patience,° patience I need!   *endurance*
270   You see me here, you gods, a poor old man,
As full of grief as age; wretched in both!
If it be you that stirs these daughters' hearts
Against their father, fool me not so much
To bear it tamely;[4] touch me with noble anger,
275   And let not women's weapons, water-drops,
Stain my man's cheeks! No, you unnatural hags,
I will have such revenges on you both,
That all the world shall—I will do such things—
What they are, yet I know not; but they shall be
280   The terrors of the earth! You think I'll weep;
No, I'll not weep.
I have full cause of weeping, but this heart
Shall break into a hundred thousand flaws°   *fragments*

1. Deserves some degree ("rank") of praise.
2. Even the lowliest beggars have something more than the barest minimum.
3. If gorgeousness in clothes is measured by the warmth they provide, your elaborate clothes are superfluous, for they barely cover your body.
4. Do not make me so foolish as to accept it meekly.

Or ere° I'll weep. O fool, I shall go mad! *before*
Exeunt LEAR, GLOUCESTER, KENT, *and* FOOL.
Storm and tempest

285 CORNWALL Let us withdraw; 't will be a storm.
REGAN This house is little; the old man and his people
Cannot be well bestowed.° *lodged*
GONERIL 'Tis his own blame; hath put himself from° rest, *deprived himself of*
And must needs taste his folly.
290 REGAN For his particular,° I'll receive him gladly, *single self*
But not one follower.
GONERIL   So am I purposed.
Where is my lord of Gloucester?
CORNWALL Followed the old man forth. He is returned.
Re-enter GLOUCESTER
GLOUCESTER The king is in high rage.
CORNWALL   Whither is he going?
295 GLOUCESTER He calls to horse, but will I know not whither.
CORNWALL 'Tis best to give him way; he leads himself.
GONERIL My lord, entreat him by no means to stay.
GLOUCESTER Alack, the night comes on, and the bleak winds
Do sorely ruffle.° For many miles about *bluster*
There's scarce a bush.
300 REGAN   O, sir, to willful men,
The injuries that they themselves procure
Must be their schoolmasters. Shut up your doors.
He is attended with a desperate° train; *violent*
And what they may incense° him to, being apt *incite*
305 To have his ear abused,° wisdom bids fear. *deceived*
CORNWALL Shut up your doors, my lord; 'tis a wild night.
My Regan counsels well. Come out o' the storm.
Exeunt

3.1

Storm still. Enter KENT *and a* GENTLEMAN, *at several*° *different*
doors
KENT Who's there, besides foul weather?
GENTLEMAN One minded like the weather, most unquietly.
KENT I know you. Where's the king?
GENTLEMAN Contending with the fretful elements;
5 Bids the wind blow the earth into the sea,
Or swell the curlèd waters 'bove the main,° *mainland*
That things might change or cease; tears his white hair,
Which the impetuous blasts, with eyeless rage,
Catch in their fury, and make nothing of;
10 Strives in his little world of man to out-scorn
The to-and-fro-conflicting wind and rain.
This night, wherein the cub-drawn bear would couch,[1]
The lion and the belly-pinchèd wolf

3.1 Location: Bare, open country.
1. In which even the bear, though starving, having
been sucked dry ("drawn") by its cub, would not go out
to forage.

Keep their fur dry, unbonneted° he runs,   *hatless; uncrowned*
And bids what will take all.

15 KENT   But who is with him?
GENTLEMAN   None but the fool, who labors to out-jest
His heart-struck injuries.[2]
KENT   Sir, I do know you;
And dare, upon the warrant of my note,[3]
Commend a dear° thing to you. There is division,   *entrust a crucial*
20 Although as yet the face of it be covered
With mutual cunning, 'twixt Albany and Cornwall;
Who have—as who have not, that their great stars
Throned and set high?[4]—servants, who seem no less,°   *who appear as such*
Which are to France the spies and speculations°   *observers*
25 Intelligent of[5] our state. What hath been seen,
Either in snuffs and packings° of the dukes,   *quarrels and plots*
Or the hard rein° which both of them have borne   *treatment*
Against the old kind king; or something deeper,
Whereof perchance these are but furnishings;°   *pretexts*
30 But, true it is, from France there comes a power
Into this scattered kingdom; who already,
Wise in° our negligence, have secret feet   *aware of*
In some of our best ports, and are at point°   *ready*
To show their open banner. Now to you:
35 If on my credit you dare build° so far   *if you trust me*
To make your speed to Dover, you shall find
Some that will thank you, making just° report   *accurate*
Of how unnatural and bemadding° sorrow   *maddening*
The king hath cause to plain.°   *complain*
40 I am a gentleman of blood and breeding;
And, from some knowledge and assurance, offer
This office° to you.   *role; duty*
GENTLEMAN   I will talk further with you.
KENT   No, do not.
For confirmation that I am much more
45 Than my out-wall,° open this purse, and take   *outward appearance*
What it contains. If you shall see Cordelia—
As fear not but you shall—show her this ring,
And she will tell you who your fellow° is   *(Kent himself)*
That yet you do not know. Fie on this storm!
50 I will go seek the king.
GENTLEMAN   Give me your hand. Have you no more to say?
KENT   Few words, but, to effect,° more than all yet;   *in importance*
That, when we have found the king—in which your pain
That way, I'll this[6]—he that first lights on him
55 Holla the other.

                                        Exeunt severally

---

2. "To out-jest": to relieve with laughter; to exorcise
through ridicule. "Heart-struck injuries": injuries (from
the betrayal of his paternal love) that penetrated to the
heart.
3. On the basis of my skill (at judging people).

4. I.e., as has everybody who has been favored by destiny.
5. Supplying intelligence about; well informed of.
6. I.e., in which effort you will go that way and I this.

3.2

Enter LEAR *and* FOOL. *Storm still*

LEAR   Blow, winds, and crack your cheeks! rage! blow!
You cataracts and hurricanoes,[1] spout
Till you have drenched our steeples, drowned the cocks!°   *weather vanes*
You sulphurous and thought-executing fires,[2]
5   Vaunt-couriers° to oak-cleaving thunderbolts,   *forerunners*
Singe my white head! And thou, all-shaking thunder,
Smite flat the thick rotundity o' the world!
Crack Nature's molds, all germens° spill at once,   *seeds*
That make ingrateful man!

10   FOOL   O nuncle, court holy-water[3] in a dry house is better
than this rain-water out o' door. Good nuncle, in, and ask
thy daughters' blessing! Here's a night pities neither wise
man nor fool.

LEAR   Rumble thy bellyful! Spit, fire! spout, rain!
15   Nor rain, wind, thunder, fire, are my daughters:
I tax° not you, you elements, with unkindness;   *blame*
I never gave you kingdom, called you children,
You owe me no subscription.° Then let fall   *obedience, allegiance*
Your horrible pleasure. Here I stand, your slave,
20   A poor, infirm, weak, and despised old man.
But yet I call you servile ministers,°   *agents*
That have with two pernicious daughters joined
Your high engendered battles° 'gainst a head   *heaven-bred forces*
So old and white as this. O! O! 't is foul!

25   FOOL   He that has a house to put 's head in has a good
headpiece.°   *hat; brain*
        The cod-piece that will house
          Before the head has any,
        The head and he shall louse;
30   So beggars marry many.[4]
        The man that makes his toe
          What he his heart should make
        Shall of a corn cry woe,
          And turn his sleep to wake.[5]
35   For there was never yet fair woman but she made mouths
in a glass.[6]

LEAR   No, I will be the pattern of all patience; I will say
nothing.

Enter KENT

KENT   Who's there?

3.2 Location: As before.
1. "Hurricanoes": waterspouts (water from both sky
and sea). "Cataracts": floodgates of the heavens.
2. Lightning that strikes as swiftly as thought.
3. Sprinkled blessings of a courtier; flattery.
4. Whoever finds his penis a lodging before providing
shelter for his head will end up in lice-infested poverty
and live in married beggary. A codpiece was a pouchlike
covering for the male genitals, often conspicuous, particularly in the costume of a fool.
5. The man who values an inferior part of his body over
the part that is truly valuable (as Lear valued Goneril
and Regan over Cordelia) will suffer from and lose sleep
over that inferior part.
6. She practiced making pretty faces in a mirror.

40   FOOL   Marry, here's grace and a cod-piece; that's a wise
       man and a fool.[7]
       KENT   Alas, sir, are you here? Things that love night
       Love not such nights as these; the wrathful skies
       Gallow° the very wanderers of the dark,   *frighten*
45   And make them keep° their caves. Since I was man,   *keep inside*
       Such sheets of fire, such bursts of horrid thunder,
       Such groans of roaring wind and rain, I never
       Remember to have heard. Man's nature cannot carry°   *bear*
       The affliction nor the fear.
       LEAR   Let the great gods,
50   That keep this dreadful pother° o'er our heads,   *commotion*
       Find out their enemies now. Tremble, thou wretch,
       That hast within thee undivulgèd crimes,
       Unwhipped of° justice. Hide thee, thou bloody hand;   *unpunished by*
       Thou perjured, and thou simular° of virtue   *simulator, pretender*
55   That are incestuous. Caitiff,° to pieces shake,   *wretch*
       That under covert and convenient seeming°   *fitting hypocrisy*
       Hast practiced on° man's life. Close° pent-up guilts   *against / secret*
       Rive° your concealing continents,° and cry   *split open / coverings*
       These dreadful summoners grace.[8] I am a man
       More sinned against than sinning.
60   KENT   Alack, bare-headed?
       Gracious my lord, hard by here is a hovel;
       Some friendship will it lend you 'gainst the tempest.
       Repose you there, while I to this hard house—
       More harder than the stones whereof 'tis raised,
65   Which[9] even but now, demanding after° you,   *inquiring about*
       Denied me to come in—return, and force
       Their scanted° courtesy.   *niggardly*
       LEAR   My wits begin to turn.
       Come on, my boy. How dost, my boy? Art cold?
       I am cold myself. Where is this straw, my fellow?
70   The art° of our necessities is strange,   *skill; alchemy*
       That can make vile things precious. Come, your hovel.
       Poor fool and knave, I have one part in my heart
       That's sorry yet for thee.
       FOOL (*singing*)[1]
             He that has and° a little tiny wit° —   *even / sense*
75   With hey, ho, the wind and the rain—
            Must make content with his fortunes fit,
            Though the rain it raineth every day.
       LEAR   True, boy. Come, bring us to this hovel.
                             Exeunt LEAR *and* KENT

---

7. The supposedly wise King is symbolized by royal grace, the Fool by his codpiece (here, slang for "penis"). The Fool speaks ironically: the King, as he has pointed out, is now the foolish one. "Marry": by the Virgin Mary (a mild oath).

8. And pray for mercy from these elements that bring you to justice.
9. I.e., the occupants of the house.
1. The following song is an adaptation of that sung by Feste at the end of *Twelfth Night*.

FOOL   This is a brave night to cool a courtesan.[2]
80   I'll speak a prophecy ere I go:[3]
            When priests are more in word than matter;°   real virtue
            When brewers mar their malt with water;
            When nobles are their tailors' tutors;[4]
            No heretics burned, but wenches' suitors;[5]
85   When every case in law is right;°   just
            No squire in debt, nor no poor knight;
            When slanders do not live in tongues,
            Nor cutpurses° come not to throngs;   pickpockets
            When usurers tell their gold i' the field,[6]
90   And bawds and whores do churches build;
            Then shall the realm of Albion°   Britain
            Come to great confusion.°   decay
            Then comes the time, who lives to see 't,
            That going° shall be used° with feet.   walking/practiced
95   This prophecy Merlin shall make; for I live before his
        time.[7]   Exit

3.3

Enter GLOUCESTER *and* EDMUND

GLOUCESTER   Alack, alack, Edmund, I like not this unnatural dealing. When I desired their leave that I might pity°   relieve
him, they took from me the use of mine own house;
charged me, on pain of their perpetual displeasure, nei-
5   ther to speak of him, entreat for him, nor any way sustain
him.
EDMUND   Most savage and unnatural!
GLOUCESTER   Go to;° say you nothing. There's a division   (an expletive)
betwixt the dukes, and a worse matter than that. I have
10   received a letter this night; 'tis dangerous to be spoken;
I have locked the letter in my closet.° These injuries the   private chamber
king now bears will be revenged home;° there's part of a   to the hilt
power already footed;[1] we must incline to[2] the king. I will
seek him, and privily° relieve him. Go you and maintain   secretly, privately
15   talk with the duke, that my charity be not of him perceived. If he ask for me, I am ill, and gone to bed. Though
I die for it, as no less is threatened me, the king my old
master must be relieved. There is some strange thing
toward,° Edmund; pray you, be careful.   Exit   coming
20   EDMUND   This courtesy, forbid[3] thee, shall the duke
Instantly know, and of that letter too.

---

2. To cool even the hot lusts of a prostitute.
3. What follows is a parody of the pseudo-Chaucerian
"Merlin's Prophecy" from George Puttenham's *The Art
of English Poesy* (1589).
4. When noblemen follow fashion more closely than
their tailors do.
5. When the only heretics burned are lovers, who burn
from venereal disease.
6. When usurers can count their profits openly

(because they have no shady dealings to hide).
7. Merlin was the great wizard at the legendary court
of King Arthur. Lear's Britain is set in an even more
distant past.
3.3 Location: At Gloucester's castle.
1. Part of an army already landed.
2. We must take the side of.
3. Forbidden. "Courtesy": act of kindness.

This seems a fair deserving,[4] and must draw me
That which my father loses—no less than all.
The younger rises when the old doth fall. *Exit*

3.4

Enter LEAR, KENT, *and* FOOL

KENT   Here is the place, my lord; good my lord, enter:
The tyranny of the open night's too rough
For nature° to endure.   *i.e., human weakness*

    Storm still

LEAR   Let me alone.
KENT   Good my lord, enter here.
5   LEAR   Wilt break my heart?
KENT   I had rather break mine own. Good my lord, enter.
LEAR   Thou think'st 'tis much that this contentious storm
Invades us to the skin. So 'tis to thee;
But where the greater malady is fixed,°   *rooted*
10   The lesser is scarce felt. Thou'dst shun a bear;
But if thy flight lay toward the raging sea,
Thou'dst meet the bear i' the mouth. When the mind's free,°   *unburdened*
The body's delicate.° The tempest in my mind   *sensitive*
Doth from my senses take all feeling else
15   Save° what beats there. Filial ingratitude!   *except*
Is it not as° this mouth should tear this hand   *as if*
For lifting food to 't? But I will punish home.°   *thoroughly*
No, I will weep no more. In such a night
To shut me out! Pour on; I will endure.
20   In such a night as this! O Regan, Goneril!
Your old kind father, whose frank heart gave all—
O, that way madness lies; let me shun that;
No more of that.
KENT   Good my lord, enter here.
LEAR   Prithee, go in thyself; seek thine own ease:
25   This tempest will not give me leave to° ponder   *allow me to*
On things would hurt me more. But I'll go in.
(*To the* FOOL) In, boy; go first. You houseless poverty°—   *poor*
Nay, get thee in. I'll pray, and then I'll sleep.

    FOOL *goes in*

Poor naked wretches, whereso'er you are,
30   That bide° the pelting of this pitiless storm,   *endure; dwell in*
How shall your houseless heads and unfed sides,°   *starved ribs*
Your looped and windowed[1] raggedness, defend you
From seasons such as these? O, I have ta'en
Too little care of this! Take physic, pomp;[2]
35   Expose thyself to feel what wretches feel,
That thou mayst shake the superflux[3] to them,

---

4. This seems an action that deserves to be rewarded.
3.4 Location: Open country, before a cattle shed.
1. I.e., full of holes and vents; "windowed" could also refer to cloth worn through to semitransparency, like
the oilcloth window "panes" of the poor.
2. Cure yourself, pompous person.
3. Superfluity; bodily discharge, suggested by "physic" (which also has the meaning of "purgative") in line 34.

And show the heavens more just.
EDGAR (*within*) Fathom and half,[4] fathom and half!
  Poor Tom!

The FOOL *runs out from the hovel*

40 FOOL Come not in here, nuncle, here's a spirit.
  Help me, help me!
  KENT Give me thy hand. Who's there?
  FOOL A spirit, a spirit! He says his name's poor Tom.
  KENT What art thou that dost grumble there i' the straw?
45 Come forth.

Enter EDGAR *disguised as a madman*

EDGAR Away! the foul fiend follows me!
  Through the sharp hawthorn blows the cold wind.[5]
  Humh! go to thy cold bed, and warm thee.[6]
LEAR Hast thou given all to thy two daughters? And art
50 thou come to this?
EDGAR Who gives any thing to poor Tom? whom the foul
  fiend hath led through fire and through flame, through
  ford and whirlpool, o'er bog and quagmire; that hath laid
  knives under his pillow and halters° in his pew; set rats-   *nooses*
55 bane° by his porridge;[7] made him proud of heart, to ride   *rat poison*
  on a bay trotting-horse over four-inched bridges,[8] to
  course° his own shadow for° a traitor. Bless thy five wits![9]   *hunt/as*
  Tom's a-cold—O, do, de, do de, do de. Bless thee from
  whirlwinds, star-blasting, and taking![1] Do poor Tom some
60 charity, whom the foul fiend vexes: there could I have
  him now—and there—and there again, and there.[2]

Storm still

LEAR What, has his daughters brought him to this pass?
  Couldst thou save nothing? Didst thou give them all?
FOOL Nay, he reserved a blanket, else we had been all
65 shamed.
LEAR Now, all the plagues that in the pendulous° air   *overhanging; portentous*
  Hang fated o'er men's faults light on thy daughters!
KENT He hath no daughters, sir.
LEAR Death, traitor! nothing could have subdued nature
70 To such a lowness but his unkind daughters.
  Is it the fashion that discarded fathers
  Should have thus little mercy on their flesh?
  Judicious punishment! 't was this flesh begot
  Those pelican[3] daughters.

4. "Nine feet," a sailor's cry when taking soundings to
gauge the depth of water.
5. Perhaps a fragment from a ballad.
6. This expression is also used by the drunken beggar
Christopher Sly in Shakespeare's *The Taming of the
Shrew*, Induction 1.
7. These are all means by which the foul fiend tempts
Tom to commit suicide.
8. Impossibly narrow, and probably suicidal to attempt
without diabolical help.
9. The five wits were common wit, imagination, fan-

tasy, estimation, and memory (from medieval and
Renaissance cognitive theory).
1. Infection; bewitchment. "Whirlwinds," "star-blasting": malign astrological influences capable of causing
sickness or death.
2. As Edgar speaks this sentence, he might kill vermin
on his body as if they were devils.
3. Greedy. Young pelicans were reputed to feed on
blood from the wounds they made in their mother's
breast; in some versions, they first killed their father.

75 EDGAR   Pillicock sat on Pillicock-hill.
Halloo, halloo, loo, loo![4]

FOOL   This cold night will turn us all to fools and madmen.

EDGAR   Take heed o' the foul fiend; obey thy parents; keep
thy word justly; swear not; commit not with man's sworn
80 spouse; set not thy sweet heart on proud array.[5] Tom's a-
cold.

LEAR   What hast thou been?

EDGAR   A serving-man, proud in heart and mind; that
curled my hair; wore gloves in my cap;[6] served the lust of
85 my mistress' heart, and did the act of darkness with her;
swore as many oaths as I spake words, and broke them
in the sweet face of heaven: one that slept in the contriving of lust, and waked to do it. Wine loved I deeply,
dice dearly; and in woman out-paramoured the Turk.[7]
90 False of heart, light of ear,° bloody of hand; hog in sloth,   *rumor-hungry*
fox in stealth, wolf in greediness, dog in madness, lion
in prey. Let not the creaking of shoes[8] nor the rustling of
silks betray thy poor heart to woman. Keep thy foot[9] out
of brothels, thy hand out of plackets,[1] thy pen from lend-
95 ers' books, and defy the foul fiend. Still through the hawthorn blows the cold wind: Says suum, mun, ha, no,
nonny. Dolphin my boy, my boy, sessa! let him trot by.[2]
        Storm still

LEAR   Why, thou wert better in thy grave than to answer°   *encounter*
with thy uncovered body this extremity of the skies.° Is   *violent weather*
100 man no more than this? Consider him well. Thou owest
the worm no silk, the beast no hide, the sheep no wool,
the cat[3] no perfume. Ha! here's three on's° are sophisti-   *of us*
cated! Thou art the thing itself; unaccommodated[4] man
is no more but such a poor, bare, forked animal as thou
105 art. Off, off, you lendings!° come unbutton here.   *borrowed clothes*
        Tearing off his clothes

FOOL   Prithee, nuncle, be contented; 'tis a naughty° night   *foul*
to swim in. Now a little fire in a wild° field were like an   *barren; lustful*
old lecher's heart; a small spark, all the rest on's° body   *of his*
cold. Look, here comes a walking fire.
        Enter GLOUCESTER, WITH A TORCH

110 EDGAR   This is the foul fiend Flibbertigibbet.[5] He begins
at curfew,° and walks till the first cock.° He gives the web   9:00 P.M./ *midnight*
and the pin,° squinies[6] the eye, and makes the hare-lip;   *cataract*

4. A fragment of an old rhyme, followed by hunting
cries or a ballad refrain; "Pillicock" was both a term of
endearment and a euphemism for "penis."
5. These are fragments from the Ten Commandments.
6. Favors from his mistress. In Petrarchan poetry, wooers are "servants" to their ladies.
7. And had more women than the sultan had in his
harem.
8. Creaking shoes were a fashionable affectation.
9. Punning on the French *foutre* ("fuck").
1. Slits in skirts or petticoats.
2. These phrases are probably snatches from songs and

proverbs. "Dolphin" is an imagined animal or devil or
the heir to the French throne ("dauphin," which Shakespeare usually Anglicized), or all three.
3. Civet cat, in Shakespeare's time the major source of
musk for perfume.
4. Naked; without the trappings of civilization.
5. A devil drawn from folk beliefs, but famous for his
prominent place in Samuel Harsnett's *Declaration of
Egregious Popish Impostures* (1603); the frequent borrowings from Harsnett in *King Lear* set the earliest possible composition date for the play.
6. Causes squints in.

mildews the white° wheat, and hurts the poor creature of   *near-ripe*
earth.

115   St. Withold footed thrice the old;[7]
        He met the night-mare[8] and her nine-fold;°   *nine familiars, demons*
        Bid her alight,
        And her troth plight,°   *and give her word*
        And, aroint thee,° witch, aroint thee!   *begone*
120 KENT   How fares your grace?
LEAR   What's° he?   *who's*
KENT   Who's there? What is't you seek?
GLOUCESTER   What are you there? Your names?
EDGAR   Poor Tom, that eats the swimming frog, the toad,
125 the tadpole, the wall-newt and the water;° that in the fury   *water newt*
of his heart, when the foul fiend rages, eats cow-dung for
sallets;° swallows the old rat and the ditch-dog;[9] drinks   *savories*
the green mantle° of the standing-pool; who is whipped   *scum*
from tithing to tithing,° and stock-punished,° and impris-   *parish / put in stocks*
130 oned; who hath had three suits to his back, six shirts to
his body, horse to ride, and weapon to wear;
        But mice and rats, and such small deer,[1]
        Have been Tom's food for seven long year.
Beware my follower. Peace, Smulkin;° peace, thou fiend!   *a Harsnett devil*
135 GLOUCESTER   What, hath your grace no better company?
EDGAR   The prince of darkness is a gentleman. Modo he's
call'd, and Mahu.[2]
GLOUCESTER   Our flesh and blood is grown so vile, my lord,
That it doth hate what gets° it.   *begets*
140 EDGAR   Poor Tom's a-cold.
GLOUCESTER   Go in with me. My duty cannot suffer°   *permit me*
To obey in all your daughters' hard commands:
Though their injunction be to bar my doors,
And let this tyrannous night take hold upon you
145 Yet have I ventured to come seek you out.
And bring you where both fire and food is ready.
LEAR   First let me talk with this philosopher.
What is the cause of thunder?
KENT   Good my lord, take his offer; go into the house.
150 LEAR   I'll take a word with this same learned Theban.°   *i.e., Greek sage*
What is your study?°   *field of expertise*
EDGAR   How to prevent the fiend, and to kill vermin.
LEAR   Let me ask you one word in private.
KENT   Importune him once more to go, my lord;
His wits begin to unsettle.
155 GLOUCESTER   Canst thou blame him?
        Storm still

---

7. St. Withold traversed the hilly countryside three times. "Old": wold, uplands.
8. A demon that is not necessarily in the shape of a horse.
9. A dog found dead in a ditch.

1. Animals. These verses are adapted from a romance popular in Shakespeare's time, *Bevis of Hampton*.
2. Modo and Mahu, more Harsnett devils, were commanding generals of the hellish troops.

His daughters seek his death; ah, that good Kent!
He said it would be thus, poor banished man!
Thou say'st the king grows mad; I'll tell thee, friend,
I am almost mad myself. I had a son,
160 Now outlawed° from my blood. He sought my life.   *disowned*
But lately, very late.° I loved him, friend;   *recently*
No father his son dearer. True to tell thee,
The grief hath crazed my wits. What a night's this!
I do beseech your grace—
LEAR   O, cry you mercy,° sir.   *beg your pardon*
165 Noble philosopher, your company.
EDGAR   Tom's a-cold.
GLOUCESTER   In, fellow, there, into the hovel; keep thee
    warm.
LEAR   Come, let's in all.
                              This way, my lord.
KENT   With him!
170 LEAR   I will keep still with my philosopher.
KENT   Good my lord, soothe° him; let him take the fellow.   *humor*
GLOUCESTER   Take him you on.°   *on ahead*
KENT   Sirrah, come on; go along with us.
LEAR   Come, good Athenian.
175 GLOUCESTER   No words, no words: hush.
EDGAR   Child Rowland³ to the dark tower came,
    His word° was still°—Fie, foh, and fum,   *motto / always*
    I smell the blood of a British⁴ man.   *Exeunt*

3.5

Enter CORNWALL *and* EDMUND

CORNWALL   I will have my revenge ere I depart his house.
EDMUND   How, my lord, I may be censured,° that nature°   *judged / kinship*
    thus gives way to loyalty, something fears me° to think of. *I am somewhat afraid*
CORNWALL   I now perceive, it was not altogether your
5   brother's evil disposition made him seek his° death; but   *(Gloucester's)*
    a provoking merit, set a-work by a reprovable badness in
    himself.¹
EDMUND   How malicious is my fortune, that I must repent
    to be just! This is the letter he spoke of, which approves
10 him an intelligent party to the advantages of France.² O
    heavens! that this treason were not, or not I the detector!
CORNWALL   Go with me to the duchess.
EDMUND   If the matter of this paper be certain, you have
    mighty business in hand.
15 CORNWALL   True or false, it hath made thee Earl of

---

3. Roland is the famous hero of the Charlemagne legends. "Child": an aspirant to knighthood. In the nineteenth century, Robert Browning built a notable poem from this line.
4. "An Englishman" usually appears in this rhyme from the cycle of tales of which "Jack and the Beanstalk" is the best-known. The alteration befits Lear's ancient

Britain.
3.5 Location: At Gloucester's castle.
1. I.e., Gloucester's own wickedness deservedly triggered the blameworthy evil in Edgar.
2. I.e., which proves him a spy and informer in the aid of France.

Gloucester. Seek out where thy father is, that he may be
ready for our apprehension.°   *arrest*
EDMUND (*aside*) If I find him comforting the king, it will
stuff his° suspicion more fully.—I will persèver in my   *(Cornwall's)*
20 course of loyalty, though the conflict be sore between
that and my blood.°   *filial duty*
CORNWALL I will lay trust upon thee, and thou shalt find
a dearer father in my love.   *Exeunt*

3.6

Enter GLOUCESTER, LEAR, KENT, FOOL, *and* EDGAR

GLOUCESTER Here is better than the open air; take it
thankfully. I will piece° out the comfort with what addi-   *pad*
tion I can; I will not be long from you.
KENT All the power of his wits have given sway to his impa-
5   tience:[1] the gods° reward your kindness!   *may the gods*

Exit GLOUCESTER

EDGAR Frateretto° calls me; and tells me Nero is an angler   *a Harsnett devil*
in the lake of darkness.[2] Pray, innocent, and beware the
foul fiend.
FOOL Prithee, nuncle, tell me whether a madman be a
10   gentleman or a yeoman?[3]
LEAR A king, a king!
FOOL No, he's a yeoman that has a gentleman to his son;
for he's a mad yeoman that sees his son a gentleman
before him.
15 LEAR To have a thousand with red burning spits
Come hissing in upon 'em—
EDGAR The foul fiend bites my back.
FOOL He's mad that trusts in the tameness of a wolf, a
horse's health, a boy's love, or a whore's oath.
20 LEAR It shall be done; I will arraign° them straight.°   *prosecute/immediately*
(*To* EDGAR) Come, sit thou here, most learned justicer;°   *judge*
(*to the* FOOL) Thou, sapient sir, sit here. Now, you she
foxes!
EDGAR Look, where he stands and glares! Wantest thou
25   eyes° at trial, madam?   *observers*
Come o'er the bourn,° Bessy, to me[4]—   *small stream*
FOOL   Her boat hath a leak,[5]
And she must not speak
Why she dares not come over to thee.
30 EDGAR The foul fiend haunts poor Tom in the voice of a
nightingale. Hopdance° cries in Tom's belly for two   *a demon*
white° herring. Croak° not, black angel; I have no food   *fresh/growl*
for thee.

3.6 Location: Within an outbuilding of Gloucester's.
1. Rage; inability to bear more suffering.
2. In Chaucer's *Monk's Tale*, the infamously cruel
Roman emperor Nero is found fishing in hell.
3. A free landowner but not a member of the gentry,
lacking official family arms and the distinctions they

confer. Shakespeare seems to have procured a coat of
arms for his father in 1596.
4. From an old song.
5. She has venereal disease; punning on "boat" as body
and "burn" as genital discomfort.

KENT   How do you, sir? Stand you not so amazed:
35   Will you lie down and rest upon the cushions?
LEAR   I'll see their trial first. Bring in the evidence.
    (*To* EDGAR) Thou robed man of justice, take thy place;
    (*to the* FOOL) And thou, his yoke-fellow of equity,°   *partner of law*
    Bench° by his side. (*To* KENT) You are o' the commission,°   *sit/judiciary*
40   Sit you too.
LEAR   Let us deal justly.
          Sleepest or wakest thou, jolly shepherd?
            Thy sheep be in the corn;°   *grain*
          And for one blast of thy minikin° mouth,   *dainty*
45   Thy sheep shall take no harm.
    Pur! the cat[6] is gray.
LEAR   Arraign her first; 'tis Goneril. I here take my oath
    before this honorable assembly, she kicked the poor king
    her father.
50 FOOL   Come hither, mistress. Is your name Goneril?
LEAR   She cannot deny it.
FOOL   Cry you mercy, I took you for a joint-stool.[7]
LEAR   And here's another, whose warped looks proclaim
    What store° her heart is made on.° Stop her there!   *material/of*
55   Arms, arms, sword, fire! Corruption in the place!
    False justicer, why hast thou let her 'scape?
EDGAR   Bless thy five wits!
KENT   O pity! Sir, where is the patience now,
    That you so oft have boasted to retain?
60 EDGAR (*aside*)   My tears begin to take his part so much,
    They'll mar my counterfeiting.
LEAR   The little dogs and all,°   *even the little dogs*
    Tray, Blanch, and Sweet-heart, see, they bark at me.
EDGAR   Tom will throw his head at° them. Avaunt,° *will threaten (?)/begone*
65 you curs!
          Be thy mouth or° black or white,   *either*
          Tooth that poisons° if it bite;   *gives rabies*
          Mastiff, greyhound, mongrel grim,
          Hound or spaniel, brach° or lym,   *bitch*
70   Or bobtail tike or trundle-tail.[8]
          Tom will make them weep and wail:
          For, with throwing thus my head,
          Dogs leap the hatch,[9] and all are fled.
    Do de, de, de. Sessa![1] Come, march to wakes° and fairs *parish festivals*
75   and market-towns. Poor Tom, thy horn is dry.[2]
LEAR   Then let them anatomize° Regan; see what breeds   *dissect*
    about her heart. Is there any cause in nature that makes
    these hard hearts? (*To* EDGAR) You, sir, I entertain° for   *retain*

---

6. Pur the cat is another devil; such devils in the shape of cats were the familiars of witches.
7. I beg your pardon, I mistook you for a stool. Here the part of Goneril is actually being played by a stool.
8. Short-tailed mongrel or long-tailed.
9. Dogs leap over the lower half of a divided door.

1. Apparently nonsense, although "Sessa" may be a version of the French *cessez* ("stop" or "hush").
2. A begging formula that refers to the horn vessel that vagabonds carried for drink; the covert sense is that Edgar has run out of Bedlamite inspiration.

one of my hundred; I do not like the fashion of your gar-
80   ments. You will say they are Persian;° but let them be   *oriental; splendid*
   changed.
   KENT   Now, good my lord, lie there and rest awhile.
   LEAR   Make no noise, make no noise; draw the curtains.°   *bed curtains*
   So, so, so. We'll go to supper i' the morning.
85   FOOL   And I'll go to bed at noon.
            [*Re-enter* GLOUCESTER]
   GLOUCESTER   Come hither, friend. Where is the king my master?
   KENT   Here, sir; but trouble him not; his wits are gone.
   GLOUCESTER   Good friend, I prithee, take him in thy arms;
   I have o'erheard a plot of death upon° him: *against*
90   There is a litter ready; lay him in 't
   And drive towards Dover, friend, where thou shalt meet
   Both welcome and protection. Take up thy master.
   If thou shouldst dally half an hour, his life,
   With thine, and all that offer to defend him,
95   Stand in assured loss.° Take up, take up!   *are certainly doomed*
   And follow me, that will to some provision
   Give thee quick conduct.³
   KENT   Oppressèd nature sleeps:
   This rest might yet have balmed° thy broken sinews,°   *soothed / nerves*
   Which, if convenience will not allow,
100   Stand in hard cure.° (*To the* FOOL) Come, help to bear   *will be hard to cure*
      thy master:
   Thou must not stay behind.
   GLOUCESTER   Come come, away.
                        Exeunt all but EDGAR
   EDGAR   When we our betters see bearing our° woes,   *our same*
   We scarcely think our miseries our foes.
   Who alone suffers suffers most i' the mind,
105   Leaving free° things and happy shows° behind: *carefree / scenes*
   But then the mind much sufferance doth o'erskip
   When grief hath mates, and bearing° fellowship.   *pain, suffering*
   How light and portable my pain seems now,
   When that which makes me bend makes the king bow;
110   He° childed as I fathered! Tom, away!   *he is*
   Mark the high noises,° and thyself bewray°   *important rumors / reveal*
   When false opinion, whose wrong thought defiles thee,
   In thy just proof repeals and reconciles thee.⁴
   What° will hap° more tonight, safe 'scape the king!   *whatever / chance*
115   Lurk, lurk.   *Exit*

3.7

   Enter CORNWALL, REGAN, GONERIL, EDMUND, *and*
   servants
   CORNWALL (*to* GONERIL)   Post° speedily to my lord your   *ride*

---

3. Who will quickly guide you to some supplies.   (with your father).
4. When true evidence pardons you and reconciles you   3.7 Location: At Gloucester's castle.

husband; show him this letter. The army of France is
landed. Seek out the villain Gloucester.

Exeunt some of the servants

REGAN   Hang him instantly.

5   GONERIL   Pluck out his eyes.

CORNWALL   Leave him to my displeasure. Edmund, keep
you our sister° company. The revenges we are bound[1] to   sister-in-law
take upon your traitorous father are not fit for your
beholding. Advise the duke, where you are going, to a
10   most festinate preparation.[2] We are bound° to the like.   committed
Our posts° shall be swift and intelligent° betwixt us.   messengers / well-informed
Farewell, dear sister: farewell, my lord of Gloucester.

Enter OSWALD

How now! Where's the king?

OSWALD   My lord of Gloucester hath conveyed him hence.
15   Some five or six and thirty of his° knights,   (Lear's)
Hot questrists° after him, met him at gate;   searchers
Who, with some other of the lord's° dependants,   (Gloucester's)
Are gone with him towards Dover; where they boast
To have well-armed friends.

CORNWALL   Get horses for your mistress.

20   GONERIL   Farewell, sweet lord, and sister.

CORNWALL   Edmund, farewell.

Exeunt GONERIL, EDMUND, *and* OSWALD

Go seek the traitor Gloucester,
Pinion him° like a thief, bring him before us.   tie his arms

Exeunt other servants

Though well we may not pass° upon his life   pass sentence
25   Without the form° of justice, yet our power   official proceedings
Shall do a courtesy[3] to our wrath, which men
May blame, but not control. Who's there? the traitor?

Enter GLOUCESTER, *brought in by two or three*

REGAN   Ingrateful fox! 'tis he.

CORNWALL   Bind fast his corky° arms.   withered

30   GLOUCESTER   What mean your graces? Good my friends,
consider
You are my guests. Do me no foul play, friends.

CORNWALL   Bind him, I say.

Servants bind him

REGAN   Hard, hard. O filthy traitor!

GLOUCESTER   Unmerciful lady as you are, I'm none.

CORNWALL   To this chair bind him. Villain, thou shalt find—

REGAN *plucks his beard*°   (an extreme insult)

35   GLOUCESTER   By the kind gods, 'tis most ignobly done
To pluck me by the beard.

REGAN   So white,° and such a traitor!   white-haired; venerable

GLOUCESTER   Naughty° lady,   wicked

---

1. Bound by duty.
2. I.e., when you reach Albany, tell the duke to prepare   quickly.
3. Shall allow a courtesy, or indulgence; shall bow to.

These hairs, which thou dost ravish from my chin,
Will quicken,° and accuse thee. I am your host.   *come alive*
40   With robbers' hands my hospitable favors°   *features*
You should not ruffle° thus. What will you do?   *snatch at*
CORNWALL   Come, sir, what letters had you late° from   *lately*
France?
REGAN   Be simple° answered, for we know the truth.   *straightforwardly*
CORNWALL   And what confederacy have you with the traitors
45   Late footed° in the kingdom?   *landed*
REGAN   To whose hands have you sent the lunatic king?
Speak.
GLOUCESTER   I have a letter guessingly set down,[4]
Which came from one that's of a neutral heart,
And not from one opposed.
CORNWALL   Cunning.
50   REGAN   And false.
CORNWALL   Where hast thou sent the king?
GLOUCESTER   To Dover.
REGAN   Wherefore° to Dover? Wast thou not charged° at   *why/commanded*
peril—
CORNWALL   Wherefore to Dover? Let him first answer
that.
55   GLOUCESTER   I am tied to the stake, and I must stand the
course.[5]
REGAN   Wherefore to Dover?
GLOUCESTER   Because I would not see thy cruel nails
Pluck out his poor old eyes; nor thy fierce sister
In his anointed[6] flesh stick boarish fangs.
60   The sea, with such a storm as his bare head
In hell-black night endured, would have buoyed° up,   *risen*
And quenched the stellèd° fires.   *stars'*
Yet, poor old heart, he holp° the heavens to rage.   *helped*
If wolves had at thy gate howled that dern° time,   *dreary, dreadful*
65   Thou shouldst have said "Good porter, turn the key."°   *(to open the door)*
All cruels else subscribed.[7] But I shall see
The wingèd vengeance[8] overtake such children.
CORNWALL   See 't shalt thou never. Fellows,° hold the   *servants*
chair.
Upon these eyes of thine I'll set my foot.
70   GLOUCESTER   He that will think° to live till he be old,   *whoever hopes*
Give me some help! O cruel! O ye gods!
REGAN   One side will mock another. The other too!
CORNWALL   If you see vengeance—
FIRST SERVANT   Hold your hand, my lord:
I have served you ever since I was a child;

---

4. Written without confirmation; speculative.
5. An image from bearbaiting, in which a bear on a short tether had to fight off the assault of dogs.
6. Consecrated with holy oils (as part of a king's coronation).

7. All other cruel creatures yielded to compassion.
8. Swift or heaven-sent revenge; either an angel of God or the Furies, who were flying executors of divine vengeance in classical myth.

75 But better service have I never done you
Than now to bid you hold.
REGAN   How now, you dog!
FIRST SERVANT   If you did wear a beard upon your chin,
I'd shake it on this quarrel.[9]
80 REGAN   What do you mean?°   *intend*
CORNWALL   My villain!°   *servant; villain*
FIRST SERVANT   Why, then, come on, and take the chance of anger.[1]
REGAN   Give me thy sword. A peasant stand up thus!
              CORNWALL *is wounded.*
              Takes a sword, and runs at him behind
FIRST SERVANT   O, I am slain! My lord, you have one eye left
85 To see some mischief° on him. O!   *Dies*   *injury*
CORNWALL   Lest it see more, prevent it. Out, vile jelly!
Where is thy luster now?
GLOUCESTER   All dark and comfortless. Where's my son Edmund?
Edmund, enkindle all the sparks of nature,[2]
To quit° this horrid act.   *requite, avenge*
90 REGAN   Out, treacherous villain!
Thou call'st on him that hates thee. It was he
That made the overture° of thy treasons to us;   *revelation*
Who is too good to pity thee.
GLOUCESTER   O my follies! Then Edgar was abused.°   *slandered*
95 Kind gods, forgive me that, and prosper him!
REGAN   Go thrust him out at gates, and let him smell
His way to Dover.   *Exit one with* GLOUCESTER
How is't, my lord? how look you?°   *how do you feel*
CORNWALL   I have received a hurt. Follow me, lady;
100 Turn out that eyeless villain. Throw this slave
Upon the dunghill. Regan, I bleed apace.
Untimely comes this hurt. Give me your arm.
              Exit CORNWALL *led by* REGAN
SECOND SERVANT   I'll never care what wickedness I do,
If this man come to good.[3]
THIRD SERVANT   If she live long,
105 And in the end meet the old° course of death,   *usual*
Woman will all turn monsters.
SECOND SERVANT   Let's follow the old earl, and get the Bedlam
To lead him where he would. His roguish madness
Allows itself to any thing.
110 THIRD SERVANT   Go thou; I'll fetch some flax and whites of eggs
To apply to his bleeding face. Now, heaven help him!
              Exeunt severally

---

9. I'd pluck it over this point; I'd issue a challenge.
1. Take the risk of fighting when angry; take the fortune of one who is governed by his anger.
2. All the warmth of filial love; all the anger that your

father has received such treatment.
3. I.e., because this may be a sign that evil goes unpunished.

4.1

Enter EDGAR

EDGAR Yet better thus, and known to be contemnèd°   *despised*
Than still° contemnèd and flattered. To be worst,   *always*
The lowest and most dejected thing of fortune,
Stands still in esperance, lives not in fear.[1]
5 The lamentable change is from the best;
The worst returns to laughter.[2] Welcome, then,
Thou unsubstantial air that I embrace!
The wretch that thou hast blown unto the worst
Owes nothing° to thy blasts. But who comes here?   *(because he can't pay)*

Enter GLOUCESTER, *led by an* OLD MAN

10 My father, parti-eyed?[3] World, world, O world!
But that thy strange mutations make us hate thee,
Life would not yield to age.[4]

OLD MAN O, my good lord, I have been your tenant, and
your father's tenant, these fourscore years.

15 GLOUCESTER Away, get thee away! Good friend, be gone.
Thy comforts° can do me no good at all;   *assistance*
Thee they may hurt.

OLD MAN Alack, sir, you cannot see your way.

GLOUCESTER I have no way, and therefore want no eyes;
20 I stumbled when I saw. Full oft 'tis seen,
Our means secure us, and our mere defects
Prove our commodities.[5] O dear son Edgar,
The food° of thy abusèd° father's wrath!   *fuel; prey/despised*
Might I but live to see thee in° my touch,   *through*
I'd say I had eyes again!

25 OLD MAN   How now! Who's there?

EDGAR (*aside*) O gods! Who is't can say "I am at the worst"?
I am worse than e'er I was.

OLD MAN   'Tis poor mad Tom.

EDGAR (*aside*) And worse I may be yet: the worst is not
So long as we can say "This is the worst."

OLD MAN Fellow, where goest?

30 GLOUCESTER   Is it a beggar-man?

OLD MAN Madman and beggar too.

GLOUCESTER He has some reason, else he could not beg.
I' the last night's storm I such a fellow saw;
Which made me think a man a worm. My son
35 Came then into my mind, and yet my mind
Was then scarce friends with him. I have heard more since.
As flies to wanton° boys are we to the gods;   *playful; careless*
They kill us for their sport.

EDGAR (*aside*)   How should this be?

4.1 Location: Open country.
1. Remains in hope ("esperance") because there is no
fear of falling further.
2. The change to be lamented is one that alters the
best of circumstances; the worst luck can only improve.
3. Multicolored like a fool's costume (red with blood

under white dressings).
4. If there were no strange reversals of fortune to make
the world hateful, we would not consent to aging and
death.
5. Our wealth makes us overconfident, and our utter
deprivation proves to be beneficial.

Bad is the trade that must play fool to sorrow,[6]
40   Angering itself and others.—Bless thee, master!
GLOUCESTER   Is that the naked fellow?
OLD MAN   Ay, my lord.
GLOUCESTER   Then, prithee, get thee gone. If, for my sake,
    Thou wilt o'ertake us, hence a mile or twain,
    I' the way toward Dover, do it for ancient love;[7]
45   And bring some covering for this naked soul,
    Who I'll entreat to lead me.
OLD MAN   Alack, sir, he is mad.
GLOUCESTER   'Tis the times' plague, when[8] madmen lead the blind.
    Do as I bid thee, or rather do thy pleasure;
    Above the rest, be gone.
50 OLD MAN   I'll bring him the best 'parel° that I have,   *apparel*
    Come on 't what will.   *Exit*
GLOUCESTER   Sirrah, naked fellow—
EDGAR   Poor Tom's a-cold. (*Aside*) I cannot daub it further.[9]
GLOUCESTER   Come hither, fellow.
55 EDGAR (*aside*)   And yet I must.—Bless thy sweet eyes, they bleed.
GLOUCESTER   Know'st thou the way to Dover?
EDGAR   Both stile and gate, horse-way and foot-path. Poor
    Tom hath been scared out of his good wits. Bless thee,
    good man's son, from the foul fiend! Five fiends have
60   been in Poor Tom at once; of lust, as Obidicut; Hobbi-
    didance, prince of dumbness; Mahu, of stealing; Modo,
    of murder; Flibbertigibbet, of mopping and mowing,° who   *making faces*
    since possesses chambermaids and waiting-women. So,
    bless thee, master!
65 GLOUCESTER   Here, take this purse, thou whom the heavens' plagues
    Have humbled to all strokes.° That I am wretched   *to accept all blows*
    Makes thee the happier. Heavens, deal so still!°   *always*
    Let the superfluous and lust-dieted man,[1]
    That slaves your ordinance,[2] that will not see
70   Because he doth not feel, feel your power quickly;
    So distribution should undo excess,
    And each man have enough. Dost thou know Dover?
EDGAR   Ay, master.
GLOUCESTER   There is a cliff, whose high and bending° head   *overhanging*
75   Looks fearfully in the confinèd deep.[3]
    Bring me but to the very brim of it,
    And I'll repair the misery thou dost bear
    With something rich about me. From that place
    I shall no leading need.
EDGAR   Give me thy arm.
80   Poor Tom shall lead thee.   *Exeunt*

---

6. It is a bad business to have to play the fool in the face of sorrow.
7. For the sake of our long and loyal relationship (as master and servant).
8. The time is truly sick when.
9. I cannot continue the charade. "Daub": mask, plaster.
1. Let the overprosperous man who indulges his appetite.
2. Makes your law subject to him.
3. Looks fearsomely into the straits below.

4.2

Enter GONERIL *and* EDMUND

GONERIL   Welcome, my lord. I marvel our mild husband
    Not° met us on the way.   *has not*
        Enter OSWALD
                              Now where's your master?
OSWALD   Madam, within, but never man so changed.
    I told him of the army that was landed;
5   He smiled at it. I told him you were coming;
    His answer was "The worse." Of Gloucester's treachery,
    And of the loyal service of his son,
    When I informed him, then he called me sot,°   *fool*
    And told me I had turned the wrong side out.[1]
10   What most he should dislike seems pleasant to him;
    What like, offensive.
GONERIL (*to* EDMUND)   Then shall you go no further.
    It is the cowish° terror of his spirit,   *cowardly*
    That dares not undertake. He'll not feel wrongs
    Which tie him to an answer.[2] Our wishes on the way
15   May prove effects.[3] Back, Edmund, to my brother;°   *brother-in-law*
    Hasten his musters° and conduct his powers.° *call-up of troops/armies*
    I must change arms at home, and give the distaff[4]
    Into my husband's hands. This trusty servant
    Shall pass between us. Ere long you are like° to hear,   *likely*
20   If you dare venture in your own behalf,
    A mistress's° command. Wear this; spare speech;   *(playing on "lover's")*
      (giving a favor)
    Decline your head. This kiss, if it durst speak,
    Would stretch thy spirits up into the air.
    Conceive,° and fare thee well.   *understand my meaning*
EDMUND   Yours in° the ranks of death.   *even in*
25 GONERIL   My most dear Gloucester!
                      Exit EDMUND
    O, the difference of man and man!
    To thee a woman's services are due:
    My fool usurps my body.[5]
OSWALD   Madam, here comes my lord.   *Exit*
        Enter ALBANY
GONERIL   I have been worth the whistling.[6]
ALBANY   O Goneril!
30   You are not worth the dust which the rude wind
    Blows in your face. I fear your disposition.
    That nature, which contemns it° origin,   *despises its*
    Cannot be bordered certain° in itself.   *be defended securely*
    She that herself will sliver and disbranch°   *split*

4.2 Location: Before Albany's castle.
1. I had reversed things (by mistaking loyalty for treachery).
2. He'll ignore insults that should provoke him to retaliate.
3. May be put into action.

4. A device used in spinning and thus emblematic of the female role.
5. My idiot husband presumes to possess me.
6. At one time, you would have come to welcome me home; referring to the proverb "It is a poor dog that is not worth the whistling."

35 From her material sap, perforce must wither
And come to deadly use.[7]
GONERIL   No more; the text is foolish.
ALBANY   Wisdom and goodness to the vile seem vile;
Filths savor but themselves. What have you done?
40 Tigers, not daughters, what have you performed?
A father, and a gracious agèd man,
Whose reverence even the head-lugged° bear would lick,   *dragged by the head*
Most barbarous, most degenerate, have you madded.
Could my good brother° suffer you to do it?   *brother-in-law*
45 A man, a prince, by him so benefited!
If that the heavens do not their visible spirits
Send quickly down to tame these vild° offenses,   *vile*
It will come,
Humanity must perforce° prey on itself,   *inevitably*
Like monsters of the deep.
50 GONERIL   Milk-livered° man!   *cowardly*
That bear'st a cheek for blows, a head for wrongs:[8]
Who hast not in thy brows an eye discerning
Thine honor from thy suffering;[9] that not know'st
Fools do those villains pity who are punished
55 Ere they have done their mischief. Where's thy drum?°   *(to muster troops)*
France spreads his banners in our noiseless° land,   *peaceful*
With plumèd helm thy state begins to threat;
Whiles thou, a moral° fool, sit'st still, and criest   *moralizing*
"Alack, why does he so?"
ALBANY   See thyself, devil!
60 Proper deformity shows not in the fiend
So horrid as in woman.[1]
GONERIL   O vain° fool!   *useless*
ALBANY   Thou changèd and self-covered[2] thing, for shame,
Be-monster not thy feature. Were't my fitness°   *if it were appropriate*
To let these hands obey my blood,
65 They are apt enough to dislocate and tear
Thy flesh and bones. Howe'er° thou art a fiend,   *although*
A woman's shape doth shield thee.
GONERIL   Marry, your manhood! mew![3]
Enter a MESSENGER
ALBANY   What news?
70 MESSENGER   O, my good lord, the Duke of Cornwall's dead;
Slain by his servant, going to put out
The other eye of Gloucester.
ALBANY   Gloucester's eyes?
MESSENGER   A servant that he bred, thrilled with remorse,°   *shaken with pity*

---

7. Be destroyed; be used for burning. The allusion is probably biblical: "But that which beareth thorns and briers is reproved, and is near unto cursing; whose end is to be burned" (Hebrews 6.8).
8. Fit for abuse; ready for cuckold's horns.
9. I.e., that can distinguish between an insult to your honor and something you should patiently endure.
1. Deformity (of morals) is appropriate in the devil and

so less horrid than in woman, from whom virtue is expected. Albany may hold a mirror in front of Goneril, since Jacobean women sometimes wore small mirrors attached to their dresses.
2. Altered and with your true (womanly) self concealed.
3. A derisive catcall. "Marry": By the Virgin Mary.

Opposed against the act, bending° his sword   *directing*
75   To° his great master; who, thereat enraged,   *against*
Flew on him, and amongst them felled him dead;
But not without that harmful stroke, which since
Hath plucked him after.[4]
ALBANY   This shows you are above,
You justicers,° that these our nether crimes[5]   *judges*
80   So speedily can venge! But, O poor Gloucester!
Lost he his other eye?
MESSENGER   Both, both, my lord.
This letter, madam, craves a speedy answer;
'Tis from your sister.
GONERIL (*aside*)   One way I like this well;[6]
85   But being° a widow, and my Gloucester with her,   *her being*
May all the building in my fancy pluck
Upon my hateful life.[7] Another way,
The news is not so tart.°—I'll read, and answer.   *Exit*   *bitter*
ALBANY   Where was his son when they did take his eyes?
MESSENGER   Come with my lady hither.
90   ALBANY   He is not here.
MESSENGER   No, my good lord; I met him back° again.   *returning*
ALBANY   Knows he the wickedness?
MESSENGER   Ay, my good lord; 'twas he informed against him;
And quit the house on purpose, that their punishment
Might have the freer course.
95   ALBANY   Gloucester, I live
To thank thee for the love thou show'dst the king,
And to revenge thine eyes. Come hither, friend.
Tell me what more thou know'st.   *Exeunt*

4.3

Enter KENT *and a* GENTLEMAN

KENT   Why the King of France is so suddenly gone back
know you the reason?
GENTLEMAN   Something he left imperfect° in the state,   *unsettled*
which since his coming forth is thought of;° which   *remembered*
5   imports° to the kingdom so much fear and danger, that   *portends*
his personal return was most required and necessary.
KENT   Who hath he left behind him general?
GENTLEMAN   The Marshall of France, Monsieur LaFar.
KENT   Did your letters pierce the queen to any demonstration of grief?
10   GENTLEMAN   Ay, sir. She took them, in my presence;
And now and then an ample tear trilled down
Her delicate cheek. It seemed she was a queen
Over her passion, who,° most rebel-like,   *which*
Sought to be king o'er her.
KENT   O, then it moved her.

---

4. Has sent him to follow his servant into death.
5. Lower crimes, and so committed on earth, but also
suggesting that the deeds smack of the netherworld of
hell.
6. Because a political rival has been eliminated.
7. May pull down all of my built-up fantasies and thus
make my life hateful.
4.3 Location: Near the French camp at Dover.

15 GENTLEMAN   Not to a rage. Patience and sorrow strove
    Who should express her goodliest.[1] You have seen
    Sunshine and rain at once: her smiles and tears
    Were like a° better way. Those happy smilets,   *were similar in a*
    That played on her ripe lip, seemed not to know
20   What guests were in her eyes, which parted thence,
    As pearls from diamonds dropped. In brief,
    Sorrow would be a rarity° most beloved,   *gem*
    If all could so become it.[2]
KENT   Made she no verbal question?
GENTLEMAN   'Faith, once or twice she heaved the name of "father"
25   Pantingly forth, as if it pressed her heart;
    Cried "Sisters! sisters! Shame of ladies! sisters!
    Kent! father! sisters! What, i' the storm? i' the night?
    Let pity not be believed!"[3] There she shook
    The holy water from her heavenly eyes,
30   And clamor moistened.[4] Then away she started°   *sprang*
    To deal with grief alone.
KENT   It is the stars,
    The stars above us, govern our conditions;
    Else one self mate and make[5] could not beget
    Such different issues.° You spoke not with her since?   *offspring*
35 GENTLEMAN   No.
KENT   Was this before the king returned?
GENTLEMAN   No, since.
KENT   Well, sir, the poor distressed Lear's i' the town;
    Who sometime, in his better tune,° remembers   *state of mind*
    What we are come about, and by no means
    Will yield° to see his daughter.   *consent*
40 GENTLEMAN   Why, good sir?
KENT   A sovereign shame so elbows° him; his own unkindness,   *prods, nudges*
    That stripped her from his benediction, turned her
    To foreign casualties,° gave her dear rights   *risks*
    To his dog-hearted daughters, these things sting
45   His mind so venomously, that burning shame
    Detains him from Cordelia.
GENTLEMAN   Alack, poor gentleman!
KENT   Of Albany's and Cornwall's powers you heard not?
GENTLEMAN   'Tis so, they are afoot.
KENT   Well, sir, I'll bring you to our master Lear,
50   And leave you to attend him. Some dear cause°   *some important reason*
    Will in concealment wrap me up awhile;
    When I am known aright, you shall not grieve°   *repent*
    Lending me this acquaintance.° I pray you, go   *news*
    Along with me.   *Exeunt*

---

1. Which should better express her feelings.
2. If everyone wore it so beautifully.
3. Never believe in pity; compassion cannot exist.
4. And moistened her anguish (with tears).
5. Or else the same pair of spouses.

4.4

Enter, with drum and colors, CORDELIA, DOCTOR,
and soldiers

CORDELIA   Alack, 'tis he! Why, he was met even now
As mad as the vexed sea; singing aloud;
Crowned with rank fumiter and furrow-weeds,[1]
With hor-docks, hemlock, nettles, cuckoo-flowers,
5   Darnel, and all the idle° weeds that grow   *useless*
In our sustaining corn. A century° send forth;   *battalion (100 men)*
Search every acre in the high-grown field,
And bring him to our eye.   *Exit an officer*
What can man's wisdom
10 In the restoring° his bereaved sense?   *do to restore*
He that helps him take all my outward° worth.   *material*
DOCTOR   There is means, madam.
Our foster-nurse of nature[2] is repose,
The which he lacks. That to provoke in him,
15 Are many simples operative,[3] whose power
Will close the eye of anguish.
CORDELIA   All blest secrets,
All you unpublished virtues° of the earth,   *obscure healing plants*
Spring with my tears! be aidant and remediate°   *healing and remedial*
In the good man's distress! Seek, seek for him;
20 Lest his ungoverned rage dissolve the life
That wants° the means to lead it.   *lacks*
Enter a MESSENGER
MESSENGER   News, madam;
The British powers° are marching hitherward.   *armies*
CORDELIA   'Tis known before; our preparation stands
In expectation of them. O dear father,
25 It is thy business that I go about;[4]
Therefore great France
My mourning and importuned° tears hath pitied.   *importunate; solicitous*
No blown° ambition doth our arms incite,   *inflated*
But love, dear love, and our aged father's right.
30 Soon may I hear and see him!   *Exeunt*

4.5

Enter REGAN *and* OSWALD

REGAN   But are my brother's powers° set forth?   *(Albany's forces)*
OSWALD   Ay, madam.
REGAN   Himself in person there?
OSWALD   Madam, with much ado.°   *trouble*
Your sister is the better soldier.
5   REGAN   Lord Edmund spake not with your lord at home?
OSWALD   No, madam.

4.4 Location: The French camp at Dover.
1. Fumiter was used against brain sickness. Furrow-
weeds, like the other weeds in the following lines, grow
in the furrows of plowed fields.
2. That which comforts and nourishes human nature.

3. To induce that ("repose") in him, there are many
effective medicinal herbs.
4. The line echoes Christ's explanation of his mission
in Luke 2.49: "I must go about my father's business."
4.5 Location: At Gloucester's castle.

REGAN   What might import° my sister's letter to him?   *mean*
OSWALD   I know not, lady.
REGAN   Faith, he is posted° hence on serious matter.   *hurried*
10   It was great ignorance, Gloucester's eyes being out,
To let him live. Where he arrives he moves
All hearts against us. Edmund, I think, is gone,
In pity of his misery,° to dispatch   *(ironic)*
His nighted° life; moreover, to descry°   *darkened / investigate*
15   The strength o' the enemy.
OSWALD   I must needs after° him, madam, with my letter.   *go after*
REGAN   Our troops set forth tomorrow. Stay with us;
The ways are dangerous.
OSWALD   I may not, madam:
My lady charged° my duty in this business.   *commanded*
20   REGAN   Why should she write to Edmund? Might not you
Transport her purposes by word? Belike,°   *perhaps*
Something—I know not what. I'll love° thee much,   *reward*
Let me unseal the letter.
OSWALD   Madam, I had rather—
REGAN   I know your lady does not love her husband;
25   I am sure of that; and at her late° being here   *recently*
She gave strange oeillades° and most speaking looks   *amorous glances*
To noble Edmund. I know you are of her bosom.°   *in her confidence*
OSWALD   I, madam?
REGAN   I speak in understanding;° y'are, I know't.   *with certainty*
30   Therefore I do advise you, take this note:°   *take note of this*
My lord is dead; Edmund and I have talked;
And more convenient° is he for my hand   *appropriate*
Than for your lady's. You may gather° more.   *infer*
If you do find him, pray you, give him this;[1]
35   And when your mistress hears thus much from you,
I pray, desire her call her wisdom to her.[2]
So, fare you well.
If you do chance to hear of that blind traitor,
Preferment falls on him that cuts him off.°   *cuts his life short*
40   OSWALD   Would I could meet him, madam! I should show
What party I do follow.
REGAN   Fare thee well.   *Exeunt*

4.6

Enter GLOUCESTER, *and* EDGAR *dressed like a peasant*
GLOUCESTER   When shall we come to the top of that same°   *agreed-upon*
hill?
EDGAR   You do climb up it now. Look how we labor.
GLOUCESTER   Methinks the ground is even.
EDGAR   Horrible steep.
Hark, do you hear the sea?

---

1. This information, but possibly another letter or   2. Tell her to come to her senses.
token.   4.6 Location: Near Dover.

GLOUCESTER   No, truly.

5 EDGAR   Why, then, your other senses grow imperfect
   By your eyes' anguish.
GLOUCESTER   So may it be, indeed.
   Methinks thy voice is altered, and thou speakest
   In better phrase and matter° than thou didst.   *sense*
EDGAR   Y'are much deceived. In nothing am I changed
   But in my garments.
10 GLOUCESTER   Methinks y'are better spoken.
EDGAR   Come on, sir; here's the place. Stand still. How fearful
   And dizzy 'tis, to cast one's eyes so low!
   The crows and choughs° that wing the midway air[1]   *jackdaws*
   Show° scarce so gross° as beetles. Halfway down   *appear/big*
15 Hangs one that gathers sampire,° dreadful trade!   *seaweed*
   Methinks he seems no bigger than his head.
   The fishermen, that walk upon the beach,
   Appear like mice; and yond tall anchoring bark,°   *ship*
   Diminished to her cock;° her cock, a buoy   *dinghy*
20 Almost too small for sight. The murmuring surge,
   That on the unnumbered° idle pebble chafes,   *innumerable*
   Cannot be heard so high. I'll look no more,
   Lest my brain turn, and the° deficient sight   *my*
   Topple° down headlong.   *topple me*
GLOUCESTER   Set me where you stand.
25 EDGAR   Give me your hand. You are now within a foot
   Of th' extreme verge. For all beneath the moon
   Would I not leap upright.[2]
GLOUCESTER   Let go my hand.
   Here, friend, 's another purse; in it a jewel
   Well worth a poor man's taking. Fairies and gods
30 Prosper it[3] with thee! Go thou farther off;
   Bid me farewell, and let me hear thee going.
EDGAR   Now fare you well, good sir.
GLOUCESTER   With all my heart.
EDGAR (*aside*)   Why I do trifle thus with his despair
   Is done to cure it.
GLOUCESTER (*kneeling*)   O you mighty gods!
35 This world I do renounce, and, in your sights,
   Shake patiently my great affliction off.
   If I could bear it longer, and not fall
   To quarrel° with your great opposeless wills,   *into conflict*
   My snuff and loathèd part of nature[4] should
40 Burn itself out. If Edgar live, O, bless him!
   Now, fellow, fare thee well.
         He falls forward and swoons
EDGAR   Gone, sir; farewell.—

---

1. The air between cliff and sea.
2. I would not jump up and down (for fear of losing my balance).
3. Make it increase. Fairies were sometimes held to hoard and multiply treasure.
4. The scorched and hateful remnant of my lifetime. "Snuff": end of a candle wick.

And yet I know not how conceit may rob
The treasury of life, when life itself
Yields to the theft.[5] Had he been where he thought,
By this° had thought been past. Alive or dead?   *now*
Ho, you sir! friend! Hear you, sir? speak!
Thus might he pass° indeed. Yet he revives.   *pass away*
What are you, sir?
GLOUCESTER   Away, and let me die.
EDGAR   Hadst thou been aught° but gossamer, feathers, air,   *anything*
So many fathom down precipitating,°   *plunging*
Thou'dst shivered° like an egg; but thou dost breathe;   *shattered*
Hast heavy substance; bleed'st not; speak'st; art sound.
Ten masts at each° make not the altitude   *end to end*
Which thou hast perpendicularly fell.
Thy life's a miracle. Speak yet again.
GLOUCESTER   But have I fallen, or no?
EDGAR   From the dread summit of this chalky bourn.[6]
Look up a-height; the shrill-gorged° lark so far   *shrill-throated*
Cannot be seen or heard. Do but look up.
GLOUCESTER   Alack, I have no eyes.
Is wretchedness deprived° that benefit,   *deprived of*
To end itself by death? 'Twas yet some comfort,
When misery could beguile° the tyrant's rage,   *cheat*
And frustrate his proud will.
EDGAR   Give me your arm.
Up—so. How is 't? Feel you your legs? You stand.
GLOUCESTER   Too well, too well.
EDGAR   This is above all strangeness.
Upon the crown o' the cliff, what thing was that
Which parted from you?
GLOUCESTER   A poor unfortunate beggar.
EDGAR   As I stood here below, methought his eyes
Were two full moons; he had a thousand noses,
Horns whelked° and waved like the enridgèd sea: *twisted*
It was some fiend. Therefore, thou happy father,°   *lucky old man*
Think that the clearest° gods, who make them honors   *purest; most illustrious*
Of men's impossibilities,[7] have preserved thee.
GLOUCESTER   I do remember now. Henceforth I'll bear
Affliction till it do cry out itself
"Enough, enough," and die. That thing you speak of,
I took it for a man; often 't would say
"The fiend, the fiend"—he led me to that place.
EDGAR   Bear free and patient thoughts. But who comes here?
        Enter LEAR, *fantastically dressed with wild flowers*
The safer sense will ne'er accommodate
His master thus.[8]

5. Edgar worries that the imagined scenario ("conceit") he has invented may be enough to kill his father, particularly as Gloucester wishes for ("yields to") his own death.
6. The white chalk cliffs of Dover, which make a boundary ("bourn") between land and sea.
7. Who attain honor for themselves by performing deeds impossible to men.
8. A sane mind would never allow its possessor to dress up this way.

LEAR   No, they cannot touch me for coining;[9] I am the king
  himself.

85 EDGAR   O thou side-piercing sight!

LEAR   Nature's above art in that respect.[1] There's your
  press-money.[2] That fellow handles his bow like a crow-
  keeper.[3] Draw me a clothier's yard.[4] Look, look, a mouse!
  Peace, peace; this piece of toasted cheese will do 't.°   *(lure the mouse)*
90 There's my gauntlet; I'll prove it on a giant.[5] Bring up the
  brown bills.[6] O, well flown, bird!° i' the clout,° i' the clout.   *arrow / bull's-eye*
  Hewgh! Give the word.°   *password*

EDGAR   Sweet marjoram.[7]

LEAR   Pass.

95 GLOUCESTER   I know that voice.

LEAR   Ha! Goneril, with a white beard! They flattered me
  like a dog;° and told me I had white hairs in my beard ere   *fawningly*
  the black ones were there.[8] To say "aye" and "no" to everything that I said!—"Aye" and "no" too was no good divin-
100 ity.[9] When the rain came to wet me once, and the wind
  to make me chatter; when the thunder would not peace
  at my bidding; there I found° 'em, there I smelt 'em out.   *understood*
  Go to, they are not men o' their words! They told me I
  was everything. 'Tis a lie, I am not ague-proof.°   *immune to illness*

105 GLOUCESTER   The trick° of that voice I do well remember.   *peculiarity*
  Is 't not the king?

LEAR   Aye, every inch a king!
  When I do stare, see how the subject quakes.
  I pardon that man's life. What was thy cause?°   *crime*
  Adultery?

110 Thou shalt not die. Die for adultery? No.
  The wren goes to 't, and the small gilded fly
  Does lecher in my sight.
  Let copulation thrive; for Gloucester's bastard son
  Was kinder to his father than my daughters
115 Got 'tween the lawful sheets. To 't luxury,° pell-mell!   *lechery*
  For I lack soldiers. Behold yond simpering dame,
  Whose face between her forks presages snow;[1]
  That minces° virtue, and does shake the head   *affects*
  To hear of° pleasure's name;   *even of*
120 The fitchew, nor the soilèd horse,[2] goes to 't
  With a more riotous appetite.

9. Because minting money was the prerogative of the
king, nobody could overtake or equal ("touch") him.
1. My true feelings will always outvalue others' hypocrisy; my natural supremacy surpasses any attempt to
create a false new reign. This image may also be based
on coining (see preceding note).
2. Fee paid to a soldier impressed, or forced, into the
army.
3. A person hired as a scarecrow, and thus unfit for
anything else.
4. Draw the bowstring the full length of the arrow (a
standard English arrow was a cloth yard—thirty-seven
inches—long).

5. I'll defend my stand even against a giant. To throw
down an armored glove ("gauntlet") was to issue a challenge.
6. Brown painted pikes; or, the soldiers carrying them.
7. Used medicinally against madness.
8. I.e., told me I had wisdom before age.
9. I.e., poor theology (because insincere); from James
5.12, "Let your yea be yea; nay, nay."
1. Whose expression implies cold chastity. "Face"
refers to the area between her legs ("forks"), as well as
to her literal facial expression as framed by the aristocratic lady's starched headpiece, also called a "fork."
2. Neither the polecat nor a horse full of fresh grass.

Down from the waist they are Centaurs,[3]
Though women all above.
But° to the girdle° do the gods inherit.°   *only/waist/own*
125   Beneath is all the fiends'; there's hell,[4] there's darkness,
There's the sulphurous pit, burning, scalding,
Stench, consumption! Fie, fie, fie! pah! pah!
Give me an ounce of civet,[5] good apothecary,
To sweeten my imagination.
130   There's money for thee.
    GLOUCESTER   O, let me kiss that hand!
    LEAR   Let me wipe it first; it smells of mortality.
    GLOUCESTER   O ruined piece° of nature! This great world   *masterpiece*
Shall so wear out to nought.[6] Dost thou know me?
135   LEAR   I remember thine eyes well enough. Dost thou
squiny° at me? No, do thy worst, blind Cupid; I'll not love.   *squint*
Read thou this challenge; mark but the penning of it.
    GLOUCESTER   Were all the letters suns, I could not see one.
    EDGAR (*aside*)   I would not take° this from report. It is,   *believe*
140   And my heart breaks at it.
    LEAR   Read.
    GLOUCESTER   What, with the case° of eyes?   *socket*
    LEAR   O, ho, are you there with me?[7] No eyes in your head,
nor no money in your purse? Your eyes are in a heavy
145   case,[8] your purse in a light. Yet you see how this world
goes.
    GLOUCESTER   I see it feelingly.°   *by touch; painfully*
    LEAR   What, art mad? A man may see how this world goes
with no eyes. Look with thine ears. See how yond justice
150   rails upon yond simple° thief. Hark, in thine ear. Change   *lowly; innocent*
places and, handy-dandy,[9] which is the justice, which is
the thief? Thou hast seen a farmer's dog bark at a beggar?
    GLOUCESTER   Aye, sir.
    LEAR   And the creature° run from the cur? There thou   *wretch*
155   mightst behold the great image of authority: a dog's
obeyed in office.
Thou rascal beadle,[1] hold° thy bloody hand!   *restrain*
Why dost thou lash that whore? Strip thine own back;
Thou hotly lusts to use her in that kind°   *way*
160   For which thou whipp'st her. The usurer hangs the cozener.[2]
Through tattered clothes small vices do appear;
Robes and furred gowns hide all. Plate° sin with gold,   *armor, gild*
And the strong lance of justice hurtless° breaks;   *harmlessly*
Arm it in rags, a pigmy's straw does pierce it.

---

3. Lecherous mythological creatures that have a human body to the waist and the legs and torso of a horse below.
4. Shakespeare's frequent term for female genitals.
5. Exotic perfume derived from the sex glands of the civet cat.
6. Shall decay to nothing in the same way. In Renaissance philosophy, humans were perfectly analogous to the cosmos, standing for the whole in miniature and as its masterpiece.
7. Is that what you are telling me?
8. In a sad condition; playing on "case" as "sockets."
9. Pick a hand, as in a child's game.
1. The parish officer responsible for whippings.
2. The ruinous moneylender, prosperous enough to be made a judge, convicts the ordinary cheat.

165 None does offend, none, I say, none; I'll able° 'em;   *authorize*
Take that of me, my friend, who have the power
To seal the accuser's lips. Get thee glass eyes;
And, like a scurvy politician,[3] seem
To see the things thou dost not. Now, now, now, now!
170 Pull off my boots. Harder, harder! So.
EDGAR   O, matter and impertinency° mixed!   *sense and nonsense*
Reason in madness!
LEAR   If thou wilt weep my fortunes, take my eyes.
I know thee well enough; thy name is Gloucester:
175 Thou must be patient. We came crying hither;
Thou knows't, the first time that we smell the air,
We wail and cry. I will preach to thee. Mark.
            LEAR *takes off his crown of weeds and flowers*[4]
GLOUCESTER   Alack, alack the day!
LEAR   When we are born, we cry that we are come
180 To this great stage of fools. This'° a good block;[5]   *this is*
It were a delicate° stratagem, to shoe   *subtle*
A troop of horse with felt.[6] I'll put 't in proof:°   *to the test*
And when I have stol'n upon these sons-in-law,
Then, kill, kill, kill, kill, kill, kill!
            Enter a GENTLEMAN, *with attendants*
185 GENTLEMAN   O, here he is; lay hand upon him. Sir,
Your most dear daughter—
LEAR   No rescue? What, a prisoner? I am even
The natural fool[7] of fortune. Use° me well;   *treat*
You shall have ransom. Let me have surgeons;
I am cut to the brains.
190 GENTLEMAN   You shall have any thing.
LEAR   No seconds?° all myself?   *supporters*
Why, this would make a man a man of salt,[8]
To use his eyes for garden water-pots,
Aye, and laying° autumn's dust.   *settling*
GENTLEMAN   Good sir—
195 LEAR   I will die bravely,[9] like a smug° bridegroom. What!   *an elegant*
I will be jovial. Come, come; I am a king,
My masters, know you that?
GENTLEMAN   You are a royal one, and we obey you.
LEAR   Then there's life° in't. Nay, if you get it, you shall get   *hope*
200 it with running. Sa, sa, sa, sa.[1]
            (*Exit running; attendants follow*)
GENTLEMAN   A sight most pitiful in the meanest wretch,
Past speaking of in a king! Thou hast one daughter,

3. A vile schemer. In early modern England, "politician" meant an ambitious, even Machiavellian, upstart.
4. Like a preacher, removing his hat in the pulpit.
5. Stage (often called "scaffold" and hence linked to
executioner's block); block used to shape a felt hat
(such as the hat removed by a preacher before a sermon); mounting block (such as the stump or stock Lear
may have sat on to remove his boots).
6. Hat material, to muffle the sound of the approaching cavalry.
7. Born plaything; playing on "natural" as "mentally
deficient."
8. A man reduced to nothing but the salt his tears
deposit.
9. With courage; showily. "Die" plays on the Renaissance sense of "have an orgasm."
1. A cry to encourage dogs in the hunt.

Who redeems nature from the general curse
Which twain have brought her to.[2]
EDGAR   Hail, gentle° sir.   *noble*
205   GENTLEMAN   Sir, speed you.° What's your will?   *God speed you*
EDGAR   Do you hear aught, sir, of a battle toward?°   *coming*
GENTLEMAN   Most sure and vulgar.° Everyone hears that,   *commonly known*
Which° can distinguish sound.   *who*
EDGAR   But, by your favor,
How near's the other army?
210   GENTLEMAN   Near and on speedy foot. The main descry°   *appearance*
Stands on the hourly thought.°   *is expected forthwith*
EDGAR   I thank you, sir. That's all.
GENTLEMAN   Though that the queen on° special cause° is   *for/reason*
here,
Her army is moved on.
EDGAR   I thank you, sir.
                                                                Exit GENTLEMAN
215   GLOUCESTER   You ever-gentle gods, take my breath from me;
Let not my worser spirit[3] tempt me again
To die before you please!
EDGAR   Well pray you, father.[4]
GLOUCESTER   Now, good sir, what are you?
EDGAR   A most poor man, made tame to fortune's blows;
220   Who, by the art of known and feeling° sorrows,   *profound*
Am pregnant to° good pity. Give me your hand,   *disposed to feel*
I'll lead you to some biding.°   *resting place*
GLOUCESTER   Hearty thanks.
The bounty and the benison of heaven
To boot, and boot!°   *as well, what's more*
                Enter OSWALD
225   OSWALD   A proclaimed prize![5] Most happy!°   *lucky*
That eyeless head of thine was first framed° flesh   *made of*
To raise my fortunes. Thou old unhappy traitor,
Briefly thyself remember.[6] The sword is out
That must destroy thee.
GLOUCESTER   Now let thy friendly hand
Put strength enough to't.
                EDGAR *interposes*
230   OSWALD   Wherefore, bold peasant.
Darest thou support a published° traitor? Hence,   *proclaimed*
Lest that the infection° of his fortune take   *(deathly) sickness*
Like° hold on thee. Let go his arm.   *the same*
EDGAR   Chill[7] not let go, zir, without vurther 'casion.°   *further occasion*
235   OSWALD   Let go, slave, or thou diest!
EDGAR   Good gentleman, go your gait,° and let poor volk   *walk on*
pass. An chud ha'° bin zwaggered out of my life, 't would   *if I could have*

---

2. I.e., who restores proper meaning and order to a
universe plagued by the crimes of the other two daughters; alluding to the fall of humankind and the natural
world caused by the sin of Adam and Eve and to the
universal redemption brought about by Christ's sacrifice.

3. Wicked inclination; bad angel.
4. A term of respect for an elderly man.
5. A wanted man, with a bounty on his life.
6. Recollect and pray forgiveness for your sins.
7. I will; dialect from Somerset was a stage convention
for peasant dialogue.

not ha' bin zo long as 'tis by a vortnight. Nay, come not
near th' old man; keep out, che vor ye, or ise try whether
240   your costard or my ballow be the harder.[8] Chill be plain
with you.
OSWALD   Out, dunghill!
EDGAR   Chill pick your teeth, zir. Come! No matter vor
your foins.°   *sword thrusts*
             They fight, and EDGAR *knocks him down*
245   OSWALD   Slave, thou hast slain me. Villain, take my purse.
If ever thou wilt thrive, bury my body;
And give the letters which thou find'st about me
To Edmund earl of Gloucester. Seek him out
Upon° the British party. O, untimely death!   *within*
250 Death!   *He dies*
EDGAR   I know thee well: a serviceable° villain;   *an officious*
As duteous to the vices of thy mistress
As badness would desire.
GLOUCESTER   What, is he dead?
EDGAR   Sit you down, father; rest you.
255 Let's see his pockets; the letters that he speaks of
May be my friends. He's dead; I am only sorry
He had no other death'sman.° Let us see.   *executioner*
Leave,° gentle wax;[9] and, manners blame us not.   *by your leave*
To know our enemies' minds, we'd rip their hearts;
260 Their° papers, is more lawful.   *to rip their*
(*Reads*) "Let our reciprocal vows be remembered. You
have many opportunities to cut him off. If your will want°   *lacks*
not, time and place will be fruitfully offered. There is
nothing done,° if he return the conqueror. Then am I the *accomplished*
265 prisoner, and his bed my jail; from the loathed warmth
whereof deliver me, and supply° the place for your   *fill*
labor.[1]
                     Your—wife, so I would say—
                         Affectionate servant,
270   Goneril."
O undistinguished space of woman's will![2]
A plot upon her virtuous husband's life;
And the exchange° my brother! Here, in the sands,   *substitute*
Thee I'll rake up,° the post unsanctified°   *cover up/unholy messenger*
275 Of murderous lechers; and in the mature time°   *when the time is ripe*
With this ungracious° paper strike the sight   *ungodly*
Of the death-practiced duke.[3] For him 'tis well
That of thy death and business I can tell.
GLOUCESTER   The king is mad. How stiff is my vile sense,[4]
280 That I stand up, and have ingenious feeling[5]
Of my huge sorrows! Better I were distract;°   *mad*

---

8. I.e., I warn you, or I shall test whether your head or
my cudgel is harder. "Costard": a kind of apple.
9. The wax seal on the letter.
1. As a reward for your endeavors and for further sexual exertion.
2. Limitless extent of woman's willfullness. As with

"hell" in line 125. "will" might also refer to a woman's
genitals.
3. Of the duke whose death is plotted.
4. How obstinate is my unwanted power of reason.
5. That I remain upright and firm in my sanity and
have rational perceptions.

So should my thoughts be severed from my griefs,
And woes by wrong° imaginations lose   *false*
The knowledge of themselves.
    Drum afar off
EDGAR   Give me your hand.
285 Far off, methinks, I hear the beaten drum.
Come, father, I'll bestow° you with a friend.   *Exeunt*   *lodge*

4.7
Enter CORDELIA, KENT, DOCTOR, *and a* GENTLEMAN

CORDELIA O thou good Kent, how shall I live and work,
To match thy goodness? My life will be too short,
And every measure° fail me.   *attempt*
KENT To be acknowledged, madam, is o'erpaid.°   *is more than enough*
5 All my reports go¹ with the modest truth;
Nor more nor clipped, but so.²
CORDELIA   Be better suited.°   *attired*
These weeds° are memories of those worser hours.   *clothes*
I prithee, put them off.
KENT   Pardon me, dear madam;
Yet to be known shortens my made intent.³
10 My boon I make it,⁴ that you know° me not   *acknowledge*
Till time and I think meet.°   *suitable*
CORDELIA Then be 't so, my good lord. (*To the* DOCTOR)
    How does the king?
DOCTOR Madam, sleeps still.
CORDELIA O you kind gods,
15 Cure this great breach in his abusèd nature!
The untuned and jarring senses, O, wind up⁵
Of this child-changèd⁶ father!
DOCTOR   So please your majesty
That we may wake the king? He hath slept long.
CORDELIA Be governed by your knowledge, and proceed
20 I' the sway° of your own will. Is he arrayed?°   *by the authority/clothed*
    Enter LEAR *in a chair carried by servants*
GENTLEMAN Aye, madam. In the heaviness of his sleep
We put fresh garments on him.
DOCTOR Be by, good madam, when we do awake him;
I doubt not of his temperance.°   *calmness*
CORDELIA   Very well.
    Music
25 DOCTOR Please you, draw near. Louder the music there!
CORDELIA O my dear father! Restoration hang
Thy medicine on my lips; and let this kiss
Repair those violent harms that my two sisters
Have in thy reverence° made!   *aged dignity*

4.7 Location: The French camp at Dover.
1. May all accounts of me agree.
2. Not greater or less, but exactly the modest amount
I deserve.
3. I.e., revealing myself now would abort my designs.

4. The reward I beg is.
5. Reorder his confused and delirious mind. The image
is of tightening the strings of a lute.
6. Changed by his children; changed into a child; playing on a musical key change.

KENT   Kind and dear princess!

CORDELIA   Had you not[7] been their father, these white

30   flakes°   *locks of hair*
      Had challenged° pity of them. Was this a face   *would have provoked*
      To be opposed against the warring winds?
      To stand against the deep dread-bolted thunder?
      In the most terrible and nimble stroke

35   Of quick, cross lightning? to watch°—poor perdu![8]—   *to stand guard*
      With this thin helm?° Mine enemy's dog,   *helmet (of hair)*
      Though he had bit me, should have stood that night
      Against my fire; and wast thou fain,° poor father,   *glad*
      To hovel thee with swine, and rogues forlorn,

40   In short° and musty straw? Alack, alack!   *scant; broken*
      'Tis wonder that thy life and wits at once
      Had not concluded all.° He wakes; speak to him.   *altogether*

DOCTOR   Madam, do you; 'tis fittest.

CORDELIA   How does my royal lord? How fares your majesty?

45 LEAR   You do me wrong to take me out o' the grave.
      Thou art a soul in bliss; but I am bound
      Upon a wheel of fire, that mine own tears
      Do scald like molten lead.[9]

CORDELIA   Sir, do you know me?

LEAR   You are a spirit, I know. When did you die?

50 CORDELIA   Still, still, far wide!°   *unbalanced*

DOCTOR   He's scarce awake. Let him alone awhile.

LEAR   Where have I been? Where am I? Fair daylight?
      I am mightily abused.° I should e'en die with pity,   *wronged; deceived*
      To see another thus. I know not what to say.

55   I will not swear these are my hands. Let's see.
      I feel this pin prick. Would I were assured
      Of my condition!

CORDELIA   O, look upon me, sir,
      And hold your hands in benediction o'er me:
      No, sir, you must not kneel.

60 LEAR   Pray, do not mock me.
      I am a very foolish fond° old man,   *silly*
      Fourscore and upward, not an hour more nor less;
      And, to deal plainly,
      I fear I am not in my perfect mind.

65   Methinks I should know you, and know this man;
      Yet I am doubtful; for I am mainly° ignorant   *entirely*
      What place this is; and all the skill I have
      Remembers not these garments; nor I know not
      Where I did lodge last night. Do not laugh at me;

70   For, as I am a man, I think this lady
      To be my child Cordelia.

7. Even if you had not.
8. Lost one; in military terminology, a dangerously
exposed sentry.

9. Lear puts himself in either hell or purgatory, both
places of such punishment in medieval accounts.

CORDELIA   And so I am, I am.
LEAR   Be your tears wet?[1] Yes, faith. I pray, weep not.
    If you have poison for me, I will drink it.
    I know you do not love me; for your sisters
75   Have, as I do remember, done me wrong.
    You have some cause, they have not.
CORDELIA   No cause, no, cause.
LEAR   Am I in France?
KENT   In your own kingdom, sir.
LEAR   Do not abuse° me.   deceive; mock
DOCTOR   Be comforted, good madam. The great rage,
80   You see, is killed in him; and yet it is danger
    To make him even o'er° the time he has lost.   go over
    Desire him to go in. Trouble him no more
    Till further settling.°   until his mind eases
CORDELIA   Will't please your highness walk?
LEAR   You must bear with me:
85   Pray you now, forget and forgive. I am old and foolish.
            Exeunt all but KENT *and* GENTLEMAN
GENTLEMAN   Holds it true, sir, that the Duke of Cornwall
    was so slain?
KENT   Most certain, sir.
GENTLEMAN   Who is conductor° of his people?   commander
90 KENT   As 'tis said, the bastard son of Gloucester.
GENTLEMAN   They say Edgar, his banished son, is with the
    earl of Kent in Germany.
KENT   Report° is changeable. 'Tis time to look about.°   rumor/prepare defenses
    The powers of the kingdom approach apace.
95 GENTLEMAN   The arbitrement° is like to be bloody. Fare   encounter
    you well, sir.   *Exit*
KENT   My point and period[2] will be throughly wrought,
    Or° well or ill, as this day's battle's fought.   *Exit*   for

5.1

Enter, with drum and colors, EDMUND, REGAN, GEN-
TLEMAN, *and soldiers*
EDMUND   Know° of the duke if his last purpose hold,[1]   inquire
    Or whether since he is advised by aught[2]
    To change the course. He's full of alteration°   indecision
    And self-reproving. Bring his constant pleasure.°   his settled intent
            To a GENTLEMAN, *who goes out*
5 REGAN   Our sister's man is certainly miscarried.[3]
EDMUND   'Tis to be doubted,° madam.   feared
REGAN   Now, sweet lord,
    You know the goodness I intend upon you.
    Tell me—but truly—but then speak the truth,
    Do you not love my sister?

1. Are your tears real?; is this really happening?
2. The purpose and end of my life; literally, the full
stop.
5.1 Location: The British camp near Dover.

1. If his previous intention (to wage war) remains firm.
2. Since then anything has persuaded him.
3. Has surely come to grief by some accident.

EDMUND	In honored° love.	*honorable*

10 REGAN   But have you never found my brother's way
    To the forfended⁴ place?

EDMUND   That thought abuses° you.   *deceives*

REGAN   I am doubtful that you have been conjunct°   *complicit*
    And bosomed with° her, as far as we call hers.⁵   *enamored of*

EDMUND   No, by mine honor, madam.

15 REGAN   I never shall endure her. Dear my lord,
    Be not familiar° with her.   *intimate*

EDMUND   Fear° me not.   *doubt*
    She and the duke her husband!

        Enter, with drum and colors, ALBANY, GONERIL, *and*
        soldiers

GONERIL (*aside*)   I had rather lose the battle than that sister
    Should loosen° him and me.   *disunite*

20 ALBANY   Our very loving sister, well be-met.
    Sir, this I hear: the king is come to his daughter,
    With others whom the rigor° of our state°   *harshness/government*
    Forced to cry out. Where I could not be honest,°   *honorable*
    I never yet was valiant. For this business,
25   It toucheth° us, as France invades our land,   *concerns*
    Not bolds the king, with others, whom, I fear,
    Most just and heavy causes make oppose.⁶

EDMUND   Sir, you speak nobly.

REGAN   Why is this reasoned?⁷

GONERIL   Combine together 'gainst the enemy;
30   For these domestic and particular broils°   *minor details*
    Are not the question here.

ALBANY   Let's then determine
    With the ancient° of war on our proceeding.   *experienced officer*

EDMUND   I shall attend you presently° at your tent.   *in a moment*

REGAN   Sister, you'll go with us?⁸

35 GONERIL   No.

REGAN   'Tis most convenient;° pray you, go with us.   *suitable*

GONERIL (*aside*)   O, ho, I know the riddle.°—I will go.   *disguised meaning*
        As they are going out, enter EDGAR *disguised*

EDGAR   If e'er your grace had speech with man so poor,
    Hear me one word.

ALBANY   I'll overtake you. Speak.
        Exeunt all but ALBANY *and* EDGAR

40 EDGAR   Before you fight the battle, ope this letter.
    If you have victory, let the trumpet sound
    For him that brought it. Wretched though I seem,
    I can produce a champion that will prove°   *defend*
    What is avouched° there. If you miscarry,°   *maintained/perish*

---

4. Forbidden (to Edmund, because it is adulterous).
5. In total intimacy; all the way.
6. This is of concern to us because France lands on
our soil, not because it emboldens the king and others,
who, I am afraid, have been provoked for good and solid
reasons.
7. What is the point of this kind of speech?
8. Regan wants Goneril to go with Albany and her,
rather than with Edmund.

45 Your business of the world hath so an end,
And machination° ceases. Fortune love you!   *plotting*
ALBANY   Stay till I have read the letter.
EDGAR   I was forbid it.
When time shall serve, let but the herald cry,
And I'll appear again.
50 ALBANY   Why, fare thee well. I will o'erlook thy paper.
                                  Exit EDGAR
      Re-enter EDMUND
EDMUND   The enemy 's in view; draw up your powers.°   *troops*
Here is the guess° of their true strength and forces   *estimate*
By diligent discovery;° but your haste   *spying*
Is now urged on you.
ALBANY   We will greet the time.[9]   *Exit*
55 EDMUND   To both these sisters have I sworn my love;
Each jealous° of the other, as the stung   *suspicious*
Are of the adder. Which of them shall I take?
Both? one? or neither? Neither can be enjoyed,
If both remain alive. To take the widow
60 Exasperates, makes mad her sister Goneril;
And hardly° shall I carry out my side,°   *with difficulty / plan*
Her husband being alive. Now then we'll use
His countenance[1] for the battle; which being done,
Let her who would be rid of him devise
65 His speedy taking off. As for the mercy
Which he intends to Lear and to Cordelia,
The battle done, and they within our power,
Shall° never see his pardon; for my state°   *they shall / condition*
Stands on° me to defend, not to debate.   *Exit*   *obliges*

5.2

      Alarum within.[1] Enter, with drum and colors, LEAR,
      CORDELIA, *and soldiers, over the stage; and exeunt*
      Enter EDGAR *and* GLOUCESTER
EDGAR   Here, father,[2] take the shadow of this tree
For your good host;° pray that the right may thrive: *shelter*
If ever I return to you again,
I'll bring you comfort.
GLOUCESTER   Grace go with you, sir!
                           Exit EDGAR
      Alarum and retreat° within. Re-enter EDGAR   *trumpet signal*
5 EDGAR   Away, old man! give me thy hand! away!
King Lear hath lost, he and his daughter ta'en.
Give me thy hand! come on!

---

9. We will be ready to meet the occasion.
1. Authority or backing; also suggesting "face," to be
used like a mask for Edmund's ambition.
5.2 Location: The rest of the play takes place near the

battlefield.
1. Trumpet call to battle (backstage).
2. See note to 4.6.217.

GLOUCESTER No farther, sir; a man may rot even° here.   *right*
EDGAR What, in ill thoughts again? Men must endure
10   Their going hence, even as their coming hither;
        Ripeness is all.[3] Come on!
GLOUCESTER   And that's true, too. *Exeunt*

5.3
Enter, in conquest, with drum and colors, EDMUND;
LEAR *and* CORDELIA, *prisoners;* CAPTAIN, *soldiers,* &C.

EDMUND Some officers take them away. Good guard,
        Until their greater pleasures[1] first be known
        That are to censure° them.   *judge*
CORDELIA   We are not the first
        Who, with best meaning,° have incurred the worst.   *intention*
5   For thee, oppressèd king, am I cast down;°   *(into unhappiness)*
        Myself could else out-frown false Fortune's frown.[2]
        Shall we not see these daughters and these sisters?
LEAR No, no, no, no! Come, let's away to prison.
        We two alone will sing like birds i' the cage.
10   When thou dost ask me blessing, I'll kneel down,
        And ask of thee forgiveness. So we'll live,
        And pray, and sing, and tell old tales, and laugh
        At gilded butterflies,[3] and hear poor rogues
        Talk of court news; and we'll talk with them too,
15   Who loses and who wins; who 's in, and who 's out;
        And take upon 's the mystery of things,
        As if we were God's spies; and we'll wear out,°   *outlast*
        In a walled prison, packs and sects of great ones,
        That ebb and flow by the moon.[4]
EDMUND   Take them away.
20   LEAR Upon such sacrifices,[5] my Cordelia,
        The gods themselves throw incense. Have I caught thee?
        He that parts us shall bring a brand from heavens,
        And fire us hence like foxes.[6] Wipe thine eyes;
        The good-years shall devour them, flesh and fell,[7]
25   Ere they shall make us weep! We'll see 'em starved first.
        Come.   *Exeunt* LEAR *and* CORDELIA, *guarded*
EDMUND Come hither, captain; hark.
        Take thou this note (*giving a paper*). Go follow them to prison:
        One step I have advanced° thee. If thou dost   *promoted*
30   As this instructs thee, thou dost make thy way
        To noble fortunes. Know thou this, that men

3. To await the destined time is the most important thing, as fruit falls only when ripe (playing on Gloucester's "rot," line 8); readiness for death is our only duty (compare *Hamlet* 5.2.160, "The readiness is all").
5.3
1. Guard them well until the desires of those greater persons.
2. Otherwise, I could be defiant in the face of bad fortune.
3. Gaudy and ephemeral courtiers; trivial matters.

4. Followers and factions of important people whose positions at court vary as the tide.
5. Upon such sacrifices as we are, or as you have made.
6. I.e., must have divine aid to do so. The image is of using a torch to smoke foxes out of their holes, or, in the case of Lear and Cordelia, prison cells.
7. Meat and skin; entirely. The precise meaning of "good-years" has not been explained; it may signify simply the passage of time or may suggest some ominous, destructive power.

Are as the time is. To be tender-minded
Does not become a sword.° Thy great employment   *befit a swordsman*
Will not bear question.° Either say thou'lt do't,   *discussion*
Or thrive by other means.
35 CAPTAIN   I'll do't, my lord.
EDMUND   About it; and write happy when thou hast done.[8]
Mark, I say, instantly; and carry it° so   *carry it out*
As I have set it down.
CAPTAIN   I cannot draw a cart, nor eat dried oats;°   *(like a horse)*
40 If it be a man's work, I'll do it.   *Exit*
          Flourish. Enter ALBANY, GONERIL, REGAN, *another*
          CAPTAIN, *and soldiers*
ALBANY   Sir, you have showed today your valiant strain,°   *qualities; birth*
And fortune led you well. You have the captives
That were the opposites° of this day's strife.   *opponents*
I do require them of you, so to use° them   *treat*
45 As we shall find their merits and our safety
May equally determine.
EDMUND   Sir, I thought it fit
To send the old and miserable king
To some retention° and appointed guard;   *confinement*
Whose° age has charms in it, whose title more,   *(Lear's)*
50 To pluck the common bosom[9] on his side,
And turn our impressed lances° in our eyes   *conscripted lancers*
Which[1] do command them. With him I sent the queen;
My reason all the same; and they are ready
Tomorrow, or at further space,° t'appear   *at a future point*
55 Where you shall hold your session.° At this time   *court of judgment*
We sweat and bleed; the friend hath lost his friend;
And the best quarrels, in the heat, are cursed
By those that feel their sharpness.[2]
The question of Cordelia and her father
Requires a fitter place.
60 ALBANY   Sir, by your patience,
I hold you but a subject of° this war,   *in waging*
Not as a brother.
REGAN   That's as we list° to grace him.   *like*
Methinks our pleasure might have been demanded,[3]
Ere you had spoken so far. He led our powers;°   *armies*
65 Bore the commission of my place and person;
The which immediacy° may well stand up,   *close connection*
And call itself your brother.
GONERIL   Not so hot!°   *not so fast*
In his own grace° he doth exalt himself,   *merit*
More than in your addition.[4]
REGAN   In my rights,

---

8. Go to it, and call yourself happy when you are done.
9. To garner the affection of the populace.
1. In the eyes of us who.
2. And in the heat of battle, even the most just wars

are cursed by those who must suffer the fighting.
3. I think you should have inquired into my wishes.
4. In the honors you confer upon him.

70   By me invested, he compeers° the best.   *equals*
GONERIL   That were the most,[5] if he should husband you.
REGAN   Jesters do oft prove prophets.
GONERIL   Holla, holla!
    That eye that told you so looked but a-squint.[6]
REGAN   Lady, I am not well; else I should answer
75   From a full-flowing stomach.° General,   *anger*
    Take thou my soldiers, prisoners, patrimony:
    Dispose of them, of me; the walls° are thine.   *fortress of my heart*
    Witness the world, that I create thee here
    My lord and master.
GONERIL   Mean you to enjoy him?
80 ALBANY   The let-alone° lies not in your good will.   *veto*
EDMUND   Nor in thine, lord.
ALBANY   Half-blooded° fellow, yes.   *bastard*
REGAN (*to* EDMUND)   Let the drum strike,[7] and prove my title thine.
ALBANY   Stay yet; hear reason. Edmund, I arrest thee
    On capital treason; and, in thine attaint,[8]
85   This gilded serpent (*pointing to* GONERIL). For your
        claim, fair sister,°   *sister-in-law*
    I bar it in the interest of my wife;
    'Tis she is sub-contracted to this lord,
    And I, her husband, contradict your banes.°   *announcement of marriage*
    If you will marry, make your loves to me,
    My lady is bespoke.
90 GONERIL   An interlude!°   *a farce*
ALBANY   Thou art armed, Gloucester. Let the trumpet sound.
    If none appear to prove upon thy head
    Thy heinous, manifest, and many treasons,
    There is my pledge (*throwing down a glove*); I'll prove it on thy heart,
95   Ere I taste bread, thou art in nothing less°   *in no way less guilty*
    Than I have proclaimed thee.
REGAN   Sick, O, sick!
GONERIL (*aside*)   If not, I'll ne'er trust medicine.°   *poison (euphemistic)*
EDMUND   There's my exchange (*throwing down a glove*).
    What° in the world he is   *whoever*
    That names me traitor, villain-like he lies.
100   Call by thy trumpet. He that dares approach,
    On him, on you, who not? I will maintain
    My truth and honor firmly.
ALBANY   A herald, ho!
EDMUND   A herald, ho, a herald!
ALBANY   Trust to thy single virtue;° for thy soldiers,   *your unassisted power*
105   All levied in my name, have in my name
    Took their discharge.
REGAN   My sickness grows upon me.

---

5. That investiture would be complete.
6. Squinting was a proverbial effect of jealousy, because of the tendency to look suspiciously at potential rivals.

7. Perhaps to announce the betrothal or a challenge.
8. And in order to accuse you; and as one who shares your corruption or crime.

ALBANY   She is not well; convey her to my tent.

Exit REGAN, *led*

Enter a HERALD

Come hither, herald—Let the trumpet sound—
And read out this.

CAPTAIN   Sound, trumpet! (*A trumpet sounds*)

110   HERALD [*reads*]   "If any man of quality or degree within the
lists of the army will maintain upon Edmund, supposed
earl of Gloucester, that he is a manifold traitor, let him
appear by the third sound of the trumpet. He is bold in
his defense."

115   EDMUND   Sound! (*First trumpet*)

HERALD   Again! (*Second trumpet*)

HERALD   Again! (*Third trumpet*)

Trumpet answers within
Enter EDGAR, *at the third sound, armed, with a trum-*
pet before him

ALBANY   Ask him his purposes, why he appears
Upon this call o' the trumpet.

HERALD   What° are you?   who

120   Your name, your quality?° and why you answer   degree, rank
This present summons?

EDGAR   Know, my name is lost;
By treason's tooth bare-gnawn and canker-bit.°   worm-eaten
Yet am I noble as the adversary
I come to cope.°   to encounter

ALBANY   Which is that adversary?

125   EDGAR   What's he that speaks for Edmund earl of Gloucester?

EDMUND   Himself. What say'st thou to him?

EDGAR   Draw thy sword,
That,° if my speech offend a noble heart,   so that
Thy arm may do thee justice. Here is mine.
Behold, it is the privilege of mine honors,

130   My oath, and my profession. I protest,
Maugre° thy strength, youth, place, and eminence,   despite
Despite thy victor sword and fire-new° fortune,   newly minted
Thy valor and thy heart,° thou art a traitor;   courage
False to thy gods, thy brother, and thy father;

135   Conspirant 'gainst this high-illustrious prince;
And, from the extremest upward° of thy head   top
To the descent° and dust below thy foot,   lowest part; sole
A most toad-spotted⁹ traitor. Say thou "No,"
This sword, this arm, and my best spirits, are bent°   ready

140   To prove upon thy heart, whereto I speak,
Thou liest.

EDMUND   In wisdom I should ask thy name;
But, since thy outside looks so fair and warlike
And that thy tongue some say of breeding breathes,

---

9. Venomous, like a toad; spotted with disgrace.

What safe and nicely I might well delay
145   By rule of knighthood, I disdain and spurn.[1]
Back do I toss these treasons to thy head;
With the hell-hated° lie o'erwhelm thy heart;   *hated as much as hell*
Which, for° they yet glance by and scarcely bruise,   *since*
This sword of mine shall give them instant way,°   *access*
150   Where they shall rest for ever. Trumpets, speak!
      Alarums. They fight. EDMUND *falls*
ALBANY   Save° him, save him!   *spare*
GONERIL   This is practice,° Gloucester: *trickery*
By the law of arms thou wast not bound to answer
An unknown opposite.° Thou art not vanquished,   *opponent*
But cozened and beguiled.°   *cheated and deceived*
ALBANY   Shut your mouth, dame,
155   Or with this paper shall I stople° it.   *plug*
Thou worse than any name, read thine own evil.
No tearing, lady! I perceive you know it.
      Gives the letter to EDMUND
GONERIL   Say, if I do, the laws are mine, not thine.
Who can arraign° me for 't?   *prosecute*
ALBANY   Most monstrous! oh!
Know'st thou this paper?
160 GONERIL   Ask me not what I know. *Exit*
ALBANY   Go after her: she's desperate; govern° her.   *restrain*
EDMUND   What you have charged me with, that have I done;
And more, much more; the time will bring it out.
'Tis past, and so am I. But what art thou
165   That hast this fortune on me?[2] If thou 'rt noble,
I do forgive thee.
EDGAR   Let's exchange charity.°   *forgiveness*
I am no less in blood than thou art, Edmund;
If more, the more thou hast wronged me.
My name is Edgar, and thy father's son.
170   The gods are just, and of our pleasant vices
Make instruments to plague us.
The dark and vicious place where thee he got°   *begot*
Cost him his eyes.
EDMUND   Thou hast spoken right, 'tis true;
The wheel° is come full circle! I am here.[3]   *fortune's wheel*
175 ALBANY   Methought thy very gait did prophesy
A royal nobleness. I must embrace thee.
Let sorrow split my heart, if ever I
Did hate thee or thy father!
EDGAR   Worthy prince. I know 't.
ALBANY   Where have you hid yourself?
180   How have you known the miseries of your father?
EDGAR   By nursing them, my lord. List° a brief tale;   *listen to*

---

1. And since your speech may suggest high birth, I will
not stick safely and meticulously to the rules of knighthood by refusing to fight you.

2. Who have this good fortune at my expense.
3. Back at the lowest point.

And when 'tis told, O, that my heart would burst!
The bloody proclamation to escape,[4]
That followed me so near—O, our lives' sweetness!
185   That we the pain of death would hourly die
Rather than die at once![5]—taught me to shift
Into a madman's rags; to assume a semblance
That very° dogs disdained; and in this habit   *even*
Met I my father with his bleeding rings,°   *sockets*
190   Their precious stones new lost; became his guide,
Led him, begged for him, saved him from despair;
Never—O fault!—revealed myself unto him
Until some half-hour past, when I was armed:
Not sure, though hoping, of this good success,°   *conclusion*
195   I asked his blessing, and from first to last
Told him my pilgrimage. But his flawed° heart—   *cracked*
Alack, too weak the conflict to support!—
'Twixt two extremes of passion, joy and grief,
Burst smilingly.

EDMUND   This speech of yours hath moved me,
200   And shall perchance do good; but speak you on;
You look as you had something more to say.

ALBANY   If there be more, more woeful, hold it in;
For I am almost ready to dissolve,°   *melt into tears*
Hearing of this.

EDGAR   This would have seemed a period°   *conclusion*
205   To such as love not sorrow; but another,
To amplify° too much would make much more,   *enlarge, extend*
And top extremity.
Whilst I was big in clamor° came there in a man,   *lamenting loudly*
Who, having seen me in my worst estate,
210   Shunned my abhorred society; but then, finding
Who 'twas that so endured, with his strong arms
He fastened on my neck, and bellowed out
As he'd burst heaven; threw him on my father;
Told the most piteous tale of Lear and him°   *himself*
215   That ever ear received; which in recounting
His grief grew puissant,° and the strings of life   *powerful*
Began to crack. Twice then the trumpets sounded,
And there I left him tranced.

ALBANY   But who was this?

EDGAR   Kent, sir, the banished Kent; who in disguise
220   Followed his enemy king,[6] and did him service
Improper° for a slave.   *unfit even*

Enter a GENTLEMAN, *with a bloody knife*

GENTLEMAN   Help, help, O, help!

EDGAR   What kind of help?

ALBANY   Speak, man.

---

4. In order to escape the sentence of death.
5. How sweet must life be that we prefer the constant pain of dying to death itself.
6. "Enemy"—that is, hostile—because Lear had previously banished him.

EDGAR   What means that bloody knife?
GENTLEMAN   'Tis hot, it smokes,
  It came even from the heart of—O, she's dead!
225 ALBANY   Who dead? speak, man.
GENTLEMAN   Your lady, sir, your lady! and her sister
  By her is poisoned; she hath confessed it.
EDMUND   I was contracted to them both. All three
  Now marry° in an instant.   unite (in death)
    Enter KENT
EDGAR   Here comes Kent.
230 ALBANY   Produce their bodies, be they alive or dead:
  This judgment of the heavens, that makes us tremble,
  Touches us not with pity.   *Exit* GENTLEMAN
                  O, is this he?
  The time will not allow the compliment
  Which very manners urges.[7]
KENT   I am come
235 To bid my king and master aye° good night.   forever
  Is he not here?
ALBANY   Great thing of° us forgot!   by
  Speak, Edmund, where's the king? and where's Cordelia?
  See'st thou this object,° Kent?   spectacle
    The bodies of GONERIL *and* REGAN *are brought in*
KENT   Alack, why thus?
EDMUND   Yet° Edmund was beloved.   despite all
240 The one the other poisoned for my sake,
  And after slew herself.
ALBANY   Even so. Cover their faces.
EDMUND   I pant for life. Some good I mean to do,
  Despite of mine own nature. Quickly send,
245 Be brief° in it, to the castle; for my writ[8]   speedy
  Is on the life of Lear and on Cordelia:
  Nay, send in time.
ALBANY   Run, run, O, run!
EDGAR   To who, my lord? Who hath the office?° send   commission
  Thy token of reprieve.
250 EDMUND   Well thought on. Take my sword,
  Give it the° captain.   to the
ALBANY   Haste thee for thy life. *Exit* EDGAR
EDMUND   He hath commission from thy wife and me
  To hang Cordelia in the prison, and
  To lay the blame upon her own despair,
255 That she fordid herself.[9]
ALBANY   The gods defend her! Bear him hence awhile.
                  EDMUND *is borne off*
    Re-enter LEAR, *with* CORDELIA *dead in his arms;*
    EDGAR, CAPTAIN, *and others following*

---

7. I.e., the ceremony that barest custom demands.
8. Order of execution.
9. Destroyed herself. In most of Shakespeare's source

texts for the play, Cordelia does in fact kill herself after
reigning for some years.

LEAR   Howl, howl, howl, howl! O, you are men of stones:
   Had I your tongues and eyes, I'd use them so
   That heaven's vault should crack. She's gone forever!
260   I know when one is dead, and when one lives;
   She's dead as earth. Lend me a looking-glass;
   If that her breath will mist or stain the stone,[1]
   Why, then she lives.
KENT   Is this the promised end?[2]
EDGAR   Or image of that horror?
ALBANY   Fall, and cease![3]
265   LEAR   This feather stirs; she lives! If it be so,
   It is a chance which does redeem all sorrows
   That ever I have felt.
KENT *(kneeling)*[4]   O my good master!
LEAR   Prithee, away.
EDGAR   'Tis noble Kent, your friend.
LEAR   A plague upon you, murderers, traitors all!
270   I might have saved her; now she's gone for ever!
   Cordelia, Cordelia! stay a little. Ha!
   What is 't thou say'st? Her voice was ever soft,
   Gentle, and low, an excellent thing in woman.
   I killed the slave that was a-hanging thee.
CAPTAIN   'Tis true, my lords, he did.
275   LEAR   Did I not, fellow?
   I have seen the day, with my good biting falchion°   *light sword*
   I would have made them skip: I am old now,
   And these same crosses spoil me.[5] Who are you?
   Mine eyes are not o' the best. I'll tell you straight.°   *recognize you soon*
280   KENT   If fortune brag of two she loved and hated,
   One of them we behold.[6]
LEAR   This is a dull sight.[7] Are you not Kent?
KENT   The same,
   Your servant Kent. Where is your servant Caius?°   *(Kent's pseudonym)*
LEAR   He's a good fellow, I can tell you that;
285   He'll strike, and quickly too. He's dead and rotten.
KENT   No, my good lord; I am the very man—
LEAR   I'll see that straight.[8]
KENT   That, from your first of difference and decay,[9]
   Have followed your sad steps.
LEAR   You are welcome hither.
290   KENT   Nor no man else.[1] All's cheerless, dark, and deadly.°   *deathly*
   Your eldest daughters have fordone° themselves,   *destroyed*

---

1. Mica, or stone polished to a mirror finish.
2. Doomsday; expected end of the play. In no version of the story previous to Shakespeare's does Cordelia die at this point.
3. Let the world collapse and end.
4. Lear probably kneels over Cordelia's body during most of the scene, and Kent kneels here partly in submission, partly to catch Lear's attention.
5. And these recent adversities have weakened me; and these parries I could once match would now destroy me.

6. If there were only two supreme examples in the world of Fortune's ability to raise up and cast down, Lear would be one; alternatively, we are each of us one (Lear and Kent are here looking at each other).
7. This is a sad sight; my vision is failing.
8. I'll attend to that shortly; I'll comprehend that in a moment.
9. Who from the beginning of your alteration and deterioration.
1. No, neither I nor anyone else is welcome—that is, this is not a welcoming sight.

And desperately° are dead.   *in despair*

LEAR   Aye, so I think.

ALBANY   He knows not what he says; and vain° it is   *in vain*
That we present us to him.

EDGAR   Very bootless.°   *futile*

Enter a CAPTAIN

CAPTAIN   Edmund is dead, my lord.

295   ALBANY   That's but a trifle here.
You lords and noble friends, know our intent.
What comfort to this great decay° may come   *ruin, destruction*
Shall be applied. For us, we will resign,
During the life of this old majesty,
300   To him our absolute power; (*to* EDGAR *and* KENT) you, to your rights;
With boot,° and such addition° as your honors   *reward/distinction*
Have more than merited. All friends shall taste
The wages of their virtue, and all foes
The cup of their deserving. O, see, see!
305   LEAR   And my poor fool² is hanged! No, no, no life!
Why should a dog, a horse, a rat, have life,
And thou no breath at all? Thou'lt come no more,
Never, never, never, never, never!
Pray you, undo this button. Thank you, sir.
310   Do you see this? Look on her, look, her lips,
Look there, look there!   *Dies*

EDGAR   He faints! My lord, my lord!

KENT   Break, heart; I prithee, break!

EDGAR   Look up, my lord.

KENT   Vex not his ghost.³ O, let him pass! He hates him much
That would upon the rack⁴ of this tough world
Stretch him out longer.

315   EDGAR   He is gone, indeed.

KENT   The wonder is, he hath endured so long.
He but usurped his life.⁵

ALBANY   Bear them from hence. Our present business
Is general woe. (*To* KENT *and* EDGAR) Friends of my soul, you twain
320   Rule in this realm, and the gored° state sustain.   *wounded; bloody*

KENT   I have a journey, sir, shortly to go;
My master calls me, I must not say no.

EDGAR   The weight of this sad time we must obey;
Speak what we feel, not what we ought to say.
325   The oldest hath borne most; we that are young
Shall never see so much, nor live so long.

Exeunt, with dead march

---

2. A term of endearment, here used for Cordelia.
3. Do not disturb his departing soul.

4. Instrument of torture, used to stretch its victims.
5. From death, which already had a claim on it.

The Two Texts of *King Lear*

The following excerpts enable readers to compare, on facing pages, a sample passage from the quarto *History of King Lear* (1608) and the Folio *Tragedy of King Lear* (1623). (On the relation between the two texts, see above, p. 1109.) The quarto version of this scene seems to emphasize a French invasion of the kingdom, while the Folio text seems to emphasize an impending civil war.

From The History of King Lear, Scene 8

[*Storm.*] *Enter* KENT [DISGUISED,] AND [FIRST] GEN-
TLEMAN, AT SEVERAL° DOORS — *different*

KENT What's here, beside foul weather?

FIRST GENTLEMAN One minded like the weather,
Most unquietly.

KENT I know you. Where's the King?

FIRST GENTLEMAN Contending with the fretful element;
Bids the wind blow the earth into the sea

5 Or swell the curlèd waters 'bove the main,° — *mainland*
That things might change or cease; tears his white hair,
Which the impetuous blasts, with eyeless rage,
Catch in their fury and make nothing of;
Strives in his little world of man to outstorm

10 The to-and-fro-conflicting wind and rain.
This night, wherein the cub-drawn bear would couch,[1]
The lion and the belly-pinchèd wolf
Keep their fur dry, unbonneted° he runs, — *hatless; uncrowned*
And bids what will take all.

KENT But who is with him?

15 FIRST GENTLEMAN None but the fool, who labors to outjest
His heart-struck injuries.[2]

KENT Sir, I do know you,
And dare upon the warrant of my art[3]
Commend a dear° thing to you. There is division, — *entrust a crucial*
Although as yet the face of it be covered

20 With mutual cunning, 'twixt Albany and Cornwall;
But true it is. From France there comes a power
Into this scattered kingdom, who already,
Wise in° our negligence, have secret feet — *aware of*
In some of our best ports, and are at point° — *ready*

25 To show their open banner. Now to you:
If on my credit you dare build° so far — *if you trust me*
To make your speed to Dover, you shall find
Some that will thank you, making just° report — *accurate*
Of how unnatural and bemadding° sorrow — *maddening*

30 The king hath cause to plain.° — *complain*
I am a gentleman of blood and breeding,
And from some knowledge and assurance offer
This office° to you. — *role; duty*

FIRST GENTLEMAN I will talk farther with you.

35 KENT No, do not.

---

1. In which even the bear, though starving, having been sucked dry ("drawn") by its cub, would not go out to forage.
2. "To outjest": to relieve with laughter; to exorcise through ridicule. "Heart-struck injuries": injuries (from the betrayal of his paternal love) that penetrated to the heart.
3. On the basis of my skill (at judging people).

From The Tragedy of King Lear 3.1

Storm still. Enter KENT [*disguised*] *and* [THE FIRST]
GENTLEMAN, *severally*

KENT   Who's there, besides foul weather?

FIRST GENTLEMAN   One minded like the weather,
  Most unquietly.

KENT   I know you. Where's the King?

FIRST GENTLEMAN   Contending with the fretful elements;
  Bids the wind blow the earth into the sea
5 Or swell the curlèd waters 'bove the main,°   *mainland*
  That things might change or cease.

KENT   But who is with him?

FIRST GENTLEMAN   None but the Fool, who labors to outjest
  His heart-struck injuries.[1]

KENT   Sir, I do know you,
  And dare upon the warrant of my note[2]
10 Commend a dear° thing to you. There is division,   *entrust a crucial*
  Although as yet the face of it is covered
  With mutual cunning, 'twixt Albany and Cornwall,
  Who have—as who have not that their great stars
  Throned and set high[3]—servants, who seem no less,°   *who appear as such*
15 Which are to France the spies and speculations°   *observers*
  Intelligent of[4] our state. What hath been seen,
  Either in snuffs and packings° of the Dukes,   *quarrels and plots*
  Or the hard rein° which both of them hath borne   *treatment*
  Against the old kind King; or something deeper,
20 Whereof perchance these are but furnishings°—   *pretexts*

FIRST GENTLEMAN   I will talk further with you.

KENT   No, do not.

1. See p. 1192, n. 2.
2. See p. 1192, n. 3.
3. I.e., as has everybody who has been favored by destiny.
4. Supplying intelligence about; well informed of.

For confirmation that I am much more
Than my out-wall,° open this purse, and take   °outward appearance
What it contains. If you shall see Cordelia—
As fear not but you shall—show her this ring
40   And she will tell you who your fellow° is,   °(Kent himself)
That yet you do not know. Fie on this storm!
I will go seek the King.
FIRST GENTLEMAN   Give me your hand.
Have you no more to say?
KENT   Few words, but to effect°   °but in importance
More than all yet: that when we have found the King—
45   In which endeavor I'll° this way, you that—   °I'll go
He that first lights on him holla the other.

                                        Exeunt severally

For confirmation that I am much more
Than my out-wall,° open this purse, and take   outward appearance
What it contains. If you shall see Cordelia—
As fear not but you shall—show her this ring
And she will tell you who that fellow° is   (Kent himself)
That yet you do not know. Fie on this storm!
I will go seek the King.
FIRST GENTLEMAN   Give me your hand. Have you no more to say?
KENT   Few words, but to effect° more than all yet: but in importance
That when we have found the King—in which your pain
That way, I'll this⁵—he that first lights on him
Holla the other.   *Exeunt [severally]*

5. In which effort you will go that way and I this.

THOMAS CAMPION
1567–1620

Thomas Campion was a law student, a physician, a composer, a writer of masques, and a poet. His first poetic attempts were in Latin. His love of quantitative versification in classical Latin poems carried over into his English poems and songs. In quantitative verse the syllables are arranged in patterns according to their length and duration (that is, according to the length of time it takes to pronounce them) rather than according to accent or stress; see, for instance, Campion's *Rose-cheeked Laura.* In his *Observations in the Art of English Poesy* he defended quantitative verse and disparaged the accentual, rhymed verse characteristic of poetry in English and the other vernacular languages. But his finest achievements as a lyric poet arise from the fact that he was both poet and composer. In the preface to one of his books, he wrote, "I have chiefly aimed to couple my words and notes lovingly together, which will be much for him to do that hath not power over both."

My sweetest Lesbia[1]

My sweetest Lesbia, let us live and love,
And though the sager sort our deeds reprove,
Let us not weigh them. Heav'n's great lamps do dive
Into their west, and straight again revive,
5   But soon as once set is our little light,
Then must we sleep one ever-during night.

If all would lead their lives in love like me,
Then bloody swords and armor should not be;
No drum nor trumpet peaceful sleeps should move,
10   Unless alarm came from the camp of love.
But fools do live, and waste their little light,
And seek with pain their ever-during night.

When timely death my life and fortune ends,
Let not my hearse be vexed with mourning friends,
15   But let all lovers, rich in triumph, come
And with sweet pastimes grace my happy tomb;
And Lesbia, close up thou my little light,
And crown with love my ever-during night.

1601

I care not for these ladies

I care not for these ladies
That must be wooed and prayed;
Give me kind Amaryllis,
The wanton country[1] maid.

---

1. Imitated and partly translated from a poem by Catullus (87–ca. 54 B.C.E.), the Latin lyric poet who often celebrated the charms of Lesbia in his verses. This and the two lyrics that follow appeared, with musical settings, in *A Book of Airs,* which contains Campion's first work as a composer.
1. With an obscene pun—as also in line 9.

5   Nature art disdaineth;
Her beauty is her own.
   Her when we court and kiss,
   She cries "Forsooth, let go!"
   But when we come where comfort is,
10   She never will say no.

If I love Amaryllis,
She gives me fruit and flowers;
But if we love these ladies,
We must give golden showers.
15   Give them gold that sell love,
Give me the nutbrown lass,
   Who when we court and kiss,
   She cries "Forsooth, let go!"
   But when we come where comfort is,
20   She never will say no.

These ladies must have pillows,
And beds by strangers wrought.
Give me a bower of willows,
Of moss and leaves unbought,
25   And fresh Amaryllis,
With milk and honey fed,
   Who when we court and kiss,
   She cries "Forsooth, let go!"
   But when we come where comfort is,
30   She never will say no.

1601

When to her lute Corinna sings

When to her lute Corinna sings,
Her voice revives the leaden° strings,   *i.e., heavy*
And doth in highest notes appear
As any challenged° echo clear;   *aroused*
5   But when she doth of mourning speak,
Ev'n with her sighs the strings do break.

And as her lute doth live or die,
Led by her passion, so must I:
For when of pleasure she doth sing,
10   My thoughts enjoy a sudden spring;
But if she doth of sorrow speak,
Ev'n from my heart the strings do break.

1601

Rose-cheeked Laura[1]

Rose-cheeked Laura, come,
Sing thou smoothly with thy beauty's
Silent music, either other°   *each the other*
    Sweetly gracing.

5   Lovely forms do flow
From concent[2] divinely framed;
Heav'n is music, and thy beauty's
    Birth is heavenly.

These dull notes we sing
10 Discords need for helps to grace them;
Only beauty purely loving
    Knows no discord,

But still moves delight,
Like clear springs renewed by flowing,
15 Ever perfect, ever in them-
    Selves eternal.

1602

Now winter nights enlarge

Now winter nights enlarge
The number of their hours,
And clouds their storms discharge
    Upon the airy towers.
5 Let now the chimneys blaze
    And cups o'erflow with wine,
Let well-tuned words amaze
    With harmony divine.
Now yellow waxen lights
10 Shall wait on honey Love,
While youthful revels, masques,° and courtly sights   *masked balls*
    Sleep's leaden spells remove.

This time doth well dispense
    With[1] lovers' long discourse;
15 Much speech hath some defense,
    Though beauty no remorse.
All do not all things well:
    Some[2] measures comely tread,
Some knotted riddles tell,

---

1. Written by Campion to illustrate his theories of versification in *Observations in the Art of English Poesy*, this song is a brilliant example of quantitative verse made musically effective in English.

2. Playing or singing together in harmony.
1. "Dispense / With": permit, allow.
2. I.e., some people. "Measures": dances; also poetic rhythms.

20   Some poems smoothly read.
    The Summer hath his joys,
      And Winter his delights;
    Though Love and all his pleasures are but toys,°   *trifles*
    They shorten tedious nights.

                            1617

There is a garden in her face

    There is a garden in her face,
    Where roses and white lilies grow;
      A heav'nly paradise is that place,
    Wherein all pleasant fruits do flow.
5   There cherries grow, which none may buy
      Till "Cherry ripe!"[1] themselves do cry.

    Those cherries fairly do enclose
    Of orient pearl a double row;
      Which when her lovely laughter shows,
10   They look like rosebuds filled with snow.
      Yet them nor° peer nor prince can buy,   *neither*
      Till "Cherry ripe!" themselves do cry.

    Her eyes like angels watch them still;
    Her brows like bended bows do stand,
15   Threatening with piercing frowns to kill
    All that attempt with eye or hand
      Those sacred cherries to come nigh,
      Till "Cherry ripe!" themselves do cry.

                            1617

Think'st thou to seduce me then[1]

    Think'st thou to seduce me then with words that have no meaning?
    Parrots so can learn to prate, our speech by pieces gleaning;
    Nurses teach their children so about the time of weaning.

    Learn to speak first, then to woo; to wooing much pertaineth:
5   He that courts us, wanting art, soon falters when he feigneth,
    Looks asquint on his discourse,[2] and smiles when he complaineth.

    Skillful anglers hide their hooks, fit baits for every season;
    But with crooked pins fish thou, as babes do that want reason:
    Gudgeons[3] only can be caught with such poor tricks of treason.

1. A familiar cry of London street vendors.
1. In this poem and the one following, Campion assumes the voice of a female speaker; the proce-dure is rare among early poets. Both poems are written in the old-fashioned metrical form known

as fourteeners—verses of fourteen or fifteen syl-lables, with seven accented beats.
2. Looks away from the lady to check on his script. "Wanting art": lacking skill.
3. Small fish.

10   Ruth[4] forgive me, if I erred from humane heart's compassion,
      When I laughed sometimes too much to see thy foolish fashion:
      But, alas, who less could do that found so good occasion?

                                                              1617

Fain would I wed

      Fain would I wed a fair young man that night and day could please me,
      When my mind or body grieved, that had the power to ease me.
      Maids are full of longing thoughts that breed a bloodless sickness,
      And that, oft I hear men say, is only cured by quickness.°   *liveliness, motion*
5   Oft have I been wooed and praised, but never could be movèd;
      Many for a day or so I have most dearly lovèd,
      But this foolish mind of mine straight° loathes the thing resolvèd;   *at once*
      If to love be sin in me, that sin is soon absolvèd.
      Sure I think I shall at last fly to some holy order;
10   When I once am settled there, then can I fly no farther.
      Yet I would not die a maid, because I had a mother,
      As I was by one brought forth, I would bring forth another.

                                                              1617

4. Pity, which misled the girl into seeming too complaisant.

THOMAS NASHE
1567–1601

Thomas Nashe, a Cambridge graduate, was a versatile writer of controversial pamphlets, satires, plays, a novel, and lyric verse. He was one of the so-called University Wits who in the late 1580s came to London and wrote for the stage and the press. They lived short and precarious lives: Nashe was about thirty-three when he died; his friend Christopher Marlowe died at twenty-nine; George Peele, at thirty; and Robert Greene, at thirty-two. Nashe's polemical enemy was an older man, Gabriel Harvey, Spenser's friend; Nashe exchanged a series of vituperative and slanderous pamphlets with Harvey in which Nashe's talent for invective and mockery was exploited to the fullest. In June 1599 the ecclesiastical authorities ordered that "all Nashe's books and Doctor Harvey's books be taken wheresoever they may be found and that none of their books be ever printed hereafter."

Nashe wrote a festive comedy, *Summer's Last Will and Testament*; an attack on women called *The Anatomy of Absurdity*; an attack on social abuses of every kind titled *Pierce Penniless, His Supplication to the Devil*; and a strident comparison between the sins of the Jews that led to the destruction of Jerusalem and the current morals and manners of London, called *Christ's Tears Over Jerusalem*. His picaresque narrative, *The Unfortunate Traveler or the Life of Jack Wilton*, recounts the adventures of the young hero all over Europe, including fictive encounters with Erasmus and the poet Surrey, the massacre of the Protestant radicals in Germany, and harrowing, melodramatic exploits in seductive, corrupt, and plague-ridden Italy. Nashe's outlook, like that of many satirists, was conservative; he attacked innovation and praised the purported stability and order of the past. But there is something wild and extreme in his vision of the world, and his prose style, which sometimes sounds like modern experimental fiction, is headlong, impatient, colloquial, and vivid.

A Litany in Time of Plague[1]

Adieu, farewell, earth's bliss,
This world uncertain is;
Fond° are life's lustful joys,   *foolish*
Death proves them all but toys,°   *trifles*
5 None from his darts can fly;
I am sick, I must die.
    Lord, have mercy on us!

Rich men, trust not in wealth,
Gold cannot buy you health;
10 Physic himself must fade,
All things to end are made.
The plague full swift goes by;
I am sick, I must die.
    Lord, have mercy on us!

15 Beauty is but a flower
Which wrinkles will devour;
Brightness falls from the air,
Queens have died young and fair,
Dust hath closèd Helen's eye.
20 I am sick, I must die.
    Lord, have mercy on us!

Strength stoops unto the grave,
Worms feed on Hector brave;
Swords may not fight with fate,
25 Earth still holds ope her gate.
"Come, come!" the bells do cry.
I am sick, I must die.
    Lord, have mercy on us!

Wit with his wantonness
30 Tasteth death's bitterness;
Hell's executioner
Hath no ears for to hear
What vain art can reply.
I am sick, I must die.
35   Lord, have mercy on us!

Haste, therefore, each degree,
To welcome destiny;
Heaven is our heritage,

1. This lyric is from *A Pleasant Comedy Called Summer's Last Will and Testament,* acted before the archbishop of Canterbury in his palace at Croydon in 1592 and published in 1600.

Earth but a player's stage;
40   Mount we unto the sky.
I am sick, I must die.
Lord, have mercy on us!

1592   1600

From Pierce Penniless, His Supplication to the Devil

[THE DEFENSE OF PLAYS]

That state or kingdom that is in league with all the world, and hath no foreign sword to vex it, is not half so strong or confirmed to endure as that which lives every hour in fear of invasion. There is a certain waste of the people for whom there is no use but war; and these men must have some employment still to cut them off; *Nam si foras hostem non habent, domi invenient.*[1] If they have no service abroad, they will make mutinies at home. Or if the affairs of the state be such as cannot exhale all these corrupt excrements, it is very expedient they have some light toys to busy their heads withal, cast before them as bones to gnaw upon, which may keep them from having leisure to intermeddle with higher matters.

To this effect, the policy of plays is very necessary, howsoever some shallow-brained censurers (not the deepest searchers into the secrets of government) mightily oppugn them. For whereas the afternoon being the idlest time of the day, wherein men that are their own masters (as gentlemen of the court, the Inns of the Court,[2] and the number of captains and soldiers about London) do wholly bestow themselves upon pleasure, and that pleasure they divide (how virtuously, it skills[3] not) either into gaming, following of harlots, drinking, or seeing a play; is it not then better (since of four extremes all the world cannot keep them but they will choose one) that they should betake them to the least, which is plays? Nay, what if I prove plays to be no extreme, but a rare exercise of virtue? First, for the subject of them, (for the most part) it is borrowed out of our English chronicles, wherein our forefathers' valiant acts (that have lain long buried in rusty brass and worm-eaten books) are revived, and they themselves raised from the grave of oblivion, and brought to plead their aged honors in open presence; than which, what can be a sharper reproof to these degenerate, effeminate days of ours?

How would it have joyed brave Talbot,[4] the terror of the French, to think that after he had lain two hundred years in his tomb he should triumph again on the stage, and have his bones new embalmed with the tears of ten thousand spectators at least (at several times), who in the tragedian that represents his person imagine they behold him fresh bleeding.

I will defend it against any collian[5] or clubfisted usurer of them all, there is no immortality can be given a man on earth like unto plays. What talk I to them of immortality, that are the only underminers of honor, and do envy

---

1. Adapted from Livy, *History* 30.9. Nashe translates.
2. Law schools.
3. Matters.
4. In the play *Harey the VI* produced by Strange's

men for Henslowe on March 3, 1592. What relation this play had to the Shakespearean *1 Henry VI* is uncertain, but Nashe's reference would fit 1.4.39–43 and 2.3.14–24.
5. Rascal (the usual form is "cullion").

any man that is not sprung up by base brokery like themselves? They care not if all the ancient houses were rooted out, so that like the burgomasters of the Low Countries they might share the government amongst them as states, and be quartermasters of our monarchy. All arts to them are vanity; and if you tell them what a glorious thing it is to have Henry the Fifth represented on the stage leading the French king prisoner, and forcing both him and the Dolphin[6] to swear fealty, "Aye, but," will they say, "what do we get by it?" Respecting neither the right of fame that is due to true nobility deceased, nor what hopes of eternity are to be proposed to adventurous minds to encourage them forward, but only their execrable lucre and filthy unquenchable avarice.

They know when they are dead they shall not be brought upon the stage for any goodness, but in a merriment of the usurer and the devil, or buying arms of the herald, who gives them the lion without tongue, tail, or talons, because his master whom he must serve is a townsman and a man of peace, and must not keep any quarreling beasts to annoy his honest neighbors.

In plays, all cozenages,[7] all cunning drifts over-gilded with outward holiness, all stratagems of war, all the cankerworms that breed on the rust of peace, are most lively anatomized; they show the ill success of treason, the fall of hasty climbers, the wretched end of usurpers, the misery of civil dissension, and how just God is evermore in punishing of murther. And to prove every one of these allegations could I propound the circumstances of this play and that play, if I meant to handle this theme otherwise than *obiter*.[8] What should I say more? They are sour pills of reprehension wrapped up in sweet words. Whereas some petitioners of the counsel against them object,[9] they corrupt the youth of the city and withdraw prentices from their work, they heartily wish they might be troubled with none of their youth nor their prentices; for some of them (I mean the ruder handicrafts' servants) never come abroad but they are in danger of undoing; and as for corrupting them when they come, that's false, for no play they have encourageth any man to tumults or rebellion, but lays before such the halter and the gallows; or praiseth or approveth pride, lust, whoredom, prodigality, or drunkenness, but beats them down utterly. As for the hindrance of trades and traders of the city by them, that is an article foisted in by the vintners, alewives, and victualers, who surmise if there were no plays they should have all the company that resort to them lie boozing and beer-bathing in their houses every afternoon. Nor so, nor so, good brother bottle-ale, for there are other places besides where money can bestow itself; the sign of the smock[1] will wipe your mouth clean; and yet I have heard ye have made her a tenant to your taphouses. But what shall he do that hath spent himself? Where shall he haunt? Faith, when dice, lust, and drunkenness, and all, have dealt upon him, if there be never a play for him to go to for his penny, he sits melancholy in his chamber, devising upon felony or treason, and how he may best exalt himself by mischief.

In Augustus' time (who was the patron of all witty sports) there happened a great fray in Rome about a player, insomuch as all the city was in an uproar; whereupon the emperor (after the broil was somewhat overblown) called the

---

6. Dauphin (son of the king of France).
7. Deceptions, cheats.
8. By the way.

9. The confutation of citizens' objections against players [Nashe's note].
1. Of a prostitute.

player before him, and asked what was the reason that a man of his quality durst presume to make such a brawl about nothing. He smilingly replied, "It is good for thee, O Caesar, that the people's heads are troubled with brawls and quarrels about us and our light matters; for otherwise they would look into thee and thy matters." Read Lipsius[2] or any profane or Christian politician, and you shall find him of this opinion. Our players are not as the players beyond sea, a sort of squirting bawdy comedians, that have whores and common courtesans to play women's parts, and forbear no immodest speech or unchaste action that may procure laughter; but our scene is more stately furnished than ever it was in the time of Roscius, our representations honorable and full of gallant resolution, not consisting like theirs of pantaloon, a whore, and a zany,[3] but of emperors, kings, and princes; whose true tragedies (*Sophocleo cothurno*[4]) they do vaunt.

Not Roscius nor Aesope,[5] those admired tragedians that have lived ever since before Christ was born, could ever perform more in action than famous Ned Allen.[6] I must accuse our poets of sloth and partiality that they will not boast in large impressions what worthy men (above all nations) England affords. Other countries cannot have a fiddler break a string but they will put it in print, and the old Romans in the writings they published thought scorn to use any but domestical examples of their own home-bred actors, scholars, and champions, and them they would extol to the third and fourth generation; cobblers, tinkers, fencers, none escaped them, but they mingled them all in one gallimaufry of glory.

Here I have used a like method, not of tying myself to mine own country, but by insisting in the experience of our time; and if I ever write anything in Latin (as I hope one day I shall), not a man of any desert here amongst us, but I will have up. Tarlton, Ned Allen, Knell, Bentley,[7] shall be made known to France, Spain, and Italy; and not a part that they surmounted in, more than other, but I will there note and set down, with the manner of their habits and attire.[8]

1592

From The Unfortunate Traveler, or The Life of Jack Wilton[1]

[ROMAN SUMMER]

I saw a summer banqueting house belonging to a merchant, that was the marvel of the world, and could not be matched except God should make another paradise. It was built round of green marble like a theater without; within there was a heaven and earth comprehended both under one roof. The heaven was a clear overhanging vault of crystal, wherein the sun and

2. Justus Lipsius (1547–1606), Belgian scholar and historian. "Politician": shrewd person.
3. Type parts in the *commedia dell' arte*.
4. With Sophoclean dignity.
5. These two Roman actors flourished about 70 B.C.E.
6. Edward Alleyn (1566–1626), the most celebrated Elizabethan actor.
7. Actors older than Alleyn and famous in the

period before 1588. Richard Tarlton (d.1588) was the most popular Elizabethan comedian.
8. Nashe never fulfilled this resolution.
1. *The Unfortunate Traveler*, published in 1594, recounts the many adventures of the scapegrace Jack Wilton. Toward the end of the book, Jack arrives at Rome, the site, in the usual English view, of roughly equal numbers of wonders and horrors.

moon and each visible star had his true similitude, shine, situation, and motion, and, by what enwrapped[2] art I cannot conceive, these spheres in their proper orbs observed their circular wheelings and turnings, making a certain kind of soft angelical murmuring music in their often windings and going about; which music the philosophers say in the true heaven,[3] by reason of the grossness of our senses, we are not capable of. For the earth, it was counterfeited in that likeness that Adam lorded over it before his fall. A wide, vast, spacious room it was, such as we would conceit[4] Prince Arthur's hall to be, where he feasted all his Knights of the Round Table together every Pentecost. The floor was painted with the beautifulest flowers that ever man's eye admired; which so lively were delineated that he that viewed them afar off and had not directly stood poringly over them, would have sworn they had lived indeed. The walls round about were hedged with olives and palm trees and all other odoriferous fruitbearing plants, which at any solemn entertainment dropped myrrh and frankincense. Other trees, that bare no fruit, were set in just order one against another, and divided the room into a number of shady lanes, leaving but one overspreading pine tree arbor where we sat and banqueted.

On the well-clothed boughs of this conspiracy of pine trees against the resembled[5] sunbeams were perched as many sorts of shrill-breasted birds as the summer hath allowed for singing men in her sylvan chapels. Who, though they were bodies without souls, and sweet-resembled substances without sense, yet by the mathematical experiments of long silver pipes secretly inrinded in the entrails of the boughs whereon they sat, and undiscernibly conveyed under their bellies into their small throats sloping, they whistled and freely caroled their natural field note. Neither went those silver pipes straight, but, by many-edged, unsundered writhings and crankled[6] wanderings aside, strayed from bough to bough into an hundred throats. But into this silver pipe so writhed and wandering aside, if any demand how the wind was breathed, forsooth the tail of the silver pipe stretched itself into the mouth of a great pair of bellows, where it was close soldered and bailed about with iron; it could not stir or have any vent betwixt. These bellows, with the rising and falling of leaden plummets wound up on a wheel, did beat up and down uncessantly, and so gathered in wind, serving with one blast all the snarled pipes to and fro of one tree at once. But so closely were all those organizing implements obscured in the corpulent trunks of the trees that every man there present renounced conjectures of art and said it was done by enchantment.

One tree for his fruit bare nothing but enchained chirping birds, whose throats being conduit-piped with squared narrow shells, and charged syringe-wise with searching sweet water driven in by a little wheel for the nonce,[7] that fed it afar off, made a spirting sound, such as chirping is, in bubbling upwards through the rough crannies of their closed bills.

Under tuition[8] of the shade of every tree that I have signified to be in this round hedge, on delightful leafy cloisters lay a wild tyrannous beast asleep all prostrate; under some, two together, as the dog nuzzling his nose under

2. I.e., concealed.
3. The music "in the true heaven" is the fabled music of the spheres.
4. Conceive, imagine.

5. Simulated. "Conspiracy": union.
6. Twisted.
7. For the purpose.
8. Protection.

the neck of the deer, the wolf glad to let the lamb lie upon him to keep him warm, the lion suffering the ass to cast his leg over him, preferring one honest unmannerly friend before a number of crouching pickthanks.[9] No poisonous beast there reposed (poison was not before our parent Adam transgressed).[1] There were no sweet-breathing panthers that would hide their terrifying heads to betray; no men-imitating hyenas that changed their sex to seek after blood. Wolves, as now when they are hungry eat earth,[2] so then did they feed on earth only and abstained from innocent flesh. The unicorn did not put his horn into the stream to chase away venom before he drank,[3] for then there was no such thing extant in the water or on the earth. Serpents were as harmless to mankind as they are still one to another; the rose had no cankers, the leaves no caterpillars, the sea no sirens, the earth no usurers. Goats then bare wool, as it is recorded in Sicily they do yet. The torrid zone was habitable; only jays loved to steal gold and silver to build their nests withal, and none cared for covetous clientry or running to the Indies. As the elephant understands his country speech, so every beast understood what man spoke. The ant did not hoard up against winter, for there was no winter, but a perpetual spring, as Ovid[4] saith. No frosts to make the green almond tree counted rash and improvident in budding soonest of all other; or the mulberry tree a strange politician[5] in blooming late and ripening early. The peach tree at the first planting was fruitful and wholesome, whereas now, till it be transplanted, it is poisonous and hateful.[6] Young plants for their sap had balm; for their yellow gum, glistering amber. The evening dewed not water on flowers, but honey. Such a golden age, such a good age, such an honest age, was set forth in this banqueting house.

Oh Rome, if thou hast in thee such soul-exalting objects, what a thing is heaven in comparison of thee, of which Mercator's globe[7] is a perfecter model than thou art? Yet this I must say to the shame of us Protestants: if good works may merit heaven, they do them, we talk of them. Whether superstition or no makes them unprofitable servants, that let pulpits decide; but there you shall have the bravest[8] ladies, in gowns of beaten gold, washing pilgrims' and poor soldiers' feet, and doing nothing, they and their waiting-maids, all the year long, but making shirts and bands for them against[9] they come by in distress. Their hospitals are more like noblemen's houses than otherwise; so richly furnished, clean kept and hot perfumed, that a soldier would think it a sufficient recompense for all his travel and his wounds, to have such a heavenly retiring place. For the pope and his pontificalibus[1] I will not deal with; only I will dilate unto you what happened whilst I was in Rome.

9. Sycophants.
1. The banqueting house represents the world before Adam's fall; thus it includes "no poisonous beast," since poison did not exist in prelapsarian Eden.
2. Both the earth-eating wolves and the sex-changing hyenas (and, below, the elephant who understands speech) derive from the collection of fabulous claims in the *Natural History* of Pliny the Elder (23–79 C.E.). The sweet-breathing panthers may have come from the same source, but the belief that the panther lures its victims by its (supposedly) sweet breath was commonplace.
3. The unicorn's horn was thought to be an anti-

dote for poison.
4. In his account of the Golden Age (*Metamorphoses* 1.89–112). Nashe's view of the prelapsarian world, like others, conflates it with the Golden Age.
5. Crafty plotter.
6. Again from Pliny.
7. The Flemish cartographer Gerardus Mercator designed terrestrial and celestial globes in 1541 and 1551, respectively; they were in common use in England when Nashe wrote.
8. Finest.
9. In case. "Bands": collars.
1. Vestments.

So it fell out that, it being a vehement hot summer when I was a sojourner there, there entered such a hotspurred[2] plague as hath not been heard of. Why, it was but a word and a blow, "Lord have mercy upon us," and he was gone. Within three quarters of a year in that one city there died of it a hundred thousand: look in Lanquet's *Chronicle*[3] and you shall find it. To smell of a nosegay that was poisoned, and turn your nose to a house that had the plague, it was all one. The clouds, like a number of cormorants that keep their corn till it stink and is musty, kept in their stinking exhalations till they had almost stifled all Rome's inhabitants. Physicians' greediness of gold made them greedy of their destiny. They would come to visit those with whose infirmity their art had no affinity; and even as[4] a man with a fee should be hired to hang himself, so would they quietly go home and die presently after they had been with their patients. All day and all night long, car-men did nothing but go up and down the streets with their carts, and cry "Have you any dead bodies to bury?" And had many times out of one house their whole loading. One grave was the sepulcher of seven score; one bed was the altar whereon whole families were offered.

The walls were hoared and furred with the moist scorching steam of their desolation. Even as, before a gun is shot off, a stinking smoke funnels out and prepares the way for him, so before any gave up the ghost, death arrayed in a stinking smoke stopped his nostrils and crammed itself full into his mouth that closed up his fellow's eyes, to give him warning to prepare for his funeral. Some died sitting at their meat, others as they were asking counsel of the physician for their friends. I saw at the house where I was hosted, a maid bring her master warm broth for to comfort him, and she sink down dead herself ere he had half eat it up.

1594

2. Fiery.
3. Wilton's travels supposedly took place early in the sixteenth century. (He meets such figures as Thomas More and Erasmus and serves as page to the poet Henry Howard, earl of Surrey.) In 1522, according to the chronicle history that Wilton cites, one of the recurrent epidemics of the Black Plague killed a hundred thousand people in Rome.
4. Just as if.

The Early Seventeenth Century
1603–1660

When Queen Elizabeth died on March 24, 1603, after more than four decades on the throne, her kinsman James VI of Scotland succeeded her as James I of England without the disruptions or attempted *coups* that had been feared. The nation breathed a sigh of relief and expected a new beginning. The change from an aged queen without progeny to a thirty-six-year-old king, with an attractive queen, Anne of Denmark, and children who could assure the succession, was cause for celebration. But there was also cause for unease, as the nation saw itself exchanging an English Deborah, whom God had favored with a miraculous victory over the Spanish Armada and who had declared herself married to her people, for an aloof Scotsman with a foreign entourage that might displace English place-seekers. The atmosphere and anxieties at the change of regimes are suggested by an entry in the diary of Lady Anne Clifford, then thirteen years old:

> About 10 o'clock King *James* was proclaimed in *Cheapside* by all the Council with great joy and triumph. I went to see and hear. This peaceable coming-in of the King was unexpected of all sorts of people. . . . At this time we used to go very much to *Whitehall*, and walked much in the garden which was frequented by lords and ladies, my Mother [Margaret Clifford, countess of Cumberland] being all full of hopes, every man expecting mountains and finding molehills. . . . We all went to *Tibbalds* [Theobalds] to see the King who used my Mother and aunt very graciously, but we all saw a great change between the fashion of the Court as it is now and of that in the Queen's time, for we were all lousy by sitting in the chamber of Sir *Thomas Erskine*. . . . About this time my Aunt *Warwick* went to meet the Queen [enroute from Scotland]. . . . Then my Mother and I went on our journey to overtake her, and killed three horses that day with extremity of heat. . . .

> Upon the 25th of July the King and Queen were crowned at *Westminster*, my Father and Mother both attended in their robes, my Aunt of *Bath* and my Uncle *Russell*, which solemn sight my Mother would not let me see because the plague was hot in *London*.

Because of the plague, public celebrations of the coronation were postponed until the following year, when the king made an elaborate progress through the City of London. He passed through ceremonial arches and viewed pageants that represented him in terms suited to his patriarchal and absolutist royal style: a Roman Augustus, a wise Solomon, a Sun King, and the ruler of a newly constituted Britain with England and Scotland linked. The progress was designed to testify to an ideal relationship between a ruler and his people, but it revealed tensions and misunderstandings on both sides. Unlike Elizabeth, James thoroughly disliked exposing himself at such close quarters to the tumultuous crowds. His plans for a full union between his two kingdoms found little favor with the English people. The relationships between the monarch and his people and between England and Scotland would be sources of deep and recurrent conflict throughout his reign, and long afterward.

Traditional literary and historical periods are arbitrary, and their association with monarchs' reigns even more so. Broad political and cultural movements—the Reformation, exploration and colonization, the rising bourgeois class in the cities, the printing press and the expansion of literacy, conflicts over gender roles, changes in perceptions of the self and of authorship—have a much longer time-frame. They span the centuries (roughly 1500–1700) that scholars refer to as the Renaissance when they mean to emphasize breaks with medieval culture and the Early Modern Period when they mean to emphasize seeds of the modern world. Nor do authors' lives and careers neatly conform to the conventional periods. Shakespeare wrote his great tragedies and romances in James I's reign; Donne wrote his elegies, satires, and some love poems in the last decade of Queen Elizabeth's. Milton completed *Paradise Lost* and wrote two other major poems in the 1660s. Yet recognizing the years 1603–60 as a period brings into focus important political, intellectual, cultural, and stylistic currents that bear directly upon literary production. It also permits attention to changes in worldview that helped shape the cultural and literary scene: Galileo's astronomy, Bacon's empiricism, justifications for revolution, and the seismic shift in consciousness that, in 1649, allowed for the formal trial, conviction, and execution of an anointed king.

STATE AND CHURCH, 1603–40

Soon after James I's ascension, the Elizabethan settlement in church and state began to unravel. By great astuteness, by appointing brilliant ministers, and by playing complex roles as female monarch and Petrarchan lady, eliciting both obedience and love, Elizabeth had managed to maintain control over her Parliaments, retain the loyalty and devotion of most of her subjects, and win respect abroad. The Stuart kings, James I and his son Charles I, were unable to do this, engaging in constant confrontations with their Parliaments and subjects over taxes, religion, unpopular ministers, and parliamentary rights. Elizabeth did not try to define precisely how power is divided in what was usually described as a "mixed" government of Monarch, Lords, and Commons. James, while yet in Scotland, published two arguments for royal absolutism, *The True Law of Free Monarchies* (1597) and *Basilikon Doran* (1598). These works, both reissued in 1603, proclaim the divine right of kings as God's deputies and as fathers of their people and explain that monarchs are "free" in that they are accountable only to God. A series of analogies is seen to structure a patriarchal social order: as God is absolute ruler of the universe, so is the king of his people and the father of his family. James also claimed a role as shaper of culture in other published works, among them original poems, a translation of the psalms, a treatise on witchcraft, and a vigorous polemic against tobacco.

By contrast with Elizabeth's, James's court was disorderly and indecorous, marked by hard drinking and late-night feasting, a craze for hunting, and great extravagance. While Elizabeth had created eight new peers, James created sixty, selling peerages and noble titles as a means of raising funds. The court was in a constant state of financial crisis. As early as 1605, the king lamented that "it is a horror to me to think of the height of my place, the greatness of my debts, and the smallness of my means." Unlike Elizabeth, James had to maintain separate households for his queen and for the heir apparent, Prince Henry. The three courts had markedly different styles. The queen's household had places for female as well as male courtiers and separate channels for patronage, the most important being the queen's favorite, Lucy Russell, countess of Bedford, who was a major patron of Donne and Jonson. Prince Henry also patronized authors and scholars (among them Sir Walter Ralegh, who was writing, in prison, his *History of the World*, and George Chapman, who was translating Homer). His household became a focus for militant Protestants who were seeking more reform at home and more vigorous support of Protestantism abroad.

James himself relied increasingly on favorites who became channels for patronage in all spheres: first Robert Car, earl of Somerset, then George Villiers, duke of Buckingham. The attachment James formed for these favorites was highly romantic. "God so love me," the king wrote to Buckingham, "as I only desire to live in the world for your sake, and that I would rather live banished in any part of the earth with you than live a sorrowful widow's life without you." Such sentiments, not surprisingly, gave rise to widespread rumors of homosexual activities at court. The rumors are certainly plausible, though the surviving evidence of same-sex relationships in Early Modern England is extremely difficult to interpret. Sodomy was a crime punishable by death, but prosecutions were extremely rare. English law simply declined to recognize the possibility of lesbian acts. From Shakespeare's sonnets to James's letters, we find avowals of love and desire between men which may sometimes be formal expressions of affection based on classical models, or, alternatively, expressions of passionate physical and spiritual love. The interpretive difficulty is compounded by the absence in the period of any clear reference to homosexual "identity," though there are many references to same-sex acts and feelings. What is clear is that male friendships at the court of James and elsewhere were suffused with an eroticism, at once delightful and threatening, that subsequent periods policed more anxiously.

Religious tensions mounted during James's reign. The divisive energies of the Reformation had been tamed under Elizabeth by the establishment of a national church that accommodated, more or less comfortably, the great majority of her subjects, whether mostly Catholic or mostly Protestant in their religious views. During the first decade of James's reign, this accommodation held. The discovery and thwarting of the "Gunpowder Plot" in 1605, in which Guy Fawkes and a band of Roman Catholic conspirators plotted to blow up the Houses of Parliament and seize control of the government, unified English Protestants in a wave of anti-Catholic sentiment and support for the monarch. James, it seemed, had been preserved by a divine miracle even as Elizabeth had been by the defeat of the Armada. Also, the king's sponsorship of the so-called King James Bible (the Authorized Version, 1611) was a powerful force for Protestant unity.

Religion was such a vital cement for maintaining social and political order that, for almost everybody, genuine separation of church and state was unthinkable. Yet Christians thought it absolutely vital for their salvation or damnation to make right decisions about controversial theological issues: what to believe about predestination? how to conduct public worship? how to read, understand, and explicate scripture? what private devotions and meditations to use? what church was established by Christ? how to know if one is saved? So it is not surprising that Roman Catholics and various kinds of Puritans resisted the Established Church and that the Established Church tried to repress that opposition.

There were still many open or covert Roman Catholics who paid stiff fines for recusancy (failing to take the sacrament in the Established Church). They were also barred from taking degrees in the universities or holding public office or practicing at the bar, since to do so required an oath recognizing the monarch's supremacy over the church. Catholic priests, if captured, might be executed as traitors in the usual grisly fashion of hanging, drawing, disemboweling, and quartering. Yet there were Catholics in high places. Some ancient noble houses held to the old religion. And when Queen Anne refused to take the sacrament at her coronation there was intense speculation that she was a covert Catholic, speculation that continued (without being actually proved) throughout the reign.

From the other side, Puritans, as they were disparagingly called, pressed for more reformation in doctrine, ritual, and especially in church government, so as to bring the English church into closer conformity with the Presbyterian Church organization in Geneva, as established by the Protestants reformer John Calvin. Theology as such was not the issue, since much of the clergy accepted some version of Calvinism, as did King James. However, within that consensus Puritans tended to hold more extreme views about predestination (God's consignment of individuals to salvation or damnation—election and reprobation—without reference to their own acts or merit) and about the total depravity of humankind after the Fall. Many Puritans sought to remain within the Established Church but wanted to eliminate what they saw as the "popish" elements in the liturgy of *The Book of Common Prayer* and the "idolatrous" religious images in churches, e.g., religious statues, stained-glass windows, and an ornate high altar. They emphasized preaching and reading the Bible, not sacraments, as the core of religious practice; they sought moral and social reform through laws governing recreation, sabbath-keeping, drunkenness, and public order; and they emphasized the individual's direct responsibility for his or her own faith and for fulfilling his or her vocation or calling in the world, counting success as a possible indicator of election to salvation. The largest Puritan denomination, the Presbyterians, held that the Bible mandated church government by Presbyters (ministers), Lay Elders, and Synods (regional and national convocations) and agitated to substitute that organization for the Established Church hierarchy of archbishops, bishops, and priests. Some separatist Puritans (Congregationalists, Brownists, Anabaptists) wanted no national church, only individual gathered churches of the elect; some of them went to Holland or New England to escape repression.

Prince Henry's sudden death in 1612 dashed the hopes of Puritans and other reformist Protestants, prompting an outpouring of funeral elegies and laments reminiscent of the response to Sir Philip Sidney's early death in 1586. Prince Charles became heir apparent, and Henry's role as a potential leader of international Protestantism was partly filled by Frederick, Elector Palatine, who married James's daughter Elizabeth in 1613. Reformist Protestants urged James to take an active military role in the Thirty-Years' War (1618–48), which erupted over Frederick's claims to Bohemia and raged all over Europe, pitting Protestant against Roman Catholic nations. But James sought, unsuccessfully, to play peacemaker in that conflict. In 1623 he set plans in motion to marry Prince Charles to the Catholic Infanta of Spain, but when those plans collapsed over religious issues the nation was overjoyed. When Charles married the French princess Henrietta Maria instead there was little objection: though Catholic, she was at least not Spanish. The English antipathy to Catholic Spain reached back to Mary Tudor's reign (with her Spanish husband, Phillip II) and it intensified to white heat with the threat of invasion by the Spanish Armada (1588).

The ascent of Charles I to the throne in 1625 brought a palpable change in monarchical style. Unlike his father, Charles was not a theorist of royal absolutism and the divine right of kings, but he acted on those principles with consistency and inflexibility. By temperament James was given to compromise, whereas Charles held out for his royal prerogatives. He dissolved Parliament three times and in 1629 began nearly a decade of "personal rule" without Parliament, raising money through special taxes that were widely denounced as illegal and governing through a much-hated cabinet council: Buckingham, the earl of Strafford, and Archbishop Laud. Religious conflicts also intensified. Queen Henrietta Maria brought with her from France to England an entourage of Roman Catholic priests and followers and promoted the conversion to Catholicism of several English noblewomen in her court. The appointment in 1633 of William Laud as archbishop of Canterbury, the ecclesiastical head of the English Church, proved to be a watershed event. Throughout the 1630s Laud promoted the rapid growth of a high Anglican faction within the church, conforming its ceremony, ritual, and doctrine more closely to Roman Catholicism. The altar rather than the pulpit again dominated the church, making the eucharist the primary element in worship, rather than preaching. Ministers of Puritan tendency were dispossessed of their livings, and the full liturgy of The Book of Common Prayer was required in every parish. In theology Laud threw down the gauntlet to much of the nation by imposing an Arminian rather than a Calvinist interpretation on the

Thirty-Nine Articles of the Church of England—a doctrine of Free Will, that is, rather than Predestination.

Through both reigns, but especially that of Charles, resistance to Stuart absolutism came from several quarters. The Commons in Parliament insisted on their own rights and powers and demanded reforms in return for voting subsidies. As the peerage grew more impoverished, due in part to changes in agriculture but also to the expense of maintaining their status in the lavish courts, many peers of ancient lineage grew increasingly disaffected. Some Puritans and reform-minded clergy found ways to urge their causes in the pulpit and the press. Also, the wealthy bourgeois in the cities gained considerable power as sources of needed funds: they often supplied loans to the Crown and also funded exploration and colonization in the New World and elsewhere through such corporations as the East and West India Companies.

As the 1630s drew to a close, Archbishop Laud and Charles attempted to impose *The Book of Common Prayer* and episcopal organization upon Presbyterian Scotland. When the Scots resisted, Charles took this as a direct challenge to his authority, being persuaded that to dismantle ecclesiastical hierarchy threatened hierarchy everywhere and ultimately the Crown: "No Bishop, No King." Charles's military action against Scotland (The First and Second Bishops' Wars in 1639–40) was funded by extra-legal taxes, but met with abject failure. Exacerbating the situation, Laud laid down new canons for the English church, requiring full conformity in liturgy and preaching and an oath from all clergy opposing any change in the church government then in place. Riots in the London streets and Scots occupation of several northern English cities forced Charles to call the so-called "Long Parliament," which would soon be managing a revolution.

LITERATURE AND CULTURE, 1603–40

The earlier seventeenth century brought old and new ideas about the nature of things into sharp opposition. An inherited body of concepts and images was still available to be used by Donne, Burton, and others, even as they were being questioned or displaced: the Ptolemaic universe with its nine concentric spheres whose movements produce music, its circling sun and fixed earth, and its assumption of perfection above the moon and corruption beneath; the four elements—fire, air, water, earth—that comprise the matter of all things; and the four humors of the body—choler, blood, phlegm, and melancholy—that determine temperament and in great imbalance make for disease, mental and physical. Jacobeans thought of themselves as especially prone to melancholy: Shakespeare's Hamlet and Jacques in *As You Like It* are melancholics, as is Bosola in Webster's *The Duchess of Malfi*. Robert Burton wrote a massive and thoroughly delightful treatise on the malady, which he thought universal, *The Anatomy of Melancholy* (1621). Milton's title figure in *Il Penseroso* is a benign exemplar of that temperament, which was commonly associated with scholars. Key concepts of this inherited system were order and analogy, often rendered in striking literary images. Donne was especially fond of the macrocosm/microcosm parallel according to which the human being is seen as "a little world" or recapitulation of the world itself; and almost everyone believed in some version of the "chain" of being that links and orders all species hierarchically.

But this system, with its *a priori* assumptions and reliance upon ancient authority, was challenged by Francis Bacon's new emphasis on scientific method, as well as by actual experiments such as Gabriel Harvey's discovery of the circulation of the blood and Galileo's telescope, which supplied evidence confirming the Copernican astronomy. Galileo dislodged the earth from its former fixed and stable position at the center of the cosmos and, in defiance of all ordinary observation, sent it whirling about the sun; he also found evidence of change and corruption in the heavens and advanced mind-boggling speculations about life on other planets and infinite universes. Donne, like other writers of his age, responded to the new ideas, giving voice to the anxieties they produced in his *Anatomy of the World*:

> And new philosophy calls all in doubt,
> The element of fire is quite put out;
> The sun is lost, and the earth, and no man's wit
> Can well direct him where to look for it.

Milton, however, embraced the new science, referring with pride to a visit during his European tour to "the famous Galileo, grown old, a prisoner to the Inquisition for thinking in astronomy otherwise than the Franciscan and Dominican licensers thought." In *Paradise Lost* he made complex poetic use of the astronomical controversy.

In both reigns, the court was an important site of literary activity. Births, marriages, and funerals in the royal family prompted celebratory or elegiac verse, as did other royal occasions. Queen Anne played a major role in giving distinctive form and prominence to the court masque, traditionally presented at Christmastide and most often on Twelfth Night (January 6). The spectacular and extravagant masques devised by Inigo Jones, written by Ben Jonson, and danced by royal and noble personages portray King James as source of all power and splendor in the kingdom. *The Masque of Blackness*, anthologized here, praises him as the Sun-King whose powers could "blanch an Ethiop" and bring other races and nations to desire and conform to the English standard of beauty. Masques customarily end with the masquers unmasking and dancing with other courtiers, symbolizing the fusion of the ideal world and the Stuart court. But masques like *Blackness* and the *Masque of Queens*, produced and danced by Queen Anne and her ladies, also served to assert their own interests and power and to enact some resistance to the king's control. Masques performed by Prince Henry display a similar tension between competing ideals and interests.

Beyond the court, some noblemen retained their status as powerful local patrons with many clients, including poets and playwrights. Especially prominent were the interrelated families of the Sidneys at Penshurst and the Herberts at Wilton. Ben Jonson's country-house poem *To Penshurst* celebrates the Sidney estate as an alternative ideal to the court, hospitable alike to poets and kings; his collection of poems *The Forest* also includes several other poems associated with the Sidney family. Aemilia Lanyer's country-house poem of about the same date, *The Description of Cooke-Ham*, celebrates the estate occupied by Margaret Clifford, countess of Cumberland, and her daughter Anne (author of the *Diary* quoted above), crediting her residence there with nurturing her poetry. Jonson's book of *Epigrams* and Lanyer's dedicatory poems construct imagined communities of worthy personages and patrons honored by and honoring the poet. Coteries of friends also promoted and circulated literary works. Donne addressed several verse letters and some of his *Songs and Sonnets* to male friends in the law courts and at court; later he became part of a coterie formed around his patron, Lucy Russell, countess of Bedford, with whom he sometimes exchanged poems.

The church also promoted writing of several kinds: treatises of devotion, meditation, and instruction; controversial tracts (like Donne's *Pseudo-Martyr* against the Roman Catholics); cases of conscience that work out difficult moral issues in complex situations; and especially sermons. This is an age in which everyone heard sermons at least once and often twice on Sunday, as well as on all days of special religious or national celebration. Sermons were at least an hour long and often much longer. Congregants, especially children, were urged to outline them, repeat them later, and meditate on them. The essence of a sermon, Protestants agreed, is the careful exposition of Scripture, and its purpose is to instruct and move. Gifted Church of England preachers like Donne and Launcelot Andrews called on all the resources of artful rhetoric and elegant style to enthrall their congregations. They probed the words and phrases of a Scripture text by wordplay, allusions, conceits, and quotations from the learned languages, but Andrews's linguistic analysis was curt and often dialogic, while Donne's was flowing and rhythmical, dense with paradoxes and graphic images. By contrast, many Puritans sought a logical, undecorated style that would display God's word in its own splendor, unadorned by human wit. In his treatise on preaching, *The Art of Prophecying*, William Perkins declared, "It is a by-word with us: It was a very plain sermon. And I say again, the plainer, the better." But other Puritans, like Richard Sibbes, used biblical metaphors and powerful, affecting rhetoric to apply the biblical text closely to their congregations, so as to move them to good.

The City of London was also an important site for literary creation. City officials commissioned Lord Mayors' pageants and other civic entertainments. Also, the numerous booksellers contracted for and published books of domestic advice, devotional treatises, "how-to-do-it" manuals, and tracts of political and religious controversy. The theaters continued to flourish in the Liberties just outside the City, and therefore not under London's jurisdiction; this was the only sphere in which authors could support themselves by writing. Shakespeare was at the height of his powers: *King Lear*, *Othello*, *Macbeth*, *Twelfth Night*, *The Tempest*, and several others were staged during the early years of James's reign. So were Ben Jonson's major comedies— *Volpone*, *The Alchemist*, and *Epicoene*—as well as *Bartholomew Fair*, Jonson's contribution to City Comedy. That new kind, practiced by Thomas Middleton, Thomas Heywood, and others, drew satirical and comic matter from the life of London. The most important new playwright was John Webster, whose dark tragedies *The Duchess of Malfi* and *The White Devil* combined gothic horror with poetry of stunning beauty.

This era saw important changes in poetic fashion. Several prominent Elizabethan genres were no longer much in evidence: long allegorical or mythological narratives, sonnet sequences, and pastoral poems. Nor were such stylistic features as nature imagery, florid ornament, and sonorous lyricism. The norm was coming to be short, very concentrated poems in a colloquial and often witty "plain style." The major poets of these years, Donne, Jonson, and George Herbert, led this shift, as well as the rise to prominence of other genres: love elegy and satire after the classical models of Ovid and Horace, epigram, verse epistle, dramatic monologue, meditative religious lyric, and country-house poem. These three poets represent three distinct modes of authorship, but have in common a pronounced anxiety about the nature of literary production and the relation of the author to society. All three exercised an important influence on poets of the next generation.

John Donne, whose imprudent marriage cost him a much-desired career in the court bureaucracy but who later became a famous preacher and dean of St. Paul's Cathedral, cast himself in the older mold of gentleman amateur, circulating his poems in manuscript to friends and coterie circles, and largely avoiding print publication (his poems were published posthumously in 1633). In both their style and their content, Donne's poems were designed to be read by a select few rather than the public at large. His best poems explore the private worlds of love and religion, often developing passionate dialectical arguments that set them in anxious opposition to the public world. His style is characterized by learned terms and images, speechlike and often unmelodic verses, and strikingly dramatic language that often evokes a scene in progress. It is also characterized by witty play with paradoxes, ironies and the conjunction of opposites, as in the so-called "metaphysical conceit"—a surprising metaphor that (as Samuel Johnson later observed) links together images from very different ranges of experience. Donne took particular delight in challenging his sophisticated readers by interchanging the vocabularies of sexual and religious love both in his love poems and in his religious poems. Donne has sometimes been regarded as the founder of a "metaphysical school" of poetry, but that classification is not very useful. We find some echoes of Donne's style in some later poets such as Thomas Carew, who praised Donne as "Monarch of wit," John Cleveland, Abraham Cowley, and Andrew Marvell. But neither they nor the other poets sometimes linked with Donne (Herbert, Vaughan, Crashaw, Traherne) can be usefully classified as members of a "school," since none of them is very like Donne, nor are they like one another.

Ben Jonson staked his claim as a new kind of professional author when he published his court masques, his plays for the public theater, and two collections of poems in an elegant folio titled *Works* in the same year (1616) that King James published his treatises and poems under the same title. Jonson's finest poems celebrate the social world of friendship and community and embody the classical values of simplicity, restraint, economy, decorum, good workmanship, and art. Important principles of his poetics can be gleaned from his comments on poets and poetry to his friend, William Drummond of Hawthornden, and from his volume of extracts from classical sources: that nature first and then art makes the poet; that the poet's formation demands wit, judgment, and the proper imitation of models; and that the ideal poetic style is strong and plain (not abstruse like Donne's): "Pure and neat language I love, yet plain and customary." A ruling principle for Jonson is decorum—the proper fit of style to subject. Another is that the best art conceals art. In contrast to Donne, Jonson cast himself as the father of a brood of poetic sons—known as the Tribe or Sons of Ben—and met regularly with some of them in the Apollo Room of the Devil Tavern in London. Robert Herrick and many of the poets known as Cavaliers for their attachment to the court—Carew, Lovelace, Suckling, Henry Vaughan in his secular verse, Thomas Randolph, Sir Charles Cotton, Edmund Waller—either acknowledged the relationship or gave some evidence of it.

George Herbert, pastor to a small country parish, was a very different kind of author from Donne, who wrote to please his friends and patrons, or Jonson, who wrote to instruct the court and country. Herbert destroyed his secular verse in English and turned his volume of religious verse over to a friend on his deathbed, desiring him to print it if he thought it would be useful "to some dejected poor soul" and otherwise to burn it. The 177 lyrics contained in that volume, *The Temple* (1633), display a complex religious sensibility and great artistic subtlety in an amazing variety of kinds, stanzaic forms, and rhythmic patterns. In several of these poems, Herbert agonized about the paradoxical necessity, and at the same time impossibility, of a Christian poet giving fit and sincere praise to God. He also questioned whether literary art is appropriate to divine praises and if so, what kind of art? Several poems renounce old poetic styles and ornaments for a new, plain, devotional, and biblical mode, exploring the question posed in *Jordan I*, "Is there in truth no beauty?" Herbert was the major influence on the next generation of religious lyric poets and was explicitly recognized as such by Thomas Vaughan and Richard Crashaw, though Crashaw's baroque, lushly sensuous poetry bears little resemblance to his. The influence of Herbert is occasionally evident in Traherne, Marvell, and the American colonial poet Edward Taylor.

The Jacobean era (so-called from King James I) also saw the emergence of what would become a major new prose genre, the familiar essay. Francis Bacon brought it to England in a form very different from the intimate, tentative, conversational essay developed some decades earlier in France by Montaigne. Bacon's fifty-eight short sketches have, by contrast, a pithy, sententious style and a tone of cool objectivity, as if presenting society's accumulated practical wisdom on such topics as *Marriage and the Single Life, Truth, Simulation and Dissimulation, Ambition, Followers and Friends,* and *Suitors.* In the final edition of the *Essays* (1625), more than half deal with public life or public affairs, written from the vantage point of the man of affairs concerned to make his way in the world. They voice precepts of moral wisdom and public virtue, though tempered by expediency and self-interest. The combination provides a penetrating insight into the interests, problems, and modes of thought of the ruling class in Jacobean society. Bacon's other works are analyses of the state of knowledge in England and proposals for placing it on a scientific basis of induction and experimentation. His fictional utopia *The New Atlantis* imagines a society based on the Baconian dream of scientific learning and research.

These years mark the entry of Englishwomen, in some numbers, into authorship and publication. Their works rewrite discourses that repress or diminish women—patriarchy, gender hierarchy, the apostle Paul's teachings on marriage—and shape several genres to women's concerns. Most of these women were from the nobility or gentry and all were educated above the norm for women in the period. While some (Anne Clifford, Margaret Hoby, Lady Mildmay, Elizabeth Melville, and Martha Moulsworth) wrote private diaries and autobiographies that remained in manuscript, Dorothy Leigh published the most popular of several mothers' manuals, extending the sphere of domestic power allotted to women in the patriarchal family. Rachel Speght, the first female polemicist who can be securely identified, published a defense of women (1617) as a riposte to a notorious Jacobean attack on "Lewd, idle, froward, and unconstant women," as well as a long meditative poem and a dream-vision poem allegorizing her education (1621). Aemilia Lanyer is the first Englishwoman to publish a substantial volume of original poems (1611), containing poetic dedications, a long poem on Christ's passion, and a country-house poem, all defending women's interests and worth. Elizabeth Cary, Lady Falkland, is the first Englishwoman to publish a tragedy, *Mariam* (1613), a Senecan closet drama that probes the situation of a queen-wife subjected to domestic and political tyranny. Lady Mary Wroth, niece of Sir Philip Sidney and the countess of Pembroke, wrote three works that are firsts for an Englishwoman. Her Petrarchan sonnet sequence *Pamphilia to Amphilanthus* (1621) gives voice and subjectivity to the woman lover-poet. It was published with her long prose romance *Urania* (1621), which presents a range of women's responses to life and love as well as many spheres for women's exercise of agency and power—as rulers, counselors, scholars, storytellers, poets, and seers. Her unpublished pastoral tragicomedy *Love's Victory* depicts a nonhierarchical pastoral world whose ideality depends on female friendships and female control.

When Charles and Henrietta Maria came to the throne in 1625, the changed court style in this Caroline era directly affected the arts and literature. As the Puritan Lucy Hutchinson recalled, "The fools and bawds, mimics and catamites of the former court grew out of fashion," to be replaced by a new sophistication and refinement and a courtly code idealizing female beauty, heterosexual love, and harmony. Charles and his queen were art collectors on a large scale and patrons of such painters as Rubens and Van Dyke; the latter portrayed Charles in magnificent, heroic poses, mounted on a splendid white stallion. A fashionable artistic and literary cult of platonic love mythologized the two monarchs as the ideal Platonic hermaphrodite, their union joining together heroic virtue and divine beauty or love. This was the dominant theme of Caroline court masques by Jonson, Thomas Carew, William Davenant, and others, also mounted by Inigo Jones. These masques were even more extravagantly hyperbolic than the Jacobean masques: though at times they alluded to contemporary problems, their primary effect was to mystify and reinforce Charles's personal rule. In this milieu several courtier-poets—Carew, Suckling, Waller—wrote playful, sophisticated, sometimes delicate and sometimes licentious love lyrics on *carpe diem* themes: seize the day, time passes swiftly, make love now.

During the 1630s, the culture wars intensified between the Caroline court and the Laudian church on the one hand and the reformist Protestant and Puritan opposition on the other. In 1633 Charles reissued James I's *Book of Sports*, prescribing the continuation of traditional holiday festivities and Sunday sports in every parish in an effort to extend the cultural control of the court throughout the country. Puritans denounced both court festivities and country sports on religious grounds: they regarded masques, maypoles, and morris dances as palpable occasions of sin and the Sunday sports as profanations of the Sabbath. Also, many saw connections between the sophisticated pastoralism, Neoplatonism, and representations of ritual in the court masques and the Queen's Roman Catholicism. William Prynne had staked out the most extreme Puritan position, publishing in November 1632 a passionate tirade of over one thousand pages against stage-plays, masques, masque dancing, maypoles, and rural festivals, country sports on the Sabbath, Laudian ritual, stained-glass windows, and much more. He associated the court arts—"effeminate mixed dancing, lascivious pictures, wanton fashions, face painting . . . amorous pastorals, lascivious effeminate music"—with licentiousness, effeminacy, and seduction to popery. Worse, his reference to "Women actors, notorious whores" was thought to refer to the queen and her ladies, then rehearsing a pastoral play at court. For this cultural critique Prynne was stripped of his academic degrees, ejected from the legal profession, set in the pillory at Westminster and Cheapside, had his books burned and his ears cut off, and was sentenced to life imprisonment. The severity of the punishment indicates the perceived danger of his book, which one judge claimed would "effect disobedience to the state, and a general dislike unto all governments."

Milton's early poems display astonishing artistic virtuosity rooted in literary and generic traditions, but they also respond to the tensions of these years. Milton repudiated courtly and Laudian aesthetics and also Prynne's wholesale prohibitions, developing reformed versions of pastoral, masque, and hymn. His lovely hymn *On the Morning of Christ's Nativity* (1629) contains a long section on the casting out of idols at Christ's birth which resonates with contemporary Puritan resistance to Laudian "idolatry." His entertainment *Arcades* (1632) and the masque known as *Comus* (1634, 1637) associate the tempter figure with the licentious Cavaliers and their *carpe diem* seductions, honoring the better values of virtuous Protestant aristocrats in their own estates as well as the curative powers of good art—poetry, song, and dance. And his magnificent pastoral funeral elegy *Lycidas* contains a vehement denunciation of the establishment clergy as "Blind Mouths"—both ignorant and greedy—who deprive their flocks of spiritual nourishment.

THE REVOLUTIONARY ERA, 1640–60

Now almost four hundred years after the execution of Charles I, the English Revolution is still not quite over. Its aftershocks can be felt in the politically heated debate over its causes, which continues to this day. On the one hand, many historians see the revolution as the consequence, at least in part, of long-term changes in the English society and economy. They point to the conflict between new (capitalist) and old (feudal) modes of production in agriculture, industry, and trade and to the rising power and ambition of the gentry, the urban bourgeoisie, and those known as the "middling sort" of people in town and country. The frustrated demands of these classes for a greater measure of economic, political, and religious freedom led to rising social tensions and eventually civil war and revolution. This view, championed by Marxists among others, has been opposed by a revisionist school which emphasizes short-term and avoidable causes of the war. These historians point to a number of unlucky chance events, personal psychological factors, and poor decisions made by a small group of individuals. The political overtones of this clash of historians are unmistakeable. The debate over whether this was Europe's first bourgeois revolution or merely the consequence (as one scholar has argued) of Charles I's attempts to compensate for a sense of masculine inadequacy is ultimately a debate about the nature of history. As such it is not only about the events of the past, but about the shape of the future.

Whatever causes contributed to the outbreak of hostilities, there is no doubt that the twenty-year revolutionary period left the English economy far more open to the development of capitalist production. It also saw the development of concepts central to bourgeois liberal thought and soon to influence John Locke and the theorists of the American and French revolutions: religious toleration, separation of church and state, social contract, popular sovereignty, representative government, and republicanism. These concepts developed out of years of prolonged and bitter dispute centering around three fundamental questions: What kind of church government is laid down in Scripture and should therefore be settled in England? What should be the relation between church and state? What is the ultimate source of political power? The theories that evolved in response to these questions contain the seeds of much that is familiar in modern thought, mixed with much that seems forbiddingly alien. It is vital to bear in mind that the participants in these debates were not working their way (vaguely and haphazardly) toward modern liberalism, but responding (clearly and powerfully) to the most fundamental problems of their day. The debate was especially bitter and the need to find the right answers particularly intense for the many Millenarians among them, who believed that their day was very near to being the last day of all.

When the so-called "Long Parliament" convened in 1640, it had no intention of mounting a revolution and executing a king, but it was intent on securing and expanding its rights in the face of the king's perceived absolutist tendencies. Parliament set about to abolish extra-legal taxes and courts; to bring to trial and at length execute the king's hated ministers, Strafford and Laud; to rein in the bishops' power; to provide for triennial parliaments; and to remain in session until they themselves agreed to disband. As Parliament debated such matters, legitimate and underground presses poured forth a flood of treatises denouncing or supporting the bishops, *The Book of Common Prayer*, and the competing ecclesiastical models, creating a lively public forum for political discussion. That forum was also shaped by the little weekly newsbooks—the ancestors of our newpapers—which reported events at home and abroad from different political perspectives: royalist, parliamentarian, republican, army. Some of these so-called "Mercuries" were official government publications; some were licensed and quasi-official; some were fly-by-night affairs that lasted a few weeks, disappeared when the censors came after them, and then reappeared under different names.

Puritans were united in passionate opposition to the bishops, associating them with popery, tyranny over conscience, evil counsel to the king, and pompous excesses in lifestyle. Many, including Milton, demanded that they be cast out of the church, "root and branch." Puritan pamphlets sounded watchwords that were to be constantly repeated over the next two decades. One such was the call for "Godly Preachers." Another was "Holy Community," which some found embodied in the nation as a whole, some in a national church, and some in gathered churches of elect "saints." Another was "Covenant," registering the Puritan sense of being in a covenantal relation with God, whether as individuals, families, church members, or nation. Still another was the reference to England as a "New Israel," a new chosen people called to reform church and state, perhaps in preparation for Christ's Millennial Kingdom—the thousand-year reign of Christ with the saints which was to follow the Last Judgment.

In late 1641 events began to move quickly, though not inevitably, toward war. As the rift widened between Parliament and the king, and mobs of London apprentices kept up the pressure, horrific news came of an uprising in Ireland, with perhaps thirty thousand English and Scottish Protestants massacred by the enraged Catholic populace which they had dispossessed, persecuted for religion, and reduced to poverty. Parliament refused to fund the king for an invasion of Ireland, fearing he would instead invade England with an Irish army. When Charles sought to arrest five members of Parliament for treason, Londoners rose in arms against him. The king soon moved to York, the queen left for Holland to sell the crown jewels and ultimately to set up a court-in-exile in France, and Presbyterian pulpits rang with calls to God's Englishmen to come to the aid of the Lord against the wicked. Negotiations for compromise broke down over the issues that would derail them at every future stage: control of the army and episcopacy. On July 12, 1642, Parliament voted to raise an army, and on August 22 the king stood before a force of some two thousand horse and foot at Nottingham, unfurled his royal standard, and summoned his liegemen to his aid. Civil war had officially begun with its agonizing divisions, not only between but within regions of the country, cities, towns, rural communities, social classes, Parliament, the army, and even families.

Parliament and the Presbyterian clergy who managed the First Civil War (1642–46) had limited aims: to secure the rights of Parliament, to limit the king's control over the army and the church, and to settle some version of Presbyterianism as the national established church. They had no desire to depose the king, and indeed both Scots and English swore in their *Solemn League and Covenant* to uphold the king's person and authority even as they also swore to advance reformation, the rights of Parliament, and the peoples' liberties. They justified taking arms against the king by the Calvinist theory of contract, according to which political power was transferred by the people to "Magistrates" generally, so that "subordinate magistrates" (Parliament) could mount resistance to a king when, like Charles, he endangered religion and his subjects' liberties. The king set up court and an alternative parliament in Oxford, to which many in the House of Lords and some in the Commons resorted. As the Puritan armies moved through the country, fighting at Edgehill, Marston Moor, Naseby, and elsewhere, they also undertook an iconoclastic crusade to stamp out idolatry, often destroying religious images and stained-glass windows and lopping the heads off of statues, as an earlier generation of radical Protestants had done at the time of the English Reformation. The effects of these ravages can still be seen in English cathedrals and churches.

The Toleration Controversy that erupted in 1643 exposed deep divisions among Puritans. Presbyterians insisted that it was the Christian magistrates' duty to settle a national Presbyterian Church and enforce conformity to it, repressing all dissent. But some secular-minded Parliamentarians thought that broad toleration was the key to civic harmony, while Congregationalists,

Independents, and Baptists in the gathered churches and in the army vehemently opposed any national church and pressed for toleration. Most, however, stopped well short of the argument in *The Bloody Tenant* (1644) by the Baptist Roger Williams, recently returned from New England, that Christ has mandated complete separation of church and state and toleration of all religions, even Roman Catholics, Jews, and Muslims. As the revolution wore on, other sects sprang up, also seeking toleration: Seekers, Finders, Antinomians, the Family of Love, Fifth Monarchists, Quakers, Muggletonians, Ranters, and more. The orthodox were aghast, attempting unsuccessfully to stem the tide with laws against blasphemy and for censorship and with treatises like Thomas Edward's massive catalogue of dangerous sects and heresies, *Gangreana* (1646). Milton joined the toleration controversy with *Areopagitica* (1644), arguing vigorously against press censorship and for a very broad though not complete religious toleration.

The defeat of the royalist army in 1646 led to difficult, protracted negotiations and a brief Second Civil War in 1648, in which the king was again beaten. When Charles was found to be negotiating with foreign governments about an invasion, the army took drastic action, purging Parliament of its royalist and Presbyterian members along with the entire House of Lords, and insisting that the king be brought to trial. That dramatic spectacle began on January 20 in the crowded Great Hall at Westminster, where Charles heard himself accused of "High Treason and other High Crimes," specifically that he had broken his coronation oath, sought "unlimited and tyrannical power," attempted to overthrow the peoples' liberties and their foundation in successive Parliaments, and "traitorously and maliciously" made war against the Parliament and people. Every day Charles wore his hat in defiance of the court's authority and refused to answer the charges, insisting that a divinely anointed king could not be judged by any earthly power. On January 27 he was sentenced to be beheaded as a "Tyrant, Traitor, Murderer, and public Enemy," with fifty-nine commissioners signing the death warrant. On January 30, on a black-draped scaffold stage erected, ironically enough, outside the Banquetting Room at Whitehall where Charles had danced so many masque roles, he now acted his last role with dignity and courage. Andrew Marvell described the execution scene memorably in *An Horatian Ode.*

The Rump Parliament, the part of the House of Commons that was allowed to remain after the army expelled royalist and Presbyterian members (Pride's Purge), immediately established a new government "in way of a republic, without King or House of Lords" and with a Council of State as executive. Some classically educated supporters of the revolution saw themselves as reviving the forms of Athenian democracy and the Roman republic. As Hobbes later remarked, these men had absorbed the works of Demosthenes, Cicero, Livy, and others in which "popular government was extolled by the glorious name of liberty, and monarchy disgraced by the name of tyranny," and so "fell in love with their forms of government." But whatever their ideals, those in power in the infant republic (1649–54) found they could not afford to be doctrinaire or hold new elections while the state was threatened on all sides. The Scots and Irish immediately proclaimed the exiled prince—in France with his mother, Henrietta Maria—as Charles II and gathered armies to invade England; invasion was also threatened from Europe. Royalist newsletters and Presbyterian pulpits exploded in fury, pronouncing it sacrilege to execute a king anointed by God. The government party, including Milton, had to argue somewhat uncomfortably that popular sovereignty for the present could only extend to the "well affected" and that the good men raised up by God to serve the cause of liberty—the Rump and the army—could act for the whole people.

But the new establishment was not threatened by royalists alone. The Rump and the army were at odds with one another, divided within themselves, and attacked by a chorus of voices demanding far more radical religious and political reform. Millenarians and Fifth Monarchists called for political power to be given to regenerate "Saints," in preparation for the last days and the thousand-year reign of Christ. Quakers were seen to defy state and church authority by refusing to take oaths or remove their hats and by denouncing ministers in their own pulpits—practices that often landed them in prison. The rank and file of the army contained many so-called Levellers, who held that "all power is originally and essentially in the whole body of the people" and insisted that voting rights should not be limited to men of property. In 1649, disaffected Levellers such as John Lilburne denounced the new government as illegitimate and were arrested and imprisoned. Still more threatening in principle if not in fact were the "True Levellers" or Diggers, a few poor men who set out on April 1, 1649, to cultivate waste lands in Surrey as a symbolic claim to rights in the common lands and, in theory, to all property; their leader, Gerrard Winstanley, wrote eloquent manifestos urging their Christian communist program. Most alarming of all, out of all proportion to their scant numbers, were the Ranters, who believed that because God dwelt in them none of their acts could be sinful; some acted on that belief by running naked in the streets, or by open sexual license, or by blaspheming and swearing (hence their name). The Ranter Abiezer Coppe published wildly imagistic and mystical tracts denouncing wrongs perpetrated against the poor and proclaiming the inner light.

The threat of invasion was dispelled by Oliver Cromwell's victories in Ireland and Scotland. The war in Ireland was especially bloody as Cromwell's army slaughtered the native Irish without quarter in a frenzy of religious hatred. The republic gained international prestige by winning notable sea victories in the Anglo-Dutch War (1652–54), which erupted over trade rivalries and supremacy in the English Channel. But, given continued popular disaffection, the republic's leaders still could not find a way to call new elections, and relations between the Rump and army grew worse. In 1653 Cromwell expelled the Rump and convened a new legislature dominated by radical sectaries and Millenarians. This so-called "Barebones" Parliament, nicknamed for a prominent member, Praisegod Barebone, self-destructed in less than six months, and at the end of the year Cromwell was sworn in as Protector for life under England's first written constitution. The transition was comparatively smooth, save for outraged republicans opposed to any "single person," Fifth Monarchists who thought Cromwell had usurped the place of "King Jesus" soon to appear, and royalists who continued to act in the interests of Charles II. Many property owners adhered to Cromwell as the only hope for stability and settlement, while others, including Milton, did so because religious liberty was more secure with him than with the Rump or the other parliaments. Quakers and Ranters continued to receive harsh treatment, though Cromwell intervened sometimes to rescue Quakers from prison. He also began a program to readmit Jews to England, partly in the interests of trade but also to open the way for their conversion, supposedly a precursor of the last days as prophesied in the New Testament Book of Revelation.

Cromwell succumbed to a virulent influenza epidemic and died on September 3, 1658. Had he lived longer he might have restored monarchy to England by having himself crowned; his last constitution contained several monarchical features. Oliver's son Richard, who inherited none of his father's leadership qualities, took over as Protector but by August 1659 he was out. In the mounting chaos, the Rump was recalled with great fanfare, only to be turned out by a faction of army officers and then recalled yet again. In early 1660, General George Monk marched from Scotland to London proclaiming his firm support for the republic, but he soon called elections for a new "full and free" parliament that everyone knew would restore the king. As Monk played out his hand and negotiated secretly with Charles, royalist and Presbyterian preachers ridiculed and denounced the republic in pulpit and press, and rumps of beef were roasted throughout the City of London. A few republicans and radicals made last-ditch efforts to stave off the inevitable: the last polemic plea for the Good Old Cause was probably Milton's *Ready and Easy Way to Establish a Free Commonwealth*, published in late April 1660. On May 8, 1660, Charles II was officially proclaimed king; he landed at Dover on May 25 and made a triumphal entry into London four days later.

Over the next few years some regicides were executed and others were imprisoned, the court and the Anglican church were restored to full glory, and Puritan dissenters were harshly repressed. But royal absolutism was not restored. Parliament was now a force to be reckoned with; and the merchant classes, filled with dissenters, had powerful economic leverage. Less than three decades after Charles II returned, his brother, the Roman Catholic King James II, who had succeeded because Charles had no legitimate progeny, was frightened into fleeing the country in the so-called "Glorious Revolution" of 1688. The throne was transferred to the Dutch Protestant William of Orange and his wife, Mary, a daughter of James II. The English revolution was apparently dismantled in 1660, but its long-term effects profoundly changed English institutions and English society.

LITERATURE AND CULTURE, 1640–60

One of Parliament's first acts after hostilities began in 1642 was to abolish public sports and stage plays as unsuited to the calamitous times, "being spectacles of pleasure, too commonly expressing lascivious mirth and levity." The last play produced was Richard Brome's *A Jovial Crew: Or, The Merry Beggars*. During the next fifteen years, London theaters were dismantled and destroyed: the Globe, Blackfriars, the Phoenix, the Fortune, and the bear-gardens. Dramatic literature continued to be published—some Caroline plays in the 1640s and Brome's play in 1652. Also, both royalists and anti-royalists wrote play-pamphlets about real-life dramas, such as *The Famous Tragedie of King Charles I. Basely Butchered* (1649). Royalist exiles in France wrote plays, among them the duke of Newcastle and his duchess, Margaret

Cavendish. Also, despite the prohibitions, some plays were put on stage in England. Beaumont and Fletcher's *Wit without Money* was performed in February 1648 at the Red Bull Theater. Under the Protectorate, some erstwhile royalist playwrights used the new fashion for opera to develop "reformed" dramas. William Davenant's *First Day's Entertainment at Rutland House* (1656) and James Shirley's *Cupid and Death* were presented in quasi-private circumstances, but Davenant's *Cruelty of the Spaniards in Peru* (1658) was performed in the more public venue of the Cockpit Theater. This and other Davenant plays of the late 1650s dramatize crusades against the Turks and the Spaniards, emphasizing colonial and imperial myths.

During the revolutionary era many royalist authors found support in hard times from circles of friends. Also, with the disruption of their usual patronage networks, many decided to publish their verse. During the 1640s the bookseller Herbert Moseley collected and published volumes of poems by the Cavalier poets Thomas Carew, Sir John Denham, Edmund Waller, Sir John Suckling, James Shirley, Richard Lovelace, and Robert Herrick. Some of these poets fought for their king; others were imprisoned or fled abroad with the queen or went into "internal exile" at home. Their poems, some dating from the 1630s, celebrate royalist culture and the courtly ideal of the good life: wine, good food, good friends, good verses, hospitality, and loyalty to the king. One characteristic genre for them is the elegant love lyric, often with a *carpe diem* theme; other common themes are friendship and retirement. Stylistically, their verses are characterized by urbanity, smoothness, and (especially with Herrick) diligent attention to classical models. Several poems in Herrick's delightful collection of short lyrics, *Hesperides* (1648), celebrate those rural, quasi-pagan harvest festivals and May-day rituals so much criticized by Puritans. Others underscore the volume's dominant theme: "time's trans-shifting," the transience of all life, beauty, and poetry. Waller and Denham helped set the fashion for melodic rhymed stanzas and iambic pentameter couplets, which were to become normative verse patterns after the Restoration. The poems of Suckling and Lovelace construct a quintessential Cavalier persona with the qualities usually associated with those supporters of the king and queen. He talks amusingly, bawdily, charmingly, and sometimes sadly about the joys and tribulations of love, the conflicts of love and honor, loyalty to friends, and the trials of the times. He presents himself as an amateur, writing verse in the midst of a life devoted to more important matters: war, love, the king's service, and the endurance of loss.

During the 1650s, royalists wrote lyric poems in places removed from the hostile centers of parliamentary power. Henry Vaughan in Wales wrote religious verse expressing his intense longing for past biblical eras of innocence and for the perfection of heaven or the millennium, and representing himself in the present as a solitary wanderer seeking out the vestiges of God in nature. Also in Wales, Katherine Philips wrote and circulated in manuscript poems that celebrate female friends in the Platonic terms normally reserved for male friendships. Their publication after the Restoration brought Philips some celebrity as "The Matchless Orinda." Richard Crashaw, an exile in Paris and Rome and a convert to Roman Catholicism, is England's only major baroque poet. His poems treat typical baroque topics—weeping Magdalens, infant Saviors, rosy cherubs, tender Virgins, tormented martyrs, ecstatic saints—in the lush, sensuous language that, according to Counter-

Reformation aesthetics, could reveal the spiritual by stimulating the senses. Margaret Cavendish, duchess of Newcastle, also in exile with the queen in Paris, published two collections of lyrics when she returned to England in 1653; a number of these poems are about her own role as poet. After the Restoration she published several dramas and her remarkable utopian romance, *The Blazing World* (1668), which imagines a world governed by an empress with absolute power to rule as she will and learn what she wishes. Cavendish claims for herself as author a comparable absolutism in creating fictional worlds.

The most important English philosopher and political theorist of the earlier seventeenth century, Thomas Hobbes, was also an exile in Paris, as long-time tutor and secretary in the Cavendish family. While there he developed his materialist philosophy and psychology, his critique of language, and, in *Leviathan* (1651), his unflinching analysis and defense of absolute and indivisible sovereignty based on social contract. As his argument validates whatever government is in power and can preserve peace and security—whether Stuart kings, the republic, or Cromwell—he was distrusted by royalists and republicans alike. Claims of royal legitimacy and assertions of the rights and liberties of the people are alike irrelevant in Hobbes's political theory.

Several prose works by royalists have become classics of their respective prose genres. They seem to have little or nothing to do with the contemporary scene but in fact they carry a political charge. In his *Life of Donne*, Izaak Walton went some distance toward producing a scholarly biography: he drew on his personal knowledge of Donne in his later years, collected facts and sometimes dubious anecdotes from those who knew him, and read his letters and personal papers. But Walton's overall design presents Donne as a latter-day St. Augustine—rakish in youth, saintly in his later life as dean of St. Paul's. Published as a preface to a collection of Donne's sermons in 1640, when religious tensions were growing and war loomed on the horizon, Walton's work makes Donne a modern "saint" of Anglicanism. Later, Walton wrote an enormously popular treatise on fishing, *The Complete Angler* (1653), presenting it as a dialogue between Walton's warm-hearted persona, Piscator the angler, and a hunter, Venator, a figure for busy, warlike Puritans. At length Venator is converted to the better values of fishing—peace, tranquility, charity, and contemplation—which are associated with Christianity and specifically with Anglicanism. The pun *angler/Anglican* is surely intended, and it is reinforced by Walton's inclusion of several poems by Herbert as well as a poem praising *The Book of Common Prayer*. Sir Thomas Browne published *Religio Medici* (A Doctor's Religion) in 1642/43, offering it as a portrait of his mind. Browne presents himself as a genial, speculative doctor who contains in himself many paradoxes and idiosyncratic views but willingly submits his judgment to the Church of England, who loves ritual and ceremony, who finds nothing human foreign to him, and who can sympathize with and worship with all Christians, even Roman Catholics. The subtext presents him as a model of Anglican inclusiveness and charity, a sharp contrast to reforming Puritans bent on ridding the church of its errors. Browne's other works published in this period display his Baconian, antiquarian, and mystical sides.

The omnipresent prose genre of the revolutionary era was the polemic tract. Tracts large and small addressed all aspects of all the religious, social, and political controversies. Many voices are memorable for their rhetorical and literary power amid that hubbub: the Leveller John Lilburne, the Digger Gerrard Winstanley, the tolerationist Roger Williams, the prophet Anna Trapnall, and Milton. The most important and rhetorically effective treatise on the royalist side was *Eikon Basilike* (1649), purportedly written by Charles I while in prison and awaiting trial and execution, though in fact the work of the Presbyterian cleric John Gauden. Within one year of its first appearance, it went through some forty editions in London and twenty-five more in Ireland and abroad. Usually published with a striking engraving of the king in prayer as a frontispiece, it presents the king's interpretation of the past two decades. The text represents him as Charles the martyr, the suffering hero of his own tragedy: Christlike in his sufferings and in his forgiveness of enemies; a second David in his psalmlike prayers; a man of culture, mildness, moderation, and peace pursued by bloodthirsty enemies; a king innocent of any deliberate wrongdoing; a man of conscience in holding firm for bishops, liturgy, and his royal prerogatives. On the revolutionary side, James Harrington's republican utopia *The Commonwealth of Oceana* (1656) was influential in its own time and important to later political theory. Addressed to Cromwell, it casts him in the fictional character of an Archon who founds a republic on scientific principles that assure its permanence: an agrarian law to regulate property distribution, a two-house legislature chosen by an elaborate rotation, and a highly complex system of elections. Harrington seeks to persuade Cromwell to imitate his fictional counterpart and establish the English government on the principles of Oceana: whereas Cromwell insisted that only good men can preserve the state, Harrington wants to convince him that good institutions will inevitably produce good men. *Oceana* ends with the Cromwell-figure resigning his extraordinary power back to the Parliament and retiring to private life—a rather obvious hint to the Protector. In the last months of the revolution, Harrington's ideas were regularly debated by members of the so-called Rota Club and repackaged in several treatises.

It is no surprise that the revolutionary era gave new impetus to women's writing. The overturning of boundaries and the circumstances of war that placed women in novel and sometimes dangerous situations gave them unusual events to chronicle and prompted self-discovery. Autobiographies of three royalist women, Lady Anne Halkett, Lady Anne Fanshaw, and Margaret Cavendish, duchess of Newcastle, all published after the Restoration, report their emotions, their love relationships, and their sometimes daring activities during those trying days. On the revolutionary side, Lucy Hutchinson's *Memoir* of her husband, Colonel John Hutchinson, treats his life with her and his significant role in the war and in government within a narrative that is also a republican history of those times; it was first published in 1806, along with an autobiographical fragment dealing with her early life. She left in manuscript several poems on personal and political themes. Leveller women joined the polemic fray, offering petitions and manifestos in support of their imprisoned husbands and their cause. Quaker women came into their own as preachers and sometimes writers of tracts, authorized by Quaker belief that all persons should testify to what the Inner Light of the Spirit communicates to them. Among the Quaker Margaret Fell's several treatises is one justifying women speaking in church. Female prophets came forth in some numbers during the revolution, their claims to divine inspiration gaining currency from the widespread belief that the Spirit was moving in unexpected ways. The published prophecies of Lady Eleanor Davies, Mary Cary, and Anna Trapnell often carried a strong political critique of Charles or Cromwell. Trapnell dictated her ecstatic visions to scribes, but she also wrote a lively autobiographical report of her adventures and persecution during a missionary journey in the west of England.

If the royalist side claimed most of the poets and the writers of literary prose during this period, the revolution could claim the best of them: Marvell and Milton. During several regimes, Andrew Marvell maintained his independent vision and his firm commitment to religious toleration. He wrote most of his supremely artful lyrics and political poems while at Nunappleton in 1650–52, tutoring the daughter of the retired parliamentary general Sir Thomas Fairfax; in 1657 he joined his friend Milton in the office of Cromwell's Latin Secretariat. All of his poems play wittily with genre and literary convention. His love poems span the spectrum from *carpe diem* invitations to love to neoplatonic affirmations of the absolute split between soul and body, to near-postmodern perceptions that what attracts love is only an unstable set of shifting images. His pastorals, spoken as dramatic monologues by such unusual figures as Damon the Mower, disrupt pastoral norms of contentment and harmony between humans and nature. Several of his political poems are praises of Cromwell, but the finest of them, *An Horatian Ode upon Cromwell's Return from Ireland,* also invites sympathy for the executed king. It recognizes Cromwell as a providential force and celebrates his Irish victory, but also indicates the potential danger in his military successes and meteoric rise to power as a kind of Caesar. Marvell's very long poem celebrating his patron's estate, *Upon Appleton House,* attains something like epic scope, as it locates the static, mythic features traditionally celebrated in country-house poems within the course of providential history in Israel and England, a history that includes the chaotic events of the English revolution.

Milton's commitment to the revolution was unwavering, early to late, despite his disillusion when it failed to realize his fundamental ideals: religious toleration for all Protestants and the free circulation of ideas without prior censorship. He argued for those ideals in the most impressive and enduring polemic of the age, his eloquent, brilliantly imagistic *Areopagitica* (1644). First as self-appointed advisor to the state, then as its official defender, he addressed the other great issues under debate and argued for his own positions: removal of the bishops "root and branch"; the necessity of divorce for incompatibility so as to relieve widespread human unhappiness; justifications for tyrannicide and republican government based on natural law and popular sovereignty; the right of those who love liberty to act, if necessary, for the whole people; denial to magistrates of any power over religion; church disestablishment; the manifest evils of kingship; and the divine preference for republican government. He was a Puritan, but both his theological heterodoxies and his poetic vision mark him as a distinctly unusual one.

During the twenty years in which he wrote polemics in support of these causes, Milton also wrote several sonnets, revising that small kind to accommodate large public and private topics: a threatened attack by the royalist army on London; praise of and advice to Cromwell about the church; agonizing questions posed by his blindness; and the massacre of the proto-Protestant Waldensians by Roman Catholic forces in the Piedmont. In 1645 he published his collected poems in a double volume, English and Latin, offering it as a counterstatement to the royalist volumes of the 1640s. He wrote some part of *Paradise Lost* in the 1650s and completed it after the Restoration, encompassing in it all he had thought, read, and experienced of tyranny, political rhetoric, evil, deception, love, the need for human companionship, the woes and the good of human life. This stunning, cosmic, blank-verse epic assimilates and critiques the epic tradition and Milton's entire intellectual and literary heritage, classical and Christian. Yet it has at its center not martial heroes but a domestic pair, whose challenge is to discover how to live the good human life day by day, in Eden and later in the fallen world, amid intense emotional pressures and the seductions of evil.

Seventeenth-century poetry and prose retains its hold on readers because so much of it is so very good, fusing (as T. S. Eliot recognized) intellectual strength, emotional passion, and linguistic artfulness. We have in Donne and Marvell love poetry at once cerebral, witty, and passionate; in Donne and Herbert religious poetry at once deeply felt and highly artful; in Jonson tough-minded analyses of what is worthy of praise and blame in the social order; in Herrick some of the most exquisite short lyrics in the English language; in Crashaw the most extravagantly baroque as well as, arguably, the most musical poet in our literature. We watch English prose become a highly flexible instrument, suited to informal essays, scientific or political treatises, religious meditation, biography and autobiography, and vigorous polemic. We observe a number of literary forms evolve for the analysis or dramatization or representation of the self: dramatic monologues portraying the self or several imagined selves in various love situations; religious meditations on the state of the soul; meditations on personal experiences like illness; intellectual or spiritual autobiographies; sermons in which the preacher takes himself as example. Finally, we have in Milton an epic poet who assumed the role of inspired prophet, envisioning a world produced by God but shaped by human choice and imagination.

THE EARLY SEVENTEENTH CENTURY

TEXTS	CONTEXTS
1603 James I, *Basilikon Doran* reissued	1603 Death of Elizabeth I; accession of James I. Plague
1604 William Shakespeare, *Othello*	
1605 Shakespeare, *King Lear*. Ben Jonson, *The Masque of Blackness*. Francis Bacon, *The Advancement of Learning*	1605 Gunpowder Plot, failed effort by Roman Catholic extremists to blow up Parliament
1606 Jonson, *Volpone*. Shakespeare, *MacBeth*	
	1607 Founding of Jamestown colony in Virginia
1609 Shakespeare, *Sonnets*	1609 Galileo's telescope
1611 "King James" Bible (Authorized Version). Shakespeare, *The Tempest*. John Donne, *The First Anniversary*. Aemilia Lanyer, *Salve Deus Rex Judaeorum*	
1612 Donne, *The Second Anniversary*	1612 Death of Prince Henry
1613 Elizabeth Cary, *The Tragedy of Mariam*	
1614 John Webster, *The Duchess of Malfi*	
1616 Jonson, *Works*. James I, *Works*	1616 Death of Shakespeare
	1618 Beginning of the Thirty Years War
	1619 First African slaves in North America exchanged by Dutch frigate for food and supplies at Jamestown
1620 Bacon, *Novum Organum*	1620 Pilgrims land at Plymouth
1621 Mary Wroth, *The Countess of Montgomery's Urania*. Robert Burton, *Anatomy of Melancholy*	1621 Donne appointed dean of St. Paul's Cathedral
1623 Shakespeare, First Folio	
	1625 Death of James I; accession of Charles I; Charles I marries Henrietta Maria
	1629 Charles I dissolves Parliament
1633 Donne, *Poems*. George Herbert, *The Temple*	1633 Galileo forced by the Inquisition to recant the Copernican theory
1637 John Milton, *Lycidas*	
1640 Thomas Carew, *Poems*	1640 Long Parliament called (1640–53). Archbishop Laud impeached
1642 Thomas Browne, *Religio Medici*. Milton, *Reason of Church Government*	1642 First Civil War begins (1642–46). Parliament closes the theaters
1643 Milton, *Doctrine and Discipline of Divorce*	1643 Accession of Louis XIV of France
1644 Milton, *Areopagitica*	
1645 Milton, *Poems*. Edmund Waller, *Poems*	1645 Archbishop Laud executed. Royalists defeated at Naseby

TEXTS	CONTEXTS
1648 Robert Herrick, *Hesperides*	**1648** Second Civil War. Pride's Purge of Parliament
1649 Milton, *Eikonoklastes*	**1649** Trial and execution of Charles I. Republic declared. Milton becomes Latin Secretary (1649–59)
1650 Henry Vaughan, *Silex Scintillans* (Part II, 1655)	
1651 Thomas Hobbes, *Leviathan*. Andrew Marvell, *Upon Appleton House* (unpublished)	
	1652 Dutch War (1652–53)
	1653 Cromwell made Lord Protector
	1658 Death of Cromwell; his son Richard made Protector
1660 Milton, *Ready and Easy Way to Establish a Free Commonwealth*	**1660** Restoration of Charles II to throne. Royal Society founded
	1662 Charles II marries Catherine of Braganza
	1665 The Great Plague
1666 Margaret Cavendish, *The Blazing World*	**1666** The Great Fire
1667 Milton, *Paradise Lost* (in ten books). Katherine Philips, *Collected Poems*. John Dryden, *Annus Mirabilis*	
1671 Milton, *Paradise Regained* and *Samson Agonistes*	
1674 Milton, *Paradise Lost* (in twelve books)	**1674** Death of Milton
1681 Marvell, *Poems,* published posthumously	

JOHN DONNE
1572–1631

Lovers' eyeballs threaded on a string. A god who assaults the human heart with a battering ram. A teardrop that encompasses and drowns the world. John Donne's poems abound with startling images, some of them exalting and others grotesque. With his strange and playful intelligence, expressed in puns, paradoxes, and the elaborately sustained metaphors known as "conceits," Donne has enthralled and sometimes enraged readers from his day to our own. The tired clichés of love poetry—cheeks like roses, hearts pierced by the arrows of love—emerge reinvigorated and radically transformed by his hand, demanding from the reader an unprecedented level of mental alertness and engagement. Donne prided himself on his wit and displayed it not only in his conceits but in his grasp of learned and obscure discourses ranging from theology to alchemy, from cosmology to law. Yet for all their ostentatious intellectuality, Donne's poems never give the impression of being academic exercises put into verse. Rather, they are intense dramatic monologues in which the speaker's ideas and feelings seem to shift and evolve from one line to the next. Donne's prosody is equally dramatic, mirroring in its variable and jagged rhythms the effect of speech (and eliciting from his classically minded contemporary Ben Jonson the gruff observation that "Donne, for not keeping of accent deserved hanging").

Donne began life as an outsider, and in some respects remained one until death. He was born in London in 1572 into a devout Roman Catholic household. The family was prosperous, but, as the poet later remarked, none had suffered more heavily for its loyalty to the Catholic Church: "I have been ever kept awake in a meditation of martyrdom." Donne was distantly related to the great Catholic humanist and martyr Sir Thomas More. Closer to home, a Jesuit uncle was executed by the brutal method of hanging, drawing, quartering, and disemboweling, and his own brother Henry, arrested for harboring a priest, died in prison of the plague. As a Catholic in Protestant England, growing up in decades when anti-Roman feeling reached new heights, Donne could not expect any kind of public career, nor even to receive a university degree (he left Oxford without one and studied law for a time at the Inns of Court). What he could reasonably expect instead was prejudice, official harrassment, and crippling financial penalties. He chose not to live under such conditions. At some point in the 1590s, having returned to London after travels abroad, and having devoted some years to studying theological issues, Donne converted to the English Church.

The poems that belong with certainty to this period of his life—the five Satires and most of the Elegies—reveal a man both fascinated by and keenly critical of English society. Four of the satires treat commonplace Elizabethan topics—foppish and obsequious courtiers, bad poets, corrupt lawyers and a corrupt court—but are unique both in their visceral revulsion and in their intellectual excitement. Donne uses striking images of pestilence, itchy lust, vomit, excrement, and pox to create a unique satiric world, busy, vibrant, and corrupt, in which his dramatic speakers have only to step outside the door to be innundated by all the fools and knaves in Christendom. By contrast, the third satire treats the quest for true religion—the question that preoccupied him above all others in these years—in terms that are serious, passionately witty, and deeply felt. Donne argues that honest doubting search is better than the facile acceptance of any religious tradition, epitomizing that point brilliantly in the image of Truth on a high and craggy hill, very difficult to climb. What is certain is that society's values are of no help whatsoever to the individual seeker—none will escape the final judgment by pleading that "A Harry, or a Martin taught [them] this." In the love Elegies Donne seems intent on making up for his social powerlessness through witty representations of mastery in the bedroom and of adventurous travel.

In *Elegy 16* he imagines his speaker embarking on a journey "O'er the white Alps" and with mingled tenderness and condescension argues down a naive mistress's proposal to accompany him. And in *Elegy 19*, his fondling of a naked lover becomes in a famous conceit the equivalent of exploration in America. Donne's interest in satire and elegy—classical Roman genres which he helped introduce to English verse—is itself significant. He wrote in English, but he reached out to other traditions.

If Donne's conversion to the Church of England promised him security, social acceptance, and the possibility of a public career, that promise was soon to be cruelly withdrawn. In 1596–97 he participated in the earl of Essex's military expeditions against Catholic Spain in Cádiz and the Azores (the experience prompted two remarkable descriptive poems of life at sea, *The Storm* and *The Calm*) and upon his return became secretary to Sir Thomas Egerton, Lord Keeper of the Great Seal. This should have been the beginning of a successful public career. But his secret marriage in 1601 to Egerton's seventeen-year-old niece Ann More enraged Donne's employer and the bride's wealthy father; Donne was briefly imprisoned and dismissed from service. The poet was reduced to a retired country life beset by financial insecurity and a rapidly increasing family; Ann bore twelve children (not counting miscarriages) by the time she died at age thirty-three. At one point, Donne wrote despairingly that while the death of a child would mean one less mouth to feed, he could not afford the burial expenses. In this bleak period, he wrote but dared not publish a paradoxical defense of suicide (*Biathanatos*).

As his family grew, Donne made every effort to reinstate himself in the favor of the great. To win the approval of James I, he penned *Pseudo-Martyr* (1610), defending the king's insistence that Catholics take the Oath of Allegiance. This set an irrevocable public stamp on his renunciation of Catholicism, and Donne followed up with a witty satire on the Jesuits, *Ignatius his Conclave* (1611). In the same period he was producing a steady stream of occasional poems for friends and patrons such as Somerset (the king's favorite), the countess of Bedford, and Magdalen Herbert, and for small coteries of courtiers and ladies. Like most gentlemen of his era, Donne saw poetry as a polite accomplishment rather than as a trade or vocation, and in consequence he circulated his poems in manuscript but left most of them uncollected and unpublished. In 1611 and 1612, however, he published the first and second *Anniversaries* on the death of the daughter of his patron, Sir Robert Drury.

For some years King James had urged an ecclesiastical career on Donne, denying him any other means of advancement. In 1615 Donne finally consented, overcoming his sense of unworthiness and the pull of other ambitions. He was ordained in the Church of England and entered upon a distinguished career as court preacher, reader in divinity at Lincoln's Inn, and dean of St. Paul's. Donne's metaphorical style, bold erudition, and dramatic wit established him as a great preacher in an age that appreciated learned sermons powerfully delivered. Some 160 of his sermons survive, preached to monarchs and courtiers, lawyers and London magistrates, city merchants and trading companies. As a distinguished clergyman in the Church of England, Donne had traveled an immense distance from the religion of his childhood and the adventurous life of his twenties. Yet in his sermons and late poems we find the same brilliant and idiosyncratic mind at work, refashioning his profane conceits to serve a new and higher purpose. In *Expostulation 19* he praises God as the greatest of literary stylists: "a figurative, a metaphorical God," imagining God as a conceit-maker like himself. In poems, meditations, and sermons, Donne came increasingly to be engaged in anxious contemplation of his own mortality. In *A Hymn to God my God in my Sickness*, Donne imagines himself spread out on his deathbed like a map showing the route to the next world. Only a few days before his death he preached *Death's Duel*, a terrifying analysis of all life as a decline toward death and dissolution which contemporaries termed his own funeral sermon. On his deathbed, according to his contemporary biographer Izaak Walton, Donne had a portrait made of himself in his shroud and meditated on it daily. Meditations upon skulls as emblems of mortality were common in the period, but nothing is more characteristic of Donne than to find a way to meditate on his own skull.

Given the shape of Donne's career, it is no surprise that his poems and prose works display an astonishing variety of attitudes, viewpoints, and feelings on the great subjects of love and religion. Yet this variety cannot be fully explained in biographical terms. The poet's own attempt to distinguish between Jack Donne, the young rake, and Dr. Donne, the grave and religious dean of St. Paul's, is (perhaps intentionally) misleading. We do not know the time and circumstances for most of Donne's verses, but it is clear that many of his finest religious poems predate his ordination, and it is possible that he continued to add to the love poems known as his *Songs and Sonnets* after he entered the Church. Theological language abounds in his love poetry, and daringly erotic images occur in his religious verse.

Although they were not widely known in his lifetime, Donne's *Songs and Sonnets* have been the cornerstone of his reputation almost since their publication in 1633. The title associates them with the popular miscellanies of love poems and sonnet sequences in the Petrarchan tradition, but they directly challenge the popular Petrarchan sonnet sequences of the 1590s. The collection contains only one formal sonnet, the "Songs" are not notably lyrical, and Donne draws upon and transforms a whole range of literary traditions concerned with love. Like Petrarch, Donne can present himself as the despairing lover of an unattainable lady (*The Funeral*); like Ovid he can be lighthearted, witty, cynical, and frankly lustful (*The Flea, The Indifferent*); like the Neoplatonists, he espouses a theory of transcendant love, but he breaks from them with his insistence in many poems on the union of physical and spiritual love. What binds these poems together and grants them enduring power is their compelling immediacy. The speaker is always in the throes of intense emotion, and that emotion is not static but constantly shifting and evolving with the turns of the poet's thought. Donne seems supremely present in these poems, standing behind their various speakers. Where Petrarchan poets exhaustively catalogue their beloved's physical features (though in highly conventional terms), Donne's speakers tell us little or nothing about the loved woman, or about the male friends imagined as audience for many poems. Donne's repeated insistence that the private world of lovers is superior to the wider public world, or that it somehow contains all of that world, or obliterates it, is understandable in light of the many disappointments of his career. Yet this was also a poet who threw himself headlong into life, love, and sexuality, and later into the very visible public role of court and city preacher.

Donne was long grouped with Herbert, Vaughan, Crashaw, Marvell, Traherne, and Cowley under the heading of "Metaphysical Poets." The expression was first employed by critics like Samuel Johnson and William Hazlitt, who found the intricate conceits and self-conscious learning of these poets incompatible with poetic beauty and sincerity. Early in the twentieth century, T. S. Eliot sought to restore their reputation, attributing to them a unity of thought and feeling which had since their time been lost. Today the term "Metaphysicals" seems more an obstacle than an aid to understanding these very different poets. There was certainly no formal "school" of metaphysical poetry, and the characteristics ascribed to it by later critics pertain chiefly to Donne. Like Ben Jonson, John Donne had a large influence on the succeeding generation, but he remains a singularity.

metaphysical: more spiritual. [handwritten]

FROM SONGS AND SONNETS[1]

The Flea[2]

she denies him the mingling of their blood [handwritten]

Mark but this flea, and mark in this,
How little that which thou deniest me is;
Me it sucked first, and now sucks thee,
And in this flea our two bloods mingled be; →*marriage* [handwritten]
5 Thou know'st that this cannot be said
A sin, or shame, or loss of maidenhead,
   Yet this enjoys before it woo,
   And pampered swells with one blood made of two,[3]
   And this, alas, is more than we would do. *this action the flea is getting is more than him.* [handwritten]

10 Oh stay, three lives in one flea spare,
Where we almost, nay more than married are.
This flea is you and I, and this *spare the flea b/c it is sacred.* [handwritten]
   Our marriage bed and marriage temple is;
when the 2 bloods mingal, they become one, then they have been married, & can have sex. [handwritten]
Though parents grudge, and you, we are met,
15 And cloistered[4] in these living walls of jet.° *the flea.*   *black habit* [handwritten]
   Though use° make you apt to kill[5] me,
   Let not to that, self-murder added be,
   And sacrilege, three sins in killing three. *killing the marriage* [handwritten]

Cruel and sudden, hast thou since
20 Purpled thy nail in blood of innocence? } *kill the flea* [handwritten]
Wherein could this flea guilty be,
Except in that drop which it sucked from thee?
Yet thou triumph'st, and say'st that thou
Find'st not thy self nor me the weaker now;
she was right, she isn't weaker [handwritten]
25 'Tis true; then learn how false fears be:
Just so much honor, when thou yield'st to me,
Will waste, as this flea's death took life from thee.

If she goes to bed w/ him she won't loose honor. [handwritten]
they kill the flea that sucked their blood. [handwritten]

1633

The Good-Morrow

I wonder, by my troth, what thou and I
Did, till we loved? Were we not weaned till then,
But sucked on country pleasures, childishly?

---

1. Donne's love poems were written over nearly two decades, beginning around 1595; they were not published in Donne's lifetime but circulated widely in manuscript. The title *Songs and Sonnets* was supplied in the second edition (1635), which grouped the poems by kind, but neither this arrangement nor the more haphazard organization of the first edition (1633) is Donne's own. In Donne's time the term *sonnet* often meant simply "love lyric," and in fact there is only one formal sonnet in this collection. For the poems we present we follow the 1635 edition, beginning with the extremely popular poem *The Flea*.
2. This insect afforded a popular erotic theme for poets all over Europe, deriving from a pseudo-Ovidian medieval poem in which a lover envies the flea for the liberties it takes with his mistress's body.
3. The swelling suggests pregnancy.
4. As in a convent or monastery.
5. "Kill" carries an allusion to sexual intercourse.

Or snorted° in the seven sleepers' den?[1]   *snored*
'Twas so; but° this, all pleasures fancies be.   *except for*
If ever any beauty I did see,
Which I desired, and got, 'twas but a dream of thee.

And now good morrow to our waking souls,
Which watch not one another out of fear;
For love all love of other sights controls,
And makes one little room an everywhere.
Let sea-discoverers to new worlds have gone,
Let maps to others, worlds on worlds have shown:
Let us possess one world;[2] each hath one, and is one.

My face in thine eye, thine in mine appears,
And true plain hearts do in the faces rest;
Where can we find two better hemispheres,
Without sharp North, without declining West?
Whatever dies was not mixed equally;[3]
If our two loves be one, or thou and I
Love so alike that none do slacken, none can die.

1633

Song

Go and catch a falling star,
    Get with child a mandrake root,[1]   *these things*
Tell me where all past years are,   *are all impossible*
    Or who cleft the Devil's foot,
Teach me to hear mermaids° singing,   *sirens*
Or to keep off envy's stinging,
        And find
        What wind
Serves to advance an honest mind.

If thou beest born to strange sights,
    Things invisible to see,
Ride ten thousand days and nights,
    Till age snow white hairs on thee,
Thou, when thou return'st, wilt tell me
All strange wonders that befell thee,
        And swear   *he is very sinical.*
        No where
Lives a woman true, and fair.

1. Cave in Ephesus where, according to legend, seven Christian youths hid from pagan persecutors and slept for 187 years.
2. "Our world" in many manuscripts.
3. Scholastic philosophy taught that when the elements were imperfectly ("not equally") mixed, matter was mutable and mortal; conversely, when the elements were perfectly mixed, matter was immutable and hence immortal.

1. The mandrake root, or mandragora, is forked like the lower part of the human body. It was thought to shriek when pulled from the ground and to kill all humans who heard it; it was also (paradoxically) thought to help women conceive.

20   If thou find'st one, let me know,
       Such a pilgrimage were sweet;
Yet do not, I would not go,
       Though at next door we might meet;
Though she were true when you met her,
And last till you write your letter,
25   Yet she
          Will be
False, ere I come, to two, or three.

1633

The Undertaking

    I have done one braver thing
       Than all the Worthies[1] did,
And yet a braver thence doth spring,
       Which is, to keep that hid.

5   It were but madness now t' impart
       The skill of specular stone,[2]
When he which can have learned the art
       To cut it, can find none.

    So, if I now should utter this,
10   Others (because no more
Such stuff to work upon, there is)
       Would love but as before.

    But he who loveliness within
       Hath found, all outward loathes,
15   For he who color loves, and skin,
       Loves but their oldest clothes.

    If, as I have, you also do
       Virtue attired in woman see,
And dare love that, and say so too,
20   And forget the He and She;

    And if this love, though placèd so,
       From profane men you hide,
Which will no faith on this bestow,
       Or, if they do, deride;

25   Then you have done a braver thing
       Than all the Worthies did;

---

1. According to medieval legend, the Nine Worthies, or supreme heroes of history, included three Jews (Joshua, David, Judas Maccabeus), three pagans (Hector, Alexander, Julius Caesar), and three Christians (Arthur, Charlemagne, Godfrey of Bouillon).

2. A transparent or translucent material, reputed to have been used in antiquity for windows, but no longer known. Great skill was needed to cut it.

And a braver thence will spring,
Which is, to keep that hid.

1633

The Sun Rising[1]

he doesn't like the sun

Busy old fool, unruly sun,
Why dost thou thus
Through windows and through curtains call on us?
Must to thy motions lovers' seasons run?
5   Saucy pedantic wretch, go chide *don't bother us / bother them*
Late schoolboys and sour prentices,
Go tell court huntsmen that the King will ride,[2]
Call country ants to harvest offices;[3]
Love, all alike, no season knows nor clime, *lovers shouldn't work*
10   Nor hours, days, months, which are the rags of time.

why would you want to tear up time.

her eyes could blind the sun

Thy beams, so reverend and strong
Why shouldst thou think?
I could eclipse and cloud them with a wink, *he can just close his eyes to not see the sun, but he wants to see his love.*
But that I would not lose her sight so long;
15   If her eyes have not blinded thine,
Look, and tomorrow late, tell me,
Whether both th' Indias of spice and mine[4]
Be where thou leftst them, or lie here with me.
Ask for those kings whom thou saw'st yesterday, *their bed is the center of the universe.*
20   And thou shalt hear, All here in one bed lay. *& the world has come to nations them.*

She is all states,° and all princes I,
Nothing else is.
Princes do but play us; compared to this,
All honor's mimic, all wealth alchemy. *all wealth is fake.*
25   Thou, sun, art half as happy as we,
In that the world's contracted thus;
Thine age asks ease, and since thy duties be *the sun should revolve around them.*
To warm the world, that's done in warming us.
Shine here to us, and thou art everywhere;
30   This bed thy center is,[5] these walls thy sphere.

1633

The Indifferent[1]

I can love both fair and brown,[2]
Her whom abundance melts, and her whom want betrays.

1. Some lines of this poem recall Ovid, *Amores*
1.13.
2. King James was very fond of hunting.
3. Autumn chores. "Country ants": farm drudges.
4. The India of "spice" is East India; that of "mine"
(gold) is the West Indies.

5. According to the old Ptolemaic astronomy, the
earth was the center of the sun's orbit, and the
sun's motion was contained within its sphere.
1. Some lines of this poem recall Ovid, *Amores*
2.4.
2. Both blond and brunet.

Her who loves loneness best, and her who masks and plays,
Her whom the country formed, and whom the town,
5   Her who believes, and her who tries,°   *tests*
Her who still weeps with spongy eyes,
And her who is dry cork, and never cries;
I can love her, and her, and you, and you,
I can love any, so she be not true.

10 Will no other vice content you?
Will it not serve your turn to do as did your mothers?
Or have you all old vices spent, and now would find out others?
Or doth a fear that men are true torment you?
O we are not, be not you so;
15 Let me, and do you, twenty know.
Rob me, but bind me not, and let me go.
Must I, who came to travail thorough³ you,
Grow your fixed subject, because you are true?

Venus heard me sigh this song,
20 And by love's sweetest part, variety, she swore,
She heard not this till now; and that it should be so no more.
She went, examined, and returned ere long,
And said, Alas, some two or three
Poor heretics in love there be,
25 Which think to 'stablish dangerous constancy.
But I have told them, Since you will be true,
You shall be true to them who are false to you.

1633

The Canonization¹

For God's sake hold your tongue, and let me love,
   Or chide my palsy, or my gout,
My five gray hairs, or ruined fortune, flout,
   With wealth your state, your mind with arts improve,
5   Take you a course, get you a place,²
      Observe His Honor, or His Grace,³
Or the King's real, or his stampèd face⁴
     Contemplate; what you will, approve,°   *try, test*
     So you will let me love.

10 Alas, alas, who's injured by my love?
   What merchant's ships have my sighs drowned?
Who says my tears have overflowed his ground?
   When did my colds a forward° spring remove?⁵   *early*
    When did the heats which my veins fill

---

3. Through. "Travail": grief, but also journey, travel.
1. The poem plays off against the Roman Catholic process of determining that certain persons are saints, proper objects of veneration and prayer.
2. An appointment, at court or elsewhere. "Take

you a course": follow some career.
3. Pay court to some lord or bishop.
4. On coins; "real" (royal) refers also to a particular Spanish coin.
5. Petrarchan lovers traditionally sigh, weep, and are frozen by their mistresses' neglect.

15   Add one man to the plaguy bill?⁶
      Soldiers find wars, and lawyers find out still
          Litigious men, which quarrels move,
          Though she and I do love.

      Call us what you will, we are made such by love;
20   Call her one, me another fly,
      We're tapers too, and at our own cost die,⁷
          And we in us find the eagle and the dove.⁸
              The phoenix riddle hath more wit
              By us: we two being one, are it.
25   So, to one neutral thing both sexes fit.
          We die and rise the same, and prove
          Mysterious by this love.

      We can die by it, if not live by love,
          And if unfit for tombs and hearse
30   Our legend be, it will be fit for verse;
          And if no piece of chronicle we prove,
              We'll build in sonnets pretty rooms;⁹
              As well a well-wrought urn becomes°   *befits*
      The greatest ashes, as half-acre tombs,
35   And by these hymns,¹ all shall approve°   *confirm*
          Us canonized for love:

      And thus invoke us: You whom reverend love
          Made one another's hermitage;
      You, to whom love was peace, that now is rage;
40   Who did the whole world's soul contract,² and drove
              Into the glasses of your eyes
              (So made such mirrors, and such spies,°   *spyglasses, telescopes*
      That they did all to you epitomize)
          Countries, towns, courts:³ Beg from above
45   A pattern of your love!

                                                          1633

6. Deaths from the plague, which raged in summer, were recorded by parish in weekly bills.
7. Flies were emblems of transience and lustfulness; tapers (candles) attract flies to their death and also consume themselves. "Die" in the punning terminology of the period means to experience orgasm, and there was a superstition that intercourse shortens life.
8. The eagle signifies strength and vision; the dove, meekness and mercy. The phoenix was a mythic Arabian bird, only one of which existed at any one time. After living five hundred years, it was consumed by fire, then rose triumphantly from its ashes a new bird. Thus it was a symbol of immortality and sometimes associated with Christ. "Eagle" and "dove" are also alchemical terms for processes leading to the rise of "phoenix," a stage in the transmutation of metals to gold.
9. "Rooms" (punning on the Italian meaning of "stanza") will contain their exploits, as prose chronicle histories contain great deeds done in the world.
1. The lover's own poems.
2. An alternative meaning is "extract."
3. "Countries, towns, courts" are objects of the verb "drove." The notion is that eyes both see and reflect the outside world, and so can contain all of it.

Song

Sweetest love, I do not go,
  For weariness of thee,
Nor in hope the world can show
  A fitter love lor me;
5   But since that I
Must die at last, 'tis best,
To use myself in jest
    Thus by fained deaths[1] to die.

Yesternight the sun went hence
10   And yet is here today,
He hath no desire nor sense,
  Nor half so short a way:
    Then fear not me,
But believe that I shall make
15 Speedier journeys, since I take
    More wings and spurs than he.

O how feeble is man's power,
  That if good fortune fall,
Cannot add another hour,
20   Nor a lost hour recall!
    But come bad chance,
And we join to'it our strength,
And we teach it art and length,
    Itself o'r us to'advance.

25 When thou sigh'st, thou sigh'st not wind,
  But sigh'st my soule away,
When thou weep'st, unkindly[2] kind,
  My life's blood doth decay.
    It cannot be
30 That thou lov'st me, as thou say'st,
If in thine my life thou waste,
    Thou art the best of me.

Let not thy divining° heart   *prophetic*
  Forethink me any ill,
35 Destiny may take thy part,
  And may thy fears fulfill;
    But think that we
Are but turned aside to sleep;
They who one another keep
40   Alive, ne'er parted be.

1633

---

1. I.e., absences.   2. Also carries the meaning "unnatural."

Air and Angels

Twice or thrice had I loved thee,
Before I knew thy face or name;
So in a voice, so in a shapeless flame,
Angels affect us oft, and worshipped be;
5   Still° when, to where thou wert, I came,   *always*
Some lovely glorious nothing[1] I did see.
    But since my soul, whose child love is,
Takes limbs of flesh, and else could nothing do,[2]
    More subtle° than the parent is   *rarified*
10 Love must not be, but take a body too;
    And therefore what thou wert, and who,
        I bid love ask, and now
That it assume thy body I allow,
And fix itself in thy lip, eye, and brow.
15 Whilst thus to ballast love I thought,
    And so more steadily to have gone,
With wares which would sink° admiration,   *overwhelm*
I saw I had love's pinnace° overfraught;°   *small boat/overballasted*
    Every thy hair for love to work upon
20 Is much too much, some fitter must be sought;
    For, nor in nothing, nor in things
Extreme and scatt'ring° bright, can love inhere. *diffused, dazzling*
    Then as an angel, face and wings
Of air, not pure as it, yet pure doth wear,
25   So thy love may be my love's sphere;[3]
        Just such disparity
As is 'twixt air and angels' purity,
'Twixt women's love and men's will ever be.[4]

1633

Break of Day[1]

'Tis true, 'tis day; what though it be?
O wilt thou therefore rise from me?
Why should we rise because 'tis light?
Did we lie down because 'twas night?
5 Love, which in spite of darkness brought us hither,
Should in despite of light keep us together.
Light hath no tongue, but is all eye;
If it could speak as well as spy,
This were the worst that it could say,
10 That being well, I fain would stay,

1. Spiritual beauty, the true object of love in Neo-platonic philosophy.
2. My soul could not function unless it were in a body.
3. Each sphere was thought to be governed by an angel (an intelligence).
4. It was commonly believed that angels, when they appeared to humans, assumed a body of air which, though pure, was less so than the angel's spiritual essence.
1. An aubade, or song of the lovers' parting at dawn, this poem is unusual for Donne in having a female speaker. The poem was given a musical setting and published in 1622, in William Corkine's *Second Book of Ayers*.

And that I loved my heart and honor so
That I would not from him, that had them, go.

Must business thee from hence remove?
O, that's the worst disease of love.
15 The poor, the foul, the false, love can
Admit, but not the busied man.
He which hath business, and makes love, doth do
Such wrong, as when a married man doth woo.

1622, 1633

A Valediction:[1] Of Weeping

Let me pour forth
My tears before thy face whilst I stay here,
For thy face coins them, and thy stamp° they bear,   *image*
And by this mintage they are something worth,
5   For thus they be
     Pregnant of thee;
Fruits of much grief they are, emblems° of more—   *symbols*
When a tear falls, that Thou falls which it bore,
So thou and I are nothing then, when on a diverse° shore.   *different*

10   On a round ball
A workman that hath copies by can lay
An Europe, Afric, and an Asia,
And quickly make that, which was nothing, all;[2]
     So doth each tear
15   Which thee doth wear,[3]
A globe, yea world, by that impression grow,
Till thy tears mixed with mine do overflow
This world; by waters sent from thee, my heaven dissolvèd so.

     O more than moon,
20 Draw not up seas to drown me in thy sphere;[4]
Weep me not dead in thine arms, but forbear
To teach the sea what it may do too soon.
     Let not the wind
     Example find
25 To do me more harm than it purposeth;
Since thou and I sigh one another's breath,
Whoe'er sighs most is cruelest, and hastes the other's death.

1633

---

1. A farewell poem, one of four so titled in the *Songs and Sonnets*. Another is *A Valediction: Forbidding Mourning*, p. 1248.
2. I.e., on a blank globe one can place maps of the continents and so convert a cypher ("nothing") into the whole world ("all").
3. Bears your image.
4. A star or planet with more power of attraction than the moon might not only affect tides but draw the very seas unto itself.

Love's Alchemy

Some that have deeper digged love's mine than I,
Say where his centric° happiness doth lie: *central*
   I have loved, and got, and told,
   But should I love, get, tell, till I were old,
5   I should not find that hidden mystery;
     O, 'tis imposture all:
And as no chemic° yet the elixir¹ got,   *alchemist*
   But glorifies his pregnant pot²
   If by the way to him befall
10 Some odoriferous thing, or medicinal;
   So lovers dream a rich and long delight,
   But get a winter-seeming summer's night.³

Our ease, our thrift, our honor, and our day,
Shall we for this vain bubble's shadow pay?
15   Ends love in this, that my man°   *servant*
Can be as happy as I can, if he can
Endure the short scorn of a bridegroom's play?
   That loving wretch that swears
'Tis not the bodies marry, but the minds,
20   Which he in her angelic finds,
   Would swear as justly that he hears,
In that day's rude hoarse minstrelsy, the spheres.⁴
   Hope not for mind in women; at their best
Sweetness and wit, they are but mummy, possessed.⁵

1633

A Nocturnal upon Saint Lucy's Day, Being the Shortest Day¹

'Tis the year's midnight and it is the day's,
Lucy's, who scarce seven hours herself unmasks;
   The sun is spent, and now his flasks²
   Send forth light squibs,° no constant rays.   *firecrackers*
5   The world's whole sap is sunk;
The general balm th' hydroptic³ earth hath drunk,
Whither, as to the bed's feet, life is shrunk,

---

1. A magic medicine sought by alchemists and reputed to heal all ills.
2. A fertile (and womb-shaped) retort, calling up the common analogy between producing the elixir of life and human generation.
3. A night cold as in winter and short as in summer.
4. The perfect harmony of the planets, moving in concentric crystalline spheres, is contrasted with the boistrous serenade of pots, pans, and trumpets, performed on the wedding night.
5. The syntax of the last two lines is unclear, and they are punctuated differently in various copies. The 1633 edition reads: "at their best, / Sweetnesse, and wit they are, but, *mummy*, possesst." Many modern editors punctuate as we do here.

"Mummy" suggests a corpselike body, without mind or spirit.
1. The nocturne, or night office of the Roman Catholic Church, is a service held in the primitive church at midnight. St. Lucy's Day fell on December 13 according to the old calendar still in use in England at the time, and its vigil (the previous day and night) is the winter solstice, the shortest day of the year. At this time of the year, the sun rises after 8 A.M. in the latitude of London and sets well before 4 P.M.
2. The stars are flasks, thought to store up light from the sun.
3. Dropsical, thus insatiably thirsty. "General balm": the supposedly life-preserving essence of all things.

Dead and interred; yet all these seem to laugh,
Compared with me, who am their epitaph.

10   Study me, then, you who shall lovers be
At the next world, that is, at the next spring;
    For I am every dead thing
    In whom love wrought new alchemy.
      For his art did express°   *extract*
15 A quintessence[4] even from nothingness,
From dull privations and lean emptiness.
He ruined me, and I am re-begot
Of absence, darkness, death: things which are not.

All others from all things draw all that's good,
20 Life, soul, form, spirit, whence they being have;
    I, by love's limbeck,[5] am the grave
    Of all that's nothing. Oft a flood
      Have we two wept, and so
Drowned the whole world, us two; oft did we grow
25 To be two chaoses when we did show
Care to aught else; and often absences
Withdrew our souls, and made us carcasses.

But I am by her death (which word wrongs her)
Of the first nothing the elixir grown;[6]
30   Were I a man, that I were one
    I needs must know; I should prefer,
      If I were any beast,
Some ends, some means; yea plants, yea stones detest
And love.[7] All, all some properties invest.
35 If I an ordinary nothing were,
As shadow, a light and body must be here.

But I am none; nor will my sun renew.
You lovers, for whose sake the lesser sun
    At this time to the Goat[8] is run
40   To fetch new lust and give it you,
      Enjoy your summer all.
Since she enjoys her long night's festival,
Let me prepare towards her, and let me call
This hour her vigil and her eve, since this
45 Both the year's and the day's deep midnight is.

1633

---

4. The reputed fifth essence, a celestial element beyond the mundane four elements, thought to be latent in all things and to be a universal cure. Alchemists sought to extract it.
5. Alembic; a vessel used in distilling.
6. I.e., the quintessence of that absolute nothing-ness that existed before the creation.
7. Beasts have intentions; plants and even stones (like lodestones) have attractions and antipathies.
8. The sign of Capricorn, which the sun enters at the winter solstice; the goat is an emblem of sexual vigor.

The Bait[1] *reply to reply of Raleigh.*

Come live with me and be my love,
And we will some new pleasures prove,
Of golden sands and crystal brooks,
With silken lines and silver hooks.

5 There will the river whispering run,
Warmed by thine eyes more than the sun.
And there the enamored fish will stay,
Begging themselves they may betray.

When thou wilt swim in that live bath,
10 Each fish, which every channel hath,
Will amorously to thee swim,
Gladder to catch thee, than thou him.

If thou, to be so seen, beest loath,
By sun or moon, thou darkenest both;
15 And if myself have leave to see,
I need not their light, having thee.

if you fall in love, it happens.

Let others freeze with angling reeds,
And cut their legs with shells and weeds,
Or treacherously poor fish beset
20 With strangling snare or windowy net;

Let coarse bold hands from slimy nest
The bedded fish in banks out-wrest,
Or curious traitors, sleave-silk flies,[2]
Bewitch poor fishes' wandering eyes.

the man is trying to get away now.

25 For thee, thou needest no such deceit,
For thou thyself art thine own bait;
That fish that is not catched thereby,
Alas, is wiser far than I.

the fish that gets away is lucky.

she is dangerous b/c no one can get away from her.

1633

The Apparition

When by thy scorn, O murderess, I am dead,
And that thou thinkst thee free
From all solicitation from me,
Then shall my ghost come to thy bed,
5 And thee, feigned vestal,[1] in worse arms shall see;

---

1. This poem is Donne's response to Marlowe's *Passionate Shepherd to His Love* (p. 989). Another of the many responses was Ralegh's *The Nymph's Reply to the Shepherd* (p. 879).

2. Flies made of unraveled silk. "Curious": exquisitely made.
1. Virgins consecrated to the Roman goddess Vesta.

Then thy sick taper will begin to wink,°   *flicker*
And he whose thou art then, being tired before,
Will, if thou stir, or pinch to wake him, think
    Thou call'st for more,
10 And in false sleep will from thee shrink,
And then, poor aspen wretch,[2] neglected thou
Bathed in a cold quicksilver sweat[3] wilt lie
    A verier° ghost than I;   *truer*
What I will say, I will not tell thee now,
15 Lest that preserve thee; and since my love is spent,
I had rather thou shouldst painfully repent,
Than by my threatenings rest still innocent.

1633

A Valediction: Forbidding Mourning[1]

[handwritten: saying goodbye to his wife.]

As virtuous men pass mildly away,
    And whisper to their souls to go,
Whilst some of their sad friends do say
    The breath goes now, and some say, No;

[handwritten: virtuous men die mildly b/c they are content]
[handwritten: he died so peaceful that they weren't sure he was dead.]

So let us melt, and make no noise,
    No tear-floods, nor sigh-tempests move;
'Twere profanation° of our joys   *desecration*
    To tell the laity our love.

[handwritten: If other people saw their love it wouldn't be holy any more]
[handwritten: secular]
[handwritten: they should part so quietly that people wouldn't notice]

Moving of th' earth brings harms and fears,   *unstable*
10   Men reckon what it did and meant;
    But trepidation of the spheres,
    Though greater far, is innocent.[2]

[handwritten: they are dedicated to love like a clergy.]
[handwritten: comparison to an earthquake instills panic, nosy movement not heavenly]

Dull sublunary[3] lovers' love   *[handwritten: earthly]*
    (Whose soul is sense) cannot admit
15 Absence, because it doth remove
    Those things which elemented° it.   *composed*

[handwritten: earthly love is superficial, but since they have heavenly love]

But we, by a love so much refined
    That our selves know not what it is,
Inter-assurèd of the mind,
20   Care less, eyes, lips, and hands to miss.

[handwritten: their love is strong no matter where or how far apart. they are]

Our two souls therefore, which are one,
    Though I must go, endure not yet

---

2. Aspen leaves flutter in the slightest breeze.
3. Sweating in terror; quicksilver (mercury) was a stock prescription for venereal disease, and sweating was part of the cure.
1. For "valediction" see p. 1244, n. 1. Izaak Walton speculated that this poem was addressed to Donne's wife on the occasion of his trip to the Continent in 1611, but there is no proof of that. Donne was, however, apprehensive about that trip; Walton also heard that, while abroad, Donne had a

startling vision of his wife holding a dead baby at about the time she gave birth to a stillborn child.
2. Earthquakes cause damage and were thought to be portentous. Trepidation (in the Ptolemaic cosmology, an oscillation of the ninth or crystalline sphere imparted to all the inner spheres), though a much more violent motion than an earthquake, is neither destructive nor sinister.
3. Beneath the moon, therefore earthly, sensual, and subject to change.

A breach, but an expansion,
  Like gold to airy thinness beat.

[handwritten: when they leave one another they are like gold that has been beaten (a very malleable metal that doesn't break) gold doesn't tarnish]

25 If they be two, they are two so
    As stiff twin compasses⁴ are two;

[handwritten: they make circles.]

  Thy soul, the fixed foot, makes no show
    To move, but doth, if th' other do.

  And though it in the center sit,
30   Yet when the other far doth roam,
  It leans and hearkens after it,
    And grows erect, as that comes home.

  Such wilt thou be to me, who must,
    Like th' other foot, obliquely run;
35 Thy firmness makes my circle just, *[handwritten: perfect]*
    And makes me end where I begun.

                                 1633

The Ecstasy¹

Where, like a pillow on a bed,
  A pregnant bank swelled up to rest
The violet's reclining head,
  Sat we two, one another's best.

5 Our hands were firmly cemented
    With a fast balm° which thence did spring,   *perspiration*
  Our eye-beams² twisted, and did thread
    Our eyes upon one double string;

  So to intergraft our hands, as yet
10   Was all our means to make us one,
  And pictures in our eyes to get°   *beget*
    Was all our propagation.³

  As 'twixt two equal armies Fate
    Suspends uncertain victory,
15 Our souls (which to advance their state
    Were gone out) hung 'twixt her and me;

  And whilst our souls negotiate there,
    We like sepulchral statues lay;   *[handwritten: statue on a tomb]*
  All day the same our postures were,
20   And we said nothing all the day.

4. The two legs of a geometer's or draughtsman's compass. This simile is the most famous example of the "metaphysical conceit" (see "Figurative language," in the "Literary Terminology" appendix to this volume).
1. From *ekstasis* (Greek), a movement of the soul outside of the body.
2. Invisible shafts of light, thought of as going out of the eyes and thereby enabling one to see things.
3. Reflections of each in the other's eyes, often called "making babies."

If any, so by love refined
    That he soul's language understood,
And by good love were grown all mind,[4]
    Within convenient distance stood,

25 He (though he know not which soul spake,
    Because both meant, both spake the same)
Might thence a new concoction[5] take,
    And part far purer than he came.

This ecstasy doth unperplex,
30   We said, and tell us what we love;
We see by this it was not sex;
    We see we saw not what did move;°   *motivate us*

But as all several° souls contain   *separate*
    Mixture of things, they know not what,
35 Love these mixed souls doth mix again,
    And makes both one, each this and that.

[handwritten: in love, two souls strengthen each other]

A single violet transplant,
    The strength, the color, and the size
    (All which before was poor and scant)
40   Redoubles still, and multiplies.

When love with one another so
    Interinanimates two souls,
That abler soul, which thence doth flow,
[handwritten: the soul created from the mix]   Defects of loneliness controls.

45 We then, who are this new soul, know
    Of what we are composed and made,
For th' atomies° of which we grow   *components*
    Are souls, whom no change can invade.

But O alas, so long, so far
50   Our bodies why do we forbear?
They are ours, though they are not we; we are
    The intelligences, they the sphere.[6]

We owe them thanks because they thus
    Did us to us at first convey,
55 Yielded their forces, sense, to us,
    Nor are dross to us, but allay.[7]

On man heaven's influence works not so
    But that it first imprints the air:[8]

---

4. On this higher love, see Bembo's ladder of love from *The Courtier*, p. 579.
5. In the alchemical sense of sublimation or purification.
6. In Ptolemaic astronomy, each planet, set in a transparent "sphere" that revolved and so carried it around the earth, was inhabited by a controlling angelic "intelligence."
7. "Dross" is an impurity that weakens metal; "allay" (alloy) strengthens it.
8. Astrological influences were thought to work on people through the medium of the surrounding air.

So soul into the soul may flow,
60   Though it to body first repair.°   *go*

As our blood labors to beget
    Spirits[9] as like souls as it can,
Because such fingers need° to knit   *are needed*
    That subtle knot which makes us man,

65 So must pure lovers' souls descend
        T' affections, and to faculties
Which sense may reach and apprehend;
        Else a great prince in prison lies.

To our bodies turn we then, that so
70   Weak men on love revealed may look;
Love's mysteries[1] in souls do grow,
        But yet the body is his book.

And if some lover, such as we,
        Have heard this dialogue of one,[2]
75 Let him still mark° us; he shall see   *observe*
        Small change when we are to bodies gone.

                                                                    1633

The Funeral

Whoever comes to shroud me, do not harm
        Nor question much
That subtle wreath of hair which crowns my arm;
The mystery, the sign you must not touch,
5   For 'tis my outward soul,
Viceroy to that, which then to heaven being gone,
        Will leave this to control,
And keep these limbs, her[1] provinces, from dissolution.

For if the sinewy thread[2] my brain lets fall
10   Through every part
Can tie those parts and make me one of all,
These hairs which upward grew, and strength and art
        Have from a better brain,
Can better do it; except° she meant that I   *unless*
15   By this should know my pain,
As prisoners then are manacled, when they're condemned to die.

Whate'er she meant by it, bury it with me,
        For since I am

9. Subtle substances thought to be produced by
the blood to serve as intermediaries between body
and soul.
1. The implied comparison is with God's mysteries, which are revealed and may be read in the book
of Nature and the book of Scripture.

2. "Dialogue of one" because "both meant, both
spake the same" (line 26).
1. The soul's, but also the mistress's (cf. "she," line
14).
2. The nervous system.

Love's martyr, it might breed idolatry,
20   If into others' hands these relics[3] came:
          As 'twas humility
      To afford to it all that a soul can do,
          So 'tis some bravery,
      That since you would save[4] none of me, I bury some of you.

                                                                    1633

The Blossom

      Little think'st thou, poor flower,
          Whom I have watched six or seven days,
      And seen thy birth, and seen what every hour
      Gave to thy growth, thee to this height to raise,
5   And now dost laugh and triumph on this bough,
              Little think'st thou
      That it will freeze anon, and that I shall
      Tomorrow find thee fall'n, or not at all.

          Little think'st thou, poor heart,
10   That labor'st yet to nestle thee,
      And think'st by hovering here to get a part
      In a forbidden or forbidding tree,[1]
      And hop'st her stiffness by long siege to bow,
              Little think'st thou
15   That thou tomorrow, ere that sun doth wake,
      Must with this sun and me a journey take.

          But thou, which lov'st to be
          Subtle to plague thyself, wilt say,
      Alas, if you must go, what's that to me?
20   Here lies my business, and here I will stay:
      You go to friends whose love and means present
              Various content
      To your eyes, ears, and tongue, and every part.
      If then your body go, what need you a heart?

25   Well, then, stay here; but know,
          When thou hast stayed and done thy most,
      A naked thinking heart that makes no show
      Is to a woman but a kind of ghost.
      How shall she know my heart; or, having none,
30   Know thee for one?
      Practice may make her know some other part,
      But take my word, she doth not know a heart.

---

3. Body parts or other objects belonging to a saint, venerated by Roman Catholics.
4. All the early printed texts read "have" (which carries sexual connotations), while many manu-scripts read "save."
1. The fruit of this tree is "forbidden" (presumably because the woman is married) or "forbidding" (because she is unwilling).

Meet me at London, then,
Twenty days hence, and thou shalt see
35   Me fresher and more fat° by being with men   *prosperous*
Than if I had stayed still with her and thee.
For God's sake, if you can, be you so too:
     I would give you
There to another friend, whom we shall find
40   As glad to have my body as my mind.

1633

The Relic

When my grave is broke up again
Some second guest to entertain
(For graves have learned that woman-head°   *female trait*
To be to more than one a bed),[1]
5   And he that digs it spies
A bracelet of bright hair about the bone,
     Will he not let us alone,
And think that there a loving couple lies,
Who thought that this device might be some way
10 To make their souls, at the last busy day,°   *Judgment Day*
Meet at this grave, and make a little stay?

If this fall in a time, or land,
Where mis-devotion[2] doth command,
Then he that digs us up will bring
15 Us to the Bishop and the King,
     To make us relics; then
Thou shalt be a Mary Magdalen, and I
     A something else thereby;
All women shall adore us, and some men;
20 And since at such times, miracles are sought,
I would have that age by this paper taught
What miracles we harmless lovers wrought.

First, we loved well and faithfully,
Yet knew not what we loved, nor why,
25 Difference of sex no more we knew,
     Than our guardian angels do;
     Coming and going, we
Perchance might kiss, but not between those meals;[3]
     Our hands ne'er touched the seals°   *sexual organs*
30 Which nature, injured by late law, sets free:[4]
These miracles we did: but now, alas,

1. Graves were often used to inter successive corpses, the bones of previous occupants being deposited in charnel houses.
2. False devotion, superstition. i.e., Roman Catholicism.
3. The kiss of salutation and parting.
4. Human law forbids the free love permitted by nature. "Late": recent (comparatively speaking).

All measure and all language I should pass,
Should I tell what a miracle she was.

1633

A Lecture upon the Shadow

Stand still, and I will read to thee
A lecture, Love, in love's philosophy.
   These three hours that we have spent
   Walking here, two shadows went
5 Along with us, which we ourselves produced;
But, now the sun is just above our head,
   We do those shadows tread
   And to brave clearness all things are reduced.
So, whilst our infant loves did grow,
10 Disguises did and shadows flow
From us and our care;° but now, 'tis not so.   *caution*

That love hath not attained the high'st degree
Which is still diligent lest others see.

Except° our loves at this noon stay,   *unless*
15 We shall new shadows make the other way.
   As the first were made to blind
   Others, these which come behind
Will work upon ourselves, and blind our eyes.
If our loves faint and westwardly decline,
20   To me thou falsely thine
   And I to thee mine actions shall disguise.
The morning shadows wear away,
But these grow longer all the day,
But, oh, love's day is short if love decay.

25 Love is a growing or full constant light,
And his first minute after noon is night.

1635

Elegy[1] 16. On His Mistress

By our first strange and fatal interview,
By all desires which thereof did ensue,
By our long starving hopes, by that remorse°   *pity*

1. In Latin poetry, an elegy is not necessarily a funeral lament but simply a discursive or reflective poem written in "elegiacs" (unrhymed couplets of alternating dactylic hexameters and pentameters). The subject matter primarily associated with this meter was sex, the most famous collection of ele- gies being Ovid's *Amores*. Several of Donne's ele- gies—almost all written in the 1590s—take Ovid as their principal model and resemble him in ingenious wit and in frank and unapologetic erot- icism. *Elegy 16* is highly dramatic.

Which my words' masculine persuasive force
5 Begot in thee, and by the memory
Of hurts which spies and rivals threatened me,
I calmly beg; but by thy father's wrath,
By all pains which want and divorcement hath,
I conjure thee; and all the oaths which I
10 And thou have sworn to seal joint constancy
Here I unswear and overswear them thus:
Thou shalt not love by ways so dangerous.
Temper, oh fair love, love's impetuous rage;
Be my true mistress still, not my feigned page.²
15 I'll go, and, by thy kind leave, leave behind
Thee, only worthy to nurse in my mind
Thirst to come back. Oh, if thou die before,
My soul from other lands to thee shall soar.
Thy (else almighty) beauty cannot move
20 Rage from the seas, nor thy love teach them love,
Nor tame wild Boreas' harshness.³ Thou hast read
How roughly he in pieces shiverèd
Fair Orithea, whom he swore he loved.
Fall ill or good, 'tis madness to have proved°   sought out
25 Dangers unurged; feed on this flattery,
That absent lovers one in th' other be.
Dissemble nothing, not a boy, nor change
Thy body's habit,° nor mind's; be not strange   clothing
To thyself only; all will spy in thy face
30 A blushing womanly discovering grace.
Richly clothed apes are called apes, and as soon
Eclipsed as bright we call the moon the moon.
Men of France, changeable chameleons,
Spitals° of diseases, shops of fashions,   hospitals
35 Love's fuellers⁴ and the rightest company
Of players which upon the world's stage be,
Will quickly know thee, and know⁵ thee; and alas!
Th' indifferent° Italian, as we pass   bisexual
His warm land, well content to think thee page,
40 Will hunt thee with such lust and hideous rage
As Lot's fair guests were vexed.⁶ But none of these
Nor spongy, hydroptic⁷ Dutch shall thee displease
If thou stay here. O stay here, for, for thee,
England is only a worthy gallery
45 To walk in expectation, till from thence
Our greatest king call thee to his presence.⁸
When I am gone, dream me some happiness,

---

2. The speaker's mistress wanted to accompany
him abroad, disguised as a page boy. Such esca-
pades occasionally took place in real life; in 1605,
Elizabeth Southwell, disguised as a page, went
abroad with Sir Robert Dudley.
3. God of the north wind; Ovid in *Metamorphoses*
6 describes the wild force with which Boreas
abducted Orithea.
4. Providers of aphrodisiacs.
5. "Know" in the sexual sense. "Alas" may pun on

"a lass."
6. The inhabitants of Sodom brought destruction
on themselves when they tried to rape two angels
who visited Lot in the guise of young men (Genesis
19.1–11).
7. Dropsical, thus insatiably thirsty.
8. Throne rooms commonly had antechambers
(galleries) where visitors waited until the monarch
was ready to see them.

Nor let thy looks our long-hid love confess;
Nor praise nor dispraise me, bless nor curse
50 Openly love's force, nor in bed fright thy nurse
With midnight's startings, crying out "Oh, oh!
Nurse, oh my love is slain, I saw him go
O'er the white Alps alone; I saw him, I,
Assailed, fight, taken, stabbed, bleed, fall, and die."
55 Augur me better chance, except dread Jove
Think it enough for me t' have had thy love.

1635

Elegy 19. To His Mistress Going to Bed[1]

Come, Madam, come, all rest my powers defy,
Until I labor, I in labor lie.[2]
The foe oft-times, having the foe in sight,
Is tired with standing though he never fight.
5 Off with that girdle,° like heaven's zone° glistering,   belt/zodiac
But a far fairer world encompassing.
Unpin that spangled breastplate[3] which you wear
That th' eyes of busy fools may be stopped there.
Unlace yourself, for that harmonious chime
10 Tells me from you that now it is bed-time.
Off with that happy busk,° which I envy,   bodice
That still can be and still can stand so nigh.
Your gown going off, such beauteous state reveals
As when from flowery meads th' hill's shadow steals.
15 Off with that wiry coronet and show
The hairy diadem which on you doth grow;
Now off with those shoes, and then safely tread
In this love's hallowed temple, this soft bed.
In such white robes, heaven's angels used to be
20 Received by men; thou, angel, bring'st with thee
A heaven like Mahomet's paradise;[4] and though
Ill spirits walk in white, we easily know
By this these angels from an evil sprite,
Those set our hairs, but these our flesh upright.
25   License my roving hands, and let them go
Before, behind, between, above, below.
O my America! my new-found-land,
My kingdom, safeliest when with one man manned,
My mine of precious stones, my empery,°   empire
30 How blest am I in this discovering thee!
To enter in these bonds is to be free;
There where my hand is set, my seal shall be.[5]

---

1. This poem reworks the central situation of Ovid's *Amores* 1.5 in much more dramatic terms.
2. Labor in the dual sense of "get to work (sexually)" and "distress."
3. The stomacher, an ornamental, often jeweled, covering for the chest, worn under the lacing of the bodice.

4. A place of sensual pleasure, thought to be populated by seductive houris for the delectation of the faithful.
5. The jokes mingle law with sex: where he has signed a document (placed his hand) he will now place his seal; and in the bonds of her arms he will find freedom.

Full nakedness! All joys are due to thee.
As souls unbodied, bodies unclothed must be,
35 To taste whole joys. Gems which you women use
Are like Atalanta's balls,[6] cast in men's views,
That when a fool's eye lighteth on a gem,
His earthly soul may covet theirs, not them.
Like pictures, or like books' gay coverings, made
40 For laymen, are all women thus arrayed;
Themselves are mystic books, which only we
(Whom their imputed grace will dignify)
Must see revealed.[7] Then since that I may know,
As liberally as to a midwife show
45 Thyself: cast all, yea, this white linen hence,
Here is no penance, much less innocence.[8]
    To teach thee, I am naked first; why then
What need'st thou have more covering than a man?

                                                    1669

Satire 3

In satire the author holds a subject up to ridicule or to scorn. Like his elegies, Donne's five verse satires were written in his twenties and are in the forefront of an effort in the 1590s (by Donne, Ben Jonson, Joseph Hall, and John Marston) to naturalize those classical forms in England. While elements of satire figure in many different kinds of literature, the great models for formal verse satire were the Roman poets Horace and Juvenal, the former for an ubanely witty style, the latter for an indignant or angry manner. While Donne's other satires call on these models, his third satire more nearly resembles a third Roman satirist, Persius, known for an abstruse style and moralizing manner. This work is a strenuous discussion of an acute theological problem, for the age and for Donne himself: How may one discover the true Christian church among so many claimants to that role? At the time Donne wrote this, he was in the process of leaving the Roman Catholic Church of his heritage for the Church of England.

Satire 3

Kind pity chokes my spleen;[1] brave scorn forbids
Those tears to issue which swell my eyelids;
I must not laugh, nor weep° sins, and be wise: *lament*
Can railing then cure these worn maladies?
5 Is not our mistress, fair Religion,
As worthy of all our souls' devotion
As virtue was to the first blinded age?[2]

6. Atalanta, running a race against her suitor Hippomenes, was beaten when he dropped golden balls (apples) for her to pick up. Donne reverses the story.
7. By granting favors to their lovers, women impute to them grace that they don't deserve, as God (in Calvinist doctrine) imputes grace to undeserving sinners. Laymen can only look at the covers of mystic books (women) but "we" elect can read them.
8. Some manuscripts read: "There is no penance due to innocence." White garments would be appropriate either for the innocent virgin or for the sinner doing formal penance.
1. The seat of bile, hence scorn and ridicule.
2. The age of paganism, blind to Christianity but capable of natural morality ("virtue").

Are not heaven's joys as valiant to assuage
Lusts, as earth's honor was to them?° Alas,   *pagans*
10   As we do them in means, shall they surpass
Us in the end, and shall thy father's spirit
Meet blind philosophers in heaven, whose merit
Of strict life may be imputed faith,[3] and hear
Thee, whom he taught so easy ways and near
15   To follow, damned? O, if thou dar'st, fear this;
This fear great courage and high valor is.
Dar'st thou aid mutinous Dutch,[4] and dar'st thou lay
Thee in ships, wooden sepulchers, a prey
To leaders' rage, to storms, to shot, to dearth?°   *famine*
20   Dar'st thou dive seas and dungeons° of the earth?   *mines, caves*
Hast thou courageous fire to thaw the ice
Of frozen North discoveries?[5] and thrice
Colder than salamanders, like divine
Children in the oven,[6] fires of Spain, and the line,
25   Whose countries limbecks to our bodies be,
Canst thou for gain bear?[7] And must every he
Which cries not "Goddess!" to thy mistress, draw,°   *fight a duel*
Or eat thy poisonous words? Courage of straw!
O desperate coward, wilt thou seem bold, and
30   To thy foes and his° (who made thee to stand   *God's*
Sentinel in his world's garrison) thus yield,
And for forbidden wars leave th' appointed field?[8]
Know thy foes: The foul Devil (whom thou
Strivest to please) for hate, not love, would allow
35   Thee fain his whole realm to be quit;° and as   *to satisfy you*
The world's all parts wither away and pass,[9]
So the world's self, thy other loved foe, is
In her decrepit wane, and thou, loving this,
Dost love a withered and worn strumpet; last,
40   Flesh (itself's death) and joys which flesh can taste
Thou lovest; and thy fair goodly soul, which doth
Give this flesh power to taste joy, thou dost loathe.
Seek true religion. O, where? Mirreus,[1]
Thinking her unhoused here, and fled from us,°
45   Seeks her at Rome; there, because he doth know
That she was there a thousand years ago.
He loves her rags so, as we here obey

3. Donne's formulation wittily turns on its head the key concept of reformed Protestant theology—that salvation is to be achieved only by imputing Christ's merits to Christians through faith—by suggesting that virtuous pagans might be saved by imputing faith to them on the basis of their moral life.
4. English volunteers took frequent part with the Dutch in their wars against Spain. Donne himself had sailed in two raiding expeditions against the Spanish (see *The Storm*, p. 1260).
5. Many explorers tried to find a northwest passage to the Pacific.
6. In the biblical story (Daniel 3), Shadrach, Meshack, and Abednego were rescued from a fiery furnace. The salamander (a lizardlike creature) was

thought to be so cold-blooded that it could live in fire.
7. The object of "bear" is "fires of Spain, and the line"—inquisitorial and equatorial heats, which roast people as chemists heat materials in "limbecks" (alembics, or vessels for distilling).
8. Of moral struggle.
9. The common belief that the world was growing old and becoming decrepit.
1. The satiric types in this passage represent different creeds: "Mirreus" is a Roman Catholic; "Crantz" an austere Calvinist Presbyterian of Geneva; "Graius" a Church of England Erastian who believes in any religion sponsored by the state; "Phrygius" a skeptic; and "Graccus" a complete relativist.

The statecloth[2] where the Prince sat yesterday.
Crantz to such brave loves will not be enthralled,
50 But loves her only, who at Geneva is called
Religion—plain, simple, sullen, young,
Contemptuous, yet unhandsome; as among
Lecherous humors,° there is one that judges   *temperaments*
No wenches wholesome but coarse country drudges.
55 Graius stays still at home here, and because
Some preachers, vile ambitious bawds, and laws
Still new, like fashions, bid him think that she
Which dwells with us is only perfect, he
Embraceth her whom his godfathers will
60 Tender to him, being tender, as wards still
Take such wives as their guardians offer, or
Pay values.[3] Careless Phrygius doth abhor
All, because all cannot be good, as one
Knowing some women whores, dares marry none.
65 Graccus loves all as one, and thinks that so
As women do in divers countries go
In divers habits, yet are still one kind,
So doth, so is religion; and this blind-
ness too much light breeds;[4] but unmoved thou
70 Of force° must one, and forced but one allow;   *necessity*
And the right; ask thy father which is she,
Let him ask his; though truth and falsehood be
Near twins, yet truth a little elder is;
Be busy to seek her, believe me this,
75 He's not of none, nor worst, that seeks the best.[5]
To adore, or scorn an image, or protest,
May all be bad; doubt wisely; in strange way
To stand inquiring right, is not to stray;
To sleep, or run wrong, is. On a huge hill,
80 Cragged and steep, Truth stands, and he that will
Reach her, about must, and about must go,
And what the hill's suddenness resists, win so;
Yet strive so, that before age, death's twilight,
Thy soul rest, for none can work in that night.[6]
85 To will° implies delay, therefore now do.   *intend a future act*
Hard deeds, the body's pains; hard knowledge too
The mind's endeavors reach,° and mysteries   *achieve*
Are like the sun, dazzling, yet plain to all eyes.
Keep the truth which thou hast found; men do not stand
90 In so ill case here, that God hath with his hand
Signed kings' blank charters to kill whom they hate,
Nor are they vicars, but hangmen to fate.[7]
Fool and wretch, wilt thou let thy soul be tied

2. The royal canopy, a symbol of kingly power.
3. If minors in care of a guardian (in wardship) rejected the wives offered ("tendered") to them they had to pay fines ("values").
4. I.e., being blind to the differences between religions, Graccus has too much light to see where truth might lie.

5. The person who seeks the best church is neither an unbeliever nor the worst sort of believer.
6. Echoes John 9.4, "the night cometh, when no man can work."
7. Kings are not God's vicars on earth, with license ("blank charters") to persecute or kill whomever they wish on grounds of religion.

To man's laws, by which she shall not be tried
95 At the last day? O, will it then boot° thee   *profit*
To say a Philip, or a Gregory,
A Harry, or a Martin taught thee this?[8]
Is not this excuse for mere° contraries   *complete*
Equally strong? Cannot both sides say so?
100 That thou mayest rightly obey power, her bounds know;
Those passed, her nature and name is changed; to be
Then humble to her is idolatry.
As streams are, power is; those blest flowers that dwell
At the rough stream's calm head, thrive and prove well,
105 But having left their roots, and themselves given
To the stream's tyrannous rage, alas, are driven
Through mills, and rocks, and woods, and at last, almost
Consumed in going, in the sea are lost:
So perish souls, which more choose men's unjust
110 Power from God claimed, than God himself to trust.

1633

The Storm[1]

To Mr. Christopher Brooke

Thou which art I[2] ('tis nothing to be so),
Thou which art still thyself, by these shalt know
Part of our passage; and a hand or eye
By Hilliard[3] drawn is worth an history
5   By a worse painter made; and (without pride)
When by thy judgment they are dignified,
My lines are such: 'tis the preeminence
Of friendship only to impute excellence.
     England, to whom we owe what we be and have,
10 Sad that her sons did seek a foreign grave
(For Fate's or Fortune's drifts° none can soothsay,°   *intentions/predict*
Honor and misery have one face° and way),   *appearance*
From out her pregnant entrails sighed a wind
Which at th' air's middle marble[4] room did find
15 Such strong resistance that itself it threw
Downward again; and so when it did view

---

8. "Philip" is Philip II of Spain, "Gregory" is Pope Gregory XIII or XIV, "Harry" is England's Henry VIII, and "Martin" is Martin Luther.
1. *The Storm* is a display of virtuoso wit, but it is also factual reporting of a historical event. In 1597, Elizabeth, alarmed by reports of a second Armada being prepared by Philip II of Spain, authorized a preemptive strike under the primary leadership of Essex and Ralegh; Donne went along as a gentleman volunteer. Having started against Cádiz, the fleet ran into a violent storm, a result of which was this verse letter; later in the summer, after refitting at Plymouth, the fleet sailed again toward the

Azores. But there the adventurers ran into exactly the opposite weather problem, a prolonged calm, about which Donne wrote a second verse letter, probably addressed, like the first, to Christopher Brooke, a close friend from the Inns of Court, who also attended Donne's clandestine marriage.
2. In Neoplatonic philosophy, friends have, as it were, one soul in two bodies.
3. Nicholas Hilliard, the most famous portrait painter and miniaturist of the Elizabethan age.
4. The coldest middle region, where hail, snow, and fierce storms took form.

How in the port our fleet dear time did leese,°   *lose*
Withering like prisoners which lie but for fees,[5]
Mildly it kissed our sails, and fresh and sweet
20   As to a stomach sterved,° whose insides meet,   *starving*
Meat[6] comes, it came; and swole our sails, when we
So joyed, as Sara her swelling joyed to see.[7]
     But 'twas but° so kind as our countrymen   *only*
Which bring friends one day's way, and leave them then.
25   Then like two mighty kings, which dwelling far
Asunder, meet against a third to war,
The south and west winds joined, and as they blew,
Waves like a rolling trench before them threw.
     Sooner than you read this line did the gale,
30   Like shot, not feared till felt, our sails assail;
And what at first was called a gust, the same
Hath now a storm's, anon a tempest's name.
Jonas, I pity thee, and curse those men
Who when the storm raged most did wake thee then;[8]
35   Sleep is pain's easiest salve, and doth fulfill
All offices of death except to kill.
But when I waked, I saw that I saw not;
I° and the sun which should teach me had forgot   *ay(?)*
East, west, day, night, and I could only say,
40   If the world had lasted, now it had been day.
Thousands our noises were, yet we 'mongst all
Could none by his right name but thunder call.
Lightning was all our light, and it rained more
Than if the sun had drunk the sea before.
45   Some coffined in their cabins lie, equally
Grieved that they are not dead and yet must die;
And as sin-burdened souls from graves will creep
At the last day, some forth their cabins peep,
And tremblingly ask what news, and do hear so
50   Like jealous husbands what they would not know.
Some sitting on the hatches would seem there°   *from that position*
With hideous gazing to fear° away fear.   *frighten*
Then note they the ship's sicknesses, the mast
Shaked with this ague, and the hold and waist°   *amidships*
55   With a salt dropsy° clogged, and all our tacklings   *excess of sea water*
Snapping, like too-high-stretched treble strings.
And from our tattered sails rags drop down so
As from one hanged in chains a year ago.[9]
Even our ordnance, placed for our defense,
60   Strive to break loose and 'scape away from thence.[1]
     Pumping hath tired our men, and what's the gain?

---

5. Prisoners often languished in jail for lack of money to pay the jailers' fees.
6. Donne's fondness for repeating in immediate proximity the same sound or word, not always as puns, is apparent here: "meat/Meet"; "comes, it came"; and in line 30, "sails assail."
7. Sarah, wife of Abraham, laughed with joy when she learned she was pregnant with Isaac at age 90; Abraham was 103 (Genesis 2.6–7).

8. Jonah, asleep in his storm-tossed vessel, was awakened and accused of bringing bad luck (Jonah 1.5–6).
9. After being executed, criminals were often left chained indefinitely on the gallows, as a warning to others.
1. Cannon ("ordnance") torn loose from their moorings were a fearful peril in a rough sea.

Seas into seas thrown we suck in again.
Hearing hath deafed our sailors, and if they
Knew how to hear, there's none knows what to say.
65 Compared to these storms, death is but a qualm,
Hell somewhat lightsome, and the Bermuda calm.[2]
Darkness, light's elder brother, his birthright
Claims o'er this world, and to heaven hath chasèd light.
All things are one, and that one none° can be,   *nothing*
70 Since all forms uniform deformity
Doth cover, so that we, except God say
Another *Fiat*, shall have no more day.[3]
So violent yet long these furies be,
That though thine absence sterve° me, I wish not thee.   *famish*

1597   1633

An Anatomy of the World   Donne composed and published this poem in
1611 to mark the first anniversary of the death of Elizabeth Drury, fifteen-year-old
daughter of his patron and friend Sir Robert Drury. On the actual occasion of her
death he composed a "Funeral Elegy," and on the second anniversary he wrote a
companion poem to this one, titled *The Progress of the Soul* (The Second Anniversary),
publishing all three poems together in 1612. The issue here is not personal grief:
responding to criticism of his wildly hyperbolic praises of Elizabeth, Donne commented that he had never met the young woman but intended rather to describe "the
Idea of a woman, and not as she was." Nor is this merely a poem to please a patron,
though Donne obviously hoped to do that. Rather, as the full title indicates, Donne
took the occasion of Elizabeth's untimely death to analyze (the term "anatomy" evokes
both a rigorous logical analysis and a medical dissection in an anatomy theater) the
corruption, decay, and disintegration of the world in all its aspects, due ultimately to
the Fall of humankind. Here, the death of the young virgin Elizabeth is made to figure
that loss and all its dire effects; in the Second Anniversary her death figures the soul's
progress to heavenly glory. For the *Anatomy*, we give the long introduction (lines 1–
90) and the first two of the four meditations (lines 91–246), each of which contains
a lament for the various aspects of humankind's and the world's deterioration, in a
eulogy of the dead girl as symbol of lost innocence, and a two-line refrain. The marginal glosses on the left-hand side are by Donne, added in 1612.

From An Anatomy of the World

From *The First Anniversary*

The entry into   When that rich soul which to her heaven is gone,
the work.   Whom all they celebrate who know they have one
                   (For who is sure he hath a soul, unless
                   It see, and judge, and follow worthiness,
                   And by deeds praise it? He who doth not this,   5

2. The Bermudas lie in a turbulent area of ocean;
compare Shakespeare, "the still-vex'd Bermoothes"
in *The Tempest* 1.2, and the modern-day "Bermuda

triangle."
3. By saying "Let there be light" (*Fiat lux*), God
created the first day (Genesis 1.3).

May lodge an inmate soul, but 'tis not his);
When that queen ended here her progress time,[1]
And, as to her standing house,[2] to heaven did climb,
Where, loath to make the saints attend° her long,   *await*
She's now a part both of the choir and song,   10
This world in that great earthquake languishèd;
For in a common bath of tears it bled,
Which drew the strongest vital spirits[3] out:
But succored° then with a perplexèd doubt,   *comforted*
Whether the world did lose or gain in this   15
(Because since now no other way there is
But goodness to see her, whom all would see,
All must endeavor to be good as she),
This great consumption to a fever turned,
And so the world had fits; it joyed, it mourned.   20
And as men think that agues physic are,[4]
And the ague being spent, give over care,
So thou, sick world, mistak'st thyself to be
Well, when, alas, thou art in a lethargy.°   *in a near-death coma*
Her death did wound and tame thee then, and then   25
Thou might'st have better spared the sun, or man;
That wound was deep, but 'tis more misery
That thou hast lost thy sense and memory.
'Twas heavy° then to hear thy voice of moan,   *sad, depressing*
But this is worse, that thou art speechless grown.   30
Thou hast forgot thy name thou hadst; thou wast
Nothing but she, and her thou hast o'erpast.°   *outlived*
For as a child kept from the font,° until   *baptismal font*
A prince, expected long, come to fulfill
The ceremonies, thou unnamed had'st laid,   35
Had not her coming, thee her palace made:[5]
Her name defined thee, gave thee form and frame,
And thou forget'st to celebrate thy name.
    Some months she hath been dead (but being dead,
Measures of times are all determinèd),°   *ceased*
But long she hath been away, long, long, yet none
Offers to tell us who it is that's gone.
But as in states doubtful of future heirs,
When sickness without remedy impairs
The present prince, they're loath it should be said   45
The prince doth languish, or the prince is dead:
So mankind, feeling now a general thaw,°   *melting, disintegration*
A strong example gone, equal to law,
The cèment which did faithfully compact
And glue all virtues, now resolved,° and slacked,   *dissolved*
Thought it some blasphemy to say she was dead,
Or that our weakness was discoverèd°   *disclosed*

1. "That queen" is Elizabeth Drury, implicitly compared to Queen Elizabeth, who liked to go on "progresses," formal visits from one country house to another.
2. I.e., her royal palace or permanent residence.
3. "Vital spirits" of the blood were mysterious agents supposed to link soul with body.
4. "Ague" is chills and fever. "Physic": medicine. Some people think the fever stage of the disease is itself a cure.
5. The sick world is still being addressed; until it was made her palace, the world was a nameless nothing.

In that confession; therefore spoke no more
Than tongues, the soul being gone, the loss deplore.
But though it be too late to succor thee,   55
Sick world, yea, dead, yea, putrefied, since she,
Thy intrinsic balm[6] and thy preservative,
Can never be renewed, thou never live,
I (since no man can make thee live) will try
What we may gain by thy anatomy.[7]   60
Her death hath taught us dearly that thou art
Corrupt and mortal in thy purest part.
   Let no man say, the world itself being dead,
'Tis labor lost to have discoverèd
The world's infirmities, since there is none   65
Alive to study this dissection;

What life the   For there's a kind of world remaining still,
world hath still.   Though she which did inanimate and fill
The world be gone, yet in this last long night,
Her ghost doth walk; that is, a glimmering light,   70
A faint weak love of virtue and of good
Reflects from her on them which understood
Her worth; and though she have shut in all day,
The twilight of her memory doth stay;
Which, from the carcass of the old world free,   75
Creates a new world; and new creatures be
Produced:[8] the matter and the stuff of this,
Her virtue, and the form our practice is;
And though to be thus elemented,° arm   *constituted*
These creatures, from home-born intrinsic harm   80
(For all assumed° unto this dignity   *raised*
So many weedless Paradises be,
Which of themselves produce no venomous sin,
Except some foreign serpent bring it in),
Yet, because outward storms the strongest break,   85
And strength itself by confidence grows weak,
This new world may be safer, being told

The sickness   The dangers and diseases of the old:
of the world.   For with due temper men do then forgo
Or covet things, when they their true worth know.   90

Impossibility of   There is no health; physicians say that we
health.   At best enjoy but a neutrality.
And can there be worse sickness than to know
That we are never well, nor can be so?
We are born ruinous;° poor mothers cry   *falling into ruin*
That children come not right, nor orderly,
Except they headlong come and fall upon
An ominous precipitation.[9]
How witty's° ruin! how importunate   *ingenious*

---

6. A medicine that preserved one in perfect health forever.
7. I.e., by dissecting and analyzing the world's corpse.
8. The sun was thought to have power to breed new life out of carcasses and mud.

9. "We do not make account that a child comes right, except it come with the head forward, and thereby prefigure that headlong falling into calamities which it must suffer after" (Donne, *Sermons*, ed. Potter & Simpson, 4.333).

Upon mankind! It labored to frustrate   100
Even God's purpose; and made Woman, sent
For man's relief, cause of his languishment.
They were to good ends, and they are so still,
But accessory, and principal in ill.[1]
For that first marriage was our funeral: 105
One woman at one blow then killed us all,
And singly, one by one, they kill us now.
We do delightfully ourselves allow
To that consumption; and profusely blind,
We kill ourselves to propagate our kind.[2]   110
   And yet we do not that; we are not men:
There is not now that mankind which was then
When as the sun and man did seem to strive

Shortness of   (Joint tenants[3] of the world) who should survive;
life.   When stag and raven and the long-lived tree,   115
Compared with man, died in minority;[4]
When, if a slow-paced star had stolen away
From the observer's marking, he might stay
Two or three hundred years to see it again,
And then make up his observation plain;   120
When, as the age was long, the size was great;
Man's growth confessed and recompensed the meat;[5]
So spacious and large, that every soul
Did a fair kingdom and large realm control;
And when the very stature, thus erect,   125
Did that soul a good way towards heaven direct,
Where is this mankind now? who lives to age
Fit to be made Methusalem his page?
Alas, we scarce live long enough to try
Whether a new-made clock run right, or lie.   130
Old grandsires talk of yesterday with sorrow,
And for our children we reserve tomorrow.
So short is life that every peasant strives,
In a torn house, or field, to have three lives.[6]
   And as in lasting, so in length is man   135

Smallness of   Contracted to an inch, who was a span;[7]
stature.   For had a man at first in forests strayed,
Or shipwrecked in the sea, one would have laid
A wager that an elephant or whale
That met him would not hastily assail   140
A thing so equal to him: now, alas,
The fairies and the pygmies well may pass
As credible; mankind decays so soon,

1. Women are only helpers in good but leaders in evil. "That first marriage" (line 105): Adam and Eve's.
2. Popular superstition had it that every act of sex shortened one's life by a day.
3. Joint owners. The survivor would enjoy sole ownership.
4. Stags, ravens, and oak trees were thought to live particularly long, but compared with early humans, they died in youth.

5. Early humans were thought to have eaten better than modern humans, lived longer, and grown to greater stature. Methuselah (below) is said to have lived 969 years (Genesis 5.27).
6. Leases of farmland were often made for "three lives," i.e., through the longest-lived of three designated persons.
7. I.e., the distance from tip of thumb to tip of little finger, about nine inches.

We're scarce our fathers' shadows cast at noon.
Only death adds to our length:[8] nor are we grown   145
In stature to be men, till we are none.
But this were light,° did our less volume hold   *a trifle*
All the old text, or had we changed to gold
Their silver; or disposed into less glass
Spirits of virtue,[9] which then scattered was.   150
But 'tis not so: we're not retired, but damped;[1]
And as our bodies, so our minds are cramped:
'Tis shrinking, not close weaving, that hath thus
In mind and body both bedwarfèd us.
We seem ambitious, God's whole work to undo;   155
Of nothing He made us, and we strive, too,
To bring ourselves to nothing back; and we
Do what we can to do it so soon as He.
With new diseases[2] on ourselves we war,
And with new physic,[3] a worse engine far.   160
    Thus man, this world's vice-emperor, in whom
All faculties, all graces are at home—
And if in other creatures they appear,
They're but man's ministers and legates there,
To work on their rebellions, and reduce   165
Them to civility, and to man's use—
This man, whom God did woo, and loath to attend°   *wait*
Till man came up, did down to man descend,
This man, so great, that all that is, is his,
Oh what a trifle, and poor thing he is!   170
If man were anything, he's nothing now:
Help, or at least some time to waste, allow[4]
To his other wants, yet when he did depart°   *part with*
With her whom we lament, he lost his heart.
    She, of whom th' ancients seemed to prophesy   175
When they called virtues by the name of *she;*[5]
She in whom virtue was so much refined
That for allay° unto so pure a mind   *alloy*
She took the weaker sex, she that could drive
The poisonous tincture, and the stain of Eve,   180
Out of her thoughts and deeds, and purify
All, by a true religious alchemy;
She, she is dead; she's dead: when thou knowest this,
Thou knowest how poor a trifling thing man is.
And learn'st thus much by our anatomy,   185
The heart being perished, no part can be free.
And that except thou feed (not banquet)[6] on
The supernatural food, religion,
Thy better growth grows witherèd and scant;
Be more than man, or thou'rt less than an ant.   190

---

8. The corpse of a person is said to measure a little
more than his or her height when alive.
9. I.e., distilled virtue, which would fit into a
smaller bottle. "Virtue" includes the sense of
"power" as well as that of "goodness."
1. I.e., not compressed but shrunk.
2. I.e., influenza, and especially syphilis.

3. New medications—said to be far worse than
the diseases they ostensibly combat.
4. One might give.
5. The virtues are all represented in Latin by feminine nouns and portrayed as female figures.
6. Taste, nibble. A banquet usually contained des-
serts and delicacies.

Then, as mankind, so is the world's whole frame
Quite out of joint, almost created lame:
For, before God had made up all the rest,
Corruption entered and depraved the best.
It seized the angels,[7] and then first of all   195
The world did in her cradle take a fall,
And turned her brains, and took a general maim,
Wronging each joint of th' universal frame.
The noblest part, man, felt it first; and then
Decay of nature Both beasts and plants, cursed in the curse of man.[8]   200
in other parts. So did the world from the first hour decay,
That evening was beginning of the day,[9]
And now the springs and summers which we see
Like sons of women after fifty be.[1]
And new philosophy calls all in doubt: 205
The element of fire is quite put out;[2]
The sun is lost, and the earth, and no man's wit°   *intellect*
Can well direct him where to look for it.
And freely men confess that this world's spent,°   *exhausted*
When in the planets and the firmament   210
They seek so many new;[3] they see that this
Is crumbled out again to his atomies.°   *atoms*
'Tis all in pieces, all coherence gone;
All just supply, and all relation:
Prince, subject; father, son,[4] are things forgot,   215
For every man alone thinks he hath got
To be° a phoenix, and that there can be   *has become*
None of that kind of which he is, but he.[5]
      This is the world's condition now, and now
She that should all parts to reunion bow,   220
She that had all magnetic force alone,
To draw and fasten sundered parts in one;
She whom wise nature had invented then
When she observed that every sort of men
Did in their voyage in this world's sea stray,   225
And needed a new compass for their way;
She that was best, and first original
Of all fair copies, and the general
Steward to Fate;[6] she whose rich eyes and breast
Gilt the West Indies, and perfumed the East;[7]   230
Whose having breathed in this world did bestow
Spice on those isles, and bade them still smell so,

7. The angels who fell from heaven with Satan and became demons. As purely intellectual beings, angels are the world's "brains" (line 197).
8. For a similar account of the way humankind's fall corrupted the physical universe, see *Paradise Lost* 10.706ff.
9. The world's day began with the darkness of sin.
1. Women giving birth after the age of fifty were thought to produce feeble or defective children.
2. The Polish astronomer Copernicus in the 16th century and the Italian Galileo in the 17th led the argument of the "new philosophy," that the sun, not the earth, is the center of the cosmos. This theory also contradicted the notion that a realm of

fire surrounded the earth beyond the air.
3. Galileo's first accounts of his telescope observations were published in 1610, intensifying speculations as to whether there are other inhabited worlds.
4. I.e., all traditional relationships.
5. Legend had it that there was only one phoenix on earth at any one time.
6. Fate or Providence disposes all things, but she was their "Steward," dispensing what has been decreed.
7. The West Indies were a source of gold, the East Indies a source of spices and perfumes.

And that rich Indie which doth gold inter
Is but as single money,° coined from her;   *small change*
She to whom this world must itself refer   235
As suburbs, or the microcosm of her,
She, she is dead; she's dead: when thou know'st this,
Thou know'st how lame a cripple this world is.
And learn'st thus much by our anatomy,
That this world's general sickness doth not lie   240
In any humor,[8] or one certain part;
But, as thou sawest it rotten at the heart,
Thou seest a hectic° fever hath got hold   *consumptive*
Of the whole substance, not to be controlled,
And that thou hast but one way not to admit   245
The world's infection, to be none of it.

*   *   *

1611

From Holy Sonnets[1]

1

Thou hast made me, and shall thy work decay?
Repair me now, for now mine end doth haste;
I run to death, and death meets me as fast,
And all my pleasures are like yesterday.
5   I dare not move my dim eyes any way,
Despair behind, and death before doth cast
Such terror, and my feeble flesh doth waste
By sin in it, which it towards hell doth weigh.°   *incline, weigh down*
Only thou art above, and when towards thee
10 By thy leave I can look, I rise again;
But our old subtle foe so tempteth me
That not one hour myself I can sustain.
Thy grace may wing° me to prevent° his art,   *give wings to/forestall*
And thou like adamant° draw mine iron heart.   *magnetic lodestone*

1635

5

I am a little world[2] made cunningly
Of elements, and an angelic sprite;°   *spirit, soul*

8. The four bodily "humors"—blood, phlegm, bile, choler—combine to make up a temperament; when they are out of balance a person is ill. So with the world.
1. Donne wrote a variety of religious poems (called "Divine Poems"), including a group of nineteen *Holy Sonnets* that reflect his interest in Jesuit and especially Protestant meditative procedures. He probably began writing them about 1609, a decade or so after leaving the Catholic church. Our

selections follow the traditional numbering established in Sir Herbert Grierson's influential edition, since for most of these sonnets we cannot tell when they were written or in what order they were intended to appear.
2. The traditional idea of the human being as microcosm (a "little world"), containing in miniature all the features of the macrocosm or great world.

But black sin hath betrayed to endless night
My world's both parts, and O, both parts must die.
5   You which beyond that heaven which was most high
Have found new spheres, and of new lands can write,[3]
Pour new seas in mine eyes, that so I might
Drown my world with my weeping earnestly,
Or wash it if it must be drowned no more.[4]
10   But O, it must be burnt! Alas, the fire
Of lust and envy have burnt it heretofore,
And made it fouler; let their flames retire,
And burn me, O Lord, with a fiery zeal
Of thee and thy house, which doth in eating heal.[5]

                                                            1635

                              7

At the round earth's imagined corners,[6] blow
Your trumpets, angels; and arise, arise
From death, you numberless infinities
Of souls, and to your scattered bodies go:
5   All whom the flood did, and fire[7] shall, o'erthrow,
All whom war, dearth,° age, agues,° tyrannies,   *famine/fevers*
Despair, law, chance hath slain, and you whose eyes
Shall behold God, and never taste death's woe.[8]
But let them sleep, Lord, and me mourn a space;
10   For, if above all these, my sins abound,
'Tis late to ask abundance of thy grace
When we are there. Here on this lowly ground,
Teach me how to repent; for that's as good
As if thou hadst sealed my pardon with thy blood.

                                                            1633

                              9

If poisonous minerals, and if that tree[9]
Whose fruit threw death on else-immortal us,
If lecherous goats, if serpents envious[1]
Cannot be damned, alas! why should I be?
5   Why should intent or reason, born in me,
Make sins, else equal, in me more heinous?
And, mercy being easy and glorious
To God, in his stern wrath why threatens he?
But who am I that dare dispute with thee

3. Astronomers, especially Galileo.
4. God promised Noah (Genesis 9.11) never to
flood the earth again.
5. See Psalm 69.9: "For the zeal of thine house
hath eaten me up." These lines refer to three kinds
of flame—those of the Last Judgment, those of lust
and envy, and those of zeal, which alone save.
6. Cf. Revelations 7.1: "I saw four angels standing
on the four corners of the earth."

7. Noah's flood, and the universal conflagration at
the end of the world (Revelation 6.11).
8. Those who will be alive at the Second Coming
(cf. Luke 9.27).
9. The Tree of Knowledge of Good and Evil,
whose fruit was forbidden to Adam and Eve in
Eden.
1. Traits commonly associated with these creatures.

10   O God? Oh, of thine only worthy blood
     And my tears, make a heavenly Lethean[2] flood,
     And drown in it my sin's black memory.
     That thou remember them some claim as debt;
     I think it mercy if thou wilt forget.[3]

                                                    1633

[handwritten: Death isn't that bad.] **10**

     Death, be not proud, though some have callèd thee
     Mighty and dreadful, for thou art not so;
     For those whom thou think'st thou dost overthrow
     Die not, poor Death, nor yet canst thou kill me.
5   From rest and sleep, which but thy pictures be,
     Much pleasure; then from thee much more must flow,
     And soonest our best men with thee do go,
     Rest of their bones, and soul's delivery.[4]
     Thou art slave to fate, chance, kings, and desperate men,
10   And dost with poison, war, and sickness dwell,
     And poppy° or charms can make us sleep as well   opium
     And better than thy stroke; why swell'st° thou then?   puff with pride
     One short sleep past, we wake eternally
     And death shall be no more; Death, thou shalt die.[5]

[handwritten annotations: he feels that he is saved; if death is like sleep, it must be good; death is freedom for the soul; death is slave to awful things; he thinks he will go to heaven; for people who believe death doesn't exist b/c after death is life; death can kill the body but not the soul.]

                                                    1633

13

     What if this present were the world's last night?
     Mark in my heart, O soul, where thou dost dwell,
     The picture of Christ crucified, and tell
     Whether that countenance can thee affright.
5   Tears in his eyes quench the amazing light,
     Blood fills his frowns, which from his pierced head fell;
     And can that tongue adjudge thee unto hell
     Which prayed forgiveness for his foes' fierce spite?
     No, no; but as in my idolatry
10   I said to all my profane° mistresses,   earthly
     Beauty of pity, foulness only is
     A sign of rigor:[6] so I say to thee,
     To wicked spirits are horrid shapes assigned,
     This beauteous form assures a piteous mind.

                                                    1633

2. In classical mythology, the waters of the river Lethe in the underworld caused total forgetfulness.
3. Cf. Jeremiah 31.34: "I will forgive their iniquity, and I will remember their sins no more."
4. I.e., to find rest for their bones and freedom ("delivery") for their souls.
5. Cf. 1 Corinthians 15.26: "The last enemy that shall be destroyed is death."
6. In Neoplatonic theory, beautiful features are the sign of a compassionate mind, while ugliness signifies the contrary.

[handwritten: to god] 14 *[handwritten: °god—king]*
[handwritten: ° viceroy— reason, needs faith]
[handwritten: but...also]

[handwritten: holy trinity]
Batter my heart, three-personed God; for you   *[handwritten: °he is asking]*
As yet but knock, breathe, shine, and seek to mend;   *[handwritten: god to have mercy on him]*
That I may rise and stand, o'erthrow me, and bend
Your force to break, blow, burn, and make me new.   *[handwritten: °2 & 4 the verbs are parallel]*
[handwritten left margin: god was to gentle.]
5   I, like an usurped town, to another due,   *[handwritten: but more violent.]*
Labor to admit you, but O, to no end;   *[handwritten: °he is trying to let God in.]*
Reason, your viceroy[7] in me, me should defend,   *[handwritten: °he is like a town that]*
But is captived, and proves weak or untrue.   *[handwritten: has gladly taken a]*
Yet dearly I love you, and would be loved fain,°   *[handwritten: °he wants god to keep him]*
10   But am betrothed[8] unto your enemy.   *[handwritten: from temptation.]*
Divorce me, untie or break that knot again;   *[handwritten: °like marriage]*
Take me to you, imprison me, for I,
Except° you enthrall me, never shall be free,   *unless / captivate*
Nor ever chaste, except you ravish[9] me.

[handwritten: being enslaved by God is ultimate freedom.]   1633

17

Since she whom I loved hath paid her last debt[1]
To Nature, and to hers, and my good is dead,
And her soul early into heaven ravishèd,
Wholly on heavenly things my mind is set.
5   Here the admiring her my mind did whet
To seek thee, God; so streams do show the head;°   *source*
But though I have found thee, and thou my thirst hast fed,
A holy thirsty dropsy melts me yet.
But why should I beg more love, whenas thou
10   Dost woo my soul, for hers offering all thine:
And dost not only fear lest I allow
My love to saints and angels, things divine,
But in thy tender jealousy dost doubt°   *fear*
Lest the world, flesh, yea, devil put thee out.

1899

18

Show me, dear Christ, thy spouse[2] so bright and clear.
What! is it she which on the other shore
Goes richly painted? or which, robbed and tore,
Laments and mourns in Germany and here?[3]

7. The governor in your stead. *[handwritten: replacement king]* 1892.
8. Humanity's relationship with God has been described in terms of marriage and adultery from the time of the Hebrew prophets.
9. Rape, also overwhelm with wonder. "Enthrall": enslave, also enchant.
1. Donne's wife died in 1617 at the age of thirty-three, having just given birth to her twelfth child. This very personal sonnet, and the following one, survive in a single manuscript discovered only in

2. The church is commonly called the bride of Christ. Cf. Revelation 19.7–8: "The marriage of the Lamb is come, and his wife hath made herself ready. / And to her was granted that she should be arrayed in fine linen, clean and white."
3. I.e., neither the painted woman (the Church of Rome) nor the ravished virgin (the Lutheran and Calvinist churches in Germany and England) seem very like a bride.

5   Sleeps she a thousand, then peeps up one year?
Is she self-truth, and errs? now new, now outwore?
Doth she, and did she, and shall she evermore
On one, on seven, or on no hill appear?[4]
Dwells she with us, or like adventuring knights
10 First travel we to seek, and then make love?
Betray, kind husband, thy spouse to our sights,
And let mine amorous soul court thy mild dove,
Who is most true and pleasing to thee then
When she is embraced and open to most men.[5]

1899

19

Oh, to vex me, contraries meet in one:
Inconstancy unnaturally hath begot
A constant habit; that when I would not
I change in vows, and in devotion.
5   As humorous is my contrition
As my profane love, and as soon forgot:
As riddlingly distempered, cold and hot,[6]
As praying, as mute, as infinite, as none.
I durst not view heaven yesterday; and today
10 In prayers, and flattering speeches I court God:
Tomorrow I quake with true fear of his rod.
So my devout fits come and go away
Like a fantastic ague:[7] save that here
Those are my best days, when I shake with fear.

1899

Good Friday, 1613. Riding Westward

Let man's soul be a sphere, and then, in this,
The intelligence that moves, devotion is,[1]
And as the other spheres, by being grown
Subject to foreign motions, lose their own,
5   And being by others hurried every day,
Scarce in a year their natural form[2] obey;
Pleasure or business, so, our souls admit
For their first mover, and are whirled by it.

4. The church on one hill is probably Solomon's temple on Mount Moriah; that on seven hills is the Church of Rome; that on no hill is the Presbyterian church of Geneva.
5. The final lines wittily rework, with startling sexual associations, Song of Solomon 5.2: "Open to me, my sister, my love, my dove, my undefiled." That biblical book was often interpreted as the song of love between Christ and the church.
6. Arising from the unbalanced humors, changeable.

7. A fever, attended with paroxysms of hot and cold and trembling fits. "Fantastic": capricious, extravagant.
1. As angelic intelligences guide the celestial spheres, so devotion is or should be the guiding principle of human life.
2. Their true moving principle or intelligence. Spheres were thought to be sometimes deflected from their orbits by outside influences and were continually directed by the Primum Mobile, or outermost sphere.

Hence is 't, that I am carried towards the West
10 This day, when my soul's form bends toward the East.
There I should see a Sun[3] by rising, set,
And by that setting endless day beget:
But that Christ on this cross did rise and fall,
Sin had eternally benighted all.
15 Yet dare I almost be glad I do not see
That spectacle, of too much weight for me.
Who sees God's face, that is self-life, must die;[4]
What a death were it then to see God die?
It made his own lieutenant,° Nature, shrink;   *deputy*
20 It made his footstool crack, and the sun wink.[5]
Could I behold those hands which span the poles,
And tune[6] all spheres at once, pierced with those holes?
Could I behold that endless height which is
Zenith to us, and t'our antipodes,[7]
25 Humbled below us? Or that blood which is
The seat° of all our souls, if not of his,   *dwelling-place*
Make dirt of dust, or that flesh which was worn
By God for his apparel, ragg'd and torn?
If on these things I durst not look, durst I
30 Upon his miserable mother cast mine eye,
Who was God's partner here, and furnished thus
Half of that sacrifice which ransomed us?
Though these things, as I ride, be from° mine eye,   *away from*
They are present yet unto my memory,
35 For that looks towards them; and thou look'st towards me,
O Savior, as thou hang'st upon the tree.
I turn my back to thee but to receive
Corrections,[8] till thy mercies bid thee leave.°   *cease*
O think me worth thine anger; punish me;
40 Burn off my rusts and my deformity;
Restore thine image so much, by thy grace,
That thou may'st know me, and I'll turn my face.

         1633

A Hymn to Christ, at the Author's Last Going into Germany[1]

In what torn ship soever I embark,
That ship shall be my emblem of thy ark;[2]
What sea soever swallow me, that flood

3. The *sun/Son* pun was an ancient one. Christ the Son of God set when he rose on the Cross, and that setting (death) gave rise to the Christian era and the promise of immortality.
4. God told Moses, "Thou canst not see my face, for there shall no man see me, and live" (Exodus 33.20).
5. An earthquake and eclipse supposedly accompanied the Crucifixion (Matthew 27.45, 51). Cf. Isaiah 66.1: "Thus saith the Lord, The heaven is my throne, and the earth is my footstool."
6. Some manuscripts read "turn."

7. God is at once the highest point for us and for our antipodes, those who live on the opposite side of the earth.
8. Suggests a flogging.
1. Donne went to Germany in 1619 as chaplain to the earl of Doncaster. The mission was a diplomatic one, to the king and queen of Bohemia, King James's son-in-law and daughter, who at that time were mainstays of the Protestant cause on the Continent.
2. Noah's ark.

Shall be to me an emblem of thy blood;
5   Though thou with clouds of anger do disguise
Thy face, yet through that mask I know those eyes,
    Which, though they turn away sometimes, they never will despise.

I sacrifice this island³ unto thee,
And all whom I loved there, and who loved me;
10   When I have put our seas twixt them and me,
Put thou thy sea⁴ betwixt my sins and thee.
As the tree's sap doth seek the root below
In winter, in my winter now I go
    Where none but thee, th' eternal root of true love, I may know.

15   Nor thou nor thy religion dost control°   *censure, restrain*
The amorousness of an harmonious soul,
But thou wouldst have that love thyself; as thou
Art jealous, Lord, so I am jealous now.
Thou lov'st not, till from loving more⁵ thou free
20   My soul; whoever gives, takes liberty;
    Oh, if thou car'st not whom I love, alas, thou lov'st not me.

Seal then this bill of my divorce to all
On whom those fainter beams of love did fall;
Marry those loves which in youth scattered be
25   On fame, wit, hopes (false mistresses) to thee.
Churches are best for prayer that have least light:
To see God only, I go out of sight,
    And to 'scape stormy days, I choose an everlasting night.

1633

Hymn to God My God, in My Sickness¹

Since I am coming to that holy room
    Where, with thy choir of saints for evermore,
I shall be made thy music; as I come
    I tune the instrument here at the door,
5   And what I must do then, think² now before.

Whilst my physicians by their love are grown
    Cosmographers, and I their map, who lie
Flat on this bed, that by them may be shown
    That this is my southwest discovery³
10   *Per fretum febris,*⁴ by these straits to die,

---

3. England.
4. Sea of Christ's blood.
5. From loving any other thing.
1. Though Izaak Walton, Donne's pious biographer, assigns this poem to the last days of his life, it was probably written in December 1623.
2. This and the previous poem are less hymns

(songs of praise) than meditations preparing (tuning the instrument) for such hymns.
3. South is the region of heat, west the region of sunset and death.
4. Through the straits of fever, with a pun on straits as sufferings, rigors, and a geographical reference to the Strait of Magellan.

I joy, that in these straits, I see my West;
  For, though their currents yield return to none,
What shall my West hurt me? As West and East
  In all flat maps (and I am one) are one,[5]
15   So death doth touch the resurrection.

Is the Pacific Sea my home? Or are
  The Eastern riches?° Is Jerusalem?   *Cathay, China*
Anyan,[6] and Magellan, and Gibraltar,
  All straits, and none but straits, are ways to them,
20   Whether where Japhet dwelt, or Cham, or Shem.[7]

We think that Paradise and Calvary,
  Christ's cross and Adam's tree, stood in one place;
Look, Lord and find both Adams[8] met in me;
  As the first Adam's sweat surrounds my face,
25   May the last Adam's blood my soul embrace.

So, in his purple wrapped,[9] receive me, Lord;
  By these his thorns give me his other crown;
And, as to others' souls I preached thy word,
  Be this my text, my sermon to mine own:
30   Therefore that he may raise the Lord throws down.

                                              1635

A Hymn to God the Father[1]

Wilt thou forgive that sin where I begun,
  Which is my sin, though it were done before?[2]
Wilt thou forgive that sin through which I run,
  And do run still, though still I do deplore?
5   When thou hast done,[3] thou hast not done,
      For I have more.

Wilt thou forgive that sin by which I have won
  Others to sin? and made my sin their door?
Wilt thou forgive that sin which I did shun
10   A year or two, but wallowed in a score?
      When thou hast done, thou hast not done,
      For I have more.

5. If a flat map is pasted on a round globe, west and east meet.
6. Anian, a strait on the west coast of America, shown on early maps as separating America from Asia.
7. The three sons of Noah by whom the world was repopulated after the Flood (Genesis 10). The descendants of Japhet were thought to inhabit Europe; those of Cham (Ham), Africa; and those of Shem, Asia.
8. Adam and Christ. Legend had it that Christ's cross was erected on the spot, or at least in the region, where the tree forbidden to Adam in Eden had stood.
9. In his blood, also in his kingly robes.
1. This hymn was used as a congregational hymn. Walton tells us that Donne wrote it during his illness of 1623, had it set to music, and was delighted to hear it performed (as it frequently was) by the choir of St. Paul's Cathedral.
2. I.e., he inherits the original sin of Adam and Eve.
3. In the refrains, Donne puns on his own name and may pun on his wife's maiden name, Ann More.

I have a sin of fear, that when I have spun
My last thread, I shall perish on the shore;
15   Swear by thy self, that at my death thy Son
Shall shine as he shines now and heretofore;
And, having done that, thou hast done,
I fear[4] no more.

1633

From Devotions upon Emergent Occasions[1]
Meditation 4

Medicusque vocatur.
The physician is sent for.[2]

It is too little to call man a little world; except God, man is a diminutive to nothing.[3] Man consists of more pieces, more parts, than the world; than the world doth, nay, than the world is. And if those pieces were extended and stretched out in man as they are in the world, man would be the giant and the world the dwarf; the world but the map, and the man the world. If all the veins in our bodies were extended to rivers, and all the sinews to veins of mines, and all the muscles that lie upon one another to hills, and all the bones to quarries of stones, and all the other pieces to the proportion of those which correspond to them in the world, the air would be too little for this orb of man to move in, the firmament would be but enough for this star. For as the whole world hath nothing to which something in man doth not answer,[4] so hath man many pieces of which the whole world hath no representation. Enlarge this meditation upon this great world, man, so far as to consider the immensity of the creatures this world produces. Our creatures are our thoughts, creatures that are born giants, that reach from east to west, from earth to heaven, that do not only bestride all the sea and land, but span the sun and firmament at once: my thoughts reach all, comprehend all.

Inexplicable mystery! I their creator am in a close prison, in a sick bed, anywhere, and any one of my creatures, my thoughts, is with the sun, and beyond the sun, overtakes the sun, and overgoes the sun in one pace, one step, everywhere. And then as the other world produces serpents and vipers, malignant and venomous creatures, and worms and caterpillars, that endeavor to devour that world which produces them, and monsters compiled and complicated[5] of divers parents and kinds, so this world, our selves, pro-

---

4. Some manuscripts read "have."
1. Donne's *Devotions* were composed in the aftermath of his serious illness in the winter of 1623, though Donne characteristically writes as if the events of the illness were happening as he describes them. The *Devotions* recount in twenty-three sections the stages ("emergent occasions") of the illness and recovery: the term associates the exercise with a popular kind of Protestant meditation on the occasions that daily life presents to us. Each section contains a "meditation upon our human condition," an "expostulation and debatement with God," and a prayer to God. The book

was published almost immediately, offering its meditation on an intensely personal experience as exemplary for others.
2. Donne's Latin epigraphs are followed by his English translations, often quite free.
3. This meditation is based on the notion that each human being is a microcosm, a little world, analogous in every respect to the macrocosm or great world. But in playing with this notion, Donne paradoxically reverses it.
4. Correspond.
5. Mixed.

duces all these in us, in producing diseases and sicknesses of all those sorts; venomous and infectious diseases, feeding and consuming diseases, and manifold and entangled diseases made up of many several ones. And can the other world name so many venomous, so many consuming, so many monstrous creatures, as we can diseases of all these kinds? O miserable abundance, O beggarly riches! How much do we lack of having remedies for every disease, when as yet we have not names for them?

But we have a Hercules against these giants, these monsters: that is the physician. He musters up all the forces of the other world to succor this, all nature to relieve man. We have the physician but we are not the physician. Here we shrink in our proportion, sink in our dignity in respect of very mean creatures who are physicians to themselves. The hart that is pursued and wounded, they say, knows an herb which, being eaten, throws off the arrow: a strange kind of vomit.[6] The dog that pursues it, though he be subject to sickness, even proverbially knows his grass that recovers him. And it may be true that the drugger[7] is as near to man as to other creatures; it may be that obvious and present simples,[8] easy to be had, would cure him; but the apothecary is not so near him, nor the physician so near him, as they two are to other creatures. Man hath not that innate instinct to apply these natural medicines to his present danger, as those inferior creatures have. He is not his own apothecary, his own physician, as they are. Call back therefore thy meditation again, and bring it down.[9] What's become of man's great extent and proportion, when himself shrinks himself and consumes himself to a handful of dust? What's become of his soaring thoughts, his compassing thoughts, when himself brings himself to the ignorance, to the thoughtlessness, of the grave? His diseases are his own, but the physician is not; he hath them at home, but he must send for the physician.

Meditation 17

Nunc lento sonitu dicunt, morieris.
Now this bell tolling softly for another, says to me, Thou must die.

Perchance he for whom this bell[1] tolls may be so ill as that he knows not it tolls for him; and perchance I may think myself so much better than I am, as that they who are about me and see my state may have caused it to toll for me, and I know not that. The church is catholic, universal, so are all her actions; all that she does belongs to all. When she baptizes a child, that action concerns me; for that child is thereby connected to that head which is my head too, and ingrafted into that body[2] whereof I am a member. And when she buries a man, that action concerns me: all mankind is of one author and is one volume; when one man dies, one chapter is not torn out of the book, but translated[3] into a better language; and every chapter must be so translated. God employs several translators; some pieces are translated by age, some by sickness, some by war, some by justice; but God's hand is in every

6. Deer supposedly expelled arrows wounding them by eating the herb dittany.
7. One who administers drugs might do this for man as well as for other creatures, but one who sells drugs ("the apothecary") and the physician do not know how to prescribe for man as well as for

other creatures.
8. Medicinal plants.
9. I.e., apply it to the present situation.
1. The "passing bell" for the dying.
2. The church.
3. Punning on the literal sense, "carried across."

translation, and his hand shall bind up all our scattered leaves again for that library where every book shall lie open to one another. As therefore the bell that rings to a sermon calls not upon the preacher only, but upon the congregation to come, so this bell calls us all; but how much more me, who am brought so near the door by this sickness. There was a contention as far as a suit[4] (in which piety and dignity, religion and estimation,[5] were mingled) which of the religious orders should ring to prayers first in the morning; and it was determined that they should ring first that rose earliest. If we understand aright the dignity of this bell that tolls for our evening prayer, we would be glad to make it ours by rising early, in that application, that it might be ours as well as his whose indeed it is. The bell doth toll for him that thinks it doth; and though it intermit again, yet from that minute that that occasion wrought upon him, he is united to God. Who casts not up his eye to the sun when it rises? but who takes off his eye from a comet when that breaks out? Who bends not his ear to any bell which upon any occasion rings? but who can remove it from that bell which is passing a piece of himself out of this world? No man is an island, entire of itself; every man is a piece of the continent, a part of the main.[6] If a clod be washed away by the sea, Europe is the less, as well as if a promontory were, as well as if a manor of thy friend's or of thine own were. Any man's death diminishes me, because I am involved in mankind; and therefore never send to know for whom the bell tolls; it tolls for thee.[7] Neither can we call this a begging of misery or a borrowing of misery, as though we were not miserable enough of ourselves but must fetch in more from the next house, in taking upon us the misery of our neighbors. Truly it were an excusable covetousness if we did; for affliction is a treasure, and scarce any man hath enough of it. No man hath affliction enough that is not matured and ripened by it, and made fit for God by that affliction. If a man carry treasure in bullion, or in a wedge of gold, and have none coined into current moneys, his treasure will not defray[8] him as he travels. Tribulation is treasure in the nature of it, but it is not current money in the use of it, except we get nearer and nearer our home, heaven, by it. Another man may be sick too, and sick to death, and this affliction may lie in his bowels as gold in a mine and be of no use to him; but this bell that tells me of his affliction digs out and applies that gold to me, if by this consideration of another's danger I take mine own into contemplation and so secure myself by making my recourse to my God, who is our only security.

From *Expostulation 19*

[THE LANGUAGE OF GOD]

My God, my God, thou art a direct God, may I not say a literal God, a God that wouldst be understood literally and according to the plain sense of all that thou sayest. But thou art also (Lord, I intend it to thy glory, and let no profane misinterpreter abuse it to thy diminution), thou art a figurative, a metaphorical God too: a God in whose words there is such a height of

---

4. Controversy that went as far as a lawsuit.
5. Self-esteem.
6. Mainland.

7. This phrase gave Hemingway the title for his novel *For Whom the Bell Tolls*.
8. Meet his expenses.

figures, such voyages, such peregrinations to fetch remote and precious metaphors, such extensions, such spreadings, such curtains of allegories, such third heavens of hyperboles, so harmonious elocutions, so retired and so reserved expressions, so commanding persuasions, so persuading commandments, such sinews even in thy milk and such things in thy words, as all profane[9] authors seem of the seed of the serpent that creeps; thou art the dove that flies. Oh, what words but thine can express the inexpressible texture and composition of thy word; in which, to one man, that argument that binds his faith to believe that to be the word of God is the reverent simplicity of the word, and to another, the majesty of the word; and in which two men, equally pious, may meet, and one wonder that all should not understand it, and the other as much that any man should. So, Lord, thou givest us the same earth to labor on and to lie in; a house and a grave of the same earth; so, Lord, thou givest us the same word for our satisfaction and for our inquisition,[1] for our instruction and for our admiration too. For there are places that thy servants Jerome and Augustine would scarce believe (when they grew warm by mutual letters) of one another that they understood them, and yet both Jerome and Augustine call upon persons whom they knew to be far weaker than they thought one another (old women and young maids) to read thy Scriptures, without confining them to these or those places.[2]

Neither art thou thus a figurative, a metaphorical God, in thy word only, but in thy works too. The style of thy works, the phrase of thine actions, is metaphorical. The institution of thy whole worship in the old law was a continual allegory; types[3] and figures overspread all, and figures flowed into figures, and poured themselves out into further figures. Circumcision carried a figure of baptism,[4] and baptism carries a figure of that purity which we shall have in perfection in the New Jerusalem. Neither didst thou speak and work in this language only in the time of the prophets; but since thou spokest in thy son it is so too. How often, how much more often, doth thy son call himself a way and a light and a gate and a vine and bread than the son of God or of man? How much oftener doth he exhibit a metaphorical Christ than a real, a literal? This hath occasioned thine ancient servants, whose delight it was to write after thy copy,[5] to proceed the same way in their expositions of the Scriptures, and in their composing both of public liturgies and of private prayers to thee, to make their accesses to thee in such a kind of language as thou wast pleased to speak to them, in a figurative, in a metaphorical language; in which manner I am bold to call the comfort which I receive now in this sickness, in the indication of the concoction[6] and maturity thereof, in certain clouds[7] and residences[8] which the physicians observe, a discovering of land from sea after a long and tempestuous voyage. * * *

1623   1624

9. Secular.
1. Investigation.
2. Saints Jerome and Augustine did in fact differ over the proper way of interpreting the Bible, yet they both encouraged its use by the unlearned.
3. Anticipations or prefigurations, especially persons and events in the Hebrew Bible that were read as prefiguring Christ, or some aspect of the New Testament or of Christian practice. For a beautiful

poem exemplifying this process, see Herbert, *The Bunch of Grapes* (p. 1607).
4. Both circumcision and baptism are rites of admission to a religious community.
5. Text.
6. Ripening.
7. Cloudy urine.
8. Residues.

From Death's Duel[1]

[Donne's last sermon, on Psalm 68.20: "And unto God the Lord belong the issues of Death"—i.e., from death.]

* * * First, then, we consider this *exitus mortis*, to be *liberatio à morte*, that with God, the Lord are the issues of death, and therefore in all our deaths, and the deadly calamities of this life, we may justly hope of a good issue from him; and all our periods and transitions in this life, are so many passages from death to death. Our very birth and entrance into this life is *exitus à morte*, an issue from death, for in our mother's womb we are dead so, as that we do not know we live, not so much as we do in our sleep, neither is there any grave so close, or so putrid a prison, as the womb would be unto us, if we stayed in it beyond our time, or died there before our time. In the grave the worms do not kill us, we breed and feed, and then kill the worms which we ourselves produced. In the womb the dead child kills the mother that conceived it, and is a murderer, nay a parricide, even after it is dead. And if we be not dead so in the womb, so as that being dead, we kill her that gave us our first life, our life of vegetation, yet we are dead so, as David's Idols are dead. In the womb we have eyes and see not, ears and hear not.[2] There in the womb we are fitted for works of darkness, all the while deprived of light: And there in the womb we are taught cruelty, by being fed with blood, and may be damned, though we be never born. * * *

But then this *exitus à morte* is but *introitus in mortem*, this issue, this deliverance from that death, the death of the womb, is an entrance, a delivering over to another death, the manifold deaths of this world. We have a winding sheet in our mother's womb, which grows with us from our conception, and we come into the world wound up in that winding sheet, for we come to seek a grave. * * *

Now this which is so singularly peculiar to him [Christ], that his flesh should not see corruption, at his second coming, his coming to Judgment, shall extend to all then alive, their flesh shall not see corruption. . . . But for us that die now and sleep in the state of the dead, we must all pass this posthume death, this death after death, nay this death after burial, this dissolution after dissolution, this death of corruption and putrifaction, of vermiculation and incineration, of dissolution and dispersion in and from the grave. When those bodies that have been the children of royal parents, and the parents of royal children, must say with Job, to corruption, thou art my father, and to the worm thou art my mother and my sister.[3] Miserable riddle, when the same worm must be my mother, and my sister, and myself. Mis-

---

1. The printed version of this sermon (1632) has the subtitle "A Consolation to the Soul, against the dying life, and living death of the body." Donne's friend and executor Henry King (later Bishop of Chichester) supplied the further information that the sermon was delivered at Whitehall, before King Charles, that it was delivered only a few days before Donne's death, and that it was fitly styled "the author's own funeral sermon." Donne was a powerful and popular preacher, and this sermon was especially moving according to the testimony of many auditors, including Izaak Walton (see his account of Donne on his deathbed, p. 1583).

Besides the personal drama of the preacher himself visibly ill and perhaps dying, the audience must have responded to the almost unbearably graphic analysis of the forms of death and decay—a theme that often preoccupied Donne. As in his poems, the language is personal, rich in learning and curious lore, dazzling in verbal ingenuity and metaphor. As in the *Devotions*, the sentences are long, sinuous, and elaborate. Typically, he uses a number of Latin phrases, but almost always translates or paraphrases them immediately.

2. Paraphrases Psalm 115.5–6.
3. Paraphrases Job 17.14.

erable incest, when I must be married to my mother and my sister, beget, and bear that worm which is all that miserable penury; when my mouth shall be filled with dust, and the worm shall feed, and feed sweetly upon me,[4] when the ambitious man shall have no satisfaction, if the poorest alive tread upon him, nor the poorest receive any contentment in being made equal to princes, for they shall be equal but in dust. One dieth at his full strength, being wholly at ease and in quiet, and another dies in the bitterness of his soul, and never eats with pleasure, but they lie down alike in the dust, and the worm covers them.[5] The worm covers them in Job, and in Esay, it covers them and is spread under them, the worm is spread under thee, and the worm covers thee.[6] There's the mats and the carpets that lie under, and there's the State and the Canopy, that hangs over the greatest of the sons of men. Even those bodies that were the temple of the Holy Ghost, come to this dilapidation, to ruin, to rubbish, to dust: even the Israel of the Lord, and Jacob himself hath no other specification, no other denomination, but that *vermis Jacob*, thou worm of Jacob.[7] Truly the consideration of this posthume death, this death after burial, that after God (with whom are the issues of death) hath delivered me from the death of the womb, by bringing me into the world, and from the manifold deaths of the world, by laying me in the grave, I must die again in an incineration of this flesh, and in a dispersion of that dust. * * *

There we leave you in that blessed dependancy, to hang upon him that hangs upon the Cross, there bathe in his tears, there suck at his wounds, and lie down in peace in his grave, till he vouchsafe you a resurrection, and an ascension into that Kingdom, which he hath purchased for you, with the inestimable price of his incorruptible blood. Amen.

1632

4. Echoes Job 24.20.
5. Echoes Job 21.23–26.

6. Echoes Isaiah 14.11.
7. That epithet is used in Isaiah 41.14.

AEMILIA LANYER
1569–1645

Aemilia Lanyer was the first Englishwoman to publish a substantial volume of original poems and the first to make an overt bid for patronage, as previously only a male poet of the era might. She was daughter to an Italian-Jewish family of court musicians (the Bassanos), and for some years the mistress of Queen Elizabeth's Lord Chamberlain, Henry Cary, Lord Hunsdon, forty-five years her senior and a notable patron of the arts, including Shakespeare's company. Apparently to cover a pregnancy by him that resulted in a son named Henry, she married into another family of gentlemen musicians attached to the courts of Elizabeth I and James I. Educated in the aristocratic household of the countess of Kent and supported in style by Hunsdon, her fortunes declined after her marriage to Alfonso Lanyer, and her efforts to find some niche at the Jacobean court came to nothing. The gossipy notebooks of the astrologer Simon Forman record some of these facts from information Lanyer provided when consulting him about her fortunes. She evidently resided for some time in the bookish and cultivated household of Margaret Clifford, countess of Cumberland, and Margaret's young daughter Anne Clifford, receiving there some encouragement in learning, piety, and poetry, as well as, perhaps, some support in the unusual venture of offering her poems for publication.

Lanyer's single volume of poems, *Salve Deus Rex Judaeorum* (1611), has a decided feminist thrust. A series of dedicatory poems to former and would-be patronesses praises them as a community of contemporary good women. The title poem, a baroque meditation on Christ's Passion which at times invites some comparison with Donne and Crashaw, contrasts the good women who are part of the Passion story with the weak and evil men portrayed there and also incorporates a defense of Eve and all women. That defense and Lanyer's prose epistle "To the Virtuous Reader" are spirited contributions to the so-called *querelle des femmes*, a massive body of writings both serious and satiric that extends over several centuries and argues the issue of women's worthiness or faultiness in several genres and languages: some examples include Chaucer's *Wife of Bath's Prologue and Tale*, John Knox's denunciation of Mary Queen of Scots, and Shakespeare's *Taming of the Shrew*. The final poem in Lanyer's volume, *The Description of Cooke-ham*, celebrates in elegiac mode the crown estate occasionally occupied by the countess of Cumberland, portraying it as an Edenic paradise of women, now lost. This poem may or may not have been written before Ben Jonson's *To Penshurst*—commonly thought to have inaugurated the "country-house" genre in English literature—but Lanyer's poem can claim priority in publication. These two poems offer an instructive comparison, constructing male and female conceptions of an idealized social order that respond in very different ways to contemporary gender ideology.

From Salve Deus Rex Judaeorum[1]

To the Doubtful Reader[2]

Gentle Reader, if thou desire to be resolved, why I give this title, *Salve Deus Rex Judaeorum*, know for certain, that it was delivered unto me in sleep many years before I had any intent to write in this manner, and was quite out of my memory, until I had written the Passion of Christ, when immediately it came into my remembrance, what I had dreamed long before. And thinking it a significant token[3] that I was appointed to perform this work, I gave the very same words I received in sleep as the fittest title I could devise for this book.

To the Queen's Most Excellent Majesty[4]

Renowned Empress, and Great Britain's Queen,
Most gracious mother of succeeding kings;
Vouchsafe° to view that which is seldom seen,   *be willing*

1. "Hail God, King of the Jews," a variant of the inscription affixed to Christ's cross.
2. Lanyer placed this explanation at the end of her volume, not the beginning, as a further authorizing gesture. Invoking the familiar genre of the dream vision, she lays claim to some kind of poetic, and even divine, inspiration. "Doubtful": doubting.
3. Sign.
4. The first of eight poems addressed to court ladies whom Lanyer seeks to attract as patrons;

such poems commonly preface literary works by male courtier-poets, though not usually in such numbers. These poems are followed by a prose address to her actual patron, the countess of Cumberland, and then by the prose epistle included here, "To the Virtuous Reader." This first poem addresses Anne of Denmark, James I's queen, patron of writers such as Ben Jonson and Samuel Daniel, and mother of Prince Henry, Princess Elizabeth, and the future Charles I.

A woman's writing of divinest things:
5   Read it fair Queen, though it defective be,
       Your Excellence can grace both it and me.

                    *   *   *

       Behold, great Queen, fair *Eve's* Apology,°   *defense*
       Which I have writ in honor of your sex,
75   And do refer unto your Majesty
       To judge if it agree not with the Text:[5]
           And if it do, why are poor women blamed,
           Or by more faulty men so much defamed.

                    *   *   *

       My weak distempered brain and feeble spirits,
140   Which all unlearned have adventured, this
       To write of Christ, and of his sacred merits,
       Desiring that this book her° hands may kiss: *the Queen's*
           And though I be unworthy of that grace,
           Yet let her blessed thoughts this book embrace.

145   And pardon me (fair Queen) though I presume
       To do that which so many better can;
       Not that I learning to myself assume,
       Or that I would compare with any man:
           But as they are scholars, and by Art do write,
150   So Nature yields my soul a sad° delight.   *solemn, serious*

       And since all Arts at first from Nature came,
       That goodly creature, mother of perfection
       Whom *Jove's*[6] almighty hand at first did frame,
       Taking both her and hers[7] in his protection:
155   Why should not she now grace my barren muse,
           And in a woman all defects excuse.

       So peerless Princess humbly I desire,
       That your great wisdom would vouchsafe t'omit°   *overlook*
       All faults; and pardon if my spirits retire,
160   Leaving° to aim at what they cannot hit: *declining*
           To write your worth, which no pen can express,
           Were but t'eclipse your fame, and make it less.[8]

To the Virtuous Reader

Often have I heard, that it is the property of some women, not only to emulate the virtues and perfections of the rest, but also by all their powers of ill speaking, to eclipse the brightness of their deserved fame: now contrary to their custom, which men I hope unjustly lay to their charge, I have written this small volume, or little book, for the general use of all virtuous ladies and

---

5. The biblical text (Genesis 1–3).
6. God as creator of Nature.
7. Nature, and those (especially women) under Nature's protection.

8. As her poetry of praise cannot possibly do justice to the queen, she abandons an attempt that would obscure rather than promote the queen's fame.

gentlewomen of this kingdom; and in commendation of some particular persons of our own sex, such as for the most part, are so well known to myself, and others, that I dare undertake Fame dares not to call any better. And this have I done, to make known to the world, that all women deserve not to be blamed though some forgetting they are women themselves, and in danger to be condemned by the words of their own mouths, fall into so great an error, as to speak unadvisedly against the rest of their sex; which if it be true, I am persuaded they can show their own imperfection in nothing more: and therefore could wish (for their own ease, modesties, and credit) they would refer such points of folly, to be practised by evil disposed men, who forgetting they were born of women, nourished of women, and that if it were not by the means of women, they would be quite extinguished out of the world, and a final end of them all, do like vipers deface the wombs wherein they were bred, only to give way and utterance to their want of discretion and goodness. Such as these, were they that dishonored Christ his Apostles and Prophets, putting them to shameful deaths. Therefore we are not to regard any imputations, that they undeservedly lay upon us, no otherwise than to make use of them to our own benefits, as spur to virtue, making us fly all occasions that may color their unjust speeches to pass current. Especially considering that they have tempted even the patience of God himself, who gave power to wise and virtuous women, to bring down their pride and arrogancy. As was cruel Cesarus by the discreet counsel of noble Deborah, judge and prophetess of Israel: and resolution of Jael wife of Heber the Kenite:[9] wicked Haman, by the divine prayers and prudent proceedings of beautiful Hester:[1] blasphemous Holofernes, by the invincible courage, rare wisdom, and confident carriage of Judith: and the unjust Judges, by the innocency of chaste Susanna:[2] with infinite others, which for brevity sake I will omit. As also in respect it pleased our Lord and Saviour Jesus Christ, without the assistance of man, being free from original and all other sins, from the time of his conception, till the hour of his death, to be begotten of a woman, born of a woman, nourished of a woman, obedient to a woman; and that he healed women, pardoned women, comforted women: yea, even when he was in his greatest agony and bloody sweat, going to be crucified, and also in the last hour of his death, took care to dispose of a woman:[3] after his resurrection, appeared first to a woman, sent a woman to declare his most glorious resurrection to the rest of his Disciples.[4] Many other examples I could allege of divers faithful and virtuous women, who have in all ages not only been confessors but also endured most cruel martyrdom for their faith in Jesus Christ. All which is sufficient to enforce all good Christians

---

9. Sisera (Canaanite leader, hence "cesarus," i.e., "caesar") was a Canaanite military commander (12th century B.C.E.) routed in battle by the Israelites under the leadership of the prophetess Deborah. Sisera was subsequently killed by the Kenite woman Jael, who enticed him to her tent and then drove a tent spike through his temples while he slept (Judges 4).
1. Esther, the Jewish wife (5th century B.C.E.) of the Persian King Ahasuerus (Xerxes I), who by her wit and courage subverted the plot of the King's minister, Haman, to annihilate the Jews (Esther 1–7). Judith in the 5th century B.C.E. delivered her Judean countrymen from the Assyrians by capti-

vating their leader, Holofernes, with her charms and then decapitating him while he was drunk (Apocrypha, Book of Judith).
2. Jewish wife and example of chastity (6th century B.C.E.). She was falsely accused of adultery by two Jewish elders, in revenge for refusing their sexual advances, and condemned to death. The wise judge Daniel saved her by uncovering the elders' perjury (Apocrypha, Book of Susanna).
3. I.e., Christ asked his apostle John to care for his mother Mary (John 19.25–27). "Dispose of": provide for.
4. Mary Magdalen (John 20.1–18).

and honorable-minded men to speak reverently of our sex, and especially of all virtuous and good women. To the modest censures of both which, I refer these my imperfect endeavors, knowing that according to their own excellent dispositions they will rather cherish, nourish, and increase the least spark of virtue where they find it, by their favorable and best interpretations, than quench it by wrong constructions. To whom I wish all increase of virtue, and desire their best opinions.

Eve's Apology in Defense of Women[5]

Now Pontius Pilate is to judge the cause°   *case*
Of faultless Jesus, who before him stands,
Who neither hath offended prince, nor laws,
Although he now be brought in woeful bands.
5 O noble governor, make thou yet a pause,
  Do not in innocent blood inbrue° thy hands;   *stain*
    But hear the words of thy most worthy wife,[6]
    Who sends to thee, to beg her Savior's life.

  Let barb'rous cruelty far depart from thee,
10 And in true justice take affliction's part;
  Open thine eyes, that thou the truth may'st see.
  Do not the thing that goes against thy heart,
  Condemn not him that must thy Savior be;
  But view his holy life, his good desert.
15 Let not us women glory in men's fall,[7]
  Who had power given to overrule us all.

  Till now your indiscretion sets us free.
  And makes our former fault much less appear;
  Our mother Eve, who tasted of the tree,
20 Giving to Adam what she held most dear,
  Was simply good, and had no power to see;[8]
  The after-coming harm did not appear:
    The subtle serpent that our sex betrayed
    Before our fall so sure a plot had laid.

25 That undiscerning ignorance perceived
  No guile or craft that was by him intended;
  For had she known of what we were bereaved,[9]
  To his request she had not condescended.

5. Lanyer supplies the title for this subsection of the *Salve Deus* on her title page. Eve is not, however, the speaker; rather, the narrator presents Eve's "Apology" (defense of her actions), which is also a defense of all women. She does so by means of an apostrophe (impassioned address) to Pilate, the Roman official who authorized the crucifixion of Jesus. Lanyer makes Pilate and Adam representatives of the male gender, whereas Eve and Pilate's wife represent womankind.
6. Pilate's wife wrote her husband a letter urging Pilate to spare Jesus, about whom she had a warning dream (Matthew 27.19).
7. The fall of Adam, and the prospective fall of

Pilate.
8. In Eden, Eve ate the forbidden fruit first, at the serpent's bidding. Genesis commentary usually emphasized Eve's full knowledge that God had forbidden them on pain of death and banishment from Eden to eat the fruit of the Tree of Knowledge of Good and Evil; her action was usually ascribed to intemperance, pride, and ambition.
9. Deprived, specifically of eternal life. In Genesis 3, Eve was enticed by the serpent to eat the forbidden fruit; she in turn enticed her husband. God expelled them from Eden, condemning Adam to hard labor, Eve to pain in childbirth and subjection to her husband, and both to suffering and death.

But she, poor soul, by cunning was deceived;
30 No hurt therein her harmless heart intended:
    For she alleged° God's word, which he° denies,   asserted / serpent
    That they should die, but even as gods be wise.

But surely Adam cannot be excused;
Her fault though great, yet he was most to blame;
35 What weakness offered, strength might have refused,
Being lord of all, the greater was his shame.
Although the serpent's craft had her abused,
God's holy word ought all his actions frame,°   determine
    For he was lord and king of all the earth,
40 Before poor Eve had either life or breath,

Who being framed° by God's eternal hand   fashioned
The perfectest man that ever breathed on earth;
And from God's mouth received that strait° command,   strict
The breach whereof he knew was present death;
45 Yea, having power to rule both sea and land,
Yet with one apple won to lose that breath[1]
Which God had breathed in his beauteous face,
Bringing us all in danger and disgrace.

And then to lay the fault on Patience' back,
50 That we (poor women) must endure it all.
We know right well he did discretion lack,
Being not persuaded thereunto at all.
If Eve did err, it was for knowledge sake;
The fruit being fair persuaded him to fall:
55 No subtle serpent's falsehood did betray him;
If he would eat it, who had power to stay° him?   prevent

Not Eve, whose fault was only too much love,
Which made her give this present to her dear,
That what she tasted he likewise might prove,°   experience
60 Whereby his knowledge might become more clear;
He never sought her weakness to reprove
With those sharp words which he of God did hear;
    Yet men will boast of knowledge, which he took
    From Eve's fair hand, as from a learned book.

65 If any evil did in her remain,
Being made of him,[2] he was the ground of all.
If one of many worlds[3] could lay a stain
Upon our sex, and work so great a fall
To wretched man by Satan's subtle train,[4]
70 What will so foul a fault amongst you all?

1. The breath of life, which would have been eternal.
2. Genesis 2.21–22 reports God's creation of Eve
from Adam's rib.
3. May allude to the commonplace that man is a

little world, applying it here to woman.
4. Tradition identifies Satan with the serpent,
although that identification is not made in Genesis.

Her weakness did the serpent's words obey,
But you in malice God's dear Son betray,

Whom, if unjustly you condemn to die,
Her sin was small to what you do commit;
75 All mortal sins[5] that do for vengeance cry
Are not to be compared unto it.
If many worlds would altogether try
By all their sins the wrath of God to get,
  This sin of yours surmounts them all as far
80   As doth the sun another little star.[6]

[handwritten: Pilate's sin is worse than eves b/c he is condeming the man who clears eve, & he knows what the consiquences are.]

Then let us have our liberty again,
And challenge° to yourselves no sovereignty.   *claim*
You came not in the world without our pain,
Make that a bar against your cruelty;
85 Your fault being greater, why should you disdain
Our being your equals, free from tyranny?
  If one weak woman simply did offend,
  This sin of yours hath no excuse nor end,

[handwritten: his sin is more tyrannous.]

To which, poor souls, we never gave consent.
90 Witness, thy wife, O Pilate, speaks for all,
Who did but dream, and yet a message sent
That thou shouldest have nothing to do at all
With that just man[7] which, if thy heart relent,
Why wilt thou be a reprobate° with Saul[8]   *damned*
95   To seek the death of him that is so good,
  For thy soul's health to shed his dearest blood?

1611

The Description of Cooke-ham[1]

Farewell (sweet *Cooke-ham*) where I first obtained
Grace[2] from that grace where perfect grace remained;
And where the muses gave their full consent,
I should have power the virtuous to content;
5 Where princely palace[3] willed me to indite,
The sacred story of the soul's delight.

---

5. Sins punishable by damnation.
6. In the Ptolemaic system, the sun was larger than the other planets and the fixed stars.
7. Christ.
8. King of Israel who sought the death of God's annointed prophet-king, David. The parallel is with Pilate, who sought Christ's death.
1. The poem was written in honor of Margaret Clifford, countess of Cumberland, and celebrates a royal estate leased to her brother, at which the countess occasionally resided. The poem should be compared with Jonson's *To Penshurst*. Lanyer's poem is based on a familiar classical topic, the "Farewell to a Place," which had its most famous

development in Virgil's *Eclogue* 1. Lanyer makes extensive use of the common pastoral motif of nature's active sympathy with and response to human emotion—which later came to be called the "pathetic fallacy."
2. Here, both God's grace and the favor of Her Grace, the Countess of Cumberland. Lanyer attributes both her religious conversion and her vocation as poet to a period of residence at Cookeham in the countess's household. We do not know how long or under what circumstances Lanyer resided there.
3. Apparently a reference to the countess as her patron, commissioning her Passion poem.

Farewell (sweet place) where virtue then did rest,
And all delights did harbor in her breast;
Never shall my sad eyes again behold
10 Those pleasures which my thoughts did then unfold.
Yet you (great Lady) Mistress of that place,
From whose desires did spring this work of grace;
Vouchsafe to think upon those pleasures past,
As fleeting worldly joys that could not last,
15 Or, as dim shadows of celestial pleasures,
Which are desired above all earthly treasures.
Oh how (methought) against° you thither came,   *in preparation for*
Each part did seem some new delight to frame!
The house received all ornaments to grace it,
20 And would endure no foulness to deface it.
And walks put on their summer liveries,[4]
And all things else did hold like similes:[5]
The trees with leaves, with fruits, with flowers clad,
Embraced each other, seeming to be glad,
25 Turning themselves to beauteous Canopies,
To shade the bright sun from your brighter eyes;
The crystal streams with silver spangles graced,
While by the glorious sun they were embraced;
The little birds in chirping notes did sing,
30 To entertain both you and that sweet spring.
And *Philomela*[6] with her sundry lays,
Both you and that delightful place did praise.
Oh how me thought each plant, each flower, each tree
Set forth their beauties then to welcome thee!
35 The very hills right humbly did descend,
When you to tread on them did intend.
And as you set your feet, they still did rise,
Glad that they could receive so rich a prize.
The gentle winds did take delight to be
40 Among those woods that were so graced by thee,
And in sad murmur uttered pleasing sound,
That pleasure in that place might more abound.
The swelling banks delivered all their pride
When such a *Phoenix*[7] once they had espied.
45 Each arbor, bank, each seat, each stately tree,
Thought themselves honored in supporting thee.
The pretty birds would oft come to attend thee,
Yet fly away for fear they should offend thee;
The little creatures in the burrough by
50 Would come abroad to sport them in your eye,
Yet fearful of the bow in your fair hand,

---

4. Distinctive garments worn by persons in the service of great families, to indicate whose servants they were.
5. Behaved in similar fashion.
6. In myth, Philomela was raped by her brother-in-law Tereus, who also tore out her tongue; the gods transformed her into a nightingale. Here the bird's song is joyous but later mournful (line 189),

associating her own woes with those of Cookeham at the women's departure.
7. Mythical bird that lived alone of its kind for five hundred years, then was consumed in flame and reborn from its own ashes; metaphorically, a person of rare excellence. "All their pride": fish (cf. *To Penshurst*, lines 31–36).

Would run away when you did make a stand.
Now let me come unto that stately tree,
Wherein such goodly prospects you did see;
55   That oak that did in height his fellows pass,
As much as lofty trees, low growing grass,
Much like a comely cedar straight and tall,
Whose beauteous stature far exceeded all.
How often did you visit this fair tree,
60   Which seeming joyful in receiving thee,
Would like a palm tree spread his arms abroad,
Desirous that you there should make abode;
Whose fair green leaves much like a comely veil,
Defended° *Phoebus* when he would assail;   *defended against, resisted*
65   Whose pleasing boughs did yield a cool fresh air,
Joying° his happiness when you were there.   *enjoying*
Where being seated, you might plainly see
Hills, vales, and woods, as if on bended knee
They had appeared, your honor to salute,
70   Or to prefer some strange unlooked-for suit;[8]
All interlaced with brooks and crystal springs,
A prospect fit to please the eyes of kings.
And thirteen shires appeared all in your sight,
Europe could not afford much more delight.
75   What was there then but gave you all content,
While you the time in meditation spent
Of their Creator's power, which there you saw,
In all his creatures held a perfect law;
And in their beauties did you plain descry°   *perceive*
80   His beauty, wisdom, grace, love, majesty.
In these sweet woods how often did you walk,
With Christ and his Apostles there to talk;
Placing his holy Writ in some fair tree
To meditate what you therein did see.
85   With *Moses* you did mount his holy hill
To know his pleasure, and perform his will.[9]
With lowly *David* you did often sing
His holy hymns to Heaven's eternal King.[1]
And in sweet music did your soul delight
90   To sound his praises, morning, noon, and night.
With blessed *Joseph* you did often feed
Your pined brethren, when they stood in need.[2]
And that sweet Lady sprung from *Clifford's* race,
Of noble *Bedford's* blood, fair stem of grace,[3]
95   To honorable *Dorset* now espoused,[4]
In whose fair breast true virtue then was housed,

8. To urge some unexpected petition, as to a monarch.
9. You sought out and followed God's law, like Moses, who received the Ten Commandments on Mount Sinai.
1. You often sang David's psalms.
2. Like Joseph, who fed the starving Israelites in Egypt, you fed the hungry.
3. Main line of the family tree. Anne Clifford, only surviving child of the seaman-adventurer George Clifford, third earl of Cumberland, and the countess, a Russell (of "Bedford's blood"). She was tutored by Samuel Daniel and her *Diary* offers interesting insights into this period.
4. Anne Clifford was married to Richard Sackville, third earl of Dorset, on February 25, 1609; the reference helps date Lanyer's poem.

Oh what delight did my weak spirits find
In those pure parts of her well framéd mind.
And yet it grieves me that I cannot be
100   Near unto her, whose virtues did agree
With those fair ornaments of outward beauty,
Which did enforce from all both love and duty.
Unconstant Fortune, thou art most to blame,
Who casts us down into so low a frame
105   Where our great friends we cannot daily see,
So great a difference is there in degree.[5]
Many are placed in those orbs of state,
Parters[6] in honor, so ordained by Fate,
Nearer in show, yet farther off in love,
110   In which, the lowest always are above.[7]
But whither am I carried in conceit,
My wit too weak to conster° of the great.   *construe*
Why not? although we are but born of earth,
We may behold the heavens, despising death;
115   And loving heaven that is so far above,
May in the end vouchsafe us entire love.[8]
Therefore sweet memory do thou retain
Those pleasures past, which will not turn again:
Remember beauteous *Dorset's* former sports,[9]
120   So far from being touched by ill reports,
Wherein myself did always bear a part,
While reverend love presented my true heart.
Those recreations let me bear in mind,
Which her sweet youth and noble thoughts did find,
125   Whereof deprived, I evermore must grieve,
Hating blind Fortune, careless to relieve.
And you sweet Cooke-ham, whom these ladies leave,
I now must tell the grief you did conceive
At their departure, when they went away,
130   How everything retained a sad dismay.
Nay long before, when once an inkling came,
Methought each thing did unto sorrow frame:
The trees that were so glorious in our view,
Forsook both flowers and fruit, when once they knew
135   Of your depart, their very leaves did wither,
Changing their colors as they grew together.
But when they saw this had no power to stay you,
They often wept, though, speechless, could not pray you,
Letting their tears in your fair bosoms fall,
140   As if they said, Why will ye leave us all?
This being vain, they cast their leaves away
Hoping that pity would have made you stay:
Their frozen tops, like age's hoary hairs,

---

5. These lines and lines 117–25 probably exaggerate Lanyer's former familiarity with Anne Clifford.
6. Separators, i.e., the various honorific ranks "orbs of state" act to separate person from person.
7. An egalitarian sentiment playing on the Christian notion that in spiritual things—love and charity—the poor and lowly surpass the great ones.
8. I.e., we (lowly) may also love God and enjoy God's love, and hence are equal to anyone.
9. As was common, Anne Clifford is here referred to by her husband's title.

Shows their disasters, languishing in fears.
145   A swarthy riveled rind° all over spread,   *bark*
      Their dying bodies half alive, half dead.
      But your occasions[1] called you so away
      That nothing there had power to make you stay.
      Yet did I see a noble grateful mind
150   Requiting each according to their kind,
      Forgetting not to turn and take your leave
      Of these sad creatures, powerless to receive
      Your favor, when with grief you did depart,
      Placing their former pleasures in your heart,
155   Giving great charge to noble memory
      There to preserve their love continually.
      But specially the love of that fair tree,
      That first and last you did vouchsafe to see,
      In which it pleased you oft to take the air
160   With noble *Dorset*, then a virgin fair,
      Where many a learned book was read and scanned,
      To this fair tree, taking me by the hand,
      You did repeat the pleasures which had passed,
      Seeming to grieve they could no longer last.
165   And with a chaste, yet loving kiss took leave,
      Of which sweet kiss I did it soon bereave,°   *take from it*
      Scorning a senseless creature should possess
      So rare a favor, so great happiness.
      No other kiss it could receive from me,
170   For fear to give back what it took of thee,
      So I ungrateful creature did deceive it
      Of that which you in love vouchsafed to leave it.
      And though it oft had given me much content,
      Yet this great wrong I never could repent;
175   But of the happiest made it most forlorn,
      To show that nothing's free from Fortune's scorne,
      While all the rest with this most beauteous tree
      Made their sad comfort sorrow's harmony.
      The flowers that on the banks and walks did grow,
180   Crept in the ground, the grass did weep for woe.
      The winds and waters seemed to chide together
      Because you went away they knew not whither;
      And those sweet brooks that ran so fair and clear,
      With grief and trouble wrinkled did appear.
185   Those pretty birds that wonted were to sing,
      Now neither sing, nor chirp, nor use their wing,
      But with their tender feet on some bare spray,
      Warble forth sorrow, and their own dismay.
      Fair *Philomela* leaves her mournful ditty,
190   Drowned in deep sleep, yet can procure no pity.
      Each arbor, bank, each seat, each stately tree
      Looks bare and desolate now for want of thee,

1. After her husband's death (1605) Margaret Clifford chiefly resided in her dower properties in the north; Anne Clifford was married in 1609.

Turning green tresses into frosty gray,
While in cold grief they wither all away.
195 The sun grew weak, his beams no comfort gave,
While all green things did make the earth their grave.
Each brier, each bramble, when you went away
Caught fast your clothes, thinking to make you stay;
Delightful Echo wonted° to reply   *was accustomed*
200 To our last words, did now for sorrow die;
The house cast off each garment that might grace it,
Putting on dust and cobwebs to deface it.
All desolation then there did appear,
When you were going whom they held so dear.
205 This last farewell to *Cooke-ham* here I give,
When I am dead thy name in this may live,
Wherein I have performed her noble hest°   *commission*
Whose virtues lodge in my unworthy breast,
And ever shall, so long as life remains,
210 Tying my life to her by those rich chains.[2]

1611

2. Her virtues.

BEN JONSON
1572–1637

In 1616 Ben Jonson published his *Works*, earning howls of derision and incredulity
from many who were astounded to see mere plays and poems collected under the
same title the king gave to his political treatises. Many of Jonson's contemporaries
shied away from publication, either because, like Donne, they wrote for small coterie
audiences, or because, like Shakespeare, they wrote for theater companies which
preferred not to let go of the scripts. Jonson knew and admired both Donne and
Shakespeare, and more than any Jacobean belonged to both of their very different
worlds, but in publishing his *Works* he broke with them and laid claim to an altogether
higher literary status. He had risen from very humble beginnings to become England's
unofficial poet laureate, with a pension from the king and honorary degrees from both
universities. If he was not the first professional author in England, he was the first to
invest that role with dignity and respectability. His published *Works*, over which he
labored with painstaking and pedantic care, are designed to testify to an extraordinary
feat of self-transformation.

Jonson's early life was tough and turbulent. The posthumous son of a London
clergyman, he was educated at Westminster school under the great antiquarian
scholar William Camden. There he developed his love of classical learning, but lacking the resources to continue his education, Jonson was forced to turn to his step-
father's trade of bricklaying, a life he "could not endure." He escaped by joining the
English forces in Flanders, where, as he later boasted, he killed a man in single combat
before the eyes of two armies. Back in London, his attempt to make a living as an
actor and playwright almost ended in early disaster. He was imprisoned in 1597 for

collaborating with Thomas Nashe on the scandalous play *The Isle of Dogs* (now lost), and shortly after his release he killed one of his fellow actors in a duel. Jonson escaped the gallows by pleading benefit of clergy (a medieval privilege allowing felons who could read Latin to be tried by a more lenient ecclesiastical court). His learning had saved his life, but he emerged from captivity branded on the thumb, and with another mark against him as well. Under the influence of a priest imprisoned with him, he had converted to Catholicism (around the time that John Donne was abandoning that faith). Jonson was now more than ever a marginal figure, distrusted by the society that he satirized brilliantly in his early plays.

Jonson's fortunes improved with the accession of James I, though not at once. In 1603 he was called before the Privy Council to answer charges of "popery and treason" found in his play *Sejanus*. Little more than a year later he was in jail again for his part in the play *Eastward Ho*, which openly mocked the king's Scots accent and propensity for selling knighthoods. But Jonson was now on the way to establishing himself at the new court. In 1605 he received the commission to organize the Twelfth Night entertainment; *The Masque of Blackness* was the first of twenty-four masques he would produce for the court, most of them in collaboration with the architect and scene designer Inigo Jones. In the same years that he was writing the masques he produced his greatest works for the public theater. His first successful play, *Every Man in His Humor* (1598), had inaugurated the so-called "comedy of humors," in which the ruling eccentricities or passions of the characters (thought to be caused by physiological imbalance) are exposed to ridicule. He capitalized on this success with the comedies *Volpone* (1606), *The Alchemist* (1610), and *Bartholomew Fair* (1614). Jonson preserved the detached, satiric perspective of an outsider, but he was rising in society and making accommodations where necessary. In 1605, when suspicion fell upon him as a Catholic following the exposure of the Gunpowder Plot, he showed his loyalty by agreeing to serve as a spy for the Privy Council. Five years later he would return to the Church of England.

Although he rose to a position of eminent respectability, Jonson seems to have been possessed all his life by an uncontrollably quarrelsome spirit. Indeed, much of his best work emerged out of fierce tensions with his collaborators and contemporaries. At the turn of the century he became embroiled in the so-called "War of the Theaters," in which he satirized and was satirized by his fellow playwrights John Marston and Thomas Dekker. Later, his long collaborative partnership with Inigo Jones was marked by ever more bitter rivalry over the relative importance of words and scenery in the making of masques. Jonson also poured scorn and invective on the public theater audiences who failed, in his view, to appreciate the classical unities he brought to his plots. The failure of his play *The New Inn* elicited his *Ode to Himself* (1629), a disgusted farewell to the "loathed stage." Yet even after a stroke in 1629 left him partially paralyzed and confined to his home, Jonson continued to write for the stage, and was at work on a new play when he died in 1637.

In spite of his antagonistic nature, Jonson had a great capacity for friendship. His friends included Shakespeare, Donne, Francis Bacon, and John Selden, and in later years he gathered about himself a group of admiring younger men known as the "Sons of Ben," whose numbers included Herrick, Carew, and Suckling. He was a fascinating and inexhaustible conversationalist, as recorded by his friend William Drummond of Hawthornden, who carefully noted down Jonson's off-the-cuff opinions on a wide variety of subjects, ranging from his fellow poets to his sexual predilictions. Jonson also moved easily among the great of the land, though in poems like *Celebration of Charis* he shows himself cutting a ridiculous figure in the fashionable world. His patrons included Lady Mary Wroth and Sir Walter Ralegh and members of the Sidney and Herbert families. In *To Penshurst*, a celebration of Robert Sidney's country estate, Jonson offers an ideal image of a social order in which a virtuous patriarchal governor offers ready hospitality to guests of all stations, from poets to kings.

To Penshurst, together with Aemilia Lanyer's *Description of Cooke-ham*, inaugurated the small genre of the "country-house poem" in England. Jonson tried his hand, usually with success, at a wide range of poetic genres, including epitaph and epigram, love and funeral elegy, verse satire and verse letter, song and ode. More often than not he looked back to classical precedents. From the Roman poets Horace and Martial he derived not only generic models but an ideal vision of the artist and society against which he measured himself and the court he served. In many poems he adopted the persona of "bluff Ben," a witty, keenly perceptive, and scrupulously honest judge of men and women. The classical values Jonson most admired are enumerated in his longest epigram, *Inviting a Friend to Supper,* which describes a dinner party characterized by moderation, civility, graciousness, and pleasure that delights without enslaving—all contrasting sharply with the excess and licentiousness that marked the banquets and entertainments of imperial Rome and Stuart England. Yet the poet who produced this image of perfect moderation was notorious in his life as a drinker and a glutton with, as he puts it in *My Picture Left in Scotland,* a "mountain belly." Jonson was a man of immense appetites, which found expression in his art as well as in his life. His best works seethe with an almost uncontrollable imaginative energy and lust for abundance. Even his profound classical learning manifests this impulse. The notes and references to learned authorities which spill across the margins of his *Works* can be seen as the literary equivalent of food and drink piled high on the poet's table. Years of hardship had taught Jonson to seek his feasts in his imagination, and he could make the most mundane object the basis for flights of high fancy. As he told Drummond, he once "consumed a whole night in lying looking to his great toe, about which he had seen Tartars and Turks, Romans and Carthaginians fight in his imagination." In Drummond's view, Jonson was "oppressed with fantasy." Perhaps it was so—but Jonson's capacity for fantasy also produced a wide variety of plays, masques, and poems, in styles ranging from witty comedy to delicate lyricism.

The Masque of Blackness

When James I and Queen Anne ascended the English throne in 1603, they presided over the development of the court masque as a major form of praise, entertainment, and political idealization, celebrating the Stuart court as the embodiment of all perfections. *Blackness* established Jonson and Inigo Jones as the chief makers of court masques for more than two decades. Jonson provided the words and Jones the spectacle; over the years their rivalry grew ever more intense. For the first decade the queen took an active role in planning and performing court masques, which were usually performed only once—most often on Twelfth Night, as in this case, or sometimes for a wedding or other special occasion. *Blackness* also began the tradition of prodigiously expensive masques: the queen's bills for it came to around £5000 (more than five hundred times what the young Jonson would have made in a year as an apprentice bricklayer). These entertainments were customarily followed by an elaborate feast and all-night dancing (the revels). On this occasion, as on many that followed, the evening was chaotic. The banquet table was overturned by the crush of diners before the meal began; guests were beaten by the palace guards; light-fingered revelers stole jewels, chains, and purses; and sexual liaisons went on in dark corners.

Court masques differed from performances in the public theater in almost every respect. Most important, the essence of the masque is dance. They were multimedia events combining songs, speech, richly ornamented costumes and masks, shifting scene panels depicting elaborate architecture and landscapes, and intricate machines in which gods and goddesses descended from the heavens. They were presented to King James, who occupied the Chair of State, which was placed in the ideal viewing position. While the speaking parts were taken by professionals, the dancers were members of the court, including—to the horror of English Puritans—women. In the reign of Charles I, William Prynne lost his ears for attacking masques and comparing the women who danced in them (including the queen) to whores.

On the surface, Blackness asserts the cultural superiority of the English over non-European peoples and celebrates the patriarchal power of James, the "Sun King" of Britain, who can turn black skin to white. But in this and other queen's masques a subversive current is evident. Jonson tells us it was "her Majesty's will" that the ladies appear as black African beauties. Their costumes designed by Inigo Jones conjoin exotic beauty and wildness, associating them with the feared and desired "others" discovered (or imagined) by contemporary explorers. The power of the supposed Sun King is further undercut by Niger's lengthy praise of black beauty and by the fact that the promised transformation of the ladies' skin is never seen (though they have become white in the sequel, The Masque of Beauty, performed three years later). Some viewers found the work unsettling, one deeming the ladies' apparel "too light and courtesan-like" and their black faces and hands "a very loathsome sight."

In many later Jacobean masques the glorification of the monarch seems less conflicted. Jonson developed a kind of prologue known as the antimasque, in which wicked, disruptive, or rustic characters played by professional actors invade the court, only to be banished by the aristocratic masquers whose dancing transforms the court into a golden world. They then enact the mixture of the ideal and real as they unmask, revealing themselves as court personages, and proceed to dance the revels with the other members of the court. Caroline court masques, in which Charles I and Queen Henrietta Maria regularly danced, tended to be longer, more elaborate, more dialogic, more spectacular, and even more hyperbolic. But early to late, many masques contain features that subtly resist the politics of Stuart absolutism.

The Masque of Blackness

*The Queen's Masques: the first
Of Blackness
Personated at the Court at Whitehall,
on the Twelfth Night, 1605.*

Pliny, Solinus, Ptolemy, and of late Leo the African,[1] remember unto us a river in Ethiopia famous by the name of Niger.[2] of which the people were called Nigritae, now Negroes, and are the blackest nation of the world. This river taketh spring out of a certain lake,[3] eastward, and after a long race, falleth into the western ocean. Hence (because it was her Majesty's will to have them blackamoors at first) the invention was derived by me, and presented thus.

First, for the scene, was drawn a Landscape[4] *consisting of small woods, and here and there a void place filled with huntings; which falling, an artificial sea was seen to shoot forth, as if it flowed to the land, raised with waves which seemed to move, and in some places the billow to break,[5] as imitating that orderly disorder, which is common in nature. In front of this sea were placed six tritons,[6] in moving*

---

1. This long introductory note is Jonson's. Leo wrote the *Description of Africa* (1526); the other three are classical authorities on geography.
2. Some, though not Pliny, identified it as the Nile. Niger means black.
3. Lake Chad.
4. Painted on the front curtain.
5. Effects created by a series of painted cloths raised and lowered by a machine.
6. Sea gods.

and sprightly actions; their upper parts human, save that their hairs were blue, as partaking of the sea-color; their desinent⁷ parts fish, mounted above their heads, and all varied in disposition. From their backs were borne out certain light pieces of taffeta, as if carried by the wind, and their music made out of wreathed shells. Behind these, a pair of sea-maids, for song, were as conspicuously seated; between which two great sea-horses, as big as the life, put forth themselves; the one mounting aloft, and writhing his head from the other, which seemed to sink forwards; so intended for variation, and that the figure behind might come off better. Upon their backs Oceanus⁸ and Niger were advanced.

Oceanus, presented in a human form, the color of his flesh blue, and shadowed with a robe of sea green; his head grey and horned, as he is described by the ancients; his beard of the like mixed color. He was garlanded with algae or sea-grass, and in his hand a trident.

Niger, in form and color of an Ethiop, his hair and rare beard curled, shadowed with a blue and bright mantle; his front, neck, and wrists adorned with pearl; and crowned with an artificial wreath of cane and paper-rush.

These induced the masquers, which were twelve nymphs, negroes, and the daughters of Niger, attended by so many of the Oceaniae,⁹ which were their light-bearers.

The masquers were placed in a great concave shell, like mother of pearl, curiously made to move on those waters, and rise with the billow; the top thereof was stuck with a chevron of lights which, indented to the proportion of the shell, struck a glorious beam upon them as they were seated one above another; so that they were all seen, but in an extravagant¹ order.

On sides of the shell did swim six huge sea-monsters, varied in their shapes and dispositions, bearing on their backs the twelve torch-bearers, who were planted there in several greces,² so as the backs of some were seen, some in purfle³ (or side), others in face, and all having their lights burning out of whelks or murex shells.

The attire of the masquers was alike in all, without difference; the colors azure and silver, their hair thick, and curled upright in tresses, like pyramids, but returned on the top with a scroll and antique dressing of feathers, and jewels interlaced with ropes of pearl. And for the front, ear, neck and wrists, the ornament was of the most choice and orient pearl, best setting off from the black.

For the light-bearers, sea-green, waved about the skirts with gold and silver; their hair loose and flowing, garlanded with sea-grass, and that stuck with branches of coral.

These thus presented, the scene behind seemed a vast sea (and united with this that flowed forth)⁴ from the termination or horizon of which (being the level of the state,⁵ which was placed in the upper end of the hall) was drawn, by the lines of perspective, the whole work, shooting downwards from the eye; which decorum made it more conspicuous, and caught the eye afar off with a wandering beauty. To which was added an obscure and cloudy night piece,⁶ that made the whole set off. So much for the bodily part, which was of Master Inigo Jones his design and act.

By this, one of the tritons, with the two sea-maids, began to sing to the others' loud music, their voices being a tenor and two trebles.

---

7. Back.
8. The Atlantic Ocean, father of the river Niger. Both ride on the backs of hippopotamuses ("sea horses," line 31).
9. Sea nymphs, daughters of Oceanus and Tethys.
1. Moving about.
2. Steps.

3. Profile.
4. The painted backdrop and the wave machine.
5. The king's throne, placed at the ideal viewing position, the vanishing point of the perspective.
6. The upper part of the scenery, through which the moon later descends.

SONG

Sound, sound aloud
The welcome of the orient flood
Into the west;
Fair Niger, son to great Oceanus,
5   Now honored thus
With all his beauteous race,
Who though but black in face,
Yet are they bright,
And full of life and light,
10   To prove that beauty best
Which not the color, but the feature
Assures unto the creature.

OCEANUS   Be silent, now the ceremony's done,
And Niger, say, how comes it, lovely son,
15   That thou, the Ethiop's river, so far east,
Art seen to fall into th'extremest west
Of me, the king of floods, Oceanus,
And in mine empire's heart salute me thus?
My ceaseless current now amazèd stands
20   To see thy labor through so many lands
Mix thy fresh billow with my brackish stream,
And in thy sweetness, stretch thy diademe°   realm, rule
To these far distant and unequalled skies,
This squarèd circle of celestial bodies.[7]
25   NIGER   Divine Oceanus, 'tis not strange at all
That, since the immortal souls of creatures mortal
Mix with their bodies, yet reserve for ever
A power of separation, I should sever
My fresh streams from thy brackish, like things fixed,
30   Though with thy powerful saltness thus far mixed.
'Virtue though chained to earth, will still live free;
And hell it self must yield to industry.'[8]
OCEANUS   But what's the end of thy Herculean labours,
Extended to these calm and blessèd shores?
35   NIGER   To do a kind and careful father's part,
In satisfying every pensive heart
Of these my daughters, my most lovèd birth;
Who, though they were the first formed dames of earth,
And in whose sparkling and refulgent° eyes   radiant
40   The glorious sun did still delight to rise,
Though he (the best judge, and most formal cause[9]
Of all dames' beauties) in their firm hues draws
Signs of his fervent'st love, and thereby shows
That in their black the perfect'st beauty grows,
45   Since the fixed color of their curlèd hair

7. The squared circle is an image of perfection, a
hyperbolic compliment to Britain.
8. Alludes to Horace, Odes 1.3.36.

9. Aristotle's formal cause produces the form or
essence of any thing.

(Which is the highest grace of dames most fair)
No cares, no age can change, or there display
The fearful tincture of abhorrèd grey,
Since Death herself (herself being pale and blue)
50 Can never alter their most faithful hue;
All which are arguments to prove how far
Their beauties conquer in great beauty's war;
And more, how near divinity they be,
That stand from passion or decay so free.
55 Yet, since the fabulous voices of some few
Poor brain-sick men, styled poets[1] here with you,
Have, with such envy of their graces, sung
The painted beauties other empires sprung,
Letting their loose and wingèd fictions fly
60 To infect all climates, yea, our purity;
As of one Phaëton, that fired the world,[2]
And that before his heedless flames were hurled
About the globe, the Ethiops were as fair
As other dames, now black with black despair,
65 And in respect of their complexions changed,
Are eachwhere, since, for luckless creatures ranged.
Which when my daughters heard (as women are
Most jealous of their beauties) fear and care
Possessed them whole; yea, and believing them,[3]
70 They wept such ceaseless tears into my stream
That it hath thus far overflowed his shore
To seek them patience; who have since e'ermore
As the sun riseth, charged his burning throne
With volleys of revilings, 'cause he shone
75 On their scorched cheeks with such intemperate fires,
And other dames made queens of all desires.
To frustrate which strange error oft I sought,
Though most in vain against a settled thought
As women's are, till they confirmed at length
80 By miracle what I wish so much strength
Of argument resisted; else they feigned:
For in the lake where their first spring they gained,
As they sat cooling their soft limbs one night,
Appeared a face all circumfused with light;
85 (And sure they saw't, for Ethiops never dream)[4]
Wherein they might decipher through the stream
These words:
    That they a land must forthwith seek,
    Whose termination (of the Greek)
90 Sounds -tania; where bright Sol, that heat

1. English Petrarchan poets, whose ideal of
beauty involves fair skin, blonde hair, and blue
eyes. See, e.g., the sonnets of Sidney and Spenser.
2. Son of Apollo the sun god, whose ill-fated
attempt to drive the sun's chariot scorched the
earth and, reportedly, turned the skin of the daughters of Niger black.
3. The poets (line 132).
4. Jonson cites Pliny for this saying.

Their bloods, doth never rise or set,
But in his journey passeth by,
And leaves that climate of the sky
To comfort of a greater light,[5]
95   Who forms all beauty with his sight.
In search of this have we three princedoms past
That speak out -tania in their accents last:
Black Mauritania[6] first, and secondly
Swarth Lusitania,[7] next we did descry
100   Rich Aquitania,[8] and yet cannot find
The place unto these longing nymphs designed.°   appointed
Instruct and aid me, great Oceanus:
What land is this that now appears to us?
OCEANUS   This land, that lifts into the temperate air
105   His snowy cliff, is Albion the fair,
So called of Neptune's son, who ruleth here;[9]
For whose dear guard, myself four thousand year,
Since old Deucalion's[1] days, have walked the round
About his empire, proud to see him crowned
Above my waves.

*At this, the moon was discovered in the upper part of the house, triumphant in
a silver throne, made in figure of a pyramis.[2] Her garments white and silver, the
dressing of her head antique, and crowned with a luminary or sphere of light,
which striking on the clouds, and heightened with silver, reflected as natural
clouds do by the splendor of the moon. The heaven about her was vaulted with
blue silk, and set with stars of silver which had in them their several lights burning. The sudden sight of which made Niger to interrupt Oceanus with this present
passion.[3]*

110   NIGER   —O see, our silver star!
Whose pure auspicious light greets us thus far!
Great Æthiopia, goddess of our shore,[4]
Since with particular worship we adore
Thy general brightness, let particular grace
115   Shine on my zealous daughters. Show the place
Which long their longings urged their eyes to see.
Beautify them, which long have deified thee.
AETHIOPIA   Niger, be glad; resume thy native cheer.
Thy daughters' labors have their period here,
120   And so thy errors. I was that bright face
Reflected by the lake, in which thy race
Read mystic lines (which skill Pythagoras[5]

5. The allusion is to James, the "Sun-King" of Britain.
6. Land of the Moors in North Africa.
7. Portugal.
8. Southwest France.
9. King James, regularly so styled because of Britain's close relationship to the sea. Albion (previous
line): ancient name for England (white land).

1. A Greek analogue to Noah, as the survivor of a
great flood.
2. Pyramid.
3. Instant outburst.
4. Jonson identifies her as the moon, worshipped
by the Ethiopians.
5. Mystical Greek philosopher, who taught men
how to read writing on the moon.

First taught to men by a reverberate° glass).　　　　　　　　*reflecting*
This blessed isle doth with that *-tania* end
125　Which there they saw inscribed, and shall extend
Wished satisfaction to their best desires.
Britannia, which the triple world admires,[6]
This isle hath now recovered for her name;
Where reign those beauties that with so much fame
130　The sacred Muses' sons have honorèd,
And from bright Hesperus to Eos spread.[7]
With that great name, Britannia, this blest isle
Hath won her ancient dignity and style,
A *world divided from the world*,[8] and tried
135　The abstract of it in his general pride.
For were the world, with all his wealth, a ring,
Britannia (whose new name makes all tongues sing)
Might be a diamond worthy to enchase it,
Ruled by a sun, that to this height doth grace it.
140　Whose beams shine day and night, and are of force
To blanch an Ethiop and revive a cor'se.[9]
His light sciental is and (past mere nature)
Can salve the rude defects of every creature.
　　Call forth thy honored daughters, then,
145　And let them 'fore the Britain men
Indent the land with those pure traces[1]
They flow with in their native graces.
Invite them boldly to the shore,
Their beauties shall be scorched no more;
150　This sun is temperate, and refines
All things on which his radiance shines.

Here the tritons sounded, and they danced on shore, every couple as they advanced severally presenting their fans,[2] in one of which were inscribed their mixed names, in the other a mute hieroglyphic, expressing their mixed qualities. Which manner of symbol I rather chose than imprese, *as well for strangeness, as relishing of antiquity, and more applying to that original doctrine of sculpture which the Egyptians are said first to have brought from the Ethiopians.*

	The Names[3]	The Symbols
The Queen	*Euphoris*	*A golden tree, laden with fruit*
Countess of Bedford	*Aglaia*	

---

6. The triple realms of heaven, earth, and underworld, admiring the three kingdoms of England, Scotland, and Wales united under James. James reintroduced the name "Britain" in 1604, to refer to the united island.
7. West to east.
8. Britain as a separate world, divided from Europe by the channel.
9. Corpse. Both are proverbial impossibilities.
1. Imprint the land with their dancing feet. This is the call for the main masque dances.
2. The women advanced in pairs holding fans to the audience: on one appeared both names; on the other, an allegorical symbol of their conjoined qualities.

3. The meaning of the pairs' names and symbols, in order: abundance and splendor, fertility symbol; transparent and flexibility, a twenty-sided water symbol; swiftness and spotless, symbol of purity; moisture and coldness, symbol, the salamander who lives in fire unharmed; sweetness and delicacy, symbol of education; weight and revolving, symbol, the earth's globe. The women are members of Queen Anne's court, two of them notable in literary circles: Donne and Jonson wrote poems about Lucy, countess of Bedford (see for Jonson, p. 1397); Lady Mary Wroth wrote poems and a romance (p. 1422), and see Jonson, p. 1408.

Lady Herbert Countess of Derby	Diaphane Eucampse	The figure icosahedron of crystal
Lady Rich Countess of Suffolk	Ocyte Kathare	A pair of naked feet in a river
Lady Bevill Lady Effingham	Notis Pscychrote	The salamander simple
Lady Elizabeth Howard Lady Susan Vere	Glycyte Malacia	A cloud full of rain dropping
Lady Wroth Lady Walsingham	Baryte Periphere	An urn, sphered with wine

The names of the Oceaniae were

Doris	Cydippe	Beroe	Ianthe
Petrae	Glauce	Acaste	Lycoris
Ocyrhoe	Tyche	Clytia	Plexaure

Their own single dance ended, as they were about to make choice of their men, one from the sea was heard to call 'em with this charm, sung by a tenor voice.

SONG

Come away, come away,
We grow jealous of your stay.
If you do not stop your ear,
We shall have more cause to fear
Sirens of the land, than they
To doubt the sirens of the sea.

155

Here they danced with their men several measures and corantos. All which ended, they were again accited[4] to sea, with a song of two trebles, whose cadences were iterated by a double echo from several parts of the land.

SONG

Daughters of the subtle flood,
Do not let earth longer entertain you;
1st ECHO   Let earth longer entertain you
2nd ECHO   Longer entertain you

160

'Tis to them enough of good
That you give this little hope to gain you.
1st ECHO   Give this little hope to gain you.
2nd ECHO   Little hope to gain you.

165

If they love
You shall quickly see;

4. Summoned.

> For when to flight you move,
> They'll follow you, the more you flee.

170   1st ECHO   Follow you, the more you flee.
    2nd ECHO   The more you flee.

> If not, impute it each to other's matter;
> They are but earth—

    1st ECHO   But earth,
175   2nd ECHO   Earth—
> And what you vowed was water.

    1st ECHO   And what you vowed was water
    2nd ECHO   You vowed was water.

AETHIOPIA   Enough, bright nymphs, the night grows old,
180   And we are grieved we cannot hold
    You longer light; but comfort take.
    Your father only to the lake
    Shall make return; yourselves, with feasts,
    Must here remain the Ocean's guests.
185   Nor shall this veil the sun hath cast
    Above your blood, more summers last.
    For which, you shall observe these rites:
    Thirteen times thrice, on thirteen nights
    (So often as I fill my sphere
190   With glorious light, throughout the year)
    You shall, when all things else do sleep
    Save your chaste thoughts, with reverence steep
    Your bodies in that purer brine
    And wholesome dew, called rosmarine;
195   Then with that soft and gentler foam,
    Of which the ocean yet yields some,
    Whereof bright Venus, beauty's queen,
    Is said to have begotten been,
    You shall your gentler limbs o'er-lave,
200   And for your pains, perfection have.
    So that, this night, the year gone round,[5]
    You do again salute this ground;
    And in the beams of yond' bright sun
    Your faces dry, and all is done.

*At which, in a dance they returned to the sea, where they took their shell, and
with this full song, went out.*

SONG

205   Now Dian,° with her burning face,   *the moon*
    Declines apace:

---

5. Jonson had probably already planned the *Masque of Beauty*, in which the women's black skins were
turned white, but intervening masques prevented its production until 1608.

By which our waters know
To ebb, that late did flow.
Back seas, back nymphs, but with a forward grace
210   Keep still your reverence to the place,
And shout with joy of favor you have won,
In sight of Albion, Neptune's son.

1605

Volpone   This dark satire on human greed is set in Venice, but its true target is the city of London, or the city that London is about to become. It is a place devoted to commerce and mired in corruption, populated by greedy fools and conniving rascals. Like Shakespeare, Donne, and Thomas More before them, Jonson was deeply disturbed by the rise of a money economy in which every aspect of life could be prostituted to commercial interest. In *Volpone*, Jonson protests the inhumanity not just of greedy people but of greedy laws—laws made by the greedy to protect the acquisitions of the greedy. In many ways the state of Venice is shown in this play to be a worse criminal than the criminals it prosecutes.

Volpone combines elements drawn from several sources and traditions. The classical satirist Lucian provided the theme of a rich old man playing with the money-grubbing scoundrels who hoped to inherit his wealth. The medieval legend of crafty Reynard the Fox contributes to the character of Volpone (the fox) and to the play's pervasive animal imagery. Such characters as Mosca the wily parasite, Voltore the unscrupulous lawyer, the avaricious dotard Corbaccio, and the voluble Lady Would-Be are drawn in part from Roman comedy. Some scenes, such as that in which Volpone disguised as a mountebank woos Celia at her window, are drawn from the Italian *commedia dell'arte*. But *Volpone* is much more than the sum of its borrowings. It is a work of wonderful comic vitality, full of wit and mischief, in which the audience cannot help but applaud the clever con artists as they play and prey upon their loathsome victims.

Volpone was first performed by the King's Men (Shakespeare's company) in the spring of 1606, at the Globe Theater. (See the illustration, in the appendices to this volume, of a contemporary popular theater constructed on similar lines, which was the model for the recently reconstructed Globe on London's Bankside.) The Globe seated some two thousand persons—aristocrats and prosperous citizens in the tiered galleries (or sometimes on the stage itself), lower-class "groundlings" in the pit in front of the stage. The play was also performed before learned audiences in Oxford and Cambridge, who no doubt appreciated its adherence to the classical unities of action, time, and place. It was first published in quarto form in 1607 and republished with a few changes in the 1616 *Works*, the basis for the present text. Stage directions and scene divisions have been added.

Volpone

or

The Fox

THE PERSONS OF THE PLAY[1]

VOLPONE, *a magnifico*
MOSCA, *his parasite*
VOLTORE, *an advocate*
CORBACCIO, *an old gentleman*
CORVINO, *a merchant*
BONARIO, *son to* CORBACCIO
SIR POLITIC WOULD-BE, *a knight*
PEREGRINE, *a gentleman traveler*
NANO, *a dwarf*
CASTRONE, *an eunuch*
ANDROGYNO, *an hermaphrodite*

GREGE (*or Mob*)
COMMENDATORI, *officers of justice*
MERCATORI, *three merchants*
AVOCATORI, *four magistrates*
NOTARIO, *the register*
LADY WOULD-BE, SIR POLITIC'S *Wife*
CELIA, CORVINO'S *Wife*
SERVITORI, *Servants, two* WAITING-WOMEN, &c.

THE SCENE, *Venice*

The Argument

V *olpone, childless, rich, feigns sick, despairs,*
O *ffers his state to hopes of several heirs,*
L *ies languishing; his parasite receives*
P *resents of all, assures, deludes; then weaves*
5 O *ther cross plots, which ope themselves, are told.*
N *ew tricks for safety are sought; they thrive: when bold,* ⎫
E *ach tempts the other again, and all are sold.*° ⎬ deceived
⎭

Prologue

Now, luck yet send us, and a little wit
Will serve to make our play hit;
According to the palates of the season,
Here is rhyme, not empty of reason.
5 *This we were bid to credit from our poet,*
Whose true scope, if you would know it,
In all his poems still hath been this measure,
To mix profit with your pleasure,[2]

---

1. Most of the names are Italian and suggest the characters' natures. Volpone: "fox." Magnifico simply means "gentleman." Mosca: "fly." Parasite implies scavenging, as well as fawning dependence. The client-patron relationship in ancient Rome fostered parasitical dependents, and Jonson saw something similar, around the English court and around the big money men of London. Voltore: "vulture." Corbaccio: "raven." Corvino: "crow." Bonario: "good." Sir Politic Would-be: the word "politic" carried overtones of devious and subtle Machiavellian calculation. Its abbreviation ("Pol") suggests further the parrot he is. Peregrine: in English, "a falcon"; but the word also associates

with "pilgrim," i.e., "traveler." Nano: "dwarf." Castrone: "gelding." Androgyno: from the Greek, "man-woman," i.e., "hermaphrodite." Grege: from the Italian, "mob" or "crowd." Commendatori: a not very distinguished title of honor: Jonson assigns them a function akin to sergeants or marshals of a court. Mercatori: "merchants." Avocatori: properly, in Italian, "prosecutors"; Jonson makes them judges. Notario: "recorder." Celia: literally, "heavenly." The "Argument" (below) is a capsule summary of the plot.

2. That the poet is to mix profit with pleasure was an idea dating back to Horace's *Art of Poetry*, lines 343–44.

  And not as some, whose throats their envy failing,
10 *Cry hoarsely, All he writes is railing;*°   *abuse, invective*
  And when his plays come forth, think they can flout them,
   With saying, He was a year about them.
  To these there needs no lie but this his creature,
   Which was, two months since, no feature;[3]
15 *And though he dares give them five lives to mend it,*
   'Tis known, five weeks fully penned it,
  From his own hand, without a coadjutor,°   *co-author*
   Novice, journey man,° *or tutor.*   *apprentice, assistant*
  Yet thus much I can give you as a token
20 *Of his play's worth: no eggs are broken,*
  Nor quaking custards with fierce teeth affrighted,[4]
   Wherewith your rout° *are so delighted*   *mob, groundlings*
  Nor hales he in a gull, old ends[5] *reciting,*
   To stop gaps in his loose writing;
25 *With such a deal of monstrous and forced action,*
   As might make Bedlam[6] *a faction;*
  Nor made he his play for jests stolen from each table,
   But makes jests to fit his fable;
  And so presents quick comedy refined,
30 *As best critics have designed;*
  The laws of time, place, persons he observeth,[7]
   From no needful rule he swerveth.
  All gall and copperas from his ink he draineth,
   Only a little salt remaineth,[8]
35 *Wherewith he'll rub your cheeks till, red with laughter,*
   They shall look fresh a week after.

Act 1

SCENE 1. *A room in* VOLPONE'*s house.*

[*Enter* VOLPONE *and* MOSCA.]

VOLPONE Good morning to the day; and next, my gold!
Open the shrine, that I may see my saint.

  [MOSCA *withdraws the curtain*[9] *and discovers piles of gold, plate, jewels,*
  &c.]

Hail the world's soul, and mine! more glad than is
The teeming earth to see the longed-for sun
5 Peep through the horns of the celestial ram,[1]
Am I, to view thy splendor darkening his;
That lying here, amongst my other hoards,

3. To deny (give the lie to) this charge it is enough to note that Jonson's creature (this play) did not exist two months ago.
4. Comic routines—thrown eggs or custard pies— that were popular on the Elizabethan stage. A giant custard pie was also served at city feasts inaugurating the lord mayor; sometimes an attendant fool jumped into it.
5. Ancient adages. "Gull": buffoon.
6. Bethlehem Hospital, the madhouse.
7. The so-called Aristotelian unities, actually imposed as prescripts by the Renaissance critics

Castelvetro and Scaliger, placed limits of time (twenty-four hours) and place (one location) on a dramatic action; comic "persons" were to be from the lower or middle classes.
8. Gall and copperas (i.e., green vitriol) are traditional ingredients of ink: both are corrosive and bitter to the taste. Salt is a classical metaphor for wit, that which gives flavor to speech or writing.
9. He uncovers a small curtained inner area of the stage.
1. The sun peeps through the horns of the Ram (Aries) late in March.

Show'st like a flame by night, or like the day
Struck out of chaos, when all darkness fled
10   Unto the center. O thou son of Sol,[2]
But brighter than thy father, let me kiss,
With adoration, thee, and every relic
Of sacred treasure in this blessèd room.
Well did wise poets by thy glorious name
15   Title that age which they would have the best[3]
Thou being the best of things, and far transcending
All style° of joy, in children, parents, friends,   *kinds*
Or any other waking dream on earth.
Thy looks when they to Venus did ascribe,
20   They should have given her twenty thousand Cupids,[4]
Such are thy beauties and our loves! Dear saint,
Riches, the dumb god,[5] that givest all men tongues,
That canst do nought, and yet mak'st men do all things;
The price of soul; even hell, with thee to boot,
25   Is made worth heaven. Thou art virtue, fame,
Honor and all things else. Who can get thee,
He shall be noble, valiant, honest, wise—
MOSCA   And what he will, sir. Riches are in fortune
A greater good than wisdom is in nature.
30   VOLPONE   True, my belovèd Mosca. Yet I glory
More in the cunning purchase° of my wealth   *acquisition*
Than in the glad possession, since I gain
No common way; I use no trade, no venture;
I wound no earth with plowshares, fat no beasts
35   To feed the shambles;° have no mills for iron,   *slaughterhouse*
Oil, corn, or men, to grind them into powder;
I blow no subtle glass,[6] expose no ships
To threat'nings of the furrow-facèd sea;
I turn no moneys° in the public bank,   *earn no interest*
Nor usure° private—   *maybe loans*
40   MOSCA   No, sir, nor devour
Soft prodigals. You shall have some will swallow
A melting heir as glibly as your Dutch
Will pills of butter, and ne'er purge[7] for it;
Tear forth the fathers of poor families
45   Out of their beds, and coffin them alive
In some kind clasping prison, where their bones
May be forth-coming when the flesh is rotten.

---

2. Gold is compared to the creation of day (Genesis 1), when darkness "fled to the center," i.e., hell. Gold is said to be "the son of Sol" (the sun) because in Renaissance lore the fertilizing rays of the sun penetrating the ground supposedly developed the "seeds of gold" found there.
3. The Golden Age.
4. Lines 16–20 are translated from a fragment of Euripides. A traditional epithet of Venus is "golden," but Volpone is not satisfied with her minting a single golden boy; he wants a lot of them.
5. Mammon, god of riches, is dumb because

"silence is golden."
6. Glass was a Venetian specialty, in Jonson's day as now. "Mills to grind men to powder" is the sort of prophetic hyperbole that would take on new meaning during the Industrial Revolution of the 18th and 19th centuries.
7. Empty the bowels. Many jokes were made in the 17th century on the Dutch appetite for butter. Loan sharks swallowed up heirs by lending them money at exorbitant rates against their future inheritance.

But your sweet nature doth abhor these courses;
You loathe the widow's or the orphan's tears
50   Should wash your pavements, or their piteous cries
Ring in your roofs, and beat the air for vengeance.
VOLPONE   Right, Mosca; I do loathe it.
MOSCA   And besides, sir,
You are not like the thresher that doth stand
With a huge flail, watching a heap of corn,
55   And, hungry, dares not taste the smallest grain,
But feeds on mallows and such bitter herbs;
Nor like the merchant who hath filled his vaults
With Romagnia and rich Candian wines,
Yet drinks the lees° of Lombard's vinegar.[8]   *dregs*
60   You will not lie in straw, whilst moths and worms
Feed on your sumptuous hangings and soft beds.
You know the use of riches, and dare give now
From that bright heap, to me, your poor observer,
Or to your dwarf, or your hermaphrodite,
65   Your eunuch, or what other household trifle
Your pleasure allows maintenance—
VOLPONE   Hold thee, Mosca, [*Gives him money.*]
Take of my hand; thou strik'st on truth in all,
And they are envious term thee parasite.
Call forth my dwarf, my eunuch, and my fool,
70   And let them make me sport. [*Exit* MOSCA.] What should I do,
But cocker up° my genius and live free   *pamper, indulge*
To all delights my fortune calls me to?
I have no wife, no parent, child, ally,
To give my substance to, but whom I make
75   Must be my heir; and this makes men observe° me.   *court*
This draws new clients daily to my house,
Women and men of every sex and age,
That bring me presents, send me plate, coin, jewels,
With hope that when I die (which they expect
80   Each greedy minute) it shall then return
Tenfold upon them; whilst some, covetous
Above the rest, seek to engross me whole,[9]
And counter-work the one unto the other,
Contend in gifts, as they would seem in love.
85   All which I suffer, playing with their hopes,
And am content to coin them into profit,
And look upon their kindness, and take more,
And look on that; still bearing them in hand,°   *deluding them*
Letting the cherry knock against their lips,
90   And draw it by their mouths, and back again.[1]—How now!

---

8. Romagnia (pronounced *rumney*) was a sweet wine from Greece; Candian is wine from Crete (Candia). French and Italian wines ('Lombard's vinegar') were not much appreciated.
9. An engrosser bought up an entire crop of grain, held it for hard times, then sold it at exorbitant prices.
1. "Chop-cherry" is a country game in which a cherry hung from a string is dangled before players who try to catch it with their teeth.

SCENE 2

[*Enter* MOSCA *with* NANO, ANDROGYNO, *and* CASTRONE.]

NANO   *Now, room for fresh gamesters, who do will you to know,*
      They do bring you neither play nor university show;
    And therefore do entreat you, that whatsoever they rehearse,
      May not fare a whit the worse, for the false pace of the verse.[2]
5   *If you wonder at this, you will wonder more ere we pass,*
      For know, here[3] *is enclosed the soul of Pythagoras,*
    That juggler divine, as hereafter shall follow;
      Which soul, fast and loose, sir, came first from Apollo,
    And was breathed into Aethalides,[4] *Mercurius his son,*
10   *Where it had the gift to remember all that ever was done,*
    From thence it fled forth, and made quick transmigration
      To goldy-locked Euphorbus,[5] *who was killed in good fashion*
    At the siege of old Troy by the cuckold of Sparta.
      Hermotimus was next (I find it in my charta)[6]
15   *To whom it did pass, where no sooner it was missing,*
      But with one Pyrrhus of Delos it learned to go a-fishing;
    And thence did it enter the sophist of Greece.
      From Pythagore, she went into a beautiful piece
    Hight°Aspasia, the meretrix;[7] *and the next toss of her*   called
20   *Was again of a whore she became a philosopher,*
    Crates the cynic,[8] *as itself doth relate it;*
      Since, kings, knights, and beggars, knaves, lords, and fools gat it,
    Besides ox and ass, camel, mule, goat, and brock,°   badger
      In all which it hath spoke, as in the cobbler's cock.[9]
25   *But I come not here to discourse of that matter,*
      Or his one, two, or three, or his great oath, BY QUATER!
    His musics, his trigon, his golden thigh,[1]
      Or his telling how elements shift; but I
    Would ask how of late thou hast suffered translation,
30   *And shifted thy coat in these days of reformation?*
ANDROGYNO   *Like one of the reformed, a fool, as you see,*
    Counting all old° doctrine heresy.   pre-Reformation
NANO   *But not on thine own forbid meats hast thou ventured?*
ANDROGYNO   *On fish, when first a Carthusian I entered.*[2]
35 NANO   *Why, then thy dogmatical silence hath left thee?*
ANDROGYNO   *Of that an obstreperous lawyer bereft me.*[3]

2. The loose, jogtrot meter recalled the four-stress line of the old morality plays.

3. He points at Androgyno. The Greek philosopher Pythagoras put forward the doctrine of transmigration of souls. Nano's comic story elaborates on the account in the life of Pythagoras by Diogenes Laertius.

4. Herald of the Argonauts.

5. Trojan hero killed by Menelaus ("the cuckold of Sparta"), whose wife, Helen, went off with Paris. Pythagoras specifically claimed to have been Euphorbus and to recall the event.

6. Hermotimus is a prophet mentioned in Nano's "charta," i.e., the text of Diogenes Laertius. Pyrrhus of Delos (line 16) is a fisherman mentioned in Diogenes. The "sophist of Greece" (line 17) is Pythagoras himself.

7. Whore. But Aspasia was simply the mistress of Pericles.

8. A disciple of Diogenes the Cynic who professed a particularly bitter brand of skepticism.

9. Lucian's comic dialogue *Gallus*, between a cobbler and a cock, reproduces much of this material about Pythagoras.

1. Pythagorean theories about music and numerology, the Pythagorean theorem about right angles, and the myth that Pythagoras had a golden thigh are glanced at here. A trigon is a triangle; the oath "By Quater" (four) is reported in Plutarch, *On the Sayings of the Philosophers.*

2. As a Carthusian monk he ate fish, forbidden to the Pythagorean.

3. Having taken the vow of silence as a Carthusian, he became a lawyer and tallied constantly.

NANO   *O wonderful change! When Sir Lawyer forsook thee,*
   For Pythagore's sake, what body then took thee?
ANDROGYNO   *A good dull mule.*
NANO   *And how! by that means*
40   *Thou wert brought to allow of the eating of beans?*[4]
ANDROGYNO   *Yes.*
NANO   *But from the mule into whom didst thou pass?*
ANDROGYNO   *Into a very strange beast, by some writers called an ass;*
   By others, a precise, pure, illuminate brother,[5]
     Of those devour flesh, and sometimes one another;
45   *And will drop you forth a libel, or a sanctified lie,*
     Betwixt every spoonful of a nativity-pie.[6]
NANO   *Now quit thee, for heaven, of that profane nation,*
   And gently report thy next transmigration.
ANDROGYNO   *To the same that I am.*
NANO   *A creature of delight,*
50   *And, what is more than a fool, an hermaphrodite!*
   Now, prithee, sweet soul, in all thy variation,
     Which body wouldst thou choose, to take up thy station?
ANDROGYNO   *Troth, this I am in, even here would I tarry.*
NANO   *'Cause here the delight of each sex thou canst vary?*
55 ANDROGYNO   *Alas, those pleasures be stale and forsaken;*
   No, 'tis your fool wherewith I am so taken,
   The only one creature that I can call blessed;
     For all other forms I have proved most distressed.
NANO   *Spoke true, as thou wert in Pythagoras still.*
60   *This learned opinion we celebrate will,*
   Fellow eunuch, as behooves us, with all our wit and art,
     To dignify that whereof ourselves are so great and special a part.
VOLPONE   Now, very, very pretty! Mosca, this
   Was thy invention?
MOSCA   If it please my patron,
   Not else.
VOLPONE   It doth, good Mosca.
65 MOSCA   Then it was, sir.
     [NANO *and* CASTRONE *sing.*]

      Fools, they are the only nation
      Worth men's envy or admiration;
      Free from care or sorrow-taking,
      Selves and others merry making,
70   *All they speak or do is sterling,*
      Your fool he is your great man's darling,
      And your ladies' sport and pleasure;
      Tongue and bauble are his treasure.
      E'en his face begetteth laughter,
75   *And he speaks truth free from slaughter;*[7]
      He's the grace of every feast,

4. Pythagoras forbade the eating of beans.
5. All these adjectives pointed at the Puritans, for whom Jonson had a standing aversion.
6. Puritans avoided the word *Christmas* because it included the "popish" word *mass*; they used the word *Nativity* instead.
7. I.e., with impunity.

And sometimes the chiefest guest;
Hath his trencher° and his stool.   dish
When wit waits upon the fool,
80   *O, who would not be*
                        He, he, he? [*Knocking without.*]
VOLPONE   Who's that? Away!   [*Exeunt* NANO *and* CASTRONE.]
                        Look, Mosca.
MOSCA   Fool, begone!   [*Exit* ANDROGYNO.]
        'Tis Signor Voltore, the advocate;
        I know him by his knock.
VOLPONE   Fetch me my gown,
85   My furs, and night-caps; say my couch is changing,
        And let him entertain himself awhile
        Without i' the gallery. [*Exit* MOSCA.] Now, now my clients
        Begin their visitation! Vulture, kite,
        Raven, and gor-crow, all my birds of prey[8]
90   That think me turning carcass, now they come;
        I am not for them yet.
                [*Re-enter* MOSCA, *with the gown, &c.*]
                        How now? The news?
MOSCA   A piece of plate,° sir.   silver platter
VOLPONE   Of what bigness?
MOSCA   Huge,
        Massy, and antique, with your name inscribed,
        And arms engraven.
VOLPONE   Good! and not a fox
95   Stretched on the earth, with fine delusive sleights
        Mocking a gaping crow?[9] ha, Mosca!
MOSCA   Sharp, sir.
VOLPONE   Give me my furs. [*Puts on his sick dress.*]
                        Why dost thou laugh so, man?
MOSCA   I cannot choose, sir, when I apprehend
        What thoughts he has without now, as he walks:
100   That this might be the last gift he should give;
        That this would fetch you; if you died today,
        And gave him all, what he should be tomorrow;
        What large return would come of all his ventures;
        How he should worshipped be, and reverenced;
105   Ride with his furs and foot-cloths[1] waited on
        By herds of fools and clients; have clear way
        Made for his mule, as lettered as himself;
        Be called the great and learnèd advocate:
        And then concludes, there's nought impossible.
VOLPONE   Yes, to be learnèd, Mosca.
110 MOSCA   O, no; rich
        Implies it. Hood an ass with reverend purple,
        So you can hide his two ambitious ears,

8. Lady Politic is the kite, Corvino the gorcrow   feigning death to catch a carrion crow.
("gor": filth). They are all carrion eaters.   1. Ornate tapestries laid on the horse.
9. Apparently an allusion to a fable about a fox

And he shall pass for a cathedral doctor.°   *doctor of theology*
VOLPONE My caps, my caps, good Mosca. Fetch him in.
MOSCA Stay, sir; your ointment for your eyes.
115 VOLPONE   That's true;
 Dispatch, dispatch!° I long to have possession   *hurry*
 Of my new present.
MOSCA   That, and thousands more,
 I hope to see you lord of.
VOLPONE   Thanks, kind Mosca.
MOSCA And that, when I am lost in blended dust,
120 And hundred such as I am, in succession—
VOLPONE Nay, that were too much, Mosca.
MOSCA   You shall live,
 Still, to delude these harpies.[2]
VOLPONE   Loving Mosca!
 'Tis well. My pillow now, and let him enter. [*Exit* MOSCA.]
 Now, my feigned cough, my phthisic,° and my gout, *consumption*
125 My apoplexy, palsy, and catarrhs,
 Help, with your forcèd functions, this my posture,
 Wherein, this three year, I have milked their hopes.
 He comes; I hear him—Uh! [*coughing*] uh! uh! uh! O—

SCENE 3

 [*Enter* MOSCA, *introducing* VOLTORE *with a piece of plate.*]
MOSCA You still are what you were, sir. Only you,
 Of all the rest, are he commands his love,
 And you do wisely to preserve it thus,
 With early visitation, and kind notes
5 Of your good meaning to him, which, I know,
 Cannot but come most grateful. Patron! Sir!
 Here's Signor Voltore is come—
VOLPONE [*faintly*]   What say you?
MOSCA Sir, Signor Voltore is come this morning
 To visit you.
VOLPONE I thank him.
MOSCA   And hath brought
10 A piece of antique plate, bought of St. Mark,[3]
 With which he here presents you.
VOLPONE   He is welcome.
 Pray him to come more often.
MOSCA   Yes.
VOLTORE   What says he?
MOSCA He thanks you, and desires you see him often.
VOLPONE Mosca.
MOSCA   My patron?
VOLPONE.   Bring him near, where is he?
 I long to feel his hand.
15 MOSCA   The plate is here, sir.

---

2. Monstrous birds of prey.   3. I.e., in St. Mark's Square.

VOLTORE   How fare you, sir?
VOLPONE   I thank you, Signor Voltore.
  Where is the plate? mine eyes are bad.
VOLTORE [*putting it into his hands*]   I'm sorry
  To see you still thus weak.
MOSCA [*aside*]   That he's not weaker.
VOLPONE   You are too munificent.
VOLTORE   No, sir; would to heaven
20   I could as well give health to you, as that plate!
VOLPONE   You give, sir, what you can; I thank you. Your love
  Hath taste in this, and shall not be unanswered;
  I pray you see me often.
VOLTORE   Yes, I shall, sir.
VOLPONE   Be not far from me.
MOSCA   Do you observe that, sir?
25   VOLPONE   Hearken unto me still; it will concern you.
MOSCA   You are a happy man, sir; know your good.
VOLPONE   I cannot now last long—
MOSCA   You are his heir, sir.
VOLTORE   Am I?
VOLPONE   I feel me going; Uh! uh! uh! uh!
  I'm sailing to my port, Uh! uh! uh! uh!
30   And I am glad I am so near my haven.
MOSCA   Alas, kind gentleman! Well, we must all go—
VOLTORE   But, Mosca—
MOSCA   Age will conquer.
VOLTORE   Pray thee, hear me:
  Am I inscribed his heir for certain?
MOSCA   Are you!
  I do beseech you, sir, you will vouchsafe
35   To write me in your family.[4] All my hopes
  Depend upon your worship. I am lost,
  Except the rising sun do shine on me.
VOLTORE   It shall both shine and warm thee, Mosca.
MOSCA   Sir,
  I am a man that have not done your love
40   All the worst offices.° Here I wear your keys,   services
  See all your coffers and your caskets locked,
  Keep the poor inventory of your jewels,
  Your plate and moneys; am your steward, sir,
  Husband° your goods here.   care for
VOLTORE   But am I sole heir?
45   MOSCA   Without a partner, sir; confirmed this morning.
  The wax is warm yet, and the ink scarce dry
  Upon the parchment.
VOLTORE.   Happy, happy me!
  By what good chance, sweet Mosca?
MOSCA   Your desert, sir;

4. I.e., inscribe me in the list of your servants.

I know no second cause.
VOLTORE   Thy modesty
50   Is loath to know it; well, we shall requite it.
MOSCA   He ever liked your course, sir; that first took him.
I oft have heard him say how he admired
Men of your large profession, that could speak
To every cause, and things mere contraries,
55   Till they were hoarse again, yet all be law;
That with most quick agility could turn
And return; make knots, and undo them;
Give forkèd counsel;° take provoking gold   *ambiguous advice*
On either hand, and put it up.⁵ These men,
60   He knew, would thrive with their humility.
And, for his part, he thought he should be blessed
To have his heir of such a suffering spirit,
So wise, so grave, of so perplexed a tongue,
And loud withal, that would not wag, nor scarce
65   Lie still, without a fee; when every word
Your worship but lets fall is a sequin!—°   *zecchino, a gold coin*
                           [*Knocking without.*]
Who's that? One knocks; I would not have you seen, sir.
And yet—pretend you came and went in haste;
I'll fashion an excuse—and, gentle sir,
70   When you do come to swim in golden lard,
Up to the arms in honey, that your chin
Is born up stiff with fatness of the flood,
Think on your vassal; but remember me:
I have not been your worst of clients.
VOLTORE   Mosca—
75   MOSCA   When will you have your inventory brought, sir?
Or see a copy of the will? [*Knocking again.*] Anon!⁶
I'll bring them to you, sir. Away, be gone;
Put business in your face.   [*Exit* VOLTORE.]
VOLPONE [*springing up*]   Excellent Mosca!
Come hither, let me kiss thee.
MOSCA   Keep you still, sir.
Here is Corbaccio.
80   VOLPONE   Set the plate away.
The vulture's gone, and the old raven's come.

SCENE 4

MOSCA   Betake you to your silence and your sleep.
[*puts the plate away*] Stand there and multiply. Now shall we see
A wretch who is indeed more impotent
Than this can feign to be; yet hopes to hop
Over his grave.
              [*Enter* CORBACCIO.]
5   Signor Corbaccio!

5. Take bribes from both sides and keep them.   6. Said in response to a rap at the door.

You're very welcome, sir.
CORBACCIO   How does your patron?
MOSCA Troth, as he did, sir; no amends.
CORBACCIO   What! mends he?
MOSCA No, sir, he's rather worse.
CORBACCIO   That's well. Where is he?
MOSCA Upon his couch, sir, newly fallen asleep.
CORBACCIO Does he sleep well?
10 MOSCA   No wink, sir, all this night,
    Nor yesterday; but slumbers.°   *dozes*
CORBACCIO   Good! He should take
    Some counsel of physicians. I have brought him
    An opiate here, from mine own doctor.
MOSCA He will not hear of drugs.
CORBACCIO   Why? I myself
15   Stood by while it was made, saw all the ingredients,
    And know it cannot but most gently work.
    My life for his, 'tis but to make him sleep.
VOLPONE [*aside*] Ay, his last sleep, if he would take it.
MOSCA   Sir,
    He has no faith in physic.
CORBACCIO   Say you, say you?
20 MOSCA He has no faith in physic. He does think
    Most of your doctors are the greater danger,
    And worse disease, t' escape. I often have
    Heard him protest that your physician
    Should never be his heir.
CORBACCIO   Not I his heir?
MOSCA Not your physician, sir.
25 CORBACCIO   O, no, no, no,
    I do not mean it.
MOSCA   No, sir, nor their fees
    He cannot brook; he says, they flay a man,
    Before they kill him.
CORBACCIO   Right, I do conceive° you.   *understand*
MOSCA And then they do it by experiment;
30   For which the law not only doth absolve them,
    But gives them great reward; and he is loath
    To hire his death so.
CORBACCIO   It is true, they kill
    With as much license as a judge.
MOSCA   Nay, more;
    For he but kills, sir, where the law condemns,
    And these can kill him too.
35 CORBACCIO   Ay, or me,
    Or any man. How does his apoplex?
    Is that strong on him still?
MOSCA   Most violent.
    His speech is broken, and his eyes are set,
    His face drawn longer than 'twas wont—

CORBACCIO   How? How?
  Stronger than he was wont?

40 MOSCA   No, sir: his face
  Drawn longer than 'twas wont.

CORBACCIO   O, good!

MOSCA   His mouth
  Is ever gaping, and his eyelids hang.

CORBACCIO   Good.

MOSCA   A freezing numbness stiffens all his joints,
  And makes the color of his flesh like lead.

CORBACCIO   'Tis good.

MOSCA   His pulse beats slow and dull.

45 CORBACCIO.   Good symptoms still.

MOSCA   And from his brain—

CORBACCIO   Ha? How? Not from his brain?

MOSCA   Yes, sir, and from his brain—

CORBACCIO   I conceive you; good.

MOSCA   Flows a cold sweat, with a continual rheum,°   *mucous discharge*
  Forth the resolvèd° corners of his eyes.   *relaxed*

50 CORBACCIO Is't possible? Yet I am better, ha!
  How does he with the swimming of his head?

MOSCA   O, sir, 'tis past the scotomy;° he now   *dizziness*
  Hath lost his feeling, and hath left to snort.
  You hardly can perceive him, that he breathes.

55 CORBACCIO Excellent, excellent! Sure I shall outlast him!
  This makes me young again, a score of years.

MOSCA   I was a-coming for you, sir.

CORBACCIO   Has he made his will?
  What has he given me?

MOSCA   No, sir.

CORBACCIO   Nothing? ha!

MOSCA   He has not made his will, sir.

CORBACCIO   Oh, oh, oh!

60 What then did Voltore, the lawyer, here?

MOSCA   He smelt a carcass, sir, when he but heard
  My master was about his testament,
  As I did urge him to it for your good.

CORBACCIO He came unto him, did he? I thought so.

65 MOSCA   Yes, and presented him this piece of plate.

CORBACCIO To be his heir?

MOSCA   I do not know, sir.

CORBACCIO   True,
  I know it too.

MOSCA [*aside*] By your own scale,° sir.   *measure*

CORBACCIO   Well,
  I shall prevent him yet. See, Mosca, look:
  Here I have brought a bag of bright sequins,
  Will quite weigh down his plate.

70 MOSCA [*taking the bag*]   Yea, marry, sir.
  This is true physic, this your sacred medicine;

No talk of opiates, to this great elixir![7]
CORBACCIO   'Tis *aurum palpabile*,[8] if not *potabile*.
MOSCA   It shall be ministered to him, in his bowl.
CORBACCIO   Ay, do, do, do.

75 MOSCA   Most blessèd cordial!
This will recover him.
CORBACCIO   Yes, do, do, do.
MOSCA   I think it were not best, sir.
CORBACCIO   What?
MOSCA   To recover him.
CORBACCIO   O, no, no, no; by no means.
MOSCA   Why, sir, this
Will work some strange effect, if he but feel it.

80 CORBACCIO   'Tis true, therefore forbear; I'll take my venture.
Give me it again.
MOSCA   At no hand; pardon me.
You shall not do yourself that wrong, sir. I
Will so advise you, you shall have it all.
CORBACCIO   How?
MOSCA   All, sir; 'tis your right, your own; no man

85 Can claim a part; 'tis yours without a rival,
Decreed by destiny.
CORBACCIO   How, how, good Mosca?
MOSCA   I'll tell you, sir. This fit he shall recover—
CORBACCIO   I do conceive you.
MOSCA   And, on first advantage
Of his gained sense, will I re-importune him

90 Unto the making of his testament,
And show him this. [*Pointing to the money.*]
CORBACCIO   Good, good.
MOSCA   'Tis better yet,
If you will hear, sir.
CORBACCIO   Yes, with all my heart.
MOSCA   Now, would I counsel you, make home with speed;
There, frame a will, whereto you shall inscribe
My master your sole heir.

95 CORBACCIO   And disinherit
My son?
MOSCA   O, sir, the better: for that color°   *appearance*
Shall make it much more taking.°   *convincing*
CORBACCIO   O, but color?
MOSCA   This will, sir, you shall send it unto me.
Now, when I come to enforce, as I will do,

100 Your cares, your watchings, and your many prayers,
Your more than many gifts, your this day's present,
And last, produce your will; where, without thought

---

7. No sedatives ("opiates") can compare with this great medicine. The elixir was supposed to be the supreme, universal medicine, capable of prolonging life indefinitely as well as of transforming baser metals to gold.
8. I.e., palpable, material gold; *aurum potabile* was drinkable gold (the elixir).

Or least regard unto your proper issue,
A son so brave and highly meriting,
105   The stream of your diverted love hath thrown you
Upon my master, and made him your heir:
He cannot be so stupid, or stone dead,
But out of conscience and mere gratitude—
CORBACCIO   He must pronounce me his?
MOSCA   'Tis true.
CORBACCIO   This plot
Did I think on before.
110   MOSCA   I do believe it.
CORBACCIO   Do you not believe it?
MOSCA   Yes, sir.
CORBACCIO   Mine own project.
MOSCA   Which, when he hath done, sir—
CORBACCIO   Published me his heir?
MOSCA   And you so certain to survive him—
CORBACCIO   Ay.
MOSCA   Being so lusty a man—
CORBACCIO   'Tis true.
MOSCA   Yes, sir—
115   CORBACCIO   I thought on that too. See, how he should be
The very organ to express my thoughts!
MOSCA   You have not only done yourself a good—
CORBACCIO   But multiplied it on my son?
MOSCA   'Tis right, sir.
CORBACCIO   Still my invention.
MOSCA   'Las, sir! heaven knows
120   It hath been all my study, all my care
(I e'en grow gray withal), how to work things—
CORBACCIO   I do conceive, sweet Mosca.
MOSCA   You are he
For whom I labor here.
CORBACCIO   Ay, do, do, do:
I'll straight about it.   [Going.]
MOSCA   Rook go with you, raven![9]
CORBACCIO   I know thee honest.
MOSCA [aside]   You do lie, sir!
125   CORBACCIO   And—
MOSCA   Your knowledge is no better than your ears, sir.
CORBACCIO   I do not doubt to be a father to thee.
MOSCA   Nor I to gull my brother of his blessing.[1]
CORBACCIO   I may have my youth restored to me, why not?
MOSCA   Your worship is a precious ass!
130   CORBACCIO   What sayest thou?
MOSCA   I do desire your worship to make haste, sir.

9. The rook is a crowlike bird, raucous and thievish, but Mosca is playing on a secondary meaning—cheat or deception.
1. Jacob robbed his brother Esau of his blessing, by impersonating him before blind old Isaac (Genesis 27), as Mosca will rob Corbaccio's son, Bonario.

CORBACCIO   'Tis done, 'tis done; I go. [*Exit.*]
VOLPONE [*leaping from his couch*]   O, I shall burst!
  Let out my sides, let out my sides—°   *loosen my clothes*
MOSCA   Contain
  Your flux of laughter, sir; you know this hope
135 Is such a bait it covers any hook.
VOLPONE   O, but thy working, and thy placing it!
  I cannot hold; good rascal, let me kiss thee:
  I never knew thee in so rare a humor.
MOSCA   Alas, sir, I but do as I am taught;
140 Follow your grave instructions; give them words;
  Pour oil° into their ears, and send them hence.   *flattery*
VOLPONE   'Tis true, 'tis true. What a rare punishment
  Is avarice to itself!²
MOSCA   Ay, with our help, sir.
VOLPONE   So many cares, so many maladies,
145 So many fears attending on old age,
  Yea, death so often called on, as no wish
  Can be more frequent with them, their limbs faint,
  Their senses dull, their seeing, hearing, going,
  All dead before them; yea, their very teeth,
150 Their instruments of eating, failing them:
  Yet this is reckoned life! Nay, here was one,
  Is now gone home, that wishes to live longer!
  Feels not his gout, nor palsy; feigns himself
  Younger by scores of years, flatters his age
155 With confident belying it, hopes he may,
  With charms, like Aeson,³ have his youth restored;
  And with these thoughts so battens,° as if fate   *thrives*
  Would be as easily cheated on, as he,
  And all turns air! [*Knocking within.*] Who's that there, now?
    a third?
160 MOSCA   Close, to your couch again; I hear his voice:
  It is Corvino, our spruce merchant.
VOLPONE [*lies down as before*]   Dead.
MOSCA   Another bout, sir, with your eyes. [*anointing them*]
    —Who's there?

                        SCENE 5

      [*Enter* CORVINO.]
    Signor Corvino! come most wished for! O,
  How happy were you, if you knew it, now!
CORVINO   Why? What? Wherein?
MOSCA   The tardy hour is come, sir.
CORVINO   He is not dead?
MOSCA   Not dead, sir, but as good;
  He knows no man.

2. Seneca, *Epistle* 115.6.
3. Jason's father, restored to youth by the magic of Medea.

CORVINO   How shall I do then?

5   MOSCA   Why, sir?

CORVINO   I have brought him here a pearl.

MOSCA   Perhaps he has

So much remembrance left as to know you, sir.

He still calls on you; nothing but your name

Is in his mouth. Is your pearl orient,[4] sir?

10   CORVINO   Venice was never owner of the like.

VOLPONE [*faintly*]   Signor Corvino!

MOSCA   Hark.

VOLPONE   Signor Corvino!

MOSCA   He calls you; step and give it him.—He's here, sir,

And he has brought you a rich pearl.

CORVINO   How do you, sir?

Tell him it doubles the twelfth carat.[5]

MOSCA   Sir,

15   He cannot understand, his hearing's gone;

And yet it comforts him to see you—

CORVINO   Say

I have a diamond for him, too.

MOSCA   Best show it, sir;

Put it into his hand; 'tis only there

He apprehends:[6] he has his feeling, yet.

See how he grasps it!

20   CORVINO   'Las, good gentleman!

How pitiful the sight is!

MOSCA   Tut! forget, sir.

The weeping of an heir should still be laughter

Under a visor.°   *mask*

CORVINO   Why, am I his heir?

MOSCA   Sir, I am sworn, I may not show the will

25   Till he be dead: but here has been Corbaccio,

Here has been Voltore, here were others too,

I cannot number 'em, they were so many,

All gaping here for legacies; but I,

Taking the vantage of his naming you,

30   *Signor Corvino, Signor Corvino*, took

Paper and pen and ink, and there I asked him

Whom he would have his heir? *Corvino*. Who

Should be executor? *Corvino*. And

To any question he was silent to,

35   I still interpreted the nods he made,

Through weakness, for consent, and sent home th' others,

Nothing bequeathed them but to cry and curse.

CORVINO   O, my dear Mosca! [*they embrace*] Does he not

perceive us?

---

4. From the East, source of the most lustrous and precious pearls.

5. I.e., weighs twenty-four carats, a huge pearl.

6. In English, "apprehends" means "to understand" but the root Latin sense is "to take hold of."

MOSCA   No more than a blind harper.[7] He knows no man,
40   No face of friend, nor name of any servant,
            Who 'twas that fed him last, or gave him drink;
            Not those he hath begotten, or brought up,
            Can he remember.
CORVINO   Has he children?
MOSCA   Bastards,
            Some dozen or more, that he begot on beggars,
45   Gypsies, and Jews, and black-moors, when he was drunk.
            Knew you not that, sir? 'Tis the common fable,°   *it's widely believed*
            The dwarf, the fool, the eunuch, are all his;
            He's the true father of his family,
            In all save me; but he has given them nothing.
50 CORVINO   That's well, that's well! Art sure he does not hear us?
MOSCA   Sure, sir! Why, look you, credit your own sense.
                              [*shouts in* VOLPONE's *ear*]
            The pox approach and add to your diseases,
            If it would send you hence the sooner, sir.
            For your incontinence, it hath deserved it
55   Throughly and throughly, and the plague to boot!—
            You may come near, sir—Would you would once close
            Those filthy eyes of yours, that flow with slime
            Like two frog-pits; and those same hanging cheeks,
            Covered with hide instead of skin—Nay, help, sir—
60   That look like frozen dish-clouts set on end!
CORVINO   Or like an old smoked wall, on which the rain
            Ran down in streaks!
MOSCA   Excellent, sir! Speak out.
            You may be louder yet; a culverin°   *cannon*
            Dischargèd in his ear would hardly bore it.
65 CORVINO   His nose is like a common sewer, still running.
MOSCA   'Tis good! And what his mouth?
CORVINO   A very draught.°   *cesspool*
MOSCA   O, stop it up—
CORVINO   By no means.
MOSCA   Pray you, let me:
            Faith, I could stifle him rarely with a pillow,
            As well as any woman that should keep him.°   *nurse*
CORVINO   Do as you will; but I'll be gone.
70 MOSCA   Be so;
            It is your presence makes him last so long.
CORVINO   I pray you, use no violence.
MOSCA   No, sir? Why?
            Why should you be thus scrupulous, pray you, sir?
CORVINO   Nay, at your discretion.
MOSCA   Well, good sir, begone.

---

7. An apparent reference to a helpless blind beggar, but alluding also to the keen insight of blind poets like Homer—hence, a hint that Volpone sees the situation clearly.

75 CORVINO I will not trouble him now, to take my pearl?
MOSCA Puh! nor your diamond. What a needless care
  Is this afflicts you? Is not all here yours?
  Am not I here? whom you have made? your creature?
  That owe my being to you?
CORVINO   Grateful Mosca!
80 Thou art my friend, my fellow, my companion,
  My partner, and shalt share in all my fortunes.
MOSCA Excepting one.
CORVINO   What's that?
MOSCA   Your gallant wife, sir.— [*Exit* CORVINO.]
  Now is he gone: we had no other means
  To shoot him hence, but this.
VOLPONE   My divine Mosca!
85 Thou hast today outgone thyself. [*Knocking within.*] Who's there?
  I will be troubled with no more. Prepare
  Me music, dances, banquets, all delights;
  The Turk is not more sensual in his pleasures
  Than will Volpone. [*Exit* MOSCA.] Let me see; a pearl!
90 A diamond! plate! sequins! Good morning's purchase.
  Why, this is better° than rob churches, yet;   *much easier*
  Or fat° by eating, once a month, a man—[*Enter* MOSCA.]   *grow fat*
  Who is 't?
MOSCA   The beauteous Lady Would-be, sir,
  Wife to the English knight, Sir Politic Would-be
, 95 (This is the style, sir, is directed me),⁸
  Hath sent to know how you have slept tonight,
  And if you would be visited?
VOLPONE   Not now:
  Some three hours hence—
MOSCA   I told the squire so much.
VOLPONE When I am high with mirth and wine, then, then.
100 'Fore heaven, I wonder at the desperate valor
  Of the bold English, that they dare let loose
  Their wives to all encounters!
MOSCA   Sir, this knight
  Had not his name for nothing: he is *politic*,°   *devious, subtle*
  And knows, howe'er his wife affect strange airs,
105 She hath not yet the face to be dishonest.⁹
  But had she Signor Corvino's wife's face—
VOLPONE Has she so rare a face?
MOSCA   O, sir, the wonder,
  The blazing star° of Italy! a wench   *comet*
  O' the first year!¹ a beauty ripe as harvest!
110 Whose skin is whiter than a swan all over,
  Than silver, snow, or lilies! a soft lip,
  Would tempt you to eternity of kissing!

---

8. I.e., "this is the way I've been told to announce
her."
9. I.e., "she's not beautiful enough to be

unchaste."
1. I.e., like the sacrificial lamb "of the first year,
without blemish" of Leviticus 9.3.

And flesh that melteth in the touch to blood!
Bright as your gold, and lovely as your gold!
VOLPONE   Why had not I known this before?
115 MOSCA   Alas, sir,
Myself but yesterday discovered it.
VOLPONE   How might I see her?
MOSCA   O, not possible;
She's kept as warily as is your gold;
Never does come abroad, never takes air,
120 But at a window. All her looks are sweet
As the first grapes or cherries, and are watched
As near as they are.
VOLPONE   I must see her.
MOSCA   Sir,
There is a guard of ten spies thick upon her,
All his whole household; each of which is set
125 Upon his fellow, and have all their charge,
When he goes out, when he comes in, examined.
VOLPONE   I will go see her, though but at her window.
MOSCA   In some disguise, then.
VOLPONE   That is true; I must
Maintain mine own shape² still the same; we'll think.
                                        [Exeunt.]

Act 2

SCENE 1. *St. Mark's Place, before* CORVINO's *house.*

[*Enter* SIR POLITIC WOULD-BE, *and* PEREGRINE.]
SIR POLITIC   Sir, to a wise man, all the world's his soil.
It is not Italy, nor France, nor Europe
That must bound me, if my fates call me forth.
Yet, I protest, it is no salt° desire   *wanton*
5   Of seeing countries, shifting a religion,
Nor any disaffection to the state
Where I was bred, and unto which I owe
My dearest plots,° hath brought me out; much less   *projects, notions*
That idle, antique, stale, gray-headed project
10   Of knowing men's minds and manners, with Ulysses!³
But a peculiar humor of my wife's,
Laid for this height° of Venice, to observe,   *latitude*
To quote, to learn the language, and so forth.—
I hope you travel, sir, with license?°   *a passport*
PEREGRINE   Yes.
15   SIR POLITIC   I dare the safelier converse—How long, sir,
Since you left England?
PEREGRINE   Seven weeks.
SIR POLITIC   So lately!

---

2. Disguise, role.
3. Ulysses (Homer says) knew the minds of many men and saw many cities.

You have not been with my lord ambassador?
PEREGRINE   Not yet, sir.
SIR POLITIC   Pray you, what news, sir, vents our climate?⁴
  I heard last night a most strange thing reported
20 By some of my lord's followers, and I long
  To hear how 'twill be seconded.
PEREGRINE   What was 't, sir?
SIR POLITIC   Marry, sir, of a raven that should build
  In a ship royal of the king's.⁵
PEREGRINE [aside]   This fellow,
  Does he gull me, trow? or is gulled?⁶—Your name, sir?
SIR POLITIC   My name is Politic Would-be.
25 PEREGRINE [aside]   O, that speaks him.—
  A knight, sir?
SIR POLITIC   A poor knight, sir.
PEREGRINE   Your lady
  Lies here in Venice for intelligence   *attires, dresses*
  Of tires° and fashions and behavior
  Among the courtesans?⁷ the fine Lady Would-be?
30 SIR POLITIC   Yes, sir; the spider and the bee ofttimes
  Suck from one flower.
PEREGRINE   Good Sir Politic,
  I cry you mercy; I have heard much of you.
  'Tis true, sir, of your raven.
SIR POLITIC   On your knowledge?
PEREGRINE   Yes, and your lion's whelping in the Tower.⁸
SIR POLITIC   Another whelp!
PEREGRINE   Another, sir.
35 SIR POLITIC   Now, heaven!
  What prodigies be these? The fires at Berwick!
  And the new star!⁹ these things concurring, strange
  And full of omen! Saw you those meteors?
PEREGRINE   I did, sir.
SIR POLITIC   Fearful! Pray you, sir, confirm me,
40 Were there three porpoises seen above the bridge,
  As they give out?¹
PEREGRINE   Six, and a sturgeon, sir.
SIR POLITIC   I am astonished!
PEREGRINE   Nay, sir, be not so;
  I'll tell you a greater prodigy than these—
SIR POLITIC   What should these things portend?
PEREGRINE   The very day
45 (Let me be sure) that I put forth from London,

---

4. I.e., "What news from home?"
5. The raven is a bird of ill omen.
6. To "gull" is to fool or deceive. 'Trow?': do you think?
7. Venetian prostitutes were for hundreds of years reputed to be the most desirable in Europe.
8. Lions were kept caged in the Tower of London. Most of the events to which Sir Politic alludes

occurred shortly before the play's first production and would have been familiar to the audience.
9. A new star was discovered by Kepler in October 1604, and the aurora borealis over Berwick in December that year was said to resemble armies of fighting men.
1. It was unusual for deep-sea creatures to venture up the Thames, past London Bridge.

There was a whale discovered in the river,
As high as Woolwich, that had waited there,
Few know how many months, for the subversion
Of the Stade fleet.[2]
SIR POLITIC   Is't possible? Believe it,
50 'Twas either sent from Spain, or the Archduke's:
Spinola's whale, upon my life, my credit![3]
Will they not leave these projects? Worthy sir,
Some other news.
PEREGRINE   Faith, Stone the fool is dead,
And they do lack a tavern fool extremely.
SIR POLITIC   Is Mas'° Stone dead?[4]   Master
55 PEREGRINE   He's dead, sir; why, I hope
You thought him not immortal? [aside] O, this knight,
Were he well known, would be a precious thing
To fit our English stage. He that should write
But such a fellow, should be thought to feign
Extremely, if not maliciously.
60 SIR POLITIC   Stone dead!
PEREGRINE   Dead. Lord! how deeply, sir, you apprehend it!
He was no kinsman to you?
SIR POLITIC   That I know of.
Well, that same fellow was an unknown fool.
PEREGRINE   And yet you knew him, it seems?
SIR POLITIC   I did so. Sir,
65 I knew him one of the most dangerous heads
Living within the state, and so I held him.
PEREGRINE   Indeed, sir?
SIR POLITIC   While he lived, in action.
He has received weekly intelligence,
Upon my knowledge, out of the Low Countries,
70 For all parts of the world, in cabbages;[5]
And those dispensed again to ambassadors,
In oranges, musk melons, apricots,
Lemons, pome-citrons,° and suchlike; sometimes   large citrons
In Colchester oysters, and your Selsey cockles.[6]
PEREGRINE   You make me wonder!
75 SIR POLITIC   Sir, upon my knowledge.
Nay, I've observed him, at your public ordinary,°   tavern
Take his advertisement° from a traveler   information
(A concealed statesman) in a trencher of meat;
And instantly, before the meal was done,
Convey an answer in a toothpick.
80 PEREGRINE   Strange!

---

2. The fleet of the English Merchant Adventurers, an import-export company based at Stade on the Elbe estuary.
3. Sir Politic believes the rumors that a whale sighted in the Thames in January 1606 had come either from Spain itself or from the Archduke Albert, ruler of the Spanish Netherlands, or from Ambrosio Spinola, general of the Spanish armies in Holland.
4. Stone the fool was an actual figure, about whom various anecdotes survive.
5. Cabbages were a recent importation from Holland.
6. The oysters and cockles specified were the best shellfish to be had in England.

How could this be, sir?

SIR POLITIC   Why, the meat was cut
So like his character, and so laid, as he
Must easily read the cipher.

PEREGRINE   I have heard
He could not read, sir.

SIR POLITIC   So 'twas given out,
85   In policy,° by those that did employ him: *as a cover*
But he could read, and had your languages,
And to 't,° as sound a noddle—   *in addition*

PEREGRINE   I have heard, sir,
That your baboons were spies, and that they were
A kind of subtle nation near to China.

90   SIR POLITIC   Ay, ay, your Mamaluchi.[7] Faith, they had
Their hand in a French plot or two; but they
Were so extremely given to women, as
They made discovery of all; yet I
Had my advices° here, on Wednesday last,   *dispatches*
95   From one of their own coat, they were returned,
Made their relations,° as the fashion is,   *reports*
And now stand fair for fresh employment.

PEREGRINE [*aside*]   'Heart!
This Sir Politic will be ignorant of nothing.
—It seems, sir, you know all.

SIR POLITIC   Not all, sir; but
100   I have some general notions. I do love
To note and to observe; though I live out,
Free from the active torrent, yet I'd mark
The currents and the passages of things
For mine own private use, and know the ebbs
And flows of state.

105   PEREGRINE   Believe it, sir, I hold
Myself in no small tie unto my fortunes
For casting me thus luckily upon you,
Whose knowledge, if your bounty equal it,
May do me great assistance in instruction
110   For my behavior and my bearing, which
Is yet so rude and raw.

SIR POLITIC   Why, came you forth
Empty of rules for travel?

PEREGRINE   Faith, I had
Some common ones from out that vulgar° grammar   *vernacular*
Which he that cried Italian to me taught me.[8]

115   SIR POLITIC   Why this it is that spoils all our brave bloods,
Trusting our hopeful gentry unto pedants,
Fellows of outside and mere bark.[9] You seem
To be a gentleman, of ingenuous race:°   *honorable stock*

---

7. *Mamelukes*, a group of warriors originally from Circassia, in Asia Minor, who held or controlled the throne of Egypt for many years. They had noth-ing to do with baboons, China, or French plots.
8. Trained me in the pronunciation of Italian.
9. Superficial and ignorant teachers.

I not profess it, but my fate hath been
120 To be where I have been consulted with,
In this high kind, touching some great men's sons,
Persons of blood and honor—
PEREGRINE [*seeing people approach*] Who be these, sir?

SCENE 2

[*Enter* MOSCA *and* NANO *disguised, followed by persons
with materials for erecting a stage.*]
MOSCA Under that window, there 't must be. The same.
SIR POLITIC Fellows to mount a bank. Did your instructor
In the dear tongues never discourse to you
Of the Italian mountebanks?[1]
PEREGRINE   Yes, sir.
SIR POLITIC   Why,
Here you shall see one.
5 PEREGRINE   They are quacksalvers,
Fellows that live by venting° oils and drugs?   *selling*
SIR POLITIC Was that the character he gave you of them?
PEREGRINE As I remember.
SIR POLITIC   Pity his ignorance.
They are the only knowing men of Europe!
10 Great general scholars, excellent physicians,
Most admired statesmen, professed favorites,
And cabinet counselors to the greatest princes;
The only languaged men of all the world![2]
PEREGRINE And I have heard they are most lewd° impostors;   *ignorant*
15 Made all of terms and shreds; no less beliers
Of great men's favors than their own vile medicines;
Which they will utter upon monstrous oaths,
Selling that drug for twopence, ere they part,
Which they have valued at twelve crowns before.
20 SIR POLITIC Sir, calumnies are answered best with silence.
Yourself shall judge.—Who is it mounts, my friends?
MOSCA Scoto of Mantua, sir.[3]
SIR POLITIC   Is't he? Nay, then
I'll proudly promise, sir, you shall behold
Another man than has been phant'sied° to you.   *described*
25 I wonder, yet, that he should mount his bank
Here in this nook, that has been wont t'appear
In face of the Piazza!—Here he comes.
[*Enter* VOLPONE *disguised as a mountebank and followed by a crowd of
people.*]
VOLPONE [*to* NANO] Mount, zany.°   *fool, clown*
MOB   Follow, follow, follow, follow, follow![4]

---

1. The word *mountebank* comes from the Italian
monta in banco, meaning "to mount the bench."
Mountebanks were a mixture of street entertainer
and patent medicine salesman.
2. The best talkers.

3. A juggler, magician, and performer at legerdemain who had performed before Queen Elizabeth.
4. The speech of the crowd is intended to mimic
a confused hubbub.

SIR POLITIC   See how the people follow him! He's a man
30   May write ten thousand crowns in bank here. Note,

                                        [VOLPONE *mounts the stage.*]

    Mark but his gesture: I do use to observe
    The state he keeps in getting up.
PEREGRINE   'Tis worth it, sir.
VOLPONE   *Most noble gentlemen, and my worthy patrons! It may seem*
    strange, that I, your Scoto Mantuano, who was ever wont to fix my bank
35   *in face of the public Piazza, near the shelter of the Portico to the Procur-*
    atia,[5] *should now, after eight months' absence from this illustrious city of*
    Venice, humbly retire myself into an obscure nook of the Piazza.
SIR POLITIC   Did not I now object the same?
PEREGRINE   Peace, sir.
VOLPONE   *Let me tell you: I am not, as your Lombard proverb saith, cold*
40   *on my feet;*[5] *or content to part with my commodities at a cheaper rate than*
    I accustomed: look not for it. Nor that the calumnious reports of that impu-
    dent detractor and shame to our profession (Alessandro Buttone, I mean),
    who gave out in public I was condemned a sforzato[7] *to the galleys, for*
    poisoning the Cardinal Bembo's—cook,[8] *hath at all attached, much less*
45   *dejected, me. No, no, worthy gentlemen; to tell you true, I cannot endure*
    to see the rabble of these ground ciarlitani,[9] *that spread their cloaks on the*
    pavement as if they meant to do feats of activity, and then come in lamely
    with their moldy tales out of Boccaccio, like stale Tabarin,[1] *the fabulist:*
    some of them discoursing their travels, and of their tedious captivity in the
50   *Turks' galley, when, indeed, were the truth known, they were the Chris-*
    tians' galleys, where very temperately they ate bread and drunk water, as a
    wholesome penance enjoined them by their confessors for base pilferies.[2]
SIR POLITIC   Note but his bearing, and contempt of these.
VOLPONE   *These turdy-facy-nasty-paty-lousy-fartical rogues, with one poor*
55   *groat's-worth of unprepared antimony, finely wrapped up in several scar-*
    toccios,[3] *are able very well to kill their twenty a week, and play; yet these*
    meager, starved spirits, who have half stopped the organs of their minds
    with earthy oppilations,[4] *want not their favorers among your shrivelled*
    salad-eating artisans, who are overjoyed that they may have their ha'p'orth[5]
60   *of physic; though it purge them into another world, it makes no matter.*
SIR POLITIC   Excellent! Have you heard better language, sir?
VOLPONE   *Well, let them go. And, gentlemen, honorable gentlemen, know*
    that for this time our bank, being thus removed from the clamors of the

---

5. The arcade along the north side of Piazza San Marco, where the Procurators (senior government officials) resided.
6. There is in fact an Italian proverb, *Haver freddo a'piedi,* meaning "to be so hard up that one has to sell one's goods at a loss."
7. Slave.
8. Alessandro Buttone is an imaginary rival who has dreamed up a slander against Scoto—but the tale is absurd, because Cardinal Bembo died in 1547, more than fifty years before the play is supposed to be taking place. The dash before "cook" suggests that the title of cook is a euphemism.
9. Charlatan.

1. Tabarine was an actual Italian comedian of the time who performed in France during the 1570s. Boccaccio's tales from the *Decameron* (14th century) were "moldy" by the 17th.
2. Venetian galleys were often operated by captive Turks or condemned criminals who were chained to the bench, fed miserable food, and whipped mercilessly.
3. Little paper envelopes in which drugs were placed. Antimony was the basis of most common emetics.
4. Obstructions.
5. Half-penny worth.

canaglia,[6] *shall be the scene of pleasure and delight; for I have nothing to*
65 *sell, little or nothing to sell.*
SIR POLITIC   I told you, sir, his end.
PEREGRINE   You did so, sir.
VOLPONE   *I protest, I and my six servants are not able to make of this pre-*
cious liquor so fast as it is fetched away from my lodging by gentlemen of
your city; strangers of the Terra-firma;[7] *worshipful merchants; ay, and sen-*
70 *ators too: who, ever since my arrival, have detained me to their uses by*
their splendidous liberalities. And worthily; for what avails your rich man
to have his magazines stuffed with moscadelli,[8] *or of the purest grape, when*
his physicians prescribe him, on pain of death, to drink nothing but water
cocted[9] *with aniseeds? O, health! health! the blessing of the rich! the riches*
75 *of the poor! who can buy thee at too dear a rate, since there is no enjoying*
this world without thee? Be not then so sparing of your purses, honorable
gentlemen, as to abridge the natural course of life—
PEREGRINE   You see his end?
SIR POLITIC   Ay, is't not good?
VOLPONE   *For when a humid flux, or catarrh,*[1] *by the mutability of air, falls*
80 *from your head into an arm or shoulder, or any other part, take you a*
ducat, or your sequin of gold, and apply to the place affected: see what
good effect it can work. No, no, tis this blessed unguento, *this rare extrac-*
tion, that hath only power to disperse all malignant humors that proceed
either of hot, cold, moist, or windy causes—
PEREGRINE   I would he had put in dry too.[2]
85 SIR POLITIC   Pray you, observe.
VOLPONE   *To fortify the most indigest and crude stomach, ay, were it of one*
that, through extreme weakness, vomited blood, applying only a warm nap-
kin to the place, after the unction and fricace;[3] *for the* vertigine *in the*
head, putting but a drop into your nostrils, likewise behind the ears; a most
90 *sovereign and approved remedy: the* Mal Caduco, *cramps, convulsions,*
paralyses, epilepsies, Tremor-Cordia, *retired nerves, ill vapors of the spleen,*
stoppings of the liver, the stone, the strangury, Hernia Ventosa, Iliaca Passio; *stops a* Dysenteria *immediately; easeth the torsion of the small guts,*
and cures Melancholia Hypochondriaca,[4] *being taken and applied,*
95 *according to my printed receipt.* [pointing to his bill and his vial] *For this*
is the physician, this the medicine; this counsels, this cures; this gives the
direction, this works the effect; and, in sum, both together may be termed
an abstract of the theoric[5] *and practic in the Aesculapian art.*[6] *'Twill cost*
you eight crowns. And, Zan Fritada,[7] *prithee sing a verse extempore in*
100 *honor of it.*
SIR POLITIC   How do you like him, sir?
PEREGRINE   Most strangely, I!

---

6. Rabble.
7. Still the Venetian term for land across the
lagoon, the mainland.
8. Muscatel wine.
9. Cooked.
1. Cold.
2. The four "humors" or ingredients of a balanced
human complexion are assigned the qualities hot,
cold, moist, and dry.
3. Anointing and massage.

4. *Melancholia Hypochondriaca* is black depression. The other ailments are *Mal Caduco*, falling
sickness, epilepsy; *Tremor-Cordia*, palpitations of
the heart; retired nerves, shrunken sinews; strangury, painful urination; *Hernia Ventosa*, gassy hernia; *Iliaca Passio*, cramps of the small intestine.
5. Theory.
6. Medicine (from Aesculapius, Greek god of
medicine).
7. Probably Nano, called "zany pancake."

SIR POLITIC   Is not his language rare?
PEREGRINE   But° alchemy,   *except for*
I never heard the like; or Broughton's books.[8]

[NANO *sings.*]

    Had old Hippocrates, or Galen,[9]
105   *That to their books put med'cines all in,*
    But known this secret, they had never
    (Of which they will be guilty ever)
    Been murderers of so much paper,
    Or wasted many a hurtless taper;
110   *No Indian drug had e'er been famed,*
    Tobacco, sassafras not named;
    Ne yet, of guacum[1] one small stick, sir,
    Nor Raymond Lully's great elixir.
    We had been known the Danish Gonswart,
115   *Or Paracelsus, with his long sword.[2]*

PEREGRINE   All this, yet, will not do; eight crowns is high.
VOLPONE   *No more. Gentlemen, if I had but time to discourse to you the miraculous effects of this my oil, surnamed* oglio del Scoto;[3] *with the countless catalogue of those I have cured of the aforesaid, and many more*
120 *diseases; the patents and privileges of all the princes and commonwealths of Christendom; or but the depositions of those that appeared on my part before the signory of the Sanita[4] and most learned College of Physicians; where I was authorized, upon notice taken of the admirable virtues of my medicaments, and mine own excellency in matter of rare and unknown*
125 *secrets, not only to disperse them publicly in this famous city, but in all the territories that happily joy under the government of the most pious and magnificent states of Italy. But may some other gallant fellow say, "O, there be divers that make profession to have as good and as experimented receipts as yours." Indeed, very many have essayed, like apes, in imitation of that*
130 *which is really and essentially in me, to make of this oil; bestowed great cost in furnaces, stills, alembics,[5] continual fires, and preparation of the ingredients (as indeed there goes to it six hundred several simples,[6] besides some quantity of human fat, for the conglutination, which we buy of the anatomists); but when these practitioners come to the last decoction, blow,*
135 *blow, puff, puff, and all flies in* fumo:[7] *ha, ha, ha! Poor wretches, I rather pity their folly and indiscretion than their loss of time and money; for those may be recovered by industry: but to be a fool born is a disease incurable.*
    For myself, I always from my youth have endeavored to get the rarest secrets, and book them, either in exchange or for money: I spared nor cost
140 *nor labor, where anything was worthy to be learned. And, gentlemen, hon-*

8. Hugh Broughton, a Puritan divine and rabbinical scholar.
9. Famous doctors of the classical world.
1. Modern guaiacum, obtained from the bark of a South American tree.
2. Raymond Lully or Lull was a Spanish mystic philosopher of the 13th century who claimed to have discovered the elixir. "The Danish Gonswart":

unidentifiable. Paracelus, the famous German doctor of the 16th century, was said to have kept medications and herbs in his sword handle.
3. Scoto's oil.
4. The board of medical examiners in Venice.
5. Distilleries.
6. Medicinal plants.
7. In smoke. "Decoction": boiling down.

orable gentlemen, I will undertake, by virtue of chemical art, out of the honorable hat that covers your head to extract the four elements; that is to say, the fire, air, water, and earth, and return you your felt without burn or stain. For, whilst others have been at the balloo,[8] I have been at my book; and am now past the craggy paths of study, and come to the flowery plains of honor and reputation.

SIR POLITIC I do assure you, sir, that is his aim.

VOLPONE *But to our price—*

PEREGRINE And that withal, Sir Pol.

VOLPONE *You all know, honorable gentlemen, I never valued this* ampulla, *or vial, at less than eight crowns; but for this time I am content to be deprived of it for six: six crowns is the price, and less in courtesy I know you cannot offer me; take it or leave it, howsoever, both it and I am at your service. I ask you not as the value of the thing, for then I should demand of you a thousand crowns: so the Cardinals Montalto, Farnese, the great Duke of Tuscany, my gossip,[9] with divers other princes, have given me; but I despise money. Only to show my affection to you, honorable gentlemen, and your illustrious state here, I have neglected the messages of these princes, mine own offices, framed my journey hither, only to present you with the fruits of my travels.* [to NANO and MOSCA]—*Tune your voices once more to the touch of your instruments, and give the honorable assembly some delightful recreation.*

PEREGRINE What monstrous and most painful circumstance
Is here, to get some three or four *gazettes*,[1]
Some three pence in the whole—for that 'twill come to.

SONG

> *You that would last long, list to my song,*
> *Make no more coil,° but buy this oil*   fuss
> *Would you be ever fair and young?*
> *Stout of teeth and strong of tongue?*
> *Tart of palate? quick of ear?*
> *Sharp of sight? of nostril clear?*
> *Moist of hand and light of foot?*
> *Or, I will come nearer to 't,*
> *Would you live free from all diseases?*
> *Do the act your mistress pleases,*
> *Yet fright all aches from your bones?*
> *Here's a med'cine for the nones.°*   purpose

VOLPONE *Well, I am in a humor at this time to make a present of the small quantity my coffer contains, to the rich in courtesy, and to the poor for God's sake. Wherefore, now mark: I asked you six crowns; and six crowns, at other times, you have paid me; you shall not give me six crowns, nor five, nor four, nor three, nor two, nor one; nor half a* ducat; *no, nor a* moccenigo.[2] *Six pence it will cost you, or six hundred pound—expect no*

---

8. A ball game.
9. Cardinal Montalto became Pope as Sixtus V in 1585; Alessandro Farnese had been Pope as Paul III in 1534; "the great Duke of Tuscany" was Cosimo de Medici, who died in 1587. "Gossip":

godfather.
1. The smallest Venetian coins, worth less than an English penny.
2. A Venetian coin, worth about nine English pennies.

lower price, for, by the banner of my front, I will not bate a bagatine[3]—
that I will have, only, a pledge of your loves, to carry something from
185 *amongst you to show I am not contemned by you. Therefore, now, toss your*
handkerchiefs, cheerfully, cheerfully;[4] and be advertised that the first
heroic spirit that deigns to grace me with a handkerchief, I will give it a
little remembrance of something beside, shall please it better than if I had
presented it with a double pistolet.[5]

190 PEREGRINE   Will you be that heroic spark, Sir Pol?
        [CELIA, *at a window above, throws down her handkerchief.*]
        O, see! the window has prevented[6] you.
        VOLPONE   *Lady, I kiss your bounty; and for this timely grace you have done*
your poor Scoto of Mantua, I will return you, over and above my oil, a
secret of that high and inestimable nature shall make you forever enamored
195 *on that minute wherein your eye first descended on so mean, yet not alto-*
gether to be despised, an object. Here is a powder concealed in this paper,
of which, if I should speak to the worth, nine thousand volumes were but
as one page, that page as a line, that line as a word; so short is this pilgrim-
age of man (which some call life) to the expressing of it. Would I reflect
200 *on the price? Why, the whole world were but as an empire, that empire as*
a province, that province as a bank, that bank as a private purse to the
purchase of it. I will only tell you: it is the powder that made Venus a
goddess (given her by Apollo), that kept her perpetually young, cleared her
wrinkles, firmed her gums, filled her skin, colored her hair; from her
205 *derived to Helen, and at the sack of Troy unfortunately lost; till now, in*
this our age, it was as happily recovered, by a studious antiquary, out of
some ruins of Asia, who sent a moiety[7] of it to the court of France (but
much sophisticated[8]), wherewith the ladies there now color their hair. The
rest, at this present, remains with me; extracted to a quintessence, so that
210 *wherever it but touches, in youth it perpetually preserves, in age restores*
the complexion; seats your teeth, did they dance like virginal jacks,[9] firm
as a wall; makes them white as ivory, that were black as—

SCENE 3

        [*Enter* CORVINO.]
CORVINO   Spite o' the devil, and my shame! [*to* VOLPONE] Come
        down here;
        Come down! No house but mine to make your scene?
        Signor Flaminio, will you down, sir? down?
        What, is my wife your Franciscina,[1] sir?
5   No windows on the whole Piazza here
        To make your properties, but mine? but mine?
        [*beats away* VOLPONE, NANO, &c.]

---

3. A tiny coin, a fraction of a cent.
4. Customers sometimes knotted their money in a handkerchief or glove and tossed it on stage; the money was taken out, replaced with the medicine, and the handkerchief tossed back to the purchaser.
5. A double pistolet was a Spanish coin of some value, worth an English pound.
6. Anticipated.
7. Portion.

8. Adulterated.
9. In virginals (early harpsichords), the strings were plucked by quills set in bits of wood called "jacks"; their leaping motion provides the term for "Scoto's" comparison.
1. Flaminio was one of the stock characters—a lover—in the *commedia dell'arte*, Franciscina the always available servant girl.

'Heart! ere tomorrow I shall be new christened,
And called the *Pantalone di Bisognosi*[2]
About the town.   [*Exit* CORVINO, *and the crowd disperses.*]
PEREGRINE   What should this mean, Sir Pol?
SIR POLITIC   Some trick of state, believe it; I will home.
PEREGRINE   It may be some design on you.
SIR POLITIC   I know not.
   I'll stand upon my guard.
PEREGRINE   It is your best, sir.
SIR POLITIC   This three weeks, all my advices, all my letters,
   They have been intercepted.
PEREGRINE   Indeed, sir!
   Best have a care.
SIR POLITIC   Nay, so I will.
PEREGRINE   This knight,
   I may not lose him, for my mirth, till night.   [*Exeunt.*]

SCENE 4. *A room in* VOLPONE's *house.*

[*Enter* VOLPONE *and* MOSCA.]
VOLPONE   O, I am wounded!
MOSCA   Where, sir?
VOLPONE   Not without;
   Those blows were nothing; I could bear them ever.
   But angry Cupid, bolting from her eyes,
   Hath shot himself into me like a flame,
   Where now he flings about his burning heat,
   As in a furnace an ambitious° fire   growing
   Whose vent is stopped. The fight is all within me.
   I cannot live, except thou help me, Mosca;
   My liver[3] melts, and I, without the hope
   Of some soft air from her refreshing breath,
   Am but a heap of cinders.
MOSCA   'Las, good sir,
   Would you had never seen her!
VOLPONE   Nay, would thou
   Hadst never told me of her!
MOSCA   Sir, 'tis true;
   I do confess I was unfortunate,
   And you unhappy: but I'm bound in conscience,
   No less than duty, to effect my best
   To your release of torment, and I will, sir.
VOLPONE   Dear Mosca, shall I hope?
MOSCA   Sir, more than dear,
   I will not bid you to despair of aught
   Within a human compass.
VOLPONE   O, there spoke
   My better angel. Mosca, take my keys,
   Gold, plate, and jewels, all's at thy devotion°   service

2. Pantaloon of the Paupers. Pantaloon, in the
commedia dell'arte, is a doddering old fool in perpetual terror of being cuckolded.
3. Traditionally, the seat of the passions.

Employ them how thou wilt; nay, coin me too,
So thou in this but crown my longings. Mosca?
MOSCA   Use but your patience.
VOLPONE   So I have.
25 MOSCA   I doubt not
To bring success to your desires.
VOLPONE   Nay, then,
I not repent me of my late disguise.
MOSCA   If you can horn° him, sir, you need not.   *cuckold*
VOLPONE   True:
Besides, I never meant him for my heir.—
30 Is not the color of my beard and eyebrows
To make me known?
MOSCA   No jot.
VOLPONE   I did it well.
MOSCA   So well, would I could follow you in mine,
With half the happiness!—and yet I would
Escape your epilogue.[4]
VOLPONE   But were they gulled
With a belief that I was Scoto?
35 MOSCA   Sir,
Scoto himself could hardly have distinguished!
I have not time to flatter you now; we'll part:
And as I prosper, so applaud my art.   [*Exeunt.*]

SCENE 5. *A room in* CORVINO's *house.*

[*Enter* CORVINO, *sword in his hand, dragging in* CELIA.]
CORVINO   Death of mine honor, with the city's fool!
A juggling, tooth-drawing, prating mountebank!
And at a public window! where, whilst he,
With his strained action and his dole[5] of faces,
5 To his drug-lecture draws your itching ears,
A crew of old, unmarried, noted lechers
Stood leering up like satyrs: and you smile
Most graciously, and fan your favors forth,
To give your hot spectators satisfaction!
10 What, was your mountebank their call?[6] their whistle?
Or were you enamored on his copper rings,
His saffron jewel with the toad-stone in 't?
Or his embroidered suit with the cope-stitch,
Made of a hearse cloth?[7] or his old tilt-feather?
15 Or his starched beard? Well! you shall have him, yes!
He shall come home and minister unto you
The fricace for the mother.[8] Or, let me see,
I think you'd rather mount;[9] would you not mount?

4. Avoid the beating you got.
5. Guile, with the suggestion of false faces or masks.
6. I.e., did you arrange the appearance of Scoto deliberately to draw a crowd?
7. Copper rings and toad-stone jewelry are Corvino's sneers at the cheap and flashy dress of the

mountebank, whose suit (he imagines) is made of coarse brown burlap ("hearse-cloth") prettied up with embroidery.
8. Massage for hysteria, thought to be caused by a wandering womb.
9. Mount the stage and the man.

Why, if you'll mount, you may; yes, truly, you may:
20 And so you may be seen down to the foot.
Get you a cittern, Lady Vanity,[1]
And be a dealer with the virtuous man;
Make one: I'll but protest myself a cuckold,
And save your dowry. I'm a Dutchman, I!
25 For if you thought me an Italian,
You would be damned ere you did this, you whore![2]
Thou'dst tremble to imagine that the murder
Of father, mother, brother, all thy race,
Should follow, as the subject of my justice.
    CELIA   Good sir, have patience.
30 CORVINO   What couldst thou propose
Less to thyself, than in this heat of wrath,
And stung with my dishonor, I should strike
This steel into thee, with as many stabs
As thou wert gazed upon with goatish° eyes?   *lascivious*
35 CELIA   Alas, sir, be appeased! I could not think
My being at the window should more now
Move your impatience than at other times.
    CORVINO   No? not to seek and entertain a parley
With a known knave, before a multitude?
40 You were an actor with your handkerchief,
Which he most sweetly kissed in the receipt,
And might, no doubt, return it with a letter,
And 'point the place where you might meet—your sister's,
Your mother's, or your aunt's might serve the turn.
45 CELIA   Why, dear sir, when do I make these excuses,
Or ever stir abroad, but to the church?
And that so seldom—
    CORVINO   Well, it shall be less;
And thy restraint before was liberty
To what I now decree: and therefore mark me.
50 First, I will have this bawdy light° dammed up;   *window*
And till 't be done, some two or three yards off,
I'll chalk a line, o'er which if thou but chance
To set thy desperate foot, more hell, more horror,
More wild remorseless rage shall seize on thee
55 Than on a conjuror that had heedless left
His circle's safety ere his devil was laid.[3]
Then, here's a lock° which I will hang up upon thee,   *chastity belts*
And, now I think on 't, I will keep thee backwards;
Thy lodging shall be backwards; thy walks backwards;
60 Thy prospect—all be backwards; and no pleasure
That thou shalt know but backwards. Nay, since you force
My honest nature, know, it is your own,

---

1. "Lady Vanity" is a stock figure out of the old morality plays. "Cittern": a kind of guitar.
2. The stolidity of Dutch men was a common theme of satire. Italians were reputed to be fiercely jealous. In the event of her infidelity, Celia's dowry would be forfeited to her husband.
3. When a warlock raised the devil, he was safe if he drew a magic circle and stayed inside it.

Being too open, makes me use you thus.
Since you will not contain your subtle nostrils
65 In a sweet room, but they must snuff the air
Of rank and sweaty passengers—[*Knocking within.*] One knocks.
Away, and be not seen, pain of thy life;
Nor look toward the window: if thou dost—
Nay, stay, hear this: let me not prosper, whore,
70 But I will make thee an anatomy,[4]
Dissect thee mine own self, and read a lecture
Upon thee to the city, and in public.
Away!—[*Exit* CELIA.] Who's there?   [*Enter* SERVANT.]
SERVANT   'Tis Signor Mosca, sir.

SCENE 6

CORVINO Let him come in. [*Exit* SERVANT.] His master's dead: there's yet
Some good to help the bad. [*Enter* MOSCA.] My Mosca, welcome!
I guess your news.
MOSCA   I fear you cannot, sir.
CORVINO Is't not his death?
MOSCA   Rather the contrary.
CORVINO Not his recovery?
MOSCA   Yes, sir.
5 CORVINO   I am cursed,
I am bewitched, my crosses meet to vex me.
How? how? how? how?
MOSCA   Why, sir, with Scoto's oil!
Corbaccio and Voltore brought of it,
Whilst I was busy in an inner room—
10 CORVINO Death! that damned mountebank! But for the law
Now I could kill the rascal: it cannot be
His oil should have that virtue.° Have not I   *efficacy*
Known him a common rogue, come fiddling in
To the *osteria,*° with a tumbling whore,   *inn*
15 And, when he has done all his forced tricks, been glad
Of a poor spoonful of dead wine, with flies in 't?
It cannot be. All his ingredients
Are a sheep's gall, a roasted bitch's marrow,
Some few sod° earwigs, pounded caterpillars,   *boiled*
20 A little capon's grease, and fasting spittle:[5]
I know them to a dram.
MOSCA   I know not, sir;
But some on 't, there, they poured into his ears,
Some in his nostrils, and recovered him,
Applying but the fricace.°   *massage*
CORVINO   Pox o' that fricace!
25 MOSCA And since, to seem the more officious
And flattering of his health, there they have had,

4. A corpse for anatomical demonstrations.   5. Spit taken from a hungry man.

At extreme fees, the college of physicians
Consulting on him, how they might restore him;
Where one would have a cataplasm° of spices   *poultice*
30 Another a flayed ape clapped to his breast,
A third would have it a dog, a fourth an oil
With wild cats' skins; at last, they all resolved
That to preserve him was no other means
But some young woman must be straight sought out,
35 Lusty, and full of juice, to sleep by him;
And to this service, most unhappily
And most unwillingly, am I now employed,
Which here I thought to pre-acquaint you with,
For your advice, since it concerns you most;
40 Because I would not do that thing might cross
Your ends, on whom I have my whole dependence, sir.
Yet, if I do it not, they may delate°   *denounce*
My slackness to my patron, work me out
Of his opinion;° and there all your hopes,   *favor*
45 Ventures, or whatsoever, are all frustrate!
I do but tell you, sir. Besides, they are all
Now striving who shall first present him; therefore—
I could entreat you, briefly conclude somewhat;
Prevent° them if you can.   *forestall*
CORVINO   Death to my hopes,
50 This is my villainous fortune! Best to hire
Some common courtesan.
MOSCA   Ay, I thought on that, sir;
But they are all so subtle, full of art,
And age, again, doting and flexible,
So as—I cannot tell—we may perchance
Light on a quean° may cheat us all.   *harlot*
55 CORVINO   'Tis true.
MOSCA No, no: it must be one that has no tricks, sir,
Some simple thing, a creature made unto it;
Some wench you may command. Have you no kinswoman?
God's so—Think, think, think, think, think, think, think, sir.
60 One o' the doctors offered there his daughter.
CORVINO How!
MOSCA   Yes, Signor Lupo,° the physician.   *wolf*
CORVINO His daughter!
MOSCA   And a virgin, sir. Why, alas,
He knows the state of 's body, what it is;
That nought can warm his blood, sir, but a fever;
65 Nor any incantation raise his spirit:[6]
A long forgetfulness hath seized that part.
Besides, sir, who shall know it? Some one or two—
CORVINO I pray thee give me leave. [*walks aside*] If any man
But I had had this luck—The thing in itself,

---

6. With a pun on *spirit*, meaning "semen."

70 I know, is nothing—Wherefore should not I
    As well command my blood and my affections
    As this dull doctor? In the point of honor,
    The cases are all one of wife and daughter.

MOSCA [aside]   I hear him coming.

CORVINO   She shall do 't: 'tis done.

75 'Slight! if this doctor, who is not engaged,
    Unless 't be for his counsel, which is nothing,
    Offer his daughter, what should I, that am
    So deeply in? I will prevent him. Wretch!
    Covetous wretch!—Mosca, I have determined.

MOSCA   How, sir?

80 CORVINO   We'll make all sure. The party you wot of°   *think of*
    Shall be mine own wife, Mosca.

MOSCA   Sir, the thing,
    But that I would not seem to counsel you,
    I should have motioned° to you at the first: *suggested*
    And, make your count, you have cut all their throats.

85 Why, 'tis directly taking a possession!
    And in his next fit, we may let him go.
    'Tis but to pull the pillow from his head,
    And he is throttled: it had been done before,
    But for your scrupulous doubts.

CORVINO   Ay, a plague on 't,

90 My conscience fools my wit! Well, I'll be brief,
    And so be thou, lest they should be before us:
    Go home, prepare him, tell him with what zeal
    And willingness I do it; swear it was
    On the first hearing, as thou mayst do truly,
95 Mine own free motion.

MOSCA   Sir, I warrant you,
    I'll so possess him with it, that the rest
    Of his starved clients shall be banished all,
    And only you received. But come not, sir,
    Until I send, for I have something else
100 To ripen for your good; you must not know it.

CORVINO   But do not you forget to send now.

MOSCA   Fear not.
                                            [*Exit* MOSCA.]

                    SCENE 7

CORVINO   Where are you, wife? my Celia! wife!
        [*Enter* CELIA, *weeping.*]
                                            What, blubbering?
    Come, dry those tears. I think thou thought'st me in earnest.
    Ha! by this light I talked so but to try thee.
    Methinks the lightness of the occasion
5   Should have confirmed° thee. Come, I am not jealous.   *reassured*

CELIA   No?

CORVINO   Faith I am not, I, nor never was;
 It is a poor unprofitable humor.
 Do not I know, if women have a will,
 They'll do° 'gainst all the watches of the world,   *have sex*
10 And that the fiercest spies are tamed with gold?[7]
 Tut, I am confident in thee, thou shalt see 't;
 And see, I'll give thee cause too, to believe it.
 Come, kiss me. Go, and make thee ready straight,
 In all thy best attire, thy choicest jewels,
15 Put them all on, and, with them, thy best looks:
 We are invited to a solemn feast
 At old Volpone's, where it shall appear
 How far I am free from jealousy or fear. [*Exeunt.*]

Act 3

SCENE 1. *A street.*

[*Enter* MOSCA.]
MOSCA   I fear I shall begin to grow in love
 With my dear self and my most prosperous parts,
 They do so spring and burgeon; I can feel
 A whimsy in my blood: I know not how,
5 Success hath made me wanton. I could skip
 Out of my skin, now, like a subtle snake,
 I am so limber. O! your parasite
 Is a most precious thing, dropped from above,
 Not bred 'mongst clods and clodpoles° here on earth. *thick heads*
10 I muse the mystery[8] was not made a science,
 It is so liberally professed! Almost
 All the wise world is little else, in nature,
 But parasites or sub-parasites. And yet
 I mean not those that have your bare town-art,
15 To know who's fit to feed them; have no house,
 No family, no care, and therefore mold
 Tales for men's ears, to bait that sense; or get
 Kitchen-invention, and some stale receipts°   *recipes*
 To please the belly, and the groin;[9] nor those,
20 With their court dog-tricks, that can fawn and fleer,° *laugh obsequiously*
 Make their revènue out of legs and faces,°   *bows and smiles*
 Echo my lord, and lick away a moth:
 But your fine elegant rascal, that can rise
 And stoop almost together, like an arrow;
25 Shoot through the air as nimbly as a star;
 Turn short as doth a swallow; and be here,
 And there, and here, and yonder, all at once;
 Present to any humor, all occasion;
 And change a visor° swifter than a thought! *mask (of his expression)*

7. Immemorial commonplaces on the lust and treachery of women.
8. Craft. Mosca is playing on the idea of the liberal arts and sciences.
9. The parasite who talks for a living "baits" (teases, gratifies) the sense of hearing; others gratify the bellies and groins of their patrons.

30   This is the creature had the art born with him;
    Toils not to learn it, but doth practice it
    Out of most excellent nature: and such sparks
    Are the true parasites, others but their zanies.°   *fools*

SCENE 2

    [*Enter* BONARIO.]
MOSCA [*aside*]   Who's this? Bonario, old Corbaccio's son?
    The person I was bound to seek.—Fair sir,
    You are happily met.
BONARIO   That cannot be by thee.
MOSCA   Why, sir?
BONARIO   Nay, pray thee know thy way, and leave me:
5   I would be loath to interchange discourse
    With such a mate as thou art.
MOSCA   Courteous sir,
    Scorn not my poverty.
BONARIO   Not I, by heaven;
    But thou shalt give me leave to hate thy baseness.
MOSCA   Baseness!
BONARIO   Ay; answer me, is not thy sloth
10   Sufficient argument? thy flattery?
    Thy means of feeding?
MOSCA   Heaven be good to me!
    These imputations are too common, sir,
    And easily stuck on virtue when she's poor.
    You are unequal to me, and howe'er
15   Your sentence may be righteous, yet you are not,
    That, ere you know me, thus proceed in censure:
    St. Mark bear witness 'gainst you, 'tis inhuman. [*Weeps.*]
BONARIO [*aside*]   What! does he weep? The sign is soft and good;
    I do repent me that I was so harsh.
20 MOSCA   'Tis true that, swayed by strong necessity,
    I am enforced to eat my careful bread
    With too much obsequy;° 'tis true, beside,   *flattery, servility*
    That I am fain to spin mine own poor raiment°   *clothing*
    Out of my mere observance,° being not born   *service*
25   To a free fortune: but that I have done
    Base offices, in rending friends asunder,
    Dividing families, betraying counsels,
    Whispering false lies, or mining men with praises,
    Trained their credulity with perjuries,
30   Corrupted chastity, or am in love
    With mine own tender ease, but would not rather
    Prove the most rugged and laborious course
    That might redeem my present estimation,
    Let me here perish in all hope of goodness.
35 BONARIO [*aside*]   This cannot be a personated° passion.—   *pretended*
    I was to blame, so to mistake thy nature;
    Pray thee forgive me and speak out thy business.

MOSCA   Sir, it concerns you; and though I may seem
    At first to make a main offense in manners,
40   And in my gratitude unto my master,
    Yet for the pure love which I bear all right,
    And hatred of the wrong, I must reveal it.
    This very hour your father is in purpose
    To disinherit you—
BONARIO   How!
MOSCA   And thrust you forth
45   As a mere stranger to his blood; 'tis true, sir.
    The work no way engageth me, but as
    I claim an interest in the general state
    Of goodness and true virtue, which I hear
    T' abound in you; and for which mere respect,
50   Without a second aim, sir, I have done it.
BONARIO   This tale hath lost thee much of the late trust
    Thou hadst with me; it is impossible.
    I know not how to lend it any thought
    My father should be so unnatural.
55 MOSCA   It is a confidence that well becomes
    Your piety; and formed, no doubt, it is
    From your own simple innocence, which makes
    Your wrong more monstrous and abhorred. But, sir,
    I now will tell you more. This very minute,
60   It is or will be doing; and, if you
    Shall be but pleased to go with me, I'll bring you,
    I dare not say where you shall see, but where
    Your ear shall be a witness of the deed;
    Hear yourself written bastard and professed
    The common issue of the earth.[1]
65 BONARIO   I'm mazed.°   *bewildered*
MOSCA   Sir, if I do it not, draw your just sword,
    And score your vengeance on my front and face;
    Mark me your villain: you have too much wrong,
    And I do suffer for you, sir. My heart
    Weeps blood in anguish—
70 BONARIO   Lead; I follow thee.   [*Exeunt.*]

SCENE 3. *A room in* VOLPONE'*s house.*

[*Enter* VOLPONE.]
VOLPONE   Mosca stays long, methinks. Bring forth your sports,
    And help to make the wretched time more sweet.
    [*Enter* NANO, ANDROGYNO, *and* CASTRONE.]
NANO   *Dwarf, fool, and eunuch, well met here we be.*
    A question it were now, whether of us three,
5   *Being, all, the known delicates° of a rich man,*   *objects of pleasure*
    In pleasing him, claim the precedency can?
CASTRONE   *I claim for myself.*
ANDROGYNO   *And so doth the fool.*

---

1. The Roman term for a bastard was *filius terrae,* "son of earth."

NANO   'Tis foolish indeed: let me set you both to school.
   First for your dwarf, he's little and witty,
10   And everything, as it is little, is pretty;
   Else why do men say to a creature of my shape,
     So soon as they see him, "It's a pretty little ape?"
   And why a pretty ape, but for pleasing imitation
     Of greater men's action, in a ridiculous fashion?
15   Beside, this feat° body of mine doth not crave   *trim*
     Half the meat, drink, and cloth one of your bulks will have.
   Admit your fool's face be the mother of laughter,
     Yet, for his brain, it must always come after:
   And though that do feed him, it's a pitiful case
20   His body is beholding to such a bad face. [*Knocking within.*]
VOLPONE   Who's there? my couch; away! Look, Nano, see—
   [*Exeunt* ANDROGYNO *and* CASTRONE.]
   Give me my caps, first—go, enquire. [*Exit* NANO.] Now, Cupid
   Send it be Mosca, and with fair return!
NANO [*within*]   It is the beauteous madam—
VOLPONE   Would-be—is it?
NANO   The same.
25 VOLPONE   Now torment on me! Squire her in;
   For she will enter, or dwell here forever:
   Nay, quickly. [*retires to his couch*]—That my fit were past! I fear
   A second hell too, that my loathing this
   Will quite expel my appetite to the other:[2]
30   Would she were taking now her tedious leave.
   Lord, how it threats me what I am to suffer!

SCENE 4

[*Enter* NANO *with* LADY POLITIC WOULD-BE.]
LADY POLITIC   I thank you, good sir. Pray you signify
   Unto your patron I am here.—This band
   Shows not my neck enough.—I trouble you, sir.
   Let me request you, bid one of my women
5   Come hither to me. In good faith, I am dressed
   Most favorably today. It is no matter;
   'Tis well enough.[3]
     [*Enter 1st* WAITING-WOMAN.]
               Look, see, these petulant° things,   *troublesome*
   How they have done this!
VOLPONE [*aside*]   I do feel the fever
   Entering in at mine ears; O, for a charm
   To fright it hence!
10 LADY POLITIC   Come nearer: is this curl
   In his right place? or this? Why is this higher
   Than all the rest? You have not washed your eyes yet?
   Or do they not stand even in your head?
   Where's your fellow? Call her.   [*Exit 1st* WOMAN.]

---

2. Celia. "This": Lady Politic.
3. The theme of talkative women was ancient and traditional.

NANO [aside]   Now, St. Mark
15   Deliver us! Anon she'll beat her women,
     Because her nose is red.
         [*Re-enter 1st with 2nd* WOMAN.]
LADY POLITIC   I pray you, view
     This tire,° forsooth: are all things apt, or no?   *headdress*
     2 WOMAN   One hair a little, here, sticks out, forsooth.
LADY POLITIC   Does 't so, forsooth! And where was your dear sight
20   When it did so, forsooth! What now! bird-eyed?[4]
     And you, too? Pray you both approach and mend it.
     Now, by that light, I muse you're not ashamed!
     I, that have preached these things so oft unto you,
     Read you the principles, argued all the grounds,
25   Disputed every fitness, every grace,
     Called you to counsel of so frequent dressings—
NANO [aside]   More carefully than of your fame or honor.
LADY POLITIC   Made you acquainted what an ample dowry
     The knowledge of these things would be unto you,
30   Able, alone, to get you noble husbands
     At your return; and you thus to neglect it!
     Besides, you seeing what a curious° nation   *fastidious*
     The Italians are, what will they say of me?
     The English lady cannot dress herself.—
35   Here's a fine imputation to our country!
     Well, go your ways, and stay in the next room.
     This fucus° was too coarse too; it's no matter.   *makeup*
     Good sir, you'll give them entertainment?
         [*Exeunt* NANO *and* WAITING-WOMEN.]
VOLPONE   The storm comes toward me.
LADY POLITIC [*goes to the couch*]   How does my Volpone?
40   VOLPONE   Troubled with noise; I cannot sleep; I dreamt
     That a strange fury entered now my house
     And with the dreadful tempest of her breath
     Did cleave my roof asunder.
LADY POLITIC   Believe me, and I
     Had the most fearful dream, could I remember 't—
45   VOLPONE [aside]   Out on my fate! I have given her the occasion
     How to torment me: she will tell me hers.
LADY POLITIC   Methought, the golden mediocrity,°   *mean*
     Polite, and delicate—
VOLPONE   O, if you do love me,
     No more; I sweat and suffer at the mention
50   Of any dream: feel how I tremble yet.
LADY POLITIC   Alas, good soul! the passion of the heart.
     Seed-pearl were good now, boiled with syrup of apples,
     Tincture of gold, and coral, citron-pills,[5]
     Your elecampane root, myrobalanes[6]—

---

4. With the look of a frightened bird.
5. Plants supposed to supply antidepressant drugs.

6. Elecampane was a stimulant; myrobalanes was for diarrhea.

55 VOLPONE [*aside*]   Ay me, I have ta'en a grasshopper by the wing!
LADY POLITIC   Burnt silk, and amber; you have muscadel
Good in the house—
VOLPONE   You will not drink and part?
LADY POLITIC   No, fear not that. I doubt we shall not get
Some English saffron—half a dram would serve;
60 Your sixteen cloves, a little musk, dried mints,
Bugloss,[7] and barley-meal—
VOLPONE   She's in again!
Before I feigned diseases, now I have one.
LADY POLITIC   And these applied with a right scarlet cloth.
VOLPONE [*aside*]   Another flood of words! a very torrent!
LADY POLITIC   Shall I, sir, make you a poultice?
65 VOLPONE   No, no, no;
I'm very well, you need prescribe no more.
LADY POLITIC   I have a little studied physic; but now,
I'm all for music, save in the forenoons
An hour or two for painting. I would have
70 A lady, indeed, to have all letters and arts,
Be able to discourse, to write, to paint,
But principal, as Plato holds,[8] your music
(And so does wise Pythagoras, I take it)
Is your true rapture, when there is consent°   *harmony, concord*
75 In face, in voice, and clothes: and is, indeed,
Our sex's chiefest ornament.
VOLPONE   The poet
As old in time as Plato, and as knowing,
Says that your highest female grace is silence.[9]
LADY POLITIC   Which of your poets? Petrarch, or Tasso, or Dante?
80 Guarini? Ariosto? Aretine?
Cieco di Hadria?[1] I have read them all.
VOLPONE [*aside*]   Is everything a cause to my destruction?
LADY POLITIC   I think I have two or three of them about me.
VOLPONE [*aside*]   The sun, the sea, will sooner both stand still
85 Than her eternal tongue! Nothing can 'scape it.
LADY POLITIC   Here's *Pastor Fido*[2]—
VOLPONE [*aside*]   Profess obstinate silence;
That's now my safest.
LADY POLITIC   All our English writers,
I mean such as are happy in th' Italian,
Will deign to steal out of this author, mainly;
90 Almost as much as from Montagnié:[3]
He has so modern and facile a vein,
Fitting the time, and catching the court-ear!

---

7. A common herb used as a mild stimulant.
8. Plato's *Republic* proposed education in music for men, not women.
9. Sophocles (*Ajax*, line 293).
1. All Lady Politic's poets are famous Italian Renaissance poets. Cieco do Hadria ("the blind man of Adria") was Luigi Groto, an actor as well

as a poet.
2. A pastoral by Giovanni Battista Guarini (1590), internationally popular.
3. Montaigne's name tended to be given three syllables; his *Essays*, first published in 1580, were translated into English by Jonson's friend John Florio (1603).

Your Petrarch is more passionate, yet he,
In days of sonneting, trusted them with much:
95   Dante is hard, and few can understand him.
But, for a desperate wit, there's Aretine;[4]
Only, his pictures are a little obscene—
You mark me not?
VOLPONE   Alas, my mind's perturbed.
LADY POLITIC   Why, in such cases, we must cure ourselves,
Make use of our philosophy—
100 VOLPONE   Oh me!
LADY POLITIC   And as we find our passions do rebel,
Encounter them with reason, or divert them
By giving scope unto some other humor
Of lesser danger; as in politic bodies,°   governments
105 There's nothing more doth overwhelm the judgment,
And cloud the understanding, than too much
Settling and fixing and, as 't were, subsiding
Upon one object. For the incorporating
Of these same outward things into that part
110 Which we call mental, leaves some certain feces°   dregs
That stop the organs and, as Plato says,
Assassinate our knowledge.[5]
VOLPONE [aside]   Now the spirit
Of patience help me!
LADY POLITIC   Come, in faith, I must
Visit you more a-days, and make you well;
Laugh and be lusty.
115 VOLPONE [aside]   My good angel save me!
LADY POLITIC   There was but one sole man in all the world
With whom I e'er could sympathize; and he
Would lie you, often[6] three, four hours together
To hear me speak; and be sometime so rapt,
120 As he would answer me quite from the purpose,
Like you, and you are like him, just. I'll discourse,
An 't be but only, sir, to bring you asleep,
How we did spend our time and loves together,
For some six years.
VOLPONE   Oh, oh, oh, oh, oh, oh!
125 LADY POLITIC   For we were coaetanei,° and brought up—   the same age
VOLPONE   Some power, some fate, some fortune rescue me!

SCENE 5

[Enter MOSCA.]
MOSCA   God save you, madam!
LADY POLITIC   Good sir.
VOLPONE   Mosca! welcome,

---

4. Aretino's dirty poems, written to accompany
some pornographic drawings by Giulio Romano,
were internationally notorious.

5. Lady Politic is into orthodox, but very verbose,
psychology.
6. Would (if you please) often lie still.

Welcome to my redemption!
MOSCA   Why, sir?
VOLPONE [*aside to* MOSCA]   O,
    Rid me of this my torture, quickly, there;
    My madam with the everlasting voice:
5   The bells in time of pestilence ne'er made
    Like noise, or were in that perpetual motion!
    The cockpit comes not near it.[7] All my house
    But now steamed like a bath with her thick breath.
    A lawyer could not have been heard; nor scarce
10   Another woman, such a hail of words
    She has let fall. For hell's sake, rid her hence.
MOSCA   Has she presented?
VOLPONE   O, I do not care;
    I'll take her absence upon any price,
    With any loss.
MOSCA   Madam—
LADY POLITIC   I have brought your patron
    A toy,° a cap here, of mine own work.   *trifle*
15 MOSCA   'Tis well.
    I had forgot to tell you, I saw your knight,
    Where you would little think it—
LADY POLITIC   Where?
MOSCA   Marry,
    Where yet, if you make haste, you may apprehend him,
    Rowing upon the water in a gondola,
20   With the most cunning courtesan of Venice.
LADY POLITIC   Is't true?
MOSCA   Pursue them, and believe your eyes:
    Leave me to make your gift. [*Exit* LADY POLITIC *hastily.*]—
      I knew 'twould take:
    For, lightly,° they that use themselves most license   *commonly*
    Are still most jealous.
VOLPONE   Mosca, hearty thanks
25   For thy quick fiction and delivery of me.
    Now to my hopes, what sayest thou?
        [*Re-enter* LADY POLITIC.]
LADY POLITIC   But do you hear, sir?—
VOLPONE   Again! I fear a paroxysm.
LADY POLITIC   Which way
    Rowed they together?
MOSCA   Toward the Rialto.
LADY POLITIC   I pray you lend me your dwarf.
MOSCA   I pray you take him—
                            [*Exit* LADY POLITIC.]
30   Your hopes, sir, are like happy blossoms: fair,
    And promise timely fruit, if you will stay

---

7. When the plague struck, church bells constantly tolled; at the cockpit, spectators constantly shout bets and encouragement to the birds.

But the maturing; keep you at your couch.
Corbaccio will arrive straight, with the will;
When he is gone, I'll tell you more.   [*Exit.*]
VOLPONE   My blood,
35   My spirits are returned; I am alive:
And, like your wanton gamester at primero,[8]
Whose thought had whispered to him, not go less,
Methinks I lie, and draw—for an encounter.
[*The bed-curtains close upon* VOLPONE.]

SCENE 6. *The passage leading to* VOLPONE's *chamber.*

[*Enter* MOSCA *and* BONARIO.]
MOSCA   Sir, here concealed, [*shows him a closet*] you may
    hear all. But, pray you,
Have patience, sir. [*Knocking within.*]—The same's your
    father knocks:
I am compelled to leave you.   [*Exit.*]
BONARIO   Do so. Yet
    Cannot my thought imagine this a truth.   [*Goes into the closet.*]

SCENE 7. *Another part of the same.*

[*Enter* MOSCA *and* CORVINO, CELIA *following.*]
MOSCA   Death on me! You are come too soon, what meant you?
    Did not I say, I would send?
CORVINO   Yes, but I feared
    You might forget it, and then they prevent° us.   forestall
MOSCA [*aside*]   Prevent! Did e'er man haste so for his horns?
5   A courtier would not ply it so, for a place.
    —Well, now there is no helping it, stay here;
    I'll presently return.
            [*Crosses stage to* BONARIO.]
CORVINO   Where are you, Celia?
    You know not wherefore I have brought you hither?
CELIA   Not well, except you told me.
CORVINO   Now, I will:
    Hark hither. [*He leads her apart, and whispers to her.*]
10   MOSCA [*to* BONARIO.]   Sir, your father hath sent word
    It will be half an hour ere he come;
    And therefore, if you please to walk the while
    Into that gallery—at the upper end
    There are some books to entertain the time;
15   And I'll take care no man shall come unto you, sir.
BONARIO   Yes, I will stay there. [*aside*]—I do doubt this fellow.
                        [*Exit* BONARIO.]
MOSCA [*looking after him*]   There, he is far enough; he can hear nothing:
    And, for his father, I can keep him off.
            [*Goes to* VOLPONE's *couch, opens the curtains, and whispers with him.*]

8. An early form of the Spanish card game later known as ombre (the game played in Pope's *The Rape of the Lock*). The phrases "go less," "draw," and "encounter" are all used in primero.

CORVINO [*to* CELIA]   Nay, now, there is no starting back, and therefore
20   Resolve upon it: I have so decreed.
      It must be done. Nor would I move 't afore,
      Because I would avoid all shifts and tricks
      That might deny me.
CELIA   Sir, let me beseech you,
      Affect not these strange trials; if you doubt
25   My chastity, why, lock me up forever;
      Make me the heir of darkness. Let me live
      Where I may please your fears, if not your trust.
CORVINO   Believe it, I have no such humor, I.
      All that I speak I mean; yet I'm not mad;
30   Not horn-mad,⁹ see you? Go to, show yourself
      Obedient, and a wife.
CELIA   O heaven!
CORVINO   I say it,
      Do so.
CELIA   Was this the train?°   *scheme*
CORVINO   I've told you reasons:
      What the physicians have set down; how much
      It may concern me; what my engagements are;
35   My means; and the necessity of those means,
      For my recovery: wherefore, if you be
      Loyal and mine, be won, respect my venture.°   *business transaction*
CELIA   Before your honor?
CORVINO   Honor! tut, a breath;¹
      There's no such thing in nature. A mere term
40   Invented to awe fools. What, is my gold
      The worse for touching, clothes for being looked on?
      Why, this 's no more. An old decrepit wretch,
      That has no sense, no sinew; takes his meat
      With others' fingers; only knows to gape
45   When you do scald his gums;² a voice; a shadow;
      And what can this man hurt you?
CELIA [*aside*]   Lord! what spirit
      Is this hath entered him?
CORVINO   And for your fame,°   *reputation*
      That's such a jig;° as if I would go tell it,   *joke*
      Cry it on the Piazza! Who shall know it,
50   But he that cannot speak it, and this fellow,
      Whose lips are in my pocket? Save yourself
      (If you'll proclaim 't, you may), I know no other
      Should come to know it.
CELIA   Are heaven and saints then nothing?
      Will they be blind or stupid?
CORVINO   How!

9. Not mad from being cuckolded, or from fearing
it.
1. Like Falstaff (*1 Henry IV* 5.1), Corvino disposes
easily of honor.

2. I.e., the old man has to be fed by others and
doesn't even know enough to open his mouth for
food.

CELIA   Good sir,
55   Be jealous still, emulate them; and think
        What hate they burn with toward every sin.
        CORVINO   I grant you; if I thought it were a sin,
        I would not urge you. Should I offer this
        To some young Frenchman, or hot Tuscan blood
60   That had read Aretine, conned all his prints,[3]
        Knew every quirk within lust's labyrinth,
        And were professed critic in lechery,
        And I would look upon him, and applaud him,
        This were a sin: but here, 'tis contrary,
65   A pious work, mere charity, for physic,°   medicine
        And honest polity to assure mine own.[4]
        CELIA   O heaven! canst thou suffer such a change?
        VOLPONE   Thou art mine honor, Mosca, and my pride,
        My joy, my tickling, my delight! Go bring them.
        MOSCA [advancing]   Please you draw near, sir.
70   CORVINO   Come on, what—
        You will not be rebellious? By that light—
        MOSCA.   Sir,
        Signor Corvino here is come to see you—
        VOLPONE   O!
        MOSCA   And hearing of the consultation had,
        So lately, for your health, is come to offer,
        Or rather, sir, to prostitute—
75   CORVINO   Thanks, sweet Mosca.
        MOSCA   Freely, unasked, or unentreated—
        CORVINO   Well.
        MOSCA   As the true fervent instance of his love,
        His own most fair and proper wife, the beauty
        Only of price in Venice—
        CORVINO   'Tis well urged.
80   MOSCA   To be your comfortress, and to preserve you.
        VOLPONE   Alas, I'm past, already! Pray you, thank him
        For his good care and promptness; but for that,
        'Tis a vain labor e'en to fight 'gainst heaven;
        Applying fire to stone—uh, uh, uh, uh! [coughing]—
85   Making a dead leaf grow again. I take
        His wishes gently, though; and you may tell him
        What I've done for him: marry, my state is hopeless.
        Will him to pray for me; and to use his fortune
        With reverence, when he comes to 't.
        MOSCA   Do you hear, sir?
        Go to him with your wife.
90   CORVINO [to CELIA]   Heart of my father!
        Wilt thou persist thus? Come, I pray thee, come.
        Thou seest 'tis nothing. Celia! By this hand,

---

3. I.e., that had read Aretino's poems and studied   4. "Honest polity" (policy, craft) is an oxymoron.
the obscene illustrations to them.

I shall grow violent. Come, do 't, I say.
CELIA   Sir, kill me, rather: I will take down poison,
 Eat burning coals,[5] do anything.
95 CORVINO   Be damned!
 'Heart! I will drag thee hence, home, by the hair;
 Cry thee a strumpet through the streets; rip up
 Thy mouth unto thine ears; and slit thy nose,
 Like a raw rochet!°—Do not tempt me; come,   *a fish*
100 Yield, I am loath—Death! I will buy some slave
 Whom I will kill, and bind thee to him, alive;[6]
 And at my window hang you forth, devising
 Some monstrous crime which I, in capital letters,
 Will eat into thy flesh with aquafortis°   *acid*
105 And burning corsives,° on this stubborn breast. *corrosives*
 Now, by the blood thou hast incensed, I'll do it!
CELIA   Sir, what you please you may, I am your martyr.
CORVINO   Be not thus obstinate, I have not deserved it:
 Think who it is entreats you. Pray thee, sweet;
110 Good faith, thou shalt have jewels, gowns, attires,
 What thou wilt think, and ask. Do but go kiss him.
 Or touch him, but. For my sake. At my suit.
 This once. No? Not? I shall remember this.
 Will you disgrace me thus? Do you thirst my undoing?
MOSCA   Nay, gentle lady, be advised.
115 CORVINO   No, no.
 She has watched her time. God's precious, this is scurvy,[7]
 'Tis very scurvy; and you are—
MOSCA   Nay, good sir.
CORVINO   An arrant locust, by heaven, a locust! Whore,
 Crocodile, that hast thy tears prepared,
 Expecting how thou 'lt bid them flow—
120 MOSCA   Nay, pray you, sir!
 She will consider.
CELIA   Would my life would serve
 To satisfy—
CORVINO 'Sdeath! If she would but speak to him,
 And save my reputation, 'twere somewhat;
 But spitefully to affect my utter ruin!
125 MOSCA   Ay, now you've put your fortune in her hands.
 Why, i 'faith, it is her modesty; I must quit° her. *acquit*
 If you were absent, she would be more coming° *forthcoming*
 I know it, and dare undertake for her.
 What woman can before her husband? Pray you,
 Let us depart, and leave her here.
130 CORVINO   Sweet Celia,
 Thou mayst redeem all yet; I'll say no more:

---

5. Portia, the virtuous wife of Brutus, killed herself in this way.
6. King Tarquin made such threats to try to gain the bed of the chaste Roman heroine, Lucretia.

7. I.e., by God's precious blood, this is villainous. For her husband, Celia is a "locust" because a devouring plague, a "crocodile" because of her hypocritical tears.

If not, esteem yourself as lost. Nay, stay there.
    [*Shuts the door and exit with* MOSCA.]
CELIA   O God, and his good angels! whither, whither,
    Is shame fled human breasts? that with such ease
135   Men dare put off your honors, and their own?
    Is that which ever was a cause of life
    Now placed beneath the basest circumstance,
    And modesty an exile made, for money?
VOLPONE   Ay, in Corvino, and such earth-fed minds,
    [*leaping from his couch*]
140   That never tasted the true heaven of love.
    Assure thee, Celia, he that would sell thee,
    Only for hope of gain, and that uncertain,
    He would have sold his part of Paradise
    For ready money, had he met a cope-man.°   *buyer*
145   Why art thou mazed to see me thus revived?
    Rather applaud thy beauty's miracle;
    'Tis thy great work: that hath, not now alone,
    But sundry times raised me, in several shapes,
    And, but this morning, like a mountebank,
150   To see thee at thy window. Ay, before
    I would have left my practice for thy love
    In varying figures I would have contended
    With the blue Proteus, or the hornèd flood.[8]
    Now art thou welcome.
CELIA   Sir!
VOLPONE   Nay, fly me not.
155   Nor let thy false imagination
    That I was bed-rid, make thee think I am so:
    Thou shalt not find it. I am now as fresh,
    As hot, as high, and in as jovial plight
    As when in that so celebrated scene
160   At recitation of our comedy,
    For entertainment of the great Valois,
    I acted young Antinous;[9] and attracted
    The eyes and ears of all the ladies present,
    To admire each graceful gesture, note, and footing.

SONG[1]
165   *Come, my Celia, let us prove,*
    While we can, the sports of love;
    Time will not be ours forever,
    He, at length, our good will sever;
    Spend not then his gifts in vain.
170   *Suns that set may rise again;*
    But if once we lose this light,

8. Proteus was a sea god who could take any shape at will. Achelous was a river god who fought with Hercules in several shapes: as a river, as a snake, and finally as a bull—hence, "the hornèd flood" (Ovid, *Metamorphoses* 9).
9. Henry of Valois, duke of Anjou and newly cre-

ated King Henry III of France, visited and was entertained in Venice in 1574. Antinous was a favorite of the Roman emperor Hadrian.
1. The opening lines are adapted from the Latin lyric poet Catullus, and the whole song treats the theme of *carpe diem* (seize the day).

'Tis with us perpetual night.
Why should we defer our joys?
Fame and rumor are but toys.
175   Cannot we delude the eyes
Of a few poor household spies?
Or his easier ears beguile,
Thus removèd by our wile?
'Tis no sin love's fruits to steal;
180   But the sweet thefts to reveal,
To be taken, to be seen,
These have crimes accounted been.

CELIA   Some sèrene° blast me, or dire lightning strike   *noxious mist*
    This my offending face!
VOLPONE   Why droops my Celia?
185   Thou hast, in place of a base husband, found
    A worthy lover: use thy fortune well,
    With secrecy and pleasure. See, behold
    What thou art queen of; not in expectation,
    As I feed others, but possessed and crowned.
190   See here a rope of pearl, and each more orient
    Than that the brave Egyptian queen caroused:[2]
    Dissolve and drink them. See, a carbuncle°   *ruby*
    May put out both the eyes of our St. Mark;
    A diamond, would have bought Lollia Paulina,
195   When she came in like starlight, hid with jewels
    That were the spoils of provinces;[3] take these,
    And wear, and lose them: yet remains an earring
    To purchase them again, and this whole state.
    A gem but worth a private patrimony
200   Is nothing: we will eat such at a meal.
    The heads of parrots, tongues of nightingales,
    The brains of peacocks, and of ostriches
    Shall be our food: and, could we get the phoenix,[4]
    Though nature lost her kind, she were our dish.
205 CELIA   Good sir, these things might move a mind affected
    With such delights; but I, whose innocence
    Is all I can think wealthy, or worth th' enjoying,
    And which, once lost, I have nought to lose beyond it,
    Cannot be taken with these sensual baits:
    If you have conscience—
210 VOLPONE   'Tis the beggar's virtue;
    If thou hast wisdom, hear me, Celia.
    Thy baths shall be the juice of gilly-flowers,[5]
    Spirit of roses, and of violets,
    The milk of unicorns, and panthers' breath
215   Gathered in bags and mixed with Cretan wines.[6]

---

2. Cleopatra reportedly dissolved a precious pearl in wine and during a banquet with Antony drank it up.
3. Lollia Paulina, wife of the Roman emperor Caligula, appeared at a banquet in jewels.

4. Only one phoenix is said to be alive at any one time; eating it would eradicate the species.
5. Clove-scented flowers used to flavor drinks and as a light perfume.
6. The most expensive known to Jonson's age.

Our drink shall be preparèd gold and amber,
Which we will take until my roof whirl round
With the vertigo; and my dwarf shall dance,
My eunuch sing, my fool make up the antic,
220 Whilst we, in changèd shapes, act Ovid's tales,[7]
Thou like Europa now, and I like Jove,
Then I like Mars and thou like Erycine:
So of the rest, till we have quite run through
And wearied all the fables of the gods.
225 Then will I have thee in more modern forms,
Attirèd like some sprightly dame of France,
Brave Tuscan lady, or proud Spanish beauty;
Sometimes, unto the Persian Sophy's wife,
Or the Grand Signor's[8] mistress; and, for change,
230 To one of our most artful courtesans,
Or some quick Negro, or cold Russian;
And I will meet thee in as many shapes:
Where we may so transfuse our wandering souls
Out at our lips, and score up sums of pleasures, [*Sings.*]

235   *That the curious shall not know*
         How to tell° them as they flow;   count
       And the envious, when they find
         What their number is, be pined.[9]

CELIA   If you have ears that will be pierced; or eyes
240 That can be opened; a heart may be touched;
Or any part that yet sounds man about you;
If you have touch of holy saints, or heaven,
Do me the grace to let me 'scape. If not,
Be bountiful and kill me. You do know
245 I am a creature hither ill betrayed
By one whose shame I would forget it were.
If you will deign me neither of these graces,
Yet feed your wrath, sir, rather than your lust
(It is a vice comes nearer manliness),
250 And punish that unhappy crime of nature,
Which you miscall my beauty; flay my face,
Or poison it with ointments for seducing
Your blood to this rebellion. Rub these hands
With what may cause an eating leprosy,
255 E'en to my bones and marrow: anything
That may disfavor° me, save in my honor—   disfigure
And I will kneel to you, pray for you, pay down
A thousand hourly vows, sir, for your health;
Report, and think you virtuous—
VOLPONE   Think me cold,

---

7. I.e., enact the shape-changing fables in the *Metamorphoses*. Jove raped Europa in the shape of a bull; Mars and Venus ("Erycine") were lovers.
8. The "Sophy" is the shah of Persia, the "Grand

Signor" the sultan of Turkey.
9. Tormented. The verses, once again, are adapted from Catullus.

260 Frozen, and impotent, and so report me?
That I had Nestor's hernia,[1] thou wouldst think.
I do degenerate, and abuse my nation,
To play with opportunity thus long;
I should have done the act, and then have parleyed.
Yield, or I'll force thee. [*Seizes her.*]

CELIA   O! just God!

265 VOLPONE   In vain—

BONARIO [*rushing in*]   Forbear, foul ravisher! libidinous swine!
Free the forced lady, or thou diest, impostor!
But that I'm loath to snatch thy punishment
Out of the hand of justice, thou shouldst yet
270 Be made the timely sacrifice of vengeance
Before this altar, and this dross, thy idol.
Lady, let's quit the place, it is the den
Of villainy; fear nought, you have a guard:
And he ere long shall meet his just reward.

                 [*Exeunt* BONARIO *and* CELIA.]

275 VOLPONE   Fall on me, roof, and bury me in ruin!
Become my grave, that wert my shelter! O!
I am unmasked, unspirited, undone,
Betrayed to beggary, to infamy—

SCENE 8

[*Enter* MOSCA, *wounded and bleeding.*]

MOSCA   Where shall I run, most wretched shame of men,
To beat out my unlucky brains?

VOLPONE   Here, here.
What! dost thou bleed?

MOSCA   O that his well-driven sword
Had been so courteous to have cleft me down
5 Unto the navel, ere I lived to see
My life, my hopes, my spirits, my patron, all
Thus desperately engagèd, by my error!

VOLPONE   Woe on thy fortune!

MOSCA   And my follies, sir.

VOLPONE   Thou hast made me miserable.

MOSCA   And myself, sir.
10 Who would have thought he would have hearkened so?

VOLPONE   What shall we do?

MOSCA   I know not; if my heart
Could expiate the mischance, I'd pluck it out.
Will you be pleased to hang me? or cut my throat?
And I'll requite you, sir. Let's die like Romans,
Since we have lived like Grecians.[2] [*Knocking within.*]

15 VOLPONE   Hark! who's there?

---

1. Nestor was the oldest of the Greek kings at the siege of Troy. Juvenal (*Satire* 6.326) said Nestor had a hernia.
2. Greeks, especially Corinthians, were famous for living in luxury; Romans, for committing suicide with dignity when life no longer appeared worthy of them.

I hear some footing; officers, the Saffi,°   police
Come to apprehend us! I do feel the brand
Hissing already at my forehead; now
Mine ears are boring.[3]

MOSCA   To your couch, sir; you
20   Make that place good, however. [VOLPONE *lies down, as*
       before.]—Guilty men
Suspect what they deserve still. Signor Corbaccio!

SCENE 9

[*Enter* CORBACCIO *with* VOLTORE *behind, unseen.*]

CORBACCIO   Why, how now, Mosca?
MOSCA   O, undone, amazed, sir.
Your son, I know not by what accident,
Acquainted with your purpose to my patron
Touching your will, and making him your heir,
5   Entered our house with violence, his sword drawn,
Sought for you, called you wretch, unnatural,
Vowed he would kill you.
CORBACCIO   Me!
MOSCA   Yes, and my patron.
CORBACCIO   This act shall disinherit him indeed:
Here is the will.
MOSCA   'Tis well, sir.
CORBACCIO   Right and well;
Be you as careful now for me.
10   MOSCA   My life, sir,
Is not more tendered; I am only yours.
CORBACCIO   How does he? Will he die shortly, think'st thou?
MOSCA   I fear
He'll outlast May.
CORBACCIO   Today?
MOSCA   No, last out May, sir.
CORBACCIO   Couldst thou not give him a dram?
MOSCA   O, by no means, sir.
CORBACCIO   Nay, I'll not bid you.
15   VOLTORE [*coming forward*]   This is a knave, I see.
MOSCA [*seeing* VOLTORE, *aside*]   How! Signor Voltore! Did he hear me?
VOLTORE   Parasite!
MOSCA   Who's that? O, sir, most timely welcome—
VOLTORE   Scarce
To the discovery of your tricks, I fear.
You are his, *only*? and mine also, are you not?
MOSCA   Who? I, sir?
20   VOLTORE   You, sir. What device is this
About a will?
MOSCA   A plot for you, sir.
VOLTORE   Come,

3. Branding on the face and boring holes in the ears were common criminal punishments.

Put not your foists° upon me; I shall scent them.   *tricks, stinks*
MOSCA   Did you not hear it?
VOLTORE   Yes, I hear Corbaccio
     Hath made your patron there his heir.
MOSCA   'Tis true,
25   By my device, drawn to it by my plot,
     With hope—
VOLTORE   Your patron should reciprocate?
     And you have promised?
MOSCA   For your good, I did, sir.
     Nay more, I told his son, brought, hid him here,
     Where he might hear his father pass the deed;
30   Being persuaded to it by this thought, sir,
     That the unnaturalness, first, of the act,
     And then his father's oft disclaiming in him
     (Which I did mean t' help on), would sure enrage him
     To do some violence upon his parent,
35   On which the law should take sufficient hold,
     And you be stated° in a double hope: *installed*
     Truth be my comfort, and my conscience,
     My only aim was to dig you a fortune
     Out of these two old rotten sepulchres—
VOLTORE   I cry thee mercy, Mosca.
40   MOSCA   Worth your patience,
     And your great merit, sir. And see the change!
VOLTORE   Why, what success?°   *outcome*
MOSCA   Most hapless! you must help, sir.
     Whilst we expected the old raven, in comes
     Corvino's wife, sent hither by her husband—
VOLTORE   What, with a present?
45   MOSCA   No, sir, on visitation
     (I'll tell you how anon); and, staying long,
     The youth he grows impatient, rushes forth,
     Seizeth the lady, wounds me, makes her swear
     (Or he would murder her, that was his vow)
50   To affirm my patron to have done her rape:
     Which how unlike it is, you see! and hence,
     With that pretext he's gone to accuse his father,
     Defame my patron, defeat you—
VOLTORE   Where's her husband?
     Let him be sent for straight.
MOSCA   Sir, I'll go fetch him.
VOLTORE   Bring him to the Scrutineo.[4]
55   MOSCA   Sir, I will.
VOLTORE   This must be stopped.
MOSCA   O, you do nobly, sir.
     Alas, 'twas labored all, sir, for your good;

---

4. The court of law, which has power to investigate possible violations of the law before any particular suit is filed.

Nor was there want of counsel in the plot:
But fortune can, at any time, o'erthrow
60 The projects of a hundred learnèd clerks,° sir.   scholars
CORBACCIO [*listening*]   What's that?
VOLTORE   Will 't please you, sir, to go along?
                  [*Exit* CORBACCIO *followed by* VOLTORE.]
MOSCA   Patron, go in, and pray for our success.
VOLPONE [*rising from his couch*]   Need makes devotion: heaven
    your labor bless!   [*Exeunt.*]

Act 4

SCENE 1. *A street.*

[*Enter* SIR POLITIC WOULD-BE *and* PEREGRINE.]
SIR POLITIC   I told you, sir, it was a plot; you see
    What observation is! You mentioned° me   asked
    For some instructions: I will tell you, sir
    (Since we are met here in this height of Venice),
5   Some few particulars I have set down
    Only for this meridian, fit to be known
    Of your crude traveler; and they are these.
    I will not touch, sir, at your phrase, or clothes,
    For they are old.
PEREGRINE   Sir, I have better.
SIR POLITIC   Pardon,
    I meant, as they are themes.
10 PEREGRINE   O, sir, proceed:
    I'll slander you no more of wit, good sir.
SIR POLITIC   First, for your garb,° it must be grave and serious,   comportment
    Very reserved and locked; not tell a secret
    On any terms, not to your father; scarce
15 A fable but with caution; make sure choice
    Both of your company and discourse; beware
    You never speak a truth—
PEREGRINE   How!
SIR POLITIC   Not to strangers,
    For those be they you must converse with most;
    Others I would not know, sir, but at distance,
20 So as I still might be a saver in them:[5]
    You shall have tricks, else, passed upon you hourly.
    And then, for your religion, profess none,
    But wonder at the diversity of all;
    And, for your part, protest, were there no other
25 But simply the laws o' th' land, you could content you.
    Nick Machiavel and Monsieur Bodin both
    Were of this mind.[6] Then must you learn the use

---

5. A gambling term, to provide against the loss of money.
6. The abbreviation "Nick Machiavel" implies casual familiarity. The political theorist Nicolo Machiavelli saw religion as useful to the state if rightly managed by it. Jean Bodin, the French

And handling of your silver fork at meals,
The metal of your glass[7] (these are main matters
30   With your Italian), and to know the hour
When you must eat your melons and your figs.
PEREGRINE   Is that a point of state too?
SIR POLITIC   Here it is:
For your Venetian, if he see a man
Preposterous in the least, he has him straight;
35   He has: he strips him. I'll acquaint you, sir.
I now have lived here, 'tis some fourteen months;
Within the first week of my landing here,
All took me for a citizen of Venice,
I knew the forms so well—
PEREGRINE [*aside*]   And nothing else.
40   SIR POLITIC   I had read Contarine, took me a house,
Dealt with my Jews[8] to furnish it with movables—
Well, if I could but find one man, one man
To mine own heart, whom I durst trust, I would—
PEREGRINE   What, what, sir?
SIR POLITIC   Make him rich; make him a fortune;
45   He should not think again. I would command it.
PEREGRINE   As how?
SIR POLITIC   With certain projects° that I have   *schemes*
Which I may not discover.°   *reveal*
PEREGRINE [*aside*]   If I had
But one to wager with, I would lay odds now,
He tells me instantly.
SIR POLITIC   One is (and that
50   I care not greatly who knows) to serve the state
Of Venice with red herrings for three years,
And at a certain rate, from Rotterdam,[9]
Where I have correspondence. There's a letter,
Sent me from one o' the States,[1] and to that purpose;
55   He cannot write his name, but that's his mark.
PEREGRINE   He is a chandler?°   *candlemaker*
SIR POLITIC   No, a cheesemonger.
There are some other too with whom I treat
About the same negotiation;
And I will undertake it: for, 'tis thus,
60   I'll do't with ease, I've cast it all.° Your hoy[2]   *figured it out*
Carries but three men in her, and a boy;
And she shall make me three returns a year.

___

political philosopher, advocated religious tolerance
as a means to prevent civil wars.
7. The composition of your glass (so as to know
what to put in it?). Handling a fork was a new experience for the English traveling abroad, as it was
not yet used in England.
8. The Jews that everybody goes to for furniture to
set up a Venetian dwelling. Contarini wrote a book
entitled, in English translation, *The Common-*

wealth and Government of Venice (1599).
9. The Venetians have plenty of fresh fish in the
Adriatic.
1. Member of the States-General, the Dutch legislature.
2. A small North Sea coastal vessel; such a boat
would have great trouble making a trip to Venice,
let alone carrying a worthwhile cargo.

So, if there come but one of three, I save;
If two, I can defalk:° but this is now   reduce the amount
If my main project fail.

65 PEREGRINE   Then you have others?

SIR POLITIC   I should be loath to draw the subtle air
Of such a place without my thousand aims.
I'll not dissemble, sir; where'er I come,
I love to be considerative; and 'tis true

70 I have at my free hours thought upon
Some certain goods unto the state of Venice,
Which I do call my *Cautions*; and, sir, which
I mean, in hope of pension, to propound
To the Great Council, then unto the Forty,

75 So to the Ten.[3] My means are made already—

PEREGRINE   By whom?

SIR POLITIC   Sir, one that, though his place be obscure,
Yet he can sway, and they will hear him. He's
A *commendatore*.

PEREGRINE   What! a common sergeant?

SIR POLITIC   Sir, such as they are put it in their mouths

80 What they should say, sometimes, as well as greater.
I think I have my notes to show you— [*Searching his pockets.*]

PEREGRINE   Good, sir.

SIR POLITIC   But you shall swear unto me, on your gentry,°   as a gentleman
Not to anticipate—

PEREGRINE.   I, sir!

SIR POLITIC.   Nor reveal
A circumstance—My paper is not with me.

PEREGRINE   O, but you can remember, sir.

85 SIR POLITIC   My first is
Concerning tinderboxes.° You must know   matchboxes
No family is here without its box.
Now, sir, it being so portable a thing,
Put case that you or I were ill affected

90 Unto the state; sir, with it in our pockets,
Might not I go into the Arsenal,[4]
Or you? come out again? and none the wiser?

PEREGRINE   Except yourself, sir.

SIR POLITIC   Go to, then. I therefore
Advertise to the state, how fit it were

95 That none but such as were known patriots,
Sound lovers of their country, should be suffered
To enjoy them in their houses; and even those
Sealed at some office, and at such a bigness
As might not lurk in pockets.

PEREGRINE   Admirable!

---

3. Representative legislative bodies of the Vene-   these eminent bodies.
tian government. "My means": my approaches to   4. The Venetian shipyard.

SIR POLITIC My next is, how to inquire, and be resolved
By present demonstration, whether a ship
Newly arrived from Syria, or from
Any suspected part of all the Levant,° *the Middle East*
Be guilty of the plague; and where they use
To lie out forty, fifty days, sometimes,
About the Lazaretto,[5] for their trial,
I'll save that charge and loss unto the merchant,
And in an hour clear the doubt.
PEREGRINE Indeed, sir!
SIR POLITIC Or—I will lose my labor.
PEREGRINE My faith, that's much.
SIR POLITIC Nay, sir, conceive me. 'Twill cost me in onions,
Some thirty livres[6]—
PEREGRINE Which is one pound sterling.
SIR POLITIC Besides my waterworks; for this I do, sir:
First, I bring in your ship 'twixt two brick walls;
But those the state shall venture. On the one
I strain° me a fair tarpaulin,° and in that *stretch / canvas*
I stick my onions, cut in halves; the other
Is full of loopholes, out at which I thrust
The noses of my bellows; and those bellows
I keep, with waterworks,[7] in perpetual motion,
Which is the easiest matter of a hundred.
Now, sir, your onion, which doth naturally
Attract the infection, and your bellows blowing
The air upon him, will show instantly,
By his changed color, if there be contagion,
Or else remain as fair as at the first.
—Now 'tis known, 'tis nothing.
PEREGRINE You are right, sir.
SIR POLITIC I would I had my note.
PEREGRINE Faith, so would I:
But you have done well for once, sir.
SIR POLITIC Were I false,
Or would be made so, I could show you reasons
How I could sell this state now to the Turk,
Spite of their galleys, or their— [*Examining his papers.*]
PEREGRINE Pray you, Sir Pol.
SIR POLITIC I have them not about me.
PEREGRINE That I feared.
They are there, sir?
SIR POLITIC No, this is my diary,
Wherein I note my actions of the day.

5. Quarantine hospital on an island outside Venice where foreign ships were held until passengers, crew, and cargo were proved to be free of disease. Bubonic plague carried by fleas living on shipboard rats was a constant peril in Venice.
6. A French coin of small value. Onions, cut open, supposedly absorbed the plague germs from the air.
7. Apparently a waterwheel arranged to operate a bellows. Of course there is no spot in the flat country around Venice where streams have enough power to turn a wheel.

135 PEREGRINE Pray you let's see, sir. What is here? [*reads*]
      Notandum,°   *it must be noted*
      A rat had gnawn my spur-leathers; notwithstanding,
      I put on new and did go forth; but first
      I threw three beans over the threshold. Item,
      I went, and bought two toothpicks, whereof one
140   *I burst immediately in a discourse*
      With a Dutch merchant 'bout ragion del stato.[8]
      From him I went and paid a moccenigo°   *coin of small worth*
      For piecing° *my silk stockings; by the way*   *mending*
      I cheapened sprats;[9] *and at St. Mark's I urined.*
      Faith, these are politic notes!
145 SIR POLITIC   Sir, I do slip
      No action of my life, thus, but I quote it.
    PEREGRINE Believe me, it is wise!
    SIR POLITIC   Nay, sir, read forth.

                         SCENE 2

       [*Enter, at a distance,* LADY POLITIC WOULD-BE, NANO, *and two*
       WAITING-WOMEN.]
    LADY POLITIC Where should this loose knight be, trow? Sure, he's housed.
    NANO Why, then he's fast.[1]
    LADY POLITIC   Ay, he plays both with me.[2]
      I pray you stay. This heat will do more harm
      To my complexion than his heart is worth.
5   (I do not care to hinder, but to take him.)
      How it[3] comes off! [*Rubbing her cheeks.*]
    1 WOMAN   My master's yonder.
    LADY POLITIC   Where?
    2 WOMAN With a young gentleman.
    LADY POLITIC   That same's the party,
      In man's apparel! Pray you, sir, jog my knight;
      I will be tender to his reputation,
      However he demerit.
    SIR POLITIC [*seeing her*] My lady!
10 PEREGRINE   Where?
    SIR POLITIC 'Tis she indeed, sir; you shall know her. She is,
      Were she not mine, a lady of that merit,
      For fashion and behavior; and for beauty
      I durst compare—
    PEREGRINE   It seems you are not jealous,
      That dare commend her.
15 SIR POLITIC   Nay, and for discourse—
    PEREGRINE Being your wife, she cannot miss that.
    SIR POLITIC [*introducing Peregrine*]   Madam,
      Here is a gentleman; pray you, use him fairly;

---

8. Reason of state. Machiavelli's justification for
whatever action is politically necessary, even if
immoral.
9. Bargained over the price of fish.

1. Implies that he's securely fastened and in fast
company.
2. Both fast and loose.
3. I.e., her makeup.

He seems a youth, but he is—
LADY POLITIC   None.
SIR POLITIC   Yes, one
   Has put his face as soon into the world—
LADY POLITIC   You mean, as early? but today?
20 SIR POLITIC   How's this?
LADY POLITIC   Why, in this habit, sir; you apprehend me.
   Well, Master Would-be, this doth not become you;
   I had thought the odor, sir, of your good name
   Had been more precious to you; that you would not
25   Have done this dire massacre on your honor;
   One of your gravity, and rank besides!
   But knights, I see, care little for the oath
   They make to ladies, chiefly, their own ladies.
SIR POLITIC   Now, by my spurs, the symbol of my knighthood[4]—
30 PEREGRINE [aside]   Lord, how his brain is humbled for an oath!
SIR POLITIC   I reach° you not.   *understand*
LADY POLITIC   Right, sir, your polity
   May bear it through thus. [to PEREGRINE]—Sir, a word with you.
   I would be loath to contest publicly
   With any gentlewoman, or to seem
35   Froward,° or violent: as *The Courtier* says,[5]   *refractory*
   It comes too near rusticity in a lady,
   Which I would shun by all means; and however
   I may deserve from Master Would-be, yet
   T' have one fair gentlewoman thus be made
40   The unkind instrument to wrong another,
   And one she knows not, ay, and to persèver;
   In my poor judgment, is not warranted
   From being a solecism[6] in our sex,
   If not in manners.
PEREGRINE   How is this!
SIR POLITIC   Sweet madam,
   Come nearer to your aim.
45 LADY POLITIC   Marry, and will, sir.
   Since you provoke me with your impudence,
   And laughter of your light land-siren here,
   Your Sporus,[7] your hermaphrodite—
PEREGRINE   What's here?
   Poetic fury and historic[3] storms!
50 SIR POLITIC   The gentleman, believe it, is of worth,
   And of our nation.
LADY POLITIC   Ay, your Whitefriars[9] nation!
   Come, I blush for you, Master Would-be, ay;

4. Because King James created knights indiscriminately at his accession, knighthood was a target for jokes during his reign.
5. I.e., Castiglione's *Il Cortegiano*, translated by Hoby (1561) as *The Courtier* (p. 578).
6. An error in language, but Lady Politic misuses the term to mean an error in behavior.

7. Sporus was a favorite catamite of Nero, who dressed him in drag and married him.
8. With reference to the historical allusion (Sporus).
9. Disreputable quarter of London, inhabited by whores.

And am ashamed you should have no more forehead°   sense of shame
Than thus to be the patron or St. George
55   To a lewd harlot, a base fricatrice,°   prostitute
A female devil in a male outside.
SIR POLITIC   Nay,
An° you be such a one, I must bid adieu   if
To your delights. The case appears too liquid.   [Exit.]
LADY POLITIC   Ay, you may carry 't clear, with your
state-face!°   solemn expression
60   But for your carnival concupiscence,¹
Who here is fled for liberty of conscience
From furious persecution of the marshal,
Her will I dis'ple.²
PEREGRINE   This is fine, i' faith,
And do you use this often? Is this part
65   Of your wit's exercise, 'gainst you have occasion?
Madam—
LADY POLITIC   Go to, sir.
PEREGRINE   Do you hear me, lady?
Why, if your knight have set you to beg shirts,
Or to invite me home, you might have done it
A nearer way, by far.³
LADY POLITIC   This cannot work you
Out of my snare.
70   PEREGRINE   Why, am I in it, then?
Indeed your husband told me you were fair,
And so you are; only your nose inclines,
That side that's next the sun, to the queen-apple.⁴
LADY POLITIC   This cannot be endured by any patience.

SCENE 3

[Enter MOSCA.]
MOSCA   What's the matter, madam?
LADY POLITIC   If the Senate
Right not my quest in this,⁵ I will protest them
To all the world no aristocracy.
MOSCA   What is the injury, lady?
LADY POLITIC   Why, the callet°   slut
5   You told me of, here I have ta'en disguised.
MOSCA   Who? this! What means your ladyship? The creature
I mentioned to you is apprehended now
Before the Senate; you shall see her—
LADY POLITIC   Where?
MOSCA   I'll bring you to her. This young gentleman,
10   I saw him land this morning at the port.
LADY POLITIC   Is't possible! How has my judgment wandered?

1. A wench as licentious as the time of Carnival.
2. Discipline; specifically, whip. In England (though not in Venice), the marshal was directly charged with catching and punishing prostitutes.
3. Peregrine implies that the knight is pimping for his wife.
4. Lady Politic has a fiery red nose.
5. Does not do me justice.

Sir, I must, blushing, say to you, I have erred,
And plead your pardon.
PEREGRINE   What, more changes yet!
LADY POLITIC   I hope you've not the malice to remember
15   A gentlewoman's passion. If you stay
In Venice here, please you to use me, sir—
MOSCA   Will you go, madam?
LADY POLITIC   Pray you, sir, use me; in faith,
The more you see me, the more I shall conceive
You have forgot our quarrel.
     [*Exeunt* LADY WOULD-BE, MOSCA, NANO, *and* WAITING-WOMEN.]
PEREGRINE   This is rare!
20   Sir Politic Would-be? No, Sir Politic Bawd!°   *pimp*
To bring me thus acquainted with his wife!
Well, wise Sir Pol, since you have practiced thus
Upon my freshman-ship,[6] I'll try your salt-head,
What proof it is against a counterplot.   [*Exit.*]

SCENE 4. *The Scrutineo.*°   Senate House

[*Enter* VOLTORE, CORBACCIO, CORVINO, *and* MOSCA.]
VOLTORE   Well, now you know the carriage of the business,
Your constancy is all that is required
Unto the safety of it.
MOSCA   Is the lie[7]
Safely conveyed amongst us? Is that sure?
Knows every man his burden?[8]
CORVINO   Yes.
5   MOSCA   Then shrink not.
CORVINO [*aside to* MOSCA]   But knows the advocate the truth?
MOSCA   O, sir,
By no means; I devised a formal tale
That salved your reputation. But be valiant, sir.
CORVINO   I fear no one but him, that this his pleading
Should make him stand for a co-heir—
10   MOSCA   Co-halter!
Hang him; we will but use his tongue, his noise,
As we do Croaker's[9] here.
CORVINO   Ay, what shall he do?
MOSCA   When we have done, you mean?
CORVINO   Yes.
MOSCA   Why, we'll think:
Sell him for mummia;[1] he's half dust already.
15   [*to* VOLTORE] Do you not smile to see this buffalo,[2]
How he doth sport it with his head? [*aside*]—I should,
If all were well and past. [*to* CORBACCIO.] Sir, only you

6. Innocence, as of a freshman, but in opposition
to Sir Politic's "salt-head" (seasoned experience,
also salaciousness).
7. Untruth, but also the shape of things, as in the
lie or lay of the land.

8. "Part," as in part singing.
9. Corbaccio's.
1. Medicine made from mummies.
2. An allusion to the cuckold's horns worn by Corvino.

Are he that shall enjoy the crop of all,
And these know not for whom they toil.

CORBACCIO   Ay, peace.

20 MOSCA [*turning to* CORVINO.]   But you shall eat it. [*aside*] Much![3]
     [*to* VOLTORE] Worshipful sir,
     Mercury sit upon your thundering tongue,
     Or the French Hercules,[4] and make your language
     As conquering as his club, to beat along,
     As with a tempest, flat, our adversaries;
     But much more yours, sir.

25 VOLTORE   Here they come, have done.

MOSCA   I have another witness, if you need, sir,
     I can produce.

VOLTORE   Who is it?

MOSCA   Sir, I have her.

SCENE 5

[*Enter* AVOCATORI *and take their seats;* BONARIO, CELIA, NOTARIO,
COMMENDATORI, SAFFI, *and other* OFFICERS OF JUSTICE.]

1 AVOCATORE   The like of this the Senate never heard of.

2 AVOCATORE   'Twill come most strange to them when we report it.

4 AVOCATORE   The gentlewoman[5] has been ever held
     Of unreprovèd name.

3 AVOCATORE   So the young man.[6]

5 4 AVOCATORE   The more unnatural part that of his father.

2 AVOCATORE   More of the husband.[7]

1 AVOCATORE   I not know to give
     His act a name, it is so monstrous!

4 AVOCATORE   But the impostor,[8] he's a thing created
     To exceed example!

1 AVOCATORE   And all aftertimes!

10 2 AVOCATORE   I never heard a true voluptuary
     Described, but him.

3 AVOCATORE   Appear yet those were cited?

NOTARIO   All but the old magnifico, Volpone.

1 AVOCATORE   Why is not he here?

MOSCA   Please your fatherhoods,
     Here is his advocate: himself's so weak,
     So feeble—

4 AVOCATORE   What are you?

15 BONARIO   His parasite,
     His knave, his pander:° I beseech the court   procurer
     He may be forced to come, that your grave eyes
     May bear strong witness of his strange impostures.

VOLTORE   Upon my faith and credit with your virtues,

20   He is not able to endure the air.

---

3. I.e., "fat chance!"
4. Both Mercury, god of thieves, and the French
Hercules were known for eloquence.
5. Celia.

6. Bonario.
7. Corvino.
8. Volpone.

2 AVOCATORE   Bring him, however.
3 AVOCATORE   We will see him.
4 AVOCATORE   Fetch him.
VOLTORE   Your fatherhoods' fit pleasures be obeyed;   [*Exeunt* OFFICERS.]
    But sure, the sight will rather move your pities
    Than indignation. May it please the court,
25   In the meantime, he may be heard in me.
    I know this place most void of prejudice,
    And therefore crave it, since we have no reason
    To fear our truth should hurt our cause.
3 AVOCATORE   Speak free.
VOLTORE   Then know, most honored fathers, I must now
30   Discover to your strangely abusèd ears,
    The most prodigious and most frontless° piece   *shameless*
    Of solid impudence and treachery
    That ever vicious nature yet brought forth
    To shame the state of Venice. This lewd woman,
35   That wants° no artificial looks or tears   *lacks*
    To help the visor° she has now put on,   *mask*
    Hath long been known a close° adulteress   *secret*
    To that lascivious youth there; not suspected,
    I say, but known, and taken in the act
40   With him; and by this man, the easy husband,
    Pardoned; whose timeless° bounty makes him now   *ill-timed*
    Stand here, the most unhappy, innocent person
    That ever man's own goodness made accused.
    For these, not knowing how to owe a gift
45   Of that dear grace but with their shame, being placed
    So above all powers of their gratitude,
    Began to hate the benefit; and, in place
    Of thanks, devise to extirp° the memory   *wipe out*
    Of such an act. Wherein, I pray your fatherhoods
50   To observe the malice, yea, the rage of creatures
    Discovered in their evils; and what heart
    Such take, even from their crimes. But that anon
    Will more appear. This gentleman, the father,
    Hearing of this foul fact, with many others
55   Which daily struck at his too tender ears,
    And grieved in nothing more than that he could not
    Preserve himself a parent (his son's ills
    Growing to that strange flood), at last decreed
    To disinherit him.
1 AVOCATORE   These be strange turns!
60 2 AVOCATORE   The young man's fame was ever fair and honest.
VOLTORE   So much more full of danger is his vice,
    That can beguile so under shade of virtue.
    But, as I said, my honored sires, his father
    Having this settled purpose, by what means
65   To him betrayed, we know not, and this day
    Appointed for the deed; that parricide—

I cannot style him better—by confederacy°   *conspiracy*
Preparing this his paramour to be there,
Entered Volpone's house (who was the man,
70   Your fatherhoods must understand, designed
For the inheritance), there sought his father;
But with what purpose sought he him, my lords?
I tremble to pronounce it, that a son
Unto a father, and to such a father,
75   Should have so foul, felonious intent:
It was to murder him! When, being prevented
By his more happy absence, what then did he?
Not check his wicked thoughts; no, now new deeds
(Mischief doth ever end where it begins);
80   An act of horror, fathers! He dragged forth
The agèd gentleman that had there lain bed-rid
Three years and more, out of his innocent couch,
Naked upon the floor, there left him; wounded
His servant in the face; and, with this strumpet,
85   The stale° to his forged practice,° who was glad   *decoy/trickery*
To be so active (I shall here desire
Your fatherhoods to note but my collections,°   *deductions*
As most remarkable), thought at once to stop
His father's ends, discredit his free choice
90   In the old gentleman, redeem themselves,
By laying infamy upon this man,⁹
To whom, with blushing, they should owe their lives.
1 AVOCATORE   What proofs have you of this?
BONARIO   Most honored fathers,
I humbly crave there be no credit given
To this man's mercenary tongue.
95   2 AVOCATORE   Forbear.
BONARIO   His soul moves in his fee.
3 AVOCATORE   O, sir!
BONARIO   This fellow,
For six sols° more, would plead against his Maker.   *coins*
1 AVOCATORE   You do forget yourself.
VOLTORE   Nay, nay, grave fathers,
Let him have scope; can any man imagine
100   That he will spare his accuser, that would not
Have spared his parent?
1 AVOCATORE   Well, produce your proofs.
CELIA   I would I could forget I were a creature.
VOLTORE   Signor Corbaccio!   [CORBACCIO *comes forward.*]
4 AVOCATORE   What is he?
VOLTORE   The father.
2 AVOCATORE   Has he had an oath?
NOTARIO   Yes.
CORBACCIO   What must I do now?

9. Corvino.

NOTARIO   Your testimony's craved.

105   CORBACCIO   Speak to the knave?
I'll have my mouth first stopped with earth; my heart
Abhors his knowledge:[1] I disclaim in him.

1 AVOCATORE   But for what cause?

CORBACCIO   The mere portent of nature!
He is an utter stranger to my loins.

BONARIO   Have they made you to this?

110   CORBACCIO   I will not hear thee,
Monster of men, swine, goat, wolf, parricide!
Speak not, thou viper.

BONARIO   Sir, I will sit down,
And rather wish my innocence should suffer,
Than I resist the authority of a father.

VOLTORE   Signor Corvino!   [CORVINO comes forward.]

2 AVOCATORE   This is strange.

115   1 AVOCATORE   Who's this?

NOTARIO   The husband.

4 AVOCATORE   Is he sworn?

NOTARIO   He is.

3 AVOCATORE   Speak, then.

CORVINO   This woman, please your fatherhoods, is a whore
Of most hot exercise, more than a partridge,[2]
Upon recòrd—

1 AVOCATORE   No more.

CORVINO   Neighs like a jennet.[3]

NOTARIO   Preserve the honor of the court.

120   CORVINO   I shall,
And modesty of your most reverend ears.
And yet I hope that I may say these eyes
Have seen her glued unto that piece of cedar,
That fine well-timbered gallant; and that here[4]

125   The letters may be read, through the horn,
That make the story perfect.

MOSCA [aside to CORVINO]   Excellent, sir!

CORVINO [aside to MOSCA]   There is no shame in this now, is there?

MOSCA   None.

CORVINO   Or if I said, I hoped that she were onward
To her damnation, if there be a hell

130   Greater than whore and woman; a good Catholic
May make the doubt.[5]

3 AVOCATORE   His grief hath made him frantic.

1 AVOCATORE   Remove him hence. [CELIA swoons.]

2 AVOCATORE   Look to the woman.

CORVINO   Rare!
Prettily feigned, again!

---

1. Shudders to recognize him.
2. The partridge was thought to vie with the sparrow as the most lustful of birds.
3. I.e., like a mare in heat.

4. Corvino holds two fingers over his head to make the horned sign of the cuckold.
5. The 1607 quarto reads "Christian"; the 1616 Folio reads "Catholic."

4 AVOCATORE   Stand from about her.

1 AVOCATORE   Give her the air.

3 AVOCATORE [*to* MOSCA]   What can you say?

MOSCA   My wound,

135   May it please your wisdoms, speaks for me, received
        In aid of my good patron, when he missed
        His sought-for father,[6] when that well-taught dame
        Had her cue given her to cry out, A rape!

BONARIO   O most laid impudence! Fathers—

3 AVOCATORE   Sir, be silent;

140   You had your hearing free, so must they theirs.

2 AVOCATORE   I do begin to doubt th' imposture here.

4 AVOCATORE   This woman has too many moods.

VOLTORE   Grave fathers,
        She is a creature of a most professed
        And prostituted lewdness.

CORVINO   Most impetuous,
        Unsatisfied, grave fathers!

145 VOLTORE   May her feignings
        Not take your wisdoms: but this day she baited
        A stranger, a grave knight, with her loose eyes
        And more lascivious kisses. This man [*indicating* MOSCA] saw them
        Together on the water, in a gondola.

150 MOSCA   Here is the lady herself, that saw them too,
        Without; who then had in the open streets
        Pursued them, but for saving her knight's honor.

1 AVOCATORE   Produce that lady.

2 AVOCATORE   Let her come.   [*Exit* MOSCA.]

4 AVOCATORE   These things,
        They strike with wonder.

3 AVOCATORE   I am turned a stone.

SCENE 6

[*Enter* MOSCA *with* LADY WOULD-BE.]

MOSCA   Be resolute, madam.

LADY POLITIC   Ay, this same is she. [*Pointing to* CELIA.]
        Out, thou chameleon[7] harlot! Now thine eyes
        Vie tears with the hyena.[8] Dar'st thou look
        Upon my wrongèd face?—I cry your pardons,

5   I fear I have forgettingly transgressed
        Against the dignity of the court—

2 AVOCATORE   No, madam.

LADY POLITIC   And been exorbitant°—   *excessive*

2 AVOCATORE   You have not, lady.

4 AVOCATORE   These proofs are strong.

LADY POLITIC   Surely, I had no purpose

---

6. Corbaccio.
7. An animal that changes colors, therefore an emblem of deceit.

8. Emblematic of treachery and an eater of carrion.

To scandalize your honors, or my sex's.
3 AVOCATORE   We do believe it.
10   LADY POLITIC   Surely, you may believe it.
2 AVOCATORE   Madam, we do.
LADY POLITIC   Indeed you may; my breeding
Is not so coarse—
4 AVOCATORE   We know it.
LADY POLITIC   To offend
With pertinacy—
3 AVOCATORE   Lady—
LADY POLITIC   Such a presence!
No, surely.
1 AVOCATORE   We well think it.
LADY POLITIC   You may think it.
15   1 AVOCATORE   Let her o'ercome. [to BONARIO] What witnesses have you,
To make good your report?
BONARIO   Our consciences.
CELIA   And heaven, that never fails the innocent.
4 AVOCATORE   These are no testimonies.
BONARIO   Not in your courts,
Where multitude, and clamor overcomes.
1 AVOCATORE   Nay, then you do wax insolent.
        [Re-enter OFFICERS, bearing VOLPONE on a couch.
        LADY POLITIC embraces him.]
20   VOLTORE   Here, here,
The testimony comes that will convince,
And put to utter dumbness their bold tongues!
See here, grave fathers, here's the ravisher,
The rider on men's wives, the great impostor,
25   The grand voluptuary! Do you not think
These limbs should affect venery?° or these eyes   lust
Covet a concubine? Pray you mark these hands;
Are they not fit to stroke a lady's breasts?
Perhaps he doth dissemble!
BONARIO   So he does.
VOLTORE   Would you have him tortured?
30   BONARIO   I would have him proved.
VOLTORE   Best try him then with goads, or burning irons;
Put him to the strappado.[9] I have heard
The rack hath cured the gout; 'faith, give it him,
And help him of a malady; be courteous.
35   I'll undertake, before these honored fathers,
He shall have yet as many left diseases
As she has known adulterers, or thou strumpets.
O, my most equal hearers, if these deeds,
Acts of this bold and most exorbitant strain,
40   May pass with sufferance, what one citizen

9. A common torture of the time: a man's hands were tied behind his back and he was hoisted by his wrists by a pulley, then dropped with a jerk, often dislocating his shoulders.

But owes the forfeit of his life, yea, fame,
To him that dares traduce him? Which of you
Are safe, my honored fathers? I would ask,
With leave of your grave fatherhoods, if their plot
45 Have any face or color like to truth?
Or if, unto the dullest nostril here,
It smell not rank and most abhorrèd slander?
I crave your care of this good gentleman,
Whose life is much endangered by their fable;
50 And as for them, I will conclude with this,
That vicious persons, when they're hot, and fleshed
In impious acts, their constancy abounds:
Damned deeds are done with greatest confidence.
1 AVOCATORE   Take them to custody, and sever them.
                              [CELIA and BONARIO are taken out.]
55 2 AVOCATORE   'Tis pity two such prodigies should live.
1 AVOCATORE   Let the old gentleman be returned with care:
                              [Exeunt OFFICERS with VOLPONE.]
I'm sorry our credulity hath wronged him.
4 AVOCATORE   These are two creatures!
3 AVOCATORE   I have an earthquake in me.
2 AVOCATORE   Their shame, even in their cradles, fled their faces.
60 4 AVOCATORE [to VOLTORE]   You have done a worthy service to the state,
    sir,
In their discovery.
1 AVOCATORE   You shall hear, ere night,
What punishment the court decrees upon them.
VOLTORE   We thank your fatherhoods. [Exeunt AVOCATORI, NOTARIO,
    and OFFICERS] [to MOSCA]—How like you it?
MOSCA   Rare.
I'd have your tongue, sir, tipped with gold for this;
65 I'd have you be the heir to the whole city;
The earth I'd have want men, ere you want living:
They're bound to erect your statue in St. Mark's.
Signor Corvino, I would have you go
And show yourself, that you have conquered.
CORVINO   Yes.
70 MOSCA [aside to CORVINO]   It was much better that you should profess
    Yourself a cuckold thus, than that the other
    Should have been proved.
CORVINO   Nay, I considered that;
Now it is her fault.
MOSCA   Then it had been yours.
CORVINO   True; I do doubt this advocate still.
MOSCA   I' faith,
75 You need not; I dare ease you of that care.
CORVINO   I trust thee, Mosca.
MOSCA   As your own soul, sir. [Exit CORVINO.]
CORBACCIO   Mosca!
MOSCA   Now for your business, sir.
CORBACCIO   How! Have you business?

MOSCA Yes, yours, sir.
CORBACCIO   O, none else?
MOSCA   None else, not I.
CORBACCIO Be careful then.
MOSCA   Rest you with both your eyes, sir.
CORBACCIO Dispatch it.[1]
MOSCA   Instantly.
80   CORBACCIO   And look that all,
      Whatever, be put in, jewels, plate, moneys,
      Household stuff, bedding, curtains.
MOSCA   Curtain-rings, sir:
      Only the advocate's fee must be deducted.
CORBACCIO I'll pay him now; you'll be too prodigal.
MOSCA Sir, I must tender it.
85   CORBACCIO   Two sequins is well?
MOSCA No, six, sir.
CORBACCIO   'Tis too much.
MOSCA   He talked a great while;
      You must consider that, sir.
CORBACCIO   Well, there's three—
MOSCA I'll give it him.
CORBACCIO   Do so, and there's for thee. [Exit.]
MOSCA Bountiful bones! What horrid strange offense
90   Did he commit 'gainst nature, in his youth,
      Worthy this age? [to VOLTORE]—You see, sir, how I work
      Unto your ends; take you no notice.
VOLTORE   No,
      I'll leave you.
MOSCA   All is yours [Exit VOLTORE.]—the devil and all,
      Good advocate!—Madam, I'll bring you home.
LADY POLITIC No, I'll go see your patron.
95   MOSCA   That you shall not.
      I'll tell you why. My purpose is to urge
      My patron to reform° his will; and for   revise
      The zeal you have shown today, whereas before
      You were but third or fourth, you shall be now
100   Put in the first; which would appear as begged,
      If you were present. Therefore—
LADY POLITIC   You shall sway me. [Exeunt.]

Act 5

SCENE 1. A room in VOLPONE's house.

[Enter VOLPONE.]
VOLPONE Well, I am here, and all this brunt° is past.   trouble
      I ne'er was in dislike with my disguise
      Till this fled moment;[2] here 'twas good, in private,
      But in your public—cavè° whilst I breathe.   beware (Latin)

---

1. I.e., get the will made, with me in it.   2. Moment just past.

5 'Fore God, my left leg 'gan to have the cramp,
   And I apprehended³ straight some power had struck me
   With a dead palsy. Well! I must be merry,
   And shake it off. A many of these fears
   Would put me into some villainous disease,
10 Should they come thick upon me: I'll prevent 'em.
   Give me a bowl of lusty wine, to fright
   This humor from my heart. [drinks]—Hum, hum, hum!
   'Tis almost gone already, I shall conquer.
   Any device, now, of rare ingenious knavery,
15 That would possess me with a violent laughter,
   Would make me up again. [drinks again]—So, so, so, so!
   This heat is life; 'tis blood by this time! Mosca!

                    SCENE 2

        [Enter MOSCA.]
   MOSCA   How now, sir? Does the day look clear again?
   Are we recovered? and wrought out of error
   Into our way, to see our path before us?
   Is our trade free once more?
   VOLPONE   Exquisite Mosca!
   MOSCA   Was it not carried learnedly?
5 VOLPONE   And stoutly.
   Good wits are greatest in extremities.
   MOSCA   It were a folly beyond thought, to trust
   Any grand act unto a cowardly spirit.
   You are not taken° with it enough, methinks.   pleased
10 VOLPONE   O, more than if I had enjoyed the wench;
   The pleasure of all womankind's not like it.
   MOSCA   Why, now you speak, sir! We must here be fixed;
   Here we must rest. This is our masterpiece;
   We cannot think to go beyond this.
   VOLPONE   True,
   Thou'st played thy prize, my precious Mosca.
15 MOSCA   Nay, sir,
   To gull the court—
   VOLPONE   And quite divert the torrent
   Upon the innocent.
   MOSCA   Yes, and to make
   So rare a music out of discords—
   VOLPONE   Right.
   That yet to me's the strangest! how thou'st borne it
20 That these, being so divided 'mongst themselves,
   Should not scent somewhat, or in me or thee,
   Or doubt their own side.
   MOSCA   True, they will not see 't.
   Too much light blinds them, I think.⁴ Each of them

_____
3. The word is printed in one text and pronounced   4. An ancient adage.
in all "apprended."

Is so possessed and stuffed with his own hopes
25   That anything unto the contrary,
Never so true, or never so apparent,
Never so palpable, they will resist it—
VOLPONE   Like a temptation of the devil.
MOSCA   Right, sir.
Merchants may talk of trade, and your great signors
30   Of land that yields well; but if Italy
Have any glebe° more fruitful than these fellows,   land
I am deceived. Did not your advocate rare?[5]
VOLPONE   O—*My most honored fathers, my grave fathers,*
Under correction of your fatherhoods,
35   *What face of truth is here? If these strange deeds*
May pass, most honored fathers—I had much ado
To forbear laughing.
MOSCA   It seemed to me you sweat, sir.
VOLPONE   In troth, I did a little.
MOSCA   But confess, sir,
Were you not daunted?
VOLPONE   In good faith, I was
40   A little in a mist, but not dejected;
Never but still myself.
MOSCA   I think it, sir.
Now, so truth help me, I must needs say this, sir,
And out of conscience for your advocate—
He has taken pains, in faith, sir, and deserved,
45   In my poor judgment (I speak it under favor,
Not to contrary you, sir) very richly—
Well—to be cozened.
VOLPONE   Troth, and I think so too,
By that I heard him, in the latter end.
MOSCA   O, but before, sir: had you heard him first
50   Draw it to certain heads, then aggravate,[6]
Then use his vehement figures°—I looked still   powerful rhetoric
When he would shift a shirt;[7] and doing this
Out of pure love, no hope of gain—
VOLPONE   'Tis right.
I cannot answer him, Mosca, as I would,
55   Not yet; but for thy sake, at thy entreaty,
I will begin e'en now to vex them all,
This very instant.
MOSCA   Good, sir.
VOLPONE   Call the dwarf
And eunuch forth.
MOSCA   Castrone, Nano!
        [*Enter* CASTRONE *and* NANO.]
NANO   Here.

5. Did not your advocate (perform) rare(ly)?
6. Terms of legal oratory.

7. I.e., he sweated so much over his speech, it
seemed he might have to change his linen.

VOLPONE   Shall we have a jig now?

MOSCA   What you please, sir.

VOLPONE   Go,

60   Straight give out about the streets, you two,
      That I am dead; do it with constancy,
      Sadly, do you hear? Impute it to the grief
      Of this late slander.   [*Exeunt* CASTRONE *and* NANO.]

MOSCA   What do you mean, sir?

VOLPONE   O,
      I shall have instantly my vulture, crow,

65   Raven, come flying hither on the news
      To peck for carrion, my she-wolf and all,
      Greedy, and full of expectation—

MOSCA   And then to have it ravished from their mouths!

VOLPONE   'Tis true. I will have thee put on a gown,

70   And take upon thee as thou wert mine heir;
      Show them a will. Open that chest and reach
      Forth one of those that has the blanks; I'll straight
      Put in thy name.

MOSCA   It will be rare, sir. [*Gives him a paper.*]

VOLPONE   Ay,
      When they e'en gape, and find themselves deluded—

MOSCA   Yes.

75   VOLPONE   And thou use them scurvily! Dispatch,
      Get on thy gown.

MOSCA   But what, sir, if they ask
      After the body?

VOLPONE   Say it was corrupted.

MOSCA   I'll say it stunk, sir; and was fain to have it
      Coffined up instantly and sent away.

80   VOLPONE   Anything, what thou wilt. Hold, here's my will.
      Get thee a cap, a count-book,° pen and ink,   *ledger*
      Papers afore thee; sit as thou wert taking
      An inventory of parcels. I'll get up
      Behind the curtain, on a stool, and hearken;

85   Sometime peep over, see how they do look,
      With what degrees their blood doth leave their faces.
      O, 'twill afford me a rare meal of laughter!

MOSCA [*putting on a cap, and setting out the table, &c.*]
      Your advocate will turn stark dull upon it.

VOLPONE   It will take off his oratory's edge.

90   MOSCA   But your clarissimo,° old round-back, he   *Venetian grandee*
      Will crump you[8] like a hog louse with the touch.

VOLPONE   And what Corvino?

MOSCA   O, sir, look for him
      Tomorrow morning with a rope and dagger
      To visit all the streets;[9] he must run mad.

8. Curl up on you; there is a species of wood louse   9. I.e., looking for a place to commit suicide.
or hog louse that curls up in a ball when touched.

95 My lady too, that came into the court
   To bear false witness for your worship—
VOLPONE   Yes,
   And kissed me 'fore the fathers, when my face
   Flowed all with oils.
MOSCA   And sweat, sir. Why, your gold
   Is such another medicine, it dries up
100 All those offensive savors; it transforms
   The most deformèd, and restores them lovely,
   As 'twere the strange poetical girdle.¹ Jove
   Could not invent t' himself a shroud more subtle
   To pass Acrisius' guards.² It is the thing
105 Makes all the world her grace, her youth, her beauty.
VOLPONE   I think she loves me.
MOSCA   Who? the lady, sir?
   She's jealous of you.
VOLPONE   Dost thou say so?   [Knocking within.]
MOSCA   Hark,
   There's some already.
VOLPONE   Look.
MOSCA   It is the vulture;
   He has the quickest scent.
VOLPONE   I'll to my place,
   Thou to thy posture.   [Goes behind the curtain.]
MOSCA   I am set.
110 VOLPONE   But, Mosca,
   Play the artificer now, torture them rarely.

SCENE 3

[Enter VOLTORE.]
VOLTORE   How now, my Mosca?
MOSCA [writing]   Turkey carpets, nine—
VOLTORE   Taking an inventory? That is well.
MOSCA   Two suits of bedding, tissue³—
VOLTORE   Where's the will?
   Let me read that the while.
      [Enter SERVANTS with CORBACCIO in a chair.]
CORBACCIO   So, set me down,
   And get you home.   [Exeunt SERVANTS.]
5 VOLTORE   Is he come now to trouble us?
MOSCA   Of cloth of gold, two more—
CORBACCIO   Is it done, Mosca?
MOSCA   Of several velvets, eight—
VOLTORE   I like his care.
CORBACCIO   Dost thou not hear?
      [Enter CORVINO.]

1. The girdle of Venus (cestus) made any wearer
irresistibly beautiful.
2. Acrisius was the father of Danaë; he locked her
up in a well-guarded tower, but Jove came to her
in the form of a shower of gold.
3. Fine fabric with threads of gold or silver interwoven.

CORVINO   Ha! is the hour come, Mosca?
VOLPONE [*peeping over the curtain*] Ay, now they muster.
CORVINO   What does the advocate here,
  Or this Corbaccio?
CORBACCIO   What do these here?
    [*Enter* LADY POLITIC WOULD-BE.]

10 LADY POLITIC   Mosca!
  Is his thread spun?[4]
MOSCA   *Eight chests of linen*—
VOLPONE   O,
  My fine Dame Would-be, too!
CORVINO   Mosca, the will,
  That I may show it these, and rid them hence.
MOSCA   *Six chests of diaper, four of damask.*[5]—There.
    [*Gives them the will carelessly, over his shoulder.*]
CORBACCIO   Is that the will?
MOSCA   *Down-beds, and bolsters*—
15 VOLPONE   Rare!
  Be busy still. Now they began to flutter:
  They never think of me. Look, see, see, see!
  How their swift eyes run over the long deed,
  Unto the name, and to the legacies,
  What is bequeathed them there—
20 MOSCA   *Ten suits of hangings*°—   *tapestries*
VOLPONE Ay, in their garters, Mosca. Now their hopes
  Are at the gasp.
VOLTORE   Mosca the heir!
CORBACCIO   What's that?
VOLPONE My advocate is dumb; look to my merchant;
  He has heard of some strange storm, a ship is lost,
25 He faints; my lady will swoon. Old glazen-eyes,[6]
  He hath not reached his despair yet.
CORBACCIO   All these
  Are out of hope; I am, sure, the man. [*Takes the will.*]
CORVINO   But, Mosca—
MOSCA *Two cabinets*—
CORVINO   Is this in earnest?
MOSCA   One
  Of ebony—
CORVINO   Or do you but delude me?
30 MOSCA *The other, mother of pearl*—I am very busy.
  Good faith, it is a fortune thrown upon me—
  Item, one salt° *of agate*—not my seeking.   *salt cellar*
LADY POLITIC Do you hear, sir?
MOSCA   A *perfumed box*—Pray you forbear,
  You see I'm troubled—*made of an onyx*—
LADY POLITIC   How!

---

4. The thread of life, spun by the Fates.
5. A rich fabric woven with many figures (from

Damascus). "Diaper": fine linen cloth.
6. Corbaccio, who wears glasses.

35   MOSCA   Tomorrow or next day I shall be at leisure
      To talk with you all.
    CORVINO   Is this my large hope's issue?
    LADY POLITIC   Sir, I must have a fairer answer.
    MOSCA   Madam!
      Marry, and shall: pray you, fairly quit my house.
      Nay, raise no tempest with your looks, but hark you:
40   Remember what your ladyship offered me
      To put you in an heir; go to, think on it,
      And what you said e'en your best madams did
      For maintenance; and why not you? Enough.
      Go home, and use the poor Sir Pol, your knight, well,
45   For fear I tell some riddles; go, be melancholic.   [*Exit* LADY POLITIC.]
    VOLPONE   O, my fine devil!
    CORVINO   Mosca, pray you a word.
    MOSCA   Lord! will not you take your dispatch hence yet?
      Methinks, of all, you should have been the example.
      Why should you stay here? With what thought, what promise?
50   Hear you: do not you know I know you an ass,
      And that you would most fain have been a wittol,[7]
      If fortune would have let you? That you are
      A declared cuckold, on good terms? This pearl,
      You'll say, was yours? Right. This diamond?
55   I'll not deny 't, but thank you. Much here else?
      It may be so. Why, think that these good works
      May help to hide your bad. I'll not betray you;
      Although you be but extraordinary,
      And have it only in title,[8] it sufficeth;
60   Go home, be melancholic too, or mad.   [*Exit* CORVINO.]
    VOLPONE   Rare Mosca! How his villainy becomes him!
    VOLTORE   Certain he doth delude all these for me.
    CORBACCIO   Mosca the heir!
    VOLPONE   O, his four eyes have found it!
    CORBACCIO   I am cozened, cheated, by a parasite slave;
      Harlot,[9] thou hast gulled me.
65   MOSCA   Yes, sir. Stop your mouth,
      Or I shall draw the only tooth is left.
      Are not you he, that filthy covetous wretch,
      With the three legs,[1] that here, in hope of prey,
      Have, any time this three year, snuffed about
70   With your most groveling nose, and would have hired
      Me to the poisoning of my patron, sir?
      Are not you he that have today in court
      Professed the disinheriting of your son?
      Perjured yourself? Go home, and die, and stink;
75   If you but croak a syllable, all comes out:

---

7. A pimp for your own wife.
8. I.e., not a full-fledged pimp or cuckold, just one who did his best to be such.

9. Frequently used of men, in the sense of "scoundrel."
1. I.e., two plus a cane or crutch.

Away, and call your porters!   [*Exit* CORBACCIO.]
                    —Go, go stink.
VOLPONE   Excellent varlet!
VOLTORE   Now, my faithful Mosca,
    I find thy constancy—
MOSCA   Sir?
VOLTORE   Sincere.
MOSCA [*writing*]   A table
    Of porphyry—I mar'l° you'll be thus troublesome.   marvel
    VOLTORE   Nay, leave off now, they are gone.
80 MOSCA   Why, who are you?
    What! Who did send for you? O, cry you mercy,
    Reverend sir! Good faith, I am grieved for you
    That any chance of mine should thus defeat
    Your (I must needs say) most deserving travails:
85 But I protest, sir, it was cast upon me,
    And I could almost wish to be without it,
    But that the will o' the dead must be observed.
    Marry, my joy is that you need it not;
    You have a gift, sir (thank your education),
90 Will never let you want while there are men
    And malice to breed causes. Would I had
    But half the like, for all my fortune, sir!
    If I have any suits (as I do hope,
    Things being so easy and direct, I shall not),
95 I will make bold with your obstreperous aid—
    Conceive me—for your fee, sir. In meantime,
    You that have so much law, I know have the conscience
    Not to be covetous of what is mine.
    Good sir, I thank you for my plate; 'twill help
100 To set up a young man. Good faith, you look
    As you were costive; best go home and purge,² sir.   [*Exit* VOLTORE.]
    VOLPONE [*comes from behind the curtain*]   Bid him eat lettuce
        well.³ My witty mischief,
    Let me embrace thee. O that I could now
    Transform thee to a Venus!—Mosca, go,
105 Straight take my habit of clarissimo,⁴
    And walk the streets; be seen, torment them more.
    We must pursue, as well as plot. Who would
    Have lost this feast?
MOSCA   I doubt it will lose them.
VOLPONE   O, my recovery shall recover all.
110 That I could now but think on some disguise
    To meet them in, and ask them questions;
    How I would vex them still at every turn!
MOSCA   Sir, I can fit you.
VOLPONE   Canst thou?
MOSCA   Yes, I know

2. Take a laxative. "Costive": constipated.   4. Mosca, in putting on the distinctive dress of a
3. Lettuce was thought to have mild purgative   patrician (*clarissimo*), disobeys the strict laws
powers.   about dressing above one's rank.

<table>
<tr><td>115</td><td>One o' the commendatori,° sir, so like you;
Him will I straight make drunk, and bring you his habit.°</td><td>sergeants
uniform</td></tr>
</table>

VOLPONE   A rare disguise, and answering thy brain!
   O, I will be a sharp disease unto them.
MOSCA   Sir, you must look for curses—
VOLPONE   Till they burst;
   The fox fares ever best when he is cursed. [*Exeunt.*]

SCENE 4. *A hall in* SIR POLITIC's *house.*

[*Enter* PEREGRINE *disguised, and three* MERCHANTS.]
PEREGRINE   Am I enough disguised?
1 MERCHANT   I warrant you.
PEREGRINE   All my ambition is to fright him only.
2 MERCHANT   If you could ship him away, 'twere excellent.
3 MERCHANT   To Zant, or to Aleppo?[5]
PEREGRINE   Yes, and have his

5   Adventures put i' the Book of Voyages,
   And his gulled story[6] registered for truth.
   Well, gentlemen, when I am in a while,
   And that you think us warm in our discourse,
   Know your approaches.
1 MERCHANT   Trust it to our care. [*Exeunt* MERCHANTS.]
      [*Enter* WAITING-WOMAN.]
10   PEREGRINE   Save you, fair lady! Is Sir Pol within?
WOMAN   I do not know, sir.
PEREGRINE   Pray you say unto him,
   Here is a merchant upon earnest business
   Desires to speak with him.
WOMAN   I will see, sir. [*Exit.*]
PEREGRINE   Pray you.—

   I see the family° is all female here.   *household*
      [*Re-enter* WAITING-WOMAN.]
15   WOMAN   He says, sir, he has weighty affairs of state
   That now require him whole; some other time
   You may possess him.
PEREGRINE   Pray you say again,
   If those require him whole, these will exact him,
   Whereof I bring him tidings. [*Exit* WOMAN.]—What might be
20   His grave affair of state now? How to make
   Bolognian sausages[7] here in Venice, sparing
   One o' the ingredients?
      [*Re-enter* WAITING-WOMAN.]
WOMAN   Sir, he says he knows
   By your word *tidings* that you are no statesman,[8]
   And therefore wills you stay.
PEREGRINE   Sweet, pray you return him;
25   I have not read so many proclamations,

5. Zant or (nowadays) Zakynthos is an Ionian island known for its currants; at that time it was part of the Venetian empire. "Aleppo" is a town in Syria.

6. The story of the trick played on him.
7. Sausages of Bologna were famous.
8. "Tidings" were what ordinary people received; a secret-service operative would get "intelligence."

And studied them for words, as he has done—
But—here he deigns to come.   [*Exit* WOMAN.]
        [*Enter* SIR POLITIC.]
SIR POLITIC   Sir, I must crave
    Your courteous pardon. There hath chanced today
    Unkind disaster 'twixt my lady and me;
30 And I was penning my apology,
    To give her satisfaction, as you came now.
PEREGRINE   Sir, I am grieved I bring you worse disaster:
    The gentleman you met at the port today,
    That told you he was newly arrived—
SIR POLITIC   Ay, was
    A fugitive punk?°   whore
35 PEREGRINE   No, sir, a spy set on you;
    And he has made relation to the Senate
    That you professed to him to have a plot
    To sell the state of Venice to the Turk.⁹
SIR POLITIC   O me!
PEREGRINE   For which, warrants are signed by this time
40 To apprehend you and to search your study
    For papers—
SIR POLITIC   Alas, sir, I have none but notes
    Drawn out of play-books—
PEREGRINE   All the better, sir.
SIR POLITIC   And some essays. What shall I do?
PEREGRINE   Sir, best
    Convey yourself into a sugar-chest;
45 Or, if you could lie round, a frail° were rare,   rush basket
    And I could send you aboard.
SIR POLITIC   Sir, I but talked so,
    For discourse' sake merely. [*Knocking within.*]
PEREGRINE   Hark! they are there.
SIR POLITIC   I am a wretch, a wretch!
PEREGRINE   What will you do, sir?
    Have you ne'er a currant-butt° to leap into?   cask for currants
50 They'll put you to the rack; you must be sudden.
SIR POLITIC   Sir, I have an engine°—   contrivance
3 MERCHANT [*within*]   Sir Politic Would-be!
2 MERCHANT [*within*]   Where is he?
SIR POLITIC   That I have thought upon before-time.
PEREGRINE   What is it?
SIR POLITIC   I shall ne'er endure the torture.
    Marry, it is, sir, of a tortoise-shell,
55 Fitted for these extremities: pray you, sir, help me.
    Here I've a place, sir, to put back my legs;
    Please you to lay it on, sir. [*Lies down while* PEREGRINE
        places the shell upon him.]—With this cap

9. See 4.1.130.

And my black gloves, I'll lie, sir, like a tortoise,
    Till they are gone.
PEREGRINE   And call you this an engine?
60 SIR POLITIC   Mine own device[1]—Good sir, bid my wife's women
    To burn my papers.   [*Exit* PEREGRINE.]
        [*The* MERCHANTS *rush in.*]
1 MERCHANT   Where is he hid?
2 MERCHANT   We must,
    And will, sure, find him.
2 MERCHANT   Which is his study?
        [*Re-enter* PEREGRINE.]
1 MERCHANT   What
    Are you, sir?
PEREGRINE   I am a merchant, that came here
    To look upon this tortoise.
3 MERCHANT   How!
1 MERCHANT   St. Mark!
    What beast is this?
PEREGRINE   It is a fish.
65 2 MERCHANT   Come out here!
PEREGRINE   Nay, you may strike him, sir, and tread upon him:
    He'll bear a cart.
1 MERCHANT   What, to run over him?
PEREGRINE   Yes.
3 MERCHANT   Let's jump upon him.
2 MERCHANT   Can he not go?
PEREGRINE   He creeps, sir.
1 MERCHANT   Let's see him creep. [*Pokes him.*]
PEREGRINE   No, good sir, you will hurt him.
70 2 MERCHANT   'Heart, I will see him creep, or prick his guts.
3 MERCHANT   Come out here!
PEREGRINE   Pray you, sir! [*aside to* SIR POLITIC]
    —Creep a little.
1 MERCHANT   Forth!
2 MERCHANT   Yet farther.
PEREGRINE   Good sir! [*aside to* SIR POLITIC]—Creep.
2 MERCHANT   We'll see his legs.
    [*They pull off the shell and discover him.*]
3 MERCHANT   God's so, he has garters!
1 MERCHANT   Ay, and gloves!
2 MERCHANT   Is this
    Your fearful tortoise?
75 PEREGRINE [*discovering himself*] Now, Sir Pol, we are even;
    For your next project I shall be prepared.
    I am sorry for the funeral of your notes, sir.
1 MERCHANT   'Twere a rare motion to be seen in Fleet Street.
2 MERCHANT   Ay, in the Term.

---

1. Contrivance. But also his self-chosen emblem. The tortoise symbolized prudence, silence, and policy.

1 MERCHANT.   Or Smithfield,[2] in the fair.

80 3 MERCHANT   Methinks 'tis but a melancholic sight.

PEREGRINE   Farewell, most politic tortoise!

    [*Exeunt* PEREGRINE, MERCHANTS.]
    [*Re-enter* WAITING-WOMAN.]

SIR POLITIC   Where's my lady?
  Knows she of this?

WOMAN   I know not, sir.

SIR POLITIC   Inquire.   [*Exit* WOMAN.]
  O, I shall be the fable of all feasts,
  The freight of the gazetti,[3] ship-boys' tale;

85   And, which is worst, even talk for ordinaries.°   *town gossip*
    [*Re-enter* WOMAN]

WOMAN   My lady's come most melancholic home,
  And says, sir, she will straight to sea, for physic.°   *for her health*

SIR POLITIC   And I, to shun this place and clime forever,
  Creeping with house on back, and think it well

90   To shrink my poor head in my politic shell.   [*Exeunt.*]

SCENE 5. *A room in* VOLPONE's *house.*

    [*Enter* MOSCA *in the habit of a clarissimo, and* VOLPONE
    in that of a commendatore.]

VOLPONE   Am I then like him?

MOSCA   O, sir, you are he.
  No man can sever° you.   *distinguish*

VOLPONE   Good.

MOSCA   But what am I?

VOLPONE   'Fore heaven, a brave *clarissimo*; thou becom'st it!
  Pity thou wert not born one.

MOSCA   If I hold
  My made one, 'twill be well.

5 VOLPONE   I'll go and see
  What news first at the court.   [*Exit.*]

MOSCA   Do so. My fox
  Is out of his hole, and ere he shall re-enter
  I'll make him languish in his borrowed case,°   *false costume*
  Except he come to composition° with me.—   *financial arrangement*
  Androgyno, Castrone, Nano!
    [*Enter* ANDROGYNO, CASTRONE, *and* NANO.]

10 ALL   Here.

MOSCA   Go, recreate yourselves abroad; go, sport.—   [*Exeunt.*]
  So, now I have the keys and am possessed.
  Since he will needs be dead afore his time,

2. A district outside London city walls, the site of the Bartholomew Fair. "Rare motion": puppet show. "Fleet Street": a street in central London

particularly busy "in the Term," when the law courts were in session.
3. Subject of the newsletters.

I'll bury him, or gain by him. I am his heir,
15 And so will keep me, till he share at least.
To cozen him of all were but a cheat
Well placed; no man would cònstrue it a sin:
Let his sport pay for 't. This is called the fox trap.   [*Exit.*]

SCENE 6. *A street.*

[*Enter* CORBACCIO *and* CORVINO.]

CORBACCIO   They say the court is set.
CORVINO   We must maintain
   Our first tale good, for both our reputations.
CORBACCIO   Why, mine's no tale; my son would there have killed me.
CORVINO   That's true, I had forgot. [*aside*]—Mine is, I'm sure.
   But for your will, sir.
5 CORBACCIO   Ay, I'll come upon him
   For that hereafter, now his patron's dead.

[*Enter* VOLPONE *in disguise.*]

VOLPONE   Signor Corvino! and Corbaccio! Sir,
   Much joy unto you.
CORVINO   Of what?
VOLPONE   The sudden good
   Dropped down upon you—
CORBACCIO   Where?
VOLPONE   And none knows how,
   From old Volpone, sir.
10 CORBACCIO   Out, arrant knave!
VOLPONE   Let not your too much wealth, sir, make you furious.
CORBACCIO   Away, thou varlet.
VOLPONE   Why, sir?
CORBACCIO   Dost thou mock me?
VOLPONE   You mock the world, sir; did you not change wills?
CORBACCIO   Out, harlot!
VOLPONE   O! belike you are the man,
15 Signor Corvino? Faith, you carry it well;
   You grow not mad withal; I love your spirit.
   You are not over-leavened[4] with your fortune.
   You should have some would swell now, like a wine-vat,
   With such an autumn—Did he give you all, sir?
CORVINO   Avoid, you rascal!
20 VOLPONE   Troth, your wife has shown
   Herself a very woman;[5] but you are well,
   You need not care, you have a good estate
   To bear it out, sir; better by this chance.
   Except Corbaccio have a share.
CORBACCIO   Hence, varlet.
25 VOLPONE   You will not be a'known, sir; why, 'tis wise.
   Thus do all gamesters, at all games, dissemble;

4. Too puffed up (like a loaf of bread).   5. I.e., promiscuous.

No man will seem to win. [*Exeunt* CORVINO *and* CORBACCIO.]
　　　　　　　　　—Here comes my vulture,
Heaving his beak up in the air, and snuffing.

SCENE 7

[*Enter* VOLTORE.]

VOLTORE　Outstripped thus, by a parasite! a slave,
　Would run on errands, and make legs° for crumbs!　　　*bow and scrape*
　Well, what I'll do—
VOLPONE　　　　　　　The court stays for your worship.
　I e'en rejoice, sir, at your worship's happiness,
5　And that it fell into so learnèd hands,
　That understand the fingering—
VOLTORE　　　　　　　　　What do you mean?
VOLPONE　I mean to be a suitor to your worship
　For the small tenement, out of reparations°—　　　*repair*
　That at the end of your long row of houses,
10　By the Pescheria;° it was, in Volpone's time,　　　*fish market*
　Your predecessor, ere he grew diseased,
　A handsome, pretty, customed° bawdyhouse　　　*well-patronized*
　As any was in Venice—none dispraised;[6]
　But fell with him. His body and that house
　Decayed together.
15　VOLTORE　　　　　　Come, sir, leave your prating.
VOLPONE　Why, if your worship give me but your hand
　That I may have the refusal, I have done.
　'Tis a mere toy to you, sir; candle-rents;[7]
　As your learned worship knows—
VOLTORE　　　　　　　　　What do I know?
20　VOLPONE　Marry, no end of your wealth, sir; God decrease it!
VOLTORE　Mistaking knave! what, mock'st thou my misfortune?
VOLPONE　His blessing on your heart, sir; would 'twere more!
　　　　　　　　　　　　　　　[*Exit* VOLTORE.]
　—Now to my first again, at the next corner.　　　[*Exit.*]

SCENE 8. *Another part of the street.*

[*Enter* CORBACCIO *and* CORVINO;—MOSCA *passes over the
stage, before them.*]

CORBACCIO　See, in our habit![8] See the impudent varlet!
CORVINO　That I could shoot mine eyes at him like gun-stones!
　[*Enter* VOLPONE.]
VOLPONE　But is this true, sir, of the parasite?
CORBACCIO　Again, to afflict us! Monster!
VOLPONE　　　　　　　　　　　In good faith, sir,
5　I'm heartily grieved a beard of your grave length
　Should be so over-reached. I never brooked°　　　*could stand*

---

6. Without prejudice to any of the other splendid
bawdy houses in Venice.
7. Rents from poor properties would only be
enough to buy candles.
8. The clothes reserved for patricians.

That parasite's hair; methought his nose should cozen.°   *deceive*
There still was somewhat in his look did promise
The bane of a clarissimo.[9]
CORBACCIO   Knave—
VOLPONE   Methinks
10 Yet you, that are so traded in the world,
 A witty merchant, the fine bird Corvino,
 That have such moral emblems on your name,
 Should not have sung your shame, and dropped your cheese,
 To let the fox laugh at your emptiness.[1]
15 CORVINO Sirrah, you think the privilege of the place,
 And your red saucy cap, that seems to me
 Nailed to your jolt-head° with those two sequins,[2]   *blockhead*
 Can warrant your abuses. Come you hither;
 You shall perceive, sir, I dare beat you; approach.
20 VOLPONE No haste, sir, I do know your valor well,
 Since you durst publish what you are, sir.[3]
CORVINO   Tarry,
 I'd speak with you.
VOLPONE   Sir, sir, another time—
CORVINO Nay, now.
VOLPONE   O God, sir! I were a wise man,
 Would stand the fury of a distracted cuckold. [*As he is*
  running off, re-enter MOSCA.]
CORBACCIO What, come again!
25 VOLPONE [*aside*]   Upon 'em, Mosca; save me.
CORBACCIO The air's infected where he breathes.
CORVINO   Let's fly him.
      [*Exeunt* CORVINO *and* CORBACCIO.]
VOLPONE Excellent basilisk![4] Turn upon the vulture.

SCENE 9

   [*Enter* VOLTORE.]
VOLTORE Well, flesh-fly, it is summer with you now;
 Your winter will come on.
MOSCA   Good advocate,
 Pray thee not rail, nor threaten out of place thus;
 Thou 'lt make a solecism, as Madam says.[5]
5 Get you a biggen[6] more; your brain breaks loose. [*Exit.*]
VOLTORE Well, sir.
VOLPONE   Would you have me beat the insolent slave,
 Throw dirt upon his first good clothes?
VOLTORE   This same
 Is doubtless some familiar.
VOLPONE   Sir, the court,

---

9. I.e., trouble for a patrician.
1. He applies Aesop's fable of the fox, the crow,
and the piece of cheese.
2. Volpone's disguise as a sergeant includes a red
cap with two brass buttons.

3. A cuckold whose horns are evident to all.
4. A mythical creature that kills with its glance.
5. The "solecism" of Lady Politic is at 4.2.23.
6. Lawyer's skullcap.

In troth, stays for you. I am mad, a mule
10 That never read Justinian[7] should get up
And ride an advocate. Had you no quirk°   *device*
To avoid gullage,° sir, by such a creature?   *trickery*
I hope you do but jest; he has not done it;
This 's but confederacy° to blind the rest.   *conspiracy*
You are the heir?
15 VOLTORE   A strange, officious,
Troublesome knave! Thou dost torment me.
VOLPONE   I know—
It cannot be, sir, that you should be cozened;
'Tis not within the wit of man to do it;
You are so wise, so prudent; and 'tis fit
20 That wealth and wisdom still should go together. [*Exeunt.*]

SCENE 10. *The Scrutineo.*

[*Enter* AVOCATORI, NOTARIO, BONARIO, CELIA, CORBACCIO,
CORVINO, COMMENDATORI, SAFFI, &c.]

1 AVOCATORE   Are all the parties here?
NOTARIO   All but the advocate.
2 AVOCATORE   And here he comes.
          [*Enter* VOLTORE *and* VOLPONE.]
1 AVOCATORE   Then bring them forth to sentence.
VOLTORE   O, my most honored fathers, let your mercy
Once win upon your justice, to forgive—
I am distracted—
VOLPONE [*aside*]   What will he do now?
5 VOLTORE   O,
I know not which to address myself to first;
Whether your fatherhoods, or these innocents—
CORVINO [*aside*]   Will he betray himself?
VOLTORE   Whom equally
I have abused, out of most covetous ends—
CORVINO   The man is mad!
CORBACCIO   What's that?
CORVINO   He is possessed.°   *by the devil*
10 VOLTORE   For which, now struck in conscience, here I prostrate
Myself at your offended feet, for pardon.
1, 2 AVOCATORI   Arise.
CELIA   O heaven, how just thou art!
VOLPONE [*aside*]   I am caught
In mine own noose—
CORVINO [*to* CORBACCIO]   Be constant, sir; naught now
Can help, but impudence.
1 AVOCATORE   Speak forward.
15 COMMENDATORE [*to the courtroom*]   Silence!
VOLTORE   It is not passion in me, reverend fathers,
But only conscience, conscience, my good sires,
That makes me now tell truth. That parasite,

7. The Roman legal codes compiled by the Emperor Justinian.

That knave, hath been the instrument of all.
1 AVOCATORE   Where is that knave? Fetch him.
VOLPONE   I go. [*Exit.*]
20   CORVINO   Grave fathers,
This man's distracted; he confessed it now;
For, hoping to be old Volpone's heir,
Who now is dead—
3 AVOCATORE   How!
2 AVOCATORE   Is Volpone dead?
CORVINO   Dead since, grave fathers.
BONARIO   O sure vengeance!
1 AVOCATORE   Stay!
Then he was no deceiver?
25   VOLTORE   O no, none;
The parasite, grave fathers.
CORVINO   He does speak
Out of mere envy, 'cause the servant's made
The thing he gaped for. Please your fatherhoods,
This is the truth, though I'll not justify
30   The other[8] but he may be some-deal faulty.
VOLTORE   Ay, to your hopes, as well as mine, Corvino.
But I'll use modesty. Pleaseth your wisdoms
To view these certain notes, and but confer them;
As I hope favor, they shall speak clear truth.
CORVINO   The devil has entered him!
35   BONARIO   Or bides in you.
4 AVOCATORE   We have done ill, by a public officer
To send for him, if he be heir.[9]
2 AVOCATORE   For whom?
4 AVOCATORE   Him that they call the parasite.
3 AVOCATORE   'Tis true,
He is a man of great estate now left.
40   4 AVOCATORE   Go you and learn his name, and say the court
Entreats his presence here, but to the clearing
Of some few doubts.   [*Exit* NOTARIO]
2 AVOCATORE   This same's a labyrinth!
1 AVOCATORE [*to* CORVINO]   Stand you unto your first report?
CORVINO   My state,
My life, my fame—
BONARIO   Where is it?
CORVINO   Are at the stake.
1 AVOCATORE [*to* CORBACCIO]   Is yours so too?
45   CORBACCIO   The advocate's a knave;
And has a forkèd tongue—
2 AVOCATORE   Speak to the point.
CORBACCIO   So is the parasite too.
1 AVOCATORE   This is confusion.
VOLTORE   I do beseech your fatherhoods, read but those—

8. I.e., Mosca.
9. As a patrician (which he automatically is if he   has a lot of money), Mosca must be accorded more
                                                       dignity.

[*Giving them papers.*]

CORVINO   And credit nothing the false spirit hath writ;
50   It cannot be but he's possessed, grave fathers.

SCENE 11. *A street.*

[*Enter* VOLPONE.]

VOLPONE   To make a snare for mine own neck! and run
My head into it, wilfully! with laughter!
When I had newly 'scaped, was free and clear!
Out of mere wantonness! O, the dull devil
5   Was in this brain of mine, when I devised it,
And Mosca gave it second; he must now
Help to sear up° this vein, or we bleed dead.   *cauterize*
        [*Enter* NANO, ANDROGYNO, *and* CASTRONE.]
How now! Who let you loose? Whither go you now?
What? to buy gingerbread, or to drown kitlings?
10 NANO   Sir, Master Mosca called us out of doors,
And bid us all go play, and took the keys.
ANDROGYNO   Yes.
VOLPONE   Did Master Mosca take the keys? Why, so!
I'm farther in. These are my fine conceits!
I must be merry, with a mischief to me!
15   What a vile wretch was I, that could not bear
My fortune soberly! I must have my crotchets,
And my conundrums! Well, go you and seek him.
His meaning may be truer than my fear.
Bid him, he straight come to me, to the court;
20   Thither will I, and, if 't be possible,
Unscrew my advocate, upon new hopes.
When I provoked him, then I lost myself.   [*Exeunt.*]

SCENE 12. *The Scrutineo.*

[AVOCATORI, BONARIO, CELIA, CORBACCIO, CORVINO,
VOLTORE, COMMENDATORI, SAFFI, &c. *as before.*]

1 AVOCATORE [*showing the papers*]
These things can ne'er be reconciled. He here
Professeth that the gentleman was wronged,
And that the gentlewoman was brought thither,
Forced by her husband, and there left.
VOLTORE   Most true.
CELIA   How ready is heaven to those that pray!
5 1 AVOCATORE   But that
Volpone would have ravished her, he holds
Utterly false, knowing his impotence.
CORVINO   Grave fathers, he's possessed; again, I say,
Possessed; nay, if there be possession and
Obsession, he has both.¹

---

1. In possession a devil controls the mind from within; in obsession, from without.

10 3 AVOCATORE   Here comes our officer.
      [*Enter* VOLPONE, *still in disguise.*]
VOLPONE   The parasite will straight be here, grave fathers.
4 AVOCATORE   You might invent some other name, sir varlet.
3 AVOCATORE   Did not the notary meet him?
VOLPONE   Not that I know.
4 AVOCATORE   His coming will clear all.
2 AVOCATORE   Yet, it is misty.
VOLTORE   May 't please your fatherhoods—
15 VOLPONE [*whispers to* VOLTORE]   Sir, the parasite
      Willed me to tell you that his master lives;
      That you are still the man; your hopes the same;
      And this was only a jest—
VOLTORE   How?
VOLPONE   Sir, to try
      If you were firm, and how you stood affected.
VOLTORE   Art sure he lives?
VOLPONE   Do I live, sir?
20 VOLTORE   O me!
      I was too violent.
VOLPONE   Sir, you may redeem it.
      They said you were possessed: fall down, and seem so.
      I'll help to make it good. [VOLTORE *falls.*]—God bless the man!
      [*aside*] Stop your wind hard, and swell.—See, see, see!
25 He vomits crooked pins!² His eyes are set,
      Like a dead hare's hung in a poulter's° shop!   *poultry merchant*
      His mouth's running away! Do you see, signor?
      Now it is in his belly.
CORVINO   Ay, the devil!
VOLPONE   Now in his throat.
CORVINO   Ay, I perceive it plain.
30 VOLPONE   'Twill out, 'twill out! Stand clear! See where it flies;
      In shape of a blue toad with a bat's wings!
      Do not you see it, sir?
CORBACCIO   What? I think I do.
CORVINO   'Tis too manifest.
VOLPONE   Look! he comes to himself!
VOLTORE   Where am I?
VOLPONE   Take good heart, the worst is past, sir.
      You are dispossessed.
35 1 AVOCATORE   What accident is this?
2 AVOCATORE   Sudden and full of wonder!
3 AVOCATORE   If he were
      Possessed, as it appears, all this is nothing. [*He waves the notes.*]
CORVINO   He has been often subject to these fits.
1 AVOCATORE   Show him that writing.—Do you know it, sir?
40 VOLPONE [*whispers to* VOLTORE]   Deny it, sir, forswear it; know it not.

---

2. The symptoms that Volpone "sees," and persuades others to see, were standard in accounts of demonic possession. The "blue toad with bat's wings" (below) is the demon himself.

VOLTORE   Yes, I do know it well, it is my hand;
But all that it contains is false.

BONARIO   O practice!°   *deceit*

2 AVOCATORE   What maze is this?

1 AVOCATORE   Is he not guilty then,
Whom you there name the parasite?

VOLTORE   Grave fathers,
45   No more than his good patron, old Volpone.

4 AVOCATORE   Why, he is dead.

VOLTORE   O no, my honored fathers,
He lives—

1 AVOCATORE   How! Lives?

VOLTORE   Lives.

2 AVOCATORE   This is subtler yet!

3 AVOCATORE   You said he was dead.

VOLTORE   Never.

3 AVOCATORE [*to* CORVINO]   You said so!

CORVINO   I heard so.

4 AVOCATORE   Here comes the gentleman; make him way.
[*Enter* MOSCA *as a clarissimo.*]

3 AVOCATORE   A stool!
50   4 AVOCATORE [*aside*]   A proper man; and, were Volpone dead,
A fit match for my daughter.

3 AVOCATORE   Give him way.

VOLPONE [*aside to* MOSCA]   Mosca, I was almost lost; the advocate
Had betrayed all; but now it is recovered;
All's on the hinge° again—say I am living.   *working well*
55   MOSCA   What busy knave is this! Most reverend fathers,
I sooner had attended your grave pleasures,
But that my order for the funeral
Of my dear patron did require me—

VOLPONE [*aside*]   Mosca!

MOSCA   Whom I intend to bury like a gentleman.

VOLPONE [*aside*]   Ay, quick,° and cozen me of all.   *alive*
60   2 AVOCATORE   Still stranger!
More intricate!

1 AVOCATORE   And come about again!

4 AVOCATORE [*aside*]   It is a match, my daughter is bestowed.

MOSCA [*aside to* VOLPONE]   Will you give me half?

VOLPONE   First I'll be hanged.

MOSCA [*aside*]   I know
Your voice is good, cry not so loud.

1 AVOCATORE   Demand
65   The advocate.—Sir, did you not affirm
Volpone was alive?

VOLPONE   Yes, and he is;
This gentleman³ told me so. [*aside to* MOSCA] Thou shalt have half.

MOSCA   Whose drunkard is this same? Speak, some that know him:

---

3. I.e., Mosca.

I never saw his face. [*aside to* VOLPONE] I cannot now
   Afford it you so cheap.
VOLPONE [*aside*]   No?
70 1 AVOCATORE [*to* VOLTORE] What say you?
VOLTORE The officer told me.
VOLPONE   I did, grave fathers,
   And will maintain he lives, with mine own life,
   And that this creature [*points to* MOSCA] told me. [*aside*] I was born
   With all good stars my enemies.
MOSCA   Most grave fathers,
75 If such an insolence as this must pass
   Upon me, I am silent: 'twas not this
   For which you sent, I hope.
2 AVOCATORE   Take him away.
VOLPONE [*aside*] Mosca!
3 AVOCATORE   Let him be whipped—
VOLPONE [*aside*]   Wilt thou betray me?
   Cozen me?
3 AVOCATORE And taught to bear himself
   Toward a person of his rank.
80   Away. [*The* OFFICERS *seize* VOLPONE.]
MOSCA I humbly thank your fatherhoods.
   Soft, soft. Whipped?
VOLPONE [*aside*]
   And lose all that I have? If I confess,
   It cannot be much more.
4 AVOCATORE [*to* MOSCA] Sir, are you married?
VOLPONE [*aside*] They'll be allied anon; I must be resolute.
   The fox shall here uncase.   [*Throws off his disguise.*]
MOSCA   Patron!
85 VOLPONE   Nay, now
   My ruins shall not come alone; your match
   I'll hinder sure: my substance shall not glue you
   Nor screw you into a family.
MOSCA   Why, patron!
VOLPONE I am Volpone, and this [*pointing to* MOSCA] is my knave;
90 This, [*to* VOLTORE] his own knave; this, [*to* CORBACCIO] avarice's fool;
   This, [*to* CORVINO] a chimera[4] of wittol, fool, and knave.
   And, reverend fathers, since we all can hope
   Nought but a sentence, let's not now despair it.
   You hear me brief.
CORVINO   May it please your fatherhoods—
COMMENDATORE Silence!
95 1 AVOCATORE   The knot is now undone by miracle!
2 AVOCATORE Nothing can be more clear.
3 AVOCATORE   Or can more prove
   These innocent.
1 ADVOCATORE Give them their liberty.

---

4. The chimera was a fantastic creature compounded of lion, goat, and serpent.

BONARIO   Heaven could not long let such gross crimes be hid.

2 AVOCATORE   If this be held the highway to get riches,
    May I be poor!

3 AVOCATORE   This is not gain, but torment.

1 AVOCATORE   These possess wealth as sick men possess fevers,
    Which trulier may be said to possess them.[5]

2 AVOCATORE   Disrobe that parasite.

CORVINO, MOSCA   Most honored fathers!

1 AVOCATORE   Can you plead aught to stay the course of justice?
    If you can, speak.

CORVINO, VOLTORE   We beg favor.

CELIA   And mercy.

1 AVOCATORE   You hurt your innocence, suing for the guilty.
    Stand forth; and first the parasite. You appear
    T' have been the chiefest minister, if not plotter,
    In all these lewd impostures; and now, lastly,
    Have with your impudence abused the court,
    And habit of a gentleman of Venice,
    Being a fellow of no birth or blood:[6]
    For which our sentence is, first, thou be whipped;
    Then live perpetual prisoner in our galleys.

VOLPONE   I thank you for him.

MOSCA   Bane° to thy wolfish nature!   *poison*

1 AVOCATORE   Deliver him to the Saffi.   [MOSCA *is led out.*]
    —Thou, Volpone,
    By blood and rank a gentleman, canst not fall
    Under like censure; but our judgment on thee
    Is that thy substance all be straight confiscate
    To the hospital of the Incurabili.[7]
    And, since the most was gotten by imposture,
    By feigning lame, gout, palsy, and such diseases,
    Thou art to lie in prison, cramped with irons,
    Till thou be'st sick and lame indeed. Remove him.   [*He is led aside.*]

VOLPONE   This is called mortifying of a fox.[8]

1 AVOCATORE   Thou, Voltore, to take away the scandal
    Thou hast given all worthy men of thy profession,
    Art banished from their fellowship, and our state.
    Corbaccio!—bring him near—we here possess
    Thy son of all thy state,° and confine thee   *estate*
    To the monastery of San Spirito;
    Where, since thou knew'st not how to live well here,
    Thou shalt be learned° to die well.   *taught*

CORBACCIO   Ha! what said he?

COMMENDATORE   You shall know anon, sir.

1 AVOCATORE   Thou, Corvino, shalt
    Be straight embarked from thine own house, and rowed

---

5. The aphorism is Seneca's (*Epistle* 119.2).
6. Mosca's sentence is most severe, because of his class.
7. The Hospital of the Incurables in Venice, for diseased orphans, beggars, and prostitutes.

8. "Mortifying": not just humiliating but killing. Both the galleys and the dungeons of Venice were widely reputed the most horrible in Europe; neither Mosca nor Volpone is long for this world.

Round about Venice, through the Grand Canal,
Wearing a cap with fair long ass's ears
Instead of horns; and so to mount, a paper
Pinned on thy breast, to the Berlina°—   pillory
CORVINO   Yes,
140   And have mine eyes beat out with stinking fish,
Bruised fruit, and rotten eggs—'Tis well: I'm glad
I shall not see my shame yet.
1 AVOCATORE   And to expiate
Thy wrongs done to thy wife, thou art to send her
Home, to her father, with her dowry trebled:
And these are all your judgments—
145   ALL   Honored fathers!
1 AVOCATORE   Which may not be revoked. Now you begin,
When crimes are done, and past, and to be punished,
To think what your crimes are: away with them!
Let all that see these vices thus rewarded,
150   Take heart, and love to study 'em! Mischiefs feed
Like beasts, till they be fat, and then they bleed.   [Exeunt.]
        [VOLPONE comes forward.]
The seasoning of a play is the applause.
Now, though the fox be punished by the laws,
He yet doth hope, there is no suffering due
155   *For any fact° which he hath done 'gainst you.*   crime
If there be, censure him; here he doubtful stands.
If not, fare jovially, and clap your hands.   [Exit.]

1606   1607

FROM EPIGRAMS[1]

To My Book

It will be looked for, book, when some but see
    Thy title, *Epigrams,* and named of me,
Thou should'st be bold, licentious, full of gall,
    Wormwood° and sulphur, sharp and toothed[2] withal,   bitter-tasting plant
5   Become a petulant thing, hurl ink and wit
    As madmen stones, not caring whom they hit.
Deceive their malice who could wish it so,
    And by thy wiser temper let men know
Thou art not covetous of least self-fame
10   Made from the hazard of another's shame[3]—

1. Epigrams are commonly thought of as brief, witty, incisive poems of personal invective, often with a surprise turn at the end. But when Jonson included in his collected *Works* of 1616 a separate section headed "Epigrams (Book 1)," he was using the word in a more liberal sense. His "epigrams" included (besides some sharp and satiric verses) several poems of compliment and courtesy, some memorial epitaphs, and a verse letter, *Inviting a Friend to Supper. To My Book* and the next several poems come from this section. The "Book 1" of Jonson's title implied a "Book 2"; there are a number of epigramlike verses scattered through his later poetry, but Jonson never assembled them under any such title.
2. The distinction between toothed (biting) and toothless (general) satires—originally made by Joseph Hall (1574–1656), who claimed to be the first English satirist—was a commonplace.
3. Here, as often elsewhere, Jonson echoes the greatest Roman epigrammatist, Martial.

Much less with lewd, profane, and beastly phrase
  To catch the world's loose laughter or vain gaze.
He that departs° with his own honesty   *parts*
  For vulgar praise, doth it too dearly buy.

                                 1616

On Something, That Walks Somewhere

At court I met it, in clothes brave° enough   *fine*
  To be a courtier, and looks grave enough
To seem a statesman: as I near it came,
  It made me a great face. I asked the name.
5 "A lord," it cried, "buried in flesh and blood,
  And such from whom let no man hope least good,
For I will do none; and as little ill,
  For I will dare none." Good lord, walk dead still.

                                 1616

To William Camden[1]

Camden, most reverend head, to whom I owe
  All that I am in arts, all that I know
(How nothing's that!), to whom my country owes
  The great renown and name wherewith she goes;[2]
5 Than thee the age sees not that thing more grave,
  More high, more holy, that she more would crave.
What name, what skill, what faith hast thou in things!
  What sight in searching the most antique springs!
What weight and what authority in thy speech!
10 Man scarce can make that doubt,[3] but thou canst teach.
Pardon free truth and let thy modesty,
  Which conquers all, be once o'ercome by thee.
Many of thine° this better could than I;   *your pupils*
  But for° their powers, accept my piety.   *in place of*

                                 1616

On My First Daughter[1]

Here lies, to each her parents' ruth,°   *grief*
Mary, the daughter of their youth;
Yet all heaven's gifts being heaven's due,
It makes the father less to rue.

---

1. Camden, a distinguished scholar and antiquary, had been Jonson's teacher at Westminster School.
2. Camden's studies of his native land in *Britannia* (1586) and *Remains of a Greater Work Concerning Britain* (1605) ran to several editions and were translated abroad.
3. I.e., raise that question.
1. Probably written in the late 1590s, in Jonson's Roman Catholic period (ca. 1598–1610).

5 At six months' end she parted hence
    With safety of her innocence;
    Whose soul heaven's queen, whose name she bears,
    In comfort of her mother's tears,
    Hath placed amongst her virgin-train:
10 Where, while that severed doth remain,
    This grave partakes the fleshly birth;°   *the body*
    Which cover lightly, gentle earth![2]

1616

To John Donne

  Donne, the delight of Phoebus° and each Muse,   *god of poetry*
  Who, to thy one, all other brains refuse;[1]
  Whose every work, of thy most early wit,
  Came forth example and remains so yet;
5 Longer a-knowing than most wits do live,
  And which no affection praise enough can give.
  To it[2] thy language, letters, arts, best life,
  Which might with half mankind maintain a strife.
  All which I meant to praise, and yet I would,
10 But leave, because I cannot as I should.

1616

On Don Surly

  Don Surly, to aspire[1] the glorious name
    Of a great man, and to be thought the same,
  Makes serious use of all great trade° he knows.   *tricks*
    He speaks to men with a Rhinocerotes' nose,[2]
5 Which he thinks great; and so reads verses too,
    And that is done as he saw great men do.
  He has timpanies[3] of business in his face,
    And can forget men's names with a great grace.
  He will both argue and discourse in oaths,
10   Both which are great; and laugh at ill-made clothes—
  That's greater yet—to cry his own up neat.
    He doth, at meals, alone his pheasant eat,
  Which is main greatness; and at his still board[4]
    He drinks to no man; that's, too, like a lord.
15 He keeps another's wife, which is a spice°   *species*
    Of solemn greatness. And he dares, at dice,

---

2. A common sentiment in Latin epitaphs.
1. I.e., the muses shower their favors exclusively on you.
2. In addition to your wit.
1. Attain. "Don" is a Spanish title, and the Spanish

were thought to have pompous manners.
2. I.e., with his nose tilted up like a rhinoceros.
3. Swellings, tumors—a figure for pride.
4. I.e., his solitary dinner table.

Blaspheme God greatly, or some poor hind° beat   *rustic*
  That breathes in his dog's way; and this is great.
Nay more, for greatness' sake, he will be one
20   May hear my epigrams, but like of none.
Surly, use other arts; these only can
  Style thee a most great fool, but no great man.

1616

On Giles and Joan

Who says that Giles and Joan at discord be?
  Th' observing neighbors no such mood can see.
Indeed, poor Giles repents he married ever,
  But that his Joan doth too. And Giles would never
5 By his free will be in Joan's company;
  No more would Joan he should. Giles riseth early,
And having got him out of doors is glad;
  The like is Joan. But turning home is sad,
And so is Joan. Ofttimes, when Giles doth find
10   Harsh sights at home, Giles wisheth he were blind:
All this doth Joan. Or that his long-yearned[1] life
  Were quite outspun. The like wish hath his wife.
The children that he keeps Giles swears are none
  Of his begetting; and so swears his Joan.
15 In all affections she concurreth still.
  If now, with man and wife, to will and nill°   *not will*
The self-same things a note of concord be,
  I know no couple better can agree.

1616

On My First Son

Farewell, thou child of my right hand,[1] and joy;
My sin was too much hope of thee, loved boy:
Seven years thou wert lent to me, and I thee pay,
Exacted by thy fate, on the just day.
5 O could I lose all father now! For why
Will man lament the state he should envy,
To have so soon 'scaped world's and flesh's rage,
And, if no other misery, yet age?
Rest in soft peace, and asked, say, "Here doth lie
10 Ben Jonson his best piece of poetry."[2]
For whose sake henceforth all his vows be such
As what he loves may never like too much.[3]

1616

---

1. Spun from long skeins of yarn.
1. A literal translation of the Hebrew name "Benjamin," which implies the meaning "dexterous" or "fortunate." The boy was born in 1596 and died on his birthday in 1603.

2. Poet and father are both makers, Jonson's favorite term for the poet.
3. The obscure grammar of the last lines allows for various readings; "like" may carry the sense of "please."

On Lucy, Countess of Bedford[1]

This morning, timely rapt with holy fire,
I thought to form unto my zealous muse,
What kind of creature I could most desire,
To honor, serve, and love; as poets use.[2]
5   I meant to make her fair, and free, and wise,
Of greatest blood, and yet more good than great;
I meant the day-star° should not brighter rise,   *the sun*
Nor lend like influence from his lucent seat.
I meant she should be courteous, facile,° sweet,   *affable*
10 Hating that solemn vice of greatness, pride;
I meant each softest virtue, there should meet,
Fit in that softer bosom to reside.
Only a learnèd, and a manly soul
I purposed her; that should, with even powers,
15 The rock, the spindle, and the shears[3] control
Of destiny, and spin her own free hours.
Such when I meant to feign, and wished to see,
My muse bad, *Bedford* write, and that was she.

1616

To Lucy, Countess of Bedford, with Mr. Donne's Satires[1]

Lucy, you brightness[2] of our sphere, who are
    Life of the Muses' day, their morning star!
If works, not th' authors, their own grace should look,°   *have regard to*
    Whose poems would not wish to be your book?
5 But these, desired by you, the maker's ends
    Crown with their own. Rare poems ask rare friends.
Yet satires, since the most of mankind be
    Their unavoided° subject, fewest see: *inevitable*
For none e'er took that pleasure in sin's sense,
10   But, when they heard it taxed, took more offense.
They then that, living where the matter is bred,[3]
    Dare for these poems yet both ask and read
And like them too, must needfully, though few,
    Be of the best: and 'mongst those, best are you;
15 Lucy, you brightness of our sphere, who are
    The Muses' evening, as their morning star.[4]

1616

1. The countess of Bedford was a famous patroness of the age, to whom Jonson, Donne, and many other poets addressed poems of compliment.
2. This elegant epigram of praise plays off against the Pygmalion story, in which the sculptor molds a statue of his ideal woman and she then comes to life.
3. Emblems of the three Fates: Clotho spun the thread of life, Lachesis decided its length, and Atropos cut the thread to end life.

1. With this poem, Jonson offered a manuscript collection of Donne's satires (see p. 1257), such as commonly passed from hand to hand in court circles.
2. Lucy's name derives from the Latin *lux*, meaning light.
3. I.e., at court.
4. The planet Venus is called Lucifer (light-bearing) when it appears before sunrise, Hesperus when it appears after sunset.

Inviting a Friend to Supper

Tonight, grave sir, both my poor house and I
   Do equally desire your company:
Not that we think us worthy such a guest,
   But that your worth will dignify our feast
5 With those that come; whose grace may make that seem
   Something, which else could hope for no esteem.
It is the fair acceptance, Sir, creates
   The entertainment perfect: not the cates.°   *food*
Yet shall you have, to rectify your palate,
10   An olive, capers, or some better salad
Ushering the mutton; with a short-legged hen,
   If we can get her, full of eggs, and then
Lemons and wine for sauce; to these, a coney°   *rabbit*
   Is not to be despaired of for our money;
15 And though fowl now be scarce, yet there are clerks,°   *scholars*
   The sky not falling, think we may have larks.
I'll tell you of more, and lie, so you will come:
   Of partridge, pheasant, woodcock, of which some
May yet be there; and godwit if we can,
20   Knot, rail, and ruff, too.[1] Howsoe'er, my man°   *servant*
Shall read a piece of Virgil, Tacitus,
   Livy, or of some better book to us,
Of which we'll speak our minds amidst our meat;
   And I'll profess° no verses to repeat: *promise*
25 To this,° if aught appear which I not know of,   *add to this*
   That will the pastry, not my paper, show of.[2]
Digestive cheese and fruit there sure will be;
   But that which most doth take my muse and me
Is a pure cup of rich Canary wine,
30   Which is the Mermaid's now, but shall be mine;
Of which, had Horace or Anacreon[3] tasted,
   Their lives, as do their lines, till now had lasted.
Tobacco, Nectar, or the Thespian spring[4]
   Are all but Luther's beer to this I sing.
35 Of this we will sup free but moderately,
   And we will have no Pooly or Parrot[5] by;
Nor shall our cups make any guilty men,
   But at our parting we will be as when
We innocently met. No simple word
40   That shall be uttered at our mirthful board
Shall make us sad next morning, or affright
   The liberty that we'll enjoy tonight.

                                   1616

---

1. All these are edible birds.
2. I.e., papers may appear, but they will be under pies (to keep them from sticking to the pan), not for declamation.
3. Horace and Anacreon (one in Latin, the other in Greek) wrote many poems in praise of wine. The Mermaid tavern was a favorite haunt of the poets; sweet wine from the Canary Islands was popular in England.

4. One of two springs on Mount Helicon, both reputed to be sources of poetic inspiration. Compared to Canary, all these other intoxicants are no better than inferior German beer.
5. Pooly and Parrot were government spies, though their conjunction also suggests a talkative bird, Poll Parrot. While a Roman Catholic and even after, Jonson had reason to be wary of undercover agents.

Epitaph on S. P., a Child of Queen Elizabeth's Chapel[1]

Weep with me, all you that read
This little story;
And know for whom a tear you shed,
Death's self is sorry.
5 'Twas a child that so did thrive
In grace and feature,
As Heaven and Nature seemed to strive
Which owned the creature.
Years he numbered scarce thirteen
10 When Fates turned cruel,
Yet three filled zodiacs had he been
The stage's jewel;[2]
And did act (what now we moan)
Old men so duly,°   *aptly*
15 As, sooth, the Parcae° thought him one,   *Fates*
He played so truly.
So, by error, to his fate
They all consented;
But, viewing him since (alas, too late),
20 They have repented,
And have sought (to give new birth)
In baths[3] to steep him;
But, being so much too good for earth,
Heaven vows to keep him.

1616

FROM THE FOREST[1]

To Penshurst[2]

Thou art not, Penshurst, built to envious show,
Of touch[3] or marble; nor canst boast a row
Of polished pillars, or a roof of gold;
Thou hast no lantern° whereof tales are told,
5 Or stair, or courts; but stand'st an ancient pile,
And, these grudged at,[4] art reverenced the while.
Thou joy'st in better marks, of soil, of air,
Of wood, of water; therein thou art fair.

[handwritten annotation: It flatters the family. It is a modest house & there is continuity between family cupola and the people]

1. Salomon Pavy, a boy actor in the troupe known as the Children of Queen Elizabeth's Chapel, who had appeared in several of Jonson's plays; he died in 1602.
2. He had been on the stage for three seasons.
3. Perhaps such magic baths as that of Medea, which restored Jason's father to his first youth (Ovid, *Metamorphoses* 7).
1. In the 1616 *Works*, Jonson grouped some of his nonepigrammatic poems under the heading *The Forest*, a translation of the term *Sylvae*, meaning a poetic miscellany. *To Penshurst* and the two follow-

ing poems are from that group.
2. Penshurst, in Kent, was the estate of Robert Sidney, Viscount Lisle (later, earl of Leicester), a younger brother of the poet Sir Philip Sidney (see p. 909). Along with Lanyer's *The Description of Cooke-ham* (p. 1287), this poem inaugurated the small genre of English "country-house" poems, which includes Marvell's *Upon Appleton House* (p. 1704).
3. Touchstone, a fine black (and expensive) variety of basalt.
4. More pretentious houses attract envy.

Thou hast thy walks for health, as well as sport;
10   Thy mount, to which the dryads° do resort,   *wood nymphs*
Where Pan and Bacchus their high feasts have made,
        Beneath the broad beech and the chestnut shade;
That taller tree, which of a nut was set
        At his great birth where all the Muses met.[5]
15   There in the writhèd bark are cut the names
        Of many a sylvan,° taken with his flames;   *countryman*
And thence the ruddy satyrs[6] oft provoke
        The lighter fauns to reach thy Lady's Oak.[7]
Thy copse° too, named of Gamage,[8] thou hast there,   *little woods*
20   That never fails to serve thee seasoned deer
When thou wouldst feast or exercise thy friends.
        The lower land, that to the river bends,
Thy sheep, thy bullocks, kine,° and calves do feed;   *cattle*
        The middle grounds thy mares and horses breed.
25   Each bank doth yield thee conies;° and the tops,°   *rabbits / high ground*
        Fertile of wood, Ashore and Sidney's copse,
To crown thy open table, doth provide
        The purpled pheasant with the speckled side;
The painted partridge lies in every field,
30   And for thy mess is willing to be killed.
And if the high-swollen Medway[9] fail thy dish,
        Thou hast thy ponds, that pay thee tribute fish:
Fat agèd carps that run into thy net,
        And pikes, now weary their own kind to eat,
35   As loath the second draught or cast to stay,
        Officiously° at first themselves betray;   *dutifully*
Bright eels that emulate them, and leap on land
        Before the fisher, or into his hand.
Then hath thy orchard fruit, thy garden flowers,
40   Fresh as the air, and new as are the hours.
The early cherry, with the later plum,
        Fig, grape, and quince, each in his time doth come;
The blushing apricot and woolly peach
        Hang on thy walls, that every child may reach.
45   And though thy walls be of the country stone,
        They're reared with no man's ruin, no man's groan;
There's none that dwell about them wish them down;
        But all come in, the farmer and the clown,°   *peasant*
And no one empty-handed, to salute
50   Thy lord and lady, though they have no suit.°   *request to make*
Some bring a capon, some a rural cake,
        Some nuts, some apples; some that think they make
The better cheeses bring them, or else send
        By their ripe daughters, whom they would commend
55   This way to husbands, and whose baskets bear

5. Sir Philip Sidney was born at Penshurst.
6. Satyrs and fauns were woodland spirits. Satyrs, with the body of a man and the legs (and horns) of a goat, were symbols of lechery. "Provokes": challenges to a race.
7. Named after a lady of the house who went into labor under its branches.
8. Lady Barbara (Gamage) Sidney, wife of Sir Robert.
9. The local river.

An emblem of themselves in plum or pear.
But what can this (more than express their love)
    Add to thy free provisions, far above
The need of such? whose liberal board doth flow
60   With all that hospitality doth know;
Where comes no guest but is allowed to eat,
    Without his fear, and of thy lord's own meat;
Where the same beer and bread, and selfsame wine,
    That is his lordship's shall be also mine,
65 And I not fain to sit (as some this day
    At great men's tables), and yet dine away.[1]
Here no man tells° my cups; nor, standing by,   *counts*
    A waiter doth my gluttony envy,
But gives me what I call, and lets me eat;
70   He knows below° he shall find plenty of meat.   *in the servants' quarters*
Thy tables hoard not up for the next day;
    Nor, when I take my lodging, need I pray
For fire, or lights, or livery; all is there,
    As if thou then wert mine, or I reigned here:
75 There's nothing I can wish, for which I stay.°
    That found King James when, hunting late this way
With his brave son, the Prince,[2] they saw thy fires
    Shine bright on every hearth, as the desires
Of thy Penates° had been set on flame   *Roman household gods*
80   To entertain them; or the country came
With all their zeal to warm their welcome here.
    What (great I will not say, but) sudden cheer
Didst thou then make 'em! and what praise was heaped
    On thy good lady then, who therein reaped
85 The just reward of her high housewifery;
    To have her linen, plate, and all things nigh,
When she was far; and not a room but dressed
    As if it had expected such a guest!
These, Penshurst, are thy praise, and yet not all.
90   Thy lady's noble, fruitful, chaste withal.
His children thy great lord may call his own,
    A fortune in this age but rarely known.
They are, and have been, taught religion; thence
    Their gentler spirits have sucked innocence.
95 Each morn and even they are taught to pray,
    With the whole household, and may, every day,
Read in their virtuous parents' noble parts
    The mysteries of manners, arms, and arts.
Now, Penshurst, they that will proportion° thee   *compare*
100   With other edifices, when they see
Those proud, ambitious heaps, and nothing else,
    May say, their lords have built, but thy lord dwells.

                                              1616

---

1. Different courses might be served to different
guests, depending on their social status. The lord
would have the best food.

2. Prince Henry, the heir apparent, who died in
November 1612.

Song: To Celia[1]

Drink to me only with thine eyes,
   And I will pledge with mine;
Or leave a kiss but in the cup,
   And I'll not look for wine.
5 The thirst that from the soul doth rise
   Doth ask a drink divine:
But might I of Jove's nectar sup,
   I would not change for thine.
I sent thee late a rosy wreath,
10   Not so much honoring thee,
As giving it a hope that there
   It could not withered be.
But thou thereon didst only breathe,
   And sent'st it back to me;
15 Since when it grows and smells, I swear,
   Not of itself, but thee.

1616

To Heaven

Good and great God, can I not think of thee
   But it must straight my melancholy be?
Is it interpreted in me disease
   That, laden with my sins, I seek for ease?
5 Oh, be thou witness, that the reins[1] dost know
   And hearts of all, if I be sad for show,
And judge me after, if I dare pretend
   To aught but grace, or aim at other end.
As thou art all, so be thou all to me,
10   First, midst, and last, converted° one and three,   *interchanging*
My faith, my hope, my love; and in this state,
   My judge, my witness, and my advocate.
Where have I been this while exiled from thee,
   And whither rapt,° now thou but stoop'st to me?   *carried off*
15 Dwell, dwell here still: Oh, being everywhere,
   How can I doubt to find thee ever here?
I know my state, both full of shame and scorn,
   Conceived in sin and unto labor born,
Standing with fear, and must with horror fall,
20   And destined unto judgment after all.
I feel my griefs too, and there scarce is ground

---

1. These famous lines are a patchwork of five separate prose passages by Philostratus, a Greek sophist (3rd century C.E.). The music that has made it a barroom favorite is by an anonymous 18th-
century composer.
1. Literally, kidneys, but also the seat of the affections, with a glance at Psalm 7.9: "the righteous God trieth the hearts and reins."

Upon my flesh to inflict another wound.
Yet dare I not complain or wish for death
With holy Paul,[2] lest it be thought the breath
25   Of discontent; or that these prayers be
For weariness of life, not love of thee.

1616

FROM UNDERWOOD

From A Celebration of Charis in Ten Lyric Pieces[1]

1. His Excuse for Loving

Let it not your wonder move,
Less your laughter, that I love.
Though I now write fifty years,
I have had, and have, my peers.
5   Poets, though divine,[2] are men;
Some have loved as old again.
And it is not always face,
Clothes, or fortune gives the grace,
Or the feature,° or the youth;   form, comeliness
10   But the language and the truth,
With the ardor and the passion,
Gives the lover weight and fashion.
If you then will read the story,
First, prepare you to be sorry
15   That you never knew till now
Either whom to love or how;
But be glad as soon with me
When you know that this is she
Of whose beauty it was sung,
20   She shall make the old man young,
Keep the middle age at stay,
And let nothing high decay,
Till she be the reason why
All the world for love may die.

2. How He Saw Her

I beheld her, on a day,
When her look out-flourished May;
And her dressing did out-brave°   surpass in finery
All the pride the fields then have;

2. "Who shall deliver me from the body of this
death?" (Roman 7.24).
1. Preparing a 2nd edition of his *Works* (published
posthumously in 1640–41), Jonson added a third
section of poems, *Underwood*, "out of the analogy
they hold to *The Forest* in my former book." Of its

eighty-nine poems, we print most of the *Celebration of Charis* and three others.
    The Greek word *charis*, from which Jonson's lady
takes her name, means "grace" or "loveliness."
2. A commonplace of literary criticism.

5 Far I was from being stupid,
 For I ran and called on Cupid:
 "Love, if thou wilt ever see
 Mark of glory, come with me;
 Where's thy quiver? Bend thy bow—
10 Here's a shaft, thou art too slow!"
 And (withal) I did untie
 Every cloud° about his eye;[3]   *clout, cloth*
 But he had not gained his sight
 Sooner than he lost his might
15 Or his courage; for away
 Straight he ran and durst not stay,
 Letting bow and arrow fall;
 Nor for any threat or call
 Could be brought once back to look.
20 I, foolhardy, there up-took
 Both the arrow he had quit
 And the bow, with thought to hit
 This my object. But she threw
 Such a lightning,[4] as I drew,
25 At my face, that took my sight
 And my motion from me quite;
 So that there I stood a stone,
 Mocked of° all, and called of° one   *by/by*
 (Which with grief and wrath I heard)
30 Cupid's statue with a beard,
 Or else one that played his ape,°   *imitated him*
 In a Hercules-his shape.[5]

3. What He Suffered

 After many scorns like these,
 Which the prouder beauties please,
 She content was to restore
 Eyes and limbs, to hurt me more;
5 And would, on conditions, be
 Reconciled to Love, and me:
 First, that I must kneeling yield
 Both the bow and shaft I held
 Unto her; which Love might take
10 At her hand, with oath to make
 Me the scope° of his next draught,°   *target/shot*
 Aimèd with that self-same shaft.
 He no sooner heard the law,
 But the arrow home did draw
15 And (to gain her by his art)

---

3. The blindness of Cupid is a Renaissance addition to the classical figure.
4. From her eyes.

5. The image is ridiculous: giant Hercules acting like the child Cupid.

Left it sticking in my heart;
Which when she beheld to bleed,
She repented of the deed,
And would fain have changed the fate,
20 But the pity comes too late.
Loser-like, now, all my wreak°   *vengeance*
Is, that I have leave to speak,
And in either prose or song
To revenge me with my tongue,
25 Which how dexterously I do,
Hear and make example too.

*   *   *

4. Her Triumph⁶

See the chariot at hand here of Love,
    Wherein my lady rideth!
Each that draws is a swan or a dove,⁷
    And well the car Love guideth.
5 As she goes, all hearts do duty
            Unto her beauty;
And enamored do wish, so they might
            But enjoy such a sight,
That they still° were to run by her side,   *always*
10 Through swords, through seas, whither she would ride.

Do but look on her eyes, they do light
    All that Love's world compriseth!
Do but look on her hair, it is bright
    As Love's star when it riseth!
15 Do but mark, her forehead's smoother
            Than words that soothe her!
And from her archèd brows, such a grace
            Sheds itself through the face,
As alone there triumphs to the life
20 All the gain, all the good, of the elements' strife.⁸

Have you seen but a bright lily grow,
    Before rude hands have touched it?
Have you marked but the fall o' the snow,
    Before the soil hath smutched it?
25 Have you felt the wool o' the beaver,
            Or swan's down ever?
Or have smelt o' the bud o' the brier,
            Or the nard i' the fire?⁹
Or have tasted the bag o' the bee?
30 O so white! O so soft! O so sweet is she!

*   *   *

6. Following Petrarch, many Renaissance poets used the figure of the triumphal procession to celebrate a person or concept—time, chastity, fame, etc. Metrically, this poem is highly complex.
7. Venus's birds.
8. The four elements—earth, water, air, fire—were thought to be in perpetual conflict.
9. Spikenard, an aromatic ointment.

7. Begging Another, on Color° of Mending the Former   *pretense*

For Love's sake, kiss me once again;
   I long, and should not beg in vain.
      Here's none to spy or see;
         Why do you doubt or stay?
5   I'll taste as lightly as the bee
That doth but touch his flower and flies away.
      Once more, and, faith, I will be gone;
      Can he that loves ask less than one?
         Nay, you may err in this,
10   And all your bounty wrong;
      This could be called but half a kiss.
What w'are but once to do, we should do long.
      I will but mend the last, and tell
      Where, how it would have relished well;
15   Join lip to lip and try;
         Each suck other's breath.
      And whilst our tongues perplexèd lie,
Let who will think us dead, or wish our death.

8. Urging Her of a Promise

Charis one day in discourse
Had of Love and of his force
Lightly promised she would tell
What a man she could love well;
5   And that promise set on fire
All that heard her, with desire.
With the rest, I long expected
When the work would be effected;
But we find that cold delay,
10   And excuse spun every day,
As, until she tell her one,
We all fear she loveth none.
Therefore, Charis, you must do't,
For I will so urge you to't,
15   You shall neither eat nor sleep,
No, nor forth your window peep
With your emissary° eye,   *spying*
To fetch in the forms go by,[1]
And pronounce which band° or lace   *collar*
20   Better fits him than his face.
Nay, I will not let you sit
'Fore your idol glass a whit,
To say over every purl°   *loop of lace*
There, or to reform a curl;
25   Or with secretary Sis
To consult if fucus° this   *cosmetic*
Be as good as was the last.

1. To observe the passing men.

All your sweet of life is past;
Make accompt,° unless you can—   *account*
30   And that quickly—speak° your man.   *describe*

9. *Her Man Described by Her Own Dictamen°*   *statement*

Of your trouble, Ben, to ease me,
I will tell what man would please me.
I would have him, if I could,
Noble, or of greater[2] blood:
5   Titles, I confess, do take me;
And a woman God did make me.
French to boot, at least in fashion,
And his manners of that nation.
    Young I'd have him, too, and fair,
10 Yet a man; with crispèd° hair   *curly*
Cast in thousand snares and rings
For Love's fingers, and his wings—
Chestnut color, or more slack°   *duller*
Gold, upon a ground° of black.   *background*
15 Venus' and Minerva's eyes,
For he must look wanton-wise.
    Eyebrows bent like Cupid's bow,
Front,° an ample field of snow;   *forehead*
Even nose, and cheek withal
20 Smooth as is the billiard ball;
Chin as woolly as the peach,
And his lip should kissing teach,
Till he cherished too much beard,
And make Love or me afeard.
25   He would have a hand as soft
As the down, and show it oft;
Skin as smooth as any rush,
And so thin, to see a blush
Rising through it e're it came;
30 All his blood should be a flame
Quickly fired, as in beginners
In love's school, and yet no sinners.
    'Twere too long to speak of all;
What we harmony do call
35 In a body, should be there.
Well he should his clothes to wear;
Yet no tailor help to make him;
Dressed, you still for man[3] should take him,
And not think h'had eat a stake,
40 Or were set up in a brake.°   *rigid framework*
    Valiant he should be as fire,
Showing danger° more than ire;   *bravery*
Bounteous as the clouds to earth,
And as honest as his birth.

---

2. I.e., royal.   3. Not a foppish clothes-horse.

45   All his actions to be such
     As to do no thing too much.
     Nor o'er-praise nor yet condemn,
     Nor out-value nor contemn,
     Nor do wrongs nor wrongs receive,
50   Nor tie knots[4] nor knots unweave;
     And from baseness to be free,
     As he durst love Truth and me.
       Such a man, with every part,
     I could give my very heart;
55   But of one, if short he came,[5]
     I can rest me where I am.

10. Another Lady's Exception Present at the Hearing

For his mind I do not care:
That's a toy that I could spare.
Let his title be but great,
His clothes rich and band sit neat,
5   Himself young and face be good:
All I wish is understood.
What you please you parts may call;
'Tis one good part I'd lie withal.

1640–41

A Sonnet, to the Noble Lady, the Lady Mary Wroth[1]

I that have been a lover, and could show it,
    Though not in these, in rhymes not wholly dumb,
    Since I exscribe° your sonnets, am become   *copy out*
A better lover, and much better poet.
5   Nor is my muse, or I ashamed to owe it
    To those true numerous graces; whereof some
    But charm the senses, others overcome
Both brains and hearts; and mine now best do know it:
For in your verse all Cupid's armory,
10   His flames, his shafts, his quiver, and his bow,
    His very eyes are yours to overthrow.
But then his mother's° sweets you so apply,   *Venus's*
    Her joys, her smiles, her loves, as readers take
    For Venus' ceston,[2] every line you make.

1640–41

4. Logical tricks or crafty devices.
5. I.e., if he fell short in one respect.
1. Mary Wroth, author of the sonnet sequence *Pamphilia to Amphilanthus* (p. 1428) and the romance *The Countess of Montgomery's Urania* (p. 1423), was the daughter of Robert Sidney and his wife, Barbara Gamage, of Penshurst, the niece of Sir Philip Sidney and the countess of Pembroke; she was the wife of Sir Robert Wroth, whose coun-

try estate Jonson also praised in *The Forest*. The poem exhibits how poems were exchanged within a coterie, though Jonson also writes as a client to a patron. This is Jonson's only sonnet, used here to pay tribute to Wroth's sequence, and notably to its erotic power.
2. Venus's girdle or belt, which had aphrodisiacal powers; it aroused passion in all beholders.

My Picture Left in Scotland[1]

I now think Love is rather deaf than blind,
    For else it could not be
        That she
Whom I adore so much should so slight me
5   And cast my love behind;
I'm sure my language to her was as sweet,
    And every close° did meet   *cadence*
    In sentence° of as subtle feet,   *wise sayings*
    As hath the youngest he
10   That sits in shadow of Apollo's tree.[2]

O, but my conscious fears
    That fly my thoughts between,
    Tell me that she hath seen
    My hundreds of gray hairs,
15   Told seven and forty years,
Read so much waist[3] as she cannot embrace
My mountain belly and my rocky face;
And all these through her eyes have stopped her ears.

1619   1640–41

The Ode on Cary and Morison

The ode, originally a classical form, is a lyric poem in an elevated style, celebrating a lofty theme, a noble personage, or a grand occasion. The Greek poet Pindar wrote many odes for winners of the Olympic games, known as "Great Odes" because of their exalted subject and style. Later, the Roman poet Horace wrote more restrained poems that came to be known as "Lesser Odes." Petrarch in Italy and Ronsard in France wrote odes in the classical manner, but Jonson is the first to do so in England. His Cary-Morison ode comes closer than any other in the language to the lofty style and manner of Pindar, while his *To Penshurst* is in the Horatian style, as is, later, Marvell's *Horatian Ode upon Cromwell's Return from Ireland*.

Pindar's odes were designed to be sung by a chorus and often followed a three-part scheme: the chorus moved in one direction while chanting the strophe, reversed direction for the antistrophe, and stood still for the epode. Jonson imitates this pattern with his triple division of turn, counterturn, and stand—the terms more or less literally translated from the original Greek. His turns and counterturns rhyme in couplets, with line lengths varying in all stanzas according to a uniform scheme; the twelve-line stands follow a more complex but equally strict design. He imitates Pindar also in his moral generalizations and lofty but impersonal praise of the two noble friends. Later in the century, under the influence of Abraham Cowley and under a misapprehension about Pindar's style, odes became more extravagant, more vehement in tone, and more irregular in form.

1. After his walking tour of Scotland in 1618–19, Jonson sent a manuscript version of this poem to William Drummond, with whom he had stayed. The woman of the poem may or may not be a real person.
2. The god of poetry.
3. With a pun on waste.

To the Immortal Memory and Friendship of That Noble Pair, Sir Lucius Cary and Sir H. Morison[1]

The Turn

Brave infant of Saguntum,[2] clear°   *explain*
Thy coming forth in that great year
When the prodigious Hannibal did crown
His rage, with razing your immortal town.
5 Thou, looking then about
Ere thou wert half got out,
Wise child, didst hastily return
And mad'st thy mother's womb thine urn.
How summed° a circle[3] didst thou leave mankind *complete*
10 Of deepest lore, could we the center find!

The Counter-Turn

Did wiser nature draw thee back
From out the horror of that sack,
Where shame, faith, honor, and regard of right
Lay trampled on?—the deeds of death and night
15 Urged, hurried forth, and hurled
Upon th' affrighted world?
Sword, fire, and famine, with fell fury met,
And all on utmost ruin set:
As, could they but life's miseries foresee,
20 No doubt all infants would return like thee.

The Stand

For what is life if measured by the space,
Not by the act?
Or maskèd man, if valued by his face,
Above his fact?°   *deeds*
25 Here's one outlived his peers
And told forth fourscore years:
He vexèd time, and busied the whole state,
Troubled both foes and friends,
But ever to no ends:
30 What did this stirrer but die late?
How well at twenty had he fall'n or stood!
For three of his four score, he did no good.

The Turn

He[4] entered well, by virtuous parts,
Got up and thrived with honest arts:

---

1. Henry Morison died in 1629 at the age of twenty. His good friend Lucius Cary (son of Elizabeth Cary, the author of *Mariam*, p. 1508) became the second Viscount Falkland. He was known for his learning, and he died fighting for King Charles in the first years of the civil war.

2. Pliny tells the story of an infant born while Sagunto, in Spain, was being assaulted by Hannibal; he dived back into his mother's womb (setting a record for brevity of life) and was buried there.
3. Emblem of perfection.
4. I.e., another man.

35　He purchased friends and fame and honors then,
　　And had his noble name advanced with men;
　　But, weary of that flight,
　　He stooped in all men's sight
　　To sordid flatteries, acts of strife,
40　And sunk in that dead sea of life
　　So deep, as he did then death's waters sup;
　　But that the cork of title buoyed him up.

The Counter-Turn

　　Alas, but Morison fell young;—
　　He never fell, thou fall'st,[5] my tongue.
45　He stood, a soldier, to the last right end,
　　A perfect patriot and a noble friend,
　　But most a virtuous son.
　　All offices° were done　　　　　　　　　　　　　*duties of life*
　　By him, so ample, full, and round
50　In weight, in measure, number, sound,
　　As, though his age imperfect might appear,
　　His life was of humanity the sphere.

The Stand

　　Go now, and tell out° days summed up with fears,　　*count*
　　And make them years;
55　Produce thy mass of miseries on the stage
　　To swell thine age;
　　Repeat of things a throng,
　　To show thou hast been long,
　　Not lived; for life doth her great actions spell,°　　*tell over*
60　By what was done and wrought
　　In season, and so brought
　　To light: her measures are, how well
　　Each syllab'e° answered, and was formed how fair;　　*syllable*
　　These make the lines of life, and that's her air.[6]

The Turn

65　It is not growing like a tree
　　In bulk, doth make man better be,
　　Or standing long an oak, three hundred year,
　　To fall a log at last, dry, bald, and sere:
　　A lily of a day
70　Is fairer far in May,
　　Although it fall and die that night;
　　It was the plant and flower of light.
　　In small proportions we just beauties see,
　　And in short measures life may perfect be.

5. Slip, with a latent pun on Latin *fallo*, "to make　　are its metrical patterns as well as the standards by
a mistake."　　　　　　　　　　　　　　　　　　　which it is judged.
6. Life is a poem set to music; life's "measures"

The Counter-Turn

75 Call, noble Lucius, then for wine,
And let thy looks with gladness shine:
Accept this garland,[7] plant it on thy head,
And think, nay, know, thy Morison's not dead.
He leaped the present age,
80 Possessed with holy rage,
To see that bright eternal day,
Of which we priests and poets say
Such truths as we expect for happy men,
And there he lives with memory: and Ben

The Stand

85 Jonson, who sung this of him ere he went
Himself to rest,
Or taste a part of that full joy he meant
To have expressed
In this bright asterism:°   constellation
90 Where it were friendship's schism
(Were not his Lucius long with us to tarry)
To separate these twi-
Lights, the Dioscuri,[8]
And keep the one half from his Harry.
95 But fate doth so alternate the design,
Whilst that in heaven, this light on earth must shine.

The Turn

And shine as you exalted are,
Two names of friendship, but one star,
Of hearts the union. And those not by chance
100 Made, or indentured,° or leased out t' advance   contracted for
The profits for a time.
No pleasures vain did chime
Of rhymes or riots at your feasts,
Orgies of drink, or feigned protests;
105 But simple love of greatness and of good
That knits brave minds and manners, more than blood.

The Counter-Turn

This made you first to know the why
You liked, then after to apply
That liking; and approach so one the tother,°   other
110 Till either grew a portion of the other;
Each stylèd by his end,
The copy of his friend.

---

7. This poem.
8. The mythical Greek twins, Castor and Pollux, the Dioscuri, were said to have exchanged places regularly, after Castor's death, between earth and the underworld. They are the principal stars of the constellation Gemini (the twins).

You lived to be the great surnames
And titles by which all made claims
115 Unto the virtue: nothing perfect done,
But as a Cary or a Morison.

The Stand

And such a force the fair example had,
As they that saw
The good and durst not practice it, were glad
120 That such a law
Was left yet to mankind;
Where they might read and find
Friendship in deed was written, not in words.
And with the heart, not pen,
125 Of two so early° men,   youthful
Whose lives her rolls were, and records,
Who, ere the first down bloomèd on the chin
Had sowed these fruits, and got the harvest in.

1629   1640–41

Slow, Slow, Fresh Fount[1]

Slow, slow, fresh fount, keep time with my salt tears;
Yet slower, yet, O faintly, gentle springs!
List to the heavy part the music bears:
Woe weeps out her division,[2] when she sings.
5   Droop herbs and flowers;
        Fall grief in showers;
        Our beauties are not ours.
            O, I could still,
Like melting snow upon some craggy hill,
10   Drop, drop, drop, drop,
Since nature's pride is now a withered daffodil.

1600

Queen and Huntress[1]

Queen and huntress, chaste and fair,
Now the sun is laid to sleep,
Seated in thy silver chair,
State in wonted manner keep;
5   Hesperus entreats thy light,
Goddess excellently bright.

---

1. From the play *Cynthia's Revels* (1.2). This lyric is a lament sung by Echo for Narcissus, who was entranced by his own reflection and who was ultimately transformed into a flower.
2. Grief at parting; also a rapid melodic passage of music.

1. Also from *Cynthia's Revels* (4.3), this song is sung by Hesperus, the evening star, to Cynthia or Diana, goddess of chastity and the moon—with whom Queen Elizabeth was constantly compared.

Earth, let not thy envious shade
Dare itself to interpose;[2]
Cynthia's shining orb was made
10   Heaven to clear, when day did close.
Bless us then with wishèd sight,
Goddess excellently bright.

Lay thy bow of pearl apart,
And thy crystal-shining quiver;
15   Give unto the flying hart
Space to breathe, how short soever.
Thou that mak'st a day of night,
Goddess excellently bright.

1600

Still to Be Neat[1]

Still to be neat, still to be dressed
As° you were going to a feast,   *as though*
Still to be powdered, still perfumed;
Lady, it is to be presumed,
5   Though art's hid causes are not found,
All is not sweet, all is not sound.

Give me a look, give me a face
That makes simplicity a grace;
Robes loosely flowing, hair as free—
10   Such sweet neglect more taketh me
Than all the adulteries of art.
They strike mine eyes, but not my heart.

1609

To the Memory of My Beloved, The Author, Mr. William Shakespeare, and What He Hath Left Us[1]

To draw no envy, Shakespeare, on thy name,
Am I thus ample° to thy book and fame,   *copious*
While I confess thy writings to be such
As neither man nor muse can praise too much.
5   'Tis true, and all men's suffrage.° But these ways   *consent*
Were not the paths I meant unto thy praise;
For silliest° ignorance on these may light,   *simplest*
Which, when it sounds at best, but echoes right;
Or blind affection, which doth ne'er advance
10   The truth, but gropes, and urgeth all by chance;
Or crafty malice might pretend this praise,

2. Eclipses were thought to portend evil.
1. Sung in the play *Epicoene*, this song concerns the art of makeup, but also art more generally.

1. This poem was prefixed to the first Folio of Shakespeare's plays (1623).

And think to ruin where it seemed to raise.
These are as° some infamous bawd or whore   *as though*
    Should praise a matron. What could hurt her more?
15 But thou art proof against them, and, indeed,
    Above th' ill fortune of them, or the need.
I therefore will begin. Soul of the age!
    The applause! delight! the wonder of our stage!
My Shakespeare, rise; I will not lodge thee by
20   Chaucer or Spenser, or bid Beaumont lie
A little further to make thee a room:[2]
    Thou art a monument without a tomb,
And art alive still while thy book doth live,
    And we have wits to read and praise to give.
25 That I not mix thee so, my brain excuses,
    I mean with great, but disproportioned° Muses;   *not comparable*
For, if I thought my judgment were of years,
    I should commit thee surely with thy peers,
And tell how far thou didst our Lyly outshine,
30   Or sporting Kyd, or Marlowe's mighty line.[3]
And though thou hadst small Latin and less Greek,[4]
    From thence to honor thee I would not seek°   *lack*
For names, but call forth thund'ring Aeschylus,
    Euripides, and Sophocles to us,
35 Pacuvius, Accius, him of Cordova dead,[5]
    To life again, to hear thy buskin° tread   *symbol of tragedy*
And shake a stage; or, when thy socks° were on,   *symbol of comedy*
    Leave thee alone for the comparison
Of all that insolent Greece or haughty Rome
40   Sent forth, or since did from their ashes come.
Triumph, my Britain; thou hast one to show
    To whom all scenes° of Europe homage owe.   *stages*
He was not of an age, but for all time!
    And all the Muses still were in their prime
45 When like Apollo he came forth to warm
    Our ears, or like a Mercury to charm.
Nature herself was proud of his designs,
    And joyed to wear the dressing of his lines,
Which were so richly spun, and woven so fit,
50   As, since, she will vouchsafe no other wit:
The merry Greek, tart Aristophanes,
    Neat Terence, witty Plautus[6] now not please,
But antiquated and deserted lie,
    As they were not of Nature's family.
55 Yet must I not give Nature all; thy Art,
    My gentle Shakespeare, must enjoy a part.

2. Chaucer, Spenser, and Francis Beaumont were buried in Westminster Abbey; Shakespeare, in Stratford.
3. John Lily, Thomas Kyd, and Christopher Marlowe were Elizabethan dramatists contemporary or nearly contemporary with Shakespeare.
4. Shakespeare's Latin was pretty good, but Jonson is judging by the standard of his own remarkable scholarship.

5. Marcus Pacuvius, Lucius Accius (2nd century B.C.E.) and "him of Cordova," Seneca the Younger (1st century C.E.), were Latin tragedians. Seneca's tragedies had a large influence on Elizabethan revenge tragedy.
6. Aristophanes, an ancient Greek satirist and writer of comedy; Terence and Plautus (2nd and 3rd centuries B.C.E.), Roman writers of comedy.

For though the poet's matter° Nature be,   *subject matter*
    His Art doth give the fashion;° and that he   *form, style*
    Who casts° to write a living line must sweat   *undertakes*
60 (Such as thine are) and strike the second heat
    Upon the Muses' anvil; turn the same,
        And himself with it, that he thinks to frame,
        Or for the laurel he may gain a scorn;
        For a good poet's made as well as born.
65 And such wert thou! Look how the father's face
        Lives in his issue; even so the race
    Of Shakespeare's mind and manners brightly shines
        In his well-turnèd and true-filèd lines,
    In each of which he seems to shake a lance,[7]
70   As brandished at the eyes of ignorance.
    Sweet swan of Avon, what a sight it were
        To see thee in our waters yet appear,
    And make those flights upon the banks of Thames
        That so did take Eliza and our James![8]
75 But stay; I see thee in the hemisphere
        Advanced and made a constellation there![9]
    Shine forth, thou star of poets, and with rage
        Or influence[1] chide or cheer the drooping stage,
    Which, since thy flight from hence, hath mourned like night,
80   And despairs day, but for thy volume's light.

                                                        1623

Ode to Himself[1]

    Come, leave the loathèd stage,
        And the more loathsome age,
    Where pride and impudence, in faction knit,
        Usurp the chair of wit,
5   Indicting and arraigning every day
        Something they call a play.
        Let their fastidious, vain
        Commission of the brain
    Run on and rage, sweat, censure, and condemn:
10 They were not made for thee, less thou for them.

        Say that thou pour'st them wheat,
        And they will acorns eat;
    'Twere simple° fury still thyself to waste   *foolish*
        On such as have no taste!
15 To offer them a surfeit of pure bread,
        Whose appetites are dead!

---

7. Pun on Shake-speare.
8. Queen Elizabeth and King James.
9. Heroes and demigods were typically exalted after death to a place among the stars.
1. "Rage" and "influence" describe the supposed effects of the planets on earthly affairs. "Rage" also implies poetic inspiration.

1. The failure of Jonson's *The New Inn* (1629) inspired this assault on criticism and the public taste. For Thomas Carew's affectionate, mocking rebuke, see p. 1659.

No, give them grains their fill,
Husks, draff to drink, and swill:[2]
If they love lees,° and leave the lusty wine,   *dregs*
20 Envy them not; their palate's with the swine.

No doubt some moldy tale
Like *Pericles*,[3] and stale
As the shrieve's° crusts, and nasty as his fish—   *sheriff's*
  Scraps, out of every dish
25 Thrown forth and raked into the common tub,[4]
  May keep up the play club:
  There, sweepings do as well
  As the best-ordered meal;
For who the relish of these guests will fit
30 Needs set them but the alms basket of wit.

And much good do 't you then:
  Brave plush and velvet men
Can feed on orts;° and, safe in your stage clothes,[5] *scraps*
  Dare quit,° upon your oaths,   *acquit*
35 The stagers and the stage-wrights[6] too, your peers,
  Of larding your large ears
With their foul comic socks,°   *symbols of comedy*
  Wrought upon twenty blocks;[7]
Which, if they're torn, and turned, and patched enough,
40 The gamesters° share your guilt,[8] and you their stuff. *gamblers*

Leave things so prostitute
And take th' Alcaic lute;[9]
Or thine own Horace, or Anacreon's lyre;
  Warm thee by Pindar's fire:
45 And though thy nerves° be shrunk, and blood be cold, *sinews*
  Ere years have made thee old,
  Strike that disdainful heat
  Throughout, to their defeat,
As curious fools, and envious of thy strain,
50 May, blushing, swear no palsy's in thy brain.

But when they hear thee sing
  The glories of thy king,
His zeal to God and his just awe o'er men,
  They may, blood-shaken then,
55 Feel such a flesh-quake to possess their powers
  As they shall cry, "Like ours,
  In sound of peace or wars,
  No harp e'er hit the stars

2. All three items are food for pigs.
3. Shakespeare's play, at least in part (printed 1609).
4. The basket outside the jail to receive food for the poor was called the sheriff's tub.
5. Actors often wore on the stage clothes cast off by the gentry; these parasites wear clothes cast off by actors.
6. Playwrights. "Stagers": actors.
7. A pun: molds/blockheads.
8. A pun: guilt/gilt.
9. Alcaeus (ca. 600 B.C.E.), Horace, Anacreon, and Pindar were among the greatest lyric poets.

In tuning forth the acts of his sweet reign,
60   And raising Charles his chariot 'bove his Wain."[1]

1629   1631, 1640–41

Timber, or Discoveries   Published posthumously in the *Works* (1640–41),
Jonson's observations on literary matters had their origins in a commonplace book
that culled extracts from Sir Philip Sidney's *Defense of Poesy*; from major classical
theorists like Aristotle, Cicero, Seneca, Quintilian, and Horace; and from recent
Dutch critics. Jonson digested all this together under various topics, setting it forth
in his own voice and intermixing some trenchant observations on his own contemporaries. Among his major precepts are that the essence of poetry is its "fiction" or
imitation; that natural wit is the major quality needed in a poet, though "art" and
practice are also necessary; that one learns to become a poet by first imitating a single
model, digesting and transforming what is taken from him; that good sense should
have priority over style; and that the language of poetry should be clear, simple, strong,
strict, and succinct. In the tradition of the Renaissance humanists, Jonson insists that
the good poet is also the good man, who properly comprehends encyclopedic wisdom
in himself, fitting him to be a counselor to rulers. Despite its disjointed form, *Timber*
is probably the most important English commentary on poetics between Sidney and
Thomas Hobbes.

From Timber,[1] or Discoveries

Poetry in this latter age hath proved but a mean mistress to such as have
wholly addicted themselves to her, or given their names up to her family.
They who have but saluted her on the by, and now and then tendered their
visits, she hath done much for, and advanced in the way of their own professions (both the law and the gospel)[2] beyond all they could have hoped, or
done for themselves without her favor. Wherein she doth emulate the judicious but preposterous bounty of the times' grandees,[3] who accumulate all
they can upon the parasite or freshman[4] in their friendship, but think an old
client or honest servant bound by his place to write and starve.

Indeed, the multitude commend writers as they do fencers or wrestlers,
who, if they come in robustiously and put for it with a deal of violence, are
received for the braver fellows; when many times their own rudeness is a
cause of their disgrace, and a slight touch of their adversary gives all that
boisterous force the foil. But in these things the unskilful are naturally
deceived, and judging wholly by the bulk think rude things greater than

---

1. Jonson's poetry will elevate the chariot of
Charles I (symbol of his royal power) above
Charles's Wain (Wagon)—the seven bright stars of
Ursa Major.

1. *Timber* carries on the string of woodland titles
Jonson adopted from Statius's *Silvae* (Trees); he
had already published two volumes of poetry under
the titles *The Forest* and *Underwoods*. "Timber"
suggests the materials out of which the poems are

crafted.

2. E.g., Sir John Davies, who prospered at the law,
and John Donne, who became a clergyman, had
their careers advanced by calling attention to
themselves through their poetry.

3. Patrons. The Spanish word *grandees* was just
coming into English use.

4. Newcomer.

polished, and scattered more numerous than composed.[5] Nor think this only to be true in the sordid multitude, but the neater sort of our gallants; for all are the multitude, only they differ in clothes, not in judgment or understanding.

I remember the players have often mentioned it as an honor to Shakespeare that in his writing, whatsoever he penned, he never blotted out a line. My answer hath been, Would he had blotted a thousand: which they thought a malevolent speech. I had not told posterity this, but for their ignorance who choose that circumstance to commend their friend by wherein he most faulted, and to justify mine own candor, for I loved the man and do honor his memory, on this side idolatry, as much as any. He was indeed honest and of an open and free nature, had an excellent fancy, brave notions, and gentle expressions, wherein he flowed with that facility that sometimes it was necessary he should be stopped: *Sufflaminandus erat,* as Augustus said of Haterius.[6] His wit was in his own power; would the rule of it had been so too. Many times he fell into those things could not escape laughter, as when he said in the person of Caesar, one speaking to him: "Caesar, thou dost me wrong," he replied: "Caesar did never wrong but with just cause," and such like, which were ridiculous.[7] But he redeemed his vices with his virtues. There was ever more in him to be praised than to be pardoned.

* * *

For a man to write well, there are required three necessaries: to read the best authors, observe the best speakers, and much exercise of his own style.[8] In style, to consider what ought to be written, and after what manner. He must first think and excogitate his matter, then choose his words and examine the weight of either. Then take care, in placing and ranking both matter and words, that the composition be comely; and to do this with diligence and often. No matter how slow the style be at first, so it be labored[9] and accurate; seek the best, and be not glad of the forward conceits[1] or first words that offer themselves to us; but judge of what we invent, and order what we approve. Repeat often what we have formerly written; which, beside that it helps the consequence and makes the juncture better, it quickens the heat of imagination, that often cools in the time of setting down, and gives it new strength, as if it grew lustier by the going back. As we see in the contention of leaping, they jump farthest that fetch their race largest; or as in throwing a dart or javelin, we force back our arms to make our loose[2] the stronger. Yet if we have a fair gale of wind, I forbid not the steering out of our sail, so the favor of the gale deceive us not. For all that we invent doth please us in the conception or birth, else we would never set it down. But the safest is to return to our judgment and handle over again those things the easiness of which might make them justly suspected. So did the best writers in their beginnings; they imposed upon themselves care and industry. They did nothing rashly. They obtained first to write well, and then custom made it easy

---

5. The paragraph up to this point is based on Quintilian.
6. "He needed damping." Haterius was a talky senator; the story is from Seneca, *Controversiae* 4.
7. The allusion is to *Julius Caesar* 3.1.47, but Jonson either misquotes, or someone corrected Shakespeare's line before it appeared in the Folio of

1623.
8. This unit on prose style is largely borrowed from Quintilian, with touches from Juan Luis Vives (1492–1540) and Justus Lipsius (1547–1606).
9. Careful.
1. Ideas.
2. Throw.

and a habit. By little and little their matter showed itself to them more plentifully, their words answered, their composition followed; and all, as in a well-ordered family, presented itself in the place. So that the sum of all is: Ready writing makes not good writing, but good writing brings on ready writing.

Yet when we think we have got the faculty, it is even then good to resist it, as to give a horse a check sometimes with [his] bit, which doth not so much stop his course as stir his mettle. Again, whither a man's genius is best able to reach, thither it should more and more contend, lift, and dilate itself; as men of low stature raise themselves on their toes, and so ofttimes get even, if not eminent. Besides, as it is fit for grown and able writers to stand of themselves and work with their own strength, to trust and endeavor by their own faculties; so it is fit for the beginner and learner to study others, and the best. For the mind and memory are more sharply exercised in comprehending another man's things than our own; and such as accustom themselves and are familiar with the best authors shall ever and anon find somewhat of them in themselves; and in the expression of their minds, even when they feel it not, be able to utter something like theirs, which hath an authority above their own. Nay, sometimes it is the reward of a man's study, the praise of quoting another man fitly. And though a man be more prone and able for one kind of writing than another, yet he must exercise all. For as in an instrument, so in style, there must be a harmony and consent of parts.

* * *

Custom is the most certain mistress of language, as the public stamp makes the current money.[3] But we must not be too frequent with the mint, every day coining; nor fetch words from the extreme and utmost ages, since the chief virtue of a style is perspicuity, and nothing so vicious in it as to need an interpreter. Words borrowed of antiquity do lend a kind of majesty to style, and are not without their delight sometimes. For they have the authority of years, and out of their intermission do win to themselves a kind of grace-like newness. But the eldest of the present and newest of the past language is the best. For what was the ancient language, which some men so dote upon, but the ancient custom? Yet when I name custom, I understand not the vulgar custom, for that were a precept no less dangerous to language than life, if we should speak or live after the manners of the vulgar. But that I call custom of speech which is the consent of the learned, as custom of life which is the consent of the good. Virgil was most loving of antiquity; yet how rarely doth he insert *aquai* and *pictai*![4] Lucretius is scabrous and rough in these; he seeks them, as some do Chaucerisms with us, which were better expunged and banished. Some words are to be culled out for ornament and color, as we gather flowers to strew houses or make garlands; but they are better when they grow to our style as in a meadow, where, though the mere grass and greenness delights, yet the variety of flowers doth heighten and beautify. Marry, we must not play or riot too much with them, as in paronomasias;[5] nor use too swelling or ill-sounding words, *quae per salebras*

---

3. The first few sentences of this unit on language are based on Quintilian, the rest on Vives, *On the Proper Method of Speaking* (1532).
4. These are ancient forms of *aquae* and *pictae*,

which do appear, once apiece, in the *Aeneid*, 7.464 and 9.26.
5. Puns, plays on words.

altaque saxa cadunt.[6] It is true, there is no sound but shall find some lovers, as the bitterest confections are grateful to some palates. Our composition must be more accurate in the beginning and end than in the midst, and in the end more than in the beginning; for through the midst the stream bears us. And this is attained by custom more than care or diligence. We must express readily and fully, not profusely. There is difference between a liberal and a prodigal hand. As it is a great point of art, when our matter requires it, to enlarge and veer out all sail, so to take it in and contract it is of no less praise when the argument doth ask it. Either of them hath their fitness in the place. A good man always profits by his endeavor, by his help; yea, when he is absent; nay, when he is dead, by his example and memory. So good authors in their style.

A strict and succinct style is that where you can take away nothing without loss, and that loss to be manifest. The brief style is that which expresseth much in little. The concise style, which expresseth not enough, but leaves somewhat to be understood. The abrupt style, which hath many breaches, and doth not seem to end but fall. The congruent and harmonious fitting of parts in a sentence hath almost the fastening and force of knitting and connection, as in stones well squared, which will rise strong a great way without mortar. Periods[7] are beautiful when they are not too long, for so they have their strength too, as in a pike or javelin. As we must take the care that our words and sense be clear, so if the obscurity happen through the hearer's or reader's want of understanding, I am not to answer for them, no more than for their not listening or marking;[8] I must neither find them ears nor mind. But a man cannot put a word so in sense but something about it will illustrate it, if the writer understand himself. For order helps much to perspicuity, as confusion hurts. *Rectitudo lucem adfert; obliquitas et circumductio offuscat.*[9] We should therefore speak what we can the nearest way, so as we keep our gait, not leap; for too short may as well not be let into the memory as too long not kept in. Whatsoever loseth the grace and clearness converts into a riddle; the obscurity is marked, but not the value. That perisheth, and is passed by, like the pearl in the fable.[1] Our style should be like a skein of silk, to be carried and found by the right thread, not ravelled and perplexed; then all is a knot, a heap.

* * *

1640–41

6. "Which fall on rough places and steep rocks." The phrase is from Martial.
7. Periodic sentences, characterized by balanced phrases and clauses with the main clause at the end.
8. Paying attention.
9. "Directness gives light; indirect and devious diction confuses things." The sentence is from Vives.
1. The fable is that of Phaedrus (3.12): a cock found a pearl on a dunghill, but as neither was interested in the other, that is where the pearl remained.

MARY WROTH
1587–1651?

Lady Mary Wroth was the most prolific, self-conscious, and impressive female author of the Jacobean era. Her published work (1621) include two firsts for an English-woman: a 558-page romance, *The Countess of Montgomery's Urania*, which includes more than fifty poems; and appended to it a Petrarchan lyric sequence that had circulated some years in manuscript, 103 sonnets and elegant songs titled *Pamphilia to Amphilanthus*. Wroth left unpublished a very long but unfinished continuation of the *Urania* and a pastoral drama, *Love's Victory*, also a first for an Englishwoman. Her achievement was fostered by her strong sense of identity as a Sidney, heir to the literary talent and cultural role of her famous uncle Sir Philip Sidney, her famous aunt Mary Sidney Herbert, countess of Pembroke, who may have served as mentor to her, and her father Robert Sidney, Viscount Lisle, author of a recently discovered sonnet sequence. But she used that heritage transgressively to replace heroes with heroines in genres employed by the male Sidney authors—notably Philip Sidney's *Astrophil and Stella* and *The Countess of Pembroke's Arcadia*—transforming their gen-der politics and exploring the poetics and situation of women writers.

As Robert Sidney's eldest daughter, she lived and was educated at Penshurst, the Sidney country house celebrated by Ben Jonson, and was often at her aunt's "little college" at Wilton. She danced at court in *The Masque of Blackness* and perhaps in other masques; she was married (incompatibly) at age seventeen to Sir Robert Wroth of Durrance and Loughton Manor, whose office it was to facilitate the king's hunting; and she was patron to several poets, including Jonson. He celebrated her in two epigrams and in a verse letter honoring her husband, dedicated his great comedy *The Alchemist* to her, and claimed in his only sonnet (p. 1408) that the artistry and erotic power of her sonnets had made him "a better lover, and much better poet." After her husband's death she carried on a long-standing love affair with her married first cousin, William Herbert, earl of Pembroke, himself a poet, a powerful courtier, and a patron of the theater and of literature. That relationship produced two children and occasioned some scandal.

The significant names in the title of Wroth's Petrarchan sequence, *Pamphilia* ("all-loving") to *Amphilanthus* ("lover of two"), are from characters in her romance who at times shadow Wroth and her lover Pembroke. Though it was passé by Wroth's time, the Petrarchan lyric sequence had long served as the major genre for analyzing a male lover's desire, passions, frustrations, and fantasies (and sometimes his career anxi-eties), so it was the obvious beginning point for a woman poet undertaking the con-struction of subjectivity in a female lover-speaker. Wroth does not, however, simply reverse roles: Pamphilia addresses very few sonnets to Amphilanthus and seldom assumes the Petrarchan lover's position of abject servitude to a cruel beloved; instead, she proclaims subjection to Cupid, usually identified with the force of her own desire. This radical revision identifies female desire as the source and center of the love relationship and celebrates the woman lover-poet's movement from the bondage of chaotic passion to the freedom of self-chosen constancy.

Wroth's romance, *Urania*, breaks the romance convention of a plot centered on courtship, portraying instead married heroines and their love relationships, both inside and outside of marriage. It is in part an idealizing fantasy in which all the principal characters are queens, kings, and emperors, with the power and comparative freedom such positions allow. However the landscape is not Arcadia or Fairyland but war-torn Europe and Asia, and the romance fantasy, with Spenserian symbolic places and knights fighting evil tyrants and monsters, only partially overlays a rigidly patri-archal Jacobean world rife with rape, incest, arranged or forced marriages, jealous husbands, tortured women, and endangered children. Those conditions, affecting all women from shepherdesses to queens, are rendered in large part through the numerous stories interpolated in romance fashion within the principal plots. The male heroes are courageous fighters and attractive lovers, but all are flawed by inconstancy. The higher heroism involves attainment or preservation of personal integrity and agency in love amid intense social and psychological pressures and constraints, and it belongs to a few women, chief among them Pamphilia, the good queen and heroine of constancy; Urania, the wise counselor who wins through to self-knowledge and makes wise choices in love; and Veralinda, who marries her true lover after great trials. A major means of self-definition and agency for almost all Wroth's female characters is storytelling and making poems. Women compose twice as many of the poems as men do, and Pamphilia (Wroth's surrogate) is singled out as a poet by vocation by the number and recognized excellence of her poems.

The *Urania* was widely assumed by contemporaries to be a *roman á clef*, alluding not only to Sidney-Pembroke-Wroth affairs but also at times to notable scandals and personages of the Jacobean court. A public outcry from one such target, Lord Edward Denny, elicited from Wroth a spirited and satiric response; she also made an offer to the king's minister Buckingham to withdraw the work from circulation. There is, however, no evidence that she actually did so, though the uproar may have discouraged her from publishing part II of the romance and her pastoral drama.

From The Countess of Montgomery's Urania[1]

From *The First Book*

When the spring began to appear like the welcome messenger of summer, one sweet (and in that more sweet) morning, after Aurora[2] had called all careful eyes to attend the day, forth came the fair shepherdess Urania[3] (fair indeed; yet that far too mean a title for her, who for beauty deserved the highest style[4] could be given by best-knowing judgments). Into the mead[5] she came, where usually she drove her flocks to feed, whose leaping and wantonness showed they were proud of such a guide: but she, whose sad thoughts led her to another manner of spending her time, made her soon leave them, and follow her late-begun custom; which was (while they delighted themselves) to sit under some shade, bewailing her misfortune; while they fed, to feed upon her own sorrow and tears, which at this time she began again to summon, sitting down under the shade of a well-spread beech; the ground (then blest) and the tree, with full and fine-leaved branches, growing proud to bear and shadow such perfections. But she regarding nothing, in comparison of her woe, thus proceeded in her grief: "Alas Urania," said she (the true servant to misfortune), "of any misery that can befall woman, is not this the most and greatest which thou art fallen into? Can there be any near the unhappiness of being ignorant, and that in the highest kind, not being certain of mine own estate or birth? Why was I

1. Wroth's title echoes *The Countess of Pembroke's Arcadia*, the romance written by her uncle, Sir Philip Sidney. The countess of Montgomery was Susan (Vere) Herbert, Wroth's close friend and the sister-in-law of her lover, William Herbert. The opening of *Urania* is meant to be compared to (and contrasted with) the opening of the *Arcadia* (p. 912), in which two shepherds lament the absence of their beloved, the mysterious shepherdess Urania.
2. The Greek goddess of the dawn.
3. The name has multiple associations: the Muse

of Astronomy, the Muse of Christian Poetry, a surname for Aphrodite (Venus) designating Heavenly Beauty. It was also an honorific commonly bestowed on Wroth's aunt, Mary Sidney, countess of Pembroke. In Wroth's romance, Urania is a foundling adopted by shepherds but actually the daughter of the king of Naples: after losing one lover and gaining another, she marries, becomes a matriarch, and is throughout (as in this episode) a counselor of others.
4. Title.
5. Meadow.

not still continued in the belief I was, as I appear, a shepherdess, and daughter to a shepherd? My ambition then went no higher than this estate, now flies it to a knowledge; then was I contented, now perplexed. O ignorance, can thy dullness yet procure so sharp a pain? and that such a thought as makes me now aspire unto knowledge? How did I joy in this poor life, being quiet? blest in the love of those I took for parents, but now by them I know the contrary, and by that knowledge, now to know myself. Miserable Urania, worse art thou now than these thy lambs; for they know their dams, while thou dost live unknown of any." By this were others come into that mead with their flocks: but she, esteeming her sorrowing thoughts her best and choicest company, left that place, taking a little path which brought her to the further side of the plain, to the foot of the rocks, speaking as she went these lines, her eyes fixed upon the ground, her very soul turned into mourning.

> Unseen, unknown, I here alone complain
>   To rocks, to hills, to meadows, and to springs,
> Which can no help return to ease my pain,
>   But back my sorrows the sad Echo[6] brings.
> 5 Thus still increasing are my woes to me,
>   Doubly resounded by that moanful voice,
> Which seems to second me in misery,
>   And answer gives like friend of mine own choice.
> Thus only she doth my companion prove,
> 10   The others silently do offer ease.
> But those that grieve, a grieving note do love;
>   Pleasures to dying eyes bring but disease:
> And such am I, who daily ending live,
>   Wailing a state which can no comfort give.

In this passion she went on, till she came to the foot of a great rock, she thinking of nothing less than ease, sought how she might ascend it; hoping there to pass away her time more peaceably with loneliness, though not to find least respite from her sorrow, which so dearly she did value, as by no means she would impart it to any. The way was hard, though by some windings making the ascent pleasing. Having attained the top, she saw under some hollow trees the entry into the rock: she fearing nothing but the continuance of her ignorance, went in; where she found a pretty room, as if that stony place had yet in pity, given leave for such perfections to come into the heart as chiefest, and most beloved place, because most loving. The place was not unlike the ancient (or the descriptions of ancient) Hermitages, instead of hangings, covered and lined with ivy, disdaining aught else should come there, that being in such perfection. This richness in Nature's plenty made her stay to behold it, and almost grudge the pleasant fulness of content that place might have, if sensible, while she must know to taste of torments. As she was thus in passion mixed with pain, throwing her eyes as wildly as timorous lovers do for fear of discovery, she perceived a little light, and such a one, as a chink doth oft discover to our sights. She curious to see what this was, with her delicate hands put the natural ornament aside, discerning

---

6. In classical mythology Echo was a wood nymph who pined away in unrequited love for the handsome Narcissus until only her voice remained (Ovid, *Metamorphoses* 3).

a little door, which she putting from her, passed through it into another room, like the first in all proportion; but in the midst there was a square stone, like to a pretty table, and on it a wax-candle burning; and by that a paper,[7] which had suffered itself patiently to receive the discovering of so much of it, as presented this sonnet (as it seemed newly written) to her sight.

> Here all alone in silence might I mourn:
>   But how can silence be where sorrows flow?
> Sighs with complaints have poorer pains out-worne;
>   But broken hearts can only true grief show.
> 5 Drops of my dearest blood shall let Love know
>   Such tears for her I shed, yet still do burn,
> As no spring can quench least part of my woe,
>   Till this live earth, again to earth doe turne.
> Hateful all thought of comfort is to me,
> 10   Despised day, let me still night possess;
> Let me all torments feel in their excesse,
>   And but this light allow my state to see.
> Which still doth waste, and wasting as this light,
> Are my sad days unto eternal night.

"Alas Urania!" sighed she. "How well do these words, this place, and all agree with thy fortune? Sure poor soul thou wert here appointed to spend they days, and these rooms ordained to keep thy tortures in; none being assuredly so matchlessly unfortunate."

Turning from the table, she discerned in the room a bed of boughs, and on it a man lying, deprived of outward sense, as she thought, and of life, as she at first did fear, which struck her into a great amazement: yet having a brave spirit, though shadowed under a mean habit,[8] she stepped unto him, whom she found not dead, but laid upon his back, his head a little to her wards, his arms folded on his breast, hair long, and beard disordered, manifesting all care;[9] but care itself had left him: curiousness thus far afforded him, as to be perfectly discerned the most exact piece of misery; apparel he had suitable to the habitation, which was a long gray[1] robe. This grieveful spectacle did much amaze the sweet and tender-hearted Shepherdess; especially, when she perceived (as she might by the help of the candle) the tears which distilled from his eyes; who seeming the image of death, yet had this sign of worldly sorrow, the drops falling in that abundance, as if there were a kind strife among them, to rid their Master first of that burdenous[2] carriage; or else meaning to make a flood, and so drown their woeful patient in his own sorrow, who yet lay still, but then fetching a deep groan from the profoundest part of his soul, he said:

"Miserable Perissus,[3] canst thou thus live, knowing she that gave thee life is gone? Gone, O me! and with her all my joy departed. Wilt thou (unblessed creature) lie here complaining for her death, and know she died for thee?

---

7. The episode alludes to an episode in Sidney's *Old Arcadia* (181) in which one of the heroines, Cleophila, enters a darkened cave illuminated by a single candle and finds a poem on top of a stone table.
8. Garment.

9. Trouble.
1. Gray is typically associated with mourning and despair.
2. Burdensome.
3. Perissus: Lost one.

Let truth and shame make thee do something worthy of such a love, ending thy days like thyself, and one fit to be her servant. But that I must not do: then thus remain and foster storms, still to torment thy wretched soul withall, since all are little, and too too little for such a loss. O dear Limena,[4] loving Limena, worthy Limena, and more rare, constant Limena: perfections delicately feigned to be in women were verified in thee, was such worthiness framed only to be wondered at by the best, but given as a prey to base and unworthy jealousy? When were all worthy parts joined in one, but in thee (my best Limena)? Yet all these grown subject to a creature ignorant of all but ill; like unto a Fool, who in a dark Cave, that hath but one way to get out, having a candle, but not the understanding what good it doth him, puts it out: this ignorant wretch not being able to comprehend thy virtues, did so by thee in thy murder, putting out the world's light, and men's admiration: Limena, Limena, O my Limena."

With that he fell from complaining into such a passion, as weeping and crying were never in so woeful a perfection, as now in him; which brought as deserved a compassion from the excellent Shepherdess, who already had her heart so tempered with grief, as that it was apt to take any impression that it would come to seal withall. Yet taking a brave courage to her, she stepped unto him, kneeling down by his side, and gently pulling him by the arm, she thus spoke.

"Sir," said she, "having heard some part of your sorrows, they have not only made me truly pity you, but wonder at you; since if you have lost so great a treasure, you should not lie thus leaving her and your love unrevenged, suffering her murderers to live, while you lie here complaining; and if such perfections be dead in her, why make you not the Phoenix[5] of your deeds live again, as to new life raised out of the revenge you should take on them? Then were her end satisfied, and you deservedly accounted worthy of her favor, if she were so worthy as you say."

"If she were, O God," cried out Perissus, "what devilish spirit art thou, that thus dost come to torture me? But now I see you are a woman; and therefore not much to be marked, and less resisted: but if you know charity, I pray now practice it, and leave me who am afflicted sufficiently without your company; or if you will stay, discourse not to me."

"Neither of these will I do," said she.

"If you be then," said he, "some fury of purpose sent to vex me, use your force to the uttermost in martyring me; for never was there a fitter subject, then the heart of poor Perissus is."

"I am no fury," replied the divine Urania, "nor hither come to trouble you, but by accident lighted on this place; my cruel hap being such, as only the like can give me content, while the solitariness of this like cave might give me quiet, though not ease. Seeking for such a one, I happened hither; and this is the true cause of my being here, though now I would use it to a better end if I might: Wherefore favor me with the knowledge of your grief; which heard, it may be I shall give you some counsel, and comfort in your sorrow."

4. Limena: Woman of home or threshold.

"Cursed may I be," cried he, "if ever I take comfort, having such cause of mourning: but because you are, or seem to be afflicted, I will not refuse to satisfy your demand, but tell you the saddest story that ever was rehearsed by dying man to living woman, and such a one, as I fear will fasten too much sadness in you; yet should I deny it, I were to blame, being so well known to these senseless places; as were they sensible of sorrow, they would condole, or else amazed at such cruelty stand dumb as they do, to find that man should be so inhuman."

* * *

SONG[6]

Love what art thou? A vain thought
In our minds by fant'sy wrought.
Idle smiles did thee beget,
While fond wishes made the net
5   Which so many fools have caught.

Love what art thou? Light and fair,
Fresh as morning, clear as th' air.
But too soon thy evening change
Makes thy worth with coldness range;
10   Still thy joy is mixt with care.

Love what art thou? A sweet flower
Once full blown,° dead in an hour.   *in full bloom*
Dust in wind as staid remains
As thy pleasure or our gains,
15   If thy humor° change, to lour.   *whim*

Love what art thou? Childish, vain,
Firm as bubbles made by rain,
Wantonness thy greatest pride.
These foul faults thy virtues hide—
20   But babes can no staidness gain.

Love what art thou? Causeless cursed,
Yet alas these not the worst:
Much more of thee may be said.
But thy law I once obeyed,
25   Therefore say no more at first.

1621

---

6. This song, one of a group of eclogues that marks the conclusion of book 1 of the *Urania*, is sung to a shepherdess by a shepherd, "being, as it seemed, fallen out with Love."

From Pamphilia to Amphilanthus[1]

1

When night's black mantle could most darkness prove,
    And sleep, death's image, did my senses hire
    From knowledge of myself, then thoughts did move
    Swifter than those most swiftness need require.
5   In sleep, a chariot drawn by winged desire
    I saw, where sat bright Venus, Queen of Love,
    And at her feet, her son,[2] still adding fire
    To burning hearts, which she did hold above.
    But one heart flaming more than all the rest
10   The goddess held, and put it to my breast.
    "Dear son, now shut,"[3] said she: "thus must we win."
He her obeyed, and martyred my poor heart.
    I, waking, hoped as dreams it would depart:
    Yet since, O me, a lover I have been.

16

Am I thus conquered? Have I lost the powers
    That to withstand, which joys to ruin me?[4]
    Must I be still while it my strength devours,
    And captive leads me prisoner, bound, unfree?
5   Love first shall leave men's fant'sies to them free,[5]
    Desire shall quench Love's flames, spring hate sweet showers,
    Love shall loose all his darts, have sight, and see
    His shame, and wishings hinder happy hours.
    Why should we not Love's purblind° charms resist?   *completely blind*
10   Must we be servile, doing what he list?°   *what pleases him*
No, seek some host to harbor thee: I fly
    Thy babish tricks, and freedom do profess.
    But O my hurt makes my lost heart confess
    I love, and must: So farewell liberty.

28

SONG[6]

Sweetest love, return again,
    Make not too long stay:
Killing mirth and forcing pain,

---

1. Pamphilia ("All-loving") is the protagonist of *Urania*. Her unfaithful beloved's name means "Lover of Two." These characters are first cousins, like Mary Wroth and William Herbert; their names adumbrate the main theme of both the romance and the appended sonnet sequence, constancy in the face of unfaithfulness.

    Pamphilia to Amphilanthus is broken into several separately numbered series (the first of which includes forty-eight sonnets, with songs inserted after every sixth sonnet except the last). In Josephine A. Roberts's edition of Wroth's poetry, the

poems are numbered consecutively throughout the work; we have adopted this convenient renumbering.

2. Cupid.
3. I.e., shut the burning heart into Pamphilia's breast.
4. I.e., have I lost the power to withstand love ("That"), which takes pleasure in ruining me?
5. I.e., this and the other impossibilities that follow will occur before I surrender to love.
6. The poem seems to revise one of Donne's songs: "Sweetest love, I do not go," p. 1242.

Sorrow leading way.
5 Let us not thus parted be:
Love and absence ne'r agree.

But since you must needs depart,
    And me hapless leave,
In your journey take my heart,
10   Which will not deceive.
Yours it is, to you it flies,
Joying in those lovèd eyes.

So in part we shall not part,
    Though we absent be:
15 Time, nor place, nor greatest smart
    Shall my bands make free.
Tied I am, yet think it gain:
In such knots I feel no pain.

But can I live, having lost
20   Chiefest part of me?
Heart is fled, and sight is crossed,
    These my fortunes be.
Yet dear heart go, soon return:
As good there as here to burn.

39

Take heed mine eyes, how you your looks do cast
    Lest they betray my heart's most secret thought,
    Be true unto yourselves, for nothing's bought
More dear than doubt which brings a lover's fast.[7]

5 Catch you all watching eyes, ere they be past,
    Or take yours fixed where your best love hath sought
    The pride of your desires; let them be taught
Their faults for shame, they could no truer last.

Then look, and look with joy for conquest won
10   Of those that searched your hurt in double kind;[8]
    So you kept safe, let them themselves look blind
Watch, gaze, and mark till they to madness run.

While you, mine eyes enjoy full sight of love
Contented that such happinesses move.

40

False hope which feeds but to destroy, and spill[9]
    What it first breeds; unnatural to the birth

---

7. Lack of nourishment for love, due to jealousy (doubt).
8. Those who spy and pry with their two eyes, to discover my secret love.
9. Kill. The image is of miscarriage or infanticide.

Of thine own womb; conceiving but to kill,
And plenty gives to make the greater dearth,[1]
5   So tyrants do who falsely ruling earth
Outwardly grace them,[2] and with profits fill,
Advance those who appointed are to death,
To make their greater fall to please their will.
Thus shadow° they their wicked vile intent,   conceal
10   Coloring evil with a show of good
While in fair shows their malice so is spent;[3]
Hope kills the heart, and tyrants shed the blood.
For hope deluding brings us to the pride
Of our desires the farther down to slide.

68

My pain, still smothered in my grievèd breast,
Seeks for some ease, yet cannot passage find
To be discharged of this unwelcome guest:
When most I strive, most fast his burdens bind,
5   Like to a ship on Goodwin's[4] cast by wind,
The more she strives, more deep in sand is pressed,
Till she be lost; so am I, in this kind,°   manner
Sunk, and devoured, and swallowed by unrest,
Lost, shipwracked, spoiled, debarred of smallest hope,
10   Nothing of pleasure left; save thoughts have scope,
Which wander may. Go then, my thoughts, and cry
Hope's perished, Love tempest-beaten, Joy lost:
Killing Despair hath all these blessings crossed.
Yet Faith still cries, Love will not falsify.

74

SONG

Love a child is ever crying,
Please him, and he straight is flying;
Give him, he the more is craving,
Never satisfied with having.

5   His desires have no measure,
Endless folly is his treasure;
What he promiseth he breaketh:
Trust not one word that he speaketh.

He vows nothing but false matter,
10   And to cozen you he'll flatter.

---

1. I.e., gives abundance only to make scarcity more painful afterward.
2. I.e., those whom they mean to destroy (see the next line).
3. Expended, employed. "Shows": appearances.
4. Goodwin Sands, a line of shoals at the entrance to the Strait of Dover.

Let him gain the hand,° he'll leave you,   *the upper hand*
     And still glory to deceive you.

He will triumph in your wailing,
     And yet cause be of your failing:
15   These his virtues are, and slighter
     Are his gifts, his favors lighter.

Feathers are as firm in staying,
     Wolves no fiercer in their preying.
     As a child then leave him crying,
20   Nor seek him, so given to flying.

From *A Crown of Sonnets Dedicated to Love*[5]
77

In this strange labyrinth how shall I turn?
     Ways° are on all sides, while the way I miss: *paths*
     If to the right hand, there in love I burn;
     Let me go forward, therein danger is;
5   If to the left, suspicion hinders bliss,
     Let me° turn back, Shame cries I ought return,   *if I*
     Nor faint though crosses[6] with my fortunes kiss;
     Stand still is harder, although sure to mourn.[7]
Then let me take the right- or left-hand way;
10   Go forward, or stand still, or back retire;
     I must these doubts endure without allay°   *abatement*
     Or help, but travail find for my best hire.[8]
Yet that which most my troubled sense doth move
Is to leave all, and take the thread of love.[9]

103

My muse now happy, lay thyself to rest,
     Sleep in the quiet of a faithful love,
     Write you no more, but let these fancies move
     Some other hearts, wake not to new unrest.

5   But if you study, be those thoughts addressed
     To truth, which shall eternal goodness prove;
     Enjoying of true joy, the most, and best,
     The endless gain which never will remove.

5. The "crown" is a difficult poetic form (originally Italian and usually known by its Italian name, *corona*) in which the last line of each poem serves as the first line of the next, until a circle is completed by the last line of the final poem, which is the same as the first line of the first one. The number of poems varies from seven to (as in Wroth's *corona*) fourteen.
In contrast to the errant-child Cupid of the preceding part of the sequence, Love in this series is a mature and just monarch, whose true service ennobles lovers. The crown is in part a recantation of the harsh judgment of love earlier in the sequence. But Pamphilia relapses into melancholy afterward.
6. Troubles, adversity. "Faint": lose heart.
7. I.e., certain to make me mourn.
8. I.e., I find travail (with a pun on "travel," the spelling in the 1621 edition) is my only reward.
9. Ariadne gave Theseus a thread to follow so as to find his way out of the Labyrinth, after killing the Minotaur at its center.

Leave the discourse of Venus, and her son
10   To young beginners,[1] and their brains inspire
With stories of great love, and from that fire
Get heat to write the fortunes they have won.

And thus leave off, what's past shows you can love,
Now let your constancy your honor prove.[2]

1621

1. In Neoplatonic love philosophy,"beginners" in
love are attracted to physical beauty and sensory
delights, while more advanced lovers love virtue
and spiritual beauty. Writing love sonnets is traditionally the business of young lovers.

2. In a symbolic episode in the *Urania*, Pamphilia
embodies the virtue of Constancy; she accepts the
keys to the Throne of Love, "at which instant *Constancy* vanished as metamorphosing herself into
her breast" (1.1.141).

JOHN WEBSTER
1580?–1625?

John Webster's fame rests on two remarkable tragedies, both set in Roman Catholic
Italy and both evoking the common Jacobean stereotype of that land as a place of
sophisticated and morbid corruption, sumptuous and evil. Both have at their center
bold and brave heroines who choose for themselves in love and refuse to submit to
male patriarchs. In *The White Devil* (1608/12), based on events that took place in
Italy in 1581–85, Vittoria Corombona boldly defies a courtroom full of corrupt magistrates who convict her of adultery and murder. In *The Duchess of Malfi* (1614/23),
based on an Italian *novella*, the spirited and noble ruler of Malfi marries her steward
Antonio secretly, for love, defying the commands of her brothers, a duke and a cardinal, that she remain a widow. Their dark motives include greed for her fortune,
overweening pride in their noble blood, and incestuous desire. The play weds sublime
poetry and lurid gothic horror in the devious machinations set in motion against the
duchess by her brothers' melancholy spy Bosola, in the macabre mental and physical
torments to which they subject her, in the desperate lunatic ravings of the duke after
having her strangled, and in the final scenes in which the stage is littered with the
slaughtered bodies of all the principal characters, as well as the small children of the
duchess and Antonio. Webster's portrayal of the independent spirit and courage of
the duchess invites comparison with the royal heroine of Elizabeth Cary's tragedy
Mariam, written at about the same date.

Webster was the son of a London tailor and a member of the Merchant Taylors'
Company, but we know little else about him. He wrote a tragicomedy, *The Devil's
Law Case* (1621), and collaborated on several plays with contemporary playwrights,
among them Thomas Dekker in *Westward Hoe* (1607) and John Marston in *The
Malcontent* (1604). Of all the Stuart dramatists, Webster is the one who comes
closest to Shakespeare in his power of tragic utterance and his flashes of poetic
brilliance.

The Duchess of Malfi

DRAMATIS PERSONAE

FERDINAND, *Duke of Calabria*
THE CARDINAL, *his brother*
ANTONIO BOLOGNA, *steward of
the household to the* DUCHESS
DELIO, *his friend*
DANIEL DE BOSOLA, *gentleman
of the horse to the* DUCHESS
CASTRUCCIO, *an old Lord*
MARQUIS OF PESCARA
COUNT MALATESTE
SILVIO, *a Lord, of Milan*
RODERIGO } *gentlemen attending*
GRISOLAN } *on the* DUCHESS

DOCTOR
Several MADMEN, PILGRIMS,
EXECUTIONERS, OFFICERS,
ATTENDANTS &c.
THE DUCHESS OF MALFI, *sister
of* FERDINAND *and the*
CARDINAL
CARIOLA, *her woman*
JULIA, CASTRUCCIO'*s wife, and
the* CARDINAL'*s mistress*
OLD LADY, LADIES, *and*
CHILDREN

SCENE. *Amalfi, Rome, Loreto, and Milan*

Act 1

SCENE 1. *Amalfi; a hall in the* DUCHESS' *palace.*

[*Enter* ANTONIO *and* DELIO.]

DELIO   You are welcome to your country, dear Antonio;
   You have been long in France, and you return
   A very formal Frenchman in your habit.[1]
   How do you like the French court?
ANTONIO   I admire it:
5   In seeking to reduce both state and people
   To a fixed order, their judicious king
   Begins at home; quits° first his royal palace   *rids*
   Of flattering sycophants, of dissolute
   And infamous persons—which he sweetly terms
10   His Master's masterpiece, the work of heaven[2]—
   Considering duly that a prince's court
   Is like a common fountain, whence should flow
   Pure silver drops in general, but if 't chance
   Some cursed example poison 't near the head,
15   Death and diseases through the whole land spread.
   And what is 't makes this blessed government
   But a most provident council; who dare freely
   Inform him the corruption of the times.
   Though some o' th' court hold it presumption
20   To instruct princes what they ought to do,
   It is a noble duty to inform them
   What they ought to foresee.—Here comes Bosola,

---

1. An absolute Frenchman in your dress.   2. Alludes to Christ ridding the temple of moneychangers.

The only court-gall;[3] yet I observe his railing
Is not for simple love of piety.
25   Indeed, he rails at those things which he wants;
Would be as lecherous, covetous, or proud,
Bloody, or envious, as any man,
If he had means to be so. Here's the Cardinal.
    [*Enter the* CARDINAL *and* BOSOLA.]
BOSOLA   I do haunt you still.
30 CARDINAL   So.
BOSOLA   I have done you better service than to be slighted thus. Miserable
age, where the only reward of doing well is the doing of it!
CARDINAL   You enforce your merit too much.
BOSOLA   I fell into the galleys[4] in your service; where, for two years
35 together, I wore two towels instead of a shirt, with a knot on the shoulder, after the fashion of a Roman mantle. Slighted thus? I will thrive
some way. Blackbirds fatten best in hard weather; why not I in these dog
days?[5]
CARDINAL   Would you could become honest!
BOSOLA   With all your divinity do but direct me the way to it. I have known
40 many travel far for it, and yet return as arrant knaves as they went forth,
because they carried themselves always along with them. [*Exit* CARDI-
NAL.] Are you gone? Some fellows, they say, are possessed with the devil,
but this great fellow were able to possess the greatest devil, and make
him worse.
45 ANTONIO   He hath denied thee some suit?
BOSOLA   He and his brother are like plum trees that grow crooked over
standing pools;[6] they are rich and o'erladen with fruit, but none but
crows, pies,[7] and caterpillars feed on them. Could I be one of their flattering panders, I would hang on their ears like a horseleech till I were
50 full and then drop off. I pray, leave me. Who would rely upon these
miserable dependencies, in expectation to be advanced tomorrow? What
creature ever fed worse than hoping Tantalus?[8] Nor ever died any man
more fearfully than he that hoped for a pardon. There are rewards for
hawks and dogs when they have done us service; but for a soldier that
55 hazards his limbs in a battle, nothing but a kind of geometry is his last
supportation.[9]
DELIO   Geometry?
BOSOLA   Aye, to hang in a fair pair of slings, take his latter swing in the
world upon an honorable pair of crutches, from hospital to hospital. Fare
60 ye well, sir: and yet do not you scorn us; for places in the court are but
like beds in the hospital, where this man's head lies at that man's foot,
and so lower and lower.   [*Exit.*]
DELIO   I knew this fellow seven years[1] in the galleys

---

3. One who frets the court, but with the overtone
of a disease, a blight.
4. Service at the oar of a Mediterranean galley was
the last penalty this side of torture and execution,
and was likely to be a death sentence.
5. The hot, sultry season of midsummer.
6. Stagnant waters.
7. Magpies, birds of evil omen like blackbirds.

8. Tantalus, in classical mythology, was "tantalized" by the constant presence of delectable food
and drink that, though desperate, he could never
reach.
9. Support.
1. In speaking to the cardinal himself (line 34),
Bosola had mentioned only two years.

For a notorious murder; and 'twas thought
65 The Cardinal suborned it. He was released
By the French general, Gaston de Foix,
When he recovered Naples.²
ANTONIO   'Tis great pity
He should be thus neglected; I have heard
He's very valiant. This foul melancholy
70 Will poison all his goodness; for, I'll tell you,
If too immoderate sleep be truly said
To be an inward rust unto the soul,
It then doth follow want of action
Breeds all black malcontents; and their close rearing,
75 Like moths in cloth, do hurt for want of wearing.³

SCENE 2

[*Enter* CASTRUCCIO, SILVIO, RODERIGO, *and* GRISOLAN.]
DELIO   The presence° 'gins to fill: you promised me   *audience hall*
To make me the partaker of the natures
Of some of your great courtiers.
ANTONIO   The Lord Cardinal's,
And other strangers' that are now in court?
5   I shall. Here comes the great Calabrian duke.
[*Enter* FERDINAND *and* ATTENDANTS.]
FERDINAND   Who took the ring oftenest?⁴
SILVIO   Antonio Bologna, my lord.
FERDINAND   Our sister duchess' great-master of her household? Give him
the jewel. When shall we leave this sportive action, and fall to action
10 indeed?
CASTRUCCIO   Methinks, my lord, you should not desire to go to war in
person.
FERDINAND   Now for some gravity. Why, my lord?
CASTRUCCIO   It is fitting a soldier arise to be a prince, but not necessary
15 a prince descend to be a captain.
FERDINAND   No?
CASTRUCCIO   No, my lord, he were far better do it by a deputy.
FERDINAND   Why should he not as well sleep or eat by a deputy? This
might take idle, offensive, and base office from him, whereas the other
20 deprives him of honor.
CASTRUCCIO   Believe my experience, that realm is never long in quiet
where the ruler is a soldier.
FERDINAND   Thou told'st me thy wife could not endure fighting.
CASTRUCCIO   True, my lord.
25 FERDINAND   And of a jest she broke of a captain she met full of wounds.
I have forgot it.

2. Gaston de Foix, French commander, was active in Italy during the early 1500s; hence, the time of the tragedy is about a hundred years before Webster wrote. Ferdinand and the cardinal are Spaniards established in Italy, like the infamous house of Borgia.
3. I.e., malcontents, being unemployed, suffer from psychic moths, like clothes not worn for a long time.
4. A common game around court, used in training for tournaments, involved catching a hanging ring on the tip of a lance. But some of Webster's audience would have caught a sexual analogy.

CASTRUCCIO   She told him, my lord, he was a pitiful fellow, to lie, like the
children of Israel, all in tents.[5]

FERDINAND   Why, there's a wit were able to undo all the chirurgeons[6] o'
30   the city; for although gallants should quarrel and had drawn their weapons and were ready to go to it, yet her persuasions would make them put
up.

CASTRUCCIO   That she would, my lord.

FERDINAND   How do you like my Spanish gennet?[7]

35   RODERIGO   He is all fire.

FERDINAND   I am of Pliny's opinion, I think he was begot by the wind; he
runs as if he were ballassed[8] with quicksilver.

SILVIO   True, my lord, he reels from the tilt often.[9]

RODERIGO and GRISOLAN   Ha, ha, ha!

40   FERDINAND   Why do you laugh? Methinks, you that are courtiers should
be my touchwood, take fire when I give fire; that is, laugh but when I
laugh, were the subject never so witty.

CASTRUCCIO   True, my lord, I myself have heard a very good jest, and have
scorned to seem to have so silly a wit as to understand it.

45   FERDINAND   But I can laugh at your fool, my lord.

CASTRUCCIO   He cannot speak, you know, but he makes faces: my lady
cannot abide him.

FERDINAND   No?

CASTRUCCIO   Nor endure to be in merry company, for she says too much
50   laughing and too much company fills her too full of the wrinkle.

FERDINAND   I would, then, have a mathematical instrument made for her
face, that she might not laugh out of compass.[1] I shall shortly visit you
at Milan, Lord Silvio.

SILVIO   Your grace shall arrive most welcome.

55   FERDINAND   You are a good horseman, Antonio. You have excellent riders
in France. What do you think of good horsemanship?

ANTONIO   Nobly, my lord: as out of the Grecian horse issued many famous
princes,[2] so out of brave horsemanship arise the first sparks of growing
resolution that raise the mind to noble action.

60   FERDINAND   You have bespoke it worthily.

SILVIO   Your brother, the Lord Cardinal, and sister duchess.
    [Re-enter CARDINAL, with DUCHESS, CARIOLA, and JULIA.]

CARDINAL   Are the galleys come about?

GRISOLAN   They are, my lord.

FERDINAND   Here's the Lord Silvio, is come to take his leave.

DELIO   Now, sir, your promise. What's that Cardinal?

65   I mean his temper? They say he's a brave fellow,
Will play[3] his five thousand crowns at tennis, dance,
Court ladies, and one that hath fought single combats.

ANTONIO   Some such flashes superficially hang on him for form; but

---

5. Lint bandages were called "tents."
6. Surgeons.
7. Sometimes "jennet": a small Spanish horse of
Arabian stock.
8. Ballasted. Pliny in his *Natural History* tells
about some Spanish horses generated by a swift
wind (8.67).

9. Recoiling from the shock of a charge.
1. Excessively; with a pun on the draftsman's compass.
2. The Trojan horse, in which the Greek warriors
hid, to overrun Troy.
3. Wager.

observe his inward character: he is a melancholy churchman; the spring
in his face is nothing but the engendering of toads; where he is jealous
of any man, he lays worse plots for them than ever was imposed on
Hercules, for he strews in his way flatterers, panders, intelligencers,[4]
atheists, and a thousand such political monsters. He should have been
Pope; but instead of coming to it by the primitive decency of the Church,
he did bestow bribes so largely and so impudently as if he would have
carried it away without heaven's knowledge. Some good he hath done—
DELIO   You have given too much of him. What's his brother?
ANTONIO   The duke there? A most perverse and turbulent nature.
What appears in him mirth is merely outside;
If he laugh heartily, it is to laugh
All honesty out of fashion.
DELIO   Twins?
ANTONIO   In quality.
He speaks with others' tongues, and hears men's suits
With others' ears; will seem to sleep o' th' bench
Only to entrap offenders in their answers;
Dooms men to death by information;°   *testimony of spies*
Rewards by hearsay.°   *random report*
DELIO   Then the law to him
Is like a foul black cobweb to a spider:
He makes of it his dwelling and a prison
To entangle those shall feed him.
ANTONIO   Most true:
He ne'er pays debts unless they be shrewd turns,°   *hurtful acts*
And those he will confess that he doth owe.
Last, for his brother there, the Cardinal,
They that do flatter him most say oracles
Hang at his lips; and verily I believe them,
For the devil speaks in them.
But for their sister, the right noble duchess,
You never fixed your eye on three fair medals
Cast in one figure, of so different temper.
For her discourse, it is so full of rapture,
You only will begin then to be sorry
When she doth end her speech, and wish, in wonder,
She held it less vainglory to talk much,
Than your penance to hear her: whilst she speaks,
She throws upon a man so sweet a look,
That it were able to raise one to a galliard°   *gay and lively dance*
That lay in a dead palsy, and to dote
On that sweet countenance; but in that look
There speaketh so divine a continence
As cuts off all lascivious and vain hope.
Her days are practiced in such noble virtue
That sure her nights, nay, more, her very sleeps,
Are more in heaven than other ladies' shrifts.°   *confessions*

4. Spies.

Let all sweet ladies break their flattering glasses,
And dress themselves in her.

DELIO   Fie, Antonio,
115   You play the wire-drawer⁵ with her commendations.
ANTONIO   I'll case° the picture up only thus much;   *frame*
All her particular worth grows to this sum:
She stains° the time past, lights the time to come.   *darkens*
CARDINAL   You must attend my lady in the gallery,
Some half an hour hence.
120   ANTONIO   I shall.   [*Exeunt* ANTONIO *and* DELIO.]
FERDINAND   Sister, I have a suit to you.
DUCHESS   To me, sir?
FERDINAND   A gentleman here, Daniel de Bosola,
One that was in the galleys—
DUCHESS   Yes, I know him.
FERDINAND   A worthy fellow he is. Pray, let me entreat for
The provisorship of your horse.
125   DUCHESS   Your knowledge of him
Commends him and prefers him.
FERDINAND   Call him hither.   [*Exit* ATTENDANT.]
We are now upon° parting. Good Lord Silvio,   *at the point of*
Do us commend to all our noble friends
At the leaguer.°   *camp*
SILVIO   Sir, I shall.
DUCHESS   You are for Milan?
SILVIO   I am.
130   DUCHESS   Bring the caroches. We'll bring you down to the haven.⁶
                  [*Exeunt all but* FERDINAND *and the* CARDINAL.]
CARDINAL   Be sure you entertain° that Bosola   *hire*
For your intelligence:° I would not be seen in 't;   *spy*
And therefore many times I have slighted him
When he did court our furtherance, as this morning.
135   FERDINAND   Antonio, the great-master of her household,
Had been far fitter.
CARDINAL   You are deceived in him:
His nature is too honest for such business.
He comes: I'll leave you.   [*Exit.*]
       [*Re-enter* BOSOLA.]
BOSOLA   I was lured to you.
FERDINAND   My brother here the Cardinal could never
Abide you.
140   BOSOLA   Never since he was in my debt.
FERDINAND   Maybe some oblique character in your face
Made him suspect you.
BOSOLA   Doth he study physiognomy?
There's no more credit to be given to th' face
Than to a sick man's urine, which some call
145   The physician's whore, because she cozens° him.   *tricks*

5. Draw out her praises excessively.   6. Harbor. "Caroches": carriages.

He did suspect me wrongfully.
FERDINAND   For that
You must give great men leave to take their times.
Distrust doth cause us seldom be deceived:
You see, the oft shaking of the cedar tree
Fastens it more at root.
150 BOSOLA   Yet, take heed;
For to suspect a friend unworthily
Instructs him the next way to suspect you,
And prompts him to deceive you.
FERDINAND [*giving him money*]   There's gold.
BOSOLA   So:
What follows? Never rained such showers as these
155 Without thunderbolts i' th' tail of them.
Whose throat must I cut?
FERDINAND   Your inclination to shed blood rides post
Before my occasion to use you. I give you that
To live i' th' court here, and observe the duchess;
160 To note all the particulars of her 'havior,
What suitors do solicit her for marriage,
And whom she best affects. She's a young widow:
I would not have her marry again.
BOSOLA   No, sir?
FERDINAND   Do not you ask the reason, but be satisfied
I say I would not.
165 BOSOLA   It seems you would create me
One of your familiars.°   diabolic spirits
FERDINAND   Familiar? What's that?
BOSOLA   Why, a very quaint invisible devil in flesh,
An intelligencer.°   spy
FERDINAND   Such a kind of thriving thing
I would wish thee, and ere long thou may'st arrive
At a higher place by 't.
170 BOSOLA   Take your devils,
Which hell calls angels;[7] these cursed gifts would make
You a corrupter, me an impudent traitor;
And should I take these, they'd take me to hell.
FERDINAND   Sir, I'll take nothing from you that I have given:
175 There is a place that I procured for you
This morning, the provisorship o' th' horse;
Have you heard on 't?
BOSOLA   No.
FERDINAND   'Tis yours. Is 't not worth thanks?
BOSOLA   I would have you curse yourself now, that your bounty,
Which makes men truly noble, e'er should make me
180 A villain. Oh, that to avoid ingratitude
For the good deed you have done me, I must do
All the ill man can invent! Thus the devil

---

7. Gold coins, marked with the image of the archangel Michael.

Candies all sins o'er; and what heaven terms vile,
That names he complimental.°   *gracious*

FERDINAND   Be yourself;
185   Keep your old garb of melancholy; 'twill express
You envy those that stand above your reach,
Yet strive not to come near 'em: this will gain
Access to private lodgings, where yourself
May, like a politic dormouse—

BOSOLA   As I have seen some
190   Feed in a lord's dish, half asleep, not seeming
To listen to any talk; and yet these rogues
Have cut his throat in a dream. What's my place?
The provisorship o' th' horse? Say, then, my corruption
Grew out of horse-dung. I am your creature.

FERDINAND   Away!
195   BOSOLA   Let good men, for good deeds, covet good fame,
Since place and riches oft are bribes of shame:
Sometimes the devil doth preach.   [*Exit.*]

SCENE 3

[*Enter* DUCHESS, CARDINAL, *and* CARIOLA.]

CARDINAL   We are to part from you, and your own discretion
Must now be your director.

FERDINAND   You are a widow:
You know already what man is; and therefore
Let not youth, high promotion, eloquence—

5   CARDINAL   No, nor any thing without the addition, honor,
Sway your high blood.

FERDINAND   Marry! They are most luxurious°   *lecherous*
Will wed twice.

CARDINAL   Oh, fie!

FERDINAND   Their livers are more spotted
Than Laban's sheep.[8]

DUCHESS   Diamonds are of most value,
They say, that have passed through most jewelers' hands.

FERDINAND   Whores by that rule are precious.

10   DUCHESS   Will you hear me?
I'll never marry.

CARDINAL   So most widows say;
But commonly that motion° lasts no longer   *impulse*
Than the turning of an hourglass; the funeral sermon
And it end both together.

FERDINAND   Now hear me:
15   You live in a rank pasture, here, i' th' court;
There is a kind of honey-dew[9] that's deadly;
'Twill poison your fame° look to 't; be not cunning;   *reputation*

8. Dividing his flock with Jacob, Laban took the
speckled sheep (Genesis 30.31–33); the liver as
seat of the passions was thought to be diseased
when discolored.
9. A sweet, sticky substance left on plants by
aphids.

For they whose faces do belie their hearts
Are witches ere they arrive at twenty years,
Aye, and give the devil suck.

20 DUCHESS   This is terrible good counsel.

FERDINAND   Hypocrisy is woven of a fine small thread,
Subtler than Vulcan's engine:[1] yet, believe 't,
Your darkest actions, nay, your privatest thoughts,
Will come to light.

CARDINAL   You may flatter yourself,

25 And take your own choice; privately be married
Under the eaves of night—

FERDINAND   Think 't the best voyage
That e'er you made; like the irregular crab,
Which, though 't goes backward, thinks that it goes right
Because it goes its own way; but observe,

30 Such weddings may more properly be said
To be executed than celebrated.

CARDINAL   The marriage night
Is the entrance into some prison.

FERDINAND   And those joys,
Those lustful pleasures, are like heavy sleeps
Which do forerun man's mischief.

CARDINAL   Fare you well.

35 Wisdom begins at the end: remember it.   *[Exit.]*

DUCHESS   I think this speech between you both was studied,
It came so roundly off.

FERDINAND   You are my sister;
This was my father's poniard,° do you see?   *dagger*
I'd be loth to see 't look rusty, 'cause 'twas his.

40 I would have you to give o'er these chargeable° revels: *expensive*
A visor[2] and a mask are whispering-rooms
That were ne'er built for goodness—fare ye well—
And women like that part which, like the lamprey,[3]
Hath never a bone in 't.

DUCHESS   Fie, sir!

FERDINAND   Nay,

45 I mean the tongue; variety of courtship.
What cannot a neat knave with a smooth tale
Make a woman believe? Farewell, lusty widow.   *[Exit.]*

DUCHESS   Shall this move me? If all my royal kindred
Lay in my way unto this marriage,

50 I'd make them my low footsteps; and even now,
Even in this hate, as men in some great battles,
By apprehending danger, have achieved
Almost impossible actions (I have heard soldiers say so),
So I through frights and threatenings will assay

55 This dangerous venture. Let old wives report

---

1. The net in which Vulcan, Venus's husband, caught her misbehaving with Mars.
2. A half-mask, worn by ladies at carnivals, thea-
ters, and other dubious resorts.
3. Lamprey eels (which are vertebrates) have a cartilaginous, not a bony, skeleton.

I winked and chose a husband. Cariola,
To thy known secrecy I have given up
More than my life—my fame.
CARIOLA   Both shall be safe,
For I'll conceal this secret from the world
60   As warily as those that trade in poison
Keep poison from their children.
DUCHESS   Thy protestation
Is ingenious° and hearty:° I believe it.   *ingenuous / sincere*
Is Antonio come?
CARIOLA   He attends you.
DUCHESS   Good dear soul,
Leave me, but place thyself behind the arras,⁴
65   Where thou mayst overhear us. Wish me good speed,
For I am going into a wilderness
Where I shall find nor path nor friendly clue
To be my guide.   [CARIOLA *goes behind the arras.*]
        [*Enter* ANTONIO]
                    I sent for you: sit down;
Take pen and ink, and write. Are you ready?
ANTONIO   Yes.
DUCHESS   What did I say?
70   ANTONIO   That I should write somewhat.
DUCHESS   Oh, I remember:
After these triumphs and this large expense,
It's fit, like thrifty husbands,⁵ we inquire
What's laid up for tomorrow.
ANTONIO   So please your beauteous excellence.
75   DUCHESS   Beauteous?
Indeed, I thank you: I look young for your sake;
You have ta'en my cares upon you.
ANTONIO   I'll fetch your grace
The particulars of your revenue and expense.
DUCHESS   Oh, you are an upright treasurer: but you mistook;
80   For when I said I meant to make inquiry
What's laid up for tomorrow, I did mean
What's laid up yonder for me.
ANTONIO   Where?
DUCHESS   In heaven.
I am making my will (as 'tis fit princes should,
In perfect memory), and I pray sir, tell me,
85   Were not one better make it smiling thus
Than in deep groans and terrible ghastly looks,
As if the gifts we parted with procured°   *brought on*
That violent distraction?
ANTONIO   O, much better.
DUCHESS   If I had a husband now, this care were quit:

---

4. Tapestries were often hung in Renaissance palaces to moderate the chill of the bare walls.
5. Though used here in its original sense of one
who preserves and safeguards property, the word
shows where the duchess's thoughts are tending.

90 But I intend to make you overseer.
    What good deed shall we first remember? Say.
ANTONIO   Begin with that first good deed begun i' th' world
    After man's creation, the sacrament of marriage:
    I'd have you first provide for a good husband;
    Give him all.
DUCHESS   All?
95 ANTONIO   Yes, your excellent self.
DUCHESS   In a winding-sheet?
ANTONIO   In a couple.
DUCHESS   Saint Winfred, that were a strange will!⁶
ANTONIO   'Twere stranger if there were no will in you
    To marry again.
DUCHESS   What do you think of marriage?
100 ANTONIO   I take 't, as those that deny purgatory;
    It locally° contains or heaven or hell;   *within itself*
    There's no third place in 't.
DUCHESS   How do you affect it?⁷
ANTONIO   My banishment, feeding my melancholy,
    Would often reason thus—
DUCHESS   Pray, let's hear it.
105 ANTONIO   Say a man never marry, nor have children,
    What takes that from him? Only the bare name
    Of being a father, or the weak delight
    To see the little wanton ride a-cock-horse
    Upon a painted stick, or hear him chatter
    Like a taught starling.
110 DUCHESS   Fie, fie, what's all this?
    One of your eyes is bloodshot; use my ring to 't,
    They say 'tis very sovereign.⁸ 'Twas my wedding-ring,
    And I did vow never to part with it
    But to my second husband.
ANTONIO   You have parted with it now.
DUCHESS   Yes, to help your eyesight.
ANTONIO   You have made me stark blind.
115 DUCHESS   How?
ANTONIO   There is a saucy and ambitious devil
    Is dancing in this circle.⁹
DUCHESS   Remove him.
ANTONIO   How?
DUCHESS   There needs small conjuration, when your finger
    May do it: thus; is it fit?   [*She puts the ring upon his finger; he kneels.*]
ANTONIO   What said you?
DUCHESS   Sir,
120 This goodly roof of yours¹ is too low built;
    I cannot stand upright in 't nor discourse,

6. Saint Winifred, Welsh virgin and martyr, is an odd saint for the duchess of Malfi to swear on. "In a couple": i.e., of sheets—but with a play on "coupling."
7. Feel about it.
8. Healing, but with an overtone implying royal power.
9. To conjure up a devil, the necromancer first draws a charmed circle on the ground—like the duchess's ring.
1. His head as he kneels.

Without I raise it higher: raise yourself;
Or, if you please, my hand to help you: so.   [*Raises him.*]
ANTONIO   Ambition, madam, is a great man's madness,
125   That is not kept in chains and close-pent rooms,
          But in fair lightsome lodgings, and is girt
          With the wild noise of prattling visitants,
          Which makes it lunatic beyond all cure.
          Conceive not I am so stupid but I aim
130   Whereto your favors tend; but he's a fool
          That, being a-cold, would thrust his hands i' th' fire
          To warm them.
DUCHESS   So, now the ground's broke,
          You may discover what a wealthy mine
          I make you lord of.
ANTONIO   O my unworthiness!
135   DUCHESS   You were ill to sell yourself:
          This darkening of your worth is not like that
          Which tradesmen use i' th' city; their false lights
          Are to rid bad wares off:[2] and I must tell you,
          If you will know where breathes a complete man
140   (I speak it without flattery), turn your eyes,
          And progress through yourself.
ANTONIO   Were there nor heaven
          Nor hell, I should be honest: I have long served virtue,
          And ne'er ta'en wages of her.
DUCHESS   Now she pays it.
          The misery of us that are born great!
145   We are forced to woo, because none dare woo us;
          And as a tyrant doubles° with his words   *speaks ambiguously*
          And fearfully equivocates, so we
          Are forced to express our violent passions
          In riddles and in dreams, and leave the path
150   Of simple virtue, which was never made
          To seem the thing it is not. Go, go brag
          You have left me heartless;° mine is in your bosom: *without a heart*
          I hope 'twill multiply love there. You do tremble:
          Make not your heart so dead a piece of flesh,
155   To fear more than to love me. Sir, be confident:
          What is 't distracts you? This is flesh and blood, sir;
          'Tis not the figure cut in alabaster
          Kneels at my husband's tomb. Awake, awake, man!
          I do here put off all vain ceremony,
160   And only do appear to you a young widow
          That claims you for her husband, and, like a widow,
          I use but half a blush in 't.
ANTONIO   Truth speak for me,
          I will remain the constant sanctuary
          Of your good name.
DUCHESS   I thank you, gentle love:

---

2. Tradesmen in the city display their goods in a poor light so the defects won't be seen.

165 And 'cause° you shall not come to me in debt,   *so that*
    Being now my steward, here upon your lips
    I sign your *Quietus est.*[3] This you should have begged now;
    I have seen children oft eat sweetmeats thus,
    As fearful to devour them too soon.
ANTONIO   But for your brothers?
170 DUCHESS   Do not think of them.
    All discord without this circumference[4]
    Is only to be pitied, and not feared;
    Yet, should they know it, time will easily
    Scatter the tempest.
ANTONIO   These words should be mine,
175 And all the parts you have spoke, if some part of it
    Would not have savored flattery.
DUCHESS   Kneel.

                  [CARIOLA *comes from behind the arras.*]
ANTONIO   Ha!
DUCHESS   Be not amazed; this woman's of my counsel:
    I have heard lawyers say, a contract in a chamber
    Per verba de presenti[5] is absolute marriage.   [*She and* ANTONIO *kneel.*]
180 Bless, heaven, this sacred gordian,° which let violence   *knot*
    Never untwine!
ANTONIO   And may our sweet affections, like the spheres,
    Be still° in motion!   *constantly*
DUCHESS   Quickening,° and make   *giving life*
    The like soft music![6]
185 ANTONIO   That we may imitate the loving palms,
    Best emblem of a peaceful marriage, that ne'er
    Bore fruit, divided!
DUCHESS   What can the Church force more?
ANTONIO   That fortune may not know an accident,
    Either of joy or sorrow, to divide
    Our fixèd wishes!
190 DUCHESS   How can the Church bind faster?°   *tighter*
    We now are man and wife, and 'tis the Church
    That must but echo this. Maid, stand apart:[7]
    I now am blind.
ANTONIO   What's your conceit° in this?   *idea*
DUCHESS   I would have you lead your fortune by the hand
195 Unto your marriage bed
    (You speak in me this, for we now are one);
    We'll only lie, and talk together, and plot
    To appease my humorous° kindred; and if you please,   *choleric*
    Like the old tale in *Alexander and Lodowick,*
200 Lay a naked sword between us, keep us chaste.[8]

---

3. The legal formula for marking a bill "paid" or "acquitted."
4. Outside this room.
5. "By words concerning the present (fact)." In canon law, the duchess is right; the agreement of two parties to consider themselves married is a valid contract with or without priest, ceremony, or

witness.
6. Like the supposed music of the spheres.
7. The phrase is addressed to Cariola as the duchess shuts her eyes and rejects all support.
8. Alexander and Lodowick were look-alike friends in an old ballad. For purely virtuous reasons, one slept with the wife of the other, but with

Oh, let me shroud my blushes in your bosom,
Since 'tis the treasury of all my secrets! [*Exeunt* DUCHESS *and* ANTONIO.]
CARIOLA   Whether the spirit of greatness or of woman
    Reign most in her, I know not; but it shows
205   A fearful madness: I owe her much of pity.   [*Exit.*]

Act 2

SCENE 1

[*Enter* BOSOLA *and* CASTRUCCIO.]
BOSOLA   You say you would fain be taken for an eminent courtier?
CASTRUCCIO   'Tis the very main of my ambition.
BOSOLA   Let me see: you have a reasonable good face for 't already, and
    your nightcap expresses your ears sufficient largely. I would have you
5   learn to twirl the strings of your band[1] with a good grace, and in a set
    speech, at th' end of every sentence, to hum three or four times, or blow
    your nose till it smart again, to recover your memory. When you come
    to be a president[2] in criminal causes, if you smile upon a prisoner, hang
    him, but if you frown upon him and threaten him, let him be sure to
10   'scape the gallows.
CASTRUCCIO   I would be a very merry president.
BOSOLA   Do not sup o' nights; 'twill beget you an admirable wit.
CASTRUCCIO   Rather it would make me have a good stomach[3] to quarrel;
    for they say, your roaring boys[4] eat meat seldom, and that makes them
15   so valiant. But how shall I know whether the people take me for an
    eminent fellow?
BOSOLA   I will teach a trick to know it: give out you lie a-dying, and if you
    hear the common people curse you, be sure you are taken for one of the
    prime nightcaps.[5]
    [*Enter an* OLD LADY.]
20   You come from painting now?
OLD LADY   From what?
BOSOLA   Why, from your scurvy face-physic. To behold thee not painted
    inclines somewhat near a miracle; these in thy face here were deep ruts
    and foul sloughs the last progress.[6] There was a lady in France that,
25   having had the smallpox, flayed the skin off her face to make it more
    level; and whereas before she looked like a nutmeg grater, after she
    resembled an abortive hedgehog.
OLD LADY   Do you call this painting?
BOSOLA   No, no, but you call it careening of an old morphewed lady, to
30   make her disembogue again: there's rough-cast phrase to your plastic.[7]
OLD LADY   It seems you are well acquainted with my closet.

---

the precaution indicated.
1. The elaborate ruff of the day had strings attached to it.
2. Presiding magistrate.
3. Disposition.
4. London town bullies.
5. Lawyers (who wore a white coif or skullcap; cf.

line 4, above).
6. A progress was a formal royal journey of state.
7. Scraping ("careening") of an old, scaly ("morphewed") ship ("lady") to fit her for the ocean ("making her disembogue") again. All these metaphors are language cast in rough bronze on the clay model ("plastic") of the lady's condition.

BOSOLA One would suspect it for a shop of witchcraft, to find in it the fat
of serpents, spawn of snakes, Jews' spittle, and their young children's
ordure; and all these for the face. I would sooner eat a dead pigeon taken
from the soles of the feet of one sick of the plague than kiss one of you
fasting.[8] Here are two of you, whose sin of your youth is the very patrimony of the physician; makes him renew his footcloth with the spring,
and change his high-prized courtesan with the fall of the leaf.[9] I do wonder you do not loathe yourselves. Observe my meditation now:

What thing is in this outward form of man
To be beloved? We account it ominous,
If nature do produce a colt, or lamb,
A fawn, or goat, in any limb resembling
A man, and fly from 't as a prodigy:
Man stands amazed to see his deformity
In any other creature but himself.
But in our own flesh, though we bear diseases
Which have their true names only ta'en from beasts—
As the most ulcerous wolf and swinish measle[1]—
Though we are eaten up of lice and worms,
And though continually we bear about us
A rotten and dead body, we delight
To hide it in rich tissue: all our fear,
Nay, all our terror, is lest our physician
Should put us in the ground to be made sweet—
Your wife's gone to Rome: you two couple, and get you
To the wells at Lucca to recover your aches.[2]

[*Exeunt* CASTRUCCIO *and* OLD LADY.]

I have other work on foot. I observe our duchess
Is sick a-days: she pukes, her stomach seethes,
The fins of her eyelids look most teeming blue,
She wanes i' th' cheek, and waxes fat i' th' flank,
And contrary to our Italian fashion,
Wears a loose-bodied gown: there's somewhat in 't.
I have a trick may chance discover it,
A pretty one; I have bought some apricocks,°   apricots
The first our spring yields.

[*Enter* ANTONIO *and* DELIO, *talking apart.*]

DELIO   And so long since married?
You amaze me.
ANTONIO   Let me seal your lips forever:
For, did I think that anything but th' air
Could carry these words from you, I should wish
You had no breath at all.   [*turning to* BOSOLA]

---

8. Centuries of traditional invective about
women's cosmetic practices, and some contemporary practices and superstitions, lie behind this
speech. Freshly killed pigeons were applied to the
feet of plague victims, and fasting was supposed to
cause bad breath.
9. The physician grows rich on those who have
outworn their youth; every spring he buys a new

harness for his horse and every fall a new mistress
for himself.
1. "Wolf" and "measle": an ulcerous skin disease
(lupus) and an infection of swine, sometimes confused with human measles.
2. The wells at Lucca are the mineral springs at
nearby Montecatini, renowned as a place to "take
the cure."

Now, sir, in your contemplation? You are studying to become a great
wise fellow?

BOSOLA   Oh, sir, the opinion of wisdom is a foul tetter[3] that runs all over
a man's body. If simplicity[4] direct us to have no evil, it directs us to a
75 happy being, for the subtlest folly proceeds from the subtlest wisdom.
Let me be simply honest.

ANTONIO   I do understand your inside.

BOSOLA   Do you so?

ANTONIO   Because you would not seem to appear to th' world
Puffed up with your preferment, you continue
80 This out-of-fashion melancholy. Leave it, leave it.

BOSOLA   Give me leave to be honest in any phrase, in any compliment
whatsoever. Shall I confess myself to you? I look no higher than I can
reach: they are the gods that must ride on winged horses. A lawyer's mule
of a slow pace will both suit my disposition and business; for, mark me,
85 when a man's mind rides faster than his horse can gallop, they quickly
both tire.

ANTONIO   You would look up to heaven, but I think
The devil, that rules i' th' air, stands in your light.

BOSOLA   Oh, sir, you are lord of the ascendant,[5] chief man with the duch-
90 ess; a duke was your cousin-german removed. Say you were lineally
descended from King Pepin,[6] or he himself, what of this? Search the
heads of the greatest rivers in the world, you shall find them but bubbles
of water. Some would think the souls of princes were brought forth by
some more weighty cause than those of meaner persons: they are
95 deceived, there's the same hand to them; the like passions sway them;
the same reason that makes a vicar go to law for a tithe-pig[7] and undo
his neighbors, makes them spoil a whole province, and batter down
goodly cities with the cannon.

[Enter DUCHESS and LADIES.]

DUCHESS   Your arm, Antonio; do I not grow fat?
100 I am exceeding short-winded. Bosola,
I would have you, sir, provide for me a litter,
Such a one as the Duchess of Florence rode in.

BOSOLA   The duchess used one when she was great with child.

DUCHESS   I think she did. Come hither, mend my ruff;
105 Here, when? Thou art such a tedious° lady, and   clumsy
Thy breath smells of lemon peels;[8] would thou hadst done;
Shall I swoon under thy fingers? I am
So troubled with the mother![9]

BOSOLA [aside]   I fear too much.

DUCHESS   I have heard you say
That the French courtiers wear their hats on 'fore
110 The king.

ANTONIO   I have seen it.

3. Scab.
4. Foolishness.
5. In astrology, the predominating influence, controlling destiny.
6. Father of Charlemagne, hence source of a great
dynasty.

7. A parson was entitled to a tenth (tithe) of his
parishioners' annual profit but was thought mean
if he sued for a petty sum.
8. Lemon peels, chewed to sweeten the breath.
9. Heartburn, but with a second meaning not lost
on Bosola.

DUCHESS   In the presence?
ANTONIO   Yes.
DUCHESS   Why should not we bring up that fashion? 'Tis
  Ceremony more than duty that consists
  In the removing of a piece of felt.
115 Be you the example to the rest o' th' court;
  Put on your hat first.
ANTONIO   You must pardon me.
  I have seen, in colder countries than in France,
  Nobles stand bare to th' prince, and the distinction
  Methought showed reverently.
BOSOLA   I have a present for your grace.
120 DUCHESS   For me, sir?
BOSOLA   Apricocks, madam.
DUCHESS   O, sir, where are they?
  I have heard of none to-year.
BOSOLA [aside]   Good: her color rises.
DUCHESS   Indeed, I thank you: they are wondrous fair ones.
  What an unskillful fellow is our gardener!
125 We shall have none this month.
BOSOLA   Will not your grace pare them?
DUCHESS   No. They taste of musk, methinks; indeed they do.
BOSOLA   I know not: yet I wish your grace had pared 'em.
DUCHESS   Why?
BOSOLA   I forgot to tell you, the knave gardener,
130 Only to raise his profit by them the sooner,
  Did ripen them in horse-dung.[1]
DUCHESS   O, you jest.
  You shall judge: pray taste one.
ANTONIO   Indeed, madam,
  I do not love the fruit.
DUCHESS   Sir, you are loath
  To rob us of our dainties: 'tis a delicate fruit;
  They say they are restorative.
135 BOSOLA   'Tis a pretty art,
  This grafting.
DUCHESS   'Tis so; a bettering of nature.
BOSOLA   To make a pippin grow upon a crab,°   crab apple
  A damson on a blackthorn. [aside] How greedily she eats them!
  A whirlwind strike off these bawd farthingales![2]
140 For, but for that and the loose-bodied gown,
  I should have discovered apparently°   certainly
  The young springal° cutting a caper in her belly.   fellow
DUCHESS   I thank you, Bosola. They were right good ones,
  If they do not make me sick.
ANTONIO   How now, madam?
145 DUCHESS   This green fruit and my stomach are not friends;

---

1. The heat of decomposing manure was widely
supposed to have special virtues.

2. Early hoopskirts, capable of concealing the figure.

How they swell me!

BOSOLA [*aside*]   Nay, you are too much swelled already.

DUCHESS   Oh, I am in an extreme cold sweat!

BOSOLA   I am very sorry.

DUCHESS   Lights to my chamber! O good Antonio,
I fear I am undone!

DELIO   Lights there, lights!

[*Exeunt* DUCHESS *and* LADIES. *Exit, on the other side,* BOSOLA.]

150   ANTONIO   O my most trusty Delio, we are lost!
I fear she's fall'n in labor; and there's left
No time for her remove.

DELIO   Have you prepared
Those ladies to attend her? and procured
That politic° safe conveyance for the midwife   secret
Your duchess plotted?

155   ANTONIO   I have.

DELIO   Make use, then, of this forced occasion:
Give out that Bosola hath poisoned her
With these apricocks; that will give some color
For her keeping close.

ANTONIO   Fie, fie, the physicians
Will then flock to her.

160   DELIO   For that you may pretend
She'll use some prepared antidote of her own,
Lest the physicians should re-poison her.

ANTONIO   I am lost in amazement: I know not what to think on 't.

[*Exeunt.*]

SCENE 2

[*Enter* BOSOLA.]

BOSOLA   So, so, there's no question but her tetchiness[3] and most vulturous
eating of the apricocks are apparent signs of breeding.

[*Enter an* OLD LADY.]

Now?

OLD LADY   I am in haste, sir.

5   BOSOLA   There was a young waiting-woman had a monstrous desire to see
the glass-house[4]—

OLD LADY   Nay, pray let me go.

BOSOLA   And it was only to know what strange instrument it was should
swell up a glass to the fashion of a woman's belly.

10   OLD LADY   I will hear no more of the glass-house. You are still abusing
women?

BOSOLA   Who, I? No; only, by the way now and then, mention your frailties. The orange tree bears ripe and green fruit and blossoms all together;
and some of you give entertainment for pure love, but more for more
15   precious reward. The lusty spring smells well, but drooping autumn

3. Irritability.
4. Where bottles were blown, near the theater in Blackfriars.

tastes well. If we have the same golden showers that rained in the time of Jupiter the thunderer, you have the same Danaës still,[5] to hold up their laps to receive them. Didst thou never study the mathematics?

OLD LADY   What's that sir?

20 BOSOLA   Why, to know the trick how to make a many lines meet in one center. Go, go, give your foster daughters good counsel: tell them that the devil takes delight to hang at a woman's girdle, like a false rusty watch, that she cannot discern how the time passes.   [*Exit* OLD LADY.]

[*Enter* ANTONIO, DELIO, RODERIGO, *and* GRISOLAN.]

ANTONIO   Shut up the court-gates.

RODERIGO   Why, sir? what's the danger?

25 ANTONIO   Shut up the posterns presently,[6] and call
All the officers o' th' court.

GRISOLAN   I shall instantly.   [*Exit.*]

ANTONIO   Who keeps the key o' th' park gate?

RODERIGO   Forobosco.

ANTONIO   Let him bring 't presently.

[*Re-enter* GRISOLAN *with* SERVANTS.]

1 SERVANT   O, gentlemen o' the court, the foulest treason!

30 BOSOLA [*aside*]   If that these apricocks should be poisoned now,
Without my knowledge!

1 SERVANT   There was taken even now
A Switzer° in the duchess' bedchamber—   *Swiss guard*

2 SERVANT   A Switzer?

1 SERVANT   With a pistol in his great codpiece.[7]

BOSOLA   Ha, ha, ha!

1 SERVANT   The codpiece was the case for 't.

2 SERVANT   There was

35 A cunning traitor: who would have searched his codpiece?

1 SERVANT   True, if he had kept out of the ladies' chambers.
And all the molds of his buttons were leaden bullets.

2 SERVANT   O wicked cannibal!
A fire-lock° in 's codpiece!   *pistol*

1 SERVANT   'Twas a French plot,
Upon my life.

40 2 SERVANT   To see what the devil can do!

ANTONIO   Are all the officers here?

SERVANTS   We are.

ANTONIO   Gentlemen,
We have lost much plate[8] you know, and but this evening
Jewels, to the value of four thousand ducats,
Are missing in the duchess' cabinet.
Are the gates shut?

SERVANT   Yes.

45 ANTONIO   'Tis the duchess' pleasure

---

5. Jupiter's success in wooing Danaë in a shower of gold traditionally illustrated female venality.
6. At once. "Posterns": outer gates.
7. An outsize flap worn on the front of men's trunk hose.
8. Massive gold and silver dishes, a frequent form of wealth in the days before banks.

Each officer be locked into his chamber
　Till the sun-rising; and to send the keys
　Of all their chests and of their outward doors
　Into her bedchamber. She is very sick.
RODERIGO　At her pleasure.
50 ANTONIO　　　　　　　　She entreats you take 't not ill:
　The innocent shall be the more approved by it.
BOSOLA　Gentlemen o' th' wood-yard, where's your Switzer now?
1 SERVANT　By this hand, 'twas credibly reported by one o' th' black
　guard.[9]　　　　　　　　[Exeunt all except ANTONIO and DELIO.]
DELIO　How fares it with the duchess?
55 ANTONIO　　　　　　　　　　　　She's exposed
　Unto the worst of torture, pain, and fear.
DELIO　Speak to her all happy comfort.
ANTONIO　How I do play the fool with mine own danger!
　You are this night, dear friend, to post to Rome;
　My life lies in your service.
60 DELIO　　　　　　　　　　Do not doubt me.
ANTONIO　Oh, 'tis far from me, and yet fear presents me
　Somewhat that looks like danger.
DELIO　　　　　　　　　　Believe it,
　'Tis but the shadow of your fear, no more;
　How superstitiously we mind our evils!
65 The throwing down salt, or crossing of a hare,
　Bleeding at nose, the stumbling of a horse,
　Or singing of a cricket, are of power
　To daunt whole man° in us. Sir, fare you well:　　　　*all courage*
　I wish you all the joys of a blessed father:
70 And, for my faith, lay this unto your breast,
　Old friends, like old swords, still are trusted best.　　[*Exit.*]
　　　[*Enter* CARIOLA.]
CARIOLA　Sir, you are the happy father of a son:
　Your wife commends him to you.
ANTONIO　　　　　　　　　Blessed comfort!
　For heaven's sake tend her well: I'll presently
75 Go set a figure for 's nativity.[1]　　　　　　　　[*Exeunt.*]

SCENE 3

　　[*Enter* BOSOLA, *with a dark lantern.*]
BOSOLA　Sure I did hear a woman shriek: list, ha!
　And the sound came, if I received it right,
　From the duchess' lodgings. There's some stratagem
　In the confining all our courtiers
5 To their several wards: I must have part of it;
　My intelligence will freeze else.[2] List, again!
　It may be 'twas the melancholy bird,
　Best friend of silence and of solitariness,

9. Kitchen scullions. The "wood-yard" is a source
of firewood for kitchen and fireplaces.

1. Cast his horoscope.
2. All my news will be cold.

The owl, that screamed so. Ha! Antonio?
[*Enter* ANTONIO *with a candle, his sword drawn.*]

10 ANTONIO   I heard some noise. Who's there? What art thou? Speak.
BOSOLA   Antonio? Put not your face nor body
  To such a forced expression of fear.
  I am Bosola, your friend.
ANTONIO   Bosola!
  [*aside*] This mole does undermine me.—Heard you not
  A noise even now?
BOSOLA   From whence?
15 ANTONIO   From the duchess' lodging.
BOSOLA   Not I. Did you?
ANTONIO   I did, or else I dreamed.
BOSOLA   Let's walk towards it.
ANTONIO   No, it may be 'twas
  But the rising of the wind.
BOSOLA   Very likely.
  Methinks 'tis very cold, and yet you sweat:
  You look wildly.
20 ANTONIO   I have been setting a figure[3]
  For the duchess' jewels.
BOSOLA   Ah, and how falls your question?
  Do you find it radical?[4]
ANTONIO   What's that to you?
  'Tis rather to be questioned what design,
  When all men were commanded to their lodgings,
  Makes you a night-walker.
25 BOSOLA   In sooth, I'll tell you:
  Now all the court's asleep, I thought the devil
  Had least to do here; I came to say my prayers;
  And if it do offend you I do so,
  You are a fine courtier.
ANTONIO [*aside*]   This fellow will undo me.
30   You gave the duchess apricocks today:
  Pray heaven they were not poisoned!
BOSOLA   Poisoned? A Spanish fig[5]
  For the imputation!
ANTONIO   Traitors are ever confident
  Till they are discovered. There were jewels stolen, too;
  In my conceit,° none are to be suspected   opinion
  More than yourself.
35 BOSOLA   You are a false steward.
ANTONIO   Saucy slave, I'll pull thee up by the roots.
BOSOLA   Maybe the ruin will crush you to pieces.
ANTONIO   You are an impudent snake indeed, sir:
  Are you scarce warm, and do you show your sting?
  You libel well, sir.

3. Establishing the loss involved. But Bosola takes the expression astrologically, as if Antonio were casting a horoscope.
4. Indicative, significant.
5. An obscene gesture, which Bosola doubtless makes onstage.

40 BOSOLA   No, sir: copy it out,
  And I will set my hand to 't.[6]
  ANTONIO [aside]   My nose bleeds.
    One that were superstitious would count
    This ominous, when it merely comes by chance:
    Two letters, that are wrought here for my name,
45 Are drowned in blood!
    Mere accident. For you, sir, I'll take order
    I' th' morn you shall be safe.[7] [aside] 'Tis that must color
    Her lying-in.—Sir, this door you pass not:
    I do not hold it fit that you come near
50 The duchess' lodgings, till you have quit yourself.
    [aside] The great are like the base, nay, they are the same,
    When they seek shameful ways to avoid shame.   [Exit.]
  BOSOLA   Antonio hereabout did drop a paper:
    Some of your help, false friend: [opening his lantern] Oh, here it is.
55 What's here? A child's nativity calculated?   [reads]
    "The duchess was delivered of a son, 'tween the hours twelve and one in
    the night, Anno Dom. 1504,"—that's this year—"decimo nono Decem-
    bris,"[8]—that's this night—"taken according to the meridian of Malfi"—
    that's our duchess: happy discovery! "The lord of the first house being
60 combust[9] in the ascendant, signifies short life; and Mars being in a
    human sign, joined to the tail of the Dragon, in the eighth house, doth
    threaten a violent death. Caetera non scrutantur."[1]
    Why, now 'tis most apparent: this precise[2] fellow
    Is the duchess' bawd:° I have it to my wish!   procurer
65 This is a parcel of intelligency
    Our courtiers were cased up for: it needs must follow
    That I must be committed on pretense
    Of poisoning her; which I'll endure, and laugh at.
    If one could find the father now! But that
70 Time will discover. Old Castruccio
    I' th' morning posts to Rome: by him I'll send
    A letter that shall make her brothers' galls
    O'erflow their livers. This was a thrifty° way.   shrewd
    Though lust do mask in ne'er so strange disguise,
75 She's oft found witty, but is never wise.   [Exit.]

SCENE 4. The palace of the CARDINAL at Rome.

[Enter CARDINAL and JULIA.]

CARDINAL   Sit. Thou art my best of wishes. Prithee, tell me
    What trick didst thou invent to come to Rome
    Without thy husband.
JULIA   Why, my lord, I told him
    I came to visit an old anchorite°   hermit

---

6. Bosola denies the charge, not by denying malignancy, but by offering to publish it.
7. Under guard.
8. December 19.
9. Burnt up; i.e., the ruling planet is close to the sun.

1. "The rest is not examined"—i.e., the horoscope is incomplete. Mars and the Dragon are sinister signs, even separately; fatal together.
2. Meticulous, fussy.

Here for devotion.

5 CARDINAL   Thou are a witty false one—
   I mean, to him.

   JULIA   You have prevailed with me
   Beyond my strongest thoughts! I would not now
   Find you inconstant.

   CARDINAL   Do not put thyself
   To such a voluntary torture, which proceeds
   Out of your own guilt.

   JULIA   How, my lord?

10 CARDINAL   You fear
   My constancy, because you have approved°   experienced
   Those giddy and wild turnings in yourself.

   JULIA Did you e'er find them?

   CARDINAL   Sooth, generally for women;
   A man might strive to make glass malleable,
   Ere he should make them fixed.

15 JULIA   So, my lord.

   CARDINAL We had need go borrow that fantastic glass
   Invented by Galileo the Florentine[3]
   To view another spacious world i' th' moon,
   And look to find a constant woman there.

   JULIA This is very well, my lord.

20 CARDINAL   Why do you weep?
   Are tears your justification? The selfsame tears
   Will fall into your husband's bosom, lady,
   With a loud protestation that you love him
   Above the world. Come, I'll love you wisely,

25 That's jealously, since I am very certain
   You cannot make me cuckold.

   JULIA   I'll go home
   To my husband.

   CARDINAL   You may thank me, lady,
   I have taken you off your melancholy perch,
   Bore you upon my fist, and showed you game,

30 And let you fly at it.[4] I pray thee, kiss me.
   When thou wast with thy husband, thou wast watched
   Like a tame elephant: still you are to thank me:
   Thou hadst only kisses from him and high feeding;
   But what delight was that? 'Twas just like one

35 That hath a little fingering on the lute,
   Yet cannot tune it: still you are to thank me.

   JULIA You told me of a piteous wound i' th' heart
   And a sick liver, when you wooed me first,
   And spake like one in physic.[5]   [A knock is heard.]

   CARDINAL   Who's that?

40 Rest firm,° for my affection to thee,   be assured

---

3. In 1504, Galileo's telescope was more than one
hundred years in the future, but the reference was
topical for Webster's audience.

4. The cardinal speaks of himself as a falconer
training a bird (Julia).
5. Like a person under a doctor's care.

Lightning moves slow to 't.°   *by comparison*
      [*Enter* SERVANT.]
SERVANT   Madam, a gentleman,
    That's come post from Malfi, desires to see you.
CARDINAL   Let him enter. I'll withdraw.   [*Exit.*]
SERVANT   He says
    Your husband, old Castruccio, is come to Rome,
45 Most pitifully tired with riding post.⁶   [*Exit.*]
      [*Enter* DELIO.]
JULIA   Signor Delio! [*aside*]—'tis one of my old suitors.
DELIO   I was bold to come and see you.
JULIA   Sir, you are welcome.
DELIO   Do you lie here?
JULIA   Sure, your own experience
    Will satisfy you no: our Roman prelates
    Do not keep lodging for ladies.
50 DELIO   Very well.
    I have brought you no commendations from your husband,
    For I know none by him.
JULIA   I hear he's come to Rome.
DELIO   I never knew man and beast, of a horse and a knight,
    So weary of each other: if he had had a good back,
55 He would have undertook to have borne his horse,
    His breech was so pitifully sore.
JULIA   Your laughter
    Is my pity.
DELIO   Lady, I know not whether
    You want money, but I have brought you some.
JULIA   From my husband?
DELIO   No, from mine own allowance.
60 JULIA   I must hear the condition, ere I be bound to take it.
DELIO   Look on 't, 'tis gold: hath it not a fine color?
JULIA   I have a bird more beautiful.
DELIO   Try the sound on 't.
JULIA   A lute string far exceeds it:
    It hath no smell, like cassia or civet;
65 Nor is it physical,° though some fond° doctors   *medicinal / foolish*
    Persuade us seethe 't in cullises:° I'll tell you,   *broth*
    This is a creature bred by—
      [*Re-enter* SERVANT.]
SERVANT   Your husband's come,
    Hath delivered a letter to the Duke of Calabria
    That, to my thinking, hath put him out of his wits.   [*Exit.*]
70 JULIA   Sir, you hear:
    Pray, let me know your business and your suit
    As briefly as can be.
DELIO   With good speed: I would wish you,

6. When riding post, one changed horses at regular intervals without stopping to rest oneself.

At such time as you are non-resident
With your husband, my mistress.
75 JULIA Sir, I'll go ask my husband if I shall,
And straight return your answer.   [*Exit.*]
DELIO   Very fine!
Is this her wit, or honesty, that speaks thus?
I heard one say the duke was highly moved
With a letter sent from Malfi. I do fear
80 Antonio is betrayed: how fearfully
Shows his ambition now! Unfortunate fortune!
They pass through whirlpools, and deep woes do shun,
Who the event weigh ere the action's done.⁷   [*Exit.*]

SCENE 5

[*Enter* CARDINAL, *and* FERDINAND *with a letter.*]
FERDINAND   I have this night digged up a mandrake.⁸
CARDINAL   Say you?
FERDINAND   And I am grown mad with 't.
CARDINAL   What's the prodigy?
FERDINAND   Read there—a sister damned: she's loose i' th' hilts;⁹
Grown a notorious strumpet.
CARDINAL   Speak lower.
FERDINAND   Lower?
5 Rogues do not whisper 't now, but seek to publish 't
(As servants do the bounty of their lords)
Aloud; and with a covetous searching eye,
To mark who note them. O, confusion seize her!
She hath had most cunning bawds to serve her turn,
10 And more secure conveyances for lust
Than towns of garrison for service.
CARDINAL   Is 't possible?
Can this be certain?
FERDINAND   Rhubarb, oh, for rhubarb
To purge this choler!¹ Here's the cursèd day
To prompt my memory, and here 't shall stick
15 Till of her bleeding heart I make a sponge
To wipe it out.
CARDINAL   Why do you make yourself
So wild a tempest?
FERDINAND   Would I could be one,
That I might toss her palace 'bout her ears,
Root up her goodly forests, blast her meads,°   *meadows*
20 And lay her general territory as waste
As she hath done her honors.
CARDINAL   Shall our blood,

---

7. I.e., who judge of actions before seeing their
final consequences.
8. A fabulous root, violently aphrodisiac but also
deadly poison. Both aspects apply to Ferdinand.
9. I.e., promiscuous.
1. Rhubarb, as a laxative, was thought curative of
the high pressures of hot rage.

The royal blood of Aragon and Castile,
Be thus attainted?
FERDINAND   Apply desperate physic:
We must not now use balsamum,° but fire,°   *balm / cautery*
25   The smarting cupping-glass,[2] for that 's the mean
To purge infected blood, such blood as hers.
There is a kind of pity in mine eye,
I'll give it to my handkercher; and now 'tis here,
I'll bequeath this to her bastard.
CARDINAL   What to do?
30   FERDINAND   Why, to make soft lint for his mother's wounds,
When I have hewed her to pieces.
CARDINAL   Cursèd creature!
Unequal nature, to place women's hearts
So far upon the left side![3]
FERDINAND   Foolish men,
That e'er will trust their honor in a bark
35   Made of so slight weak bulrush as is woman,
Apt every minute to sink it!
CARDINAL   Thus ignorance, when it hath purchased honor,
It cannot wield it.
FERDINAND   Methinks I see her laughing—
Excellent hyena! Talk to me somewhat, quickly,
40   Or my imagination will carry me
To see her in the shameful act of sin.
CARDINAL   With whom?
FERDINAND   Haply° with some strong-thighed bargeman,   *perhaps*
Or one o' th' wood-yard that can quoit° the sledge   *throw*
45   Or toss the bar,[4] or else some lovely squire
That carries coal up to her privy lodgings.
CARDINAL   You fly beyond your reason.
FERDINAND   Go to, mistress!
'Tis not your whore's milk that shall quench my wild fire,
But your whore's blood.
50   CARDINAL   How idly shows this rage, which carries you,
As men conveyed by witches through the air,
On violent whirlwinds! This intemperate noise
Fitly resembles deaf men's shrill discourse,
Who talk aloud, thinking all other men
To have their imperfection.
55   FERDINAND   Have not you
My palsy?
CARDINAL   Yes, I can be angry, but
Without this rupture: there is not in nature
A thing that makes man so deformed, so beastly,
As doth intemperate anger. Chide yourself.
60   You have divers men who never yet expressed

---

2. By which people were bled.
3. The left is the sinister side, associated with bad

luck, deceit, and passion.
4. Gross tests of strength.

Their strong desire of rest but by unrest,
By vexing of themselves. Come, put yourself
In tune.
FERDINAND   So; I will only study to seem
The thing I am not. I could kill her now,
65   In you, or in myself; for I do think
It is some sin in us heaven doth revenge
By her.
CARDINAL   Are you stark mad?
FERDINAND   I would have their bodies
Burnt in a coal-pit with the ventage° stopped,   chimney
That their cursed smoke might not ascend to heaven;
70   Or dip the sheets they lie in in pitch or sulphur,
Wrap them in 't, and then light them like a match;
Or else to boil their bastard to a cullis,°   broth
And give 't his lecherous father to renew°   repair
The sin of his back.⁵
CARDINAL   I'll leave you.
FERDINAND   Nay, I have done.
75   I am confident, had I been damned in hell,
And should have heard of this, it would have put me
Into a cold sweat. In, in; I'll go sleep.
Till I know who leaps my sister, I'll not stir:
That known, I'll find scorpions to string my whips,⁶
80   And fix her in a general eclipse.   [Exeunt.]

Act 3

SCENE 1. Amalfi.

[Enter ANTONIO and DELIO.]
ANTONIO   Our noble friend, my most belovèd Delio!
Oh, you have been a stranger long at court;
Came you along with the Lord Ferdinand?
DELIO   I did, sir. And how fares your noble duchess?
5   ANTONIO   Right fortunately well: she's an excellent
Feeder of pedigrees; since you last saw her,
She hath had two children more, a son and daughter.
DELIO   Methinks 'twas yesterday: let me but wink,
And not behold your face, which to mine eye
10   Is somewhat leaner, verily I should dream
It were within this half-hour.
ANTONIO   You have not been in law, friend Delio,
Nor in prison, nor a suitor at the court,
Nor begged the reversion of some great man's place,
15   Nor troubled with an old wife, which doth make
Your time so insensibly° hasten.   imperceptively

5. As Atreus did to Thyestes in Greek legend.
6. Tipping the thongs of a whip with "scorpions"
(tips of jagged steel or lead that sting and bite the

flesh) is an old metaphor for aggravated punishment.

DELIO   Pray, sir, tell me,
　　Hath not this news arrived yet to the ear
　　Of the Lord Cardinal?
ANTONIO   I fear it hath:
　　The Lord Ferdinand, that's newly come to court,
　　Doth bear himself right dangerously.
20 DELIO   Pray, why?
ANTONIO   He is so quiet that he seems to sleep
　　The tempest out, as dormice do in winter.
　　Those houses that are haunted are most still
　　Till the devil be up.
DELIO   What say the common people?
25 ANTONIO   The common rabble do directly say
　　She is a strumpet.
DELIO   And your graver heads,
　　Which would be politic,° what censure° they?   statesmanlike / opine
ANTONIO   They do observe I grow to infinite purchase,
　　The left-hand way,[7] and all suppose the duchess
30 Would amend it, if she could; for, say they,
　　Great princes, though they grudge their officers
　　Should have such large and unconfinèd means
　　To get wealth under them, will not complain,
　　Lest thereby they should make them odious
35 Unto the people; for other obligation
　　Of love or marriage between her and me
　　They never dream of.
DELIO   The Lord Ferdinand
　　Is going to bed.
　　　　　[Enter DUCHESS, FERDINAND, and BOSOLA.]
FERDINAND   I'll instantly to bed,
　　For I am weary.—I am to bespeak
　　A husband for you.
40 DUCHESS   For me, sir? Pray, who is 't?
FERDINAND   The great Count Malateste.
DUCHESS   Fie upon him!
　　A count? He's a mere stick of sugar candy;
　　You may look quite through him. When I choose
　　A husband, I will marry for your honor.
45 FERDINAND   You shall do well in 't.—How is 't, worthy Antonio?
DUCHESS   But, sir, I am to have private conference with you
　　About a scandalous report is spread
　　Touching mine honor.
FERDINAND   Let me be ever deaf to 't:
　　One of Pasquil's paper bullets,[8] court-calumny,
50 A pestilent air, which princes' palaces
　　Are seldom purged of. Yet, say that it were true,
　　I pour it in your bosom, my fixed love

---

7. I.e., they think I am getting rich dishonestly.
8. Anonymous satires were traditionally pasted on

the statue of Pasquillo, or Pasquino, near Piazza
Navona in Rome, and attributed to his authorship.

Would strongly excuse, extenuate, nay, deny
Faults, were they apparent in you. Go, be safe
In your own innocency.
55 DUCHESS [*aside*]   O blessèd comfort!
This deadly air is purged.

[*Exeunt* DUCHESS, ANTONIO, *and* DELIO.]

FERDINAND   Her guilt treads on
Hot-burning coulters.[9] Now, Bosola,
How thrives our intelligence?°   *detective work*
BOSOLA   Sir, uncertainly:
'Tis rumored she hath had three bastards, but
By whom, we may go read i' th' stars.
60 FERDINAND   Why, some
Hold opinion all things are written there.
BOSOLA   Yes, if we could find spectacles to read them.
I do suspect there hath been some sorcery
Used on the duchess.
FERDINAND   Sorcery? To what purpose?
65 BOSOLA   To make her dote on some desertless fellow
She shames to acknowledge.
FERDINAND   Can your faith give way
To think there's power in potions or in charms,
To make us love whether we will or no?
BOSOLA   Most certainly.
70 FERDINAND   Away! These are mere gulleries,[1] horrid things,
Invented by some cheating mountebanks
To abuse us. Do you think that herbs or charms
Can force the will? Some trials have been made
In this foolish practice, but the ingredients
75 Were lenitive[2] poisons, such as are of force
To make the patient mad; and straight the witch
Swears by equivocation they are in love.
The witchcraft lies in her rank° blood. This night   *wanton*
I will force confession from her. You told me
80 You had got, within these two days, a false key
Into her bedchamber.
BOSOLA   I have.
FERDINAND   As I would wish.
BOSOLA   What do you intend to do?
FERDINAND   Can you guess?
BOSOLA   No.
FERDINAND   Do not ask, then:
He that can compass° me, and know my drifts,°   *comprehend / purposes*
85 May say he hath put a girdle 'bout the world,
And sounded all her quicksands.
BOSOLA   I do not
Think so.

---

9. Medieval chastity inquests customarily   1. Deceits.
required the questioned lady to walk barefoot over   2. Softening, slow-working.
red-hot plowshares ("coulters").

FERDINAND What do you think, then, pray?

BOSOLA That you
Are your own chronicle too much, and grossly
Flatter yourself.

FERDINAND Give me thy hand; I thank thee:
90   I ne'er gave pension but to flatterers,
Till I entertained thee. Farewell.
That friend a great man's ruin strongly checks,
Who rails into his belief all his defects. [*Exeunt.*]

SCENE 2. *The Bedchamber of the* DUCHESS.

[*Enter* DUCHESS, ANTONIO, *and* CARIOLA.]

DUCHESS Bring me the casket hither, and the glass.
You get no lodging here tonight, my lord.

ANTONIO Indeed, I must persuade one.

DUCHESS Very good:
I hope in time 'twill grow into a custom,
5   That noblemen shall come with cap and knee
To purchase a night's lodging of their wives.

ANTONIO I must lie here.

DUCHESS Must! You are a lord of misrule.[3]

ANTONIO Indeed, my rule is only in the night.

DUCHESS To what use will you put me?

ANTONIO We'll sleep together.

10 DUCHESS Alas, what pleasure can two lovers find in sleep?

CARIOLA My lord, I lie with her often, and I know
She'll much disquiet you.

ANTONIO See, you are complained of.

CARIOLA For she's the sprawling'st bedfellow.

ANTONIO I shall like her
The better for that.

CARIOLA Sir, shall I ask you a question?

ANTONIO I pray thee, Cariola.

15 CARIOLA Wherefore still, when you lie with my lady,
Do you rise so early?

ANTONIO Laboring men
Count the clock oftenest, Cariola,
Are glad when their task's ended.

DUCHESS I'll stop your mouth. [*Kisses him.*]

ANTONIO Nay, that's but one; Venus had two soft doves
20   To draw her chariot; I must have another— [*She kisses him again.*]
When wilt thou marry, Cariola?

CARIOLA Never, my lord.

ANTONIO Oh, fie upon this single life! Forgo it.
We read how Daphne, for her peevish flight,
Became a fruitless bay tree; Syrinx turned
25   To the pale empty reed; Anaxarete
Was frozen into marble: whereas those

---

3. The mock-monarch of a carnival festival.

Which married, or proved kind unto their friends,
Were by a gracious influence trans-shaped
Into the olive, pomegranate, mulberry,
30 Became flowers, precious stones, or eminent stars.[4]
CARIOLA   This is a vain poetry, but I pray you tell me,
If there were proposed me, wisdom, riches, and beauty,
In three several young men, which should I choose?
ANTONIO   'Tis a hard question: this was Paris' case,
35 And he was blind in 't, and there was great cause;
For how was 't possible he could judge right,
Having three amorous goddesses in view,
And they stark naked? 'Twas a motion[5]
Were able to benight the apprehension
40 Of the severest counselor of Europe.
Now I look on both your faces so well formed,
It puts me in mind of a question I would ask.
CARIOLA   What is 't?
ANTONIO   I do wonder why hard-favored ladies,
For the most part, keep worse-favored waiting-women
45 To attend them, and cannot endure fair ones.
DUCHESS   Oh, that's soon answered.
Did you ever in your life know an ill painter
Desire to have his dwelling next door to the shop
Of an excellent picture-maker? 'Twould disgrace
50 His face-making, and undo him. I prithee,
When were we so merry?—My hair tangles.
ANTONIO   Pray thee, Cariola, let's steal forth the room,
And let her talk to herself: I have divers times
Served her the like, when she hath chafed extremely.
55 I love to see her angry. Softly, Cariola.   [Exeunt ANTONIO and CARIOLA.]
DUCHESS   Doth not the color of my hair 'gin to change?
When I wax gray, I shall have all the court
Powder their hair with arras,[6] to be like me.
You have cause to love me; I entered you into my heart
60 Before you would vouchsafe to call for the keys.
       [Enter FERDINAND behind.]
We shall one day have my brothers take you napping;
Methinks his presence, being now in court,
Should make you keep your own bed; but you'll say
Love mixed with fear is sweetest. I'll assure you,
65 You shall get no more children till my brothers
Consent to be your gossips.[7] Have you lost your tongue?
       [She turns and sees FERDINAND.]
'Tis welcome:

4. The olive was created by Athena; the mulberry gained its color from the blood of Pyramus and Thisbe; the pomegranate seems to have no particular mythological origin. Most of the other stories of ladies being transformed for complying, or not complying, with the solicitations of a god are from Ovid's *Metamorphoses*.
5. Spectacle. Paris had to choose among Hera, Athena, and Aphrodite, goddesses of marriage, wisdom, and love; his selecting the third led to the Trojan war.
6. Orris root, used in powdered form to make hair artificially gray.
7. Sponsors in baptism.

For know, whether I am doomed to live or die,
I can do both like a prince.

FERDINAND   Die, then, quickly! [*Giving her a poniard.*]

70 Virtue, where art thou hid? What hideous thing
Is it that doth eclipse thee?

DUCHESS   Pray, sir, hear me.

FERDINAND Or is it true thou art but a bare name,
And no essential thing?

DUCHESS   Sir—

FERDINAND   Do not speak.

DUCHESS No, sir: I will plant my soul in mine ears, to hear you.

75 FERDINAND O most imperfect light of human reason,
That mak'st us so unhappy to foresee
What we can least prevent! Pursue thy wishes,
And glory in them: there's in shame no comfort
But to be past all bounds and sense of shame.

DUCHESS I pray, sir, hear me. I am married.

80 FERDINAND   So!

DUCHESS Haply,° not to your liking: but for that,   *perhaps*
Alas, your shears do come untimely now
To clip the bird's wings that's already flown!
Will you see my husband?

FERDINAND   Yes, if I could change
Eyes with a basilisk.[8]

85 DUCHESS   Sure, you came hither
By his confederacy.

FERDINAND   The howling of a wolf
Is music to thee, screech-owl: prithee, peace.
Whate'er thou art that hast enjoyed my sister,
For I am sure thou hear'st me, for thine own sake

90 Let me not know thee. I came hither prepared
To work thy discovery; yet am now persuaded
It would beget such violent effects
As would damn us both. I would not for ten millions
I had beheld thee: therefore use all means

95 I never may have knowledge of thy name;
Enjoy thy lust still, and a wretched life,
On that condition. And for thee, vile woman,
If thou do wish thy lecher may grow old
In thy embracements, I would have thee build

100 Such a room for him as our anchorites
To holier use inhabit. Let not the sun
Shine on him till he's dead; let dogs and monkeys
Only converse with him, and such dumb things
To whom nature denies use to sound his name;

105 Do not keep a paraquito,° lest she learn it;   *parrot*
If thou do love him, cut out thine own tongue,

---

8. Monster that was fabled to kill with a glance.

Lest it bewray him.

DUCHESS   Why might not I marry?
I have not gone about in this to create
Any new world or custom.

FERDINAND   Thou art undone;
110   And thou hast ta'en that massy sheet of lead
That hid thy husband's bones, and folded it
About my heart.

DUCHESS   Mine bleeds for 't.

FERDINAND   Thine? Thy heart?
What should I name 't unless a hollow bullet
Filled with unquenchable wildfire?

DUCHESS   You are in this
115   Too strict, and were you not my princely brother,
I would say, too willful. My reputation
Is safe.

FERDINAND   Dost thou know what reputation is?
I'll tell thee—to small purpose, since the instruction
Comes now too late.
120   Upon a time, Reputation, Love, and Death
Would travel o'er the world; and it was concluded
That they should part, and take three several ways.
Death told them, they should find him in great battles,
Or cities plagued with plagues. Love gives them counsel
125   To inquire for him 'mongst unambitious shepherds,
Where dowries were not talked of, and sometimes
'Mongst quiet kindred that had nothing left
By their dead parents. "Stay," quoth Reputation,
"Do not forsake me; for it is my nature,
130   If once I part from any man I meet,
I am never found again." And so for you:
You have shook hands° with Reputation,   *parted*
And made him invisible. So, fare you well.
I will never see you more.

DUCHESS   Why should only I,
135   Of all the other princes of the world,
Be cased up, like a holy relic? I have youth
And a little beauty.

FERDINAND   So you have some virgins
That are witches. I will never see thee more.   [*Exit.*]
       [*Enter* ANTONIO *with a pistol, and* CARIOLA.]

DUCHESS   You saw this apparition?

ANTONIO   Yes. We are
140   Betrayed. How came he hither? I should turn
This to thee, for that.   [*Pointing the pistol at* CARIOLA.]

CARIOLA   Pray, sir, do; and when
That you have cleft my heart, you shall read there
Mine innocence.

DUCHESS   That gallery gave him entrance.

ANTONIO   I would this terrible thing would come again,
145   That, standing on my guard, I might relate
           My warrantable[9] love.   [*She shows the poniard.*]
                              Ha! What means this?
DUCHESS   He left this with me.
ANTONIO   And it seems did wish
           You would use it on yourself.
DUCHESS   His action seemed
           To intend so much.
ANTONIO   This hath a handle to 't
150   As well as a point: turn it towards him, and
           So fasten the keen edge in his rank gall.   [*Knocking within.*]
           How now! Who knocks? More earthquakes?
DUCHESS   I stand
           As if a mine beneath my feet were ready
           To be blown up.
CARIOLA   'Tis Bosola.
DUCHESS   Away!
155   O misery! Methinks unjust actions
           Should wear these masks and curtains, and not we.
           You must instantly part hence: I have fashioned it already. [*Exit* ANTONIO.]
                  [*Enter* BOSOLA.]
BOSOLA   The duke your brother is ta'en up in a whirlwind,
           Hath took horse, and 's rid post to Rome.
DUCHESS   So late?
160   BOSOLA   He told me, as he mounted into th' saddle,
           You were undone.
DUCHESS   Indeed, I am very near it.
BOSOLA   What's the matter?
DUCHESS   Antonio, the master of our household,
           Hath dealt so falsely with me in 's accounts:
165   My brother stood engaged with me for money
           Ta'en up of certain Neapolitan Jews,
           And Antonio lets the bonds be forfeit.[1]
BOSOLA   Strange!—[*aside*] This is cunning.
DUCHESS   And hereupon
           My brother's bills at Naples are protested
           Against.[2]—Call up our officers.
170   BOSOLA   I shall.   [*Exit.*]
                  [*Re-enter* ANTONIO.]
DUCHESS   The place that you must fly to is Ancona:[3]
           Hire a house there; I'll send after you
           My treasure and my jewels. Our weak safety
           Runs upon enginous wheels: short syllables
175   Must stand for periods.[4] I must now accuse you

---

9. Legitimate, defensible.
1. I.e., my brother stood security for some money I borrowed from Neapolitan moneylenders; now Antonio has let them call on the duke for payment.
2. I.e., Duke Ferdinand's checks have bounced.
3. On the Adriatic coast of Italy, across the pen-

insula from Amalfi and well to the north.
4. Full sentences. "Enginous": delicately balanced, as in clockwork. The allusion to Tasso (next line) is literally accurate (*Jerusalem Delivered* 2.22) but anachronistic, since Tasso's poem was not published until 1574.

Of such a feignèd crime as Tasso calls
Magnanima menzogna, a noble lie,
'Cause it must shield our honors. Hark! They are coming.
        [*Re-enter* BOSOLA *and* OFFICERS.]
ANTONIO   Will your grace hear me?
180   DUCHESS   I have got well by you; you have yielded me
        A million of loss: I am like to inherit
        The people's curses for your stewardship.
        You had the trick in audit-time to be sick,
        Till I had signed your *quietus;*° and that cured you   *receipt*
185   Without help of a doctor.—Gentlemen,
        I would have this man be an example to you all;
        So shall you hold my favor; I pray, let him;°   *release him*
        For he's done that, alas, you would not think of,
        And, because I intend to be rid of him,
190   I mean not to publish. [*to* ANTONIO] Use your fortune elsewhere.
ANTONIO   I am strongly armed to brook my overthrow;
        As commonly men bear with a hard year,
        I will not blame the cause on 't; but do think
        The necessity of my malevolent star
195   Procures this, not her humor. Oh, the inconstant
        And rotten ground of service! You may see,
        'Tis even like him that in a winter night
        Takes a long slumber o'er a dying fire,
        As loth to part from 't; yet parts thence as cold
        As when he first sat down.
200   DUCHESS   We do confiscate,
        Towards the satisfying of your accounts,
        All that you have.
ANTONIO   I am yours, and 'tis very fit
        All mine should be so.
DUCHESS   So, sir, you have your pass.°   *passport*
ANTONIO   You may see, gentlemen, what 'tis to serve
205   A prince with body and soul.   [*Exit.*]
BOSOLA   Here's an example for extortion: what moisture is drawn out of
        the sea, when foul weather comes, pours down, and runs into the sea
        again.
DUCHESS   I would know what are your opinions of this Antonio.
210   SECOND OFFICER   He could not abide to see a pig's head gaping: I thought
        your grace would find him a Jew.[5]
THIRD OFFICER   I would you had been his officer, for your own sake.
FOURTH OFFICER   You would have had more money.
FIRST OFFICER   He stopped his ears with black wool, and to those came
215   to him for money said he was thick of hearing.
SECOND OFFICER   Some said he was an hermaphrodite, for he could not
        abide a woman.

---

5. Jews were identified by their antipathy to pork, but the assumptions here are deliberately ridiculous.

FOURTH OFFICER   How scurvy proud he would look when the treasury was full! Well, let him go!

220 FIRST OFFICER   Yes, and the chippings of the buttery fly after him, to scour his gold chain![6]

DUCHESS   Leave us. [*Exeunt* OFFICERS.] What do you think of these?

BOSOLA   That these are rogues that in 's prosperity, but to have waited on his fortune, could have wished his dirty stirrup riveted through their
225 noses, and followed after 's mule, like a bear in a ring; would have prostituted their daughters to his lust; made their first-born intelligencers;[7] thought none happy but such as were born under his blessed planet, and wore his livery: and do these lice drop off now? Well, never look to have the like again:[8] he hath left a sort of flattering rogues behind him; their
230 doom must follow. Princes pay flatterers in their own money: flatterers dissemble their vices, and they dissemble their lies; that's justice. Alas, poor gentleman!

DUCHESS   Poor? He hath amply filled his coffers.

BOSOLA   Sure, he was too honest. Pluto, the god of riches, when he 's sent
235 by Jupiter to any man, he goes limping, to signify that wealth that comes on God's name comes slowly; but when he's sent on the devil's errand, he rides post and comes in by scuttles. Let me show you what a most unvalued[9] jewel you have in a wanton humor thrown away, to bless the man shall[1] find him. He was an excellent courtier and most faithful; a
240 soldier that thought it as beastly to know his own value too little as devilish to acknowledge it too much. Both his virtue and form deserved a far better fortune: his discourse rather delighted to judge itself than show itself; his breast was filled with all perfection, and yet it seemed a private whispering-room, it made so little noise of 't.

245 DUCHESS   But he was basely descended.

BOSOLA   Will you make yourself a mercenary herald, rather to examine men's pedigrees than virtues? You shall want[2] him: for know, an honest statesman to a prince is like a cedar planted by a spring; the spring bathes the tree's root, the grateful tree rewards it with his shadow: you have not
250 done so. I would sooner swim to the Bermoothes[3] on two politicians' rotten bladders, tied together with an intelligencer's[4] heartstring, than depend on so changeable a prince's favor. Fare thee well, Antonio! Since the malice of the world would needs down with thee, it cannot be said yet that any ill happened unto thee, considering thy fall was accompanied
255 with virtue.

DUCHESS   Oh, you render me excellent music!

BOSOLA   Say you?

DUCHESS   This good one that you speak of is my husband.

BOSOLA   Do I not dream? Can this ambitious age
Have so much goodness in 't as to prefer
260 A man merely for worth, without these shadows
Of wealth and painted honors? Possible?

---

6. A gold chain was the steward's traditional badge of office. Bread crumbs (the "chippings of the buttery") were used to polish gold and silver plate.
7. Spies.
8. I.e., a servant as good as he was.
9. Invaluable. "By scuttles": in haste.

1. Who shall.
2. Miss.
3. The Bermudas, unknown at the time of the action, but very topical a hundred years later, when the play was written.
4. Spy's.

DUCHESS   I have had three children by him.

BOSOLA   Fortunate lady!
> For you have made your private nuptial bed
> The humble and fair seminary of peace.
265   No question but many an unbeneficed scholar[5]
> Shall pray for you for this deed, and rejoice
> That some preferment in the world can yet
> Arise from merit. The virgins of your land
> That have no dowries shall hope your example
270   Will raise them to rich husbands. Should you want
> Soldiers, 'twould make the very Turks and Moors
> Turn Christians, and serve you for this act.
> Last, the neglected poets of your time,
> In honor of this trophy of a man,
275   Raised by that curious[c] engine, your white hand,   *exquisite*
> Shall thank you, in your grave, for 't; and make that
> More reverend than all the cabinets[6]
> Of living princes. For Antonio,
> His fame shall likewise flow from many a pen,
280   When heralds shall want coats to sell to men.[7]

DUCHESS   As I taste comfort in this friendly speech,
> So would I find concealment.

BOSOLA   Oh, the secret of my prince,
> Which I will wear on th' inside of my heart!

285 DUCHESS   You shall take charge of all my coin and jewels,
> And follow him; for he retires himself
> To Ancona.

BOSOLA   So.

DUCHESS   Whither, within few days,
> I mean to follow thee.

BOSOLA   Let me think:
> I would wish your grace to feign a pilgrimage
290   To our Lady of Loreto,[8] scarce seven leagues
> From fair Ancona; so may you depart
> Your country with more honor, and your flight
> Will seem a princely progress, retaining
> Your usual train about you.

DUCHESS   Sir, your direction
> Shall lead me by the hand.

295 CARIOLA   In my opinion,
> She were better progress to the baths at Lucca,
> Or go visit the Spa in Germany;
> For, if you will believe me, I do not like
> This jesting with religion, this feigned
> Pilgrimage.

300 DUCHESS   Thou art a superstitious fool.

---

5. A scholar without an official appointment.
6. Council chambers. She will be more honored in her grave than living princes in their courts.
7. The Heralds' College (an English royal corpo-ration) carried on a brisk trade in coats of arms.
8. The shrine of the Virgin at Loreto was famous throughout Europe.

Prepare us instantly for our departure.
Past sorrows, let us moderately lament them;
For those to come, seek wisely to prevent them.

                              [Exit DUCHESS, *with* CARIOLA.*]*

BOSOLA   A politician° is the devil's quilted anvil;   *crafty intriguer*
305   He fashions all sins on him, and the blows
       Are never heard: he may work in a lady's chamber,
       As here for proof. What rests° but I reveal   *remains*
       All to my lord? Oh, this base quality
       Of intelligencer! Why, every quality° i' th' world   *profession*
310   Prefers° but gain or commendation: *offers*
       Now for this act I am certain to be raised,
       And men that paint weeds to the life are praised.   *[Exit.]*

SCENE 3. *Rome.*

    [Enter CARDINAL, FERDINAND, MALATESTE, PESCARA, SILVIO, DELIO.*]*
CARDINAL   Must we turn soldier, then?
MALATESTE   The Emperor,[9]
       Hearing your worth that way, ere you attained
       This reverend garment, joins you in commission
       With the right fortunate soldier the Marquis of Pescara,
       And the famous Lannoy.
5   CARDINAL   He that had the honor
       Of taking the French king prisoner?[1]
MALATESTE   The same.
       Here's a plot drawn for a new fortification
       At Naples.   *[They talk apart.]*
FERDINAND   This great Count Malateste, I perceive,
       Hath got employment?
DELIO   No employment, my lord;
10   A marginal note in the muster-book, that he is
       A voluntary lord.
FERDINAND   He's no soldier?
DELIO   He has worn gunpowder in 's hollow tooth for the toothache.[2]
SILVIO   He comes to the leaguer with a full intent
       To eat fresh beef and garlic, means to stay
15   Till the scent be gone, and straight return to court.
DELIO   He hath read all the late service[3] as the city chronicle relates it,
       and keeps two painters going, only to express battles in model.
SILVIO   Then he'll fight by the book.
DELIO   By the almanac, I think, to choose good days and shun the critical.
20   That's his mistress' scarf.
SILVIO   Yes, he protests he would do much for that taffeta.
DELIO   I think he would run away from a battle, to save it from taking[4]
       prisoner.

---

9. The Spanish emperor, Charles V.
1. Charles de Lannoy, Belgian by origin, did indeed capture Francis I at Pavia in 1525, about two decades after the date of the play's supposed action. "Pescara": also a commander at Pavia.

2. Saltpeter was sometimes used to relieve a toothache. "Leaguer" (next line): gathering of the armies.
3. Recent military operations.
4. Being taken.

SILVIO He is horribly afraid gunpowder will spoil the perfume on 't.

25 DELIO I saw a Dutchman break his pate once for calling him pot-gun;[5] he made his head have a bore in 't like a musket.

SILVIO I would he had made a touchhole to 't. He is indeed a guarded sumpter-cloth, only for the remove of the court.[6]

[*Enter* BOSOLA *and speaks to* FERDINAND *and the* CARDINAL.]

PESCARA Bosola arrived? What should be the business?

30 Some falling out amongst the cardinals.
These factions amongst great men, they are like
Foxes; when their heads are divided,
They carry fire in their tails, and all the country
About them goes to wrack for 't.[7]

SILVIO   What's that Bosola?

35 DELIO I knew him in Padua—a fantastical scholar, like such who study to know how many knots were in Hercules' club, of what color Achilles' beard was, or whether Hector were not troubled with the toothache. He hath studied himself half blear-eyed to know the true symmetry of Caesar's nose by a shoeing-horn; and this he did to gain the name of a
40 speculative[8] man.

PESCARA Mark Prince Ferdinand:
A very salamander lives in 's eye,
To mock the eager violence of fire.[9]

SILVIO That Cardinal hath made more bad faces with his oppression than
45 ever Michael Angelo[1] made good ones: he lifts up 's nose, like a foul porpoise before a storm.

PESCARA The Lord Ferdinand laughs.

DELIO Like a deadly cannon that lightens ere it smokes.

PESCARA These are your true pangs of death,
50 The pangs of life, that struggle with great statesmen.

DELIO In such a deformed silence witches whisper
Their charms.

CARDINAL   Doth she make religion her riding hood
To keep her from the sun and tempest?

FERDINAND   That,
That damns her. Methinks her fault and beauty,
55 Blended together, show like leprosy,
The whiter, the fouler. I make it a question
Whether her beggarly brats were ever christened.

CARDINAL I will instantly solicit the state of Ancona
To have them banished.

FERDINAND   You are for Loreto?
60 I shall not be at your ceremony; fare you well.
Write to the Duke of Malfi, my young nephew

5. Popgun.
6. Decorated saddlecloth used only when the court is changing its residence; i.e., he's only for show. "Touchhole": where the match was applied to set off a cannon.
7. Samson once tied some foxes together by the tail and set them afire to burn down the cornfields of the Philistines (Judges 15).
8. Profound, given to abstruse thoughts. Intense

and especially fantastical scholarship was thought to be a cause of melancholy—Bosola's temperament—caused by an imbalance of black bile.
9. The salamander was supposed to be so cold and wet of constitution that it could live in fire.
1. Michelangelo Buonarroti (1475–1564), the great Florentine painter and sculptor. Another anachronism.

She had by her first husband, and acquaint him
With 's mother's honesty.
BOSOLA   I will.
FERDINAND   Antonio!
A slave that only smelled of ink and counters,
65 And never in 's life looked like a gentleman,
But in the audit-time. Go, go presently,°   at once
Draw me out an hundred and fifty of our horse,
And meet me at the fort-bridge.[2]   [*Exeunt.*]

SCENE 4. *The Shrine of Our Lady of Loreto.*

[*Enter* TWO PILGRIMS.]
FIRST PILGRIM   I have not seen a goodlier shrine than this;
Yet I have visited many.
SECOND PILGRIM   The Cardinal of Aragon
Is this day to resign his cardinal's hat:
His sister duchess likewise is arrived
5   To pay her vow of pilgrimage. I expect
A noble ceremony.
FIRST PILGRIM   No question. They come.
[*Here the ceremony of the* CARDINAL's *installment in the habit of a sol-
dier: performed in delivering up his cross, hat, robes, and ring at the
shrine, and investing him with sword, helmet, shield, and spurs; then*
ANTONIO, *the* DUCHESS, *and their children, having presented themselves
at the shrine, are, by a form of banishment in dumb show expressed
towards them by the* CARDINAL *and the state of Ancona, banished: during
all which ceremony, this ditty is sung, to very solemn music, by divers
churchmen.*]

Arms and honors deck thy story,
To thy fame's eternal glory!
Adverse fortune ever fly thee;
10 No disastrous fate come nigh thee!

I alone will sing thy praises,
Whom to honor virtue raises;
And thy study, that divine is,
Bent to martial discipline is.
15 Lay aside all those robes lie by thee;
Crown thy arts with arms, they'll beautify thee.[3]

O worthy of worthiest name, adorned in this manner,
Lead bravely thy forces on under war's warlike banner!
Oh, mayst thou prove fortunate in all martial courses!
20 Guide thou still by skill in arts and forces!
Victory attend thee nigh, whilst fame sings loud thy powers;
Triumphant conquest crown thy head, and blessings pour down showers!

2. Drawbridge.
3. This song is not very suitable to the scene, and Webster, in the edition of 1623, denied writing it.

[*Exeunt all except the* TWO PILGRIMS.]

FIRST PILGRIM   Here's a strange turn of state! Who would have thought
So great a lady would have matched herself

25 Unto so mean a person? Yet the Cardinal
Bears himself much too cruel.
SECOND PILGRIM   They are banished.
FIRST PILGRIM   But I would ask what power hath this state
Of Ancona to determine⁴ of a free prince?
SECOND PILGRIM   They are a free state, sir, and her brother showed

30 How that the Pope, fore-hearing of her looseness,
Hath seized into the protection of the Church
The dukedom which she held as dowager.⁵
FIRST PILGRIM   But by what justice?
SECOND PILGRIM   Sure, I think by none,
Only her brother's instigation.

35 FIRST PILGRIM   What was it with such violence he took
Off from her finger?
SECOND PILGRIM   'Twas her wedding ring,
Which he vowed shortly he would sacrifice
To his revenge.
FIRST PILGRIM   Alas, Antonio!
If that a man be thrust into a well,

40 No matter who sets hands to 't, his own weight
Will bring him sooner to th' bottom. Come, let's hence.
Fortune makes this conclusion general,
All things do help th' unhappy man to fall.   [*Exeunt.*]

SCENE 5. *Near Loreto.*

[*Enter* DUCHESS, ANTONIO, CHILDREN, CARIOLA, *and* SERVANTS.]
DUCHESS   Banished Ancona!
ANTONIO   Yes, you see what power
Lightens in great men's breath.
DUCHESS   Is all our train
Shrunk to this poor remainder?
ANTONIO   These poor men,
Which have got little in your service, vow

5 To take your fortune, but your wiser buntings,⁶
Now they are fledged, are gone.
DUCHESS   They have done wisely.
This puts me in mind of death: physicians thus,
With their hands full of money, use to give o'er
Their patients.
ANTONIO   Right° the fashion of the world: *exactly*

10 From decayed fortunes every flatterer shrinks;
Men cease to build where the foundation sinks.
DUCHESS   I had a very strange dream tonight.°   *last night*

4. Pass judgment on.   son, the still youthful duke.
5. The duchess held Malfi only as guardian for her   6. Migratory birds. "Take": accept.

ANTONIO   What was 't?

DUCHESS   Methought I wore my coronet of state,
    And on a sudden all the diamonds
    Were changed to pearls.

15 ANTONIO   My interpretation
    Is, you'll weep shortly, for to me the pearls
    Do signify your tears.

DUCHESS   The birds that live
    I' th' field on the wild benefit of nature
    Live happier than we; for they may choose their mates,

20   And carol their sweet pleasures to the spring.
            [*Enter* BOSOLA *with a letter.*]

BOSOLA   You are happily o'erta'en.

DUCHESS   From my brother?

BOSOLA   Yes, from the Lord Ferdinand your brother
    All love and safety.

DUCHESS   Thou dost blanch° mischief,   *whitewash*
    Wouldst make it white. See, see, like to calm weather

25   At sea before a tempest, false hearts speak fair
    To those they intend most mischief.   [*reads*]
    "Send Antonio to me; I want his head in a business."
    A politic equivocation!
    He doth not want your counsel, but your head;

30   That is, he cannot sleep till you be dead.
    And here's another pitfall that's strewed o'er
    With roses: mark it, 'tis a cunning one:
    "I stand engaged for your husband for several debts at Naples: let not
    that trouble him; I had rather have his heart than his money."
    And I believe so too.

35 BOSOLA   What do you believe?

DUCHESS   That he so much distrusts my husband's love,
    He will by no means believe his heart is with him
    Until he see it: the devil is not cunning
    Enough to circumvent us in riddles.

40 BOSOLA   Will you reject that noble and free league
    Of amity and love which I present you?

DUCHESS   Their league is like that of some politic° kings,   *crafty*
    Only to make themselves of strength and power
    To be our after-ruin: tell them so.

BOSOLA   And what from you?

45 ANTONIO   Thus tell him: I will not come.

BOSOLA   And what of this?   [*Pointing to the letter.*]

ANTONIO   My brothers have dispersed
    Bloodhounds abroad; which till I hear are muzzled,
    No truce, though hatched with ne'er such politic skill,
    Is safe, that hangs upon our enemies' will.
    I'll not come at° them.   *to*

50 BOSOLA   This proclaims your breeding:
    Every small thing draws a base mind to fear,

As the adamant° draws iron. Fare you well, sir;   *lodestone*
You shall shortly hear from 's.   [*Exit.*]
DUCHESS   I suspect some ambush;
  Therefore, by all my love I do conjure you
55 To take your eldest son, and fly towards Milan.
  Let us not venture all this poor remainder
  In one unlucky bottom.[7]
ANTONIO   You counsel safely.
  Best of my life, farewell. Since we must part,
  Heaven hath a hand in 't, but no otherwise
60 Than as some curious artist takes in sunder
  A clock or watch, when it is out of frame,[8]
  To bring 't in better order.
DUCHESS   I know not which is best,
  To see you dead, or part with you. Farewell, boy:
65 Thou art happy that thou hast not understanding
  To know thy misery; for all our wit
  And reading brings us to a truer sense
  Of sorrow. In the eternal church, sir,
  I do hope we shall not part thus.
ANTONIO   Oh, be of comfort!
70 Make patience a noble fortitude,
  And think not how unkindly we are used:
  Man, like to cassia, is proved best being bruised.[9]
DUCHESS   Must I, like to a slave-born Russian,
  Account it praise to suffer tyranny?
75 And yet, O heaven, thy heavy hand is in 't!
  I have seen my little boy oft scourge his top,[1]
  And compared myself to 't: naught made me e'er
  Go right but heaven's scourge-stick.
ANTONIO   Do not weep:
  Heaven fashioned us of nothing, and we strive
80 To bring ourselves to nothing. Farewell, Cariola,
  And thy sweet armful. If I do never see thee more,
  Be a good mother to your little ones,
  And save them from the tiger. Fare you well.
DUCHESS   Let me look upon you once more, for that speech
85 Came from a dying father. Your kiss is colder
  Than that I have seen an holy anchorite
  Give to a dead man's skull.
ANTONIO   My heart is turned to a heavy lump of lead,
  With which I sound my danger. Fare you well.
                            [*Exeunt* ANTONIO *and his son.*]
90 DUCHESS   My laurel is all withered.
  CARIOLA   Look, madam, what a troop of armèd men

---

7. The metaphor is mercantile: let's not load all
our cargo in one ship ("bottom").
8. Not working. "Curious artist": clever craftsman.
9. Cinnamon bark ("cassia") is most aromatic (virtuous) when pressed.
1. Children used to make tops spin by whipping
them.

Make toward us.

DUCHESS   Oh, they are very welcome:
When Fortune's wheel² is over-charged with princes,
The weight makes it move swift: I would have my ruin
Be sudden.

        [*Enter* BOSOLA *vizarded,*° *with a guard.*]   *masked*

95   I am your adventure,³ am I not?

BOSOLA   You are. You must see your husband no more.

DUCHESS   What devil art thou that counterfeits heaven's thunder?

BOSOLA   Is that terrible? I would have you tell me whether
Is that note worse that frights the silly birds
100   Out of the corn, or that which doth allure them
To the nets? You have hearkened to the last too much.

DUCHESS   Oh, misery! Like to a rusty o'erchargèd cannon,
Shall I never fly in pieces?—Come, to what prison?

BOSOLA   To none.

DUCHESS   Whither, then?

BOSOLA   To your palace.

DUCHESS   I have heard
105   That Charon's boat serves to convey all o'er
The dismal lake,⁴ but brings none back again.

BOSOLA   Your brothers mean you safety and pity.

DUCHESS   Pity!
With such a pity men preserve alive
Pheasants and quails, when they are not fat enough
110   To be eaten.

BOSOLA   These are your children?

DUCHESS   Yes.

BOSOLA   Can they prattle?

DUCHESS   No.
But I intend, since they were born accursed,
Curses shall be their first language.

BOSOLA   Fie, madam!
Forget this base, low fellow—

DUCHESS   Were I a man,
115   I'd beat that counterfeit face° into thy other.   *mask*

BOSOLA   One of no birth.⁵

DUCHESS   Say that he was born mean,
Man is most happy when 's own actions
Be arguments and examples of his virtue.

BOSOLA   A barren, beggarly virtue!

120 DUCHESS   I prithee, who is greatest? Can you tell?
Sad tales befit my woe: I'll tell you one.
A salmon, as she swam unto the sea,
Met with a dogfish, who encounters her
With this rough language: "Why art thou so bold

---

2. The wheel of fortune is an ancient emblem of
mutability; people have their fixed positions on it
and rise or fall as it turns.
3. Object of your journey.

4. In classical mythology, Charon transports the
souls of the dead across the river Styx to Hades.
5. Of low rank by birth.

125　　To mix thyself with our high state of floods,
　　　　Being no eminent courtier, but one
　　　　That for the calmest and fresh time o' th' year
　　　　Dost live in shallow rivers, rank'st thyself
　　　　With silly smelts and shrimps? And darest thou
130　　Pass by our dog-ship without reverence?"
　　　　"Oh!" quoth the salmon, "sister, be at peace:
　　　　Thank Jupiter we both have passed the net!
　　　　Our value never can be truly known,
　　　　Till in the fisher's basket we be shown:
135　　I' th' market then my price may be the higher,
　　　　Even when I am nearest to the cook and fire."
　　　　So to great men the moral may be stretchèd:
　　　　Men oft are valued high, when they're most wretched.
　　　　But come, whither you please. I am armed 'gainst misery;
140　　Bent to all sways of the oppressor's will:
　　　　There's no deep valley but near some great hill.　　　　[Exeunt.]

Act 4

SCENE 1. *Amalfi.*

　　　　　[*Enter* FERDINAND *and* BOSOLA.]
FERDINAND　How doth our sister duchess bear herself
　　　　In her imprisonment?
BOSOLA　　　　　　　　Nobly. I'll describe her.
　　　　She's sad as one long used to 't, and she seems
　　　　Rather to welcome the end of misery
5　　　Than shun it; a behavior so noble
　　　　As gives a majesty to adversity:
　　　　You may discern the shape of loveliness
　　　　More perfect in her tears than in her smiles;
　　　　She will muse four hours together; and her silence,
10　　Methinks, expresseth more than if she spake.
FERDINAND　Her melancholy seems to be fortified
　　　　With a strange disdain.
BOSOLA　　　　　　　　'Tis so; and this restraint,
　　　　Like English mastiffs that grow fierce with tying,
　　　　Makes her too passionately apprehend
　　　　Those pleasures she's kept from.
15　FERDINAND　　　　　　　　Curse upon her!
　　　　I will no longer study in the book
　　　　Of another's heart. Inform her what I told you.　　　　[*Exit.*]
　　　　　　[*Enter* DUCHESS.]
BOSOLA　All comfort to your grace!
DUCHESS　　　　　　　　　I will have none.
　　　　Pray thee, why dost thou wrap thy poisoned pills
20　　In gold and sugar?
BOSOLA　Your elder brother, the Lord Ferdinand,
　　　　Is come to visit you, and sends you word,

'Cause once he rashly made a solemn vow
Never to see you more, he comes i' th' night,
25   And prays you gently neither torch nor taper
Shine in your chamber. He will kiss your hand
And reconcile himself, but for his vow
He dares not see you.
DUCHESS   At his pleasure.
Take hence the lights: he's come.
         [*Enter* FERDINAND.]
FERDINAND   Where are you?
30   DUCHESS   Here, sir.
FERDINAND   This darkness suits you well.
DUCHESS   I would ask your pardon.
FERDINAND   You have it;
For I account it the honorabl'st revenge,
Where I may kill, to pardon. Where are your cubs?
DUCHESS   Whom?
35   FERDINAND   Call them your children;
For though our national law distinguish bastards
From true legitimate issue, compassionate nature
Makes them all equal.
DUCHESS   Do you visit me for this?
You violate a sacrament o' th' Church
Shall make you howl in hell for 't.
40   FERDINAND   It had been well
Could you have lived thus always; for, indeed,
You were too much i' th' light—but no more—
I come to seal my peace with you. Here's a hand
                         [*Gives her a dead man's hand.*]
To which you have vowed much love; the ring upon 't
45   You gave.
DUCHESS   I affectionately kiss it.
FERDINAND   Pray, do, and bury the print of it in your heart.
I will leave this ring with you for a love-token,
And the hand as sure as the ring; and do not doubt
50   But you shall have the heart, too. When you need a friend,
Send it to him that owed° it; you shall see   owned
Whether he can aid you.
DUCHESS   You are very cold;
I fear you are not well after your travel.
Ha! Lights! Oh, horrible!
FERDINAND   Let her have lights enough.   [*Exit.*]
55   DUCHESS   What witchcraft doth he practice, that he hath left
A dead man's hand here?
         [*Here is discovered, behind a traverse,*[6] *the artificial figures of Antonio
         and his children, appearing as if they were dead.*]
BOSOLA   Look you, here's the piece from which 'twas ta'en.
He doth present you this sad spectacle,

6. Curtain.

That, now you know directly they are dead,
60   Hereafter you may wisely cease to grieve
For that which cannot be recovered.
DUCHESS   There is not between heaven and earth one wish
I stay for after this: it wastes[7] me more
Than were 't my picture, fashioned out of wax,
65   Stuck with a magical needle, and then buried
In some foul dunghill; and yond's an excellent property[8]
For a tyrant, which I would account mercy.
BOSOLA   What's that?
DUCHESS   If they would bind me to that lifeless trunk
And let me freeze to death.
BOSOLA   Come, you must live.
70   DUCHESS   That's the greatest torture souls feel in hell,
In hell: that they must live, and cannot die.
Portia,[9] I'll new-kindle thy coals again,
And revive the rare and almost dead example
Of a loving wife.
BOSOLA   Oh, fie! Despair? Remember
You are a Christian.
75   DUCHESS   The Church enjoins fasting:
I'll starve myself to death.
BOSOLA   Leave this vain sorrow.
Things being at the worst begin to mend: the bee
When he hath shot his sting into your hand, may then
Play with your eyelid.
DUCHESS   Good comfortable fellow,
80   Persuade a wretch that's broke upon the wheel[1]
To have all his bones new set; entreat him live
To be executed again. Who must dispatch me?
I account this world a tedious theater,
For I do play a part in 't 'gainst my will.
BOSOLA   Come, be of comfort; I will save your life.
85   DUCHESS   Indeed,
I have not leisure to tend so small a business.
BOSOLA   Now, by my life, I pity you.
DUCHESS   Thou art a fool, then,
To waste thy pity on a thing so wretched
As cannot pity itself. I am full of daggers.
90   Puff, let me blow these vipers from me.
        [*Enter* SERVANT.]
What are you?
SERVANT   One that wishes you long life.
DUCHESS   I would thou wert hanged for the horrible curse
Thou hast given me. I shall shortly grow one
Of the miracles of pity. I'll go pray—

7. Consumes, as by secret disease; witches were
supposed to be able to "waste" their enemies by
making wax images and tormenting them as indicated below.

8. Appropriate act.
9. Portia, the wife of Brutus, committed suicide
by holding hot coals in her mouth.
1. Rack.

No, I'll go curse.

BOSOLA   Oh, fie!

95 DUCHESS   I could curse the stars—

BOSOLA   Oh, fearful!

DUCHESS   And those three smiling seasons of the year
    Into a Russian winter,[2] nay, the world
    To its first chaos.

BOSOLA   Look you, the stars shine still.

100 DUCHESS   Oh, but you must
    Remember, my curse hath a great way to go.
    Plagues, that make lanes through largest families,
    Consume them!

BOSOLA   Fie, lady!

DUCHESS   Let them, like tyrants,
    Never be remembered but for the ill they have done;
105   Let all the zealous prayers of mortified
    Churchmen forget them!

BOSOLA   Oh, uncharitable!

DUCHESS   Let Heaven a little while cease crowning martyrs
    To punish them!
    Go, howl them this, and say, I long to bleed:
110   It is some mercy when men kill with speed.

                       [*Exeunt* DUCHESS *and* SERVANT.]

      [*Re-enter* FERDINAND.]

FERDINAND   Excellent, as I would wish; she's plagued in art:
    These presentations are but framed in wax
    By the curious master in that quality,
    Vincentio Lauriola,[3] and she takes them
    For true substantial bodies.

115 BOSOLA   Why do you do this?

FERDINAND   To bring her to despair.

BOSOLA   'Faith, end here,
    And go no farther in your cruelty.
    Send her a penitential garment to put on
    Next to her delicate skin, and furnish her
    With beads and prayer books.

120 FERDINAND   Damn her! That body of hers,
    While that my blood ran pure in 't, was more worth
    Than that which thou wouldst comfort, called a soul.
    I will send her masks of common courtesans,
    Have her meat served up by bawds and ruffians,
125   And, 'cause she'll needs be mad, I am resolved
    To remove forth the common hospital
    All the mad-folk, and place them near her lodging;
    There let them practice together, sing and dance,
    And act their gambols to the full o' th' moon:
130   If she can sleep the better for it, let her.

---

2. A Russian winter would last all year long.
3. The art of wax modeling was common enough, but the name of the artist seems to be imaginary.

Your work is almost ended.
BOSOLA   Must I see her again?
FERDINAND   Yes.
BOSOLA   Never.
FERDINAND   You must.
BOSOLA   Never in mine own shape;
   That's forfeited by my intelligence°   *betrayal*
135 And this last cruel lie. When you send me next,
   The business shall be comfort.
FERDINAND   Very likely.
   Thy pity is nothing of kin to thee.⁴ Antonio
   Lurks about Milan: thou shalt shortly thither
   To feed a fire as great as my revenge,
140 Which ne'er will slack till it have spent his fuel.
   Intemperate agues⁵ make physicians cruel.   [*Exeunt.*]

SCENE 2

[*Enter* DUCHESS *and* CARIOLA.]
DUCHESS   What hideous noise was that?
CARIOLA   'Tis the wild consort°   *band*
   Of madmen, lady, which your tyrant brother
   Hath placed about your lodging. This tyranny,
   I think, was never practiced till this hour.
5 DUCHESS   Indeed, I thank him. Nothing but noise and folly
   Can keep me in my right wits, whereas reason
   And silence make me stark mad. Sit down;
   Discourse to me some dismal tragedy.
CARIOLA   Oh, 'twill increase your melancholy.
DUCHESS   Thou art deceived:
10 To hear of greater grief would lessen mine.
   This is a prison?
CARIOLA   Yes, but you shall live
   To shake this durance off.
DUCHESS   Thou art a fool:
   The robin redbreast and the nightingale
   Never live long in cages.
CARIOLA   Pray, dry your eyes.
   What think you of, madam?
15 DUCHESS   Of nothing:
   When I muse thus, I sleep.
CARIOLA   Like a madman, with your eyes open?
DUCHESS   Dost thou think we shall know one another in th' other world?
CARIOLA   Yes, out of question.
DUCHESS   Oh that it were possible we might
20 But hold some two days' conference with the dead!
   From them I should learn somewhat, I am sure,
   I never shall know here. I'll tell thee a miracle;
   I am not mad yet, to my cause of sorrow:

4. I.e., pity doesn't suit you very well.   5. Fevers that cannot be controlled.

Th' heaven o'er my head seems made of molten brass,
25 The earth of flaming sulphur, yet I am not mad.
I am acquainted with sad misery
As the tanned galley slave is with his oar;
Necessity makes me suffer constantly,
And custom makes it easy. Who do I look like now?
30 CARIOLA   Like to your picture in the gallery,
A deal of life in show, but none in practice;
Or rather like some reverend monument
Whose ruins are even pitied.
DUCHESS   Very proper.
And Fortune seems only to have her eyesight
35 To behold my tragedy.
How now! What noise is that?
[*Enter* SERVANT.]
SERVANT   I am come to tell you
Your brother hath intended you some sport.
A great physician, when the Pope was sick
Of a deep melancholy, presented him
40 With several sorts of madmen, which wild object
Being full of change and sport, forced him to laugh,
And so the imposthume° broke. The self-same cure   abscess
The duke intends on you.
DUCHESS   Let them come in.
SERVANT   There's a mad lawyer; and a secular priest;[6]
45 A doctor that hath forfeited his wits
By jealousy; an astrologian
That in his works said such a day o' the' month
Should be the day of doom, and, failing of 't,
Ran mad; an English tailor crazed i' th' brain
50 With the study of new fashions; a gentleman-usher[7]
Quite beside himself with care to keep in mind
The number of his lady's salutations
Or "How do you's" she employed him in each morning;
A farmer, too, an excellent knave in grain,
55 Mad 'cause he was hindered transportation:[8]
And let one broker that's mad loose to these,
You'd think the devil were among them.
DUCHESS   Sit, Cariola. Let them loose when you please,
For I am chained to endure all your tyranny.
[*Enter* MADMEN.]
[*Here by a* MADMAN *this Song is sung to a dismal kind of music.*]

60   Oh, let us howl some heavy note,
                                 Some deadly dogged howl,
                          Sounding as from the threatening throat
                                 Of beasts and fatal fowl!
                          As ravens, screech owls, bulls, and bears,
65   We'll bell[9] and bawl our parts,

6. One serving a parish, not a member of an order.   8. Forbidden to export.
7. Doorkeeper.   9. Cry.

Till irksome noise have cloyed your ears
And corrosived your hearts.
At last, whenas our choir wants breath,
Our bodies being blest,
70   We'll sing, like swans, to welcome death,
And die in love and rest.

FIRST MADMAN   Doomsday not come yet? I'll draw it nearer by a perspective,[1] or make a glass that shall set all the world on fire upon an instant. I cannot sleep; my pillow is stuffed with a litter of porcupines.

75 SECOND MADMAN   Hell is a mere glass-house, where the devils are continually blowing up women's souls on hollow irons, and the fire never goes out.

THIRD MADMAN   I will lie with every woman in my parish the tenth night; I will tithe them over like haycocks.

80 FOURTH MADMAN   Shall my pothecary outgo me because I am a cuckold? I have found out his roguery; he makes alum of his wife's urine, and sells it to puritans that have sore throats with overstraining.

FIRST MADMAN   I have skill in heraldry.

SECOND MADMAN   Hast?

85 FIRST MADMAN   You do give for your crest a woodcock's[2] head with the brains picked out on 't; you are a very ancient gentleman.

THIRD MADMAN   Greek is turned Turk: we are only to be saved by the Helvetian translation.[3]

FIRST MADMAN   Come on, sir, I will lay the law to you.

90 SECOND MADMAN   Oh, rather lay a corrosive: the law will eat to the bone.

THIRD MADMAN   He that drinks but to satisfy nature is damned.

FOURTH MADMAN   If I had my glass[4] here, I would show a sight should make all the women here call me mad doctor.

FIRST MADMAN   What's he? A rope maker?

95 SECOND MADMAN   No, no, no, a snuffling knave that, while he shows the tombs, will have his hand in a wench's placket.

THIRD MADMAN   Woe to the caroche[5] that brought home my wife from the masque at three o'clock in the morning! It had a large featherbed in it.

100 FOURTH MADMAN   I have pared the devil's nails forty times, roasted them in raven's eggs, and cured agues with them.

THIRD MADMAN   Get me three hundred milchbats, to make possets[6] to procure sleep.

FOURTH MADMAN   All the college may throw their caps[7] at me: I have made
105   a soap boiler costive;[8] it was my masterpiece.

    [*Here the dance, consisting of eight* MADMEN, *with music answerable thereunto; after which* BOSOLA, *like an old man, enters.*]

DUCHESS   Is he mad too?

SERVANT   Pray, question him. I'll leave you.

                                   [*Exeunt* SERVANT *and* MADMEN.]

BOSOLA   I am come to make thy tomb.

1. Telescope.
2. A proverbially stupid bird.
3. The Geneva Bible; but how it would help with the Greeks and Turks is clear only to the lunatic.
4. Looking glass.
5. Carriage. "Placket": slit in a skirt.
6. Sedative drafts, here made of bat's milk.
7. Despair of emulating.
8. Constipated.

DUCHESS   Ha! My tomb?
  Thou speak'st as if I lay upon my deathbed,
  Gasping for breath. Dost thou perceive me sick?
110 BOSOLA Yes, and the more dangerously, since thy sickness is insensible.[9]
DUCHESS Thou art not mad, sure. Dost know me?
BOSOLA Yes.
DUCHESS   Who am I?
BOSOLA Thou art a box of worm-seed, at best but a salvatory of green
  mummy. What's this flesh? A little crudded[1] milk, fantastical puff paste.
115 Our bodies are weaker than those paper prisons boys use to keep flies
  in, more contemptible, since ours is to preserve earthworms. Didst thou
  ever see a lark in a cage? Such is the soul in the body: this world is like
  her little turf of grass, and the heaven o'er our heads, like her looking
  glass, only gives us a miserable knowledge of the small compass of our
120 prison.
DUCHESS Am not I thy duchess?
BOSOLA Thou art some great woman, sure, for riot[2] begins to sit on thy
  forehead, clad in gray hairs, twenty years sooner than on a merry milkmaid's. Thou sleep'st worse than if a mouse should be forced to take
125 up her lodging in a cat's ear: a little infant that breeds its teeth,[3] should
  it lie with thee, would cry out, as if thou wert the more unquiet bed-
  fellow.
DUCHESS I am Duchess of Malfi still.
BOSOLA That makes thy sleep so broken:
130 Glories, like glowworms, afar off shine bright,
  But, looked to near, have neither heat nor light.
DUCHESS Thou art very plain.
BOSOLA My trade is to flatter the dead, not the living; I am a tomb-maker.
DUCHESS And thou com'st to make my tomb?
135 BOSOLA Yes.
DUCHESS Let me be a little merry. Of what stuff wilt thou make it?
BOSOLA Nay, resolve° me first, of what fashion?   *inform*
DUCHESS Why, do we grow fantastical in our deathbed? Do we affect
  fashion in the grave?
140 BOSOLA Most ambitiously. Princes' images on their tombs do not lie, as
  they were wont, seeming to pray up to heaven, but with their hands under
  their cheeks, as if they died of the toothache. They are not carved with
  their eyes fixed upon the stars, but as their minds were wholly bent upon
  the world, the self-same way they seem to turn their faces.
145 DUCHESS Let me know fully therefore the effect
  Of this thy dismal preparation,
  This talk fit for a charnel.
BOSOLA   Now I shall.
  [*Enter* EXECUTIONERS, *with a coffin, cords, and a bell.*]
  Here is a present from your princely brothers;

---

9. Imperceptible.
1. Curdled. "Worm-seed" is a matter whose ultimate end is the generation of worms. "A salvatory
of green mummy": the substance of mummified
bodies was considered medicinal. The living body

is a box ("salvatory") of such medicine, only not yet
ready for use.
2. Debauchery.
3. A teething infant.

And may it arrive welcome, for it brings
Last benefit, last sorrow.
150 DUCHESS   Let me see it:
I have so much obedience in my blood,
I wish it in their veins to do them good.
BOSOLA   This is your last presence-chamber.[4]
CARIOLA   O my sweet lady!
DUCHESS   Peace, it affrights not me.
155 BOSOLA   I am the common bellman,
That usually is sent to condemned persons
The night before they suffer.
DUCHESS   Even now thou said'st
Thou wast a tomb-maker.
BOSOLA   'Twas to bring you
By degrees to mortification.[5] Listen.   [*rings the bell*]

160   Hark, now everything is still
The screech owl and the whistler[6] shrill
Call upon our dame aloud,
And bid her quickly don her shroud!
Much you had of land and rent:
165   Your length in clay's now competent.[7]
A long war disturbed your mind:
Here your perfect peace is signed.
Of what is 't fools make such vain keeping?
Sin their conception, their birth weeping,
170   Their life a general mist of error,
Their death a hideous storm of terror.
Strew your hair with powders sweet,
Don clean linen, bathe your feet,
And (the foul fiend more to check)
175   A crucifix let bless your neck:
'Tis now full tide 'tween night and day;
End your groan, and come away.

CARIOLA   Hence, villains, tyrants, murderers! Alas!
What will you do with my lady? Call for help.
180 DUCHESS   To whom? To our next neighbors? They are mad-folks.
BOSOLA   Remove that noise.
DUCHESS   Farewell, Cariola.
In my last will I have not much to give:
A many hungry guests have fed upon me;
Thine will be a poor reversion.°   *inheritance*
CARIOLA   I will die with her.
185 DUCHESS   I pray thee, look thou giv'st my little boy
Some syrup for his cold, and let the girl
Say her prayers ere she sleep.
                         [CARIOLA *is forced out by the* EXECUTIONERS.]

---

4. A noble person's reception room.   6. A bird premonitory of death.
5. Repentance, also death and decomposition.   7. Sufficient.

Now what you please.
What death?
BOSOLA   Strangling: here are your executioners.
DUCHESS   I forgive them:
190   The apoplexy, catarrh, or cough o' th' lungs
Would do as much as they do.
BOSOLA   Doth not death fright you?
DUCHESS   Who would be afraid on 't,
Knowing to meet such excellent company
In th' other world?
BOSOLA   Yet, methinks,
195   The manner of your death should much afflict you:
This cord should terrify you.
DUCHESS   Not a whit.
What would it pleasure me to have my throat cut
With diamonds? Or to be smothered
With cassia?° Or to be shot to death with pearls?   *cinnamon*
200   I know death hath ten thousand several doors
For men to take their exits, and 'tis found
They go on such strange geometrical hinges,
You may open them both ways.—Any way, for heaven sake,
So I were out of your whispering. Tell my brothers
205   That I perceive death, now I am well awake,
Best gift is they can give or I can take.
I would fain put off my last woman's fault,
I'd not be tedious to you.
EXECUTIONER   We are ready.
DUCHESS   Dispose my breath how please you, but my body
Bestow upon my women, will you?
210   EXECUTIONER   Yes.
DUCHESS   Pull, and pull strongly, for your able strength
Must pull down heaven upon me—
Yet stay; heaven-gates are not so high arched
As princes' palaces; they that enter there
215   Must go upon their knees. [*kneels*] Come, violent death.
Serve for mandragora[8] to make me sleep!
Go tell my brothers, when I am laid out,
They then may feed in quiet.   [*They strangle her.*]
BOSOLA   Where's the waiting woman?
220   Fetch her. Some other strangle the children.
                    [*Exeunt* EXECUTIONERS, *some of whom return with* CARIOLA.]
Look you, there sleeps your mistress.
CARIOLA   Oh, you are damned
Perpetually for this! My turn is next.
Is 't not so ordered?
BOSOLA   Yes, and I am glad
You are so well prepared for 't.
CARIOLA   You are deceived, sir,

8. The word is used loosely for a stupefying drug.

225 I am not prepared for 't, I will not die;
I will first come to my answer, and know
How I have offended.
BOSOLA   Come, dispatch her.
You kept her counsel; now you shall keep ours.
CARIOLA   I will not die, I must not; I am contracted
To a young gentleman.
230 EXECUTIONER   Here's your wedding ring.
CARIOLA   Let me but speak with the Duke; I'll discover
Treason to his person.
BOSOLA   Delays! Throttle her.
EXECUTIONER   She bites and scratches.
CARIOLA   If you kill me now,
I am damned; I have not been at confession
This two years.
BOSOLA [to EXECUTIONERS]   When!
CARIOLA   I am quick with child.
235 BOSOLA   Why, then,
Your credit's saved.[9]   [They strangle CARIOLA.]
            Bear her into th' next room;
Let this lie still.   [Exeunt the EXECUTIONERS with the body of CARIOLA.]
        [Enter FERDINAND.]
FERDINAND   Is she dead?
BOSOLA   She is what
You'd have her. But here begin your pity. [Shows the children strangled.]
Alas, how have these offended?
FERDINAND   The death
Of young wolves is never to be pitied.
240 BOSOLA   Fix
Your eye here.
FERDINAND   Constantly.
BOSOLA   Do you not weep?
Other sins only speak; murder shrieks out:
The element of water moistens the earth,
But blood flies upwards and bedews the heavens.
245 FERDINAND   Cover her face; mine eyes dazzle: she died young.
BOSOLA   I think not so; her infelicity°   unhappiness
Seemed to have years too many.
FERDINAND   She and I were twins;
And should I die this instant, I had lived
Her time to a minute.
BOSOLA   It seems she was born first:
250 You have bloodily approved[1] the ancient truth,
That kindred commonly do worse agree
Than remote strangers.
FERDINAND   Let me see her face again.
Why didst not thou pity her? What an excellent
Honest man mightst thou have been,

9. Your reputation will now be safe.   1. Given proof of.

255 If thou hadst borne her to some sanctuary!
Or, bold in a good cause, opposed thyself,
With thy advancèd sword above thy head,
Between her innocence and my revenge!
I bade thee, when I was distracted of my wits,
260 Go kill my dearest friend, and thou hast done 't.
For let me but examine well the cause:
What was the meanness of her match to me?
Only I must confess I had a hope,
Had she continued widow, to have gained
265 An infinite mass of treasure by her death:
And that was the main cause, her marriage,
That drew a stream of gall quite through my heart.
For thee, as we observe in tragedies
That a good actor many times is cursed
270 For playing a villain's part, I hate thee for 't,
And, for my sake, say thou hast done much ill well.
BOSOLA   Let me quicken your memory, for I perceive
You are falling into ingratitude: I challenge
The reward due to my service.
FERDINAND   I'll tell thee
What I'll give thee.
BOSOLA   Do.
275 FERDINAND   I'll give thee a pardon
For this murder.
BOSOLA   Ha!
FERDINAND   Yes, and 'tis
The largest bounty I can study to do thee.
By what authority didst thou execute
This bloody sentence?
BOSOLA   By yours.
FERDINAND   Mine! Was I her judge?
280 Did any ceremonial form of law
Doom her to not-being? Did a complete jury
Deliver her conviction up i' th' court?
Where shalt thou find this judgment registered,
Unless in hell? See, like a bloody fool,
285 Thou'st forfeited thy life, and thou shalt die for 't.
BOSOLA   The office of justice is perverted quite
When one thief hangs another. Who shall dare
To reveal this?
FERDINAND   Oh, I'll tell thee;
The wolf shall find her grave, and scrape it up,
290 Not to devour the corpse, but to discover
The horrid murder.
BOSOLA   You, not I, shall quake for 't.
FERDINAND   Leave me.
BOSOLA   I will first receive my pension.
FERDINAND   You are a villain.
BOSOLA   When your ingratitude

Is judge, I am so.

FERDINAND   Oh, horror!

295   That not the fear of Him which binds the devils
    Can prescribe man obedience!
    Never look upon me more.

BOSOLA   Why, fare thee well.
    Your brother and your self are worthy men:
    You have a pair of hearts are rotten graves,

300   Rotten, and rotting others; and your vengeance,
    Like two chained bullets, still goes arm in arm.
    You may be brothers, for treason, like the plague,
    Doth take much in a blood.[2] I stand like one
    That long hath ta'en a sweet and golden dream.

305   I am angry with myself, now that I wake.

FERDINAND   Get thee into some unknown part o' th' world,
    That I may never see thee.

BOSOLA   Let me know
    Wherefore I should be thus neglected. Sir,
    I served your tyranny, and rather strove

310   To satisfy yourself than all the world,
    And though I loathed the evil, yet I loved
    You that did counsel it; and rather sought
    To appear a true servant than an honest man.

FERDINAND   I'll go hunt the badger by owl-light:

315   'Tis a deed of darkness.   *[Exit.]*

BOSOLA   He's much distracted. Off, my painted honor!
    While with vain hopes our faculties we tire,
    We seem to sweat in ice and freeze in fire.
    What would I do, were this to do again?

320   I would not change my peace of conscience
    For all the wealth of Europe.—She stirs; here's life.
    Return, fair soul, from darkness, and lead mine
    Out of this sensible° hell.—She's warm, she breathes.   *living*
    Upon thy pale lips I will melt my heart,

325   To store them with fresh color.—Who's there!
    Some cordial° drink!—Alas! I dare not call: *restorative*
    So pity would destroy pity.—Her eye opes,
    And heaven in it seems to ope, that late was shut,
    To take me up to mercy.

DUCHESS   Antonio!

330 BOSOLA   Yes, madam, he is living;
    The dead bodies you saw were but feigned statues:
    He's reconciled to your brothers: the Pope hath wrought
    The atonement.

DUCHESS   Mercy!   *[She dies.]*

BOSOLA   Oh, she's gone again! There the cords of life broke.

335   Oh, sacred innocence, that sweetly sleeps
    On turtles'[3] feathers, whilst a guilty conscience

---

2. Treason and plague run in certain families.   3. Turtledoves, emblems of a loving couple.

Is a black register wherein is writ
All our good deeds and bad, a perspective°   telescope
That shows us hell! That we cannot be suffered
340   To do good when we have a mind to it!
This is manly sorrow:
These tears, I am very certain, never grew
In my mother's milk. My estate is sunk
Below the degree of fear. Where were
345   These penitent fountains while she was living?
Oh, they were frozen up! Here is a sight
As direful to my soul as is the sword
Unto a wretch hath slain his father. Come,
I'll bear thee hence,
350   And execute thy last will; that's deliver
Thy body to the reverend dispose°   disposition
Of some good women: that the cruel tyrant
Shall not deny me. Then I'll post to Milan,
Where somewhat I will speedily enact
355   Worth⁴ my dejection.   [Exit with the body.]

Act 5

SCENE 1. *A public place in Milan.*

[*Enter* ANTONIO *and* DELIO.]
ANTONIO   What think you of my hope of reconcilement
To the Aragonian brethren?
DELIO   I misdoubt it;
For though they have sent their letters of safe conduct
For your repair to Milan, they appear
5   But nets to entrap you. The Marquis of Pescara,
Under whom you hold certain land in cheat,⁵
Much 'gainst his noble nature hath been moved
To seize those lands, and some of his dependents
Are at this instant making it their suit
10   To be invested in your revenues.⁶
I cannot think they mean well to your life
That do deprive you of your means of life,
Your living.
ANTONIO   You are still an heretic°   skeptic
To any safety I can shape myself.
15   DELIO   Here comes the Marquis. I will make myself
Petitioner for some part of your land,
To know whither it is flying.
ANTONIO   I pray do.   [*Withdraws.*]
       [*Enter* PESCARA.]

---

4. Worthy of.
5. Escheat, i.e., subject to forfeiture under certain

conditions.
6. I.e., to be given your rents.

DELIO   Sir, I have a suit to you.

PESCARA   To me?

DELIO   An easy one.

20   There is the citadel of Saint Bennet,
      With some demesnes,[7] of late in the possession
      Of Antonio Bologna; please you bestow them on me.

PESCARA   You are my friend, but this is such a suit,
      Nor fit for me to give, nor you to take.

DELIO   No, sir?

25 PESCARA   I will give you ample reason for 't
      Soon in private.—Here's the Cardinal's mistress.
            [Enter JULIA.]

JULIA   My lord, I am grown your poor petitioner,
      And should be an ill beggar, had I not
      A great man's letter here, the Cardinal's,
      To court you in my favor.   [Gives a letter.]

30 PESCARA   He entreats for you
      The citadel of Saint Bennet, that belonged
      To the banished Bologna.

JULIA   Yes.

PESCARA   I could not
      Have thought of a friend I could rather pleasure with it;
      'Tis yours.

JULIA   Sir, I thank you; and he shall know

35   How doubly I am engaged both in your gift,
      And speediness of giving, which makes your grant
      The greater.   [Exit.]

ANTONIO [aside]   How they fortify themselves
      With my ruin!

DELIO   Sir, I am little bound to you.

PESCARA   Why?

DELIO   Because you denied this suit to me, and gave 't
      To such a creature.

40 PESCARA   Do you know what it was?
      It was Antonio's land, not forfeited
      By course of law, but ravished from his throat
      By the Cardinal's entreaty. It were not fit
      I should bestow so main° a piece of wrong   egregious

45   Upon my friend; 'tis a gratification
      Only due to a strumpet, for it is injustice.
      Shall I sprinkle the pure blood of innocents
      To make those followers I call my friends
      Look ruddier[8] upon me? I am glad

50   This land, ta'en from the owner by such wrong,
      Returns again unto so foul an use
      As salary for his lust. Learn, good Delio,
      To ask noble things of me, and you shall find

---

7. Associated estates. "Saint Bennet": St. Bene-   8. More agreeably, literally with a healthier
dict.   (ruddy) complexion.

I'll be a noble giver.

DELIO   You instruct me well.

55 ANTONIO [aside]   Why, here's a man now would fright impudence
     From saucist beggars.

PESCARA   Prince Ferdinand's come to Milan,
     Sick, as they give out, of an apoplexy,
     But some say 'tis a frenzy. I am going
     To visit him.   [Exit.]

ANTONIO   'Tis a noble old fellow.

60 DELIO   What course do you mean to take, Antonio?

ANTONIO   This night I mean to venture all my fortune,
     Which is no more than a poor lingering life,
     To the Cardinal's worst of malice. I have got
     Private access to his chamber, and intend
65   To visit him about the mid of night,
     As once his brother did our noble duchess.
     It may be that the sudden apprehension
     Of danger—for I'll go in mine own shape—
     When he shall see it fraught with love and duty,
70   May draw the poison out of him, and work
     A friendly reconcilement. If it fail,
     Yet it shall rid me of this infamous calling,
     For better fall once than be ever falling.

DELIO   I'll second you in all danger, and, howe'er,
75 My life keeps rank with yours.

ANTONIO   You are still my loved and best friend.   [Exeunt.]

SCENE 2

[Enter PESCARA and DOCTOR.]

PESCARA   Now, doctor, may I visit your patient?

DOCTOR   If 't please your lordship: but he's instantly°   *very shortly*
     To take the air here in the gallery
     By my direction.

PESCARA   Pray thee, what's his disease?

5 DOCTOR   A very pestilent disease, my lord,
     They call lycanthropia.

PESCARA   What's that?
     I need a dictionary to 't.

DOCTOR   I'll tell you.
     In those that are possessed with 't there o'erflows
     Such melancholy humor, they imagine
10   Themselves to be transformèd into wolves;
     Steal forth to churchyards in the dead of night,
     And dig dead bodies up: as two nights since
     One met the Duke 'bout midnight in a lane
     Behind Saint Mark's Church, with the leg of a man
15   Upon his shoulder; and he howled fearfully;
     Said he was a wolf, only the difference
     Was, a wolf's skin was hairy on the outside,

His on the inside; bade them take their swords,
Rip up his flesh, and try. Straight I was sent for,
20 And, having ministered to him, found his grace
Very well recovered.
PESCARA   I'm glad on 't.
DOCTOR   Yet not without some fear
Of a relapse. If he grow to his fit again,
I'll go a nearer way to work with him
25 Than ever Paracelsus[5] dreamed of: if
They'll give me leave, I'll buffet his madness
Out of him. Stand aside; he comes.
        [*Enter* FERDINAND, MALATESTE, CARDINAL, *and* BOSOLA *apart.*]
FERDINAND   Leave me.
MALATESTE   Why doth your lordship love this solitariness?
FERDINAND   Eagles commonly fly alone: they are crows, daws, and star-
30 lings that flock together. Look, what's that follows me?
MALATESTE   Nothing, my lord.
FERDINAND   Yes.
MALATESTE   'Tis your shadow.
FERDINAND   Stay it; let it not haunt me.
35 MALATESTE   Impossible, if you move, and the sun shine.
FERDINAND   I will throttle it.   [*Throws himself on the ground.*]
MALATESTE   O, my lord, you are angry with nothing.
FERDINAND   You are a fool: how is 't possible I should catch my shadow,
unless I fall upon 't? When I go to hell, I mean to carry a bribe; for, look
40 you, good gifts evermore make way for the worst persons.
PESCARA   Rise, good my lord.
FERDINAND   I am studying the art of patience.
PESCARA   'Tis a noble virtue.
FERDINAND   To drive six snails before me from this town to Moscow; nei-
45 ther use goad nor whip to them, but let them take their own time—the
patient'st man i' th' world match me for an experiment—and I'll crawl
after like a sheep-biter.[1]
CARDINAL   Force him up.   [*They raise him.*]
FERDINAND   Use me well, you were best. What I have done, I have done:
50 I'll confess nothing.
DOCTOR   Now let me come to him. Are you mad, my lord? Are you out of
your princely wits?
FERDINAND   What's he?
PESCARA   Your doctor.
55 FERDINAND   Let me have his beard sawed off, and his eyebrows filed more
civil.
DOCTOR   I must do mad tricks with him, for that's the only way on 't.[2] I
have brought your grace a salamander's skin to keep you from sunburn-
ing.
60 FERDINAND   I have cruel sore eyes.
DOCTOR   The white of a cockatrix's[3] egg is present remedy.

9. Paracelsus, the great Swiss alchemist, famous
for his cures by sympathetic magic.
1. A sheepdog that bites or worries sheep.

2. I.e., to cure him.
3. A fabulous, and deadly poisonous, serpent, supposed to be hatched of a cock's egg.

FERDINAND   Let it be a new-laid one, you were best. Hide me from him: physicians are like kings—they brook no contradiction.

DOCTOR   Now he begins to fear me: now let me alone with him.

65 CARDINAL   How now? Put off your gown?

DOCTOR   Let me have some forty urinals filled with rosewater: he and I'll go pelt one another with them. Now he begins to fear me. Can you fetch a frisk, sir?[4] Let him go, let him go, upon my peril: I find by his eye he stands in awe of me; I'll make him as tame as a dormouse.

70 FERDINAND   Can you fetch your frisks, sir? I will stamp him into a cullis,[5] flay off his skin, to cover one of the anatomies[6] this rogue hath set i' th' cold yonder in Barber-Chirurgeons'[7] Hall. Hence, hence! You are all of you like beasts for sacrifice: there's nothing left of you but tongue and belly, flattery and lechery.   [Exit.]

PESCARA   Doctor, he did not fear you throughly.

75 DOCTOR   True;
I was somewhat too forward.

BOSOLA [aside]   Mercy upon me,
What a fatal judgment hath fall'n upon this Ferdinand!

PESCARA   Knows your grace what accident hath brought
Unto the prince this strange distraction?

80 CARDINAL [aside]   I must feign somewhat.—Thus they say it grew:
You have heard it rumored, for these many years
None of our family dies but there is seen
The shape of an old woman, which is given
By tradition to us to have been murdered

85 By her nephews for her riches. Such a figure
One night, as the prince sat up late at 's book,
Appeared to him; when, crying out for help,
The gentlemen of 's chamber found his grace
All on a cold sweat, altered much in face

90 And language; since which apparition,
He hath grown worse and worse, and I much fear
He cannot live.

BOSOLA   Sir, I would speak with you.

PESCARA   We'll leave your grace,
Wishing to the sick prince, our noble lord,
All health of mind and body.

95 CARDINAL   You are most welcome.
[Exeunt PESCARA, MALATESTE, and DOCTOR.]
Are you come? So. [aside] This fellow must not know
By any means I had intelligence°   was accessory
In our duchess' death; for, though I counseled it,
The full of all th' engagement seemed to grow

100 From Ferdinand.—Now, sir, how fares our sister?
I do not think but sorrow makes her look
Like to an oft-dyed garment: she shall now
Taste comfort from me. Why do you look so wildly?
Oh, the fortune of your master here the prince

---

4. Cut a caper, dance a jig.
5. Broth.
6. Anatomical skeletons hung up in the surgeon's

college, which Ferdinand proposes to cover with the doctor's flayed skin.
7. Surgeons.

105 Dejects you, but be you of happy comfort:
     If you'll do one thing for me I'll entreat,
     Though he had a cold tombstone o'er his bones,
     I'll make you what you would be.
BOSOLA   Anything;
     Give it me in a breath, and let me fly to 't:
110 They that think long, small expedition win,
     For musing much o' th' end cannot begin.
          [Enter JULIA.]
JULIA   Sir, will you come in to supper?
CARDINAL   I am busy;
     Leave me.
JULIA [aside]   What an excellent shape hath that fellow!   [Exit.]
115 CARDINAL   'Tis thus. Antonio lurks here in Milan:
     Inquire him out, and kill him. While he lives,
     Our sister cannot marry, and I have thought
     Of an excellent match for her. Do this, and style me
     Thy advancement.[8]
120 BOSOLA   But by what means shall I find him out?
     CARDINAL   There is a gentleman called Delio
     Here in the camp, that hath been long approved
     His loyal friend. Set eye upon that fellow;
     Follow him to mass; maybe Antonio,
125 Although he do account religion
     But a school-name,° for fashion of the world   an idle phrase
     May accompany him; or else go inquire out
     Delio's confessor, and see if you can bribe
     Him to reveal it. There are a thousand ways
130 A man might find to trace him; as to know
     What fellows haunt the Jews for taking up
     Great sums of money, for sure he's in want;
     Or else to go to th' picture-makers, and learn
     Who bought her picture lately. Some of these
     Haply may take.
135 BOSOLA   Well, I'll not freeze i' th' business:
     I would see that wretched thing, Antonio,
     Above all sights i' th' world.
CARDINAL   Do, and be happy.   [Exit.]
BOSOLA   This fellow doth breed basilisks in 's eyes,
     He's nothing else but murder; yet he seems
140 Not to have notice of the duchess' death.
     'Tis his cunning: I must follow his example;
     There cannot be a surer way to trace
     Than that of an old fox.
          [Re-enter JULIA, with a pistol.]
JULIA   So, sir, you are well met.
BOSOLA   How now?
JULIA   Nay, the doors are fast enough.
145 Now, sir, I will make you confess your treachery.

8. Look to me for your promotion.

BOSOLA   Treachery?

JULIA   Yes, confess to me
   Which of my women 'twas, you hired to put
   Love-powder into my drink?

BOSOLA   Love-powder?

JULIA   Yes, when I was at Malfi.
150   Why should I fall in love with such a face else?
   I have already suffered for thee so much pain,
   The only remedy to do me good
   Is to kill my longing.

BOSOLA   Sure, your pistol holds
   Nothing but perfumes or kissing-comfits.[9]
155   Excellent lady! You have a pretty way on 't
   To discover your longing. Come, come, I'll disarm you,
   And arm you thus:[1] yet this is wondrous strange.

JULIA   Compare thy form and my eyes together, you'll find
   My love no such great miracle. Now you'll say
160   I am wanton: this nice modesty in ladies
   Is but a troublesome familiar[2] that haunts them.

BOSOLA   Know you me, I am a blunt soldier.

JULIA   The better:
   Sure, there wants° fire where there are no lively sparks   *lacks*
   Of roughness.

BOSOLA   And I want compliment.[3]

JULIA   Why, ignorance
165   In courtship cannot make you do amiss,
   If you have a heart to do well.

BOSOLA   You are very fair.

JULIA   Nay, if you lay beauty to my charge,
   I must plead unguilty.

BOSOLA   Your bright eyes
   Carry a quiver of darts in them, sharper
   Than sunbeams.

170 JULIA   You will mar me with commendation,
   Put yourself to the charge of courting me,
   Whereas now I woo you.

BOSOLA [*aside*]   I have it, I will work upon this creature.—
   Let us grow most amorously familiar.
175   If the great Cardinal now should see me thus,
   Would he not count me a villain?

JULIA   No, he might count me a wanton,
   Not lay a scruple of offence on you;
   For if I see and steal a diamond,
180   The fault is not i' th' stone, but in me the thief
   That purloins it. I am sudden with you.
   We that are great women of pleasure, use to cut off
   These uncertain wishes and unquiet longings,

9. Candies to sweeten the breath.   2. Attendant spirit or demon.
1. Disarm (by taking away her pistol); arm (by   3. I don't have the gift of flattery.
embracing her).

And in an instant join the sweet delight
185 And the pretty excuse together. Had you been i' th' street,
Under my chamber window, even there
I should have courted you.
BOSOLA   Oh, you are an excellent lady!
JULIA   Bid me do somewhat for you presently°   *right away*
To express I love you.
BOSOLA   I will, and if you love me,
190 Fail not to effect it.
The Cardinal is grown wondrous melancholy;
Demand the cause, let him not put you off
With feigned excuse; discover the main ground on 't.
JULIA   Why would you know this?
BOSOLA   I have depended on him,
195 And I hear he is fallen in some disgrace
With the Emperor: if he be, like the mice
That forsake falling houses, I would shift
To other dependence.
JULIA   You shall not need follow the wars;
I'll be your maintenance.
200 BOSOLA   And I your loyal servant;
But I cannot leave my calling.
JULIA   Not leave
An ungrateful general for the love of a sweet lady?
You are like some cannot sleep in featherbeds,
But must have blocks for their pillows.
BOSOLA   Will you do this?
JULIA   Cunningly.
205 BOSOLA   Tomorrow I'll expect th' intelligence.
JULIA   Tomorrow? Get you into my cabinet,
You shall have it with you. Do not delay me,
No more than I do you. I am like one
That is condemned: I have my pardon promised,
210 But I would see it sealed. Go, get you in;
You shall see me wind my tongue about his heart
Like a skein of silk.   [*Exit* BOSOLA.]
          [*Re-enter* CARDINAL.]
CARDINAL   Where are you?
          [*Enter* SERVANTS.]
SERVANTS   Here.
CARDINAL   Let none, upon your lives,
Have conference with the Prince Ferdinand,
215 Unless I know it. [*aside*] In this distraction
He may reveal the murder.   [*Exeunt* SERVANTS.]
Yond's my lingering consumption:
I am weary of her, and by any means
Would be quit of.
JULIA   How now, my lord?
What ails you?
CARDINAL   Nothing.

220 JULIA   Oh, you are much altered:
    Come, I must be your secretary, and remove
    This lead from off your bosom.[4] What's the matter?
CARDINAL   I may not tell you.
JULIA   Are you so far in love with sorrow
225   You cannot part with part of it? Or think you
    I cannot love your grace when you are sad
    As well as merry? Or do you suspect
    I, that have been a secret to your heart
    These many winters, cannot be the same
    Unto your tongue?
230 CARDINAL   Satisfy thy longing—
    The only way to make thee keep my counsel
    Is not to tell thee.
JULIA   Tell your echo this,
    Or flatterers, that like echoes still report
    What they hear though most imperfect, and not me;
235   For if that you be true unto yourself,
    I'll know.
CARDINAL   Will you rack me?[5]
JULIA   No, judgment shall
    Draw it from you: it is an equal fault,
    To tell one's secrets unto all or none.
CARDINAL   The first argues folly.
JULIA   But the last, tyranny.
240 CARDINAL   Very well. Why, imagine I have committed
    Some secret deed which I desire the world
    May never hear of.
JULIA   Therefore may not I know it?
    You have concealed for me as great a sin
    As adultery. Sir, never was occasion
245   For perfect trial of my constancy
    Till now: sir, I beseech you—
CARDINAL   You'll repent it.
JULIA   Never.
CARDINAL   It hurries thee to ruin: I'll not tell thee.
    Be well advised, and think what danger 'tis
250   To receive a prince's secrets: they that do,
    Had need have their breasts hooped with adamant
    To contain them. I pray thee, yet be satisfied;
    Examine thine own frailty; 'tis more easy
    To tie knots than unloose them: 'tis a secret
255   That, like a lingering poison, may chance lie
    Spread in thy veins, and kill thee seven year hence.
JULIA   Now you dally with me.
CARDINAL   No more; thou shalt know it.
    By my appointment the great Duchess of Malfi
    And two of her young children, four nights since,

---

4. Secretaries opened letters addressed to their   5. Will you torture me?
masters by removing the heavy lead seals.

Were strangled.

260 JULIA   O Heaven! Sir, what have you done?

CARDINAL   How now? How settles this? Think you your bosom
     Will be a grave dark and obscure enough
     For such a secret?

JULIA   You have undone yourself, sir.

CARDINAL   Why?

JULIA   It lies not in me to conceal it.

CARDINAL   No?

265   Come, I will swear you to 't upon this book.

JULIA   Most religiously.

CARDINAL   Kiss it.   [*She kisses the book.*]
                     Now you shall
     Never utter it; thy curiosity
     Hath undone thee: thou'rt poisoned with that book.
     Because I knew thou couldst not keep my counsel,
     I have bound thee to 't by death.
       [*Re-enter* BOSOLA.]

270 BOSOLA   For pity sake,
   Hold!

CARDINAL   Ha! Bosola?

JULIA   I forgive you
     This equal piece of justice you have done;
     For I betrayed your counsel to that fellow:
     He overheard it; that was the cause I said
     It lay not in me to conceal it.

275 BOSOLA   O foolish woman,
   Couldst not thou have poisoned him?

JULIA   'Tis weakness,
     Too much to think what should have been done. I go
     I know not whither.   [*Dies.*]

CARDINAL   Wherefore com'st thou hither?

BOSOLA   That I might find a great man like yourself,

280   Not out of his wits as the Lord Ferdinand,
     To remember my service.

CARDINAL   I'll have thee hewed in pieces.

BOSOLA   Make not yourself such a promise of that life
     Which is not yours to dispose of.

CARDINAL   Who placed thee here?

BOSOLA   Her lust, as she intended.

CARDINAL   Very well.

285   Now you know me for your fellow murderer.

BOSOLA   And wherefore should you lay fair marble colors[6]
     Upon your rotten purposes to me?
     Unless you imitate some that do plot great treasons,
     And when they have done, go hide themselves i' th' graves
     Of those were actors in 't?

290 CARDINAL   No more; there is
   A fortune attends thee.

---

6. Plaster was often painted to look like marble.

BOSOLA   Shall I go sue to Fortune any longer?
  'Tis the fool's pilgrimage.
CARDINAL   I have honors in store for thee.
BOSOLA   There are a many ways that conduct to seeming
  Honor, and some of them very dirty ones.
295 CARDINAL   Throw to the devil
  Thy melancholy; the fire burns well,
  What need we keep a stirring of 't, and make
  A greater smother? Thou wilt kill Antonio?
BOSOLA   Yes.
CARDINAL   Take up that body.
BOSOLA   I think I shall
300 Shortly grow the common bier for churchyards!
CARDINAL   I will allow thee some dozen of attendants
  To aid thee in the murder.
BOSOLA   Oh, by no means. Physicians that apply horseleeches to any rank
  swelling use to cut off their tails, that the blood may run through them
305 the faster. Let me have no train[7] when I go to shed blood, lest it make
  me have a greater when I ride to the gallows.[8]
CARDINAL   Come to me after midnight, to help to remove that body to her
  own lodging. I'll give out she died of the plague; 'twill breed the less
  inquiry after her death.
310 BOSOLA   Where's Castruccio her husband?
CARDINAL   He's rode to Naples to take possession of Antonio's citadel.
BOSOLA   Believe me, you have done a very happy turn.
CARDINAL   Fail not to come. There is the master key of our lodgings, and
  by that you may conceive what trust I plant in you.
315 BOSOLA   You shall find me ready.   [Exit CARDINAL.]
  Oh poor Antonio, though nothing be so needful
  To thy estate as pity, yet I find
  Nothing so dangerous. I must look to my footing;
  In such slippery ice-pavements men had need
320 To be frost-nailed well; they may break their necks else;
  The precedent's here afore me. How this man
  Bears up in blood! Seems fearless! Why, 'tis well:
  Security some men call the suburbs of hell,
  Only a dead° wall between. Well, good Antonio,   bare
325 I'll seek thee out, and all my care shall be
  To put thee into safety from the reach
  Of these most cruel biters that have got
  Some of thy blood already. It may be,
  I'll join with thee in a most just revenge:
330 The weakest arm is strong enough that strikes
  With the sword of justice. Still methinks the duchess
  Haunts me. There, there, 'tis nothing but my melancholy.
  O Penitence, let me truly taste thy cup,
  That throws men down only to raise them up!   [Exit.]

7. Followers.
8. Criminals, carted through the streets to be

hanged at Tyburn, were followed by crowds of the idle, the sadistic, and their own fellow criminals.

SCENE 3. *A Fortification at Milan.*

[*Enter* ANTONIO *and* DELIO. *Echo from the* DUCHESS' *grave.*]

DELIO   Yond's the Cardinal's window. This fortification
    Grew from the ruins of an ancient abbey;
    And to yond side o' th' river lies a wall,
    Piece of a cloister, which in my opinion
5   Gives the best echo that you ever heard,
    So hollow and so dismal, and withal
    So plain in the distinction of our words,
    That many have supposed it is a spirit
    That answers.
ANTONIO   I do love these ancient ruins.
10   We never tread upon them but we set
    Our foot upon some reverend history:
    And, questionless, here in this open court,
    Which now lies naked to the injuries
    Of stormy weather, some men lie interred
15   Loved the church so well, and gave so largely to 't,
    They thought it should have canopied their bones
    Till doomsday; but all things have their end:
    Churches and cities, which have diseases like to men,
    Must have like death that we have.
ECHO   "Like death that we have."
DELIO   Now the echo hath caught you.
20 ANTONIO   It groaned, methought, and gave
    A very deadly accent.
ECHO   "Deadly accent."
DELIO   I told you 'twas a pretty one: you may make it
    A huntsman, or a falconer, a musician,
    Or a thing of sorrow.
ECHO   "A thing of sorrow."
ANTONIO   Aye, sure, that suits it best.
25 ECHO   "That suits it best."
ANTONIO   'Tis very like my wife's voice.
ECHO   "Aye, wife's voice."
DELIO   Come, let's walk further from 't. I would not have you
    Go to th' Cardinal's tonight: do not.
ECHO   "Do not."
DELIO   Wisdom doth not more moderate wasting sorrow
30   Than time: take time for 't; be mindful of thy safety.
ECHO   "Be mindful of thy safety."
ANTONIO   Necessity compels me:
    Make° scrutiny throughout the passes   *if you make*
    Of your own life, you'll find it impossible
    To fly your fate.
ECHO   "Oh, fly your fate."
35 DELIO   Hark! The dead stones seem to have pity on you,
    And give you good counsel.
ANTONIO   Echo, I will not talk with thee,

For thou art a dead thing.
ECHO   "Thou art a dead thing."
ANTONIO   My duchess is asleep now,
40   And her little ones, I hope sweetly: O heaven,
      Shall I never see her more?
ECHO   "Never see her more."
ANTONIO   I marked not one repetition of the echo
      But that, and on the sudden a clear light
      Presented me a face folded in sorrow.
DELIO   Your fancy merely.
45 ANTONIO   Come, I'll be out of this ague,°   *fever*
      For to live thus is not indeed to live;
      It is a mockery and abuse of life.
      I will not henceforth save myself by halves;
      Lose all, or nothing.
DELIO   Your own virtue save you!
50 I'll fetch your eldest son, and second[9] you:
      It may be that the sight of his own blood
      Spread in so sweet a figure° may beget   *face*
      The more compassion.
ANTONIO   However, fare you well.
      Though in our miseries Fortune have a part,
55 Yet in our noble sufferings she hath none:
      Contempt of pain, that we may call our own.   *[Exeunt.]*

SCENE 4. *A room in the* CARDINAL'*s palace.*

[*Enter* CARDINAL, PESCARA, MALATESTE, RODERIGO, *and* GRISOLAN.]

CARDINAL   You shall not watch tonight by the sick prince;
      His grace is very well recovered.
MALATESTE   Good my lord, suffer° us.   *allow*
CARDINAL   Oh, by no means;
      The noise and change of object in his eye
5   Doth more distract him. I pray, all to bed;
      And though you hear him in his violent fit,
      Do not rise, I entreat you.
PESCARA   So, sir; we shall not.
CARDINAL   Nay, I must have you promise upon your honors,
      For I was enjoined to 't by himself; and he seemed
      To urge it sensibly.°   *with strong feeling*
10 PESCARA   Let our honors bind
      This trifle.
CARDINAL   Nor any of your followers.
MALATESTE   Neither.
CARDINAL   It may be, to make trial of your promise,
      When he's asleep, myself will rise and feign
      Some of his mad tricks, and cry out for help,
      And feign myself in danger.
15 MALATESTE   If your throat were cutting,
      I'd not come at you, now I have protested against it.

9. Back you up.

CARDINAL   Why, I thank you.   [*Withdraws.*]
GRISOLAN   'Twas a foul storm tonight.
RODERIGO   The Lord Ferdinand's chamber shook like an osier.[1]
MALATESTE   'Twas nothing but pure kindness in the devil,
20   To rock his own child.   [*Exeunt all except the* CARDINAL.]
CARDINAL   The reason why I would not suffer these
    About my brother is because at midnight
    I may with better privacy convey
    Julia's body to her own lodging. Oh, my conscience!
25   I would pray now, but the devil takes away my heart
    For having any confidence in prayer.
    About this hour I appointed Bosola
    To fetch the body: when he hath served my turn,
    He dies.   [*Exit.*]
         [*Enter* BOSOLA.]
30 BOSOLA   Ha! 'Twas the Cardinal's voice; I heard him name
    Bosola and my death. Listen! I hear
    One's footing.
         [*Enter* FERDINAND.]
FERDINAND   Strangling is a very quiet death.
BOSOLA [*aside*]   Nay, then, I see I must stand upon my guard.
FERDINAND   What say to that? Whisper softly; do you agree to 't? So; it
35   must be done i' th' dark: the Cardinal would not for a thousand pounds
    the doctor should see it.   [*Exit.*]
BOSOLA   My death is plotted; here's the consequence of murder.
    We value not desert nor Christian breath,
    When we know black deeds must be cured with death.
         [*Enter* ANTONIO *and* SERVANT.]
40 SERVANT   Here stay, sir, and be confident, I pray:
    I'll fetch you a dark lantern.   [*Exit.*]
ANTONIO   Could I take him at his prayers,
    There were hope of pardon.
BOSOLA   Fall right, my sword!   [*Stabs him.*]
    I'll not give thee so much leisure as to pray.
45 ANTONIO   Oh, I am gone! Thou hast ended a long suit[2]
    In a minute.
BOSOLA   What art thou?
ANTONIO   A most wretched thing,
    That only have thy benefit in death,
    To appear myself.
         [*Re-enter* SERVANT *with a lantern.*]
SERVANT   Where are you, sir?
ANTONIO   Very near my home. Bosola?
SERVANT   Oh, misfortune!
50 BOSOLA   Smother thy pity; thou art dead else. Antonio?
    The man I would have saved 'bove mine own life!
    We are merely the stars' tennis balls, struck and bandied
    Which way please them.[3] O good Antonio,

1. A willow wand.
2. Antonio thinks it is the cardinal, to whom he came to address a plea ("suit"), who has stabbed him.
3. The power of the stars over people's lives was a Renaissance commonplace.

I'll whisper one thing in thy dying ear
55 Shall make thy heart break quickly! Thy fair duchess
And two sweet children—

ANTONIO   Their very names
Kindle a little life in me.

BOSOLA   Are murdered.

ANTONIO   Some men have wished to die
At the hearing of sad tidings; I am glad
60 That I shall do 't in sadness: I would not now
Wish my wounds balmed nor healed, for I have no use
To put my life to. In all our quest of greatness,
Like wanton boys, whose pastime is their care,
We follow after bubbles blown in th' air.
65 Pleasure of life, what is't? Only the good hours
Of an ague; merely a preparative to rest,
To endure vexation. I do not ask
The process° of my death; only commend me   reason, circumstances
To Delio.

BOSOLA   Break, heart!

70 ANTONIO   And let my son fly the courts of princes.   [*Dies.*]

BOSOLA   Thou seem'st to have loved Antonio?

SERVANT   I brought him hither
To have reconciled him to the Cardinal.

BOSOLA   I do not ask thee that.
Take him up, if thou tender thine own life,
75 And bear him where the lady Julia
Was wont to lodge. Oh, my fate moves swift;
I have this Cardinal in the forge already;
Now I'll bring him to th' hammer. Oh direful misprision!⁴
I will not imitate things glorious,
80 No more than base; I'll be mine own example.
On, on, and look thou represent,° for silence,   *imitate*
The thing thou bear'st.⁵   [*Exeunt.*]

SCENE 5

[*Enter* CARDINAL, *with a book.*]

CARDINAL   I am puzzled in a question about hell:
He says, in hell there's one material fire,
And yet it shall not burn all men alike.
Lay him by. How tedious is a guilty conscience!
5 When I look into the fish ponds in my garden,
Methinks I see a thing armed with a rake,
That seems to strike at me.

[*Enter* BOSOLA, *and* SERVANT *bearing* ANTONIO's *body.*]
                              Now, art thou come?
Thou look'st ghastly:
There sits in thy face some great determination
Mixed with some fear.

---

4. Misunderstanding.   5. The corpse.

10 BOSOLA   Thus it lightens into action:
   I am come to kill thee.
   CARDINAL   Ha! Help! Our guard!
   BOSOLA   Thou art deceived; they are out of thy howling.
   CARDINAL   Hold; and I will faithfully divide
   Revenues with thee.
   BOSOLA   Thy prayers and proffers
   Are both unseasonable.
15 CARDINAL   Raise the watch!
   We are betrayed!
   BOSOLA   I have confined your flight:[6]
   I'll suffer your retreat to Julia's chamber,
   But no further.
   CARDINAL   Help! We are betrayed!
       [*Enter, above,* PESCARA, MALATESTE, RODERIGO, *and* GRISOLAN.]
   MALATESTE   Listen.
   CARDINAL   My dukedom for rescue!
   RODERIGO   Fie upon his counterfeiting!
   MALATESTE   Why, 'tis not the Cardinal.
20 RODERIGO   Yes, yes, 'tis he,
   But I'll see him hanged ere I'll go down to him.
   CARDINAL   Here's a plot upon me. I am assaulted! I am lost,
   Unless some rescue.
   GRISOLAN   He doth this pretty well,
   But it will not serve to laugh me out of my honor.
   CARDINAL   The sword's at my throat!
25 RODERIGO   You would not bawl so loud then.
   MALATESTE   Come, come, let's go to bed. He told us thus much aforehand.
   PESCARA   He wished you should not come at him; but, believe 't,
   The accent of the voice sounds not in jest:
   I'll down to him, howsoever, and with engines.[7]
   Force ope the doors.   [*Exit above.*]
30 RODERIGO   Let's follow him aloof,[8]
   And note how the Cardinal will laugh at him.
                [*Exeunt, above,* MALATESTE, RODERIGO, *and* GRISOLAN.]
   BOSOLA   There's for you first,   [*He kills the* SERVANT.]
   'Cause you shall not unbarricade the door
   To let in rescue.
   CARDINAL   What cause hast thou to pursue my life?
35 BOSOLA   Look there.
   CARDINAL   Antonio?
   BOSOLA   Slain by my hand unwittingly.
   Pray, and be sudden: when thou killed'st thy sister,
   Thou took'st from Justice her most equal balance,
   And left her naught but her sword.
   CARDINAL   Oh, mercy!
40 BOSOLA   Now it seems thy greatness was only outward;

6. Cut off your escape.   8. At a distance.
7. Bars and beams.

For thou fall'st faster of thyself than calamity
Can drive thee. I'll not waste longer time: there!   [*Stabs him.*]
CARDINAL   Thou hast hurt me.
BOSOLA   Again!   [*Stabs him again.*]
CARDINAL   Shall I die like a leveret,[9]
Without any resistance? Help, help, help!
45   I am slain!
        [*Enter* FERDINAND.]
FERDINAND   Th' alarum? Give me a fresh horse;
Rally the vaunt-guard, or the day is lost.
Yield, yield! I give you the honor of arms,
Shake my sword over you; will you yield?[1]
CARDINAL   Help me; I am your brother!
50   FERDINAND   The devil!
My brother fight upon the adverse party?
        [*He wounds the* CARDINAL, *and, in the scuffle, gives* BOSOLA *his death-
        wound.*]
There flies your ransom.
CARDINAL   O justice!
I suffer now for what hath former° been: *earlier*
Sorrow is held the eldest child of sin.
55   FERDINAND   Now you're brave fellows. Caesar's fortune was harder than
Pompey's; Caesar died in the arms of prosperity, Pompey at the feet
of disgrace. You both died in the field. The pain's nothing: pain many
times is taken away with the apprehension of greater, as the toothache
with the sight of a barber that comes to pull it out: there's philosophy
60   for you.
BOSOLA   Now my revenge is perfect. Sink, thou main cause
                                                        [*He kills* FERDINAND.]
Of my undoing! The last part of my life
Hath done me best service.
FERDINAND   Give me some wet hay; I am broken-winded.[2] I do account
65   this world but a dog-kennel: I will vault credit and affect high pleasures
beyond death.
BOSOLA   He seems to come to himself, now he's so near
The bottom.
FERDINAND   My sister, O my sister! There's the cause on 't.
70   Whether we fall by ambition, blood, or lust,
Like diamonds we are cut with our own dust.   [*Dies.*]
CARDINAL   Thou hast thy payment, too.
BOSOLA   Yes, I hold my weary soul in my teeth.
'Tis ready to part from me. I do glory
75   That thou, which stood'st like a huge pyramid
Begun upon a large and ample base,
Shalt end in a little point, a kind of nothing.
        [*Enter, below,* PESCARA, MALATESTE, RODERIGO, *and* GRISOLAN.]
PESCARA   How now, my lord?
MALATESTE   O sad disaster!

---

9. A baby hare.
1. Ferdinand thinks he's on the field of battle and
offering the "honor of arms" (liberal surrender

terms) to his foes. "Vaunt-guard": vanguard.
2. Worn-out horses are said to be broken-winded.

RODERIGO   How comes this?

BOSOLA   Revenge for the Duchess of Malfi murdered

80   By th' Aragonian brethren; for Antonio
    Slain by this hand; for lustful Julia
    Poisoned by this man; and lastly for myself,
    That was an actor in the main of all,
    Much 'gainst mine own good nature, yet i' th' end
    Neglected.

PESCARA   How now, my lord?

85 CARDINAL   Look to my brother:
    He gave us these large wounds as we were struggling
    Here i' the rushes.[3] And now, I pray,
    Let me be laid by and never thought of.   [*Dies.*]

PESCARA   How fatally, it seems, he did withstand
    His own rescue!

90 MALATESTE   Thou wretched thing of blood,
    How came Antonio by his death?

BOSOLA   In a mist: I know not how;
    Such a mistake as I have often seen
    In a play. Oh, I am gone!

95   We are only like dead walls or vaulted graves,
    That, ruined, yield no echo. Fare you well.
    It may be pain, but no harm to me to die
    In so good a quarrel. Oh, this gloomy world,
    In what a shadow or deep pit of darkness

100   Doth, womanish and fearful, mankind live!
    Let worthy minds ne'er stagger in distrust
    To suffer death or shame for what is just:
    Mine is another voyage.   [*Dies.*]

PESCARA   The noble Delio, as I came to the palace,

105   Told me of Antonio's being here, and showed me
    A pretty gentleman, his son and heir.

        [*Enter* DELIO *with* ANTONIO's SON.]

MALATESTE   O, sir, you come too late.

DELIO   I heard so, and
    Was armed° for it ere I came. Let us make noble use   *prepared*
    Of this great ruin, and join all our force

110   To establish this young hopeful° gentleman   *promising*
    In 's mother's right. These wretched eminent things
    Leave no more fame behind 'em, than should one
    Fall in a frost, and leave his print in snow;
    As soon as the sun shines, it ever melts

115   Both form and matter. I have ever thought
    Nature doth nothing so great for great men
    As when she's pleased to make them lords of truth:
    Integrity of life is fame's best friend,
    Which nobly, beyond death, shall crown the end.   [*Exeunt.*]

performed 1613   *published* 1623

---

3. Leafy plants, strewn over Elizabethan floors in lieu of carpets.

ELIZABETH CARY
1585?–1639

Elizabeth (Tanfield) Cary was the first Englishwoman to write and publish a drama, *The Tragedy of Mariam* (1613); it was probably composed between 1602 and 1609 and invites comparison with Webster's *Duchess of Malfi*, performed in 1613. Both plays have as protagonists forceful queens who insist on preserving the integrity of their own emotional lives in regard to marriage and who otherwise flout gender expectations; both queens are murdered by violently jealous men who then go mad. Cary's play, however, was not intended for the stage: it is a Senecan closet drama, a genre that dramatizes the clash of ideological positions. *Mariam* explores issues important in Cary's own life and controverted in the Jacobean state: the claims of conscience, the analogy of domestic and state tyranny, the power of kings and husbands, the rights and duties of wives and subjects, the justifications for resistance to tyrants, and the possibility and power of passive resistance.

The major source for Cary's life is a memoir by one of her daughters written about 1655. Though conceived as an exemplary biography or saint's life, it shows Cary continually caught between pressures to conform and submit and an inner imperative to resist and challenge authority. Daughter of a successful lawyer and judge, Sir Lawrence Tanfield, and of a mother descended from the country gentry, she grew up in Oxfordshire as a precocious only child, reading omnivorously, learning languages, translating Seneca's epistles and Ortelius's geography, and writing verses. The memoir claims that she learned, chiefly on her own, French, Spanish, Italian, Latin, and Hebrew (though her tutor John Davies of Hereford probably helped); that she often read all night, bribing the servants for candles her mother refused; and that at age twelve she regaled her father with arguments against Calvin's *Institutes*. In 1602, at age seventeen, she married Sir Henry Cary, a successful courtier who was at length appointed Privy Councillor (1618), Viscount Falkland in the Scottish peerage (1620), and Lord Deputy of Ireland (1622).

The memoir portrays Elizabeth struggling to conform her own inclinations and "strong will" to the will of her "very absolute" husband." She bore eleven children between 1609 and 1624 and nursed all but one; she read continually in history, poetry, moral philosophy, and the Church Fathers; and in 1626, now back in England, she converted openly to Catholicism—a move that left her isolated, attacked, cast off by husband and family, and in acute financial distress. (A covert profession would have caused no trouble in the court of the Catholic queen Henrietta Maria, but an open avowal was especially threatening to her husband as governor of Ireland.) Ultimately, she brought six of her children to Catholicism, spiriting two sons abroad in the dead of night to receive a Jesuit education, and leading four daughters to join a Benedictine convent at Cambray. Her eldest son, Lucius, celebrated in Ben Jonson's Cary-Morison ode as the embodiment of Cavalier virtues, became the center of a noted intellectual circle at his estate, Great Tew.

Most of Cary's other writing did not survive, apparently: the memoir attributes to her a verse "Life of Tamurlane," several saints' lives in verse, an answer to a controversial Protestant tract by her son Lucius, and translations of the works of Cardinal Perron and other French divines; she and her tutor Davies also refer to an earlier tragedy set in Sicily. We do have her epitaph on Buckingham (ca. 1628), several trenchant letters to Charles I and others seeking redress after Falkland cast her off, and a translation (1630) of Cardinal Perron's answer to a treatise by King James. Also, she is probably (but not certainly) the author of a remarkable *History of the Life, Reign, and Death of Edward II* (ca. 1627–28); if so, she is the first Englishwoman to write a full-scale history.

The Tragedy of Mariam, the Fair Queen of Jewry

Cary supplied an Argument to the play, but the modern reader may be better served by a succinct summary of the historical situation and the play. Observing the unity of time, Cary brings the pressure of antecedent events and incorporates materials from other parts of the Herod story (drawn chiefly from Josephus's *Antiquities*) to heighten dramatic tension. Before the play begins, Herod the Great, with the aid of Rome, has (in 39 B.C.E.) supplanted Hircanus, the hereditary king and priest in Israel, divorced his first wife, Doris, and married Hircanus's granddaughter, the singularly beautiful Mariam, whom he loves with fierce intensity and jealous passion. To secure his throne he arranged a drowning accident to remove the new high priest, Mariam's brother Aristobolus (35 B.C.E.), and had old Hircanus executed (30 B.C.E.). Cary's play reverses these two events. Called to Rome to answer accusations leveled by Alexandra, the mother of Mariam and Aristobolus, Herod left orders with his uncle Josephus, who is also the husband of his sister Salome, to kill Mariam in the event of his death so no other man could possess her. Reinstated as king, Herod had Josephus killed for telling Mariam about the decree for her death, taking that as evidence supporting Salome's false charge that the two were lovers. He then married Salome to Constabarus, who, unknown to Herod, had hidden away the sons of Babas, under sentence of death for their opposition to Herod. The play begins with Herod again in Rome, in danger of death as a partisan of the defeated and recently deceased Mark Antony. Before departing, he had left with his officer Sohemus another order for Mariam to be killed in the event of his death; Sohemus also reveals the decree to her.

The play begins as news comes of Herod's death, causing (during three acts) a sense of relief, liberation, and new beginnings under the joint rule of Mariam and her mother, Alexandra (in the minority of Mariam's son). Mariam is at first torn between grief and joy but is relieved that the tyrant who murdered her kin and decreed her death will not return. Pheroras, Herod's brother, who had been under command to marry an infant, now marries his true love, Graphina. The sons of Babas now come out of hiding to serve the state, and Constabarus is no longer in peril for having concealed them. Sohemus will not suffer for his decision to let Mariam live in defiance of Herod's command. Even those who regret Herod's death benefit from it: his sister Salome, who had first plotted to have her second husband, Constabarus, killed by Herod so she might marry a new lover, now determines upon divorce instead— scandalous for a woman in Israel but hardly so wicked as murder.

At Herod's unexpected return, all these hopeful new beginnings are crushed: Babas's sons are executed; Sohemus is accused by Salome of adultery with Mariam and is executed for that (and for revealing Herod's instructions); Mariam refuses Herod's sexual advances and berates him for murdering her kin; Salome engineers a plot by which Mariam's servant offers (supposedly from her) a cup of poison to Herod and then goads Herod to command her death. A messenger recounts the details of Mariam's noble death, and Herod runs mad with grief and remorse, persuaded at last of her innocence and inestimable worth.

In the scenes presented here, the plotlines with Graphina/Pheroras and the sons of Babas are omitted, but Mariam is positioned against her chief foils. One is the chorus, which in this kind of Senecan tragedy speak from a partial, not an authoritative, vantage point: as a company of Jews, they judge Mariam by their own very conservative notion of a wife's duty, that she owes entire subjection of mind and body to her husband. Another is Salome, who speaks forcefully for a woman's right to divorce and for evenhanded justice for unhappy wives—though she herself is thoroughly wicked, denouncing the innocent Mariam for marital infidelity while she flaunts her illicit affairs and has two husbands killed when she is ready to replace them. Mariam herself recognizes that she has brought her death on herself by refusing to live by the accepted female triad of virtues: she is chaste, but manifestly not silent or obedient. She challenges patriarchal control within the institution of marriage, claiming a wife's right to her own speech—public and private—as well as to the integrity of her own emotional life and self-definition.

From The Tragedy of Mariam, the Fair Queen of Jewry

Act 1

SCENE 1[1]

[MARIAM *alone.*]

MARIAM   How oft have I with public voice run on
To censure Rome's last hero[2] for deceit:
Because he wept when Pompey's life was gone,
Yet when he lived, he thought his name too great.
5   But now I do recant, and, Roman lord,
Excuse too rash a judgement in a woman:
My sex pleads pardon, pardon then afford,
Mistaking is with us but too too common.
Now do I find, by self-experience taught,
10   One object yields both grief and joy:
You wept indeed, when on his worth you thought,
But joyed that slaughter did your foe destroy.
So at his death your eyes true drops did rain,
Whom dead, you did not wish alive again.
15   When Herod lived, that now is done to death,
Oft have I wished that I from him were free:
Oft have I wished that he might lose his breath,
Oft have I wished his carcass dead to see.
Then rage and scorn had put my love to flight,
20   That love which once on him was firmly set:
Hate hid his true affection from my sight,
And kept my heart from paying him his debt.
And blame me not, for Herod's jealousy
Had power even constancy itself to change:
25   For he, by barring me from liberty,
To shun° my ranging, taught me first to range.   prevent
But yet too chaste a scholar was my heart,
To learn to love another than my lord:
To leave his love, my lesson's former part,
30   I quickly learned, the other I abhorred.
But now his death to memory doth call
The tender love that he to Mariam bare.°   bore
And mine to him; this makes those rivers fall,
Which by another thought unmoistened are.
35   For Aristobulus, the lowliest youth[3]
That ever did in angel's shape appear,

---

1. The first edition, 1613, contains some obvious misprints here silently corrected.
2. Julius Caesar. At line 5 Mariam addresses the absent Caesar in apostrophe.
3. Some editors emend to "loveliest," given the great emphasis on his beauty.

The cruel Herod was not moved to ruth;°   *pity*
Then why grieves Mariam Herod's death to hear?
Why joy I not the tongue no more shall speak,
40   That yielded forth my brother's latest° doom: *final*
Both youth and beauty might thy° fury break,   *Herod's*
And both in him did ill befit a tomb.
And, worthy grandsire,[4] ill did he requite
His high ascent, alone by thee procured,
45   Except° he murdered thee to free the sprite°   *unless/spirit*
Which still he thought on earth too long immured.
How happy was it that Sohemus' mind
Was moved to pity my distressed estate!
Might Herod's life a trusty servant find,[5]
50   My death to his had been unseparate.
These thoughts have power, his death to make me bear,
Nay more, to wish the news may firmly hold:
Yet cannot this repulse some falling tear,
That will against my will some grief unfold.
55   And more I owe him for his love to me,
The deepest love that ever yet was seen:
Yet had I rather much a milkmaid be,
Than be the monarch of Judea's queen.
It was for nought but love he wished his end
60   Might to my death but the vaunt-courier° prove: *forerunner*
But I had rather still be foe than friend,
To him that saves for hate, and kills for love.
Hard-hearted Mariam, at thy discontent
What floods of tears have drenched his manly face!
65   How canst thou then so faintly now lament
They truest lover's death, a death's disgrace:[6]
Ay, now, mine eyes, you do begin to right
The wrongs of your admirer and my lord.[7]
Long since you should have put your smiles to flight,
70   Ill doth a widowed eye with joy accord.
Why, now methinks the love I bare° him then,   *bore*
When virgin freedom left me unrestrained,
Doth to my heart begin to creep again,
My passion[8] now is far from being feigned.

*   *   *

SCENE 4

*   *   *

[SALOME *alone.*]
SALOME   Lives Salome to get so base a style°   *name*
As "foot" to the proud Mariam? Herod's spirit

---

4. Mariam here addresses the murdered Hircanus.
5. I.e., if Herod alive had been able to find trustworthy servants to kill me, my death had been joined to his
6. I.e., her faint laments dishonor his death.
7. Herod.
8. Emotion of grief.

In happy time for her endured exile,
For did he live, she should not miss her merit:[9]
265 But he is dead: and though he were my brother,
His death such store of cinders cannot cast
My coals of love to quench: for though they smother
The flames a while, yet will they out at last.
Oh blest Arabia,[1] in best climate place,
270 I by the fruit will censure° of the tree: judge
'Tis not in vain they happy name thou hast,
If all Arabians like Silleus be.
Had not my fate been too too contrary,
When I on Constabarus first did gaze,
275 Silleus had been object to mine eye:
Whose looks and personage must all eyes amaze.
But now, ill-fated Salome, thy tongue
To Constabarus by itself is tied:
And now, except I do the Hebrew wrong,
280 I cannot be the fair Arabian's bride:
What childish lets° are these? Why stand I now   obstacles
On honorable points? 'Tis long ago
Since shame was written on my tainted brow:[2]
And certain 'tis, that shame is honor's foe.
285 Had I upon my reputation stood,
Had I affected° an unspotted life,   desired
Josephus' veins had still been stuffed with blood,
And I to him had lived a sober wife.
Then had I never cast an eye of love
290 On Constabarus' now detested face,
Then had I kept my thoughts without remove:
And blushed at motion of the least disgrace:
But shame is gone, and honor wiped away,
And impudency on my forehead sits:
295 She bids me work my will without delay,
And for my will I will employ my wits.
He loves, I love; what then can be the cause
Keeps me [from] being the Arabian's wife?
It is the principles of Moses' laws,
300 For Constabarus still remains in life.
If he to me did bear as earnest hate,
As I to him, for him there were an ease;
A separating bill[3] might free his fate
From such a yoke that did so much displease.
305 Why should such privilege to man be given?
Or given to them, why barred from women then?
Are men than we in greater grace with Heaven?
Or cannot women hate as well as men?

I'll be the custom-breaker: and begin
310 To show my sex the way to freedom's door,
And with an off'ring will I purge my sin;
The law was made for none but who are poor.[4]
If Herod had lived, I might to him accuse
My present lord. But for the future's sake[5]
315 Then would I tell the king he did refuse
The sons of Babas in his power to take.
But now I must divorce him from my bed,
That my Silleus may possess his room:°   place
Had I not begged his life, he had been dead,[6]
320 I curse my tongue, the hind'rer of his doom,
But then my wand'ring heart to him was fast,
Nor did I dream of change: Silleus said,
He would be here, and see, he comes at last.
Had I not named him, longer had he stayed.

* * *

SCENE 6

* * *

[SALOME. CONSTABARUS.]
375 CONSTABARUS   Oh Salome, how much you wrong your name,
Your race, your country, and your husband most!
A stranger's private conference[7] is shame,
I blush for you, that have your blushing lost.
Oft have I found, and found you to my grief,
380 Consorted with this base Arabian here:
Heaven knows that you have been my comfort chief,
Then do not now my greater plague appear.
Now by the stately carvèd edifice
That on Mount Sion makes so fair a show,[8]
385 And by the altar fit for sacrifice,
I love thee more than thou thyself dost know.
Oft with a silent sorrow have I heard
How ill Judea's mouth doth censure thee:
And did I not thine honor much regard,
390 Thou shouldst not be exhorted thus for me.
Didst thou but know the worth of honest fame,
How much a virtuous woman is esteemed,
Thou wouldest like hell eschew deservèd shame,
And seek to be both chaste and chastely deemed.
395 Our wisest prince did say, and true he said,
A virtuous woman crowns her husband's head.[9]

4. The opening chapters of Leviticus prescribe specific offerings for specific sins; Salome's cynical comment is that the wealthy can afford such offerings, and so buy release from any sin.
5. I.e., for the sake of my future husband, I would have told (next lines) Herod that Constabarus did not kill Herod's enemies, the sons of Babas, but instead hid them.
6. Constabarus, while governor of Idumaea under Herod, sought to obtain that kingdom for himself; only Salome was able to persuade Herod to spare his life.
7. For a woman to talk privately with a stranger is shameful.
8. The Temple of Jerusalem.
9. Proverbs 12.4, attributed to King Solomon.

SALOME   Did I for this uprear thy low estate?
　　Did I for this requital beg thy life,
　　That thou hadst forfeited to hapless fate,
400　　To be to such a thankless wretch the wife?
　　This hand of mine hath lifted up thy head,
　　Which many a day ago had fallen full low,
　　Because the sons of Babas are not dead;
　　To me thou dost both life and fortune owe.
405　CONSTABARUS   You have my patience often exercised,
　　Use make my choler keep within the banks:[1]
　　Yet boast no more, but be by me advised.
　　A benefit upbraided° forfeits thanks:　　　　　　　　　　　reproached
　　I prithee, Salome, dismiss this mood,
410　　Thou dost not know how ill it fits thy place:
　　My words were all intended for thy good,
　　To raise thine honor and to stop disgrace.
　　SALOME   To stop disgrace? Take thou no care for me,
　　Nay, do thy worst, thy worst I set not by:°　　　　　　　care not for
415　　No shame of mine is like to light on thee,
　　Thy love and admonitions I defy.
　　Thou shalt no hour longer call me wife,
　　Thy jealousy procures my hate so deep:
　　That I from thee do mean to free my life,
420　　By a divorcing bill before I sleep.
　　CONSTABARUS   Are Hebrew women now transformed to men?
　　Why do you not as well our battles fight,
　　And wear our armor? Suffer this, and then
　　Let all the world be topsy-turvèd° quite.　　　　　turned upside down
425　　Let fishes graze, beasts swim[2] and birds descend,
　　Let fire burn downwards whilst the earth aspires:
　　Let winter's heat and summer's cold offend,
　　Let thistles grow on vines, and grapes on briars,
　　Set us to spin or sew, or at the best
430　　Make us wood-hewers, water-bearing wights:°　　　　creatures
　　For sacred service let us take no rest,
　　Use us as Joshua did the Gibonites.[3]
　　SALOME   Hold on your talk, till it be time to end,
　　For me I am resolved it shall be so:
435　　Though I be first that to this course do bend,
　　I shall not be the last, full well I know.
　　CONSTABARUS   Why then be witness Heav'n, the judge of sins,
　　Be witness spirits that eschew the dark:
　　Be witness angels, witness cherubins,
440　　Whose semblance sits upon the holy Ark:[4]
　　Be witness earth, be witness Palestine,

1. I.e., may habit ("use") make me control my anger ("choler").
2. The 1613 edition reads "swine," but the context dictates this emendation.
3. That is, make us into women ("spin or sew") or

slaves (hewers of wood and drawers of water) such as Joshua made of the Gibeonites (Joshua 9.21).
4. Two gold cherubim were to adorn the mercy seat, placed above the ark of the covenant (Exodus 25.18–20).

Be witness David's city,° if my heart   *Jerusalem*
Did ever merit such an act of thine:
Or if the fault be mine that makes us part.
445 Since mildest Moses, friend unto the Lord,
Did work his wonders in the land of Ham,
And slew the first-born babes without a sword,
In sign whereof we eat the holy lamb:[5]
Till now that fourteen hundred years are past,
450 Since first the Law[6] with us hath been in force.
You are the first, and will, I hope, be last,
That ever sought her husband to divorce.
SALOME   I mean not to be led by precedent,
My will shall be to me instead of Law.
455 CONSTABARUS   I fear me much you will too late repent,
That you have ever lived so void of awe:
This is Silleus' love that makes you thus
Reverse all order: you must next be his.
But if my thoughts aright the cause discuss,
460 In winning you, he gains no lasting bliss;
I was Silleus, and not long ago
Josephus then was Constabarus now:
When you became my friend° you proved his foe,   *lover*
As now for him you break to me your vow.[7]
465 SALOME   If once I loved you, greater is your debt:
For certain 'tis that you deserved it not.
And undeservèd love we soon forget,
And therefore that to me can be no blot.
But now fare ill,[8] my once belovèd lord,
470 Yet never more belovèd than now abhorred.   [*Exit* SALOME.]
CONSTABARUS   Yet Constabarus biddeth thee farewell.
Farewell, light creature. Heaven forgive thy sin:
My prophesying spirit doth foretell
Thy wavering thoughts do yet but new begin.
475 Yet I have better scaped than Joseph did,
But if our Herod's death had been delayed,
The valiant youths that I so long have hid,
Had been by her, and I for them, betrayed.[9]
Therefore in happy hour did Caesar give
480 The fatal blow to wanton Anthony:
For had he lived, our Herod then should live,
But great Anthonius' death made Herod die.
Had he enjoyed his breath, not I alone
Had been in danger of a deadly fall:
485 But Mariam had the way of peril gone,
Though by the tyrant most belov'd of all—

5. Passover celebrates this last of the ten plagues by which Moses delivered the Israelites from slavery in Egypt (the "land of Ham," line 446).
6. The Law of Moses.
7. I.e., not long ago I was in Silleus's place as your lover and Josephus in my place as your husband; now for Silleus you break your marriage vow to me.
8. As opposed to "farewell."
9. Babas's sons.

The sweet-faced Mariam, as free from guilt
As Heaven from spots, yet had her lord come back,
Her purest blood had been unjustly spilt,
490   And Salome it was would work her wrack.°   destruction
Though all Judea yield her innocent,
She often hath been near to punishment.   [*Exit.*]

* * *

Act 3

SCENE 3

* * *

[MARIAM. SOHEMUS.]
MARIAM   Sohemus, tell me what the news may be
120   That makes your eyes so full, your cheeks so blue?
SOHEMUS   I know not now how to call them. Ill for me
'Tis sure they are: not so, I hope, for you.
Herod—
MARIAM   Oh, what of Herod?
SOHEMUS   Herod lives.
[MARIAM] How! Lives? What, in some cave or forest hid?
125   SOHEMUS   Nay, back returned with honor. Caesar gives
Him greater grace than e'er Anthonius did.
MARIAM   Foretell the ruin of my family,
Tell me that I shall see our city burned:
Tell me I shall a death disgraceful die,
130   But tell me not that Herod is returned.
SOHEMUS   Be not impatient, madam, be but mild,
His love to you again will soon be bred.
MARIAM   I will not to his love be reconciled,
With solemn vows I have forsworn his bed.
SOHEMUS   But you must break those vows.
135   MARIAM   I'll rather break
The heart of Mariam. Cursed is my fate:
But speak no more to me, in vain ye speak°   advise me
To live with him I so profoundly hate.
SOHEMUS   Great queen, you must to me your pardon give,
140   Sohemus cannot now your will obey:
If your command should me to silence drive,
It were not to obey, but to betray.
Reject and slight my speeches, mock my faith,
Scorn my observance, call my counsel nought:
145   Though you regard not what Sohemus saith,
Yet will I ever freely speak my thought.
I fear ere long I shall fair Mariam see
In woeful state, and by herself undone:
Yet for your issue's sake[1] more temp'rate be,

1. Mariam's sons by Herod, Alexander and Aristobulus.

150   The heart by affability is won.

    MARIAM   And must I to my prison turn again?

       Oh, now I see I was an hypocrite:

       I did this morning for his death complain,

       And yet do mourn, because he lives, ere night.

155   When I his death believed, compassion wrought,

       And was the stickler° 'twixt my heart and him: *mediator*

       But now that curtain's drawn from off my thought,

       Hate doth appear again with visage grim:

       And paints the face of Herod in my heart,

160   In horrid colors with detested look:

       Then fear would come, but scorn doth play her part,

       And saith that scorn with fear can never brook.°   *put up with*

       I know I could enchain him with a smile:

       And lead him captive with a gentle word,

165   I scorn my look should ever man beguile,

       Or other speech than meaning° to afford.   *what I mean*

       Else Salome in vain might spend her wind,

       In vain might Herod's mother whet her tongue:

       In vain had they complotted and combined,

170   For I could overthrow them all ere long.

       Oh, what a shelter is mine innocence,

       To shield me from the pangs of inward grief:

       'Gainst all mishaps it is my fair defence,

       And to my sorrows yields a large relief.

175   To be commandress of the triple earth,[2]

       And sit in safety from a fall secure:

       To have all nations celebrate my birth,

       I would not that my spirit were impure.

       Let my distressèd state unpitied be,

180   Mine innocence is hope enough for me. [*Exit.*]

    SOHEMUS   Poor guiltless queen! Oh, that my wish might place

       A little temper° now about thy heart: *moderation*

       Unbridled speech is Mariam's worst disgrace,°   *fault*

       And will endanger her without desert.°   *her deserving it*

185   I am in greater hazard. O'er my head,

       The fatal axe doth hang unsteadily:[3]

       My disobedience once discoverèd

       Will shake it down: Sohemus so shall die.

       For when the King shall find, we thought his death

190   Had been as certain as we see his life:

       And marks withal I slighted so his breath,°   *command*

       As to preserve alive his matchless wife—

       Nay more, to give to Alexander's hand[4]

       The regal dignity; the sovereign power,

2. Probably Rome, Egypt, and Jerusalem.
3. An allusion to the sword of Damocles; Damocles was a courtier to Dionysius of Syracuse, who suspended a sword by a single hair over Damocles' head to illustrate the precariousness of a king's fortunes.
4. Mariam's son.

195 How I had yielded up at her command,
The strength of all the city, David's Tower[5]—
What more than common death may I expect,
Since I too well do know his cruelty?
'Twere death a word of Herod's to neglect;
200 What then to do directly contrary?
Yet, life, I quit thee with a willing spirit,
And think thou could'st not better be employed:
I forfeit thee for her that more doth merit,
Ten such° were better dead than she destroyed.   such as I
205 But fare thee well, chaste queen, well may I see
The darkness palpable, and rivers part:[6]
The sun stand still, nay more, retorted be,[7]
But never woman with so pure a heart.
Thine eyes' grave majesty keeps all in awe,
210 And cuts the wings of every loose desire:
Thy brow is table to the modest law;[8]
Yet though we dare not love, we may admire.[9]
And if I die, it shall my soul content,
My breath in Mariam's service shall be spent.

215 CHORUS   'Tis not enough for one that is a wife
To keep her spotless from an act of ill:
But from suspicion she should free her life,
And bare° herself of power as well as will.   strip
   'Tis not so glorious for her to be free,
220 As by her proper° self restrained to be.   own

When she hath spacious ground to walk upon,
Why on the ridge should she desire to go?
It is no glory to forbear alone°   only
Those things that may her honor overthrow.
225 But 'tis thankworthy if she will not take
All lawful liberties for honor's sake.

That wife her hand against her fame doth rear,
That more than to her lord alone will give
A private word to any second ear,
230 And though she may with reputation live,[1]
   Yet though most chaste, she doth her glory blot,
   And wounds her honor, though she kills it not.

When to their husbands they themselves do bind,
Do they not wholly give themselves away?
235 Or give they but their body, not their mind,

---

5. A fort Herod built by the western wall of Jerusalem; it was named David's Tower later, by the
crusaders.
6. Darkness was one of the ten plagues called
down on Israel by Moses; "rivers part" refers to the
parting of the Red Sea that enabled the Israelites
to escape from Pharaoh (Exodus 14.21–22).
7. Joshua commanded the sun to stand still
(Joshua 10.12–14); Herod imagines it traveling

backward.
8. Sohemus compares Mariam's brow to the tablets ("tables") on which the Ten Commandments
were engraved.
9. Cf. the speech which Antonio speaks of the
duchess of Malfi (p. 1437).
1. I.e., the wife that gives a private word to any
besides her husband may not lose her reputation
but blots it.

Reserving that, though best, for others' prey?
  No sure, their thoughts no more can be their own,
  And therefore should to none but one be known.

  Then she usurps upon another's right,
240 That seeks to be by public language graced;
  And though her thoughts reflect with purest light,
  Her mind if not peculiar° is not chaste.   *exclusive*
    For in a wife it is no worse to find,
    A common° body than a common mind.   *shared, public*

245 And every mind, though free from thought of ill,
  That out of glory° seeks a worth to show,   *desire of praise*
  When any's ears but one therewith they fill,[2]
  Doth in a sort her pureness overthrow.
    Now Mariam had (but that to this she bent)[3]
250   Been free from fear, as well as innocent.

Act 4

SCENE 3

*   *   *

[HEROD. MARIAM.]
HEROD   And here she comes indeed: happily met,
  My best and dearest half: what ails my dear?
  Thou dost the difference° certainly forget   *disparity*
90 'Twixt dusky habits° and a time so clear.°   *clothes / favorable*
MARIAM   My lord, I suit my garment to my mind,
  And there no cheerful colors can I find.
HEROD   Is this my welcome? Have I longed so much
  To see my dearest Mariam discontent?
95 What is't that is the cause thy heart to touch?
  Oh speak, that I thy sorrow may prevent.
  Art thou not Jewry's queen, and Herod's too?
  Be my commandress, be my sovereign guide:
  To be by thee directed I will woo,
100 For in thy pleasure lies my highest pride.
  Or if thou think Judea's narrow bound
  Too strict a limit for thy great command:
  Thou shalt be empress of Arabia crowned,
  For thou shalt rule, and I will win the land.
105 I'll rob the holy David's sepulchre
  To give thee wealth, if thou for wealth do care:
  Thou shalt have all they did with him inter,
  And I for thee will make the Temple bare.
MARIAM   I neither have of power[4] nor riches want,
110 I have enough, nor do I wish for more:

2. I.e., when they fill any other ears (besides the husband's) with speech to show their worth.
3. Except that she talked too freely to others.

4. I.e., I neither have [desire] of power, nor want riches.

Your offers to my heart no ease can grant,
Except they could my brother's life restore.
No, had you wished the wretched Mariam glad,
Or had your love to her been truly tied:
115 Nay, had you not desired to make her sad,
My brother nor my grandsire had not died.
HEROD   Wilt thou believe no oaths to clear thy lord?
How oft have I with execration° sworn: *curse*
Thou art by me belovèd, by me adored,
120 Yet are my protestations heard with scorn.
Hircanus plotted to deprive my head
Of this long-settled honor that I wear:
And therefore I did justly doom him dead,
To rid the realm from peril, me from fear.
125 Yet I for Mariam's sake do so repent
The death of one whose blood she did inherit:
I wish I had a kingdom's treasure spent,
So I had ne'er expelled Hircanus' spirit.
As I affected that same noble youth,[5]
130 In lasting infamy my name enroll
If I not mourned his death with hearty truth.
Did I not show to him my earnest love,
When I to him the priesthood did restore,
And did for him a living priest remove,
135 Which never had been done but once before?[6]
MARIAM   I know that, moved by importunity,
You made him priest, and shortly after die.
HEROD   I will not speak, unless to be believed,
This froward° humor will not do you good: *peevish*
140 It hath too much already Herod grieved,
To think that you on terms of hate have stood.
Yet smile, my dearest Mariam, do but smile,
And I will all unkind conceits exile.
MARIAM   I cannot frame disguise, nor never taught
145 My face a look dissenting from my thought.
HEROD   By Heaven, you vex me, build° not on my love.   *rely*
MARIAM   I will not build on so unstable ground.
HEROD   Nought is so fixed, but peevishness may move.°   *dislodge*
MARIAM   'Tis better slightest cause than none were found.
150 HEROD   Be judge yourself, if ever Herod sought
Or would be moved a cause of change to find:
Yet let your look declare a milder thought,
My heart again you shall to Mariam bind.
How oft did I for you my mother chide,
155 Revile my sister, and my brother rate:°   *berate*
And tell them all my Mariam they belied;
Distrust me still, if these be signs of hate.

---

5. I.e., since I was fond of Aristobolus (Mariam's brother, murdered by Herod's plot). There may be a line missing here, since the rhyme scheme is disrupted.

6. Herod removed Ananelus from the priesthood to give it to Aristobolus; but such a removal had happened twice before.

SCENE 4

* * *

[*Enter* BUTLER.]

HEROD   What hast thou here?

BUTLER   A drink procuring love,

160   The queen desired me to deliver it.

MARIAM   Did I? Some hateful practice° this will prove,   plot
Yet can it be no worse than Heavens permit.

HEROD [*To the* BUTLER.]   Confess the truth, thou wicked instrument
To her outrageous will, 'tis [poison] sure:

165   Tell true, and thou shalt scape the punishment,
Which, if thou do conceal, thou shalt endure.

BUTLER   I know not, but I doubt it be no less,
Long since the hate of you her heart did seize.

HEROD   Know'st thou the cause thereof?

BUTLER   My lord, I guess

170   Sohemus told the tale that did displease.

HEROD   Oh Heaven! Sohemus false! Go, let him die,
Stay not to suffer him to speak a word: [*Exit* BUTLER.]
Oh damnèd villain, did he falsify
The oath he swore ev'n of his own accord?

175   Now do I know thy falsehood, painted devil,
Thou white enchantress. Oh, thou art so foul,
That hyssop[7] cannot cleanse thee, worst of evil.
A beauteous body hides a loathsome soul.
Your love Sohemus, moved by his affection,

180   Though he have ever heretofore been true,
Did blab forsooth, that I did give direction,
If we were put to death to slaughter you.
And you in black revenge attended° now   waited
To add a murder to your breach of vow.

MARIAM   Is this a dream?

185   HEROD   Oh Heaven, that 'twere no more,
I'll give my realm to who can prove it so:
I would I were like any beggar poor,
So I for false my Mariam did not know—
Foul pith contained in the fairest rind

190   That ever graded a cedar. Oh, thine eye
Is pure as Heaven, but impure thy mind,
And for impurity shall Mariam die.
Why didst thou love Sohemus?

MARIAM   They can tell
That say I loved him, Mariam says not so.

195   HEROD   Oh, cannot impudence the coals expel,
That for thy love in Herod's bosom glow?
It is as plain as water, and denial
Makes of thy falsehood but a greater trial.
Hast thou beheld thyself, and could'st thou stain

7. An herb used to treat lepers. "White enchantress" may allude to the Renaissance idea of a white devil, a fair-seeming hypocrite.

200 So rare perfection? Even for love of thee
I do profoundly hate thee. Wert thou plain,
Thou should'st the wonder of Judea be.
But oh, thou art not. Hell itself lies hid
Beneath thy heavenly show. Yet never wert thou chaste:
205 Thou might'st exalt, pull down, command, forbid,
And be above the wheel of fortune placed.[8]
Hadst thou complotted Herod's massacre,
That so thy son a monarch might be styled,
Not half so grievous such an action were,
210 As once to think, that Mariam is defiled.
Bright workmanship of nature sullied o'er,
With pitchèd° darkness now thine end shall be: pitch-black
Thou shalt not live, fair fiend, to cozen more,
With heavenly[9] semblance, as thou cozen'dst me.
215 Yet must I love thee in despite of death,
And thou shalt die in the despite of love:
For neither shall my love prolong thy breath,
Nor shall thy loss of breath my love remove.
I might have seen thy falsehood in thy face;
220 Where could'st thou get thy stars that served for eyes
Except by theft, and theft is foul disgrace?
This had appeared before, were Herod wise,
But I'm a sot, a very sot, no better:
My wisdom long ago a-wand'ring fell,
225 Thy face, encount'ring it, my wit did fetter,
And made me for delight my freedom sell.
Give me my heart, false creature, 'tis a wrong,
My guiltless heart should now with thine be slain:
Thou hadst no right to lock it up so long,
230 And with usurper's name I Mariam stain.
        [*Enter* BUTLER.]
HEROD   Have you designed° Sohemus to his end?   *dispatched*
BUTLER   I have, my lord.
HEROD   Then call our royal guard
To do as much for Mariam. [*Exit* BUTLER.] They offend
Leave[1] ill unblamed, or good without reward. [*Enter* SOLDIERS.]
235 Here, take her to her death. Come back, come back,
What meant I to deprive the world of light:
To muffle Jewry in the foulest black,
That ever was an opposite to white?
Why, whither would you carry her?
SOLDIER   You bade
240 We should conduct her to her death, my lord.
HEROD   Why, sure I did not, Herod was not mad.
Why should she feel the fury of the sword?
Oh, now the grief returns into my heart,

8. I.e., you might have been able to do whatever you would, and been exempt from the turns of fortune's wheel.

9. The 1613 text reads "heavy," but this emendation seems called for by the context.
1. Who leave.

And pulls me piecemeal: love and hate do fight:
245 And now hath love acquired the greater part,
Yet now hath hate affection conquered quite.
And therefore bear her hence: and, Hebrew, why
Seize you with lion's paws the fairest lamb
Of all the flock? She must not, shall not, die.
250 Without her I most miserable am,
And with her more than most. Away, away,
But bear her but to prison, not to death:
And is she gone indeed? Stay, villains, stay,
Her looks alone preserved your sovereign's breath.
255 Well, let her go, but yet she shall not die;
I cannot think she meant to poison me:
But certain 'tis she lived too wantonly,
And therefore shall she never more be free.   [*Exeunt.*]

*   *   *

SCENE 8

*   *   *

525 MARIAM   Am I the Mariam that presumed so much,
And deemed my face must needs preserve my breath?
Ay, I it was that thought my beauty such,
As it alone could countermand my death.
Now death will teach me: he can pale as well
530 A cheek of roses as a cheek less bright,
And dim an eye whose shine doth most excel,
As soon as one that casts a meaner light.
Had not myself against myself conspired,
No plot, no adversary from without
535 Could Herod's love from Mariam have retired,
Or from his heart have thrust my semblance out.
The wanton queen that never loved for love,
False Cleopatra, wholly set on gain,
With all her sleights did prove,° yet vainly prove,   °try
540 For her the love of Herod to obtain.
Yet her allurements, all her courtly guile,
Her smiles, her favors, and her smooth deceit
Could not my face from Herod's mind exile,
But were with him of less than little weight.
545 That face and person that in Asia late
For beauty's goddess, Paphos' queen,[2] was ta'en:
That face that did captive° great Julius' fate,   °take captive
That very face that was Anthonius' bane,°   °destruction
That face that to be Egypt's pride was born,
550 That face that all the world esteemed so rare:[3]
Did Herod hate, despise, neglect, and scorn,

---

2. Venus.
3. The Egyptian queen Cleopatra was the beauty

who captivated both Julius Caesar and Mark
Antony (lines 547–48).

When with the same, he Mariam's did compare.
This made that I improvidently wrought,
And on the wager even my life did pawn:
555 Because I thought, and yet but truly thought,
That Herod's love could not from me be drawn.
But now, though out of time,° I plainly see   too late
It could be drawn, though never drawn from me,
Had I but with humility been graced,
560 As well as fair I might have proved me wise:
But I did think because I knew me chaste,
One virtue for a woman might suffice.
That mind for glory of our sex might stand,
Wherein humility and chastity
565 Doth march with equal paces hand in hand.
But one, if single seen, who setteth by?°   takes account
And I had singly one, but 'tis my joy,
That I was ever innocent, though sour:
And therefore can they but my life destroy,
570 My soul is free from adversary's power.
You princes great in power, and high in birth,
Be great and high, I envy not your hap.°   lot
Your birth must be from dust, your power on earth;
In Heav'n shall Mariam sit in Sara's lap.[4]

*   *   *

Act 5

SCENE 1

*   *   *

55 [NUNTIO]   She came unmoved, with pleasant grace,
As if to triumph her arrival were:
In stately habit, and with cheerful face:
Yet ev'ry eye was moist but Mariam's there.
When justly° opposite to me she came,   exactly
60 She picked me out from all the crew:
She beckoned to me, called me by my name,
For she my name, my birth, and fortune knew.
HEROD   What, did she name thee? Happy, happy man,
Wilt thou not ever love that name the better?
65 But what sweet tune did this fair dying swan[5]
Afford thine ear? Tell all, omit no letter.
NUNTIO   "Tell thou my lord," said she—
HEROD   Me, meant she me?
Is't true,° the more my shame: I was her lord,   if it is true
Were I not mad, her lord I still should be:[6]

4. Mariam envisions herself not in Abraham's
bosom but in its female counterpart, the lap of
Abraham's wife, Sarah.
5. The swan was thought to sing most sweetly (or

only) before its own death.
6. I.e., if I had not been her (tyrannical) lord, I
still would be her husband and lord.

70   But now her name must be by me adored.
             Oh say, what said she more? Each word she said
             Shall be the food whereon my heart is fed.
           NUNTIO   "Tell thou my lord thou saw'st me loose my breath."
           HEROD   Oh, that I could that sentence now control.°   *overrun*
75   NUNTIO   "If guiltily, eternal be my death"—
           HEROD   I hold her chaste ev'n in my inmost soul.
           NUNTIO   "By three days hence, if wishes could revive,
             I know himself would make me oft alive."[7]
           HEROD   Three days: three hours, three minutes, not so much,
80   A minute in a thousand parts divided;
             My penitency for her death is such,
             As in the first[8] I wished she had not died.
             But forward in thy tale.
           NUNTIO   Why, on she went,
             And after she some silent prayer had said,
85   She died as if to die she were content,
             And thus to Heav'n her heav'nly soul is fled.
           HEROD   But art thou sure there doth no life remain?
             Is't possible my Mariam should be dead?
             Is there no trick to make her breathe again?
90   NUNTIO   Her body is divided from her head.
           HEROD   Why, yet methinks there might be found by art
             Strange ways of cure; 'tis sure rare things are done
             By an inventive head, and willing heart.
           NUNTIO   Let not, my lord, your fancies idly run.
95   It is as possible it should be seen,
             That we should make the holy Abraham live,
             Though he entombed two thousand years had been,
             As breath again to slaughtered Mariam give.
             But now for more assaults prepare your ears—
100   HEROD   There cannot be a further cause of moan,
             This accident shall shelter me from fears:
             What can I fear? Already Mariam's gone.
             Yet tell ev'n what you will.
           NUNTIO   As I came by,
             From Mariam's death, I saw upon a tree
105   A man that to his neck a cord did tie:[9]
             Which cord he had designed his end to be.
             When me he once discerned, he downwards bowed,
             And thus with fearful voice he cried aloud,
             "Go tell the King he trusted ere he tried,°   *tested*
110   I am the cause that Mariam causeless died."
           HEROD   Damnation take him, for it was the slave
             That said she meant with poison's deadly force

---

7. Mariam predicts that Herod will wish her alive after three days, with apparent allusion to Jesus' prediction that he would rise from the dead after three days.

8. In the first thousandth of a minute.

9. Recalls the manner of Judas's suicide after his betrayal of Jesus (Matthew 27.5).

To end my life that she the crown might have:
Which tale did Mariam from herself divorce.[1]
115 Oh, pardon me, thou pure unspotted ghost,
My punishment must needs sufficient be,
In missing that content I valued most:
Which was thy admirable face to see.
I had but one inestimable jewel,[2]
120 Yet one I had no monarch had the like,
And therefore may I curse myself as cruel:
'Twas broken by a blow myself did strike.
I gazed thereon and never thought me blessed,
But when on it my dazzled eye might rest,
125 A precious mirror made by wondrous art,
I prized it ten times dearer than my crown,
And laid it up fast folded in my heart:
Yet I in sudden choler° cast it down,   anger
And pash'd° it all to pieces.   smashed

* * *

HEROD   She's dead, hell take her murderers, she was fair,[3]
150 Oh, what a hand she had, it was so white,
It did the whiteness of the snow impair:°   darken
I never more shall see so sweet a sight.
NUNTIO   'Tis true, her hand was rare.
HEROD   Her hand? her hands;
She had not singly one of beauty rare,
155 But such a pair as here where Herod stands,
He dares the world to make to both compare.[4]
Accursèd Salome, hadst thou been still,°   silent
My Mariam had been breathing by my side:
Oh, never had I, had I had my will,
160 Sent forth command, that Mariam should have died.
But, Salome, thou didst with envy vex,°   fret
To see thyself outmatchèd in thy sex:
Upon your sex's forehead Mariam sat,
To grace you all like an imperial crown,
165 But you, fond fool, have rudely pushed thereat,
And proudly pulled your proper glory down.
One smile of hers—nay, not so much—a look
Was worth a hundred thousand such as you.
Judea, how canst thou the wretches brook,°   endure
170 That robbed from thee the fairest of the crew?
You dwellers in the now deprivèd land,
Wherein the matchless Mariam was bred:

---

1. The Butler's accusation that Mariam was plotting to take over the throne from Herod is not in Cary's chief source, Josephus's *Antiquities*.
2. Proverbs 31.10 calls a good wife more precious than jewels. Cf. *Othello* 5.2.346–47: "one whose hand / (Like the base Indian) threw a pearl away/

Richer than all his tribe."
3. The rhythm of the line invites comparison with *The Duchess of Malfi* 4.2.245: "Cover her face. / Mine eyes dazzle. She died young" (p. 1487).
4. I.e., Herod dares the world to find any comparable two hands anywhere.

Why grasp not each of you a sword in hand,
To aim at me your cruel sovereign's head?
175 Oh, when you think of Herod as your king,
And owner of the pride of Palestine,
This act to your remembrance likewise bring:
'Tis I have overthrown your royal line.

                    *   *   *

Why shine you, sun, with an aspect so clear?
I tell you once again my Mariam's dead.
195 You could but shine, if some Egyptian blowse,
Or Aethiopian dowdy lose her life:[5]
This was—then wherefore bend you not your brows?—
The King of Jewry's fair and spotless wife.
Deny thy beams, and, moon, refuse thy light,
200 Let all the stars be dark, let Jewry's eye
No more distinguish which is day and night:
Since her best birth did in her bosom die.

                    *   *   *

If she had been like an Egyptian[6] black,
240 And not so fair, she had been longer lived:
Her overflow of beauty turnèd back,
And drowned the spring from whence it was derived.
Her heav'nly beauty 'twas that made me think
That it with chastity could never dwell:[7]
245 But now I see that Heav'n in her did link
A spirit and a person° to excel.   body
I'll muffle up myself in endless night,
And never let mine eyes behold the light.
Retire thyself, vile monster, worse than he[8]
250 That stained the virgin earth with brother's blood.[9]
Still in some vault or den enclosèd be,
Where with thy tears thou may'st beget a flood,
Which flood in time may drown thee: happy day
When thou at once shalt die and find a grave;
255 A stone upon the vault someone shall lay,
Which monument shall an inscription have,
And these shall be the words it shall contain:
Here Herod lies, that hath his Mariam slain. [*Exit.*]

                                                    1613

---

5. I.e., you [sun] could only shine in the same way
if a beggar's prostitute [blowse] or shabby old
woman [dowdy] died; "Egyptian" and "Aethiopian"
mark them as dark-skinned (not fair like Mariam)
and may allude to Cleopatra.

6. Another allusion to Cleopatra.
7. The idea that chastity and beauty cannot coexist is a misogynistic commonplace.
8. Herod addresses himself.
9. Cain, who murdered Abel.

The Science of Self
and World

The seventeenth century saw writers developing new genres to fashion a self, to describe other persons, or to present a personal vision of the world. Literary fictions and poetry in all eras deal with such matters, but they are pursued with a new immediacy and seeming realism in the self-probing lyrics of Donne and Herbert. New kinds emerged to accommodate a new focus on real people and the actual contemporary world, and new methods were devised for analyzing both of these subjects. The works produced are often intimate and personal but at the same time serve political or public purposes. These genres are chiefly (but not exclusively) prose kinds; in them, we can watch the remarkable development of English prose, as it became a flexible instrument that could take various forms (or combine them) for diverse purposes and could employ several styles: plain and direct, curt and epigrammatic, homely and vulgar, witty and boldly imagistic, irregular and energetic, learned and allusive, ornate and Latinate. In general, we can mark a movement away from Ciceronean balanced rhythms, *copia* (abundance), *pleonism* (elegant restatement), and complex sentence structure marked by subordination, toward what was generally known as "Senecan" style in either a curt and aphoristic version or a loose variety, the latter marked by broken rhythms and more loosely organized sentences.

Autobiography came into its own in this period, emerging out of the numerous diaries, memoirs, and journals kept by individuals. The tendency to self-analysis was strengthened by Protestant and especially Puritan directives to keep a careful, daily account of how it stands between God and one's own soul and to write up at evening what things of spiritual significance have occurred during the day. It was also promoted by the practice of meditation on events in one's life that are taken to be providential: an example is Donne's *Devotions upon Emergent Occasions*, a meditation on the various stages of an illness that threatened to be fatal. The move toward formal autobiography occurs when a unifying structure and perspective are imposed on some part of a life. The speaker may be a close version of the author, as in Martha Moulsworth's poetic *Memorandum*, which reviews the principal events in her life on the occasion of her fifty-fifth birthday, and in the autobiographical accounts by Margaret Cavendish or Anne Halkett. Alternatively, the author may look back to older allegorical modes, as in Rachel Speght's *Dream*, a dream-vision poem allegorizing the obstacles and delights the speaker Rachel encountered in her pursuit of learning. In another vein, Sir Thomas Browne's intellectual autobiography, *Religio Medici*, sets forth in intimate but elegant prose the personal and sometimes eccentric religious views of a carefully constructed version of Browne as genial, tolerant, speculative doctor. In the seventeenth century, biography also became newly important, nourished in part by the sense that the lives of notable contemporaries should be recorded for history. Biographies had been written before (e.g., Thomas More's *Life of Richard III* or the short biographies often appended to funeral sermons), but Izaak Walton's several *Lives* achieved a new sophistication and completeness, while still bearing the imprint of the old model of the saint's life; the survival of this model is especially evident in the *Life of Donne*.

Short essays and treatises of all kinds in English came to be primary vehicles for analyzing aspects of the external world, though Latin remained important for scholarly discourse. With Bacon the essay is not an intimate, personal confession (as it was for the French writer Montaigne), but rather the aphoristic voice of accumulated public wisdom delivered from the perspective of a man of affairs eager to make his way in the world of Jacobean court culture. In longer treatises, Bacon proposed methods for the radical reform of knowledge; he also devised a fictional scientific utopia, *The New Atlantis*. Richard Burton's massive and continually digressive treatise *Anatomy of Melancholy* analyzes in elaborate detail and in a loose, galloping style all aspects of a psychological malady Burton thought universal; he adopted the name Democritus Junior, offering thereby to take on the nature and role of the Greek satirist Democritus. In a very different vein and in a forthright, analytic style, Hobbes's lengthy treatise *Leviathan* develops a comprehensive theory of human nature and of the commonwealth. For Hobbes, absolute sovereignty flows directly from the irrevocable compact humans are forced by their own natures to make, since such absolutism alone can save them from what would otherwise be a war of every man against every man. During the English Civil War, prose treatises proliferated, composed by all kinds and classes of writers and on every conceivable subject, though chiefly on how to reform the church and the state. These treatises democritized prose, using it not simply to represent but also to reform radically or overturn institutions of the social world: the church, the state, the universities, the family. Such polemic generally advanced the movement toward the style valued in the Restoration era, characterized by clarity, smoothness, and artful simplicity.

FRANCIS BACON

Francis Bacon's writings focus on the world rather than on the self, dealing chiefly with issues of practical morality, politics, and the theory of knowledge. As a literary figure Bacon (1561–1626) played a central role in developing the English essay and English prose styles, as well as in inaugurating the genre of the scientific utopia in his *New Atlantis*. He was even more important to the intellectual and cultural history of the earlier seventeenth century for his treatises that aimed to reform and promote learning through experiment and induction. His lifespan closely overlaps that of Donne and Jonson, but unlike those writers he came from a noble family close to the center of government and power; he was also nephew by marriage to William Cecil, Lord Burghley, Queen Elizabeth's most trusted advisor. During Elizabeth's reign, Bacon studied law, entered Parliament, and took an active part in prosecuting his friend and patron, the earl of Essex, who was charged by the queen with treason. But his political fortunes took off under James I: Bacon was knighted in 1603, became attorney general in 1613, lord chancellor (the highest judicial post) and Baron Verulam in 1618, and Viscount St. Albans in 1621. That same year, however, he fell from the heights to the nadir: he was convicted on twenty-three counts of corruption and accepting bribes, fined, imprisoned, and forced from office. Bacon admitted the truth of the charges (though they were in part politically motivated), merely observing that everyone took bribes and that bribery never influenced his judgment. He later commented: "I was the justest judge that was in England these fifty years, but it was the justest censure in Parliament that was these 200 years."

As an essayist, Bacon stands at almost the opposite pole from his great French predecessor Michel de Montaigne (1533–1592), who proposed to learn about humankind in general by intensive analysis of his own body and mind and by exploring the full range of his sensations, emotions, attitudes, and ideas. Bacon's essays are instead on topics "Civil and Moral," as his title has it. Montaigne's essays are tentative in structure, witty, expansive, and reflective in style, intimate, candid, and affable in tone; he speaks constantly in the first person. Bacon adopts an aphoristic structure and a curt and often disjunctive version of what was then labeled the Senecan style, as well as a tone of cool objectivity and weighty sententiousness; he seldom uses "I," but instead presents himself as the mouthpiece for society's accumulated practical wisdom. The ten short essays of the first edition of essays (1597) are little more than collections of maxims placed in sequence; the thirty-eight of the second edition (1612) are longer and looser; the fifty-eight of the final edition (1625) are smoother in texture, use more figurative language, and are more unified. In that last edition, more than half of the essays deal with public life, and many of the others—even on such topics as "Truth," "Marriage," and "Love"—are written from the vantage point of a man of affairs concerned to make his way in the world, rather than that of a profound moralist. They evoke a general atmosphere of expediency and self-interest but also voice precepts of moral wisdom and public virtue, offering penetrating insights into the interests, problems, and thinking of the Jacobean ruling class.

Bacon saw his proposals for the reform of knowledge as central to his sense of self: early on he told Lord Burghley, "I have taken all knowledge to be my province." Whereas Donne in the *First Anniversary* saw human history as a process of inevitable degeneration and decay, Bacon saw it as progressive and believed that his new "scientific" method would lead humankind to a better future. In *The Advancement of Learning* (1605), he attempted a preliminary survey of the entire field of learning, by analyzing the principal obstacles to its advancement: rhetoric, which prompts the study of words rather than things; medieval Scholasticism, which ignores nature and promotes a barren rationalism; and pseudosciences such as astrology and alchemy. He then diagnosed what remains to be learned. In 1623 he set forth a reworked and greatly expanded Latin version of this treatise. Also in Latin, Bacon's *Novum Organum* (1620) urged induction—combining the empirical and the rational—as the correct method of investigating nature: the title challenges Aristotle's *Organon* (which was still the basis of university education) with its heavy reliance on deduction. The *Novum Organum* includes a trenchant analysis of four kinds of "Idols" or images to which we give false worship: these are the psychological dispositions and fears that hold humankind back in its quest for truth and cause it to cling obstinately to the past. Bacon did not himself make a major contribution to science, and despite his emphasis on experiment he for the most part ignored the major scientific breakthroughs of his age, which grew out of experiment: the astronomy of Galileo, William Harvey's discovery of the circulation of the blood, William Gilbert's observations on magnetism. Bacon's true role was as a herald of the modern age; despite his critique of rhetoric he used the rich resources of figurative language—and of utopian fiction in *New Atlantis*—forcefully to call his countrymen to a new faith in experiment and science. The thrust of his method was to segregate theology and science as "two truths"—a separation that freed science to go its own way unhampered by the old dogmas and creeds, but left it unrestrained by the morality such creeds supported. Bacon is a primary creator of the myth of science as pathway to Utopia; late in the seventeenth century the Royal (scientific) Society honored him as a prophet.

FROM ESSAYS[1]

Of Truth

"What is truth?" said jesting Pilate; and would not stay for an answer.[2] Certainly there be that delight in giddiness,[3] and count it a bondage to fix a belief; affecting free will in thinking, as well as in acting. And though the sects of philosophers of that kind be gone, yet there remain certain discoursing wits,[4] which are of the same veins, though there be not so much blood in them as was in those of the ancients. But it is not only the difficulty and labor which men take in finding out of truth; nor again, that when it is found, it imposeth upon[5] men's thoughts, that doth bring lies in favor; but a natural though corrupt love of the lie itself. One of the later school of the Grecians examineth the matter, and is at a stand[6] to think what should be in it, that men should love lies, where neither they make for pleasure, as with poets, nor for advantage, as with the merchant, but for the lie's sake. But I cannot tell: this same truth is a naked and open daylight, that doth not show the masks and mummeries and triumphs of the world half so stately and daintily as candlelights. Truth may perhaps come to the price of a pearl, that showeth best by day, but it will not rise to the price of a diamond or carbuncle,[7] that showeth best in varied lights. A mixture of a lie doth ever add pleasure. Doth any man doubt that if there were taken out of men's minds vain opinions, flattering hopes, false valuations, imaginations as one would, and the like, but it would leave the minds of a number of men poor shrunken things, full of melancholy and indisposition, and unpleasing to themselves? One of the fathers, in great severity, called poesy *vinum daemonum*,[8] because it filleth the imagination, and yet it is but with the shadow of a lie. But it is not the lie that passeth through the mind, but the lie that sinketh in, and settleth in it, that doth the hurt, such as we spake of before. But howsoever these things are thus in men's depraved judgments and affections, yet truth, which only doth judge itself, teacheth that the inquiry of truth, which is the love-making or wooing of it, the knowledge of truth, which is the presence of it, and the belief of truth, which is the enjoying of it, is the sovereign good of human nature. The first creature[9] of God, in the works of the days, was the light of the sense; the last was the light of reason; and his sabbath work ever since is the illumination of his Spirit. First he breathed light upon the face of the matter, or chaos; then he breathed light into the face of man; and still he breatheth and inspireth light into the face of his chosen. The poet that beautified the sect that was otherwise inferior to the rest[1] saith yet excellently well: "It is a pleasure to stand upon the shore, and to see ships tossed upon

1. Bacon's essays appeared in three editions, 1597 (10 essays), 1612 (38 essays), and 1625 (58 essays); we illustrate the very considerable stylistic differences between the earliest and latest collections by presenting two versions of *Of Studies* (p. 1541). Otherwise all selections are from the 1625 collection, in which *Of Truth* stands first.
2. See John 18.38 for Pilate's idle query to Jesus.
3. Foolish changeability. "That": those who.
4. Discursive minds. "Philosophers of that kind": the Greek Skeptics, who taught the uncertainty of all things.
5. Restricts, controls.
6. I.e., is baffled.
7. Ruby.
8. The wine of devils; St. Augustine is probably being cited.
9. Creation.
1. Lucretius's *On the Nature of Things* expressed the Epicurean creed, which Bacon thought inferior because it emphasized pleasure.

the sea; a pleasure to stand in the window of a castle, and to see a battle, and the adventures thereof below; but no pleasure is comparable to the standing upon the vantage ground of truth" (a hill not to be commanded,[2] and where the air is always clear and serene), "and to see the errors, and wanderings, and mists, and tempests, in the vale below": so always that this prospect[3] be with pity, and not with swelling or pride. Certainly, it is heaven upon earth to have a man's mind move in charity, rest in providence, and turn upon the poles of truth.

To pass from theological and philosophical truth to the truth of civil business, it will be acknowledged even by those that practice it not, that clear and round dealing[4] is the honor of man's nature, and that mixture of falsehood is like alloy in coin of gold and silver, which may make the metal work the better, but it embaseth[5] it. For these winding and crooked courses are the goings of the serpent; which goeth basely upon the belly, and not upon the feet. There is no vice that doth so cover a man with shame as to be found false and perfidious. And therefore Montaigne saith prettily, when he inquired the reason why the word of the lie should be such a disgrace, and such an odious charge, saith he, "If it be well weighed, to say that a man lieth is as much to say as that he is brave towards God and a coward towards men."[6] For a lie faces God, and shrinks from man. Surely the wickedness of falsehood and breach of faith cannot possibly be so highly expressed, as in that it shall be the last peal to call the judgments of God upon the generations of men, it being foretold that when Christ cometh, he shall not "find faith upon the earth."[7]

1625

Of Marriage and Single Life

He that hath wife and children hath given hostages to fortune; for they are impediments to great enterprises, either of virtue or mischief. Certainly the best works, and of greatest merit for the public, have proceeded from the unmarried or childless men, which both in affection and means have married and endowed the public. Yet it were great reason that those that have children should have greatest care of future times, unto which they know they must transmit their dearest pledges. Some there are who, though they lead a single life, yet their thoughts do end with themselves, and account future times impertinences.[1] Nay, there are some other that account wife and children but as bills of charges. Nay more, there are some foolish rich covetous men that take a pride in having no children, because they may be thought so much the richer. For perhaps they have heard some talk, "Such an one is a great rich man," and another except to it, "Yea, but he hath a great charge of children"; as if it were an abatement to his riches. But the most ordinary cause of a single life is liberty, especially in certain self-pleasing and humorous[2] minds, which are so sensible of every restraint, as they will go near to

2. Dominated.
3. I.e., provided always that this observation.
4. Upright.
5. Debases.

6. *Essays* 2.18.
7. Luke 18.8.
1. Irrelevant concerns.
2. Unbalanced, whimsical.

think their girdles and garters to be bonds and shackles. Unmarried men are best friends, best masters, best servants, but not always best subjects, for they are light to run away, and almost all fugitives are of that condition. A single life doth well with churchmen, for charity will hardly water the ground where it must first fill a pool. It is indifferent for judges and magistrates, for if they be facile[3] and corrupt, you shall have a servant five times worse than a wife. For soldiers, I find the generals commonly in their hortatives[4] put men in mind of their wives and children; and I think the despising of marriage amongst the Turks maketh the vulgar soldier more base. Certainly wife and children are a kind of discipline of humanity; and single men, though they be many times more charitable, because their means are less exhaust,[5] yet, on the other side, they are more cruel and hardhearted (good to make severe inquisitors), because their tenderness is not so oft called upon. Grave natures, led by custom, and therefore constant, are commonly loving husbands, as was said of Ulysses, *Vetulam suam praetulit immortalitati.*[6] Chaste women are often proud and froward,[7] as presuming upon the merit of their chastity. It is one of the best bonds, both of chastity and obedience, in the wife if she think her husband wise, which she will never do if she find him jealous. Wives are young men's mistresses, companions for middle age, and old men's nurses; so as a man may have a quarrel[8] to marry when he will. But yet he was reputed one of the wise men that made answer to the question when a man should marry: "A young man not yet, an elder man not at all."[9] It is often seen that bad husbands have very good wives; whether it be that it raiseth the price of their husbands' kindness when it comes, or that the wives take a pride in their patience. But this never fails, if the bad husbands were of their own choosing, against their friends' consent; for then they will be sure to make good their own folly.

1612, 1625

Of Great Place

Men in great place are thrice servants: servants of the sovereign or state, servants of fame, and servants of business. So as they have no freedom, neither in their persons, nor in their actions, nor in their times. It is a strange desire, to seek power and to lose liberty, or to seek power over others and to lose power over a man's self. The rising unto place is laborious, and by pains men come to greater pains; and it is sometimes base, and by indignities men come to dignities. The standing is slippery, and the regress is either a downfall or at least an eclipse, which is a melancholy thing: *Cum non sis qui fueris, non esse cur velis vivere.*[1] Nay, retire men cannot when they would, neither will they when it were reason; but are impatient of privateness, even in age and sickness, which require the shadow;[2] like old townsmen, that will be still

3. Pliable.
4. Exhortations.
5. Exhausted.
6. "He preferred his old wife to immortality." Ulysses might have had immortality with the nymph Calypso, but preferred to go back to Penelope.
7. Ill-tempered.

8. Pretext.
9. Thales (6th century B.C.E.), one of the Seven Sages of Greece.
1. "When you aren't what you were, there's no reason to live" (Cicero, *Familiar Letters* 7.3).
2. "The shadow" of retirement, out of the glare of public life.

sitting at their street door, though thereby they offer age to scorn. Certainly great persons had need to borrow other men's opinions to think themselves happy; for if they judge by their own feeling, they cannot find it; but if they think with themselves what other men think of them, and that other men would fain be as they are, then they are happy, as it were by report; when perhaps they find the contrary within. For they are the first that find their own griefs, though they be the last that find their own faults. Certainly men in great fortunes are strangers to themselves, and while they are in the puzzle of business they have no time to tend their health, either of body or mind. *Illi mors gravis incubat, qui notus nimis omnibus, ignotus moritur sibi.*[3] In place there is license to do good and evil, whereof the latter is a curse; for in evil the best condition is not to will, the second not to can.[4] But power to do good is the true and lawful end of aspiring; for good thoughts (though God accept them) yet towards men are little better than good dreams, except they be put in act; and that cannot be without power and place, as the vantage and commanding ground. Merit and good works is the end of man's motion, and conscience[5] of the same is the accomplishment of man's rest; for if a man can be partaker of God's theater,[6] he shall likewise be partaker of God's rest. *Et conversus Deus, ut aspiceret opera quae fecerunt manus suae, vidit quod omnia essent bona nimis;*[7] and then the sabbath.

In the discharge of thy place set before thee the best examples, for imitation is a globe[8] of precepts. And after a time set before thee thine own example; and examine thyself strictly, whether thou didst not best at first. Neglect not also the examples of those that have carried themselves ill in the same place; not to set off thyself by taxing[9] their memory, but to direct thyself what to avoid. Reform, therefore, without bravery, or scandal[1] of former times and persons; but yet set it down to thyself, as well to create good precedents as to follow them. Reduce things to the first institution,[2] and observe wherein and how they have degenerate; but yet ask counsel of both times; of the ancient time what is best, and of the latter time what is fittest. Seek to make thy course regular, that men may know beforehand what they may expect; but be not too positive and peremptory, and express thyself well when thou digressest from thy rule. Preserve the right of thy place, but stir not questions of jurisdiction; and rather assume thy right in silence and *de facto,*[3] than voice it with claims and challenges. Preserve likewise the rights of inferior places, and think it more honor to direct in chief than to be busy in all. Embrace and invite helps and advices touching the execution of thy place, and do not drive away such as bring thee information as meddlers, but accept of them in good part. The vices of authority are chiefly four: delays, corruption, roughness, and facility.[4] For delays, give easy access, keep times appointed, go through with that which is in hand, and interlace not business[5] but of necessity. For corruption, do not only bind thine own hands or thy servants' hands from taking, but bind the hands of suitors also from offering. For integrity used doth the one; but integrity professed, and with a

---

3. "Death lies heavily on him who, while too well known to everyone else, dies unknown to himself" (Seneca, *Thyestes*).
4. Be able.
5. Consciousness.
6. Actions in the world.
7. "And God saw every thing that he had made, and, behold, it was very good" (Genesis 1.31).

8. World.
9. Blaming.
1. Defaming. "Bravery": ostentation.
2. To their original form.
3. Without debate, as a matter of course.
4. Docility, too great obligingness.
5. I.e., do not carry on different businesses at the same time.

manifest detestation of bribery, doth the other. And avoid not only the fault, but the suspicion. Whosoever is found variable and changeth manifestly, without manifest cause, giveth suspicion of corruption. Therefore, always when thou changest thine opinion or course, profess it plainly and declare it, together with the reasons that move thee to change; and do not think to steal it.[6] A servant or a favorite, if he be inward,[7] and no other apparent cause of esteem, is commonly thought but a by-way to close[8] corruption. For roughness, it is a needless cause of discontent; severity breedeth fear, but roughness breedeth hate. Even reproofs from authority ought to be grave, and not taunting. As for facility, it is worse than bribery; for bribes come but now and then, but if importunity or idle respects[9] lead a man, he shall never be without. As Solomon saith, "To respect persons is not good, for such a man will transgress for a piece of bread."[1]

It is most true that was anciently spoken, "A place showeth the man"; and it showeth some to the better and some to the worse. *Omnium consensu capax imperii, nisi imperasset,*[2] saith Tacitus of Galba; but of Vespasian he saith, *Solus imperantium Vespasianus mutatus in melius:*[3] though the one was meant of sufficiency, the other of manners and affection. It is an assured sign of a worthy and generous spirit, whom honor amends.[4] For honor is, or should be, the place of virtue; and as in nature things move violently to their place and calmly in their place, so virtue in ambition is violent, in authority settled and calm. All rising to great place is by a winding stair; and if there be factions, it is good to side a man's self[5] whilst he is in the rising, and to balance himself when he is placed. Use the memory of thy predecessor fairly and tenderly; for if thou dost not, it is a debt will sure be paid when thou art gone. If thou have colleagues, respect them, and rather call them when they look not for it, than exclude them when they have reason to look to be called. Be not too sensible[6] or too remembering of thy place in conversation and private answers to suitors; but let it rather be said, "When he sits in place he is another man."

1612, 1625

Of Superstition[1]

It were better to have no opinion of God at all than such an opinion as is unworthy of him. For the one is unbelief, the other is contumely:[2] and certainly superstition is the reproach of the deity. Plutarch saith well to that purpose: "Surely" (saith he) "I had rather a great deal men should say there was no such man at all as Plutarch, than that they should say that there was one Plutarch that would eat his children as soon as they were born"—as the poets speak of Saturn.[3] And as the contumely is greater towards God, so the

---

6. Change your mind without its being noticed.
7. In his master's confidence.
8. Secret.
9. Irrelevant considerations.
1. Cf. Proverbs 28.21.
2. "Everyone would have thought him a good ruler, if he had not ruled."
3. "Of all the emperors, only Vespasian changed for the better." "Sufficiency": abilities. "Affection": disposition.

4. I.e., whom promotion improves.
5. For a man to take sides.
6. Sensitive.
1. Irrational religious practices founded on fear or ignorance.
2. Contempt.
3. Saturn (Cronos), god of time (among other things), was reputed to eat all his children, as time does. Many of the sentiments in Bacon's essay come from Plutarch's essay *On Superstition.*

danger is greater towards men. Atheism leaves a man to sense, to philosophy, to natural piety, to laws, to reputation, all which may be guides to an outward moral virtue, though religion were not. But superstition dismounts all these, and erecteth an absolute monarchy in the minds of men. Therefore atheism did never perturb states, for it makes men wary of themselves as looking no further;[4] and we see the times inclined to atheism (as the time of Augustus Caesar) were civil times. But superstition hath been the confusion of many states, and bringeth in a new *primum mobile*, that ravisheth all the spheres of government.[5] The master of superstition is the people, and in all superstition wise men follow fools, and arguments are fitted to practice in a reversed order. It was gravely said by some of the prelates in the council of Trent, where the doctrine of the schoolmen bare great sway, *that the schoolmen were like astronomers, which did feign eccentrics and epicycles and such engines of orbs to save the phenomena, though they knew there were no such things;*[6] and in like manner that the schoolmen had framed a number of subtle and intricate axioms and theorems to save the practice of the church.

The causes of superstition are: pleasing and sensual rites and ceremonies; excess of outward and pharisaical holiness;[7] over-great reverence of traditions, which cannot but load the church; the stratagems of prelates for their own ambition and lucre; the favoring too much of good intentions, which openeth the gate to conceits[8] and novelties; the taking an aim at divine matters by human, which cannot but breed mixture of imaginations; and lastly barbarous times, especially joined with calamities and disasters. Superstition without a veil is a deformed thing, for as it addeth deformity to an ape to be so like a man, so the similitude of superstition to religion makes it the more deformed. And as wholesome meat corrupteth to little worms, so good forms and orders corrupt into a number of petty observances. There is a superstition in avoiding superstition, when men think to do best if they go furthest from the superstition formerly received; therefore care would be had that (as it fareth in ill purgings) the good be not taken away with the bad, which commonly is done when the people is the reformer.[9]

1612, 1625

Of Plantations[1]

Plantations are amongst ancient, primitive, and heroical works. When the world was young it begat more children; but now it is old it begets fewer: for

4. I.e., not looking beyond their own personal lifetimes. The rule of Augustus Caesar was marked by general peace and civil quiet (i.e., civilized). Why Bacon thinks they "inclined to atheism" is less clear.

5. The prime mover (*primum mobile*) was supposed to control the motions of the other heavenly spheres; superstition is a second (and contrary) mover.

6. "Saving the phenomena" means explaining appearances, as did the elaborate theories of pre-Copernican astronomers (epicycles, trepidation, and such concepts). So with the Scholastic philosophers ("schoolmen").

7. The Pharisees were the strict party among the Jews of Christ's time; they taught precise observance of the letter of Mosaic law.

8. Fancies.

9. The final sentence is directed against Puritan reformers, who loathed ceremonies, traditions, liturgy, and images, which they considered "superstitions."

1. The planting of colonies was a standard topic of political theory since Plato, with attention focused on such matters as the choice of site, the best mix of population, and the treatment of indigenous peoples. Sir Thomas More considered the matter in his *Utopia* (p. 506), and it took on increased practical importance in the narratives of English explorers such as Sir Walter Ralegh (p. 885), and especially in the early 17th century, with the establishment of the first permanent English settlements in the New World. Bacon's essay completely avoids the most acute moral

I may justly account new plantations to be the children of former kingdoms. I like a plantation in a pure soil; that is, where people are not displanted to the end to plant in others. For else it is rather an extirpation than a plantation. Planting of countries is like planting of woods; for you must make account to leese[2] almost twenty years profit, and expect your recompense in the end. For the principal thing that hath been the destruction of most plantations hath been the base and hasty drawing of profit in the first years. It is true, speedy profit is not to be neglected, as far as may stand[3] with the good of the plantation, but no further. It is a shameful and unblessed thing to take the scum of people, and wicked condemned men, to be the people with whom you plant; and not only so, but it spoileth the plantation, for they will ever live like rogues, and not fall to work, but be lazy, and do mischief, and spend victuals, and be quickly weary, and then certify over[4] to their country, to the discredit of the plantation. The people wherewith you plant ought to be gardeners, plowmen, laborers, smiths, carpenters, joiners,[5] fishermen, fowlers, with some few apothecaries, surgeons, cooks, and bakers.

In a country of plantation, first look about what kind of victual the country yields of itself to hand, as chestnuts, walnuts, pineapples, olives, dates, plums, cherries, wild honey, and the like, and make use of them. Then consider what victual or esculent[6] things there are which grow speedily and within the year, as parsnips, carrots, turnips, onions, radish, artichokes of Jerusalem,[7] maize, and the like. For wheat, barley, and oats, they ask[8] too much labor; but with peas and beans you may begin, both because they ask less labor and because they serve for meat[9] as well as for bread. And of rice likewise cometh a great increase, and it is a kind of meat. Above all, there ought to be brought store of biscuit, oatmeal, flour, meal, and the like in the beginning, till bread may be had. For beasts or birds, take chiefly such as are least subject to diseases, and multiply fastest, as swine, goats, cocks, hens, turkeys, geese, house doves, and the like. The victual in plantations ought to be expended almost as in a besieged town; that is, with certain[1] allowance. And let the main part of the ground employed to gardens or corn be to[2] a common stock, and to be laid in and stored up and then delivered out in proportion; besides some spots of ground that any particular person will manure[3] for his own private. Consider likewise what commodities the soil where the plantation is doth naturally yield, that they may some way help to defray the charge of the plantation (so it be not, as was said, to the untimely prejudice of the main business), as it hath fared with tobacco in Virginia. Wood commonly aboundeth but too much, and therefore timber is fit to be one. If there be iron ore and streams whereupon to set the mills, iron is a brave[4] commodity, where wood aboundeth. Making of bay-salt, if the climate be proper for it, would be put in experience.[5] Growing silk likewise, if any be, is a likely commodity. Pitch and tar, where store of firs and pines are,

---

issues English colonization was posing: English participation in the brutal African slave trade; and the stocking of "plantations" in Ireland with Scottish Presbyterian settlers (to supplement genocidal policies that were starving out the indigenous Roman Catholics). These policies sowed the seeds of slavery in America and civil war in Ireland.
2. Lose.
3. Be consistent.
4. Report.
5. Joiners build (wooden) furnishings.
6. Edible.

7. Jerusalem artichokes, a species of sunflower having an edible root. "Jerusalem" is a mistranslation of the Italian word for sunflower, girasole.
8. Require. "For": as for.
9. I.e., as a main dish.
1. Fixed.
2. For. "Corn": grain.
3. Cultivate.
4. Excellent.
5. I.e., should be tried. "Bay-salt" is a coarse salt obtained by evaporating seawater. "Growing silk" (next sentence): vegetable silk.

will not fail; so drugs and sweet woods, where they are, cannot but yield great profit. Soap ashes[6] likewise, and other things that may be thought of. But moil not too much under ground, for the hope of mines is very uncertain, and useth to make the planters lazy in other things.

For government, let it be in the hands of one, assisted with some counsel; and let them have commission to exercise martial laws, with some limitation. And above all, let men make that profit of being in the wilderness, as they have God always, and his service, before their eyes. Let not the government of the plantation depend upon too many counselors and undertakers[7] in the country that planteth, but upon a temperate number; and let those be rather noblemen and gentlemen than merchants, for they look ever to the present gain. Let there be freedoms from custom[8] till the plantation be of strength; and not only freedom from custom, but freedom to carry their commodities where they may make their best of them, except there be some special cause of caution. Cram not in people by sending too fast, company after company, but rather harken how they waste,[9] and send supplies proportionably, but so as the number may live well in the plantation, and not by surcharge[1] be in penury.

It hath been a great endangering to the health of some plantations, that they have built along the sea and rivers, in marish[2] and unwholesome grounds. Therefore, though you begin there, to avoid carriage and other like discommodities,[3] yet build still rather upwards from the streams than along. It concerneth likewise the health of the plantation that they have good store of salt with them, that they may use it in their victuals when it shall be necessary. If you plant where savages are, do not only entertain them with trifles and jingles, but use them justly and graciously, with sufficient guard nevertheless; and do not win their favor by helping them to invade their enemies, but for their defense it is not amiss. And send oft of them over to the country that plants, that they may see a better condition than their own, and commend it when they return. When the plantation grows to strength, then it is time to plant with women as well as with men, that the plantation may spread into generations and not be ever pieced from without. It is the sinfullest thing in the world to forsake or destitute a plantation once in forwardness; for besides the dishonor it is the guiltiness of blood of many commiserable[4] persons.

1625

Of Negotiating

It is generally better to deal by speech than by letter, and by the mediation of a third than by a man's self. Letters are good when a man would draw an answer by letter back again, or when it may serve for a man's justification afterwards to produce his own letter, or where it may be danger to be interrupted or heard by pieces. To deal in person is good when a man's face

---

6. Ashes used for making soap.
7. Investors holding shares in the enterprise.
8. Customs duties.
9. I.e., observe at what rate the population declines.

1. I.e., by being overpopulated.
2. Marshy.
3. Disadvantages, inconveniences.
4. Worthy of compassion. "Destitute": abandon.

breedeth regard, as commonly with inferiors, or in tender[1] cases, where a man's eye upon the countenance of him with whom he speaketh may give him a direction how far to go; and generally, where a man will reserve to himself liberty either to disavow or to expound. In choice of instruments, it is better to choose men of a plainer sort, that are like to do that that is committed to them, and to report back again faithfully the success,[2] than those that are cunning to contrive out of other men's business somewhat to grace themselves, and will help the matter in report for satisfaction sake. Use also such persons as affect[3] the business wherein they are employed, for that quickeneth much; and such as are fit for the matter, as bold men for expostulation, fair-spoken men for persuasion, crafty men for inquiry and observation, froward and absurd men for business that doth not well bear out itself.[4] Use also such as have been lucky, and prevailed before in things wherein you have employed them; for that breeds confidence, and they will strive to maintain their prescription.[5] It is better to sound a person with whom one deals afar off, than to fall upon the point at first, except you mean to surprise him by some short question. It is better dealing with men in appetite,[6] than with those that are where they would be. If a man deal with another upon conditions, the start or first performance is all, which a man cannot reasonably demand,[7] except either the nature of the thing be such which must go before, or else a man can persuade the other party that he shall still need him in some other thing, or else that he be counted the honester man. All practice is to discover or to work.[8] Men discover themselves in trust, in passion, at unawares, and of necessity, when they would have somewhat done and cannot find an apt pretext. If you would work any man, you must either know his nature and fashions, and so lead him; or his ends, and so persuade him; or his weakness and disadvantages, and so awe him; or those that have interest in him, and so govern him. In dealing with cunning persons, we must ever consider their ends, to interpret their speeches; and it is good to say little to them, and that which they least look for. In all negotiations of difficulty, a man may not look to sow and reap at once, but must prepare business, and so ripen it by degrees.

1597, 1625

Of Masques and Triumphs[1]

These things are but toys to come amongst such serious observations; but yet, since princes will have such things, it is better they should be graced with elegancy, than daubed with cost. Dancing to song is a thing of great state and pleasure. I understand it that the song be in choir, placed aloft, and accompanied with some broken music,[2] and the ditty fitted to the device.

1. Delicate.
2. Result.
3. Like.
4. I.e., when your business is less than honest, use an ill-tempered or foolish person.
5. Keep up their reputation.
6. Hungry, i.e., ambitious men.
7. You cannot reasonably make special conditions favorable to you, except in the circumstances noted.
8. All sharp bargaining aims to find out what men are up to or to make use of them. "Discover" (next sentence): reveal.
1. For an example of court masques, see Jonson, *The Masque of Blackness* (p. 1294).
2. Part-music, for different voices and different kinds of instruments.

Acting in song, especially in dialogues, hath an extreme good grace; I say acting, not dancing (for that is a mean and vulgar thing);[3] and the voices of the dialogue would be strong and manly (a base and tenor, no treble), and the ditty high and tragical, not nice or dainty. Several choirs, placed one over against another, and taking the voices by catches anthem-wise, give great pleasure. Turning dances into figure[4] is a childish curiosity; and, generally, let it be noted, that those things which I here set down are such as to naturally take the sense, and not respect petty wonderments. It is true, the alterations of scenes, so it be quietly and without noise, are things of great beauty and pleasure for they feed and relieve the eye before it be full of the same object. Let the scenes abound with light, specially colored and varied; and let the masquers, or any other that are to come down from the scene,[5] have some motions upon the scene itself before their coming down; for it draws the eye strangely, and makes it with great pleasure to desire to see that it cannot perfectly discern. Let the songs be loud and cheerful, and not chirpings or pulings; let the music, likewise, be sharp and loud, and well placed. The colors that show best by candlelight[6] are white, carnation, and a kind of sea-water green; and oes or spangs,[7] as they are of no great cost, so they are of most glory. As for rich embroidery, it is lost and not discerned. Let the suits of the masquers be graceful, and such as become the person when the vizors are off; not after examples of known attires, Turks, soldiers, mariners, and the like. Let anti-masques[8] not be long; they have been commonly of fools, satyrs, baboons, wild men, antics, beasts, sprites, witches, Ethiopes, pigmies, turquets,[9] nymphs, rustics, Cupids, statues moving, and the like. As for angels, it is not comical enough to put them in anti-masques; and any thing that is hideous, as devils, giants, is, on the other side, as unfit; but, chiefly, let the music of them be recreative, and with some strange changes. Some sweet odors suddenly coming forth, without any drops falling, are, in such a company as there is steam and heat, things of great pleasure and refreshment. Double masques, one of men, another of ladies, addeth state and variety; but all is nothing, except the room be kept clear and neat.

For justs, and tourneys, and barriers,[1] the glories of them are chiefly in the chariots, wherein the challengers make their entry; especially if they be drawn with strange beasts, as lions, bears, camels, and the like; or in the devices of their entrance, or in the bravery of their liveries, or in the goodly furniture of their horses and armor. But enough of these toys.

1625

---

3. Bacon's emphasis on dialogue and song (as opposed to dance) is in keeping with the increased emphasis on dialogue in later Jacobean and Caroline masques; dance, however, is traditionally at the center of both early and late masques.
4. Patterns with allegorical or numerological significance.
5. To unmask at the end and come onto the floor, so as to take part in the general dancing (the revels) with members of the court.
6. The Banqueting Hall at Whitehall, the site of many court masques, was lit only by candlelight; viewers complained that some masques were hard to see.
7. Spangles shaped like the letter "O."
8. The antic dances (presented by professionals) that precede the main masque dances and represent the vices, follies, or disorders that are to be dispelled with the arrival of the main masques (royal and noble personages).
9. Turkish dwarfs.
1. One form of masque was the joust ("just") or barriers, which chiefly involved knights, who represent allegorical qualities, tilting lances against each other.

Of Studies

[1597 version]¹

Studies serve for pastimes, for ornaments, and for abilities. Their chief use for pastime is in privateness² and retiring; for ornament, is in discourse; and for ability, is in judgment. For expert men³ can execute, but learned men are fittest to judge or censure. To spend too much time in them is sloth; to use them too much for ornament is affectation; to make judgment wholly by their rules is the humor⁴ of a scholar. They perfect nature, and are perfected by experience. Crafty men contemn them, simple men admire them, wise men use them, for they teach not their own use; but that⁵ is a wisdom without them, and above them, won by observation. Read not to contradict nor to believe, but to weigh and consider. Some books are to be tasted, others to be swallowed, and some few to be chewed and digested; that is, some books are to be read only in parts; others to be read but cursorily; and some few to be read wholly, and with diligence and attention. Reading maketh a full man, conference⁶ a ready man, and writing an exact man. And therefore, if a man write little, he had need have a great memory; if he confer little, he had need have a present wit;⁷ and if he read little, he had need have much cunning, to seem to know that⁸ he doth not. Histories make men wise; poets, witty;⁹ the mathematics, subtle; natural philosophy,¹ deep; moral, grave; logic and rhetoric, able to contend.

Of Studies

[1625 version]

Studies serve for delight, for ornament, and for ability. Their chief use for delight is in privateness¹ and retiring; for ornament, is in discourse; and for ability, is in the judgment and disposition of business. For expert men² can execute, and perhaps judge of particulars, one by one; but the general counsels, and the plots and marshaling of affairs, come best from those that are learned. To spend too much time in studies is sloth; to use them too much for ornament is affectation; to make judgment wholly by their rules is the humor³ of a scholar. They perfect nature, and are perfected by experience; for natural abilities are like natural plants, that need pruning by study; and studies themselves do give forth directions too much at large, except they be bounded in by experience. Crafty men contemn studies, simple men admire them, and wise men use them, for they teach not their own use; but that⁴ is

1. This version of the essay illustrates Bacon's early epigrammatic, aphoristic style, featuring balance, parallelism, disjunction between sentences, and a curtness that is occasionally cryptic. The 1625 version keeps some aphoristic elements unchanged but provides more connectives and transitions, resulting in a smoother, more flowing style.
2. Private life.
3. Men of experience.
4. Disposition, implying folly.
5. I.e., the knowledge of how to use them. "Without": outside.
6. Conversation.
7. Lively intelligence.
8. That which.
9. Clever.
1. Science. "Moral": moral philosophy.
1. Private life.
2. Men of experience.
3. Mannerism.
4. I.e., the knowledge of how to use them. "Without": outside.

a wisdom without them, and above them, won by observation. Read not to contradict and confute, nor to believe and take for granted, nor to find talk and discourse, but to weigh and consider. Some books are to be tasted, others to be swallowed, and some few to be chewed and digested; that is, some books are to be read only in parts; others to be read, but not curiously;[5] and some few to be read wholly, and with diligence and attention. Some books also may be read by deputy and extracts made of them by others, but that would be only in the less important arguments and the meaner sort of books; else distilled books are like common distilled waters,[6] flashy things. Reading maketh a full man, conference[7] a ready man, and writing an exact man. And therefore, if a man write little, he had need have a great memory; if he confer little, he had need have a present wit;[8] and if he read little, he had need have much cunning, to seem to know that[9] he doth not. Histories make men wise; poets, witty;[1] the mathematics, subtle; natural philosophy,[2] deep; moral, grave; logic and rhetoric, able to contend. *Abeunt studia in mores.*[3] Nay, there is no stond or impediment in the wit but may be wrought out by fit studies, like as diseases of the body may have appropriate exercises. Bowling is good for the stone and reins,[4] shooting for the lungs and breast, gentle walking for the stomach, riding for the head, and the like. So if a man's wit be wandering, let him study the mathematics; for in demonstrations, if his wit be called away never so little, he must begin again. If his wit be not apt to distinguish or find differences, let him study the schoolmen, for they are *cumini sectores.*[5] If he be not apt to beat over matters[6] and to call up one thing to prove and illustrate another, let him study the lawyer's cases. So every defect of the mind may have a special receipt.[7]

From The Advancement of Learning

[THE ABUSES OF LANGUAGE][1]

Martin Luther, conducted (no doubt) by an higher providence, but in discourse of reason finding what a province[2] he had undertaken against the bishop of Rome and the degenerate traditions of the church, and finding his own solitude being no ways aided by the opinions of his own time, was enforced to awake all antiquity and to call former times to his succor to make a party against the present time, so that the ancient authors both in divinity and in humanity which had long time slept in libraries began generally to be read and revolved.[3] This by consequence did draw on a necessity of a more

5. Attentively.
6. Used as home remedies, without real value.
7. Conversations.
8. Lively intelligence.
9. That which.
1. Clever.
2. Science. "Moral": i.e., moral philosophy.
3. "Studies culminate in manners" (Ovid, *Heroides*). "Stond": difficulty.
4. Gallbladder and kidneys.
5. "Dividers of cuminseed," i.e., hairsplitters. "Schoolmen": Scholastic philosophers.
6. Discuss a subject thoroughly.
7. Cure, prescription.
1. Among the "three distempers of learning" that

Bacon proposes to cure in this work, the most important involves "vain imaginations, vain altercations, and vain affectations"; to help explain these he offers a concise history of changes in the language of learned discourse since the Reformation.
2. Task.
3. Considered. Luther (1483–1546) indeed looked back to the original languages of the Bible and to ancient authors in "divinity" (chiefly Augustine), but he was not involved in the efforts of the humanists (including Erasmus and Sir Thomas More) to revive the classical languages and authors.

exquisite travail in the languages original wherein those authors did write,[4] for the better understanding of those authors and the better advantage of pressing and applying their words. And thereof grew again a delight in their manner of style and phrase, and an admiration of that kind of writing, which was much furthered and precipitated by the enmity and opposition that the propounders of those (primitive but seeming new) opinions had against the schoolmen, who were generally of the contrary part, and whose writings were altogether in a differing style and form, taking liberty to coin and frame new terms of art to express their own sense and to avoid circuit of speech, without regard to the pureness, pleasantness, and (as I may call it) lawfulness of the phrase or word.[5] And again, because the greatest labor then was with the people (of whom the Pharisees were wont to say, *Execrabilis ista turba, quae non novit legem*[6]), for the winning and persuading of them there grew of necessity in chief price and request[7] eloquence and variety of discourse, as the fittest and forciblest access into the capacity of the vulgar sort. So that these four causes concurring (the admiration of ancient authors, the hate of the schoolmen, the exact study of languages, and the efficacy of preaching) did bring in an affectionate study of eloquence and copy[8] of speech, which then began to flourish. This grew speedily to an excess, for men began to hunt more after words than matter, and more after the choiceness of the phrase, and the round and clean composition of the sentence, and the sweet falling of the clauses, and the varying and illustration of their works with tropes and figures[9] than after the weight of matter, worth of subject, soundness of argument, life of invention, or depth of judgment. Then grew the flowing and watery vein of Osorius, the Portugal bishop, to be in price.[1] Then did Sturmius spend such infinite and curious pains upon Cicero the orator and Hermogenes the rhetorician, besides his own books of periods and imitation and the like. Then did Carr of Cambridge and Ascham[2] with their lectures and writings almost deify Cicero and Demosthenes, and allure all young men that were studious unto that delicate and polished kind of learning. Then did Erasmus take occasion to make the scoffing echo, *Decem annos consumpsi in legendo Cicerone,* and the echo answered in Greek, *one, Asine.*[3] Then grew the learning of the schoolmen to be utterly despised as barbarous. In sum, the whole inclination and bent of those times was rather towards copy than weight.

Here therefore is the first distemper of learning, when men study words and not matter, whereof though I have represented an example of late times, yet it hath been and will be *secundum maius et minus*[4] in all time. And how is it possible but this should have an operation to discredit learning, even

4. Classical Greek and Latin, and Biblical Hebrew. "Travail": labor.
5. The Scholastic philosophers ("schoolmen") used the living Latin of the Middle Ages, wrenching the language yet further from classical norms in applying it to subtle philosophical matters; the humanists denounced the Scholastics' Latin as barbarous and sought instead to imitate classical models, especially Cicero.
6. "The people who knoweth not the law are cursed" (John 7.49).
7. Worth and demand.
8. Copiousness. "Affectionate": devoted.
9. Figurative language.
1. Jeronimo Osorio (1506–1580) wrote a history

of Portuguese conquests in a "flowing and watery vein" that caused him to be known as "the Portuguese Cicero." His contemporary, Johann Sturm, edited texts of Cicero and the Greek rhetorician Hermogenes; his "book of periods" was a rhetorical handbook.
2. Nicholas Carr was professor of Greek at Cambridge; Roger Ascham was tutor to Queen Elizabeth and author of *The Schoolmaster* (p. 565). Both admired the balanced and polished sentences of Ciceronian style.
3. "I spent ten years in reading Cicero." Echo answers, "Ass!" The joke is in the *Colloquies* of Erasmus.
4. More or less.

with vulgar capacities, when they see learned men's works like the first letter of a patent or limned[5] book, which though it hath large flourishes, yet it is but a letter? It seems to me that Pygmalion's frenzy[6] is a good emblem or portraiture of this vanity, for words are but the images of matter, and except they have life of reason and invention, to fall in love with them is all one as to fall in love with a picture.

But yet notwithstanding, it is a thing not hastily to be condemned to clothe and adorn the obscurity even of philosophy itself with sensible and plausible elocution. For hereof we have great examples in Xenophon, Cicero, Seneca, Plutarch, and of Plato also in some degree; and hereof likewise there is great use, for surely to the severe inquisition of truth and the deep progress into philosophy it is some hindrance, because it is too early satisfactory to the mind of man, and quencheth the desire of further search before we come to a just period; but then if a man be to have any use of such knowledge in civil occasions of conference, counsel, persuasion, discourse, or the like, then shall he find it prepared to his hands in those authors which write in that manner. But the excess of this is so justly contemptible that as Hercules, when he saw the image of Adonis, Venus' minion, in a temple, said in disdain, *Nil sacri es;*[7] so there is none of Hercules' followers in learning, that is, the more severe and laborious sort of inquirers into truth,[8] but will despise those delicacies and affectations as indeed capable of no divineness.

1605

From Novum Organum[1]

[THE IDOLS]

52

Such then are the idols which I call *Idols of the Tribe;*[2] and which take their rise either from the homogeneity of the substance of the human spirit, or from its preoccupation, or from its narrowness, or from its restless motion, or from an infusion of the affections, or from the incompetency of the senses, or from the mode of impression.

53

The *Idols of the Cave* take their rise in the peculiar constitution, mental or bodily, of each individual; and also in education, habit, and accident. Of this kind there is a great number and variety; but I will instance those the

5. Illuminated, i.e., illustrated, as with elaborate initial capitals. Royal grants ("patents") were also engrossed with fancy initial letters.
6. Pygmalion's "frenzy" (delirium) was to fall in love with a statue he had carved of a beautiful woman.
7. "You're nothing holy." Adonis was the lover ("minion") of Venus, deified after his death while boarhunting.
8. Hercules early in life was offered a choice between an existence of ignoble ease and sensory delights and one of strenuous virtue. He chose the latter, and so do his followers in learning.
1. *Novum Organum,* or "The New Instrument of

Learning," was not written in English but in Latin, for an international scholarly audience. Nonetheless it requires our attention here, as it is the keystone of Bacon's vast project to reform the structure of human learning from the ground up. His reform called for careful observation of all aspects of nature and controlled experiment, but the first part of the book analyzes the stumbling blocks in the way—among them, famously, the various idols or delusive images of truth that lead people away from the exact knowledge of science.
2. By "Idols of the Tribe" Bacon means the common human tendency to generalize on the basis of inadequate facts and unreliable sense impressions.

pointing out of which contains the most important caution, and which have most effect in disturbing the clearness of the understanding.

* * *

58 *Let such then be our provision and contemplative prudence for keeping off and dislodging the Idols of the Cave*, which grow for the most part either out of the predominance of a favorite subject, or out of an excessive tendency to compare or to distinguish, or out of partiality for particular ages, or out of the largeness or minuteness of the objects contemplated. And generally let every student of nature take this as a rule—that whatever his mind seizes and dwells upon with peculiar satisfaction is to be held in suspicion, and that so much the more care is to be taken in dealing with such questions to keep the understanding even and clear.

59

But the *Idols of the Marketplace* are the most troublesome of all: idols which have crept into the understanding through the alliances of words and names. For men believe that their reason governs words; but it is also true that words react on the understanding; and this it is that has rendered philosophy and the sciences sophistical and inactive. Now words, being commonly framed and applied according to the capacity of the vulgar, follow those lines of division which are most obvious to the vulgar understanding. And whenever an understanding of greater acuteness or a more diligent observation would alter those lines to suit the true divisions of nature, words stand in the way and resist the change. Whence it comes to pass that the high and formal discussions of learned men end oftentimes in disputes about words and names; with which (according to the use[3] and wisdom of the mathematicians) it would be more prudent to begin, and so by means of definitions reduce them to order. Yet even definitions cannot cure this evil in dealing with natural and material things; since the definitions themselves consist of words, and those words beget others; so that it is necessary to recur to individual instances, and those in due series and order; as I shall say presently when I come to the method and scheme for the formation of notions and axioms.[4]

60

The idols imposed by words on the understanding are of two kinds. They are either names of things which do not exist (for as there are things left unnamed through lack of observation, so likewise are there names which result from fantastic suppositions and to which nothing in reality corresponds), or they are names of things which exist, but yet confused and ill-defined, and hastily and irregularly derived from realities. Of the former kind are Fortune, the Prime Mover, Planetary Orbits, Element of Fire, and like fictions which owe their origin to false and idle theories.[5] And this class of

3. Custom.
4. Bacon's mistrust of words helped to prompt the Royal Society to cultivate a plain, stripped prose style for purposes of scientific communication.
5. The "Prime Mover" was a transparent sphere on the outside of the universe, supposed to move all the other spheres; the "Element of Fire" was an area of pure, invisible fire, supposed to exist above the atmosphere. Obviously, these concepts could be based on no observation. By "Planetary Orbits"

idols is more easily expelled, because to get rid of them it is only necessary that all theories should be steadily rejected and dismissed as obsolete.[6]

But the other class, which springs out of a faulty and unskillful abstraction, is intricate and deeply rooted. Let us take for example such a word as *humid*; and see how far the several things which the word is used to signify agree with each other; and we shall find the word *humid* to be nothing else than a mark loosely and confusedly applied to denote a variety of actions which will not bear to be reduced to any constant meaning. For it both signifies that which easily spreads itself round any other body; and that which in itself is indeterminate and cannot solidize; and that which readily yields in every direction; and that which easily divides and scatters itself; and that which easily unites and collects itself; and that which readily flows and is put in motion; and that which readily clings to another body and wets it; and that which is easily reduced to a liquid, or being solid easily melts. Accordingly when you come to apply the word—if you take it in one sense, flame is humid; if in another, air is not humid; if in another, fine dust is humid; if in another, glass is humid. So that it is easy to see that the notion is taken by abstraction only from water and common and ordinary liquids, without any due verification.

There are however in words certain degrees of distortion and error. One of the least faulty kinds is that of names of substances, especially of lowest species and well-deduced (for the notion of *chalk* and of *mud* is good, of *earth* bad); a more faulty kind is that of actions, as *to generate, to corrupt, to alter*; the most faulty is of qualities (except such as are the immediate objects of the sense), as *heavy, light, rare, dense*, and the like. Yet in all these cases some notions are of necessity a little better than others, in proportion to the greater variety of subjects that fall within the range of the human sense.

61

But the *Idols of the Theater*[7] are not innate, nor do they steal into the understanding secretly, but are plainly impressed and received into the mind from the playbooks of philosophical systems and the perverted rules of demonstration. To attempt refutations in this case would be merely inconsistent with what I have already said: for since we agree neither upon principles nor upon demonstrations, there is no place for argument. And this is so far well, inasmuch as it leaves the honor of the ancients untouched. For they are no wise disparaged—the question between them and me being only as to the way. For as the saying is, the lame man who keeps the right road outstrips the runner who takes a wrong one. Nay, it is obvious that when a man runs the wrong way, the more active and swift he is the further he will go astray.

But the course I propose for the discovery of sciences is such as leaves but little to the acuteness and strength of wits, but places all wits and understandings nearly on a level. For as in the drawing of a straight line or a perfect circle, much depends on the steadiness and practice of the hand, if it be done by aim of hand only, but if with the aid of rule or compass, little or nothing; so is it exactly with my plan. But though particular confutations

---

6. Bacon may be referring to the old notion of crystalline spheres in which the planets were supposed to be set.
6. Bacon does not mean "theories" in the inclusive modern sense, but "abstractions loosely invoked to explain particular facts."

7. I.e., those derived from previous philosophical systems, which misrepresent life and mislead people by pretending to show them reality itself.

would be of no avail, yet touching the sects and general divisions of such systems I must say something; something also touching the external signs which show that they are unsound; and finally something touching the causes of such great infelicity and of such lasting and general agreement in error; that so the access to truth may be made less difficult, and the human understanding may the more willingly submit to its purgation and dismiss its idols.

62

Idols of the Theater, or of systems, are many, and there can be and perhaps will be yet many more. For were it not that now for many ages men's minds have been busied with religion and theology; and were it not that civil governments, especially monarchies, have been averse to such novelties, even in matters speculative, so that men labor therein to the peril and harming of their fortunes, not only unrewarded, but exposed also to contempt and envy; doubtless there would have arisen many other philosophical sects like to those which in great variety flourished once among the Greeks. For as on the phenomena of the heavens many hypotheses may be constructed, so likewise (and more also) many various dogmas may be set up and established on the phenomena of philosophy. And in the plays of this philosophical theater you may observe the same thing which is found in the theater of the poets, that stories invented for the stage are more compact and elegant, and more as one would wish them to be, than true stories out of history.

In general, however, there is taken for the material of philosophy either a great deal out of a few things, or a very little out of many things; so that on both sides philosophy is based on too narrow a foundation of experiment and natural history, and decides on the authority of too few cases. For the rational school of philosophers snatches from experience a variety of common instances, neither duly ascertained nor diligently examined and weighed, and leaves all the rest to meditation and agitation of wit.[8]

There is also another class of philosophers, who having bestowed much diligent and careful labor on a few experiments, have thence made bold to educe and construct systems; wresting all other facts in a strange fashion to conformity therewith.

And there is yet a third class, consisting of those who out of faith and veneration mix their philosophy with theology and traditions; among whom the vanity of some has gone so far aside as to seek the origin of sciences among spirits and genii. So that this parent stock of errors—this false philosophy—is of three kinds: the sophistical, the empirical, and the superstitious.

* * *

68

So much concerning the several classes of idols, and their equipage: all of which must be renounced and put away with a fixed and solemn determination, and the understanding thoroughly freed and cleansed; the entrance into the kingdom of man, founded on the sciences, being not much other

---

8. Bacon's enthusiasm for experiment at times led him to denigrate the value of reason, but what he chiefly opposes here is the excessive concern with logic he finds in the Scholastic philosophers.

than the entrance into the kingdom of heaven, whereinto none may enter except as a little child.

1620

From The New Atlantis[1]

[SOLOMON'S HOUSE]

We came at our day and hour, and I was chosen by my fellows for the private access.[2] We found him in a fair chamber, richly hanged, and carpeted under foot, without any degrees to the state.[3] He was set upon a low throne richly adorned, and a rich cloth of state over his head, of blue satin embroidered. He was alone, save that he had two pages of honor, on either hand one, finely attired in white. His under-garments were the like that we saw him wear in the chariot;[4] but instead of his gown, he had on him a mantle with a cape of the same fine black, fastened about him. When we came in, as we were taught, we bowed low at our first entrance, and when we were come near his chair, he stood up, holding forth his hand ungloved and in posture of blessing; and we every one of us stooped down, and kissed the hem of his tippet.[5] That done, the rest departed, and I remained. Then he warned the pages forth of the room, and caused me to sit down beside him, and spake to me thus in the Spanish tongue:

"God bless thee, my son; I will give thee the greatest jewel I have. For I will impart unto thee, for the love of God and men, a relation of the true state of Solomon's House. Son, to make you know the true state of Solomon's House, I will keep this order. First, I will set forth unto you the end of our foundation. Secondly, the preparations and instruments we have for our works. Thirdly, the several employments and functions whereto our fellows are assigned. And fourthly, the ordinances and rites which we observe.

"The end of our foundation is the knowledge of causes, and secret motions of things; and the enlarging of the bounds of human empire, to the effecting of all things possible.

"The preparations and instruments are these. We have large and deep caves of several depths: the deepest are sunk six hundred fathom; and some of them are digged and made under great hills and mountains; so that if you reckon together the depth of the hill and the depth of the cave, they are, some of them, above three miles deep. For we find that the depth of a hill, and the depth of a cave from the flat, is the same thing; both remote alike from the sun and heaven's beams, and from the open air. These caves we

---

1. Thomas More's *Utopia* (1516) set a fashion for accounts of imaginary communities with more or less ideal forms of government (see pp. 506–23). Bacon's imaginary community has at its center an account of a research establishment, Solomon's House, that could exist in any society; indeed a version of it was established in England in 1662 as the Royal Society. Bacon's title alludes to the legendary island and ideal commonwealth in the Atlantic Ocean described by Plato in *Critias*; in the 17th century it was sometimes located in the New World. Bacon places his island, Bensalem, in the Pacific, roughly where the Solomon Islands had

been discovered in 1568. After an imaginary journey the nameless narrator and his shipmates discover an island cut off from Hebrew and Greek civilization (though given a special revelation of Christianity) and thereby freed to focus on the development of science.
2. Audience with one of the scientific "Fathers" of Solomon's House.
3. Without stairs leading up to the dais.
4. He had made a triumphal entry into the city the previous day, wearing an undergarment of white linen and a black robe.
5. Scarf.

call the Lower Region, and we use them for all coagulations, indurations,[6] refrigerations, and conservations of bodies. We use them likewise for the imitation of natural mines, and the producing also of new artificial metals, by compositions and materials which we use, and lay there for many years. We use them also sometimes (which may seem strange) for curing of some diseases, and for prolongation of life in some hermits that choose to live there, well accommodated of[7] all things necessary, and indeed live very long; by whom also we learn many things.

"We have burials in several earths, where we put divers cements,[8] as the Chinese do their porcelain. But we have them in greater variety, and some of them more fine. We have also great variety of composts and soils, for the making of the earth fruitful.

"We have high towers, the highest about half a mile in height, and some of them likewise set upon high mountains, so that the vantage of the hill, with the tower, is in the highest of them three miles at least. And these places we call the Upper Region, accounting the air between the high places and the low as a Middle Region. We use these towers, according to their several heights and situations, for insolation,[9] refrigeration, conservation, and for the view of divers meteors—as winds, rain, snow, hail; and some of the fiery meteors[1] also. And upon them, in some places, are dwellings of hermits, whom we visit sometimes, and instruct what to observe.

"We have great lakes, both salt and fresh, whereof we have use for the fish and fowl. We use them also for burials of some natural bodies, for we find a difference in things buried in earth, or in air below the earth, and things buried in water. We have also pools, of which some do strain fresh water out of salt, and others by art do turn fresh water into salt. We have also some rocks in the midst of the sea, and some bays upon the shore, for some works wherein is required the air and vapor of the sea. We have likewise violent streams and cataracts, which serve us for many motions; and likewise engines for multiplying and enforcing[2] of winds to set also on going divers motions.

"We have also a number of artificial wells and fountains, made in imitation of the natural sources and baths, as tincted upon[3] vitriol, sulphur, steel, brass, lead, niter, and other minerals; and again, we have little wells for infusions of many things, where the waters take the virtue[4] quicker and better than in vessels or basins. And amongst them we have a water which we call Water of Paradise, being by that we do to it, made very sovereign[5] for health and prolongation of life.

"We have also great and spacious houses, where we imitate and demonstrate meteors—as snow, hail, rain, some artificial rains of bodies and not of water, thunders, lightnings; also generations of bodies in air—as frogs, flies, and divers others.

"We have also certain chambers, which we call Chambers of Health, where we qualify[6] the air as we think good and proper for the cure of divers diseases and preservation of health.

"We have also fair and large baths, of several mixtures, for the cure of

6. Hardenings.
7. Provided with.
8. Clays and pottery mixtures.
9. Exposure to the sun.
1. Anything that fell from the sky was, in Renaissance terminology, a meteor.

2. Reinforcing, strengthening.
3. Tinctured with.
4. Property (of the substances put into water).
5. Efficacious.
6. Modify.

diseases and the restoring of man's body from arefaction;[7] and others for the confirming of it in strength of sinews, vital parts, and the very juice and substance of the body.

"We have also large and various orchards and gardens, wherein we do not so much respect beauty as variety of ground and soil, proper for divers trees and herbs, and some very spacious, where trees and berries are set, whereof we make divers kinds of drinks, besides the vineyards. In these we practice likewise all conclusions[8] of grafting and inoculating, as well of wild trees as fruit trees, which produceth many effects. And we make (by art) in the same orchards and gardens trees and flowers to come earlier or later than their seasons, and to come up and bear more speedily than by their natural course they do. We make them also by art greater much than their nature; and their fruit greater and sweeter, and of differing taste, smell, color, and figure, from their nature. And many of them we so order as they become of medicinal use.

"We have also means to make divers plants rise by mixtures of earths without seeds, and likewise to make divers new plants, differing from the vulgar,[9] and to make one tree or plant turn into another.

"We have also parks and enclosures of all sorts of beasts and birds; which we use not only for view or rareness, but likewise for dissections and trials,[1] that thereby we may take light what may be wrought upon the body of man. Wherein we find many strange effects: as continuing life in them, though divers parts, which you account vital, be perished and taken forth; resuscitating of some that seem dead in appearance; and the like. We try also all poisons and other medicines upon them, as well of chirurgery[2] as physic. By art likewise, we make them greater or taller than their kind is, and contrariwise dwarf them and stay their growth; we make them more fruitful and bearing than their kind is, and contrariwise barren and not generative. Also, we make them differ in color, shape, activity, many ways. We find means to make commixtures and copulations of different kinds, which have produced many new kinds,[3] and them not barren, as the general opinion is. We make a number of kinds of serpents, worms, fishes, flies, of putrefaction, whereof some are advanced (in effect) to be perfect creatures, like beasts or birds, and have sexes, and do propagate. Neither do we this by chance, but we know beforehand of what matter and commixture what kind of those creatures will arise.

"We have also particular pools where we make trials upon fishes, as we have said before of beasts and birds.

"We have also places for breed and generation of those kinds of worms and flies which are of special use; such as are with you your silkworms and bees."[4]

*　*　*

"For the several employments and offices of our fellows, we have twelve that sail into foreign countries under the names of other nations (for our

---

7. Drying up.
8. Experiments.
9. Ordinary.
1. Experiments.
2. Surgery.
3. Species. It was commonly supposed that all hybrids were sterile.

4. The narrator continues to describe the various bakeries, vineyards, breweries, and kitchens operated by Solomon's House. He enumerates the medicines discovered there, as well as various experiments with heat. The researchers study light, sound, perfumes, mechanics, mathematics, and all ways of deceiving the senses.

own we conceal), who bring us the books and abstracts and patterns of experiments of all other parts. These we call Merchants of Light.

"We have three that collect the experiments which are in all books. These we call Depredators.

"We have three that collect the experiments of all mechanical arts, and also of liberal sciences, and also of practices which are not brought into arts. These we call Mystery-men.

"We have three that try new experiments, such as themselves think good. These we call Pioneers or Miners.

"We have three that draw the experiments of the former four into titles and tables, to give the better light for the drawing of observations and axioms out of them. These we call Compilers.

"We have three that bend themselves, looking into the experiments of their fellows, and cast about how to draw out of them things of use and practice for man's life and knowledge, as well for works as for plain demonstration of causes, means of natural divinations, and the easy and clear discovery of the virtues and parts of bodies. These we call Dowry-men or Benefactors.

"Then after divers meetings and consults of our whole number, to consider of the former labors and collections, we have three that take care out of them to direct new experiments, of a higher light, more penetrating into nature than the former. These we call Lamps.

"We have three others that do execute the experiments so directed, and report them. These we call Inoculators.

"Lastly, we have three that raise the former discoveries by experiments into greater observations, axioms, and aphorisms. These we call Interpreters of Nature.

"We have also, as you must think, novices and apprentices, that the succession of the former employed men do not fail; besides a great number of servants and attendants, men and women. And this we do also: we have consultations, which of the inventions and experiences which we have discovered shall be published, and which not; and take all an oath of secrecy for the concealing of those which we think fit to keep secret; though some of those we do reveal sometimes to the State, and some not.[5]

"For our ordinances and rites, we have two very long and fair galleries: in one of these we place patterns and samples of all manner of the more rare and excellent inventions; in the other we place the statues of all principal inventors. There we have the statue of your Columbus, that discovered the West Indies; also the inventor of ships; your monk that was the inventor of ordnance and of gunpowder;[6] the inventor of music; the inventor of letters; the inventor of printing; the inventor of observations of astronomy; the inventor of works in metal; the inventor of glass; the inventor of silk of the worm; the inventor of wine; the inventor of corn and bread; the inventor of sugars; and all these by more certain tradition than you have. Then we have divers inventors of our own, of excellent works, which since you have not seen, it were too long to make descriptions of them; and besides, in the right understanding of those descriptions you might easily err. For upon every invention of value we erect a statue to the inventor, and give him a liberal and honorable reward. These statutes are some of brass, some of marble and touch-

5. Bacon allows his scientists considerable autonomy in relation to the state.

6. Tradition credits Roger Bacon, a 13th-century monk, with the discovery of gunpowder.

stone,[7] some of cedar and other special woods gilt and adorned; some of iron, some of silver, some of gold.

"We have certain hymns and services, which we say daily, of laud and thanks to God for his marvelous works; and forms of prayer, imploring his aid and blessing for the illumination of our labors, and the turning of them into good and holy uses.

"Lastly, we have circuits or visits of divers principal cities of the kingdom; where, as it cometh to pass, we do publish such new profitable inventions as we think good. And we do also declare natural divinations of diseases, plagues, swarms of hurtful creatures, scarcity, tempests, earthquakes, great inundations, comets, temperature of the year, and divers other things; and we give counsel thereupon, what the people shall do for the prevention and remedy of them."

And when he had said this he stood up; and I, as I had been taught, kneeled down; and he laid his right hand upon my head, and said, "God bless thee, my son, and God bless this relation which I have made. I give thee leave to publish it, for the good of other nations; for we here are in God's bosom, a land unknown." And so he left me; having assigned a value of about two thousand ducats for a bounty to me and my fellows. For they give great largesses, where they come, upon all occasions.

The rest was not perfected.

1627

7. A hard basaltic-type rock.

MARTHA MOULSWORTH

In her *Memorandum*, carefully dated November 10, 1632, Moulsworth (1577–16??) represents herself as a fifty-five-year-old English widow of the gentry class, taking stock of her life and finding it generally satisfactory. This verse autobiography (unpublished, and only recently discovered in manuscript at the Beinecke Library, Yale, Osborn Ms. fb 150) is remarkable for its early date, its balanced structure (fifty-five couplets for her fifty-five years), its careful patterning, and its wryly judicious tone in presenting the pleasures and pains, the satisfactions and injustices of her own and the general female lot. At moments her tone and stance recall Chaucer's Wife of Bath. Moulsworth counts herself generally fortunate. Her father, Robert Dorsett, was a gentleman cleric educated at Oxford and a canon of Christ Church College, where he tutored both Sir Philip Sidney and his brother Robert of Penshurst. She credits him with educating her in Latin and other learning, as she puts it, "beyond my sex." However, as he died before she was three years old, she must mean that he arranged for that education. She had three husbands, all associated with London guilds, and enjoyed them all (the suggestion of sexual satisfaction is clear); but she delighted most and longest in the last husband (Bevill Moulsworth), who gave her large control over their household. Yet she also greatly enjoys her current freedom of widowhood and intends to keep that status. Her satisfaction, however, is tempered by a keen awareness of loss: she has forgotten all her Latin from disuse, all her children have died (another evidence of the period's shocking infant mortality), and she still grieves for her last husband. At one point, she takes on the role of spokesperson for all women, urging university education for them and claiming—with bold over-statement—that given such opportunity women would outstrip men in both intellectual development and languages ("wit and tongues"). That is a thoroughly radical proposition, almost if not entirely without parallel at this early date.

The marginal references in brackets are Moulsworth's own.

The Memorandum of Martha Moulsworth, Widow

November the 10th, 1632

The tenth day of the winter month November
A day which I must duly still remember,
Did open first these eyes, and showed this light,
Now on that day, upon that day I write. [*November the 10th, 1632*]
5   This season fitly willingly combines
The birthday of myself, and of these lines.
The time the clock, the yearly stroke is one [*My muse is a tell clock,*
That clock by fifty five returns hath gone *and echoes every stroke*
How few, how many warnings it will give *with a coupled rhyme so*
many times, viz. 55. Acts
10   He only knows, in whom we are, and live. *17.28 &*]
In carnal state of sin original
I did not stay one whole day natural.
The seal of grace in sacramental water
So soon had I, so soon become the daughter
15   Of earthly parents, and of heavenly Father.
Some christen late for state,° the wiser rather.° *pomp / earlier*

My name was Martha. Martha took much pain [*Luke 10.14*][1]
Our Savior Christ her guest to entertain.
God give me grace my inward house to dight° *decorate*
20   That he with me may sup, and stay all night. [*Revelation 3.20*]
My father was a man of spotless fame [*Luke 24.29*]
Of gentle birth, and Dorset was his name.
He had, and left lands of his own possession;
He was of Levi's tribe by his profession.[2]
25   His mother Oxford knowing well his worth,
Arrayed in scarlet robe[3] did send him forth.
By him I was brought up in godly piety,
In modest cheerfulness, and sad° sobriety. *grave*
Nor only so, beyond my sex and kind
30   He did with learning Latin deck [my] mind.

1. Moulsworth evidently miscopied the reference to Martha, the sister who tended to her house-keeping while her sister Mary sat at Jesus' feet; it should be Luke 10.41.
2. Among the ancient Hebrews, the tribe of Levi performed religious duties and had no portion of land in Canaan; Moulsworth's father was a clergyman, but she claims he owned land, though his will does not substantiate that.
3. He graduated from Oxford in the scarlet robes of a doctor of divinity.

And why not so? The muses females are,
And therefore of us females take some care.
Two universities we have of men,
O that we had but one of women then!
35 O then that would in wit, and tongues surpass
All art of men that is, or ever was.
But I of Latin have no cause to boast
For want of use, I long ago it lost.   [*Latin is not the most marketable marriage metal*]

Had I no other portion to my dower
40 I might have stood a virgin to this hour,
But though the virgin Muses I love well,
I have long since bid virgin life farewell.
Thrice this right hand did holy wedlock plight
And thrice this left with pledged ring was dight.°   *adorned*
45 Three husbands me, and I have them enjoyed,[4]
Nor I by them, nor they by me annoyed.
All lovely, loving all, some more, some less,
Though gone, their love and memory I bless.
Until my one and twentieth yeare of age   [*1 husband, Mr. Nicholas Prynne, April 18, 1598*]
50 I did not bind myself in marriage
My spring was late, some think that sooner love
But backward° springs do oft the kindest prove.   *delayed*
My first knot° held five years, and eight months more,   *marriage bond*
Then was a year set on my mourning score.°   *account*
55 My second bond ten years nine months did last
Three years eight months I kept a widow's fast.[5]   [*2nd Mr. Thomas Throughood, February 3, 1604*]
The third I took a lovely man, and kind,
Such comeliness in age we seldom find.
From Mortimers[6] he drew his pedegree.   [*3rd Mr. Bevill Moulsworth, June 15, 1619*]
60 Their arms he bore, not bought with herald's fee.
Third wife I was to him, as he to me
Third husband was, in number we agree.
Eleven years and eight months his autumn[7] lasted
A second spring, too soon away it hasted.
65 Was never man so buxom° to his wife,   *affable, indulgent*
With him I led an easy darling's life.
I had my will in house, in purse, in store,[8]
What would a woman old or young have more?

Two years almost outwearing since he died,
70 And yet, and yet my tears for him not dried.
I by the first, and last, some issue had
But root and fruit[9] is dead, which makes me sad.
My husbands all on holydays did die
Such day, such way, they to the saints did hie.
75 This life is workday[1] even at the best,

4. Moulsworth asserts her own pleasure first, implying also sexual pleasure.
5. Period of abstinence (from marital comforts and pleasures) as a widow.
6. An ancient noble family. "Herald's fee" (next line): he did not buy, as many did, a phony pedigree and coat of arms from a corrupt official.

7. Though aging ["autumn"], he enjoyed in marriage a renewed youth ["second spring," next line].
8. Provision of household goods.
9. All her children, as well as their fathers ["root"].
1. Days of labor or work, as opposed to eternal holidays in heaven after death.

But Christian death, an holy day of rest.
The first, the first of Martyrs did befall.
St. Stephen's feast[2] to him was funeral.
The morrow after Christ our flesh did take,
80 This husband did his mortal flesh forsake.
The second on a double sainted day
To Jude, and Simon,[3] took his happy way.
This Simon as an ancient story saith
Did first in England plant the Christian faith.[4]   [Nicephorus, History]
85 Most sure it is that Jude in holy writ   [Jude, verse 3][5]
Doth warn us to maintain, and fight for it,
In which all those that live, and die, may well
Hope with the saints eternally to dwell.
The last on St. Matthias day[6] did wend
90 Unto his home, and pilgrimage's end.
This feast comes in that season which doth bring
Upon dead winter's cold, a lively spring.
His body wintering in the lodge of death,
Shall feel a spring, with bud of life and breath,
95 And rise in incorruption, glory, power.   [1 Corinthians 15.42][7]
Like to the body of our Savior.   [Philippians 3.21][8]

In vain it were, profane it were for me
With sadness to ask which of these three   [Matthew 22.18][9]
I shall call husband in the Resurrection.
100 For then shall all in glorious perfection,
Like to th'immortal heavenly angels live
Who wedlock's bonds do neither take nor give.   [[Matthew 22] verse
But in the meantime this must be my care   30][1]
Of knitting here a fourth knot to beware.
105 A threefold cord though hardly yet is broken,   [Ecclesiastes 4.12][2]
Another ancient story doth betoken
That seldom comes a better.[3] Why should I
Then put my widowhood in jeopardy?
The virgin's life is gold, as clerks us tell,
110 The widow's silver. I love silver well!

1632   1993

2. December 26; for his martyrdom see Acts 7.54–60.
3. October 28. The evangelical missions of the two apostles were linked in the records.
4. Nicephorus Callistus (ca. 1256–1335), a Byzantine historian, author of an 18-volume church history. The story of Simon planting Christianity in England is repeated by Thomas Fuller in his *Church History of Britain*.
5. "Ye should earnestly contend for the faith which was once delivered unto the saints" (Jude 1.3).
6. February 24.
7. The body is said to be "sown in corruption" and "raised in incorruption" at the resurrection of the dead (1 Corinthians 15.42).
8. Christ is said to change "our vile body, that it may be fashioned like his glorious body" (Philippians 3.21).
9. Jesus denounced the "wickedness" of a question by the Philistines in Matthew 22.18.
1. Asked about a woman married successively to seven husbands, Jesus replied that "in the resurrection they neither marry, nor are given in marriage, but are like the angels of God in heaven" (Matthew 22.30).
2. "A threefold cord is not quickly broken" (Ecclesiastes 4.12).
3. This proverb, "seldom comes the better," was widely current in the period.

RACHEL SPEGHT

In *A Dream,* Rachel Speght (ca. 1597–16??) employs the device of the dream vision to represent, in allegory, the obstacles she encountered and the rapturous delight she experienced in her pursuit of learning. She describes her three-hundred-line poem as substantially autobiographical, "imaginary in manner, real in matter," but she gives her own story a general application by putting into the mouth of Truth a strong defense of women's education. The allegory plays off the medieval dream vision, the *Romance of the Rose,* whose lover-hero is variously hindered or helped by personifications of psychological faculties and forces, in his attempts to enter the Garden of Love. In *A Dream,* Rachel meets personifications of psychological and societal forces who either hinder or help her to enter the Garden of Erudition. The poem concludes with a reprise of the controversy Speght engaged in four years earlier and with a reference to her mother's death, the occasion for the longer meditative poem, *Mortality's Memorandum,* to which *A Dream* stands as preface.

Speght was a tolerably well-educated young woman of the London middle class; her father, who was a Calvinist clergyman and an author, provided her with some classical education—very rare for seventeenth-century women of any class. In her writings she both claims and displays a knowledge of Latin, a degree of training in logic and rhetoric, and familiarity with a wide range of learned authorities—a foundation that was probably derived from the popular handbooks, anthologies, or commonplace books widely used by writers of the era. Her tract defending women, *A Muzzle for Melastomus* [black mouth] (1617), is a response to the rambling, boistrous, tonally confused, but lively attack on women by Joseph Swetnam, *Arraignment of Lewd, Idle, Froward, and Unconstant Women* (1615). Speght's work may be the only contribution by a woman to the vigorous Jacobean pamphlet war touched off by Swetnam over woman's place and role; there were at least eight texts, including two satires on cross-dressing. Of these pamphlets' authors, only Speght published under her own name and insisted on her authorial identity, thus becoming the first Englishwoman to claim the role of polemicist and critic of contemporary gender ideology. While she engages effectively in the railing attacks and witty repostes expected in such controversy, most of her treatise consists of serious argument, in which Speght reinterprets often-discussed biblical texts (especially Genesis 1–3) and presses them to yield a more expansive and equitable concept of gender.

From A Dream[1]

[Rachel, asleep, has a dream which causes her to gaze upon the world and recognize with grief that she understands nothing of it. *Thought* asks why she is distressed.]

> My grief, quoth I, is called *Ignorance,*
> Which makes me differ little from a brute,
> For animals are led by nature's lore,
> Their seeming science is but custom's fruit;
> 5 When they are hurt they have a sense of pain,
> But want the sense to cure themselves again.
>
> And ever since this grief did me oppress,
> Instinct of nature is my chiefest guide.

---

1. The eight stanzas preceding this extract describe the circumstances of Rachel's dream vision.

I feel disease, yet know not what I ail,
10　I find a sore, but can no salve provide:
　　I hungry am, yet cannot seek for food,
　　Because I know not what is bad or good.

　　And sometimes when I seek the golden mean,
　　My weakness makes me fail of mine intent,
15　That suddenly I fall into extremes,
　　Nor can I see a mischief to prevent,
　　But see the pain when I the peril find,
　　Because my malady doth make me blind.

　　What is without the compass of my braine,
20　My sickness makes me say it cannot be;
　　What I conceive not, cannot come to pass,
　　Because for it I can no reason see.
　　I measure all men's feet by mine own shoe,
　　And count all well, which I appoint or do.

25　The pestilent effects of my disease
　　Exceed report, their number is so great;
　　The evils, which through it I do incur,
　　Are more than I am able to repeat.
　　Wherefore, good *Thought* I sue to thee again,
30　To tell me how my cure I may obtain.

[Thought sends her to *Age*, to get help from *Experience*. *Age* says the remedy for her disease is *Knowledge*, found in *Erudition's* Garden, and sends *Industry* to lead her there.]

*　*　*

　　Dissuasion hearing her assign my help,
　　(And seeing that consent I did detect)
105　Did many remoras° to me propose,　　　　　　　　　*hindrances*
　　As dulness, and my memory's defect,
　　The difficulty of attaining lore,°　　　　　　　　　　*learning*
　　My time, and sex, with many others more.

　　Which when I heard, my mind was much perplexed,
110　And as a horse new come into the field,
　　Who with a Harquebus[2] at first doth start,
　　So did this shot make me recoil and yield.
　　But of my fear when some did notice take,
　　In my behalf they this reply did make.

115　First quoth *Desire, Dissuasion*, hold thy peace,
　　These oppositions come not from above:
　　Quoth *Truth*, they cannot spring from reason's root,
　　And therefore now thou shalt no victor prove,

2. An early type of portable gun, mounted on a tripod or carriage in the field.

No, quoth *Industry*, be assured this,
120   Her friends shall make thee of thy purpose miss.

For with my sickle I will cut away
All obstacles, that in her way can grow;
And by the issue of her own attempt,
I'll make thee *labor omnia vincet*[3] know.
125   Quoth *Truth*, and since her sex thou do'st object,
Thy folly I by reason will detect.

Both man and woman of three parts consist,
Which *Paul* doth body, soul, and spirit call: [*1 Thess.* 5.24][4]
And from the soul three faculties arise,
130   The mind, the will, the power; then wherefore shall
A woman have her intellect in vain,
Or not endeavor *Knowledge* to attain?

The talent God doth give, must be employed,   [*Luke* 19.23]
His own with vantage he must have again:
135   All parts and faculties were made for use;
The God of *Knowledge* nothing gave in vain.
'Twas *Mary's* choice our Savior did approve,   [*Luke* 10.42]
Because that she the better part did love.

Cleobulina and *Demophila*,[5]
140   With *Telesilla*, as historians tell,
(Whose fame doth live, though they have long been dead)
Did all of them in Poetry excell.
A Roman matron that *Cornelia*[6] hight,°   *was named*
An eloquent and learned style did write.

145   *Hypatia*[7] in Astronomy had skill,
Aspatia was in Rhetoric so expert,
As that Duke *Pericles* of her did learn;
Arete[8] did devote herself to art,
And by consent (which shows she was no foole)
150   She did succeed her father in his school.

---

3. "Labor will conquer all," an allusion to Virgil's *Georgics* 1.145, "*labor omnia vincit*," labor conquered all things. Speght's transformed romance garden also recalls Virgil's *Eclogue* 10.69, "*omnia vincit amor*," love conquers all, and the ambiguous motto of Chaucer's Prioress, "*Amor vincit omnia*," *Canterbury Tales*, General Prologue, line 162 (p. 219).
4. The bracketed biblical references in the margins are Speght's.
5. Speght refers to learned women from classical times often cited in defenses of women. Cleobulina or Eumerus (fl. 6th century B.C.E.), named for her father, Cleobulus of Rhodes, one of the seven sages, was celebrated for composing riddles in hexameter verse and for learning medical arts. Demophyle (ca. 600 B.C.E.), pupil and companion of Sappho, wrote erotic poems and hymns to Artemis. Telesilla (fl. ca. 510 B.C.E.), one of the so-called nine lyric muses, wrote odes, hymns, and battle songs and reportedly led a band of Athenian women to fight against Sparta in the Peloponne-

sian War. The "historians" are Plutarch and Philostratus.
6. Daughter of P. Scipio Africanus and mother of the two Gracchi tribunes, she was often identified as the source of their virtue and oratory.
7. Hypatia (ca. C.E. 370), instructed by her father Theon in philosophy and mathematics, presided over the Neoplatonic school of Plotinus in Alexandria and wrote on astronomy, algebra, conic sections, and other topics. Aspasia (470–410 B.C.E.), Pericles' mistress, was described by Socrates in Plato's *Menexenus* (probably ironically) as his own teacher, as teacher of rhetoric to Pericles, and as the composer of his famous funeral oration honoring the fallen in the Peloponnesian War. Speght's honorific, "Duke," plays on the Latin *dux*, leader, commander.
8. Arete (fl. 370–340 B.C.E.) succeeded her father Aristippus, founder of the Cyrenian school of philosophy, where she reportedly taught natural science, moral philosophy, and ethics for thirty-five years and wrote more than forty books.

* * *

When *Truth* had ended what she meant to say,[9]
Desire did move me to obey her will,
Whereto consenting I did soon proceed,
Her counsel and my purpose to fulfill;
185 And by the help of *Industry* my friend,
I quickly did attain my journey's end.

Where being come, *Instruction's* pleasant air
Refreshed my senses which were almost dead,
And fragrant flowers of sage and fruitful plants
190 Did send sweet savors up into my head.
And taste of science appetite did move,
To augment *Theory* of things above.[1]

There did the harmony of those sweet birds[2]
(Which higher soar with Contemplation's wings,
195 Then barely with a superficial view,
Denote the value of created things)
Yield such delight as made me to implore
That I might reap this pleasure more and more.

And as I walked wand'ring with *Desire*,
200 To gather that, for which I thither came,
(Which by the help of *Industry* I found)
I met my old acquaintance, *Truth* by name;
Whom I requested briefly to declare,
The virtue of that plant I found so rare.

205 Quoth she, by it God's image man doth bear,   [*Col. 3.10*]
Without it he is but a human shape
Worse than the Devil, for he knoweth much:
Without it who can any ill escape?
By virtue of it evils are withstood;
210 *The mind without it is not counted good.*   [*Prov. 19.2*]

Who wanteth *Knowledge* is a Scripture fool,
Against the *Ignorant* the Prophets pray;
And *Hosea*[3] threatens judgment unto those
Whom want of *Knowledge* made to run astray.
215 Without it thou no practique good canst show,
More than by hap,° as blind men hit a crow.   chance

True *Knowledge* is the window of the soul,
Through which her objects she doth speculate;°   view
It is the mother of faith, hope, and love,
220 Without it who can virtue estimate?

9. In the five omitted stanzas, Truth refers in general terms to other learned women and urges Rachel to stand firm against Dissuasion.
1. I.e., the taste of learning whetted my longing ("appetite") to increase my conception ("theory") of higher things.

2. I.e., the song of birds (which through contemplation I am led to value more highly than a superficial view would provide, as evidence of the value of the creation) "yields such delight . . ."
3. Hosea 4.1–6.

By it, in grace thou shalt desire to grow;
'Tis life eternal God and Christ to *Know*.   [*John* 17.3]

Great *Alexander*[4] made so great account,
Of *Knowledge*, that he oftentimes would say,
225   That he to *Aristotle* was more bound
For *Knowledge*, upon which *Death* could not prey,
Than to his father *Phillip* for his life,
Which was uncertain, irksome, full of strife.

This true report put edge unto *Desire*,
230   Which did incite me to increse my store,
And told me 'twas a lawful avarice
To covet *Knowledge* daily more and more.
This counsel I did willingly obey,
Till some occurrence[5] called me away,

235   And made me rest content with that I had,
Which was but little, as effect doth show,
And quenched hope for gaining any more,
For I my time must other-wayes bestow.
I therefore to that place returned again
240   From whence I came, and where I must remain.

But by the way I saw a full fed Beast,[6]
Which roared like some monster, or a Devil,
And on *Eve's* sex he foamed filthy froth,
As if that he had had the falling evil;°   *epilepsy*
245   To whom I went to free them from mishaps,
And with a *Muzzle* sought to bind his chaps.

1621

4. Aristotle directed the education of Alexander the Great, son of Philip of Macedon.
5. The specific occasion is not clear but the following stanzas date it just before Speght's answer to Swetnam, i.e., about 1616, when Speght was eighteen or nineteen. At this point her formal education ended and she was recalled to domestic duties, though she was not married until four years later.
6. Swetnam, whose treatise attacking women she answered with her tract, *A Muzzle for Melastomus*. The remaining portion of the poem comments on that controversy, other answers to Swetnam, and the death of Speght's mother, which occasioned this volume.

ROBERT BURTON

Robert Burton's *Anatomy of Melancholy* focuses sharply on the self: unlike Bacon, Burton assumes that knowledge of psychology, not natural science, is humankind's greatest need. His enormous but delightful treatise analyzes in encyclopedic detail that ubiquitous Jacobean malady, melancholy, supposedly caused, according to contemporary humor theory, by an excess of black bile. Melancholy was responsible, according to Burton and others, for the wild passions and despair of lovers, the agonies and ecstasies of religious devotees, the frenzies of madmen, and the studious abstraction exemplified by scholars such as Shakespeare's *Hamlet* or Milton's *Il Penseroso*. But for Burton melancholy is more than a particular temperament or disease: it encompasses all the folly and madness intrinsic to the fallen human condition and so afflicts the whole world—necessarily including Burton himself.

Burton (1577–1640) was a scholar and cleric who lived in Christ Church College, Oxford, all his life: he never married, never traveled, never sought sucess in the world, but, as he says of himself in his Preface, he lived a "silent, sedentary, solitary, private life," researching his great book in the Bodleian Library and reading omniverously on other topics. First published in 1621, the *Anatomy* went through five editions during the author's life, each much augmented over the last. In his Preface, Burton creates a persona for himself, Democritus Junior, who proposes to complete the supposedly lost book on melancholy and madness by the Greek "laughing philosopher" Democritus. As Democritus Junior he promises not only to laugh but also to scoff, satirize, and lament.

The title term "Anatomy" invites expectations of a clear, logical, ordered treatment of a medical subject after the manner of Vesalius, expectations also evoked by Donne in his *First Anniversary, An Anatomy of the World*. Burton's subtitle promises an analysis of "all the kinds, causes, symptoms, prognostics, and several cures" of melancholy and proposes a division into three parts—the Causes and Effects of melancholy; its Cures; and its two principal kinds, Love Melancholy and Religious Melancholy—as well as various "sections, members, and subsections." But instead of such clarity and rigidity of structure in the course of the treatise, the categories collapse into each other. Since the psychic disorder he discusses is universal, Burton feels justified in being all-inclusive and digressive, taking us in picaresque disorder from one subject to the next, moving readily from the inner landscape to the world outside. The work contains a utopia, a treatise on climatology, and discourses on geography and meteorology, as well as case sudies of various sufferers from melancholy: a man who thought he was glass, a man who thought he was butter, the sorry predicament of maids, nuns, and widows suffering sexual deprivation, etc. Also, Burton cites every authority who wrote about any aspect of melancholy, from classical times to his present, but in no special order and without privileging any citations, including those quoted from scripture; this randomness and the resulting internal contradictions undercut the authorities, collapsing them all into the idiosyncratic voice of Burton/Democritus Jr. The prose style of long, loose sentences thrusting forward, as of thoughts rushing pell-mell beyond the author's control, reinforces the impression of a disorderly world not at all amenable to Baconian logical thought and scientific categories. Burton concludes his massive exploration by offering as the only remedy against melancholy the pragmatic advice, "Be not idle." His book, were we to read it all, would keep us from idleness for a good long time.

From The Anatomy[1] of Melancholy

Democritus[2] Junior to the Reader

Gentle Reader, I presume thou wilt be very inquisitive to know what antic or personate[3] actor this is, that so insolently intrudes upon this common

1. A logical dissection of a topic into its several parts, on an analogy with a medical anatomy. (See also Donne, *An Anatomy of the World*, p. 1262.) Burton's full title plays wittily with the term while pointing to the massive scope of his work: *The Anatomy of Melancholy. What it is, with all the kinds, causes, symptoms, prognostics, & several cures of it. In three Partitions, with their several sections,* members, & subsections. Philosophically, medicinally, historically opened & cut up.

2. In this extract Burton describes Democritus (ca. 460–370 B.C.E.), the Greek philosopher known as a founder of atomism and as the "laughing philsopher," and explains why he constructs himself as his son and intellectual heir.

3. Clownish or masked (impersonating).

theatre to the world's view, arrogating another man's name; whence he is, why he doth it, and what he hath to say. Although, as he said,[4] *Primum si noluero, non respondebo, quis coacturus est?* I am a free man born, and may choose whether I will tell; who can compel me? If I be urged, I will as readily reply as that Egyptian in Plutarch,[5] when a curious fellow would needs know what he had in his basket, *Quum vides velatam, quid inquiris in rem absconditam?* It was therefore covered, because he should not know what was in it. Seek not after that which is hid; if the contents please thee, "and be for thy use, suppose the Man in the Moon, or whom thou wilt, to be the author"; I would not willingly be known. Yet in some sort to give thee satisfaction, which is more than I need, I will show a reason, both of this usurped name, title, and subject. And first of the name of Democritus; lest any man by reason of it should be deceived, expecting a pasquil,[6] a satire, some ridiculous treatise (as I myself should have done), some prodigious tenent, or paradox of the earth's motion, of infinite worlds, *in infinito vacuo, ex fortuita atomorum collisione*, in an infinite waste, so caused by an accidental collision of motes in the sun, all which Democritus held, Epicurus and their master Leucippus[7] of old maintained, and are lately revived by Copernicus, Brunus,[8] and some others. Besides, it hath been always an ordinary custom, as Gellius observes, "for later writers and impostors to broach many absurd and insolent fictions under the name of so noble a philosopher as Democritus, to get themselves credit, and by that means the more to be respected," as artificers usually do, *Novo qui marmori ascribunt Praxitelen suo.*[9] 'Tis not so with me.

> *Non hic Centauros, non Gorgonas, Harpyasque*
> *Invenies, hominem pagina nostra sapit.*

> No Centaurs here, or Gorgons look to find,
> My subject is of man and humankind.

Thou thyself art the subject of my discourse.

> *Quicquid agunt homines, votum, timor, ira, voluptas,*
> *Gaudia, discursus, nostri farrago libelli.*

> Whate'er men do, vows, fears, in ire, in sport,
> Joys, wand'rings, are the sum of my report.

My intent is no otherwise to use his name, than Mercurius Gallobelgicus, Mercurius Britannicus, use the name of Mercury, Democritus Christianus, etc.; although there be some other circumstances for which I have masked myself under this vizard, and some peculiar respects which I cannot so well express, until I have set down a brief character of this our Democritus, what he was, with an epitome of his life.

4. Burton's marginal note identifies this passage as from Seneca's satire on the death of Claudius Caesar: "In the first place, if I don't want to answer, I won't; who will make me?" Here, as often elsewhere, Burton provides his own translation or paraphrase just before or after the Latin quotes which he sprinkles in liberally as they occur to him; in such cases no translation will be supplied. The notes that follow will not identify every quotation and allusion but only supply what is needed for comprehension.

5. Plutarch, "On Curiosity," *Moralia:* "Seeing the cover, why do you ask what is concealed?"
6. Lampoon.
7. Leucippus of Miletus was, with Democritus, the founder of the atomistic philosophy that Epicurus adopted.
8. Giordano Bruno (1548–1600), an Italian priest who was executed for advocating Copernican astronomy and other advanced opinions.
9. "Who sign their own new statues with the name of Praxitiles," the famous Greek sculptor.

Democritus, as he is described by Hippocrates and Laertius, was a little wearish[1] old man, very melancholy by nature, averse from company in his latter days, and much given to solitariness, a famous philosopher in his age, coævus[2] with Socrates, wholly addicted to his studies at the last, and to a private life: writ many excellent works, a great divine, according to the divinity of those times, an expert physician, a politician, an excellent mathematician, as *Diacosmus* and the rest of his works do witness. He was much delighted with the studies of husbandry, saith Columella, and often I find him cited by Constantinus and others treating of that subject. He knew the natures, differences of all beasts, plants, fishes, birds; and, as some say, could understand the tunes and voices of them. In a word, he was *omnifariam doctus*, a general scholar, a great student; and to the intent he might better contemplate, I find it related by some, that he put out his eyes, and was in his old age voluntarily blind, yet saw more than all Greece besides, and writ of every subject, *Nihil in toto opificio naturæ, de quo non scripsit.*[3] A man of an excellent wit, profound conceit; and to attain knowledge the better in his younger years he travelled to Egypt and Athens, to confer with learned men, "admired of some, despised of others." After a wandering life, he settled at Abdera, a town in Thrace, and was sent for thither to be their law-maker, recorder, or town clerk as some will; or as others, he was there bred and born. Howsoever it was, there he lived at last in a garden in the suburbs, wholly betaking himself to his studies and a private life, "saving that sometimes he would walk down to the haven, and laugh heartily at such variety of ridiculous objects, which there he saw." Such a one was Democritus.

But in the meantime, how doth this concern me, or upon what reference do I usurp his habit? I confess, indeed, that to compare myself unto him for aught I have yet said, were both impudency and arrogancy. I do not presume to make any parallel, *antistat mihi millibus trecentis, parvus sum, nullus sum, altum nec spiro, nec spero.*[4] Yet thus much I will say of myself, and that I hope without all suspicion of pride, or self-conceit, I have lived a silent, sedentary, solitary, private life, *mihi et musis*[5] in the university, as long almost as Xenocrates in Athens, *ad senectam fere*[6] to learn wisdom as he did, penned up most part in my study. For I have been brought up a student in the most flourishing college of Europe, *augustissimo collegio,*[7] and can brag with Jovius, almost, *in ea luce domicilii Vaticani, totius orbis celeberrimi, per 37 annos multa opportunquè didici;*[8] for thirty years I have continued (having the use of as good libraries as ever he had) a scholar, and would be therefore loath, either by living as a drone to be an unprofitable or unworthy member of so learned and noble a society, or to write that which should be anyway dishonourable to such a royal and ample foundation. Something I have done, though by my profession a divine, yet *turbine raptus ingenii*, as he[9] said, out of a running wit, an unconstant, unsettled mind. I had a great desire (not

1. Wizened.
2. Coeval; contemporary.
3. "There is nothing in the whole range of nature's works about which he has not written."
4. "He is immeasurably superior to me. I am insignificant, a nobody, with little ambition and small prospects."
5. "For myself and my studies."
6. "Virtually to old age."
7. Christ's Church College, Oxford.

8. "In the splendor of my Vatican residence, the most famous [library] in the world, I have spent thirty-seven full and advantageous years." Paolo Giovio (Jovius 1483–1552) wrote the history of his own time in 45 volumes, under the patronage of Pope Clement VII.
9. Julius-Caesar Scaliger, an Italian scholar (1484–1558) of encyclopedic learning, a neo-Latin poet, and a literary critic whose *Poetics* is a massive commentary on Aristotle's *Poetics*.

able to attain to a superficial skill in any) to have some smattering in all, to be *aliquis in omnibus, nullus in singulis*,[1] which Plato commends, out of him Lipsius approves and furthers, "as fit to be imprinted in all curious wits, not to be a slave of one science, or dwell altogether in one subject, as most do, but to rove abroad, *centum puer artium*,[2] to have an oar in every man's boat, to taste of every dish, and sip of every cup," which, saith Montaigne, was well performed by Aristotle and his learned countryman Adrian Turnebos. This roving humour (though not with like success) I have ever had, and like a ranging spaniel, that barks at every bird he sees, leaving his game, I have followed all, saving that which I should, and may justly complain, and truly, *qui ubique est, nusquam est*,[3] which Gesner did in modesty, that I have read many books, but to little purpose, for want of good method; I have confusedly tumbled over divers authors in our libraries, with small profit for want of art, order, memory, judgment. I never travelled but in map or card, in which my unconfined thoughts have freely expatiated, as having ever been especially delighted with the study of cosmography. Saturn was lord of my geniture, culminating, etc., and Mars principal significator of manners, in partile conjunction with mine ascendant; both fortunate in their houses, etc.[4] I am not poor, I am not rich; *nihil est, nihil deest*, I have little, I want nothing: all my treasure is in Minerva's[5] tower. Greater preferment as I could never get, so am I not in debt for it, I have a competency (*laus Deo*)[6] from my noble and munificent patrons, though I live still a collegiate student, as Democritus in his garden, and lead a monastic life, *ipse mihi theatrum*,[7] sequestered from those tumults and troubles of the world, *et tanquam in specula positus* (as he[8] said), in some high place above you all, like *Stoicus sapiens, omnia sæcula præterita præsentiaque videns, uno velut intuitu*,[9] I hear and see what is done abroad, how others run, ride, turmoil, and macerate themselves in court and country, far from those wrangling lawsuits, *aulæ vanitatem, fori ambitionem, ridere mecum soleo*,[1] I laugh at all; "only secure lest my suit go amiss, my ships perish," corn and cattle miscarry, trade decay, "I have no wife nor children good or bad to provide for." A mere spectator of other men's fortunes and adventures, and how they act their parts, which methinks are diversely presented unto me, as from a common theatre or scene. I hear new news every day, and those ordinary rumours of war, plagues, fires, inundations, thefts, murders, massacres, meteors, comets, spectrums, prodigies, apparitions, of towns taken, cities besieged in France, Germany, Turkey, Persia, Poland, etc., daily musters and preparations, and such-like, which these tempestuous times afford, battles fought, so many men slain, monomachies,[2] shipwrecks, piracies, and sea-fights, peace, leagues, stratagems, and fresh alarums. A vast confusion of vows, wishes, actions, edicts, petitions, lawsuits, pleas; laws, proclamations, complaints, grievances are daily brought to our ears. New books every day, pamphlets, currantoes,[3] stories, whole catalogues

---

1. "Competent in all [subjects], insignificant in any one."
2. "The servant of a hundred arts."
3. "He who is everywhere is nowhere."
4. He was born under the gloomy planet Saturn (his ascendant), whose influence was somewhat modified by the fiery and energetic planet Mars; and he was fortunate in the houses (parts of the heavens) those planets occupied.
5. Goddess of wisdom.
6. "Praise be to God."
7. "A theater to myself."
8. Daniel Heinsius (1580–1655), one of the most famous classical scholars of the Dutch Renaissance and a neo-Latin poet and dramatist.
9. "The Stoic sage seeing all past and present ages simultaneously, and at a single glance."
1. "I laugh to myself at the vanity of the court, the ambition of public life."
2. Single combats.
3. Newspapers.

of volumes of all sorts, new paradoxes, opinions, schisms, heresies, controversies in philosophy, religion, etc. Now come tidings of weddings, maskings, mummeries, entertainments, jubilees, embassies, tilts and tournaments, trophies, triumphs, revels, sports, plays: then again, as in a new shifted scene, treasons, cheating tricks, robberies, enormous villainies in all kinds, funerals, burials, deaths of princes, new discoveries, expeditions: now comical, then tragical matters. To-day we hear of new lords and officers created, to-morrow of some great men deposed, and then again of fresh honours conferred; one is let loose, another imprisoned; one purchaseth, another breaketh; he thrives, his neighbour turns bankrupt; now plenty, then again dearth and famine; one runs, another rides, wrangles, laughs, weeps, etc. Thus I daily hear, and such-like, both private and public news; amidst the gallantry and misery of the world—jollity, pride, perplexities and cares, simplicity and villainy; subtlety, knavery, candour and integrity, mutually mixed and offering themselves—I rub on *privus privatus*;[4] as I have still lived, so I now continue, *statu quo prius*,[5] left to a solitary life and mine own domestic discontents: saving that sometimes, *ne quid mentiar*,[6] as Diogenes went into the city and Democritus to the haven to see fashions, I did for my recreation now and then walk abroad, look into the world, and could not choose but make some little observation.

From *Love Melancholy*

PART 3, SECTION 2, MEMBER 1, SUBSECTION 2: HOW LOVE TYRANNIZETH OVER MEN. LOVE, OR HEROICAL MELANCHOLY, HIS DEFINITION, PART AFFECTED.

'Tis a happy state this[1] indeed, when the fountain is blessed (saith Solomon, Proverbs v.18), "and he rejoiceth with the wife of his youth, and she is to him as the loving hind and pleasant roe,[2] and he delights in her continually." But this love of ours is immoderate, inordinate, and not to be comprehended in any bounds. It will not contain itself within the union of marriage or apply to one object, but is a wandering, extravagant, a domineering, a boundless, an irrefragable, a destructive passion; sometimes this burning lust rageth after marriage, and then it is properly called jealousy; sometimes before, and then it is called heroical melancholy; it extends sometimes to corrivals, etc., begets rapes, incests, murders: *Marcus Antoninus compressit Faustinam sororem, Caracalla Juliam novercam, Nero matrem, Caligula sorores, Cinyras Myrrham filiam*, etc.[3] But it is confined within no terms of blood, years, sex, or whatsoever else. Some furiously rage before they come to discretion or age. Quartilla in Petronius[4] never remembered she was a maid; and the Wife of Bath in Chaucer cracks,

> Since I was twelve years old, believe,
> Husbands at kirk-door had I five.[5]

4. "In complete privacy."
5. "In the same condition as before."
6. "Not to conceal anything." "Diogenes": Cynic philosopher, noted for his moroseness and austerity of life.
1. I.e., the state of matrimony.
2. The hind is a female and the roebuck (roe) a male deer.

3. "Marc Antony slept with his sister Faustina, Caracalla with his stepmother Julia, Nero with his mother, Caligula with his sisters, Cinyras with his daughter Myrrha."
4. A character in the *Satyricon* of Petronius Arbiter (1st century C.E.).
5. Burton cites from memory, and inaccurately (cf. p. 253).

Aretine's Lucretia sold her maidenhead a thousand times before she was twenty-four years old, *plus millies vendideram virginitatem, etc., neque te celabo, non deerant qui ut integram ambirent.*[6] Rahab, that harlot, began to be a professed quean at ten years of age, and was but fifteen when she hid the spies, as Hugh Broughton proves, to whom Serrarius the Jesuit, *quaest.* 6 *in cap.* 2 Josue, subscribes. Generally women begin *pubescere* as they call it, or *catulire* as Julius Pollux cites, *lib.* 2, *cap.* 3 *Onomast.* out of Aristophanes, at fourteen years old, then they do offer themselves, and some plainly rage. Leo Afer[7] saith that in Africa a man shall scarce find a maid at fourteen years of age, they are so forward, and many amongst us after they come into the teens do not live without husbands, but linger. What pranks in this kind the middle age have played is not to be recorded, *si mihi sint centum linguae, sint oraque centum,*[8] no tongue can sufficiently declare, every story is full of men and women's insatiable lust, Neros, Heliogabali, Bonosi, etc.[9] *Coelius Aufilenum, et Quintius Aufilenam depereunt,*[1] etc. They neigh after other men's wives (as Jeremy, *cap.* v.8 complaineth) like fed horses, or range like town bulls, *raptores virginum et viduarum,*[2] as many of our great ones do. Solomon's wisdom was extinguished in this fire of lust, Samson's strength enervated, piety in Lot's daughters quite forgot, gravity of priesthood in Eli's sons, reverend old age in the elders that would violate Susanna, filial duty in Absalom to his stepmother, brotherly love in Amnon towards his sister. Human, divine laws, precepts, exhortations, fear of God and men, fair, foul means, fame, fortunes, shame, disgrace, honor cannot oppose, stave off, or withstand the fury of it, *omnia vincit amor, etc.*[3] No cord nor cable can so forcibly draw, or hold so fast, as love can do with a twined thread. The scorching beams under the equinoctial or extremity of cold within the circle Arctic, where the very seas are frozen, cold or torrid zone cannot avoid or expel this heat, fury, and rage of mortal men.

> *Quo fugis? ah, demens! nulla est fuga, tu licet usque*
> *Ad Tanaim fugias, usque sequetur amor.*[4]

Of women's unnatural, unsatiable lust, what country, what village doth not complain? Mother and daughter sometimes dote on the same man; father and son, master and servant on one woman.

> *Sed amor, sed ineffrenata libido,*
> *Quid castum in terris intentatumque reliquit?*[5]

---

6. "Moreover, there were those who could restore it." The tale of Lucretia comes from a set of dialogues published by Pietro Aretino in 1534; they parody the dialogues of Plato and are set in a brothel. The whore Rahab appears in Joshua 2. Hugh Broughton (below) was a biblical scholar of Burton's day.
7. Leo Afer or Africanus was a 16th-century Spanish Moor who wrote one of the first accounts of Africa. "Pubescere": mature sexually. "Catulire": desire a male. Julius Pollux compiled a dictionary (*Onomasticon*) that Burton cites frequently.
8. "If I had a hundred tongues, a hundred mouths."
9. Nero and Heliogabalus were corrupt Roman emperors, their vices described in lurid detail by Roman historians and moralists.
1. "Coelius had an itch for Aufilenus, Quintius for Aufilena." From Catullus, the Roman erotic poet.
2. "Ravishers of maids and widows." "Jeremy" is St. Jerome.
3. "Love conquers all."
4. "Whither away? ah, madman! there is no escape. Flee to the remotest districts of the river Don, love will still follow." From Propertius, the Latin elegist.
5. "But love, unbridled passion, leaves nothing on earth untempted, nothing chaste." From Euripides, the Greek tragedian.

What breach of vows and oaths, fury, dotage, madness might I reckon up! Yet this is more tolerable in youth, and such as are still in their hot blood; but for an old fool to dote, to see an old lecher, what more odious, what can be more absurd? and yet what so common? who so furious? *Amare ea aetate si occeperint, multo insaniunt acrius.*[6] Some dote then more than ever they did in their youth. How many decrepit, hoary, harsh, writhen, bursten-bellied, crooked, toothless, bald, blear-eyed, impotent, rotten old men shall you see flickering still in every place? One gets him a young wife, another a courtesan, and when he can scarce lift his leg over a sill and hath one foot already in Charon's boat,[7] when he hath the trembling in his joints, the gout in his feet, a perpetual rheum in his head, a continuate cough, "his sight fails him, thick of hearing, his breath stinks,"[8] all his moisture is dried up and gone, may not spit from him, a very child again, that cannot dress himself or cut his own meat, yet he will be dreaming of and honing after wenches; what can be more unseemly? Worse it is in women than in men; when she is *aetate declivis, diu vidua, mater olim, parum decore matrimonium sequi videtur,* an old widow, a mother so long since (in Pliny's opinion),[9] she doth very unseemly seek to marry; yet whilst she is so old, a crone, a beldam, she can neither see nor hear, go nor stand, a mere carcass, a witch, and scarce feel, she caterwauls and must have a stallion, a champion, she must and will marry again, and betroth herself to some young man that hates to look on her but for her goods, abhors the sight of her, to the prejudice of her good name, her own undoing, grief of friends, and ruin of her children.

But to enlarge or illustrate this power and effects of love is to set a candle in the sun. It rageth with all sorts and conditions of men, yet is most evident among such as are young and lusty, in the flower of their years, nobly descended, high fed, such as live idly and at ease; and for that cause (which our divines call burning lust) this *ferinus insanus amor,* this mad and beastly passion, as I have said, is named by our physicians heroical love, and a more honorable title put upon it, *amor nobilis* as Savonarola[1] styles it, because noble men and women make a common practice of it and are so ordinarily affected with it. Avicenna,[2] *lib.* 3, *fen.* 1, *tract.* 4, *cap.* 23, calleth this passion *Ilishi* and defines it to be "a disease or melancholy vexation or anguish of mind, in which a man continually meditates of the beauty, gesture, manners of his mistress, and troubles himself about it"; "desiring" (as Savonarola adds) "with all intentions and eagerness of mind to compass or enjoy her; as commonly hunters trouble themselves about their sports, the covetous about their gold and goods, so is he tormented still about his mistress." Arnoldus Villanovanus[3] in his book of heroical love defines it "a continual cogitation of that which he desires, with a confidence or hope of compassing it"; which definition his commentator cavils at. For continual cogitation is not the *genus* but a symptom of love; we continually think of that which we hate and abhor,

---

6. "When they start loving at that age, the madness takes them worse." From Plautus, the Roman comic dramatist.
7. Charon ferries the souls of the dead across the river Styx.
8. Quoted from Cyprian, 3rd-century bishop of Carthage.
9. Pliny, *Natural History* 8. The Latin is translated by Burton.

1. Not the Florentine reformer, but his grandfather Michele, a Paduan physician.
2. An encyclopedic Arabian physician of the 11th century.
3. Arnold of Villanova was a Spanish doctor, astrologer, and alchemist of the 13th and early 14th centuries.

as well as that which we love; and many things we covet and desire without all hope of attaining. Carolus à Lorme in his *Questions* makes a doubt *an amor sit morbus*, whether this heroical love be a disease: Julius Pollux, *Onomast*. lib. 6, *cap.* 44, determines it. They that are in love are likewise sick; *lascivus, salax, lasciviens, et qui in venerem furit, vere est aegrotus.*[4] Arnoldus will have it improperly so called, and a malady rather of the body than mind. Tully,[5] in his *Tusculans*, defines it a furious disease of the mind; Plato, madness itself; Ficinus, his commentator, *cap.* 12, a species of madness, "for many have run mad for women" (I Esdras iv.26); but Rhasis,[6] "a melancholy passion"; and most physicians make it a species or kind of melancholy (as will appear by the symptoms), and treat of it apart; whom I mean to imitate, and to discuss it in all his kinds, to examine his several causes, to show his symptoms, indications, prognostics, effects, that so it may be with more facility cured.

The part affected in the meantime, as Arnoldus supposeth, "is the former part of the head for want of moisture," which his commentator rejects. Langius, *Med. epist. lib.* 1, *cap.* 24, will have this passion sited in the liver, and to keep residence in the heart, "to proceed first from the eyes so carried by our spirits, and kindled with imagination in the liver and heart"; *cogit amare iecur,*[7] as the saying is. *Medium ferit per hepar,* as Cupid in Anacreon. For some such cause belike, Homer feigns Titius' liver (who was enamored of Latona) to be still gnawed by two vultures day and night in hell, "for that young men's bowels thus enamored are so continually tormented by love."[8] Gordonius, *cap.* 2, *part.* 2, "will have the testicles an immediate subject or cause, the liver an antecedent." Fracastorius agrees in this with Gordonius,[9] *inde primitus imaginatio venerea, erectio, etc.; titillatissimam partem vocat, ita ut nisi extruso semine gestiens voluptas non cessat, nec assidua veneris recordatio, addit Guastavinius, Comment.,* 4 *sect.,* prob. 27 Arist.[1] But properly it is a passion of the brain, as all other melancholy, by reason of corrupt imagination, and so doth Jason Pratensis, *cap.* 19, *De morb. cerebri* (who writes copiously of this erotical love), place and reckon it amongst the affections of the brain. Melanchthon, *De anima,* confutes those that make the liver a part affected, and Guianerius, *tract.* 15, *cap.* 13 *et* 17, though many put all the affections in the heart, refers it to the brain. Ficinus, *cap.* 7, *In Convivium Platonis,* "will have the blood to be the part affected." Jo. Freitagius, *cap.* 14, *Noct. med.,* supposeth all four affected, heart, liver, brain, blood; but the major part concur upon the brain, 'tis *imaginatio laesa,*[2] and both imagination and reason are misaffected; because of his corrupt judgment and continual meditation of that which he desires, he may truly be said to be melancholy. If it be violent, or his disease inveterate, as I have deter-

4. "One who is lustful, lecherous, lascivious, and mad with desire is really sick."
5. I.e., Cicero.
6. Rhasis or Rhazes was an Arab physician of the 10th century.
7. "The liver compels one to love"; and in the next phrase, "Love strikes through the liver." Anacreon was a Greek lyric poet.
8. *Odyssey* 11.
9. Gordonius, Guastavinius, Jason Pratensis, Guianerius, Freitagius et al. are Renaissance physicians from the ragbag of Burton's encyclopedic

reading. Two who stand out are Girolamo Fracastoro and Marsilio Ficino—the former a physician still remembered for his work on communicable diseases, the latter known mostly for his learned commentaries on the dialogues of Plato.
1. "Whence at first come erotic imaginings, erection, etc.; it so rouses the most excitable part, adds Guastavinius, that until emission takes place, the longing pleasure does not cease, nor the constant recollection of lovemaking."
2. A wounded imagination.

mined in the precedent partitions, both imagination and reason are misaffected, first one, then the other.

1621, 1651

SIR THOMAS BROWNE

Thomas Browne (1605–1682) presents his best-known work, *Religio Medici* (A doctor's religion), as a species of intellectual autobiography, terming it "the true Anatomy
of myself." Unlike the spiritual autobiographies common in the period, *Religio Medici*
does not tell a story of conversion or providential experiences, and it bears no sign of
the angst, melancholy, fear of damnation, and dread of death that such works often
record. Nor does Browne report the facts of his life (as Martha Moulsworth does in
her poem): that he was born into the family of a cloth merchant, attended Winchester
school and Pembroke College, Oxford, studied at the best medical schools (Mont-
pelier, Padua, Leyden), practiced medicine in Yorkshire and Norwich, married in
1641, and fathered twelve children. Instead he lays out—as an exercise in delighted
self-analysis and self-portrayal—his personal and sometimes eccentric views on a wide
variety of topics pertaining to religious doctrine and practice. In this two-part treatise
divided into many numbered paragraphs, he voices his fondness for Anglo-Catholic
ritual but also his belief in Calvinist predestination; he denounces religious persecution but thinks many religious martyrs were not particularly admirable; he believes
in witches but is skeptical of latter-day miracles. He emphasizes especially his love of
mystery and wonder, such that (in contrast with Bacon) he revels in metaphor and
takes positive joy in accepting things contrary to reason: "I love to lose myself in a
mystery, to pursue my reason to an *O altitudo*."

For this unusual autobiography, Browne constructs a curious and engaging persona: the genial, speculative doctor who finds nothing human foreign to him and so
is the very personification of charity and inclusiveness. He can readily participate in
the customs of others in food, drink, or religion (even in certain Roman Catholic
practices) but yet value his own customs. According to his preface, he wrote the work
around 1636 for himself only and circulated it in manuscript to a few friends, but
then was forced by a pirated edition (1642) to print a correct version (1643). His
decision to publish, however, just as King and Parliament took to the battlefield in
the Civil War was hardly coincidental, and the treatise has subtle political resonance.
Disparaging dogmatism and holding up to gentle irony those who claim exclusive
possession of the path to salvation, Browne portrays himself as a model Anglican, one
who is tolerant of and has himself held erroneous or heretical views (e.g., he can
hardly bring himself to believe that anyone, even the devil, is eternally damned), but
also someone who deplores schism and is ready to conform his mind to the teachings
of his church. His exercise in self-analysis comments on the wider world of church
and state, setting his own example of Anglican comprehensiveness against reforming
Puritans eager to rid the church of its errors.

In his other works Browne shows other sides of his multifaceted self and explores
other aspects of his world. *Pseudodoxia Epidemica*, or *Vulgar Errors* (1646) shows
Browne on his Baconian side, analyzing the causes of popular errors in a wide variety
of fields and the authors who perpetuate them. *Hydrotaphia, or Urn-Burial* (1658)
shows Browne as a passionate antiquarian, prompted to study and comment on the

funeral customs of various peoples by the discovery near Norwich of funeral urns that were thought (erroneously) to be of Roman origin. That work culminates in a sonorous meditation on mortality and the futility of all such commemorations, given the inevitable obliteration of all human fame. It was published with an even more curious work, *The Garden of Cyrus*, named after the Persian emperor who supposedly constructed the famous Hanging Gardens of Babylon. This work displays Browne the naturalist treating the history of horticulture, and also the mystical and neoplatonic Browne who finds quincunxes (shapes with five members or parts) everywhere in nature. Browne was a favorite prose stylist of many later writers, among them Coleridge, Lamb, De Quincy, and Melville: polysyllabic and Latinate, his prose mixes wit and sumptuous rhetoric, rising often to a resonant poetry.

From Religio Medici[1]

From *Part 1*

1. For my religion, though there be several circumstances that might persuade the world I have none at all—as the general scandal of my profession,[2] the natural course of my studies, the indifferency[3] of my behavior and discourse in matters of religion, neither violently defending one, nor with that common ardor and contention opposing another—yet in despite hereof I dare without usurpation assume the honorable style of a Christian. Not that I merely owe this title to the font,[4] my education, or clime wherein I was born, as being bred up either to confirm those principles my parents instilled into my unwary understanding, or by a general consent proceed in the religion of my country; but having in my riper years and confirmed judgment seen and examined all, I find myself obliged by the principles of grace and the law of mine own reason to embrace no other name but this. Neither doth herein my zeal so far make me forget the general charity I owe unto humanity, as rather to hate than pity Turks, infidels, and (what is worse) Jews;[5] rather contenting myself to enjoy that happy style than maligning those who refuse so glorious a title.

2. But because the name of a Christian is become too general to express our faith—there being a geography of religions as well as lands, and every clime distinguished not only by their laws and limits, but circumscribed by their doctrines and rules of faith—to be particular, I am of that reformed new-cast religion wherein I mislike nothing but the name;[6] of the same belief our Savior taught, the Apostles disseminated, the Fathers authorized, and the Martyrs confirmed; but by the sinister ends of princes, the ambition and avarice of prelates, and the fatal corruption of times, so decayed, impaired, and fallen from its native beauty that it required the careful and charitable

---

1. The Religion of a Doctor. Browne presents himself as a sound Church of England man, who accepts all its teachings and practices but has wide sympathy for other religious practices (even Roman Catholicism). He avoids any conflict between his scientific and his religious self by a forthright "fideism"—entirely separating reason from faith and thereby exempting faith from any critique by reason, or any support from it. This was also the stance of some contemporary Roman Catholic skeptics, notably Montaigne and Pierre

Charron.
2. Doctors were popularly reputed to be irreligious or atheistic.
3. Impartiality.
4. The baptismal font.
5. Browne thought them worse because they had been given a better chance than the others to know and accept Christianity.
6. Protestantism, for its connotations of contentiousness.

hands of these times to restore it to its primitive integrity. Now the accidental occasion whereon, the slender means whereby, the low and abject condition of the person by whom so good a work was set on foot,[7] which in our adversaries beget contempt and scorn, fills me with wonder, and is the very same objection the insolent pagans first cast at Christ and his disciples.

3. Yet have I not so shaken hands with those desperate resolutions—who had rather venture at large their decayed bottom[8] than bring her in to be new trimmed in the dock, who had rather promiscuously retain all than abridge any, and obstinately be what they are than what they have been—as to stand in diameter and sword's point with them. We have reformed from them, not against them; for, omitting those improperations and terms of scurrility betwixt us, which only difference[9] our affections and not our cause, there is between us one common name and appellation, one faith and necessary body of principles common to us both; and therefore I am not scrupulous to converse and live with them, to enter their churches in defect of ours, and either pray with them or for them. I could never perceive any rational consequence from those many texts which prohibit the children of Israel to pollute themselves with the temples of the heathens; we being all Christians, and not divided by such detested impieties as might profane our prayers or the place wherein we make them; or that a resolved conscience may not adore her Maker anywhere, especially in places devoted to his service; where, if their devotions offend him, mine may please him, if theirs profane it, mine may hallow it. Holy water and crucifix, dangerous to the common people, deceive not my judgment nor abuse my devotion at all. I am, I confess, naturally inclined to that which misguided zeal terms superstition.[1] My common conversation I do acknowledge austere, my behavior full of rigor, sometimes not without morosity; yet at my devotion I love to use the civility of my knee, my hat, and hand, with all those outward and sensible motions which may express or promote my invisible devotion. I should violate my own arm rather than a church, nor willingly deface the memory of saint or martyr. At the sight of a cross or crucifix I can dispense with my hat, but scarce with the thought and memory of my Savior. I cannot laugh at, but rather pity, the fruitless journeys of pilgrims, or contemn the miserable condition of friars; for though misplaced in circumstance, there is somewhat in it of devotion. I could never hear the Ave-Maria bell without an elevation,[2] or think it a sufficient warrant, because they erred in one circumstance, for me to err in all—that is, in silence and dumb contempt. Whilst, therefore, they directed their devotions to her, I offered mine to God, and rectified the errors of their prayers by rightly ordering mine own. At a solemn procession I have wept abundantly while my consorts,[3] blind with opposition and prejudice, have fallen into an excess of scorn and laughter. There are questionless, both in Greek, Roman, and African churches, solemnities and ceremonies whereof the wiser zeals do make a Christian use; and stand condemned by us, not as evil in themselves, but as allurements and

7. Luther, who was a miner's son, began the Reformation.
8. The leaky ship of the Roman Catholic Church. "Shaken hands": parted from.
9. Differentiate. "Improperations": reproaches.
1. He defines himself here and in the next few

lines against Puritan iconoclasts who would uproot all such "superstitions."
2. Exaltation of mind. "Ave-Maria bell": Angelus, rung daily at 6:00 and 12:00, morning and night.
3. Companions.

baits of superstition to those vulgar heads that look asquint on the face of truth, and those unstable judgments that cannot consist[4] in the narrow point and center of virtue without a reel or stagger to the circumference.

4. As there were many reformers, so likewise many reformations; every country proceeding in a particular way and method, according as their national interest together with their constitution and clime inclined them: some angrily and with extremity, others calmly and with mediocrity,[5] not rending but easily dividing the community, and leaving an honest possibility of a reconciliation; which, though peaceable spirits do desire, and may conceive that revolution of time and the mercies of God may effect, yet that judgment that shall consider the present antipathies between the two extremes, their contrarieties in condition, affection, and opinion, may with the same hopes expect an union in the poles of heaven.

5. But—to difference myself nearer, and draw into a lesser circle—there is no church whose every part so squares unto my conscience, whose articles, constitutions, and customs seem so consonant unto reason, and as it were framed to my particular devotion, as this whereof I hold my belief: the Church of England, to whose faith I am a sworn subject, and therefore in a double obligation subscribe unto her articles and endeavor to observe her constitutions. Whatsoever is beyond, as points indifferent, I observe according to the rules of my private reason or the humor and fashion of my devotion; neither believing this because Luther affirmed it nor disapproving that because Calvin hath disavouched it. I condemn not all things in the council of Trent nor approve all in the synod of Dort.[6] In brief, where the Scripture is silent, the church is my text; where that speaks, 'tis but my comment; where there is a joint silence of both, I borrow not the rules of my religion from Rome or Geneva, but the dictates of my own reason. It is an unjust scandal of our adversaries and a gross error in ourselves to compute the nativity of our religion from Henry the Eighth, who, though he rejected the Pope, refused not the faith of Rome, and effected no more than what his own predecessors desired and essayed in ages past, and was conceived the state of Venice would have attempted in our days.[7] It is as uncharitable a point in us to fall upon those popular scurrilities and opprobrious scoffs of the bishop of Rome, to whom as a temporal prince we owe the duty of good language. I confess there is cause of passion between us. By his sentence I stand excommunicated: "heretic" is the best language he affords me; yet can no ear witness I ever returned to him the name of "Antichrist," "Man of Sin," or "Whore of Babylon."[8] It is the method of charity to suffer without reaction. Those usual satires and invectives of the pulpit may perchance produce a good effect on the vulgar, whose ears are opener to rhetoric than logic; yet do they in no wise confirm the faith of wiser believers, who know that a good cause needs not to be patroned by a passion, but can sustain itself upon a temperate dispute.

---

4. Stand firm.
5. Moderation. "Extremity": violence.
6. The Council of Trent (1545–63) in Italy defined Catholic dogma after the Reformation; the Council of Dort (1618–19) in Holland defined Calvinist doctrine.

7. Though he repudiated the Pope, Henry VIII was for long an ambiguous Protestant. Venice was excommunicated in 1606 for challenging papal authority.
8. Stock terms of anti-Catholic abuse.

6. I could never divide myself from any man upon the difference of an opinion, or be angry with his judgment for not agreeing with me in that from which perhaps within a few days I should dissent myself. I have no genius to disputes in religion, and have often thought it wisdom to decline them, especially upon a disadvantage, or when the cause of truth might suffer in the weakness of my patronage. Where we desire to be informed, 'tis good to contest with men above ourselves; but to confirm and establish our opinions, 'tis best to argue with judgments below our own, that the frequent spoils and victories over their reasons may settle in ourselves an esteem and confirmed opinion of our own. Every man is not a proper champion for truth, nor fit to take up the gauntlet in the cause of verity. Many, from the ignorance of these maxims and an inconsiderate zeal unto truth, have too rashly charged the troops of error, and remain as trophies unto the enemies of truth. A man may be in as just possession of truth as of a city, and yet be forced to surrender. 'Tis therefore far better to enjoy her with peace than to hazard her on a battle. If therefore there rise any doubts in my way, I do forget them or at least defer them till my better settled judgment and more manly reason be able to resolve them; for I perceive every man's own reason is his best Oedipus,[9] and will upon a reasonable truce find a way to loose those bonds wherewith the subtleties of error have enchained our more flexible and tender judgments. In philosophy, where truth seems double-faced, there is no man more paradoxical than myself, but in divinity I love to keep the road; and, though not in an implicit, yet an humble faith, follow the great wheel of the church, by which I move, not reserving any proper poles or motion from the epicycle of my own brain.[1] By this means I leave no gap for heresies, schisms, or errors, of which at present I hope I shall not injure truth to say I have no taint or tincture. I must confess my greener studies have been polluted with two or three—not any begotten in the latter centuries, but old and obsolete, such as could never have been revived but by such extravagant and irregular heads as mine. For indeed heresies perish not with their authors, but like the river Arethusa, though they lose their currents in one place, they rise up again in another.[2] One general council is not able to extirpate one singular heresy. It may be canceled for the present, but revolution of time and the like aspects from heaven will restore it, when it will flourish till it be condemned again; for as though there were a metempsychosis, and the soul of one man passed into another, opinions do find after certain revolutions men and minds like those that first begat them. To see ourselves again we need not look for Plato's year.[3] Every man is not only himself; there have been many Diogenes and as many Timons,[4] though but few of that name. Men are lived over again; the world is now as it was in ages past. There was none then but there hath been someone since that parallels him, and is as it were his revived self.

* * *

9. Solver of riddles, as Oedipus solved that of the Sphinx.
1. In Ptolemaic astronomy, an "epicycle" is a small circle centered on the largest circle of a planet's orbit, hypothesized to account for inexplicable variations in the planet's motion.
2. In myth, when the fountain Arethusa, in Greece, was pursued by the river god Alpheus she dived into the sea and came up again in Sicily.
3. Browne's note on this reads: "A revolution of certain thousand years, when all things should return unto their former estate."
4. Diogenes was a Cynic philosopher, Timon a noted misanthrope, both Greek.

9. As for those wingy mysteries in divinity and airy subtleties in religion, which have unhinged the brains of better heads, they never stretched the *pia mater*[5] of mine. Methinks there be not impossibilities enough in religion for an active faith. The deepest mysteries ours contains have not only been illustrated but maintained by syllogism and the rule of reason. I love to lose myself in a mystery, to pursue my reason to an O *altitudo!*[6] 'Tis my solitary recreation to pose my apprehension with those involved enigmas and riddles of the Trinity, with Incarnation and Resurrection. I can answer all the objections of Satan and my rebellious reason with that odd resolution I learned of Tertullian, *Certum est quia impossibile est.*[7] I desire to exercise my faith in the difficultest points, for to credit ordinary and visible objects is not faith but persuasion. Some believe the better for seeing Christ his sepulcher, and when they have seen the Red Sea doubt not of the miracle. Now, contrarily, I bless myself and am thankful that I lived not in the days of miracles, that I never saw Christ nor his disciples. I would not have been one of those Israelites that passed the Red Sea, nor one of Christ's patients on whom he wrought his wonders: then had my faith been thrust upon me, nor should I enjoy that greater blessing pronounced to all that believe and saw not. 'Tis an easy and necessary belief to credit what our eye and sense hath examined. I believe he was dead, buried, and rose again; and desire to see him in his glory rather than to contemplate him in his cenotaph or sepulcher. Nor is this much to believe. As we have reason, we owe this faith unto history; they only had the advantage of a bold and noble faith who lived before his coming, who upon obscure prophecies and mystical types[8] could raise a belief and expect apparent impossibilities.

*   *   *

15. * * * I could never content my contemplation with those general pieces of wonder, the flux and reflux of the sea, the increase of Nile, the conversion of the needle to the north; and have studied to match and parallel those in the more obvious and neglected pieces of nature, which without further travel I can do in the cosmography of myself. We carry with us the wonders we seek without us: there is all Africa and her prodigies[9] in us. We are that bold and adventurous piece of nature which he that studies wisely learns in a compendium what others labor at in a divided piece and endless volume.

16. Thus are there two books from whence I collect my divinity: besides that written one of God, another of his servant nature, that universal and public manuscript that lies expansed unto the eyes of all. Those that never saw him in the one have discovered him in the other. This was the scripture and theology of the heathens: the natural motion of the sun made them more admire him than its supernatural station[1] did the children of Israel; the ordinary effects of nature wrought more admiration in them than in the other

---

5. A membrane covering the brain, often used for the brain itself.
6. From Romans 11.33: "O the depth [Latin Vulgate, *altitudo*] of the riches both of the wisdom and knowledge of God! How unsearchable are his judgments, and his ways past finding out!" The Latin term can also mean "heights."

7. Tertullian commenting on the Resurrection, "It is certain because it is impossible."
8. Foreshadowings of Christ in the Old Testament.
9. Marvels.
1. Standing still, as at the battle of Gibeon (Joshua 10.13).

all his miracles. Surely the heathens knew better how to join and read these mystical letters than we Christians, who cast a more careless eye on these common hieroglyphics, and disdain to suck divinity from the flowers of nature. Nor do I so forget God as to adore the name of nature; which I define not, with the schools, the principle of motion and rest, but that straight and regular line, that settled and constant course the wisdom of God hath ordained the actions of his creatures according to their several kinds. To make a revolution every day is the nature of the sun, because that necessary course which God hath ordained it, from which it cannot swerve but by a faculty[2] from that voice which first did give it motion. Now this course of nature God seldom alters or perverts, but like an excellent artist hath so contrived his work that with the selfsame instrument, without a new creation, he may effect his obscurest designs. Thus he sweetened the water with a wood;[3] preserved the creatures in the Ark, which the blast of his mouth might have as easily created: for God is like a skillful geometrician, who when more easily and with one stroke of his compass he might describe or divide a right line, had yet rather do this in a circle or longer way according to the constituted and forelaid principles of his art. Yet this rule of his he doth sometimes pervert, to acquaint the world with his prerogative, lest the arrogancy of our reason should question his power and conclude he could not. And thus I call the effects of nature the works of God, whose hand and instrument she only is; and therefore to ascribe his actions unto her is to devolve the honor of the principal agent upon the instrument: which if with reason we may do, then let our hammers rise up and boast they have built our houses, and our pens receive the honor of our writings. I hold there is a general beauty in the works of God, and therefore no deformity in any kind or species of creature whatsoever. I cannot tell by what logic we call a toad, a bear, or an elephant ugly; they being created in those outward shapes and figures which best express the actions of their inward forms, and having passed that general visitation of God, who saw that all that he had made was good[4]—that is, conformable to his will, which abhors deformity and is the rule of order and beauty. There is therefore no deformity but in monstrosity; wherein notwithstanding there is a kind of beauty, nature so ingeniously contriving the irregular parts as they become sometimes more remarkable than the principal fabric. To speak yet more narrowly, there was never anything ugly or misshapen but the chaos; wherein notwithstanding (to speak strictly) there was no deformity because no form, nor was it yet impregnate by the voice of God. Now, nature is not at variance with art nor art with nature, they both being the servants of his providence: art is the perfection of nature. Were the world now as it was the sixth day, there were yet a chaos: nature hath made one world and art another. In brief, all things are artificial, for nature is the art of God.

* * *

34. These[5] are certainly the magisterial and master pieces of the creator; the flower or (as we may say) the best part of nothing; actually existing what

2. Authority.
3. Exodus 15.25 tells how the Lord sweetened the bitter waters of Marah with a special tree.

4. Genesis 1.31.
5. The angels.

we are but in hopes and probability. We are only that amphibious piece between a corporal and spiritual essence; that middle form that links those two together, and makes good the method of God and nature, that jumps not from extremes but unites the incompatible distances by some middle and participating natures. That we are the breath and similitude of God it is indisputable and upon record of holy Scripture; but to call ourselves a microcosm or little world I thought it only a pleasant trope of rhetoric[6] till my nearer judgment and second thoughts told me there was a real truth therein. For first we are a rude mass and in the rank of creatures which only are and have a dull kind of being not yet privileged with life or preferred to sense or reason. Next we live the life of plants, the life of animals, the life of men, and at last the life of spirits; running on, in one mysterious nature, those five kinds of existences which comprehend the creatures not only of the world but of the universe. Thus is man that great and true amphibium whose nature is disposed to live not only like other creatures in divers elements but in divided and distinguished worlds. For though there be but one world to sense, there are two to reason; the one visible, the other invisible, whereof Moses seems to have left no description, and of the other[7] so obscurely that some parts thereof are yet in controversy: and truly for the first chapters of Genesis I must confess a great deal of obscurity. Though divines have, to the power of human reason, endeavored to make all go in a literal meaning, yet those allegorical interpretations are also probable, and perhaps the mystical method of Moses bred up in the hieroglyphical schools of the Egyptians.[8]

* * *

59. Again, I am confident and fully persuaded, yet dare not take my oath of my salvation. I am as it were sure, and do believe without all doubt, that there is such a city as Constantinople; yet for me to take my oath thereon were a kind of perjury, because I hold no infallible warrant from my own sense to confirm me in the certainty thereof. And truly, though many pretend an absolute certainty of their salvation, yet when an humble soul shall contemplate her own unworthiness she shall meet with many doubts and suddenly find how little we stand in need of the precept of St. Paul, *Work out your salvation with fear and trembling.*[9] That which is the cause of my election I hold to be the cause of my salvation, which was the mercy and beneplacit[1] of God before I was or the foundation of the world. *Before Abraham was, I am,* is the saying of Christ;[2] yet is it true in some sense if I say it of myself, for I was not only before myself but Adam, that is, in the idea of God and the decree of that synod held from all eternity. And in this sense, I say, the world was before the creation and at an end before it had a beginning; and thus was I dead before I was alive. Though my grave be England, my dying place was Paradise, and Eve miscarried of me before she conceived of Cain.

* * *

6. Figure of speech.
7. The visible world.
8. Some Neoplatonists thought that Moses, reared among the Egyptians, understood their hieroglyphic symbolism and imitated it in his own

writing of Scripture.
9. Philippians 2.12.
1. Good pleasure.
2. John 8.58.

From *Part 2*

1. Now for that other virtue of charity,[3] without which faith is mere notion, and of no existence, I have ever endeavored to nourish the merciful disposition and humane inclination I borrowed from my parents, and regulate it to the written and prescribed laws of charity; and if I hold the true anatomy of myself,[4] I am delineated and naturally framed to such a piece of virtue. For I am of a constitution so general that it comforts and sympathizeth with all things; I have no antipathy, or rather idiosyncrasy, in diet, humor, air, anything. I wonder not at the French for their dishes of frogs, snails, and toadstools, nor at the Jews for locusts and grasshoppers; but being amongst them, make them my common viands, and I find they agree with my stomach as well as theirs. I could digest a salad gathered in a churchyard as well as in a garden. I cannot start at the presence of a serpent, scorpion, lizard, or salamander, at the sight of a toad or viper I find in me no desire to take up a stone to destroy them. I feel not in myself those common antipathies that I can discover in others: those national repugnances do not touch me, nor do I behold with prejudice the French, Italian, Spaniard, or Dutch; but where I find their actions in balance with my countrymen's, I honor, love and embrace them in the same degree. I was born in the eighth climate,[5] but seem for to be framed and constellated unto all. I am no plant that will not prosper out of a garden. All places, all airs make unto me one country; I am in England everywhere and under any meridian. I have been shipwrackt,[6] yet am not enemy with the sea or winds; I can study, play, or sleep in a tempest. In brief, I am averse from nothing; my conscience would give me the lie if I should say I absolutely detest or hate any essence but the devil, or so at least abhor anything but that we might come to composition.[7] If there be any among those common objects of hatred I do contemn and laugh at, it is that great enemy of reason, virtue, and religion, the multitude—that numerous piece of monstrosity which, taken asunder, seem men and the reasonable creatures of God, but confused together make but one great beast, and a monstrosity more prodigious than Hydra.[8] It is no breach of charity to call these fools; it is the style all holy writers have afforded them, set down by Solomon in canonical Scripture[9] and a point of our faith to believe so. Neither in the name of multitude do I only include the base and minor sort of people; there is a rabble even amongst the gentry, a sort of plebeian heads whose fancy moves with the same wheel as these; men in the same level with mechanics, though their fortunes do somewhat guild their infirmities, and their purses compound for their follies.[1] But as in casting account, three or four men together come short in account of one man placed by himself below them, so neither are a troop of these ignorant dorados[2] of that true esteem and value as many a forlorn person whose condition doth place him below

3. Like many theological manuals, Browne's first book concerns faith, the second, charity.
4. If I have properly analyzed myself. See Donne, *Anatomy of the World*, and Burton, *Anatomy of Melancholy*, for the way this term is used. "Delineated": designed.
5. In the eighth of the twenty-four regions between the equator and the poles.
6. Browne was shipwrecked returning to England from Ireland in 1630.

7. Reach an agreement.
8. In Greek mythology, a nine-headed serpent that grew two heads for every one that was cut off.
9. E.g., Proverbs 1.7, "fools despise wisdom and instruction."
1. With the growing rebelliousness of the Puritan merchants and even some of the aristocracy as his point of reference, Browne redefines the rabble in terms of attitude and moral worth, not class.
2. Wealthy persons.

their feet. Let us speak like politicians, there is a nobility without heraldry, a natural dignity whereby one man is ranked with another, another filed before him, according to the quality of his desert, and preeminence of his good parts. Though the corruption of these times and the bias of present practice wheel another way, thus it was in the first and primitive commonwealths, and is yet in the integrity and cradle of well-ordered polities, till corruption getteth ground, ruder desires laboring after that which wiser considerations contemn, everyone having a liberty to amass and heap up riches, and they a license or faculty to do or purchase anything.

*　*　*

1642 (pirated)
1643 (authorized)

From Hydriotaphia, or Urn-Burial[1]

From *Chapter 5*

Now since these dead bones have already outlasted the living ones of Methuselah,[2] and in a yard under ground, and thin walls of clay, outworn all the strong and specious buildings above it, and quietly rested under the drums and tramplings of three conquests;[3] what prince can promise such diuturnity unto his relics, or might not gladly say,

Sic ego componi versus in ossa velim?[4]

Time, which antiquates antiquities, and hath an art to make dust of all things, hath yet spared these minor monuments.* * *

Circles and right lines limit and close all bodies, and the mortal right-lined circle must conclude and shut up all.[5] There is no antidote against the opium of time, which temporally considereth all things: our fathers find their graves in our short memories, and sadly tell us how we may be buried in our survivors. Gravestones tell truth scarce forty years.[6] Generations pass while some trees stand, and old families last not three oaks. To be read by bare inscriptions like many in Gruter,[7] to hope for eternity by enigmatical epithets or first letters of our names, to be studied by antiquaries, who we were, and have new names given us like many of the mummies, are cold consolations unto the students of perpetuity, even by everlasting languages.

To be content that times to come should only know there was such a man, not caring whether they knew more of him, was a frigid ambition in Cardan;[8] disparaging his horoscopal inclination and judgment of himself. Who cares to subsist like Hippocrates' patients, or Achilles' horses in Homer, under

1. The subtitle indicates the occasion of the work: *A Discourse of the Sepulchral Urns lately found in Norfolk.* The discovery of some forty or fifty ancient urns in a Norfolk field prompted this discourse on ancient funerary customs and at length on death and immortality.
2. Methuselah lived 969 years (Genesis 5.27).
3. If the bones were Roman (as Browne thought) the conquests would be Saxon, Danish, and Norman. "Diuturnity": long life.
4. Thus I, when dead, should wish to go to rest (Tibullus).
5. Browne's note equates "the mortal right-lined

circle" with the Greek letter theta (θ), the first letter of the word for death (*thanatos*) and a symbol of it.
6. Because old corpses are dug up and replaced with new (see Donne, *The Relic*, lines 3–4, p. 1253).
7. Jan Gruter (1560–1627), a Dutch scholar who published a collection of inscriptions.
8. Girolamo Cardano, an Italian mathematician and occultist of the 16th century, declared, "I want it to be known that I exist, I do not wish to be known what [kind of person] I am."

naked nominations, without deserts and noble acts, which are the balsam of our memories, the *entelechia*[9] and soul of our subsistences? To be nameless in worthy deeds exceeds[1] an infamous history. The Canaanitish woman lives more happily without a name than Herodias with one. And who had not rather have been the good thief than Pilate?[2]

But the iniquity of oblivion blindly scattereth her poppy,[3] and deals with the memory of men without distinction to merit of perpetuity. Who can but pity the founder of the pyramids? Herostratus lives that burnt the temple of Diana;[4] he is almost lost that built it. Time hath spared the epitaph of Adrian's horse,[5] confounded that of himself. In vain we compute our felicities by the advantage of our good names, since bad have equal durations, and Thersites is like to live as long as Agamemnon.[6] Who knows whether the best of men be known, or whether there be not more remarkable persons forgot than any that stand remembered in the known account of time? Without the favor of the everlasting register,[7] the first man had been as unknown as the last, and Methuselah's long life had been his only chronicle.

Oblivion is not to be hired: the greater part must be content to be as though they had not been, to be found in the register of God, not in the record of man. Twenty-seven names make up the first story, and the recorded names ever since contain not one living century.[8] The number of the dead long exceedeth all that shall live. The night of time far surpasseth the day, and who knows when was the equinox? Every hour adds unto that current arithmetic, which scarce stands one moment. And since death must be the Lucina[9] of life, and even pagans could doubt whether thus to live were to die; since our longest sun sets at right descensions, and makes but winter arches,[1] and therefore it cannot be long before we lie down in darkness, and have our light in ashes;[2] since the brother of death daily haunts us with dying mementos, and time that grows old itself bids us hope no long duration; diuturnity is a dream and folly of expectation.

Darkness and light divide the course of time, and oblivion shares with memory a great part even of our living beings; we slightly remember our felicities, and the smartest strokes of affliction leave but short smart upon us. Sense endureth no extremities, and sorrows destroy us or themselves. To weep into stones are fables.[3] Afflictions induce callosities;[4] miseries are slippery, or fall like snow upon us, which notwithstanding is no unhappy stupidity. To be ignorant of evils to come, and forgetful of evils past, is a merciful provision in nature, whereby we digest the mixture of our few and evil days, and, our delivered senses not relapsing into cutting remembrances, our sor-

9. Essence, perfection.
1. Is better than.
2. The woman of Canaan offered water to Christ (Matthew 15.22); Herodias demanded the head of John the Baptist (Mark 22–25); the good thief crucified beside Christ was promised paradise; Pontius Pilate, procurator of Judea, refused to intervene to save Christ.
3. Opiate. "Iniquity" inequity.
4. We remember Herostratus, who burned the great temple of Diana at Ephesus, one of the seven wonders of the world, but scarcely remember the builder (Chersiphon, according to Pliny).
5. Hadrian, emperor of Rome in the 2nd century, erected an inscribed monument to his horse.
6. Thersites, the scurrilous scoffer of the *Iliad*;

Agamemnon, leader of the Greek forces.
7. The Bible.
8. Genesis 1–5 tells the story of the human race from the creation to the flood in twenty-seven names; of all the names since the flood, not one hundred ("century") are really living ones.
9. Roman goddess of childbirth. "That current arithmetic": that continual addition.
1. I.e., even the longest human life is like a short winter's day (in which the sun traces a low "arch").
2. At funerals, Browne's note says, the Jews place a wax candle in a pot of ashes beside the corpse. The "brother of death" (next line) is sleep.
3. Like Niobe, whose grief turned her to stone.
4. Calluses, hardness, indifference.

rows are not kept raw by the edge of repetitions. A great part of antiquity contented their hopes of subsistency with a transmigration of their souls: a good way to continue their memories, while, having the advantage of plural successions, they could not but act something remarkable in such variety of beings, and enjoying the fame of their passed selves, make accumulation of glory unto their last durations. Others, rather than be lost in the uncomfortable night of nothing, were content to recede into the common being, and make one particle of the public soul of all things, which was no more than to return into their unknown and divine original again. Egyptian ingenuity was more unsatisfied, contriving their bodies in sweet consistencies,[5] to attend the return of their souls. But all was vanity, feeding the wind, and folly. The Egyptian mummies, which Cambyses or time hath spared, avarice now consumeth.[6] Mummy is become merchandise, Mizraim cures wounds, and Pharaoh is sold for balsams.

In vain do individuals hope for immortality, or any patent[7] from oblivion, in preservations below the moon; men have been deceived even in their flatteries above the sun, and studied conceits to perpetuate their names in heaven. The various cosmography of that part hath already varied the names of contrived constellations: Nimrod is lost in Orion, and Osiris in the Dog Star.[8] While we look for incorruption in the heavens, we find they are but like the earth, durable in their main bodies, alterable in their parts: whereof beside comets and new stars, perspectives[9] begin to tell tales, and the spots that wander about the sun, with Phaëthon's favor,[1] would make clear conviction.

There is nothing strictly immortal but immortality. Whatever hath no beginning may be confident of no end; all others have a dependent being and within the reach of destruction; which is the peculiar[2] of that necessary essence that cannot destroy itself; and the highest strain of omnipotency, to be so powerfully constituted as not to suffer even from the power of itself. But the sufficiency of Christian immortality frustrates all earthly glory, and the quality of either state after death makes a folly of posthumous memory. God, who can only[3] destroy our souls, and hath assured our resurrection, either of our bodies or names hath directly promised no duration. Wherein there is so much of chance that the boldest expectants have found unhappy frustration; and to hold long subsistence seems but a scape[4] in oblivion. But man is a noble animal, splendid in ashes and pompous in the grave, solemnizing nativities and deaths with equal luster, nor omitting ceremonies of bravery[5] in the infamy of his nature.

Life is a pure flame, and we live by an invisible sun within us. A small fire sufficeth for life, great flames seemed too little after death, while men vainly affected precious pyres, and to burn like Sardanapalus;[6] but the wisdom of

5. The reference is to embalming practices.
6. The story of Cambyses ravaging Egypt is told in Herodotus 3. Powdered mummy was sold in the 17th century as medicine (see Donne, *Love's Alchemy*, line 24, p. 1245). "Mizraim": i.e., Egypt; Mizraim was a son of Ham (Genesis 10.6–14).
7. Protection.
8. The names of the stars and constellations change—Osiris to Sirius, Nimrod to Orion.
9. Telescopes.
1. Phaëthon's foolish attempt to drive the chariot

of his father, the sun god Helios (Apollo), nearly set the world on fire. His erratic course suggests to Browne the wandering sunspots recently charted by astronomers.
2. Characteristic.
3. Who alone can.
4. Weak trick.
5. Splendor.
6. Sardanapalus burned up a palace full of eunuchs, concubines, and treasures as his funeral pyre.

funeral laws found the folly of prodigal blazes, and reduced undoing fires unto the rule of sober obsequies, wherein few could be so mean as not to provide wood, pitch, a mourner, and an urn.

Five languages secured not the epitaph of Gordianus.[7] The man of God[8] lives longer without a tomb than any by one, invisibly interred by angels, and adjudged to obscurity, though not without some marks directing human discovery. Enoch and Elias,[9] without either tomb or burial, in an anomalous state of being, are the great examples of perpetuity, in their long and living memory, in strict account being still on this side death, and having a late part yet to act upon this stage of earth. If in the decretory term of the world[1] we shall not all die but be changed, according to received translation, the last day will make but few graves; at least quick resurrections will anticipate lasting sepultures; some graves will be opened before they be quite closed, and Lazarus be no wonder.[2] When many that feared to die shall groan that they can die but once, the dismal state is the second and living death, when life puts despair on the damned; when men shall wish the coverings of mountains, not of monuments, and annihilations shall be courted.[3]

While some have studied monuments, others have studiously declined them; and some have been so vainly boisterous that they durst not acknowledge their graves, wherein Alaricus[4] seems most subtle, who had a river turned to hide his bones at the bottom. Even Sulla,[5] that thought himself safe in his urn, could not prevent revenging tongues, and stones thrown at his monument. Happy are they whom privacy makes innocent, who deal so with men in this world that they are not afraid to meet them in the next; who, when they die, make no commotion among the dead, and are not touched with that poetical taunt of Isaiah.[6]

Pyramids, arches, obelisks were but the irregularities of vainglory, and wild enormities of ancient magnanimity. But the most magnanimous resolution rests in the Christian religion, which trampleth upon pride, and sits on the neck of ambition, humbly pursuing that infallible perpetuity unto which all others must diminish their diameters, and be poorly seen in angles of contingency.[7]

Pious spirits who passed their days in raptures of futurity made little more of this world than the world that was before it, while they lay obscure in the chaos of pre-ordination and night of their fore-beings. And if any have been so happy as truly to understand Christian annihilation, ecstasy, exolution,[8] liquefaction, transformation, the kiss of the spouse, gustation of God, and ingression into the divine shadow, they have already had an handsome anticipation of heaven; the glory of the world is surely over, and the earth in ashes unto them.

To subsist in lasting monuments, to live in their productions, to exist in

7. The epitaph of this emperor of Rome (238–44), though written in five languages, was obliterated.
8. Moses (Deuteronomy 34).
9. Enoch and Elijah ("Elias") were translated straight to heaven (Genesis 5.24, 2 Kings 2.11); they are sometimes identified with the "witnesses" who are to return to earth in the last days (Revelation 11.5).
1. The decreed end of the world, the Last Judgment.
2. Lazarus, the dead man raised by Christ (John 11).

3. The damned souls will shriek for mountains to shield him from the wrath of God (Luke 23.30; Revelation 6.16).
4. Alaric, the Gothic invader, was buried in the bed of the river Busento (410 C.E.).
5. Roman politician and general, who died 78 B.C.E.
6. In Isaiah 14 the mighty ones of the earth are taunted with their approaching downfall into hell.
7. The smallest possible angle.
8. The loosening or freeing of the spirit.

their names and predicament of chimeras,[9] was large satisfaction unto old expectations, and made one part of their Elysiums.[1] But all this is nothing in the metaphysics of true belief. To live indeed is to be again ourselves, which being not only an hope but an evidence in noble believers, 'tis all one to lie in St. Innocent's churchyard, as in the sands of Egypt:[2] ready to be anything, in the ecstasy of being ever, and as content with six foot as the *moles* of Adrianus.[3]

—*Tabesne cadavera solvat,*
An rogus, haud refert.

—LUCAN

1658

9. In the condition of phantasms.
1. The pagan afterworld.
2. In Paris, where bodies soon consume, contrasted with the desert, where they last a long time.
3. Adrian's (Hadrian's) tomb, now Castel San

Angelo in Rome, the type of a magnificent mausoleum. The Latin tag is translated, "By the swift funeral pyre or slow decay / (No matter which) the bodies pass away" (Lucan, *Pharsalia* 7.809–10).

IZAAK WALTON

Walton's *Life of Donne*, first published in 1640 as a biographical introduction to Donne's collected sermons, was the most artistic and accurate English biography to date. Walton (1593–1683) drew on his personal knowledge of and friendship with Donne in his later years, talked with others who knew him, and looked over his poems, letters, and papers; but he enlivens his narrative with anecdotes that are often questionably accurate, and he quotes conversations that he could not have heard. While Walton made an effort to research his facts, his is not a scholarly biography, written in accord with the canons of evidence that have evolved since Walton's time. Rather, it is shaped by the great models of life-writing to which everyone in that age looked: Plutarch's *Lives*, portraying subjects as examples of virtue and vice; and hagiography or saints' lives exemplified by Augustine's autobiographical *Confessions* (ca. 400) and by Foxe's *Book of Martyrs*. The influence of hagiography on Walton is evident as he explicitly reads Donne's life against that of St. Augustine: rakish in youth and saintly in age. It is especially evident in the passage below, on Donne's remarkable preparations for death. It is no accident that this biography, published just as religious tensions were growing acute and Civil War loomed on the horizon, represented Donne as a "saint" of Anglicanism. The other lives Walton wrote—of George Herbert, Richard Hooker, Henry Wotton, and Bishop Robert Sanderson—presented them as exemplary Anglican worthies to the triumphant Anglican church after the Restoration.

A prosperous merchant in the clothing trade, Walton lived for several years in the parish of St. Dunstans in the West, where Donne was vicar. He was a staunch royalist, credited with smuggling one of Prince Charles's jewels out of the country, but his life was otherwise unremarkable, save for his wildly popular book on fishing, *The Compleat Angler* (1653). Written during the Cromwellian ascendancy, this series of dialogues between a fisherman and a hunter (and briefly a falconer) creates for Walton a fascinating surrogate self, Piscator, the angler. Setting the representative values of fishermen—moderation, peacefulness, generosity, thankfulness, contemplation— over against the contrasting values assigned to hunters and falconers, Walton makes "angling" stand in for the ceremonious, peaceful, ordered life of royalist Anglicans, now so violently disrupted. As a stylist Walton writes prose that is easy and colloquial but graceful and polished.

From The Life of Dr. John Donne[1]

[DONNE ON HIS DEATHBED]

It is observed that a desire of glory or commendation is rooted in the very nature of man; and that those of the severest and most mortified[2] lives, though they may become so humble as to banish self-flattery, and such weeds as naturally grow there; yet they have not been able to kill this desire of glory, but that like our radical heat,[3] it will both live and die with us; and many think it should do so; and we want not sacred examples to justify the desire of having our memory to outlive our lives; which I mention, because Dr. Donne, by the persuasion of Dr. Fox, easily yielded at this very time[4] to have a monument made for him; but Dr. Fox undertook not to persuade him how, or what monument it should be; that was left to Dr. Donne himself.

A monument being resolved upon, Dr. Donne sent for a carver to make for him in wood the figure of an urn, giving him directions for the compass and height of it; and to bring with it a board, of the just[5] height of his body. These being got, then without delay a choice painter was got to be in readiness to draw his picture, which was taken as followeth. Several charcoal fires being first made in his large study, he brought with him into that place his winding-sheet in his hand, and having put off all his clothes, had this sheet put on him, and so tied with knots at his head and feet, and his hands so placed, as dead bodies are usually fitted to be shrouded and put into their coffin or grave. Upon this urn he thus stood with his eyes shut and with so much of the sheet turned aside as might show his lean, pale, and deathlike face, which was purposely turned toward the east, from whence he expected the second coming of his and our Savior Jesus. In this posture he was drawn at his just height; and when the picture was fully finished, he caused it to be set by his bedside, where it continued and became his hourly object till his death, and was then given to his dearest friend and executor Dr. Henry King,[6] then chief residentiary of St. Paul's, who caused him to be thus carved in one entire piece of white marble, as it now stands in that church;[7] and by Dr. Donne's own appointment, these words were to be affixed to it as his epitaph:

JOHANNES DONNE
Sac. Theol. Profess.

Post varia studia quibus ab annis tenerrimis
fideliter, nec infeliciter incubuit,

1. See Donne's sermon, *Death's Duel* (p. 1280), preached on February 25, 1631; he died on March 31 and was buried in St. Paul's on April 3.
2. Self-denying.
3. Bodily warmth.
4. His physician, Dr. Simeon Fox.

5. Exact.
6. Poet, canon of St. Paul's ("residentiary"), and later bishop of Chichester. "Object": of meditation.
7. The statue on Donne's tomb, executed by the well-known sculptor Nicholas Stone, survived the great fire and may still be seen in St. Paul's.

> *instinctu et impulsu Sp. Sancti, monitu*
> *et hortatu*
>
> REGIS JACOBI, *ordines sacros*
> *amplexus, anno sui Jesu, 1614, et suae aetatis 42,*
> *decanatu huius ecclesiae indutus 27*
> *Novembris, 1621,*
>
> *exutus morte ultimo die Martii, 1631,*
> *hic licet in occiduo cinere aspicit eum*
> *cuius nomen est Oriens.*[8]

And now, having brought him through the many labyrinths and perplexities of a various life, even to the gates of death and the grave, my desire is he may rest till I have told my reader that I have seen many pictures of him in several habits and at several ages and in several postures; and I now mention this because I have seen one picture of him, drawn by a curious[9] hand, at his age of eighteen, with his sword and what other adornments might then suit with the present fashions of youth and the giddy gaieties of that age;[1] and his motto then was—

> How much shall I be changed,
> Before I am changed!

And if that young and his now dying picture were at this time set together, every beholder might say, "Lord! how much is Dr. Donne already changed, before he is changed!" And the view of them might give my reader occasion to ask himself with some amazement, "Lord! how much may I also, that am now in health, be changed before I am changed; before this vile, this changeable body shall put off mortality!" and therefore to prepare for it. But this is not writ so much for my reader's memento[2] as to tell him that Dr. Donne would often in his private discourses, and often publicly in his sermons, mention the many changes both of his body and mind; especially of his mind from a vertiginous giddiness; and would as often say, "his great and most blessed change was from a temporal to a spiritual employment"; in which he was so happy, that he accounted the former part of his life to be lost; and the beginning of it to be from his first entering into sacred orders and serving his most merciful God at his altar.

Upon Monday after the drawing this picture, he took his last leave of his beloved study; and being sensible of his hourly decay, retired himself to his bedchamber; and that week sent at several[3] times for many of his most considerable friends, with whom he took a solemn and deliberate farewell, commending to their considerations some sentences useful for the regulation of their lives; and then dismissed them, as good Jacob did his sons, with a

8. "John Donne, Professor of Sacred Theology. After various studies, which he plied from his tenderest youth faithfully and not unsuccessfully, moved by the instinct and impulse of the Holy Spirit and the admonition and encouragement of King James, he took holy orders in the year of his Jesus 1614 and the year of his age forty-two. On the 27th of November 1621, he was invested as dean of this church; and divested by death, the last day of March 1631. Here in the decline of ashes he looks to One whose name is a Rising Sun."
9. Skillful. "Habits": garbs.
1. The picture is reproduced as the frontispiece to the second edition (1635) of Donne's *Poems*. It bears the Spanish motto *Antes muerto que mudado* (rather dead than changed, i.e., constant until death), which Walton mistranslates below.
2. *Memento mori*, remembrance of death.
3. Separate.

spiritual benediction. The Sunday following, he appointed his servants, that if there were any business yet undone that concerned him or themselves, it should be prepared against Saturday next; for after that day he would not mix his thoughts with anything that concerned this world; nor ever did; but, as Job, so he "waited for the appointed day of his dissolution."[4]

And now he was so happy as to have nothing to do but to die, to do which he stood in need of no longer time; for he had studied it long and to so happy a perfection that in a former sickness he called God to witness, "he was that minute ready to deliver his soul into his hands, if that minute God would determine his dissolution."[5] In that sickness he begged of God the constancy to be preserved in that estate forever; and his patient expectation to have his immortal soul disrobed from her garment of mortality makes me confident he now had a modest assurance that his prayers were then heard and his petition granted. He lay fifteen days earnestly expecting his hourly change; and in the last hour of his last day, as his body melted away and vapored into spirit, his soul having, I verily believe, some revelation of the beatifical vision, he said, "I were miserable if I might not die"; and after those words, closed many periods of his faint breath by saying often, "Thy kingdom come, thy will be done." His speech, which had long been his ready and faithful servant, left him not till the last minute of his life, and then forsook him, not to serve another master (for who speaks like him), but died before him; for that it was then become useless to him that now conversed with God on earth as angels are said to do in heaven, only by thoughts and looks. Being speechless, and seeing heaven by that illumination by which he saw it, he did, as St. Stephen, "look steadfastly into it, till he saw the Son of Man standing at the right hand of God his Father";[6] and being satisfied with this blessed sight, as his soul ascended and his last breath departed from him, he closed his own eyes; and then disposed his hands and body into such a posture as required not the least alteration by those that came to shroud him.

Thus variable, thus virtuous was the life; thus excellent, thus exemplary was the death of this memorable man.

He was buried in that place of St. Paul's Church which he had appointed for that use some years before his death; and by which he passed daily to pay his public devotions to Almighty God (who was then served twice a day by a public form of prayer and praises in that place): but he was not buried privately, though he desired it; for, beside an unnumbered number of others, many persons of nobility, and of eminency for learning, who did love and honor him in his life, did show it at his death by a voluntary and sad attendance of his body to the grave, where nothing was so remarkable as a public sorrow.

To which place of his burial some mournful friends repaired, and, as Alexander the Great did to the grave of the famous Achilles,[7] so they strewed his with an abundance of curious and costly flowers; which course they (who were never yet known) continued morning and evening for many days, not ceasing till the stones that were taken up in that church to give his body admission into the cold earth (now his bed of rest) were again by the mason's

4. Job 14.14.
5. Walton paraphrases from Donne's *Devotions upon Emergent Occasions*, Prayer 23.
6. Acts 7.55.
7. Plutarch, "Alexander," sect. 15.

art so leveled and firmed as they had been formerly, and his place of burial undistinguishable to common view.

The next day after his burial, some unknown friend, some one of the many lovers and admirers of his virtue and learning, wrote this epitaph with a coal on the wall over his grave:

> Reader! I am to let thee know,
> Donne's body only lies below;
> For, could the grave his soul comprise,
> Earth would be richer than the skies!

Nor was this all the honor done to his reverend ashes; for, as there be some persons that will not receive a reward for that for which God accounts himself a debtor, persons that dare trust God with their charity and without a witness; so there was by some grateful unknown friend that thought Dr. Donne's memory ought to be perpetuated, an hundred marks sent to his two faithful friends and executors,[8] towards the making of his monument. It was not for many years known by whom; but after the death of Dr. Fox, it was known that it was he that sent it; and he lived to see as lively a representation of his dead friend as marble can express: a statue indeed so like Dr. Donne, that (as his friend Sir Henry Wotton hath expressed himself) "it seems to breathe faintly, and posterity shall look upon it as a kind of artificial miracle."

He was of stature moderately tall; of a straight and equally proportioned body, to which all his words and actions gave an unexpressible addition of comeliness.

The melancholy and pleasant humor were in him so contempered that each gave advantage to the other, and made his company one of the delights of mankind.

His fancy was unimitably high, equaled only by his great wit;[9] both being made useful by a commanding judgment.

His aspect was cheerful, and such as gave a silent testimony of a clear knowing soul, and of a conscience at peace with itself.

His melting eye showed that he had a soft heart, full of noble compassion; of too brave a soul to offer injuries and too much a Christian not to pardon them in others.

He did much contemplate (especially after he entered into his sacred calling) the mercies of Almighty God, the immortality of the soul, and the joys of heaven; and would often say, in a kind of sacred ecstasy, "Blessed be God that he is God, only and divinely like himself."

He was by nature highly passionate, but more apt to reluct at[1] the excesses of it. A great lover of the offices of humanity, and of so merciful a spirit that he never beheld the miseries of mankind without pity and relief.

He was earnest and unwearied in the search of knowledge, with which his vigorous soul is now satisfied, and employed in a continual praise of that God that first breathed it into his active body: that body, which once was a

---

8. Henry King and Dr. John Monfort.
9. Mental acuity. "Fancy": imagination.

1. Struggle, strive against.

temple of the Holy Ghost and is now become a small quantity of Christian dust:

But I shall see it reanimated.

Feb. 15, 1640   I.W.

1640, 1675

THOMAS HOBBES

Thomas Hobbes's masterwork *Leviathan* is the most important work of English political theory to appear up to that time (1651), notable especially for grounding its political vision upon a comprehensive philosophy of nature and of knowledge. A thoroughgoing materialist, Hobbes (1588–1679) held that everything in the universe, including God and the human mind, is composed only of matter; spirit does not exist. All knowledge is gained through sensory impressions, which (like mind itself) are nothing but matter in motion; and what we call the self is simply a tissue of sensory impressions—clear and immediate in the presence of the objects that evoke them, vague and less vivid in their absence. An iron determinism of cause and effect governs everything in the universe, including human action. Humans beings, Hobbes thought, seek self-preservation as a primary goal and seek power as the means to secure that goal. His politics springs directly from his dark vision of human nature: all humans have sufficient equality of physical and mental powers to have equal hopes of goods and equal fears of danger from others, so that in the state of nature, before the foundation of some sovereign power to keep them all in awe, they exist in a continual state of war—the war of every man against every man in which life, in Hobbes's memorable phrase, is "solitary, poor, nasty, brutish, and short." To escape this condition, humans covenant with each other to establish an absolute sovereign government over all of them: that sovereign power (which need not be a king, but is always indivisible) then incorporates the wills and persons of them all, so they no longer have wills or rights or liberties apart from the sovereign's will; it is the sovereign's right also to pronounce on all matters of religion and doctrine. The four parts of Hobbes's long treatise deal, respectively, with the nature of human beings, the creation of the state, the proper subordination of the church to the sovereign power of the state, and what Hobbes labels the "kingdom of darkness" (the Roman Catholic Church).

In Hobbes's system, the founding political covenant, once made, cannot be revoked; revolution or resistance to the sovereign for any reason is absurd, since no tyranny can be so evil as the state of war the sovereign power prevents. But if he should be overthrown, the individual sovereign has no further claim, and people, for their safety, must accept the new sovereign power unconditionally. While Hobbes was generally associated with the royalist cause—as a tutor in the Cavendish family and as an exile in Paris from 1640 to 1651 where he tutored the future Charles II—his argument disturbed royalists since it made no real distinction between a legitimate monarch and a successful usurper (like Cromwell). It scandalized Puritans by its materialism, rationalism, and secularism (Hobbes was falsely denounced as an atheist), and by its argument for an absolutism that cannot be modified or qualified, even on religious grounds. Other versions of covenant theory, developed by the various parties who carried out the revolution and the regicide, insisted that the power transferred by the people to the sovereign could be limited or revoked. An example is Milton's *Tenure of Kings and Magistrates.*

While in Paris and after, Hobbes studied mathematics, especially geometry, and published a number of other works (in Latin and English) on physics, psychology, and politics. Like Bacon, he also concerned himself with the slipperiness of language, especially figurative language, which, to his thinking, clouds or perverts truth; he recommended clear definitions and the removal of all ambiguities. After the Restoration, he wrote a history of the causes of the civil wars in England entitled *Behemoth* (1679).

From Leviathan[1]

From *The Introduction*

[THE ARTIFICIAL MAN]

Nature (the art whereby God hath made and governs the world) is by the art of man, as in many other things, so in this also imitated, that it can make an artificial[2] animal. For seeing life is but a motion of limbs, the beginning whereof is in some principal part within, why may we not say that all automata (engines that move themselves by springs and wheels as doth a watch) have an artificial life?[3] For what is the heart but a spring; and the nerves but so many strings; and the joints but so many wheels, giving motion to the whole body such as was intended by the artificer? Art goes yet further, imitating that rational and most excellent work of nature, man. For by art is created that great Leviathan called a Common-Wealth or State (in Latin, *Civitas*), which is but an artificial man, though of greater stature and strength than the natural, for whose protection and defense it was intended; and in which the sovereignty is an artificial soul, as giving life and motion to the whole body; the magistrates and other officers of judicature and execution, artificial joints; reward and punishment (by which, fastened to the seat of the sovereignty, every joint and member is moved to perform his duty) are the nerves, that do the same in the body natural; the wealth and riches of all the particular members are the strength; *salus populi* (the people's safety) its business; counselors, by whom all things needful for it to know are suggested unto it, are the memory; equity and laws an artificial reason and will; concord, health; sedition, sickness; and civil war, death. Lastly, the pacts and covenants by which the parts of this body politic were at first made, set together, and united, resemble that *Fiat* or the "let us make man," pronounced by God in the creation.[4]

* * *

1. The title refers to the primordial sea creature Leviathan, described in Job 41 as the prime evidence of and analogue to God's power, beyond all human measure and comprehension. Hobbes takes him as figure for the sovereign power in the state. Leviathan was also sometimes taken as a figure for Satan, on the basis of Job 41.33: "He is a

king over all the children of pride."
2. Made by art.
3. Hobbes's definition of life as motion collapses the distinction between the life of humans and the life of machines or institutions.
4. Genesis 1.26.

From *Part 1*

CHAPTER 1. OF SENSE

Concerning the thoughts of man, I will consider them first singly and afterwards in train or dependence upon one another. Singly, they are every one a representation or appearance of some quality or other accident of a body without us, which is commonly called an object. Which object worketh on the eyes, ears, and other parts of man's body, and by diversity of working produceth diversity of appearances.

The original of them all is that which we call sense. (For there is no conception in a man's mind which hath not at first, totally or by parts, been begotten upon the organs of sense.)[5] The rest are derived from that original.

To know the natural cause of sense is not very necessary to the business now in hand, and I have elsewhere written of the same at large. Nevertheless, to fill each part of my present method, I will briefly deliver the same in this place.

The cause of sense is the external body or object which presseth the organ proper to each sense, either immediately as in the taste and touch, or mediately, as in seeing, hearing, and smelling; which pressure, by the mediation of nerves and other strings and membranes of the body continued inwards to the brain and heart, causeth there a resistance or counter-pressure or endeavor of the heart to deliver itself;[6] which endeavor, because outward, seemeth to be some matter without. And this seeming or fancy is that which men call sense; and consisteth, as to the eye, in a light or color figured; to the ear, in a sound; to the nostril in an odor; to the tongue and palate in a savor; and to the rest of the body in heat, cold, hardness, softness, and such other qualities as we discern by feeling. All which qualities called "sensible"[7] are, in the object that causeth them, but so many several motions of the matter by which it presseth our organs diversely. Neither, in us that are pressed, are they anything else but diverse motions; for motion produceth nothing but motion. But their appearance to us is fancy, the same waking, that dreaming. And as pressing, rubbing, or striking the eye makes us fancy a light; and pressing the ear produceth a din; so do the bodies also we see or hear produce the same by their strong though unobserved actions. For if those colors and sounds were in the bodies or objects that cause them, they could not be severed from them, as by glasses[8] and in echoes by reflection we see they are; where we know the thing we see is in one place, the appearance in another. And though at some certain distance the real and very object seem invested with the fancy it begets in us, yet still the object is one thing, the image or fancy is another. So that sense in all cases is nothing else but original fancy, caused (as I have said) by the pressure, that is by the motion, of external things upon our eyes, ears, and other organs thereunto ordained.

But the philosophy-schools[9] through all the universities of Christendom, grounded upon certain texts of Aristotle, teach another doctrine, and say for the cause of vision, that the thing seen sendeth forth on every side a visible

5. This view of the mind as a blank sheet written on by physical experience leaves no room for the influence of genetic inheritance.
6. Hobbes's physiology of sense is, in keeping with his premises, strictly mechanical.
7. I.e., accessible through the senses.
8. Mirrors.
9. The Scholastic philosophers (Schoolmen).

species—in English, a visible show, apparition, or aspect, or a being seen—the receiving whereof into the eye is seeing. And for the cause of hearing, that the thing heard sendeth forth an audible species, that is an audible aspect or audible being seen, which entering at the ear maketh hearing. Nay for the cause of understanding also they say the thing understood sendeth forth intelligible species, that is an intelligible being seen, which coming into the understanding makes us understand. I say not this as disapproving the use of universities, but because I am to speak hereafter of their office in a commonwealth, I must let you see on all occasions by the way what things would be amended in them; amongst which the frequency of insignificant[1] speech is one.

CHAPTER 13. OF THE NATURAL CONDITION OF MANKIND AS CONCERNING THEIR FELICITY AND MISERY

Nature hath made men so equal in the faculties of body and mind as that, though there be found one man sometimes manifestly stronger in body or of quicker mind than another, yet when all is reckoned together, the difference between man and man is not so considerable as that one man can thereupon claim to himself any benefit, to which another may not pretend as well as he. For as to the strength of body, the weakest has strength enough to kill the strongest, either by secret machination, or by confederacy[2] with others that are in the same danger with himself.

And as to the faculties of the mind—setting aside the arts grounded upon words, and especially that skill of proceeding upon general and infallible rules, called science; which very few have, and but in few things; as being not a native faculty, born with us; nor attained, as prudence, while we look after somewhat else—I find yet a greater equality amongst men than that of strength. For prudence is but experience, which equal time equally bestows on all men, in those things they equally apply themselves unto. That which may perhaps make such equality incredible is but a vain conceit of one's own wisdom, which almost all men think they have in a greater degree than the vulgar—that is, than all men but themselves and a few others, whom by fame, or for concurring with themselves, they approve. For such is the nature of men, that howsoever they may acknowledge many others to be more witty, or more eloquent, or more learned, yet they will hardly believe there be many so wise as themselves; for they see their own wit at hand, and other men's at a distance. But this proveth rather that men are in that point equal, than unequal. For there is not ordinarily a greater sign of the equal distribution of anything than that every man is contented with his share.

From this equality of ability ariseth equality of hope in the attaining of our ends. And therefore if any two men desire the same thing, which nevertheless they cannot both enjoy, they become enemies; and in the way to their end (which is principally their own conservation, and sometimes their delectation[3] only) endeavor to destroy or subdue one another. And from hence it comes to pass, that where an invader hath no more to fear than another man's single power, if one plant, sow, build, or possess a convenient seat, others may probably be expected to come prepared with forces united,

1. Unmeaningful speech.
2. Alliance.
3. Pleasure.

to dispossess and deprive him, not only of the fruit of his labor, but also of his life or liberty. And the invader again is in the like danger of another.

And from this diffidence[4] of one another, there is no way for any man to secure himself so reasonable as anticipation; that is, by force or wiles to master the persons of all men he can, so long, till he see no other power great enough to endanger him; and this is no more than his own conservation requireth, and is generally allowed. Also because there be some, that taking pleasure in contemplating their own power in the acts of conquest, which they pursue farther than their security requires; if others that otherwise would be glad to be at ease within modest bounds, should not by invasion increase their power, they would not be able long time, by standing only on their defense, to subsist. And by consequence, such augmentation of dominion over men being necessary to a man's conservation, it ought to be allowed him.

Again, men have no pleasure, but on the contrary a great deal of grief, in keeping company, where there is no power able to overawe them all. For every man looketh that his companion should value him at the same rate he sets upon himself; and upon all signs of contempt, or undervaluing, naturally endeavors, as far as he dares (which amongst them that have no common power to keep them in quiet, is far enough to make them destroy each other), to extort a greater value from his contemners[5] by damage, and from others by the example.

So that in the nature of man, we find three principal causes of quarrel. First, competition; secondly, diffidence; thirdly, glory.

The first maketh men invade for gain; the second, for safety; and the third, for reputation. The first use violence to make themselves masters of other men's persons, wives, children, and cattle; the second, to defend them; the third, for trifles, as a word, a smile, a different opinion, and any other sign of undervalue, either direct in their persons, or by reflection in their kindred, their friends, their nation, their profession, or their name.

Hereby it is manifest that during the time men live without a common power to keep them all in awe, they are in that condition which is called war; and such a war as is of every man against every man. For war consisteth not in battle only, or the act of fighting, but in a tract of time wherein the will to contend by battle is sufficiently known; and therefore the notion of time is to be considered in the nature of war, as it is in the nature of weather. For as the nature of foul weather lieth not in a shower or two of rain, but in an inclination thereto of many days together; so the nature of war consisteth not in actual fighting, but in the known disposition thereto, during all the time there is no assurance to the contrary. All other time is peace.

Whatsoever therefore is consequent to a time of war, where every man is enemy to every man, the same is consequent to the time wherein men live without other security than what their own strength and their own invention shall furnish them withal. In such condition there is no place for industry, because the fruit thereof is uncertain, and consequently no culture of the earth; no navigation, nor use of the commodities that may be imported by sea; no commodious building; no instruments of moving, and removing, such things as require much force; no knowledge of the face of the earth; no

---

4. Lack of faith, mistrust.   5. Scorners.

account of time; no arts; no letters; no society; and, which is worst of all, continual fear, and danger of violent death; and the life of man, solitary, poor, nasty, brutish, and short.

It may seem strange to some man that has not well weighed these things, that nature should thus dissociate and render men apt to invade and destroy one another; and he may therefore, not trusting to this inference, made from the passions, desire perhaps to have the same confirmed by experience. Let him therefore consider with himself, when taking a journey, he arms himself and seeks to go well accompanied; when going to sleep, he locks his doors; when even in his house he locks his chests; and this when he knows there be laws, and public officers, armed, to revenge all injuries shall be done him; what opinion he has of his fellow subjects, when he rides armed; of his fellow citizens, when he locks his doors; and of his children and servants, when he locks his chests. Does he not there as much accuse mankind by his actions, as I do by my words? But neither of us accuse man's nature in it. The desires and other passions of man are in themselves no sin. No more are the actions that proceed from those passions, till they know a law that forbids them, which, till laws be made, they cannot know; nor can any law be made, till they have agreed upon the person that shall make it.

It may peradventure be thought there was never such a time nor condition of war as this; and I believe it was never generally so, over all the world; but there are many places where they live so now. For the savage people in many places of America, except the government of small families, the concord whereof dependeth on natural lust, have no government at all and live at this day in that brutish manner as I said before. Howsoever, it may be perceived what manner of life there would be, where there were no common power to fear, by the manner of life which men that have formerly lived under a peaceful government use to degenerate into in a civil war.[6]

But though there had never been any time wherein particular men were in a condition of war one against another, yet in all times, kings and persons of sovereign authority, because of their independency, are in continual jealousies, and in the state and posture of gladiators; having their weapons pointing, and their eyes fixed on one another; that is, their forts, garrisons, and guns upon the frontiers of their kingdoms, and continual spies upon their neighbors, which is a posture of war. But because they uphold thereby the industry of their subjects, there does not follow from it that misery which accompanies the liberty of particular men.

To this war of every man against every man, this also is consequent: that nothing can be unjust. The notions of right and wrong, justice and injustice, have there no place. Where there is no common power, there is no law; where no law, no injustice. Force and fraud are in war the two cardinal virtues. Justice and injustice are none of the faculties neither of the body nor mind. If they were, they might be in a man that were alone in the world, as well as his senses and passions. They are qualities that relate to men in society, not in solitude. It is consequent also to the same condition that there be no propriety,[7] no dominion, no *mine* and *thine* distinct; but only that to be every man's, that he can get; and for so long as he can keep it. And thus

---

6. Hobbes is thinking of the recent civil wars in England, and perhaps also of the Greek civil wars described by Thucydides (whom he translated).
7. Property.

much for the ill condition which man by mere nature is actually placed in; though with a possibility to come out of it, consisting partly in the passions, partly in his reason.

The passions that incline men to peace are fear of death, desire of such things as are necessary to commodious living, and a hope by their industry to obtain them. And reason suggesteth convenient articles of peace, upon which men may be drawn to agreement. These articles are they which otherwise are called the Laws of Nature, whereof I shall speak more particularly in the two following chapters.

FROM CHAPTER 14. OF THE FIRST AND SECOND NATURAL LAWS

The Right of Nature, which writers commonly call *ius naturale,* is the liberty each man hath to use his own power as he will himself for the preservation of his own nature, that is to say, of his own life; and consequently of doing anything which in his own judgment and reason he shall conceive to be the aptest means thereunto.

By Liberty is understood, according to the proper signification of the word, the absence of external impediments, which impediments may oft take away part of a man's power to do what he would, but cannot hinder him from using the power left him according as his judgment and reason shall dictate to him.

A Law of Nature *(lex naturalis)* is a precept or general rule found out by reason, by which a man is forbidden to do that which is destructive of his life or taketh away the means of preserving the same; and to omit that by which he thinketh it may be best preserved. For though they that speak of this subject use to confound[8] *Ius* and *Lex, Right* and *Law,* yet they ought to be distinguished, because Right consisteth in liberty to do or to forbear, whereas Law determineth and bindeth to one of them: so that Law and Right differ as much as obligation and liberty, which in one and the same matter are inconsistent.

And because the condition of man (as hath been declared in the precedent chapter) is a condition of war of every one against every one, in which case every one is governed by his own reason, and there is nothing he can make use of that may not be a help unto him in preserving his life against his enemies: it followeth that in such a condition every man has a right to every thing, even to one another's body. And therefore as long as this natural right of every man to every thing endureth, there can be no security to any man (how strong or wise soever he be) of living out the time which nature ordinarily alloweth men to live. And consequently it is a precept or general rule of reason, *That every man ought to endeavor peace, as far as he has hope of obtaining it; and when he cannot obtain it, that he may seek and use all helps and advantages of war.* The first branch of which rule containeth the first and fundamental law of nature, which is *to seek peace and follow it.* The second, the sum of the right of nature, which is, *by all means we can to defend ourselves.*

From this fundamental law of nature, by which men are commanded to endeavor peace, is derived this second law: *That a man be willing, when others are so too, as far-forth as*[9] *for peace and defense of himself he shall think*

8. Confuse.   9. Insofar as.

*it necessary, to lay down this right to all things, and be contented with so much
liberty against other men as he would allow other men against himself.* For as
long as any man holdeth this right of doing anything he liketh, so long are
all men in the condition of war. But if other men will not lay down their
right, as well as he, then there is no reason for anyone to divest himself of
his. For that were to expose himself to prey (which no man is bound to)
rather than to dispose himself to peace. This is that law of the Gospel: *Whatsoever you require that others should do to you, that do ye to them.*[1]

FROM CHAPTER 15. OF OTHER LAWS OF NATURE

From that law of nature by which we are obliged to transfer to another
such rights as, being retained, hinder the peace of mankind, there followeth
a third, which is this: *That men perform their covenants made:*[2] without
which, covenants are in vain, and but empty words; and, the right of all men
to all things remaining, we are still in the condition of war.

And in this law of nature consisteth the fountain and original of Justice.
For where no covenant hath preceded, there hath no right been transferred,
and every man has right to every thing; and consequently no action can be
unjust. But when a covenant is made, then to break it is unjust; and the
definition of injustice is no other than *the not performance of covenant.* And
whatsoever is not unjust is just.* * *

For the question is not of promises mutual where there is no security of
performance on either side, as when there is no civil power erected over the
parties promising; for such promises are no covenants. But either where one
of the parties has performed already, or where there is a power to make him
perform: there is the question whether it be against reason, that is against
the benefit of the other, to perform or not. And I say it is not against reason.[3]
For the manifestation whereof, we are to consider: first, that when a man
doth a thing which (notwithstanding anything can be foreseen and reckoned
on) tendeth to his own destruction, howsoever[4] some accident, which he
could not expect, arriving may turn it to his benefit; yet such events do not
make it reasonably or wisely done. Secondly, that in a condition of war,
wherein every man to every man, for want of a common power to keep them
all in awe, is an enemy, there is no man can hope by his own strength or wit
to defend himself from destruction without the help of confederates; where
everyone expects the same defense by the confederation that anyone else
does. And therefore he which declares he thinks it reason to deceive those
that help him can in reason expect no other means of safety than what can
be had from his own single power. He therefore that breaketh his covenant,
and consequently declareth that he thinks he may with reason do so, cannot
be received into any society that unite themselves for peace and defense, but
by the error of them that receive him; nor when he is received be retained
in it without seeing the danger of their error; which errors a man cannot
reasonably reckon upon as the means of his security. And therefore if he be

---

1. The Golden Rule: Matthew 7.12, Luke 6.31.
2. Though the terms are general, Hobbes refers in
this chapter especially to the covenants men make
with each other when they transfer power to the
sovereign. Milton makes very different use of cov-

enant theory to justify the rebellion and regicide in
The Tenure of Kings and Magistrates.
3. I.e., to perform the promise.
4. Even though.

left or cast out of society, he perisheth; and if he live in society, it is by the errors of other men, which he could not foresee nor reckon upon; and consequently against the reason of his preservation; and so as all men that contribute not to his destruction forbear him only out of ignorance of what is good for themselves.

As for the instance of gaining the secure and perpetual felicity of heaven by any way, it is frivolous: there being but one way imaginable, and that is not breaking, but keeping of covenant.

And for the other instance of attaining sovereignty by rebellion, it is manifest that though the event follow, yet because it cannot reasonably be expected, but rather the contrary; and because by gaining it so others are taught to gain the same in like manner, the attempt thereof is against reason. Justice therefore, that is to say, keeping of covenant, is a rule of reason, by which we are forbidden to do anything destructive to our life, and consequently a law of nature.

*   *   *

1651

GEORGE HERBERT
1593–1633

Unlike the learned and witty style of the work of his friend John Donne, Herbert's style in his single volume of religious poetry, *The Temple*, is deceptively simple, marked by ease and grace. But it is also marked by self-irony, a remarkable intellectual and emotional range, and a highly conscious artistry that is evident in the poems' tight construction, exact diction, perfect control of tone, and great variety of stanzaic forms and rhythmic patterns. As well, these poems reflect Herbert's struggle to define his relationship to God through biblical metaphors that are also invested with the tensions and anxieties those relationships held in his own society: king and subject, lord and courtier, master and servant, father and child, bridegroom and bride, friend to friend of inferior status. None of Herbert's secular English poems survives, so his reputation rests on this single volume, published posthumously. *The Temple* contains a long prefatory poem, *The Church-Porch*, and a long concluding poem, *Church Militant*, which together enclose a collection of 177 short lyrics entitled *The Church*, among which are sonnets, songs, hymns, laments, meditative poems, dialogue poems, acrostic poems, emblematic poems, and more. Herbert's own description of the collection is apt: "a picture of the many spiritual conflicts that have passed between God and my soul." Izaak Walton reports that Herbert gave the manuscript to his friend Nicholas Farrar, head of a quasi-monastic community at Little Gidding, with instructions to publish it if he thought it would "turn to the advantage of any dejected poor soul" and otherwise to burn it. Fortunately, Farrar chose to publish, and *The Temple* became the major influence on the religious lyric poets of the Caroline age: Henry Vaughan, Richard Crashaw, Thomas Traherne, and even Edward Taylor, the American colonial poet.

The fifth son of an eminent Welsh family, Herbert's upbringing and that of his nine siblings was carefully monitored by his mother, Magdalen Herbert, patron and friend of Donne and several other scholars and poets. Herbert was educated at Westminster School and at Trinity College, Cambridge, where he subsequently held a fellowship and wrote Latin poetry: elegies on the death of Prince Henry (1612), witty epigrams, poems on Christ's passion and death, and poems defending the rites of the English Church. In 1620 he was appointed "public orator," the official spokesman and correspondent for the university; this was a step toward a career at court or in public service, as was his election as Member of Parliament from Montgomery in 1624. But that route was closed off by the death of influential patrons and the change of monarchs. Like Donne, Herbert hesitated for some years before being ordained, but in 1630 he took up pastoral duties in the small country parish at Bemerton in Wiltshire. Whereas Donne preached to monarchs and statesmen, Herbert ministered to a few cottagers and none of his sermons survive. His small book on the duties of his new life, *A Priest to the Temple; or, The Country Parson*, testifies to the earnestness and joy (but also to the aristocratic uneasiness) with which he embraced that role. In chronic bad health he lived only three more years—performing pastoral duties assiduously, writing and revising his poems, playing music, and listening to organ and choir at nearby Salisbury cathedral.

Herbert locates himself in the church through many poems that treat church liturgy, architecture, and art—e.g., *Church Monuments* and *The Windows*—but his primary emphasis is always on the soul's inner architecture. Unlike Donne's poems, Herbert's poems do not voice anxious fears about his salvation or about his desperate sins and helplessness; his anxieties center rather on his relationship with Christ, most often represented as that of friend with friend. Many poems register the speaker's distress over the vacillations and regressions in this relationship, over his lack of "fruition" in God's service, and over the instability in his own nature, purposes, and temperament. In several dialogic poems the speaker's difficulties and anxieties are alleviated or resolved by the voice of a divine friend heard within or recalled through a scripture text (as in *The Collar*). In poem after poem he resists but has to come to terms with the fact that his relationship with Christ is always radically unequal, that Christ must both initiate it and make possible his own response. He struggles constantly with the paradox that, as the works of a Christian poet, his poems ought to give fit and sincere praise to God but that they cannot possibly do so—an issue explored in *The Altar*, the two *Jordan* poems, *Easter*, *The Forerunners*, and many more.

His recourse is to develop a biblical poetics that renounces conventional poetic styles—"fiction and false hair"—so as to depend on God's "art" wrought in his own soul and displayed in the language, metaphors, and symbolism of the Bible. He makes scant use of Donnean learned imagery drawn from such areas as cosmology or medicine or Scholastic philosophy, but his allusions carry profound significances. A biblical metaphor provides the unifying motif for the volume: the New Testament temple in the human heart (1 Corinthians 3.16). Another recurring biblical metaphor represents the Christian as plant or tree or flower in God's garden, needing pruning, rain, and nurture. Many poems are related to religious emblems: shaped poems like *The Altar* that present image and picture at once, or others like *Life* that might stand as commentaries on an emblem, here, a posy. Other poems allude to typological symbolism, which reads persons and events in the Old Testament as types or foreshadowings of Christ, the fulfillment or antitype; often, as in *The Bunch of Grapes*, Herbert locates both type and antitype in the speaker's soul.

FROM *THE TEMPLE*[1]

The Altar[2]

A broken A L T A R , Lord, thy servant rears,
Made of a heart, and cemented with tears:
  Whose parts are as thy hand did frame;
  No workman's tool hath touched the same.[3]
5   A   H E A R T   alone
              Is   such   a   stone,
              As   nothing   but
              Thy power doth cut.
              Wherefore each part
10   Of   my hard heart
              Meets in this frame,
              To praise thy Name:
That, if I chance to hold my peace,
These stones to praise thee may not cease.[4]
15 Oh let thy blessed S A C R I F I C E be mine,
And   sanctify   this   A L T A R   to   be   thine.

Redemption[1]

Having been tenant long to a rich lord,
  Not thriving, I resolvèd to be bold,
And make a suit unto him, to afford
  A new small-rented lease, and cancel th' old.[2]

5 In heaven at his manor I him sought:
  They told me there that he was lately gone
About some land which he had dearly bought
  Long since on earth, to take possession.

I straight returned, and knowing his great birth,
10   Sought him accordingly in great resorts—
In cities, theaters, gardens, parks, and courts:
  At length I heard a ragged noise and mirth

Of thieves and murderers; there I him espied,
Who straight, "Your suit is granted," said, and died.

---

1. The title of Herbert's volume sets his poems in relation to David's Psalms for the Temple at Jerusalem; his are new covenant "psalms" for the New Testament temple in the heart. All of the following poems come from this volume, published in 1633.
2. A variety of emblem poem. Emblems customarily have three parts: a picture, a motto, and a poem. This kind collapses picture and poem into one, presenting the emblem image by its very shape. Shaped poems have been used by the occasional author from Hellenistic times to Dylan Thomas.
3. A reference to Exodus 20.25, in which the Lord enjoins Moses to build an altar of uncut stones,
not touched by any tool, and also to Psalm 51.7: "A broken and the contrite heart, O God, thou wilt not despise."
4. A reference to Luke 19.40: "I tell you that, if these should hold their peace, the stones would immediately cry out." Herbert's poems obtain much of their resonance from the biblical echoes they incorporate.
1. Literally, "buying back." In this beautifully concise sonnet Herbert figures God as a landlord, himself as a discontented tenant.
2. I.e., to ask him for a new lease, with a smaller rent; the figure points to the New Testament supplanting the Old.

Easter[1]

Rise, heart, thy lord is risen. Sing his praise
   Without delays,
Who takes thee by the hand, that thou likewise
   With him may'st rise;
5 That, as his death calcinèd[2] thee to dust,
His life may make thee gold, and, much more, just.

Awake, my lute, and struggle for thy part
   With all thy art.
The cross taught all wood to resound his name
10   Who bore the same.
His stretchèd sinews taught all strings what key
Is best to celebrate this most high day.

Consort, both heart and lute, and twist[3] a song
   Pleasant and long;
15 Or, since all music is but three parts vied[4]
   And multiplied,
Oh let thy blessèd spirit bear a part,
And make up our defects with his sweet art.

The Song

  I got me flowers to straw° thy way,[5]   *strew*
20 I got me boughs off many a tree;
  But thou wast up by break of day
  And brought'st thy sweets along with thee.

  The sun arising in the east,
  Though he give light and th' east perfume,
25 If they should offer to contest
  With thy arising, they presume.

  Can there be any day but this,
  Though many suns to shine endeavor?
  We count three hundred, but we miss:°   *misunderstand*
30 There is but one, and that one ever.

---

1. The first three stanzas work out the poetics of writing hymns; then comes the hymn itself.
2. Burnt to powder.
3. Weave. "Consort": harmonize.

4. Increased by repetition. Harmony is based on the triad, the chord.
5. Evokes the scene of Christ's entry into Jerusalem (Matthew 21.8).

Easter Wings[1]

creation Lord, who createdst man in wealth and store,°   *abundance*
the fall Though foolishly he lost the same,
    things became worse Decaying more and more
      Till he became   *genesis*
5 *(Noah, Babble)* *waiting for a messiah* Most poor:
        With thee
          O let me rise
Jesus As larks, harmoniously,
    And sing this day thy victories:
10 Then shall the fall further the flight in me.[2] *fortunate fall.*

    My tender age in sorrow did begin: *now it is*
    And still with sicknesses and shame   *personal*
      Thou didst so punish sin,
        That I became *(I was weak, unhealthy)*
15   Most thin.
        With thee
      Let me combine,
    And feel this day thy victory;
  For, if I imp[3] my wing on thine,
20 Affliction shall advance the flight in me. *on to Jesus' wing, he can't do it by himself, he needs the wing of Jesus*

Affliction (1)[1]

When first thou didst entice to thee my heart,
    I thought the service brave:°   *splendid*
So many joys I writ down for my part,
    Besides what I might have
5 Out of my stock of natural delights,
Augmented with thy gracious benefits.

I lookèd on thy furniture so fine,
    And made it fine to me;
Thy glorious household stuff did me entwine,
10   And 'tice° me unto thee.   *entice*
Such stars I counted mine: both heaven and earth
Paid me my wages in a world of mirth.

What pleasures could I want,° whose king I served,   *lack*
    Where joys my fellows were?
15 Thus argued into hopes, my thoughts reserved
    No place for grief or fear;
Therefore my sudden soul caught at the place,
And made her youth and fierceness seek thy face.

1. Another emblem poem whose shape presents the emblem picture; the lines, increasing and decreasing, imitate flight, and also the spiritual experience of falling and rising. Early editions printed the poem with the lines running vertically, making the wing shape more apparent.

2. The idea of the "Fortunate Fall," which brought humankind so great a redeemer.
3. In falconry, to insert feathers in a bird's wing.
1. Herbert sometimes uses the same title for several poems, thereby associating them; editors distinguish them by adding numbers.

At first thou gav'st me milk and sweetnesses;
20   I had my wish and way:
My days were strawed° with flowers and happiness;   *strewn*
        There was no month but May.
But with my years sorrow did twist and grow,
And made a party unawares° for woe.   *unwittingly*

25 My flesh began unto² my soul in pain,
        Sicknesses cleave° my bones;   *penetrate*
Consuming agues° dwell in every vein,   *fevers with convulsions*
        And tune my breath to groans.
Sorrow was all my soul; I scarce believed,
30 Till grief did tell me roundly, that I lived.

When I got health, thou took'st away my life,
        And more; for my friends die:
My mirth and edge was lost: a blunted knife
        Was of more use than I.
35 Thus thin and lean without a fence or friend,
I was blown through with every storm and wind.

Whereas my birth and spirit rather took
        The way that takes the town,
Thou didst betray me to a lingering book,
40   And wrap me in a gown.³
I was entangled in the world of strife,
Before I had the power to change my life.

Yet, for I threatened oft the siege to raise,
        Not simpering all mine age,
45 Thou often didst with academic praise
        Melt and dissolve my rage.
I took thy sweetened pill, till I came where
I could not go away, nor persevere.

Yet lest perchance I should too happy be
50   In my unhappiness,
Turning my purge° to food, thou throwest me   *laxative*
        Into more sicknesses.
Thus doth thy power cross-bias° me, not making   *turn me from my aim*
Thine own gift good, yet me from my ways taking.

55 Now I am here, what thou wilt do with me
        None of my books will show:
I read, and sigh, and wish I were a tree,
        For sure then I should grow
To fruit or shade; at least, some bird would trust
60 Her household to me, and I should be just.

Yet, though thou troublest me, I must be meek;
        In weakness must be stout.

---

2. Complained to.   3. Cleric's garb.

Well, I will change the service, and go seek
      Some other master out.
65 Ah, my dear God! though I am clean forgot,
Let me not love thee, if I love thee not.

Prayer (1)[1]

Prayer, the church's banquet; angels' age,
    God's breath in man returning to his birth;
The soul in paraphrase,° heart in pilgrimage;   *clarifying by expansion*
    The Christian plummet,[2] sounding heaven and earth;

5 Engine against th' Almighty, sinner's tower,
    Reversèd thunder, Christ-side-piercing spear,
The six-days' world transposing[3] in an hour;
    A kind of tune which all things hear and fear:

Softness and peace and joy and love and bliss;
10   Exalted manna,[4] gladness of the best;
Heaven in ordinary,[5] man well dressed,
The milky way, the bird of paradise,

    Church bells beyond the stars heard, the soul's blood,
    The land of spices; something understood.

Jordan (1)[1]

Who says that fictions only and false hair
Become a verse? Is there in truth no beauty?
Is all good structure in a winding stair?
May no lines pass, except they do their duty°   *pay reverence to*
5   Not to a true, but painted chair?[2]

Is it no verse, except enchanted groves
And sudden arbors shadow coarse-spun lines?[3]
Must purling° streams refresh a lover's loves?   *rippling*
Must all be veiled,[4] while he that reads, divines,
10   Catching the sense at two removes?

Shepherds[5] are honest people: let them sing;
Riddle who list,° for me, and pull for prime:[6]   *wishes*

1. This extraordinary sonnet is a series of epithets without a verb, defining prayer by metaphor.
2. A weight used to measure (sound) the depth of water.
3. A musical term indicating sounds produced at another pitch from the original.
4. The food God supplied to the Israelites in the wilderness.
5. I.e., "everyday heaven."
1. The river Jordan, which the Israelites crossed to enter the promised land, was also taken as a symbol for baptism.

2. It was the custom for men to bow before a throne, whether it was occupied or not (see Donne, *Satire* 3, lines 47–48, p. 1257), but to require bowing before a throne in a painting would be ridiculous.
3. "Sudden,' i.e., that appear unexpectedly (an artificial effect much sought after in landscape gardening). "Shadow": shade.
4. As in allegory.
5. Conventional pastoral poets.
6. To draw a lucky card in the game of primero. "For me": as far as I am concerned.

I envy no man's nightingale or spring;
Nor let them punish me with loss of rhyme,
15   Who plainly say, *My God, My King.*[7]

Church Monuments[1]

While that my soul repairs to her devotion,
Here I entomb my flesh, that it betimes
May take acquaintance of this heap of dust
To which the blast of death's incessant motion,
5   Fed with the exhalation of our crimes,
Drives all at last. Therefore I gladly trust

My body to this school, that it may learn
To spell his elements and find his birth
Written in dusty heraldry and lines°   *engraving, genealogy*
10   Which dissolution sure doth best discern,
Comparing dust with dust and earth with earth.[2]
These[3] laugh at jet and marble, put for signs

To sever the good fellowship of dust
And spoil the meeting. What shall point out them[4]
15   When they shall bow and kneel and fall down flat
To kiss those heaps which now they have in trust?
Dear flesh, while I do pray, learn here thy stem
And true descent, that, when thou shalt grow fat

And wanton in thy cravings, thou mayest know
20   That flesh is but the glass which holds the dust
That measures all our time, which also shall
Be crumbled into dust. Mark here below
How tame these ashes are, how free from lust,
That thou mayest fit thyself against thy fall.

The Windows[1]

Lord, how can man preach thy eternal word?
He is a brittle, crazy° glass,   *flawed, distorting*
Yet in thy temple thou dost him afford
This glorious and transcendent place,
5   To be a window through thy grace.

But when thou dost anneal[2] in glass thy story,
Making thy life to shine within

---

7. Echoes Psalm 145.1: "my God, O king."
1. The earlier, manuscript version of the poem does not divide it into stanzas.
2. Alludes to Genesis 3.19: "For dust thou art and to dust shalt thou return."
3. I.e., dust and earth.
4. The inhabitants of the tombs.

1. From his little parish at Bemerton, Herbert used to walk twice a week across Salisbury Plain to the great cathedral, where he delighted not only in the music but in the stained-glass windows. This poem explores how the preacher himself may become such a window.
2. To burn colors into glass.

The holy preachers, then the light and glory
    More reverend grows, and more doth win,
10   Which else shows wat'rish, bleak, and thin.

Doctrine and life, colors and light, in one
    When they combine and mingle, bring
A strong regard and awe; but speech alone
    Doth vanish like a flaring thing,
15   And in the ear, not conscience, ring.

Denial

When my devotions could not pierce
    Thy silent ears,
Then was my heart broken, as was my verse;
    My breast was full of fears
5   And disorder;[1]

My bent thoughts, like a brittle bow,
    Did fly asunder:
Each took his way; some would to pleasures go,
    Some to the wars and thunder
10   Of alarms.

As good go anywhere, they say,
    As to benumb
Both knees and heart in crying night and day,
    Come, come, my God, O come!
15   But no hearing.

O that thou shouldst give dust a tongue
    To cry to thee,
And then not hear it crying! All day long
    My heart was in my knee,
20   But no hearing.

Therefore my soul lay out of sight,
    Untuned, unstrung;
My feeble spirit, unable to look right,
    Like a nipped blossom, hung
25   Discontented.

O cheer and tune my heartless breast;
    Defer no time,
That so thy favors granting my request,
    They and my mind may chime,°   ring together, agree
30   And mend my rhyme.

1. Unrhymed, as are all the concluding lines of each stanza except the last.

Virtue

Sweet day, so cool, so calm, so bright,
    The bridal of the earth and sky:
The dew shall weep thy fall tonight,
        For thou must die.

5 Sweet rose, whose hue, angry and brave,[1]
    Bids the rash gazer wipe his eye:
Thy root is ever in its grave,
        And thou must die.

Sweet spring, full of sweet days and roses,
10 A box where sweets° compacted lie;   *perfumes*
My music shows ye have your closes,[2]
        And all must die.

Only a sweet and virtuous soul,
    Like seasoned timber, never gives;
15 But though the whole world turn to coal,[3]
        Then chiefly lives.

Man

My God, I heard this day
That none doth build a stately habitation,
    But he that means to dwell therein.
    What house more stately hath there been,
5 Or can be, than is man? to[1] whose creation
        All things are in decay.

For man is every thing
And more; he is a tree, yet bears more[2] fruit;
    A beast, yet is or should be more;
10 Reason and speech we only bring.[3]
Parrots may thank us, if they are not mute:
        They go upon the score.[4]

Man is all symmetry,
Full of proportions, one limb to another,
15 And all to all the world besides;[5]
    Each part may call the farthest, brother;
For head with foot hath private amity,
        And both with moons and tides.

---

1. Splendid. "Angry": having the hue of anger, red.
2. Concluding cadences in music. This poem has often been set to music.
3. Be reduced to a cinder at the Last Judgment.
1. Compared to.
2. An alternative reading is "no."
3. Man has a vegetable, an animal, and a spiritual nature; he is the only creature that speaks and reasons.
4. Parrots are indebted to us for speech.
5. The notion of man as microcosm, whose parts all correspond to features of the great world. Cf. Donne, *Anatomy of the World*, p. 1262.

Nothing hath got so far
20 But man hath caught and kept it as his prey.
His eyes dismount° the highest star: *bring down to earth*
He is in little all the sphere.°   *the universe*
Herbs gladly cure our flesh; because that they
Find their acquaintance there.

25 For us the winds do blow,
The earth doth rest, heav'n move, and fountains flow;
Nothing we see but means our good,
As our delight, or as our treasure.
The whole is either our cupboard of food,
30 Or cabinet of pleasure.

The stars have us to bed;
Night draws the curtain which the sun withdraws,
Music and light attend our head.
All things unto our flesh are kind°   *akin*
35 In their descent and being; to our mind
In their ascent and cause.

Each thing is full of duty.
Waters united are our navigation,
Distinguished,° our habitation;   *separated*
40 Below, our drink; above, our meat;⁶
Both are our cleanliness. Hath one such beauty?
Then how are all things neat!

More servants wait on man
Than he'll take notice of; in every path,
45 He treads down that which doth befriend him,
When sickness makes him pale and wan.⁷
O mighty love! Man is one world, and hath
Another to attend him.

Since then, my God, thou hast
50 So brave a palace built, O, dwell in it,
That it may dwell with thee at last!
Till then, afford us so much wit,
That, as the world serves us, we may serve thee,
And both thy servants be.

Jordan (2)¹

When first my lines of heavenly joys made mention,
Such was their luster, they did so excel,
That I sought out quaint words and trim invention;

---

6. Oceans are valuable for navigation; the earth was created by dividing waters from waters (Genesis 1.6–7); on earth water is drink, from above (as dew or manna), food.

7. The herb that will cure him when he's sick.
1. Cf. *Jordan (1)* (p. 1601), and Sidney, *Astrophil and Stella* 1 (p. 917).

My thoughts began to burnish,° sprout, and swell,   *burgeon*
5 Curling with metaphors a plain intention,
Decking the sense, as if it were to sell.°   *for sale*

Thousands of notions in my brain did run,
Offering their service, if I were not sped:° *supplied, satisfied*
I often blotted what I had begun;
10 This was not quick[2] enough, and that was dead.
Nothing could seem too rich to clothe the sun,
Much less those joys which trample on his head.[3]

As flames do work and wind when they ascend,
So did I weave myself into the sense;
15 But while I bustled, I might hear a friend
Whisper, "How wide[4] is all this long pretense!
There is in love a sweetness ready penned:
Copy out only that, and save expense."

Time

Meeting with Time, "Slack thing," said I,[1]
"Thy scythe is dull; whet it for shame."
"No marvel, sir," he did reply,
"If it at length deserve some blame;
5 But where one man would have me grind it,
  Twenty for one too sharp do find it."

"Perhaps some such of old did pass,
Who above all things loved this life;
To whom thy scythe a hatchet was,
10 Which now is but a pruning knife.[2]
  Christ's coming hath made man thy debtor,
  Since by thy cutting he grows better.

"And in his blessing thou art blessed,
For where thou only wert before
15 An executioner at best,
Thou art a gardener now, and more,
  An usher to convey our souls
  Beyond the utmost stars and poles.

"And this is that makes life so long,
20 While it detains us from our God.
Ev'n pleasures here increase the wrong,
And length of days lengthens the rod.° *used for blows*
  Who wants° the place where God doth dwell *lacks*
  Partakes already half of hell.

---

2. Lively.
3. The "joys which trample on" the sun's head are
those of the Son.
4. Irrelevant, wide of the mark.

1. Herbert is the speaker in stanzas 1, 2, 3, 4, and
the first two lines of stanza 5.
2. A hatchet kills, a pruning knife improves growing things.

25   "Of what strange length must that needs be,
Which ev'n eternity excludes!"—
Thus far Time heard me patiently,
Then chafing said, "This man deludes:
What do I here before his door?
30   He doth not crave less time, but more."

The Bunch of Grapes[1]

Joy, I did lock thee up;° but some bad man   *take secure possession*
      Hath let thee out again,
And now methinks I am where I began
      Sev'n years ago: one vogue° and vein,   *tendency*
5   One air of thoughts usurps my brain.
I did towards Canaan draw, but now I am
Brought back to the Red Sea, the sea of shame.[2]

For as the Jews of old by God's command
      Traveled, and saw no town,
10 So now each Christian hath his journeys spanned;
      Their story pens and sets us down.[3]
      A single deed is small renown.
God's works are wide, and let in future times;
His ancient justice overflows our crimes.

15 Then have we too our guardian fires and clouds;
      Our Scripture-dew[4] drops fast;
We have our sands and serpents, tents and shrouds;[5]
      Alas! our murmurings come not last.
      But where's the cluster? where's the taste
20 Of mine inheritance? Lord, if I must borrow,
Let me as well take up their joy as sorrow.

But can he want° the grape who hath the wine?   *lack*
      I have their fruit and more.
Blessèd be God, who prospered Noah's vine[6]
25   And made it bring forth grapes good store.
      But much more him I must adore
Who of the Law's sour juice[7] sweet wine did make,
Even God himself being pressèd for my sake.

1. When the children of Israel almost lost hope in the wilderness, God inspired Moses to send forth scouts, who returned to report that Canaan was a land of milk and honey. In evidence they brought back a single bunch of grapes so big they had to carry it between them on a pole (Numbers 13.23).
2. The Red Sea's color suggests blushing for shame. Because the Israelites complained about their long ordeal in the wilderness after leaving Egypt, God drove them back toward the Red Sea.
3. The wandering of the Israelites in the wilderness was taken to be a type (prefiguration) of the Christian's trials on the path of salvation. "Spanned": measured out.
4. I.e., manna.
5. Temporary shelters.
6. Noah's vine (Genesis 9) was taken as a type of the earth replenished by God after the Flood.
7. The severe rules of the Old Testament as contrasted with the sweeter and more liberal covenant of the New Testament, which Christ's crucifixion established.

The Pilgrimage

I traveled on, seeing the hill where lay
    My expectation.
A long it was and weary way.
The gloomy cave of desperation
5 I left on th' one, and on the other side
    The rock of pride.[1]

And so I came to fancy's meadow, strowed
    With many a flower;
Fain would I here have made abode,
10   But I was quickened by my hour.[2]
So to care's copse I came, and there got through
    With much ado.

That led me to the wild of passion, which
    Some call the wold°—   *treeless plain, moor*
15   A wasted place but sometimes rich.
Here I was robbed of all my gold
Save one good angel,[3] which a friend had tied
    Close to my side.

At length I got unto the gladsome hill
20   Where lay my hope,
Where lay my heart; and, climbing still,
    When I had gained the brow and top,
A lake of brackish waters on the ground
    Was all I found.

25 With that abashed, and struck with many a sting
    Of swarming fears,
I fell, and cried, "Alas, my king!
    Can both the way and end be tears?"
Yet taking heart I rose, and then perceived
30   I was deceived:

My hill was further; so I flung away,
    Yet heard a cry,
Just as I went: *None goes that way*
    And lives: "If that be all," said I,
35 "After so foul a journey, death is fair,
    And but a chair."[4]

---

1. The rock and cave allude to Scylla and Charybdis, perils faced by Odysseus and often allegorized. The spiritual pilgrimage through allegorical perils was a frequent literary motif: cf. Bunyan's *Pilgrim's Progress* (p. 2137), and Henry Vaughan's *Regeneration* (p. 1617).

2. Short span of life.
3. A golden coin as well as (punningly) a guardian angel.
4. "Chair" implies rest and immobility but also a conveyance (a sedan chair).

The Holdfast[1]

I threatened to observe the strict decree
   Of my dear God with all my power and might.
   But I was told by one, it could not be;
Yet I might trust in God to be my light.

5   Then will I trust, said I, in him alone.
    Nay, ev'n to trust in him, was also his;
    We must confess, that nothing is our own.
   Then I confess that he my succor is.

   But to have nought is ours, not to confess
10   That we have nought. I stood amazed at this,
    Much troubled, till I heard a friend express,
That all things were more ours by being his.
   What Adam had, and forfeited for all,
   Christ keepeth now, who cannot fail or fall.

The Collar[1]

I struck the board[2] and cried, "No more;
        I will abroad!
What? shall I ever sigh and pine?
My lines and life are free, free as the road,
5   Loose as the wind, as large as store.
        Shall I be still in suit?[3]
Have I no harvest but a thorn
To let me blood, and not restore
What I have lost with cordial° fruit?   *restorative to the heart*
10   Sure there was wine
   Before my sighs did dry it; there was corn
   Before my tears did drown it.
Is the year only lost to me?
       Have I no bays[4] to crown it,
15   No flowers, no garlands gay? all blasted?
        All wasted?
Not so, my heart; but there is fruit,
        And thou hast hands.
   Recover all thy sigh-blown age
20   On double pleasures: leave thy cold dispute
Of what is fit and not. Forsake thy cage,
       Thy rope of sands,
Which petty thoughts have made, and made to thee

---

1. Alludes to Psalm 73.27 in the *Book of Common Prayer*: "It is good for me to hold me fast by God." The poem dramatizes the entire reliance on grace—and the abnegation of any human capacity to cooperate with it or claim any merit—that was a cornerstone of Calvinist theology.
1. The emblematic title at first suggests a clerical collar that has become a slave's collar; also, punningly, it comes to suggest the speaker's choler (anger) and, perhaps, the caller that he at last hears.
2. Table, with perhaps an allusion to the communion table.
3. In attendance, waiting on someone for a favor.
4. The poet's laurel wreath, symbol of recognized accomplishment.

Good cable,[5] to enforce and draw,
25   And be thy law,
While thou didst wink and wouldst not see.
    Away! take heed;
    I will abroad.
Call in thy death's-head[6] there; tie up thy fears.
30   He that forbears
    To suit and serve his need,
    Deserves his load."
But as I raved and grew more fierce and wild
    At every word,
35 Methoughts I heard one calling, *Child!*[7]
    And I replied, *My Lord.*

The Pulley[1]

When God at first made man,
Having a glass of blessings standing by,
"Let us," said he, "pour on him all we can:
Let the world's riches, which dispersèd lie,
5 Contract into a span."

So strength first made a way;
Then beauty flowed, then wisdom, honor, pleasure.
When almost all was out, God made a stay,
Perceiving that, alone of all his treasure,
10 Rest in the bottom lay.[2]

"For if I should," said he,
"Bestow this jewel also on my creature,
He would adore my gifts instead of me,
And rest in Nature, not the God of Nature;
15 So both should losers be.

"Yet let him keep the rest,
But keep them with repining restlessness:
Let him be rich and weary, that at least,
If goodness lead him not, yet weariness
20 May toss him to my breast."

The Flower

 How fresh, O Lord, how sweet and clean
Are thy returns! even as the flowers in spring,
 To which, besides their own demesne,°   *domain, demeanor*

---

5. Christian restrictions on behavior, which the "petty thoughts" of the docile believer have made into strong bonds.
6. Skull, emblem of human mortality, and often used as an object for meditation.
7. The call "Child" reminds the speaker of Paul's words (Romans 8.14–17) that Christians are not in "bondage again to fear" but are children of God, "and if children, then heirs."
1. The poem inverts the legend of Pandora's box, which released all manner of evils when opened, but left Hope trapped inside.
2. "Rest" has two senses: "remainder" and "repose."

The late-past frosts tributes of pleasure bring.
Grief melts away
Like snow in May,
As if there were no such cold thing.

Who would have thought my shriveled heart
Could have recovered greenness? It was gone
Quite underground; as flowers depart
To see their mother-root, when they have blown,°   *bloomed*
Where they together
All the hard weather,
Dead to the world, keep house unknown.

These are thy wonders, Lord of power,
Killing and quickening, bringing down to hell
And up to heaven in an hour,
Making a chiming of a passing-bell.[1]
We say amiss
This or that is:
Thy word is all, if we could spell.

O that I once past changing were,
Fast in thy Paradise, where no flower can wither!
Many a spring I shoot up fair,
Offering° at heaven, growing and groaning thither;   *aiming*
Nor doth my flower
Want a spring shower,[2]
My sins and I joining together.

But while I grow in a straight line,
Still upwards bent, as if heaven were mine own,
Thy anger comes, and I decline:
What frost to that? what pole is not the zone
Where all things burn,
When thou dost turn,
And the least frown of thine is shown?[3]

And now in age I bud again,
After so many deaths I live and write;
I once more smell the dew and rain,
And relish versing. O my only light,
It cannot be
That I am he
On whom thy tempests fell all night.

These are thy wonders, Lord of love,
To make us see we are but flowers that glide;°   *slip silently away*
Which when we once can find and prove,[4]
Thou hast a garden for us where to bide;

5
10
15
20
25
30
35
40
45

---

1. The "passing-bell," intended to mark the death of a parishioner, is tolled in a monotone; a chiming bell offers pleasant variety.
2. Tears of contrition.
3. I.e., compared with God's wrath, what polar chill would not seem like the heat of the equator?
4. Experience.

Who would be more,
Swelling through store,
Forfeit their Paradise by their pride.

The Forerunners

The harbingers are come: see, see their mark;
White is their color,[1] and behold my head.
But must they have my brain? must they dispark°   *turn out*
Those sparkling notions which therein were bred?
5   Must dullness turn me to a clod?
Yet have they left me "Thou art still my God."[2]

Good men ye be to leave me my best room,
Even all my heart and what is lodgèd there:
I pass not,° I, what of the rest become,   *care not*
10   So "Thou art still my God" be out of fear.
    He will be pleasèd with that ditty;
And if I please Him, I write fine and witty.

Farewell, sweet phrases, lovely metaphors:
But will ye leave me thus? when ye before
15   Of stews and brothels only knew the doors,
Then did I wash you with my tears, and more,
    Brought you to church well-dressed and clad:
My God must have my best, even all I had.

Lovely enchanting language, sugarcane,
20   Honey of roses, whither wilt thou fly?
Hath some fond lover 'ticed° thee to thy bane?   *enticed*
And wilt thou leave the church and love a sty?
    Fie! thou wilt soil thy 'broidered coat,
And hurt thyself and him that sings the note.

25   Let foolish lovers, if they will love dung,
With canvas, not with arras,° clothe their shame: *fine cloth*
Let Folly speak in her own native tongue.
True Beauty dwells on high; ours is a flame
    But borrowed thence to light us thither:
30   Beauty and beauteous words should go together.

Yet, if you go, I pass not; take your way.
For "Thou art still my God" is all that ye
Perhaps with more embellishment can say.
Go, birds of spring; let winter have his fee;
35   Let a bleak paleness chalk the door,
So all within be livelier than before.

---

1. Harbingers rode ahead of a royal traveling party to requisition lodgings, marking the doors with chalk.

2. Echoes Psalm 31.14: "But I trusted in thee, O Lord: I said, Thou art my God."

Discipline

Throw away thy rod,
Throw away thy wrath:
   O my God,
Take the gentle path.

5 For my heart's desire
Unto thine is bent:
   I aspire
To a full consent.

Not a word or look
10 I affect to own,
   But by book,[1]
And thy book alone.

Though I fail, I weep:
Though I halt in pace,
15   Yet I creep
To the throne of grace.

Then let wrath remove;
Love will do the deed:
   For with love
20 Stony hearts will bleed.

Love is swift of foot;
Love's a man of war,[2]
   And can shoot,
And can hit from far.

25 Who can 'scape his bow?
That which wrought on thee,
   Brought thee low,
Needs must work on me.

Throw away thy rod;
30 Though man frailties hath,
   Thou art God:
Throw away thy wrath.

Death

Death, thou wast once an uncouth, hideous thing,
   Nothing but bones,

1. I.e., like an actor who follows his playbook.
2. The jubilant song sung by Moses in Exodus 15

calls the Lord "a man of war," but Herbert also
alludes to Cupid, another divine bowman.

The sad effect of sadder groans:
Thy mouth was open, but thou couldst not sing.

5   For we considered thee as at some six
Or ten years hence,
After the loss of life and sense,
Flesh being turned to dust and bones to sticks.

We looked on this side of thee, shooting short,
10   Where we did find
The shells of fledge-souls left behind—
Dry dust, which sheds no tears, but may extort.[1]

But since our Savior's death did put some blood
Into thy face,
15   Thou art grown fair and full of grace,
Much in request, much sought for as a good.

For we do now behold thee gay and glad
As at doomsday,
When souls shall wear their new array,
20   And all thy bones with beauty shall be clad.

Therefore we can go die as sleep, and trust
Half that we have
Unto an honest faithful grave,
Making our pillows either down or dust.

Love (3)

Love bade me welcome: yet my soul drew back,
Guilty of dust and sin.
But quick-eyed Love, observing me grow slack°   *hesitant*
From my first entrance in,
5   Drew nearer to me, sweetly questioning
If I lacked anything.[1]

"A guest," I answered, "worthy to be here":
Love said, "You shall be he."
"I, the unkind, ungrateful? Ah, my dear,
10   I cannot look on thee."
Love took my hand, and smiling did reply,
"Who made the eyes but I?"

"Truth, Lord; but I have marred them; let my shame
Go where it doth deserve."
15   "And know you not," says Love, "who bore the blame?"

1. Souls that have left the body and gone to heaven are like fledgling chicks that have left the shell behind; that corpse ("dry dust") sheds no tears but may draw ("extort") from the survivors.

1. The first question of shopkeepers and tavern waiters to an entering customer would be "What d'ye lack?" (i.e., want).

"My dear, then I will serve."
"You must sit down," says Love, "and taste my meat."
So I did sit and eat.[2]

2. In addition to the sacrament of Communion, the reference is especially to the final communion in heaven, when the Lord "shall gird himself, and make them to sit down to meat, and will come forth and serve them" (Luke 12.37).

HENRY VAUGHAN
1621–1695

Born to a Welsh family of modest means but considerable antiquity, Henry Vaughan claimed his Welsh heritage by terming himself "The Silurist" in a volume of verse published in 1651, *Olor Iscanus (The Swan of Usk)*. The Silures were an ancient British tribe from southeast Wales. The Welsh language accounts for some features of Vaughan's poetry: the frequency of assonance and consonance rhymes and alliteration, the multiplication of comparisons and similes (*dyfalu*), and a sensitivity to nature, especially the countryside around the Usk River. In his secular volumes—*Olor Iscanus, Poems with the Tenth Satire of Juvenal Englished* (1646), and a late-published collection of earlier verse, *Thalia Rediviva* (1678)—Vaughan often presented himself as one of the "Sons of Ben Jonson."

After his education at Oxford and the Inns of Court, Vaughan returned to Wales at the outbreak of the Civil War (1642), served as secretary to the Welsh circuit courts until 1645, briefly fought for King Charles at Chester, and published his major collection of religious verse, *Silex Scintillans* (The Flashing Flint), in 1650; it was republished in 1655 with a second book added. The turn to religious subjects may have been prompted by a conversion experience: the title is explicated by an emblem of a flintlike heart struck by a bolt of lightning from the hand of God. Several of these poems voice Vaughan's dismay over the dismantling by Puritans of the liturgy, rituals, and festivals of the English Church, and others reveal his animus toward the new government: "I'll not stuff my story / With your Commonwealth and glory." In his later years Vaughan took up the practice of medicine without much formal study, and in 1655 translated a volume of medical lore, *Hermitical Physic*.

In his book of prose meditations, *Mount of Olives* (1652), Vaughan quotes or commends several of Herbert's poems, and in the preface to *Silex Scintillans* he presents himself as a "son of Herbert," placing himself among the many "pious converts" gained by Herbert's "holy life and verse." Herbert's influence is second only to that of the Bible in *Silex Scintillans*: some twenty-six poems have titles appropriated from *The Temple*, several owe their metrical form to Herbert, many begin with an exact or nearly exact quotation of a line from Herbert (compare Vaughan's *Unprofitableness* with Herbert's *The Flower*), and Herbertian echoes, allusions, and quotations are pervasive. Yet no one with an ear for poetry will mistake Vaughan's long, loose, free-flowing poetic lines for Herbert's artful precision. Vaughan's religious sensibility is also very different from Herbert's: his speaker cannot locate himself in the physical church (now dismantled) nor does he encounter Christ as friend; instead he wanders solitary through a landscape at once biblical, emblematic, and contemporary, mourning lost innocence. He finds vestiges of the divine everywhere, but is consumed with longing for the full relationship with the divine yet to come, at the last day.

A unifying motif of Vaughan's volume is pilgrimage, and many poems are meditations—on a personal experience, or a biblical text, or on one of the creatures of nature. Also, image clusters originating in the Bible carry over symbolic meaning from that source. Images of dawn, beam, star, ray, candle, shining, cloud, veil, and mist variously suggest spiritual illumination and mortal opaqueness. This light/darkness dichotomy receives expecially complex treatment in *The Night*, where Vaughan identifies in God "a deep but dazzling darkness." Another cluster renders the vitality and sentience of nature in images of green, white, quickness, flowers, roses, buds, and lilies. Vaughan's twin brother Thomas brought him in contact with Hermetic philosophy, an esoteric brand of Neoplatonism attributed to a mythical Egyptian magus, Hermes Trismagistus, and based on occult correspondences in nature. This influence is most apparent in the poem *Cock-Crowing*.

FROM POEMS

A Song to Amoret[1]

If I were dead, and in my place,
    Some fresher youth designed,
To warm thee with new fires, and grace
    Those arms I left behind;

5 Were he as faithful as the Sun,
    That's wedded to the Sphere;[2]
His blood as chaste, and temperate run,
    As April's mildest tear;

Or were he rich, and with his heaps,
10   And spacious share of Earth,
Could make divine affection cheap,
    And court° his golden birth: *pay court to*

For all these arts I'ld not believe,
    (No though he should be thine)
15 The mighty Amorist could give
    So rich a heart as mine.

Fortune and beauty thou mightst find,
    And greater men then I:
But my true resolved mind,
20   They never shall come nigh.

For I not for an hour did love,
    Or for a day desire,

1. This poem comes from Vaughan's first collection, all on worldly themes and many on love. Amoret has sometimes been identified with Vaughan's first wife, but on no secure ground. Amoret (formed from *amor*, love) is a traditional name for a poet's beloved from classical literature; note Spenser's use of the name in *Faerie Queene* 3, and the variation on it in his sonnet sequence *Amoretti*.
2. In the Ptolemaic scheme, each of the planets (including the sun, which was regarded as a planet) occupied one of the spheres revolving around the earth.

But with my soul had from above,
This endless holy fire.

1646

FROM SILEX SCINTILLANS

Regeneration[1]

A ward, and still in bonds,[2] one day
    I stole abroad;
It was high spring, and all the way
    Primrosed[3] and hung with shade;
5   Yet was it frost within,
      And surly winds
Blasted my infant buds, and sin
    Like clouds eclipsed my mind.

Stormed thus, I straight perceived my spring
10   Mere stage and show,
My walk a monstrous, mountained thing,
    Roughcast with rocks and snow;
    And as a pilgrim's eye,
      Far from relief,
15 Measures the melancholy sky,
    Then drops and rains for grief.

So sighed I upwards still; at last
    'Twixt steps and falls
I reached the pinnacle, where placed
20   I found a pair of scales;
I took them up and laid
    In th' one, late pains;
The other smoke and pleasures weighed,
    But proved the heavier grains.[4]

25 With that, some cried, "Away!" Straight I
    Obeyed, and led
Full east, a fair, fresh field could spy;
    Some called it Jacob's bed,[5]
    A virgin soil which no
30   Rude feet ere trod,

1. The poem allegorizes in rather precise Calvinist terms the experience of God's grace calling the elect and distinguishing between the regenerate and the unregenerate.
2. He begins as one in the Pauline "spirit of bondage" to fear because of sin and as one still in his minority (wardship) under the Old Testament law. This contrasts with the "spirit of adoption" whereby we are children of God: "And if children then heirs; heirs of God and joint-heirs with Christ" (Romans 8.14–17).

3. Alluding to the adage that the "primrose path" leads to perdition.
4. He climbs Mount Sinai (tries to live by the Old Testament law) but finds his sins and follies far outweigh those efforts.
5. Jacob slept in an open field where he had a vision of a ladder leading to heaven (Genesis 28.11–19); that place, Bethel, was taken as a type or figure for the church. Vaughan's poem *Jacobs Pillow, and Pillar* works out this allegory.

Where, since he stepped there, only go
        Prophets and friends of God.

Here I reposed; but scarce well set,
        A grove descried
35 Of stately height, whose branches met
        And mixed on every side;
        I entered, and once in,
            Amazed to see 't,
Found all was changed, and a new spring[6]
40   Did all my senses greet.

The unthrift sun shot vital gold,
        A thousand pieces,
And heaven its azure did unfold,
        Checkered with snowy fleeces;
45 The air was all in spice,
        And every bush
A garland wore; thus fed my eyes,
        But all the ear lay hush.°   quiet

Only a little fountain[7] lent
50   Some use for ears,
And on the dumb shades language spent
        The music of her tears;
        I drew her near, and found
            The cistern full
55 Of divers stones, some bright and round,
        Others ill-shaped and dull.[8]

The first, pray mark, as quick as light
        Danced through the flood;
But the last, more heavy than the night,
60   Nailed to the center stood.
        I wondered much, but tired
            At last with thought,
My restless eye that still desired
        As strange an object brought:

65 It was a bank of flowers, where I descried,
        Though 'twas midday,
Some fast asleep, others broad-eyed
        And taking in the ray;
        Here musing long, I heard
70   A rushing wind
Which still increased, but whence it stirred
        Nowhere I could not find.

---

6. Imagery in the following lines—spring, perfumes, flowers—alludes to the Song of Solomon (Canticles) in which the bride is traditionally allegorized as the church or the beloved soul.
7. In the Song of Solomon 4.15 the "fountain of waters, a well of living waters" was traditionally allegorized as Christ.
8. Alludes to 1 Peter 2.5, which refers to the faithful as "lively stones." The different sorts of stones and flowers here suggest the elect and the reprobate.

I turned me round, and to each shade
            Dispatched an eye
75 To see if any leaf had made
            Least motion or reply;
      But while I listening sought
            My mind to ease
      By knowing where 'twas, or where not,
80   It whispered, "Where I please."[9]

"Lord," then said I, "on me one breath,
And let me die before my death!"

"Arise O North, and come thou South wind,
and blow upon my garden, that the spices
thereof may flow out."[1]

1650

The Retreat

Happy those early days! when I
Shined in my angel infancy.
Before I understood this place
Appointed for my second race.[1]
5 Or taught my soul to fancy aught
But a white, celestial thought;
When yet I had not walked above
A mile or two from my first love,
And looking back, at that short space,
10 Could see a glimpse of His bright face;
When on some gilded cloud or flower
My gazing soul would dwell an hour,
And in those weaker glories spy
Some shadows of eternity;
15 Before I taught my tongue to wound
My conscience with a sinful sound,
Or had the black art to dispense
A several° sin to every sense,   *different*
But felt through all this fleshly dress
20 Bright shoots of everlastingness.
      O, how I long to travel back,
And tread again that ancient track!
That I might once more reach that plain
Where first I left my glorious train,
25 From whence th' enlightened spirit sees
That shady city of palm trees.[2]

9. John 3.8: "The wind bloweth where it listeth, and thou hearest the sound thereof, but canst not tell whence it cometh, and whither it goeth, so is every one that is born of the Spirit."
1. Vaughan identifies this verse as Canticles (Song of Solomon) 5.17; it is properly 4.16.
1. The poem alludes throughout to the Platonic doctrine of pre-existence, in conjunction with Christ's words (Mark 10.15): "Whosoever shall not receive the kingdom of God as a little child, he shall not enter therein." Comparisons are often made to Wordsworth's *Ode: Intimations of Immortality.*
2. The New Jerusalem, the Heavenly City (for its identification with Jericho, the "city of Palm Trees") (Deuteronomy 34.3).

But, ah! my soul with too much stay°   *delay*
Is drunk, and staggers in the way.
Some men a forward motion love;
30   But I by backward steps would move,
And when this dust falls to the urn,
In that state I came, return.

                                        1650

Silence, and Stealth of Days!

Silence, and stealth of days! 'tis now
    Since thou art gone[1]
Twelve hundred hours, and not a brow[2]
    But clouds hang on.
5 As he that in some cave's thick damp,
    Locked from the light,
Fixeth a solitary lamp
    To brave the night,
And walking from his sun, when past
10   That glimmering ray,
Cuts through the heavy mists in haste
    Back to his day,[3]
So o'er fled minutes I retreat
    Unto that hour
15 Which showed thee last, but did defeat
    Thy light and power;
I search and rack my soul to see
    Those beams again,
But nothing but the snuff[4] to me
20   Appeareth plain,
That dark and dead sleeps in its known
    And common urn;
But those[5] fled to their maker's throne,
    There shine and burn.
25 O could I track them! but souls must
    Track one the other,
And now the spirit, not the dust,
    Must be thy brother.
Yet I have one Pearl,[6] by whose light
30   All things I see,
And in the heart of earth and night,
    Find heaven and thee.

1648   1650

---

1. As indicated in lines 27–28, the poem is on the loss of Vaughan's brother—not his twin brother, Thomas, the hermetic philosopher, who did not die until 1666, but his younger brother, William, who died in July 1648.
2. Mountain ridge, or forehead.
3. The miner fixes his lamp halfway down the dark shaft, ventures a little beyond it, but then beats a hasty retreat.
4. The burnt wick of the lamp or candle.
5. The reference is back to "light and power."
6. Probably the Bible. The reference is to Matthew 13.45–46, to the merchant who sold all he had to buy a pearl of great price, there likened to the Kingdom of Heaven.

Corruption

Sure it was so. Man in those early days
    Was not all stone and earth;
He shined a little, and by those weak rays
    Had some glimpse of his birth.
5   He saw heaven o'er his head, and knew from whence
    He came, condemnèd, hither;
And, as first love draws strongest, so from hence
    His mind sure progressed thither.
Things here were strange unto him: sweat and till,
10   All was a thorn or weed:[1]
Nor did those last, but (like himself) died still
    As soon as they did seed.
They seemed to quarrel with him, for that act
    That felled him foiled them all:
15   He drew the curse upon the world, and cracked
    The whole frame with his fall.[2]
This made him long for home, as loath to stay
    With murmurers and foes;
He sighed for Eden, and would often say,
20   "Ah! what bright days were those!"
Nor was heaven cold unto him; for each day
    The valley or the mountain
Afforded visits, and still Paradise lay
    In some green shade or fountain.
25   Angels lay lieger[3] here; each bush and cell,
    Each oak and highway knew them:
Walk but the fields, or sit down at some well,
    And he was sure to view them.
Almighty Love! where art thou now? Mad man
30   Sits down and freezeth on;
He raves, and swears to stir nor fire, nor fan,
    But bids the thread° be spun.   *thread of Fate*
I see, thy curtains are close-drawn; thy bow[4]
    Looks dim, too, in the cloud;
35   Sin triumphs still, and man is sunk below
    The center, and his shroud.
All's in deep sleep and night: thick darkness lies
    And hatcheth o'er thy people—
But hark! what trumpet's that? what angel cries,
40   "Arise! thrust in thy sickle"?[5]

1650

---

1. God's curse on Adam for eating the forbidden fruit included a curse on the earth: "Thorns also and thistles shall it bring forth to thee" (Genesis 3.18).
2. Cf. Donne, *Anatomy of the World*, lines 199–200 (p. 1262).
3. As resident ambassadors (from heaven).

4. The rainbow, God's covenant with Noah after the Flood (Genesis 9.13).
5. Alludes to Revelation 14.15: "And another angel came out of the temple, crying with a loud voice to him that sat on the cloud, 'Thrust in thy sickle, and reap, for the harvest of the earth is now.'"

Unprofitableness

How rich, O Lord! how fresh thy visits are![1]
'Twas but just now my bleak leaves hopeless hung,
    Sullied with dust and mud;
Each snarling blast shot through me, and did share°   *shear off*
5   Their youth and beauty; cold showers nipped and wrung
    Their spiciness and blood.
But since thou didst in one sweet glance survey
Their sad decays, I flourish, and once more
    Breathe all perfumes and spice;
10 I smell a dew like myrrh, and all the day
Wear in my bosom a full sun; such store
    Hath one beam from thy eyes.
But, ah, my God! what fruit hast thou of this?
What one poor leaf did ever I let[2] fall
15   To wait upon thy wreath?
Thus thou all day a thankless weed dost dress,
And when th' hast done, a stench or fog is all
    The odor I bequeath.

                                1650

The World

I saw eternity the other night,
Like a great ring of pure and endless light,
    All calm as it was bright;
And round beneath it, Time, in hours, days, years,
5   Driven by the spheres,[1]
Like a vast shadow moved, in which the world
    And all her train were hurled.
The doting lover in his quaintest° strain   *most ingenious*
    Did there complain;
10 Near him, his lute, his fancy, and his flights,
    Wit's sour delights,
With gloves and knots,° the silly snares of pleasure,   *love knots*
    Yet his dear treasure,
All scattered lay, while he his eyes did pour
15   Upon a flower.

The darksome statesman hung with weights and woe
Like a thick midnight fog moved there so slow
    He did nor stay nor go;
Condemning thoughts, like sad eclipses, scowl
20   Upon his soul,
And clouds of crying witnesses without
    Pursued him with one shout.

---

1. Compare Herbert's *The Flower* (p. 1610).
2. The original printed text reads "yet," emended here.

1. The concentric spheres of Ptolemaic astronomy.

Yet digged the mole, and, lest his ways be found,
   Worked underground,[2]
25 Where he did clutch his prey. But one did see
      That policy:°   strategy
Churches and altars fed him; perjuries
      Were gnats and flies;
It rained about him blood and tears: but he
30   Drank them as free.[3]

The fearful miser on a heap of rust
Sat pining all his life there, did scarce trust
      His own hands with the dust;
Yet would not place° one piece above, but lives   invest
35   In fear of thieves.
Thousands there were as frantic as himself,
      And hugged each one his pelf:
The downright epicure placed heaven in sense,°   the senses
      And scorned pretense;
40 While others, slipped into a wide excess,
      Said little less;
The weaker sort slight, trivial wares enslave,
      Who think them brave°   fine, showy
And poor, despisèd Truth sat counting by°   recording
45   Their victory.

Yet some, who all this while did weep and sing,
And sing and weep, soared up into the ring;
      But most would use no wing.
"O fools!" said I, "thus to prefer dark night
50   Before true light!
To live in grots and caves, and hate the day
      Because it shows the way,
The way which from this dead and dark abode
      Leads up to God,
55 A way where you might tread the sun and be
      More bright than he!"
But as I did their madness so discuss,
      One whispered thus:
"This ring the bridegroom did for none provide,
60   But for his bride."[4]

John Chap. 2. ver. 16, 17

All that is in the world, the lust of the flesh, the lust
of the eyes, and the pride of life, is not of the father,
but is of the world.
    And the world passeth away, and the lusts thereof,
but he that doth the will of God abideth forever.

1650

2. I.e., the "darksome statesman" (line 16).
3. I.e., as freely as they rained.
4. Alludes to Revelation 19.7–9, the marriage of
the Lamb and his Bride, allegorized as Christ and
the church or Christ and the regenerate soul:
"Blessed are they which are called unto the marriage supper of the Lamb."

They Are All Gone into the World of Light!

They are all gone into the world of light!
   And I alone sit ling'ring here;
Their very memory is fair and bright,
   And my sad thoughts doth clear.

5 It glows and glitters in my cloudy breast
   Like stars upon some gloomy grove,
Or those faint beams in which this hill is dressed
   After the sun's remove.

I see them walking in an air of glory,
10   Whose light doth trample on my days;
My days, which are at best but dull and hoary,
   Mere glimmering and decays.

O holy hope, and high humility,
   High as the heavens above!
15 These are your walks, and you have showed them me
   To kindle my cold love.

Dear, beauteous death! the jewel of the just,
   Shining nowhere but in the dark;
What mysteries do lie beyond thy dust,
20   Could man outlook that mark!°   *boundary*

He that hath found some fledged bird's nest may know
   At first sight if the bird be flown;
But what fair well° or grove he sings in now,   *spring*
   That is to him unknown.

25 And yet, as angels in some brighter dreams
   Call to the soul when man doth sleep,
So some strange thoughts transcend our wonted themes,
   And into glory peep.

If a star were confined into a tomb,
30   Her captive flames must needs burn there;
But when the hand that locked her up gives room,
   She'll shine through all the sphere.

O Father of eternal life, and all
   Created glories under thee!
35 Resume thy spirit from this world of thrall°   *slavery*
   Into true liberty!

Either disperse these mists, which blot and fill
    My pèrspective[1] still as they pass,
Or else remove me hence unto that hill
40   Where I shall need no glass.

1655

Cock-Crowing[1]

Father of lights! what sunny seed,[2]
What glance of day hast thou confined
Into this bird? To all the breed
This busy ray thou hast assigned;
5   Their magnetism works all night,
        And dreams of Paradise and light.

Their eyes watch for the morning hue,
Their little grain expelling night
So shines and sings, as if it knew
10   The path unto the house of light.
        It seems their candle, howe'r done,
        Was tinned° and lighted at the sun.   *kindled*

If such a tincture,[3] such a touch,
So firm a longing can impower,
15   Shall they own image[4] think it much
To watch for thy appearing hour?
        If a mere blast so fill the sail,
        Shall not the breath of God[5] prevail?

O thou immortal light and heat!
20   Whose hand so shines through all this frame,[6]
That by the beauty of the seat,
We plainly see, who made the same.
        Seeing thy seed abides in me,
        Dwell thou in it, and I in thee.

25   To sleep without thee, is to die;
Yea, 'tis a death partakes of hell:
For where thou dost not close the eye

1. Literally, telescope, but more freely, distant vision.
1. The poem calls upon the Hermetical notion of sympathetic attraction between earthly and heavenly bodies, e.g., the cock whose crowing announces the sun's rising because it bears within itself a "seed" of the sun. Vaughan finds here an analogy for the attraction the soul has for its Maker.
2. The opening lines recall a passage from Henry's brother, the Hermetic philosopher Thomas Vaughan: "For she [the Anima or Soul] is guided in her operations by a spiritual metaphysical grain, a seed or glance of light . . . descending from the Father of lights." That term for God is from James

1.17. "Seed," "glance," "ray," and "grain" in line 8 are almost synonymous Hermetical terms for the bit of the sun implanted in the cock. "Magnetism" (line 5) refers to the attraction between the cock's "seed" and its source, the sun.
3. Alchemical term for a spiritual principle whose quality may be infused into material things.
4. Alludes to Genesis 1.27: "So God created man in his own image."
5. Alludes to Genesis 2.7: "And the Lord God formed man of the dust of the ground, and breathed into his nostrils the breath of life; and man became a living soul."
6. Universe.

It never opens, I can tell.
      In such a dark, Egyptian border,
30   The shades of death dwell and disorder.[7]

If joys, and hopes, and earnest throes,
And hearts, whose pulse beats still for light
Are given to birds; who, but thee, knows
A love-sick soul's exalted flight?
35   Can souls be tracked by any eye
      But his, who gave them wings to fly?

Only this veil[8] which thou hast broke,
And must be broken yet in me,
This veil, I say, is all the cloak
40 And cloud which shadows thee from me.
      This veil thy full-eyed love denies,
      And only gleams and fractions spies.

O take it off! make no delay,
But brush me with thy light, that I
45 May shine unto a perfect day,
And warm me at thy glorious Eye!
      O take it off! or till it flee,
      Though with no lily,[9] stay with me!

1655

The Night

John 3.2[1]

Through that pure virgin-shrine,
That sacred veil drawn o'er thy glorious noon,
That men might look and live as glowworms shine
      And face the moon,
5 Wise Nicodemus saw such light
As made him know his God by night.

      Most blest believer he!
Who in that land of darkness and blind eyes
Thy long-expected healing wings[2] could see,
10   When thou didst rise,
And what can never more be done,
Did at midnight speak with the Sun!

      O who will tell me where
He found thee at that dead and silent hour?

---

7. Alludes to Exodus 10.21, Moses bringing down the plague of "darkness over the land of Egypt, even darkness which may be felt."
8. Echoes Hebrews 10.20: "By a new and living way, which he [Christ] hath consecrated for us, through the veil, that is to say, his flesh."
9. Echoes Song of Solomon 2.16: "My beloved is mine, and I am his: he feedeth among the lilies."
1. John 3.2 describes how a Pharisee named Nicodemus came to Jesus by night and said, "Rabbi, we know that thou art a teacher come from God."
2. Echoes Malachi 4.2: "The Son of righteousness [shall] arise with healing in his wings."

15 What hallowed solitary ground did bear
　　　　　So rare a flower,
　　　Within whose sacred leaves did lie
　　　The fullness of the Deity?

　　　　　No mercy seat of gold,
20 No dead and dusty cherub nor carved stone,[3]
　　　But his own living works did my Lord hold
　　　　　And lodge alone;
　　　Where trees and herbs did watch and peep
　　　And wonder while the Jews did sleep.

25 　　　Dear night! this world's defeat,[4]
　　　The stop to busy fools; care's check and curb;
　　　The day of spirits; my soul's calm retreat
　　　　　Which none disturb!
　　　Christ's progress and his prayer time;
30 　　The hours to which high heaven doth chime;

　　　　　God's silent, searching flight,
　　　When my Lord's head is filled with dew, and all
　　　His locks are wet with the clear drops of night;
　　　　　His still, soft call;[5]
35 　　His knocking time; the soul's dumb watch,
　　　When spirits their fair kindred catch.

　　　　　Were all my loud, evil days
　　　Calm and unhaunted as is thy dark tent,
　　　Whose peace but by some angel's wing or voice
40 　　　　Is seldom rent,
　　　Then I in heaven all the long year
　　　Would keep, and never wander here.

　　　　　But living where the sun
　　　Doth all things wake, and where all mix and tire
45 Themselves and others, I consent and run
　　　　　To every mire,
　　　And by this world's ill-guiding light
　　　Err more than I can do by night.

　　　　　There is in God (some say)[6]
50 A deep but dazzling darkness, as men here
　　　Say it is late and dusky, because they
　　　　　See not all clear.

3. God commanded the Israelites to cover the Ark of the Covenant with "a mercy seat of pure gold . . . and . . . two cherubims of gold, of beaten work . . . in the two ends of the mercy seat" (Exodus 25.17–18).
4. The style of this stanza and the next deliberately echoes Herbert's *Prayer* (1) (p. 1601).
5. Echoes Song of Solomon 5.2: "I sleep, but my heart waketh: it is the voice of my beloved that knocketh, saying, Open to me, my sister, my love, my dove, my undefiled: for my head is filled with dew, and my locks with the drops of the night." For the allegory see *The World*, note 4.
6. Dionysius the Areopagite (ca. 5th century) deals with concepts of divine darkness, which Nicholas of Cusa later developed, referring to the "Darkness where truly dwells . . . the one who is beyond all" and "the superessential Darkness which is hidden by all the light that is in existing things."

Oh for that night, where I in him
Might live invisible and dim!

1655

The Waterfall

With what deep murmurs through time's silent stealth
Doth thy transparent, cool, and watery wealth
   Here flowing fall,
    And chide, and call,
5 As if his liquid, loose retinue stayed
Ling'ring, and were of this steep place afraid,[1]
   The common pass
   Where, clear as glass,
   All must descend,
10   Not to an end,
But quickened by this steep and rocky grave,
Rise to a longer course more bright and brave.°   *resplendent*

Dear stream! dear bank! where often I
Have sat and pleased my pensive eye—
15 Why, since each drop of thy quick[2] store
Runs thither whence it flowed before,
Should poor souls fear a shade or night,
Who came, sure, from a sea of light?
Or since those drops are all sent back
20 So sure to thee that none doth lack,
Why should frail flesh doubt any more
That what God takes he'll not restore?
O useful element and clear!
My sacred wash and cleanser here,
25 My first consigner[3] unto those
Fountains of life where the Lamb goes![4]
What sublime truths and wholesome themes
Lodge in thy mystical deep streams!
Such as dull man can never find
30 Unless that Spirit lead his mind
Which first upon thy face did move
And hatched all with his quickening love.[5]
As this loud brook's incessant fall
In streaming rings restagnates° all   *makes still again*
35 Which reach by course the bank, and then
Are no more seen, just so pass men.
Oh my invisible estate,

---

1. The water, with its startling descent in a water-fall but ultimate circularity to its source, is for Vaughan an emblem of death and restoration of the soul to its source.
2. Living.
3. In baptism.

4. Echoes Revelation 7.17: "For the Lamb . . . shall lead them unto living fountains of waters."
5. Alludes to Genesis 1.2: "And the Spirit of God moved upon the face of the earth." The Latin Vulgate version, "*incubabant*," is closer to Vaughan's "hatched."

My glorious liberty,[6] still late!
Thou art the channel my soul seeks,
40   Not this with cataracts and creeks.

1655

6. Alludes to Romans 8.21, promising deliverance "from the bondage of corruption into the glorious liberty of the children of God."

RICHARD CRASHAW
ca. 1613–1649

Richard Crashaw titled his first and second collections of sacred poems *Steps to the Temple* (1646, 1648), a gesture that acknowledges Herbert's leadership of the movement to reclaim poetry for God. But he does not claim discipleship. Indeed Crashaw differs greatly from Herbert and from every other English religious poet of the period in religious and aesthetic sensibility. He converted to Roman Catholicism and was deeply committed to its rituals and devotions. Also, he is the only major English poet in the tradition of the continental baroque, influenced by the poetics of the Catholic Counter-Reformation and its attempt to render the spiritual in and through the senses. In the visual arts and in literature the baroque style is exuberant, rhetorical, florid, sensuous, and elaborately ornamented; it uses sensuous metaphors for spiritual themes and objects, dissolves lines and forms, and seeks to transcend the limits of each genre or medium. Crashaw's favorite subjects are the baroque artists' favorites: angels and cherubs, the infant Jesus, the wounds and streaming blood of the crucified savior, the sorrows and sufferings of the Virgin, the tears of the penitent Magdalen, the agonies of the martyrs, the love-wounds and ecstasies of the mystic Teresa. Crashaw's version of the baroque, especially his favorite images and rhymes—breasts and nests, wounds and swoons, darts and hearts, kisses, blood, tears, sweet, dear, delicious, milky, rosy—prompted one critic to observe that in Crashaw "over-ripeness is all." Others have pronounced some of his sensuous comparisons grotesque, as when, in *The Weeper*, he describes the Magdalen's tears as "portable and compendious oceans" and as a breakfast for cherubs. But Crashaw is also alone among English poets in rendering the experience of rapture and religious ecstasy, in such remarkable poems as *Music's Duel* and a few hymns.

Crashaw's attraction to Roman Catholicism was a natural expression of his temperament, though without the catalyst of the Civil War he might not have converted. The son of a Puritan divine noted for hatred of popery and the Jesuits, he was educated at the Charterhouse and Pembroke College, Cambridge, both of them centers of Laudian Anglicanism. In 1636 he was elected a fellow of Peterhouse, and by 1639 he had become an Anglican priest, curate of Little St. Mary's, and college lecturer; a contemporary wrote that his sermons "ravished more like poems" but apparently none survive. He called Peterhouse his "little contentful kingdom," but his life there was violently disrupted in 1643 when the Puritans occupied Cambridge. He fled to Paris and the English court in exile, became a Roman Catholic in 1645, and was saved from destitution by obtaining various minor posts through the queen's influence, the last one at Loreto—thought to be Jesus' house at Nazareth, miraculously transported to Italy.

Crashaw's Latin epigrams, published as *Epigrammatica Sacra* (1634), were much influenced by Jesuit epigram style and are among the best by an Englishman. In their

Latin and later English versions, they are characterized by sophisticated rhetoric, puns, paradoxes, antitheses, metallic wit, and sometimes grotesque metaphors, as in the epigram on Luke II. In 1646 he published with the first version of *Steps to the Temple* a book of secular poems, *The Delight of the Muses*, some of them in Jonson's restrained plain style. But the masterpiece of this book is *Music's Duel*, a much elaborated version of a poem by the Jesuit Famianus Strada about a contest between a nightingale and a lutenist, melody and harmony. Crashaw imitates musical sounds by means of liquid vowels, smooth and gliding syntax, sound repetitions, and onomatopoeia, but beyond that he renders the ecstasy and rapture of listening to music by blending sounds and collapsing one sense into another (synesthesia), creating an effect of phantasmagoria or continual metamorphosis.

Crashaw constantly revised his religious poems, usually making them longer. His last (posthumous) volume, *Carmen Deo Nostro* (1652), includes emblems he may have executed himself, among them the padlocked heart prefixed to a poem urging the countess of Denbigh to convert to Catholicism. Especially notable are the final versions of several hymns, ranging from the soft prettiness and melting sweetness of the pastoral antiphon *In the Holy Nativity* to the vigorous and witty praise of St. Teresa, *The Flaming Heart*. Part "Advice to a Painter" (a genre important for political commentary after the Restoration), and part ecstatic hymn, the latter poem sharply critiques a painting of St. Teresa and the Seraph conceived in the manner of Bernini's famous sculpture.

FROM DELIGHTS OF THE MUSES

Music's Duel[1]

      Now westward *Sol* had spent the richest beams
      Of noon's high glory, when hard by the streams
      Of *Tiber*, on the scene of a green plat,
      Under protection of an oak, there sat
 5   A sweet Lute's-master: in whose gentle airs
      He lost the day's heat, and his own hot cares.
         Close in the covert of the leaves there stood
      A Nightingale, come from the neighboring wood:
      (The sweet inhabitant of each glad tree,
 10   Their Muse, their *Siren*, harmless *Siren* she)
      There stood she listening, and did entertain
      The Music's soft report: and mold the same
      In her own murmurs, that whatever mood
      His curious fingers lent, her voice made good:
 15   The man perceived his rival, and her art,
      Disposed to give the light-foot Lady sport
      Awakes his Lute, and 'gainst the fight to come
      Informs it, in a sweet *Praeludium*°   prelude, introduction
      Of closer strains, and ere the war begin,
 20   He lightly skirmishes on every string

1. Based on a much shorter Latin poem by the Jesuit Famianus Strada (1617), which also relates a contest between a nightingale and a lutenist, as a version of the contest between nature and art. Crashaw's poem also represents the contest of two kinds of music, melody (monody) and harmony (polyphony). The poem is especially remarkable for synesthesia, the blending of sensory images into one another, and sometimes the representation of one sense in the imagery of another.

Charged with a flying touch: and straightway she
Carves out her dainty voice as readily,
Into a thousand sweet distinguished tones,
And reckons up in soft divisions,°   *rapid melodic passages*
25   Quick volumes of wild notes; to let him know
By that shrill taste, she could do something too.
    His nimble hands instinct then taught each string
A cap'ring cheerfulness; and made them sing
To their own dance; now negligently rash
30   He throws his arm, and with a long drawn dash
Blends all together; then distinctly trips
From this to that; then quick returning skips
And snatches this again, and pauses there.
She measures every measure, every where
35   Meets art with art; sometimes as if in doubt
Not perfect yet, and fearing to be out
Trails her plain² ditty in one long-spun note
Through the sleek passage of her open throat:
A clear unwrinkled song, then doth she point it
40   With tender accents, and severely joint it
By short diminutives, that being reared
In controverting warbles evenly shared,
With her sweet self she wrangles; he amazed
That from so small a channel should be raised
45   The torrent of a voice, whose melody
Could melt into such sweet variety,
Strains higher yet; that tickled with rare art
The tattling° strings (each breathing in his part)   *prattling*
Most kindly do fall out; the grumbling bass
50   In surly groans disdains the treble's grace.
The high-perched treble chirps at this, and chides,
Until his finger (moderator) hides
And closes the sweet quarrel, rousing all
Hoarse, shrill, at once; as when the trumpets call
55   Hot Mars to th'harvest of Death's field, and woo
Men's hearts into their hands; this lesson too
She gives him back; her supple breast thrills out
Sharp airs, and staggers in a warbling doubt
Of dallying sweetness, hovers o'er her skill,
60   And folds in waved notes with a trembling bill,
The pliant series of her slippery song.
Then starts she suddenly into a throng
Of short thick sobs, whose thundering volleys float,
And roll themselves over her lubric° throat   *smooth*
65   In panting murmurs, stilled° out of her breast,   *distilled*
That ever-bubbling spring; the sugared nest
Of her delicious soul, that there does lie
Bathing in streams of liquid melody;
Music's best seed-plot, whence in ripened airs
70   A golden-headed harvest fairly rears

2. Simple melody, without divisions.

His honey-dropping tops, plowed by her breath
Which there reciprocally laboreth
In that sweet soil. It seems a holy choir
Founded to th'name of great *Apollo's*[3] lyre.
75 Whose silver-roof rings with the sprightly notes
Of sweet-lipped Angel-Imps, that swill their throats
In cream of morning *Helicon*,[4] and then
Prefer soft anthems to the ears of men,
To woo them from their beds, still murmuring
80 That men can sleep while they their Matins sing:
(Most divine service) whose so early lay
Prevents° the eyelids of the blushing day.   *comes before*
There might you hear her kindle her soft voice,
In the close murmur of a sparkling noise,
85 And lay the groundwork of her hopeful song,
Still keeping in the forward stream, so long
Till a sweet whirlwind (striving to get out)
Heaves her soft bosom, wanders round about,
And makes a pretty earthquake in her breast,
90 Till the fledged notes at length forsake their nest;
Fluttering in wanton shoals, and to the sky
Winged with their own wild echoes prattling fly.
She opes the floodgate, and lets loose a tide
Of streaming sweetness, which in state doth ride
95 On the waved back of every swelling strain,
Rising and falling in a pompous train.
And while she thus discharges a shrill peal
Of flashing airs, she qualifies° their zeal   *moderates*
With the cool epode of a graver note,
100 Thus high, thus low, as if her silver throat
Would reach the brazen voice of war's hoarse bird;°   *the raven*
Her little soul is ravished: and so poured
Into loose ecstasies, that she is placed
Above herself, Music's *Enthusiast*.
105   Shame now and anger mixed a double stain
In the Musician's face; yet once again
(Mistress) I come; now reach a strain, my Lute,
Above her mock, or be forever mute.
Or tune a song of victory to me,
110 Or to thyself sing thine own obsequy;°   *funeral song*
So said, his hands sprightly as fire he flings,
And with a quavering coyness tastes the strings.
The sweet-lipped sisters° musically frighted,   *the Muses*
Singing their fears are fearfully delighted.
115 Trembling as when *Apollo's* golden hairs
Are fanned and frizzled, in the wanton airs
Of his own breath: which married to his lyre
Doth tune the *Spheres*, and make Heaven's self look higher.

---

3. God of music and poetry, father of the Muses.
4. Mountain in Greece, home of the Muses; sometimes, the fountains there.

From this to that, from that to this he flies,
120　Feels Music's pulse in all her arteries,
　　Caught in a net which there *Apollo* spreads,
　　His fingers struggle with the vocal threads,
　　Following those little rills,[5] he sinks into
　　A Sea of *Helicon*; his hand does go
125　Those parts of sweetness, which with *Nectar* drop,
　　Softer than that which pants in *Hebe's*[6] cup.
　　The humorous strings expound his learned touch
　　By various glosses; now they seem to grutch°　　　　　　*grumble*
　　And murmur in a buzzing din, then jingle
130　In shrill tongued accents: striving to be single.
　　Every smooth turn, every delicious stroke
　　Gives life to some new Grace; thus doth h'invoke
　　Sweetness by all her names; thus, bravely thus
　　(Fraught with a fury so harmonious)
135　The Lute's light *Genius* now does proudly rise,
　　Heaved on the surges of swollen rhapsodies.
　　Whose flourish (meteor-like) doth curl the air
　　With flash of high-borne fancies; here and there
　　Dancing in lofty measures, and anon
140　Creeps on the soft touch of a tender tone:
　　Whose trembling murmurs melting in wild airs
　　Runs to and fro, complaining his sweet cares
　　Because those precious mysteries that dwell,
　　In music's ravished soul he dare not tell,
145　But whisper to the world: thus do they vary
　　Each string his note, as if they meant to carry
　　Their master's blest soul (snatched out at his ears
　　By a strong ecstasy) through all the spheres
　　Of Music's heaven; and seat it there on high
150　In th' *Empyraeum*° of pure harmony.　　　　　　*highest heaven*
　　At length (after so long, so loud a strife
　　Of all the strings, still breathing the best life
　　Of blest variety attending on
　　His finger's fairest revolution
155　In many a sweet rise, many as sweet a fall)
　　A full-mouthed *Diapason*[7] swallows all.
　　　　This done, he lists what she would say to this,
　　And she although her breath's late exercise
　　Had dealt too roughly with her tender throat,
160　Yet summons all her sweet powers for a note
　　Alas! in vain! for while (sweet soul) she tries
　　To measure all those wild diversities
　　Of chatt'ring strings, by the small size of one
　　Poor simple voice, raised in a natural tone,
165　She fails, and failing grieves, and grieving dies.
　　She dies; and leaves her life the victor's prize,

5. Small streams; also, passages of liquid notes.　　7. A grand burst of harmony through all the notes
6. Greek goddess of youth and cupbearer to the　　of the scale.
gods.

Falling upon his Lute; o fit to have
(That lived so sweetly) dead, so sweet a Grave!

1646

FROM STEPS TO THE TEMPLE

To the Infant Martyrs[1]

Go, smiling souls, your new-built cages[2] break:
In heaven you'll learn to sing, ere here to speak.[3]
Nor let the milky fonts that bathe your thirst
    Be your delay;
5 The place that calls you hence is, at the worst,
    Milk all the way.[4]

1646

I Am the Door[1]

And now th' art set wide ope, the spear's sad art,
Lo! hath unlocked thee at the very heart;
  He to himself (I fear the worst)
    And his own hope
5 Hath shut these doors of heaven, that durst
    Thus set them ope.

1646

On the Wounds of Our Crucified Lord

O these wakeful wounds of thine!
  Are they mouths? or are they eyes?
Be they mouths, or be they eyne,[1]
  Each bleeding part some one supplies.[2]

5 Lo! a mouth, whose full-bloomed lips
    At too dear a rate are roses.
Lo! a bloodshot eye! that weeps
    And many a cruel tear discloses.

1. This epigram and the three following were originally written in Latin in a volume of Sacred Epigrams and then rendered in English versions. Epigrams are brief, pithy, witty poems with, as was often said, "a sting in the tail." This poem addresses the Holy Innocents, the infants murdered by Herod in an effort to destroy the newborn Jesus, who was honored as King of the Jews by the Magi (Matthew 2.16–18).

2. Their bodies.
3. Infant comes from the Latin *infans*, meaning "unable to speak."
4. The Milky Way will replace their mothers' milk.
1. "I am the door; by me if any man enter in, he shall be saved" (1 John 10.9).
1. Eyes, an old plural form.
2. I.e., each wound of Christ is either an eye or a mouth.

O thou that on this foot hast laid
10   Many a kiss and many a tear,
Now thou shalt have all repaid.
    Whatsoe'er thy charges were.

This foot hath got a mouth and lips
    To pay the sweet sum of thy kisses;
15 To pay thy tears, an eye that weeps
    Instead of tears such gems as this is.

The difference only this appears
    (Nor can the change offend).
The debt is paid in ruby-tears
20   Which thou in pearls didst lend.

1646

Luke 11.[27][1]
Blessed be the paps which Thou hast sucked

Suppose he had been tabled at thy teats,
    Thy hunger feels not what he eats:
He'll have his teat e're long (a bloody one)[2]
    The Mother then must suck the Son.

1646

FROM CARMEN DEO NOSTRO

In the Holy Nativity of Our Lord God: A Hymn Sung as by the Shepherds[1]

CHORUS   Come we shepherds whose blest sight
          Hath met Love's noon in Nature's night;
              Come lift we up our loftier song,
          And wake the sun that lies too long.

5   To all our world of well-stol'n joy
              He° slept, and dreamt of no such thing,   *the sun*
          While we found out Heaven's fairer Eye,
              And kissed the cradle of our King.

1. The verse identifies the addressee: "And it came to pass, as he [Jesus] spake these words, a certain woman of the company lifted up her voice, and said unto him, 'Blessed is the womb that bare thee, and the paps which thou hast sucked.' "
2. The wound in Christ's side, making his breast (the fountain of all graces) bloody.
1. The poem's form, the interweaving of chorus and alternating soloists, is structurally comparable to an oratorio, an Italian musical form which Crashaw may well have known from his sojourns on the Continent. Its form invites comparison with Dryden's *Alexander's Feast*; and its subject with Milton's *On the Morning of Christ's Nativity*. The last version of this poem (1652), printed here, differs considerably from the first version (1646).

Tell him he rises now too late
To show us aught worth looking at.

Tell him we now can show him more
    Than he e'er showed to mortal sight;
Than he himself e'er saw before,
    Which to be seen needs not his light.
Tell him, Tityrus, where th' hast been;
Tell him, Thyrsis,² what th' hast seen.

TITYRUS   Gloomy night embraced the place
    Where the noble infant lay.
The babe looked up and showed his face:
    In spite of darkness, it was day.
It was thy day, Sweet! and did rise,
Not from the East, but from thine eyes.
    CHORUS It was thy day, Sweet, *etc.*

THYRSIS   Winter chid aloud, and sent
    The angry North to wage his wars;
The North forgot his fierce intent,
    And left perfumes instead of scars.
By those sweet eyes' persuasive powers,
Where he meant frost, he scattered flowers.
    CHORUS By those sweet eyes', *etc.*

BOTH   We saw thee in thy balmy° nest,   *Eastern, perfumed*
    Young dawn of our eternal day!
We saw thine eyes break from their East
    And chase the trembling shades away.
We saw thee; and we blessed the sight.
We saw thee by thine own sweet light.

TITYRUS   Poor world (said I), what wilt thou do
    To entertain this starry stranger?
Is this the best thou canst bestow,
    A cold, and not too cleanly, manger?
Contend, ye powers of heaven and earth,
To fit a bed for this huge birth.
    CHORUS Contend, ye powers, *etc.*

THYRSIS   Proud world (said I), cease your contèst,
    And let the Mighty Babe alone.
The phoenix³ builds the phoenix' nest;
    Love's architecture is his own.

---

2. Tityrus and Thyrsis are typical names for shepherds in classical pastoral poetry; Crashaw here identifies such pastoral figures with the biblical shepherds from the hillsides around Bethlehem.
3. The legendary bird of ancient Egypt, often taken as a symbol for Christ. Only one phoenix

existed at any one time; after it had lived five hundred years, it was consumed in flame and a new phoenix rose from the ashes. Christ as Son of God took part in the making of the world long before his incarnation.

The Babe whose birth embraves° this morn   *makes splendid*
Made his own bed ere he was born.
     CHORUS   The Babe whose, *etc.*

50

TITYRUS   I saw the curl'd drops, soft and slow,
     Come hovering o'er the place's head,
Offering their whitest sheets of snow
     To furnish the fair Infant's bed:

55

Forbear (said I), be not too bold;
Your fleece is white, but 'tis too cold.
     CHORUS   Forbear (said I), *etc.*

THYRSIS   I saw the obsequious Seraphims[4]
     Their rosy fleece of fire bestow,

60

For well they now can spare their wings
     Since Heaven itself lies here below.
Well done (said I), but are you sure
Your down so warm will pass for pure?
     CHORUS.   Well done (said I), *etc.*

65   TITYRUS   No, no; your King's not yet to seek
     Where to repose his royal head;
See, see; how soon his new-bloomed cheek
     Twixt mother's breasts is gone to bed.
Sweet choice (said we), no way but so

70

Not to lie cold, yet sleep in snow.
     CHORUS   Sweet choice (said we), *etc.*

BOTH   We saw thee in thy balmy nest,
     Bright dawn of our eternal day!
We saw thine eyes break from their East

75

     And chase the trembling shades away.
We saw thee; and we blessed the sight.
We saw thee, by thine own sweet light.
     CHORUS   We saw thee, *etc.*

FULL CHORUS
Welcome, all wonders in one sight!
     Eternity shut in a span.

80

Summer in winter. Day in night.
     Heaven in earth, and God in man.
Great little one! whose all-embracing birth
Lifts earth to heaven, stoops heaven to earth.

85   Welcome! though not to gold nor silk,
     To more than Caesar's birthright is;
Two sister-seas of Virgin-milk,
     With many a rarely-tempered kiss

---

4. The highest order of angels, associated with fire because of their ardent love of God.

That breathes at once both maid and mother,
90   Warms in the one, cools in the other.

Welcome! though not to those gay flies[5]
     Gilded i' th' beams of earthly kings—
Slippery souls in smiling eyes;
     But to poor shepherds, homespun things,
95   Whose wealth's their flock, whose wit to be
Well read in their simplicity.

Yet when young April's husband showers
     Shall bless the fruitful Maia's bed,[6]
We'll bring the first-born of her flowers
100   To kiss thy feet and crown thy head.
To thee, dread Lamb! whose love must keep
The shepherds more than they the sheep.

To Thee, meek Majesty! soft King
     Of simple graces and sweet loves,
105   Each of us his lamb will bring,
     Each his pair of silver doves,
Till burnt at last in fire of Thy fair eyes,
Ourselves become our own best sacrifice.

1646, 1652

NON VI.[1]

'Tis not the work of force but skill
To find the way into man's will.
'Tis love alone can hearts unlock.
Who knows the WORD, he needs not knock.

5. Courtiers, stigmatized in three compressed lines as ephemeral, worldly, and hypocritical.
6. The showers of April make fruitful the bed of May (from Maia, identified with an ancient Italian goddess of the spring).
1. Not by force. "Emblems" were popular throughout Europe in the late Renaissance. Their elements were generally three: an image, an adage, and a poem explaining the relation of the other two. The image was often an enigma, with the poem often moralizing its various elements. Crashaw's poem to the countess of Denbigh takes its departure from an enigmatic image, but, like the best of the emblem poems, goes far beyond it. The heart here has a hinge on the right, to show that it can be opened, but is sealed on the left with a scroll or phylactery inscribed with letters standing for the Word, which alone enables one to open the heart. Crashaw is said to have engraved this image himself.

TO THE
Noblest & best of Ladies, the
Countess of Denbigh.

Persuading her to Resolution in Religion, & to render herself without further delay into the Communion of the Catholic Church.[2]

What heaven-entreated heart is this,
Stands trembling at the gate of bliss,
Holds fast the door, yet dares not venture
Fairly to open it, and enter?
5   Whose definition is a doubt
'Twixt life and death, 'twixt in and out.
Say, lingering fair! why comes the birth
Of your brave soul so slowly forth?
Plead your pretenses (O you strong
10   In weakness!) why you choose so long
In labor of your self to lie,
Not daring quite to live nor die.
Ah, linger not, loved soul! a slow
And late consent was a long no;
15   Who grants at last, long time tried
And did his best to have denied.
What magic bolts, what mystic bars,
Maintain the will in these strange wars!
What fatal yet fantastic bands
20   Keep the free heart from its own hands!
So when the year takes cold, we see
Poor waters their own prisoners be;
Fettered and locked up fast they lie
In a sad self-captivity.
25   Th' astonished nymphs their flood's strange fate deplore,
To see themselves their own severer shore.
   Thou that alone canst thaw this cold,
And fetch the heart from its stronghold,
Almighty Love! end this long war,
30   And of a meteor make a star.[3]
O fix this fair Indefinite;
And 'mongst thy shafts of sovereign light
Choose out that sure decisive dart

---

2. Susan, countess of Denbigh, had been widowed in 1643, when her husband was killed fighting for the king. She went to Paris into exile with Queen Henrietta Maria in 1644 and, along with some other ladies attached to the court of that Roman Catholic queen, was herself attracted to that religion. Crashaw himself was a new convert; here he engages in a poetic version of the pressure often exerted by both Catholic priests and Anglican clergy on influential court ladies. As usual, he calls upon the imagery of erotic persuasion to urge her conversion.

3. Meteors were sublunary and therefore irregular and transient; stars, located above the moon, were regular, fixed, and permanent.

Which has the key of this close heart,
35   Knows all the corners of 't, and can control
The self-shut cabinet of an unsearched soul.
O let it be at last love's hour!
Raise this tall trophy of thy power;
Come once the conquering way, not to confute,
40   But kill this rebel-word, *irresolute,*
That so, in spite of all this peevish strength
Of weakness, she may write, *resolved at length.*
    Unfold at length, unfold, fair flower,
And use the season of love's shower.
45   Meet his well-meaning wounds, wise heart,
And haste to drink the wholesome dart,
That healing shaft which heaven till now
Hath in love's quiver hid for you.
O dart of love! arrow of light!
50   O happy you, if it hit right;
It must not fall in vain, it must
Not mark the dry, regardless dust.
Fair one, it is your fate, and brings
Eternal worlds upon its wings.
55   Meet it with wide-spread arms, and see
Its seat your soul's just center be.
Disband dull fears; give faith the day.
To save your life, kill your delay.
It is love's siege, and sure to be
60   Your triumph, though his victory.
'Tis cowardice that keeps this field,
And want of courage not to yield.
Yield, then, O yield, that love may win
The fort at last, and let life in.
65   Yield quickly, lest perhaps you prove
Death's prey before the prize of love.
This fort of your fair self, if 't be not won,
He is repulsed indeed; but you are undone.

                                     1652

The Flaming Heart

St. Teresa of Avila, a sixteenth-century Spanish mystic and founder of an ascetic order of barefoot Carmelite nuns, was one of the great figures of the Catholic Counter-Reformation. Her autobiography, popular throughout Europe and translated into English in 1642 as *The Flaming Heart*, describes not only her practical problems in establishing her order but also a series of ecstatic trances and visitations that represent union with the divine in sensual, indeed erotic, imagery. The great Italian sculptor and architect Bernini portrayed a famous mystical experience described in Teresa's autobiography, in a stunning baroque statue still in the church of Santa Maria della Vittoria, in Rome. It shows the saint in an attitude of ecstatic, swooning abandonment while a somewhat juvenile seraph stands over her, in the act of plunging a golden arrow in her heart. Crashaw may or may not have seen this statue while Bernini was at work on it (it was installed only after Crashaw's death), but his poem addresses a painter who has produced a picture of this episode conceived much as Bernini presented it. Such use of the sensory and sensual to render the spiritual is a cornerstone of Counter-Reformation aesthetics and of baroque art.

THE

FLAMING HEART
UPON THE BOOK AND
Picture of the seraphical saint

TERESA,

(AS SHE IS USUALLY EX-
pressed with a SERAPHIM
biside her.)[1]

Well-meaning readers! you that come as friends,
And catch the precious name this piece pretends,°   *puts forward*
Make not too much haste to admire
That fair-cheeked fallacy of fire.
5   That is a Seraphim, they say,
And this the great Teresia.
Readers, be ruled by me, and make
Here a well-placed and wise mistake:
You must transpose the picture quite
10   And spell it wrong to read it right;
Read *him* for *her* and *her* for *him*,
And call the Saint the Seraphim.
   Painter, what didst thou understand,
To put her dart into his hand!
15   See, even the years and size of him
Shows this the Mother Seraphim.
This is the mistress-flame; and duteous he,
Her happy fire-works here comes down to see.
O most poor-spirited of men!
20   Had thy cold pencil kissed her pen[2]
Thou couldst not so unkindly err
To show us this faint shade for her.
Why, man, this speaks pure mortal frame,
And mocks with female frost love's manly flame.
25   One would suspect thou meant'st to paint
Some weak, inferior, woman saint.
But had thy pale-faced purple took
Fire from the burning cheeks of that bright book,
Thou wouldst on her have heaped up all

---

1. "Seraphim" is in fact the plural form of seraph. This highest order of angels was thought to burn continually in the fire of divine love.

2. I.e., if you'd only been properly inspired by her book.

30 That could be found seraphical:
Whate'er this youth of fire wears fair,
Rosy fingers, radiant hair,
Glowing cheek and glistering wings,
All those fair and flagrant° things,   *burning*
35 But before all, that fiery dart
Had filled the hand of this great heart.
    Do then as equal right requires,
Since his the blushes be, and hers the fires,
Resume and rectify thy rude design,
40 Undress thy seraphim into mine.
Redeem this injury of thy art,
Give him the veil, give her the dart.
    Give him the veil, that he may cover
The red cheeks° of a rivaled lover,   *blushes*
45 Ashamed that our world now can show
Nests of new Seraphims here below.[3]
    Give her the dart, for it is she
(Fair youth) shoots both thy shaft and thee.
Say, all ye wise and well-pierced hearts
50 That live and die amidst her darts,°   *i.e., her writings*
What is 't your tasteful spirits do prove°   *experience*
In that rare life of her and love?
Say and bear witness. Sends she not
A Seraphim at every shot?
55 What magazines of immortal arms there shine!
Heaven's great artillery in each love-spun line.
Give then the dart to her who gives the flame,
Give him the veil who kindly takes the shame.
    But if it be the frequent fate
60 Of worst faults to be fortunate;
If all's prescription,[4] and proud wrong
Hearkens not to an humble song,
For all the gallantry of him,
Give me the suffering Seraphim.[5]
65 His be the bravery of all those bright things,
The glowing cheeks, the glistering wings,
The rosy hand, the radiant dart;
Leave her alone the Flaming Heart.
    Leave her that, and thou shalt leave her
70 Not one loose shaft, but love's whole quiver.
For in love's field was never found
A nobler weapon than a wound.
Love's passives are his activ'st part,
The wounded is the wounding heart.
75 O heart! the equal poise of love's both parts,
Big alike with wounds and darts,
Live in these conquering leaves,[6] live all the same;

---

3. Teresa burns on earth in love, as seraphim do
in heaven.
4. I.e., settled beforehand, by the decision of the
artist.

5. If Teresa can't be transformed into the angel,
as he would like, Crashaw prefers her as the "suffering" lover.
6. I.e., the leaves of St. Teresa's book.

And walk through all tongues one triumphant flame.
Live here, great heart; and love and die and kill,
80   And bleed and wound; and yield and conquer still.
Let this immortal life, where'er it comes,
Walk in a crowd of loves and martyrdoms.
Let mystic deaths wait on 't, and wise souls be
The love-slain witnesses of this life of thee.
85   O sweet incendiary! show here thy art,
Upon this carcass of a hard, cold heart;°   *Crashaw's heart*
Let all thy scattered shafts of light, that play
Among the leaves of thy large books of day,[7]
Combined against this breast, at once break in
90   And take away from me myself and sin!
This gracious robbery shall thy bounty be,
And my best fortunes such fair spoils of me.[8]
O thou undaunted daughter of desires!
By all thy dower of lights and fires;
95   By all the eagle in thee, all the dove;[9]
By all thy lives and deaths of love;
By thy large draughts of intellectual day,
And by thy thirsts of love more large than they;
By all thy brim-filled bowls of fierce desire,
100 By thy last morning's draught of liquid fire;
By the full kingdom of that final kiss
That seized thy parting soul, and sealed thee His;
By all the heavens thou hast in Him,
Fair sister of the seraphim,
105 By all of Him we have in thee,
Leave nothing of myself in me!
Let me so read thy life that I
Unto all life of mine may die!

1652

---

7. Books filled with intellectual and spiritual light.
8. I.e., my best fortune will be to be despoiled in this way.
9. The eagle suggests wisdom and power, for its

lofty flight and ability to look into the sun's eye; the dove suggests mercy and gentleness. Cf. Donne's *The Canonization*, line 22 (p. 1240).

ROBERT HERRICK
1591–1674

Robert Herrick is the most devoted of the Sons of Ben, though his epigrams and lyrics (like Jonson's) also show the direct influence of classical poets: Horace, Anacreon, Catullus, Tibullus, Ovid, and Martial. Born in London the son of a goldsmith and apprenticed for some years in that craft, Herrick took B.A. and M.A. degrees at Cambridge and consorted in the early 1620s with Jonson and his "tribe," meeting regularly at the Apollo Room. After his ordination in 1623, he apparently served as chaplain to various noblemen and in that role joined Buckingham's failed military expedition to rescue French Protestants at Rhé in 1627. In 1630 he was installed as vicar of Dean Prior in Devonshire but found much to dislike about rural life in the West Country. Expelled as a royalist in 1647, he apparently lived in and about London until the Restoration, when he was reinstated at Dean Prior and lived there until his death.

His single volume of poems, *Hesperides* (1648), with its appended book of religious poems, *Noble Numbers*, contains over four hundred short poems which, at first glance, seem mostly playful and charming, remarkable for their exquisite and unerring artistry and perfect decorum. Many are love poems on the *Carpe Diem* theme—seize the day, time is fleeting, make love now; a famous example is the elegant song *To the Virgins, to Make Much of Time*. But Herrick's range is much wider than is sometimes recognized: he moves from the pastoral to the cynical, from an almost rococo elegance to coarse, even vulgar, epigrams, and from the didactic to the dramatic. Also, he derives mythic energy and power from certain recurring motifs. One is metamorphosis, "times trans-shifting," the transience of all natural things. Another is celebration—festivals and feasts—evoking the social, ritualistic, and even anthropological signficances and energies contained in rural harvest festivals (*The Hock-Cart*) or the May Day rituals described in what is perhaps his finest poem, *Corinna's Going A-Maying*. Yet another is the classical but also perennial ideal of the "good life," defined in his terms as "cleanly wantonness." For Herrick this involves love devoid of high passion (the several mistresses he addresses seem interchangeable and not very real); the pleasures of food, drink, and song; delight in the beauty of surfaces (as in *Upon Julia's Clothes*); and finally, the creation of poetry as some ballast against the ravages of time.

These poems, published just months before the execution of Charles I, seem almost oblivious to the catastrophes of the war and the political turmoil. But they are not. Poems celebrating rural feasts and festivals, ceremonial social occasions, and the rituals of good fellowship reinforce the old conservative values of social stability, tradition, and order threatened by the Puritan revolution. Several poems that draw upon the Celtic mythology of fairy folk make their feasts, temples, worship, and ceremonies stand in for the forbidden ceremonies of the Laudian church and a life governed by ritual. Still other poems, like *The Hock-Cart* and *Corinna's Going A-Maying*, celebrate the kind of rural festivals that were at the center of the culture wars between royalists and Puritans. Both James I and Charles I urged such activities in their *Book of Sports* as a means of reinforcing hierarchical relations and traditional institutions in the countryside and deflecting discontent, while Puritans vigorously opposed these activities on those accounts and as occasions for drunkenness and licentiousness.

FROM HESPERIDES[1]

The Argument[2] of His Book

I sing of brooks, of blossoms, birds, and bowers,
Of April, May, of June, and July flowers.
I sing of Maypoles, hock carts, wassails, wakes,[3]

---

1. The Hesperides, or Western Maidens, guarded an orchard and garden, also called Hesperides, in which grew a tree bearing golden apples. Herrick's title suggests that his poems are golden apples from his residence in western Devonshire; the following poems are all from that volume, published in 1648.

2. Subject matter, themes.
3. Festive, not funerary occasions, to celebrate the dedication of a new church. "Hock carts" carried home the last load of the harvest, so they were adorned and celebrated. "Wassails" were Twelfth Night celebrations.

Of bridegrooms, brides, and of their bridal cakes.
5   I write of youth, of love, and have access
By these to sing of cleanly wantonness.
I sing of dews, of rains, and, piece by piece,
Of balm, of oil, of spice, and ambergris.[4]
I sing of times trans-shifting,° and I write   *transcience*
10   How roses first came red and lilies white.
I write of groves, of twilights, and I sing
The court of Mab and of the fairy king.[5]
I write of hell; I sing (and ever shall)
Of heaven, and hope to have it after all.

Upon the Loss of His Mistresses[1]

I have lost, and lately, these
Many dainty mistresses:
Stately Julia, prime of all;
Sappho next, a principal;
5   Smooth Anthea, for a skin
White and heaven-like crystalline;
Sweet Electra, and the choice
Myrrha, for the lute and voice;
Next Corinna for her wit
10   And the graceful use of it,
With Perilla; all are gone,
Only Herrick's left alone,
For to number sorrows by
Their departures hence, and die.

The Vine

I dreamed this mortal part of mine
Was metamorphosed to a vine,
Which, crawling one and every way,
Enthralled my dainty Lucia.[1]
5   Methought, her long small legs and thighs
I with my tendrils did surprise;
Her belly, buttocks, and her waist
By my soft nervelets were embraced.
About her head I writhing hung,
10   And with rich clusters (hid among
The leaves) her temples I behung,
So that my Lucia seemed to me
Young Bacchus ravished by his tree.°   *the grapevine*

---

4. A secretion of the sperm whale which is used
in making perfume—hence it suggests something
rare and delectable.
5. Mab was queen of the fairies and wife of their
king, Oberon.
1. The ladies are imaginary, and their names are

traditional in classical love poetry and pastoral
poetry.
1. For the sake of both rhyme and meter, the
name of this lady is given three syllables here; in
line 12 it has only two.

My curls about her neck did crawl,
15 And arms and hands they did enthrall,
So that she could not freely stir
(All parts there made one prisoner).
But when I crept with leaves to hide
Those parts which maids keep unespied,
20 Such fleeting pleasures there I took
That with the fancy I awoke,
And found (ah me!) this flesh of mine
More like a stock than like a vine.

Dreams

Here we are all, by day; by night, we're hurled
By dreams, each one into a several° world.   *separate*

Delight in Disorder[1]

A sweet disorder in the dress
Kindles in clothes a wantonness.
A lawn° about the shoulders thrown   *fine linen scarf*
Into a fine distraction;
5 An erring° lace, which here and there   *wandering*
Enthralls the crimson stomacher;[2]
A cuff neglectful, and thereby
Ribbons to flow confusedly;
A winning wave, deserving note,
10 In the tempestuous petticoat;
A careless shoestring, in whose tie
I see a wild civility:
Do more bewitch me than when art
Is too precise[3] in every part.

His Farewell to Sack[1]

Farewell, thou thing, time-past so known, so dear
To me as blood to life and spirit; near,
Nay, thou more near than kindred, friend, man, wife,
Male to the female, soul to body, life
5 To quick action, or the warm soft side
Of the resigning yet resisting bride.
The kiss of virgins; first-fruits of the bed;

---

1. One of several poems in this period in which women's dress is a means by which to explore the relation of nature and art. See Jonson's *Still to Be Neat*, p. 1414.
2. An ornamental covering of the chest, worn under the laces of the bodice.

3. "Precise" and "precision" were terms used satirically about Puritans. Herrick, in praising feminine disarray, is at one level praising the "sprezzatura" or careless grace of Cavalier art.
1. Sack is sherry wine, imported from Spain.

Soft speech, smooth touch, the lips, the maidenhead;
These and a thousand sweets could never be
10 So near or dear as thou wast once to me.
O thou, the drink of gods and angels! Wine
That scatterest spirit and lust;° whose purest shine   *pleasure*
More radiant than the summer's sunbeams shows,
Each way illustrious, brave;° and like to those   *splendid*
15 Comets we see by night, whose shagg'd² portents
Foretell the coming of some dire events,
Or° some full flame which with a pride aspires,   *or like to*
Throwing about his wild and active fires.
'Tis thou, above nectar, O divinest soul!
20 (Eternal in thyself) that canst control
That which subverts whole nature: grief and care,
Vexation of the mind, and damned despair.
'Tis thou alone who with thy mystic fan³
Work'st more than wisdom, art, or nature can
25 To rouse the sacred madness,⁴ and awake
The frost-bound blood and spirits, and to make
Them frantic with thy raptures, flashing through
The soul like lightning, and as active too.
'Tis not Apollo can, or those thrice three
30 Castalian sisters sing,⁵ if wanting thee.
Horace, Anacreon both had lost their fame
Had'st thou not filled them with thy fire and flame.⁶
Phoebean splendor! and thou Thespian spring!⁷
Of which sweet swans must drink before they sing
35 Their true-paced numbers and their holy lays
Which makes them worthy cedar and the bays.⁸
But why? why longer do I gaze upon
Thee with the eye of admiration?
Since I must leave thee, and enforced must say
40 To all thy witching beauties, Go, Away.
But if thy whimpering looks do ask me why,
Then know that nature bids thee go, not I.
'Tis her erroneous self has made a brain
Uncapable of such a sovereign
45 As is thy powerful self. Prithee not smile,
Or smile more inly, lest thy looks beguile
My vows denounced° in zeal, which thus much show thee,   *proclaimed*
That I have sworn but by thy looks to know thee.
Let others drink thee freely, and desire
50 Thee and their lips espoused, while I admire

2. Hairy, referring to a comet's tail.
3. Instrument for winnowing grain; associated with Bacchus, god of wine.
4. Poetic inspiration or frenzy, often likened to intoxication.
5. I.e., Apollo, god of poetry, and the Nine Muses; the Castalian spring on Mount Parnassus was sacred to them.
6. Both Horace and Anacreon wrote about the

pleasures of wine.
7. In addition to being an epithet of Apollo, *phoebus* in Greek means bright, pure. The inhabitants of Thespiae in Boeotia worshiped the muses and held an annual festival in their honor at the spring of Hippocrene, nearby.
8. Cedar oil was used to preserve papyrus; the poet's crown is woven of bay (i.e., laurel) leaves.

And love thee but not taste thee. Let my muse
Fail of thy former helps, and only use
Her inadulterate strength. What's done by me
Hereafter shall smell of the lamp, not thee.[9]

Corinna's Going A-Maying

Get up! get up for shame! the blooming morn
Upon her wings presents the god unshorn.[1]
   See how Aurora throws her fair
   Fresh-quilted colors through the air:[2]
5   Get up, sweet slug-a-bed, and see
   The dew bespangling herb and tree.
Each flower has wept and bowed toward the east
Above an hour since, yet you not dressed;
   Nay, not so much as out of bed?
10   When all the birds have matins° said,   *morning prayer*
   And sung their thankful hymns, 'tis sin,
   Nay, profanation° to keep in,   *impiety*
Whenas a thousand virgins on this day
Spring, sooner than the lark, to fetch in May.[3]

15 Rise, and put on your foliage, and be seen
To come forth, like the springtime, fresh and green,
   And sweet as Flora.[4] Take no care
   For jewels for your gown or hair;
   Fear not; the leaves will strew
20   Gems in abundance upon you;
Besides, the childhood of the day has kept,
Against° you come, some orient pearls[5] unwept;   *until*
   Come and receive them while the light
   Hangs on the dew-locks of the night,
25   And Titan° on the eastern hill   *the sun*
   Retires himself, or else stands still
Till you come forth. Wash, dress, be brief in praying:
Few beads[6] are best when once we go a-Maying.

Come, my Corinna, come; and, coming, mark
30 How each field turns° a street, each street a park   *turns into*
   Made green and trimmed with trees; see how
   Devotion gives each house a bough
   Or branch: each porch, each door ere this,
   An ark, a tabernacle is,[7]

---

9. To "smell of the lamp" is a proverbial expression for a laborious and uninspired literary production.
1. Apollo, the sun god; sunbeams are seen as his flowing locks.
2. Aurora is goddess of the dawn.
3. On May Day morning, it was the custom to gather whitethorn blossoms and trim the house with them.
4. Flora, Italian goddess of flowers, had her festival in the spring.

5. Pearls from the orient were especially lustrous, like drops of dew.
6. Rosary beads of the "old" Catholic religion, but more generally, a casual term for prayers.
7. The doorways, ornamented with whitethorn, are like the Hebrew Ark of the Covenant, or the sanctuary that housed it (Leviticus 23.40–42: "Ye shall take you on the first day the boughs of goodly trees . . . ").

³⁵ Made up of whitethorn neatly interwove,
As if here were those cooler shades of love.
  Can such delights be in the street
  And open fields, and we not see 't?
  Come, we'll abroad; and let's obey
⁴⁰ The proclamation[8] made for May,
And sin no more, as we have done, by staying;
But, my Corinna, come, let's go a-Maying.

There's not a budding boy or girl this day
But is got up and gone to bring in May;
⁴⁵ A deal of youth, ere this, is come
  Back, and with whitethorn laden, home.
  Some have dispatched their cakes and cream
  Before that we have left to dream;
And some have wept, and wooed, and plighted troth,
⁵⁰ And chose their priest, ere we can cast off sloth.
  Many a green-gown[9] has been given,
  Many a kiss, both odd and even;[1]
  Many a glance, too, has been sent
  From out the eye, love's firmament;
⁵⁵ Many a jest told of the keys betraying
This night, and locks picked; yet we're not a-Maying.

Come, let us go while we are in our prime,
And take the harmless folly of the time.
  We shall grow old apace, and die
⁶⁰ Before we know our liberty.
  Our life is short, and our days run
  As fast away as does the sun;
And, as a vapor or a drop of rain,
Once lost, can ne'er be found again,
⁶⁵ So when or you or I are made
  A fable, song, or fleeting shade,
  All love, all liking, all delight
  Lies drowned with us in endless night.[2]
Then while time serves, and we are but decaying,
⁷⁰ Come, my Corinna, come, let's go a-Maying.

To the Virgins, to Make Much of Time

  Gather ye rosebuds while ye may,
    Old time is still a-flying;[1]
  And this same flower that smiles today,
    Tomorrow will be dying.

8. Probably a reference to Charles I's "Declaration to his subjects concerning lawful sports."
9. Got by rolling in the grass.
1. Kisses are odd and even in kissing games.
2. Some echoes of the apocryphal book Wisdom of Solomon 2.1–8: "For the ungodly said . . . the breath of our nostrils is as smoke, and a little spark . . . and our life shall pass away as the trace of a cloud. . . . Come on therefore . . . Let us crown ourselves with rose buds before they be withered." This *carpe diem* sentiment is a frequent theme in classical love poetry.
1. Translates the Latin *tempus fugit*.

5   The glorious lamp of heaven, the sun,
          The higher he's a-getting,
       The sooner will his race be run,[2]
          And nearer he's to setting.

       That age is best which is the first,
10   When youth and blood are warmer;
       But being spent, the worse, and worst
          Times still succeed the former.

       Then be not coy, but use your time,
          And while ye may, go marry;
15   For having lost but once your prime,
          You may forever tarry.

The Hock-Cart,[1] or Harvest Home

to the Right Honorable Mildmay, Earl of Westmoreland

       Come, sons of summer, by whose toil
       We are the lords of wine and oil;[2]
       By whose tough labors and rough hands
       We rip up first, then reap our lands.
5   Crowned with the ears of corn, now come
       And, to the pipe, sing harvest home.
       Come forth, my Lord, and see the cart
       Dressed up with all the country art.
       See here a maukin,° there a sheet,   scarecrow
10   As spotless pure as it is sweet,
       The horses, mares, and frisking fillies
       Clad all in linen, white as lilies,
       The harvest swains and wenches bound
       For joy to see the hock-cart crowned.
15   About the cart, hear how the rout
       Of rural younglings raise the shout,
       Pressing before, some coming after,
       Those with a shout and these with laughter.
       Some bless the cart, some kiss the sheaves,
20   Some prank° them up with oaken leaves;   adorn
       Some cross the fill-horse, some with great
       Devotion[3] stroke the home-borne wheat;
       While other rustics, less attent
       To prayers than to merriment,
25   Run after with their breeches rent.
          Well, on, brave boys, to your Lord's hearth,
       Glittering with fire; where, for your mirth,

2. In classical myth, the sun was taken to be the chariot of Phoebus Apollo, which he drove across the heavens daily.
1. The last cart carrying home the harvest; hence the occasion for a rural festival, traditional throughout Europe. Mildmay Fane, earl of West-moreland (1628–1660), was one of Herrick's patrons.

2. Wine and oil are the yields of Mediterranean farming. Herrick uses them to relate the local English feast to classical pastoral.
3. The fill-horse is harnessed between the shafts of the cart. Crossing the horse and kissing the sheaves are Catholic practices; Puritans would see them as superstitious, not as "Devotion."

Ye shall see first the large and chief
Foundation of your feast, fat beef;
30   With upper stories, mutton, veal,
And bacon,° which makes full the meal,   *pork*
With several dishes standing by,
As here a custard, there a pie,
And here all-tempting frumenty.°   *pudding*
35   And for to make the merry cheer,
If smirking° wine be wanting° here,   *sparkling / lacking*
There's that which drowns all care, stout beer:
Which freely drink to your Lord's health,
Then to the plow (the common-wealth),
40   Next to your flails, your fans,⁴ your vats,
Then to the maids with wheaten hats,
To the rough sickle and crook'd scythe,
Drink, frolic boys, till all be blithe.
     Feed, and grow fat; and, as ye eat,
45   Be mindful that the lab'ring neat,°   *cattle*
As you, may have their fill of meat.⁵
And know, besides, ye must revoke°   *call back*
The patient ox unto his yoke,
And all go back unto the plow
50   And harrow, though they're hanged up now.
And you must know, your Lord's word's true,
Feed him ye must whose food fills you,
And that this pleasure is like rain,
Not sent ye for to drown your pain
55   But for to make it spring again.⁶

How Roses Came Red¹

Roses at first were white,
     Till they could not agree,
Whether my *Sappho's* breast,
     Or they more white should be.

5   But being vanquished quite,
     A blush their cheeks bespread;
Since which (believe the rest)
     The roses first came red.

Upon the Nipples of Julia's Breast

Have ye beheld (with much delight)
A red rose peeping through a white?

---

4. "Flails" are threshing instruments; "fans" are
used to winnow grain from chaff. The plow is the
common source of everybody's wealth. In line with
the anti-Puritan sentiments of the whole poem, the
word *commonwealth*, in this communal and earthy
sense, invites a contrast with Puritan republican
theories.

5. The cattle's "meat," of course, is grain or hay.
6. Spring is heralded by rain, but the lines also
point to the continual renewal of the agricultural
worker's pain and labor.
1. This poem, and several others in the collection,
present minitransformations in witty allusion to
Ovid's epic-like *Metamorphoses*.

Or else a cherry (double graced)
Within a lily center-placed?
5   Or ever marked the pretty beam
A strawberry shows half drowned in cream?
Or seen rich rubies blushing through
A pure smooth pearl, and orient too?
So like to this, nay all the rest,
10   Is each neat niplet of her breast.

Upon Jack and Jill. Epigram[2]

When Jill complains to Jack for want of meat,
Jack kisses Jill, and bids her freely eat.
Jill says, Of what? Says Jack, On that sweet kiss,
Which full of nectar and ambrosia is,
5   The food of poets. So I thought, says Jill;
That makes them look so lank, so ghost-like still.
Let poets feed on air or what they will;
Let me feed full till that I fart, says Jill.

To Marygolds

Give way, an° ye be ravished by the sun,   *if*
And hang the head whenas the act is done.
Spread as he spreads; wax less as he does wane,
And as he shuts, close up to maids again.

His Prayer to Ben Jonson

When I a verse shall make,
Know I have prayed thee,
For old religion's sake,[3]
Saint Ben to aid me.

5   Make the way smooth for me
When I, thy Herrick,
Honoring thee, on my knee,
Offer my lyric.

Candles I'll give to thee
10   And a new altar;
And thou Saint Ben shalt be
Writ in my psalter.

---

2. Cf. Jonson, *On Giles and Joan,* p. 1396.
3. Herrick plays on the fact that Jonson was for a while a Catholic (of the "old religion"), as well as a saint in the mock religion of poetry. Protestants disapproved of prayers to saints.

The Bad Season Makes the Poet Sad[1]

Dull to myself and almost dead to these
My many fresh and fragrant mistresses,
Lost to all music now, since every thing
Puts on the semblance here of sorrowing.
5   Sick is the land to the heart, and doth endure
More dangerous faintings by her desperate cure.
But if that golden age would come again,
And Charles here rule as he before did reign,
If smooth and unperplexed the seasons were,
10   As when the sweet Maria livèd here,
I should delight to have my curls half drowned
In Tyrian dews,[2] and head with roses crowned,
And once more yet (ere I am laid out dead)
Knock at a star with my exalted head.[3]

The Night-Piece, to Julia

Her eyes the glowworm lend thee,
The shooting stars attend thee;
   And the elves also,
   Whose little eyes glow
5   Like the sparks of fire, befriend thee.

No Will-o'th'-Wisp mislight thee,[1]
Nor snake or slowworm° bite thee;   *adder*
   But on, on thy way,
   Not making a stay,
10   Since ghost there's none to affright thee.

Let not the dark thee cumber;
What though the moon does slumber?
   The stars of the night
   Will lend thee their light
15   Like tapers clear without number.

Then, Julia, let me woo thee,
Thus, thus to come unto me:
   And when I shall meet
   Thy silv'ry feet,
20   My soul I'll pour into thee.

1. The bad season is evidently political, not mete-orological. If line 10 refers to Charles's queen, Henrietta Maria, the poem must have been written after 1644, when she was forced to retire to France.
2. Perfume from Tyre was one of many Middle Eastern luxuries proverbial in Roman times.

3. The last line translates literally the last line of Horace's first ode, to his patron, Maecenas. Herrick hopes once more to have enlightened readers and an enlightened patron, so that he can feel something of Horace's exaltation.
1. Will-o'-the-wisp traditionally draws travelers astray with false lights.

Upon His Verses

What offspring other men have got,
The how, where, when I question not.
These are the children I have left;
Adopted some, none got by theft.
5　But all are touched (like lawful plate)[1]
And no verse illegitimate.

His Return to London

From the dull confines of the drooping West,[1]
To see the day spring from the pregnant East,
Ravished in spirit, I come, nay more, I fly
To thee, blest place of my nativity!
5　Thus, thus with hallowed foot I touch the ground
With thousand blessings by thy fortune crowned.
O fruitful Genius![2] that bestowest here
An everlasting plenty, year by year.
O place! O people! Manners! framed to please
10　All nations, customs, kindreds, languages!
I am a free-born Roman;[3] suffer then
That I amongst you live a citizen.
London my home is, though by hard fate sent
Into a long and irksome banishment;
15　Yet since called back, henceforward let me be,
O native country, repossessed by thee!
For, rather than I'll to the West return,
I'll beg of thee first here to have mine urn.
Weak I am grown, and must in short time fall;
20　Give thou my sacred relics burial.

1647?

Upon Julia's Clothes

Whenas in silks my Julia goes,
Then, then, methinks, how sweetly flows
That liquefaction of her clothes.

Next, when I cast mine eyes and see
5　That brave[1] vibration each way free,
Oh, how that glittering taketh me!

---

1. A special variety of quartz, known as basanite, was used to test gold and silver objects; the color of the smear left on the touchstone revealed its purity.
1. Devonshire, where his parish, Dean Prior, was located.

2. In classical Rome, the genius of a place was its guardian deity.
3. An ancient Roman born in the city was said to be "free of it," i.e., entitled to its special rights and privileges, including residence there.
1. Splendid, glorious.

Upon Prue, His Maid[2]

In this little urn is laid
Prudence Baldwin, once my maid,
From whose happy spark here let
Spring the purple violet.

To His Book's End[3]

To his book's end this last line he'd have placed:
Jocund° his muse was, but his life was chaste.   *merry, sprightly*

FROM NOBLE NUMBERS

To His Conscience[1]

Can I not sin, but thou wilt be
My private protonotary?[2]
Can I not woo thee to pass by
A short and sweet iniquity?
5 I'll cast a mist and cloud upon
My delicate transgression
So utter dark as that no eye
Shall see the hugged° impiety.   *cherished*
Gifts blind the wise,[3] and bribes do please
10 And wind° all other witnesses: *pervert*
And wilt not thou with gold be tied
To lay thy pen and ink aside?
That in the mirk° and tongueless night   *black, murky*
Wanton I may, and thou not write?
15 It will not be; and therefore now
For times to come I'll make this vow,
From aberrations to live free,
So I'll not fear the Judge, or thee.

Another Grace for a Child

Here a little child I stand,
Heaving up my either hand;
Cold as paddocks° though they be,   *frogs*
Here I lift them up to thee,
5 For a benison° to fall   *blessing*
On our meat and on us all. *Amen.*

2. This is an odd epitaph, since Prudence Baldwin
died four years after Herrick.
3. The last poem of *Hesperides.*
1. This and the following poem are from *Noble
Numbers,* the collection of Herrick's religious

poems that was bound together with *Hesperides.*
2. Chief recording clerk of a court.
3. Echoes Deuteronomy 16.19: "A gift doth blind
the eyes of a wise man."

THOMAS CAREW
1595–1640

Thomas Carew (pronounced *Carey*) is perhaps the Cavalier poet with the greatest range and complexity. He gained his B.A. at Merton College, Oxford, studied law (his father's profession), held several minor positions in the diplomatic and court bureaucracy, fought for his King in the ill-fated expedition against the Scots (The First Bishops War, 1638–39), and died of syphilis. A brilliant and dissolute young man, he was a great favorite with Charles I and Henrietta Maria.

His *Poems* (1640), published posthumously, are witty and often outrageous, but their emphasis on natural sensuality and the need for union between king and subjects encodes a serious critique of the Neoplatonic artifice of the Caroline court. Carew's spectacular court masque, *Coelum Britannicum*, performed at the Banqueting Hall at Whitehall on February 18, 1633, was based on a philosophic dialogue by Giordano Bruno; it combines wildly hyperbolic praise of the monarchs with (in the antimasques) a dramatization of several social and moral problems. As a love poet Carew sometimes plays off Donnean situations and poems; elsewhere, as in "Ask me no more where Jove bestows," he imitates Jonson's most purely lyrical vein. But his characteristic note is one of frank sexuality and emotional realism: in *The Rapture*, probably the most erotic poem of the era, he describes the sexual act in highly evocative terms under the sustained metaphor of a voyage. He also wrote country-house poems that, unlike Jonson's *To Penshurst*, describe Saxham and Wrest as places of refuge from the court and the mounting dangers outside their gates. Carew's poems of literary criticism provide astute commentary on contemporary authors. *To Ben Jonson* evaluates Jonson with Jonsonian precision, measure, and judiciousness in weighing out praise and blame. His famous *Elegy* on Donne praises Donne's innovation, reformation of style, avoidance of classical tags, "giant fancy," and especially his tough masculinity of style, a feature Carew imitates in this poem's energetic run-over couplets, quick changes of rhythms and images, and vigorous "strong lines."

An Elegy upon the Death of the Dean of Paul's, Dr. John Donne[1]

Can we not force from widowed poetry,
Now thou art dead, great Donne, one elegy
To crown thy hearse? Why yet dare we not trust,
Though with unkneaded dough-baked[2] prose, thy dust,
5   Such as the unscissored[3] churchman from the flower
Of fading rhetoric, short-lived as his hour,
Dry as the sand that measures it,[4] should lay
Upon thy ashes on the funeral day?
Have we no voice, no tune? Didst thou dispense°   *lay out, use up*
10   Through all our language both the words and sense?
'Tis a sad truth. The pulpit may her plain
And sober Christian precepts still retain;
Doctrines it may, and wholesome uses, frame,

---

1. First appearing with a number of other elegies in the 1633 edition of Donne's poems, then reprinted in 1640 with some changes, Carew's tribute is notable among 17th-century poems on poetry for its technical precision.

2. I.e., tedious and flat.
3. With uncut hair.
4. The hourglass was used by preachers to keep track of time.

Grave homilies and lectures; but the flame
15 Of thy brave soul, that shot such heat and light
    As burnt our earth and made our darkness bright,
    Committed holy rapes upon our will,
    Did through the eye the melting heart distill,
    And the deep knowledge of dark truths so teach
20 As sense might judge what fancy could not reach,[5]
    Must be desired° forever. So the fire   missed
    That fills with spirit and heat the Delphic choir,[6]
    Which, kindled first by thy Promethean[7] breath,
    Glowed here a while, lies quenched now in thy death.
25 The Muses' garden, with pedantic weeds
    O'erspread, was purged by thee; the lazy seeds
    Of servile imitation thrown away,
    And fresh invention planted; thou didst pay
    The debts of our penurious bankrupt age—
30 Licentious thefts, that make poetic rage
    A mimic fury, when our souls must be
    Possessed or with Anacreon's ecstasy,
    Or Pindar's,[8] not their own. The subtle cheat
    Of sly exchanges, and the juggling feat
35 Of two-edged words,[9] or whatsoever wrong
    By ours was done the Greek or Latin tongue,
    Thou hast redeemed, and opened us a mine
    Of rich and pregnant fancy, drawn a line
    Of masculine expression, which had good
40 Old Orpheus[1] seen, or all the ancient brood
    Our superstitious fools admire, and hold
    Their lead more precious than thy burnished gold,
    Thou hadst been their exchequer, and no more
    They in each other's dust had raked for ore.
45 Thou shalt yield no precedence but of time
    And the blind fate of language, whose tuned chime°   rhyme
    More charms the outward sense; yet thou mayest claim
    From so great disadvantage greater fame,
    Since to the awe of thy imperious wit
50 Our stubborn language bends, made only fit
    With her tough thick-ribbed hoops to gird about
    Thy giant fancy, which had proved too stout
    For their soft melting phrases. As in time
    They had the start, so did they cull the prime
55 Buds of invention many a hundred year,
    And left the rifled fields, besides the fear
    To touch their harvest; yet from those bare lands
    Of what is purely thine, thy only hands

---

5. I.e., so that things too abstract to be imagined might be made plain to sense.
6. The choir of poets, inspired by Apollo, whose oracle used to be at Delphi.
7. Prometheus stole fire from heaven to aid humankind.
8. Anacreon (6th and 5th centuries B.C.E.) and Pindar (first half of the 5th century B.C.E.) were

famous Greek lyric poets.
9. "Sly exchanges": Carew seems to refer to the habit of using English words in their Latin senses. "Two-edged words" might be puns, but these were a favorite device of Donne's.
1. Ancient Greek poet and prophet, often used as the type of all poets.

(And that thy smallest work) have gleanèd more
60 Than all those times and tongues could reap before.
     But thou art gone, and thy strict laws will be
Too hard for libertines in poetry.
They will repeal° the goodly exiled train   *recall from banishment*
Of gods and goddesses, which in thy just reign
65 Were banished nobler poems; now with these
The silenced tales o' th' *Metamorphoses*²
Shall stuff their lines and swell the windy page,
Till verse, refined by thee in this last age,
Turn ballad-rhyme, or those old idols be
70 Adored again with new apostasy.
     O pardon me, that break with untuned verse
The reverend silence that attends thy hearse,
Whose awful° solemn murmurs were to thee,   *awesome*
More than these faint lines, a loud elegy,
75 That did proclaim in a dumb eloquence
The death of all of the arts, whose influence,
Grown feeble, in these panting numbers lies
Gasping short-winded accents, and so dies:
So doth the swiftly turning wheel not stand
80 In th' instant we withdraw the moving hand,
But some small time maintain a faint weak course
By virtue of the first impulsive force;
And so whilst I cast on thy funeral pile
Thy crown of bays,° oh, let it crack awhile   *poet's crown*
85 And spit disdain, till the devouring flashes
Suck all the moisture up; then turn to ashes.
     I will not draw the envy to engross
All thy perfections, or weep all our loss;
Those are too numerous for an elegy,
90 And this too great to be expressed by me.
Though every pen should take a distinct part,
Yet art thou theme enough to tire° all art.³   *exhaust*
Let others carve the rest; it shall suffice
I on thy tomb this epitaph incise:

95   *Here lies a king, that ruled as he thought fit*
     The universal monarchy of wit;
     Here lie two flamens,⁴ and both those the best:
     Apollo's⁵ first, at last the true God's priest.

                                                    1633, 1640

---

2. Ovid's tales in the *Metamorphoses* had been a
favorite stockpile of poetical properties for Renaissance poets; Donne did not use them.
3. This line and the preceding one were omitted

in the 1640 edition.
4. Priests of the Roman religion.
5. God of poetry.

To Ben Jonson

*Upon occasion of his Ode of Defiance
annexed to his play of* The New Inn[1]

'Tis true, dear Ben, thy just chastising hand
Hath fixed upon the sotted age a brand
To their swoll'n pride and empty scribbling due.
It can nor judge nor write; and yet 'tis true
5   Thy comic Muse from the exalted line
Touched by thy *Alchemist*[2] doth since decline
From that her zenith,° and foretells a red   *highest point*
And blushing evening when she goes to bed—
Yet such as shall outshine the glimmering light
10   With which all stars shall gild the following night.
Nor think it much (since all thy eaglets may
Endure the sunny trial)[3] if we say,
This hath the stronger wing, or that doth shine
Tricked up in fairer plumes, since all are thine.
15   Who hath his flock of cackling geese compared
With thy tuned choir of swans? or who hath dared
To call thy births deformed? But if thou bind
By city-custom, or by gavel-kind,[4]
In equal shares thy love to all thy race,
20   We may distinguish of their sex and place:
Though one hand shape them and though one brain strike
Souls into all, they are not all alike.
Why should the follies then of this dull age
Draw from thy pen such an immodest rage
25   As seems to blast thy else-immortal bays,°   *the poet's crown*
When thine own tongue proclaims thy itch of praise?
Such thirst will argue drought. No, let be hurled
Upon thy works by the detracting world
What malice can suggest; let the rout° say   *rabble*
30   The running sands that, ere thou make a play,
Count the slow minutes might a Goodwin frame[5]
To swallow when th' hast done thy shipwrecked name.
Let them the dear° expense of oil upbraid,   *extravagant*
Sucked by thy watchful lamp that hath betrayed
35   To theft the blood of martyred authors, spilt
Into thy ink, while thou growest pale with guilt.[6]
Repine not at the taper's thrifty waste,
That sleeks thy terser poems; nor is haste

---

1. Jonson's late play *The New Inn* was hissed from the stage in 1629 and published in 1631 with an angry *Ode to Himself* prefixed. Carew's remonstration must have been written close to that event.
2. Jonson's play (1610) about three confidence tricksters.
3. To make sure the young birds in his nest are genuine eaglets, the eagle is reputed to fly with them up toward the sun; true eagles will not be blinded by the rays.
4. "City-custom" (i.e., London City custom) and "gavel-kind" (a system of land tenure once com-

mon in Kent) were two legal ways of dividing an estate equally among all the heirs—as opposed to the normal English rule of primogeniture (everything to the eldest son).
5. Goodwin Sands were shoals in the Strait of Dover, shifty and treacherous, on which many ships were lost. Jonson's slowness in composition was proverbial.
6. The other great charge against Jonson was that he copied or translated too liberally from other authors.

Praise, but excuse; and if thou overcome
40   A knotty writer, bring the booty home;
Nor think it theft if the rich spoils so torn
From conquered authors be as trophies worn.
Let others glut on the extorted praise
Of vulgar breath: trust thou to after days.
45   Thy labored works shall live when Time devours
Th' abortive offspring of their hasty hours.
Thou art not of their rank, the quarrel lies
Within thine own verge[7]—then let this suffice,
The wiser world doth greater thee confess
50   Than all men else, than thy self only less.

ca. 1631   1640

A Song[1]

Ask me no more where Jove bestows,
When June is past, the fading rose;
For in your beauties orient° deep,   *lustrous*
These flowers, as in their causes, sleep.[2]

5   Ask me no more whither do stray
The golden atoms of the day;
For in pure love heaven did prepare
Those powders to enrich your hair.

Ask me no more whither doth haste
10   The nightingale when May is past;
For in your sweet dividing[3] throat
She winters, and keeps warm her note.

Ask me no more where those stars light,
That downwards fall in dead of night;
15   For in your eyes they sit, and there
Fixèd become, as in their sphere.

Ask me no more if east or west
The phoenix builds her spicy nest;[4]
For unto you at last she flies,
20   And in your fragrant bosom dies.

1640

7. I.e., within your own territory, against yourself.
Duels cannot properly take place between two men
of different rank, and as Jonson is out of everyone
else's class, he can only fight himself.
1. Widely popular and several times set to music,
this poem exists in different forms. Like Donne's
Go and catch a falling star (p. 1237), this poem is
built around a series of impossibilities.

2. Aristotelian philosophy suggested that objects
often lay latent in their causes. The lady is a sum-
mation of last summer and cause of the next one.
3. Harmonious (from "division," or rapid melodic
passage).
4. The phoenix, an Arabian bird, builds her nest
from spicy shrubs. She dies every five hundred
years and a new bird springs from her ashes.

A Rapture

I will enjoy thee now, my Celia, come
And fly with me to love's Elysium.[1]
The giant, Honor, that keeps cowards out,
Is but a masquer,° and the servile rout°   *actor/rabble*
5 Of baser subjects only bend in vain
To the vast idol, whilst the nobler train
Of valiant lovers daily sail between
The huge Colossus' legs,[2] and pass unseen
Unto the blissful shore. Be bold and wise,
10 And we shall enter; the grim Swiss[3] denies
Only tame fools a passage, that not know
He is but form and only frights in show
The duller eyes that look from far; draw near,
And thou shalt scorn what we were wont to fear.
15 We shall see how the stalking pageant[4] goes
With borrowed legs, a heavy load to those
That made and bear him—not as we once thought
The seed of gods, but a weak model wrought
By greedy men, that seek to enclose the common,
20 And within private arms empale free woman.[5]
  Come then, and mounted on the wings of love,
We'll cut the flitting air and soar above
The monster's head, and in the noblest seats
Of those blessed shades, quench and renew our heats.
25 There shall the Queens of Love and Innocence,
Beauty, and Nature banish all offense
From our close ivy twines, there I'll behold
Thy barèd snow and thy unbraided gold.
There my enfranchised hand on every side
30 Shall o'er thy naked polished ivory slide.
No curtain there, though of transparent lawn,°   *fine linen*
Shall be before thy virgin treasure drawn,
But the rich mine to the enquiring eye
Exposed, shall ready still for mintage lie,
35 And we will coin young Cupids.[6] There a bed
Of roses and fresh myrtles shall be spread
Under the cooler shade of cypress groves;
Our pillows, of the down of Venus' doves,[7]
Whereon our panting limbs we'll gently lay
40 In the faint respites of our active play,
That so our slumbers may in dreams have leisure
To tell the nimble fancy our past pleasure,

---

1. In classical mythology, the abode of the blessed spirits.
2. The ancient Colossus of Rhodes bestrode the entrance to that harbor, so that ships entering or leaving passed between its legs.
3. The Pope's Swiss Guard were renowned for their height.
4. Figure in a pageant, make-believe giant.

5. To "empale" is to surround with a fence, but the word has phallic overtones as well.
6. Behind this metaphor of mine-mint-and-coin lies the ancient belief that in the creation of children woman contributes matter, and man, form (*materia* and *forma*).
7. Venus rides in a chariot drawn by a yoke of doves.

And so our souls that cannot be embraced
Shall the embraces of our bodies taste.
45 Meanwhile the bubbling stream shall court the shore,
Th' enamored chirping wood-choir shall adore
In varied tunes the Deity of Love;
The gentle blasts of western winds shall move
The trembling leaves, and through their close boughs breathe
50 Still music, while we rest ourselves beneath
Their dancing shade; till a soft murmur, sent
From souls entranced in amorous languishment
Rouse us, and shoot into our veins fresh fire
Till we in their sweet ecstasy expire.
55   Then, as the empty bee, that lately bore
Into the common treasure all her store,
Flies 'bout the painted field with nimble wing,
Deflowering the fresh virgins of the spring,
So will I rifle all the sweets that dwell
60 In my delicious paradise, and swell
My bag with honey, drawn forth by the power
Of fervent kisses from each spicy flower.
I'll seize the rosebuds in their perfumed bed,
The violet knots, like curious mazes spread
65 O'er all the garden, taste the ripened cherry,
The warm, firm apple, tipped with coral berry.
Then will I visit with a wandering kiss
The vale of lilies and the bower of bliss,
And where the beauteous region both divide
70 Into two milky ways, my lips shall slide
Down those smooth alleys, wearing as I go
A track° for lovers on the printed snow.   path
Thence climbing o'er the swelling Apennine,
Retire into thy grove of eglantine,°   sweetbriar
75 Where I will all those ravished sweets distill
Through love's alembic,[8] and with chemic skill
From the mixed mass one sovereign balm[9] derive,
Then bring that great elixir to thy hive.
    Now in more subtle wreaths I will entwine
80 My sinewy thighs, my legs and arms with thine;
Thou like a sea of milk shalt lie displayed,
Whilst I the smooth, calm Ocèan invade
With such a tempest as when Jove of old
Fell down on Danaë in a storm of gold.[1]
85 Yet my tall pine shall in the Cyprian[2] strait
Ride safe at anchor and unlade her freight;
My rudder with thy bold hand like a tried
And skillful pilot thou shalt steer, and guide
My bark° into love's channel, where it shall   vessel

8. I.e., retort—a vessel used for distilling.
9. According to alchemical doctrine, skilled distillation could extract from common metals not only the philosopher's stone but an ointment ("sovereign balm"), good to prevent as well as to cure all diseases whatever.

1. Zeus (or Jove) wooed Danaë in a shower of gold, begetting Perseus.
2. Cyprus was reputed the birthplace of the goddess of love, sometimes called simply "the Cyprian." "Pine": mast, and by metonymy, ship.

90   Dance as the bounding waves do rise or fall.
    Then shall thy circling arms embrace and clip
    My naked body, and thy balmy lip
    Bathe me in juice of kisses, whose perfume
    Like a religious incense shall consume
95   And send up holy vapors to those powers
    That bless our loves and crown our sportful hours,
    That with such halcyon[3] calmness fix our souls
    In steadfast peace, as no affright controls.
    There no rude sounds shake us with sudden starts,
100   No jealous ears, when we unrip our hearts,
    Suck our discourse in, no observing spies
    This blush, that glance traduce; no envious eyes
    Watch our close meetings, nor are we betrayed
    To rivals by the bribèd chambermaid.
105   No wedlock bonds unwreathe our twisted loves,
    We seek no midnight arbor, no dark groves
    To hide our kisses; there the hated name
    Of husband, wife, lust, modest, chaste, or shame
    Are vain and empty words, whose very sound
110   Was never heard in the Elysian ground.
    All things are lawful there that may delight
    Nature or unrestrainèd appetite.
    Like and enjoy, to will and act is one;
    We only sin when love's rites are not done.
115   The Roman Lucrece there reads the divine
    Lectures of love's great master, Aretine,
    And knows as well as Laïs how to move
    Her pliant body in the act of love.[4]
    To quench the burning ravisher, she hurls
120   Her limbs into a thousand winding curls,
    And studies artful postures, such as be
    Carved on the bark of every neighboring tree
    By learnèd hands, that so adorned the rind
    Of those fair plants, which, as they lay entwined
125   Have fanned their glowing fires. The Grecian dame
    That in her endless web toiled for a name
    As fruitless as her work doth there display
    Herself before the youth of Ithaca,
    And th' amorous sport of gamesome nights prefer
130   Before dull dreams of the lost traveler.[5]
    Daphne hath broke her bark, and that swift foot
    Which th' angry gods had fastened with a root
    To the fixed earth, doth now unfettered run

3. While the halcyon (a legendary sea bird) nests on the waves, the ocean remains calm.

4. In Elysium, Lucrece (chastest of Roman matrons, who committed suicide to atone for the disgrace of her rape by Tarquin) reads Aretino (bawdiest of Italian pornographers) to provoke her attacker to new efforts. Laïs was a famous prostitute of Corinth.

5. Penelope was the faithful wife of Odysseus ("the lost traveler"); during the twenty years he was away (at Troy, and on the way back), she fended off her importunate suitors by weaving an endless web—she unwove by night what she wove by day—which she said she had to finish before she could marry again. But in Elysium, she welcomes "the youth of Ithaca" (the suitors) and enjoys "gamesome nights" with them.

To meet th' embraces of the youthful sun.[6]
135 She hangs upon him like his Delphic lyre,[7]
Her kisses blow the old and breathe new fire;
Full of her god, she sings inspired lays,
Sweet odes of love, such as deserve the bays
Which she herself was.[8] Next her, Laura lies
140 In Petrarch's learnèd arms, drying those eyes
That did in such sweet smooth-paced numbers flow,
As made the world enamored of his woe.[9]
These and ten thousand beauties more, that died
Slave to the tyrant,[1] now enlarged, deride
145 His canceled laws, and for their time misspent
Pay into love's exchequer double rent.
　　Come then, my Celia, we'll no more forbear
To taste our joys, struck with a panic fear,
But will depose from his imperious sway
150 This proud usurper and walk free as they,
With necks unyoked; nor is it just that he
Should fetter your soft sex with chastity,
Which Nature made unapt for abstinence;
When yet this false impostor can dispense
155 With human justice and with sacred right,
And maugre° both their laws, command me fight　　*in spite of*
With rivals or with emulous loves, that dare
Equal with thine their mistress' eyes or hair.
If thou complain of wrong, and call my sword
160 To carve out thy revenge, upon that word
He° bids me fight and kill, or else he brands　　*i.e., Honor*
With marks of infamy my coward hands.
And yet religion bids from bloodshed fly,
And damns me for that act. Then tell me why
165 This goblin Honor which the world adores
Should make men atheists and not women whores.

1640

6. Closely pursued by Apollo, god of poetry and the sun, Daphne turned into a laurel bush or bay tree to get away from him.
7. The shrine of Apollo was at Delphi; he carries a lyre as an emblem of poetic harmony.
8. The songs she sings deserve the laurel crown of poetry, which she herself was.

9. Petrarch (1304–1374) wrote his celebrated sonnet sequence to Laura, mourning his unsatisfied desire in the first part, and Laura's death in the second.
1. Honor; the inhabitants of Elysium are liberated ("enlarged") from his prison.

SIR JOHN SUCKLING
1609–1642

The Cavalier ideal is perhaps best seen in the life and poetry of John Suckling—
"natural, easy Suckling" as Congreve's heroine Millimant termed him in *The Way of
the World* several decades later. Born of an aristocratic Norfolk family, Suckling was

educated at Cambridge, took the Grand Tour, fought in the Thirty Years' War, spent a small fortune to outfit a troop of horses in white doublets and scarlet breeches and coats to fight for the king in Scotland in 1639 (they were ignominiously defeated), took part in an unsuccessful royalist plot to free the king's minister Strafford from execution in 1641, and then fled to Paris where, a year later, he died bankrupt. He was described as a Don Juan and a wit, as well as "the greatest gallant of his time and the greatest gamester" for bowling and cards. His poems and songs adopt several stances toward love: cynical debunking of love myths, frank enjoyment of sensual pleasure, invitations to love, and also poems *Against Fruition* that claim the greatest delights are in the chase. His witty satire on his contemporaries, *A Session of the Poets*, describes a contest for the position of poet laureate. And his playful epithalamium, *A Ballad upon a Wedding*, demystifies the usual celebration of the cosmic and religious significances of marriage (as in Spenser's sublime pastoral *Epithalamion*) by detailing comic rustic parallels and identifying sex as the great leveler.

Song[1]

Why so pale and wan, fond lover?
   Prithee, why so pale?
Will, when looking well can't move her,
   Looking ill prevail?
5   Prithee, why so pale?

Why so dull and mute, young sinner?
   Prithee, why so mute?
Will, when speaking well can't win her,
   Saying nothing do 't?
10   Prithee, why so mute?

Quit, quit, for shame; this will not move,
   This cannot take her.
If of herself she will not love,
   Nothing can make her:
15   The devil take her!

1638

FROM FRAGMENTA AUREA[1]

Loving and Beloved

There never yet was honest man
   That ever drove the trade of love.
It is impossible, nor can
   Integrity our ends promove;°   promote
5 For kings and lovers are alike in this,
   That their chief art in reign dissembling is.

---

1. This song was first printed in Suckling's play   1. *Golden Remains* (1646).
Aglaura (1638).

Here we are loved and there we love:
    Good nature now and passion strive
    Which of the two should be above
10   And laws unto the other give.
So we false fire with art sometimes discover,
And the true fire with the same art do cover.

    What rack² can fancy find so high?
    Here we must court and here engage,
15   Though in the other place we die.
        O! 'tis torture all and cozenage:°   *trickery*
And which the harder is I cannot tell,
To hide true love, or make false love look well.

    Since it is thus, god of desire,°   *Cupid*
20   Give me my honesty again,
    And take thy brands back and thy fire;
      I'm weary of the state I'm in:
Since (if the very best should now befall)
Love's triumph must be Honor's funeral.

1646

A Ballad upon a Wedding[1]

I tell thee, Dick, where I have been,
Where I the rarest things have seen,
    Oh, things without compare!
Such sights again cannot be found
5 In any place on English ground,
    Be it at wake° or fair.   *a parish festival*

At Charing Cross,² hard by the way
Where we, thou know'st, do sell our hay,
    There is a house with stairs;
10 And there did I see coming down
Such folk as are not in our town,
    Forty, at least, in pairs.

Amongst the rest, one pest'lent fine
(His beard no bigger, though, than thine)
15   Walked on before the rest:
Our landlord looks like nothing to him;
The King (God bless him!), 'twould undo him,
    Should he go still° so dressed.   *continually*

At course-a-park,³ without all doubt,
20 He should have first been taken out

2. An instrument of torture designed to stretch, or even pull apart, the bodies of those bound on it.
1. The poem is a comic epithalamium (wedding poem) which wittily burlesques such solemn and lofty exemplars of the genre as Spenser's *Epithalamion* (p. 868), turning pastoral into rude rusticity. This poem probably celebrates the wedding of John Lord Lovelace to Anne Wentworth (July 11,

1638); "Dick" may be the poet Richard Lovelace, the groom's brother.
2. Originally a stone cross erected by Edward I, it became a busy center of trade in the city of Westminster; the Haymarket is nearby.
3. A country game, in which a girl calls out a boy to choose her.

By all the maids i'th' town,
Though lusty Roger there had been,
Or little George upon the Green,
    Or Vincent of the Crown.[4]

25 But wot° you what? the youth was going   *know*
To make an end of all his wooing;
    The parson for him stayed;
Yet by his leave, for all his haste,
He did not so much wish all past,
30   Perchance, as did the maid.

The maid (and thereby hangs a tale,
For such a maid no Whitsun-ale[5]
    Could ever yet produce):
No grape that's kindly° ripe could be   *naturally*
35 So round, so plump, so soft as she,
    Nor half so full of juice.

Her finger was so small, the ring
Would not stay on which they did bring,
    It was too wide a peck;°   *much too large*
40 And stay truth (for out it must),
It looked like the great collar (just)
    About our young colt's neck.

Her feet beneath her petticoat
Like little mice stole in and out,
45   As if they feared the light;
But oh! she dances such a way,
No sun upon an Easter day
    Is half so fine a sight.

He would have kissed her once or twice,
50 But she would not, she was so nice,°   *demure*
    She would not do't in sight;
And then she looked as who should say,
I will do what I list today,
    And you shall do't at night.

55 Her cheeks so rare a white was on,
No daisy makes comparison
    (Who sees them is undone°),   *overcome*
For streaks of red were mingled there,
Such as are on a Katherine pear[6]
60   (The side that's next the sun).

Her lips were red, and one was thin,
Compared to that was next her chin

---

4. "As good as George of Green" was a folk saying suggesting male prowess; the other names probably have the same import.
5. Festivals for Whitsuntide or Pentecost (the seventh Sunday after Easter) were occasions for merrymaking and, especially, drinking.
6. A small, early variety of pear.

(Some bee had stung it newly);
But, Dick, her eyes so guard her face,
65 I durst no more upon them gaze
Than on the sun in July.

Her mouth so small, when she does speak,
Thou'dst swear her teeth her words did break,
That they might passage get;
70 But she so handled still the matter,
They came as good as ours, or better,
And are not spent a whit.

If wishing should be any sin,
The parson himself had guilty been
75 (She looked that day so purely);
And did the youth so oft the feat
At night, as some did in conceit,°   *fancy*
It would have spoiled him, surely.

Passion, oh me! how I run on!
80 There's that that would be thought upon,
I trow,° besides the bride: *reckon*
The business of the kitchen's great,
For it is fit that men should eat,
Nor was it there denied.

85 Just in the nick the cook knocked thrice,
And all the waiters in a trice
His summons did obey;
Each servingman, with dish in hand,
Marched boldly up, like our trained band,[7]
90   Presented, and away.

When all the meat was on the table,
What man of knife or teeth was able
To stay to be entreated?
And this the very reason was,
95 Before the parson could say grace,
The company was seated.

Now hats fly off, and youths carouse;
Healths first go round, and then the house,
The bride's came thick and thick;
100 And when 'twas named another's health,
Perhaps he made it hers by stealth;
And who could help it, Dick?

O'th' sudden up they rise and dance;
Then sit again, and sigh, and glance;
105   Then dance again and kiss;

---

7. Our village militia, trained in the rudiments of drill and the use of firearms.

Thus several ways the time did pass,
Whilst every woman wished her place,
    And every man wished his.

By this time all were stol'n aside
110 To counsel and undress the bride,
    But that he must not know;
But yet 'twas thought he guessed her mind,
And did not mean to stay behind
    Above an hour or so.

115 When in he came, Dick, there she lay
Like new-fall'n snow melting away
    ('Twas time, I trow, to part);
Kisses were now the only stay,
Which soon she gave, as who would say,
120   "Good Boy!" with all my heart.[8]

But just as heav'ns would have, to cross it,
In came the bridesmaids with the posset;[9]
    The bridegroom eat° in spite,   *ate*
For had he left the women to't,
125 It would have cost two hours to do't,
    Which were too much that night.

At length the candle's out, and now
All that they had not done, they do:
    What that is, who can tell?
130 But I believe it was no more
Than thou and I have done before
    With Bridget and with Nell.

                               1646

FROM THE LAST REMAINS OF SIR JOHN SUCKLING

Out upon It!

Out upon it! I have loved
    Three whole days together;
And am like to love three more,
    If it prove fair weather.

5   Time shall molt away his wings,
    Ere he shall discover
In the whole wide world again
    Such a constant lover.

8. Some manuscripts read, "God b'w'y" (God be with you).
9. A mixture of spiced hot milk curdled with sherry wine, traditionally offered to the bridegroom on his wedding night.

But the spite on 't is, no praise
10 Is due at all to me:
Love with me had made no stays,
  Had it any been but she.

Had it any been but she,
  And that very face,[1]
15 There had been at least ere this
  A dozen dozen in her place.

1659

1. Other versions of the poem give the line as "that very very face."

RICHARD LOVELACE
1618–1657

Usually linked with Suckling as a quintessential Cavalier, Richard Lovelace was described by a contemporary as "the most amiable and beautiful person that ever eye beheld." Born into a wealthy Kentish family, he was educated at Oxford, and, like Suckling, fought for his king in Scotland (in both expeditions, 1639 and 1640). But he was not a libertine and his poems, in contrast with Suckling's, often exalt women, love, and honor. Also, he shared with his king a serious interest in art, especially the paintings of Rubens, Van Dyke, and Lely. He was imprisoned for a few months in 1642 for supporting the "Kentish Petition" that urged restoration of the king to his ancient rights; in To Althea, from Prison, he finds freedom from external bondage in the Cavalier ideals of women, wine, and royalism. During 1643–46 he fought in Holland and France and in the king's armies in England, and was wounded abroad. In a general roundup of known royalists in 1648 he was imprisoned for ten months, and while there prepared his poems for publication under the title Lucasta (1649). Besides witty and charming love songs, that volume includes the plaintive ballad about the conflict between love and honor, To Lucasta, Going to the Wars, and also a poem that presents the Cavalier ideal at its most attractive: The Grasshopper. That emblematic summer creature is taken to symbolize the loss of the king and the carefree Cavalier life in the Puritan "winter," but Lovelace finds in the fellowship of Cavalier friends a nobler version of the good life and a truer kingship. After 1649 he endured a decade of penury, largely dependent on the largess of his friend and fellow royalist, Charles Cotton. His remaining poems appeared in 1659 as Lucasta: Postume Poems.

FROM LUCASTA

To Lucasta, Going to the Wars

Tell me not, sweet, I am unkind,
  That from the nunnery

Of thy chaste breast and quiet mind
　　To war and arms I fly.

5　True, a new mistress now I chase,
　　The first foe in the field;
And with a stronger faith embrace
　　A sword, a horse, a shield.

Yet this inconstancy is such
10　As you too shall adore;
I could not love thee, dear, so much,
　　Loved I not honor more.

1649

The Grasshopper[1]

To My Noble Friend, Mr. Charles Cotton

O thou that swing'st upon the waving hair
　　Of some well-fillèd oaten beard,
Drunk every night with a delicious tear
　　Dropped thee from heav'n, where now th' art reared,

5　The joys of earth and air are thine entire,
　　That with thy feet and wings dost hop and fly;
And when thy poppy° works thou dost retire　　　　*opiate*
　　To thy carved acorn bed to lie.

Up with the day, the sun thou welcom'st then,
10　Sport'st in the gilt-plats° of his beams,　　　　*golden fields*
And all these merry days mak'st merry men,
　　Thyself, and melancholy streams.[2]

But ah, the sickle! golden ears are cropped,
　　Ceres and Bacchus[3] bid goodnight;
15　Sharp frosty fingers all your flow'rs have topped,
　　And what scythes spared, winds shave off quite.

Poor verdant fool! and now green ice! thy joys,
　　Large and as lasting as thy perch of grass,
Bid us lay in 'gainst winter rain, and poise°　　　　*counterbalance*
20　Their floods with an o'erflowing glass.

Thou best of men and friends! we will create
　　A genuine summer in each other's breast;
And spite of this cold time and frozen fate
　　Thaw us a warm seat to our rest.

1. The grasshopper is traditionally a figure for a life of improvident, carefree pleasure, in contrast with the industrious ant who lays up stores for the winter. The circumstances of the poem are those of the interregnum, when a winter of Puritanism seemed, to royalists, to be settling over England and obliterating their mode of life; the grasshopper may also allude to the recently executed king, Charles I.
2. The three objects of "mak'st merry" are "men," "thyself," and "melancholy streams."
3. Goddess of grain and god of wine.

25   Our sacred hearths shall burn eternally
          As vestal flames;⁴ the North Wind, he
      Shall strike his frost-stretched wings, dissolve, and fly
          This Etna in epitome.⁵

      Dropping December shall come weeping in,
30   Bewail th' usurping of his reign;
      But when in showers of old Greek we begin,
          Shall cry, he hath his crown again!⁶

      Night as clear Hesper° shall our tapers whip   the evening star
          From the light casements where we play,
35   And the dark hag⁷ from her black mantle strip,
          And stick there everlasting day.

      Thus richer than untempted kings are we,
          That asking nothing, nothing need:
      Though lord of all that seas embrace, yet he
40   That wants himself is poor indeed.

                                                            1649

To Althea, from Prison

      When Love with unconfinèd wings
          Hovers within my gates,
      And my divine Althea brings
          To whisper at the grates;
5   When I lie tangled in her hair
          And fettered to her eye,
      The gods¹ that wanton° in the air   play
          Know no such liberty.

      When flowing cups run swiftly round,
10   With no allaying Thames,²
      Our careless heads with roses bound,
          Our hearts with loyal flames;
      When thirsty grief in wine we steep,
          When healths and draughts go free,
15   Fishes that tipple in the deep
          Know no such liberty.

      When, like committed linnets,³ I
          With shriller throat shall sing

---

4. The Vestal Virgins, in Rome, were responsible for tending an eternal flame in the Temple of Vesta.
5. Boreas, the north wind, folding up ("striking") his wings, flees from the heat of the volcano within Mount Etna, a figure for the fires of friendship.
6. Greek wine was especially favored in the classical world. "Crown" here has multiple associa-
tions: the crown worn by "King Christmas" at the festivities banned by Puritans; and the crown Cavaliers hoped would soon be restored to Charles II.
7. Hecate, a daughter of Night.
1. Some versions read "birds" instead of "gods."
2. No mixture of water (as from the River Thames) in the wine.
3. Caged finches.

The sweetness, mercy, majesty,
20 And glories of my king;
When I shall voice aloud how good
 He is, how great should be,
Enlargèd winds, that curl the flood,
 Know no such liberty.

25 Stone walls do not a prison make,
 Nor iron bars a cage;
Minds innocent and quiet take
 That for an hermitage.
If I have freedom in my love,
30 And in my soul am free,
Angels alone, that soar above,
 Enjoy such liberty.

1649

Love Made in the First Age.[1] To Chloris

In the nativity of time,
Chloris, it was not thought a crime
 In direct Hebrew for to woo.[2]
Now we make love as all on fire,
5 Ring retrograde[3] our loud desire,
 And court in English backward too.

Thrice happy was that golden age,
When compliment was construed rage,[4]
 And fine words in the center hid;
10 When cursèd *No* stained no maid's bliss,
And all discourse was summed in *Yes,*
 And nought forbade, but to forbid.

Love then unstinted, love did sip,
And cherries plucked fresh from the lip,
15 On cheeks and roses free he fed;
Lasses like autumn plums did drop,
And lads indifferently° did crop   *without preference*
 A flower and a maidenhead.

Then unconfinèd each did tipple
20 Wine from the bunch, milk from the nipple;
 Paps tractable as udders were;
Then equally the wholesome jellies

1. The Golden Age.
2. Hebrew, supposed to be the original human language, is read from right to left; we have reversed this.
3. Backwards, in reverse. The term also has musi-
cal connotations, perhaps referring here to a pattern of bell-ringing.
4. Passion. Compliments in the Golden Age were understood as ardent propositions.

Were squeezed from olive trees and bellies,
   Nor suits of trespass did they fear.

25 A fragrant bank of strawberries,
   Diapered° with violet's eyes,   *decorated, dappled*
      Was table, tablecloth, and fare;
   No palace to the clouds did swell,
   Each humble princess then did dwell
30   In the piazza⁵ of her hair.

   Both broken faith and th' cause of it,
   All-damning gold, was damned to th' pit;
      Their troth, sealed with a clasp and kiss,
   Lasted until that extreme day
35 In which they smiled their souls away,
      And, in each other, breathed new bliss.

   Because no fault, there was no tear;
   No groan did grate the granting ear,
      No false foul breath their del'cate smell:
40 No serpent kiss poisoned the taste,
   Each touch was naturally chaste,
      And their mere sense a miracle.

   Naked as their own innocence,
   And unembroidered⁶ from offense
45   They went, above poor riches, gay;
   On softer than the cygnet's° down,   *young swan*
   In beds they tumbled of their own;
      For each within the other lay.

   Thus did they live; thus did they love,
50 Repeating only joys above;
      And angels were, but with clothes on,
   Which they would put off cheerfully,
   To bathe them in the galaxy,°   *the Milky Way*
      Then gird them with the heavenly zone.⁷

55 Now, Chloris, miserably crave
   The offered bliss you would not have,
      Which evermore I must deny,
   Whilst ravished with these noble dreams
   And crownèd with mine own soft beams,
60   Enjoying of my self I lie.

                                                     1659

---

5. Arcade, hence an artful structure.
6. I.e., without the stiff gold braid of rank or
authority.
7. The zodiac of stars.

EDMUND WALLER
1606–1687

Poets of the Restoration and Augustan age regularly identified Edmund Waller as a model, paired as such with Sir John Denham, author of a royalist landscape poem, *Cooper's Hill*. These two poets were rightly seen as innovators in the use of smooth, often end-stopped, and antithetically balanced couplets, which anticipated the metrical norm of the next age, the heroic couplet. They were also praised for "correct," natural, and graceful diction. The son of a very wealthy father, Waller studied at Eton, Cambridge, and Lincoln's Inn, married a wealthy lady who died young, and courted in artful verse the celebrated beauty Dorothy Sidney (as "Sacharissa"). A Parliamentarian at first, he participated in a royalist plot to seize London for the Crown and upon discovery was thought to have saved his life by informing on his co-conspirators. Exiled to Paris in 1643, he was pardoned in 1651. After the Restoration he took an active part in court life and wrote panegyrics on Charles II. His first volume of *Poems* (1645) was published a few months before Milton's first volume and by the same bookseller, who noted that both poets' songs had been set to music by the famous court musician, Henry Lawes.

The Story of Phoebus and Daphne Applied[1]

  Thyrsis, a youth of the inspirèd train,°   *company of poets*
  Fair Sacharissa loved, but loved in vain;[2]
  Like Phoebus sung the no less amorous boy;
  Like Daphne she, as lovely and as coy.°   *reluctant*
5 With numbers° he the flying nymph pursues,   *verses*
  With numbers such as Phoebus' self might use.
  Such is the chase when love and fancy leads
  O'er craggy mountains and through flowery meads,°   *meadows*
  Invoked to testify the lover's care
10 Or form some image of his cruel fair.
  Urged with his fury, like a wounded deer,
  O'er these he fled; and now approaching near,
  Had reached the nymph with his harmonious lay,°   *song*
  Whom all his charms could not incline to stay.
15 Yet what he sung in his immortal strain,
  Though unsuccessful, was not sung in vain.
  All but the nymph that should redress his wrong
  Attend his passion and approve his song.
  Like Phoebus thus, acquiring unsought praise,
20 He catched at love, and filled his arms with bays.

1645

---

1. Phoebus (Apollo), god of poetry, fell in love with Daphne and pursued her until, in answer to her prayer, she was turned into a laurel or bay tree, which became an emblem of poetic fame. Successful poets are crowned with laurel (bay) leaves.
2. Sacharissa (from the Latin for sugar, hence, sweetest) alludes here and in other Waller poems to Lady Dorothy Sidney of Penshurst, eldest daughter of the earl of Leicester (the son of that Robert Sidney for whom Jonson wrote *To Penshurst*). Waller courted her unsuccessfully for some years; here he alludes to himself as Thyrsis.

Song

Go, lovely rose!
Tell her that wastes her time and me
That now she knows,
When I resemble° her to thee,   *compare*
5   How sweet and fair she seems to be.

Tell her that's young,
And shuns to have her graces spied,
That hadst thou sprung
In deserts, where no men abide,
10   Thou must have uncommended died.

Small is the worth
Of beauty from the light retired;
Bid her come forth,
Suffer herself to be desired,
15   And not blush so to be admired.

Then die! that she
The common fate of all things rare
May read in thee;
How small a part of time they share
20   That are so wondrous sweet and fair!

1645

ABRAHAM COWLEY
1618–1667

Abraham Cowley (pronounced *Cooley*) published his first volume of verse, *Poetical Blossoms* (1633), at fifteen; it sold well enough to justify two enlarged editions (1636; 1637). Educated at Westminster School and Trinity College, Cambridge, he became a fellow of that college, wrote a Latin comedy for student production, and composed many of the lyric poems later published under the title *The Mistress* (1647). In his *Life of Cowley*, Samuel Johnson based his definition of the so-called "metaphysical" style chiefly on the extravagant conceits in these poems. As a royalist Cowley was ejected from his fellowship in 1644; he then joined the court at Oxford and followed the queen to Paris, serving her as courtier, spy, and confidential scribe. Returning to England in 1654, he brought out a volume of *Poems* (1656) that included several Pindaric odes. Cowley's pindarics are more irregular and more exalted than Jonson's great Pindaric ode on Cary and Morison, though the *Ode: Of Wit*, included here, is more regular and restrained, closer to a Horatian ode. Setting aside some of the many current meanings of "wit" (among them, genius, learning, skill at discovering unexpected comparisons, quickness of repartee, imagination, a style based on antithesis, and verbal cleverness including puns and smart sexual inuendos), Cowley urges a more comprehensive, albeit undefinable, conception of that quality. The 1656 volume also contained an unfinished biblical epic, *Davideis*, and an essay about writing biblical epic that no doubt interested Milton, who was then at work on *Paradise Lost*. Though Cowley's preface records a defeated royalist's wish "to retire myself to some of our American plantations" and "forsake this world forever," he settled near London and took a degree in medicine from Oxford. After the Restoration he studied and published on botany and wrote a famous ode on the newly formed Royal Society.

Ode: Of Wit

Tell me, O tell, what kind of thing is Wit,
  Thou who master art of it.[1]
For the First Matter loves variety less;
Less women love 't,[2] either in love or dress.
5   A thousand different shapes it bears,
    Comely in thousand shapes appears.
Yonder we saw it plain; and here 'tis now,
Like spirits in a place, we know not how.

London, that vents° of false ware so much store,   *sells*
10 In no ware deceives us more.
For men, led by the color and the shape,
Like Zeuxis' birds, fly to the painted grape;[3]
    Some things do through our judgment pass
    As through a multiplying° glass,   *magnifying*
15 And sometimes, if the object be too far,
We take a falling meteor for a star.

Hence 'tis, a Wit, that greatest word of fame,
  Grows such a common name;
And wits by our creation they become
20 Just so as tit'lar bishops made at Rome.[4]
    'Tis not a tale, 'tis not a jest
    Admired with laughter at a feast,
Nor florid talk which can that title gain;
The proofs of Wit forever must remain.

25 'Tis not to force some lifeless verses meet
  With their five gouty feet.
All everywhere, like man's, must be the soul,[5]
And reason the inferior powers control.
    Such were the numbers which could call
30   The stones into the Theban wall.[6]
Such miracles are ceased, and now we see
No towns or houses raised by poetry.

1. The addressee is unknown. "The First Matter" (line 3): the basic material of the universe, given a multiplicity of shapes by the Deity.
2. I.e., women love variety less than wit does.
3. Zeuxis, a Greek painter of the 5th century B.C.E., reportedly painted grapes so realistic that birds came to peck at them.
4. Certain churches in Rome have as their titular incumbents cardinals whose real duties are elsewhere.
5. An old formula from Plotinus has it that the soul is all in every part.
6. When Amphion and Zethus were fortifying Thebes, Amphion's performance on the lyre was so moving that the stones rose into place of their own accord.

Yet 'tis not to adorn and gild each part;
   That shows more cost than art.
35 Jewels at nose and lips but ill appear;
Rather than all things Wit, let none be there.
   Several° lights will not be seen,   *separate*
   If there be nothing else between.
Men doubt because they stand so thick i' th' sky
40 If those be stars which paint the galaxy.

'Tis not when two like words make up one noise,
   Jests for Dutch men and English boys,[7]
In which who finds out Wit, the same may see
In an'grams and acrostics, poetry.[8]
45   Much less can that have any place
   At which a virgin hides her face.
Such dross the fire must purge away; 'tis just
The author blush there where the reader must.

'Tis not such lines as almost crack the stage
50   When Bajazet begins to rage;[9]
Nor a tall met'phor in the bombast way,
Nor the dry chips of short-lunged Seneca.[1]
   Nor upon all things to obtrude
   And force some odd similitude.
55 What is it then, which like the power divine
   We only can by negatives define?

In a true piece of Wit all things must be,
   Yet all things there agree,
As in the ark, joined without force or strife,
60 All creatures dwelt: all creatures that had life;
   Or as the primitive forms of all
   (If we compare great things with small)
Which without discord or confusion lie
In that strange mirror of the Deity.[2]

65 But love, that molds one man up out of two,
   Makes me forget and injure you.
I took you for myself, sure, when I thought
That you in anything were to be taught.
   Correct my error with thy pen,
70   And if any ask me then
What thing right Wit and height of genius is,
I'll only show your lines, and say, *'Tis this.*

1656, 1668

---

7. Scorn for a pun mingles with contempt for the Dutch.
8. Cf. the famous essay on wit by Joseph Addison (p. 2494).
9. Bajazet was a grandiloquent character in Marlowe's *Tamburlaine*.

1. The Senecan style tended toward terse, epigrammatic statements.
2. As in line 3, Cowley posits a kind of first matter that contains potentially all the objects of the world.

KATHERINE PHILIPS
1632–1664

The best-known woman poet of her own and the next generation, Katherine Philips was honored as "The Matchless Orinda," the classical name she chose for herself in her poetic addresses to a coterie of chiefly female friends, especially Mary Aubrey (M. A.) and Anne Owen (Lucasia). Sometimes reminiscent of Donne's love lyrics and sometimes of the ancient Greek Sappho's erotic lyrics to women, these poems develop an exalted ideal of female friendship as a Platonic union of souls. Born to a well-to-do Presbyterian family and educated at Mrs. Salmon's Presbyterian school, Philips was taken to Wales when her mother remarried. In 1648 at age seventeen she was married to James Philips, thirty-eight years her senior and a prominent Presbyterian magistrate and Member of Parliament. They lived together twelve years, chiefly in the small Welsh town of Cardigan, and had two children: Hector, whose death a few days after birth prompted one of her most moving poems, and Katherine, who lived to adulthood. A royalist despite her Puritan family connections, Philips forged connections with other displaced royalists. Her poems circulated in manuscript and elicited high praise from Vaughan in *Olor Iscanus*. They include elegies, epitaphs, poems at parting, and friendship poems to women and men, but also poetry on political themes: a denunciation of the regicide, *Upon the Double Murder of King Charles*, and panegyrics on the restored Stuarts. At the Restoration, James Philips barely escaped execution as a regicide, had his estates confiscated, and lost his seat in parliament, but Katherine became a favorite at Court, promoted by her friend Sir Charles Cotterell ("Poliarchus"), who was master of ceremonies. In Ireland attempting (unsuccessfully) to redeem an investment, she translated Corneille's *Pompey* and her friend the earl of Orrery produced and printed it in Dublin in 1663. The first edition of her poems, apparently pirated, appeared in 1664, the same year she died of smallpox. Her friend Cotterell brought out an authorized edition in 1667.

A Married State[1]

A married state affords but little ease
The best of husbands are so hard to please.
This in wives' careful° faces you may spell   *full of cares*
Though they dissemble their misfortunes well.
5 A virgin state is crowned with much content;[2]
It's always happy as it's innocent.
No blustering husbands to create your fears;
No pangs of childbirth to extort your tears;
No children's cries for to offend your ears;
10 Few worldly crosses to distract your prayers:
Thus are you freed from all the cares that do
Attend on matrimony and a husband too.
Therefore Madam, be advised by me
Turn, turn apostate to love's levity,

1. In a manuscript (Orielton MSS Box 24 at the National Library of Wales) this poem appears with another by Philips, addressed to Anne Barlow (whom she probably met in 1646); this one is probably also for Barlow. Both are signed by her maiden name, C. Fowler, so were evidently written before her marriage in 1648.
2. Praise of the single life is a common topic in women's poetry.

15 Suppress wild nature if she dare rebel.
　　There's no such thing as leading apes in hell.[3]

ca. 1646　　　　　　　　　　　　　　　　　　　　　　Ms; 1988

Upon the Double Murder of King Charles

In Answer to a Libelous Rhyme made by V. P.[1]

I think not on the state, nor am concerned
Which way soever that great helm[2] is turned,
But as that son whose father's danger nigh
Did force his native dumbness, and untie
5　His fettered organs: so here is a cause
That will excuse the breach of nature's laws.[3]
Silence were now a sin: nay passion now
Wise men themselves for merit would allow.[4]
What noble eye could see (and careless pass)
10　The dying lion kicked by every ass?
Hath Charles so broke God's laws, he must not have
A quiet crown, nor yet a quiet grave?
Tombs have been sanctuaries; thieves lie here
Secure from all their penalty and fear.
15　Great Charles his double misery was this,
Unfaithful friends, ignoble enemies;
Had any heathen been this prince's foe,
He would have wept to see him injured so.
His title was his crime, they'd reason good
20　To quarrel at the right they had withstood.
He broke God's laws, and therefore he must die,
And what shall then become of thee and I?
Slander must follow treason; but yet stay,
Take not our reason with our king away.
25　Though you have seized upon all our defense,
Yet do not sequester° our common sense.　　　　　　　　*confiscate*
But I admire not at this new supply:
No bounds will hold those who at scepters fly.
Christ will be King, but I ne'er understood,
30　His subjects built his kingdom up with blood
(Except their own) or that he would dispense
With his commands, though for his own defense.
Oh! to what height of horror are they come
Who dare pull down a crown, tear up a tomb![5]

1649?　　　　　　　　　　　　　　　　　　　　　　　　　1664

---

3. Proverbially, the fate of spinsters.
1. The itinerant Welsh preacher Vavasour Powell was a Fifth Monarchist and an ardent republican who justified the regicide on the ground that Christ's second coming was imminent, when he would rule with his saints, putting down all earthly kings. His poem, which Philips is answering, has not survived, but the likelihood is that both were written shortly after Charles I's execution (January 30, 1649).

2. Steering wheel for the "ships" of state.
3. Breaking the supposed law of nature that excludes women from speaking about public affairs.
4. Wise men, especially Stoic philosophers, normally counsel the firm control or elimination of passions.
5. Their slanders tear up Charles's tomb after his death.

Friendship's Mystery, To My Dearest *Lucasia*[1]

1

Come, my *Lucasia*, since we see
    That Miracles Men's faith do move,
By wonder and by prodigy
    To the dull angry world let's prove
5   There's a Religion in our Love.

2

For though we were designed t' agree,
    That Fate no liberty destroys,
But our Election is as free
    As Angels, who with greedy choice
10   Are yet determined to their joys[2]

3

Our hearts are doubled by the loss,
    Here Mixture is Addition grown;
We both diffuse,° and both engross:°   *spread out/collect*
    And we whose minds are so much one,
15   Never, yet ever are alone.

4

We court our own Captivity
    Than Thrones more great and innocent:
'Twere banishment to be set free,
    Since we wear fetters whose intent
20   Not bondage is, but Ornament.

5

Divided joys are tedious found,
    And griefs united easier grow:
We are selves but by rebound,
    And all our Titles shuffled so,
25   Both Princes, and both Subjects too.[3]

6

Our Hearts are mutual Victims laid,
    While they (such power in Friendship lies)
Are Altars, Priests, and Off'rings made:
    And each Heart which thus kindly° dies,   *benevolently, naturally*
30   Grows deathless by the Sacrifice.

1655, 1664

---

1. This poem was first printed, with a musical setting by the royalist musician and composer Henry Lawes, as "Mutual Affection betweene *Orinda* and *Lucasia*" in Lawes's *The Second Book of Ayres* (1655); our text is from *Poems by the most deservedly admired Mrs. Katherine Philips, the matchless Orinda* (1667). Lucasia is Philips's name for her friend Anne Owen.
2. Angels, though created with free will, were thought to have become fixed in goodness when they turned toward God in the first moments after their creation.
3. Compare Donne, *The Sun Rising*, lines 21–22: "She is all states, and all princes, I" (p. 1239).

To Mrs. M. A.[1] at Parting

I have examined and do find,
 Of all that favor me
There's none I grieve to leave behind
 But only only thee.
5 To part with thee I needs must die,
Could parting separate thee and I.

But neither chance nor compliment
 Did element our love:
'Twas sacred sympathy was lent
10 Us from the choir above.
(That friendship fortune did create,
Still fears a wound from time or fate.)

Our changed and mingled souls are grown
 To such acquaintance now,
15 That if each would resume their own,
 Alas! we know not how.
We have each other so engrossed
That each is in the union lost.[2]

And thus we can no absence know,
20 Nor shall we be confined;
Our active souls will daily go
 To learn each other's mind.
Nay, should we never meet to sense,
Our souls would hold intelligence.°   would still commune

25 Inspirèd with a flame divine,
 I scorn to court a stay;[3]
For from that noble soul of thine
 I ne'er can be away.
But I shall weep when thou dost grieve;
30 Nor can I die whilst thou dost live.

By my own temper I shall guess
 At thy felicity,
And only like my happiness
 Because it pleaseth thee.
35 Our hearts at any time will tell
If thou or I be sick or well.

All honor, sure, I must pretend,°   aspire to
All that is good or great:
She that would be Rosania's[4] friend

---

1. M. A. was Mary Aubrey, the first and, until she married, the dearest member of Philips's "Society of Friendship." Orinda's valedictory poem to her—which Keats admired enough to copy it out in full in an early letter—recalls some of Donne's lyrics, especially *A Valediction: Forbidding Mourning*

(p. 1248).
2. These lines play upon the Neoplatonic idea of friendship and spiritual love—two souls become one.
3. Postponement (of their parting).
4. The poetic name Philips gave to Mary Aubrey.

40   Must be at least complete.
If I have any bravery,
'Tis cause I have so much of thee.

Thy leiger° soul in me shall lie,   *ambassadorial*
    And all thy thoughts reveal;
45   Then back again with mine shall fly,
    And thence to me shall steal.
Thus still to one another tend:
Such is the sacred name of friend.

Thus our twin souls in one shall grow,
50   And teach the world new love,
Redeem the age and sex, and show
    A flame fate dares not move:
And courting death to be our friend,
Our lives, together too, shall end.

55 A dew shall dwell upon our tomb
    Of such a quality
That fighting armies, thither come,
    Shall reconcilèd be.
We'll ask no epitaph, but say:
60 ORINDA and ROSANIA.

                                      1664

On the Death of My First and Dearest Child,
Hector Philips[1]

Twice forty months in wedlock[2] I did stay,
    Then had my vows crowned with a lovely boy.
And yet in forty days[3] he dropped away;
    O swift vicissitude of human joy!

5 I did but see him, and he disappeared,
    I did but touch the rosebud, and it fell;
A sorrow unforeseen and scarcely feared,
    So ill can mortals their afflictions spell.°   *discern*

And now, sweet babe, what can my trembling heart
10   Suggest to right my doleful fate or thee?
Tears are my muse, and sorrow all my art,
    So piercing groans must be thy elegy.

Thus whilst no eye is witness of my moan,
    I grieve thy loss (Ah, boy too dear to live!),

1. In a manuscript the subtitle reads, "born the 23d of April, and died the 2d of May 1655. Set by Mr. Lawes." There is however no extant musical setting.

2. Philips was married in August 1648.
3. The subtitle indicates that he lived barely ten days; the change here is clearly for the parallelism.

15 And let the unconcernèd world alone,
Who neither will, nor can, refreshment give.

An off'ring too for thy sad tomb I have,
Too just a tribute to thy early hearse.
Receive these gasping numbers to thy grave,
20 The last of thy unhappy mother's verse.[4]

1655   1667

4. This was not in fact Philips's last poem, but the sentiment is both true to human feeling and common in elegy. She had one other child, a year later—a daughter, Katherine, who survived her.

ANDREW MARVELL
1621–1678

Andrew Marvell's finest poems are second to none in this or any other period. He wrote less than Donne, Jonson, and Herbert did, but his range is in some ways greater, as he claimed both the private worlds of love and religion and the public worlds of political and satirical poetry and prose. His overriding concern with art, his elegant, well-crafted, limpid style, and the cool balance and reserve of some poems align him with Ben Jonson, but his paradoxes and complexities of tone, his use of dramatic monologue, and his witty, dialectical arguments associate him with Donne. Above all, he is a supremely original poet, so complex and elusive that it is often hard to know what he really thought about the subjects he treats. Many of his poems were published posthumously in 1681, some thirty years after they were written, by a woman who claimed to be his widow but was probably his housekeeper. So their date and order of composition is often in doubt, as is his authorship of some anonymous works.

The son of a Church of England clergyman, Marvell grew up in Yorkshire, attended Trinity College, Cambridge (perhaps deriving the persistant strain of Neoplatonism in his poetry from the academics known as the Cambridge Platonists), ran off to London, and converted to Roman Catholicism until his father put an end to both ventures. He returned to Cambridge, took his degree in 1639, and stayed on as a scholar until his father's death in 1641. During the years of the Civil Wars (1642–47), he traveled in France, Italy, Holland and Spain; much later he said of the Puritan "Good Old Cause" that it was "too good to have been fought for." While his earliest poems associate him with royalists, those after 1649 celebrate the Commonwealth and Cromwell, sometimes with ambivalence but recognizing divine providence in the political changes. From 1650 to 1652 he lived at Nunappleton as tutor to the twelve-year-old daughter of Thomas Fairfax, who had given over his command of the Parliamentary army to Cromwell because he was unwilling to invade Scotland. In these years of retirement and ease, Marvell probably wrote most of his love lyrics and pastorals as well as *Upon Appleton House*. Subsequently he was tutor to Cromwell's ward, William Dutton, and traveled with him on the Continent; in 1657 he joined the blind Milton, at Milton's request, in the post of Latin secretary to Cromwell's Council of State. Marvell accepted the Restoration but maintained his own independent vision and his abiding belief in religious toleration, a mixed state, and constitutional government. He helped his friend Milton avoid execution for his revolutionary polemics and helped negotiate Milton's release from a brief imprisonment. Elected a Member of Parliament in 1659 from his hometown, Hull in Yorkshire, he held that post until 1678, focusing his attention on the needs of his district; on two occasions he went on diplomatic missions—to Holland and Russia. His (necessarily anonymous) anti-royalist polemics of these years include his best-known prose work, *The Rehearsal Transprosed* (1672–73), which defends Puritan dissenters and denounces censorship with verve and wit, and several verse satires that ridicule Charles II and his ministers. He also wrote a brilliant poem of criticism and interpretation on Milton's *Paradise Lost* that was prefixed to the second edition (1674).

Many of Marvell's poems explore the human condition in terms of fundamental dichotomies that resist resolution. In religious or philosophical poems like *The Coronet* or *The Dialogue Between the Soul and Body*, the conflict is between nature and grace, or body and soul, or poetic creation and sacrifice. In love poems such as *The Definition of Love* or *To His Coy Mistress* it is often between flesh and spirit, or physical sex and platonic love, or idealizing courtship and the ravages of time. In pastorals like the Mower poems and *The Garden* the opposition is between nature and art, or the fallen and Edenic state, or violent passion and contentment. Marvell's most subtle and complex political poem, *An Horatian Ode upon Cromwell's Return from Ireland*, sets stable traditional order and ancient right against providential revolutionary change, and the goods and costs of retirement and peace against those of action and war. *Upon Appleton House* also opposes the attractions of various kinds of retirement to the duties of action and reformation.

Marvell's stylistic experiments and transformations of genres produce striking aesthetic effects. Many of his dramatic monologues are voiced by named, naive personas—the Mower, the Nymph complaining—who stand at some remove from the author. One of his most remarkable figures—the phrase "Like a green thought in a green shade" from *The Garden*—derives its power from the unanalyzable suggestiveness the entire poem invests in the term "green." *To His Coy Mistress*, perhaps the best known of the century's *carpe diem* poems, is voiced by a witty and urbane speaker in balanced and artful couplets, but its rapid shifts from the world of fantasy to the charnal house of reality raise questions as to whether this is a clever seduction poem or a probing of existential angst, and whether Marvell intends to endorse or critique this speaker's view of passion and sex. In *Upon Appleton House* Marvell transforms the static, mythic features of Jonson's country-house poem *To Penshurst* to create a poem of epic-like scope that incorporates history and the conflicts of contemporary society. It assimilates to the course of providential history the topographical features of the Fairfax estate, the myth of origin of the Fairfax family, the experiences of the poet-tutor on his progress around the estate, and the activities and projected future of the daughter of the house. In the poem's rich symbolism, biblical events—Eden, the first temptation, the Fall, the wilderness experience of the Israelites—find echoes in the experiences of the Fairfax family, the speaker, the history of the English Reformation, and the wanton destruction of the recent Civil Wars.

FROM POEMS[1]

The Coronet[2]

When for the thorns with which I long, too long,
    With many a piercing wound,
    My Savior's head have crowned,

---

1. Marvell's lyrics were all published posthumously in 1681.

2. A floral wreath, also a garland of poems of praise.

I seek with garlands to redress that wrong,
5   Through every garden, every mead,
I gather flowers (my fruits are only flowers),
     Dismantling all the fragrant towers°   *high headdress*
That once adorned my shepherdess's head:
And now, when I have summed up all my store,
10   Thinking (so I myself deceive)
     So rich a chaplet° thence to weave   *wreath*
As never yet the King of Glory wore,
     Alas! I find the serpent old,[3]
     That, twining° in his speckled breast,   *entwining*
15   About the flowers disguised does fold
     With wreaths of fame and interest.[4]
Ah, foolish man, that wouldst debase with them,
     And mortal glory, heaven's diadem!
But thou who only couldst the serpent tame,
20   Either his slippery knots at once untie,
     And disentangle all his winding snare,
Or shatter too with him my curious frame,°   *elaborate construction*
     And let these wither, so that he may die,
     Though set with skill and chosen out with care;
25   That they, while thou on both their spoils dost tread,
     May crown thy feet, that could not crown thy head.[5]

Bermudas[1]

Where the remote Bermudas ride
   In th' ocean's bosom unespied,
From a small boat that rowed along,
   The listening winds received this song:

5   "What should we do but sing his praise
   That led us through the wat'ry maze
Unto an isle so long unknown,
   And yet far kinder than our own?
Where he the huge sea monsters wracks,[2]
10   That lift the deep upon their backs;
He lands us on a grassy stage,
   Safe from the storms, and prelate's rage.[3]
He gave us this eternal spring
   Which here enamels everything,
15   And sends the fowls to us in care,
   On daily visits through the air;

---

3. Alludes to the serpent that tempted Eve (Genesis 3), traditionally understood to be an instrument for Satan.
4. Self-glorification, self-advancement.
5. See the curse on the serpent (Genesis 3.15), that the seed of Eve will bruise his head.
1. Otherwise known as the "Summer Isles," the Bermudas were described in travel books like John Smith's *The General History of Virginia, New England and the Summer Isles* (1624) as an Edenic

paradise. The poem was probably written after 1653, when Marvell took up residence in the house of John Oxenbridge, who had twice visited the Bermudas.
2. Probably an allusion to the event described in Edmund Waller's mock epic, a battle between the Bermudans and two stranded whales.
3. The Puritan settlers in Bermuda have escaped both the dangers of the sea voyage and religious persecution at home.

He hangs in shades the orange bright,
Like golden lamps in a green night,
And does in the pomegranates close
20   Jewels more rich than Ormus[4] shows;
He makes the figs our mouths to meet,
And throws the melons at our feet;
But apples° plants of such a price,   pineapples
No tree could ever bear them twice;
25   With cedars, chosen by his hand
From Lebanon, he stores the land;
And makes the hollow seas that roar
Proclaim the ambergris[5] on shore;
He cast (of which we rather° boast)   more properly
30   The Gospel's pearl upon our coast,
And in these rocks for us did frame
A temple, where to sound his name.
O let our voice his praise exalt
Till it arrive at heaven's vault,
35   Which, thence (perhaps) rebounding, may
Echo beyond the Mexique Bay."°   Gulf of Mexico

        Thus sung they in the English boat
        An holy and a cheerful note;
        And all the way, to guide their chime,
40   With falling oars they kept the time.

A Dialogue Between the Soul and Body[1]

SOUL.   O, who shall from this dungeon raise
        A soul enslaved so many ways?[2]
        With bolts of bones, that fettered stands
        In feet, and manacled in hands.
5   Here blinded with an eye, and there
        Deaf with the drumming of an ear;
        A soul hung up, as 'twere, in chains
        Of nerves, and arteries, and veins;
        Tortured, besides each other part,
10   In a vain head and double heart.

BODY.   O, who shall me deliver whole
        From bonds of this tyrannic soul?
        Which, stretched upright, impales me so
        That mine own precipice[3] I go;
15   And warms and moves this needless° frame   without needs
        (A fever could but do the same),

---

4. Hormuz, a pearl- and jewel-trading center in
the Persian Gulf.
5. A substance found in sperm whales, used in the
manufacture of expensive perfume.
1. The poem derives from the medieval *debat* on
this theme but alters the usual ending, which gives

a clear victory to soul.
2. The soul echoes Romans 7.24: "O wretched
man that I am! who shall deliver me from the body
of this death?"
3. Having a soul allows humans to walk erect and
so face the danger of falling.

And, wanting where° its spite to try,   *lacking an object*
Has made me live to let me die.
A body that could never rest
20   Since this ill spirit it possessed.

SOUL.   What magic could me thus confine
Within another's grief to pine?
Where, whatsoever it complain,°   *suffer, complain of*
I feel, that cannot feel,⁴ the pain;
25   And all my care itself employs,
That to preserve which me destroys;
Constrained not only to endure
Diseases, but, what's worse, the cure;
And, ready oft the port to gain,
30   Am shipwrecked into health again.

BODY.   But physic° yet could never reach   *medicine*
The maladies thou me dost teach:
Whom first the cramp of hope does tear,
And then the palsy shakes of fear;
35   The pestilence of love does heat,
Or hatred's hidden ulcer eat;
Joy's cheerful madness does perplex,
Or sorrow's other madness vex;
Which knowledge forces me to know,
40   And memory will not forego.
What but a soul could have the wit
To build me up for sin so fit?
So architects do square and hew
Green trees that in the forest grew.

The Nymph Complaining for the Death of Her Fawn¹

The wanton troopers² riding by
Have shot my fawn, and it will die.
Ungentle men! They cannot thrive
To kill thee. Thou ne'er didst alive
5   Them any harm; alas, nor could
Thy death yet do them any good.
I'm sure I never wished them ill,
Nor do I for all this, nor will:
But if my simple prayers may yet
10   Prevail with heaven to forget
Thy murder, I will join my tears
Rather than fail. But, O my fears!

4. The soul can sympathize ("feel") though it has
no power of physical sensation.
1. The lament for the death of a pet is an ancient
topic dating back to Catullus and Ovid; the closest
analogue may be Virgil's story of Sylvia's deer killed
wantonly by the Trojans (*Aeneid* 7.475ff). John
Skelton (p. 499) has a mock-heroic poem on *Philip
Sparrow*. There are also echoes of the Song of

Songs, which have prompted critical debate as to
whether Marvell uses them with serious allegorical
import or the nymph uses them quite inappropriately.
2. Soldiers of the invading Scots army were called
"troopers" (ca. 1640), as were, sometimes, soldiers
of Cromwell's New Model army.

It cannot die so. Heaven's king
Keeps register of everything,
15 And nothing may we use in vain.
Even beasts must be with justice slain,
Else men are made their deodands.³
Though they should wash their guilty hands
In this warm lifeblood, which doth part
20 From thine, and wound me to the heart,
Yet could they not be clean; their stain
Is dyed in such a purple grain.
There is not such another in
The world to offer for their sin.
25   Unconstant Sylvio, when yet
I had not found him counterfeit,°   false, deceitful
One morning (I remember well),
Tied in this silver chain and bell,
Gave it to me; nay, and I know
30 What he said then, I'm sure I do.
Said he, Look how your huntsman here
Hath taught a fawn to hunt his dear.
But Sylvio soon had me beguiled;
This waxéd tame, while he grew wild,
35 And quite regardless of my smart,
Left me his fawn, but took his heart.⁴
      Thenceforth I set myself to play
My solitary time away
With this; and very well content
40 Could so mine idle life have spent.
For it was full of sport, and light
Of foot and heart, and did invite
Me to its game. It seemed to bless
Itself in me; how could I less
45 Than love it? O I cannot be
Unkind t' a beast that loveth me.
      Had it lived long, I do not know
Whether it too might have done so
As Sylvio did; his gifts might be
50 Perhaps as false or more than he.
But I am sure, for aught that I
Could in so short a time espy,
Thy love was far more better than
The love of false and cruel men.
55   With sweetest milk and sugar first
I it at mine own fingers nursed.
And as it grew, so every day
It waxed more sweet and white than they.
It had so sweet a breath! and oft
60 I blushed to see its foot more soft
And white—shall I say than my hand?—

3. In English law, objects forfeit (literally, to God) because they caused a human being's death. The nymph applies the term to persons.

4. A pun: heart/hart (a deer); line 32 also puns on dear/deer.

Nay, any lady's of the land.
   It is a wondrous thing how fleet
'Twas on those little silver feet,
65 With what a pretty skipping grace
It oft would challenge me the race;
And when it had left me far away,
'Twould stay, and run again, and stay.
For it was nimbler much than hinds,[5]
70 And trod, as on the four winds.
   I have a garden of my own
But so with roses overgrown
And lilies that you would it guess
To be a little wilderness.
75 And all the springtime of the year
It only lovèd to be there.
Among the beds of lilies, I
Have sought it oft where it should lie,
Yet could not, till itself would rise,
80 Find it, although before mine eyes.
For in the flaxen lilies' shade
It like a bank of lilies laid.
Upon the roses it would feed,
Until its lips ev'n seemed to bleed;
85 And then to me 'twould boldly trip
And print those roses on my lip.
But all its chief delight was still
On roses thus itself to fill,
And its pure virgin limbs to fold
90 In whitest sheets of lilies cold.
Had it lived long, it would have been
Lilies without, roses within.
   O help! O help! I see it faint,
And die as calmly as a saint.
95 See how it weeps. The tears do come
Sad, slowly dropping like a gum.
So weeps the wounded balsam, so
The holy frankincense[6] doth flow.
The brotherless Heliades
100 Melt in such amber tears as these.[7]
   I in a golden vial will
Keep these two crystal tears, and fill
It till it do o'erflow with mine,
Then place it in Diana's shrine.
105   Now my sweet fawn is vanished to
Whither the swans and turtles° go,   *turtledoves*
In fair Elysium[8] to endure
With milk-white lambs and ermines pure.

5. I.e., full-grown deer.
6. Both balsam and frankincense are fragrant resins obtained a drop at a time from trees with holes bored in them.
7. The three daughters of the sun (Helios), grieving the death of their rash brother Phaethon, were transformed to black poplar trees dropping "tears" of amber.
8. The Elysian fields, a pagan version of heaven.

O do not run too fast, for I
110   Will but bespeak thy grave, and die.
          First my unhappy statue shall
Be cut in marble, and withal,
Let it be weeping too; but there
Th' engraver sure his art may spare,
115   For I so truly thee bemoan
That I shall weep, though I be stone:[9]
Until my tears, still dropping, wear
My breast, themselves engraving there.
There at my feet shalt thou be laid,
120   Of purest alabaster made;
For I would have thine image be
White as I can, though not as thee.

To His Coy Mistress[1]

shy, standoffish.   _Carpe diem._ _"seize the day"_

Had we but world enough, and time,
This coyness, lady, were no crime.
We would sit down, and think which way   _he wishes he had enough time to love her properly._
To walk, and pass our long love's day.
5   Thou by the Indian Ganges' side
Shouldst rubies find; I by the tide
Of Humber would complain.[2] I would
Love you ten years before the Flood,
And you should, if you please, refuse
10   Till the conversion of the Jews.[3]
My vegetable love should grow
Vaster than empires, and more slow;
An hundred years should go to praise   _It is impossible._
Thine eyes, and on thy forehead gaze;
15   Two hundred to adore each breast,
But thirty thousand to the rest:
An age at least to every part,   _he wants to spend eternity with her._
And the last age should show your heart.
For, lady, you deserve this state,°
20   Nor would I love at lower rate.
        But at my back I always hear
Time's wingèd chariot hurrying near;   _now he says that time won't let them spend eternity with eachother_
And yonder all before us lie
Deserts of vast eternity.
25   Thy beauty shall no more be found,
Nor, in thy marble vault, shall sound
My echoing song; then worms shall try

° dignity

9. Niobe, lamenting the death of her many children, in whom she took inordinate pride, was turned to stone.
1. One of the most famous _carpe diem_ (seize the day) poems of the period, it develops the motifs of time and space, introduced in line 1.
2. The exotic river Ganges is on one side of the world, the Humber river flows past Marvell's city,
Hull, on the opposite side. Complaints are poems of plaintive, unavailing love.
3. Popular belief had it that the Jews were to be converted just before the Last Judgment. The exaggerated offers in this stanza play off against conventional hyperbolic declarations of love in Petrarchan poetry.

That long-preserved virginity,
And your quaint[4] honor turn to dust,
30 And into ashes all my lust:
The grave's a fine and private place,
But none, I think, do there embrace.
    Now therefore, while the youthful hue
Sits on thy skin like morning dew,[5]
35 And while thy willing soul transpires
At every pore with instant fires,[6]
Now let us sport us while we may,
And now, like amorous birds of prey,
Rather at once our time devour
40 Than languish in his slow-chapped[7] power.
Let us roll all our strength and all
Our sweetness up into one ball,
And tear our pleasures with rough strife
Thorough° the iron gates of life:[8]   through
45 Thus, though we cannot make our sun
Stand still, yet we will make him run.[9]

handwritten margin notes:
they will die & their love with it.
or he & the worms. If she doesn't yeild to him, the worms will ~~have~~ take her virginity.
now he says that they should have sex
more aggresive

The Definition of Love

My Love is of a birth as rare
As 'tis, for object, strange and high;
It was begotten by Despair
Upon Impossibility.

5 Magnanimous Despair alone
Could show me so divine a thing,
Where feeble Hope could ne'er have flown
But vainly flapped its tinsel wing.

And yet I quickly might arrive
10 Where my extended soul is fixed;[1]
But Fate does iron wedges drive,
And always crowds itself betwixt.

For Fate with jealous eye does see
Two perfect loves, nor lets them close;°   unite
15 Their union would her ruin be,
And her tyrannic power depose.[2]

And therefore her decrees of steel
Us as the distant poles have placed

4. "Quaint" puns on "out of date" and *queynte*, a term for the female genitals.
5. The text reads "glew," which could be correct, but "dew" is a common emendation.
6. Urgent, sudden enthusiasm. "Transpires": breathes forth.
7. Slowly devouring jaws.
8. One manuscript reads "grates," a somewhat dif-

ferent figure for the sexual act proposed.
9. The sun stood still for Joshua (Joshua 10.12) in his war against Gibeon; see the very different resolution in Donne's *The Sun Rising* (p. 1239).
1. The soul has extended itself from the speaker's body and fixed itself to his lover.
2. Two perfections, united, would not be subject to change and thereby to Fate.

(Though Love's whole world on us doth wheel),[3]
20   Not by themselves to be embraced,

Unless the giddy heaven fall,
And earth some new convulsion tear,
And, us to join, the world should all
Be cramped into a planisphere.[4]

25   As lines, so loves oblique may well
Themselves in every angle greet;[5]
But ours, so truly parallel,
Though infinite, can never meet.

Therefore the love which us doth bind,
30   But Fate so enviously debars,
Is the conjunction of the mind,
And opposition of the stars.[6]

The Picture of Little T. C. in a Prospect of Flowers[1]

See with what simplicity
This nymph begins her golden days!
In the green grass she loves to lie,
And there with her fair aspect tames
5   The wilder flowers and gives them names,
But only with the roses plays,
        And them does tell
What color best becomes them and what smell.

Who can foretell for what high cause
10   This darling of the gods was born?
Yet this is she whose chaster laws
The wanton Love shall one day fear,
And under her command severe
See his bow broke and ensigns° torn.   *flags, pennants*
15   Happy who can
Appease this virtuous enemy of man!

O then let me in time compound°   *come to terms*
And parley with those conquering eyes
Ere they have tried their force to wound,
20   Ere with their glancing wheels they drive
In triumph over hearts that strive
And them that yield but more despise:

3. Rotates as on its axis.
4. A two-dimensional map of the world; Marvell images a round globe collapsed into a flat pancake shape, top to bottom, which would bring the two poles together.
5. Oblique lines can touch in angles, as might "oblique" lovers that (in one meaning of the term)

"deviate from right conduct or thought."
6. Conjunction is the coming together of two heavenly bodies in the same sign of the zodiac; "opposition" places them at diametrical opposites.
1. The little girl, T. C., has not been identified with any certainty. "Prospect": landscape.

Let me be laid
Where I may see thy glories from some shade.

25 Meantime, whilst every verdant thing
Itself does at thy beauty charm,
Reform the errors of the spring;
Make that the tulips may have share
Of sweetness, seeing they are fair;
30 And roses of their thorns disarm:
   But most procure
That violets may a longer age endure.

But O, young beauty of the woods,
Whom Nature courts with fruit and flowers,
35 Gather the flowers but spare the buds,
Lest Flora,[2] angry at thy crime
To kill her infants in their prime,
Do quickly make th' example yours;
   And ere we see,
40 Nip in the blossom all our hopes and thee.

The Mower Against Gardens[1]

Luxurious° man, to bring his vice in use,[2]   *voluptuous*
   Did after him the world seduce,
And from the fields the flowers and plants allure,
   Where Nature was most plain and pure.
5 He first enclosed within the garden's square
   A dead and standing pool of air,
And a more luscious earth for them did knead,
   Which stupefied them while it fed.
The pink grew then as double as his mind;[3]
10   The nutriment did change the kind.
With strange perfumes he did the roses taint;
And flowers themselves were taught to paint.
The tulip white did for complexion seek,
   And learned to interline its cheek;
15 Its onion root they then so high did hold,
   That one was for a meadow sold;[4]
Another world was searched through oceans new,
   To find the marvel of Peru;[5]
And yet these rarities might be allowed
20   To man, that sovereign thing and proud,
Had he not dealt between the bark and tree,[6]

[handwritten marginalia: he doesn't like his job.]

[handwritten marginalia: they started to create flowers]

2. Roman goddess of flowers.
1. The four Mower poems are linked by their treatment of a distinctly unusual pastoral figure, a mower rather than a shepherd or goatherd, who provides a singular perspective on those familiar pastoral topics, nature versus art and nature's sympathy for man (the pathetic fallacy). As mower wielding a scythe, he evokes other figures (Time, Death).
2. Into common practice.

3. The double pink or carnation is a product of sophisticated ("double") minds.
4. A highly lucrative trade in Dutch tulip bulbs flourished during the 17th century.
5. *Mirabilis jalapa*, the four o'clock, was an exotic, multicolored flower found originally in tropical America.
6. An adage for interfering between husband and wife, in reference, apparently, to grafting.

Forbidden mixtures there to see.
No plant now knew the stock from which it came;
    He grafts upon the wild the tame,
25   That the uncertain and adult'rate fruit
        Might put the palate in dispute.
His green seraglio[7] has its eunuchs too,
        Lest any tyrant him outdo;
And in the cherry he does Nature vex,
30   To procreate without a sex.[8]
'Tis all enforced, the fountain and the grot,
        While the sweet fields do lie forgot,
Where willing Nature does to all dispense
        A wild and fragrant innocence;
35   And fauns and fairies do the meadows till
        More by their presence than their skill.
Their statues polished by some ancient hand
        May to adorn the gardens stand;
But, howsoe'er the figures do excel,
40   The gods themselves with us do dwell.

they see this as unnatural.

Damon the Mower

Hark how the mower Damon sung,
With love of Juliana stung![1]
While everything did seem to paint
The scene more fit for his complaint.[2]
5   Like her fair eyes the day was fair,
But scorching like his amorous care;
Sharp, like his scythe, his sorrow was,
And withered, like his hopes, the grass.

"Oh what unusual heats are here,
10   Which thus our sunburned meadows sear!
The grasshopper its pipe gives o'er,
And hamstinged° frogs can dance no more: disabled
But in the brook the green frog wades,
And grasshoppers seek out the shades.
15   Only the snake, that kept within,
Now glitters in its second skin.

"This heat the sun could never raise,
Nor dog star so inflame the days;[3]
It from an higher beauty grow'th,
20   Which burns the fields and mower both;
Which mads the dog, and makes the sun
Hotter than his own Phaëton.[4]

---

7. Enclosure, a harem in a sultan's palace.
8. Cherries were commonly propagated by grafting.
1. Damon is a familiar classical name in pastoral; Juliana gets her name from July (lines 23–24).
2. The plaintive love song of an unrequited lover.

3. The dog star (Sirius in the constellation Canis Major) rises with the sun in late summer, producing the heats of "dog days."
4. Son of Helios, the sun god of Greek mythology, he tried to drive his father's chariot but let the horses run away and scorched the world.

Not July causeth these extremes,
But Juliana's scorching beams.

25 "Tell me where I may pass the fires
Of the hot day or hot desires,
To what cool cave shall I descend,
Or to what gelid° fountain bend?   icy
Alas! I look for ease in vain,
30 When remedies themselves complain:[5]
No moisture but my tears do rest,
No cold but in her icy breast.

"How long wilt thou, fair shepherdess,
Esteem me and my presents less?
35 To thee the harmless snake I bring,
Disarmèd of its teeth and sting:
To thee chameleons, changing hue,
And oak leaves tipped with honeydew;
Yet thou, ungrateful, hast not sought
40 Nor what they are, nor who them brought.

"I am the mower Damon, known
Through all the meadows I have mown.
On me the morn her dew distills
Before her darling daffodils,
45 And if at noon my toil me heat,
The sun himself licks off my sweat;
While, going home, the evening sweet
In cowslip-water bathes my feet.

"What though the piping shepherd stock
50 The plains with an unnumbered flock?
This scythe of mine discovers wide
More ground than all his sheep do hide.
With this the golden fleece I shear
Of all these closes every year,[6]
55 And though in wool more poor than they,
Yet I am richer far in hay.

"Nor am I so deformed to sight
If in my scythe I lookèd right;
In which I see my picture done
60 As in a crescent moon the sun.
The deathless fairies take me oft
To lead them in their dances soft,
And when I tune myself to sing,
About me they contract their ring.[7]

65 "How happy might I still have mowed,
Had not Love here his thistles sowed!

---

5. I.e., fountain and cave themselves complain of
unusual heat.
6. Hay is the "wool" of the fields ("closes").

7. I.e., the "fairy ring," a discolored circle of grass
popularly supposed to result from fairies dancing
there.

But now I all the day complain,
Joining my labor to my pain;
And with my scythe cut down the grass,
70   Yet still my grief is where it was;
But when the iron blunter grows,
Sighing, I whet my scythe and woes."

While thus he threw his elbow round,
Depopulating all the ground,
75   And with his whistling scythe does cut
Each stroke between the earth and root,
The edgèd steel, by careless chance,
Did into his own ankle glance,
And there among the grass fell down[8]
80   By his own scythe the mower mown.

"Alas!" said he, "these hurts are slight
To those that die by Love's despite.
With shepherd's purse and clown's all-heal[9]
The blood I stanch and wound I seal.
85   Only for him no cure is found
Whom Juliana's eyes do wound.
'Tis Death alone that this must do;
For, Death, thou art a mower too."

The Mower to the Glowworms

Ye living lamps, by whose dear light
The nightingale does sit so late,
And studying all the summer night
Her matchless songs does meditate,

5   Ye country comets, that portend
No war nor prince's funeral,
Shining unto no higher end
Than to presage the grass's fall;

Ye glowworms, whose officious° flame   *zealous, attentive*
10   To wand'ring mowers shows the way,
That in the night have lost their aim,
And after foolish fires° do stray;   *will-o-the-wisps*

Your courteous fires in vain you waste,
Since Juliana here is come,
15   For she my mind hath so displaced
That I shall never find my home.

8. Evokes the biblical phrase "All flesh is grass" (Isaiah 40.6).

9. Folk names for popular remedies to heal wounds, found in fields and hedges.

The Mower's Song

My mind was once the true survey
Of all these meadows fresh and gay,
And in the greenness of the grass
Did see its hopes[1] as in a glass;°   mirror
5   When Juliana came, and she,
What I do to the grass, does to my thoughts and me.[2]

But these, while I with sorrow pine,
Grew more luxuriant still and fine,
That not one blade of grass you spied
10 But had a flower on either side;
When Juliana came, and she,
What I do to the grass, does to my thoughts and me.

Unthankful meadows, could you so
A fellowship so true forego,
15 And in your gaudy May-games[3] meet,
While I lay trodden under feet?
When Juliana came, and she,
What I do to the grass, does to my thoughts and me.

But what you in compassion ought
20 Shall now by my revenge be wrought,
And flowers, and grass, and I, and all,
Will in one common ruin fall;
For Juliana comes, and she,
What I do to the grass, does to my thoughts and me.

25 And thus ye meadows, which have been
Companions of my thoughts more green,
Shall now the heraldry become
With which I shall adorn my tomb;
For Juliana comes, and she,
30 What I do to the grass, does to my thoughts and me.

The Garden

How vainly men themselves amaze°   bewilder
To win the palm, the oak, or bays,[1]
And their uncessant labors see
Crowned from some single herb or tree,
5   Whose short and narrow-vergèd° shade   edged
Does prudently their toils upbraid;
While all flowers and all trees do close°   unite, agree
To weave the garlands of repose!

1. Green is the color of hope.
2. The alexandrine (12-syllable line) used here is
the only example of a refrain in Marvell.
3. Festivals and merrymaking marked the first of
May.
1. Honors, respectively, for military, civic, and
poetic achievement.

Fair Quiet, have I found thee here,
10 And Innocence, thy sister dear?
Mistaken long, I sought you then
In busy companies of men.
Your sacred plants, if here below,°   *on earth*
Only among the plants will grow;
15 Society is all but rude,
To° this delicious solitude.   *compared to*

No white nor red[2] was ever seen
So amorous as this lovely green.
Fond lovers, cruel as their flame,
20 Cut in these trees their mistress' name:
Little, alas, they know or heed
How far these beauties hers exceed!
Fair trees, wheresoe'er your barks I wound,
No name shall but your own be found.[3]

25 When we have run our passion's heat,
Love hither makes his best retreat.
The gods, that mortal beauty chase,
Still in a tree did end their race:
Apollo hunted Daphne so,
30 Only that she might laurel grow;
And Pan did after Syrinx speed,
Not as a nymph, but for a reed.[4]

What wondrous life in this I lead!
Ripe apples drop about my head;
35 The luscious clusters of the vine
Upon my mouth do crush their wine;
The nectarine and curious° peach   *exquisite*
Into my hands themselves do reach;
Stumbling on melons[5] as I pass,
40 Insnared with flowers, I fall on grass.

Meanwhile the mind, from pleasure less,[6]
Withdraws into its happiness;
The mind, that ocean where each kind
Does straight° its own resemblance find;[7]   *immediately*
45 Yet it creates, transcending these,
Far other worlds and other seas,
Annihilating all that's made
To a green thought in a green shade.

2. Colors traditionally associated with female beauty.
3. Marvell proposes to carve in the bark of trees, not *Sylvia* or *Laura*, but *Beech* and *Oak*.
4. Apollo, the god of poetry, chased Daphne until she turned into a laurel (the emblematic reward of poets); Pan pursued Syrinx until she became a reed, out of which he made panpipes. The gods' motives were, of course, sexual, not horticultural.

5. "Melons," with etymological roots in the Greek word for *apple*, may recall the apple over which all humankind stumbled.
6. "Less" may modify either "pleasure" or "mind."
7. As the ocean supposedly contained a counterpart of every creature on land, so the ocean of the mind holds the innate ideas of all things (in Neoplatonic philosophy).

Here at the fountain's sliding foot,
50　Or at some fruit tree's mossy root,
　　Casting the body's vest° aside,　　　　　　　　　　*garment*
　　My soul into the boughs does glide:
　　There like a bird it sits and sings,
　　Then whets° and combs its silver wings,　　　　　*preen*
55　And, till prepared for longer flight,
　　Waves in its plumes the various light.[8]

　　Such was that happy garden-state,
　　While man there walked without a mate:
　　After a place so pure and sweet,
60　What other help could yet be meet![9]
　　But 'twas beyond a mortal's share
　　To wander solitary there:
　　Two paradises 'twere in one
　　To live in paradise alone.

65　How well the skillful gardener drew
　　Of flowers and herbs this dial new,[1]
　　Where from above the milder sun
　　Does through a fragrant zodiac run;
　　And as it works, th' industrious bee
70　Computes its time[2] as well as we!
　　How could such sweet and wholesome hours
　　Be reckoned but with herbs and flowers?

An Horatian Ode

Upon Cromwell's Return from Ireland[1]

　　The forward° youth that would appear　　　　　*eager, ambitious*
　　Must now forsake his Muses dear,
　　　　Nor in the shadows sing
　　　　His numbers languishing:

5　'Tis time to leave the books in dust
　　And oil th' unusèd armor's rust,
　　　　Removing from the wall
　　　　The corselet° of the hall.[2]　　　　　　　　*upper body armor*

　　So restless Cromwell could not cease
10　In the inglorious arts of peace,

---

8. The multicolored light of this world, contrasted with the white radiance of eternity.
9. Genesis 2.18 recounts the Lord's decision to make a "help meet" for Adam, Eve.
1. The garden itself is laid out as a sundial.
2. With a pun on thyme.
1. Cromwell returned from conquering Ireland in May 1650, about eighteen months after the execution of Charles I. The two events were persistently connected, in that Cromwell's notable success in Ireland was taken as a sign of God's favor to the new republican regime and to Crom-

well as his chosen instrument. Pindaric odes (like Jonson's Cary–Morison ode, p. 1409) are heroic and ecstatic; Horatian odes are poems of cool and balanced judgment, as this one is in its representations of Cromwell, Charles I, and the issues of power and providence.
2. Here as elsewhere there are allusions to Lucan's *Pharsalia*, a poem of civil war whose sympathies are with Pompey, Cato, and the Roman Republic against Caesar and the empire. The poem's allusions to Caesar are most often to Charles I, but sometimes to Cromwell.

But through adventurous war
Urgèd his active star;[3]

And, like the three-forked lightning, first
Breaking the clouds where it was nursed,
15   Did thorough his own side
His fiery way divide:[4]

For 'tis all one to courage high,
The emulous, or enemy;
And with such, to enclose
20   Is more than to oppose.

Then burning through the air he went,
And palaces and temples rent;
And Caesar's head at last
Did through his laurels blast.[5]

25 'Tis madness to resist or blame
The force of angry heaven's flame;
And if we would speak true,
Much to the man is due,

Who from his private gardens, where
30 He lived reservèd and austere
(As if his highest plot
To plant the bergamot[6]),

Could by industrious valor climb
To ruin the great work of Time,
35   And cast the kingdom old
Into another mold;

Though Justice against Fate complain,
And plead the ancient rights in vain:
But those do hold or break,
40   As men are strong or weak.

Nature that hateth emptiness,
Allows of penetration[7] less,
And therefore must make room
Where greater spirits come.

45 What field of all the civil wars
Where his were not the deepest scars?

---

3. Cromwell's brilliance as a military commander—he was primarily responsible for the victory
of Parliament's forces in the Civil War—solidified
his power.
4. The "three-forked lightning" identifies him with
Zeus, suggesting the elemental force by which he
surpassed all those in his own party ("side") of radical Independents; the imagery of giving birth to

himself also suggests going Caesar (born by cae-
sarian section) one better.
5. Royal crowns were made of laurel because they
were supposed to protect from lightning.
6. A variety of pear (from the Turkish, "prince's
pear").
7. Nature abhors a vacuum, but even more, the
penetration of one body's space by another body.

> And Hampton shows what part
> He had of wiser art;[8]
>
> Where, twining subtle fears with hope,
> 50 He wove a net of such a scope
> That Charles himself might chase
> To Caresbrooke's narrow case,
>
> That thence the royal actor[9] borne,
> The tragic scaffold might adorn;
> 55 While round the armèd bands
> Did clap their bloody hands.
>
> *He* nothing common did or mean
> Upon that memorable scene,
> But with his keener eye
> 60 The ax's edge did try;[1]
>
> Nor called the gods with vulgar spite
> To vindicate his helpless right;
> But bowed his comely head
> Down, as upon a bed.
>
> 65 This was that memorable hour,
> Which first assured the forcèd power;
> So when they did design
> The Capitol's first line,
>
> A bleeding head where they begun
> 70 Did fright the architects to run;
> And yet in that the state
> Foresaw its happy fate.[2]
>
> And now the Irish are ashamed
> To see themselves in one year tamed;
> 75 So much one man can do,
> That does both act and know.
>
> They can affirm his praises best,
> And have, though overcome, confessed
> How good he is, how just,
> 80 And fit for highest trust.[3]

8. Charles was confined at Hampton Court after his defeat, as Parliament attempted to negotiate terms for his restoration. Cromwell was rumored to have connived at his escape to Carisbrooke Castle on the Isle of Wight in order to convince Parliament that he could not be trusted and must be executed. Cromwell has shown himself master of the two "arts" of rule defined by Machiavelli, namely, force and craft.
9. The theater metaphors used for Charles are even more powerful because the "tragic scaffold" was erected outside Whitehall, where so many royal masques were produced.

1. A play on the Latin *acies*, which means the edge of a sword or ax, a keen glance, and the vanguard of a battle.
2. Livy and Pliny record that the workmen digging the foundations for a temple of Jupiter at Rome uncovered a bloody head which they were persuaded to take as an omen that Rome would be head (*caput*) of a great empire; the temple and the hill took the name Capitoline from that event.
3. Cromwell conducted a particularly brutal campaign in Ireland, and the Irish had no such testimonials for him; the lines are deeply equivocal.

Nor yet grown stiffer with command,
But still in the republic's hand—
  How fit he is to sway,
  That can so well obey.[4]

85 He to the Commons' feet presents
A kingdom for his first year's rents;
  And, what he may, forbears
  His fame to make it theirs;[5]

And has his sword and spoils ungirt,
90 To lay them at the public's skirt:
  So, when the falcon high
  Falls heavy from the sky,

She, having killed, no more does search,
But on the next green bough to perch;
95   Where, when he first does lure,
  The falconer has her sure.

What may not then our isle presume,
While victory his crest does plume!
  What may not others fear,
100   If thus he crown each year!

A Caesar he ere long to Gaul,
To Italy an Hannibal,
  And to all states not free,
  Shall climactèric be.[6]

105 The Pict no shelter now shall find
Within his party-colored mind,
  But from this valor sad,°   *severe, solemn*
  Shrink underneath the plaid;[7]

Happy if in the tufted brake
110 The English hunter him mistake,
  Nor lay his hounds in near
  The Caledonian° deer.   *Scottish*

But thou, the war's and Fortune's son,
March indefatigably on;

4. The maxim about obedience fitting one to rule is a commonplace. The implications of "yet" and "still," along with the next stanza, suggest a Caesar-figure who has not—but might—cross the Rubicon and defy the Republic, as Julius Caesar did.
5. Thus far, Cromwell gives the Republic credit for his victories.
6. It was thought that Cromwell's military acumen might subdue France and Italy (who threatened to attack the new republic to restore Charles II), just as did Caesar and Hannibal of old. "Climacteric":

a period of crucial, epochal change—here, the expectation that the example of a successful English republic would topple absolute monarchs abroad.
7. Early Scots were called Picts (from the Latin *pictus*, painted), because the warriors painted themselves many colors; contemporary Scots are particolored (divided into many factions) like a scotch plaid. Cromwell was about to go to subdue Scotland, which had declared for Charles II.

115   And for the last effect,
         Still keep thy sword erect;

         Besides the force it has to fright
         The spirits of the shady night,[8]
         The same arts that did gain
120   A power must it maintain.[9]

1650

Upon Appleton House[1]

To My Lord Fairfax

I

Within this sober frame expect
Work of no foreign Architect,
That unto caves the quarries drew,
And forests did to pastures hew;
5   Who of his great design in pain
Did for a model vault his brain,[2]
Whose columns should so high be raised
To arch the brows that on them gazed.

2

Why should of all things man unruled
10   Such unproportioned dwellings build?
The beasts are by their dens exprest,
And birds contrive an equal[3] nest;
The low-roofed tortoises do dwell
In cases fit of tortoise-shell:
15   No creature loves an empty space;
Their bodies measure out their place.

3

But he, superfluously spread,
Demands more room alive than dead;

8. A sword carried with the blade upright evokes the classical tradition that underworld spirits (here, the slain king and his followers) are frightened off by raised weapons.

9. The maxim alludes to Machiavelli's advice that a kingdom won by force must for some time be maintained by force.

1. From 1651 to 1653, Marvell served as tutor to Mary Fairfax, daughter of Ann Vere and Thomas Fairfax, commander in chief of the parliamentary army throughout the civil wars. Fairfax opposed the regicide and in 1650 resigned his command rather than lead a preemptive strike against Scotland (which had declared for Charles II). Cromwell took over as Fairfax retired to his country estates in Yorkshire, especially Nunappleton, a comparatively simple brick structure on the site of a former

Cistercian priory dissolved by Henry VIII along with all monasteries in 1542. The poem makes the house and its history figure the progress of the Reformation and the recent civil wars, played off against the Fall, the conflicts of the Israelites in the Wilderness, and other biblical moments. The poem is structured as a journey around the estate, intersected by a long passage of family history. It was apparently written in the summer of 1651, when Mary Fairfax was twelve.

2. Design in his brain its absurdly high vaulted ceilings. This poem invites comparison and contrast with other country-house poems and the houses, estates, and society they describe: Jonson's *To Penshurst* (p. 1399) and Lanyer's *Cooke-ham* (p. 1287).

3. I.e., a nest proportioned to their size.

And in his hollow palace goes
20 Where winds as he themselves may lose.
What need of all this marble crust
T' impark the wanton mote of dust,
That thinks by breadth the world t' unite
Though the first builders[4] failed in height?

4

25 But all things are composed here
Like Nature, orderly and near:
In which we the dimensions find
Of what more sober age and mind,
When larger sized men did stoop
30 To enter at a narrow loop;
As practicing, in doors so strait,
To strain themselves through Heaven's Gate.

5

And surely when the after age
Shall hither come in pilgrimage,
35 These sacred places to adore,
By Vere and Fairfax trod before,
Men will dispute how their extent
Within such dwarfish confines went;
And some will smile at this as well
40 As Romulus his bee-like cell.[5]

6

Humility alone designs
Those short but admirable lines,
By which, ungirt and unconstrained,
Things greater are in less contained.
45 Let other vainly strive t'immure
The circle in the quadrature![6]
These holy mathematics can
In ev'ry figure equal man.[7]

7

Yet thus the laden house does sweat,
50 And scarce endures the Master great:
But where he comes the swelling hall
Stirs, and the square grows spherical;[8]
More by his magnitude distressed,
Than he is by its straitness pressed;
55 And too officiously° it slights   overeagerly
That in itself which him delights.

---

4. The proud builders of the Tower of Babel, who thought to make it reach to heaven (Genesis 11).
5. The thatched hut of the legendary founder of Rome.
6. To square the circle.
7. The circle symbolized perfection, the square variously virtue, justice, and prudence.
8. The square hall rises up into a domed cupola.

8

So honor better lowness bears,
Than that unwonted greatness wears.
Height with a certain grace does bend,
60 But low things clownishly ascend.
And yet what needs there here excuse,
Where ev'ry thing does answer use?
Where neatness nothing can condemn,
Nor pride invent° what to contemn?   *find out*

9

65 A stately frontispiece of poor[9]
Adorns without the open door;
Nor less the rooms within commends
Daily new furniture of friends.
The house was built upon the place
70 Only as for a mark of grace;
And for an Inn to entertain
Its Lord a while, but not remain.[1]

10

Him Bishops-Hill, or Denton may,
Or Bilbrough, better hold than they;
75 But Nature here hath been so free
As if she said, Leave this to me.
Art would more neatly° have defaced   *elegantly*
What she had laid so sweetly waste;
In fragrant gardens, shady woods,
80 Deep meadows, and transparent floods.

11

While with slow eyes we these survey,
And on each pleasant footstep stay,
We opportunely may relate
The progress of this house's fate.
85 A Nunnery first gave it birth
For Virgin Buildings oft brought forth.
And all that neighbor-ruin shows
The quarries whence this dwelling rose.

12

Near to this gloomy cloister's gates
90 There dwelt the blooming virgin Thwaites[2]
Fair beyond measure, and an heir
Which might deformity make fair.
And oft she spent the summer suns

9. Poor people awaiting Fairfax's alms.
1. The house is described as an inn, with an allusion to Hebrews 11.13–16 and the faithful who proclaim themselves "strangers and pilgrims on the earth" as they "desire a better country, that is, an heavenly."

2. In 1518 the heiress Isabel Thwaites was to marry Thomas Fairfax's ancestor, William, but was confined by her guardian, the prioress of Nunappleton; William obtained an order for her release and then seized her by force and married her.

Discoursing with the subtle nuns.
95 Whence in these words one to her weaved
(As 'twere by chance) thoughts long conceived.

13

"Within this holy leisure we
Live innocently as you see.
These walls restrain the world without,
100 But hedge° our liberty about.   *defend*
These bars inclose that wider den
Of those wild creatures, called men;
The cloister outward shuts its gates,
And, from us, locks on them the grates.

14

105 "Here we, in shining armor white,°   *nun's habit*
Like Virgin Amazons do fight:
And our chaste lamps we hourly trim,
Lest the great Bridegroom find them dim.[3]
Our orient° breaths perfumed are   *fresh*
110 With incense of incessant pray'r.
And holy-water of our tears
Most strangely our complexion clears:

15

"Not tears of grief; but such as those
With which calm pleasure overflows;
115 Or pity, when we look on you
That live without this happy vow.
How should we grieve that must be seen
Each one a Spouse, and each a Queen;
And can in Heaven hence behold
120 Our brighter robes and crowns of gold?

16

"When we have prayed all our beads,
Some one the holy Legend° reads;   *a saint's life*
While all the rest with needles paint
The face and graces of the Saint.
125 But what the linen can't receive
They in their lives do interweave.
This work the Saints best represents;
That serves for Altar's ornaments.

17

"But much it to our work would add
130 If here your hand, your face we had.
By it we would our Lady touch;[4]

3. Matthew 25.1–13 contrasts the wise virgins who kept their lamps lit for the Bridegroom (Christ) and the foolish ones who did not and so were excluded from the marriage feast (heaven).
4. We could come close to representing the Virgin Mary in our designs, with you as model.

Yet thus she you resembles much.
Some of your features, as we sewed,
Through every Shrine should be bestowed:
135 And in one beauty we would take
Enough a thousand Saints to make.

18

"And (for I dare not quench the fire
That me does for your good inspire)
'Twere sacrilege a man t' admit
140 To holy things, for Heaven fit.
I see the angels in a crown
On you the lilies show'ring down;
And round about you glory breaks,
That something more than human speaks.

19

145 "All beauty, when at such a height,
Is so already consecrate.
Fairfax I know; and long ere this
Have marked the youth, and what he is.
But can he such a rival seem
150 For whom you Heav'n should disesteem?
Ah, no! and 'twould more honor prove
He your Devoto° were, than Love.   *devotee*

20

"Here live beloved, and obeyed,
Each one your sister, each your maid.
155 And, if our Rule seem strictly penned,
The Rule itself to you shall bend.
Our Abbess too, now far in age,
Doth your succession near presage.
How soft the yoke on us would lie,
160 Might such fair hands as yours it tie!

21

"Your voice, the sweetest of the choir,
Shall draw Heav'n nearer, raise us higher:
And your example, if our head,
Will soon us to perfection lead.
165 Those virtues to us all so dear,
Will straight grow sanctity when here:
And that, once sprung, increase so fast
Till miracles it work at last.

22

"Nor is our Order yet so nice,°   *precise*
170 Delight to banish as a vice.
Here pleasure piety doth meet,
One perfecting the other sweet.

So through the mortal fruit we boil
The sugar's uncorrupting oil;
175 And that which perished while we pull,
Is thus preserved clear and full.

23

"For such indeed are all our arts;
Still handling Nature's finest parts.
Flow'rs dress the altars; for the clothes,
180 The sea-born amber⁵ we compose;
Balms for the grieved° we draw; and pastes   *injured*
We mold, as baits for curious tastes.
What need is here of man? unless
These as sweet sins we should confess.

24

185 "Each night among us to your side
Appoint a fresh and virgin bride;
Whom if our Lord at midnight find,
Yet neither should be left behind.
Where you may lie as chaste in bed,
190 As pearls together billeted,
All night embracing arm in arm,
Like chrystal pure with cotton warm.

25

"But what is this to all the store
Of joys you see, and may make more!
195 Try but a while, if you be wise:
The trial neither costs, nor ties."
Now Fairfax seek her promised faith:°   *promise to wed*
Religion that dispensed hath;
Which she henceforward does begin:⁶
200 The nun's smooth tongue has sucked her in.

26

Oft, though he knew it was in vain,
Yet would he valiantly complain:
"Is this that Sanctity so great,
An art by which you finelier cheat?
205 Hypocrite witches, hence avant,
Who though in prison yet enchant!
Death only can such thieves make fast,
As rob though in the dungeon cast.

27

"Were there but, when this house was made,
210 One stone that a just hand had laid,

---

5. Ambergris from the sperm whale supplies the rich perfume for our altarcloths.

6. She now begins her "religious" life in the convent.

It must have fall'n upon her head
Who first thee from thy faith misled.
And yet, how well soever meant,
With them 'twould soon grow fraudulent:
215   For like themselves they alter all,
And vice infects the very wall.

28

"But sure those buildings last not long,
Founded by folly, kept by wrong.
I know what fruit their gardens yield,
220   When they it think by night concealed.
Fly from their vices. 'Tis thy state,°   estate
Not thee, that they would consecrate.
Fly from their ruin. How I fear
Though guiltless lest thou perish there!"

29

225   What should he do? He would respect
Religion, but not Right neglect;
For first Religion taught him Right,
And dazzled not but cleared his sight.
Sometimes resolved his sword he draws,
230   But reverenceth then the laws:
For Justice still that Courage led;
First from a judge, then soldier bred.[7]

30

Small honor would be in the storm.°   storming the priory
The Court him grants the lawful form;
235   Which licensed either peace or force,
To hinder the unjust divorce.
Yet still the nuns his right debarred,
Standing upon their holy guard.
Ill-counseled women, do you know
240   Whom you resist, or what you do?

31

Is not this he whose offspring fierce
Shall fight through all the Universe;
And with successive valor try
France, Poland, either Germany;
245   Till one, as long since prophesied,
His horse through conquered Britain ride?
Yet, against Fate, his spouse they kept,
And the great race would intercept.[8]

---

7. His father was judge of the Common Pleas; his maternal grandfather was a heroic soldier.
8. Thomas Fairfax, son of William and Isabel Thwaites, fought in Italy and Germany; his descendants were also honored soldiers; the present Fairfax fulfilled the prophecy by his victories in the civil war.

32

Some to the breach against their foes
250   Their Wooden Saints in vain oppose.
Another bolder stands at push
With their old holy-water brush.
While the disjointed° Abbess threads   *distracted*
The jingling chain-shot of her beads.
255   But their loud'st cannon were their lungs;
And sharpest weapons were their tongues.

33

But, waving these aside like flies,
Young Fairfax through the wall does rise.
Then th' unfrequented vault appeared,
260   And superstitions vainly feared.
The Relics false were set to view;
Only the jewels there were true—
But truly bright and holy Thwaites
That weeping at the altar waits.

34

265   But the glad youth away her bears
And to the Nuns bequeaths her tears:
Who guiltily their prize bemoan,
Like gypsies that a child had stol'n.
Thenceforth (as when th' enchantment ends
270   The castle vanishes or rends)
The wasting cloister with the rest
Was in one instant dispossesed.[9]

35

At the demolishing, this seat
To Fairfax fell as by escheat.[1]
275   And what both Nuns and Founders willed
'Tis likely better thus fulfilled:
For if the Virgin proved not theirs,
The Cloister yet remained hers;
Though many a Nun there made her vow,
280   'Twas no Religious House till now.

36

From that blest bed the hero came,
Whom France and Poland yet does fame;
Who, when retired here to peace,
His warlike studies could not cease;
285   But laid these gardens out in sport
In the just figure of a fort;

9. An allusion to Henry VIII's dissolution of the monasteries.
1. Legally, in the absence of an heir, the property reverted to him as lord of the manor; Henry gave monastery lands to his nobles.

And with five bastions it did fence,
As aiming one for ev'ry sense.[2]

37

      When in the East the morning ray
290 Hangs out the colors of the day,
      The bee through these known alleys hums,
      Beating the dian° with its drums.   *reveille*
      Then flow'rs their drowsy eyelids raise,
      Their silken ensigns each displays,
295 And dries its pan[3] yet dank with dew,
      And fills its flask° with odors new.   *powder flask*

38

      These, as their Governor goes by,
      In fragrant volleys they let fly;
      And to salute their Governess
300 Again as great a charge they press:
      None for the Virgin Nymph;[4] for she
      Seems with the flow'rs a flow'r to be.
      And think so still! though not compare[5]
      With breath so sweet, or cheek so fair.

39

305 Well shot ye firemen!° Oh how sweet,   *shooters*
      And round your equal fires do meet;
      Whose shrill report no ear can tell,
      But echoes to the eye and smell.
      See how the flow'rs, as at Parade,
310 Under their Colors stand displayed:
      Each Regiment in order grows,
      That of the tulip, pink, and rose.

40

      But when the vigilant patrol
      Of stars walks round about the Pole,
315 Their leaves, that to the stalks are curled,
      Seem to their staves the ensigns furled.
      Then in some flow'r's beloved hut
      Each bee as sentinel is shut;
      And sleeps so too: but, if once stirred,
320 She runs you through, nor asks the word.°   *password*

41

      Oh thou,° that dear and happy isle   *England*
      The garden of the world ere while,
      Thou Paradise of four[6] seas,

---

2. The garden's five (seeming) bulwarks or fortifications aim at the five senses.
3. Where the powder is kept in a musket.
4. Mary Fairfax (Maria)—Marvell's pupil at
    Nunappleton.
5. The imperatives are addressed to the flowers.
6. Pronounced with two syllables.

Which Heaven planted us to please,
325 But, to exclude the world, did guard
With wat'ry if not flaming sword:[7]
What luckless apple did we taste,
To make us mortal, and thee waste?

42

Unhappy! shall we never more
330 That sweet Militia restore,
When gardens only had their tow'rs,
And all the garrisons were flow'rs;
When roses only arms might bear,
And men did rosy garlands wear?
335 Tulips, in several colors barred,
Were then the Switzers[8] of our Guard.

43

The gardener had the soldier's place,
And his more gentle forts did trace.
The nursery of all things green
340 Was then the only magazine.
The winter quarters were the stoves°   *hothouses*
Where he the tender plants removes.
But war all this doth overgrow;
We ordnance plant, and power sow.

44

345 And yet there walks one on the sod
Who, had it pleased him and God,
Might once have made our gardens spring
Fresh as his own and flourishing.
But he preferred to the Cinque Ports[9]
350 These five imaginary forts;
And, in those half-dry trenches, spanned°   *restrained*
Pow'r which the ocean might command.

45

For he did, with his utmost skill,
Ambition weed, but Conscience till.
355 Conscience, that Heaven-nursed plant,
Which most our earthly gardens want.°   *lack, need*
A prickling leaf it bears, and such
As that which shrinks at every touch;
But flow'rs eternal, and divine,
360 That in the crowns of saints do shine.

7. Eden after the Fall was guarded by angels with flaming swords.
8. The papal Swiss guards wore multicolored uniforms.

9. The Five Ports on the southeast coast of England, of which Fairfax was warden for a time; the "imaginary forts" are the five bastions of line 287.

46

The sight does from these bastions ply
Th' invisible Artillery;
And at proud Cawood Castle[1] seems
To point the Batt'ry of its beams,
365 As if it quarreled° in the seat   *found fault with*
Th' ambition of its Prelate great;
But o'er the meads below it plays,
Or innocently seems to gaze.

47

And now to the abyss I pass
370 Of that unfathomable grass,
Where men like grasshoppers appear,
But grasshoppers are giants[2] there:
They, in their squeaking laugh, contemn
Us as we walk more low than them:
375 And, from the precipices tall
Of the green spires, to us do call.

48

To see men through this meadow dive,
We wonder how they rise alive;
As, under water, none does know
380 Whether he fall through it or go;°   *move forward*
But as the mariners that sound
And show upon their lead the ground,[3]
They bring up flow'rs so to be seen,
And prove they've at the bottom been.

49

385 No scene° that turns with engines strange   *stage set*
Does oft'ner than these meadows change:
For when the sun the grass hath vexed,
The tawny mowers enter next;
Who seem like Israelites to be
390 Walking on foot through a green sea.
To them the grassy deeps divide
And crowd a lane to either side.[4]

50

With whistling scythe and elbow strong,
These massacre the grass along:
395 While one, unknowing, carves the rail,[5]
Whose yet unfeathered quills her fail.
The edge all bloody from its breast

---

1. Seat of the archbishop of York, two miles from Appleton House.
2. Cf. Numbers 13.33: "And there we saw the giants . . . and we were in our own sight as grasshoppers, and so we were in their sight."
3. Show the nature of the ground below.
4. The mowers produce a lane in the grassy meadow, like that formed when the Red Sea parted to allow the Israelites passage.
5. The corn crake (land rail), a field bird.

He draws, and does his stroke detest;
Fearing the flesh untimely mowed
400　To him a fate as black forebode.

51

But bloody Thestylis[6] that waits
To bring the mowing camp their cates,°　　　　　　　　*food*
Greedy as kites has trussed it up,
And forthwith means on it to sup;
405　When on another quick° she lights,　　　　　　　　*line*
And cries, he[7] called us Israelites;
But now, to make his saying true.[8]
Rains rain for quails, for manna dew.

52

Unhappy birds! what does it boot
410　To build below the grasses' root,
When lowness is unsafe as height,
And chance o'ertakes what scapeth spite?
And now your orphan parents' call
Sounds your untimely funeral.
415　Death-trumpets creak in such a note,
And 'tis the sourdine[9] in their throat.

53

Or° sooner hatch or higher build:　　　　　　　　　*either*
The mower now commands the field;
In whose new traverse° seemeth wrought　　　　　　　*track*
420　A camp of battle newly fought:
Where, as the meads with hay, the plain
Lies quilted o'er with bodies slain;
The women that with forks it fling,
Do represent the pillaging.

54

425　And now the careless victors play,
Dancing the triumphs of the Hay;[1]
Where every mower's wholesome heat
Smells like an Alexander's sweat,[2]
Their females fragrant as the mead
430　Which they in Fairy Circles tread:
When at their dance's end they kiss,
Their new-made hay not sweeter is.

6. A camp follower comically given the name of a classical shepherdess. The harvest activities allude at times to the civil war.
7. The author, at line 389. The Puritans constantly compared themselves and their revolution to the Israelites battling enemies and wandering in the wilderness en route to Canaan, the Promised Land.
8. Exodus 13–15 describes the quails and manna

(left after the dew evaporated) with which the Israelites were miraculously fed after crossing the Red Sea.
9. A small pipe put into the mouth of a trumpet to produce a low sound.
1. A country dance (with a pun).
2. Plutarch wrote that Alexander the Great's sweat smelled sweet.

55

When after this 'tis piled in cocks,
Like a calm sea it shows the rocks:
435 We wond'ring in the river near
How boats among them safely steer.
Or, like the desert Memphis[3] sand,
Short Pyramids of hay do stand.
And such the Roman camps do rise[4]
440 In hills for soldiers' obsequies.

56

This Scene° again withdrawing brings   *stage set*
A new and empty face of things;
A leveled space, as smooth and plain,
As cloths for Lely[5] stretched to stain.
445 The world when first created sure
Was such a table rase[6] and pure;
Or rather such is the toril
Ere the bulls enter at Madril.[7]

57

For to this naked equal flat,
450 Which Levellers[8] take pattern at,
The villagers in common° chase   *common pasture*
Their cattle, which it closer rase;°   *crops*
And what below the scythe increased°   *grew*
Is pinched yet nearer by the beast.
455 Such, in the painted world, appeared,
Davenant with th' Universal Herd.[9]

58

They seem within the polished grass
A landskip drawn in looking glass;
And shrunk in the huge pasture show
460 As spots, so shaped, on faces do.[1]
Such fleas, ere they approach the eye,
In multiplying° glasses lie.   *magnifying*
They feed so wide, so slowly move,
As Constellations do above.

59

465 Then, to conclude these pleasant Acts,
Denton sets ope' its cataracts;[2]

3. An ancient Egyptian city near the pyramids.
4. Hillocks that served as burial mounds; they were actually British in origin, not Roman.
5. Canvases for the Dutch portrait painter Sir Peter Lely, who came to England in 1643.
6. *Tabula rasa* (Latin): a clean or blank slate.
7. Madrid. "Toril": bull ring.
8. A radical faction (actually the Diggers or True Levellers) who sought social and economic equality. A group of Diggers began to put their tenets into practice by taking over and cultivating the land

on St. George Hill, part of Fairfax's domain. See Gerrard Winstanley (p. 1739).
9. William D'Avenant, in his heroic poem *Gondibert* (2.6), describes a painting of creation, where on the sixth day "an universal herd" of animals appeared.
1. A landscape (or painted landscape) reflected in a mirror would be reduced in size.
2. Small waterfalls or dams. Denton, also a Fairfax estate (see line 73), was located on the Wharfe River thirty miles from Nunappleton.

And makes the meadow truly be
(What it but seemed before) a sea.
For, jealous of its Lord's long stay,
470   It tries t' invite him thus away.
The river in it self is drowned
And isles th' astonished cattle round.

60

Let others tell the Paradox,
How eels now bellow in the ox;[3]
475   How horses at their tails do kick,
Turned as they hang to leeches quick;[4]
How boats can over bridges sail,
And fishes do the stables scale;
How salmons trespassing are found,
480   And pikes are taken in the pound.°   *cattle pen*

61

But I, retiring from the flood,
Take sanctuary in the wood;
And, while it lasts, my self embark
In this yet green, yet growing ark;
485   Where the first Carpenter[5] might best
Fit timber for his keel have pressed;°   *obtained*
And where all creatures might have shares,
Although in armies, not in pairs.

62

The double wood of ancient stocks
490   Linked in so thick an union locks,
It like two Pedigrees[6] appears,
On one hand Fairfax, th' other Veres:
Of whom though many fell in war,
Yet more to Heaven shooting are:
495   And, as they Nature's cradle decked,
Will in green age her hearse expect.

63

When first the eye this forest sees
It seems indeed as Wood not Trees;
As if their neighborhood° so old   *nearness*
500   To one great trunk them all did mold.
There the huge bulk takes place, as meant
To thrust up a Fifth Element;[7]
And stretches still so closely wedged
As if the Night within were hedged.

3. Because the ox swallowed them.
4. In popular superstition horse hairs in water become live leeches or eels.
5. Noah, who built an ark to escape a flood covering the earth (Genesis 6).

6. Genealogical trees, of the Fairfax and Vere families.
7. The so-called quintessence, beyond and superior to fire, air, water, and earth.

64

505 Dark all without it knits; within
It opens passable and thin;
And in as loose an order grows
As the Corinthian porticoes.[8]
The arching boughs unite between
510 The columns of the temple green;
And underneath the winged choirs
Echo about their tuned fires.

65

The Nightingale does here make choice
To sing the trials of her voice.
515 Low shrubs she sits in, and adorns
With music high the squatted thorns.
But highest oaks stoop down to hear,
And list'ning elders prick the ear.
The thorn, lest it should hurt her, draws
520 Within the skin its shrunken claws.

66

But I have for my music found
A sadder, yet more pleasing sound:
The stock doves,° whose fair necks are graced   *turtledoves*
With nuptial rings, their ensigns chaste;
525 Yet always, for some cause unknown,
Sad pair, unto the elms they moan.
O why should such a couple mourn,
That in so equal flames do burn!

67

Then as I careless on the bed
530 Of gelid strawberries do tread,
And through the hazels thick espy
The hatching throstle's shining eye,
The heron from the ash's top
The eldest of its young lets drop,
535 As if it stork-like[9] did pretend
That tribute to its Lord to send.

68

But most the Hewel's° wonders are,   *green woodpecker's*
Who here has the Holt-felster's° care.   *woodcutter's*
He walks still upright from the root,
540 Meas'ring the timber with his foot;
And all the way, to keep it clean,
Doth from the bark the wood-moths glean.
He, with his beak, examines well
Which fit to stand and which to fell.

8. The most elaborate order of Greek columns.
9. The stork upon leaving a nest was believed to
leave behind one of its young as a tribute to the
householder.

69

545   The good he numbers up, and hacks;
      As if he marked them with the ax.
      But where he, tinkling with his beak,
      Does find the hollow oak[1] to speak,
      That for his building he designs,
550   And through the tainted side he mines.
      Who could have thought the tallest Oak
      Should fall by such a feeble stroke!

70

      Nor would it, had the tree not fed
      A Traitor-worm, within it bred.
555   (As first our Flesh corrupt within
      Tempts impotent and bashful Sin)
      And yet that Worm triumphs not long,
      But serves to feed the Hewel's young;
      While the oak seems to fall content,
560   Viewing the treason's punishment.

71

      Thus I, easy Philosopher,
      Among the Birds and Trees confer;
      And little now to make me, wants°   *lacks*
      Or° of the Fowls, or of the Plants.   *either*
565   Give me but wings as they, and I
      Straight floating on the air shall fly:
      Or turn me but, and you shall see
      I was but an inverted tree.[2]

72

      Already I begin to call
570   In their most learned original:
      And where I language want, my signs
      The bird upon the bough divines;
      And more attentive there doth sit
      Than if she were with lime twigs knit.
575   No leaf does tremble in the wind
      Which I returning cannot find.

73

      Out of these scattered Sibyl's Leaves[3]
      Strange Prophecies my fancy weaves:
      And in one history consumes,
580   Like Mexique paintings, all the Plumes.°   *feathers*
      What Rome, Greece, Palestine, ere said
      I in this light Mosaic[4] read.

---

1. The "royal" oak was traditionally an emblem of monarchy.
2. Originally classical, this is a widely used metaphor in the Renaissance.
3. The Cumaean Sibyl, in Virgil, committed her prophecies to leaves which Aeneas fears might be scattered (*Aeneid* 6.77).
4. The pattern formed by the trembling leaves; also the books of Moses.

Thrice happy he who, not mistook,
Hath read in Nature's mystic Book.[5]

74

585   And see how chance's better wit
Could with a mask[6] my studies hit!
The oak-leaves me embroider all,
Between which caterpillars crawl;
And ivy, with familiar trails,
590   Me licks, and clasps, and curls, and hales.
Under this antic cope[7] I move
Like some great Prelate of the Grove.

75

Then, languishing with ease, I toss
On pallets swoln of velvet moss;
595   While the wind, cooling through the boughs,
Flatters with air my panting brows.
Thanks for my rest, ye mossy banks,
And unto you, cool Zephyrs,° thanks,   *gentle west winds*
Who, as my hair, my thoughts too shed,°   *part*
600   And winnow from the chaff my head.

76

How safe, methinks, and strong, behind
These trees have I encamped my mind;
Where Beauty, aiming at the heart,
Bends in some tree its useless° dart;   *harmless*
605   And where the world no certain shot
Can make, or me it toucheth not.
But I on it securely play,
And gall its horsemen all the day.

77

Bind me ye Woodbines in your twines,
610   Curl me about ye gadding Vines,
And O so close your circles lace,
That I may never leave this place:
But, lest your fetters prove too weak,
Ere I your silken bondage break,
615   Do you, O Brambles, chain me too,
And courteous Briars, nail me through.[8]

78

Here in the morning tie my chain,
Where the two woods have made a lane;
While, like a Guard on either side,
620   The trees before their Lord divide;

5. The book of the creatures, or the book of God's works.
6. Masque costume or disguise appropriate to the speaker's studies.
7. Comic ecclesiastical vestment.
8. The imagery evokes imprisonment and crucifixion.

This, like a long and equal thread,
Betwixt two Labyrinths does lead.
But, where the floods did lately drown,
There at the evening stake me down.

79

625 For now the waves are fall'n and dried,
And now the meadows fresher dyed;
Whose grass, with moister color dashed,
Seems as green silks but newly washed.
No Serpent new nor Crocodile
630 Remains behind our little Nile;[9]
Unless it self you will mistake,
Among these meads° the only snake.   meadows

80

See in what wanton harmless folds
It ev'ry where the meadow holds;
635 And its yet muddy back doth lick.
Till as a crystal mirror slick;°   smooth
Where all things gaze themselves, and doubt
If they be in it or without.
And for his shade° which therein shines,   shadow
640 Narcissus like,[1] the Sun too pines.

81

Oh what a pleasure 'tis to hedge
My temples here with heavy sedge;
Abandoning my lazy side,
Stretched as a bank unto the tide;
645 Or to suspend my sliding foot
On th' osier's undermined root,
And in its branches tough to hang,
While at my lines the fishes twang!

82

But now away my hooks, my quills,°   floats
650 And angles, idle utensils.
The young Maria walks tonight:
Hide trifling youth thy pleasures slight.
'Twere shame that such judicious eyes
Should with such toys a man surprise;
655 She that already is the Law
Of all her Sex, her Age's Awe.

83

See how loose Nature, in respect
To her, it self doth recollect;
And everything so whisht° and fine,   hushed

9. Our river; serpents and crocodiles were thought
to be bred by spontaneous generation from the
mud of the Nile.

1. Narcissus lay beside water, staring at his reflection.

660   Starts forthwith to its Bonne Mine.°   *good appearance*
       The Sun himself, of Her aware,
       Seems to descend with greater care;
       And lest She see him go to bed,
       In blushing clouds conceals his head.

84

665   So when the shadows laid asleep
       From underneath these banks do creep,
       And on the river as it flows
       With ebon shuts° begin to close;   *black shutters*
       The modest halcyon[2] comes in sight,
670   Flying betwixt the day and night;
       And such an horror calm and dumb,
       Admiring Nature does benumb.

85

       The viscous° air, wheresoe'r she fly,   *thick*
       Follows and sucks her azure dye;
675   The jellying stream compacts° below,   *solidifies*
       If it might fix her shadow so;
       The stupid° fishes hang, as plain   *stupefied*
       As flies in crystal overta'en;
       And men the silent Scene assist,°   *attend*
680   Charmed with the Sapphire-winged Mist.[3]

86

       Maria such, and so° doth hush   *in like fashion*
       The World, and through the Ev'ning rush.
       No new-born Comet such a train
       Draws through the sky, nor star new-slain.[4]
685   For straight those giddy rockets fail,
       Which from the putrid earth exhale,[5]
       But by her flames, in Heaven tried,
       Nature is wholly vitrified.°   *turned to glass*

87

       'Tis she that to these gardens gave
690   That wondrous beauty which they have;
       She straightness on the woods bestows;
       To her the meadow sweetness owes;
       Nothing could make the river be
       So crystal-pure but only she;
695   She yet more pure, sweet, straight, and fair,
       Than gardens, woods, meads, rivers are.

88

       Therefore what first she on them spent,
       They gratefully again present:

---

2. The kingfisher, who by nesting on the waves brought absolute calm to the sea.
3. The bird in its flight.
4. Meteor, or shooting star.
5. Vapors exhaled from the earth.

The meadow, carpets where to tread;
700 The garden, flow'rs to crown her head;
And for a glass, the limpid brook,
Where she may all her beauties look;
But, since she would not have them seen,
The wood about her draws a screen.

89

705 For she, to higher beauties raised,
Disdains to be for lesser praised.
She counts her beauty to converse
In all the languages as hers;
Nor yet in those her self employs
710 But for the Wisdom, not the Noise;
Nor yet that Wisdom would affect,
But as 'tis Heaven's Dialect.

90

Blest Nymph! that couldst so soon prevent
Those trains° by youth against thee meant: *artillery*
715 Tears (wat'ry shot that pierce the mind)
And sighs (Love's cannon charged with wind)
True praise (that breaks through all defense)
And feigned complying innocence;
But knowing where this ambush lay,
720 She scaped the safe, but roughest way.

91

This 'tis to have been from the first
In a domestic heaven nursed,
Under the discipline severe
Of Fairfax, and the starry Vere;
725 Where not one object can come nigh
But pure, and spotless as the eye;
And goodness doth itself entail
On females, if there want a male.⁶

92

Go now fond° sex that on your face   *foolish*
730 Do all your useless study place,
Nor once at vice your brows dare knit
Lest the smooth forehead wrinkled sit;
Yet your own face shall at you grin,
Thorough° the black-bag° of your skin;   *through / mask*
735 When knowledge only could have filled
And Virtue all those furrows tilled.

93

Hence she with graces more divine
Supplies beyond her sex the line;
And, like a sprig of mistletoe,

6. Maria was the only child and heir of the Fairfaxes.

740   On the Fairfacian Oak doth grow;
      Whence, for some universal good,
      The Priest shall cut the sacred bud;[7]
      While her glad Parents most rejoice,
      And make their Destiny their Choice.

94

745   Mean time ye fields, springs, bushes, flow'rs,
      Where yet she leads her studious hours
      (Till Fate her worthily translates,
      And find a Fairfax for our Thwaites),
      Employ the means you have by her,
750   And in your kind yourselves prefer;[8]
      That, as all Virgins she precedes,
      So you all Woods, Streams, Gardens, Meads.

95

      For you Thessalian Tempe's[9] seat
      Shall now be scorned as obsolete;
755   Aranjuez, as less, disdained;
      The Bel-Retiro[1] as constrained;
      But name not the Idalian Grove,[2]
      For 'twas the seat of wanton Love;
      Much less the dead's Elysian Fields,[3]
760   Yet nor to them your Beauty yields.

96

      'Tis not, what once it was, the World,
      But a rude heap together hurled;
      All negligently overthrown,
      Gulfs, deserts, precipices, stone.
765   Your lesser World[4] contains the same,
      But in more decent order tame;
      You Heaven's Center, Nature's Lap,
      And Paradise's only Map.

97

      But now the Salmon-Fishers moist
770   Their Leathern Boats begin to hoist;
      And, like Antipodes in shoes,[5]
      Have shod their heads in their canoes.
      How Tortoise-like, but not so slow,
      These rational Amphibii[6] go!
775   Let's in; for the dark Hemisphere
      Does now like one of them appear.

1651

---

7. Maria is, of course, intended for marriage.
8. Make yourselves the best you can.
9. The Vale of Tempe, in Greece, was a kind of paradise.
1. Spanish palaces.
2. A favorite haunt of Aphrodite (Venus), goddess of love, on Cyprus.
3. The pleasant habitation of the good in the clas-
sical underworld.
4. Appleton House.
5. The men who dwell on the other side of the world are sometimes said to wear their shoes on their heads; these English fishermen transport their leathern boats on their heads.
6. As men, the fishermen are "rational"; and they live in two elements, land and water.

Voices of the War

If the Puritan Revolution of 1640–60 was the political storm center of the seventeenth century, the execution of Charles I on January 30, 1649, was the eye of that storm. By what right did the judicial body that passed judgment on Charles take that action? Who were they and whom did they represent? What political body could henceforth claim to exercise legitimate power? In executing Charles, the Puritans had cut off not just the life of a man but the line of Stuart kings and perhaps the entire monarchical line reaching back to William the Conqueror. The successive governments—a republic "without King or House of Lords" (1649–53), a Protectorate under Oliver Cromwell (1654–58), and then a hodgepodge of makeshift arrangements (1658–60)—were unable to achieve the authority, unity, and widespread support necessary for a permanent settlement.

As the storm clouds gathered leading to the outbreak of hostilities in August 1642, and throughout the period of the Civil Wars and Interregnum until Charles II was restored in May 1660, English men and some women, of every class and condition, began expressing themselves in little booklets called tracts. Thousands were printed and sold for a penny or two on the streets. At the outset they mainly addressed ecclesiastical issues: abolition of the bishops, reformation of liturgy, remodeling the institution of the church. But efforts to settle a new national church along Presbyterian lines broke down under the pressure of widespread demands for toleration of the rapidly proliferating Independent congregations and sects. Other polemicists offered new models of the state: a constitutional monarchy, a republic, a theocracy, a democracy of sorts, a communist utopia. Many tracts gave voice to the frustrations and wrongs of the lower classes: some urged the abolition of tithes, some demanded reform of the law and penal system, some thought the distribution of property manifestly unjust, some advocated free love, some looked for Christ's imminent return to earth to rule with his saints, and some proclaimed themselves the Messiah. Prophets and visionaries, male and female, raised their voices and spoke by God's direction. In the religious movements and the social upheavals of the period, some women found unusual opportunities for action and expression. Only a few women had sufficient education, or opportunity, to engage in the polemic controversies, but in letters, memoirs, and occasionally in print some found ways to protest domestic tyranny and women's usual exclusion from the public realm. In brief, England experienced in the years from 1640 to 1660 a stirring of the spirit such as no European society had yet known, and the range of English prose expanded in so many different directions as to defy coherent description.

The extracts included here are intended to sample some of these directions. In a broader sense, most of the poets and prose writers who published during the revolutionary period could also be called voices in the war, in that they register, sometimes obliquely but nonetheless surely, their responses to the conflicts swirling about them: poets like Vaughan, Herrick, Carew, Lovelace, Suckling, Marvell, and Milton; prose writers like Thomas Hobbes, Sir Thomas Browne, Izaak Walton, and again Milton. But most of the men and women sampled here (the exception is Clarendon) are drawn from the newly articulate classes of English society, and their texts speak directly from and about the battlefields of ideas. Out of the maelstrom of proposals that were promoted by these various radical groups were some tenets that have helped shape modern free societies: complete religious toleration; the idea of one man (not, alas, one woman), one vote; an uncensored press; the concept of a reformed, humane, penal system; church disestablishment; educational reform; and popular sovereignty.

LUCY HUTCHINSON

Lucy Hutchinson (née Apsley) (1620–after 1675), whose life centered in the North Country city of Nottingham, was a staunch republican, memoirist, poet, biographer, and historian of the revolutionary period. In a fragmentary autobiography, she relates that she could read English perfectly by the age of four, and that "having a great memory, I was carried to sermons, and while I was very young could remember and repeat them . . . exactly." Her parents allowed her to receive at home as good an education as her brothers got at school. She reports that her future husband learned of her existence by noticing some of her Latin books. At age eighteen, she was married to John Hutchinson, a man of unyielding conviction and courage: he fought in the Puritan armies, served as governor of Nottingham Castle, sat in the Long Parliament, voted for the execution of Charles I, supported the republican commonwealth (1649–53), and withdrew support from Cromwell when he overrode and dismissed parliaments. Hutchinson was arrested after the Restoration and died in prison in 1664. After his death his devoted wife of twenty-six years wrote her *Memoirs of Colonel John Hutchinson*, purportedly to preserve his memory for her children. But within that memoir and eyewitness account of the remarkable period they had lived through, she enfolded a broad history of and commentary upon the Puritan movement and the revolution. Almost certainly she hoped for a broader audience of nonconformists and republicans who might someday revive the Good Old Cause, though because of its politics her work was not published until 1806.

The extract below is from a private diary upon which her memoir/history is based; in it she reconstructs a dramatic scene in Nottingham in April 1642, as parliamentary and royalist adherents, now on the brink of war, were maneuvering for support and military power in the countryside. (Hostilities broke out in late August.) She reconstructs a dialogue between her husband, not yet a colonel but already a Puritan leader sympathetic to Parliament (designated as H.) and his kinsman, Lord Newark, lord lieutenant of the county (designated as N.). Norfolk is under orders from the king to acquire gunpowder stored in the town hall; Hutchinson, passing through Nottingham, is asked to intervene and prevent the removal of the gunpowder its militia may soon need and want to use against the king. The discourse between the two distantly related gentlemen remains polite, even courtly, but the subtext of threat is evident, a foretaste of the antagonisms that will soon split families apart. At one point Lucy Hutchinson represents the "voice" of the country populace, who make clear their readiness to speak in far different accents.

From Memoirs of Colonel Hutchinson

[A CONFRONTATION]

Mr. Hutchinson asking who were above,[1] he was told that the lord lieu-tenant, my Lord Newark, was there, to whom he sent his name and de-sired to speak with him; and being come up found in the room where the powder was weighing, my Lord Newark, the sheriff Sir John Digby, and two or three captains. Mr. Hutchinson, addressing himself to my lord only, spoke to him:

H. My lord, hearing that there was some question concerning the county's powder, I am come to kiss your lordship's hands,[2] and to beseech you that I may know what your desires and intents are concerning it?

N. Cousin, the king desires to borrow it of the country,[3] to supply his great necessities.

H. I beseech your lordship, what commission have you to demand this?

N. Upon my honor, I have a commission from his majesty, but it is left behind me; but I will engage my honor, it shall be repaid the country.

H. Your lordship's honor is an engagement would be accepted for more than I am worth; but in such an occasion as this, the greatest man's engage-ment in the kingdom cannot be a satisfaction to the country.

N. The king's intents are only to borrow it, and if the country will not lend it he will pay for it.

H. My lord, 'tis not the value of the powder we endeavor to preserve, but in times of danger, as these are, those things which serve for our defense are not valuable at any price, should you give us as many barrels of gold as you take barrels of powder.

N. Upon my faith and honor, cousin, it shall be restored in ten days.

H. My lord, such is the danger of the times that for aught we know we may in less than four days be ruined for want of it: and I beseech your lordship to consider how sad a thing it is in these times of war to leave a poor country and the people in it naked and open to the injury of every passenger;[4] for if you take our powder, you may as well take our arms, without which we are unable to make use of them, and I hope your lordship will not disarm the country.

N. Why, who should the country fear? I am their lord lieutenant and engaged with my life and honor to defend them! What danger are they in?

H. Danger! yes, my lord, great danger; there is a troop of horse now in the town, and it hath often happened so that they have committed great out-rages and insolencies, calling divers honest men Puritans and rogues, with divers other provoking terms and carriages. I myself was abused by some of them as I passed on the road. I chanced to meet some of these gentle-men, who, as soon as I was past, inquired my name, and being told it, gave me another, saying among themselves that I was a Puritan and a traitor; as two or three honest men that came behind told me. Besides, your lordship

1. On the second floor of the town hall.
2. Kissing hands is a courtly ceremonial gesture, often metaphorical rather than physical, but expressing obeisance.

3. I.e., the rural districts surrounding the county seat. *Country* and *county* are often inter-changeably.
4. Passerby.

may be far off, and we ruined before you can come to us, being unarmed and not able to defend ourselves from anybody, and this country being a road through which under the name of soldiers rude people daily pass from the north to south, and terrify the country; which if they knew to be naked and unarmed, they would thereby be encouraged to greater insolencies and mischiefs.

N. The king's occasions are such and so urgent as I cannot dispense with it for any reasons, but must needs have it.

H. I hope your lordship will not deny that the country hath a right, interest, and property in it.

N. I do not deny it.

H. Then, my lord, I hope his majesty will not command it from them.

N. No, he doth but desire to borrow it.

H. Then I hope if he do but desire to borrow it, his majesty hath signified his request to those that have interest in it, under his hand.

N. Upon my honor he hath, but I left it behind me.

H. I beseech your lordship, then, that you would not take it away till you have acquainted the country with it, who only have power to lend it; and if your lordship be pleased to do this, I will engage myself that by tomorrow at twelve of the clock, that part of the country who have interest in the powder shall all wait on your lordship, and give you their resolutions.

N. The king's occasions cannot admit of that delay.

H. I beseech of your lordship, yet be pleased to consider the dangerous consequence of taking it without the country's consent, and be pleased but to stay till they can come in.

N. That time is more than his majesty's necessities can dispense withal.

With that Mr. Hutchinson went downstairs, where by that time a good company of the country were gathered together, to whom Mr. Hutchinson told what my lord had said to him; and they desired him that he would but stand to them, and they would part with every drop of blood out of their bodies before he should have it; and said besides, that they would go up and break my lord's neck and the sheriff's out of the windows; but Mr. Hutchinson desired them to stay below till he had once more spoken to my lord; and then, taking only one or two more with him, went in and spoke to my lord.

H. My lord, I am again, at the request of the country that are below, come to your lordship, and do once more humbly beseech you to consider the business you are about before you proceed further in it, for it may prove of dangerous consequence if you go on.

N. Cousin,[5] I am confident it cannot, for the country will not deny this to the king.

H. It's very probable they will not, if your lordship please to have patience till they can be called in, that they may be acquainted with his majesty's desires.

N. His majesty is very well assured of the willingness and cheerfulness of the greater part of the country to it.

---

5. A general term for kinsman, of whatever relationship.

H. My lord, I do not know what assurance his majesty hath of it, but if you please to look out of this window (pointing to the countrymen below in the streets) you will see no inconsiderable number gathered who, I fear, will not be willing to part with it.

N. Those are but some few factious men, not to be considered.

H. My lord, we have been happy yet, in these unhappy differences, to have had no blood shed, and I am confident your lordship is so noble and tender of your country that it would very much trouble you to have a hand in the first man's blood that should be spent in this quarrel.

N. Cousin, it cannot come to that, fear it not (this was spoken very slightly and contemptuously); his majesty's occasions are urgent, and must be served.

(With that, the country came very fast up, which when the cavalier captains saw, they slunk down.)

H. Why then, my lord, I must plainly tell you, not one here but will lose every drop of blood in his body before he will part with one corn of it, without your lordship can show either a command or a request for it under his majesty's hand and seal, or that the country be called together to give their free consent to it; for we have all property and interest in it, being members of this county, and it being bought with our money for the particular defense and safety of the same.

My lord desired to borrow part of it, but that being denied, he turned to Sir John Digby and took him to the window, where, after he had whispered with him a while, Sir John Digby laid down his pen, ink, and paper, with which he had been taking an account of the powder, match,[6] and bullet. The countrymen desired my lord aloud that he would not take away their powder out of the country; upon which, turning to them, he thus spoke:

"Gentlemen, his majesty was assured by some of the cheerfulness of this country's affections to him, which I am very sorry to see so much failing in, and that the country should come so much short of this town,[7] which hath cheerfully lent his majesty one barrel of powder; but it seems he can have none from you. I pray God you do not repent this carriage of yours toward his majesty, which he must be acquainted withal."

A countryman, standing forth, asked his lordship this question, "Whether, if he were to take a journey into a place where probably he might be set upon by thieves and robbers, and having a charge[8] about him, if any friend should ask him to lend his sword, he would part with it and go himself without? My lord, the case is ours; our wives, children, and estates all depend upon this country's safety; and how can it be safe in these dangerous times, when so many troops and companies pass through and commit outrages and abuses among us, if we have not arms and powder wherewith to defend us?"

My lord made no reply, but bade the men whom he had employed to weigh up the powder desist, and so went down the stairs. Mr. Hutchinson followed him, and as he went, an ancient gentleman who was with my lord, whose face and name were both unknown to him, came to him, and said these

6. Slow-burning fuses for discharging cannon.
7. The town of Nottingham proper, as distinct from the rest of the county.
8. Money or valuables.

words: "Stand to it; I'll warrant you gentlemen it is well done." And as they passed through a low room, my lord took Mr. Hutchinson aside and said:

N. Cousin, I must acquaint the king with this.

H. My lord, it's very likely you must, being employed upon his majesty's service, give him an account.

N. Nay, cousin (smiling), I mean not so, but I must acquaint him, and I am sorry I must, that you are the head and ringleader of a faction, whereby you hinder his majesty's service.

H. My lord, I do not conceive how this can be a faction, I speaking only (out of the noble respect and honor I bear your lordship, in private to you, to prevent a mischief) the sense of these men, who I perceived were come to know by what authority, and why, their powder, which is their proper[9] goods and only means of safety in these times of danger, should be taken from them. And if it were a faction, I am not the head of it—I accidentally coming to town from Sir John Biron's last night, and neither knowing nor imagining any of this business, was this morning importuned to wait on your lordship at the town's hall, by many countrymen who informed me you were taking away their powder out of the country.

N. Cousin, if you can answer it, I shall be glad of it; but I'll assure you, I must let his majesty know.

H. If his majesty must know it, I am very happy I spoke to none but your lordship, who, I am confident, is so noble that you will neither add nor diminish anything to my prejudice; and then I am confident the justice and reasonableness of what I have said, with my own innocency in speaking it, will bear me out.

N. Ay, cousin, but your name is up already.[1]

H. It may be so, my lord; and I believe those that set it up had no good wishes to me; and as it rose, so, in the name of God, let it fall; for I know my own clearness and innocency in anything that can be objected against me.

N. Well, cousin, well; I am glad of your good resolution.

And so my lord left him. The gentlemen of the country that were there, upon consideration what they should do with their powder, determined to return my lord thanks for sparing it and to lock it up with two locks, whereof the sheriff should have one key and the mayor another; which accordingly was done; but Mr. Hutchinson came no more at my lord.

1642   1806

9. Their own.
1. I.e., you are already singled out as a Puritan leader.

LADY ANNE HALKETT

Lady Anne Halkett, née Anne Murray (1622–1699), was born into a family of the royal household; her father was a tutor to Prince Charles, later Charles I. Thus was determined her allegiance to the royalist cause, an attachment by comparison with which her several sentimental love affairs were mere incidents. She was a tough and active partisan, and more directly than most women of her day engaged in the intrigues of the civil wars. With one of her particular admirers, Colonel Bamfield, she assisted the young duke of York (future King James II of England) in making his escape from parliamentary custody. Her account of this adventure appeared in her memoirs, published many years later. We pick up the story in April 1648, with the question of Colonel Bamfield's intentions.

From The Memoirs

[SPRINGING THE DUKE]

This gentleman came to see me sometimes in the company of ladies who had been my mother's neighbors in St. Martin's Lane, and sometimes alone, but whenever he came his discourse was serious, handsome, and tending to impress the advantages of piety, loyalty, and virtue; and these subjects were so agreeable to my own inclination that I could not but give them a good reception, especially from one that seemed to be so much an owner of them himself. After I had been used to freedom of discourse with him, I told him I approved much of his advice to others, but I thought his own practice contradicted much of his profession, for one of his acquaintance had told me he had not seen his wife in a twelvemonth, and it was impossible in my opinion for a good man to be an ill husband; and therefore he must defend himself from one before I could believe the other of him. He said it was not necessary to give everyone that might condemn him the reason of his being so long from her, yet to satisfy me he would tell me the truth, which was that, he being engaged in the king's service, he was obliged to be at London where it was not convenient for her to be with him, his stay in any place being uncertain; besides, she lived amongst her friends who, though they were kind to her, yet were not so to him, for most of that country had declared for the Parliament and were enemies to all that had or did serve the king, and therefore his wife, he was sure, would not condemn him for what he did by her own consent. This seeming reasonable, I did insist no more upon that subject.

At this time he had frequent letters from the king,[1] who employed him in several affairs, but that of the greatest concern which he was employed in was to contrive the duke of York's escape out of St. James[2] (where His Highness and the duke of Gloucester and the Princess Elizabeth lived under the care of the earl of Northumberland and his lady). The difficulties of it was represented by Colonel Bamfield; but His Majesty still pressed it, and I remember this expression was in one of the letters: "I believe it will be difficult, and if he miscarry in the attempt, it will be the greatest affliction that can arrive to me; but I look upon James's escape as Charles's preservation,[3] and nothing can content me more; therefore be careful what you do."

1. Charles I, currently close prisoner of the parliamentary army under Cromwell. In less than a year he would be executed.
2. St. James's Palace, the present royal residence. The two named below were other children of Charles I.

3. Charles I must have feared the capture or assassination of the heir apparent, Prince Charles, then in France with his mother, Queen Henrietta Maria. If the younger son, James, were alive and at liberty, there would be no point in such an attempt to cut off the succession.

This letter, amongst others, he showed me, and where the king approved of his choice of me to entrust with it, for to get the duke's clothes made and to dress him in his disguise. So now all Colonel Bamfield's business and care was how to manage this business of so important concern, which could not be performed without several persons' concurrence in it, for he being generally known as one whose stay at London was in order to serve the king, few of those who were entrusted by the Parliament in public concerns durst own converse or hardly civility to him, lest they should have been suspect by their party, which made it difficult for him to get access to the duke. But, to be short, having communicated the design to a gentleman attending His Highness who was full of honor and fidelity, by his means he had private access to the duke, to whom he presented the king's letter and order to His Highness for consenting to act what Colonel Bamfield should contrive for his escape, which was so cheerfully entertained and so readily obeyed, that being once designed there was nothing more to do than to prepare all things for the execution. I had desired him to take a ribbon with him and bring me the bigness of the duke's waist and his length, to have clothes made fit for him. In the meantime, Colonel Bamfield was to provide money for all necessary expense, which was furnished by an honest citizen. When I gave the measure to my tailor to inquire how much mohair would serve to make a petticoat and waistcoat to a young gentlewoman of that bigness and stature, he considered it a long time, and said he had made many gowns and suits, but he had never made any to such a person in his life. I thought he was in the right; but his meaning was he had never seen any woman of so low a stature have so big a waist. However, he made it as exactly fit as if he had taken the measure himself. It was a mixed mohair of a light hair color and black, and the under-petticoat was scarlet.

All things being now ready, upon the 20th of April 1648 in the evening was the time resolved for the duke's escape. And in order to that, it was designed for a week before every night as soon as the duke had supped he and those servants that attended His Highness (till the earl of Northumberland and the rest of the house had supped) went to a play called *hide and seek*,[4] and sometimes he would hide himself so well that in half an hour's time they could not find him. His Highness had so used them to this that when he went really away they thought he was but at the usual sport. A little before the duke went to supper that night, he called for the gardener, who only had a treble key besides that which the duke had, and bid him give him that key till his own was mended, which he did. And after His Highness had supped, he immediately called to go to the play, and went down the privy stairs into the garden, and opened the gate that goes into the park, treble locking all the doors behind him. And at the garden gate Colonel Bamfield waited for His Highness, and putting on a cloak and periwig, hurried him away to the park gate, where a coach waited that carried them to the waterside, and, taking the boat that was appointed for that service, they rowed to the stairs next the bridge, where I and Miriam[5] waited in a private house hard by that Colonel Bamfield had prepared for dressing His Highness, where all things were in a readi-

---

4. As a boy of fourteen, James could play such a game without arousing suspicion and could be disguised without too much difficulty in women's clothes.

5. Anne Murray's personal maidservant.

ness. But I had many fears, for Colonel Bamfield had desired me, if they came not there precisely by ten o'clock, to shift for myself, for then I might conclude they were discovered, and so my stay there could do no good but prejudice myself. Yet this did not make me leave the house though ten o'clock did strike, and he that was entrusted often went to the landing place and saw no boat coming was much discouraged, and asked me what I would do. I told him I came there with a resolution to serve His Highness, and I was fully determined not to leave that place till I was out of hopes of doing what I came there for, and would take my hazard. He left me to go again to the waterside, and while I was fortifying myself against what might arrive to me, I heard a great noise of many as I thought coming upstairs, which I expected to be soldiers to take me, but it was a pleasing disappointment, for the first that came in was the duke, who with much joy I took in my arms and gave God thanks for his safe arrival. His Highness called "Quickly, quickly, dress me!"; and, putting off his clothes, I dressed him in the women's habit that was prepared, which fitted His Highness very well, and was very pretty in it.

After he had eaten something I made ready while I was idle, lest His Highness should be hungry, and having sent for a Wood-street cake (which I knew he loved) to take in the barge, with as much haste as could be His Highness went cross the bridge to the stairs where the barge lay, Colonel Bamfield leading him; and immediately the boatmen plied the oar so well that they were soon out of sight, having both wind and tide with them. But I afterwards heard the wind changed, and was so contrary that Colonel Bamfield told me he was terribly afraid they should have been blown back again. And the duke said, "Do anything with me rather than let me go back again," which put Colonel Bamfield to seek help where it was only to be had, and, after he had most fervently supplicated assistance from God, presently the wind blew fair, and they came safely to their intended landing place. But I heard there was some difficulty before they got to the ship at Gravesend, which had like to have discovered them had not Colonel Washington's lady assisted them.

After the duke's barge was out of sight of the bridge, I and Miriam went where I appointed the coach to stay for me, and made drive as fast as the coachman could to my brother's house, where I stayed. I met none in the way that gave me any apprehension that the design was discovered, nor was it noised abroad till the next day, for (as I related before) the duke having used to play at hide and seek, and to conceal himself a long time, when they missed him at the same play, thought he would have discovered himself as formerly when they had given over seeking him. But a much longer time being passed than usually was spent in that divertissement, some began to apprehend that His Highness was gone in earnest past their finding, which made the earl of Northumberland (to whose care he was committed), after strict search made in the house of St. James and all thereabouts to no purpose, to send and acquaint the Speaker of the House of Commons that the duke was gone, but how or by what means he knew not, but desired that there might be orders sent to the Cinque Ports[6] for stopping all ships going

---

6. A group of channel ports, originally five in number (hence the name); most English shipping to or from the Continent passed through them.

out till the passengers were examined and search made in all suspected places where His Highness might be concealed.

Though this was gone about with all the vigilancy imaginable, yet it pleased God to disappoint them of their intention by so infatuating those several persons who were employed for writing orders that none of them were able to write one right, but ten or twelve of them were cast by before one was according to their mind. This account I had from Mr. N. who was mace-bearer to the Speaker all that time and a witness of it. This disorder of the clerks contributed much to the duke's safety, for he was at sea before any of the orders came to the ports, and so was free from what was designed if they had taken His Highness. Though several were suspected for being accessory to the escape, yet they could not charge any with it but the person who went away, and he being out of their reach, they took no notice as either to examine or imprison others.[7]

1778

7. Despite this romantic beginning to their friendship, Colonel Bamfield and Murray never did get together. His wife was the problem; he never could discover for sure whether she was alive or dead. In 1656, Murray married Sir James Halkett.

JOHN LILBURNE

John Lilburne (1615?–1657) was a natural-born agitator who had suffered for his polemics against the bishops, and who had fought in the parliamentary army against the king. More important, he was a prime mover in the Leveller movement (a name given them originally in derision for their democratic principles). They believed in extending the suffrage to all men by eliminating the usual property qualifications and the new political tests. More radically, they believed that to reconstitute a legal government in England would require a new social contract or Agreement of the People, spelling out as in a constitution the specific powers of government and the rights and liberties of the people. Among these were free elections, freedom of speech and religion, reform of the law and the courts, relief to debtors, and other social reforms for which, in their view, the revolution had been mounted. In the early months of 1649, after the execution of Charles I, Lilburne came into direct conflict with Cromwell and his coalition of army officers and trusted allies in the "Rump" House of Commons (purged to a fraction of its traditional size) over elections and the legal status of the new commonwealth. Cromwell and his party backed away from free elections, certain that they would bring back the monarchy and destroy the infant republic, established "without King or House of Lords"; also, they thought the Levellers' radical reforms would surely destabilize the state. In turn, the Levellers thought Cromwell was motivated solely by personal ambition. After Lilburne vigorously denounced Cromwell's betrayal of the revolution in a pamphlet entitled *Englands New Chains Discovered*, at the end of March Cromwell ordered troops to arrest the four leading Levellers (Lilburne, Prince, Overton, and Walwyn) and bring them before the Council of State for examination. That action prompted the confrontation excerpted below, from Lilburne's long and passionate pamphlet titled *Picture of the Council of State*.

Lilburne's fundamental ground of argument in this confrontation is from the legal rights traditionally assured to Englishmen and violated by these arbitrary procedures.

He challenged the new authorities to show any authority for their actions against him, putting the council itself on trial. A fearless, melodramatic speaker and writer, he lectured his judges unmercifully. The blunt, hammerlike phrases of Lilburne's prose strike with the force of a man driving spikes. Like John Bunyan, Lilburne is a prose artist in the grip of a moral idea.

From The Picture of the Council of State

[LILBURNE DEFIES THE AUTHORITIES]

* * * "Well, then, Mr. Bradshaw," said I, "if it please you and these gentlemen to afford me the same liberty and privilege that the cavaliers did at Oxford, when I was arraigned before them for my life, for levying war in the quarrel of the commonwealth against the late king and his party (which was liberty of speech, to speak my mind freely without interruption), I shall speak and go on; but without the grant of liberty of speech, I shall not say a word more to you."

To which he replied, "That is already granted you, and therefore you may go on to speak what you can or will say for yourself, if you please; or if you will not, you may hold your peace and withdraw."

"Well, then," said I, "Mr. Bradshaw, with your favor, thus. I am an Englishman born, bred, and brought up, and England is a nation governed, bounded, and limited by laws and liberties: and for the liberties of England I have both fought and suffered much. But truly, sir, I judge it now infinitely below me, and the glory and excellency of my late actions, now to plead merit or desert unto you, as though I were forced to fly to the merit of my former actions, to lay in a counter-scale, to weigh down your indignation against me for my pretended late offenses. No, sir, I scorn it, I abhor it. And therefore, sir, I now stand before you upon the bare, naked, and single account of an Englishman, as though I had never said, done, or acted anything that tended to the preservation of the liberties thereof; but yet, have never done any act that did put me out of a legal capacity to claim the utmost punctilio,[1] benefit, and privilege that the laws and liberties of England will afford to any of you here present, or any other man in the whole nation. And the laws and liberties of England are my inheritance and birthright.

"And in your late declaration, published about four or five days ago, wherein you lay down the grounds and reasons (as I remember) of your doing justice upon the late king, and why you have abolished kingly government and the House of Lords, you declare in effect the same, and promise to maintain the laws of England in reference to the people's liberties and freedoms. And amongst other things therein contained, you highly commend and extol the Petition of Right,[2] made in the third year of the late king, as one of the most excellent and glorious laws in reference to the people's liberties that ever was made in this nation; and you there very much blame and cry out upon the king for robbing and denying the people of England the benefit of that law. And sure I am (for I have read and studied it), there is

---

1. Point, particular.
2. In the Petition of Right (1628), Parliament drew up and presented to Charles I a formal statement of the rights and privileges to which they laid claim in the name of the people of England.

one clause in it that saith expressly, That no freeman of England ought to be adjudged for life, limb, liberty, or estate but by the laws already in being established and declared. And truly, sir, if this be good and sound legal doctrine (as undoubtedly it is, or else your own declarations are false and lies), I wonder what you gentlemen are. For the declared and known laws of England know you not, neither by names nor qualifications, as persons endowed with any power either to imprison or try me, or the meanest freeman of England. And truly, were it not that I know the faces of divers of you, and honor the persons of some of you, as members of the House of Commons that have stood pretty firm in shaking times to the interest of the nation, I should wonder what you are, or before whom I am, and should not in the least honor or reverence you so much as with civil respect, especially considering the manner of my being brought before you, with armed men, and the manner of your close[3] sitting, contrary to all courts of justice. * * *

"Sir, by the law of England, let me tell you, what the House votes, orders, and enacts within their walls is nothing to me, I am not at all bound by them, nor in law can take any cognizance of them as laws, although twenty members come out of the House and tell me such things are done, till they be published and declared by sound of trumpet, proclamation, or the like, by a public officer or magistrate, in the public and open places of the nation. But truly, sir, I never saw any law in print or writing that declares your power so proclaimed or published. And therefore, sir, I know not what more to make of you than a company of private men, being neither able to own you as a court of justice, because the law speaks nothing of you; nor as a council of state, till I see and read or hear your commission, which I desire (if you please) to be acquainted with."[4]

* * *

Mr. Bradshaw * * * said unto me to this effect: "Lieut. Colonel Lilburne, this Council hath considered what you have said, and what they have been informed of concerning you, and also of that duty that lies upon them by the command of the House, which enjoins them to improve their utmost ability to find out the author of this book; and therefore to effect that end, they judge themselves bound to demand of you this question: Whether you made not this book, or were privy to the making of it, or no?"

And after some pause, and wondering at the strangeness of the question, I answered, and said: "Mr. Bradshaw, I cannot but stand amazed that you should ask me such a question as this, at this time of the day, considering what you said unto me at my first being before you; and considering it is now about eight years ago since this very Parliament annihilated the court of Star Chamber, Council Board, and High Commission,[5] and that for such proceedings as these. And truly, sir, I have been a contestor and sufferer for the liberties of England these twelve years together, and I should now look upon myself as the basest fellow in the world if now in one moment I should undo

---

3. Closed, secret.
4. After a great deal of haggling over whether the council really exists in a legal sense, Bradshaw finally gets around to asking the question that is at the root of the whole affair, Lilburne's authorship of *Legal Fundamental Liberties*.
5. These were all courts that had become infa-

mous under the eleven-year period of unparliamentary government (1629–40). Star Chamber and High Commission were particularly hateful as ecclesiastical courts that reminded their victims of the Inquisition. Lilburne had suffered imprisonment and whipping at their hands.

all that I have been doing all this while, which I must of necessity do if I should answer to you questions against myself. For in the first place, by answering this question against myself, I should betray the liberties of England in acknowledging you to have a legal jurisdiction over me to try and adjudge me; which I have already proved to your faces you have not in the least. And if you have forgot what you said to me thereupon, yet I have not forgot what I said to you. And secondly, sir, if I should answer to questions against myself and to betray myself, I should do that which not only law but nature abhors. And therefore I cannot but wonder that you yourselves are not ashamed to demand so illegal and unworthy a thing of me as this is. And therefore in short were it that I owned your power (which I do not in the least) I would be hanged before I would do so base and un-Englishman-like an action, to betray my liberty, which I must of necessity do in answering questions to accuse myself. But, sir, this I will say to you, my late actions have not been done in a hole or a corner, but on the housetop in the face of the sun, before hundreds and some thousands of people. And therefore why ask you me any questions? Go to those that have heard me and seen me, and it is possible you may find some hundreds of witnesses to tell you what I have said and done. For I hate holes and corners. My late actions need no covers nor hidings, they have been more honest than so, and I am not sorry for what I have done, for I did look well about me before I did what I did, and I am ready to lay down my life to justify what I have done. And so much in answer to your question.

"But now, sir, with your favor one word more, to mind you again of what I said before, in reference to my martial imprisonment. And truly, sir, I must tell you, circumstantials of my liberty at this time I shall not much dispute, but for the essentials of them I shall die. I am now in the soldiers' custody, where to continue in silence and patience is absolutely to betray my liberty. For they have nothing to do with me, nor the meanest freeman in England in this case. And besides, sir, they have no rules to walk by but their wills and their swords, which are two dangerous things. It may be I may be of an hasty, choleric temper, and not able nor willing to bear their affronts; and peradventure[6] they may be as willing to put them upon me as I am unwilling to bear them. And for you in this case to put fire and tinder together, to burn up one another, will not be much commendable, nor tend much to the accomplishment of your ends. But if for all this you shall send me back to the military sword again, either to Whitehall or any other suchlike garrisoned place in England, I do solemnly protest before the Eternal God of Heaven and Earth, I will fire it and burn it down to the ground, if possibly I can, although I be burnt to ashes with the flames thereof. For, sir, I say again, the soldiers have nothing to do to be my jailers; and besides, it is a maxim among the soldiers, that they must obey without dispute all the commands of their officers, be they right or wrong; and it is also the maxim amongst the officers, that if they do not do it, they must hang for it. Therefore if the officers command them to cut my throat, they must either do it or hang for it. And truly, sir (looking wishfully upon Cromwell, that sat just against[7] me), I must be plain with you, I have not found so much honor, honesty, justice, or conscience in any of the principal officers of the army as to trust my life

6. Perhaps.

7. Opposite. "Wishfully": intently.

under their protection or to think it can be safe under their immediate fingers. And therefore, not knowing nor very much caring what you will do with me, I earnestly entreat you, if you will again imprison me, send me to a civil jail that the law knows, as Newgate, the Fleet, or the Gatehouse."[8]

* * *

So after we were all come out, and all four in a room close by them, all alone, I laid my ear to their door and heard Lieutenant General Cromwell (I am sure of it) very loud, thumping his fist upon the council table till it rang again, and heard him speak in these very words or to this effect: "I tell you, sir, you have no other way to deal with these men but to break them in pieces." And thumping upon the council table again, he said: "Sir, let me tell you that which is true, if you do not break them, they will break you; yea, and bring all the guilt of the blood and treasure shed and spent in this kingdom upon your head and shoulders; and frustrate and make void all that work that with so many years' industry, toil, and pains you have done, and so render you to all rational men in the world as the most contemptiblest generation of silly, low-spirited men in the earth, to be broken and routed by such a despicable contemptible generation of men as they are; and therefore, sir, I tell you again, you are necessitated to break them." * * * Upon which discourse of Cromwell's, the blood run up and down my veins, and I heartily wished myself in again amongst them (being scarce able to contain myself), that so I might have gone five or six stories higher than I did before.[9]

* * *

I know they have an army at command, but if every hair on the head of that officer or soldier they have at their command were a legion of men, I would fear them no more than so many straws, for the Lord Jehovah is my rock and defense, under the assured shelter of whose wings I am safe and secure, and therefore will sing and be merry; and do hereby sound an eternal trumpet of defiance to all the men and devils in earth and hell, but[1] only those men that have the image of God in them, and demonstrate it among men by their just, honest, merciful, and righteous actions. And as for all those vile actions their saint-like agents have fixed upon me[2] of late, I know before God that none is righteous, no, not one, but only he that is clothed with the glorious righteousness of Jesus Christ, which I assuredly know my soul hath been, and now is clothed with, in the strength of which I have walked for above twelve years together, and through the strength of which I have been able at any time in all that time to lay down my life on a quarter of an hour's warning. But as to man, I bid defiance to all my adversaries upon earth, to search my ways and goings with a candle and to lay any one base action to my charge in any kind whatsoever, since the first day that I visibly made profession of the fear of God, which is now above twelve years. Yea, I bid defiance to him or them to proclaim it upon the housetops, pro-

8. After being questioned by the council, and continually refusing to answer, Lilburne and his three associates are shut up in a room alongside the council chamber.

9. Lilburne concludes his narration with a direct personal appeal to his reader and to his own religious conscience.

1. Except.

2. Attributed to me.

vided he will set his hand to it, and proclaim a public place where before indifferent men in the face of the sun his accusation may be scanned. Yea, I here declare that if any man or woman in England, either in reference to my public actions, to the state's money, or in reference to my private dealings in the world, shall come in and prove against me that ever I defrauded him or her of twelvepence, and for every twelvepence that I have so done, I will make him or her twenty shillings worth of amends, so far as all the estate I have in the world will extend.

Courteous reader and dear countryman, excuse I beseech thee my boasting and glorying, for I am necessitated to it, my adversaries' base and lying calumniations putting me upon it, and Paul and Samuel did it before me: and so I am thine, if thou art for the just freedoms and liberties of the land of thy nativity.

> JOHN LILBURNE, that never yet changed his principles from better to worse, nor could never be threatened out of them, nor courted from them, that never feared the rich nor mighty, nor never despised the poor nor needy, but always hath, and hopes by God's goodness to continue, *semper idem.*[3]

From the Tower of London, April 3, 1649

1649

3. Ever the same.

GERRARD WINSTANLEY

Besides the political threat they posed, the Levellers' demand for democratic elections raised the fear in Cromwell and his conservative associates that, with unpropertied voters outnumbering the propertied by five to one, they might divide or even abolish private property. That was in fact the program of a small group calling themselves True Levellers or, later, Diggers, who were a group of Christian communists. Their leader was Gerrard Winstanley (1609–1676?), a failed businessman and subsequently a hired laborer, who began to publish tracts in 1648, became notorious in 1649 with the attempted enactment of the Diggers' program, and lapsed back into obscurity after his last published work in 1652.

In the spring of 1649 the Diggers began to put their ideals into practice, digging up the wasteland of St. George's Hill in Surrey and preparing it for crops. Though this land was not enclosed, all over England landowners claimed property rights in such common land, and the Diggers' gesture of cultivation here and in a few other Digger communities made a threatening counterclaim on behalf of the poor and propertyless. Their aim was at one level practical: at least one-third of England, they claimed, was barren waste, and if properly cultivated it could vastly increase the quantity and lower the price of food, to the great benefit of the poor. At another level it was ideological, a fundamental challenge to the very concept of private ownership of land. The army and the civil authorities were not very hard on the Diggers but the local landholders were, beating them up, expelling them, and destroying their several settlements. But their often-eloquent tracts survived to inspire later communes. In the tract excerpted here, Winstanley reworks biblical imagery and prophecy to produce a strikingly original religious-political-economic allegory of human society as it is and as it might be.

From The True Levellers' Standard Advanced

A DECLARATION TO THE POWERS OF ENGLAND AND TO ALL THE POWERS OF THE WORLD, *showing the cause why the common people of England have begun and gives consent to dig up, manure, and sow corn upon George Hill in Surrey; by those that have subscribed, and thousands more that gives consent*

In the beginning of time, the great creator Reason made the earth to be a common treasury to preserve beasts, birds, fishes, and man, the lord that was to govern this creation; for man had domination given to him over the beasts, birds, and fishes; but not one word was spoken in the beginning that one branch of mankind should rule over another.

And the reason is this: Every single man, male and female, is a perfect creature of himself; and the same spirit that made the globe dwells in man to govern the globe; so that the flesh of man, being subject to Reason his maker, hath him to be his teacher and ruler within himself, therefore needs not run abroad after any teacher or ruler without[1] him; for he needs not that any man should teach him, for the same anointing that ruled in the Son of Man teacheth him all things.

But since human flesh (that king of beasts) began to delight himself in the objects of the creation more than in the Spirit Reason and Righteousness, who manifests himself to be the indweller in the five senses of hearing, seeing, tasting, smelling, feeling, then he fell into blindness of mind and weakness of heart, and runs abroad for a teacher and ruler.[2] And so selfish Imagination taking possession of the five senses, and ruling as king in the room of Reason therein, and working with Covetousness, did set up one man to teach and rule over another; and thereby the Spirit was killed, and man was brought into bondage and became a greater slave to such of his own kind than the beasts of the field were to him.

And hereupon the earth (which was made to be a common treasury of relief for all, both beasts and men) was hedged into enclosures[3] by the teachers and rulers, and the others were made servants and slaves; and that earth, that is within this creation made a common storehouse for all, is bought and sold and kept in the hands of a few, whereby the great Creator is mightily dishonored, as if he were a respecter of persons, delighting in the comfortable livelihood of some and rejoicing in the miserable poverty and straits of others. From the beginning it was not so.

* * *

O thou Powers of England, though thou hast promised to make this people a free people, yet thou hast so handled the matter through thy self-seeking

---

1. Outside.
2. I.e., clergyman and king.
3. For centuries, ambitious farmers and greedy landlords had been trying to expand their holdings by "enclosing" (i.e., fencing in) lands that had previously been waste or common. Poor folk naturally resented the process.

humor that thou hast wrapped us up more in bondage, and oppression lies heavier upon us; not only bringing thy fellow-creatures the commoners to a morsel of bread, but by confounding all sorts of people by thy government of doing and undoing.

First, thou hast made the people to take a covenant and oaths to endeavor a reformation and to bring in liberty every man in his place; and yet while a man is in pursuing of that covenant, he is imprisoned and oppressed by thy officers, courts, and justices, so called.

Thou hast made ordinances to cast down oppressing, popish, episcopal, self-willed, and prerogative laws; yet we see that self-will and prerogative power is the great standing law that rules all in action, and others in words.

Thou hast made many promises and protestations to make the land a free nation; and yet at this very day the same people to whom thou hast made such protestations of liberty are oppressed by thy courts, sizes,[4] sessions, by thy justices and clerks of the peace, so called, bailiffs, committees, are imprisoned and forced to spend that bread that should save their lives from famine.

And all this because they stand to maintain an universal liberty and freedom which not only is our birthright, which our Maker gave us, but which thou hast promised to restore unto us, from under the former oppressing powers that are gone before, and which likewise we have bought with our money in taxes, free-quarter, and bloodshed; all which sums thou hast received at our hands, and yet thou hast not given us our bargain.[5]

* * *

The work we are going about is this, to dig up George Hill and the waste ground thereabouts, and to sow corn, and to eat our bread together by the sweat of our brows.

And the first reason is this, That we may work in righteousness, and lay the foundation of making the earth a common treasury for all, both rich and poor, that everyone that is born in the land may be fed by the earth his mother that brought him forth, according to the Reason that rules in the creation. Not enclosing any part into any particular hand, but all as one man working together and feeding together as sons of one father, members of one family; not one lording over another, but all looking upon each other as equals in the creation; so that our Maker may be glorified in the work of his own hands, and that everyone may see he is no respecter of persons but equally loves his whole creation, and hates nothing but the Serpent, which is covetousness, branching forth into selfish imagination, pride, envy, hypocrisy, uncleanness; all seeking the ease and honor of flesh, and fighting against the Spirit Reason that made the creation; for that is the corruption, the curse, the devil, the father of lies; death and bondage that serpent and dragon that the creation is to be delivered from.

* * *

* * * If you cast your eye a little backward, you shall see that this outward teaching and ruling power is the Babylonish yoke laid upon Israel of old

4. Assizes.
5. The war against Charles Stuart had been successfully concluded by the parliamentary armies without any clear agreement on its aims. The more radical partisans of the cause were bound to feel betrayed when the new society proved to be much like the old one. "Free-quarter": free board and lodging for soldiers.

under Nebuchadnezzar;[6] and so successively from that time, the conquering enemy have still laid these yokes upon Israel to keep Jacob down.[7] And the last enslaving conquest which the enemy got over Israel was the Norman over England; and from that time, kings, lords, judges, justices, bailiffs, and the violent bitter people that are freeholders, are and have been successively: the Norman bastard William himself, his colonels, captains, inferior officers, and common soldiers, who still are from that time to this day in pursuit of that victory, imprisoning, robbing, and killing the poor enslaved English Israelites.

And this appears clear, for when any trustee or state officer is to be chosen, the freeholders or landlords must be the choosers, who are the Norman common soldiers spread abroad in the land; and who must be chosen but some very rich man, who is the successor of the Norman colonels or high officers? And to what end have they been thus chosen, but to establish that Norman power the more forcibly over the enslaved English, and to beat them down again whenas they gather heart to seek for Liberty?

For what are all those binding and restraining laws that have been made from one age to another since that Conquest, and are still upheld by fury over the people? I say, What are they but the cords, bonds, manacles, and yokes that the enslaved English, like Newgate prisoners, wears upon their hands and legs as they walk the streets; by which those Norman oppressors and these their successors from age to age have enslaved the poor people, killed their younger brother, and would not suffer Jacob to arise.

O what mighty delusion do you, who are the powers of England, live in! That while you pretend to throw down that Norman yoke and Babylonish power, and have promised to make the groaning people of England a free people, yet you still lift up that Norman yoke and slavish tyranny, and hold the people as much in bondage as the bastard Conqueror himself and his council of war.

* * *

Therefore, if thou wilt find mercy, *Let Israel go free*; break in pieces quickly the bond of particular property, disown this oppressing murder, oppression, and thievery of buying and selling of land, owning of landlords,[8] and paying of rents, and give thy free consent to make the earth a common treasury, without grumbling; that the younger brethren may live comfortably upon earth, as well as the elder; that all may enjoy the benefit of their creation.

And hereby thou wilt *Honor thy father and thy mother*: thy Father, which is the Spirit of Community that made all and that dwells in all; thy Mother, which is the earth, that brought us all forth, that as a true mother loves all her children. Therefore do not thou hinder the Mother Earth from giving all her children suck by thy enclosing it into particular hands, and holding up that cursed bondage of enclosure by thy power.

And then thou wilt repent of thy theft, in maintaining the breach of the eighth commandment by stealing the land, as I say, from thy fellow-creatures

---

6. The Babylonian Captivity lamented by Jeremiah was seen as a "type" or foreshadowing of subsequent repressions of God's people, including the poor English "Israelites" of 1649. Such typological reading of the Bible and of history, with application to the present, was common with Puritan groups,

who continually drew parallels between England and Israel.
7. Esau, the older son of Isaac, and Jacob, the younger, stand, respectively, for the domineering and the exploited members of the human family.
8. Owning by landlords.

or younger brothers; which thou and all thy landlords have and do live in the breach of that commandment.

Then thou wilt *Own no other God* or ruling power, *but one,* which is the King of Righteousness, ruling and dwelling in everyone and in the whole; whereas now thou hast many gods: for covetousness is thy god, pride, and an envious murdering humor (to kill one by prison or gallows that crosses thee, though their cause be pure, sound, and good reason) is thy god, self-love and slavish fear (lest others serve thee as thou hast served them) is thy god; hypocrisy, fleshly imagination that keeps no promise, covenant, nor protestation is thy god; love of money, honor, and ease is thy god. And all these and the like ruling powers makes thee blind and hard-hearted, that thou does not nor cannot lay to heart the affliction of others, though they die for want of bread in that rich city, undone under your eyes.

Therefore once more, *Let Israel go free,*[9] that the poor may labor the waste-land and suck the breasts of their Mother Earth, that they starve not: and in so doing, thou wilt keep the *Sabbath day,* which is a day of rest, sweetly enjoying the peace of the Spirit of Righteousness, and find peace by living among a people that live in peace; this will be a day of rest which thou never knew yet.

But I do not entreat thee, for thou art not to be entreated, but in the *Name of the Lord* that hath drawn me forth to speak to thee; I, yea I say, I command thee to *let Israel go free* and quietly *to gather together into the place where I shall appoint; and hold them no longer in bondage.*

And * * * if thou wilt not *let Israel go free* (for thou being the antitype[1] will be more stout and lusty than the *Egyptian Pharaoh* of old, who was thy type), then know that whereas I brought ten plagues upon him, I will multiply my plagues upon thee, till I make thee weary and miserably ashamed: And *I will bring out my people with a strong hand and stretched-out arm.*

Thus we have discharged our souls in declaring the cause of our digging upon George Hill in Surrey, that the great council and army of the land may take notice of it, that there is no intent of tumult or fighting, but only to get bread to eat with the sweat of our brows, working together in righteousness and eating the blessings of the earth in peace.[2]

* * *

1649

---

9. Repeated use of the phrase "Let Israel go free" emphasizes the typological relationship between the Jews in Egypt before the Exodus (the type or foreshadowing) and the oppressed English people (the antitype or fulfillment).
1. The Egyptian Pharoah is the type of the oppres-

sive English landlords, and Winstanley is a new Moses ("antitype", calling down new plagues upon them.
2. The tract was signed at the end by Winstanley and fourteen others.

ANNA TRAPNEL

Anna Trapnel (1620?–1660?) is one of several remarkable female prophets who burst into speech and print among the sects that proliferated during the Interregnum. She was a Fifth Monarchist, one who believed in and sought to prepare for the imminent Second Coming, when Christ would reign in person with his saints for a thousand years. She was also an itinerant preacher, who traveled about the countryside delivering, sometimes in trances, prophecies that were often politically charged. A short pamphlet, *Strange and Wonderful News from Whitehall* (1654), describes her falling into a trance on January 11 and prophesying for eleven days and twelve nights to the crowds that came to hear her. A detailed rendering of some of those prophecies, in verse, was published as *The Cry of a Stone* (1654), the text of which was apparently taken down when she was speaking. In it she (like other Fifth Monarchists) denounces the newly formed Protectorate as a usurping of Christ's rightful reign. Targeting Cromwell as the "little horn" of Daniel's prophecy which must be overthrown before Christ's "Fifth Monarchy" arrives, she calls on him to renounce his title and his great revenue "whilst the poor are ready to starve," and to acknowledge Christ as the only real Protector. In the *Report and Plea* she describes her call from the Lord to travel and preach in Cornwall and her experiences there, including her arrest and interrogation before a tribunal in Truro, which thought at first to convict her as a witch. This is not mystical prophecy taken down by others, but her own lively narrative. The excerpt below is a vivid reconstruction, mostly as a dramatic scene, of her bold and witty defense of herself before the justices. Claiming the role of prophet allowed her, as it did some other women, to venture far outside the usual gender norms.

Anna Trapnel's Report and Plea, or, a Narrative of Her Journey from London into Cornwall.

* * * After that day wherein I was thus carried forth to speak for Christ's interest, the clergy, with all their might, rung their jangling bells against me, and called to the Rulers to take me up. That I heard was the speech of Mr. Welstead: and others said, "The people would be drawn away, if the rulers did not take some course with me." . . . But while I was singing praises to the Lord for his love to me, the justices sent their constable to fetch me; who came, and said, "He must have me with him": and he pulled, and called me, they said that were by, but I was not capable thereof. . . . Then a friend persuaded them to see whether they could put me out of that condition [a trance], and told them "I was never known to be put out of it."[1] So they came. Justice Launce, now a parliament-man, was one of them, I was told. These justices that came to fetch me out of my bed, they made a great tumult, them and their followers, in the house, and some came upstairs, crying, "A witch, a witch"; making a great stir on the stairs; and a poor honest man rebuking such that said so, he was tumbled downstairs and beaten too, by one of the justices' followers. And the justices made a great noise, in putting out of my chamber where I lay, many of my friends; and they said, "If my friends would not take me up, they would have some should take me up." One of my friends told them, "that they must fetch their silk gowns[2] to do it then, for the poor would not do it." And they threatened much, but the Lord overruled them. They caused my eyelids to be pulled up, for they said, "I held them fast, because I would deceive the people": they spoke to this pur-

---

1. I.e., on other occasions no one was ever able to bring her out of such a trance.   2. The justices.

pose. One of the justices pinched me by the nose, and caused my pillow to be pulled from under my head, and kept pulling me, and calling me; but I heard none of all this stir and bustle.

* * *

And when I came before them [at the court session], Lobb being the mouth of the court, as he was foreman of the jury, he represented the whole court. And he first demanded of me my name, and I told him; and he said, "Anna Trapnel, Here is a Bill of Indictment to be read, for you to give in your answer concerning." Then Justice Lobb said, "Read the Bill": so it was read to me. And Lobb said, "Are you guilty, or no?" I had no word to say at the present; but the Lord said to me, "Say not guilty, according to the form of the Bill"; so I spoke it as from the Lord, who knew I was not guilty of such an indictment. Then said Lobb, "Traverse the Bill to the next assizes," so that was done. . . .

And I thought they had done with me at that time; so they had, if they had gone according to true law, which was, not to have brought their inter-rogatories then. But the report was, that I would discover myself to be a witch when I came before the justices, by having never a word to answer for myself; for it used to be so among the witches, they could not speak before the magistrates. And so they said, it would be so with me; but the Lord quickly defeated them herein, and caused many to be of another mind. Then Lobb said, "Tender her the book which was written from something said at Whitehall." So the book was reached out to me, and Justice Lobb said, "What say you to that book? will you own it? is it yours?"[3]

A. T. "I am not careful to answer you in that matter."

Then they said, "She denies her book." They they whispered with those behind them. Then spake Justice Lobb again, and said, "Read a vision of the horns out of the book." So that was read. Then Justice Lobb said, "What say you to that? Is it yours?"

A. T. "I am not careful to answer you in that matter, touching the whole book, as I told you before, so I say again. For what was spoken, was at Whitehall, at a place of concourse of people, and near a council,[4] I suppose wise enough to call me into question if I offended, and unto them I appeal. But though it was said I *appealed unto Caesar, and unto Caesar should I go*, yet I have not been brought before him which is called Caesar." So much by the by.

Again, I said, "I supposed they had not power to question me for that which was spoke in another county." They said, "Yes, that they had." Then the book was put by; and they again whispered.

Then Justice Lobb asked me about my coming into that country, "How it came to pass, that I came into that country."[5]

I answered, "I came as others did, that were minded to go into the country."

Lobb. "But why did you come into this country?"

---

3. *The Cry of a Stone*. She never directly answers the question about authorship, presumably because the work was the product of a trance, divinely inspired.

4. Presumably, the magistrates at Whitehall, who could have called her before them if they thought they had cause.

5. "Country" is often used for "county" in seventeenth-century texts.

A. T. "Why might not I come here, as well as into another country?"

Lobb. "But you have no lands, nor livings, nor acquaintance to come to in this country."

A. T. "What though I had not, I am a single person, and why may I not be with my friends anywhere."

Lobb. "I understand you are not married."

A. T. "Then having no hindrance, why may not I go where I please, if the Lord so will?"

The spoke Jutice Launce. "But did not some desire you to come down?" And this Lobb asked me too: but I told them, "I would accuse none, I was there to answer, as to what they should charge my own particular with."[6]

Launce said, "Pray Mistress tell us, what moved you to come such a journey?"

A. T. "The Lord gave me leave to come. Asking of him leave, whithersoever I went, I used still to pray for his direction in all I do. And so I suppose ought you," I said.

Justice Launce. "But pray tell us, what moved you to come such a journey?"

A. T. "The Lord moved me, and gave me leave."

Launce. "But had you not some of extraordinary impulses [of] Spirit, that brought you down? Pray tell us what these were."

A. T. "When you are capable of extraordinary impulses of Spirit, I will tell you. But I suppose you are not in a capacity now," for I saw how deridingly he spoke. And for answering him thus, he said, "I was one of a bold Spirit; but he soon took me down." So he himself said, but some said, "I took them down." For the Lord carried me so to speak, that they were in a hurry and confusion, and sometimes would speak all together. That I was going to say, "What, are you like women, all speakers and no hearers?" But I said thus, "Why do you speak all at a time? I cannot answer all, when speaking at once; I appeal to the civillest of you." And I directed my speech to Justice Lobb, who spake very moderately, and gave me a civil answer, saying, "You are not acquainted with the manner of the Court, which is to give in their sayings."

A. T. "But I cannot answer all at once; indeed I do not know the manner of the Court, for I never was before any till now."

Justice Lobb. "You prophesy against Truro."

A. T. "Indeed, I pray against the sins of the people of Truro, and for their souls' welfare. Are you angry for that?"

Lobb. "But you must not judge Authority, but pray for them, and not speak so suspiciously of them." And more to this purpose he spoke to me.

A. T. "I will take up your word, in which you said, I was not to judge: you said well, for so saith the Scripture, *Who art thou that judgest another man's servant? to his own master he standeth or falleth; yea, he shall be holden up, for God is able to make him stand.* But you have judged me, and never heard me speak: you have not dealt so well by me as Agrippa dealt by Paul. Though Agrippa was an heathen, he would have Paul speak before he gave in his judgement concerning him."[7]

6. A neat evasion to avoid naming others or giving any color to notions of a conspiracy.
7. The story of Paul invited to speak for himself

before Agrippa is recounted in Acts 25.13 to 26.1–32.

Justice Tregegle. "Oh you are a dreamer."

A. T. "So they called Joseph, therefore I wonder not that you call me so."

* * *

I seeing they were very willing to be gone, I said, "Have you done with me?" Answer was, "I might now go away," but I said, "Pray what is it to break the good behavior you have bound me over to? I know not what you may make a breaking of it: is it breaking the good behavior, to pray and sing?"

Justice Travel said, "No so I did it at the habitation where I abode."

"It's well," said I, "you will give leave it shall be anywhere."[8] I said, "I will leave one word with you, and that is this: A time will come when you and I shall appear before the great Judge of the tribunal seat of the Most High, and then I think you will hardly be able to give an account for this day's work before the Lord, at that day of true Judgement."

Said Tregegle, "Take you no care for us."

So they were willing to have no more discourse with me.

1654

8. Because she proposes to continue traveling about.

ABIEZER COPPE

When Winstanley declared that "every single man, male and female, is a perfect creature of himself," needing no teacher or ruler other than the spirit within, the individualist strain of Puritanism might seem to have reached its limit. But there was another impulse at work also, antinomianism, the belief that the Mosaic law (the Ten Commandments) and the moral law itself are abrogated for the elect, who are saved by grace alone. Less extreme antinomians (like Milton) held that Christians were freed from the law in order to follow the law of love written in the heart, an even higher moral standard. But extremists, like Abiezer Coppe (1619–1672) and his fellow Ranters, held that the elect, saved by grace and inhabited by God, are perfect, are incapable of sin, and have a religious duty, by sinning freely, frequently and publicly, to demonstrate their sanctity. Drawn largely from the ranks of apprentices, distressed urban artisans, and itinerants of various sorts, Ranters flourished from 1649 to about 1654: some cursed and blasphemed constantly, others drank to excess, smoked strong tobacco in their meetings, ran naked in the streets, and fornicated openly, often, and with multiple mates. They earned their name, Ranters, by their random, hectic, "inspired" discourse, rooted heavily in the Bible and the experiential; the Ranter prophetic voice attempts to escape from the usual forms and conventions of language. Abiezer Coppe, perhaps the most notorious Ranter, spent some time at Oxford University, then became an itinerant preacher: between jail terms he produced two tracts in 1649, both titled *A Fiery Flying Roll*, from which these extracts are taken.

From A Fiery Flying Roll

* * * Behold, behold, behold, I the eternal God, the Lord of Hosts, who am that mighty Leveller, am coming (yea, even at the doors) to level in good earnest, to level to some purpose, to level with a witness, to level the hills with the valleys, and to lay the mountains low.[1]

High mountains! lofty cedars! it's high time for you to enter into the rocks and to hide you in the dust for fear of the Lord and for the glory of his majesty. For the lofty looks of man shall be humbled and the haughtiness of men shall be bowed down, and the Lord ALONE shall be exalted in that day. * * *

Hills! Mountains! Cedars! Mighty men! Your breath is in your nostrils.

Those that have admired, adored, idolized, magnified, set you up, fought for you, ventured goods and good name, limb and life for you, shall cease from you.

You shall not at all be accounted of (not one of you), ye sturdy oaks who bow not down before eternal Majesty—Universal Love, whose service is perfect freedom, and who hath put down the mighty (remember, remember your forerunner),[2] and who is putting down the mighty from their seats, and exalting them of low degree. * * *

And the prime leveling is laying low the mountains and leveling the hills in Man.

* * *

The eternal God, the mighty Leveler is coming, yea come, even at the door; and what will you do in that day? * * *

Mine ears are filled brimful with cries of poor prisoners, Newgate, Ludgate cries (of late) are seldom out of mine ears. Those doleful cries, *Bread, bread, bread for the Lord's sake*, pierce mine ears and heart, I can no longer forbear.

Wherefore hie you apace to all prisons in the kingdom,

Bow before those poor, nasty, lousy, ragged wretches, say to them, your humble servants, sirs (without a compliment), we let you go free and serve you, &c.

Do this or (as I live, saith the Lord) thine eyes (at least) shall be bored out, and thou carried captive into a strange land.

* * * Loose the bonds of wickedness, undo the heavy burdens, let the oppressed go free, and break every yoke. Deal thy bread to the hungry, and bring the poor that are cast out (both of houses and synagogues) to thy house. Cover the naked: hide not thyself from thine own flesh, from a cripple, a rogue, a beggar, he's thine own flesh. From a whoremonger, a thief, &c., he's flesh of thy flesh, and his flesh and whoredom is flesh of thy flesh also, thine own flesh. Thou mayest have ten times more of each within thee than he that acts outwardly in either. Remember, turn not away thine eyes from thine OWN FLESH.

Give over, give over thy midnight mischief.

Let branding with the letter B[3] alone.

Be no longer so horridly, hellishly, impudently, arrogantly wicked as to judge what is sin, what not, what evil and what not, what blasphemy and what not.

For thou and all thy reverend divines, so-called (who divine for tithes, hire,

---

1. Coppe's prose is too saturated with biblical phrases and echoes to be fully annotated; here the phrasing is from Isaiah 40.

2. Given the date of Coppe's *Roll*, he may be alluding to Charles I.

3. For Blasphemer. "Let": cease.

and money, and serve the Lord Jesus Christ for their own bellies), are ignorant of this one thing:

That sin and transgression is finished, it's a mere riddle that they with all their human learning can never read.

Neither can they understand what pure honor is wrapped up in the king's motto, *Honi soit qui mal y pense*. Evil to him that evil thinks.[4]

Some there are who are accounted the offscouring of all things, who are Noble Knights of the Garter. Since which—they could see no evil, think no evil, do no evil, know no evil.

ALL is religion that they speak, and honor that they do.

* * *

A strange yet most true story; under which is couched that Lion whose roaring shall make all the beasts of the field tremble, and all the kingdoms of the earth quake. * * *

Follow me, who last Lord's day, Septem. 30, 1649, met him in open field, a most strange deformed man, clad with patched clouts; who looking wishly[5] on me, mine eye pitied him; and my heart, or the day of the Lord, which burned as an oven in me, set my tongue on flame to speak to him, as followeth:

How now friend, art thou poor?

He answered, yea Master very poor.

Whereupon my bowels trembled within me, and quivering fell upon the worm-eaten chest (my corpse,[6] I mean), that I could not hold a joint still.

And my great love within me (who is the great God within that chest or corpse) was burning hot toward him; and made the lock-hole of the chest, to wit the mouth of the corpse, again to open, thus:

Art poor?

Yea, very poor, said he.

Whereupon the strange woman who flattereth with her lips and is subtle of heart said within me,

It's a poor wretch, give him twopence.

But my EXCELLENCY and MAJESTY (in me) scorned her words, confounded her language, and kicked her out of his presence.

But immediately the WELL-FAVORED HARLOT,[7] whom I carried not upon my horse behind me, but who rose up in me, said:

—It's a poor wretch, give him sixpence and that's enough for a squire or knight to give to one poor body.

—Besides (saith the holy Scripturian whore), he's worse than an infidel that provides not for his own family.

—True love begins at home, &c.

—Thou and thy family are fed as the young ravens, strangely, though thou hast been a constant preacher, yet thou hast abhorred both tithes and hire; and thou knowest not aforehand who will give thee the worth of a penny.

---

4. The motto of the Order of the Garter delights Coppe because it implies that evil exists only in the eye of the beholder.
5. Intently.
6. Coppe puns on Latin *Corpus* and English *corpse.*
7. The two women within Coppe may indicate, respectively, simple greed and hypocritical self-interest.

—Have a care of the main chance.

And thus she flattereth with her lips and her words being smoother than oil; and her lips dropping as the honeycomb, I was fired to hasten my hand into my pocket; and, pulling out a shilling, said to the poor wretch, Give me sixpence, here's a shilling for thee.[8]

He answered, I cannot, I have never a penny.

Whereupon I said, I would fain have given thee something if thou couldst have changed my money.

Then saith he, God bless you.

Whereupon with much reluctancy, with much love, and with amazement (of the right stamp) I turned my horse head from him, riding away. But a while after I was turned back (being advised by my Demilance[9]) to wish him call for sixpence, which I would leave at the next town at one's house, which I thought he might know—Sapphira-like,[1] keeping back part.

But (as God judged me) I, as she, was struck down dead.

And behold the plague of God fell into my pocket, and the rust of my silver rose up against me and consumed my flesh as with fire; so that I and my money perished with me.

I being cast into that lake of fire and brimstone.

And all the money I had about me to a penny (though I thought through the instigation of my *quondam Mistress* to have reserved some, having rode about 8 miles, not eating one mouthful of bread that day, and had drunk but one small draught of drink, and had between 8 and 9 miles more to ride ere I came to my journey's end; my horse being lame, the ways dirty, it raining all the way, and I not knowing what extraordinary occasion I might have for money). Yet (I say) the rust of my silver did so rise up in judgment against me, and burnt my flesh like fire; and the 5th of James[2] thundered such an alarm in mine ears, that I was fain to cast all I had into the hands of him, whose visage was more marred than any man's that I ever saw.

This is a true story, most true in the history.

It's true also in the mystery.

And there are deep ones couched under it, for it's a shadow of various, glorious (though strange) good things to come.

Well!—to return—after I had thrown my rusty cankered money into the poor wretch's hands, I rode away from him, being filled with trembling, joy, and amazement, feeling the sparkles of a great glory arising up from under these ashes.

After this, I was made (by that divine power which dwelleth in this Ark or chest) to turn my horse head—whereupon I beheld this poor deformed wretch looking earnestly after me; and upon that, was made to put off my hat, and bow to him seven times, and was (at that strange posture) filled with trembling and amazement, some sparkles of glory arising up also from under this, as also from under these ashes; yet I rode back once more to the poor wretch, saying, Because I am a King I have done this, but you need not tell anyone.

---

8. Give me change. A shilling was equivalent to twelve pence.
9. Possibly a misprint for Delilah.
1. Sapphira, wife of Ananias, tried to cheat the Apostles out of their just due (Acts 5).

2. James 5.1–6 fiercely denounces the wealthy: "Your gold and silver is cankered; and the rust of them shall be a witness against you, and shall eat your flesh as it were fire" (5.3).

The day's our own.

This was done on the last LORD'S DAY, Septem. 30 in the year 1649, which is the year of the Lord's recompenses for Zion, and the day of his Vengeance,[3] the dreadful day of Judgment. But I have done (for the present) with this story, for it is the latter end of the year 1649.

1649

3. Coppe may be recalling that January 30, just eight months before, was the day of King Charles's execution.

EDWARD HYDE, EARL OF CLARENDON

Edward Hyde (1609–1674) was educated at Oxford and during the 1630s practiced law. From about 1641 onward, he was among the chief supporters and advisers of Charles I; he went into exile with the boy who was to become Charles II and was privy to the various plots and plans of the royalists to restore him to power. After the Restoration he became lord chancellor and prime minister to Charles II, and he was instrumental in enacting the so-called Clarendon Code, a series of harsh penal laws against all nonconformists to the Anglican church. He was impeached in 1667, owing partly to England's ill success in the Dutch War, and spent the last seven years of his life in France.

Clarendon's great *History of the Rebellion* was written in part amid the events it describes. For the Muse of History such a short view can be a mixed blessing. But Clarendon's learning—legal, classical, and historical—and the formality of his method save him from many of the failings of partisanship. He wrote with dignity and for posterity. His *History*, which first appeared in print thirty years after his death, was remarkable not only for the largeness of its canvas but also for the force and coherence of the social philosophy informing it, which retains its influence under the name of Toryism. As a historian and rhetorician Clarendon invites comparison with his models, Thucydides and Tacitus; as an evaluator of character he invites comparison with Plutarch, whose judicious balance and careful assessment of good and bad qualities are replicated in Clarendon's "Character" of Oliver Cromwell given here.

From The History of the Rebellion

[THE CHARACTER OF OLIVER CROMWELL][1]

About the middle of August he was seized on by a common tertian ague,[2] from which he believed a little ease and divertissement at Hampton Court[3] would have freed him; but the fits grew stronger and his spirits much abated, so that he returned again to Whitehall,[4] when his physicians began to think him in danger, though the preachers who prayed always about him and told

1. After the manner of ancient historians, Clarendon describes the last days, sickness, and death of Cromwell, then summarizes his character. The Protector, who had been depressed for some time by the death of a favorite daughter, first grew ill in the summer of 1658.
2. An acute fever, with paroxysms recurring every third day.
3. Hampton Court, built by Cardinal Wolsey and ceded by him to Henry VIII, is a splendid old palace up the Thames from London. "Divertissement": diversion.
4. Whitehall, in London, was the traditional residence of the head of state.

God Almighty what great things he had done for Him, and how much more need He had still of his service, declared as from God that he should recover, and he himself did not think he should die, till even the time that his spirits failed him, and then declared to them that he did appoint his son to succeed him, his eldest son Richard. And so expired upon the third day of September (a day he thought always very propitious to him, and on which he had triumphed for several victories),[5] 1658, a day very memorable for the greatest storm of wind that had been ever known for some hours before and after his death, which overthrew trees, houses, and made great wrecks at sea, and was so universal that there were terrible effects of it both in France and Flanders, where all people trembled at it, besides the wrecks all along the coast, many boats having been cast away in the very rivers; and within few days after, that circumstance of his death that accompanied that storm was known.

He was one of those men *quos vituperare ne inimici quidem possunt, nisi ut simul laudent,*[6] for he could never have done half that mischief without great parts of courage and industry and judgment, and he must have had a wonderful understanding in the natures and humors of men, and as great a dexterity in the applying them, who from a private and obscure birth (though of a good family), without interest of estate, alliance, or friendships, could raise himself to such a height, and compound and knead such opposite and contradictory tempers, humors, and interests into a consistence that contributed to his designs and to their own destruction, whilst himself grew insensibly powerful enough to cut off those by whom he had climbed, in the instant that they projected to demolish their own building.[7] What Velleius Paterculus said of Cinna may very justly be said of him, *Ausum eum quae nemo auderet bonus, perfecisse quae a nullo nisi fortissimo perfici possunt.*[8] Without doubt no man with more wickedness ever attempted anything, or brought to pass what he desired more wickedly, more in the face and contempt of religion and moral honesty; yet wickedness as great as his could never have accomplished those trophies without the assistance of a great spirit, an admirable circumspection and sagacity, and a most magnanimous resolution. When he appeared first in the Parliament he seemed to have a person in no degree gracious, no ornament of discourse, none of those talents which use to reconcile the affections of the standers-by; yet as he grew into place and authority, his parts[9] seemed to be renewed, as if he had concealed faculties till he had occasion to use them, and when he was to act the part of a great man, he did it without any indecency[1] through the want of custom.

After he was confirmed and invested Protector by the Humble Petition and Advice,[2] he consulted with very few upon any action of importance, nor

---

5. Dunbar and Worcester were important battles that Cromwell had won on September 3.
6. "Whom not even his enemies could curse without praising him." The source of the phrase is unknown.
7. Clarendon's judgment can be compared with that of Marvell in *An Horatian Ode* (p. 1700). "Insensibly": imperceptively.
8. "He dared undertake what no good man would have tried, and triumphed where only the strongest of men could have succeeded." Velleius Paterculus

(died 30 C.E.) wrote a concise *History of Rome;* the quotation is from 2.24.
9. Personal qualities.
1. Indecorum.
2. In December 1653, Cromwell was invested as Protector under a written constitution called the Instrument of Government. In 1657 another constitution, *The Humble Petition and Advice,* invested him with quasi-monarchical powers and restored the House of Lords.

communicated any enterprise he resolved upon with more than those who were to have principal parts in the execution of it, nor to them sooner than was absolutely necessary. What he once resolved, in which he was not rash, he would not be dissuaded from, nor endure any contradiction of his power and authority, but extorted obedience from them who were not willing to yield it.

When he had laid some very extraordinary tax upon the city, one Cony, an eminent fanatic,[3] and one who had heretofore served him very notably, positively refused to pay his part and loudly dissuaded others from submitting to it, as an imposition notoriously against the law and the property of the subject, which all honest men were bound to defend. Cromwell sent for him and cajoled him with the memory of the old kindness and friendship that had been between them, and that of all men he did not expect this opposition from him in a matter that was so necessary for the good of the commonwealth. But it was always his fortune to meet with the most rude and obstinate behavior from those who had formerly been absolutely governed by him, and they commonly put him in mind of some expressions and sayings of his own in cases of the like nature. So this man remembered[4] him how great an enemy he had expressed himself to such grievances, and declared that all who submitted to them and paid illegal taxes were more to blame, and greater enemies to their country, than they who imposed them; and that the tyranny of princes could never be grievous but by the tameness and stupidity of the people.

When Cromwell saw that he could not convert him, he told him that he had a will as stubborn as his, and he would try which of them two should be master, and thereupon with some terms of reproach and contempt he committed the man to prison—whose courage was nothing abated by it, but as soon as the term came, he brought his *habeas corpus*[5] in the King's Bench, which they then called the Upper Bench. Maynard, who was of counsel with the prisoner, demanded his liberty with great confidence, both upon the illegality of the commitment and the illegality of the imposition,[6] as being laid without any lawful authority. The judges could not maintain or defend either, but enough declared what their sentence would be, and therefore the Protector's attorney required a further day to answer what had been urged. Before that day, Maynard was committed to the Tower for presuming to question or make doubt of his authority, and the judges were sent for and severely reprehended for suffering that license; and when they with all humility mentioned the law, and Magna Charta, Cromwell told them their Magna Farta should not control his actions, which he knew were for the safety of the commonwealth. He asked them who made them judges; whether they had any authority to sit there but what he gave them, and that if his authority were at an end, they knew well enough what would become of themselves. And therefore advised them to be more tender of that which could only preserve them, and so dismissed them with caution that they should not suffer the lawyers to prate what it would not become them to hear.

Thus he subdued a spirit that had been often troublesome to the most

3. In Clarendon's vocabulary, a radical Puritan.   5. Writ to release a prisoner.
"The city": the city of London.   6. I.e., the original tax.
4. Reminded.

sovereign power, and made Westminster Hall[7] as obedient and subservient to his commands as any of the rest of his quarters. In all other matters which did not concern the life of his jurisdiction, he seemed to have great reverence for the law, and rarely interposed between party and party; and as he proceeded with this kind of indignation and haughtiness with those who were refractory and dared to contend with his greatness, so towards those who complied with his good pleasure and courted his protection he used a wonderful civility, generosity, and bounty.

To reduce three nations which perfectly hated him to an entire obedience to all his dictates, to awe and govern those nations by an army that was indevoted to him and wished his ruin, was an instance of a very prodigious address;[8] but his greatness at home was but a shadow of the glory he had abroad. It was hard to discover which feared him most, France, Spain, or the Low Countries, where his friendship was current at the value he put upon it; and as they did all sacrifice their honor and their interest to his pleasure, so there is nothing he could have demanded that either of them would have denied him.

* * *

He was not a man of blood, and totally declined Machiavel's method, which prescribes upon any alteration of a government, as a thing absolutely necessary, to cut off all the heads of those, and extirpate their families, who are friends to the old;[9] and it was confidently reported in the Council of Officers, it was more than once proposed that there might be a general massacre of all the royal party as the only expedient to secure the government, but Cromwell would never consent to it, it may be out of too much contempt of his enemies. In a word, as he had all the wickednesses against which damnation is denounced and for which hellfire is prepared, so he had some virtues which have caused the memory of some men in all ages to be celebrated, and he will be looked upon by posterity as a brave, bad man.

1702–04

---

7. The center of the law courts and legal profession. Clarendon never tells us what happened to poor George Cony; the lawyer and judges made their submission and got off, but the fate of the plaintiff remains obscure.

8. Skill. "Indevoted": Clarendon's word, carefully coined to express the far from unanimous feelings of the army.
9. See *The Prince:* chap. 3 for the precept, chap. 7 for the example.

THOMAS TRAHERNE
1637–1674

Thomas Traherne's most remarkable works—his stanzaic poems, free verse *Thanksgivings*, and the brilliant prose meditative sequence *Centuries of Meditation*—were lost for over two centuries and with them access to a unique religious and aesthetic sensibility, one that conceives of heavenly felicity as a state that can be enjoyed in this world by recovering the perspective of lost childhood innocence. Traherne published in 1673 a polemic against Roman Catholics (*Roman Forgeries*), and some works of moral philosophy, meditation, and devotion received posthumous publication over the next several years, but his poems and the *Centuries* were only discovered in manuscript in 1896–97, and at first his poems were attributed to Vaughan. Little is known of Traherne's life: the son of a Herefordshire shoemaker, he received a degree from Brasenose College, Oxford, took orders and became rector of Credenhill in Herefordshire in 1661, became chaplain about 1660 to Sir Orlando Bridgeman, Lord Keeper of the Great Seal, and spent his last years in and near London. The *Centuries*, four books of one hundred items each and a fifth unfinished, contain prose meditations (which are often ecstatic prose poems) and some interpolated poems; the work was addressed to his good friend Mrs. Susanna Hopton, to help her attain "felicity." The poems render moments of spiritual experience pertaining to the speaker's enjoyment of a wondrous heavenly felicity in childhood, his painful loss of it in maturity, and his successful efforts to recover that heavenly perspective.

From Centuries of Meditation

From *The Third Century*

3

The Corn was Orient and Immortal Wheat, which never should be reaped, nor was ever sown. I thought it had stood from everlasting to everlasting. The Dust and Stones of the Street were as Precious as GOLD. The Gates were at first the End of the World, The Green Trees when I saw them first through one of the Gates Transported and Ravished me; their Sweetnes and unusual Beauty made my Heart to leap, and almost mad with Extasie, they were such strange and Wonderfull Thing: The Men! O what Venerable and Reverend Creatures did the Aged seem! Immortal Cherubims! And yong Men Glittering and Sparkling Angels and Maids strange Seraphick Pieces of Life and Beauty! Boys and Girles Tumbling in the Street, and Playing, were moving Jewels. I knew not that they were Born or should Die. But all things abided Eternaly as they were in their Proper Places. Eternity was Manifest in the Light of the Day, and som thing infinit Behind evry thing appeared: which talked with my Expectation and moved my Desire. The Citie seemed to stand in Eden, or to be Built in Heaven. The Streets were mine, the Temple was mine, the People were mine, their Clothes and Gold and Silver was mine, as much as their Sparkling Eys Fair Skins and ruddy faces. The Skies were mine, and so were the Sun and Moon and Stars, and all the World was mine, and I the only Spectator and Enjoyer of it. I knew no Churlish Proprieties, nor Bounds nor Divisions: but all Proprieties and Divisions were mine: all Treasures and the Possessors of them. So that with much adoe I was corrupted; and made to learn the Dirty Devices of this World. Which now I unlearn, and becom as it were a little Child again, that I may enter into the Kingdom of GOD.

1908

Wonder

How like an angel came I down!
　　How bright are all things here!
When first among his works I did appear,
　　O how their glory me did crown!
5　　The world resembled his eternity,
　　　　In which my soul did walk,
　　And everything that I did see
　　　　Did with me talk.

　　The skies in their magnificence,
10　　　The lively, lovely air;
O how divine, how soft, how sweet, how fair!
　　The stars did entertain my sense,[1]
And all the works of God so bright and pure,
　　　　So rich and great did seem,
15　　As if they ever must endure,
　　　　In my esteem.

　　A native health and innocence
　　　　Within my bones did grow,
And while my God did all his glories show,
20　　I felt a vigor in my sense
That was all Spirit. I within did flow
　　　　With seas of life like wine;
　　I nothing in the world did know
　　　　But 'twas divine.

25　　Harsh ragged objects were concealed,
　　　　Oppression's tears and cries,
Sins, griefs, complaints, dissensions, weeping eyes,
　　Were hid; and only things revealed
Which heavenly spirits and the angels prize.
30　　　The state of innocence
　　And bliss, not trades and poverties,
　　　　Did fill my sense.

　　The streets were paved with golden stones,
　　　　The boys and girls were mine,
35　　O how did all their lovely faces shine!
　　The sons of men were holy ones.
Joy, beauty, welfare did appear to me
　　　　And everything which here I found
　　While like an angel I did see,
40　　　　Adorned the ground.

　　Rich diamond and pearl and gold
　　　　In every place was seen;
Rare splendors, yellow, blue, red, white, and green,

1. Sight, especially.

Mine eyes did everywhere behold.
45 Great wonders clothed with glory did appear,
      Amazement was my bliss.
    That and my wealth was everywhere:
      No joy to this!°   compared to this

    Cursed and devised proprieties,[2]
50   With envy, avarice,
  And fraud, those fiends that spoil even paradise,
    Fled from the splendor of mine eyes.
  And so did hedges, ditches, limits, bounds:
      I dreamed not aught of those,
55   But wandered over all men's grounds,
        And found repose.

    Proprieties themselves were mine,
      And hedges ornaments;
  Walls, boxes, coffers, and their rich contents
60   Did not divide my joys, but shine.
  Clothes, ribbons, jewels, laces, I esteemed
      My joys by others worn;
    For me they all to wear them seemed
        When I was born.

                                                          1903

On Leaping over the Moon

    I saw new worlds beneath the water lie,
      New people, and another sky
        And sun, which seen by day
        Might things more clear display.
5   Just such another[1]
          Of late my brother[2]
    Did in his travel see, and saw by night,
      A much more strange and wondrous sight;
    Nor could the world exhibit such another
10   So great a sight, but in a brother.

    Adventure strange! no such in story we
      New or old, true or feignèd see.
        On earth he seemed to move,
        Yet heaven went above;[3]
15   Up in the skies
          His body flies,
    In open, visible, yet magic sort:
      As he along the way did sport,
    Like Icarus[4] over the flood he soars
20   Without the help of wings or oars.

2. Legally willed properties.
1. Another world.
2. Traherne's brother Philip.

3. I.e., yet went above the heavens.
4. The waxen wings of Icarus melted in the sun
and dropped him fatally into the sea.

As he went tripping o'er the king's highway,
  A little pearly river lay
    O'er which, without a wing
    Or oar, he dared to swim,
25   Swim through the air
      On body fair;
He would not use nor trust Icarian wings[5]
  Lest they should prove deceitful things;
For had he fallen, it had been wondrous high,
30   Not from, but from above, the sky.

He might have dropped through that thin element
  Into a fathomless descent
    Unto the nether sky
    That did beneath him lie
35   And there might tell
      What wonders dwell
On earth above. Yet bold he briskly runs,
  And soon the danger overcomes,
Who, as he leapt, with joy related soon
40   How happy he o'erleaped the moon.

What wondrous things upon the earth are done
  Beneath and yet above the sun!
    Deeds all appear again
    In higher spheres; remain
45   In clouds as yet:
      But there they get
Another light, and in another way
  Themselves to us above display.
The skies themselves this earthly globe surround;
50   We're even here within them found.

On heavenly ground within the skies we walk,
  And in this middle center talk:
    Did we but wisely move
    On earth in heaven above,
55   We then should be
      Exalted high
Above the sky: from whence whoever falls,
  Through a long dismal precipice,
Sinks to the deep abyss where Satan crawls,
60   Where horrid Death and Dèspair lies.

As much as others thought themselves to lie
  Beneath the moon, so much more high
    Himself he thought to fly
    Above the starry sky,
65   As that he spied
      Below the tide.
Thus did he yield me in the shady night
  A wondrous and instructive light,

---

5. The wings of Icarus.

Which taught me that under our feet there is,
70   As o'er our heads, a place of bliss.

                                        1910

MARGARET CAVENDISH
1623–1673

Margaret (Lucas) Cavendish, duchess of Newcastle, wrote and published numerous works during the Interregnum and Restoration era, in a great variety of genres: poetry (*Poems and Fancies*, 1653), essays (*Philosophical Fancies*, 1653, *The World's Olio*, 1655), short fiction (*Nature's Pictures*, 1656), autobiography (*A True Relation of My Birth, Breeding, and Life*, 1656), utopian romance (*The Blazing World*, 1666), scientific essays chiefly critical of the new science, letters, a biography of her husband (*The Life of . . . William Cavendish*, 1667), and some eighteen plays, of which one, *The Forced Marriage*, was produced in 1670. Most were published in lavish editions, at the Newcastles' own expense, and at the time they elicited more derision than praise: for a woman, especially an aristocratic woman, to publish works dealing so intimately with her desires, opinions, personal circumstances, and aspirations to fame and authorship was seen by many as disgraceful. Samuel Pepys concluded, after reading her life of her husband the duke, that she was "a mad, conceited, ridiculous woman, and he an ass to suffer [her] to write what she writes to him and of him." Her fantastic dress and sometimes idiosyncratic social behavior abetted that characterization: she took pride in "singularity" and even insisted on paying a visit to the all-male Royal Society. But the philosopher Thomas Hobbes thought well of her, and her rediscoverers in recent decades have been impressed by her works and her self-construction as a female author.

Her autobiography analyzes her responses to the circumstances of her life: born into a wealthy royalist family that encouraged her disposition to read and write; accepted as maid of honor by Queen Henrietta Maria, whom she followed into exile in Paris; married there (1645) to the widowed William Cavendish, thirty years her senior, who was one of Charles I's generals and later duke of Newcastle; exiled with him for fifteen years on the Continent, where (his estates having been sequestered) they ran up exorbitant debts; and restored to status and fortune after the Restoration. The duke, who was himself something of a poet, playwright, and philosopher, encouraged, supported, and promoted Margaret's literary endeavors—for which she was profoundly grateful. In polemical prefaces to her several works, she develops a fragmentary poetics, trenchantly defends her right to publish and to participate in contemporary intellectual exchange, defends women's rational powers, and decries their educational disadvantages and exclusion from the public domain.

From Poems and Fancies

The Poetess's Hasty Resolution

Reading my verses, I liked them so well,
Self-love did make my judgment to rebel.

Thinking them so good, I thought more to write;
Considering not how others would them like.
5   I writ so fast, I thought, if I lived long,
A pyramid of fame[1] to build thereon.
Reason observing which way I was bent,
Did stay my hand, and asked me what I meant;
Will you, said she, thus waste your time in vain,
10 On that which in the world small praise shall gain?
For shame, leave off, said she, the printer spare,
He'll lose by your ill poetry, I fear.
Besides the world hath already such a weight
Of useless books, as it is overfraught.[2]
15 Then pity take, do the world a good turn,
And all you write cast in the fire, and burn.
Angry I was, and Reason struck away,
When I did hear, what she to me did say.
Then all in haste I to the press it sent,
20 Fearing persuasion might my book prevent.
But now 'tis done, with grief repent do I,
Hang down my head with shame, blush, sigh, and cry.
Take pity, and my drooping spirits raise,
Wipe off my tears with handkerchiefs of praise.

1653

The Hunting of the Hare

Betwixt two ridges of plowed land lay Wat,[1]
Pressing his body close to earth lay squat.
His nose upon his two forefeet close lies,
Glazing obliquely with his great gray eyes.
5   His head he always sets against the wind,
If turn his tail, his hairs blow up behind:
Which he too cold will grow, but he is wise,
And keeps his coat still down, so warm he lies.
Then resting all the day, till, sun doth set,
10 Then riseth up, his relief for to get.
Walking about until the sun doth rise,
Then back returns, down in his form he lies.
At last, poor Wat was found, as he there lay,
By huntsmen, with their dogs which came that way.
15 Seeing, gets up, and fast begins to run,
Hoping some ways the cruel dogs to shun.
But they by nature have so quick a scent,
That by their nose they trace what way he went.
And with their deep, wide mouths set forth a cry,
20 Which answered was by echoes in the sky.
Then Wat was struck with terror, and with fear,
Thinks every shadow still the dogs they were.

1. A poetic monument.
2. Like a ship with too heavy a cargo, in danger of

sinking.
1. Conventional name for a hare.

And running out some distance from the noise,
To hide himself, his thoughts he new employs.
25 Under a clod of earth in sand pit wide,
Poor Wat sat close, hoping himself to hide.
There long he had not sat, but straight his ears
The winding° horns and crying dogs he hears: *blowing*
Staring with fear, up leaps, then doth he run,
30 And with such speed, the ground scarce treads upon.
Into a great thick wood he straightway gets.
Where underneath a broken bough he sits.
At every leaf that with the wind did shake,
Did bring such terror, made his heart to ache.
35 That place he left, to champaign° plains he went, *open*
Winding about, for to deceive their scent.
And while they snuffling were, to find his track,
Poor Wat, being weary, his swift pace did slack.
On his two hinder legs for ease did sit,
40 His forefeet rubbed his face from dust, and sweat.
Licking his feet, he wiped his ears so clean,
That none could tell that Wat had hunted been.
But casting round about his fair great eyes,
The hounds in full career he near him spies:
45 To Wat it was so terrible a sight,
Fear gave him wings, and made his body light.
Though weary was before, by running long,
Yet now his breath he never felt more strong.
Like those that dying are, think health returns,
50 When tis but a faint blast, which life out burns.
For spirits seek to guard the heart about,
Striving with death, but death doth quench them out.
Thus they so fast came on, with such loud cries,
That he no hopes hath left, nor help espies.
55 With that the winds did pity poor Wat's case,
And with their breath the scent blew from the place.
Then every nose is busily employed,
And every nostril is set open wide,
And every head doth seek a several way,
60 To find what grass, or track, the scent on lay.
Thus quick industry° that is not slack, *clever work*
Is like to witchery,° brings lost things back. *witchcraft*
For though the wind had tied the scent up close,
A busy dog thrust in his snuffling nose
65 And drew it out, with it did foremost run,
Then horns blew loud, for th'rest to follow on.
The great slow hounds, their throats did set a base,
The fleet swift hounds, as tenors next in place,
The little beagles they a treble sing,
70 And through the air their voices round did ring.
Which made a consort, as they ran along;
If they but words could speak, might sing a song.
The horns kept time, the hunters shout for joy,
And valiant seem, poor Wat for to destroy:

75 Spurring their horses to a full career,
    Swim rivers deep, leap ditches without fear;
    Endanger life and limbs so fast will ride,
    Only to see how patiently Wat died.
    At last,[2] the dogs so near his heels did get,
80 That they their sharp teeth in his breech did set;
    Then tumbling down, did fall with weeping eyes,
    Gives up his ghost, and thus poor Wat he dies.
    Men whooping loud, such acclamations make,
    As if the Devil they did prisoner take.
85 When they do but a shiftless creature kill;
    To hunt, there needs no valiant soldier's skill.
    But man doth think that exercise and toil,
    To keep their health, is best, which makes most spoile.
    Thinking that food and nourishment so good,
90 And appetite, that feeds on flesh and blood.
    When they do lions, wolves, bears, tigers see,
    To kill poor sheep, straight say, they cruel be,
    But for themselves all creatures think too few
    For luxury, wish God would make them new.
95 As if that God made creatures for man's meat,
    To give them life and sense, for man to eat;
    Or else for sport, or recreation's sake,
    Destroy those lives that God saw good to make:
    Making their stomachs, graves, which full they fill
100 With murdered bodies that in sport they kill.
    Yet man doth think himself so gentle, mild,
    When he of creatures is most cruel wild.
    And is so proud, thinks only he shall live,
    That God a God-like nature did him give.
105 And that all creatures for his sake alone
    Was made for him, to tyrannize upon.

                                        1653, 1664

From A True Relation of My Birth, Breeding, and Life[1]

As for my breeding, it was according to my birth and the nature of my sex, for my birth was not lost in my breeding; for as my sisters had been bred, so was I in plenty, or rather with superfluity. . . . 'Tis true my mother might have increased her daughters' portions by a thrifty sparing, yet she chose to bestow it on our breeding, honest pleasures, and harmless delight, out of an opinion that if she bred us with needy necessity it might chance to create in us sharking[2] qualities, mean thoughts, and base actions, which she knew my

---

2. From 1664 edition; 1653 has "For why."
1. Cavendish's autobiography is a concise account, factual and at times self-reflective, of her early life. It comprises the final section of *Nature's Pictures* (1656), a collection of her fiction written

during the Newcastles' exile in Antwerp during the Cromwell regime. Many of her works, like this one, were privately printed in elegant format at the author's expense.
2. Greedy.

father as well as herself did abhor. Likewise we were bred tenderly, for my mother naturally did strive to please and delight her children, not to cross or torment them, terrifying them with threats or lashing them with slavish whips. But instead of threats, reason was used to persuade us, and instead of lashes, the deformities of vices was discovered, and the graces and virtues were presented unto us.

* * *

After the Queen went from Oxford, and so out of England, I was parted from them.[3] For when the Queen was in Oxford I had a great desire to be one of her Maids of Honor. . . . And though I might have learned more wit, and advanced my understanding by living in a court, yet being dull, fearful, and bashful, I neither heeded what was said or practiced, but just what belonged to my loyal duty and my own honest reputation. And indeed I was so afraid to dishonor my friends and family by my indiscreet actions that I rather chose to be accounted a fool than to be thought rude or wanton. In truth my bashfulness and fears made me repent my going from home to see the world abroad. . . .

So I continued almost two years, until such time as I was married from thence. For my Lord the Marquis of Newcastle[4] did approve of those bashful fears which many condemned, and would choose such a wife as he might bring to his own humors,[5] and not such an one as was wedded to self-conceit, or one that had been tempered to the humors of another, for which he wooed me for his wife. And though I did dread marriage, and shunned men's companies as much as I could, yet I could not nor had not the power to refuse him, by reason my affections were fixed on him, and he was the only person I ever was in love with. Neither was I ashamed to own it, but gloried therein, for it was not amorous love. I never was infected therewith—it is a disease, or a passion, or both, I know by relation, not by experience. Neither could title, wealth, power, or person entice me to love. But my love was honest and honorable, being placed upon merit; which affection joyed at the fame of his worth, pleased with delight in his wit, proud of the respects he used to me, and triumphing in the affections he professed for me. . . . And though my Lord hath lost his estate, and banished out of his country for his loyalty to his King and country, yet neither despised poverty nor pinching necessity could make him break the bonds of friendship, or weaken his loyal duty to his King or country.

* * *

When I am writing any sad feigned stories or serious humors or melancholy passions, I am forced many times to express them with the tongue before I can write them with the pen, by reason those thoughts that are sad, serious, and melancholy are apt to contract and to draw back too much, which oppression doth as it were overpower or smother the conception in the brain. But when some of those thoughts are sent out in words, they give

---

3. Her mother and family; her father had died when she was two years old. In 1643 Charles I moved his family and court to Oxford, where Margaret became maid of honor to Queen Henrietta Maria; in 1644 the queen fled with some supporters, Margaret among them, to her native Paris, to urge support for the royalist cause.
4. William Cavendish (1593–1676), a general in the king's army, fled to the Continent in 1644. Margaret was his second wife, married in 1645 in Paris.
5. Inclination, disposition.

the rest more liberty to place themselves in a more methodical order, marching more regularly with my pen on the ground of white paper. But my letters seem rather as a ragged rout, than a well-armed body, for the brain being quicker in creating than the hand in writing, or the memory in retaining, many fancies are lost by reason they of times outrun the pen. Where I, to keep speed in the race, write so fast as I stay not so long as to write my letters plain, insomuch as some have taken my handwriting for some strange character.[6] . . . My only trouble is lest my brain should grow barren, or that the root of my fancies should become insipid, withering into a dull stupidity, for want of maturing subjects to write on.

* * *

Since I have writ in general thus far of my life, I think it fit, I should speak something of my humor, particular practice, and disposition. As for my humor, I was from my childhood given to contemplation, being more taken or delighted with thoughts then in conversation with a society, in so much as I would walk two or three hours, and never rest, in a musing, considering, contemplating manner, reasoning with myself of everything my senses did present. . . . Likewise I had a natural stupidity towards the learning of any other language than my native tongue, for I could sooner and with more facility understand the sense than remember the words, and for want of such memory makes me so unlearned in foreign languages as I am: as for my practice,[7] I was never very active, by reason I was given so much to contemplation. . . . As for my study of books it was little, yet I chose rather to read, than to employ my time in any other work, or practice, and when I read what I understood not, I would ask my brother, the Lord Lucas, he being learned, the sense of meaning thereof; but my serious study could not be much, by reason I took great delight in attiring, fine dressing, and fashions, especially such fashions as I did invent myself, not taking that pleasure in such fashions as was invented by others: also I did dislike any should follow my fashions, for I always took delight in a singularity, even in the accoutrements of habits, but whatsoever I was addicted to, either in fashion of clothes, contemplations of thoughts, actions of life, they were lawful, honorable, and modest, of which I can avouch to the world with a great confidence, because it is a pure truth.

* * *

I am a great emulator; for though I wish none worse than they are, yet it is lawful for me to wish myself the best, and to do my honest endeavor thereunto; for I think it no crime to wish myself the exactest[8] of Nature's works, my thread of life the longest, my chain of destiny the strongest, my mind the peaceablest, my life the pleasantest, my death the easiest, and the greatest saint in Heaven. Also to do my endeavor, so far as honor and honesty doth allow of, to be the highest on Fortune's wheel, and to hold the wheel from turning if I can; and if it be commendable to wish another's good, it were a sin not to wish my own; for as envy is a vice, so emulation is a virtue, but emulation is in the way to ambition, or indeed it is a noble ambition.

---

6. Code.
7. Refers, probably, to practicing a musical instrument, music being an accomplishment cultivated

in high-born young ladies.
8. Most perfect.

But I fear my ambition inclines to vainglory, for I am very ambitious; yet 'tis neither for beauty, wit, titles, wealth, or power, but as they are steps to raise me to fame's tower, which is to live by remembrance on after-ages. . . . But I hope my readers will not think me vain for writing my life, since there have been many that have done the like, as Caesar,[9] Ovid, and many more, both men and women, and I know no reason I may not do it as well as they: but I verily believe some censuring readers will scornfully say, Why hath this lady writ her own life? since none cares to know whose daughter she was, or whose wife she is, or how she was bred, or what fortunes she had, or how she lived, or what humor or disposition she was of? I answer that it is true, that 'tis to no purpose to the readers, but it is to the authoress, because I write it for my own sake, not theirs; neither did I intend this piece for to delight, but to divulge; not to please the fancy but to tell the truth, lest after-ages should mistake, in not knowing I was daughter to one Master Lucas[1] of St. Johns, near Colchester, in Essex, second wife to the Lord Marquis of Newcastle; for My Lord having had two wives, I might easily have been mistaken, especially if I should die and My Lord marry again.

1656

The Blazing World   Part romance, part utopia, and part science fiction, *The Blazing World* is also an idealized version of Cavendish's own ideas and fantasies in that it portrays the effortless rise of a woman to absolute power. It begins in the vein of romance: a young woman is abducted and miraculously saved as a tempest carries the abductors' boat to the North Pole and on to another universe, the Blazing World, whose emperor promptly marries her and turns over the entire government of the realm to her. It takes on a utopian character, as the new Empress learns from the fantastically diverse inhabitants about their numerous scientific experiments and about the royalist politics and religious uniformity of the place. She then brings Margaret Cavendish to be her scribe and returns with Margaret (in the state of disembodied spirits and platonic friends) to visit and learn about Margaret's world and Margaret's husband, the duke; she also puts down a rebellion at home and subjects other nations to her beneficent rule. Cavendish's preface makes a bold claim for authorial self-sufficiency, equating her creation and rule over her textual world with the conquering and ruling of empires by Caesar and Alexander. She undertakes to emphasize the satisfactions of authorship, but in doing so she also underscores the social and political restrictions on women that have confined her sphere of action to an imagined world.

The Description of a New World, Called The Blazing World[1]

To the Reader

* * * This is the reason, why I added this piece of fancy to my philosophical observations, and joined them as two worlds at the ends of their poles; both

9. Julius Caesar wrote an account of his military campaigns (*Commentaries*); the Roman poet Ovid wrote poems ostensibly about his own life and loves.
1. Thomas Lucas (ca. 1573–1625), a gentleman of large fortune and estates. Margaret describes

him as "not a peer of the realm, yet there were few peers who had much greater estates, or lived more noble therewith."
1. *The Blazing World* was published in 1666 and 1668, together with Newcastle's *Observations upon Experimental Philosophy*, a critique of the new sci-

for my own sake, to divert my studious thoughts, which I employed in the contemplation thereof, and to delight the reader with variety, which is always pleasing. But lest my fancy should stray too much, I chose such a fiction as would be agreeable to the subject treated of in the former parts; it is a description of a *new world*, not such as *Lucian*'s or the *French*-man's world in the moon;[2] but a world of my own creating, which I call the *Blazing World*: the first part whereof is *romancical*, the second philosophical, and the third is merely *fancy*, or (as I may call it) *fantastical*, which if it add any satisfaction to you, I shall account my self a happy *creatoress*; if not, I must be content to live a melancholy life in my own world; I cannot call it a poor world, if poverty be only want of gold, silver, and jewels; for there is more gold in it than all the chemists ever did, and (as I verily believe) will ever be able to make. As for the rocks of diamonds, I wish with all my soul they might be shared amongst my noble female friends, and upon that condition, I would willingly quit my part; and of the gold I should only desire so much as might suffice to repair my noble lord and husband's losses:[3] for I am not covetous, but as ambitious as ever any of my sex was, is, or can be; which makes, that though I cannot be *Henry* the Fifth, or *Charles* the Second, yet I endeavor to be *Margaret* the *First*; and although I have neither power, time nor occasion to conquer the world as *Alexander* and *Caesar* did; yet rather than not to be mistress of one, since Fortune and the Fates would give me none, I have made a world of my own: for which no body, I hope, will blame me, since it is in every one's power to do the like.

---

* * * No sooner was the Lady brought before the Emperor, but he conceived her to be some goddess, and offered to worship her; which she refused, telling him, (for by that time she had pretty well learned their language) that although she came out of another world, yet was she but a mortal; at which the Emperor rejoicing, made her his wife, and gave her an absolute power to rule and govern all that world as she pleased. But her subjects, who could hardly be persuaded to believe her mortal, tendered her all the veneration and worship due to a deity . . .

Their priests and governors were princes of the imperial blood, and made eunuchs for that purpose; and as for the ordinary sort of men in that part of the world where the Emperor resided, they were of several complexions; not white, black, tawny, olive or ash-coloured; but some appeared of an azure, some of a deep purple, some of a grass-green, some of a scarlet, some of an orange color, etc. Which colors and complexions, whether they were made by the bare reflection of light, without the assistance of small particles, or by the help of well-ranged and ordered atoms; or by a continual agitation of little globules; or by some pressing and reacting motion, I am not able to determine. The rest of the inhabitants of that world, were men of several different sorts, shapes, figures, dispositions, and humors, as I have already

---

ence emphasizing the limitations of experiment founded on human perception, and such machines as the microscope and telescope.
2. Cyrano de Bergerac (1620–1655), author of *Histoire comique conenant les états et empires de la lune* (1657). The Greek satirist Lucian of Samosata (125–200? C.E.) wrote dialogues about an

imaginary voyage, translated in 1634.
3. Cavendish's husband, William, was formally banished from England and his estates confiscated in 1649; they were all restored after the Restoration. During his banishment Margaret estimated that he suffered financial losses of around £940,000.

made mention heretofore; some were bear-men, some worm-men, some fish-
or mear-men,[4] otherwise called sirens; some bird-men, some fly-men, some
ant-men, some geese-men, some spider-men, some lice-men, some fox-men,
some ape-men, some jackdaw-men, some magpie-men, some parrot-men,
some satyrs, some giants, and many more, which I cannot all remember; and
of these several sorts of men, each followed such a profession as was most
proper for the nature of their species, which the Empress encouraged them
in, especially those that had applied themselves to the study of several arts
and sciences; for they were as ingenious and witty in the invention of profitable and useful arts, as we are in our world, nay, more; and to that end she
erected schools, and founded several societies. The bear-men were to be her
experimental philosophers, the bird-men her astronomers, the fly-, worm-
and fish-men her natural philosophers, the ape-men her chemists, the satyrs
her Galenic physicians, the fox-men her politicians, the spider- and lice-men
her mathematicians, the jackdaw-, magpie- and parrot-men her orators and
logicians, the giants her architects, etc. But before all things, she having got
a sovereign power from the Emperor over all the world, desired to be
informed both of the manner of their religion and government, and to that
end she called the priests and statesmen, to give her an account of either.
Of the statesmen she enquired, first, why they had so few laws? To which
they answered, that many laws made many divisions, which most commonly
did breed factions, and at last break out into open wars. Next, she asked,
why they preferred the monarchical form of government before any other?
They answered, that as it was natural for one body to have but one head, so
it was also natural for a politic body to have but one governor; and that a
commonwealth, which had many governors was like a monster with many
heads: besides, said they, a monarchy is a divine form of government, and
agrees most with our religion; for as there is but one God, whom we all
unanimously worship and adore with one faith, so we are resolved to have
but one Emperor, to whom we all submit with one obedience.

Then the Empress seeing that the several sorts of her subjects had each
their churches apart, asked the priests whether they were of several religions?
They answered her Majesty, that there was no more but one religion in all
that world, nor no diversity of opinions in that same religion; for though
there were several sorts of men, yet had they all but one opinion concerning
the worship and adoration of God. The Empress asked them, whether they
were Jews, Turks, or Christians? We do not know, said they, what religions
those are; but we do all unanimously acknowledge, worship and adore the
only, omnipotent, and eternal God, with all reverence, submission, and duty.
Again, the Empress enquired, whether they had several forms of worship?
They answered, no: for our devotion and worship consists only in prayers,
which we frame according to our several necessities, in petitions, humiliations, thanksgiving, etc. Truly, replied the Empress, I thought you had been
either Jews, or Turks, because I never perceived any women in your congregations; but what is the reason, you bar them from your religious assemblies?
It is not fit, said they, that men and women should be promiscuously together
in time of religious worship; for their company hinders devotion, and makes
many, instead of praying to God, direct their devotion to their mistresses.

4. Mermen, the male counterparts of mermaids.

But, asked the Empress, have they no congregation of their own, to perform the duties of divine worship, as well as men? No, answered they: but they stay at home, and say their prayers by themselves in their closets.[5] Then the Empress desired to know the reason why the priests and governors of their world were made eunuchs? They answered, to keep them from marriage: for women and children most commonly make disturbance both in church and state. But, said she, women and children have no employment in church or state. 'Tis true, answered they; but although they are not admitted to public employments, yet are they so prevalent[6] with their husbands and parents, that many times by their importunate persuasions, they cause as much, nay, more mischief secretly, than if they had the management of public affairs.

* * *

[THE EMPRESS BRINGS THE DUCHESS OF NEWCASTLE TO THE BLAZING WORLD]

After some time, when the spirits had refreshed themselves in their own vehicles, they sent one of their nimblest spirits, to ask the Empress, whether she would have a scribe. * * * Then the spirit asked her, whether she would have the soul of a living or a dead man? Why, said the Empress, can the soul quit a living body, and wander or travel abroad? Yes, answered he, for according to Plato's doctrine, there is a conversation of souls, and the souls of lovers live in the bodies of their beloved. Then I will have, answered she, the soul of some ancient famous writer, either of Aristotle, Pythagoras, Plato, Epicurus,[7] or the like. The spirit said, that those famous men were very learned, subtle, and ingenious writers, but they were so wedded to their own opinions, that they would never have the patience to be scribes. Then, said she, I'll have the soul of one of the most famous modern writers, as either of Galileo, Gassendus, Descartes, Helmont, Hobbes, H. More, etc.[8] The spirit answered, that they were fine ingenious writers, but yet so self-conceited, that they would scorn to be scribes to a woman. But, said he, there's a lady, the Duchess of Newcastle, which although she is not one of the most learned, eloquent, witty and ingenious, yet is she a plain and rational writer, for the principle of her writings, is sense and reason, and she will without question, be ready to do you all the service she can. This lady then, said the Empress, will I choose for my scribe, neither will the Emperor have reason to be jealous, she being one of my own sex. In truth, said the spirit, husbands have reason to be jealous of platonic lovers, for they are very dangerous, as being not only very intimate and close, but subtle and insinuating. You say well, replied the Empress; wherefore I pray send me the Duchess of Newcastle's soul; which the spirit did; and after she came to wait on the Empress, at her first arrival the Empress embraced and saluted her with a spiritual kiss.

* * *

5. Private chambers.
6. I.e., they prevail so much.
7. Classical philosophers and founders, respectively, of schools of philosophy: the Peripatetics, the Pythagoreans, the Academics, the Epicureans.
8. Galileo Galilei (1564–1642), Italian astronomer and defender of the Copernican system; Pierre Gassendi (1592–1655), proponent of a mechanistic theory of matter; René Descartes (1596–1650), French mathematician and philosopher who had a major influence on the new science; Jan Baptista Van Helmont (1577–1644), Flemish chemist; Thomas Hobbes, English mechanistic philosopher and political scientist, author of Leviathan (see p. 1587); Henry More (1614–1687), one of the antimaterialist Cambridge Platonists.

[THE DUCHESS WANTS A WORLD TO RULE]

Well, said the Duchess, setting aside this dispute, my ambition is, that I would fain be as you are, that is, an Empress of a world, and I shall never be at quiet until I be one. I love you so well, replied the Empress, that I wish with all my soul, you had the fruition of your ambitious desire, and I shall not fail to give you my best advice how to accomplish it; the best informers are the immaterial spirits, and they'll soon tell you, whether it be possible to obtain your wish. But, said the Duchess, I have little acquaintance with them, for I never knew any before the time you sent for me. They know you, replied the Empress; for they told me of you, and were the means and instrument of your coming hither: wherefore I'll confer with them, and enquire whether there be not another world, whereof you may be Empress as well as I am of this? No sooner had the Empress said this, but some immaterial spirits came to visit her, of whom she enquired, whether there were but there worlds in all, to wit, the Blazing World where she was in, the world which she came from, and the world where the Duchess lived? The spirits answered, that there were more numerous worlds than the stars which appeared in these three mentioned worlds. Then the Empress asked, whether it was not possible, that her dearest friend the Duchess of Newcastle, might be Empress of one of them?[9] Although there be numerous, nay, infinite worlds, answered the spirits, yet none is without government. But is none of these worlds so weak, said she, that it may be surprised or conquered? The spirits answered, that Lucian's world of lights, had been for some time in a snuff, but of late years one Helmont had got it, who since he was Emperor of it, had so strengthened the immortal parts thereof with mortal out-works, as it was for the present impregnable. Said the Empress, if there be such an infinite number of worlds, I am sure, not only my friend, the Duchess, but any other might obtain one. Yes, answered the spirits, if those worlds were uninhabited; but they are as populous as this, your Majesty governs. Why, said the Empress, it is not impossible to conquer a world. No, answered the spirits, but, for the most part, conquerors seldom enjoy their conquest, for they being more feared than loved, most commonly come to an untimely end. If you will but direct me, said the Duchess to the spirits, which world is easiest to be conquered, her Majesty will assist me with means, and I will trust to fate and fortune; for I had rather die in the adventure of noble achievements, than live in obscure and sluggish security; since by the one, I may live in a glorious fame, and by the other I am buried in oblivion. The spirits answered, that the lives of fame were like other lives; for some lasted long, and some died soon. 'Tis true, said the Duchess; but yet the shortest-lived fame lasts longer than the longest life of man. But, replied the spirits, if occasion does not serve you, you must content yourself to live without such achievements that may gain you a fame: but we wonder, proceeded the spirits, that you desire to be Empress of a terrestrial world, whenas you can create yourself a celestial world if you please. What, said the Empress, can any mortal be a creator? Yes, answered the spirits; for every human creature can create an immaterial world fully inhabited by immaterial creatures, and populous of immaterial subjects, such as we are, and all this within the compass of the head or skull; nay, not only so, but he may create a world of

9. Speculation about multiple inhabited worlds was an occasional topic in texts on the new astronomy. Milton's Raphael introduces the idea to Adam (*Paradise Lost* 8.148–52).

what fashion and government he will, and give the creatures thereof such motions, figures, forms, colors, perceptions, etc. as he pleases, and make whirlpools, lights, pressures and reactions, etc. as he thinks best; nay, he may make a world full of veins, muscles, and nerves, and all these to move by one jolt or stroke: also he may alter that world as often as he pleases, or change it from a natural world, to an artificial; he may make a world of ideas, a world of atoms, a world of lights, or whatsoever his fancy leads him to. And since it is in your power to create such a world, what need you to venture life, reputation and tranquility, to conquer a gross material world? . . . You have converted me, said the Duchess to the spirits, from my ambitious desire; wherefore I'll take your advice, reject and despise all the worlds without me, and create a world of my own.

* * *

The Epilogue to the Reader

By this poetical description, you may perceive, that my ambition is not only to be Empress, but Authoress of a whole world; and that the worlds I have made, both the Blazing and the other Philosophical World, mentioned in the first part of this description, are framed and composed of the most pure, that is, the rational parts of matter, which are the parts of my mind; which creation was more easily and suddenly effected, than the conquests of the two famous monarchs of the world, Alexander and Caesar:[1] neither have I made such disturbances, and caused so many dissolutions of particulars, otherwise named deaths, as they did; for I have destroyed but some few men in a little boat, which died through the extremity of cold, and that by the hand of Justice, which was necessitated to punish their crime of stealing away a young and beauteous lady.[2] And in the formation of those worlds, I take more delight and glory, than ever Alexander or Caesar did in conquering this terrestrial world; and though I have made my Blazing World, a peaceable world, allowing it but one religion, one language, and one government; yet could I make another world, as full of factions, divisions, and wars, as this is of peace and tranquility; and the rational figures of my mind might express as much courage to fight, as Hector and Achilles[3] had; and be as wise as Nestor, as eloquent as Ulysses, and as beautiful as Helen. But I esteeming peace before war, wit before policy, honesty before beauty; instead of the figures of Alexander, Caesar, Hector, Achilles, Nestor, Ulysses, Helen, etc. chose rather the figure of honest Margaret Newcastle, which now I would not change for all this terrestrial world; and if any should like the world I have made, and be willing to be my subjects, they may imagine themselves such, and they are such, I mean, in their minds, fancies or imaginations; but if they cannot endure to be subjects, they may create worlds of their own, and govern themselves as they please: but yet let them have a care, not to prove unjust usurpers, and to rob me of mine; for concerning the Philosophical World, I am Empress of it myself; and as for the Blazing

---

1. Alexander the Great and Julius Caesar were both famed as conquerors of much of the world known to them.
2. A reference to the romancelike incident with which *The Blazing World* begins, the abduction of a young woman by a party of adventurers, whose boat was blown in a tempest to the North Pole, where they perished (except for the woman, who entered into the Blazing World).

3. The principal heroes of Homer's *Iliad*, Hector the Trojan and Achilles the Greek. "Nestor": wise advisor to the Greeks. "Ulysses": hero of Homer's *Odyssey*. "Helen": her beauty caused the Trojan War, as it prompted the Trojan Paris to steal her away from her Greek husband, Menelaus.

World, it having an Empress already, who rules it with great wisdom and conduct, which Empress is my dear Platonic friend; I shall never prove so unjust, treacherous and unworthy to her, as to disturb her government, much less to depose her from her imperial throne, for the sake of any other; but rather choose to create another world for another friend.

1666, 1668

JOHN MILTON
1608–1674

When he was thirty, John Milton proclaimed himself the future author of a great English epic. He promised a poem devoted to the glory of the nation, centering around the deeds of King Arthur or some other ancient hero. When Milton finally published his epic thirty years later, readers found instead a poem set in Heaven, Hell, and the garden of Eden, in which traditional heroism is denigrated and England not once mentioned. What lay between the youthful promise and the eventual fulfillment was a career marked by private tragedy and public controversy. Milton tells us much about both these experiences in his works, which combine an intense self-scrutiny and concern with authorship with urgent intervention in the great questions of his time. It is scarcely possible to treat Milton's career separately from the history of England in his lifetime, not only because he was an active participant in public affairs but also because he himself refused to distinguish between his private life and affairs of church and state. When he signed himself, as he often did, "John Milton, Englishman," he did not simply mean *an* Englishman. As England's self-appointed prophetic bard, Milton saw himself as spokesman for the nation as a whole, even when he found himself in a minority of one. Milton was a man who devoted his life to public causes, but whose understanding of those causes often arose out of the most personal concerns.

The young Milton self-consciously set out to follow the steps of the ideal poetic career—beginning with pastoral and ending with epic—modeled on that of the Roman poet Virgil. In this approach to his vocation, he stood at the opposite end of the spectrum from such Cavalier contemporaries as Suckling and Lovelace, who turned to verse with an air of studied carelessness. Milton began by writing occasional poems in Latin and several English poems in the pastoral mode: lyrics, the masque *Comus* (1634), and the pastoral elegy *Lycidas* (1683). These are extraordinary works in their own right, which crown and transform their respective genres, but Milton also undertook them as preparation for the greater genres of tragedy and epic. He was embarking on a road previously traveled by Edmund Spenser, whom he called "a better teacher than Scotus or Aquinas." Milton resembles Spenser in certain ways, above all in his constant use of myth and archetype, alluding to and juxtaposing biblical and classical stories. But Milton's learning was greater than Spenser's. As part of his preparation for a poetic career, he undertook a six-year program of self-directed reading in ancient and modern theology, philosophy, history, science, politics, and literature. His command of languages included Latin, Greek, Hebrew and its dialects, Italian, French, Spanish, and Dutch. The sum of the western literary and intellectual heritage impinged on his writing as immediately and directly as the circumstances of his own life, but he continually reconceived the ideas, literary forms, and values of this heritage to make them relevant to himself and his age.

For Milton to devote six years of his adult life to an obscure course of private study required extraordinary confidence in the service he hoped to perform for God and country. It also, of course, required money, which was provided by his father, who was a successful scrivener—a combination of solicitor, investment advisor, and money lender. Although Milton enjoyed the company of some aristocrats and was profoundly grateful that his father spared him from the grubby business of making money, he belonged to the London bourgeoisie. His father's business dealings and loans at interest paid for private tutors in his youth, for his education at St. Paul's, one of the finest schools in the land, for his seven years at Cambridge and the six years of reading that followed, and for his "grand tour" of France, Italy, and Switzerland at the age of thirty. Yet Milton's connection with the class that stood to benefit most directly from Europe's first bourgeois revolution does not account for his passionate political views. His brother, Christopher, fought on the royalist side. For the Milton brothers, as for most of their contemporaries, the civil wars did not appear as a confrontation of class interests, but as a conflict between radically differing theories of government and, above all, religion.

From the outbreak of the conflict until his death, Milton was allied with the Puritan cause. Yet his religious opinions developed throughout his life, from relative orthodoxy in his youth to ever more heretical positions in his later years. Milton went up to Cambridge in 1625 with every intention of taking orders in the Church of England. In the hindsight of 1642, he blamed the lack of reformation and the corruption in the English Church under Archbishop Laud for forcing him to abandon that goal, proclaiming himself "church-outed by the Prelates." Milton's change of direction must also have been linked to the fastidious contempt he expressed for the ignorant and clownish clergymen-in-making who were his fellow students at Cambridge: "They thought themselves gallant men, and I thought them fools." Those fellow students dubbed Milton "The Lady of Christ's College." Above all, Milton came to believe that he was destined to serve his language, his country, and his God as a poet. In his first major English poem, the hymn *On the Morning of Christ's Nativity* (written at the age of twenty-one), Milton had already begun to construct himself as a prophetic bard. His sense of poetic mission grew over the next decade, accompanied by growing disillusion with the Church of England. Both are present in *Lycidas* (1638), written to lament the untimely death of his Cambridge contemporary Edward King. The figure of King recedes in the poem next to Milton's anxious contemplation of poetry as a vocation and his furious diatribe against the corrupt Anglican clergy who leave their charges prey to the "grim wolf" of Catholicism. Yet while he was in Italy on the Grand Tour (1638–39), Milton delighted in exchanging verses and learned compliments with various Catholic intellectuals and men of letters, some of whom became friends. Milton could always maintain friendships and family relationships across ideological divides.

Upon his return to England, Milton opened a school and was soon involved in Presbyterian efforts to depose the bishops and reform Church liturgy, writing five "Antiprelatical" tracts denouncing and satirizing bishops. These were the first in a remarkable series of political interventions which occupied Milton for the next twenty years, until the disaster (for him) of the Restoration. He wrote successively on church government, divorce, education, freedom of the press, regicide, and republicanism. He also served as Latin Secretary to the Commonwealth Government (1649–53) and to Oliver Cromwell's Protectorate (1654–58), writing the official letters—mostly in Latin—to foreign governments and heads of state. Yet Milton was the very opposite of a faceless spokesman for a party line. From the beginning to the end of his polemical career, his publications show an extraordinary courage and independence of thought. In his tracts advocating divorce on the grounds of incompatibility and with the right to remarry, he adopted and vigorously defended a position almost unheard of at the time, one which required a boldly antiliteral reading of the gospels. In *Areopagitica*, he put forward an impassioned defense of a free press against a Parliament determined to restore effective censorship. And just as he was among the first to attack the power of the bishops, so he was virtually the last defender of the "Good Old Cause" of the Revolution; the second edition of his *Ready and Easy Way to Establish a Free Commonwealth* appeared in late April 1660, scarcely two weeks before the Restoration.

Several of these treatises were also prompted by personal concerns or crises. In his polemical tract *The Reason of Church Government Urged Against Prelaty*, Milton devoted several pages to a discussion of his poetic vocation and the great works he might produce in the future. His writings on divorce, which can hardly have seemed the most pressing of issues in the strife-torn years 1643–45, were motivated by his personal experience of a disastrous marriage. Aged thirty-three, inexperienced with women, and idealistic about marriage as in essence a union of minds and spirits, he had wedded a young woman of seventeen, Mary Powell, who returned to her royalist family just a few months after the marriage. Milton responded by turning his private grief into a matter of public controversy. The fact that his tracts on divorce could not be licensed and were roundly denounced in Parliament, from pulpits, and in print prompted him in turn to write *Areopagitica*, his famous defense of a free press and the free commerce in ideas. Yet he saw all these personal issues—a reformed poetry, the domestic liberty to be achieved through needful divorce, and a free press—as vital to the creation of a reformed English culture.

In the years that followed, Milton suffered a series of agonizing tragedies. Mary Powell returned to him in 1645, but died in childbirth in 1652, leaving four children; the only son, John, died a few months later. In the same year, Milton became totally blind. Whatever the medical causes, Milton himself attributed his blindness to late nights of reading in his youth and his exertions in writing defenses of the execution of Charles I and the new republic. Milton married again in 1656, apparently happily, but his new wife, Katherine Woodcock, was dead two years later, along with their infant daughter. Katherine is probably the subject of his sonnet *Methought I Saw My Late Espousèd Saint*, a moving dream-vision poignant with the sense of loss—both of sight and of love. Milton had little time for poetry in these years, but his few sonnets revolutionized the genre, overlaying the Petrarchan metrical structure with an urgent rhetorical voice and using the small sonnet form, hitherto confined mainly to matters of love, for new and grand subjects: praise of Cromwell mixed with admonition and political advice; a prophetic denunciation calling down God's vengeance for Protestants massacred in Piedmont; an emotion-filled account of his continuing struggle to come to terms with his blindness as part of God's providence.

Milton's courageous defense of the Revolution down to the last possible moment could have spelled disaster for him upon the return of Charles II. For several months after that event, he was in hiding, his life in danger, but friends, especially the poet Andrew Marvell, managed his pardon and later his release from a brief imprisonment. He lived out his last years in reduced circumstances, plagued by ever more serious attacks of gout but grateful for the domestic comforts provided by his third wife, Elizabeth Minshull, whom he married in 1663 and who survived him. In such conditions, dismayed by the defeat of his political and religious cause, totally blind and often ill, threatened by the horrific plague of 1665 and the great fire of 1666, and entirely dependent on amanuenses and friends to transcribe his dictation, he completed the great epic poem that undertakes to "justify the ways of God to men." *Paradise Lost* radically reconceives the epic genre and epic heroism, choosing as protagonists a domestic couple rather than martial heroes, and degrading the military glory celebrated in epic tradition in favor of the "better fortitude / Of patience and heroic martyrdom." Michael's prophecy to Adam makes clear that the course of human history is tragic, that the world will remain "to good malignant, to bad men benign" until the Second Coming of Christ. Yet it also makes clear that throughout history God will raise up prophets and heroes to resist wicked tyrants and corrupt societies.

In his final years, Milton continued to pursue subjects that had interested him from his youth, publishing works on grammar and logic chiefly written during his days as schoolmaster, a *History of Britain* (1670) from earliest times to the Norman Conquest, and a treatise urging toleration for Puritan dissenters (1673). He also continued work on his *Christian Doctrine*, a Latin treatise which reveals how far Milton had moved from the orthodoxies of his day. The work denies the Trinity (making Christ and the Holy Spirit much inferior to God the Father), insists upon free will (against Calvinist predestination), and privileges the inspiration of the Spirit over the Scriptures and the Ten Commandments. Such radical and heterodox positions could not be made public in his lifetime, certainly not in the repressive conditions of the Restoration, and Milton's *Christian Doctrine* was lost to view for over 150 years.

In 1671 Milton published two poems which resonate with echoes of the harsh repression and the moral and political challenges Puritan dissenters faced after the Restoration. *Paradise Regained*, a brief epic in four books, treats Jesus' Temptation in the Wilderness as a hard intellectual struggle through which the hero comes to understand himself and his mission and defeats Satan by renouncing the whole panoply of false or faulty versions of the good life and of his kingdom. *Samson Agonistes*, a classical tragedy, is the more harrowing for the resemblances between its tragic hero and its author. The deeply flawed, pain-wracked, blind, and defeated Samson struggles, in dialogues with his visitors, to gain self-knowledge, discovering at last a desperate way to triumph over his captors and offer his people a chance to regain their freedom. In these last poems, Milton sought to educate his readers in moral and political wisdom and virtue. Only through such inner transformation, Milton now firmly believed, would men and women come to value—and so perhaps reclaim—the intellectual, religious, and political freedom he so vigorously promoted in his prose and poetry.

FROM POEMS

On the Morning of Christ's Nativity[1]

1

This is the month, and this the happy morn
Wherein the son of Heaven's eternal King,
Of wedded maid and virgin mother born,
Our great redemption from above did bring;
5 For so the holy sages once did sing,
    That he our deadly forfeit[2] should release,
And with his Father work us a perpetual peace.

2

That glorious form, that light unsufferable,°   *unable to be endured*
And that far-beaming blaze of majesty
10 Wherewith he wont at Heaven's high council-table
To sit the midst of Trinal Unity,[3]

---

1. This ode was written on Christmas 1629, a few weeks after Milton's twenty-first birthday. He placed it first in the 1645 edition of his poems, claiming in it his vocation as inspired poet. The poem often looks back to Spenser: the first four stanzas are an adaptation of the Spenserian stanza; there are several Spenserian archaisms (*y*- prefixes) and some Spenser-like onamatopoeia (lines 156, 172). Comparison with Crashaw's nativity poem

(p. 1635) will highlight some important differences between Roman Catholic and Puritan aesthetics in this period.
2. The sentence of death consequent on the Fall. "Holy sages": for example, the prophet Isaiah (chaps. 9 and 40) and Job (chap. 19) were thought to have foretold Christ as Messiah.
3. The Trinity: Father, Son (incarnate in Christ), and Holy Ghost.

He laid aside; and here with us to be,
  Forsook the courts of everlasting day,
And chose with us a darksome house of mortal clay.

3

15 Say, heavenly Muse, shall not thy sacred vein
Afford a present to the infant God?
Hast thou no verse, no hymn, or solemn strain,
To welcome him to this his new abode,
Now while the heaven by the sun's team untrod[4]
20   Hath took no print of the approaching light,
And all the spangled host° keep watch in squadrons bright?   *angels*

4

See how from far upon the eastern road
The star-led wizards[5] haste with odors sweet:
O run, prevent° them with thy humble ode,   *anticipate*
25 And lay it lowly at his blessèd feet;
Have thou the honor first thy Lord to greet,
  And join thy voice unto the angel choir,
From out his secret altar touched with hallowed fire.[6]

The Hymn

1

It was the winter wild
30 While the Heaven-born child
  All meanly wrapped in the rude manger lies;
Nature in awe to him
Had doffed her gaudy trim[7]
  With her great Master so to sympathize;
35 It was no season then for her
To wanton with the sun, her lusty paramour.

2

Only with speeches fair
She woos the gentle air
  To hide her guilty front with innocent snow,
40 And on her naked shame,
Pollute with sinful blame,
  The saintly veil of maiden white to throw,[8]
Confounded that her Maker's eyes
Should look so near upon her foul deformities.

---

4. In classical myth, the sun (Phoebus Apollo) drove across heaven in a chariot drawn by horses.
5. The Magi who followed the star of Bethlehem to find and adore the infant Christ.
6. Isaiah's lips were touched by a burning coal from the altar, purifying him and confirming him as a prophet (Isaiah 6.7).
7. Put off her garments of leaves and flowers.
8. Nature fell also with the Fall, so she is a harlot (line 36), not a pure maiden, despite her white garment of snow.

3

45   But he her fears to cease
    Sent down the meek-eyed Peace;
      She, crowned with olive green, came softly sliding
    Down through the turning sphere,[9]
    His ready harbinger,°   *forerunner*
50   With turtle[1] wing the amorous clouds dividing,
    And waving wide her myrtle wand,
    She strikes a universal peace through sea and land.

4

    No war or battle's sound
    Was heard the world around;[2]
55   The idle spear and shield were high up-hung;
    The hookèd chariot[3] stood
    Unstained with hostile blood,
      The trumpet spake not to the armèd throng,
    And kings sat still with aweful° eye,   *filled with awe*
60   As if they surely knew their sovereign Lord was by.

5

    But peaceful was the night
    Wherein the Prince of Light
      His reign of peace upon the earth began:
    The winds, with wonder whist,°   *hushed*
65   Smoothly the waters kissed,
      Whispering new joys to the mild oceàn,
    Who now hath quite forgot to rave,
    While birds of calm[4] sit brooding on the charmèd wave.

6

    The stars with deep amaze
70   Stand fixed in steadfast gaze,
      Bending one way their precious influence,
    And will not take their flight
    For all the morning light,
      Or Lucifer[5] that often warned them thence;
75   But in their glimmering orbs did glow
    Until their Lord himself bespake,° and bid them go.   *spoke out*

7

    And though the shady gloom
    Had given day her room,

---

9. The Ptolemaic spheres, revolving around the earth.

1. Like a turtledove, which, like the myrtle, is an emblem of Venus as the olive crown is of peace. Love is hereby associated with peace.

2. Around the time of Christ's birth, the "Peace of Augustus" held, during which no major wars dis-

turbed the Roman Empire; that peace was sometimes attributed to Christ.

3. War chariots were built with scythelike hooks on the axles, to wound and kill.

4. Kingfishers (halcyons) were thought to calm the seas during the time they nested on its waves.

5. Not Satan but the morning star, Venus.

The sun himself withheld his wonted speed,
80 And hid his head for shame
        As° his inferior flame   *as if*
    The new-enlightened world no more should need;
He saw a greater Sun[6] appear
Than his bright throne or burning axletree° could bear.   *chariot axle*

8

85 The shepherds on the lawn
    Or ere the point of dawn
        Sat simply chatting in a rustic row;
    Full little thought they than°   *then*
    That the mighty Pan[7]
90   Was kindly[8] come to live with them below;
    Perhaps their loves or else their sheep
    Was all that did their silly° thoughts so busy keep.   *simple, humble*

9

    When such music sweet
    Their hearts and ears did greet
95   As never was by mortal finger struck,
    Divinely warbled voice
    Answering the stringèd noise,
        As all their souls in blissful rapture took;
    The air, such pleasure loath to lose,
100 With thousand echoes still prolongs each heavenly close.°   *cadence*

10

    Nature that heard such sound
    Beneath the hollow round
        Of Cynthia's seat,[9] the airy region thrilling,°   *piercing; delighting*
    Now was almost won
105 To think her part was done,
        And that her reign had here its last fulfilling;
    She knew such harmony alone
    Could hold all heaven and earth in happier union.

11

    At last surrounds their sight
110 A globe of circular light
        That with long beams the shamefaced night arrayed;°   *adorned with rays*
    The helmèd cherubim
    And sworded seraphim[1]
        Are seen in glittering ranks with wings displayed,

6. The familiar Son/sun pun.
7. Pan, patron of shepherds, is a merry, goat-footed god, but he was often conceived in more exalted terms and identified with Christ, because his name in Greek means "all."
8. By nature; also, benevolently.
9. Cynthia is the moon. Nature rules below the moon (the region of the four elements and subject to decay). The unchanging, perfect region above the moon is normally the only place one could hear either angels' hymnody or the music of the spheres.
1. Seraphim and cherubim are the highest of the traditional nine orders of angels; they are often portrayed in martial attire.

115   Harping in loud and solemn choir
      With unexpressive° notes to Heaven's newborn heir.   *inexpressible*

12

      Such music (as 'tis said)
      Before was never made,
          But when of old the sons of morning sung,[2]
120   While the Creator great
      His constellations set,
          And the well-balanced world on hinges° hung,   *the two poles*
      And cast the dark foundations deep,
      And bid the welt'ring waves their oozy channel keep.

13

125   Ring out, ye crystal spheres,
      Once bless our human ears
          (If ye have power to touch our senses so),
      And let your silver chime
      Move in melodious time,
130   And let the bass of Heaven's deep organ blow;
      And with your ninefold harmony[3]
      Make up full consort to th' angelic symphony.

14

      For if such holy song
      Enwrap our fancy long,
135   Time will run back and fetch the age of gold;[4]
      And speckled Vanity
      Will sicken soon and die,
          And leprous Sin will melt from earthly mold,
      And Hell itself will pass away,
140   And leave her dolorous mansions to the peering day.

15

      Yea, Truth and Justice then
      Will down return to men,
          Th' enameled arras° of the rainbow wearing,   *brightly colored fabric*
      And Mercy set between,[5]
145   Throned in celestial sheen,
          With radiant feet the tissued[6] clouds down steering;

2. Job 38.4–7: "Where wast thou when I laid the foundations of the earth? . . . / When the morning stars sang together and all the sons of God shouted for joy."
3. In Pythagorean theory, each of the nine moving spheres sounds a distinctive note (the tenth, the *primum mobile*, does not move). It was supposed that, after the Fall, this harmonious music of the spheres could not be heard on earth. Earth would be the "bass" of the cosmic organ, sounding under that planetary harmony.
4. The first age, of human innocence, classical mythology's equivalent to the Garden of Eden.

5. This allegorical scene, suggesting a masque descent, alludes to Psalm 85.10, part of the liturgy for Christmas: "Mercy and truth are met together; righteousness and peace have kissed each other." Peace, in the poem, has already descended (lines 45–52). The lines also evoke the flight of Astraea, the classical goddess of Justice, at the end of the Golden Age, and her return with its restoration, celebrated by Virgil in his 4th eclogue, applied by him to the birth of Pollio, but by Christians to Christ.
6. Cloth woven with silver and gold.

And Heaven, as at some festival,
Will open wide the gates of her high palace hall.

16

But wisest Fate says no,
150 This must not yet be so;
    The Babe lies yet in smiling infancy[7]
That on the bitter cross
Must redeem our loss,
    So both himself and us to glorify;
155 Yet first to those ychained[8] in sleep
The wakeful trump of doom must thunder through the deep,

17

With such a horrid clang
As on Mount Sinai rang
    While the red fire and smoldering clouds outbrake;[9]
160 The agèd earth, aghast
With terror of that blast,
    Shall from the surface to the center shake,
When at the world's last sessiòn,
The dreadful Judge in middle air shall spread his throne.

18

165 And then at last our bliss
Full and perfect is,
    But now begins; for from this happy day
Th' old dragon under ground,[1]
In straiter limits bound,
170   Not half so far casts his usurpèd sway,
And wroth to see his kingdom fail,
Swinges° the scaly horror of his folded tail.   lashes

19

The oracles are dumb;[2]
No voice or hideous hum
175   Runs through the archèd roof in words deceiving.
Apollo from his shrine
Can no more divine,
    With hollow shriek the steep of Delphos leaving.[3]
No nightly trance or breathèd spell
180 Inspires the pale-eyed priest from the prophetic cell.

7. The Latin word, *infans*, means, literally, non-speaking.
8. One of Spenser's archaic y- prefixes.
9. Moses received the Ten Commandments amid thunder and lightning atop Mount Sinai (Exodus 19); the Last Judgment will take place amid similar uproar.

1. The Devil (Revelation 20.2).
2. An ancient tradition held that pagan oracles ceased with the coming of Christ; another identified the pagan gods with the fallen angels.
3. Apollo's main shrine was at Delphi, on the slopes of Mount Parnassus.

20

The lonely mountains o'er
And the resounding shore
   A voice of weeping heard and loud lament;
From haunted spring and dale
185   Edged with the poplar pale,
   The parting Genius[4] is with sighing sent;
With flower-inwoven tresses torn
The nymphs in twilight shade of tangled thickets mourn.

21

In consecrated earth
190   And on the holy hearth,
   The Lars and Lemures[5] moan with midnight plaint;
In urns and altars round
A drear and dying sound
   Affrights the flamens[6] at their service quaint;
195   And the chill marble seems to sweat,
While each peculiar power forgoes his wonted seat.

22

Peor and Baalim[7]
Forsake their temples dim,
   With that twice-battered god of Palestine,[8]
200   And moonèd Ashtaroth,[9]
Heaven's queen and mother both,
   Now sits not girt with tapers' holy shine;
The Libyc Hammon[1] shrinks° his horn;   *draws in*
In vain the Tyrian maids their wounded Thammuz mourn.[2]

23

205   And sullen Moloch,[3] fled,
Hath left in shadows dread
   His burning idol all of blackest hue;
In vain with cymbals' ring
They call the grisly king
210   In dismal dance about the furnace blue;
The brutish gods of Nile as fast,[4]
Isis and Orus and the dog Anubis haste.

---

4. A local deity guarding a particular place.
5. Spirits of the dead. "Lars": household gods.
6. Roman priests.
7. Other manifestations of Baal. "Baal-Peor": a Canaanite sun-god.
8. Dagon, the Philistine god whose image at Ashdod was twice thrown down when the Ark of the Covenant was placed beside it (1 Samuel 5.2–4).
9. Ashtaroth, also known as Astarte, was a Phoenician fertility goddess identified with the moon.
1. Hammon, also Ammon, an Egyptian and Libyan god, depicted as a ram.

2. Thammuz, lover of Astaroth, was killed by a boar and lamented by the Phoenician women; he was taken into the Greek pantheon as Adonis.
3. Moloch was a Phoenician fire god, a brazen idol with a human body and a calf's head; the statue was heated flaming hot and children were thrown into its embrace, with cymbals drowning out their cries (2 Kings 22.10).
4. Egyptian gods had some features of animals: Isis was represented with cow's horns, Orus or Horus with a hawk's head, Osiris (lines 213–15) sometimes had the shape of a bull.

24

Nor is Osiris seen
In Memphian grove or green,
215 Trampling the unshowered° grass with lowings loud,   *rainless*
Nor can he be at rest
Within his sacred chest;
     Naught but profoundest Hell can be his shroud.
In vain with timbreled anthems dark
220 The sable-stolèd sorcerers bear his worshipped ark.⁵

25

He feels from Judah's land
The dreaded Infant's hand,
     The rays of Bethlehem blind his dusky eyn;°   *eyes*
Nor all the gods beside
225 Longer dare abide,
     Not Typhon huge, ending in snaky twine:
Our Babe, to show his godhead true,
Can in his swaddling bands control the damnèd crew.⁶

26

So when the sun in bed,
230 Curtained with cloudy red,
     Pillows his chin upon an orient° wave,   *eastern, bright*
The flocking shadows pale
Troop to th' infernal jail;
     Each fettered ghost slips to his several grave;
235 And the yellow-skirted fays
Fly after the night-steeds, leaving their moon-loved maze.⁷

27

But see! the Virgin blessed
Hath laid her Babe to rest.
     Time is our tedious song should here have ending.
240 Heaven's youngest-teemèd° star   *latest born*
Hath fixed her polished car,°   *gleaming chariot*
     Her sleeping Lord with handmaid lamp attending:
And all about the courtly stable
Bright-harnessed° angels sit in order serviceàble.   *bright-armored*

1629   1645

5. Osiris's image was carried from temple to temple in a wooden chest, and his priests accompanied it with tambourines ("timbrels").
6. "Typhon" was a hundred-headed monster who was a serpent below the waist, a figure for the Devil. The infant Christ controlling him calls up (as a foreshadowing) the story of the infant Hercules strangling two giant serpents in his cradle.
7. Fairy rings. "Yellow-skirted fays": horses drawing Night's chariot.

On Shakespeare[1]

What needs my Shakespeare for his honored bones
The labor of an age in pilèd stones,
Or that his hallowed relics should be hid
Under a star-ypointing[2] pyramid?
5   Dear son of memory,[3] great heir of fame,
What° need'st thou such weak witness of thy name?   *why*
Thou in our wonder and astonishment
Hast built thyself a livelong° monument.   *enduring*
For whilst to th' shame of slow-endeavoring art
10 Thy easy numbers flow, and that each heart
Hath from the leaves of thy unvalued° book   *invaluable*
Those Delphic[4] lines with deep impression took,
Then thou, our fancy of itself bereaving,
Dost make us marble with too much conceiving;[5]
15 And so sepùlchered in such pomp dost lie,
That kings for such a tomb would wish to die.

1630   1632

L'Allegro[1]

Hence loathèd Melancholy,[2]
Of Cerberus[3] and blackest midnight born,
In Stygian[4] cave forlorn
'Mongst horrid shapes, and shrieks, and sights unholy,
5   Find out some uncouth° cell,   *desolate*
Where brooding Darkness spreads his jealous wings,
And the night-raven sings;
There under ebon shades and low-browed rocks,
As ragged as thy locks,
10 In dark Cimmerian[5] desert ever dwell.
But come thou goddess fair and free,

1. This tribute, Milton's first published poem, appeared in the Second Folio of Shakespeare's plays (1632).
2. A Spenserian archaism.
3. As "son of memory" Shakespeare is a brother of the Muses, who are the daughters of Mnemosyne (Memory).
4. Apollo, god of poetry, had his oracle at Delphi.
5. Shakespeare's mesmerized readers are themselves his (marble) monument.
1. The companion poems L'Allegro and Il Penseroso are both written in tetrameter couplets, but Milton's virtuosity produces entirely different tempos and sound qualities in the two poems. The Italian titles name, respectively, the cheerful, mirthful man and the melancholy, contemplative man. The poems are carefully balanced and their different values celebrated, though Penseroso's greater

length and final coda may intimate that life's superiority. Mirth, the presiding deity of Allegro, is described in terms that evoke Botticelli's presentation of the Grace Euphrosone (youthful mirth) and her sisters in his Primavera.
2. The black Melancholy recognized and here exorcized by Mirth's man is a disease leading to madness; Il Penseroso celebrates melancholy as the temperament of the scholarly, contemplative man, represented in Durer's famous engraving Melancholy. Burton's Anatomy of Melancholy (p. 1561) treats the entire range of possibilities.
3. The three-headed hellhound of classical mythology.
4. Near the river Styx, in the underworld.
5. Homer's Cimmereans (Odyssey 11.13–19) live on the outer edge of the world, in perpetual darkness.

In heaven yclept Euphrosyne,[6]
And by men, heart-easing Mirth,
Whom lovely Venus at a birth
15 With two sister Graces more
To ivy-crownèd Bacchus bore;
Or whether (as some sager sing)
The frolic wind that breathes the spring,
Zephyr with Aurora playing,
20 As he met her once a-Maying,
There on beds of violets blue,
And fresh-blown° roses washed in dew,   *newly opened*
Filled her with thee a daughter fair,
So buxom,° blithe, and debonair.   *lively*
25 Haste thee nymph, and bring with thee
Jest and youthful Jollity,
Quips° and Cranks,° and wanton Wiles,   *witty sayings/jokes*
Nods, and Becks,° and wreathèd Smiles,   *beckonings*
Such as hang on Hebe's[7] cheek,
30 And love to live in dimple sleek;
Sport that wrinkled Care derides,
And Laughter holding both his sides.
Come, and trip it° as ye go   *dance*
On the light fantastic toe,
35 And in thy right hand lead with thee
The mountain nymph, sweet Liberty;
And if I give thee honor due,
Mirth, admit me of thy crew
To live with her and live with thee,
40 In unreprovèd° pleasures free;   *irreproachable*
To hear the lark begin his flight,
And, singing, startle the dull night,
From his watch-tower in the skies,
Till the dappled dawn doth rise;
45 Then to come in spite of° sorrow,   *in defiance of*
And at my window bid good morrow,
Through the sweetbriar or the vine,
Or the twisted eglantine.
While the cock with lively din
50 Scatters the rear of darkness thin,
And to the stack or the barn door,
Stoutly struts his dames before;
Oft listening how the hounds and horn
Cheerly rouse the slumbering morn,
55 From the side of some hoar hill,
Through the high wood echoing shrill.
Sometime walking not unseen

---

6. The three Graces—Euphrosyne (four syllables) figuring Youthful Mirth, Aglaia, Brilliance, and Thalia, Bloom—were commonly taken to be offspring of Venus (Love and Beauty) and Bacchus (god of wine). Milton proceeds, however, to devise another, more innocent parentage for Euphrosyne (ascribing it to "some sager," lines 17–24): Zephyr, the West Wind, and Aurora, goddess of the Dawn.
7. Goddess of youth and cupbearer to the gods.

By hedgerow elms, on hillocks green,
Right against the eastern gate,
60   Where the great sun begins his state,[8]
Robed in flames and amber light,
The clouds in thousand liveries dight;°   dressed
While the plowman near at hand
Whistles o'er the furrowed land,
65   And the milkmaid singeth blithe,
And the mower whets his scythe,
And every shepherd tells his tale
Under the hawthorn in the dale.
Straight mine eye hath caught new pleasures
70   Whilst the landscape round it measures;
Russet lawns and fallows° gray,   plowed land
Where the nibbling flocks do stray,
Mountains on whose barren breast
The laboring clouds do often rest;
75   Meadows trim with daisies pied,°   multicolored
Shallow brooks, and rivers wide.
Towers and battlements it sees
Bosomed high in tufted trees,
Where perhaps some beauty lies,
80   The cynosure[9] of neighboring eyes.
Hard by, a cottage chimney smokes
From betwixt two agèd oaks,
Where Corydon and Thyrsis met
Are at their savory dinner set
85   Of herbs and other country messes,
Which the neat-handed° Phyllis dresses;   dexterous
And then in haste her bower she leaves,
With Thestylis[1] to bind the sheaves;
Or if the earlier season lead
90   To the tanned° haycock in the mead.   sun-dried
Sometimes with secure° delight   careless
The upland hamlets will invite,
When the merry bells ring round
And the jocund rebecks[2] sound
95   To many a youth and many a maid,
Dancing in the checkered shade;
And young and old come forth to play
On a sunshine holiday,
Till the livelong daylight fail;
100   Then to the spicy nut-brown ale,
With stories told of many a feat,
How fairy Mab the junkets[3] eat;
She was pinched and pulled, she said,

8. Stately procession, as by a monarch.
9. Literally, the bright polestar, by which mariners
steer; here, a splendid object, much gazed at.
1. Milton uses traditional names from classical
pastoral—"Corydon," "Thyrsis," "Phyllis," "Thestylis"—for his rustic English shepherds.

2. A small three-stringed fiddle. "Jocund": merry,
sprightly.
3. Sweetmeats, especially with cream. Queen
Mab is the fairy queen, consort of Oberon. "She"
and "he" in the next two lines are country folk telling of their experiences with fairies.

And he, by friar's lantern led,
105 Tells how the drudging goblin⁴ sweat
To earn his cream-bowl duly set,
When in one night, ere glimpse of morn,
His shadowy flail hath threshed the corn
That ten day-laborers could not end;
110 Then lies him down the lubber fiend,⁵
And stretched out all the chimney's° length,   *fireplace's*
Basks at the fire his hairy strength;
And crop-full out of doors he flings
Ere the first cock his matin rings.
115 Thus done the tales, to bed they creep,
By whispering winds soon lulled asleep.
Towered cities please us then,
And the busy hum of men,
Where throngs of knights and barons bold
120 In weeds of peace high triumphs⁶ hold,
With store of ladies, whose bright eyes
Rain influence,⁷ and judge the prize
Of wit or arms, while both contend
To win her grace, whom all commend.
125 There let Hymen⁸ oft appear
In saffron robe, with taper clear,
And pomp and feast and revelry,
With masque and antique° pageantry;   *ancient, also antic*
Such sights as youthful poets dream
130 On summer eves by haunted stream.
Then to the well-trod stage anon,
If Jonson's learned sock be on,
Or sweetest Shakespeare, fancy's child,
Warble his native wood-notes wild.⁹
135 And ever against eating cares;¹
Lap me in soft Lydian airs,²
Married to immortal verse
Such as the meeting soul may pierce
In notes with many a winding bout°   *circuit*
140 Of linkèd sweetness long drawn out,
With wanton heed and giddy cunning,
The melting voice through mazes running,
Untwisting all the chains that tie
The hidden soul of harmony;
145 That Orpheus' self may heave his head

4. Robin Goodfellow, alias Puck, Pook, or Hob-goblin. "Friar's lantern": will-o-the-wisp.
5. Robin traditionally did all manner of drudging work for people, to be rewarded with a bowl of cream.
6. Pageants. "Weeds of peace": courtly raiment.
7. The ladies' eyes are stars and so have astrological influence over the men.
8. Roman god of marriage. An orange-yellow (saffron) robe and a torch are his attributes.
9. It was conventional to contrast Jonson as a

"learned" poet and Shakespeare as a "natural" one, but L'Allegro's views and choices of literature also suits with his nature. "Sock": the comedian's low-heeled slipper, contrasted with the tragedian's buskin, a high-heeled boot.
1. "Eating cares" (Horace, *Odes* 2.11.18) is one of many classical echoes in the poem.
2. Plato considered "Lydian airs" to be enervating, soft, and sensual; he preferred the solemn Doric mode. Some others thought Lydian airs relaxing and delightful.

From golden slumber on a bed
Of heaped Elysian flowers, and hear
Such strains as would have won the ear
Of Pluto, to have quite set free
150 His half-regained Eurydice.[3]
These delights if thou canst give,
Mirth, with thee I mean to live.[4]

ca. 1631   1645

Il Penseroso[1]

Hence vain deluding Joys,[2]
   The brood of Folly without father bred,
How little you bestead,°   avail
   Or fill the fixèd mind with all your toys°   trifles
5   Dwell in some idle brain,
   And fancies fond° with gaudy shapes possess,   foolish
As thick and numberless
   As the gay motes that people the sunbeams,
Or likest hovering dreams,
10   The fickle pensioners of Morpheus'[3] train.
But hail thou Goddess sage and holy,
Hail, divinest Melancholy,
   Whose saintly visage is too bright
To hit° the sense of human sight,   suit
15 And therefore to our weaker view
O'erlaid with black, staid Wisdom's hue;[4]
Black, but such as in esteem,
Prince Memnon's sister[5] might beseem,
Or that starred Ethiope queen[6] that strove
20 To set her beauty's praise above
The sea nymphs, and their powers offended.
Yet thou art higher far descended;
Thee bright-haired Vesta long of yore
To solitary Saturn bore;[7]
25 His daughter she (in Saturn's reign
Such mixture was not held a stain).

3. Orpheus's music so moved Pluto that he agreed to release his dead wife Eurydice (four syllables, accent on the second) from the underworld, but he violated the condition set—that he not look back at her—and so lost her again. Milton often uses Orpheus as a figure for the poet.
4. The final lines echo Marlowe's *The Passionate Shepherd to His Love* (p. 990): "If these delights thy mind may move, / Then live with me, and be my love."
1. Melancholy's man celebrates a melancholy that does not produce madness but the scholarly temperament, ruled by Saturn. See note 2 to *L'Allegro*.
2. For Melancholy's man, Mirth is not the innocent joys of *L'Allegro*, but "vain deluding Joys."
3. Morpheus is the god of sleep. "Pensioners": followers.
4. The melancholy humor, caused by black bile,

was thought to make the face dark or saturnine—from the ancient god, Saturn, allegorized in Neoplatonic philosophy as "the collective angelic mind."
5. Memnon, in *Odyssey* 11, was a handsome Ethiopian prince; his sister Himera's beauty was mentioned by later commentators. Cf. Song of Solomon 1.5, "I am black but comely."
6. Cassiopeia was turned into a constellation ("starred") for bragging that she was more beautiful than the sea nymphs.
7. Vesta, daughter of Saturn, was goddess of the household and a virgin, as were her priestesses. Milton invented the story of her sexual congress with Saturn on Mount Ida, resulting in Melancholy's birth. Saturn ruled the gods and the world during the Golden Age, which ended when he was murdered by his son Jove.

Oft in glimmering bowers and glades
He met her, and in secret shades
Of woody Ida's inmost grove,
30 While yet there was no fear of Jove.
Come pensive nun, devout and pure,
Sober, steadfast, and demure,
All in a robe of darkest grain,°   color
Flowing with majestic train,
35 And sable stole[8] of cypress lawn
Over thy decent° shoulders drawn.   comely, modestly covered
Come, but keep thy wonted state,
With even step and musing gait,
And looks commercing with the skies,
40 Thy rapt soul sitting in thine eyes:
There held in holy passion still,
Forget thyself to marble,[9] till
With a sad° leaden downward cast°   grave, dignified / glance
Thou fix them on the earth as fast.
45 And join with thee calm Peace and Quiet,
Spare Fast, that oft with gods doth diet,
And hears the Muses in a ring
Aye° round about Jove's altar sing.   continually
And add to these retired Leisure,
50 That in trim gardens takes his pleasure:
But first, and chiefest, with thee bring
Him that yon soars on golden wing,
Guiding the fiery-wheelèd throne,
The cherub Contemplatiòn;[1]
55 And the mute Silence hist° along,   summon
'Less Philomel[2] will deign a song,
In her sweetest, saddest plight,
Smoothing the rugged brow of night,
While Cynthia[3] checks her dragon yoke
60 Gently o'er th' accustomed oak;
Sweet bird that shunn'st the noise of folly,
Most musical, most melancholy!
Thee chantress oft the woods among
I woo to hear thy evensong;[4]
65 And missing thee, I walk unseen
On the dry smooth-shaven green,
To behold the wandering moon,
Riding near her highest noon,
Like one that had been led astray
70 Through the heaven's wide pathless way;
And oft as if her head she bowed,

8. A delicate black cloth.
9. Still as a statue.
1. The special function of cherubim is contemplation of God; Milton alludes also (line 53) to their identification with the wheels of the mystical chariot/throne of God described by Ezekiel (Ezekiel 10).
2. The nightingale (the bird into which Philomela was transformed after her rape by her brother-in-law Tereus) traditionally sings a mournful song.
3. Goddess of the moon, also associated with Hecate, goddess of the underworld, who drives a pair of sleepless dragons.
4. The evening liturgy traditionally sung by cloistered monks and nuns ("chantress" evokes such a singer); L'Allegro's cock, by contrast, calls hearers to the morning liturgy, matins (line 114).

Stooping through a fleecy cloud.
Oft on a plat° of rising ground,   *plot, open field*
I hear the far-off curfew sound
75 Over some wide-watered shore,
Swinging slow with sullen° roar;   *deep, mournful*
Or if the air will not permit,
Some still removèd place will fit,
Where glowing embers through the room
80 Teach light to counterfeit a gloom,
Far from all resort of mirth,
Save the cricket on the hearth,
Or the bellman's;[5] drowsy charm,
To bless the doors from nightly harm;
85 Or let my lamp at midnight hour
Be seen in some high lonely tower,
Where I may oft outwatch the Bear,[6]
With thrice-great Hermes,[7] or unsphere
The spirit of Plato to unfold
90 What words or what vast regions hold
The immortal mind that hath forsook
Her mansion in this fleshly nook;
And of those demons[8] that are found
In fire, air, flood, or under ground,
95 Whose power hath a true consent°   *agreement*
With planet, or with element.
Sometime let gorgeous Tragedy
In sceptered pall[9] come sweeping by,
Presenting Thebes, or Pelops' line,
100 Or the tale of Troy divine,[1]
Or what (though rare) of later age
Ennobled hath the buskined[2] stage.
But, O sad virgin, that thy power
Might raise Musaeus[3] from his bower,
105 Or bid the soul of Orpheus[4] sing
Such notes as, warbled to the string,
Drew iron tears down Pluto's cheek,
And made Hell grant what Love did seek.
Or call up him[5] that left half told
110 The story of Cambuscan bold,
Of Camball and of Algarsife,
And who had Canacee to wife,

---

5. Night watchman who rang a bell to mark the hours.

6. The Great Bear constellation never sets in northern skies.

7. Various esoteric books (actually written in the 3rd and 4th centuries) were attributed to an ancient Egyptian, Hermes Trismegistus ("thrice great"). Neoplatonists made him the father of all knowledge; later he became a patron of magicians and alchemists. To "unsphere" Plato is to bring him magically back to earth from whatever sphere he now inhabits—in practical terms, by reading his books.

8. Demons, halfway between gods and men, pre-side over the four elements.

9. Royal robe, worn by tragic actors.

1. Tragedies about Thebes include Sophocles' *Oedipus* cycle, those about the line of Pelops, Aeschylus's *Oresteia*, and those about Troy, Euripedes' *Trojan Women*.

2. The buskin (high boot) of tragedy, constrasted with the sock of comedy (*L'Allegro*, line 132).

3. Mythical poet-priest of the pre-Homeric age, supposedly a son or pupil of Orpheus.

4. For the story of Orpheus, see *L'Allegro*, line 145, and note.

5. Chaucer, whose *Squire's Tale* is unfinished.

That owned the virtuous° ring and glass,   *having magical powers*
And of the wondrous horse of brass,
115 On which the Tartar king did ride;
And if aught else great bards beside
In sage and solemn tunes have sung,
Of tourneys and of trophies hung,
Of forests and enchantments drear,
120 Where more is meant than meets the ear.[6]
Thus, Night, oft see me in thy pale career,
Till civil-suited Morn[7] appear,
Not tricked and frounced as she was wont
With the Attic boy to hunt,
125 But kerchiefed in a comely cloud,
While rocking winds are piping loud,
Or ushered with a shower still,°   *gentle*
When the gust hath blown his fill,
Ending on the rustling leaves,
130 With minute drops from off the eaves.
And when the sun begins to fling
His flaring beams, me, Goddess, bring
To archèd walks of twilight groves,
And shadows brown that Sylvan[8] loves
135 Of pine or monumental oak,
Where the rude ax with heavèd stroke
Was never heard the nymphs to daunt,
Or fright them from their hallowed haunt.
There in close covert° by some brook,   *hidden place*
140 Where no profaner eye may look,
Hide me from day's garish eye,
While the bee with honeyed thigh,
That at her flowery work doth sing,
And the waters murmuring
145 With such consort° as they keep,   *musical harmony*
Entice the dewy-feathered sleep;
And let some strange mysterious dream
Wave at his wings in airy stream
Of lively portraiture displayed
150 Softly on my eyelids laid.
And as I wake, sweet music breathe
Above, about, or underneath,
Sent by some spirit to mortals good,
Or th' unseen genius° of the wood.   *guardian deity*
155 But let my due feet never fail
To walk the studious cloister's pale,°   *enclosure*
And love the high embowèd roof,
With antic pillars massy proof,[9]
And storied windows richly dight,[1]

6. A capsule definition of allegory.
7. The now soberly dressed Aurora, goddess of the dawn, once fell in love with Cephalus ("the Attic boy") and hunted with him. "Tricked and frounced": adorned and with frizzled hair.

8. Roman god of woodlands.
9. Massive and strong. "Antic": covered with quaint or grotesque carvings, also antique.
1. Dressed. "Storied windows": stained-glass windows depicting biblical stories.

160 Casting a dim religious light.
    There let the pealing organ blow
    To the full-voiced choir below,
    In service high and anthems clear,
    As may with sweetness, through mine ear,
165 Dissolve me into ecstasies,
    And bring all heaven before mine eyes.
    And may at last my weary age
    Find out the peaceful hermitage,
    The hairy gown and mossy cell,
170 Where I may sit and rightly spell°   *study*
    Of every star that heaven doth shew,
    And every herb that sips the dew,
    Till old experience do attain
    To something like prophetic strain.
175 These pleasures, Melancholy, give,[2]
    And I with thee will choose to live.

ca. 1631   1645

Lycidas   Milton wrote this pastoral elegy for a volume of Latin, Greek, and English poems, *Justa Eduourdo King Naufrago* (1638), commemorating the death by shipwreck of his college classmate Edward King, three years younger than himself. King was not a close friend, but Milton's deepest emotions, anxieties, and fears are engaged here because, as poet and minister, King could serve him as a kind of alter ego. Still engaged in preparing himself, at the age of twenty-nine, for his projected poetic career, Milton was forced to recognize the uncertainty of all human endeavors. King's death posed the problem of mortality in its most agonizing form: the death of the young, the unfulfilled, the good, seems to deny all meaning to life, to demonstrate the uselessness of exceptional talent, lofty ambition, and noble ideals of service to God.

While the poem expresses Milton's anxieties, it also serves as an announcement of his grand ambitions. Like Edmund Spenser, Milton saw mastery of pastoral mode as the first step in a great poetic career. In *Lycidas* that mastery is complete. In the tradition which Milton received from classical and Renaissance predecessors, including Theocritus, Virgil, Petrarch, and Spenser, the pastoral landscape was invested with profound significances that had little indeed to do with the hard life of agricultural labor. The carefree shepherds who engage in singing contests, watch contentedly over their grazing sheep, fall in love, and write poetry offer an image or human life in harmony with nature and the seasonal processes of fruition and mellowing before the winter of death. The classical image of the shepherd as poet is mingled with the Christian understanding of the shepherd as pastor (Christ is the Good Shepherd), and sometimes as the prophet called to his mission from the fields, like David or Isaiah. Milton calls on all these associations, along with other motifs specific to pastoral funeral elegy: the recollection of past friendship, a questioning of destiny for cutting short this life, a procession of mourners (often mythological figures), and a "flower passage" in which nature pays tribute to the dead shepherd.

Lycidas uses but continually tests and challenges the assumptions and conventions

2. Compare this version of the echo from Marlowe's *Passionate Shepherd* with that with which *L'Allegro* ends.

of pastoral elegy, making for profound tensions and clashes of tone. The pastoral "oaten flute" is interrupted by divine pronouncements and bitter invective; nature seems rife with examples of meaningless waste and early death; the "blind Fury" often cuts off the poet's "thin-spun life" before he can win fame; good pastors die young while corrupt "Blind Mouths" remain; and Nature cannot even pay her tribute of flowers to Lycidas's funeral bier since he welters in the deep, his bones hurled to the "bottom of the monstrous world." In response to these fierce challenges come pronouncements by Apollo and St. Peter, and images of protection and resurrection in nature and myth, culminating in a new vision of pastoral: in heaven Lycidas enjoys a perfected pastoral existence, and in the coda, the consoled shepherd arises and carries his song to "pastures new." Milton's questioning thus leads to a final reassertion of confidence in his calling as national poet. Moreover, in the headnote added in the 1645 volume of his *Poems*, he lays claim to prophetic authority, for the Anglican clergy he denounced as corrupt in 1638 had mostly been expelled from their livings by Puritan reformers in 1645.

Lycidas

IN THIS MONODY[1] THE AUTHOR BEWAILS A LEARNED FRIEND,
UNFORTUNATELY DROWNED IN HIS PASSAGE FROM CHESTER ON THE
IRISH SEAS, 1637. AND BY OCCASION FORETELLS THE RUIN OF OUR
CORRUPTED CLERGY, THEN IN THEIR HEIGHT.

Yet once more, O ye laurels, and once more		
Ye myrtles brown, with ivy never sere,[2]		
I come to pluck your berries harsh and crude,°		*unripe*
And with forced fingers rude,°		*unskilled*
5 Shatter your leaves before the mellowing year.		
Bitter constraint, and sad occasion dear,°		*heartfelt, also dire*
Compels me to disturb your season due;		
For Lycidas is dead, dead ere his prime,[3]		
Young Lycidas, and hath not left his peer.		
10 Who would not sing for Lycidas? He knew		
Himself to sing, and build the lofty rhyme.[4]		
He must not float upon his watery bier		
Unwept, and welter° to the parching wind,		*be tossed about*
Without the meed° of some melodious tear.°		*reward / elegy*
15 Begin then, sisters of the sacred well[5]		
That from beneath the seat of Jove doth spring,		
Begin, and somewhat loudly sweep the string.		
Hence with denial vain, and coy excuse;		
So may some gentle Muse[6]		
20 With lucky words favor my destined urn,		
And as he passes turn,		

1. A dirge sung by a single voice, though this one incorporates several other voices. This Miltonic headnote was added in the edition of 1645; it identifies Milton as a prophet in the passage denouncing the clergy in this 1638 poem (lines 112–31) and invites the reader to remember Milton's 1641–42 polemics against the English bishops and church government (now dismantled).
2. "Laurels," associated with Apollo and poetry; "myrtle," associated with Venus and love; "ivy,"

associated with Bacchus and frenzy (also learning). All three are evergreens ("never sere") linked to poetic inspiration.
3. King was twenty-five.
4. King had written several poems of compliment in the patronage mode, chiefly on members of the royal family.
5. The nine (sister) Muses called (probably) from the fountain Aganippe, near Mount Helicon.
6. Here, some kindly poet.

And bid fair peace be to my sable shroud.
For we were nursed upon the selfsame hill,
Fed the same flock, by fountain, shade, and rill.
25 Together both, ere the high lawns° appeared   *upland pastures*
Under the opening eyelids of the morn,
We drove afield, and both together heard
What time the grayfly winds her sultry horn,[7]
Battening our flocks with the fresh dews of night,
30 Oft till the star that rose at evening bright
Toward heaven's descent had sloped his westering wheel.[8]
Meanwhile the rural ditties were not mute,
Tempered to th' oaten flute,[9]
Rough satyrs danced, and fauns with cloven heel
35 From the glad sound would not be absent long,
And old Damoetas[1] loved to hear our song.
     But O the heavy change, now thou art gone,
Now thou art gone, and never must return!
Thee, shepherd, thee the woods and desert caves,
40 With wild thyme and the gadding° vine o'ergrown,   *wandering*
And all their echoes mourn.
The willows and the hazel copses green
Shall now no more be seen,
Fanning their joyous leaves to thy soft lays.
45 As killing as the canker° to the rose,   *cankerworm*
Or taint-worm[2] to the weanling herds that graze,
Or frost to flowers that their gay wardrobe wear
When first the white-thorn blows;[3]
Such, Lycidas, thy loss to shepherd's ear.
50 Where were ye, nymphs,[4] when the remorseless deep
Closed o'er the head of your loved Lycidas?
For neither were ye playing on the steep
Where your old bards, the famous Druids,[5] lie,
Nor on the shaggy top of Mona high,
55 Nor yet where Deva spreads her wizard stream:[6]
Ay me! I fondly dream—
Had ye been there—for what could that have done?
What could the Muse[7] herself that Orpheus bore,
The Muse herself, for her enchanting[8] son
60 Whom universal Nature did lament,
When by the rout[9] that made the hideous roar

7. I.e., heard the grayfly when she buzzes. "Battening" (next line): feeding.
8. Hesperus, the evening star.
9. Panpipes, played traditionally by shepherds in pastoral.
1. A type name from pastoral poetry, possibly referring to some particular tutor at Cambridge. "Satyrs": goat-legged woodland creatures, Pan's boisterous attendants.
2. Internal parasite fatal to newly weaned lambs.
3. Hawthorne in bloom.
4. Nature deities.
5. Priestly poet-kings of Celtic Britain, who worshiped the forces of nature. They are buried on the mountain ("steep") Kerig-y-Druidion in Wales.
6. Deva, the river Dee in Cheshire, was magic

("wizard") because its shifting stream foretold prosperity or dearth for the land. "Mona" is the island of Anglesey. All these places are in the West Country, near where King drowned.
7. Calliope, Muse of epic poetry, was the mother of Orpheus.
8. Implies both song and magic; the root word survives in "incantation."
9. Orpheus's song was drowned out by the screams of a mob ("rout") of Thracian women, the Bacchantes, who then were able to tear him to pieces and throw his gory head into the river Hebrus, which carried it—still singing—to the island of Lesbos, bringing that island the gift of poetry.

His gory visage down the stream was sent,
Down the swift Hebrus to the Lesbian shore?
   Alas! What boots° it with incessant care   *profits*
65 To tend the homely slighted shepherd's trade,
And strictly meditate the thankless Muse?¹
Were it not better done as others use,
To sport with Amaryllis in the shade,
Or with the tangles of Neaera's hair?²
70 Fame is the spur that the clear spirit doth raise
(That last infirmity of noble mind)
To scorn delights, and live laborious days;
But the fair guerdon° when we hope to find,   *reward*
And think to burst out into sudden blaze,
75 Comes the blind Fury³ with th' abhorrèd shears,
And slits the thin-spun life. "But not the praise,"
Phoebus replied, and touched my trembling ears;⁴
"Fame is no plant that grows on mortal soil,
Nor in the glistering foil⁵
80 Set off to th' world, nor in broad rumor lies,
But lives and spreads aloft by those pure eyes,
And perfect witness of all-judging Jove;
As he pronounces lastly on each deed,
Of so much fame in heaven expect thy meed."°   *reward*
85   O fountain Arethuse, and thou honored flood,
Smooth-sliding Mincius, crowned with vocal reeds,
That strain I heard was of a higher mood.⁶
But now my oat° proceeds,   *pastoral flute*
And listens to the herald of the sea⁷
90 That came in Neptune's plea.
He asked the waves, and asked the felon° winds,   *savage*
"What hard mishap hath doomed this gentle swain?"
And questioned every gust of rugged° wings   *stormy*
That blows from off each beakèd promontory;
95 They knew not of his story,
And sage Hippotades⁸ their answer brings,
That not a blast was from his dungeon strayed;
The air was calm, and on the level brine,
Sleek Panope⁹ with all her sisters played.
100 It was that fatal and perfidious bark,
Built in th' eclipse,¹ and rigged with curses dark,
That sunk so low that sacred head of thine.
   Next Camus,² reverend sire, went footing slow,

1. I.e., study to write poetry (a Virgilian phrase).
2. "Amaryllis" and "Neaera" (*Nee-eye-ra*), conventional names for pretty shepherdesses wooed in song by pastoral shepherds.
3. Atropos, one of the three Fates, whose scissors cuts the thread of human life after her sisters spin and measure it. Milton makes her a savage, and blind, Fury.
4. Phoebus Apollo, god of poetic inspiration. In *Eclogue* 6.3–4 he plucked Virgil's ears, warning him against impatient ambition.
5. Flashy, glittering metal foil, set under a gem to enhance its brilliance.

6. Arethusa was a fountain in Sicily associated with Greek pastoral poetry (Theocritus), Mincius a river in Lombardy associated with Latin pastoral (Virgil); Milton invokes them as a return to the pastoral after the "higher mood" of Apollo's speech.
7. Triton, who comes gathering evidence about the accident for Neptune's court.
8. Aeolus, god of winds.
9. The chief Nereid or sea nymph.
1. Eclipses were taken as evil omens.
2. God of the river Cam, representing Cambridge University.

His mantle hairy, and his bonnet sedge,°   *formed of reeds*
105 Inwrought with figures dim, and on the edge
    Like to that sanguine flower inscribed with woe.[3]
    "Ah! who hath reft," quoth he, "my dearest pledge?"
    Last came and last did go
    The pilot of the Galilean lake;[4]
110 Two massy keys he bore of metals twain
    (The golden opes, the iron shuts amain).°   *forever*
    He shook his mitered locks, and stern bespake:
    "How well could I have spared for° thee, young swain,   *in place of*
    Enow° of such as for their bellies' sake   *enough (plural)*
115 Creep and intrude and climb into the fold![5]
    Of other care they little reckoning make,
    Than how to scramble at the shearers' feast,[6]
    And shove away the worthy bidden guest.
    Blind mouths![7] that scarce themselves know how to hold
120 A sheep-hook, or have learned aught else the least
    That to the faithful herdsman's art belongs!
    What recks it them? What need they? They are sped;[8]
    And when they list,° their lean° and flashy songs   *choose / meager*
    Grate on their scrannel° pipes of wretched straw.   *harsh, thin*
125 The hungry sheep look up, and are not fed,
    But swoln with wind, and the rank mist they draw,°   *inhale*
    Rot inwardly,[9] and foul contagion sp.ead,
    Besides what the grim wolf with privy paw[1]
    Daily devours apace, and nothing said.
130 But that two-handed engine at the door[2]
    Stands ready to smite once, and smite no more."
      Return, Alpheus,[3] the dread voice is past,
    That shrunk thy streams; return, Sicilian muse,
    And call the vales, and bid them hither cast
135 Their bells and flowerets of a thousand hues.[4]
    Ye valleys low where the mild whispers use,°   *frequent*

---

3. Like the *AI AI* cry of grief supposedly found on the hyacinth, a "sanguine flower" sprung from the blood of the youth Hyacinthus, beloved of Apollo and accidentally killed by him.
4. St. Peter, originally a fisherman on the sea of Galilee, was Christ's chief apostle; his keys open and shut the gates of heaven. He wears a bishop's miter (line 112): Milton in his antiprelatical tracts allows for a special role for apostles but denies any distinction in office between bishops and ministers in the later church.
5. Cf. John 10.1: "He that entereth not by the door into the sheepfold, but climbeth up some other way, the same is a thief and a robber."
6. Festive suppers for the sheepshearers (hence, the material rewards of their ministry). "Worthy bidden guest": cf. Matthew 22.8, the parable of the marriage feast, "they which were bidden were not worthy."
7. This audacious metaphor collapses them into these reprehensible qualities, blindness, as opposed to the oversight the term *episcopus* (bishop) signifies; gluttony, as opposed to the feeding of flocks proper to pastors. "Sheep-hook" (line

120): the bishop's staff is in the form of a shepherd's crook.
8. Provided for. "What recks it them?": what do they care?
9. Sheep-rot is used as an allegory of church corruption by both Petrarch and Dante.
1. I.e., Roman Catholicism, whose agents operated in secret ("privy"). Conversions in the court of the Roman Catholic queen Henrietta Maria were notorious.
2. A celebrated crux, variously explained as the two houses of Parliament, St. Peter's keys, the two-edged sword of the gospel, a sword wielded by two hands, and by other guesses; what is clear is the denunciation of impending, apocalyptic vengeance. In Matthew 24.33 the Last Judgment is said to be "even at the doors."
3. A river in Arcadia, fabled to pass unmixed through the sea before mixing its waters with the "fountain Arethuse" in Sicily, again reviving the pastoral mode after the fierce denunciation of Peter (see lines 85–87).
4. A catalogue of flowers was a common pastoral topic. "Bells": bell-shaped flowers.

Of shades and wanton winds, and gushing brooks,
On whose fresh lap the swart star sparely looks,[5]
Throw hither all your quaint enameled eyes,[6]
140 That on the green turf suck the honeyed showers,
And purple all the ground with vernal flowers.
Bring the rathe° primrose that forsaken dies,   *early*
The tufted crow-toe, and pale jessamine,[7]
The white pink, and the pansy freaked° with jet,   *flecked*
145 The glowing violet,
The musk-rose, and the well-attired woodbine,
With cowslips wan° that hang the pensive head,   *pale*
And every flower that sad embroidery wears:
Bid amaranthus[8] all his beauty shed,
150 And daffadillies fill their cups with tears,
To strew the laureate hearse° where Lycid lies.   *laurel-decked bier*
For so to interpose a little ease,
Let our frail thoughts dally with false surmise.[9]
Ay me! whilst thee the shores and sounding seas
155 Wash far away, where'er thy bones are hurled,
Whether beyond the stormy Hebrides,[1]
Where thou perhaps under the whelming° tide   *roaring, overwhelming*
Visit'st the bottom of the monstrous world;
Or whether thou, to our moist vows denied,
160 Sleep'st by the fable of Bellerus old,[2]
Where the great vision of the guarded mount
Looks toward Namancos and Bayona's hold;[3]
Look homeward angel now, and melt with ruth:°   *pity*
And, O ye dolphins,[4] waft the hapless youth.
165   Weep no more, woeful shepherds, weep no more,
For Lycidas your sorrow is not dead,
Sunk though he be beneath the wat'ry floor;
So sinks the day-star° in the ocean bed,   *the sun*
And yet anon repairs his drooping head,
170 And tricks° his beams, and with new-spangled ore   *adorns, trims*
Flames in the forehead of the morning sky:
So Lycidas sunk low, but mounted high,
Through the dear might of him[5] that walked the waves,
Where, other groves and other streams along,[6]
175 With nectar pure his oozy° locks he laves,   *moist*

---

5. The Dog Star, Sirius, associated with the heats of late summer.
6. Flowers curiously patterned and adorned with many colors.
7. White jasmine. "Tufted crow-toe": hyacinth or buttercup, growing in clusters. "Woodbine" (line 146): honeysuckle.
8. In Greek, "unfading," a legendary flower of immortality, one that never fades.
9. False, because Lycidas's body is not here to receive floral and poetic tributes.
1. Islands off the coast of Scotland, the northern terminus of the Irish Sea.
2. A fabulous giant invented by Milton as the origin of the Latin name for Land's End in Cornwall, *Bellerium*. "Monstrous world" (line 158): filled

with monsters, also, immense.
3. St. Michael's Mount in Cornwall, where the archangel was said to have appeared to fishermen in 495, and from which he is envisioned as looking over the Atlantic toward a region and fortress (Bayona's hold) in northern Spain, thereby guarding Protestant England against the continuing Roman Catholic threat.
4. Dolphins brought the Greek poet Arion safely ashore, for love of his verse, and also performed other sea rescues.
5. Christ, who rescued Peter when he tried and failed to do so (Matthew 14.25–31).
6. See Revelation 22.1–2, on the "pure river of water of life," and the "tree of life, which bare twelve manner of fruits."

And hears the unexpressive nuptial song,[7]
In the blest kingdoms meek of joy and love.
There entertain him all the saints above,
In solemn troops and sweet societies
180   That sing, and singing in their glory move,
And wipe the tears forever from his eyes.
Now, Lycidas, the shepherds weep no more;
Henceforth thou art the genius[8] of the shore,
In thy large recompense, and shalt be good
185   To all that wander in that perilous flood.
       Thus sang the uncouth swain[9] to th' oaks and rills,
While the still morn went out with sandals gray;
He touched the tender stops of various quills,[1]
With eager thought warbling his Doric[2] lay:
190   And now the sun had stretched out all the hills,
And now was dropped into the western bay;
At last he rose, and twitched his mantle blue:[3]
Tomorrow to fresh woods, and pastures new.

November 1637   1638

From The Reason of Church Government
Urged Against Prelaty[1]

[PLANS AND PROJECTS]

* * * Concerning therefore this wayward subject against prelaty,[2] the
touching whereof is so distasteful and disquietous[3] to a number of men, as
by what hath been said I may deserve of charitable readers to be credited
that neither envy nor gall hath entered me upon this controversy, but the
enforcement of conscience only and a preventive fear lest the omitting of
this duty should be against me when I would store up to myself the good
provision of peaceful hours; so lest it should be still imputed to me, as I have
found it hath been, that some self-pleasing humor of vainglory hath incited
me to contest with men of high estimation, now while green years are upon
my head;[4] from this needless surmisal I shall hope to dissuade the intelligent
and equal auditor, if I can but say successfully that which in this exigent[5]

7. Inexpressible hymn of joy sung "at the marriage
supper of the Lamb" (Revelation 19).
8. Local guardian spirit.
9. Another voice now seems to take over from the
previously heard voice of the "uncouth swain"
(unknown, unskilled shepherd).
1. The oaten stalks of panpipes.
2. Rustic, the dialect of Theocritus and other
famous Greek pastoral poets.
3. The color of hope. "Twitched": pulled up
around his shoulders.
1. This was the fourth of five tracts Milton published attacking the bishops, liturgy, and church
government of the Church of England, in support
of Presbyterian reform, though these tracts also
show signs of the more radical positions he will
soon adopt. This 1642 treatise is the first one to
carry his name, so the autobiographical passage is
in part to introduce himself to the reader and

explain why, though a layman and a young man,
he feels himself called, and well prepared, to write
on theology and ecclesiastical order. Beyond that
rhetorical purpose, this is also the fullest account
Milton ever set forth of his poetics: his sense of the
poet's calling, of the nature and multiple uses of
poetry, and of the several genres each has
employed or hopes to attempt. It also registers his
inner conflict between duty (to serve God and his
church with his learning) and desire (to write
poetry).
2. Government by prelates (bishops). "Wayward";
untoward, unpromising.
3. Distressing.
4. Milton's opponents, Bishops Joseph Hall,
James Ussher, and Lancelot Andrewes, were
famous and he was still almost unknown, at age
thirty-four.
5. Urgent occasion. "Equal": impartial.

behooves me; although I would be heard only, if it might be, by the elegant and learned reader, to whom principally for a while I shall beg leave I may address myself. To him it will be no new thing though I tell him that if I hunted after praise by the ostentation of wit and learning, I should not write thus out of mine own season when I have neither yet completed to my mind the full circle of my private studies,[6] although I complain not of any insufficiency to the matter in hand; or, were I ready to my wishes, it were a folly to commit anything elaborately composed to the careless and interrupted listening of these tumultuous times. Next, if I were wise only to mine own ends, I would certainly take such a subject as of itself might catch applause, whereas this hath all the disadvantages on the contrary, and such a subject as the publishing whereof might be delayed at pleasure, and time enough to pencil it over with all the curious touches of art, even to the perfection of a faultless picture; whenas in this argument the not deferring is of great moment to the good speeding,[7] that if solidity have leisure to do her office, art cannot have much. Lastly, I should not choose this manner of writing, wherein knowing myself inferior to myself, led by the genial[8] power of nature to another task, I have the use, as I may account it, but of my left hand. And though I shall be foolish in saying more to this purpose, yet, since it will be such a folly as wisest men going about to commit have only confessed and so committed, I may trust with more reason, because with more folly, to have courteous pardon. For although a poet, soaring in the high region of his fancies with his garland and singing robes about him, might without apology speak more of himself than I mean to do, yet for me sitting here below in the cool element of prose, a mortal thing among many readers of no empyreal conceit,[9] to venture and divulge unusual things of myself, I shall petition to the gentler sort, it may not be envy[1] to me.

I must say, therefore, that after I had from my first years by the ceaseless diligence and care of my father (whom God recompense) been exercised to the tongues and some sciences, as my age would suffer,[2] by sundry masters and teachers both at home and at the schools, it was found that whether aught was imposed me by them that had the overlooking, or betaken to of mine own choice in English or other tongue, prosing or versing (but chiefly this latter), the style, by certain vital signs it had, was likely to live. But much latelier in the private academies of Italy,[3] whither I was favored to resort—perceiving that some trifles which I had in memory, composed at under twenty or thereabout (for the manner is that everyone must give some proof of his wit[4] and reading there) met with acceptance above what was looked for, and other things which I had shifted in scarcity of books and conveniences to patch up amongst them, were received with written encomiums,[5] which the Italian is not forward to bestow on men of this side the Alps—I

6. After taking his B.A. and M.A. degrees from Cambridge, Milton spent nearly six more years in private study at home; he was still continuing that program of reading.
7. Prompt publication is essential in polemic, so substance rather than art must be the priority. "Office": duty.
8. Intellectual gifts or natural disposition.
9. Without sublime and elevated conceits.
1. Cause for odium or disrespect.
2. Admit. "Tongue": foreign language. In *Ad*

Patrem Milton says that as a boy he learned Latin, Greek, French, Italian, and Hebrew.
3. When on the grand tour of the Continent (1638–39) Milton enjoyed attending academies in Rome and especially Florence, which were centers for literary, scientific, and social exchange.
4. Ingenuity, creative powers; Milton read some of his Latin poems to the Academies.
5. Praises. Milton published five of these, in Latin, as prefatory material to the Latin part of his 1645 *Poems*.

began thus far to assent both to them and divers of my friends here at home, and not less to an inward prompting which now grew daily upon me, that by labor and intent study (which I take to be my portion in this life) joined with the strong propensity of nature, I might perhaps leave something so written to aftertimes, as they should not willingly let it die. These thoughts at once possessed me, and these other: that if I were certain to write as men buy leases, for three lives and downward,[6] there ought no regard be sooner had than to God's glory by the honor and instruction of my country. For which cause, and not only for that I knew it would be hard to arrive at the second rank among the Latins, I applied myself to that resolution which Ariosto followed against the persuasions of Bembo,[7] to fix all the industry and art I could unite to the adorning of my native tongue; not to make verbal curiosities the end—that were a toilsome vanity—but to be an interpreter and relater of the best and sagest things among mine own citizens throughout this island in the mother dialect. That what the greatest and choicest wits of Athens, Rome, or modern Italy, and those Hebrews of old did for their country, I, in my proportion, with this over and above of being a Christian,[8] might do for mine; not caring to be once named abroad, though perhaps I could attain to that, but content with these British islands as my world; whose fortune hath hitherto been that if the Athenians, as some say, made their small deeds great and renowned by their eloquent writers, England hath had her noble achievements made small by the unskillful handling of monks and mechanics.

Time serves not now, and perhaps I might seem too profuse to give any certain account of what the mind at home in the spacious circuits of her musing hath liberty to propose to herself, though of highest hope and hardest attempting: whether that epic form whereof the two poems of Homer and those other two of Virgil and Tasso are a diffuse, and the book of Job a brief, model;[9] or whether the rules of Aristotle herein are strictly to be kept, or nature to be followed,[1] which in them that know art and use judgment is no transgression but an enriching of art; and lastly, what king or knight before the conquest[2] might be chosen in whom to lay the pattern of a Christian hero. And as Tasso gave to a prince of Italy his choice whether he would command him to write of Godfrey's expedition against the infidels, or Belisarius against the Goths, or Charlemagne against the Lombards;[3] if to the instinct of nature and the emboldening of art aught may be trusted, and that there be nothing adverse in our climate[4] or the fate of this age, it haply would be no rashness from an equal diligence and inclination to present the like offer in our own ancient stories; or whether those dramatic consti-

---

6. Leases were often drawn for a tenancy to run through the longest-lived of three named persons.
7. Rejecting Cardinal Bembo's advice, Ariosto said he would rather be first among the Italian poets than second among those writing Latin.
8. The advantage would be in having "true" subjects to write about.
9. The great models for the "diffuse" or long epic were Homer's Iliad and Odyssey, Virgil's Aeneid, and Torquato Tasso's Gerusalemme Liberata; there was also a long tradition of reading the Book of Job as a "brief" epic, a moral conflict between Job and Satan. Milton's brief epic, Paradise Regained (1671), makes some use of that model. For all the genres he discusses, Milton cites both classical and

biblical models.
1. One contemporary debate concerned whether the Aristotelian rule of beginning in medias res was to be followed, or Ariosto's "natural" method of beginning at the beginning of the story.
2. At first Milton considered as potential epic subjects King Arthur, who fought against invading Saxons, and King Alfred, who warred with invading Danes; he excluded those after the Norman Conquest.
3. Tasso offered this choice to his patron, Alfonso II d'Este, duke of Ferrara.
4. Milton often speculated that the cold climate of England might not be conducive to poetry as the warmer climate of Italy and Greece had been.

tutions[5] wherein Sophocles and Euripides reign shall be found more doctrinal and exemplary to a nation. The Scripture also affords us a divine pastoral drama in the Song of Solomon, consisting of two persons and a double chorus, as Origen rightly judges. And the Apocalypse of St. John is the majestic image of a high and stately tragedy, shutting up and intermingling her solemn scenes and acts with a sevenfold chorus of hallelujahs and harping symphonies; and this my opinion the grave authority of Paraeus, commenting that book, is sufficient to confirm. Or if occasion shall lead to imitate those magnific odes and hymns wherein Pindarus and Callimachus[6] are in most things worthy, some others in their frame judicious, in their matter most an end[7] faulty. But those frequent songs throughout the law and prophets beyond all these, not in their divine argument alone, but in the very critical art of composition, may be easily made appear over all the kinds of lyric poesy to be incomparable.[8] These abilities, wheresoever they be found, are the inspired gift of God rarely bestowed, but yet to some (though most abuse) in every nation; and are of power beside the office of a pulpit to inbreed and cherish in a great people the seeds of virtue and public civility, to allay the perturbations of the mind and set the affections in right tune, to celebrate in glorious and lofty hymns the throne and equipage of God's almightiness, and what he works and what he suffers to be wrought with high providence in his church, to sing the victorious agonies of martyrs and saints, the deeds and triumphs of just and pious nations doing valiantly through faith against the enemies of Christ, to deplore the general relapses of kingdoms and states from justice and God's true worship. Lastly, whatsoever in religion is holy and sublime, in virtue amiable or grave, whatsoever hath passion or admiration in all the changes of that which is called fortune from without or the wily subtleties and refluxes of man's thoughts from within, all these things with a solid and treatable smoothness to paint out and describe.[9] Teaching over the whole book of sanctity and virtue through all the instances of example, with such delight to those especially of soft and delicious temper,[1] who will not so much as look upon truth herself unless they see her elegantly dressed, that whereas the paths of honesty and good life appear now rugged and difficult, though they be indeed easy and pleasant, they would then appear to all men both easy and pleasant, though they were rugged and difficult indeed. And what a benefit this would be to our youth and gentry may be soon guessed by what we know of the corruption and bane which they suck in daily from the writings and interludes of libidinous and ignorant poetasters,[2] who, having scarce ever heard of that which is the main consistence of a true poem, the choice of such persons as they ought to introduce, and what is moral and decent to each one, do for the most part lap up vicious

---

5. Plays. Sophocles and Euripedes are supreme examples of Greek tragedy; the scripture models for drama are the Song of Solomon as a "divine pastoral drama" (Milton cites Origen, an Alexandrine Father of the 3rd century), and the Book of Revelation as a "high and stately tragedy" (he cites David Paraeus, a German theologian of the 16th and 17th centuries).
6. Pindar, a 5th century B.C.E. Greek poet, wrote numerous odes especially on winners of the Olympic games; Callimachus, a 3rd century B.C.E. Alexandrine Greek, wrote elegant elegiac verse on the origin of various myths and rituals.

7. Almost entirely.
8. He thinks especially of the Psalms, often compared to classical lyric.
9. See the wide range of kinds and subjects and functions suggested for the serious national poet.
1. Temperament. Milton here paraphrases Horace's formula, that poetry is to teach and delight, and Sidney's notion that it makes truth palatable by the delightful covering.
2. Some of the pseudo-poets of the Cavalier court who wrote on lascivious topics.

principles in sweet pills to be swallowed down, and make the taste of virtuous documents harsh and sour.

But because the spirit of man cannot demean[3] itself lively in this body without some recreating intermission of labor and serious things, it were happy for the commonwealth if our magistrates, as in those famous governments of old, would take into their care, not only the deciding of our contentious law cases and brawls, but the managing of our public sports and festival pastimes, that they might be, not such as were authorized a while since,[4] the provocations of drunkenness and lust, but such as may inure and harden our bodies by martial exercises to all warlike skill and performance, and may civilize, adorn, and make discreet our minds by the learned and affable meeting of frequent academies, and the procurement of wise and artful recitations sweetened with eloquent and graceful enticements to the love and practice of justice, temperance, and fortitude, instructing and bettering the nation at all opportunities, that the call of wisdom and virtue may be heard everywhere, as Solomon saith: "She crieth without, she uttereth her voice in the streets, in the top of high places, in the chief concourse, and in the openings of the gates."[5] Whether this may not be, not only in pulpits, but after another persuasive method,[6] at set and solemn panegyries, in theaters, porches,[7] or what other place or way may win most upon the people to receive at once both recreation and instruction, let them in authority consult.

The thing which I had to say, and those intentions which have lived within me ever since I could conceive myself anything worth to my country, I return to crave excuse that urgent reason hath plucked from me by an abortive and foredated discovery.[8] And the accomplishment of them lies not but in a power above man's to promise; but that none hath by more studious ways endeavored, and with more unwearied spirit that none shall, that I dare almost aver of myself as far as life and free leisure will extend; and that the land had once enfranchised herself from this impertinent[9] yoke of prelaty, under whose inquisitorious and tyrannical duncery no free and splendid wit can flourish. Neither do I think it shame to covenant with any knowing reader that for some few years yet I may go on trust with him toward the payment of what I am now indebted, as being a work not to be raised from the heat of youth or the vapors of wine, like that which flows at waste from the pen of some vulgar amorist or the trencher fury of a rhyming parasite, nor to be obtained by the invocation of Dame Memory and her siren daughters,[1] but by devout prayer to that Eternal Spirit who can enrich with all utterance and knowledge, and sends out his seraphim with the hallowed fire of his altar to touch and purify the lips of whom he pleases.[2] To this must be added

---

3. Comport.
4. Charles I's republication (1633) of James I's *Book of Sports*, encouraging sports, dancing, and rural festivals on Sundays—anathama to Puritans.
5. The phrases are from Proverbs 1.29–21 and 8.2–3. Milton would not ban recreation or festival pastimes, but reform them: his models are the lofty encomiastic poems and recitations Plato would admit into his *Republic*, the literary and social exchanges of the Italian academies, and martial exercises (to prepare the citizenry for war, now imminent).

6. I.e., poetry.
7. Porticos. "Panegyries": solemn public meetings.
8. I.e., I have been forced to write for my country's sake and to reveal my poetic plans before I was ready to do either.
9. Not rightly pertaining to.
1. True poetry comes, not from youth, wine, a full plate, or even Memory (and her daughters the Muses): tradition alone does not make a poet.
2. The coal from the altar that purifies the prophet's lips (Isaiah 6.6–7): the passage makes poetry first and foremost the product of inspira-

industrious and select reading, steady observation, insight into all seemly and generous arts and affairs; till which in some measure be compassed, at mine own peril and cost I refuse not to sustain this expectation. * * * But were it the meanest under-service, if God by his secretary conscience enjoin it, it were sad for me if I should draw back; for me especially, now when all men offer their aid to help ease and lighten the difficult labors of the church, to whose service by the intentions of my parents and friends I was destined of a child, and in mine own resolutions: till coming to some maturity of years and perceiving what tyranny had invaded the church, that he who would take orders must subscribe slave and take an oath withal,[3] which, unless he took with a conscience that would retch, he must either straight perjure or split his faith; I thought it better to prefer a blameless silence before the sacred office of speaking, bought and begun with servitude and forswearing. Howsoever, thus church-outed by the prelates, hence may appear the right I have to meddle in these matters, as before the necessity and constraint appeared.

1642

Areopagitica

Areopagitica   In this most literary of his tracts, Milton sets forth a trenchant defense of intellectual liberty that has had a powerful influence on the evolving liberal conception of the freedom of speech, press, and thought. His target is the Press Ordinance of June 14, 1643, Parliament's attempt to crack down on the flood of pamphlets (including Milton's own controversial treatises on divorce) that poured forth both from legal and from underground presses as the Civil War raged. Like Tudor and Stuart censorship laws, Parliament's ordinance demanded that works be registered with the Stationers and licensed by the censors before publication, and that both author and publisher be identified, on pain of fines and imprisonment for both. Milton vigorously protests the prepublication licensing of books, arguing that such measures have only been used by, and are only fit for, degenerate cultures. In the regenerate English nation, now "rousing herself like a strong man after sleep," men and women must be allowed to develop in virtue by participating in the clash and conflict of ideas. Truth will always overcome falsehood in reasoned debate. Thus, in opposition to the Presbyterians then in power, Milton defends widespread religious toleration, though with restrictions on Roman Catholicism, which, like most of his Protestant contemporaries, he viewed as a political threat and a tyranny binding individual conscience to the Pope.

The title associates the tract with the speech of the Greek orator Isocrates to the Areopagus, the Council of the Wise in Athens. Learned readers would have recognized the irony of this; while Isocrates instructed the council to reform Athens by careful supervision of the private lives of citizens, Milton argues that only liberty and removal of censorship can advance reformation. This association explains the oratorical tone of the tract, which was, in fact, subtitled "A Speech." Milton's style is elevated, eloquent, dense with poetic figures, and ranges in tone from satire and ridicule to urgent pleading and florid praise. His arguments and principles are often couched

tion, but Milton also insists on his need to attain well-nigh universal knowledge and experience.

3. Milton was not willing to subscribe the oath affirming that the Book of Common Prayer and the present government of the church by bishops were according to the word of God; still less was he will-

ing to subscribe the notorious "etcetera" oath required in 1640, that the minister would never seek to alter the government of the church "by Archbishops, Bishops, Deacons, and Archdeacons, etc."

in striking images and phrases. One example is his passionate testimony to the potency and inestimable value of books: "As good almost kill a man as kill a good book . . ." Most memorable is his ringing credo that echoes down the centuries to protest every new tyranny: "Give me the liberty to know, to utter, and to argue freely according to conscience, above all liberties."

From Areopagitica

I deny not, but that it is of greatest concernment in the Church and Commonwealth, to have a vigilant eye how Books demean[1] themselves as well as men; and thereafter to confine, imprison, and do sharpest justice on them as malefactors:[2] For Books are not absolutely dead things, but do contain a potency of life in them to be as active as that soul was whose progeny they are; nay they do preserve as in a vial the purest efficacy and extraction of that living intellect that bred them. I know they are as lively, and as vigorously productive, as those fabulous Dragon's teeth; and being sown up and down, may chance to spring up armed men.[3] And yet on the other hand unless wariness be used, as good almost kill a Man as kill a good Book; who kills a Man kills a reasonable creature, God's Image; but he who destroys a good Book, kills reason it self, kills the Image of God, as it were in the eye. Many a man lives a burden to the Earth; but a good Book is the precious life-blood of a master spirit, embalmed and treasured up on purpose to a life beyond life. 'Tis true, no age can restore a life, whereof perhaps there is no great loss; and revolutions of ages do not oft recover the loss of a rejected truth, for the want of which whole Nations fare the worse. We should be wary therefore what persecution we raise against the living labors of public men, how we spill that seasoned life of man preserved and stored up in Books; since we see a kind of massacre, whereof the execution ends not in the slaying of an elemental life, but strikes at that ethereal and fifth essence,[4] the breath of reason it self, slays an immortality rather then a life. But lest I should be condemned of introducing licence, while I oppose Licensing, I refuse not the pains to be so much Historical, as will serve to show what hath been done by ancient and famous Commonwealths, against this disorder, till the very time that this project of licensing crept out of the *Inquisition*,[5] was catched up by our Prelates, and hath caught some of our Presbyters.[6] * * *

* * * Good and evil we know in the field of this world grow up together almost inseparably; and the knowledge of good is so involved and interwoven with the knowledge of evil, and in so many cunning resemblances hardly to be discerned, that those confused seeds which were imposed on Psyche as

1. Behave.
2. Milton allows that books may be called to account after publication, if they are proved to contain libels or other manifest crimes (he leaves this quite vague).
3. After Cadmus killed a dragon on his way to founding Thebes, on a god's advice he sowed the dragon's teeth, which sprang up as an army, the belligerent forefathers of Sparta.
4. Quintessence, a pure, mystical substance above the four elements (fire, air, water, earth).

5. The Roman Catholic institution for suppressing heresy, especially strong in Spain.
6. The Presbyterians, powerful in the Parliament, were striving to establish theirs as the national church and suppress others; Milton, who began by supporting them in *The Reason of Church Government* (p. 1796) and his other antiprelatical tracts (1641–42), now rejects them, in large part because they seek to supplant one repressive church with another.

an incessant labor to cull out and sort asunder[7] were not more intermixed. It was from out the rind of one apple tasted, that the knowledge of good and evil, as two twins cleaving together, leaped forth into the world. And perhaps this is that doom which Adam fell into of knowing good and evil, that is to say of knowing good by evil.

As therefore the state of man now is, what wisdom can there be to choose, what continence to forbear, without the knowledge of evil? He that can apprehend and consider vice with all her baits and seeming pleasures, and yet abstain, and yet distinguish, and yet prefer that which is truly better, he is the true wayfaring[8] Christian. I cannot praise a fugitive and cloistered virtue, unexercised and unbreathed,[9] that never sallies out and sees her adversary, but slinks out of the race where that immortal garland is to be run for, not without dust and heat. Assuredly we bring not innocence into the world, we bring impurity much rather; that which purifies us is trial, and trial is by what is contrary. That virtue therefore which is but a youngling in the contemplation of evil, and knows not the utmost that vice promises to her followers, and rejects it, is but a blank virtue, not a pure; her whiteness is but an excremental[1] whiteness; which was the reason why our sage and serious poet Spenser (whom I dare be known to think a better teacher than Scotus or Aquinas[2]), describing true temperance under the person of Guyon, brings him in with his palmer through the cave of Mammon and the bower of earthly bliss, that he might see and know, and yet abstain.

Since therefore the knowledge and survey of vice is in this world so necessary to the constituting of human virtue, and the scanning of error to the confirmation of truth, how can we more safely, and with less danger, scout into the regions of sin and falsity than by reading all manner of tractates and hearing all manner of reason? And this is the benefit which may be had of books promiscuously read.

But of the harm that may result hence, three kinds are usually reckoned. First is feared the infection that may spread; but then all human learning and controversy in religious points must remove out of the world, yea, the Bible itself; for that ofttimes relates blasphemy not nicely,[3] it describes the carnal sense of wicked men not unelegantly, it brings in holiest men passionately murmuring against providence through all the arguments of Epicurus;[4] in other great disputes it answers dubiously and darkly to the common reader.[5]

* * *

7. Angry at her son Cupid's love for Psyche, Venus set the girl many trials, among them to sort out a vast mound of mixed seeds, but the ants took pity on her and did the work.
8. The printed text reads "wayfaring," calling up the image of the Christian pilgrim; several presentation copies correct it (by hand) to "warfaring," calling up the image of the Christian warrior. Both suit the passage.
9. Not forced by exertion to breathe hard. "Immortal garland" (next line): the prize for the winner of a race, as figure for the "crown of life" promised to those who endure temptation (James 1.12).
1. Exterior only.
2. Duns Scotus and Thomas Aquinas, major Scholastic theologians. Guyon, the hero of Book II of the Faerie Queene, passes through the Cave

of Mammon (symbolic of all worldly goods and honors) without his Palmer-guide, but that figure does accompany him through the Bower of Bliss.
3. Daintily.
4. Greek philosopher (342–270 B.C.E.) who taught that happiness is the greatest good, and that virtue should be practiced because it brings happiness; some of his followers equated happiness with sensual enjoyment. Milton may be thinking of the biblical book of Ecclesiastes.
5. Milton goes on to argue that a fool can find material for folly in the best books, and a wise person material for wisdom in the worst. Also, one cannot remove evil by censoring books without also censoring ballads, fiddlers, clothing, conversation, and all social life.

To sequester out of the world into Atlantic and Utopian politics,[6] which never can be drawn into use, will not mend our condition, but to ordain wisely as in this world of evil, in the midst whereof God hath placed us unavoidably. . . . Impunity and remissness, for certain, are the bane of a commonwealth; but here the great art lies, to discern in what the law is to bid restraint and punishment, and in what things persuasion only is to work. If every action which is good or evil in man at ripe years were to be under pittance[7] and prescription and compulsion, what were virtue but a name, what praise could be then due to well-doing, what gramercy[8] to be sober, just, or continent?

Many there be that complain of divine providence for suffering Adam to transgress; foolish tongues! when God gave him reason, he gave him freedom to choose, for reason is but choosing; he had been else a mere artificial Adam, such an Adam as he is in the motions.[9] We ourselves esteem not of that obedience, or love, or gift, which is of force: God therefore left him free, set before him a provoking object, ever almost in his eyes; herein consisted his merit, herein the right of his reward, the praise of his abstinence.[1] Wherefore did he create passions within us, pleasures round about us, but that these rightly tempered are the very ingredients of virtue? They are not skillful considerers of human things, who imagine to remove sin by removing the matter of sin; for, besides that it is a huge heap increasing under the very act of diminishing, though some part of it may for a time be withdrawn from some persons, it cannot from all, in such a universal thing as books are; and when this is done, yet the sin remains entire. Though ye take from a covetous man all his treasure, he has yet one jewel left: ye cannot bereave him of his covetousness. Banish all objects of lust, shut up all youth into the severest discipline that can be exercised in any hermitage, ye cannot make them chaste that came not thither so: such great care and wisdom is required to the right managing of this point.

Suppose we could expel sin by this means; look how much we thus expel of sin, so much we expel of virtue: for the matter of them both is the same; remove that, and ye remove them both alike. This justifies the high providence of God, who, though he commands us temperance, justice, continence, yet pours out before us, even to a profuseness, all desirable things, and gives us minds that can wander beyond all limit and satiety. Why should we then affect a rigor contrary to the manner of God and of nature, by abridging or scanting those means, which books freely permitted are, both to the trial of virtue and the exercise of truth? It would be better done to learn that the law must needs be frivolous which goes to restrain things uncertainly and yet equally working to good and to evil. And were I the chooser, a dram of well-doing should be preferred before many times as much the forcible hindrance of evil-doing. For God sure esteems the growth and completing of one virtuous person more than the restraint of ten vicious.

* * *

6. Milton alludes to More's *Utopia* and Bacon's *New Atlantis* (pp. 506 and 1548).
7. Rationing.
8. Reward, thanks.

9. Puppet shows.
1. Compare Milton's representation of Adam and Eve in Eden in *Paradise Lost*.

What advantage is it to be a man over it is to be a boy at school, if we have only scaped the ferula[2] to come under the fescue of an Imprimatur; if serious and elaborate writings, as if they were no more than the theme of a grammar-lad under his pedagogue, must not be uttered without the cursory eyes of a temporizing and extemporizing licenser?[3] He who is not trusted with his own actions, his drift not being known to be evil, and standing to the hazard of law and penalty, has no great argument to think himself reputed, in the commonwealth wherein he was born, for other than a fool or a foreigner.

When a man writes to the world, he summons up all his reason and deliberation to assist him; he searches, meditates, is industrious, and likely consults and confers with his judicious friends, after all which done he takes himself to be informed in what he writes, as well as any that writ before him. If in this the most consummate act of his fidelity and ripeness, no years, no industry, no former proof of his abilities can bring him to that state of maturity as not to be still mistrusted and suspected (unless he carry all his considerate diligence, all his midnight watchings, and expense of Palladian[4] oil, to the hasty view of an unleisured licenser, perhaps much his younger, perhaps far his inferior in judgment, perhaps one who never knew the labor of book-writing), and if he be not repulsed, or slighted, must appear in print like a puny[5] with his guardian, and his censor's hand on the back of his title to be his bail and surety that he is no idiot, or seducer; it cannot be but a dishonor and derogation to the author, to the book, to the privilege and dignity of learning. * * *

And how can a man teach with authority, which is the life of teaching, how can he be a doctor in his book as he ought to be, or else had better be silent, whenas all he teaches, all he delivers, is but under the tuition, under the correction of his patriarchal[6] licenser to blot or alter what precisely accords not with the hide-bound humor which he calls his judgment? When every acute reader upon the first sight of a pedantic license, will be ready with these like words to ding the book a quoit's[7] distance from him: "I hate a pupil teacher, I endure not an instructor that comes to me under the wardship of an overseeing fist. I know nothing of the licenser, but that I have his own hand here for his arrogance; who shall warrant me his judgment?" "The State, sir," replies the stationer, but has a quick return: "The State shall be my governors, but not my critics; they may be mistaken in the choice of a licenser, as easily as this licenser may be mistaken in an author."

* * *

Well knows he who uses to consider, that our faith and knowledge thrives by exercise, as well as our limbs and complexion.[8] Truth is compared in Scripture to a streaming fountain;[9] if her waters flow not in a perpetual progression, they sicken into a muddy pool of conformity and tradition. A man may be a heretic in the truth; and if he believe things only because his

2. "Ferula": a schoolmaster's rod; "fescue": a pointer. Milton's keen sense of the affront to scholars and scholarship, and to himself, is evident in this passage.
3. He temporizes in following the times, and acts by whim (extemporizes).
4. Pertaining to Pallas Athena, goddess of wisdom.
5. A minor, hence, young, unseasoned.

6. Taking on the role of a father: also, standing in for ecclesiastical patriarchs or prelates (like Archbishop Laud).
7. A flat disc of stone or metal, thrown as an exercise of strength or skill.
8. Constitution, the proper mingling of qualities in the body.
9. In Psalm 85.11.

pastor says so, or the Assembly[1] so determines, without knowing other reason, though his belief be true, yet the very truth he holds becomes his heresy.

* * *

Truth indeed came once into the world with her Divine Master, and was a perfect shape most glorious to look on: but when he ascended, and his apostles after him were laid asleep, then straight arose a wicked race of deceivers, who, as that story goes of the Egyptian Typhon with his conspirators, how they dealt with the good Osiris,[2] took the virgin Truth, hewed her lovely form into a thousand pieces, and scattered them to the four winds. From that time ever since, the sad friends of Truth, such as durst appear, imitating the careful search that Isis made for the mangled body of Osiris, went up and down gathering up limb by limb, still as they could find them. We have not yet found them all, Lords and Commons, nor ever shall do, till her Master's second coming; he shall bring together every joint and member, and shall mold them into an immortal feature of loveliness and perfection. Suffer not these licensing prohibitions to stand at every place of opportunity, forbidding and disturbing them that continue seeking, that continue to do our obsequies[3] to the torn body of our martyred saint.

We boast our light; but if we look not wisely on the sun itself, it smites us into darkness. Who can discern those planets that are oft combust,[4] and those stars of brightest magnitude that rise and set with the sun, until the opposite motion of their orbs bring them to such a place in the firmament where they may be seen evening or morning? The light which we have gained was given us, not to be ever staring on, but by it to discover onward things more remote from our knowledge. It is not the unfrocking of a priest, the unmitering of a bishop, and the removing him from off the Presbyterian shoulders, that will make us a happy nation. No, if other things as great in the church, and in the rule of life both economical and political, be not looked into and reformed, we have looked so long upon the blaze that Zwinglius and Calvin[5] hath beaconed up to us, that we are stark blind.

There be who perpetually complain of schisms and sects, and make it such a calamity that any man dissents from their maxims. 'Tis their own pride and ignorance which causes the disturbing, who neither will hear with meekness, nor can convince; yet all must be suppressed which is not found in their syntagma.[6] They are the troublers, they are the dividers of unity, who neglect and permit not others to unite those dissevered pieces which are yet wanting to the body of Truth. To be still searching what we know not by what we know, still closing up truth to truth as we find it (for all her body is homogeneal and proportional), this is the golden rule in theology as well as in arithmetic, and makes up the best harmony in a church; not the forced and outward union of cold and neutral and inwardly divided minds.

Lords and Commons of England, consider what nation it is whereof ye are, and whereof ye are the governors: a nation not slow and dull, but of a

---

1. The Westminster Assembly, convened by Parliament in 1643 to reorganize the English church along Presbyterian lines.
2. Plutarch tells, in Isis and Osiris, of Typhon's scattering the fragments of his brother Osiris and of Isis's efforts to recover them.
3. Funeral or commemorative rites.

4. Burned up; in astrology, so close to the sun as not to be visible.
5. Zwingli and Calvin, famous Protestant reformers, were mainstays of the Presbyterian cause. "Economical": domestic.
6. Compilations of beliefs, creeds.

quick, ingenious, and piercing spirit, acute to invent, subtle and sinewy to discourse, not beneath the reach of any point the highest that human capacity can soar to. Therefore the studies of learning in her deepest sciences have been so ancient and so eminent among us, that writers of good antiquity and ablest judgment have been persuaded that even the school of Pythagoras and the Persian wisdom took beginning from the old philosophy of this island.[7] And that wise and civil Roman, Julius Agricola, who governed once here for Caesar, preferred the natural wits of Britain before the labored studies of the French. Nor is it for nothing that the grave and frugal Transylvanian sends out yearly from as far as the mountainous borders of Russia, and beyond the Hercynian wilderness, not their youth, but their staid men, to learn our language and our theologic arts.[8]

Yet that which is above all this, the favor and the love of heaven we have great argument to think in a peculiar manner propitious and propending[9] towards us. Why else was this nation chosen before any other, that out of her, as out of Zion,[1] should be proclaimed and sounded forth the first tidings and trumpet of Reformation to all Europe? And had it not been the obstinate perverseness of our prelates against the divine and admirable spirit of Wycliffe to suppress him as a schismatic and innovator, perhaps neither the Bohemian Huss and Jerome,[2] no, nor the name of Luther or of Calvin, had been ever known: the glory of reforming all our neighbors had been completely ours. But now, as our obdurate clergy have with violence demeaned the matter, we are become hitherto the latest and the backwardest scholars of whom[3] God offered to have made us the teachers.

Now once again by all concurrence of signs, and by the general instinct of holy and devout men, as they daily and solemnly express their thoughts, God is decreeing to begin some new and great period in his church, even to the reforming of Reformation itself; what does he then but reveal himself to his servants, and as his manner is, first to his Englishmen? I say, as his manner is, first to us, though we mark not the method of his counsels, and are unworthy. Behold now this vast city: a city of refuge,[4] the mansion house of liberty, encompassed and surrounded with his protection; the shop of war hath not there more anvils and hammers waking, to fashion out the plates[5] and instruments of armed justice in defense of beleaguered truth, than there be pens and heads there, sitting by their studious lamps, musing, searching, revolving new notions and ideas wherewith to present, as with their homage and their fealty, the approaching Reformation: others as fast reading, trying all things, assenting to the force of reason and convincement.

What could a man require more from a nation so pliant and so prone to

7. Some speculation existed as to whether the Pythagorean notion of the transmigration of souls might trace back to the Druids, but the notion was mostly denied.
8. The "civil" (cultured, civilized) Agricola's opinion of the British intellect (referred to next) is found in Tacitus's *Life of Agricola*. Transylvania (now Romania) was an independent Protestant country whose citizens sometimes came to England to study. "Hercynian wilderness": Roman name for a forested and mountainous region of Germany.
9. Inclining, favorable. "Argument": reason.
1. Mount Zion, in Jerusalem, the site of the Tem-

ple.
2. John Wycliffe was a 14th-century English reformer and translator of the Bible, whose books were forbidden by Pope Alexander V in 1409. John Huss spread Wycliffe's doctrines on the Continent; he was burned at the stake in 1415, as was (the next year) his follower Jerome of Prague.
3. Of those whom. "Demeaned": conducted, degraded.
4. Numbers 35 instructs the Jews to establish "cities of refuge" where those accused of crimes are protected from "revengers of blood."
5. Plate mail, for armor.

seek after knowledge? What wants there to such a towardly[6] and pregnant soil, but wise and faithful laborers, to make a knowing people, a nation of prophets,[7] of sages, and of worthies? We reckon more than five months yet to harvest; there need not be five weeks; had we but eyes to lift up, the fields are white already.[8] Where there is much desire to learn, there of necessity will be much arguing, much writing, many opinions; for opinion in good men is but knowledge in the making. Under these fantastic terrors of sect and schism we wrong the earnest and zealous thirst after knowledge and understanding which God hath stirred up in this city.

What some lament of, we rather should rejoice at, should rather praise this pious forwardness among men, to reassume the ill-deputed care of their religion into their own hands again. A little generous prudence, a little forbearance of one another, and some grain of charity might win all these diligences to join, and unite into one general and brotherly search after truth; could we but forego this prelatical tradition of crowding free consciences and Christian liberties into canons and precepts of men. I doubt not, if some great and worthy stranger should come among us, wise to discern the mold and temper of a people, and how to govern it, observing the high hopes and aims, the diligent alacrity of our extended thoughts and reasonings in the pursuance of truth and freedom, but that he would cry out as Pyrrhus did, admiring the Roman docility and courage: "If such were my Epirots, I would not despair the greatest design that could be attempted, to make a church or kingdom happy."[9] Yet these are the men cried out against for schismatics and sectaries;[1] as if, while the temple of the Lord was building, some cutting, some squaring the marble, others hewing the cedars, there should be a sort of irrational men, who could not consider there must be many schisms and many dissections[2] made in the quarry and in the timber, ere the house of God can be built. And when every stone is laid artfully together, it cannot be united into a continuity, it can but be contiguous in this world; neither can every piece of the building be of one form; nay rather the perfection consists in this, that out of many moderate varieties and brotherly dissimilitudes that are not vastly disproportional, arises the goodly and the graceful symmetry that commends the whole pile and structure. Let us therefore be more considerate builders, more wise in spiritual architecture, when great reformation is expected. For now the time seems come, wherein Moses the great prophet may sit in heaven rejoicing to see that memorable and glorious wish of his fulfilled, when not only our seventy elders, but all the Lord's people, are become prophets.[3]

* * *

6. Favorable.
7. In Numbers 11.29 Moses reproaches Joshua, who complained of the presence of other prophets: "Enviest thou for my sake? Would God that all the Lord's people were prophets."
8. Milton is paraphrasing Christ's words to his disciples (John 4.35): "Lift up your eyes, and look on the fields: for they are white already to harvest."
9. Though King Pyrrhus of Epirus beat the Roman armies at Heraclea in 280 B.C.E., he was much impressed by their discipline.

1. "Schismatics": those who cut up or divide the church; "sectaries": members of Protestant communions outside the national church.
2. Milton is playing on the literal meaning of "schism," cutting up or dividing.
3. Again alluding to Numbers 11.29, Milton equates the English assembly of clergy to set doctrine and church order (the Westminster Assembly) with the Jewish Sanhedrin of seventy elders.

Methinks I see in my mind a noble and puissant nation rousing herself like a strong man after sleep, and shaking her invincible locks:[4] methinks I see her as an eagle mewing[5] her mighty youth, and kindling her undazzled eyes at the full midday beam; purging and unscaling her long-abused sight at the fountain itself of heavenly radiance; while the whole noise of timorous and flocking birds, with those also that love the twilight, flutter about, amazed at what she means, and in their envious gabble would prognosticate[6] a year of sects and schisms.

What should ye do then, should ye suppress all this flowery crop of knowledge and new light sprung up and yet springing daily in this city? Should ye set an oligarchy of twenty engrossers[7] over it, to bring a famine upon our minds again, when we shall know nothing but what is measured to us by their bushel? Believe it, Lords and Commons, they who counsel ye to such a suppressing do as good as bid ye suppress yourselves; and I will soon show how.[8]

* * *

And now the time in special is by privilege to write and speak what may help to the further discussing of matters in agitation. The temple of Janus with his two controversial faces might now not unsignificantly be set open.[9] And though all the winds of doctrine were let loose to play upon the earth, so Truth be in the field, we do injuriously by licensing and prohibiting to misdoubt her strength. Let her and Falsehood grapple; who ever knew Truth put to the worse in a free and open encounter? Her[1] confuting is the best and surest suppressing. He who hears what praying there is for light and clearer knowledge to be sent down among us would think of other matters to be constituted beyond the discipline of Geneva framed and fabricked already to our hands.[2]

Yet when the new light which we beg for shines in upon us, there be who envy and oppose if it come not first in at their casements. What a collusion is this, whenas we are exhorted by the wise man to use diligence, to seek for wisdom as for hidden treasures early and late,[3] that another order shall enjoin us to know nothing but by statute. When a man hath been laboring the hardest labor in the deep mines of knowledge, hath furnished out his findings in all their equipage, drawn forth his reasons as it were a battle[4] ranged, scattered and defeated all objections in his way, calls out his adversary into the plain, offers him the advantage of wind and sun if he please, only that he may try the matter by dint of argument; for his opponents then to skulk, to lay ambushments, to keep a narrow bridge of licensing where the chal-

4. The allusion is to Samson, whose uncut hair made him invincible, when he frustrated the first three attempts of Delilah and the Philistines to subdue him in sleep (Judges 16.6–14).
5. Molting, when the eagle sheds it feathers and thereby renews its coat; eagles were thought to be able to look directly at the sun.
6. Predict.
7. Engrossers, much hated in the English countryside, bought up great quantities of grain and held it for times of famine, selling it at high prices; Milton equates them with the twenty authorized printers, the stationers.
8. Milton argues that Parliament, by its own liberalizing reforms to date, has created the vigorous

and inquiring minds it now seeks to suppress.
9. Janus, as god of beginnings and endings, had two faces looking in opposite directions; a door dedicated to him in Rome was kept open in time of war, closed in time of peace.
1. I.e., Falsehood's.
2. Milton was already disenchanted with Genevan "Discipline" (Presbyterian church government) and within a year or so would be writing, "New Presbyter is but Old Priest, writ large." "Fabricked": fabricated.
3. Solomon s advice in Proverbs 8.11.
4. Line of battle. Wind and sun (below) were significant advantages in a fight with swords.

lenger should pass, though it be valor enough in soldiership, is but weakness and cowardice in the wars of Truth.

For who knows not that Truth is strong, next to the Almighty? She needs no policies nor stratagems nor licensings to make her victorious—those are the shifts and the defenses that error uses against her power. Give her but room, and do not bind her when she sleeps, for then she speaks not true, as the old Proteus[5] did, who spake oracles only when he was caught and bound, but then rather she turns herself into all shapes except her own, and perhaps tunes her voice according to the time, as Micaiah did before Ahab,[6] until she be adjured into her own likeness.

Yet it is not impossible that she may have more shapes than one. What else is all that rank of things indifferent, wherein Truth may be on this side or on the other without being unlike herself? What but a vain shadow else is the abolition of those ordinances, that handwriting nailed to the cross?[7] what great purchase is this Christian liberty which Paul so often boasts of? His doctrine is that he who eats or eats not, regards a day or regards it not, may do either to the Lord.[8] How many other things might be tolerated in peace and left to conscience, had we but charity, and were it not the chief stronghold of our hypocrisy to be ever judging one another? I fear yet this iron yoke of outward conformity hath left a slavish print upon our necks; the ghost of a linen decency[9] yet haunts us. We stumble and are impatient at the least dividing of one visible congregation from another, though it be not in fundamentals; and through our forwardness to suppress and our backwardness to recover any enthralled piece of truth out of the grip of custom, we care not[1] to keep truth separated from truth, which is the fiercest rent and disunion of all. We do not see that while we still affect by all means a rigid and external formality, we may as soon fall again into a gross conforming stupidity, a stark and dead congealment of "wood and hay and stubble," forced and frozen together, which is more to the sudden degenerating of a church than many sub-dichotomies of petty schisms.

Not that I can think well of every light separation, or that all in a church is to be expected "gold and silver and precious stones."[2] It is not possible for man to sever the wheat from the tares, the good fish from the other fry; that must be the angels' ministry at the end of mortal things.[3] Yet if all cannot be of one mind—as who looks they should be?—this doubtless is more wholesome, more prudent, and more Christian, that many be tolerated rather than all compelled. I mean not tolerated popery and open superstition, which, as it extirpates all religions and civil supremacies, so itself should be extirpate, provided first that all charitable and compassionate means be used to win and regain the weak and the misled; that also which is impious or evil absolutely, either against faith or manners,[4] no law can possibly permit that

---

5. The sea god who could change shape at will, to avoid capture (*Odyssey* 4).

6. Micaiah, a prophet of God, tried for a time to disguise an unpleasant prophecy from King Ahab but then spoke truth when adjured to do so (1 Kings 22.10–28).

7. The locution, from Colossians 2.14, implies that the crucifixion canceled all the rules and penalties of the Mosaic law. Paul's doctrine of Christian liberty is expressed in Galatians 5 and elsewhere.

8. In the Lord's service.

9. The scraps of white linen around the necks and wrists of gentlemen (and white bands around the necks of clergymen) are made emblems of formal piety.

1. Scruple not.

2. The contrast between "wood, hay, stubble" and "gold, silver, precious stones" is from 1 Corinthians 3.12.

3. In Matthew 13.24–30, 36–43, Christ in a parable tells his disciples to let the wheat and tares (weeds) grow up together till harvest time.

4. Morals.

intends not to unlaw itself; but those neighboring differences or rather indifferences are what I speak of, whether in some point of doctrine or of discipline, which though they may be many yet need not interrupt "the unity of spirit," if we could but find among us the "bond of peace."[5]

In the meanwhile, if anyone would write and bring his helpful hand to the slow-moving reformation which we labor under, if truth have spoken to him before others, or but seemed at least to speak, who hath so bejesuited[6] us that we should trouble that man with asking license to do so worthy a deed? And not consider this, that if it come to prohibiting, there is not aught more likely to be prohibited than truth itself; whose first appearance to our eyes bleared and dimmed with prejudice and custom is more unsightly and unplausible than many errors, even as the person is of many a great man slight and contemptible to see to. And what do they tell us vainly of new opinions, when this very opinion of theirs, that none must be heard but whom they like, is the worst and newest opinion of all others, and is the chief cause why sects and schisms do so much abound, and true knowledge is kept at distance from us; besides yet a greater danger which is in it. For when God shakes a kingdom[7] with strong and healthful commotions to a general reforming, it is not untrue that many sectaries and false teachers are then busiest in seducing; but yet more true it is that God then raises to his own work men of rare abilities and more than common industry, not only to look back and revise what hath been taught heretofore, but to gain further and go on some new enlightened steps in the discovery of truth.

* * *

1644

Sonnets
Between 1630 and 1658 Milton wrote twenty-four sonnets. Five in Italian constitute a mini-Petrarchan sequence on a perhaps imaginary Italian lady. The rest, in English, are individual poems on a wide variety of topics and occasions though not on the usual sonnet topics (love, as in the sequences of Sidney, Spenser, and Shakespeare, or religious devotion, as in that of Donne). Milton writes sometimes about personal crises (his blindness, the death of his wife), sometimes about political issues or personages (Cromwell, the persecuting Parliament), sometimes about friends and friendship (Cyriack Skinner, Lady Margaret Ley), sometimes about historical events (a threatened royalist attack on London, the massacre of Protestants in Piedmont); and his tone ranges from Jonsonian urbanity to prophetic denunciation. The form of the sonnets is Petrarchan (see "Poetic Forms and Literary Terminology," in the appendices to this volume), but in the later sonnets especially (e.g., the Blindness and Piedmont sonnets) the sense runs on from line to line, overriding the expected end-stopped lines and the octave/sestet shift. There is some precedent for this in the Italian sonneteer Giovanni Della Casa, but not for the powerful tension Milton creates as meaning and emotion strive within and against the metrical form of the Petrarchan sonnet. Milton's new ways with the sonnet had a profound and acknowledged influence on the Romantic poets, especially Wordsworth and Shelley.

5. The quoted phrases are from Ephesians 4.3.
6. Imposed on us Jesuit ideas (of censorship).
7. Milton alludes to Haggai 2.7: "I will shake all

nations, and the desire of all nations shall come, and I will fill this house with glory, saith the Lord of hosts."

SONNETS

How Soon Hath Time

How soon hath Time, the subtle thief of youth,
   Stol'n on his wing my three and twentieth year!
   My hasting days fly on with full career,
   But my late spring no bud or blossom shew'th.
5 Perhaps my semblance might deceive[1] the truth,
   That I to manhood am arrived so near,
   And inward ripeness doth much less appear,
   That some more timely-happy spirits endu'th.°   *endows*
   Yet be it less or more, or soon or slow,
10   It shall be still in strictest measure even[2]
   To that same lot, however mean or high,
Toward which Time leads me, and the will of Heaven;
   All is, if I have grace to use it so,
   As ever in my great Taskmaster's eye.[3]

1632?   1645

On the New Forcers of Conscience Under the Long Parliament[1]

Because you have thrown off your prelate lord,[2]
   And with stiff vows renounced his liturgy,
   To seize the widowed whore Plurality[3]
   From them whose sin ye envied, not abhorred,
5 Dare ye for this adjure the civil sword[4]
   To force our consciences that Christ set free,
   And ride us with a classic hierarchy[5]
   Taught ye by mere A. S. and Rutherford?[6]
Men whose life, learning, faith, and pure intent
10   Would have been held in high esteem with Paul
   Must now be named and printed heretics

---

1. Misrepresent. "Semblance": appearance.
2. Equal, adequate. "It": Milton's inner growth. "Even / To that same lot": conformed to the appointed destiny.
3. The final lines allow for various readings. "Taskmaster" identifies God with the parable (Matthew 20.1–16) in which a vineyard keeper takes on workers throughout the day, paying the same wages to those hired at the first and at the eleventh hour.
1. The sonnet targets the Presbyterians, whom Milton in *The Reason of Church Government* (p. 1796) and other antiprelatical tracts of 1641–42 had supported against the bishops. Now that they have overthrown the bishops and dominate the Long Parliament, they seek to become the national church, repressing all others. This *sonetto*

cauduto or "tailed sonnet" (an Italian form) has the usual fourteen lines followed by two "tails" of three lines each.
2. Bishops and the ecclesiastical church structure.
3. The practice of holding several benefices at once; she is a "widowed whore" because her earlier lovers, the Anglican clergy, can no longer possess her.
4. State authority.
5. The Presbyterian church order comprised of synods and classes as governing boards and disciplinary courts.
6. Adam Stuart and Samuel Rutherford, Scottish Presbyterian pamphleteers who urged the establishment of an English national Presbyterian church on the Scottish model.

By shallow Edwards and Scotch what-d'ye-call:[7]
   But we do hope to find out all your tricks,
   Your plots and packing° worse than those of Trent,[8]   *fraudulent dealings*
15   That so the Parliament[9]
May with their wholesome and preventive shears
Clip your phylacteries,[1] though balk your ears,[2]
             And succor our just fears
When they shall read this clearly in your charge:
20 New *presbyter* is but old *priest* writ large.[3]

ca. 1646   1673

To the Lord General Cromwell, May 1652[1]

Cromwell, our chief of men, who through a cloud
   Not of war only, but detractions[2] rude,
   Guided by faith and matchless fortitude
   To peace and truth[3] thy glorious way hast ploughed,
5 And on the neck of crownèd Fortune proud
   Hast reared God's trophies,[4] and his work pursued,
   While Darwen stream with blood of Scots imbrued[5]
   And Dunbar field resounds thy praises loud,
And Worcester's laureate wreath;[6] yet much remains
10   To conquer still; peace hath her victories
   No less renowned than war; new foes arise,
Threatening to bind our souls with secular chains:[7]
   Help us to save free conscience from the paw
   Of hireling wolves[8] whose gospel is their maw.°   *belly*

1652   1694

7. Thomas Edwards analyzed hundreds of so-called "heresies" in a book picturesquely titled *Gangraena* (1645, 1646). It even identifies Milton as the founder of a sect of Divorcers, promoting "divorce at pleasure." "Scotch what-d'ye-call" may refer to another Scots cleric, Robert Baillie, or may simply be a sneer at the unpronounceability of Scottish names.
8. The Council of Trent, held by the Roman Church to deal with the Protestant Reformation, was notorious as a scene of political jockeying.
9. In the previous few months Independents and more secular-minded republicans had gained some strength in the Parliament, so Milton could hope they might weigh in against Presbyterian repression.
1. Little scrolls containing texts from the Pentateuch, worn on the forehead by orthodox Jews; Milton takes them as a symbol of self-righteous ostentation.
2. "Balk": spare. Mutilation by cutting off the ears was a punishment formerly suffered by several Presbyterian leaders, as Milton hereby reminds them. Milton changed the rather cruel manuscript version of this line—"Crop ye as close as marginal P———'s ears"—alluding to the ultraprolific pamphleteer William Prynne, who stuffed his margins with citations, and who had his ears cropped twice.
3. "Priest" is, etymologically, a contracted form of "Presbyter."

1. The sonnet appeals to Cromwell, a longtime supporter of religious toleration but also of some kind of loosely defined national church, to oppose recent proposals by Independents to set up a national church with a paid clergy and some limits to toleration. This is the only Milton sonnet to end with an epigrammatic couplet. It could not be published in the 1673 *Poems* of Milton, because of the subject.
2. Cromwell was a target of slander and vituperation from royalists and from extreme radicals.
3. The words "Truth and Peace" were on a coin issued by Parliament to honor Cromwell's victories over the Scots at Preston (1648), Dunbar (1650), and Worcester (1651).
4. Alluding to the ancient Greek custom of erecting trophies of victory on the battlefield.
5. Stained with blood. The river Darwen runs through Preston, site of a major victory by Cromwell over the Scots.
6. Cromwell described his victory at Worcester as his "crowning mercy."
7. Alluding to the new proposals that Parliament, the secular power, repress heresies and blasphemy.
8. Milton fiercely opposed a paid clergy, believing they should support themselves or be supported by their congregations.

When I Consider How My Light Is Spent[1]

When I consider how my light is spent,°   *extinguished*
Ere half my days,[2] in this dark world and wide,
And that one talent which is death to hide[3]
Lodged with me useless, though my soul more bent
5 To serve therewith my Maker, and present
My true account, lest he returning chide;
"Doth God exact day-labor, light denied?"[4]
I fondly° ask; but Patience to prevent°   *foolishly / forestall*
That murmur, soon replies, "God doth not need
10 Either man's work or his own gifts; who best
Bear his mild yoke, they serve him best. His state°   *splendor*
Is kingly.[5] Thousands at his bidding speed
And post o'er land and ocean without rest:
They also serve who only stand and wait."

1652?   1673

On the Late Massacre in Piedmont[1]

Avenge,[2] O Lord, thy slaughtered saints, whose bones
Lie scattered on the Alpine mountains cold;
Even them who kept thy truth so pure of old
When all our fathers worshiped stocks and stones,[3]
5 Forget not: in thy book[4] record their groans
Who were thy sheep and in their ancient fold
Slain by the bloody Piemontese that rolled
Mother with infant down the rocks. Their moans
The vales redoubled to the hills, and they

1. Apparently written soon after Milton lost his sight entirely in 1652.
2. Milton was forty-three in 1652; he is obviously not thinking of the biblical lifespan of seventy, but perhaps of that of his father, who died at eighty-four.
3. In the parable of the talents (Matthew 25.14–30), a crucial text for Puritans, the servants who put their master's money ("talents") to earn interest for him were praised while the servant who buried the single talent he was given was deprived of it and cast into outer darkness. Milton puns on "literary talent." "Useless" (line 4) carries a pun on usury, the return expected by the Master.
4. Milton also alludes here to the parable of the vineyard keeper (see *How Soon Hath Time*, n. 3). Also to John 9.4, spoken by Jesus before curing a blind man: "I must work the works of him that sent me, while it is day: the night cometh, when no man can work."
5. The changed metaphor for God—from master who needs to profit from his workers to King—allows the inference that those who "stand and wait" may be placed nearest the throne.
1. The Waldensians (or Vaudois) were a proto-Protestant sect dating to the 12th century, who lived in the valleys of northern Italy (the Piedmont)

and southern France; Protestants considered them a remnant retaining Apostolic purity, free of Catholic superstitions and graven images ("stocks and stones"). The treaty that had allowed them freedom of worship was bypassed in 1655 when the armies of the Catholic duke of Savoy conducted a massacre, razing villages, committing unspeakable atrocities, and hurling women and children from the mountaintops. Protestant Europe was outraged, and in his capacity as Cromwell's Latin secretary Milton translated and wrote several letters about the episode. The sonnet incorporates details from such letters and the contemporary newsbooks. Here Milton transforms the sonnet into a prophetic denunciation.
2. Cf. Revelation 6.9–10: "The souls of them that were slain for the word of God . . . cried with a loud voice, saying 'How long, O Lord, holy and true, dost thou not judge and avenge our blood?' "
3. Pagan gods of wood and stone, but with allusion to Roman Catholic "idols."
4. Cf. Revelation 20.12: "The dead were judged out of those things which were written in the books, according to their works." "Sheep": echoes Romans 8.36: "We are accounted as sheep for the slaughter."

10   To heaven. Their martyred blood and ashes sow
         O'er all th' Italian fields, where still doth sway
         The triple tyrant:[5] that from these may grow
         A hundredfold, who having learnt thy way
         Early may fly the Babylonian woe.[6]

1655   1673

Methought I Saw My Late Espousèd Saint[1]

         Methought I saw my late espousèd saint
             Brought to me like Alcestis[2] from the grave,
             Whom Jove's great son to her glad husband gave,
             Rescued from death by force though pale and faint.
5   Mine, as whom[3] washed from spot of childbed taint,
             Purification in the old law did save,[4]
             And such, as yet once more I trust to have
             Full sight of her in heaven without restraint,
         Came vested all in white, pure as her mind.
10   Her face was veiled, yet to my fancied sight[5]
             Love, sweetness, goodness, in her person shined
         So clear, as in no face with more delight.
             But O, as to embrace me she inclined,
             I waked, she fled, and day brought back my night.

1658   1673

Paradise Lost   The setting of Milton's great epic encompasses Heaven, Hell, primordial Chaos, and the planet Earth. It features battles among immortal spirits, voyages through space, and lakes of fire. Yet its protagonists are a married couple living in a garden, and its climax consists in the eating of a piece of fruit. *Paradise Lost* is ultimately about the human condition, the Fall that caused "all our woe," and the promise and means of restoration. It is also about knowing and choosing, about free will. In the opening passages of Books 1, 3, 7, and 9, Milton highlights the choices and difficulties he faced in creating his poem. His central characters—Satan, Beelzebub, Abdiel, Adam, and Eve—are confronted with hard choices under the pressure of powerful desires and sometimes devious temptations. Milton's readers, too, are continually challenged to choose and to reconsider their most basic assumptions

5. The pope, wearing his tiara with three crowns. The passage alludes to Tertullian's maxim that "the blood of the martyrs is the seed of the church"; also to the parable of the sower (Matthew 13.3), some of whose seed brought forth fruit "an hundredfold"; and also to Cadmus, who sowed dragon's teeth that sprang forth armed men.
6. Protestants often identified the Roman Church with the whore of Babylon (Revelation 17–18).
1. There is some critical debate as to whether this poem refers to Milton's first wife, Mary Powell, who died in May 1652 three days after giving birth to her third daughter, or his second wife, Katherine Woodcock, who died in February 1658, after giving birth (in October 1657) to a daughter. The text

can support either, but the latter seems more likely. The sonnet is couched as a dream vision.
2. In Euripedes' *Alcestis*, Alcestis, wife of Admetus, is rescued from the underworld by Hercules ("Jove's great son") and restored, veiled, to Admetus; he is overjoyed when he lifts the veil, but she must remain silent until she is ritually cleansed.
3. As one whom.
4. The Mosaic Law (Leviticus 12.4–8) prescribed periods for the purification of women after childbirth (eighty days for a daughter).
5. She is veiled like Alcestes and Milton's sight of her is only "fancied"; he never saw the face of his second wife, Katherine.

about freedom, heroism, work, pleasure, language, nature, and love. The great themes of *Paradise Lost* are intimately linked to the political questions at stake in the English Revolution and Restoration, but the connection is by no means simple or straightforward. This is a poem in which Satan leads a revolution against an absolute monarch and in which questions of tyranny, servitude, and liberty are debated in a Parliament in Hell. Milton's readers are hereby challenged to rethink these topics and, like Abdiel debating with Satan in Books 5 and 6, to make crucial distinctions.

In Milton's time, the conventions of epic poetry comprised a familiar recipe. The action should begin *in medias res* (in the middle of things), following the poet's statement of his theme and invocation of his Muse. The reader could expect grand battles and love affairs, supernatural intervention, a descent into the underworld, catalogs of warriors, and epic similes. Milton had absorbed the epic tradition in its entirety, and his poem abounds with echoes of Homer and Virgil, the fifteenth-century Italians Tasso and Ariosto, and the English Spenser. But in *Paradise Lost* he at once heightens epic conventions and values and utterly transforms them. This is the epic to end all epics. Milton gives us the first and greatest of all wars (between God and Satan) and the first and greatest of love affairs (between Adam and Eve). His theme is the destiny of the entire human race, caught up in the temptation and Fall of our first "grand parents."

Milton challenges his readers in *Paradise Lost*, at once fulfilling and defying all of our expectations. Nothing in the epic tradition or in biblical interpretation can prepare us for the Satan who hurtles into view in Book 1, with his awesome energy and defiance, incredible fortitude, and, above all, magnificent rhetoric. For some readers, including Blake and Shelley, Satan has been the true hero of the poem. But Milton is engaged in a radical re-evaluation of epic values, and Satan's version of heroism must be contrasted with those of the loyal Abdiel and the Son of God. Moreover, the poem's truly epic action takes place not on the battlefield but in the moral and domestic arena. Milton's Adam and Eve are not conventional epic heroes, but neither are they the conventional Adam and Eve. Their state of innocence is not childlike, tranquil, and free of sexual desire. Instead, the first couple enjoy sex, experience tension and passion, make mistakes of judgment, and grow in knowledge. Their task is to prune what is unruly in their own natures as they prune the vegetation in their garden, for both have the capacity to grow wild. Their relationship exhibits gender hierarchy, but Milton's early readers may have been surprised by the fullness and complexity of Eve's character and the centrality of her role, not only in the Fall but in the promised restoration.

We expect in epics a grand style, and Milton's style engulfs us from the outset with its energy and power, as those rushing, enjambed, blank-verse lines propel us along with only a few pauses for line endings or grammar (there is only one fullstop in the first twenty-six lines). The elevated diction and complex syntax, the sonorities and patternings, make a magnificent music. But that music is an entire orchestra of tones, including the high political rhetoric of Satan in Books 1 and 2, the evocative sensuousness of the descriptions of Eden, the delicacy of Eve's love lyric to Adam in Book 4, the relatively plain speech of God in Book 3, and the speech rhythms of Adam and Eve's marital quarrel in Book 9. This majestic achievement depends on the poet's rejection of heroic couplets, the norm for epic and tragedy in the Restoration, vigorously defended by Dryden, but denounced by Milton in his note on "The Verse." The choice of verse form was, like so many other things in Milton's life, in part a question of politics. Milton's terms associate the "troublesome and modern bondage of rhyming" with Restoration monarchy and repression of dissidents and present his use of unrhymed blank verse as a recovery of "ancient liberty."

The first edition (1667) presented *Paradise Lost* in ten books; the second (1674) recast it into twelve books after the Virgilian model, splitting the original Books 7 and 10. We present the twelve-book epic in its entirety, to allow readers to experience the impact of the whole.

PARADISE LOST

SECOND EDITION (1674)

The Verse

The measure is English heroic verse without rhyme, as that of Homer in Greek and of Virgil in Latin; rhyme being no necessary adjunct or true ornament of poem or good verse, in longer works especially, but the invention of a barbarous age, to set off wretched matter[1] and lame meter; graced indeed since by the use of some famous modern poets,[2] carried away by custom, but much to their own vexation, hindrance, and constraint to express many things otherwise, and for the most part worse than else they would have expressed them. Not without cause therefore some both Italian[3] and Spanish poets of prime note have rejected rhyme both in longer and shorter works, as have also long since our best English tragedies, as a thing of itself, to all judicious ears, trivial and of no true musical delight; which consists only in apt numbers,[4] fit quantity of syllables, and the sense variously drawn out from one verse into another, not in the jingling sound of like endings, a fault avoided by the learned ancients both in poetry and all good oratory. This neglect then of rhyme so little is to be taken for a defect, though it may seem so perhaps to vulgar readers, that it rather is to be esteemed an example set, the first in English, of ancient liberty recovered to heroic poem from the troublesome and modern bondage of rhyming.

Book 1

The Argument[1]

This first book proposes, first in brief, the whole subject, man's disobedience, and the loss thereupon of Paradise wherein he was placed: then touches the prime cause of his fall, the Serpent, or rather Satan in the Serpent; who revolting from God, and drawing to his side many legions of angels, was by the command of God driven out of Heaven with all his crew into the great deep. Which action passed over, the poem hastes into the midst of things,[2] presenting Satan with his angels now fallen into Hell, described here, not in the center[3] (for Heaven and Earth may be supposed as yet not made, certainly not yet accursed) but in a place of utter darkness, fitliest called Chaos: here Satan with his angels lying on the burning lake, thunderstruck and astonished, after a certain space recovers, as from confusion, calls up him who next in order and dignity lay by him; they confer of their miserable fall. Satan awakens all his legions, who lay till then in the same manner confounded; they rise, their numbers, array of battle, their chief leaders named, according to the idols known afterwards in Canaan and the

---

1. Perhaps the bawdy content of the Latin songs composed by Goliardic poets of the Middle Ages; they learned rhyme from medieval hymns.
2. Notably, Dryden. See his *Essay of Dramatic Poesy*, p. 2114.
3. Trissino and Tasso.
4. Appropriate rhythm.
1. *Paradise Lost* appeared originally without any

sort of prose aid to the reader, but the printer asked Milton for some "Arguments," or summary explanations of the action in the various books, and these were prefixed to later issues of the poem. We reprint the "Argument" for the first book.
2. According to Horace, the epic poet should begin, "*in medias res.*"
3. I.e., of the earth.

countries adjoining. To these Satan directs his speech, comforts them with hope yet of regaining Heaven, but tells them lastly of a new world and new kind of creature to be created, according to an ancient prophecy or report in Heaven; for that angels were long before this visible creation, was the opinion of many ancient Fathers.[4] To find out the truth of this prophecy, and what to determine[5] thereon he refers to a full council. What his associates thence attempt. Pandemonium the palace of Satan rises, suddenly built out of the deep: the infernal peers there sit in council.

Of man's first disobedience, and the fruit[1]
Of that forbidden tree, whose mortal° taste
Brought death into the world, and all our woe,
With loss of Eden, till one greater Man[2]
Restore us, and regain the blissful seat,
Sing Heav'nly Muse,[3] that on the secret top
Of Oreb, or of Sinai, didst inspire
That shepherd, who first taught the chosen seed,
In the beginning how the heav'ns and earth
10 Rose out of Chaos: or if Sion hill[4]
Delight thee more, and Siloa's brook that flowed
Fast by the oracle of God; I thence
Invoke thy aid to my advent'rous song,
That with no middle flight intends to soar
15 Above th' Aonian mount,[5] while it pursues
Things unattempted yet in prose or rhyme.[6]
And chiefly thou O Spirit,[7] that dost prefer
Before all temples th' upright heart and pure,
Instruct me, for thou know'st; thou from the first
20 Wast present, and with mighty wings outspread
Dove-like sat'st brooding[8] on the vast abyss
And mad'st it pregnant: what in me is dark
Illumine, what is low raise and support;
That to the height of this great argument°   subject, theme
25 I may assert Eternal Providence,
And justify° the ways of God to men.   show the justice of
    Say first, for Heav'n hides nothing from thy view
Nor the deep tract of Hell, say first what cause[9]
Moved our grand parents in that happy state,
30 Favored of Heav'n so highly, to fall off

4. Church Fathers, the Christian writers of the first centuries.
5. I.e., what action to take.
1. Eve's apple, and all the consequences of eating it. This first Proem (lines 1–26) combines the epic statement of theme and invocation.
2. Christ, the second Adam.
3. In Greek mythology, Urania, Muse of astronomy; here, however, by the references to Oreb and Sinai, identified with the Muse who inspired Moses ("that shepherd") to write Genesis and the other four books of the Pentateuch for the instruction of the Jews ("the chosen seed").
4. Mount Zion: the site of Solomon's Temple. "Siloa's Brook": a spring near the Temple where Christ cured a blind man.
5. Helicon, home of the classical Muses. Milton

will attempt to surpass Homer and Virgil.
6. Paradoxically, Milton vaunts his originality in a translated line from Ariosto's Orlando Furioso 1.2. The allusion also challenges the romantic epic in Ariosto's tradition.
7. An impulse or voice or power of God.
8. A composite of phrases and ideas from Genesis 1.2 ("And the earth was without form, and void, and darkness was upon the face of the deep. And the Spirit of God moved upon the face of the waters"). Only a small number of Milton's many allusions to the Bible (in many versions) can be indicated in the notes. Milton's brooding dove image comes from the Latin (Tremellius) Bible version, "incubabat."
9. An opening question like this is an epic convention.

From their Creator, and transgress his will
For° one restraint, lords of the world besides?°   *because of / otherwise*
Who first seduced them to that foul revolt?
Th' infernal Serpent; he it was, whose guile
35   Stirred up with envy and revenge, deceived
The mother of mankind, what time° his pride   *when*
Had cast him out from Heav'n, with all his host
Of rebel angels, by whose aid aspiring
To set himself in glory above his peers,°   *equals*
40   He trusted to have equaled the Most High,
If he opposed; and with ambitious aim
Against the throne and monarchy of God
Raised impious war in Heav'n and battle proud
With vain attempt. Him the Almighty Power
45   Hurled headlong flaming from th' ethereal sky
With hideous ruin and combustion down
To bottomless perdition, there to dwell
In adamantine[1] chains and penal fire,
Who durst defy th' Omnipotent to arms.
50   Nine times the space[2] that measures day and night
To mortal men, he with his horrid crew
Lay vanquished, rolling in the fiery gulf
Confounded though immortal: but his doom
Reserved him to more wrath; for now the thought
55   Both of lost happiness and lasting pain
Torments him; round he throws his baleful° eyes   *malignant*
That witnessed huge affliction and dismay
Mixed with obdúrate pride and steadfast hate:
At once as far as angels ken° he views   *range of sight*
60   The dismal situation waste and wild,
A dungeon horrible, on all sides round
As one great furnace flamed, yet from those flames
No light,[3] but rather darkness visible
Served only to discover sights of woe,
65   Regions of sorrow, doleful shades, where peace
And rest can never dwell, hope never comes
That comes to all;[4] but torture without end
Still urges,° and a fiery deluge, fed   *always provokes*
With ever-burning sulphur unconsumed:
70   Such place Eternal Justice had prepared
For those rebellious, here their prison ordained
In utter darkness, and their portion set
As far removed from God and light of Heav'n
As from the center thrice to th' utmost pole.[5]
75   O how unlike the place from whence they fell!

1. A mythical substance of great hardness.
2. Extent of time, linear distances.
3. Omitting the verb conveys abruptly the paradox, fire without light.
4. The phrase alludes to Dante ("All hope abandon, ye who enter here").
5. Milton makes use of various images of the cosmos in *Paradise Lost*: (1) The earth is the center of the (Ptolemaic) cosmos of ten concentric spheres; (2) The earth and the whole cosmos are an appendage hanging from Heaven by a golden chain; (3) The cosmos seems Copernican from the angels' perspective (see Book 8). Here, the fall from Heaven to Hell is described as thrice as far as the distance from the center (earth) to the outermost sphere.

There the companions of his fall, o'erwhelmed
With floods and whirlwinds of tempestuous fire,
He soon discerns, and welt'ring° by his side   rolling in the waves
One next himself in power, and next in crime,
80 Long after known in Palestine, and named
Beëlzebub,[6] To whom th' Arch-Enemy,
And thence in Heav'n called Satan,[7] with bold words
Breaking the horrid silence thus began.
  "If thou beest he; but O how fall'n![8] how changed
85 From him, who in the happy realms of light
Clothed with transcendent brightness didst outshine
Myriads though bright: if he whom mutual league,
United thoughts and counsels, equal hope
And hazard in the glorious enterprise,
90 Joined with me once, now misery hath joined
In equal ruin: into what pit thou seest
From what height fall'n, so much the stronger proved
He with his thunder:° and till then who knew   thunderbolt
The force of those dire arms? Yet not for those,
95 Nor what the potent victor in his rage
Can else inflict, do I repent or change,
Though changed in outward luster, that fixed mind
And high disdain, from sense of injured merit,
That with the mightiest raised me to contend,
100 And to the fierce contention brought along
Innumerable force of Spirits armed
That durst dislike his reign, and me preferring,
His utmost power with adverse power opposed
In dubious° battle on the plains of Heav'n,   of uncertain outcome
105 And shook his throne. What though the field be lost?
All is not lost; the unconquerable will,
And study° of revenge, immortal hate,   intense consideration
And courage never to submit or yield:
And what is else not to be overcome?[9]
110 That glory never shall his wrath or might
Extort from me. To bow and sue for grace
With suppliant knee, and deify his power
Who from the terror of this arm so late
Doubted° his empire, that were low indeed,   feared for
115 That were an ignominy and shame beneath
This downfall; since by fate the strength of gods[1]
And this empyreal substance cannot fail,°   cease to exist
Since through experience of this great event
In arms not worse, in foresight much advanced,
120 We may with more successful hope resolve

6. A Phoenician deity, or Baal (the name means
"Lord of Flies"). He is called the prince of devils
in Matthew 12.24. As with the other fallen angels,
his angelic name has been obliterated, and he is
now called by the name he will bear as a pagan
deity. That literary strategy evokes all the evil associations attaching to those names in human history.
7. In Hebrew the name means "adversary."

8. Alludes to Isaiah 14.12: "How art thou fallen
from heaven, O Lucifer, Son of the morning."
9. I.e., what else does it mean not to be overcome?
1. A term commonly used in the poem for angels.
But to Satan and his followers it means more, as
Satan claims the position of a god, subject to fate
but nothing else. Their substance is "empyreal" (of
the empyrean).

To wage by force or guile eternal war
Irreconcilable, to our grand foe,
Who now triúmphs, and in th' excess of joy
Sole reigning holds the tyranny of Heav'n."
125   So spake th' apostate angel, though in pain,
Vaunting aloud, but racked with deep despair:
And him thus answered soon his bold compeer.°   *comrade, equal*
   "O Prince, O Chief of many thronéd Powers,
That led th' embattled Seraphim² to war
130 Under thy conduct, and in dreadful deeds
Fearless, endangered Heav'ns perpetual King;
And put to proof his high supremacy,
Whether upheld by strength, or chance, or fate;
Too well I see and rue the dire event,°   *outcome*
135 That with sad overthrow and foul defeat
Hath lost us Heav'n, and all this mighty host
In horrible destruction laid thus low,
As far as gods and heav'nly essences
Can perish: for the mind and spirit remains
140 Invincible, and vigor soon returns,
Though all our glory extinct, and happy state
Here swallowed up in endless misery.
But what if he our conqueror (whom I now
Of force° believe almighty, since no less   *necessarily*
145 Than such could have o'erpow'red such force as ours)
Have left us this our spirit and strength entire
Strongly to suffer and support our pains,
That we may so suffice° his vengeful ire,   *satisfy*
Or do him mightier service as his thralls
150 By right of war, whate'er his business be
Here in the heart of Hell to work in fire,
Or do his errands in the gloomy deep;
What can it then avail though yet we feel
Strength undiminished, or eternal being
155 To undergo eternal punishment?"
Whereto with speedy words th' Arch-Fiend replied.
   "Fall'n Cherub, to be weak is miserable
Doing or suffering: but of this be sure,
To do aught good never will be our task,
160 But ever to do ill our sole delight,
As being the contrary to his high will
Whom we resist. If then his providence
Out of our evil seek to bring forth good,
Our labor must be to pervert that end,
165 And out of good still to find means of evil;
Which ofttimes may succeed, so as perhaps
Shall grieve him, if I fail° not, and disturb   *err*
His inmost counsels from their destined aim.
But see the angry victor hath recalled

[Handwritten margin note lines 124–133: "he is saying that God is in heaven boasting — to go back to heaven would be cowardly, unforgiving—unchristian"]

[Handwritten margin note lines 138–146: "god is claiming that they don't need heaven if they still have their spirit"]

[Handwritten margin note lines 157–164: "dedicating themselves to implacating evil. the best bad guys they can be"]

2. According to tradition, there were nine orders of angels, arranged hierarchically—seraphim, cherubim, thrones, dominions, virtues, powers, principalities, archangels, and angels. The poem makes use of some of these titles, but does not keep this hierarchy.

170 His ministers of vengeance and pursuit
    Back to the gates of Heav'n: the sulphurous hail
    Shot after us in storm, o'erblown hath laid°   *calmed*
    The fiery surge, that from the precipice
    Of Heav'n received us falling, and the thunder,
175 Winged with red lightning and impetuous rage,
    Perhaps hath spent his shafts, and ceases now
    To bellow through the vast and boundless deep.
    Let us not slip° th' occasion, whether scorn,   *let slip*
    Or satiate fury yield it from our foe.
180 Seest thou yon dreary plain, forlorn and wild,
    The seat of desolation, void of light,
    Save what the glimmering of these livid° flames   *bluish*
    Casts pale and dreadful? Thither let us tend
    From off the tossing of these fiery waves,
185 There rest, if any rest can harbor there,
    And reassembling our afflicted powers,°   *armies*
    Consult how we may henceforth most offend°   *harm, vex*
    Our enemy, our own loss how repair,
    How overcome this dire calamity,
190 What reinforcement we may gain from hope,
    If not what resolution from despair."[3]
      Thus Satan talking to his nearest mate
    With head uplift above the wave, and eyes
    That sparkling blazed, his other parts besides
195 Prone on the flood, extended long and large
    Lay floating many a rood,[4] in bulk as huge
    As whom° the fables name of monstrous size,   *as those whom*
    Titanian, or Earth-born, that warred on Jove,
    Briareos or Typhon,[5] whom the den
200 By ancient Tarsus held, or that sea-beast
    Leviathan,[6] which God of all his works
    Created hugest that swim th' ocean stream:
    Him haply slumb'ring on the Norway foam
    The pilot of some small night-foundered° skiff,   *overcome by night*
205 Deeming some island, oft, as seamen tell,[7]
    With fixèd anchor in his scaly rind
    Moors by his side under the lee,° while night   *out of the wind*
    Invests° the sea, and wishèd morn delays: *covers*
    So stretched out huge in length the Arch-Fiend lay
210 Chained on the burning lake, nor ever thence
    Had ris'n or heaved his head, but that the will
    And high permission of all-ruling Heaven
    Left him at large to his own dark designs,

---

3. Five of the last nine lines of Satan's speech rhyme.
4. An old unit of measure, between six and eight yards.
5. Both the Titans, led by Briareos (said to have had a hundred hands), and the earth-born Giants, represented by Typhon (who lived in Cilicea near Tarsus and was said to have had a hundred heads), fought with Jove. They were punished by being thrown into the underworld. Christian mythogra-phers found in these stories an analogy to Satan's revolt and punishment.
6. The whale, often identified with the great sea-monster and enemy of the Lord in Isaiah 17.1 and the crocodilelike dragon of Job 41. Both were also identified with Satan.
7. The story of the deceived sailor and the illusory island was a commonplace, but the reference to Norway suggests a 16th-century version by Olaus Magnus, a Swedish historian.

That with reiterated crimes he might
215 Heap on himself damnation, while he sought
Evil to others, and enraged might see
How all his malice served but to bring forth
Infinite goodness, grace and mercy shown
On man by him seduced, but on himself
220 Treble confusion, wrath and vengeance poured.
Forthwith upright he rears from off the pool
His mighty stature; on each hand the flames
Driv'n backward slope their pointing spires,° and rolled   *points of flames*
In billows, leave i' th' midst a horrid° vale.   *dreadful, bristling*
225 Then with expanded wings he steers his flight
Aloft, incumbent on° the dusky air   *resting on*
That felt unusual weight, till on dry land
He lights,° if it were land that ever burned   *alights*
With solid, as the lake with liquid fire,
230 And such appeared in hue; as when the force
Of subterranean wind transports a hill
Torn from Pelorus, or the shattered side
Of thund'ring Etna,[8] whose combustible
And fueled entrails thence conceiving fire,
235 Sublimed° with mineral fury, aid the winds,   *vaporized*
And leave a singèd bottom all involved°   *enveloped*
With stench and smoke: such resting found the sole
Of unblest feet. Him followed his next mate,
Both glorying to have scaped the Stygian° flood   *Styxlike, hellish*
240 As gods, and by their own recovered strength,
Not by the sufferance° of supernal power.   *permission*
    "Is this the region, this the soil, the clime,"
Said then the lost Archangel, "this the seat°   *estate*
That we must change for Heav'n, this mournful gloom
245 For that celestial light? Be it so, since he
Who now is sovran can dispose and bid
What shall be right: farthest from him is best
Whom reason hath equaled, force hath made supreme
Above his equals. Farewell happy fields
250 Where joy for ever dwells: Hail horrors, hail
Infernal world, and thou profoundest Hell
Receive thy new possessor: one who brings
A mind not to be changed by place or time.
The mind is its own place, and in itself
255 Can make a Heav'n of Hell, a Hell of Heav'n.[9]
What matter where, if I be still the same,
And what I should be, all but less than° he   *barely less than*
Whom thunder hath made greater? Here at least
We shall be free; th' Almighty hath not built
260 Here for his envy,[1] will not drive us hence:
Here we may reign secure, and in my choice
To reign is worth ambition though in Hell:

8. Pelorus and Etna are volcanic mountains in
Siciy.

9. Compare Satan's soliloquy, 4.33–113.
1. I.e., because he desires this place.

Better to reign in Hell, than serve in Heav'n.[2]
But wherefore let we then our faithful friends,
265 Th' associates and copartners of our loss
Lie thus astonished° on th' oblivious pool,[3]   stunned
And call them not to share with us their part
In this unhappy mansion, or once more
With rallied arms to try what may be yet
270 Regained in Heav'n, or what more lost in Hell?"
       So Satan spake, and him Beëlzebub
Thus answered. "Leader of those armies bright,
Which but th' Omnipotent none could have foiled,
If once they hear that voice, their liveliest pledge
275 Of hope in fears and dangers, heard so oft
In worst extremes, and on the perilous edge°   front lines
Of battle when it raged, in all assaults
Their surest signal, they will soon resume
New courage and revive, though now they lie
280 Groveling and prostrate on yon lake of fire,
As we erewhile, astounded and amazed,
No wonder, fall'n such a pernicious highth."
       He scarce had ceased when the superior Fiend
Was moving toward the shore; his ponderous shield
285 Ethereal temper,[4] massy, large and round,
Behind him cast; the broad circumference
Hung on his shoulders like the moon, whose orb
Through optic glass the Tuscan artists views[5]
At evening from the top of Fesole,
290 Or in Valdarno, to descry new lands,
Rivers or mountains in her spotty globe.
His spear, to equal which the tallest pine
Hewn on Norwegian hills, to be the mast
Of some great ammiral,° were but a wand,   admiral's ship
295 He walked with to support uneasy steps
Over the burning marl,° not like those steps   soil
On heaven's azure; and the torrid clime
Smote on him sore besides, vaulted with fire;
Nathless° he so endured, till on the beach   nevertheless
300 Of that inflamed° sea, he stood and called   flaming
His legions, angel forms, who lay entranced
Thick as autumnal leaves that strow the brooks
In Vallombrosa,[6] where th' Etrurian shades
High overarched embow'r;° or scattered sedge°   form bowers/seaweed
305 Afloat, when with fierce winds Orion[7] armed
Hath vexed the Red Sea coast, whose waves o'erthrew

2. An ironic echo of *Odyssey* 11.489–91, where
the shade of Achilles tells Odysseus that it is better
to be a farmhand on earth than king among the
dead.
3. The epithet "oblivious" is transferred from the
fallen angels to the pool in which they have fallen.
4. I.e., tempered in celestial fire.
5. Galileo, who looked through a telescope ("optic
glass") from the hill town of Fiesole outside Florence, in the valley of the Arno river ("Valdarno,"

val d'Arno). In 1610 he published a book describing the mountains on the moon.
6. The name means "shady valley," a region high
in the Apennines, about twenty miles from Florence, in Tuscany ("Etruria"). Similes comparing
the numberless dead to falling leaves are frequent
in epic (e.g., *Aeneid* 6.309–10).
7. Orion is a constellation whose rising near sunset in late summer and autumn was associated with
storms in the Red Sea.

Busiris[8] and his Memphian chivalry,
While with perfidious hatred they pursued
The sojourners of Goshen, who beheld
310 From the safe shore their floating carcasses
And broken chariot wheels; so thick bestrown
Abject and lost lay these, covering the flood,
Under amazement of their hideous change.
He called so loud, that all the hollow deep
315 Of Hell resounded. "Princes, Potentates,
Warriors, the flow'r of heav'n, once yours, now lost,
If such astonishment as this can seize
Eternal Spirits: or have ye chos'n this place
After the toil of battle to repose
320 Your wearied virtue,° for the ease you find   strength, valor
To slumber here, as in the vales of Heav'n?
Or in this abject posture have ye sworn
To adore the conqueror? who now beholds
Cherub and Seraph rolling in the flood
325 With scattered arms and ensigns,° till anon   battle flags
His swift pursuers from Heav'n gates discern
Th' advantage, and descending tread us down
Thus drooping, or with linkèd thunderbolts
Transfix us to the bottom of this gulf.
330 Awake, arise, or be for ever fall'n."
      They heard, and were abashed, and up they sprung
Upon the wing, as when men wont to watch
On duty, sleeping found by whom they dread,
Rouse and bestir themselves ere well awake.
335 Nor did they not perceive° the evil plight
In which they were, or the fierce pains not feel;
Yet to their general's voice they soon obeyed
Innumerable. As when the potent rod
Of Amram's son[1] in Egypt's evil day
340 Waved round the coast, up called a pitchy cloud
Of locusts, warping° on the eastern wind,
That o'er the realm of impious Pharaoh hung
Like night, and darkened all the land of Nile:
So numberless were those bad angels seen
345 Hovering on wing under the cope° of Hell
'Twixt upper, nether, and surrounding fires;
Till, as a signal giv'n, th' uplifted spear
Of their great Sultan[2] waving to direct
Their course, in even balance down they light
350 On the firm brimstone, and fill all the plain;
A multitude, like which the populous North
Poured never from her frozen loins, to pass
Rhene or the Danaw, when her barbarous sons

[Handwritten annotations in margins:]
the men get up as if they are sleeping night watchmen. They were surprised & scared.

they are like a swarm of locust. they black the floating sky. like the plagues in Egypt. when they go to earth they will kill the roof humans.

the barbarians sacked & plundered Rome & pushed them into the dark ages.

---

8. Mythical Egyptian pharaoh, whom Milton associates with the pharaoh of Exodus 14 who pursued the Israelites ("sojourners of Goshen") into the Red Sea, which God parted for them. His "chivalry" are horsemen from Memphis.
9. The double negatives make a positive: they did perceive both plight and pain.
1. Moses, who drew down a plague of locusts on Egypt (Exodus 10.12–15).
2. A first use of this description of Satan as an Oriental despot.

Came like a deluge on the South, and spread
355 Beneath Gibraltar to the Libyan sands.³
Forthwith from every squadron and each band
The heads and leaders thither haste where stood
Their great commander; godlike shapes and forms
Excelling human, princely dignities,
360 And powers that erst in Heaven sat on thrones;
Though of their names in heav'nly records now
Be no memorial, blotted out and razed°   *erased*
By their rebellion, from the Books of Life.
Nor had they yet among the sons of Eve
365 Got them new names, till wand'ring o'er the earth,
Through God's high sufferance for the trial of man,
By falsities and lies the greatest part
Of mankind they corrupted to forsake
God their Creator, and th' invisible
370 Glory of him that made them, to transform
Oft to the image of a brute, adorned
With gay religions° full of pomp and gold,   *showy rites*
And devils to adore for deities:
Then were they known to men by various names,
375 And various idols through the heathen world.
     Say, Muse, their names then known, who first, who last,⁴
Roused from the slumber on that fiery couch,
At their great emperor's call, as next in worth
Came singly° where he stood on the bare strand,   *one at a time*
380 While the promiscuous° crowd stood yet aloof.   *mixed*
     The chief were those who from the pit of Hell
Roaming to seek their prey on earth, durst fix
Their seats long after next the seat of God,⁵
Their altars by his altar, gods adored
385 Among the nations round, and durst abide
Jehovah thund'ring out of Zion, throned
Between the Cherubim;⁶ yea, often placed
Within his sanctuary itself their shrines,
Abomination; and with cursèd things
390 His holy rites, and solemn feasts profaned,
And with their darkness durst affront his light.
First Moloch,⁷ horrid king besmeared with blood
Of human sacrifice, and parents' tears,
Though for the noise of drums and timbrels° loud   *tambourines*
395 Their children's cries unheard, that passed through fire
To his grim idol. Him the Ammonite⁸
Worshiped in Rabba and her wat'ry plain,

---

3. The barbarian invasions of Rome began with
crossings of the Rhine ("Rhene") and Danube
("Danaw") rivers and spread across Spain, via Gibraltar, to North Africa.
4. The catalog of gods here is an epic convention;
Homer catalogs ships; Virgil, warriors.
5. The first group of devils come from the Middle
East, close neighbors of Jehovah "throned" in his
sanctuary in Jerusalem.
6. Golden cherubim adorned opposite ends of the

gold cover on the Ark of the Covenant.
7. Moloch was a sun god, sometimes represented
as a roaring bull or with a calf's head, within whose
brazen image living children were supposedly
burned as sacrifices.
8. The Ammonites lived east of the Jordan.
"Rabba" is modern Amman, in Jordan; "Argob,"
"Basan," "utmost Arnon" are lands east of the Dead
Sea.

In Argob and in Basan, to the stream
Of Utmost Arnon. Nor content with such
400 Audacious neighborhood, the wisest heart
Of Solomon he led by fraud to build
His temple right against the temple of God
On that opprobrious hill, and made his grove
The pleasant valley of Hinnom, Tophet thence
405 And black Gehenna called, the type of Hell.[9]
Next Chemos,[1] th' obscene dread of Moab's sons,
From Aroer to Nebo, and the wild
Of southmost Abarim; in Hesebon
And Horanaim, Seon's realm, beyond
410 The flow'ry dale of Sibma clad with vines,
And Elealè to th' Asphaltic Pool.[2]
Peor[3] his other name, when he enticed
Israel in Sittim on their march from Nile
To do him wanton rites, which cost them woe.
415 Yet thence his lustful orgies he enlarged
Even to that hill of scandal,[4] by the grove
Of Moloch homicide, lust hard by hate;
Till good Josiah drove them thence to Hell.
With these came they, who from the bord'ring flood
420 Of old Euphrates to the brook that parts
Egypt from Syrian ground,[5] had general names
Of Baalim and Ashtaroth, those male,
These feminine.[6] For Spirits when they please
Can either sex assume, or both; so soft
425 And uncompounded is their essence pure,
Not tied or manacled with joint or limb,
Nor founded on the brittle strength of bones,
Like cumbrous flesh; but in what shape they choose
Dilated or condensed, bright or obscure,
430 Can execute their airy purposes,
And works of love or enmity fulfill.
For those the race of Israel oft forsook
Their Living Strength, and unfrequented left
His righteous altar, bowing lowly down
435 To bestial gods; for which their heads as low
Bowed down in battle, sunk before the spear
Of despicable foes. With these in troop
Came Astoreth, whom the Phoenicians called
Astartè, queen of Heav'n, with crescent horns;

---

9. The rites of Moloch on "that opprobrious hill"
(the Mount of Olives), just opposite the Jewish
temple, and in the valley of Hinnom so polluted
those places that they were turned into the refuse
dump of Jerusalem. Under the name "Tophet" and
"Gehenna," Hinnom became a type of Hell.
1. Chemos or Chemosh, associated with Moloch
in 1 Kings 11.7, was the god of the Moabites,
whose lands (many drawn from Isaiah 15–16) are
mentioned in the following lines.
2. The Dead Sea.
3. The story of Peor seducing the Israelites in Sit-

tim is told in Numbers 15.
4. The Mount of Olives where Solomon built temples for Chemos and Moloch (1 Kings 11.7); epithets were commonly attached to the names of
gods, as here, Moloch "homicide." Josiah (next
line) destroyed pagan idols in Jerusalem and other
cities (2 Chronicles 34).
5. Palestine lies between the Euphrates and "the
brook of Besor" (1 Samuel 30.10).
6. Plural forms, masculine and feminine, respectively, denoting aspects of the sun god Baal and
the moon goddess Astarte.

440 To whose bright image nightly by the moon
     Sidonian virgins[7] paid their vows and songs,
     In Sion also not unsung, where stood
     Her temple on th' offensive mountain,[8] built
     By that uxorious king, whose heart though large,
445 Beguiled by fair idolatresses, fell
     To idols foul. Thammuz[9] came next behind,
     Whose annual wound in Lebanon allured
     The Syrian damsels to lament his fate
     In amorous ditties all a summer's day,
450 While smooth Adonis[1] from his native work
     Ran purple to the sea, supposed with blood
     Of Thammuz yearly wounded: the love-tale
     Infected Sion's daughters with like heat,
     Whose wanton passions in the sacred porch
455 Ezekiel[2] saw, when by the vision led
     His eye surveyed the dark idolatries
     Of alienated Judah. Next came one
     Who mourned in earnest, when the captive ark
     Maimed his brute image, head and hands lopped off
460 In his own temple, on the grunsel edge,[3]
     Where he fell flat, and shamed his worshipers:
     Dagon his name, sea monster, upward man
     And downward fish: yet had his temple high
     Reared in Azotus, dreaded through the coast
465 Of Palestine, in Gath and Ascalon[4]
     And Accaron and Gaza's frontier bounds.
     Him followed Rimmon,[5] whose delightful seat
     Was fair Damascus, on the fertile banks
     Of Abbana and Pharphar, lucid streams.
470 He also against the house of God was bold:
     A leper once he lost and gained a king,[6]
     Ahaz his sottish conqueror, whom he drew
     God's altar to disparage and displace
     For one of Syrian mode, whereon to burn
475 His odious off'rings, and adore the gods
     Whom he had vanquished. After these appeared
     A crew who under names of old renown,
     Osiris, Isis, Orus[7] and their train

7. Sidon and Tyre were the chief cities of Phoenicia.
8. The Mount of Olives again. "That uxorious king" (next line) is Solomon, who "loved many strange women" (2 Kings 11.1–8).
9. A Syrian god, supposedly killed by a boar in Lebanon; his Greek form was Adonis, beloved of Aphrodite and god of the solar year. Annual festivals mourned his death and celebrated his revival as signifying the death and rebirth of vegetation.
1. Here, the Lebanese river named for the deity because every spring it turned blood-red from sedimentary mud.
2. The prophet complained that Jewish women were worshipping Thammuz (Ezekiel 8.14).
3. When the Philistines stole the ark of God, they placed it in the temple of their sea god, Dagon, but

in the morning the mutilated statue of Dagon was found on the threshhold ("grunsel edge") (1 Samuel 5.1–5).
4. The five chief cities of the Philistines, sites of Dagon's worship.
5. A Phoenician god whose temple was in Damascus.
6. A Syrian general, Naaman, was cured of leprosy and converted from worship of Rimmon by the waters of the Jordan (2 Kings 5), while King Ahaz, an Israelite monarch who conquered Damascus, was converted there to Rimmon's worship.
7. The second group of devils include the Egyptian gods driven from Heaven by the revolt of the giants (Ovid, Metamorphoses 5) and forced to wander in "monstrous" (next line) animal disguises.

With monstrous shapes and sorceries abused
480 Fanatic Egypt and her priests, to seek
Their wand'ring gods disguised in brutish forms
Rather than human. Nor did Israel scape
Th' infection when their borrowed gold composed
The calf in Oreb:⁸ and the rebel king
485 Doubled that sin in Bethel and in Dan,
Lik'ning his Maker to the grazèd ox,⁹
Jehovah, who in one night when he passed
From Egypt marching, equaled° with one stroke   levelled
Both her first-born and all her bleating gods.¹
490 Belial came last,² than whom a spirit more lewd
Fell not from Heaven, or more gross to love
Vice for itself: to him no temple stood
Or altar smoked; yet who more oft than he
In temples and at altars, when the priest
495 Turns atheist, as did Eli's sons,³ who filled
With lust and violence the house of God.
In courts and palaces he also reigns
And in luxurious cities, where the noise
Of riot ascends above their loftiest tow'rs,
500 And injury and outrage: and when night
Darkens the streets, then wander forth the sons
Of Belial, flown° with insolence and wine.⁴   flushed
Witness the streets of Sodom, and that night
In Gibeah,⁵ when the hospitable door
505 Exposed a matron to avoid worse rape.
      These were the prime in order and in might;
The rest were long to tell, though far renowned,
Th' Ionian gods, of Javan's issue held
Gods, yet confessed later than Heav'n and Earth
510 Their boasted parents;⁶ Titan Heav'n's first-born
With his enormous brood, and birthright seized
By younger Saturn, he from mightier Jove,
His own and Rhea's son, like measure found;
So Jove usurping reigned:⁷ these first in Crete
515 And Ida known, thence on the snowy top
Of cold Olympus ruled the middle air
Their highest heav'n; or on the Delphian cliff,

8. In the wilderness of Egypt, while Moses was receiving the Law, Aaron made a golden calf, thought to be an idol of the Egyptian god Apis and made of ornaments brought out of Egypt (Exodus 32).
9. Jereboam, "the rebel king" who led the ten tribes of Israel in revolt against Solomon's son, Reheboam; he doubled Aaron's sin by making two golden calves (1 Kings 12–30).
1. Jehovah smote the firstborn of all Egyptian families as well as their gods (Exodus 12.12).
2. Belial was never worshiped as a god; his name means "wickedness," but its use in phrases like "sons of Belial" encouraged personification.
3. Priests who were termed "sons of Belial" because they seized for themselves offerings made to God and lay with prostitutes (1 Samuel 2.12–

22).
4. This passage, with its present-tense verbs, invites application to current examples—like Cavaliers at court and Restoration London.
5. Lot begged the Sodomites to rape his daughter rather than his (male) angel guests (Genesis 19); in Gibeah a Levite avoided worse (homosexual) rape by surrendering his concubine to riotous "sons of Belial" (Judges 19.21–30).
6. The Ionian Greeks ("Javan's issue," i.e., of the line of Javan, grandson of Noah) regarded the Titans as gods; their supposed parents were Heaven (Uranus) and Earth (Gaea).
7. The Titan Chronos, or Saturn, deposed his elder brother, married his sister Rhea, and ruled until he was deposed by his son, Zeus (Jove), who had been reared in secret on Mount Ida in Crete.

Or in Dodona, and through all the bounds
Of Doric land;[8] or who with Saturn old
520 Fled over Adria to th' Hesperian fields,
And o'er the Celtic roamed the utmost isles.[9]
   All these and more came flocking; but with looks
Downcast and damp,° yet such wherein appeared   *depressed, dazed*
Obscure some glimpse of joy, to have found their chief
525 Not in despair, to have found themselves not lost
In loss itself; which on his count'nance cast
Like doubtful hue:[1] but he his wonted pride
Soon recollecting, with high words, that bore
Semblance of worth, not substance, gently raised
530 Their fainting courage, and dispelled their fears.
Then straight commands that at the warlike sound
Of trumpets loud and clarions be upreared
His mighty standard; that proud honor claimed
Azazel[2] as his right, a Cherub tall:
535 Who forthwith from the glittering staff unfurled
Th' imperial ensign, which full high advanced
Shone like a meteor streaming to the wind
With gems and golden luster rich emblazed,
Seraphic arms and trophies:[3] all the while
540 Sonorous metal° blowing martial sounds: *trumpets*
At which the universal host upsent
A shout that tore Hell's concave,° and beyond   *vault*
Frighted the reign of Chaos and old Night.[4]
All in a moment through the gloom were seen
545 Ten thousand banners rise into the air   *they are very organized.*
With orient° colors waving: with them rose   *lustrous*
A forest huge of spears: and thronging helms
Appeared, and serried° shields in thick array   *pushed close together*
Of depth immeasurable: anon they move
550 In perfect phalanx to the Dorian[5] mood
Of flutes and soft recorders; such as raised
To highth of noblest temper heroes old
Arming to battle, and instead of rage   *they know they have lost but*
Deliberate valor breathed, firm and unmoved   *they are still*
555 With dread of death to flight or foul retreat, *proud & see*
Nor wanting power to mitigate and swage°   *assuage* *their cause*
With solemn touches, troubled thoughts, and chase *as richeous.*
Anguish and doubt and fear and sorrow and pain
From mortal or immortal minds. Thus they
560 Breathing united force with fixèd thought
Moved on in silence to soft pipes that charmed

8. Zeus and the other Olympian gods had their seat on Mount Olympus, in "middle air"; they were worshiped in Delphi, Dodona, and throughout Greece ("Doric lands").
9. Saturn, after his downfall, fled over "Adria" (the Adriatic Sea) to "the Hesperian fields" (Italy), crossed the "Celtic" fields of France, and thence to Britain, the "utmost isles."
1. Satan's face reflected the same mixed emotions.
2. Traditionally, one of the four standard-bearers

in Satan's army. "Clarions" (line 532): small, shrill trumpets.
3. Their flags bear the heraldic arms of the various orders of angels and memorials of their battles.
4. In *Paradise Lost* 2.894–909, 959–70 Chaos and Night rule the region of unformed matter between Heaven and earth.
5. Severe, martial music used by the Spartans marching to battle. "Phalanx": battle formation.

Their painful steps o'er the burnt soil; and now
Advanced in view they stand, a horrid° front   *bristling with spears*
Of dreadful length and dazzling arms, in guise
565 Of warriors old with ordered spear and shield,
Awaiting what command their mighty chief
Had to impose. He through the armèd files
Darts his experienced eye, and soon traverse°   *across*
The whole battalion views, their order due,
570 Their visages and stature as of gods,
Their number last he sums. And now his heart
Distends with pride, and hard'ning in his strength
Glories: for never since created man[6]
Met such embodied force, as named° with these   *composed*
575 Could merit more than that small infantry[7]
Warred on by cranes: though all the giant brood
Of Phlegra with th' heroic race were joined
That fought at Thebes and Ilium,[8] on each side
Mixed with auxiliar° gods; and what resounds   *allied*
580 In fable or romance of Uther's son
Begirt with British and Armoric knights;
And all who since, baptized or infidel
Jousted in Aspramont or Montalban,
Damasco, or Marocco, or Trebisond,
585 Or whom Biserta sent from Afric shore
When Charlemain with all his peerage fell
By Fontarabbia.[9] Thus far these beyond
Compare of mortal prowess, yet observed°   *obeyed*
Their dread commander: he above the rest
590 In shape and gesture proudly eminent
Stood like a tow'r; his form had yet not lost
All her[1] original brightness, nor appeared
Less than Archangel ruined, and th' excess
Of glory obscured: as when the sun new-ris'n
595 Looks through the horizontal° misty air   *on the horizon*
Shorn of his beams, or from behind the moon
In dim eclipse° disastrous twilight sheds   *ill-starred*
On half the nations, and with fear of change
Perplexes monarchs. Darkened so, yet shone
600 Above them all th' Archangel: but his face
Deep scars of thunder had intrenched,° and care   *furrowed*
Sat on his faded cheek, but under brows
Of dauntless courage, and considerate° pride   *conscious, deliberate*
Waiting revenge: cruel his eye, but cast
605 Signs of remorse and passion° to behold   *compassion, pain*

[Handwritten annotations in right margin:]
he is filled with pride for what he has created. he has no remourse, & he is comitting the same sin as before.

like Zeus. he could continue to rebel or ask for forgiveness. he becomes dark & loses his heavenly glow.

6. I.e., since the creation of man.
7. Pygmies (little people, with a pun on *infants*) had periodic fights with the cranes, in Pliny's account. Compared with Satan's forces, all other armies are puny.
8. In Greek mythology, the Giants fought the gods at Phlegra in Macedonia; in Roman myth, it was at Phlegra in Italy. Satan's forces surpass them, even if joined with the Seven who fought against Thebes and the whole Greek host that besieged

Troy ("Illium").
9. Satan's forces also surpass the "British or Armoric" (from Brittany) knights who fought with King Arthur ("Uther's son"), and all the romance knights who fought at the famous named sites in the following lines. Roncevalles, near Fontarabba, was the place where Charlemagne's "peerage," including his best knight, Roland, were defeated in battle (though not Charlemagne himself).
1. "Forma" in Latin is feminine.

The fellows of his crime, the followers rather
(Far other once beheld in bliss) condemned
For ever now to have their lot in pain,
Millions of Spirits for his fault amerced°   *deprived*
610 Of Heav'n, and from eternal splendors flung
For his revolt, yet faithful how they stood,
Their glory withered: as when Heaven's fire
Hath scathed the forest oaks, or mountain pines,
With singèd top their stately growth though bare
615 Stands on the blasted heath. He now prepared
To speak; whereat their doubled ranks they bend
From wing to wing, and half enclose him round
With all his peers: attention held them mute.
Thrice he essayed, and thrice, in spite of scorn,
620 Tears such as angels weep burst forth: at last
Words interwove with sighs found out their way.
    "O myriads of immortal Spirits, O Powers
Matchless, but with th' Almighty, and that strife
Was not inglorious, though th' event° was dire,   *outcome*
625 As this place testifies, and this dire change
Hateful to utter: but what power of mind
Foreseeing or presaging, from the depth
Of knowledge past or present, could have feared,
How such united force of gods, how such
630 As stood like these, could ever know repulse?
For who can yet believe, though after loss,
That all these puissant° legions, whose exile   *potent, powerful*
Hath emptied Heav'n, shall fail to reascend
Self-raised, and repossess their native seat?
635 For me, be witness all the host of Heav'n,
If counsels different,° or danger shunned   *contradictory*
By me, have lost our hopes. But he who reigns
Monarch in Heav'n, till then as one secure
Sat on his throne, upheld by old repute,
640 Consent or custom, and his regal state
Put forth at full, but still his strength concealed,
Which tempted our attempt,² and wrought our fall.
Henceforth his might we know, and know our own
So as not either to provoke, or dread
645 New war, provoked; our better part remains
To work in close design, by fraud or guile
What force effected not: that he no less
At length from us may find, who overcomes
By force, hath overcome but half his foe.
650 Space may produce new worlds; whereof so rife°   *common*
There went a fame° in Heav'n that he ere long   *rumor*
Intended to create, and therein plant
A generation, whom his choice regard
Should favor equal to the sons of Heaven:
655 Thither, if but to pry, shall be perhaps

---

2. Satan is an inveterate punster.

Our first eruption,° thither or elsewhere: *breaking out*
For this infernal pit shall never hold
Celestial Spirits in bondage, not th' abyss
Long under darkness cover. But these thoughts
660 Full counsel must mature: peace is despaired,
For who can think submission? War then, war
Open or understood° must be resolved."   *covert*
    He spake: and to confirm his words, out flew
Millions of flaming swords, drawn from the thighs
665 Of mighty Cherubim; the sudden blaze
Far round illumined Hell: highly they raged
Against the Highest, and fierce with graspèd arms
Clashed on their sounding shields the din of war,[3]
Hurling defiance toward the vault of Heav'n.
670   There stood a hill not far whose grisly top
Belched fire and rolling smoke; the rest entire
Shone with a glossy scurf,° undoubted sign   *crust*
That in his womb was hid metallic ore,
The work of sulphur.[4] Thither winged with speed
675 A numerous brígade hastened. As when bands
Of pioneers° with spade and pickax armed   *military engineers*
Forerun the royal camp, to trench a field,
Or cast a rampart. Mammon[5] led them on,
Mammon, the least erected Spirit that fell
680 From Heav'n, for ev'n in Heav'n his looks and thoughts
Were always downward bent, admiring more
The riches of Heav'n's pavement, trodden gold,
Than aught divine or holy else enjoyed
In vision beatific: by him first
685 Men also, and by his suggestion taught,
Ransacked the center, and with impious hands
Rifled the bowels of their mother earth
For treasures better hid. Soon had his crew
Opened into the hill a spacious wound
690 And digged out ribs of gold. Let none admire°   *wonder*
That riches grow in Hell; that soil may best
Deserve the precious bane.° And here let those   *poison*
Who boast in mortal things, and wond'ring tell
Of Babel, and the works of Memphian kings,[6]
695 Learn how their greatest monuments of fame,
And strength and art are easily outdone
By Spirits reprobate, and in an hour
What in an age they with incessant toil
And hands innumerable scarce perform.
700 Nigh on the plain in many cells prepared,
That underneath had veins of liquid fire
Sluiced from the lake, a second multitude

3. Like Roman legionaires, the fallen angels applaud by beating swords on shields.
4. Sulfur and mercury were considered the basic substances of all metals.
5. Mammon, an abstract word for riches, came to be personified and associated with the god of wealth, Plutus, and so with Pluto, god of the underworld. Cf. Matthew 6.24: 'Ye cannot serve God and Mammon.'
6. The Tower of Babel and the pyramids of Egypt.

With wondrous art founded° the massy ore,　　　　　　　　　　*melted*
Severing° each kind, and scummed the bullion dross:°　*separating/boiling dregs*
705　A third as soon had formed within the ground
A various mold, and from the boiling cells
By strange conveyance filled each hollow nook,
As in an organ from one blast of wind
To many a row of pipes the soundboard breathes.
710　Anon out of the earth a fabric huge
Rose like an exhalation, with the sound
Of dulcet symphonies and voices sweet,[7]
Built like a temple, where pilasters° round　　　*columns set in a wall*
Were set, and Doric pillars[8] overlaid
715　With golden architrave; nor did there want
Cornice or frieze, with bossy° sculptures grav'n;　　*embossed*
The roof was fretted° gold. Not Babylon,　　*richly ornamented*
Nor great Alcairo such magnificence
Equaled in all their glories, to enshrine
720　Belus or Serapis[9] their gods, or seat
Their kings, when Egypt with Assyria strove
In wealth and luxury. Th' ascending pile
Stood fixed° her stately height, and straight° the doors　*complete/at once*
Opening their brazen folds discover wide
725　Within, her ample spaces, o'er the smooth
And level pavement: from the archèd roof
Pendent by subtle magic many a row
Of starry lamps and blazing cressets[1] fed
With naphtha and asphaltus yielded light
730　As from a sky. The hasty multitude
Admiring entered, and the work some praise
And some the architect: his hand was known
In Heav'n by many a towered structure high,
Where sceptered angels held their residence,
735　And sat as princes, whom the Súpreme King
Exalted to such power, and gave to rule,
Each in his hierarchy, the orders bright.
Nor was his name unheard or unadored
In ancient Greece and in Ausonian land
740　Men called him Mulciber[2] and how he fell
From Heav'n, they fabled, thrown by angry Jove
Sheer o'er the crystal battlements: from morn
To noon he fell, from noon to dewy eve,
A summer's day; and with the setting sun
745　Dropped from the zenith like a falling star,
On Lemnos th' Aégean isle: thus they relate,
Erring; for he with this rebellious rout

---

7. After melting the gold with fire from the lake
and pouring it into molds, the devils cause their
building to rise as by magic, to the sounds of marvelous music.
8. Doric pillars are severe and plain. The devils'
palace combines classical architectural features
with elaborate ornamentation, suggesting, perhaps, St. Peter's in Rome.

9. At Babylon in Assyria there were temples to
"Belus" or Baal; at Alcairo (modern Cairo, ancient
Memphis) in Egypt they were to Osiris ("Serapis").
1. Basketlike lamps, hung from the ceiling.
2. Hephaestus, or Vulcan, was sometimes known
in "Ausonian land" (Italy) as "Mulciber." The story
of Jove's tossing him out of heaven is told in book
1 of the *Iliad*.

Fell long before; nor aught availed him now
To have built in Heav'n high tow'rs; nor did he scape
750   By all his engines, but was headlong sent
With his industrious crew to build in Hell.
      Meanwhile the wingèd heralds by command
Of sovran power, with awful ceremony
And trumpet's sound throughout the host proclaim
755   A solemn council forthwith to be held
At Pandemonium,³ the high capitol
Of Satan and his peers:° their summons called   *nobles*
From every band and squarèd regiment
By place° or choice° the worthiest; they anon   *rank/election*
760   With hundreds and with thousands trooping came
Attended: all access was thronged, the gates
And porches wide, but chief the spacious hall
(Though like a covered field, where champions bold
Wont ride in armed, and at the Soldan's° chair   *sultan's*
765   Defied the best of paynim° chivalry   *pagan*
To mortal combat or career with lance)
Thick swarmed, both on the ground and in the air,
Brushed with the hiss of rustling wings. As bees
In springtime, when the sun with Taurus⁴ rides,
770   Pour forth their populous youth about the hive
In clusters; they among fresh dews and flowers
Fly to and fro, or on the smoothèd plank,
The suburb of their straw-built citadel,
New rubbed with balm, expatiate and confer⁵
775   Their state affairs. So thick the aery crowd
Swarmed and were straitened; till the signal giv'n,
Behold a wonder! They but now who seemed
In bigness to surpass Earth's giant sons
Now less than smallest dwarfs, in narrow room
780   Throng numberless, like that Pygmean race
Beyond the Indian mount,⁶ or fairy elves,
Whose midnight revels, by a forest side
Or fountain some belated peasant sees,
Or dreams he sees, while overhead the moon
785   Sits arbitress,° and nearer to the earth   *witness*
Wheels her pale course: they on their mirth and dance
Intent, with jocund° music charm his ear;⁷   *merry*
At once with joy and fear his heart rebounds.
Thus incorporeal Spirits to smallest forms
790   Reduced their shapes immense, and were at large,
Though without number still amidst the hall
Of that infernal court. But far within
And in their own dimensions like themselves

3. "Pandemonium" (a Miltonic coinage) means literally "All-Demons," an inversion of Pantheon, "All Gods."
4. The sun is in the zodiacal sign of Taurus from about April 19 to May 20.
5. Spread out and discuss. Bee similes were common in epic from Homer on; also, the bees' (roy-

alist) society was often cited in political argument. The simile prepares for the sudden contraction of the devils, who can shrink or dilate at will.
6. The pygmies were supposed to live beyond the Himalayas.
7. The belated peasant's.

The great Seraphic Lords and Cherubim
795 In close recess and secret conclave sat,
A thousand demi-gods on golden seats,
Frequent and full.[8] After short silence then
And summons read, the great consult[9] began.

[handwritten margin note: they shrunk down so they could all fit into the building & decide what to do next]

Book 2

High on a throne of royal state, which far
Outshone the wealth of Ormus and of Ind,[1]
Or where the gorgeous East with richest hand
Show'rs on her kings barbaric pearl and gold,
5 Satan exalted sat, by merit raised
To that bad eminence; and from despair
Thus high uplifted beyond hope, aspires
Beyond thus high, insatiate to pursue
Vain war with Heav'n, and by success° untaught
10 His proud imaginations° thus displayed.
    "Powers and Dominions,[2] deities of Heaven,
For since no deep within her gulf can hold
Immortal vigor, though oppressed and fall'n,
I give not Heav'n for lost. From this descent
15 Celestial Virtues rising, will appear
More glorious and more dread than from no fall,
And trust themselves to fear no second fate.
Me though just right, and the fixed laws of Heav'n
Did first create your leader, next, free choice,
20 With what besides, in counsel or in fight,
Hath been achieved of merit, yet this loss
Thus far at least recovered, hath much more
Established in a safe unenvied throne
Yielded with full consent. The happier state
25 In Heaven, which follows dignity, might draw
Envy from each inferior; but who here
Will envy whom the highest place exposes
Foremost to stand against the Thunderer's aim
Your bulwark, and condemns to greatest share
30 Of endless pain? Where there is then no good
For which to strive, no strife can grow up there
From faction; for none sure will claim in Hell
Precédence, none, whose portion is so small
Of present pain, that with ambitious mind
35 Will covet more. With this advantage then
To union, and firm faith, and firm accord,
More than can be in Heav'n, we now return
To claim our just inheritance of old,
Surer to prosper than prosperity
40 Could have assured us;[3] and by what best way,

[handwritten margin notes:
5 main speakers.
Beelzebub — this is a place they are free
Mammon — greedy
Belial — coward / the outcome schemes
Satan — he is the one who doesn't want to stay
Moloch — wants war]

8. Crowded together, and in full complement.
9. Consultation, often secret and seditious.
1. India. "Ormus": an island in the Persian Gulf, modern Hormuz, famous for pearls.
2. Angelic orders.
3. Note the play on "sure—prosper—prosperity—assure," a favorite device of Milton's.

Whether of open war or covert guile,[4]
We now debate; who can advise, may speak."
   He ceas'd, and next him Moloch, sceptered king
Stood up, the strongest and the fiercest Spirit
45 That fought in Heav'n; now fiercer by despair:
His trust was with th' Eternal to be deemed
Equal in strength, and rather than be less
Cared not to be at all; with that care lost
Went all his fear: of God, or Hell, or worse
50 He recked° not, and these words thereafter spake.   *cared*
   "My sentence° is for open war: of wiles,   *judgment*
More unexpert,° I boast not: them let those   *less experienced*
Contrive who need, or when they need, not now.
For while they sit contriving, shall the rest,
55 Millions that stand in arms, and longing wait
The signal to ascend, sit lingering here
Heav'n's fugitives, and for their dwelling-place
Accept this dark opprobrious den of shame,
The prison of his tyranny who reigns
60 By our delay? No, let us rather choose
Armed with Hell flames and fury all at once
O'er Heav'n's high tow'rs to force resistless way,
Turning our tortures into horrid° arms   *bristling, horrifying*
Against the Torturer; when to meet the noise
65 Of his almighty engine° he shall hear   *the thunderbolt*
Infernal thunder, and for lightning see
Black fire and horror shot with equal rage
Among his angels; and his throne itself
Mixed with Tartarean[5] sulfur, and strange fire,
70 His own invented torments. But perhaps
The way seems difficult and steep to scale
With upright wing against a higher foe.
Let such bethink them, if the sleepy drench°   *large draught*
Of that forgetful° lake benumb not still,   *causing oblivion*
75 That in our proper° motion we ascend   *natural*
Up to our native seat: descent and fall
To us is adverse. Who but felt of late
When the fierce foe hung on our broken rear
Insulting,[6] and pursued us through the deep,
80 With what compulsion and laborious flight
We sunk thus low? Th' ascent is easy then;
Th' event° is feared; should we again provoke   *outcome*
Our stronger, some worse way his wrath may find
To our destruction: if there be in Hell
85 Fear to be worse destroyed: what can be worse
Than to dwell here, driven out from bliss, condemned
In this abhorrèd deep to utter woe;
Where pain of unextinguishable fire

---

4. A typical epic convention (in Homer, Virgil,
Tasso, and elsewhere) involved councils debating
war or peace, with spokesmen on each side. Satan
offers only the option of war, open or covert.

5. Tartarus is a classical name for hell.
6. With the Latin sense of stamping on; also, triumphantly scorning.

Must exercise° us without hope of end   *vex, afflict*
90   The vassals[7] of his anger, when the scourge
Inexorably, and the torturing hour
Calls us to penance? More destroyed than thus
We should be quite abolished and expire.
What fear we then? What° doubt we to incense   *why*
95   His utmost ire? which to the high enraged,
Will either quite consume us, and reduce
To nothing this essential,° happier far   *essence*
Than miserable to have eternal being:
Or if our substance be indeed divine,
100   And cannot cease to be, we are at worst
On this side nothing;[8] and by proof we feel
Our power sufficient to disturb his Heav'n,
And with perpetual inroads to alarm,
Though inaccessible, his fatal[9] throne:
105   Which if not victory is yet revenge."
    He ended frowning, and his look, denounced°   *portended*
Desperate revenge, and battle dangerous
To less than gods. On th' other side up rose
Belial, in act more graceful and humane;   *civil, polite*
110   A fairer person lost not Heav'n; he seemed
For dignity composed and high exploit:
But all was false and hollow; though his tongue
Dropped manna, and could make the worse appear
The better reason,[1] to perplex and dash°   *confuse*
115   Maturest counsels: for his thoughts were low;
To vice industrious, but to nobler deeds
Timorous and slothful: yet he pleased the ear,
And with persuasive accent thus began.
    "I should be much for open war, O Peers,
120   As not behind in hate; if what was urged
Main reason to persuade immediate war,
Did not dissuade me most, and seem to cast
Ominous conjecture on the whole success:
When he who most excells in fact° of arms,   *feat*
125   In what he counsels and in what excels
Mistrustful, grounds his courage on despair
And utter dissolution, as the scope
Of all his aim, after some dire revenge.
First, what revenge? The tow'rs of Heav'n are filled
130   With armèd watch, that render all access
Impregnable; oft on the bordering deep
Encamp their legions, or with obscure wing
Scout far and wide into the realm of Night,
Scorning surprise. Or could we break our way
135   By force, and at our heels all Hell should rise

[handwritten margin notes: he enjoys war & knows things can't get worse, so he wants to fight God]

[handwritten margin note: Belial]

[handwritten margin notes: he is lazy, slothful & a good talker]

---

7. Servants, but perhaps also, vessels.
8. I.e., we cannot be worse off than we are now, and still live.
9. Established by Fate; also, deadly.
1. The Sophists, mercenary teachers of rhetoric in ancient Greece, were denounced by Plato for making "the worse appear / The better reason." "His tongue / Dropped manna": his honeyed words seemed like the manna supplied to the Israelites in the desert.

With blackest insurrection, to confound
Heav'n's purest light, yet our great enemy
All incorruptible would on his throne
Sit unpolluted, and th' ethereal mold[2]
140　Incapable of stain would soon expel
Her mischief, and purge off the baser fire
Victorious. Thus repulsed, our final hope
Is flat despair: we must exasperate
Th' almighty victor to spend all his rage,
145　And that must end us, that must be our cure,
To be no more; sad cure; for who would lose,
Though full of pain, this intellectual being,
Those thoughts that wander through eternity,
To perish rather, swallowed up and lost
150　In the wide womb of uncreated night,
Devoid of sense and motion? And who knows,
Let this be good, whether our angry foe
Can give it, or will ever? How he can
Is doubtful; that he never will is sure.
155　Will he, so wise, let loose at once his ire,
Belike° through impotence, or unaware,　　　　　*perhaps*
To give his enemies their wish, and end
Them in his anger, whom his anger saves
To punish endless? 'Wherefore cease we then?'
160　Say they who counsel war, 'We are decreed,
Reserved and destined to eternal woe;
Whatever doing, what can we suffer more,
What can we suffer worse?' Is this then worst,
Thus sitting, thus consulting, thus in arms?
165　What when we fled amain,° pursued and strook°　*headlong/struck*
With Heav'n's afflicting thunder, and besought
The deep to shelter us? This Hell then seemed
A refuge from those wounds. Or when we lay
Chained on the burning lake? That sure was worse.
170　What if the breath that kindled those grim fires
Awaked should blow them into sevenfold rage
And plunge us in the flames? Or from above
Should intermitted° vengeance arm again　　　　　*suspended*
His red right hand to plague us? What if all
175　Her° stores were opened, and this firmament　　　*Hell's*
Of Hell should spout her cataracts° of fire,　　　*cascades*
Impendent[3] horrors, threat'ning hideous fall
One day upon our heads; while we perhaps
Designing or exhorting glorious war,
180　Caught in a fiery tempest shall be hurled
Each on his rock transfixed, the sport and prey
Of racking whirlwinds, or for ever sunk
Under yon boiling ocean, wrapped in chains;
There to converse with everlasting groans,

2. Heavenly substance, derived from "ether," the
fifth and purest element, thought to be incorruptible.
3. In the Latin sense, hanging down, threatening.

[handwritten: mind is its own place. make a heaven of hell. or a hell of heaven]

185 Unrespited, unpitied, unreprieved,
     Ages of hopeless end; this would be worse.
     War therefore, open or concealed, alike
     My voice dissuades; for what can force or guile[4]
     With him, or who deceive his mind, whose eye
190 Views all things at one view? He from Heav'n's high
     All these our motions° vain, sees and derides;   *proposals*
     Not more almighty to resist our might
     Than wise to frustrate all our plots and wiles.
     Shall we then live thus vile, the race of Heav'n
195 Thus trampled, thus expelled to suffer here
     Chains and these torments? Better these than worse
     By my advice; since fate inevitable
     Subdues us, and omnipotent decree,
     The victor's will. To suffer, as to do,
200 Our strength is equal, nor the law unjust
     That so ordains: this was at first resolved,
     If we were wise, against so great a foe
     Contending, and so doubtful what might fall.
     I laugh, when those who at the spear are bold
205 And vent'rous, if that fail them, shrink and fear
     What yet they know must follow, to endure
     Exile, or ignominy, or bonds, or pain,
     The sentence of their conqueror: This is now
     Our doom; which if we can sustain and bear,
210 Our Supreme Foe in time may much remit
     His anger, and perhaps thus far removed
     Not mind us not offending, satisfied
     With what is punished; whence these raging fires
     Will slacken, if his breath stir not their flames.

[handwritten: god might not be as angry in time]

215 Our purer essence then will overcome
     Their noxious vapor, or inured° not feel,   *accustomed*
     Or changed at length, and to the place conformed
     In temper and in nature, will receive
     Familiar the fierce heat, and void of pain;
220 This horror will grow mild, this darkness light,
     Besides what hope the never-ending flight
     Of future days may bring, what chance, what change
     Worth waiting, since our present lot appears
     For happy though but ill, for ill not worst,[5]
225 If we procure not to ourselves more woe."
         Thus Belial, with words clothed in reason's garb,
     Counseled ignoble ease and peaceful sloth,
     Not peace: and after him thus Mammon spake.

[handwritten: he might make hell more like heaven]

[handwritten: satan won't listen b/c he sees Belial as lower than he.]

         "Either to disenthrone the King of Heav'n
230 We war, if war be best, or to regain
     Our own right lost: him to unthrone we then
     May hope when everlasting fate shall yield
     To fickle chance, and Chaos judge the strife:

---

4. The verb "accomplish" or "achieve" is understood.
5. I.e., from the point of view of happiness, the

devils are in ill state; from the point of view of evil, they could be worse.

The former vain to hope argues° as vain   *proves*
235 The latter: for what place can be for us
Within Heav'n's bound, unless Heav'n's Lord supreme
We overpower? Suppose he should relent
And publish grace to all, on promise made
Of new subjection; with what eyes could we
240 Stand in his presence humble, and receive
Strict laws imposed, to celebrate his throne
With warbled hymns, and to his Godhead sing
Forced hallelujahs; while he lordly sits
Our envied Sovran, and his altar breathes
245 Ambrosial° odors and ambrosial flowers,   *fragrant, immortal*
Our servile offerings. This must be our task
In Heav'n, this our delight; how wearisome
Eternity so spent in worship paid
To whom we hate. Let us not then pursue
250 By force impossible, by leave obtained
Unacceptable, though in Heav'n, our state
Of splendid vassalage,° but rather seek   *servitude*
Our own good from ourselves, and from our own
Live to ourselves, though in this vast recess,
255 Free, and to none accountable, preferring
Hard liberty before the easy yoke
Of servile pomp. Our greatness will appear
Then most conspicuous, when great things of small,
Useful of hurtful, prosperous of adverse
260 We can create, and in what place soe'er
Thrive under evil, and work ease out of pain
Through labor and endurance. This deep world
Of darkness do we dread? How oft amidst
Thick clouds and dark doth Heav'n's all-ruling Sire
265 Choose to reside, his glory unobscured,
And with the majesty of darkness round
Covers his throne; from whence deep thunders roar
Must'ring their rage, and Heav'n resembles Hell?
As he our darkness, cannot we his light
270 Imitate when we please? This desert soil
Wants° not her hidden luster, gems and gold;   *lacks*
Nor want we skill or art, from whence to raise
Magnificence; and what can Heav'n show more?
Our torments also may in length of time
275 Become our elements, these piercing fires
As soft as now severe, our temper° changed   *constitution*
Into their temper; which must needs remove
The sensible of pain.[6] All things invite
To peaceful counsels, and the settled state
280 Of order, how in safety best we may
Compose° our present evils, with regard   *come to terms with*
Of what we are and where, dismissing quite
All thoughts of war: ye have what I advise."

6. Pain felt by the senses.

He scarce had finished, when such murmur filled
285   Th' assembly, as when hollow rocks retain
The sound of blust'ring winds, which all night long
Had roused the sea, now with hoarse cadence lull
Seafaring men o'erwatched,° whose bark by chance   *worn out from watching*
Or pinnace° anchors in a craggy bay   *boat*
290   After the tempest: such applause was heard
As Mammon ended, and his sentence pleased,
Advising peace: for such another field°   *battlefield*
They dreaded worse than Hell: so much the fear
Of thunder and the sword of Michaël[7]
295   Wrought still within them; and no less desire
To found this nether empire, which might rise
By policy,° and long process of time,   *statecraft*
In emulation opposite to Heav'n.
Which then Beëlzebub perceived, than whom,
300   Satan except, none higher sat, with grave
Aspect he rose, and in his rising seemed
A pillar of state; deep on his front° engraven   *brow*
Deliberation sat and public care;
And princely counsel in his face yet shone,
305   Majestic though in ruin: sage he stood
With Atlantean[8] shoulders fit to bear
The weight of mightiest monarchies; his look
Drew audience and attention still as night
Or summer's noontide air, while thus he spake.
310   "Thrones and imperial Powers, offspring of Heav'n
Ethereal Virtues; or these titles[9] now
Must we renounce, and changing style be called
Princes of Hell? for so the popular vote
Inclines, here to continue, and build up here
315   A growing empire. Doubtless! while we dream,
And know not that the King of Heav'n hath doomed
This place our dungeon, not our safe retreat
Beyond his potent arm, to live exempt
From Heav'n's high jurisdiction, in new league
320   Banded against his throne, but to remain
In strictest bondage, though thus far removed,
Under th' inevitable curb, reserved
His captive multitude: for he, be sure,
In height or depth, still first and last will reign
325   Sole King, and of his kingdom lose no part
By our revolt, but over Hell extend
His empire, and with iron scepter rule
Us here, as with his golden those in Heav'n.
What° sit we then projecting peace and war?   *why*
330   War hath determined us,[1] and foiled with loss
Irreparable; terms of peace yet none

[Handwritten margin notes: "he is reminding them that they are in gods prison"; "they will go to earth insted of heaven"; "Adam & Eve"; "they want to destroy something god loves"]

7. The warrior angel, chief of the angelic armies.
8. Worthy of Atlas, the Titan who as a punishment
for rebellion was condemned to hold up the heavens on his shoulders.

9. The official titles of angelic orders.
1. I.e., war has decided the question for us, but
also limited us.

Vouchsafed or sought; for what peace will be giv'n
To us enslaved, but custody severe,
And stripes, and arbitrary punishment
335 Inflicted? And what peace can we return,
But, to our power,[2] hostility and hate,
Untamed reluctance,° and revenge though slow,   *resistance*
Yet ever plotting how the conqueror least
May reap his conquest, and may least rejoice
340 In doing what we most in suffering feel?
Nor will occasion want,° nor shall we need   *be lacking*
With dangerous expedition to invade
Heav'n, whose high walls fear no assault or siege,
Or ambush from the deep. What if we find
345 Some easier enterprise? There is a place
(If ancient and prophetic fame° in Heav'n   *rumor*
Err not) another world, the happy seat   earth
Of some new race called Man, about this time
To be created like to us, though less
350 In power and excellence, but favored more
Of him who rules above; so was his will
Pronounced among the gods, and by an oath,
That shook Heav'n's whole circumference, confirmed.
Thither let us bend all our thoughts, to learn
355 What creatures there inhabit, of what mold,
Or substance, how endued,° and what their power,   *endowed*
And where their weakness, how attempted° best,   *attacked, tempted*
By force or subtlety. Though Heav'n be shut,   an indirect
And Heav'n's high arbitrator sit secure   attack
360 In his own strength, this place may lie exposed,
The utmost border of his kingdom, left
To their defense who hold it:[3] here perhaps
Some advantageous act may be achieved
By sudden onset, either with Hell fire
365 To waste° his whole creation, or possess   *lay waste*
All as our own, and drive as we were driven,
The puny habitants, or if not drive,
Seduce them to our party, that their God   if god gets angry
May prove their foe, and with repenting hand   enough then man
370 Abolish his own works.[4] This would surpass   will join satan
Common revenge, and interrupt his joy   this will make
In our confusion, and our joy upraise   them more
In his disturbance; when his darling sons   powerful
Hurled headlong to partake with us, shall curse
375 Their frail original,° and faded bliss,   *originator, parent*
Faded so soon. Advise° if this be worth   this shou*consider*
Attempting, or to sit in darkness here   they a jelous
Hatching vain empires." Thus Beëlzebub   of man
Pleaded his devilish counsel, first devised
380 By Satan, and in part proposed: for whence,

2. I.e., to the best of our power.
3. To be defended by the occupants.
4. Cf. Genesis 6.7: "And the Lord said, I will

destroy man [and all other creatures]; for it repenteth me that I have made them."

But from the author of all ill could spring
So deep a malice, to confound° the race   ruin
Of mankind in one root,[5] and earth with Hell
To mingle and involve, done all to spite
385 The great Creator? But their spite still serves
His glory to augment. The bold design
Pleased highly those infernal States,° and joy   nobles
Sparkled in all their eyes; with full assent
They vote: whereat his speech he thus renews.
390   "Well have ye judged, well ended long debate,
Synod of gods, and like to what ye are,
Great things resolved, which from the lowest deep
Will once more lift us up, in spite of fate,
Nearer our ancient seat; perhaps in view
395 Of those bright confines, whence with neighboring arms
And opportune excursion we may chance
Re-enter Heav'n; or else in some mild zone
Dwell not unvisited of Heav'n's fair light
Secure, and at the bright'ning orient beam
400 Purge off this gloom; the soft delicious air,
To heal the scar of these corrosive fires
Shall breathe her balm. But first whom shall we send
In search of this new world, whom shall we find
Sufficient? Who shall tempt° with wand'ring feet   attempt, venture
405 The dark unbottomed infinite abyss
And through the palpable obscure[6] find out
His uncouth° way, or spread his aery flight   unknown
Upborne with indefatigable wings
Over the vast abrupt,[7] ere he arrive
410 The happy isle? what strength, what art can then
Suffice, or what evasion bear him safe
Through the strict senteries° and stations thick   sentries
Of angels watching round? Here he had need
All circumspection, and we now no less
415 Choice° in our suffrage; for on whom we send,   discrimination
The weight of all and our last hope relies."
    This said, he sat; and expectation held
His look suspense,[8] awaiting who appeared
To second, or oppose, or undertake
420 The perilous attempt: but all sat mute,
Pondering the danger with deep thoughts; and each
In other's count'nance read his own dismay
Astonished. None among the choice and prime
Of those Heav'n-warring champions could be found
425 So hardy as to proffer or accept
Alone the dreadful voyage; till at last
Satan, whom now transcendent glory raised
Above his fellows, with monarchal pride

---

5. Adam, the first man, is the "root" of the human
race.
6. Darkness so thick it can be felt (cf. Exodus
10.21).

7. Chaos, a striking example of sound imitating
sense.
8. I.e., everyone sat waiting in suspense.

Conscious of highest worth, unmoved thus spake.
430   "O progeny of Heav'n, empyreal Thrones,
With reason hath deep silence and demur°   *hesitation*
Seized us, though undismayed: long is the way
And hard, that out of Hell leads up to light;
Our prison strong, this huge convex of fire,
435   Outrageous to devour, immures us round
Ninefold,⁹ and gates of burning adamant
Barred over us prohibit all egress.
These passed, if any pass, the void profound
Of unessential Night receives him next
440   Wide gaping, and with utter loss of being
Threatens him, plunged in that abortive gulf.¹
If thence he scape into whatever world,
Or unknown region, what remains him less°   *awaits him except*
Than unknown dangers and as hard escape?
445   But I should ill become this throne, O Peers,
And this imperial sovranty, adorned
With splendor, armed with power, if aught proposed
And judged of public moment,° in the shape   *importance*
Of difficulty or danger could deter
450   Me from attempting. Wherefore do I assume
These royalties, and not refuse to reign,
Refusing° to accept as great a share   *if I refuse*
Of hazard as of honor, due alike
To him who reigns, and so much to him due
455   Of hazard more, as he above the rest
High honored sits? Go therefore mighty Powers,
Terror of Heav'n, though fall'n; intend° at home,   *consider*
While here shall be our home, what best may ease
The present misery, and render Hell
460   More tolerable; if there be cure or charm
To respite or deceive, or slack the pain
Of this ill mansion: intermit no watch
Against a wakeful foe, while I abroad
Through all the coasts of dark destruction seek
465   Deliverance for us all: this enterprise
None shall partake with me." Thus saying rose
The monarch, and prevented° all reply,   *forestalled*
Prudent, lest from his resolution raised°   *roused*
Others among the chief might offer now
470   (Certain to be refused) what erst they feared;
And so refused might in opinion stand
His rivals, winning cheap the high repute
Which he through hazard huge must earn. But they
Dreaded not more th' adventure than his voice
475   Forbidding; and at once with him they rose;
Their rising all at once was as the sound
Of thunder heard remote. Towards him they bend

[handwritten marginal annotations:]
he is doing this but he is taking a risk
he is a hero like Jesus he is making a sacrifice for them like Jesus did for man. he also goes alone so that if he succedes he will have all the glory.

---

9. Hell's fiery walls and gate have nine thicknesses
(see lines 645ff.).
1. Chaos is a womb in which all potential forms

fragment (see lines 900ff.) "Unessential" (line
439): i.e., having no real essence.

With awful° reverence prone; and as a god   *full of awe*
Extol him equal to the Highest in Heav'n:
480   Nor failed they to express how much they praised,
That for the general safety he despised
His own: for neither do the Spirits damned
Lose all their virtue; lest bad men should boast
Their specious° deeds on earth, which glory excites,   *pretending to worth*
485   Or close° ambition varnished o'er with zeal.   *secret*
      Thus they their doubtful consultations dark
Ended rejoicing in their matchless chief:
As when from mountain tops the dusky clouds
Ascending, while the north wind sleeps, o'erspread
490   Heav'n's cheerful face, the louring element°   *threatening sky*
Scowls o'er the darkened landscape snow, or show'r;
If chance the radiant sun with farewell sweet
Extend his evening beam, the fields revive,
The birds their notes renew, and bleating herds
495   Attest their joy, that hill and valley rings.
O shame to men! Devil with devil damned
Firm concord holds, men only disagree
Of creatures rational, though under hope
Of heavenly grace: and God proclaiming peace,
500   Yet live in hatred, enmity, and strife
Among themselves, and levy cruel wars,
Wasting the earth, each other to destroy:
As if (which might induce us to accord)
Man had not hellish foes enow° besides,   *enough*
505   That day and night for his destruction wait.
      The Stygian council thus dissolved; and forth
In order came the grand infernal peers:
Midst came their mighty paramount,° and seemed   *supreme ruler*
Alone th' antagonist of Heav'n, nor less
510   Than Hell's dread emperor with pomp supreme,
And god-like imitated state; him round
A globe° of fiery Seraphim enclosed   *band, circle*
With bright emblazonry and horrent² arms.
Then of their session ended they bid cry
515   With trumpet's regal sound the great result:
Toward the four winds four speedy Cherubim
Put to their mouths the sounding alchemy³
By herald's voice explained; the hollow abyss
Heard far and wide, and all the host of hell
520   With deaf'ning shout, returned them loud acclaim.
Thence more at ease their minds and somewhat raised
By false presumptuous hope, the rangèd° powers   *arrayed in ranks*
Disband, and wand'ring, each his several way
Pursues, as inclination or sad choice
525   Leads him perplexed, where he may likeliest find
Truce to his restless thoughts, and entertain°   *while away*
The irksome hours, till his great chief return.

---

2. Bristling. "Emblazonry": decorated shields.   3. Trumpets (made of the goldlike alloy, brass).

Part on the plain, or in the air sublime°   aloft
Upon the wing, or in swift race contend,
530 As at th' Olympian games or Pythian fields;[4]
Part curb their fiery steeds, or shun the goal[5]
With rapid wheels, or fronted° brigades form.   confronting
As when to warn proud cities war appears
Waged in the troubled sky, and armies rush
535 To battle in the clouds,[6] before each van°   vanguard
Prick° forth the aery knights, and couch their spears   spur
Till thickest legions close; with feats of arms
From either end of Heav'n the welkin° burns.   sky
Others with vast Typhoean[7] rage more fell
540 Rend up both rocks and hills, and ride the air
In Whirlwind; Hell scarce holds the wild uproar.
As when Alcides from Oechalia crowned
With conquest, felt th' envenomed robe, and tore
Through pain up by the roots Thessalian pines,
545 And Lichas from the top of Oeta threw
Into th' Euboic sea.[8] Others more mild,
Retreated in a silent valley, sing
With notes angelical to many a harp
Their own heroic deeds and hapless fall
550 By doom of battle; and complain that fate
Free virtue should enthrall to force or chance.
Their song was partial,° but the harmony   prejudiced
(What could it less when Spirits immortal sing?)
Suspended° Hell, and took with ravishment   held in suspense
555 The thronging audience. In discourse more sweet
(For eloquence the soul, song charms the sense)
Others apart sat on a hill retired,
In thoughts more elevate, and reasoned high
Of providence, foreknowledge, will, and fate,
560 Fixed fate, free will, foreknowledge absolute,
And found no end, in wand'ring mazes lost.
Of good and evil much they argued then,
Of happiness and final misery,
Passion and apathy,[9] and glory and shame,
565 Vain wisdom all, and false philosophy:
Yet with a pleasing sorcery could charm
Pain for a while or anguish, and excite
Fallacious hope, or arm th' obdurèd° breast   hardened
With stubborn patience as with triple steel.
570 Another part in squadrons and gross° bands,   solid, dense
On bold adventure to discover wide
That dismal world, if any clime perhaps

4. The Olympic games were held at Olympia, the Pythian games at Delphi. Games celebrating a (usually dead) hero are an epic convention.
5. To drive a chariot as close as possible around a column without hitting it.
6. The appearance of warfare in the skies, reported before several notable battles, portends trouble on earth.

7. Like that of Typhon, the hundred-headed Titan (see 1.199)
8. Wearing a poisoned robe given him in a deception, Hercules in his dying agonies threw his beloved companion Lichas, along with a good part of Mount Oeta, into the sea of Euboea, near Thermopylae.
9. The Stoic goal of freedom from passion.

Might yield them easier habitation, bend
Four ways their flying march, along the banks
575   Of four infernal rivers that disgorge
Into the burning lake their baleful streams:[1]
Abhorrèd Styx the flood of deadly hate,
Sad Acheron of sorrow, black and deep;
Cocytus, named of lamentation loud
580   Heard on the rueful stream; fierce Phlegethon
Whose waves of torrent fire inflame with rage.
Far off from these a slow and silent stream,
Lethe the river of oblivion rolls
Her wat'ry labyrinth, whereof who drinks,
585   Forthwith his former state and being forgets,
Forgets both joy and grief, pleasure and pain.
Beyond this flood a frozen continent
Lies dark and wild, beat with perpetual storms
Of whirlwind and dire hail, which on firm land
590   Thaws not, but gathers heap,[2] and ruin seems
Of ancient pile; all else deep snow and ice,
A gulf profound as that Serbonian bog[3]
Betwixt Damiata and Mount Casius old,
Where armies whole have sunk: the parching air
595   Burns frore,° and cold performs th' effect of fire.   *frozen*
Thither by harpy-footed[4] Furies haled,
At certain revolutions° all the damned   *recurring times*
Are brought: and feel by turns the bitter change
Of fierce extremes, extremes by change more fierce,
600   From beds of raging fire to starve° in ice   *make numb*
Their soft ethereal warmth, and there to pine
Immovable, infixed, and frozen round,
Periods of time; thence hurried back to fire.
They ferry over this Lethean sound
605   Both to and fro, their sorrow to augment,
And wish and struggle, as they pass, to reach
The tempting stream, with one small drop to lose
In sweet forgetfulness all pain and woe,
All in one moment, and so near the brink;
610   But fate withstands, and to oppose th' attempt
Medusa[5] with Gorgonian terror guards
The ford, and of itself the water flies
All taste of living wight, as once it fled
The lip of Tantalus.[6] Thus roving on
615   In cónfused march forlorn, th' advent'rous bands
With shudd'ring horror pale, and eyes aghast

1. These four rivers are traditional in hellish geography. Milton distinguishes them by the original meanings of their Greek names: Styx means "hateful," Acheron "woeful," etc. Lethe is "far off" and quite different from the others, oblivion being a desired state in Hell.
2. In a heap, resembling the ruin of an old building ("ancient pile").
3. Lake Serbonis, once famous for its quicksands, lies near the city of Damiata, just east of the Nile.

4. Taloned. In Greek mythology the harpies (monsters with women's faces) carried off individuals to the Furies, who avenged crimes.
5. One of the three Gorgons, women with snaky hair, scaly bodies, and boar's tusks, the sight of whose faces changed men to stone.
6. Tantalus, afflicted with a raging thirst, stood in the middle of a lake, the water of which always receded when he tried to drink (hence, "tantalize").

Viewed first their lamentable lot, and found
No rest: through many a dark and dreary vale
They passed, and many a region dolorous,
620 O'er many a frozen, many a fiery alp,°   *volcano*
Rocks, caves, lakes, fens, bogs, dens, and shades of death,
A universe of death, which God by curse
Created evil, for evil only good,
Where all life dies, death lives, and nature breeds,
625 Perverse, all monstrous, all prodigious things,
Abominable, inutterable, and worse
Than fables yet have feigned, or fear conceived,
Gorgons and Hydras, and Chimeras[7] dire.
  Meanwhile the Adversary of God and man,
630 Satan, with thoughts inflamed of highest design,
Puts on swift wings,° and towards the gates of hell   *flies swiftly*
Explores his solitary flight; sometimes
He scours the right-hand coast, sometimes the left,
Now shaves with level wing the deep, then soars
635 Up to the fiery concave° tow'ring high.   *vault*
As when far off at sea a fleet descried
Hangs on the clouds, by equinoctial winds°   *from the equator*
Close sailing from Bengala,° or the isles   *Bengal*
Of Ternate and Tidore,[8] whence merchants bring
640 Their spicy drugs: they on the trading flood
Through the wide Ethiopian to the Cape
Ply stemming nightly toward the pole:[9] so seemed
Far off the flying Fiend. At last appear
Hell bounds high reaching to the horrid roof,
645 And thrice threefold the gates; three folds were brass,
Three iron, three of adamantine rock,
Impenetrable, impaled with circling fire,
Yet unconsumed. Before the gates there sat
On either side a formidable shape;[1]
650 The one seemed woman to the waist, and fair,
But ended foul in many a scaly fold
Voluminous and vast, a serpent armed
With mortal sting: about her middle round
A cry° of hell-hounds never ceasing barked   *pack*
655 With wide Cerberean[2] mouths full loud, and rung
A hideous peal: yet, when they list, would creep,
If aught disturbed their noise, into her womb,
And kennel there, yet there still barked and howled,
Within unseen. Far less abhorred than these
660 Vexed Scylla[3] bathing in the sea that parts

---

7. The Hydra was a serpent whose multiple heads grew back when severed; the Chimera was a fire-breathing creature, part lion, part dragon, part goat.
8. Two of the Molucca or "Spice" Islands, modern Indonesia.
9. The South Pole. "Ethiopian": the Indian Ocean. "The Cape" is the Cape of Good Hope.
1. The allegorical figures of Sin and Death are founded on James 1.15: "Then when lust hath con-

ceived, it bringeth forth sin: and sin, when it is finished, bringeth forth death." But the incestuous relations of Sin and Death are Milton's own invention. Physically, Sin is modeled on Virgil's or Ovid's Scylla, with some touches adopted from Spenser's Error. Death is a traditional figure, vague and vast.
2. Like Cerberus, the multiheaded hound of Hell.
3. Circe, out of jealousy, threw poison into the water where Scylla bathed, in the straits between Calabria and Sicily ("Trinacria"); the poison

Calabria from the hoarse Trinacrian shore:
Nor uglier follow the night-hag,[4] when called
In secret, riding through the air she comes
Lured with the smell of infant blood, to dance
665   With Lapland witches, while the laboring° moon   *troubled*
Eclipses at their charms.° The other shape,   *magic*
If shape it might be called that shape had none
Distinguishable in member, joint, or limb,
Or substance might be called that shadow seemed,
670   For each seemed either; black it stood as night,
Fierce as ten Furies, terrible as hell,
And shook a dreadful dart; what seemed his head
The likeness of a kingly crown had on.
Satan was now at hand, and from his seat
675   The monster moving onward came as fast
With horrid strides. Hell trembled as he strode.
Th' undaunted Fiend what this might be admired,°   *wondered*
Admired, not feared; God and his Son except,
Created thing naught valued he nor shunned;
680   And with disdainful look thus first began.
      "Whence and what art thou, execrable shape,
That dar'st, though grim and terrible, advance
Thy miscreated front° athwart my way   *misshapen face*
To yonder gates? Through them I mean to pass,
685   That be assured, without leave asked of thee:
Retire, or taste° thy folly, and learn by proof,   *experience*
Hell-born, not to contend with Spirits of Heav'n."
      To whom the goblin full of wrath replied:
"Art thou that traitor angel, art thou he,
690   Who first broke peace in Heav'n and faith, till then
Unbroken, and in proud rebellious arms
Drew after him the third part of Heav'n's sons
Conjured° against the Highest, for which both thou   *sworn together*
And they outcast from God, are here condemned
695   To waste eternal days in woe and pain?
And reckon'st thou thyself with Spirits of Heav'n,
Hell-doomed, and breath'st defiance here and scorn,
Where I reign king, and to enrage thee more,
Thy king and lord? Back to thy punishment,
700   False fugitive, and to thy speed add wings,
Lest with a whip of scorpions I pursue
Thy ling'ring, or with one stroke of this dart
Strange horror seize thee, and pangs unfelt before."
      So spake the grisly terror, and in shape,
705   So speaking and so threat'ning, grew tenfold
More dreadful and deform: on th' other side
Incensed with indignation Satan stood
Unterrified, and like a comet burned
That fires the length of Ophiuchus[5] huge

---

caused Scylla to develop a ring of barking, snapping dogs around her waist.
4. Hecate (three syllables), goddess of sorcery.
She attends orgies of witches in Lapland (famous

for witchcraft), drawn by the blood of babies sacrificed for the occasion.
5. A vast northern constellation, "The Serpent
Bearer."

710 In th' arctic sky, and from his horrid° hair   *bristling*
Shakes pestilence and war. Each at the head
Leveled his deadly aim; their fatal hands
No second stroke intend, and such a frown
Each cast at th' other, as when, two black clouds
715 With Heav'n's artillery fraught,[6] come rattling on
Over the Caspian,[7] then stand front to front
Hov'ring a space, till winds the signal blow
To join their dark encounter in mid-air:
So frowned the mighty combatants, that Hell
720 Grew darker at their frown, so matched they stood;
For never but once more was either like
To meet so great a foe.[8] And now great deeds
Had been achieved, whereof all Hell had rung,
Had not the snaky sorceress that sat
725 Fast by Hell gate, and kept the fatal key,
Ris'n, and with hideous outcry rushed between.
    "O father, what intends thy hand," she cried,
"Against thy only son?[9] What fury O son,
Possesses thee to bend that mortal dart
730 Against thy father's head? And know'st for whom;
For him who sits above and laughs the while
At thee ordained his drudge, to execute
Whate'er his wrath, which he calls justice, bids,
His wrath which one day will destroy ye both."
735   She spake, and at her words the hellish pest
Forbore, then these to her Satan returned.
    "So strange thy outcry, and thy words so strange
Thou interposest, that my sudden hand
Prevented° spares to tell thee yet by deeds   *forestalled*
740 What it intends; till first I know of thee,
What thing thou art, thus double-formed, and why
In this infernal vale first met thou call'st
Me father, and that phantasm call'st my son?
I know thee not, nor ever saw till now
745 Sight more detestable than him and thee."
    T' whom thus the portress of Hell gate replied:
"Hast thou forgot me then, and do I seem
Now in thine eye so foul, once deemed so fair
In Heav'n, when at th' assembly, and in sight
750 Of all the Seraphim with thee combined
In bold conspiracy against Heav'n's King,
All on a sudden miserable pain
Surprised thee, dim thine eyes, and dizzy swum
In darkness, while thy head flames thick and fast
755 Threw forth, till on the left side op'ning wide,
Likest to thee in shape and count'nance bright,
Then shining heav'nly fair, a goddess armed
Out of thy head I sprung:[1] amazement seized

6. Loaded with thunderbolts.
7. The Caspian is a particularly stormy area.
8. I.e., the Son of God.
9. Sin, Death, and Satan, in their various inter-
relations, parody obscenely the relations between
God and the Son, Adam and Eve.
1. As Athena sprang full-grown from the head of
Zeus.

All th' host of Heav'n; back they recoiled afraid
760 At first, and called me Sin, and for a sign
Portentous held me; but familiar grown,
I pleased, and with attractive graces won
The most averse, thee chiefly, who full oft
Thyself in me thy perfect image viewing
765 Becam'st enamored, and such joy thou took'st
With me in secret, that my womb conceived
A growing burden. Meanwhile war arose,
And fields were fought in Heav'n; wherein remained
(For what could else) to our almighty foe
770 Clear victory, to our part loss and rout
Through all the empyrean: down they fell
Driv'n headlong from the pitch° of Heaven, down   summit
Into this deep, and in the general fall
I also; at which time this powerful key
775 Into my hand was giv'n, with charge to keep
These gates for ever shut, which none can pass
Without my op'ning. Pensive here I sat
Alone, but long I sat not, till my womb
Pregnant by thee, and now excessive grown
780 Prodigious motion felt and rueful throes.
At last this odious offspring whom thou seest
Thine own begotten, breaking violent way
Tore through my entrails, that with fear and pain
Distorted, all my nether shape thus grew
785 Transformed: but he my inbred enemy
Forth issued, brandishing his fatal dart
Made to destroy: I fled, and cried out 'Death';
Hell trembled at the hideous name, and sighed
From all her caves, and back resounded 'Death.'
790 I fled, but he pursued (though more, it seems,
Inflamed with lust than rage) and swifter far,
Me overtook his mother all dismayed,
And in embraces forcible and foul
Engend'ring with me, of that rape begot
795 These yelling monsters that with ceaseless cry
Surround me, as thou saw'st, hourly conceived
And hourly born, with sorrow infinite
To me, for when they list,° into the womb   wish
That bred them they return, and howl and gnaw
800 My bowels, their repast; then bursting forth
Afresh with conscious terrors vex me round,
That rest or intermission none I find.
Before mine eyes in opposition sits
Grim Death my son and foe, who sets them on,
805 And me his parent would full soon devour
For want of other prey, but that he knows
His end with mine involved; and knows that I
Should prove a bitter morsel, and his bane,
Whenever that shall be; so fate pronounced.
810 But thou O father, I forewarn thee, shun

His deadly arrow; neither vainly hope
To be invulnerable in those bright arms,
Though tempered heav'nly, for that mortal dint,°   *blow*
Save he who reigns above, none can resist."

815   She finished, and the subtle Fiend his lore°   *lesson*
Soon learned, now milder, and thus answered smooth.
"Dear daughter, since thou claim'st me for thy sire,
And my fair son here show'st me, the dear pledge
Of dalliance had with thee in Heav'n, and joys
820 Then sweet, now sad to mention, through dire change
Befall'n us unforeseen, unthought of, know
I come no enemy, but to set free
From out this dark and dismal house of pain,
Both him and thee, and all the heav'nly host
825 Of Spirits that in our just pretenses° armed   *claims*
Fell with us from on high: from them I go
This uncouth errand sole,[2] and one for all
Myself expose, with lonely steps to tread
Th' unfounded° deep, and through the void immense   *bottomless*
830 To search with wand'ring quest a place foretold
Should be, and, by concurring signs, ere now
Created vast and round, a place of bliss
In the purlieus° of Heav'n, and therein placed   *outskirts*
A race of upstart creatures, to supply
835 Perhaps our vacant room, though more removed,
Lest Heav'n surcharged° with potent multitude   *overcrowded*
Might hap to move new broils:° be this or aught   *controversies*
Than this more secret now designed, I haste
To know, and this once known, shall soon return,
840 And bring ye to the place where thou and Death
Shall dwell at ease, and up and down unseen
Wing silently the buxom° air, embalmed°   *yielding / made fragrant*
With odors; there ye shall be fed and filled
Immeasurably, all things shall be your prey."
845 He ceased, for both seemed highly pleased, and Death
Grinned horrible a ghastly smile, to hear
His famine° should be filled, and blessed his maw   *ravenous hunger*
Destined to that good hour: no less rejoiced
His mother bad, and thus bespake her sire.
850   "The key of this infernal pit by due,
And by command of Heav'n's all-powerful King
I keep, by him forbidden to unlock
These adamantine gates; against all force
Death ready stands to interpose his dart,
855 Fearless to be o'ermatched by living might.
But what owe I to his commands above
Who hates me, and hath hither thrust me down
Into this gloom of Tartarus profound,
To sit in hateful office here confined,
860 Inhabitant of Heav'n, and heav'nly-born,

2. Unknown journey—a parody of Christ's errand on earth (3.236–65).

Here in perpetual agony and pain,
With terrors and with clamors compassed round
Of mine own brood, that on my bowels feed?
Thou art my father, thou my author, thou
865   My being gav'st me; whom should I obey
But thee, whom follow? Thou wilt bring me soon
To that new world of light and bliss, among
The gods who live at ease, where I shall reign
At thy right hand voluptuous,[3] as beseems
870   Thy daughter and thy darling, without end."
     Thus saying, from her side the fatal key,
Sad instrument of all our woe, she took;
And towards the gate rolling her bestial train,[4]
Forthwith the huge portcullis high up drew,
875   Which but herself not all the Stygian powers°   *armies of Hell*
Could once have moved; then in the key-hole turns
Th' intricate wards, and every bolt and bar
Of massy iron or solid rock with ease
Unfastens: on a sudden open fly
880   With impetuous recoil and jarring sound
Th' infernal doors, and on their hinges grate
Harsh thunder, that the lowest bottom shook
Of Erebus.° She opened, but to shut   *Hell*
Excelled° her power; the gates wide open stood,   *exceeded*
885   That with extended wings a bannered host
Under spread ensigns° marching might pass through   *flags, standards*
With horse and chariots ranked in loose array;
So wide they stood, and like a furnace mouth
Cast forth redounding° smoke and ruddy flame.   *billowing*
890   Before their eyes in sudden view appear
The secrets of the hoary deep, a dark
Illimitable° ocean without bound,   *without limit*
Without dimension, where length, breadth, and height,
And time and place are lost; where eldest Night
895   And Chaos, ancestors of Nature, hold
Eternal anarchy, amidst the noise
Of endless wars, and by confusion stand.
For Hot, Cold, Moist, and Dry, four champions fierce
Strive here for mastery, and to battle bring
900   Their embryon atoms;[5] they around the flag
Of each his faction, in their several clans,
Light-armed or heavy, sharp, smooth, swift or slow,
Swarm populous, unnumbered as the sands
Of Barca or Cyrene's torrid soil,[6]
905   Levied to side with warring winds, and poise[7]

3. As the Son sits at God's right hand, Sin will at
Satan's, a blasphemous parody of the Creed and of
Paradise Lost 3.250–80.
4. I.e. accompanied by her yelping offspring.
5. These subatomic qualities combine together in
nature to form the four elements, fire, earth, water,
and air, but they struggle endlessly in Chaos,
where the atoms of these elements remain undeveloped (in "embryo").
6. Cities built on the shifting sands of North
Africa.
7. Give weight to. "Levied": both enlisted and
raised up.

Their lighter wings. To whom these most adhere,
He rules a moment; Chaos⁸ umpire sits,
And by decision more embroils the fray
By which he reigns: next him high arbiter
910 Chance governs all. Into this wild abyss,
The womb of Nature and perhaps her grave,
Of neither sea, nor shore, nor air, nor fire,
But all these in their pregnant causes° mixed   *seeds*
Confus'dly, and which thus must ever fight,
915 Unless th' Almighty Maker them ordain
His dark materials to create more worlds,
Into this wild abyss the wary Fiend
Stood on the brink of Hell and looked a while,
Pondering his voyage; for no narrow frith°   *channel, firth*
920 He had to cross. Nor was his ear less pealed°   *dinned*
With noises loud and ruinous (to compare
Great things with small) than when Bellona⁹ storms,
With all her battering engines bent to raze
Some capital city; or less than if this frame°   *structure*
925 Of Heav'n were falling, and these elements
In mutiny had from her axle torn
The steadfast earth. At last his sail-broad vans°   *wings*
He spreads for flight, and in the surging smoke
Uplifted spurns the ground, thence many a league
930 As in a cloudy chair ascending rides
Audacious, but that seat soon failing, meets
A vast vacuity: all unawares
Flutt'ring his pennons¹ vain plumb down he drops
Ten thousand fathom deep, and to this hour
935 Down had been falling, had not by ill chance
The strong rebuff° of some tumultuous cloud   *counterblast*
Instinct° with fire and niter° hurried him   *filled / saltpeter*
As many miles aloft: that fury stayed,
Quenched in a boggy Syrtis,² neither sea,
940 Nor good dry land: night foundered on he fares,
Treading the crude consistence, half on foot,
Half flying; behoves° him now both oar and sail   *befits*
As when a gryphon through the wilderness
With wingèd course o'er hill or moory° dale,   *marshy*
945 Pursues the Arimaspian, who by stealth
Had from his wakeful custody purloined
The guarded gold:³ so eagerly the Fiend
O'er bog or steep, through strait, rough, dense, or rare,
With head, hands, wings, or feet pursues his way,
950 And swims or sinks, or wades, or creeps, or flies:
At length a universal hubbub wild

8. Chaos is both the place where confusion reigns
and personified confusion itself.
9. Goddess of war.
1. Useless wings ("pinions").
2. Quicksand in North African gulfs, famous for

their shifting sandbars.
3. Gryphons, fabulous creatures, half-eagle, half-
lion, hoarded gold which was stolen from them by
the one-eyed Arimaspians.

Of stunning sounds and voices all confused
Borne through the hollow dark assaults his ear
With loudest vehemence: thither he plies,
955 Undaunted to meet there whatever Power
Or Spirit of the nethermost abyss
Might in that noise reside, of whom to ask
Which way the nearest coast of darkness lies
Bordering on light; when straight behold the throne
960 Of Chaos, and his dark pavilion spread
Wide on the wasteful deep; with him enthroned
Sat sable-vested Night, eldest of things,
The consort of his reign; and by them stood
Orcus and Ades,⁴ and the dreaded name
965 Of Demogorgon,⁵ Rumor next and Chance,
And Tumult and Confusion all embroiled,
And Discord with a thousand various mouths.
　　T' whom Satan turning boldly, thus. "Ye Powers
And Spirits of this nethermost abyss,
970 Chaos and ancient Night, I come no spy,
With purpose to explore or to disturb
The secrets of your realm, but by constraint
Wand'ring this darksome desert, as my way
Lies through your spacious empire up to light,
975 Alone, and without guide, half lost, I seek
What readiest path leads where your gloomy bounds
Confine with° Heav'n; or if some other place　　　*border on*
From your dominion won, th' Ethereal King
Possesses lately, thither to arrive
980 I travel this profound;° direct my course;　　　*deep pit*
Directed, no mean recompense it brings
To your behoof,° if I that region lost,　　　*on your behalf*
All usurpation thence expelled, reduce
To her original darkness and your sway
985 (Which is my present journey)⁶ and once more
Erect the standard there of ancient Night;
Yours be th' advantage all, mine the revenge."
　　Thus Satan; and him thus the anarch⁷ old
With falt'ring speech and visage incomposed°　　　*disordered*
990 Answered. "I know thee, stranger, who thou art,
That mighty leading angel, who of late
Made head against Heav'n's King, though overthrown.
I saw and heard, for such a numerous host
Fled not in silence through the frighted deep
995 With ruin upon ruin, rout on rout,
Confusion worse confounded; and Heav'n gates
Poured out by millions her victorious bands
Pursuing. I upon my frontiers here
Keep residence; if all I can will serve,
1000 That little which is left so to defend,

---

4. Latin and Greek names of Pluto, god of Hell.
5. A mysterious deity associated with Fate; Milton elsewhere identifies him with Chaos.

6. The purpose of my present journey.
7. Chaos is not monarch of his realm but, appropriately, "anarch," nonruler.

Encroached on still° through our intestine broils°   *constantly/civil wars*
Weak'ning the scepter of old Night: first Hell
Your dungeon stretching far and wide beneath;
Now lately heaven and earth,[8] another world
1005 Hung o'er my realm, linked in a golden chain
To that side Heav'n from whence your legions fell:
If that way be your walk, you have not far;
So much the nearer danger; go and speed;
Havoc and spoil and ruin are my gain."
1010   He ceased; and Satan stayed not to reply,
But glad that now his sea should find a shore,
With fresh alacrity and force renewed
Springs upward like a pyramid of fire
Into the wild expanse, and through the shock
1015 Of fighting elements, on all sides round
Environed wins his way; harder beset
And more endangered, than when Argo passed
Through Bosporus betwixt the justling rocks:[9]
Or when Ulysses on the larboard shunned
1020 Charybdis, and by th' other whirlpool steered.[1]
So he with difficulty and labor hard
Moved on, with difficulty and labor he;
But he once passed, soon after when man fell,
Strange alteration! Sin and Death amain°   *at full speed*
1025 Following his track, such was the will of Heav'n,
Paved after him a broad and beaten way
Over the dark abyss, whose boiling gulf
Tamely endured a bridge of wondrous length
From Hell continued reaching th' utmost orb[2]
1030 Of this frail world; by which the Spirits perverse
With easy intercourse pass to and fro
To tempt or punish mortals, except whom
God and good angels guard by special grace.
But now at last the sacred influence
1035 Of light appears, and from the walls of Heav'n
Shoots far into the bosom of dim Night
A glimmering dawn; here Nature first begins
Her farthest verge,° and Chaos to retire   *threshold*
As from her outmost works a broken foe
1040 With tumult less and with less hostile din,
That° Satan with less toil, and now with ease   *so that*
Wafts on the calmer wave by dubious light
And like a weather-beaten vessel holds°   *makes for*
Gladly the port, though shrouds and tackle torn;
1045 Or in the emptier waste, resembling air
Weighs° his spread wings, at leisure to behold   *balances*
Far off th' empyreal Heav'n, extended wide

---

8. The cosmos, with its own "heaven" (not the empyrean, the Heaven of God and the angels).
9. Jason and his fifty Argonauts, sailing through the Bosporus to the Black Sea in pursuit of the Golden Fleece, had to pass through the Symplegades, or clashing rocks.

1. Homer's Ulysses, sailing where Italy almost touches Sicily, had to pass between Charybdis, a whirlpool, and Scylla, a monster who devoured six of his men (not another whirlpool, as used here).
2. The bridge ends on the outermost sphere of the ten concentric spheres making up the universe.

In circuit, undetermined square or round,
With opal tow'rs and battlements adorned
1050 Of living sapphire, once his native seat;
And fast by hanging in a golden chain
This pendent world,° in bigness as a star
Of smallest magnitude close by the moon.
Thither full fraught with mischievous revenge,
1055 Accursed, and in a curséd hour, he hies.

Book 3

Hail holy Light, offspring of Heav'n first-born,
Or of th' Eternal coeternal beam
May I express thee unblamed?[1] Since God is light,
And never but in unapproachèd light
5 Dwelt from eternity, dwelt then in thee,
Bright effluence of bright essence increate.°   uncreated, eternal
Or hear'st thou rather[2] pure ethereal stream,
Whose fountain who shall tell? Before the sun,
Before the heavens thou wert, and at the voice
10 Of God, as with a mantle didst invest°   cover
The rising world of waters dark and deep,
Won from the void and formless infinite.
Thee I revisit now with bolder wing,
Escaped the Stygian pool, though long detained
15 In that obscure sojourn, while in my flight
Through utter and through middle darkness[3] borne
With other notes than to th' Orphéan lyre[4]
I sung of Chaos and eternal Night,
Taught by the Heav'nly Muse[5] to venture down
20 The dark descent, and up to reascend,
Though hard and rare: thee I revisit safe,
And feel thy sovran vital lamp; but thou
Revisit'st not these eyes, that roll in vain
To find thy piercing ray, and find no dawn;
25 So thick a drop serene hath quenched their orbs,
Or dim suffusion[6] veiled. Yet not the more
Cease I to wander where the Muses haunt
Clear spring, or shady grove, or sunny hill,
Smit with the love of sacred song; but chief
30 Thee Sion[7] and the flow'ry brooks beneath
That wash thy hallowed feet, and warbling flow,

1. This second Proem or invocation (3.1–55) is a hymn to Light, addressed either as the first creature of God or as coeternal with God, with allusion to 1 John 1.5, "God is Light, and in him is no darkness at all."
2. I.e., would you rather be called (a Latinism).
3. Hell is "utter" (i.e., outer) darkness; Chaos is middle darkness.
4. One of the so-called Orphic Hymns is *To Night*, and Orpheus himself visited the underworld. But Milton's song, Christian and epic, is of a different kind.
5. Urania (though not named until 7.1).
6. Cataract—*suffusio nigra*. "Drop serene": *gutta serena*, the medical term for Milton's kind of blindness.
7. The mountain of scriptural inspiration, with its brooks Siloa and Kidron.

Nightly I visit: nor sometimes forget°   *always remember*
Those other two equaled with me in fate,[8]
So were I equaled with them in renown,
35 Blind Thamyris and blind Maeonides,
And Tiresias and Phineus prophets old,[9]
Then feed on thoughts, that voluntary move
Harmonious numbers;° as the wakeful bird°   *verses / nightingale*
Sings darkling,° and in shadiest covert hid   *in the dark*
40 Tunes her nocturnal note. Thus with the year
Seasons return, but not to me returns
Day, or the sweet approach of ev'n or morn,
Or sight of vernal bloom, or summer's rose,
Or flocks, or herds, or human face divine;
45 But cloud instead, and ever-during dark
Surrounds me, from the cheerful ways of men
Cut off, and for the book of knowledge° fair   *Book of Nature*
Presented with a universal blank
Of nature's works to me expunged and razed,°   *erased*
50 And wisdom at one entrance quite shut out.
So much the rather thou celestial Light
Shine inward, and the mind through all her powers
Irradiate, there plant eyes, all mist from thence
Purge and disperse, that I may see and tell
55 Of things invisible to mortal sight.
     Now had the Almighty Father from above,
From the pure empyrean where he sits
High throned above all height, bent down his eye,
His own works and their works at once to view:
60 Above him all the sanctities° of Heaven   *angels*
Stood thick as stars, and from his sight received
Beatitude past utterance; on his right
The radiant image of his glory sat,
His only Son; on earth he first beheld
65 Our two first parents, yet the only two
Of mankind, in the happy garden placed,
Reaping immortal fruits of joy and love,
Uninterrupted joy, unrivaled love
In blissful solitude; he then surveyed
70 Hell and the gulf between, and Satan there
Coasting the wall of Heav'n on this side Night
In the dun° air sublime,° and ready now   *dusky / above*
To stoop with wearied wings, and willing feet
On the bare outside of this world,° that seemed   *universe*
75 Firm land embosomed without firmament,°   *atmosphere*
Uncertain which, in ocean or in air.
Him God beholding from his prospect high,
Wherein past, present, future he beholds,
Thus to his only Son foreseeing spake.
80   "Only begotten Son, seest thou what rage

8. I.e., blind like me.
9. Thamyris was a blind Thracian poet, who lived
before Homer; "Maeonides" is an epithet of
Homer; Tiresias was the blind prophet of Thebes;
Phineus was a blind king and seer (*Aeneid* 3).

Transports our Adversary, whom no bounds
Prescribed, no bars of Hell, nor all the chains
Heaped on him there, nor yet the main° abyss   vast
Wide interrupt[1] can hold; so bent he seems
85   On desperate revenge, that shall redound
Upon his own rebellious head. And now
Through all restraint broke loose he wings his way
Not far off Heav'n, in the precincts of light,
Directly towards the new-created world,
90   And man there placed, with purpose to essay
If him by force he can destroy, or worse,
By some false guile pervert; and shall pervert;
For man will hearken to his glozing° lies,   *flattering*
And easily transgress the sole command,
95   Sole pledge of his obedience: so will fall
He and his faithless progeny: whose fault?
Whose but his own? Ingrate, he had of me
All he could have; I made him just and right,
Sufficient to have stood, though free to fall.
100 Such I created all th' ethereal Powers
And Spirits, both them who stood and them who failed;
Freely they stood who stood, and fell who fell.
Not free, what proof could they have giv'n sincere
Of true allegiance, constant faith or love,
105 Where only what they needs must do, appeared,
Not what they would? What praise could they receive?
What pleasure I from such obedience paid,
When will and reason (reason also is choice)
Useless and vain, of freedom both despoiled,
110 Made passive both, had served necessity,
Not me. They therefore as to right belonged,
So were created, nor can justly accuse
Their Maker, or their making, or their fate,
As if predestination overruled
115 Their will, disposed by absolute decree
Or high foreknowledge; they themselves decreed
Their own revolt, not I: if I foreknew,
Foreknowledge had no influence on their fault,
Which had no less proved certain unforeknown.[2]
120 So without least impulse or shadow of fate,
Or aught by me immutably foreseen,
They trespass, authors to themselves in all
Both what they judge and what they choose; for so
I formed them free, and free they must remain,
125 Till they enthrall themselves: I else must change
Their nature, and revoke the high decree
Unchangeable, eternal, which ordained
Their freedom, they themselves ordained their fall.
The first sort[3] by their own suggestion fell,

[Handwritten annotation, right margin: It is man's own fault, they should have been strong enough]

[Handwritten annotation, right margin: god asks the angels for a voluntere to go down & bring man back to god. he has forgiven them before they have fallen.]

---

1. Forming a wide breach between Heaven and
Hell.

2. I.e., if I had not foreknown it.
3. Satan and his crew.

130   Self-tempted, self-depraved: man falls deceived
       By the other first: man therefore shall find grace,
       The other none: in mercy and justice both,
       Through Heav'n and earth, so shall my glory excel,
       But mercy first and last shall brightest shine."
135   Thus while God spake, ambrosial fragrance filled
       All Heav'n, and in the blessèd Spirits elect°   *unfallen*
       Sense of new joy ineffable diffused:
       Beyond compare the Son of God was seen
       Most glorious, in him all his Father shone
140   Substantially expressed, and in his face
       Divine compassion visibly appeared,
       Love without end, and without measure grace,
       Which uttering thus he to his Father spake.
           "O Father, gracious was that word which closed
145   Thy sovran sentence, that man should find grace;
       For which both Heav'n and earth shall high extol
       Thy praises, with th' innumerable sound
       Of hymns and sacred songs, wherewith thy throne
       Encompassed shall resound thee ever blessed.
150   For should man finally be lost, should man
       Thy creature late so loved, thy youngest son
       Fall circumvented thus by fraud, though joined
       With his own folly? That be from thee far,
       That far be from thee, Father, who art judge
155   Of all things made, and judgest only right.[4]
       Or shall the Adversary[5] thus obtain
       His end, and frustrate thine, shall he fulfill
       His malice, and thy goodness bring to naught,
       Or proud return though to his heavier doom,
160   Yet with revenge accomplished, and to Hell
       Draw after him the whole race of mankind,
       By him corrupted? Or wilt thou thyself
       Abolish thy creation, and unmake,
       For him, what for thy glory thou hast made?
165   So should thy goodness and thy greatness both
       Be questioned and blasphemed° without defense."   *reviled*
           To whom the great Creator thus replied.
       "O Son, in whom my soul hath chief delight,
       Son of my bosom, Son who art alone
170   My Word, my wisdom, and effectual might,[6]
       All hast thou spoken as my thoughts are, all
       As my eternal purpose hath decreed:
       Man shall not quite be lost, but saved who will,
       Yet not of will in him, but grace in me
175   Freely vouchsafed; once more I will renew
       His lapsèd powers, though forfeit and enthralled

---

4. The Son echoes (or rather foreshadows) Abraham pleading with the Lord to spare Sodom: "That be far from thee to do after this manner, to slay the righteous with the wicked . . . that be far from thee. Shall not the Judge of all the earth do right?" (Genesis 18.25).
5. *Satan* in Hebrew means "adversary."
6. God's speech is rhythmic and sometimes rhymed.

By sin to foul exorbitant desires;
Upheld by me, yet once more he shall stand
On even ground against his mortal foe,
180 By me upheld, that he may know how frail
His fall'n condition is, and to me owe
All his deliv'rance, and to none but me.
Some I have chosen of peculiar grace
Elect above the rest;[7] so is my will:
185 The rest shall hear me call, and oft be warned°   warned about
Their sinful state, and to appease betimes
Th' incensèd Deity, while offered grace
Invites; for I will clear their senses dark,
What may suffice, and soften stony hearts
190 To pray, repent, and bring obedience due.
To prayer, repentance, and obedience due,
Though but endeavored with sincere intent,
Mine ear shall not be slow, mine eye not shut.
And I will place within them as a guide
195 My umpire conscience, whom if they will hear,
Light after light well used they shall attain,[8]
And to the end persisting, safe arrive.
This my long sufferance and my day of grace
They who neglect and scorn, shall never taste;
200 But hard be hardened, blind be blinded more,
That they may stumble on, and deeper fall;
And none but such from mercy I exclude.
But yet all is not done; man disobeying,
Disloyal breaks his fealty, and sins
205 Against the high supremacy of Heav'n,
Affecting° Godhead, and so losing all,   aspiring to
To expiate his treason hath naught left,
But to destruction sacred and devote,°   consecrated
He with his whole posterity must die,
210 Die he or justice must; unless for him
Some other able, and as willing, pay
The rigid satisfaction, death for death.
Say heav'nly Powers, where shall we find such love,
Which of ye will be mortal to redeem
215 Man's mortal crime,[9] and just th' unjust to save,
Dwells in all heaven charity so dear?"
    He asked, but all the heav'nly choir stood mute,[1]
And silence was in Heav'n; on man's behalf
Patron or intercessor none appeared,
220 Much less that durst upon his own head draw
The deadly forfeiture, and ransom set.

---

7. In this speech, Milton's God rejects the Calvinist doctrine that he had from the beginning predestined the damnation or salvation of each individual soul; he claims rather that grace sufficient for salvation is offered to all, enabling everyone, if they choose to do so, to believe and persevere. He does, however, assert his right to give special grace to some.
8. By using the light of conscience well they will gain more light.
9. "Mortal" means "human" in line 214, but "deadly" in line 215.
1. Compare the devils in the Great Consult, 2.420–26.

And now without redemption all mankind
Must have been lost, adjudged to death and Hell
By doom severe, had not the Son of God,
225 In whom the fullness dwells of love divine,
His dearest mediation° thus renewed.   *intercession*

    "Father, thy word is passed, man shall find grace;
And shall grace not find means, that finds her way,
The speediest of thy wingèd messengers,
230 To visit all thy creatures, and to all
Comes unprevented,° unimplored, unsought,   *unanticipated*
Happy for man, so coming; he her aid
Can never seek, once dead in sins and lost;
Atonement for himself or offering meet,
235 Indebted and undone, hath none to bring:
Behold me then, me for him, life for life
I offer, on me let thine anger fall;
Account me man; I for his sake will leave
Thy bosom, and this glory next to thee
240 Freely put off, and for him lastly die
Well pleased, on me let Death wreck all his rage;
Under his gloomy power I shall not long
Lie vanquished; thou hast giv'n me to possess
Life in myself forever, by thee I live,
245 Though now to Death I yield, and am his due
All that of me can die, yet that debt paid,
Thou wilt not leave me in the loathsome grave
His prey, nor suffer my unspotted soul
Forever with corruption there to dwell;
250 But I shall rise victorious, and subdue
My vanquisher, spoiled of his vaunted spoil;
Death his death's wound shall then receive, and stoop
Inglorious, of his mortal sting disarmed.
I through the ample air in triumph high
255 Shall lead Hell captive maugre° Hell, and show   *in spite of*
The powers of darkness bound.[2] Thou at the sight
Pleased, out of Heaven shalt look down and smile,
While by thee raised I ruin[3] all my foes,
Death last, and with his carcass glut the grave:
260 Then with the multitude of my redeemed
Shall enter Heaven long absent, and return,
Father, to see thy face, wherein no cloud
Of anger shall remain, but peace assured,
And reconcilement; wrath shall be no more
265 Thenceforth, but in thy presence joy entire."

    His words here ended, but his meek aspéct
Silent yet spake, and breathed immortal love
To mortal men, above which only shone
Filial obedience: as a sacrifice

---

2. The Son's triumph is represented in a series of paradoxes—a vanquisher vanquished, a spoiler spoiled, Death dead, Hell captured in all Hell's

despite.
3. In the Latin sense, throw down.

270 Glad to be offered, he attends the will
Of his great Father. Admiration° seized   *wonder*
All Heav'n, what this might mean, and wither tend
Wond'ring; but soon th' Almighty thus replied:
  "O thou in Heav'n and earth the only peace
275 Found out for mankind under wrath, O thou
My sole complacence!° well thou know'st how dear   *pleasure, delight*
To me are all my works, nor man the least
Though last created, that for him I spare
Thee from my bosom and right hand, to save,
280 By losing thee a while, the whole race lost.
Thou therefore whom⁴ thou only canst redeem,
Their nature also to thy nature join;
And be thy self man among men on earth,
Made flesh, when time shall be, of virgin seed,
285 By wondrous birth: be thou in Adam's room
The head of all mankind, though Adam's son.⁵
As in him perish all men, so in thee
As from a second root shall be restored,
As many as are restored, without thee none.
290 His crime makes guilty all his sons; thy merit
Imputed shall absolve them who renounce
Their own both righteous and unrighteous deeds,⁶
And live in thee transplanted, and from thee
Receive new life. So man, as is most just,
295 Shall satisfy for man, be judged and die,
And dying rise, and rising with him raise
His brethren, ransomed with his own dear life.
So heav'nly love shall outdo hellish hate,
Giving to death, and dying to redeem,
300 So dearly to redeem what hellish hate
So easily destroyed, and still destroys
In those who, when they may, accept not grace.
Nor shalt thou by descending to assume
Man's nature, lessen or degrade thine own.
305 Because thou hast, though throned in highest bliss
Equal to God, and equally enjoying
God-like fruition,° quitted all to save   *state*
A world from utter loss, and hast been found
By merit more than birthright Son of God,⁷
310 Found worthiest to be so by being good,
Far more than great or high; because in thee
Love hath abounded more than glory abounds.
Therefore thy humiliation shall exalt
With thee thy manhood also to this throne;

---

4. The antecedent of "whom" is, loosely construed, the "their nature" that follows it.
5. The Son of God, who long antedates the creation of Adam and who is actually the first created being (3.383), is later incarnated in Jesus Christ; he is called Second Adam and "Son of Man" by reason of his descent from the first man, Adam. Cf. 1 Corinthians 15.22: "For as in Adam all die,

even so in Christ shall all be made alive."
6. The merit of Christ attributed vicariously ("imputed") to human beings frees from original sin those who renounce their own deeds, good and bad, and hope to be saved by faith.
7. A heterodox doctrine, that Christ was Son of God by merit. Compare with Satan (2.5).

315 Here shalt thou sit incarnate, here shalt reign
Both God and man, Son both of God and man,
Anointed[8] universal King; all power
I give thee, reign forever, and assume
Thy merits; under thee as Head Supreme
320 Thrones, Princedoms, Powers, Dominions[9] I reduce:
All knees to thee shall bow, of them that bide
In Heaven, or earth, or under earth in Hell;
When thou attended gloriously from Heav'n
Shalt in the sky appear, and from thee send
325 The summoning Archangels to proclaim
Thy dread tribunal: forthwith from all winds°   directions
The living, and forthwith the cited° dead   summoned
Of all past ages to the general doom
Shall hasten, such a peal shall rouse their sleep.
330 Then all thy saints assembled, thou shalt judge
Bad men and angels, they arraigned° shall sink   accursed
Beneath thy sentence; Hell, her numbers full,
Thenceforth shall be forever shut. Meanwhile
The world shall burn, and from her ashes spring
335 New Heav'n and earth, wherein the just shall dwell,[1]
And after all their tribulations long
See golden days, fruitful of golden deeds,
With joy and love triumphing, and fair truth.
Then thou thy regal scepter shalt lay by,
340 For regal scepter then no more shall need,°   be needed
God shall be all in all. But all ye gods,°   angels
Adore him, who to compass all this dies,
Adore the Son, and honor him as me."
    No sooner had th' Almighty ceased, but all
345 The multitude of angels with a shout
Loud as from numbers without number, sweet
As from blest voices, uttering joy, Heav'n rung[2]
With jubilee, and loud hosannas filled
Th' eternal regions: lowly reverent
350 Towards either throne[3] they bow, and to the ground
With solemn adoration down they cast
Their crowns inwove with amarant[4] and gold,
Immortal amarant, a flow'r which once
In Paradise, fast by the Tree of Life
355 Began to bloom, but soon for man's offense
To Heav'n removed where first it grew, there grows,
And flow'rs aloft shading the Fount of Life,
And where the river of bliss through midst of Heav'n
Rolls o'er Elysian[5] flow'rs her amber° stream;   pure

[handwritten marginal note: "there is a great contrast to hell. they don't fight, they cheer for each other, here they applaud Jesus' valor."]

---

8. "The Anointed" in Hebrew means messiah.
9. Orders of angels.
1. Milton's description of the Last Judgment draws on several biblical texts, including Matthew 24.30–31, and 25.31–32; the account of the burning and re-creation of Heaven and earth is from 2 Peter 3.12–13.
2. "Multitude" (line 345) is the subject of the sen-

tence, "rung" the verb, and "Heav'n" the object.
3. Thrones of God and the Son.
4. In Greek, "unfading," a legendary immortal flower.
5. Milton draws freely, for his Christian Heaven, on descriptions of the classical paradisal place, the Elysian Fields.

360 With these that never fade the Spirits elect
Bind their resplendent locks inwreathed with beams,
Now in loose garlands thick thrown off, the bright
Pavement that like a sea of jasper shone
Impurpled with celestial roses smiled.
365 Then crowned again their golden harps they took,
Harps ever tuned, that glittering by their side
Like quivers hung, and with preamble sweet
Of charming symphony they introduce
Their sacred song, and waken raptures high;
370 No voice exempt,° no voice but well could join   *excluded*
Melodious part, such concord is in Heav'n.
   Thee Father first they sung omnipotent,
Immutable, immortal, infinite,
Eternal King; thee Author of all being,
375 Fountain of light, thyself invisible
Amidst the glorious brightness where thou sitt'st
Throned inaccessible, but when thou shad'st
The full blaze of thy beams, and through a cloud
Drawn round about thee like a radiant shrine,[6]
380 Dark with excessive bright thy skirts appear,
Yet dazzle Heav'n, that brightest Seraphim
Approach not, but with both wings veil their eyes.
Thee next they sang of all creation first,[7]
Begotten Son, Divine Similitude,
385 In whose conspicuous count'nance, without cloud
Made visible, th' Almighty Father shines,
Whom else no creature can behold;[8] on thee
Impressed th' effulgence of his glory abides,
Transfused on thee his ample spirit rests.
390 He Heav'n of heavens and all the Powers therein
By thee created, and by thee threw down
Th' aspiring Dominations.[9] Thou that day
Thy Father's dreadful thunder didst not spare,
Nor stop thy flaming chariot wheels, that shook
395 Heav'n's everlasting frame, while o'er the necks
Thou drov'st of warring angels disarrayed.
Back from pursuit thy Powers° with loud acclaim   *angels*
Thee only extolled, Son of thy Father's might,
To execute fierce vengeance on his foes,
400 Not so on man; him through their malice fall'n,
Father of mercy and grace, thou didst not doom
So strictly, but much more to pity incline:
No sooner did thy dear and only Son
Perceive thee purposed not to doom° frail man   *judge*
405 So strictly, but much more to pity inclined,
He to appease thy wrath, and end the strife
Of mercy and justice in thy face discerned,

---

6. Note the turn from theological debate to images
that evoke a more mystical aspect of God.
7. The Son is not eternal, as in Trinitarian doctrine, but rather, God's first creation.

8. If it were not for the Son who is God's image,
no creature could see God.
9. The rebel angels.

Regardless of the bliss wherein he sat
Second to thee, offered himself to die
410 For man's offense. O unexampled love,
Love nowhere to be found to be found less than divine!
Hail Son of God, Saviour of men, thy name
Shall be the copious matter of my[1] song
Henceforth, and never shall my harp thy praise
415 Forget, nor from thy Father's praise disjoin.
    Thus they in Heav'n, above the starry sphere,
Their happy hours in joy and hymning spent.
Meanwhile upon the firm opacous° globe   *opaque*
Of this round world, whose first convex divides
420 The luminous inferior orbs, enclosed
From Chaos and th' inroad of Darkness old,
Satan alighted walks:[2] a globe far off
It seemed, now seems a boundless continent
Dark, waste, and wild, under the frown of Night
425 Starless exposed, and ever-threatening storms
Of Chaos blust'ring round, inclement sky;
Save on that side which from the wall of Heav'n
Though distant far some small reflection gains
Of glimmering air less vexed with tempest loud:
430 Here walked the Fiend at large in spacious field.
As when a vulture on Imaus bred,
Whose snowy ridge the roving Tartar bounds,[3]
Dislodging from a region scarce of prey
To gorge the flesh of lambs or yeanling° kids   *newborn*
435 On hills where flocks are fed, flies toward the springs
Of Ganges or Hydaspes, Indian streams;[4]
But in his way lights on the barren plains
Of Sericana, where Chineses drive
With sails and wind their cany wagons light:
440 So on this windy sea of land, the Fiend
Walked up and down alone bent on his prey,
Alone, for other creature in this place
Living or lifeless to be found was none,
None yet, but store hereafter from the earth
445 Up hither like aërial vapors flew
Of all things transitory and vain, when sin
With vanity had filled the works of men:
Both all things vain, and all who in vain things
Built their fond hopes of glory or lasting fame,
450 Or happiness in this or th' other life;
All who have their reward on earth, the fruits
Of painful superstition and blind zeal,
Naught seeking but the praise of men, here find
Fit retribution, empty as their deeds;

---

1. Either Milton here quotes the angels singing as a single chorus, or he associates himself with their song, or both.
2. Satan is on the outermost of the ten concentric spheres that make up the cosmos.
3. Imaus, a ridge of mountains beyond the modern

Himalayas, runs north through Asia from modern Afghanistan to the Arctic Circle.
4. Both the Ganges and Hydaspes (a tributary of the Indus) rise from the mountains of northern India. Sericana (line 438) is a region in Northwest China.

455   All th' unaccomplished° works of nature's hand,   *imperfect*
         Abortive, monstrous, or unkindly° mixed,   *unnatural*
         Dissolved on earth, fleet° hither, and in vain,   *float*
         Till final dissolution, wander here,
         Not in the neighboring moon, as some[5] have dreamed;
460   Those argent° fields more likely habitants,   *silver*
         Translated saints,[6] or middle Spirits hold
         Betwixt th' angelical and human kind:
         Hither of ill-joined sons and daughters born
         First from the ancient world those giants came
465   With many a vain exploit, though then renowned:[7]
         The builders next of Babel on the plain
         Of Sennaär,[8] and still with vain design
         New Babels, had they wherewithal, would build:
         Others came single; he who to be deemed
470   A god, leaped fondly° into Etna flames,   *foolishly*
         Empedocles, and he who to enjoy
         Plato's Elysium, leaped into the sea,
         Cleombrotus, and many more too long,[9]
         Embryos and idiots, eremites° and friars   *hermits*
475   White, black, and gray, with all their trumpery.[1]
         Here pilgrims roam, that strayed so far to seek
         In Golgotha[2] him dead, who lives in Heav'n;
         And they who to be sure of paradise
         Dying put on the weeds° of Dominic,   *garments*
480   Or in Franciscan think to pass disguised;[3]
         They pass the planets seven, and pass the fixed,
         And that crystálline sphere whose balance weighs
         The trepidation talked, and that first moved;[4]
         And now Saint Peter at Heav'n's wicket seems
485   To wait them with his keys, and now at foot
         Of Heav'n's ascent they lift their feet, when lo
         A violent crosswind from either coast
         Blows them transverse ten thousand leagues awry
         Into the devious° air. Then might ye see   *erratic*
490   Cowls, hoods and habits[5] with their wearers tossed
         And fluttered into rags; then relics, beads,
         Indulgences, dispenses, pardons, bulls,
         The sport of winds: all these upwhirled aloft

---

5. Milton's Paradise of Fools (named in line 496) was inspired by Ariosto's Limbo of Vanity in *Orlando Furioso* (book 34, lines 73ff.); Milton's region is reserved for deluded victims of misplaced devotion, chiefly Roman Catholics.
6. Holy men like Enoch and Elijah, transported to Heaven while yet alive.
7. Giants, born of unnatural marriages between the "sons of God" and the daughters of men (Genesis 6.4), are creatures unkindly mixed.
8. Shinar, the plain of Babel (Genesis 11.2–9); the Tower of Babel is an emblem of human pride and folly.
9. I.e., it would take too long to name them. Both Empedocles and Cleombrotus foolishly carried piety to the point of suicide.
1. The white friars are Carmelites; the black,

Dominicans; and the gray, Franciscans. "Trumpery": religious paraphernalia.
2. Place where Christ was crucified.
3. Some try to trick God into granting them salvation by wearing on their deathbeds the garb of various religious orders.
4. Milton follows their souls through the spheres of the moon and sun, the five then-known planets, the fixed stars, and the sphere responsible for the "trepidation" (a periodic corrective shudder of the cosmos), up to the *primum mobile* or prime mover. The next step seems to be the empyreal Heaven.
5. The dress of religious orders, together with (next lines) rosary beads, saints' relics, various kinds of pardon for sins, and papal decrees ("bulls").

Fly o'er the backside° of the world far off   *rump*
495 Into a limbo large and broad, since called
The Paradise of Fools, to few unknown
Long after, now unpeopled, and untrod;
All this dark globe the Fiend found as he passed,
And long he wandered, till at last a gleam
500 Of dawning light turned thitherward in haste
His traveled° steps; far distant he descries   *travel-weary*
Ascending by degrees° magnificent   *steps*
Up to the wall of heaven a structure high,
At top whereof, but far more rich appeared
505 The work as of a kingly palace gate
With frontispiece° of diamond and gold   *pediment*
Embellished; thick with sparkling orient° gems   *lustrous*
The portal shone, inimitable on earth,
By model, or by shading pencil drawn.
510 The stairs were such as whereon Jacob saw
Angels ascending and descending, bands
Of guardians bright, when he from Esau fled
To Padan-Aram in the field of Luz,
Dreaming by night under the open sky,
515 And waking cried, "This is the gate of Heav'n."[6]
Each stair mysteriously was meant, nor stood
There always, but drawn up to Heav'n sometimes
Viewless,° and underneath a bright sea flowed   *invisible*
Of jasper, or of liquid pearl, whereon
520 Who after came from earth, sailing arrived,
Wafted by angels, or flew o'er the lake
Rapt in a chariot drawn by fiery steeds.[7]
The stairs were then let down, whether to dare
The Fiend by easy ascent, or aggravate
525 His sad exclusion from the doors of bliss.
Direct against which opened from beneath,
Just o'er the blissful seat of Paradise,
A passage down to th' earth, a passage wide,[8]
Wider by far than that of aftertimes
530 Over Mount Zion, and, though that were large,
Over the Promised Land to God so dear,
By which, to visit oft those happy tribes,
On high behests his angels to and fro
Passed frequent, and his eye with choice° regard *discriminating*
535 From Paneas the fount of Jordan's flood
To Beërsaba, where the Holy Land
Borders on Egypt and the Arabian shore;[9]
So wide the op'ning seemed, where bounds were set
To darkness, such as bound the ocean wave.
540 Satan from hence now on the lower stair

---

6. The story of Jacob's vision is summarized from
Genesis 28.1–19; the stairs of the ladder allegorically ("mysteriously") represent stages of spiritual
growth.
7. Elijah was wafted to heaven in a chariot.

8. A passage through the crystalline spheres, otherwise impenetrable.
9. From Paneas (or Dan) in northern Palestine to
Beersaba, or Beersheba, near the Egyptian border—
the entire land of Israel.

That scaled by steps of gold to Heaven gate
Looks down with wonder at the sudden view
Of all this world at once. As when a scout
Through dark and desert ways with peril gone
545 All night; at last by break of cheerful dawn
Obtains° the brow of some high-climbing hill,   *gains*
Which to his eye discovers unaware
The goodly prospect of some foreign land
First seen, or some renowned metropolis
550 With glistering spires and pinnacles adorned,
Which now the rising sun gilds with his beams.
Such wonder seized, though after Heaven seen,
The Spirit malign, but much more envy seized
At sight of all this world beheld so fair.
555 Round he surveys, and well might, where he stood
So high above the circling canopy
Of night's extended shade; from eastern point
Of Libra to the fleecy star that bears
Andromeda far off Atlantic seas[1]
560 Beyond th' horizon; then from pole to pole
He views in breadth, and without longer pause
Down right into the world's first region throws
His flight precipitant, and winds with ease
Through the pure marble° air his oblique way   *sparkling*
565 Amongst innumerable stars, that shone
Stars distant, but nigh hand seemed other worlds,
Or other worlds they seemed, or happy isles,
Like those Hesperian gardens famed of old,
Fortunate fields, and groves and flow'ry vales,[2]
570 Thrice happy isles, but who dwelt happy there
He stayed not to inquire: above them all
The golden sun in splendor likest Heaven
Allured his eye: thither his course he bends
Through the calm firmament; but up or down
575 By center, or eccentric, hard to tell,
Or longitude,[3] where the great luminary
Aloof the vulgar constellations thick,
That from his lordly eye keep distance due,
Dispenses light from far; they as they move
580 Their starry dance in numbers that compute
Days, months, and years, towards his all-cheering lamp
Turn swift their various motions, or are turned
By his magnetic beam, that gently warms
The universe, and to each inward part
585 With gentle penetration, though unseen,
Shoots invisible virtue° even to the deep: *influence, strength*
So wondrously was set his station bright.
  There lands the Fiend, a spot like which perhaps

1. In the zodiac, Libra is diametrically opposite Aries, or the Ram ("the fleecy star"), which seems to carry the constellation Andromeda on its back. 2. The gardens of the Hesperides and the "fortu-

nate isles" of Greek mythology, classical versions of paradise, lay far out in the Atlantic. 3. Milton leaves open whether the sun or the earth is at the center of the cosmos.

Astronomer in the sun's lucent orb
590   Through his glazed optic tube yet never saw.[4]
The place he found beyond expression bright,
Compared with aught on earth, metal or stone;
Not all parts like, but all alike informed
With radiant light, as glowing iron with fire;
595   If metal, part seemed gold, part silver clear;
If stone, carbuncle most or chrysolite,[5]
Ruby or topaz, to the twelve that shone
In Aaron's breastplate,[6] and a stone besides
Imagined rather oft than elsewhere seen,[7]
600   That stone, or like to that which here below
Philosophers in vain so long have sought,[8]
In vain, though by their powerful art they bind
Volátile Hermes, and call up unbound
In various shapes old Proteus from the sea,
605   Drained through a limbec to his native form.[9]
What wonder then if fields and regions here
Breathe forth elixir pure,[1] and rivers run
Potable° gold, when with one virtuous° touch   *drinkable / powerful*
Th' arch-chemic° sun so far from us remote   *chief alchemist*
610   Produces with terrestrial humor° mixed   *earth's moisture*
Here in the dark so many precious things
Of color glorious and effect so rare?
Here matter new to gaze the Devil met
Undazzled, far and wide his eye commands,
615   For sight no obstacle found here, nor shade,
But all sunshine, as when his beams at noon
Culminate from th' equator, as they now
Shot upward still direct, whence no way round
Shadow from body opaque can fall,[2] and the air,
620   Nowhere so clear, sharpened his visual ray
To objects distant far,[3] whereby he soon
Saw within ken° a glorious angel stand,   *range of vision*
The same whom John saw also in the sun:[4]
His back was turned, but not his brightness hid;
625   Of beaming sunny rays, a golden tiar°   *tiara, crown*
Circled his head, nor less his locks behind
Illustrious° on his shoulders fledge° with wings   *lustrous / feathered*
Lay waving round; on some great charge employed
He seemed, or fixed in cogitation deep.

---

4. Galileo first observed sunspots through his telescope in 1609.
5. Any green stone. "Carbuncle": any red stone.
6. In Exodus 28.15–20, Aaron's "breastplate" is described as decorated with twelve different gems, of which Milton lists the first four.
7. I.e., elsewhere imagined more often than seen.
8. Alchemists had identified the "philosophers'" stone with the *urim* on Aaron's breastplace (Exodus 28.30); that stone reputedly could heal all diseases, restore paradise, and transmute base metals to gold.
9. "Hermes": the winged god and the element mercury, which evaporated readily ("volatile").

"Proteus": the shape-shifting sea-god, a symbol of matter. Alchemists would "bind" (solidify) mercury and dissolve or refine matter to its "native form" in a vessel (alembic, "limbec").
1. The liquid form of the philosopher's stone. "Here": in the sun.
2. Before the Fall (and the consequent tipping of the earth's axis) the sun at noon, on the equator, never cast a shadow. "Culminate": reach their zenith.
3. The eye was thought to emit a beam into the object perceived.
4. "I saw an angel standing in the sun" (Revelation 19.17).

630 Glad was the Spirit impure; as now in hope
  To find who might direct his wand'ring flight
  To Paradise the happy seat of man,
  His journey's end and our beginning woe.
  But first he casts° to change his proper shape,   *contrives*
635 Which else might work him danger or delay:
  And now a stripling Cherub he appears,
  Not of the prime,[5] yet such as in his face
  Youth smiled celestial, and to every limb
  Suitable grace diffused, so well he feigned;
640 Under a coronet his flowing hair
  In curls on either cheek played, wings he wore
  Of many a colored plume sprinkled with gold,
  His habit fit for speed succinct,° and held   *close-fitting*
  Before his decent° steps a silver wand.   *comely*
645 He drew not nigh unheard; the angel bright,
  Ere he drew nigh, his radiant visage turned,
  Admonished by his ear, and straight was known
  Th' Archangel Uriel, one of the sev'n
  Who in God's presence, nearest to his throne[6]
650 Stand ready at command, and are his eyes
  That run through all the heav'ns, or down to th' earth
  Bear his swift errands over moist and dry,
  O'er sea and land: him Satan thus accosts:
  "Uriel, for thou of those sev'n Spirits that stand
655 In sight of God's high throne, gloriously bright,
  The first art wont his great authentic° will   *authoritative*
  Interpreter through highest Heav'n to bring,
  Where all his sons thy embassy attend;
  And here art likeliest by supreme decree
660 Like honor to obtain, and as his eye
  To visit oft this new creation round;
  Unspeakable desire to see, and know
  All these his wondrous works, but chiefly man,
  His chief delight and favor,° him for whom   *favorite*
665 All these his works so wondrous he ordained,
  Hath brought me from the choirs of Cherubim
  Alone thus wand'ring. Brightest Seraph tell
  In which of all these shining orbs hath man
  His fixèd seat, or fixèd seat hath none,
670 But all these shining orbs his choice to dwell;
  That I may find him, and with secret gaze,
  Or open admiration him behold
  On whom the great Creator hath bestowed
  Worlds, and on whom hath all these graces poured;
675 That both in him and all things, as is meet,
  The Universal Maker we may praise;
  Who justly hath driv'n out his rebel foes
  To deepest Hell, and to repair that loss

---

5. Not yet in the prime of life, or, not of the prime
rank of angels.
6. Uriel—in Hebrew, "Light" (or fire) of God—is

the angel named first (in 1 Enoch) among the
seven angels who stood before God's throne.

Created this new happy race of men
680   To serve him better: wise are all his ways."
      So spake the false dissembler unperceived;
      For neither man nor angel can discern
      Hypocrisy, the only evil that walks
      Invisible, except to God alone,
685   By his permissive will, through Heav'n and earth:
      And oft though wisdom wake, suspicion sleeps
      At wisdom's gate, and to simplicity
      Resigns her charge, while goodness thinks no ill
      Where no ill seems: which now for once beguiled
690   Uriel, though regent of the sun, and held
      The sharpest-sighted Spirit of all in Heav'n;
      Who to the fraudulent impostor foul
      In his uprightness answer thus returned:
      "Fair angel, thy desire which tends° to know   *inclines*
695   The works of God, thereby to glorify
      The great Work-Master, leads to no excess
      That reaches blame, but rather merits praise
      The more it seems excess, that led thee hither
      From thy empyreal mansion thus alone,
700   To witness with thine eyes what some perhaps
      Contented with report hear only in Heav'n:
      For wonderful indeed are all his works,
      Pleasant to know, and worthiest to be all
      Had in remembrance always with delight;
705   But what created mind can comprehend
      Their number, or the wisdom infinite
      That brought them forth, but hid their causes deep.
      I saw when at his word the formless mass,
      This world's material mold,° came to a heap: *substance*
710   Confusion heard his voice, and wild uproar
      Stood ruled, stood vast infinitude confined;
      Till at his second bidding darkness fled,
      Light shone, and order from disorder sprung:
      Swift to their several quarters hasted then
715   The cumbrous elements, earth, flood, air, fire,
      And this ethereal quíntessence[7] of Heav'n
      Flew upward, spirited with various forms,
      That rolled orbicular,[8] and turned to stars
      Numberless, as thou seest, and how they move;
720   Each had his place appointed, each his course,
      The rest in circuit walls this universe.
      Look downward on that globe whose hither side
      With light from hence, though but reflected, shines;
      That place is earth the seat of man, that light
725   His day, which else as th' other hemisphere
      Night would invade, but there the neighboring moon
      (So call that opposite fair star) her aid

7. The fifth element, of which the incorruptible heavenly bodies were made.
8. The spherical shape of the stars and their orbits. "Spirited with various forms": presided over or inhabited by various angelic spirits or intelligences (Plato, *Timaeus* 41E).

Timely interposes, and her monthly round
Still ending, still renewing through mid-Heav'n,
730 With borrowed light her countenance triform⁹
Hence¹ fills and empties to enlighten th' earth,
And in her pale dominion checks the night.
That spot to which I point is Paradise,
Adam's abode, those lofty shades his bow'r.
735 Thy way thou canst not miss, me mine requires."
⁣   Thus said, he turned, and Satan bowing low,
As to superior Spirits is wont in Heav'n,
Where honor due and reverence none neglects,
Took leave, and toward the coast of earth beneath,
740 Down from th' ecliptic,° sped with hoped success,   *the sun's orbit*
Throws his steep flight in many an airy wheel,
Nor stayed, till on Niphates' top² he lights.

Book 4

O for that warning voice, which he who saw
Th' Apocalypse, heard cry in heaven aloud,
Then when the Dragon, put to second rout,
Came furious down to be revenged on men,
5 "Woe to the inhabitants on earth!"¹ that now,
While time was, our first parents had been warned
The coming of their secret foe, and scaped
Haply° so scaped his mortal° snare; for now   *happily / deadly*
Satan, now first inflamed with rage, came down,
10 The tempter ere° th' accuser of mankind,   *before being*
To wreck° on innocent frail man his loss   *avenge, wreak*
Of that first battle, and his flight to Hell:
Yet not rejoicing in his speed, though bold,
Far off and fearless, nor with cause to boast,
15 Begins his dire attempt, which nigh the birth
Now rolling, boils in his tumultuous breast,
And like a devilish engine back recoils
Upon himself; horror and doubt distract
His troubled thoughts, and from the bottom stir
20 The Hell within him, for within him Hell
He brings, and round about him, nor from Hell
One step no more than from himself can fly
By change of place: now conscience wakes despair
That slumbered, wakes the bitter memory
25 Of what he was, what is, and what must be
Worse; of worse deeds worse sufferings must ensue.
Sometimes towards Eden which now in his view
Lay pleasant, his grieved look he fixes sad,
Sometimes towards Heav'n and the full-blazing sun,
30 Which now sat high in his meridian tow'r:²

---

9. The moon was said to have a triple nature: Luna
in heaven, Diana on earth, and Hecate in Hell.
1. From here (the sun).
2. A mountain in Assyria.

1. John of Patmos, in Revelation 12.3–12, hears
such a cry during a second war in Heaven, between
the Dragon and the angels.
2. Midday, the height of noon.

Then much revolving,° thus in sighs began. *pondering*
   "O thou that with surpassing glory crowned,[3]
Look'st from thy sole dominion like the god
Of this new world: at whose sight all the stars
35 Hide their diminished heads; to thee I call,
But with no friendly voice, and add thy name
O sun, to tell thee how I hate thy beams
That bring to my remembrance from what state
I fell, how glorious once above thy sphere;
40 Till pride and worse ambition threw me down
Warring in Heav'n against Heav'n's matchless King:
Ah wherefore! he deserved no such return
From me, whom he created what I was
In that bright eminence, and with his good
45 Upbraided none,[4] nor was his service hard.
What could be less than to afford him praise,
The easiest recompense, and pay him thanks,
How due! yet all his good proved ill in me,
And wrought but malice; lifted up so high
50 I 'sdained° subjection, and thought one step higher *disdained*
Would set me highest, and in a moment quit° *pay*
The debt immense of endless gratitude,
So burthensome still° paying, still to owe; *always*
Forgetful what from him I still received,
55 And understood not that a grateful mind
By owing owes not, but still pays, at once
Indebted and discharged; what burden then?
O had his powerful destiny ordained
Me some inferior angel, I had stood
60 Then happy; no unbounded hope had raised
Ambition. Yet why not? some other Power° *angel*
As great might have aspired, and me though mean
Drawn to his part; but other Powers as great
Fell not, but stand unshaken, from within
65 Or from without, to all temptations armed.
Hadst thou[5] the same free will and power to stand?
Thou hadst: whom hast thou then or what to accuse,
But Heav'n's free love dealt equally to all?
Be then his love accursed, since love or hate,
70 To me alike, it deals eternal woe.
Nay cursed be thou; since against his thy will
Chose freely what it now so justly rues.
Me miserable![6] which way shall I fly
Infinite wrath, and infinite despair?
75 Which way I fly is Hell; myself am Hell;[7]
And in the lowest deep a lower deep
Still threat'ning to devour me opens wide,

---

3. Milton's nephew, Edward Phillips, said that this soliloquy was written "several years before the poem was begun," and was intended to begin a drama on the topic, *Adam Unparadised*.
4. Demanded no return for his benefits (James 1.5).
5. Compare Satan's address to himself here with Adam's soliloquy in parallel circumstances (10.758ff.).
6. A Latinism, *me miserum!*
7. Compare Satan's earlier claim that "the mind is its own place" (1.254).

To which the Hell I suffer seems a Heav'n.
O then at last relent! is there no place
80 Left for repentance, none for pardon left?
None left but by submission; and that word
Disdain forbids me, and my dread of shame
Among the Spirits beneath, whom I seduced
With other promises and other vaunts
85 Than to submit, boasting I could subdue
Th' Omnipotent. Ay me, they little know
How dearly I abide° that boast so vain,   *pay the penalty for*
Under what torments inwardly I groan:
While they adore me on the throne of hell,
90 With diadem and scepter high advanced
The lower still I fall, only supreme
In misery; such joy ambition finds.
But say I could repent and could obtain
By act of grace⁸ my former state; how soon
95 Would hight recall high thoughts, how soon unsay
What feigned submission swore: ease would recant
Vows made in pain, as violent° and void.   *forced*
For never can true reconcilement grow
Where wounds of deadly hate have pierced so deep:
100 Which would but lead me to a worse relapse,
And heavier fall: so should I purchase dear
Short intermission bought with double smart.
This knows my punisher; therefore as far
From granting he, as I from begging peace:
105 All hope excluded thus, behold instead
Of us outcast, exiled, his new delight,
Mankind created, and for him this world.
So farewell hope, and with hope farewell fear,
Farewell remorse: all good to me is lost;
110 Evil be thou my good; by thee at least
Divided empire with Heav'n's King I hold
By thee, and more than half perhaps will reign;
As man ere long, and this new world shall know."
       Thus while he spake, each passion dimmed his face
115 Thrice changed with pale,° ire, envy and despair,   *pallor*
Which marred his borowed visage, and betrayed
Him counterfeit, if any eye beheld.
For heav'nly minds from such distempers foul
Are ever clear. Whereof he soon aware,
120 Each perturbation smoothed with outward calm,
Artificer of fraud; and was the first
That practiced falsehood under saintly show,
Deep malice to conceal, couched° with revenge: *hidden*
Yet not enough had practiced to deceive
125 Uriel once warned; whose eye pursued him down
The way he went, and on th' Assyrian mount°   *Niphates*
Saw him disfigured, more than could befall

8. The technical term for a formal pardon.

Spirit of happy sort: his gestures fierce
He marked and mad demeanor, then alone,
130 As he supposed, all unobserved, unseen.
    So on he fares, and to the border comes
Of Eden, where delicious Paradise,⁹
Now nearer, crowns with her enclosure green,
As with a rural mound the champaign head°   *open summit*
135 Of a steep wilderness, whose hairy sides
With thicket overgrown, grotesque¹ and wild,
Access denied; and overhead up grew
Insuperable highth of loftiest shade,
Cedar, and pine, and fir, and branching palm,
140 A sylvan scene, and as the ranks ascend
Shade above shade, a woody theater²
Of stateliest view. Yet higher than their tops
The verdurous wall of Paradise up sprung:
Which to our general sire gave prospect large
145 Into his nether empire neighboring round.
And higher than that wall a circling row
Of goodliest trees loaden with fairest fruit,
Blossoms and fruits at once of golden hue
Appeared, with gay enameled° colors mixed: *bright*
150 On which the sun more glad impressed his beams
Than in fair evening cloud, or humid bow,°   *rainbow*
When God hath show'red the earth; so lovely seemed
That landscape: and of pure now purer air³
Meets his approach, and to the heart inspires°   *infuses*
155 Vernal delight and joy, able to drive°   *drive out*
All sadness but despair: now gentle gales
Fanning their odoriferous° wings dispense   *fragrance-bearing*
Native perfumes, and whisper whence they stole
Those balmy spoils. As when to them who sail
160 Beyond the Cape of Hope,° and now are past   *Cape of Good Hope*
Mozambic, off at sea northeast winds blow
Sabean odors from the spicy shore
Of Araby the Blest,⁴ with such delay
Well pleased they slack their course, and many a league
165 Cheered with the grateful° smell old Ocean smiles.   *pleasing*
So entertained those odorous sweets the Fiend
Who came their bane, though with them better pleased
Than Asmodeus with the fishy fume,
That drove him, though enamored, from the spouse
170 Of Tobit's son,⁵ and with a vengeance sent
From Media post to Egypt, there fast bound.
    Now to th'ascent of that steep savage° hill   *wooded, wild*

9. Paradise is a delightful ("delicious") garden on top of a steep hill situated in the east of the land of Eden.
1. Characterized by interwoven, tangled vines and branches.
2. As if in a Greek amphitheater, the trees are set row on row.
3. The air becomes still purer.
4. *Arabia Felix* (modern Yemen). "Sabean": the biblical Sheba.
5. The Apocryphal book of Tobit tells of Tobias, Tobit's son, who married Sara and avoided the fate of her previous seven husbands (killed on their wedding night by the demon Asmodeus) by following the instructions of the angel Raphael and making a fishy smell to drive him off; Asmodeus then fled to Egypt where Raphael bound him.

Satan had journeyed on, pensive and slow;
But further way found none, so thick entwined,
175 As one continued brake,° the undergrowth   *thicket*
Of shrubs and tangling bushes had perplexed
All path of man or beast that passed that way:
One gate there only was, and that looked east
On th' other side: which when th' arch-felon saw
180 Due entrance he disdained, and in contempt,
At one slight bound high overleaped all bound
Of hill or highest wall, and sheer within
Lights on his feet. As when a prowling wolf,
Whom hunger drives to seek new haunt for prey,
185 Watching where shepherds pen their flocks at eve
In hurdled cotes° amid the field secure,   *pens of woven reeds*
Leaps o'er the fence with ease into the fold:
Or as a thief bent to unhoard the cash
Of some rich burgher, whose substantial doors,
190 Cross-barred and bolted fast, fear no assault,
In at the window climbs, or o'er the tiles;
So clomb° this first grand thief into God's fold: *climbed*
So since into his church lewd hirelings[6] climb.
Thence up he flew, and on the Tree of Life,
195 The middle tree and highest there that grew,
Sat like a cormorant;[7] yet not true life
Thereby regained, but sat devising death
To them who lived; nor on the virtue° thought   *power*
Of that life-giving plant, but only used
200 For prospect,° what well used had been the pledge   *as a lookout*
Of immortality. So little knows
Any, but God alone, to value right
The good before him, but perverts best things
To worst abuse, or to their meanest use.
205   Beneath him with new wonder now he views
To all delight of human sense exposed
In narrow room nature's whole wealth, yea more,
A heav'n on earth: for blissful Paradise
Of God the garden was, by him in the east
210 Of Eden planted; Eden stretched her line
From Auran eastward to the royal tow'rs
Of great Seleucia, built by Grecian kings,
Or where the sons of Eden long before
Dwelt in Telassar:[8] in this pleasant soil
215 His far more pleasant garden God ordained;
Out of the fertile ground he caused to grow
All trees of noblest kind for sight, smell, taste;
And all amid them stood the Tree of Life,
High eminent, blooming ambrosial° fruit   *divinely fragrant*

[Handwritten annotations: "Satan is a wolf & are sheep" (beside lines 182–185); "this makes the tone more ominous" (beside lines 189–193).]

---

6. Base men interested only in money; Milton would have clergymen not paid by the state, to ensure their purity of motive.
7. A sea bird, noted for gluttony.
8. "Auran" is the province of Hauran on the east-

ern border of Israel. "Selucia," a powerful city on the Tigris, near modern Baghdad, was founded by one of Alexander's generals ("built by Grecian kings"). "Telassar" is another Near Eastern kingdom.

220 Of vegetable gold; and next to life
Our death the Tree of Knowledge grew fast by,
Knowledge of good bought dear by knowing ill.
Southward through Eden⁹ went a river large,
Nor changed his course, but through the shaggy hill
225 Passed underneath engulfed, for God had thrown
That mountain as his garden mold° high raised   *rich earth*
Upon the rapid current, which through veins
Of porous earth with kindly° thirst up drawn,   *natural*
Rose a fresh fountain, and with many a rill
230 Watered the garden; thence united fell
Down the steep glade, and met the nether flood,
Which from his darksome passage now appears,
And now divided into four main streams,
Runs diverse, wand'ring many a famous realm
235 And country whereof here needs no account,
But rather to tell how, if art could tell,
How from that sapphire fount the crispèd° brooks,   *wavy, rippling*
Rolling on orient pearl and sands of gold,
With mazy error¹ under pendent shades
240 Ran nectar, visiting each plant, and fed
Flow'rs worthy of Paradise which not nice° art   *fastidious*
In beds and curious knots, but nature boon°   *bounteous*
Poured forth profuse on hill and dale and plain,
Both where the morning sun first warmly smote
245 The open field, and where the unpierced shade
Embrowned° the noontide bow'rs. Thus was this place,   *darkened*
A happy rural seat of various view,²
Groves whose rich trees wept odorous gums and balm,
Others whose fruit burnished with golden rind
250 Hung amiable,° Hesperian fables true,³   *lovely*
If true, here only, and of delicious taste:
Betwixt them lawns, or level downs, and flocks
Grazing the tender herb, were interposed,
Or palmy hillock, or the flow'ry lap
255 Of some irriguous° valley spread her store,   *well-watered*
Flow'rs of all hue, and without thorn the rose:
Another side, umbrageous° grots and caves   *shady*
Of cool recess, o'er which the mantling° vine   *enveloping*
Lays forth her purple grape, and gently creeps
260 Luxuriant; meanwhile murmuring waters fall
Down the slope hills, dispersed, or in a lake,
That to the fringèd bank with myrtle crowned,
Her crystal mirror holds, unite their streams.
The birds their choir apply; airs,⁴ vernal airs,
265 Breathing the smell of field and grove, attune
The trembling leaves, while universal Pan⁵

---

9. The Tigris (identified at 9.71) flowed under the
hill.
1. From Latin *errare*, wandering.
2. Like a country estate, with a variety of prospects.
3. These were real golden apples, by contrast to

those feigned golden apples of the Hesperides,
fabled paradisal islands in the Western Ocean.
4. Both breezes and melodies. "Their choir apply":
practice their songs.
5. The god of all nature—"pan" in Greek means
"all."

Knit° with the Graces and the Hours in dance   *clasping hands*
Led on th' eternal spring. Not that fair field
Of Enna, where Proserpine gathering flow'rs
270 Herself a fairer flow'r by gloomy Dis
Was gathered, which cost Ceres all that pain
To seek her through the world; nor that sweet grove
Of Daphne by Orontes, and th' inspired
Castalian spring,[6] might with this Paradise
275 Of Eden strive; nor that Nyseian isle
Girt with the river Triton, where old Cham,
Whom Gentiles Ammon call and Libyan Jove,
Hid Amalthea and her florid° son   *wine-flushed*
Young Bacchus from his stepdame Rhea's eye;[7]
280 Nor where Abassin kings their issue guard,
Mount Amara,[8] though this by some supposed
True Paradise under the Ethiop line°   *equator*
By Nilus'° head, enclosed with shining rock,   *Nile's*
A whole day's journey high, but wide remote
285 From this Assyrian garden,° where the Fiend   *Eden*
Saw undelighted all delight, all kind
Of living creatures new to sight and strange:
    Two of far nobler shape erect and tall,
God-like erect, with native honor clad
290 In naked majesty seemed lords of all,
And worthy seemed, for in their looks divine
The image of their glorious Maker shone,
Truth, wisdom, sanctitude severe and pure,
Severe but in true filial freedom placed;
295 Whence true authority in men;[9] though both
Not equal, as their sex not equal seemed;
For contemplation he and valor formed,
For softness she and sweet attractive grace,
He for God only, she for God in him:[1]   *she is subservient*
300 His fair large front° and eye sublime declared   *forehead*
Absolute rule; and hyacinthine[2] locks
Round from his parted forelock manly hung   *eve is*
Clust'ring, but not beneath his shoulders broad: *not as*
She as a veil down to the slender waist   *smart*
305 Her unadorned golden tresses wore   *as adam*
Disheveled, but in wanton ringlets waved
As the vine curls her tendrils,[3] which implied
Subjection, but required with gentle sway,°   *persuasion*

---

6. Milton compares Paradise with famous beauty spots of antiquity. Enna in Sicily was a lovely meadow from which "Proserpine" was kidnapped by "gloomy Dis" (i.e., Pluto); her mother Ceres sought her throughout the world. The grove of Daphne, near Antioch and the Orontes River in the Near East, had a spring called "Castalia" after the Muses' fountain near Parnassus.
7. The isle of Nysa in the river Triton in Tunisia was where Ammon (an Egyptian god, identified with Cham or Ham, the son of Noah) hid Bacchus, his child by Amalthea (who later became the god of wine), away from the eyes of his wife Rhea.

8. Atop Mount Amara, the "Abassin" (Abyssinian) king had a splendid palace in a paradisal garden.
9. This phrase underscores Milton's idea that true freedom involves obedience to natural superiors (i.e., God).
1. The phrase has as its context 1 Corinthians 11.3: "The head of every man is Christ; and the head of the woman is the man."
2. A classical metaphor for hair curled in the form of hyacinth petals, and perhaps also implying dark or flowing.
3. Eve's hair is curly, abundant, not subjected to rigid control, like the vegetation in Paradise.

And by her yielded, by him best received,

310　Yielded with coy° submission, modest pride, *shyly reserved*

And sweet reluctant amorous delay.

Nor those mysterious parts were then concealed,

Then was not guilty shame, dishonest° shame *unchaste*

Of nature's works, honor dishonorable,

315　Sin-bred, how have ye troubled all mankind

With shows instead, mere shows of seeming pure,

And banished from man's life his happiest life,

Simplicity and spotless innocence.

So passed they naked on, nor shunned the sight

320　Of God or angel, for they thought no ill:

So hand in hand they passed, the loveliest pair

That ever since in love's embraces met,

Adam the goodliest man of men since born

His sons, the fairest of her daughters Eve.

325　Under a tuft of shade that on a green

Stood whispering soft, by a fresh fountain side

They sat them down, and after no more toil

Of their sweet gard'ning labor than sufficed

To recommend cool Zephyr,[4] and made ease

330　More easy, wholesome thirst and appetite

More grateful, to their supper fruits they fell,

Nectarine° fruits which the compliant boughs *sweet as nectar*

Yielded them, sidelong as they sat recline

On the soft downy bank damasked with flow'rs:

335　The savory pulp they chew, and in the rind

Still as they thirsted scoop the brimming stream;

Nor gentle purpose,° nor endearing smiles *conversation*

Wanted,° nor youthful dalliance as beseems *lacked*

Fair couple, linked in happy nuptial league,

340　Alone as they. About them frisking played

All beasts of th' earth, since wild, and of all chase° *a game preserve*

In wood or wilderness, forest or den;

Sporting the lion ramped,° and in his paw *stood on hind legs*

Dandled the kid; bears, tigers, ounces,° pards° *lynxes / leopards*

345　Gamboled before them; th' unwieldy elephant

To make them mirth used all his might, and wreathed

His lithe proboscis;° close the serpent sly *trunk*

Insinuating,° wove with Gordian twine *writhing, twisting*

His braided train,[5] and of his fatal guile

350　Gave proof unheeded; others on the grass

Couched, and now filled with pasture gazing sat,

Or bedward ruminating:° for the sun *chewing the cud*

Declined was hasting now with prone° career *sinking*

To th' Ocean Isles,° and in th' ascending scale *the Azores*

355　Of Heav'n the stars that usher evening rose:

When Satan still in gaze, as first he stood,

Scarce thus at length failed speech recovered sad.

---

4. I.e., to make a cool breeze welcome.

5. Checkered body. "Gordian twine": cords as convoluted as the Gordian knot which Alexander the Great had to cut with his sword.

[handwritten marginal notes: "he lays out a heirarchy / God ↓ Adam ↓ Eve"; "Satan is trying to make Adam & Eve feel the same way about god that he does."; "this eludes to the question, 'who is equal to whom?'"; "this is an image of peace and happiness"]

"O Hell! what do mine eyes with grief behold,
Into our room of bliss thus high advanced
360 Creatures of other mold, earth-born perhaps,
Not Spirits, yet to heav'nly Spirits bright
Little inferior; whom my thoughts pursue
With wonder, and could love, so lively shines
In them divine resemblance, and such grace
365 The hand that formed them on their shape hath poured.
Ah gentle pair, ye little think how nigh   *he is very gentel*
Your change approaches, when all these delights
Will vanish and deliver ye to woe,   *crocidile tears*
More woe, the more your taste is now of joy;
370 Happy, but for so happy° ill secured   *it is ~~good~~*   *such happiness*
Long to continue, and this high seat your heav'n   *god's faul t*
Ill fenced for heav'n to keep out such a foe   *they are going*
As now is entered; yet no purposed foe   *to fail, he should*
To you whom I could pity thus forlorn   *have protected*
375 Though I unpitied: league with you I seek,   *them better*
And mutual amity so strait,° so close,   *intimate*
That I with you must dwell, or you with me
Henceforth; my dwelling haply may not please
Like this fair Paradise, your sense, yet such
380 Accept your Maker's work; he gave it me,
Which I as freely give; Hell shall unfold,
To entertain you two, her widest gates,
And send forth all her kings; there will be room,
Not like these narrow limits, to receive
385 Your numerous offspring; if no better place,
Thank him who puts me loath to this revenge
On you who wrong me not for° him who wronged.   *in place of*
And should I at your harmless innocence
Melt, as I do, yet public reason just,
390 Honor and empire with revenge enlarged
By conquering this new world, compels me now
To do what else though damned I should abhor."[6]
    So spake the Fiend, and with necessity,
The tyrant's plea, excused his devilish deeds.
395 Then from his lofty stand on that high tree
Down he alights among the sportful herd
Of those four-footed kinds, himself now one,
Now other, as their shape served best his end
Nearer to view his prey, and unespied
400 To mark what of their state he more might learn
By word or action marked: about them round
A lion now he stalks with fiery glare,
Then as a tiger, who by chance hath spied
In some purlieu° two gentle fawns at play,   *outskirts of a forest*
405 Straight couches close, then rising changes oft
His couchant watch, as one who chose his ground
Whence rushing he might surest seize them both

---

6. Satan's excuse—reason of state, public interest, empire, etc.—is called "the tyrant's plea" in line 394.

Gripped in each paw: when Adam first of men
To first of women Eve thus moving speech
410   Turned him all ear to hear new utterance flow:
     "Sole partner and sole° part of all these joys,   *chief*
Dearer thyself than all; needs must the Power
That made us, and for us this ample world
Be infinitely good, and of his good
415   As liberal and free as infinite,
That raised us from the dust and placed us here
In all this happiness, who at his hand
Have nothing merited, nor can perform
Aught whereof he hath need, he who requires
420   From us no other service than to keep
This one, this easy charge, of all the trees
In Paradise that bear delicious fruit
So various, not to taste that only Tree
Of Knowledge, planted by the Tree of Life,
425   So near grows death to life, whate'er death is,
Some dreadful thing no doubt; for well thou know'st
God hath pronounced it death to taste that Tree,
The only sign of our obedience left
Among so many signs of power and rule
430   Conferred upon us, and dominion giv'n
Over all other creatures that possess
Earth, air, and sea. Then let us not think hard
One easy prohibition, who enjoy
Free leave so large to all things else, and choice
435   Unlimited of manifold delights:
But let us ever praise him, and extol
His bounty, following our delightful task
To prune these growing plants, and tend these flow'rs,
Which were it toilsome, yet with thee were sweet."
440   To whom thus Eve replied. "O thou for whom
And from whom I was formed flesh of thy flesh,
And without whom am to no end, my guide
And head, what thou hast said is just and right.
For we to him indeed all praises owe,
445   And daily thanks, I chiefly who enjoy
So far the happier lot, enjoying thee
Preeminent by so much odds,° while thou   *advantage*
Like consort to thyself canst nowhere find.
That day I oft remember, when from sleep
450   I first awaked, and found myself reposed°   *resting*
Under a shade on flowers, much wond'ring where
And what I was, whence thither brought, and how.
Not distant far from thence a murmuring sound
Of waters issued from a cave and spread
455   Into a liquid plain, then stood unmoved
Pure as th' expanse of Heav'n; I thither went
With unexperienced thought, and laid me down
On the green bank, to look into the clear
Smooth lake, that to me seemed another sky.

460 As I bent down to look, just opposite,
A shape within the wat'ry gleam appeared
Bending to look on me, I started back,
It started back, but pleased I soon returned.
Pleased it returned as soon with answering looks   *she is seeing her reflection (narcissus)*
465 Of sympathy and love; there I had fixed
Mine eyes till now, and pined with vain° desire,[7]   futile
Had not a voice thus warned me, 'What thou seest,
What there thou seest fair creature is thyself,
With thee it came and goes: but follow me,
470 And I will bring thee where no shadow stays°   hinders
Thy coming, and thy soft embraces, he   *saying that*
Whose image thou art, him thou shalt enjoy   *Adam is better*
Inseparably thine, to him shalt bear   *looking than*
Multitudes like thyself, and thence be called   *she.*
475 Mother of human race': what could I do,
But follow straight° invisibly thus led?   at once
Till I espied thee, fair indeed and tall,
Under a platan,° yet methought less fair,   plane tree
Less winning soft, less amiably mild,
480 Than that smooth wat'ry image; back I turned,
Thou following cried'st aloud, 'Return fair Eve,
Whom fli'st thou? Whom thou fli'st, of him thou art,
His flesh, his bone; to give thee being I lent
Out of my side to thee, nearest my heart
485 Substantial life, to have thee by my side
Henceforth an individual° solace dear;   inseparable, distinct
Part of my soul I seek thee, and thee claim
My other half': with that thy gentle hand
Seized mine, I yielded, and from that time see
490 How beauty is excelled by manly grace
And wisdom, which alone is truly fair."
     So spake our general mother, and with eyes
Of conjugal attraction unreproved,
And meek surrender, half embracing leaned
495 On our first father, half her swelling breast
Naked met his under the flowing gold
Of her loose tresses hid: he in delight
Both of her beauty and submissive charms
Smiled with superior love, as Jupiter
500 On Juno smiles, when he impregns° the clouds   impregnates
That shed May flowers; and pressed her matron lip
With kisses pure: aside the Devil turned
For envy, yet with jealous leer malign
Eyed them askance, and to himself thus plained.°   complained
505   "Sight hateful, sight tormenting! thus these two
Imparadised in one another's arms
The happier Eden, shall enjoy their fill
Of bliss on bliss, while I to Hell am thrust,

7. Eve's experience reprises (but with significant differences) the story of Narcissus, who fell in love with his own reflection and was transformed into a flower.

Where neither joy nor love, but fierce desire,
510 Among our other torments not the least,
Still° unfulfilled with pain of longing pines;   *always*
Yet let me not forget what I have gained
From their own mouths; all is not theirs it seems:
One fatal tree there stands of Knowledge called,
515 Forbidden them to taste: Knowledge forbidden?
Suspicious, reasonless. Why should their Lord
Envy° them that? Can it be sin to know,   *begrudge*
Can it be death? And do they only stand
By ignorance, is that their happy state,
520 The proof of their obedience and their faith? *he wanted to*
O fair foundation laid whereon to build *figure out who*
Their ruin! Hence I will excite their minds *& how to manipulate.*
With more desire to know, and to reject
Envious commands, invented with design
525 To keep them low whom knowledge might exalt
Equal with gods; aspiring to be such,
They taste and die: what likelier can ensue?
But first with narrow search I must walk round
This garden, and no corner leave unspied;
530 A chance, but chance⁸ may lead where I may meet
Some wand'ring Spirit of Heav'n, by fountain side,
Or in thick shade retired, from him to draw
What further would be learnt. Live while ye may,
Yet happy pair; enjoy, till I return,
535 Short pleasures, for long woes are to succeed."
       So saying, his proud step he scornful turned,
But with sly circumspection, and began
Through wood, through waste, o'er hill, o'er dale his roam.°   *act of wandering*
Meanwhile in utmost longitude, where Heav'n
540 With earth and ocean meets, the setting sun
Slowly descended, and with right aspéct
Against the eastern gate of Paradise
Leveled his evening rays.⁹ it was a rock
Of alabaster,¹ piled up to the clouds,
545 Conspicuous far, winding with one ascent
Accessible from earth, one entrance high;
The rest was craggy cliff, that overhung
Still as it rose, impossible to climb.
Betwixt these rocky pillars Gabriel² sat
550 Chief of th' angelic guards, awaiting night;
About him exercised heroic games
Th' unarmèd youth of Heav'n, but nigh at hand
Celestial armory, shields, helms, and spears
Hung high with diamond flaming, and with gold.
555 Thither came Uriel, gliding through the even
On a sunbeam, swift as a shooting star
In autumn thwarts° the night, when vapors fired   *passes across*

8. An opportunity, even if only by luck.
9. Setting in the west, the sun struck the eastern
gate from the inside, at a 90-degree angle.

1. White, translucent marble veined with colors.
2. In Hebrew, "Strength of God." A tradition (cf.
Enoch 20.7) gave Gabriel charge of Paradise.

Impress the air, and shows the mariner
From what point of his compass to beware
560 Impetuous winds:[3] he thus began in haste.
    "Gabriel, to thee thy course by lot hath giv'n
Charge and strict watch that to this happy place
No evil thing approach or enter in;
This day at hight of noon came to my sphere
565 A Spirit, zealous, as he seemed, to know
More of th' Almighty's works, and chiefly man
God's latest image: I described° his way   descried, observed
Bent all on speed, and marked his airy gait;°   path
But in the mount that lies from Eden north,
570 Where he first lighted, soon discerned his looks
Alien from Heav'n, with passions foul obscured:
Mine eye pursued him still, but under shade°   trees
Lost sight of him; one of the banished crew
I fear, hath ventured from the deep, to raise
575 New troubles; him thy care must be to find."
    To whom the wingèd warrior thus returned:
"Uriel, no wonder if thy perfect sight,
Amid the sun's bright circle where thou sitt'st,
See far and wide. In at this gate none pass
580 The vigilance here placed, but such as come
Well known from Heav'n; and since meridian hour°   noon
No creature thence: if Spirit of other sort,
So minded, have o'erleaped these earthy bounds
On purpose, hard thou know'st it to exclude
585 Spiritual substance with corporeal bar.
But if within the circuit of these walks,
In whatsoever shape he lurk, of whom
Thou tell'st, by morrow dawning I shall know."
    So promised he, and Uriel to his charge
590 Returned on that bright beam, whose point now raised
Bore him slope downward to the sun now fall'n
Beneath th' Azorès; whether the prime orb,
Incredible how swift, had thither rolled
Diurnal,° or this less volúble° earth   daily / swift-turning
595 By shorter flight to th' east,[4] had left him there
Arraying with reflected purple and gold
The clouds that on his western throne attend.
Now came still evening on, and twilight gray
Had in her sober livery all things clad;
600 Silence accompanied, for beast and bird,
They to their grassy couch, these to their nests
Were slunk, all but the wakeful nightingale;
She all night long her amorous descant° sung;   melody
Silence was pleased: now glowed the firmament
605 With living sapphires: Hesperus[5] that led

---

3. Shooting stars were thought to indicate by the
direction of their fall the source of oncoming
storms. "Vapors fired": heat lightning.
4. Here and elsewhere Milton leaves open the

question of whether the sun moves around the
earth, or vice versa.
5. The evening star, Venus.

The starry host, rode brightest, till the moon
Rising in clouded majesty, at length
Apparent° queen unveiled her peerless light,   *clearly seen*
And o'er the dark her silver mantle threw.
610   When Adam thus to Eve: "Fair consort, th' hour
Of night, and all things now retired to rest
Mind us of like repose, since God hath set
Labor and rest, as day and night to men
Successive, and the timely dew of sleep
615   Now falling with soft slumbrous weight inclines
Our eyelids; other creatures all day long
Rove idle unemployed, and less need rest;
Man hath his daily work of body or mind
Appointed, which declares his dignity,
620   And the regard of Heav'n on all his ways;
While other animals unactive range,
And of their doings God takes no account.
Tomorrow ere fresh morning streak the east
With first approach of light, we must be ris'n,
625   And at our pleasant labor, to reform
Yon flow'ry arbors, yonder alleys green,
Our walk at noon, with branches overgrown,
That mock our scant manuring,° and require   *cultivating*
More hands than ours to lop their wanton growth:
630   Those blossoms also, and those dropping gums,
That lie bestrown unsightly and unsmooth,
Ask riddance,° if we mean to tread with ease;   *need to be cleared*
Meanwhile, as nature wills, night bids us rest."
    To whom thus Eve with perfect beauty adorned.
635   "My author and disposer, what thou bidd'st
Unargued I obey; so God ordains,
God is thy law, thou mine: to know no more
Is woman's happiest knowledge and her praise.
With thee conversing I forget all time.
640   All seasons° and their change, all please alike.   *times of day*
Sweet[6] is the breath of morn, her rising sweet,
With charm[7] of earliest birds; pleasant the sun
When first on this delightful land he spreads
His orient beams, on herb, tree, fruit, and flow'r,
645   Glist'ring with dew; fragrant the fertile earth
After soft showers; and sweet the coming on
Of grateful evening mild, then silent night
With this her solemn bird° and this fair moon,   *the nightingale*
And these the gems of heav'n, her starry train:
650   But neither breath of morn when she ascends
With charm of earliest birds, nor rising sun
On this delightful land, nor herb, fruit, flow'r,
Glist'ring with dew, nor fragrance after showers,
Nor grateful evening mild, nor silent night

---

6. With this embedded lyric, Eve displays her literary talents as author of an elegant love song, sonnetlike and replete with striking rhetorical figures of circularity and repetition.
7. Blended singing of many birds.

655 With this her solemn bird, nor walk by moon,
Or glittering starlight without thee is sweet.
But wherefore all night long shine these, for whom
This glorious sight, when sleep hath shut all eyes?"
    To whom our general ancestor replied.
660 "Daughter of God and man, accomplished Eve,[8]
Those have their course to finish, round the earth,
By morrow evening, and from land to land
In order, though to nations yet unborn,
Minist'ring light prepared, they set and rise;
665 Lest total darkness should by night regain
Her old possession, and extinguish life
In nature and all things, which these soft° fires   *agreeable*
Not only enlighten, but with kindly° heat   *natural, benevolent*
Of various influence foment and warm,
670 Temper or nourish, or in part shed down
Their stellar virtue on all kinds that grow
On earth, made hereby apter to receive
Perfection from the sun's more potent ray.[9]
These then, though unbeheld in deep of night,
675 Shine not in vain, nor think, though men were none,
That Heav'n would want spectators, God want praise;
Millions of spiritual creatures walk the earth
Unseen, both when we wake, and when we sleep:
All these with ceaseless praise his works behold
680 Both day and night: how often from the steep
Of echoing hill or thicket have we heard
Celestial voices to the midnight air,
Sole, or responsive each to other's note
Singing their great Creator: oft in bands
685 While they keep watch, or nightly rounding walk,
With heav'nly touch of instrumental sounds
In full harmonic number joined, their songs
Divide[1] the night, and lift our thoughts to Heaven."
    Thus talking hand in hand alone they passed
690 On to their blissful bower; it was a place
Chos'n by the sovran Planter, when he framed°   *fashioned*
All things to man's delightful use; the roof
Of thickest covert was inwoven shade
Laurel and myrtle, and what higher grew
695 Of firm and fragrant leaf; on either side
Acanthus, and each odorous bushy shrub
Fenced up the verdant wall; each beauteous flow'r,
Iris all hues, roses, and jessamine°   *jasmine*
Reared high their flourished° heads between, and wrought   *flowering*
700 Mosaic; underfoot the violet,
Crocus, and hyacinth with rich inlay
Broidered the ground, more colored than with stone

---

8. Having many talents and achievements; perfect, complete.
9. The stars were thought to have their own occult influence, and also to moderate that of the sun.
1. Mark the watches of the night; also, perform musical "divisions," elaborate melodic passages.

Of costliest emblem:° other creature here   *inlaid work*
Beast, bird, insect, or worm durst enter none,
705 Such was their awe of man. In shadier bower
More sacred and sequestered,° though but feigned,   *secluded*
Pan or Silvanus never slept, nor nymph,
Nor Faunus[2] haunted. Here in close recess
With flowers, garlands, and sweet-smelling herbs
710 Espousèd Eve decked first her nuptial bed,
And heav'nly choirs the hymenean° sung,   *wedding song*
What day the genial[3] angel to our sire
Brought her in naked beauty more adorned,
More lovely than Pandora, whom the gods
715 Endowed with all their gifts, and O too like
In sad event,° when to the unwiser son   *outcome*
Of Japhet brought by Hermes, she ensnared
Mankind with her fair looks, to be avenged
On him who had stole Jove's authentic fire.[4]
720   Thus at their shady lodge arrived, both stood,
Both turned, and under open sky adored
The God that made both sky, air, earth and Heav'n
Which they beheld, the moon's resplendent globe
And starry pole:° "Thou also mad'st the night,   *sky*
725 Maker Omnipotent, and thou the day,
Which we in our appointed work employed
Have finished happy in our mutual help
And mutual love, the crown of all our bliss
Ordained by thee, and this delicious place
730 For us too large, where thy abundance wants
Partakers, and uncropped falls to the ground.
But thou hast promised from us two a race
To fill the earth, who shall with us extol
Thy goodness infinite, both when we wake,
735 And when we seek, as now, thy gift of sleep."
        This said unanimous, and other rites
Observing none, but adoration pure
Which God likes best,[5] into their inmost bow'r
Handed° they went; and eased° the putting off   *hand in hand / spared*
740 These troublesome disguises which we wear,
Straight side by side were laid, nor turned I ween°   *surmise*
Adam from his fair spouse, nor Eve the rites
Mysterious[6] of connubial love refused:
Whatever hypocrites austerely talk
745 Of purity and place and innocence,

---

2. Forest and field divinities of classical mythology.
3. Presiding over marriage and generation.
4. Pandora (the name means "all gifts") was an artificial woman, molded of clay, bestowed by the gods on Epimetheus, brother of Prometheus (who angered Jove by stealing fire from heaven). She brought a box that foolish Epimetheus opened, releasing all the ills of the human race, leaving only hope inside. The brothers were sons of Iapetos,

whom Milton identifies with Japhet, Noah's third son. The Eve-Pandora parallel was often noted.
5. Like many Puritans, Milton objected to set forms of prayer, so Adam and Eve pray spontaneously (therefore sincerely), but also, paradoxically, together. Their prayer develops variations on Psalm 104.20–24.
6. Awe-inspiring. St. Paul (Ephesians 5.32) calls the union of man and woman a "mystery" paralleling that of Christ and the Church.

Defaming as impure what God declares
Pure, and commands to some, leaves free to all.
Our Maker bids increase,[7] who bids abstain
But our destroyer, foe to God and man?
750 Hail wedded Love, mysterious law, true source
Of human offspring, sole propriety°   *private property*
In Paradise of all things common else.
By thee adulterous lust was driv'n from men
Among the bestial herds to range, by thee
755 Founded in reason, loyal, just, and pure,
Relations dear, and all the charities°   *loves*
Of father, son, and brother first were known.
Far be it, that I should write thee sin or blame,
Or think thee unbefitting holiest place,
760 Perpetual fountain of domestic sweets,
Whose bed is undefiled and chaste pronounced,
Present, or past, as saints and patriarchs used.[8]
Here Love his golden shafts employs, here lights
His constant lamp, and waves his purple wings,
765 Reigns here and revels;[9] not in the bought smile
Of harlots, loveless, joyless, unendeared,
Casual fruition, nor in court amours,
Mixed dance, or wanton masque, or midnight ball,
Or serenade, which the starved° lover sings   *perished with cold*
770 To his proud fair, best quitted with disdain.
These lulled by nightingales embracing slept,
And on their naked limbs the flow'ry roof
Show'red roses, which the morn repaired.° Sleep on,   *replaced*
Blest pair; and O yet happiest if ye seek
775 No happier state, and know to know no more.[1]
    Now had night measured with her shadowy cone
Half way up hill this vast sublunar vault,[2]
And from their ivory port the Cherubim
Forth issuing at th' accustomed hour stood armed
780 To their night-watches in warlike parade,
When Gabriel to his next in power thus spake:
    "Uzziel, half these draw off, and coast[3] the south
With strictest watch; these other wheel[4] the north,
Our circuit meets full west." As flame they part
785 Half wheeling to the shield, half to the spear.
From these, two strong and subtle Spirits he called
That near him stood, and gave them thus in charge:
    "Ithuriel and Zephon,[5] with winged speed
Search through this garden, leave unsearched no nook,
790 But chiefly where those two fair creatures lodge,

---

7. Genesis 1.28.
8. Throughout history ("present or past"), Old and New Testament worthies have "used" matrimony as a noble estate.
9. The "golden shafts" (arrows) of Cupid produce true love, his lead-tipped arrows, hate.
1. Know enough to be content with what you know.
2. The conical shadow cast by the earth has moved halfway up to its zenith, so it is 9 P.M., the end of the first three-hour watch.
3. Follow the coastline. "Uzziel": Hebrew, "My strength is God."
4. "Wheel": (military term), turn to; "shield" (line 785) is left, "spear" is right.
5. Hebrew, "A looking out." "Ithuriel": Hebrew, "Discovery of God."

Now laid perhaps asleep secure of° harm. *from*
This evening from the sun's decline arrived
Who° tells of some infernal Spirit seen *one who*
Hitherward bent who could have thought? escaped
795 The bars of Hell, on errand bad no doubt:
Such where ye find, seize fast, and hither bring."
    So saying, on he led his radiant files,
Dazzling the moon; these to the bower direct
In search of whom they sought: him there they found
800 Squat like a toad, close at the ear of Eve;
Assaying by his devilish art to reach
The organs of her fancy,⁶ and with them forge
Illusions as he list, phantasms and dreams;
Or if, inspiring° venom, he might taint *breathing*
805 Th' animal spirits that from pure blood arise
Like gentle breaths from rivers pure, thence raise
At least distempered,° discontented thoughts, *disordered*
Vain hopes, vain aims, inordinate desires
Blown up with high conceits° engend'ring pride. *notions*
810 Him thus intent Ithuriel with his spear
Touched lightly; for no falsehood can endure
Touch of celestial temper,⁷ but returns
Of force to its own likeness: up he starts
Discovered and surprised. As when a spark
815 Lights on a heap of nitrous powder,⁸ laid
Fit for the tun some magazine to store
Against a rumored war, the smutty° grain *black*
With sudden blaze diffused, inflames the air:
So started up in his own shape the Fiend.
820 Back stepped those two fair angels half amazed
So sudden to behold the grisly king;
Yet thus, unmoved with fear, accost him soon:
    "Which of those rebel Spirits adjudged to Hell
Com'st thou, escaped thy prison; and transformed,
825 Why sat'st thou like an enemy in wait
Here watching at the head of these that sleep?"
    "Know ye not then," said Satan, filled with scorn,
"Know ye not me? Ye knew me once no mate
For you, there sitting where ye durst not soar;
830 Not to know me argues° yourselves unknown, *proves*
The lowest of your throng; or if ye know,
Why ask ye, and superfluous begin
Your message, like to end as much in vain?"
    To whom thus Zephon, answering scorn with scorn:
835 "Think not, revolted Spirit, thy shape the same,
Or undiminished brightness, to be known
As when thou stood'st in Heav'n upright and pure;
That glory then, when thou no more wast good,

---

6. The faculty of forming mental images.
7. Anything, like the spear, made ("tempered") in heaven.
8. Alights or kindles ("lights") gunpowder

("nitrous powder"), ready (next lines) to be stored in some barrel ("tun") laid up in some storehouse ("magazine"), in preparation for ("against") rumors of war.

Departed from thee, and thou resembl'st now
840   Thy sin and place of doom obscure° and foul.   *dark*
But come, for thou, be sure, shalt give account
To him who sent us, whose charge is to keep
This place inviolable, and these from harm."
    So spake the Cherub, and his grave rebuke
845   Severe in youthful beauty, added grace
Invincible: abashed the Devil stood,
And felt how awful goodness is, and saw
Virtue in her shape how lovely, saw, and pined°   *mourned*
His loss; but chiefly to find here observed
850   His luster visibly impaired; yet seemed
Undaunted. "If I must contend," said he,
"Best with the best, the sender not the sent,
Or all at once; more glory will be won,
Or less be lost." "Thy fear," said Zephon bold,
855   "Will save us trial what the least can do
Single° against thee wicked, and thence weak."   *in single combat*
    The Fiend replied not, overcome with rage;
But like a proud steed reined, went haughty on,
Champing his iron curb: to strive or fly
860   He held it vain; awe from above had quelled
His heart, not else dismayed. Now drew they nigh
The western point, where those half-rounding guards
Just met, and closing stood in squadron joined
Awaiting next command. To whom their chief
865   Gabriel from the front thus called aloud:
    "O friends, I hear the tread of nimble feet
Hasting this way, and now by glimpse discern
Ithuriel and Zephon through the shade,°   *trees*
And with them comes a third of regal port,°   *bearing*
870   But faded splendor wan;° who by his gait   *faint, dark*
And fierce demeanor seems the Prince of Hell,
Not likely to part hence without contést;
Stand firm, for in his look defiance lours."
    He scarce had ended, when those two approached
875   And brief related whom they brought, where found,
How busied, in what form and posture couched.
    To whom with stern regard thus Gabriel spake:
"Why hast thou, Satan, broke the bounds prescribed
To thy transgressions, and disturbed the charge°   *responsibility*
880   Of others, who approve not to transgress
By thy example, but have power and right
To question thy bold entrance on this place;
Employed it seems to violate sleep, and those
Whose dwelling God hath planted here in bliss?"
885   To whom thus Satan, with contemptuous brow:
"Gabriel, thou hadst in Heav'n th' esteem° of wise,   *reputation of being*
And such I held thee; but this question asked
Puts me in doubt. Lives there who loves his pain?
Who would not, finding way, break loose from Hell,
890   Though thither doomed? Thou wouldst thyself, no doubt,

And boldly venture to whatever place
Farthest from pain, where thou mightst hope to change°   *exchange*
Torment with ease, and soonest recompense
Dole° with delight, which in this place I sought;   *pain, grief*
895   To thee no reason, who know'st only good,
But evil hast not tried: and wilt object⁹
His will who bound us? Let him surer bar
His iron gates, if he intends our stay
In that dark durance:° thus much what was asked.¹   *confinement*
900   The rest is true, they found me where they say;
But that implies not violence or harm."
      Thus he in scorn. The warlike angel moved,
Disdainfully half smiling thus replied:
"O loss of one in Heav'n to judge of wise,²
905   Since Satan fell, whom folly overthrew,
And now returns him from his prison scaped,
Gravely in doubt whether to hold them wise
Or not, who ask what boldness brought him hither
Unlicensed from his bounds in Hell prescribed;
910   So wise he judges it to fly from pain
However,° and to scape his punishment.   *howsoever*
So judge thou still, presumptuous, till the wrath,
Which thou incurr'st by flying, meet thy flight
Sevenfold, and scourge that wisdom back to Hell,
915   Which taught thee yet no better, that no pain
Can equal anger infinite provoked.
But wherefore thou alone? Wherefore with thee
Came not all Hell broke loose? Is pain to them
Less pain, less to be fled, or thou than they
920   Less hardy to endure? Courageous chief,
The first in flight from pain, hadst thou alleged
To thy deserted host this cause of flight,
Thou surely hadst not come sole fugitive."
      To which the Fiend thus answered frowning stern:
925   "Not that I less endure, or shrink from pain,
Insulting angel, well thou know'st I stood°   *withstood*
Thy fiercest, when in battle to thy aid
The blasting volleyed thunder made all speed
And seconded thy else not dreaded spear.
930   But still thy words at random, as before,
Argue thy inexperience what behoves
From° hard assays° and ill successes past   *after/attacks*
A faithful leader, not to hazard all
Through ways of danger by himself untried.
935   I therefore, I alone first undertook
To wing the desolate abyss, and spy
This new-created world, whereof in Hell
Fame° is not silent, here in hope to find   *rumor*

9. Put forward as an objection.
1. I.e., thus much (answers) what was asked.
2. Irony: "O what a loss to Heaven to lose such a

judge of wisdom as Satan, whose folly led to his
fall."

Better abode, and my afflicted powers°   *downcast armies*
940   To settle here on earth, or in mid-air;[3]
       Though for possession put° to try once more   *forced*
       What thou and thy gay° legions dare against;   *showy*
       Whose easier business were to serve their Lord
       High up in Heav'n, with songs to hymn his throne,
945   And practiced distances to cringe, not fight."[4]
            To whom the warrior angel soon replied:
       "To say and straight unsay, pretending first
       Wise to fly pain, professing next the spy,
       Argues no leader, but a liar traced,°   *found out*
950   Satan, and couldst thou faithful add? O name,
       O sacred name of faithfulness profaned!
       Faithful to whom? To thy rebellious crew?
       Army of fiends, fit body to fit head;
       Was this your discipline and faith engaged,
955   Your military obedience, to dissolve
       Allegiance to th' acknowledged Power Supreme?
       And thou sly hypocrite, who now wouldst seem
       Patron of liberty, who more than thou
       Once fawned, and cringed, and servilely adored
960   Heav'n's awful Monarch?[5] Wherefore but in hope
       To dispossess him, and thyself to reign?
       But mark what I areed° thee now, avaunt;°   *advise / be gone*
       Fly thither whence thou fledd'st: if from this hour
       Within these hallowed limits thou appear,
965   Back to th' infernal pit I drag thee chained,
       And seal thee so, as henceforth not to scorn
       The facile° gates of Hell too slightly barred."   *easily moved*
            So threatened he, but Satan to no threats
       Gave heed, but waxing° more in rage replied: *growing*
970   "Then when I am thy captive talk of chains,
       Proud limitary[6] Cherub, but ere then
       Far heavier load thyself expect to feel
       From my prevailing arm, though Heaven's King
       Ride on thy wings, and thou with thy compeers,
975   Used to the yoke, draw'st his triumphant wheels
       In progress through the road of heav'n star-paved."
            While thus he spake, th' angelic squadron bright
       Turned fiery red, sharp'ning in moonèd horns[7]
       Their phalanx, and began to hem him round
980   With ported[8] spears, as thick as when a field
       Of Ceres[9] ripe for harvest waving bends
       Her bearded grove of ears, which way the wind
       Sways them; the careful ploughman doubting stands

3. Satan will become "prince of the power of the air" (Ephesians 2.2).
4. Satan contemptuously parallels the angels' courtly deference (distance) before God's throne and keeping a safe distance from battle. "Cringe": bow or kneel in fear or servility.
5. See 5.617 for Satan's "servile" adoration on the day of the Son's exaltation, when he "seemed well pleased" but was not.
6. Frontier guard, also, one of limited authority.
7. A crescent-shaped military formation.
8. Held slantwise in front.
9. Roman goddess of grain; here, the grain itself. A Homeric simile compares an excited army to windswept corn (*Iliad* 2.147–50).

Lest on the threshing-floor his hopeful sheaves
985 Prove chaff. On th' other side Satan alarmed°   *called to arms*
Collecting all his might dilated stood,
Like Teneriffe or Atlas[1] unremoved:°   *unremovable*
His stature reached the sky, and on his crest
Sat Horror plumed; nor wanted in his grasp
990 What seemed both spear and shield: now dreadful deeds
Might have ensued, nor only Paradise
In this commotion, but the starry cope°   *vault*
Of Heav'n perhaps, or all the elements
At least had gone to wrack, disturbed and torn
995 With violence of this conflict, had not soon
Th' Eternal to prevent such horrid fray
Hung forth in Heav'n his golden scales, yet seen
Betwixt Astraea and the Scorpion sign,[2]
Wherein all things created first he weighed,
1000 The pendulous round earth with balanced air
In counterpoise, now ponders all events,
Battles and realms: in these he put two weights
The sequel each of parting and of fight;[3]
The latter quick up flew, and kicked the beam;
1005 Which Gabriel spying, thus bespake the Fiend:
   "Satan, I know thy strength, and thou know'st mine,
Neither our own but giv'n; what folly then
To boast what arms can do, since thine no more
Than Heav'n permits, nor mine, though doubled now
1010 To trample thee as mire: for proof look up,
And read thy lot in yon celestial sign
Where thou art weighed, and shown how light, how weak,[4]
If thou resist." The Fiend looked up and knew
His mounted scale aloft: nor more; but fled
1015 Murmuring, and with him fled the shades of night.

Book 5

Now Morn her rosy steps in th' eastern clime   *this echos an*
Advancing, sowed the earth with orient pearl,° *epic, things* *sparkling dew* *are going to get bad.*
When Adam waked, so customed, for his sleep
Was aery light, from pure digestion bred,   *"red sky at night, sailor*
5 And temperate vapors bland,° which th' only sound   *delight, red sky at morn,*   *gentle, balmy*
Of leaves and fuming rills, Aurora's fan,[1]   *sailor take warn"*
Lightly dispersed, and the shrill matin° song   *morning*
Of birds on every bough; so much the more
His wonder was to find unawakened Eve
10 With tresses discomposed, and glowing cheek,

1. A mountain in Morocco. "Teneriffe": a mountain in the Canary Islands.
2. The zodiac sign Libra is between Virgo (identified with Astraea, goddess of Justice, who fled the earth at the end of the Golden Age) and Scorpio.
3. In several classical epic similes the fates of opposing heroes are weighed in scales by the gods, but here God "ponders" (weighs the consequences

of) all events, including parting or fighting. Battle, desired by Satan, proves lighter ("kicked the beam," line 1004).
4. Cf. Daniel 5.27: "Thou art weighed in the balances, and art found wanting."
1. Rustling leaves stirred by Aurora, goddess of the dawn.

As through unquiet rest: he on his side
Leaning half-raised, with looks of cordial° love   *heartfelt*
Hung over her enamored, and beheld
Beauty, which whether waking or asleep,
15 Shot forth peculiar° graces; then with voice   *its own*
Mild, as when Zephyrus on Flora[2] breathes,
Her hand soft touching, whispered thus: "Awake
My fairest, my espoused, my lastest found,
Heav'n's last best gift, my ever new delight,
20 Awake, the morning shines, and the fresh field
Calls us, we lose the prime, to mark how spring
Our tended plants, how blows° the citron grove,   *blooms*
What drops the myrrh, and what the balmy reed,°   *balsam*
How nature paints her colors, how the bee
25 Sits on the bloom extracting liquid sweet."[3]
    Such whispering waked her, but with startled eye
On Adam, whom embracing, thus she spake:
    "O sole in whom my thoughts find all repose,
My glory, my perfection, glad I see
30 Thy face, and morn returned, for I this night,
Such night till this I never passed, have dreamed,
If dreamed, not as I oft am wont, of thee,
Works of day past, or morrow's next design,
But of offense and trouble, which my mind
35 Knew never till this irksome night. Methought
Close at mine ear one called me forth to walk
With gentle voice, I thought it thine; it said,
'Why sleep'st thou Eve? now is the pleasant time,
The cool, the silent, save where silence yields
40 To the night-warbling bird, that now awake
Tunes sweetest his love-labored song; now reigns
Full-orbed the moon, and with more pleasing light
Shadowy sets off the face of things, in vain,
If none regard; heav'n wakes with all his eyes,°   *stars*
45 Whom to behold but thee, nature's desire,
In whose sight all things joy, with ravishment
Attracted by thy beauty still° to gaze.'   *continually*
I rose as at thy call, but found thee not;
To find thee I directed then my walk;
50 And on, me thought, alone I passed through ways
That brought me on a sudden to the tree
Of interdicted knowledge: fair it seemed,
Much fairer to my fancy than by day:
And as I wond'ring looked, beside it stood
55 One shaped and winged like one of those from Heav'n
By us oft seen; his dewy locks distilled
Ambrosia;° on that tree he also gazed;   *heavenly fragrance*

[handwritten annotations: a dream from Satan. he is whispering in her ear. she thinks the dream is sinful & she is at fault. never is watching her because she is so beautiful. he is trying to re-awaken her pride.]

---

2. Zephyrus is god of the gentle west wind, Flora
goddess of flowers.
3. Adam sings a morning love song (*aubade*) to
Eve, which works variations on Song of Solomon
2.10–12: "Rise up, my love, my fair one, and come

away. . . . The flowers appear on the earth; the
time of the singing of birds is come." Compare
Satan's serenade (5.38–47), a parody of Adam's
aubade and the Song of Solomon. "Prime" (line
21): first hour of the day.

And 'O fair plant,' said he, with fruit surcharged,

Deigns none to ease thy load and taste thy sweet,

60   Nor god,° nor man; is knowledge so despised?

Or envy, or what reserve forbids to taste?[4]

Forbid who will, none shall from me withhold

Longer thy offered good, why else set here?'

This said he paused not, but with vent'rous arm

65   He plucked, he tasted; me damp horror chilled

At such bold words vouched with° a deed so bold: *backed by*

But he thus overjoyed, 'O fruit divine,

Sweet of thyself, but much more sweet thus cropped,

Forbidden here, it seems, as only fit

70   For gods, yet able to make gods of men:

And why not gods of men, since good, the more

Communicated, more abundant grows,

The author not impaired,° but honored more?   *injured, diminished*

Here, happy creature, fair angelic Eve,

75   Partake thou also; happy though thou art,

Happier thou may'st be, worthier canst not be:

Taste this, and be henceforth among the gods

Thyself a goddess, not to earth confined,

But sometimes in the air, as we, sometimes

80   Ascend to Heav'n, by merit thine, and see

What life the gods live there, and such live thou.'

So saying, he drew nigh, and to me held,

Even to my mouth of that same fruit held part

Which he had plucked; the pleasant savory smell

85   So quickened appetite, that I, me thought,

Could not but taste. Forthwith up to the clouds

With him I flew, and underneath beheld

The earth outstretched immense, a prospect wide

And various: wond'ring at my flight and change

90   To this high exaltation: suddenly

My guide was gone, and I, methought, sunk down,

And fell asleep; but O how glad I waked

To find this but a dream!" Thus Eve her night

Related, and thus Adam answered sad.°   *gravely, soberly*

95   "Best image of myself and dearer half,

The trouble of thy thoughts this night in sleep

Affects me equally; nor can I like

This uncouth° dream, of evil sprung I fear;   *strange, unpleasant*

Yet evil whence? in thee can harbor none,

100   Created pure. But know that in the soul

Are many lesser faculties[5] that serve

Reason as chief: among these fancy next

Her office holds; of all external things,

Which the five watchful senses represent,

105   She forms imaginations,° aery shapes,   *images*

---

4. I.e., does envy or some other barrier ("reserve") forbid your being tasted?

5. Adam's explanation of the dream (lines 100–113) summarizes the orthodox faculty psychology and dream theory of Milton's time—one among many kinds of knowledge with which unfallen man was endowed.

[Handwritten annotations:]

the tree is heavy w/ fruit, she should angel help it.

he eats from the tree, & he becomes a god

if she eats it she will be a god & go up to heaven.

there is more to life than just being added to it by Adam, she should aim higher

she flies w/ satan. like when satan tempts Jesus on the mountain, he tells them they can have all they can see. she sinks down when the archangel sees satan & kicks him out.

Adam doesn't criticize her

fantasy comes out in dreams

Which reason joining or disjoining, frames
All what we affirm or what deny, and call
Our knowledge or opinion; then retires
Into her private cell when nature rests.
110 Oft in her absence mimic fancy wakes
To imitate her; but misjoining shapes,
Wild work produces oft, and most in dreams,
Ill matching words and deeds long past or late.
Some such resemblances methinks I find
115 Of our last evening's talk in this thy dream,[6]
But with addition strange; yet be not sad.
Evil into the mind of god[7] or man
May come and go, so unapproved,[8] and leave
No spot or blame behind: which gives me hope
120 That what in sleep thou didst abhor to dream,
Waking thou never wilt consent to do.
Be not disheartened then, nor cloud those looks
That wont to be more cheerful and serene
Than when fair morning first smiles on the world,
125 And let us to our fresh employments rise
Among the groves, the fountains, and the flow'rs
That open now their choicest bosomed smells
Reserved from night, and kept for thee in store."
      So cheered he his fair spouse, and she was cheered,
130 But silently a gentle tear let fall
From either eye, and wiped them with her hair;
Two other precious drops that ready stood,
Each in their crystal sluice, he ere they fell
Kissed as the gracious signs of sweet remorse
135 And pious° awe, that feared to have offended.   dutiful
      So all was cleared, and to the field they haste.
But first from under shady arborous° roof,   consisting of trees
Soon as they forth were come to open sight
Of day-spring,° and the sun, who scarce up risen   daybreak
140 With wheels yet hov'ring o'er the ocean brim,
Shot parallel to the earth his dewy ray,
Discovering in wide landscape all the east
Of Paradise and Eden's happy plains,
Lowly they bowed adoring, and began
145 Their orisons,° each morning duly paid   prayers
In various style, for neither various style
Nor holy rapture° wanted they to praise   ecstasy
Their Maker, in fit strains pronounced or sung
Unmeditated,[9] such prompt eloquence
150 Flowed from their lips, in prose or numerous° verse,   rhythmic
More tuneable° than needed lute or harp   melodious
To add more sweetness, and they thus began:
      "These are thy glorious works, Parent of good,[1]

---

6. Adam recalls his own words in 4.411–39.
7. Probably "angel" as elsewhere, but perhaps God, whose omniscience must encompass knowledge of evil as well as good.
8. If not approved of, or not acted on (put to the proof).

9. In a variety of styles or forms of speech and song, which harmonize together but are at the same time impromptu, spontaneous, and ecstatic.
1. Their morning hymn works variations on Psalms 148, 104, and 19, as well as the Canticle Benedicite.

Almighty, thine this universal frame,
155 Thus wondrous fair; thyself how wondrous then!
Unspeakable, who sitt'st above these heavens,
To us invisible or dimly seen
In these thy lowest works, yet these declare
Thy goodness beyond thought, and power divine:
160 Speak ye who best can tell, ye sons of light,
Angels, for ye behold him, and with songs
And choral symphonies, day without night,
Circle his throne rejoicing, ye in Heav'n,
On earth join all ye creatures to extol
165 Him first, him last, him midst, and without end.
Fairest of stars,[2] last in the train of night,
If better thou belong not to the dawn,
Sure pledge of day, that crown'st the smiling morn
With thy bright circlet, praise him in thy sphere
170 While day arises, that sweet hour of prime.
Thou sun, of this great world both eye and soul,
Acknowledge him thy greater, sound his praise
In thy eternal course, both when thou climb'st,
And when high noon hast gained, and when thou fall'st.
175 Moon, that now meet'st the orient sun, now fli'st
With the fixed stars, fixed in their orb that flies,
And ye five other wand'ring fires that move
In mystic dance not without song,[3] resound
His praise, who out of darkness called up light.
180 Air, and ye elements the eldest birth
Of nature's womb, that in quaternion[4] run
Perpetual circle, multiform, and mix
And nourish all things, let your ceaseless change
Vary to our great Maker still new praise.
185 Ye mists and exhalations that now rise
From hill or steaming lake, dusky or gray,
Till the sun paint your fleecy skirts with gold,
In honor to the world's great Author rise,
Whether to deck with clouds the uncolored sky,
190 Or wet the thirsty earth with falling showers,
Rising or falling still advance his praise.
His praise ye winds, that from four quarters blow,
Breathe soft or loud; and wave your tops, ye pines,
With every plant, in sign of worship wave.
195 Fountains and ye, that warble, as ye flow,
Melodious murmurs, warbling tune his praise.
Join voices all ye living souls: ye birds,
That singing up to heaven gate ascend,
Bear on your wings and in your notes his praise.
200 Ye that in waters glide, and ye that walk
The earth, and stately tread, or lowly creep;
Witness if I be silent, morn or even,

2. Venus, the morning star and (as Hesperus) the evening star.
3. The planets, unlike the fixed stars, change their relative positions; their motion produces the music of the spheres, audible to unfallen humans.
4. The fourfold changing relationship of the four elements.

To hill, or valley, fountain, or fresh shade
Made vocal by my song, and taught his praise.
205 Hail universal Lord, be bounteous still°   *always*
To give us only good; and if the night
Have gathered aught of evil or concealed,
Disperse it, as now light dispels the dark."
    So prayed they innocent, and to their thoughts
210 Firm peace recovered soon and wonted calm.
On to their morning's rural work they haste
Among sweet dews and flow'rs; where any row
Of fruit trees over-woody° reached too far   *too bushy*
Their pampered boughs, and needed hands to check
215 Fruitless embraces: or they led the vine
To wed her elm;[5] she spoused about him twines
Her marriageable arms, and with her brings
Her dow'r th' adopted clusters, to adorn
His barren leaves. Them thus employed beheld
220 With pity Heav'n's high King, and to him called
Raphael, the sociable Spirit, that deigned
To travel with Tobias, and secured
His marriage with the seven-times-wedded maid.[6]
    "Raphael," said he, "thou hear'st what stir on earth
225 Satan from Hell scaped through the darksome gulf
Hath raised in Paradise, and how disturbed
This night the human pair, how he designs
In them at once to ruin all mankind.
Go therefore, half this day as friend with friend
230 Converse with Adam, in what bow'r or shade
Thou find'st him from the heat of noon retired,
To respite his day-labor with repast,
Or with repose; and such discourse bring on,
As may advise him of his happy state,
235 Happiness in his power left free to will,
Left to his own free will, his will though free,
Yet mutable; whence warn him to beware
He swerve not too secure:° tell him withal   *overconfident*
His danger, and from whom, what enemy
240 Late fall'n himself from Heav'n, is plotting now
The fall of others from like state of bliss;
By violence, no, for that shall be withstood,
But by deceit and lies; this let him know,
Lest wilfully transgressing he pretend°   *plead*
245 Surprisal, unadmonished, unforewarned."
    So spake th' Eternal Father, and fulfilled
All justice: nor delayed the wingèd saint°   *angel*
After his charge received; but from among
Thousand celestial ardors,[7] where he stood

5. A familiar emblem of matrimony, the elm symbolizing masculine strength and the vine, feminine
fruitfulness, softness, and sweetness; note, however, the matriarchal implications of "adopted
clusters."

6. Raphael (in Hebrew, "Health of God") was the
advisor of Tobias in winning his wife (see 4.168–
71 and note).
7. Bright spirits burning in love; the Hebrew "seraph" means "to burn."

250 Veiled with his gorgeous wings, up springing light
Flew through the midst of Heav'n; th' angelic choirs
On each hand parting, to his speed gave way
Through all th' empyreal road; till at the gate
Of Heav'n arrived, the gate self-opened wide
255 On golden hinges turning, as by work°   *mechanism*
Divine the sovran Architect had framed.
From hence, no cloud, or, to obstruct his sight,
Star interposed, however small he sees,
Not unconform to other shining globes,
260 Earth and the gard'n of God, with cedars crowned
Above all hills. As when by night the glass°   *telescope*
Of Galileo, less assured, observes
Imagined lands and regions in the moon:
Or pilot from amidst the Cyclades[8]
265 Delos or Samos first appearing kens°   *discerns*
A cloudy spot. Down thither prone° in flight   *bent forward*
He speeds, and through the vast ethereal sky
Sails between worlds and worlds, with steady wing
Now on the polar wings, then with quick fan
270 Winnows the buxom° air; till within soar   *yielding*
Of tow'ring eagles,[9] to all the fowls he seems
A phoenix, gazed by all, as that sole bird
When to enshrine his relics in the sun's
Bright temple, to Egyptian Thebes he flies.[1]
275 At once on th' eastern cliff of Paradise
He lights, and to his proper shape returns
A Seraph winged; six wings he wore, to shade
His lineaments° divine; the pair that clad   *parts of the body*
Each shoulder broad, came mantling° o'er his breast   *draping*
280 With regal ornament; the middle pair
Girt like a starry zone° his waist, and round   *belt*
Skirted his loins and thighs with downy gold
And colors dipped in Heav'n; the third his feet
Shadowed from either heel with feathered mail[2]
285 Sky-tinctured grain.° Like Maia's son[3] he stood,   *dye*
And shook his plumes, that heav'nly fragrance filled
The circuit wide. Straight knew him all the bands
Of angels under watch; and to his state,°   *rank*
And to his message° high in honor rise;   *mission*
290 For on some message high they guessed him bound.
Their glittering tents he passed, and now is come
Into the blissful field; through groves of myrrh,
And flow'ring odors, cassia, nard, and balm;[4]

8. A circular group of islands in the south Aegean Sea; the two islands seen as "spots" from within the archipelago are Delos (the traditional center but famous for having floated adrift) and Samos (outside the group).
9. Raphael sails with steady wing, turns at the pole, beats ("fans") with his wings the yielding ("buxom") air, and then comes within range of the eagle's soaring flight.
1. The phoenix was a mythical, unique bird ("sole") who lived five hundred years, was consumed by fire, and was reborn from the ashes, which it then carried to the temple of the sun at Heliopolis in Egypt.
2. Plumage suggesting scale-armor.
3. Mercury, messenger of the gods.
4. "Odors": aromatic substances; "cassia": cinnamon; "nard": spikenard; "balm"; balsam—all were used to make perfumed ointments.

A wilderness of sweets; for nature here
295 Wantoned° as in her prime, and played° at will   *reveled/acted out*
Her virgin fancies, pouring forth more sweet,
Wild above rule or art; enormous° bliss.   *immense, beyond rule*
Him through the spicy forest onward come
Adam discerned, as in the door he sat[5]
300 Of his cool bow'r, while now the mounted sun
Shot down direct his fervid rays, to warm
Earth's inmost womb, more warmth than Adam needs;
And Eve within, due° at her hour prepared   *fittingly*
For dinner savory fruits, of taste to please
305 True appetite and not disrelish thirst,
Of nectarous draughts between, from milky stream,
Berry or grape: to whom thus Adam called:
    "Haste hither Eve, and worth thy sight behold
Eastward among those trees, what glorious shape
310 Comes this way moving; seems another morn
Ris'n on mid-noon; some great behest from Heav'n
To us perhaps he brings, and will vouchsafe
This day to be our guest. But go with speed,
And what thy stores contain, bring forth and pour
315 Abundance, fit to honor and receive
Our heav'nly stranger; well we may afford
Our givers their own gifts, and large bestow
From large bestowed, where nature multiplies
Her fertile growth, and by disburd'ning grows
320 More fruitful, which instructs us not to spare."
    To whom thus Eve. "Adam, earth's hallowed mold,°   *model, earth*
Of God inspired, small store will serve, where store,[6]
All seasons, ripe for use hangs on the stalk;
Save what by frugal storing firmness gains
325 To nourish, and superfluous moist consumes:
But I will haste and from each bough and brake
Each plant and juiciest gourd will pluck such choice
To entertain our angel guest, as he
Beholding shall confess that here on earth
330 God hath dispensed his bounties as in Heav'n."
    So saying, with dispatchful looks in haste
She turns, on hospitable thoughts intent
What choice to chose for delicacy best,
What order, so contrived as not to mix
335 Tastes, not well joined, inelegant, but bring
Taste after taste upheld° with kindliest° change,   *maintained/most natural*
Bestirs her then, and from each tender stalk
Whatever earth all-bearing mother yields
In India east or west, or middle shore
340 In Pontus or the Punic coast,[7]or where
Alcinous reigned, fruit of all kinds, in coat,

5. Raphael's visit to Adam is modeled on Abraham's entertainment of three angels (Genesis 18. 1–16).
6. A great quantity. "Small store": few stored foods.
7. The "middle shore" includes "Pontus," the

south coast of the Black Sea famous for nuts and fruits, and the "Punic" (Carthaginian) coast of North Africa on the Mediterranean, famous for figs; the gardens of Alcinous (next line) are described in *Odyssey* 7.113–21 as perpetually fruitful.

Rough, or smooth-rined, or bearded husk, or shell
She gathers, tribute large, and on the board
Heaps with unsparing hand; for drink the grape
345 She crushes, inoffensive must, and meaths[8]
From many a berry, and from sweet kernels pressed
She tempers° dulcet creams, nor these to hold   *blends*
Wants° her fit vessels pure, then strews the ground   *lacks*
With rose and odors from the shrub unfumed.[9]
350 Meanwhile our primitive° great sire, to meet   *original*
His godlike guest, walks forth, without more train
Accompanied than with his own complete
Perfections, in himself was all his state,°   *dignity, authority*
More solemn° than the tedious pomp that waits   *awe-inspiring*
355 On princes, when their rich retínue long
Of horses led, and grooms besmeared with gold
Dazzles the crowd, and sets them all agape.
Nearer his presence Adam though not awed,
Yet with submiss approach and reverence meek,
360 As to a superior nature, bowing low,
      Thus said: "Native of Heav'n, for other place:
None can than Heav'n such glorious shape contain;
Since by descending from the thrones above,
Those happy places thou hast deigned a while
365 To want,° and honor these, vouchsafe with us   *be parted from*
Two only, who yet by sovran gift possess
This spacious ground, in yonder shady bow'r
To rest, and what the garden choicest bears
To sit and taste, till this meridian° heat   *noontime*
370 Be over, and the sun more cool decline."
      Whom thus the angelic Virtue[1] answered mild:
"Adam, I therefore came, nor art thou such
Created, or such place hast here to dwell,
As may not oft invite, though Spirits of Heav'n
375 To visit thee; lead on then where thy bow'r
O'ershades; for these mid-hours, till evening rise
I have at will." So to the sylvan lodge
They came, that like Pomona's[2] arbor smiled
With flow'rets decked° and fragrant smells; but Eve   *covered*
380 Undecked, save with herself more lovely fair
Than wood-nymph, or the fairest goddess feigned
Of three that in Mount Ida naked strove,[3]
Stood to entertain her guest from Heav'n; no veil
She needed, virtue-proof,° no thought infirm   *armored in virtue*
385 Altered her cheek. On whom the Angel "Hail"
Bestowed, the holy salutation used
Long after to blest Mary, second Eve.[4]

8. Meads, drinks sweetened with honey. "Must": unfermented fruit juice.
9. Naturally scented, not burned for incense.
1. Milton uses these angelic titles freely, in the Protestant manner, not as designations of the nine traditional orders (Raphael was called "Seraph" at line 277).
2. The Roman goddess of fruit trees.
3. On Mount Ida, Venus, Juno, and Minerva

"strove" naked for the title of the most beautiful; Paris awarded the prize (the apple of discord) to Venus, which led to the rape of Helen and the Trojan War.
4. Cf. the angel's words to Mary announcing that she would bear a son, Jesus (Luke 1.28): "Hail, thou that art highly favored, the Lord is with thee: blessed art thou among women."

"Hail mother of mankind, whose fruitful womb
Shall fill the world more numerous with thy sons
390   Than with these various fruits the trees of God
Have heaped this table." Raised of grassy turf
Their table was, and mossy seats had round,
And on her ample square from side to side
All autumn piled, though spring and autumn here
395   Danced hand in hand. A while discourse they hold;
No fear lest dinner cool; when thus began
Our author:° "Heav'nly stranger, please to taste   *forefather*
These bounties which our Nourisher, from whom
All perfect good unmeasured out, descends,
400   To us for food and for delight hath caused
The earth to yield; unsavory food perhaps
To spiritual natures; only this I know,
That one Celestial Father gives to all."
   To whom the angel: "Therefore what he gives
405   (Whose praise be ever sung) to man in part
Spiritual, may of° purest Spirits be found   *by*
No ingrateful food: and food alike those pure
Intelligential substances require⁵
As doth your rational; and both contain
410   Within them every lower faculty
Of sense, whereby they hear, see, smell, touch, taste,
Tasting concoct, digest, assimilate,⁶
And corporeal to incorporeal turn.
For know, whatever was created, needs
415   To be sustained and fed; of elements
The grosser feeds the purer, earth the sea,
Earth and the sea feed air, the air those fires
Ethereal, and as lowest first the moon;
Whence in her visage round those spots, unpurged
420   Vapors not yet into her substance turned.⁷
Nor doth the moon no nourishment exhale
From her moist continent to higher orbs.⁸
The sun that light imparts to all, receives
From all his alimental° recompense   *nourishing*
425   In humid exhalations, and at even
Sups with the ocean:⁹ though in Heav'n the trees
Of life ambrosial fruitage bear, and vines
Yield nectar,¹ though from off the boughs each morn
We brush mellifluous° dews, and find the ground   *honey-flowing*
430   Covered with pearly grain; yet God hath here

---

5. Milton's angels ("intelligential substances") require real food, even as "rational" men do (see below, lines 430–38). As a monist (believer that all creation is of one matter), Milton denied the more common (dualistic) idea that angels are pure spirit, holding instead that they are of a very highly refined material substance.
6. Three stages in digestion.
7. Here Raphael describes lunar spots as still-undigested vapors (in keeping with his exposition of the universal need of nourishment); in 1.287–

91 he referred to moonspots in Galileo's terms, as landscape features.
8. A double negative: the moon does exhale such nourishment to other planets.
9. Milton explains evaporation as the sun dining off moisture exhaled from the oceans.
1. Ambrosia is the food and nectar the drink of the classical gods; Milton adds "pearly grain" (line 430), like the manna showered on the Israelites in the desert (Exodus 16.14).

Varied his bounty so with new delights,
As may compare with Heaven; and to taste
Think not I shall be nice."° So down they sat,   *fastidious, finicky*
And to their viands fell, nor seemingly°   *in show*
435 The angel, nor in mist, the common gloss°   *explanation*
Of theologians, but with keen dispatch
Of real hunger, and concoctive° heat   *digestive*
To transubstantiate;[2] what redounds, transpires
Through Spirits with ease; nor wonder, if by fire
440 Of sooty coal the empiric° alchemist   *experimental*
Can turn, or holds it possible to turn
Metals of drossiest ore to perfect gold
As from the mine. Meanwhile at table Eve
Ministered naked, and their flowing cups
445 With pleasant liquors crowned.° O innocence   *filled to the brim*
Deserving Paradise! if ever, then,
Then had the Sons of God excuse t' have been
Enamored at that sight,[3] but in those hearts
Love unlibidinous° reigned, nor jealousy   *without lust*
450 Was understood, the injured lover's hell.
     Thus when with meats and drinks they had sufficed,
Not burdened nature, sudden mind arose
In Adam, not to let th' occasion pass
Given him by this great conference to know
455 Of things above his world, and of their being
Who dwell in Heav'n, whose excellence he saw
Transcend his own so far, whose radiant forms
Divine effulgence,° whose high power so far   *shining forth*
Exceeded human, and his wary speech
460 Thus to th' empyreal minister he framed:
    "Inhabitant with God, now know I well
Thy favor, in this honor done to man,
Under whose lowly roof thou hast vouchsafed
To enter and these earthly fruits to taste,
465 Food not of angels, yet accepted so,
As that more willingly thou couldst not seem
At Heav'n's high feasts t' have fed: yet what compare?"
    To whom the wingèd Hierarch replied:
"O Adam, one Almighty is, from whom
470 All things proceed, and up to him return,
If not depraved from good, created all
Such to perfection, one first matter all,[4]
Endued with various forms, various degrees

2. In common theological use, transubstantiation is the Roman Catholic doctrine that the bread and wine of the eucharist become the body and blood of Christ. Milton vigorously denied that doctrine, but he describes the angels' transforming of earthly food into their more highly refined spiritual substance as a true transubstantiation. The excess ("what redounds") is exhaled ("transpires") through angelic pores.
3. Genesis 6.2 tells of the marriage of the daughters of men with the sons of God, usually identified as sons of Seth, but a patristic tradition (alluded to here) identifies them as angels.
4. Milton held that the universe was created out of Chaos, not out of nothing: the primal matter of Chaos had its origin in God, who subsequently created all things from that matter (see 7.168–73, 210–42). This materialist "monism" denies sharp distinctions between angels and men, spirit and matter: all beings are of one substance, of varying degrees of refinement and life.

Of substance, and in things that live, of life;
475　But more refined, more spiritous, and pure,
As nearer to him placed or nearer tending
Each in their several active spheres assigned,
Till body up to spirit work, in bounds
Proportioned to each kind.⁵ So from the root
480　Springs lighter the green stalk, from thence the leaves
More airy, last the bright consummate flow'r
Spirits odórous breathes:⁶ flow'rs and their fruit
Man's nourishment, by gradual scale sublimed°　　　　　*purified*
To vital spirits aspire, to animal,
485　To intellectual, give both life and sense,
Fancy° and understanding, whence the soul　　　　　*imagination*
Reason receives, and reason is her being,
Discursive, or intuitive;⁷ discourse
Is oftest yours, the latter most is ours,
490　Differing but in degree, of kind the same.
Wonder not then, what God for you saw good
If I refuse not, but convert, as you,
To proper° substance; time may come when men　　　　　*our own*
With angels may participate, and find
495　No inconvenient diet, nor too light fare:
And from these corporal nutriments perhaps
Your bodies may at last turn all to spirit,
Improved by tract° of time, and winged ascend　　　　　*passage*
Ethereal as we, or may at choice
500　Here or in heav'nly paradises dwell;
If ye be found obedient, and retain
Unalterably firm his love entire
Whose progeny you are. Meanwhile enjoy
Your fill what happiness this happy state
505　Can comprehend, incapable° of more."　　　　　*unable to contain*
　　　To whom the patriarch of mankind replied:
"O favorable Spirit, propitious guest,
Well hast thou taught the way that might direct
Our knowledge, and the scale of nature set
510　From center to circumference, whereon
In contemplation of created things
By steps we may ascend to God. But say,
What meant that caution joined, 'If ye be found
Obedient'? Can we want obedience then
515　To him, or possibly his love desert

5. Milton's version of the chain of being qualifies natural hierarchy by allowing for movement up or down; beings may become increasingly "spiritual" or increasingly gross (as the rebel angels do), depending on their moral choices—"nearer tending."
6. The plant figure—root, stalk, leaves, flowers, and fruit—provides an illustration of the dynamism of being in the universe and further explains why Raphael can eat the fruit. Such food is then transformed (next lines) into various orders of "spirits"—"vital," "animal," and "intellectual" (flu-

ids in the blood that sustain life, sensation, motion, and finally intellect and its functions, "fancy," "understanding," and "reason"), indicating that the soul is also material.
7. Traditionally, on the dualist assumption that angels are pure spirit and humans a combination of matter and spirit, angelic intuition (immediate apprehension of truth) was absolutely distinguished from human "discourse" of reason (arguing from premises to conclusions). Milton, denying that assumption, makes the distinction only relative, a matter of "degree" (line 490).

Who formed us from the dust, and placed us here
Full to the utmost measure of what bliss
Human desires can seek or apprehend?"
        To whom the angel: "Son of Heav'n and earth,
520   Attend: that thou art happy, owe° to God;   *attribute*
That thou continu'st such, owe to thyself,
That is, to thy obedience; therein stand.
This was that caution giv'n thee; be advised.
God made thee perfect, not immutable;°   *unchangeable*
525   And good he made thee, but to persevere
He left it in thy power, ordained thy will
By nature free, not overruled by fate
Inextricable, or strict necessity;
Our voluntary service he requires,
530   Not our necessitated, such with him
Finds no acceptance, nor can find, for how
Can hearts, not free, be tried whether they serve
Willing or no, who will but what they must
By destiny, and can no other choose?
535   Myself and all th' angelic host that stand
In sight of God enthroned, our happy state
Hold, as you yours, while our obedience holds;
On other surety° none; freely we serve,   *guarantee*
Because we freely love, as in our will
540   To love or not; in this we stand or fall:
And some are fall'n, to disobedience fall'n,
And so from Heav'n to deepest Hell; O fall
From what high state of bliss into what woe!"
        To whom our great progenitor: "Thy words
545   Attentive, and with more delighted ear,
Divine instructor, I have heard, than when
Cherubic songs° by night from neighboring hills   *songs of Cherubim*
Aerial music send: nor knew I not[8]
To be both will and deed created free;
550   Yet that we never shall forget to love
Our Maker, and obey him whose command
Single, is yet° so just, my constant thoughts   *also*
Assured me, and still assure: though what thou tell'st
Hath passed in Heav'n, some doubt within me move,
555   But more desire to hear, if thou consent,
The full relation, which must needs be strange,
Worthy of sacred silence to be heard;
And we have yet large° day, for scarce the sun   *ample*
Hath finished half his journey, and scarce begins
560   His other half in the great zone of Heav'n."
        Thus Adam made request, and Raphael
After short pause assenting, thus began:
        "High matter[9] thou enjoin'st me. O prime of men,

---

8. A double negative; i.e., "I did know."
9. Raphael's account of the war in Heaven is an
epic device, a narrative of past action; it is also a
mini-epic itself, with traditional battles, challenges, and single combats. As an "epic" poet
treating sacred matter, Raphael confronts a narrative challenge similar to Milton's own.

Sad task and hard, for how shall I relate
565 To human sense th' invisible exploits
Of warring Spirits; how without remorse
The ruin of so many glorious once
And perfect while they stood; how last unfold
The secrets of another world, perhaps
570 Not lawful to reveal? Yet for thy good
This is dispensed, and what surmounts the reach
Of human sense, I shall delineate so,
By lik'ning spiritual to corporal forms,
As may express them best, though what if earth
575 Be but the shadow of Heav'n, and things therein
Each to other like, more than on earth is thought?
      "As yet this world was not, and Chaos wild
Reigned where these heav'ns now roll, where earth now rests
Upon her center poised, when on a day
580 (For time, though in eternity, applied
To motion, measures all things durable
By present, past, and future)[1] on such day
As Heav'n's great year[2] brings forth, th' empyreal host
Of angels by imperial summons called,
585 Innumerable before th' Almighty's throne
Forthwith from all the ends of Heav'n appeared
Under their hierarchs° in orders bright.   *leaders*
Ten thousand thousand ensigns high advanced,
Standards, and gonfalons[3] twixt van and rear
590 Stream in the air, and for distinction serve
Of hierarchies, of orders, and degrees;
Or in their glittering tissues° bear emblazed   *cloth*
Holy memorials, acts of zeal and love
Recorded eminent. Thus when in orbs
595 Of circuit° inexpressible they stood,   *circumference*
Orb within orb, the Father Infinite,
By whom in bliss embosomed sat the Son,
Amidst as from a flaming mount, whose top
Brightness had made invisible, thus spake:
600   " 'Hear all ye Angels, progeny of Light,
Thrones, Dominations, Princedoms, Virtues, Powers,
Hear my decree, which unrevoked shall stand.
This day I have begot whom I declare
My only Son, and on this holy hill
605 Him have anointed,[4] whom ye now behold
At my right hand; your head I him appoint;
And by my Self have sworn to him shall bow
All knees in Heav'n, and shall confess him Lord:
Under his great vicegerent[5] reign abide

---

1. Countering a long philosophical tradition, Milton asserts the existence of time in Heaven, before the creation of the universe.
2. Plato and others defined the "great year" as the cycle completed when all the heavenly bodies simultaneously return to the positions they held at the cycle's beginning.
3. Banners fastened to crosspieces or frames.
4. Cf. Psalm 2.7: "I will declare the decree . . .

Thou art my Son: this day have I begotten thee." The episode refers to the exaltation of the Son as King, not his actual begetting, since he is elsewhere described as "of all creation first" (3.383) and as God's agent in creating the angels and everything else.
5. Vice-regent, one appointed by the supreme ruler (here, God) to wield his authority.

610 United as one individual° soul   *indivisible*
    Forever happy: him who° disobeys   *whoever*
    Me disobeys, breaks union, and that day
    Cast out from God and blessèd vision, falls
    Into utter° darkness, deep engulfed, his place   *outer, total*
615 Ordained without redemption, without end.'
        "So spake th' Omnipotent, and with his words
    All seemed well pleased, all seemed, but were not all.
    That day, as other solemn° days, they spent   *ceremonial*
    In song and dance about the sacred hill,
620 Mystical dance, which yonder starry sphere
    Of planets and of fixed° in all her wheels   *fixed stars*
    Resembles nearest, mazes intricate,
    Eccentric,° intervolved,° yet regular   *off center / intertwined*
    Then most, when most irregular they seem:
625 And in their motions harmony divine
    So smooths her charming tones,⁶ that God's own ear
    Listens delighted. Evening now approached
    (For we have also our evening and our morn,
    We ours for change delectable, not need)
630 Forthwith from dance to sweet repast they turn
    Desirous; all in circles as they stood,
    Tables are set, and on a sudden piled
    With angels' food, and rubied nectar flows
    In pearl, in diamond, and massy gold,
635 Fruit of delicious vines, the growth of Heav'n.
    On flow'rs reposed, and with fresh flow'rets crowned,
    They eat, they drink, and in communion sweet
    Quaff immortality and joy, secure
    Of surfeit where full measure only bounds
640 Excess, before th' all-bounteous King, who show'red
    With copious hand, rejoicing in their joy.
    Now when ambrosial° night with clouds exhaled   *fragrant*
    From that high mount of God, whence light and shade
    Spring both, the face of brightest Heav'n had changed
645 To grateful° twilight (for night comes not there   *pleasing*
    In darker veil) and roseate° dews disposed   *rose-scented*
    All but the unsleeping eyes of God to rest,
    Wide over all the plain, and wider far
    Than all this globous earth in plain outspread,
650 (Such are the courts of God) th' angelic throng
    Dispersed in bands and files their camp extend
    By living streams among the trees of life,
    Pavilions numberless, and sudden reared,
    Celestial tabernacles, where they slept
655 Fanned with cool winds, save those who in their course
    Melodious hymns about the sovran throne
    Alternate all night long: but not so waked
    Satan, so call him now, his former name
    Is heard no more in Heav'n; he of the first,

6. The movements of the angels in their dance produce harmony, like those of the planets in the Pythagorean theory of the music of the spheres.

660 If not the first Archangel, great in power,
     In favor and pre-eminence, yet fraught
     With envy against the Son of God, that day
     Honored by his great Father, and proclaimed
     Messiah[7] King anointed, could not bear
665 Through pride that sight, and thought himself impaired.
     Deep malice thence conceiving and disdain,
     Soon as midnight brought on the dusky hour
     Friendliest to sleep and silence, he resolved
     With all his legions to dislodge,° and leave   leave camp
670 Unworshiped, unobeyed the throne supreme
     Contemptuous, and his next subordinate[8]
     Awak'ning, thus to him in secret spake:
          " 'Sleep'st thou companion dear, what sleep can close
     Thy eyelids? and remember'st what decree
675 Of yesterday, so late hath passed the lips
     Of Heav'n's Almighty. Thou to me thy thoughts
     Wast wont,° I mine to thee was wont to impart;   in the habit of
     Both waking we were one; how then can now
     Thy sleep dissent? New laws thou seest imposed;
680 New laws from him who reigns, new minds° may raise   purposes
     In us who serve, new counsels, to debate
     What doubtful may ensue, more in this place
     To utter is not safe. Assemble thou
     Of all those myriads which we lead the chief;
685 Tell them that by command, ere yet dim night
     Her shadowy cloud withdraws, I am to haste,
     And all who under me their banners wave,
     Homeward with flying march where we possess
     The quarters of the north, there to prepare
690 Fit entertainment to receive our King
     The great Messiah, and his new commands,
     Who speedily through all the hierarchies
     Intends to pass triumphant, and give laws.'
          "So spake the false Archangel, and infused
695 Bad influence into th' unwary breast
     Of his associate; he together calls,
     Or several one by one, the regent powers,
     Under him regent, tells, as he was taught,
     That the Most High commanding, now ere night,
700 Now ere dim night had disencumbered Heav'n,
     The great hierarchal standard was to move;
     Tells the suggested° cause, and casts between   insinuated
     Ambitious words and jealousies, to sound°   make trials of
     Or taint integrity; but all obeyed
705 The wonted signal, and superior voice
     Of their great potentate° for great indeed   ruler
     His name, and high was his degree in Heav'n;
     His count'nance as° the morning star that guides   like

---

7. Hebrew, "anointed."
8. His original name in Heaven is lost (1.350–66),
but he will come to be known as Beelzebub
(2.299–300).

The starry flock, allured them, and with lies
710　Drew after him the third part of Heav'n's host:
Meanwhile, th' Eternal eye, whose sight discerns
Abstrusest° thoughts, from forth his holy mount　　　*most secret*
And from within the golden lamps that burn
Nightly before him, saw without their light
715　Rebellion rising, saw in whom, how spread
Among the sons of morn, what multitudes
Were banded to oppose his high decree;
And smiling to his only Son thus said:
　　" 'Son, thou in whom my glory I behold
720　In full resplendence, heir of all my might,
Nearly it now concerns us to be sure
Of our omnipotence, and with what arms
We mean to hold what anciently we claim
Of deity or empire, such a foe
725　Is rising, who intends to erect his throne
Equal to ours, throughout the spacious north;
Nor so content, hath in his thought to try
In battle, what our power is, or our right.
Let us advise, and to this hazard draw
730　With speed what force is left, and all employ
In our defense, lest unawares we lose
This our high place, our sanctuary, our hill.'
　　"To whom the Son with calm aspect and clear
Lightning divine, ineffable, serene,
735　Made answer: 'Mighty Father, thou thy foes
Justly hast in derision, and secure
Laugh'st at their vain designs and tumults vain,[9]
Matter to me of glory, whom their hate
Illustrates,° when they sell all regal power　　　*makes illustrious*
740　Giv'n me to quell their pride, and in event°　　　*in the outcome*
Know whether I be dextrous to subdue
Thy rebels, or be found the worst in Heav'n.'
　　"So spake the Son, but Satan with his powers°　　　*armies*
Far was advanced on wingèd speed, an host
745　Innumerable as the stars of night,
Or stars of morning, dewdrops, which the sun
Impearls on every leaf and every flower.
Regions they passed, the mighty regencies°　　　*dominions*
Of Seraphim and Potentates and Thrones
750　In their triple degrees, regions to° which　　　*compared to*
All they dominion, Adam, is no more
Than what this garden is to all the earth,
And all the sea, from one entire globose°　　　*globe*
Stretched into longitude° which having passed　　　*spread out flat*
755　At length into the limits° of the north　　　*regions*
They came, and Satan to his royal seat
High on a hill, far blazing, as a mount
Raised on a mount, with pyramids and tow'rs

9. Cf. Psalm 2.4: "He that sitteth in the heavens shall laugh: / The Lord shall have them in derision."

From diamond quarries hewn, and rocks of gold,
760 The palace of great Lucifer (so call
That structure in the dialect of men
Interpreted) which not long after, he
Affecting° all equality with God,   *arrogating*
In imitation of that mount whereon
765 Messiah was declared in sight of Heav'n,
The Mountain of the Congregation called;
For thither he assembled all his train,
Pretending so commanded to consult
About the great reception of their King,
770 Thither to come, and with calumnious art
Of counterfeited truth thus held their ears:
    " 'Thrones, Dominations, Princedoms, Virtues, Powers,
If these magnific titles yet remain
Not merely titular, since by decree
775 Another now hath to himself engrossed°   *monopolized*
All power, and us eclipsed under the name
Of King anointed, for whom all this haste
Of midnight march, and hurried meeting here,
This only to consult how we may best
780 With what may be devised of honors new
Receive him coming to receive from us
Knee-tribute yet unpaid, prostration vile,
Too much to one, but double how endured,
To one and to his image now proclaimed?
785 But what if better counsels might erect
Our minds and teach us to cast off this yoke?
Will ye submit your necks, and choose to bend
The supple knee? Ye will not, if I trust
To know ye right, or if ye know yourselves
790 Natives and sons of Heav'n possessed before
By none, and if not equal all, yet free,
Equally free; for orders and degrees
Jar not with liberty, but well consist.
Who can in reason then or right assume
795 Monarchy over such as live by right
His equals,[1] if in power and splendor less,
In freedom equal? or can introduce
Law and edíct on us, who without law
Err not, much less for this to be our Lord,
800 And look for adoration to th' abuse
Of those imperial titles which assert
Our being ordained to govern, not to serve?'
    "Thus far his bold discourse without control
Had audience, when among the Seraphim
805 Abdiel,[2] than whom none with more zeal adored
The Deity, and divine commands obeyed,

---

1. Satan here paraphrases republican theory against earthly monarchy like that urged by Milton in his *Tenure of Kings and Magistrates* (1649); Abdiel, however, insists (lines 809–33) that the argument from equality cannot pertain to God and the angels.
2. Hebrew, "Servant of God."

Stood up, and in a flame of zeal severe
The current of his fury thus opposed:
   " 'O argument blasphémous, false and proud!
810 Words which no ear ever to hear in Heav'n
Expected, least of all from thee, ingrate,
In place thyself so high above thy peers.
Canst thou with impious obloquy condemn
The just decree of God, pronounced and sworn,
815 That to his only Son by right endued
With regal scepter, every soul in Heav'n
Shall bend the knee, and in that honor due
Confess him rightful King? Unjust thou says't,
Flatly unjust, to bind with laws the free,
820 And equal over equals to let reign,
One over all with unsucceeded° power.   *without successor*
Shalt thou give law to God, shalt thou dispute
With him the points of liberty, who made
Thee what thou art, and formed the pow'rs of Heav'n
825 Such as he pleased, and circumscribed their being?
Yet by experience taught we know how good,
And of our good, and of our dignity
How provident he is, how far from thought
To make us less, bent rather to exalt
830 Our happy state under one head more near
United. But to grant it thee unjust,
That equal over equals monarch reign:
Thyself though great and glorious dost thou count,
Or all angelic nature joined in one,
835 Equal to him begotten Son, by whom
As by his Word the mighty Father made
All things, ev'n thee, and all the Spirits of Heav'n
By him created in their bright° degrees,   *illustrious*
Crowned them with glory, and to their glory named
840 Thrones, Dominations, Princedoms, Virtues, Powers,
Essential Powers, nor by his reign obscured,
But more illustrious made, since he the head
One of our number thus reduced becomes,[3]
His laws our laws, all honor to him done
845 Returns our own. Cease then this impious rage,
And tempt not these; but hasten to appease
Th' incensèd Father and th' incensèd Son,
While pardon may be found in time besought.'
   "So spake the fervent angel, but his zeal
850 None seconded, as out of season judged,
Or singular and rash, whereat rejoiced
Th' Apostate, and more haughty thus replied.
'That we were formed then say'st thou? and the work
Of secondary hands, by task transferred
855 From Father to his Son? Strange point and new!

---

3. Abdiel suggests that the Son's appointment as the angels' King is something like an "incarnation" for them.

Doctrine which we would know whence learnt: who saw
When this creation was? Remember'st thou
Thy making, while the Maker gave thee being?
We know no time when we were not as now;
860 Know none before us, self-begot, self-raised,[4]
By our own quick'ning power, when fatal course°   the course of fate
Had circled his full orb, the birth mature
Of this our native Heav'n, ethereal sons.
Our pussiance is our own, our own right hand
865 Shall teach us highest deeds, by proof to try
Who is our equal: then thou shalt behold
Whether by supplication we intend
Address, and to begirt th' Almighty throne
Beseeching or besieging. This report,
870 These tidings carry to th' anointed King;
And fly, ere evil intercept thy flight.'
    "He said, and as the sound of waters deep
Hoarse murmur echoed to his words applause
Through the infinite host, nor less for that
875 The flaming Seraph fearless, though alone
Encompassed round with foes, thus answered bold:
    " 'O alienate from God, O Spirit accurst,
Forsaken of all good; I see thy fall
Determined, and thy hapless crew involved
880 In this perfidious fraud, contagion spread
Both of thy crime and punishment: henceforth
No more be troubled how to quit the yoke
Of God's Messiah; those indulgent laws
Will not be now vouchsafed, other decrees
885 Against thee are gone forth without recall;
That golden scepter which thou didst reject
Is now an iron rod to bruise and break
Thy disobedience. Well thou didst advise,
Yet not for thy advice or threats I fly
890 These wicked tents devoted,° lest the wrath   doomed
Impendent,° raging into sudden flame   impending
Distinguish not: for soon expect to feel
His thunder on thy head, devouring fire.
Then who created thee lamenting learn,
895 When who can uncreate thee thou shalt know.'
    "So spake the Seraph Abdiel faithful found,
Among the faithless, faithful only he;
Among innumerable false, unmoved,
Unshaken, unseduced, unterrified
900 His loyalty he kept, his love, his zeal;
Nor number, nor example with him wrought
To swerve from truth, or change his constant mind
Though single. From amidst them forth he passed,
Long way through hostile scorn, which he sustained

---

4. Satan's (illogical) argument is that since the angels cannot remember their creation they created themselves. Cf. Adam's comment on his recollection of origins (8.250–51).

905　Superior, nor of violence feared aught;
　　And with retorted scorn his back he turned
　　On those proud tow'rs to swift destruction doomed."

Book 6

　　All night the dreadless angel[1] unpursued
　　Through Heav'n's wide champaign° held his way, till Morn,　　　　*plain*
　　Waked by the circling Hours,[2] with rosy hand
　　Unbarred the gates of light. There is a cave
5　Within the mount of God, fast by his throne,
　　Where light and darkness in perpetual round
　　Lodge and dislodge by turns, which makes through Heav'n
　　Grateful vicissitude,° like day and night;　　　　*delightful change*
　　Light issues forth, and at the other door
10　Obsequious° darkness enters, till her hour　　　　*compliant*
　　To veil the Heav'n, though darkness there might well
　　Seem twilight here; and now went forth the Morn
　　Such as in highest Heav'n, arrayed in gold
　　Empyreal;° from before her vanished night,　　　　*heavenly*
15　Shot through with orient beams: when all the plain
　　Covered with thick embattled° squadrons bright,　　　　*in battle array*
　　Chariots and flaming arms, and fiery steeds
　　Reflecting blaze on blaze, first met his view:
　　War he perceived, war in procinct,° and found　　　　*preparation*
20　Already known what he for news had thought
　　To have reported: gladly then he mixed
　　Among those friendly Powers who him received
　　With joy and acclamations loud, that one
　　That of so many myriads fall'n, yet one
25　Returned not lost: on to the sacred hill
　　They led him high applauded, and present
　　Before the seat supreme; from whence a voice:
　　From midst a golden cloud thus mild was heard.
　　" 'Servant of God,[3] well done, well hast thou fought
30　The better fight, who single hast maintained
　　Against revolted multitudes the cause
　　Of truth, in word mightier than they in arms;
　　And for the testimony of truth hast borne
　　Universal reproach, far worse to bear
35　Than violence: for this was all thy care
　　To stand approved in sight of God, though worlds
　　Judged thee perverse: the easier conquest now
　　Remains thee, aided by this host of friends,
　　Back on thy foes more glorious to return
40　Than scorned thou didst depart, and to subdue
　　By force, who reason for their law refuse,
　　Right reason° for their law, and for their King　　　　*upright, true reason*
　　Messiah, who by right of merit reigns.

1. I.e., Abdiel.
2. Daughters of Jove, who control the seasons and guard the gates of Heaven. "Morn": Aurora, goddess of dawn.
3. The literal meaning (Hebrew) of the name Abdiel.

Go Michael of celestial armies prince,
45 And thou in military prowess next
Gabriel, lead forth to battle these my sons°   *angels*
Invincible, lead forth my armèd saints
By thousands and by millions ranged for fight;
Equal[4] in number to that godless crew
50 Rebellious, them with fire and hostile arms
Fearless assault, and to the brow of Heav'n
Pursuing drive them out from God and bliss,
Into their place of punishment, the gulf
Of Tartarus,° which ready opens wide   *Hell*
55 His fiery chaos to receive their fall.'
   "So spake the Sovran Voice, and clouds began
To darken all the hill, and smoke to roll
In dusky wreaths reluctant° flames, the sign   *writhing*
Of wrath awaked: nor with less dread the loud
60 Ethereal trumpet from on high gan° blow: *began to*
At which command the powers militant,
That stood for Heav'n, in mighty quadrate[5] joined
Of union irresistible, moved on
In silence their bright legions, to the sound
65 Of instrumental harmony that breathed
Heroic ardor to advent'rous deeds
Under their godlike leaders, in the cause
Of God and his Messiah. On they move
Indissolubly firm; nor obvious° hill,   *standing in the way*
70 Nor strait'ning vale,[6] nor wood, nor stream divides
Their perfect ranks; for high above the ground
Their march was, and the passive air upbore
Their nimble tread; as when the total kind
Of birds in orderly array on wing
75 Came summoned over Eden to receive
Their names of thee; so over many a tract
Of Heav'n they marched, and many a province wide
Tenfold the length of this terrene:° at last   *earth, terrain*
Far in th' horizon to the north appeared
80 From skirt to skirt a fiery region, stretched
In battailous° aspéct, and nearer view   *warlike*
Bristled with upright beams innumerable
Of rigid spears, and helmets thronged, and shields
Various, with boastful argument° portrayed,   *heraldic devices*
85 The banded powers of Satan hasting on
With furious expedition;° for they weened°   *speed/thought*
That selfsame day by fight, or by surprise
To win the mount of God, and on his throne
To set the envier of his state, the proud
90 Aspirer, but their thoughts proved fond° and vain   *foolish*
In the mid-way: though strange to us it seemed

4. God sends out only an equal force to match the one-third of the angelic host that rebelled, not the two-thirds that remained loyal.

5. A square military formation.
6. A narrow valley would force other armies to march in a file.

At first, that angel should with angel war,
And in fierce hosting meet, who wont[7] to meet
So oft in festivals of joy and love
95   Unanimous, as sons of one great Sire
Hymning th' Eternal Father: but the shout
Of battle now began, and rushing sound
Of onset ended soon each milder thought.
High in the midst exalted as a god
100 Th' Apostate in his sun-bright chariot sat
Idol of majesty divine, enclosed
With flaming Cherubim, and golden shields;
Then lighted from his gorgeous throne, for now
'Twixt host and host but narrow space was left,
105 A dreadful interval, and front to front
Presented stood in terrible array
Of hideous length: before the cloudy van,°   *frowning vanguard*
On the rough edge of battle° ere it joined,   *front line*
Satan with vast and haughty strides advanced,
110 Came tow'ring, armed in adamant and gold;
Abdiel that sight endured not, where he stood
Among the mightiest, bent on highest deeds,
And thus his own undaunted heart explores:
    " 'O Heav'n! that such resemblance of the Highest
115 Should yet remain, where faith and realty°   *sincerity*
Remain not; wherefore should not strength and might
There fail where virtue fails, or weakest prove
Where boldest; though to sight° unconquerable?   *seemingly*
His puissance, trusting in th' Almighty's aid,
120 I mean to try, whose reason I have tried°   *proved by trial*
Unsound and false; nor is it aught but just,
That he who in debate of truth hath won,
Should win in arms, in both disputes alike
Victor; though brutish that contést and foul,
125 When reason hath to deal with force, yet so
Most reason is that reason overcome.'
    "So pondering, and from his armèd peers
Forth stepping opposite, half-way he met
His daring foe, at this prevention° more   *obstruction*
130 Incensed, and thus securely° him defied: *confidently*
    " 'Proud, art thou met? Thy hope was to have reached
The highth of thy aspiring unopposed,
The throne of God unguarded, and his side
Abandoned at the terror of thy power
135 Or potent tongue; fool, not to think how vain
Against the Omnipotent to rise in arms;
Who out of smallest things could without end
Have raised incessant armies to defeat
Thy folly; or with solitary hand
140 Reaching beyond all limit at one blow

7. Were accustomed to. "Hosting": hostile encounter.

Unaided could have finished thee, and whelmed
Thy legions under darkness; but thou seest
All are not of thy train; there be° who faith   *there are those*
Prefer, and piety° to God, though then   *devotion*
145   To thee not visible, when I alone
Seemed in thy world erroneous to dissent
From all: my sect[8] thou seest, now learn too late
How few sometimes may know, when thousand err.'
    "Whom the grand Foe with scornful eye askance
150   Thus answered. 'Ill for thee, but in wished hour
Of my revenge, first sought for thou return'st
From flight, seditious angel, to receive
Thy merited reward, the first assay
Of this right hand provoked, since first that tongue
155   Inspired with contradiction durst oppose
A third part of the gods, in synod met
Their deities to assert, who while they feel
Vigor divine within them, can allow
Omnipotence to none. But well thou com'st
160   Before thy fellows, ambitious to win
From me some plume, that thy success[9] may show
Destruction to the rest: this pause between
(Unanswered lest thou boast)[1] to let thee know;
At first I thought that liberty and Heav'n
165   To heav'nly souls had been all one;° but now   *one and the same*
I see that most through sloth had rather serve,
Minist'ring Spirits, trained up in feast and song;
Such hast thou armed, the minstrelsy[2] of heav'n,
Servility° with freedom to contend,   *bondage, obsequiousness*
170   As both their deeds compared this day shall prove.'
    "To whom in brief thus Abdiel stern replied:
'Apostate, still thou err'st, nor end wilt find
Of erring, from the path of truth remote:
Unjustly thou deprav'st° it with the name   *vilify*
175   Of servitude to serve whom God ordains,
Or nature; God and nature bid the same,
When he who rules is worthiest, and excels
Them whom he governs.[3] This is servitude,
To serve th' unwise, or him who hath rebelled
180   Against his worthier, as thine now serve thee,
Thyself not free, but to thyself enthralled;

---

8. The term carries political resonance, since the national English church, Anglican or (during the revolution) Presbyterian, sought to suppress and persecute the sects who separated from it (Baptists, Quakers, Socinians, and others), often denouncing them as heretics. Satan claims that a "synod" (line 156, term for a Presbyterian assembly) has proclaimed the truth of the rebel angels' case; Abdiel insists that truth may rather reside (as here) with a single "dissenter" or sect of a few.
9. The outcome of your action. "Plume": token of

victory.
1. I.e., lest thou boast that I did not answer your argument.
2. Satan's contemptuous pun links together the loyal angels' service ("Minist'ring," line 167) with their song, likened to the street songs of minstrels.
3. Abdiel cites the "natural law" principle that rule rightly belongs to the best or worthiest, and that tyrants are enslaved to their own passions (next line).

Yet lewdly° dar'st our minist'ring upbraid.   *ignorantly, basely*
Reign thou in Hell thy kingdom, let me serve
In Heav'n God ever blest, and his divine
185 Behests obey, worthiest to be obeyed;
Yet chains in Hell, not realms expect: meanwhile
From me returned, as erst thou saidst, from flight,
This greeting on thy impious crest receive.'
　　"So saying, a noble stroke he lifted high,
190 Which hung not, but so swift with tempest fell
On the proud crest of Satan, that no sight,
Nor motion of swift thought, less could his shield
Such ruin intercept: ten paces huge
He back recoiled; the tenth on bended knee
195 His massy spear upstayed: as if on earth
Winds under ground or waters forcing way
Sidelong, had pushed a mountain from his seat
Half sunk with all his pines. Amazement seized
The rebel Thrones,⁴ but greater rage to see
200 Thus foiled their mightiest: ours joy filled, and shout,
Presage of victory and fierce desire
Of battle: whereat Michaël bid sound
Th' Archangel trumpet; through the vast of Heav'n
It sounded, and the faithful armies rung
205 Hosanna to the Highest: nor stood at gaze
The adverse legions, nor less hideous joined
The horrid shock: now storming fury rose,
And clamor such as heard in Heav'n till now
Was never, arms on armor clashing brayed⁵
210 Horrible discord, and the madding° wheels   *whirling madly*
Of brazen chariots raged; dire was the noise
Of conflict; overhead the dismal° hiss   *dreadful*
Of fiery darts in flaming volleys flew,
And flying vaulted either host with fire.
215 So under fiery cope° together rushed   *sky*
Both battles main,⁶ with ruinous assault
And inextinguishable rage; all Heav'n
Resounded, and had earth been then, all earth
Had to her center shook. What wonder? when
220 Millions of fierce encount'ring angels fought
On either side, the least of whom could wield
These elements,⁷ and arm him with the force
Of all their regions: how much more of power
Army against army numberless to raise
225 Dreadful combustion° warring, and disturb,   *tumult*
Though not destroy, their happy native seat;

---

4. Here as elsewhere Milton uses the name of one
angelic order to stand for all. But the choice of
"Thrones" here carries political resonance, linking
monarchs with rebels against God's kingdom.
5. Made a harsh, jarring sound.

6. The principal body of an army, as opposed to
the van, rear, and wing.
7. The four elements—fire, air, water, earth—that
constitute the several "regions" (next line) of planet
earth.

Had not th' Eternal King Omnipotent
From his stronghold of Heav'n high overruled
And limited their might; though numbered such
230 As each divided legion might have seemed
A numerous host, in strength each armèd hand
A legion; led in fight, yet leader seemed
Each warrior single as in chief,[8] expert
When to advance, or stand, or turn the sway°   force
235 Of battle, open when, and when to close
The ridges° of grim war; no thought of flight,   ranks
None of retreat, no unbecoming deed
That argued fear; each on himself relied,
As° only in his arm the moment[9] lay   as if
240 Of victory; deeds of eternal fame
Were done, but infinite: for wide was spread
That war and various; sometimes on firm ground
A standing fight, then soaring on main° wing   strong, powerful
Tormented° all the air; all air seemed then   agitated
245 Conflicting fire: long time in even scale
The battle hung; till Satan, who that day
Prodigious power had shown, and met in arms
No equal, ranging through the dire attack
Of fighting Seraphim confused, at length
250 Saw where the sword of Michael smote, and felled
Squadrons at once; with huge two-handed sway
Brandished aloft the horrid edge came down
Wide-wasting; such destruction to withstand
He hasted, and opposed the rocky orb
255 Of tenfold adamant, his ample shield[1]
A vast circumference: at his approach
The great Archangel from his warlike toil
Surceased, and glad as hoping here to end
Intestine war° in Heav'n, the Arch-Foe subdued   civil war
260 Or captive dragged in chains, with hostile frown
And visage all inflamed first thus began:
    " 'Author of evil, unknown till thy revolt,
Unnamed in Heav'n, now plenteous, as thou seest
These acts of hateful strife, hateful to all,
265 Though heaviest by just measure on thyself
And thy adherents: how hast thou disturbed
Heav'n's blessèd peace, and into nature brought
Misery, uncreated till the crime
Of thy rebellion! how hast thou instilled
270 Thy malice into thousands, once upright
And faithful, now proved false! But think not here
To trouble holy rest; Heav'n casts thee out
From all her confines. Heav'n the seat of bliss
Brooks° not the works of violence and war.   endures

---

8. I.e., the angelic legions had leaders, yet each single warrior seemed like such a leader.
9. Weight that will tip the scales.

1. Satan's shield is a rocklike ("rocky") circle, made of impenetrable "adamant" (probably diamond), ten layers thick.

275 Hence then, and evil go with thee along
Thy offspring, to the place of evil, Hell,
Thou and thy wicked crew; there mingle° broils,   *concoct*
Ere this avenging sword begin thy doom,
Or some more sudden vengeance winged from God
280 Precipitate thee with augmented pain.'
"So spake the Prince of Angels; to whom thus
The Adversary:[2] 'Nor think thou with wind
Of airy threats to awe whom yet with deeds
Thou canst not. Hast thou turned the least of these
285 To flight, or if to fall, but that they rise
Unvanquished, easier to transact with me
That thou shouldst hope, imperious, and with threats
To chase me hence?[3] Err not that so shall end
The strife which thou call'st evil, but we style
290 The strife of glory: which we mean to win,
Or turn this Heav'n itself into the Hell
Thou fablest, here however to dwell free,
If not to reign: meanwhile thy utmost force,
And join him named Almighty to thy aid,
295 I fly not, but have sought thee far and nigh.'
"They ended parle,° and both addressed° for fight   *parlay/prepared*
Unspeakable; for who, though with the tongue
Of angels, can relate, or to what things
Liken on earth conspicuous, that may lift
300 Human imagination to such hight
Of godlike power: for likest gods they seemed,
Stood they or moved, in stature, motion, arms
Fit to decide the empire of great Heav'n.
Now waved their fiery swords, and in the air
305 Made horrid circles; two broad suns their shields
Blazed opposite, while Expectation stood[4]
In horror; from each hand with speed retired
Where erst° was thickest fight, th' angelic throng,   *ever*
And left large field, unsafe within the wind
310 Of such commotion, such as to set forth
Great things by small,[5] if nature's concord broke,
Among the constellations war were sprung,
Two planets rushing from aspéct malign
Of fiercest opposition in mid sky,
315 Should combat, and their jarring spheres confound.
Together both with next to almighty arm,
Uplifted imminent one stroke they aimed
That might determine,° and not need repeat,°   *end/repetition*
As not of power,[6] at once; nor odds° appeared   *inequality*

2. A literal translation of the name "Satan."
3. I.e., Have you made even the least of my followers flee, or seen them fall and fail to rise, that
you would hope "imperiously" to deal ("transact")
otherwise with me, driving me off by mere threats?
"Err not": don't falsely suppose.
4. Personifying the angels' apprehension.
5. An epic simile comparing the clash of these

armies ("great things") with war among the planets, in which two planets clashing together from
diametrically opposed positions ("aspect malign,"
line 313), would cast the planetary system and its
music ("jarring spheres") into confusion ("confound," line 315).
6. I.e., because they would not have power to
repeat the blow.

320　In might or swift prevention;° but the sword　　　　　　　　*anticipation*
　　　Of Michael from the armory of God
　　　Was giv'n him tempered so, that neither keen
　　　Nor solid might resist that edge: it met
　　　The sword of Satan with steep force to smite
325　Descending, and in half cut sheer, nor stayed,
　　　But with swift wheel reverse, deep ent'ring shared°　　　　　*cut off*
　　　All his right side; then Satan first knew pain,
　　　And writhed him to and fro convolved;° so sore　　　　　　*contorted*
　　　The griding° sword with discontinuous° wound　　*keenly cutting/gaping*
330　Passed through him, but th' ethereal substance closed
　　　Not long divisible, and from the gash
　　　A stream of nectarous humor issuing flowed
　　　Sanguine,° such as celestial Spirits may bleed,　　　　　　*blood-red*
　　　And all his armor stained erewhile so bright.
335　Forthwith on all sides to his aid was run
　　　By angels many and strong, who interposed
　　　Defense, while others bore him on their shields
　　　Back to his chariot, where it stood retired
　　　From off the files of war; there they him laid
340　Gnashing for anguish and despite and shame
　　　To find himself not matchless, and his pride
　　　Humbled by such rebuke, so far beneath
　　　His confidence to equal God in power.
　　　Yet soon he healed; for Spirits that live throughout
345　Vital in every part, not as frail man
　　　In entrails, heart or head, liver or reins,°　　　　　　　　*kidneys*
　　　Cannot but by annihilating die;
　　　Nor in their liquid texture mortal wound
　　　Receive, no more than can the fluid air:
350　All heart they live, all head, all eye, all ear,
　　　All intellect, all sense, and as they please,
　　　They limb themselves,7 and color, shape, or size
　　　Assume, as likes° them best, condense or rare.　　　　　　　*please*
　　　　"Meanwhile in other parts like deeds deserved
355　Memorial, where the might of° Gabriel fought,　　　　　　　*mighty*
　　　And with fierce ensigns pierced the deep array8
　　　Of Moloch furious king, who him defied,
　　　And at his chariot wheels to drag him bound
　　　Threatened, nor from the Holy One of Heav'n
360　Refrained his tongue blasphémous; but anon
　　　Down clov'n to the waist, with shattered arms
　　　And uncouth° pain fled bellowing. On each wing　　　　　*unfamiliar*
　　　Uriel and Raphael his vaunting foe,
　　　Though huge, and in a rock of diamond armed,
365　Vanquished Adramelech, and Asmadai,9
　　　Two potent Thrones, that to be less than gods

---

7. I.e., provide themselves with limbs. "Condense or rare" (line 352): dense or airy.
8. With his companies ("ensigns") he pierced Moloch's troops in their dense formation ("deep

array").
9. Asmodeus, a Persian god (cf. 4.167–71). "Adramelech": "King of Fire," a god worshipped at Samaria with human sacrifice.

Disdained, but meaner thoughts learned in their flight,
Mangled with ghastly wounds through plate and mail.
Nor stood unmindful Abdiel to annoy°   *injure*
370 The atheist° crew, but with redoubled blow   *impious*
Ariel and Arioch, and the violence
Of Ramiel[1] scorched and blasted overthrew.
I might relate of thousands, and their names
Eternize here on earth; but those elect
375 Angels contented with their fame in Heav'n
Seek not the praise of men: the other sort
In might though wondrous and in acts of war,
Nor of renown less eager, yet by doom
Cancelled from Heav'n and sacred memory,
380 Nameless in dark oblivion let them dwell.
For strength from truth divided and from just,
Illaudable,° naught merits but dispraise   *unworthy of praise*
And ignominy, yet to glory aspires
Vainglorious, and through infamy seeks fame:
385 Therefore eternal silence be their doom.
    "And now their mightiest quelled, the battle swerved,[2]
With many an inroad gored; deformèd rout
Entered, and foul disorder; all the ground
With shivered armor strown, and on a heap
390 Chariot and charioteer lay overturned
And fiery foaming steeds; what° stood, recoiled   *those who*
O'erwearied, through the faint Satanic host
Defensive scarce,[3] or with pale fear surprised,°   *seized unexpectedly*
Then first with fear surprised and sense of pain
395 Fled ignominious, to such evil brought
By sin of disobedience, till that hour
Not liable to fear or flight or pain.
Far otherwise th' inviolable saints
In cubic phalanx firm advanced entire,
400 Invulnerable, impenetrably armed:
Such high advantages their innocence
Gave them above their foes, not to have sinned,
Not to have disobeyed; in fight they stood
Unwearied, unobnoxious° to be pained   *not liable*
405 By wound, though from their place by violence moved.
    "Now night her course began, and over Heav'n
Inducing darkness, grateful truce imposed,
And silence on the odious din of war:
Under her cloudy covert both retired,
410 Victor and vanquished: on the foughten field
Michaël and his angels prevalent°   *victorious*
Encamping, placed in guard their watches round,
Cherubic waving fires: on th' other part
Satan with his rebellious disappeared,

---

1. "Ramiel": "Thunder of God." "Ariel": "Lion of
God." "Arioch": "Lionlike."

2. I.e., the army gave way.
3. Scarcely defending themselves.

415   Far in the dark dislodged,° and void of rest,   *shifted quarters*
    His potentates to council called by night;
    And in the midst thus undismayed began:
      " 'O now in danger tried, now known in arms
    Not to be overpowered, companions dear,
420   Found worthy not of liberty alone,
    Too mean pretense,° but what we more affect,[4]   *low aim*
    Honor, dominion, glory, and renown,
    Who have sustained one day in doubtful° fight,   *indecisive*
    (And if one day, why not eternal days?)
425   What Heaven's Lord had powerfullest to send
    Against us from about his throne, and judged
    Sufficient to subdue us to his will,
    But proves not so: then fallible, it seems,
    Of future° we may deem him, though till now   *in the future*
430   Omniscient thought. True is, less firmly armed,
    Some disadvantage we endured and pain,
    Till now not known, but known as soon contemned,[5]
    Since now we find this our empyreal form
    Incapable of mortal injury
435   Imperishable, and though pierced with wound,
    Soon closing, and by native vigor healed.
    Of evil then so small as easy think
    The remedy; perhaps more valid° arms,   *powerful*
    Weapons more violent, when next we meet,
440   May serve to better us, and worse° our foes,   *injure*
    Or equal what between us made the odds,
    In nature none: if other hidden cause
    Left them superior, while we can preserve
    Unhurt our minds, and understanding sound,
445   Due search and consultation will disclose.'
      "He sat; and in th' assembly next upstood
    Nisroch,[6] of Principalities the prime;
    As one he stood escaped from cruel fight,
    Sore toiled, his riven arms to havoc hewn,°   *cut to pieces*
450   And cloudy in aspéct thus answering spake:
    'Deliverer from new lords, leader to free
    Enjoyment of our right as gods; yet hard
    For gods, and too unequal work we find
    Against unequal arms to fight in pain,
455   Against unpained, impassive;[7] from which evil
    Ruin must needs ensue; for what avails
    Valor or strength, though matchless, quelled with pain
    Which all subdues, and makes remiss° the hands   *slack, weak*
    Of mightiest. Sense of pleasure we may well
460   Spare out of life perhaps, and not repine,
    But live content, which is the calmest life:
    But pain is perfect misery, the worst
    Of evils, and excessive, overturns

---

4. Aspire to.
5. No sooner known than despised.
6. An Assyrian god; the Hebrew name means "del-

icate temptation."
7. Not liable to suffering.

All patience. He who therefore can invent
465 With what more forcible we may offend°   *attack*
Our yet unwounded enemies, or arm
Ourselves with like defense, to me° deserves   *in my opinion*
No less than for deliverance what we owe.'[8]
    "Whereto with look composed Satan replied.
470 'Not uninvented that, which thou aright
Believ'st so main° to our success, I bring;   *essential*
Which of us who beholds the bright surfáce
Of this ethereous mold° whereon we stand,   *ethereal matter*
This continent of spacious Heav'n, adorned
475 With plant, fruit, flow'r ambrosial, gems and gold,
Whose eye so superfically surveys
These things, as not to mind° from whence they grow *consider*
Deep under ground, materials dark and crude,
Of spiritous and fiery spume,° till touched   *frothy matter*
480 With Heav'n's ray, and tempered they shoot forth
So beauteous, op'ning to the ambient° light.   *enveloping*
These in their dark nativity the deep
Shall yield us, pregnant with infernal° flame,   *from underground*
Which into hollow engines° long and round   *cannon*
485 Thick-rammed, at th' other bore[9] with touch of fire
Dilated and infuriate° shall send forth   *raging*
From far with thund'ring noise among our foes
Such implements of mischief as shall dash
To pieces, and o'erwhelm whatever stands
490 Adverse, that they shall fear we have disarmed
The Thunderer of his only° dreaded bolt.   *unique*
Nor long shall be our labor, yet ere dawn,
Effect shall end our wish. Meanwhile revive;
Abandon fear; to strength and counsel joined
495 Think nothing hard, much less to be despaired.'
    He ended, and his words their drooping cheer°   *spirits*
Enlightened, and their languished hope revived.
Th' invention all admired,° and each, how he   *marveled at*
To be th' inventor missed, so easy it seemed
500 Once found, which yet unfound most would have thought
Impossible: yet haply° of thy race   *by chance*
In future days, if malice should abound,
Some one intent on mischief, or inspired
With dev'lish machination might devise
505 Like instrument to plague the sons of men
For sin, on war and mutual slaughter bent.
Forthwith from council to the work they flew,
None arguing stood, innumerable hands
Were ready, in a moment up they turned
510 Wide the celestial soil, and saw beneath
Th' originals° of nature in their crude   *original elements*
Conception; sulphurous and nitrous foam[1]
They found, they mingled, and with subtle art,

---

8. I.e., we would owe such a one our deliverance.
9. The touchhole into which fine powder was poured to serve as fuse for the charge. "Thick": compactly.
1. Saltpeter ("nitrous foam") and sulphur are the ingredients of gunpowder.

Concocted° and adjusted° they reduced   *heated/dried*
515 To blackest grain, and into store conveyed:
Part hidden veins digged up (nor hath this earth
Entrails unlike) of mineral and stone,
Whereof to found° their engines and their balls   *cast*
Of missive° ruin; part incentive° reed   *missile/kindling*
520 Provide, pernicious° with one touch to fire.   *quick, destructive*
So all ere day-spring,° under conscious[2] night   *dawn*
Secret they finished, and in order set,
With silent circumspection unespied.
Now when fair morn orient in Heav'n appeared
525 Up rose the victor angels, and to arms
The matin° trumpet sung: in arms they stood   *morning*
Of golden panoply, refulgent° host,   *shining*
Soon banded; others from the dawning hills
Looked round, and scouts each coast light-armèd scour,
530 Each quarter, to descry the distant foe,
Where lodged, or whither fled, or if for fight,
In motion or in alt:° him soon they met   *halt*
Under spread ensigns moving nigh, in slow
But firm battalion; back with speediest sail
535 Zophiel,[3] of Cherubim the swiftest wing,
Came flying, and in mid-air aloud thus cried:
" 'Arm, warriors, arm for fight, the foe at hand,
Whom fled we thought, will save us long pursuit
This day, fear not his flight; so thick a cloud
540 He comes, and settled in his face I see
Sad° resolution and secure:° let each   *sober/confident*
His adamantine coat gird well, and each
Fit well his helm, gripe fast his orbèd shield,
Borne ev'n° or high, for this day will pour down,   *straight out*
545 If I conjecture° aught, no drizzling shower,   *interpret signs*
But rattling storm of arrows barbed with fire.'
So warned he them aware themselves, and soon
In order, quit of all impediment;°   *hindrance*
Instant without disturb° they took alarm,   *disorder*
550 And onward move embattled;° when behold   *in battle order*
Not distant far the heavy pace the foe
Approaching gross° and huge; in hollow cube   *compact*
Training° his devilish enginry, impaled°   *hauling/fenced in*
On every side with shadowing squadrons deep,
555 To hide the fraud. At interview° both stood   *at mutual view*
A while, but suddenly at head appeared
Satan: and thus was heard commanding loud:
" 'Vanguard, to right and left the front unfold;
That all may see who hate us, how we seek
560 Peace and composure,° and with open breast   *agreement*
Stand ready to receive them, if they like
Our overture,[4] and turn not back perverse;

2. Aware, as an accessory to a crime.
3. Hebrew, "Spy of God."
4. A pun on "offer to negotiate" and "opening"

(aperture), the hole or muzzle of the cannon. The passage is full of puns: e.g., "perverse" (line 562, peevish, turned the wrong way), "discharge" (line

But that I doubt, however witness Heaven,
Heav'n witness thou anon, while we discharge
565 Freely our part: ye who appointed stand
Do as you have in charge, and briefly touch
What we propound, and loud that all may hear.'
    "So scoffing in ambiguous words, he scarce
Had ended; when to right and left the front
570 Divided, and to either flank retired.
Which to our eyes discovered new and strange,
A triple-mounted° row of pillars laid   *in three rows*
On wheels (for like to pillars most they seemed
Or hollowed bodies made of oak or fir
575 With branches lopped, in wood or mountain felled)
Brass, iron, stony mold,° had not their mouths   *matter*
With hideous orifice gaped on us wide,
Portending hollow truce; at each behind
A Seraph stood, and in his hand a reed
580 Stood waving tipped with fire; while we suspense,°   *in suspense*
Collected stood within our thoughts amused,°   *puzzled*
Not long, for sudden all at once their reeds
Put forth, and to a narrow vent applied
With nicest touch. Immediate in a flame,
585 But soon obscured with smoke, all Heav'n appeared,
From those deep-throated engines belched,[5] whose roar
Emboweled° with outrageous noise the air,   *disemboweled*
And all her entrails tore, disgorging foul
Their devilish glut, chained[6] thunderbolts and hail
590 Of iron globes, which on the victor host
Leveled, with such impetuous fury smote,
That whom they hit, none on their feet might stand,
Though standing else as rocks, but down they fell
By thousands, Angel on Archangel rolled,
595 The sooner for their arms; unarmed they might
Have easily as Spirits evaded swift
By quick contraction or remove; but now
Foul dissipation° followed and forced rout;   *dispersal*
Nor served it to relax their serried files.[7]
600 What should they do? If on they rushed, repulse
Repeated, and indecent° overthrow   *shameful*
Doubled, would render them yet more despised,
And to their foes a laughter; for in view
Stood ranked of Seraphim another row
605 In posture to displode° their second dire°   *explode/volley*
Of thunder: back defeated to return
They worse abhorred. Satan beheld their plight,
And to his mates thus in derision called:
    " 'O friends, why come not on these victors proud?

---

564), "charge," "touch," "propound," "loud" (lines
566–67), "hollow" (line 578).
5. See the sustained debased imagery relating to
bodily functions, e.g., "belched," "embowelled,"
"entrails," and other terms suggestive of vomiting
and defecating.
6. Chainshot, which was linked cannonballs.
7. I.e., nor did it do any good ("served it") to loosen
up ("relax") their rows pressed close together ("serried files").

610 Erewhile they fierce were coming, and when we,
To entertain them fair with open front°   *candid face*
And breast,° (what could we more?) propounded[8] terms   *heart*
Of composition, straight they changed their minds,
Flew off, and into strange vagaries° fell,   *eccentric notions*
615 As they would dance, yet for a dance they seemed
Somewhat extravagant and wild, perhaps
For joy of offering peace: but I suppose
If our proposals once again were heard
We should compel them to a quick result.'
620   "To whom thus Belial in like gamesome mood:
'Leader, the terms we sent were terms of weight,
Of hard contents, and full of force urged home,
Such as we might perceive amused[9] them all,
And stumbled many: who receives them right,
625 Had need from head to foot well understand;
Not understood, this gift they have besides,
They show us when our foes walk not upright.'"
    "So they among themselves in pleasant° vein   *jesting*
Stood scoffing, hightened in their thoughts beyond
630 All doubt of victory, Eternal Might
To match with their inventions they presumed
So easy, and of his thunder made a scorn,
And all his host derided, while they stood
A while in trouble; but they stood not long,
635 Rage prompted them at length, and found them arms
Against such hellish mischief fit to oppose.
Forthwith (behold the excellence, the power,
Which God hath in his mighty angels placed)
Their arms away they threw, and to the hills
640 (For earth hath this variety from Heav'n
Of pleasure situate in hill and dale)
Light as the lightning glimpse they ran, they flew,
From their foundations loos'ning to and fro
They plucked the seated hills with all their load,[1]
645 Rocks, waters, woods, and by the shaggy tops
Uplifting bore them in their hands: amaze,°   *astonishment, panic*
Be sure, and terror seized the rebel host,
When coming towards them so dread they saw
The bottom of the mountains upward turned,
650 Till on those cursèd engines' triple-row
They saw them whelmed, and all their confidence
Under the weight of mountains buried deep,
Themselves invaded° next, and on their heads   *attacked*
Main° promontories flung, which in the air   *great, solid*
655 Came shadowing, and oppressed° whole legions armed.   *pressed down*
Their armor helped their harm, crushed in and bruised
Into their substance pent,° which wrought them pain   *closely confined*

---

8. More puns, on "propounded," "terms of composition," "flew off."
9. A pun on "held their attention" and "bewildered them." Belial also puns on (among other terms) "stumbled" ("nonplussed" and "tripped up") and

"understand" ("comprehend" and "prop up").
1. The hurling of hills as missiles is taken from the war between the Olympian gods and the Giants, in Hesiod's *Theogony*.

Implacable, and many a dolorous groan,
Long struggling underneath, ere they could wind
660 Out of such prison, though Spirits of purest light,
Purest at first, now gross by sinning grown.
The rest in imitation to like arms
Betook them, and the neighboring hills uptore;
So hills amid the air encountered hills
665 Hurled to and fro with jaculation° dire,   *hurling*
That underground they fought in dismal shade;
Infernal noise; war seemed a civil° game   *humane, refined*
To° this uproar; horrid confusion heaped   *compared to*
Upon confusion rose: and now all Heav'n
670 Had gone to wrack, with ruin overspread,
Had not th' Almighty Father where he sits
Shrined in his sanctuary of Heav'n secure,
Consulting° on the sum of things, foreseen   *considering*
This tumult, and permitted all, advised:°   *deliberately*
675 That his great purpose he might so fulfill,
To honor his anointed Son avenged
Upon his enemies, and to declare
All power on him transferred: whence to his Son
Th' assessor[2] of his throne he thus began:
680   " 'Effulgence° of my glory, Son beloved,   *radiance*
Son in whose face invisible is beheld
Visibly,[3] what by Deity I am,
And in whose hand what by decree I do,
Second Omnipotence,[4] two days are passed,
685 Two days, as we compute the days of Heav'n,
Since Michael and his powers went forth to tame
These disobedient; sore hath been their fight,
As likeliest was, when two such foes met armed;
For to themselves I left them, and thou know'st,
690 Equal in their creation they were formed,
Save what sin hath impaired, which yet hath wrought
Insensibly,° for I suspend their doom;   *imperceptively*
Whence in perpetual fight they needs must last
Endless, and no solution will be found:
695 War wearied hath performed what war can do,
And to disordered rage let loose the reins,
With mountains as with weapons armed, which makes
Wild work in Heav'n, and dangerous to the main.°   *whole continent*
Two days are therefore passed, the third is thine;
700 For thee I have ordained it, and thus far
Have suffered,° that the glory may be thine   *permitted*
Of ending this great war, since none but thou
Can end it. Into thee such virtue and grace
Immense I have transfused, that all may know
705 In Heav'n and Hell thy power above compare,

2. One who sits beside, an associate.
3. Cf. Colossians 1.15: "Who is the image of the invisible God."
4. Two omnipotences are a logical impossibility; the phrase underscores Milton's view that the Son

receives all power from the Father. Cf. John 5.19, "The Son can do nothing of himself, but what he seeth the Father do," which Milton cites in *Christian Doctrine* 1.5 to argue that the Son derives all power from the Father.

And this perverse commotion governed thus,
To manifest thee worthiest to be heir
Of all things, to be heir and to be King
By sacred unction,° thy deservèd right.   anointing
710 Go then thou mightiest in thy Father's might,
Ascend my chariot, guide the rapid wheels
That shake heav'n's basis, bring forth all my war,°   instruments of war
My bow and thunder, my almighty arms
Gird on, and sword upon thy puissant thigh;
715 Pursue these sons of darkness, drive them out
From all Heav'n's bounds into the utter° deep: outer
There let them learn, as likes them, to despise
God and Messiah his anointed King.'5
    "He said, and on his Son with rays direct
720 Shone full, he all his Father full expressed
Ineffably into his face received,
And thus the Filial Godhead answering spake:
    " 'O Father, O Supreme of heav'nly Thrones,
First, highest, holiest, best, thou always seek'st
725 To glorify thy Son, I always thee,
As is most just; this I my glory account,
My exaltation, and my whole delight,
That thou in me well pleased, declar'st thy will
Fulfilled, which to fulfill is all my bliss.
730 Scepter and power, thy giving, I assume,
And gladlier shall resign, when in the end
Thou shalt be all in all, and I in thee
Forever, and in me all whom thou lov'st:
But whom thou hat'st, I hate, and can put on
735 Thy terrors, as I put thy mildness on,
Image of thee in all things; and shall soon,
Armed with thy might, rid Heav'n of these rebelled,
To their prepared ill mansion driven down
To chains of darkness, and th' undying worm,
740 That from thy just obedience could revolt,
Whom to obey is happiness entire.
Then shall thy saints unmixed, and from th' impure
Far separate, circling thy holy mount
Unfeignèd hallelujahs to thee sing,
745 Hymns of high praise, and I among them chief.'
So said, he o'er his scepter bowing, rose
From the right hand of Glory where he sat,
And the third sacred morn began to shine
Dawning through Heav'n: forth rushed with whirlwind sound
750 The chariot of Paternal Deity,
Flashing thick flames, wheel within wheel undrawn,
Itself instinct with° spirit, but convoyed   animated by
By four Cherubic shapes, four faces each6
Had wondrous, as with stars their bodies all
755 And wings were set with eyes, with eyes the wheels

5. The literal meaning of "Messiah."
6. The Son's living chariot, with its four-faced
Cherubim—the faces being man, lion, ox, and

eagle—is taken from Ezekiel 1 (especially 1.10)
and 10.

Of beryl, and careering fires between;[7]
Over their heads a crystal firmament,
Whereon a sapphire throne, inlaid with pure
Amber, and colors of the show'ry arch.°   *rainbow*
760   He in celestial panoply all armed
Of radiant Urim,[8] work divinely wrought,
Ascended, at his right hand Victory
Sat eagle-winged,[9] beside him hung his bow
And quiver with three-bolted thunder stored,
765   And from about him fierce effusion° rolled   *copious emission*
Of smoke and bickering° flame, and sparkles dire;   *flickering*
Attended with ten thousand thousand saints,
He onward came, far off his coming shone,
And twenty thousand[1] (I their number heard)
770   Chariots of God, half on each hand were seen:
He on the wings of Cherub rode sublime°   *lifted up*
On the crystálline sky, in sapphire throned,
Illustrious° far and wide, but by his own   *shining*
First seen: them unexpected joy surprised,
775   When the great ensign of Messiah blazed
Aloft by angels borne, his sign in Heav'n:
Under whose conduct Michael soon reduced°   *led back*
His army, circumfused° on either wing,   *spread around*
Under their Head embodied all in one.
780   Before him Power Divine his way prepared;
At his command the uprooted hills retired
Each to his place, they heard his voice and went
Obsequious, Heav'n his wonted face renewed,
And with fresh flow'rets hill and valley smiled.
785   This saw his hapless foes but stood obdured,°   *hardened*
And to rebellious fight rallied their powers
Insensate, hope conceiving from despair.
In heav'nly Spirits could such perverseness dwell?
But to convince the proud what signs avail,
790   Or wonders move th' obdúrate to relent?
They hardened more by what might most reclaim,
Grieving° to see his glory, at the sight   *aggrieved*
Took envy, and aspiring to his height,
Stood re-embattled[2] fierce, by force or fraud
795   Weening° to prosper, and at length prevail   *thinking*
Against God and Messiah, or to fall
In universal ruin last, and now
To final battle drew; disdaining flight,
Or faint retreat; when the great Son of God
800   To all his host on either hand thus spake:
    " 'Stand still in bright array ye saints, here stand
Ye angels armed, this day from battle rest;[3]

---

7. Cf. Ezekiel 10.12: "And their whole body and their hands, and their wings, and the wheels, were full of eyes round about, even the wheels that they four had."
8. Gems worn by Aaron in his "breastplate of judgement" (Exodus 28.30).
9. Jove's bird was the eagle; his weapon was the thunderbolt.
1. Cf. Psalm 68.17: "The chariots of God are twenty thousand, even thousands of angels: the Lord is among them."
2. Drawn up again in battle formation.
3. Echoes Moses' words when God destroyed the Egyptians in the Red Sea (Exodus 14.13): "Fear ye

Faithful hath been your warfare, and of God
Accepted, fearless in his righteous cause,
805 And as ye have received, so have ye done
Invincibly; but of this cursèd crew
The punishment to other hand belongs,
Vengeance is his,[4] or whose he sole appoints;
Number to this day's work is not ordained
810 Nor multitude, stand only and behold
God's indignation on these godless poured
By me, not you but me they have despised,
Yet envied; against me is all their rage,
Because the Father, t' whom in Heav'n supreme
815 Kingdom and power and glory appertains,
Hath honored me according to his will.
Therefore to me their doom he hath assigned;
That they may have their wish, to try with me
In battle which the stronger proves, they all,
820 Or I alone against them, since by strength
They measure all, of other excellence
Not emulous, nor care who them excels;
Nor other strife with them do I vouchsafe."°   grant
    "So spake the Son, and into terror changed
825 His count'nance too severe to be beheld
And full of wrath bent on his enemies.
At once the Four[5] spread out their starry wings
With dreadful shade contiguous, and the orbs
Of his fierce chariot rolled, as with the sound
830 Of torrent floods, or of a numerous host.
He on his impious foes right onward drove,
Gloomy as night; under his burning wheels
The steadfast empyrean shook throughout,
All but the throne itself of God. Full soon
835 Among them he arrived; in his right hand
Grasping ten thousand thunders, which he sent
Before him, such as in their souls infixed
Plagues; they astonished° all resistance lost,   struck with fear
All courage; down their idle weapons dropped;
840 O'er shields and helms, and helmèd heads he rode
Of Thrones and mighty Seraphim prostráte,
That wished the mountains now might be again
Thrown on them as a shelter from his ire.
Nor less on either side tempestuous fell
845 His arrows, from the fourfold-visaged Four,
Distinct° with eyes, and from the living wheels,   adorned
Distinct alike with multitude of eyes;
One spirit in them ruled, and every eye
Glared lightning, and shot forth pernicious° fire   deadly
850 Among th' accursed, that withered all their strength,
And of their wonted vigor left them drained,

---

not, stand still, and see the salvation of the Lord
which he will show to you this day."
4. Cf. Romans 12.19: "Vengeance is mine; I will

repay, saith the Lord."
5. The four "Cherubic shapes" of line 753.

Exhausted, spiritless, afflicted, fall'n.
Yet half his strength he put not forth, but checked
His thunder in mid-volley, for he meant
855 Not to destroy, but root them out of Heav'n:
The overthrown he raised, and as a herd
Of goats or timorous flock together thronged
Drove them before him thunderstruck, pursued
With terrors and with furies to the bounds
860 And crystal wall of Heav'n, which op'ning wide,
Rolled inward, and a spacious gap disclosed
Into the wasteful° deep; the monstrous sight   desolate
Strook them with horror backward, but far worse
Urged them behind; headlong themselves they threw
865 Down from the verge of Heav'n, eternal wrath
Burnt after them to the bottomless pit.
     "Hell heard th' unsufferable noise, Hell saw
Heav'n ruining° from Heav'n, and would have fled   falling headlong
Affrighted; but strict fate had cast too deep
870 Her dark foundations, and too fast had bound.
Nine days they fell; confounded Chaos roared,
And felt tenfold confusion in their fall
Through his wild anarchy, so huge a rout°   defeated army
Encumbered° him with ruin: Hell at last   burdened
875 Yawning received them whole, and on them closed,
Hell their fit habitation fraught with fire
Unquenchable, the house of woe and pain.
Disburdened Heav'n rejoiced, and soon repaired
Her mural° breach, returning whence it rolled.   in the wall
880 Sole victor from th' expulsion of his foes
Messiah his triumphal chariot turned:
To meet him all his saints, who silent stood
Eye-witnesses of his almighty acts,
With jubilee° advanced; and as they went,   joyful shouts
885 Shaded with branching palm, each order bright
Sung triumph, and him sung victorious King,
Son, Heir, and Lord, to him dominion giv'n,
Worthiest to reign: he celebrated rode
Triumphant through mid-Heav'n, into the courts
890 And temple of his mighty Father throned
On high: who into glory him received,
Where now he sits at the right hand of bliss.
     "Thus measuring things in Heav'n by things on earth
At thy request, and that thou may'st beware
895 By what is past, to thee I have revealed
What might have else to human race been hid;
The discord which befell, and war in Heav'n
Among th' angelic powers,° and the deep fall   armies
Of those too high aspiring, who rebelled
900 With Satan, he who envies now thy state,
Who now is plotting how he may seduce
Thee also from obedience, that with him
Bereaved of happiness thou may'st partake

His punishment, eternal misery;
905   Which would be all his solace and revenge,
As a despite done against the Most High,
Thee once to gain companion of his woe.
But listen not to his temptations, warn
Thy weaker;[6] let it profit thee to have heard
910   By terrible example the reward
Of disobedience; firm they might have stood,
Yet fell; remember, and fear to transgress."

Book 7

Descend from Heav'n Urania,[1] by that name
If rightly thou art called, whose voice divine
Following, above th' Olympian hill I soar,
Above the flight of Pegasean wing.[2]
5   The meaning, not the name I call: for thou
Nor of the muses nine, nor on the top
Of old Olympus dwell'st, but heav'nly born,
Before the hills appeared, or fountain flowed,
Thou with eternal Wisdom[3] didst converse,°   associate
10   Wisdom thy sister, and with her didst play
In presence of th' Almighty Father, pleased
With thy celestial song. Up led by thee
Into the Heav'n of Heav'ns I have presumed,
An earthly guest, and drawn empyreal air,
15   Thy temp'ring;° with like safety guided down   made suitable by thee
Return me to my native element:
Lest from this flying steed unreined (as once
Bellerophon,[4] though from a lower clime)°   region
Dismounted, on th' Aleian field I fall
20   Erroneous° there to wander and forlorn.   straying
Half yet remains unsung, but narrower bound
Within the visible diurnal sphere;[5]
Standing on earth, not rapt° above the pole,   transported, enraptured
More safe I sing with mortal voice, unchanged
25   To hoarse or mute, though fall'n on evil days,
On evil days though fall'n on evil tongues;
In darkness, and with dangers compassed round,[6]

---

6. Eve, who is, however, present for this story.
1. Urania, the Greek Muse of Astronomy, had been made into the Muse of Christian Poetry by DuBartas and other religious poets. Milton, however, constructs another definition for her (line 5ff.). Milton begins Book 7 with a third Proem (lines 1–39).
2. Pegasus, the flying horse of inspired poetry, suggests (in connection with Bellerophon, line 18) Milton's sense of perilous audacity in writing this poem.
3. In Proverbs 8.24–31 Wisdom tells of her activities before the Creation: "Then I was by him [God], as one brought up with him; and I was daily his delight, rejoicing always before him." Milton describes "eternal Wisdom" as a "daughter" of God (personification of his wisdom), and devises a myth

in which the Muse of Divine Poetry ("celestial song," line 12) is Wisdom's "sister"—also, thereby, originating from God.
4. Bellerophon incurred the gods' anger when he tried to fly to heaven upon Pegasus; Zeus sent an insect to sting the horse, and Bellerophon fell down to the "Aleian field" (plain of error), where he wandered alone and blind until his death.
5. The universe, which appears to rotate daily.
6. After the Restoration of Charles II (May 1660) and until the passage of the Act of Oblivion (August 1660), Milton was in danger of death and dismemberment (like Orpheus, lines 34–35); several of his republican colleagues were hanged, drawn, and quartered for their part in the revolution and regicide.

And solitude; yet not alone, while thou
Visit'st my slumbers nightly, or when morn
30 Purples the east: still govern thou my song,
Urania, and fit audience find, though few.
But drive far off the barbarous dissonance
Of Bacchus and his revelers,[7] the race
Of that wild rout that tore the Thracian bard
35 In Rhodope, where woods and rocks had ears
To rapture, till the savage clamor drowned
Both harp and voice; nor could the Muse[8] defend
Her son. So fail not thou, who thee implores:
For thou art heav'nly, she an empty dream.
40　　Say goddess, what ensued when Raphael,
The affable Archangel, had forewarned
Adam by dire example to beware
Apostasy, by what befell in Heaven
To those apostates, lest the like befall
45 In Paradise to Adam or his race,
Charged not to touch the interdicted tree,
If they transgress, and slight that sole command,
So easily obeyed amid the choice
Of all tastes else to please their appetite,
50 Though wand'ring. He with his consorted° Eve　　*wedded*
The story heard attentive, and was filled
With admiration,° and deep muse to hear　　*amazement*
Of things so high and strange, things to their thought
So unimaginable as hate in Heav'n,
55 And war so near the peace of God in bliss
With such confusion: but the evil soon
Driv'n back redounded° as a flood on those　　*flowed back*
From whom it sprung, impossible to mix
With blessedness. Whence Adam soon repealed°　　*abandoned*
60 The doubts that in his heart arose: and now
Led on, yet sinless, with desire to know
What nearer might concern him, how this world
Of Heav'n and earth conspicuous° first began,　　*visible*
When, and whereof created, for what cause,
65 What within Eden or without was done
Before his memory, as one whose drouth°　　*thirst*
Yet scarce allayed still eyes the current° stream,　　*flowing*
Whose liquid murmur heard new thirst excites,
Proceeded thus to ask his heav'nly guest:
70　　"Great things, and full of wonder in our ears,
Far differing from this world, thou hast revealed
Divine interpreter, by favor sent
Down from the empyrean to forewarn
Us timely of what might else have been our loss,

---

7. The music of the "Thracian Bard" Orpheus, type of the poet, charmed even "woods and rocks," but his song was drowned out by the Bacchantes, a "wild rout" of screaming women who murdered and dismembered him and threw his body parts into the Hebrus River, which rises in the "Rhod-ope" mountains. Milton fears that a similar "barbarous dissonance" unleashed by the Restoration will drown out his voice and threaten his life.
8. Orpheus's mother is Calliope, Muse of Epic Poetry.

75   Unknown, which human knowledge could not reach:
     For which to the Infinitely Good we owe
     Immortal thanks, and his admonishment
     Receive with solemn purpose to observe
     Immutably his sovran will, the end°   *purpose*
80   Of what we are. But since thou hast vouchsafed
     Gently for our instruction to impart
     Things above earthly thought, which yet concerned
     Our knowing, as to Highest Wisdom seemed,
     Deign to descend now lower, and relate
85   What may no less perhaps avail us known,
     How first began this Heav'n which we behold
     Distant so high, with moving fires adorned
     Innumerable, and this which yields or fills
     All space, the ambient° air wide interfused   *yielding*
90   Embracing round this florid° earth, what cause   *flowery*
     Moved the Creator in his holy rest
     Through all eternity so late to build
     In Chaos,⁹ and the work begun, how soon
     Absolved,° if unforbid thou may'st unfold   *finished*
95   What we, not to explore the secrets ask
     Of his eternal empire, but the more
     To magnify° his works, the more we know.   *glorify*
     And the great light of day yet wants to run
     Much of his race though steep, suspense° in Heav'n   *attentive, suspended*
100 Held by thy voice, thy potent voice he hears,
     And longer will delay to hear thee tell
     His generation,° and the rising birth   *creation*
     Of nature from the unapparent deep:¹
     Or if the star of evening and the moon
105 Haste to thy audience, night with her will bring
     Silence, and sleep list'ning to thee will watch,°   *stay awake*
     Or we can bid his absence, till thy song
     End, and dismiss thee ere the morning shine."
         Thus Adam his illustrious guest besought:
110   And thus the godlike angel answered mild:
     "This also thy request with caution asked
     Obtain: though to recount almighty works
     What words or tongue of Seraph can suffice,
     Or heart of man suffice to comprehend?
115 Yet what thou canst attain, which best may serve
     To glorify the Maker, and infer°   *make, render*
     Thee also happier, shall not be withheld
     Thy hearing, such commission from above
     I have received, to answer thy desire
120 Of knowledge within bounds; beyond abstain
     To ask, nor let thine own inventions° hope   *speculations*
     Things not revealed, which th' invisible King,
     Only omniscient, hath suppressed in night,

---

9. Adam's question about God's actions before the creation was often cited as an example of presumptuous and dangerous speculation, especially when, as here, it implies mutability in God. But in Milton's Eden, error that is not deliberate is not sinful.

1. Invisible, because dark and without form.

To none communicable in earth or heaven:
125 Enough is left besides to search and know.
But knowledge is as food, and needs no less
Her temperance over appetite, to know
In measure what the mind may well contain,
Oppresses else with surfeit, and soon turns
130 Wisdom to folly, as nourishment to wind.
     "Know then, that after Lucifer from Heav'n
(So call him, brighter once amidst the host
Of angels, than that star the stars among)[2]
Fell with his flaming legions through the deep
135 Into his place, and the great Son returned
Victorious with his saints, th' Omnipotent
Eternal Father from his throne beheld
Their multitude, and to his Son thus spake:
     " 'At least our envious foe hath failed, who thought
140 All like himself rebellious, by whose aid
This inaccessible high strength, the seat
Of Deity supreme, us dispossessed,[3]
He trusted to have seized, and into fraud°   *deception, error*
Drew many, whom their place knows here no more;
145 Yet far the greater part have kept, I see,
Their station, Heav'n yet populous retains
Number sufficient to possess her realms
Though wide, and this high temple to frequent
With ministeries due and solemn rites:
150 But lest his heart exalt him in the harm
Already done, to have dispeopled Heav'n,
My damage fondly° deemed, I can repair   *foolishly*
That detriment, if such it be to lose
Self-lost, and in a moment will create
155 Another world, out of one man a race
Of men innumerable, there to dwell,
Not here, till by degrees of merit raised
They open to themselves at length the way
Up hither, under long obedience tried,
160 And earth be changed to Heav'n and Heav'n to earth,
One kingdom, joy and union without end.
Meanwhile inhabit lax,° ye Powers of Heav'n;   *spread out*
And thou my Word, begotten Son, by thee
This I perform, speak thou, and be it done:[4]
165 My overshadowing Spirit and might with thee
I send along, ride forth, and bid the deep
Within appointed bounds be heav'n and earth,
Boundless the deep, because I am who fill
Infinitude, nor vacuous the space.
170 Though I uncircumscribed myself retire,
And put not forth my goodness, which is free
To act or not,[5] necessity and chance

2. I.e., Lucifer (Satan) was once brighter among the angels than the star bearing his name is among the stars.
3. I.e., once he had dispossessed us.

4. God identifies himself as Creator, the Son as his agent to speak his creating Word.
5. Milton's God creates out of Chaos, not out of nothing; the matter of Chaos emanated from God,

Approach not me, and what I will is fate.'
    "So spake th' Almighty and to what he spake
175 His Word, the Filial Godhead, gave effect.
    Immediate are the acts of God, more swift
    Than time or motion, but to human ears
    Cannot without process of speech be told,[6]
    So told as earthly notion° can receive.   *human understanding*
180 Great triumph and rejoicing was in Heav'n
    When such was heard declared the Almighty's will;
    'Glory' they sung to the Most High, 'good will
    To future men, and in their dwellings peace:
    Glory to him whose just avenging ire
185 Had driven out th' ungodly from his sight
    And th' habitations of the just; to him
    Glory and praise, whose wisdom had ordained
    Good out of evil to create, instead
    Of Spirits malign a better race to bring
190 Into their vacant room, and thence diffuse
    His good to worlds and ages infinite.'
    So sang the hierarchies: meanwhile the Son
    On his great expedition now appeared,
    Girt with omnipotence, with radiance crowned
195 Of majesty divine, sapience and love
    Immense, and all his Father in him shone.
    About his chariot numberless were poured
    Cherub and Seraph, Potentates and Thrones,
    And Virtues, winged Spirits, and chariots winged,
200 From the armory of God, where stand of old
    Myriads between two brazen mountains lodged
    Against° a solemn day, harnessed at hand,   *in preparation for*
    Celestial equipage; and now came forth
    Spontaneous, for within them spirit lived,
205 Attendant on their Lord: Heav'n opened wide
    Her ever-during° gates, harmonious sound   *lasting*
    On golden hinges moving, to let forth
    The King of Glory[7] in his powerful Word
    And Spirit coming to create new worlds.
210 On heav'nly ground they stood, and from the shore
    They viewed the vast immeasurable abyss
    Outrageous° as a sea, dark, wasteful, wild,   *enormous, violent*
    Up from the bottom turned by furious winds
    And surging waves, as mountains to assault
215 Heav'n's height, and with the center mix the pole.
        " 'Silence, ye troubled waves, and thou deep, peace,'
    Said then th' Omnific° Word, 'your discord end:'   *all-creating*
        "Nor stayed, but on the wings of Cherubim
    Uplifted, in paternal glory rode

---

and Chaos is therefore "infinite" because God fills
it even while he withholds his "goodness" (creating
power) from it. Neither necessity nor chance affect
in any way God's freely willed creative act.
6. Raphael explains the principle of accommodation, whereby God's acts are said to be translated
into terms humans can understand: here, a six-day
creation. This principle allows for an escape from
biblical literalism.
7. Cf. Psalm 24.9: "Lift up your heads, O ye gates;
even lift them up, ye everlasting doors; and the
King of glory shall come in."

220   Far into Chaos, and the world unborn;
     For Chaos heard his voice: him all his train
     Followed in bright procession to behold
     Creation, and the wonders of his might.
     Then stayed the fervid° wheels, and in his hand   *burning*
225   He took the golden compasses, prepared
     In God's eternal store, to circumscribe
     This universe, and all created things:
     One foot he centered, and the other turned
     Round through the vast profundity obscure,
230   And said, 'Thus far extend, thus far thy bounds,
     This be thy just° circumference O world.'   *exact*
     Thus God the heav'n created, thus the earth,
     Matter unformed and void: darkness profound
     Covered th' abyss: but on the wat'ry calm
235   His brooding wings the Spirit of God outspread,
     And vital virtue° infused, and vital warmth   *power*
     Throughout the fluid mass, but downward purged
     The black tartareous cold infernal dregs[8]
     Adverse to life: then founded, then conglobed
240   Like things to like, the rest to several place
     Disparted, and between spun out the air,
     And earth self-balanced on her center hung.
       " 'Let there be light,' said God,[9] and forthwith light
     Ethereal, first of things, quintessence[1] pure
245   Sprung from the deep, and from her native east
     To journey through the airy gloom began,
     Sphered in a radiant cloud, for yet the sun
     Was not; she in a cloudy tabernacle
     Sojourned the while. God saw the light was good;
250   And light from darkness by the hemisphere
     Divided: light the day, and darkness night
     He named. Thus was the first day ev'n and morn:[2]
     Nor passed uncelebrated, nor unsung
     By the celestial choirs, when orient light
255   Exhaling° first from darkness they beheld;   *rising as vapor*
     Birthday of heav'n° and earth; with joy and shout   *the sky*
     The hollow universal orb they filled,
     And touched their golden harps, and hymning praised
     God and his works, Creator him they sung,
260   Both when first evening was, and when first morn.
       "Again, God said, 'Let there be firmament
     Amid the waters, and let it divide
     The waters from the waters': and God made
     The firmament, expanse of liquid,° pure,   *clear, bright*
265   Transparent, elemental air diffused
     In circuit to the uttermost convex°   *vault*

---

8. Crusty, gritty stuff left over from the elements infused with life that make up the universe; it is associated with Hell ("infernal," "tartarous") and presumably used in its composition.
9. God's creating words, here and later, are quoted from Genesis 1–2, but Milton freely elaborates the

creatures' responses to those words.
1. Ether was thought to be a fifth element or "quintessence," the substance of the celestial bodies above the moon.
2. One twenty-four-hour period measured in the Hebrew manner from sundown to sundown.

Of this great round:° partition firm and sure,   *universe*
The waters underneath from those above
Dividing: for as earth, so he the world
270 Built on circumfluous waters calm, in wide
Crystálline ocean, and the loud misrule
Of Chaos far removed, lest fierce extremes
Contiguous might distemper³ the whole frame:
And heav'n° he named the firmament: so ev'n   *the sky*
275 And morning chorus sung the second day.
    "The earth was formed, but in the womb as yet
Of waters, embryon⁴ immature involved°   *enfolded*
Appeared not: over all the face of earth
Main° ocean flowed, not idle, but with warm   *of great expanse*
280 Prolific humor° soft'ning all her globe,   *generative moisture*
Fermented the great mother to conceive,
Satiate with genial° moisture, when God said,   *generative*
'Be gathered now ye waters under heav'n
Into one place, and let dry land appear.'
285 Immediately the mountains huge appear
Emergent, and their broad bare backs upheave
Into the clouds, their tops ascend the sky:
So high as heaved the tumid° hills, so low   *swollen*
Down sunk a hollow bottom broad and deep,
290 Capacious bed of waters: thither they
Hasted with glad precipitance,° uprolled   *headlong fall*
As drops on dust conglobing from the dry;
Part rise in crystal wall or ridge direct°   *surge forward*
For haste; such flight the great command impressed
295 On the swift floods: as armies at the call
Of trumpet (for of armies thou hast heard)
Troop to their standard, so the wat'ry throng,
Wave rolling after wave, where° way they found,
If steep, with torrent rapture,° if through plain,   *force*
300 Soft-ebbing; nor withstood them rock or hill,
But they, or under ground, or circuit wide
With serpent error° wand'ring, found their way,   *winding course*
And on the washy ooze deep channels wore;
Easy, ere God had bid the ground be dry,
305 All but within those banks, where rivers now
Stream, and perpetual draw their humid train.
The dry land, earth, and the great receptacle
Of congregated waters he called seas:
And saw that it was good, and said, 'Let th' earth
310 Put forth the verdant grass, herb yielding seed,
And fruit-tree yielding fruit after her kind;
Whose seed is in herself upon the earth.'
He scarce had said, when the bare earth, till then
Desert and bare, unsightly, unadorned,

---

3. Disturb the order and mixture of the elements and the created "frame" of the universe.
4. The earth is at first the "embryo" enveloped in a "womb of waters" and is then herself the "great mother" (line 281), made ready ("fermented") to conceive and bear every other being.

315 Brought forth the tender grass, whose verdure clad
Her universal face with pleasant green,
Then herbs of every leaf, that sudden flow'red
Op'ning their various colors, and made gay
Her bosom smelling sweet: and these scarce blown,°   *blossomed*
320 Forth flourished thick the clust'ring vine, forth crept
The swelling gourd, up stood the corny° reed   *hard as horn*
Embattled in her field: add the humble° shrub,   *low-growing*
And bush with frizzled hair implicit:° last   *tangled*
Rose as in dance the stately trees, and spread
325 Their branches hung with copious fruit; or gemmed°   *put forth buds*
Their blossoms: with high woods the hills were crowned,
With tufts the valleys and each fountain side,
With borders long the rivers. That earth now
Seemed like to Heav'n, a seat where gods might dwell,
330 Or wander with delight, and love to haunt
Her sacred shades: though God had yet not rained
Upon the earth, and man to till the ground
None was, but from the earth a dewy mist
Went up and watered all the ground, and each
335 Plant of the field, which ere it was in the earth
God made, and every herb, before it grew
On the green stem; God saw that it was good:
So ev'n and morn recorded the third day.
    "Again th' Almighty spake: 'Let there be lights
340 High in th' expanse of heaven° to divide   *the sky*
The day from night; and let them be for signs,
For seasons, and for days, and circling years,
And let them be for lights as I ordain
Their office in the firmament of heav'n
345 To give light on the earth'; and it was so.
And God made two great lights, great for their use
To man, the greater to have rule by day,
The less by night altern:° and made the stars,   *in turns*
And set them in the firmament of heav'n
350 To illuminate the earth, and rule the day
In their vicissitude,° and rule the night,   *regular alternation*
And light from darkness to divide. God saw,
Surveying his great work, that it was good:
For of celestial bodies first the sun
355 A mighty sphere he framed, unlightsome first,
Though of ethereal mold:° then formed the moon   *fashioned from ether*
Globose, and every magnitude of stars,
And sowed with stars the heav'n thick as a field:
Of light by far the greater part he took,
360 Transplanted from her cloudy shrine,[5] and placed
In the sun's orb, made porous to receive
And drink the liquid light, firm to retain
Her gathered beams, great palace now of light.

5. The "cloudy tabernacle" of line 248.

Hither as to their fountain other stars
365   Repairing, in their golden urns draw light,
And hence the morning planet gilds her horns;[6]
By tincture° or reflection they augment   absorption
Their small peculiar,° though from human sight   own small light
So far remote, with dimunition seen.
370   First in his east the glorious lamp was seen,
Regent of day, and all th' horizon round
Invested with bright rays, jocund° to run   merry
His longitude° through heav'n's high road: the gray   distance
Dawn, and the Pleiades before him danced
375   Shedding sweet influence: less bright the moon,
But opposite in leveled west was set
His mirror, with full face borrowing her light
From him, for other light she needed none
In that aspect,° and still that distance keeps   when full
380   Till night, then in the east her turn she shines,
Revolved on heav'n's great axle, and her reign
With thousand lesser lights dividual° holds,   divided
With thousand thousand stars, that then appeared
Spangling the hemisphere: then first adorned
385   With their bright luminaries that set and rose,
Glad° evening and glad morn crowned the fourth day.   bright, gay
      And God said, 'Let the waters generate
Reptile° with spawn abundant, living soul: creeping animals
And let fowl fly above the earth, with wings
390   Displayed° on the op'n firmament of heav'n.'   spread out
And God created the great whales, and each
Soul living, each that crept, which plenteously
The waters generated by their kinds,
And every bird of wing after his kind;
395   And saw that it was good, and blessed them, saying,
'Be fruitful, multiply, and in the seas
And lakes and running streams the waters fill;
And let the fowl be multiplied on the earth.'
Forthwith the sounds and seas, each creek and bay
400   With fry° innumerable swarm, and shoals   young fish
Of fish that with their fins and shining scales
Glide under the green wave, in sculls that oft
Bank the mid-sea:[7] part single or with mate
Graze the seaweed their pasture, and through groves
405   Of coral stray, or sporting with quick glance
Show to the sun their waved° coats dropped° with gold,   striped/flecked
Or in their pearly shells at ease, attend°   watch for
Moist nutriment, or under rocks their food
In jointed armor watch: on smooth the seal,
410   And bended[8] dolphins play: part huge of bulk

6. Venus, which Galileo's telescope found to be
crescent-shaped in her first quarter.
7. The fishes' darting motions resemble boats
oared now on one side, now on the other ("sculls");
as they turn they seem to form banks within the
sea.
8. Curved in leaping. "Smooth": a stretch of calm
water.

Wallowing unwieldy, enormous in their gait
Tempest° the ocean: there leviathan⁹   *stir up*
Hugest of living creatures, on the deep
Stretched like a promontory sleeps or swims,
415 And seems a moving land, and at his gills
Draws in, and at his trunk spouts out a sea.
Meanwhile the tepid caves, and fens and shores
Their brood as numerous hatch, from th' egg that soon
Bursting with kindly° rupture forth disclosed   *natural*
420 Their callow° young, but feathered soon and fledge   *without feathers*
They summed their pens,¹ and soaring th' air sublime
With clang° despised the ground, under a cloud   *harsh cry*
In prospect;² there the eagle and the stork
On cliffs and cedar tops their eyries build:
425 Part loosely° wing the region,° part more wise   *separately/sky*
In common, ranged in figure wedge³ their way,
Intelligent° of seasons, and set forth   *understanding*
Their aery caravan high over seas
Flying, and over lands with mutual wing
430 Easing their flight;⁴ so steers the prudent crane
Her annual voyage, borne on winds; the air
Floats,° as they pass, fanned with unnumbered plumes: *undulates*
From branch to branch the smaller birds with song
Solaced the woods, and spread their painted wings
435 Till ev'n, nor then the solemn nightingale
Ceased warbling, but all night tuned her soft lays:
Others on silver lakes and rivers bathed
Their downy breast; the swan, with archèd neck
Between her white wings mantling proudly, rows
440 Her state with oary feet:⁵ yet oft they quit
The dank,° and rising on stiff pennons, tow'r°   *pool/soar into*
The mid-aerial sky: others on ground
Walked firm; the crested cock whose clarion sounds
The silent hours, and th' other° whose gay train   *the peacock*
445 Adorns him, colored with the florid hue
Of rainbows and starry eyes. The waters thus
With fish replenished,° and the air with fowl,   *fully supplied*
Evening and morn solemnized the fifth day.
        "The sixth, and of creation last arose
450 With evening harps and matin,° when God said,   *morning*
'Let th' earth bring forth soul living in her kind,
Cattle and creeping things, and beast of the earth,
Each in their kind.' The earth obeyed, and straight
Op'ning her fertile womb teemed° at a birth   *brought forth*
455 Innumerous living creatures, perfect forms,
Limbed and full grown: out of the ground up rose

---

9. The great whale (see 1.200–208).
1. Brought their feathers to full growth.
2. The ground seems covered by a cloud of birds.
3. Fly in a wedge formation.
4. Birds were thought to support each other with

their wings when they fly in formation.
5. The swan's outstretched ("mantling," line 439) wings form a mantle, and it seems like a monarch on a royal barge rowed by its own "oary" feet.

As from his lair the wild beast where he wons°   *dwells*
In forest wild, in thicket, brake, or den;
Among the trees in pairs they rose, they walked:
460   The cattle in the fields and meadows green:
Those rare and solitary, these⁶ in flocks
Pasturing at once, and in broad herds unsprung.
The grassy clods° now calved, now half appeared   *mounds of earth*
The tawny lion, pawing to get free
465   His hinder parts, then springs as broke from bonds,
And rampant shakes his brinded° mane; the ounce,°   *streaked/lynx*
The libbard,° and the tiger, as the mole   *leopard*
Rising, the crumbled earth above them threw
In hillocks; the swift stag from under ground
470   Bore up his branching head: scarce from his mold
Behemoth⁷ biggest born of earth upheaved
His vastness: fleeced the flocks and bleating rose,
As plants: ambiguous between sea and land
The river-horse⁸ and scaly crocodile.
475   At once came forth whatever creeps the ground,
Insect or worm;⁹ those waved their limber fans
For wings, and smallest lineaments exact
In all the liveries decked of summer's pride
With spots of gold and purple, azure and green:
480   These as a line their long dimension drew,
Streaking the ground with sinuous trace; not all
Minims° of nature; some of serpent kind   *smallest animals*
Wondrous in length and corpulence involved°   *coiled*
Their snaky folds, and added wings. First crept
485   The parsimonious emmet,° provident   *thrifty ant*
Of future, in small room large heart° enclosed,   *great wisdom*
Pattern of just equality perhaps
Hereafter, joined in her popular tribes
Of commonalty:¹ swarming next appeared
490   The female bee that feeds her husband drone
Deliciously, and builds her waxen cells
With honey stored: the rest are numberless,
And thou their natures know'st, and gav'st them names,²
Needless to thee repeated; nor unknown
495   The serpent subtlest beast of all the field,
Of huge extent sometimes, with brazen eyes
And hairy mane³ terrific,° though to thee.   *terrifying*
Not noxious, but obedient at thy call.
Now heav'n in all her glory shone, and rolled

---

6. "These" are the domestic cattle who come forth
in "flocks" and "herds" in pastures; "those" are the
wild beasts who come forth "in pairs" (line 459),
and spread out ("rare") at wide intervals.
7. A huge biblical beast (Job 40.15), often identified with the elephant.
8. Translates the Greek name "hippopotamus."
9. Any creeping creature, including serpents.
1. The ant will become the symbol of a frugal and
self-governing republic ("pattern of just equality")

with the "popular" (populous, plebian) tribes of
common people ("commonalty") joined in rule
(lines 486–89); Milton made it such a symbol in
his prose tract *The Ready and Easy Way*. Bees here
(lines 489–93) suggest delightful ease but are not
yet (as in 1.768–75) a symbol of monarchy and
associated with Hell.
2. See 8.342–54, and Genesis 2.19–20.
3. Sea serpents were so described in *Aeneid*
2.203–7.

500 Her motions, as the great First Mover's hand
First wheeled their course; earth in her rich attire
Consummate° lovely smiled; air, water, earth,   *complete, perfect*
By fowl, fish, beast, was flown, was swum, was walked
Frequent;° and of the sixth day yet remained;   *in throngs*
505 There wanted yet the master work, the end°   *purpose*
Of all yet done: a creature who not prone
And brute as other creatures, but endued
With sanctity of reason, might erect
His stature,[4] and upright with front° serene   *brow, face*
510 Govern the rest, self-knowing, and from thence
Magnanimous to correspond[5] with Heav'n,
But grateful to acknowledge whence his good
Descends, thither with heart and voice and eyes
Directed in devotion, to adore
515 And worship God supreme, who made him chief
Of all his works: therefore th' Omnipotent
Eternal Father (for where is not he
Present) thus to his Son audibly spake:
    " 'Let us make now man in our image, man
520 In our similitude, and let them rule
Over the fish and fowl of sea and air,
Beast of the field, and over all the earth,
And every creeping thing that creeps the ground.'
This said, he formed thee, Adam, thee O man
525 Dust of the ground, and in thy nostrils breathed
The breath of life; in his own image he
Created thee, in the image of God
Express,° and thou becam'st a living soul.   *exact*
Male he created thee, but thy consort
530 Female for race; then blessed mankind, and said,
'Be fruitful, multiply, and fill the earth,
Subdue it, and throughout dominion hold
Over fish of the sea, and fowl of the air,
And every living thing that moves on the earth.'
535 Wherever thus created, for no place
Is yet distinct by name, thence,° as thou know'st   *from there*
He brought thee into this delicious° grove,   *delightful*
This garden, planted with the trees of God,
Delectable both to behold and taste;
540 And freely all their pleasant fruit for food
Gave thee, all sorts are here that all th' earth yields,
Variety without end; but of the tree
Which tasted works knowledge of good and evil,
Thou may'st not: in the day thou eat'st, thou di'st;
545 Death is the penalty imposed, beware,
And govern well thy appetite, lest Sin
Surprise thee, and her black attendant Death.

---

4. Both "stand erect" and "elevate his condition":   was created for Heaven.
his erect stance was understood to signify that he   5. Both "be in harmony" and "communicate."

Here finished he, and all that he had made
Viewed, and behold all was entirely good;
550　So ev'n and morn accomplished the sixth day:
Yet not till the Creator from his work
Desisting, though unwearied, up returned
Up to the Heav'n of Heav'ns his high abode,
Thence to behold his new-created world
555　Th' addition of his empire, how it showed
In prospect from his throne, how good, how fair,
Answering his great Idea.[6] Up he rode
Followed with acclamation and the sound
Symphonious of ten thousand harps that tuned°　　　　　　*performed*
560　Angelic harmonies: the earth, the air
Resounded (thou remember'st, for thou heard'st),
The heav'ns and all the constellations rung,
The planets in their stations list'ning stood,
While the bright pomp° ascended jubilant.　　　　　*triumphal procession*
565　　" 'Open, ye everlasting gates,' they sung,
'Open, ye Heav'ns, your living doors; let in
The great Creator from his work returned
Magnificent,[7] his six days' work, a world;
Open, and henceforth oft; for God will deign
570　To visit oft the dwellings of just men
Delighted, and with frequent intercourse
Thither will send his wingèd messengers
On errands of supernal grace.' So sung
The glorious train ascending: he through Heav'n,
575　That opened wide her blazing° portals, led　　　　　*radiant*
To God's eternal house direct the way,
A broad and ample road, whose dust is gold
And pavement stars, as stars to thee appear,
Seen in the Galaxy, that Milky Way
580　Which nightly as a circling zone° thou seest　　　　　*belt*
Powdered with stars. And now on earth the seventh
Evening arose in Eden, for the sun
Was set, and twilight from the east came on,
Forerunning night; when at the holy mount
585　Of Heav'n's high-seated top, th' imperial throne
Of Godhead, fixed forever firm and sure,
The Filial Power arrived, and sat him down
With his great Father, for he[8] also went
Invisible, yet stayed (such privilege
590　Hath Omnipresence) and the work ordained,°　　　　　*ordered, enacted*
Author and end of all things, and from work
Now resting, blessed and hallowed the sev'nth day,
As resting on that day from all his work,
But not in silence holy kept; the harp

6. Eternal archetype or pattern, as in Plato: concept in the mind of God.
7. Cf. Psalm 24.7: "Lift up your heads, O ye gates; and be ye lift up, ye everlasting doors; and the King of glory shall come in."
8. The Father.

595   Had work and rested not, the solemn pipe,
And dulcimer, all organs° of sweet stop,   *wind instruments*
All sounds on fret[9] by string or golden wire
Tempered° soft tunings, intermixed with voice   *brought into harmony*
Choral[c] or unison: of incense clouds   *in parts*
600   Fuming from golden censers hid the mount.
     "Creation and the six day's acts they sung:
'Great are thy works, Jehovah, infinite
Thy power; what thought can measure thee or tongue
Relate thee; greater now in thy return
605   Than from the giant[1] angels; thee that day
Thy thunders magnified; but to create
Is greater than created to destroy.
Who can impair thee, mighty king, or bound
Thy empire? Easily the proud attempt
610   Of Spirits apostate and their counsels vain
Thou hast repelled, while impiously they thought
Thee to diminish, and from thee withdraw
The number of thy worshipers. Who seeks
To lessen thee, against his purpose serves
615   To manifest the more thy might: his evil
Thou usest, and from thence creat'st more good.
Witness this new-made world, another heav'n
From Heaven gate not far, founded in view
On the clear hyaline,[2] the glassy sea;
620   Of amplitude almost immense,° with stars   *immeasurable*
Numerous, and every star perhaps a world
Of destined habitation; but thou know'st
Their seasons: among these the seat of men,
Earth with her nether ocean circumfused,
625   Their pleasant dwelling-place. Thrice happy men,
And sons of men, whom God hath thus advanced,
Created in his image, there to dwell
And worship him, and in reward to rule
Over his works, on earth, in sea, or air,
630   And multiply a race of worshipers
Holy and just: thrice happy if they know
Their happiness, and persevere upright.'
     "So sung they, and the empyrean rung,
With hallelujahs:[3] thus was Sabbath kept.
635   And thy request think now fulfilled, that asked
How first this world and face of things began,
And what before thy memory was done
From the beginning, that posterity
Informed by thee might know; if else thou seek'st
640   Aught, not surpassing human measure, say."

---

9. Bar on the fingerboard of a stringed instrument.
"Dulciner": the Hebrew bagpipe (Daniel 3.5).
1. The allusion implies that the myth of the
Giants' revolt against Jove is a classical type or version of the angels' rebellion.

2. From the Greek word for glass (Revelation 4.6),
the waters above the firmament as contrasted with
the "nether ocean" (line 624), the earth's seas.
3. Hebrew, "praise the Lord."

Book 8

The angel ended, and in Adam's ear
So charming° left his voice, that he a while   *spell-binding*
Thought him still speaking, still stood fixed to hear;
Then as new-waked thus gratefully replied:[1]
5   "What thanks sufficient, or what recompense
Equal have I to render thee, divine
Historian, who thus largely hast allayed
The thirst I had of knowledge, and vouchsafed
This friendly condescension to relate
10 Things else by me unsearchable, now heard
With wonder, but delight, and, as is due,
With glory attribúted to the high
Creator; something yet of doubt remains,
Which only thy solution° can resolve.   *explanation*
15 When I behold this goodly frame,° this world   *the universe*
Of heav'n and earth consisting, and compute
Their magnitudes, this earth a spot, a grain,
An atom, with the firmament compared
And all her numbered° stars, that seem to roll   *numerous*
20 Spaces incomprehensible (for such
Their distance argues and their swift return
Diurnal°) merely to officiate° light   *daily / supply*
Round this opacous° earth, this punctual° spot,   *dark / pointlike*
One day and night; in all their vast survey
25 Useless besides; reasoning I oft admire,°   *wonder*
How Nature wise and frugal could commit
Such disproportions, with superfluous hand
So many nobler bodies to create,
Greater so manifold,° to this one use,   *so much greater*
30 For aught appears,° and on their orbs impose   *as it seems*
Such restless revolution day by day
Repeated, while the sedentary° earth,   *motionless*
That better might with far less compass° move,   *circular course*
Served by more noble than herself, attains
35 Her end without least motion, and receives,
As tribute such a sumless° journey brought   *incalculable*
Of incorporeal speed, her warmth and light;
Speed, to describe whose swiftness number fails."
      So spake our sire, and by his count'nance seemed
40 Ent'ring on studious thoughts abstruse, which Eve
Perceiving where she sat retired in sight,
With lowliness majestic from her seat,
And grace that won who saw to wish her stay,
Rose, and went forth among her fruits and flow'rs,
45 To visit° how they prospered, bud and bloom,   *see*
Her nursery;[2] they at her coming sprung

---

1. When Milton divided Book 7 of the ten-book version of 1667 into the present Books 7 and 8, he replaced a line reading "To whom thus Adam gratefully replied" with these introductory lines.
2. Her garden, where she "nurses" her flowers and plants.

And touched by her fair tendance gladlier grew.
Yet went she not as not with such discourse
Delighted, or not capable her ear
50 Of what was high: such pleasure she reserved,
Adam relating, she sole auditress;
Her husband the relater she preferred
Before the angel, and of him to ask
Chose rather;[3] he, she knew, would intermix
55 Grateful digressions, and solve high dispute
With conjugal caresses, from his lip
Not words alone pleased her. O when meet now
Such pairs, in love and mutual honor joined?
With goddess-like demeanor forth she went;
60 Not unattended, for on her as queen
A pomp° of winning Graces[4] waited still,   *procession*
And from about her shot darts of desire
Into all eyes to wish her still in sight.
And Raphael now to Adam's doubt proposed
65 Benevolent and facile° thus replied.   *easy, affable*
     "To ask or search I blame thee not, for heav'n
Is as the book of God before thee set,
Wherein to read his wondrous works, and learn
His seasons, hours, or days, or months, or years:
70 This to attain, whether heav'n move or earth,
Imports not, if thou reckon right; the rest[5]
From man or angel the great Architect
Did wisely to conceal, and not divulge
His secrets to be scanned° by them who ought   *judged critically*
75 Rather admire;° or if they list to try   *marvel*
Conjecture, he his fabric° of the heav'ns   *design*
Hath left to their disputes, perhaps to move
His laughter at their quaint opinions wide°   *wide of the mark*
Hereafter, when they come to model heav'n
80 And calculate the stars, how they will wield
The mighty frame, how build, unbuild, contrive
To save appearances,[6] how gird the sphere
With centric and eccentric scribbled o'er,
Cycle and epicycle,[7] orb in orb:
85 Already by thy reasoning this I guess,
Who art to lead thy offspring, and supposest
That bodies bright and greater should not serve
The less not bright, nor heav'n such journeys run,
Earth sitting still, when she alone receives

---

3. The emphasis on choice suggests that Eve is not
bound in Eden by the Pauline directive (1 Corinthians 14–35) that women refrain from speaking
in church and instead learn at home from their
husbands, but she voluntarily and for her own
pleasure observes this hierarchical decorum.
4. The Graces attended on Venus.
5. Presumably, God's ways with other worlds and
other creatures inhabiting them (if any).
6. To find ways of explaining discrepancies

between their hypotheses and observed facts.
7. In the Ptolemaic system, observed irregularities
in the motion of heavenly bodies were first
explained by hypothesizing eccentric orbits, then
by adding epicycles, which were smaller orbits
whose centers ride on the circumference of the
main eccentric circles and carry the planets. The
Copernican system also had some recourse to epicycles.

90　The benefit: consider first, that great
　　Or bright infers° not excellence: the earth　　　　　　　　　*implies*
　　Though, in comparison of heav'n, so small,
　　Nor glistering, may of solid good contain
　　More plenty than the sun that barren shines,
95　Whose virtue on itself works no effect,
　　But in the fruitful earth; there first received
　　His beams, unactive° else, their vigor find.　　　　　　　　*ineffective*
　　Yet not to earth are those bright luminaries
　　Officious,° but to thee earth's habitant.　　　　　　　　*attentive, dutiful*
100　And for the heav'n's wide circuit, let it speak
　　The Maker's high magnificence, who built
　　So spacious, and his line stretched out so far;
　　That man may know he dwells not in his own;
　　An edifice too large for him to fill,
105　Lodged in a small partition, and the rest
　　Ordained for uses to his Lord best known.
　　The swiftness of those circles° áttribute,　　　　　　　　*orbits*
　　Though numberless,° to his omnipotence,　　　　　　　　*innumerable*
　　That to corporeal substances could add
110　Speed almost spiritual;° me thou think'st not slow,　　　　*that of angels*
　　Who since the morning hour set out from Heav'n
　　Where God resides, and ere mid-day arrived
　　In Eden, distance inexpressible
　　By numbers that have name. But this I urge,
115　Admitting motion in the heav'ns, to show
　　Invalid that which thee to doubt it moved;
　　Not that I so affirm, though so it seem
　　To thee who hast thy dwelling here on earth.[8]
　　God to remove his ways from human sense,
120　Placed heav'n from earth so far, that earthly sight,
　　If it presume, might err in things too high,
　　And no advantage gain. What if the sun
　　Be center to the world, and other stars
　　By his attractive virtue° and their own　　　　　　　　*magnetism*
125　Incited, dance about him various rounds?°　　　　　　　　*circles*
　　Their wand'ring course now high, now low, then hid,
　　Progressive, retrograde,° or standing still,　　　　　　　*backward*
　　In six thou seest,[9] and what if sev'nth to these
　　The planet earth, so steadfast though she seem,
130　Insensibly three difference motions move?[1]
　　Which else to several spheres thou must ascribe,
　　Moved contrary with thwart obliquities,[2]

8. Raphael declines to "reveal" astronomical truth to Adam, leaving that matter open to human scientific speculation. He suggests here that Adam's Ptolemaic assumptions result from his earthbound perspective, and he implies that angels see the universe in different terms. In the following lines (122–58) he sets forth advanced scientific notions Adam had not imagined: not only Copernican astronomy but multiple universes and other inhabited planets.
9. Mercury, Venus, Mars, Jupiter, Saturn, and the moon. In the Ptolemaic system the "seventh" is the sun, in the Copernican, earth.
1. Copernicus described the three motions as daily, annual, and "motion in declination" whereby the earth's axis swerved so as always to point in the same direction.
2. Oblique paths that cross each other.

Or save the sun his labor, and that swift
Nocturnal and diurnal rhomb[3] supposed,
135 Invisible else above all stars, the wheel
Of day and night; which needs not thy belief,
If earth industrious of herself fetch day
Traveling east, and with her part averse
From the sun's beam meet night, her other part
140 Still luminous by his ray. What if that light
Sent from her through the wide transpicuous° air,   *transparent*
To the terrestrial moon be as a star
Enlight'ning her by day, as she by night
This earth? Reciprocal, if land be there,
145 Fields and inhabitants: her spots thou seest
As clouds, and clouds may rain, and rain produce
Fruits in her softened soil, for some to eat
Allotted there; and other suns perhaps
With their attendant moons thou wilt descry
150 Communicating male° and female° light,   *original/reflected*
Which two great sexes animate° the world,   *endow with life*
Stored in each orb perhaps with some that live.
For such vast room in nature unpossessed
By living soul, desert and desolate,
155 Only to shine, yet scarce to cóntribute
Each orb a glimpse of light, conveyed so far
Down to this habitable,° which returns   *inhabited place*
Light back to them, is obvious to dispute.°   *open to dispute*
But whether thus these things, or whether not,
160 Whether the sun predominant in heav'n
Rise on the earth, or earth rise on the sun,
He from the east his flaming road begin,
Or she from west her silent course advance
With inoffensive° pace that spinning sleeps   *unobstructed, harmless*
165 On her soft axle, while she paces ev'n,
And bears thee soft with the smooth air along,
Solicit° not thy thoughts with matters hid,   *disturb*
Leave them to God above, him serve and fear;
Of other creatures, as him pleases best,
170 Wherever placed, let him dispose: joy thou
In what he gives to thee, this Paradise
And thy fair Eve; heav'n is for thee too high
To know what passes there; be lowly wise:
Think only what concerns thee and thy being;
175 Dream not of other worlds, what creatures there
Live, in what state, condition, or degree,
Contented that thus far hath been revealed
Not of earth only but of highest Heav'n."
    To whom thus Adam cleared of doubt, replied:
180 "How fully hast thou satisfied me, pure

---

3. Wheel, that is, the *primum mobile*, which (if we accept the Ptolemaic system and "save the sun his labor") revolves around the universe every twenty-four hours, carrying the planets and their spheres with it.

Intelligence° of Heav'n, angel serene,   *spirit*
And freed from intricacies, taught to live
The easiest way, nor with perplexing thoughts
To interrupt the sweet of life, from which
185   God hath bid dwell far off all anxious cares,
And not molest us, unless we ourselves
Seek them with wand'ring thoughts, and notions vain.
But apt the mind or fancy is to rove
Unchecked, and of her roving is no end;
190   Till warned, or by experience taught, she learn,
That not to know at large of things remote
From use, obscure and subtle, but to know
That which before us lies in daily life,
Is the prime wisdom; what is more, is fume,°   *vapor*
195   Or emptiness, or fond impertinence,°   *foolish irrelevance*
And renders us in things that most concern
Unpracticed, unprepared, and still to seek.°   *always searching*
Therefore from this high pitch let us descend
A lower flight, and speak of things at hand
200   Useful, whence haply mention may arise
Of something not unseasonable to ask
By sufferance,° and thy wonted favor deigned.   *permission*
Thee I have heard relating what was done
Ere my remembrance: now hear me relate
205   My story, which perhaps thou hast not heard;
And day is yet not spent; till then thou seest
How subtly to detain thee I devise,
Inviting thee to hear while I relate,
Fond,° were it not in hope of thy reply: *foolish*
210   For while I sit with thee, I seem in Heav'n,
And sweeter thy discourse is to my ear
Than fruits of palm-tree pleasantest to thirst
And hunger both, from labor, at the hour
Of sweet repast; they satiate, and soon fill,
215   Though pleasant, but thy words with grace divine
Imbued, bring to their sweetness no satiety."
        To whom thus Raphael answered heav'nly meek:
"Nor are thy lips ungraceful, sire of men,
Nor tongue ineloquent; for God on thee
220   Abundantly his gifts hath also poured
Inward and outward both, his image fair:
Speaking or mute all comeliness and grace
Attends thee, and each word, each motion forms.
Nor less think we in Heav'n of thee on earth
225   Than of our fellow-servant, and inquire
Gladly into the ways of God with man:
For God we see hath honored thee, and set
On man his equal love: say therefore on;
For I that day was absent, as befell,
230   Bound on a voyage uncouth° and obscure,   *strange*
Far on excursion toward the gates of Hell;
Squared in full legion (such command we had)

To see that none thence issued forth a spy,
Or enemy, while God was in his work,
235 Lest he incensed at such eruption bold,
Destruction with creation might have mixed.
Not that they durst without his leave attempt,
But us he sends upon his high behests
For state,° as sovran King, and to inure°   *ceremony/strengthen*
240 Our prompt obedience. Fast we found, fast shut
The dismal gates, and barricadoed strong;
But long ere our approaching heard within
Noise, other than the sound of dance or song,
Torment, and loud lament, and furious rage.
245 Glad we returned up to the coasts of light
Ere Sabbath evening: so we had in charge.
But thy relation now; for I attend,
Pleased with thy words no less than thou with mine."
        So spake the godlike Power, and thus our sire:
250 "For man to tell how human life began
Is hard: for who himself beginning knew?[4]
Desire with thee still longer to converse
Induced me. As new-waked from soundest sleep
Soft on the flow'ry herb I found me laid
255 In balmy sweat, which with his beams the sun
Soon dried, and on the reeking° moisture fed.   *steaming*
Straight toward heav'n my wond'ring eyes I turned,
And gazed a while the ample sky, till raised
By quick instinctive motion up I sprung
260 As thitherward endeavoring, and upright
Stood on my feet; about me round I saw
Hill, dale, and shady woods, and sunny plains,
And liquid lapse° of murmuring streams; by these,   *flow*
Creatures that lived, and moved, and walked, or flew,
265 Birds on the branches warbling; all things smiled,
With fragrance and with joy my heart o'erflowed.
Myself I then perused, and limb by limb
Surveyed, and sometimes went,° and sometimes ran   *walked*
With supple joints, as lively vigor led:
270 But who I was, or where, or from what cause,
Knew not; to speak I tried, and forthwith spake,
My tongue obeyed and readily could name
Whate'er I saw.[5] 'Thou sun,' said I, 'fair light,
And thou enlightened earth, so fresh and gay,
275 Ye hills and dales, ye rivers, woods, and plains,
And ye that live and move, fair creatures, tell,
Tell, if ye saw, how came I thus, how here?
Not of myself; by some great Maker then,
In goodness and in power preeminent;
280 Tell me, how may I know him, how adore,

4. Compare Satan's inability to remember his origins (5.859–63) from which he infers self-creation, whereas Adam infers a Maker (278).

5. Adam's ability to name the creatures was said to signify his intuitive understanding of their natures.

From whom I have that thus I move and live,
And feel that I am happier than I know.'
While thus I called, and strayed I knew not whither,
From where I first drew air, and first beheld
285 This happy light, when answer none returned,
On a green shady bank profuse of flow'rs
Pensive I sat me down; there gentle sleep
First found me, and with soft oppression seized
My drowsèd sense, untroubled, though I thought
290 I then was passing to my former state
Insensible, and forthwith to dissolve:
When suddenly stood at my head a dream,
Whose inward apparition gently moved
My fancy to believe I yet had being,
295 And lived: one came, methought, of shape divine,
And said, 'Thy mansion° wants° thee, Adam, rise,   *habitation/lacks*
First man, of men innumerable ordained
First father, called by thee I come thy guide
To the garden of bliss, thy seat° prepared.'   *residence*
300 So saying, by the hand he took me raised,
And over fields and waters, as in air
Smooth sliding without step, last led me up
A woody mountain whose high top was plain,
A circuit wide, enclosed, with goodliest trees
305 Planted, with walks, and bowers, that what I saw
Of earth before scarce pleasant seemed. Each tree
Load'n with fairest fruit, that hung to the eye
Tempting, stirred in me sudden appetite
To pluck and eat; whereat I waked, and found
310 Before mine eyes all real, as the dream
Had lively° shadowed: here had new begun   *vividly*
My wand'ring, had not he who was my guide
Up hither, from among the trees appeared,
Presence Divine. Rejoicing, but with awe
315 In adoration at his feet I fell
Submiss:° he reared me, and 'Whom thou sought'st I am,'   *submissive*
Said mildly, 'Author of all this thou seest
Above, or round about thee or beneath.
This paradise I give thee, count it thine
320 To till and keep,° and of the fruit to eat: *care for*
Of every tree that in the garden grows
Eat freely with glad heart; fear here no dearth:
But of the tree whose operation° brings   *action*
Knowledge of good and ill, which I have set
325 The pledge of thy obedience and thy faith,
Amid the garden by the Tree of Life,
Remember what I warn thee, shun to taste,
And shun the bitter consequence: for know,
The day thou eat'st thereof, my sole command
330 Transgressed, inevitably thou shalt die;
From that day mortal, and this happy state
Shalt lose, expelled from hence into a world

Of woe and sorrow.'[6] Sternly he pronounced
The rigid interdiction,° which resounds   *prohibition*
335 Yet dreadful in mine ear, though in my choice
Not to incur; but soon his clear aspéct
Returned and gracious purpose° thus renewed: *speech*
'Not only these fair bounds, but all the earth
To thee and to thy race I give; as lords
340 Possess it, and all things that therein live,
Or live in sea, or air, beast, fish, and fowl.
In sign whereof each bird and beast behold
After their kinds; I bring them to receive
From thee their names, and pay thee fealty
345 With low subjection; understand the same
Of fish within their wat'ry residence,
Not hither summoned, since they cannot change
Their element to draw the thinner air.'
As thus he spake, each bird and beast behold
350 Approaching two and two, these° cow'ring low   *the beasts*
With blandishment,° each bird stooped on his wing.   *flattering gesture*
I named them, as they passed, and understood
Their nature, with such knowledge God endued
My sudden apprehension:[7] but in these
355 I found not what methought I wanted still;
And to the heav'nly Vision thus presumed:
   " 'O by what name, for thou above all these,
Above mankind, or aught than mankind higher,
Surpassest far my naming,[8] how may I
360 Adore thee, Author of this universe,
And all this good to man, for whose well-being
So amply, and with hands so liberal
Thou hast provided all things: but with me
I see not who partakes. In solitude
365 What happiness, who can enjoy alone,
Or all enjoying, what contentment find?'
Thus I presumptuous; and the Vision bright,
As with a smile more brightened, thus replied:
   " 'What call'st thou solitude? Is not the earth
370 With various living creatures, and the air
Replenished,° and all these at thy command   *fully stocked*
To come and play before thee? Know'st thou not
Their language and their ways? They also know,°   *have understanding*
And reason not contemptibly; with these
375 Find pastime, and bear rule; thy realm is large.'
So spake the Universal Lord, and seemed
So ordering. I with leave of speech implored,
And humble deprecation thus replied:
   " 'Let not my words offend thee, Heav'nly Power,

[Handwritten margin note: Adam says he is lonly, god says he has the creatures, Adam is sad he can't talk to them, and they all have mates to talk to.]

6. Compare God's commands to Adam (Genesis
1.28–39, 2.16–17) with Milton's elaboration here.
7. Adam had already begun naming the sun and
features of the earth (lines 72–73), but here he
names (and thereby shows he understands) all living creatures.
8. Adam reasons, as the Scholastics did, from the
creatures to the fact of a Creator, but he cannot
name (and so indicates that he cannot understand)
God, except as God reveals himself.

380 My Maker, be propitious while I speak.
Hast thou not made me here thy substitute,
And these inferior far beneath me set?
Among unequals what society
Can sort,° what harmony or true delight?   *agree*
385 Which must be mutual, in proportion due
Giv'n and received; but in disparity
The one intense, the other still remiss[9]
Cannot well suit with either, but soon prove
Tedious alike. Of fellowship I speak
390 Such as I seek, fit to participate°   *partake of*
All rational delight, wherein the brute
Cannot be human consort; they rejoice
Each with their kind, lion with lioness;
So fitly them in pairs thou hast combined;
395 Much less can bird with beast, or fish with fowl
So well converse,° nor with the ox the ape;   *associate*
Worse then can man with beast, and least of all.'
    "Whereto th' Almighty answered, not displeased:
'A nice° and subtle happiness I see   *fastidious*
400 Thou to thyself proposest, in the choice
Of thy associates, Adam, and wilt taste
No pleasure, though in pleasure, solitary.
What think'st thou then of me, and this my state?
Seem I to thee sufficiently possessed
405 Of happiness, or not? who am alone
From all eternity, for none I know
Second to me or like, equal much less.
How have I then with whom to hold converse
Save with the creatures which I made, and those
410 To me inferior, infinite descents
Beneath what other creatures are to thee?'
    "He ceased, I lowly answered: 'To attain
The height and depth of thy eternal ways
All human thoughts come short, Supreme of things;
415 Thou in thyself art perfect, and in thee
Is no deficience found; not so is man,
But in degree, the cause of his desire
By conversation with his like to help,
Or solace his defects.[1] No need that thou
420 Shouldst propagate, already infinite;
And through all numbers absolute, though One;[2]
But man by number is to manifest
His single imperfection, and beget
Like of his like, his image multiplied,
425 In unity defective, which requires

---

9. As with poorly matched musical instruments,
Adam's string is too taut ("intense") and the animals' is too slack ("remiss") to be in harmony
("suit").
1. God is absolutely perfect, man only relatively so
("in degree"), and thereby needs companionship
with a fit mate to assuage ("solace") the "defects"

arising from solitariness.
2. God, though One, contains all numbers, but
man has to remedy the "imperfection" of being single (line 423) by procreating and thereby multiplying his single and thereby "defective" image (line
425).

Collateral° love, and dearest amity.   *mutual*
Thou in thy secrecy° although alone,   *seclusion*
Best with thyself accompanied, seek'st not
Social communication, yet so pleased,
430 Canst raise thy creature to what height thou wilt
Of union or communion, deified;
I by conversing cannot these erect
From prone, nor in their ways complacence° find.'   *satisfaction*
Thus I emboldened spake, and freedom used
435 Permissive,° and acceptance found, which gained   *permitted*
This answer from the gracious Voice Divine:
    " 'Thus far to try thee, Adam, I was pleased,
And find thee knowing not of beasts alone,
Which thou hast rightly named, but of thyself,
440 Expressing well the spirit within thee free,
My image, not imparted to the brute,
Whose fellowship therefore unmeet for thee
Good reason was thou freely shouldst dislike,
And be so minded still. I, ere thou spak'st,
445 Knew it not good for man to be alone,
And no such company as then thou saw'st
Intended thee, for trial only brought,
To see how thou couldst judge of fit and meet:
What next I bring shall please thee, be assured,
450 Thy likeness, thy fit help, thy other self,
Thy wish, exactly to thy heart's desire.'[3]
    "He ended, or I heard no more, for now
My earthly by his heav'nly overpowered,
Which it had long stood under,° strained to the height   *been exposed to*
455 In that celestial colloquy sublime,
As with an object that excels° the sense,   *exceeds*
Dazzled and spent, sunk down, and sought repair
Of sleep, which instantly fell on me, called
By nature as in aid, and closed mine eyes.
460 Mine eyes he closed, but open left the cell
Of fancy° my internal sight, by which   *imagination*
Abstract° as in a trance methought I saw.   *withdrawn*
Though sleeping, where I lay, and saw the shape
Still glorious before whom awake I stood;
465 Who stooping opened my left side, and took
From thence a rib, with cordial° spirits warm,   *from the heart*
And life-blood streaming fresh; wide was the wound,
But suddenly with flesh filled up and healed:
The rib he formed and fashioned with his hands;
470 Under his forming hands a creature grew,[4]
Manlike, but different sex, so lovely fair
That what seemed fair in all the world seemed now
Mean, or in her summed up, in her contained
And in her looks, which from that time infused

[handwritten margin note: God is testing Adam to see if he is intelligent enough to know he wanted a mate.]

[handwritten margin note: God is single, but he is perfect]

---

3. Compare the account in Genesis 2.18 with Milton's elaboration.

4. Compare the *Creation of Eve* by the Italian painter Paolo Veronese (1528–1588).

475   Sweetness into my heart, unfelt before,
And into all things from her air° inspired   *mien, look*
The spirit of love and amorous delight.
She disappeared, and left me dark, I waked
To find her, or for ever to deplore
480   Her loss, and other pleasures all abjure:
When out of hope, behold her, not far off,
Such as I saw her in my dream, adorned
With what all earth or heaven could bestow
To make her amiable:° on she came,   *lovely*
485   Led by her heav'nly Maker, though unseen,[5]
And guided by his voice, nor uninformed
Of nuptial sanctity and marriage rites:
Grace was in all her steps, Heav'n in her eye,
In every gesture dignity and love.
490   I overjoyed could not forbear aloud:
    " 'This turn hath made amends; thou hast fulfilled
Thy words, Creator bounteous and benign,
Giver of all things fair, but fairest this
Of all thy gifts, nor enviest.° I now see   *give reluctantly*
495   Bone of my bone, flesh of my flesh, my self
Before me; woman is her name, of man
Extracted; for this cause he shall forgo
Father and mother, and to his wife adhere;
And they shall be one flesh, one heart, one soul.'[6]
500   "She heard me thus, and though divinely brought,
Yet innocence and virgin modesty,
Her virtue and the conscience°   *consciousness*
That would be wooed, and not unsought be won,
Not obvious,° not obtrusive,° but retired,   *bold/forward*
505   The more desirable, or to say all,
Nature herself, though pure of sinful thought,
Wrought in her so that, seeing me, she turned;
I followed her, she what was honor knew,
And with obsequious° majesty approved   *compliant*
510   My pleaded reason. To the nuptial bow'r
I led her blushing like the morn: all heav'n,
And happy constellations on that hour
Shed their selectest influence; the earth
Gave sign of gratulation,° and each hill;   *rejoicing, congratulation*
515   Joyous the birds; fresh gales and gentle airs[7]
Whispered it to the woods, and from their wings
Flung rose, flung odors from the spicy shrub,
Disporting,° till the amorous bird of night°   *frolicking/nightingale*
Sung spousal, and bid haste the evening star°   *Venus*
520   On his hill top, to light the bridal lamp.
    Thus I have told thee all my state, and brought
My story to the sum of earthly bliss
Which I enjoy, and must confess to find
In all things else delight indeed, but such

---

5. Compare Eve's version of these events (4.440–91).

6. Compare the account in Genesis 2.23–24.
7. Both breezes and melodies. "Gales": winds.

525   As used or not, works in the mind no change,
      Nor vehement desire, these delicacies
      I mean of taste, sight, smell, herbs, fruits, and flow'rs,
      Walks, and the melody of birds; but here
      Far otherwise, transported° I behold,   *enraptured*
530   Transported touch; here passion first I felt,
      Commotion° strange, in all enjoyments else   *mental agitation*
      Superior and unmoved, here only weak
      Against the charm of beauty's powerful glance.
      Or° nature failed in me, and left some part   *either*
535   Not proof enough such object to sustain,°   *withstand*
      Or from my side subducting,° took perhaps   *subtracting*
      More than enough; at least on her bestowed
      Too much of ornament, in outward show
      Elaborate, of inward less exact.
540   For well I understand in the prime end
      Of nature her th' inferior, in the mind
      And inward faculties, which most excel,
      In outward also her resembling less
      His image who made both, and less expressing
545   The character of that dominion giv'n
      O'er other creatures; yet when I approach
      Her loveliness, so absolute° she seems   *perfect, independent*
      And in herself complete, so well to know
      Her own, that what she wills to do or say,
550   Seems wisest, virtuousest, discreetest, best;
      All higher knowledge in her presence falls
      Degraded, wisdom in discourse with her
      Loses discount'nanced,° and like folly shows;   *disconcerted, abashed*
      Authority and reason on her wait,
555   As one intended first, not after made
      Occasionally;° and to consúmmate all,   *incidentally*
      Greatness of mind and nobleness their seat
      Build in her loveliest, and create an awe
      About her, as a guard angelic placed."
560   To whom the angel with contracted brow:
      "Accuse not nature, she hath done her part;
      Do thou but thine, and be not diffident°   *mistrustful*
      Of wisdom, she deserts thee not, if thou
      Dismiss not her, when most thou need'st her nigh,
565   By áttributing overmuch to things
      Less excellent, as thou thyself perceiv'st.
      For what admir'st thou, what transports thee so,
      An outside? Fair no doubt, and worthy well
      Thy cherishing, thy honoring, and thy love,
570   Not thy subjection: weigh with her thyself;
      Then value: ofttimes nothing profits more
      Than self-esteem, grounded on just and right
      Well managed; of that skill the more thou know'st,
      The more she will acknowledge thee her head,[8]

[Handwritten annotations in right margin:]
Adam speaking to the archangel about Eve. he is saying Eve is better than me. then he gets slapped down he is so in love that he is tounge tied.

Milton is saying that women are dangerous.

it is good to honor her but don't let her rule. you are in charge & not she. the angel is like Milton's concious.

---

8. See 1 Corinthians 11.31: "The head of every man is Christ; and the head of the woman is the man; and the head of Christ is God."

575 And to realities yield all her shows:
Made so adorn for thy delight the more,
So awful,° that with honor thou may'st love   *awe-inspiring*
Thy mate, who sees when thou art seen least wise.
But if the sense of touch whereby mankind
580 Is propagated seem such dear delight
Beyond all other, think the same vouchsafed
To cattle and each beast; which would not be
To them made common and divulged,° if aught   *imparted generally*
Therein enjoyed were worthy to subdue
585 The soul of man, or passion in him move.
What higher in her society thou find'st
Attractive, human, rational, love still;
In loving thou dost well, in passion not,
Wherein true love consists not; love refines
590 The thoughts, and heart enlarges, hath his seat
In reason, and is judicious, is the scale⁹
By which to heav'nly love thou may'st ascend,
Not sunk in carnal pleasure, for which cause
Among the beasts no mate for thee was found."
595   To whom thus half abashed Adam replied.
"Neither her outside formed so fair, nor aught
In procreation common to all kinds
(Though higher of the genial¹ bed by far,
And with mysterious reverence I deem)
600 So much delights me, as those graceful acts,
Those thousand decencies° that daily flow   *fitting acts*
From all her words and actions, mixed with love
And sweet compliance, which declare unfeigned
Union of mind, or in us both one soul;
605 Harmony to behold in wedded pair
More grateful than harmonious sound to the ear.
Yet these subject not; I to thee disclose
What inward thence I feel, not therefore foiled,°   *overcome*
Who meet with various objects, from the sense
610 Variously representing;² yet still free
Approve the best, and follow what I approve.
To love thou blam'st me not, for love thou say'st
Leads up to Heav'n, is both the way and guide;
Bear with me then, if lawful what I ask;
615 Love not the heav'nly Spirits, and how their love
Express they, by looks only, or do they mix
Irradiance, virtual or immediate° touch?"   *actual*
    To whom the angel with a smile that glowed
Celestial rosy red, love's proper hue,³

[Marginal handwritten annotations:]
even though he loves her she doesn't control him.
Milton is more like God than Adam, but he wants to be like Adam

---

9. The ladder of love, a Neoplatonic concept for
the movement from sensual love to higher forms,
and ultimately to love of God (see Castiglione's
Courtier, p. 578).
1. Both nuptial and generative. Adam takes
respectful issue with the apparent denigration of
human sex in Raphael's account of the Neoplatonic ladder, which prompts his question about

angelic sex (lines 615–17).
2. I.e., various objects, variously represented to
me by my senses.
3. This is not likely to be an embarrassed blush:
red is the color traditionally associated with Seraphim who burn with ardor. Raphael's smile also
glows with friendship for Adam and appreciation
of his perceptive inference about angelic love.

620 Answered. "Let it suffice thee that thou know'st
    Us happy, and without love no happiness.
    Whatever pure thou in the body enjoy'st
    (And pure thou wert created) we enjoy
    In eminence,° and obstacle find none   *surprisingly*
625 Of membrane, joint, or limb, exclusive bars:
    Easier than air with air, if Spirits embrace,
    Total they mix, union of pure with pure
    Desiring; nor restrained conveyance need
    As flesh to mix with flesh, or soul with soul.
630 But I can now no more; the parting sun
    Beyond the earth's green cape[4] and verdant isles
    Hesperian sets, my signal to depart.
    Be strong, live happy, and love, but first of all
    Him whom to love is to obey, and keep
635 His great command; take heed lest passion sway
    Thy judgment to do aught, which else free will
    Would not admit;° thine and of all thy sons   *permit*
    The weal or woe in thee is placed; beware.
    I in thy persevering shall rejoice,
640 And all the blest: stand fast; to stand or fall
    Free in thine own arbitrament° it lies.   *determination*
    Perfect within, no outward aid require;°   *depend on*
    And all temptation to transgress repel."
       So saying, he arose; whom Adam thus
645 Followed with benediction. "Since to part,
    Go heavenly guest, ethereal messenger,
    Sent from whose sovran goodness I adore.
    Gentle to me and affable hath been
    Thy condescension, and shall be honored ever
650 With grateful memory: thou to mankind
    Be good and friendly still, and oft return."
       So parted they, the angel up to Heav'n
    From the thick shade, and Adam to his bow'r.

Book 9   the fall

No more of talk where God or angel guest
    With man, as with his friend, familiar used
    To sit indulgent, and with him partake
    Rural repast, permitting him the while
5 Venial° discourse unblamed: I now must change   *pardonable*
    Those notes to tragic; foul distrust, and breach
    Disloyal on the part of man, revolt,
    And disobedience: on the part of Heav'n
    Now alienated, distance and distaste,°   *aversion*
10 Anger and just rebuke, and judgment giv'n,
    That brought into this world a world of woe,
    Sin and her shadow Death, and misery
    Death's harbinger: sad task, yet argument

---

4. Cape Verde near Dakar and the islands off that coast are the westernmost ("Hesperian") points of Africa.

Not less but more heroic than the wrath
15 Of stern Achilles on his foe pursued
Thrice fugitive about Troy wall; or rage
Of Turnus for Lavinia disespoused,
Or Neptune's ire or Juno's, that so long
Perplexed the Greek and Cytherea's son;[1]
20 If answerable° style I can obtain   *fitting*
Of my celestial patroness, who deigns
Her nightly visitation unimplored,[2]
And dictates to me slumb'ring, or inspires
Easy my unpremeditated verse:
25 Since first this subject for heroic song
Pleased me long choosing, and beginning late;
Not sedulous° by nature to indite   *eager*
Wars, hitherto the only argument°   *subject*
Heroic deemed, chief mastery to dissect
30 With long and tedious havoc fabled knights
In battles feigned; the better fortitude
Of patience and heroic martyrdom
Unsung; or to describe races and games,
Or tilting furniture,[3] emblazoned shields,
35 Impresses quaint, caparisons and steeds;
Bases and tinsel trappings, gorgeous knights
At joust and tournament; then marshaled feast
Served up in hall with sewers,° and seneschals;°   *waiters/stewards*
The skill of artifice° or office mean,   *mechanic art*
40 Not that which justly gives heroic name
To person or to poem. Me of these
Nor skilled nor studious, higher argument
Remains,[4] sufficient of itself to raise
That name, unless an age too late, or cold
45 Climate, or years damp my intended wing
Depressed, and much they may, if all be mine,
Not hers who brings it nightly to my ear.
  The sun was sunk, and after him the star
Of Hesperus,[5] whose office is to bring
50 Twilight upon the earth, short arbiter
'Twixt day and night, and now from end to end
Night's hemisphere had veiled the horizon round:
When Satan who late fled[6] before the threats

1. In this fourth proem (lines 1–47), after signaling his change from pastoral to tragic mode (lines 1–6), Milton emphasizes tragic elements in several classical epics: Achilles pursuing Hector three times around Troy wall before killing him (*Iliad* 22); Turnus fighting Aeneas over the loss of his betrothed Lavinia and killed by him; Odysseus ("the Greek") and Aeneas ("Cytherea's son," i.e., Venus's son) tormented ("perplexed") by Neptune (Poseidon) and Juno, respectively.
2. Milton does not here invoke the Muse but testifies to her customary nightly visits. Milton's nephew reports that he often awoke in the morning with lines of poetry fully formed in his head, ready to dictate them to an amanuensis.

3. Equipment for jousting; "impresses quaint": cunningly designed heraldic devices on shields; "caparisons": ornamental trappings or armor for horses; "bases": cloth coverings for horses. After rejecting the classical epic subjects, Milton here rejects the familiar topics of romance.
4. For a heroic poem. He proceeds to recap worries he has voiced before: that the times might not be receptive to such poems ("age too late"), that the "cold/Climate" of England or his own advanced age might "damp" (benumb, dampen) his "intended wing/Depressed" (poetic flights held down, kept from soaring).
5. Venus, the Evening Star.
6. At the end of Book 4.

Of Gabriel out of Eden, now improved°   *increased*
55 In meditated fraud and malice, bent
On man's destruction, maugre what might hap
Of heavier on himself,[7] fearless returned.
By night he fled, and at midnight returned
From compassing the earth, cautious of day,
60 Since Uriel regent of the sun descried
His entrance, and forewarned the Cherubim
That kept their watch; thence full of anguish driv'n,
The space of seven continued nights he rode
With darkness, thrice the equinoctial line°   *equator*
65 He circled, four times crossed the car of Night
From pole to pole, traversing each colure;[8]
On the eighth returned, and on the coast averse°   *turned away*
From entrance on Cherubic watch, by stealth
Found unsuspected way. There was a place,
70 Now not, though sin, not time, first wrought the change,
Where Tigris at the foot of Paradise
Into a gulf shot under ground, till part
Rose up a fountain by the Tree of Life;
In with the river sunk, and with it rose
75 Satan involved in rising mist, then sought
Where to lie hid. Sea he had searched and land
From Eden over Pontus,[9] and the pool
Maeotis, up beyond the river Ob;
Downward as far Antarctic; and in length
80 West from Orontes to the ocean barred
At Darien, thence to the land where flows
Ganges and Indus: thus the orb he roamed
With narrow search; and with inspection deep
Considered every creature, which of all   *he choses the*
85 Most opportune might serve his wiles, and found   *snake as his*
The serpent subtlest beast of all the field.[1]   *vessel.*
Him after long debate, irresolute°   *undecided*
Of° thoughts revolved, his final sentence° chose   *among/decision*
Fit vessel, fittest imp° of fraud, in whom   *offshoot*
90 To enter, and his dark suggestions hide
From sharpest sight: for in the wily snake,
Whatever sleights° none would suspicious mark,   *artifices*
As from his wit and native subtlety
Proceeding, which in other beasts observed
95 Doubt° might beget of diabolic pow'r   *suspicion*
Active within beyond the sense of brute.
Thus he resolved, but first from inward grief
His bursting passion into plaints thus poured:

7. I.e., despite ("maugre") what might result in
heavier punishments for himself.
8. The colures are two great circles that intersect
at right angles at the poles. By circling the globe
from east to west at the equator and then over the
north and south poles, Satan can remain in darkness, keeping the earth between himself and the
sun. "Car of Night" (line 65): the earth's shadow,
imagined as the chariot of the goddess Night.

9. The Black Sea. Satan's journey (lines 77–82)
takes him from there to the Sea of Azov in Russia
("Maeotis"), beyond the river "Ob" in Siberia,
which flows into the Arctic Ocean, then south to
Antarctica; thence west from "Orontes" (a river in
Syria) across the Atlantic to "Darien" (the Isthmus
of Panama), then across the Pacific and Asia to
India where the "Ganges" and "Indus" rivers flow.
1. The serpent is so described in Genesis 3.1.

"O earth, how like to Heav'n, if not preferred
100 More justly, seat worthier of gods, as built
With second thoughts, reforming what was old!
For what God after better worse would build?
Terrestrial heav'n, danced round by other heav'ns
That shine, yet bear their bright officious° lamps, *dutiful*
105 Light above light, for thee alone, as seems,[2]
In thee concent'ring all their precious beams
Of sacred influence: as God in Heav'n
Is center, yet extends to all, so thou
Centring receiv'st from all those orbs; in thee,
110 Not in themselves, all their known virtue appears
Productive in herb, plant, and nobler birth
Of creatures animate with gradual life
Of growth, sense, reason,[3] all summed up in man.
With what delight could I have walked thee round,
115 If I could joy in aught, sweet interchange
Of hill and valley, rivers, woods and plains,
Now land, now sea, and shores with forest crowned,
Rocks, dens, and caves; but I in none of these
Find place or refuge; and the more I see
120 Pleasures about me, so much more I feel
Torment within me, as from the hateful siege°   *conflict*
Of contraries; all good to me becomes
Bane,° and in Heav'n much worse would be my state.   *poison*
But neither here seek I, no nor in Heav'n
125 To dwell, unless by mastering Heav'n's Supreme;
Nor hope to be myself less miserable
By what I seek, but others to make such
As I, though thereby worse to me redound:
For only in destroying I find ease
130 To my relentless thoughts; and him[4] destroyed,
Or won to what may work his utter loss,
For whom all this was made, all this will soon
Follow, as to him linked in weal or woe:
In woe then; that destruction wide may range:
135 To me shall be the glory sole among
The infernal Powers, in one day to have marred
What he Almighty styled, six nights and days
Continued making, and who knows how long
Before had been contriving, though perhaps
140 Not longer than since I in one night freed
From servitude inglorious well-nigh half
Th' angelic name, and thinner left the throng
Of his adorers. He to be avenged,
And to repair his numbers thus impaired,
145 Whether such virtue° spent of old now failed   *power*
More angels to create, if they at least

2. Like Adam (8.15ff.) and Eve (4.657) but not
Raphael (8.114–78), Satan assumes a Ptolemaic
universe centered on the earth and humankind.
3. Graduated in steps ("gradual," line 113) from

vegetable to animal to rational forms (souls); cf.
5.469–90.
4. Adam. "This" (line 132): the universe.

Are his created, or to spite us more,
Determined to advance into our room
A creature formed of earth, and him endow,
150 Exalted from so base original,°   *origin*
With heav'nly spoils, our spoils: what he decreed
He effected; man he made, and for him built
Magnificent this world, and earth his seat,
Him lord pronounced, and, O indignity!
155 Subjected to his service angel wings,
And flaming ministers to watch and tend
Their earthy charge: of these the vigilance
I dread, and to elude, thus wrapped in mist
Of midnight vapor glide obscure, and pry
160 In every bush and brake, where hap° may find   *luck*
The serpent sleeping, in whose mazy folds
To hide me, and the dark intent I bring.
O foul descent!⁵ that I who erst contended
With gods to sit the highest, am now constrained
165 Into a beast, and mixed with bestial slime,
This essence to incarnate and imbrute,
That to the height of deity aspired;
But what will not ambition and revenge
Descend to? Who aspires must down as low
170 As high he soared, obnoxious° first or last   *exposed*
To basest things. Revenge, at first though sweet,
Bitter ere long back on itself recoils;
Let it; I reck° not, so it light well aimed,   *care*
Since higher I fall short, on him who next
175 Provokes my envy, this new favorite
Of Heav'n, this man of clay, son of despite,
Whom us the more to spite his Maker raised
From dust: spite then with spite is best repaid.'
    So saying, through each thicket dank or dry,
180 Like a black mist low creeping, he held on
His midnight search, where soonest he might find
The serpent: him fast sleeping soon he found
In labyrinth of many a round self-rolled,
His head the midst, well stored with subtle wiles:
185 Not yet in horrid shade or dismal den,
Nor nocent° yet, but on the grassy herb   *harmful, guilty*
Fearless unfeared he slept: in at his mouth
The Devil entered, and his brutal° sense,   *animal*
In heart or head, possessing soon inspired
190 With act intelligential: but his sleep
Disturbed not, waiting close° th' approach of morn.   *hidden*
Now whenas sacred light began to dawn
In Eden on the humid flow'rs, that breathed
Their morning incense, when all things that breathe
195 From th' earth's great altar send up silent praise

---

5. Satan "imbruting" himself in a snake parodies, grotesquely, the Son's incarnation in human form, as Christ.

To the Creator, and his nostrils fill
With grateful° smell, forth came the human pair   *pleasing*
And joined their vocal worship to the choir
Of creatures wanting° voice; that done, partake   *lacking*
200 The season, prime° for sweetest scents and airs: *best*
Then cómmune how that day they best may ply
Their growing work; for much their work outgrew
The hands' dispatch of two gard'ning so wide.
And Eve first to her husband thus began:
205 "Adam, well may we labor still° to dress   *continually*
This garden, still to tend plant, herb and flow'r,
Our pleasant task enjoined, but till more hands
Aid us, the work under our labor grows,
Luxurious° by restraint; what we by day   *luxuriant*
210 Lop overgrown, or prune, or prop, or bind,
One night or two with wanton growth derides,
Tending to wild. Thou therefore now advise
Or hear what to my mind first thoughts present,
Let us divide our labors, thou where choice
215 Leads thee, or where most needs, whether to wind
The woodbine round this arbor, or direct
The clasping ivy where to climb, while I
In yonder spring° of roses intermixed   *growth*
With myrtle, find what to redress° till noon: *set upright*
220 For while so near each other thus all day
Our task we choose, what wonder if so near
Looks intervene and smiles, or object new
Casual discourse draw on, which intermits
Our day's work brought to little, though begun
225 Early, and th' hour of supper comes unearned.
To whom mild answer Adam thus returned:
"Sole Eve, associate sole,[6] to me beyond
Compare above all living creatures dear,
Well hast thou motioned,° well thy thoughts employed   *proposed*
230 How we might best fulfill the work which here
God hath assigned us, nor of me shalt pass
Unpraised: for nothing lovelier can be found
In woman, than to study household good,
And good works in her husband to promote.[7]
235 Yet not so strictly hath our Lord imposed
Labor, as to debar us when we need
Refreshment, whether food, or talk between,
Food of the mind, or this sweet intercourse
Of looks and smiles, for smiles from reason flow,
240 To brute denied, and are of love the food,
Love not the lowest end of human life.
For not to irksome toil, but to delight
He made us, and delight to reason joined.
These paths and bowers doubt not but our joint hands

[handwritten margin notes: "they should work separately to get more work done, they didn't work for their food." "now she wants to have a voice, she wants Adam to respect & be proud of her." "women are only there for their men. he said they weren't put there to work, but to be happy."]

---

6. Adam puns on "sole" as "unrivaled" and "only" (cf. 4.411).

7. Adam's compliments owe something to the praises of a good wife in Proverbs 31.

245 Will keep from wilderness with ease, as wide
As we need walk, till younger hands ere long
Assist us: but if much convérse perhaps
Thee satiate, to short absence I could yield.
For solitude sometimes is best society,
250 And short retirement urges sweet return.
But other doubt possesses me, lest harm
Befall thee severed from me; for thou know'st
What hath been warned us, what malicious foe
Envying our happiness, and of his own
255 Despairing, seeks to work us woe and shame
By sly assault; and somewhere nigh at hand
Watches, no doubt, with greedy hope to find
His wish and best advantage, us asunder,
Hopeless to circumvent us joined, where each
260 To other speedy aid might lend at need;
Whether his first design be to withdraw
Our fealty from God, or to disturb
Conjugal love, than which perhaps no bliss
Enjoyed by us excites his envy more;
265 Or° this, or worse, leave not the faithful side   °whether
That gave thee being, still shades thee and protects.
The wife, where danger or dishonor lurks,
Safest and seemliest by her husband stays,
Who guards her, or with her the worst endures."
270   To whom the virgin[8] majesty of Eve,
As one who loves, and some unkindness meets,
With sweet austere composure thus replied.
    "Offspring of Heav'n and earth, and all earth's lord,
That such an enemy we have, who seeks
275 Our ruin, both by thee informed I learn,
And from the parting angel overheard
As in a shady nook I stood behind,
Just then returned at shut of evening flow'rs.[9]
But that thou shouldst my firmness therefore doubt
280 To God or thee, because we have a foe
May tempt it, I expected not to hear.
His violence thou fear'st not, being such,
As we, not capable of death or pain,
Can either not receive, or can repel.
285 His fraud is then thy fear, which plain infers
Thy equal fear that my firm faith and love
Can by his fraud be shaken or seduced;
Thoughts, which how found they harbor in thy breast,
Adam, misthought of° her to thee so dear?"   °misapplied to
290   To whom with healing words Adam replied.
    "Daughter of God and man, immortal Eve,

---

8. The term here means unspotted or peerless; Milton has insisted at the end of Books 4 and 8 that Adam and Eve have sex.
9. Somewhat confusing, since Eve heard the full story of the war in Heaven and Raphael's earlier warnings; Raphael's parting words (8.630–43) overheard by Eve do not mention Satan but warn Adam to resist his passion for Eve. He does, however, reiterate the charge to obey the "great command" and repel temptation.

For such thou art, from sin and blame entire:°   *untouched*
Not diffident° of thee do I dissuade   *distrustful*
Thy absence from my sight, but to avoid
295 Th' attempt itself, intended by our foe.
For he who tempts, though in vain, at least asperses°   *bespatters*
The tempted with dishonor foul, supposed
Not incorruptible of faith, not proof
Against temptation: thou thyself with scorn
300 And anger wouldst resent the offered wrong,
Though ineffectual found; misdeem not then,
If such affront I labor to avert
From thee alone, which on us both at once
The enemy, though bold, will hardly dare,
305 Or daring, first on me th' assault shall light.
Nor thou his malice and false guile contemn;
Subtle he needs must be, who could seduce
Angels, nor think superfluous others' aid.
I from the influence of thy looks receive
310 Access° in every virtue, in thy sight   *increase*
More wise, more watchful, stronger, if need were
Of outward strength; while shame, thou looking on,
Shame to be overcome or overreached°   *outwitted*
Would utmost vigor raise, and raised unite.
315 Why shouldst not thou like sense within thee feel
When I am present, and thy trial choose
With me, best witness of thy virtue tried."
   So spake domestic Adam in his care
And matrimonial love; but Eve, who thought
320 Less° attribúted to her faith sincere,   *too little*
Thus her reply with accent sweet renewed.
  "If this be our condition, thus to dwell
In narrow circuit straitened° by a foe,   *confined*
Subtle or violent, we not endued
325 Single with like defense, wherever met,
How are we happy, still° in fear of harm?   *always*
But harm precedes not sin: only our foe
Tempting affronts us with his foul esteem
Of our integrity: his foul esteem
330 Sticks no dishonor on our front,° but turns   *forehead*
Foul on himself; then wherefore shunned or feared
By us? who rather double honor gain
From his surmise proved false, find peace within,
Favor from Heav'n, our witness from th' event.°   *outcome*
335 And what is faith, love, virtue unassayed
Alone, without exterior help sustained?[1]
Let us not then suspect our happy state
Left so imperfect by the Maker wise,
As not secure to single° or combined.   *one alone*
340 Frail is our happiness, if this be so,
And Eden were no Eden thus exposed."

1. Compare and contrast *Areopagitica*, p. 1801.

To whom thus Adam fervently replied.
"O woman, best are all things as the will
Of God ordained them, his creating hand
345 Nothing imperfect or deficient left
Of all that he created, much less man,
Or aught that might his happy state secure,
Secure from outward force; within himself
The danger lies, yet lies within his power:
350 Against his will he can receive no harm.
But God left free the will, for what obeys
Reason, is free, and reason he made right,[2]
But bid her well beware, and still erect,°   alert
Lest by some fair appearing good surprised
355 She dictate false, and misinform the will
To do what God expressly hath forbid.
Not then mistrust, but tender love enjoins,
That I should mind° thee oft, and mind thou me.   remind, pay heed to
Firm we subsist,° yet possible to swerve,   stand, exist
360 Since reason not impossibly may meet
Some specious° object by the foe suborned,   deceptively attractive
And fall into deception unaware,
Not keeping strictest watch, as she was warned.
Seek not temptation then, which to avoid
365 Were better, and most likely if from me
Thou sever not: trial will come unsought.
Wouldst thou approve° thy constancy, approve   prove
First thy obedience; th' other who can know,
Not seeing thee attempted, who attest?
370 But if thou think, trial unsought may find
Us both securer° than thus warned thou seem'st,   overconfident
Go; for thy stay, not free, absents thee more;
Go in thy native innocence, rely
On what thou hast of virtue, summon all,
375 For God towards thee hath done his part, do thine."
    So spake the patriarch of mankind, but Eve
Persisted, yet submiss, though last, replied:
    "With thy permission then, and thus forewarned
Chiefly by what thy own last reasoning words
380 Touched only, that our trial, when least sought,
May find us both perhaps far less prepared,
The willinger I go, nor much expect
A foe so proud will first the weaker seek;
So bent, the more shall shame him his repulse."
385 Thus saying, from her husband's hand her hand
Soft she withdrew, and like a wood-nymph light[3]
Oread or Dryad, or of Delia's train,
Betook her to the groves, but Delia's self
In gait surpassed and goddess-like deport,°   bearing

2. Right reason, a classical concept accommodated to Christian thought, is the God-given power
to apprehend truth and moral law.
3. Light-footed, with overtones of "fickle" or "frivolous." "Oread": a mountain nymph. "Dryad": a
wood nymph. "Delia": Diana, born on the isle of
Delos, hunted with a "train" of nymphs.

390 Though not as she with bow and quiver armed,
But with such gardening tools as art yet rude,
Guiltless of fire[4] had formed, or angels brought.
To Pales, or Pomona, thus adorned,
Likest she seemed[5] Pomona when she fled
395 Vertumnus, or to Ceres in her prime,
Yet virgin of Proserpina from Jove.
Her long with ardent look his eye pursued
Delighted, but desiring more her stay.
Oft he to her his charge of quick return
400 Repeated, she to him as oft engaged
To be returned by noon amid the bow'r,
And all things in best order to invite
Noontide repast, or afternoon's repose.
O much deceived, much failing,° hapless° Eve,   *erring/unlucky*
405 Of thy presumed return! event perverse!
Thou never from that hour in Paradise
Found'st either sweet repast, or sound repose;
Such ambush hid among sweet flow'rs and shades
Waited with hellish rancor imminent
410 To intercept thy way, or send thee back
Despoiled of innocence, of faith, of bliss.
For now, and since first break of dawn the Fiend,
Mere serpent in appearance, forth was come,
And on his quest, where likeliest he might find
415 The only two of mankind, but in them
The whole included race, his purposed prey.
In bow'r and field he sought, where any tuft
Of grove or garden-plot more pleasant lay,
Their tendance or plantation[6] for delight,
420 By fountain or by shady rivulet
He sought them both, but wished his hap° might find   *luck*
Eve separate; he wished, but not with hope
Of what so seldom chanced, when to his wish,
Beyond his hope, Eve separate he spies,
425 Veiled in a cloud of fragrance, where she stood,
Half spied, so thick the roses bushing round
About her glowed, oft stooping to support
Each flow'r of slender stalk, whose head though gay
Carnation, purple, azure, or specked with gold,
430 Hung drooping unsustained, them she upstays
Gently with myrtle band, mindless° the while,   *heedless*
Herself, though fairest unsupported flow'r
From her best prop so far, and storm so nigh.[7]
Nearer he drew, and many a walk traversed

---

4. Having no experience of fire, not needed in Paradise. Milton may be alluding to the guilt of Prometheus, who stole fire from heaven.
5. These goddesses, like Eve, are associated with agriculture (lines 393–96)—Pales, with flocks and pastures; Pomona, with fruit trees, Ceres with harvests—and the latter two foreshadow Eve's situation. Pomona was chased by the wood god

"Vertumnus" in many guises before surrendering to him; Ceres was impregnated by Jove with Proserpina—later carried off to Hades by Pluto.
6. I.e., which they had cultivated or planted for their pleasure.
7. The conceit of the flower-gatherer who is herself gathered evokes the story of Proserpina, to whom it was applied in 4.269–71.

435 Of stateliest covert, cedar, pine, or palm,
Then voluble° and bold, now hid, now seen   *undulating*
Among thick-woven arborets° and flow'rs   *small trees*
Embordered on each bank, the hand° of Eve: *handiwork*
Spot more delicious than those gardens feigned
440 Or of revived Adonis, or renowned
Alcinous, host of old Laertes' son,
Or that, not mystic, where the sapient king
Held dalliance with his fair Egyptian spouse.[8]
Much he the place admired, the person more.
445 As one who long in populous city pent,
Where houses thick and sewers annoy° the air,   *make noisome, befoul*
Forth issuing on a summer's morn to breathe
Among the pleasant villages and farms
Adjoined, from each thing met conceives delight,
450 The smell of grain, or tedded grass, or kine,[9]
Or dairy, each rural sight, each rural sound;
If chance with nymph-like step fair virgin pass,
What pleasing seemed, for° her now pleases more,   *because of*
She most, and in her look sums all delight.
455 Such pleasure took the Serpent to behold
This flow'ry plat,° the sweet recess° of Eve   *plot/retreat*
Thus early, thus alone; her heav'nly form
Angelic, but more soft, and feminine,
Her graceful innocence, her every air°   *manner*
460 Of gesture or least action overawed
His malice, and with rapine sweet[1] bereaved
His fierceness of the fierce intent it brought:
That space the Evil One abstracted° stood   *withdrawn*
From his own evil, and for the time remained
465 Stupidly good,° of enmity disarmed,   *good because stupefied*
Of guile, of hate, of envy, of revenge;
But the hot hell that always in him burns,
Though in mid-heav'n, soon ended his delight,
And tortures him now more, the more he sees
470 Of pleasure not for him ordained: then soon
Fierce hate he recollects, and all his thoughts
Of mischief gratulating,° thus excites: *greeting*
   "Thoughts, whither have ye led me, with what sweet
Compulsion thus transported to forget
475 What hither brought us, hate, not love, nor hope
Of Paradise for Hell, hope here to taste
Of pleasure, but all pleasure to destroy,
Save what is in destroying, other joy
To me is lost. Then let me not let pass
480 Occasion which now smiles, behold alone
The woman, opportune° to all attempts,   *open*

8. The gardens of Adonis were beauty spots named for the lovely youth loved by Venus, killed by a boar, and subsequently revived; Odysseus ("Laertes' son") was entertained by "Alcinous" in his beautiful gardens. Solomon ("the sapient king") entertained his "fair Egyptian spouse," the Queen of Sheba, in a real garden (not "mystic," or "feigned," as the others were).
9. Cattle. "Tedded": spread out to dry, like hay.
1. From Latin "rapere," to seize, the root of both "rape" and "rapture," underscoring the paradox of the ravisher (temporarily) ravished.

Her husband, for I view far round, not nigh,
Whose higher intellectual more I shun,
And strength, of courage haughty,° and of limb   *exalted*
485 Heroic built, though of terrestrial° mold,   *earthly*
Foe not informidable, exempt from wound,
I not; so much hath Hell debased, and pain
Enfeebled me, to what I was in Heav'n.
She fair, divinely fair, fit love for gods,
490 Not terrible,° though terror be in love   *terrifying*
And beauty, not° approached by stronger hate,   *unless*
Hate stronger, under show of love well feigned,
The way which to her ruin now I tend."
    So spake the Enemy of mankind, enclosed
495 In serpent, inmate bad, and toward Eve
Addressed his way, not with indented° wave,   *zigzag*
Prone on the ground, as since, but on his rear,
Circular base of rising folds, that tow'red
Fold above fold a surging maze, his head
500 Crested aloft, and carbuncle° his eyes;   *deep red*
With burnished neck of verdant gold, erect
Amidst his circling spires,° that on the grass   *coils*
Floated redundant:° pleasing was his shape,   *in swelling waves*
And lovely, never since of serpent kind
505 Lovelier, not those that in Illyria changed
Hermione and Cadmus, or the god
In Epidaurus;² nor to which transformed
Ammonian Jove, or Capitoline was seen,
He with Olympias, this with her who bore
510 Scipio, the height of Rome.³ With tract° oblique   *course*
At first, as one who sought access, but feared
To interrupt, sidelong he works his way.
As when a ship by skilful steersman wrought
Nigh river's mouth or foreland, where the wind
515 Veers oft, as oft so steers, and shifts her sail;
So varied he, and of his tortuous train
Curled many a wanton° wreath in sight of Eve,   *luxuriant, sportive*
To lure her eye; she busied heard the sound
Of rustling leaves, but minded not, as used
520 To such disport before her through the field,
From every beast, more duteous at her call,
Than at Circean⁴ call the herd disguised.
He bolder now, uncalled before her stood;
But as in gaze admiring: oft he bowed
525 His turret crest, and sleek enameled° neck,   *multicolored*
Fawning, and licked the ground whereon she trod.
His gentle dumb expression turned at length

[Handwritten marginal notes: "he aproaches her slowly b/c she is cautious & this will make her less suspicious"; "he fawns on her to instil pride"]

2. The legendary founder of Thebes, "Cadmus," and his wife Harmonia (Milton's "Hermione") were changed to serpents when they went to "Illyria" in old age; Aesculapius, god of healing, sometimes came forth as a serpent fron his temple in "Epidaurus."
3. Jupiter Ammon ("Ammonian Jove") made love to "Olympias" in the form of a snake, and sired Alexander the Great; the Jupiter worshipped in Rome ("Capitoline") also in serpent form, sired Scipio Africanus, the savior and great leader ("height") of Rome.
4. Circe, in the *Odyssey*, transformed men to beasts and was attended by an obedient herd.

The eye of Eve to mark his play; he glad
Of her attention gained, with serpent tongue
530 Organic, or impulse of vocal air,[5]
His fraudulent temptation thus began.
     "Wonder not, sovran mistress, if perhaps
Thou canst, who art sole wonder, much less arm
Thy looks, the heav'n of mildness, with disdain,
535 Displeased that I approach thee thus, and gaze
Insatiate, I thus single, nor have feared
Thy awful brow, more awful thus retired.
Fairest resemblance of thy Maker fair,
Thee all things living gaze on, all things thine
540 By gift, and thy celestial beauty adore
With ravishment beheld, there best beheld
Where universally admired; but here.
In this enclosure wild, these beasts among,
Beholders rude, and shallow to discern
545 Half what in thee is fair, one man except,
Who sees thee? (and what is one?) who shouldst be seen
A goddess among gods, adored and served
By angels numberless, thy daily train."[6]
     So glozed° the Tempter, and his proem° tuned;   *flattered / prelude*
550 Into the heart of Eve his words made way,
Though at the voice much marveling; at length
Not unamazed she thus in answer spake.
"What may this mean? Language of man pronounced
By tongue of brute, and human sense expressed?
555 The first at least of these I thought denied
To beasts, whom God on their creation-day
Created mute to all articulate sound;
The latter I demur,° for in their looks   *hesitate about*
Much reason, and in their actions oft appears.
560 Thee, serpent, subtlest beast of all the field
I knew, but not with human voice endued;°   *endowed*
Redouble then this miracle, and say,
How cam'st thou speakable° of mute, and how   *able to speak*
To me so friendly grown above the rest
565 Of brutal kind, that daily are in sight?
Say, for such wonder claims attention due."
     To whom the guileful Tempter thus replied:
"Empress of this fair world, resplendent Eve,
Easy to me it is to tell thee all
570 What thou command'st, and right thou shouldst be obeyed:
I was at first as other beasts that graze
The trodden herb, of abject thoughts and low,
As was my food, nor aught but food discerned
Or sex, and apprehended nothing high:
575 Till on a day roving the field, I chanced
A goodly tree far distant to behold

---

5. Satan either used the actual tongue of the serpent or impressed the air with his own voice.

6. Satan's entire speech is couched in the extravagant praises of the Petrarchan love convention.

Loaden with fruit of fairest colors mixed,
Ruddy and gold: I nearer drew to gaze;
When from the boughs a savory odor blown,
580 Grateful to appetite, more pleased my sense
Than smell of sweetest fennel, or the teats
Of ewe or goat dropping with milk at ev'n,[7]
Unsucked of lamb or kid, that tend their play.
To satisfy the sharp desire I had
585 Of tasting those fair apples, I resolved
Not to defer;° hunger and thirst at once,   delay
Powerful persuaders, quickened at the scent
Of that alluring fruit, urged me so keen.
About the mossy trunk I wound me soon,
590 For high from ground the branches would require
Thy utmost reach or Adam's: round the tree
All other beasts that saw, with like desire
Longing and envying stood, but could not reach.
Amid the tree now got, where plenty hung
595 Tempting so nigh, to pluck and eat my fill
I spared° not, for such pleasure till that hour   refrained
At feed or fountain never had I found.
Sated at length, ere long I might perceive
Strange alteration in me, to degree
600 Of reason in my inward powers,[8] and speech
Wanted° not long, though to this shape retained.   lacked
Thenceforth to speculations high or deep
I turned my thoughts, and with capacious mind
Considered all things visible in Heav'n,
605 Or earth, or middle,° all things fair and good;   regions between
But all that fair and good in thy divine
Semblance, and in thy beauty's heav'nly ray
United I beheld; no fair° to thine   beauty
Equivalent or second, which compelled
610 Me thus, though importune° perhaps, to come   inopportunely
And gaze, and worship thee of right declared
Sovran of creatures, universal dame."[9]
        So talked the spirited[1] sly snake; and Eve
Yet more amazed unwary thus replied:
615 "Serpent, thy overpraising leaves in doubt
The virtue° of that fruit, in thee first proved: power
But say, where grows the tree, from hence how far?
For many are the trees of God that grow
In Paradise, and various, yet unknown
620 To us, in such abundance lies our choice,
As leaves a greater store of fruit untouched,

---

7. According to Pliny, serpents ate fennel to aid in shedding their skins and to sharpen their eyesight; folklore had it that they drank the milk of sheep and goats.
8. There is no precedent in Genesis or the interpretative tradition for Satan's powerfully persuasive argument by analogy based on the snake's supposed experience of attaining to reason and speech by eating the forbidden fruit.
9. Satan continues his Petrarchan language of courtship.
1. Both inspired by and possessed by an evil spirit, Satan.

Still hanging incorruptible, till men
Grow up to their provision,[2] and more hands
Help to disburden nature of her birth."
625   To whom the wily adder, blithe and glad:
"Empress, the way is ready, and not long,
Beyond a row of myrtles, on a flat,
Fast by a fountain, one small thicket past
Of blowing myrrh and balm;[3] if thou accept
630 My conduct,° I can bring thee thither soon."   *guidance*
    "Lead then," said Eve. He leading swiftly rolled
In tangles, and made intricate seem straight,
To mischief swift. Hope elevates, and joy
Brightens his crest, as when a wand'ring fire,°   *will-o'-the-wisp*
635 Compact° of unctuous° vapor, which the night   *composed/oily*
Condenses, and the cold environs round,
Kindled through agitation to a flame,
Which oft, they say, some evil spirit attends,
Hovering and blazing with delusive light,
640 Misleads th' amazed° night-wanderer from his way   *bewildered*
To bogs and mires, and oft through pond or pool,
There swallowed up and lost, from succor far.
So glistered the dire snake, and into fraud
Led Eve our credulous mother, to the tree
645 Of prohibition, root of all our woe;
Which when she saw, thus to her guide she spake:
    "Serpent, we might have spared our coming hither,
Fruitless to me, though fruit be here to excess,
The credit of whose virtue° rest with thee,   *power*
650 Wondrous indeed, if cause of such effects.
But of this tree we may not taste nor touch;
God so commanded, and left that command
Sole daughter of his voice;[4] the rest, we live
Law to ourselves, our reason is our law."
655   To whom the Tempter guilefully replied:
"Indeed? hath God then said that of the fruit
Of all these garden trees ye shall not eat,
Yet lords declared of all in earth or air?"
    To whom thus Eve yet sinless: "Of the fruit
660 Of each tree in the garden we may eat,
But of the fruit of this fair tree amidst
The garden, God hath said, 'Ye shall not eat
Thereof, nor shall ye touch it, lest ye die,' "[5]
    She scarce had said, though brief, when now more bold
665 The Tempter, but with show of zeal and love
To man, and indignation at his wrong,
New part puts on, and as to passion moved,

2. I.e., until the numbers of the human race are
such as to consume the food God has provided.
3. Blooming trees that exude the aromatic gums,
myrrh and balm (balsam).
4. God's only direct commandment (in Hebrew,
Bath Kol, "daughter of a voice" from heaven). Oth-

erwise, they follow the moral law of nature, known
to them perfectly by their unfallen reason, "our
reason is our law."
5. Eve's formulation indicates her "sufficient"
understanding of the prohibition and the conditions of life in Eden.

Fluctuates disturbed, yet comely, and in act
Raised,[6] as of some great matter to begin.
670 As when of old some orator renowned
In Athens or free Rome, where eloquence
Flourished, since mute, to some great cause addressed,
Stood in himself collected, while each part,
Motion, each act won audience ere the tongue,
675 Sometimes in high began, as no delay
Of preface brooking[7] through his zeal of right.
So standing, moving, or to high upgrown
The Tempter all impassioned thus began:
    "O sacred, wise, and wisdom-giving plant,
680 Mother of science,° now I feel thy power   knowledge
Within me clear, not only to discern
Things in their causes, but to trace the ways
Of highest agents, deemed however wise.
Queen of this universe, do not believe
685 Those rigid threats of death; ye shall not die:
How should ye? By the fruit? It gives you life
To knowledge.[8] By the Threat'ner? Look on me,
Me who have touched and tasted, yet both live,
And life more perfect have attained than fate
690 Meant me, by vent'ring higher than my lot.
Shall that be shut to man, which to the beast
Is open? Or will God incense his ire
For such a petty trespass, and not praise
Rather your dauntless virtue,° whom the pain   courage
695 Of death denounced,° whatever thing death be,   threatened
Deterred not from achieving what might lead
To happier life, knowledge of good and evil;
Of good, how just?[9] Of evil, if what is evil
Be real, why not known, since easier shunned?
700 God therefore cannot hurt ye, and be just;
Not just, not God;[1] not feared then, nor obeyed:
Your fear itself of death removes the fear.
Why then was this forbid? Why but to awe,
Why but to keep ye low and ignorant,
705 His worshipers; he knows that in the day
Ye eat thereof, your eyes that seem so clear,
Yet are but dim, shall perfectly be then
Opened and cleared, and ye shall be as gods,
Knowing both good and evil as they know.
710 That ye should be as gods, since I as man,
Internal man, is but proportion meet,
I of brute human, ye of human gods.[2]

---

6. Drawn up to full dignity. Satan as the snake takes on the role of a Greek or Roman orator defending liberty (lines 671–72), a Demosthenes or a Cicero.

7. Bursting into the middle of his speech without a preface, and "upgrown" to the impassioned high style ("high") at once (lines 675–78).

8. I.e., life as well as knowledge, and a better life enhanced by knowledge, which Satan in the snake presents as a "magical" property of the tree.

9. I.e., how can it be just to forbid the knowledge of good?

1. Satan's sophism invites atheism: if God forbids knowledge of good and evil he is not just, therefore not God, therefore his threat of death need not be feared.

2. Satan invites the aspiration to divinity, based on analogy to the supposed experience of the snake.

So ye shall die perhaps, by putting off
Human, to put on gods, death to be wished,
715 Though threatened, which no worse than this can bring.
And what are gods that man may not become
As they, participating° godlike food?
The gods[3] are first, and that advantage use
On our belief, that all from them proceeds;
720 I question it, for this fair earth I see,
Warmed by the sun, producing every kind,
Them nothing; if they all° things, who enclosed
Knowledge of good and evil in this tree,
That whoso eats thereof, forthwith attains
725 Wisdom without their leave? And wherein lies
Th' offense, that man should thus attain to know?
What can your knowledge hurt him, or this tree
Impart against his will if all be his?
Or is it envy, and can envy dwell
730 In heav'nly breasts? These, these and many more
Causes import° your need of this fair fruit.
Goddess humane,[4] reach then, and freely taste."
    He ended, and his words replete with guile
Into her heart too easy entrance won:
735 Fixed on the fruit she gazed, which to behold
Might tempt alone, and in her ears the sound
Yet rung of his persuasive words, impregned°
With reason, to her seeming, and with truth;
Meanwhile the hour of noon drew on, and waked
740 An eager appetite, raised by the smell
So savory of that fruit, which with desire,
Inclinable now grown to touch or taste,
Solicited her longing eye;[5] yet first
Pausing a while, thus to herself she mused:
745   "Great are thy virtues,° doubtless, best of fruits,
Though kept from man, and worthy to be admired,
Whose taste, too long forborne, at first assay°
Gave elocution to the mute, and taught
The tongue not made for speech to speak thy praise:
750 Thy praise he also who forbids thy use,
Conceals not from us, naming thee the Tree
Of Knowledge, knowledge both of good and evil;
Forbids us then to taste, but his forbidding
Commends thee more, while it infers° the good
755 By thee communicated, and our want:°
For good unknown, sure is not had, or had
And yet unknown, is as not had at all,
In plain° then, what forbids he but to know,
Forbids us good, forbids us to be wise?
760 Such prohibitions bind not. But if death
Bind us with after-bands,° what profits then

participating — *partaking of*
all — *produce all*
import — *prove*
virtues — *powers*
assay — *try*
infers — *implies*
want — *lack*
plain — *in plain words*
after-bands — *later bonds*

Handwritten annotations:
death = advancement
They will advance to gods. If Eve improves she will be better than Adam. The flaw is that he never died.

She is trying to sound like a philosopher, but she is just getting confused. Why would the tree be there if they weren't meant to eat. She sees what she thinks happened to the snake. She is starting to see god like satan. God is mean. He doesn't want them to succeed.

3. Hereafter, Satan speaks of "gods," not God.
4. Both "human" and "gracious" or "kindly."
5. All Eve's senses—sight, hearing, smell, taste, and touch—are solicited by the fruit.

Our inward freedom? In the day we eat
Of this fair fruit, our doom is, we shall die.
How dies the serpent? He hath eat'n and lives,
765 And knows, and speaks, and reasons, and discerns,
Irrational till then. For us alone
Was death invented? Or to us denied
This intellectual food, for beasts reserved?
For beasts it seems: yet that one beast which first
770 Hath tasted, envies° not, but brings with joy
The good befall'n him, author unsuspect,[6]
Friendly to man, far from deceit or guile.
What fear I then, rather what know to fear
Under this ignorance of good and evil,
775 Of God or death, of law or penalty?
Here grows the cure of all, this fruit divine,
Fair to the eye, inviting to the taste,
Of virtue° to make wise: what hinders then   *power*
To reach, and feed at once both body and mind?"
780   So saying, her rash hand in evil hour
Forth reaching to the fruit, she plucked, she eat.[7]
Earth felt the wound, and nature from her seat
Sighing through all her works gave signs of woe,
That all was lost. Back to the thicket slunk
785 The guilty serpent, and well might, for Eve
Intent now wholly on her taste, naught else
Regarded, such delight till then, as seemed,
In fruit she never tasted, whether true
Or fancied so, through expectation high
790 Of knowledge, nor was Godhead from her thought.
Greedily she engorged without restraint,
And knew not eating death:[8] satiate at length,
And heightened as with wine, jocund° and boon,°   *merry/jolly*
Thus to herself she pleasingly began:
795   "O sovran, virtuous, precious of all trees
In Paradise, of operation blest
To sapience, hitherto obscured, infamed,[9]
And thy fair fruit let hang, as to no end
Created; but henceforth my early care,
800 Not without song, each morning, and due praise
Shall tend thee, and the fertile burden ease
Of thy full branches offered free to all;
Till dieted by thee I grow mature
In knowledge, as the gods who all things know;
805 Though others envy what they cannot give;
For had the gift been theirs,[1] it had not here
Thus grown. Experience, next to thee I owe,
Best guide; not following thee, I had remained

[handwritten marginalia: She is convincing herself to do this, she thinks god is not good & they don't need to listen / begrudges]

[handwritten marginalia: the fall]

[handwritten marginalia: pathetic fallacy: nature reflects our mood. as she falls, nature responds.]

[handwritten marginalia: the snake feels guilty]

[handwritten marginalia: she becomes drunk.]

---

6. An authority or informant beyond suspicion.
7. Ate: an accepted past tense, pronounced *et*.
8. I.e., she is eating death and doesn't know it, or
experience it yet, but also, punning, death is eating
her too.

9. Slandered. "Sapience": both knowledge and
tasting (Latin, *sapere*).
1. Like Satan, Eve now conflates gods and God,
ascribing envy but also lack of power to "them."

In ignorance, thou open'st wisdom's way,
810 And giv'st accéss, though secret° she retire.   *hidden*
And I perhaps am secret° Heav'n is high,   *unseen*
High and remote to see from thence distinct
Each thing on earth; and other care perhaps
May have diverted from continual watch
815 Our great Forbidder, safe with all his spies
About him. But to Adam in what sort°   *guise*
Shall I appear? shall I to him make known
As yet my change, and give him to partake
Full happiness with me, or rather not,
820 But keep the odds° of knowledge in my power   *advantage*
Without copartner? so to add what wants°   *lacks*
In female sex, the more to draw his love,
And render me more equal, and perhaps,
A thing not undesirable, sometime
825 Superior; for inferior who is free?[2]
This may be well: but what if God have seen,
And death ensue? Then I shall be no more,
And Adam wedded to another Eve,
Shall live with her enjoying, I extinct;
830 A death to think. Confirmed then I resolve,
Adam shall share with me in bliss or woe:
So dear I love him, that with him all deaths
I could endure, without him live no life."
    So saying, from the tree her step she turned,
835 But first low reverence done, as to the power
That dwelt within,[3] whose presence had infused
Into the plant sciential° sap, derived   *knowledge-producing*
From nectar, drink of gods. Adam the while
Waiting desirous her return, had wove
840 Of choicest flow'rs a garland to adorn
Her tresses, and her rural labors crown,
As reapers oft are wont their harvest queen.
Great joy he promised to his thoughts, and new
Solace in her return, so long delayed;
845 Yet oft his heart, divine of° something ill,   *foreboding*
Misgave him; he the falt'ring measure° felt;   *heartbeat*
And forth to meet her went, the way she took
That morn when first they parted; by the Tree
Of Knowledge he must pass; there he her met,
850 Scarce from the tree returning; in her hand
A bough of fairest fruit that downy smiled,
New gathered, and ambrosial smell diffused.
To him she hasted, in her face excuse
Came prologue,[4] and apology to prompt,
855 Which with bland° words at will she thus addressed.   *mild, coaxing*
    "Hast thou not wondered, Adam, at my stay?
Thee I have missed, and thought it long, deprived

2. Cf. Satan, 1.248–63, 5.790–97.
3. Eve ends with idolatry, worship of the tree.
4. I.e., excuse came like the prologue in a play,
and apology (justification, self-defense) served as
prompter.

Thy presence, agony of love till now
Not felt, nor shall be twice, for never more
860 Mean I to try, what rash untried I sought,
The pain of absence from thy sight. But strange
Hath been the cause, and wonderful to hear:
This tree is not as we are told, a tree
Of danger tasted,° nor to evil unknown   *if tasted*
865 Op'ning the way, but of divine effect
To open eyes, and make them gods who taste;
And hath been tasted such: the serpent wise,
Or° not restrained as we, or not obeying,   *either*
Hath eaten of the fruit, and is become,
870 Not dead, as we are threatened, but thenceforth
Endued with human voice and human sense,
Reasoning to admiration,° and with me   *cause wonder*
Persuasively° hath so prevailed, that I   *by persuasion*
Have also tasted, and have also found
875 Th' effects to correspond, opener mine eyes,
Dim erst,° dilated spirits, ampler heart,   *before*
And growing up to godhead; which for thee
Chiefly I sought, without thee can despise.
For bliss, as thou hast part, to me is bliss,
880 Tedious, unshared with thee, and odious soon.
Thou therefore also taste, that equal lot
May join us, equal joy, as equal love;
Lest thou not tasting, different degree°   *rank*
Disjoin us, and I then too late renounce
885 Deity for thee, when fate will not permit."[5]
    Thus Eve with count'nance blithe her story told;
But in her cheek distemper[6] flushing glowed.
On th' other side, Adam, soon as he heard
The fatal trespass done by Eve, amazed,°   *stunned*
890 Astonied° stood and blank, while horror chill   *petrified*
Ran through his veins, and all his joints relaxed;
From his slack hand the garland wreathed for Eve
Down dropped, and all the faded roses shed:
Speechless he stood and pale, till thus at length
895 First to himself he inward silence broke:
    "O fairest of creation, last and best
Of all God's works, creature in whom excelled
Whatever can to sight or thought be formed,
Holy, divine, good, amiable, or sweet!
900 How art thou lost, how on a sudden lost,
Defaced, deflow'red, and now to death devote?°   *doomed*
Rather how hast thou yielded to transgress
The strict forbiddance, how to violate
The sacred° fruit forbidd'n! some cursèd fraud   *consecrated*
905 Of enemy hath beguiled thee, yet unknown,
And me with thee hath ruined, for with thee

---

5. Compare Eve in soliloquy, lines 817–31.
6. I.e., disorder arising from disturbance of the balance of humors in the body, intoxication.

Certain my resolution is to die; *he will die w/ her*
How can I live without thee, how forgo *b/c he loves her*
Thy sweet converse and love so dearly joined,
910 To live again in these wild woods forlorn?
Should God create another Eve, and I
Another rib afford, yet loss of thee
Would never from my heart; no no, I feel
The link of nature draw me: flesh of flesh, *wedding vows.*
915 Bone of my bone thou art,[7] and from thy state *he eats the fruit*
Mine never shall be parted, bliss or woe." *for a different*
  So having said, as one from sad dismay *reason.*
Recomforted, and after thoughts disturbed *she is motivated*
Submitting to what seemed remédiless, *by power & he*
920 Thus in calm mood his words to Eve he turned: *by love.*
  "Bold deed thou hast presumed, advent'rous Eve,
And peril great provoked, who thus hast dared
Had it been only coveting to eye
That sacred fruit, sacred° to abstinence,   *set apart*
925 Much more to taste it under ban to touch.
But past who can recall, or done undo?
Not God omnipotent, nor fate; yet so
Perhaps thou shalt not die, perhaps the fact°   *deed*
Is not so heinous now, foretasted fruit,
930 Profaned first by the serpent, by him first
Made common and unhallowed ere our taste;
Nor yet on him found deadly, he yet lives,
Lives, as thou saidst, and gains to live as man
Higher degree of life, inducement strong
935 To us, as likely tasting to attain
Proportional ascent, which cannot be
But to be gods, or angels demi-gods.
Nor can I think that God, Creator wise,
Though threat'ning, will in earnest so destroy
940 Us his prime creatures, dignified so high,
Set over all his works, which in our fall,
For us created, needs with us must fail,
Dependent made; so God shall uncreate,
Be frustrate, do, undo, and labor lose,
945 Not well conceived of God, who though his power
Creation could repeat, yet would be loath
Us to abolish, lest the Adversary°   *Satan*
Triumph and say; 'Fickle their state whom God
Most favors, who can please him long? Me first
950 He ruined, now mankind; whom will he next?'
Matter of scorn, not to be given the Foe.
However I with thee have fixed my lot,
Certain° to undergo like doom; if death   *resolved*
Consort° with thee, death is to me as life;   *associate*
955 So forcible within my heart I feel
The bond of nature draw me to my own,

7. Adam echoes Genesis 2.23–24.

My own in thee, for what thou art is mine;
Our state cannot be severed, we are one,
One flesh; to lose thee were to lose myself."
960   So Adam, and thus Eve to him replied:
"O glorious trial of exceeding[8] love,
Illustrious evidence, example high!
Engaging me to emulate, but short
Of thy perfection, how shall I attain,
965   Adam, from whose dear side I boast me sprung,
And gladly of our union hear thee speak,
One heart, one soul in both; whereof good proof
This day affords, declaring thee resolved,
Rather than death or aught° than death more dread   anything other
970   Shall separate us, linked in love so dear,
To undergo with me one guilt, one crime,
If any be, of tasting this fair fruit,
Whose virtue,° for of good still good proceeds,   power
Direct, or by occasion° hath presented   indirectly
975   This happy trial of thy love, which else
So eminently never had been known.
Were it° I thought death menaced would ensue°   if/result from
This my attempt, I would sustain alone
The worst, and not persuade thee, rather die
980   Deserted, than oblige° thee with a fact°   bind/deed
Pernicious to thy peace, chiefly assured
Remarkably so late of thy so true,
So faithful love unequaled;[9] but I feel
Far otherwise th' event,° not death, but life   result
985   Augmented, opened eyes, new hopes, new joys,
Taste so divine, that what of sweet before
Hath touched my sense, flat seems to this, and harsh.
On my experience, Adam, freely taste,
And fear of death deliver to the winds."
990   So saying, she embraced him, and for joy
Tenderly wept, much won that he his love
Had so ennobled, as of choice to incur
Divine displeasure for her sake, or death.
In recompense (for such compliance bad
995   Such recompense best merits) from the bough
She gave him of that fair enticing fruit
With liberal hand: he scrupled not to eat
Against his better knowledge, not deceived,[1]
But fondly° overcome with female charm.   foolishly
1000   Earth trembled from her entrails, as again
In pangs, and nature gave a second groan;
Sky loured, and muttering thunder, some sad drops
Wept at completing of the mortal sin
Original;[2] while Adam took no thought,

---

8. The word, which Eve intends as praise, carries the implication of "excessive."
9. I.e., since I have so recently been assured of your unparalleled love.
1. Cf. 1 Timothy 2.14: "And Adam was not deceived, but the woman being deceived was in the transgression."
2. The theological doctrine that all Adam's descendants are stained by Adam's sin, and are thereby subject to physical death and (unless saved by grace) to damnation.

1005 Eating his fill, nor Eve to iterate°   *repeat*
Her former trespass feared, the more to soothe
Him with her loved society, that now
As with new wine intoxicated both
They swim in mirth, and fancy that they feel
1010 Divinity within them breeding wings
Wherewith to scorn the earth: but that false fruit
Far other operation first displayed,
Carnal desire inflaming, he on Eve
Began to cast lascivious eyes, she him
1015 As wantonly repaid; in lust they burn:
Till Adam thus 'gan Eve to dalliance move:
    "Eve, now I see thou art exact of taste,
And elegant, of sapience³ no small part,
Since to each meaning savor we apply,
1020 And palate call judicious; I the praise
Yield thee, so well this day thou hast purveyed.°   *provided*
Much pleasure we have lost, while we abstained
From this delightful fruit, nor known till now
True relish, tasting; if such pleasure be
1025 In things to us forbidden, it might be wished,
For this one tree had been forbidden ten.
But come, so well refreshed, now let us play,
As meet° is, after such delicious fare;   *appropriate*
For never did thy beauty since the day
1030 I saw thee first and wedded thee, adorned
With all perfections, so inflame my sense
With ardor to enjoy thee, fairer now
Than ever, bounty of this virtuous tree."
    So said he, and forbore not glance or toy°   *caress*
1035 Of amorous intent, well understood
Of° Eve, whose eye darted contagious fire.   *by*
Her hand he seized, and to a shady bank,
Thick overhead with verdant roof embow'red
He led her nothing loath; flow'rs were the couch,
1040 Pansies, and violets, and asphodel,
And hyacinth, earth's freshest softest lap.
There they their fill of love and love's disport
Took largely, of their mutual guilt the seal,
The solace of their sin, till dewy sleep
1045 Oppressed them, wearied with their amorous play.
Soon as the force of that fallacious fruit,
That with exhilarating vapor bland°   *pleasing*
About their spirits had played, and inmost powers
Made err, was now exhaled, and grosser sleep
1050 Bred of unkindly° fumes,° with conscious dreams   *unnatural / vapors*
Encumbered,° now had left them, up they rose   *oppressed*
As from unrest, and each the other viewing,
Soon found their eyes how opened, and their minds
How darkened; innocence, that as a veil

---

3. Adam commends Eve for her fine ("exact") and discriminating ("elegant") taste, as a part of "sapience," which means both "taste" and "wisdom."

1055   Had shadowed them from knowing ill, was gone,
        Just confidence, and native righteousness,
        And honor from about them, naked left
        To guilty shame: he° covered, but his robe   *shame*
        Uncovered more. So rose the Danite strong
1060   Hercúlean Samson from the harlot-lap
        Of Philistéan Dálilah, and waked
        Shorn of his strength,[4] they destitute and bare
        Of all their virtue: silent, and in face
        Confounded long they sat, as strucken mute,
1065   Till Adam, though not less than Eve abashed,
        At length gave utterance to these words constrained:°   *forced*
            "O Eve, in evil[5] hour thou didst give ear
        To that false worm, of whomsoever taught
        To counterfeit man's voice, true in our fall,
1070   False in our promised rising; since our eyes
        Opened we find indeed, and find we know
        Both good and evil, good lost and evil got,[6]
        Bad fruit of knowledge, if this be to know,
        Which leaves us naked thus, of honor void,
1075   Of innocence, of faith, of purity,
        Our wonted° ornaments now soiled and stained,   *former*
        And in our faces evident the signs
        Of foul concupiscence;[7] whence evil store;
        Even shame, the last of evils; of the first
1080   Be sure then. How shall I behold the face
        Henceforth of God or angel, erst with joy
        And rapture so oft beheld? Those heav'nly shapes
        Will dazzle now this earthly, with their blaze
        Insufferably bright. O might I here
1085   In solitude live savage, in some glade
        Obscured, where highest woods impenetrable
        To star or sunlight, spread their umbrage° broad,   *shadow, foliage*
        And brown as evening: cover me ye pines,
        Ye cedars, with innumerable boughs
1090   Hide me, where I may never see them more.
        But let us now, as in bad plight, devise
        What best may for the present serve to hide
        The parts of each from other, that seem most
        To shame obnoxious,° and unseemliest seen,   *exposed*
1095   Some tree whose broad smooth leaves together sewed,
        And girded on our loins, may cover round
        Those middle parts, that this newcomer, shame,
        There sit not, and reproach us as unclean."
            So counseled he, and both together went

---

4. Samson, of the tribe of Dan, told the "harlot"
Philistine Delilah that the secret of his strength
(like that of Hercules) lay in his hair; she sheared
it off while he slept, and when he awoke he was
easily captured and blinded by his enemies.
5. Adam's bitter pun—Eve, evil—repudiates the
actual etymology of Eve, "life," which Adam will
later reaffirm (11.159–61).

6. Milton, like most commentators, derives the
tree's name from the event (4.222, 11.84–89).
7. The theological term for the unruly human passions and desires seen as one effect of the Fall, a
sign of abundance ("store") of evils. If "shame" is
the "last" evil, the "first" is probably the guiltiness
that produces it, according to Milton's *Christian
Doctrine* (1.12).

1100 Into the thickest wood, there soon they chose
The fig tree,[8] not that kind for fruit renowned,
But such as at this day to Indians known
In Malabar or Deccan spreads her arms
Branching so broad and long, that in the ground
1105 The bended twigs take root, and daughters grow
About the mother tree, a pillared shade
High overarched, and echoing walks between;
There oft the Indian herdsman shunning heat
Shelters in cool, and tends his pasturing herds
1110 At loopholes cut through thickest shade: those leaves
They gathered, broad as Amazonian targe,°   *shields*
And with what skill they had, together sewed,
To gird their waist, vain covering if to hide
Their guilt and dreaded shame. O how unlike
1115 To that first naked glory. Such of late
Columbus found th' American so girt
With feathered cincture,° naked else and wild,   *belt*
Among the trees on isles and woody shores.
Thus fenced, and as they thought, their shame in part
1120 Covered, but not at rest or ease of mind,
They sat them down to weep, nor only tears
Rained at their eyes, but high winds worse within
Began to rise, high passions, anger, hate,
Mistrust, suspicion, discord, and shook sore
1125 Their inward state of mind, calm region once
And full of peace, now tossed and turbulent:
For understanding ruled not, and the will
Heard not her lore, both in subjection now
To sensual appetite, who from beneath
1130 Usurping over sovran reason claimed
Superior sway: from thus distempered breast,[9]
Adam, estranged° in look and altered style,   *unlike himself*
Speech intermitted thus to Eve renewed:
        "Would thou hadst hearkened to my words, and stayed
1135 With me, as I besought thee, when that strange
Desire of wand'ring this unhappy morn,
I know not whence possessed thee; we had then
Remained still happy, not as now, despoiled
Of all our good, shamed, naked, miserable.
1140 Let none henceforth seek needless cause to approve°   *prove*
The faith they owe; when earnestly they seek
Such proof, conclude, they then begin to fail."
        To whom soon moved with touch of blame thus Eve:
"What words have passed thy lips, Adam severe,
1145 Imput'st thou that to my default, or will
Of wand'ring, as thou call'st it, which who knows
But might as ill have happened thou being by,

[handwritten margin note: he is beginning to berate Eve. He is blaming her for their state.]

---

8. The banyan, or Indian fig, has small leaves, but the account Milton draws on from Gerard's *Herbal* (1597) contains the details of lines 1104–11; "Malabar" and "Deccan" are in southern India.

9. The immediate psychological effects of the Fall are evident in the subjection of reason to the lower faculties of sensual appetite.

Or to thyself perhaps: hadst thou been there,
Or here th' attempt, thou couldst not have discerned
1150 Fraud in the serpent, speaking as he spake;
No ground of enmity between us known,
Why he should mean me ill, or seek to harm.
Was I to have never parted from thy side?
As good have grown there still a lifeless rib.
1155 Being as I am, why didst not thou the head
Command me absolutely not to go,
Going into such danger as thou saidst?
Too facile° then thou didst not much gainsay,   easy, mild
Nay didst permit, approve, and fair dismiss.
1160 Hadst thou been firm and fixed in thy dissent,
Neither had I transgressed, nor thou with me."
    To whom then first incensed Adam replied.
"Is this the love, is this the recompense
Of mine to thee, ingrateful Eve, expressed°   demonstrated
1165 Immutable when thou wert lost, not I,
Who might have lived and joyed immortal bliss,
Yet willingly chose rather death with thee:
And am I now upbraided, as the cause
Of thy transgressing? not enough severe,
1170 It seems, in thy restraint: what could I more?
I warned thee, I admonished thee, foretold
The danger, and the lurking enemy
That lay in wait; beyond this had been force,
And force upon free will hath here no place.
1175 But confidence then bore thee on, secure°   self-assured
Either to meet no danger, or to find
Matter of glorious trial; and perhaps
I also erred in overmuch admiring
What seemed in thee so perfect, that I thought
1180 No evil durst attempt thee, but I rue
That error now, which is become my crime,
And thou th' accuser. Thus it shall befall
Him who to worth in women overtrusting
Lets her will rule; restraint she will not brook,°   accept
1185 And left to herself, if evil thence ensue,
She first his weak indulgence will accuse."
    Thus they in mutual accusation spent
The fruitless hours, but neither self-condemning,
And of their vain contést appeared no end.

Book 10

Meanwhile the heinous and despiteful act
Of Satan done in Paradise, and how
He in the serpent had perverted Eve,
Her husband she, to taste the fatal fruit,
5 Was known in Heav'n; for what can scape the eye

Of God all-seeing, or deceive his heart
Omniscient, who in all things wise and just,
Hindered not Satan to attempt the mind
Of man, with strength entire,° and free will armed,   *fully equipped*
10 Complete to have discovered and repulsed
Whatever wiles of foe or seeming friend.
For still they knew, and ought to have still° remembered   *always*
The high injunction not to taste that fruit,
Whoever tempted; which they not obeying,
15 Incurred, what could they less, the penalty,
And manifold in sin, deserved to fall.
Up into Heav'n from Paradise in haste
Th' angelic guards ascended, mute and sad
For man, for of his state by this° they knew,   *this time*
20 Much wond'ring how the subtle Fiend had stol'n
Entrance unseen. Soon as th' unwelcome news
From earth arrived at Heaven gate, displeased
All were who heard, dim sadness did not spare
That time celestial visages, yet mixed
25 With pity, violated not their bliss.
About the new-arrived, in multitudes
Th' ethereal people ran, to hear and know
How all befell: they[1] towards the throne supreme
Accountable made haste to make appear
30 With righteous plea, their utmost vigilance,
And easily approved; when the Most High
Eternal Father from his secret cloud,
Amidst in thunder uttered thus his voice:
    "Assembled Angels, and ye Powers returned
35 From unsuccessful charge, be not dismayed,
Nor troubled at these tidings from the earth,
Which your sincerest care could not prevent,
Foretold so lately what would come to pass,
When first this tempter crossed the gulf from Hell.
40 I told ye then he should prevail and speed°   *succeed*
On his bad errand, man should be seduced
And flattered out of all, believing lies
Against his Maker; no decree of mine
Concurring to necessitate his fall,
45 Or touch with lightest moment[2] of impulse
His free will, to her own inclining left
In even scale. But fall'n he is, and now
What rests,° but that the mortal sentence pass   *remains*
On his transgression, death denounced that day,
50 Which he presumes already vain and void,
Because not yet inflicted, as he feared,
By some immediate stroke; but soon shall find
Forbearance no acquittance ere day end.[3]

1. The angels, "accountable" for guarding Eden, rush to God's throne to explain that they had exercised "utmost vigilance"; their plea is readily accepted ("easily approved," line 31).

2. The smallest weight that would tip the scales.
3. A proverb: "Abstinence from enforcing a debt is not release from it." Next line: My justice must not be scorned as my generosity has been.

Justice shall not return as bounty scorned.
55 But whom send I to judge them? Whom but thee
Vicegerent Son, to thee I have transferred
All judgment, whether in Heav'n, or earth, or Hell.[4]
Easy it may be seen that I intend
Mercy colleague with justice, sending thee
60 Man's friend, his mediator, his designed
Both ransom and redeemer voluntary,
And destined man himself to judge man fall'n."
    So spake the Father, and unfolding bright
Toward the right hand his glory, on the Son
65 Blazed forth unclouded deity; he full
Resplendent all his Father manifest
Expressed, and thus divinely answered mild:
    "Father Eternal, thine is to decree,
Mine both in Heav'n and earth to do thy will
70 Supreme, that thou in me thy Son beloved
May'st ever rest well pleased. I go to judge
On earth these thy transgressors; but thou know'st,
Whoever judged, the worst on me must light,
When time shall be, for so I undertook
75 Before thee; and not repenting, this obtain
Of right, that I may mitigate their doom
On me derived,° yet I shall temper so   *diverted*
Justice with mercy, as may illustrate most°   *best show*
Them fully satisfied, and thee appease.
80 Attendance none shall need, nor train,° where none   *attendants*
Are to behold the judgment, but the judged,
Those two; the third best absent is condemned,
Convict° by flight, and rebel to all law: *proved guilty*
Conviction to the serpent none belongs."
85   Thus saying, from his radiant seat he rose
Of high collateral° glory: him Thrones and Powers,   *placed side by side*
Princedoms, and Dominations ministrant
Accompanied to Heaven gate, from whence
Eden and all the coast° in prospect lay.   *region*
90 Down he descended straight; the speed of gods
Time counts not,[5] though with swiftest minutes winged.
Now was the sun in western cadence° low   *falling*
From noon, and gentle airs due at their hour
To fan the earth now waked, and usher in
95 The evening cool, when he from wrath more cool
Came the mild judge and intercessor both
To sentence man: the voice of God they heard
Now walking in the garden, by soft winds
Brought to their ears, while day declined; they heard,
100 And from his presence hid themselves among
The thickest trees, both man and wife, till God
Approaching, thus to Adam called aloud.

4. Cf. John 5.22: "For the Father judgeth no man,   taken much of the morning to travel from heaven
but hath committed all judgment unto the Son."   to earth (8.110–15).
5. The Son's descent is immediate; Raphael had

"Where art thou Adam, wont° with joy to meet   *used before*
My coming seen far off? I miss thee here,
105 Not pleased, thus entertained with solitude,
Where obvious duty erewhile appeared unsought:
Or come I less conspicuous, or what change
Absents thee, or what chance detains? Come forth."
He came, and with him Eve, more loth, though first
110 To offend, discount'nanced both, and discomposed;
Love was not in their looks, either to God
Or to each other, but apparent° guilt,   *easily seen*
And shame, and perturbation, and despair,
Anger, and obstinacy, and hate, and guile.
115 Whence Adam falt'ring long, thus answered brief:
"I heard thee in the garden, and of thy voice
Afraid, being naked, hid myself." To whom
The gracious Judge without revile° replied: *abuse*
"My voice thou oft hast heard, and hast not feared,
120 But still° rejoiced, how is it now become   *always*
So dreadful to thee? That thou art naked, who
Hath told thee? Hast thou eaten of the tree
Whereof I gave thee charge thou shouldst not eat?"
To whom thus Adam sore beset replied.
125 "O Heav'n! in evil strait this day I stand
Before my Judge, either to undergo
Myself the total crime, or to accuse
My other self, the partner of my life;
Whose failing, while her faith to me remains,
130 I should conceal, and not expose to blame
By my complaint; but strict necessity
Subdues me, and calamitous constraint,
Lest on my head both sin and punishment,
However insupportable, be all
135 Devolved;° though should I hold my peace, yet thou   *fallen on*
Wouldst easily detect what I conceal.
This woman whom thou mad'st to be my help,
And gav'st me as thy perfect gift, so good,
So fit, so acceptáble, so divine,
140 That from her hand I could suspect no ill,
And what she did, whatever in itself,
Her doing seemed to justify the deed;
She gave me of the tree, and I did eat."[6]
To whom the Sovran Presence thus replied.
145 "Was she thy God, that her thou didst obey
Before his voice, or was she made thy guide,
Superior, or but equal, that to her
Thou didst resign thy manhood, and the place
Wherein God set thee above her made of thee,
150 And for thee,[7] whose perfection far excelled

6. Compare Adam's speech in Genesis 3.12, and the elements Milton adds of complaint, veiled accusation of God, and self-exculpation; also compare Eve's answer in Genesis and in lines 159–60.

7. Cf. 1 Corinthians 11.8–9: "For the man is not of the woman; but the woman of the man. Neither was the man created for the woman; but the woman for the man."

Hers in all real dignity: adorned
She was indeed, and lovely to attract
Thy love, not thy subjection, and her gifts
Were such as under government well seemed,

155 Unseemly to bear rule, which was thy part
And person,[8] hadst thou known thyself aright."
    So having said, he thus to Eve in few°   *few words*
"Say woman, what is this which thou hast done?"
    To whom sad Eve with shame nigh overwhelmed,

160 Confessing soon, yet not before her judge
Bold or loquacious, thus abashed replied:
"The serpent me beguiled and I did eat."
    Which when the Lord God heard, without delay
To judgment he proceeded on th' accused

165 Serpent though brute, unable to transfer
The guilt on him who made him instrument
Of mischief, and polluted from the end°   *purpose*
Of his creation; justly then accursed,
As vitiated in nature:[9] more to know

170 Concerned not man (since he no further knew)
Nor altered his offense; yet God at last
To Satan first in sin his doom applied,
Though in mysterious terms, judged as then best:
And on the serpent thus his curse let fall.

175   "Because thou hast done this, thou art accursed
Above all cattle, each beast of the field;
Upon thy belly groveling thou shalt go,
And dust shalt eat all the days of thy life.
Between thee and the woman I will put

180 Enmity, and between thine and her seed;
Her seed shall bruise thy head, thou bruise his heel."[1]
    So spake this oracle, then verified
When Jesus son of Mary second Eve,
Saw Satan fall like lightning down from Heav'n,[2]

185 Prince of the air; then rising from his grave
Spoiled principalities and powers, triumphed
In open show, and with ascension bright
Captivity led captive through the air,
The realm itself of Satan long usurped,

190 Whom he shall tread at last under our feet;
Ev'n he who now foretold his fatal bruise,
And to the woman thus his sentence turned.
    "Thy sorrow I will greatly multiply
By thy conception; children thou shalt bring

195 In sorrow forth, and to thy husband's will
Thine shall submit, he over thee shall rule."

---

8. Role and character (persona), as in a drama.
9. The serpent was "unable to transfer" (line 165)
his own guilt in being "polluted" from his proper
end and nature onto Satan, who made him "instrument," so he was "justly . . . accused," but the
terms of that judgment have a "mysterious" (line
173) or hidden meaning that applies to Satan.

1. This is the so-called "protoevangelion" or judgment of Satan that contains at the same time the
promise of the redeemer; Adam and Eve are led to
understand it by degrees.
2. Cf. Christ's comment to his disciples (Luke
10.18: "I beheld Satan as lightning fall from
heaven").

On Adam last thus judgment he pronounced.
"Because thou hast hearkened to the voice of thy wife,
And eaten of the tree concerning which
200 I charged thee, saying: Thou shalt not eat thereof,
Cursed is the ground for thy sake, thou in sorrow
Shalt eat thereof all the days of thy life;
Thorns also and thistles it shall bring thee forth
Unbid, and thou shalt eat th' herb of the field,
205 In the sweat of thy face shalt thou eat bread,
Till thou return unto the ground, for thou
Out of the ground wast taken: know thy birth,
For dust thou art, and shalt to dust return."
    So judged he man, both judge and savior sent,
210 And th' instant stroke of death denounced° that day   *announced*
Removed far off; then pitying how they stood
Before him naked to the air, that now
Must suffer change, disdained not to begin
Thenceforth the form of servant to assume,
215 As when he washed his servants' feet,[3] so now
As father of his family he clad
Their nakedness with skins of beasts, or° slain,   *either*
Or as the snake with youthful coat repaid;
And thought not much° to clothe his enemies: *too much*
220 Nor he their outward only with the skins
Of beasts, but inward nakedness, much more
Opprobrious, with his robe of righteousness,
Arraying covered from his Father's sight.
To him with swift ascent he up returned,
225 Into his blissful bosom reassumed
In glory as of old, to him appeased
All, though all-knowing, what had passed with man
Recounted, mixing intercession sweet.
Meanwhile ere thus was sinned and judged on earth,
230 Within the gates of Hell sat Sin and Death,
In counterview within the gates, that now
Stood open wide, belching outrageous° flame   *unrestrained*
Far into Chaos, since the fiend passed through,
Sin opening, who thus now to Death began:
235   "O son, why sit we here each other viewing
Idly, while Satan our great author° thrives   *father*
In other worlds, and happier seat provides
For us his offspring dear? It cannot be,
But that success attends him; if mishap,
240 Ere this he had returned, with fury driv'n
By his avengers, since no place like° this   *as well as*
Can fit his punishment, or their revenge.
Methinks I feel new strength within me rise,
Wings growing, and dominion giv'n me large
245 Beyond this deep; whatever draws me on,

---

3. Cf. Philamon 2.7: "[Christ] . . . took upon him the form of a servant"; John 13.5: "He poureth water into a basin, and began to wash the disciples' feet."

Or sympathy,[4] or some connatural force
Powerful at greatest distance to unite
With secret amity things of like kind
By secretest conveyance. Thou my shade
250 Inseparable must with me along:
For Death from Sin no power can separate.
But lest the difficulty of passing back
Stay his return perhaps over this gulf
Impassable, impervious,° let us try   impenetrable
255 Advent'rous work, yet to thy power and mine
Not unagreeable, to found° a path   establish
Over this main from Hell to that new world
Where Satan now prevails, a monument
Of merit high to all th' infernal host,
260 Easing their passage hence, for intercourse,°   passing back and forth
Or transmigration,° as their lot shall lead.   emigration
Nor can I miss the way, so strongly drawn
By this new-felt attraction and instínct."
     Whom thus the meager° shadow answered soon: emaciated
265 "Go whither fate and inclination strong
Leads thee, I shall not lag behind, nor err
The way, thou leading, such a scent I draw
Of carnage, prey innumerable, and taste
The savor of death from all things there that live:
270 Nor shall I to the work thou enterprisest
Be wanting, but afford thee equal aid."
     So saying, with delight he snuffed the smell
Of mortal change on earth. As when a flock
Of ravenous fowl, though many a league remote,
275 Against° the day of battle, to a field,   anticipating
Where armies lie encamped, come flying, lured
With scent of living carcasses designed°   marked out
For death, the following day, in bloody fight.
So scented the grim feature,° and upturned   form, shape
280 His nostril wide into the murky air,
Sagacious° of his quarry from so far.   keenly smelling, wise
Then both from out Hell gates into the waste
Wide anarchy of Chaos damp and dark
Flew diverse,° and with power (their power was great)   in different directions
285 Hovering upon the water, what they met
Solid or slimy, as in raging sea
Tossed up and down, together crowded drive
From each side shoaling° towards the mouth of Hell.   assembling
As when two polar winds blowing adverse
290 Upon the Cronian Sea,[5] together drive
Mountains of ice, that stop th' imagined way
Beyond Petsora eastward, to the rich
Cathaian coast. The aggregated soil

---

4. Sin feels an attraction ("sympathy") drawing
two things together, or an innate ("connatural")
force, linking her to Satan.
5. The Arctic Ocean; the "imagined way" (lines

291–93) is the northeast passage to North China
("Cathay") from Pechora ("Petsora"), a river in
Siberia, which Henry Hudson could only imagine
(in 1608) because it was blocked with ice.

Death with his mace petrific,[6] cold and dry,
295 As with a trident smote, and fixed as firm
As Delos floating once; the rest his look
Bound with Gorgonian rigor[7] not to move,
And with asphaltic slime;° broad as the gate,   *pitch*
Deep to the roots of Hell the gathered beach
300 They fastened, and the mole° immense wrought on   *pier*
Over the foaming deep high-arched, a bridge
Of length prodigious joining to the wall°   *outer shell*
Immovable of this now fenceless world
Forfeit to Death; from hence a passage broad,
305 Smooth, easy, inoffensive° down to Hell.   *free from obstacle*
So, if great things to small may be compared,
Xerxes,[8] the liberty of Greece to yoke,
From Susa his Memnonian palace high
Came to the sea, and over Hellespont
310 Bridging his way, Europe with Asia joined,
And scourged with many a stroke th' indignant waves.
Now had they brought the work by wondrous art
Pontifical,[9] a ridge of pendent rock
Over the vexed° abyss, following the track   *stormy*
315 Of Satan, to the selfsame place where he
First lighted from his wing, and landed safe
From out of Chaos to the outside bare
Of this round world: with pins of adamant
And chains they made all fast, too fast they made
320 And durable; and now in little space
The confines° met of empyrean Heav'n   *boundaries*
And of this world, and on the left hand Hell
With long reach interposed; three sev'ral ways
In sight, to each of these three places led.[1]
325 And now their way to earth they had descried,
To Paradise first tending, when behold
Satan in likeness of an angel bright
Betwixt the Centaur and the Scorpion[2] steering
His zenith, while the sun in Aries rose:
330 Disguised he came, but those his children dear
Their parent soon discerned, though in disguise.
He, after Eve seduced, unminded° slunk   *unnoticed*
Into the wood fast by, and changing shape
To observe the sequel, saw his guileful act
335 By Eve, though all unweeting,° seconded   *unaware*
Upon her husband, saw their shame that sought
Vain covertures;° but when he saw descend   *garments*

6. Turning things to stone. Death's materials are the "cold and dry" elements; his mace is associated with Neptune's "trident," which was said to have "fixed" the floating Greek island of Delos.
7. Anything the Gorgon Medusa looked upon turned to stone.
8. The Persian king Xerxes ordered the sea whipped when it destroyed the bridge of ships he built over the Hellespont (linking Europe and Asia) so as to invade Greece. "Susa": Xerxes' winter residence, founded by the mythical Prince Memnon.
9. Bridge-building, with a pun on "papal" (the Pope had the title "pontifex maximus").
1. The golden staircase or chain linking the universe to Heaven, the new bridge linking it to Hell, and the passage through the spheres down to earth.
2. Satan steered between Sagittarius (the Centaur) and Scorpio, thereby passing through Anguis, the constellation of the Serpent.

The Son of God to judge them, terrified
He fled, not hoping to escape, but shun
340 The present, fearing guilty what his wrath
Might suddenly inflict; that past, returned
By night, and list'ning where the hapless pair
Sat in their sad discourse, and various plaint,
Thence gathered his own doom, which understood
345 Not instant, but of future time.[3] With joy
And tidings fraught, to Hell he now returned,
And at the brink of Chaos, near the foot
Of this new wondrous pontifice,° unhoped   bridge
Met who to meet him came, his offspring dear.
350 Great joy was at their meeting, and at sight
Of that stupendous bridge his joy increased.
Long he admiring stood, till Sin, his fair
Enchanting daughter, thus the silence broken:
    "O Parent, these are thy magnific deeds,
355 Thy trophies,[4] which thou view'st as not thine own,
Thou art their author and prime architect:
For I no sooner in my heart divined,
My heart, which by a secret harmony
Still moves with thine, joined in connection sweet,
360 That thou on earth hadst prospered, which thy looks
Now also evidence, but straight I felt
Though distant from thee worlds between, yet felt
That I must after thee with this thy son;
Such fatal consequence[5] unites us three:
365 Hell could no longer hold us in her bounds,
Nor this unvoyageable gulf obscure
Detain from following thy illustrious track.
Thou hast achieved our liberty, confined
Within Hell gates till now, thou us empow'red
370 To fortify thus far, and overlay
With this portentous° bridge the dark abyss.   marvelous, ominous
Thine now is all this world, thy virtue° hath won   power, courage
What thy hands builded not, thy wisdom gained
With odds° what war hath lost, and fully avenged   advantage
375 Our foil in Heav'n; here thou shalt monarch reign,
There didst not; there let him still victor sway,
As battle hath adjudged, from this new world
Retiring, by his own doom alienated,
And henceforth monarchy with thee divide
380 Of all things parted by th' empyreal bounds,
His quadrature,[6] from thy orbicular world,
Or try thee now more dangerous to his throne."
    Whom thus the Prince of Darkness answered glad:

3. This evidently refers to the plaints and discourse of Adam and Eve (lines 720–1104), which
therefore precede Satan's return to Hell (lines
345–609).
4. Objects or persons captured in battle were displayed in the Triumphs accorded Roman generals
and emperors who had won a great military victory;
the term casts Satan's conquests in Eden in such

terms.
5. Connection of cause and effect.
6. Revelation 21.16 describes the City of God as
"four-square, and the length is as large as the
breadth"; Satan's new conquest, earth, is an orb.
Sin may imply its superiority (being a sphere).
"Try": discover by experience.

"Fair daughter, and thou son and grandchild both,
385 High proof ye now have giv'n to be the race
Of Satan (for I glory in the name,
Antagonist⁷ of Heav'n's Almighty King)
Amply have merited of me, of all
Th' infernal empire, that so near Heav'n's door
390 Triumphal with triumphal act⁸ have met,
Mine with this glorious work, and made one realm
Hell and this world, one realm, one continent
Of easy thoroughfare. Therefore while I
Descend through darkness, on your road with ease
395 To my associate powers, them to acquaint
With these successes, and with them rejoice,
You two this way, among those numerous orbs
All yours, right down to Paradise descend;
There dwell and reign in bliss, thence on the earth
400 Dominion exercise and in the air,
Chiefly on man, sole lord of all declared,
Him first make sure your thrall, and lastly kill.
My substitutes I send ye, and create
Plenipotent° on earth, of matchless might   *with full power*
405 Issuing from me: on your joint vigor now
My hold of this new kingdom all depends,
Through Sin to Death exposed by my exploit.
If your joint power prevail, th' affairs of Hell
No detriment need fear, go and be strong."
410   So saying he dismissed them, they with speed
Their course through thickest constellations held
Spreading their bane;° the blasted° stars looked wan,   *poison / ruined*
And planets, planet-strook,⁹ real eclipse
Then suffered. Th' other way Satan went down
415 The causey° to Hell gate; on either side   *causeway*
Disparted Chaos over-built exclaimed,
And with rebounding surge the bars assailed,
That scorned his indignation.¹ Through the gate,
Wide open and unguarded, Satan passed,
420 And all about found desolate; for those²
Appointed to sit there, had left their charge,
Flown to the upper world; the rest were all
Far to the inland retired, about the walls
Of Pandemonium, city and proud seat
425 Of Lucifer, so by allusion° called,   *metaphor*
Of that bright star³ to Satan paragoned.
There kept their watch the legions, while the grand⁴
In council sat, solicitous° what chance   *anxious*

7. The name "Satan" means "adversary" or "antagonist."
8. The repeated word emphasizes that Satan is
enacting a Triumph, passing over a triumphal
bridge rather than through triumphal arches; the
scene would likely evoke the "Roman" Triumph
and triumphal arches celebrating the Restoration
of Charles II.
9. Suffering not merely a temporary eclipse but a
real loss of light, as from the malign influence of

an adverse planet.
1. Chaos is the instinctive enemy of all order, so
hostile to the bridge built over it.
2. Sin and Death.
3. Satan before his fall was Lucifer, the Light-
bringer, and the Morning Star is named Lucifer
because it is compared ("paragoned") to him.
4. The "grand infernal peers" who govern (cf.
2.507).

Might intercept their emperor sent, so he
430 Departing gave command, and they observed.
As when the Tartar⁵ from his Russian foe
By Astracan over the snowy plains
Retires, or Bactrian Sophi from the horns
Of Turkish crescent, leaves all waste beyond
435 The realm of Aladule, in his retreat
To Tauris or Casbeen: so these the late
Heav'n-banished host, left desert utmost Hell
Many a dark league, reduced° in careful watch   *drawn together*
Round their metropolis, and now expecting
440 Each hour their great adventurer from the search
Of foreign worlds: he through the midst unmarked,°   *unnoticed*
In show plebeian angel militant
Of lowest order,° passed; and from the door   *private*
Of that Plutonian⁶ hall, invisible
445 Ascended his high throne, which under state°   *canopy*
Of richest texture spread, at th' upper end
Was placed in regal luster. Down a while
He sat, and round about him saw unseen:
At last as from a cloud his fulgent head
450 And shape star-bright appeared, or brighter, clad
With what permissive° glory since his fall   *permitted*
Was left him, or false glitter: all amazed
At that so sudden blaze the Stygian⁷ throng
Bent their aspéct, and whom they wished beheld,
455 Their mighty chief returned: loud was th' acclaim:
Forth rushed in haste the great consulting peers,
Raised from their dark divan,⁸ and with like joy
Congratulant approached him, who with hand
Silence, and with these words attention won:
460   "Thrones, Dominations, Princedoms, Virtues, Powers,
For in possession such, not only of right,
I call ye⁹ and declare ye now, returned
Successful beyond hope, to lead ye forth
Triumphant out of this infernal pit
465 Abominable, accurst, the house of woe,
And dungeon of our tyrant now possess,
As lords, a spacious world, to our native heaven
Little inferior, by my adventure hard
With peril great achieved. Long were to tell
470 What I have done, what suffered, with what pain
Voyaged th' unreal,° vast, unbounded deep   *unformed*
Of horrible confusion, over which
By Sin and Death a broad way now is paved

5. The simile compares the fallen angels, withdrawn from other regions of Hell to guard their
metropolis, to Tartars retiring before attacking
Russians and Persians before the attacking Turks
(lines 431–39). "Astracan": a region west of the
Caspian Sea inhabited by Russia and defended
against Turks and Tartars; "Aladule": the region of
Armenia, from which the last Persian ruler, called
"Anadule," a "Bactrian Sophi" (Persian Shah), was

forced to retreat from the Turks, to Tabriz
("Tauris") and Kazvin ("Casbeen").
6. Pertaining to Pluto, ruler of the classical underworld.
7. Of the river Styx in Hades, the river of hate.
8. The Turkish Council of State (continuing the
comparisons with oriental despotism).
9. I.e., you now have these titles not only by right
but by possession (from the conquest on earth).

To expedite your glorious march; but I
475 Toiled out my uncouth° passage, forced to ride   *strange*
Th' untractable abyss, plunged in the womb
Of unoriginal¹ Night and Chaos wild,
That jealous of their secrets fiercely opposed
My journey strange, with clamorous uproar
480 Protesting² Fate supreme; thence how I found
The new-created world, which fame in Heav'n
Long had foretold, a fabric wonderful
Of absolute perfection, therein man
Placed in a paradise, by our exile
485 Made happy: him by fraud I have seduced
From his Creator, and the more to increase
Your wonder, with an apple. He thereat
Offended, worth your laughter, hath giv'n up
Both his beloved man and all his world,
490 To Sin and Death a prey, and so to us,
Without our hazard, labor, or alarm,
To range in, and to dwell, and over man
To rule, as over all he should have ruled.
True is, me also he hath judged, or rather
495 Me not, but the brute serpent in whose shape
Man I deceived; that which to me belongs,
Is enmity, which he will put between
Me and mankind; I am to bruise his heel;
His seed, when is not set, shall bruise my head:
500 A world who would not purchase with a bruise,
Or much more grievous pain? Ye have th' account
Of my performance: what remains, ye gods,
But up and enter now into full bliss."³
       So having said, a while he stood, expecting
505 Their universal shout and high applause.
To fill his ear, when contrary he hears
On all sides, from innumerable tongues
A dismal universal hiss, the sound
Of public scorn; he wondered, but not long
510 Had leisure, wond'ring at himself now more;
His visage drawn he felt to sharp and spare,
His arms clung to his ribs, his legs entwining
Each other, till supplanted° down he fell   *tripped up*
A monstrous serpent on his belly prone,
515 Reluctant,° but in vain, a greater power   *struggling*
Now ruled him, punished in the shape he sinned,
According to his doom: he would have spoke,
But hiss for hiss returned with forkèd tongue
To forkèd tongue, for now were all transformed
520 Alike, to serpents⁴ all as accessories

---

1. Having no origin, uncreated.
2. Protesting both to, and against, Fate.
3. Ironically, the final word of Satan's proud, triumphal speech rhymes with and so prepares for the "hiss" that will soon greet him, as his would-

be triumph is turned by God to abject humiliation.
4. The scene recalls Dante's vivid description of the thieves metamorphosed to snakes in *Inferno* 24–25.

To his bold riot:° dreadful was the din   *revolt*
Of hissing through the hall, thick swarming now
With complicated° monsters, head and tail,   *tangled*
Scorpion[5] and asp, and amphisbaena dire,
525   Cerastes horned, hydrus, and ellops drear,
And dipsas (not so thick swarmed once the soil
Bedropped with blood of Gorgon,[6] or the isle
Ophiusa) but still greatest he the midst,
Now dragon grown, larger than whom the sun
530   Engendered in the Pythian vale on slime,
Huge Python,[7] and his power no less he seemed
Above the rest still to retain; they all
Him followed issuing forth to th' open field,
Where all yet left of that revolted rout
535   Heav'n-fall'n, in station stood or just array,[8]
Sublime° with expectation when to see   *raised up*
In triumph issuing forth their glorious chief;
They saw, but other sight instead, a crowd
Of ugly serpents; horror on them fell,
540   And horrid sympathy; for what they saw,
They felt themselves now changing; down their arms,
Down fell both spear and shield, down they as fast,
And the dire hiss renewed, and the dire form
Catched by contagion, like in punishment,
545   As in their crime. Thus was th' applause they meant,
Turned to exploding hiss, triumph to shame
Cast on themselves from their own mouths. There stood
A grove hard by, sprung up with this their change,
His will who reigns above, to aggravate
550   Their penance,° laden with fair fruit, like that   *punishment*
Which grew in Paradise, the bait of Eve
Used by the Tempter: on that prospect strange
Their earnest eyes they fixed, imagining
For one forbidden tree a multitude
555   Now ris'n, to work them further woe or shame;
Yet parched with scalding thirst and hunger fierce,
Though to delude them sent, could not abstain,
But on they rolled in heaps, and up the trees
Climbing, sat thicker than the snaky locks
560   That curled Megaera:[9] greedily they plucked
The fruitage fair to sight, like that which grew
Near that bituminous lake where Sodom flamed;[1]
This more delusive, not the touch, but taste
Deceived; they fondly° thinking to allay   *foolishly*

5. The "Scorpion" has a venomous sting at the tip of the tail; "asp" is a small Egyptian viper; "amphisbaena" supposedly had a head at each end; "Cerastes" is an asp with horny projections over each eye; "hydrus" and "ellops" were mythical water snakes; "dipsas" was a mythical snake whose bite caused raging thirst.
6. Drops of blood from the Gorgon Medusa's severed head turned into snakes; "Ophiusa" in Greek means "isle of snakes."

7. A gigantic serpent engendered from the slime left by Deucalion's flood; Apollo slew him and appropriated the "Pythian" vale and shrine at Delphi.
8. I.e., at their posts or on parade.
9. One of three Furies with snaky hair.
1. Sodom apples reputedly grew on the spot where the accursed city once stood, now the Dead Sea ("that bituminous lake"); the apples look good, but dissolve into ashes when eaten.

565 Their appetite with gust,° instead of fruit   *relish*
     Chewed bitter ashes, which th' offended taste
     With spattering noise rejected: oft they assayed,°   *attempted*
     Hunger and thirst constraining, drugged as oft,
     With hatefulest disrelish writhed their jaws
570 With soot and cinders filled; so oft they fell
     Into the same illusion, not as man
     Whom they triumphed once lapsed.[2] Thus were they plagued
     And worn with famine, long and ceaseless hiss,
     Till their lost shape, permitted, they resumed,[3]
575 Yearly enjoined, some say, to undergo
     This annual humbling certain numbered days,
     To dash their pride, and joy for man seduced.
     However some tradition they dispersed
     Among the heathen of their purchase° got,   *plunder*
580 And fabled how the serpent, whom they called
     Ophion with Eurynome,[4] the wide-
     Encroaching Eve perhaps, had first the rule
     Of high Olympus, thence by Saturn driv'n
     And Ops, ere yet Dictaean Jove was born.
585 Meanwhile in Paradise the hellish pair
     Too soon arrived, Sin there in power before,
     Once actual, now in body,[5] and to dwell
     Habitual habitant; behind her Death
     Close following pace for pace, not mounted yet
590 On his pale horse:[6] to whom Sin thus began:
       "Second of Satan sprung, all-conquering Death,
     What think'st thou of our empire now, though earned
     With travail° difficult, not better far   *labor*
     Than still at Hell's dark threshold to have sat watch,
595 Unnamed, undreaded, and thyself half-starved?"
       Whom thus the Sin-born monster answered soon:
     "To me, who with eternal famine pine,
     Alike is Hell, or Paradise, or Heaven,
     There best, where most with ravin° I may meet;   *prey*
600 Which here, though plenteous, all too little seems
     To stuff this maw, this vast unhidebound corpse."[7]
       To whom th' incestuous mother thus replied:
     "Thou therefore on these herbs, and fruits, and flow'rs
     Feed first, on each beast next, and fish, and fowl,
605 No homely morsels, and whatever thing
     Thy scythe of Time mows down, devour unspared,

---

2. Unlike man who fell once, they try to eat the dissolving apples over and over again.
3. God permitted them to regain their "lost form" as fallen angels; but they are undergoing a slower, natural metamorphosis into grosser substance by their continuing commitment to and choice of evil.
4. The Titan "Ophion" (whose name means "snake") and his wife "Eurynome" ("the wide-reacher") ruled Olympus until driven away by "Saturn" and his wife "Ops," who were in turn overthrown by "Jove," who lived on the mountain

"Dicte." Milton suggests that these may represent versions of the story transmitted by the fallen angels to the pagans (lines 578–84).
5. Sin was present in Eden in the actual sins committed by Adam and Eve; now she will dwell there in her own body and in all other bodies.
6. Cf. Revelation 6.8: "Behold a pale horse, and his name that sat on him was Death, and Hell followed with him."
7. Its hide does not cling close to its bones: Death's hunger is such that it can never fill its skin.

Till I in man residing through the race,
His thoughts, his looks, words, actions all infect,
And season him thy last and sweetest prey."
610   This said, they both betook them several ways,
Both to destroy, or unimmortal make
All kinds, and for destruction to mature
Sooner or later; which th' Almighty seeing,
From his transcendent seat the saints among,
615   To those bright orders uttered thus his voice:
    "See with what heat these dogs of Hell advance
To waste and havoc° yonder world, which I   *plunder*
So fair and good created, and had still
Kept in that state, had not the folly of man
620   Let in these wasteful furies, who impute
Folly to me, so doth the Prince of Hell
And his adherents, that with so much ease
I suffer them to enter and possess
A place so heav'nly, and conniving seem
625   To gratify my scornful enemies,
That laugh, as if transported with some fit
Of passion, I to them had quitted all,°   *handed everything over*
At random yielded up to their misrule;
And know not that I called and drew them thither
630   My hell-hounds, to lick up the draff° and filth   *dregs*
Which man's polluting sin with taint hath shed
On what was pure, till crammed and gorged, nigh burst
With sucked and glutted offal, at one sling
Of thy victorious arm, well-pleasing Son,
635   Both Sin, and Death, and yawning grave at last
Through Chaos hurled, obstruct the mouth of Hell
For ever, and seal up his ravenous jaws.
Then Heav'n and earth renewed shall be made pure
To sanctity that shall receive no stain:
640   Till then the curse pronounced on both precedes."°   *takes precedence*
    He ended, and the heav'nly audience loud
Sung halleluiah, as the sound of seas,
Through multitude that sung: "Just are thy ways,
Righteous are thy decrees on all thy works;
645   Who can extenuate° thee? Next, to the Son,   *disparage*
Destined restorer of mankind, by whom
New heav'n and earth shall to the ages rise,
Or down from Heav'n descend." Such was their song,
While the Creator calling forth by name
650   His mighty angels gave them several charge,
As sorted° best with present things. The sun   *suited*
Had first his precept so to move, so shine,
As might affect the earth with cold and heat
Scarce tolerable, and from the north to call
655   Decrepit winter, from the south to bring
Solstitial summer's heat. To the blank° moon   *white, pale*
Her office they prescribed, to th' other five

Their planetary motions and aspécts[8]
In sextile, square, and trine, and opposite,
660 Of noxious efficacy, and when to join
In synod° unbenign, and taught the fixed°   *conjunction/fixed stars*
Their influence malignant when to show'r,
Which of them rising with the sun, or falling,
Should prove tempestuous:° to the winds they set   *productive of storms*
665 Their corners, when with bluster to confound
Sea, air, and shore, the thunder when to roll
With terror through the dark aerial hall.
Some say[9] he bid his angels turn askance
The poles of earth twice ten degrees and more
670 From the sun's axle; they with labor pushed
Oblique the centric globe:° some say the sun   *the earth*
Was bid turn reins from th' equinoctial road°   *the equator*
Like distant breadth to Taurus[1] with the sev'n
Atlantic Sisters, and the Spartan Twins
675 Up to the Tropic Crab; thence down amain°   *at full speed*
By Leo and the Virgin and the Scales,
As deep as Capricorn, to bring in change
Of seasons to each clime; else had the spring
Perpetual smiled on earth with vernant° flow'rs,   *spring*
680 Equal in days and nights, except to those
Beyond the polar circles; to them day
Had unbenighted° shone, while the low sun   *without any night*
To recompense his distance, in their sight
Had rounded still° th' horizon, and not known   *always*
685 Or° east or west, which had forbid the snow   *either*
From cold Estotiland, and south as far
Beneath Magellan.[2] At that tasted fruit
The sun, as from Thyestean banquet,[3] turned
His course intended; else how had the world
690 Inhabited, though sinless, more than now,
Avoided pinching cold and scorching heat?
These changes in the heav'ns, though slow, produced
Like change on sea and land, sideral blast,
Vapor, and mist, and exhalation hot,
695 Corrupt and pestilent: now from the north
Of Norumbega, and the Samoed shore
Bursting their brazen dungeon, armed with ice
And snow and hail and stormy gust and flaw,°   *squall*
Boreas and Caecias and Argestes loud

---

8. Astrological positions. The next line names
positions of 60, 90, 120, and 180 degrees, respectively.
9. The poem offers both a Ptolemaic and a Copernican explanation of the shifts made in the cosmic
order so as to change the prelapsarian eternal
spring. The Copernican explanation (offered first)
proposes that the earth's axis is now tilted (lines
668–71); the Ptolemaic explanation is that the
plane of the Sun's orbit is tilted (lines 671–78).
1. Lines 673–78 trace the sun's apparent (Ptole-

maic) journey from Aries through Taurus and the
rest of the zodiac over the course of the year.
2. The region of the Straits of Magellan, at the tip
of South America. "Estotiland" (line 686): northern Labrador.
3. As a revenge, Atreus killed one of the sons of
his brother Thyestes and served him in a banquet
to that brother; the sun changed course to avoid
the sight. "Sideral blast" (line 694): malevolent
stellar influences.

700 And Thrascias rend the woods and seas upturn;
With adverse blast upturns them from the south
Notus and Afer black with thund'rous clouds
From Serraliona,[4] thwart of these as fierce
Forth rush the Levant and the ponent winds
705 Eurus and Zephyr with their lateral noise,
Sirocco and Libecchio.[5] Thus began
Outrage from lifeless things; but Discord first
Daughter of Sin, among th' irrational,
Death introduced through fierce antipathy:[6]
710 Beast now with beast gan war, and fowl with fowl,
And fish with fish; to graze the herb° all leaving,   *grass*
Devour'd each other; nor stood much in awe
Of man, but fled him, or with count'nance grim
Glared on him passing: these were from without
715 The growing miseries, which Adam saw
Already in part, though hid in gloomiest shade,
To sorrow abandoned, but worse felt within,
And in a troubled sea of passion tossed,
Thus to disburden sought with sad complaint:
720   "O miserable of happy![7] Is this the end
Of this new glorious world, and me so late
The glory of that glory, who now become
Accurst of blessèd, hide me from the face
Of God, whom to behold was then my height
725 Of happiness: yet well, if here would end
The misery, I deserved it, and would bear
My own deservings; but this will not serve;
All that I eat or drink, or shall beget,
Is propagated[8] curse. O voice once heard
730 Delightfully, 'Increase and multiply,'
Now death to hear! For what can I increase
Or multiply, but curses on my head?
Who of all ages to succeed, but feeling
The evil on him brought by me, will curse
735 My head: 'Ill fare our ancestor impure,
For this we may thank Adam'; but his thanks
Shall be the execration; so besides
Mine own that bide upon[9] me, all from me
Shall with a fierce reflux on me redound,

---

4. Winds (701–06) from the south ("Notus," "Afer") come from Sierra Leone ("Serraliona") on the west coast of Africa; "Boreas," "Caecias," "Argestes," and "Thrascias" are all winds that blow from the north, northeast, and northwest, bursting from the cave ("brazen dungeon") in which Aeolus imprisoned the winds (line 695–700); "Norumbega" (line 696) is northeastern North America, including New England and maritime Canada; "Samoed" is Siberia.
5. Crossing the north and south winds ("thwart," line 703) are (from the east) the "Levant" (from the Levant) and "Eurus" (east southeast); from the west ("ponent"), "Zephyr" the west wind; "Sirocco" and "Libecchio" come from the southeast and

southwest, respectively.
6. "Discord" (personified as daughter of Sin) introduced Death among the animals ("the irrational") by stirring up "antipathy" among them.
7. Adam's complaint begins with the classical formula for a tragic fall or *peripeteia*, the change from happiness to misery.
8. Handed down from one generation to the next.
9. I.e., Adam's "own" curse will remain ("bide") with him, and the curse ("execration") of "all" who descend from him will "redound" on him as to their natural "center"; objects so placed ("in their place," line 741) were thought to be weightless ("light") but these curses will be "heavy."

740 On me as on their natural center light
Heavy, though in their place. O fleeting joys
Of Paradise, dear bought with lasting woes!
Did I request thee, Maker, from my clay
To mold me man, did I solicit thee
745 From darkness to promote me, or here place
In this delicious garden? As my will
Concurred not to my being, it were but right
And equal° to reduce me to my dust,   *just*
Desirous to resign, and render back
750 All I received, unable to perform
Thy terms too hard, by which I was to hold
The good I sought not. To the loss of that,
Sufficient penalty, why hast thou added
The sense of endless woes? Inexplicable
755 Thy justice seems; yet to say truth, too late
I thus contest; then should have been refused
Those terms whatever, when they were proposed:
Thou[1] didst accept them; wilt thou enjoy the good,
Then cavil the conditions? And though God
760 Made thee without thy leave, what if thy son
Prove disobedient, and reproved, retort,
'Wherefore didst thou beget me? I sought it not:'
Wouldst thou admit for his contempt of thee
That proud excuse? Yet him not thy election,°   *choice*
765 But natural necessity begot.
God made thee of choice his own, and of his own
To serve him, thy reward was of his grace,
Thy punishment then justly is at his will.
Be it so, for I submit, his doom is fair,
770 That dust I am, and shall to dust return:
O welcome hour whenever! Why delays
His hand to execute what his decree
Fixed on this day? Why do I overlive,
Why am I mocked with death, and lengthened out
775 To deathless pain? How gladly would I meet
Mortality my sentence, and be earth
Insensible, how glad would lay me down
As in my mother's lap! There I should rest
And sleep secure; his dreadful voice no more
780 Would thunder in my ears, no fear of worse
To me and to my offspring would torment me
With cruel expectation. Yet one doubt
Pursues me still, lest all I° cannot die,   *all of me*
Lest that pure breath of life, the spirit of man
785 Which God inspired, cannot together perish
With this corporeal clod; then in the grave,
Or in some other dismal place, who knows
But I shall die a living death? O thought
Horrid, if true! Yet why? It was but breath

[handwritten annotations: "they are seeing that God may have a plan." and "like Satan."]

---

1. Adam turns from addressing God to address himself.

790 Of life that sinned; what dies but what had life
And sin? The body properly hath neither.
All of me then shall die:² let this appease
The doubt, since human reach no further knows.
For though the Lord of all be infinite,
795 Is his wrath also? Be it, man is not so,
But mortal doomed. How can he exercise
Wrath without end on man whom death must end?
Can he make deathless death? That were to make
Strange contradiction, which to God himself
800 Impossible is held, as argument
Of weakness, not of power. Will he draw out,
For anger's sake, finite to infinite
In punished man, to satisfy his rigor
Satisfied never; that were to extend
805 His sentence beyond dust and nature's law,
By which all causes else according still
To the reception of their matter act,
Not to th' extent of their own sphere.³ But say
That death be not one stroke, as I supposed,
810 Bereaving° sense, but endless misery   *taking away*
From this day onward, which I feel begun
Both in me, and without° me, and so last   *outside of*
To perpetuity; ay me, that fear
Comes thund'ring back with dreadful revolution°   *recurrence*
815 On my defenseless head; both Death and I
Am found eternal, and incorporate° both,   *made one body*
Nor I on my part single, in me all
Posterity stands cursed: fair patrimony
That I must leave ye, sons; O were I able
820 To waste it all myself, and leave ye none!
So disinherited how would ye bless
Me now your curse! Ah, why should all mankind
For one man's fault thus guiltless be condemned,
If guiltless? But from me what can proceed,
825 But all corrupt, both mind and will depraved,
Not to do° only, but to will the same   *act*
With me? How can they then acquitted stand
In sight of God? Him after all disputes
Forced I absolve: all my evasions vain
830 And reasonings, though through mazes, lead me still
But to my own conviction: first and last
On me, me only, as the source and spring
Of all corruption, all the blame lights due;
So might the wrath.⁴ Fond° wish! Couldst thou support   *foolish*
835 That burden heavier than the earth to bear,
Than all the world much heavier, though divided

2. After debating the matter, Adam concludes that the soul dies with the body; Milton in his *Christian Doctrine* worked out this "mortalist" doctrine, with its corollary, that both soul and body rise at the Last Judgment.
3. Adam convinces himself that "finite" matter

(line 802) cannot suffer "infinite" punishment by an axiom of traditional philosophy, that by "nature's law" (line 805) the actions of agents are limited by the nature of the object they act upon.
4. Cf. the Son's offer to accept all humankind's guilt (3.236), and Eve's similar offer (10.935–36).

With that bad woman? Thus what thou desir'st,
And what thou fear'st, alike destroys all hope
Of refuge, and concludes thee miserable
840 Beyond all past example and future,
To Satan only like both crime and doom.
O conscience, into what abyss of fears
And horrors hast thou driv'n me; out of which
I find no way, from deep to deeper plunged!"
845   Thus Adam to himself lamented loud
Through the still night, not now, as ere man fell,
Wholesome and cool, and mild, but with black air
Accompanied, with damps° and dreadful gloom,   *noxious vapors*
Which to his evil conscience represented
850 All things with double terror: on the ground
Outstretched he lay, on the cold ground, and oft
Cursed his creation, Death as oft accused
Of tardy execution, since denounced°   *pronounced*
The day of his offense: "Why comes not Death,"
855 Said he, "with one thrice-accéptáble stroke
To end me? Shall Truth fail to keep her word,
Justice divine not hasten to be just?
But Death comes not at call, Justice divine
Mends not her slowest pace for prayers or cries.
860 O woods, O fountains, hillocks, dales and bow'rs,
With other echo late I taught your shades
To answer, and resound far other song."[5]
Whom thus afflicted when sad Eve beheld,
Desolate where she sat, approaching nigh,
865 Soft words to his fierce passion she assayed;
But her with stern regard he thus repelled:
    "Out of my sight, thou serpent,[6] that name best   *he calls her a*
Befits thee with him leagued, thyself as false   *serpent, he feels,*
And hateful; nothing wants,° but that thy shape,   *she isn't greatful*
                                                                that he fell is lacking
870 Like his, and color serpentine may show   *w/ her*
Thy inward fraud, to warn all creatures from thee
Henceforth; lest that too heav'nly form, pretended[7]
To hellish falsehood, snare them. But° for thee   *except*
I had persisted happy, had not thy pride
875 And wand'ring vanity, when least was safe,
Rejected my forewarning, and disdained
Not to be trusted, longing to be seen
Though by the Devil himself, him overweening°   *overconfident*
To overreach, but with the serpent meeting
880 Fooled and beguiled, by him thou, I by thee,
To trust thee from my side, imagined wise,
Constant, mature, proof against all assaults,
And understood not all was but a show
Rather than solid virtue, all but a rib
885 Crooked by nature, bent, as now appears,

5. Cf. their morning hymn (5.153–208).   aspirated, means "serpent."
6. Adam's bitter, misogynistic outcry begins with 7. Held in front of, as a cover or mask.
reference to the patristic notion that the name Eve,

More to the part siníster° from me drawn,   *the left side*
Well if thrown out, as supernumerary[8]
To my just number found. O why did God,
Creator wise, that peopled highest heav'n
890 With Spirits masculine,[9] create at last
This novelty on earth, this fair defect
Of nature,[1] and not fill the world at once
With men as angels without feminine,
Or find some other way to generate
895 Mankind? This mischief had not then befall'n,
And more that shall befall, innumerable
Disturbances on earth through female snares,
And strait conjunction[2] with this sex: for either
He never shall find out fit mate, but such
900 As some misfortune brings him, or mistake,
Or whom he wishes most shall seldom gain
Through her perverseness, but shall see her gained
By a far worse, or if she love, withheld
By parents, or his happiest choice too late
905 Shall meet, already linked and wedlock-bound
To a fell° adversary, his hate or shame: *bitter*
Which infinite calamity shall cause
To human life, and household peace confound."
    He added not, and from her turned, but Eve
910 Not so repulsed, with tears that ceased not flowing,
And tresses all disordered, at his feet
Fell humble, and embracing them, besought
His peace, and thus proceeded in her plaint:
    "Forsake me not thus, Adam, witness Heav'n
915 What love sincere, and reverence in my heart
I bear thee, and unweeting° have offended,   *unintentionally*
Unhappily deceived; thy suppliant
I beg, and clasp thy knees;[3] bereave me not,
Whereon I live, thy gentle looks, thy aid,
920 Thy counsel in this uttermost distress,
My only strength and stay: forlorn of thee,
Whither shall I betake me, where subsist?
While yet we live, scarce one short hour perhaps,
Between us two let there be peace, both joining,
925 As joined in injuries, one enmity
Against a foe by doom express° assigned us,   *explicit judgment*
That cruel serpent: on me exercise not
Thy hatred for this misery befall'n,
On me already lost, me than thyself
930 More miserable; both have sinned, but thou

---

8. It was supposed that Adam had thirteen ribs on the left side, so he could spare one for the creation of Eve and still retain the proper ("just") number, twelve.
9. The Miltonic Bard indicated that angels can assume at will "either sex . . . or both" (1.424).
1. Aristotle had claimed that the female is a defec-

tive male.
2. Close, hard-pressing, binding union: Adam goes on to project the problems of future marriages.
3. Eve assumes the posture of the classical suppliant, clasping the knees of the one she begs from.

Against God only, I against God and thee,
And to the place of judgment will return,
There with my cries importune Heaven, that all
The sentence from thy head removed may light
935 On me, sole cause to thee of all this woe,
Me me only just object of his ire."[4]
    She ended weeping, and her lowly plight,°   *posture*
Immovable till peace obtained from fault
Acknowledged and deplored, in Adam wrought
940 Commiseration; soon his heart relented
Towards her, his life so late and sole delight,
Now at his feet submissive in distress,
Creature so fair his reconcilement seeking,
His counsel whom she had displeased, his aid;
945 As one disarmed, his anger all he lost,
And thus with peaceful words upraised her soon:
    "Unwary, and too desirous, as before,
So now of what thou know'st not, who desir'st
The punishment all on thyself; alas!
950 Bear thine own first, ill able to sustain
His full wrath whose thou feel'st as yet least part,[5]
And my displeasure bear'st so ill. If prayers
Could alter high decrees, I to that place
Would speed before thee, and be louder heard,
955 That on my head all might be visited,
Thy frailty and infirmer sex forgiv'n,
To me committed and by me exposed.
But rise, let us no more contend, nor blame
Each other, blamed enough elsewhere, but strive
960 In offices of love, how we may light'n
Each other's burden in our share of woe;
Since this day's death denounced, if aught I see,
Will prove no sudden, but a slow-paced evil,
A long day's dying to augment our pain,
965 And to our seed (O hapless seed!) derived."°   *passed on*
    To whom thus Eve, recovering heart, replied:
"Adam, by sad experiment I know
How little weight my words with thee can find,
Found so erroneous, thence by just event°   *consequence*
970 Found so unfortunate; nevertheless,
Restored by thee, vile as I am, to place
Of new acceptance, hopeful to regain
Thy love, the sole contentment of my heart
Living or dying, from thee I will not hide
975 What thoughts in my unquiet breast are ris'n,
Tending to some relief of our extremes,
Or end, though sharp and sad, yet tolerable,
As in our evils, and of easier choice.

---

4. Eve also echoes the Son's offer (3.236). Cf.
Adam's cry (10.832).
5. I.e., you could hardly bear God's "full wrath"

since you are so distraught when you feel only the
smallest part of it, and you can "ill" bear my displeasure (line 952).

If care of our descent perplex us most,[6]
980 Which must be born to certain woe, devoured
By Death at last, and miserable it is
To be to others cause of misery,
Our own begotten, and of our loins to bring
Into this cursèd world a woeful race,
985 That after wretched life must be at last
Food for so foul a monster, in thy power
It lies, yet ere conception to prevent
The race unblest, to being yet unbegot.
Childless thou art, childless remain; so Death
990 Shall be deceived° his glut, and with us two   *cheated of*
Be forced to satisfy his rav'nous maw.
But if thou judge it hard and difficult,
Conversing, looking, loving, to abstain
From love's due rites, nuptial embraces sweet,
995 And with desire to languish without hope,
Before the present object[7] languishing
With like desire, which would be misery
And torment less than none of what we dread,
Then both ourselves and seed at once to free
1000 From what we fear for both, let us make short,°   *lose no time*
Let us seek Death, or he not found, supply
With our own hands his office on ourselves;
Why stand we longer shivering under fears,
That show no end but death, and have the power,
1005 Of many ways to die the shortest choosing,
Destruction with destruction to destroy."
   She ended here, or vehement despair
Broke off the rest; so much of death her thoughts
Had entertained, as dyed her cheeks with pale.
1010 But Adam with such counsel nothing swayed,
To better hopes his more attentive mind
Laboring had raised, and thus to Eve replied.
   "Eve thy contempt of life and pleasure seems
To argue in thee something more sublime
1015 And excellent than what thy mind contemns;°   *despises*
But self-destruction therefore sought, refutes
That excellence thought in thee, and implies,
Not thy contempt, but anguish and regret
For loss of life and pleasure overloved.
1020 Or if thou covet death, as utmost end
Of misery, so thinking to evade
The penalty pronounced, doubt not but God
Hath wiselier armed his vengeful ire than so
To be forestalled; much more I fear lest death
1025 So snatched will not exempt us from the pain
We are by doom to pay: rather such acts
Of contumácy° will provoke the Highest   *contempt*

---

6. I.e., if concern for our descendants most torment ("perplex") us.

7. I.e., Eve herself, who then projects her own
frustrated desire if they were to forgo sex.

To make death in us live. Then let us seek
Some safer resolution, which methinks
1030 I have in view, calling to mind with heed
Part of our sentence, that thy seed shall bruise
The serpent's head; piteous amends, unless
Be meant, whom I conjecture, our grand foe
Satan, who in the serpent hath contrived
1035 Against us this deceit: to crush his head
Would be revenge indeed; which will be lost
By death brought on ourselves, or childless days
Resolved, as thou proposest; so our foe
Shall scape his punishment ordained, and we
1040 Instead shall double ours upon our heads.
No more be mentioned then of violence
Against ourselves, and wilful barrenness,
That cuts us off from hope, and savors only
Rancor and pride, impatience and despite,
1045 Reluctance° against God and his just yoke   resistance
Laid on our necks. Remember with what mild
And gracious temper he both heard and judged
Without wrath or reviling: we expected
Immediate dissolution, which we thought
1050 Was meant by death that day, when lo, to thee
Pains only in child-bearing were foretold,
And bringing forth, soon recompensed with joy,
Fruit of thy womb:[8] on me the curse aslope
Glanced on the ground,[9] with labor I must earn
1055 My bread; what harm? Idleness had been worse;
My labor will sustain me; and lest cold
Or heat should injure us, his timely care
Hath unbesought provided, and his hands
Clothed us unworthy, pitying while he judged;
1060 How much more, if we pray him, will his ear
Be open, and his heart to pity incline,
And teach us further by what means to shun
Th' inclement seasons, rain, ice, hail and snow,
Which now the sky with various face begins
1065 To show us in this mountain, while the winds
Blow moist and keen, shattering° the graceful locks   scattering
Of these fair spreading trees; which bids us seek
Some better shroud,° some better warmth to cherish   shelter
Our limbs benumbed, ere this diurnal star°   the sun
1070 Leave cold the night, how we his gathered beams
Reflected, may with matter sere foment,
Or by collision of two bodies grind
The air attrite to fire,[1] as late the clouds
Justling or pushed with winds rude in their shock

---

8. Adam's unconscious echo of Elizabeth's address to Mary, mother of Jesus (Luke 1.41–42), "Blessed is the fruit of thy womb," lays the ground for their fuller understanding of the promise about the "seed" of the woman.
9. I.e., the curse, like a spear that almost missed its target, glanced aside and hit the ground.
1. Adam projects the invention of fire: they might, by striking two bodies together, rub ("attrite") the air into fire by fiction; or else (line 1070) focus reflected sunbeams (through some equivalent of glass) on dry ("sere") matter.

1075 Tine° the slant lightning, whose thwart° flame driv'n down   *ignite/slanting*
Kindles the gummy bark of fir or pine,
And sends a comfortable heat from far,
Which might supply° the sun: such fire to use,   *take the place of*
And what may else be remedy or cure
1080 To evils which our own misdeeds have wrought,
He will instruct us praying, and of grace
Beseeching him, so as we need not fear
To pass commodiously this life, sustained
By him with many comforts, till we end
1085 In dust, our final rest and native home.
What better can we do, than to the place
Repairing where he judged us, prostrate fall
Before him reverent, and there confess
Humbly our faults, and pardon beg, with tears
1090 Watering the ground, and with our sighs the air
Frequenting,° sent from hearts contrite, in sign   *filling*
Of sorrow unfeigned, and humiliation meek.
Undoubtedly he will relent and turn
From his displeasure; in whose look serene,
1095 When angry most he seemed and most severe,
What else but favor, grace, and mercy shone?"
    So spake our father penitent, nor Eve
Felt less remorse: they forthwith to the place
Repairing where he judged them prostrate fell
1100 Before him reverent, and both confessed
Humbly their faults, and pardon begged, with tears
Watering the ground, and with their sighs the air
Frequenting, sent from hearts contrite, in sign
Of sorrow unfeigned, and humiliation meek.[2]

humble is the
opposite of pride

Book 11

Thus they in lowliest plight repentant stood[1]
Praying, for from the mercy-seat above
Prevenient grace[2] descending had removed
The stony from their hearts, and made new flesh
5 Regenerate grow instead, that sighs now breathed
Unutterable, which the spirit of prayer
Inspired, and winged for Heav'n with speedier flight
Than loudest oratory: yet their port
Not of mean suitors, nor important[3] less
10 Seemed their petition, than when th' ancient pair
In fables old, less ancient yet than these,

2. The final six lines repeat, almost word for word, lines 1086–92, with only six lines separating them; this provides strong closure, as the poet describes Adam's proposed gesture of repentance carried out in every detail.
1. "Stood" may mean "remained," or that, after prostrating themselves (10.1099) they prayed standing upright; their demeanor ("port") was "Not of mean suitors" (11.8–9), and they had stood to pray before (4.720).
2. Grace given before the human will can turn from sin, enabling it to do so.
3. See the wordplay on "port" and "important."

Deucalion and chaste Pyrrha to restore
The race of mankind drowned, before the shrine
Of Themis stood devout.⁴ To Heav'n their prayers
15 Flew up, nor missed the way, by envious winds
Blown vagabond or frustrate:⁵ in they passed
Dimensionless through heav'nly doors; then clad
With incense, where the golden altar fumed,
By their great Intercessor, came in sight
20 Before the Father's throne: them the glad° Son   *pleased*
Presenting, thus to intercede began:
      "See Father, what first-fruits on earth are sprung
From thy implanted grace in man, these sighs
And prayers, which in this golden censer, mixed
25 With incense, I thy priest before thee bring,
Fruits of more pleasing savor from thy seed
Sown with contrition in his heart, than those
Which his own hand manuring° all the trees   *cultivating*
Of Paradise could have produced, ere fall'n
30 From innocence. Now therefore bend thine ear
To supplication, hear his sighs though mute;
Unskilful with what words to pray, let me
Interpret for him, me his advocate
And propitiation, all his works on me
35 Good or not good ingraft,⁶ my merit those
Shall perfect, and for these my death shall pay.
Accept me, and in me from these receive
The smell of peace toward mankind, let him live
Before thee reconciled, at least his days
40 Numbered, though sad, till death, his doom (which I
To mitigate thus plead, not to reverse)
To better life shall yield him, where with me
All my redeemed may dwell in joy and bliss,
Made one with me as I with thee am one."
45   To whom the Father, without cloud, serene:
"All thy request for man, accepted Son,
Obtain, all thy request was my decree:
But longer in that Paradise to dwell,
The law I gave to nature him forbids:
50 Those pure immortal elements that know
No gross, no unharmonious mixture foul,
Eject him tainted now, and purge him off
As a distemper, gross to air as gross,
And mortal food,⁷ as may dispose him best

---

4. In Greek myth, when "Deucalion" and his wife
"Pyrrha" (like Noah's family) alone survived a universal flood, they sought direction from "Themis,"
goddess of Justice; she told them to throw stones
behind them, which became men and women.
5. I.e., their prayers were not scattered ("blown
vagabond") by spiteful ("envious") winds, or prevented ("frustrate") from reaching their goal.
"Dimensionless": without physical extension.
6. The theological term for Christ's standing in

the place of humankind, taking onto himself all
their deeds, perfecting the good by his merit, and,
by his death, "paying" the debt due God's justice
for their evil deeds.
7. The pure elements of the Garden of Eden will
themselves "purge" Adam and Eve as an impurity
or disorder ("distemper"), ejecting them to a place
where the air and food are more gross, like themselves.

55　For dissolution° wrought by sin, that first　　　　　　　　　*death*
　　Distempered all things, and of incorrupt
　　Corrupted. I at first with two fair gifts
　　Created him endowed, with happiness
　　And immortality: that fondly° lost,　　　　　　　　　　　*foolishly*
60　This other served but to eternize woe;
　　Till I provided death; so death becomes
　　His final remedy, and after life
　　Tried in sharp tribulation, and refined
　　By faith and faithful works, to second life,
65　Waked in the renovation⁸ of the just,
　　Resigns him up with Heav'n and earth renewed.
　　But let us call to synod° all the blest　　　　　　　　　*assembly*
　　Through Heav'n's wide bounds; from them I will not hide
　　My judgments, how with mankind I proceed,
70　As how with peccant° angels late they saw;　　　　　　　*sinning*
　　And in their state, though firm, stood more confirmed."
　　　　He ended, and the Son gave signal high
　　To the bright minister that watched, he blew
　　His trumpet, heard in Oreb⁹ since perhaps
75　When God descended, and perhaps once more
　　To sound at general doom. Th' angelic blast
　　Filled all the regions: from their blissful bow'rs
　　Of amarantine° shade, fountain or spring,　　　　　　　*unfading*
　　By the waters of life, where'er they sat
80　In fellowships of joy, the sons of light
　　Hasted, resorting to the summons high,
　　And took their seats; till from his throne supreme
　　Th' Almighty thus pronounced his sovran will:
　　　　"O sons, like one of us man is become
85　To know both good and evil, since his taste
　　Of that defended° fruit; but let him boast　　　　　　　*forbidden*
　　His knowledge of good lost, and evil got,
　　Happier, had it sufficed him to have known
　　Good by itself, and evil not at all.
90　He sorrows now, repents, and prays contrite,
　　My motions in him; longer than they move,
　　His heart I know, how variable and vain
　　Self-left.¹ Lest therefore his now bolder hand
　　Reach also of the Tree of Life, and eat,
95　And live forever, dream at least to live
　　Forever,² to remove him I decree,
　　And send him from the garden forth to till
　　The ground whence he was taken, fitter soil.
　　　　"Michael, this my behest have thou in charge,
100　Take to thee from among the Cherubim

---

8. The resurrection and renewal of body and soul on the Last Day.
9. Where God delivered the Ten Commandments to the sound of a trumpet (Exodus 19.19); it will sound again at the Last Judgment ("general doom," line 76).
1. Left to itself, without my continual promptings

("motions," line 91), I know his heart to be "variable and vain."
2. Milton adds the phrase "dream at least to live forever" to suggest that parts of God's speech (especially lines 84–85, 93–96, closely quoted from Genesis 3.22) are ironic.

Thy choice of flaming warriors, lest the Fiend
Or° in behalf of man, or to invade   *either*
Vacant possession some new trouble raise:
Haste thee, and from the Paradise of God
105   Without remorse° drive out the sinful pair,   *pity*
From hallowed ground th' unholy, and denounce
To them and to their progeny from thence
Perpetual banishment. Yet lest they faint°   *lose courage*
At the sad sentence rigorously urged,
110   For I behold them softened and with tears
Bewailing their excess,° all terror hide.   *violation of law*
If patiently thy bidding they obey,
Dismiss them not disconsolate; reveal
To Adam what shall come in future days,
115   As I shall thee enlighten,³ intermix
My cov'nant in the woman's seed renewed;
So send them forth, though sorrowing, yet in peace:
And on the east side of the garden place,
Where entrance up from Eden easiest climbs,
120   Cherubic watch,⁴ and of a sword the flame
Wide-waving, all approach far off to fright,
And guard all passage to the Tree of life:
Lest Paradise a receptácle prove
To spirits foul, and all my trees their prey,
125   With whose stol'n fruit man once more to delude."
          He ceased; and th' archangelic power prepared
For swift descent, with him the cohort bright
Of watchful Cherubim; four faces each
Had, like a double Janus,⁵ all their shape
130   Spangled with eyes more numerous than those
Of Argus, and more wakeful than to drowse,
Charmed with Arcadian pipe, the pastoral reed
Of Hermes, or his opiate rod. Meanwhile
To resalute the world with sacred light
135   Leucóthea⁶ waked, and with fresh dews embalmed
The earth, when Adam and first matron Eve
Had ended now their orisons, and found
Strength added from above, new hope to spring
Out of despair, joy, but with fear yet linked;
140   Which thus to Eve his welcome words renewed:
          "Eve, easily may faith admit, that all
The good which we enjoy, from Heav'n descends;
But that from us aught should ascend to Heav'n

---

3. God, it seems, has to "enlighten" Michael with
knowledge of humankind's future at the same time
Michael presents that future to Adam (cf. 12.128);
Michael is told to "intermix" in his account God's
"cov'nant in the woman's seed" (line 116), the
"mysterious" promise of the redeemer hinted when
the Son pronounced judgment on the serpent
(10.179–81).
4. Cf. Genesis 3.24: "He placed at the east of the
garden of Eden Cherubims, and a flaming sword
which turned every way, to keep the way of the tree

of life."
5. Janus, the Roman god of doorways, had two
faces; in one version he had four, corresponding to
the four seasons and the four quarters of the earth.
"Argus" (line 131), a giant with one hundred eyes,
was set by Juno to watch Jove's mistress Io, but
Hermes (Mercury) put all of his eyes to sleep with
his music ("pipe") and his sleep-producing caduceus ("opiate rod").
6. Roman goddess of the dawn.

So prevalent° as to concern the mind   *influential*
145 Of God high-blest, or to incline his will,
   Hard to belief may seem; yet this will prayer,
   Or one short sigh of human breath, upborne
   Ev'n to the seat of God. For since I sought
   By prayer th' offended Deity to appease,
150 Kneeled and before him humbled all my heart,
   Methought I saw him placable and mild,
   Bending his ear; persuasion in me grew
   That I was heard with favor; peace returned
   Home to my breast, and to my memory
155 His promise, that thy seed shall bruise our foe;
   Which then not minded in dismay, yet now
   Assures me that the bitterness of death
   Is past, and we shall live. Whence Hail to thee,
   Eve rightly called,[7] mother of all mankind,
160 Mother of all things living, since by thee
   Man is to live, and all things live for man."
     To whom thus Eve with sad demeanor meek:
   "Ill-worthy I such title should belong
   To me transgressor, who for thee ordained
165 A help, became thy snare; to me reproach
   Rather belongs, distrust and all dispraise:
   But infinite in pardon was my Judge,
   That I who first brought death on all, am graced
   The source of life; next favorable thou,
170 Who highly thus to entitle me vouchsaf'st,
   Far other name deserving. But the field
   To labor calls us now with sweat imposed,
   Though after sleepless night; for see the morn,
   All unconcerned with our unrest, begins
175 Her rosy progress smiling; let us forth,
   I never from thy side henceforth to stray,
   Where'er our day's work lies, though now enjoined
   Laborious, till day droop; while here we dwell,
   What can be toilsome in these pleasant walks?
180 Here let us live, though in fall'n state, content."
     So spake, so wished much-humbled Eve, but fate
   Subscribed not; nature first gave signs,° impressed   *omens*
   On bird, beast, air, air suddenly eclipsed°   *darkened*
   After short blush of morn; nigh in her sight
185 The bird of Jove, stooped from his airy tow'r,[8]
   Two birds of gayest plume before him drove;
   Down from a hill the beast that reigns[9] in woods,
   First hunter then, pursued a gentle brace,°   *pair*
   Goodliest of all the forest, hart and hind;
190 Direct to th' eastern gate was bent their flight.
   Adam observed, and with his eye the chase

---

7. The name Eve is cognate with the Hebrew word meaning life. In Genesis 3.20 Adam names his wife Eve only after the Fall; Milton's Adam has named her before (4.481) and now affirms that that name is right.
8. The eagle swooped ("stooped") from his soaring flight ("tow'r").
9. The lion.

Pursuing, not unmoved to Eve thus spake:
  "O Eve, some further change awaits us nigh,
Which Heaven by these mute signs in nature shows
195 Forerunners of his purpose, or to warn
Us haply too secure° of our discharge   *overconfident*
From penalty, because from death released
Some days; how long, and what till then our life,
Who knows, or more than this, that we are dust,
200 And thither must return and be no more.
Why else this double object in our sight
Of flight pursued in th' air and o'er the ground
One way the selfsame hour? Why in the east
Darkness ere day's mid-course, and morning light
205 More orient° in yon western cloud that draws   *bright*
O'er the blue firmament a radiant white,
And slow descends, with something heav'nly fraught."°   *stored*
  He erred not, for by this° the heav'nly bands   *by this time*
Down from a sky of jasper lighted° now   *alighted, shone*
210 In Paradise, and on a hill made alt,°   *halt*
A glorious apparition, had not doubt
And carnal fear that day dimmed Adam's eye.
Not that more glorious, when the angels met
Jacob in Mahanaim,[1] where he saw
215 The field pavilioned with his guardians bright;
Nor that which on the flaming mount appeared
In Dothan, covered with a camp of fire,
Against the Syrian king,[2] who to surprise
One man, assassin-like had levied war,
220 War unproclaimed. The princely hierarch[3]
In their bright stand, there left his powers to seize
Possession of the garden; he alone,
To find where Adam sheltered, took his way,
Not unperceived of Adam, who to Eve,
225 While the great visitant approached, thus spake:
  "Eve, now expect great tidings, which perhaps
Of us will soon determine,° or impose   *make an end*
New laws to be observed; for I descry
From yonder blazing cloud that veils the hill
230 One of the heav'nly host, and by his gait
None of the meanest, some great potentate
Or of the Thrones above, such majesty
Invests him coming; yet not terrible,
That I should fear, nor sociably mild,
235 As Raphael, that I should much confide,
But solemn and sublime, whom not to offend,
With reverence I must meet, and thou retire."
He ended; and th' Archangel soon drew nigh,

---

1. Jacob gave that name, meaning "armies" or "camps" ("field pavilioned," line 215) to a place where he saw an army of angels.
2. He had levied war against "Dothan" (line 217) in order to capture Elisha the prophet ("one man"),
but the Lord saved him by sending "horses and chariots of fire" (2 Kings 6.8ff.).
3. Michael, who left his angelic forces ("powers") in their formation ("stand") to take possession of the garden (lines 221–22).

Not in his shape celestial, but as man
240 Clad to meet man; over his lucid arms
A military vest of purple flowed
Livelier than Meliboean, or the grain
Of Sarra,[4] worn by kings and heroes old
In time of truce; Iris had dipped the woof;
245 His starry helm unbuckled showed him prime
In manhood where youth ended; by his side
As in a glistering zodiac° hung the sword,   belt
Satan's dire dread, and in his hand the spear.
Adam bowed low, he kingly from his state°   stately bearing
250 Inclined not, but his coming thus declared:
    "Adam, Heav'n's high behest no preface needs:
Sufficient that thy prayers are heard, and Death,
Then due by sentence when thou didst transgress,
Defeated° of his seizure° many days   cheated/possession
255 Giv'n thee of grace, wherein thou may'st repent,
And one bad act with many deeds well done
May'st cover: well may then thy Lord appeased
Redeem thee quite from Death's rapacious claim;
But longer in this Paradise to dwell
260 Permits not; to remove thee I am come,
And send thee from the garden forth to till
The ground whence thou wast taken, fitter soil."
    He added not, for Adam at the news
Heart-strook with chilling gripe° of sorrow stood,   spasm
265 That all his senses bound; Eve, who unseen
Yet all had heard, with audible lament
Discovered° soon the place of her retire: revealed
    "O unexpected stroke, worse than of Death!
Must I thus leave thee Paradise? thus leave
270 Thee native soil,[5] these happy walks and shades,
Fit haunt of gods? where I had hope to spend,
Quiet though sad, the respite° of that day   delay
That must be mortal to us both. O flow'rs,
That never will in other climate grow,
275 My early visitation, and my last
At ev'n which I bred up with tender hand
From the first op'ning bud, and gave ye names,[6]
Who now shall rear ye to the sun, or rank
Your tribes,° and water from th' ambrosial fount?   species
280 Thee lastly nuptial bower, by me adorned
With what to sight or smell was sweet; from thee
How shall I part, and whither wander down
Into a lower world, to° this obscure   compared to
And wild, how shall we breathe in other air
285 Less pure, accustomed to immortal fruits?"

---

4. Both Tyre ("Sarra") and "Meliboea" (line 242) in Thessaly were famous for purple dye.
5. Unlike Adam, Eve was created in the Paradise of Eden.
6. Departing from Genesis 2.19, in which Adam alone gives names, Milton has Eve name the flowers, an action that signifies (like Adam's naming of the beasts, 8.352–54) intuitive knowledge of their nature.

Whom thus the Angel interrupted mild:
"Lament not Eve, but patiently resign
What justly thou hast lost; nor set thy heart,
Thus over-fond, on that which is not thine;
290 Thy going is not lonely, with thee goes
Thy husband, him to follow thou art bound;
Where he abides, think there thy native soil."
    Adam by this from the cold sudden damp°   *dejection*
Recovering, and his scattered spirits returned,
295 To Michael thus his humble words addressed:
    "Celestial, whether among the Thrones, or named
Of them the highest, for such of shape may seem
Prince above princes, gently hast thou told
Thy message, which might else in telling wound,
300 And in performing end us; what besides
Of sorrow and dejection and despair
Our frailty can sustain, thy tidings bring,
Departure from this happy place, our sweet
Recess, and only consolation left
305 Familiar to our eyes, all places else
Inhospitable appear and desolate,
Nor knowing us nor known: and if by prayer
Incessant I could hope to change the will
Of him who all things can,° I would not cease   *knows, can do*
310 To weary him with my assiduous cries:
But prayer against his absolute decree
No more avails than breath against the wind,
Blown stifling back on him that breathes it forth:
Therefore to his great bidding I submit.
315 This most afflicts me, that departing hence,
As from his face I shall be hid, deprived
His blessed count'nance; here I could frequent,
With worship, place by place where he vouchsafed
Presence Divine, and to my sons relate:
320 'On this mount he appeared, under this tree
Stood visible, among these pines his voice
I heard, here with him at this fountain talked:'
So many grateful altars I would rear
Of grassy turf, and pile up every stone
325 Of luster from the brook, in memory,
Or monument to ages, and thereon
Offer sweet-smelling gums and fruits and flow'rs:
In yonder nether world where shall I seek
His bright appearances, or footstep trace?
330 For though I fled him angry, yet recalled
To life prolonged and promised race,[7] I now
Gladly behold though but his utmost skirts
Of glory, and far off his steps adore."
    To whom thus Michael with regard benign:
335 "Adam, thou know'st Heav'n his, and all the earth,

7. His descendants, from whom will spring the "promised Seed."

Not this rock only; his omnipresence fills
Land, sea, and air, and every kind that lives,
Fomented° by his virtual° power and warmed: *nurtured/potent*
All th' earth he gave thee to possess and rule,
340   No despicable gift; surmise not then
His presence to these narrow bounds confined
Of Paradise or Eden: this had been
Perhaps thy capital seat, from whence had spread
All generations, and had hither come
345   From all the ends of th' earth, to celebrate
And reverence thee their great progenitor.
But this preeminence thou hast lost, brought down
To dwell on even ground now with thy sons:
Yet doubt not but in valley and in plain
350   God is as here, and will be found alike
Present, and of his presence many a sign
Still following thee, still compassing thee round
With goodness and paternal love, his face
Express, and of his steps the track divine.
355   Which that thou may'st believe, and be confirmed,
Ere thou from hence depart, know I am sent
To show thee what shall come in future days
To thee and to thy offspring,[8] good with bad
Expect to hear, supernal grace contending
360   With sinfulness of men; thereby to learn
True patience, and to temper joy with fear
And pious sorrow, equally inured°   *tempered*
By moderation either state to bare,
Prosperous or adverse: so shalt thou lead
365   Safest thy life, and best prepared endure
Thy mortal passage when it comes. Ascend
This hill; let Eve (for I have drenched her eyes)[9]
Here sleep below while thou to foresight wak'st,
As once thou slept'st while she to life was formed."
370   To whom thus Adam gratefully replied:
"Ascend, I follow thee, safe guide, the path
Thou lead'st me, and to the hand of Heav'n submit,
However chast'ning, to the evil turn
My obvious° breast, arming to overcome   *exposed*
375   By suffering, and earn rest from labor won,
If so I may attain." So both ascend
In the visions of God: it was a hill
Of Paradise the highest, from whose top
The hemisphere of earth in clearest ken°   *view*
380   Stretched out to amplest reach of prospect lay.
Not higher that hill nor wider looking round,
Whereon for different cause the Tempter set
Our second Adam in the wilderness,
To show him all earth's kingdoms and their glory.[1]

---

8. Prophetic visions are a common feature in epic, e.g., Aeneas's vision of his descendants culminating in the Roman Empire (Virgil, *Aeneid* 6.754–854).

9. Put a soporific liquid ("drench") in her eyes.

1. When Satan tempted Christ (the subject of Milton's "brief epic" *Paradise Regained*), he took him up to "an exceeding high mountain" and

385   His eye might there command wherever stood
      City of old or modern fame, the seat
      Of mightiest empire, from the destined walls
      Of Cambalu, seat of Cathaian Can,
      And Samarkand by Oxus, Temir's throne,
390   To Paquin of Sinaean kings, and thence
      To Agra and Lahore of Great Mogul
      Down to the golden Chersonese,[2] or where
      The Persian in Ecbatan sat, or since
      In Hispahan, or where the Russian Czar
395   In Moscow, or the Sultan in Bizance,
      Turkéstan-born;[3] nor could his eye not ken°   *view*
      Th' empire of Negus to his utmost port
      Ercoco and the less maritime kings
      Mombaza, and Quiloa, and Melind,
400   And Sofala thought Ophir, to the realm
      Of Congo, and Angola farthest south;[4]
      Or thence from Niger flood to Atlas mount
      The kingdoms of Almansor, Fez and Sus,
      Marocco and Algiers, and Tremisen;[5]
405   On Europe thence, and where Rome was to sway
      The world: in spirit perhaps he also saw
      Rich Mexico the seat of Motezume,
      And Cusco in Peru, the richer seat
      Of Atabalipa, and yet unspoiled
410   Guiana, whose great city Geryon's sons
      Call El Dorado:[6] but to nobler sights
      Michael from Adam's eyes the film removed
      Which that false fruit that promised clearer sight
      Had bred; then purged with euphrasy and rue[7]
415   The visual nerve, for he had much to see;
      And from the well of life three drops instilled.
      So deep the power of these ingredients pierced,
      Ev'n to the inmost seat of mental sight,

showed him "all the kingdoms of the world, and the glory of them" (Matthew 4.8). The passage that follows details the places "he" (Christ and/or Adam) might see (lines 386–412).

2. His first views are of "destined" (yet to come) great kingdoms in Asia: "Cambalu," capital of "Cathay," the region of North China ruled by such khans as Genghis and Kublai; "Samarkand," ruled by Tamburlaine ("Temir"), near the "Oxus" river near modern Uzbekistan; Beijing ("Paquin," Peking," ruled by Chinese ("Sinaean") kings; "Agra" and "Lahore," capitals in northern India ruled by the "Great Mogul"; "golden Chersonese," an area sometimes identified with the Malay Peninsula.

3. Next, Persian and Turkish kingdoms. From Persia (Iran): Ecbatana ("Echatan"), a summer residence of Persian kings, and the 16th-century Persian capital Isfahan ("Hispahan"); and Byzantium ("Bizance," Constantinople, Istanbul), capital of the Ottoman Empire after falling to the Turks in 1453.

4. From Africa: Abyssinia (empire of King "Negus"); Arkiko ("Ercoco") in Ethiopia, a Red Sea port; Mombasa ("Mombaza") and Malindi ("Melind") in Kenya; Kilwa ("Quiloa") in Tanzania; "Sofala," sometimes identified with the biblical

"Ophir" from which Solomon took gold for his Temple (1 Kings 9.28); and "Congo" and "Angola" on the west coast.

5. In North Africa: the kingdoms of Almansor (the name shared by various Muslim rulers, here referring probably to Abu-Amir al Ma-Ma'afiri, Caliph of Cordova) reached from the "Niger" river in northern Morocco to the "Atlas" mountains in Algeria, taking in Morocco (and its capital, "Fez"), Tunis ("Sus"), and part of Algeria called Tiemecen ("Tremisen").

6. Because they lay on the other side of the spherical earth, Christ and/or Adam could only see places in the New World "in spirit" (line 406): Mexico, the seat of Montezuma ("Motezume"), the last Aztec emperor; "Cusco in Peru," seat of Atahualpa ("Atabalipa"), the last Incan emperor (murdered by Pizarro), and "Guiana" (a region including Surinam, Guyana, and parts of Venezuela and Brazil). Unlike Mexico and Peru it was "yet unspoiled" by the Spaniards (sons of the evil monster Geryon, in Spenser an allegory of the great power and oppression of Spain), though they identified its chief city, Manoa, with the fabled city of gold, "El Dorado."

7. Both herbs were thought to sharpen eyesight.

That Adam now enforced to close his eyes,
420 Sunk down and all his spirits became entranced:
But him the gentle angel by the hand
Soon raised, and his attention thus recalled:
    "Adam, now ope thine eyes, and first behold
Th' effects which thy original crime hath wrought
425 In some to spring from thee, who never touched
Th' excepted° tree, nor with the snake conspired,   *forbidden*
Nor sinned thy sin, yet from that sin derive
Corruption to bring forth more violent deeds."
    His eyes he opened, and beheld a field,
430 Part arable and tilth,° whereon were sheaves   *cultivated*
New-reaped, the other part sheep-walks and folds;
I' th' midst an altar as the landmark° stood   *boundary marker*
Rustic, of grassy sord;° thither anon   *turf*
A sweaty reaper from his tillage brought
435 First-fruits, the green ear, and the yellow sheaf,
Unculled,° as came to hand; a shepherd next   *picked at random*
More meek came with the firstlings of his flock
Choicest and best; then sacrificing, laid
The inwards and their fat, with incense strewed,
440 On the cleft wood, and all due rites performed.
His off'ring soon propitious fire from heav'n
Consumed with nimble glance, and grateful steam;[8]
The other's not, for his was not sincere;
Whereat he inly raged, and as they talked,
445 Smote him into the midriff with a stone
That beat out life; he fell, and deadly pale
Groaned out his soul with gushing blood effused.
Much at that sight was Adam in his heart
Dismayed, and thus in haste to th' angel cried:
450   "O teacher, some great mischief hath befall'n
To that meek man, who well had sacrificed;
Is piety thus and pure devotion paid?"
    T' whom Michael thus, he also moved, replied:
"These two are brethren, Adam, and to come
455 Out of thy loins;[9] th' unjust the just hath slain,
For envy that his brother's offering found
From Heav'n acceptance; but the bloody fact°   *crime*
Will be avenged, and th' other's faith approved
Lose no reward, though here thou see him die,
460 Rolling in dust and gore." To which our sire:
    "Alas, both for the deed and for the cause!
But have I now seen death? Is this the way
I must return to native dust? O sight
Of terror, foul and ugly to behold,
465 Horrid to think, how horrible to feel!"
    To whom thus Michaël: "Death thou hast seen
In his first shape on man; but many shapes

---

8. Milton's version of the Cain and Abel story
(Genesis 4.1–16) provides a clear reason for God's
rejection of Cain's sacrifice.

9. Adam has to be told that these are his own sons,
not simply descendants.

Of Death, and many are the ways that lead
To his grim cave, all dismal; yet to sense
470 More terrible at th' entrance than within.
Some, as thou saw'st, by violent stroke shall die,
By fire, flood, famine; by intemperance more
In meats and drinks, which on the earth shall bring
Diseases dire, of which a monstrous crew
475 Before thee shall appear; that thou may'st know
What misery th' inabstinence of Eve
Shall bring on men." Immediately a place[1]
Before his eyes appeared, sad,° noisome, dark,   *lamentable*
A lazar-house it seemed, wherein were laid
480 Numbers of all diseased, all maladies
Of ghastly spasm, or racking torture, qualms
Of heart-sick agony, all feverous kinds,
Convulsions, epilepsies, fierce catarrhs,
Intestine stone and ulcer, colic pangs,
485 Demoniac frenzy, moping melancholy
And moon-struck madness,° pining atrophy,   *lunacy*
Marasmus, and wide-wasting pestilence,[2]
Dropsies, and asthmas, and joint-racking rheums.
Dire was the tossing, deep the groans, Despair
490 Tended the sick busiest from couch to couch;
And over them triumphant Death his dart
Shook, but delayed to strike, though oft invoked
With vows, as their chief good, and final hope.
Sight so deform what heart of rock could long
495 Dry-eyed behold? Adam could not, but wept,
Though not of woman born; compassion quelled
His best of man,° and gave him up to tears   *manliness, courage*
A space, till firmer thoughts restrained excess,
And scarce recovering words his plaint renewed:
500 "O miserable mankind, to what fall
Degraded, to what wretched state reserved!
Better end here unborn. Why is life giv'n
To be thus wrested from us? Rather why
Obtruded on us thus? who if we knew
505 What we receive, would either not accept
Life offered, or soon beg to lay it down,
Glad to be so dismissed in peace. Can thus
Th' image of God in man created once
So goodly and erect, though faulty since,
510 To such unsightly sufferings be debased
Under inhuman pains? Why should not man,
Retaining still divine similitude
In part, from such deformities be free,
And for his Maker's image sake exempt?"
515 "Their Maker's image," answered Michael, "then
Forsook them, when themselves they vilified°   *debased*

---

1. This is the only nonbiblical sight shown to
Adam, a "lazar-house" (line 479)—a hospital for
leprosy and infectious diseases—described in

partly realistic, partly allegorical terms.
2. The plague. "Marasmus": a wasting disease of
the body.

To serve ungoverned appetite, and took°   *took away*
His image whom they served, a brutish vice,
Inductive° mainly to° the sin of Eve.   *produced/from*
520 Therefore so abject is their punishment,
Disfiguring not God's likeness, but their own,
Or if his likeness, by themselves defaced
While they pervert pure nature's healthful rules
To loathsome sickness, worthily,° since they   *deservedly*
525 God's image did not reverence in themselves."
    "I yield it just," said Adam, "and submit.
But is there yet no other way, besides
These painful passages, how we may come
To death, and mix with our connatural dust?"
530   "There is," said Michael, "if thou well observe
The rule of not too much, by temperance taught
In what thou eat'st and drink'st, seeking from thence
Due nourishment, not gluttonous delight,
Till many years over thy head return:
535 So may'st thou live, till like ripe fruit thou drop
Into thy mother's[3] lap, or be with ease
Gathered, not harshly plucked, for death mature:
This is old age; but then thou must outlive
Thy youth, thy strength, thy beauty, which will change
540 To withered weak and gray; thy senses then
Obtuse, all taste of pleasure must forgo,
To what thou hast, and for the air of youth
Hopeful and cheerful, in thy blood will reign
A melancholy damp° of cold and dry   *depression of spirits*
545 To weigh thy spirits down, and last consume
The balm° of life." To whom our ancestor: *preservative essence*
    "Henceforth I fly not death, nor would prolong
Life much, bent rather how I may be quit
Fairest and easiest of this cumbrous charge,
550 Which I must keep till my appointed day
Of rend'ring up, and patiently attend°   *await*
My dissolution." Michaël replied:
    "Nor love thy life, nor hate; but what thou liv'st
Live well, how long or short permit to Heav'n:
555 And now prepare thee for another sight."
    He looked and saw a spacious plain,[4] whereon
Were tents of various hue; by some were herds
Of cattle grazing: others, whence the sound
Of instruments that made melodious chime
560 Was heard, of harp and organ; and who moved
Their stops and chords was seen:[5] his volant touch
Instinct through all proportions low and high
Fled and pursued transverse the resonant fugue.
In other part stood one[6] who at the forge

3. "Mother" earth.
4. Adam's third vision is based on Genesis 4.19–22; "tents" identifies these as the descendants of Cain, described as "such as dwell in tents."
5. Genesis 4.21 describes Cain's descendant Jubel as "father of all such as handle the harp and organ." "Volant": nimble; "instinct": instinctive; "proportions": ratios of pitches; "fugue": musical form in which one statement of the theme seems to chase another.
6. Tubal-cain, "instructor of every artificer in brass and iron" (Genesis 4.22).

565 Laboring, two massy clods of iron and brass
    Had melted (whether found where casual° fire   *accidental*
    Had wasted woods on mountain or in vale,
    Down to the veins of earth, thence gliding hot
    To some cave's mouth, or whether washed by stream
570 From underground) the liquid ore he drained
    Into fit molds prepared; from which he formed
    First his own tools; then, what might else be wrought
    Fusile° or grav'n in metal. After these,   *cast*
    But on the hither side a different sort[7]
575 From the high neighboring hills, which was their seat,
    Down to the plain descended: by their guise
    Just men they seemed, and all their study bent
    To worship God aright, and know his works
    Not hid,[8] nor those things last which might preserve
580 Freedom and peace to men: they on the plain
    Long had not walked, when from the tents behold
    A bevy of fair women, richly gay
    In gems and wanton dress; to the harp they sung
    Soft amorous ditties, and in dance came on:
585 The men though grave, eyed them, and let their eyes
    Rove without rein, till in the amorous net
    Fast caught, they liked, and each his liking chose;
    And now of love they treat till th' evening star[9]
    Love's harbinger appeared; then all in heat
590 They light the nuptial torch, and bid invoke
    Hymen,[1] then first to marriage rites invoked;
    With feast and music all the tents resound.
    Such happy interview and fair event°   *outcome*
    Of love and youth not lost, songs, garlands, flow'rs,
595 And charming symphonies attached° the heart   *seized*
    Of Adam, soon° inclined to admit delight,   *easily*
    The bent of nature; which he thus expressed:
       "True opener of mine eyes, prime angel blest,
    Much better seems this vision, and more hope
600 Of peaceful days portends, than those two past;
    Those were of hate and death, or pain much worse,
    Here nature seems fulfilled in all her ends."
       To whom thus Michael: "Judge not what is best
    By pleasure, though to nature seeming meet,
605 Created, as thou art, to nobler end
    Holy and pure, conformity divine.
    Those tents thou saw'st so pleasant, were the tents
    Of wickedness, wherein shall dwell his race
    Who slew his brother; studious they appear
610 Of arts that polish life, inventors rare,
    Unmindful of their Maker, though his spirit
    Taught them, but they his gifts acknowledged none.
    Yet they a beauteous offspring shall beget;

7. The descendants of Seth, Adam's third son (Genesis 4.16); "hither side": away from the "East" where Cain's sons lived.
8. They studied God's visible works, not the "mat-ters hid" that Raphael had warned Adam against.
9. Venus.
1. God of marriage.

For that fair female troop thou saw'st, that seemed
615 Of goddesses, so blithe, so smooth, so gay,
Yet empty of all good wherein consists
Woman's domestic honor and chief praise;
Bred only and completed° to the taste   *accomplished*
Of lustful appetence,° to sing, to dance,   *desire*
620 To dress, and troll° the tongue, and roll the eye.   *move*
To these that sober race of men, whose lives
Religious titled them the Sons of God,[2]
Shall yield up all their virtue, all their fame
Ignobly, to the trains° and to the smiles   *wiles, snares*
625 Of these fair atheists, and now swim in joy,
(Erelong to swim at large) and laugh; for which
The world erelong a world of tears must weep."
    To whom thus Adam of short joy bereft:
"O pity and shame, that they who to live well
630 Entered so fair, should turn aside to tread
Paths indirect, or in the mid way faint!
But still I see the tenor of man's woe
Holds on the same, from woman to begin."
    "From man's effeminate slackness it begins,"
635 Said th' angel, "who should better hold his place
By wisdom, and superior gifts received.
But now prepare thee for another scene."
    He looked and saw wide territory spread
Before him, towns, and rural works between,
640 Cities of men with lofty gates and tow'rs,
Concourse° in arms, fierce faces threat'ning war,   *encounters*
Giants[3] of mighty bone, and bold emprise;°   *chivalric adventure*
Part wield their arms, part curb the foaming steed,
Single or in array of battle ranged°   *drawn up in ranks*
645 Both horse and foot, nor idly must'ring stood;
One way a band select from forage drives
A herd of beeves, fair oxen and fair kine
From a fat meadow ground; or fleecy flock,
Ewes and their bleating lambs over the plain,
650 Their booty; scarce with life the shepherds fly,
But call in aid, which makes a bloody fray;
With cruel tournament the squadrons join;
Where cattle pastured late, now scattered lies
With carcasses and arms th' ensanguined° field   *blood-stained*
655 Deserted: others to a city strong
Lay siege, encamped; by battery, scale, and mine,[4]
Assaulting; others from the wall defend
With dart and jav'lin, stones and sulphurous fire;
On each hand slaughter and gigantic deeds.

---

2. Like many exegetes, Milton identifies the "sons of God" as the descendants of Seth, and the "daughters of men" whom they wed (Genesis 6.2) as the descendants of Cain.
3. Adam's fourth vision, based on Genesis 6.4, is of the "Giant" offspring of the previous marriages

(identified at lines 683–84); Milton makes them exemplify false heroism and false glory sought through military might and conquest (lines 689–99).
4. I.e., by battering, scaling, and tunneling under the walls.

660   In other part the sceptered heralds call
      To council in the city gates: anon
      Gray-headed men and grave, with warriors mixed,
      Assemble, and harangues are heard, but soon
      In factious opposition, till at last
665   Of middle age one[5] rising eminent
      In wise deport, spake much of right and wrong,
      Of justice, of religion, truth and peace,
      And judgment from above: him old and young
      Exploded,° and had seized with violent hands,   *mocked*
670   Had not a cloud descending snatched him thence
      Unseen amid the throng: so violence
      Proceeded, and oppression, and sword-law
      Through all the plain, and refuge none was found.
      Adam was all in tears, and to his guide
675   Lamenting turned full sad; "O what are these,
      Death's ministers, not men, who thus deal death
      Inhumanly to men, and multiply
      Ten-thousandfold the sin of him who slew
      His brother; for of whom such massacre
680   Make they but of their brethren, men of men?
      But who was that just man, whom had not Heav'n
      Rescued, had in his righteousness been lost?"
        To whom thus Michael: "These are the product
      Of those ill-mated marriages thou saw'st:
685   Where good with bad were matched, who of themselves
      Abhor to join; and by imprudence mixed,
      Produce prodigious births of body or mind.
      Such were these giants, men of high renown;
      For in those days might only shall be admired,
690   And valor and heroic virtue called;
      To overcome in battle, and subdue
      Nations, and bring home spoils with infinite
      Manslaughter, shall be held the highest pitch
      Of human glory, and for glory done
695   Of triumph, to be styled great conquerors,
      Patrons of mankind, gods, and sons of gods,
      Destroyers rightlier called and plagues of men.
      Thus fame shall be achieved, renown on earth,
      And what most merits fame in silence hid.
700   But he the sev'nth from thee,[6] whom thou beheld'st
      The only righteous in a world perverse,
      And therefore hated, therefore so beset
      With foes for daring single to be just,
      And utter odious truth, that God would come
705   To judge them with his saints: him the Most High
      Rapt in a balmy cloud with winged steeds

---

5. Enoch, who "walked with God; and he was not, for God took him" (Genesis 5.24); Milton elaborates on the story.
6. Here Enoch is more precisely identified by generation, but neither he nor the other biblical personages in these pageants are named. Apparently, Michael and Adam together see the pageants, and Michael (by God's illumination) can interpret them rightly, but neither of the two knows the names these persons will later bear.

Did, as thou saw'st, receive, to walk with God
High in salvation and the climes of bliss,
Exempt from death; to show thee what reward
710 Awaits the good, the rest what punishment;
Which now direct thine eyes and soon behold."
     He looked, and saw the face of things quite changed;
The brazen throat of war had ceased to roar,
All now was turned to jollity and game,
715 To luxury° and riot,° feast and dance,   lust/debauchery
Marrying or prostituting, as befell,
Rape or adultery, where passing fair°   surpassing beauty
Allured them; thence from cups to civil broils.
At length a reverend sire[7] among them came,
720 And of their doings great dislike declared,
And testified against their ways; he oft
Frequented their assemblies, whereso met,
Triumphs or festivals, and to them preached
Conversion and repentance, as to souls
725 In prison under judgments imminent:
But all in vain: which when he saw, he ceased
Contending, and removed his tents far off;
Then from the mountain hewing timber tall,
Began to build a vessel of huge bulk,
730 Measured by cubit, length, and breadth, and height,
Smeared round with pitch, and in the side a door
Contrived, and of provisions laid in large
For man and beast: when lo a wonder strange!
Of every beast, and bird, and insect small
735 Came sevens and pairs, and entered in, as taught
Their order: last the sire and his three sons
With their four wives; and God made fast the door.
Meanwhile the southwind rose, and with black wings
Wide hovering, all the clouds together drove
740 From under heav'n; the hills to their supply°   assistance
Vapor, and exhalation dusk° and moist,   dark mist
Sent up amain;° and now the thickened sky   with main force
Like a dark ceiling stood; down rushed the rain
Impetuous, and continued till the earth
745 No more was seen; the floating vessel swum
Uplifted; and secure with beakèd prow
Rode tilting o'er the waves, all dwellings else
Flood overwhelmed, and them with all their pomp
Deep under water rolled; sea covered sea,
750 Sea without shore;[8] and in their palaces
Where luxury late reigned, sea-monsters whelped
And stabled; of mankind, so numerous late,
All left, in one small bottom° swum embarked.   boat
How didst thou grieve then, Adam, to behold

---

7. Noah. Milton's account is based on Genesis
6–9.
8. The "sea without shore" and some other fea-

tures of this description are taken from Ovid's
account of Deucalion's Flood (*Metamorphoses*
1.292–300, Sandys translation).

755   The end of all thy offspring, end so sad,
       Depopulation; thee another flood,
       Of tears and sorrow a flood thee also drowned,
       And sunk thee as thy sons; till gently reared
       By th' angel, on thy feet thou stood'st at last,
760   Though comfortless, as when a father mourns
       His children, all in view destroyed at once;
       And scarce to th' angel untter'dst thus thy plaint:
         "O visions ill foreseen! Better had I
       Lived ignorant of future, so had borne
765   My part of evil only, each day's lot
       Enough to bear; those now, that were dispensed
       The burd'n of many ages, on me light
       At once, by my foreknowledge[9] gaining birth
       Abortive, to torment me ere their being,
770   With thought that they must be. Let no man seek
       Henceforth to be foretold what shall befall
       Him or his children, evil he may be sure,
       Which neither his foreknowing can prevent,
       And he the future evil shall no less
775   In apprehension than in substance feel
       Grievous to bear: but that care now is past,
       Man is not whom to warn:[1] those few escaped
       Famine and anguish will at last consume
       Wand'ring that wat'ry desert: I had hope
780   When violence was ceased, and war on earth,
       All would have then gone well, peace would have crowned
       With length of happy days the race of man;
       But I was far deceived; for now I see
       Peace to corrupt no less than war to waste.
785   How comes it thus? unfold, celestial guide,
       And whether here the race of man will end."
         To whom thus Michael: "Those whom last thou saw'st
       In triumph and luxurious wealth, are they
       First seen in acts of prowess eminent
790   And great exploits, but of true virtue void;
       Who having spilt much blood, and done much waste
       Subduing nations, and achieved thereby
       Fame in the world, high titles, and rich prey,
       Shall change their course to pleasure, ease, and sloth,
795   Surfeit, and lust, till wantonness and pride
       Raise out of friendship hostile deeds in peace.
       The conquered also, and enslaved by war
       Shall with their freedom lost all virtue lose
       And fear of God, from whom their piety feigned
800   In sharp contést of battle found no aid
       Against invaders; therefore cooled in zeal
       Thenceforth shall practice how to live secure,

9. The term suggests that Adam is experiencing
something akin to God's foreknowledge, which the
poem insists is not predestination. Adam knows

what is to happen but can neither cause it nor prevent it.
1. I.e., There is no man to warn, all will die.

Worldly or dissolute, on what their lords
Shall leave them to enjoy,[2] for th' earth shall bear
805 More than enough, that temperance may be tried:
So all shall turn degenerate, all depraved,
Justice and temperance, truth and faith forgot;
One man except, the only son of light
In a dark age, against example good,
810 Against allurement, custom, and a world
Offended;° fearless of reproach and scorn,   hostile
Or violence, he of their wicked ways
Shall them admonish, and before them set
The paths of righteousness, how much more safe,
815 And full of peace, denouncing° wrath to come   proclaiming
On their impenitence; and shall return
Of them derided, but of God observed
The one just man alive; by his command
Shall build a wondrous ark, as thou beheld'st,
820 To save himself and household from amidst
A world devote° to universal wrack.   doomed
No sooner he with them of man and beast
Select for life shall in the ark be lodged,
And sheltered round, but all the cataracts°   floodgates
825 Of heav'n set open on the earth shall pour
Rain day and night, all fountains of the deep
Broke up, shall heave the ocean to usurp
Beyond all bounds, till inundation rise
Above the highest hills: then shall this mount
830 Of Paradise by might of waves be moved
Out of his place, pushed by the hornèd flood,[3]
With all his verdure spoiled, and trees adrift
Down the great river to the op'ning gulf,[4]
And there take root an island salt and bare,
835 The haunt of seals and orcs,° and sea-mews'° clang. sea monsters/gulls
To teach thee that God áttributes to place
No sanctity, if none be thither brought
By men who there frequent, or therein dwell.
And now what further shall ensue, behold."
840   He looked, and saw the ark hull° on the flood,   drift
Which now abated, for the clouds were fled,
Driv'n by a keen north wind, that blowing dry
Wrinkled the face of deluge, as decayed;
And the clear sun on his wide wat'ry glass
845 Gazed hot, and of the fresh wave largely drew,
As after thirst, which made their flowing shrink
From standing lake to tripping° ebb, that stole   running
With soft foot towards the deep, who now had stopped
His sluices, as the heav'n his windows shut.
850 The ark no more now floats, but seems on ground

---

2. This passage (lines 797–806) may also allude
to the backsliding Puritans who betrayed the Commonwealth in 1660 and have now taken on the
vices of the restored royalists.

3. Classical river gods were often depicted as
horned.
4. I.e., down the Euphrates River to the Persian
Gulf.

Fast on the top of some high mountain fixed.[5]
And now the tops of hills as rocks appear;
With clamor thence the rapid currents drive
Towards the retreating sea their furious tide.
855 Forthwith from out the ark a raven flies,
And after him, the surer messenger,
A dove sent forth once and again to spy
Green tree or ground whereon his foot may light;
The second time returning, in his bill
860 An olive leaf he brings, pacific sign:
Anon dry ground appears, and from his ark
The ancient sire descends with all his train;
Then with uplifted hands, and eyes devout,
Grateful to Heav'n, over his head beholds
865 A dewy cloud, and in the cloud a bow
Conspicuous with three listed colors gay,[6]
Betok'ning peace from God, and cov'nant new.
Whereat the heart of Adam erst so sad
Greatly rejoiced, and thus his joy broke forth:
870 "O thou who future things canst represent
As present, heav'nly instructor, I revive
At this last sight, assured that man shall live
With all the creatures, and their seed preserve.
Far less I now lament for one whole world
875 Of wicked sons destroyed, than I rejoice
For one man found so perfect and so just,
That God vouchsafes to raise another world
From him, and all his anger to forget.[7]
But say, what mean those colored streaks in heav'n,
880 Distended° as the brow of God appeased,   *spread out*
Or serve they as a flow'ry verge to bind
The fluid skirts of that same wat'ry cloud,
Lest it again dissolve and show'r the earth?"
To whom th' Archangel: "Dextrously thou aim'st;
885 So willingly doth God remit his ire,
Though late repenting him of man depraved,
Grieved at his heart, when looking down he saw
The whole earth filled with violence, and all flesh
Corrupting each their way; yet those removed,
890 Such grace shall one just man find in his sight,
That he relents, not to blot out mankind,
And makes a cov'nant[8] never to destroy
The earth again by flood, nor let the sea
Surpass his bounds, nor rain to drown the world
895 With man therein or beast; but when he brings
Over the earth a cloud, will therein set
His triple-colored bow, whereon to look

5. Mount Ararat (Genesis 8.4).
6. The primary colors, red, yellow, and blue.
7. The language invites recognition of Noah as a type (foreshadowing) of Christ, the one "perfect" and "just" who will cause God to forget his anger.

8. The language of covenant makes this promise— that God will not again destroy the earth by flood— a type of the "covenant of grace" through which God will save humankind.

And call to mind his cov'nant: day and night,
Seed-time and harvest, heat and hoary frost
900   Shall hold their course, till fire purge all things new,
Both Heav'n and earth, wherein the just shall dwell."[9]

Book 12

As one who in his journey bates° at noon,   *stops for refreshment*
Though bent on speed, so here the Archangel paused
Betwixt the world destroyed and world restored,
If Adam aught perhaps might interpose;
5   Then with transition sweet new speech resumes:[1]
    "Thus thou hast seen one world begin and end;
And man as from a second stock proceed.
Much thou hast yet to see, but I perceive
Thy mortal sight to fail; objects divine
10   Must needs impair and weary human sense:
Henceforth what is to come I will relate,[2]
Thou therefore give due audience, and attend.
This second source of men, while yet but few,
And while the dread of judgment past remains
15   Fresh in their minds, fearing the Deity,
With some regard to what is just and right
Shall lead their lives, and multiply apace,
Laboring the soil, and reaping plenteous crop,
Corn wine and oil; and from the herd or flock,
20   Oft sacrificing bullock, lamb, or kid,
With large wine-offerings poured, and sacred feast,
Shall spend their days in joy unblamed, and dwell
Long time in peace by families and tribes
Under paternal rule; till one[3] shall rise
25   Of proud ambitious heart, who not content
With fair equality, fraternal state,
Will arrogate dominion undeserved
Over his brethren, and quite dispossess
Concord and law of nature from the earth;
30   Hunting (and men not beasts shall be his game)
With war and hostile snare such as refuse
Subjection to his empire tyrannous:
A mighty hunter thence he shall be styled
Before the Lord, as in despite of Heav'n,
35   Or from Heav'n claiming second sovranty;[4]

---

9. The restoration of the orderly processes of nature after the Flood is identified as a type (foreshadowing) of the final renewal of all things after the final conflagration at the Last Judgment.
1. The first five lines were added when Book 10 of the 1667 edition was divided to make Books 11 and 12 of the 1674 edition.
2. Adam no longer sees visions or pageants, as before, but simply listens to Michael's narration.
3. Nimrod (Genesis 10.8–10) is described as the first king, in terms that equate kingship itself with tyranny (lines 25–29).

4. Milton offers two explanations of the biblical phrase "Before the Lord": either he openly defied God ("despite") or he claimed divine right ("second sovranty") like the Stuart kings. Drawing on the (false) etymology linking the name Nimrod with the Hebrew "to rebel," Milton implies that the paradox developed in the next two lines (that he accuses others of rebellion but is himself a rebel against God) extends to other kings, especially Charles I, who accused his opponents in the Civil War of rebellion.

And from rebellion shall derive his name,
Though of rebellion others he accuse.
He with a crew, whom like ambition joins
With him or under him to tyrannize,
40   Marching from Eden towards the west, shall find
The plain, wherein a black bituminous gurge°   *whirlpool*
Boils out from under ground, the mouth of Hell;
Of brick, and of that stuff they cast° to build   *decide*
A city and tow'r,[5] whose top may reach to Heav'n;
45   And get themselves a name, lest far dispersed
In foreign lands their memory be lost,
Regardless whether good or evil fame.
But God who oft descends to visit men
Unseen, and through their habitations walks
50   To mark their doings, them beholding soon,
Comes down to see their city, ere the tower
Obstruct Heav'n tow'rs, and in derision sets
Upon their tongues a various° spirit to raze   *divisive*
Quite out their native language, and instead
55   To sow a jangling noise of words unknown:
Forthwith a hideous gabble[6] rises loud
Among the builders; each to other calls
Not understood, till hoarse, and all in rage,
As mocked they storm; great laughter was in Heav'n
60   And looking down, to see the hubbub strange
And hear the din; thus was the building left
Ridiculous, and the work Confusion[7] named."
    Whereto thus Adam fatherly displeased:
"O execrable son so to aspire
65   Above his brethren, to himself assuming
Authority usurped, from God not giv'n:
He gave us only over beast, fish, fowl
Dominion absolute; that right we hold
By his donation; but man over men
70   He made not lord; such title to himself
Reserving, human left from human free.[8]
But this usurper his encroachment proud
Stays not on man; to God his tower intends
Siege and defiance: wretched man! What food
75   Will he convey up thither to sustain
Himself and his rash army, where thin air
Above the clouds will pine° his entrails gross,   *waste away*
And famish him of breath, if not of bread?"
    To whom thus Michael: "Justly thou abhorr'st
80   That son, who on the quiet state of men
Such trouble brought, affecting° to subdue   *aspiring*
Rational liberty; yet know withal,

---

5. Babylon is the city, Babel the Tower.
6. Genesis 11.1–9 recounts the building of the Tower of Babel reaching to Heaven; God punished this presumption by confounding the builders' original language into multiple languages.

7. "Confusion" was taken to be the meaning of "Babel."
8. Adam states the assumption Milton often invokes to support republicanism.

Since thy original lapse, true liberty
Is lost, which always with right reason dwells
85 Twinned, and from her hath no dividual° being:[9]   *separate*
Reason in man obscured, or not obeyed,
Immediately inordinate desires
And upstart passions catch the government
From reason, and to servitude reduce
90 Man till then free. Therefore since he permits
Within himself unworthy powers to reign
Over free reason, God in judgment just
Subjects him from without to violent lords;
Who oft as undeservedly enthrall
95 His outward freedom: tyranny must be,
Though to the tyrant thereby no excuse.
Yet sometimes nations will decline so low
From virtue, which is reason, that no wrong,
But justice, and some fatal curse annexed
100 Deprives them of their outward liberty,
Their inward lost: witness th' irreverent son[1]
Of him who built the ark, who for the shame
Done to his father, heard this heavy curse,
'Servant of servants,' on his vicious race.[2]
105 Thus will this latter, as the former world,
Still tend from bad to worse, till God at last
Wearied with their iniquities, withdraw
His presence from among them, and avert
His holy eyes; resolving from thenceforth
110 To leave them to their own polluted ways;
And one peculiar° nation to select   *special*
From all the rest, of whom to be invoked,
A nation from one faithful man[3] to spring:
Him on this side Euphrates yet residing,
115 Bred up in idol-worship; O that men
(Canst thou believe?) should be so stupid grown,
While yet the patriarch[4] lived, who scaped the Flood,
As to forsake the living God, and fall
To worship their own work in wood and stone
120 For gods! Yet him God the Most High vouchsafes
To call by vision from his father's house,
His kindred and false gods, into a land
Which he will show him, and from him will raise
A mighty nation, and upon him show'r

9. As Milton (following classical theorists) often
did, and as Abdiel did earlier (6.179–81), Michael
links political to psychological servitude, and
political liberty to inner freedom, i.e., the exercise
of "right reason" and the control of passion. Loss
of liberty is often (though not always) God's just
punishment for national decline (lines 81–100).
The long passage alludes to the "baseness" of the
English in restoring monarchy in 1660.
1. Ham, son of Noah, who looked on the nakedness of his father and brought down the curse that
his descendants would be "servant of servants" to

their brethren (Genesis 9.24–25).
2. Tribe. "Race" did not then bear its modern
sense, so Milton is probably thinking of the
Canaanites (descendants of Ham's son Canaan)
rather than black Africans; blacks were, however,
classed among Ham's descendants and this biblical
text was used to justify slavery.
3. Abraham, whose name means "Father of many
nations"; the passage is based on Genesis 11.27 to
25.10.
4. Noah, who lived for 350 years after the Flood.

125　His benediction so, that in his seed
　　All nations shall be blest; he straight obeys,
　　Not knowing to what land, yet firm believes:
　　I see him, but thou canst not,⁵ with what faith
　　He leaves his gods, his friends, and native soil
130　Ur⁶ of Chaldaea, passing now the ford
　　To Haran, after him a cumbrous train
　　Of herds and flocks, and numerous servitude;° *servants and slaves*
　　Not wand'ring poor, but trusting all his wealth
　　With God, who called him, in a land unknown.
135　Canaan he now attains, I see his tents
　　Pitched about Sechem, and the neighboring plain
　　Of Moreh; there by promise he receives
　　Gift to his progeny of all that land;
　　From Hamath⁷ northward to the desert south
140　(Things by their names I call, though yet unnamed)
　　From Hermon east to the great western sea,
　　Mount Hermon, yonder sea, each place behold
　　In prospect, as I point them; on the shore
　　Mount Carmel;⁸ here the double-founted stream
145　Jordan, true limit eastward; but his sons
　　Shall dwell to Senir, that long ridge of hills.
　　This ponder, that all nations of the earth
　　Shall in his seed be blessed; by that seed
　　Is meant thy great Deliverer,⁹ who shall bruise
150　The Serpent's head; whereof to thee anon
　　Plainlier shall be revealed. This patriarch blest,
　　Whom 'faithful Abraham'¹ due time shall call,
　　A son, and of his son a grandchild leaves,
　　Like him in faith, in wisdom, and renown;
155　The grandchild with twelve sons increased, departs
　　From Canaan, to a land hereafter called
　　Egypt, divided by the river Nile;
　　See where it flows,² disgorging at seven mouths
　　Into the sea: to sojourn in that land
160　He comes invited by a younger son³
　　In time of dearth,° a son whose worthy deeds *famine*
　　Raise him to be the second in that realm
　　Of Pharaoh: there he dies, and leaves his race
　　Growing into a nation, and now grown

---

5. Michael evidently continues to see the stories he recounts as visionary scenes or pageants; Adam must accept the story of Abraham "by faith," analogous to the faith Abraham himself displays.
6. Ur was on one bank of the Euphrates, "Haran" (line 131) on the other, to the northwest.
7. The Promised Land was bounded on the north by "Hamath," a city on the Orontes River in west Syria; on the south by the wilderness "desert" of Zin; on the east by "Mount Hermon"; and on the west by the Mediterranean, the "great western sea" (lines 139–42).
8. A mountain range near Haifa, on the Mediterranean coast of Israel; "Jordan," the river thought incorrectly to have two sources ("double-

founted"), the Jor and the Dan; Senir (line 146), a peak of Mount Hermon.
9. Michael interprets the promise to Abraham (Genesis 17.5, "a father of many nations have I made thee") typologically, as to be fulfilled in Christ, the "woman's seed."
1. Echoes Galatians 3.9: "So then they which be of faith are blessed with faithful Abraham." His son (line 153) is Isaac and his grandson, Jacob.
2. Adam can apparently see geographical features, though not the scenes Michael sees and describes.
3. Joseph, the next youngest of Jacob's twelve sons, invited the Israelites to Egypt to escape famine, but they were subsequently made slaves (Genesis 21–50).

165 Suspected to° a sequent° king, who seeks   *by/successive*
    To stop their overgrowth, as inmate° guests   *foreign*
    Too numerous; whence of guests he makes them slaves
    Inhospitably, and kills their infant males:
    Till by two brethren (those two brethren call
170 Moses and Aaron) sent from God to claim
    His people from enthralment,[4] they return
    With glory and spoil back to their promised land.
    But first the lawless tyrant, who denies°   *refuses*
    To know their God, or message to regard,
175 Must be compelled by signs and judgments dire;[5]
    To blood unshed the rivers must be turned,
    Frogs, lice and flies must all his palace fill
    With loathed intrusion, and fill all the land;
    His cattle must of rot and murrain° die,   *cattle plague*
180 Botches[6] and blains must all his flesh emboss,
    And all his people; thunder mixed with hail,
    Hail mixed with fire must rend th' Egyptian sky
    And wheel on th' earth, devouring where it rolls;
    What it devours not, herb, or fruit, or grain,
185 A darksome cloud of locusts swarming down
    Must eat, and on the ground leave nothing green:
    Darkness must overshadow all his bounds,
    Palpable darkness, and blot out three days;
    Last with one midnight stroke all the first-born
190 Of Egypt must lie dead. Thus with ten wounds°   *plagues*
    The river-dragon[7] tamed at length submits
    To let his sojourners depart, and oft
    Humbles his stubborn heart, but still as ice
    More hardened after thaw, till in his rage
195 Pursuing whom he late dismissed, the sea
    Swallows him with his host, but them lets pass
    As on dry land[8] between two crystal walls,
    Awed by the rod of Moses so to stand
    Divided, till his rescued gain their shore:
200 Such wondrous power God to his saint will lend,
    Though present in his angel,[9] who shall go
    Before them in a cloud, and pillar of fire,
    By day a cloud, by night a pillar of fire,
    To guide them in their journey, and remove
205 Behind them, while th' obdúrate king pursues:
    All night he will pursue, but his approach
    Darkness defends° between till morning watch;   *prevents*
    Then through the fiery pillar and the cloud
    God looking forth will trouble all his host

---

4. The story of Moses and Aaron leading the Israelites from captivity to the Promised Land is told in Exodus and Deuteronomy.

5. The ten plagues, recounted in lines 175–90.

6. Boils; "blains": blisters; "emboss": cover as with studs.

7. The Egyptian Pharaoh is termed "the great dragon that lieth in the midst of his rivers" (Ezekiel 29.3).

8. The Red Sea was parted by the rod of Moses; the Israelites passed through but Pharoah's pursuing forces drowned as the water rushed back (Exodus 13.17–22 and 14.5–31).

9. Milton repeats here a view developed in his *Christian Doctrine*, that God was "present in his angel," not in his own person, in the cloud and pillar of fire that led the Israelites on their journey (Exodus 13.21–24).

210　And craze° their chariot wheels: when by command　　　　　*shatter*
　　　Moses once more his potent rod extends
　　　Over the sea; the sea his rod obeys;
　　　On their embattled ranks the waves return,
　　　And overwhelm their war:° the race elect　　　　　　　　　*armies*
215　Safe towards Canaan from the shore advance
　　　Through the wild desert, not the readiest way,
　　　Lest ent'ring on the Canaanite alarmed°　　　　　　　*prepared to fight*
　　　War terrify them inexpert, and fear
　　　Return them back to Egypt, choosing rather
220　Inglorious life with servitude; for life
　　　To noble and ignoble is more sweet
　　　Untrained in arms, where rashness leads not on.[1]
　　　This also shall they gain by their delay
　　　In the wide wilderness, there they shall found
225　Their government, and their great senate[2] choose
　　　Through the twelve tribes, to rule by laws ordained:
　　　God from the mount of Sinai, whose gray top
　　　Shall tremble, he descending, will himself
　　　In thunder, lightning and loud trumpet's sound
230　Ordain them laws;[3] part such as appertain
　　　To civil justice, part religious rites
　　　Of sacrifice, informing them, by types
　　　And shadows,[4] of that destined Seed to bruise
　　　The Serpent, by what means he shall achieve
235　Mankind's deliverance. But the voice of God
　　　To mortal ear is dreadful; they beseech
　　　That Moses might report to them his will,
　　　And terror cease; he grants what they besought
　　　Instructed that to God is no access
240　Without mediator, whose high office now
　　　Moses in figure[5] bears, to introduce
　　　One greater, of whose day he shall foretell,
　　　And all the Prophets in their age the times
　　　Of great Messiah shall sing. Thus laws and rites
245　Established, such delight hath God in men
　　　Obedient to his will, that he vouchsafes
　　　Among them to set up his tabernacle,
　　　The Holy One with mortal men to dwell:
　　　By his prescript a sanctuary is framed
250　Of cedar, overlaid with gold, therein
　　　An ark, and in the ark his testimony,
　　　The records of his cov'nant, over these
　　　A mercy-seat of gold between the wings
　　　Of two bright Cherubim, before him burn
255　Seven lamps as in a zodiac° representing　　　　　　*like the planets*

1. I.e., unless prompted by "rashness," those "untrained in arms" will choose servitude rather than battle.
2. The "Seventy Elders" of the Sanhedrin, whom Milton cites as a model for republican government in his *Ready and Easy Way*.
3. God delivered ceremonial, civil, and moral/religious laws (the Ten Commandments) to Moses on

Mount Sinai, with thunder and lightning (lines 227–32; Exodus 19–31).
4. The principle of typology, whereby persons and events in the Old Testament are seen to prefigure Christ or matters pertaining to his life or the Christian church.
5. Moses is a type of Christ in his role as mediator between the people and God.

345　The space of seventy years, then brings them back,
　　　Rememb'ring mercy, and his cov'nant sworn
　　　To David, stablished as the days of Heav'n.
　　　Returned from Babylon by leave of kings[8]
　　　Their lords, whom God disposed,° the house of God　　　*made well-disposed*
350　They first re-edify, and for a while
　　　In mean estate live moderate, till grown
　　　In wealth and multitude, factious they grow;
　　　But first among the priests dissension springs,
　　　Men who attend the altar, and should most
355　Endeavor peace: their strife pollution brings
　　　Upon the temple itself: at last they seize
　　　The scepter, and regard not David's sons,°　　　*descendants*
　　　Then lose it to a stranger,[9] that the true
　　　Anointed King Messiah might be born
360　Barred of his right; yet at his birth a star
　　　Unseen before in heav'n proclaims him come,
　　　And guides the eastern sages,° who inquire　　　*the Magi*
　　　His place, to offer incense, myrrh, and gold;
　　　His place of birth a solemn° angel tells　　　*awe-inspiring*
365　To simple shepherds, keeping watch by night;
　　　They gladly thither haste, and by a choir
　　　Of squadroned angels hear his carol sung.
　　　A virgin is his mother, but his sire
　　　The Power of the Most High; he shall ascend
370　The throne hereditary, and bound his reign
　　　With earth's wide bounds, his glory with the heav'ns."
　　　　　He ceased, discerning Adam with such joy
　　　Surcharged,° as had like grief been dewed in tears,　　　*overwhelmed*
　　　Without the vent of words, which these he breathed:
375　　　"O prophet of glad tidings, finisher
　　　Of utmost hope! now clear I understand
　　　What oft my steadiest thoughts have searched in vain,
　　　Why our great expectation should be called
　　　The Seed of Woman: Virgin Mother, hail,
380　High in the love of Heav'n, yet from my loins
　　　Thou shalt proceed, and from thy womb the Son
　　　Of God Most High; so God with man unites.
　　　Needs must the Serpent now his capital° bruise　　　*on the head, fatal*
　　　Expect with mortal pain: say where and when
385　Their fight, what stroke shall bruise the Victor's heel."
　　　　　To whom thus Michael: "Dream not of their fight,
　　　As of a duel, or the local wounds
　　　Of head or heel: not therefore joins the Son
　　　Manhood to Godhead, with more strength to foil
390　Thy enemy; nor so is overcome
　　　Satan, whose fall from Heav'n, a deadlier bruise,

8. The Persian kings Cyrus the Great, Darius, and
Artaxerxes allowed the Jews to return from Babylon
and rebuild the Temple.
9. Antiochus, father of Herod the Great (who
ruled at the time of Christ's birth), was made governor of Jerusalem in 61 B.C.E. by the Romans, and

procurator of Judaea in 47 B.C.E. Prior to this (lines
353–57), strife among the priests allowed the Sel-
ucid king Antiochus IV to sack Jerusalem and pollute the Temple; then one of the Maccabees seized
the throne, disregarding the claims of David's
dynasty.

Disabled not to give thee thy death's wound:
Which he who comes thy Savior, shall recure,°   *heal*
Not by destroying Satan, but his works
395   In thee and in thy seed: nor can this be,
But by fulfilling that which thou didst want,°   *lack*
Obedience to the law of God, imposed
On penalty of death, and suffering death,
The penalty to thy transgression due,
400   And due to theirs which out of thine will grow:
So only can high justice rest apaid.°   *satisfied*
The law of God exact he shall fulfill
Both by obedience and by love, though love
Alone fulfill the law; thy punishment
405   He shall endure by coming in the flesh
To a reproachful life and cursèd death,
Proclaiming life to all who shall believe
In his redemption, and that his obedience
Imputed becomes theirs by faith, his merits
410   To save them, not their own, though legal works.[1]
For this he shall live hated, be blasphemed,
Seized on by force, judged, and to death condemned
A shameful and accursed, nailed to the Cross
By his own nation, slain for bringing life;
415   But to the Cross he nails thy enemies,
The law that is against thee, and the sins
Of all mankind, with him there crucified,
Never to hurt them more who rightly trust
In this his satisfaction; so he dies,
420   But soon revives, Death over him no power
Shall long usurp; ere the third dawning light
Return, the stars of morn shall see him rise
Out of his grave, fresh as the dawning light,
Thy ransom paid, which man from Death redeems,
425   His death for man, as many as offered life[2]
Neglect not, and the benefit embrace
By faith not void of works: this God-like act
Annuls thy doom, the death thou shouldst have died,
In sin for ever lost from life; this act
430   Shall bruise the head of Satan, crush his strength
Defeating Sin and Death, his two main arms,
And fix far deeper in his head their stings
Than temporal death shall bruise the Victor's heel,
Or theirs whom he redeems, a death like sleep,
435   A gentle wafting to immortal life.
Nor after resurrection shall he stay
Longer on earth than certain times to appear
To his disciples, men who in his life
Still followed him; to them shall leave in charge

---

1. Michael restates the theological doctrine that humans can only be saved by Christ's merits attributed to them vicariously ("imputed"), not by their own good works performed according to God's law ("legal").

2. I.e., for as many as accept ("neglect not") his offer of life.

440 To teach all nations what of him they learned
And his salvation, them who shall believe
Baptizing in the profluent° stream, the sign   *flowing*
Of washing them from guilt of sin to life
Pure, and in mind prepared, if so befall,
445 For death, like that which the Redeemer died.
All nations they shall teach; for from that day
Not only to the sons of Abraham's loins
Salvation shall be preached, but to the sons
Of Abraham's faith wherever through the world;
450 So in his seed all nations shall be blest.[3]
Then to the Heav'n of Heav'ns he shall ascend
With victory, triumphing through the air
Over his foes and thine; there shall surprise
The Serpent, prince of air, and drag in chains
455 Through all his realm, and there confounded leave;
Then enter into glory, and resume
His seat at God's right hand, exalted high
Above all names in Heav'n; and thence shall come,
When this world's dissolution shall be ripe
460 With glory and power to judge both quick° and dead,   *living*
To judge th' unfaithful dead, but to reward
His faithful, and receive them into bliss,
Whether in Heav'n or earth, for then the earth
Shall all be paradise, far happier place
465 Than this of Eden, and far happier days."
      So spake th' Archangel Michaël, then paused,
As at the world's great period;° and our sire   *consummation*
Replete with joy and wonder thus replied:
      "O goodness infinite, goodness immense!
470 That all this good of evil shall produce,
And evil turn to good; more wonderful
Than that which by creation first brought forth
Light out of darkness! Full of doubt I stand,
Whether I should repent me now of sin
475 By me done and occasioned, or rejoice
Much more, that much more good thereof shall spring,
To God more glory, more good will to men
From God, and over wrath grace shall abound.[4]
But say, if our Deliverer up to Heav'n
480 Must reascend, what will betide the few
His faithful, left among th' unfaithful herd,
The enemies of truth; who then shall guide
His people, who defend? Will they not deal
Worse with his followers than with him they dealt?"
485   "Be sure they will," said th' angel; "but from Heav'n
He to his own a Comforter will send,[5]

---

3. Michael spells out the application to Christ of the promise offered typologically to Abraham's seed.

4. These lines do not formulate the medieval idea of the *felix culpa*—that the Fall was fortunate in bringing humans greater happiness than they would otherwise have enjoyed—only that the Fall

has provided God an occasion to bring still greater good out of evil. The poem makes clear that Adam and Eve would have grown in perfection and advanced to Heaven had they not sinned.

5. The Holy Spirit, who for Milton is much subordinate to both Father and Son.

The promise of the Father, who shall dwell
His Spirit within them, and the law of faith
Working through love, upon their hearts shall write,
490 To guide them in all truth, and also arm
With spiritual armor, able to resist
Satan's assaults, and quench his fiery darts,[6]
What° man can do against them, not afraid,   *as much as*
Though to the death, against such cruelties
495 With inward consolations recompensed,
And oft supported so as shall amaze
Their proudest persecutors: for the Spirit
Poured first on his apostles, whom he sends
To evangelize the nations, then on all
500 Baptized, shall them with wondrous gifts endue°   *endow*
To speak all tongues, and do all miracles,
As did their Lord before them. Thus they win
Great numbers of each nation to receive
With joy the tidings brought from Heav'n: at length
505 Their ministry performed, and race well run,
Their doctrine and their story written left,[7]
They die; but in their room, as they forewarn,
Wolves shall succeed for teachers, grievous wolves,
Who all the sacred mysteries of Heav'n
510 To their own vile advantages shall turn
Of lucre and ambition, and the truth
With superstitions and traditions taint,[8]
Left only in those written records pure,
Though not but by the Spirit understood.
515 Then shall they seek to avail themselves of names,°   *honors*
Places° and titles, and with these to join   *offices*
Secular power, though feigning still to act
By spiritual, to themselves appropriating
The Spirit of God, promised alike and giv'n
520 To all believers;[9] and from that pretense,
Spiritual laws by carnal° power shall force   *fleshly, worldly*
On every conscience; laws which none shall find
Left them enrolled, or what the Spirit within
Shall on the heart engrave.[1] What will they then
525 But force the Spirit of Grace itself, and bind
His consort Liberty; what, but unbuild
His living temples,[2] built by faith to stand,

[handwritten marginal note:] wolves = bad priests. the church becomes corrupt, things don't always get better.

6. Cf. Ephesians 6.11–16: "Put on the whole armor of God, that ye may be able to stand against the wiles of the devil. . . . Above all, taking the shield of faith, wherewith ye shall be able to quench all the fiery darts of the wicked." The subsequent history (lines 493–505) is that of the early Christian church in apostolic times.
7. I.e., in the Gospels and Epistles.
8. The history summarized in lines 510–40 is of the corruption of the Christian church by superstitions, traditions, and persecutions of conscience in patristic times under the popes and the Christian emperors, but also extending to the Last Day. The terms point especially to what Milton saw as the revival of "popish" superstitions in the English Church of the Restoration, and to the fierce persecution of Dissenters.
9. These lines affirm the Protestant principle of every Christian's right to interpret Scripture according to the "inner light" of the Spirit, and denounce (as Milton consistently did in his tracts) the use of civil ("carnal") power to enforce orthodoxy.
1. I.e., there is nothing in Scripture or in the Spirit's inner teaching that sanctions persecution for conscience.
2. Cf. 1 Corinthians 3.16: "Know ye not that ye are the temple of God?" "His consort Liberty": Milton typically insists that Christ's gospel and the Spirit of God teach liberty, religious and civil, alluding as here to 2 Corinthians 3.17: 'Where the Spirit of the Lord is, there is Liberty."

Their own faith not another's: for on earth
Who against faith and conscience can be heard
530 Infallible?[3] Yet many will presume:
Whence heavy persecution shall arise
On all who in the worship persevere
Of Spirit and Truth; the rest, far greater part,
Will deem in outward rites and specious forms
535 Religion satisfied; Truth shall retire
Bestuck with sland'rous darts, and works of faith
Rarely be found: so shall the world go on,
To good malignant, to bad men benign,
Under her own weight groaning, till the day
540 Appear of respiration° to the just,   respite
And vengeance to the wicked, at return
Of him so lately promised to thy aid,
The Woman's Seed,[4] obscurely then foretold,
Now amplier known thy Saviour and thy Lord,
545 Last in the clouds from Heav'n to be revealed
In glory of the Father, to dissolve
Satan with his perverted world, then raise
From the conflagrant mass,° purged and refined,   the burning world
New heav'ns, new earth, ages of endless date
550 Founded in righteousness and peace of love,
To bring forth fruits joy and eternal bliss."
He ended; and thus Adam last replied:
"How soon hath thy prediction, seer blest,
Measured this transient world, the race of time,
555 Till time stand fixed: beyond is all abyss,
Eternity, whose end no eye can reach.
Greatly instructed I shall hence depart,
Greatly in peace of thought, and have my fill
Of knowledge, what° this vessel can contain;   as much as
560 Beyond which was my folly to aspire.
Henceforth I learn, that to obey is best,
And love with fear the only God, to walk
As in his presence, ever to observe
His providence, and on him sole depend,
565 Merciful over all his works, with good
Still overcoming evil, and by small
Accomplishing great things, by things deemed weak
Subverting worldly strong, and worldly wise
By simply meek; that suffering for truth's sake
570 Is fortitude to highest victory,
And to the faithful death the gate of life;
Taught this by his example whom I now
Acknowledge my Redeemer ever blest."
To whom thus also th' angel last replied:
575 "This having learnt, thou hast attained the sum
Of wisdom; hope no higher, though all the stars

---

3. An attack on papal claims to infallibility, asserted though not yet proclaimed as doctrine.
4. Michael's story ends with the full explication of the promised "Woman's Seed" as Christ, and with the renewal of all things after the Last Judgment (lines 545–51).

Thou knew'st by name,[5] and all th' ethereal powers,
All secrets of the deep, all nature's works,
Or works of God in heav'n, air, earth, or sea,
580 And all the riches of this world enjoy'dst,
And all the rule, one empire; only add
Deeds to thy knowledge answerable,° add faith,   *corresponding*
Add virtue, patience, temperance, add love,
By name to come called charity, the soul
585 Of all the rest: then wilt thou not be loath
To leave this Paradise, but shalt possess
A paradise within thee, happier far.
Let us descend now therefore from this top
Of speculation;° for the hour precise   *hill of speculation*
590 Exacts° our parting hence; and see the guards,   *requires*
By me encamped on yonder hill, expect
Their motion,° at whose front a flaming sword,   *await their orders*
In signal of remove, waves fiercely round;
We may no longer stay: go, waken Eve;
595 Her also I with gentle dreams have calmed
Portending good, and all her spirits composed
To meek submission: thou at season fit
Let her with thee partake what thou hast heard,
Chiefly what may concern her faith to know,
600 The great deliverance by her seed to come
(For by the Woman's Seed) on all mankind.
That ye may live, which will be many days,
Both in one faith unanimous though sad,
With cause for evils past, yet much more cheered
605 With meditation on the happy end."
    He ended, and they both descend the hill;
Descended, Adam to the bow'r where Eve
Lay sleeping ran before, but found her waked;
And thus with words not sad she him received:
610   "Whence thou return'st, and whither went'st, I know;
For God is also in sleep, and dreams advise,[6]
Which he hath sent propitious, some great good
Presaging, since with sorrow and heart's distress
Wearied I fell asleep: but now lead on;
615 In me is no delay; with thee to go,
Is to stay here; without thee here to stay,
Is to go hence unwilling; thou to me
Art all things under heav'n,[7] all places thou,
Who for my wilful crime art banished hence.
620 This further consolation yet secure
I carry hence; though all by me is lost,

---

5. Michael glances back at Raphael's warning in Book 8 that Adam should concern himself first with matters pertaining to his own life and world, rather than speculating overmuch about the cosmos.

6. The lines suggest that Eve's dream has provided her a parallel (if lesser) prophecy to Adam's visions and instruction. Cf. Numbers 12.6: "If there be a prophet among you, I the Lord will make myself known unto him in a vision, and will speak to him in a dream."

7. Eve has the last word in the poem, a love-song recalling her lovely prelapsarian lyric (4.641ff.). Her language also recalls Ruth's promise to accompany her mother-in-law, Naomi (Ruth 1.16). In her last lines (621–23) she rather surprisingly characterizes herself as the central epic protagonist of Milton's poem.

Such favor I unworthy am vouchsafed,
By me the Promised Seed shall all restore."
So spake our mother Eve, and Adam heard
625 Well pleased, but answered not; for now too nigh
Th' Archangel stood, and from the other hill
To their fixed station, all in bright array
The Cherubim descended; on the ground
Gliding metéorous,° as evening mist   *like a meteor*
630 Ris'n from a river o'er the marish° glides,   *marsh*
And gathers ground fast at the laborer's heel
Homeward returning. High in front advanced,
The brandished sword of God before them blazed
Fierce as a comet; which with torrid heat,
635 And vapor° as the Libyan air adust,°   *smoke / parched*
Began to parch that temperate clime; whereat
In either hand the hast'ning angel caught
Our ling'ring parents, and to th' eastern gate
Led them direct, and down the cliff as fast
640 To the subjected° plain; then disappeared.   *low-lying*
They looking back, all th' eastern side beheld
Of Paradise, so late their happy seat,°   *estate*
Waved over by that flaming brand,° the gate   *sword*
With dreadful faces thronged and fiery arms:
645 Some natural tears they dropped, but wiped them soon;
The world was all before them, where to choose
Their place of rest, and Providence their guide:
They hand in hand with wand'ring steps and slow,
Through Eden took their solitary way.[8]

1674

---

8. The paradox, "hand in hand" / "solitary," is especially resonant.

The Restoration and the Eighteenth Century 1660–1785

1660:   Charles II restored to the English throne
1688–89:   The Glorious Revolution: deposition of James II and accession
            of William of Orange
1700:   Death of John Dryden
1707:   Act of Union unites Scotland and England, which thus become
            "Great Britain"
1714:   Rule by House of Hanover begins with accession of George I
1744–45:   Deaths of Alexander Pope and Jonathan Swift
1784:   Death of Samuel Johnson

The Restoration and the eighteenth century were times of enormous growth and change in England—or Great Britain, as the nation came to be called after 1707, when the Act of Union joined Scotland to England and Wales. Britain became a world power, an empire on which the sun never set. But it also changed internally. England had always been an agricultural nation; most people were farmers who spent their lives in the neighborhoods where they were born. Gradually their horizons expanded. As the population doubled, to more than ten million, the balance of power shifted toward cities, while trades and industries multiplied and standards of living rose. Moreover, Great Britain became a literate nation, a nation of readers. Almost everyone read the new periodicals and novels that reflected the lives of ordinary women and men, and writers learned to cater to the public. Common interests linked the British Isles; among major authors, Jonathan Swift, Edmund Burke, Richard Sheridan, and Oliver Goldsmith came from Ireland, and James Thomson, David Hume, and James Boswell came from Scotland. Britons also ventured abroad. In a series of wars against France from 1689 to 1763, colonies were annexed around the world, from Canada in the west to India in the east, and an aggressive market economy—including a lucrative slave trade—brought in unprecedented wealth. At the same time, such developments strained the old ways of life. The gulf widened between rich and poor; individual interests and rights took the place of hierarchical values; and new class conflicts turned people against one another. Regret for what had been lost—the communities and beliefs that gave each person a place to belong to—competed with an eagerness for what had been gained—new ideas and pleasures, new chances to rise. The struggle between these opposing visions affects every phase of eighteenth-century life.

RELIGION AND POLITICS

The Restoration of 1660—the return of Charles Stuart to England—brought hope to a nation divided against itself, exhausted by twenty years of civil wars. Almost all of Charles's subjects welcomed him home, for after the abdication of Richard Cromwell in 1659 the country had seemed at the brink of chaos, and Britons were eager to believe that their king would bring order and law and a spirit of mildness back into the national life. But no political settlement could be stable until religious issues had been resolved. The restoration of the monarchy meant that the established church would also be restored, and though Charles was willing to pardon or ignore many former enemies (such as Milton), the bishops and Anglican clergy were less tolerant of dissent. When Parliament reimposed the Book of Common Prayer in 1662, and then in 1664 barred Nonconformists from religious meetings outside the established church, thousands of clergyman resigned their livings, and the jails were filled with preachers like John Bunyan who refused to be silenced. In 1673 the Test Act required all holders of civil and military offices to take the sacrament in an Anglican Church and to deny belief in transubstantiation. Thus Protestant Dissenters and Roman Catholics were largely excluded from public life; for instance, Alexander Pope, a Catholic, could not attend a university, own land, or vote. The scorn of Anglicans for Nonconformist zeal or "enthusiasm" (a belief in private revelation) bursts out in Samuel Butler's popular *Hudibras* (1663), a caricature of Presbyterians and Independents. And English Catholics were widely regarded as potential traitors who had probably set the great fire that destroyed much of London in 1666.

Yet the triumph of the established church did not resolve the constitutional issues that had divided Charles I and Parliament. Charles II had promised to govern through Parliament, but slyly tried to consolidate royal power. Steering away from crises, he hid his Catholic sympathies and avoided a test of strength with Parliament—except on one occasion. In 1678 the report of the Popish Plot, in which Catholics would rise and murder their Protestant foes, terrified London; and though the charge turned out to be a fraud, the House of Commons exploited the fear by trying to force Charles to exclude his Catholic brother, James, duke of York, from succession to the throne. The turmoil of this period is captured brilliantly by Dryden's *Absalom and Achitophel* (1681). Finally, Charles defeated the Exclusion Bill by dissolving Parliament. But the crisis resulted in a basic division of the country between two new political parties. The party that supported the king came to be called Tories; the king's opponents, Whigs. By the end of the century the two parties had developed opposing attitudes on most important issues. The Tories, who drew their strength from the landed gentry and country clergy, represented conservative values; they strongly supported the Crown and the Anglican Church as the pillars of social and political stability. Convinced that only those with local ties and deep roots in the land could rule responsibly, they were hostile to the rising influence of the new moneyed interests. The Whigs were more progressive and diverse: many powerful nobles, jealous of the powers of the Crown; the merchants and financiers of London; a number of bishops and low-church clergymen; and the Dissenters. What held them together were policies of toleration and support of commerce.

Neither party could live with James II. After he came to the throne in 1685, he claimed the right to make his own laws, suspended the Test Act, and began to fill the army and government with fellow Catholics. Matters came to a head in 1688, when the birth of a son confronted the nation with the prospect of a Catholic dynasty. Secret negotiations paved the way for the Dutchman William of Orange, a champion of Protestantism and the husband of James's Protestant daughter Mary. William landed with a small army in southwestern England and marched toward London. As he advanced, the king's allies faded away, and James fled to a permanent exile in France. The house of Stuart would be heard from again. For more than half a century some loyal Jacobites (from the Latin *Jacobus,* "James"), especially in Scotland, supported James, his son ("the Old Pretender"), and his grandson ("the Young Pretender" or "Bonnie Prince Charlie") as the legitimate rulers of Britain. Moreover, a good many writers, from Aphra Behn and Dryden (and arguably Pope and Johnson) to Robert Burns, privately sympathized with Jacobitism. But after the failure of one last rising in 1745, the cause would dwindle gradually into a wistful sentiment. In retrospect, the coming of William and Mary in 1688—the Glorious, or Bloodless, Revolution—had calmed the fierce divisions within the nation and prepared the way for a unified Great Britain.

A lasting settlement followed. In 1689 a Bill of Rights revoked James's actions; it limited the powers of the Crown, reaffirmed the supremacy of Parliament, and guaranteed some individual rights. The same year the Toleration Act relaxed the strain of religious conflict by granting a limited freedom of worship to Dissenters (although not to Catholics or Jews) so long as they swore allegiance to the Crown. This proved to be a workable compromise; and with the passage of the Act of Settlement in 1701, putting Sophia, electress of Hanover, and her descendants in line for the throne (as the granddaughter of James I, she was the closest Protestant relative of Princess Anne, James II's younger daughter, whose sole surviving child died in that year), the difficult problems that had so long divided England seemed resolved. The principles established in 1689 endured unaltered in essentials until the Reform Bill of 1832.

During Anne's reign (1702–14), new political tensions embittered the nation. England and its allies defeated France and Spain in the War of the Spanish Succession (1702–13)—a Whig war, supported by Whig lords and London merchants, who grew rich on war profits and gained by weakening the power of France and Spain. The spoils included new colonies and the *asiento,* a contract to supply slaves to the Spanish Empire. The hero of the war, Captain-General John Churchill, duke of Marlborough, won the famous victory of Blenheim; was showered with honors and wealth; and with his duchess, dominated the queen until 1710. But the Whigs and Marlborough pushed their luck too hard. When the Whigs tried to reward the Dissenters for their loyalty by removing the Test, Anne fought back to defend the established church. She dismissed her Whig ministers and the Marlboroughs and called in Robert Harley and the brilliant young Henry St. John to form a Tory ministry. These ministers were popular with writers; they employed Defoe and Swift and commissioned Matthew Prior to negotiate the Peace of Utrecht (1713). But to Swift's despair—he later burlesqued events at court in *Gulliver's Travels*—a bitter rivalry broke out between Harley (then earl of Oxford) and St. John (then Viscount Bolingbroke). Though Bolingbroke succeeded in ousting Oxford, the death of Anne in 1714 reversed his fortunes. George I (Sophia's son) became the first Hanoverian king, and the vindictive Whigs returned to power. Harley was imprisoned in the Tower of London until 1717; and Bolingbroke, charged with being a Jacobite traitor, fled to France. Pardoned in 1723, he came back to England and directed the opposition to Robert Walpole, while playing the gentleman-philosopher-farmer and helping Pope to plan *An Essay on Man*. Government was now securely in the hands of the Whigs.

The three Georges who occupied the throne during the rest of the century presided over a nation that grew increasingly prosperous through war, trade, colonization, consumer capitalism, and the beginnings of industrialism. George I (reigned 1714–27) and George II (reigned 1727–60) were German at heart; they spoke broken English and took little interest in England's affairs. Hence ministers became more important and more independent of the Crown than they had ever been before. Through royal indifference and the ambition and skill of Walpole, the first "prime minister," the modern system of ministerial government began to develop. Walpole rose to power as a result of the "South Sea bubble" (1720), a stock market crash; and his ability to restore confidence and keep the country running smoothly—as well as to juggle money—would mark his long ascendancy (1721–42). He was a master of the patronage system, installing his dependents in government offices and controlling the House of Commons by buying off its members. But he did not buy off the wits, and they were offended. Gay's *Beggar's Opera* (1728) and Fielding's *Jonathan Wild* (1743) draw interesting parallels between great criminals and great politicians, and Pope's *Dunciad* uses Walpole as an emblem of the corruption and commercialization of the whole social fabric. Yet Pope himself had made a fortune by marketing his poems as cleverly as he wrote them. Increasingly, authors, like politicians, rose in the world by giving the public what it wanted. Walpole was unwilling to go to war (and fell because he managed it badly); but the next major English statesman, William Pitt the Elder, appealed to the patriotism of common people and called for the expansion of British power and commerce overseas. The defeat of the French in the Seven Years' War (1756–63), especially in North America, was largely his doing.

The long reign of George III (1760–1820) was dominated by two great concerns: the emergence of Britain as a colonial power and the cry for a new social order based on liberty and radical reform. In 1763 the Peace of Paris consolidated British rule over Canada and India, and not even the later loss of the American colonies could stem the rise of the empire. Great Britain was no longer an isolated island but a nation with interests and responsibilities around the world. At home, however, there was discontent. The wealth brought to England by industrialism and foreign trade had not spread to the working classes. It seemed to many that the bonds of custom that once held people together had broken, and now money alone was respected. Protestants turned against Catholics; in 1780 the Gordon Riots put London temporarily under mob rule. The king was popular with his subjects and tried to take government into his own hands, rising above all parties, but his efforts often backfired—as when the American colonists mistook him for a tyrant. From 1788 to the end of his life, moreover, an inherited disease (porphyria) periodically unhinged his mind, as in a memorable scene described by

Frances Burney. Meanwhile, reformers such as John Wilkes and Richard Price called for a new political democracy. Fear of their radicalism would contribute to the British reaction against the French Revolution. In the last decades of the century, British authors would be torn between two opposing attitudes: loyalty to the old traditions of subordination, mutual obligations, and local self-sufficiency; and yearning for a new dispensation founded on principles of liberty, the rule of reason, and human rights.

THE CONTEXT OF IDEAS

The political turbulence of the seventeenth century subsided only gradually during the period after the Restoration (1660–1700), and literature also registered a conflict of values. John Milton's major poems, a culmination of Renaissance art, appeared at the same time that John Dryden was leading the way to a new age of elegance. Bunyan's *Pilgrim's Progress* expressed the Nonconformist conscience at the same time that the earl of Rochester expressed the creed of a libertine and rake. In the theater, witty, bawdy comedies—written and acted by women as well as men—reflected the style of a fun-loving, dissolute court. But country people kept their old ways of life, and respectable London citizens were scandalized by the behavior of aristocratic rakes who regarded them with contempt and considered their wives and daughters fair game. Even good Royalists like John Evelyn and Samuel Pepys, in their diaries, often worry about the moral laxity of the court and the king.

Charles set a mixed example for the nation. A lover of pleasure and women, he was always ready to sacrifice principles to live in comfort. But he also took a genuine interest in new ideas and supported the arts and sciences. French and Italian musicians, as well as painters from the Low Countries, migrated to England; and playhouses—closed by the Puritans since 1642—sprang back to life. In 1660 Charles authorized two new companies of actors: the King's Players and the Duke's. Two years later he chartered the Royal Society of London for the Improving of Natural Knowledge, thus giving official approval to the scientific revolution that was reshaping views of the world. Early in the century, Francis Bacon had called for an advancement of learning based on direct observations of nature; and two wonderful inventions, the microscope and telescope, had begun to reveal that nature is more extravagant—teeming with tiny creatures and boundless galaxies—than anyone had ever imagined. Now experiments came into vogue, in thought and morals as well as science and art. The sense that new worlds were being discovered could be unnerving, but it was also exciting.

Skepticism and freethinking flourished during the late seventeenth century. The civil wars had turned the world upside down; if a king could be executed, what authority was safe? Even after the Restoration, the question remained. One answer had been offered by Thomas Hobbes, whose *Leviathan* (1651) had argued that only an absolute government could check the "perpetual and restless desire of power" in all human beings, a competition that would lead to the "war of every man against every man" unless the final power were vested in some sovereign. Hobbes's emphasis on the predatory passions that drive both human nature and society was detested by the

church and attacked on all sides. Yet his ideas influenced many young people, especially the libertines who devoted their lives to a quest for pleasure
and power. His pessimistic view of human nature also provoked, by way of
reaction, an optimistic insistence on the natural goodness of humanity,
which would become an article of faith for many in the eighteenth century.
Another influential point of view was philosophic skepticism. Originating in
ancient Greece, skepticism revived in the all-questioning essays of the
Frenchman Michel de Montaigne (1533–1592). The skeptic argued that all
knowledge derives from our senses but that, because our senses do not report
the world accurately, reliable knowledge is impossible to achieve. The safest
course is to remember that most beliefs rest on opinion and not to hunger
for some ultimate, inaccessible truth. Butler, Dryden, and Rochester were
among those who followed this doctrine. But though skeptics might doubt
the results of human reasoning, they were not precluded from religious
beliefs. As Dryden asserted after converting to Catholicism, to accept the
mysteries of Christianity one needs faith alone.

The new science also encouraged a challenge to traditional wisdom and
learning. The ancients (and the fathers of the church) had not known about
the solar system, the circulation of the blood, the existence of microscopic
organisms, or the law of gravity. In this respect the moderns were much
wiser. But the school curriculum still began with years of Latin and Greek.
Humanistic education had long relied on standard ancient texts, which were
supposed to teach the student everything necessary for understanding life.
Hence a battle of books broke out in the late seventeenth century between
the champions of ancient and of modern learning; Swift, Pope, and other
British writers fought for the ancients. Nevertheless, modern habits of
thought began to dominate intellectual life. In assessing the probability of
some argument, for instance, a debater could no longer settle the issue by
citing authorities; now experts had to calculate the odds. New fields like
statistics and economics were developed by one member of the Royal Society,
Sir William Petty. In tune with the times, Swift's *Modest Proposal* adopts the
statistical and economic model of proof, even while satirizing it. Moreover,
the weakening of authority allowed independent voices—amateurs as well
as professionals, and women as well as men—to try their own ideas. Margaret
Cavendish, duchess of Newcastle, and Behn were not afraid to publish original speculations on philosophic or scientific theories. One book that stayed
popular for more than a century, Fontenelle's *Conversations on the Plurality
of Worlds* (1686; translated from French by Behn and later by Burney), suggested that an infinite number of alternate worlds and living creatures might
exist, not only in outer space but under our feet, invisibly small. A similar
train of thought would suggest that our own world is plural (or multicultural)
and that its most basic institutions—systems of government, marriage, the
church, the distribution of wealth—could always be organized in some different way. Schemes for reforming society preoccupied many writers. Both
Mary Astell and Daniel Defoe, for instance, proposed model schools for the
education of women.

As views of nature changed, so did philosophy and religion. What we call
"science" today was then grouped under "natural history" (the collection and
description of facts of nature), "natural philosophy" (the study of the causes
of what happens in nature), and "natural religion" (the study of nature as a
book written by God). And the discovery of laws of nature, such as Boyle's

law (the pressure and volume of a gas are inversely proportional) or Newton's laws of optics and celestial mechanics, seemed evidence of a universal order in creation. Theologically, the elegant simplicity of that order supported the idea of a divine intelligence whose presence might be deduced from his works, as a watch implies a watchmaker. For Deists like Bolingbroke, religion did not depend on mystery or superstition. Enlightened minds relied only on reason, which taught the goodness and wisdom of natural law and its creator. Natural religion could not, however, discern an active god who punished vice and rewarded virtue in this life; evidently the First Cause had withdrawn from the universe He set in motion. Many orthodox Christians shuddered at the vision of a vast, impersonal machine of nature. Instead they rested their faith on the revelation of Scripture, the scheme of salvation in which Christ died to redeem our sins. Newton himself spent much of his life exploring mysteries of Scripture. Yet many others, like Pope in *An Essay on Man* or Thomson in *The Seasons,* insisted that they saw no contradiction between the books of nature and Relevation.

Philosophers also claimed to be following nature. The main line of British philosophy—which runs from Bacon and Hobbes through John Locke, George Berkeley, and David Hume—can be characterized broadly as empiricism, the doctrine that regards all knowledge as derived from experience. However much they disagree with one another, eighteenth-century philosophers typically shun metaphysics—the search for essential or ultimate principles of reality, transcending the physical—in favor of more practical concerns: how do we know what we know, and how can we best put that knowledge to use? Reasoning from what they know most immediately, their own minds and perceptions, they draw conclusions about the natural basis of the ways that human beings behave, especially in morals and politics. Nor do they suppose that reason alone can account for what we believe. Berkeley's famous paradox—that we know the world only through our senses and thus cannot prove that any material thing exists—is intended to demonstrate the necessity of faith, because reality amounts to no more than a perception in the mind of God; and Hume's famous argument about causation—that "causes and effects are discoverable, not by reason but by experience"— implies that our sense of the world derives not from logical thought but from beliefs and feelings. British philosophers like to appeal to common sense. Accepting the limits of human intelligence and power, they settle for the possible. Thus Locke, the philosopher who most influenced others, expresses the temper of his times in the *Essay Concerning Human Understanding* (1690):

> If by this inquiry into the nature of the understanding, I can discover the powers thereof; how far they reach; to what things they are in any degree proportionate; and where they fail us, I suppose it may be of use, to prevail with the busy mind of man to be more cautious in meddling with things exceeding its comprehension; to stop when it is at the utmost extent of its tether; and to sit down in a quiet ignorance of those things which, upon examination, are found to be beyond the reach of our capacities. . . . Our business here is not to know all things, but those which concern our conduct.

These words might be taken as the creed of eighteenth-century England. Such a position is Swift's, when he inveighs against metaphysics, abstract logical deductions, and theoretical science. It is similar to Pope's warning against human presumption in *An Essay on Man*. It prompts Johnson to talk of "the business of living" and to restrain the flights of unbridled imagination. And it helps account for the Anglican clergy's dislike of emotion and "enthusiasm" in religion, and for their emphasis on good works, rather than faith, as the way to salvation. Locke's empiricism pervaded eighteenth-century British thought on politics, education, and morals as well as philosophy; Johnson's great *Dictionary* (1755) uses more than fifteen hundred illustrations from his writings.

During the early eighteenth century, the most heated challenges to authority tended to cool. The Act of Settlement and the Act of Union, reducing some tensions within the nation, seemed paralleled by a growing consensus in manners and ideas. Addison and Steele are the masters of that consensus. Attracting a national audience, the *Tatler* (1709–11) and the *Spectator* (1711–12; 1714) both produced and reflected an urbane social ideal, an intellectual life in which all sorts of people could mingle, as in the streets and parks of a thriving city like London. Here a large middle-class public learned to think and behave politely. The pressure to be respectable was especially strong on women. The freedom of thought that some had begun to exercise in the Restoration gradually diminished into a regime of the proper lady. Yet most people believed that their lives were getting better. Potentially threatening sources of change—not only new ideas but new ways of living, secular, urban, and market-driven—were smoothed by Addison and his successors into examples of the variety that is the spice of life. There were more goods, more pleasures to taste, more opportunities to rise, than ever before. Through most of the century, as prosperity grew, the rifts in the nation seemed patched. In the provinces as well as in London, in Scotland as well as in England, a standard of good manners came to be shared.

An optimistic view of the ties that bind people together extended to human nature. Rejecting Hobbes, and minimizing original sin, some eighteenth-century thinkers asserted that human beings are naturally good and find their highest happiness by being good to others. In midcentury a new word, *sentimental*, suddenly came into fashion. Those who trusted humanity looked for virtue in instinctive and social impulses rather than in a code of conduct sanctioned by divine law. Religion itself, according to Laurence Sterne, might be a "Great Sensorium," a sort of central nervous system that connects the feelings of all living creatures in one great benevolent soul. And people began to feel—or to fancy they felt—exquisite pleasure in the exercise of charity. The cult of sensibility fostered a philanthropy that led to social reforms seldom envisioned in earlier times—to the improvement of jails, the relief of imprisoned debtors, the establishment of foundling hospitals and homes for penitent prostitutes, and ultimately the abolition of the slave trade. And it also loosed a ready flow of feeling and tears, sympathetic responses to the joys and sorrows of fellow human beings. The doctrine of natural goodness, popularized by Rousseau, suggested that civilization corrupts us and that if we lived in a state of nature, like "noble savages," we might retain a childlike innocence and virtue. Such notions encouraged an interest in primitive societies and in poets who were reputed to draw their inspiration directly from nature, like the thresher Stephen Duck, the milkmaid Ann Yearsley, and the plowman Robert Burns. William Wordsworth's fascination with children and simple, rural people grows out of the eighteenth-century wish to believe in natural goodness and genius.

As the wave of sentimentalism mounted, it was balanced by a rise of religious feeling. The evangelical revival known as Methodism began in the 1730s, led by three Oxford graduates: John Wesley (1703–1791), his brother Charles (1707–1788), and George Whitefield (1714–1770). The Methodists took their gospel to the common people, warning that all were sinners and damned, unless they accepted "amazing grace," salvation through faith. Often denied the privilege of preaching in village churches, evangelicals preached to thousands in barns or the open fields. The emotionalism of such revival meetings repelled the somnolent Anglican Church and the upper classes, who feared that the fury and zeal of the Puritan sects were returning. Methodism was sometimes related to madness; convinced that he was damned forever, the poet William Cowper broke down and became a recluse. But the religious awakening persisted and affected many clergymen and laymen within the Establishment, who reanimated the church and promoted unworldliness and piety. Nor did the insistence of Methodists on faith over works as the way to salvation prevent them or their Anglican allies from fighting for social reforms. The campaign to abolish slavery and the slave trade was driven largely by a passion to save souls.

Both sentimentalism and evangelicalism placed a new importance on individuals—their private encounters with one another or with a personal god. The older hierarchical system had tended to subordinate individuals to their social rank or station. In the eighteenth century that fixed system began to break down, and people's sense of themselves began to change. Locke argued that personal identity rests on nothing more secure than consciousness, not on any "pure substance" such as a soul; we know who we are today because we remember who we were yesterday. In that case, the self seems frail, because memories cannot always be trusted. Yet such views provoked many people to reexamine themselves. The difference between the self as it appears to us in introspection and the identity that others fasten on us—for instance, between the person a woman feels herself to be and the generic "woman" whose role she is supposed to fill—becomes a major interest of eighteenth-century writing. Anne Finch, Lady Mary Wortley Montagu, and Burney all grapple, in their own ways, with the problem of how to stay true to their own core of feelings in spite of social expectations. Similarly, a new kind of fiction, the novel, devotes unprecedented attention to what particular characters are thinking and feeling. In such a world, an institution like marriage begins to be defined as a means to self-fulfillment and personal happiness rather than as a family alliance. By the end of the century many issues of politics and the law revolve around rights, not traditions. The modern individual had been invented; no product of the age is more enduring.

LITERARY PRINCIPLES

The literature of the period between 1660 and 1785 divides conveniently into three lesser periods of about forty years each. The first, extending to the death of Dryden in 1700, is characterized by an effort to bring a new refinement to English literature according to sound critical principles of what is

fitting and right; the second, ending with the deaths of Pope in 1744 and
Swift in 1745, extends that effort to a wider circle of readers, with special
satirical attention to what is unfitting and wrong; the third, concluding with
the death of Johnson in 1784 and the publication of Cowper's *The Task* in
1785, confronts the old principles with revolutionary ideas that would come
to the fore in the Romantic movement of the late eighteenth and early nineteenth centuries.

Apparently, a sudden change of taste took place about 1660. The change
had been long prepared, however, by a trend in European culture, especially
in seventeenth-century France: the desire for an elegant simplicity. Reacting
against the difficulty and occasional extravagance of late Renaissance literature, writers and critics called for a new restraint, clarity, regularity, and
good sense. Donne's "metaphysics" and Milton's bold storming of heaven,
for instance, seemed overdone to some Restoration readers. Hence Dryden
and Andrew Marvell both were tempted to revise *Paradise Lost,* smoothing
away its sublime but arduous idiosyncrasies. The "easy, natural" wit that such
writers prefer, surprising but seldom shocking, may well reflect a yearning
for peace and order after the violent extremism of the civil wars. Postwar
writing aims to be disarming, to counsel a middle way among opposing parties.

This movement produced in France an impressive body of classical literature that distinguished the age of Louis XIV. In England it produced a
literature often termed "Augustan," after the writers who flourished during
the reign of Augustus Caesar, the first Roman emperor. Rome's Augustan
Age reestablished stability after the civil war that followed the assassination
of Julius Caesar. Its chief poets, Virgil, Horace, and Ovid, addressed their
polished works to a sophisticated aristocracy among whom they looked for
patrons. Dryden's generation took advantage of the analogy between post–
civil war England and Augustan Rome. Later generations would be suspicious of that analogy; after 1700 most writers stressed that Augustus had
been a tyrant who thought himself greater than the law. But in 1660 there
was hope that Charles would be a better Augustus, bringing England the
civilized virtues of an Augustan age without its vices.

Charles and his followers brought back from exile an admiration of French
literature as well as French fashions, and the theoretical "correctness" of
such writers as Pierre Corneille, René Rapin, and Nicolas Boileau came into
vogue. The effort to formulate rules of good writing appealed to Dryden and
later to Pope. Even Shakespeare had sometimes been careless; and although
writers could not expect to surpass his genius, they might hope to avoid his
faults. But "neoclassical" English literature aimed to be not only classical
but *new.* When Dryden and Pope make use of Greek or Latin or French
poets, they convert them to English traditions of variety, freewheeling fancy,
and humor. Chaucer, Spenser, Shakespeare, Jonson, and Milton (as well as
Homer, Virgil, Horace, Longinus, and Corneille) helped form the literary
consciousness of the new age.

If Charles had never lived abroad, English literature would probably still
have turned toward an ideal of elegant simplicity. Jonson's poems and criticism had brought the classicizing tendencies of the English Renaissance to
a focus. His closed heroic couplets set an example for Edmund Waller and
Sir John Denham, whom Dryden considered the principal "refiners" of

English metrics. By 1625 one "son of Ben," Sir John Beaumont, anticipated the critical standards of Dryden and Pope, in couplets very much like theirs:

> Pure phrase, fit epithets, a sober care
> Of metaphors, descriptions clear, yet rare,
> Similitudes contracted, smooth and round,
> Not vexed by learning, but with Nature crowned:
> Strong figures drawn from deep inventions, springs,
> Consisting less in words, and more in things:
> A language not affecting ancient times,
> Nor Latin shreds, by which the pedant climbs.
> (*To His Late Majesty, Concerning the True Form of*
> *English Poetry*)

Such standards, alien to the verse of Donne, Richard Crashaw, or Milton, suggest that a native classicism, serene and graceful, existed side by side with metaphysical poetry. The emphasis on the correct ("pure"), the appropriate ("fit"), restraint and discipline ("sober care"), clarity, the fresh and surprising ("rare"), nature, strength, freedom from pedantry indicates exactly the direction English poets were to follow after the Restoration.

Above all, the new simplicity of style aimed to give pleasure to readers— to write about passions that everyone could recognize in language that everyone could understand. According to Dryden, Donne's amorous verse mistakenly "perplexes the minds of the fair sex with nice speculations of philosophy, when he should engage their hearts, and entertain them with the softnesses of love." Dryden's poems would not make that mistake; like subsequent English critics, he values poetry according to its power to move an audience. Thus Timotheus, in Dryden's *Alexander's Feast,* is not only a musician but an archetypal poet who can make Alexander tearful or loving or angry at will. Readers, in turn, were supposed to cooperate with authors through the exercise of their own imaginations, creating pictures in the mind. When Timotheus describes vengeful ghosts holding torches, Alexander hallucinates in response and seizes a torch "with zeal to destroy." Much eighteenth-century poetry demands to be visualized. A phrase from Horace's *Art of Poetry, ut pictura poesis* (as in painting, so in poetry), was interpreted to mean that poetry ought to be a visual as well as verbal art. Pope's *Eloisa to Abelard,* for instance, begins by picturing two rival female personifications: "heavenly-pensive contemplation" and "ever-musing melancholy." Readers were expected to *see* these figures: Contemplation, in the habit of a nun, whose eyes roll upward toward heaven; and the black goddess Melancholy, in wings and drapery, who broods upon the darkness. These two competing visions fight for Eloisa's soul throughout the poem, which we see entirely through her perspective. Eighteenth-century readers knew how to translate words into pictures, and modern readers can share their pleasure by learning to see poetic images in the mind's eye.

What poets most tried to see and represent was *Nature*—a word of many meanings. The Augustans focused especially on one meaning: Nature as the universal and permanent elements in human experience. External nature— the landscape—attracted attention throughout the eighteenth century as a source of pleasure and an object of inquiry. But as Finch muses on the landscape, in *A Nocturnal Reverie,* it is her own soul she discovers. Pope's injunction to the critic, "First follow Nature," has primarily *human* nature in view. Nature consists of the enduring, general truths that have been, are, and will be true for everyone in all times, everywhere. Hence the business of the poet, according to Johnson's *Rasselas*, is not "to number the streaks of the tulip" but "to examine, not the individual, but the species; to remark general properties and large appearances . . . to exhibit in his portraits of nature such prominent and striking features as recall the original to every mind." Yet if human nature was held to be uniform, human beings were known to be infinitely varied. Pope praises Shakespeare's characters as "Nature herself," but continues that "every single character in Shakespeare is as much an individual as those in life itself; it is . . . impossible to find any two alike." The general need not exclude the particular. In *The Vanity of Human Wishes*, Johnson describes the sorrows of an old woman: "Now kindred Merit fills the sable Bier, / Now lacerated Friendship claims a tear." Here "kindred Merit" refers particularly to a worthy relative who has died, and "lacerated Friendship" refers to a friend who has been wasted by violence or disease. Yet Merit and Friendship are also personifications, and the lines imply that the woman may be mourning the passing of goodness like her own or a broken friendship; values and sympathies can die as well as people. This play on words is not a pun. Rather, it indicates a state of mind in which life assumes the form of a perpetual allegory and some abiding truth shines through each circumstance and moment as it passes. The particular is already the general, in good eighteenth-century verse.

To study Nature was also to study the ancients. Nature and Homer, according to Pope, were the same; and both Pope and his readers applied Horace's satires on Rome to their own world, because Horace had expressed the perennial forms of life. Moreover, modern writers could learn from the ancients how to practice their craft. If a poem is an object to be made, the *poet* (a word derived from the Greek for "maker") must make the object to proper specifications. Thus poets were taught to plan their works in one of the classical "kinds" or genres—epic, tragedy, comedy, pastoral, satire, or ode—to choose a language appropriate to that genre, and to select the right style and tone and rhetorical figures. Even when Henry Fielding experimented with a modern form, the novel, in *Joseph Andrews* (1742), he claimed to follow an ancient model, the "comic epic-poem in prose." The rules of art, as Pope had said, "are Nature methodized." At the same time, however, writers needed *wit*: quickness of mind, inventiveness, a knack for conceiving images and metaphors and for perceiving resemblances between things apparently unlike. Shakespeare had surpassed the ancients themselves in wit, and no one could deny that Pope was witty. Hence a major project of the age was to combine good method with wit, or judgment with fancy. Nature intended them to be one, and the role of judgment was not to suppress passion, energy, and originality but to make them more effective through discipline: "The wingèd courser, like a generous horse, / Shows most true mettle when you check his course."

The test of a poet's true mettle is language. When Wordsworth, in the preface to *Lyrical Ballads* (1800), declared that he wrote "in a selection of the language really used by men," he went on to attack eighteenth-century poets for their use of an artificial and stock "poetic diction." Many poets did employ a special language. It is characterized by personification, representing a thing or abstraction in human form, as when an "Ace of Hearts steps forth" or "Melancholy frowns"; by periphrasis (a roundabout way of avoiding homely words: "finny tribes" for *fish*, or "household feathery people" for *chickens*); by stock phrases such as "shining sword," "verdant mead," "bounding main," and "checkered shade"; by words used in their original Latin sense, such as "genial," "gelid," and "horrid"; and by English sentences forced into Latin syntax ("Here rests his head upon the lap of Earth / A youth to Fortune and to Fame unknown," where *youth* is the subject of the verb *rests*). This language originated in the attempt of Renaissance poets to rival the elegant diction of Virgil and other Roman writers, and Milton depended on it to help him obtain "answerable style" for the lofty theme of *Paradise Lost*. When used mechanically it could become a mannerism. But Thomas Gray contrives subtle, expressive effects from artificial diction and syntax, as in the ironic inflation of *Ode on the Death of a Favorite Cat* or a famous stanza from *Elegy Written in a Country Churchyard*:

> The boast of heraldry, the pomp of power,
> And all that beauty, all that wealth e'er gave,
> Awaits alike the inevitable hour.
> The paths of glory lead but to the grave.

It is easy to misread the first sentence. What is the subject of *awaits*? The answer must be *hour* (the only available singular noun), which lurks at the end of the sentence, ready to spring a trap not only on the reader but on all those aristocratic, powerful, beautiful, wealthy people who forget that their hour will come. Moreover, the intricacy of that sentence sets off the simplicity of the next, which says the same thing with deadly directness. The artful mix in the *Elegy* of a special poetic language—a language that nobody speaks—with sentiments that everybody feels helps account for the poem's enduring popularity.

Versification also tests a poet's skill. The heroic couplet was brought to such perfection by Pope, Johnson thought, that "to attempt any further improvement of versification will be dangerous." Pope's couplets, in rhymed iambic pentameter, typically present a complete statement, closed by a punctuation mark. Within the binary system of these two lines, as in a digital computer, a world of distinctions can be compressed. The second line of the couplet might closely parallel the first in structure and meaning, for instance, or the two lines might antithetically play against each other. Similarly, because normally the length of a pentameter line requires a slight pause called a "caesura" ("Know then thyself, presume not God to scan"), one part of the line can be made parallel with or antithetical to the other or even to one part of the following line. Sir John Denham's *Cooper's Hill* (1642) includes a passage, quoted and parodied for many years, that illustrates these effects. The poem addresses the Thames and builds up a witty comparison between the flow of a river and the flow of verse (italics are added to highlight the terms compared):

	O could I flow like thee, | and make thy stream
Parallelism:	*My great example,* | as it is *my theme!*
Double balance:	Though *deep,* yet *clear,* | though *gentle,* yet not *dull,*
Double balance:	*Strong* without *rage,* | without *o'erflowing, full.*

Once Dryden and Pope had bound such passages more tightly together with alliteration and assonance, the typical metrical-rhetorical wit of the new age had been perfected. For most of the eighteenth century its only metrical rival was blank verse: iambic pentameter that does not rhyme and is not closed in couplets. Milton's blank verse in *Paradise Lost* provided one model, and the dramatic blank verse of Shakespeare and Dryden provided another. This more expansive form appealed to poets who cared less for wit than for stories and thoughts with plenty of room to develop. Blank verse was favored as the best medium for philosophical poems, descriptive poems, meditative poems, and original or translated epics, from Thomson's *Seasons* (1726–30) to Cowper's *The Task* (1785), and the tradition continued in Wordsworth's *Tintern Abbey* and *Prelude*.

Yet not all poets chose to compete with Pope's wit or Milton's heroic striving. Ordinary people also wrote and read verse, and many of them neither knew nor regarded the classics. Only a minority of men, and very few women, had the chance to study Latin and Greek, but that did not keep a good many from playing with verse as a pastime or writing about their own lives. Hence the eighteenth century is the first age to reflect the modern tension between "high" and "low" art. While the heroic couplet was being perfected, doggerel also thrived, and Milton's blank verse was sometimes reduced to describing a drunk or an oyster. Burlesque and broad humor characterize the common run of eighteenth-century verse. As the audience for poetry became more diversified, so did the subject matter. No readership was too small to address; Isaac Watts, and later Anna Laetitia Barbauld and William Blake, wrote songs for children. The rise of unconventional forms and topics of verse subverted an older poetic ideal: the Olympian art that only a handful of the elect could possibly master. The eighteenth century brought poetry down to earth. In the future, art that claimed to be high would have to find ways to distinguish itself from the low.

RESTORATION LITERATURE, 1660–1700

Dryden brought England a *modern* literature between 1660 and 1700. He combined a cosmopolitan outlook on the latest European trends with some of the richness and variety he admired in Chaucer and Shakespeare. In most of the important contemporary forms—occasional verse, comedy, tragedy, heroic play, ode, satire, translation, and critical essay—both his example and his precepts influenced others. As a critic, he spread the word that English literature, particularly his own, could vie with the best of the past. As a translator, he made such classics as Ovid and Virgil available to a wide public; for the first time, a large number of women and men without a formal education could feel included in the literary world.

The effort to reach a new audience is clearly marked by Restoration prose. The styles of Donne's sermons, of Milton's pamphlets, or of Browne's treatises now seemed too elaborate and rhetorical for simple communication. By contrast, Pepys and Behn head straight to the point, informally and unselfconsciously. The Royal Society asked its members to employ a plain, utilitarian prose style that spelled out scientific truths; rhetorical flourishes and striking metaphors might be acceptable in poetry, which engaged the emotions, but they had no place in rational discourse. In polite literature, exemplified by Cowley, Dryden, and Sir William Temple, the ideal of good prose came to be a style with the ease and poise of well-bred urbane conversation. This is a social prose for a sociable age. Later, it became the mainstay of essayists like Addison and Steele, of eighteenth-century novelists, and of the host of brilliant eighteenth-century letter writers, including Montagu, Horace Walpole, Gray, Cowper, and Burney, who still give readers the sense of being their intimate friends.

Yet despite its broad appeal to the public, Restoration literature kept its ties to an aristocratic heroic ideal. The "fierce wars and faithful loves" of epic poems were expected to offer patterns of virtue for noble emulation. These ideals lived on in popular French prose romances and in Behn's *Oroonoko*. But the ideal was most fully expressed in heroic plays like those written by Dryden, which push to extremes the conflict between love and honor in the hearts of impossibly valiant heroes and impossibly high-minded and attractive heroines. Dryden's best serious drama, however, was his blank verse tragedy *All for Love* (produced 1677), based on the story of Antony and Cleopatra. Instead of Shakespeare's worldwide panorama, his rapid shifts of scene and complex characters, this version follows the unities of time, place, and action, compressing the plot to the tragic last hours of the lovers. Two other tragic playwrights were celebrated in the Restoration and for a long time to come: Nathaniel Lee (ca. 1649–1692), known for violent plots and wild ranting, and the pathetic Thomas Otway (1652–1685).

But comedy was the real distinction of Restoration drama. The best plays of Sir George Etherege (*The Man of Mode*, 1676), William Wycherley (*The Country Wife*, 1675), Aphra Behn (*The Rover*, 1677), William Congreve (*Love for Love*, 1695; *The Way of the World*, 1700), and later George Farquhar (*The Beaux' Stratagem*, 1707) can still hold the stage today. These "comedies of manners" pick social behavior apart, exposing the nasty struggles for power among the upper classes, who use wit and manners as weapons. Human nature in these plays often conforms to the worst fears of Hobbes; sensual, false-hearted, selfish characters prey on each other. The male hero lives for pleasure and for the money and women that he can conquer. The object of his game of sexual intrigue is a beautiful, witty, pleasure-loving, and emancipated lady, every bit his equal in the strategies of love. What makes them stand out is the true wit and well-bred grace with which they step through the minefield of the plot.

During the 1690s "Societies for the Reformation of Manners" began to attack the blasphemy and obscenity they detected on stage, and they sometimes brought offenders to trial. The clergyman Jeremy Collier bore down hard on Dryden, Wycherley, and Congreve in *A Short View of the Immorality and Profaneness of the English Stage* (1698), which spoke for the moral outrage of the pious middle classes. The wits retreated. Although lying and sexual appetite drive *The Way of the World*, prudence and love win the day. The temper of comedy softened; at the end of the century, the heroes and heroines were often good-natured and decent. Ladies could safely attend the theater, where several of the leading playwrights were women, such as Mary Pix, Susanna Centlivre, and Catharine Trotter. When Dryden died in 1700, a more respectable society was coming into being. One of the tasks that, early in the next century, Steele and Addison undertook in the *Tatler* and

Spectator and Pope in *An Essay on Criticism* was to rehabilitate "wit" by making it the servant of social and moral decorum.

Decorum was also enforced by the clubs where literary people gathered. The coffeehouses of London served as informal meeting places; first founded in 1652, they numbered in the hundreds by the turn of the century. Collectively they functioned as a new kind of national forum, a public sphere. There men could smoke, drink chocolate or coffee, read newspapers, write and receive letters, gossip, do business, argue, and observe the oddities of character for which the English were famous. Eventually clubs like Addison's imaginary Spectator Club came to preside over literary life. Their members helped determine the tone of literature, the reputations of writers, the success or failure of plays, and the character of the *Spectator* itself. At first women were excluded. Around 1750, however, some intellectual women (known as bluestockings because they wore homely worsted hose instead of black silk) established clubs of their own under the leadership of Elizabeth Montagu, and gradually men joined them for literary conversation.

EIGHTEENTH-CENTURY LITERATURE, 1700–45

Early in the century a new and brilliant group of writers took the stage: Swift, with *A Tale of a Tub* (1704–10); Addison, with *The Campaign* (1705), a poetic celebration of the battle of Blenheim; Prior, with *Poems on Several Occasions* (1707); Steele, with the *Tatler* (1709); and the youthful Pope, in the same year, with his *Pastorals*. These writers consolidate and popularize the social graces of the previous age. Determined to preserve good sense and civilized values, they turn their wit against fanaticism and innovation. Hence this is a great age of satire. Deeply conservative but also playful, the finest works often cast a strange light on modern times by viewing them through the screen of classical myths and classical forms. Thus Pope exposes the frivolity of fashionable London, in *The Rape of the Lock,* through the incongruity of verse that casts the idle rich as epic heroes. Similarly, Swift uses epic similes to mock the moderns in *The Battle of the Books,* and John Gay's *Trivia, or the Art of Walking the Streets of London* (1716) uses mock georgics to order his tour of the city. Such incongruities are not entirely negative. They also provide a fresh perspective on things that had once seemed too low for poetry to notice them—for instance, in *The Rape of the Lock,* a girl putting on her makeup. In this way a parallel with classical literature can show not only how far the modern world has fallen but also how much has stayed the same in the lives of ordinary, unheroic people.

At the same time, a new sort of reading matter began to appeal to an audience eager to be entertained. The reading public expanded dramatically during the eighteenth century, and its recruits included upper-class women and the prosperous men and women of the growing middle class. These readers liked to participate in print culture. One bookseller, John Dunton, brought out a series of periodicals, beginning with *The Athenian Mercury* in 1691, that invited questions and contributions from the public, like an Internet chat room. Later the popular press churned out a succession of newspapers; periodical essays in the manner of the *Tatler;* miscellaneous collections of verse and prose; and finally, in 1731, the first magazine, the

Gentleman's Magazine, followed not only by imitations but also by successful literary journals like the *Monthly Review* (1749) and the *Critical Review* (1756). Each audience attracted some periodical tailored to it, as with the *Female Tatler* (1709) and Eliza Haywood's *Female Spectator* (1744–46). The new journalism satisfied a hunger for information about politics, science, philosophy, and literature as well as for scandal and gossip. Early in the century the notorious *New Atalantis* (1709), by Delariviere Manley, caused a sensation by disguising the "secret memoirs" of real people as fiction; and although Manley and her publishers were arrested, the racy mixture of fact and fiction would play a major part in the rise of the novel, especially in the works of Daniel Defoe. As the number of readers grew, so did the demand for writers. Grub Street, where many poor London writers lived, became a synonym for hacks and scandal mongers. To Pope and Swift, these drudges represented a serious threat to the dignity of authorship and humanistic learning. But it was the public, not a few wealthy patrons, that eighteenth-century writers had to please. Johnson began his career as an employee of the *Gentleman's Magazine,* then took the job of putting together a dictionary, and only gradually emerged as a major author. Nor could the novel have come into being without the new customers for print, who wanted to read about people whose lives were like their own.

As the readership changed, so did kinds of literature. Lyric poetry, one of the glories of the late sixteenth and early seventeenth centuries, became in the Restoration a minor, graceful mode, often used to flatter a patron or mistress. Between 1700 and 1740, however, the forms of poetry shifted. The sonnet now seemed an archaic, courtly form; lyrics went out of fashion, replaced by descriptive and didactic verse, along with such popular genres as the ballad, the hymn, the burlesque. A similar shift in taste occurred in the drama. The moral reform of the 1690s, together with an increasingly optimistic view of human nature, made Restoration rakes seem libels on humanity. The old comedy of manners was replaced by a new kind, later called "sentimental" not only because goodness triumphs over vice but also because it deals in high moral sentiments rather than witty dialogue and because the embarrassments of its heroines and heroes move the audience not to laughter but to tears. Middle-class virtue refuses to bow to aristocratic codes. In one crucial scene of Steele's influential play *The Conscious Lovers* (1722), for instance, the hero would rather accept dishonor than fight a duel with a friend. Piety and middle-class values typify tragedies such as George Lillo's *London Merchant* (1731). One luxury invented in eighteenth-century Europe was the delicious pleasure of weeping, and comedies as well as tragedies brought that pleasure to playgoers through many decades. Some plays resisted the tide. Gay's cynical *Beggar's Opera* (1728) was a tremendous success, and later in the century the comedies of Goldsmith and Sheridan proved that sentiment is not necessarily an enemy to wit and laughter. Yet larger and larger audiences responded more to spectacles and special effects than to sophisticated writing. Although the *stage* prospered during the eighteenth century, and the star system produced idolized actors and actresses (such as David Garrick and Sarah Siddons), the authors of *drama* tended to fade to the background.

The rising tide of popular taste also provoked a reaction. Pope and Swift and other satirists turned their weapons against what they perceived as the coarsening and corruption of public life and the arts. Early in his career, Pope (like Dryden before him) had set out to make the texts and principles of classical literature available to everyone who could read English. His translations of Homer brought the epic tradition home to Britain, earning him enormous profits. But eventually he came to fear that the barbarians were winning. Politics contributed to this despair; both Pope and Swift were Tory satirists in an age of Whig domination. Tories stood fast against the social and economic changes that were transforming Britain from an island kingdom into a world power and from an agrarian into a mercantile society. A new nexus of cash and credit seemed to be driving out the civic humanism that put the nation ahead of private interests. Moral revulsion—especially against the wheeling and dealing perfected by Walpole—fueled the satirists' rage. In his last great work, *The Dunciad*, Pope imagines the tragic victory of Chaos and Night over Order and Art. Swift emphasizes that the world is going mad. The abandonment of practical reality to crackbrained theories of science, religious fanaticism, and romantic illusions leaves no recourse—except a saving remnant of laughter.

A wholly different sort of poetry accompanied the age of satire. Since the seventeenth century, no poems had been more popular than those about the pleasures of retirement, which invited the reader to dream about a safe retreat in the country or to meditate, like Finch, on scenery and the soul. But after 1726, when Thomson published *Winter*, the first of his cycle on the seasons, the poetry of natural description came into its own. A taste for gentle, picturesque beauty found expression not only in verse but in the elaborate, cultivated art of landscape gardening, and finally in the cherished English art of landscape painting in watercolor or oils (often illustrating Thomson's *Seasons*). Tourists as well as poets roamed the countryside, frequently quoting verse as they gazed at some evocative scene. Wordsworth's love of external nature draws on eighteenth-century sources; *Tintern Abbey* is very much a poem of the century in which it was written.

During the course of the century, Britons learned to enjoy not only the tamed and gentrified nature of landscape gardens and fields but also a thrilling pleasure or fear in the presence of "the sublime" in nature: rushing waters, wild prospects, and mountains shrouded in mist. Whether enthusiasts went to the landscape in search of God or merely of heightened sensations, they came back feeling that they had been touched by something beyond the life they knew, by something that could hardly be expressed. Even before the deaths of Pope and Swift, a literature of feeling vied with the literature of wit. A partiality for the sublime passed from Thomson to Collins and eventually to the excited and ecstatic style of Christopher Smart. Pope had written of "a grace beyond the reach of art, / Which, without passing through the judgment, gains / The heart, and all its end at once attains"; but many of his successors identified that appeal to feeling—and avoidance of judgment—with poetry itself. The presence of the sublime in nature, as well as in the emotions of writers and readers, would be a staple of literature for decades to come.

THE EMERGENCE OF NEW LITERARY THEMES AND MODES, 1740–85

When Matthew Arnold called the eighteenth century an "age of prose," he meant to belittle its poetry, but he also stated a significant fact: great prose does dominate the age. Until the 1740s, poetry tended to set the standards of literature. But the growth of new kinds of prose took the initiative away from verse. Novelists became better known than poets; no writers of mid-century were more admired or popular than Samuel Richardson and Henry Fielding. And intellectual prose also flourished, with the achievements of Johnson in the essay and literary criticism; of Boswell in biography; of Hume in philosophy; of Burke in politics; of Edward Gibbon in history; of Sir Joshua Reynolds in aesthetics; of Gilbert White in natural history; and of Adam Smith in economics. Each of these authors is a master stylist, whose effort to express himself clearly and fully demands an art as carefully wrought as poetry. Other writers of prose were more informal. The memoirs of such women as Laetitia Pilkington, Charlotte Charke, Hester Thrale Piozzi, and Frances Burney bring each reader into their private lives and also remind us that the new print culture created celebrities, who wrote not only about themselves but about other celebrities they knew. The interest of readers in Samuel Johnson helped to sell his own books as well as a host of books that quoted his sayings. But the prose of the age also had to do justice to difficult and complicated ideas. Swift's prose, Johnson thought, was easy—perhaps too easy—to understand; "it instructs, but does not persuade." Johnson's prose, and that of his time, had higher ambitions. An unprecedented effort to formulate the first principles of philosophy, history, psychology, and art required a new style of persuasion.

Johnson helped codify that language, not only with his writings but with the first great English *Dictionary* (1755). This work established him as a national man of letters; eventually the period would be known as "the Age of Johnson." But his dominance was based on an ideal of service to others. The *Dictionary* illustrates its definitions with more than 114,000 quotations from the best English writers, thus building a bridge from past to present usage; and Johnson's essays, poems, and criticism also reflect his desire to preserve the lessons of the past. Yet he looks to the future as well, trying both to reach and to mold a nation of readers. If Johnson speaks for his age, one reason is his faith in common sense and the common reader. "By the common sense of readers uncorrupted with literary prejudices," he wrote in the last of his *Lives of the Poets* (1781), "must be finally decided all claim to poetical honors." A similar respect for the good judgment of ordinary people, and for standards of taste and behavior that anyone can share, marks many writers of the age. Both Burke, the great conservative statesman and author, and Thomas Paine, his radical adversary, proclaim themselves apostles of common sense. Moreover, the poets whom everyone read relied on verse that could do justice to the feelings of simple people. Gray's *Elegy*, Goldsmith's *The Deserted Village*, Crabbe's *The Village*, and the lyrics of Burns all strive to make poetry from and for the lives of common men and women.

Nevertheless, an age of great prose can burden its poets. The generation of talented young poets who emerged about the time of Pope's death, a group that includes Gray, William Collins, Mark Akenside, and the brothers Joseph and Thomas Warton, seems afraid that the spirit of poetry might be dying, driven out by the spirit of prose, by uninspiring truth, by the end of superstitions that had once peopled the land with poetic fairies and demons. In an age barren of magic, they ask, where has poetry gone? That question haunts many poems, suffusing them with melancholy. The prototype of the mid-eighteenth-century poet was Milton's *Il Penseroso,* a night-loving solitary who broods on the "far-off curfew" or the plangent organ in the twilight of a Gothic church. Such a figure has little in common with poets like Dryden and Pope, social beings who live in a crowded world and seldom confess their private feelings in public. The melancholy poet withdraws into himself and yearns to be living in some other time and place.

Poets who muse in silence are never far from thoughts of death, and a morbid fascination with suicide and the grave preoccupies many midcentury poets. Pope's *Essay on Man* had taken a sunny view of providence; Edward Young's *The Complaint: or Night Thoughts on Life, Death, and Immortality* (1742–46), an immensely long poem in blank verse, is darkened by Christian fear of the life to come. But the "graveyard school" pays less attention to religion than to images of decay. Surrounded by medieval ruins and tombs, the spirits of graveyard poets tremble and sink. The revival of Gothic architectural styles, most famously in Horace Walpole's tiny pseudo-Gothic castle, Strawberry Hill, influenced literary styles as well. The Gothic vogue, along with a vogue for Chinese decor, suggested that classical canons of taste—simplicity and harmonious balance—might count for less than the pleasures of fancy—intricate puzzles and a willful excess. Poets began to cultivate archaic language and antique forms. Inspired by Thomas Percy's edition of *Reliques of Ancient English Poetry* (1765), Thomas Chatterton passed off his own ballads as medieval; he died at seventeen, soon after his forgeries were exposed, but the Romantics later idolized his precocious genius. The most remarkable consequence of the medieval revival, however, was the invention of the Gothic romance. Walpole's *Castle of Otranto* (1765), a dreamlike tale of terror set in a simulacrum of Strawberry Hill, created a mode of fiction that retains its popularity to the present day. In a typical Gothic romance, amid the glooms and secret passages of some remote castle, the laws of nightmare replace the laws of probability. Forbidden themes—incest, murder, necrophilia, atheism, and the torments of sexual desire—are allowed free play; repressed anxieties and terrors rise to the surface of the narrative. Most such romances, like William Beckford's *Vathek* (1786) and Matthew Lewis's *The Monk* (1796), revel in sensationalism and the grotesque. But Gothicism also resulted in works, like Ann Radcliffe's, that temper romance with reality, as well as in serious novels of social purpose, like William Godwin's *Caleb Williams* (1794) and Mary Wollstonecraft's *Maria, or The Wrongs of Woman* (1798); and Mary Shelley, the daughter of Wollstonecraft and Godwin, eventually composed a romantic nightmare, *Frankenstein* (1818), that continues to haunt our dreams.

When poets looked for a renewal of poetry, however, they sought it not so much in the Gothic as in their own imaginations and feelings. In his *Ode to Fancy* (1746), Joseph Warton associated "fancy" with visions in the wilderness and spontaneous passions; the true poet was no longer defined as a craftsman or maker but as a seer or nature's priest. "The public has seen all that art can do," William Shenstone wrote in 1761, welcoming James Macpherson's *Ossian*, "and they want the more striking efforts of wild, original, enthusiastic genius." Macpherson filled the bill. His primitive, sentimental epics, supposedly translated from an ancient Gaelic warrior-bard, won the hearts of readers around the world; Napoleon and Thomas Jefferson, for instance, both thought that Ossian was greater than Homer. At the same time, many of the best poets of the period identified with the recluse or the outcast. Collins, Smart, and Cowper all were isolated from society by fits of madness, and only a handful of readers noticed the extraordinary work of Smart or later of William Blake.

Meanwhile, a different sort of poetry flourished: humorous, personal, and down to earth. As the reading public expanded, so did the number of people who tried their hand at verse; and they wrote about whatever interested them. Women and men described the details of their lives in homely images and graphic language. Such poets were not afraid to deal with beggars and barbers and chimney sweeps, or to sing the joys of village sports or the bustle of washing day. For much of the public, poetry offered the pleasures of self-expression and companionship. Cowper, the most popular poet of the later part of the century, won his readers with a modest, intimate kind of verse, seldom departing far from the accents of friendly conversation. Women especially prized his poems, and poets like Anna Seward and Charlotte Smith helped revive the lyric. Amid revolutions in society and thought, poets were asked to teach their readers how to respond—above all, how to feel. The next generation would try to answer that call.

THE BEGINNING OF THE NOVEL

The modern novel came into its own in the 1740s. Prose fiction had existed, to be sure, since ancient times; the Greeks and Romans wrote stories about the tribulations of love, and narrative traditions lie behind the Bible and most other sacred writings. Other early types of prose fiction include Sir Philip Sidney's courtly *Arcadia* and Lady Mary Wroth's *Urania*; the earthy tales of Thomas Nashe and Thomas Deloney; the long French romances of the seventeenth century, blending chivalric adventure and courtly love; and in a world apart, Bunyan's vivid allegories of the spiritual quests and battles of wayfaring Christians. Nor were clear distinctions drawn between history and fiction; Behn's *Oroonoko* is both. In the early eighteenth century, writers often mixed facts with their fiction, as when they whipped up scandalous versions of current events or reported some famous criminal's "true story." The master of this genre was Daniel Defoe. A middle-class writer, he did not seek upper-class readers (though *Robinson Crusoe*, 1719, appealed to all classes). Instead he aimed at shopkeepers, apprentices, and servants, a readership avid for racy stories, usually laced with moral indignation. Defoe shows his readers a world that they know, where unheroic people try to cope with practical problems, like finding a trustworthy spouse or simply staying alive. Nor was he alone in writing about and for women. For the first time in British history, a critical mass of female readers and writers carried weight with publishers. Jane Barker and Mary Davys, along with many others, brought women's work and daily lives as well as love affairs to fiction. Such stories were not only amusing but also served as models of conduct; they influenced the stories that real people told about themselves.

Samuel Richardson conceived the idea of *Pamela, or Virtue Rewarded* (1740) while compiling a little book of model letters. The letters grew into a story about a captivating young servant who resists her master's base designs on her virtue until he gives up and marries her. The combination of a high moral tone with sexual titillation and a minute analysis of the heroine's emotions and state of mind proved irresistible to readers. Richardson caught the attention of all literate Europe and once and for all established the novel as we know it: a serious form that can also be a popular success. He topped that success with *Clarissa* (1747–48). In the conflict between the libertine Lovelace, an attractive and diabolical aristocrat, and the angelic Clarissa, a middle-class paragon who struggles to stay pure, Richardson caught the ideals and tensions of a society whose values were in flux. No earlier author had involved readers so much in the feelings and motives of characters, examined minute by minute—this is the longest novel in English—until they seem more real than people we meet every day. The sympathy that readers felt for Clarissa was magnified by a host of sentimental novels, including Frances Sheridan's *Memoirs of Miss Sidney Bidulph* (1761), Rousseau's *Julie, or The New Heloise* (1761), and Henry Mackenzie's *The Man of Feeling* (1771). But Richardson also contributed to the art of the novel; he worked to make every detail contribute to the whole. Such later novelists as Burney and Jane Austen profited from his example.

Like Richardson, Henry Fielding had a gift for writing dramatic scenes; in the 1730s he had been the best comic playwright in England. But Fielding looked down on Richardson's pious middle-class values. *Joseph Andrews* (1742) begins by turning *Pamela* farcically upside-down, as Joseph (Pamela's brother) defends his chastity from the lewd advances of Lady Booby. Fielding's true model, however, is Cervantes' great *Don Quixote* (1605–15), from which he took an ironic, antiromantic style, a plot of wandering around the countryside, and an idealistic central character (Parson Adams) who keeps mistaking appearances for reality. The ambition of writing what Fielding called "a comic epic-poem in prose" went still further in *The History of Tom Jones, A Foundling* (1749). Crowded with incidents and comments on the state of England, the novel contrasts a good-natured, generous, wayward hero (who needs to learn prudence) with cold-hearted people who use moral codes and the law for their own selfish interests. This emphasis on instinctive virtue and vice, instead of Richardson's devotion to good principles, put off respectable readers like Johnson and Burney. But Coleridge thought that *Tom Jones* (along with *Oedipus Rex* and Jonson's *Alchemist*) was one of "the three most perfect plots ever planned."

Remarkable experiments in fiction run through the later part of the century, anticipating many of the forms that novelists still use today. Tobias Smollett's picaresque *Roderick Random* (1748) and *Humphry Clinker* (1771) delight in coarse practical jokes, the freaks and strong odors of life. But the most *novel* novelist of the age was Laurence Sterne, a humorous, sentimental clergyman who loves to play tricks on his readers. *The Life and Opinions of Tristram Shandy* (1760–67) abandons clock time for psychological time, whimsically follows chance associations, interrupts its own stories, violates the conventions of print by putting chapters 18 and 19 after chapter 25, sneaks in double entendres, and seems ready to go on forever. And yet these games get us inside the characters' minds, as if the world were as capricious as our thoughts. Sterne's self-conscious art implies that people's private obsessions shape their lives—or help create reality itself. Present-day novelists still play the games he invented.

At the same time, the focus on eccentric or individual points of view, along with the popularity of fiction—Gothic or sentimental—that indulged in extreme states of feeling, freed many writers to question the norms of behavior. Identifying with characters in novels, readers might find themselves. That seems to have been especially true for women. By the end of the century most of the leading British novelists were women—Burney, Radcliffe, and later Maria Edgeworth—and the novel was often considered a feminine preserve. For that reason, perhaps, it lost some prestige. When two young women spend their time reading novels together, in *Northanger Abbey,* the young Jane Austen defends them against some critic (presumably male) who might accuse them of frivolity: " 'It is only a novel!' . . . only some work in which the greatest powers of the mind are displayed, in which the most thorough knowledge of human nature, the happiest delineation of its varieties, the liveliest effusions of wit and humour, are conveyed to the world in the best chosen language." Novels, she argues, not only give pleasure to women but foster their education. Yet men were already beginning to take back the novel. Although today no English novelist of manners seems greater than Austen, early in the nineteenth century it was Walter Scott whose novels everyone read; and the historical novel, filled with scenes of men at work and war, largely superseded more intimate forms. That broader canvas would mark out the future of fiction.

CONTINUITY AND REVOLUTION

The history of eighteenth-century literature was first composed by the Romantics, who wrote it to serve their own interests. Prizing originality, they naturally preferred to stress how different they were from writers of the previous age. Later historians have tended to follow their lead, competing to prove that everything changed in 1776, or 1789, or 1798. This revolutionary view of history accounts for what happened to the word *revolution.* The older meaning referred to a movement around a point, a recurrence or cycle, as in the revolutions of the planets; the newer meaning signified a violent break with the past, an overthrow of the existing order, as in the Big Bang or the French Revolution. Romantic rhetoric made heavy use of such dramatic upheavals. Yet every history devoted to truth must take account of both sorts of revolution, of continuities as well as changes. The ideals that many Romantics made their own—the passion for liberty and equality, the founding of justice on individual rights, the distrust of institutions, the love of nature, the reverence for imagination, and even the embrace of change— were grown from seeds that had been planted long before. Nor did Augustan literature abruptly vanish on that day in 1798 when Wordsworth and Coleridge anonymously published a small and unsuccessful volume of poems called *Lyrical Ballads.* Even when they rebel against the work of Pope and Johnson and Gray, Romantic writers incorporate much of their language and values.

What Restoration and eighteenth-century literature passed on to the future, in fact, was chiefly a set of unresolved problems. The age of Enlightenment was also, in England, an age that insisted on holding fast to older beliefs and customs; the age of population explosion was also an age of individualism; the age that developed the slave trade was also the age that gave rise to the abolitionist movement; the age that codified rigid standards of conduct for women was also an age when many women took the chance to read and write and think for themselves; the age of reason was also the age when sensibility flourished; the last classical age was also the first modern age. These contradictions are far from abstract; writers were forced to choose their own directions. When young James Boswell looked for a mentor whose biography he might write, he considered not only Samuel Johnson but also David Hume, whose skeptical views of morality, truth, and religion were everything Johnson abhorred. The two writers seem to inhabit different worlds, yet Boswell traveled freely between them. That was exciting and also instructive. "Without Contraries is no progression," according to one citizen of Johnson's London, William Blake, who also thought that "Opposition is true Friendship." Good conversation was a lively eighteenth-century art, and sharp disagreements did not keep people from talking. The conversations the period started have not ended yet.

THE RESTORATION AND THE EIGHTEENTH CENTURY

TEXTS	CONTEXTS
1660 Samuel Pepys begins his diary.	1660 Charles II restored to the throne. Reopening of the theaters
1662 Samuel Butler, *Hudibras*, part 1	1662 Act of Uniformity requires all clergy to obey the Church of England. Chartering of the Royal Society
	1666 Fire destroys the City of London
1667 John Milton, *Paradise Lost*	
1668 John Dryden, *Essay of Dramatic Poesy*	1668 Dryden becomes Poet Laureate
	1673 Test Act requires all officeholders to swear allegiance to Anglicanism
1678 John Bunyan, *Pilgrim's Progress,* part 1	1678 The "Popish Plot" inflames anti-Catholic feeling
1681 Dryden, *Absalom and Achitophel*	1681 Charles II dissolves Parliament
	1685 Death of Charles II. James II, his Catholic brother, takes the throne
1687 Sir Isaac Newton, *Principia Mathematica*	
1688 Aphra Behn, *Oroonoko*	1688–89 The Glorious Revolution; James II exiled and succeeded by his Protestant daughter, Mary, and her husband, William of Orange
1690 John Locke, *An Essay Concerning Human Understanding*	
1700 William Congreve, *The Way of the World.* Mary Astell, *Some Reflections upon Marriage*	
	1702 Death of William III; succession of Anne (Protestant daughter of James II)
1704 Jonathan Swift, *A Tale of a Tub.* Newton, *Opticks*	
	1707 Act of Union with Scotland
	1710 Tories take power
1711 Alexander Pope, *An Essay on Criticism.* Joseph Addison and Sir Richard Steele, *The Spectator* (1711–12, 1714)	
	1714 Death of Queen Anne; George I (great-grandson of James I) becomes the first Hanoverian king; Tory government replaced by Whigs
1716 Lady Mary Wortley Montagu writes her letters from Turkey (1716–18)	
1717 Pope, *The Rape of the Lock*	
1719 Daniel Defoe, *Robinson Crusoe*	
	1720 South Sea Bubble collapses
	1721 Robert Walpole comes to power

TEXTS	CONTEXTS
1726 Swift, *Gulliver's Travels*	
	1727 George I dies; George II succeeds
1728 John Gay, *The Beggar's Opera*	
1733 Pope, *An Essay on Man*	
	1737 Licensing Act censors the stage
1740 Samuel Richardson, *Pamela*	
1742 Henry Fielding, *Joseph Andrews*	1742 Walpole resigns
1743 Pope, *The Dunciad* (final version). William Hogarth, *Marriage A-la-Mode*	
1746 William Collins's *Odes*	1746 Charles Edward Stuart's defeat at Culloden ends the last Jacobite rebellion
1747 Richardson, *Clarissa*	
	1748 Treaty of Aix-la-Chapelle
1749 Fielding, *Tom Jones*	
1751 Thomas Gray, *Elegy Written in a Country Churchyard*	1751 Robert Clive seizes Arcot, the prelude to English control of India
1755 Samuel Johnson, *Dictionary*	
	1756 Beginning of Seven Years War
1759 Johnson, *Rasselas*. Voltaire, *Candide*	1759 James Wolfe's capture of Quebec assures British control of Canada
1760 Laurence Sterne, *Tristram Shandy* (1760–67)	1760 George III succeeds to the throne
1765 Johnson's edition of Shakespeare	
	1768 Captain James Cook voyages to Australia and New Zealand
1770 Oliver Goldsmith, *The Deserted Village*	
	1775 American Revolution (1775–83). James Watt produces steam engines
1776 Adam Smith, *The Wealth of Nations*	
1778 Frances Burney, *Evelina*	
1779 Johnson, *Lives of the Poets* (1779–81)	
	1780 Gordon Riots in London
1783 George Crabbe, *The Village*	1783 William Pitt becomes Prime Minister
1785 William Cowper, *The Task*	

JOHN DRYDEN
1631–1700

Although John Dryden's parents seem to have sided with Parliament against the king, there is no evidence that the poet grew up in a strict Puritan family. His father, a country gentleman of moderate fortune, gave his son a gentleman's education at Westminster School, under the renowned Dr. Richard Busby, who used the rod as a pedagogical aid in imparting a sound knowledge of the learned languages and literatures to his charges (among others John Locke and Matthew Prior). From Westminster, Dryden went to Trinity College, Cambridge, where he took his A.B. in 1654. His first important poem, *Heroic Stanzas* (1659), was written to commemorate the death of Cromwell. The next year, however, in *Astraea Redux,* Dryden joined his countrymen in celebrating the return of Charles II to his throne. During the rest of his life Dryden was to remain entirely loyal to Charles and to his successor, James II.

Dryden is the commanding literary figure of the last four decades of the seventeenth century. Every important aspect of the life of his times—political, religious, philosophical, artistic—finds expression somewhere in his writings. Dryden is the least personal of poets. He is not at all the solitary, subjective poet listening to the murmur of his own voice and preoccupied with his own feelings, but rather a citizen of the world commenting publicly on matters of public concern.

From the beginning to the end of his literary career, Dryden's nondramatic poems are most typically occasional poems, which celebrate particular events of a public character—a coronation, a military victory, a death, or a political crisis. Such poems are social and ceremonial, written not for the self but for the nation. Dryden's principal achievements in this form are the two poems on the king's return and his coronation; *Annus Mirabilis* (1667), which celebrates the English naval victory over the Dutch and the fortitude of the people of London and the king during the Great Fire, both events of that "wonderful year," 1666; the political poems; the lines on the death of Oldham (1684); and odes such as *Alexander's Feast.*

Between 1664 and 1681, however, Dryden was mainly a playwright. The newly chartered theaters needed a modern repertory, and he set out to supply the need. Dryden wrote his plays, as he frankly confessed, to please his audiences, which were not heterogeneous like Shakespeare's but were largely drawn from the court and from people of fashion. In the style of the time, he produced rhymed heroic plays, in which incredibly noble heroes and heroines face incredibly difficult choices between love and honor; comedies, in which male and female rakes engage in intrigue and bright repartee; and later, libretti for the newly introduced dramatic form, the opera. His one great tragedy, *All for Love* (1677), in blank verse, adapts Shakespeare's *Antony and Cleopatra* to the unities of time, place, and action. As his *An Essay of Dramatic Poesy* (1668) shows, Dryden had studied the works of the great playwrights of Greece and Rome, of the English Renaissance, and of contemporary France, seeking sound theoretical principles on which to construct the new drama that the age demanded. Indeed, his fine critical intelligence always supported his creative powers, and because he took literature seriously and enjoyed discussing it, he became, almost casually, what Samuel Johnson called him: "the father of English criticism." His abilities as both poet and dramatist brought him to the attention of the king, who in 1668 made him poet laureate. Two years later the post of historiographer royal was added to the laureateship at a combined stipend of £200, enough money to live on.

Between 1678 and 1681, when he was nearing fifty, Dryden discovered his great gift for writing formal verse satire. A quarrel with the playwright Thomas Shadwell prompted the mock-heroic episode *Mac Flecknoe,* probably written in 1678 or 1679 but not published until 1682. Out of the stresses occasioned by the Popish Plot (1678) and its political aftermath came his major political satires, *Absalom and Ach-*

itophel (1681), and *The Medal* (1682), his final attack on the villain of *Absalom and Achitophel,* the earl of Shaftesbury. Twenty years' experience as poet and playwright had prepared him technically for the triumph of *Absalom and Achitophel.* He had mastered the heroic couplet, having fashioned it into an instrument suitable in his hands for every sort of discourse from the thrust and parry of quick logical argument, to lyric feeling, rapid narrative, or forensic declamation. Thanks to this long discipline, he was able in one stride to rival the masters of verse satire: Horace, Juvenal, Persius, in ancient Rome, and Boileau, his French contemporary.

The consideration of religious and political questions that the events of 1678–81 forced on Dryden brought a new seriousness to his mind and works. In 1682 he published *Religio Laici,* a poem in which he examined the grounds of his religious faith and defended the middle way of the Anglican Church against the rationalism of Deism on the one hand and the authoritarianism of Rome on the other. But he had moved closer to Rome than he perhaps realized when he wrote the poem. Charles II died in 1685 and was succeeded by his Catholic brother, James II. Within a year Dryden and his two sons were converted to Catholicism. Though his enemies accused him of opportunism, he proved his sincerity by his steadfast loyalty to the Roman Church after James abdicated and the Protestant William and Mary came in; as a result he was to lose his offices and their much-needed stipends. From his new position as a Roman Catholic, Dryden wrote in 1687 *The Hind and the Panther,* in which a milk-white Hind (the Roman Church) and a spotted Panther (the Anglican Church) eloquently debate theology. The Hind has the better of the argument, but Dryden already knew that James's policies were failing, and with them the Catholic cause in England.

Dryden was now nearing sixty, with a family to support on a much-diminished income. To earn a living, he resumed writing plays and turned to translations. In 1693 appeared his versions of Juvenal and Persius, with the long dedicatory epistle on satire; and in 1697, his greatest achievement in this mode, the works of Virgil. At the very end, two months before his death, came the *Fables Ancient and Modern,* prefaced by one of the finest of his critical essays and made up of translations from Ovid, Boccaccio, and Chaucer.

What was the nature of Dryden's achievement? First and foremost, he brought the pleasures of literature to the ever-increasing reading public of Britain. As a critic and translator, he made many classics available to men and women who lacked a classical education. His canons of taste and theoretical principles would set the standard for the next generation. As a writer of prose, he helped establish a popular new style, shaped to the cadences of good conversation. Johnson praised its apparent artlessness: "every word seems to drop by chance, though it falls into its proper place. Nothing is cold or languid; the whole is airy, animated, and vigorous . . . though all is easy, nothing is feeble; though all seems careless, there is nothing harsh." Although Dryden's plays went out of fashion, his poems did not. His satire inspired the most brilliant verse satirist of the next century, Alexander Pope, and the energy and variety of his metrics launched the long-standing vogue of heroic couplets. Augustan style is at its best in his poems: lively, dignified, precise, and always musical—a flexible instrument of public speech. "By him we were taught *sapere et fari,* to think naturally and express forcibly," Johnson concluded. "What was said of Rome, adorned by Augustus, may be applied by an easy metaphor to English poetry embellished by Dryden, *lateritiam invenit, marmoream reliquit,* he found it brick, and he left it marble."

From Annus Mirabilis[1]

* * *

[LONDON REBORN]

845 Yet London, empress of the northern clime,
　　By an high fate thou greatly didst expire;
　　Great as the world's, which at the death of time
　　Must fall, and rise a nobler frame by fire.[2]

　　As when some dire usurper Heaven provides,
850 　　To scourge his country with a lawless sway:[3]
　　His birth, perhaps, some petty village hides,
　　And sets his cradle out of fortune's way:

　　Till fully ripe his swelling fate breaks out,
　　And hurries him to mighty mischiefs on:
855 His Prince, surprised at first, no ill could doubt,°　　　　　*fear*
　　And wants the power to meet it when 'tis known:

　　Such was the rise of this prodigious fire,
　　Which in mean buildings first obscurely bred,
　　From thence did soon to open streets aspire,
860 　　And straight to palaces and temples spread.

* * *

　　Me-thinks already, from this chymic[4] flame,
1170 　　I see a city of more precious mold:
　　Rich as the town which gives the Indies name,°　　　　　*Mexico*
　　With silver paved, and all divine with gold.

　　Already, laboring with a mighty fate,
　　She shakes the rubbish from her mounting brow,
1175 And seems to have renewed her charter's date,
　　Which Heaven will to the death of time allow.

　　More great than human, now, and more August,[5]
　　New deified she from her fires does rise:
　　Her widening streets on new foundations trust,
1180 　　And, opening, into larger parts she flies.

1. 1666 was a "year of wonders" (*annus mirabilis*): war, plague, and the Great Fire of London. According to the enemies of Charles II, God was visiting His wrath on the English people to signify that the reign of an unholy king would soon come to an end. Dryden's long "historical poem" *Annus Mirabilis*, written the same year, interprets the wonders differently: as trials sent by God to punish rebellious spirits and to bind the king and his people together. "Never had prince or people more mutual reason to love each other," Dryden wrote, "if suffering for each other can endear affection." Charles had endured rejection and exile, England had been torn by civil wars. Dryden views these sufferings as a covenant, a pledge of better times to come. Out of Charles's troubles, he predicts in heroic stanzas modeled on Virgil, the king shall arise like a new Augustus, the ruler of a great empire, and out of fire, London shall arise like the phoenix, ready to take its place as trade center for the world, in the glory of a new Augustan age.
2. Ovid, whom Dryden quotes, foretells, in *The Metamorphoses* 1, that the world will be purged by fire.
3. Probably a reference to Oliver Cromwell.
4. Alchemic or transmuting. The fire of London, which utterly consumed the central city, burned for four days, September 2–6. By September 10, Christopher Wren had already submitted a plan, much of it later adopted, for rebuilding the city on a grander scale.
5. Augusta, the old name of London [Dryden's note].

Before, she like some shepherdess did show,
    Who sat to bathe her by a river's side:
Not answering to her fame, but rude and low,
    Nor taught the beauteous arts of modern pride.

1185 Now, like a Maiden Queen, she will behold,
    From her high turrets, hourly suitors come:
The East with incense, and the West with gold,
    Will stand, like suppliants, to receive her doom.°   *judgment, decree*

The silver Thames, her own domestic flood,
1190   Shall bear her vessels like a sweeping train;
And often wind (as of his mistress proud)
    With longing eyes to meet her face again.

The wealthy Tagus, and the wealthier Rhine,
    The glory of their towns no more shall boast;
1195 And Seine, that would with Belgian rivers join,[6]
    Shall find her luster stained, and traffic lost.

The venturous merchant, who designed[7] more far,
    And touches on our hospitable shore,
Charmed with the splendor of this northern star,
1200   Shall here unlade him, and depart no more.

Our powerful navy shall no longer meet,
    The wealth of France or Holland to invade;
The beauty of this Town, without a fleet,
    From all the world shall vindicate° her trade.   *defend, protect*

1205 And while this famed emporium we prepare,
    The British ocean shall such triumphs boast,
That those who now disdain our trade to share,
    Shall rob like pirates on our wealthy coast.

Already we have conquered half the war,
1210   And the less dangerous part is left behind:
Our trouble now is but to make them dare,
    And not so great to vanquish as to find.

Thus to the eastern wealth through storms we go,
    But now, the Cape once doubled,° fear no more;   *sailed around*
1215 A constant trade-wind will securely blow,
    And gently lay us on the spicy shore.

1666   1667

6. France and Holland (which then included Bel-gium) had made an alliance for trade, as well as war, against England. The river Tagus flows into the Atlantic at Lisbon.
7. Intended to go.

Song from *Marriage à la Mode*

I

Why should a foolish marriage vow,
    Which long ago was made,
Oblige us to each other now,
    When passion is decayed?
5   We loved, and we loved, as long as we could,
    Till our love was loved out in us both;
But our marriage is dead when the pleasure is fled:
    'Twas pleasure first made it an oath.

2

If I have pleasures for a friend,
10   And farther love in store,
What wrong has he whose joys did end,
    And who could give no more?
'Tis a madness that he should be jealous of me,
    Or that I should bar him of another:
15 For all we can gain is to give ourselves pain,
    When neither can hinder the other.

ca. 1672   1673

Absalom and Achitophel In 1678 a dangerous crisis, both religious and political, threatened to undo the Restoration settlement and to precipitate England once again into civil war. The Popish Plot and its aftermath not only whipped up extreme anti-Catholic passions, but led between 1679 and 1681 to a bitter political struggle between Charles II (whose adherents came to be called Tories) and the earl of Shaftesbury (whose followers were termed Whigs). The issues were nothing less than the prerogatives of the crown and the possible exclusion of the king's Catholic brother, James, duke of York, from his position as heir-presumptive to the throne. Charles's cool courage and brilliant, if unscrupulous, political genius saved the throne for his brother and gave at least temporary peace to his people.

Charles was a Catholic at heart—he received the last rites of that church on his deathbed—and was eager to do what he could do discreetly for the relief of his Catholic subjects, who suffered severe civil and religious disabilities imposed by their numerically superior Protestant compatriots. James openly professed the Catholic religion, an awkward fact politically, for he was next in line of succession because Charles had no legitimate children. The household of the duke, as well as that of Charles's neglected queen, Catherine of Braganza, inevitably became the center of Catholic life and intrigue at court and consequently of Protestant prejudice and suspicion.

No one understood, however, that the situation was explosive until 1678, when Titus Oates (a renegade Catholic convert of infamous character) offered sworn testimony of the existence of a Jesuit plot to assassinate the king, burn London, massacre Protestants, and reestablish the Roman Church.

The country might have kept its head and come to realize (what no historian has doubted) that Oates and his confederates were perjured rascals, as Charles himself quickly perceived. But panic was created by the discovery of the body of a prominent London justice of the peace, Sir Edmund Berry Godfrey, who a few days before had received for safekeeping a copy of Oates's testimony. The murder, immediately ascribed to the Catholics, has never been solved. Fear and indignation reached a hysterical pitch when the seizure of the papers of the duke of York's secretary revealed that he had been in correspondence with the confessor of Louis XIV regarding the reestablishment of the Roman Church in England. Before the terror subsided many innocent men were executed on the increasingly bold and always false evidence of Oates and his accomplices.

The earl of Shaftesbury, the duke of Buckingham, and others quickly took advantage of the situation. With the support of the Commons and the City of London, they moved to exclude the duke of York from the succession. Between 1679 and 1681 Charles and Shaftesbury were engaged in a mighty struggle. The Whigs found a candidate of their own in the king's favorite illegitimate son, the handsome and engaging duke of Monmouth, whom they advanced as a proper successor to his father. They urged Charles to legitimize him, and when he refused, they whispered that there was proof that the king had secretly married Monmouth's mother. The young man allowed himself to be used against his father. He was sent on a triumphant progress through western England, where he was enthusiastically received. Twice an Exclusion Bill nearly passed both houses. But by early 1681 Charles had secured his own position by secretly accepting from Louis XIV a three-year subsidy that made him independent of Parliament, which had tried to force his hand by refusing to vote him funds. He summoned Parliament to meet at Oxford in the spring of 1681, and a few moments after the Commons had passed the Exclusion Bill, in a bold stroke he abruptly dissolved Parliament, which never met again during his reign. Already, as Charles was aware, a reaction had set in against the violence of the Whigs. In midsummer, when he felt it safe to move against his enemies, Shaftesbury was sent to the Tower of London, charged with high treason. In November, the grand jury, packed with Whigs, threw out the indictment, and the earl was free, but his power was broken, and he lived only two more years.

Shortly before the grand jury acted, Dryden published anonymously the first part of *Absalom and Achitophel*, apparently hoping to influence their verdict. The issues in question were grave; the chief actors, the most important men in the realm. Dryden, therefore, could not use burlesque and caricature as had Butler, or the mock heroic as he himself had done in *Mac Flecknoe*. Only a heroic style and manner were appropriate to his weighty material, and the poem is most original in its blending of the heroic and the satiric. Dryden's task called for all his tact and literary skill; he had to mention, but to gloss over, the king's faults: his indolence and love of pleasure; his neglect of his wife, and his devotion to his mistresses—conduct that had left him with many children, but no heir except his Catholic brother. He had to deal gently with Monmouth, whom Charles still loved. And he had to present, or appear to present, the king's case objectively.

The remarkable parallels between the rebellion of Absalom against his father King David (2 Samuel 13–18) had already been remarked in sermons, satires, and pamphlets. Dryden took the hint and gave contemporary events a due distance and additional dignity by approaching them indirectly through their biblical analogues. The poem is famous for its brilliant portraits of the king's enemies and friends, but equally admirable are the temptation scene (which, like other passages, is indebted to *Paradise Lost*) and the remarkably astute analysis of the Popish Plot itself.

A second part of *Absalom and Achitophel* appeared in 1682. Most of it is the work of Nahum Tate, but lines 310–509, which include the devastating portraits of Doeg and Og (two Whig poets, Elkanah Settle and Thomas Shadwell), are certainly by Dryden.

Absalom and Achitophel: A Poem

In pious times, ere priestcraft did begin,
Before polygamy was made a sin;
When man on many multiplied his kind,
Ere one to one was cursedly confined;
5 When nature prompted and no law denied
Promiscuous use of concubine and bride;
Then Israel's monarch after Heaven's own heart,[1]
His vigorous warmth did variously impart
To wives and slaves; and, wide as his command,
10 Scattered his Maker's image through the land.
Michal,[2] of royal blood, the crown did wear,
A soil ungrateful to the tiller's care:
Not so the rest; for several mothers bore
To godlike David several sons before.
15 But since like slaves his bed they did ascend,
No true succession could their seed attend.
Of all this numerous progeny was none
So beautiful, so brave, as Absalom:[3]
Whether, inspired by some diviner lust,
20 His father got him with a greater gust,°   *relish, pleasure*
Or that his conscious destiny made way,
By manly beauty, to imperial sway.
Early in foreign fields he won renown,
With kings and states allied to Israel's crown:[4]
25 In peace the thoughts of war he could remove,
And seemed as he were only born for love.
Whate'er he did, was done with so much ease,
In him alone 'twas natural to please;
His motions all accompanied with grace;
30 And paradise was opened in his face.
With secret joy indulgent David viewed
His youthful image in his son renewed:
To all his wishes nothing he denied;
And made the charming Annabel[5] his bride.
35 What faults he had (for who from faults is free?)
His father could not, or he would not see.
Some warm excesses which the law forbore,
Were construed youth that purged by boiling o'er:
And Amnon's murther,[6] by a specious name,
40 Was called a just revenge for injured fame.
Thus praised and loved the noble youth remained,
While David, undisturbed, in Sion° reigned.   *London*

1. David ("a man after [God's] own heart," according to 1 Samuel 13.14) represents Charles II.
2. One of David's wives, who represents the childless queen, Catherine of Braganza.
3. James Scott, duke of Monmouth (1649–1685).
4. Monmouth had won repute as a soldier fighting for France against Holland and for Holland against France.

5. Anne Scott, duchess of Buccleuch (pronounced *Bue-cloo*), a beauty and a great heiress.
6. Absalom killed his half-brother Amnon, who had raped Absalom's sister Tamar (2 Samuel 13.28–29). The parallel with Monmouth is vague. He is known to have committed acts of violence in his youth, but certainly not fratricide.

But life can never be sincerely° blest;   *wholly*
Heaven punishes the bad, and proves° the best.   *tests*
45   The Jews,° a headstrong, moody, murmuring race,   *English*
As ever tried the extent and stretch of grace;
God's pampered people, whom, debauched with ease,
No king could govern, nor no God could please
(Gods they had tried of every shape and size
50   That god-smiths could produce, or priests devise);[7]
These Adam-wits, too fortunately free,
Began to dream they wanted liberty;[8]
And when no rule, no precedent was found,
Of men by laws less circumscribed and bound,
55   They led their wild desires to woods and caves,
And thought that all but savages were slaves.
They who, when Saul was dead, without a blow,
Made foolish Ishbosheth[9] the crown forgo;
Who banished David did from Hebron[1] bring,
60   And with a general shout proclaimed him king:
Those very Jews, who, at their very best,
Their humor° more than loyalty expressed,   *caprice*
Now wondered why so long they had obeyed
An idol monarch, which their hands had made;
65   Thought they might ruin him they could create,
Or melt him to that golden calf,[2] a state.°   *republic*
But these were random bolts;° no formed design   *shots*
Nor interest made the factious crowd to join:
The sober part of Israel, free from stain,
70   Well knew the value of a peaceful reign;
And, looking backward with a wise affright,
Saw seams of wounds, dishonest° to the sight: *disgraceful*
In contemplation of whose ugly scars
They cursed the memory of civil wars.
75   The moderate sort of men, thus qualified,°   *assuaged*
Inclined the balance to the better side;
And David's mildness managed it so well,
The bad found no occasion to rebel.
But when to sin our biased[3] nature leans,
80   The careful Devil is still at hand with means;
And providently pimps for ill desires:
The Good Old Cause[4] revived, a plot requires.
Plots, true or false, are necessary things,
To raise up commonwealths and ruin kings.
85   The inhabitants of old Jerusalem
Were Jebusites;[5] the town so called from them;

---

7. Dryden recalls the political and religious controversies that, since the Reformation, had divided
England and finally caused civil wars.
8. Adam rebelled because he felt that he lacked
("wanted") liberty, because he was forbidden to eat
the fruit of one tree.
9. Saul's son; he stands for Richard Cromwell,
who succeeded his father as lord protector. "Saul":
Oliver Cromwell.
1. Where David reigned over Judah after the death
of Saul and before he became king of Israel (2

Samuel 1–5). Charles had been crowned in Scotland in 1651.
2. The image worshiped by the children of Israel
during the period that Moses spent on Mount
Sinai, receiving the law from God.
3. Inclined (cf. *Mac Flecknoe*, line 189 and n. 5,
p. 2105).
4. The Commonwealth. Dryden stigmatizes the
Whigs by associating them with subversion.
5. Roman Catholics. The original name of Jerusalem (here, London) was Jebus.

And theirs the native right.
But when the chosen people° grew more strong,   *Protestants*
The rightful cause at length became the wrong;
90   And every loss the men of Jebus bore,
They still were thought God's enemies the more.
Thus worn and weakened, well or ill content,
Submit they must to David's government:
Impoverished and deprived of all command,
95   Their taxes doubled as they lost their land;
And, what was harder yet to flesh and blood,
Their gods disgraced, and burnt like common wood.[6]
This set the heathen priesthood[7] in a flame;
For priests of all religions are the same:
100   Of whatsoe'er descent their godhead be,
Stock, stone, or other homely pedigree.
In his defense his servants are as bold,
As if he had been born of beaten gold.
The Jewish rabbins,[8] though their enemies,
105   In this conclude them honest men and wise:
For 'twas their duty, all the learned think,
To espouse his cause, by whom they eat and drink.
From hence began that Plot, the nation's curse,
Bad in itself, but represented worse;
110   Raised in extremes, and in extremes decried;
With oaths affirmed, with dying vows denied;
Not weighed or winnowed by the multitude;
But swallowed in the mass, unchewed and crude.
Some truth there was, but dashed° and brewed with lies,   *adulterated*
115   To please the fools, and puzzle all the wise.
Succeeding times did equal folly call,
Believing nothing, or believing all.
The Egyptian rites the Jebusites embraced,
Where gods were recommended by their taste.[9]
120   Such savory deities must needs be good,
As served at once for worship and for food.
By force they could not introduce these gods,
For ten to one in former days was odds;
So fraud was used (the sacrificer's trade):
125   Fools are more hard to conquer than persuade.
Their busy teachers mingled with the Jews,
And raked for converts even the court and stews:°   *brothels*
Which Hebrew priests the more unkindly took,
Because the fleece accompanies the flock.[1]
130   Some thought they God's anointed° meant to slay   *the king*
By guns, invented since full many a day:
Our author swears it not; but who can know
How far the Devil and Jebusites may go?
This Plot, which failed for want of common sense,

---

6. Such oppressive laws against Roman Catholics date from the time of Elizabeth I.
7. Roman Catholic clergy.
8. Anglican clergy.
9. Here Dryden sneers at the doctrine of transubstantiation. "Egyptian": French, therefore Catho-lic.
1. Dryden charges that the Anglican clergy ("Hebrew priests") resented proselytizing by Catholics chiefly because they stood to lose their tithes ("fleece").

135 Had yet a deep and dangerous consequence:
For, as when raging fevers boil the blood,
The standing lake soon floats into a flood,
And every hostile humor, which before
Slept quiet in its channels, bubbles o'er;
140 So several factions from this first ferment
Work up to foam, and threat the government.
Some by their friends, more by themselves thought wise,
Opposed the power to which they could not rise.
Some had in courts been great, and thrown from thence,
145 Like fiends were hardened in impenitence;
Some, by their monarch's fatal mercy, grown
From pardoned rebels kinsmen to the throne,
Were raised in power and public office high;
Strong bands, if bands ungrateful men could tie.
150 Of these the false Achitophel[2] was first;
A name to all succeeding ages cursed:
For close designs, and crooked counsels fit;
Sagacious, bold, and turbulent of wit;°   unruly imagination
Restless, unfixed in principles and place;
155 In power unpleased, impatient of disgrace:
A fiery soul, which, working out its way, ⎫
Fretted the pygmy body to decay,   ⎬
And o'er-informed the tenement of clay.[3] ⎭
A daring pilot in extremity;
160 Pleased with the danger, when the waves went high,
He sought the storms; but, for a calm unfit,
Would steer too nigh the sands, to boast his wit.
Great wits are sure to madness near allied,[4]
And thin partitions do their bounds divide;
165 Else why should he, with wealth and honor blest,
Refuse his age the needful hours of rest?
Punish a body which he could not please;
Bankrupt of life, yet prodigal of ease?
And all to leave what with his toil he won,
170 To that unfeathered two-legged thing,[5] a son;
Got, while his soul did huddled° notions try;   confused, hurried
And born a shapeless lump, like anarchy.
In friendship false, implacable in hate,
Resolved to ruin or to rule the state.
175 To compass this the triple bond[6] he broke, ⎫
The pillars of the public safety shook,   ⎬
And fitted Israel for a foreign yoke;   ⎭

---

2. Anthony Ashley Cooper, first earl of Shaftesbury (1621–1683). He had served in the parliamentary army and been a member of Cromwell's council of state. He later helped bring back Charles and, in 1670, was made a member of the notorious Cabal Ministry, which formed an alliance with Louis XIV in which England betrayed her ally, Holland, and joined France in war against that country. In 1672 he became lord chancellor, but with the dissolution of the cabal in 1673, he was removed from office. Lines 146–49 apply perfectly to him.

3. The soul is thought of as the animating principle, the force that puts the body in motion. Shaftesbury's body seemed too small to house his fiery, energetic soul.
4. "Great wits": men of genius. That genius and madness are akin is a very old idea.
5. Cf. Plato's definition of a human: "a featherless biped."
6. The triple alliance of England, Sweden, and Holland against France, 1668. Shaftesbury helped to bring about the war against Holland in 1672.

Then seized with fear, yet still affecting fame,
Usurped a patriot's all-atoning name.
180 So easy still it proves in factious times,
With public zeal to cancel private crimes.
How safe is treason, and how sacred ill,
Where none can sin against the people's will!
Where crowds can wink, and no offense be known,
185 Since in another's guilt they find their own!
Yet fame deserved, no enemy can grudge;
The statesman we abhor, but praise the judge.
In Israel's courts ne'er sat an Abbethdin[7]
With more discerning eyes, or hands more clean;
190 Unbribed, unsought, the wretched to redress;
Swift of dispatch, and easy of access.
Oh, had he been content to serve the crown,
With virtues only proper to the gown;
Or had the rankness of the soil been freed
195 From cockle, that oppressed the noble seed;
David for him his tuneful harp had strung,
And Heaven had wanted one immortal song.[8]
But wild Ambition loves to slide, not stand,
And Fortune's ice prefers to Virtue's land.
200 Achitophel, grown weary to possess
A lawful fame, and lazy happiness,
Disdained the golden fruit to gather free,
And lent the crowd his arm to shake the tree.
Now, manifest of° crimes contrived long since,   *detected in*
205 He stood at bold defiance with his prince;
Held up the buckler of the people's cause
Against the crown, and skulked behind the laws.
The wished occasion of the Plot he takes;
Some circumstances finds, but more he makes.
210 By buzzing emissaries fills the ears
Of listening crowds with jealousies° and fears   *suspicions*
Of arbitrary counsels brought to light,
And proves the king himself a Jebusite.
Weak arguments! which yet he knew full well
215 Were strong with people easy to rebel.
For, governed by the moon, the giddy Jews
Tread the same track when she the prime renews;
And once in twenty years, their scribes record,[9]
By natural instinct they change their lord.
220 Achitophel still wants a chief, and none
Was found so fit as warlike Absalom:
Not that he wished his greatness to create
(For politicians neither love nor hate),

7. The chief of the seventy elders who composed the Jewish supreme court. The allusion is to Shaftesbury's serving as lord chancellor from 1672 to 1673. Dryden's praise of Shaftesbury's integrity in this office, by suggesting a balanced judgment, makes his condemnation of the statesman more effective than it might otherwise have been.
8. I.e., David would have had occasion to write one fewer song of praise to heaven. The reference may be to 2 Samuel 22 or to Psalm 4.
9. The moon "renews her prime" when its several phases recur on the same day of the solar calendar—i.e., complete a cycle—as happens approximately every twenty years. The crisis between Charles I and Parliament began to grow acute about 1640; Charles II returned in 1660; it is now 1680 and a full cycle has been completed.

But, for he knew his title not allowed,
225   Would keep him still depending on the crowd,
That kingly power, thus ebbing out, might be
Drawn to the dregs of a democracy.[1]
Him he attempts with studied arts to please,
And sheds his venom in such words as these:
230   "Auspicious prince, at whose nativity
Some royal planet[2] ruled the southern sky;
Thy longing country's darling and desire;
Their cloudy pillar and their guardian fire:
Their second Moses, whose extended wand
235   Divides the seas, and shows the promised land;[3]
Whose dawning day in every distant age
Has exercised the sacred prophet's rage:
The people's prayer, the glad diviners' theme,
The young men's vision, and the old men's dream![4]
240   Thee, savior, thee, the nation's vows[5] confess,
And, never satisfied with seeing, bless:
Swift unbespoken pomps thy steps proclaim,
And stammering babes are taught to lisp thy name.
How long wilt thou the general joy detain,
245   Starve and defraud the people of thy reign?
Content ingloriously to pass thy days
Like one of Virtue's fools that feeds on praise;
Till thy fresh glories, which now shine so bright,
Grow stale and tarnish with our daily sight.
250   Believe me, royal youth, thy fruit must be
Or gathered ripe, or rot upon the tree.
Heaven has to all allotted, soon or late,
Some lucky revolution of their fate;
Whose motions if we watch and guide with skill
255   (For human good depends on human will),
Our Fortune rolls as from a smooth descent,
And from the first impression takes the bent;
But, if unseized, she glides away like wind,
And leaves repenting Folly far behind.
260   Now, now she meets you with a glorious prize,
And spreads her locks before her as she flies.[6]
Had thus old David, from whose loins you spring,
Not dared, when Fortune called him, to be king,
At Gath[7] an exile he might still remain,
265   And heaven's anointing[8] oil had been in vain.

---

1. To Dryden, "democracy" meant popular government. The "dregs of a democracy" would be mob rule.
2. A planet whose influence destines him to kingship.
3. After their exodus from Egypt under the leadership of Moses, whose "extended wand" separated the waters of the Red Sea so that they crossed over on dry land, the Israelites were led in their forty-year wandering in the wilderness by a pillar of cloud by day and a pillar of fire by night (Exodus 13–14).

4. Cf. Joel 2.28.
5. Solemn promises of fidelity.
6. Achitophel gives to Fortune the traditional attributes of the allegorical personification of Opportunity: bald except for a forelock, she can be seized only as she approaches.
7. Brussels, where Charles spent his last years in exile. David took refuge from Saul in Gath (1 Samuel 27.4).
8. After God rejected Saul, he sent Samuel to anoint the boy David, as a token that he should finally come to the throne (1 Samuel 16.1–13).

Let his successful youth your hopes engage;
But shun the example of declining age;
Behold him setting in his western skies,
The shadows lengthening as the vapors rise.
270   He is not now, as when on Jordan's sand⁹
      The joyful people thronged to see him land,
      Covering the beach, and blackening all the strand;
      But, like the Prince of Angels, from his height
      Comes tumbling downward with diminished light;¹
275   Betrayed by one poor plot to public scorn
      (Our only blessing since his cursed return),
      Those heaps of people which one sheaf did bind,
      Blown off and scattered by a puff of wind.
      What strength can he to your designs oppose,
280   Naked of friends, and round beset with foes?
      If Pharaoh's² doubtful succor he should use,
      A foreign aid would more incense the Jews:
      Proud Egypt would dissembled friendship bring;
      Foment the war, but not support the king:
285   Nor would the royal party e'er unite
      With Pharaoh's arms to assist the Jebusite;
      Or if they should, their interest soon would break,
      And with such odious aid make David weak.
      All sorts of men by my successful arts,
290   Abhorring kings, estrange their altered hearts
      From David's rule: and 'tis the general cry,
      'Religion, commonwealth, and liberty.'³
      If you, as champion of the public good,
      Add to their arms a chief of royal blood,
295   What may not Israel hope, and what applause
      Might such a general gain by such a cause?
      Not barren praise alone, that gaudy flower
      Fair only to the sight, but solid power;
      And nobler is a limited command,
300   Given by the love of all your native land,
      Than a successive title,⁴ long and dark,
      Drawn from the moldy rolls of Noah's ark."
          What cannot praise effect in mighty minds,
      When flattery soothes, and when ambition blinds!
305   Desire of power, on earth a vicious weed,
      Yet, sprung from high, is of celestial seed:
      In God 'tis glory; and when men aspire,
      'Tis but a spark too much of heavenly fire.
      The ambitious youth, too covetous of fame,
310   Too full of angels' metal⁵ in his frame,
      Unwarily was led from virtue's ways,

9. The seashore at Dover, where Charles landed
(May 25, 1660).
1. Cf. the fall of Satan in *Paradise Lost* 1.50–124,
which dims the brightness of the archangel. The
choice of the undignified word *tumbling* is deliberate.
2. Louis XIV of France.

3. Cf. line 82 and n. 4.
4. A title to the crown based on succession.
5. An alternative spelling of *mettle* (i.e., spirit).
But a pun on "metal" is intended, as is obvious
from the pun "angel" (a purely intellectual being
and a coin). Ambition caused the revolt of the
angels in heaven.

Made drunk with honor, and debauched with praise.
Half loath, and half consenting to the ill
(For loyal blood within him struggled still),
315 He thus replied: "And what pretense have I
To take up arms for public liberty?
My father governs with unquestioned right;
The faith's defender, and mankind's delight,
Good, gracious, just, observant of the laws:
320 And heaven by wonders has espoused his cause.
Whom has he wronged in all his peaceful reign?
Who sues for justice to his throne in vain?
What millions has he pardoned of his foes,
Whom just revenge did to his wrath expose?
325 Mild, easy, humble, studious of our good,
Inclined to mercy, and averse from blood;
If mildness ill with stubborn Israel suit,
His crime is God's beloved attribute.
What could he gain, his people to betray,
330 Or change his right for arbitrary sway?
Let haughty Pharaoh curse with such a reign
His fruitful Nile, and yoke a servile train.
If David's rule Jerusalem displease,
The Dog Star[6] heats their brains to this disease.
335 Why then should I, encouraging the bad,
Turn rebel and run popularly mad?
Were he a tyrant, who, by lawless might
Oppressed the Jews, and raised the Jebusite,
Well might I mourn; but nature's holy bands
340 Would curb my spirits and restrain my hands:
The people might assert° their liberty,   claim
But what was right in them were crime in me.
His favor leaves me nothing to require,
Prevents my wishes, and outruns desire.
345 What more can I expect while David lives?
All but his kingly diadem he gives:
And that"—But there he paused; then sighing, said—
"Is justly destined for a worthier head.
For when my father from his toils shall rest
350 And late augment the number of the blest,
His lawful issue shall the throne ascend,
Or the collateral line,[7] where that shall end.
His brother, though oppressed with vulgar spite,
Yet dauntless, and secure of native right,
355 Of every royal virtue stands possessed;
Still dear to all the bravest and the best.
His courage foes, his friends his truth proclaim;
His loyalty the king, the world his fame.
His mercy even the offending crowd will find,

---

6. Sirius, which in midsummer rises and sets with the sun and is thus associated with the maddening heat of the "dog days."
7. In the event of Charles's dying without legiti-

mate issue, the throne would constitutionally pass to his brother, James, or his descendants, the "collateral line."

360   For sure he comes of a forgiving kind.[8]
   Why should I then repine at heaven's decree,
   Which gives me no pretense to royalty?
   Yet O that fate, propitiously inclined,
   Had raised my birth, or had debased my mind;
365   To my large soul not all her treasure lent,
   And then betrayed it to a mean descent!
   I find, I find my mounting spirits bold,
   And David's part disdains my mother's mold.
   Why am I scanted by a niggard birth?[9]
370   My soul disclaims the kindred of her earth;
   And, made for empire, whispers me within,
   'Desire of greatness is a godlike sin.' "
     Him staggering so when hell's dire agent found,[1]
   While fainting Virtue scarce maintained her ground,
375   He pours fresh forces in, and thus replies:
   "The eternal god, supremely good and wise,
   Imparts not these prodigious gifts in vain:
   What wonders are reserved to bless your reign!
   Against your will, your arguments have shown,
380   Such virtue's only given to guide a throne.
   Not that your father's mildness I contemn,
   But manly force becomes the diadem.
   'Tis true he grants the people all they crave;
   And more, perhaps, than subjects ought to have:
385   For lavish grants suppose a monarch tame,
   And more his goodness than his wit° proclaim.   *intelligence*
   But when should people strive their bonds to break,
   If not when kings are negligent or weak?
   Let him give on till he can give no more,
390   The thrifty Sanhedrin[2] shall keep him poor;
   And every shekel which he can receive,
   Shall cost a limb of his prerogative.[3]
   To ply him with new plots shall be my care;
   Or plunge him deep in some expensive war;
395   Which when his treasure can no more supply,
   He must, with the remains of kingship, buy.
   His faithful friends our jealousies and fears
   Call Jebusites, and Pharaoh's pensioners;
   Whom when our fury from his aid has torn,
400   He shall be naked left to public scorn.
   The next successor, whom I fear and hate,
   My arts have made obnoxious to the state;
   Turned all his virtues to his overthrow,
   And gained our elders[4] to pronounce a foe.
405   His right, for sums of necessary gold,

---

8. Race, in the sense of family.
9. I.e., why am I limited by a sordid birth?
1. Observe the Miltonic inversion, which helps maintain the epic tone.
2. The highest judicial counsel of the Jews, here, Parliament.
3. The Whigs hoped to limit the special privileges

of the Crown (the royal "prerogative") by refusing to vote money to Charles. He circumvented them by living on French subsidies and refusing to summon Parliament.
4. The chief magistrates and rulers of the Jews. Shaftesbury had won over ("gained") country gentlemen and nobles to his hostile view of James.

Shall first be pawned, and afterward be sold;
Till time shall ever-wanting David draw,
To pass your doubtful title into law:
If not, the people have a right supreme
410 To make their kings; for kings are made for them.
All empire is no more than power in trust,
Which, when resumed, can be no longer just.
Succession, for the general good designed,
In its own wrong a nation cannot bind;
415 If altering that the people can relieve,
Better one suffer than a nation grieve.
The Jews well know their power: ere Saul they chose,[5]
God was their king, and God they durst depose.
Urge now your piety,[6] your filial name,
420 A father's right and fear of future fame;
The public good, that universal call,
To which even heaven submitted, answers all.
Nor let his love enchant your generous mind;
'Tis Nature's trick to propagate her kind.
425 Our fond begetters, who would never die,
Love but themselves in their posterity.
Or let his kindness by the effects be tried,
Or let him lay his vain pretense aside.
God said he loved your father; could he bring
430 A better proof than to anoint him king?
It surely showed he loved the shepherd well,
Who gave so fair a flock as Israel.
Would David have you thought his darling son?
What means he then, to alienate[7] the crown?
435 The name of godly he may blush to bear:
'Tis after God's own heart[8] to cheat his heir.
He to his brother gives supreme command;
To you a legacy of barren land,[9]
Perhaps the old harp, on which he thrums his lays,
440 Or some dull Hebrew ballad in your praise.
Then the next heir, a prince severe and wise,
Already looks on you with jealous eyes;
Sees through the thin disguises of your arts,
And marks your progress in the people's hearts.
445 Though now his mighty soul its grief contains,
He meditates revenge who least complains;
And, like a lion, slumbering in the way,
Or sleep dissembling, while he waits his prey,
His fearless foes within his distance draws,
450 Constrains his roaring, and contracts his paws;
Till at the last, his time for fury found,

5. Before Saul, the first king of Israel, came to the throne, the Jews were governed by judges. Similarly Oliver Cromwell ("Saul") as lord protector took over the reins of government, after he had dissolved the Rump Parliament in 1653.
6. Dutifulness to a parent.

7. In law, to convey the title to property to another person.
8. An irony (cf. line 7 and n. 1).
9. James was given the title of generalissimo in 1678. In 1679 Monmouth was banished and withdrew to Holland.

He shoots with sudden vengeance from the ground;
The prostrate vulgar° passes o'er and spares,   *common people*
But with a lordly rage his hunters tears.
455 Your case no tame expedients will afford:
Resolve on death, or conquest by the sword,
Which for no less a stake than life you draw;
And self-defense is nature's eldest law.
Leave the warm people no considering time;
460 For then rebellion may be thought a crime.
Prevail yourself of what occasion gives,
But try your title while your father lives;
And that your arms may have a fair pretense,°   *pretext*
Proclaim you take them in the king's defense:
465 Whose sacred life each minute would expose
To plots, from seeming friends, and secret foes.
And who can sound the depth of David's soul?
Perhaps his fear his kindness may control.
He fears his brother, though he loves his son,
470 For plighted vows too late to be undone.
If so, by force he wishes to be gained,
Like women's lechery, to seem constrained.°   *forced*
Doubt not; but when he most affects the frown,
Commit a pleasing rape upon the crown.
475 Secure his person to secure your cause:
They who possess the prince, possess the laws."
     He said, and this advice above the rest
With Absalom's mild nature suited best:
Unblamed of life (ambition set aside),
480 Not stained with cruelty, nor puffed with pride,
How happy had he been, if destiny
Had higher placed his birth, or not so high!
His kingly virtues might have claimed a throne,
And blest all other countries but his own.
485 But charming greatness since so few refuse,
'Tis juster to lament him than accuse.
Strong were his hopes a rival to remove,
With blandishments to gain the public love;
To head the faction while their zeal was hot,
490 And popularly prosecute the Plot.
To further this, Achitophel unites
The malcontents of all the Israelites;
Whose differing parties he could wisely join,
For several ends, to serve the same design:
495 The best (and of the princes some were such),
Who thought the power of monarchy too much;
Mistaken men, and patriots in their hearts;
Not wicked, but seduced by impious arts.
By these the springs of property were bent,
500 And wound so high, they cracked the government.
The next for interest sought to embroil the state,
To sell their duty at a dearer rate;

And make their Jewish markets of the throne,
Pretending public good, to serve their own.
505 Others thought kings an useless heavy load,
Who cost too much, and did too little good.
These were for laying honest David by,
On principles of pure good husbandry.°   *economy*
With them joined all the haranguers of the throng,
510 That thought to get preferment by the tongue.
Who follow next, a double danger bring,
Not only hating David, but the king:
The Solymaean rout,[1] well-versed of old
In godly faction, and in treason bold;
515 Cowering and quaking at a conqueror's sword,
But lofty to a lawful prince restored;
Saw with disdain an ethnic[2] plot begun,
And scorned by Jebusites to be outdone.
Hot Levites[3] headed these; who, pulled before
520 From the ark, which in the Judges' days they bore,
Resumed their cant, and with a zealous cry
Pursued their old beloved theocracy:
Where Sanhedrin and priest enslaved the nation,
And justified their spoils by inspiration:[4]
525 For who so fit for reign as Aaron's race,[5]
If once dominion they could found in grace?
These led the pack; though not of surest scent,
Yet deepest-mouthed[6] against the government.
A numerous host of dreaming saints succeed,
530 Of the true old enthusiastic breed:[7]
'Gainst form and order they their power employ,
Nothing to build, and all things to destroy.
But far more numerous was the herd of such,
Who think too little, and who talk too much.
535 These out of mere instinct, they knew not why,
Adored their fathers' God and property;
And, by the same blind benefit of fate,
The Devil and the Jebusite did hate:
Born to be saved, even in their own despite,
540 Because they could not help believing right.
Such were the tools; but a whole Hydra more
Remains, of sprouting heads too long to score.
Some of their chiefs were princes of the land:

---

1. I.e., London rabble. Solyma was a name for
Jerusalem.
2. Gentile; here, Roman Catholic.
3. I.e., Presbyterian clergymen. The tribe of Levi,
assigned to duties in the tabernacle, carried the ark
of the covenant during the forty-year sojourn in the
wilderness (Numbers 4). Under the Commonwealth ("in the Judges' days") Presbyterianism
became the state religion, and its clergy, therefore,
"bore the ark." The Act of Uniformity (1662)
forced the Presbyterian clergy out of their livings:
in short, before the Popish Plot, they had been
"pulled from the ark." They are represented here
as joining the Whigs in the hope of restoring the

commonwealth, "their old beloved theocracy."
4. Observe in these lines the cluster of disparaging
words: "cant," "zealous," "inspiration." Dryden
shared Samuel Butler's contempt for the irration-
ality of Dissenters.
5. Priests had to be descendants of Aaron (Exodus
28.1, Numbers 18.7).
6. Loudest. The phrase is applied to hunting dogs.
"Pack" and "scent" sustain the image.
7. "Dreaming saints": a term used by certain Dissenters for those elected to salvation. The extreme
fanaticism of the "saints" and their claims to inspiration are characterized as a form of religious madness ("enthusiastic").

In the first rank of these did Zimri[8] stand;
545　A man so various, that he seemed to be
Not one, but all mankind's epitome:
Stiff in opinions, always in the wrong;
Was everything by starts, and nothing long;
But, in the course of one revolving moon,
550　Was chymist,° fiddler, statesman, and buffoon:　　　　*chemist*
Then all for women, painting, rhyming, drinking,
Besides ten thousand freaks that died in thinking.
Blest madman, who could every hour employ,
With something new to wish, or to enjoy!
555　Railing° and praising were his usual themes;　　　　*reviling, abusing*
And both (to show his judgment) in extremes:
So over-violent, or over-civil,
That every man, with him, was God or Devil.
In squandering wealth was his peculiar art:
560　Nothing went unrewarded but desert.
Beggared by fools, whom still° he found° too late,　*constantly/found out*
He had his jest, and they had his estate.
He laughed himself from court; then sought relief
By forming parties, but could ne'er be chief;
565　For, spite of him, the weight of business fell
On Absalom and wise Achitophel:
Thus, wicked but in will, of means bereft,
He left not faction, but of that was left.
　　　Titles and names 'twere tedious to rehearse
570　Of lords, below the dignity of verse.
Wits, warriors, Commonwealth's men, were the best;
Kind husbands, and mere nobles, all the rest.
And therefore, in the name of dullness, be
The well-hung Balaam and cold Caleb, free;
575　And canting Nadab let oblivion damn,
Who made new porridge for the paschal lamb.[9]
Let friendship's holy band some names assure;
Some their own worth, and some let scorn secure.
Nor shall the rascal rabble here have place,
580　Whom kings no titles gave, and God no grace:
Not bull-faced Jonas,[1] who could statutes draw
To mean rebellion, and make treason law.
But he, though bad, is followed by a worse,

8. George Villiers, second duke of Buckingham (1628–1687), wealthy, brilliant, dissolute, and unstable. He had been an influential member of the cabal, but after 1673 had joined Shaftesbury in opposition to the court party. This is the least political of the satirical portraits in the poem. Buckingham had been the chief author of *The Rehearsal* (1671), the play that satirized the heroic play and ridiculed Dryden in the character of Mr. Bayes. Politics gave Dryden an opportunity to retaliate. He comments on this portrait in his *A Discourse Concerning the Original and Progress of Satire*. Dryden had two biblical Zimris in mind: the Zimri destroyed for his lustfulness and blasphemy (Numbers 25) and the conspirator and regicide of 1 Kings 16.8–20 and 2 Kings 9.31.

9. The lamb slain during Passover; here, Christ. The identities of Balaam, Caleb, and Nadab have not been certainly established, although various Whig nobles have been suggested. For Balaam see Numbers 22–24; for Caleb, Numbers 13–14; and for Nadab, Leviticus 10.1–2. "Well-hung": fluent of speech or sexually potent or both. "Cold" would contrast with the second meaning of well-hung. "Canting" points to a Nonconformist, as does "new porridge," for Dissenters referred to the Book of Common Prayer contemptuously as "porridge," a hodgepodge, unsubstantial stuff.
1. Sir William Jones, attorney general, had been largely responsible for the passage of the first Exclusion Bill by the House of Commons. He prosecuted the accused in the Popish Plot.

The wretch who heaven's anointed dared to curse:
585   Shimei,[2] whose youth did early promise bring
Of zeal to God and hatred to his king,
Did wisely from expensive sins refrain,
And never broke the Sabbath, but for gain;
Nor ever was he known an oath to vent,
590   Or curse, unless against the government.
Thus heaping wealth, by the most ready way
Among the Jews, which was to cheat and pray,
The city, to reward his pious hate
Against his master, chose him magistrate.
595   His hand a vare° of justice did uphold;   *staff*
His neck was loaded with a chain of gold.
During his office, treason was no crime;
The sons of Belial[3] had a glorious time;
For Shimei, though not prodigal of pelf,
600   Yet loved his wicked neighbor as himself.
When two or three were gathered to declaim ⎫
Against the monarch of Jerusalem,   ⎬
Shimei was always in the midst of them; ⎭
And if they cursed the king when he was by,
605   Would rather curse than break good company.
If any durst his factious friends accuse,
He packed a jury of dissenting Jews;
Whose fellow-feeling in the godly cause
Would free the suffering saint from human laws.
610   For laws are only made to punish those
Who serve the king, and to protect his foes.
If any leisure time he had from power
(Because 'tis sin to misemploy an hour),
His business was, by writing, to persuade
615   That kings were useless, and a clog to trade;
And, that his noble style he might refine,
No Rechabite[4] more shunned the fumes of wine.
Chaste were his cellars, and his shrieval board[5]
The grossness of a city feast abhorred:
620   His cooks, with long disuse, their trade forgot;
Cool was his kitchen, though his brains were hot,
Such frugal virtue malice may accuse,
But sure 'twas necessary to the Jews:
For towns once burnt[6] such magistrates require
625   As dare not tempt God's providence by fire.
With spiritual food he fed his servants well,

---

2. Shimei cursed and stoned David when he fled into the wilderness during Absalom's revolt (2 Samuel 16.5–14). His name is used here for one of the two sheriffs of London: Slingsby Bethel, a Whig, former republican, and virulent enemy of Charles. He packed juries with Whigs and so secured the acquittal of enemies of the court, among them Shaftesbury himself.
3. Sons of wickedness (cf. Milton, *Paradise Lost*

1.490–505). Dryden probably intended a pun on Balliol, the Oxford college in which leading Whigs stayed during the brief and fateful meeting of Parliament at Oxford in 1681.
4. An austere Jewish sect that drank no wine (Jeremiah 35.2–19).
5. Sheriff's dinner table.
6. London burned in 1666.

But free from flesh that made the Jews rebel;
And Moses' laws he held in more account,
For forty days of fasting in the mount.[7]
630   To speak the rest, who better are forgot,
Would tire a well-breathed witness of the Plot.
Yet, Corah,[8] thou shalt from oblivion pass:
Erect thyself, thou monumental brass,
High as the serpent of thy metal made,[9]
635   While nations stand secure beneath thy shade.
What though his birth were base, yet comets rise
From earthy vapors, ere they shine in skies.
Prodigious actions may as well be done
By weaver's issue,[1] as by prince's son.
640   This arch-attestor for the public good
By that one deed ennobles all his blood.
Who ever asked the witnesses' high race
Whose oath with martyrdom did Stephen[2] grace?
Ours was a Levite, and as times went then,
645   His tribe were God Almighty's gentlemen.
Sunk were his eyes, his voice was harsh and loud,
Sure signs he neither choleric[3] was nor proud:
His long chin proved his wit; his saintlike grace
A church vermilion, and a Moses' face.[4]
650   His memory, miraculously great,
Could plots, exceeding man's belief, repeat;
Which therefore cannot be accounted lies,
For human wit could never such devise.
Some future truths are mingled in his book;
655   But where the witness failed, the prophet spoke:
Some things like visionary flights appear;
The spirit caught him up, the Lord knows where,
And gave him his rabbinical degree,
Unknown to foreign university.[5]
660   His judgment yet his memory did excel;
Which pieced his wondrous evidence so well,
And suited to the temper of the times,
Then groaning under Jebusitic crimes.
Let Israel's foes suspect his heavenly call,
665   And rashly judge his writ apocryphal;[6]
Our laws for such affronts have forfeits made:
He takes his life, who takes away his trade.

---

7. Mount Sinai, where, during a fast of forty days, Moses received the law (Exodus 34.28).
8. Or Korah, a rebellious Levite, swallowed up by the earth because of his crimes (Numbers 16). Corah is Titus Oates, the self-appointed, perjured, and "well-breathed" (long-winded) witness of the plot.
9. Moses erected a brazen serpent to heal the Jews bitten by fiery serpents (Numbers 21.4–9). "Brass" also means impudence or shamelessness.
1. Oates's father, a clergyman, belonged to an obscure family of ribbon weavers.

2. The first Christian martyr, accused by false witnesses (Acts 6–7).
3. Prone to anger.
4. Moses' face shone when he came down from Mount Sinai with the tables of the law (Exodus 34.29–30). Oates's face suggests high living, not spiritual illumination.
5. Oates falsely claimed to be a doctor of divinity in the University of Salamanca.
6. Not inspired and hence excluded from Holy Writ.

Were I myself in witness Corah's place,
The wretch who did me such a dire disgrace
670 Should whet my memory, though once forgot,
To make him an appendix of my plot.
His zeal to heaven made him his prince despise,
And load his person with indignities;
But zeal peculiar privilege affords,
675 Indulging latitude to deeds and words;
And Corah might for Agag's murder⁷ call,
In terms as coarse as Samuel used to Saul.
What others in his evidence did join
(The best that could be had for love or coin),
680 In Corah's own predicament will fall;
For *witness* is a common name to all.
　　Surrounded thus with friends of every sort,
Deluded Absalom forsakes the court:
Impatient of high hopes, urged with renown,
685 And fired with near possession of a crown.
The admiring crowd are dazzled with surprise,
And on his goodly person feed their eyes:
His joy concealed, he sets himself to show,
On each side bowing popularly⁸ low;
690 His looks, his gestures, and his words he frames,
And with familiar ease repeats their names.
Thus formed by nature, furnished out with arts,
He glides unfelt into their secret hearts.
Then, with a kind compassionating look,
695 And sighs, bespeaking pity ere he spoke,
Few words he said; but easy those and fit,
More slow than Hybla-drops,⁹ and far more sweet.
　　"I mourn, my countrymen, your lost estate;
Though far unable to prevent your fate:
700 Behold a banished man, for your dear cause
Exposed a prey to arbitrary laws!
Yet oh! that I alone could be undone,
Cut off from empire, and no more a son!
Now all your liberties a spoil are made;
705 Egypt° and Tyrus° intercept your trade,　　　　*France/Holland*
And Jebusites your sacred rites invade.
My father, whom with reverence yet I name,
Charmed into ease, is careless of his fame;
And, bribed with petty sums of foreign gold,
710 Is grown in Bathsheba's¹ embraces old;
Exalts his enemies, his friends destroys;
And all his power against himself employs.
He gives, and let him give, my right away;

---

7. Agag is probably one of the five Catholic peers executed for the Popish Plot in 1680, most likely Lord Stafford, against whom Oates fabricated testimony; he is almost certainly not, as is usually suggested, Sir Edmund Berry Godfrey (see headnote, p. 2076). "Agag's murder" and Samuel's coarse terms to Saul are in 1 Samuel 15.

8. "So as to please the crowd" (Johnson's *Dictionary*).
9. The famous honey of Hybla in Sicily.
1. With whom David committed adultery (2 Samuel 11); here, Charles II's French mistress, Louise de Keroualle, duchess of Portsmouth.

But why should he his own, and yours betray?
715 He only, he can make the nation bleed,
And he alone from my revenge is freed.
Take then my tears (with that he wiped his eyes),
'Tis all the aid my present power supplies:
No court-informer can these arms accuse;
720 These arms may sons against their fathers use:
And 'tis my wish, the next successor's reign
May make no other Israelite complain."
    Youth, beauty, graceful action seldom fail;
But common interest always will prevail;
725 And pity never ceases to be shown
To him who makes the people's wrongs his own.
The crowd (that still believe their kings oppress)
With lifted hands their young Messiah bless:
Who now begins his progress to ordain
730 With chariots, horsemen, and a numerous train;
From east to west his glories he displays,[2]
And, like the sun, the promised land surveys.
Fame runs before him as the morning star,
And shouts of joy salute him from afar:
735 Each house receives him as a guardian god,
And consecrates the place of his abode:
But hospitable treats did most commend
Wise Issachar,[3] his wealthy western friend.
This moving court, that caught the people's eyes,
740 And seemed but pomp, did other ends disguise:
Achitophel had formed it, with intent
To sound the depths, and fathom, where it went,
The people's hearts; distinguish friends from foes,
And try their strength, before they came to blows.
745 Yet all was colored with a smooth pretense
Of specious love, and duty to their prince.
Religion, and redress of grievances,
Two names that always cheat and always please,
Are often urged; and good King David's life
750 Endangered by a brother and a wife.[4]
Thus, in a pageant show, a plot is made,
And peace itself is war in masquerade.
O foolish Israel! never warned by ill,
Still the same bait, and circumvented still!
755 Did ever men forsake their present ease,
In midst of health imagine a disease;
Take pains contingent mischiefs to foresee,
Make heirs for monarchs, and for God decree?
What shall we think![5] Can people give away

2. In 1680 Monmouth made a progress through the west of England, seeking popular support for his cause.
3. Thomas Thynne of Longleat. He entertained Monmouth on his journey in the west. "Wise" is, of course, ironic.
4. Titus Oates had sworn that both James, duke of York, and the queen were involved in a similar plot to poison Charles II.
5. In the passage that follows, Dryden states his political philosophy. He bases the royal authority on a covenant entered into by the governor and the governed.

760 Both for themselves and sons, their native sway?
Then they are left defenseless to the sword
Of each unbounded, arbitrary lord:
And laws are vain, by which we right enjoy,
If kings unquestioned can those laws destroy.
765 Yet if the crowd be judge of fit and just,
And kings are only officers in trust,
Then this resuming covenant was declared
When kings were made, or is forever barred.
If those who gave the scepter could not tie
770 By their own deed their own posterity,
How then could Adam bind his future race?
How could his forfeit on mankind take place?
Or how could heavenly justice damn us all,
Who ne'er consented to our father's fall?
775 Then kings are slaves to those whom they command,
And tenants to their people's pleasure stand.
Add, that the power for property allowed
Is mischievously seated in the crowd;
For who can be secure of private right,
780 If sovereign sway may be dissolved by might?
Nor is the people's judgment always true:
The most may err as grossly as the few;
And faultless kings run down, by common cry,
For vice, oppression, and for tyranny.
785 What standard is there in a fickle rout,
Which, flowing to the mark,° runs faster out?   °highwater mark
Nor only crowds, but Sanhedrins may be
Infected with this public lunacy,[6]
And share the madness of rebellious times,
790 To murder monarchs for imagined crimes.[7]
If they may give and take whene'er they please,
Not kings alone (the Godhead's images),
But government itself at length must fall
To nature's state, where all have right to all.
795 Yet, grant our lords the people kings can make,
What prudent men a settled throne would shake?
For whatsoe'er their sufferings were before,
That change they covet makes them suffer more.
All other errors but disturb a state,
800 But innovation is the blow of fate.
If ancient fabrics nod, and threat to fall,
To patch the flaws, and buttress up the wall,
Thus far 'tis duty; but here fix the mark;
For all beyond it is to touch our ark.[8]
805 To change foundations, cast the frame anew,
Is work for rebels, who base ends pursue,
At once divine and human laws control,

---

6. The fickle crowd flows and ebbs like the tide, which is pulled back and forth by the moon (hence "lunacy," after the Latin *luna*, or "moon").
7. An allusion to the execution of Charles I.

8. Uzzah was struck dead because he sacrilegiously touched the Ark of the Covenant (2 Samuel 6.6–7).

And mend the parts by ruin of the whole.
The tampering world is subject to this curse,
810 To physic their disease into a worse.
　　Now what relief can righteous David bring?
How fatal 'tis to be too good a king!
Friends he has few, so high the madness grows:
Who dare be such, must be the people's foes:
815 Yet some there were, even in the worst of days;
Some let me name, and naming is to praise.
　　In this short file Barzillai⁹ first appears;
Barzillai, crowned with honor and with years:
Long since, the rising rebels he withstood
820 In regions waste, beyond the Jordan's flood:
Unfortunately brave to buoy the State;
But sinking underneath his master's fate:
In exile with his godlike prince he mourned;
For him he suffered, and with him returned.
825 The court he practiced, not the courtier's art:
Large was his wealth, but larger was his heart:
Which well the noblest objects knew to choose,
The fighting warrior, and recording Muse.
His bed could once a fruitful issue boast;
830 Now more than half a father's name is lost.
His eldest hope,¹ with every grace adorned,
By me (so Heaven will have it) always mourned,
And always honored, snatched in manhood's prime
By unequal fates, and Providence's crime:
835 Yet not before the goal of honor won, ⎫
All parts fulfilled of subject and of son; ⎬
Swift was the race, but short the time to run. ⎭
O narrow circle, but of power divine,
Scanted in space, but perfect in thy line!
840 By sea, by land, thy matchless worth was known,
Arms thy delight, and war was all thy own:
Thy force, infused, the fainting Tyrians° propped;   *the Dutch*
And haughty Pharaoh found his fortune stopped.
Oh ancient honor! Oh unconquered hand,
845 Whom foes unpunished never could withstand!
But Israel was unworthy of thy name:
Short is the date of all immoderate fame.
It looks as Heaven our ruin had designed,
And durst not trust thy fortune and thy mind.
850 Now, free from earth, thy disencumbered soul
Mounts up, and leaves behind the clouds and starry pole:
From thence thy kindred legions mayst thou bring,
To aid the guardian angel of thy king.
Here stop my Muse, here cease thy painful flight;

---

9. James Butler, duke of Ormond (1610–1688). He was famous for his loyalty to the Stuart cause. He fought for Charles I in Ireland, and when that cause was hopeless, he joined Charles II in his exile abroad. He spent a large fortune on behalf of the king and continued to serve him loyally after the Restoration.
1. Ormond's son, Thomas, earl of Ossory (1634–1680), a famous soldier and like his father devoted to Charles II.

855 No pinions can pursue immortal height:
Tell good Barzillai thou canst sing no more,
And tell thy soul she should have fled before:
Or fled she with his life, and left this verse
To hang on her departed patron's hearse?
860 Now take thy steepy flight from heaven, and see
If thou canst find on earth another *he*:
Another *he* would be too hard to find;
See then whom thou canst see not far behind.
Zadoc the priest, whom, shunning power and place,
865 His lowly mind advanced to David's grace:
With him the Sagan of Jerusalem,
Of hospitable soul, and noble stem;
Him of the western dome, whose weighty sense
Flows in fit words and heavenly eloquence.
870 The prophets' sons,[2] by such example led,
To learning and to loyalty were bred:
For colleges on bounteous kinds depend,
And never rebel was to arts a friend.
To these succeed the pillars of the laws,
875 Who best could plead, and best can judge a cause.
Next them a train of loyal peers ascend;
Sharp-judging Adriel, the Muses' friend,
Himself a Muse—in Sanhedrin's debate
True to his prince, but not a slave of state:
880 Whom David's love with honors did adorn,
That from his disobedient son were torn.
Jotham of piercing wit, and pregnant thought,
Indued by nature, and by learning taught
To move assemblies, who but only tried
885 The worse a while, then chose the better side;
Nor chose alone, but turned the balance too;
So much the weight of one brave man can do.
Hushai,[3] the friend of David in distress,
In public storms, of manly steadfastness:
890 By foreign treaties he informed his youth,
And joined experience to his native truth.
His frugal care supplied the wanting throne,
Frugal for that, but bounteous of his own:
'Tis easy conduct when exchequers flow,
895 But hard the task to manage well the low;
For sovereign power is too depressed or high,
When kings are forced to sell, or crowds to buy.
Indulge one labor more, my weary Muse,
For Amiel:[4] who can Amiel's praise refuse?
900 Of ancient race by birth, but nobler yet
In his own worth, and without title great:

2. The boys of Westminster School, which Dryden had attended. "Zadoc": William Sancroft, archbishop of Canterbury. "Sagan": Henry Compton, bishop of London. "Him of the western dome": John Dolben, dean of Westminster.

3. Laurence Hyde, earl of Rochester. "Adriel": John Sheffield, earl of Mulgrave. "Jotham": George Savile, marquis of Halifax.
4. Edward Seymour, speaker of the House of Commons.

The Sanhedrin long time as chief he ruled,
Their reason guided, and their passion cooled:
So dexterous was he in the crown's defense,
905   So formed to speak a loyal nation's sense,
That, as their band was Israel's tribes in small,
So fit was he to represent them all.
Now rasher charioteers the seat ascend,
Whose loose careers his steady skill commend:
910   They like the unequal ruler of the day,
Misguide the seasons, and mistake the way;
While he withdrawn at their mad labor smiles,
And safe enjoys the sabbath of his toils.
     These were the chief, a small but faithful band ⎫
915   Of worthies, in the breach who dared to stand, ⎬
And tempt the united fury of the land. ⎭
With grief they viewed such powerful engines bent,
To batter down the lawful government:
A numerous faction, with pretended frights,
920   In Sanhedrins to plume the regal rights;
The true successor from the court removed:[5]
The Plot, by hireling witnesses, improved.
These ills they saw, and, as their duty bound,
They showed the king the danger of the wound:
925   That no concessions from the throne would please,
But lenitives[6] fomented the disease;
That Absalom, ambitious of the crown,
Was made the lure to draw the people down;
That false Achitophel's pernicious hate
930   Had turned the Plot to ruin Church and State:
The council violent, the rabble worse;
That Shimei taught Jerusalem to curse.
     With all these loads of injuries oppressed,
And long revolving, in his careful breast,
935   The event of things, at last, his patience tired,
Thus from his royal throne, by Heaven inspired,
The godlike David spoke: with awful fear
His train their Maker in their master hear.
     "Thus long have I, by native mercy swayed,
940   My wrongs dissembled, my revenge delayed:
So willing to forgive the offending age,
So much the father did the king assuage.
But now so far my clemency they slight,
The offenders question my forgiving right.
945   That one was made for many, they contend;
But 'tis to rule; for that's a monarch's end.
They call my tenderness of blood, my fear;
Though manly tempers can the longest bear.
Yet, since they will divert my native course,
950   'Tis time to show I am not good by force.

---

5. The duke of York had been banished from England.   6. Any medicine that relieves pain.

Those heaped affronts that haughty subjects bring,
Are burdens for a camel, not a king:
Kings are the public pillars of the State,
Born to sustain and prop the nation's weight:
955   If my young Samson will pretend a call
To shake the column, let him share the fall:[7]
But, oh, that yet he would repent and live!
How easy 'tis for parents to forgive!
With how few tears a pardon might be won
960   From nature, pleading for a darling son!
Poor pitied youth, by my paternal care
Raised up to all the height his frame could bear:
Had God ordained his fate for empire born,
He would have given his soul another turn:
965   Gulled° with a patriot's name, whose modern sense   *deceived*
Is one that would by law supplant his prince:
The people's brave, the politician's tool;
Never was patriot yet, but was a fool.
Whence comes it that religion and the laws
970   Should more be Absalom's than David's cause?
His old instructor, ere he lost his place,
Was never thought indued with so much grace.[8]
Good heavens, how faction can a patriot paint!
My rebel ever proves my people's saint:
975   Would *they* impose an heir upon the throne?
Let Sanhedrins be taught to give their own.
A king's at least a part of government,
And mine as requisite as their consent;
Without my leave a future king to choose,
980   Infers a right the present to depose:
True, they petition me to approve their choice;
But Esau's hands suit ill with Jacob's voice.[9]
My pious subjects for my safety pray,
Which to secure, they take my power away.
985   From plots and treasons Heaven preserve my years,
But save me most from my petitioners.
Unsatiate as the barren womb or grave;
God cannot grant so much as they can crave.
What then is left but with a jealous eye
990   To guard the small remains of royalty?
The law shall still direct my peaceful sway,
And the same law teach rebels to obey:
Votes shall no more established power control—
Such votes as make a part exceed the whole:
995   No groundless clamors shall my friends remove,
Nor crowds have power to punish ere they prove:
For gods and godlike kings, their care express,
Still to defend their servants in distress.

---

7. Judges 16.
8. The earl of Shaftesbury.

9. Genesis 27.22.

O that my power to saving were confined:
1000 Why am I forced, like Heaven, against my mind,
To make examples of another kind?
Must I at length the sword of justice draw?
O curst effects of necessary law!
How ill my fear they by my mercy scan!
1005 Beware the fury of a patient man.
Law they require, let Law then show her face;
They could not be content to look on Grace,
Her hinder parts, but with a daring eye
To tempt the terror of her front and die.[1]
1010 By their own arts, 'tis righteously decreed,
Those dire artificers of death shall bleed.
Against themselves their witnesses will swear,
Till viper-like their mother Plot they tear:
And suck for nutriment that bloody gore,
1015 Which was their principle of life before.
Their Belial with their Belzebub[2] will fight;
Thus on my foes, my foes shall do me right:
Nor doubt the event; for factious crowds engage,
In their first onset, all their brutal rage.
1020 Then let 'em take an unresisted course,
Retire and traverse, and delude their force:
But when they stand all breathless, urge the fight,
And rise upon 'em with redoubled might:
For lawful power is still superior found,
1025 When long driven back, at length it stands the ground."
He said. The Almighty, nodding, gave consent;
And peals of thunder shook the firmament.
Henceforth a series of new time began,
The mighty years in long procession ran:
1030 Once more the godlike David was restored,
And willing nations knew their lawful lord.

1681

Mac Flecknoe The target of this superb satire, which is cast in the form of a
mock-heroic episode, is Thomas Shadwell (1640–1692), the playwright, with whom
Dryden had been on good terms for a number of years, certainly as late as March
1678. Shadwell considered himself the successor of Ben Jonson and the champion
of the type of comedy that Jonson had written, the "comedy of humors," in which
each character is presented under the domination of a single psychological trait or
eccentricity, his humor. His plays are not without merit, but they are often clumsy
and prolix and certainly much inferior to Jonson's. For many years he had conducted
a public argument with Dryden on the merits of Jonson's comedies, which he thought
Dryden undervalued. Exactly what moved Dryden to attack him is a matter of con-

---

1. Moses was not allowed to see the countenance
of Jehovah (Exodus 33.20–23).

2. A god of the Philistines. "Belial": the incarnation of all evil.

jecture: he may simply have grown progressively bored and irritated by Shadwell and his tedious argument. The poem seems to have been written in late 1678 or 1679 and to have circulated only in manuscript until it was printed in 1682 in a pirated edition by an obscure publisher. By that time, the two playwrights were alienated by politics as well as by literary quarrels. Shadwell was a violent Whig and the reputed author of a sharp attack on Dryden as the Tory author of *Absalom and Achitophel* and *The Medal*. It was probably for this reason that the printer added the subtitle referring to Shadwell's Whiggism in the phrase "true-blue-Protestant poet." Political passions were running high, and sales would be helped if the poem seemed to refer to the events of the day.

Whereas Butler had debased and degraded his victims by using burlesque, caricature, and the grotesque, Dryden exposed Shadwell to ridicule by using the devices of mock epic, which treats the low, mean, or absurd in the grand language, lofty style, and solemn tone of epic poetry. The obvious disparity between subject and style makes the satiric point. In 1678, a prolific, untalented writer, Richard Flecknoe, died. Dryden conceived the idea of presenting Shadwell (the self-proclaimed heir of Ben Jonson, the laureate) as the son and successor of Flecknoe—hence *Mac* (i.e., son of) *Flecknoe*—from whom he inherits the throne of dullness. Flecknoe in the triple role of king, priest, and poet hails his successor, pronounces a panegyric on his perfect fitness for the throne, anoints and crowns him, foretells his glorious reign, and as he sinks (leaden dullness cannot soar), leaves his mantle to fall symbolically on Shadwell's shoulders. The poem abounds in literary allusions—to Roman legend and history and to the *Aeneid*, to Cowley's fragmentary epic *The Davideis*, to *Paradise Lost*, and to Shadwell's own plays. Biblical allusions add an unexpected dimension of incongruous dignity to the low scene. The coronation takes place in the City, to the plaudits of the citizens, who are fit to admire only what is dull. In 217 lines, Dryden created an image of Shadwell that has fixed his reputation to this day.

Mac Flecknoe

Or a Satire upon the True-Blue-Protestant Poet, T. S.

All human things are subject to decay,
And when fate summons, monarchs must obey.
This Flecknoe found, who, like Augustus,[1] young
Was called to empire, and had governed long;
5   In prose and verse, was owned, without dispute,
Through all the realms of Nonsense, absolute.
This aged prince, now flourishing in peace,
And blest with issue of a large increase,
Worn out with business, did at length debate
10 To settle the succession of the state;
And, pondering which of all his sons was fit
To reign, and wage immortal war with wit,
Cried: " 'Tis resolved; for nature pleads that he
Should only rule, who most resembles me.
15 Sh——[2] alone my perfect image bears,
Mature in dullness from his tender years:

---

1. In 31 B.C.E. Octavian became the first Roman emperor at the age of thirty-two. He assumed the title Augustus in 27 B.C.E.
2. Thomas Shadwell. The initial and second letter of the name followed by a dash give the appearance, but only the appearance, of protecting Dryden's victim by concealing his name. A common device in the satire of the period.

Sh—— alone, of all my sons, is he
Who stands confirmed in full stupidity.
The rest to some faint meaning make pretense,
20 But Sh—— never deviates into sense.
Some beams of wit on other souls may fall,
Strike through, and make a lucid interval;
But Sh——'s genuine night admits no ray,
His rising fogs prevail upon the day.
25 Besides, his goodly fabric³ fills the eye,
And seems designed for thoughtless majesty:
Thoughtless as monarch oaks that shade the plain,
And, spread in solemn state, supinely reign.
Heywood and Shirley were but types of thee,⁴
30 Thou last great prophet of tautology.⁵
Even I, a dunce of more renown than they,
Was sent before but to prepare thy way;
And, coarsely clad in Norwich drugget,⁶ came
To teach the nations in thy greater name.⁷
35 My warbling lute, the lute I whilom° strung,   *formerly*
When to King John of Portugal⁸ I sung,
Was but the prelude to that glorious day,
When thou on silver Thames didst cut thy way,
With well-timed oars before the royal barge,
40 Swelled with the pride of thy celestial charge;
And big with hymn, commander of a host,
The like was ne'er in Epsom blankets tossed.⁹
Methinks I see the new Arion¹ sail,
The lute still trembling underneath thy nail.
45 At thy well-sharpened thumb from shore to shore
The treble squeaks for fear, the basses roar;
Echoes from Pissing Alley Sh—— call,
And Sh—— they resound from Aston Hall.
About thy boat the little fishes throng,
50 As at the morning toast° that floats along.   *sewage*
Sometimes, as prince of thy harmonious band,
Thou wield'st thy papers in thy threshing hand,
St. André's² feet ne'er kept more equal time,
Not ev'n the feet of thy own *Psyche's* rhyme;
55 Though they in number as in sense excel:

3. His body. Shadwell was a corpulent man.
4. Thomas Heywood (ca. 1570–1641) and James Shirley (1596–1666), playwrights popular before the closing of the theaters in 1642 but now out of fashion. They are introduced here as "types" (i.e., prefigurings) of Shadwell, in the sense that Solomon was regarded as an Old Testament prefiguring of Christ, the "last [final] great prophet."
5. Unnecessary repetition of meaning in different words.
6. A coarse woolen cloth. Flecknoe was a Catholic priest.
7. The parallel between Flecknoe, as forerunner of Shadwell, and John the Baptist, as forerunner of Jesus, is made plain in lines 32–34 by the use of details and even words taken from Matthew 3.3–4 and John 1.23.
8. Flecknoe boasted of the patronage of the Portuguese king.
9. A reference to Shadwell's comedy *Epsom Wells* and to the farcical scene in his *Virtuoso*, in which Sir Samuel Hearty is tossed in a blanket.
1. A legendary Greek poet. Returning home by sea, he was robbed and thrown overboard by the sailors, but saved by a dolphin that had been charmed by his music.
2. A French dancer who designed the choreography of Shadwell's opera *Psyche* (1675). Dryden's sneer at the mechanical metrics of the songs in *Psyche* is justified.

So just, so like tautology, they fell,
That, pale with envy, Singleton[3] forswore
The lute and sword, which he in triumph bore,
And vowed he ne'er would act Villerius[4] more."
60 Here stopped the good old sire, and wept for joy
In silent raptures of the hopeful boy.
All arguments, but most his plays, persuade,
That for anointed dullness[5] he was made.
     Close to the walls which fair Augusta° bind   *London*
65 (The fair Augusta much to fears inclined),[6]
An ancient fabric,° raised to inform the sight,   *building*
There stood of yore, and Barbican it hight:
A watchtower once; but now, so fate ordains,
Of all the pile an empty name remains.
70 From its old ruins brothel houses rise,
Scenes of lewd loves, and of polluted joys,
Where their vast courts the mother-strumpets keep,
And, undisturbed by watch, in silence sleep.
Near these a Nursery[7] erects its head,
75 Where queens are formed, and future heroes bred;
Where unfledged actors learn to laugh and cry,
Where infant punks° their tender voices try,   *prostitutes*
And little Maximins[8] the gods defy.
Great Fletcher never treads in buskins here,
80 Nor greater Jonson dares in socks[9] appear;
But gentle Simkin[1] just reception finds
Amidst this monument of vanished minds:
Pure clinches° the suburbian Muse affords,   *puns*
And Panton[2] waging harmless war with words.
85 Here Flecknoe, as a place to fame well known,
Ambitiously design'd his Sh——'s throne;
For ancient Dekker[3] prophesied long since,
That in this pile would reign a mighty prince,
Born for a scourge of wit, and flail of sense;
90 To whom true dullness should some *Psyches* owe,
But worlds of *Misers* from his pen should flow;
Humorists and *Hypocrites*[4] it should produce,
Whole Raymond families, and tribes of Bruce.
     Now Empress Fame had published the renown
95 Of Sh——'s coronation through the town.
Roused by report of Fame, the nations meet,

3. John Singleton (d. 1686), a musician at the
Theatre Royal.
4. A character in Sir William Davenant's *Siege of
Rhodes* (1656), the first English opera.
5. The anticipated phrase is "anointed *majesty*."
English kings are anointed with oil at their coronations.
6. This line alludes to the fears excited by the Popish Plot (cf. *Absalom and Achitophel*, p. 2075).
7. The name of a training school for young actors.
8. Maximin is the cruel emperor in Dryden's
Tyrannic Love (1669), notorious for his bombast.
9. "Buskins" and "socks" were the symbols of trag-

edy and comedy. John Fletcher (1579–1625), the
playwright and collaborator with Francis Beaumont (ca. 1584–1616).
1. A popular character in low farces.
2. Said to have been a celebrated punster.
3. Thomas Dekker (ca. 1572–1632), the playwright, whom Jonson had satirized in *The Poetaster*.
4. Three of Shadwell's plays; *The Hypocrite*, a failure, was not published. "Raymond" and "Bruce"
(line 93) are characters in *The Humorists* and *The
Virtuoso*, respectively.

From near Bunhill, and distant Watling Street.[5]
No Persian carpets spread the imperial way,
But scattered limbs of mangled poets lay;
100   From dusty shops neglected authors come,
Martyrs of pies, and relics of the bum.[6]
Much Heywood, Shirley, Ogilby[7] there lay,
But loads of Sh—— almost choked the way.
Bilked stationers for yeomen stood prepared,
105   And Herringman was captain of the guard.[8]
The hoary prince in majesty appeared,
High on a throne of his own labors reared.
At his right hand our young Ascanius sate,
Rome's other hope, and pillar of the state.
110   His brows thick fogs, instead of glories, grace,
And lambent dullness played around his face.[9]
As Hannibal did to the altars come,
Sworn by his sire a mortal foe to Rome,[1]
So Sh—— swore, nor should his vow be vain,
115   That he till death true dullness would maintain;
And, in his father's right, and realm's defense,
Ne'er to have peace with wit, nor truce with sense.
The king himself the sacred unction[2] made,
As king by office, and as priest by trade.
120   In his sinister° hand, instead of ball,   *left*
He placed a mighty mug of potent ale;
Love's Kingdom to his right he did convey,
At once his scepter, and his rule of sway;
Whose righteous lore the prince had practiced young,
125   And from whose loins recorded *Psyche* sprung.
His temples, last, with poppies were o'erspread,
That nodding seemed to consecrate his head.[3]
Just at that point of time, if fame not lie,
On his left hand twelve reverend owls did fly.[4]
130   So Romulus, 'tis sung, by Tiber's brook,
Presage of sway from twice six vultures took.
The admiring throng loud acclamations make,
And omens of his future empire take.
The sire then shook the honors[5] of his head,

---

5. Because Bunhill is about a quarter of a mile and Watling Street little more than half a mile from the site of the Nursery, where the coronation is held, Shadwell's fame is narrowly circumscribed. Moreover, his subjects live in the heart of the City, regarded by men of wit and fashion as the abode of bad taste and middle-class vulgarity.
6. Unsold books eventually went to bakers' shops and privies.
7. John Ogilby, a translator of Homer and Virgil, ridiculed by both Dryden and Pope as a bad poet.
8. "Bilked stationers": cheated publishers, acting as "yeomen" of the guard, led by Henry Herringman, who until 1679 was the publisher of both Shadwell and Dryden.
9. "Ascanius": or Iulus, son of Aeneas. Virgil referred to him as *"spes altera Romae"* ("Rome's other hope," *Aeneid* 12.168). As Troy fell, he was marked as favored by the gods when a flickering

("lambent") flame played round his head (*Aeneid* 2.680–84).
1. Hannibal, who almost conquered Rome in 216 B.C.E., during the second Punic War, took this oath at the age of nine (Livy 21.1).
2. The sacramental oil, used in the coronation.
3. During the coronation a British monarch holds two symbols of the throne: a globe ("ball") representing the world in the left hand and a scepter in the right. Shadwell's symbols of monarchy are a mug of ale; Flecknoe's dreary play *Love's Kingdom*; and a crown of poppies, which suggest heaviness, dullness, and drowsiness. The poppies also refer obliquely to Shadwell's addiction to opium.
4. Birds of night, appropriate substitutes for the twelve vultures whose flight confirmed to Romulus the destined site of Rome, of which he was founder and king.
5. Ornaments, hence locks.

135   And from his brows damps of oblivion shed
      Full on the filial dullness: long he stood,
      Repelling from his breast the raging god;
      At length burst out in this prophetic mood:
        "Heavens bless my son, from Ireland let him reign
140   To far Barbadoes on the western main;[6]
      Of his dominion may no end be known,
      And greater than his father's be his throne;
      Beyond *Love's Kingdom* let him stretch his pen!"
      He paused, and all the people cried, "Amen."
145   Then thus continued he: "My son, advance
      Still in new impudence, new ignorance.
      Success let others teach, learn thou from me
      Pangs without birth, and fruitless industry.
      Let *Virtuosos* in five years be writ;
150   Yet not one thought accuse thy toil of wit.
      Let gentle George[7] in triumph tread the stage,
      Make Dorimant betray, and Loveit rage;
      Let Cully, Cockwood, Fopling, charm the pit,
      And in their folly show the writer's wit.
155   Yet still thy fools shall stand in thy defense,
      And justify their author's want of sense.
      Let 'em be all by thy own model made
      Of dullness, and desire no foreign aid;
      That they to future ages may be known,
160   Not copies drawn, but issue of thy own.
      Nay, let thy men of wit too be the same,
      All full of thee, and differing but in name.
      But let no alien S—dl—y[8] interpose,
      To lard with wit[9] thy hungry *Epsom* prose.
165   And when false flowers of rhetoric thou wouldst cull,
      Trust nature, do not labor to be dull;
      But write thy best, and top; and, in each line,
      Sir Formal's[1] oratory will be thine:
      Sir Formal, though unsought, attends thy quill,
170   And does thy northern dedications[2] fill.
      Nor let false friends seduce thy mind to fame,
      By arrogating Jonson's hostile name.
      Let father Flecknoe fire thy mind with praise,
      And uncle Ogilby thy envy raise.
175   Thou art my blood, where Jonson has no part:
      What share have we in nature, or in art?
      Where did his wit on learning fix a brand,
      And rail at arts he did not understand?
      Where made he love in Prince Nicander's vein,[3]

---

6. Shadwell's empire is vast but empty.
7. Sir George Etherege (ca. 1635–1691), a writer of brilliant comedies. In the next couplet Dryden names characters from his plays.
8. Sir Charles Sedley (1638–1701), wit, rake, poet, and playwright. Dryden hints that he contributed more than the prologue to Shadwell's *Epsom Wells*.

9. This phrase recalls a sentence in Burton's *Anatomy of Melancholy*: "They lard their lean books with the fat of others' works."
1. Sir Formal Trifle, the ridiculous and vapid orator in *The Virtuoso*.
2. Shadwell frequently dedicated his works to the duke of Newcastle and members of his family.
3. In *Psyche*.

180   Or swept the dust in *Psyche's* humble strain?
       Where sold he bargains, 'whip-stitch,[4] kiss my arse,'
       Promised a play and dwindled to a farce?[5]
       When did his Muse from Fletcher scenes purloin,
       As thou whole Eth'rege dost transfuse to thine?
185   But so transfused, as oil on water's flow,
       His always floats above, thine sinks below.
       This is thy province, this thy wondrous way,
       New humors to invent for each new play:
       This is that boasted bias[6] of thy mind,
190   By which one way, to dullness, 'tis inclined;
       Which makes thy writings lean on one side still,
       And, in all changes, that way bends thy will.
       Nor let thy mountain-belly make pretense
       Of likeness; thine's a tympany[7] of sense.
195   A tun° of man in thy large bulk is writ,   *large cask*
       But sure thou'rt but a kilderkin° of wit.   *small cask*
       Like mine, thy gentle numbers feebly creep;
       Thy tragic Muse gives smiles, thy comic sleep.
       With whate'er gall thou sett'st thyself to write,
200   Thy inoffensive satires never bite.
       In thy felonious heart though venom lies,
       It does but touch thy Irish pen,[8] and dies.
       Thy genius calls thee not to purchase fame
       In keen iambics,° but mild anagram.   *sharp satire*
205   Leave writing plays, and choose for thy command
       Some peaceful province in acrostic land.
       There thou may'st wings display and altars raise,
       And torture one poor word ten thousand ways.[9]
       Or, if thou wouldst thy different talent suit,
210   Set thy own songs, and sing them to thy lute."
          He said: but his last words were scarcely heard⎫
       For Bruce and Longville had a trap prepared, ⎬
       And down they sent the yet declaiming bard.[1] ⎭
       Sinking he left his drugget robe behind,
215   Borne upwards by a subterranean wind.
       The mantle fell to the young prophet's part,[2]
       With double portion of his father's art.

ca. 1679   1682

4. A nonsense word frequently used by Sir Samuel Hearty in *The Virtuoso.* To "sell bargains" is to answer an innocent question with a coarse or indecent phrase, as in this line.

5. Low comedy that depends largely on situation rather than wit, consistently condemned by Dryden and other serious playwrights.

6. In bowling, the spin given to the bowl that causes it to swerve. Dryden closely parodies a passage in Shadwell's epilogue to *The Humorists.*

7. A swelling in some part of the body caused by wind.

8. Dryden accuses Flecknoe and his "son" of being Irish. Ireland suggested only poverty, superstition, and barbarity to 17th-century Londoners.

9. "Wings" and "altars" refer to poems in the shape of these objects as in George Herbert's *Easter Wings* (p. 1599) and *The Altar* (p. 1597). "Anagram": the transposition of letters in a word so as to make a new one. "Acrostic": a poem in which the first letter of each line, read downward, makes up the name of the person or thing that is the subject of the poem. Dryden is citing instances of triviality and overingenuity in literature.

1. In *The Virtuoso,* Bruce and Longville play this trick on Sir Formal Trifle while he makes a speech.

2. When the prophet Elijah was carried to heaven in a chariot of fire borne on a whirlwind, his mantle fell on his successor, the younger prophet Elisha (2 Kings 2.8–14). Flecknoe, prophet of dullness, naturally cannot ascend, but must sink.

To the Memory of Mr. Oldham[1]

Farewell, too little, and too lately known,
Whom I began to think and call my own:
For sure our souls were near allied, and thine
Cast in the same poetic mold with mine.
5   One common note on either lyre did strike,
And knaves and fools[2] we both abhorred alike.
To the same goal did both our studies drive;
The last set out the soonest did arrive.
Thus Nisus fell upon the slippery place,
10 While his young friend[3] performed and won the race.
O early ripe! to thy abundant store
What could advancing age have added more?
It might (what nature never gives the young)
Have taught the numbers° of thy native tongue.   *metrics, verse*
15 But satire needs not those, and wit will shine
Through the harsh cadence of a rugged line.[4]
A noble error, and but seldom made,
When poets are by too much force betrayed.
Thy generous fruits, though gathered ere their prime, ⎫
20 Still showed a quickness;[5] and maturing time ⎬
But mellows what we write to the dull sweets of rhyme. ⎭
Once more, hail and farewell;[6] farewell, thou young,
But ah too short, Marcellus[7] of our tongue;
Thy brows with ivy, and with laurels bound;[8]
25 But fate and gloomy night encompass thee around.

1684

A Song for St. Cecilia's Day[1]

I

From harmony, from heavenly harmony
This universal frame began:

---

1. John Oldham (1653–1683), the young poet whose *Satires upon the Jesuits* (1681) won Dryden's admiration. This elegy was published in Oldham's *Remains in Verse and Prose* (1684).
2. The objects of satire.
3. Nisus, on the point of winning a footrace, slipped in a pool of blood. His "young friend" was Euryalus (Virgil's *Aeneid* 5.315–39).
4. Dryden repeats the Renaissance idea that the satirist should avoid smoothness and affect rough meters ("harsh cadence").
5. Sharpness of flavor.
6. Dryden echoes the famous words that conclude Catullus's elegy to his brother: "*Atque in perpetuum, frater, ave atque vale*" ("And forever, brother, hail and farewell!").
7. The nephew of Augustus, adopted by him as his successor. After winning military fame as a youth, he died at the age of twenty. Virgil celebrated him in the *Aeneid* 6.854–86. The last line of Dryden's poem is a reminiscence of *Aeneid* 6.866.
8. The poet's wreath (cf. Milton's *Lycidas*, lines 1–

2, p. 1790).
1. St. Cecilia, a Roman lady, was an early Christian martyr. She has long been regarded as the patroness of music and the supposed inventor of the organ. Celebrations of her festival day (November 22) in England were usually devoted to music and the praise of music, and from about 1683 to 1703 the Musical Society in London annually commemorated it with a religious service and a public concert. This concert always included an ode written and set to music for the occasion, of which the two by Dryden (*A Song for St. Cecilia's Day*, 1687, and *Alexander's Feast*, 1697) are the most distinguished. G. B. Draghi, an Italian brought to England by Charles II, set this ode to music; but Handel's fine score, composed in 1739, has completely obscured the original setting. This is an irregular ode in the manner of Cowley. In stanzas 3–6, Dryden boldly attempted to suggest in the sounds of his words the characteristic tones of the instruments mentioned.

When Nature underneath a heap
       Of jarring atoms lay,
5   And could not heave her head,
The tuneful voice was heard from high:
       "Arise, ye more than dead."
Then cold, and hot, and moist, and dry,[2]
In order to their stations leap,
10   And Music's power obey.
From harmony, from heavenly harmony
       This universal frame began:
       From harmony to harmony
Through all the compass of the notes it ran,
15   The diapason[3] closing full in man.

2

What passion cannot Music raise and quell![4]
       When Jubal struck the corded shell,[5]
       His listening brethren stood around,
       And, wondering, on their faces fell
20   To worship that celestial sound.
Less than a god they thought there could not dwell
       Within the hollow of that shell
       That spoke so sweetly and so well.
What passion cannot Music raise and quell!

3

25   The trumpet's loud clangor
          Excites us to arms,
       With shrill notes of anger,
          And mortal alarms.
       The double double double beat
30   Of the thundering drum
Cries: "Hark! the foes come;
Charge, charge, 'tis too late to retreat."

4

       The soft complaining flute
       In dying notes discovers
35   The woes of hopeless lovers,
Whose dirge is whispered by the warbling lute.

2. "Nature": created nature, ordered by the Divine
Wisdom out of chaos, which Dryden, adopting the
physics of the Greek philosopher Epicurus,
describes as composed of the warring and discor-
dant ("jarring") atoms of the four elements: earth,
fire, water, and air ('cold," "hot," "moist," and
"dry").
3. The entire compass of tones in the scale. Dryden is thinking of the Chain of Being, the ordered
creation from inanimate nature up to humans,
God's latest and final work. The just gradations of
notes in a scale are analogous to the equally just

gradations in the ascending scale of created beings.
Both are the result of harmony.
4. The power of music to describe, evoke, or subdue emotion ("passion") is a frequent theme in
17th-century literature. In stanzas 2–6, the poet
considers music as awakening religious awe, warlike courage, sorrow for unrequited love, jealousy
and fury, and the impulse to worship God.
5. According to Genesis 4.21, Jubal was the inventor of the lyre and the pipe. Dryden imagines
Jubal's lyre to have been made of a tortoise shell
("corded shell").

5

Sharp violins[6] proclaim
Their jealous pangs, and desperation,
Fury, frantic indignation,
40   Depth of pains, and height of passion,
For the fair, disdainful dame.

6

But O! what art can teach,
What human voice can reach,
The sacred organ's praise?
45   Notes inspiring holy love,
Notes that wing their heavenly ways
To mend the choirs above.

7

Orpheus[7] could lead the savage race;
And trees unrooted left their place,
50   Sequacious of° the lyre;   *following*
But bright Cecilia raised the wonder higher:
When to her organ vocal breath was given,
An angel heard, and straight appeared,[8]
Mistaking earth for heaven.

GRAND CHORUS

55   *As from the power of sacred lays*
       The spheres began to move,
And sung the great Creator's praise[9]
       To all the blest above;
So, when the last and dreadful hour
60   *This crumbling pageant*[1] *shall devour,*
The trumpet shall be heard on high, ⎫
The dead shall live, the living die, ⎬
And Music shall untune the sky.[2] ⎭

1687

Epigram on Milton[1]

Three poets,[2] in three distant ages born,
Greece, Italy, and England did adorn.

6. A reference to the bright tone of the modern violin, introduced into England at the Restoration. The tone of the old-fashioned viol is much duller.
7. Legendary poet, son of one of the Muses, who played so wonderfully on the lyre that wild beasts ("the savage race") grew tame and followed him, as did even rocks and trees.
8. According to the legend, it was Cecilia's piety, not her music, that brought an angel to visit her.
9. As it was harmony that ordered the universe, so it was angelic song ("sacred lays") that put the celestial bodies ("spheres") in motion. The harmonious chord that results from the traditional

"music of the spheres" is a hymn of "praise" sung by created nature to its "Creator."
1. The universe: the stage on which the drama of human salvation has been acted out.
2. The "last trump" of 1 Corinthians 15.52, which will announce the Resurrection and the Last Judgment. Dryden develops his theme of harmony as order in such a way as to give full emphasis of the splendid paradox ("Music shall *untune*") in the final line of the ode.
1. Engraved beneath the portrait of Milton in Jacob Tonson's edition of *Paradise Lost* (1688).
2. I.e., Homer, Virgil, and Milton.

The first in loftiness of thought surpassed,
The next in majesty, in both the last:
5   The force of Nature could no farther go;
To make a third, she joined the former two.

1688

Alexander's Feast[1]

Or the Power of Music; An Ode in Honor of St. Cecilia's Day

I

'Twas at the royal feast, for Persia won
        By Philip's[2] warlike son:
    Aloft in awful state
    The godlike hero sate
5   On his imperial throne;
His valiant peers were placed around;
Their brows with roses and with myrtles[3] bound:
    (So should desert in arms be crowned).
    The lovely Thaïs, by his side,
10   Sate like a blooming Eastern bride
In flower of youth and beauty's pride.
        Happy, happy, happy pair!
        None but the brave,
        None but the brave,
15   None but the brave deserves the fair.

CHORUS

Happy, happy, happy pair!
None but the brave,
None but the brave,
None but the brave deserves the fair.

2

20 Timotheus, placed on high
        Amid the tuneful choir,
    With flying fingers touched the lyre:
    The trembling notes ascend the sky,
        And heavenly joys inspire.

1. In Dryden's earlier poem for St. Cecilia's Day, music was celebrated primarily as harmony and order, though its power over the passions was also praised. *Alexander's Feast* is devoted entirely to the second theme. It is based on a well-known episode in the life of Alexander the Great. After the defeat of the Persian emperor Darius III and the fall of the Persian capital Persepolis (331 B.C.E.), Alexander held a great feast for his officers. Thaïs, his Athenian mistress, persuaded him to set fire to the palace in revenge for the burning of Athens by the Persians under Xerxes in 480 B.C.E. According to Plutarch, Alexander was moved by love and wine, not by music, but Dryden, perhaps altering an old tradition that Alexander's musician Timotheus once by his flute-playing caused the hero to start up and arm himself, attributes the burning of Persepolis to the power of music. The original music was by Jeremiah Clarke, but Handel's score of 1736 is better known.
2. King Philip II of Macedonia, father of Alexander the Great.
3. Emblems of love. The Greeks and Romans wore wreaths of flowers at banquets.

25 The song began from Jove,
  Who left his blissful seats above
  (Such is the power of mighty love).
  A dragon's fiery form belied the god:[4]
  Sublime on radiant spires[5] he rode,
30   When he to fair Olympia pressed;
   And while he sought her snowy breast:
  Then, round her slender waist he curled,
  And stamped an image of himself, a sovereign of the world.
  The listening crowd admire° the lofty sound: *wonder at*
35 "A present deity," they shout around;
  "A present deity," the vaulted roofs rebound.
   With ravished ears
   The monarch hears,
   Assumes the god,
40   Affects to nod,
  And seems to shake the spheres.[6]

CHORUS

* With ravished ears*
* The monarch hears,*
* Assumes the god,*
45 *Affects to nod,*
  And seems to shake the spheres.

3

  The praise of Bacchus° then the sweet musician sung, *god of wine*
   Of Bacchus ever fair and ever young:
   The jolly god in triumph comes;
50   Sound the trumpets; beat the drums;
    Flushed with a purple grace
    He shows his honest face:
  Now give the hautboys;° breath; he comes, he comes!   *oboes*
   Bacchus, ever fair and young
55   Drinking joys did first ordain;
  Bacchus' blessings are a treasure,
  Drinking is a soldier's pleasure;
   Rich the treasure,
   Sweet the pleasure,
60   Sweet is pleasure after pain.

CHORUS

* Bacchus' blessings are a treasure,*
* Drinking is the soldier's pleasure;*
* Rich the treasure,*

---

4. An oracle had declared that Alexander was the son of Zeus ("Jove") by Philip's wife Olympias (not, as Dryden calls her in line 30, "Olympia"), thus conferring on him that semidivinity often claimed by heroes. Zeus habitually conducted his amours with mortals in the guise of an animal: in this case a dragon.

5. High on shining coils ("radiant spires"). "Spires" for the coils of a serpent is derived from the Latin word *spira*, which Virgil uses in this sense, *Aeneid* 2.217 (cf. *Paradise Lost* 9.502).
6. According to Virgil (*Aeneid* 10.115) the nod of Jove causes earthquakes.

Sweet the pleasure,
65 *Sweet is pleasure after pain.*

4

Soothed with the sound, the king grew vain;
Fought all his battles o'er again,
And thrice he routed all his foes, and thrice he slew the slain.
The master saw the madness rise,
70 His glowing cheeks, his ardent eyes;
And, while he° heaven and earth defied,   *Alexander*
Changed his° hand, and checked his° pride.   *Timotheus's/Alexander's*
He chose a mournful Muse,
Soft pity to infuse:
75 He sung Darius great and good,
By too severe a fate
Fallen, fallen, fallen, fallen,
Fallen from his high estate,
And weltering in his blood;
80 Deserted at his utmost need
By those his former bounty fed;
On the bare earth exposed he lies,
With not a friend to close his eyes.[7]
With downcast looks the joyless victor sate,
85 Revolving° in his altered soul   *pondering*
The various turns of chance below;
And, now and then, a sigh he stole,
And tears began to flow.

CHORUS

Revolving in his altered soul
90 *The various turns of chance below;*
And, now and then, a sigh he stole,
And tears began to flow.

5

The mighty master smiled to see
That love was in the next degree;
95 'Twas but[8] a kindred sound to move,
For pity melts the mind to love.
Softly sweet, in Lydian[9] measures,
Soon he soothed his soul to pleasures.
"War," he sung, "is toil and trouble;
100 Honor, but an empty bubble.
Never ending, still beginning,
Fighting still, and still destroying:
If the world be worth thy winning,
Think, O think it worth enjoying.
105 Lovely Thaïs sits beside thee,

7. After his final defeat by Alexander, Darius was
assassinated by his own followers.
8. I.e., it was necessary only.

9. In Greek music the Lydian mode expressed the
plaintive and the sad.

Take the good the gods provide thee."
The many[1] rend the skies with loud applause;
So Love was crowned, but Music won the cause.
The prince, unable to conceal his pain,
110   Gazed on the fair
        Who caused his care,
And sighed and looked, sighed and looked,
Sighed and looked, and sighed again:
At length, with love and wine at once oppressed,
115 The vanquished victor sunk upon her breast.

CHORUS

The prince, unable to conceal his pain,
      Gazed on the fair
      Who caused his care,
And sighed and looked, sighed and looked,
120 *Sighed and looked, and sighed again:*
    At length, with love and wine at once oppressed,
    The vanquished victor sunk upon her breast.

6

Now strike the golden lyre again:
A louder yet, and yet a louder strain.
125 Break his bands of sleep asunder,
And rouse him, like a rattling peal of thunder.
      Hark, hark, the horrid° sound   *rough*
      Has raised up his head:
      As waked from the dead,
130   And amazed, he stares around,
"Revenge, revenge!" Timotheus cries,
    "See the Furies[2] arise!
See the snakes that they rear,
How they hiss in their hair,
135 And the sparkles that flash from their eyes!
    Behold a ghastly band,
    Each a torch in his hand!
Those are Grecian ghosts, that in battle were slain,
    And unburied remain[3]
140   Inglorious on the plain:
    Give the vengeance due
    To the valiant crew.
Behold how they toss their torches on high,
  How they point to the Persian abodes,
145 And glittering temples of their hostile gods!"
The princes applaud, with a furious joy;
And the king seized a flambeau° with zeal to destroy;   *torch*
    Thaïs led the way,

---

1. As G. R. Noyes points out, "many" means *meiny*, "a retinue," a spelling that Dryden used elsewhere in his work.
2. The Erinyes of the Greeks, avengers of crimes against the natural and the social orders. They are described as women with snakes in their hair and wrapped around their waists and arms.
3. According to Greek beliefs, the shades of the dead could not rest until their bodies were buried.

> To light him to his prey,
> 150   And, like another Helen, fired another Troy.[4]

CHORUS

> *And the king seized a flambeau with zeal to destroy;*
> *Thaïs led the way,*
> *To light him to his prey,*
> *And, like another Helen, fired another Troy.*

7

> 155   Thus long ago,
> Ere heaving bellows learned to blow,
> While organs yet were mute;
> Timotheus, to his breathing flute,
> And sounding lyre,
> 160   Could swell the soul to rage, or kindle soft desire.
> At last, divine Cecilia came,
> Inventress of the vocal frame;°   organ
> The sweet enthusiast,[5] from her sacred store,
> Enlarged the former narrow bounds,
> 165   And added length to solemn sounds,
> With nature's mother wit, and arts unknown before.
> Let old Timotheus yield the prize,
> Or both divide the crown:
> He raised a mortal to the skies;
> 170   She drew an angel down.

GRAND CHORUS

> *At last, divine Cecilia came,*
> *Inventress of the vocal frame;*
> *The sweet enthusiast, from her sacred store,*
> *Enlarged the former narrow bounds,*
> 175   *And added length to solemn sounds,*
> *With nature's mother wit, and arts unknown before.*
> *Let old Timotheus yield the prize,*
> *Or both divide the crown:*
> *He raised a mortal to the skies;*
> 180   *She drew an angel down.*

1697

4. Helen's elopement to Troy with Paris brought on the Trojan War and the ultimate destruction of the city by the Greeks.
5. Usually at this time a disparaging word, frequently, though not always, applied to a religious zealot or fanatic. Here it is used approvingly and in its literal sense, "possessed by a god," an allusion to Cecilia's angelic companion referred to in line 170 (but see *Song for St. Cecilia's Day*, line 53 and n. 8, p. 2108).

CRITICISM

Because Dryden liked to talk about literature, he became a critic, indeed the first comprehensive critic in England. The Elizabethans, largely impelled by the example of Italian humanists, had produced an interesting but unsystematic body of critical writings. Dryden could look back to such pioneer works as George Puttenham's *Art of English Poesy* (1589), Sir Philip Sidney's *Defense of Poesy* (1595), Samuel Daniel's *Defense of Rhyme* (ca. 1603), and Ben Jonson's *Timber, or Discoveries* (1641). These and later writings Dryden knew, as he knew the ancients and the important contemporary French critics, notably Pierre Corneille, Fr. René Rapin, and Nicolas Boileau. Taken as a whole, his critical prefaces and dedications, which appeared between 1664 and 1700, are the work of a man of independent mind who has made his own synthesis of critical canons from wide reading, a great deal of thinking, and the constant practice of the art of writing. As a critic he is no one's disciple, and he has the saving grace of being always willing to change his mind.

All but a very few of Dryden's critical works (most notably *An Essay of Dramatic Poesy*) grew out of the works to which they served as prefaces: comedies, heroic plays, tragedies, translations, and poems of various sorts. Each work posed problems that Dryden was eager to discuss with his readers, and the topics that he treated proved to be important in the development of the new literature of which he was the principal apologist. He dealt with the processes of literary creation, the poet's relation to tradition, the forms of modern drama, the craft of poetry, and above all the genius of earlier poets: Shakespeare, Jonson, Chaucer, Juvenal, Horace, Homer, and Virgil. For nearly forty years this voice was heard in the land; and when it was finally silenced, a set of critical standards had come into existence and a new age had been given its direction.

From An Essay of Dramatic Poesy[1]

[TWO SORTS OF BAD POETRY]

* * * "I have a mortal apprehension of two poets,[2] whom this victory, with the help of both her wings, will never be able to escape." " 'Tis easy to guess whom you intend," said Lisideius; "and without naming them, I ask you if one of them does not perpetually pay us with clenches[3] upon words, and a

---

1. With the reopening of the theaters in 1660, older plays were revived, but despite their power and charm, they seemed old-fashioned. Although new playwrights, ambitious to create a modern English drama, soon appeared, they were uncertain of their direction. What, if anything, useful could they learn from the dramatic practice of the ancients? Should they ignore the English dramatists of the late 16th and early 17th centuries? Should they make their example the vigorous contemporary drama of France? Dryden addresses himself to these and other problems in this essay, his first extended piece of criticism. Its purpose, he tells us, was "chiefly to vindicate the honor of our English writers from the censure of those who unjustly prefer the French before them." Its method is skeptical: Dryden presents several points of view, but imposes none. The form is a dialogue among friends, like the *Tusculan Disputations* or the *Brutus* of Cicero. Crites praises the drama of the ancients; Eugenius protests against their authority and argues for the idea of progress in the arts; Lisideius urges the excellence of French

plays; and Neander, speaking in the climactic position, defends the native tradition and the greatness of Shakespeare, Fletcher, and Jonson. The dialogue takes place on June 3, 1665, in a boat on the Thames. The four friends are rowed downstream to listen to the cannonading of the English and Dutch fleets, engaged in battle off the Suffolk coast. As the gunfire recedes they are assured of victory and order their boatman to return to London, and naturally enough they fall to discussing the number of bad poems that the victory will evoke.

2. Probably Robert Wilde and possibly Richard Flecknoe, whom Dryden later ridiculed in *Mac Flecknoe*. Their actual identity is unimportant, for they merely represent two extremes in poetry, both deplorable: the fantastic and extravagant manner of decadent metaphysical wit and its opposite, the flat and the dull. The new poetry was to seek a mean between these extremes (cf. Pope, *An Essay on Criticism* 2.239–42 and 289–300, pp. 2514 and 2515).

3. Puns.

certain clownish kind of raillery?[4] if now and then he does not offer at a catachresis or Clevelandism,[5] wresting and torturing a word into another meaning: in fine, if he be not one of those whom the French would call *un mauvais buffon;*[6] one who is so much a well-willer to the satire, that he spares no man; and though he cannot strike a blow to hurt any, yet ought to be punished for the malice of the action, as our witches are justly hanged, because they think themselves so, and suffer deservedly for believing they did mischief, because they meant it." "You have described him," said Crites, "so exactly that I am afraid to come after you with my other extremity of poetry. He is one of those who, having had some advantage of education and converse, knows better than the other what a poet should be, but puts it into practice more unluckily than any man; his style and matter are everywhere alike: he is the most calm, peaceable writer you ever read: he never disquiets your passions[7] with the least concernment, but still[8] leaves you in as even a temper as he found you; he is a very Leveller[9] in poetry: he creeps along with ten little words in every line, and helps out his numbers with *for to,* and *unto,* and all the pretty expletives[1] he can find, till he drags them to the end of another line; while the sense is left tired halfway behind it: he doubly starves all his verses, first for want of thought, and then of expression; his poetry neither has wit in it, nor seems to have it; like him in Martial:

Pauper videri Cinna vult, et est pauper.[2]

"He affects plainness, to cover his want of imagination: when he writes the serious way, the highest flight of his fancy is some miserable antithesis, or seeming contradiction; and in the comic he is still reaching at some thin conceit, the ghost of a jest, and that too flies before him, never to be caught; these swallows which we see before us on the Thames are the just resemblance of his wit: you may observe how near the water they stoop, how many proffers they make to dip, and yet how seldom they touch it; and when they do, it is but the surface: they skim over it but to catch a gnat, and then mount into the air and leave it."

[THE WIT OF THE ANCIENTS: THE UNIVERSAL]

* * * "A thing well said will be wit in all languages; and though it may lose something in the translation, yet to him who reads it in the original, 'tis still the same: he has an idea of its excellency, though it cannot pass from his mind into any other expression or words than those in which he finds it. When Phaedria, in the *Eunuch,*[3] had a command from his mistress to be absent two days, and, encouraging himself to go through with it, said, '*Tan-*

---

4. Boorish banter.
5. "Catachresis": the use of a word in a sense remote from its normal meaning: a legitimate figure of speech used by all poets, it had been abused by John Cleveland (1613–1658), who was at first admired for his ingenuity, but whose reputation declined rapidly after the Restoration. A Clevelandism: "The marigold, whose courtier's face/ *Echoes* the sun."
6. A malicious jester (French).
7. Emotions.

8. Always.
9. The Levellers were radical egalitarians and republicans, a powerful political force in the Puritan army about 1648. They were suppressed by Cromwell.
1. Words used merely to fill out a line of verse (cf. Pope, *An Essay on Criticism* 2.346–47, p. 2516).
2. Cinna wishes to seem poor, and he is poor (Latin; *Epigrams* 8.19).
3. A comedy by the Roman poet Terence (ca. 185–159 B.C.E.).

dem ego non illa caream, si sit opus, vel totum triduum?'[4]—Parmeno, to mock
the softness of his master, lifting up his hands and eyes, cries out, as it were
in admiration, *'Hui! universum triduum!'*[5] the elegancy of which *universum,*
though it cannot be rendered in our language, yet leaves an impression on
our souls: but this happens seldom in him; in Plautus[6] oftener, who is infinitely too bold in his metaphors and coining words, out of which many times
his wit is nothing; which questionless was one reason why Horace falls upon
him so severely in those verses:

> *Sed proavi nostri Plautinos et numeros et*
> *Laudavere sales, nimium patienter utrumque,*
> *Ne dicam stolide.*[7]

For Horace himself was cautious to obtrude a new word on his readers, and
makes custom and common use the best measure of receiving it into our
writings:

> *Multa renascentur quae nunc cecidere, cadentque*
> *Quae nunc sunt in honore vocabula, si volet usus,*
> *Quem penes arbitrium est, et jus, et norma loquendi.*[8]

"The not observing this rule is that which the world has blamed in our
satirist, Cleveland: to express a thing hard and unnaturally is his new way of
elocution. 'Tis true no poet but may sometimes use a catachresis: Virgil does
it—

> *Mistaque ridenti colocasia fundet acantho*—[9]

in his eclogue of Pollio; and in his seventh *Aeneid:*

> *mirantur et undae,*
> *Miratur nemus insuetum fulgentia longe*
> *Scuta virum fluvio pictasque innare carinas.*[1]

And Ovid once so modestly that he asks leave to do it:

> *quem, si verbo audacia detur,*
> *Haud metuam summi dixisse Palatia caeli.*[2]

calling the court of Jupiter by the name of Augustus his palace; though in
another place he is more bold, where he says, *'et longas visent Capitolia
pompas.'*[3] But to do this always, and never be able to write a line without it,
though it may be admired by some few pedants, will not pass upon those

4. Shall I not then do without her, if need be, for
three whole days? (Latin).
5. The wit of Parmeno's exclamation, "Oh, three
entire days," depends on *universum,* which suggests that a lover may regard three days as an eternity. "Admiration": wonder.
6. Titus Maccus Plautus, Roman comic poet (ca.
254–184 B.C.E.).
7. But our ancestors too tolerantly (I do not say
foolishly) praised both the verse and the wit of
Plautus (Latin; *Art of Poetry,* lines 270–72). Dryden misquotes slightly.
8. Many words that have perished will be born
again, and those shall perish that are now
esteemed, if usage wills it, in whose power are the
judgment, the law, and the pattern of speech

(Latin; *Art of Poetry,* lines 70–72).
9. [The earth] shall give forth the Egyptian bean,
mingled with the smiling acanthus (Latin;
Eclogues 4.20). "Smiling acanthus" is a catachresis.
1. Actually *Aeneid* 8.91–93. Dryden's paraphrase
makes the point clearly: "The woods and waters
wonder at the gleam / Of shields and painted ships
that stem the stream" (Latin; *Aeneid* 8.125–26).
"Wonder" is a catachresis.
2. [This is the place] which, if boldness of expression be permitted, I shall not hesitate to call the
Palace of high heaven (Latin; *Metamorphoses*
1.175–76).
3. And the Capitol shall see the long processions
(Latin; *Metamorphoses* 1.561).

who know that wit is best conveyed to us in the most easy language; and is most to be admired when a great thought comes dressed in words so commonly received that it is understood by the meanest apprehensions, as the best meat is the most easily digested: but we cannot read a verse of Cleveland's without making a face at it, as if every word were a pill to swallow: he gives us many times a hard nut to break our teeth, without a kernel for our pains. So that there is this difference betwixt his satires and Doctor Donne's; that the one gives us deep thoughts in common language, though rough cadence; the other gives us common thoughts in abstruse words: 'tis true in some places his wit is independent of his words, as in that of the *Rebel Scot:*

> Had Cain been Scot, God would have changed his doom;
> Not forced him wander, but confined him home.[4]

"*Si sic omnia dixisset!*[5] This is wit in all languages: it is like mercury, never to be lost or killed: and so that other—

> For beauty, like white powder, makes no noise,
> And yet the silent hypocrite destroys.[6]

You see that the last line is highly metaphorical, but it is so soft and gentle that it does not shock us as we read it."

[SHAKESPEARE AND BEN JONSON COMPARED]

"To begin, then, with Shakespeare. He was the man who of all modern, and perhaps ancient poets, had the largest and most comprehensive soul. All the images of Nature were still present to him, and he drew them, not laboriously, but luckily; when he describes anything, you more than see it, you feel it too. Those who accuse him to have wanted learning, give him the greater commendation: he was naturally learned; he needed not the spectacles of books to read Nature; he looked inwards, and found her there. I cannot say he is everywhere alike; were he so, I should do him injury to compare him with the greatest of mankind. He is many times flat, insipid; his comic wit degenerating into clenches, his serious swelling into bombast. But he is always great when some great occasion is presented to him; no man can say he ever had a fit subject for his wit and did not then raise himself as high above the rest of poets,

Quantum lenta solent inter viburna cupressi[7]

The consideration of this made Mr. Hales[8] of Eton say that there was no subject of which any poet ever writ, but he would produce it much better treated of in Shakespeare; and however others are now generally preferred before him, yet the age wherein he lived, which had contemporaries with him Fletcher and Jonson, never equaled them to him in their esteem: and in the last king's[9] court, when Ben's reputation was at highest, Sir John

4. Lines 63–64.
5. Had he said everything thus! (Latin; Juvenal's *Satires* 10.123–24).
6. From *Rupertismus,* lines 39–40. Mercury is said to be "killed" if its fluidity is destroyed.
7. As do cypresses among the bending shrubs

(Latin; Virgil's *Eclogues* 1.25).
8. The learned John Hales (1584–1656), provost of Eton. He is reputed to have said this to Jonson himself.
9. Charles I.

Suckling,[1] and with him the greater part of the courtiers, set our Shakespeare far above him. . . .

"As for Jonson, to whose character I am now arrived, if we look upon him while he was himself (for his last plays were but his dotages), I think him the most learned and judicious writer which any theater ever had. He was a most severe judge of himself, as well as others. One cannot say he wanted wit, but rather that he was frugal of it. In his works you find little to retrench[2] or alter. Wit, and language, and humor also in some measure, we had before him; but something of art[3] was wanting to the drama till he came. He managed his strength to more advantage than any who preceded him. You seldom find him making love in any of his scenes or endeavoring to move the passions; his genius was too sullen and saturnine[4] to do it gracefully, especially when he knew he came after those who had performed both to such an height. Humor was his proper sphere:[5] and in that he delighted most to represent mechanic people.[6] He was deeply conversant in the ancients, both Greek and Latin, and he borrowed boldly from them: there is scarce a poet or historian among the Roman authors of those times whom he has not translated in *Sejanus* and *Catiline*.[7] But he has done his robberies so openly, that one may see he fears not to be taxed by any law. He invades authors like a monarch; and what would be theft in other poets is only victory in him. With the spoils of these writers he so represents old Rome to us, in its rites, ceremonies, and customs, that if one of their poets had written either of his tragedies, we had seen less of it than in him. If there was any fault in his language, 'twas that he weaved it too closely and laboriously, in his serious plays:[8] perhaps, too, he did a little too much Romanize our tongue, leaving the words which he translated almost as much Latin as he found them: wherein, though he learnedly followed the idiom of their language, he did not enough comply with the idiom of ours. If I would compare him with Shakespeare, I must acknowledge him the more correct poet, but Shakespeare the greater wit.[9] Shakespeare was the Homer, or father of our dramatic poets; Jonson was the Virgil, the pattern of elaborate writing; I admire him, but I love Shakespeare. To conclude of him; as he has given us the most correct plays, so in the precepts which he has laid down in his *Discoveries,* we have as many and profitable rules for perfecting the stage, as any wherewith the French can furnish us."

1668

---

1. Courtier, poet, playwright, much admired in Dryden's time for his wit and the easy naturalness of his style.
2. Delete.
3. Craftsmanship.
4. Heavy.
5. In Jonson's comedies the characters are seen under the domination of some psychological trait, ruling passion, or affectation—i.e., some "hu-

mor"—that makes them unique and ridiculous.
6. I.e., artisans.
7. Jonson's two Roman plays, dated 1605 and 1611, respectively.
8. This is the reading of the first edition. Curiously enough, in the second edition Dryden altered the phrase to "in his comedies especially."
9. Genius.

From The Author's Apology for Heroic Poetry and Heroic License[1]

["BOLDNESS" OF FIGURES AND TROPES DEFENDED:
THE APPEAL TO "NATURE"]

* * * They, who would combat general authority with particular opinion, must first establish themselves a reputation of understanding better than other men. Are all the flights of heroic poetry to be concluded bombast, unnatural, and mere madness, because they are not affected with their excellencies? It is just as reasonable as to conclude there is no day, because a blind man cannot distinguish of light and colors. Ought they not rather, in modesty, to doubt of their own judgments, when they think this or that expression in Homer, Virgil, Tasso, or Milton's *Paradise* to be too far strained, than positively to conclude that 'tis all fustian and mere nonsense? 'Tis true there are limits to be set betwixt the boldness and rashness of a poet; but he must understand those limits who pretends to judge as well as he who undertakes to write: and he who has no liking to the whole ought, in reason, to be excluded from censuring of the parts. He must be a lawyer before he mounts the tribunal; and the judicature of one court, too, does not qualify a man to preside in another. He may be an excellent pleader in the Chancery, who is not fit to rule the Common Pleas. But I will presume for once to tell them that the boldest strokes of poetry, when they are managed artfully, are those which most delight the reader.

Virgil and Horace, the severest writers of the severest age, have made frequent use of the hardest metaphors and of the strongest hyperboles; and in this case the best authority is the best argument, for generally to have pleased, and through all ages, must bear the force of universal tradition. And if you would appeal from thence to right reason, you will gain no more by it in effect than, first, to set up your reason against those authors, and, secondly, against all those who have admired them. You must prove why that ought not to have pleased which has pleased the most learned and the most judicious; and, to be thought knowing, you must first put the fool upon all mankind. If you can enter more deeply than they have done into the causes and resorts[2] of that which moves pleasure in a reader, the field is open, you may be heard: but those springs of human nature are not so easily discovered by every superficial judge: it requires philosophy, as well as poetry, to sound the depth of all the passions, what they are in themselves, and how they are to be provoked; and in this science the best poets have excelled. * * * From hence have sprung the tropes and figures,[3] for which they wanted a name who first practiced them and succeeded in them. Thus I grant you that the knowledge of Nature was the original rule, and that all poets ought to study

---

1. This essay was prefixed to Dryden's *State of Innocence,* the libretto for an opera (never produced), based on *Paradise Lost.* Dryden had been ridiculed for the extravagant and bold imagery and rhetorical figures that are typical of the style of his rhymed heroic plays. This preface is a defense not only of his own predilection for what Samuel Johnson described as "wild and daring sallies of sentiment, in the irregular and eccentric violence of

wit" but also of the theory that heroic and idealized materials should be treated in lofty and boldly metaphorical style; hence his definition of wit as propriety.
2. Mechanical springs that set something in motion.
3. I.e., such figures of speech as metaphors and similes. "Tropes": the uses of words in a figurative sense.

her, as well as Aristotle and Horace, her interpreters.[4] But then this also undeniably follows, that those things which delight all ages must have been an imitation of Nature—which is all I contend. Therefore is rhetoric made an art; therefore the names of so many tropes and figures were invented, because it was observed they had such and such effect upon the audience. Therefore catachreses and hyperboles[5] have found their place amongst them; not that they were to be avoided, but to be used judiciously and placed in poetry as heightenings and shadows are in painting, to make the figure bolder, and cause it to stand off to sight. * * *

[WIT AS "PROPRIETY"]

* * * [Wit] is a propriety of thoughts and words; or, in other terms, thought and words elegantly adapted to the subject. If our critics will join issue on this definition, that we may *convenire in aliquo tertio;*[6] if they will take it as a granted principle, it will be easy to put an end to this dispute. No man will disagree from another's judgment concerning the dignity of style in heroic poetry; but all reasonable men will conclude it necessary that sublime subjects ought to be adorned with the sublimest, and, consequently, often with the most figurative expressions. * * *

1677

From A Discourse Concerning the Original and Progress of Satire[1]

[THE ART OF SATIRE]

* * * How easy is it to call rogue and villain, and that wittily! But how hard to make a man appear a fool, a blockhead, or a knave without using any of those opprobrious terms! To spare the grossness of the names, and to do the thing yet more severely, is to draw a full face, and to make the nose and cheeks stand out, and yet not to employ any depth of shadowing.[2] This is the mystery of that noble trade, which yet no master can teach to his apprentice; he may give the rules, but the scholar is never the nearer in his practice. Neither is it true that this fineness of raillery[3] is offensive. A witty man is tickled while he is hurt in this manner, and a fool feels it not. The occasion of an offense may possibly be given, but he cannot take it. If it be granted

---

4. In the words of the French critic René Rapin, the rules (largely derived from Aristotle's *Poetics* and Horace's *Art of Poetry*) were made to "reduce Nature to method" (cf. Pope, *An Essay on Criticism* 1.88–89, p. 2511).
5. Deliberate overstatement or exaggeration. "Catachresis": the use of a word in a sense remote from its normal meaning.
6. To find some means of agreement, in a third term, between the two opposites [Latin; W. P. Ker's note].
1. This passage is an excerpt from the long and rambling preface that served as the dedication of a translation of the satires of the Roman satirists Juvenal and Persius to Charles Sackville, sixth earl of Dorset. The translations were made by Dryden

and other writers, among them William Congreve. Dryden traces the origin and development of verse satire in Rome and in a very fine passage contrasts Horace and Juvenal as satiric poets. It is plain that he prefers the "tragic" satire of Juvenal to the urbane and laughing satire of Horace. But in the passage printed here, he praises his own satiric character of Zimri (the duke of Buckingham) in *Absalom and Achitophel* for the very reason that it is modeled on Horatian "raillery," not Juvenalian invective.
2. Early English miniaturists prided themselves on the art of giving roundness to the full face without painting in shadows.
3. Satirical mirth, good-natured satire.

that in effect this way does more mischief; that a man is secretly wounded, and though he be not sensible himself, yet the malicious world will find it out for him; yet there is still a vast difference betwixt the slovenly butchering of a man, and the fineness of a stroke that separates the head from the body, and leaves it standing in its place. A man may be capable, as Jack Ketch's[4] wife said of his servant, of a plain piece of work, a bare hanging; but to make a malefactor die sweetly was only belonging to her husband. I wish I could apply it to myself, if the reader would be kind enough to think it belongs to me. The character of Zimri in my *Absalom*[5] is, in my opinion, worth the whole poem: it is not bloody, but it is ridiculous enough; and he, for whom it was intended, was too witty to resent it as an injury. If I had railed,[6] I might have suffered for it justly; but I managed my own work more happily, perhaps more dexterously. I avoided the mention of great crimes, and applied myself to the representing of blindsides, and little extravagancies; to which, the wittier a man is, he is generally the more obnoxious.[7] It succeeded as I wished; the jest went round, and he was laughed at in his turn who began the frolic. * * *

1693

From The Preface to *Fables Ancient and Modern*[1]

[IN PRAISE OF CHAUCER]

In the first place, as he is the father of English poetry, I hold him in the same degree of veneration as the Grecians held Homer, or the Romans Virgil. He is a perpetual fountain of good sense; learned in all sciences;[2] and, therefore, speaks properly on all subjects. As he knew what to say, so he knows also when to leave off; a continence which is practiced by few writers, and scarcely by any of the ancients, excepting Virgil and Horace. * * *

Chaucer followed Nature everywhere, but was never so bold to go beyond her; and there is a great difference of being *poeta* and *nimis poeta*,[3] if we may believe Catullus, as much as betwixt a modest behavior and affectation. The verse of Chaucer, I confess, is not harmonious to us; but 'tis like the eloquence of one whom Tacitus commends, it was *auribus istius temporis accommodata:*[4] they who lived with him, and some time after him, thought it musical; and it continues so, even in our judgment, if compared with the numbers of Lydgate and Gower,[5] his contemporaries; there is the rude sweet-

---

4. A notorious public executioner of Dryden's time (d. 1686). His name later became a generic term for all members of his profession.
5. *Absalom and Achitophel*, lines 544–68 (p. 2089).
6. Reviled, abused. Observe that the verb differed in meaning from its noun, defined above.
7. Liable.
1. Dryden's final work, published in the year of his death, was a collection of translations from Homer, Ovid, Boccaccio, and Chaucer, and one or two other pieces. The *Preface* is Dryden's ripest and finest critical essay. He is not concerned here with critical theory or with a formalistic approach to literature but is simply a man, grown old in the reading and writing of poetry, who is eager to talk informally with his readers about some of his favorite authors. His praise of Chaucer (unusually sympathetic and perceptive for 1700) is animated by that love of great literature that is manifest in everything that Dryden wrote.
2. Branches of learning.
3. A poet ("*poeta*") and too much of a poet ("*nimis poeta*"). The phrase is not from Catullus but from Martial (*Epigrams* 3.44).
4. Suitable to the ears of that time (Latin). Tacitus was a Roman historian and writer on oratory (ca. 55–ca. 117).
5. John Gower (d. 1408) was a poet and friend of Chaucer. "Numbers": versification. John Lydgate (ca. 1370–ca. 1449) wrote poetry that shows the influence of Chaucer.

ness of a Scotch tune in it, which is natural and pleasing, though not perfect. 'Tis true I cannot go so far as he who published the last edition of him;[6] for he would make us believe the fault is in our ears, and that there were really ten syllables in a verse where we find but nine; but this opinion is not worth confuting; 'tis so gross and obvious an error that common sense (which is a rule in everything but matters of faith and revelation) must convince the reader that equality of numbers in every verse which we call heroic[7] was either not known, or not always practiced in Chaucer's age. It were an easy matter to produce some thousands of his verses which are lame for want of half a foot, and sometimes a whole one, and which no pronunciation can make otherwise. We can only say that he lived in the infancy of our poetry, and that nothing is brought to perfection at the first. * * *

He must have been a man of a most wonderful comprehensive nature, because, as it has been truly observed of him, he has taken into the compass of his *Canterbury Tales* the various manners and humors (as we now call them) of the whole English nation in his age. Not a single character has escaped him. All his pilgrims are severally distinguished from each other; and not only in their inclinations but in their very physiognomies and persons. Baptista Porta[8] could not have described their natures better than by the marks which the poet gives them. The matter and manner of their tales, and of their telling, are so suited to their different educations, humors, and callings that each of them would be improper in any other mouth. Even the grave and serious characters are distinguished by their several sorts of gravity: their discourses are such as belong to their age, their calling, and their breeding; such as are becoming of them, and of them only. Some of his persons are vicious, and some virtuous; some are unlearned, or (as Chaucer calls them) lewd, and some are learned. Even the ribaldry of the low characters is different: the Reeve, the Miller, and the Cook are several[9] men, and distinguished from each other as much as the mincing Lady Prioress and the broad-speaking, gap-toothed Wife of Bath. But enough of this; there is such a variety of game springing up before me that I am distracted in my choice, and know not which to follow. 'Tis sufficient to say, according to the proverb, that here is God's plenty. * * *

1700

---

6. Thomas Speght's Chaucer, which Dryden used, was first published in 1598; the second edition, published in 1602, was reprinted in 1687.
7. The pentameter line. In Dryden's time few readers knew how to pronounce Middle English, especially the syllabic *e*. Moreover, Chaucer's works were known only in corrupt printed texts. As a consequence Chaucer's verse seemed rough and irregular.
8. Giambattista della Porta (ca. 1535–1615), author of a Latin treatise on physiognomy.
9. Different.

SAMUEL PEPYS
1633–1703

Samuel Pepys (pronounced "Peeps") was the son of a London tailor. With the help of a scholarship he took a degree at Cambridge; with the help of a cousin he found a place in the Navy Office. Eventually, through hard work and an eye for detail, he rose to secretary of the Admiralty. His defense of the Navy Office and himself before Parliament in 1668 won him a reputation as a good administrator, and his career continued to prosper until it was broken, first by false accusations of treason in 1679 and finally by the deposition of James II in 1688. But Pepys was more than a bureaucrat. A Londoner to his core, he was interested in all the activities of the city: the theater, music, the social whirl, business, religion, literary life, and the scientific experiments of the Royal Society (which he served as president from 1684 to 1686). He also found plenty of chances to indulge his two obsessions: chasing after women and making money.

Pepys kept his diary from 1660 to 1669 (when his eyesight began to fail). Writing in shorthand and sometimes in code, he was utterly frank in recording the events of his day, both public and private, the major affairs of state or his quarrels with his wife. Altogether he wrote about 1.3 million words. When the diary was first deciphered and published in the nineteenth century, it made him newly famous. As a document of social history it is unsurpassed for its rich detail, honesty, and immediacy. But more than that, it gives us a sense of somebody else's world: what it was like to live in the Restoration, and what it was like to see through the eyes of Pepys.

From The Diary

[THE GREAT FIRE]

September 2, 1666

Lords day. Some of our maids sitting up late last night to get things ready against our feast today, Jane called us up, about 3 in the morning, to tell us of a great fire they saw in the City.[1] So I rose, and slipped on my nightgown and went to her window, and thought it to be on the back side of Mark Lane[2] at the furthest; but being unused to such fires as followed, I thought it far enough off, and so went to bed again and to sleep. About 7 rose again to dress myself, and there looked out at the window and saw the fire not so much as it was, and further off. So to my closet[3] to set things to rights after yesterday's cleaning. By and by Jane comes and tells me that she hears that above 300 houses have been burned down tonight by the fire we saw, and that it was now burning down all Fish Street by London Bridge. So I made myself ready presently,[4] and walked to the Tower and there got up upon one of the high places, Sir J. Robinson's little son going up with me; and there I did see the houses at that end of the bridge all on fire, and an infinite great fire on this and the other side the end of the bridge—which, among other people, did trouble me for poor little Michell and our Sarah[5] on the Bridge. So down, with my heart full of trouble, to the Lieutenant of the Tower, who tells me that it begun this morning in the King's baker's house in Pudding Lane, and that it hath burned down St. Magnus' Church and most part of Fish Street already. So I down to the waterside and there got a boat and through bridge, and there saw a lamentable fire. Poor Michell's house, as far as the Old Swan,[6] already burned that way and the fire running further, that in a very little time it got as far as the Steelyard while I was there. Everybody endeavoring to remove their goods, and flinging into the river or bringing

1. The fire of London, which was to destroy four-fifths of the central city, had begun an hour earlier. For another description see Dryden's *Annus Mirabilis* (p. 2073).
2. Near Pepys's own house in Seething Lane.
3. A small private room or study.

4. Immediately.
5. William Michell and his wife, Betty, one of Pepys's old flames, lived near London Bridge. Sarah had been a maid of the Pepys's.
6. A tavern in Thames Street, near the source of the fire.

them into lighters[7] that lay off. Poor people staying in their houses as long as till the very fire touched them, and then running into boats or clambering from one pair of stair by the waterside to another. And among other things, the poor pigeons I perceive were loath to leave their houses, but hovered about the windows and balconies till they were some of them burned, their wings, and fell down.

Having stayed, and in an hour's time seen the fire rage every way, and nobody to my sight endeavoring to quench it, but to remove their goods and leave all to the fire; and having seen it get as far as the Steelyard, and the wind mighty high and driving it into the city, and everything, after so long a drought, proving combustible, even the very stones of churches, and among other things, the poor steeple by which pretty Mrs.   [8] lives, and whereof my old school-fellow Elborough is parson, taken fire in the very top and there burned till it fell down—I to Whitehall[9] with a gentleman with me who desired to go off from the Tower to see the fire in my boat—to Whitehall, and there up to the King's closet in the chapel, where people came about me and I did give them an account dismayed them all; and word was carried in to the King, so I was called for and did tell the King and Duke of York what I saw, and that unless his Majesty did command houses to be pulled down, nothing could stop the fire. They seemed much troubled, and the King commanded me to go to my Lord Mayor from him and command him to spare no houses but to pull down before the fire every way. The Duke of York bid me tell him that if he would have any more soldiers, he shall; and so did my Lord Arlington afterward, as a great secret. Here meeting with Captain Cocke, I in his coach, which he lent me, and Creed with me, to Paul's;[1] and there walked along Watling Street as well as I could, every creature coming away loaden with goods to save—and here and there sick people carried away in beds. Extraordinary good goods carried in carts and on backs. At last met my Lord Mayor in Canning Street, like a man spent, with a hankercher[2] about his neck. To the King's message, he cried like a fainting woman, "Lord, what can I do? I am spent. People will not obey me. I have been pulling down houses. But the fire overtakes us faster than we can do it." That he needed no more soldiers; and that for himself, he must go and refresh himself, having been up all night. So he left me, and I him, and walked home— seeing people all almost distracted and no manner of means used to quench the fire. The houses too, so very thick thereabouts, and full of matter for burning, as pitch and tar, in Thames Street—and warehouses of oil and wines and brandy and other things. Here I saw Mr. Isaak Houblon, that handsome man—prettily dressed and dirty at his door at Dowgate, receiving some of his brothers' things whose houses were on fire; and as he says, have been removed twice already, and he doubts[3] (as it soon proved) that they must be in a little time removed from his house also—which was a sad consideration. And to see the churches all filling with goods, by people who themselves should have been quietly there at this time.

By this time it was about 12 o'clock, and so home and there find my guests, which was Mr. Wood and his wife, Barbary Shelden, and also Mr. Moone— she mighty fine, and her husband, for aught I see, a likely[4] man. But Mr.

---

7. Barges.
8. Mrs. Horsely, a beauty admired and pursued by Pepys.
9. Palace in central London.

1. St. Paul's Cathedral, later ravaged by the fire.
2. Handkerchief.
3. Fears.
4. Promising.

Moone's design and mine, which was to look over my closet and please him with the sight thereof, which he hath long desired, was wholly disappointed, for we were in great trouble and disturbance at this fire, not knowing what to think of it. However, we had an extraordinary good dinner, and as merry as at this time we could be.

While at dinner, Mrs. Batelier came to enquire after Mr. Woolfe and Stanes (who it seems are related to them), whose houses in Fish Street are all burned, and they in a sad condition. She would not stay in the fright.

As soon as dined, I and Moone away and walked through the City, the streets full of nothing but people and horses and carts loaden with goods, ready to run over one another, and removing goods from one burned house to another—they now removing out of Canning Street (which received goods in the morning) into Lumbard Street and further; and among others, I now saw my little goldsmith Stokes receiving some friend's goods, whose house itself was burned the day after. We parted at Paul's, he home and I to Paul's Wharf, where I had appointed a boat to attend me; and took in Mr. Carcasse and his brother, whom I met in the street, and carried them below and above bridge, to and again, to see the fire, which was now got further, both below and above, and no likelihood of stopping it. Met with the King and Duke of York in their barge, and with them to Queenhithe and there called Sir Rd. Browne[5] to them. Their order was only to pull down houses apace, and so below bridge at the waterside; but little was or could be done, the fire coming upon them so fast. Good hopes there was of stopping it at the Three Cranes above, and at Buttolph's Wharf below bridge, if care be used; but the wind carries it into the City, so as we know not by the waterside what it doth there. River full of lighters and boats taking in goods, and good goods swimming in the water; and only, I observed that hardly one lighter or boat in three that had the goods of a house in, but there was a pair of virginals[6] in it. Having seen as much as I could now, I away to Whitehall by appointment, and there walked to St. James's Park, and there met my wife and Creed and Wood and his wife and walked to my boat, and there upon the water again, and to the fire up and down, it still increasing and the wind great. So near the fire as we could for smoke; and all over the Thames, with one's face in the wind you were almost burned with a shower of firedrops—this is very true—so as houses were burned by these drops and flakes of fire, three or four, nay five or six houses, one from another. When we could endure no more upon the water, we to a little alehouse on the Bankside over against the Three Cranes, and there stayed till it was dark almost and saw the fire grow; and as it grew darker, appeared more and more, and in corners and upon steeples and between churches and houses, as far as we could see up the hill of the City, in a most horrid malicious bloody flame, not like the fine flame of an ordinary fire. Barbary[7] and her husband away before us. We stayed till, it being darkish, we saw the fire as only one entire arch of fire from this to the other side the bridge, and in a bow up the hill, for an arch of above a mile long. It made me weep to see it. The churches, houses, and all on fire and flaming at once, and a horrid noise the flames made, and the cracking of houses at their ruin. So home with a sad heart, and there find everybody discoursing and lamenting the fire; and poor Tom Hater came

5. Sir Richard Browne was a former lord mayor. "Queenhithe": harbor in Thames Street.
6. Table-size harpsichord, popular at the time.

7. The actress Elizabeth Knepp, another of Pepys's mistresses. He calls her "Barbary" because she had enchanted him by singing *Barbary Allen*.

with some few of his goods saved out of his house, which is burned upon Fish Street hill. I invited him to lie at my house, and did receive his goods: but was deceived in his lying there,[8] the noise coming every moment of the growth of the fire, so as we were forced to begin to pack up our own goods and prepare for their removal. And did by moonshine (it being brave,[9] dry, and moonshine and warm weather) carry much of my goods into the garden, and Mr. Hater and I did remove my money and iron chests into my cellar—as thinking that the safest place. And got my bags of gold into my office ready to carry away, and my chief papers of accounts also there, and my tallies[1] into a box by themselves. So great was our fear, as Sir W. Batten had carts come out of the country to fetch away his goods this night. We did put Mr. Hater, poor man, to bed a little; but he got but very little rest, so much noise being in my house, taking down of goods.

September 5, 1666

I lay down in the office again upon W. Hewer's[2] quilt, being mighty weary and sore in my feet with going till I was hardly able to stand. About 2 in the morning my wife calls me up and tells of new cries of "Fire!"—it being come to Barking Church, which is the bottom of our lane. I up; and finding it so, resolved presently to take her away; and did, and took my gold (which was about £2350), W. Hewer, and Jane down by Poundy's boat to Woolwich.[3] But Lord, what a sad sight it was by moonlight to see the whole City almost on fire—that you might see it plain at Woolwich, as if you were by it. There when I came, I find the gates[4] shut, but no guard kept at all; which troubled me, because of discourses now begun that there is plot in it and that the French had done it.[5] I got the gates open, and to Mr. Shelden's,[6] where I locked up my gold and charged my wife and W. Hewer never to leave the room without one of them in it night nor day. So back again, by the way seeing my goods well in the lighters at Deptford and watched well by people. Home, and whereas I expected to have seen our house on fire, it being now about 7 o'clock, it was not. But to the fire, and there find greater hopes than I expected; for my confidence of finding our office on fire was such, that I durst not ask anybody how it was with us, till I came and saw it not burned. But going to the fire, I find, by the blowing up of houses and the great help given by the workmen out of the King's yards,[7] sent up by Sir W. Penn, there is a good stop given to it, as well at Mark Lane end as ours—it having only burned the dial[8] of Barking Church, and part of the porch, and was there quenched. I up to the top of Barking steeple, and there saw the saddest sight of desolation that I ever saw. Everywhere great fires. Oil cellars and brimstone and other things burning. I became afeared to stay there long; and therefore down again as fast as I could, the fire being spread as far as I could see it, and to Sir W. Penn's and there eat a piece of cold meat, having eaten nothing since Sunday but the remains of Sunday's dinner.

8. I.e., mistaken in asking him to stay.
9. Fine.
1. Receipts notched on sticks.
2. William Hewer, Pepys's chief clerk. Pepys had packed or sent away all his own goods.
3. Suburb on the east side of London.
4. Dockyard gates.

5. There were rumors that the French had set the fire and were invading the city.
6. William Shelden, a Woolwich official at whose home Mrs. Pepys had stayed the year before, during the plague.
7. Dockyards.
8. Clock.

Here I met with Mr. Young and Whistler; and having removed all my things, and received good hopes that the fire at our end is stopped, they and I walked into the town and find Fanchurch Street, Gracious Street, and Lumbard Street all in dust. The Exchange a sad sight, nothing standing there of all the statues or pillars but Sir Tho. Gresham's picture in the corner.[9] Walked into Moorefields (our feet ready to burn, walking through the town among the hot coals) and find that full of people, and poor wretches carrying their goods there, and everybody keeping his goods together by themselves (and a great blessing it is to them that it is fair weather for them to keep abroad[1] night and day); drank there, and paid twopence for a plain penny loaf.

Thence homeward, having passed through Cheapside and Newgate Market, all burned—and seen Anthony Joyce's house in fire. And took up (which I keep by me) a piece of glass of Mercer's Chapel in the street, where much more was, so melted and buckled with the heat of the fire, like parchment. I also did see a poor cat taken out of a hole in the chimney joining to the wall of the Exchange, with the hair all burned off the body and yet alive. So home at night, and find there good hopes of saving our office—but great endeavors of watching all night and having men ready; and so we lodged them in the office and had drink and bread and cheese for them. And I lay down and slept a good night about midnight—though when I rose, I hear that there had been a great alarm of French and Dutch being risen—which proved nothing. But it is a strange thing to see how long this time did look since Sunday, having been always full of variety of actions, and little sleep, that it looked like a week or more. And I had forgot almost the day of the week.[2]

[THE DEB WILLET AFFAIR]

October 25, 1668

Lords day. Up, and discoursing with my wife about our house and many new things we are doing of; and so to church I, and there find Jack Fen come, and his wife, a pretty black[3] woman; I never saw her before, nor took notice of her now. So home and to dinner; and after dinner, all the afternoon got my wife and boy[4] to read to me. And at night W. Batelier comes and sups with us; and after supper, to have my head combed by Deb,[5] which occasioned the greatest sorrow to me that ever I knew in this world; for my wife, coming up suddenly, did find me embracing the girl con my hand sub su coats; and indeed, I was with my main in her cunny.[6] I was at a wonderful loss upon it, and the girl also; and I endeavored to put it off, but my wife was struck mute and grew angry, and as her voice came to her, grew quite out of order; and I do say little, but to bed; and my wife said little also, but could not sleep all night; but about 2 in the morning waked me and cried, and fell to tell me as a great secret that she was a Roman Catholic and had

9. Sir Thomas Gresham had founded the Royal Exchange, a center for shopping and trading, in 1568. It was rebuilt in 1669.
1. Out of doors.
2. A day later the fire was under control. Pepys's own house was spared.
3. Dark-haired.
4. Servant. Pepys had no children.
5. Deborah Willett, Mrs. Pepys's maid.
6. With his hand under her skirts and in her vulva.

received the Holy Sacrament;[7] which troubled me but I took no notice of it, but she went on from one thing to another, till at last it appeared plainly her trouble was at what she saw; but yet I did not know how much she saw and therefore said nothing to her. But after her much crying and reproaching me with inconstancy and preferring a sorry girl before her, I did give her no provocations but did promise all fair usage to her, and love, and foreswore any hurt that I did with her—till at last she seemed to be at ease again; and so toward morning, a little sleep; [*Oct. 26*] and so I, with some little repose and rest, rose, and up and by water to Whitehall, but with my mind mightily troubled for the poor girl, whom I fear I have undone by this, my wife telling me that she would turn her out of door. However, I was obliged to attend the Duke of York, thinking to have had a meeting of Tanger[8] today, but had not; but he did take me and Mr. Wren into his closet, and there did press me to prepare what I had to say upon the answers of my fellow-officers to his great letter; which I promised to do against[9] his coming to town again the next week; and so to other discourse, finding plainly that he is in trouble and apprehensions of the reformers, and would be found to do what he can towards reforming himself. And so thence to my Lord Sandwich; where after long stay, he being in talk with others privately, I to him; and there he taking physic and keeping his chamber, I had an hour's talk with him about the ill posture of things at this time, while the King gives countenance to Sir Ch. Sidly and Lord Buckhurst,[1] telling him their late story of running up and down the streets a little while since all night, and their being beaten and clapped up all night by the constable, who is since chid and imprisoned for his pains.

He tells me that he thinks his matters do stand well with the King—and hopes to have dispatch to his mind;[2] but I doubt it, and do see that he doth fear it too. He told me my Lady Carteret's trouble about my writing of that letter of the Duke of York's lately to the office; which I did not own, but declared to be of no injury to G. Carteret,[3] and that I would write a letter to him to satisfy him therein. But this I am in pain how to do without doing myself wrong, and the end I had, of preparing a justification to myself hereafter, when the faults of the Navy come to be found out. However, I will do it in the best manner I can.

Thence by coach home and to dinner, finding my wife mightily discontented and the girl sad, and no words from my wife to her. So after dinner, they out[4] with me about two or three things; and so home again, I all the evening busy and my wife full of trouble in her looks; and anon to bed—where about midnight, she wakes me and there falls foul on me again, affirming that she saw me hug and kiss the girl; the latter I denied, and truly; the other I confessed and no more. And upon her pressing me, did offer to give her under my hand that I would never see Mrs. Pierce more, nor Knepp, but did promise her particular demonstrations of my true love to her, owning some indiscretion in what I did, but that there was no harm in it. She at last on these promises was quiet, and very kind we were, and so to sleep; [*Oct. 27*] and in the morning up, but with my mind troubled for the poor girl, with whom I could not get opportunity to speak; but to the office, my mind mighty full of sorrow for her, where all the morning, and to dinner with my people and to the office all the afternoon; and so at night home and there busy to get some things ready against tomorrow's meeting of Tanger; and that being done and my clerks gone, my wife did towards bedtime begin to be in a mighty rage from some new matter that she had got in her head, and did most part of the night in bed rant at me in most high terms, of threats of publishing[5] my shame; and when I offered to rise, would have rose too, and caused a candle to be lit, to burn by her all night in the chimney while she ranted; while I, that knew myself to have given some grounds for it, did make it my business to appease her all I could possibly, and by good words and fair promises did make her very quiet; and so rested all night and rose with perfect good peace, being heartily afflicted for this folly of mine that did occasion it; but was forced to be silent about the girl, which I have no mind to part with, but much less that the poor girl should be undone by my folly. [*Oct. 28*] So up, with mighty kindness from my wife and a thorough peace; and being up, did by a note advise the girl what I had done and owned, which note I was in pain for till she told me that she had burned it. This evening, Mr. Spong came and sat late with me, and first told me of the instrument called Parrallogram,[6] which I must have one of, showing me his practice thereon by a map of England.

November 14, 1668

Up, and had a mighty mind to have seen or given a note to Deb or to have given her a little money; to which purpose I wrapped up 40s in a paper, thinking to give her; but my wife rose presently, and would not let me be out of her sight; and went down before me into the kitchen, and came up and told me that she was in the kitchen, and therefore would have me go round the other way; which she repeating, and I vexed at it, answered her a little angrily; upon which she instantly flew out into a rage, calling me dog and rogue, and that I had a rotten heart; all which, knowing that I deserved it, I bore with; and word being brought presently up that she was gone away by coach with her things, my wife was friends; and so all quiet, and I to the office with my heart sad, and find that I cannot forget the girl, and vexed I know not where to look for her—and more troubled to see how my wife is by this means likely for ever to have her hand over me, that I shall for ever be a slave to her; that is to say, only in matters of pleasure, but in other things she will make her business, I know, to please me and to keep me right to her—which I will labor to be indeed, for she deserves it of me, though it will be I fear a little time before I shall be able to wear Deb out of my mind. At the office all the morning, and merry at noon at dinner; and after dinner to the office, where all the afternoon and doing much business late; my mind being free of all troubles, I thank God, but[7] only for my thoughts of this girl, which hang after her. And so at night home to supper, and there did sleep

5. Making public.
6. The pantograph, a mechanism for copying
maps or plans.
7. Except.

with great content with my wife. I must here remember that I have lain with my moher[8] as a husband more times since this falling-out then in I believe twelve months before—and with more pleasure to her then I think in all the time of our marriage before.

November 18, 1668

Lay long in bed, talking with my wife, she being unwilling to have me go abroad, being and declaring herself jealous of my going out, for fear of my going to Deb; which I do deny—for which God forgive me, for I was no sooner out about noon but I did go by coach directly to Somerset House and there inquired among the porters there for Dr. Allbun;[9] and the first I spoke with told me he knew him, and that he was newly gone into Lincoln's Inn fields, but whither he could not tell me, but that one of his fellows, not then in the way, did carry a chest of drawers thither with him, and that when he comes he would ask him. This put me in some hopes; and I to Whitehall and thence to Mr. Povy's, but he at dinner; and therefore I away and walked up and down the Strand between the two turnstiles,[1] hoping to see her out of a window; and then employed a porter, one Osbeston, to find out this doctor's lodgings thereabouts; who by appointment comes to me to Hercules' Pillars, where I dined alone, but tells me that he cannot find out any such but will inquire further. Thence back to Whitehall to the treasury a while, and thence to the Strand; and towards night did meet with the porter that carried the chest of drawers with this doctor, but he would not tell me where he lived, being his good master he told me; but if I would have a message to him, he would deliver it. At last, I told him my business was not with him, but a little gentlewoman, one Mrs. Willet, that is with him; and sent him to see how she did, from her friend in London, and no other token. He goes while I walk in Somerset House walk there in the court; at last he comes back and tells me she is well, and that I may see her if I will—but no more. So I could not be commanded by my reason, but I must go this very night; and so by coach, it being now dark, I to her, close by my tailor's; and there she came into the coach to me, and yo did besar her and tocar her thing, but ella[2] was against it and labored with much earnestness, such as I believed to be real; and yet at last yo did make her tener mi cosa in her mano, while mi mano was sobra her pectus, and so did hazer with grand delight.[3] I did nevertheless give her the best counsel I could, to have a care of her honor and to fear God and suffer no man para haver to do con her—as yo have done—which she promised. Yo did give her 20s and directions para laisser[4] sealed in paper at any time the name of the place of her being, at Herringman's my bookseller in the Change[5]—by which I might go para her. And so bid her good-night, with much content to my mind and resolution to look after her no more till I heard from her. And so home, and there told my wife a fair tale, God knows, how I spent the whole day; with which the poor wretch was satisfied, or at least seemed so; and so to supper and to bed, she having been mighty busy

8. Woman or wife (*mujer* in Spanish).
9. Pepys's wife had told him that Deb was staying with a man named Allbon.
1. To keep traffic, except for pedestrians, out of the street.
2. She. "Besar": kiss. "Tocar": touch.

3. Carry on. "Tener mi cosa in her mano": take my thing in her hand.
4. To leave.
5. The Royal Exchange was a center for shopping, business, and trade.

all day in getting of her house in order against tomorrow, to hang up our new hangings and furnishing our best chamber.

November 19, 1668

Up, and at the office all the morning, with my heart full of joy to think in what a safe condition all my matters now stand between my wife and Deb and me; and at noon, running upstairs to see the upholsters, who are at work upon hanging my best room and setting up my new bed, I find my wife sitting sad in the dining-room; which inquiring into the reason of, she begun to call me all the false, rotten-hearted rogues in the world, letting me understand that I was with Deb yesterday; which, thinking impossible for her ever to understand, I did a while deny; but at last did, for the ease of my mind and ·hers, and for ever to discharge my heart of this wicked business, I did confess all; and above-stairs in our bed-chamber there, I did endure the sorrow of her threats and vows and curses all the afternoon. And which was worst, she swore by all that was good that she would slit the nose of this girl, and be gone herself this very night from me; and did there demand 3 or 400*l* of me to buy my peace, that she might be gone without making any noise, or else protested that she would make all the world know of it. So, with most perfect confusion of face and heart, and sorrow and shame, in the greatest agony in the world, I did pass this afternoon, fearing that it will never have an end; but at last I did call for W. Hewer, who I was forced to make privy now to all; and the poor fellow did cry like a child and obtained what I could not, that she would be pacified, upon condition that I would give it under my hand never to see or speak with Deb while I live, as I did before of Pierce and Knepp; and which I did also, God knows, promise for Deb too, but I have the confidence to deny it, to the perjuring of myself. So before it was late, there was, beyond my hopes as well as desert, a tolerable peace; and so to supper, and pretty kind words, and to bed, and there yo did hazer con ella to her content; and so with some rest spent the night in bed, being most absolutely resolved, if ever I can master this bout, never to give her occasion while I live of more trouble of this or any other kind, there being no curse in the world so great as this of the difference between myself and her; and therefore I do by the grace of God promise never to offend her more, and did this night begin to pray to God upon my knees alone in my chamber; which God knows I cannot yet do heartily, but I hope God will give me the grace more and more every day to fear Him, and to be true to my poor wife. This night the upholsters did finish the hanging of my best chamber, but my sorrow and trouble is so great about this business, that put me out of all joy in looking upon it or minding how it was.[6]

6. Despite his promises, Pepys continued to hanker for Deb, and they had a few brief encounters. Mrs. Pepys accused him of talking to Deb in his dreams, and once threatened him with red-hot tongs. But so far as is known the affair was never consummated.

JOHN BUNYAN
1628–1688

John Bunyan is one of the most remarkable figures in seventeenth-century literature. The son of a poor Bedfordshire tinker (a maker and mender of metal pots), he received only meager schooling and then learned his father's craft. Nothing in the circumstances of his early life could have suggested that he would become a writer known the world over.

Grace Abounding to the Chief of Sinners (1666), his spiritual autobiography, was written to show the way by which a sinner is led by God's grace through the agonies of spiritual crises to a new birth and the assurance of salvation and to record his transformation into an eloquent and fearless Baptist preacher. Preachers, both male and female, often even less educated than Bunyan, were common phenomena among the sects during the Commonwealth. They wished no ordination but the "call," and they could dispense with learning because they abounded in inspiration, inner light, and the gifts conferred by the Holy Spirit. In November 1660, the Anglican Church began to persecute and silence the dissenting sects. Jails filled with unlicensed Nonconformist preachers, and Bunyan was one of the prisoners. Refusing to keep silent, he chose imprisonment and so for twelve years remained in Bedford jail, preaching to his fellow prisoners and writing religious books. Upon his release, he was called to the pastorate of a Nonconformist group in Bedford. It was during a second imprisonment, in 1675, when the Test Act was once again rigorously enforced against Nonconformists, that he wrote his greatest work, *The Pilgrim's Progress from This World to That Which Is to Come* (1678), revised and augmented in the third edition (1679). Bunyan was a prolific writer: part 2 of *The Pilgrim's Progress*, dealing with the journey of Christian's wife and children, appeared in 1684; *The Life and Death of Mr. Badman*, in 1680; *The Holy War*, in 1682. And these major works form only a small part of all his writings.

The Pilgrim's Progress is the most popular allegory in English. Its basic metaphor—life is a journey—is simple and familiar; the objects that the pilgrim Christian meets are homely and commonplace: a quagmire, the highway, the bypaths and shortcuts through pleasant meadows, the inn, the steep hill, the town fair on market day, and the river that must be forded. As in the equally homely parables of Jesus, however, these simple things are charged with spiritual significance. Moreover, this is a tale of adventure. If the road that Christian travels is the King's Highway, it is also a perilous path along which we encounter giants, wild beasts, hobgoblins, and the terrible Apollyon, "the angel of the bottomless pit," with whom Christian must fight. Bunyan keeps the tale firmly based on human experience, and his style, modeled on the prose of the English Bible, together with his concrete language and carefully observed details, enables even the simplest reader to share the experiences of the characters. What could be better than the following sentence? "Some cry out against sin even as the mother cries out against her child in her lap, when she calleth it slut and naughty girl, and then falls to hugging and kissing it." In a secular age, *The Pilgrim's Progress* is no longer a household book, but it survives in the phrases it gave to our language: "the slough of despond," "the house beautiful," "Mr. Worldly-Wiseman," and "Vanity Fair." And it lives again for anyone who reads beyond the first page.

From Grace Abounding to the Chief of Sinners

It would be too long for me here to stay, to tell you in particular how God did set me down in all the things of Christ, and how he did, that he might so do, lead me into his words, yea and also how he did open them unto me, make them shine before me, and cause them to dwell with me and comfort me over and over, both of his own being, and the being of his Son, and Spirit, and Word, and Gospel.

Only this, as I said before I will say unto you again, that in general he was pleased to take this course with me, first, to suffer me to be afflicted with temptation concerning them, and then reveal them to me; as sometimes I should lie under great guilt for sin, even crushed to the ground therewith, and then the Lord would shew me the death of Christ, yea and so sprinkle my Conscience with his Blood, that I should find, and that before I was aware, that in that Conscience where but just now did reign and rage the Law, even there would rest and abide the Peace and Love of God through Christ.

Now had I an evidence, as I thought, of my salvation from Heaven, with many golden Seals thereon, all hanging in my sight; now could I remember this manifestation, and the other discovery of grace with comfort; and should often long and desire that the last day were come, that I might forever be inflamed with the sight, and joy, and communion of him, whose Head was crowned with Thorns, whose Face was spit on, and Body broken, and Soul made an offering for my sins: for whereas before I lay continually trembling at the mouth of Hell; now me thought I was got so far therefrom, that I could not, when I looked back, scarce discern it; and O thought I, that I were fourscore years old now, that I might die quickly, that my soul might be gone to rest.

But before I had got thus far out of these my temptations, I did greatly long to see some ancient Godly man's Experience, who had writ some hundred of years before I was born; for, for those who had writ in our days, I thought (but I desire them now to pardon me) that they had Writ only that which others felt, or else had, through the strength of their Wits and Parts, studied to answer such Objections as they perceived others were perplexed with, without going down themselves into the deep. Well, after many such longings in my mind, the God in whose hands are all our days and ways, did cast into my hand, one day, a book of *Martin Luther,* his comment on the *Galathians,* so old that it was ready to fall piece from piece, if I did but turn it over. Now I was pleased much that such an old book had fallen into my hand; the which, when I had but a little way perused, I found my condition in his experience, so largely and profoundly handled, as if his Book had been written out of my heart; this made me marvel: for thus thought I, this man could not know anything of the state of Christians now, but must needs write and speak of the Experience of former days.

Besides, he doth most gravely also, in that book debate of the rise of these temptations, namely, Blasphemy, Desperation, and the like, shewing that the law of *Moses,* as well as the Devil, Death, and Hell, hath a very great hand therein; the which at first was very strange to me, but considering and watching, I found it so indeed. But of Particulars here I intend nothing, only this methinks I must let fall before all men, I do prefer this book of Mr. *Luther* upon the *Galathians,* (excepting the Holy Bible) before all the books that ever I have seen, as most fit for a wounded Conscience.

* * *

And now I found, as I thought, that I loved Christ dearly. O me thought my soul cleaved unto him, my affections cleaved unto him. I felt love to him as hot as fire, and now, as Job said, I thought I should die in my nest; but I did quickly find that my great love was but little, and that I, who had as I thought such burning love to Jesus Christ, could let him go again for a trifle. God can tell how to abase us, and can hide pride from man. Quickly after this my love was tried to purpose.

For after the Lord had in this manner thus graciously delivered me from this great and sore temptation, and had set me down so sweetly in the faith of his holy gospel, and had given me such strong consolation and blessed evidence from heaven touching my interest in his love through Christ; the Tempter came upon me again, and that with a more grievous and dreadful temptation than before.

And that was to sell and part with this most blessed Christ, to exchange him for the things of this life, for any thing: the temptation lay upon me for the space of a year, and did follow me so continually that I was not rid of it one day in a month, no not sometimes one hour in many days together, unless I was asleep.

And though in my judgment I was persuaded that those who were once effectually in Christ (as I hoped, through his grace, I had seen myself) could never lose him forever . . . yet it was a continual vexation to me to think I should have so much as one such thought within me against a Christ, a Jesus, that had done for me as he had done; and yet then I had almost none others, but such blasphemous ones.

But it was neither my dislike of the thought, nor yet any desire and endeavor to resist it, that in the least did shake or abate the continuation or force and strength thereof; for it did always in almost whatever I thought intermix itself therewith, in such sort that I could neither eat my food, stoop for a pin, chop a stick, or cast mine eye to look on this or that, but still the temptation would come, *Sell Christ for this, or sell Christ for that; sell him, sell him.*

Sometimes it would run in my thoughts not so little as a hundred times together, Sell him, sell him, sell him; against which, I may say, for whole hours together, I have been forced to stand as continually leaning and forcing my spirit against it, lest haply before I were aware, some wicked thought might arise in my heart that might consent thereto; and sometimes also the Tempter would make me believe I had consented to it, then should I be as tortured on a rack for whole days together.

This temptation did put me to such scares lest I should sometimes, I say, consent thereto and be overcome therewith, that by the very force of my mind in laboring to gainsay and resist this wickedness, my very body also would be put into action or motion, by way of pushing or thrusting with my hands or elbows; still answering, as fast as the destroyer said *Sell him:* I will not, I will not, I will not, I will not, no, not for thousands, thousands, thousands of worlds, thus reckoning lest I should in the midst of these assaults set too low a value of him, even until I scarce well knew where I was, or how to be composed again.

At these seasons he would not let me eat my food at quiet, but forsooth when I was set at the table at my meat, I must go hence to pray, I must leave my food now, just now, so counterfeit holy would this Devil be. When I was thus tempted, I should say in myself, *Now I am at my meat, let me make an end. No,* said he, *you must do it now, or you will displease God and despise*

Christ. Wherefore I was much afflicted with these things; and because of the sinfulness of my nature (imagining that these things were impulses from God), I should deny to do it as if I denied God; and then should I be as guilty because I did not obey a temptation of the Devil, as if I had broken the law of God indeed.

But to be brief, one morning, as I did lie in my bed, I was, as at other times, most fiercely assaulted with this temptation, to *sell and part with Christ;* the wicked suggestion still running in my mind, *Sell him, sell him, sell him,* as fast as a man could speak; against which also in my mind, as at other times, I answered, No, no, not for thousands, thousands, thousands, at least twenty times together; but at last, after much striving, even until I was almost out of breath, I felt this thought pass through my heart, *Let him go if he will!* and I thought also that I felt my heart freely consent thereto. Oh, the diligence of Satan! Oh, the desperateness of man's heart!

Now was the battle won, and down I fell, as a bird that is shot from the top of a tree, into great guilt and fearful despair; thus getting out of my bed, I went moping into the field; but God knows with as heavy a heart as mortal man, I think, could bear; where for the space of two hours, I was like a man bereft of life, and as now past all recovery, and bound over to eternal punishment.

* * *

Now was I as one bound, I felt myself shut up unto the judgment to come; nothing now for two years together would abide with me but damnation and an expectation of damnation: I say nothing now would abide with me but this, save some few moments for relief, as in the sequel you will see.

These words were to my soul like fetters of brass to my legs, in the continual sound of which I went for several months together. But about ten or eleven a clock one day, as I was walking under a hedge, full of sorrow and guilt, God knows, and bemoaning myself for this hard hap, that such a thought should arise within me, suddenly this sentence bolted in upon me, *The blood of Christ remits all guilt;* at this I made a stand in my spirit: with that, this word took hold upon me, *The blood of Jesus Christ his son cleanseth us from all sin.*

Now I began to conceive peace in my soul, and methought I saw as if the tempter did leer and steal away from me, as being ashamed of what he had done. At the same time also I had my sin and the blood of Christ thus represented to me, That my sin when compared to the blood of Christ was no more to it than this little clot or stone before me is to this vast and wide field that here I see. This gave me good encouragement for the space of two or three hours, in which time also methought I saw by faith the son of God as suffering for my sins. But because it tarried not, I therefore sunk in my spirit under exceeding guilt again.

* * *

And now I was both a burden and a terror to myself, nor did I ever so know, as now, what it was to be weary of my life and yet afraid to die. Oh, how gladly now would I have been anybody but myself! Anything but a man! and in any condition but mine own! for there was nothing did pass more frequently over my mind, than that it was impossible for me to be forgiven my transgression, and to be saved from the wrath to come.

* * *

Once as I was walking to and fro in a good man's shop, bemoaning to myself in my sad and doleful state, afflicting myself with self-abhorrence for this wicked and ungodly thought, lamenting also for this hard hap of mine, for that I should commit so great a sin, greatly fearing I should not be pardoned; praying also in my heart, That if this sin of mine did differ from that against the Holy Ghost, the Lord would show it to me: and being now ready to sink with fear, suddenly there was as if there had rushed in at the window the noise of wind upon me, but very pleasant, and as if I had heard a voice speaking, *Didst ever refuse to be justified by the blood of Christ?* and withal my whole life of profession[1] past was in a moment opened to me, wherein I was made to see that designedly I had not; so my heart answered groaningly, *No.* Then fell with power that word of God upon me, *See that ye refuse not him that speaketh* (Hebrews 12.25). This made a strange seizure upon my spirit; it brought light with it, and commanded a silence in my heart of all those tumultuous thoughts that before did use, like masterless hellhounds to roar and bellow and make a hideous noise within me. It showed me also that Jesus Christ had yet a work of grace and mercy for me, that he had not, as I had feared, quite forsaken and cast off my soul; yea, this was a kind of chide for my proneness to desperation; a kind of threatening me if I did not, notwithstanding my sins and the heinousness of them, venture my salvation upon the son of God. . . . This lasted in the savor of it, for about three or four days, and then I began to mistrust and to despair again.

* * *

At another time I remember I was again much under the question, Whether the blood of Christ was sufficient to save my soul? In which doubt I continued from morning till about seven or eight at night; and at last when I was, as it were, quite worn out with fear lest it should not lay hold on me, these words did sound suddenly within me, *He is able:* but me thought this word *able* was spoke so loud unto me, it showed such a *great* word, it seemed to be writ in *great* letters, and gave such a justle to my fear and doubt (I mean for the time it tarried with me, which was about a day) as I never had from that, all my life either before or after that.

But one morning when I was again at prayer and trembling under the fear of this, that no word of God could help me, that piece of a sentence darted in upon me, *My grace is sufficient.* At this me thought I felt some stay, as if there might be hopes. But O how good a thing is it for God to send his word! for about a fortnight before, I was looking on this very place, and then I thought it could not come near my soul with comfort, and threw down my book in a pet. Then I thought it was not large enough for me; no, not large enough; but now it was as if it had arms of grace so wide that it could not only enclose me, but many more besides.

By these words I was sustained, yet not without exceeding conflicts, for the space of seven or eight weeks: for my peace would be in and out some-

---

1. My life as a believing (professing) Christian.

times twenty times a day. Comfort now and trouble presently; peace now, and before I could go a furlong, as full of fear and guilt as ever heart could hold. And this was not only now and then, but my whole seven weeks' experience; for this about the sufficiency of grace and that of Esau's parting with his birthright[2] would be like a pair of scales within my mind, sometimes one end would be uppermost and sometimes again the other, according to which would be my peace or trouble.

1666

From The Pilgrim's Progress

From this World to That Which Is to Come:
Delivered under the Similitude of a Dream

[CHRISTIAN SETS OUT FOR THE CELESTIAL CITY]

As I walked through the wilderness of this world, I lighted on a certain place where was a Den, and I laid me down in that place to sleep; and, as I slept, I dreamed a dream. I dreamed, and behold I saw a man clothed with rags, standing in a certain place, with his face from his own house, a book in his hand, and a great burden upon his back (Isaiah lxiv.6; Luke xiv.33; Psalms xxxviii.4; Habakkuk ii.2; Acts xvi.31). I looked and saw him open the book and read therein; and, as he read, he wept, and trembled; and not being able longer to contain, he brake out with a lamentable cry, saying, "What shall I do?" (Acts ii.37).

In this plight, therefore, he went home and refrained himself as long as he could, that his wife and children should not perceive his distress; but he could not be silent long, because that his trouble increased. Wherefore at length he brake his mind to his wife and children; and thus he began to talk to them. O my dear wife, said he, and you the children of my bowels, I your dear friend am in myself undone by reason of a burden that lieth hard upon me; moreover, I am for certain informed that this our city will be burned with fire from heaven, in which fearful overthrow both myself, with thee, my wife, and you, my sweet babes, shall miserably come to ruin, except (the which yet I see not) some way of escape can be found, whereby we may be delivered. At this his relations were sore amazed; not for that they believed that what he had said to them was true, but because they thought that some frenzy distemper[1] had got into his head; therefore, it drawing towards night, and they hoping that sleep might settle his brains, with all haste they got him to bed; but the night was as troublesome to him as the day; wherefore, instead of sleeping, he spent it in sighs and tears. So when the morning was come, they would know how he did. He told them, Worse and worse; he also set to talking to them again, but they began to be hardened. They also thought to drive away his distemper by harsh and surly carriages[2] to him: sometimes they would deride, sometimes they would chide, and sometimes

2. Bunyan believed that when the fatal phrase about "letting Christ go if he would" flashed through his mind, all power to share in the Christian blessing was eternally lost to him, as Esau sold his birthright irrevocably, irretrievably, forever.

1. A malady causing madness. The use of *frenzy* as an adjective was not uncommon in the 17th century.
2. Behavior.

they would quite neglect him. Wherefore he began to retire himself to his chamber, to pray for and pity them, and also to condole his own misery; he would also walk solitarily in the fields, sometimes reading, and sometimes praying; and thus for some days he spent his time.

Now I saw, upon a time, when he was walking in the fields, that he was (as he was wont) reading in this book, and greatly distressed in his mind; and as he read, he burst out, as he had done before, crying, "What shall I do to be saved?"

I saw also that he looked this way and that way, as if he would run; yet he stood still, because (as I perceived) he could not tell which way to go. I looked then, and saw a man named Evangelist[3] coming to him, who asked, Wherefore dost thou cry? (Job xxxiii.23). He answered, Sir, I perceive by the book in my hand that I am condemned to die, and after that to come to judgment (Hebrews ix.27), and I find that I am not willing to do the first (Job xvi.21), nor able to do the second (Ezekiel xxii.14). . . .

Then said Evangelist, Why not willing to die, since this life is attended with so many evils? The man answered, Because I fear that this burden that is upon my back will sink me lower than the grave, and I shall fall into Tophet[4] (Isaiah xxx.33). And, sir, if I be not fit to go to prison, I am not fit to go to judgment, and from thence to execution; and the thoughts of these things make me cry.[5]

Then said Evangelist, If this be thy condition, why standest thou still? He answered, Because I know not whither to go. Then he gave him a parchment roll, and there was written within, "Fly from the wrath to come" (Matthew iii.7).

The man therefore read it, and looking upon Evangelist very carefully,[6] said, Whither must I fly? Then said Evangelist, pointing with his finger over a very wide field, Do you see yonder wicketgate?[7] (Matthew vii.13, 14.) The man said, No. Then said the other, Do you see yonder shining light? (Psalms cxix.105; II Peter i.19.) He said, I think I do. Then said Evangelist, Keep that light in your eye, and go up directly thereto; so shalt thou see the gate; at which when thou knockest it shall be told thee what thou shalt do.

So I saw in my dream that the man began to run. Now, he had not run far from his own door, but his wife and children perceiving it, began to cry after him to return; but the man put his fingers in his ears, and ran on, crying, Life! life! eternal life! (Luke xiv.26.) So he looked not behind him, but fled towards the middle of the plain (Genesis xix.17).

The neighbors also came out to see him run (Jeremiah xx.10); and as he ran some mocked, others threatened, and some cried after him to return; and, among those that did so, there were two that resolved to fetch him back by force. The name of the one was Obstinate, and the name of the other Pliable. Now by this time the man was got a good distance from them; but, however, they were resolved to pursue him, which they did, and in a little time they overtook him. Then said the man, Neighbors, wherefore are ye come? They said, To persuade you to go back with us. But he said, That can by no means be; you dwell, said he, in the City of Destruction (the place also

---

3. A preacher of the Gospel; literally, a bearer of good news.
4. The place near Jerusalem where bodies and filth were burned; hence, by association, a name

for hell.
5. Cry out.
6. Sorrowfully.
7. A small gate in or beside a larger gate.

where I was born) I see it to be so; and, dying there, sooner or later, you will sink lower than the grave, into a place that burns with fire and brimstone; be content, good neighbors, and go along with me.

OBST. What! said Obstinate, and leave our friends and our comforts behind us?

CHR. Yes, said Christian (for that was his name), because that ALL which you shall forsake is not worthy to be compared with a little of that which I am seeking to enjoy (II Corinthians v.17); and, if you will go along with me, and hold it, you shall fare as I myself; for there, where I go, is enough and to spare (Luke xv.17). Come away, and prove my words.

OBST. What are the things you seek, since you leave all the world to find them?

CHR. I seek an inheritance incorruptible, undefiled, and that fadeth not away (I Peter i.4), and it is laid up in heaven, and safe there (Hebrews xi.16), to be bestowed, at the time appointed, on them that diligently seek it. Read it so, if you will, in my book.

OBST. Tush! said Obstinate, away with your book; will you go back with us or no?

CHR. No, not I, said the other, because I have laid my hand to the plow (Luke ix.62).

OBST. Come, then, neighbor Pliable, let us turn again, and go home without him; there is a company of these crazed-headed coxcombs, that, when they take a fancy[8] by the end, are wiser in their own eyes than seven men that can render a reason (Proverbs xxvi.16).

PLI. Then said Pliable, Don't revile; if what the good Christian says is true, the things he looks after are better than ours; my heart inclines to go with my neighbor.

OBST. What! more fools still? Be ruled by me, go back; who knows whither such a brain-sick fellow will lead you? Go back, go back, and be wise.

CHR. Nay, but do thou come with thy neighbor, Pliable; there are such things to be had which I spoke of, and many more glories besides. If you believe not me, read here in this book; and for the truth of what is expressed therein, behold, all is confirmed by the blood of Him that made it (Hebrews ix.17–22; xiii.20).

PLI. Well, neighbor Obstinate, said Pliable, I begin to come to a point,[9] I intend to go along with this good man, and to cast in my lot with him: but, my good companion, do you know the way to this desired place?

CHR. I am directed by a man, whose name is Evangelist, to speed me to a little gate that is before us, where we shall receive instructions about the way.

PLI. Come, then, good neighbor, let us be going. Then they went both together. * * *

[THE SLOUGH OF DESPOND]

Now I saw in my dream, that just as they had ended this talk they drew near to a very miry slough,[1] that was in the midst of the plain; and they,

---

8. Delusion. "Coxcombs": fools.
9. Decision.

1. Pronounce to rhyme with *now*.

being heedless, did both fall suddenly into the bog. The name of the slough was Despond. Here, therefore, they wallowed for a time, being grievously bedaubed with dirt; and Christian, because of the burden that was on his back, began to sink in the mire.

PLI. Then said Pliable, Ah, neighbor Christian, where are you now?

CHR. Truly, said Christian, I do not know.

PLI. At that Pliable began to be offended, and angrily said to his fellow, Is this the happiness you have told me all this while of? If we have such ill speed at our first setting out, what may we expect 'twixt this and our journey's end? May I get out again with my life, you shall possess the brave country alone for me. And, with that, he gave a desperate struggle or two, and got out of the mire on that side of the slough which was next[2] to his own house: so away he went, and Christian saw him no more.

Wherefore Christian was left to tumble in the Slough of Despond alone: but still he endeavored to struggle to that side of the slough that was further from his own house, and next to the wicket-gate; the which he did, but could not get out, because of the burden that was upon his back: but I beheld in my dream, that a man came to him, whose name was Help, and asked him what he did there?

CHR. Sir, said Christian, I was bid go this way by a man called Evangelist, who directed me also to yonder gate, that I might escape the wrath to come; and as I was going thither I fell in here.

HELP. But why did not you look for the steps?

CHR. Fear followed me so hard that I fled the next way, and fell in.

HELP. Then said he, Give me thy hand; so he gave him his hand, and he drew him out, and set him upon sound ground, and bid him go on his way.

Then I stepped to him that plucked him out, and said, Sir, wherefore, since over this place is the way from the City of Destruction to yonder gate, is it that this plat[3] is not mended, that poor travelers might go thither with more security? And he said unto me, This miry slough is such a place as cannot be mended; it is the descent whither the scum and filth that attends conviction for sin doth continually run, and therefore it was called the Slough of Despond; for still, as the sinner is awakened about his lost condition, there ariseth in his soul many fears, and doubts, and discouraging apprehensions, which all of them get together, and settle in his place. And this is the reason of the badness of this ground. * * *

[VANITY FAIR][4]

Then I saw in my dream, that when they were got out of the wilderness, they presently saw a town before them, and the name of that town is Vanity; and at the town there is a fair kept, called Vanity Fair; it is kept all the year

---

2. Nearest.
3. A plot of ground.
4. In this, perhaps the best-known episode in the book, Bunyan characteristically turns one of the most familiar institutions in contemporary England—annual fairs—into an allegory of universal spiritual significance. Christian and his companion Faithful pass through the town of Vanity at the season of the local fair. *Vanity* means "emptiness" or "worthlessness," and hence the fair is an allegory of worldliness and the corruption of the religious life through the attractions of the world. From earliest times numerous fairs were held for stated periods throughout Britain; to them the most important merchants from all over Europe brought their wares. The serious business of buying and selling was accompanied by all sorts of diversions—eating, drinking, and other fleshly pleasures, as well as spectacles of strange animals, acrobats, and other wonders.

long; it beareth the name of Vanity Fair because the town where it is kept is lighter than vanity; and also because all that is there sold, or that cometh thither, is vanity. As is the saying of the wise. "All that cometh is vanity" (Ecclesiastes i.2, 14; ii.11, 17; xi.8; Isaiah xl.17).

This fair is no new-erected business, but a thing of ancient standing; I will show you the original of it.

Almost five thousand years agone, there were pilgrims walking to the Celestial City, as these two honest persons are; and Beelzebub, Apollyon, and Legion,[5] with their companions, perceiving by the path that the pilgrims made, that their way to the city lay through this town of Vanity, they contrived here to set up a fair; a fair wherein should be sold all sorts of vanity, and that it should last all the year long. Therefore at this fair are all such merchandise sold, as houses, lands, trades, places, honors, preferments,[6] titles, countries, kingdoms, lusts, pleasures, and delights of all sorts, as whores, bawds, wives, husbands, children, masters, servants, lives, blood, bodies, souls, silver, gold, pearls, precious stones, and what not.

And, moreover, at this fair there is at all times to be seen jugglings, cheats, games, plays, fools, apes, knaves, and rogues, and that of every kind.

Here are to be seen, too, and that for nothing, thefts, murders, adulteries, false swearers, and that of a blood-red color.

And as in other fairs of less moment, there are the several rows and streets, under their proper names, where such and such wares are vended; so here likewise you have the proper places, rows, streets (viz., countries and kingdoms), where the wares of this fair are soonest to be found. Here is the Britain Row, the French Row, the Italian Row, the Spanish Row, the German Row, where several sorts of vanities are to be sold. But, as in other fairs, some one commodity is as the chief of all the fair, so the ware of Rome and her merchandise[7] is greatly promoted in this fair; only our English nation, with some others, have taken a dislike thereat.

Now, as I said, the way to the Celestial City lies just through this town where this lusty[8] fair is kept; and he that will go to the City, and yet not go through this town, must needs "go out of the world" (I Corinthians v.10). The Prince of princes himself, when here, went through this town to his own country, and that upon a fair-day too,[9] yea, and as I think, it was Beelzebub, the chief lord of this fair, that invited him to buy of his vanities; yea, would have made him lord of the fair, would he but have done him reverence as he went through the town. (Matthew iv.8; Luke iv.5–7.) Yea, because he was such a person of honor, Beelzebub had him from street to street, and showed him all the kingdoms of the world in a little time, that he might, if possible, allure the Blessed One to cheapen[1] and buy some of his vanities; but he had no mind to the merchandise, and therefore left the town, without laying out so much as one farthing upon these vanities. This fair, therefore, is an ancient thing, of long standing, and a very great fair.

Now these pilgrims, as I said, must needs go through this fair. Well, so they did; but, behold, even as they entered into the fair, all the people in the

---

5. The "unclean spirit" sent by Jesus into the Gadarene swine (Mark 5.9). Beelzebub, prince of the devils (Matthew 12.24). Apollyon, the destroyer, "the Angel of the bottomless pit" (Revelation 9.11).
6. Appointments and promotions to political or ecclesiastical positions.

7. The usages and the temporal power of the Roman Catholic Church.
8. Merry.
9. The temptation of Jesus in the wilderness (Matthew 4.1–11).
1. Ask the price of.

fair were moved, and the town itself as it were in a hubbub about them; and that for several reasons: for

First, The pilgrims were clothed with such kind of raiment as was diverse from the raiment of any that traded in that fair. The people, therefore, of the fair, made a great gazing upon them: some said they were fools, some they were bedlams, and some they are outlandish[2] men. (I Corinthians ii.7, 8.)

Secondly, And as they wondered at their apparel, so they did likewise at their speech; for few could understand what they said; they naturally spoke the language of Canaan,[3] but they that kept the fair were the men of this world; so that, from one end of the fair to the other, they seemed barbarians[4] each to the other.

Thirdly, But that which did not a little amuse the merchandisers was that these pilgrims set very light by all their wares; they cared not so much as to look upon them; and if they called upon them to buy, they would put their fingers in their ears, and cry, "Turn away mine eyes from beholding vanity," and look upwards, signifying that their trade and traffic was in heaven. (Psalms cxix.37; Philippians iii.19, 20.)

One chanced mockingly, beholding the carriages of the men, to say unto them, What will ye buy? But they, looking gravely upon him, said, "We buy the truth" (Proverbs xxiii.23). At that there was an occasion taken to despise the men the more; some mocking, some taunting, some speaking reproachfully, and some calling upon others to smite them. At last things came to an hubbub and great stir in the fair, insomuch that all order was confounded. Now was word presently brought to the great one of the fair, who quickly came down, and deputed some of his most trusty friends to take these men into examination, about whom the fair was almost overturned. So the men were brought to examination; and they that sat upon them[5] asked them whence they came, whither they went, and what they did there, in such an unusual garb? The men told them that they were pilgrims and strangers in the world, and that they were going to their own country, which was the Heavenly Jerusalem (Hebrews xi.13–16); and that they had given no occasion to the men of the town, nor yet to the merchandisers, thus to abuse them, and to let[6] them in their journey, except it was for that, when one asked them what they would buy, they said they would buy the truth. But they that were appointed to examine them did not believe them to be any other than bedlams and mad, or else such as came to put all things into a confusion in the fair. Therefore they took them and beat them, and besmeared them with dirt, and then put them into the cage, that they might be made a spectacle to all the men of the fair. * * *

---

2. Foreign. "Bedlams": lunatics from Bethlehem Hospital, the insane asylum in London.
3. The Promised Land, ultimately conquered by the Children of Israel (Joshua 4) and settled by them; hence the pilgrims speak the language of the Bible and of the true religion. Dissenters were notorious for their habitual use of biblical language.
4. The Greeks and Romans so designated all those who spoke a foreign tongue.
5. Interrogated and tried them.
6. Hinder.

[THE RIVER OF DEATH AND THE CELESTIAL CITY]

So I saw that when they[7] awoke, they addressed themselves to go up to the City; but, as I said, the reflection of the sun upon the City (for the City was pure gold, Revelation xxi.18) was so extremely glorious, that they could not, as yet, with open face behold it, but through an instrument made for that purpose. (II Corinthians iii.18.) So I saw that as I went on, there met them two men, in raiment that shone like gold; also their faces shone as the light.

These men asked the pilgrims whence they came; and they told them. They also asked them where they had lodged, what difficulties and dangers, what comforts and pleasures they had met in the way; and they told them. Then said the men that met them, You have but two difficulties more to meet with, and then you are in the City.

Christian then and his companion asked the men to go along with them; so they told them they would. But, said they, you must obtain it by your own faith. So I saw in my dream that they went on together till they came in sight of the gate.

Now I further saw that betwixt them and the gate was a river, but there was no bridge to go over; the river was very deep. At the sight, therefore, of this river, the pilgrims were much stunned;[8] but the men that went with them said, You must go through, or you cannot come at the gate.

The pilgrims then began to inquire if there was no other way to the gate; to which they answered, Yes; but there hath not any, save two, to wit, Enoch and Elijah,[9] been permitted to tread that path, since the foundation of the world, nor shall, until the last trumpet shall sound. (I Corinthians xv.51, 52.) The pilgrims then, especially Christian, began to despond in his mind, and looked this way and that, but no way could be found by them by which they might escape the river. Then they asked the men if the waters were all of a depth. They said no; yet they could not help them in that case; for, said they, you shall find it deeper or shallower, as you believe in the King of the place.

They then addressed themselves to the water; and entering, Christian began to sink, and crying out to his good friend Hopeful, he said, I sink in deep waters; the billows go over my head, all his waves go over me! Selah.[1]

Then said the other, Be of good cheer, my brother, I feel the bottom, and it is good. Then said Christian, Ah, my friend, the sorrows of death have compassed me about; I shall not see the land that flows with milk and honey. And with that a great darkness and horror fell upon Christian, so that he could not see before him. Also here he in great measure lost his senses, so that he could neither remember nor orderly talk of any of those sweet refreshments that he had met with in the way of his pilgrimage. But all the words that he spake still tended to discover that he had horror of mind, and heart-fears that he should die in that river, and never obtain entrance in at the gate. Here also, as they that stood by perceived, he was much in the troublesome thoughts of the sins that he had committed, both since and before

7. Christian and his companion, Hopeful. Ignorance, who appears tragically in the final paragraph, had tried to accompany the two pilgrims, but had dropped behind because of his hobbling gait.
8. Amazed.

9. Both were "translated" alive to heaven (Genesis 5.24, Hebrews 11.5, 2 Kings 2.11–12).
1. A word of uncertain meaning that occurs frequently at the end of a verse in the Psalms. Bunyan may have supposed it to signify the end.

he began to be a pilgrim. 'Twas also observed that he was troubled with apparitions of hobgoblins and evil spirits; for ever and anon he would intimate so much by words. Hopeful, therefore, here had much ado to keep his brother's head above water; yea, sometimes he would be quite gone down, and then, ere a while, he would rise up again half dead. Hopeful also would endeavor to comfort him, saying, Brother, I see the gate and men standing by to receive us; but Christian would answer, 'Tis you, 'tis you they wait for; you have been Hopeful ever since I knew you. And so have you, said he to Christian. Ah, brother, said he, surely if I was right he would now arise to help me; but for my sins he hath brought me into the snare, and hath left me. Then said Hopeful, My brother, you have quite forgot the text, where it is said of the wicked, "There are no bands in their death, but their strength is firm. They are not in trouble as other men, neither are they plagued like other men" (Psalms lxxiii.4, 5). These troubles and distresses that you go through in these waters are no sign that God hath forsaken you, but are sent to try you, whether you will call to mind that which heretofore you have received of his goodness, and live upon him in your distresses.

Then I saw in my dream that Christian was as in a muse[2] a while, to whom also Hopeful added this word, Be of good cheer. Jesus Christ maketh thee whole. And with that Christian brake out with a loud voice, Oh, I see him again! and he tells me, "When thou passest through the waters, I will be with thee; and through the rivers, they shall not overflow thee" (Isaiah xliii.2). Then they both took courage, and the Enemy was after that as still as a stone, until they were gone over. Christian therefore presently found ground to stand upon, and so it followed that the rest of the river was but shallow. Thus they got over. Now, upon the bank of the river on the other side, they saw the two Shining Men again, who there waited for them. Wherefore, being come out of the river, they saluted them saying, We are ministering spirits, sent forth to minister for those that shall be heirs of salvation. Thus they went along towards the gate. * * *

Now when they were come up to the gate, there was written over it in letters of gold, "Blessed are they that do his commandments, that they may have right to the tree of life, and may enter in through the gates into the city" (Revelation xxii.14).

Then I saw in my dream, that the Shining Men bid them call at the gate; the which, when they did, some from above looked over the gate, to wit, Enoch, Moses, and Elijah, etc., to whom it was said, These pilgrims are come from the City of Destruction, for the love that they bear to the King of this place; and then the pilgrims gave in unto them each man his certificate, which they had received in the beginning; those, therefore, were carried in to the King, who, when he had read them, said, Where are the men? To whom it was answered, They are standing without the gate. The King then commanded to open the gate, "That the righteous nation," said he, "which keepeth the truth, may enter in" (Isaiah xxvi.2).

Now I saw in my dream that these two men went in at the gate; and lo, as they entered, they were transfigured, and they had raiment put on that shone like gold. There was also that met them with harps and crowns, and gave them to them: the harps to praise withal, and the crowns in token of honor. Then I heard in my dream that all the bells in the city rang again for joy, and

2. A deep meditation.

that it was said unto them, "ENTER YE INTO THE JOY OF OUR LORD" (Matthew xxv.21). I also heard the men themselves, that they sang with a loud voice, saying, "BLESSING AND HONOR, GLORY AND POWER, BE TO HIM THAT SITTETH UPON THE THRONE, AND TO THE LAMB FOREVER AND EVER" (Revelation v.13).

Now just as the gates were opened to let in the men, I looked in after them, and, behold, the City shone like the sun; the streets also were paved with gold, and in them walked many men, with crowns on their heads, palms in their hands, and golden harps to sing praises withal.

There were also of them that had wings, and they answered one another without intermission, saying, "Holy, holy, holy is the Lord" (Revelation iv.8). And after that they shut up the gates, which when I had seen I wished myself among them.

Now while I was gazing upon all these things, I turned my head to look back, and saw Ignorance come up to the riverside; but he soon got over, and that without half that difficulty which the other two men met with. For it happened that there was then in that place one Vain-hope, a ferryman, that with his boat helped him over; so he, as the other, I saw, did ascend the hill to come up to the gate, only he came alone; neither did any man meet him with the least encouragement. When he was come up to the gate, he looked up to the writing that was above, and then began to knock, supposing that entrance should have been quickly administered to him; but he was asked by the men that looked over the top of the gate, Whence came you? and what would you have? He answered, I have eat and drank in the presence of the King, and he has taught in our streets. Then they asked him for his certificate, that they might go in and show it to the King; so he fumbled in his bosom for one, and found none. Then said they, Have you none? But the man answered never a word. So they told the King, but he would not come down to see him, but commanded the two Shining Ones that conducted Christian and Hopeful to the City, to go out and take Ignorance, and bind him hand and foot, and have him away. Then they took him up, and carried him through the air, to the door that I saw in the side of the hill, and put him in there. Then I saw that there was a way to hell, even from the gates of heaven, as well as from the City of Destruction. So I awoke, and behold it was a dream.

1678

JOHN LOCKE
1632–1704

John Locke's *Essay Concerning Human Understanding* (1690) is "a history-book," according to Laurence Sterne, "of what passes in a man's own mind." Like Montaigne's essays, it aims to explore the human mind in general by closely watching one particular mind. When Locke analyzed his ideas, the ways they were acquired and put together, he found they were clear when they were based on direct experience and adequate when they were clear. Usually, it appeared, problems occurred when basic ideas were blurred or confused or did not refer to anything determinate. Thus a critical analysis of the ideas in an individual mind could lead straight to a rule about adequate ideas in general and the sort of subject where adequate ideas were possible. On the basis of such a limitation, individuals might reach rational agreement with one another and so set up an area of natural law, within which a common rule of understanding was available.

The clergy were naturally upset over Locke's new "way of ideas," which invited people to discard from their minds any ideas that they could not reduce to clear, distinct—that is, determinate—form. "Mysteries of faith" were essential to the mental economy of churchmen. How could the Trinity or the doctrine of predestination be reduced to clear, distinct ideas? If they couldn't, must one then discard them? On this last point, Locke was polite but very firm. Yes, if one wanted to discourse reasonably and understandably, one really must discard any idea that could not be given a determinate shape and meaning. The philosopher had evidently performed this operation on any unclear and indistinct ideas he found in his own mind. What was left of Christianity when one got rid of all its "unreasonable" elements was a cool, general, undemanding creed, which did not commit one to much more than a belief in the existence of God, and was, therefore, known as "Deism." Locke did not like labels, but he was a kind of Deist. Though a scandalous idea in the late seventeenth century, Deism was a quite respectable creed by the time of Pope.

Locke spent his life in thought. His background and connections were all with the Puritan movement, but he was disillusioned early with the enthusiastic moods and persecutions to which he found the Puritans prone. Having a small but steady private income, he became a student, chiefly at Oxford, learning enough medicine to act as a physician, holding an occasional appointive office, but never allowing any of these activities to limit his controlling passion: the urge to think. After 1667, he was personal physician and tutor in the household of a violent, crafty politician, the first earl of Shaftesbury (Dryden's "Achitophel"). But Locke himself was always a grave, dispassionate man. On one occasion, Shaftesbury's political enemies at Oxford had Locke watched for several years on end, during which he was not heard to say one word either critical of the government or favorable to it. When times are turbulent, so much discretion is suspicious in itself, and Locke found it convenient to go abroad for several years during the 1680s. He lived quietly in Holland and pursued his thoughts. The Glorious Revolution of 1688–89 and the accession of William III brought him back to England and made possible the publication of the *Essay*, on which he had been working for many years. Its publication foreshadowed the coming age, not only in the positive ideas that the book advanced but in the quiet way it set aside as insoluble a range of problems about absolute authority and absolute assurance to which the seventeenth century had prodigally sacrificed its best resources of mind and heart.

From An Essay Concerning Human Understanding

From *The Epistle to the Reader*

Reader,

I here put into thy hands what has been the diversion of some of my idle and heavy hours; if it has the good luck to prove so of any of thine, and thou hast but half so much pleasure in reading as I had in writing it, thou wilt as little think thy money, as I do my pains, ill-bestowed. Mistake not this for a commendation of my work; nor conclude, because I was pleased with the doing of it, that therefore I am fondly taken with it now it is done. He that hawks at larks and sparrows, has no less sport, though a much less considerable quarry, than he that flies at nobler game: and he is little acquainted with the subject of this treatise, the Understanding, who does not know, that as it is the most elevated faculty of the soul, so it is employed with a greater and more constant delight than any of the other. Its searches after truth are a sort of hawking and hunting, wherein the very pursuit makes a great part of the pleasure. Every step the mind takes in its progress towards knowledge makes some discovery, which is not only new, but the best, too, for the time at least.

For the understanding, like the eye, judging of objects only by its own sight, cannot but be pleased with what it discovers, having less regret for what has escaped it, because it is unknown. Thus he who has raised himself above the alms-basket, and, not content to live lazily on scraps of begged opinions, sets his own thoughts on work to find and follow truth, will (whatever he lights on) not miss the hunter's satisfaction; every moment of his pursuit will reward his pains with some delight, and he will have reason to think his time not ill-spent, even when he cannot much boast of any great acquisition.

This, reader, is the entertainment of those who let loose their own thoughts, and follow them in writing; which thou oughtest not to envy them, since they afford thee an opportunity of the like diversion, if thou wilt make use of thy own thoughts in reading. It is to them, if they are thy own, that I refer myself; but if they are taken upon trust from others, it is no great matter what they are, they not following truth, but some meaner consideration; and it is not worthwhile to be concerned what he says or thinks, who says or thinks only as he is directed by another. If thou judgest for thyself, I know thou wilt judge candidly; and then I shall not be harmed or offended, whatever be thy censure. For, though it be certain that there is nothing in this treatise of the truth whereof I am not fully persuaded, yet I consider myself as liable to mistakes as I can think thee; and know that this book must stand or fall with thee, not by any opinion I have of it, but thy own. If thou findest little in it new or instructive to thee, thou art not to blame me for it. It was not meant for those that had already mastered this subject, and made a thorough acquaintance with their own understandings, but for my own information, and the satisfaction of a few friends, who acknowledged themselves not to have sufficiently considered it. Were it fit to trouble thee with the history of this Essay, I should tell thee, that five or six friends, meeting at my chamber, and discoursing on a subject very remote from this, found themselves quickly at a stand by the difficulties that rose on every side. After we had awhile puzzled ourselves, without coming any nearer a resolution of those doubts which perplexed us, it came into my thoughts, that we took a wrong course; and that, before we set ourselves upon inquiries of that nature, it was necessary to examine our own abilities, and see what objects our understandings were or were not fitted to deal with. This I proposed to the company, who all readily assented; and thereupon it was agreed, that this should be our first inquiry. Some hasty and undigested thoughts, on a subject I had never before considered, which I set down against[1] our next meeting, gave the first entrance into this discourse, which, having been thus begun by chance, was continued by entreaty; written by incoherent parcels; and, after long intervals of neglect, resumed again, as my humor or occasions

---

1. Before.

permitted; and at last, in a retirement, where an attendance on my health gave me leisure, it was brought into that order thou now seest it.

This discontinued way of writing may have occasioned, besides others, two contrary faults; viz., that too little and too much may be said in it. If thou findest anything wanting, I shall be glad that what I have writ gives thee any desire that I should have gone farther: if it seems too much to thee, thou must blame the subject; for when I first put pen to paper, I thought all I should have to say on this matter would have been contained in one sheet of paper; but the farther I went, the larger prospect I had: new discoveries led me still on, and so it grew insensibly to the bulk it now appears in. I will not deny but possibly it might be reduced to a narrower compass than it is; and that some parts of it might be contracted; the way it has been writ in, by catches,[2] and many long intervals of interruption, being apt to cause some repetitions. But, to confess the truth, I am now too lazy or too busy to make it shorter.

* * * I pretend not to publish this Essay for the information of men of large thoughts and quick apprehensions; to such masters of knowledge, I profess myself a scholar, and therefore warn them beforehand not to expect anything here but what, being spun out of my own coarse thoughts,[3] is fitted to men of my own size, to whom, perhaps, it will not be unacceptable that I have taken some pains to make plain and familiar to their thoughts some truths, which established prejudice or the abstractness of the ideas themselves might render difficult. * * *

* * * The commonwealth of learning is not at this time without master-builders, whose mighty designs in advancing the sciences will leave lasting monuments to the admiration of posterity: but everyone must not hope to be a Boyle or a Sydenham; and in an age that produces such masters as the great Huygenius, and the incomparable Mr. Newton,[4] with some other of that strain, it is ambition enough to be employed as an under-laborer in clearing the ground a little, and removing some of the rubbish that lies in the way to knowledge; which certainly had been very much more advanced in the world, if the endeavors of ingenious and industrious men had not been much cumbered with the learned but frivolous use of uncouth, affected, or unintelligible terms introduced into the sciences, and there made an art of to that degree that philosophy, which is nothing but the true knowledge of things, was thought unfit or uncapable to be brought into well-bred company and polite conversation.[5] Vague and insignificant forms of speech, and abuse of language, have so long passed for mysteries of science; and hard or mis-applied words, with little or no meaning, have, by prescription, such a right to be mistaken for deep learning and height of speculation; that it will not

2. Fragments.

3. Locke's mock-modest confession that his philosophy had been "spun out of his own coarse thoughts" gave rise to a good deal of critical ridicule, echoes of which are heard in the debate between the spider and the bee in Swift's *Battle of the Books*.

4. Sir Isaac Newton. Robert Boyle, the great Anglo-Irish chemist and physicist. Thomas Sydenham was a physician and authority on the treatment of fevers. Christiaan Huygens was a Dutch mathematician and astronomer. Locke's choice of scientists to illustrate the great minds of

his time is certainly tendentious. A generation or two earlier a list of "great men" would have consisted largely of theologians and perhaps lawyers.

5. Locke was tutor to Anthony Ashley Cooper, third earl of Shaftesbury, whose philosophical writings make of genteel social conversation and civilized good humor something like guides to ultimate truth. Whatever can't be spoken in a drawing room without exposing a gentleman to ridicule—so Shaftesbury comes close to saying—is not likely to be true. Locke's basic hostility to cant and jargon has been extended by Shaftesbury, but its original source is apparent.

be easy to persuade either those who speak or those who hear them, that they are but the covers of ignorance, and hindrance of true knowledge. * * *

The booksellers, preparing for the fourth edition of my Essay, gave me notice of it, that I might, if I had leisure, make any additions or alterations I should think fit. Whereupon I thought it convenient to advertise the reader, that besides several corrections I had made here and there, there was one alteration which it was necessary to mention, because it ran through the whole book, and is of consequence to be rightly understood. What I thereupon said, was this:—

"Clear and distinct ideas" are terms which, though familiar and frequent in men's mouths, I have reason to think everyone who uses does not perfectly understand. And possibly it is but here and there one who gives himself the trouble to consider them so far as to know what he himself or others precisely mean by them. I have therefore, in most places, chose to put "determinate" or "determined,"[6] instead of "clear" and "distinct," as more likely to direct men's thoughts to my meaning in this matter. By those denominations, I mean some object in the mind, and consequently determined, i.e., such as it is there seen and perceived to be. This, I think, may fitly be called a "determinate" or "determined" idea, when such as it is at any time objectively in the mind, and so determined there, it is annexed, and without variation determined, to a name or articulate sound which is to be steadily the sign of that very same object of the mind, or determinate idea.

To explain this a little more particularly: By "determinate," when applied to a simple idea, I mean that simple appearance which the mind has in its view, or perceives in itself, when that idea is said to be in it. By "determined," when applied to a complex idea, I mean such an one as consists of a determinate number of certain simple or less complex ideas, joined in such a proportion and situation as the mind has before its view, and sees in itself, when that idea is present in it, or should be present in it, when a man gives a name to it. I say "should be"; because it is not everyone, nor perhaps anyone, who is so careful of his language as to use no word till he views in his mind the precise determined idea which he resolves to make it the sign of. The want of this is the cause of no small obscurity and confusion in men's thoughts and discourses.

I know there are not words enough in any language to answer all the variety of ideas that enter into men's discourses and reasonings. But this hinders not but that when anyone uses any term, he may have in his mind a determined idea which he makes it the sign of, and to which he should keep it steadily annexed during that present discourse. Where he does not or cannot do this, he in vain pretends to clear or distinct ideas: it is plain his are not so; and therefore there can be expected nothing but obscurity and confusion, where such terms are made use of which have not such a precise determination.

Upon this ground I have thought "determined ideas" a way of speaking less liable to mistake than "clear and distinct"; and where men have got such determined ideas of all that they reason, inquire, or argue about, they will find a great part of their doubts and disputes at an end; the greatest part of

6. Definite, limited, fixed in value.

the questions and controversies that perplex mankind depending on the doubtful and uncertain use of words, or (which is the same) indetermined ideas, which they are made to stand for. I have made choice of these terms to signify, 1. Some immediate object of the mind, which it perceives and has before it, distinct from the sound it uses as a sign of it. 2. That this idea, thus determined, i.e., which the mind has in itself, and knows and sees there, be determined without any change to that name, and that name determined to that precise idea. If men had such determined ideas in their inquiries and discourses, they would both discern how far their own inquiries and discourses went, and avoid the greatest part of the disputes and wranglings they have with others.

* * *

1690, 1700

SIR ISAAC NEWTON
1642–1727

Isaac Newton was the posthumous son of a Lincolnshire farmer. As a boy, he invented machines; as an undergraduate, he made major discoveries in optics and mathematics; and in 1667—at twenty-five—he was elected a fellow of Trinity College, Cambridge. Two years later his teacher, Isaac Barrow, resigned the Lucasian Chair of Mathematics in his favor. By then, in secret, Newton had already begun to rethink the universe. His mind worked incessantly, at the highest level of insight, both theoretical and experimental. He designed the first reflecting telescope and explained why the sky looks blue; along with Leibniz, he invented calculus; he revolutionized the study of mechanics and physics with three basic laws of motion; and as everyone knows, he discovered the universal law of gravity. Although Newton's *Principia* (*Mathematical Principles of Natural Philosophy,* 1687) made possible the modern understanding of the cosmos, his *Opticks* (1704) had a still greater impact on his contemporaries, not only for its discoveries about light and color but also for its formulation of a proper scientific method.

Newton reported most of his scientific findings in Latin, the language of international scholarship; but when he chose, he could express himself in crisp and vigorous English. His early experiments on light and color were described in a letter to Henry Oldenburg, secretary of the Royal Society, and quickly published in the society's journal. By analyzing the spectrum, Newton had discovered something amazing, the "oddest if not the most considerable detection, which hath hitherto been made in the operations of nature": light is not homogeneous, as everyone thought, but a compound of heterogeneous rays, and white is not the absence of color but a composite of all sorts of colors. Newton assumes that a clear account of his experiments and reasoning will compel assent; when, at the end of his summary, he drops a very heavy word, he clinches the point like a carpenter nailing a box shut. But other scientists resisted the theory. In years to come, Newton would be more wary; eventually he would leave the university to become master of the mint in London and to devote himself to religious studies. Yet all the while his fame would continue to grow. "There could be only one Newton," Napoleon was told a century later: "there was only one world to discover."

From A Letter of Mr. Isaac Newton, Professor of the Mathematics in the University of Cambridge, Containing His New Theory about Light and Colors

Sent by the Author to the Publisher from Cambridge, Febr. 6, 1672, in order to Be Communicated to the Royal Society

Sir,

To perform my late promise to you, I shall without further ceremony acquaint you that in the beginning of the year 1666 (at which time I applied myself to the grinding of optic glasses of other figures than spherical) I procured me a triangular glass prism to try therewith the celebrated phenomena of colors. And in order thereto having darkened my chamber and made a small hole in my window-shuts to let in a convenient quantity of the sun's light, I placed my prism at his entrance that it might be thereby refracted to the opposite wall. It was at first a very pleasing divertissement to view the vivid and intense colors produced thereby; but after a while, applying myself to consider them more circumspectly, I became surprised to see them in an *oblong* form, which according to the received laws of refraction I expected should have been *circular*.

They were terminated at the sides with straight lines, but at the ends the decay of light was so gradual that it was difficult to determine justly what was their figure; yet they seemed *semicircular*.

Comparing the length of this colored spectrum with its breadth, I found it about five times greater, a disproportion so extravagant that it excited me to a more than ordinary curiosity of examining from whence it might proceed. I could scarce think that the various thickness of the glass or the termination with shadow or darkness could have any influence on light to produce such an effect; yet I thought it not amiss first to examine those circumstances, and so tried what would happen by transmitting light through parts of the glass of divers thicknesses, or through holes in the window of divers bignesses, or by setting the prism without, so that the light might pass through it and be refracted before it was terminated by the hole. But I found none of those circumstances material. The fashion of the colors was in all these cases the same.

Then I suspected whether by any unevenness in the glass or other contingent irregularity these colors might be thus dilated. And to try this, I took another prism like the former and so placed it that the light, passing through them both, might be refracted contrary ways, and so by the latter returned into that course from which the former had diverted it. For by this means I thought the regular effects of the first prism would be destroyed by the second prism, but the irregular ones more augmented by the multiplicity of refractions. The event was that the light, which by the first prism was diffused into an oblong form, was by the second reduced into an orbicular one with as much regularity as when it did not at all pass through them. So that, whatever was the cause of that length, 'twas not any contingent irregularity.[1]

---

1. Newton goes on to describe several experiments and calculations by which he disposed of alternative theories—that rays coming from different parts of the sun caused the diffusion of light into an oblong, or that the rays of light traveled in curved paths after leaving the prism.

* * *

The gradual removal of these suspicions at length led me to the *experimentum crucis*,[2] which was this: I took two boards, and placed one of them close behind the prism at the window, so that the light might pass through a small hole made in it for the purpose and fall on the other board, which I placed at about 12 foot distance, having first made a small hole in it also, for some of that incident[3] light to pass through. Then I placed another prism behind this second board so that the light, trajected through both the boards, might pass through that also, and be again refracted before it arrived at the wall. This done, I took the first prism in my hand, and turned it to and fro slowly about its axis, so much as to make the several parts of the image, cast on the second board, successively pass through the hole in it, that I might observe to what places on the wall the second prism would refract them. And I saw by the variation of those places that the light, tending to that end of the image towards which the refraction of the first prism was made, did in the second prism suffer a refraction considerably greater than the light tending to the other end. And so the true cause of the length of that image was detected to be no other than that light consists of *rays differently refrangible*, which, without any respect to a difference in their incidence, were, according to their degrees of refrangibility, transmitted towards divers parts of the wall.[4]

* * *

I shall now proceed to acquaint you with another more notable difformity[5] in its rays, wherein the *origin of colors* is infolded. A naturalist[6] would scarce expect to see the science of those become mathematical, and yet I dare affirm that there is as much certainty in it as in any other part of optics. For what I shall tell concerning them is not an hypothesis but most rigid consequence, not conjectured by barely inferring 'tis thus because not otherwise or because it satisfied all phenomena (the philosophers' universal topic) but evinced by the mediation of experiments concluding directly and without any suspicion of doubt. * * *

The doctrine you will find comprehended and illustrated in the following propositions.

1. As the rays of light differ in degrees of refrangibility, so they also differ in their disposition to exhibit this or that particular color. Colors are not *qualifications of light*, derived from refractions or reflections of natural bodies (as 'tis generally believed), but *original and connate properties* which in divers rays are divers. Some rays are disposed to exhibit a red color and no other; some a yellow and no other, some a green and no other, and so of the rest. Nor are there only rays proper and particular to the more eminent colors, but even to all their intermediate gradations.

2. To the same degree of refrangibility ever belongs the same color, and to the same color ever belongs the same degree of refrangibility. The least refrangible rays are all disposed to exhibit a red color, and contrarily those

---

2. Crucial experiment (Latin); turning point.
3. From the Latin *incidere*, to fall into or onto. Newton uses it of light striking an obstacle.
4. This insight enables Newton to design a greatly improved telescope, which uses reflections to correct the distortions caused by the scattering of

refracted rays. He adds in passing that his experiments were interrupted for two years by the plague; but at last he returns to some further and even more important characteristics of light.
5. Diversity of forms.
6. A student of physics or "natural philosophy."

rays which are disposed to exhibit a red color are all the least refrangible. So the most refrangible rays are all disposed to exhibit a deep violet color, and contrarily those which are apt to exhibit such a violet color are all the most refrangible. And so to all the intermediate colors in a continued series belong intermediate degrees of refrangibility. And this analogy 'twixt colors and refrangibility is very precise and strict; the rays always either exactly agreeing in both or proportionally disagreeing in both.

3. The species of color and degree of refrangibility proper to any particular sort of rays is not mutable by refraction, nor by reflection from natural bodies, nor by any other cause that I could yet observe. When any one sort of rays hath been well parted from those of other kinds, it hath afterwards obstinately retained its color, notwithstanding my utmost endeavors to change it. I have refracted it with prisms and reflected it with bodies which in daylight were of other colors; I have intercepted it with the colored film of air interceding two compressed plates of glass; transmitted it through colored mediums and through mediums irradiated with other sorts of rays, and diversely terminated it; and yet could never produce any new color out of it. It would by contracting or dilating become more brisk or faint and by the loss of many rays in some cases very obscure and dark; but I could never see it changed *in specie*.[7]

4. Yet seeming transmutations of colors may be made, where there is any mixture of divers sorts of rays. For in such mixtures, the component colors appear not, but by their mutual allaying each other constitute a middling color. And therefore, if by refraction or any other of the aforesaid causes the difform rays latent in such a mixture be separated, there shall emerge colors different from the color of the composition. Which colors are not new generated, but only made apparent by being parted; for if they be again entirely mixed and blended together, they will again compose that color which they did before separation. And for the same reason, transmutations made by the convening of divers colors are not real; for when the difform rays are again severed, they will exhibit the very same colors which they did before they entered the composition—as you see blue and yellow powders when finely mixed appear to the naked eye green, and yet the colors of the component corpuscles are not thereby transmuted, but only blended. For, when viewed with a good microscope, they still appear blue and yellow interspersedly.

5. There are therefore two sorts of colors: the one original and simple, the other compounded of these. The original or primary colors are red, yellow, green, blue, and a violet-purple, together with orange, indigo, and an indefinite variety of intermediate graduations.

6. The same colors *in specie* with these primary ones may be also produced by composition. For a mixture of yellow and blue makes green; of red and yellow makes orange; of orange and yellowish green makes yellow. And in general, if any two colors be mixed which, in the series of those generated by the prism, are not too far distant one from another, they by their mutual alloy compound that color which in the said series appeareth in the mid-way between them. But those which are situated at too great a distance, do not so. Orange and indigo produce not the intermediate green, nor scarlet and green the intermediate yellow.

7. But the most surprising and wonderful composition was that of *white-*

7. In kind.

ness. There is no one sort of rays which alone can exhibit this. 'Tis ever compounded, and to its composition are requisite all the aforesaid primary colors, mixed in a due proportion. I have often with admiration beheld that all the colors of the prism, being made to converge, and thereby to be again mixed as they were in the light before it was incident upon the prism, reproduced light entirely and perfectly white, and not at all sensibly differing from a direct light of the sun, unless when the glasses I used were not sufficiently clear; for then they would a little incline it to *their* color.

8. Hence therefore it comes to pass that *whiteness* is the usual color of light, for light is a confused aggregate of rays endued with all sorts of colors, as they are promiscuously darted from the various parts of luminous bodies. And of such a confused aggregate, as I said, is generated whiteness, if there be a due proportion of the ingredients; but if any one predominate, the light must incline to that color, as it happens in the blue flame of brimstone, the yellow flame of a candle, and the various colors of the fixed stars.

9. These things considered, the manner how colors are produced by the prism is evident. For of the rays constituting the incident light, since those which differ in color proportionally differ in refrangibility, they by their unequal refractions must be severed and dispersed into an oblong form in an orderly succession from the least refracted scarlet to the most refracted violet. And for the same reason it is that objects, when looked upon through a prism, appear colored. For the difform rays, by their unequal refractions, are made to diverge towards several parts of the retina, and there express the images of things colored, as in the former case they did the sun's image upon a wall. And by this inequality of refractions they become not only colored, but also very confused and indistinct.

10. Why the colors of the rainbow appear in falling drops of rain is also from hence evident. For those drops which refract the rays disposed to appear purple in greatest quantity to the spectator's eye, refract the rays of other sorts so much less as to make them pass beside it;[8] and such are the drops on the inside of the primary bow and on the outside of the secondary or exterior one. So those drops which refract in greatest plenty the rays apt to appear red toward the spectator's eye, refract those of other sorts so much more as to make them pass beside it; and such are the drops on the exterior part of the primary and interior part of the secondary bow.

* * *

13. I might add more instances of this nature, but I shall conclude with this general one, that the colors of all natural bodies have no other origin than this, that they are variously qualified to reflect one sort of light in greater plenty than another. And this I have experimented in a dark room by illuminating those bodies with uncompounded light of divers colors. For by that means any body may be made to appear of any color. They have there no appropriate color, but ever appear of the color of the light cast upon them, but yet with this difference, that they are most brisk and vivid in the light of their own daylight color. *Minium* appeareth there of any color indifferently with which 'tis illustrated, but yet most luminous in red, and so *Bise*[9] appear-

8. I.e., disappear alongside it.
9. Azurite blue. "Minium": red lead. "Illustrated": illuminated.

eth indifferently of any color with which 'tis illustrated, but yet most luminous in blue. And therefore *minium* reflecteth rays of any color, but most copiously those endued with red; and consequently when illustrated with daylight, that is, with all sorts of rays promiscuously blended, those qualified with red shall abound most in the reflected light, and by their prevalence cause it to appear of that color. And for the same reason *bise*, reflecting blue most copiously, shall appear blue by the excess of those rays in its reflected light; and the like of other bodies. And that this is the entire and adequate cause of their colors is manifest, because they have no power to change or alter the colors of any sort of rays incident apart, but put on all colors indifferently with which they are enlightened.

These things being so, it can no longer be disputed whether there be colors in the dark, nor whether they be the qualities of the objects we see, no, nor perhaps whether light be a body. For since colors are the qualities of light, having its rays for their entire and immediate subject,[1] how can we think those rays qualities also, unless one quality may be the subject of and sustain another—which in effect is to call it substance. We should not know bodies for substances were it not for their sensible qualities, and the principal of those being now found due to something else, we have as good reason to believe that to be a substance also.[2]

Besides, who ever thought any quality to be a heterogeneous aggregate, such as light is discovered to be? But to determine more absolutely what light is, after what manner refracted, and by what modes or actions it produceth in our minds the phantasms of colors, is not so easy. And I shall not mingle conjectures with certainties.

* * *

1672

1. That of which a thing consists.
2. I.e., the only way we know bodies are substances is that our senses perceive their qualities. The chief of these qualities, color, is now known to be a quality of light, not body; our conclusion can perfectly well be that light is a form of substance, as well as body, and that we know it to be so through its quality, color.

SAMUEL BUTLER
1612–1680

Samuel Butler passed his middle years during the fury of the civil wars and under the Commonwealth, sardonically observing the behavior and lovingly memorizing the faults of the Puritan rulers. He despised them and found relief for his feelings by satirizing them, though, naturally enough, he could not publish while they were in power. He served as clerk to several Puritan justices of the peace in the west of England, one of whom, according to tradition, was the original of Sir Hudibras (the *s* is pronounced). *Hudibras*, part 1, was published late in 1662 (the edition bears the date 1663) and pleased the triumphant Royalists. King Charles II admired and often quoted the poem and rewarded its author with a gift of £300; it was, after all, a relief to laugh at what he had earlier hated and feared. The first part, attacking Presbyterians and Independents, proved more vigorous and effective than parts 2 and 3, which followed in 1664 and 1678, respectively. After his initial success, Butler was neglected by the people he had pleased. He died in poverty, and not until 1721 was a monument to his memory erected in Westminster Abbey.

Hudibras is a travesty, or burlesque: it takes a serious subject and debases it by using a low style or distorts it by grotesque exaggeration. Butler carried this mode even into his verse, for he reduced the iambic tetrameter line (used subtly and seriously by such seventeenth-century poets as John Donne, John Milton, and Andrew Marvell) to something approaching doggerel, and his boldly comic rhymes add to the effect of broad comedy that he sought to create. Burlesque was a popular form of satire during the seventeenth century, especially after the French poet Paul Scarron published his Virgile Travesti (1648), which retells the Aeneid in slang. Butler's use of burlesque expresses his contempt for the Puritans and their commonwealth; the history of England from 1642 to 1660 is made to appear mere sound and fury.

Butler took his hero's name from Spenser's Faerie Queene 2.2, where Sir Huddibras appears briefly as a rash adventurer and lover. The questing knight of chivalric romance is degraded into the meddling, hypocritical busybody Hudibras, who goes out, like an officer in Cromwell's army, "a-coloneling" against the popular sport of bear baiting. The knight and his squire, Ralph, suggest Don Quixote and Sancho Panza, but the temper of Butler's mind is as remote from Cervantes's warm humanity as it is from Spenser's ardent idealism. Butler had no illusions; he was skeptical in philosophy and conservative in politics, distrusting theoretical reasoning and the new science, disdainful of claims of inspiration and illumination, contemptuous of Catholicism and dubious of bishops, Anglican no less than Roman. It is difficult to think of anything that he approved unless it was peace, common sense, and the wisdom that emerges from the experience of humankind through the ages.

From Hudibras

From Part 1, Canto 1

THE ARGUMENT

Sir Hudibras, his passing worth,
The manner how he sallied forth,
His arms and equipage are shown,
His horse's virtues and his own:
The adventure of the Bear and Fiddle
Is sung, but breaks off in the middle.

When civil fury[1] first grew high,
And men fell out, they knew not why;
When hard words, jealousies, and fears
Set folks together by the ears
5   And made them fight, like mad or drunk,
For Dame Religion as for punk,°   *prostitute*
Whose honesty they all durst swear for,
Though not a man of them knew wherefore;
When gospel-trumpeter, surrounded
10 With long-eared rout,[2] to battle sounded,

1. The civil wars between Royalists and Parliamentarians (1642–49).
2. A mob of Puritans or Roundheads, so called because they wore their hair short instead of in flowing curls and thus exposed their ears, which to many satirists suggested the long ears of the ass. "Gospel-trumpeter": a Presbyterian minister vehemently preaching rebellion.

And pulpit, drum ecclesiastic,[3]
Was beat with fist instead of a stick;
Then did Sir Knight abandon dwelling,
And out he rode a-coloneling.[4]
15   A wight° he was whose very sight would   *creature*
Entitle him Mirror of Knighthood;
That never bent his stubborn knee
To anything but chivalry,
Nor put up blow but that which laid
20   Right worshipful on shoulder blade;[5]
Chief of domestic knights and errant,
Either for chartel or for warrant;[6]
Great on the bench, great in the saddle,[6]
That could as well bind o'er as swaddle.[7]
25   Mighty he was at both of these,
And styled of war as well as peace.
(So some rats of amphibious nature
Are either for the land or water.)
But here our authors make a doubt
30   Whether he were more wise or stout.
Some hold the one and some the other;
But howsoe'er they make a pother,
The difference was so small his brain
Outweighed his rage but half a grain;
35   Which made some take him for a tool
That knaves do work with, called a fool,
And offer to lay wagers that,
As Montaigne, playing with his cat,
Complains she thought him but an ass,[8]
40   Much more she would Sir Hudibras
(For that's the name our valiant knight
To all his challenges did write).
But they're mistaken very much,
'Tis plain enough he was no such.
45   We grant, although he had much wit,
He was very shy of using it;
As being loath to wear it out,
And therefore bore it not about,
Unless on holidays, or so,
50   As men their best apparel do.
Beside, 'tis known he could speak Greek
As naturally as pigs squeak;
That Latin was no more difficile
Than to a blackbird 'tis to whistle.

3. The Presbyterian clergy were said to have preached the country into the civil wars. Hence, in pounding their pulpits with their fists, they are said to beat their ecclesiastical drums.
4. Here pronounced *có-lo-nel-ing*.
5. When a man is knighted he kneels and is tapped on the shoulder by his overlord's sword.
6. "Chartel": a written challenge to combat, such as a knight-errant sends. But Hudibras, as justice of the peace ("domestic knight"), could also issue a "warrant" (a writ authorizing an arrest, a seizure,

or a search). Hence he is satirically called "great on the [justice's] bench" as well as in the saddle. "Errant" was spelled and pronounced *arrant*.
7. Both justice of the peace and soldier, he is equally able to "bind over" a malefactor to be tried at the next sessions or, in his role of colonel, to beat ("swaddle") him.
8. In his *Apology for Raymond Sebond*, Michel de Montaigne (1533–1592), French skeptic and essayist, wondered whether he played with his cat or his cat played with him.

55 Being rich in both, he never scanted
His bounty unto such as wanted,
But much of either would afford
To many that had not one word.
For Hebrew roots, although they're found
60 To flourish most in barren ground,[9]
He had such plenty as sufficed
To make some think him circumcised;
And truly so perhaps he was,
'Tis many a pious Christian's case.
65   He was in logic a great critic,
Profoundly skilled in analytic.
He could distinguish and divide
A hair 'twixt south and southwest side;
On either which he would dispute,
70 Confute, change hands, and still confute.
He'd undertake to prove, by force
Of argument, a man's no horse;
He'd prove a buzzard is no fowl,
And that a lord may be an owl,
75 A calf an alderman, a goose a justice,
And rooks committee-men and trustees.[1]
He'd run in debt by disputation,
And pay with ratiocination.
All this by syllogism true,
80 In mood and figure,[2] he would do.
     For rhetoric, he could not ope
His mouth but out there flew a trope;[3]
And when he happened to break off
In the middle of his speech, or cough,[4]
85 He had hard words ready to show why,
And tell what rules he did it by.
Else, when with greatest art he spoke,
You'd think he talked like other folk;
For all a rhetorician's rules
90 Teach nothing but to name his tools.
His ordinary rate of speech
In loftiness of sound was rich,
A Babylonish dialect,[5]
Which learned pedants much affect.
95 It was a parti-colored dress
Of patched and piebald languages;
'Twas English cut on Greek and Latin,
Like fustian heretofore on satin.[6]
It had an odd promiscuous tone,

---

9. Hebrew, the language of Adam, was thought of as the primitive language, the one that people in a state of nature would naturally speak.
1. Committees were set up in the counties by Parliament and given authority to imprison Royalists and to sequestrate their estates. "Rooks": a kind of blackbird; here, cheats (slang).
2. The "figure" of a syllogism is "the proper disposition of the middle term with the parts of the

question." "Mood": the form of an argument.
3. Figure of speech.
4. Some pulpit orators regarded hemming and coughing as ornaments of speech.
5. Pedants affected the use of foreign words. The allusion is to the Tower of Babel (Genesis 11.4–9).
6. Clothes made of coarse cloth ("fustian") were slashed to display the richer satin lining.

100 As if he had talked three parts in one;
     Which made some think, when he did gabble,
     They had heard three laborers of Babel,
     Or Cerberus himself pronounce
     A leash of languages at once.[7]
105 This he as volubly would vent
     As if his stock would ne'er be spent;
     And truly, to support that charge,
     He had supplies as vast and large.
     For he could coin or counterfeit
110 New words with little or no wit;[8]
     Words so debased and hard no stone
     Was hard enough to touch them on.
     And when with hasty noise he spoke 'em,
     The ignorant for current took 'em;
115 That had the orator, who once
     Did fill his mouth with pebble-stones
     When he harangued,[9] but known his phrase,
     He would have used no other ways.
         In mathematics he was greater
120 Than Tycho Brahe, or Erra Pater:[1]
     For he, by geometric scale,
     Could take the size of pots of ale;
     Resolve by sines and tangents straight,
     If bread or butter wanted weight;
125 And wisely tell what hour o' the day
     The clock does strike, by algebra.
         Beside, he was a shrewd philosopher,
     And had read every text and gloss over;
     Whate'er the crabbed'st author hath,
130 He understood by implicit faith;
     Whatever skeptic could inquire for,
     For every *why* he had a *wherefore*;
     Knew more than forty of them do,
     As far as words and terms could go.
135 All which he understood by rote
     And, as occasion served, would quote,
     No matter whether right or wrong;
     They might be either said or sung.
     His notions fitted things so well
140 That which was which he could not tell,
     But oftentimes mistook the one
     For the other, as great clerks° have done.[2]   scholars
     He could reduce all things to acts,
     And knew their natures by abstracts;

7. The sporting term "leash" denotes a group of three dogs, hawks, deer, etc., hence, three in general. Cerberus was the three-headed dog that guarded the entrance to Hades.
8. The Presbyterians and other sects invented a special religious vocabulary, much ridiculed by Anglicans: *out-goings, workings-out, gospel-walking-times*, etc.
9. Demosthenes cured a stutter by speaking with pebbles in his mouth.

1. Butler's contemptuous name for the popular astrologer William Lilly (1602–1681). Brahe (1546–1601), a Danish astronomer.
2. Elsewhere Butler wrote, "Notions are but pictures of things in the imagination of man, and if they agree with their originals in nature, they are true, and if not, false."

145   Where entity and quiddity,
       The ghosts of defunct bodies,[3] fly;
       Where truth in person does appear,
       Like words congealed in northern air.[4]
       He knew what's what, and that's as high
150   As metaphysic wit can fly.
         In school-divinity° as able   *scholastic theology*
       As he that hight Irrefragable;
       Profound in all the nominal
       And real ways beyond them all;[5]
155   And with as delicate a hand
       Could twist as tough a rope of sand;
       And weave fine cobwebs, fit for skull
       That's empty when the moon is full;[6]
       Such as take lodgings in a head
160   That's to be let unfurnishèd
       He could raise scruples dark and nice,[7]
       And after solve 'em in a trice;
       As if divinity had catched
       The itch on purpose to be scratched,
165   Or, like a mountebank,[8] did wound
       And stab herself with doubts profound,
       Only to show with how small pain
       The sores of faith are cured again;
       Although by woeful proof we find
170   They always leave a scar behind.
       He knew the seat of paradise,[9]
       Could tell in what degree it lies;
       And, as he was disposed, could prove it
       Below the moon, or else above it;
175   What Adam dreamt of when his bride
       Came from her closet in his side;
       Whether the devil tempted her
       By a High Dutch interpreter;
       If either of them had a navel;
180   Who first made music malleable;[1]
       Whether the serpent at the fall
       Had cloven feet or none at all:
       All this without a gloss or comment
       He could unriddle in a moment,
185   In proper terms, such as men smatter

---

3. In the hairsplitting logic of medieval Scholastic philosophy, a distinction was drawn between the "entity," or *being*, and the "quiddity," or *essence*, of bodies. Butler calls entity and quiddity "ghosts" because they were held to be independent realities and so to survive the bodies in which they lodge.

4. The notion, as old as the Greek wit Lucian, that in arctic regions words freeze as they are uttered and become audible only when they thaw.

5. These lines refer to the debate, continuous throughout the Middle Ages, about whether the objects of our concepts exist in nature or are mere intellectual abstractions. The "nominalists" denied their objective reality, the "realists" affirmed it. Alexander of Hales (d. 1245) was called "Irrefra-

gable," i.e., unanswerable, because his system seemed incontrovertible.

6. The frenzies of the insane were supposed to wax and wane with the moon (hence "lunatic").

7. Obscure ("dark") and subtle ("nice") intellectual perplexities ("scruples").

8. A seller of quack medicines.

9. The problem of the precise location of the Garden of Eden and the similar problems listed in the ensuing dozen lines had all been the subject of controversy among theologians.

1. Capable of being fashioned into form. Pythagoras is said to have organized sounds into the musical scale.

When they throw out and miss the matter.
    For his religion, it was fit
To match his learning and his wit:
'Twas Presbyterian true blue,[2]
190 For he was of that stubborn crew
Of errant saints[3] whom all men grant
To be the true church militant,
Such as do build their faith upon
The holy text of pike and gun;
195 Decide all controversies by
Infallible artillery,
And prove their doctrine orthodox
By apostolic blows and knocks;
Call fire, and sword, and desolation
200 A godly, thorough reformation,
Which always must be carried on
And still be doing, never done;
As if religion were intended
For nothing else but to be mended.
205 A sect whose chief devotion lies
In odd, perverse antipathies;[4]
In falling out with that or this,
And finding somewhat still amiss;
More peevish, cross, and splènetic
210 Than dog distract or monkey sick:
That with more care keep holiday
The wrong, than others the right way;
Compound for sins they are inclined to
By damning those they have no mind to;
215 Still so perverse and opposite
As if they worshiped God for spite.
The selfsame thing they will abhor
One way and long another for.
Free-will they one way disavow,[5]
220 Another, nothing else allow:
All piety consists therein
In them, in other men all sin.
Rather than fail, they will defy
That which they love most tenderly;
225 Quarrel with minced pies and disparage
Their best and dearest friend, plum-porridge;
Fat pig and goose itself oppose,
And blaspheme custard through the nose.[6]

1663

---

2. The Scotch Covenanters adopted blue as their color, in contrast to the Royalist red. Blue is the color of constancy; hence, "true blue," staunch, unwavering. This and the next five couplets bitterly recall the violence and fanaticism of the parliamentary armies in attempting to reform the Anglican Church.

3. A pun: *arrant*, meaning "unmitigated," and *errant*, meaning "wandering," were both pronounced *arrant*. The Puritans frequently called themselves "saints."

4. The hostility of the sects to everything Anglican or Roman Catholic laid them open to the charge of opposing innocent practices out of mere perverse antipathy. Some extreme Presbyterians fasted at Christmas, instead of following the old custom of feasting and rejoicing (cf. lines 211–12).

5. By the doctrine of predestination.

6. A reference to the nasal whine of the pious sectarians.

JOHN WILMOT, SECOND EARL OF ROCHESTER
1647–1680

John Wilmot, second earl of Rochester, was the precocious son of one of Charles II's most loyal followers in exile. He won the king's favor at the Restoration and, in 1664, after education at Oxford and on the Continent, took a place at court, at the age of seventeen. There he soon distinguished himself as "the man who has the most wit and the least honor in England." For one escapade, the abduction of Elizabeth Malet, an heiress, he was imprisoned in the Tower of London. But he regained his position by courageous service in the naval war against the Dutch, and in 1667 he married Malet. The rest of his career was no less stormy. His satiric wit, directed not only at ordinary mortals but at Dryden and Charles II himself, embroiled him in constant quarrels and exiles; his practical jokes, his affairs, and his dissipation were legendary. He told his biographer, Gilbert Burnet, that "for five years together he was continually drunk." Just before his death, however, he was converted to Christian repentance, and for posterity, Rochester became a favorite moral topic: the libertine who had seen the error of his ways.

Wit, in the Restoration, meant not only a clever turn of phrase but mental capacity and intellectual power. Rochester was famous for both kinds of wit. His fierce intelligence, impatient of sham and convention, helped design a way of life based on style, cleverness, and self-interest—a way of life observable in Restoration plays (Dorimant, in Etherege's *The Man of Mode,* strongly resembles Rochester). Philosophically, such behavior may be seen as an experiment in living the life of a "natural man," in accord with Hobbes's doctrine that all laws, even our notions of good and evil, are artificial social checks on natural human desires. *The Disabled Debauchee,* composed in "heroic stanzas" like those of Dryden's *Annus Mirabilis,* subverts the very notion of heroism by turning conventions upside down. Yet everything is kept plausible by Rochester's special gift for impersonation, the same talent, according to one enemy, that made him a dangerous seducer—"He enters into all your tastes and your feelings, and makes you believe everything he says, though not a single word is sincere."

The Disabled Debauchee

> As some brave admiral, in former war
>   Deprived of force, but pressed with courage still,
> Two rival fleets appearing from afar,
>   Crawls to the top of an adjacent hill;
>
> 5 From whence, with thoughts full of concern, he views
>   The wise and daring conduct of the fight,
> Whilst each bold action to his mind renews
>   His present glory and his past delight;
>
> From his fierce eyes flashes of fire he throws,
> 10   As from black clouds when lightning breaks away;
> Transported, thinks himself amidst the foes,
>   And absent, yet enjoys the bloody day;
>
> So, when my days of impotence approach,
>   And I'm by pox° and wine's unlucky chance   *venereal disease*
> 15 Forced from the pleasing billows of debauch
>   On the dull shore of lazy temperance,

My pains at least some respite shall afford
    While I behold the battle you maintain
    When fleets of glasses sail about the board,°   *table*
20   From whose broadsides[1] volleys of wit shall rain.

Nor let the sight of honorable scars,
    Which my too forward valor did procure,
    Frighten new-listed° soldiers from the wars: *newly enlisted*
    Past joys have more than paid what I endure.

25 Should any youth (worth being drunk) prove nice,°   *coy, fastidious*
    And from his fair inviter meanly shrink,
    'Twill please the ghost of my departed vice
    If, at my counsel, he repent and drink.

Or should some cold-complexioned sot forbid,
30   With his dull morals, our bold night-alarms,
    I'll fire his blood by telling what I did
    When I was strong and able to bear arms.

I'll tell of whores attacked, their lords at home;
    Bawds' quarters beaten up, and fortress won;
35   Windows demolished, watches° overcome;   *watchmen*
    And handsome ills by my contrivance done.

Nor shall our love-fits, Chloris, be forgot,
    When each the well-looked linkboy[2] strove t' enjoy,
    And the best kiss was the deciding lot
40   Whether the boy used you, or I the boy.

With tales like these I will such thoughts inspire
    As to important mischief shall incline:
    I'll make him long some ancient church to fire,
    And fear no lewdness he's called to by wine.

45 Thus, statesmanlike, I'll saucily impose,
    And safe from action, valiantly advise;
    Sheltered in impotence, urge you to blows,
    And being good for nothing else, be wise.

                                           1680

The Imperfect Enjoyment[1]

Naked she lay, clasped in my longing arms,
I filled with love, and she all over charms;
Both equally inspired with eager fire,
Melting through kindness, flaming in desire.
5 With arms, legs, lips close clinging to embrace,
She clips° me to her breast, and sucks me to her face.   *hugs*

---

1. The sides of the table; artillery on a ship; sheets
on which satirical verses were printed.
2. Good-looking boy employed to light the way
with a link or torch.
1. The genre of poems about the downfall of male

"pride"—not only a swelled head but an erection—
derives from Ovid's *Amores* 3.7. For a woman's
treatment of this situation, see Aphra Behn's *The
Disappointment* (p. 2167).

Her nimble tongue, Love's lesser lightning, played
Within my mouth, and to my thoughts conveyed
Swift orders that I should prepare to throw
10   The all-dissolving thunderbolt below.
My fluttering soul, sprung² with the pointed kiss,
Hangs hovering o'er her balmy brinks of bliss.
But whilst her busy hand would guide that part
Which should convey my soul up to her heart,
15   In liquid raptures I dissolve all o'er,
Melt into sperm, and spend at every pore.
A touch from any part of her had done 't:
Her hand, her foot, her very look's a cunt.
     Smiling, she chides in a kind murmuring noise,
20   And from her body wipes the clammy joys,
When, with a thousand kisses wandering o'er
My panting bosom, "Is there then no more?"
She cries. "All this to love and rapture's due;
Must we not pay a debt to pleasure too?"
25   But I, the most forlorn, lost man alive,
To show my wished obedience vainly strive:
I sigh, alas! and kiss, but cannot swive.°   screw
Eager desires confound my first intent,
Succeeding shame does more success prevent,
30   And rage at last confirms me impotent.
Ev'n her fair hand, which might bid heat return
To frozen age, and make cold hermits burn,
Applied to my dead cinder, warms no more
Than fire to ashes could past flames restore.
35   Trembling, confused, despairing, limber, dry,
A wishing, weak, unmoving lump I lie.
This dart of love, whose piercing point, oft tried,
With virgin blood ten thousand maids have dyed;
Which nature still directed with such art
40   That it through every cunt reached every heart—
Stiffly resolved, 'twould carelessly invade
Woman or man, nor ought its fury stayed:
Where'er it pierced, a cunt it found or made—
Now languid lies in this unhappy hour,
45   Shrunk up and sapless like a withered flower.
     Thou treacherous, base deserter of my flame,
False to my passion, fatal to my fame,
Through what mistaken magic dost thou prove
So true to lewdness, so untrue to love?
50   What oyster-cinder-beggar-common whore
Didst thou e'er fail in all thy life before?
When vice, disease, and scandal lead the way,
With what officious haste dost thou obey!
Like a rude, roaring hector° in the streets   bully
55   Who scuffles, cuffs, and justles all he meets,
But if his King or country claim his aid,

2. Startled from cover, like a game bird.

The rakehell villain shrinks and hides his head;
Ev'n so thy brutal valor is displayed,
Breaks every stew,° does each small whore invade,   *brothel*
60   But when great Love the onset does command,
Base recreant to thy prince, thou dar'st not stand.
Worst part of me, and henceforth hated most,
Through all the town a common fucking post,
On whom each whore relieves her tingling cunt
65   As hogs on gates do rub themselves and grunt,
Mayst thou to ravenous chancres be a prey,
Or in consuming weepings waste away;
May strangury and stone[3] thy days attend;
May'st thou ne'er piss, who didst refuse to spend
70   When all my joys did on false thee depend.
    And may ten thousand abler pricks agree
    To do the wronged Corinna right for thee.

1680

---

3. "Strangury" and "stone" cause slow and painful urination. "Chancres" and "weepings" are signs of venereal disease.

APHRA BEHN
1640?–1689

"A woman wit has often graced the stage," Dryden wrote in 1681. Soon after actresses first appeared in English public theaters, there was an even more striking debut by a woman writer who boldly signed her plays and talked back to her critics. In a dozen years, Aphra Behn turned out at least that many plays, discovering fresh dramatic possibilities in casts that included women with warm bodies and clever heads. She also drew attention as a warm and witty poet of love. When writing for the stage became less profitable, she turned to the emerging field of prose fiction, composing a pioneering epistolary novel, *Love Letters Between a Nobleman and His Sister*, and diverse short tales—not to mention a raft of translations from the French, pindarics to her beloved Stuart rulers, compilations, prologues, complimentary verses, all the piecework and puffery that were the stock in trade of the Restoration town wit. She worked in haste and with flair for nearly two decades and more than held her own as a professional writer. In the end, no author of her time—except Dryden himself—proved more versatile, more alive to new currents of thought, or more inventive in recasting fashionable forms.

Much of Behn's life remains a mystery. Although her books have been accompanied—and often all but buried—by volumes of rumor, hard facts are elusive. She was almost certainly from East Kent; she may well have been named Johnson. But she herself seems to have left no record of her date and place of birth, her family name and upbringing, or the identity of the shadowy Mr. Behn whom she reportedly married. Her many references to nuns and convents, as well as praise for prominent Catholic lords (*Oroonoko* is dedicated to one), have prompted speculation that she may have been raised as a Catholic and educated in a convent abroad. Without doubt, she drew on a range of worldly experience that would be closed to women in the more genteel ages to come. The circumstantial detail of *Oroonoko* supports her claim that she was in the new sugar colony of Surinam early in 1664. Perhaps she exaggerated her social position to enhance her tale, but many particulars—from dialect words and the location of plantations to methods of selling and torturing slaves—can be authenticated. During the trade war that broke out in 1665—which left her "vast and charming world" a Dutch prize—Behn traveled to the Low Countries on a spying mission for King Charles II. The king could be lax about payment, however, and Behn had to petition desperately to escape debtor's prison. In 1670 she brought out her first plays, "forced to write for bread," she confessed, "and not ashamed to own it."

In London, Behn flourished in the cosmopolitan world of the playhouse and the court. Dryden and other wits encouraged her; she mixed with actresses and managers and playwrights and exchanged verses with a lively literary set that she called her "cabal." Surviving letters record a passionate, troubled attachment to a lawyer named John Hoyle, a bisexual with libertine views. She kept up with the most advanced thinking and joined public debates with pointed satire against the Whigs. But the festivity of the Restoration world was fading out in bitter party acrimony. In 1682 Behn was placed under arrest for "abusive reflections" on the king's illegitimate son, the Whig duke of Monmouth (Dryden's Absalom). Her Royalist opinions and the immodesty of her public role made her a target; gleeful lampoons declared that she was aging and ill and once again poor. She responded by bringing out her works at a still faster rate, composing *Oroonoko*, her dedication claims, "in a few hours . . . for I never rested my pen a moment for thought." In some last works she recorded her hope that her writings would live: "I value fame as much as if I had been born a hero." When she died she was buried in Westminster Abbey.

"All women together ought to let flowers fall upon the grave of Aphra Behn," Virginia Woolf wrote, "for it was she who earned them the right to speak their minds." Behn herself spoke her mind. She scorned hypocrisy and calculation in her society and commented freely on religion, science, and philosophy. Moreover, she spoke as a woman. Denied the classical education of most male authors, she dismissed "musty rules" and lessons and relished the immediate human appeal of popular forms. Her first play, *The Forced Marriage,* exposes the bondage of matches arranged for money and status, and many later works invoke the powerful natural force of love, whose energy breaks through conventions. In a range of genres, from simple pastoral songs to complex plots of intrigue, she candidly explores the sexual feelings of women, their schooling in disguise, their need to "love upon the honest square" (for this her work was later denounced as coarse and impure). *Oroonoko* represents another departure for Behn and prose fiction. It achieves something new both in its narrative form and in extending some of her favorite themes to an original subject: the destiny of a black male hero on a world historical stage.

Oroonoko cannot be classified as fact or fiction, realism or romance. In the still unshaped field of prose narrative—where a "history" could mean any story, true or false—Behn combined the attractions of three older forms. First, she presents the work as a memoir, a personal account of what she has heard and seen. According to a friend, Behn had told this tale over and over; perhaps that explains the conversational ease with which she turns back and forth, interpreting faraway scenes for her readers at home. Second, *Oroonoko* is a travel narrative in three parts. It turns west to a new world often extolled as a paradise, then east to Africa and the amorous intrigues of a corrupt old-world court (popular reading fare), then finally west again with its hero across the infamous "Middle Passage"—over which millions of slaves would be transported during the next century—to the conflicts of a raw colonial world. Exotic scenes fascinate Behn, but she wants even more to talk to people and learn about their ways of life. As in imaginary voyages, from Sir Thomas More's *Utopia* to *Gulliver's Travels* and *Rasselas,* encounters with foreign cultures sharply challenge Europeans to reexamine themselves. Behn's primitive Indians and noble Africans live by a code of virtue, by principles of fidelity and honor, that "civilized" Christians often ignore or betray. Oroonoko embodies this code. Above all, the book is his biography. Courageous, high-minded, and great hearted, he rivals the heroes of classical epics and Plutarch's *Lives* and is equally worthy of fame. Nor does he lack gentler virtues. Like the heroes of seventeenth-century heroic dramas and romances, he shines in the company of women and proves his nobility by his passionate and constant love for Imoinda, his ideal counterpart. Yet finally a contradiction dooms Oroonoko: he is at once prince and chattel, a "royal slave."

Behn handles her forms dynamically, drawing out their inner discords and tensions. In the biography, Oroonoko's deepest values are turned against him. His trust in friendship and scrupulous truth to his word expose him to the treachery of Europeans who calculate human worth on a yardstick of profit. A hero cannot survive in such a world. His self-respect demands action, even when he can find no clear path through the tangle of assurances and lies. Moreover, the colony too seems tangled in contradictions. Behn's travel narrative reveals a broken paradise where, in the absence of secure authority, the settlers descend into a series of unstable alliances, improvised power relations, and escalating suspicions. Here every term—friend and foe, tenderness and brutality, savagery and civilization—can suddenly turn into its opposite. And the author also seems caught between worlds. The cultivated Englishwoman who narrates and acts in this memoir thinks highly of her hero's code of honor and shares his contempt for the riffraff who plague him. Yet her own role is ambiguous: she lacks the power to save Oroonoko and might even be viewed as implicated in his downfall. Only as a writer can she take control, preserving the hero in her work.

The story of Oroonoko did not end with Behn. Compassion for the royal slave and outrage at his fate were enlisted in the long battle against the slave trade. Reprinted, translated, serialized, dramatized, and much imitated, *Oroonoko* helped teach a mass audience to feel for all victims of the brutal commerce in human beings. A hundred years later, the popular writer Hannah More testified to the widening influence of the story: "No individual griefs my bosom melt, / For millions feel what Oroonoko felt." Women especially identified with the experience of personal injustice and everyday indignity—the pain of being treated as something less than fully human. Perhaps it is appropriate that the writer who made the suffering of the royal slave famous had known the pride and lowliness of being "a female pen."

The Disappointment[1]

> One day the amorous Lysander,
> By an impatient passion swayed,
> Surprised fair Cloris, that loved maid,
> Who could defend herself no longer.
> 5 All things did with his love conspire;
> The gilded planet of the day,°   *the sun*
> In his gay chariot drawn by fire,
> Was now descending to the sea,
> And left no light to guide the world
> 10 But what from Cloris' brighter eyes was hurled.
>
> In a lone thicket made for love,
> Silent as yielding maid's consent,

1. This variation on the "imperfect enjoyment" genre compares with Rochester's (p. 2163); it first appeared in a collection of his poems. But Behn gives the theme of impotence her own twist. Freely translating a French poem, Cantenac's *The Lost* *Chance Recovered*, she cuts the conclusion, in which the French lover regained his potency, and she highlights the woman's feelings as well as the man's.

She with a charming languishment,
Permits his force, yet gently strove;
15   Her hands his bosom softly meet,
But not to put him back designed,
Rather to draw 'em on inclined:
Whilst he lay trembling at her feet,
Resistance 'tis in vain to show:
20   She wants° the power to say—*Ah! what d'ye do?*   lacks

Her bright eyes sweet and yet severe,
Where love and shame confusedly strive,
Fresh vigor to Lysander give;
And breathing faintly in his ear,
25   She cried—*Cease, cease—your vain desire,*
Or I'll call out—what would you do?
My dearer honor even to you
I cannot, must not give—Retire,
Or take this life, whose chiefest part
30   *I gave you with the conquest of my heart.*

But he as much unused to fear,
As he was capable of love,
The blessed minutes to improve
Kisses her mouth, her neck, her hair;
35   Each touch her new desire alarms;
His burning, trembling hand he pressed
Upon her swelling snowy breast,
While she lay panting in his arms.
All her unguarded beauties lie
40   The spoils and trophies of the enemy.

And now without respect or fear
He seeks the object of his vows
(His love no modesty allows)
By swift degrees advancing—where
45   His daring hand that altar seized,
Where gods of love do sacrifice:
That awful throne, that paradise
Where rage is calmed, and anger pleased;
That fountain where delight still flows,
50   And gives the universal world respose.

Her balmy lips encountering his,
Their bodies, as their souls, are joined;
Where both in transports unconfined
Extend themselves upon the moss.
55   Cloris half dead and breathless lay;
Her soft eyes cast a humid light
Such as divides the day and night;
Or falling stars, whose fires decay:
And now no signs of life she shows,
60   But what in short-breathed sighs returns and goes.

He saw how at her length she lay;
He saw her rising bosom bare;
Her loose thin robes, through which appear
A shape designed for love and play;
65   Abandoned by her pride and shame
She does her softest joys dispense,
Offering her virgin innocence
A victim to love's sacred flame;
While the o'er-ravished shepherd lies
70   Unable to perform the sacrifice.

Ready to taste a thousand joys,
The too transported hapless swain
Found the vast pleasure turned to pain;
Pleasure which too much love destroys:
75   The willing garments by he laid,[2]
And heaven all opened to his view.
Mad to possess, himself he threw
On the defenseless lovely maid.
But oh what envying god conspires
80   To snatch his power, yet leave him the desire!

Nature's support (without whose aid
She can no human being give)
Itself now wants the art[3] to live;
Faintness its slackened nerves invade:
85   In vain th'enraged youth essayed
To call its fleeting vigor back;
No motion 'twill from motion take;
Excess of love his love betrayed:
In vain he toils, in vain commands:
90   The insensible[4] fell weeping in his hand.

In this so amorous cruel strife,
Where love and fate were too severe,
The poor Lysander in despair
Renounced his reason with his life:
95   Now all the brisk and active fire
That should the nobler part inflame
Served to increase his rage and shame,
And left no spark for new desire:
Not all her naked charms could move
100 Or calm that rage that had debauched his love.

Cloris returning from the trance
Which love and soft desire had bred,
Her timorous hand she gently laid
(Or guided by design or chance)
105 Upon that fabulous Priapus,[5]
That potent god, as poets feign:

2. He took off her compliant clothes.
3. Lacks the capacity.
4. Devoid of feeling and too small to be noticed.

5. Phallus. The ancient god Priapus is always pictured with an outstanding erection.

But never did young shepherdess,
Gathering the fern upon the plain,
More nimbly draw her fingers back,
110 Finding beneath the verdant leaves a snake,

Than Cloris her fair hand withdrew,
Finding that god of her desires
Disarmed of all his awful fires,
And cold as flowers bathed in the morning dew.
115 Who can the nymph's confusion guess?
The blood forsook the hinder place,
And strewed with blushes all her face,
Which both disdain and shame expressed:
And from Lysander's arms she fled,
120 Leaving him fainting on the gloomy bed.

Like lightning through the grove she hies,
Or Daphne from the Delphic god;[6]
No print upon the grassy road
She leaves, to instruct pursuing eyes.
125 The wind that wantoned in her hair
And with her ruffled garments played,
Discovered in the flying maid
All that the gods e'er made, if fair.
So Venus, when her love[7] was slain,
130 With fear and haste flew o'er the fatal plain.

The nymph's resentments none but I
Can well imagine or condole:
But none can guess Lysander's soul,
But those who swayed his destiny.
135 His silent griefs swell up to storms,
And not one god his fury spares;
He cursed his birth, his fate, his stars;
But more the shepherdess's charms,
Whose soft bewitching influence
140 Had damned him to the hell of impotence.[8]

1680

Oroonoko, or The Royal Slave[1]

I do not pretend, in giving you the history of this royal slave, to entertain my reader with the adventures of a feigned hero, whose life and fortunes

6. Apollo, from whom the Greek nymph Daphne fled until she turned into a laurel tree.
7. Adonis, who was killed by a boar.
8. Blaming the woman for an imperfect enjoyment is typical of the genre.
1. The text, prepared by Joanna Lipking, is based

on the 1688 edition, the sole edition published during Behn's lifetime. The critical edition of G. C. Duchovnay (diss., Indiana, 1971), which collates the four 17th-century editions, has been consulted.

fancy may manage at the poet's pleasure; nor in relating the truth, design to adorn it with any accidents but such as arrived in earnest to him. And it shall come simply into the world, recommended by its own proper merits and natural intrigues, there being enough of reality to support it, and to render it diverting, without the addition of invention.

I was myself an eyewitness to a great part of what you will find here set down, and what I could not be witness of, I received from the mouth of the chief actor in this history, the hero himself, who gave us the whole transactions of his youth; and though I shall omit for brevity's sake a thousand little accidents of his life, which, however pleasant to us, where history was scarce and adventures very rare, yet might prove tedious and heavy to my reader, in a world where he finds diversions for every minute, new and strange. But we who were perfectly charmed with the character of this great man were curious to gather every circumstance of his life.

The scene of the last part of his adventures lies in a colony in America called Surinam,[2] in the West Indies.

But before I give you the story of this gallant slave, 'tis fit I tell you the manner of bringing them to these new colonies, for those they make use of there are not natives of the place; for those we live with in perfect amity, without daring to command 'em, but on the contrary caress 'em with all the brotherly and friendly affection in the world, trading with 'em for their fish, venison, buffaloes,[3] skins, and little rarities; as marmosets, a sort of monkey as big as a rat or weasel but of a marvelous and delicate shape, and has face and hands like a human creature, and *cousheries*,[4] a little beast in the form and fashion of a lion, as big as a kitten, but so exactly made in all parts like that noble beast, that it is it in miniature. Then for little parakeetoes, great parrots, macaws, and a thousand other birds and beasts of wonderful and surprising forms, shapes, and colors. For skins of prodigious snakes, of which there are some threescore yards in length, as is the skin of one that may be seen at his Majesty's antiquaries'; where are also some rare flies[5] of amazing forms and colors, presented to 'em by myself, some as big as my fist, some less, and all of various excellencies, such as art cannot imitate. Then we trade for feathers, which they order into all shapes, make themselves little short habits of 'em, and glorious wreaths for their heads, necks, arms and legs, whose tinctures are unconceivable. I had a set of these presented to me, and I gave 'em to the King's theater, and it was the dress of the Indian Queen,[6] infinitely admired by persons of quality, and were unimitable. Besides these, a thousand little knacks and rarities in nature, and some of art, as their baskets, weapons, aprons, et cetera. We dealt with 'em with beads of all colors, knives, axes, pins and needles, which they used only as tools to drill holes with in their ears, noses, and lips, where they hang a great many little things, as long beads, bits of tin, brass, or silver beat thin, and any shining trinket. The beads they weave into aprons about a quarter of an ell long, and of the same breadth,[7] working them very prettily in flowers of

---

2. A British sugar colony on the South American coast east of Venezuela; later Dutch Guiana.
3. Wild oxen of various species.
4. A name appearing in local descriptions, but the animal is not clearly identified; probably the lion-headed marmoset or perhaps the *cujara* (Portuguese), a rodent known as the rice rat.

5. Butterflies.
6. The title character in the 1664 heroic play by Sir Robert Howard and John Dryden, which was noted for its lavish production. There are contemporary records of "speckled plumes" and feather headdresses.
7. About a foot square.

several colors of beads; which apron they wear just before 'em, as Adam and Eve did the fig leaves, the men wearing a long stripe of linen which they deal with us for. They thread these beads also on long cotton threads and make girdles to tie their aprons to, which come twenty times or more about the waist, and then cross, like a shoulder belt, both ways, and round their necks, arms, and legs. This adornment, with their long black hair, and the face painted in little specks or flowers here and there, makes 'em a wonderful figure to behold.

Some of the beauties which indeed are finely shaped, as almost all are, and who have pretty features, are very charming and novel; for they have all that is called beauty, except the color, which is a reddish yellow; or after a new oiling, which they often use to themselves, they are of the color of a new brick, but smooth, soft, and sleek. They are extreme[8] modest and bashful, very shy and nice of being touched. And though they are all thus naked, if one lives forever among 'em there is not to be seen an indecent action or glance; and being continually used to see one another so unadorned, so like our first parents before the Fall, it seems as if they had no wishes; there being nothing to heighten curiosity, but all you can see you see at once, and every moment see, and where there is no novelty there can be no curiosity. Not but I have seen a handsome young Indian dying for love of a very beautiful young Indian maid; but all his courtship was to fold his arms, pursue her with his eyes, and sighs were all his language; while she, as if no such lover were present, or rather, as if she desired none such, carefully guarded her eyes from beholding him, and never approached him but she looked down with all the blushing modesty I have seen in the most severe and cautious of our world. And these people represented to me an absolute idea of the first state of innocence, before man knew how to sin. And 'tis most evident and plain that simple Nature is the most harmless, inoffensive, and virtuous mistress. 'Tis she alone, if she were permitted, that better instructs the world than all the inventions of man. Religion would here but destroy that tranquillity they possess by ignorance, and laws would but teach 'em to know offense, of which now they have no notion. They once made mourning and fasting for the death of the English governor, who had given his hand to come on such a day to 'em and neither came nor sent, believing when once a man's word was passed, nothing but death could or should prevent his keeping it. And when they saw he was not dead, they asked him what name they had for a man who promised a thing he did not do. The governor told them, such a man was a liar, which was a word of infamy to a gentleman. Then one of 'em replied, "Governor, you are a liar, and guilty of that infamy." They have a native justice which knows no fraud, and they understand no vice or cunning, but when they are taught by the white men. They have plurality of wives, which, when they grow old, they serve those that succeed 'em, who are young, but with a servitude easy and respected; and unless they take slaves in war, they have no other attendants.

Those on that continent where I was had no king, but the oldest war captain was obeyed with great resignation. A war captain is a man who has led them on to battle with conduct[9] and success, of whom I shall have occasion to speak more hereafter, and of some other of their customs and manners, as they fall in my way.

---

8. Extremely. 9. Capacity to lead.

With these people, as I said, we live in perfect tranquillity and good understanding, as it behooves us to do, they knowing all the places where to seek
the best food of the country and the means of getting it, and for very small
and unvaluable trifles, supply us with what 'tis impossible for us to get; for
they do not only in the wood and over the savannas, in hunting, supply the
parts of hounds, by swiftly scouring through those almost impassable places,
and by the mere activity of their feet run down the nimblest deer and other
eatable beasts; but in the water one would think they were gods of the rivers,
or fellow citizens of the deep, so rare an art they have in swimming, diving,
and almost living in water, by which they command the less swift inhabitants
of the floods. And then for shooting, what they cannot take, or reach with
their hands, they do with arrows, and have so admirable an aim that they
will split almost a hair; and at any distance that an arrow can reach, they
will shoot down oranges and other fruit, and only touch the stalk with the
dart's point, that they may not hurt the fruit. So that they being, on all
occasions, very useful to us, we find it absolutely necessary to caress 'em as
friends, and not to treat 'em as slaves; nor dare we do other, their numbers
so far surpassing ours in that continent.

Those then whom we make use of to work in our plantations of sugar are
Negroes, black slaves altogether, which are transported thither in this manner. Those who want slaves make a bargain with a master or captain of a
ship and contract to pay him so much apiece, a matter of twenty pound a
head for as many as he agrees for, and to pay for 'em when they shall be
delivered on such a plantation. So that when there arrives a ship laden with
slaves, they who have so contracted go aboard and receive their number by
lot; and perhaps in one lot that may be for ten, there may happen to be three
or four men, the rest women and children. Or be there more or less of either
sex, you are obliged to be contented with your lot.

Coramantien,[1] a country of blacks so called, was one of those places in
which they found the most advantageous trading for these slaves, and thither
most of our great traders in that merchandise trafficked; for that nation is
very warlike and brave, and having a continual campaign, being always in
hostility with one neighboring prince or other, they had the fortune to take
a great many captives; for all they took in battle were sold as slaves, at least
those common men who could not ransom themselves. Of these slaves so
taken, the general only has all the profit; and of these generals, our captains
and masters of ships buy all their freights.

The King of Coramantien was himself a man of a hundred and odd years
old, and had no son, though he had many beautiful black wives; for most
certainly there are beauties that can charm of that color. In his younger years
he had had many gallant men to his sons, thirteen of which died in battle,
conquering when they fell; and he had only left him for his successor one
grandchild, son to one of these dead victors, who, as soon as he could bear
a bow in his hand and a quiver at his back, was sent into the field, to be
trained up by one of the oldest generals to war; where, from his natural
inclination to arms and the occasions given him, with the good conduct of
the old general, he became, at the age of seventeen, one of the most expert

---

1. Not a country but a British-held fort and slave
market on the Gold Coast of Africa, in modern-day
Ghana. As the slave trade expanded, the slaves and
workers shipped out from the region (who came to
be called Cormantines) impressed many European
observers by their beauty and bearing, their fierceness in war, and their extreme dignity under captivity or torture.

captains and bravest soldiers that ever saw the field of Mars. So that he was adored as the wonder of all that world, and the darling of the soldiers. Besides, he was adorned with a native beauty so transcending all those of his gloomy race that he struck an awe and reverence even in those that knew not his quality; as he did in me, who beheld him with surprise and wonder, when afterwards he arrived in our world.

He had scarce arrived at his seventeenth year, when fighting by his side, the general was killed with an arrow in his eye, which the Prince Oroonoko (for so was this gallant Moor[2] called) very narrowly avoided; nor had he, if the general, who saw the arrow shot, and perceiving it aimed at the Prince, had not bowed his head between, on purpose to receive it in his own body rather than it should touch that of the Prince, and so saved him.

'Twas then, afflicted as Oroonoko was, that he was proclaimed general in the old man's place; and then it was, at the finishing of that war, which had continued for two years, that the Prince came to court, where he had hardly been a month together from the time of his fifth year to that of seventeen; and 'twas amazing to imagine where it was he learned so much humanity; or to give his accomplishments a juster name, where 'twas he got that real greatness of soul, those refined notions of true honor, that absolute generosity, and that softness that was capable of the highest passions of love and gallantry, whose objects were almost continually fighting men, or those mangled or dead; who heard no sounds but those of war and groans. Some part of it we may attribute to the care of a Frenchman of wit and learning, who, finding it turn to very good account to be a sort of royal tutor to this young black, and perceiving him very ready, apt, and quick of apprehension, took a great pleasure to teach him morals, language, and science, and was for it extremely beloved and valued by him. Another reason was, he loved, when he came from war, to see all the English gentlemen that traded thither, and did not only learn their language but that of the Spaniards also, with whom he traded afterwards for slaves.

I have often seen and conversed with this great man, and been a witness to many of his mighty actions, and do assure my reader the most illustrious courts could not have produced a braver man, both for greatness of courage and mind, a judgment more solid, a wit more quick, and a conversation more sweet and diverting. He knew almost as much as if he had read much. He had heard of and admired the Romans; he had heard of the late civil wars in England, and the deplorable death of our great monarch,[3] and would discourse of it with all the sense and abhorrence of the injustice imaginable. He had an extreme good and graceful mien, and all the civility of a well-bred great man. He had nothing of barbarity in his nature, but in all points addressed himself as if his education had been in some European court.

This great and just character of Oroonoko gave me an extreme curiosity to see him, especially when I knew he spoke French and English, and that I could talk with him. But though I had heard so much of him, I was as greatly surprised when I saw him as if I had heard nothing of him, so beyond all report I found him. He came into the room and addressed himself to me,

---

2. Loosely used for any black-skinned person.
3. Charles I, beheaded in 1649 during the civil wars between Royalists and Parliamentarians. In 1688, this remark and others would have signaled

Behn's ardent support of James II, the last of the Stuart kings, who would be forced into exile within the year.

and some other women, with the best grace in the world. He was pretty tall, but of a shape the most exact that can be fancied. The most famous statuary[4] could not form the figure of a man more admirably turned from head to foot. His face was not of that brown, rusty black which most of that nation are, but a perfect ebony or polished jet. His eyes were the most awful that could be seen, and very piercing, the white of 'em being like snow, as were his teeth. His nose was rising and Roman, instead of African and flat; his mouth the finest shaped that could be seen, far from those great turned lips which are so natural to the rest of the Negroes. The whole proportion and air of his face was so noble and exactly formed that, bating[5] his color, there could be nothing in nature more beautiful, agreeable, and handsome. There was no one grace wanting that bears the standard of true beauty. His hair came down to his shoulders by the aids of art; which was by pulling it out with a quill and keeping it combed, of which he took particular care. Nor did the perfections of his mind come short of those of his person, for his discourse was admirable upon almost any subject; and whoever had heard him speak would have been convinced of their errors, that all fine wit is confined to the white men, especially to those of Christendom, and would have confessed that Oroonoko was as capable even of reigning well, and of governing as wisely, had as great a soul, as politic[6] maxims, and was as sensible of power, as any prince civilized in the most refined schools of humanity and learning, or the most illustrious courts.

This prince, such as I have described him, whose soul and body were so admirably adorned, was (while yet he was in the court of his grandfather), as I said, as capable of love as 'twas possible for a brave and gallant man to be; and in saying that, I have named the highest degree of love, for sure, great souls are most capable of that passion.

I have already said, the old general was killed by the shot of an arrow, by the side of this prince, in battle, and that Oroonoko was made general. This old dead hero had one only daughter left of his race, a beauty that, to describe her truly, one need say only she was female to the noble male, the beautiful black Venus to our young Mars, as charming in her person as he, and of delicate virtues. I have seen an hundred white men sighing after her, and making a thousand vows at her feet, all vain and unsuccessful. And she was, indeed, too great for any but a prince of her own nation to adore.

Oroonoko coming from the wars (which were now ended), after he had made his court to his grandfather, he thought in honor he ought to make a visit to Imoinda, the daughter of his foster-father, the dead general; and to make some excuses to her, because his preservation was the occasion of her father's death; and to present her with those slaves that had been taken in this last battle, as the trophies of her father's victories. When he came, attended by all the young soldiers of any merit, he was infinitely surprised at the beauty of this fair queen of night, whose face and person was so exceeding all he had ever beheld; that lovely modesty with which she received him; that softness in her look, and sighs, upon the melancholy occasion of this

4. Sculptor.
5. Except for. The singling out of Africans with European looks or moral values is by no means unique to Behn; for example, Edward Long's 1774 *History of Jamaica* reports of the Cormantines that

"their features are very different from the rest of the African Negroes, being smaller, and more of the European turn."
6. Shrewd, sagacious.

honor that was done by so great a man as Oroonoko, and a prince of whom she had heard such admirable things: the awfulness[7] wherewith she received him, and the sweetness of her words and behavior while he stayed, gained a perfect conquest over his fierce heart, and made him feel the victor could be subdued. So that having made his first compliments, and presented her a hundred and fifty slaves in fetters, he told her with his eyes that he was not insensible of her charms; while Imoinda, who wished for nothing more than so glorious a conquest, was pleased to believe she understood that silent language of newborn love, and from that moment put on all her additions to beauty.

The Prince returned to court with quite another humor than before; and though he did not speak much of the fair Imoinda, he had the pleasure to hear all his followers speak of nothing but the charms of that maid, insomuch that, even in the presence of the old king, they were extolling her and heightening, if possible, the beauties they had found in her. So that nothing else was talked of, no other sound was heard in every corner where there were whisperers, but "Imoinda! Imoinda!"

'Twill be imagined Oroonoko stayed not long before he made his second visit, nor, considering his quality, not much longer before he told her he adored her. I have often heard him say that he admired[8] by what strange inspiration he came to talk things so soft and so passionate, who never knew love, nor was used to the conversation[9] of women; but (to use his own words) he said, most happily some new and till then unknown power instructed his heart and tongue in the language of love, and at the same time, in favor of him, inspired Imoinda with a sense of his passion. She was touched with what he said, and returned it all in such answers as went to his very heart, with a pleasure unknown before. Nor did he use those obligations[1] ill that love had done him, but turned all his happy moments to the best advantage; and as he knew no vice, his flame aimed at nothing but honor, if such a distinction may be made in love; and especially in that country, where men take to themselves as many as they can maintain, and where the only crime and sin with woman is to turn her off, to abandon her to want, shame, and misery. Such ill morals are only practiced in Christian countries, where they prefer the bare name of religion, and, without virtue or morality, think that's sufficient. But Oroonoko was none of those professors, but as he had right notions of honor, so he made her such propositions as were not only and barely such; but contrary to the custom of his country, he made her vows she should be the only woman he would possess while he lived; that no age or wrinkles should incline him to change, for her soul would be always fine and always young, and he should have an eternal idea in his mind of the charms she now bore, and should look into his heart for that idea when he could find it no longer in her face.

After a thousand assurances of his lasting flame, and her eternal empire over him, she condescended to receive him for her husband, or rather, received him as the greatest honor the gods could do her.

There is a certain ceremony in these cases to be observed, which I forgot to ask him how performed; but 'twas concluded on both sides that, in obe-

---

7. Reverence.
8. Marveled.
9. Company.
1. Benefits.

dience to him, the grandfather was to be first made acquainted with the design, for they pay a most absolute resignation to the monarch, especially when he is a parent also.

On the other side, the old king, who had many wives and many concubines, wanted not court flatterers to insinuate in his heart a thousand tender thoughts for this young beauty, and who represented her to his fancy as the most charming he had ever possessed in all the long race of his numerous years. At this character his old heart, like an extinguished brand, most apt to take fire, felt new sparks of love and began to kindle; and now grown to his second childhood, longed with impatience to behold this gay thing, with whom, alas! he could but innocently play. But how he should be confirmed she was this wonder, before he used his power to call her to court (where maidens never came, unless for the King's private use), he was next to consider; and while he was so doing, he had intelligence brought him that Imoinda was most certainly mistress to the Prince Oroonoko. This gave him some chagrin; however, it gave him also an opportunity, one day when the Prince was a-hunting, to wait on a man of quality, as his slave and attendant, who should go and make a present to Imoinda as from the Prince; he should then, unknown, see this fair maid, and have an opportunity to hear what message she would return the Prince for his present, and from thence gather the state of her heart and degree of her inclination. This was put in execution, and the old monarch saw, and burned. He found her all he had heard, and would not delay his happiness, but found he should have some obstacle to overcome her heart; for she expressed her sense of the present the Prince had sent her in terms so sweet, so soft and pretty, with an air of love and joy that could not be dissembled, insomuch that 'twas past doubt whether she loved Oroonoko entirely. This gave the old king some affliction, but he salved it with this, that the obedience the people pay their king was not at all inferior to what they paid their gods; and what love would not oblige Imoinda to do, duty would compel her to.

He was therefore no sooner got to his apartment but he sent the royal veil to Imoinda, that is, the ceremony of invitation: he sends the lady he has a mind to honor with his bed a veil, with which she is covered, and secured for the King's use; and 'tis death to disobey, besides held a most impious disobedience.

'Tis not to be imagined the surprise and grief that seized this lovely maid at this news and sight. However, as delays in these cases are dangerous and pleading worse than treason, trembling, and almost fainting, she was obliged to suffer herself to be covered and led away.

They brought her thus to court; and the King, who had caused a very rich bath to be prepared, was led into it, where he sat under a canopy, in state, to receive this longed-for virgin; whom he having commanded should be brought to him, they (after disrobing her) led her to the bath, and making fast the doors, left her to descend. The King, without more courtship, bade her throw off her mantle and come to his arms. But Imoinda, all in tears, threw herself on the marble, on the brink of the bath, and besought him to hear her. She told him, as she was a maid, how proud of the divine glory she should have been, of having it in her power to oblige her king; but as by the laws he could not, and from his royal goodness would not, take from any man his wedded wife, so she believed she should be the occasion of making him commit a great sin, if she did not reveal her state and condition, and tell him she was another's, and could not be so happy to be his.

The King, enraged at this delay, hastily demanded the name of the bold man that had married a woman of her degree without his consent. Imoinda, seeing his eyes fierce and his hands tremble (whether with age or anger, I know not, but she fancied the last), almost repented she had said so much, for now she feared the storm would fall on the Prince. She therefore said a thousand things to appease the raging of his flame, and to prepare him to hear who it was with calmness; but before she spoke, he imagined who she meant, but would not seem to do so, but commanded her to lay aside her mantle and suffer herself to receive his caresses; or by his gods, he swore that happy man whom she was going to name should die, though it were even Oroonoko himself. "Therefore," said he, "deny this marriage, and swear thyself a maid." "That," replied Imoinda, "by all our powers I do, for I am not yet known to my husband." " 'Tis enough," said the King; " 'tis enough to satisfy both my conscience and my heart." And rising from his seat, he went and led her into the bath, it being in vain for her to resist.

In this time the Prince, who was returned from hunting, went to visit his Imoinda, but found her gone; and not only so, but heard she had received the royal veil. This raised him to a storm, and in his madness they had much ado to save him from laying violent hands on himself. Force first prevailed, and then reason. They urged all to him that might oppose his rage, but nothing weighed so greatly with him as the King's old age, uncapable of injuring him with Imoinda. He would give way to that hope, because it pleased him most, and flattered best his heart. Yet this served not altogether to make him cease his different passions, which sometimes raged within him, and sometimes softened into showers. 'Twas not enough to appease him, to tell him his grandfather was old and could not that way injure him, while he retained that awful duty which the young men are used there to pay to their grave relations. He could not be convinced he had no cause to sigh and mourn for the loss of a mistress he could not with all his strength and courage retrieve. And he would often cry, "O my friends! Were she in walled cities or confined from me in fortifications of the greatest strength, did enchantments or monsters detain her from me, I would venture through any hazard to free her. But here, in the arms of a feeble old man, my youth, my violent love, my trade in arms, and all my vast desire of glory avail me nothing. Imoinda is as irrecoverably lost to me as if she were snatched by the cold arms of Death. Oh! she is never to be retrieved. If I would wait tedious years, till fate should bow the old king to his grave, even that would not leave me Imoinda free; but still that custom that makes it so vile a crime for a son to marry his father's wives or mistresses would hinder my happiness, unless I would either ignobly set an ill precedent to my successors, or abandon my country and fly with her to some unknown world, who never heard our story."

But it was objected to him that his case was not the same; for Imoinda being his lawful wife, by solemn contract, 'twas he was the injured man and might if he so pleased take Imoinda back, the breach of the law being on his grandfather's side; and that if he could circumvent him and redeem her from the Otan, which is the palace of the King's women, a sort of seraglio, it was both just and lawful for him so to do.

This reasoning had some force upon him, and he should have been entirely comforted, but for the thought that she was possessed by his grandfather. However, he loved so well that he was resolved to believe what most favored his hope, and to endeavor to learn from Imoinda's own mouth what only she could satisfy him in, whether she was robbed of that blessing which was only due to his faith and love. But as it was very hard to get a sight of the women (for no men ever entered into the Otan but when the King went to entertain himself with some one of his wives or mistresses, and 'twas death at any other time for any other to go in), so he knew not how to contrive to get a sight of her.

While Oroonoko felt all the agonies of love, and suffered under a torment the most painful in the world, the old king was not exempted from his share of affliction. He was troubled for having been forced by an irresistible passion to rob his son[2] of a treasure he knew could not but be extremely dear to him, since she was the most beautiful that ever had been seen, and had besides all the sweetness and innocence of youth and modesty, with a charm of wit surpassing all. He found that, however she was forced to expose her lovely person to his withered arms, she could only sigh and weep there, and think of Oroonoko; and oftentimes could not forbear speaking of him, though her life were, by custom, forfeited by owning her passion. But she spoke not of a lover only, but of a prince dear to him to whom she spoke, and of the praises of a man who, till now, filled the old man's soul with joy at every recital of his bravery, or even his name. And 'twas this dotage on our young hero that gave Imoinda a thousand privileges to speak of him without offending, and this condescension in the old king that made her take the satisfaction of speaking of him so very often.

Besides, he many times inquired how the Prince bore himself; and those of whom he asked, being entirely slaves to the merits and virtues of the Prince, still answered what they thought conduced best to his service; which was to make the old king fancy that the Prince had no more interest in Imoinda, and had resigned her willingly to the pleasure of the King; that he diverted himself with his mathematicians, his fortifications, his officers, and his hunting.

This pleased the old lover, who failed not to report these things again to Imoinda, that she might, by the example of her young lover, withdraw her heart, and rest better contented in his arms. But however she was forced to receive this unwelcome news, in all appearance with unconcern and content, her heart was bursting within, and she was only happy when she could get alone, to vent her griefs and moans with sighs and tears.

What reports of the Prince's conduct were made to the King, he thought good to justify as far as possibly he could by his actions, and when he appeared in the presence of the King, he showed a face not at all betraying his heart. So that in a little time, the old man being entirely convinced that he was no longer a lover of Imoinda, he carried him with him in his train to the Otan, often to banquet with his mistress. But as soon as he entered, one day, into the apartment of Imoinda with the King, at the first glance from her eyes, notwithstanding all his determined resolution, he was ready to sink in the place where he stood, and had certainly done so but for the support of Aboan, a young man who was next to him; which, with his change of

2. I.e., grandson.

countenance, had betrayed him, had the King chanced to look that way. And I have observed, 'tis a very great error, in those who laugh when one says a Negro can change color, for I have seen 'em as frequently blush, and look pale, and that as visibly as ever I saw in the most beautiful white. And 'tis certain that both these changes were evident, this day, in both these lovers. And Imoinda, who saw with some joy the change in the Prince's face, and found it in her own, strove to divert the King from beholding either by a forced caress, with which she met him, which was a new wound in the heart of the poor dying Prince. But as soon as the King was busied in looking on some fine thing of Imoinda's making, she had time to tell the Prince with her angry but love-darting eyes that she resented his coldness, and bemoaned her own miserable captivity. Nor were his eyes silent, but answered hers again, as much as eyes could do, instructed by the most tender and most passionate heart that ever loved. And they spoke so well and so effectually, as Imoinda no longer doubted but she was the only delight and the darling of that soul she found pleading in 'em its right of love, which none was more willing to resign than she. And 'twas this powerful language alone that in an instant conveyed all the thoughts of their souls to each other, that[3] they both found there wanted but opportunity to make them both entirely happy. But when he saw another door opened by Onahal, a former old wife of the King's who now had charge of Imoinda, and saw the prospect of a bed of state made ready with sweets and flowers for the dalliance of the King, who immediately led the trembling victim from his sight into that prepared repose, what rage, what wild frenzies seized his heart! which forcing to keep within bounds, and to suffer without noise, it became the more insupportable, and rent his soul with ten thousand pains. He was forced to retire to vent his groans, where he fell down on a carpet and lay struggling a long time, and only breathing now and then, "—O Imoinda!"

When Onahal had finished her necessary affair within, shutting the door, she came forth to wait till the King called; and hearing someone sighing in the other room, she passed on, and found the Prince in that deplorable condition, which she thought needed her aid. She gave him cordials, but all in vain, till finding the nature of his disease by his sighs and naming Imoinda. She told him, he had not so much cause as he imagined to afflict himself, for if he knew the King so well as she did, he would not lose a moment in jealousy, and that she was confident that Imoinda bore, at this minute, part in his affliction. Aboan was of the same opinion, and both together persuaded him to reassume his courage; and all sitting down on the carpet, the Prince said so many obliging things to Onahal that he half persuaded her to be of his party. And she promised him she would thus far comply with his just desires, that she would let Imoinda know how faithful he was, what he suffered, and what he said.

This discourse lasted till the King called, which gave Oroonoko a certain satisfaction, and with the hope Onahal had made him conceive, he assumed a look as gay as 'twas possible a man in his circumstances could do; and presently after, he was called in with the rest who waited without. The King commanded music to be brought, and several of his young wives and mistresses came all together by his command to dance before him; where

3. So that.

Imoinda performed her part with an air and grace so passing all the rest as her beauty was above 'em, and received the present ordained as a prize. The Prince was every moment more charmed with the new beauties and graces he beheld in this fair one. And while he gazed, and she danced, Onahal was retired to a window with Aboan.

This Onahal, as I said, was one of the cast[4] mistresses of the old king; and 'twas these (now past their beauty) that were made guardians or governants[5] to the new and the young ones, and whose business it was to teach them all those wanton arts of love with which they prevailed and charmed heretofore in their turn; and who now treated the triumphing happy ones with all the severity, as to liberty and freedom, that was possible, in revenge of those honors they rob them of; envying them those satisfactions, those gallantries and presents, that were once made to themselves, while youth and beauty lasted, and which they now saw pass regardless by, and paid only to the bloomings. And certainly nothing is more afflicting to a decayed beauty than to behold in itself declining charms that were once adored, and to find those caresses paid to new beauties to which once she laid a claim; to hear 'em whisper as she passes by, "That once was a delicate woman." These abandoned ladies therefore endeavor to revenge all the despites[6] and decays of time on these flourishing happy ones. And 'twas this severity that gave Oroonoko a thousand fears he should never prevail with Onahal to see Imoinda. But, as I said, she was now retired to a window with Aboan.

This young man was not only one of the best quality,[7] but a man extremely well made and beautiful; and coming often to attend the King to the Otan, he had subdued the heart of the antiquated Onahal, which had not forgot how pleasant it was to be in love. And though she had some decays in her face, she had none in her sense and wit; she was there agreeable still, even to Aboan's youth, so that he took pleasure in entertaining her with discourses of love. He knew also that to make his court to these she-favorites was the way to be great, these being the persons that do all affairs and business at court. He had also observed that she had given him glances more tender and inviting than she had done to others of his quality. And now, when he saw that her favor could so absolutely oblige the Prince, he failed not to sigh in her ear and to look with eyes all soft upon her, and give her hope that she had made some impressions on his heart. He found her pleased at this, and making a thousand advances to him; but the ceremony ending and the King departing broke up the company for that day, and his conversation.

Aboan failed not that night to tell the Prince of his success, and how advantageous the service of Onahal might be to his amour with Imoinda. The Prince was overjoyed with this good news and besought him, if it were possible, to caress her so as to engage her entirely, which he could not fail to do, if he complied with her desires. "For then," said the Prince, "her life lying at your mercy, she must grant you the request you make in my behalf." Aboan understood him, and assured him he would make love so effectually that he would defy the most expert mistress of the art to find out whether he dissembled it or had it really. And 'twas with impatience they waited the next opportunity of going to the Otan.

4. Cast-off.
5. Female teachers or chaperones.
6. Insults.
7. Rank.

The wars came on, the time of taking the field approached, and 'twas impossible for the Prince to delay his going at the head of his army to encounter the enemy. So that every day seemed a tedious year till he saw his Imoinda, for he believed he could not live if he were forced away without being so happy. 'Twas with impatience, therefore, that he expected the next visit the King would make, and according to his wish, it was not long.

The parley of the eyes of these two lovers had not passed so secretly but an old jealous lover could spy it; or rather, he wanted not flatterers who told him they observed it. So that the Prince was hastened to the camp, and this was the last visit he found he should make to the Otan; he therefore urged Aboan to make the best of this last effort, and to explain himself so to Onahal that she, deferring her enjoyment of her young lover no longer, might make way for the Prince to speak to Imoinda.

The whole affair being agreed on between the Prince and Aboan, they attended the King, as the custom was, to the Otan, where, while the whole company was taken up in beholding the dancing and antic postures the women-royal made to divert the King, Onahal singled out Aboan, whom she found most pliable to her wish. When she had him where she believed she could not be heard, she sighed to him, and softly cried, "Ah, Aboan! When will you be sensible of my passion? I confess it with my mouth, because I would not give my eyes the lie; and you have but too much already perceived they have confessed my flame. Nor would I have you believe that because I am the abandoned mistress of a king, I esteem myself altogether divested of charms. No, Aboan; I have still a rest[8] of beauty enough engaging, and have learned to please too well not to be desirable. I can have lovers still, but will have none but Aboan." "Madam," replied the half-feigning youth, "you have already, by my eyes, found you can still conquer, and I believe 'tis in pity of me you condescend to this kind confession. But, Madam, words are used to be so small a part of our country courtship, that 'tis rare one can get so happy an opportunity as to tell one's heart, and those few minutes we have are forced to be snatched for more certain proofs of love than speaking and sighing; and such I languish for."

He spoke this with such a tone that she hoped it true, and could not forbear believing it; and being wholly transported with joy, for having subdued the finest of all the King's subjects to her desires, she took from her ears two large pearls and commanded him to wear 'em in his. He would have refused 'em, crying, "Madam, these are not the proofs of your love that I expect; 'tis opportunity, 'tis a lone hour only, that can make me happy." But forcing the pearls into his hand, she whispered softly to him, "Oh! Do not fear a woman's invention, when love sets her a-thinking." And pressing his hand, she cried, "This night you shall be happy. Come to the gate of the orange groves behind the Otan, and I will be ready, about midnight, to receive you." 'Twas thus agreed, and she left him, that no notice might be taken of their speaking together.

The ladies were still dancing, and the King, laid on a carpet, with a great deal of pleasure was beholding them, especially Imoinda, who that day appeared more lovely than ever, being enlivened with the good tidings Onahal had brought her of the constant passion the Prince had for her. The

8. Remnant.

Prince was laid on another carpet at the other end of the room, with his eyes fixed on the object of his soul; and as she turned or moved, so did they, and she alone gave his eyes and soul their motions. Nor did Imoinda employ her eyes to any other use than in beholding with infinite pleasure the joy she produced in those of the Prince. But while she was more regarding him than the steps she took, she chanced to fall, and so near him as that, leaping with extreme force from the carpet, he caught her in his arms as she fell; and 'twas visible to the whole presence[9] the joy wherewith he received her. He clasped her close to his bosom, and quite forgot that reverence that was due to the mistress of a king, and that punishment that is the reward of a boldness of this nature; and had not the presence of mind of Imoinda (fonder of his safety than her own) befriended him, in making her spring from his arms and fall into her dance again, he had at that instant met his death; for the old king, jealous to the last degree, rose up in rage, broke all the diversion, and led Imoinda to her apartment, and sent out word to the Prince to go immediately to the camp, and that if he were found another night in court he should suffer the death ordained for disobedient offenders.

You may imagine how welcome this news was to Oroonoko, whose unseasonable transport and caress of Imoinda was blamed by all men that loved him; and now he perceived his fault, yet cried that for such another moment, he would be content to die.

All the Otan was in disorder about this accident; and Onahal was particularly concerned, because on the Prince's stay depended her happiness, for she could no longer expect that of Aboan. So that ere they departed, they contrived it so that the Prince and he should come both that night to the grove of the Otan, which was all of oranges and citrons, and that there they should wait her orders.

They parted thus, with grief enough, till night, leaving the King in possession of the lovely maid. But nothing could appease the jealousy of the old lover. He would not be imposed on, but would have it that Imoinda made a false step on purpose to fall into Oroonoko's bosom, and that all things looked like a design on both sides; and 'twas in vain she protested her innocence. He was old and obstinate, and left her more than half assured that his fear was true.

The King going to his apartment sent to know where the Prince was, and if he intended to obey his command. The messenger returned and told him, he found the Prince pensive and altogether unpreparing for the campaign, that he lay negligently on the ground, and answered very little. This confirmed the jealousy of the King, and he commanded that they should very narrowly and privately watch his motions, and that he should not stir from his apartment but one spy or other should be employed to watch him. So that the hour approaching wherein he was to go to the citron grove, and taking only Aboan along with him, he leaves his apartment, and was watched to the very gate of the Otan, where he was seen to enter, and where they left him, to carry back the tidings to the King.

Oroonoko and Aboan were no sooner entered but Onahal led the Prince to the apartment of Imoinda, who, not knowing anything of her happiness, was laid in bed. But Onahal only left him in her chamber, to make the best

9. Company.

of his opportunity, and took her dear Aboan to her own, where he showed the heighth of complaisance for his prince, when, to give him an opportunity, he suffered himself to be caressed in bed by Onahal.

The Prince softly wakened Imoinda, who was not a little surprised with joy to find him there; and yet she trembled with a thousand fears. I believe he omitted saying nothing to this young maid that might persuade her to suffer him to seize his own, and take the rights of love; and I believe she was not long resisting those arms where she so longed to be; and having opportunity, night and silence, youth, love and desire, he soon prevailed, and ravished in a moment what his old grandfather had been endeavoring for so many months.

'Tis not to be imagined the satisfaction of these two young lovers; nor the vows she made him that she remained a spotless maid till that night, and that what she did with his grandfather had robbed him of no part of her virgin honor, the gods in mercy and justice having reserved that for her plighted lord, to whom of right it belonged. And 'tis impossible to express the transports he suffered, while he listened to a discourse so charming from her loved lips, and clasped that body in his arms for whom he had so long languished; and nothing now afflicted him but his sudden departure from her; for he told her the necessity and his commands, but should depart satisfied in this, that since the old king had hitherto not been able to deprive him of those enjoyments which only belonged to him, he believed for the future he would be less able to injure him; so that abating the scandal of the veil, which was no otherwise so than that she was wife to another, he believed her safe, even in the arms of the King, and innocent; yet would he have ventured at the conquest of the world, and have given it all, to have had her avoided that honor of receiving the royal veil. 'Twas thus, between a thousand caresses, that both bemoaned the hard fate of youth and beauty, so liable to that cruel promotion. 'Twas a glory that could well have been spared here, though desired and aimed at by all the young females of that kingdom.

But while they were thus fondly employed, forgetting how time ran on, and that the dawn must conduct him far away from his only happiness, they heard a great noise in the Otan, and unusual voices of men; at which the Prince, starting from the arms of the frighted Imoinda, ran to a little battle-ax he used to wear by his side, and having not so much leisure as to put on his habit, he opposed himself against some who were already opening the door; which they did with so much violence that Oroonoko was not able to defend it, but was forced to cry out with a commanding voice, "Whoever ye are that have the boldness to attempt to approach this apartment thus rudely, know that I, the Prince Oroonoko, will revenge it with the certain death of him that first enters. Therefore stand back, and know, this place is sacred to love and me this night; tomorrow 'tis the King's."

This he spoke with a voice so resolved and assured that they soon retired from the door, but cried, " 'Tis by the King's command we are come; and being satisfied by thy voice, O Prince, as much as if we had entered, we can report to the King the truth of all his fears, and leave thee to provide for thy own safety, as thou art advised by thy friends."

At these words they departed, and left the Prince to take a short and sad leave of his Imoinda, who, trusting in the strength of her charms, believed she should appease the fury of a jealous king by saying she was surprised, and that it was by force of arms he got into her apartment. All her concern now was for his life, and therefore she hastened him to the camp, and with much ado prevailed on him to go. Nor was it she alone that prevailed; Aboan and Onahal both pleaded, and both assured him of a lie that should be well enough contrived to secure Imoinda. So that at last, with a heart sad as death, dying eyes, and sighing soul, Oroonoko departed and took his way to the camp.

It was not long after the King in person came to the Otan, where, beholding Imoinda with rage in his eyes, he upbraided her wickedness and perfidy, and threatening her royal lover, she fell on her face at his feet, bedewing the floor with her tears and imploring his pardon for a fault which she had not with her will committed, as Onahal, who was also prostrate with her, could testify; that unknown to her, he had broke into her apartment, and ravished her. She spoke this much against her conscience, but to save her own life 'twas absolutely necessary she should feign this falsity. She knew it could not injure the Prince, he being fled to an army that would stand by him against any injuries that should assault him. However, this last thought of Imoinda's being ravished changed the measures of his revenge; and whereas before he designed to be himself her executioner, he now resolved she should not die. But as it is the greatest crime in nature amongst 'em to touch a woman after having been possessed by a son, a father, or a brother, so now he looked on Imoinda as a polluted thing, wholly unfit for his embrace; nor would he resign her to his grandson, because she had received the royal veil. He therefore removes her from the Otan, with Onahal; whom he put into safe hands, with order they should be both sold off as slaves to another country, either Christian or heathen; 'twas no matter where.

This cruel sentence, worse than death, they implored might be reversed; but their prayers were vain, and it was put in execution accordingly, and that with so much secrecy that none, either without or within the Otan, knew anything of their absence or their destiny.

The old king, nevertheless, executed this with a great deal of reluctancy; but he believed he had made a very great conquest over himself, when he had once resolved, and had performed what he resolved. He believed now that his love had been unjust, and that he could not expect the gods, or Captain of the Clouds (as they call the unknown power), should suffer a better consequence from so ill a cause. He now begins to hold Oroonoko excused, and to say he had reason for what he did. And now everybody could assure the King how passionately Imoinda was beloved by the Prince; even those confessed it now, who said the contrary before his flame was abated. So that the King being old, and not able to defend himself in war, and having no sons of all his race remaining alive but only this, to maintain him on his throne; and looking on this as a man disobliged, first by the rape of his mistress, or rather wife; and now by depriving of him wholly of her, he feared, might make him desperate and do some cruel thing, either to himself or his old grandfather, the offender: he began to repent him extremely of the contempt he had, in his rage, put on Imoinda. Besides, he considered he ought in honor to have killed her for this offense, if it had been one. He ought to have had so much value and consideration for a maid of her quality as to have nobly put her to death, and not to have sold her like a common slave, the greatest revenge and the most disgraceful of any; and to which they a thousand times prefer death, and implore it, as Imoinda did, but could not obtain that honor. Seeing therefore it was certain that Oroonoko would highly resent this affront, he thought good to make some excuse for his rashness to him; and to that end he sent a messenger to the camp, with orders to treat with him about the matter, to gain his pardon, and to endeavor to mitigate his grief; but that by no means he should tell him she was sold, but secretly put to death, for he knew he should never obtain his pardon for the other.

When the messenger came, he found the Prince upon the point of engaging with the enemy; but as soon as he heard of the arrival of the messenger, he commanded him to his tent, where he embraced him and received him with joy; which was soon abated by the downcast looks of the messenger, who was instantly demanded the cause by Oroonoko, who, impatient of delay, asked a thousand questions in a breath, and all concerning Imoinda. But there needed little return, for he could almost answer himself of all he demanded, from his sighs and eyes. At last, the messenger casting himself at the Prince's feet, and kissing them with all the submission of a man that had something to implore which he dreaded to utter, he besought him to hear with calmness what he had to deliver to him, and to call up all his noble and heroic courage to encounter with his words, and defend himself against the ungrateful[1] things he must relate. Oroonoko replied, with a deep sigh and a languishing voice, "I am armed against their worst efforts—; for I know they will tell me, Imoinda is no more—and after that, you may spare the rest." Then, commanding him to rise, he laid himself on a carpet, under a rich pavilion, and remained a good while silent, and was hardly heard to sigh. When he was come a little to himself, the messenger asked him leave to deliver that part of his embassy which the Prince had not yet divined. And the Prince cried, "I permit thee—." Then he told him the affliction the old king was in, for the rashness he had committed in his cruelty to Imoinda; and how he deigned to ask pardon for his offense, and to implore the Prince would not suffer that loss to touch his heart too sensibly, which now all the gods could not restore him, but might recompense him in glory, which he begged he would pursue; and that Death, that common revenger of all injuries, would soon even the account between him and a feeble old man.

Oroonoko bade him return his duty to his lord and master, and to assure him, there was no account of revenge to be adjusted between them; if there were, 'twas he was the aggressor, and that Death would be just and, maugre[2] his age, would see him righted; and he was contented to leave his share of glory to youths more fortunate and worthy of that favor from the gods. That henceforth he would never lift a weapon or draw a bow, but abandon the small remains of his life to sighs and tears, and the continual thoughts of what his lord and grandfather had thought good to send out of the world, with all that youth, that innocence, and beauty.

After having spoken this, whatever his greatest officers and men of the best rank could do, they could not raise him from the carpet, or persuade him to action and resolutions of life; but commanding all to retire, he shut himself into his pavilion all that day, while the enemy was ready to engage;

1. Offensive.
2. In spite of. Oroonoko is saying that he will die first.

and wondering at the delay, the whole body of the chief of the army then addressed themselves to him, and to whom they had much ado to get admittance. They fell on their faces at the foot of his carpet, where they lay and besought him with earnest prayers and tears to lead 'em forth to battle, and not let the enemy take advantages of them; and implored him to have regard to his glory, and to the world, that depended on his courage and conduct. But he made no other reply to all their supplications but this, that he had now no more business for glory; and for the world, it was a trifle not worth his care. "Go," continued he, sighing, "and divide it amongst you; and reap with joy what you so vainly prize, and leave me to my more welcome destiny."

They then demanded what they should do, and whom he would constitute in his room, that the confusion of ambitious youth and power might not ruin their order and make them a prey to the enemy. He replied, he would not give himself the trouble—; but wished 'em to choose the bravest man amongst 'em, let his quality or birth be what it would. "For, O my friends!" said he, "it is not titles make men brave or good, or birth that bestows courage and generosity, or makes the owner happy. Believe this, when you behold Oroonoko, the most wretched and abandoned by fortune of all the creation of the gods." So turning himself about, he would make no more reply to all they could urge or implore.

The army, beholding their officers return unsuccessful, with sad faces and ominous looks that presaged no good luck, suffered a thousand fears to take possession of their hearts, and the enemy to come even upon 'em, before they would provide for their safety by any defense; and though they were assured by some, who had a mind to animate 'em, that they should be immediately headed by the Prince, and that in the meantime Aboan had orders to command as general, yet they were so dismayed for want of that great example of bravery that they could make but a very feeble resistance; and at last downright fled before the enemy, who pursued 'em to the very tents, killing 'em. Nor could all Aboan's courage, which that day gained him immortal glory, shame 'em into a manly defense of themselves. The guards that were left behind about the Prince's tent, seeing the soldiers flee before the enemy and scatter themselves all over the plain, in great disorder, made such outcries as roused the Prince from his amorous slumber, in which he had remained buried for two days without permitting any sustenance to approach him. But in spite of all his resolutions, he had not the constancy of grief to that degree, as to make him insensible of the danger of his army; and in that instant he leaped from his couch and cried, "—Come, if we must die, let us meet Death the noblest way; and 'twill be more like Oroonoko to encounter him at an army's head, opposing the torrent of a conquering foe, than lazily on a couch to wait his lingering pleasure, and die every moment by a thousand wrecking³ thoughts; or be tamely taken by an enemy, and led a whining, lovesick slave to adorn the triumphs of Jamoan, that young victor, who already is entered beyond the limits I had prescribed him."

While he was speaking, he suffered his people to dress him for the field, and sallying out of his pavilion, with more life and vigor in his countenance than ever he showed, he appeared like some divine power descended to save his country from destruction; and his people had purposely put on him all

3. Racking.

things that might make him shine with most splendor, to strike a reverend awe into the beholders. He flew into the thickest of those that were pursuing his men, and being animated with despair, he fought as if he came on purpose to die, and did such things as will not be believed that human strength could perform, and such as soon inspired all the rest with new courage and new order. And now it was that they began to fight indeed, and so as if they would not be outdone even by their adored hero; who, turning the tide of the victory, changing absolutely the fate of the day, gained an entire conquest; and Oroonoko having the good fortune to single out Jamoan, he took him prisoner with his own hand, having wounded him almost to death.

This Jamoan afterwards became very dear to him, being a man very gallant and of excellent graces and fine parts; so that he never put him amongst the rank of captives, as they used to do, without distinction, for the common sale or market; but kept him in his own court, where he retained nothing of the prisoner but the name, and returned no more into his own country, so great an affection he took for Oroonoko; and by a thousand tales and adventures of love and gallantry flattered[4] his disease of melancholy and languishment, which I have often heard him say had certainly killed him, but for the conversation of this prince and Aboan, and the French governor he had from his childhood, of whom I have spoken before, and who was a man of admirable wit, great ingenuity and learning, all which he had infused into his young pupil. This Frenchman was banished out of his own country for some heretical notions he held, and though he was a man of very little religion, he had admirable morals and a brave soul.

After the total defeat of Jamoan's army, which all fled, or were left dead upon the place, they spent some time in the camp, Oroonoko choosing rather to remain a while there in his tents than enter into a palace or live in a court where he had so lately suffered so great a loss. The officers, therefore, who saw and knew his cause of discontent, invented all sorts of diversions and sports to entertain their prince; so that what with those amusements abroad and others at home, that is, within their tents, with the persuasions, arguments, and care of his friends and servants that he more peculiarly prized, he wore off in time a great part of that chagrin and torture of despair which the first efforts of Imoinda's death had given him. Insomuch as having received a thousand kind embassies from the King, and invitations to return to court, he obeyed, though with no little reluctancy; and when he did so, there was a visible change in him, and for a long time he was much more melancholy than before. But time lessens all extremes, and reduces 'em to mediums and unconcern; but no motives or beauties, though all endeavored it, could engage him in any sort of amour, though he had all the invitations to it, both from his own youth and others' ambitions and designs.

Oroonoko was no sooner returned from this last conquest, and received at court with all the joy and magnificence that could be expressed to a young victor, who was not only returned triumphant but beloved like a deity, when there arrived in the port an English ship.

This person[5] had often before been in these countries and was very well known to Oroonoko, with whom he had trafficked for slaves, and had used to do the same with his predecessors.

---

4. Soothed.   5. The ship's captain.

This commander was a man of a finer sort of address and conversation, better bred and more engaging than most of that sort of men are, so that he seemed rather never to have been bred out of a court than almost all his life at sea. This captain therefore was always better received at court than most of the traders to those countries were; and especially by Oroonoko, who was more civilized, according to the European mode, than any other had been, and took more delight in the white nations, and above all men of parts and wit. To this captain he sold abundance of his slaves, and for the favor and esteem he had for him, made him many presents, and obliged him to stay at court as long as possibly he could. Which the captain seemed to take as a very great honor done him, entertaining the Prince every day with globes and maps, and mathematical discourses and instruments; eating, drinking, hunting, and living with him with so much familiarity that it was not to be doubted but he had gained very greatly upon the heart of this gallant young man. And the captain, in return of all these mighty favors, besought the Prince to honor his vessel with his presence, some day or other, to dinner, before he should set sail; which he condescended to accept, and appointed his day. The captain, on his part, failed not to have all things in a readiness, in the most magnificent order he could possibly. And the day being come, the captain in his boat, richly adorned with carpets and velvet cushions, rowed to the shore to receive the Prince, with another longboat where was placed all his music and trumpets, with which Oroonoko was extremely delighted; who met him on the shore attended by his French governor, Jamoan, Aboan, and about a hundred of the noblest of the youths of the court. And after they had first carried the Prince on board, the boats fetched the rest off; where they found a very splendid treat, with all sorts of fine wines, and were as well entertained as 'twas possible in such a place to be.

The Prince, having drunk hard of punch and several sorts of wine, as did all the rest (for great care was taken they should want nothing of that part of the entertainment), was very merry, and in great admiration of the ship, for he had never been in one before; so that he was curious of beholding every place where he decently might descend. The rest, no less curious, who were not quite overcome with drinking, rambled at their pleasure fore and aft, as their fancies guided 'em. So that the captain, who had well laid his design before, gave the word, and seized on all his guests; they clapping great irons suddenly on the Prince, when he was leaped down in the hold to view that part of the vessel, and locking him fast down, secured him. The same treachery was used to all the rest; and all in one instant, in several places of the ship, were lashed fast in irons, and betrayed to slavery. That great design over, they set all hands to work to hoise[6] sail; and with as treacherous and fair a wind, they made from the shore with this innocent and glorious prize, who thought of nothing less than such an entertainment.

Some have commended this act as brave in the captain; but I will spare my sense of it, and leave it to my reader to judge as he pleases.

It may be easily guessed in what manner the Prince resented this indignity, who may be best resembled to a lion taken in a toil; so he raged, so he struggled for liberty, but all in vain; and they had so wisely managed his fetters that he could not use a hand in his defense, to quit himself of a life

6. Hoist.

that would by no means endure slavery, nor could he move from the place where he was tied to any solid part of the ship, against which he might have beat his head, and have finished his disgrace that way. So that being deprived of all other means, he resolved to perish for want of food. And pleased at last with that thought, and toiled and tired by rage and indignation, he laid himself down, and sullenly resolved upon dying, and refused all things that were brought him.

This did not a little vex the captain, and the more so because he found almost all of 'em of the same humor; so that the loss of so many brave slaves, so tall and goodly to behold, would have been very considerable. He therefore ordered one to go from him (for he would not be seen himself) to Oroonoko, and to assure him he was afflicted for having rashly done so unhospitable a deed, and which could not be now remedied, since they were far from shore; but since he resented it in so high a nature, he assured him he would revoke his resolution, and set both him and his friends ashore on the next land they should touch at; and of this the messenger gave him his oath, provided he would resolve to live. And Oroonoko, whose honor was such as he never had violated a word in his life himself, much less a solemn asseveration, believed in an instant what this man said, but replied, he expected for a confirmation of this to have his shameful fetters dismissed. This demand was carried to the captain, who returned him answer that the offense had been so great which he had put upon the Prince that he durst not trust him with liberty while he remained in the ship, for fear lest by a valor natural to him, and a revenge that would animate that valor, he might commit some outrage fatal to himself and the King his master, to whom his vessel did belong. To this Oroonoko replied, he would engage his honor to behave himself in all friendly order and manner, and obey the command of the captain, as he was lord of the King's vessel and general of those men under his command.

This was delivered to the still doubting captain, who could not resolve to trust a heathen, he said, upon his parole,[7] a man that had no sense or notion of the God that he worshipped. Oroonoko then replied, he was very sorry to hear that the captain pretended to the knowledge and worship of any gods who had taught him no better principles than not to credit as he would be credited; but they told him the difference of their faith occasioned that distrust. For the captain had protested to him upon the word of a Christian, and sworn in the name of a great god, which if he should violate, he would expect eternal torment in the world to come. "Is that all the obligation he has to be just to his oath?" replied Oroonoko. "Let him know I swear by my honor; which to violate, would not only render me contemptible and despised by all brave and honest men, and so give myself perpetual pain, but it would be eternally offending and diseasing all mankind, harming, betraying, circumventing and outraging all men; but punishments hereafter are suffered by one's self, and the world takes no cognizances whether this god have revenged 'em or not, 'tis done so secretly and deferred so long. While the man of no honor suffers every moment the scorn and contempt of the honester world, and dies every day ignominiously in his fame, which is more valuable than life. I speak not this to move belief, but to show you how you mistake, when you imagine that he who will violate his honor will keep his

7. Word of honor.

word with his gods." So turning from him with a disdainful smile, he refused to answer him, when he urged him to know what answer he should carry back to his captain; so that he departed without saying any more.

The captain pondering and consulting what to do, it was concluded that nothing but Oroonoko's liberty would encourage any of the rest to eat, except the Frenchman, whom the captain could not pretend to keep prisoner, but only told him he was secured because he might act something in favor of the Prince, but that he should be freed as soon as they came to land. So that they concluded it wholly necessary to free the Prince from his irons, that he might show himself to the rest; that they might have an eye upon him, and that they could not fear a single man.

This being resolved, to make the obligation the greater, the captain himself went to Oroonoko; where after many compliments, and assurances of what he had already promised, he receiving from the Prince his parole and his hand for his good behavior, dismissed his irons and brought him to his own cabin; where after having treated and reposed him a while, for he had neither eat[8] nor slept in four days before, he besought him to visit those obstinate people in chains, who refused all manner of sustenance, and entreated him to oblige 'em to eat, and assure 'em of their liberty the first opportunity.

Oroonoko, who was too generous not to give credit to his words, showed himself to his people, who were transported with excess of joy at the sight of their darling prince, falling at his feet and kissing and embracing 'em, believing, as some divine oracle, all he assured 'em. But he besought 'em to bear their chains with that bravery that became those whom he had seen act so nobly in arms; and that they could not give him greater proofs of their love and friendship, since 'twas all the security the captain (his friend) could have, against the revenge, he said, they might possibly justly take for the injuries sustained by him. And they all with one accord assured him, they could not suffer enough, when it was for his repose and safety.

After this they no longer refused to eat, but took what was brought 'em, and were pleased with their captivity, since by it they hoped to redeem the Prince, who, all the rest of the voyage, was treated with all the respect due to his birth, though nothing could divert his melancholy; and he would often sigh for Imoinda, and think this a punishment due to his misfortune, in having left that noble maid behind him that fatal night, in the Otan, when he fled to the camp.

Possessed with a thousand thoughts of past joys with this fair young person, and a thousand griefs for her eternal loss, he endured a tedious voyage, and at last arrived at the mouth of the river of Surinam, a colony belonging to the King of England, and where they were to deliver some part of their slaves. There the merchants and gentlemen of the country going on board to demand those lots of slaves they had already agreed on, and, amongst those, the overseers of those plantations where I then chanced to be, the captain, who had given the word, ordered his men to bring up those noble slaves in fetters whom I have spoken of; and having put 'em some in one and some in other lots, with women and children (which they call pickaninnies), they sold 'em off as slaves to several merchants and gentlemen; not putting any two in one lot, because they would separate 'em far from each other, not

8. The past form of *eat*.

daring to trust 'em together, lest rage and courage should put 'em upon contriving some great action, to the ruin of the colony.

Oroonoko was first seized on, and sold to our overseer, who had the first lot, with seventeen more of all sorts and sizes, but not one of quality with him. When he saw this, he found what they meant, for, as I said, he understood English pretty well; and being wholly unarmed and defenseless, so as it was in vain to make any resistance, he only beheld the captain with a look all fierce and disdainful, upbraiding him with eyes that forced blushes on his guilty cheeks; he only cried, in passing over the side of the ship, "Farewell, sir. 'Tis worth my suffering, to gain so true a knowledge both of you and of your gods by whom you swear." And desiring those that held him to forbear their pains, and telling 'em he would make no resistance, he cried, "Come, my fellow slaves; let us descend, and see if we can meet with more honor and honesty in the next world we shall touch upon." So he nimbly leaped into the boat, and showing no more concern, suffered himself to be rowed up the river with his seventeen companions.

The gentleman that bought him was a young Cornish gentleman whose name was Trefry, a man of great wit and fine learning, and was carried into those parts by the Lord——, Governor,[9] to manage all his affairs. He reflecting on the last words of Oroonoko to the captain, and beholding the richness of his vest,[1] no sooner came into the boat but he fixed his eyes on him; and finding something so extraordinary in his face, his shape and mien, a greatness of look and haughtiness in his air, and finding he spoke English, had a great mind to be inquiring into his quality and fortune; which, though Oroonoko endeavored to hide, by only confessing he was above the rank of common slaves, Trefry soon found he was yet something greater than he confessed, and from that moment began to conceive so vast an esteem for him that he ever after loved him as his dearest brother, and showed him all the civilities due to so great a man.

Trefry was a very good mathematician and a linguist, could speak French and Spanish; and in the three days they remained in the boat (for so long were they going from the ship to the plantation) he entertained Oroonoko so agreeably with his art and discourse, that he was no less pleased with Trefry than he was with the Prince; and he thought himself at least fortunate in this, that since he was a slave, as long as he would suffer himself to remain so, he had a man of so excellent wit and parts for a master. So that before they had finished their voyage up the river, he made no scruple of declaring to Trefry all his fortunes, and most part of what I have here related, and put himself wholly into the hands of his new friend, whom he found resenting all the injuries were done him, and was charmed with all the greatness of his actions; which were recited with that modesty and delicate sense as wholly vanquished him, and subdued him to his interest. And he promised him on his word and honor, he would find the means to reconduct him to his own country again, assuring him, he had a perfect abhorrence of so dishonorable an action, and that he would sooner have died than have been the author of such a perfidy. He found the Prince was very much concerned to know what became of his friends, and how they took their slavery; and

---

9. Lord Willoughby of Parham, coproprietor of Surinam by royal grant. John Treffry was his plan-tation overseer.
1. An outer garment or robe.

Trefry promised to take care about the inquiring after their condition, and that he should have an account of 'em.

Though, as Oroonoko afterwards said, he had little reason to credit the words of a *backearary*,[2] yet he knew not why, but he saw a kind of sincerity and awful truth in the face of Trefry; he saw an honesty in his eyes, and he found him wise and witty enough to understand honor; for it was one of his maxims, a man of wit could not be a knave or villain.

In their passage up the river they put in at several houses for refreshment, and ever when they landed, numbers of people would flock to behold this man; not but their eyes were daily entertained with the sight of slaves, but the fame of Oroonoko was gone before him, and all people were in admiration of his beauty. Besides, he had a rich habit on, in which he was taken, so different from the rest, and which the captain could not strip him of, because he was forced to surprise his person in the minute he sold him. When he found his habit made him liable, as he thought, to be gazed at the more, he begged Trefry to give him something more befitting a slave, which he did, and took off his robes. Nevertheless, he shone through all; and his osenbrigs (a sort of brown holland[3] suit he had on) could not conceal the graces of his looks and mien, and he had no less admirers than when he had his dazzling habit on. The royal youth appeared in spite of the slave, and people could not help treating him after a different manner, without designing it. As soon as they approached him, they venerated and esteemed him; his eyes insensibly commanded respect, and his behavior insinuated it into every soul. So that there was nothing talked of but this young and gallant slave, even by those who yet knew not that he was a prince.

I ought to tell you that the Christians never buy any slaves but they give 'em some name of their own, their native ones being likely very barbarous and hard to pronounce; so that Mr. Trefry gave Oroonoko that of Caesar, which name will live in that country as long as that (scarce more) glorious one of the great Roman; for 'tis most evident, he wanted[4] no part of the personal courage of that Caesar, and acted things as memorable, had they been done in some part of the world replenished with people and historians that might have given him his due. But his misfortune was to fall in an obscure world, that afforded only a female pen to celebrate his fame; though I doubt not but it had lived from others' endeavors, if the Dutch, who immediately after his time took that country,[5] had not killed, banished, and dispersed all those that were capable of giving the world this great man's life, much better than I have done. And Mr. Trefry, who designed it, died before he began it, and bemoaned himself for not having undertook it in time.

For the future, therefore, I must call Oroonoko Caesar, since by that name only he was known in our western world, and by that name he was received on shore at Parham House, where he was destined a slave. But if the King himself (God bless him) had come ashore, there could not have been greater expectations by all the whole plantation, and those neighboring ones, than was on ours at that time; and he was received more like a governor than a

2. White person or master; a variant of *backra*, from an Ibo word transported with the slaves to Surinam and the Caribbean.
3. Coarse cotton or linen, sometimes called osnaburg, after a German cloth-manufacturing town.
4. Lacked.
5. In 1667 the Dutch attacked and conquered Surinam, and England ceded it by treaty in exchange for New York.

slave. Notwithstanding, as the custom was, they assigned him his portion of land, his house, and his business, up in the plantation. But as it was more for form than any design to put him to his task, he endured no more of the slave but the name, and remained some days in the house, receiving all visits that were made him, without stirring towards that part of the plantation where the Negroes were.

At last he would needs go view his land, his house, and the business assigned him. But he no sooner came to the houses of the slaves, which are like a little town by itself, the Negroes all having left work, but they all came forth to behold him, and found he was that prince who had, at several times, sold most of 'em to these parts; and from a veneration they pay to great men, especially if they know 'em, and from the surprise and awe they had at the sight of him, they all cast themselves at his feet, crying out in their language, "Live, O King! Long live, O King!" and kissing his feet, paid him even divine homage.

Several English gentleman were with him; and what Mr. Trefry had told 'em was here confirmed, of which he himself before had no other witness than Caesar himself. But he was infinitely glad to find his grandeur confirmed by the adoration of all the slaves.

Caesar, troubled with their over-joy and over-ceremony, besought 'em to rise and to receive him as their fellow slave, assuring them he was no better. At which they set up with one accord a most terrible and hideous mourning and condoling, which he and the English had much ado to appease; but at last they prevailed with 'em, and they prepared all their barbarous music, and everyone killed and dressed something of his own stock (for every family has their land apart, on which, at their leisure times, they breed all eatable things), and clubbing it together,[6] made a most magnificent supper, inviting their *Grandee Captain*, their prince, to honor it with his presence; which he did, and several English with him; where they all waited on him, some playing, others dancing before him all the time, according to the manners of their several nations, and with unwearied industry endeavoring to please and delight him.

While they sat at meat Mr. Trefry told Caesar that most of these young slaves were undone in love with a fine she-slave, whom they had had about six months on their land. The Prince, who never heard the name of love without a sigh, nor any mention of it without the curiosity of examining further into that tale, which of all discourses was most agreeable to him, asked how they came to be so unhappy as to be all undone for one fair slave. Trefry, who was naturally amorous and loved to talk of love as well as anybody, proceeded to tell him, they had the most charming black that ever was beheld on their plantation, about fifteen or sixteen years old, as he guessed; that for his part, he had done nothing but sigh for her ever since she came, and that all the white beauties he had seen never charmed him so absolutely as this fine creature had done; and that no man, of any nation, ever beheld her that did not fall in love with her; and that she had all the slaves perpetually at her feet, and the whole country resounded with the fame of Clemene, "for so," said he, "we have christened her. But she denies us all with such a noble disdain, that 'tis a miracle to see that she, who can give such eternal

6. Contributing jointly.

desires, should herself be all ice and all unconcern. She is adorned with the most graceful modesty that ever beautified youth; the softest sigher—that, if she were capable of love, one would swear she languished for some absent happy man; and so retired, as if she feared a rape even from the god of day,[7] or that the breezes would steal kisses from her delicate mouth. Her task of work some sighing lover every day makes it his petition to perform for her, which she accepts blushing and with reluctancy, for fear he will ask her a look for a recompense, which he dares not presume to hope, so great an awe she strikes into the hearts of her admirers." "I do not wonder," replied the Prince, "that Clemene should refuse slaves, being as you say so beautiful, but wonder how she escapes those who can entertain her as you can do; or why, being your slave, you do not oblige her to yield." "I confess," said Trefry, "when I have, against her will, entertained her with love so long as to be transported with my passion, even above decency, I have been ready to make use of those advantages of strength and force nature has given me. But oh! she disarms me with that modesty and weeping, so tender and so moving that I retire, and thank my stars she overcame me." The company laughed at his civility to a slave, and Caesar only applauded the nobleness of his passion and nature, since that slave might be noble or, what was better, have true notions of honor and virtue in her. Thus passed they this night, after having received from the slaves all imaginable respect and obedience.

The next day Trefry asked Caesar to walk, when the heat was allayed, and designedly carried him by the cottage of the fair slave, and told him she whom he spoke of last night lived there retired. "But," says he, "I would not wish you to approach, for I am sure you will be in love as soon as you behold her." Caesar assured him he was proof against all the charms of that sex, and that if he imagined his heart could be so perfidious to love again, after Imoinda, he believed he should tear it from his bosom. They had no sooner spoke, but a little shock dog[8] that Clemene had presented her, which she took great delight in, ran out; and she, not knowing anybody was there, ran to get it in again, and bolted out on those who were just speaking of her. When seeing them, she would have run in again, but Trefry caught her by the hand and cried, "Clemene, however you fly a lover, you ought to pay some respect to this stranger" (pointing to Caesar). But she, as if she had resolved never to raise her eyes to the face of a man again, bent 'em the more to the earth when he spoke, and gave the Prince the leisure to look the more at her. There needed no long gazing or consideration to examine who this fair creature was; he soon saw Imoinda all over her; in a minute he saw her face, her shape, her air, her modesty, and all that called forth his soul with joy at his eyes, and left his body destitute of almost life; it stood without motion, and for a minute knew not that it had a being; and I believe he had never come to himself, so oppressed he was with over-joy, if he had not met with this allay, that he perceived Imoinda fall dead in the hands of Trefry. This awakened him, and he ran to her aid and caught her in his arms, where by degrees she came to herself; and 'tis needless to tell with what transports, what ecstasies of joy, they both a while beheld each other, without speaking; then snatched each other to their arms; then gaze again, as if they still

7. The sun.
8. A long-haired dog or poodle, especially associated with women of fashion.

doubted whether they possessed the blessing they grasped; but when they recovered their speech, 'tis not to be imagined what tender things they expressed to each other, wondering what strange fate had brought 'em again together. They soon informed each other of their fortunes, and equally bewailed their fate; but at the same time they mutually protested that even fetters and slavery were soft and easy, and would be supported with joy and pleasure, while they could be so happy to possess each other and to be able to make good their vows. Caesar swore he disdained the empire of the world while he could behold his Imoinda; and she despised grandeur and pomp, those vanities of her sex, when she could gaze on Oroonoko. He adored the very cottage where she resided, and said that little inch of the world would give him more happiness than all the universe could do; and she vowed it was a palace, while adorned with the presence of Oroonoko.

Trefry was infinitely pleased with this novel,[9] and found this Clemene was the fair mistress of whom Caesar had before spoke; and was not a little satisfied that heaven was so kind to the Prince as to sweeten his misfortunes by so lucky an accident; and leaving the lovers to themselves, was impatient to come down to Parham House (which was on the same plantation) to give me an account of what had happened. I was as impatient to make these lovers a visit, having already made a friendship with Caesar, and from his own mouth learned what I have related; which was confirmed by his Frenchman, who was set on shore to seek his fortunes, and of whom they could not make a slave, because a Christian, and he came daily to Parham Hill to see and pay his respects to his pupil prince. So that concerning and interesting myself in all that related to Caesar, whom I had assured of liberty as soon as the Governor arrived, I hasted presently to the place where the lovers were, and was infinitely glad to find this beautiful young slave (who had already gained all our esteems, for her modesty and her extraordinary prettiness) to be the same I had heard Caesar speak so much of. One may imagine then we paid her a treble respect; and though, from her being carved in fine flowers and birds all over her body, we took her to be of quality before, yet when we knew Clemene was Imoinda, we could not enough admire her.

I had forgot to tell you that those who are nobly born of that country are so delicately cut and rased[1] all over the forepart of the trunk of their bodies, that it looks as if it were japanned, the works being raised like high point round the edges of the flowers. Some are only carved with a little flower or bird at the sides of the temples, as was Caesar; and those who are so carved over the body resemble our ancient Picts,[2] that are figured in the chronicles, but these carvings are more delicate.

From that happy day Caesar took Clemene for his wife, to the general joy of all people; and there was as much magnificence as the country would afford at the celebration of this wedding: and in a very short time after she conceived with child, which made Caesar even adore her, knowing he was the last of his great race. This new accident made him more impatient of liberty, and he was every day treating with Trefry for his and Clemene's liberty, and offered either gold or a vast quantity of slaves, which should be paid before they let him go, provided he could have any security that he

9. Novel event or piece of news.
1. Incised. The carving is likened to figured lacquerwork in the Japanese style and to elaborate

"high point" lace.
2. A North British people appearing in histories of England and Scotland.

should go when his ransom was paid. They fed him from day to day with promises, and delayed him till the Lord Governor should come; so that he began to suspect them of falsehood, and that they would delay him till the time of his wife's delivery and make a slave of that too, for all the breed is theirs to whom the parents belong. This thought made him very uneasy, and his sullenness gave them some jealousies[3] of him; so that I was obliged, by some persons who feared a mutiny (which is very fatal sometimes in those colonies, that abound so with slaves that they exceed the whites in vast numbers), to discourse with Caesar, and to give him all the satisfaction I possibly could; they knew he and Clemene were scarce an hour in a day from my lodgings, that they eat with me, and that I obliged 'em in all things I was capable of. I entertained him with the lives of the Romans, and great men, which charmed him to my company, and her with teaching her all the pretty works[4] that I was mistress of, and telling her stories of nuns, and endeavoring to bring her to the knowledge of the true God. But of all discourses Caesar liked that the worst, and would never be reconciled to our notions of the Trinity, of which he ever made a jest; it was a riddle, he said, would turn his brain to conceive, and one could not make him understand what faith was. However, these conversations failed not altogether so well to divert him that he liked the company of us women much above the men, for he could not drink, and he is but an ill companion in that country that cannot. So that obliging him to love us very well, we had all the liberty of speech with him, especially myself, whom he called his Great Mistress; and indeed my word would go a great way with him. For these reasons, I had opportunity to take notice to him that he was not well pleased of late as he used to be, was more retired and thoughtful; and told him I took it ill he should suspect we would break our words with him, and not permit both him and Clemene to return to his own kingdom, which was not so long a way but when he was once on his voyage he would quickly arrive there. He made me some answers that showed a doubt in him, which made me ask him what advantage it would be to doubt. It would but give us a fear of him, and possibly compel us to treat him so as I should be very loath to behold; that is, it might occasion his confinement. Perhaps this was not so luckily spoke of me, for I perceived he resented that word, which I strove to soften again in vain. However, he assured me that whatsoever resolutions he should take, he would act nothing upon the white people; and as for myself and those upon that plantation where he was, he would sooner forfeit his eternal liberty, and life itself, than lift his hand against his greatest enemy on that place. He besought me to suffer no fears upon his account, for he could do nothing that honor should not dictate; but he accused himself for having suffered slavery so long; yet he charged that weakness on Love alone, who was capable of making him neglect even glory itself, and for which now he reproaches himself every moment of the day. Much more to this effect he spoke, with an air impatient enough to make me know he would not be long in bondage; and though he suffered only the name of a slave, and had nothing of the toil and labor of one, yet that was sufficient to render him uneasy; and he had been too long idle, who used to be always in action and in arms. He had a spirit all rough and fierce, and that could not be tamed to lazy rest; and though all endeavors

3. Suspicions.   4. Decorative needlework or other handiwork.

were used to exercise himself in such actions and sports as this world afforded, as running, wrestling, pitching the bar,[5] hunting and fishing, chasing and killing tigers[6] of a monstrous size, which this continent affords in abundance, and wonderful snakes, such as Alexander is reported to have encountered at the river of Amazons,[7] and which Caesar took great delight to overcome, yet these were not actions great enough for his large soul, which was still panting after more renowned action.

Before I parted that day with him, I got, with much ado, a promise from him to rest yet a little longer with patience, and wait the coming of the Lord Governor, who was every day expected on our shore; he assured me he would, and this promise he desired me to know was given perfectly in complaisance to me, in whom he had an entire confidence.

After this, I neither thought it convenient to trust him much out of our view, nor did the country, who feared him; but with one accord it was advised to treat him fairly, and oblige him to remain within such a compass, and that he should be permitted as seldom as could be to go up to the plantations of the Negroes or, if he did, to be accompanied by some that should be rather in appearance attendants than spies. This care was for some time taken, and Caesar looked upon it as a mark of extraordinary respect, and was glad his discontent had obliged 'em to be more observant to him. He received new assurance from the overseer, which was confirmed to him by the opinion of all the gentlemen of the country, who made their court to him. During this time that we had his company more frequently than hitherto we had had, it may not be unpleasant to relate to you the diversions we entertained him with, or rather he us.

My stay was to be short in that country, because my father died at sea, and never arrived to possess the honor was designed him (which was lieutenant general of six and thirty islands, besides the continent[8] of Surinam) nor the advantages he hoped to reap by them; so that though we were obliged to continue on our voyage, we did not intend to stay upon the place. Though, in a word, I must say thus much of it, that certainly had his late Majesty, of sacred memory, but seen and known what a vast and charming world he had been master of in that continent, he would never have parted so easily with it to the Dutch. 'Tis a continent whose vast extent was never yet known, and may contain more noble earth than all the universe besides, for, they say, it reaches from east to west, one way as far as China and another to Peru. It affords all things both for beauty and use; 'tis there eternal spring, always the very months of April, May, and June; the shades are perpetual, the trees bearing at once all degrees of leaves and fruit, from blooming buds to ripe autumn: groves of oranges, lemons, citrons, figs, nutmegs, and noble aromatics, continually bearing their fragrancies. The trees appearing all like nosegays adorned with flowers of different kinds; some are all white, some purple, some scarlet, some blue, some yellow; bearing, at the same time, ripe fruit and blooming young, or producing every day new. The very wood of all these trees has an intrinsic value above common timber, for they are, when

5. A game in which players compete in throwing a heavy bar or rod.
6. Wild cats, including the South American jaguar and cougar.
7. Alexander the Great is supposed to have encountered both snakes and Amazons in a campaign against India.
8. "Land not disjoined by the sea from other lands" (Johnson's *Dictionary*).

cut, of different colors, glorious to behold, and bear a price considerable, to inlay withal. Besides this they yield rich balm and gums, so that we make our candles of such an aromatic substance as does not only give a sufficient light, but, as they burn, they cast their perfumes all about. Cedar is the common firing, and all the houses are built with it. The very meat we eat, when set on the table, if it be native, I mean of the country, perfumes the whole room; especially a little beast called an armadilly, a thing which I can liken to nothing so well as a rhinoceros; 'tis all in white armor, so jointed that it moves as well in it as if it had nothing on; this beast is about the bigness of a pig of six weeks old. But it were endless to give an account of all the diverse wonderful and strange things that country affords, and which we took a very great delight to go in search of, though those adventures are oftentimes fatal and at least dangerous. But while we had Caesar in our company on these designs we feared no harm, nor suffered any.

As soon as I came into the country, the best house in it was presented me, called St. John's Hill. It stood on a vast rock of white marble, at the foot of which the river ran a vast depth down, and not to be descended on that side; the little waves still dashing and washing the foot of this rock made the softest murmurs and purlings in the world; and the opposite bank was adorned with such vast quantities of different flowers eternally blowing,[9] and every day and hour new, fenced behind 'em with lofty trees of a thousand rare forms and colors, that the prospect was the most ravishing that fancy can create.[1] On the edge of this white rock, towards the river, was a walk or grove of orange and lemon trees, about half the length of the Mall[2] here, whose flowery and fruit-bearing branches met at the top and hindered the sun, whose rays are very fierce there, from entering a beam into the grove; and the cool air that came from the river made it not only fit to entertain people in, at all the hottest hours of the day, but refreshed the sweet blossoms and made it always sweet and charming; and sure the whole globe of the world cannot show so delightful a place as this grove was. Not all the gardens of boasted Italy can produce a shade to outvie this, which nature had joined with art to render so exceeding fine; and 'tis a marvel to see how such vast trees, as big as English oaks, could take footing on so solid a rock and in so little earth as covered that rock; but all things by nature there are rare, delightful, and wonderful. But to our sports.

Sometimes we would go surprising,[3] and in search of young tigers in their dens, watching when the old ones went forth to forage for prey; and oftentimes we have been in great danger and have fled apace for our lives when surprised by the dams. But once, above all other times, we went on this design, and Caesar was with us, who had no sooner stolen a young tiger from her nest but, going off, we encountered the dam, bearing a buttock of a cow which he[4] had torn off with his mighty paw, and going with it towards his den. We had only four women, Caesar, and an English gentleman, brother to Harry Martin, the great Oliverian;[5] we found there was no escaping this

9. Blooming.
1. The original editions read "the most raving that sands can create," altered to "ravishing" in the third edition, which also corrects the next sentence, "fruity bear branches."
2. Fashionable walk in St. James's Park in London.

3. A military term for making sudden raids.
4. The jarring mixture of pronouns in the two accounts of the tigers (wild cats) may suggest a reluctance to use a feminine pronoun in moments of extreme violence. The first account was left uncorrected in all four 17th-century editions.
5. Supporter of Oliver Cromwell.

enraged and ravenous beast. However, we women fled as fast as we could from it; but our heels had not saved our lives if Caesar had not laid down his cub, when he found the tiger quit her prey to make the more speed towards him, and taking Mr. Martin's sword, desired him to stand aside, or follow the ladies. He obeyed him, and Caesar met this monstrous beast of might, size, and vast limbs, who came with open jaws upon him; and fixing his awful stern eyes full upon those of the beast, and putting himself into a very steady and good aiming posture of defense, ran his sword quite through his breast down to his very heart, home to the hilt of the sword. The dying beast stretched forth her paw, and going to grasp his thigh, surprised with death in that very moment, did him no other harm than fixing her long nails in his flesh very deep, feebly wounded him, but could not grasp the flesh to tear off any. When he had done this, he hallooed to us to return, which, after some assurance of his victory, we did, and found him lugging out the sword from the bosom of the tiger, who was laid in her blood on the ground; he took up the cub, and with an unconcern that had nothing of the joy or gladness of a victory, he came and laid the whelp at my feet. We all extremely wondered at his daring, and at the bigness of the beast, which was about the heighth of a heifer but of mighty, great, and strong limbs.

Another time, being in the woods, he killed a tiger which had long infested that part, and borne away abundance of sheep and oxen, and other things that were for the support of those to whom they belonged; abundance of people assailed this beast, some affirming they had shot her with several bullets quite through the body at several times, and some swearing they shot her through the very heart, and they believed she was a devil rather than a mortal thing. Caesar had often said he had a mind to encounter this monster, and spoke with several gentlemen who had attempted her, one crying, "I shot her with so many poisoned arrows," another with his gun in this part of her, and another in that; so that he, remarking all these places where she was shot, fancied still he should overcome her by giving her another sort of a wound than any had yet done; and one day said (at the table), "What trophies and garlands, ladies, will you make me, if I bring you home the heart of this ravenous beast that eats up all your lambs and pigs?" We all promised he should be rewarded at all our hands. So taking a bow, which he choosed out of a great many, he went up in the wood, with two gentlemen, where he imagined this devourer to be; they had not passed very far in it but they heard her voice, growling and grumbling, as if she were pleased with something she was doing. When they came in view, they found her muzzling in the belly of a new ravished sheep, which she had torn open; and seeing herself approached, she took fast hold of her prey with her forepaws and set a very fierce raging look on Caesar, without offering to approach him, for fear at the same time of losing what she had in possession. So that Caesar remained a good while, only taking aim, and getting an opportunity to shoot her where he designed; 'twas some time before he could accomplish it, and to wound her and not kill her would but have enraged her more, and endangered him. He had a quiver of arrows at his side, so that if one failed he could be supplied; at last, retiring a little, he gave her opportunity to eat, for he found she was ravenous, and fell to as soon as she saw him retire, being more eager of her prey than of doing new mischiefs. When he going softly to one side of her, and hiding his person behind certain herbage that grew high and thick, he took so good aim that, as he intended, he shot her just into the eye, and the arrow was sent with so good a will and so sure a hand that it stuck in her brain, and made her caper and become mad for a moment or two; but being seconded by another arrow, he fell dead upon the prey. Caesar cut him open with a knife, to see where those wounds were that had been reported to him, and why he did not die of 'em. But I shall now relate a thing that possibly will find no credit among men, because 'tis a notion commonly received with us, that nothing can receive a wound in the heart and live; but when the heart of this courageous animal was taken out, there were seven bullets of lead in it, and the wounds seamed up with great scars, and she lived with the bullets a great while, for it was long since they were shot. This heart the conqueror brought up to us, and 'twas a very great curiosity, which all the country came to see, and which gave Caesar occasion of many fine discourses, of accidents in war and strange escapes.

At other times he would go a-fishing; and discoursing on that diversion, he found we had in that country a very strange fish, called a numb eel[6] (an eel of which I have eaten), that while it is alive, it has a quality so cold, that those who are angling, though with a line of never so great a length with a rod at the end of it, it shall, in the same minute the bait is touched by this eel, seize him or her that holds the rod with benumbedness, that shall deprive 'em of sense for a while; and some have fallen into the water, and others dropped as dead on the banks of the rivers where they stood, as soon as this fish touches the bait. Caesar used to laugh at this, and believed it impossible a man could lose his force at the touch of a fish, and could not understand that philosophy,[7] that a cold quality should be of that nature. However, he had a great curiosity to try whether it would have the same effect on him it had on others, and often tried, but in vain. At last the sought for fish came to the bait, as he stood angling on the bank; and instead of throwing away the rod or giving it a sudden twitch out of the water, whereby he might have caught both the eel and have dismissed the rod, before it could have too much power over him, for experiment sake he grasped it but the harder, and fainting fell into the river; and being still possessed of the rod, the tide carried him, senseless as he was, a great way, till an Indian boat took him up, and perceived when they touched him a numbness seize them, and by that knew the rod was in his hand; which with a paddle (that is, a short oar) they struck away, and snatched it into the boat, eel and all. If Caesar were almost dead with the effect of this fish, he was more so with that of the water, where he had remained the space of going a league, and they found they had much ado to bring him back to life. But at last they did, and brought him home, where he was in a few hours well recovered and refreshed, and not a little ashamed to find he should be overcome by an eel, and that all the people who heard his defiance would laugh at him. But we cheered him up; and he being convinced, we had the eel at supper, which was a quarter of an ell about and most delicate meat, and was of the more value, since it cost so dear as almost the life of so gallant a man.

About this time we were in many mortal fears about some disputes the English had with the Indians, so that we could scarce trust ourselves, without

6. Electric eel.
7. "Hypothesis or system upon which natural effects are explained" (Johnson's *Dictionary*).

great numbers, to go to any Indian towns or place where they abode, for fear they should fall upon us, as they did immediately after my coming away; and that it was in the possession of the Dutch, who used 'em not so civilly as the English, so that they cut in pieces all they could take, getting into houses and hanging up the mother and all her children about her, and cut a footman I left behind me all in joints, and nailed him to trees.

This feud began while I was there, so that I lost half the satisfaction I proposed, in not seeing and visiting the Indian towns. But one day, bemoaning of our misfortunes upon this account, Caesar told us we need not fear, for if we had a mind to go, he would undertake to be our guard. Some would, but most would not venture; about eighteen of us resolved and took barge, and after eight days arrived near an Indian town. But approaching it, the hearts of some of our company failed, and they would not venture on shore; so we polled who would and who would not. For my part, I said if Caesar would, I would go; he resolved; so did my brother and my woman, a maid of good courage. Now none of us speaking the language of the people, and imagining we should have a half diversion in gazing only and not knowing what they said, we took a fisherman that lived at the mouth of the river, who had been a long inhabitant there, and obliged him to go with us. But because he was known to the Indians, as trading among 'em, and being by long living there become a perfect Indian in color, we, who resolved to surprise 'em by making 'em see something they never had seen (that is, white people), resolved only myself, my brother and woman should go; so Caesar, the fisherman, and the rest, hiding behind some thick reeds and flowers that grew on the banks, let us pass on towards the town, which was on the bank of the river all along. A little distant from the houses, or huts, we saw some dancing, others busied in fetching and carrying of water from the river. They had no sooner spied us but they set up a loud cry, that frighted us at first; we thought it had been for those that should kill us, but it seems it was of wonder and amazement. They were all naked, and we were dressed so as is most commode[8] for the hot countries, very glittering and rich, so that we appeared extremely fine; my own hair was cut short, and I had a taffety cap with black feathers on my head; my brother was in a stuff[9] suit, with silver loops and buttons and abundance of green ribbon. This was all infinitely surprising to them, and because we saw them stand still till we approached 'em, we took heart and advanced, came up to 'em, and offered 'em our hands; which they took, and looked on us round about, calling still for more company; who came swarming out, all wondering and crying out *"Tepeeme,"* taking their hair up in their hands and spreading it wide to those they called out to, as if they would say (as indeed it signified) "Numberless wonders," or not to be recounted, no more than to number the hair of their heads. By degrees they grew more bold, and from gazing upon us round, they touched us, laying their hands upon all the features of our faces, feeling our breasts and arms, taking up one petticoat, then wondering to see another; admiring our shoes and stockings, but more our garters, which we gave 'em, and they tied about their legs, being laced with silver lace at the ends, for they much esteem any shining things. In fine, we suffered 'em to survey us as they pleased, and we thought they would never have done admiring us. When Caesar and the rest

8. Suitable.   9. Woven fabric, worsted.

saw we were received with such wonder, they came up to us; and finding the Indian trader whom they knew (for 'tis by these fishermen, called Indian traders, we hold a commerce with 'em, for they love not to go far from home, and we never go to them), when they saw him therefore they set up a new joy, and cried, in their language, "Oh! here's our *tiguamy,* and we shall now know whether those things can speak." So advancing to him, some of 'em gave him their hands and cried, "*Amora tiguamy,*" which is as much as, "How do you?" or "Welcome, friend," and all with one din began to gabble to him, and asked if we had sense and wit; if we could talk of affairs of life and war, as they could do; if we could hunt, swim, and do a thousand things they use. He answered 'em, we could. Then they invited us into their houses, and dressed venison and buffalo for us; and going out, gathered a leaf of a tree called a *sarumbo* leaf, of six yards long, and spread it on the ground for a tablecloth; and cutting another in pieces instead of plates, setting us on little bow Indian stools, which they cut out of one entire piece of wood and paint in a sort of japan work. They serve everyone their mess on these pieces of leaves, and it was very good, but too high seasoned with pepper. When we had eat, my brother and I took out our flutes and played to 'em, which gave 'em new wonder; and I soon perceived, by an admiration that is natural to these people, and by the extreme ignorance and simplicity of 'em, it were not difficult to establish any unknown or extravagant religion among them, and to impose any notions or fictions upon 'em. For seeing a kinsman of mine set some paper afire with a burning glass, a trick they had never before seen, they were like to have adored him for a god, and begged he would give them the characters or figures of his name, that they might oppose it against winds and storms; which he did, and they held it up in those seasons, and fancied it had a charm to conquer them, and kept it like a holy relic. They are very superstitious, and called him the great *Peeie,* that is, prophet. They showed us their Indian *Peeie,* a youth of about sixteen years old, as handsome as nature could make a man. They consecrate a beautiful youth from his infancy, and all arts are used to complete him in the finest manner, both in beauty and shape. He is bred to all the little arts and cunning they are capable of, to all the legerdemain tricks and sleight of hand, whereby he imposes upon the rabble, and is both a doctor in physic and divinity; and by these tricks makes the sick believe he sometimes eases their pains, by drawing from the afflicted part little serpents, or odd flies, or worms, or any strange thing; and though they have besides undoubted good remedies for almost all their diseases, they cure the patient more by fancy than by medicines, and make themselves feared, loved, and reverenced. This young *Peeie* had a very young wife, who seeing my brother kiss her, came running and kissed me; after this they kissed one another, and made it a very great jest, it being so novel; and new admiration and laughing went round the multitude, that they never will forget that ceremony, never before used or known. Caesar had a mind to see and talk with their war captains, and we were conducted to one of their houses, where we beheld several of the great captains, who had been at council. But so frightful a vision it was to see 'em no fancy can create; no such dreams can represent so dreadful a spectacle. For my part I took 'em for hobgoblins or fiends rather than men; but however their shapes appeared, their souls were very humane and noble; but some wanted their noses, some their lips, some both noses and lips, some their ears, and others cut through each cheek with long slashes, through which their teeth appeared; they had other several formidable wounds and scars, or rather dismemberings. They had *comitias* or little aprons before 'em, and girdles of cotton, with their knives naked, stuck in it; a bow at their backs and a quiver of arrows on their thighs; and most had feathers on their heads of diverse colors. They cried "*Amora tiguamy*" to us at our entrance, and were pleased we said as much to 'em; they seated us, and gave us drink of the best sort, and wondered, as much as the others had done before, to see us. Caesar was marveling as much at their faces, wondering how they should all be so wounded in war; he was impatient to know how they all came by those frightful marks of rage or malice, rather than wounds got in noble battle. They told us, by our interpreter, that when any war was waging, two men chosen out by some old captain whose fighting was past, and who could only teach the theory of war, these two men were to stand in competition for the generalship, or great war captain; and being brought before the old judges, now past labor, they are asked what they dare do to show they are worthy to lead an army. When he who is first asked, making no reply, cuts off his nose, and throws it contemptibly[1] on the ground; and the other does something to himself that he thinks surpasses him, and perhaps deprives himself of lips and an eye; so they slash on till one gives out, and many have died in this debate. And 'tis by a passive valor they show and prove their activity, a sort of courage too brutal to be applauded by our black hero; nevertheless he expressed his esteem of 'em.

In this voyage Caesar begot so good an understanding between the Indians and the English that there were no more fears or heart-burnings during our stay, but we had a perfect, open, and free trade with 'em. Many things remarkable and worthy reciting we met with in this short voyage, because Caesar made it his business to search out and provide for our entertainment, especially to please his dearly adored Imoinda, who was a sharer in all our adventures; we being resolved to make her chains as easy as we could, and to compliment the Prince in that manner that most obliged him.

As we were coming up again, we met with some Indians of strange aspects; that is, of a larger size and other sort of features than those of our country. Our Indian slaves that rowed us asked 'em some questions, but they could not understand us; but showed us a long cotton string with several knots on it, and told us, they had been coming from the mountains so many moons as there were knots. They were habited in skins of a strange beast, and brought along with 'em bags of gold dust, which, as well as they could give us to understand, came streaming in little small channels down the high mountains when the rains fell; and offered to be the convoy to any body or persons that would go to the mountains. We carried these men up to Parham, where they were kept till the Lord Governor came. And because all the country was mad to be going on this golden adventure, the Governor by his letters commanded (for they sent some of the gold to him) that a guard should be set at the mouth of the river of Amazons[2] (a river so called, almost as broad as the river of Thames) and prohibited all people from going up that river, it conducting to those mountains of gold. But we going off for England before

1. With contempt.
2. The mouth of the Amazon, in Brazil, is far distant from Surinam.

the project was further prosecuted, and the Governor being drowned in a hurricane, either the design died, or the Dutch have the advantage of it. And 'tis to be bemoaned what his Majesty lost by losing that part of America.

Though this digression is a little from my story, however since it contains some proofs of the curiosity and daring of this great man, I was content to omit nothing of his character.

It was thus for some time we diverted him; but now Imoinda began to show she was with child, and did nothing but sigh and weep for the captivity of her lord, herself, and the infant yet unborn, and believed if it were so hard to gain the liberty of two, 'twould be more difficult to get that for three. Her griefs were so many darts in the great heart of Caesar; and taking his opportunity one Sunday when all the whites were overtaken in drink, as there were abundance of several trades and slaves for four years[3] that inhabited among the Negro houses, and Sunday was their day of debauch (otherwise they were a sort of spies upon Caesar), he went pretending out of goodness to 'em to feast amongst 'em; and sent all his music, and ordered a great treat for the whole gang, about three hundred Negroes; and about a hundred and fifty were able to bear arms, such as they had, which were sufficient to do execution[4] with spirits accordingly. For the English had none but rusty swords that no strength could draw from a scabbard, except the people of particular quality, who took care to oil 'em and keep 'em in good order. The guns also, unless here and there one, or those newly carried from England, would do no good or harm; for 'tis the nature of that country to rust and eat up iron, or any metals but gold and silver. And they are very unexpert at the bow, which the Negroes and Indians are perfect masters of.

Caesar, having singled out these men from the women and children, made an harangue to 'em of the miseries and ignominies of slavery, counting up all their toils and sufferings, under such loads, burdens, and drudgeries as were fitter for beasts than men, senseless brutes than human souls. He told 'em, it was not for days, months, or years, but for eternity; there was no end to be of their misfortunes. They suffered not like men, who might find a glory and fortitude in oppression, but like dogs that loved the whip and bell,[5] and fawned the more they were beaten. That they had lost the divine quality of men and were become insensible asses, fit only to bear; nay, worse: an ass, or dog, or horse, having done his duty, could lie down in retreat and rise to work again, and while he did his duty endured no stripes; but men, villainous, senseless men such as they, toiled on all the tedious week till Black Friday;[6] and then, whether they worked or not, whether they were faulty or meriting, they promiscuously, the innocent with the guilty, suffered the infamous whip, the sordid stripes, from their fellow slaves, till their blood trickled from all parts of their body, blood whose every drop ought to be revenged with a life of some of those tyrants that impose it. "And why," said he, "my dear friends and fellow sufferers, should we be slaves to an unknown people? Have they vanquished us nobly in fight? Have they won us in honorable battle? And are we by the chance of war become their slaves? This would not anger

---

3. Tradesmen, and whites who for crimes or debt were indentured for a fixed period.
4. Harm, slaughter.
5. Proverbial for something that distracts from comfort or pleasure, from the protective charm on

chariots of triumphing generals in ancient Rome.
6. Here a day of customary beating; more widely, a Friday bringing some notable disaster, from students' slang for examination day.

a noble heart, this would not animate a soldier's soul; no, but we are bought and sold like apes or monkeys, to be the sport of women, fools, and cowards, and the support of rogues, runagades,[7] that have abandoned their own countries for rapine, murders, thefts, and villainies. Do you not hear every day how they upbraid each other with infamy of life, below the wildest savages; and shall we render obedience to such a degenerate race, who have no one human virtue left to distinguish 'em from the vilest creatures? Will you, I say, suffer the lash from such hands?" They all replied, with one accord, "No, no, no; Caesar has spoke like a great captain, like a great king."

After this he would have proceeded, but was interrupted by a tall Negro of some more quality than the rest; his name was Tuscan; who bowing at the feet of Caesar, cried, "My lord, we have listened with joy and attention to what you have said, and, were we only men, would follow so great a leader through the world. But oh! consider, we are husbands and parents too, and have things more dear to us than life, our wives and children, unfit for travel in these unpassable woods, mountains, and bogs; we have not only difficult lands to overcome, but rivers to wade, and monsters to encounter, ravenous beasts of prey—." To this, Caesar replied that honor was the first principle in nature that was to be obeyed; but as no man would pretend to that, without all the acts of virtue, compassion, charity, love, justice, and reason, he found it not inconsistent with that to take an equal care of their wives and children as they would of themselves; and that he did not design, when he led them to freedom and glorious liberty, that they should leave that better part of themselves to perish by the hand of the tyrant's whip. But if there were a woman among them so degenerate from love and virtue to choose slavery before the pursuit of her husband, and with the hazard of her life to share with him in his fortunes, that such a one ought to be abandoned, and left as a prey to the common enemy.

To which they all agreed—and bowed. After this, he spoke of the impassable woods and rivers, and convinced 'em, the more danger, the more glory. He told them that he had heard of one Hannibal, a great captain, had cut his way through mountains of solid rocks;[8] and should a few shrubs oppose them, which they could fire before 'em? No, 'twas a trifling excuse to men resolved to die or overcome. As for bogs, they are with a little labor filled and hardened; and the rivers could be no obstacle, since they swam by nature, at least by custom, from their first hour of their birth. That when the children were weary they must carry them by turns, and the woods and their own industry would afford them food. To this they all assented with joy.

Tuscan then demanded what he would do. He said, they would travel towards the sea, plant a new colony, and defend it by their valor; and when they could find a ship, either driven by stress of weather or guided by Providence that way, they would seize it and make it a prize, till it had transported them to their own countries; at least, they should be made free in his kingdom, and be esteemed as his fellow sufferers, and men that had the courage and the bravery to attempt, at least, for liberty; and if they died in the attempt it would be more brave than to live in perpetual slavery.

They bowed and kissed his feet at this resolution, and with one accord

---

7. Renegades or fugitives.
8. The Carthaginian general and his troops liter-ally hacked their way down the Alps into Italy to attack Rome.

vowed to follow him to death. And that night was appointed to begin their march; they made it known to their wives, and directed them to tie their hamaca[9] about their shoulder and under their arm like a scarf, and to lead their children that could go, and carry those that could not. The wives, who pay an entire obedience to their husbands, obeyed, and stayed for 'em where they were appointed. The men stayed but to furnish themselves with what defensive arms they could get; and all met at the rendezvous, where Caesar made a new encouraging speech to 'em, and led 'em out.

But as they could not march far that night, on Monday early, when the overseers went to call 'em all together to go to work, they were extremely surprised to find not one upon the place, but all fled with what baggage they had. You may imagine this news was not only suddenly spread all over the plantation, but soon reached the neighboring ones; and we had by noon about six hundred men they call the militia of the county, that came to assist us in the pursuit of the fugitives. But never did one see so comical an army march forth to war. The men of any fashion would not concern themselves, though it were almost the common cause; for such revoltings are very ill examples, and have very fatal consequences oftentimes in many colonies. But they had a respect for Caesar, and all hands were against the Parhamites, as they called those of Parham plantation, because they did not, in the first place, love the Lord Governor, and secondly they would have it that Caesar was ill used, and baffled with;[1] and 'tis not impossible but some of the best in the country was of his counsel in this flight, and depriving us of all the slaves; so that they of the better sort would not meddle in the matter. The deputy governor,[2] of whom I have had no great occasion to speak, and who was the most fawning fair-tongued fellow in the world and one that pretended the most friendship to Caesar, was now the only violent man against him; and though he had nothing, and so need fear nothing, yet talked and looked bigger than any man. He was a fellow whose character is not fit to be mentioned with the worst of the slaves. This fellow would lead his army forth to meet Caesar, or rather to pursue him; most of their arms were of those sort of cruel whips they call cat with nine tails; some had rusty useless guns for show, others old basket hilts[3] whose blades had never seen the light in this age, and others had long staffs and clubs. Mr. Trefry went along, rather to be a mediator than a conqueror in such a battle; for he foresaw and knew, if by fighting they put the Negroes into despair, they were a sort of sullen fellows that would drown or kill themselves before they would yield; and he advised that fair means was best. But Byam was one that abounded in his own wit and would take his own measures.

It was not hard to find these fugitives; for as they fled they were forced to fire and cut the woods before 'em, so that night or day they pursued 'em by the light they made and by the path they had cleared. But as soon as Caesar found he was pursued, he put himself in a posture of defense, placing all the women and children in the rear, and himself with Tuscan by his side, or next to him, all promising to die or conquer. Encouraged thus, they never stood to parley, but fell on pell-mell upon the English, and killed some and wounded a good many, they having recourse to their whips as the best of

9. Hammock.
1. Cheated.
2. William Byam. There are recorded complaints

against him for high-handedness and from him about insubordination by settlers and slaves.
3. Swords with protective hilt guards.

their weapons. And as they observed no order, they perplexed the enemy so sorely with lashing 'em in the eyes; and the women and children seeing their husbands so treated, being of fearful cowardly dispositions, and hearing the English cry out, "Yield and live, yield and be pardoned," they all run in amongst their husbands and fathers, and hung about 'em, crying out, "Yield, yield; and leave Caesar to their revenge"; that by degrees the slaves abandoned Caesar, and left him only Tuscan and his heroic Imoinda; who, grown big as she was, did nevertheless press near her lord, having a bow and a quiver full of poisoned arrows, which she managed with such dexterity that she wounded several, and shot the governor into the shoulder; of which wound he had like to have died, but that an Indian woman, his mistress, sucked the wound and cleansed it from the venom. But however, he stirred not from the place till he had parleyed with Caesar, who he found was resolved to die fighting, and would not be taken; no more would Tuscan, or Imoinda. But he, more thirsting after revenge of another sort than that of depriving him of life, now made use of all his art of talking and dissembling, and besought Caesar to yield himself upon terms which he himself should propose, and should be sacredly assented to and kept by him. He told him, it was not that he any longer feared him, or could believe the force of two men, and a young heroine, could overcome all them, with all the slaves now on their side also; but it was the vast esteem he had for his person, the desire he had to serve so gallant a man, and to hinder himself from the reproach hereafter of having been the occasion of the death of a prince whose valor and magnanimity deserved the empire of the world. He protested to him, he looked upon this action as gallant and brave, however tending to the prejudice of his lord and master, who would by it have lost so considerable a number of slaves; that this flight of his should be looked on as a heat of youth, and rashness of a too forward courage, and an unconsidered impatience of liberty, and no more; and that he labored in vain to accomplish that which they would effectually perform as soon as any ship arrived that would touch on his coast. "So that if you will be pleased," continued he, "to surrender yourself, all imaginable respect shall be paid you; and yourself, your wife, and child, if it be here born, shall depart free out of our land."

But Caesar would hear of no composition;[4] though Byam urged, if he pursued and went on in his design, he would inevitably perish, either by great snakes, wild beasts, or hunger; and he ought to have regard to his wife, whose condition required ease, and not the fatigues of tedious travel, where she could not be secured from being devoured. But Caesar told him, there was no faith in the white men or the gods they adored, who instructed 'em in principles so false that honest men could not live amongst 'em; though no people professed so much, none performed so little; that he knew what he had to do when he dealt with men of honor, but with them a man ought to be eternally on his guard, and never to eat and drink with Christians without his weapon of defense in his hand; and for his own security, never to credit one word they spoke. As for the rashness and inconsiderateness of his action, he would confess the governor is in the right; and that he was ashamed of what he had done, in endeavoring to make those free who were by nature slaves, poor wretched rogues, fit to be used as Christians' tools;

4. Settlement.

dogs, treacherous and cowardly, fit for such masters; and they wanted only but to be whipped into the knowledge of the Christian gods to be the vilest of all creeping things, to learn to worship such deities as had not power to make 'em just, brave, or honest. In fine, after a thousand things of this nature, not fit here to be recited, he told Byam he had rather die than live upon the same earth with such dogs. But Trefry and Byam pleaded and protested together so much that Trefry, believing the governor to mean what he said, and speaking very cordially himself, generously put himself into Caesar's hands, and took him aside and persuaded him, even with tears, to live, by surrendering himself, and to name his conditions. Caesar was overcome by his wit and reasons, and in consideration of Imoinda; and demanding what he desired, and that it should be ratified by their hands in writing, because he had perceived that was the common way of contract between man and man, amongst the whites. All this was performed, and Tuscan's pardon was put in, and they surrender to the governor, who walked peaceably down into the plantation with 'em, after giving order to bury their dead. Caesar was very much toiled with the bustle of the day, for he had fought like a fury; and what mischief was done he and Tuscan performed alone, and gave their enemies a fatal proof that they durst do anything and feared no mortal force.

But they were no sooner arrived at the place where all the slaves receive their punishments of whipping, but they laid hands on Caesar and Tuscan, faint with heat and toil; and surprising them, bound them to two several stakes, and whipped them in a most deplorable and inhuman manner, rending the very flesh from their bones; especially Caesar, who was not perceived to make any moan or to alter his face, only to roll his eyes on the faithless governor, and those he believed guilty, with fierceness and indignation; and to complete his rage, he saw every one of those slaves, who but a few days before adored him as something more than mortal, now had a whip to give him some lashes, while he strove not to break his fetters; though if he had, it were impossible. But he pronounced a woe and revenge from his eyes, that darted fire that 'twas at once both awful and terrible to behold.

When they thought they were sufficiently revenged on him, they untied him, almost fainting with loss of blood from a thousand wounds all over his body, from which they had rent his clothes, and led him bleeding and naked as he was, and loaded him all over with irons; and then rubbed his wounds, to complete their cruelty, with Indian pepper, which had like to have made him raving mad; and in this condition made him so fast to the ground that he could not stir, if his pains and wounds would have given him leave. They spared Imoinda, and did not let her see this barbarity committed towards her lord, but carried her down to Parham and shut her up; which was not in kindness to her, but for fear she should die with the sight, or miscarry, and then they should lose a young slave and perhaps the mother.

You must know, that when the news was brought on Monday morning that Caesar had betaken himself to the woods and carried with him all the Negroes, we were possessed with extreme fear, which no persuasions could dissipate, that he would secure himself till night, and then that he would come down and cut all our throats. This apprehension made all the females of us fly down the river, to be secured; and while we were away they acted this cruelty. For I suppose I had authority and interest enough there, had I suspected any such thing, to have prevented it; but we had not gone many leagues but the news overtook us that Caesar was taken and whipped like a common slave. We met on the river with Colonel Martin, a man of great gallantry, wit, and goodness, and whom I have celebrated in a character of my new comedy[5] by his own name, in memory of so brave a man. He was wise and eloquent and, from the fineness of his parts, bore a great sway over the hearts of all the colony. He was a friend to Caesar, and resented this false dealing with him very much. We carried him back to Parham, thinking to have made an accommodation; when we came, the first news we heard was that the governor was dead of a wound Imoinda had given him; but it was not so well. But it seems he would have the pleasure of beholding the revenge he took on Caesar, and before the cruel ceremony was finished, he dropped down; and then they perceived the wound he had on his shoulder was by a venomed arrow, which, as I said, his Indian mistress healed by sucking the wound.

We were no sooner arrived but we went up to the plantation to see Caesar, whom we found in a very miserable and unexpressible condition; and I have a thousand times admired how he lived, in so much tormenting pain. We said all things to him that trouble, pity, and good nature could suggest, protesting our innocency of the fact and our abhorrence of such cruelties; making a thousand professions of services to him and begging as many pardons for the offenders, till we said so much that he believed we had no hand in his ill treatment; but told us he could never pardon Byam; as for Trefry, he confessed he saw his grief and sorrow for his suffering, which he could not hinder, but was like to have been beaten down by the very slaves for speaking in his defense. But for Byam, who was their leader, their head—and should, by his justice and honor, have been an example to 'em—for him, he wished to live, to take a dire revenge of him, and said, "It had been well for him if he had sacrificed me, instead of giving me the contemptible[6] whip." He refused to talk much, but begging us to give him our hands, he took 'em, and protested never to lift up his to do us any harm. He had a great respect for Colonel Martin, and always took his counsel like that of a parent, and assured him he would obey him in anything but his revenge on Byam. "Therefore," said he, "for his own safety, let him speedily dispatch me; for if I could dispatch myself I would not, till that justice were done to my injured person, and the contempt of a soldier. No, I would not kill myself, even after a whipping, but will be content to live with that infamy, and be pointed at by every grinning slave, till I have completed my revenge; and then you shall see that Oroonoko scorns to live with the indignity that was put on Caesar." All we could do could get no more words from him; and we took care to have him put immediately into a healing bath to rid him of his pepper, and ordered a chirurgeon[7] to anoint him with healing balm, which he suffered; and in some time he began to be able to walk and eat. We failed not to visit him every day, and to that end had him brought to an apartment at Parham.

The governor was no sooner recovered, and had heard of the menaces of Caesar, but he called his council; who (not to disgrace them, or burlesque the government there) consisted of such notorious villains as Newgate[8] never

5. *The Younger Brother, or The Amorous Jilt*, not produced until 1696 despite this piece of promotion.
6. Showing contempt.

7. Surgeon.
8. The major London prison, from which criminals were transported to the colonies.

transported; and possibly originally were such who understood neither the laws of God or man, and had no sort of principles to make 'em worthy the name of men; but at the very council table would contradict and fight with one another, and swear so bloodily that 'twas terrible to hear and see 'em. (Some of 'em were afterwards hanged when the Dutch took possession of the place, others sent off in chains.) But calling these special rulers of the nation together, and requiring their counsel in this weighty affair, they all concluded that (Damn 'em) it might be their own cases; and that Caesar ought to be made an example to all the Negroes, to fright 'em from daring to threaten their betters, their lords and masters; and at this rate no man was safe from his own slaves; and concluded, *nemine contradicente*,[9] that Caesar should be hanged.

Trefry then thought it time to use his authority, and told Byam his command did not extend to his lord's plantation, and that Parham was as much exempt from the law as Whitehall;[1] and that they ought no more to touch the servants of the Lord——(who there represented the King's person) than they could those about the King himself; and that Parham was a sanctuary; and though his lord were absent in person, his power was still in being there, which he had entrusted with him as far as the dominions of his particular plantations reached, and all that belonged to it; the rest of the country, as Byam was lieutenant to his lord, he might exercise his tyranny upon. Trefry had others as powerful, or more, that interested themselves in Caesar's life, and absolutely said he should be defended. So turning the governor and his wise council out of doors (for they sat at Parham House), they set a guard upon our landing place, and would admit none but those we called friends to us and Caesar.

The governor having remained wounded at Parham till his recovery was completed, Caesar did not know but he was still there; and indeed, for the most part his time was spent there, for he was one that loved to live at other people's expense; and if he were a day absent, he was ten present there, and used to play and walk and hunt and fish with Caesar. So that Caesar did not at all doubt, if he once recovered strength, but he should find an opportunity of being revenged on him. Though after such a revenge, he could not hope to live, for if he escaped the fury of the English mobile,[2] who perhaps would have been glad of the occasion to have killed him, he was resolved not to survive his whipping; yet he had, some tender hours, a repenting softness, which he called his fits of coward, wherein he struggled with Love for the victory of his heart, which took part with his charming Imoinda there; but for the most part his time was passed in melancholy thought and black designs. He considered, if he should do this deed and die, either in the attempt or after it, he left his lovely Imoinda a prey, or at best a slave, to the enraged multitude; his great heart could not endure that thought. "Perhaps," said he, "she may be first ravished by every brute, exposed first to their nasty lusts and then a shameful death." No; he could not live a moment under that apprehension, too insupportable to be borne. These were his thoughts and his silent arguments with his heart, as he told us afterwards; so that now resolving not only to kill Byam but all those he thought had enraged him, pleasing his great heart with the fancied slaughter he should make over the

9. No one disagreeing (Latin).
1. The king's palace in London. Treffry stands as Lord Willoughby's deputy on his private land,
Byam in the colony at large.
2. Common people or mob.

whole face of the plantation, he first resolved on a deed, that (however horrid it at first appeared to us all), when we had heard his reasons, we thought it brave and just. Being able to walk and, as he believed, fit for the execution of his great design, he begged Trefry to trust him into the air, believing a walk would do him good, which was granted him; and taking Imoinda with him, as he used to do in his more happy and calmer days, he led her up into a wood, where, after (with a thousand sighs, and long gazing silently on her face, while tears gushed, in spite of him, from his eyes) he told her his design first of killing her, and then his enemies, and next himself, and the impossibility of escaping, and therefore he told her the necessity of dying, he found the heroic wife faster pleading for death than he was to propose it, when she found his fixed resolution, and on her knees besought him not to leave her a prey to his enemies. He (grieved to death) yet pleased at her noble resolution, took her up, and embracing her with all the passion and languishment of a dying lover, drew his knife to kill this treasure of his soul, this pleasure of his eyes; while tears trickled down his cheeks, hers were smiling with joy she should die by so noble a hand, and be sent in her own country (for that's their notion of the next world) by him she so tenderly loved and so truly adored in this; for wives have a respect for their husbands equal to what any other people pay a deity, and when a man finds any occasion to quit his wife, if he love her, she dies by his hand; if not, he sells her, or suffers some other to kill her. It being thus, you may believe the deed was soon resolved on; and 'tis not to be doubted but the parting, the eternal leave-taking of two such lovers, so greatly born, so sensible,[3] so beautiful, so young, and so fond, must be very moving, as the relation of it was to me afterwards.

All that love could say in such cases being ended, and all the intermitting irresolutions being adjusted, the lovely, young, and adored victim lays herself down before the sacrificer; while he, with a hand resolved and a heart breaking within, gave the fatal stroke; first cutting her throat, and then severing her yet smiling face from that delicate body, pregnant as it was with fruits of tenderest love. As soon as he had done, he laid the body decently on leaves and flowers, of which he made a bed, and concealed it under the same coverlid of nature; only her face he left yet bare to look on. But when he found she was dead and past all retrieve, never more to bless him with her eyes and soft language, his grief swelled up to rage; he tore, he raved, he roared, like some monster of the wood, calling on the loved name of Imoinda. A thousand times he turned the fatal knife that did the deed toward his own heart, with a resolution to go immediately after her; but dire revenge, which now was a thousand times more fierce in his soul than before, prevents him; and he would cry out, "No; since I have sacrificed Imoinda to my revenge, shall I lose that glory which I have purchased so dear as at the price of the fairest, dearest, softest creature that ever nature made? No, no!" Then, at her name, grief would get the ascendant of rage, and he would lie down by her side and water her face with showers of tears, which never were wont to fall from those eyes. And however bent he was on his intended slaughter, he had not power to stir from the sight of this dear object, now more beloved and more adored than ever.

He remained in this deploring condition for two days, and never rose from

---

3. Sensitive.

the ground where he had made his sad sacrifice. At last, rousing from her side, and accusing himself with living too long now Imoinda was dead, and that the deaths of those barbarous enemies were deferred too long, he resolved now to finish the great work; but offering to rise, he found his strength so decayed that he reeled to and fro, like boughs assailed by contrary winds; so that he was forced to lie down again, and try to summons all his courage to his aid. He found his brains turned round, and his eyes were dizzy, and objects appeared not the same to him they were wont to do; his breath was short, and all his limbs surprised with a faintness he had never felt before. He had not eat in two days, which was one occasion of this feebleness, but excess of grief was the greatest; yet still he hoped he should recover vigor to act his design, and lay expecting it yet six days longer, still mourning over the dead idol of his heart, and striving every day to rise, but could not.

In all this time you may believe we were in no little affliction for Caesar and his wife, some were of opinion he was escaped never to return; others thought some accident had happened to him. But however, we failed not to send out an hundred people several ways to search for him; a party of about forty went that way he took, among whom was Tuscan, who was perfectly reconciled to Byam. They had not gone very far into the wood but they smelt an unusual smell, as of a dead body; for stinks must be very noisome that can be distinguished among such a quantity of natural sweets as every inch of that land produces. So that they concluded they should find him dead, or somebody that was so. They passed on towards it, as loathsome as it was, and made such a rustling among the leaves that lie thick on the ground, by continual falling, that Caesar heard he was approached; and though he had during the space of these eight days endeavored to rise, but found he wanted strength, yet looking up and seeing his pursuers, he rose and reeled to a neighboring tree, against which he fixed his back; and being within a dozen yards of those that advanced and saw him, he called out to them and bid them approach no nearer, if they would be safe. So that they stood still, and hardly believing their eyes, that would persuade them that it was Caesar that spoke to 'em, so much was he altered, they asked him what he had done with his wife, for they smelt a stink that almost struck them dead. He, pointing to the dead body, sighing, cried, "Behold her there." They put off the flowers that covered her with their sticks, and found she was killed, and cried out, "Oh, monster! that hast murdered thy wife." Then asking him why he did so cruel a deed, he replied, he had no leisure to answer impertinent questions. "You may go back," continued he, "and tell the faithless governor he may thank fortune that I am breathing my last, and that my arm is too feeble to obey my heart in what it had designed him." But his tongue faltering, and trembling, he could scarce end what he was saying. The English, taking advantage by his weakness, cried, "Let us take him alive by all means." He heard 'em; and as if he had revived from a fainting, or a dream, he cried out, "No, gentlemen, you are deceived; you will find no more Caesars to be whipped, no more find a faith in me. Feeble as you think me, I have strength yet left to secure me from a second indignity." They swore all anew, and he only shook his head and beheld them with scorn. Then they cried out, "Who will venture on this single man? Will nobody?" They stood all silent while Caesar replied, "Fatal will be the attempt to the first adventurer, let him assure himself," and at that word, held up his knife in a menacing posture. "Look ye, ye faithless crew," said he, " 'tis not life I seek, nor am I afraid of dying," and at that word cut a piece of flesh from his own throat, and threw it at 'em; "yet still I would live if I could, till I had perfected my revenge. But oh! it cannot be; I feel life gliding from my eyes and heart, and if I make not haste, I shall yet fall a victim to the shameful whip." At that, he ripped up his own belly, and took his bowels and pulled 'em out, with what strength he could; while some, on their knees imploring, besought him to hold his hand. But when they saw him tottering, they cried out, "Will none venture on him?" A bold English cried, "Yes, if he were the devil" (taking courage when he saw him almost dead); and swearing a horrid oath for his farewell to the world, he rushed on him; Caesar, with his armed hand, met him so fairly as stuck him to the heart, and he fell dead at his feet. Tuscan, seeing that, cried out, "I love thee, O Caesar, and therefore will not let thee die, if possible." And running to him, took him in his arms; but at the same time warding a blow that Caesar made at his bosom, he received it quite through his arm; and Caesar having not the strength to pluck the knife forth, though he attempted it, Tuscan neither pulled it out himself nor suffered it to be pulled out, but came down with it sticking in his arm; and the reason he gave for it was, because the air should not get into the wound. They put their hands across, and carried Caesar between six of 'em, fainted as he was, and they thought dead, or just dying; and they brought him to Parham, and laid him on a couch, and had the chirurgeon immediately to him, who dressed his wounds and sewed up his belly, and used means to bring him to life, which they effected. We ran all to see him, and if before we thought him so beautiful a sight, he was now so altered that his face was like a death's head blacked over, nothing but teeth and eyeholes. For some days we suffered nobody to speak to him, but caused cordials to be poured down his throat, which sustained his life; and in six or seven days he recovered his senses. For you must know that wounds are almost to a miracle cured in the Indies, unless wounds in the legs, which rarely ever cure.

When he was well enough to speak, we talked to him, and asked him some questions about his wife, and the reasons why he killed her; and he then told us what I have related of that resolution, and of his parting; and he besought us we would let him die, and was extremely afflicted to think it was possible he might live; he assured us if we did not dispatch him, he would prove very fatal to a great many. We said all we could to make him live, and gave him new assurances; but he begged we would not think so poorly of him, or of his love to Imoinda, to imagine we could flatter him to life again; but the chirurgeon assured him he could not live, and therefore he need not fear. We were all (but Caesar) afflicted at this news; and the sight was gashly;[4] his discourse was sad, and the earthly smell about him so strong that I was persuaded to leave the place for some time (being myself but sickly, and very apt to fall into fits of dangerous illness upon any extraordinary melancholy). The servants and Trefry and the chirurgeons promised all to take what possible care they could of the life of Caesar, and I, taking boat, went with other company to Colonel Martin's, about three days' journey down the river; but I was no sooner gone, but the governor taking Trefry about some pretended

4. Ghastly.

earnest business a day's journey up the river, having communicated his design to one Banister, a wild Irishman and one of the council, a fellow of absolute barbarity, and fit to execute any villainy, but was rich: he came up to Parham, and forcibly took Caesar, and had him carried to the same post where he was whipped; and causing him to be tied to it, and a great fire made before him, he told him he should die like a dog, as he was. Caesar replied, this was the first piece of bravery that ever Banister did, and he never spoke sense till he pronounced that word; and if he would keep it, he would declare, in the other world, that he was the only man of all the whites that ever he heard speak truth. And turning to the men that bound him, he said, "My friends, am I to die, or to be whipped?" And they cried, "Whipped! No, you shall not escape so well." And then he replied, smiling, "A blessing on thee," and assured them they need not tie him, for he would stand fixed like a rock, and endure death so as should encourage them to die. "But if you whip me," said he, "be sure you tie me fast."

He had learned to take tobacco; and when he was assured he should die, he desired they would give him a pipe in his mouth, ready lighted, which they did; and the executioner came, and first cut off his members,[5] and threw them into the fire; after that, with an ill-favored knife, they cut his ears, and his nose, and burned them; he still smoked on, as if nothing had touched him. Then they hacked off one of his arms, and still he bore up, and held his pipe; but at the cutting off the other arm, his head sunk, and his pipe dropped, and he gave up the ghost, without a groan or a reproach. My mother and sister were by him all the while, but not suffered to save him, so rude and wild were the rabble, and so inhuman were the justices, who stood by to see the execution, who after paid dearly enough for their insolence. They cut Caesar in quarters, and sent them to several of the chief plantations. One quarter was sent to Colonel Martin, who refused it, and swore he had rather see the quarters of Banister and the governor himself than those of Caesar on his plantations, and that he could govern his Negroes without terrifying and grieving them with frightful spectacles of a mangled king.

Thus died this great man, worthy of a better fate, and a more sublime wit than mine to write his praise; yet, I hope, the reputation of my pen is considerable enough to make his glorious name to survive to all ages, with that of the brave, the beautiful, and the constant Imoinda.

1688

5. Genitals.

WILLIAM CONGREVE
1670–1729

On both sides of his family William Congreve was descended from well-to-do and prominent county families. His father, a younger son, obtained a commission as lieutenant in the army and moved to Ireland in 1674. There the future playwright was educated at Kilkenny School and Trinity College, Dublin; at both places he was a younger contemporary of Swift. In 1691 he took rooms in the Middle Temple and began to study law, but soon found he preferred the wit of the coffeehouses and the theater. Within a year he had so distinguished himself at Will's Coffeehouse that he had become intimate with the great Dryden himself, and his brief career as a dramatist began shortly thereafter.

The success of *The Old Bachelor* (produced in 1693) immediately established him as the most promising young dramatist in London. It had the then phenomenally long run of fourteen days, and Dryden declared it the best first play he had ever read. *The Double Dealer* (produced in 1693) was a near failure, though it evoked one of Dryden's most graceful and gracious poems, in which he praised Congreve as the superior of Jonson and Fletcher and the equal of Shakespeare. *Love for Love* (produced in 1695) was an unqualified success and remains Congreve's most frequently revived play. In 1697 he brought out a tragedy, *The Mourning Bride*, which enjoyed great popular esteem. Congreve's most elegant comedy of manners, *The Way of the World*, received a brilliant production in 1700. But it did not succeed with audiences, and subsequently he gave up the stage. He held a minor government post, which, although a Whig, he was allowed to keep during the Tory ministry of Oxford and Bolingbroke; after the accession of George I he was given a more lucrative government sinecure. Despite the political animosities of the first two decades of the century, he managed to remain on friendly terms with Swift and Pope, and Pope dedicated to him his translation of the *Iliad*. His final years were perplexed by poor health, but were made bearable by the love of Henrietta, duchess of Marlborough, whose last child, a daughter, was in all probability the playwright's.

The Way of the World is one of the wittiest plays ever written, a play to read slowly and savor. Like an expert jeweler, Congreve polished the Restoration comedy of manners to its ultimate sparkle and gloss. The dialogue is epigrammatic and brilliant, the plot is an intricate puzzle, and the characters shine with surprisingly complex facets. Yet the play is not all dazzling surface; it also has depths. Most Restoration comedies begin with the struggle for power, sex, and money and end with a marriage. In an age that viewed property, not romance, as the basis of marriage, the hero shows his prowess by catching an heiress. *The Way of the World* reflects that standard plot; it is a battle more over a legacy than over a woman, a battle in which sexual attraction is used as a weapon. Yet Congreve, writing late in the period, reveals the weakness of those who treat love as a war or a game: "each deceiver to his cost may find / That marriage frauds too oft are paid in kind." If "the way of the world" is cynical self-interest, it is also the worldly prudence that sees through the ruses of power and turns them to better ends. In this world generosity and affection win the day and true love conquers—with the help of some clever plotting.

At the center of the action are four fully realized characters—Mirabell and Millamant, the hero and heroine, and Fainall and Mrs. Marwood, the two villains—whose stratagems and relations move the play. Around them are characters who serve in one way or another as foils: Witwoud, the would-be wit, with whom we contrast the true wit of Mirabell and Millamant; Petulant, a "humor" character, who affects bluff candor and cynical realism, but succeeds only in being offensive; and Sir Wilfull Witwoud, the booby squire from the country, who serves with Petulant to throw into relief the high good breeding and fineness of nature of the hero and heroine. Finally there is one of Congreve's finest creations, Lady Wishfort ("wish for it"), who though aging and ugly still longs for love, gallantry, and courtship and who is led by her appetites into the trap that Mirabell lays for her.

Because of the complexity of the plot, a summary of the situation at the rise of the curtain may prove helpful. Mirabell (a reformed rake) is sincerely in love with and wishes to marry Millamant, who, though a coquette and a highly sophisticated wit, is a virtuous woman. Mirabell some time before has married off his former mistress, the daughter of Lady Wishfort, to his friend Fainall. Fainall has grown tired of his

wife and has been squandering her money on his mistress, Mrs. Marwood. In order
to gain access to Millamant, Mirabell has pretended to pay court to the elderly and
amorous Lady Wishfort, who is the guardian of Millamant and as such controls half
her fortune. But his game has been spoiled by Mrs. Marwood, who nourishes a secret
love for Mirabell and, to separate him from Millamant, has made Lady Wishfort aware
of Mirabell's duplicity. Lady Wishfort now loathes Mirabell for making a fool of her—
an awkward situation, because if Millamant should marry without her guardian's
consent she would lose half her fortune, and Mirabell cannot afford to marry any but
a rich wife. It is at this point that the action begins. Mirabell perfects a plot to get
such power over Lady Wishfort as to force her to agree to the marriage, while Millamant continues to doubt whether she wishes to marry at all.

The Way of the World

DRAMATIS PERSONAE[1]

Men

FAINALL, *in love with* MRS. MARWOOD
MIRABELL, *in love with* MRS. MILLAMANT
WITWOUD
PETULANT } *followers of* MRS. MILLAMANT
SIR WILFULL WITWOUD, *half brother to* WITWOUD, *and nephew to*
   LADY WISHFORT
WAITWELL, *servant to* MIRABELL

Women

LADY WISHFORT, *enemy to* MIRABELL, *for having falsely pretended love to her*
MRS. MILLAMANT, *a fine lady, niece to* LADY WISHFORT, *and loves* MIRABELL
MRS. MARWOOD, *friend to* MR. FAINALL, *and likes* MIRABELL
MRS. FAINALL, *daughter to* LADY WISHFORT, *and wife to* FAINALL, *formerly friend*
   to MIRABELL
FOIBLE, *woman to* LADY WISHFORT
MINCING, *woman to* MRS. MILLAMANT
BETTY, *waitress at the chocolate house*
PEG, *under-servant to* LADY WISHFORT
DANCERS, FOOTMEN, *and* ATTENDANTS

SCENE—*London.*

Prologue

SPOKEN BY MR. BETTERTON[2]

Of those few fools, who with ill stars are cursed,
  Sure scribbling fools, called poets, fare the worst:
  For they're a sort of fools which Fortune makes,

---

1. The names of the principal characters reveal
their dominant traits: for example, Fainall would
fain have *all,* with perhaps also the suggestion that
he is the complete hypocrite, who *feigns;* Witwoud
is the *would-be wit;* Wishfort suggests *wish for it;*
Millamant is the lady with a thousand lovers (*mille
amants*); Marwood *would* willingly *mar* (injure) the
lovers; Mincing has an air of affected gentility (i.e.,

she *minces*), which sorts ill with her vulgar English.
"Mrs." is "Mistress," a title then used by young
unmarried ladies as well as by the married Mrs.
Fainall.
2. Thomas Betterton (ca. 1635–1710), the
greatest actor of the period, played Fainall in the
original production of this play.

And after she has made 'em fools, forsakes.
5   With nature's oafs 'tis quite a different case,
For Fortune favors all her idiot race.
In her own nest the cuckoo eggs we find,
O'er which she broods to hatch the changeling kind.[3]
No portion for her own she has to spare,
10   So much she dotes on her adopted care.
     Poets are bubbles,° by the town drawn in,   *dupes*
Suffered at first some trifling stakes to win:
But what unequal hazards do they run!
Each time they write they venture all they've won: ⎫
15   The squire that's buttered still,° is sure to be undone. ⎭ *constantly flattered*
This author, heretofore, has found your favor,
But pleads no merit from his past behavior;
To build on that might prove a vain presumption,
Should grants to poets made, admit resumption:[4]
20   And in Parnassus he must lose his seat,
If that be found a forfeited estate.[5]
     He owns, with toil he wrought the following scenes,
But if they're naught ne'er spare him for his pains:
Damn him the more; have no commiseration
25   For dullness on mature deliberation.
He swears he'll not resent one hissed-off scene ⎫
Nor, like those peevish wits, his play maintain, ⎬
Who, to assert their sense, your taste arraign. ⎭
Some plot we think he has, and some new thought;
30   Some humor too, no farce; but that's a fault.
Satire, he thinks, you ought not to expect,
For so reformed a town,[6] who dares correct?
To please, this time, has been his sole pretense,
He'll not instruct, lest it should give offense.
35   Should he by chance a knave or fool expose,
That hurts none here; sure here are none of those.
In short, our play shall (with your leave to show it)
Give you one instance of a passive poet
Who to your judgments yields all resignation;
40   So save or damn after your own discretion.

Act 1—A chocolate house.

SCENE 1

MIRABELL *and* FAINALL *rising from cards,* BETTY *waiting.*

MIRABELL   You are a fortunate man, Mr. Fainall.
FAINALL   Have we done?

---

3. Simpletons; children supposed to have been secretly exchanged in infancy for others. The "cuckoo" lays its eggs in the nests of other birds.
4. The Crown could both grant and take back ("resume") estates.
5. *Seat* rhymed with *estate*; in the next couplet, *scenes* and *pains* rhymed. A few lines later *scene* is

similarly pronounced to rhyme with *maintain,* and *fault* (the *l* being silent) is rhymed with *thought.*
6. A sarcasm, directed against the general movement to reform manners and morals and, more particularly, against Jeremy Collier's attack on actors and playwrights in his *Short View of the Profaneness and Immorality of the English Stage* (1698).

MIRABELL   What you please. I'll play on to entertain you.

FAINALL   No, I'll give you your revenge another time, when you are not so indifferent; you are thinking of something else now, and play too negligently. The coldness of a losing gamester lessens the pleasure of the winner. I'd no more play with a man that slighted his ill fortune than I'd make love to a woman who undervalued the loss of her reputation.

MIRABELL   You have a taste extremely delicate, and are for refining on your pleasures.

FAINALL   Prithee, why so reserved? Something has put you out of humor.

MIRABELL   Not at all. I happen to be grave today, and you are gay; that's all.

FAINALL   Confess, Millamant and you quarreled last night after I left you; my fair cousin has some humors that would tempt the patience of a stoic. What, some coxcomb came in, and was well received by her, while you were by?

MIRABELL   Witwoud and Petulant; and what was worse, her aunt, your wife's mother, my evil genius; or to sum up all in her own name, my old Lady Wishfort came in.

FAINALL   O, there it is then—she has a lasting passion for you, and with reason. What, then my wife was there?

MIRABELL   Yes, and Mrs. Marwood and three or four more, whom I never saw before. Seeing me, they all put on their grave faces, whispered one another; then complained aloud of the vapors,[7] and after fell into a profound silence.

FAINALL   They had a mind to be rid of you.

MIRABELL   For which good reason I resolved not to stir. At last the good old lady broke through her painful taciturnity, with an invective against long visits. I would not have understood her, but Millamant joining in the argument, I rose and with a constrained smile told her I thought nothing was so easy as to know when a visit began to be troublesome. She reddened and I withdrew, without expecting[8] her reply.

FAINALL   You were to blame to resent what she spoke only in compliance with her aunt.

MIRABELL   She is more mistress of herself than to be under the necessity of such a resignation.

FAINALL   What? though half her fortune depends upon her marrying with my lady's approbation?

MIRABELL   I was then in such a humor that I should have been better pleased if she had been less discreet.

FAINALL   Now I remember, I wonder not they were weary of you: last night was one of their cabal[9] nights; they have 'em three times a week, and meet by turns, at one another's apartments, where they come together like the coroner's inquest, to sit upon the murdered reputations of the week. You and I are excluded; and it was once proposed that all the male sex should be excepted; but somebody moved that to avoid scandal there might be one man of the community; upon which Witwoud and Petulant were enrolled members.

7. Melancholy, the blues.
8. Awaiting.

9. Secret organization designed for intrigue.

MIRABELL And who may have been the foundress of this sect? My Lady Wishfort, I warrant, who publishes her detestation of mankind, and full of the vigor of fifty-five, declares for a friend and ratafia;[1] and let posterity shift for itself, she'll breed no more.

FAINALL The discovery of your sham addresses to her, to conceal your love to her niece, has provoked this separation. Had you dissembled better, things might have continued in the state of nature.

MIRABELL I did as much as man could, with any reasonable conscience: I proceeded to the very last act of flattery with her, and was guilty of a song in her commendation. Nay, I got a friend to put her into a lampoon and compliment her with the imputation of an affair with a young fellow, which I carried so far that I told her the malicious town took notice that she was grown fat of a sudden; and when she lay in of a dropsy, persuaded her she was reported to be in labor. The devil's in't, if an old woman is to be flattered further, unless a man should endeavor downright personally to debauch her; and that my virtue forbade me. But for the discovery of this amour, I am indebted to your friend, or your wife's friend, Mrs. Marwood.

FAINALL What should provoke her to be your enemy, unless she has made you advances, which you have slighted? Women do not easily forgive omissions of that nature.

MIRABELL She was always civil to me, till of late. I confess I am not one of those coxcombs who are apt to interpret a woman's good manners to her prejudice, and think that she who does not refuse 'em everything, can refuse 'em nothing.

FAINALL You are a gallant man, Mirabell; and though you may have cruelty enough not to satisfy a lady's longing, you have too much generosity not to be tender of her honor. Yet you speak with an indifference which seems to be affected, and confesses you are conscious of a negligence.

MIRABELL You pursue the argument with a distrust that seems to be unaffected, and confesses you are conscious of a concern for which the lady is more indebted to you than is your wife.

FAINALL Fie, fie, friend, if you grow censorious I must leave you.—I'll look upon the gamesters in the next room.

MIRABELL Who are they?

FAINALL Petulant and Witwoud.—Bring me some chocolate.

MIRABELL Betty, what says your clock?

BETTY Turned of the last canonical hour,[2] sir.

MIRABELL How pertinently the jade answers me! Ha? almost one a clock! [*Looking on his watch.*]—O, y'are come—

SCENE 2

MIRABELL *and* FOOTMAN.

MIRABELL Well, is the grand affair over? You have been something tedious.

1. A liqueur flavored with fruit kernels (pronounced *rat-a-fé-a*).
2. The hours in which marriage can legally be performed in the Anglican Church, then eight to twelve noon.

FOOTMAN   Sir, there's such coupling at Pancras[3] that they stand behind one another, as 'twere in a country dance. Ours was the last couple to lead up; and no hopes appearing of dispatch, besides, the parson growing hoarse, we were afraid his lungs would have failed before it came to our turn; so we drove around to Duke's Place, and there they were riveted in a trice.

MIRABELL   So, so, you are sure they are married?

FOOTMAN   Married and bedded, sir. I am witness.

MIRABELL   Have you the certificate?

FOOTMAN   Here it is, sir.

MIRABELL   Has the tailor brought Waitwell's clothes home, and the new liveries?

FOOTMAN   Yes, sir.

MIRABELL   That's well. Do you go home again, d'ye hear, and adjourn the consummation till farther order. Bid Waitwell shake his ears, and Dame Partlet rustle up her feathers, and meet me at one a clock by Rosamond's Pond,[4] that I may see her before she returns to her lady: and as you tender your ears, be secret.

SCENE 3

MIRABELL, FAINALL, BETTY.

FAINALL   Joy of your success, Mirabell; you look pleased.

MIRABELL   Aye, I have been engaged in a matter of some sort of mirth, which is not yet ripe for discovery. I am glad this is not a cabal night. I wonder, Fainall, that you who are married, and of consequence should be discreet, will suffer your wife to be of such a party.

FAINALL   Faith, I am not jealous. Besides, most who are engaged are women and relations; and for the men, they are of a kind too contemptible to give scandal.

MIRABELL   I am of another opinion. The greater the coxcomb, always the more the scandal: for a woman who is not a fool can have but one reason for associating with a man who is one.

FAINALL   Are you jealous as often as you see Witwoud entertained by Millamant?

MIRABELL   Of her understanding I am, if not of her person.

FAINALL   You do her wrong; for to give her her due, she has wit.

MIRABELL   She has beauty enough to make any man think so; and complaisance enough not to contradict him who shall tell her so.

FAINALL   For a passionate lover, methinks you are a man somewhat too discerning in the failings of your mistress.

MIRABELL   And for a discerning man, somewhat too passionate a lover; for I like her with all her faults, nay, like her for her faults. Her follies are so natural, or so artful, that they become her, and those affections

3. The Church of St. Pancras, like that of St. James in Duke's Place (referred to later in the same speech), was notorious for a thriving trade in unlicensed marriages.

4. In St. James's Park. "Dame Partlet": Pertelote, the hen-wife of the cock Chauntecleer in Chaucer's *The Nun's Priest's Tale*.

which in another woman would be odious, serve but to make her more agreeable. I'll tell thee, Fainall, she once used me with that insolence that in revenge I took her to pieces; sifted her, and separated her failings; I studied 'em, and got 'em by rote. The catalogue was so large that I was not without hopes, one day or other, to hate her heartily: to which end I so used myself to think of 'em that at length, contrary to my design and expectation, they gave me every hour less and less disturbance, till in a few days it became habitual to me to remember 'em without being displeased. They are now grown as familiar to me as my own frailties, and in all probability in a little time longer I shall like 'em as well.

FAINALL   Marry her, marry her; be half as well acquainted with her charms as you are with her defects, and my life on't, you are your own man again.

MIRABELL   Say you so?

FAINALL   Aye, aye, I have experience; I have a wife, and so forth.

SCENE 4

[*To them*] MESSENGER.

MESSENGER   Is one Squire Witwoud here?

BETTY   Yes. What's your business?

MESSENGER   I have a letter for him, from his brother Sir Wilfull, which I am charged to deliver into his own hands.

BETTY   He's in the next room, friend—that way.

SCENE 5

MIRABELL, FAINALL, BETTY.

MIRABELL   What, is the chief of that noble family in town, Sir Wilfull Witwoud?

FAINALL   He is expected today. Do you know him?

MIRABELL   I have seen him. He promises to be an extraordinary person; I think you have the honor to be related to him.

FAINALL   Yes; he is half brother to this Witwoud by a former wife, who was sister to my Lady Wishfort, my wife's mother. If you marry Millamant, you must call cousins too.

MIRABELL   I had rather be his relation than his acquaintance.

FAINALL   He comes to town in order to equip himself for travel.

MIRABELL   For travel! Why the man that I mean is above forty.[5]

FAINALL   No matter for that; 'tis for the honor of England that all Europe should know that we have blockheads of all ages.

MIRABELL   I wonder there is not an Act of Parliament to save the credit of the nation, and prohibit the exportation of fools.

FAINALL   By no means, 'tis better as 'tis; 'tis better to trade with a little loss than to be quite eaten up with being overstocked.

MIRABELL   Pray, are the follies of this knight-errant, and those of the squire his brother, anything related?

5. The grand tour of the Continent was rapidly becoming a part of the education of gentlemen, but it was usually made in company with a tutor after a young man had graduated from a university, not after a man had passed the age of forty.

FAINALL   Not at all. Witwoud grows by the knight, like a medlar grafted on a crab.[6] One will melt in your mouth, and t'other set your teeth on edge; one is all pulp, and the other all core.

MIRABELL   So one will be rotten before he be ripe, and the other will be rotten without ever being ripe at all.

FAINALL   Sir Wilfull is an odd mixture of bashfulness and obstinacy. But when he's drunk, he's as loving as the monster in the *Tempest;*[7] and much after the same manner. To give t'other his due, he has something of good nature, and does not always want wit.

MIRABELL   Not always; but as often as his memory fails him, and his commonplace of comparisons.[8] He is a fool with a good memory, and some few scraps of other folks' wit. He is one whose conversation can never be approved, yet it is now and then to be endured. He has indeed one good quality, he is not exceptious,[9] for he so passionately affects the reputation of understanding raillery that he will construe an affront into a jest; and call downright rudeness and ill language, satire and fire.

FAINALL   If you have a mind to finish his picture, you have an opportunity to do it at full length. Behold the original.

SCENE 6

[*To them*] WITWOUD.

WITWOUD   Afford me your compassion, my dears; pity me, Fainall, Mirabell, pity me.

MIRABELL   I do from my soul.

FAINALL   Why, what's the matter?

WITWOUD   No letters for me, Betty?

BETTY   Did not a messenger bring you one but now, sir?

WITWOUD   Aye, but no other?

BETTY   No, sir.

WITWOUD   That's hard, that's very hard. A messenger, a mule, a beast of burden, he has brought me a letter from the fool my brother, as heavy as a panegyric in a funeral sermon, or a copy of commendatory verses from one poet to another. And what's worse, 'tis as sure a forerunner of the author as an epistle dedicatory.

MIRABELL   A fool, and your brother, Witwoud!

WITWOUD   Aye, aye, my half brother. My half brother he is, no nearer upon honor.

MIRABELL   Then 'tis possible he may be but half a fool.

WITWOUD   Good, good, Mirabell, *le drôle!*[1] Good, good. Hang him, don't let's talk of him. Fainall, how does your lady? Gad, I say anything in the world to get this fellow out of my head. I beg pardon that I should ask a man of pleasure and the town a question at once so foreign and domestic.

---

6. Crabapple. "Medlar": a fruit eaten when it is overripe.
7. Trinculo, in the adaptation of Shakespeare's *Tempest* by Sir William Davenant and Dryden (1667), having made Caliban drunk, says, "The poor monster is loving in his drink" (2.2).
8. One recognized sign of wit was the ability to

quickly discover resemblances between objects apparently unlike. Witwoud specializes in this kind of wit, but Mirabell suggests that they are all obvious and collected from others, like observations copied in a notebook, or "commonplace" book.
9. Quarrelsome.
1. The witty fellow (French).

But I talk like an old maid at a marriage, I don't know what I say: but she's the best woman in the world.

FAINALL   'Tis well you don't know what you say, or else your commendation would go near to make me either vain or jealous.

WITWOUD   No man in town lives well with a wife but Fainall. Your judgment, Mirabell?

MIRABELL   You had better step and ask his wife, if you would be credibly informed.

WITWOUD   Mirabell.

MIRABELL   Aye.

WITWOUD   My dear, I ask ten thousand pardons—gad, I have forgot what I was going to say to you.

MIRABELL   I thank you heartily, heartily.

WITWOUD   No, but prithee excuse me—my memory is such a memory.

MIRABELL   Have a care of such apologies, Witwoud—for I never knew a fool but he affected to complain, either of the spleen or his memory.

FAINALL   What have you done with Petulant?

WITWOUD   He's reckoning his money—my money it was.—I have no luck today.

FAINALL   You may allow him to win of you at play—for you are sure to be too hard for him at repartee. Since you monopolize the wit that is between you, the fortune must be his of course.

MIRABELL   I don't find that Petulant confesses the superiority of wit to be your talent, Witwoud.

WITWOUD   Come, come, you are malicious now, and would breed debates.—Petulant's my friend, and a very honest fellow, and a very pretty fellow, and has a smattering—faith and troth a pretty deal of an odd sort of a small wit: nay, I'll do him justice. I'm his friend, I won't wrong him.—And if he had any judgment in the world—he would not be altogether contemptible. Come, come, don't detract from the merits of my friend.

FAINALL   You don't take your friend to be over-nicely bred.

WITWOUD   No, no, hang him, the rogue has no manners at all, that I must own—no more breeding than a bum-bailey,[2] that I grant you.—'Tis pity; the fellow has fire and life.

MIRABELL   What, courage?

WITWOUD   Hum, faith I don't know as to that—I can't say as to that.— Yes, faith, in a controversy he'll contradict anybody.

MIRABELL   Though 'twere a man whom he feared, or a woman whom he loved.

WITWOUD   Well, well, he does not always think before he speaks—we have all our failings; you are too hard upon him, you are, faith. Let me excuse him—I can defend most of his faults, except one or two. One he has, that's the truth on't, if he were my brother, I could not acquit him.— That indeed I could wish were otherwise.

MIRABELL   Aye marry, what's that, Witwoud?

WITWOUD   O, pardon me—expose the infirmities of my friend?—No, my dear, excuse me there.

---

2. Bumbailiff, the lowest kind of arresting officer.

FAINALL   What, I warrant he's unsincere, or 'tis some such trifle.

WITWOUD   No, no, what if he be? 'Tis no matter for that, his wit will excuse that. A wit should no more be sincere than a woman constant; one argues a decay of parts, as t'other of beauty.

MIRABELL   Maybe you think him too positive?

WITWOUD   No, no, his being positive is an incentive to argument, and keeps up conversation.

FAINALL   Too illiterate.

WITWOUD   That! that's his happiness.—His want of learning gives him the more opportunities to show his natural parts.

MIRABELL   He wants words.

WITWOUD   Aye; but I like him for that now; for his want of words gives me the pleasure very often to explain his meaning.

FAINALL   He's impudent.

WITWOUD   No, that's not it.

MIRABELL   Vain.

WITWOUD   No.

MIRABELL   What, he speaks unseasonable truths sometimes, because he has not wit enough to invent an evasion.

WITWOUD   Truths! Ha, ha, ha! No, no, since you will have it—I mean, he never speaks truth at all—that's all. He will lie like a chambermaid, or a woman of quality's porter. Now that is a fault.

SCENE 7

[To them] COACHMAN.

COACHMAN   Is Master Petulant here, mistress?

BETTY   Yes.

COACHMAN   Three gentlewomen in a coach would speak with him.

FAINALL   O brave Petulant, three!

BETTY   I'll tell him.

COACHMAN   You must bring two dishes of chocolate and a glass of cinnamon water.

SCENE 8

MIRABELL, FAINALL, WITWOUD.

WITWOUD   That should be for two fasting strumpets, and a bawd troubled with wind. Now you may know what the three are.

MIRABELL   You are free with your friend's acquaintance.

WITWOUD   Aye, aye, friendship without freedom is as dull as love without enjoyment, or wine without toasting; but to tell you a secret, these are trulls whom he allows coach-hire, and something more by the week, to call on him once a day at public places.

MIRABELL   How!

WITWOUD   You shall see he won't go to 'em because there's no more company here to take notice of him.—Why this is nothing to what he used to do, before he found out this way. I have known him call for himself.—

FAINALL   Call for himself? What dost thou mean?

WITWOUD   Mean? Why he would slip you out of this chocolate house, just when you had been talking to him.—As soon as your back was turned—whip he was gone—then trip to his lodging, clap on a hood and scarf, and a mask, slap into a hackney coach, and drive hither to the door again in a trice; where he would send in for himself, that I mean, call for himself, wait for himself, nay and what's more, not finding himself, sometimes leave a letter for himself.

MIRABELL   I confess this is something extraordinary.—I believe he waits for himself now, he is so long a-coming. O, I ask his pardon.

SCENE 9

PETULANT, MIRABELL, FAINALL, WITWOUD, BETTY.

BETTY   Sir, the coach stays.

PETULANT   Well, well; I come.—'Sbud,[3] a man had as good be a professed midwife, as a professed whoremaster, at this rate; to be knocked up and raised at all hours, and in all places. Pox on 'em, I won't come.—D'ye hear, tell 'em I won't come.—Let 'em snivel and cry their hearts out.

FAINALL   You are very cruel, Petulant.

PETULANT   All's one, let it pass—I have a humor to be cruel.

MIRABELL   I hope they are not persons of condition[4] that you use at this rate.

PETULANT   Condition, condition's a dried fig, if I am not in humor.—By this hand, if they were your—a—a—your what-dee-call-'ems themselves, they must wait or rub off,[5] if I want appetite.

MIRABELL   What-de-call-ems! What are they, Witwoud?

WITWOUD   Empresses, my dear.—By your what-dee-call-'ems he means sultana queens.

PETULANT   Aye, Roxolanas.[6]

MIRABELL   Cry you mercy,

FAINALL   Witwoud says they are—

PETULANT   What does he say th' are?

WITWOUD   I? Fine ladies I say.

PETULANT   Pass on, Witwoud.—Harkee, by this light his relations—two co-heiresses his cousins, and an old aunt, who loves caterwauling better than a conventicle.[7]

WITWOUD   Ha, ha, ha; I had a mind to see how the rogue would come off.—Ha, ha, ha; gad, I can't be angry with him, if he had said they were my mother and my sisters.

MIRABELL   No!

WITWOUD   No; the rogue's wit and readiness of invention charm me, dear Petulant.

BETTY   They are gone, sir, in great anger.

PETULANT   Enough, let 'em trundle. Anger helps complexion, saves paint.

3. God's body.
4. Rank.
5. Make off.
6. "Empresses," "sultana queens," and "Roxo-
lanas," were terms for prostitutes. Roxolana is the wife of the Sultan in Davenant's *Siege of Rhodes* (1656).
7. Nonconformist religious meeting.

FAINALL   This continence is all dissembled; this is in order to have something to brag of the next time he makes court to Millamant, and swear
he had abandoned the whole sex for her sake.

MIRABELL   Have you not left off your impudent pretensions there yet? I
shall cut your throat, sometime or other, Petulant, about that business.

PETULANT   Aye, aye, let that pass.—There are other throats to be cut.—

MIRABELL   Meaning mine, sir?

PETULANT   Not I—I mean nobody—I know nothing. But there are uncles
and nephews in the world—and they may be rivals—What then? All's
one for that—

MIRABELL   How! Harkee, Petulant, come hither—explain, or I shall call
your interpreter.

PETULANT   Explain? I know nothing.—Why, you have an uncle, have you
not, lately come to town, and lodges by my Lady Wishfort's?

MIRABELL   True.

PETULANT   Why, that's enough.—You and he are not friends; and if he
should marry and have a child, you may be disinherited, ha?

MIRABELL   Where hast thou stumbled upon all this truth?

PETULANT   All's one for that; why, then, say I know something.

MIRABELL   Come, thou art an honest fellow, Petulant, and shalt make love
to my mistress, thou sha't, faith. What hast thou heard of my uncle?

PETULANT   I, nothing, I. If throats are to be cut, let swords clash; snug's
the word, I shrug and am silent.

MIRABELL   O raillery, raillery. Come, I know thou art in the women's
secrets.—What, you're a cabalist. I know you stayed at Millamant's last
night, after I went. Was there any mention made of my uncle or me?
Tell me; if thou hadst but good nature equal to thy wit, Petulant, Tony
Witwoud, who is now thy competitor in fame, would show as dim by thee
as a dead whiting's eye by a pearl of Orient. He would no more be seen
by thee than Mercury is by the sun: come, I'm sure thou wo't tell me.

PETULANT   If I do, will you grant me common sense then, for the future?

MIRABELL   Faith, I'll do what I can for thee, and I'll pray that Heaven may
grant it thee in the meantime.

PETULANT   Well, harkee.

FAINALL   Petulant and you both will find Mirabell as warm a rival as a
lover.

WITWOUD   Pshaw, pshaw, that she laughs at Petulant is plain. And for my
part—but that it is almost a fashion to admire her, I should—harkee—
to tell you a secret, but let it go no further—between friends, I shall
never break my heart for her.

FAINALL   How!

WITWOUD   She's handsome; but she's a sort of an uncertain woman.

FAINALL   I thought you had died for her.

WITWOUD   Umh—no—

FAINALL   She has wit.

WITWOUD   'Tis what she will hardly allow anybody else.—Now, demme, I
should hate that, if she were as handsome as Cleopatra. Mirabell is not
so sure of her as he thinks for.

FAINALL   Why do you think so?

WITWOUD   We stayed pretty late there last night, and heard something of

an uncle to Mirabell, who is lately come to town—and is between him
and the best part of his estate. Mirabell and he are at some distance, as
my Lady Wishfort has been told; and you know she hates Mirabell, worse
than a Quaker hates a parrot, or than a fishmonger hates a hard frost.
Whether this uncle has seen Mrs. Millamant or not, I cannot say; but
there were items of such a treaty being in embryo; and if it should come
to life, poor Mirabell would be in some sort unfortunately fobbed[8] i' faith.

FAINALL 'Tis impossible Millamant should harken to it.

WITWOUD Faith, my dear, I can't tell; she's a woman and a kind of a
humorist.[9]

MIRABELL And this is the sum of what you could collect last night.

PETULANT The quintessence. Maybe Witwoud knows more, he stayed
longer.—Besides they never mind him; they say anything before him.

MIRABELL I thought you had been the greatest favorite.

PETULANT Aye, *tête à tête*;[1] but not in public, because I make remarks.

MIRABELL You do?

PETULANT Aye, aye, pox, I'm malicious, man. Now he's soft, you know,
they are not in awe of him.—The fellow's well bred, he's what you call
a—what-d'ye-call-'em. A fine gentleman, but he's silly withal.

MIRABELL I thank you, I know as much as my curiosity requires. Fainall,
are you for the Mall?[2]

FAINALL Aye, I'll take a turn before dinner.

WITWOUD Aye, we'll all walk in the park, the ladies talked of being there.

MIRABELL I thought you were obliged to watch for your brother Sir Wilfull's arrival.

WITWOUD No, no, he's come to his aunt's, my Lady Wishfort. Pox on him,
I shall be troubled with him too. What shall I do with the fool?

PETULANT Beg him for his estate, that I may beg you afterwards, and so
have but one trouble with you both.

WITWOUD O rare Petulant; thou art as quick as fire in a frosty morning;
thou shalt to the Mall with us; and we'll be very severe.

PETULANT Enough, I'm in a humor to be severe.

MIRABELL Are you? Pray then walk by yourselves.—Let not us be accessory to your putting the ladies out of countenance with your senseless
ribaldry, which you roar out aloud as often as they pass by you; and when
you have made a handsome woman blush, then you think you have been
severe.

PETULANT What, what? Then let 'em either show their innocence by not
understanding what they hear, or else show their discretion by not hearing what they would not be thought to understand.

MIRABELL But hast not thou then sense enough to know that thou
ought'st to be most ashamed thyself, when thou hast put another out of
countenance?

PETULANT Not I, by this hand.—I always take blushing either for a sign
of guilt, or ill breeding.

MIRABELL I confess you ought to think so. You are in the right, that you
may plead the error of your judgment in defense of your practice.

8. Tricked.
9. A capricious person.
1. Face to face (French); i.e., in private.

2. A walk in St. James's Park, one of the fashionable resorts of the day.

Where modesty's ill manners, 'tis but fit
That impudence and malice pass for wit.

Act 2—St. James's Park.

SCENE 1

MRS. FAINALL *and* MRS. MARWOOD.

MRS. FAINALL   Aye, aye, dear Marwood, if we will be happy, we must find
the means in ourselves, and among ourselves. Men are ever in extremes;
either doting or averse. While they are lovers, if they have fire and sense,
their jealousies are insupportable: and when they cease to love (we ought
to think at least) they loathe. They look upon us with horror and distaste;
they meet us like the ghosts of what we were, and as from such, fly from
us.

MRS. MARWOOD   True, 'tis an unhappy circumstance of life that love
should ever die before us; and that the man so often should outlive the
lover. But say what you will, 'tis better to be left than never to have been
loved. To pass over youth in dull indifference, to refuse the sweets of life
because they once must leave us, is as preposterous as to wish to have
been born old, because we one day must be old. For my part, my youth
may wear and waste, but it shall never rust in my possession.

MRS. FAINALL   Then it seems you dissemble an aversion to mankind only
in compliance to my mother's humor.

MRS. MARWOOD   Certainly. To be free, I have no taste of those insipid dry
discourses with which our sex of force must entertain themselves apart
from men. We may affect endearments to each other, profess eternal
friendships, and seem to dote like lovers: but 'tis not in our natures long
to persevere. Love will resume his empire in our breasts, and every heart,
or soon or late, receive and readmit him as its lawful tyrant.

MRS. FAINALL   Bless me, how have I been deceived! Why, you profess a
libertine.

MRS. MARWOOD   You see my friendship by my freedom. Come, be as sincere, acknowledge that your sentiments agree with mine.

MRS. FAINALL   Never.

MRS. MARWOOD   You hate mankind?

MRS. FAINALL   Heartily, inveterately.

MRS. MARWOOD   Your husband?

MRS. FAINALL   Most transcendently; aye, though I say it, meritoriously.

MRS. MARWOOD   Give me your hand upon it.

MRS. FAINALL   There.

MRS. MARWOOD   I join with you. What I have said has been to try you.

MRS. FAINALL   Is it possible? Dost thou hate those vipers men?

MRS. MARWOOD   I have done hating 'em, and am now come to despise
'em; the next thing I have to do is eternally to forget 'em.

MRS. FAINALL   There spoke the spirit of an Amazon, a Penthesilea.[3]

MRS. MARWOOD   And yet I am thinking sometimes to carry my aversion
further.

3. Queen of the Amazons (a legendary nation of women warriors).

MRS. FAINALL   How?

MRS. MARWOOD   Faith, by marrying. If I could but find one that loved me very well, and would be thoroughly sensible of ill usage, I think I should do myself the violence of undergoing the ceremony.

MRS. FAINALL   You would not make him a cuckold?

MRS. MARWOOD   No; but I'd make him believe I did, and that's as bad.

MRS. FAINALL   Why had not you as good do it?

MRS. MARWOOD   O, if he should ever discover it, he would then know the worst, and be out of his pain; but I would have him ever to continue upon the rack of fear and jealousy.

MRS. FAINALL   Ingenious mischief! Would thou wert married to Mirabell.

MRS. MARWOOD   Would I were.

MRS. FAINALL   You change color.

MRS. MARWOOD   Because I hate him.

MRS. FAINALL   So do I; but I can hear him named. But what reason have you to hate him in particular?

MRS. MARWOOD   I never loved him; he is and always was insufferably proud.

MRS. FAINALL   By the reason you give for your aversion, one would think it dissembled; for you have laid a fault to his charge of which his enemies must acquit him.

MRS. MARWOOD   O then it seems you are one of his favorable enemies. Methinks you look a little pale, and now you flush again.

MRS. FAINALL   Do I? I think I am a little sick o' the sudden.

MRS. MARWOOD   What ails you?

MRS. FAINALL   My husband. Don't you see him? He turned short upon me unawares, and has almost overcome me.

SCENE 2

[*To them*] FAINALL *and* MIRABELL.

MRS. MARWOOD   Ha, ha, ha; he comes opportunely for you.

MRS. FAINALL   For you, for he has brought Mirabell with him.

FAINALL   My dear.

MRS. FAINALL   My soul.

FAINALL   You don't look well today, child.

MRS. FAINALL   D'ye think so?

MIRABELL   He is the only man that does, madam.

MRS. FAINALL   The only man that would tell me so at least; and the only man from whom I could hear it without mortification.

FAINALL   O my dear, I am satisfied of your tenderness; I know you cannot resent anything from me, especially what is an effect of my concern.

MRS. FAINALL   Mr. Mirabell, my mother interrupted you in a pleasant relation last night. I would fain hear it out.

MIRABELL   The persons concerned in that affair have yet a tolerable reputation.—I am afraid Mr. Fainall will be censorious.

MRS. FAINALL   He has a humor more prevailing than his curiosity, and will willingly dispense with the hearing of one scandalous story to avoid giving an occasion to make another by being seen to walk with his wife. This way, Mr. Mirabell, and I dare promise you will oblige us both.

SCENE 3

FAINALL, MRS. MARWOOD.

FAINALL   Excellent creature! Well, sure if I should live to be rid of my wife, I should be a miserable man.

MRS. MARWOOD   Aye!

FAINALL   For having only that one hope, the accomplishment of it of consequence must put an end to all my hopes; and what a wretch is he who must survive his hopes! Nothing remains when that day comes but to sit down and weep like Alexander, when he wanted other worlds to conquer.

MRS. MARWOOD   Will you not follow 'em?

FAINALL   Faith, I think not.

MRS. MARWOOD   Pray let us; I have a reason.

FAINALL   You are not jealous?

MRS. MARWOOD   Of whom?

FAINALL   Of Mirabell.

MRS. MARWOOD   If I am, is it inconsistent with my love to you that I am tender of your honor?

FAINALL   You would intimate then, as if there were a fellow-feeling between my wife and him.

MRS. MARWOOD   I think she does not hate him to that degree she would be thought.

FAINALL   But he, I fear, is too insensible.

MRS. MARWOOD   It may be you are deceived.

FAINALL   It may be so. I do now begin to apprehend it.

MRS. MARWOOD   What?

FAINALL   That I have been deceived, Madam, and you are false.

MRS. MARWOOD   That I am false! What mean you?

FAINALL   To let you know I see through all your little arts.—Come, you both love him; and both have equally dissembled your aversion. Your mutual jealousies of one another have made you clash till you have both struck fire. I have seen the warm confession reddening on your cheeks, and sparkling from your eyes.

MRS. MARWOOD   You do me wrong.

FAINALL   I do not.—'Twas for my ease to oversee[4] and willfully neglect the gross advances made him by my wife; that by permitting her to be engaged I might continue unsuspected in my pleasures; and take you oftener to my arms in full security. But could you think, because the nodding husband would not wake, that e'er the watchful lover slept?

MRS. MARWOOD   And wherewithal can you reproach me?

FAINALL   With infidelity, with loving another, with love of Mirabell.

MRS. MARWOOD   'Tis false. I challenge you to show an instance that can confirm your groundless accusation. I hate him.

FAINALL   And wherefore do you hate him? He is insensible, and your resentment follows his neglect. An instance! The injuries you have done him are a proof: your interposing in his love. What cause had you to make discoveries of his pretended passion? To undeceive the credulous aunt, and be the officious obstacle of his match with Millamant?

4. Overlook.

MRS. MARWOOD   My obligations to my lady urged me. I had professed a friendship to her, and could not see her easy nature so abused by that dissembler.

FAINALL   What, was it conscience then? Professed a friendship! O the pious friendships of the female sex!

MRS. MARWOOD   More tender, more sincere, and more enduring than all the vain and empty vows of men, whether professing love to us, or mutual faith to one another.

FAINALL   Ha, ha, ha; you are my wife's friend too.

MRS. MARWOOD   Shame and ingratitude! Do you reproach me? You, you upbraid me! Have I been false to her, through strict fidelity to you, and sacrificed my friendship to keep my love inviolate? And have you the baseness to charge me with the guilt, unmindful of the merit! To you it should be meritorious that I have been vicious: and do you reflect that guilt upon me, which should lie buried in your bosom?

FAINALL   You misinterpret my reproof. I meant but to remind you of the slight account you once could make of strictest ties, when set in competition with your love to me.

MRS. MARWOOD   'Tis false, you urged it with deliberate malice.—'Twas spoke in scorn, and I never will forgive it.

FAINALL   Your guilt, not your resentment, begets your rage. If yet you loved, you could forgive a jealousy, but you are stung to find you are discovered.

MRS. MARWOOD   It shall be all discovered. You too shall be discovered; be sure you shall. I can but be exposed.—If I do it myself, I shall prevent[5] your baseness.

FAINALL   Why, what will you do?

MRS. MARWOOD   Disclose it to your wife; own what has passed between us.

FAINALL   Frenzy!

MRS. MARWOOD   By all my wrongs I'll do't—I'll publish to the world the injuries you have done me, both in my fame and fortune: with both I trusted you, you bankrupt in honor, as indigent of wealth.

FAINALL   Your fame[6] I have preserved. Your fortune has been bestowed as the prodigality of your love would have it, in pleasures which we both have shared. Yet, had not you been false, I had e'er this repaid it.—'Tis true—had you permitted Mirabell with Millamant to have stolen their marriage, my lady had been incensed beyond all means of reconcilement: Millamant had forfeited the moiety[7] of her fortune, which then would have descended to my wife—and wherefore did I marry, but to make lawful prize of a rich widow's wealth, and squander it on love and you?

MRS. MARWOOD   Deceit and frivolous pretense.

FAINALL   Death, am I not married? What's pretense? Am I not imprisoned, fettered? Have I not a wife? Nay, a wife that was a widow, a young widow, a handsome widow; and would be again a widow, but that I have a heart of proof,[8] and something of a constitution to bustle through the ways of wedlock and this world. Will you yet be reconciled to truth and me?

---

5. Anticipate.
6. Good name.

7. Half.
8. I.e., a proved or tempered heart.

MRS. MARWOOD   Impossible. Truth and you are inconsistent—I hate you, and shall forever.

FAINALL   For loving you?

MRS. MARWOOD   I loathe the name of love after such usage; and next to the guilt with which you would asperse me, I scorn you most. Farewell.

FAINALL   Nay, we must not part thus.

MRS. MARWOOD   Let me go.

FAINALL   Come, I'm sorry.

MRS. MARWOOD   I care not.—Let me go.—Break my hands, do—I'd leave 'em to get loose.

FAINALL   I would not hurt you for the world. Have I no other hold to keep you here?

MRS. MARWOOD   Well, I have deserved it all.

FAINALL   You know I love you.

MRS. MARWOOD   Poor dissembling!—O that—Well, it is not yet—

FAINALL   What? What is it not? What is it not yet? It is not yet too late—

MRS. MARWOOD   No, it is not yet too late—I have that comfort.

FAINALL   It is, to love another.

MRS. MARWOOD   But not to loathe, detest, abhor mankind, myself, and the whole treacherous world.

FAINALL   Nay, this is extravagance.—Come, I ask your pardon.—No tears.—I was to blame. I could not love you and be easy in my doubts.— Pray forbear.—I believe you; I'm convinced I've done you wrong; and any way, every way will make amends.—I'll hate my wife yet more, damn her, I'll part with her, rob her of all she's worth, and we'll retire some- where, anywhere, to another world. I'll marry thee.—Be pacified.— 'Sdeath, they come, hide your face, your tears.—You have a mask,[9] wear it a moment. This way, this way, be persuaded.

SCENE 4

MIRABELL *and* MRS. FAINALL.

MRS. FAINALL   They are here yet.

MIRABELL   They are turning into the other walk.

MRS. FAINALL   While I only hated my husband, I could bear to see him, but since I have despised him, he's too offensive.

MIRABELL   O, you should hate with prudence.

MRS. FAINALL   Yes, for I have loved with indiscretion.

MIRABELL   You should have just so much disgust for your husband as may be sufficient to make you relish your lover.

MRS. FAINALL   You have been the cause that I have loved without bounds, and would you set limits to that aversion, of which you have been the occasion? Why did you make me marry this man?

MIRABELL   Why do we daily commit disagreeable and dangerous actions? To save that idol, reputation. If the familiarities of our loves had pro- duced that consequence, of which you were apprehensive, where could

9. Often worn in public places by fashionable women of the time to preserve their complexions; they were also useful to disguise a woman and so to protect her reputation when she was carrying on an illicit affair.

you have fixed a father's name with credit, but on a husband? I knew Fainall to be a man lavish of his morals, an interested and professing friend, a false and a designing lover; yet one whose wit and outward fair behavior have gained a reputation with the town, enough to make that woman stand excused who has suffered herself to be won by his addresses. A better man ought not to have been sacrificed to the occasion; a worse had not answered to the purpose. When you are weary of him, you know your remedy.

MRS. FAINALL   I ought to stand in some degree of credit with you, Mirabell.

MIRABELL   In justice to you, I have made you privy to my whole design, and put it in your power to ruin or advance my fortune.

MRS. FAINALL   Whom have you instructed to represent your pretended uncle?

MIRABELL   Waitwell, my servant.

MRS. FAINALL   He is an humble servant to Foible,[1] my mother's woman, and may win her to your interest.

MIRABELL   Care is taken for that.—She is won and worn by this time. They were married this morning.

MRS. FAINALL   Who?

MIRABELL   Waitwell and Foible. I would not tempt my servant to betray me by trusting him too far. If your mother, in hopes to ruin me, should consent to marry my pretended uncle, he might, like Mosca in *The Fox*, stand upon terms;[2] so I made him sure beforehand.

MRS. FAINALL   So, if my poor mother is caught in a contract, you will discover the imposture betimes; and release her by producing a certificate of her gallant's former marriage.

MIRABELL   Yes, upon condition that she consent to my marriage with her niece, and surrender the moiety of her fortune in her possession.

MRS. FAINALL   She talked last night of endeavoring at a match between Millamant and your uncle.

MIRABELL   That was by Foible's direction, and my instruction, that she might seem to carry it more privately.

MRS. FAINALL   Well, I have an opinion of your success, for I believe my lady will do anything to get an husband; and when she has this, which you have provided for her, I suppose she will submit to anything to get rid of him.

MIRABELL   Yes, I think the good lady would marry anything that resembled a man, though 'twere no more than what a butler could pinch out of a napkin.

MRS. FAINALL   Female frailty! We must all come to it, if we live to be old, and feel the craving of a false appetite when the true is decayed.

MIRABELL   An old woman's appetite is depraved like that of a girl—'tis the greensickness[3] of a second childhood; and like the faint offer of a latter spring, serves but to usher in the fall and withers in an affected bloom.

MRS. FAINALL   Here's your mistress.

---

1. I.e., he is Foible's lover.
2. To insist on conditions; here, to blackmail. "Mosca": the scheming parasite in Ben Jonson's *Volpone*, who in the end tries to blackmail Volpone.
3. The anemia that sometimes affects girls at puberty.

SCENE 5

[*To them*] MRS. MILLAMANT, WITWOUD, MINCING.

MIRABELL   Here she comes, i'faith, full sail, with her fan spread and streamers out, and a shoal of fools for tenders.—Ha, no, I cry her mercy.

MRS. FAINALL   I see but one poor empty sculler, and he tows her woman after him.

MIRABELL   You seem to be unattended, madam.—You used to have the *beau monde* throng after you; and a flock of gay fine perukes[4] hovering round you.

WITWOUD   Like moths about a candle—I had like to have lost my comparison for want of breath.

MILLAMANT   O, I have denied myself airs today. I have walked as fast through the crowd—

WITWOUD   As a favorite just disgraced; and with as few followers.

MILLAMANT   Dear Mr. Witwoud, truce with your similitudes: For I am as sick of 'em—

WITWOUD   As a physician of a good air—I cannot help it, madam, though 'tis against myself.

MILLAMANT   Yet again! Mincing, stand between me and his wit.

WITWOUD   Do, Mrs. Mincing, like a screen before a great fire. I confess I do blaze today, I am too bright.

MRS. FAINALL   But dear Millamant, why were you so long?

MILLAMANT   Long! Lord, have I not made violent haste? I have asked every living thing I met for you; I have inquired after you, as after a new fashion.

WITWOUD   Madam, truce with your similitudes.—No, you met her husband, and did not ask him for her.

MIRABELL   By your leave, Witwoud, that were like inquiring after an old fashion, to ask a husband for his wife.

WITWOUD   Hum, a hit, a hit, a palpable hit,[5] I confess it.

MRS. FAINALL   You were dressed before I came abroad.

MILLAMANT   Aye, that's true.—O, but then I had—Mincing, what had I? Why was I so long?

MINCING   O mem, your la'ship stayed to peruse a packet of letters.

MILLAMANT   O, aye, letters—I had letters—I am persecuted with letters—I hate letters.—Nobody knows how to write letters; and yet one has 'em, one does not know why.—They serve one to pin up one's hair.

WITWOUD   Is that the way? Pray, madam, do you pin up your hair with all your letters? I find I must keep copies.

MILLAMANT   Only with those in verse, Mr. Witwoud. I never pin up my hair with prose. I think I tried once, Mincing.

MINCING   O mem, I shall never forget it.

MILLAMANT   Aye, poor Mincing tiffed[6] and tiffed all the morning.

MINCING   Till I had the cramp in my fingers, I'll vow, mem. And all to no purpose. But when your la'ship pins it up with poetry, it sits so pleasant the next day as anything, and is so pure and so crips.[7]

---

4. Periwigs, worn by fashionable men (cf. Pope's *Rape of the Lock* 1.101, p. 2529). "*Beau monde*": fashionable world (French).

5. An allusion to the dueling scene in *Hamlet* 5.2.
6. Dressed the hair.
7. A dialectal form of "crisp," curly.

WITWOUD   Indeed, so crips?

MINCING   You're such a critic, Mr. Witwoud.

MILLAMANT   Mirabell, did not you take exceptions last night? O, aye, and went away.—Now I think on't I'm angry.—No, now I think on't I'm pleased—for I believe I gave you some pain.

MIRABELL   Does that please you?

MILLAMANT   Infinitely; I love to give pain.

MIRABELL   You would affect a cruelty which is not in your nature; your true vanity is in the power of pleasing.

MILLAMANT   O, I ask your pardon for that—one's cruelty is one's power, and when one parts with one's cruelty, one parts with one's power; and when one has parted with that, I fancy one's old and ugly.

MIRABELL   Aye, aye, suffer your cruelty to ruin the object of your power, to destroy your lover.—And then how vain, how lost a thing you'll be! Nay, 'tis true: you are no longer handsome when you've lost your lover; your beauty dies upon the instant: for beauty is the lover's gift; 'tis he bestows your charms—your glass is all a cheat. The ugly and the old, whom the looking glass mortifies, yet after commendation can be flattered by it, and discover beauties in it: for that reflects our praises, rather than your face.

MILLAMANT   O, the vanity of these men! Fainall, d'ye hear him? If they did not commend us, we were not handsome! Now you must know they could not commend one, if one was not handsome. Beauty the lover's gift?—Lord, what is a lover, that it can give? Why, one makes lovers as fast as one pleases, and they live as long as one pleases, and they die as soon as one pleases: and then if one pleases one makes more.

WITWOUD   Very pretty. Why, you make no more of making of lovers, madam, than of making so many card-matches.[8]

MILLAMANT   One no more owes one's beauty to a lover than one's wit to an echo.—They can but reflect what we look and say; vain empty things if we are silent or unseen, and want a being.

MIRABELL   Yet, to those two vain empty things, you owe two of the greatest pleasures of your life.

MILLAMANT   How so?

MIRABELL   To your lover you owe the pleasure of hearing yourselves praised; and to an echo the pleasure of hearing yourselves talk.

WITWOUD   But I know a lady that loves talking so incessantly she won't give an echo fair play; she has that everlasting rotation of tongue, that an echo must wait till she dies before it can catch her last words.

MILLAMANT   O, fiction; Fainall, let us leave these men.

MIRABELL [Aside to MRS. FAINALL.]   Draw off Witwoud.

MRS. FAINALL   Immediately; I have a word or two for Mr. Witwoud.

SCENE 6

MILLAMANT, MIRABELL, MINCING.

MIRABELL   I would beg a little private audience too.—You had the tyranny to deny me last night, though you knew I came to impart a secret to you that concerned my love.

8. Matches made by dipping pieces of card in melted sulfur.

MILLAMANT You saw I was engaged.

MIRABELL Unkind. You had the leisure to entertain a herd of fools, things who visit you from their excessive idleness, bestowing on your easiness that time, which is the encumbrance of their lives. How can you find delight in such society? It is impossible they should admire you, they are not capable: or if they were, it should be to you as a mortification; for sure to please a fool is some degree of folly.

MILLAMANT I please myself—besides, sometimes to converse with fools is for my health.

MIRABELL Your health! Is there a worse disease than the conversation of fools?

MILLAMANT Yes, the vapors; fools are physic for it, next to asafetida.

MIRABELL You are not in a course[9] of fools?

MILLAMANT Mirabell, if you persist in this offensive freedom, you'll displease me. I think I must resolve after all not to have you.—We shan't agree.

MIRABELL Not in our physic, it may be.

MILLAMANT And yet our distemper in all likelihood will be the same, for we shall be sick of one another. I shan't endure to be reprimanded nor instructed; 'tis so dull to act always by advice, and so tedious to be told of one's faults.—I can't bear it. Well, I won't have you, Mirabell—I'm resolved—I think—you may go—ha, ha, ha. What would you give that you could help loving me?

MIRABELL I would give something that you did not know I could not help it.

MILLAMANT Come, don't look grave then. Well, what do you say to me?

MIRABELL I say that a man may as soon make a friend by his wit, or a fortune by his honesty, as win a woman with plain-dealing and sincerity.

MILLAMANT Sententious Mirabell! prithee don't look with that violent and inflexible wise face, like Solomon at the dividing of the child in an old tapestry hanging.[1]

MIRABELL You are merry, madam, but I would persuade you for a moment to be serious.

MILLAMANT What, with that face? No, if you keep your countenance, 'tis impossible I should hold mine. Well, after all, there is something very moving in a lovesick face. Ha, ha, ha.—Well I won't laugh, don't be peevish—heigho! Now I'll be melancholy, as melancholy as a watchlight.[2] Well, Mirabell, if ever you will win me, woo me now. Nay, if you are so tedious, fare you well; I see they are walking away.

MIRABELL Can you not find in the variety of your disposition one moment—

MILLAMANT To hear you tell me Foible's married and your plot like to speed.—No.

MIRABELL But how you came to know it—

MILLAMANT Without the help of the devil, you can't imagine; unless she should tell me herself. Which of the two it may have been, I will leave you to consider; and when you have done thinking of that, think of me.

SCENE 7

MIRABELL alone.

MIRABELL   I have something more.—Gone!—Think of you! To think of a whirlwind, though 'twere in a whirlwind, were a case of more steady contemplation, a very tranquility of mind and mansion. A fellow that lives in a windmill has not a more whimsical dwelling than the heart of a man that is lodged in a woman. There is no point of the compass to which they cannot turn, and by which they are not turned; and by one as well as another, for motion, not method, is their occupation. To know this, and yet continue to be in love, is to be made wise from the dictates of reason, and yet persevere to play the fool by the force of instinct. O, here come my pair of turtles[3]—what, billing so sweetly! Is not Valentine's Day over with you yet?

SCENE 8

[To him] WAITWELL, FOIBLE.

MIRABELL   Sirrah Waitwell, why sure you think you were married for your own recreation and not for my conveniency.

WAITWELL   Your pardon, sir. With submission, we have indeed been solacing in lawful delights, but still with an eye to business, sir. I have instructed her as well as I could. If she can take your directions as readily as my instructions, sir, your affairs are in a prosperous way.

MIRABELL   Give you joy, Mrs. Foible.

FOIBLE   O-las, sir, I'm so ashamed—I'm afraid my lady has been in a thousand inquietudes for me. But I protest, sir, I made as much haste as I could.

WAITWELL   That she did indeed, sir. It was my fault that she did not make more.

MIRABELL   That I believe.

FOIBLE   But I told my lady as you instructed me, sir. That I had a prospect of seeing Sir Rowland your uncle, and that I would put her ladyship's picture in my pocket to show him; which I'll be sure to say has made him so enamored of her beauty that he burns with impatience to lie at her ladyship's feet and worship the original.

MIRABELL   Excellent, Foible! Matrimony has made you eloquent in love.

WAITWELL   I think she has profited, sir. I think so.

FOIBLE   You have seen Madam Millamant, sir?

MIRABELL   Yes.

FOIBLE   I told her, sir, because I did not know that you might find an opportunity; she had so much company last night.

MIRABELL   Your diligence will merit more—in the meantime—

[Gives money.]

---

3. Turtledoves, remarkable for their affectionate billing and cooing. Birds were popularly supposed to choose their mates on St. Valentine's Day.

FOIBLE   O dear sir, your humble servant.

WAITWELL   Spouse.

MIRABELL   Stand off, sir, not a penny. Go on and prosper, Foible. The lease shall be made good and the farm stocked if we succeed.

FOIBLE   I don't question your generosity, sir. And you need not doubt of success. If you have no more commands, sir, I'll be gone; I'm sure my lady is at her toilet, and can't dress till I come. O dear, I'm sure that [*Looking out.*] was Mrs. Marwood that went by in a mask; if she has seen me with you I'm sure she'll tell my lady. I'll make haste home and prevent her. Your servant, sir. B'w'y,[4] Waitwell.

MIRABELL, WAITWELL.

WAITWELL   Sir Rowland, if you please. The jade's so pert upon her preferment she forgets herself.

MIRABELL   Come, sir, will you endeavor to forget yourself—and transform into Sir Rowland.

WAITWELL   Why, sir, it will be impossible I should remember myself—married, knighted, and attended all in one day! 'Tis enough to make any man forget himself. The difficulty will be how to recover my acquaintance and familiarity with my former self; and fall from my transformation to a reformation into Waitwell. Nay, I shan't be quite the same Waitwell neither—for now I remember me, I'm married and can't be my own man again.

Aye, there's my grief; that's the sad change of life;
To lose my title, and yet keep my wife.

Act 3—A room in LADY WISHFORT's *house.*

SCENE 1

LADY WISHFORT *at her toilet,* PEG *waiting.*

LADY WISHFORT   Merciful, no news of Foible yet?

PEG   No, madam.

LADY WISHFORT   I have no more patience. If I have not fretted myself till I am pale again, there's no veracity in me. Fetch me the red—the red, do you hear, sweetheart? An errant ash color, as I'm a person. Look you how this wench stirs! Why dost thou not fetch me a little red? Didst thou not hear me, mopus?[5]

PEG   The red ratafia does your ladyship mean, or the cherry brandy?

LADY WISHFORT   Ratafia, fool. No, fool. Not the ratafia, fool. Grant me patience! I mean the Spanish paper,[6] idiot—complexion, darling. Paint, paint, paint, dost thou understand that, changeling, dangling thy hands like bobbins before thee? Why dost thou not stir, puppet? Thou wooden thing upon wires.

4. A shortened form of "God be with you" (our word *good-bye*). "Prevent her": arrive before she does.
5. Dull, stupid person.
6. Rouge.

PEG   Lord, madam, your ladyship is so impatient.—I cannot come at the paint, madam. Mrs. Foible has locked it up and carried the key with her.

LADY WISHFORT   A pox take you both!—Fetch me the cherry brandy then.

SCENE 2

LADY WISHFORT.

I'm as pale and as faint, I look like Mrs. Qualmsick, the curate's wife, that's always breeding. Wench, come, come, wench, what art thou doing? Sipping? Tasting? Save thee, dost thou not know the bottle?

SCENE 3

LADY WISHFORT, PEG *with a bottle and china cup.*

PEG   Madam, I was looking for a cup.

LADY WISHFORT   A cup, save thee, and what a cup hast thou brought! Dost thou take me for a fairy, to drink out of an acorn? Why didst thou not bring thy thimble? Hast thou ne'er a brass thimble clinking in thy pocket with a bit of nutmeg? I warrant thee. Come, fill, fill.—So—again. See who that is.—[*One knocks.*]—Set down the bottle first. Here, here, under the table.—What, wouldst thou go with the bottle in thy hand like a tapster? As I'm a person, this wench has lived in an inn upon the road before she came to me, like Maritornes the Asturian[7] in *Don Quixote.* No Foible yet?

PEG   No, madam, Mrs. Marwood.

LADY WISHFORT   O Marwood, let her come in. Come in, good Marwood.

SCENE 4

[*To them*] MRS. MARWOOD.

MRS. MARWOOD   I'm surprised to find your ladyship in *deshabillé*[8] at this time of day.

LADY WISHFORT   Foible's a lost thing; has been abroad since morning, and never heard of since.

MRS. MARWOOD   I saw her but now, as I came masked through the park, in conference with Mirabell.

LADY WISHFORT   With Mirabell! you call my blood into my face, with mentioning that traitor. She durst not have the confidence. I sent her to negotiate an affair, in which if I'm detected I'm undone. If that wheedling villain has wrought upon Foible to detect me, I'm ruined. O my dear friend, I'm a wretch of wretches if I'm detected.

MRS. MARWOOD   O madam, you cannot suspect Mrs. Foible's integrity.

LADY WISHFORT   O, he carries poison in his tongue that would corrupt integrity itself. If she has given him an opportunity, she has as good as put her integrity into his hands. Ah dear Marwood, what's integrity to an opportunity? Hark! I hear her—dear friend, retire into my closet,[9] that I

7. The servant at the inn where the Don and Sancho Panza are succored.

8. In negligee (French).

9. Private retiring room.

may examine her with more freedom. You'll pardon me, dear friend, I can make bold with you. There are books over the chimney—Quarles and Prynne, and the *Short View of the Stage*,[1] with Bunyan's works to entertain you. [*To* PEG.] Go, you thing, and send her in.

SCENE 5

LADY WISHFORT, FOIBLE.

LADY WISHFORT O Foible, where hast thou been? What hast thou been doing?

FOIBLE Madam, I have seen the party.

LADY WISHFORT But what hast thou done?

FOIBLE Nay, 'tis your ladyship has done, and are to do; I have only promised. But a man so enamored—so transported! Well, if worshiping of pictures be a sin—poor Sir Rowland, I say.

LADY WISHFORT The miniature has been counted like[2]—but hast thou not betrayed me, Foible? Hast thou not detected me to that faithless Mirabell?—What hadst thou to do with him in the park? Answer me, has he got nothing out of thee?

FOIBLE [*Aside.*] So, the devil has been beforehand with me. What shall I say?—Alas, madam, could I help it if I met that confident thing? Was I in fault? If you had heard how he used me, and all upon your ladyship's account, I'm sure you would not suspect my fidelity. Nay, if that had been the worst I could have borne; but he had a fling at your ladyship too; and then I could not hold; but i' faith I gave him his own.

LADY WISHFORT Me? What did the filthy fellow say?

FOIBLE O madam; 'tis a shame to say what he said—with his taunts and his fleers, tossing up his nose. Humh (says he) what, you are a-hatching some plot (says he) you are so early abroad, or catering (says he), ferreting for some disbanded[3] officer, I warrant—half pay is but thin subsistence (says he).—Well, what pension does your lady propose? Let me see (says he) what, she must come down pretty deep now, she's superannuated (says he) and—

LADY WISHFORT Ods my life, I'll have him—I'll have him murdered. I'll have him poisoned. Where does he eat? I'll marry a drawer to have him poisoned in his wine. I'll send for Robin from Locket's[4]—immediately.

FOIBLE Poison him? Poisoning's too good for him. Starve him, madam, starve him; marry Sir Rowland, and get him disinherited. O, you would bless yourself, to hear what he said.

LADY WISHFORT A villain!—superannuated!

FOIBLE Humh (says he) I hear you are laying designs against me too (says

1. By Collier; see n. 6, p. 2218. Francis Quarles (1592–1644), a religious poet, by 1700 regarded with contempt, but formerly greatly admired, especially among the Puritans. William Prynne (1600–1669), Puritan pamphleteer, author of *Histriomastix* (1632), a violent attack on the stage. Congreve, who had been the object of much of Collier's vituperation, slyly identifies his enemy with Puritans and Nonconformists, whom Collier, an ardent high churchman, despised.
2. Considered a likeness.
3. When a regiment was "disbanded," its officers went on half pay, often for life. "Catering": procuring (i.e., pimping for Lady Wishfort).
4. Locket's was a fashionable tavern near Charing Cross. "Drawer": one who draws wine from casks and serves it.

he) and Mrs. Millamant is to marry my uncle; (he does not suspect a word of your ladyship) but (says he) I'll fit you for that, I warrant you (says he) I'll hamper you for that (says he) you and your old frippery[5] too (says he). I'll handle you—

LADY WISHFORT Audacious villain! handle me, would he durst—frippery? old frippery! Was there ever such a foul-mouthed fellow? I'll be married tomorrow, I'll be contracted tonight.

FOIBLE The sooner the better, madam.

LADY WISHFORT Will Sir Rowland be here, say'st thou? When, Foible?

FOIBLE Incontinently, madam. No new sheriff's wife expects the return of her husband after knighthood, with that impatience in which Sir Rowland burns for the dear hour of kissing your ladyship's hand after dinner.

LADY WISHFORT Frippery! Superannuated frippery! I'll frippery the villain, I'll reduce him to frippery and rags. A tatterdemalion—I hope to see him hung with tatters, like a Long Lane penthouse,[6] or a gibbet-thief. A slander-mouthed railer—I warrant the spendthrift prodigal's in debt as much as the million lottery, or the whole court upon a birthday. I'll spoil his credit with his tailor. Yes, he shall have my niece with her fortune, he shall.

FOIBLE He! I hope to see him lodge in Ludgate first, and angle into Blackfriars for brass farthings with an old mitten.[7]

LADY WISHFORT Aye, dear Foible; thank thee for that, dear Foible. He has put me out of all patience. I shall never recompose my features to receive Sir Rowland with any economy of face. This wretch has fretted me that I am absolutely decayed. Look, Foible.

FOIBLE Your ladyship has frowned a little too rashly, indeed, madam. There are some cracks discernible in the white varnish.

LADY WISHFORT Let me see the glass.—Cracks, say'st thou? Why I am arrantly flayed—I look like an old peeled wall. Thou must repair me, Foible, before Sir Rowland comes, or I shall never keep up to my picture.

FOIBLE I warrant you, madam; a little art once made your picture like you and now a little of the same art must make you like your picture. Your picture must sit for you, madam.

LADY WISHFORT But art thou sure Sir Rowland will not fail to come? Or will a' not fail[8] when he does come? Will he be importunate, Foible, and push? For if he should not be importunate—I shall never break decorums.—I shall die with confusion, if I am forced to advance.—Oh, no, I can never advance.—I shall swoon if he should expect advances. No, I hope Sir Rowland is better bred than to put a lady to the necessity of breaking her forms. I won't be too coy neither—I won't give him despair—but a little disdain is not amiss; a little scorn is alluring.

FOIBLE A little scorn becomes your ladyship.

LADY WISHFORT Yes, but tenderness becomes me best.—A sort of dyingness—You see that picture has a sort of a—Ha, Foible? A swimmingness

---

5. Old, cast-off clothes; an insulting metaphor to apply to Lady Wishfort.
6. A shed, supported by the wall toward which it is inclined. Long Lane was a street where old clothes were sold. "Tatterdemalion": ragamuffin.
7. Prisoners begged by letting down a mitten on a string; passers-by dropped coins into it. Ludgate was a debtor's prison, adjoining the district of Blackfriars in London.
8. I.e., will *he* not fail?

in the eyes—Yes, I'll look so—my niece affects it; but she wants features. Is Sir Rowland handsome? Let my toilet be removed—I'll dress above. I'll receive Sir Rowland here. Is he handsome? Don't answer me. I won't know: I'll be surprised. I'll be taken by surprise.

FOIBLE   By storm, madam. Sir Rowland's a brisk man.

LADY WISHFORT   Is he! O, then he'll importune, if he's a brisk man, I shall save decorums if Sir Rowland importunes. I have a mortal terror at the apprehension of offending against decorums. O, I'm glad he's a brisk man. Let my things be removed, good Foible.

SCENE 6

MRS. FAINALL, FOIBLE.

MRS. FAINALL   O Foible, I have been in a fright, lest I should come too late. That devil Marwood saw you in the park with Mirabell, and I'm afraid will discover it to my lady.

FOIBLE   Discover what, madam?

MRS. FAINALL   Nay, nay, put not on that strange face. I am privy to the whole design and know Waitwell, to whom thou wert this morning married, is to personate Mirabell's uncle, and as such, winning my lady, to involve her in those difficulties from which Mirabell only must release her, by his making his conditions to have my cousin and her fortune left to her own disposal.

FOIBLE   O dear madam, I beg your pardon. It was not my confidence in your ladyship that was deficient, but I thought the former good correspondence between your ladyship and Mr. Mirabell might have hindered his communicating this secret.

MRS. FAINALL   Dear Foible, forget that.

FOIBLE   O dear madam, Mr. Mirabell is such a sweet winning gentleman—but your ladyship is the pattern of generosity. Sweet lady, to be so good! Mr. Mirabell cannot choose but to be grateful. I find your ladyship has his heart still. Now, madam, I can safely tell your ladyship our success. Mrs. Marwood had told my lady; but I warrant I managed myself. I turned it all for the better. I told my lady that Mr. Mirabell railed at her. I laid horrid things to his charge, I'll vow; and my lady is so incensed that she'll be contracted to Sir Rowland tonight, she says—I warrant I worked her up, that he may have her for asking for, as they say of a Welsh maidenhead.

MRS. FAINALL   O rare Foible!

FOIBLE   Madam, I beg your ladyship to acquaint Mr. Mirabell of his success. I would be seen as little as possible to speak to him—besides, I believe Madam Marwood watches me. She has a month's mind;[9] but I know Mr. Mirabell can't abide her.—[Calls.]—John—remove my lady's toilet. Madam, your servant. My lady is so impatient, I fear she'll come for me if I stay.

MRS. FAINALL   I'll go with you up the back stairs, lest I should meet her.

9. An inclination (toward Mirabell).

SCENE 7

MRS. MARWOOD *alone.*

MRS. MARWOOD   Indeed, Mrs. Engine,[1] is it thus with you? Are you become a go-between of this importance? Yes, I shall watch you. Why, this wench is the *passe-partout,* a very master key to everybody's strongbox. My friend Fainall,[2] have you carried it so swimmingly? I thought there was something in it; but it seems it's over with you. Your loathing is not from a want of appetite, then, but from a surfeit. Else you could never be so cool to fall from a principal to be an assistant; to procure for him! A pattern of generosity, that I confess. Well, Mr. Fainall, you have met with your match. O, man, man! Woman, woman! The devil's an ass: If I were a painter, I would draw him like an idiot, a driveler with a bib and bells. Man should have his head and horns, and woman the rest of him. Poor simple fiend! Madam Marwood has a month's mind, but he can't abide her.—'Twere better for him you had not been his confessor in that affair without you could have kept his counsel closer. I shall not prove another pattern of generosity.—He has not obliged me to that with those excesses of himself; and now I'll have none of him. Here comes the good lady, panting ripe, with a heart full of hope and a head full of care, like any chemist upon the day of projection.[3]

SCENE 8

[*To her*] LADY WISHFORT.

LADY WISHFORT   O dear Marwood, what shall I say for this rude forgetfulness—but my dear friend is all goodness.

MRS. MARWOOD   No apologies, dear madam. I have been very well entertained.

LADY WISHFORT   As I'm a person I am in a very chaos to think I should so forget myself—but I have such an olio[4] of affairs really I know not what to do—[*Calls.*] Foible—I expect my nephew Sir Wilfull every moment too.—Why, Foible!—He means to travel for improvement.

MRS. MARWOOD   Methinks Sir Wilfull should rather think of marrying than traveling at his years. I hear he is turned of forty.

LADY WISHFORT   O, he's in less danger of being spoiled by his travels.—I am against my nephew's marrying too young. It will be time enough when he comes back and has acquired discretion to choose for himself.

MRS. MARWOOD   Methinks Mrs. Millamant and he would make a very fit match. He may travel afterwards. 'Tis a thing very usual with young gentlemen.

LADY WISHFORT   I promise you I have thought on't—and since 'tis your judgment, I'll think on't again. I assure you I will; I value your judgment extremely. On my word I'll propose it.

---

1. A person who serves as an instrument or tool of others in an intrigue.
2. I.e., Mrs. Fainall.

3. An alchemical term denoting the final step in the transmutation of baser metals into gold.
4. Hodgepodge.

SCENE 9

[*To them*] FOIBLE.

LADY WISHFORT   Come, come Foible—I had forgot my nephew will be here before dinner.—I must make haste.

FOIBLE   Mr. Witwoud and Mr. Petulant are come to dine with your ladyship.

LADY WISHFORT   O dear, I can't appear till I am dressed. Dear Marwood, shall I be free with you again and beg you to entertain 'em? I'll make all imaginable haste. Dear friend, excuse me.

SCENE 10

MRS. MARWOOD, MRS. MILLAMANT, MINCING.

MILLAMANT   Sure never anything was so unbred as that odious man.—Marwood, your servant.

MRS. MARWOOD   You have a color. What's the matter?

MILLAMANT   That horrid fellow Petulant has provoked me into a flame—I have broke my fan.—Mincing, lend me yours; is not all the powder out of my hair?

MRS. MARWOOD   No. What has he done?

MILLAMANT   Nay, he has done nothing; he has only talked.—Nay, he has said nothing neither; but he has contradicted everything that has been said. For my part, I thought Witwoud and he would have quarreled.

MINCING   I vow, mem, I thought once they would have fit.

MILLAMANT   Well, 'tis a lamentable thing. I swear, that one has not the liberty of choosing one's acquaintance as one does one's clothes.

MRS. MARWOOD   If we had that liberty, we should be as weary of one set of acquaintance, though never so good, as we are of one suit, though never so fine. A fool and a doily stuff[5] would now and then find days of grace, and be worn for variety.

MILLAMANT   I could consent to wear 'em, if they would wear alike; but fools never wear out—they are such drap-de-Berry[6] things! Without one could give 'em to one's chambermaid after a day or two.

MRS. MARWOOD   'Twere better so indeed. Or what think you of the play house?[7] A fine gay glossy fool should be given there, like a new masking habit after the masquerade is over, and we have done with the disguise. For a fool's visit is always a disguise, and never admitted by a woman of wit, but to blind her affair with a lover of sense. If you would but appear barefaced now and own Mirabell, you might as easily put off Petulant and Witwoud as your hood and scarf. And indeed 'tis time, for the town has found it: the secret is grown too big for the pretense: 'tis like Mrs. Primly's great belly; she may lace it down before, but it burnishes[8] on her hips. Indeed, Millamant, you can no more conceal it than my Lady

5. A woolen cloth.
6. Coarse woolen cloth, made in the Berry district of France.
7. Fine gentlemen and ladies sometimes donated their old clothes to the playhouses.
8. Spreads out.

Strammel can her face, that goodly face, which in defiance of her Rhenish-wine tea will not be comprehended in a mask.[9]

MILLAMANT   I'll take my death, Marwood, you are more censorious than a decayed beauty, or a discarded toast.[1] Mincing, tell the men they may come up. My aunt is not dressing here; their folly is less provoking than your malice.

SCENE 11

MILLAMANT, MARWOOD.

MILLAMANT   "The town has found it." What has it found? That Mirabell loves me is no more a secret than it is a secret that you discovered it to my aunt, or than the reason why you discovered it is a secret.

MRS. MARWOOD   You are nettled.

MILLAMANT   You're mistaken. Ridiculous!

MRS. MARWOOD   Indeed, my dear, you'll tear another fan if you don't mitigate those violent airs.

MILLAMANT   O silly! Ha, ha, ha. I could laugh immoderately. Poor Mirabell! His constancy to me has quite destroyed his complaisance for all the world beside. I swear, I never enjoined it him, to be so coy.—If I had the vanity to think he would obey me, I would command him to show more gallantry.—'Tis hardly well bred to be so particular on one hand and so insensible on the other. But I despair to prevail, and so let him follow his own way. Ha, ha, ha. Pardon me, dear creature, I must laugh, ha, ha, ha; though I grant you 'tis a little barbarous, ha, ha, ha.

MRS. MARWOOD   What pity 'tis, so much fine raillery, and delivered with so significant gesture, should be so unhappily directed to miscarry.

MILLAMANT   Hae? Dear creature, I ask your pardon—I swear I did not mind you.

MRS. MARWOOD   Mr. Mirabell and you both may think it a thing impossible, when I shall tell him by telling you—

MILLAMANT   O dear, what? For it is the same thing, if I hear it—Ha, ha, ha.

MRS. MARWOOD   That I detest him, hate him, madam.

MILLAMANT   O madam, why so do I—and yet the creature loves me, ha, ha, ha. How can one forbear laughing to think of it?—I am a sibyl[2] if I am not amazed to think what he can see in me. I'll take my death, I think you are handsomer—and within a year or two as young. If you could but stay for me, I should overtake you.—But that cannot be.—Well, that thought makes me melancholy.—Now I'll be sad.

MRS. MARWOOD   Your merry note may be changed sooner than you think.

MILLAMANT   D'ye say so? Then I'm resolved I'll have a song to keep up my spirits.

9. Lady Strammel (the name means "a lean, ill-favored person") reduces by drinking Rhenish wine, but still her face is too large to be contained ("comprehended") in a mask.
1. A lady to whom toasts are no longer drunk.
2. A prophetess.

SCENE 12

[*To them*] MINCING.

MINCING The gentlemen stay but to comb,[3] madam, and will wait on you.
MILLAMANT Desire Mrs.———[4] that is in the next room to sing the song
I would have learnt yesterday. You shall hear it, madam—not that there's
any great matter in it—But 'tis agreeable to my humor.

[SONG. SET BY MR. JOHN ECCLES]

1

Love's but the frailty of the mind,
    When 'tis not with ambition joined;
A sickly flame, which if not fed expires;
And feeding, wastes in self-consuming fires.

2

5   'Tis not to wound a wanton boy
Or amorous youth, that gives the joy;
But 'tis the glory to have pierced a swain,
For whom inferior beauties sighed in vain.

3

Then I alone the conquest prize,
10   When I insult a rival's eyes:
If there's delight in love, 'tis when I see
That heart which others bleed for, bleed for me.

SCENE 13

[*To them*] PETULANT, WITWOUD.

MILLAMANT Is your animosity composed, gentlemen?
WITWOUD Raillery, raillery, madam, we have no animosity. We hit off a
little wit now and then, but no animosity. The falling out of wits is like
the falling out of lovers—we agree in the main, like treble and bass. Ha,
Petulant!
PETULANT Aye, in the main. But when I have a humor to contradict—
WITWOUD. Aye, when he has a humor to contradict, then I contradict too.
What, I know my cue. Then we contradict one another like two battle-
dores;[5] for contradictions beget one another like Jews.
PETULANT If he says black's black—if I have a humor to say 'tis blue—let
that pass.—All's one for that. If I have a humor to prove it, it must be
granted.
WITWOUD Not positively must—but it may—it may.
PETULANT Yes, it positively must, upon proof positive.

3. I.e., to comb their periwigs.
4. The name of the singer was to be inserted. The
music was by John Eccles (d. 1735), a popular
composer for the theater.

5. Rackets used to strike the shuttlecock, or bird,
in the old game from which badminton is
descended.

WITWOUD   Aye, upon proof positive it must; but upon proof presumptive it only may. That's a logical distinction now, madam.

MRS. MARWOOD   I perceive your debates are of importance and very learnedly handled.

PETULANT   Importance is one thing, and learning's another; but a debate's a debate, that I assert.

WITWOUD   Petulant's an enemy to learning; he relies altogether on his parts.[6]

PETULANT   No, I'm no enemy to learning; it hurts not me.

MRS. MARWOOD   That's a sign indeed it's no enemy to you.

PETULANT   No, no, it's no enemy to anybody but them that have it.

MILLAMANT   Well, an illiterate man's my aversion. I wonder at the impudence of any illiterate man, to offer to make love.

WITWOUD   That I confess I wonder at too.

MILLAMANT   Ah! to marry an ignorant! that can hardly read or write.

PETULANT   Why should a man be any further from being married though he can't read than he is from being hanged. The ordinary's[7] paid for setting the Psalm, and the parish priest for reading the ceremony. And for the rest which is to follow in both cases, a man may do it without book.—So all's one for that.

MILLAMANT   D'ye hear the creature? Lord, here's company, I'll be gone.

SCENE 14

SIR WILFULL WITWOUD *in a riding dress,* MRS. MARWOOD, PETULANT, WITWOUD, FOOTMAN.

WITWOUD   In the name of Bartlemew and his Fair,[8] what have we here?

MRS. MARWOOD   'Tis your brother, I fancy. Don't you know him?

WITWOUD   Not I.—Yes, I think it is he—I've almost forgot him; I have not seen him since the Revolution.[9]

FOOTMAN   Sir, my lady's dressing. Here's company; if you please to walk in, in the meantime.

SIR WILFULL   Dressing! What, it's but morning here, I warrant, with you in London; we should count it towards afternoon in our parts, down in Shropshire. Why, then belike my aunt han't dined yet—ha, friend?

FOOTMAN   Your aunt, Sir?

SIR WILFULL   My aunt, sir, yes, my aunt, sir, and your lady, sir; your lady is my aunt, sir.—Why, what do'st thou not know me, friend? Why, then send somebody hither that does. How long hast thou lived with thy lady, fellow, ha?

FOOTMAN   A week, sir; longer than anybody in the house, except my lady's woman.

SIR WILFULL   Why, then belike thou dost not know thy lady, if thou see'st her, ha, friend?

FOOTMAN   Why truly, sir, I cannot safely swear to her face in a morning,

---

6. Native abilities.
7. The clergyman appointed to prepare condemned prisoners for death.
8. A feature of St. Bartholomew's Fair, held during August in Smithfield, London, was the exhibition of monsters and freaks of nature.
9. The Glorious Revolution of 1688, which forced the abdication of James II.

before she is dressed. 'Tis like I may give a shrewd guess at her by this time.

SIR WILFULL   Well, prithee try what thou canst do; if thou canst not guess, inquire her out, do'st hear, fellow? And tell her her nephew, Sir Wilfull Witwoud, is in the house.

FOOTMAN   I shall, sir.

SIR WILFULL   Hold ye, hear me, friend; a word with you in your ear. Prithee who are these gallants?

FOOTMAN   Really, sir, I can't tell; there come so many here, 'tis hard to know 'em all.

SCENE 15

SIR WILFULL WITWOUD, PETULANT, WITWOUD, MRS. MARWOOD.

SIR WILFULL   Oons,[1] this fellow knows less than a starling; I don't think a'knows his own name.

MRS. MARWOOD   Mr. Witwoud, your brother is not behind hand in forgetfulness—I fancy he has forgot you too.

WITWOUD   I hope so.—The devil take him that remembers first, I say.

SIR WILFULL   Save you, gentlemen and lady.

MRS. MARWOOD   For shame, Mr. Witwoud; why don't you speak to him?— And you, sir.

WITWOUD   Petulant, speak.

PETULANT   And you, sir.

SIR WILFULL   [Salutes[2] MARWOOD.]   No offense, I hope.

MRS. MARWOOD   No sure, sir.

WITWOUD   This is a vile dog, I see that already. No offense! Ha, ha, ha, to him; to him, Petulant, smoke him.[3]

PETULANT   [Surveying him round.]   It seems as if you had come a journey, sir. Hem, hem.

SIR WILFULL   Very likely, sir, that it may seem so.

PETULANT   No offense, I hope, sir.

WITWOUD   Smoke the boots, the boots, Petulant, the boots. Ha, ha, ha.

SIR WILFULL   Maybe not, sir; thereafter as 'tis meant, sir.

PETULANT   Sir, I presume upon the information of your boots.

SIR WILFULL   Why, 'tis like you may, sir: If you are not satisfied with the information of my boots, sir, if you will step to the stable, you may inquire further of my horse, sir.

PETULANT   Your horse, sir! Your horse is an ass, sir!

SIR WILFULL   Do you speak by way of offense, sir?

MRS. MARWOOD   The gentleman's merry, that's all, sir.—[Aside.] 'Slife,[4] we shall have a quarrel betwixt an horse and an ass, before they find one another out. [Aloud.] You must not take anything amiss from your friends, sir. You are among your friends, here, though it may be you don't know it.—If I am not mistaken, you are Sir Wilfull Witwoud.

SIR WILFULL   Right, lady; I am Sir Wilfull Witwoud, so I write myself; no

---

1. An uncouth oath: God's wounds.
2. Kisses.
3. Make fun of him.
4. God's life.

offense to anybody, I hope; and nephew to the Lady Wishfort of this mansion.

MRS. MARWOOD   Don't you know this gentleman, sir?

SIR WILFULL   Hum! What, sure, 'tis not—yea by'r Lady, but 'tis—'sheart, I know not whether 'tis or no.—Yea but 'tis, by the Wrekin.[5] Brother Antony! What, Tony, i'faith! What, do'st thou not know me? By'r Lady, nor I thee, thou art so becravated and so beperriwigged—'sheart, why do'st not speak? Art thou o'erjoyed?

WITWOUD   Odso, brother, is it you? Your servant, brother.

SIR WILFULL   Your servant! Why, yours, sir. Your servant again—'sheart, and your friend and servant to that—and a—[*Puff.*]—and a flapdragon for your service, sir: and a hare's foot, and a hare's scut[6] for your service, sir; an you be so cold and so courtly!

WITWOUD   No offense, I hope, brother.

SIR WILFULL   'Sheart, sir, but there is, and much offense. A pox, is this your Inns o'Court[7] breeding, not to know your friends and your relations, your elders and your betters?

WITWOUD   Why, Brother Wilfull of Salop, you may be as short as a Shrewsbury cake,[8] if you please. But I tell you 'tis not modish to know relations in town. You think you're in the country, where great lubberly brothers slabber and kiss one another when they meet, like a call of sergeants.[9]—'Tis not the fashion here; 'tis not indeed, dear brother.

SIR WILFULL   The fashion's a fool; and you're a fop, dear brother. 'Sheart, I've suspected this—by'r Lady, I conjectured you were a fop, since you began to change the style of your letters and write in a scrap of paper gilt round the edges, no bigger than a subpoena. I might expect this when you left off "Honored Brother" and "hoping you are in good health," and so forth—to begin with a "Rat me, knight, I'm so sick of a last night's debauch"—'od's heart, and then tell a familiar tale of a cock and bull, and a whore and a bottle, and so conclude—You could write news before you were out of your time, when you lived with honest Pumple-Nose, the attorney of Furnival's Inn[1]—You could entreat to be remembered then to your friends round the Wrekin. We could have gazettes then, and Dawks's *Letter,* and the Weekly Bill,[2] till of late days.

PETULANT   'Slife, Witwoud, were you ever an attorney's clerk? Of the family of the Furnivals. Ha, ha, ha!

WITWOUD   Aye, aye, but that was but for a while. Not long, not long; pshaw, I was not in my own power then. An orphan, and this fellow was my guardian; aye, aye, I was glad to consent to that man to come to London. He had the disposal of me then. If I had not agreed to that, I

---

5. A solitary mountain peak in Shropshire, near the Welsh border. " 'Sheart": God's heart.
6. Rabbit's tail. "Flapdragon": something worthless.
7. The buildings—Gray's Inn, Lincoln's Inn, the Inner Temple, the Middle Temple—housing the four legal societies that have the sole right to admit persons to the practice of law.
8. Shortcake, in the modern meaning of the term. Witwoud puns, using "short" also in the sense of "abrupt." "Salop": ancient name of Shropshire.
9. Witwoud refers to the mutual greetings and

felicitations of a group of barristers ("sergeants") newly admitted to the bar.
1. One of the inns of Chancery, attached to Lincoln's Inn. Attorneys were looked down on socially; hence Petulant's ill-natured mirth in his next speech. "Before you were out of your time": before you had served out your apprenticeship.
2. The official list of the deaths occurring in London. "Gazettes": newspapers. "Dawks's *Letter*" (*News Letter*): a popular source of news in the country.

might have been bound 'prentice to a felt-maker in Shrewsbury; this fellow would have bound me to a maker of felts.

SIR WILFULL   'Sheart, and better than to be bound to a maker of fops; where, I suppose, you have served your time; and now you may set up for yourself.

MRS. MARWOOD   You intend to travel, sir, as I'm informed.

SIR WILFULL   Belike I may, madam. I may chance to sail upon the salt seas, if my mind hold.

PETULANT   And the wind serve.

SIR WILFULL   Serve or not serve, I shan't ask license of you, sir; nor the weather-cock your companion. I direct my discourse to the lady, sir. 'Tis like my aunt may have told you, madam—Yes, I have settled my concerns, I may say now, and am minded to see foreign parts. If an' how that the peace[3] holds, whereby, that is, taxes abate.

MRS. MARWOOD   I thought you had designed for France at all adventures.

SIR WILFULL   I can't tell that; 'tis like I may and 'tis like I may not. I am somewhat dainty in making a resolution, because when I make it I keep it, I don't stand shill I, shall I,[4] then; if I say't, I'll do't. But I have thoughts to tarry a small matter in town, to learn somewhat of your lingo first, before I cross the seas. I'd gladly have a spice of your French as they say, whereby to hold discourse in foreign countries.

MRS. MARWOOD   Here's an academy in town for that use.

SIR WILFULL   There is? 'Tis like there may.

MRS. MARWOOD   No doubt you will return very much improved.

WITWOUD   Yes, refined like a Dutch skipper from a whale-fishing.

SCENE 16

[To them] LADY WISHFORT *and* FAINALL.

LADY WISHFORT   Nephew, you are welcome.

SIR WILFULL   Aunt, your servant.

FAINALL   Sir Wilfull, your most faithful servant.

SIR WILFULL   Cousin Fainall, give me your hand.

LADY WISHFORT   Cousin Witwoud, your servant; Mr. Petulant, your servant.—Nephew, you are welcome again. Will you drink anything after your journey, nephew, before you eat? Dinner's almost ready.

SIR WILFULL   I'm very well, I thank you, aunt. However, I thank you for your courteous offer. 'Sheart, I was afraid you would have been in the fashion too, and have remembered to have forgot your relations. Here's your cousin Tony, belike, I mayn't call him brother for fear of offense.

LADY WISHFORT   O, he's a rallier, nephew—my cousin's a wit; and your great wits always rally their best friends to choose.[5] When you have been abroad, nephew, you'll understand raillery better.

[FAINALL *and* MRS. MARWOOD *talk apart.*]

---

3. The peace established by the Treaty of Ryswick in 1697, which concluded the war against France waged under the leadership of William III by England, the Empire, Spain, and Holland. It endured until the spring of 1702, when the War of the Spanish Succession began.
4. Shilly-shally. "Dainty": scrupulous, cautious.
5. By choice.

SIR WILFULL   Why then let him hold his tongue in the meantime, and rail when that day comes.

SCENE 17

[To them] MINCING.

MINCING   Mem, I come to acquaint your la'ship that dinner is impatient.

SIR WILFULL   Impatient? Why then belike it won't stay till I pull off my boots. Sweetheart, can you help me to a pair of slippers?—My man's with his horses, I warrant.

LADY WISHFORT   Fie, fie, nephew, you would not pull off your boots here. Go down into the hall.—Dinner shall stay for you. My nephew's a little unbred; you'll pardon him, madam.—Gentlemen, will you walk? Marwood?

MRS. MARWOOD   I'll follow you, madam—before Sir Wilfull is ready.

SCENE 18

MARWOOD, FAINALL.

FAINALL   Why then Foible's a bawd, an errant, rank, match-making bawd. And I it seems am a husband, a rank husband; and my wife a very errant, rank wife—all in the way of the world. 'Sdeath, to be a cuckold by anticipation, a cuckold in embryo? Sure I was born with budding antlers like a young satyr, or a citizen's child.[6] 'Sdeath, to be outwitted, to be outjilted—outmatrimonied. If I had kept my speed like a stag, 'twere somewhat, but to crawl after, with my horns like a snail, and be outstripped by my wife—'tis scurvy wedlock.

MRS. MARWOOD   Then shake it off. You have often wished for an opportunity to part, and now you have it. But first prevent their plot.—The half of Millamant's fortune is too considerable to be parted with to a foe, to Mirabell.

FAINALL   Damn him, that had been mine—had you not made that fond[7] discovery.—That had been forfeited, had they been married. My wife had added luster to my horns. By that increase of fortune, I could have worn 'em tipped with gold, though my forehead had been furnished like a Deputy-Lieutenant's hall.[8]

MRS. MARWOOD   They may prove a cap of maintenance[9] to you still, if you can away with your wife. And she's no worse than when you had her—I dare swear she had given up her game, before she was married.

FAINALL   Hum! That may be—She might throw up her cards; but I'll be hanged if she did not put Pam[1] in her pocket.

MRS. MARWOOD   You married her to keep you, and if you can contrive to

---

6. "Satyr": a sylvan deity, usually represented with a goat's legs and horns. A cuckold is said to wear horns. Because the wives of "citizens" (merchants living in the old city of London, not the fashionable suburbs) were regarded by the rakes as their natural and easy prey, a "citizen's child" was born to be cuckolded.

7. Foolish.

8. I.e., the great hall in the house of the deputy lieutenant of a shire. Fainall imagines it ornamented with numerous antlers taken from deer slain in the hunt.

9. In heraldry, a cap with two points like horns.

1. Jack of clubs, high card in the game of loo.

have her keep you better than you expected, why should you not keep her longer than you intended?

FAINALL   The means, the means.

MRS. MARWOOD   Discover to my lady your wife's conduct; threaten to part with her.—My lady loves her and will come to any composition to save her reputation. Take the opportunity of breaking it, just upon the discovery of this imposture. My lady will be enraged beyond bounds and sacrifice niece and fortune and all at that conjuncture. And let me alone to keep her warm; if she should flag in her part, I will not fail to prompt her.

FAINALL   Faith, this has an appearance.

MRS. MARWOOD   I'm sorry I hinted to my lady to endeavor a match between Millamant and Sir Wilfull. That may be an obstacle.

FAINALL   O, for that matter leave me to manage him; I'll disable him for that; he will drink like a Dane; after dinner, I'll set his hand in.

MRS. MARWOOD   Well, how do you stand affected towards your lady?

FAINALL   Why, faith, I'm thinking of it. Let me see—I am married already; so that's over. My wife has placed the jade with me—well, that's over too. I never loved her, or if I had, why that would have been over too by this time. Jealous of her I cannot be, for I am certain; so there's an end of jealousy. Weary of her I am and shall be—no, there's no end of that; no, no, that were too much to hope. Thus far concerning my repose. Now for my reputation. As to my own, I married not for it; so that's out of the question. And as to my part in my wife's—why, she had parted with hers before; so bringing none to me, she can take none from me; 'tis against all rule of play that I should lose to one who has not wherewithal to stake.

MRS. MARWOOD   Besides you forget, marriage is honorable.

FAINALL   Hum! Faith, and that's well thought on; marriage is honorable, as you say; and if so, wherefore should cuckoldom be a discredit, being derived from so honorable a root?

MRS. MARWOOD   Nay, I know not; if the root be honorable, why not the branches?[2]

FAINALL   So, so, why this point's clear. Well, how do we proceed?

MRS. MARWOOD   I will contrive a letter which shall be delivered to my lady at the time when that rascal who is to act Sir Rowland is with her. It shall come as from an unknown hand—for the less I appear to know of the truth, the better I can play the incendiary. Besides, I would not have Foible provoked if I could help it, because you know she knows some passages—nay, I expect all will come out. But let the mine be sprung first, and then I care not if I am discovered.

FAINALL   If the worst come to the worst, I'll turn my wife to grass[3]—I have already a deed of settlement of the best part of her estate, which I wheedled out of her; and that you shall partake at least.

MRS. MARWOOD   I hope you are convinced that I hate Mirabell now: you'll be no more jealous?

2. I.e., of the cuckold's horns.
3. Turn out to pasture. A "grass widow" is divorced or separated from her husband.

FAINALL   Jealous, no—by this kiss.—Let husbands be jealous, but let the
lover still believe. Or if he doubt, let it be only to endear his pleasure
and prepare the joy that follows, when he proves his mistress true. But
let husbands' doubts convert to endless jealousy; or if they have belief,
let it corrupt to superstition and blind credulity. I am single, and will
herd no more with 'em. True, I wear the badge, but I'll disown the order.
And since I take my leave of 'em, I care not if I leave 'em a common
motto to their common crest.

> All husbands must, or pain, or shame, endure;
> The wise too jealous are, fools too secure.

Act 4—Scene continues.

SCENE 1

LADY WISHFORT and FOIBLE.

LADY WISHFORT   Is Sir Rowland coming, say'st thou, Foible? and are
things in order?
FOIBLE   Yes, madam. I have put wax lights in the sconces, and placed the
footmen in a row in the hall, in their best liveries, with the coachman
and postilion to fill up the equipage.
LADY WISHFORT   Have you pulvilled[4] the coachman and postilion, that
they may not stink of the stable, when Sir Rowland comes by?
FOIBLE   Yes, madam.
LADY WISHFORT   And are the dancers and the music ready, that he may
be entertained in all points with correspondence to his passion?
FOIBLE   All is ready, madam.
LADY WISHFORT   And—well—and how do I look, Foible?
FOIBLE   Most killing well, madam.
LADY WISHFORT   Well, and how shall I receive him? In what figure shall I
give his heart the first impression? There is a great deal in the first
impression. Shall I sit?—No, I won't sit—I'll walk.—Aye, I'll walk from
the door upon his entrance; and then turn full upon him.—No, that will
be too sudden. I'll lie—aye, I'll lie down—I'll receive him in my little
dressing-room, there's a couch.—Yes, yes, I'll give the first impression
on a couch.—I won't lie neither, but loll and lean upon one elbow; with
one foot a little dangling off, jogging in a thoughtful way—yes—and then
as soon as he appears, start, aye, start and be surprised, and rise to meet
him in a pretty disorder—yes. O, nothing is more alluring than a levee[5]
from a couch in some confusion. It shows the foot to advantage and
furnishes with blushes and recomposing airs beyond comparison. Hark!
There's a coach.
FOIBLE   'Tis he, madam.
LADY WISHFORT   O dear, has my nephew made his addresses to Millamant? I ordered him.
FOIBLE   Sir Wilfull is set in to drinking, madam, in the parlor.

---

4. Sprinkled with perfumed powder.   5. A rising.

LADY WISHFORT 'Ods my life, I'll send him to her. Call her down, Foible; bring her hither. I'll send him as I go.—When they are together, then come to me, Foible, that I may not be too long alone with Sir Rowland.

SCENE 2

MRS. MILLAMANT, MRS. FAINALL, FOIBLE.

FOIBLE Madam, I stayed here to tell your ladyship that Mr. Mirabell has waited this half hour for an opportunity to talk with you. Though my lady's orders were to leave you and Sir Wilfull together. Shall I tell Mr. Mirabell that you are at leisure?

MILLAMANT No—What would the dear man have? I am thoughtful and would amuse myself.—Bid him come another time.

> There never yet was woman made,
> Nor shall, but to be cursed.[6]

[*Repeating and walking about.*]

That's hard!

MRS. FAINALL You are very fond of Sir John Suckling today, Millamant, and the poets.

MILLAMANT He? Aye, and filthy verses—so I am.

FOIBLE Sir Wilfull is coming, madam. Shall I send Mr. Mirabell away?

MILLAMANT Aye, if you please, Foible, send him away—or send him hither, just as you will, dear Foible. I think I'll see him—Shall I? Aye, let the wretch come.

> Thyrsis, a youth of the inspirèd train.[7]

[*Repeating.*]

Dear Fainall, entertain Sir Wilfull.—Thou hast philosophy to undergo a fool, thou art married and hast patience.—I would confer with my own thoughts.

MRS. FAINALL I am obliged to you that you would make me your proxy in this affair, but I have business of my own.

SCENE 3

[*To them*] SIR WILFULL.

MRS. FAINALL O Sir Wilfull; you are come at the critical instant. There's your mistress up to the ears in love and contemplation. Pursue your point, now or never.

SIR WILFULL Yes; my aunt will have it so.—I would gladly have been encouraged with a bottle or two, because I'm somewhat wary at first, before I am acquainted; [*This while* MILLAMANT *walks about repeating to herself.*]—but I hope, after a time, I shall break my mind—that is upon

---

6. The opening lines of a poem by Sir John Suckling. Impelled by her love to accept Mirabell, but reluctant to give herself, Millamant broods over poems that speak of the brief happiness of lovers and the falseness of men.

7. The first line of Edmund Waller's *The Story of Phoebus and Daphne Applied.* In the flight of the virgin nymph from the embraces of the amorous god, Millamant finds an emblem of her relations with Mirabell.

further acquaintance.—So for the present, cousin, I'll take my leave.—
If so be you'll be so kind to make my excuse, I'll return to my company.—

MRS. FAINALL   O fie, Sir Wilfull! What, you must not be daunted.

SIR WILFULL   Daunted, no, that's not it; it is not so much for that—for if
so be that I set on't, I'll do't. But only for the present, 'tis sufficient till
further acquaintance, that's all.—Your servant.

MRS. FAINALL   Nay, I'll swear you shall never lose so favorable an opportunity if I can help it. I'll leave you together and lock the door.

SCENE 4

SIR WILFULL, MILLAMANT.

SIR WILFULL   Nay, nay, cousin—I have forgot my gloves.—What d'ye do?
'Sheart, a'has locked the door indeed, I think.—Nay, cousin Fainall, open
the door.—Pshaw, what a vixen trick is this? Nay, now a'has seen me
too.—Cousin, I made bold to pass through, as it were.—I think this
door's enchanted.—

MILLAMANT [*Repeating.*]

> I prithee spare me, gentle boy,
> Press me no more for that slight toy.[8]

SIR WILFULL   Anan?[9] Cousin, your servant.

MILLAMANT.—"That foolish trifle of a heart"—Sir Wilfull!

SIR WILFULL   Yes—your servant. No offense I hope, cousin.

MILLAMANT [*Repeating.*]

> I swear it will not do its part,
> Though thou dost thine, employ'st thy power and art.

Natural, easy Suckling!

SIR WILFULL   Anan? Suckling? No such suckling neither, cousin, nor stripling: I thank heaven I'm no minor.

MILLAMANT   Ah rustic, ruder than Gothic.[1]

SIR WILFULL   Well, well, I shall understand your lingo one of these days,
cousin. In the meanwhile I must answer in plain English.

MILLAMANT   Have you any business with me, Sir Wilfull?

SIR WILFULL   Not at present, cousin.—Yes, I made bold to see, to come
and know if that how you were disposed to fetch a walk this evening, if
so be that I might not be troublesome, I would have sought a walk with
you.

MILLAMANT   A walk? What then?

SIR WILFULL   Nay nothing—only for the walk's sake, that's all—

MILLAMANT   I nauseate walking; 'tis a country diversion. I loathe the country and everything that relates to it.

SIR WILFULL   Indeed! Hah! Look ye, look ye, you do? Nay, 'tis like you
may.—Here are choice of pastimes here in town, as plays and the like;
that must be confessed indeed.—

MILLAMANT   Ah, *l'étourdi.*[2] I hate the town too.

---

8. The first lines of a song by Suckling.
9. How's that?
1. To the new age with its classical taste, medieval

art, especially architecture, seemed crude ("rude").
2. Oh, the silly fellow! (French); also the title of a
comedy by Molière.

SIR WILFULL   Dear heart, that's much—Hah! that you should hate 'em both! Hah! 'tis like you may; there are some can't relish the town, and others can't away with the country—'tis like you may be one of those, cousin.

MILLAMANT   Ha, ha, ha. Yes, 'tis like I may. You have nothing further to say to me?

SIR WILFULL   Not at present, cousin. 'Tis like when I have an opportunity to be more private, I may break my mind in some measure.—I conjecture you partly guess—however, that's as time shall try; but spare to speak and spare to speed, as they say.

MILLAMANT   If it is of no great importance, Sir Wilfull, you will oblige me to leave me. I have just now a little business.

SIR WILFULL   Enough, enough, cousin. Yes, yes, all a case—when you're disposed, when you're disposed. Now's as well as another time; and another time as well as now. All's one for that.—Yes, yes, if your concerns call you, there's no haste; it will keep cold as they say.—Cousin, your servant. I think this door's locked.

MILLAMANT   You may go this way, sir.

SIR WILFULL   Your servant—then with your leave I'll return to my company.

MILLAMANT   Aye, aye. Ha, ha, ha.

Like Phoebus sung the no less amorous Boy.[3]

SCENE 5

MILLAMANT, MIRABELL.

MIRABELL

Like Daphne she, as lovely and as coy.

Do you lock yourself up from me, to make my search more curious?[4] Or is this pretty artifice contrived to signify that here the chase must end, and my pursuit be crowned, for you can fly no further?

MILLAMANT   Vanity! No—I'll fly and be followed to the last moment. Though I am upon the very verge of matrimony, I expect you should solicit me as much as if I were wavering at the grate of a monastery,[5] with one foot over the threshold. I'll be solicited to the very last, nay and afterwards.

MIRABELL   What, after the last?

MILLAMANT   O, I should think I was poor and had nothing to bestow, if I were reduced to an inglorious ease; and freed from the agreeable fatigues of solicitation.

MIRABELL   But do not you know that when favors are conferred upon instant and tedious solicitation, that they diminish in their value and that both the giver loses the grace, and the receiver lessens his pleasure?

MILLAMANT   It may be in things of common application, but never sure in love. O, I hate a lover that can dare to think he draws a moment's air,

---

3. This, and the line that Mirabell caps it with, are from *The Story of Fhoebus and Daphne Applied*.

4. Intricate, laborious.
5. The grated door of a convent.

independent on the bounty of his mistress. There is not so impudent a thing in nature as the saucy look of an assured man, confident of success. The pedantic arrogance of a very husband has not so pragmatical[6] an air. Ah! I'll never marry, unless I am first made sure of my will and pleasure.

MIRABELL   Would you have 'em both before marriage? Or will you be contented with the first now, and stay for the other till after grace?

MILLAMANT   Ah, don't be impertinent.—My dear liberty, shall I leave thee? My faithful solitude, my darling contemplation, must I bid you then adieu? Ay-h adieu—My morning thoughts, agreeable wakings, indolent slumbers, all ye *douceurs,* ye *sommeils du matin,*[7] adieu.—I can't do't, 'tis more than impossible.—Positively, Mirabell, I'll lie abed in a morning as long as I please.

MIRABELL   Then I'll get up in a morning as early as I please.

MILLAMANT   Ah, idle creature, get up when you will.—and d'ye hear? I won't be called names after I'm married; positively I won't be called names.

MIRABELL   Names!

MILLAMANT   Aye, as wife, spouse, my dear, joy, jewel, love, sweetheart, and the rest of that nauseous cant, in which men and their wives are so fulsomely familiar—I shall never bear that.—Good Mirabell, don't let us be familiar or fond, nor kiss before folks, like my Lady Fadler[8] and Sir Francis; nor go to Hyde Park together the first Sunday in a new chariot, to provoke eyes and whispers; and then never be seen there together again, as if we were proud of one another the first week, and ashamed of one another ever after. Let us never visit together, nor go to a play together, but let us be very strange[9] and well bred; let us be as strange as if we had been married a great while; and as well bred as if we were not married at all.

MIRABELL   Have you any more conditions to offer? Hitherto your demands are pretty reasonable.

MILLAMANT   Trifles—as liberty to pay and receive visits to and from whom I please; to write and receive letters, without interrogatories or wry faces on your part; to wear what I please; and choose conversation with regard only to my own taste; to have no obligation upon me to converse with wits that I don't like, because they are your acquaintance; or to be intimate with fools, because they may be your relations. Come to dinner when I please, dine in my dressing room when I'm out of humor, without giving a reason. To have my closet inviolate; to be sole empress of my tea table, which you must never presume to approach without first asking leave. And lastly, wherever I am, you shall always knock at the door before you come in. These articles subscribed, if I continue to endure you a little longer, I may by degrees dwindle into a wife.

MIRABELL   Your bill of fare is something advanced in this latter account. Well, have I liberty to offer conditions—that when you are dwindled into a wife, I may not be beyond measure enlarged into a husband?

MILLAMANT   You have free leave, propose your utmost, speak and spare not.

MIRABELL   I thank you. *Imprimis*[1] then, I covenant that your acquaintance

---

6. Self-assured, conceited.
7. Soft (pleasures) and morning naps (French).
8. I.e., Fondler.

9. Reserved.
1. In the first place (Latin), as in legal documents.

be general; that you admit no sworn confidante or intimate of your own sex; no she-friend to screen her affairs under your countenance and tempt you to make trial of a mutual secrecy. No decoy duck to wheedle you a fop—scrambling to the play in a mask—then bring you home in a pretended fright, when you think you shall be found out—and rail at me for missing the play, and disappointing the frolic which you had to pick me up and prove my constancy.

MILLAMANT   Detestable *imprimis!* I go to the play in a mask!

MIRABELL   *Item,* I article,[2] that you continue to like your own face as long as I shall; and while it passes current with me, that you endeavor not to new coin it. To which end, together with all vizards for the day, I prohibit all masks for the night, made of oiled-skins and I know not what—hog's bones, hare's gall, pig water, and the marrow of a roasted cat.[3] In short, I forbid all commerce with the gentlewoman in what-d'ye-call-it court. *Item,* I shut my doors against all bawds with baskets, and pennyworths of muslin, china, fans, atlases,[4] etc. *Item,* when you shall be breeding—

MILLAMANT   Ah! Name it not.

MIRABELL   Which may be presumed, with a blessing on our endeavors—

MILLAMANT   Odious endeavors!

MIRABELL   I denounce against all strait lacing, squeezing for a shape, till you mold my boy's head like a sugar loaf; and instead of a man-child, make me father to a crooked billet.[5] Lastly, to the dominion of the tea table I submit.—But with proviso that you exceed not in your province; but restrain yourself to native and simple tea-table drinks, as tea, chocolate, and coffee. As likewise to genuine and authorized tea-table talk— such as mending of fashions, spoiling reputations, railing at absent friends, and so forth—but that on no account you encroach upon the men's prerogative, and presume to drink healths, or toast fellows; for prevention of which, I banish all foreign forces, all auxiliaries to the tea table, as orange brandy, all aniseed, cinnamon, citron and Barbados waters, together with ratafia and the most noble spirit of clary.[6]—But for cowslip-wine, poppy water, and all dormitives,[7] those I allow. These provisos admitted, in other things I may prove a tractable and complying husband.

MILLAMANT   O, horrid provisos! filthy strong waters! I toast fellows, odious men! I hate your odious provisos.

MIRABELL   Then we're agreed. Shall I kiss your hand upon the contract? And here comes one to be a witness to the sealing of the deed.

SCENE 6

[*To them*] MRS. FAINALL.

MILLAMANT   Fainall, what shall I do? Shall I have him? I think I must have him.

MRS. FAINALL   Aye, aye, take him, take him. What should you do?

2. I stipulate. "Item": used to introduce each item in a list.
3. Cosmetics were made of materials as repulsive as those that Mirabell names. "Vizards": masks.
4. Rich silk fabrics.

5. I.e., a crooked piece of firewood.
6. A sweet liqueur made of wine, honey, and spices. "Aniseed, cinnamon, citron and Barbados waters': alcoholic drinks.
7. Sleeping draughts.

MILLAMANT   Well then—I'll take my death I'm in a horrid fright—Fainall, I shall never say it—well—I think—I'll endure you.

MRS. FAINALL   Fy, fy, have him, have him, and tell him so in plain terms: for I am sure you have a mind to him.

MILLAMANT   Are you? I think I have—and the horrid man looks as if he thought so too.—Well, you ridiculous thing you, I'll have you.—I won't be kissed, nor I won't be thanked.—Here kiss my hand though.—So, hold your tongue now, don't say a word.

MRS. FAINALL   Mirabell, there's a necessity for your obedience—you have neither time to talk nor stay. My mother is coming; and in my conscience if she should see you, would fall into fits, and maybe not recover, time enough to return to Sir Rowland; who, as Foible tells me, is in a fair way to succeed. Therefore spare your ecstasies for another occasion, and slip down the back stairs, where Foible waits to consult you.

MILLAMANT   Aye, go, go. In the meantime I suppose you have said something to please me.

MIRABELL   I am all obedience.

SCENE 7

MILLAMANT, MRS. FAINALL.

MRS. FAINALL   Yonder Sir Wilfull's drunk, and so noisy that my mother has been forced to leave Sir Rowland to appease him; but he answers her only with singing and drinking.—What they may have done by this time I know not, but Petulant and he were upon quarreling as I came by.

MILLAMANT   Well, if Mirabell should not make a good husband, I am a lost thing; for I find I love him violently.

MRS. FAINALL   So it seems, for you mind not what's said to you.—If you doubt him, you had best take up with Sir Wilfull.

MILLAMANT   How can you name that superannuated lubber? foh!

SCENE 8

[To them] WITWOUD from drinking.

MRS. FAINALL   So, is the fray made up, that you have left 'em?

WITWOUD   Left 'em? I could stay no longer—I have laughed like ten christenings—I am tipsy with laughing.—If I had stayed any longer, I should have burst—I must have been let out and pieced in the sides like an unsized camlet.[8]—Yes, yes, the fray is composed; my lady came in like a *nolle prosequi*[9] and stopped the proceedings.

MILLAMANT   What was the dispute?

WITWOUD   That's the jest; there was no dispute. They could neither of 'em speak for rage; and so fell a-sputtering at one another like two roasting apples.

8. A fabric made by mixing wool and silk; "unsized" because not stiffened with some glutinous substance.

9. A Latin phrase indicating the withdrawal of a lawsuit.

SCENE 9

[*To them*] PETULANT *drunk.*

WITWOUD   Now, Petulant? All's over, all's well? Gad, my head begins to whim it about.—Why dost thou not speak? Thou art both as drunk and as mute as a fish.

PETULANT   Look you, Mrs. Millamant—if you can love me, dear nymph— say it—and that's the conclusion—pass on, or pass off—that's all.

WITWOUD   Thou hast uttered volumes, folios, in less than decimo sexto, my dear Lacedemonian.[1] Sirrah Petulant, thou art an epitomizer of words.

PETULANT   Witwoud—You are an annihilator of sense.

WITWOUD   Thou art a retailer of phrases, and dost deal in remnants of remnants, like a maker of pincushions. Thou art in truth (metaphorically speaking) a speaker of shorthand.

PETULANT   Thou art (without a figure) just one-half of an ass, and Baldwin yonder, thy half brother, is the rest.—A Gemini[2] of asses split, would make just four of you.

WITWOUD   Thou dost bite, my dear mustard-seed; kiss me for that.

PETULANT   Stand off—I'll kiss no more males.—I have kissed your twin yonder in a humor of reconciliation, till he—[*Hiccup.*]—rises upon my stomach like a radish.

MILLAMANT   Eh! filthy creature.—What was the quarrel?

PETULANT   There was no quarrel—there might have been a quarrel.

WITWOUD   If there had been words enow between 'em to have expressed provocation, they had gone together by the ears like a pair of castanets.

PETULANT   You were the quarrel.

MILLAMANT   Me!

PETULANT   If I have a humor to quarrel, I can make less matters conclude premises.—If you are not handsome, what then, if I have a humor to prove it?—If I shall have my reward, say so; if not, fight for your face the next time yourself.—I'll go sleep.

WITWOUD   Do, wrap thyself up like a woodlouse, and dream revenge— and hear me, if thou canst learn to write by tomorrow morning, pen me a challenge.—I'll carry it for thee.

PETULANT   Carry your mistress's monkey a spider—go flea dogs, and read romances—I'll go to bed to my maid.[3]

MRS. FAINALL   He's horridly drunk—how came you all in this pickle?

WITWOUD   A plot, a plot, to get rid of the knight—your husband's advice; but he sneaked off.

---

1. Spartans; people of few words. "Folios": books of the largest size. "Decimo sexto": a book of the smallest size.
2. The two Roman deities, the twins Castor and Pollux, for whom one of the signs of the zodiac is named. "Baldwin": the name of the ass in the beast

epic, *Reynard the Fox* (ca. 1175–1250).
3. Monkeys were supposed to eat spiders. Petulant scornfully contrasts what he imagines to be Witwoud's technique with his lady with his own more vigorous and direct program for the rest of the evening.

SCENE 10

SIR WILFULL *drunk*, LADY WISHFORT, WITWOUD, MILLAMANT, MRS. FAINALL.

LADY WISHFORT Out upon't, out upon't! At years of discretion, and comport yourself at this rantipole[4] rate!

SIR WILFULL No offense, aunt.

LADY WISHFORT Offense? As I'm a person, I'm ashamed of you.—Fogh! how you stink of wine! D'ye think my niece will ever endure such a borachio![5] you're an absolute borachio.

SIR WILFULL Borachio!

LADY WISHFORT At a time when you should commence an amour, and put your best foot foremost—

SIR WILFULL 'Sheart, an you grutch[6] me your liquor, make a bill.—Give me more drink, and take my purse.

[*Sings.*] Prithee fill me the glass
　　　　　'Till it laugh in my face,
　　With ale that is potent and mellow;
　　　　　He that whines for a lass
5　　　　　Is an ignorant ass,
　　For a bumper[7] has not its fellow.

But if you would have me marry my cousin—say the word and I'll do't— Wilfull will do't, that's the word—Wilfull will do't, that's my crest—my motto I have forgot.[8]

LADY WISHFORT My nephew's a little overtaken, cousin—but 'tis with drinking your health—O' my word you are obliged to him—

SIR WILFULL *In vino veritas,*[9] aunt.—If I drunk your health today, cousin—I am a borachio. But if you have a mind to be married, say the word, and send for the piper; Wilfull will do't. If not, dust it away, and let's have t'other round.—Tony, 'ods heart, where's Tony?—Tony's an honest fellow, but he spits after a bumper, and that's a fault—

[*Sings.*] We'll drink and we'll never ha' done, boys,
　　Put the glass then around with the sun, boys,
　　Let Apollo's example invite us;
　　　　　For he's drunk every night,
5　　　　　And that makes him so bright,
　　That he's able next morning to light us.

The sun's a good pimple,[1] an honest soaker, he has a cellar at your Antipodes. If I travel, aunt, I touch at your Antipodes.—Your Antipodes are a good rascally sort of topsy-turvy fellows.—If I had a bumper, I'd stand upon my head and drink a health to 'em.—A match or no match, cousin, with the hard name?—aunt, Wilfull will do't. If she has her maidenhead, let her look to't; if she has not, let her keep her own counsel in the meantime, and cry out at the nine months' end.

_____

4. Rakish.
5. Drunkard (spanish).
6. Grudge.
7. A wineglass filled to the brim. The word comes from the custom of touching (bumping) glasses when drinking toasts.

8. A coat of arms had a crest—a helmet surmounting the shield—and a motto. In his drunkenness, Sir Wilfull confuses the two.
9. In wine [there is] truth (Latin).
1. Boon companion.

MILLAMANT   Your pardon, madam, I can stay no longer—Sir Wilfull grows very powerful. Egh! how he smells! I shall be overcome if I stay. Come, cousin.

SCENE 11

LADY WISHFORT, SIR WILFULL WITWOUD, MR. WITWOUD, FOIBLE.

LADY WISHFORT   Smells! he would poison a tallow-chandler and his family. Beastly creature, I know not what to do with him. Travel, quoth a'; aye, travel, travel, get thee gone, get thee but far enough, to the Saracens, or the Tartars, or the Turks—for thou art not fit to live in a Christian commonwealth, thou beastly pagan.

SIR WILFULL   Turks, no; no Turks, aunt. Your Turks are infidels, and believe not in the grape. Your Mahometan, your Mussulman is a dry stinkard.—No offense, aunt. My map says that your Turk is not so honest a man as your Christian.—I cannot find by the map that your Mufti[2] is orthodox—whereby it is a plain case, that orthodox is a hard word, aunt, and—[Hiccup.]—Greek for claret.

[Sings.]   To drink is a Christian diversion.
                     Unknown to the Turk or the Persian:
                        Let Mahometan fools
                        Live by heathenish rules,
5   And be damned over tea cups and coffee.
                        But let British lads sing,
                        Crown a health to the king,
                        And a fig for your sultan and sophy.[3]

Ah, Tony!   [FOIBLE whispers LADY WISHFORT.]

LADY WISHFORT   Sir Rowland impatient? Good lack! what shall I do with this beastly tumbrel?—Go lie down and sleep, you sot—or as I'm a person, I'll have you bastinadoed[4] with broomsticks. Call up the wenches with broomsticks.

SIR WILFULL   Ahay? Wenches, where are the wenches?

LADY WISHFORT   Dear cousin Witwoud, get him away, and you will bind me to you inviolably. I have an affair of moment that invades me with some precipitation—you will oblige me to all futurity.

WITWOUD   Come, knight.—Pox on him, I don't know what to say to him.—Will you go to a cockmatch?

SIR WILFULL   With a wench, Tony? Is she a shakebag,[5] sirrah? Let me bite your cheek for that.

WITWOUD   Horrible! He has a breath like a bagpipe.—Aye, aye, come, will you march, my Salopian?[6]

SIR WILFULL   Lead on, little Tony—I'll follow thee, my Anthony, my Tantony. Sirrah, thou shalt be my Tantony, and I'll be thy pig.[7]

---

2. The Grand Mufti, head of the state religion of Turkey. Muslims do not drink alcohol.
3. The shah of Persia.
4. Punished by beating the soles of the feet. "Tumbrel": dung cart.

5. Gamecock.
6. Inhabitant of Shropshire.
7. St. Anthony (hence "Tantony"), the patron of swineherds, was represented accompanied by a pig.

—And a fig for your sultan and sophy.

LADY WISHFORT   This will never do. It will never make a match—at least before he has been abroad.

SCENE 12

LADY WISHFORT, WAITWELL *disguised as for* SIR ROWLAND.

LADY WISHFORT   Dear Sir Rowland, I am confounded with confusion at the retrospection of my own rudeness—I have more pardons to ask than the Pope distributes in the Year of Jubilee. But I hope where there is likely to be so near an alliance—we may unbend the severity of decorum—and dispense with a little ceremony.

WAITWELL   My impatience, madam, is the effect of my transport—and till I have the possession of your adorable person, I am tantalized on the rack; and do but hang, madam, on the tenter[8] of expectation.

LADY WISHFORT   You have excess of gallantry, Sir Rowland; and press things to a conclusion, with a most prevailing vehemence.—But a day or two for decency of marriage.—

WAITWELL   For decency of funeral, madam. The delay will break my heart—or if that should fail, I shall be poisoned. My nephew will get an inkling of my designs, and poison me—and I would willingly starve him before I die—I would gladly go out of the world with that satisfaction.— That would be some comfort to me, if I could but live so long as to be revenged on that unnatural viper.

LADY WISHFORT   Is he so unnatural, say you? Truly I would contribute much both to the saving of your life and the accomplishment of your revenge—Not that I respect[9] myself; though he has been a perfidious wretch to me.

WAITWELL   Perfidious to you!

LADY WISHFORT   O Sir Rowland, the hours that he has died away at my feet, the tears that he has shed, the oaths that he has sworn, the palpitations that he has felt, the trances and the tremblings, the ardors and the ecstasies, the kneelings, and the risings, the heart-heavings and the hand-gripings, the pangs and the pathetic regards of his protesting eyes! Oh, no memory can register.

WAITWELL   What, my rival! Is the rebel my rival? a'dies.

LADY WISHFORT   No, don't kill him at once, Sir Rowland, starve him gradually inch by inch.

WAITWELL   I'll do't. In three weeks he shall be barefoot; in a month out at knees with begging an alms—he shall starve upward and upward, till he has nothing living but his head, and then go out in a stink like a candle's end upon a saveall.[1]

LADY WISHFORT   Well, Sir Rowland, you have the way.—You are no novice in the labyrinth of love—you have the clue—but as I am a person, Sir Rowland, you must not attribute my yielding to any sinister appetite, or indigestion of widowhood; nor impute my complacency to any lethargy

---

8. A frame for stretching cloth on hooks so that it may dry without losing its original shape (cf. the phrase "to be on tenterhooks").

9. Consider.
1. A small pan inserted into a candlestick to catch the drippings of the candle.

of continuence.—I hope you do not think me prone to any iteration of
nuptials.—

WAITWELL   Far be it from me—

LADY WISHFORT   If you do, I protest I must recede—or think that I have
made a prostitution of decorums, but in the vehemence of compassion,
and to save the life of a person of so much importance—

WAITWELL   I esteem it so—

LADY WISHFORT   Or else you wrong my condescension—

WAITWELL   I do no, I do not—

LADY WISHFORT   Indeed you do.

WAITWELL   I do not, fair shrine of virtue.

LADY WISHFORT   If you think the least scruple of carnality was an ingredient—

WAITWELL   Dear madam, no. You are all camphire[2] and frankincense, all
chastity and odor.

LADY WISHFORT   Or that—

SCENE 13

[To them] FOIBLE.

FOIBLE   Madam, the dancers are ready, and there's one with a letter, who
must deliver it into your own hands.

LADY WISHFORT   Sir Rowland, will you give me leave? Think favorably,
judge candidly, and conclude you have found a person who would suffer
racks in honor's cause, dear Sir Rowland, and will wait on you incessantly.[3]

SCENE 14

WAITWELL, FOIBLE.

WAITWELL   Fie, fie!—What a slavery have I undergone; spouse, hast thou
any cordial? I want spirits.

FOIBLE   What a washy rogue art thou, to pant thus for a quarter of an
hour's lying and swearing to a fine lady?

WAITWELL   O, she is the antidote to desire. Spouse, thou wilt fare the
worse for't—I shall have no appetite for iteration of nuptials—this eight
and forty hours—by this hand I'd rather be a chairman in the dog days[4]—
than act Sir Rowland till this time tomorrow.

SCENE 15

[To them] LADY WISHFORT *with a letter.*

LADY WISHFORT   Call in the dancers.—Sir Rowland, we'll sit, if you please,
and see the entertainment.

[Dance.]

2. Camphor was considered an effective antidote
to sexual desire.
3. Immediately.
4. I.e., one who carries a sedan chair during the

hottest part of the summer. July and August are
called the "dog days" becuase during these months
the Dog Star, Sirius, rises and sets with the sun.

Now with your permission, Sir Rowland, I will peruse my letter.—I would open it in your presence, because I would not make you uneasy. If it should make you uneasy, I would burn it—speak if it does—but you may see, the superscription is like a woman's hand.

FOIBLE [*To him.*] By heaven! Mrs. Marwood's, I know it—my heart aches—get it from her.—

WAITWELL A woman's hand? No, madam, that's no woman's hand, I see that already. That's somebody whose throat must be cut.

LADY WISHFORT Nay, Sir Rowland, since you give me a proof of your passion by your jealousy, I promise you I'll make a return, by a frank communication—you shall see it—we'll open it together—look you here.—[*Reads.*]—*Madam, though unknown to you* (Look you there, 'tis from nobody that I know.)—*I have that honor for your character, that I think myself obliged to let you know you are abused. He who pretends to be Sir Rowland is a cheat and a rascal*—O Heavens! what's this?

FOIBLE Unfortunate, all's ruined.

WAITWELL How, how, let me see, let me see—[*Reads.*]—*A rascal and disguised, and suborned for that imposture*—O villainy! O villainy!—*by the contrivance of*—

LADY WISHFORT I shall faint, I shall die, oh!

FOIBLE [*To him.*] Say, 'tis your nephew's hand.—Quickly, his plot, swear, swear it.—

WAITWELL Here's a villain! Madam, don't you perceive it, don't you see it?

LADY WISHFORT Too well, too well. I have seen too much.

WAITWELL I told you at first I knew the hand—A woman's hand? The rascal writes a sort of a large hand, your Roman hand—I saw there was a throat to be cut presently. If he were my son, as he is my nephew, I'd pistol him—

FOIBLE O treachery! But are you sure, Sir Rowland, it is his writing?

WAITWELL Sure? Am I here? Do I live? Do I love this pearl of India? I have twenty letters in my pocket from him in the same character.

LADY WISHFORT How!

FOIBLE O, what luck it is, Sir Rowland, that you were present at this juncture! This was the business that brought Mr. Mirabell disguised to Madam Millamant this afternoon. I thought something was contriving, when he stole by me and would have hid his face.

LADY WISHFORT How, how!—I heard the villain was in the house indeed; and now I remember, my niece went away abruptly, when Sir Wilfull was to have made his addresses.

FOIBLE Then, then, madam, Mr. Mirabell waited for her in her chamber; but I would not tell your ladyship to discompose you when you were to receive Sir Rowland.

WAITWELL Enough, his date is short.

FOIBLE No, good Sir Rowland, don't incur the law.

WAITWELL Law! I care not for law. I can but die, and 'tis in a good cause— my lady shall be satisfied of my truth and innocence, though it cost me my life.

LADY WISHFORT No, dear Sir Rowland, don't fight. If you should be killed I must never show my face—or be hanged—O, consider my reputation,

Sir Rowland—no, you shan't fight—I'll go and examine my niece; I'll make her confess. I conjure you, Sir Rowland, by all your love not to fight.

WAITWELL   I am charmed, madam, I obey. But some proof you must let me give you—I'll go for a black box, which contains the writings of my whole estate, and deliver that into your hands.

LADY WISHFORT   Aye, dear Sir Rowland, that will be some comfort. Bring the black box.

WAITWELL   And may I presume to bring a contract to be signed this night? May I hope so far?

LADY WISHFORT   Bring what you will; but come alive, pray come alive. O, this is a happy discovery.

WAITWELL   Dead or alive I'll come—and married we will be in spite of treachery; aye, and get an heir that shall defeat the last remaining glimpse of hope in my abandoned nephew. Come, my buxom widow:

> E'er long you shall substantial proof receive
> That I'm an arrant[5] knight———

FOIBLE.   Or arrant knave.

Act 5—Scene continues.

SCENE 1

LADY WISHFORT and FOIBLE.

LADY WISHFORT   Out of my house, out of my house, thou viper, thou serpent, that I have fostered; thou bosom traitress, that I raised from nothing.—Begone, begone, begone, go, go—that I took from washing of old gauze and weaving of dead hair,[6] with a bleak blue nose over a chafing dish of starved embers, and dining behind a traverse rag,[7] in a shop no bigger than a bird cage—go, go, starve again, do, do.

FOIBLE   Dear madam, I'll beg pardon on my knees.

LADY WISHFORT   Away, out, out, go set up for yourself again.—Do, drive a trade, do, with your three-pennyworth of small ware, flaunting upon a packthread, under a brandy-seller's bulk or against a dead wall by a ballad-monger. Go, hang out an old frisoneer-gorget, with a yard of yellow colberteen[8] again; do; an old gnawed mask, two rows of pins and a child's fiddle; a glass necklace with the beads broken, and a quilted nightcap with one ear. Go, go, drive a trade—these were your commodities, you treacherous trull, this was the merchandise you dealt in when I took you into my house, placed you next myself, and made you governante[9] of my whole family. You have forgot this, have you, now you have feathered your nest?

FOIBLE   No, no, dear madam. Do but hear me, have but a moment's

---

5. The two words errant ("wandering," as in "knight-errant") and arrant ("thorough-going," "notorious") were originally the same and were still pronounced alike. This makes possible Foible's pun.
6. Foible had been a wigmaker.

7. A worn cloth, used to curtain off part of a room.
8. A French imitation of Italian lace. "Frisoneer-gorget: a woolen garment that covers the neck and breast.
9. Housekeeper.

patience—I'll confess all. Mr. Mirabell seduced me; I am not the first
that he has wheedled with his dissembling tongue. Your ladyship's own
wisdom has been deluded by him, then how should I, a poor ignorant,
defend myself? O madam, if you knew but what he promised me, and
how he assured me your ladyship should come to no damage—or else
the wealth of the Indies should not have bribed me to conspire against
so good, so sweet, so kind a lady as you have been to me.

LADY WISHFORT No damage? What, to betray me, to marry me to a cast[1]
servingman; to make me a receptacle, an hospital for a decayed pimp?
No damage? O, thou frontless[2] impudence, more than a big-bellied
actress.

FOIBLE Pray do but hear me, madam. He could not marry your ladyship,
madam.—No, indeed, his marriage was to have been void in law; for he
was married to me first, to secure your ladyship. He could not have bedded your ladyship; for if he had consummated with your ladyship, he
must have run the risk of the law, and been put upon his clergy.[3]—Yes,
indeed, I inquired of the law in that case before I would meddle or make.[4]

LADY WISHFORT What, then I have been your property, have I? I have
been convenient to you, it seems.—While you were catering for Mirabell,
I have been broker for you? What, have you made a passive bawd of
me?—This exceeds all precedent; I am brought to fine uses, to become
a botcher of second-hand marriages between Abigails and Andrews![5] I'll
couple you. Yes, I'll baste you together, you and your philander. I'll
Duke's-Place[6] you, as I'm a person. Your turtle is in custody already: you
shall coo in the same cage, if there be constable or warrant in the parish.

FOIBLE O, that ever I was born, O, that I was ever married.—A bride, aye,
I shall be a Bridewell-bride.[7] Oh!

SCENE 2

MRS. FAINALL, FOIBLE.

MRS. FAINALL Poor Foible, what's the matter?

FOIBLE O madam, my lady's gone for a constable. I shall be had to a
justice, and put to Bridewell to beat hemp; poor Waitwell's gone to prison
already.

MRS. FAINALL Have a good heart, Foible. Mirabell's gone to give security
for him. This is all Marwood's and my husband's doing.

FOIBLE Yes, yes, I know it, madam; she was in my lady's closet, and overheard all that you said to me before dinner. She sent the letter to my
lady; and that missing effect, Mr. Fainall laid this plot to arrest Waitwell,
when he pretended to go for the papers; and in the meantime Mrs. Marwood declared all to my lady.

1. Cast off, discharged.
2. Shameless.
3. I.e., pleaded Æenefit of clergy," originally the
privilege of the clergy to be tried for felony before
ecclesiastical, not secular, courts; by Congreve's
time it had become the privilege to plead exemption from a penal sentence granted a person who
could read and was a first offender.
4. A dialectal phrase; the two words mean approximately the same thing.
5. "Abigail" and "Andrew" were generic names for
maidservants and servingmen. "Botcher": a
mender of old clothes. Lady Wishfort means something like "a patcher-up of marriages."
6. Notorious for its thriving trade in unlicensed
marriages. "Philander": lover.
7. Bridewell was the house of correction for
women in London.

MRS. FAINALL Was there no mention made of me in the letter?—My mother does not suspect my being in the confederacy? I fancy Marwood has not told her, though she has told my husband.

FOIBLE Yes, madam; but my lady did not see that part. We stifled the letter before she read so far. Has that mischievous devil told Mr. Fainall of your ladyship then?

MRS. FAINALL Aye, all's out, my affair with Mirabell, everything discovered. This is the last day of our living together, that's my comfort.

FOIBLE Indeed, madam, and so 'tis a comfort if you knew all.—He has been even with your ladyship; which I could have told you long enough since, but I love to keep peace and quietness by my good will. I had rather bring friends together than set 'em at distance. But Mrs. Marwood and he are nearer related than ever their parents thought for!

MRS. FAINALL Say'st thou so, Foible? Canst thou prove this?

FOIBLE I can take my oath of it, madam. So can Mrs. Mincing; we have had many a fair word from Madam Marwood, to conceal something that passed in our chamber one evening when you were at Hyde Park—and we were thought to have gone a-walking; but we went up unawares— though we were sworn to secrecy too; Madam Marwood took a book and swore us upon it, but it was but a book of poems.—So long as it was not a Bible-oath, we may break it with a safe conscience.

MRS. FAINALL This discovery is the most opportune thing I could wish. Now, Mincing?

SCENE 3

[To them] MINCING.

MINCING My lady would speak with Mrs. Foible, mem. Mr. Mirabell is with her; he has set your spouse at liberty, Mrs. Foible, and would have you hide yourself in my lady's closet, till my old lady's anger is abated. O, my old lady is in a perilous passion, at something Mr. Fainall has said; he swears, and my old lady cries. There's a fearful hurricane, I vow. He says, mem, how that he'll have my lady's fortune made over to him, or he'll be divorced.

MRS. FAINALL Does your lady or Mirabell know that?

MINCING Yes, mem, they have sent me to see if Sir Wilfull be sober, and to bring him to them. My lady is resolved to have him, I think, rather than lose such a vast sum as six thousand pound. O, come, Mrs. Foible, I hear my old lady.

MRS. FAINALL Foible, you must tell Mincing that she must prepare to vouch when I call her.

FOIBLE Yes, yes, madam.

MINCING O yes, mem, I'll vouch anything for your ladyship's service, be what it will.

SCENE 4

MRS. FAINALL, LADY WISHFORT, MARWOOD.

LADY WISHFORT O my dear friend, how can I enumerate the benefit that I have received from your goodness? To you I owe the timely discovery of the false vows of Mirabell; to you I owe the detection of the imposter Sir Rowland. And now you are become an intercessor with my son-in-law, to save the honor of my house, and compound for the frailties of my daughter. Well, friend, you are enough to reconcile me to the bad world, or else I would retire to deserts and solitudes, and feed harmless sheep by groves and purling streams. Dear Marwood, let us leave the world and retire by ourselves and be shepherdesses.

MRS. MARWOOD Let us first dispatch the affair in hand, madam. We shall have leisure to think of retirement afterwards. Here is one who is concerned in the treaty.

LADY WISHFORT O daughter, daughter, is it possible thou should'st be my child, bone of my bone, and flesh of my flesh, and as I may say, another me, and yet transgress the most minute particle of severe virtue? Is it possible you should lean aside to iniquity, who have been cast in the direct mold of virtue? I have not only been a mold but a pattern for you, and a model for you, after you were brought into the world.

MRS. FAINALL I don't understand your ladyship.

LADY WISHFORT Not understand? Why, have you not been naught? Have you not been sophisticated? Not understand? Here I am ruined to compound[8] for your caprices and your cuckoldoms. I must pawn my plate and my jewels, and ruin my niece, and all little enough—

MRS. FAINALL I am wronged and abused, and so are you. 'Tis a false accusation, as false as hell, as false as your friend there, aye, or your friend's friend, my false husband.

MRS. MARWOOD My friend, Mrs. Fainall? Your husband my friend, what do you mean?

MRS. FAINALL I know what I mean, madam, and so do you; and so shall the world at a time convenient.

MRS. MARWOOD I am sorry to see you so passionate, madam. More temper[9] would look more like innocence. But I have done. I am sorry my zeal to serve your ladyship and family should admit of misconstruction, or make me liable to affront. You will pardon me, madam, if I meddle no more with an affair in which I am not personally concerned.

LADY WISHFORT O dear friend, I am so ashamed that you should meet with such returns.—You ought to ask pardon on your knees, ungrateful creature; she deserves more from you than all your life can accomplish— O, don't leave me destitute in this perplexity—no, stick to me, my good genius.

MRS. FAINALL I tell you, madam, you're abused—Stick to you? aye, like a leech, to suck your best blood—She'll drop off when she's full. Madam, you shan't pawn a bodkin, nor part with a brass counter,[1] in composition for me. I defy 'em all. Let 'em prove their aspersions; I know my own innocence, and dare stand a trial.

8. I.e., come to terms by making a monetary settlement. "Naught": wicked. "Sophisticated": corrupted.

9. Moderation
1. An imitation coin, used in games of chance. "Bodkin": ornamental hairpin.

SCENE 5

LADY WISHFORT, MARWOOD.

LADY WISHFORT   Why, if she should be innocent, if she should be wronged after all, ha? I don't know what to think—and I promise you, her education has been unexceptionable—I may say it; for I chiefly made it my own care to initiate her very infancy in the rudiments of virtue, and to impress upon her tender years a young odium and aversion to the very sight of men.—Aye, friend, she would have shrieked if she had but seen a man, till she was in her teens. As I'm a person, 'tis true—she was never suffered to play with a male child, though but in coats. Nay, her very babies[2] were of the feminine gender—O, she never looked a man in the face but her own father, or the chaplain, and him we made a shift to put upon her for a woman, by the help of his long garments, and his sleek face; till she was going in her fifteen.

MRS. MARWOOD   'Twas much she should be deceived so long.

LADY WISHFORT   I warrant you, or she would never have borne to have been catechized by him; and have heard his long lectures against singing and dancing, and such debaucheries; and going to filthy plays; and profane music-meetings, where the lewd trebles squeek nothing but bawdry, and the basses roar blasphemy. O, she would have swooned at the sight or name of an obscene play-book—and can I think after all this, that my daughter can be naught? What, a whore? And thought it excommunication to set her foot within the door of a playhouse? O dear friend, I can't believe it, no, no; as she says, let him prove it, let him prove it.

MRS. MARWOOD   Prove it, madam? What, and have your name prostituted in a public court; yours and your daughter's reputation worried at the bar by a pack of bawling lawyers? To be ushered in with an O Yes[3] of scandal; and have your case opened by an old fumbler lecher in a quoif[4] like a man midwife, to bring your daughter's infamy to light; to be a theme for legal punsters, and quibblers by the statute; and become a jest, against a rule of court, where there is no precedent for a jest in any record, not even in Doomsday Book;[5] to discompose the gravity of the bench, and provoke naughty interrogatories in more naughty law-Latin; while the good judge, tickled with the proceeding, simpers under a gray beard, and fidges off and on his cushion as if he had swallowed cantharides, or sate upon cowhage.[6]

LADY WISHFORT   O, 'tis very hard!

MRS. MARWOOD   And then to have my young revelers of the Temple[7] take notes, like 'prentices at a conventicle; and after talk it over again in commons, or before drawers in an eating house.

LADY WISHFORT   Worse and worse.

MRS. MARWOOD   Nay, this is nothing; if it would end here 'twere well. But it must after this be consigned by the shorthand writers to the public

2. Dolls.
3. The formula for opening court, a variant of Old French *Oyez,* "Hear ye."
4. The cap of a sergeant-at-law.
5. Or Domesday Book, the survey of England made in 1085–86 by William the Conqueror.

6. A plant that causes intolerable itching. "Fidges": fidgets. "Cantharides": Spanish fly, an irritant.
7. The law students at the Temple, one of the Inns of Court.

press; and from thence be transferred to the hands, nay into the throats and lungs of hawkers, with voices more licentious than the loud flounderman's or the woman that cries gray peas;[8] and this you must hear till you are stunned; nay, you must hear nothing else for some days.

LADY WISHFORT   O, 'tis insupportable. No, no, dear friend, make it up, make it up; aye, aye, I'll compound. I'll give up all, myself and my all, my niece and her all—anything, everything for composition.

MRS. MARWOOD   Nay, madam, I advise nothing; I only lay before you, as a friend, the inconveniencies which perhaps you have overseen.[9] Here comes Mr. Fainall. If he will be satisfied to huddle up all in silence, I shall be glad. You must think I would rather congratulate than condole with you.

SCENE 6

FAINALL, LADY WISHFORT, MRS. MARWOOD.

LADY WISHFORT   Aye, aye, I do not doubt it, dear Marwood. No, no, I do not doubt it.

FAINALL   Well, madam; I have suffered myself to be overcome by the importunity of this lady, your friend, and am content you shall enjoy your own proper estate during life; on condition you oblige yourself never to marry, under such penalty as I think convenient.

LADY WISHFORT   Never to marry?

FAINALL   No more Sir Rowlands—the next imposture may not be so timely detected.

MRS. MARWOOD   That condition, I dare answer, my lady will consent to, without difficulty; she has already but too much experienced the perfidiousness of men. Besides, madam, when we retire to our pastoral solitude we shall bid adieu to all other thoughts.

LADY WISHFORT   Aye, that's true; but in case of necessity; as of health, or some such emergency—

FAINALL   O, if you are prescribed marriage, you shall be considered; I will only reserve to myself the power to choose for you. If your physic be wholesome, it matters not who is your apothecary. Next, my wife shall settle on me the remainder of her fortune, not made over already; and for her maintenance depend entirely on my discretion.

LADY WISHFORT   This is most inhumanly savage; exceeding the barbarity of a Muscovite husband.

FAINALL   I learned it from His Czarish Majesty's retinue,[1] in a winter evening's conference over brandy and pepper, amongst other secrets of matrimony and policy, as they are at present practiced in the northern hemisphere. But this must be agreed unto, and that positively. Lastly, I will be endowed, in right of my wife, with that six thousand pound, which is the moiety of Mrs. Millamant's fortune in your possession; and which she has forfeited (as will appear by the last will and testament of your deceased husband, Sir Jonathan Wishfort) by her disobedience in contracting herself against your consent or knowledge; and by refusing the

8. Street vendors celebrated for their stridency.
9. Overlooked.

1. Peter the Great of Russia visited London in 1698.

offered match with Sir Wilfull Witwoud, which you, like a careful aunt, had provided for her.

LADY WISHFORT My nephew was *non compos*,[2] and could not make his addresses.

FAINALL I come to make demands—I'll hear no objections.

LADY WISHFORT You will grant me time to consider?

FAINALL Yes, while the instrument is drawing, to which you must set your hand till more sufficient deeds can be perfected: which I will take care shall be done with all possible speed. In the meanwhile I will go for the said instrument, and till my return you may balance this matter in your own discretion.

SCENE 7

LADY WISHFORT, MRS. MARWOOD.

LADY WISHFORT This insolence is beyond all precedent, all parallel; must I be subject to this merciless villain?

MRS. MARWOOD 'Tis severe indeed, madam, that you should smart for your daughter's wantonness.

LADY WISHFORT 'Twas against my consent that she married this barbarian, but she would have him, though her year was not out.[3]—Ah! her first husband, my son Languish, would not have carried it thus. Well, that was my choice, this is hers; she is matched now with a witness[4]—I shall be mad, dear friend. Is there no comfort for me? Must I live to be confiscated at this rebel-rate?—Here comes two more of my Egyptian plagues,[5] too.

SCENE 8

[*To them*] MILLAMANT, SIR WILFULL.

SIR WILFULL Aunt, your servant.

LADY WISHFORT Out, caterpillar, call not me aunt; I know thee not.

SIR WILFULL I confess I have been a little in disguise,[6] as they say— 'Sheart! and I'm sorry for't. What would you have? I hope I committed no offense, aunt—and if I did, I am willing to make satisfaction; and what can a man say fairer? If I have broke anything, I'll pay for't, an' it cost a pound. And so let that content for what's past, and make no more words. For what's to come, to pleasure you I'm willing to marry my cousin. So, pray, let's all be friends. She and I are agreed upon the matter before a witness.

LADY WISHFORT How's this, dear niece? Have I any comfort? Can this be true?

MILLAMANT I am content to be a sacrifice to your repose, madam; and to convince you that I had no hand in the plot, as you were misinformed,

2. I.e., *non compos mentis*: of unsound mind (Latin).
3. The conventional period of mourning for a widow was one year.
4. With a vengeance.

5. The plagues visited by God on Pharaoh until he agreed to release the Israelites from bondage (Exodus 7–12).
6. Drunk.

I have laid my commands on Mirabell to come in person, and be a witness that I give my hand to this flower of knighthood; and for the contract that passed between Mirabell and me, I have obliged him to make a resignation of it in your ladyship's presence.—He is without, and waits your leave for admittance.

LADY WISHFORT   Well, I'll swear I am something revived at this testimony of your obedience; but I cannot admit that traitor—I fear I cannot fortify myself to support his appearance. He is as terrible to me as a Gorgon;[7] if I see him, I fear I shall turn to stone, petrify incessantly.

MILLAMANT   If you disoblige him, he may resent your refusal, and insist upon the contract still. Then 'tis the last time he will be offensive to you.

LADY WISHFORT   Are you sure it will be the last time?—If I were sure of that—Shall I never see him again?

MILLAMANT   Sir Wilfull, you and he are to travel together, are you not?

SIR WILFULL   'Sheart, the gentleman's a civil gentleman, aunt, let him come in; why, we are sworn brothers and fellow travelers. We are to be Pylades[8] and Orestes, he and I. He is to be my interpreter in foreign parts. He has been overseas once already; and with proviso that I marry my cousin, will cross 'em once again, only to bear my company.—'Sheart, I'll call him in—an I set on't once, he shall come in; and see who'll hinder him.   [Goes to the door and hems.]

MRS. MARWOOD   This is precious fooling, if it would pass; but I'll know the bottom of it.

LADY WISHFORT   O dear Marwood, you are not going?

MARWOOD   Not far, madam; I'll return immediately.

SCENE 9

LADY WISHFORT, MILLAMANT, SIR WILFULL, MIRABELL.

SIR WILFULL [Aside.]   Look up, man, I'll stand by you. 'Sbud an she do frown, she can't kill you—besides—harkee, she dare not frown desperately, because her face is none of her own. 'Sheart, an she should her forehead would wrinkle like the coat of a cream cheese; but mum for that, fellow traveler.

MIRABELL   If a deep sense of the many injuries I have offered to so good a lady, with a sincere remorse, and a hearty contrition, can but obtain the least glance of compassion, I am too happy—Ah madam, there was a time—but let it be forgotten—I confess I have deservedly forfeited the high place I once held of sighing at your feet. Nay kill me not by turning from me in disdain—I come not to plead for favor—nay not for pardon. I am a suppliant only for pity—I am going where I never shall behold you more—

SIR WILFULL [Aside.]   How, fellow traveler!—You shall go by yourself then.

MIRABELL   Let me be pitied first, and afterwards forgotten—I ask no more.

SIR WILFULL   By'r Lady a very reasonable request, and will cost you nothing, aunt.—Come, come, forgive and forget, aunt. Why you must, an you are a Christian.

---

7. In Greek mythology, a hideous monster with snakes in her hair. Her glance turned people to stone.

8. The constant friend who journeyed with Orestes, the son and avenger of the murdered king Agamemnon.

MIRABELL Consider, madam, in reality you could not receive much prejudice; it was an innocent device, though I confess it had a face of guiltiness.—It was at most an artifice which love contrived—and errors which love produces have ever been accounted venial. At least think it is punishment enough that I have lost what in my heart I hold most dear, that to your cruel indignation, I have offered up this beauty, and with her my peace and quiet; nay, all my hopes of future comfort.

SIR WILFULL An he does not move me, would I may never be o' the quorum[9]—An it were not as good a deed as to drink, to give her to him again—I would I might never take shipping.—Aunt, if you don't forgive quickly I shall melt, I can tell you that. My contract went no farther than a little mouth glue,[1] and that's hardly dry.—One doleful sigh more from my fellow traveler and 'tis dissolved.

LADY WISHFORT Well, nephew, upon your account—Ah, he has a false insinuating tongue.—Well, sir, I will stifle my just resentment at my nephew's request. I will endeavor what I can to forget—but on proviso that you resign the contract with my niece immediately.

MIRABELL It is in writing and with papers of concern, but I have sent my servant for it and will deliver it to you, with all acknowledgements for your transcendent goodness.

LADY WISHFORT [Aside.] O, he has witchcraft in his eyes and tongue; when I did not see him I could have bribed a villain to his assassination; but his appearance rakes the embers which have so long lain smothered in my breast.—

SCENE 10

[To them] FAINALL, MRS. MARWOOD.

FAINALL Your date of deliberation, madam, is expired. Here is the instrument; are you prepared to sign?

LADY WISHFORT If I were prepared, I am not empowered. My niece exerts a lawful claim, having matched herself by my direction to Sir Wilfull.

FAINALL That sham is too gross to pass on me—though 'tis imposed on you, madam.

MILLAMANT Sir, I have given my consent.

MIRABELL And, sir, I have resigned my pretensions.

SIR WILFULL And, sir, I assert my right; and will maintain it in defiance of you, sir, and of your instrument. 'Sheart, an you talk of an instrument, sir, I have an old fox by my thigh shall hack your instrument of ram vellum[2] to shreds, sir. It shall not be sufficient for a *mittimus*[3] or a tailor's measure; therefore withdraw your instrument, sir, or by'r Lady I shall draw mine.

LADY WISHFORT Hold, nephew, hold.

MILLAMANT Good Sir Wilfull, respite your valor.

FAINALL Indeed? Are you provided of your guard, with your single beefeater[4] there? But I'm prepared for you; and insist upon my first proposal.

9. Justices of the peace, who were required to be present at the sessions of a court.
1. Literally, glue to be used by moistening with the tongue; but here, "glue made of mere words" and therefore not binding.

2. The legal instrument to be signed is written on vellum. "Fox": a kind of sword.
3. A warrant, committing a felon to jail.
4. Yeoman of the guard.

You shall submit your own estate to my management and absolutely make over my wife's to my sole use, as pursuant to the purport and tenor of this other covenant. I suppose, madam, your consent is not requisite in this case; nor, Mr. Mirabell, your resignation; nor, Sir Wilfull, your right—You may draw your fox if you please, sir, and make a bear garden[5] flourish somewhere else: for here it will not avail. This, my Lady Wishfort, must be subscribed, or your darling daughter's turned adrift, like a leaky hulk to sink or swim, as she and the current of this lewd town can agree.

LADY WISHFORT   Is there no means, no remedy, to stop my ruin? Ungrateful wretch! Dost thou not owe thy being, thy subsistence to my daughter's fortune?

FAINALL   I'll answer you when I have the rest of it in my possession.

MIRABELL   But that you would not accept of a remedy from my hands—I own I have not deserved you should owe any obligation to me; or else perhaps I could advise—

LADY WISHFORT   O, what? what? to save me and my child from ruin, from want, I'll forgive all that's past; nay, I'll consent to anything to come, to be delivered from this tyranny.

MIRABELL   Aye, madam, but that is too late; my reward is intercepted. You have disposed of her who only could have made me a compensation for all my services; but be it as it may, I am resolved I'll serve you. You shall not be wronged in this savage manner.

LADY WISHFORT   How! Dear Mr. Mirabell, can you be so generous at last! But it is not possible. Harkee, I'll break my nephew's match, you shall have my niece yet, and all her fortune, if you can but save me from this imminent danger.

MIRABELL   Will you? I take you at your word. I ask no more. I must have leave for two criminals to appear.

LADY WISHFORT   Aye, aye, anybody, anybody.

MIRABELL   Foible is one, and a penitent.

SCENE 11

[*To them*] MRS. FAINALL, FOIBLE, MINCING.

MRS. MARWOOD   O, my shame! These corrupt things are brought hither to expose me.

[MIRABELL *and* LADY WISHFORT *go to* MRS. FAINALL *and* FOIBLE.]

FAINALL   If it must all come out, why let 'em know it, 'tis but *the way of the world*. That shall not urge me to relinquish or abate one tittle of my terms; no, I will insist the more.

FOIBLE   Yes, indeed, madam, I'll take my Bible-oath of it.

MINCING   And so will I, mem.

LADY WISHFORT   O Marwood, Marwood, art thou false? My friend deceive me? Hast thou been a wicked accomplice with that profligate man?

MRS. MARWOOD   Have you so much ingratitude and injustice, to give credit against your friend to the aspersions of two such mercenary trulls?

MINCING   Mercenary, mem? I scorn your words. 'Tis true we found you

5. The place for bear baiting, frequented by a vulgar and unruly crowd.

and Mr. Fainall in the blue garret; by the same token, you swore us to secrecy upon Messalina's[6] poems. Mercenary? No, if we would have been mercenary, we should have held our tongues; you would have bribed us sufficiently.

FAINALL Go, you are an insignificant thing. Well, what are you the better for this! Is this Mr. Mirabell's expedient? I'll be put off no longer. You, thing that was a wife, shall smart for this. I will not leave thee wherewithal to hide thy shame: your body shall be naked as your reputation.

MRS. FAINALL I despise you and defy your malice.—You have aspersed me wrongfully.—I have proved your falsehood.—Go, you and your treacherous—I will not name it, but starve together—perish.

FAINALL Not while you are worth a groat, indeed, my dear. Madam, I'll be fooled no longer.

LADY WISHFORT Ah, Mr. Mirabell, this is small comfort, the detection of this affair.

MIRABELL O, in good time—Your leave for the other offender and penitent to appear, madam.

SCENE 12

[To them] WAITWELL with a box of writings.

LADY WISHFORT O Sir Rowland—Well, rascal.

WAITWELL What your ladyship pleases—I have brought the black box at last, madam.

MIRABELL Give it me. Madam, you remember your promise.

LADY WISHFORT Aye, dear sir.

MIRABELL Where are the gentlemen?

WAITWELL At hand, sir, rubbing their eyes, just risen from sleep.

FAINALL 'Sdeath, what's this to me? I'll not wait your private concerns.

SCENE 13

[To them] PETULANT, WITWOUD.

PETULANT How now? What's the matter? Who's hand's out?

WITWOUD Heyday! What, are you all got together, like players at the end of the last act?

MIRABELL You may remember, gentlemen, I once requested your hands as witnesses to a certain parchment.

WITWOUD Aye, I do, my hand I remember—Petulant set his mark.

MIRABELL You wrong him, his name is fairly written, as shall appear. You do not remember, gentlemen, anything of what that parchment contained— [Undoing the box.]

WITWOUD No.

PETULANT Not I. I writ, I read nothing.

MIRABELL Very well, now you shall know. Madam, your promise.

6. Mincing means *Miscellany*, a collection of poems by various writers, such as Dryden's popular *Miscellanies*. Messalina was the viciously debauched wife of the Roman emperor Claudius.

LADY WISHFORT   Aye, aye, sir, upon my honor.

MIRABELL   Mr. Fainall, it is now time that you should know that your lady, while she was at her own disposal, and before you had by your insinuations wheedled her out of a pretended settlement of the greatest part of her fortune—

FAINALL   Sir! Pretended!

MIRABELL   Yes, sir. I say that this lady while a widow, having, it seems, received some cautions respecting your inconstancy and tyranny of temper, which from her own partial opinion and fondness of you she could never have suspected—she did, I say, by the wholesome advice of friends and of sages learned in the laws of this land, deliver this same as her act and deed to me in trust, and to the uses within mentioned. You may read if you please—[*Holding out the parchment.*]—though perhaps what is written on the back may serve your occasions.

FAINALL   Very likely, sir. What's here? Damnation!—[*Reads.*] A *deed of conveyance of the whole estate real of Arabella Languish, widow, in trust to Edward Mirabell.* Confusion!

MIRABELL   Even so, sir, 'tis the way of the world, sir; of the widows of the world. I suppose this deed may bear an elder date than what you have obtained from your lady.

FAINALL   Perfidious fiend! Then thus I'll be revenged.

[*Offers to run at* MRS. FAINALL.]

SIR WILFULL   Hold, sir, now you may make your bear garden flourish somewhere else, sir.

FAINALL   Mirabell, you shall hear of this, sir, be sure you shall. Let me pass, oaf.

MRS. FAINALL   Madam, you seem to stifle your resentment: you had better give it vent.

MRS. MARWOOD   Yes, it shall have vent—and to your confusion, or I'll perish in the attempt.

SCENE THE LAST

LADY WISHFORT, MILLAMANT, MIRABELL, MRS. FAINALL, SIR WILFULL, PETULANT, WITWOUD, FOIBLE, MINCING, WAITWELL.

LADY WISHFORT   O daughter, daughter, 'tis plain thou hast inherited thy mother's prudence.

MRS. FAINALL   Thank Mr. Mirabell, a cautious friend, to whose advice all is owing.

LADY WISHFORT   Well, Mr. Mirabell, you have kept your promise and I must perform mine. First I pardon for your sake Sir Rowland there and Foible.—The next thing is to break the matter to my nephew—and how to do that—

MIRABELL   For that, madam, give yourself no trouble—let me have your consent.—Sir Wilfull is my friend; he has had compassion upon lovers, and generously engaged a volunteer in this action, for our service; and now designs to prosecute his travels.

SIR WILFULL   'Sheart, aunt, I have no mind to marry. My cousin's a fine lady, and the gentleman loves her, and she loves him, and they deserve one another. My resolution is to see foreign parts—I have set on't—and when I'm set on't, I must do't. And if these two gentlemen would travel too, I think they may be spared.

PETULANT   For my part, I say little—I think things are best off or on.

WITWOUD   Igad, I understand nothing of the matter—I'm in a maze yet; like a dog in a dancing school.

LADY WISHFORT   Well, sir, take her, and with her all the joy I can give you.

MILLAMANT   Why does not the man take me? Would you have me give myself to you over again?

MIRABELL   Aye, and over and over again—[*Kisses her hand.*]—I would have you as often as possibly I can. Well, Heaven grant I love you not too well, that's all my fear.

SIR WILFULL   'Sheart, you'll have time enough to toy after you're married; or if you will toy now, let us have a dance in the meantime; that we who are not lovers may have some other employment, besides looking on.

MIRABELL   With all my heart, dear Sir Wilfull. What shall we do for music?

FOIBLE   O, sir, some that were provided for Sir Rowland's entertainment are yet within call.

[A DANCE.]

LADY WISHFORT   As I am a person I can hold out no longer.—I have wasted my spirits so today already, that I am ready to sink under the fatigue; and I cannot but have some fears upon me yet, that my son Fainall will pursue some desperate course.

MIRABELL   Madam, disquiet not yourself on that account; to my knowledge his circumstances are such, he must of force comply. For my part, I will contribute all that in me lies to a reunion: in the meantime, madam—[*To* MRS. FAINALL.]—let me before these witnesses restore to you this deed of trust; it may be a means, well managed, to make you live easily together.

> From hence let those be warned, who mean to wed;
> Lest mutual falsehood stain the bridal bed:
> For each deceiver to his cost may find,
> That marriage frauds too oft are paid in kind

[*Exeunt omnes.*]

Epilogue

SPOKEN BY MRS. BRACEGIRDLE[7]

> After our Epilogue this crowd dismisses,
> I'm thinking how this play'll be pulled to pieces.
> But pray consider, e'er you doom its fall,
> How hard a thing 'twould be to please you all.
> 5   There are some critics so with spleen diseased,
> They scarcely come inclining to be pleased;
> And sure he must have more than mortal skill,

7. Anne Bracegirdle (ca. 1663–1748), the most brilliant actress of her generation. She created the role of Millamant. Congreve loved her, and it was rumored that they were secretly married.

Who pleases anyone against his will.
Then, all bad poets we are sure are foes,
10 And how their number's swelled the town well knows:
In shoals, I've marked 'em judging in the pit; ⎫
Though they're on no pretence for judgment fit, ⎬
But that they have been damned for want of wit. ⎭
Since when, they by their own offenses taught
15 Set up for spies on plays, and finding fault.
Others there are whose malice we'd prevent; ⎫
Such, who watch plays, with scurrilous intent ⎬
To mark out who by characters are meant. ⎭
And though no perfect likeness they can trace,
20 Yet each pretends to know the copied face.
These, with false glosses feed their own ill-nature,
And turn to libel, what was meant a *satire*.[8]
May such malicious fops this fortune find,
To think themselves alone the fools designed:
25 If any are so arrogantly vain, ⎫
To think they singly can support a scene, ⎬
And furnish fool enough to entertain. ⎭
For well the learn'd and the judicious know, ⎫
That satire scorns to stoop so meanly low, ⎬
30 As any one abstracted fop to show. ⎭
For, as when painters form a matchless face,
They from each fair one catch some different grace,
And shining features in one portrait blend,
To which no single beauty must pretend:
35 So poets oft do in one piece expose
Whole *belles assemblées* of coquettes and beaux.

1700

8. Pronounce *nā-ter* and *sā-ter*.

MARY ASTELL
1666–1731

Daughter of a Newcastle merchant, Mary Astell was encouraged and educated by her
uncle, a clergyman. She never forgot what he taught her: a confidence in her own
reason and a religious faith entirely compatible with reason. In her twenties she
moved to Chelsea, on the outskirts of London, where she spent the rest of her life.
There she championed the causes of women and the Church of England, and her
vigorous way of arguing (not only in print but in person) won her many admirers,
both male and female, as well as a few enemies. Her best-known work, *A Serious
Proposal to the Ladies* (1694), was, like the rest of her writings, published anonymously ("by a Lover of her Sex"). It advocates the founding of a monastic school or
retreat for women, where a rigorous, wide-ranging education could be combined with
moral and religious discipline. Though the idea was never carried out, it had a broad

influence on later plans for educating women, as well as on literature. At the end of Johnson's *Rasselas*, both Pekuah's dream of leading a religious order and Nekayah's desire to found a college of learned women owe something to Astell.

To question the customs and laws of marriage is to question society itself, its distribution of money and power and love. During the eighteenth century many of the terms of marriage were renegotiated. The older view of the wife as a chattel, bound by contract to a husband whom others had chosen for her and whom she was sworn to obey, was hotly debated and challenged. The witty arguments of Congreve's *The Way of the World* (1700) reflect this growing debate between the sexes. Another work published in the same year, *Some Reflections upon Marriage*, takes a more independent position. Marriage, according to Astell, is all too often a trap. She insists that a woman should be guided by reason, not only in choosing a mate but in choosing whether or not to marry at all (Astell herself never married). So long as the institution of marriage perpetuates inequality rather than a true partnership of minds, women had better beware of flattery and look to themselves or to God, not to men, for the hope of a better life. The debate on marriage continued throughout the century in works such as Defoe's *Roxana*, Hogarth's *Marriage A-la-Mode*, the novels of Samuel Richardson, *Rasselas*, and eventually the writings of Mary Wollstonecraft and William Godwin. It still continues today. In her sharp, lively style and the pertinent questions she raised, Astell has come to be seen as ahead of her time.

From Some Reflections upon Marriage[1]

If marriage be such a blessed state, how comes it, may you say, that there are so few happy marriages? Now in answer to this, it is not to be wondered that so few succeed; we should rather be surprised to find so many do, considering how imprudently men engage, the motives they act by, and the very strange conduct they observe throughout.

For pray, what do men propose to themselves in marriage? What qualifications do they look after in a spouse? What will she bring? is the first enquiry: How many acres? Or how much ready coin? Not that this is altogether an unnecessary question, for marriage without a competency,[2] that is, not only a bare subsistence, but even a handsome and plentiful provision, according to the quality[3] and circumstances of the parties, is no very comfortable condition. They who marry for love, as they call it, find time enough to repent their rash folly, and are not long in being convinced, that whatever fine speeches might be made in the heat of passion, there could be no *real kindness* between those who can agree to make each other miserable. But as an estate is to be considered, so it should not be the *main*, much less the *only* consideration; for happiness does not depend on wealth.

* * *

But suppose a man does not marry for money, though for one that does not, perhaps there are thousands that do; suppose he marries for love, an heroic action, which makes a mighty noise in the world, partly because of its rarity, and partly in regard of its extravagancy, and what does his marrying for love amount to? There's no great odds between his marrying for the love

1. The text is excerpted from the first edition.
2. Sufficient income.
3. Social position.

of money, or for the love of beauty; the man does not act according to reason in either case, but is governed by irregular appetites. But he loves her wit perhaps, and this, you'll say, is more spiritual, more refined: not at all, if you examine it to the bottom. For what is that which nowadays passes under the name of wit? A bitter and ill-natured raillery, a pert repartee, or a confident talking at all; and in such a multitude of words, it's odds if something or other does not pass that is surprising, though every thing that surprises does not please; some things are wondered at for their ugliness, as well as others for their beauty. True wit, durst one venture to describe it, is quite another thing; it consists in such a sprightliness of imagination, such a reach and turn of thought, so properly expressed, as strikes and pleases a judicious taste.[4]

* * *

Thus, whether it be wit or beauty that a man's in love with, there's no great hopes of a lasting happiness; beauty, with all the helps of art, is of no very lasting date; the more it is helped, the sooner it decays; and he, who only or chiefly chose for beauty, will in a little time find the same reason for another choice. Nor is that sort of wit which he prefers, of a more sure tenure; or allowing it to last, it will not always please. For that which has not a real excellency and value in itself, entertains no longer than that giddy humor which recommended it to us holds; and when we can like on no just, or on very little ground, 'tis certain a dislike will arise, as lightly and as unaccountably. And it is not improbable that such a husband may in a little time, by ill usage, provoke such a wife to exercise her wit, that is, her spleen on him, and then it is not hard to guess how very agreeable it will be to him.

* * *

But do the women never choose amiss? Are the men only in fault? That is not pretended; for he who will be just, must be forced to acknowledge, that neither sex is always in the right. A woman, indeed, can't properly be said to choose; all that is allowed her, is to refuse or accept what is offered. And when we have made such reasonable allowances as are due to the sex, perhaps they may not appear so much in fault as one would at first imagine, and a generous spirit will find more occasion to pity than to reprove. But sure I transgress—it must not be supposed that the ladies can do amiss he is but an ill-bred fellow who pretends that they need amendment! They are, no doubt on't, always in the right, and most of all when they take pity on distressed lovers; whatever they *say* carries an authority that no reason can resist, and all that they *do* must needs be exemplary! This is the modish language, nor is there a man of honor amongst the whole tribe that would not venture his life, nay and his salvation too, in their defense, if any but himself attempts to injure them. But I must ask pardon if I can't come up to these heights, nor flatter them with the having no faults, which is only a malicious way of continuing and increasing their mistakes.

* * *

But, alas! what poor woman is ever taught that she should have a higher design than to get her a husband? Heaven will fall in of course; and if she

4. Cf. Pope's *An Essay on Criticism* 2.297–304 (p. 2515).

make but an obedient and dutiful wife, she cannot miss of it. A husband indeed is thought by both sexes so very valuable, that scarce a man who can keep himself clean and make a bow, but thinks he is good enough to pretend[5] to any woman; no matter for the difference of birth or fortune, a husband is such a wonder-working name as to make an equality, or something more, whenever it is pronounced.

* * *

To wind up this matter: if a woman were duly principled and taught to know the world, especially the true sentiments that men have of her, and the traps they lay for her under so many gilded compliments, and such a seemingly great respect, that disgrace would be prevented which is brought upon too many families; women would marry more discreetly, and demean[6] themselves better in a married state than some people say they do.

* * *

But some sage persons may perhaps object, that were women allowed to improve themselves, and not, amongst other discouragements, driven back by the wise jests and scoffs that are put upon a woman of sense or learning, a philosophical lady, as she is called by way of ridicule, they would be too wise, and too good for the men. I grant it, for vicious and foolish men. Nor is it to be wondered that he is afraid he should not be able to govern them were their understandings improved, who is resolved not to take too much pains with his own. But these, 'tis to be hoped, are no very considerable number, the foolish at least; and therefore this is so far from being an argument against their improvement, that it is a strong one for it, if we do but suppose the men to be as capable of improvement as the women; but much more if, according to tradition, we believe they have greater capacities. This, if anything, would stir them up to be what they ought, not permit them to waste their time and abuse their faculties in the service of their irregular appetites and unreasonable desires, and so let poor contemptible women, who have been their slaves, excel them in all that is truly excellent. This would make them blush at employing an immortal mind no better than in making provision for the flesh to fulfill the lusts thereof, since women, by a wiser conduct, have brought themselves to such a reach of thought, to such exactness of judgment, such clearness and strength of reasoning, such purity and elevation of mind, such command of their passions, such regularity of will and affection, and, in a word, to such a pitch of perfection as the human soul is capable of attaining even in this life by the grace of God; such true wisdom, such real greatness, as though it does not qualify them to make a noise in this world, to found or overturn empires, yet it qualifies them for what is infinitely better, a Kingdom that cannot be moved, an incorruptible crown of glory.

* * *

Again, it may be said, if a wife's case be as it is here represented, it is not good for a woman to marry, and so there's an end of human race. But this

5. Aspire or lay claim.   6. Behave.

is no fair consequence, for all that can justly be inferred from hence is that a woman has no mighty obligations to the man who makes love to her; she has no reason to be fond of being a wife, or to reckon it a piece of preferment when she is taken to be a man's upper-servant;[7] it is no advantage to her in this world; if rightly managed it may prove one as to the next. For she who marries purely to do good, to educate souls for heaven, who can be so truly mortified as to lay aside her own will and desires, to pay such an entire submission for life, to one whom she cannot be sure will always deserve it, does certainly perform a more heroic action than all the famous masculine heroes can boast of, she suffers a continual martyrdom to bring glory to God, and benefit to mankind; which consideration indeed may carry her through all difficulties, I know not what else can, and engage her to love him who proves perhaps so much worse than a brute, as to make this condition yet more grievous than it needed to be. She has need of a strong reason, of a truly christian and well-tempered spirit, of all the assistance the best education can give her, and ought to have some good assurance of her own firmness and virtue, who ventures on such a trial; and for this reason 'tis less to be wondered at that women marry off in haste, for perhaps if they took time to consider and reflect upon it, they seldom would.

1700

7. High-ranking servant. "Preferment": advancement in rank.

DANIEL DEFOE
ca. 1660–1731

By birth, education, and occupations Daniel Defoe was a stranger to the sphere of refined tastes and classical learning that dominated polite literature during his lifetime. Middle class in his birth, Presbyterian in his religion, he belonged among the hardy Nonconformist tradesfolk who, after the Restoration, slowly increased their wealth and toward the end of the seventeenth century began to achieve political importance.

He began adult life as a small merchant and for a while prospered, but he was not overscrupulous in his dealings, and in 1692 he found himself bankrupt, with debts amounting to £17,000. This was the first of his many financial crises, crises that drove him to make his way, like his own heroes and heroines, by whatever means presented themselves. And however double his dealings, he seems always to have found the way to reconcile them with his genuine Nonconformist piety. His restless mind was fertile in "projects," both for himself and for the country, and his itch for politics made the role of passive observer impossible for him.

An ardent Whig, he first gained notoriety by political verses and pamphlets, and for one of them, *The Shortest Way with the Dissenters* (1702), in which he ironically defended Anglican oppression, he stood in the pillory three times and was sentenced to jail. He was released through the influence of Robert Harley (later earl of Oxford), who recognized in Defoe, as he was to do in Swift, a useful ally. For the next eleven years Defoe served his benefactor secretly as a political spy and confidential agent, traveling throughout England and Scotland, reporting and perhaps influencing opinion. As founder and editor of the *Review,* his job was to gain support for Harley's policies, even when, in 1710, Harley became head of a Tory ministry. It is characteristic of Defoe that, after the fall of the Tories in 1714, he went over to the triumphant Whigs and served them as loyally as he had their enemy.

When he was nearly sixty, Defoe's energy and inventiveness enabled him to break new ground, indeed to begin a new career. *Robinson Crusoe,* which appeared in 1719, is the first of a series of tales of adventure for which Defoe is now admired, but which brought him little esteem from the polite world, however much they gratified the less-cultivated readers in the City or the servants' hall. In this and other tales that followed, Defoe was able to use all his greatest gifts: the ability to re-create a milieu vividly, through the cumulative effect of carefully observed, often petty details; a special skill in writing easygoing prose, the language of actual speech, which seems to reveal the consciousness of the first-person narrator; a wide knowledge of the society in which he lived, both the trading bourgeoisie and the rogues who preyed on them; and an absorption in the spectacle of lonely human beings, whether Crusoe on his island or Moll Flanders in England and Virginia, somehow bending a stubborn and indifferent environment to their own ends of survival or profits. There is something of himself in all his protagonists: enormous vitality, humanity, and a scheming and sometimes sneaky ingenuity. In these fictitious autobiographies of adventurers or rogues—*Captain Singleton* (1720), *Moll Flanders* (1722), *Colonel Jack* (1722), and *Roxana* (1724)—Defoe spoke for and to the members of his own class. Like them, he was engrossed by property and success, and his way of writing made all he touched seem true.

From Roxana[1]

[THE CONS OF MARRIAGE]

One morning, in the middle of our unlawful freedoms—that is to say, when we were in bed together—he sighed, and told me he desired my leave to ask me one question, and that I would give him an answer to it with the same ingenuous freedom and honesty that I had used to[2] treat him with. I told him I would. Why, then, his question was, why I would not marry him, seeing I allowed him all the freedom of a husband. "Or," says he, "my dear, since you have been so kind as to take me to your bed, why will you not make me your own, and take me for good and all, that we may enjoy ourselves without any reproach to one another?"

I told him, that as I confessed it was the only thing I could not comply with him in, so it was the only thing in all my actions that I could not give him a reason for; that it was true I had let him come to bed to me, which was supposed to be the greatest favor a woman could grant; but it was evident, and he might see it, that as I was sensible of the obligation I was under to him for saving me from the worst circumstance it was possible for me to be brought to, I could deny him nothing; and if I had had any greater favor

---

1. *Roxana, or The Fortunate Mistress,* is the story, told by herself, of a beautiful and ambitious courtesan. A bad marriage and early poverty drive her to a career of prostitution, at which she succeeds brilliantly until eventually her past catches up with her. The story is set in the Restoration, and even the title reflects the decadence associated with the period: admirers give "Roxana" her name after she has displayed herself provocatively in Turkish costume at a ball (Roxalana, a sultana in Sir William Davenant's *The Siege of Rhodes,* 1656, had come to mean "whore"). In this excerpt the narrator, who has been saved from ruin and allowed herself to be seduced by an honest Dutch merchant, expresses her liberated views of marriage.

2. Been accustomed to.

to yield him, I should have done it, *that of matrimony only excepted,* and he could not but see that I loved him to an extraordinary degree, in every part of my behavior to him; but that as to marrying, which was giving up my liberty, it was what once he knew I had done, and he had seen how it had hurried me up and down in the world, and what it had exposed me to;[3] that I had an aversion to it, and desired he would not insist upon it. He might easily see I had no aversion to him; and that, if I was with child by him, he should see a testimony of my kindness to the father, for that I would settle all I had in the world upon the child.

He was mute a good while. At last says he, "Come, my dear, you are the first woman in the world that ever lay with a man and then refused to marry him, and therefore there must be some other reason for your refusal; and I have therefore one other request, and that is, if I guess at the true reason, and remove the objection, will you then yield to me?" I told him, if he removed the objection I must needs comply, for I should certainly do everything that I had no objection against.

"Why then, my dear, it must be that either you are already engaged or married to some other man, or you are not willing to dispose of your money to me, and expect to advance yourself higher with your fortune. Now, if it be the first of these, my mouth will be stopped, and I have no more to say; but if it be the last, I am prepared effectually to remove the objection, and answer all you can say on that subject."

I took him up short at the first of these, telling him he must have base thoughts of me indeed, to think that I could yield to him in such a manner as I had done, and continue it with so much freedom as he found I did, if I had a husband, or were engaged to any other man; and that he might depend upon it that was not my case, nor any part of my case.

"Why then," said he, "as to the other, I have an offer to make to you that shall take off all the objections, viz., that I will not touch one pistole[4] of your estate more than shall be with your own voluntary consent, neither now or at any other time, but you shall settle it as you please for your life, and upon who you please after your death." That I should see he was able to maintain me without it; and that it was not for that that he followed me from Paris.

I was indeed surprised at that part of his offer, and he might easily perceive it; it was not only what I did not expect, but it was what I knew not what answer to make to. He had, indeed, removed my principal objection, nay, all my objections, and it was not possible for me to give any answer; for, if upon so generous an offer I should agree with him, I then did as good as confess that it was upon the account of my money that I refused him; and that though I could give up my virtue, and expose myself, yet I would not give up my money, which, though it was true, yet was really too gross for me to acknowledge, and I could not pretend to marry him upon that principle neither. Then as to having him, and make over all my estate out of his hands, so as not to give him the management of what I had, I thought it would be not only a little Gothic[5] and inhumane, but would be always a foundation of unkindness between us, and render us suspected one to another; so that, upon the whole,

---

3. The Dutch merchant thinks that Roxana is the widow of a jeweler, whose death had left her alone and friendless; actually she was the jeweler's mistress and has since been the lover of a French prince.
4. A Spanish coin.
5. Barbaric.

I was obliged to give a new turn to it, and talk upon a kind of an elevated strain, which really was not in my thoughts, at first, at all; for I own, as above, the divesting myself of my estate and putting my money out of my hand was the sum of the matter that made me refuse to marry; but, I say, I gave it a new turn upon this occasion, as follows.

I told him I had, perhaps, different notions of matrimony from what the received custom had given us of it; that I thought a woman was a free agent as well as a man, and was born free, and could she manage herself suitably, might enjoy that liberty to as much purpose as the men do; that the laws of matrimony were indeed otherwise, and mankind at this time acted quite upon other principles, and those such that a woman gave herself entirely away from herself, in marriage, and capitulated only to be, at best, but an upper[6] servant, and from the time she took the man she was no better or worse than the servant among the Israelites, who had his ears bored—that is, nailed to the doorpost—who by that act gave himself up to be a servant during life. That the very nature of the marriage contract was, in short, nothing but giving up liberty, estate, authority, and everything to the man, and the woman was indeed a mere woman ever after—that is to say, a slave.

He replied, that though in some respects it was as I had said, yet I ought to consider that, as an equivalent to this, the man had all the care of things devolved upon him; that the weight of business lay upon his shoulders, and as he had the trust, so he had the toil of life upon him; his was the labor, his the anxiety of living; that the woman had nothing to do but to eat the fat and drink the sweet; to sit still and look around her, be waited on and made much of, be served and loved and made easy, especially if the husband acted as became him; and that, in general, the labor of the man was appointed to make the woman live quiet and unconcerned in the world; that they had the name of subjection without the thing; and if in inferior families they had the drudgery of the house and care of the provisions upon them, yet they had indeed much the easier part; for in general, the women had only the care of managing—that is, spending what their husbands get—and that a woman had the name of subjection, indeed, but that they very generally commanded not the men only, but all they had; managed all for themselves; and where the man did his duty, the woman's life was all ease and tranquility, and that she had nothing to do but to be easy, and to make all that were about her both easy and merry.

I returned, that while a woman was single, she was a masculine in her politic capacity;[7] that she had then the full command of what she had, and the full direction of what she did; that she was a man in her separated capacity, to all intents and purposes that a man could be so to himself; that she was controlled by none, because accountable to none, and was in subjection to none. So I sung these two lines of Mr——'s:[8]

> Oh! 'tis pleasant to be free,
> The sweetest Miss is Liberty.

I added, that whoever the woman was that had an estate, and would give it up to be the slave of *a great man*, that woman was a fool, and must be fit

---

6. High-ranking.
7. A male in her function of making prudent decisions.

8. Unidentified; Defoe himself may have written the lines.

for nothing but a beggar; that it was my opinion a woman was as fit to govern and enjoy her own estate without a man as a man was without a woman; and that, if she had a mind to gratify herself as to sexes, she might entertain a man as a man does a mistress; that while she was thus single she was her own, and if she gave away that power she merited to be as miserable as it was possible that any creature could be.

All he could say could not answer the force of this, as to argument; only this, that the other way was the ordinary method that the world was guided by; that he had reason to expect I should be content with that which all the world was contented with; that he was of the opinion that a sincere affection between a man and his wife answered all the objections that I had made about the being a slave, a servant, and the like; and where there was a mutual love, there could be no bondage, but that there was but one interest, one aim, one design, and all conspired to make both very happy.

"Aye," said I, "that is the thing I complain of. The pretense of affection takes from a woman everything that can be called *herself*; she is to have no interest, no aim, no view, but all is the interest, aim, and view of the husband; she is to be the passive creature you spoke of," said I. "She is to lead a life of perfect indolence, and living by faith (not in God, but) in her husband, she sinks or swims, as he is either fool or wise man, unhappy or prosperous; and in the middle of what she thinks is her happiness and prosperity, she is engulfed in misery and beggary, which she had not the least notice, knowledge, or suspicion of. How often have I seen a woman living in all the splendor that a plentiful fortune ought to allow her, with her coaches and equipages, her family and rich furniture, her attendants and friends, her visitors and good company, all about her today; tomorrow surprised with a disaster, turned out of all by a commission of bankrupt, stripped to the clothes on her back; her jointure,[9] suppose she had it, is sacrificed to the creditors so long as her husband lived, and she turned into the street, and left to live on the charity of her friends, *if she has any*, or follow the monarch, her husband, into the Mint,[1] and live there on the wreck of his fortunes, till he is forced to run away from her even there; and then she sees her children starve, herself miserable, breaks her heart, and cries herself to death! This," says I, "is the state of many a lady that has had ten thousand pound to her portion."

He did not know how feelingly I spoke this, and what extremities I had gone through of this kind; how near I was to the very last article above, viz., crying myself to death; and how I really starved for almost two years together.[2]

But he shook his head, and said, where had I lived? and what dreadful families had I lived among, that had frighted me into such terrible apprehensions of things? that these things indeed might happen where men run into hazardous things in trade, and without prudence or due consideration, launched their fortunes in a degree beyond their strength, grasping at adventures beyond their stocks, and the like; but that, as he was stated[3] in the world, if I would embark with him, he had a fortune equal with mine; that

---

9. Property settled on a wife. "A commission": a writ.
1. Debtors took refuge in the area near the Mint, where they could not be arrested.

2. Roxana's first husband, a profligate brewer, had run off, leaving her destitute.
3. Established, a person of standing.

together we should have no occasion of engaging in business any more; but that in any part of the world where I had a mind to live, whether England, France, Holland, or where I would, we might settle, and live as happily as the world could make any one live; that if I desired the management of our estate, when put together, if I would not trust him with mine, he would trust me with his; that we would be upon one bottom,[4] and I should steer. "Ay," says I, "you'll allow me to steer—that is, hold the helm—but you'll con[5] the ship, as they call it; that is, as at sea, a boy serves to stand at the helm, but he that gives him the orders is pilot."

He laughed at my simile. "No," says he; "you shall be pilot then; you shall con the ship." "Ay," says I, "as long as you please, but you can take the helm out of my hand when you please, and bid me go spin. It is not you," says I, "that I suspect, but the laws of matrimony puts the power into your hands, bids you do it, commands you to command, and binds me, forsooth, to obey. You, that are now upon even terms with me, and I with you," says I, "are the next hour set up upon the throne, and the humble wife placed at your footstool; all the rest, all that you call oneness of interest, mutual affection, and the like, is courtesy and kindness then, and a woman is indeed infinitely obliged where she meets with it; but can't help herself where it fails."

Well, he did not give it over yet, but came to the serious part, and there he thought he should be too many for me. He first hinted, that marriage was decreed by Heaven; that it was the fixed state of life, which God had appointed for man's felicity, and for establishing a legal posterity; that there could be no legal claim of estates by inheritance but by children born in wedlock; that all the rest was sunk under scandal and illegitimacy; and very well he talked upon that subject indeed.

But it would not do; I took him short there. "Look you, sir," said I, "you have an advantage of me there indeed, in my particular case; but it would not be generous to make use of it. I readily grant that it were better for me to have married you than to admit you to the liberty I have given you; but as I could not reconcile my judgment to marriage, for the reasons above, and had kindness enough for you, and obligation too much on me to resist you, I suffered your rudeness and gave up my virtue. But I have two things before me to heal up that breach of honor without that desperate one of marriage, and those are, repentance for what is past, and putting an end to it for time to come."

He seemed to be concerned to think that I should take him in that manner. He assured me that I misunderstood him; that he had more manners as well as more kindness for me, and more justice, than to reproach me with what he had been the aggressor in, and had surprised me into; that what he spoke referred to my words above, that the woman, if she thought fit, might entertain a man, as a man did a mistress; and that I seemed to mention that way of living as justifiable, and setting it as a lawful thing, and in the place of matrimony.

Well, we strained some compliments upon those points, not worth repeating; and I added, I supposed when he got to bed to me he thought himself sure of me; and indeed, in the ordinary course of things, after he had lain with me he ought to think so; but that, upon the same foot of argument

4. One ship (literally, lowest part of a hull).   5. Direct the steering of.

which I had discoursed with him upon, it was just the contrary; and when a woman had been weak enough to yield up the last point before wedlock, it would be adding one weakness to another to take the man afterwards, to pin down the shame of it upon herself all the days of her life, and bind herself to live all her time with the only man that could upbraid her with it; that in yielding at first, she must be a fool, but to take the man is to be sure to be called fool; that to resist a man is to act with courage and vigor, and to cast off the reproach, which, in the course of things, drops out of knowledge and dies. The man goes one way and the woman another, as fate and the circumstances of living direct; and if they keep one another's counsel, the folly is heard no more of. "But to take the man," says I, "is the most preposterous thing in nature, and (saving your presence) is to befoul one's self, and live always in the smell of it. No, no," added I; "after a man has lain with me as a mistress, he ought never to lie with me as a wife; that's not only preserving the crime in memory, but it is recording it in the family. If the woman marries the man afterwards, she bears the reproach of it to the last hour; if her husband is not a man of a hundred thousand, he some time or other upbraids her with it. If he has children, they fail not one way or other to hear of it. If the children are virtuous, they do their mother the justice to hate her for it; if they are wicked, they give her the mortification of doing the like, and giving her for the example. On the other hand, if the man and the woman part, there is an end of the crime and an end of the clamor. Time wears out the memory of it; or a woman may remove but a few streets, and she soon outlives it, and hears no more of it."

He was confounded at this discourse, and told me he could not say but I was right in the main. That as to that part relating to managing estates, it was arguing *à la cavalier;*[6] it was in some sense right, if the woman were able to carry it on so, but that in general the sex were not capable of it; their heads were not turned for it, and they had better choose a person capable and honest, that knew how to do them justice as women, as well as to love them; and that then the trouble was all taken off of their hands.

I told him it was a dear way of purchasing their ease; for very often when the trouble was taken off of their hands, so was their money too; and that I thought it was far safer for the sex not to be afraid of the trouble, but to be really afraid of their money; that if nobody was trusted, nobody would be deceived; and the staff in their own hands was the best security in the world.

He replied, that I had started a new thing in the world; that however I might support it by subtle reasoning, yet it was a way of arguing that was contrary to the general practice, and that he confessed he was much disappointed in it; that had he known I would have made such a use of it, he would never have attempted what he did, which he had no wicked design in, resolving to make me reparation, and that he was very sorry he had been so unhappy;[7] that he was very sure he should never upbraid me with it hereafter, and had so good an opinion of me as to believe I did not suspect him; but seeing I was positive in refusing him, notwithstanding what had passed, he had nothing to do but secure me from reproach by going back again to Paris, that so, according to my own way of arguing, it might die out of memory, and I might never meet with it again to my disadvantage.

6. Cavalierly, rashly (French).   7. Troublesome.

* * *

Thus blinded by my own vanity, I threw away the only opportunity I then had to have effectually settled my fortunes, and secured them for this world; and I am a memorial to all that shall read my story, a standing monument of the madness and distraction which pride and infatuations from hell run us into; how ill our passions guide us; and how dangerously we act, when we follow the dictates of an ambitious mind.

1724

ANNE FINCH,
COUNTESS OF WINCHILSEA
1661–1720

Born into an ancient country family, Anne Kingsmill became a maid of honor at the court of Charles II. There she met Colonel Heneage Finch; in 1684 they married. During the short reign of James II they prospered at court, but at the king's fall in 1688 they were forced to retire, eventually settling on a beautiful family estate at Eastwell, in Kent, near the south coast of England. Here Colonel Finch became, in 1712, earl of Winchilsea, and here Lady Winchilsea wrote most of her poems, influenced, she said, by "the solitude and security of the country," and by "objects naturally inspiring soft and poetical imaginations." Her *Miscellany Poems on Several Occasions, Written by a Lady* were published in 1713. One poem, *The Spleen,* a description of the mysterious melancholic illness from which she and many other fashionable people suffered, achieved some fame; Pope seems to refer to it when he invokes the goddess Spleen in *The Rape of the Lock.* But Winchilsea's larger reputation began only a century later, when Wordsworth praised her for keeping her eye on external nature and for a style "often admirable, chaste, tender, and vigorous."

Three things conspired to keep Winchilsea's poems in the shade: she was an aristocrat, her nature was retiring, and she was a woman. Any one of these might have made her shrink from exposing herself to the jeers that still, at the turn of the century, greeted any effort by a "scribbling lady." Many of her best poems, for instance *The Petition for an Absolute Retreat,* celebrate the joys of solitude. Nevertheless, remarkably, she chose to publish. The reason may be found in her contempt for the notion that women are fit for nothing but trivial pursuits. In *The Introduction* (to her poems) she insists that women are "education's, more than nature's fools," and she often comments on the damaging exclusion of half the human race from public life. But Winchilsea is her own best example of what a woman can be: keen-eyed and self-sufficient and a poet.

The Introduction[1]

Did I my lines intend for public view,
How many censures would their faults pursue!

---

1. This preface to Winchilsea's work was never published during her lifetime, for reasons explained in the poem itself.

Some would, because such words they do affect,
Cry they're insipid, empty, uncorrect.
5   And many have attained, dull and untaught,
The name of wit, only by finding fault.[2]
True judges might condemn their want of wit;
And all might say, they're by a woman writ.
Alas! a woman that attempts the pen,
10   Such an intruder on the rights of men,
Such a presumptuous creature is esteemed,
The fault can by no virtue be redeemed.
They tell us we mistake our sex and way;
Good breeding, fashion, dancing, dressing, play
15   Are the accomplishments we should desire;
To write, or read, or think, or to enquire,
Would cloud our beauty, and exhaust our time,
And interrupt the conquests of our prime;
Whilst the dull manage of a servile house
20   Is held by some our utmost art and use.
     Sure 'twas not ever thus, nor are we told
Fables,[3] of women that excelled of old;
To whom, by the diffusive hand of heaven,
Some share of wit and poetry was given.
25   On that glad day on which the Ark[4] returned,
The holy pledge for which the land had mourned,
The joyful tribes attend it on the way,
The Levites do the sacred charge convey,
Whilst various instruments before it play;
30   Here holy virgins in the concert join,[5]
The louder notes to soften and refine,
And with alternate verse[6] complete the hymn divine.
     Lo! the young poet,° after God's own heart,   David
By Him inspired and taught the Muses' art,
35   Returned from conquest a bright chorus meets,
That sing his slain ten thousand in the streets.[7]
In such loud numbers[8] they his acts declare,
Proclaim the wonders of his early war,
That Saul upon the vast applause does frown,
40   And feels its mighty thunder shake the crown.
What can the threatened judgment now prolong?[9]
Half of the kingdom is already gone;
The fairest half, whose influence guides the rest,
Have David's empire o'er their hearts confessed.
45   A woman here leads fainting Israel on,
She fights, she wins, she triumphs with a song,[1]
Devout, majestic, for the subject fit,

2. Pronounced *fawt*.
3. Idle stories or lies.
4. The Ark of the Covenant, restored to Jerusalem by David (1 Chronicles 15).
5. Pronounced *jine*.
6. A series of couplets. The choir of virgins, not mentioned in Chronicles, is imagined by Winchilsea as chanting every other line, responsively, as in some of the Psalms.

7. 1 Samuel 18.6–7.
8. Measures of music and verse.
9. What can now stave off the threatened judgment? Saul's doom ("judgment") had been prophesied: God would replace him with a better king.
1. The prophet and judge Deborah sang to praise the Lord for the victory she herself had brought about (Judges 4–5).

And far above her arms, exalts her wit,
Then to the peaceful, shady palm withdraws,
50   And rules the rescued nation with her laws.
How are we fallen! fallen by mistaken rules,
And education's, more than nature's fools;
Debarred from all improvements of the mind,
And to be dull, expected and designed;°   *intended*
55   And if some one would soar above the rest,
With warmer fancy and ambition pressed,
So strong the opposing faction still appears,
The hopes to thrive can ne'er outweigh the fears.
Be cautioned, then, my Muse, and still retired;
60   Nor be despised, aiming to be admired;
Conscious of wants, still with contracted wing,
To some few friends and to thy sorrows sing.
For groves of laurel thou wert never meant;
Be dark enough thy shades, and be thou there content.

1689?   1903

A Nocturnal Reverie

In such a night,[1] when every louder wind
Is to its distant cavern safe confined;
And only gentle Zephyr fans his wings,
And lonely Philomel,° still waking, sings;   *nightingale*
5   Or from some tree, famed for the owl's delight,
She, hollowing clear, directs the wanderer right:
In such a night, when passing clouds give place,
Or thinly veil the heavens' mysterious face;
When in some river, overhung with green,
10   The waving moon and trembling leaves are seen;
When freshened grass now bears itself upright,
And makes cool banks to pleasing rest invite,
Whence springs the woodbind, and the bramble-rose,
And where the sleepy cowslip sheltered grows;
15   Whilst now a paler hue the foxglove takes,
Yet checkers still with red the dusky brakes:
When scattered glow-worms, but in twilight fine,
Show trivial beauties watch their hour to shine;
Whilst Salisbury[2] stands the test of every light,
20   In perfect charms, and perfect virtue bright:
When odors, which declined repelling day,
Through temperate air uninterrupted stray;
When darkened groves their softest shadows wear,
And falling waters we distinctly hear;
25   When through the gloom more venerable shows

1. This phrase, repeated twice below, echoes the same repeated phrase in the night piece that opens act 5 of *The Merchant of Venice*.
2. Probably Lady Salisbury, the daughter of a friend. The sense is that this lady differs from others more trivial, who like glowworms look fine only one hour a day.

Some ancient fabric,° awful in repose,   edifice
While sunburnt hills their swarthy looks conceal,
And swelling haycocks thicken up the vale:
When the loosed horse now, as his pasture leads,
30   Comes slowly grazing through the adjoining meads,
Whose stealing pace, and lengthened shade we fear,
Till torn-up forage in his teeth we hear:
When nibbling sheep at large pursue their food,
And unmolested kine rechew the cud;
35   When curlews cry beneath the village walls,
And to her straggling brood the partridge calls;
Their shortlived jubilee the creatures keep,
Which but endures, whilst tyrant man does sleep;
When a sedate content the spirit feels,
40   And no fierce light disturbs, whilst it reveals;
But silent musings urge the mind to seek
Something, too high for syllables to speak;
Till the free soul to a composedness charmed,
Finding the elements of rage disarmed,
45   O'er all below a solemn quiet grown,
Joys in the inferior world,[3] and thinks it like her own:
In such a night let me abroad remain,
Till morning breaks, and all's confused again;
Our cares, our toils, our clamors are renewed,
50   Or pleasures, seldom reached, again pursued.

1713

3. The world of nature (compared to the world of the soul).

MATTHEW PRIOR
1664–1721

Matthew Prior was a public man. He became a diplomat when appointed secretary
to the embassy at The Hague through the patronage of Dryden's friend the earl of
Dorset. His public career culminated in his negotiating for Oxford's Tory ministry the
Treaty of Utrecht (1713), which ended the War of the Spanish Succession. But after
the fall of the Tories in 1714, Prior was recalled from Paris, placed under house arrest
for more than a year, and frequently interrogated in the hope that his evidence could
be used to bring Oxford to trial as a traitor. Upon his release he found himself out of
place and broken in fortune. But the extraordinary success of such friends as Swift
and Pope in supporting the publication by subscription of his *Poems on Several Occasions* (1718) secured him a profit of four thousand guineas, a very large sum at that
time, which enabled him to end his life in comfort.

   Prior's poetry was the by-product of a busy life—"the fruits of [his] vacant hours,"
as he once wrote. As a lyric poet he stands at the end of the long tradition of *vers de
société*, humorous light verse such as was written by the "mob of gentlemen who
wrote with ease" at the courts of Charles and James. But Prior was no careless writer:

his grace and colloquial simplicity of language are the effects of studied art. His finest pieces are his lyrics, not his official odes and panegyrics. Of his two philosophical poems it is not the serious *Solomon* that attracts readers today but rather the skeptical and witty *Alma* (written during his arrest in 1715) in deft octosyllabic couplets and homely conversational language that suggest Swift at his best. William Cowper admired Prior's ability to "make verse speak the language of prose, without being prosaic—to marshal the words of it in such an order as they might naturally take in falling from the lips of an extemporary speaker, yet without meanness, harmoniously, elegantly, and without seeming to displace a syllable for the sake of the rhyme."

No poems were more popular, in the seventeenth and eighteenth centuries, than those that praised the virtues of a modest, retired life, sequestered from the ambitions of city and court. According to Johnson, "Perhaps no composition in our language has been oftener perused than Pomfret's *Choice*" (1700), which chooses the Golden Mean: a small estate, old books and wines, a few friends, a prudent female companion, a peaceful death. Yet Prior, who knew well enough the disappointments of public life, also knew that simple country living did not guarantee virtue. *An Epitaph* satirizes not the quiet but the unexamined life. For an epigraph, Prior took a chorus from Senecca's *Thyestes*—"All I seek is to lie still"—to which we might add Tolstoy's judgment of Ivan Ilych, whose "life was most ordinary and most simple and therefore most terrible."

An Epitaph

Interred beneath this marble stone
Lie sauntering Jack and idle Joan.
While rolling threescore years and one
Did round this globe their courses run;
5   If human things went ill or well;
If changing empires rose or fell;
The morning passed, the evening came,
And found this couple still the same.
They walked and ate, good folks: what then?
10   Why then they walked and ate again.
They soundly slept the night away;
They did just nothing all the day;
And having buried children four,
Would not take pains to try for more.
15   Nor sister either had, nor brother:
They seemed just tallied for each other.
    Their moral° and economy[1]   morality
Most perfectly they made agree:
Each virtue kept its proper bound,
20   Nor trespassed on the other's ground.
Nor fame, nor censure they regarded:
They neither punished, nor rewarded.
He cared not what the footmen did;
Her maids she neither praised, nor chid:
25   So every servant took his course;
And bad at first, they all grew worse.
Slothful disorder filled his stable,

1. Household management.

And sluttish plenty decked her table.
Their beer was strong; their wine was port;
30   Their meal was large; their grace was short.
They gave the poor the remnant-meat
Just when it grew not fit to eat.
    They paid the church and parish rate,°   *tax*
And took, but read not the receipt;
35   For which they claimed their Sunday's due
Of slumbering in an upper pew.
    No man's defects sought they to know,
So never made themselves a foe.
No man's good deeds did they commend,
40   So never raised themselves a friend.
Nor cherished they relations poor:
That might decrease their present store;
Nor barn nor house did they repair:
That might oblige their future heir.
45   They neither added, nor confounded;°   *wasted*
They neither wanted, nor abounded.
Each Christmas they accompts° did clear;   *accounts*
And wound their bottom² round the year.
Nor tear nor smile did they employ
50   At news of public grief or joy.
When bells were rung and bonfires made,
If asked, they ne'er denied their aid;
Their jug was to the ringers carried,
Whoever either died, or married.
55   Their billet° at the fire was found,   *firewood*
Whoever was deposed, or crowned.
    Nor good, nor bad, nor fools, nor wise;
They would not learn, nor could advise;
Without love, hatred, joy, or fear,
60   They led—a kind of—as it were;
Nor wished, nor cared, nor laughed, nor cried;
And so they lived; and so they died.

1718

A True Maid

"No, no; for my virginity,
    When I lose that," says Rose, "I'll die."
"Behind the elms, last night," cried Dick,
    "Rose, were you not extremely sick?"

1718

2. Wound up their skein of thread; i.e., they set the year nicely to rights.

A Better Answer

To Cloe Jealous

Dear Cloe, how blubbered is that pretty face!
Thy cheek all on fire, and thy hair all uncurled!
Prithee quit this caprice; and (as old Falstaff says)
Let us e'en talk a little like folks of this world.[1]

5   How canst thou presume thou hast leave to destroy
The beauties which Venus but lent to thy keeping?
Those looks were designed to inspire love and joy;
More ord'nary eyes may serve people for weeping.

To be vexed at a trifle or two that I writ,
10   Your judgment at once and my passion you wrong:
You take that for fact which will scarce be found wit:
Od's life! must one swear to the truth of a song?

What I speak, my fair Cloe, and what I write, shows
The difference there is betwixt nature and art;
15   I court others in verse, but I love thee in prose;
And they have my whimsies, but thou hast my heart.

The god of us verse-men (you know, child) the Sun,
How after his journeys he sets up his rest;
If at morning o'er earth 'tis his fancy to run,
20   At night he reclines on his Thetis's breast.[2]

So when I am wearied with wandering all day,
To thee, my delight, in the evening I come;
No matter what beauties I saw in my way—
They were but my visits, but thou art my home.

25   Then finish, dear Cloe, this pastoral war;
And let us like Horace and Lydia agree:[3]
For thou art a girl as much brighter than her,
As he was a poet sublimer than me.

1718

---

1. Cf. *2 Henry IV* 5.3.101–02.
2. Apollo, god of poetry and of the sun, is said to recline at night on the breast of Thetis, one of the Nereids or sea spirits, because the sun seems to sink into the western ocean.
3. In Horace's *Odes* 3.9, the poet, who has been dallying with a girl named Cloe, makes up with Lydia, his former love.

JONATHAN SWIFT
1667–1745

Jonathan Swift—a posthumous child—was born of English parents in Dublin. Through the generosity of an uncle he was educated at Kilkenny School and Trinity College, Dublin, but before he could fix on a career, the troubles that followed upon James II's abdication and subsequent invasion of Ireland drove Swift along with other Anglo-Irish to England. Between 1689 and 1699 he was more or less continuously a member of the household of his kinsman Sir William Temple, an urbane, civilized man, a retired diplomat, and a friend of King William. During these years Swift read widely, rather reluctantly decided on the church as a career and so took orders, and discovered his astonishing gifts as a satirist. About 1696–97 he wrote his powerful satires on corruptions in religion and learning, A Tale of a Tub and The Battle of the Books, which were published in 1704 and reached their final form only in the fifth edition of 1710. These were the years in which he slowly came to maturity. When, at the age of thirty-two, he returned to Ireland as chaplain to the lord justice, the earl of Berkeley, he had a clear sense of his genius.

For the rest of his life, Swift devoted his talents to politics and religion—not clearly separated at the time—and most of his works in prose were written to further a specific cause. As a clergyman, a spirited controversialist, and a devoted supporter of the Anglican Church he was hostile to all who seemed to threaten it—Deists, free-thinkers, Roman Catholics, Nonconformists, or merely Whig politicians. In 1710 he abandoned the Whigs, because he opposed their indifference to the welfare of the Anglican Church in Ireland and their desire to repeal the Test Act, which required all holders of offices of state to take the Sacrament according to the Anglican rites, thus excluding Roman Catholics and Dissenters. Welcomed by the Tories, he became the most brilliant political journalist of the day, serving the government of Oxford and Bolingbroke as editor of the party organ, the Examiner, and as author of its most powerful articles, as well as writing longer pamphlets in support of important policies, such as that favoring the Peace of Utrecht (1713). He was greatly valued by the two ministers, who admitted him to social intimacy, although never to their counsels. The reward of his services was not the English bishopric that he had a right to expect, but the deanship of St. Patrick's Cathedral in Dublin, which came to him in 1713, a year before the death of Queen Anne and the fall of the Tories put an end to all his hopes of preferment in England.

In Ireland, where he lived unwillingly, he became not only an efficient ecclesiastical administrator but also, in 1724, the leader of Irish resistance to English oppression. Under the pseudonym "M. B. Drapier," he published the famous series of public letters that aroused the country to refuse to accept £100,000 in new copper coins (minted in England by William Wood, who had obtained his patent through court corruption), which, it was feared, would further debase the coinage of the already poverty-stricken kingdom. Although his authorship of the letters was known to all Dublin, no one could be found to earn the £300 offered by the government for infor-mation as to the identity of the drapier. Swift is still venerated in Ireland as a national hero. He earned the right to refer to himself in the epitaph that he wrote for his tomb as a vigorous defender of liberty.

His last years were less happy. Swift had suffered most of his adult life from what we now recognize as Ménière's disease, which affects the inner ear, causing dizziness, nausea, and deafness. After 1739, when he was seventy-two years old, his infirmities cut him off from his duties as dean, and from then on his social life dwindled. In 1742 guardians were appointed to administer his affairs, and his last three years were spent in gloom and lethargy. But this dark ending should not put his earlier life, so full of energy and humor, into a shadow. The writer of the satires was a man in full control of great intellectual powers.

He also had a gift for friendship. Swift was admired and loved by many of the distinguished men of his time. His friendships with Joseph Addison, Alexander Pope, John Arbuthnot, John Gay, Matthew Prior, Lord Oxford, and Lord Bolingbroke, not to mention those in his less brilliant but amiable Irish circle, bear witness to his moral integrity and social charm. Nor was he, despite some of his writings, indifferent to women. Esther Johnson (Swift's "Stella") was the daughter of Temple's steward, and when Swift first knew her, she was little more than a child. He educated her, formed her character, and came to love her as he was to love no other person. After Temple's death she moved to Dublin, where she and Swift met constantly, but never alone. While working with the Tories in London, he wrote letters to her, later published as *The Journal to Stella* (1766), and they exchanged poems as well. Whether they were secretly married or never married—and in either case why—has been often debated. A marriage of any sort seems most unlikely; and however perplexing their relationship was to others, it seems to have satisfied them. Not even the violent passion that Swift awakened, no doubt unwittingly, in the much younger woman Hester Vanhomrigh (pronounced *Van-úm-mer-y*)—with her pleadings and reproaches and early death— could unsettle his devotion to Stella. An enigmatic account of his relations with "Vanessa," as he called Vanhomrigh, is given in his poem *Cadenus and Vanessa*.

For all his involvement in public affairs, Swift seems to stand apart from his contemporaries—a striking figure among the statesmen of the time, a writer who towered above others by reason of his imagination, mordant wit, and emotional intensity. He has been called a misanthrope, a hater of humanity, and *Gulliver's Travels* has been considered an expression of savage misanthropy. It is true that Swift proclaimed himself a misanthrope in a letter to Pope, declaring that though he loved individuals, he hated "that animal called man" in general, and offering a new definition of the species as not *animal rationale* ("a rational animal") but as merely *animal rationis capax* ("an animal *capable* of reason"). This, he declared, is the "great foundation" on which his "misanthropy" was erected. Swift was stating not his hatred of his fellow creatures but his antagonism to the current optimistic view that human nature is essentially good. To the "philanthropic" flattery that sentimentalism and Deistic rationalism were paying to human nature, Swift opposed a more ancient and plausible view: that human nature is deeply and permanently flawed and that we can do nothing with or for the human race until we recognize its moral and intellectual limitations. In his epitaph he spoke of the "fierce indignation" that had torn his heart, an indignation that found superb expression in his greatest satires. It was provoked by the constant spectacle of creatures capable of reason, and therefore of reasonable conduct, steadfastly refusing to live up to their capabilities.

Swift is a master of prose. He defined a good style as "proper words in proper places," a more complex and difficult saying than at first appears. Clear, simple, concrete diction, uncomplicated syntax, economy and conciseness of language mark all his writings. His is a style that shuns ornaments and singularity of all kinds, a style that grows more tense and controlled the more fierce the indignation that it is called on to express. The virtues of his prose are those of his poetry, which shocks us with its hard look at the facts of life and the body. It is unpoetic poetry, devoid of, indeed as often as not mocking at, inspiration, romantic love, cosmetic beauty, easily assumed literary attitudes, and conventional poetic language. Like the prose, it is predominantly satiric in purpose, but not without its moments of comedy and light-heartedness, though written most often not so much to divert as to reform the reader.

A Description of a City Shower

Careful observers may foretell the hour
(By sure prognostics) when to dread a shower:
While rain depends,[1] the pensive cat gives o'er
Her frolics, and pursues her tail no more.
5   Returning home at night, you'll find the sink°   *sewer*
Strike your offended sense with double stink.
If you be wise, then go not far to dine;
You'll spend in coach hire more than save in wine.
A coming shower your shooting corns presage,
10   Old achés throb, your hollow tooth will rage.
Sauntering in coffeehouse is Dulman seen;
He damns the climate and complains of spleen.[2]
    Meanwhile the South, rising with dabbled wings,
A sable cloud athwart the welkin flings,
15   That swilled more liquor than it could contain,
And, like a drunkard, gives it up again.
Brisk Susan whips her linen from the rope,
While the first drizzling shower is borne aslope:
Such is that sprinkling which some careless quean°   *wench, slut*
20   Flirts on you from her mop, but not so clean:
You fly, invoke the gods; then turning, stop
To rail; she singing, still whirls on her mop.
Not yet the dust had shunned the unequal strife,
But, aided by the wind, fought still for life,
25   And wafted with its foe by violent gust,
'Twas doubtful which was rain and which was dust.
Ah! where must needy poet seek for aid,
When dust and rain at once his coat invade?
Sole coat, where dust cemented by the rain
30   Erects the nap, and leaves a mingled stain.
    Now in contiguous drops the flood comes down,
Threatening with deluge this devoted town.
To shops in crowds the daggled° females fly,   *mud-spattered*
Pretend to cheapen° goods, but nothing buy.   *bargain for*
35   The Templar spruce, while every spout's abroach,[3]
Stays till 'tis fair, yet seems to call a coach.
The tucked-up sempstress walks with hasty strides,
While streams run down her oiled umbrella's sides.
Here various kinds, by various fortunes led,
40   Commence acquaintance underneath a shed.
Triumphant Tories and desponding Whigs
Forget their feuds,[4] and join to save their wigs.

---

1. Impends, is imminent. An example of elevated diction used frequently throughout the poem to gain a mock dignity, comically inappropriate to the homely and realistic subject.
2. It was commonly believed at this time that the Englishman's tendency to melancholy ("the spleen") was attributable to the rainy climate. "Dulman": a type name (from "dull man"), like Congreve's "Petulant" or "Witwoud."
3. Pouring out water. "The Templar": a young man engaged in studying law. In the literature of the period the Templar is usually depicted as neglecting his professional studies for the sake of dissipation and the pursuit of literature. Cf. the Member of the Inner Temple in *Spectator* 2 (p. 2485).
4. The Whig ministry had just fallen and the Tories, led by Harley and St. John, were forming the government with which Swift was to be closely associated until the death of the queen in 1714.

Boxed in a chair° the beau impatient sits,   sedan chair
While spouts run clattering o'er the roof by fits,
45 And ever and anon with frightful din
The leather sounds;[5] he trembles from within.
So when Troy chairmen bore the wooden steed,
Pregnant with Greeks impatient to be freed
(Those bully Greeks, who, as the moderns do,
50 Instead of paying chairmen, run them through),[6]
Laocoön struck the outside with his spear,
And each imprisoned hero quaked for fear.[7]
    Now from all parts the swelling kennels[8] flow,
And bear their trophies with them as they go:
55 Filth of all hues and odors seem to tell
What street they sailed from, by their sight and smell.
They, as each torrent drives with rapid force,
From Smithfield or St. Pulchre's shape their course,
And in huge confluence joined at Snow Hill ridge,
60 Fall from the conduit prone to Holborn Bridge.[9]
Sweepings from butchers' stalls, dung, guts, and blood,
Drowned puppies, stinking sprats,° all drenched in mud,   } small herrings
Dead cats, and turnip tops, come tumbling down the flood.[1] ⌡

1710

Verses on the Death of Dr. Swift

Occasioned by Reading a Maxim in Rochefoucauld[1]

*Dans l'adversité de nos meilleurs amis nous trouvons toujours quelque
chose, qui ne nous déplaît pas.*[2]

As Rochefoucauld his maxims drew
From nature, I believe 'em true:
They argue no corrupted mind
In him; the fault is in mankind.
5   This maxim more than all the rest
Is thought too base for human breast:
"In all distresses of our friends
We first consult our private ends,
While Nature, kindly bent to ease us,

5. The roof of the sedan chair was made of leather.
6. Run them through with their swords. The bully, always prone to violence, was a familiar figure in London streets and places of amusement.
7. *Aeneid* 2.40–53.
8. The open gutters in the middle of the street.
9. An accurate description of the drainage system of this part of London—the eastern edge of Holborn and West Smithfield, which lie outside the old walls west and east of Newgate. The great cattle and sheep markets were in Smithfield. The church of St. Sepulchre ("St. Pulchre's") stood opposite Newgate Prison. Holborn Conduit was at the foot of Snow Hill. It drained into Fleet Ditch, an evil-smelling open sewer, at Holborn Bridge.
1. In Falkner's edition of Swift's *Works* (Dublin,

1735) a note almost certainly suggested by Swift points to the concluding triplet, with its resonant final alexandrine, as a burlesque of a mannerism of Dryden and other Restoration poets and claims that Swift's ridicule banished the triplet from contemporary poetry.
1. François de la Rochefoucauld (1613–1680), writer of witty, cynical maxims. Writing to Pope (November 26, 1725), Swift, opposing the optimistic philosophy that Pope and Bolingbroke were at that time developing, professed to have founded his whole character on these maxims.
2. In the misfortune of our best friends we always find something that does not displease us (French).

10   Points out some circumstance to please us."
      If this perhaps your patience move,°   *should agitate*
    Let reason and experience prove.
      We all behold with envious eyes
    Our equal raised above our size.
15   Who would not at a crowded show
    Stand high himself, keep others low?
    I love my friend as well as you,
    But why should he obstruct my view?
    Then let me have the higher post;
20   I ask but for an inch at most.
      If in a battle you should find
    One, whom you love of all mankind,
    Had some heroic action done,
    A champion killed, or trophy won;
25   Rather than thus be overtopped,
    Would you not wish his laurels cropped?
      Dear honest Ned is in the gout,
    Lies racked with pain, and you without:
    How patiently you hear him groan!
30   How glad the case is not your own!
      What poet would not grieve to see
    His brethren write as well as he?
    But rather than they should excel,
    He'd wish his rivals all in hell.
35   Her end when Emulation misses,
    She turns to envy, stings, and hisses:
    The strongest friendship yields to pride,
    Unless the odds be on our side.
      Vain humankind! fantastic race!
40   Thy various follies who can trace?
    Self-love, ambition, envy, pride,
    Their empire in our hearts divide.
    Give others riches, power, and station;
    'Tis all on me an usurpation;
45   I have no title to aspire,
    Yet, when you sink, I seem the higher.
    In Pope I cannot read a line,
    But with a sigh I wish it mine:
    When he can in one couplet fix
50   More sense than I can do in six,
    It gives me such a jealous fit,
    I cry, "Pox take him and his wit!"
      I grieve to be outdone by Gay
    In my own humorous biting way.
55   Arbuthnot[3] is no more my friend,
    Who dares to irony pretend,
    Which I was born to introduce,
    Refined it first, and showed its use.

---

3. A physician and wit, friend of Swift and Pope
(see Pope's *Epistle to Dr. Arbuthnot*, p. 2562).
Gay is the author of the famous *Beggar's Opera*
(1728), intimate friend of Swift and Pope. His
Trivia, or the Art of Walking the Streets of London
(1716) owes something to Swift's *City Shower.*

St. John, as well as Pulteney,[4] knows
60 That I had some repute for prose;
And, till they drove me out of date,
Could maul a minister of state.
If they have mortified my pride,
And made me throw my pen aside;
65 If with such talents Heaven hath blessed 'em,
Have I not reason to detest 'em?
        To all my foes, dear Fortune, send
Thy gifts, but never to my friend:
I tamely can endure the first,
70 But this with envy makes me burst.
        Thus much may serve by way of proem;
Proceed we therefore to our poem.
        The time is not remote, when I
Must by the course of nature die;
75 When, I foresee, my special friends
Will try to find their private ends:
Though it is hardly understood
Which way my death can do them good;
Yet thus, methinks, I hear 'em speak:
80 "See how the Dean begins to break!
Poor gentleman! he droops apace!
You plainly find it in his face.
That old vertigo[5] in his head
Will never leave him till he's dead.
85 Besides, his memory decays;
He recollects not what he says;
He cannot call his friends to mind;
Forgets the place where last he dined;
Plies you with stories o'er and o'er;
90 He told them fifty times before.
How does he fancy we can sit
To hear his out-of-fashion'd wit?
But he takes up with younger folks,
Who for his wine will bear his jokes.
95 Faith, he must make his stories shorter,
Or change his comrades once a quarter;
In half the time, he talks them round;
There must another set be found.
        "For poetry, he's past his prime;
100 He takes an hour to find a rhyme;
His fire is out, his wit decayed,
His fancy sunk, his Muse a jade.[6]
I'd have him throw away his pen—

4. Henry St. John, Lord Bolingbroke (see head-note to *An Essay on Man*, p. 2554), though debarred from the House of Lords and from public office, had become the center of a group of Tories and discontented young Whigs (of whom William Pulteney was one) who united in opposing Sir Robert Walpole, the chief minister. They published a political periodical, the *Craftsman*, thus rivaling Swift in his role of political pamphleteer and enemy of Sir Robert.
5. Johnson in his *Dictionary* authorizes Swift's pronunciation: *ver-ti-go.*
6. A worn-out horse, in contrast to Pegasus, the winged horse of Greek mythology, emblem of poetic inspiration.

But there's no talking to some men."
105   And then their tenderness appears
By adding largely to my years:
"He's older than he would be reckoned,
And well remembers Charles the Second.
He hardly drinks a pint of wine;
110   And that, I doubt, is no good sign.
His stomach, too, begins to fail;
Last year we thought him strong and hale;
But now he's quite another thing;
I wish he may hold out till spring."
115   Then hug themselves, and reason thus:
"It is not yet so bad with us."
    In such a case they talk in tropes,°   *figures of speech*
And by their fears express their hopes.
Some great misfortune to portend
120   No enemy can match a friend.
With all the kindness they profess,
The merit of a lucky guess
(When daily how-d'ye's come of course,
And servants answer, "Worse and worse!")
125   Would please 'em better, than to tell
That God be praised! the Dean is well.
Then he who prophesied the best,
Approves his foresight to the rest:
"You know I always feared the worst,
130   And often told you so at first."
He'd rather choose that I should die,
Than his prediction prove a lie.
Not one foretells I shall recover,
But all agree to give me over.
135   Yet, should some neighbor feel a pain
Just in the parts where I complain,
How many a message would he send?
What hearty prayers that I should mend?
Inquire what regimen I kept;
140   What gave me ease, and how I slept,
And more lament, when I was dead,
Than all the snivelers round my bed.
    My good companions, never fear;
For though you may mistake a year,
145   Though your prognostics run too fast,
They must be verified at last.
    Behold the fatal day arrive!
"How is the Dean?"—"He's just alive."
Now the departing prayer is read.
150   "He hardly breathes"—"The Dean is dead."
Before the passing bell begun,
The news through half the town has run.
"Oh! may we all for death prepare!
What has he left? and who's his heir?"
155   "I know no more than what the news is;

'Tis all bequeathed to public uses."
"To public use! a perfect whim!
What had the public done for him?
Mere envy, avarice, and pride:
160 He gave it all—but first he died.
And had the Dean in all the nation
No worthy friend, no poor relation?
So ready to do strangers good,
Forgetting his own flesh and blood?"
165 Now Grub Street[7] wits are all employed;
With elegies the town is cloyed;
Some paragraph in every paper
To curse the Dean, or bless the Drapier.[8]
The doctors, tender of their fame,
170 Wisely on me lay all the blame.
"We must confess his case was nice;[9]
But he would never take advice.
Had he been ruled, for aught appears,
He might have lived these twenty years:
175 For, when we opened him, we found,
That all his vital parts were sound."
From Dublin soon to London spread,
'Tis told at court, "The Dean is dead."
Kind Lady Suffolk, in the spleen,[1]
180 Runs laughing up to tell the Queen.
The Queen, so gracious, mild and good,
Cries, "Is he gone? 'tis time he should.
He's dead, you say; why, let him rot:
I'm glad the medals were forgot.[2]
185 I promised him, I own; but when?
I only was the Princess then;
But now, as consort of the King,
You know, 'tis quite a different thing."
Now Chartres, at Sir Robert's[3] levee,
190 Tells with a sneer the tidings heavy:
"Why, is he dead without his shoes?"
Cries Bob, "I'm sorry for the news:
Oh, were the wretch but living still,
And in his place my good friend Will![4]
195 Or had a miter on his head,
Provided Bolingbroke were dead!"
Now Curll his shop from rubbish drains:[5]

7. Originally a street in London largely inhabited by hack writers; later, a generic term applied to all such writers.
8. It was in the character of M. B., a Dublin drapier, that Swift aroused the Irish people to resistance against the importation of Wood's halfpence (see headnote to "Jonathan Swift," p. 2298).
9. Delicate; hence demanding careful diagnosis and treatment.
1. In low spirits. The phrase is ironic, as "laughing" makes clear. "Lady Suffolk": George II's mistress, with whom Swift became friendly during his visit to Pope in 1726.
2. Queen Caroline had promised Swift some medals when she was Princess of Wales during the same year.
3. Walpole. Colonel Francis Chartres was a debauchee, often satirized by Pope.
4. William Pulteney (see n. 4, p. 2303).
5. Edmund Curll, shrewd and disreputable bookseller, published pirated works, scandalous biographies, and works falsely ascribed to notable writers of the time.

Three genuine tomes of Swift's remains.
And then, to make them pass the glibber,
200   Revised by Tibbalds, Moore, and Cibber.[6]
He'll treat me as he does my betters,
Publish my will, my life, my letters;
Revive the libels born to die,
Which Pope must bear, as well as I.
205   Here shift the scene, to represent
How those I love, my death lament.
Poor Pope will grieve a month, and Gay
A week, and Arbuthnot a day.
    St. John himself will scarce forbear
210   To bite his pen, and drop a tear.
The rest will give a shrug, and cry,
"I'm sorry—but we all must die."
    Indifference clad in wisdom's guise
All fortitude of mind supplies:
215   For how can stony bowels melt
In those who never pity felt?
When *we* are lashed, *they* kiss the rod,
Resigning to the will of God.
    The fools, my juniors by a year,
220   Are tortured with suspense and fear;
Who wisely thought my age a screen,
When death approached, to stand between:
The screen removed, their hearts are trembling;
They mourn for me without dissembling.
225   My female friends, whose tender hearts
Have better learned to act their parts,
Receive the news in doleful dumps:
"The Dean is dead (and what is trumps?)
Then, Lord have mercy on his soul!
230   (Ladies, I'll venture for the vole.)[7]
Six deans, they say, must bear the pall.
(I wish I knew what king to call.)
Madam, your husband will attend
The funeral of so good a friend?"
235   "No, madam, 'tis a shocking sight;
And he's engaged tomorrow night:
My Lady Club would take it ill,
If he should fail her at quadrille.
He loved the Dean—(I lead a heart)
240   But dearest friends, they say, must part.
His time was come; he ran his race;
We hope he's in a better place."
    Why do we grieve that friends should die?
No loss more easy to supply.

---

6. Lewis Theobald (1688–1744), Shakespeare scholar and editor, already enthroned as king of the Dunces in Pope's *The Dunciad* (1728). Like Pope, Swift spells the name phonetically. James Moore-Smyth, poetaster and playwright, an enemy of Pope. Colley Cibber (1671–1757), comic actor, playwright, and supremely untalented poet laureate. He succeeded Theobald as king of the Dunces in the *The Dunciad* of 1743.
7. The equivalent in the card game quadrille of bidding a grand slam in bridge.

245 One year is past; a different scene;
No further mention of the Dean,
Who now, alas! no more is missed,
Than if he never did exist.
Where's now this favorite of Apollo?
250 Departed—and his works must follow,
Must undergo the common fate;
His kind of wit is out of date.
 Some country squire to Lintot[8] goes,
Inquires for *Swift* in verse and prose.
255 Says Lintot, "I have heard the name;
He died a year ago."—"The same."
He searches all his shop in vain.
"Sir, you may find them in Duck Lane:[9]
I sent them, with a load of books,
260 Last Monday to the pastry-cook's.[1]
To fancy they could live a year!
I find you're but a stranger here.
The Dean was famous in his time,
And had a kind of knack at rhyme.
265 His way of writing now is past:
The town has got a better taste.
I keep no antiquated stuff;
But spick and span I have enough.
Pray do but give me leave to show 'em:
270 Here's Colley Cibber's birthday poem.
This ode you never yet have seen
By Stephen Duck[2] upon the Queen.
Then here's a letter finely penned.
Against the *Craftsman*[3] and his friend;
275 It clearly shows that all reflection
On ministers is disaffection.
Next, here's Sir Robert's vindication,[4]
And Mr. Henley's last oration.[5]
The hawkers have not got 'em yet:
280 Your honor please to buy a set?
 "Here's Woolston's[6] tracts, the twelfth edition;
'Tis read by every politician:
The country members, when in town,
To all their boroughs send them down;
285 You never met a thing so smart;
The courtiers have them all by heart;
Those maids of honor (who can read)
Are taught to use them for their creed.

8. Bernard Lintot, a bookseller and the publisher
of Pope's Homer and some of his early poems.
9. London street where secondhand books and
publishers's remainders were sold.
1. To be used as waste paper for lining baking
dishes and wrapping parcels.
2. "The thresher poet," an agricultural laborer
whose verse brought him to the notice and patronage of Queen Caroline.
3. See n. 4, p. 2302.

4. Walpole hires a string of party scribblers who
do nothing else but write in his defense [Swift's
note].
5. "Orator" John Henley, an Independent
preacher who dazzled unlearned audiences with
his oratory and who wrote treatises on elocution.
6. Thomas Woolston (1670–1733), a freethinker
whose *Discourses on the Miracles of Our Saviour*
had recently earned him notoriety.

The reverend author's good intention
290 Has been rewarded with a pension.
He does an honor to his gown,
By bravely running priestcraft down;
He shows, as sure as God's in Gloucester,[7]
That Jesus was a grand impostor;
295 That all his miracles were cheats,
Performed as jugglers do their feats:
The Church had never such a writer;
A shame he hath not got a miter!"
    Suppose me dead; and then suppose
300 A club assembled at the Rose;[8]
Where, from discourse of this and that,
I grow the subject of their chat:
And while they toss my name about,
With favor some, and some without,
305 One, quite indifferent in the cause,
My character impartial draws:
    "The Dean, if we believe report,
Was never ill received at court.
As for his works in verse and prose,
310 I own myself no judge of those;
Nor can I tell what critics thought 'em:
But this I know, all people bought 'em,
As with a moral view designed
To cure the vices of mankind.
315   "His vein, ironically grave,
Exposed the fool and lashed the knave;
To steal a hint was never known,
But what he writ was all his own.
    "He never thought an honor done him,
320 Because a duke was proud to own him;
Would rather slip aside and choose
To talk with wits in dirty shoes;
Despised the fools with stars and garters,
So often seen caressing Chartres.
325 He never courted men in station,
Nor persons held in admiration;
Of no man's greatness was afraid,
Because he sought for no man's aid.
Though trusted long in great affairs,
330 He gave himself no haughty airs;
Without regarding private ends,
Spent all his credit for his friends;
And only chose the wise and good;
No flatterers, no allies in blood;
335 But succored virtue in distress,
And seldom failed of good success;
As numbers in their hearts must own,
Who, but for him, had been unknown.

---

7. Proverbially, Gloucestershire was full of monks.   8. A fashionable tavern in Covent Garden.

"With princes kept a due decorum,
340   But never stood in awe before 'em.
He followed David's lesson just;
In princes never put thy trust:[9]
And would you make him truly sour,
Provoke him with a slave in power.
345   The Irish senate if you named,
With what impatience he declaimed!
Fair Liberty was all his cry,
For her he stood prepared to die;
For her he boldly stood alone;
350   For her he oft exposed his own.
Two kingdoms, just as faction led,
Had set a price upon his head,
But not a traitor could be found,
To sell him for six hundred pound.[1]
355   "Had he but spared his tongue and pen,
He might have rose like other men;
But power was never in his thought,
And wealth he valued not a groat:
Ingratitude he often found,
360   And pitied those who meant the wound;
But kept the tenor of his mind,
To merit well of human kind:
Nor made a sacrifice of those
Who still were true, to please his foes.
365   He labored many a fruitless hour,
To reconcile his friends in power;
Saw mischief by a faction brewing,
While they pursued each other's ruin.
But, finding vain was all his care,
370   He left the court in mere despair.[2]
"And, oh! how short are human schemes!
Here ended all our golden dreams.
What St. John's skill in state affairs,
What Ormonde's[3] valor, Oxford's cares,
375   To save their sinking country lent,
Was all destroyed by one event.[4]
Too soon that precious life was ended,
On which alone our weal depended.
When up a dangerous faction starts,[5]

9. Psalm 146.3.
1. In 1714 the government offered £300 for the discovery of the author of Swift's *Public Spirit of the Whigs*, and in 1724 the Irish government offered a similar amount for the discovery of the author of the fourth of Swift's *Drapier's Letters*.
2. The antagonism between the two chief ministers (his dear friends), Robert Harley, earl of Oxford, and Bolingbroke, paralyzed the Tory ministry in the crucial last months of Queen Anne's life and drove Swift to retirement in Ireland, whence he returned in 1714 to make a final effort to heal the breach and save the government. He failed and retired to the country in despair. There

he received the news of Anne's death on August 1. The Hanoverian succession brought the Whigs back in triumph, ruined Swift's friends, and brought Swift's public life to a close.
3. James Butler, duke of Ormonde, who succeeded to the command of the English armies on the Continent when, in 1711, the duke of Marlborough was stripped of his offices by Anne. He went into exile in 1714 and was active in Jacobite intrigue.
4. The death of Queen Anne.
5. Swift's view of the policies of the "dangerous faction" (the Whig party) is hardly impartial. He feared it especially because of its toleration of Dis-

380   With wrath and vengeance in their hearts;
      By solemn League and Covenant bound,
      To ruin, slaughter, and confound;
      To turn religion to a fable,
      And make the government a Babel;
385   Pervert the laws, disgrace the gown,
      Corrupt the senate, rob the crown;
      To sacrifice old England's glory,
      And make her infamous in story:
      When such a tempest shook the land,
390   How could unguarded Virtue stand?
      With horror, grief, despair, the Dean
      Beheld the dire destructive scene:
      His friends in exile, or the Tower,[6]
      Himself within the frown of power,
395   Pursued by base envenomed pens,
      Far to the land of slaves and fens;°   *Ireland*
      A servile race in folly nursed,
      Who truckle most, when treated worst.
        "By innocence and resolution,
400   He bore continual persecution;
      While numbers to preferment rose,
      Whose merits were to be his foes;
      When even his own familiar friends,
      Intent upon their private ends,
405   Like renegadoes now he feels,
      Against him lifting up their heels.
        "The Dean did, by his pen, defeat
      An infamous destructive cheat;[7]
      Taught fools their interest how to know,
410   And gave them arms to ward the blow.
      Envy has owned it was his doing,
      To save that hapless land from ruin;
      While they who at the steerage[8] stood,
      And reaped the profit, sought his blood.
415   "To save them from their evil fate,
      In him was held a crime of state.
      A wicked monster on the bench,[9]
      Whose fury blood could never quench;
      As vile and profligate a villain,
420   As modern Scroggs, or old Tresilian;[1]
      Who long all justice had discarded,

---

senters, and so as an enemy of the Church of
England.
6. Bolingbroke was in exile; Oxford was sent to the
Tower of London by the Whigs.
7. The scheme to introduce Wood's copper halfpence into Ireland in 1723–24.
8. Literally the steering of a ship. Here the direction and management of public affairs in Ireland.
9. William Whitshed, lord chief justice of the
King's Bench of Ireland. In 1720, when the jury
refused to find Swift's anonymous pamphlet *Proposal for the Universal Use of Irish Manufacture*
wicked and seditious, Whitshed sent them back

nine times, hoping to force them to another verdict. In 1724 he presided over the trial of Harding,
the printer of Swift's fourth *Drapier's Letter*, but
again was unable, despite bullying, to force a verdict of guilty.
1. In 1381, Sir Robert Tresilian punished with
great severity men who had participated in the
Peasants' Revolt; he was impeached and in 1387
was hanged. Sir William Scroggs, lord chief justice
of England at the time of the Popish Plot, 1678
(see Dryden's *Absalom and Achitophel*, p. 2075),
was impeached for his misdemeanors in office in
1680.

Nor feared he God, nor man regarded;
Vowed on the Dean his rage to vent,
And make him of his zeal repent:
425   But Heaven his innocence defends,
The grateful people stand his friends;
Not strains of law, nor judge's frown,
Nor topics brought to please the crown,
Nor witness hired, nor jury picked,
430   Prevail to bring him in convict.
      "In exile, with a steady heart,
He spent his life's declining part;
Where folly, pride, and faction sway,
Remote from St. John, Pope, and Gay.
435   "His friendships there, to few confined,
Were always of the middling kind;
No fools of rank, a mongrel breed,
Who fain would pass for lords indeed:
Where titles give no right or power,
440   And peerage is a withered flower;
He would have held it a disgrace,
If such a wretch had known his face.
On rural squires, that kingdom's bane,
He vented oft his wrath in vain;
445   Biennial squires[2] to market brought:
Who sell their souls and votes for naught;
The nation stripped, go joyful back,
To rob the church, their tenants rack,
Go snacks with rogues and rapparees;°   *highwaymen*
450   And keep the peace to pick up fees;
In every job to have a share,
A jail or barrack to repair;
And turn the tax for public roads
Commodious to their own abodes.
455   "Perhaps I may allow the Dean
Had too much satire in his vein;
And seemed determined not to starve it,
Because no age could more deserve it.
Yet malice never was his aim;
460   He lashed the vice, but spared the name;
No individual could resent,
Where thousands equally were meant;
His satire points at no defect,
But what all mortals may correct;
465   For he abhorred that senseless tribe
Who call it humor when they gibe:
He spared a hump, or crooked nose,
Whose owners set not up for beaux.
True genuine dullness moved his pity,
470   Unless it offered to be witty.
Those who their ignorance confessed,

2. Members of the Irish Parliament.

He ne'er offended with a jest;
But laughed to hear an idiot quote
A verse from Horace learned by rote.
475   "He knew an hundred pleasant stories,
With all the turns of Whigs and Tories:
Was cheerful to his dying day;
And friends would let him have his way.
   "He gave the little wealth he had
480 To build a house for fools and mad;[3]
And showed by one satiric touch,
No nation wanted it so much.
That kingdom he hath left his debtor,
I wish it soon may have a better."

1731   1739

From A Tale of a Tub

A Digression Concerning the Original, the Use, and Improvement of Madness in a Commonwealth[1]

Nor shall it any ways detract from the just reputation of this famous sect,[2] that its rise and institution are owing to such an author as I have described Jack to be, a person whose intellectuals were overturned, and his brain shaken out of its natural position; which we commonly suppose to be a distemper, and call by the name of madness or frenzy. For, if we take a survey of the greatest actions that have been performed in the world, under the influence of single men, which are the establishment of new empires by conquest, the advance and progress of new schemes in philosophy, and the contriving, as well as the propagating, of new religions, we shall find the authors of them all to have been persons whose natural reason had admitted great revolutions from their diet, their education, the prevalency of some certain temper, together with the particular influence of air and climate. Besides, there is something individual in human minds, that easily kindles at the accidental approach and collision of certain circumstances, which, though of paltry and mean appearance, do often flame out into the greatest emergencies of life. For great turns are not always given by strong hands, but by lucky adaption, and at proper seasons; and it is of no import where the fire was kindled, if the vapor has once got up into the brain. For the upper region of man is furnished like the middle region of the air; the mate-

3. Swift left funds to endow a hospital for the insane.
1. *A Tale of a Tub,* Swift's first major work, recounts the adventures of three brothers: Peter (Roman Catholicism), Martin (Luther, here regarded as inspiring the Church of England), and Jack (Calvin, the spirit of Protestant dissent). But the most memorable character of the book is its narrator, who interrupts the story with numerous digressions (including even "A Digression in Praise of Digressions") and whose pride in learning and lack of common sense represent the zealous modern insanity that Swift takes as his target for satire.

"A Digression Concerning Madness," this narrator's masterpiece, is based on Swift's ironical doctrine of "the mechanical operation of the spirit": the notion that all spiritual and mental states derive from physical causes—in this case, the ascent of "vapors" to the brain. Beneath his whimsy, however, the author raises a fearful question: what right has any human being to trust that he or she is sane?
2. The Aeolists, who "maintain the original cause of all things to be wind," are equated by Swift with religious dissenters who believe themselves to be inspired.

rials are formed from causes of the widest difference, yet produce at last the same substance and effect. Mists arise from the earth, steams from dunghills, exhalations from the sea, and smoke from fire; yet all clouds are the same in composition as well as consequences, and the fumes issuing from a jakes[3] will furnish as comely and useful a vapor as incense from an altar. Thus far, I suppose, will easily be granted me; and then it will follow, that as the face of nature never produces rain but when it is overcast and disturbed, so human understanding, seated in the brain, must be troubled and overspread by vapors, ascending from the lower faculties to water the invention and render it fruitful. Now, although these vapors (as it hath been already said) are of as various original as those of the skies, yet the crop they produce differs both in kind and degree, merely according to the soil. I will produce two instances to prove and explain what I am now advancing.

A certain great prince[4] raised a mighty army, filled his coffers with infinite treasures, provided an invincible fleet, and all this without giving the least part of his design to his greatest ministers or his nearest favorites. Immediately the whole world was alarmed; the neighboring crowns in trembling expectation towards what point the storm would burst; the small politicians everywhere forming profound conjectures. Some believed he had laid a scheme for universal monarchy; others, after much insight, determined the matter to be a project for pulling down the Pope, and setting up the reformed religion, which had once been his own. Some again, of a deeper sagacity, sent him into Asia to subdue the Turk, and recover Palestine. In the midst of all these projects and preparations, a certain state-surgeon,[5] gathering the nature of the disease by these symptoms, attempted the cure, at one blow performed the operation, broke the bag, and out flew the vapor; nor did anything want to render it a complete remedy, only that the prince unfortunately happened to die in the performance. Now, is the reader exceeding curious to learn whence this vapor took its rise, which had so long set the nations at a gaze? What secret wheel, what hidden spring, could put into motion so wonderful an engine? It was afterwards discovered that the movement of this whole machine had been directed by an absent female, whose eyes had raised a protuberancy, and before emission, she was removed into an enemy's country. What should an unhappy prince do in such ticklish circumstances as these? He tried in vain the poet's never-failing receipt of *corpora quaeque;*[6] for,

> *Idque petit corpus mens unde est saucia amore:*
> *Unde feritur, eo tendit, gestitque coire.*—LUCRETIUS[7]

Having to no purpose used all peaceable endeavors, the collected part of the semen, raised and inflamed, became adust,[8] converted to choler, turned head upon the spinal duct, and ascended to the brain. The very same principle that influences a bully to break the windows of a whore who has jilted

---

3. Latrine.
4. "This was Harry the Great of France" [Swift's note]. Henry IV (1553–1610), infatuated with the princesse de Condé, whose husband had removed her to the Spanish Netherlands, prepared an expedition to bring her back.
5. Ravillac, who stabbed Henry the Great in his

coach [Swift's note].
6. Any available bodies (Latin).
7. The body strives for that which sickens the mind with love. . . . Stretches out toward that which smites it, and yearns to couple (Latin; *De Rerum Natura* 4.1048ff.).
8. Burned up.

him, naturally stirs up a great prince to raise mighty armies, and dream of nothing but sieges, battles, and victories.

——*Teterrima belli*
Causa——⁹

The other instance is what I have read somewhere in a very ancient author, of a mighty king,¹ who, for the space of above thirty years, amused himself to take and lose towns, beat armies, and be beaten, drive princes out of their dominions; fright children from their bread and butter; burn, lay waste, plunder, dragoon, massacre subject and stranger, friend and foe, male and female. 'Tis recorded, that the philosophers of each country were in grave dispute upon causes natural, moral, and political, to find out where they should assign an original solution of this phenomenon. At last the vapor or spirit, which animated the hero's brain, being in perpetual circulation, seized upon that region of the human body, so renowned for furnishing the *zibeta occidentalis*,² and gathering there into a tumor, left the rest of the world for that time in peace. Of such mighty consequence it is where those exhalations fix, and of so little from whence they proceed. The same spirits which, in their superior progress, would conquer a kingdom, descending upon the anus, conclude in a fistula.³

Let us next examine the great introducers of new schemes in philosophy, and search till we can find from what faculty of the soul the disposition arises in mortal man, of taking it into his head to advance new systems with such an eager zeal, in things agreed on all hands impossible to be known; from what seeds this disposition springs, and to what quality of human nature these grand innovators have been indebted for their number of disciples. Because it is plain, that several of the chief among them, both ancient and modern, were usually mistaken by their adversaries, and indeed by all except their own followers, to have been persons crazed, or out of their wits; having generally proceeded, in the common course of their words and actions, by a method very different from the vulgar dictates of unrefined reason; agreeing for the most part in their several models, with their present undoubted successors in the academy of modern Bedlam⁴ (whose merits and principles I shall farther examine in due place). Of this kind were *Epicurus, Diogenes, Apollonius, Lucretius, Paracelsus, Descartes*,⁵ and others, who, if they were now in the world, tied fast, and separate from their followers, would, in this our undistinguishing age, incur manifest danger of phlebotomy,⁶ and whips, and chains, and dark chambers, and straw. For what man, in the natural state or course of thinking, did ever conceive it in his power to reduce the notions of all mankind exactly to the same length, and breadth, and height of his own? Yet this is the first humble and civil design of all innovators in the empire of reason. Epicurus modestly hoped, that one time or other a

9. "The most abominable cause of war" (Latin) in olden days, according to Horace, *Satires* 1.3.107–08, was a whore.
1. This is meant of the present French king [Louis XIV] [Swift's note].
2. Paracelsus, who was so famous for chemistry, tried an experiment upon human excrement, to make a perfume of it, which when he had brought to perfection, he called *zibeta occidentalis*, or west-

ern-civet, the back parts of man . . . being the west [Swift's note].
3. Ulcer shaped like a pipe.
4. Bethlehem hospital, London's lunatic asylum.
5. Each of these famous speculative thinkers was known as a materialist, hence suspected by Swift of encouraging atheism.
6. Medical bloodletting.

certain fortuitous concourse of all men's opinions, after perpetual justlings, the sharp with the smooth, the light and the heavy, the round and the square, would by certain *clinamina*[7] unite in the notions of atoms and void, as these did in the originals of all things. Cartesius reckoned to see, before he died, the sentiments of all philosophers, like so many lesser stars in his romantic system, wrapped and drawn within his own vortex.[8] Now, I would gladly be informed, how it is possible to account for such imaginations as these in particular men without recourse to my phenomenon of vapors, ascending from the lower faculties to overshadow the brain, and there distilling into conceptions for which the narrowness of our mother-tongue has not yet assigned any other name beside that of madness or frenzy. Let us therefore now conjecture how it comes to pass, that none of these great prescribers do ever fail providing themselves and their notions with a number of implicit disciples. And, I think, the reason is easy to be assigned: for there is a peculiar string in the harmony of human understanding, which in several individuals is exactly of the same tuning. This, if you can dexterously screw up to its right key, and then strike gently upon it, whenever you have the good fortune to light among those of the same pitch, they will, by a secret necessary sympathy, strike exactly at the same time. And in this one circumstance lies all the skill or luck of the matter; for if you chance to jar the string among those who are either above or below your own height, instead of subscribing to your doctrine, they will tie you fast, call you mad, and feed you with bread and water. It is therefore a point of the nicest conduct to distinguish and adapt this noble talent, with respect to the differences of persons and of times. Cicero understood this very well, when writing to a friend in England, with a caution, among other matters, to beware of being cheated by our hackney-coachmen (who, it seems, in those days were as arrant rascals as they are now), has these remarkable words: *Est quod gaudeas te in ista loca venisse, ubi aliquid sapere viderere*.[9] For, to speak a bold truth, it is a fatal miscarriage so ill to order affairs, as to pass for a fool in one company, when in another you might be treated as a philosopher. Which I desire some certain gentlemen of my acquaintance to lay up in their hearts, as a very seasonable *innuendo*.

This, indeed, was the fatal mistake of that worthy gentleman, my most ingenious friend, Mr. W—tt—n,[1] a person, in appearance, ordained for great designs, as well as performances; whether you will consider his notions or his looks. Surely no man ever advanced into the public with fitter qualifications of body and mind, for the propagation of a new religion. Oh, had those happy talents, misapplied to vain philosophy, been turned into their proper channels of dreams and visions, where distortion of mind and countenance are of such sovereign use, the base detracting world would not then have dared to report that something is amiss, that his brain has under-

7. Swerves. The Greek philosopher Epicurus held that the universe was formed by atoms swerving together; Swift implies that a similar miracle would be required for people to join in agreement with Epicurus.
8. The physics of René Descartes (1596–1650) is based on a theory of vortices; Swift considered the theory pure romance.

9. It is ground for rejoicing that you have come to such places, where anyone can seem wise (Latin; Cicero's *Familiar Epistles* 7.10).
1. William Wotton (who had championed modern authors against Swift's patron, Sir William Temple, a spokesman for the ancients) is ridiculed in Swift's *The Battle of the Books*, published in the same volume as *A Tale of a Tub* (1704).

gone an unlucky shake; which even his brother modernists themselves, like ungrates, do whisper so loud, that it reaches up to the very garret I am now writing in.

Lastly, whosoever pleases to look into the fountains of enthusiasm,[2] from whence, in all ages, have eternally proceeded such fattening streams, will find the springhead to have been as troubled and muddy as the current. Of such great emolument is a tincture of this vapor, which the world calls madness, that without its help, the world would not only be deprived of those two great blessings, conquests and systems, but even all mankind would unhappily be reduced to the same belief in things invisible. Now, the former *postulatum* being held, that it is of no import from what originals this vapor proceeds, but either in what angles it strikes and spreads over the understanding, or upon what species of brain it ascends; it will be a very delicate point to cut the feather, and divide the several reasons to a nice and curious reader, how this numerical difference in the brain can produce effects of so vast a difference from the same vapor, as to be the sole point of individuation between Alexander the Great, Jack of Leyden[3] and Monsieur Descartes. The present argument is the most abstracted that ever I engaged in; it strains my faculties to their highest stretch; and I desire the reader to attend with utmost perpensity;[4] for I now proceed to unravel this knotty point.

There is in mankind a certain[5]   •   •   •   •   •

•   •   •   •   •   •   •   •

Hic multa   •   •   •   •   •

desiderantur.   •   •   •   •   •

•   •   •   •   •   • And this I take to be a clear solution of the matter.

Having therefore so narrowly passed through this intricate difficulty, the reader will, I am sure, agree with me in the conclusion, that if the moderns mean by madness, only a disturbance or transposition of the brain, by force of certain vapors issuing up from the lower faculties, then has this madness been the parent of all those mighty revolutions that have happened in empire, in philosophy, and in religion. For the brain, in its natural position and state of serenity, disposeth its owner to pass his life in the common forms, without any thought of subduing multitudes to his own power, his reasons, or his visions; and the more he shapes his understanding by the pattern of human learning, the less he is inclined to form parties after his particular notions, because that instructs him in his private infirmities, as well as in the stubborn ignorance of the people. But when a man's fancy gets astride on his reason, when imagination is at cuffs with the senses, and common understanding, as well as common sense, is kicked out of doors, the first proselyte he makes is himself; and when that is once compassed, the difficulty is not so great in

---

2. For much of the 18th century the word *enthusiasm* (literally, "possessed by a god") signified a deluded belief in personal revelation.
3. John of Leyden, a tailor and prophet, briefly established a revolutionary Anabaptist community, the "New Jerusalem," in the city of Münster early in the 16th century.
4. Consideration.

5. "Here is another defect in the manuscript, but I think the author did wisely, and that the matter which thus strained his faculties, was not worth a solution; and it were well if all metaphysical cobweb problems were no otherwise answered" [Swift's note]. The Latin phrase ("Much is missing here") indicates a gap in the text Swift pretends to be "editing."

bringing over others; a strong delusion always operating from without as vigorously as from within. For cant[6] and vision are to the ear and the eye, the same that tickling is to the touch. Those entertainments and pleasures we most value in life, are such as dupe and play the wag with the senses. For, if we take an examination of what is generally understood by happiness, as it has respect either to the understanding or the senses, we shall find all its properties and adjuncts will herd under this short definition, that it is a perpetual possession of being well deceived. And first, with relation to the mind or understanding, 'tis manifest what mighty advantages fiction has over truth; and the reason is just at our elbow, because imagination can build nobler scenes, and produce more wonderful revolutions, than fortune or nature will be at expense to furnish. Nor is mankind so much to blame in his choice thus determining him, if we consider that the debate merely lies between things past and things conceived; and so the question is only this: whether things that have place in the imagination, may not as properly be said to exist, as those that are seated in the memory; which may be justly held in the affirmative, and very much to the advantage of the former, since this is acknowledged to be the womb of things, and the other allowed to be no more than the grave. Again, if we take this definition of happiness, and examine it with reference to the senses, it will be acknowledged wonderfully adapt. How fading and insipid do all objects accost us, that are not conveyed in the vehicle of delusion! How shrunk is everything, as it appears in the glass of nature! So that if it were not for the assistance of artificial mediums, false lights, refracted angles, varnish, and tinsel, there would be a mighty level in the felicity and enjoyments of mortal men. If this were seriously considered by the world, as I have a certain reason to suspect it hardly will, men would no longer reckon among their high points of wisdom, the art of exposing weak sides, and publishing infirmities; an employment, in my opinion, neither better nor worse than that of unmasking, which, I think, has never been allowed[7] fair usage, either in the world, or the playhouse.

In the proportion that credulity is a more peaceful possession of the mind than curosity, so far preferable is that wisdom, which converses about the surface, to that pretended philosophy which enters into the depth of things, and then comes gravely back with informations and discoveries, that in the inside they are good for nothing. The two senses, to which all objects first address themselves, are the sight and the touch; these never examine farther than the color, the shape, the size, and whatever other qualities dwell, or are drawn by art upon the outward of bodies; and then comes reason officiously with tools for cutting, and opening, and mangling, and piercing, offering to demonstrate, that they are not of the same consistence quite through. Now I take all this to be the last degree of perverting nature; one of whose eternal laws it is, to put her best furniture forward. And therefore, in order to save the charges of all such expensive anatomy for the time to come, I do here think fit to inform the reader, that in such conclusions as these, reason is certainly in the right, and that in most corporeal beings, which have fallen under my cognizance, the outside has been infinitely preferable to the in;

---

6. "Sudden exclamations, whining, unusual tones, and in fine all praying and preaching like the unlearned of the Presbyterians" (*Spectator* 147).

7. Admitted to be.

whereof I have been farther convinced from some late experiments. Last week I saw a woman flayed, and you will hardly believe how much it altered her person for the worse. Yesterday I ordered the carcass of a beau to be stripped in my presence; when we were all amazed to find so many unsuspected faults under one suit of clothes. Then I laid open his brain, his heart, and his spleen; but I plainly perceived at every operation, that the farther we proceeded, we found the defects increase upon us in number and bulk; from all which, I justly formed this conclusion to myself: that whatever philosopher or projector[8] can find out an art to solder and patch up the flaws and imperfections of nature, will deserve much better of mankind, and teach us a more useful science, than that so much in present esteem, of widening and exposing them (like him who held anatomy to be the ultimate end of physic).[9] And he, whose fortunes and dispositions have placed him in a convenient station to enjoy the fruits of this noble art; he that can with Epicurus content his ideas with the films and images that fly off upon his senses from the superficies[1] of things; such a man, truly wise, creams off nature, leaving the sour and the dregs for philosophy and reason to lap up. This is the sublime and refined point of felicity, called the possession of being well deceived; the serene peaceful state of being a fool among knaves.

But to return to madness. It is certain, that according to the system I have above deduced, every species thereof proceeds from a redundancy of vapors; therefore, as some kinds of frenzy give double strength to the sinews, so there are of other species, which add vigor, and life, and spirit to the brain. Now, it usually happens, that these active spirits, getting possession of the brain, resemble those that haunt other waste and empty dwellings, which for want of business, either vanish, and carry away a piece of the house, or else stay at home and fling it all out of the windows. By which are mystically displayed the two principal branches of madness, and which some philosophers, not considering so well as I, have mistaken to be different in their causes, overhastily assigning the first to deficiency, and the other to redundance.

I think it therefore manifest, from what I have here advanced, that the main point of skill and address is to furnish employment for this redundancy of vapor, and prudently to adjust the season of it; by which means it may certainly become of cardinal and catholic emolument, in a commonwealth. Thus one man, choosing a proper juncture, leaps into a gulf, from thence proceeds a hero, and is called the saver of his country; another achieves the same enterprise, but unluckily timing it, has left the brand of madness fixed as a reproach upon his memory; upon so nice a distinction, are we taught to repeat the name of Curtius with reverence and love, that of Empedocles[2] with hatred and contempt. Thus also it is usually conceived, that the elder Brutus only personated the fool and madman for the good of the public; but this was nothing else than a redundancy of the same vapor long misapplied, called by the Latins, *ingenium par negotiis;*[3] or (to translate it as nearly as I can) a sort of frenzy, never in its right element, till you take it up in business of the state.

---

8. Someone given to speculative experiments.
9. Medical practice.
1. Surfaces. Epicurus considered the senses, directly affected by objects, more trustworthy than reason.
2. The Roman hero Marcus Curtius appeased the

gods by hurling himself into an ominous crack in the earth of the Forum; Empedocles committed suicide by leaping into the crater of Mount Etna.
3. A talent for business (Latin). Lucius Junius Brutus, like Hamlet, pretended madness to deceive his murderous uncle, Tarquin the Proud.

Upon all which, and many other reasons of equal weight, though not equally curious, I do here gladly embrace an opportunity I have long sought for, of recommending it as a very noble undertaking to Sir Edward Seymour, Sir Christopher Musgrave, Sir John Bowls, John How, Esq.,[4] and other patriots concerned, that they would move for leave to bring in a bill for appointing commissioners to inspect into Bedlam, and the parts adjacent; who shall be empowered to send for persons, papers, and records, to examine into the merits and qualifications of every student and professor, to observe with utmost exactness their several dispositions and behavior, by which means, duly distinguishing and adapting their talents, they might produce admirable instruments for the several offices in a state, . . . ,[5] civil, and military, proceeding in such methods as I shall here humbly propose. And I hope the gentle reader will give some allowance to my great solicitudes in this important affair, upon account of the high esteem I have borne that honorable society, whereof I had some time the happiness to be an unworthy member.

Is any student tearing his straw in piece-meal, swearing and blaspheming, biting his grate, foaming at the mouth, and emptying his piss-pot in the spectators' faces? Let the right worshipful the commissioners of inspection give him a regiment of dragoons, and send him into Flanders among the rest. Is another eternally talking, sputtering, gaping, bawling in a sound without period or article? What wonderful talents are here mislaid! Let him be furnished immediately with a green bag and papers, and threepence in his pocket,[6] and away with him to Westminster Hall. You will find a third gravely taking the dimensions of his kennel, a person of foresight and insight, though kept quite in the dark; for why, like Moses, *ecce cornuta erat ejus facies.*[7] He walks duly in one pace, entreats your penny with due gravity and ceremony, talks much of hard times, and taxes, and the whore of Babylon, bars up the wooden window of his cell constantly at eight o'clock, dreams of fire, and shoplifters, and court-customers, and privileged places. Now, what a figure would all these acquirements amount to, if the owner were sent into the city[8] among his brethren! Behold a fourth, in much and deep conversation with himself, biting his thumbs at proper junctures, his countenance checkered with business and design, sometimes walking very fast, with his eyes nailed to a paper that he holds in his hands; a great saver of time, somewhat thick of hearing, very short of sight, but more of memory; a man ever in haste, a great hatcher and breeder of business, and excellent at the famous art of whispering nothing; a huge idolator of monosyllables and procrastination, so ready to give his word to everybody, that he never keeps it; one that has forgot the common meaning of words, but an admirable retainer of the sound; extremely subject to the looseness,[9] for his occasions are perpetually calling him away. If you approach his grate in his familiar intervals, "Sir," says he, "give me a penny, and I'll sing you a song; but give me the penny first." (Hence comes the common saying, and commoner practice, of parting with money for a song.) What a complete system of court skill is here

---

4. Members of Parliament.
5. Swift omits the third office, ecclesiastical. "Instruments": useful persons.
6. "A lawyer's coach-hire" [Swift's note] from the Inns of Court to Westminster. Most lawyers carried green bags.
7. "Cornutus is either horned or shining, and by

this term, Moses is described in the vulgar Latin of the Bible" [Swift's note]. Swift puns on the Latin phrase (behold his face was shining) by suggesting someone kept in the dark through being "horned," i.e., a cuckold.
8. The commercial center of London.
9. Diarrhea.

described in every branch of it, and all utterly lost with wrong application! Accost the hole of another kennel, first stopping your nose, you will behold a surly, gloomy, nasty, slovenly mortal, raking in his own dung, and dabbling in his urine. The best part of his diet is the reversion of his own ordure, which expiring into steams, whirls perpetually about, and at last re-infunds.[1] His complexion is of a dirty yellow, with a thin scattered beard, exactly agreeable to that of his diet upon its first declination, like other insects, who having their birth and education in an excrement, from thence borrow their color and their smell. The student of this apartment is very sparing of his words, but somewhat over-liberal of his breath; he holds his hand out ready to receive your penny, and immediately upon receipt withdraws to his former occupations. Now, is it not amazing to think, the society of Warwick-lane[2] should have no more concern for the recovery of so useful a member, who, if one may judge from these appearances, would become the greatest ornament to that illustrious body? Another student struts up fiercely to your teeth, puffing with his lips, half squeezing out his eyes, and very graciously holds you out his hand to kiss. The keeper desires you not to be afraid of this professor, for he will do you no hurt; to him alone is allowed the liberty of the antechamber, and the orator of the place gives you to understand, that this solemn person is a tailor run mad with pride. This considerable student is adorned with many other qualities, upon which at present I shall not farther enlarge.————*Hark in your ear*[3]————I am strangely mistaken, if all his address, his motions, and his airs, would not then be very natural, and in their proper element.

I shall not descend so minutely, as to insist upon the vast number of beaux, fiddlers, poets, and politicians, that the world might recover by such a reformation; but what is more material, besides the clear gain redounding to the commonwealth, by so large an acquisition of persons to employ, whose talents and acquirements, if I may be so bold as to affirm it, are now buried, or at least misapplied; it would be a mighty advantage accruing to the public from this inquiry, that all these would very much excel, and arrive at great perfection in their several kinds; which, I think, is manifest from what I have already shown, and shall enforce by this one plain instance: that even I myself, the author of these momentous truths, am a person, whose imaginations are hard-mouthed,[4] and exceedingly disposed to run away with his reason, which I have observed from long experience to be a very light rider, and easily shook off; upon which account, my friends will never trust me alone, without a solemn promise to vent my speculations in this, or the like manner, for the universal benefit of human kind; which perhaps the gentle, courteous, and candid reader, brimful of that modern charity and tenderness usually annexed to his office, will be very hardly persuaded to believe.

1704

---

1. Pours in again.
2. Royal College of Physicians.
3. I cannot conjecture what the author means here, or how this chasm could be filled, though it is capable of more than one interpretation [Swift's note].
4. (Of a horse) apt to reject control by the bit.

AN ARGUMENT TO PROVE THAT THE

Abolishing of Christianity in England

MAY, AS THINGS NOW STAND, BE ATTENDED WITH SOME
INCONVENIENCES, AND PERHAPS NOT PRODUCE THOSE MANY GOOD
EFFECTS PROPOSED THEREBY.[1]

I am very sensible what a weakness and presumption it is, to reason against the general humor and disposition of the world. I remember it was with great justice, and a due regard to the freedom both of the public and the press, forbidden upon several penalties to write, or discourse, or lay wagers against the Union,[2] even before it was confirmed by Parliament, because that was looked upon as a design to oppose the current of the people, which, besides the folly of it, is a manifest breach of the fundamental law that makes this majority of opinion the voice of God. In like manner, and for the very same reasons, it may perhaps be neither safe nor prudent to argue against the abolishing of Christianity at a juncture when all parties appear so unanimously determined upon the point, as we cannot but allow from their actions, their discourses, and their writings. However, I know not how, whether from the affectation of singularity, or the perverseness of human nature, but so it unhappily falls out that I cannot be entirely of this opinion. Nay, though I were sure an order were issued for my immediate prosecution by the attorney-general, I should still confess that in the present posture of our affairs at home or abroad, I do not yet see the absolute necessity of extirpating the Christian religion from among us.

This perhaps may appear too great a paradox even for our wise and paradoxical age to endure: therefore I shall handle it with all tenderness, and with the utmost deference to that great and profound majority which is of another sentiment.

And yet the curious may please to observe how much the genius of a nation is liable to alter in half an age: I have heard it affirmed for certain by some very old people that the contrary opinion was even in their memories as much in vogue as the other is now; and that a project for the abolishing of Christianity would then have appeared as singular, and been thought as absurd, as it would be at this time to write or discourse in its defense.

Therefore I freely own that all appearances are against me. The system of the Gospel, after the fate of other systems, is generally antiquated and exploded; and the mass or body of the common people, among whom it seems to have had its latest credit, are now grown as much ashamed of it as their betters; opinions, like fashions, always descending from those of quality to the middle sort, and thence to the vulgar, where at length they are dropped and vanish.

1. The Test Act of 1673 required all holders of public office to take the Sacrament of the Lord's Supper according to the usage of the Church of England; it was directed against Dissenters and Roman Catholics. In 1708 the Whigs (with whom Swift was then allied) were seeking to repeal the Test Act in Ireland and eventually in England in an effort to consolidate the support of the Dissenters. Swift believed that repeal would do great harm to the established church, and as a good Anglican priest he opposed it with this essay.

Swift's technique is to assume blandly that to argue against the Test Act is to argue against Christianity and the church, and he constructs his essay accordingly. The basic satiric principle is, therefore, that of the *reductio ad absurdum*, but this device is surrounded by a host of other ironies.
2. The union of Scotland and England under one crown in 1707.

But here I would not be mistaken, and must therefore be so bold as to borrow a distinction from the writers on the other side, when they make a difference between nominal and real Trinitarians. I hope no reader imagines me so weak to stand up in the defense of real Christianity, such as used in primitive times (if we may believe the authors of those ages) to have an influence upon men's belief and actions: to offer at the restoring of that would indeed be a wild project; it would be to dig up foundations; to destroy at one blow all the wit, and half the learning of the kingdom; to break the entire frame and constitution of things; to ruin trade, extinguish arts and sciences with the professors of them; in short, to turn our courts, exchanges, and shops into deserts; and would be full as absurd as the proposal of Horace,[3] where he advises the Romans all in a body to leave their city and seek a new seat in some remote part of the world, by way of cure for the corruption of their manners.

Therefore I think this caution was in itself altogether unnecessary (which I have inserted only to prevent all possibility of caviling), since every candid reader will easily understand my discourse to be intended only in defense of nominal Christianity, the other having been for some time wholly laid aside by general consent as utterly inconsistent with all other present schemes of wealth and power.

But why we should therefore cast off the name and title of Christians, although the general opinion and resolution be so violent for it, I confess I cannot (with submission) apprehend the consequence necessary. However, since the undertakers propose such wonderful advantages to the nation by this project, and advance many plausible objections against the system of Christianity, I shall briefly consider the strength of both, fairly allow them their greatest weight, and offer such answers as I think most reasonable. After which I will beg leave to show what inconveniences may possibly happen by such an innovation, in the present posture of our affairs.

First, one great advantage proposed by the abolishing of Christianity is that it would very much enlarge and establish liberty of conscience, that great bulwark of our nation, and of the protestant religion, which is still too much limited by priestcraft, notwithstanding all the good intentions of the legislature, as we have lately found by a severe instance. For it is confidently reported that two young gentlemen of real hopes, bright wit, and profound judgment, who upon a thorough examination of causes and effects, and by the mere force of natural abilities, without the least tincture of learning, having made a discovery that there was no God, and generously communicating their thoughts for the good of the public, were some time ago, by an unparalleled severity, and upon I know not what obsolete law, broke only for blasphemy. And as it hath been wisely observed, if persecution once begins, no man alive knows how far it may reach, or where it will end.

In answer to all which, with deference to wiser judgments, I think this rather shows the necessity of a nominal religion among us. Great wits love to be free with the highest objects; and if they cannot be allowed a God to revile or renounce, they will speak evil of dignities, abuse the government, and reflect upon the ministry; which I am sure few will deny to be of much

3. Epode 16.

more pernicious consequence, according to the saying of Tiberius, *Deorum offensa diis curae.*[4] As to the particular fact related, I think it is not fair to argue from one instance; perhaps another cannot be produced; yet (to the comfort of all those who may be apprehensive of persecution) blasphemy we know is freely spoken a million of times in every coffeehouse and tavern, or wherever else good company meet. It must be allowed indeed, that to break an English freeborn officer only for blasphemy, was, to speak the gentlest of such an action, a very high strain of absolute power. Little can be said in excuse for the general; perhaps he was afraid it might give offense to the allies[5] among whom, for aught we know, it may be the custom of the country to believe a God. But if he argued, as some have done, upon a mistaken principle, that an officer who is guilty of speaking blasphemy may some time or other proceed so far as to raise a mutiny, the consequence is by no means to be admitted: for, surely the commander of an English army is likely to be but ill obeyed whose soldiers fear and reverence him as little as they do a deity.

It is further objected against the gospel system that it obliges men to the belief of things too difficult for freethinkers, and such who have shaken off the prejudices that usually cling to a confined education. To which I answer that men should be cautious how they raise objections which reflect upon the wisdom of the nation. Is not everybody freely allowed to believe whatever he pleases, and to publish his belief to the world whenever he thinks fit, especially if it serves to strengthen the party which is in the right? Would any indifferent foreigner who should read the trumpery lately written by Asgil, Tindal, Toland, Coward,[6] and forty more, imagine the Gospel to be our rule of faith, and confirmed by parliaments? Does any man either believe, or say he believes, or desire to have it thought that he says he believes one syllable of the matter? And is any man worse received upon that score, or does he find his want of nominal faith a disadvantage to him in the pursuit of any civil or military employment? What if there be an old dormant statute or two against him? Are they not now obsolete to a degree that Empson and Dudley[7] themselves, if they were now alive, would find it impossible to put them in execution?

It is likewise urged that there are by computation in this kingdom above ten thousand parsons whose revenues, added to those of my lords the bishops, would suffice to maintain at least two hundred young gentlemen of wit and pleasure, and freethinking enemies to priestcraft, narrow principles, pedantry, and prejudices; who might be an ornament to the court and town. And then again, so great a number of able (bodied) divines might be a recruit to our fleet and armies. This indeed appears to be a consideration of some weight; but then, on the other side, several things deserve to be considered likewise: as, first, whether it may not be thought necessary that in certain tracts of country, like what we call parishes, there shall be one man at least of abilities to read and write. Then it seems a wrong computation that the

---

4. Offenses against the gods are the concern of the gods (Tacitus, *Annals* 1.73).
5. England's principal allies against France in the War of the Spanish Succession were Holland, Austria, Prussia, Portugal, and Savoy.

6. Deistic writers.
7. Two corrupt ministers of Henry VII, notorious for reviving obsolete statutes in subservience to that king's greed.

revenues of the Church throughout this island would be large enough to maintain two hundred young gentlemen, or even half that number, after the present refined way of living; that is, to allow each of them such a rent[8] as, in the modern form of speech, would make them easy. But still there is in this project a greater mischief behind; and we ought to beware of the woman's folly who killed the hen that every morning laid her a golden egg. For, pray, what would become of the race of men in the next age if we had nothing to trust to beside the scrofulous, consumptive productions, furnished by our men of wit and pleasure, when, having squandered away their vigor, health, and estates, they are forced by some disagreeable marriage to piece up their broken fortunes, and entail rottenness and politeness on their posterity? Now here are ten thousand persons reduced by the wise regulations of Henry the Eighth to the necessity of a low diet and moderate exercise,[9] who are the only great restorers of our breed, without which the nation would in an age or two become one great hospital.

Another advantage proposed by the abolishing of Christianity is the clear gain of one day in seven, which is now entirely lost, and consequently the kingdom one-seventh less considerable in trade, business, and pleasure; besides the loss to the public of so many stately structures now in the hands of the clergy, which might be converted into playhouses, exchanges, market-houses, common dormitories, and other public edifices.

I hope I shall be forgiven a hard word, if I call this a perfect cavil. I readily own there hath been an old custom, time out of mind, for people to assemble in the churches every Sunday, and that shops are still frequently shut, in order, as it is conceived, to preserve the memory of that ancient practice; but how this can prove a hindrance to business or pleasure is hard to imagine. What if the men of pleasure are forced, one day in the week, to game at home instead of the chocolatehouse? Are not the taverns and coffeehouses open? Can there be a more convenient season for taking a dose of physic? Are fewer claps got upon Sundays than other days? Is not that the chief day for traders to sum up the accounts of the week and for lawyers to prepare their briefs? But I would fain know how it can be pretended that the churches are misapplied? Where are more appointments and rendezvouses of gallantry? Where more care to appear in the foremost box with greater advantage of dress? Where more meetings for business? Where more bargains driven of all sorts? And where so many conveniences or incitements to sleep?

There is one advantage greater than any of the foregoing proposed by the abolishing of Christianity: that it will utterly extinguish parties among us by removing those factious distinctions of High and Low Church, of Whig and Tory, Presbyterian and Church of England, which are now so many mutual clogs upon public proceedings, and dispose men to prefer the gratifying themselves, or depressing their adversaries, before the most important interest of the state.

I confess, if it were certain that so great an advantage would redound to the nation by this expedient, I would submit and be silent: but will any man

8. Income.
9. Swift refers ironically to Henry VIII's expropriation of church lands at the time of the Reformation. Instead of giving them to the church for the support of the clergy, as Swift thought he should

have done, he bestowed them on laymen, thus impoverishing the lower clergy, who were deprived of the tithes that would otherwise have been their due.

say that if the words *whoring, drinking, cheating, lying, stealing,* were by act of Parliament ejected out of the English tongue and dictionaries, we should all awake next morning chaste and temperate, honest and just, and lovers of truth? Is this a fair consequence? Or, if the physicians would forbid us to pronounce the words *pox, gout, rheumatism,* and *stone,* would that expedient serve like so many talismans to destroy the diseases themselves? Are party and faction rooted in men's hearts no deeper than phrases borrowed from religion, or founded upon no firmer principles? And is our language so poor that we cannot find other terms to express them? Are *envy, pride, avarice,* and *ambition* such ill nomenclators that they cannot furnish appellations for their owners? Will not *heydukes* and *mamalukes, mandarins* and *patshaws,* or any other words formed at pleasure, serve to distinguish those who are in the ministry from others who would be in it if they could? What, for instance, is easier than to vary the form of speech, and instead of the *church,* make it a question in politics whether the Monument[1] be in danger? Because religion was nearest at hand to furnish a few convenient phrases, is our invention so barren we can find no others? Suppose, for argument sake, that the Tories favored Margarita, the Whigs Mrs. Tofts, and the Trimmers Valentini,[2] would not *Margaritians, Toftians,* and *Valentinians* be very tolerable marks of distinction? The *Prasini* and *Veniti,*[3] two most virulent factions in Italy, began (if I remember right) by a distinction of colors in ribbons, which we might do with as good a grace about the dignity of the blue and the green, and would serve as properly to divide the court, the Parliament, and the kingdom between them, as any terms of art whatsoever borrowed from religion. Therefore I think there is little force in this objection against Christianity, or prospect of so great an advantage as is proposed in the abolishing of it.

'Tis again objected as a very absurd, ridiculous custom that a set of men should be suffered, much less employed and hired, to bawl one day in seven against the lawfulness of those methods most in use toward the pursuit of greatness, riches, and pleasure, which are the constant practice of all men alive on the other six. But this objection is, I think, a little unworthy so refined an age as ours. Let us argue this matter calmly; I appeal to the breast of any polite freethinker whether in the pursuit of gratifying a predominant passion he hath not always felt a wonderful incitement, by reflecting it was a thing forbidden; and therefore we see, in order to cultivate this taste, the wisdom of the nation hath taken special care that the ladies should be furnished with prohibited silks and the men with prohibited wine. And indeed, it were to be wished that some other prohibitions were promoted in order to improve the pleasures of the town; which, for want of such expedients begin already, as I am told, to flag and grow languid, giving way daily to cruel inroads from the spleen.[4]

'Tis likewise proposed as a great advantage to the public that if we once discard the system of the Gospel, all religion will of course be banished for ever; and consequently, along with it, those grievous prejudices of education, which under the names of *virtue, conscience, honor, justice,* and the like, are

1. The column that commemorates the Great Fire of London, 1666.
2. Singers in the popular Italian opera.
3. Rival factions in the Roman chariot races, vio-

lently supported by the populace.
4. Melancholy; often a real affliction, but as often affected as a fashionable ailment.

so apt to disturb the peace of human minds, and the notions whereof are so hard to be eradicated by right reason or freethinking, sometimes during the whole course of our lives.

Here first I observe how difficult it is to get rid of a phrase which the world is once grown fond of, though the occasion that first produced it be entirely taken away. For several years past, if a man had but an ill-favored nose, the deep thinkers of the age would some way or other contrive to impute the cause to the prejudice of his education. From this fountain were said to be derived all our foolish notions of justice, piety, love of our country, all our opinions of God, or a future state, heaven, hell, and the like: and there might formerly perhaps have been some pretense for this charge. But so effectual care hath been since taken to remove those prejudices by an entire change in the methods of education that (with honor I mention it to our polite innovators) the young gentlemen who are now on the scene seem to have not the least tincture of those infusions, or string of those weeds; and, by consequence, the reason for abolishing nominal Christianity upon that pretext is wholly ceased.

For the rest, it may perhaps admit a controversy whether the banishing of all notions of religion whatsoever would be convenient for the vulgar. Not that I am in the least of opinion with those who hold religion to have been the invention of politicians to keep the lower part of the world in awe by the fear of invisible powers; unless mankind were then very different from what it is now: for I look upon the mass or body of our people here in England to be as freethinkers, that is to say, as staunch unbelievers, as any of the highest rank. But I conceive some scattered notions about a superior power to be of singular use for the common people, as furnishing excellent materials to keep children quiet when they grow peevish, and providing topics of amusement in a tedious winter night.

Lastly, it is proposed as a singular advantage that the abolishing of Christianity will very much contribute to the uniting of Protestants, by enlarging the terms of communion so as to take in all sorts of Dissenters, who are now shut out of the pale upon account of a few ceremonies which all sides confess to be things indifferent; that this alone will effectually answer the great ends of a scheme for comprehension, by opening a large noble gate, at which all bodies may enter: whereas the chaffering with Dissenters, and dodging about this or t' other ceremony, is but like opening a few wickets[5] and leaving them at jar, by which no more than one can get in at a time, and that, not without stooping, and sideling, and squeezing his body.

To all this I answer that there is one darling inclination of mankind, which usually affects to be a retainer to religion, though she be neither its parent, its godmother, or its friend; I mean the spirit of opposition, that lived long before Christianity, and can easily subsist without it. Let us, for instance, examine wherein the opposition of sectaries[6] among us consists; we shall find Christianity to have no share in it at all. Does the Gospel any where prescribe a starched, squeezed countenance, a stiff, formal gait, a singularity of manners and habit, or any affected modes of speech different from the reasonable part of mankind? Yet, if Christianity did not lend its name to stand in the gap, and to employ or divert these humors, they must of necessity

---

5. Small gates.   6. Adherents of one of the dissenting sects.

be spent in contraventions to the laws of the land, and disturbance of the public peace. There is a portion of enthusiasm assigned to every nation, which, if it hath not proper objects to work on, will burst out, and set all in a flame. If the quiet of state can be bought by only flinging men a few ceremonies to devour, it is a purchase no wise man would refuse. Let the mastiffs amuse themselves about a sheepskin stuffed with hay, provided it will keep them from worrying the flock. The institution of convents abroad seems in one point a strain of great wisdom, there being few irregularities in human passions that may not have recourse to vent themselves in some of those orders, which are so many retreats for the speculative, the melancholy, the proud, the silent, the politic and the morose, to spend themselves, and evaporate the noxious particles; for each of whom we in this island are forced to provide a several sect of religion, to keep them quiet. And whenever Christianity shall be abolished, the legislature must find some other expedient to employ and entertain them. For what imports it how large a gate you open if there will be always left a number who place a pride and merit in refusing to enter?

Having thus considered the most important objections against Christianity and the chief advantages proposed by the abolishing thereof, I shall now with equal deference and submission to wiser judgments as before, proceed to mention a few inconveniences that may happen if the Gospel should be repealed; which perhaps the projectors may not have sufficiently considered.

And first, I am very sensible how much the gentlemen of wit and pleasure are apt to murmur, and be choked at the sight of so many daggled-tail parsons who happen to fall in their way, and offend their eyes. But at the same time, these wise reformers do not consider what an advantage and felicity it is for great wits to be always provided with objects of scorn and contempt, in order to exercise and improve their talents, and divert their spleen from falling on each other or on themselves; especially when all this may be done without the least imaginable danger to their persons.

And to urge another argument of a parallel nature: if Christianity were once abolished, how could the freethinkers, the strong reasoners, and the men of profound learning, be able to find another subject so calculated in all points whereon to display their abilities? What wonderful productions of wit should we be deprived of from those whose genius by continual practice hath been wholly turned upon raillery and invectives against religion, and would therefore never be able to shine or distinguish themselves upon any other subject! We are daily complaining of the great decline of wit among us, and would we take away the greatest, perhaps the only, topic we have left? Who would ever have suspected Asgil for a wit, or Toland for a philosopher, if the inexhaustible stock of Christianity had not been at hand to provide them with materials? What other subject, through all art or nature, could have produced Tindal for a profound author, or furnished him with readers? It is the wise choice of the subject that alone adorns and distinguishes the writer. For had a hundred such pens as these been employed on the side of religion, they would have immediately sunk into silence and oblivion.

Nor do I think it wholly groundless, or my fears altogether imaginary, that the abolishing of Christianity may perhaps bring the Church in danger, or at least put the senate to the trouble of another securing vote. I desire I may not be mistaken; I am far from presuming to affirm or think that the Church is in danger at present, or as things now stand; but we know not how soon it may be so when the Christian religion is repealed. As plausible as this project seems, there may a dangerous design lurk under it. Nothing can be more notorious than that the atheists, deists, Socinians,[7] Antitrinitarians, and other subdivisions of freethinkers are persons of little zeal for the present ecclesiastical establishment: their declared opinion is for repealing the Sacramental Test; they are very indifferent with regard to ceremonies; nor do they hold the *jus divinum* of Episcopacy.[8] Therefore this may be intended as one politic step toward altering the constitution of the Church established, and setting up Presbytery[9] in the stead, which I leave to be further considered by those at the helm.

In the last place, I think nothing can be more plain than that by this expedient, we shall run into the evil we chiefly pretend to avoid; and that the abolishment of the Christian religion will be the readiest course we can take to introduce popery. And I am the more inclined to this opinion because we know it has been the constant practice of the Jesuits to send over emissaries with instructions to personate themselves members of the several prevailing sects among us. So it is recorded that they have at sundry times appeared in the guise of Presbyterians, Anabaptists, Independents, and Quakers, according as any of these were most in credit; so, since the fashion hath been taken up of exploding religion, the popish missionaries have not been wanting to mix with the freethinkers; among whom, Toland, the great oracle of the Antichristians, is an Irish priest, the son of an Irish priest; and the most learned and ingenious author of a book called *The Rights of the Christian Church,* was in a proper juncture reconciled to the Romish faith, whose true son, as appears by an hundred passages in his treatise, he still continues. Perhaps I could add some others to the number; but the fact is beyond dispute, and the reasoning they proceed by is right: for, supposing Christianity to be extinguished, the people will never be at ease till they find out some other method of worship; which will as infallibly produce superstition as this will end in popery.

And therefore, if notwithstanding all I have said, it still be thought necessary to have a bill brought in for repealing Christianity, I would humbly offer an amendment; that instead of the word *Christianity* may be put *religion* in general; which I conceive will much better answer all the good ends proposed by the projectors of it. For, as long as we leave in being a God and his providence, with all the necessary consequences which curious and inquisitive men will be apt to draw from such premises, we do not strike at the root of the evil, though we should ever so effectually annihilate the present scheme of the Gospel. For of what use is freedom of thought, if it will not produce freedom of action, which is the sole end, how remote soever in appearance, of all objections against Christianity? And, therefore, the freethinkers consider it as a sort of edifice wherein all the parts have such a mutual dependence on each other that if you happen to pull out one single nail, the whole fabric must fall to the ground. This was happily expressed by him who had heard of a text brought for proof of the Trinity, which in an

---

7. The Socinians denied the divinity of Jesus.
8. The divine authority of Anglican bishops, derived from apostolic succession.

9. The Presbyterians opposed episcopacy and set up a democratic form of church government.

ancient manuscript was differently read; he thereupon immediately took the hint, and by a sudden deduction of a long *sorites*,[1] most logically concluded, "Why, if it be as you say, I may safely whore and drink on, and defy the parson." From which, and many the like instances easy to be produced, I think nothing can be more manifest than that the quarrel is not against any particular points of hard digestion in the Christian system, but against religion in general; which, by laying restraints on human nature, is supposed the great enemy to the freedom of thought and action.

Upon the whole, if it shall still be thought for the benefit of Church and State that Christianity be abolished, I conceive, however, it may be more convenient to defer the execution to a time of peace, and not venture in this conjuncture to disoblige our allies, who, as it falls out, are all Christians; and many of them, by the prejudices of their education, so bigoted as to place a sort of pride in the appellation. If upon being rejected by them, we are to trust to an alliance with the Turk, we shall find ourselves much deceived: for, as he is too remote, and generally engaged in war with the Persian emperor, so his people would be more scandalized at our infidelity than our Christian neighbors. Because the Turks are not only strict observers of religious worship, but what is worse, believe a God; which is more than is required of us even while we preserve the name of Christians.

To conclude: whatever some may think of the great advantages to trade by this favorite scheme, I do very much apprehend that in six months time after the act is passed for the extirpation of the Gospel, the Bank and East-India Stock may fall at least one per cent. And since that is fifty times more than ever the wisdom of our age thought fit to venture for the preservation of Christianity, there is no reason we should be at so great a loss merely for the sake of destroying it.

1708   1711

Gulliver's Travels

Gulliver's Travels is Swift's most enduring satire. Although full of allusions to recent and current events, it still rings true today, for its objects are human failings and the defective political, economic, and social institutions that they call into being. Swift adopts an ancient satirical device: the imaginary voyage. Lemuel Gulliver, the narrator, is a ship's surgeon, a moderately well educated man, kindly, resourceful, cheerful, inquiring, patriotic, truthful, and rather unimaginative—in short, a reasonably decent example of humanity, with whom a reader can readily identify. He undertakes four voyages, all of which end disastrously among "several remote nations of the world." In the first, Gulliver is shipwrecked in the empire of Lilliput, where he finds himself a giant among a diminutive people, charmed by their miniature city and amused by their toylike prettiness. But in the end they prove to be treacherous, malicious, ambitious, vengeful, and cruel. As we read we grow disenchanted with the inhabitants of this fanciful kingdom, and then gradually we begin to recognize our likeness to them, especially in the disproportion between our natural pettiness and our boundless and destructive passions. In the second voyage, Gulliver is abandoned by his shipmates in Brobdingnag, a land of giants, creatures ten times

---

1. "An argument when one proposition is accumulated on another" (Johnson's *Dictionary*).

as large as Europeans. Though he fears that such monsters must be brutes, the reverse proves to be the case. Brobdingnag is something of a utopia, governed by a humane and enlightened prince who is the embodiment of moral and political wisdom. In the long interview in which Gulliver pridefully enlarges on the glories of England and its political institutions, the king reduces him to resentful silence by asking questions that reveal the difference between what England is and what it ought to be. In Brobdingnag, Gulliver finds himself a Lilliputian, his pride humbled by his helpless state and his human vanity diminished by the realization that his body must have seemed as disgusting to the Lilliputians as do the bodies of the Brobdingnagians to him.

In the third voyage, to Laputa, Swift is chiefly concerned with attacking extremes of theoretical and speculative reasoning, whether in science, politics, or economics. Much of this voyage is an allegory of political life under the administration of the Whig minister, Sir Robert Walpole. The final voyage sets Gulliver between a race of horses, Houyhnhnms (prounced *Hwín-ims*), who live entirely by reason except for a few well-controlled and muted social affections, and their slaves, the Yahoos, whose bodies are obscene caricatures of the human body and who have no glimmer of reason but are mere creatures of appetite and passion.

When *Gulliver's Travels* first appeared, everyone read it—children for the story and politicians for the satire of current affairs—and ever since it has retained a hold on readers of every kind. Almost unique in world literature, it is simple enough for children, complex enough to carry adults beyond their depth. Swift's art works on many levels. First of all, there is the sheer playfulness of the narrative. Through Gulliver's eyes, we gaze on marvel after marvel: a tiny girl who threads an invisible needle with invisible silk or a white mare who threads a needle between pastern and hoof. The travels, like a fairy story, transport us to imaginary worlds that function with a perfect, fantastic logic different from our own; Swift exercises our sense of vision. But beyond that, he exercises our perceptions of meaning. In *Gulliver's Travels,* things are seldom what they seem; irony, probing or corrosive, underlies almost every word. In the last chapter, Gulliver insists that the example of the Houyhnhnms has made him incapable of telling a lie—but the oath he swears is quoted from Sinon, whose lies to the Trojans persuaded them to accept the Trojan *horse*. Swift trains us to read alertly, to look beneath the surface. Yet on its deepest level, the book does not offer final meanings, but a question: What is a human being? Voyaging through imaginary worlds, we try to find ourselves. Are we prideful insects or lords of creation? brutes or reasonable beings? In the last voyage, Swift pushes such questions, and Gulliver himself, almost beyond endurance; hating his own humanity, Gulliver forgets who he is. For the reader, however, the outcome cannot be so clear. Swift does not set out to satisfy our minds but to vex and unsettle them. And he leaves us at the moment when the mixed face of humanity—the pettiness of the Lilliputians, the savagery of the Yahoos, the innocence of Gulliver himself—begins to look strangely familiar, like our own faces in a mirror.

Swift's full title for this work was *Travels into Several Remote Nations of the World. In Four Parts. By Lemuel Gulliver, First a Surgeon, and then a Captain of several Ships.* In the first edition (1726), either the bookseller or Swift's friends Charles Ford, Pope, and others, who were concerned in getting the book anonymously into print, altered and omitted so much of the original manuscript (because of its dangerous political implications) that Swift was seriously annoyed. When, in 1735, the Dublin bookseller George Faulkner brought out an edition of Swift's works, the dean seems to have taken pains, surreptitiously, to see that a more authentic version of the work was published. This text is the basis of modern editions.

From Gulliver's Travels

A Letter from Captain Gulliver to His Cousin Sympson[1]

I hope you will be ready to own publicly, whenever you shall be called to it, that by your great and frequent urgency you prevailed on me to publish a very loose and uncorrect account of my travels; with direction to hire some young gentlemen of either University to put them in order, and correct the style, as my Cousin Dampier[2] did by my advice, in his book called *A Voyage round the World*. But I do not remember I gave you power to consent that anything should be omitted, and much less that anything should be inserted: therefore, as to the latter, I do here renounce everything of that kind; particularly a paragraph about her Majesty the late Queen Anne, of most pious and glorious memory; although I did reverence and esteem her more than any of human species. But you, or your interpolator, ought to have considered that as it was not my inclination, so was it not decent to praise any animal of our composition before my master Houyhnhnm; and besides, the fact was altogether false; for to my knowledge, being in England during some part of her Majesty's reign, she did govern by a chief Minister; nay, even by two successively; the first whereof was the Lord of Godolphin, and the second the Lord of Oxford; so that you have made me *say the thing that was not*. Likewise, in the account of the Academy of Projectors, and several passages of my discourse to my master Houyhnhnm, you have either omitted some material circumstances, or minced or changed them in such a manner, that I do hardly know mine own work. When I formerly hinted to you something of this in a letter, you were pleased to answer that you were afraid of giving offense; that people in power were very watchful over the press; and apt not only to interpret, but to punish everything which looked like an *innuendo* (as I think you called it). But pray, how could that which I spoke so many years ago, and at above five thousand leagues distance, in another reign, be applied to any of the Yahoos, who now are said to govern the herd; especially, at a time when I little thought on or feared the unhappiness of living under them. Have not I the most reason to complain, when I see these very Yahoos carried by Houyhnhnms in a vehicle, as if these were brutes, and those the rational creatures? And, indeed, to avoid so monstrous and detestable a sight was one principal motive of my retirement hither.[3]

Thus much I thought proper to tell you in relation to yourself, and to the trust I reposed in you.

I do in the next place complain of my own great want of judgment, in being prevailed upon by the intreaties and false reasonings of you and some others, very much against mine own opinion, to suffer my travels to be published. Pray bring to your mind how often I desired you to consider, when you insisted on the motive of public good, that the Yahoos were a species of animals utterly incapable of amendment by precepts or examples; and so it

---

1. In this letter, first published in 1735, Swift complains, among other matters, of the alterations in his original text made by the publisher, Benjamin Motte, in the interest of what he considered political discretion.

2. William Dampier (1652–1715), the explorer, whose account of his circumnavigation of the globe Swift had read.
3. To Nottinghamshire.

hath proved; for instead of seeing a full stop put to all abuses and corruptions, at least in this little island, as I had reason to expect, behold, after above six months warning, I cannot learn that my book hath produced one single effect according to mine intentions; I desired you would let me know by a letter, when party and faction were extinguished; judges learned and upright; pleaders honest and modest, with some tincture of common sense; and Smithfield[4] blazing with pyramids of law books; the young nobility's education entirely changed; the physicians banished; the female Yahoos abounding in virtue, honor, truth, and good sense; courts and levees of great ministers thoroughly weeded and swept; wit, merit, and learning rewarded; all disgracers of the press in prose and verse, condemned to eat nothing but their own cotton,[5] and quench their thirst with their own ink. These, and a thousand other reformations, I firmly counted upon by your encouragement; as indeed they were plainly deducible from the precepts delivered in my book. And, it must be owned that seven months were a sufficient time to correct every vice and folly to which Yahoos are subject; if their natures had been capable of the least disposition to virtue or wisdom; yet so far have you been from answering mine expectation in any of your letters, that on the contrary, you are loading our carrier every week with libels, and keys, and reflections, and memoirs, and second parts; wherein I see myself accused of reflecting upon great statesfolk; of degrading human nature (for so they have still the confidence to style it) and of abusing the female sex. I find likewise, that the writers of those bundles are not agreed among themselves; for some of them will not allow me to be author of mine own travels; and others make me author of books to which I am wholly a stranger.

I find likewise that your printer hath been so careless as to confound the times, and mistake the dates of my several voyages and returns; neither assigning the true year, or the true month, or day of the month; and I hear the original manuscript is all destroyed, since the publication of my book. Neither have I any copy left; however, I have sent you some corrections, which you may insert, if ever there should be a second edition; and yet I cannot stand to them, but shall leave that matter to my judicious and candid readers, to adjust it as they please.

I hear some of our sea Yahoos find fault with my sea language, as not proper in many parts, nor now in use. I cannot help it. In my first voyages, while I was young, I was instructed by the oldest mariners, and learned to speak as they did. But I have since found that the sea Yahoos are apt, like the land ones, to become new fangled in their words; which the latter change every year; insomuch, as I remember upon each return to mine own country, their old dialect was so altered, that I could hardly understand the new. And I observe, when any Yahoo comes from London out of curiosity to visit me at mine own house, we neither of us are able to deliver our conceptions in a manner intelligible to the other.[6]

If the censure of Yahoos could any way affect me, I should have great reason to complain that some of them are so bold as to think my book of travels a mere fiction out of mine own brain; and have gone so far as to drop

4. A part of London containing many bookshops.   6. Swift was the inveterate enemy of slang.
5. Presumably their paper.

hints that the Houyhnhnms, and Yahoos have no more existence than the inhabitants of Utopia.

Indeed I must confess that as to the people of Lilliput, Brobdingrag (for so the word should have been spelled, and not erroneously Brobdingnag) and Laputa, I have never yet heard of any Yahoo so presumptuous as to dispute their being, or the facts I have related concerning them; because the truth immediately strikes every reader with conviction. And, is there less probability in my account of the Houyhnhnms or Yahoos, when it is manifest as to the latter, there are so many thousands even in this city, who only differ from their brother brutes in Houyhnhnmland, because they use a sort of a jabber, and do not go naked. I wrote for their amendment, and not their approbation. The united praise of the whole race would be of less consequence to me, than the neighing of those two degenerate Houyhnhnms I keep in my stable; because, from these, degenerate as they are, I still improve in some virtues, without any mixture of vice.

Do these miserable animals presume to think that I am so far degenerated as to defend my veracity; Yahoo as I am, it is well known through all Houyhnhnmland, that by the instructions and example of my illustrious master, I was able in the compass of two years (although I confess with the utmost difficulty) to remove that infernal habit of lying, shuffling, deceiving, and equivocating, so deeply rooted in the very souls of all my species; especially the Europeans.

I have other complaints to make upon this vexatious occasion; but I forbear troubling myself or you any further. I must freely confess that since my last return, some corruptions of my Yahoo nature have revived in me by conversing with a few of your species, and particularly those of mine own family, by an unavoidable necessity; else I should never have attempted so absurd a project as that of reforming the Yahoo race in this kingdom; but I have now done with all such visionary schemes for ever.

1727?   1735

The Publisher to the Reader

The author of these travels, Mr. Lemuel Gulliver, is my ancient and intimate friend; there is likewise some relation between us by the mother's side. About three years ago Mr. Gulliver, growing weary of the concourse of curious people coming to him at his house in Redriff,[7] made a small purchase of land, with a convenient house, near Newark, in Nottinghamshire, his native country; where he now lives retired, yet in good esteem among his neighbors.

Although Mr. Gulliver were born in Nottinghamshire, where his father dwelt, yet I have heard him say his family came from Oxfordshire; to confirm which, I have observed in the churchyard at Banbury, in that county, several tombs and monuments of the Gullivers.

Before he quitted Redriff, he left the custody of the following papers in my hands, with the liberty to dispose of them as I should think fit. I have carefully perused them three times; the style is very plain and simple; and

7. Rotherhithe, a district in southern London, below Tower Bridge, then frequented by sailors.

the only fault I find is that the author, after the manner of travelers, is a little too circumstantial. There is an air of truth apparent through the whole; and indeed the author was so distinguished for his veracity, that it became a sort of proverb among his neighbors at Redriff, when anyone affirmed a thing, to say, it was as true as if Mr. Gulliver had spoke it.

By the advice of several worthy persons, to whom, with the author's permission, I communicated these papers, I now venture to send them into the world; hoping they may be, at least for some time, a better entertainment to our young noblemen, than the common scribbles of politics and party.

This volume would have been at least twice as large, if I had not made bold to strike out innumerable passages relating to the winds and tides, as well as to the variations and bearings in the several voyages; together with the minute descriptions of the management of the ship in storms, in the style of sailors; likewise the account of the longitudes and latitudes, wherein I have reason to apprehend that Mr. Gulliver may be a little dissatisfied; but I was resolved to fit the work as much as possible to the general capacity of readers. However, if my own ignorance in sea affairs shall have led me to commit some mistakes, I alone am answerable for them; and if any traveler hath a curiosity to see the whole work at large, as it came from the hand of the author, I will be ready to gratify him.

As for any further particulars relating to the author, the reader will receive satisfaction from the first pages of the book.

RICHARD SYMPSON

Part 1. A Voyage to Lilliput

CHAPTER 1. *The author gives some account of himself and family; his first inducements to travel. He is shipwrecked, and swims for his life; gets safe on shore in the country of Lilliput; is made a prisoner, and carried up the country.*

My father had a small estate in Nottinghamshire; I was the third of five sons. He sent me to Emanuel College in Cambridge, at fourteen years old, where I resided three years, and applied myself close to my studies: but the charge of maintaining me (although I had a very scanty allowance) being too great for a narrow fortune, I was bound apprentice to Mr. James Bates, an eminent surgeon in London, with whom I continued four years; and my father now and then sending me small sums of money, I laid them out in learning navigation, and other parts of the mathematics, useful to those who intend to travel, as I always believed it would be some time or other my fortune to do. When I left Mr. Bates, I went down to my father; where, by the assistance of him and my uncle John, and some other relations, I got forty pounds, and a promise of thirty pounds a year to maintain me at Leyden: there I studied physic[8] two years and seven months, knowing it would be useful in long voyages.

Soon after my return from Leyden, I was recommended by my good master Mr. Bates, to be surgeon to the *Swallow*, Captain Abraham Pannell commander; with whom I continued three years and a half, making a voyage or

8. The University of Leyden, in Holland, was a center for the study of "physic" (medicine).

two into the Levant[9] and some other parts. When I came back, I resolved to settle in London, to which Mr. Bates, my master, encouraged me; and by him I was recommended to several patients. I took part of a small house in the Old Jury; and being advised to alter my condition, I married Mrs.[1] Mary Burton, second daughter to Mr. Edmond Burton, hosier, in Newgate Street, with whom I received four hundred pounds for a portion.

But, my good master Bates dying in two years after, and I having few friends, my business began to fail; for my conscience would not suffer me to imitate the bad practice of too many among my brethren. Having therefore consulted with my wife, and some of my acquaintance, I determined to go again to sea. I was surgeon successively in two ships, and made several voyages, for six years, to the East and West Indies; by which I got some addition to my fortune. My hours of leisure I spent in reading the best authors, ancient and modern, being always provided with a good number of books; and when I was ashore, in observing the manners and dispositions of the people, as well as learning their language; wherein I had a great facility by the strength of my memory.

The last of these voyages not proving very fortunate, I grew weary of the sea, and intended to stay at home with my wife and family. I removed from the Old Jury to Fetter Lane, and from thence to Wapping, hoping to get business among the sailors; but it would not turn to account. After three years' expectation that things would mend, I accepted an advantageous offer from Captain William Prichard, master of the *Antelope*, who was making a voyage to the South Sea. We set sail from Bristol, May 4th, 1699, and our voyage at first was very prosperous.

It would not be proper, for some reasons, to trouble the reader with the particulars of our adventures in those seas: let it suffice to inform him, that in our passage from thence to the East Indies we were driven by a violent storm to the northwest of Van Diemen's Land.[2] By an observation, we found ourselves in the latitude of 30 degrees 2 minutes south. Twelve of our crew were dead by immoderate labor, and ill food, the rest were in a very weak condition. On the fifth of November, which was the beginning of summer in those parts, the weather being very hazy, the seamen spied a rock, within half a cable's length of the ship; but the wind was so strong, that we were driven directly upon it, and immediately split. Six of the crew, of whom I was one, having let down the boat into the sea, made a shift to get clear of the ship, and the rock. We rowed by my computation about three leagues, till we were able to work no longer, being already spent with labor while we were in the ship. We therefore trusted ourselves to the mercy of the waves; and in about half an hour the boat was overset by a sudden flurry from the north. What became of my companions in the boat, as well as of those who escaped on the rock, or were left in the vessel, I cannot tell; but conclude they were all lost. For my own part, I swam as fortune directed me, and was pushed forward by wind and tide. I often let my legs drop, and could feel no bottom; but when I was almost gone, and able to struggle no longer, I found myself within my depth; and by this time the storm was much abated. The declivity was so small, that I walked near a mile before I got to the shore,

9. The eastern Mediterranean.
1. "Mrs." (pronounced "Mistress") designated any woman, married or unmarried. "Old Jury": a street (once "Old Jewry") in the City of London.
2. Tasmania.

which I conjectured was about eight o'clock in the evening. I then advanced forward near half a mile, but could not discover any sign of houses or inhabitants; at least I was in so weak a condition, that I did not observe them. I was extremely tired, and with that, and the heat of the weather, and about half a pint of brandy that I drank as I left the ship, I found myself much inclined to sleep. I lay down on the grass, which was very short and soft, where I slept sounder than ever I remember to have done in my life, and as I reckoned, above nine hours; for when I awaked, it was just daylight. I attempted to rise, but was not able to stir: for as I happened to lie on my back, I found my arms and legs were strongly fastened on each side to the ground; and my hair, which was long and thick, tied down in the same manner. I likewise felt several slender ligatures across my body, from my armpits to my thighs. I could only look upwards; the sun began to grow hot, and the light offended my eyes. I heard a confused noise about me, but in the posture I lay, could see nothing except the sky. In a little time I felt something alive moving on my left leg, which advancing gently forward over my breast, came almost up to my chin; when bending my eyes downwards as much as I could, I perceived it to be a human creature not six inches high,[3] with a bow and arrow in his hands, and a quiver at his back. In the meantime, I felt at least forty more of the same kind (as I conjectured) following the first. I was in the utmost astonishment, and roared so loud, that they all ran back in a fright; and some of them, as I was afterwards told, were hurt with the falls they got by leaping from my sides upon the ground. However, they soon returned; and one of them, who ventured so far as to get a full sight of my face, lifting up his hands and eyes by way of admiration,[4] cried out in a shrill, but distinct voice, *Hekinah Degul*: the others repeated the same words several times, but I then knew not what they meant. I lay all this while, as the reader may believe, in great uneasiness; at length, struggling to get loose, I had the fortune to break the strings, and wrench out the pegs that fastened my left arm to the ground; for, by lifting it up to my face, I discovered the methods they had taken to bind me; and, at the same time, with a violent pull, which gave me excessive pain, I a little loosened the strings that tied down my hair on the left side; so that I was just able to turn my head about two inches. But the creatures ran off a second time, before I could seize them; whereupon there was a great shout in a very shrill accent; and after it ceased, I heard one of them cry aloud, *Tolgo phonac*; when in an instant I felt above an hundred arrows discharged on my left hand, which pricked me like so many needles; and besides they shot another flight into the air, as we do bombs in Europe, whereof many, I suppose, fell on my body (though I felt them not) and some on my face, which I immediately covered with my left hand. When this shower of arrows was over, I fell a groaning with grief and pain; and then striving again to get loose, they discharged another volley larger than the first, and some of them attempted with spears to stick me in the sides; but, by good luck, I had on me a buff jerkin,[5] which they could not pierce. I thought it the most prudent method to lie still; and my design was to continue so till night, when, my left hand being already loose, I could easily free myself: and as for the inhabitants, I had reason to believe I might be a match for the greatest armies they could bring against me, if they were

3. Lilliput is scaled, fairly consistently, at one-twelfth of Gulliver's world.

4. Wonderment.
5. Leather jacket.

all of the same size with him that I saw. But fortune disposed otherwise of me. When the people observed I was quiet, they discharged no more arrows: but by the noise increasing, I knew their numbers were greater; and about four yards from me, over-against my right ear, I heard a knocking for above an hour, like people at work; when turning my head that way, as well as the pegs and strings would permit me, I saw a stage erected about a foot and a half from the ground, capable of holding four of the inhabitatnts, with two or three ladders to mount it: from whence one of them, who seemed to be a person of quality, made me a long speech, whereof I understood not one syllable. But I should have mentioned, that before the principal person began his oration, he cried out three times, *Langro Dehul san*: (these words and the former were afterwards repeated and explained to me). Whereupon immediately about fifty of the inhabitants came, and cut the strings that fastened the left side of my head, which gave me the liberty of turning it to the right, and of observing the person and gesture of him who was to speak. He appeared to be of a middle age, and taller than any of the other three who attended him; whereof one was a page who held up his train, and seemed to be somewhat longer than my middle finger; the other two stood one on each side to support him. He acted every part of an orator, and I could observe many periods[6] of threatenings, and others of promises, pity and kindness. I answered in a few words, but in the most submissive manner, lifting up my left hand and both my eyes to the sun, as calling him for a witness; and being almost famished with hunger, having not eaten a morsel for some hours before I left the ship, I found the demands of nature so strong upon me, that I could not forbear showing my impatience (perhaps against the strict rules of decency) by putting my finger frequently on my mouth, to signify that I wanted food. The Hurgo (for so they call a great lord, as I afterwards learned) understood me very well. He descended from the stage, and commanded that several ladders should be applied to my sides, on which above an hundred of the inhabitants mounted, and walked towards my mouth, laden with baskets full of meat, which had been provided and sent thither by the King's orders upon the first intelligence he received of me. I observed there was the flesh of several animals, but could not distinguish them by the taste. There were shoulders, legs, and loins shaped like those of mutton, and very well dressed, but smaller than the wings of a lark. I eat them by two or three at a mouthful, and took three loaves at a time, about the bigness of musket bullets. They supplied me as fast as they could, showing a thousand marks of wonder and astonishment at my bulk and appetite. I then made another sign that I wanted drink. They found by my eating that a small quantity would not suffice me; and being a most ingenious people, they slung up with great dexterity one of their largest hogsheads; then rolled it towards my hand, and beat out the top; I drank it off at a draught, which I might well do, for it hardly held half a pint, and tasted like a small wine of Burgundy, but much more delicious. They brought me a second hogshead, which I drank in the same manner, and made signs for more, but they had none to give me. When I had performed these wonders, they shouted for joy, and danced upon my breast, repeating several times as they did at first, *Hekinah Degul*. They made me a sign that I should throw down the two hogsheads, but first warned the people below to stand out of the way, crying

6. In rhetoric, complete, well-constructed sentences.

aloud, *Borach Mivola,* and when they saw the vessels in the air, there was an universal shout of *Hekinah Degul.* I confess I was often tempted, while they were passing backwards and forwards on my body, to seize forty or fifty of the first that came in my reach, and dash them against the ground. But the remembrance of what I had felt, which probably might not be the worst they could do; and the promise of honor I made them, for so I interpreted my submissive behavior, soon drove out those imaginations. Besides, I now considered myself as bound by the laws of hospitality to a people who had treated me with so much expense and magnificence. However, in my thoughts I could not sufficiently wonder at the intrepidity of these diminutive mortals, who durst venture to mount and walk on my body, while one of my hands was at liberty, without trembling at the very sight of so prodigious a creature as I must appear to them. After some time, when they observed that I made no more demands for meat, there appeared before me a person of high rank from his Imperial Majesty. His Excellency, having mounted on the small of my right leg, advanced forwards up to my face, with about a dozen of his retinue. And producing his credentials under the Signet Royal, which he applied[7] close to my eyes, spoke about ten minutes, without any signs of anger, but with a kind of determinate resolution; often pointing forwards, which, as I afterwards found, was towards the capital city, about half a mile distant, whither it was agreed by his Majesty in council that I must be conveyed. I answered in a few words, but to no purpose, and made a sign with my hand that was loose, putting it to the other (but over his Excellency's head, for fear of hurting him or his train) and then to my own head and body, to signify that I desired my liberty. It appeared that he understood me well enough; for he shook his head by way of disapprobation, and held his hand in a posture to show that I must be carried as a prisoner. However, he made other signs to let me understand that I should have meat and drink enough, and very good treatment. Whereupon I once more thought of attempting to break my bonds; but again, when I felt the smart of their arrows upon my face and hands, which were all in blisters, and many of the darts still sticking in them; and observing likewise that the number of my enemies increased; I gave tokens to let them know that they might do with me what they pleased. Upon this the *Hurgo* and his train withdrew, with much civility and cheerful countenances. Soon after I heard a general shout, with frequent repetitions of the words, *Peplom Selan,* and I felt great numbers of the people on my left side relaxing the cords to such a degree, that I was able to turn upon my right, and to ease myself with making water; which I very plentifully did, to the great astonishment of the people, who conjecturing by my motions what I was going to do, immediately opened to the right and left on that side, to avoid the torrent which fell with such noise and violence from me. But before this, they had daubed my face and both my hands with a sort of ointment very pleasant to the smell, which in a few minutes removed all the smart of their arrows. These circumstances, added to the refreshment I had received by their victuals and drink, which were very nourishing, disposed me to sleep. I slept about eight hours, as I was afterwards assured; and it was no wonder; for the physicians, by the Emperor's order, had mingled a sleeping potion in the hogsheads of wine.

7. Brought.

It seems that upon the first moment I was discovered sleeping on the ground after my landing, the Emperor had early notice of it by an express; and determined in council that I should be tied in the manner I have related (which was done in the night while I slept), that plenty of meat and drink should be sent me, and a machine prepared to carry me to the capital city.

This resolution perhaps may appear very bold and dangerous, and I am confident would not be imitated by any prince in Europe on the like occasion; however, in my opinion it was extremely prudent as well as generous. For supposing these people had endeavored to kill me with their spears and arrows while I was asleep; I should certainly have awaked with the first sense of smart, which might so far have roused my rage and strength, as to enable me to break the strings wherewith I was tied; after which, as they were not able to make resistance, so they could expect no mercy.

These people are most excellent mathematicians, and arrived to a great perfection in mechanics by the countenance and encouragement of the Emperor, who is a renowned patron of learning. This prince hath several machines fixed on wheels, for the carriage of trees and other great weights. He often builds his largest men of war, whereof some are nine foot long, in the woods where the timber grows, and has them carried on these engines[8] three or four hundred yards to the sea. Five hundred carpenters and engineers were immediately set at work to prepare the greatest engine they had. It was a frame of wood raised three inches from the ground, about seven foot long and four wide, moving upon twenty-two wheels. The shout I heard was upon the arrival of this engine, which it seems set out in four hours after my landing. It was brought parallel to me as I lay. But the principal difficulty was to raise and place me in this vehicle. Eighty poles, each of one foot high, were erected for this purpose, and very strong cords of the bigness of packthread were fastened by hooks to many bandages, which the workmen had girt round my neck, my hands, my body, and my legs. Nine hundred of the strongest men were employed to draw up these cords by many pulleys fastened on the poles; and thus, in less than three hours, I was raised and slung into the engine, and there tied fast. All this I was told, for while the whole operation was performing, I lay in a profound sleep, by the force of that soporiferous[9] medicine infused into my liquor. Fifteen hundred of the Emperor's largest horses, each about four inches and a half high, were employed to draw me towards the metropolis, which, as I said, was half a mile distant.

About four hours after we began our journey, I awaked by a very ridiculous accident; for, the carriage being stopped a while to adjust something that was out of order, two or three of the young natives had the curiosity to see how I looked when I was asleep; they climbed up into the engine, and advancing very softly to my face, one of them, an officer in the guards, put the sharp end of his half-pike a good way up into my left nostril, which tickled my nose like a straw, and made me sneeze violently: whereupon they stole off unperceived, and it was three weeks before I knew the cause of my awaking so suddenly. We made a long march the remaining part of the day, and rested at night with five hundred guards on each side of me half with torches, and half with bows and arrows, ready to shoot me if I should offer to stir. The

---

8. Contrivances.   9. Inducing unnatural sleep.

next morning at sunrise we continued our march, and arrived within two hundred yards of the city gates about noon. The Emperor and all his court came out to meet us, but his great officers would by no means suffer his Majesty to endanger his person by mounting on my body.

At the place where the carriage stopped, there stood an ancient temple, esteemed to be the largest in the whole kingdom, which having been polluted some years before by an unnatural murder,[1] was, according to the zeal of those people, looked on as profane, and therefore had been applied to common use, and all the ornaments and furniture carried away. In this edifice it was determined I should lodge. The great gate fronting to the north was about four foot high, and almost two foot wide, through which I could easily creep. On each side of the gate was a small window not above six inches from the ground: into that on the left side, the King's smiths conveyed fourscore and eleven chains, like those that hang to a lady's watch in Europe, and almost as large, which were locked to my left leg with six and thirty padlocks. Over against this temple, on the other side of the great highway, at twenty foot distance, there was a turret at least five foot high. Here the Emperor ascended with many principal lords of his court, to have an opportunity of viewing me, as I was told, for I could not see them. It was reckoned that above an hundred thousand inhabitants came out of the town upon the same errand; and in spite of my guards, I believe there could not be fewer than ten thousand, at several times, who mounted upon my body by the help of ladders. But a proclamation was soon issued to forbid it upon pain of death. When the workmen found it was impossible for me to break loose, they cut all the strings that bound me; whereupon I rose up with as melancholy a disposition as ever I had in my life. But the noise and astonishment of the people at seeing me rise and walk are not to be expressed. The chains that held my left leg were about two yards long, and gave me not only the liberty of walking backwards and forwards in a semicircle; but, being fixed within four inches of the gate, allowed me to creep in, and lie at my full length in the temple.

CHAPTER 2. *The Emperor of Lilliput, attended by several of the nobility, comes to see the author in his confinement. The Emperor's person and habit described. Learned men appointed to teach the author their language. He gains favor by his mild disposition. His pockets are searched, and his sword and pistols taken from him.*

When I found myself on my feet, I looked about me, and must confess I never beheld a more entertaining prospect. The country round appeared like a continued garden, and the inclosed fields, which were generally forty foot psquare, resembled so many beds of flowers. These fields were intermingled with woods of half a stang,[2] and the tallest trees, as I could judge, appeared to be seven foot high. I viewed the town on my left hand, which looked like the painted scene of a city in a theater.

I had been for some hours extremely pressed by the necessities of nature; which was no wonder, it being almost two days since I had last disburthened myself. I was under great difficulties between urgency and shame. The best

---

1. Presumably a reference to the execution of Charles I, who was sentenced in Westminster Hall.

2. A quarter of an acre.

expedient I could think on, was to creep into my house, which I accordingly did; and shutting the gate after me, I went as far as the length of my chain would suffer; and discharged my body of that uneasy load. But this was the only time I was ever guilty of so uncleanly an action; for which I cannot but hope the candid reader will give some allowance, after he hath maturely and impartially considered my case, and the distress I was in. From this time my constant practice was, as soon as I rose, to perform that business in open air, at the full extent of my chain, and due care was taken every morning before company came, that the offensive matter should be carried off in wheelbarrows by two servants appointed for that purpose. I would not have dwelt so long upon a circumstance, that perhaps at first sight may appear not very momentous, if I had not thought it necessary to justify my character in point of cleanliness to the world; which I am told some of my maligners have been pleased, upon this and other occasions, to call in question.

When this adventure was at an end, I came back out of my house, having occasion for fresh air. The Emperor was already descended from the tower, and advancing on horseback towards me, which had like to have cost him dear; for the beast, although very well trained, yet wholly unused to such a sight, which appeared as if a mountain moved before him, reared up on his hinder feet: but that prince, who is an excellent horseman, kept his seat, until his attendants ran in, and held the bridle, while his Majesty had time to dismount. When he alighted, he surveyed me round with great admiration, but kept beyond the length of my chains. He ordered his cooks and butlers, who were already prepared, to give me victuals and drink, which they pushed forward in a sort of vehicles upon wheels until I could reach them. I took these vehicles, and soon emptied them all; twenty of them were filled with meat, and ten with liquor; each of the former afforded me two or three good mouthfuls, and I emptied the liquor of ten vessels, which was contained in earthen vials, into one vehicle, drinking it off at a draught; and so I did with the rest. The Empress, and young princes of the blood, of both sexes, attended by many ladies, sat at some distance in their chairs; but upon the accident that happened to the Emperor's horse, they alighted, and came near his person; which I am now going to describe. He is taller, by almost the breadth of my nail, than any of his court, which alone is enough to strike an awe into the beholders. His features are strong and masculine, with an Austrian lip, and arched nose, his complexion olive, his countenance[3] erect, his body and limbs well proportioned, all his motions graceful, and his deportment majestic. He was then past his prime, being twenty-eight years and three quarters old, of which he had reigned about seven, in great felicity, and generally victorious. For the better convenience of beholding him, I lay on my side, so that my face was parallel to his, and he stood but three yards off: however, I have had him since many times in my hand, and therefore cannot be deceived in the description. His dress was very plain and simple, the fashion of it between the Asiatic and the European; but he had on his head a light helmet of gold, adorned with jewels, and a plume on the crest. He held his sword drawn in his hand, to defend himself, if I should happen to break loose; it was almost three inches long, the hilt and scabbard were gold enriched with diamonds. His voice was shrill, but very clear and artic-

3. Bearing, appearance. Swift may be satirically idealizing George I, whom most of the British thought gross.

ulate, and I could distinctly hear it when I stood up. The ladies and courtiers were all most magnificently clad, so that the spot they stood upon seemed to resemble a petticoat spread on the ground, embroidered with figures of gold and silver. His Imperial Majesty spoke often to me, and I returned answers, but neither of us could understand a syllable. There were several of his priests and lawyers present (as I conjectured by their habits) who were commanded to address themselves to me, and I spoke to them in as many languages as I had the least smattering of, which were High and Low Dutch, Latin, French, Spanish, Italian, and Lingua Franca;[4] but all to no purpose. After about two hours the court retired, and I was left with a strong guard, to prevent the impertinence, and probably the malice of the rabble, who were very impatient to crowd about me as near as they durst; and some of them had the impudence to shoot their arrows at me as I sat on the ground by the door of my house, whereof one very narrowly missed my left eye. But the colonel ordered six of the ringleaders to be seized, and thought no punishment so proper as to deliver them bound into my hands, which some of his soldiers accordingly did, pushing them forwards with the butt-ends of their pikes into my reach; I took them all in my right hand, put five of them into my coat-pocket; and as to the sixth, I made a countenance as if I would eat him alive. The poor man squalled terribly, and the colonel and his officer were in much pain, especially when they saw me take out my penknife: but I soon put them out of fear; for, looking mildly, and immediately cutting the strings he was bound with, I set him gently on the ground, and away he ran. I treated the rest in the same manner, taking them one by one out of my pocket, and I observed both the soldiers and people were highly obliged at this mark of my clemency, which was represented very much to my advantage at court.

Towards night I got with some difficulty into my house, where I lay on the ground, and continued to do so about a fortnight; during which time the Emperor gave orders to have a bed prepared for me. Six hundred beds of the common measure were brought in carriages, and worked up in my house; an hundred and fifty of their beds sewn together made up the breadth and length, and these were four double, which however kept me but very indifferently from the hardness of the floor, that was of smooth stone. By the same computation they provided me with sheets, blankets, and coverlets, tolerable enough for one who had been so long enured to hardships as I.

As the news of my arrival spread through the kingdom, it brought prodigious numbers of rich, idle, and curious people to see me; so that the villages were almost emptied, and great neglect of tillage and household affairs must have ensued, if his Imperial Majesty had not provided by several proclamations and orders of state against this inconveniency. He directed that those who had already beheld me should return home, and not presume to come within fifty yards of my house without license from court; whereby the secretaries of state got considerable fees.

In the mean time, the Emperor held frequent councils to debate what course should be taken with me; and I was afterwards assured by a particular friend, a person of great quality, who was as much in the secret as any, that the court was under many difficulties concerning me. They apprehended[5]

---

4. A jargon, based on Italian, used by traders in the Mediterranean. "High and Low Dutch": German and Dutch.
5. Anticipated with fear.

my breaking loose, that my diet would be very expensive, and might cause a famine. Sometimes they determined to starve me, or at least to shoot me in the face and hands with poisoned arrows, which would soon dispatch me: but again they considered, that the stench of so large a carcass might produce a plague in the metropolis, and probably spread through the whole kingdom. In the midst of these consultations, several officers of the army went to the door of the great council chamber; and two of them being admitted, gave an account of my behavior to the six criminals above-mentioned; which made so favorable an impression in the breast of his Majesty, and the whole board, in my behalf, that an imperial commission was issued out, obliging all the villages nine hundred yards round the city to deliver in every morning six beeves, forty sheep, and other victuals for my sustenance; together with a proportionable quantity of bread and wine, and other liquors: for the due payment of which his Majesty gave assignments[6] upon his treasury. For this prince lives chiefly upon his own demesnes; seldom except upon great occasions raising any subsidies upon his subjects, who are bound to attend him in his wars at their own expense. An establishment was also made of six hundred persons to be my domestics, who had board-wages allowed for their maintenance, and tents built for them very conveniently on each side of my door. It was likewise ordered, that three hundred tailors should make me a suit of clothes after the fashion of the country: that six of his Majesty's greatest scholars should be employed to instruct me in their language: and, lastly, that the Emperor's horses, and those of the nobility, and troops of guards, should be exercised in my sight, to accustom themselves to me. All these orders were duly put in execution; and in about three weeks I made a great progress in learning their language; during which time the Emperor frequently honored me with his visits, and was pleased to assist my masters in teaching me. We began already to converse together in some sort; and the first words I learned, were to express my desire that he would please to give me my liberty; which I every day repeated on my knees.[7] His answer, as I could apprehend, was, that this must be a work of time, not to be thought on without the advice of his council; and that first I must *Lumos kelmin pesso desmar lon emposo;* that is, swear a peace with him and his kingdom. However, that I should be used with all kindness; and he advised me to acquire by my patience and discreet behavior, the good opinion of himself and his subjects. He desired I would not take it ill, if he gave orders to certain proper officers to search me; for probably I might carry about me several weapons, which must needs be dangerous things, if they answered the bulk of so prodigious a person.[8] I said, his Majesty should be satisfied, for I was ready to strip myself, and turn up my pockets before him. This I delivered part in words, and part in signs. He replied, that by the laws of the kingdom, I must be searched by two of his officers; that he knew this could not be done without my consent and assistance; that he had so good an opinion of my generosity and justice, as to trust their persons in my hands; that whatever they took from me should be returned when I left the country, or paid for at the rate which I would set upon them. I took up the two officers in my hands,

6. Formal mandates of revenue.
7. Gulliver's plea for liberty and the threat of starvation or rebellion he represents to his captors suggest the situation of Ireland with respect to England.

8. When the Whigs came into power in 1715, the leading Tories, who included Swift's friends Oxford and Bolingbroke (Robert Harley and Henry St. John) as well as Swift himself, were investigated by a committee of secrecy.

put them first into my coat-pockets, and then into every other pocket about me, except my two fobs, and another secret pocket which I had no mind should be searched, wherein I had some little necessaries of no consequence to any but myself. In one of my fobs there was a silver watch, and in the other a small quantity of gold in a purse. These gentlemen, having pen, ink, and paper about them, made an exact inventory of everything they saw; and when they had done, desired I would set them down, that they might deliver it to the Emperor. This inventory I afterwards translated into English, and is word for word as follows.

Imprimis, In the right coat-pocket of the Great Man-Mountain (for so I interpret the words *Quinbus Flestrin*) after the strictest search, we found only one great piece of coarse cloth, large enough to be a foot-cloth for your Majesty's chief room of state. In the left pocket, we saw a huge silver chest, with a cover of the same metal, which we the searchers were not able to lift. We desired it should be opened; and one of us, stepping into it, found himself up to the mid leg in a sort of dust, some part whereof flying up to our faces, set us both a sneezing for several times together. In his right waistcoat-pocket, we found a prodigious bundle of white thin substances, folded one over another, about the bigness of three men, tied with a strong cable, and marked with black figures; which we humbly conceive to be writings; every letter almost half as large as the palm of our hands. In the left there was a sort of engine, from the back of which were extended twenty long poles, resembling the palisados[9] before your Majesty's court; wherewith we conjecture the Man-Mountain combs his head; for we did not always trouble him with questions, because we found it a great difficulty to make him understand us. In the large pocket on the right side of his middle cover (so I translate the word *ranfu-lo*, by which they meant my breeches) we saw a hollow pillar of iron, about the length of a man, fastened to a strong piece of timber, larger than the pillar; and upon one side of the pillar were huge pieces of iron sticking out, cut into strange figures; which we know not what to make of. In the left pocket, another engine of the same kind. In the smaller pocket on the right side, were several round flat pieces of white and red metal, of different bulk; some of the white, which seemed to be silver, were so large and heavy, that my comrade and I could hardly lift them. In the left pocket were two black pillars irregularly shaped: we could not, without difficulty, reach the top of them as we stood at the bottom of his pocket. One of them was covered, and seemed all of a piece; but at the upper end of the other, there appeared a white round substance, about twice the bigness of our heads. Within each of these was inclosed a prodigious plate of steel; which, by our orders, we obliged him to show us, because we apprehended they might be dangerous engines. He took them out of their cases, and told us, that in his own country his practice was to shave his beard with one of these, and to cut his meat with the other. There were two pockets which we could not enter: these he called his fobs; they were two large slits cut into the top of his middle cover, but squeezed close by the pressure of his belly. Out

9. Fences of stakes.

of the right fob hung a great silver chain, with a wonderful kind of engine at the bottom. We directed him to draw out whatever was at the end of the chain, which appeared to be a globe, half silver, and half of some transparent metal: for on the transparent side we saw certain strange figures circularly drawn, and thought we could touch them, until we found our fingers stopped with that lucid substance. He put this engine to our ears, which made an incessant noise like that of a watermill. And we conjecture it is either some unknown animal, or the god that he worships: but we are more inclined to the latter opinion, because he assured us (if we understood him right, for he expressed himself very imperfectly), that he seldom did any thing without consulting it. He called it his oracle, and said it pointed out the time for every action of his life. From the left fob he took out a net almost large enough for a fisherman, but contrived to open and shut like a purse, and served him for the same use: we found therein several massy pieces of yellow metal, which if they be of real gold, must be of immense value.

Having thus, in obedience to your Majesty's commands, diligently searched all his pockets, we observed a girdle[1] about his waist made of the hide of some prodigious animal; from which, on the left side, hung a sword of the length of five men; and on the right, a bag or pouch divided into cells; each cell capable of holding three of your Majesty's subjects. In one of these cells were several globes or balls of a most ponderous metal, about the bigness of our heads, and required a strong hand to lift them: the other cell contained a heap of certain black grains, but of no great bulk or weight, for we could hold above fifty of them in the palms of our hands.

This is an exact inventory of what we found about the body of the Man-Mountain; who used us with great civility, and due respect to your Majesty's commission. Signed and sealed on the fourth day of the eighty-ninth moon of your Majesty's auspicious reign.

CLEFREN FRELOCK, MARSI FRELOCK.

When this inventory was read over to the Emperor, he directed me to deliver up the several particulars. He first called for my scimitar, which I took out, scabbard and all. In the meantime he ordered three thousand of his choicest troops (who then attended him) to surround me at a distance, with their bows and arrows just ready to discharge: but I did not observe it; for my eyes were wholly fixed upon his Majesty. He then desired me to draw my scimitar, which, although it had got some rust by the sea water, was in most parts exceeding bright. I did so, and immediately all the troops gave a shout between terror and surprise; for the sun shone clear, and the reflection dazzled their eyes, as I waved the scimitar to and fro in my hand. His Majesty, who is a most magnanimous[2] prince, was less daunted than I could expect; he ordered me to return it into the scabbard, and cast it on the ground as gently as I could, about six foot from the end of my chain. The next thing he demanded was one of the hollow iron pillars, by which he meant my pocket-pistols. I drew it out, and at his desire, as well as I could, expressed to him

---

1. Belt.
2. Courageous, great-spirited. Magnanimity, the relation (direct or inverse) between the size of the

body and the soul, is a central concern of the first two parts of the *Travels*.

the use of it, and charging it only with powder, which by the closeness of my pouch happened to escape wetting in the sea (an inconvenience that all prudent mariners take special care to provide against), I first cautioned the Emperor not to be afraid; and then I let it off in the air. The astonishment here was much greater than at the sight of my scimitar. Hundreds fell down as if they had been struck dead; and even the Emperor, although he stood his ground, could not recover himself in some time. I delivered up both my pistols in the same manner as I had done my scimitar, and then my pouch of powder and bullets; begging him that the former might be kept from fire; for it would kindle with the smallest spark, and blow up his imperial palace into the air. I likewise delivered up my watch, which the Emperor was very curious to see; and commanded two of his tallest yeomen of the guards to bear it on a pole upon their shoulders, as draymen in England do a barrel of ale. He was amazed at the continual noise it made, and the motion of the minute-hand, which he could easily discern; for their sight is much more acute than ours: he asked the opinions of his learned men about him, which were various and remote, as the reader may well imagine without my repeating; although indeed I could not very perfectly understand them. I then gave up my silver and copper money, my purse with nine large pieces of gold, and some smaller ones; my knife and razor, my comb and silver snuffbox, my handkerchief and journal book. My scimitar, pistols, and pouch, were conveyed in carriages to his Majesty's stores; but the rest of my goods were returned me.

I had, as I before observed, one private pocket which escaped their search, wherein there was a pair of spectacles (which I sometimes use for the weakness of my eyes), a pocket perspective,[3] and several other little conveniences; which, being of no consequence to the Emperor, I did not think myself bound in honor to discover, and I apprehended they might be lost or spoiled if I ventured them out of my possession.

CHAPTER 3. *The author diverts the Emperor and his nobility of both sexes in a very uncommon manner. The diversions of the court of Lilliput described. The author hath his liberty granted him upon certain conditions.*

My gentleness and good behavior had gained so far on the Emperor and his court, and indeed upon the army and people in general, that I began to conceive hopes of getting my liberty in a short time. I took all possible methods to cultivate this favorable disposition. The natives came by degrees to be less apprehensive of any danger from me. I would sometimes lie down, and let five or six of them dance on my hand. And at last the boys and girls would venture to come and play at hide-and-seek in my hair. I had now made a good progress in understanding and speaking their language. The Emperor had a mind one day to entertain me with several of the country shows; wherein they exceed all nations I have known, both for dexterity and magnificence. I was diverted with none so much as that of the rope-dancers, performed upon a slender white thread, extended about two foot, and twelve inches from the ground. Upon which I shall desire liberty, with the reader's patience, to enlarge a little.

This diversion is only practiced by those persons who are candidates for

_____

3. Telescope.

great employments, and high favor, at court. They are trained in this art from their youth, and are not always of noble birth, or liberal education. When a great office is vacant either by death or disgrace (which often happens) five or six of those candidates petition the Emperor to entertain his Majesty and the court with a dance on the rope; and whoever jumps the highest without falling, succeeds in the office. Very often the chief ministers themselves are commanded to show their skill, and to convince the Emperor that they have not lost their faculty. Flimnap,[4] the Treasurer, is allowed to cut a caper on the strait rope, at least an inch higher than any other lord in the whole empire. I have seen him do the summerset several times together upon a trencher[5] fixed on the rope, which is no thicker than a common packthread in England. My friend Reldresal, Principal Secretary for Private Affairs, is, in my opinion, if I am not partial, the second after the Treasurer; the rest of the great officers are much upon a par.

These diversions are often attended with fatal accidents, whereof great numbers are on record. I myself have seen two or three candidates break a limb. But the danger is much greater when the ministers themselves are commanded to show their dexterity; for, by contending to excel themselves and their fellows, they strain so far, that there is hardly one of them who hath not received a fall; and some of them two or three. I was assured, that a year or two before my arrival, Flimnap would have infallibly broke his neck, if one of the King's cushions,[6] that accidentally lay on the ground, had not weakened the force of his fall.

There is likewise another diversion, which is only shown before the Emperor and Empress, and first minister, upon particular occasions. The Emperor lays on a table three fine silken threads of six inches long. One is blue, the other red, and the third green.[7] These threads are proposed as prizes for those persons whom the Emperor hath a mind to distinguish by a peculiar mark of his favor. The ceremony is performed in his Majesty's great chamber of state; where the candidates are to undergo a trial of dexterity very different from the former, and such as I have not observed the least resemblance of in any other country of the old or the new world. The Emperor holds a stick in his hands, both ends parallel to the horizon, while the candidates, advancing one by one, sometimes leap over the stick, sometimes creep under it backwards and forwards several times, according as the stick is advanced or depressed. Sometimes the Emperor holds one end of the stick, and his first minister the other; sometimes the minister has it entirely to himself. Whoever performs his part with most agility, and holds out the longest in *leaping* and *creeping*, is rewarded with the blue-colored silk; the red is given to the next, and the green to the third, which they all wear girt twice round about the middle; and you see few great persons about this court who are not adorned with one of these girdles.

The horses of the army, and those of the royal stables, having been daily led before me, were no longer shy, but would come up to my very feet, without starting. The riders would leap them over my hand as I held it on the ground; and one of the Emperor's huntsmen, upon a large courser, took[8]

---

4. Sir Robert Walpole, the Whig head of the government, was notorious in Swift's circle for his political acrobatics.
5. Plate. "Summerset": somersault.
6. A mistress of George I was supposed to have helped restore Walpole to office in 1721.
7. The Orders of the Garter, the Bath, and the Thistle, conferred for services to the king.
8. Jumped over.

my foot, shoe and all; which was indeed a prodigious leap. I had the good fortune to divert the Emperor one day after a very extraordinary manner. I desired he would order several sticks of two foot high, and the thickness of an ordinary cane, to be brought me; whereupon his Majesty commanded the master of his woods to give directions accordingly; and the next morning six woodmen arrived with as many carriages, drawn by eight horses to each. I took nine of these sticks, and fixing them firmly in the ground in a quadrangular figure, two foot and a half square, I took four other sticks, and tied them parallel at each corner, about two foot from the ground; then I fastened my handkerchief to the nine sticks that stood erect, and extended it on all sides till it was as tight as the top of a drum; and the four parallel sticks, rising about five inches higher than the handkerchief, served as ledges on each side. When I had finished my work, I desired the Emperor to let a troop of his best horse, twenty-four in number, come and exercise upon this plain. His Majesty approved of the proposal, and I took them up one by one in my hands, ready mounted and armed, with the proper officers to exercise them. As soon as they got into order, they divided into two parties, performed mock skirmishes, discharged blunt arrows, drew their swords, fled and pursued, attacked and retired; and in short discovered the best military discipline I ever beheld. The parallel sticks secured them and their horses from falling over the stage; and the Emperor was so much delighted, that he ordered this entertainment to be repeated several days; and once was pleased to be lifted up, and give the word of command; and, with great difficulty, persuaded even the Empress herself to let me hold her in her close chair[9] within two yards of the stage, from whence she was able to take a full view of the whole performance. It was my good fortune that no ill accident happened in these entertainments, only once a fiery horse that belonged to one of the captains pawing with his hoof struck a hole in my handkerchief, and his foot slipping, he overthrew his rider and himself; but I immediately relieved them both; for covering the hole with one hand, I set down the troop with the other, in the same manner as I took them up. The horse that fell was strained in the left shoulder, but the rider got no hurt, and I repaired my handkerchief as well as I could; however, I would not trust to the strength of it any more in such dangerous enterprises.

About two or three days before I was set at liberty, as I was entertaining the court with these kinds of feats, there arrived an express to inform his Majesty that some of his subjects, riding near the place where I was first taken up, had seen a great black substance lying on the ground, very oddly shaped, extending its edges round as wide as his Majesty's bedchamber, and rising up in the middle as high as a man; that it was no living creature, as they at first apprehended, for it lay on the grass without motion, and some of them had walked round it several times; that by mounting upon each other's shoulders, they had got to the top, which was flat and even; and stamping upon it they found it was hollow within; that they humbly conceived it might be something belonging to the Man-Mountain, and if his Majesty pleased, they would undertake to bring it with only five horses. I presently[1] knew what they meant; and was glad at heart to receive this intelligence. It seems upon my first reaching the shore after our shipwreck, I was in such confusion, that before I came to the place where I went to sleep, my

9. An enclosed or sedan chair.   1. Immediately.

hat, which I had fastened with a string to my head while I was rowing, and had stuck on all the time I was swimming, fell off after I came to land; the string, as I conjecture, breaking by some accident which I never observed, but thought my hat had been lost at sea. I intreated his Imperial Majesty to give orders it might be brought to me as soon as possible, describing to him the use and the nature of it: and the next day the wagoners arrived with it, but not in a very good condition; they had bored two holes in the brim, within an inch and half of the edge, and fastened two hooks in the holes; these hooks were tied by a long cord to the harness, and thus my hat was dragged along for above half an English mile: but the ground in that country being extremely smooth and level, it received less damage than I expected.

Two days after this adventure, the Emperor, having ordered that part of his army which quarters in and about his metropolis to be in a readiness, took a fancy of diverting himself in a very singular manner. He desired I would stand like a colossus, with my legs as far asunder as I conveniently could. He then commanded his general (who was an old experienced leader, and a great patron of mine) to draw up the troops in close order, and march them under me; the foot[2] by twenty-four in a breast, and the horse by sixteen, with drums beating, colors flying, and pikes advanced. This body consisted of three thousand foot, and a thousand horse. His Majesty gave orders, upon pain of death, that every soldier in his march should observe the strictest decency with regard to my person; which, however, could not prevent some of the younger officers from turning up their eyes as they passed under me. And, to confess the truth, my breeches were at that time in so ill a condition, that they afforded some opportunities for laughter and admiration.

I had sent so many memorials and petitions for my liberty, that his Majesty at length mentioned the matter first in the cabinet, and then in a full council; where it was opposed by none, except Skyresh Bolgolam,[3] who was pleased, without any provocation, to be my mortal enemy. But it was carried against him by the whole board, and confirmed by the Emperor. That minister was *Galbet,* or Admiral of the Realm; very much in his master's confidence, and a person well versed in affairs, but of a morose and sour complexion.[4] However, he was at length persuaded to comply; but prevailed that the articles and conditions upon which I should be set free, and to which I must swear, should be drawn up by himself. These articles were brought to me by Skyresh Bolgolam in person, attended by two under-secretaries, and several persons of distinction. After they were read, I was demanded to swear to the performance of them; first in the manner of my own country, and afterwards in the method prescribed by their laws; which was to hold my right foot in my left hand, to place the middle finger of my right hand on the crown of my head, and my thumb on the tip of my right ear. But because the reader may perhaps be curious to have some idea of the style and manner of expression peculiar to that people, as well as to know the articles upon which I recovered my liberty, I have made a translation of the whole instrument,[5] word for word, as near as I was able; which I here offer to the public.

GOLBASTO MOMAREN EVLAME GURDILO SHEFIN MULLY ULLY GUE, most mighty Emperor of Lilliput, delight and terror of the universe, whose dominions extend five thousand blustrugs (about twelve miles in

---

2. Foot soldiers or infantry.
3. The earl of Nottingham, an enemy of Swift.
4. Disposition.
5. A formal legal document.

circumference) to the extremities of the globe; Monarch of all Monarchs; taller than the sons of men; whose feet press down to the center, and whose head strikes against the sun; at whose nod the princes of the earth shake their knees; pleasant as the spring, comfortable as the summer, fruitful as autumn, dreadful as winter. His most sublime Majesty proposeth to the Man-Mountain, lately arrived at our celestial dominions, the following articles, which by a solemn oath he shall be obliged to perform.

First, The Man-Mountain shall not depart from our dominions, without our license under our great seal.

Secondly, He shall not presume to come into our metropolis, without our express order; at which time the inhabitants shall have two hours warning, to keep within their doors.

Thirdly, The said Man-Mountain shall confine his walks to our principal high roads; and not offer to walk or lie down in a meadow, or field of corn.

Fourthly, As he walks the said roads, he shall take the utmost care not to trample upon the bodies of any of our loving subjects, their horses, or carriages, nor take any of our said subjects into his hands, without their own consent.

Fifthly, If an express require extraordinary dispatch, the Man-Mountain shall be obliged to carry in his pocket the messenger and horse, a six days' journey once in every moon, and return the said messenger back (if so required) safe to our Imperial Presence.

Sixthly, He shall be our ally against our enemies in the island of Blefuscu, and do his utmost to destroy their fleet, which is now preparing to invade us.

Seventhly, That the said Man-Mountain shall, at his times of leisure, be aiding and assisting to our workmen, in helping to raise certain great stones, towards covering the wall of the principal park, and other our royal buildings.

Eighthly, That the said Man-Mountain shall, in two moons' time, deliver in an exact survey of the circumference of our dominions by a computation of his own paces round the coast.

Lastly, That upon his solemn oath to observe all the above articles, the said Man-Mountain shall have a daily allowance of meat and drink sufficient for the support of 1,728 of our subjects; with free access to our Royal Person, and other marks of our favor. Given at our palace at Belfaborac the twelfth day of the ninety-first moon of our reign.

I swore and subscribed to these articles with great cheerfulness and content, although some of them were not so honorable as I could have wished; which proceeded wholly from the malice of Skyresh Bolgolam the High Admiral: whereupon my chains were immediately unlocked, and I was at full liberty: the Emperor himself in person did me the honor to be by at the whole ceremony. I made my acknowledgements by prostrating myself at his Majesty's feet: but he commanded me to rise; and after many gracious expressions, which, to avoid the censure of vanity, I shall not repeat, he added, that he hoped I should prove a useful servant, and well deserve all the favors he had already conferred upon me, or might do for the future.

The reader may please to observe, that in the last article for the recovery of my liberty, the Emperor stipulates to allow me a quantity of meat and drink, sufficient for the support of 1,728 Lilliputians. Some time after, asking a friend at court how they came to fix on that determinate number, he told me, that his Majesty's mathematicians, having taken the height of my body by the help of a quadrant, and finding it to exceed theirs in the proportion of twelve to one, they concluded from the similarity of their bodies, that mine must contain at least 1,728 of theirs, and consequently would require as much food as was necessary to support that number of Lilliputians. By which, the reader may conceive an idea of the ingenuity of that people, as well as the prudent and exact economy of so great a prince.

CHAPTER 4. *Mildendo, the metropolis of Lilliput, described, together with the Emperor's palace. A conversation between the author and a principal secretary, concerning the affairs of that empire; the author's offers to serve the Emperor in his wars.*

The first request I made after I had obtained my liberty, was, that I might have license to see Mildendo, the metropolis; which the Emperor easily granted me, but with a special charge to do no hurt, either to the inhabitants, or their houses. The people had notice by proclamation of my design to visit the town. The wall which encompassed it is two foot and an half high, and at least eleven inches broad, so that a coach and horses may be driven very safely round it; and it is flanked with strong towers at ten foot distance. I stepped over the great western gate, and passed very gently, and sideling[6] through the two principal streets, only in my short waistcoat, for fear of damaging the roofs and eaves of the houses with the skirts of my coat. I walked with the utmost circumspection, to avoid treading on any stragglers, who might remain in the streets, although the orders were very strict, that all people should keep in their houses, at their own peril. The garret windows and tops of houses were so crowded with spectators, that I thought in all my travels I had not seen a more populous place. The city is an exact square, each side of the wall being five hundred foot long. The two great streets, which run cross and divide it into four quarters, are five foot wide. The lanes and alleys, which I could not enter, but only viewed them as I passed, are from twelve to eighteen inches. The town is capable of holding five hundred thousand souls. The houses are from three to five stories. The shops and markets well provided.

The Emperor's palace is in the center of the city, where the two great streets meet. It is enclosed by a wall of two foot high, and twenty foot distant from the buildings. I had his Majesty's permission to step over this wall; and the space being so wide between that and the palace, I could easily view it on every side. The outward court is a square of forty foot, and includes two other courts: in the inmost are the royal apartments, which I was very desirous to see, but found it extremely difficult; for the great gates, from one square into another, were but eighteen inches high, and seven inches wide. Now the buildings of the outer court were at least five foot high; and it was impossible for me to stride over them, without infinite damage to the pile,

6. Sideways.

although the walls were strongly built of hewn stone, and four inches thick. At the same time the Emperor had a great desire that I should see the magnificence of his palace; but this I was not able to do till three days after, which I spent in cutting down with my knife some of the largest trees in the royal park, about an hundred yards distance from the city. Of these trees I made two stools, each about three foot high, and strong enough to bear my weight. The people having received notice a second time, I went again through the city to the palace, with my two stools in my hands. When I came to the side of the outer court, I stood upon one stool, and took the other in my hand: this I lifted over the roof, and gently set it down on the space between the first and second court, which was eight foot wide. I then stepped over the buildings very conveniently from one stool to the other, and drew up the first after me with a hooked stick. By this contrivance I got into the inmost court; and lying down upon my side, I applied my face to the windows of the middle stories, which were left open on purpose, and discovered the most splendid apartments that can be imagined. There I saw the Empress, and the young princes in their several lodgings, with their chief attendants about them. Her Imperial Majesty was pleased to smile very graciously upon me and gave me out of the window her hand to kiss.

But I shall not anticipate the reader with farther descriptions of this kind, because I reserve them for a greater work, which is now almost ready for the press; containing a general description of this empire, from its first erection, through a long series of princes, with a particular account of their wars and politics, laws, learning, and religion; their plants and animals, their peculiar manners and customs, with other matters very curious and useful; my chief design at present being only to relate such events and transactions as happened to the public, or to myself, during a residence of about nine months in that empire.

One morning, about a fortnight after I had obtained my liberty, Reldresal, Principal Secretary (as they style him) of Private Affairs, came to my house, attended only by one servant. He ordered his coach to wait at a distance, and desired I would give him an hour's audience; which I readily consented to, on account of his quality, and personal merits, as well as of the many good offices he had done me during my solicitations at court. I offered to lie down, that he might the more conveniently reach my ear; but he chose rather to let me hold him in my hand during our conversation. He began with compliments on my liberty, said he might pretend to some merit in it; but, however, added, that if it had not been for the present situation of things at court, perhaps I might not have obtained it so soon. For, said he, as flourishing a condition as we appear to be in to foreigners, we labor under two mighty evils; a violent faction at home, and the danger of an invasion by a most potent enemy from abroad. As to the first, you are to understand, that for above seventy moons past, there have been two struggling parties in the empire, under the names of *Tramecksan,* and *Slamecksan,*[7] from the high and low heels on their shoes, by which they distinguish themselves.

It is alleged indeed, that the high heels are most agreeable to our ancient constitution: but however this be, his Majesty hath determined to make use

---

7. Tory (High Church) and Whig (Low Church).

of only low heels in the administration of the government and all offices in the gift of the crown; as you cannot but observe; and particularly, that his Majesty's imperial heels are lower at least by a *drurr* than any of his court; (*drurr* is a measure about the fourteenth part of an inch). The animosities between these two parties run so high, that they will neither eat nor drink, nor talk with each other. We compute the *Tramecksan,* or High-Heels, to exceed us in number; but the power is wholly on our side. We apprehend his Imperial Highness, the heir to the crown, to have some tendency towards the High-Heels; at least we can plainly discover one of his heels higher than the other, which gives him a hobble in his gait.[8] Now, in the midst of these intestine disquiets, we are threatened with an invasion from the island of Blefuscu,[9] which is the other great empire of the universe, almost as large and powerful as this of his Majesty. For as to what we have heard you affirm, that there are other kingdoms and states in the world, inhabited by human creatures as large as yourself, our philosophers are in much doubt; and would rather conjecture that you dropped from the moon, or one of the stars; because it is certain, that an hundred mortals of your bulk would, in a short time, destroy all the fruits and cattle of his Majesty's dominions. Besides, our histories of six thousand moons make no mention of any other regions, than the two great empires of Lilliput and Blefuscu. Which two mighty powers have, as I was going to tell you, been engaged in a most obstinate war for six and thirty moons past. It began upon the following occasion. It is allowed on all hands, that the primitive way of breaking eggs before we eat them, was upon the larger end: but his present Majesty's grandfather, while he was a boy, going to eat an egg, and breaking it according to the ancient practice, happened to cut one of his fingers. Whereupon the Emperor his father published an edict, commanding all his subjects, upon great penalties, to break the smaller end of their eggs. The people so highly resented this law, that our histories tell us there have been six rebellions raised on that account; wherein one emperor lost his life, and another his crown.[1] These civil commotions were constantly fomented by the monarchs of Blefuscu; and when they were quelled, the exiles always fled for refuge to that empire. It is computed, that eleven thousand persons have, at several times, suffered death, rather than submit to break their eggs at the smaller end. Many hundred large volumes have been published upon this controversy: but the books of the Big-Endians have been long forbidden, and the whole party rendered incapable by law of holding employments.[2] During the course of these troubles, the emperors of Blefuscu did frequently expostulate by their ambassadors, accusing us of making a schism in religion, by offending against a fundamental doctrine of our great prophet Lustrog, in the fifty-fourth chapter of the *Brundecral* (which is their Alcoran[3]). This, however, is thought to be a mere strain upon the text: for the words are these; *That all true believers shall break their eggs at the convenient end:* and which is the convenient end, seems, in my humble opinion, to be left to every man's conscience, or at

---

8. The Prince of Wales (later George II) had friends in both parties.
9. France.
1. Swift's satirical allegory of the strife between Catholics (Big-Endians) and Protestants (Little-Endians) touches on Henry VIII (who "broke" with

the Pope), Charles I (who lost his life), and James II (who lost his crown).
2. The Test Act (1673) prevented Catholics and Nonconformists from holding office unless they accepted the Anglican Sacrament.
3. Koran.

least in the power of the chief magistrate[4] to determine. Now the Big-Endian exiles have found so much credit in the Emperor of Blefuscu's court, and so much private assistance and encouragement from their party here at home, that a bloody war hath been carried on between the two empires for six and thirty moons with various success;[5] during which time we have lost forty capital ships, and a much greater number of smaller vessels, together with thirty thousand of our best seamen and soldiers; and the damage received by the enemy is reckoned to be somewhat greater than ours. However, they have now equipped a numerous fleet, and are just preparing to make a descent upon us; and his Imperial Majesty, placing great confidence in your valor and strength, hath commanded me to lay this account of his affairs before you.

I desired the Secretary to present my humble duty to the Emperor, and to let him know, that I thought it would not become me, who was a foreigner, to interfere with parties; but I was ready, with the hazard of my life, to defend his person and state against all invaders.

CHAPTER 5. *The author by an extraordinary stratagem prevents an invasion. A high title of honor is conferred upon him. Ambassadors arrive from the Emperor of Blefuscu, and sue for peace. The Empress's apartment on fire by an accident; the author instrumental in saving the rest of the palace.*

The empire of Blefuscu is an island situated to the north north-east side of Lilliput, from whence it is parted only by a channel of eight hundred yards wide. I had not yet seen it, and upon this notice of an intended invasion, I avoided appearing on that side of the coast, for fear of being discovered by some of the enemy's ships, who had received no intelligence of me; all intercourse between the two empires having been strictly forbidden during the war, upon pain of death; and an embargo laid by our Emperor upon all vessels whatsoever. I communicated to his Majesty a project I had formed of seizing the enemy's whole fleet; which, as our scouts assured us, lay at anchor in the harbor ready to sail with the first fair wind. I consulted the most experienced seamen upon the depth of the channel, which they had often plumbed; who told me, that in the middle at high water it was seventy *glumgluffs* deep, which is about six foot of European measure; and the rest of it fifty *glumgluffs* at most. I walked to the northeast coast over against Blefuscu; where, lying down behind a hillock, I took out my small pocket perspective glass, and viewed the enemy's fleet at anchor, consisting of about fifty men of war, and a great number of transports: I then came back to my house, and gave order (for which I had a warrant) for a great quantity of the strongest cable and bars of iron. The cable was about as thick as packthread and the bars of the length and size of a knitting-needle. I trebled the cable to make it stronger, and for the same reason I twisted three of the iron bars together, bending the extremities into a hook. Having thus fixed fifty hooks to as many cables, I went back to the northeast coast, and putting off my coat, shoes, and stockings, walked into the sea in my leathern jerkin, about half an hour before high water. I waded with what haste I could, and swam

---

4. Ruler, sovereign. Swift himself accepted the right of the king to determine religious observances.

5. Reminiscent of the War of the Spanish Succession (1701–13).

in the middle about thirty yards until I felt the ground; I arrived at the fleet in less than half an hour. The enemy was so frighted when they saw me, that they leaped out of their ships, and swam to shore, where there could not be fewer than thirty thousand souls. I then took my tackling, and fastening a hook to the hole at the prow of each, I tied all the cords together at the end. While I was thus employed, the enemy discharged several thousand arrows, many of which stuck in my hands and face; and besides the excessive smart, gave me much disturbance in my work. My greatest apprehension was for my eyes, which I should have infallibly lost, if I had not suddenly thought of an expedient. I kept, among other little necessaries, a pair of spectacles in a private pocket, which, as I observed before, had escaped the Emperor's searchers. These I took out, and fastened as strongly as I could upon my nose; and thus armed went on boldly with my work in spite of the enemy's arrows; many of which struck against the glasses of my spectacles, but without any other effect, further than a little to discompose them. I had now fastened all the hooks, and taking the knot in my hand, began to pull; but not a ship would stir, for they were all too fast by their anchors, so that the boldest part of my enterprise remained. I therefore let go the cord, and leaving the hooks fixed to the ships, I resolutely cut with my knife the cables that fastened the anchors, receiving about two hundred shots in my face and hands; then I took up the knotted end of the cables to which my hooks were tied; and with great ease drew fifty of the enemy's largest men-of-war after me.

The Blefuscudians, who had not the least imagination of what I intended, were at first confounded with astonishment. They had seen me cut the cables, and thought my design was only to let the ships run adrift, or fall foul on each other: but when they perceived the whole fleet moving in order, and saw me pulling at the end, they set up such a scream of grief and despair, that it is almost impossible to describe or conceive. When I had got out of danger, I stopped a while to pick out the arrows that stuck in my hands and face, and rubbed on some of the same ointment that was given me at my first arrival, as I have formerly mentioned. I then took off my spectacles, and waiting about an hour until the tide was a little fallen, I waded through the middle with my cargo, and arrived safe at the royal port of Lilliput.

The Emperor and his whole court stood on the shore, expecting the issue of this great adventure. They saw the ships move forward in a large half-moon, but could not discern me, who was up to my breast in water. When I advanced to the middle of the channel, they were yet more in pain, because I was under water to my neck. The Emperor concluded me to be drowned, and that the enemy's fleet was approaching in a hostile manner: but he was soon eased of his fears, for the channel growing shallower every step I made, I came in a short time within hearing; and holding up the end of the cable by which the fleet was fastened, I cried in a loud voice, Long live the most puissant Emperor of Lilliput! This great prince received me at my landing with all possible encomiums, and created me a *Nardac* upon the spot, which is the highest title of honor among them.

His Majesty desired I would take some other opportunity of bringing all the rest of his enemy's ships into his ports. And so unmeasurable is the ambition of princes, that he seemed to think of nothing less than reducing the whole empire of Blefuscu into a province, and governing it by a viceroy;

of destroying the Big-Endian exiles, and compelling that people to break the smaller end of their eggs, by which he would remain sole monarch of the whole world. But I endeavored to divert him from this design, by many arguments drawn from the topics of policy as well as justice: and I plainly protested, that I would never be an instrument of bringing a free and brave people into slavery. And when the matter was debated in council, the wisest part of the ministry were of my opinion.

This open bold declaration of mine was so opposite to the schemes and politics of his Imperial Majesty, that he could never forgive me; he mentioned it in a very artful manner at council, where I was told that some of the wisest appeared, at least by their silence, to be of my opinion; but others, who were my secret enemies, could not forbear some expressions, which by a side-wind[6] reflected on me. And from this time began an intrigue between his Majesty and a junta of ministers maliciously bent against me, which broke out in less than two months, and had like to have ended in my utter destruction. Of so little weight are the greatest services to princes, when put into the balance with a refusal to gratify their passions.[7]

About three weeks after this exploit, there arrived a solemn embassy from Blefuscu, with humble offers of a peace; which was soon concluded upon conditions very advantageous to our Emperor; wherewith I shall not trouble the reader. There were six ambassadors, with a train of about five hundred persons; and their entry was very magnificent, suitable to the grandeur of their master, and the importance of their business. When their treaty was finished, wherein I did them several good offices by the credit I now had, or at least appeared to have at court, their Excellencies, who were privately told how much I had been their friend, made me a visit in form. They began with many compliments upon my valor and generosity; invited me to that kingdom in the Emperor their master's name; and desired me to show them some proofs of my prodigious strength, of which they had heard so many wonders; wherein I readily obliged them, but shall not interrupt the reader with the particulars.

When I had for some time entertained their Excellencies to their infinite satisfaction and surprise, I desired they would do me the honor to present my most humble respects to the Emperor their master, the renown of whose virtues had so justly filled the whole world with admiration, and whose royal person I resolved to attend before I returned to my own country. Accordingly, the next time I had the honor to see our Emperor, I desired his general license to wait on the Blefuscudian monarch, which he was pleased to grant me, as I could plainly perceive, in a very cold manner; but could not guess the reason, till I had a whisper from a certain person, that Flimnap and Bolgolam had represented my intercourse with those ambassadors as a mark of disaffection, from which I am sure my heart was wholly free. And this was the first time I began to conceive some imperfect idea of courts and ministers.

It is to be observed, that these ambassadors spoke to me by an interpreter; the languages of both empires differing as much from each other as any two in Europe, and each nation priding itself upon the antiquity, beauty, and

6. Indirectly.
7. After a series of British naval victories, the Treaty of Utrecht (1713) had ended the war with France, but the Tory ministers who engineered the peace were subsequently accused of having sold out to the enemy.

energy of their own tongues, with an avowed contempt for that of their neighbor; yet our Emperor, standing upon the advantage he had got by the seizure of their fleet, obliged them to deliver their credentials, and make their speech, in the Lilliputian tongue. And it must be confessed, that from the great intercourse of trade and commerce between both realms, from the continual reception of exiles, which is mutual among them, and from the custom in each empire to send their young nobility and richer gentry to the other, in order to polish themselves, by seeing the world, and understanding men and manners, there are few persons of distinction, or merchants, or seamen, who dwell in the maritime parts, but what can hold conversation in both tongues; as I found some weeks after, when I went to pay my respects to the Emperor of Blefuscu, which in the midst of great misfortunes, through the malice of my enemies, proved a very happy adventure to me, as I shall relate in its proper place.

The reader may remember, that when I signed those articles upon which I recovered my liberty, there were some which I disliked upon account of their being too servile, neither could any thing but an extreme necessity have forced me to submit. But being now a *Nardac,* of the highest rank in that empire, such offices[8] were looked upon as below my dignity, and the Emperor (to do him justice) never once mentioned them to me. However, it was not long before I had an opportunity of doing his Majesty, at least as I then thought, a most signal service. I was alarmed at midnight with the cries of many hundred people at my door; by which being suddenly awaked, I was in some kind of terror. I heard the word *burglum* repeated incessantly; several of the Emperor's court, making their way through the crowd, intreated me to come immediately to the palace, where her Imperial Majesty's apartment was on fire, by the carelessness of a maid of honor, who fell asleep while she was reading a romance. I got up in an instant; and orders being given to clear the way before me, and it being likewise a moonshine night, I made a shift to get to the palace without trampling on any of the people. I found they had already applied ladders to the walls of the apartment, and were well provided with buckets, but the water was at some distance. These buckets were about the size of a large thimble, and the poor people supplied me with them as fast as they could; but the flame was so violent, that they did little good. I might easily have stifled it with my coat, which I unfortunately left behind me for haste, and came away only in my leathern jerkin. The case seemed wholly desperate and deplorable; and this magnificent palace would have infallibly been burnt down to the ground, if, by a presence of mind, unusual to me, I had not suddenly thought of an expedient. I had the evening before drank plentifully of a most delicious wine, called *glimigrim* (the Blefuscudians call it *flunec,* but ours is esteemed the better sort), which is very diuretic. By the luckiest chance in the world, I had not discharged myself of any part of it. The heat I had contracted by coming very near the flames, and by my laboring to quench them, made the wine begin to operate by urine; which I voided in such a quantity, and applied so well to the proper places, that in three minutes the fire was wholly extinguished; and the rest of that noble pile, which had cost so many ages in erecting, preserved from destruction.

It was now daylight, and I returned to my house, without waiting to con-

8. Duties.

gratulate with the Emperor; because, although I had done a very eminent piece of service, yet I could not tell how his Majesty might resent the manner by which I had performed it: for, by the fundamental laws of the realm, it is capital[9] in any person, of what quality soever, to make water within the precincts of the palace. But I was a little comforted by a message from his Majesty, that he would give orders to the Grand Justiciary for passing my pardon in form; which, however, I could not obtain. And I was privately assured, that the Empress, conceiving the greatest abhorrence of what I had done,[1] removed to the most distant side of the court, firmly resolved that those buildings should never be repaired for her use; and, in the presence of her chief confidents, could not forbear vowing revenge.

CHAPTER 6. *Of the inhabitants of Lilliput; their learning, laws, and customs, the manner of educating their children. The author's way of living in that country. His vindication of a great lady.*

Although I intend to leave the description of this empire to a particular treatise, yet in the mean time I am content to gratify the curious reader with some general ideas. As the common size of the natives is somewhat under six inches, so there is an exact proportion in all other animals, as well as plants and trees: for instance, the tallest horses and oxen are between four and five inches in height, the sheep an inch and a half, more or less; their geese about the bigness of a sparrow; and so the several gradations downwards, till you come to the smallest, which, to my sight, were almost invisible; but nature hath adapted the eyes of the Lilliputians to all objects proper for their view: they see with great exactness, but at no great distance. And to show the sharpness of their sight towards objects that are near, I have been much pleased with observing a cook pulling[2] a lark, which was not so large as a common fly; and a young girl threading an invisible needle with invisible silk. Their tallest trees are about seven foot high; I mean some of those in the great royal park, the tops whereof I could but just reach with my fist clinched. The other vegetables[3] are in the same proportion; but this I leave to the reader's imagination.

I shall say but little at present of their learning, which for many ages hath flourished in all its branches among them: but their manner of writing is very peculiar; being neither from the left to the right, like the Europeans; nor from the right to the left, like the Arabians; nor from up to down, like the Chinese; nor from down to up, like the Cascagians;[4] but aslant from one corner of the paper to the other, like ladies in England.

They bury their dead with their heads directly downwards; because they hold an opinion that in eleven thousand moons they are all to rise again; in which period, the earth (which they conceive to be flat) will turn upside down, and by this means they shall, at their resurrection, be found ready standing on their feet. The learned among them confess the absurdity of this doctrine; but the practice still continues, in compliance to the vulgar.

There are some laws and customs in this empire very peculiar; and if they

---

were not so directly contrary to those of my own dear country, I should be tempted to say a little in their justification. It is only to be wished, that they were as well executed. The first I shall mention relateth to informers. All crimes against the state are punished here with the utmost severity; but if the person accused make his innocence plainly to appear upon his trial, the accuser is immediately put to an ignominious death; and out of his goods or lands, the innocent person is quadruply recompensed for the loss of his time, for the danger he underwent, for the hardship of his imprisonment, and for all the charges he hath been at in making his defense. Or, if that fund be deficient, it is largely[5] supplied by the crown. The Emperor doth also confer on him some public mark of his favor; and proclamation is made of his innocence through the whole city.

They look upon fraud as a greater crime than theft, and therefore seldom fail to punish it with death; for they allege, that care and vigilance, with a very common understanding, may preserve a man's goods from thieves; but honesty hath no fence against superior cunning: and since it is necessary that there should be a perpetual intercourse of buying and selling, and dealing upon credit, where fraud is permitted or connived at, or hath no law to punish it, the honest dealer is always undone, and the knave gets the advantage. I remember when I was once interceding with the King for a criminal who had wronged his master of a great sum of money, which he had received by order, and ran away with; and happening to tell his Majesty, by way of extenuation, that it was only a breach of trust, the Emperor thought it monstrous in me to offer, as a defense, the greatest aggravation of the crime: and truly, I had little to say in return, farther than the common answer, that different nations had different customs; for, I confess, I was heartily ashamed.

Although we usually call reward and punishment the two hinges upon which all government turns, yet I could never observe this maxim to be put in practice by any nation, except that of Lilliput. Whoever can there bring sufficient proof that he hath strictly observed the laws of his country for seventy-three moons, hath a claim to certain privileges, according to his quality[6] and condition of life, with a proportionable sum of money out of a fund appropriated for that use: he likewise acquires the title of *Snilpall*, or *Legal*, which is added to his name, but doth not descend to his posterity. And these people thought it a prodigious defect of policy among us, when I told them that our laws were enforced only by penalties, without any mention of reward. It is upon this account that the image of Justice, in their courts of judicature, is formed with six eyes, two before, as many behind, and on each side one, to signify circumspection; with a bag of gold open in her right hand, and a sword sheathed in her left, to show she is more disposed to reward than to punish.

In choosing persons for all employments, they have more regard to good morals than to great abilities; for, since government is necessary to mankind, they believe that the common size of human understandings is fitted to some station or other; and that Providence never intended to make the management of public affairs a mystery, to be comprehended only by a few persons of sublime genius, of which there seldom are three born in an age: but they

5. Fully.   6. Social position.

suppose truth, justice, temperance, and the like, to be in every man's power; the practice of which virtues, assisted by experience and a good intention, would qualify any man for the service of his country, except where a course of study is required. But they thought the want of moral virtues was so far from being supplied by superior endowments of the mind, that employments could never be put into such dangerous hands as those of persons so qualified; and at least, that the mistakes committed by ignorance in a virtuous disposition would never be of such fatal consequence to the public weal, as the practices of a man whose inclinations led him to be corrupt, and had great abilities to manage, to multiply, and defend his corruptions.

In like manner, the disbelief of a divine Providence renders a man uncapable of holding any public station; for since kings avow themselves to be the deputies of Providence, the Lilliputians think nothing can be more absurd than for a prince to employ such men as disown the authority under which he acteth.

In relating these and the following laws, I would only be understood to mean the original institutions, and not the most scandalous corruptions into which these people are fallen by the degenerate nature of man. For as to that infamous practice of acquiring great employments by dancing on the ropes, or badges of favor and distinction by leaping over sticks, and creeping under them, the reader is to observe, that they were first introduced by the grandfather of the Emperor now reigning; and grew to the present height by the gradual increase of party and faction.

Ingratitude is among them a capital crime, as we read it to have been in some other countries; for they reason thus, that whoever makes ill returns to his benefactor, must needs be a common enemy to the rest of mankind, from whom he hath received no obligation; and therefore such a man is not fit to live.

Their notions relating to the duties of parents and children differ extremely from ours. For, since the conjunction of male and female is founded upon the great law of nature, in order to propagate and continue the species, the Lilliputians will needs have it, that men and women are joined together like other animals, by the motives of concupiscence; and that their tenderness towards their young proceedeth from the like natural principle: for which reason they will never allow, that a child is under any obligation to his father for begetting him, or to his mother for bringing him into the world; which, considering the miseries of human life, was neither a benefit in itself, nor intended so by his parents, whose thoughts in their love-encounters were otherwise employed. Upon these, and the like reasonings, their opinion is, that parents are the last of all others to be trusted with the education of their own children: and therefore they have in every town public nurseries, where all parents, except cottagers[7] and laborers, are obliged to send their infants of both sexes to be reared and educated when they come to the age of twenty moons; at which time they are supposed to have some rudiments of docility. These schools are of several kinds, suited to different qualities, and to both sexes. They have certain professors[8] well skilled in preparing children for such a condition of life as befits the rank of their parents, and their own capacities as well as inclinations. I shall first say something of the male nurseries, and then of the female.

---

7. Agricultural workers, peasants. 8. Professional teachers.

The nurseries for males of noble or eminent birth are provided with grave and learned professors, and their several deputies. The clothes and food of the children are plain and simple. They are bred up in the principles of honor, justice, courage, modesty, clemency, religion, and love of their country; they are always employed in some business, except in the times of eating and sleeping, which are very short, and two hours for diversions, consisting of bodily exercises. They are dressed by men until four years of age, and then are obliged to dress themselves, although their quality be ever so great; and the women attendants, who are aged proportionably to ours at fifty, perform only the most menial offices. They are never suffered to converse with servants, but go together in small or greater numbers to take their diversions, and always in the presence of a professor, or one of his deputies; whereby they avoid those early bad impressions of folly and vice to which our children are subject. Their parents are suffered to see them only twice a year; the visit is not to last above an hour; they are allowed to kiss the child at meeting and parting; but a professor, who always standeth by on those occasions, will not suffer them to whisper, or use any fondling expressions, or bring any presents of toys, sweetmeats, and the like.

The pension from each family for the education and entertainment[9] of a child, upon failure of due payment, is levied by the Emperor's officers.

The nurseries for children of ordinary gentlemen, merchants, traders, and handicrafts, are managed proportionably after the same manner; only those designed for trades are put out apprentices at seven years old; whereas those of persons of quality continue in their exercises until fifteen, which answers to one and twenty with us: but the confinement is gradually lessened for the last three years.

In the female nurseries, the young girls of quality are educated much like the males, only they are dressed by orderly servants of their own sex, but always in the presence of a professor or deputy, until they come to dress themselves, which is at five years old. And if it be found that these nurses ever presume to entertain the girls with frightful or foolish stories, or the common follies practiced by chambermaids among us, they are publicly whipped thrice about the city, imprisoned for a year, and banished for life to the most desolate parts of the country. Thus the young ladies there are as much ashamed of being cowards and fools as the men; and despise all personal ornaments beyond decency and cleanliness: neither did I perceive any difference in their education, made by their difference of sex, only that the exercises of the females were not altogether so robust; and that some rules were given them relating to domestic life, and a smaller compass of learning was enjoined them: for their maxim is, that among people of quality, a wife should be always a reasonable and agreeable companion, because she cannot always be young. When the girls are twelve years old, which among them is the marriageable age, their parents or guardians take them home, with great expressions of gratitude to the professors, and seldom without tears of the young lady and her companions.

In the nurseries of females of the meaner sort, the children are instructed in all kinds of works proper for their sex, and their several degrees:[1] those intended for apprentices are dismissed at seven years old, the rest are kept to eleven.

9. Sustenance.   1. Various social ranks.

The meaner families who have children at these nurseries are obliged, besides their annual pension, which is as low as possible, to return to the steward of the nursery a small monthly share of their gettings, to be a portion for the child; and therefore all parents are limited in their expenses by the law. For the Lilliputians think nothing can be more unjust, than that people, in subservience to their own appetites, should bring children into the world, and leave the burthen of supporting them on the public. As to persons of quality, they give security to appropriate a certain sum for each child, suitable to their condition; and these funds are always managed with good husbandry, and the most exact justice.

The cottagers and laborers keep their children at home, their business being only to till and cultivate the earth; and therefore their education is of little consequence to the public; but the old and diseased among them are supported by hospitals: for begging is a trade unknown in this empire.

And here it may perhaps divert the curious reader, to give some account of my domestic,[2] and my manner of living in this country, during a residence of nine months and thirteen days. Having a head mechanically turned, and being likewise forced by necessity, I had made for myself a table and chair convenient enough, out of the largest trees in the royal park. Two hundred sempstresses were employed to make me shirts, and linen for my bed and table, all of the strongest and coarsest kind they could get; which, however, they were forced to quilt together in several folds; for the thickest was some degrees finer than lawn. Their linen is usually three inches wide, and three foot make a piece. The sempstresses took my measure as I lay on the ground, one standing at my neck, and another at my mid-leg, with a strong cord extended, that each held by the end, while the third measured the length of the cord with a rule of an inch long. Then they measured my right thumb, and desired no more; for by a mathematical computation, that twice round the thumb is one round the wrist, and so on to the neck and the waist; and by the help of my old shirt, which I displayed on the ground before them for a pattern, they fitted me exactly. Three hundred tailors were employed in the same manner to make me clothes; but they had another contrivance for taking my measure. I kneeled down, and they raised a ladder from the ground to my neck; upon this ladder one of them mounted, and let fall a plumb-line from my collar to the floor, which just answered the length of my coat; but my waist and arms I measured myself. When my clothes were finished, which was done in my house (for the largest of theirs would not have been able to hold them), they looked like the patchwork made by the ladies in England, only that mine were all of a color.

I had three hundred cooks to dress my victuals, in little convenient huts built about my house, where they and their families lived, and prepared me two dishes apiece. I took up twenty waiters in my hand, and placed them on the table; an hundred more attended below on the ground, some with dishes of meat, and some with barrels of wine, and other liquors, slung on their shoulders; all which the waiters above drew up as I wanted, in a very ingenious manner, by certain cords, as we draw the bucket up a well in Europe. A dish of their meat was a good mouthful, and a barrel of their liquor a reasonable draught. Their mutton yields to ours, but their beef is excellent.

2. Household.

I have had a sirloin so large, that I have been forced to make three bites of it; but this is rare. My servants were astonished to see me eat it bones and all, as in our country we do the leg of a lark. Their geese and turkeys I usually eat at a mouthful, and I must confess they far exceed ours. Of their smaller fowl I could take up twenty or thirty at the end of my knife.

One day his Imperial Majesty, being informed of my way of living, desired that himself and his royal consort, with the young princes of the blood of both sexes, might have the happiness (as he was pleased to call it) of dining with me. They came accordingly, and I placed them upon chairs of state on my table, just over against me, with their guards about them. Flimnap the Lord High Treasurer attended there likewise, with his white staff; and I observed he often looked on me with a sour countenance, which I would not seem to regard, but eat more than usual, in honor to my dear country, as well as to fill the court with admiration. I have some private reasons to believe, that this visit from his Majesty gave Flimnap an opportunity of doing me ill offices to his master. That minister had always been my secret enemy, although he outwardly caressed me more than was usual to the moroseness of his nature. He represented to the Emperor the low condition of his treasury; that he was forced to take up money at great discount; that exchequer bills[3] would not circulate under nine per cent below par; that I had cost his Majesty above a million and a half of *sprugs* (their greatest gold coin, about the bigness of a spangle); and upon the whole, that it would be advisable in the Emperor to take the first fair occasion of dismissing me.

I am here obliged to vindicate the reputation of an excellent lady, who was an innocent sufferer upon my account. The Treasurer took a fancy to be jealous of his wife, from the malice of some evil tongues, who informed him that her Grace had taken a violent affection for my person; and the court-scandal ran for some time that she once came privately to my lodging. This I solemnly declare to be a most infamous falsehood, without any grounds, farther than that her Grace was pleased to treat me with all innocent marks of freedom and friendship. I own she came often to my house, but always publicly, nor ever without three more in the coach, who were usually her sister and young daughter, and some particular acquaintance; but this was common to many other ladies of the court. And I still appeal to my servants round, whether they at any time saw a coach at my door without knowing what persons were in it. On those occasions, when a servant had given me notice, my custom was to go immediately to the door; and, after paying my respects, to take up the coach and two horses very carefully in my hands (for if there were six horses, the postillion always unharnessed four) and place them on a table, where I had fixed a moveable rim quite round, of five inches high, to prevent accidents. And I have often had four coaches and horses at once on my table full of company, while I sat in my chair leaning my face towards them; and when I was engaged with one set, the coachmen would gently drive the others round my table. I have passed many an afternoon very agreeably in these conversations. But I defy the Treasurer, or his two informers (I will name them, and let them make their best of it) Clustril and Drunlo, to prove that any person ever came to me *incognito,* except the Secretary Reldresal, who was sent by express command of his Imperial Majesty, as I

---

3. Government bills of credit. Walpole was noted as a canny financier.

have before related. I should not have dwelt so long upon this particular, if it had not been a point wherein the reputation of a great lady is so nearly concerned, to say nothing of my own; although I had the honor to be a *Nardac*, which the Treasurer himself is not; for all the world knows he is only a *Clumglum*, a title inferior by one degree, as that of a marquis is to a duke in England; yet I allow he preceded me in right of his post. These false informations, which I afterwards came to the knowledge of, by an accident not proper to mention, made the Treasurer show his lady for some time an ill countenance, and me a worse; for although he was at last undeceived and reconciled to her, yet I lost all credit with him; and found my interest decline very fast with the Emperor himself, who was indeed too much governed by that favorite.

CHAPTER 7. *The author, being informed of a design to accuse him of high treason, makes his escape to Blefuscu. His reception there.*

Before I proceed to give an account of my leaving this kingdom, it may be proper to inform the reader of a private intrigue which had been for two months forming against me.

I had been hitherto all my life a stranger to courts, for which I was unqualified by the meanness of my condition. I had indeed heard and read enough of the dispositions of great princes and ministers; but never expected to have found such terrible effects of them in so remote a country, governed, as I thought, by very different maxims from those in Europe.

When I was just preparing to pay my attendance on the Emperor of Blefuscu, a considerable person at court (to whom I had been very serviceable at a time when he lay under the highest displeasure of his Imperial Majesty) came to my house very privately at night in a close chair, and without sending his name, desired admittance. The chairmen were dismissed; I put the chair, with his Lordship in it, into my coat-pocket; and giving orders to a trusty servant to say I was indisposed and gone to sleep, I fastened the door of my house, placed the chair on the table, according to my usual custom, and sat down by it. After the common salutations were over, observing his Lordship's countenance full of concern, and enquiring into the reason, he desired I would hear him with patience, in a matter that highly concerned my honor and my life. His speech was to the following effect, for I took notes of it as soon as he left me.

You are to know, said he, that several committees of council have been lately called in the most private manner on your account: and it is but two days since his Majesty came to a full resolution.

You are very sensible that Skyresh Bolgolam (*Galbet*, or High Admiral) hath been your mortal enemy almost ever since your arrival. His original reasons I know not; but his hatred is much increased since your great success against Blefuscu, by which his glory, as Admiral, is obscured. This lord, in conjunction with Flimnap the High Treasurer, whose enmity against you is notorious on account of his lady, Limtoc the General, Lalcon the Chamberlain, and Balmuff the Grand Justiciary, have prepared articles of impeachment against you, for treason, and other capital crimes.[4]

---

4. After the Whigs had investigated Oxford and Bolingbroke, both were impeached for high treason, on charges of being sympathetic to the Jacobites and the French.

This preface made me so impatient, being conscious of my own merits and innocence, that I was going to interrupt; when he entreated me to be silent, and thus proceeded.

Out of gratitude for the favors you have done me, I procured information of the whole proceedings, and a copy of the articles, wherein I venture my head for your service.

Articles of Impeachment against Quinbus Flestrin (the Man-Mountain).

ARTICLE 1

Whereas, by a statute made in the reign of his Imperial Majesty Calin Deffar Plune, it is enacted, that whoever shall make water within the precincts of the royal palace shall be liable to the pains and penalties of high treason: notwithstanding, the said Quinbus Flestrin, in open breach of the said law, under color of extinguishing the fire kindled in the apartment of his Majesty's most dear imperial consort, did maliciously, traitorously, and devilishly, by discharge of his urine, put out the said fire kindled in the said apartment, lying and being within the precincts of the said royal palace; against the statute in that case provided, etc., against the duty, etc.

ARTICLE 2

That the said Quinbus Flestrin, having brought the imperial fleet of Blefuscu into the royal port, and being afterwards commanded by his Imperial Majesty to seize all the other ships of the said empire of Blefuscu, and reduce that empire to a province, to be governed by a viceroy from hence; and to destroy and put to death not only all the Big-Endian exiles, but likewise all the people of that empire who would not immediately forsake the Big-Endian heresy: he, the said Flestrin, like a false traitor against his most auspicious, serene, Imperial Majesty, did petition to be excused from the said service, upon pretense of unwillingness to force the consciences, or destroy the liberties and lives of an innocent people.

ARTICLE 3

That, whereas certain ambassadors arrived from the court of Blefuscu to sue for peace in his Majesty's court: he the said Flestrin did, like a false traitor, aid, abet, comfort, and divert the said ambassadors; although he knew them to be servants to a prince who was lately an open enemy to his Imperial Majesty, and in open war against his said Majesty.

ARTICLE 4

That the said Quinbus Flestrin, contrary to the duty of a faithful subject, is now preparing to make a voyage to the court and empire of Blefuscu, for which he hath received only verbal license from his Imperial Majesty; and under color of the said license, doth falsely and traitorously intend to take the said voyage, and thereby to aid, comfort, and abet the Emperor of Blefuscu, so late an enemy, and in open war with his Imperial Majesty aforesaid.

There are some other articles, but these are the most important, of which I have read you an abstract.

In the several debates upon this impeachment, it must be confessed that his Majesty gave many marks of his great *lenity;* often urging the services you had done him, and endeavoring to extenuate your crimes. The Treasurer and Admiral insisted that you should be put to the most painful and ignominious death, by setting fire on your house at night; and the General was to attend with twenty thousand men armed with poisoned arrows, to shoot you on the face and hands. Some of your servants were to have private orders to strew a poisonous juice on your shirts and sheets, which would soon make you tear your own flesh, and die in the utmost torture. The General came into the same opinion; so that for a long time there was a majority against you. But his Majesty resolving, if possible, to spare your life, at last brought off[5] the Chamberlain.

Upon this incident, Reldresal, Principal Secretary for Private Affairs, who always approved[6] himself your true friend, was commanded by the Emperor to deliver his opinion, which he accordingly did; and therein justified the good thoughts you have of him. He allowed your crimes to be great; but that still there was room for mercy, the most commendable virtue in a prince, and for which his Majesty was so justly celebrated. He said, the friendship between you and him was so well known to the world, that perhaps the most honorable board might think him partial: however, in obedience to the command he had received, he would freely offer his sentiments. That if his Majesty, in consideration of your services, and pursuant to his own merciful disposition, would please to spare your life, and only give order to put out both your eyes, he humbly conceived, that by this expedient justice might in some measure be satisfied, and all the world would applaud the *lenity* of the Emperor, as well as the fair and generous proceedings of those who have the honor to be his counselors. That the loss of your eyes would be no impediment to your bodily strength, by which you might still be useful to his Majesty. That blindness is an addition to courage, by concealing dangers from us; that the fear you had for your eyes was the greatest difficulty in bringing over the enemy's fleet; and it would be sufficient for you to see by the eyes of the ministers, since the greatest princes do no more.

This proposal was received with the utmost disapprobation by the whole board. Bolgolam, the Admiral, could not preserve his temper; but rising up in fury, said, he wondered how the Secretary durst presume to give his opinion for preserving the life of a traitor: that the services you had performed were, by all true reasons of state, the great aggravation of your crimes; that you, who were able to extinguish the fire by discharge of urine in her Majesty's apartment (which he mentioned with horror), might, at another time, raise an inundation by the same means, to drown the whole palace; and the same strength which enabled you to bring over the enemy's fleet might serve, upon the first discontent, to carry it back: that he had good reasons to think

5. Won over.   6. Proved.

you were a Big-Endian in your heart; and as treason begins in the heart before it appears in overt acts, so he accused you as a traitor on that account, and therefore insisted you should be put to death.

The Treasurer was of the same opinion; he showed to what straits his Majesty's revenue was reduced by the charge of maintaining you, which would soon grow insupportable: that the Secretary's expedient of putting out your eyes was so far from being a remedy against this evil, that it would probably increase it; as it is manifest from the common practice of blinding some kind of fowl, after which they fed the faster, and grew sooner fat: that his sacred Majesty, and the council, who are your judges, were in their own consciences fully convinced of your guilt; which was a sufficient argument to condemn you to death, without the formal proofs required by the strict letter of the law.

But his Imperial Majesty, fully determined against capital punishment, was graciously pleased to say, that since the council thought the loss of your eyes too easy a censure, some other may be inflicted hereafter. And your friend the Secretary humbly desiring to be heard again, in answer to what the Treasurer had objected concerning the great charge his Majesty was at in maintaining you, said, that his Excellency, who had the sole disposal of the Emperor's revenue, might easily provide against this evil, by gradually lessening your establishment; by which, for want of sufficient food, you would grow weak and faint, and lose your appetite, and consequently decay and consume in a few months; neither would the stench of your carcass be then so dangerous, when it should become more than half diminished; and immediately upon your death, five or six thousand of his Majesty's subjects might, in two or three days, cut your flesh from your bones, take it away by cart-loads, and bury it in distant parts to prevent infection; leaving the skeleton as a monument of admiration to posterity.

Thus by the great friendship of the Secretary, the whole affair was compromised. It was strictly enjoined, that the project of starving you by degrees should be kept a secret; but the sentence of putting out your eyes was entered on the books; none dissenting except Bolgolam the Admiral, who being a creature of the Empress, was perpetually instigated by her Majesty to insist upon your death; she having borne perpetual malice against you, on account of that infamous and illegal method you took to extinguish the fire in her apartment.

In three days your friend the Secretary will be directed to come to your house, and read before you the articles of impeachment; and then to signify the great lenity and favor of his Majesty and council; whereby you are only condemned to the loss of your eyes, which his Majesty doth not question you will gratefully and humbly submit to; and twenty of his Majesty's surgeons will attend, in order to see the operation well performed, by discharging very sharp-pointed arrows into the balls of your eyes, as you lie on the ground.

I leave to your prudence what measures you will take; and to avoid suspicion, I must immediately return in as private a manner as I came.

His Lordship did so, and I remained alone, under many doubts and perplexities of mind.

It was a custom introduced by this prince and his ministry (very different, as I have been assured, from the practices of former times), that after the court had decreed any cruel execution, either to gratify the monarch's resentment, or the malice of a favorite, the Emperor always made a speech to his whole council, expressing his great lenity and tenderness, as qualities known and confessed by all the world. This speech was immediately published through the kingdom; nor did any thing terrify the people so much as those encomiums on his Majesty's mercy; because it was observed, that the more these praises were enlarged and insisted on, the more inhuman was the punishment, and the sufferer more innocent. Yet as to myself, I must confess, having never been designed for a courtier, either by my birth or education, I was so ill a judge of things, that I could not discover the lenity and favor of this sentence, but conceived it (perhaps erroneously) rather to be rigorous than gentle. I sometimes thought of standing my trial; for although I could not deny the facts alleged in the several articles, yet I hoped they would admit of some extenuations. But having in my life perused many state trials, which I ever observed to terminate as the judges thought fit to direct, I durst not rely on so dangerous a decision, in so critical a juncture, and against such powerful enemies. Once I was strongly bent upon resistance: for while I had liberty, the whole strength of that empire could hardly subdue me, and I might easily with stones pelt the metropolis to pieces; but I soon rejected that project with horror, by remembering the oath I had made to the Emperor, the favors I received from him, and the high title of *Nardac* he conferred upon me. Neither had I so soon learned the gratitude of courtiers, to persuade myself that his Majesty's present severities acquitted me of all past obligations.

At last I fixed upon a resolution, for which it is probable I may incur some censure, and not unjustly; for I confess I owe the preserving my eyes, and consequently my liberty, to my own great rashness and want of experience: because if I had then known the nature of princes and ministers, which I have since observed in many other courts, and their methods of treating criminals less obnoxious than myself, I should with great alacrity and readiness have submitted to so *easy* a punishment. But hurried on by the precipitancy of youth, and having his Imperial Majesty's license to pay my attendance upon the Emperor of Blefuscu, I took this opportunity, before the three days were elapsed, to send a letter to my friend the Secretary, signifying my resolution of setting out that morning for Blefuscu,[7] pursuant to the leave I had got; and without waiting for an answer, I went to that side of the island where our fleet lay. I seized a large man of war, tied a cable to the prow, and lifting up the anchors, I stripped myself, put my clothes (together with my coverlet, which I carried under my arm) into the vessel; and drawing it after me, between wading and swimming, arrived at the royal port of Blefuscu, where the people had long expected me. They lent me two guides to direct me to the capital city, which is of the same name; I held them in my hands until I came within two hundred yards of the gate; and desired them to signify my arrival to one of the secretaries, and let him know, I there waited his Majesty's commands. I had an answer in about an hour, that his Majesty, attended by the royal family, and great officers of the court, was coming out to receive me. I advanced a hundred yards; the Emperor, and his train, alighted from their horses, the Empress and ladies from their

---

7. Before his trial for treason could be held, Bolingbroke had escaped to France.

coaches; and I did not perceive they were in any fright or concern. I lay on the ground to kiss his Majesty's and the Empress's hand. I told his Majesty that I was come according to my promise, and with the license of the Emperor my master, to have the honor of seeing so mighty a monarch, and to offer him any service in my power, consistent with my duty to my own prince; not mentioning a word of my disgrace, because I had hitherto no regular information of it, and might suppose myself wholly ignorant of any such design; neither could I reasonably conceive that the Emperor would discover the secret while I was out of his power: wherein, however, it soon appeared I was deceived.

I shall not trouble the reader with the particular account of my reception at this court, which was suitable to the generosity of so great a prince; nor of the difficulties I was in for want of a house and bed, being forced to lie on the ground, wrapped up in my coverlet.

CHAPTER 8. *The author, by a lucky accident, finds means to leave Blefuscu; and, after some difficulties, returns safe to his native country.*

Three days after my arrival, walking out of curiosity to the northeast coast of the island, I observed, about half a league off, in the sea, somewhat that looked like a boat overturned. I pulled off my shoes and stockings, and wading two or three hundred yards, I found the object to approach nearer by force of the tide; and then plainly saw it to be a real boat, which I supposed might, by some tempest, have been driven from a ship. Whereupon I returned immediately towards the city, and desired his Imperial Majesty to lend me twenty of the tallest vessels he had left after the loss of his fleet, and three thousand seamen under the command of his Vice Admiral. This fleet sailed round, while I went back the shortest way to the coast where I first discovered the boat; I found the tide had driven it still nearer; the seamen were all provided with cordage, which I had beforehand twisted to a sufficient strength. When the ships came up, I stripped myself, and waded till I came within an hundred yards of the boat; after which I was forced to swim till I got up to it. The seamen threw me the end of the cord, which I fastened to a hole in the fore-part of the boat, and the other end to a man of war: but I found all my labor to little purpose; for being out of my depth, I was not able to work. In this necessity, I was forced to swim behind, and push the boat forwards as often as I could, with one of my hands; and the tide favoring me, I advanced so far, that I could just hold up my chin and feel the ground. I rested two or three minutes, and then gave the boat another shove, and so on till the sea was no higher than my armpits. And now the most laborious part being over, I took out my other cables which were stowed in one of the ships, and fastening them first to the boat, and then to nine of the vessels which attended me, the wind being favorable, the seamen towed, and I shoved till we arrived within forty yards of the shore; and waiting till the tide was out, I got dry to the boat, and by the assistance of two thousand men, with ropes and engines, I made a shift to turn it on its bottom, and found it was but little damaged.

I shall not trouble the reader with the difficulties I was under by the help of certain paddles, which cost me ten days making, to get my boat to the royal port of Blefuscu; where a mighty concourse of people appeared upon my arrival, full of wonder at the sight of so prodigious a vessel. I told the Emperor that my good fortune had thrown this boat in my way, to carry me to some place from whence I might return into my native country; and begged his Majesty's orders for getting materials to fit it up, together with license to depart; which, after some kind expostulations, he was pleased to grant.

I did very much wonder, in all this time, not to have heard of any express relating to me from our Emperor to the court of Blefuscu. But I was afterwards given privately to understand, that his Imperial Majesty, never imagining I had the least notice of his designs, believed I was only gone to Blefuscu in performance of my promise, according to the license he had given me, which was well known at our court; and would return in a few days when that ceremony was ended. But he was at last in pain at my long absence; and, after consulting with the Treasurer, and the rest of that cabal, a person of quality was dispatched with the copy of the articles against me. This envoy had instructions to represent to the monarch of Blefuscu the great lenity of his master, who was content to punish me no further than with the loss of my eyes; that I had fled from justice, and if I did not return in two hours, I should be deprived of my title of *Nardac,* and declared a traitor. The envoy further added, that in order to maintain the peace and amity between both empires, his master expected, that his brother of Blefuscu would give orders to have me sent back to Lilliput, bound hand and foot, to be punished as a traitor.

The Emperor of Blefuscu, having taken three days to consult, returned an answer consisting of many civilities and excuses. He said, that as for sending me bound, his brother knew it was impossible; that although I had deprived him of his fleet, yet he owed great obligations to me for many good offices I had done him in making the peace. That however, both their Majesties would soon be made easy; for I had found a prodigious vessel on the shore, able to carry me on the sea, which he had given order to fit up with my own assistance and direction; and he hoped in a few weeks both empires would be freed from so insupportable an incumbrance.

With this answer the envoy returned to Lilliput, and the monarch of Blefuscu related to me all that had passed, offering me at the same time (but under the strictest confidence) his gracious protection, if I would continue in his service; wherein although I believed him sincere, yet I resolved never more to put any confidence in princes or ministers, where I could possibly avoid it; and therefore, with all due acknowledgements for his favorable intentions, I humbly begged to be excused. I told him, that since fortune, whether good or evil, had thrown a vessel in my way, I was resolved to venture myself in the ocean, rather than be an occasion of difference between two such mighty monarchs. Neither did I find the Emperor at all displeased; and I discovered by a certain accident, that he was very glad of my resolution, and so were most of his ministers.

These considerations moved me to hasten my departure somewhat sooner than I intended; to which the court, impatient to have me gone, very readily contributed. Five hundred workmen were employed to make two sails to my boat, according to my directions, by quilting thirteen fold of their strongest linen together. I was at the pains of making ropes and cables, by twisting ten, twenty or thirty of the thickest and strongest of theirs. A great stone that I happened to find, after a long search by the seashore, served me for an anchor. I had the tallow of three hundred cows for greasing my boat, and other uses. I was at incredible pains in cutting down some of the largest timber trees for oars and masts, wherein I was, however, much assisted by his Majesty's ship-carpenters, who helped me in smoothing them, after I had done the rough work.

In about a month, when all was prepared, I sent to receive his Majesty's commands, and to take my leave. The Emperor and royal family came out of the palace; I lay down on my face to kiss his hand, which he very graciously gave me: so did the Empress, and young princes of the blood. His Majesty presented me with fifty purses of two hundred *sprugs* apiece, together with his picture at full length, which I put immediately into one of my gloves, to keep it from being hurt. The ceremonies at my departure were too many to trouble the reader with at this time.

I stored the boat with the carcasses of an hundred oxen, and three hundred sheep, with bread and drink proportionable, and as much meat ready dressed as four hundred cooks could provide. I took with me six cows and two bulls alive, with as many ewes and rams, intending to carry them into my own country, and propagate the breed. And to feed them on board, I had a good bundle of hay, and a bag of corn.[8] I would gladly have taken a dozen of the natives; but this was a thing the Emperor would by no means permit; and besides a diligent search into my pockets, his Majesty engaged my honor not to carry away any of his subjects, although with their own consent and desire.

Having thus prepared all things as well as I was able, I set sail on the twenty-fourth day of September, 1701, at six in the morning; and when I had gone about four leagues to the northward, the wind being at southeast, at six in the evening, I descried a small island about half a league to the northwest. I advanced forward, and cast anchor on the lee-side of the island, which seemed to be uninhabited. I then took some refreshment, and went to my rest. I slept well, and as I conjecture at least six hours; for I found the day broke in two hours after I awaked. It was a clear night; I eat my breakfast before the sun was up; and heaving anchor, the wind being favorable, I steered the same course that I had done the day before, wherein I was directed by my pocket compass. My intention was to reach, if possible, one of those islands which I had reason to believe lay to the northeast of Van Diemen's Land. I discovered nothing all that day; but upon the next, about three in the afternoon, when I had by my computation made twenty-four leagues from Blefuscu, I descried a sail steering to the southeast; my course was due east. I hailed her, but could get no answer; yet I found I gained upon her, for the wind slackened. I made all the sail I could, and in half an hour she spied me, then hung out her ancient,[9] and discharged a gun. It is not easy to express the joy I was in upon the unexpected hope of once more seeing my beloved country, and the dear pledges[1] I had left in it. The ship slackened her sails, and I came up with her between five and six in the evening, September 26; but my heart leapt within me to see her English colors. I put my cows and sheep into my coat-pockets and got on board with all my little cargo of provisions. The vessel was an English merchantman, returning from Japan by the North and South Seas;[2] the captain, Mr. John Biddel of Deptford, a very civil man, and an excellent sailor. We were now

8. Wheat, not maize.
9. Flag.

1. Hostages (i.e., his family).
2. North and South Pacific.

in the latitude of 30 degrees south; there were about fifty men in the ship; and here I met an old comrade of mine, one Peter Williams, who gave me a good character to the captain. This gentleman treated me with kindness, and desired I would let him know what place I came from last, and whither I was bound; which I did in few words; but he thought I was raving, and that the dangers I underwent had disturbed my head; whereupon I took my black cattle and sheep out of my pocket, which, after great astonishment, clearly convinced him of my veracity. I then showed him the gold given me by the Emperor of Blefuscu, together with his Majesty's picture at full length, and some other rarities of that country. I gave him two purses of two hundred *sprugs* each, and promised, when we arrived in England, to make him a present of a cow and a sheep big with young.

I shall not trouble the reader with a particular account of this voyage; which was very prosperous for the most part. We arrived in the Downs[3] on the 13th of April, 1702. I had only one misfortune, that the rats on board carried away one of my sheep; I found her bones in a hole, picked clean from the flesh. The rest of my cattle I got safe on shore, and set them a grazing in a bowling-green at Greenwich, where the fineness of the grass made them feed very heartily, though I had always feared the contrary; neither could I possibly have preserved them in so long a voyage, if the captain had not allowed me some of his best biscuit, which rubbed to powder, and mingled with water, was their constant food. The short time I continued in England, I made a considerable profit by showing my cattle to many persons of quality, and others: and before I began my second voyage, I sold them for six hundred pounds. Since my last return, I find the breed is considerably increased, especially the sheep; which I hope will prove much to the advantage of the woolen manufacture, by the fineness of the fleeces.

I stayed but two months with my wife and family; for my insatiable desire of seeing foreign countries would suffer me to continue no longer. I left fifteen hundred pounds with my wife, and fixed her in a good house at Redriff. My remaining stock I carried with me, part in money, and part in goods, in hopes to improve my fortunes. My eldest uncle, John, had left me an estate in land, near Epping, of about thirty pounds a year; and I had a long lease of the Black Bull in Fetter Lane, which yielded me as much more: so that I was not in any danger of leaving my family upon the parish.[4] My son Johnny, named so after his uncle, was at the grammar school, and a towardly[5] child. My daughter Betty (who is now well married, and has children) was then at her needlework. I took leave of my wife, and boy and girl, with tears on both sides; and went on board the *Adventure*, a merchant-ship of three hundred tons, bound for Surat, Captain John Nicholas of Liverpool, Commander. But my account of this voyage must be referred to the second part of my *Travels*.

Part 2. A Voyage to Brobdingnag

CHAPTER 1. *A great storm described. The longboat sent to fetch water; the Author goes with it to discover the country. He is left on shore, is seized by one*

3. A rendezvous for ships off the southeast coast of England.
4. On welfare (living on charity given by the parish).
5. Promising.

of the natives, and carried to a farmer's house. His reception there, with several accidents that happened there. A description of the inhabitants.

Having been condemned by nature and fortune to an active and restless life, in ten months after my return I again left my native country, and took shipping in the Downs on the 20th day of June, 1702, in the *Adventure*, Captain John Nicholas, a Cornish man, Commander, bound for Surat.[6] We had a very prosperous gale till we arrived at the Cape of Good Hope, where we landed for fresh water, but discovering a leak we unshipped our goods and wintered there; for the Captain falling sick of an ague, we could not leave the Cape till the end of March. We then set sail, and had a good voyage till we passed the Straits of Madagascar; but having got northward of that island, and to about five degrees south latitude, the winds, which in those seas are observed to blow a constant equal gale between the north and west from the beginning of December to the beginning of May, on the 19th of April began to blow with much greater violence and more westerly than usual, continuing so far twenty days together, during which time we were driven a little to the east of the Molucca Islands and about three degrees northward of the Line, as our Captain found by an observation he took the 2nd of May, at which time the wind ceased, and it was a perfect calm, whereat I was not a little rejoiced. But he, being a man well experienced in the navigation of those seas, bid us all prepare against a storm, which accordingly happened the day following: for a southern wind, called the southern monsoon, began to set in.

Finding it was likely to overblow,[7] we took in our spritsail, and stood by to hand the foresail; but making foul weather, we looked the guns were all fast, and handed the mizzen. The ship lay very broad off, so we thought it better spooning before the sea, than trying or hulling. We reefed the foresail and set him, we hauled aft the foresheet; the helm was hard aweather. The ship wore bravely. We belayed the fore-downhaul; but the sail was split, and we hauled down the yard and got the sail into the ship, and unbound all the things clear of it. It was a very fierce storm; the sea broke strange and dangerous. We hauled off upon the lanyard of the whipstaff, and helped the man at helm. We would not get down our topmast, but let all stand, because she scudded before the sea very well, and we knew that the topmast being aloft, the ship was the wholesomer, and made better way through the sea, seeing we had searoom. When the storm was over, we set foresail and mainsail, and brought the ship to. Then we set the mizzen, main topsail and the fore topsail. Our course was east-northeast, the wind was at southwest. We got the starboard tacks aboard, we cast off our weather braces and lifts; we set in the lee braces, and hauled forward by the weather bowlings, and hauled them tight, and belayed them, and hauled over the mizzen tack to windward, and kept her full and by as near as she would lie.

During this storm, which was followed by a strong wind west-southwest,

6. In India. The geography of the voyage (described next) is simple: The *Adventure*, after sailing up the east coast of Africa to about five degrees south of the equator (the "Line"), is blown past India into the Malay Archipelago, north of the islands of Buru and Ceram. The storm then drives the ship northward and eastward, away from the coast of Siberia ("Great Tartary") into the northeast Pacific, at that time unexplored. Brobdingnag lies somewhere in the vicinity of Alaska.

7. This paragraph is taken almost literally from Samuel Sturmy's *Mariner's Magazine* (1669). Swift is ridiculing the use of technical terms by writers of popular voyages.

we were carried by my computation about five hundred leagues to the east, so that the oldest sailor on board could not tell in what part of the world we were. Our provisions held out well, our ship was staunch, and our crew all in good health; but we lay in the utmost distress for water. We thought it best to hold on the same course rather than turn more northerly, which might have brought us to the northwest parts of Great Tartary, and into the frozen sea.

On the 16th day of June, 1703, a boy on the topmast discovered land. On the 17th we came in full view of a great island or continent (for we knew not whether) on the south side whereof was a small neck of land jutting out into the sea, and a creek[8] too shallow to hold a ship of above one hundred tons. We cast anchor within a league of this creek, and our Captain sent a dozen of his men well armed in the longboat, with vessels for water if any could be found. I desired his leave to go with them that I might see the country and make what discoveries I could. When we came to land we saw no river or spring, nor any sign of inhabitants. Our men therefore wandered on the shore to find out some fresh water near the sea, and I walked alone about a mile on the other side, where I observed the country all barren and rocky. I now began to be weary, and seeing nothing to entertain my curiosity, I returned gently down towards the creek; and the sea being full in my view, I saw our men already got into the boat, and rowing for life to the ship. I was going to hollow after them, although it had been to little purpose, when I observed a huge creature walking after them in the sea as fast as he could; he waded not much deeper than his knees and took prodigious strides, but our men had the start of him half a league, and the sea thereabouts being full of sharp-pointed rocks, the monster was not able to overtake the boat. This I was afterwards told, for I durst not stay to see the issue of that adventure, but ran as fast as I could the way I first went, and then climbed up a steep hill, which gave me some prospect of the country. I found it fully cultivated; but that which first surprised me was the length of the grass, which, in those grounds that seemed to be kept for hay, was about twenty foot high.[9]

I fell into a highroad, for so I took it to be, although it served to the inhabitants only as a footpath through a field of barley. Here I walked on for some time, but could see little on either side, it being now near harvest, and the corn[1] rising at least forty foot. I was an hour walking to the end of this field, which was fenced in with a hedge of at least one hundred and twenty foot high, and the trees so lofty that I could make no computation of their altitude. There was a stile to pass from this field into the next: it had four steps, and a stone to cross over when you came to the utmost. It was impossible for me to climb this stile, because every step was six foot high, and the upper stone above twenty. I was endeavoring to find some gap in the hedge when I discovered one of the inhabitants in the next field advancing towards the stile, of the same size with him whom I saw in the sea pursuing our boat. He appeared as tall as an ordinary spire-steeple, and took about ten yards at every stride, as near as I could guess. I was struck with the utmost fear and astonishment, and ran to hide myself in the corn, from whence I saw him at

8. A small bay or cove, affording anchorage.
9. Swift's intention, not always carried out accurately, is that everything in Brobdingnag should be,

in relation to our familiar world, on a scale of ten to one.
1. Wheat.

the top of the stile, looking back into the next field on the right hand; and heard him call in a voice many degrees louder than a speaking trumpet; but the noise was so high in the air that at first I certainly thought it was thunder. Whereupon seven monsters like himself came towards him with reaping hooks in their hands, each hook about the largeness of six scythes. These people were not so well clad as the first, whose servants or laborers they seemed to be. For, upon some words he spoke, they went to reap the corn in the field where I lay. I kept from them at as great a distance as I could, but was forced to move with extreme difficulty, for the stalks of the corn were sometimes not above a foot distant, so that I could hardly squeeze my body betwixt them. However, I made a shift to go forward till I came to a part of the field where the corn had been laid by the rain and wind; here it was impossible for me to advance a step, for the stalks were so interwoven that I could not creep through, and the beards of the fallen ears so strong and pointed that they pierced through my clothes into my flesh. At the same time I heard the reapers not above an hundred yards behind me. Being quite dispirited with toil, and wholly overcome by grief and despair, I lay down between two ridges and heartily wished I might there end my days. I bemoaned my desolate widow and fatherless children; I lamented my own folly and willfulness in attempting a second voyage against the advice of all my friends and relations. In this terrible agitation of mind, I could not forbear thinking of Lilliput, whose inhabitants looked upon me as the greatest prodigy that ever appeared in the world; where I was able to draw an imperial fleet in my hand, and perform those other actions which will be recorded forever in the chronicles of that empire, while posterity shall hardly believe them, although attested by millions. I reflected what a mortification it must prove to me to appear as inconsiderable in this nation as one single Lilliputian would be among us. But this I conceived was to be the least of my misfortunes; for as human creatures are observed to be more savage and cruel in proportion to their bulk, what could I expect but to be a morsel in the mouth of the first among these enormous barbarians who should happen to seize me? Undoubtedly philosophers are in the right when they tell us that nothing is great or little otherwise than by comparison. It might have pleased fortune to let the Lilliputians find some nation where the people were as diminutive with respect to them as they were to me. And who knows but that even this prodigious race of mortals might be equally overmatched in some distant part of the world, whereof we have yet no discovery?

Scared and confounded as I was, I could not forbear going on with these reflections; when one of the reapers approaching within ten yards of the ridge where I lay, made me apprehend that with the next step I should be squashed to death under his foot, or cut in two with his reaping hook. And therefore when he was again about to move, I screamed as loud as fear could make me. Whereupon the huge creature trod short, and looking round about under him for some time, at last espied me as I lay on the ground. He considered a while with the caution of one who endeavors to lay hold on a small dangerous animal in such a manner that it shall not be able either to scratch or to bite him, as I myself have sometimes done with a weasel in England. At length he ventured to take me up behind by the middle between his forefinger and thumb, and brought me within three yards of his eyes, that he might behold my shape more perfectly. I guessed his meaning, and my good fortune gave me so much presence of mind that I resolved not to struggle in the least as he held me in the air about sixty foot from the ground, although he grievously pinched my sides, for fear I should slip through his fingers. All I ventured was to raise mine eyes towards the sun, and place my hands together in a supplicating posture, and to speak some words in an humble melancholy tone, suitable to the condition I then was in. For I apprehended every moment that he would dash me against the ground, as we usually do any little hateful animal which we have a mind to destroy. But my good star would have it that he appeared pleased with my voice and gestures, and began to look upon me as a curiosity, much wondering to hear me pronounce articulate words, although he could not understand them. In the meantime I was not able to forbear groaning and shedding tears and turning my head towards my sides, letting him know, as well as I could, how cruelly I was hurt by the pressure of his thumb and finger. He seemed to apprehend my meaning; for, lifting up the lappet[2] of his coat, he put me gently into it, and immediately ran along with me to his master, who was a substantial farmer, and the same person I had first seen in the field.

The farmer having (as I supposed by their talk) received such an account of me as his servant could give him, took a piece of a small straw about the size of a walking staff, and therewith lifted up the lappets of my coat, which it seems he thought to be some kind of covering that nature had given me. He blew my hairs aside to take a better view of my face. He called his hinds[3] about him, and asked them (as I afterwards learned) whether they had ever seen in the fields any little creature that resembled me. He then placed me softly on the ground upon all four; but I got immediately up, and walked slowly backwards and forwards, to let those people see I had no intent to run away. They all sat down in a circle about me, the better to observe my motions. I pulled off my hat, and made a low bow towards the farmer; I fell on my knees, and lifted up my hands and eyes, and spoke several words as loud as I could; I took a purse of gold out of my pocket, and humbly presented it to him. He received it on the palm of his hand, then applied it close to his eye to see what it was, and afterwards turned it several times with the point of a pin (which he took out of his sleeve), but could make nothing of it. Whereupon I made a sign that he should place his hand on the ground; I then took the purse, and opening it, poured all the gold into his palm. There were six Spanish pieces of four pistoles each, beside twenty or thirty smaller coins. I saw him wet the tip of his little finger upon his tongue, and take up one of my largest pieces, and then another; but he seemed to be wholly ignorant what they were. He made me a sign to put them again into my purse, and the purse again into my pocket, which after offering to him several times, I thought it best to do.

The farmer by this time was convinced I must be a rational creature. He spoke often to me, but the sound of his voice pierced my ears like that of a water mill, yet his words were articulate enough. I answered as loud as I could in several languages, and he often laid his ear within two yards of me, but all in vain, for we were wholly unintelligible to each other. He then sent his servants to their work, and taking his handkerchief out of his pocket, he doubled and spread it on his hand, which he placed flat on the ground with

---

2. Flap or fold.   3. Farm servants.

the palm upwards, making me a sign to step into it, as I could easily do, for it was not above a foot in thickness. I thought it my part to obey, and for fear of falling, laid myself at full length upon the handkerchief, with the remainder of which he lapped me up to the head for further security, and in this manner carried me home to his house. There he called his wife, and showed me to her; but she screamed and ran back as women in England do at the sight of a toad or a spider. However, when she had a while seen my behavior, and how well I observed the signs her husband made, she was soon reconciled, and by degrees grew extremely tender of me.

It was about twelve at noon, and a servant brought in dinner. It was only one substantial dish of meat (fit for the plain condition of an husbandman) in a dish of about four-and-twenty foot diameter. The company were the farmer and his wife, three children, and an old grandmother. When they were sat down, the farmer placed me at some distance from him on the table, which was thirty foot high from the floor. I was in a terrible fright, and kept as far as I could from the edge, for fear of falling. The wife minced a bit of meat, then crumbled some bread on a trencher, and placed it before me. I made her a low bow, took out my knife and fork, and fell to eat; which gave them exceeding delight. The mistress sent her maid for a small dram cup, which held about two gallons, and filled it with drink; I took up the vessel with much difficulty in both hands, and in a most respectful manner drank to her ladyship's health, expressing the words as loud as I could in English; which made the company laugh so heartily that I was almost deafened with the noise. This liquor tasted like a small cider,[4] and was not unpleasant. Then the master made me a sign to come to his trencher side; but as I walked on the table, being in great surprise all the time, as the indulgent reader will easily conceive and excuse, I happened to stumble against a crust, and fell flat on my face, but received no hurt. I got up immediately, and observing the good people to be in much concern, I took my hat (which I held under my arm out of good manners) and waving it over my head, made three huzzas to show I had got no mischief by my fall. But advancing forwards toward my master (as I shall henceforth call him), his youngest son who sat next him, an arch boy of about ten years old, took me up by the legs, and held me so high in the air that I trembled every limb; but his father snatched me from him, and at the same time gave him such a box on the left ear as would have felled an European troop of horse to the earth, ordering him to be taken from the table. But being afraid the boy might owe me a spite, and well remembering how mischievous all children among us naturally are to sparrows, rabbits, young kittens, and puppy dogs, I fell on my knees, and pointing to the boy, made my master to understand, as well as I could, that I desired his son might be pardoned. The father complied, and the lad took his seat again; whereupon I went to him and kissed his hand, which my master took, and made him stroke me gently with it.

In the midst of dinner, my mistress's favorite cat leaped into her lap. I heard a noise behind me like that of a dozen stocking weavers at work; and turning my head, I found it proceeded from the purring of this animal, who seemed to be three times larger than an ox, as I computed by the view of her head and one of her paws, while her mistress was feeding and stroking her.

4. I.e., weak cider.

The fierceness of this creature's countenance altogether discomposed me, although I stood at the farther end of the table, about fifty foot off, and although my mistress held her fast for fear she might give a spring and seize me in her talons. But it happened there was no danger, for the cat took not the least notice of me when my master placed me within three yards of her. And as I have been always told, and found true by experience in my travels, that flying or discovering[5] fear before a fierce animal is a certain way to make it pursue or attack you, so I resolved in this dangerous juncture to show no manner of concern. I walked with intrepidity five or six times before the very head of the cat, and came within half a yard of her; whereupon she drew herself back, as if she were more afraid of me. I had less apprehension concerning the dogs, whereof three or four came into the room, as it is usual in farmers' houses; one of which was a mastiff, equal in bulk to four elephants, and a greyhound, somewhat taller than the mastiff, but not so large.

When dinner was almost done, the nurse came in with a child of a year old in her arms, who immediately spied me, and began a squall that you might have heard from London Bridge to Chelsea, after the usual oratory of infants, to get me for a plaything. The mother out of pure indulgence took me up, and put me towards the child, who presently seized me by the middle, and got my head in his mouth, where I roared so loud that the urchin was frighted and let me drop; and I should infallibly have broke my neck if the mother had not held her apron under me. The nurse to quiet her babe made use of a rattle, which was a kind of hollow vessel filled with great stones, and fastened by a cable to the child's waist: but all in vain, so that she was forced to apply the last remedy by giving it suck. I must confess no object ever disgusted me so much as the sight of her monstrous breast, which I cannot tell what to compare with so as to give the curious reader an idea of its bulk, shape, and color. It stood prominent six foot, and could not be less than sixteen in circumference. The nipple was about half the bigness of my head, and the hue both of that and the dug so varified with spots, pimples, and freckles that nothing could appear more nauseous: for I had a near sight of her, she sitting down the more conveniently to give suck, and I standing on the table. This made me reflect upon the fair skins of our English ladies, who appear so beautiful to us, only because they are of our own size, and their defects not to be seen but through a magnifying glass, where we find by experiment that the smoothest and whitest skins look rough and coarse and ill colored.

I remember when I was at Lilliput, the complexion of those diminutive people appeared to me the fairest in the world; and talking upon this subject with a person of learning there, who was an intimate friend of mine, he said that my face appeared much fairer and smoother when he looked on me from the ground than it did upon a nearer view when I took him up in my hand and brought him close, which he confessed was at first a very shocking sight. He said he could discover great holes in my skin; that the stumps of my beard were ten times stronger than the bristles of a boar, and my complexion made up of several colors altogether disagreeable: although I must beg leave to say for myself that I am as fair as most of my sex and country and very little sunburnt by all my travels. On the other side, discoursing of

5. Revealing.

the ladies in that Emperor's court, he used to tell me one had freckles, another too wide a mouth, a third too large a nose; nothing of which I was able to distinguish. I confess this reflection was obvious enough; which however I could not forbear, lest the reader might think those vast creatures were actually deformed: for I must do them justice to say they are a comely race of people; and particularly the features of my master's countenance, although he were but a farmer, when I beheld him from the height of sixty foot, appeared very well proportioned.

When dinner was done, my master went out to his laborers; and as I could discover by his voice and gesture, gave his wife a strict charge to take care of me. I was very much tired and disposed to sleep, which my mistress perceiving, she put me on her own bed, and covered me with a clean white handkerchief, but larger and coarser than the mainsail of a man-of-war.

I slept about two hours, and dreamed I was at home with my wife and children, which aggravated my sorrows when I awaked and found myself alone in a vast room, between two and three hundred foot wide, and above two hundred high, lying in a bed twenty yards wide. My mistress was gone about her household affairs, and had locked me in. The bed was eight yards from the floor. Some natural necessities required me to get down; I durst not presume to call, and if I had, it would have been in vain with such a voice as mine at so great a distance from the room where I lay to the kitchen where the family kept. While I was under these circumstances, two rats crept up the curtains, and ran smelling backwards and forwards on the bed. One of them came up almost to my face; whereupon I rose in a fright, and drew out my hanger[6] to defend myself. These horrible animals had the boldness to attack me on both sides, and one of them held his forefeet at my collar; but I had the good fortune to rip up his belly before he could do me any mischief. He fell down at my feet; and the other seeing the fate of his comrade, made his escape, but not without one good wound on the back, which I gave him as he fled, and made the blood run trickling from him. After this exploit I walked gently to and fro on the bed, to recover my breath and loss of spirits. These creatures were of the size of a large mastiff, but infinitely more nimble and fierce; so that if I had taken off my belt before I went to sleep, I must have infallibly been torn to pieces and devoured. I measured the tail of the dead rat, and found it to be two yards long, wanting an inch; but it went against my stomach to drag the carcass off the bed, where it lay still bleeding; I observed it had yet some life, but with a strong slash cross the neck, I thoroughly dispatched it.

Soon after, my mistress came into the room, who seeing me all bloody, ran and took me up in her hand. I pointed to the dead rat, smiling and making other signs to show I was not hurt, whereat she was extremely rejoiced, calling the maid to take up the dead rat with a pair of tongs, and throw it out of the window. Then she set me on a table, where I showed her my hanger all bloody, and wiping it on the lappet of my coat, returned it to the scabbard. I was pressed to do more than one thing, which another could not do for me, and therefore endeavored to make my mistress understand that I desired to be set down on the floor; which after she had done, my bashfulness would not suffer me to express myself farther than by pointing to the door,

---

6. A short, broad sword.

and bowing several times. The good woman with much difficulty at last perceived what I would be at, and taking me up again in her hand, walked into the garden, where she set me down. I went on one side about two hundred yards; and beckoning to her not to look or to follow me, I hid myself between two leaves of sorrel, and there discharged the necessities of nature.

I hope the gentle reader will excuse me for dwelling on these and the like particulars, which however insignificant they may appear to groveling vulgar minds, yet will certainly help a philosopher[7] to enlarge his thoughts and imagination, and apply them to the benefit of public as well as private life, which was my sole design in presenting this and other accounts of my travels to the world; wherein I have been chiefly studious of truth, without affecting any ornaments of learning or of style. But the whole scene of this voyage made so strong an impression on my mind, and is so deeply fixed in my memory, that in committing it to paper I did not omit one material circumstance; however, upon a strict review, I blotted out several passages of less moment which were in my first copy, for fear of being censured as tedious and trifling, whereof travelers are often, perhaps not without justice, accused.

CHAPTER 2. *A description of the farmer's daughter. The Author carried to a market town, and then to the metropolis. The particulars of his journey.*

My mistress had a daughter of nine years old, a child of towardly parts for her age, very dexterous at her needle, and skillful in dressing her baby.[8] Her mother and she contrived to fit up the baby's cradle for me against night: the cradle was put into a small drawer of a cabinet, and the drawer placed upon a hanging shelf for fear of the rats. This was my bed all the time I stayed with those people, although made more convenient by degrees as I began to learn their language, and make my wants known. This young girl was so handy, that after I had once or twice pulled off my clothes before her, she was able to dress and undress me, although I never gave her that trouble when she would let me do either myself. She made me seven shirts, and some other linen of as fine cloth as could be got, which indeed was coarser than sackcloth, and these she constantly washed for me with her own hands. She was likewise my schoolmistress to teach me the language: when I pointed to anything, she told me the name of it in her own tongue, so that in a few days I was able to call for whatever I had a mind to. She was very good-natured, and not above forty foot high, being little for her age. She gave me the name of *Grildrig,* which the family took up, and afterwards the whole kingdom. The word imports what the Latins call *nanunculus,* the Italian *homunceletino,*[9] and the English *mannikin.* To her I chiefly owe my preservation in that country: we never parted while I was there; I called her my *Glumdalclitch,* or little nurse: and I should be guilty of great ingratitude if I omitted this honorable mention of her care and affection towards me, which I heartily wish it lay in my power to requite as she deserves, instead of being the innocent but unhappy instrument of her disgrace, as I have too much reason to fear.

7. "Vulgar": commonplace, uncultivated, in contrast to the scientist ("philosopher"); an irony.
8. Doll. "Towardly parts": promising abilities.

9. The Latin and Italian words are Swift's own coinages, as, of course, are the various words from the Brobdingnagian language.

It now began to be known and talked of in the neighborhood that my master had found a strange animal in the field, about the bigness of a *splacknuck*, but exactly shaped in every part like a human creature, which it likewise imitated in all its actions: seemed to speak in a little language of its own, had already learned several words of theirs, went erect upon two legs, was tame and gentle, would come when it was called, do whatever it was bid, had the finest limbs in the world, and a complexion fairer than a nobleman's daughter of three years old. Another farmer who lived hard by, and was a particular friend of my master, came on a visit on purpose to inquire into the truth of this story. I was immediately produced, and placed upon a table, where I walked as I was commanded, drew my hanger, put it up again, made my reverence to my master's guest, asked him in his own language how he did, and told him he was welcome, just as my little nurse had instructed me. This man, who was old and dimsighted, put on his spectacles to behold me better, at which I could not forbear laughing very heartily, for his eyes appeared like the full moon shining into a chamber at two windows. Our people, who discovered the cause of my mirth, bore me company in laughing, at which the old fellow was fool enough to be angry and out of countenance. He had the character of a great miser, and to my misfortune he well deserved it by the cursed advice he gave my master to show me as a sight upon a market day in the next town, which was half an hour's riding, about two and twenty miles from our house. I guessed there was some mischief contriving when I observed my master and his friend whispering long together, sometimes pointing at me; and my fears made me fancy that I overheard and understood some of their words. But the next morning Glumdalclitch, my little nurse, told me the whole matter, which she had cunningly picked out from her mother. The poor girl laid me on her bosom, and fell a weeping with shame and grief. She apprehended some mischief would happen to me from rude vulgar folks, who might squeeze me to death, or break one of my limbs by taking me in their hands. She had also observed how modest I was in my nature, how nicely I regarded my honor, and what an indignity I should conceive it to be exposed for money as a public spectacle to the meanest of the people. She said her papa and mamma had promised that Grildrig should be hers; but now she found they meant to serve her as they did last year, when they pretended to give her a lamb, and yet, as soon as it was fat, sold it to a butcher. For my own part, I may truly affirm that I was less concerned than my nurse. I had a strong hope, which never left me, that I should one day recover my liberty; and as to the ignominy of being carried about for a monster, I considered myself to be a perfect stranger in the country, and that such a misfortune could never be charged upon me as a reproach, if ever I should return to England; since the King of Great Britain himself, in my condition, must have undergone the same distress.

My master, pursuant to the advice of his friend, carried me in a box the next market day to the neighboring town, and took along with him his little daughter, my nurse, upon a pillion[1] behind him. The box was close on every side, with a little door for me to go in and out, and a few gimlet holes to let in air. The girl had been so careful to put the quilt of her baby's bed into it, for me to lie down on. However, I was terribly shaken and discomposed in

1. A pad attached to the hinder part of a saddle, on which a second person, usually a woman, could ride.

this journey, although it were but of half an hour. For the horse went about forty foot at every step, and trotted so high that the agitation was equal to the rising and falling of a ship in a great storm, but much more frequent. Our journey was somewhat further than from London to St. Albans. My master alighted at an inn which he used to frequent; and after consulting a while with the innkeeper, and making some necessary preparations, he hired the *Grultrud*, or crier, to give notice through the town of a strange creature to be seen at the Sign of the Green Eagle, not so big as a *splacknuck* (an animal in that country very finely shaped, about six foot long), and in every part of the body resembling an human creature; could speak several words and perform an hundred diverting tricks.

I was placed upon a table in the largest room of the inn, which might be near three hundred foot square. My little nurse stood on a low stool close to the table, to take care of me, and direct what I should do. My master, to avoid a crowd, would suffer only thirty people at a time to see me. I walked about on the table as the girl commanded; she asked me questions as far as she knew my understanding of the language reached, and I answered them as loud as I could. I turned about several times to the company, paid my humble respects, said they were welcome, and used some other speeches I had been taught. I took up a thimble filled with liquor, which Glumdalclitch had given me for a cup, and drank their health. I drew out my hanger, and flourished with it after the manner of fencers in England. My nurse gave me part of a straw, which I exercised as pike, having learned the art in my youth. I was that day shown to twelve sets of company, and as often forced to go over again with the same fopperies, till I was half dead with weariness and vexation. For those who had seen me made such wonderful reports that the people were ready to break down the doors to come in. My master for his own interest would not suffer anyone to touch me except my nurse; and, to prevent danger, benches were set round the table at such a distance as put me out of everybody's reach. However, an unlucky schoolboy aimed a hazel-nut directly at my head, which very narrowly missed me; otherwise, it came with so much violence that it would have infallibly knocked out my brains, for it was almost as large as a small pumpion:[2] but I had the satisfaction to see the young rogue well beaten, and turned out of the room.

My master gave public notice that he would show me again the next market day, and in the meantime he prepared a more convenient vehicle for me, which he had reason enough to do; for I was so tired with my first journey, and with entertaining company for eight hours together, that I could hardly stand upon my legs or speak a word. It was at least three days before I recovered my strength; and that I might have no rest at home, all the neighboring gentlemen from an hundred miles round, hearing of my fame, came to see me at my master's own house. There could not be fewer than thirty persons with their wives and children (for the country is very populous); and my master demanded the rate of a full room whenever he showed me at home, although it were only to a single family. So that for some time I had but little ease every day of the week (except Wednesday, which is their Sabbath) although I were not carried to the town.

My master finding how profitable I was like to be, resolved to carry me to

2. Pumpkin.

the most considerable cities of the kingdom. Having therefore provided himself with all things necessary for a long journey, and settled his affairs at home, he took leave of his wife; and upon the 17th of August, 1703, about two months after my arrival, we set out for the metropolis, situated near the middle of that empire, and about three thousand miles distance from our house. My master made his daughter Glumdalclitch ride behind him. She carried me on her lap in a box tied about her waist. The girl had lined it on all sides with the softest cloth she could get, well quilted underneath, furnished it with her baby's bed, provided me with linen and other necessaries, and made everything as convenient as she could. We had no other company but a boy of the house, who rode after us with the luggage.

My master's design was to show me in all the towns by the way, and to step out of the road for fifty or an hundred miles to any village or person of quality's house where he might expect custom. We made easy journeys of not above seven or eight score miles a day: for Glumdalclitch, on purpose to spare me, complained she was tired with the trotting of the horse. She often took me out of my box at my own desire, to give me air and show me the country, but always held me fast by leading strings. We passed over five or six rivers many degrees broader and deeper than the Nile or the Ganges; and there was hardly a rivulet so small as the Thames at London Bridge. We were ten weeks in our journey, and I was shown in eighteen large towns, besides many large villages and private families.

On the 26th day of October, we arrived at the metropolis, called in their language *Lorbrulgrud*, or Pride of the Universe. My master took a lodging in the principal street of the city, not far from the royal palace, and put out bills in the usual form, containing an exact description of my person and parts. He hired a large room between three and four hundred foot wide. He provided a table sixty foot in diameter, upon which I was to act my part, and palisadoed it round three foot from the edge, and as many high, to prevent my falling over. I was shown ten times a day to the wonder and satisfaction of all people. I could now speak the language tolerably well, and perfectly understood every word that was spoken to me. Besides, I had learned their alphabet, and could make a shift to explain a sentence here and there; for Glumdalclitch had been my instructor while we were at home, and at leisure hours during our journey. She carried a little book in her pocket, not much larger than a Sanson's *Atlas*;[3] it was a common treatise for the use of young girls, giving a short account of their religion: out of this she taught me my letters, and interpreted the words.

CHAPTER 3. *The Author sent for to Court. The Queen buys him of his master, the farmer, and presents him to the King. He disputes with his Majesty's great scholars. An apartment at Court provided for the Author. He is in high favor with the Queen. He stands up for the honor of his own country. His quarrels with the Queen's dwarf.*

The frequent labors I underwent every day made in a few weeks a very considerable change in my health: the more my master got by me, the more unsatiable he grew. I had quite lost my stomach, and was almost reduced to

3. I.e., over two feet long and about two feet wide.

a skeleton. The farmer observed it, and concluding I soon must die, resolved to make as good a hand of me as he could. While he was thus reasoning and resolving with himself, a *Slardral*, or Gentleman Usher, came from Court, commanding my master to carry me immediately thither for the diversion of the Queen and her ladies. Some of the latter had already been to see me and reported strange things of my beauty, behavior, and good sense. Her Majesty and those who attended her were beyond measure delighted with my demeanor. I fell on my knees and begged the honor of kissing her Imperial foot; but this gracious princess held out her little finger towards me (after I was set on a table), which I embraced in both my arms, and put the tip of it, with the utmost respect, to my lip. She made me some general questions about my country and my travels, which I answered as distinctly and in as few words as I could. She asked whether I would be content to live at Court. I bowed down to the board of the table, and humbly answered that I was my master's slave, but if I were at my own disposal, I should be proud to devote my life to her Majesty's service. She then asked my master whether he were willing to sell me at a good price. He, who apprehended I could not live a month, was ready enough to part with me, and demanded a thousand pieces of gold, which were ordered him on the spot, each piece being about the bigness of eight hundred moidores;[4] but, allowing for the proportion of all things between that country and Europe, and the high price of gold among them, was hardly so great a sum as a thousand guineas would be in England. I then said to the Queen, since I was now her Majesty's most humble creature and vassal, I must beg the favor that Glumdalclitch, who had always tended me with so much care and kindness, and understood to do it so well, might be admitted into her service, and continue to be my nurse and instructor. Her Majesty agreed to my petition, and easily got the farmer's consent, who was glad enough to have his daughter preferred at Court; and the poor girl herself was not able to hide her joy. My late master withdrew, bidding me farewell, and saying he had left me in a good service; to which I replied not a word, only making him a slight bow.

The Queen observed my coldness, and when the farmer was gone out of the apartment, asked me the reason. I made bold to tell her Majesty that I owed no other obligation to my late master than his not dashing out the brains of a poor harmless creature found by chance in his field; which obligation was amply recompensed by the gain he had made in showing me through half the kingdom, and the price he had now sold me for. That the life I had since led was laborious enough to kill an animal of ten times my strength. That my health was much impaired by the continual drudgery of entertaining the rabble every hour of the day; and that if my master had not thought my life in danger, her Majesty perhaps would not have got so cheap a bargain. But as I was out of all fear of being ill treated under the protection of so great and good an Empress, the Ornament of Nature, the Darling of the World, the Delight of her Subjects, the Phoenix of the Creation; so I hoped my late master's apprehensions would appear to be groundless, for I already found my spirits to revive by the influence of her most august presence.

4. Portuguese coins.

This was the sum of my speech, delivered with great improprieties and hesitation; the latter part was altogether framed in the style peculiar to that people, whereof I learned some phrases from Glumdalclitch, while she was carrying me to Court.

The Queen, giving great allowance for my defectiveness in speaking, was however surprised at so much wit and good sense in so diminutive an animal. She took me in her own hand, and carried me to the King, who was then retired to his cabinet.[5] His Majesty, a prince of much gravity, and austere countenance, not well observing my shape at first view, asked the Queen after a cold manner how long it was since she grew fond of a *splacknuck;* for such it seems he took me to be, as I lay upon my breast in her Majesty's right hand. But this princess, who hath an infinite deal of wit and humor, set me gently on my feet upon the scrutore,[6] and commanded me to give his Majesty an account of myself, which I did in a very few words; and Glumdalclitch, who attended at the cabinet door, and could not endure I should be out of her sight, being admitted, confirmed all that had passed from my arrival at her father's house.

The King, although he be as learned a person as any in his dominions, had been educated in the study of philosophy and particularly mathematics; yet when he observed my shape exactly, and saw me walk erect, before I began to speak, conceived I might be a piece of clockwork (which is in that country arrived to a very great perfection) contrived by some ingenious artist. But when he heard my voice, and found what I delivered to be regular and rational, he could not conceal his astonishment. He was by no means satisfied with the relation I gave him of the manner I came into his kingdom, but thought it a story concerted between Glumdalclitch and her father, who had taught me a set of words to make me sell at a higher price. Upon this imagination he put several other questions to me, and still received rational answers, no otherwise defective than by a foreign accent, and an imperfect knowledge in the language, with some rustic phrases which I had learned at the farmer's house, and did not suit the polite style of a court.

His Majesty sent for three great scholars who were then in their weekly waiting (according to the custom in that country). These gentlemen, after they had a while examined my shape with much nicety, were of different opinions concerning me. They all agreed that I could not be produced according to the regular laws of nature, because I was not framed with a capacity of preserving my life, either by swiftness, or climbing of trees, or digging holes in the earth. They observed by my teeth, which they viewed with great exactness, that I was a carnivorous animal; yet most quadrupeds being an overmatch for me, and field mice, with some others, too nimble, they could not imagine how I should be able to support myself, unless I fed upon snails and other insects; which they offered, by many learned arguments, to evince that I could not possibly do. One of them seemed to think that I might be an embryo, or abortive birth. But this opinion was rejected by the other two, who observed my limbs to be perfect and finished, and that I had lived several years, as it was manifested from my beard, the stumps whereof they plainly discovered through a magnifying glass. They would not

5. Private apartment.　　　　　　6. Writing desk.

allow me to be a dwarf, because my littleness was beyond all degrees of comparison; for the Queen's favorite dwarf, the smallest ever known in that kingdom, was nearly thirty foot high. After much debate, they concluded unanimously that I was only *relplum scalcath*, which is interpreted literally, *lusus naturae*; a determination exactly agreeable to the modern philosophy of Europe, whose professors, disdaining the old evasion of *occult causes*, whereby the followers of Aristotle endeavor in vain to disguise their ignorance, have invented this wonderful solution of all difficulties, to the unspeakable advancement of human knowledge.[7]

After this decisive conclusion, I entreated to be heard a word or two. I applied myself to the King, and assured his Majesty that I came from a country which abounded with several millions of both sexes, and of my own stature, where the animals, trees, and houses were all in proportion, and where by consequence I might be as able to defend myself, and to find sustenance, as any of his Majesty's subjects could do here; which I took for a full answer to those gentlemen's arguments. To this they only replied with a smile of contempt, saying that the farmer had instructed me very well in my lesson. The King, who had a much better understanding, dismissing his learned men, sent for the farmer, who by good fortune was not yet gone out of town; having therefore first examined him privately, and then confronted him with me and the young girl, his Majesty began to think that what we told him might possibly be true. He desired the Queen to order that a particular care should be taken of me, and was of opinion that Glumdalclitch should still continue in her office of tending me, because he observed we had a great affection for each other. A convenient apartment was provided for her at Court; she had a sort of governess appointed to take care of her education, a maid to dress her, and two other servants for menial offices; but the care of me was wholly appropriated to herself. The Queen commanded her own cabinetmaker to contrive a box that might serve me for a bedchamber, after the model that Glumdalclitch and I should agree upon. This man was a most ingenious artist, and according to my directions, in three weeks finished for me a wooden chamber of sixteen foot square and twelve high, with sash windows, a door, and two closets, like a London bedchamber. The board that made the ceiling was to be lifted up and down by two hinges, to put in a bed ready furnished by her Majesty's upholsterer, which Glumdalclitch took out every day to air, made it with her own hands, and letting it down at night, locked up the roof over me. A nice[8] workman, who was famous for little curiosities, undertook to make me two chairs, with backs and frames, of a substance not unlike ivory, and two tables, with a cabinet to put my things in. The room was quilted on all sides, as well as the floor and the ceiling, to prevent any accident from the carelessness of those who carried me, and to break the force of a jolt when I went in a coach. I desired a lock for my door to prevent rats and mice from coming in: the smith, after several attempts, made the smallest that ever was seen among them, for I have known a larger at the gate of a gentleman's house in England.

---

7. Swift had contempt for both the medieval Schoolmen, who discussed "occult causes," the unknown causes of observable effects, and modern scientists, who, he believed, often concealed their ignorance by using equally meaningless terms. "*Lusus naturae*": one of nature's sports, or roughly, freaks.
8. Exact.

I made a shift[9] to keep the key in a pocket of my own, fearing Glumdalclitch might lose it. The Queen likewise ordered the thinnest silks that could be gotten, to make me clothes, not much thicker than an English blanket, very cumbersome till I was accustomed to them. They were after the fashion of the kingdom, partly resembling the Persian, and partly the Chinese, and are a very grave, decent habit.

The Queen became so fond of my company that she could not dine without me. I had a table placed upon the same at which her Majesty ate, just at her left elbow, and a chair to sit on. Glumdalclitch stood upon a stool on the floor, near my table, to assist and take care of me. I had an entire set of silver dishes and plates, and other necessaries, which, in proportion to those of the Queen, were not much bigger than what I have seen of the same kind in a London toyshop,[1] for the furniture of a baby-house: these my little nurse kept in her pocket in a silver box and gave me at meals as I wanted them, always cleaning them herself. No person dined with the Queen but the two Princesses Royal, the elder sixteen years old, and the younger at that time thirteen and a month. Her Majesty used to put a bit of meat upon one of my dishes, out of which I carved for myself; and her diversion was to see me eat in miniature. For the Queen (who had indeed but a weak stomach) took up at one mouthful as much as a dozen English farmers could eat at a meal, which to me was for some time a very nauseous sight. She would craunch the wing of a lark, bones and all, between her teeth, although it were nine times as large as that of a full-grown turkey; and put a bit of bread into her mouth as big as two twelve-penny loaves. She drank out of a golden cup, above a hogshead at a draught. Her knives were twice as long as a scythe set straight upon the handle. The spoons, forks, and other instruments were all in the same proportion. I remember when Glumdalclitch carried me out of curiosity to see some of the tables at Court, where ten or a dozen of these enormous knives and forks were lifted up together, I thought I had never till then beheld so terrible a sight.

It is the custom that every Wednesday (which, as I have before observed, was their Sabbath) the King and Queen, with the royal issue of both sexes, dine together in the apartment of his Majesty, to whom I was now become a favorite; and at these times my little chair and table were placed at his left hand, before one of the salt-cellars. This prince took a pleasure in conversing with me, inquiring into the manners, religion, laws, government, and learning of Europe; wherein I gave him the best account I was able. His apprehension was so clear, and his judgment so exact, that he made very wise reflections and observations upon all I said. But I confess that after I had been a little too copious in talking of my own beloved country, of our trade and wars by sea and land, of our schisms in religion and parties in the state, the prejudices of his education prevailed so far that he could not forbear taking me up in his right hand, and stroking me gently with the other, after an hearty fit of laughing, asked me whether I were a Whig or a Tory. Then turning to his first minister, who waited behind him with a white staff, near as tall as the mainmast of the *Royal Sovereign*,[2] he observed how contemptible a thing was human grandeur, which could be mimicked by such dimin-

9. Contrived.
1. A shop for selling knickknacks.
2. One of the largest ships in the Royal Navy. At the English court the lord treasurer bore a white staff as the symbol of his office.

utive insects as I: "and yet," said he, "I dare engage, these creatures have their titles and distinctions of honor; they contrive little nests and burrows, that they call houses and cities; they make a figure in dress and equipage; they love, they fight, they dispute, they cheat, they betray." And thus he continued on, while my color came and went several times with indignation to hear our noble country, the mistress of arts and arms, the scourge of France, the arbitress of Europe, the seat of virtue, piety, honor, and truth, the pride and envy of the world, so contemptuously treated.

But as I was not in a condition to resent injuries, so, upon mature thoughts, I began to doubt whether I were injured or no. For, after having been accustomed several months to the sight and converse of this people, and observed every object upon which I cast my eyes to be of proportionable magnitude, the horror I had first conceived from their bulk and aspect was so far worn off that if I had then beheld a company of English lords and ladies in their finery and birthday clothes,[3] acting their several parts in the most courtly manner of strutting and bowing and prating, to say the truth, I should have been strongly tempted to laugh as much at them as this King and his grandees did at me. Neither indeed could I forbear smiling at myself when the Queen used to place me upon her hand towards a looking glass, by which both our persons appeared before me in full view together; and there could be nothing more ridiculous than the comparison; so that I really began to imagine myself dwindled many degrees below my usual size.

Nothing angered and mortified me so much as the Queen's dwarf, who being of the lowest stature that was ever in that country (for I verily think he was not full thirty foot high) became so insolent at seeing a creature so much beneath him that he would always affect to swagger and look big as he passed by me in the Queen's antechamber, while I was standing on some table talking with the lords or ladies of the court; and he seldom failed of a smart word or two upon my littleness, against which I could only revenge myself by calling him brother, challenging him to wrestle, and such repartees as are usual in the mouths of Court pages. One day at dinner this malicious little cub was so nettled with something I had said to him that, raising himself upon the frame of Her Majesty's chair, he took me up by the middle, as I was sitting down, not thinking any harm, and let me drop into a large silver bowl of cream, and then ran away as fast as he could. I fell over head and ears, and if I had not been a good swimmer, it might have gone very hard with me; for Glumdalclitch in that instant happened to be at the other end of the room, and the Queen was in such a fright that she wanted presence of mind to assist me. But my little nurse ran to my relief, and took me out, after I had swallowed above a quart of cream. I was put to bed; however, I received no other damage than the loss of a suit of clothes, which was utterly spoiled. The dwarf was soundly whipped, and as further punishment, forced to drink up the bowl of cream into which he had thrown me; neither was he ever restored to favor: for soon after the Queen bestowed him to a lady of high quality, so that I saw him no more, to my very great satisfaction; for I could not tell to what extremity such a malicious urchin might have carried his resentment.

He had before served me a scurvy trick, which set the Queen a laughing,

---

3. Courtiers dressed with special splendor on the monarch's birthday.

although at the same time she were heartily vexed, and would have immediately cashiered him, if I had not been so generous as to intercede. Her Majesty had taken a marrow bone upon her plate, and after knocking out the marrow, placed the bone again in the dish, erect as it stood before; the dwarf watching his opportunity, while Glumdalclitch was gone to the sideboard, mounted upon the stool she stood on to take care of me at meals, took me up in both hands, and squeezing my legs together, wedged them into the marrow bone above my waist, where I stuck for some time, and made a very ridiculous figure. I believe it was near a minute before anyone knew what was become of me, for I thought it below me to cry out. But, as princes seldom get their meat hot, my legs were not scalded, only my stockings and breeches in a sad condition. The dwarf at my entreaty had no other punishment than a sound whipping.

I was frequently rallied by the Queen upon account of my fearfulness, and she used to ask me whether the people of my country were as great cowards as myself. The occasion was this. The kingdom is much pestered with flies in summer, and these odious insects, each of them as big as a Dunstable lark, hardly gave me any rest while I sat at dinner, with their continual humming and buzzing about my ears. They would sometimes alight upon my victuals, and leave their loathsome excrement or spawn behind, which to me was very visible, although not to the natives of that country, whose large optics were not so acute as mine in viewing smaller objects. Sometimes they would fix upon my nose or forehead, where they stung me to the quick, smelling very offensively; and I could easily trace that viscous matter, which our naturalists tell us enables those creatures to walk with their feet upwards upon a ceiling. I had much ado to defend myself against these detestable animals, and could not forbear starting when they came on my face. It was the common practice of the dwarf to catch a number of these insects in his hand, as schoolboys do among us, and let them out suddenly under my nose, on purpose to frighten me, and divert the Queen. My remedy was to cut them in pieces with my knife as they flew in the air, wherein my dexterity was much admired.

I remember one morning when Glumdalclitch had set me in my box upon a window, as she usually did in fair days to give me air (for I durst not venture to let the box be hung on a nail out of the window, as we do with cages in England), after I had lifted up one of my sashes, and sat down at my table to eat a piece of sweet cake for my breakfast, above twenty wasps, allured by the smell, came flying into the room, humming louder than the drones of as many bagpipes. Some of them seized my cake, and carried it piecemeal away; others flew about my head and face, confounding me with the noise, and putting me in the utmost terror of their stings. However, I had the courage to rise and draw my hanger, and attack them in the air. I dispatched four of them, but the rest got away, and I presently shut my window. These insects were as large as partridges; I took out their stings, found them an inch and a half long, and as sharp as needles. I carefully preserved them all, and having since shown them with some other curiosities in several parts of Europe, upon my return to England I gave three of them to Gresham College,[4] and kept the fourth for myself.

4. The Royal Society, in its earliest years, met in Gresham College.

CHAPTER 4. *The country described. A proposal for correcting modern maps. The King's palace, and some account of the metropolis. The Author's way of traveling. The chief temple described.*

I now intend to give the reader a short description of this country, as far as I had traveled in it, which was not above two thousand miles round Lorbrulgrud the metropolis. For the Queen, whom I always attended, never went further when she accompanied the King in his progresses, and there stayed till his Majesty returned from viewing his frontiers. The whole extent of this prince's dominions reacheth about six thousand miles in length, and from three to five in breadth. From whence I cannot but conclude that our geographers of Europe are in a great error by supposing nothing but sea between Japan and California: for it was ever my opinion that there must be a balance of earth to counterpoise the great continent of Tartary; and therefore they ought to correct their maps and charts by joining this vast tract of land to the northwest parts of America, wherein I shall be ready to lend them my assistance.

The kingdom is a peninsula, terminated to the northeast by a ridge of mountains thirty miles high, which are altogether impassable by reason of the volcanoes upon the tops. Neither do the most learned know what sort of mortals inhabit beyond those mountains, or whether they be inhabited at all. On the three other sides it is bounded by the ocean. There is not one seaport in the whole kingdom; and those parts of the coasts into which the rivers issue are so full of pointed rocks, and the sea generally so rough, that there is no venturing with the smallest of their boats; so that these people are wholly excluded from any commerce with the rest of the world. But the large rivers are full of vessels, and abound with excellent fish, for they seldom get any from the sea, because the sea fish are of the same size with those in Europe, and consequently not worth catching; whereby it is manifest that nature, in the production of plants and animals of so extraordinary a bulk, is wholly confined to this continent, of which I leave the reasons to be determined by philosophers. However, now and then they take a whale that happens to be dashed against the rocks, which the common people feed on heartily. These whales I have known so large that a man could hardly carry one upon his shoulders; and sometimes for curiosity they are brought in hampers to Lorbrulgrud: I saw one of them in a dish at the King's table, which passed for a rarity, but I did not observe he was fond of it; for I think indeed the bigness disgusted him, although I have seen one somewhat larger in Greenland.

The country is well inhabited, for it contains fifty-one cities, near an hundred walled towns, and a great number of villages. To satisfy my curious reader, it may be sufficient to describe Lorbrulgrud. This city stands upon almost two equal parts on each side the river that passes through. It contains above eight thousand houses, and about six hundred thousand inhabitants. It is in length three *glonglungs* (which make about fifty-four English miles) and two and a half in breadth, as I measured it myself in the royal map made by the King's order, which was laid on the ground on purpose for me, and extended an hundred feet; I paced the diameter and circumference several times barefoot, and computing by the scale, measured it pretty exactly.

The King's palace is no regular edifice, but an heap of buildings about seven miles round: the chief rooms are generally two hundred and forty foot high, and broad and long in proportion. A coach was allowed to Glumdalclitch and me, wherein her governess frequently took her out to see the town, or go among the shops; and I was always of the party, carried in my box, although the girl at my own desire would often take me out, and hold me in her hand, that I might more conveniently view the houses and the people as we passed along the streets. I reckoned our coach to be about a square of Westminster Hall,[5] but not altogether so high; however, I cannot be very exact. One day the governess ordered our coachman to stop at several shops, where the beggars, watching their opportunity, crowded to the sides of the coach, and gave me the most horrible spectacles that ever an English eye beheld. There was a woman with a cancer in her breast, swelled to a monstrous size, full of holes, in two or three of which I could have easily crept, and covered my whole body. There was a fellow with a wen in his neck, larger than five woolpacks, and another with a couple of wooden legs, each about twenty foot high. But the most hateful sight of all was the lice crawling on their clothes. I could see distinctly the limbs of these vermin with my naked eye, much better than those of an European louse through a microscope, and their snouts with which they rooted like swine. They were the first I had ever beheld; and I should have been curious enough to dissect one of them if I had proper instruments (which I unluckily left behind me in the ship), although indeed the sight was so nauseous that it perfectly turned my stomach.

Besides the large box in which I was usually carried, the Queen ordered a smaller one to be made for me, of about twelve foot square and ten high, for the convenience of traveling, because the other was somewhat too large for Glumdalclitch's lap, and cumbersome in the coach; it was made by the same artist, whom I directed in the whole contrivance. This traveling closet was an exact square with a window in the middle of three of the squares, and each window was latticed with iron wire on the outside, to prevent accidents in long journeys. On the fourth side, which had no windows, two strong staples were fixed, through which the person that carried me, when I had a mind to be on horseback, put in a leathern belt, and buckled it about his waist. This was always the office of some grave trusty servant in whom I could confide, whether I attended the King and Queen in their progresses, or were disposed to see the gardens, or pay a visit to some great lady or minister of state in the court, when Glumdalclitch happened to be out of order: for I soon began to be known and esteemed among the greatest officers, I suppose more upon account of their Majesties' favor than any merit of my own. In journeys, when I was weary of the coach, a servant on horseback would buckle my box, and place it on a cushion before him; and there I had a full prospect of the country on three sides from my three windows. I had in this closet a field bed and a hammock hung from the ceiling, two chairs and a table, neatly screwed to the floor to prevent being tossed about by the agitation of the horse or the coach. And having been long used to sea voyages, those motions, although sometimes very violent, did not much discompose me.

5. The ancient hall, now incorporated into the Houses of Parliament, where the law courts then sat. Swift presumably means the square of its breadth (just under sixty-eight feet).

When I had a mind to see the town, it was always in my traveling closet, which Glumdalclitch held in her lap in a kind of open sedan, after the fashion of the country, borne by four men, and attended by two others in the Queen's livery. The people, who had often heard of me, were very curious to crowd about the sedan; and the girl was complaisant enough to make the bearers stop, and to take me in her hand that I might be more conveniently seen.

I was very desirous to see the chief temple, and particularly the tower belonging to it, which is reckoned the highest in the kingdom. Accordingly one day my nurse carried me thither, but I may truly say I came back disappointed; for the height is not above three thousand foot, reckoning from the ground to the highest pinnacle top; which, allowing for the difference between the size of those people and us in Europe, is no great matter for admiration, nor at all equal in proportion (if I rightly remember) to Salisbury steeple.[6] But, not to detract from a nation to which during my life I shall acknowledge myself extremely obliged, it must be allowed that whatever this famous tower wants in height is amply made up in beauty and strength. For the walls are near an hundred foot thick, built of hewn stone, whereof each is about forty foot square, and adorned on all sides with statues of gods and emperors cut in marble larger than the life, placed in their several niches. I measured a little finger which had fallen down from one of these statues, and lay unperceived among some rubbish, and found it exactly four foot and an inch in length. Glumdalclitch wrapped it up in a handkerchief, and carried it home in her pocket to keep among other trinkets, of which the girl was very fond, as children at her age usually are.

The King's kitchen is indeed a noble building, vaulted at top, and about six hundred foot high. The great oven is not so wide by ten paces as the cupola at St. Paul's:[7] for I measured the latter on purpose after my return. But if I should describe the kitchen grate, the prodigious pots and kettles, the joints of meat turning on the spits, with many other particulars, perhaps I should be hardly believed; at least a severe critic would be apt to think I enlarged a little, as travelers are often suspected to do. To avoid which censure, I fear I have run too much into the other extreme, and that if this treatise should happen to be translated into the language of Brobdingnag (which is the general name of that kingdom) and transmitted thither, the King and his people would have reason to complain that I had done them an injury by a false and diminutive representation.

His Majesty seldom keeps above six hundred horses in his stables: they are generally from fifty-four to sixty foot high. But when he goes abroad on solemn days, he is attended for state by a militia guard of five hundred horse, which indeed I thought was the most splendid sight that could be ever beheld, till I saw part of his army in battalia,[8] whereof I shall find another occasion to speak.

CHAPTER 5. *Several adventures that happened to the Author. The execution of a criminal. The Author shows his skill in navigation.*

I should have lived happy enough in that country if my littleness had not exposed me to several ridiculous and troublesome accidents, some of which

6. One of the most beautiful Gothic steeples in England is that of Salisbury Cathedral, 404 feet high.

7. The cupola of St. Paul's Cathedral in London is 108 feet in diameter.

8. Battle array.

I shall venture to relate. Glumdalclitch often carried me into the gardens of the court in my smaller box, and would sometimes take me out of it and hold me in her hand, or set me down to walk. I remember, before the dwarf left the Queen, he followed us one day into those gardens; and my nurse having set me down, he and I being close together near some dwarf apple trees, I must needs show my wit by a silly allusion between him and the trees, which happens to hold in their language as it doth in ours. Whereupon, the malicious rogue watching his opportunity, when I was walking under one of them, shook it directly over my head, by which a dozen apples, each of them near as large as a Bristol barrel, came tumbling about my ears; one of them hit me on the back as I chanced to stoop, and knocked me down flat on my face, but I received no other hurt; and the dwarf was pardoned at my desire, because I had given the provocation.

Another day Glumdalclitch left me on a smooth grassplot to divert myself while she walked at some distance with her governess. In the meantime there suddenly fell such a violent shower of hail that I was immediately by the force of it struck to the ground: and when I was down, the hailstones gave me such cruel bangs all over the body as if I had been pelted with tennis balls;[9] however I made a shift to creep on all four, and shelter myself by lying on my face on the lee side of a border of lemon thyme, but so bruised from head to foot that I could not go abroad in ten days. Neither is this at all to be wondered at, because nature in that country observing the same proportion through all her operations, a hailstone is near eighteen hundred times as large as one in Europe; which I can assert upon experience, having been so curious to weigh and measure them.

But a more dangerous accident happened to me in the same garden when my little nurse, believing she had put me in a secure place, which I often entreated her to do that I might enjoy my own thoughts, and having left my box at home to avoid the trouble of carrying it, went to another part of the garden with her governess and some ladies of her acquaintance. While she was absent and out of hearing, a small white spaniel belonging to one of the chief gardeners, having got by accident into the garden, happened to range near the place where I lay. The dog following the scent, came directly up, and taking me in his mouth, ran straight to his master, wagging his tail, and set me gently on the ground. By good fortune he had been so well taught that I was carried between his teeth without the least hurt, or even tearing my clothes. But the poor gardener, who knew me well, and had a great kindness for me, was in a terrible fright. He gently took me up in both his hands, and asked me how I did; but I was so amazed and out of breath that I could not speak a word. In a few minutes I came to myself, and he carried me safe to my little nurse, who by this time had returned to the place where she left me, and was in cruel agonies when I did not appear nor answer when she called; she severely reprimanded the gardener on account of his dog. But the thing was hushed up and never known at court; for the girl was afraid of the Queen's anger; and truly, as to myself, I thought it would not be for my reputation that such a story should go about.

This accident absolutely determined Glumdalclitch never to trust me abroad for the future out of her sight. I had been long afraid of this resolution, and therefore concealed from her some little unlucky adventures that

---

9. Eighteenth-century tennis balls, unlike the modern, were very hard.

happened in those times when I was left by myself. Once a kite hovering over the garden made a stoop[1] at me, and if I had not resolutely drawn my hanger, and run under a thick espalier, he would have certainly carried me away in his talons. Another time walking to the top of a fresh molehill, I fell to my neck in the hole through which that animal had cast up the earth, and coined some lie, not worth remembering, to excuse myself for spoiling my clothes. I likewise broke my right shin against the shell of a snail, which I happened to stumble over, as I was walking alone, and thinking on poor England.

I cannot tell whether I were more pleased or mortified to observe in those solitary walks that the smaller birds did not appear to be at all afraid of me; but would hop about within a yard distance, looking for worms and other food with as much indifference and security as if no creature at all were near them. I remember a thrush had the confidence to snatch out of my hand with his bill a piece of cake that Glumdalclitch had just given me for my breakfast. When I attempted to catch any of these birds, they would boldly turn against me, endeavoring to pick my fingers, which I durst not venture within their reach; and then they would hop back unconcerned to hunt for worms or snails, as they did before. But one day I took a thick cudgel, and threw it with all my strength so luckily at a linnet that I knocked him down, and seizing him by the neck with both my hands, ran with him in triumph to my nurse. However, the bird, who had only been stunned, recovering himself, gave me so many boxes with his wings on both sides of my head and body, though I held him at arm's length, and was out of the reach of his claws, that I was twenty times thinking to let him go. But I was soon relieved by one of our servants, who wrung off the bird's neck, and I had him next day for dinner, by the Queen's command. This linnet, as near as I can remember, seemed to be somewhat larger than an English swan.

The Maids of Honor often invited Glumdalclitch to their apartments, and desired she would bring me along with her, on purpose to have the pleasure of seeing and touching me. They would often strip me naked from top to toe and lay me at full length in their bosoms; wherewith I was much disgusted, because, to say the truth, a very offensive smell came from their skins, which I do not mention or intend to the disadvantage of those excellent ladies, for whom I have all manner of respect; but I conceive that my sense was more acute in proportion to my littleness, and that those illustrious persons were no more disagreeable to their lovers, or to each other, than people of the same quality are with us in England. And, after all, I found their natural smell was much more supportable than when they used perfumes, under which I immediately swooned away. I cannot forget that an intimate friend of mine in Lilliput took the freedom in a warm day, when I had used a good deal of exercise, to complain of a strong smell about me, although I am as little faulty that way as most of my sex: but I suppose his faculty of smelling was as nice with regard to me as mine was to that of this people. Upon this point, I cannot forbear doing justice to the Queen, my mistress, and Glumdalclitch, my nurse, whose persons were as sweet as those of any lady in England.

That which gave me most uneasiness among these Maids of Honor, when

---

1. Swoop. "Kite": a bird of prey.

my nurse carried me to visit them, was to see them use me without any manner of ceremony, like a creature who had no sort of consequence. For they would strip themselves to the skin and put on their smocks in my presence, while I was placed on their toilet[2] directly before their naked bodies; which, I am sure, to me was very far from being a tempting sight, or from giving me any other emotions than those of horror and disgust. Their skins appeared so coarse and uneven, so variously colored, when I saw them near, with a mole here and there as broad as a trencher, and hairs hanging from it thicker than pack-threads, to say nothing further concerning the rest of their persons. Neither did they at all scruple, while I was by, to discharge what they had drunk, to the quantity of at least two hogsheads, in a vessel that held above three tuns. The handsomest among these Maids of Honor, a pleasant frolicsome girl of sixteen, would sometimes set me astride upon one of her nipples, with many other tricks, wherein the reader will excuse me for not being over particular. But I was so much displeased that I entreated Glumdalclitch to contrive some excuse for not seeing that young lady any more.

One day a young gentleman, who was nephew to my nurse's governess, came and pressed them both to see an execution. It was of a man who had murdered one of that gentleman's intimate acquaintance. Glumdalclitch was prevailed on to be of the company, very much against her inclination, for she was naturally tender-hearted: and as for myself, although I abhorred such kind of spectacles, yet my curiosity tempted me to see something that I thought must be extraordinary. The malefactor was fixed in a chair upon a scaffold erected for the purpose, and his head cut off at a blow with a sword of about forty foot long. The veins and arteries spouted up such a prodigious quantity of blood, and so high in the air, that the great *jet d'eau* at Versailles was not equal for the time it lasted; and the head, when it fell on the scaffold floor, gave such a bounce,[3] as made me start, although I were at least half an English mile distant.

The Queen, who often used to hear me talk of my sea voyages, and took all occasions to divert me when I was melancholy, asked me whether I understood how to handle a sail or an oar, and whether a little exercise of rowing might not be convenient for my health. I answered that I understood both very well. For although my proper employment had been to be surgeon or doctor to the ship, yet often, upon a pinch, I was forced to work like a common mariner. But I could not see how this could be done in their country, where the smallest wherry was equal to a first-rate man-of-war among us, and such a boat as I could manage would never live in any of their rivers. Her Majesty said, if I would contrive a boat, her own joiner should make it, and she would provide a place for me to sail in. The fellow was an ingenious workman and, by my instructions, in ten days finished a pleasure boat with all its tackling, able conveniently to hold eight Europeans. When it was finished, the Queen was so delighted that she ran with it in her lap to the King, who ordered it to be put in a cistern full of water, with me in it, by way of trial; where I could not manage my two sculls, or little oars, for want of room. But the Queen had before contrived another project. She ordered the joiner

2. Toilet table.
3. A sudden noise. "*Jet d'eau* at Versailles": this fountain rose over forty feet in the air.

to make a wooden trough of three hundred foot long, fifty broad, and eight deep; which being well pitched to prevent leaking, was placed on the floor along the wall in an outer room of the palace. It had a cock near the bottom to let out the water when it began to grow stale, and two servants could easily fill it in half an hour. Here I often used to row for my own diversion, as well as that of the Queen and her ladies, who thought themselves well entertained with my skill and agility. Sometimes I would put up my sail, and then my business was only to steer, while the ladies gave me a gale with their fans; and when they were weary, some of the pages would blow my sail forward with their breath, while I showed my art by steering starboard or larboard as I pleased. When I had done, Glumdalclitch always carried my boat into her closet, and hung it on a nail to dry.

In this exercise I once met an accident which had like to have cost me my life. For one of the pages having put my boat into the trough, the governess who attended Glumdalclitch very officiously[4] lifted me up to place me in the boat; but I happened to slip through her fingers, and should have infallibly fallen down forty foot upon the floor, if by the luckiest chance in the world I had not been stopped by a corking-pin that stuck in the good gentlewoman's stomacher;[5] the head of the pin passed between my shirt and the waistband of my breeches, and thus I was held by the middle in the air until Glumdalclitch ran to my relief.

Another time, one of the servants, whose office it was to fill my trough every third day with fresh water, was so careless to let a huge frog (not perceiving it) slip out of his pail. The frog lay concealed till I was put into my boat, but then seeing a resting place, climbed up, and made it lean so much on one side that I was forced to balance it with all my weight on the other, to prevent overturning. When the frog was got in, it hopped at once half the length of the boat, and then over my head, backwards and forwards, daubing my face and clothes with its odious slime. The largeness of its features made it appear the most deformed animal that can be conceived. However, I desired Glumdalclitch to let me deal with it alone. I banged it a good while with one of my sculls, and at last forced it to leap out of the boat.

But the greatest danger I ever underwent in that kingdom was from a monkey, who belonged to one of the clerks of the kitchen. Glumdalclitch had locked me up in her closet, while she went somewhere upon business or a visit. The weather being very warm, the closet window was left open, as well as the windows in the door of my bigger box, in which I usually lived, because of its largeness and conveniency. As I sat quietly meditating at my table, I heard something bounce in at the closet window, and skip about from one side to the other, whereat, although I was much alarmed, yet I ventured to look out, but stirred not from my seat; and then I saw this frolicsome animal, frisking and leaping up and down, till at last he came to my box, which he seemed to view with great pleasure and curiosity, peeping in at the door and every window. I retreated to the farther corner of my room, or box, but the monkey looking in at every side, put me into such a fright that I wanted presence of mind to conceal myself under the bed, as I might easily have done. After some time spent in peeping, grinning, and chattering,

---

4. Kindly, dutifully.
5. An ornamental covering for the front and upper part of the body. "Corking-pin": a pin of the largest size.

he at last espied me, and reaching one of his paws in at the door, as a cat does when she plays with a mouse, although I often shifted place to avoid him, he at length seized the lappet of my coat (which, being made of that country cloth, was very thick and strong) and dragged me out. He took me up in his right forefoot, and held me as a nurse does a child she is going to suckle, just as I have seen the same sort of creature do with a kitten in Europe: and when I offered to struggle, he squeezed me so hard that I thought it more prudent to submit. I have good reason to believe that he took me for a young one of his own species, by his often stroking my face very gently with his other paw. In these diversions he was interrupted by a noise at the closet door, as if somebody were opening it, whereupon he suddenly leaped up to the window at which he had come in, and thence upon the leads and gutters, walking upon three legs, and holding me in the fourth, till he clambered up to a roof that was next to ours. I heard Glumdalclitch give a shriek at the moment he was carrying me out. The poor girl was almost distracted: that quarter of the palace was all in an uproar; the servants ran for ladders; the monkey was seen by hundreds in the court, sitting upon the ridge of a building, holding me like a baby in one of his forepaws and feeding me with the other, by cramming into my mouth some victuals he had squeezed out of the bag on one side of his chaps, and patting me when I would not eat; whereat many of the rabble below could not forebear laughing; neither do I think they justly ought to be blamed, for without question the sight was ridiculous enough to everybody but myself. Some of the people threw up stones, hoping to drive the monkey down; but this was strictly forbidden, or else very probably my brains had been dashed out.

The ladders were now applied, and mounted by several men; which the monkey observing, and finding himself almost encompassed, not being able to make speed enough with his three legs, let me drop on a ridge tile, and made his escape. Here I sat for some time three hundred yards from the ground, expecting every moment to be blown down by the wind, or to fall by my own giddiness, and come tumbling over and over from the ridge to the eaves. But an honest lad, one of my nurse's footmen, climbed up, and putting me into his breeches pocket, brought me down safe.

I was almost choked with the filthy stuff the monkey had crammed down my throat; but my dear little nurse picked it out of my mouth with a small needle, and then I fell a vomiting, which gave me great relief. Yet I was so weak and bruised in the sides with the squeezes given me by this odious animal that I was forced to keep my bed a fortnight. The King, Queen, and all the Court sent every day to inquire after my health, and her Majesty made me several visits during my sickness. The monkey was killed, and an order made that no such animal should be kept about the palace.

When I attended the King after my recovery, to return him thanks for his favors, he was pleased to rally me a good deal upon this adventure. He asked me what my thoughts and speculations were while I lay in the monkey's paw, how I liked the victuals he gave me, his manner of feeding, and whether the fresh air on the roof had sharpened my stomach. He desired to know what I would have done upon such an occasion in my own country. I told his Majesty that in Europe we had no monkeys, except such as were brought for curiosities from other places, and so small that I could deal with a dozen of them together, if they presumed to attack me. And as for that monstrous animal with whom I was so lately engaged (it was indeed as large as an elephant), if my fears had suffered me to think so far as to make use of my hanger (looking fiercely and clapping my hand upon the hilt as I spoke) when he poked his paw into my chamber, perhaps I should have given him such a wound as would have made him glad to withdraw it with more haste than he put it in. This I delivered in a firm tone, like a person who was jealous lest his courage should be called in question. However, my speech produced nothing else besides a loud laughter, which all the respect due to his Majesty from those about him could not make them contain. This made me reflect how vain an attempt it is for a man to endeavor doing himself honor among those who are out of all degree of equality or comparison with him. And yet I have seen the moral of my own behavior very frequent in England since my return, where a little contemptible varlet, without the least title to birth, person, wit, or common sense, shall presume to look with importance, and put himself upon a foot with the greatest persons of the kingdom.

I was every day furnishing the court with some ridiculous story; and Glumdalclitch, although she loved me to excess, yet was arch enough to inform the Queen whenever I committed any folly that she thought would be diverting to her Majesty. The girl, who had been out of order, was carried by her governess to take the air about an hour's distance, or thirty miles from town. They alighted out of the coach near a small footpath in a field, and Glumdalclitch setting down my traveling box, I went out of it to walk. There was a cow dung in the patch, and I must needs try my activity by attempting to leap over it. I took a run, but unfortunately jumped short, and found myself just in the middle up to my knees. I waded through with some difficulty, and one of the footmen wiped me as clean as he could with his handkerchief; for I was filthily bemired, and my nurse confined me to my box till we returned home, where the Queen was soon informed of what had passed and the footmen spread it about the Court, so that all the mirth, for some days, was at my expense.

CHAPTER 6. *Several contrivances of the Author to please the King and Queen. He shows his skill in music. The King inquires into the state of Europe, which the Author relates to him. The King's observations thereon.*

I used to attend the King's levee once or twice a week, and had often seen him under the barber's hand, which indeed was at first very terrible to behold. For the razor was almost twice as long as an ordinary scythe. His Majesty, according to the custom of the country, was only shaved twice a week. I once prevailed on the barber to give me some of the suds or lather, out of which I picked forty or fifty of the strongest stumps of hair. I then took a piece of fine wood, and cut it like the back of a comb, making several holes in it at equal distance with as small a needle as I could get from Glumdalclitch. I fixed in the stumps so artificially,[6] scraping and sloping them with my knife towards the points, that I made a very tolerable comb; which was a seasonable supply, my own being so much broken in the teeth that it was almost useless; neither did I know any artist in that country so nice and exact as would undertake to make me another.

6. Skillfully.

And this puts me in mind of an amusement wherein I spent many of my leisure hours. I desired the Queen's woman to save for me the combings of her Majesty's hair, whereof in time I got a good quantity; and consulting with my friend the cabinetmaker, who had received general orders to do little jobs for me, I directed him to make two chair frames, no larger than those I had in my box, and then to bore little holes with a fine awl round those parts where I designed the backs and seats; through these holes I wove the strongest hairs I could pick out, just after the manner of cane chairs in England. When they were finished, I made a present of them to her Majesty, who kept them in her cabinet, and used to show them for curiosities, as indeed they were the wonder of every one that beheld them. The Queen would have made me sit upon one of these chairs, but I absolutely refused to obey her, protesting I would rather die a thousand deaths than place a dishonorable part of my body on those precious hairs that once adorned her Majesty's head. Of these hairs (as I had always a mechanical genius) I likewise made a neat little purse above five foot long, with her Majesty's name deciphered in gold letters, which I gave to Glumdalclitch by the Queen's consent. To say the truth, it was more for show than use, being not of strength to bear the weight of the larger coins; and therefore she kept nothing in it but some little toys[7] that girls are fond of.

The King, who delighted in music, had frequent consorts[8] at court, to which I was sometimes carried, and set in my box on a table to hear them; but the noise was so great that I could hardly distinguish the tunes. I am confident that all the drums and trumpets of a royal army, beating and sounding together just at your ears, could not equal it. My practice was to have my box removed from the places where the performers sat, as far as I could, then to shut the doors and windows of it, and draw the window curtains, after which I found their music not disagreeable.

I had learned in my youth to play a little upon the spinet. Glumdalclitch kept one in her chamber, and a master attended twice a week to teach her: I call it a spinet, because it somewhat resembled that instrument, and was played upon in the same manner. A fancy came into my head that I would entertain the King and Queen with an English tune upon this instrument. But this appeared extremely difficult: for the spinet was near sixty foot long, each key being almost a foot wide; so that, with my arms extended, I could not reach to above five keys, and to press them down required a good smart stroke with my fist, which would be too great a labor and to no purpose. The method I contrived was this: I prepared two round sticks about the bigness of common cudgels; they were thicker at one end than the other, and I covered the thicker ends with a piece of a mouse's skin, that by rapping on them I might neither damage the tops of the keys, nor interrupt the sound. Before the spinet a bench was placed, about four foot below the keys, and I was put upon the bench. I ran sideling upon it that way and this, as fast as I could, banging the proper keys with my two sticks; and made a shift to play a jig, to the great satisfaction of both their Majesties: but it was the most violent exercise I ever underwent, and yet I could not strike above sixteen keys, nor, consequently, play the bass and treble together, as other artists do; which was a great disadvantage to my performance.

---

7. Trifles. 　　　　　　　　　　8. Concerts.

The King, who, as I before observed, was a prince of excellent understanding, would frequently order that I should be brought in my box and set upon the table in his closet. He would then command me to bring one of my chairs out of the box, and sit down within three yards distance upon the top of the cabinet, which brought me almost to a level with his face. In this manner I had several conversations with him. I one day took the freedom to tell his Majesty that the contempt he discovered towards Europe, and the rest of the world, did not seem answerable to those excellent qualities of mind that he was master of. That reason did not extend itself with the bulk of the body: on the contrary, we observed in our country that the tallest persons were usually least provided with it. That among other animals, bees and ants had the reputation of more industry, art, and sagacity than many of the larger kinds; and that, as inconsiderable as he took me to be, I hoped I might live to do his Majesty some signal service. The King heard me with attention, and began to conceive a much better opinion of me than he had before. He desired I would give him as exact an account of the government of England as I possibly could; because, as fond as princes commonly are of their own customs (for so he conjectured of other monarchs, by my former discourses), he should be glad to hear of anything that might deserve imitation.

Imagine with thyself, courteous reader, how often I then wished for the tongue of Demosthenes or Cicero, that might have enabled me to celebrate the praise of my own dear native country in a style equal to its merits and felicity.

I began my discourse by informing his Majesty that our dominions consisted of two islands, which composed three mighty kingdoms under one sovereign, beside our plantations in America. I dwelt long upon the fertility of our soil, and the temperature[9] of our climate. I then spoke at large upon the constitution of an English Parliament, partly made up of an illustrious body called the House of Peers, persons of the noblest blood, and of the most ancient and ample patrimonies. I described that extraordinary care always taken of their education in arts and arms, to qualify them for being counselors born to the king and kingdom; to have a share in the legislature, to be members of the highest Court of Judicature, from whence there could be no appeal; and to be champions always ready for the defense of their prince and country, by their valor, conduct, and fidelity. That these were the ornament and bulwark of the kingdom, worthy followers of their most renowned ancestors, whose honor had been the reward of their virtue, from which their posterity were never once known to degenerate. To these were joined several holy persons, as part of that assembly, under the title of Bishops, whose peculiar business it is to take care of religion, and of those who instruct the people therein. These were searched and sought out through the whole nation, by the prince and his wisest counselors, among such of the priesthood as were most deservedly distinguished by the sanctity of their lives and the depth of their erudition, who were indeed the spiritual fathers of the clergy and the people.

That the other part of the Parliament consisted of an assembly called the House of Commons, who were all principal gentlemen, freely picked and culled out by the people themselves, for their great abilities and love of their

9. Temperateness.

country, to represent the wisdom of the whole nation. And these two bodies make up the most august assembly in Europe, to whom, in conjunction with the prince, the whole legislature is committed.

I then descended to the Courts of Justice, over which the Judges, those venerable sages and interpreters of the law, presided, for determining the disputed rights and properties of men, as well as for the punishment of vice, and protection of innocence. I mentioned the prudent management of our treasury, the valor and achievements of our forces by sea and land. I computed the number of our people, by reckoning how many millions there might be of each religious sect, or political party among us. I did not omit even our sports and pastimes, or any other particular which I thought might redound to the honor of my country. And I finished all with a brief historical account of affairs and events in England for about an hundred years past.

This conversation was not ended under five audiences, each of several hours, and the King heard the whole with great attention, frequently taking notes of what I spoke, as well as memorandums of several questions he intended to ask me.

When I had put an end to these long discourses, his Majesty in a sixth audience consulting his notes, proposed many doubts, queries, and objections, upon every article. He asked what methods were used to cultivate the minds and bodies of our young nobility, and in what kind of business they commonly spent the first and teachable part of their lives. What course was taken to supply that assembly when any noble family became extinct. What qualifications were necessary in those who were to be created new lords. Whether the humor[1] of the prince, a sum of money to a Court lady or a prime minister, or a design of strengthening a party opposite to the public interest, ever happened to be motives in those advancements. What share of knowledge these lords had in the laws of their country, and how they came by it, so as to enable them to decide the properties of their fellow subjects in the last result. Whether they were always so free from avarice, partialities, or want that a bribe or some other sinister view could have no place among them. Whether those holy lords I spoke of were constantly promoted to that rank upon account of their knowledge in religious matters, and the sanctity of their lives; had never been compliers with the times while they were common priests, or slavish prostitute chaplains to some nobleman, whose opinions they continued servilely to follow after they were admitted into that assembly.

He then desired to know what arts were practiced in electing those whom I called Commoners. Whether a stranger with a strong purse might not influence the vulgar voters to choose him before their own landlord or the most considerable gentleman in the neighborhood. How it came to pass that people were so violently bent upon getting into this assembly, which I allowed to be a great trouble and expense, often to the ruin of their families, without any salary or pension: because this appeared such an exalted strain of virtue and public spirit that his Majesty seemed to doubt it might possibly not be always sincere; and he desired to know whether such zealous gentlemen could have any views of refunding themselves for the charges and trouble they were at, by sacrificing the public good to the designs of a weak and

1. Whim.

vicious prince in conjunction with a corrupted ministry. He multiplied his questions, and sifted me thoroughly upon every part of this head, proposing numberless inquiries and objections, which I think it not prudent or convenient to repeat.

Upon what I said in relation to our Courts of Justice, his Majesty desired to be satisfied in several points: and this I was the better able to do, having been formerly almost ruined by a long suit in chancery, which was decreed for me with costs. He asked what time was usually spent in determining between right and wrong, and what degree of expense. Whether advocates and orators had liberty to plead in causes manifestly known to be unjust, vexatious, or oppressive. Whether party in religion or politics were observed to be of any weight in the scale of justice. Whether those pleading orators were persons educated in the general knowledge of equity, or only in provincial, national, and other local customs. Whether they or their judges had any part in penning those laws which they assumed the liberty of interpreting and glossing upon at their pleasure. Whether they had ever at different times pleaded for and against the same cause, and cited precedents to prove contrary opinions. Whether they were a rich or a poor corporation. Whether they received any pecuniary reward for pleading or delivering their opinions. And particularly whether they were ever admitted as members in the lower senate.

He fell next upon the management of our treasury, and said he thought my memory had failed me, because I computed our taxes at about five or six millions a year, and when I came to mention the issues,[2] he found they sometimes amounted to more than double, for the notes he had taken were very particular in this point; because he hoped, as he told me, that the knowledge of our conduct might be useful to him, and he could not be deceived in his calculations. But if what I told him were true, he was still at a loss how a kingdom could run out of its estate like a private person. He asked me, who were our creditors? and where we should find money to pay them? He wondered to hear me talk of such chargeable and extensive wars; that certainly we must be a quarrelsome people, or live among very bad neighbors, and that our generals must needs be richer than our kings.[3] He asked what business we had out of our own islands, unless upon the score of trade or treaty or to defend the coasts with our fleet. Above all, he was amazed to hear me talk of a mercenary standing army[4] in the midst of peace, and among a free people. He said if we were governed by our own consent in the persons of our representatives, he could not imagine of whom we were afraid, or against whom we were to fight; and would hear my opinion whether a private man's house might not better be defended by himself, his children, and family, than by half a dozen rascals picked up at a venture[5] in the streets for small wages, who might get an hundred times more by cutting their throats.

He laughed at my odd kind of arithmetic (as he was pleased to call it) in reckoning the numbers of our people by a computation drawn from the several sects among us in religion and politics. He said he knew no reason why those who entertain opinions prejudicial to the public should be obliged to

---

2. Expenditures.
3. An allusion to the enormous fortune gained by the duke of Marlborough, formerly captain-general of the army, whom Swift detested.
4. Since the declaration of the Bill of Rights

(1689), a standing army without authorization by Parliament had been illegal. Swift and the Tories in general were vigilant in their opposition to such an army.
5. By chance.

change, or should not be obliged to conceal them. And as it was tyranny in any government to require the first, so it was weakness not to enforce the second: for a man may be allowed to keep poisons in his closet, but not to vend them about for cordials.[6]

He observed that among the diversions of our nobility and gentry I had mentioned gaming. He desired to know at what age this entertainment was usually taken up, and when it was laid down; how much of their time it employed; whether it ever went so high as to affect their fortunes; whether mean, vicious people, by their dexterity in that art, might not arrive at great riches, and sometimes keep our very nobles in dependence, as well as habituate them to vile companions, wholly take them from the improvement of their minds, and force them, by the losses they received, to learn and practice that infamous dexterity upon others.

He was perfectly astonished with the historical account I gave him of our affairs during the last century, protesting it was only an heap of conspiracies, rebellions, murders, massacres, revolutions, banishments, the very worst effects that avarice, faction, hypocrisy, perfidiousness, cruelty, rage, madness, hatred, envy, lust, malice, or ambition could produce.

His Majesty in another audience was at the pains to recapitulate the sum of all I had spoken; compared the questions he made with the answers I had given; then taking me into his hands, and stroking me gently, delivered himself in these words, which I shall never forget, nor the manner he spoke them in. "My little friend Grildrig, you have made a most admirable panegyric upon your country. You have clearly proved that ignorance, idleness, and vice are the proper ingredients for qualifying a legislator. That laws are best explained, interpreted, and applied by those whose interests and abilities lie in perverting, confounding, and eluding them. I observe among you some lines of an institution which in its original might have been tolerable; but these half erased, and the rest wholly blurred and blotted by corruptions. It doth not appear from all you have said how any one virtue is required towards the procurement of any one station among you; much less that men are ennobled on account of their virtue, that priests are advanced for their piety or learning, soldiers for their conduct or valor, judges for their integrity, senators for the love of their country, or counselors for their wisdom. As for yourself," continued the King, "who have spent the greatest part of your life in traveling, I am well disposed to hope you may hitherto have escaped many vices of your country. But by what I have gathered from your own relation, and the answers I have with much pains wringed and extorted from you, I cannot but conclude the bulk of your natives to be the most pernicious race of little odious vermin that nature ever suffered to crawl upon the surface of the earth."

CHAPTER 7. *The Author's love of his country. He makes a proposal of much advantage to the King; which is rejected. The King's great ignorance in politics. The learning of that country very imperfect and confined. Their laws, and military affairs, and parties in the State.*

Nothing but an extreme love of truth could have hindered me from concealing this part of my story. It was in vain to discover my resentments, which

---

6. Medicines to stimulate the heart, or, equally commonly, liqueurs.

were always turned into ridicule: and I was forced to rest with patience while my noble and most beloved country was so injuriously treated. I am heartily sorry as any of my readers can possibly be that such an occasion was given, but this prince happened to be so curious and inquisitive upon every particular that it could not consist either with gratitude or good manners to refuse giving him what satisfaction I was able. Yet thus much I may be allowed to say in my own vindication: that I artfully eluded many of his questions, and gave to every point a more favorable turn by many degrees than the strictness of truth would allow. For I have always borne that laudable partiality to my own country, which Dionysius Halicarnassensis[7] with so much justice recommends to an historian. I would hide the frailties and deformities of my political mother, and place her virtues and beauties in the most advantageous light. This was my sincere endeavor in those many discourses I had with that mighty monarch, although it unfortunately failed of success.

But great allowances should be given to a King who lives wholly secluded from the rest of the world, and must therefore be altogether unacquainted with the manners and customs that most prevail in other nations: the want of which knowledge will ever produce many *prejudices*, and a certain *narrowness of thinking*, from which we and the politer countries of Europe are wholly exempted. And it would be hard indeed if so remote a prince's notions of virtue and vice were to be offered as a standard for all mankind.

To confirm what I have now said, and further to show the miserable effects of a *confined education*, I shall here insert a passage which will hardly obtain belief. In hopes to ingratiate myself farther into his Majesty's favor, I told him of an invention discovered between three and four hundred years ago, to make a certain powder, into an heap of which the smallest spark of fire falling would kindle the whole in a moment, although it were as big as a mountain, and make it all fly up in the air together, with a noise and agitation greater than thunder. That a proper quantity of this powder rammed into an hollow tube of brass or iron, according to its bigness, would drive a ball of iron or lead with such violence and speed as nothing was able to sustain its force. That the largest balls thus discharged would not only destroy whole ranks of an army at once, but batter the strongest walls to the ground; sink down ships with a thousand men in each, to the bottom of the sea; and, when linked together by a chain, would cut through masts and rigging; divide hundreds of bodies in the middle, and lay all waste before them. That we often put this powder into large hollow balls of iron, and discharged them by an engine into some city we were besieging; which would rip up the pavements, tear the houses to pieces, burst and throw splinters on every side, dashing out the brains of all who came near. That I knew the ingredients very well, which were cheap and common; I understood the manner of compounding them, and could direct his workmen how to make those tubes of a size proportionable to all other things in his Majesty's kingdom, and the largest need not be above two hundred foot long; twenty or thirty of which tubes, charged with the proper quantity of powder and balls, would batter down the walls of the strongest town in his dominions in a few hours; or destroy the whole metropolis, if ever it should pretend to dispute his absolute commands. This I humbly offered to his Majesty as a small tribute of

---

7. A Greek rhetorician and historian, who flourished ca. 25 B.C.E. His history of Rome was written to reconcile the Greeks to their Roman masters.

acknowledgement in return of so many marks that I had received of his royal favor and protection.

The King was struck with horror at the description I had given of those terrible engines and the proposal I had made. He was amazed how so impotent and groveling an insect as I (these were his expressions) could entertain such inhuman ideas, and in so familiar a manner as to appear wholly unmoved at all the scenes of blood and desolation which I had painted as the common effects of those destructive machines; whereof he said some evil genius, enemy to mankind, must have been the first contriver. As for himself, he protested that although few things delighted him so much as new discoveries in art or in nature, yet he would rather lose half his kingdom than be privy to such a secret, which he commanded me, as I valued my life, never to mention any more.

A strange effect of *narrow principles* and *short views!* that a prince possessed of every quality which procures veneration, love, and esteem; of strong parts, great wisdom, and profound learning; endued with admirable talents for government, and almost adored by his subjects; should from a *nice, unnecessary scruple,* whereof in Europe we can have no conception, let slip an opportunity put into his hands that would have made him absolute master of the lives, the liberties, and the fortunes of his people. Neither do I say this with the least intention to detract from the many virtues of that excellent King, whose character I am sensible will on this account be very much lessened in the opinion of an English reader: but I take this defect among them to have risen from their ignorance; they not having hitherto reduced politics into a science, as the more acute wits of Europe have done. For I remember very well, in a discourse one day with the King, when I happened to say there were several thousand books among us written upon the art of government, it gave him (directly contrary to my intention) a very mean opinion of our understandings. He professed both to abominate and despise all *mystery, refinement, and intrigue,* either in a prince or a minister. He could not tell what I meant by *secrets of state,* where an enemy or some rival nation were not in the case. He confined the knowledge of governing within very *narrow bounds:* to common sense and reason, to justice and lenity, to the speedy determination of civil and criminal causes, with some other obvious topics which are not worth considering. And he gave it for his opinion that whoever could make two ears of corn or two blades of grass to grow upon a spot of ground where only one grew before would deserve better of mankind and do more essential service to his country than the whole race of politicians[8] put together.

The learning of this people is very defective, consisting only in morality, history, poetry, and mathematics; wherein they must be allowed to excel. But the last of these is wholly applied to what may be useful in life, to the improvement of agriculture and all mechanical arts; so that among us it would be little esteemed. And as to ideas, entities, abstractions, and transcendentals,[9] I could never drive the least conception into their heads.

No law of that country must exceed in words the number of letters in their alphabet, which consists only in two and twenty. But indeed few of them extend even to that length. They are expressed in the most plain and simple

---

8. By *politicians,* Swift means something like our modern political scientists or theorists.

9. In Swift's time, *transcendental* was practically synonymous with *metaphysical.*

terms, wherein those people are not mercurial enough to discover above one interpretation. And to write a comment upon any law is a capital crime. As to the decision of civil causes, or proceedings against criminals, their precedents are so few that they have little reason to boast of any extraordinary skill in either.

They have had the art of printing as well as the Chinese, time out of mind. But their libraries are not very large; for that of the King's, which is reckoned the biggest, doth not amount to above a thousand volumes, placed in a gallery of twelve hundred foot long, from whence I had liberty to borrow what books I pleased. The Queen's joiner had contrived in one of the Glumdalclitch's rooms a kind of wooden machine five and twenty foot high, formed like a standing ladder; the steps were each fifty foot long. It was indeed a movable pair of stairs, the lowest end placed at ten foot distance from the wall of the chamber. The book I had a mind to read was put up leaning against the wall. I first mounted to the upper step of the ladder, and turning my face towards the book began at the top of the page, and so walking to the right and left about eight or ten paces according to the length of the lines, till I had gotten a little below the level of mine eyes, and then descending gradually till I came to the bottom: after which I mounted again, and began the other page in the same manner, and so turned over the leaf, which I could easily do with both my hands, for it was as thick and stiff as a pasteboard, and in the largest folios not above eighteen or twenty foot long.

Their style is clear, masculine, and smooth, but not florid; for they avoid nothing more than multiplying unnecessary words or using various expressions. I have perused many of their books, especially those in history and morality. Among the rest, I was much diverted with a little old treatise, which always lay in Glumdalclitch's bedchamber, and belonged to her governess, a grave elderly gentlewoman, who dealt in writings of morality and devotion. The book treats of the weakness of human kind, and is in little esteem, except among the women and the vulgar. However, I was curious to see what an author of that country could say upon such a subject. This writer went through all the usual topics of European moralists: showing how diminutive, contemptible, and helpless an animal was man in his own nature; how unable to defend himself from the inclemencies of the air, or the fury of wild beasts; how much he was excelled by one creature in strength, by another in speed, by a third in foresight, by a fourth in industry. He added that nature was degenerated in these latter declining ages of the world, and could now produce only small abortive births in comparison of those in ancient times. He said it was very reasonable to think, not only that the species of men were originally much larger, but also that there must have been giants in former ages; which, as it is asserted by history and tradition, so it hath been confirmed by huge bones and skulls casually dug up in several parts of the kingdom, far exceeding the common dwindled race of man in our days. He argued that the very laws of nature absolutely required we should have been made in the beginning of a size more large and robust, not so liable to destruction from every little accident of a tile falling from a house, or a stone cast from the hand of a boy, or of being drowned in a little brook. From this way of reasoning, the author drew several moral applications useful in the conduct of life, but needless here to repeat. For my own part, I could not avoid reflecting how universally this talent was spread, of drawing lectures in morality, or indeed rather matter of discontent and repining, from the quarrels we raise with nature. And I believe, upon a strict inquiry, those quarrels might be shown as ill grounded among us as they are among that people.

As to their military affairs, they boast that the King's army consists of an hundred and seventy-six thousand foot and thirty-two thousand horse: if that may be called an army which is made up of tradesmen in the several cities, and farmers in the country, whose commanders are only the nobility and gentry, without pay or reward. They are indeed perfect enough in their exercises, and under very good discipline, wherein I saw no great merit; for how should it be otherwise, where every farmer is under the command of his own landlord, and every citizen under that of the principal men in his own city, chosen after the manner of Venice by ballot?

I have often seen the militia of Lorbrulgrud drawn out to exercise in a great field near the city, of twenty miles square. They were in all not above twenty-five thousand foot, and six thousand horse; but it was impossible for me to compute their number, considering the space of ground they took up. A cavalier mounted on a large steed might be about an hundred foot high. I have seen this whole body of horse, upon a word of command, draw their swords at once, and brandish them in the air. Imagination can figure nothing so grand, so surprising, and so astonishing. It looked as if ten thousand flashes of lightning were darting at the same time from every quarter of the sky.

I was curious to know how this prince, to whose dominions there is no access from any other country, came to think of armies, or to teach his people the practice of military discipline. But I was soon informed, both by conversation and reading their histories. For in the course of many ages they have been troubled with the same disease to which the whole race of mankind is subject: the nobility often contending for power, the people for liberty, and the King for absolute dominion. All which, however happily tempered by the laws of the kingdom, have been sometimes violated by each of the three parties, and have more than once occasioned civil wars, the last whereof was happily put an end to by this prince's grandfather in a general composition;[1] and the militia, then settled with common consent, hath been ever since kept in the strictest duty.

CHAPTER 8. *The King and Queen make a progress to the frontiers. The Author attends them. The manner in which he leaves the country very particularly related. He returns to England.*

I had always a strong impulse that I should some time recover my liberty, though it were impossible to conjecture by what means, or to form any project with the least hope of succeeding. The ship in which I sailed was the first ever known to be driven within sight of that coast; and the King had given strict orders that if at any time another appeared, it should be taken ashore, and with all its crew and passengers brought in a tumbrel[2] to Lorbrulgrud. He was strongly bent to get me a woman of my own size, by whom I might propagate the breed: but I think I should rather have died than undergone the disgrace of leaving a posterity to be kept in cages like tame

1. A political settlement based on general agreement of all parties.

2. A farm wagon.

canary birds, and perhaps in time sold about the kingdom to persons of quality for curiosities. I was indeed treated with much kindness: I was the favorite of a great King and Queen, and the delight of the whole Court, but it was upon such a foot as ill became the dignity of human kind. I could never forget those domestic pledges I had left behind me. I wanted to be among people with whom I could converse upon even terms, and walk about the streets and fields without fear of being trod to death like a frog or a young puppy. But my deliverance came sooner than I expected, and in a manner not very common; the whole story and circumstances of which I shall faithfully relate.

I had now been two years in this country; and about the beginning of the third, Glumdalclitch and I attended the King and Queen in progress to the south coast of the kingdom. I was carried as usual in my traveling box, which, as I have already described, was a very convenient closet of twelve foot wide. I had ordered a hammock to be fixed by silken ropes from the four corners at the top, to break the jolts when a servant carried me before him on horseback, as I sometimes desired; and would often sleep in my hammock while we were upon the road. On the roof of my closet, set not directly over the middle of the hammock, I ordered the joiner to cut out a hole of a foot square to give me air in hot weather as I slept, which hole I shut at pleasure with a board that drew backwards and forwards through a groove.

When we came to our journey's end, the King thought proper to pass a few days at a palace he hath near Flanflasnic, a city within eighteen English miles of the seaside. Glumdalclitch and I were much fatigued; I had gotten a small cold, but the poor girl was so ill as to be confined to her chamber. I longed to see the ocean, which must be the only scene of my escape, if ever it should happen. I pretended to be worse than I really was, and desired leave to take the fresh air of the sea with a page whom I was very fond of, and who had sometimes been trusted with me. I shall never forget with what unwillingness Glumdalclitch consented, nor the strict charge she gave the page to be careful of me, bursting at the same time into a flood of tears, as if she had some foreboding of what was to happen. The boy took me out in my box about half an hour's walk from the palace, towards the rocks on the seashore. I ordered him to set me down, and lifting up one of my sashes, cast many a wistful melancholy look towards the sea. I found myself not very well, and told the page that I had a mind to take a nap in my hammock, which I hoped would do me good. I got in, and the boy shut the window close down, to keep out the cold. I soon fell asleep: and all I can conjecture is that while I slept, the page, thinking no danger could happen, went among the rocks to look for birds' eggs; having before observed him from my window searching about, and picking up one or two in the clefts. Be that as it will, I found myself suddenly awaked with a violent pull upon the ring which was fastened at the top of my box for the conveniency of carriage. I felt my box raised very high in the air, and then borne forward with prodigious speed. The first jolt had like to have shaken me out of my hammock, but afterwards the motion was easy enough. I called out several times as loud as I could raise my voice, but all to no purpose. I looked towards my windows, and could see nothing but the clouds and sky. I heard a noise just over my head like the clapping of wings, and then began to perceive the woeful condition I was in; that some eagle had got the ring of my box in his beak, with an intent to let it fall on a rock, like a tortoise in a shell, and then pick out my body and devour it. For the sagacity and smell of this bird enable him to discover his quarry at a great distance, although better concealed than I could be within a two-inch board.

In a little time I observed the noise and flutter of wings to increase very fast, and my box was tossed up and down like a signpost in a windy day. I heard several bangs or buffets, as I thought, given to the eagle (for such I am certain it must have been that held the ring of my box in his beak), and then all on a sudden felt myself falling perpendicularly down for above a minute, but with such incredible swiftness that I almost lost my breath. My fall was topped by a terrible squash, that sounded louder to mine ears than the cataract of Niagara; after which I was quite in the dark for another minute, and then my box began to rise so high that I could see light from the tops of my windows. I now perceived that I was fallen into the sea. My box, by the weight of my body, the goods that were in, and the broad plates of iron fixed for strength at the four corners of the top and bottom, floated above five foot deep in water. I did then and do now suppose that the eagle which flew away with my box was pursued by two or three others, and forced to let me drop while he was defending himself against the rest, who hoped to share in the prey. The plates of iron fastened at the bottom of the box (for those were the strongest) preserved the balance while it fell, and hindered it from being broken on the surface of the water. Every joint of it was well grooved, and the door did not move on hinges, but up and down like a sash; which kept my closet so tight that very little water came in. I got with much difficulty out of my hammock, having first ventured to draw back the slip-board on the roof already mentioned, contrived on purpose to let in air, for want of which I found myself almost stifled.

How often did I then wish myself with my dear Glumdalclitch, from whom one single hour had so far divided me! And I may say with truth that in the midst of my own misfortune, I could not forbear lamenting my poor nurse, the grief she would suffer for my loss, the displeasure of the Queen, and the ruin of her fortune. Perhaps many travelers have not been under greater difficulties and distress than I was at this juncture, expecting every moment to see my box dashed in pieces, or at least overset by the first violent blast or a rising wave. A breach in one single pane of glass would have been immediate death, nor could anything have preserved the windows but the strong lattice wires placed on the outside against accidents in traveling. I saw the water ooze in at several crannies, although the leaks were not considerable, and I endeavored to stop them as well as I could. I was not able to lift up the roof of my closet, which otherwise I certainly should have done, and sat on the top of it, where I might at least preserve myself from being shut up, as I may call it, in the hold. Or, if I escaped these dangers for a day or two, what could I expect but a miserable death of cold and hunger! I was four hours under these circumstances, expecting and indeed wishing every moment to be my last.

I have already told the reader that there were two strong staples fixed upon that side of my box which had no window and into which the servant, who used to carry me on horseback, would put a leathern belt, and buckle it about his waist. Being in this disconsolate state, I heard, or at least thought I heard, some kind of grating noise on that side of my box where the staples were fixed; and soon after I began to fancy that the box was pulled or towed along in the sea; for I now and then felt a sort of tugging, which made the waves rise near the tops of my windows, leaving me almost in the dark. This gave me some faint hopes of relief, although I was not able to imagine how it could be brought about. I ventured to unscrew one of my chairs, which were always fastened to the floor; and having made a hard shift to screw it down again directly under the slipping-board that I had lately opened, I mounted on the chair, and putting my mouth as near as I could to the hole, I called for help in a loud voice, and in all the languages I understood. I then fastened my handkerchief to a stick I usually carried, and thrusting it up the hole, waved it several times in the air, that if any boat or ship were near, the seamen might conjecture some unhappy mortal to be shut up in the box.

I found no effect from all I could do, but plainly perceived my closet to be moved along; and in the space of an hour or better, that side of the box where the staples were, and had no window, struck against something that was hard. I apprehended it to be a rock, and found myself tossed more than ever. I plainly heard a noise upon the cover of my closet, like that of a cable, and the grating of it as it passed through the ring. I then found myself hoisted up by degrees at least three foot higher than I was before. Whereupon I again thrust up my stick and handkerchief, calling for help till I was almost hoarse. In return to which, I heard a great shout repeated three times, giving me such transports of joy as are not to be conceived but by those who feel them. I now heard a trampling over my head, and somebody calling through the hole with a loud voice in the English tongue: "If there be anybody below, let them speak." I answered, I was an Englishman, drawn by ill fortune into the greatest calamity that ever any creature underwent, and begged, by all that was moving, to be delivered out of the dungeon I was in. The voice replied, I was safe, for my box was fastened to their ship; and the carpenter should immediately come and saw an hole in the cover, large enough to pull me out. I answered, that was needless and would take up too much time, for there was no more to be done but let one of the crew put his finger into the ring, and take the box out of the sea into the ship, and so into the captain's cabin. Some of them, upon hearing me talk so wildly, thought I was mad; others laughed; for indeed it never came into my head that I was now got among people of my own stature and strength. The carpenter came, and in a few minutes sawed a passage about four foot square; then let down a small ladder, upon which I mounted, and from thence was taken into the ship in a very weak condition.

The sailors were all in amazement, and asked me a thousand questions, which I had no inclination to answer. I was equally confounded at the sight of so many pygmies, for such I took them to be, after having so long accustomed my eyes to the monstrous objects I had left. But the Captain, Mr. Thomas Wilcocks, an honest, worthy Shropshire man, observing I was ready to faint, took me into his cabin, gave me a cordial to comfort me, and made me turn in upon his own bed, advising me to take a little rest, of which I had great need. Before I went to sleep I gave him to understand that I had some valuable furniture in my box, too good to be lost, a fine hammock, an handsome field bed, two chairs, a table, and a cabinet; that my closet was hung on all sides, or rather quilted with silk and cotton; that if he would let one of the crew bring my closet into his cabin, I would open it before him and show him my goods. The Captain, hearing me utter these absurdities, concluded I was raving; however (I suppose to pacify me), he promised to give order as I desired, and going upon deck, sent some of his men down into my closet, from whence (as I afterwards found) they drew up all my goods and stripped off the quilting; but the chairs, cabinet, and bedstead, being screwed to the floor, were much damaged by the ignorance of the seamen, who tore them up by force. Then they knocked off some of the boards for the use of the ship; and when they had got all they had a mind for, let the hulk drop into the sea, which, by reason of many breaches made in the bottom and sides, sunk to rights.[3] And indeed I was glad not to have been a spectator of the havoc they made, because I am confident it would have sensibly touched me, by bringing former passages into my mind, which I had rather forget.

I slept some hours, but perpetually disturbed with dreams of the place I had left, and the dangers I had escaped. However, upon waking, I found myself much recovered. It was now about eight o'clock at night, and the Captain ordered supper immediately, thinking I had already fasted too long. He entertained me with great kindness, observing me not to look wildly, or talk inconsistently; and when we were left alone, desired I would give him a relation of my travels, and by what accident I came to be set adrift in that monstrous wooden chest. He said that about twelve o'clock at noon, as he was looking through his glass, he spied it at a distance, and thought it was a sail, which he had a mind to make,[4] being not much out of his course, in hopes of buying some biscuit, his own beginning to fall short. That, upon coming nearer, and finding his error, he sent out his longboat to discover what I was; that his men came back in a fright, swearing they had seen a swimming house. That he laughed at their folly, and went himself in the boat, ordering his men to take a strong cable along with them. That the weather being calm, he rowed round me several times, observed my windows, and the wire lattices that defended them. That he discovered two staples upon one side, which was all of boards, without any passage for light. He then commanded his men to row up to that side, and fastening a cable to one of the staples, ordered his men to tow my chest (as he called it) towards the ship. When it was there, he gave directions to fasten another cable to the ring fixed in the cover, and to raise up my chest with pulleys, which all the sailors were not able to do above two or three foot. He said they saw my stick and handkerchief thrust out of the hole, and concluded that some unhappy man must be shut up in the cavity. I asked whether he or the crew had seen any prodigious birds in the air about the time he first discovered me. To which he answered that, discoursing this matter with the sailors while I was asleep, one of them said he had observed three eagles flying towards the north, but remarked nothing of their being larger than the usual size (which I suppose must be imputed to the great height they were at), and he could not guess the reason of my question. I then asked the Captain how far he reckoned we might be from land; he said, by the best computation he could make, we were at least an hundred leagues. I assured him that he must be mistaken by almost half; for I had not left the country from whence I

---

3. At once; altogether.   4. Overtake.

came above two hours before I dropped into the sea. Whereupon he began again to think that my brain was disturbed, of which he gave me a hint, and advised me to go to bed in a cabin he had provided. I assured him I was well refreshed with his good entertainment and company, and as much in my senses as ever I was in my life. He then grew serious and desired to ask me freely whether I were not troubled in mind by the consciousness of some enormous crime, for which I was punished at the command of some prince, by exposing me in that chest, as great criminals in other countries have been forced to sea in a leaky vessel without provisions; for although he should be sorry to have taken so ill[5] a man into his ship, yet he would engage his word to set me safe on shore in the first port where we arrived. He added that his suspicions were much increased by some very absurd speeches I had delivered at first to the sailors, and afterwards to himself, in relation to my closet or chest, as well as by my odd looks and behavior while I was at supper.

I begged his patience to hear me tell my story, which I faithfully did from the last time I left England to the moment he first discovered me. And as truth always forceth its way into rational minds, so this honest, worthy gentleman, who had some tincture of learning, and very good sense, was immediately convinced of my candor and veracity. But further to confirm all I had said, I entreated him to give order that my cabinet should be brought, of which I kept the key in my pocket (for he had already informed me how the seamen disposed of my closet). I opened it in his presence and showed him the small collection of rarities I made in the country from whence I had been so strangely delivered. There was the comb I had contrived out of the stumps of the King's beard, and another of the same materials, but fixed into a paring of her Majesty's thumbnail, which served for the back. There was a collection of needles and pins from a foot to half a yard long; four wasp-stings, like joiners' tacks; some combings of the Queen's hair; a gold ring which one day she made me a present of in a most obliging manner, taking it from her little finger, and throwing it over my head like a collar. I desired the Captain would please to accept this ring in return for his civilities, which he absolutely refused. I showed him a corn that I had cut off with my own hand from a Maid of Honor's toe; it was about the bigness of a Kentish pippin, and grown so hard that, when I returned to England, I got it hollowed into a cup and set in silver. Lastly, I desired him to see the breeches I had then on, which were made of a mouse's skin.

I could force nothing on him but a footman's tooth, which I observed him to examine with great curiosity, and found he had a fancy for it. He received it with abundance of thanks, more than such a trifle could deserve. It was drawn by an unskillful surgeon in a mistake from one of Glumdalclitch's men, who was afflicted with the toothache; but it was as sound as any in his head. I got it cleaned, and put it into my cabinet. It was about a foot long, and four inches in diameter.

The Captain was very well satisfied with this plain relation I had given him, and said he hoped when we returned to England I would oblige the world by putting it in paper and making it public. My answer was that I thought we were already overstocked with books of travels; that nothing could now pass which was not extraordinary; wherein I doubted some authors less consulted truth than their own vanity or interest, or the diversion

5. Evil.

of ignorant readers. That my story could contain little besides common events, without those ornamental descriptions of strange plants, trees, birds, and other animals, or the barbarous customs and idolatry of savage people, with which most writers abound. However, I thanked him for his good opinion, and promised to take the matter into my thoughts.

He said he wondered at one thing very much, which was to hear me speak so loud, asking me whether the King or Queen of that country were thick of hearing. I told him it was what I had been used to for above two years past, and that I admired[6] as much at the voices of him and his men, who seemed to me only to whisper, and yet I could hear them well enough. But, when I spoke in that country, it was like a man talking in the street to another looking out from the top of a steeple, unless when I was placed on a table, or held in any person's hand. I told him I had likewise observed another thing: that when I first got into the ship, and the sailors stood all about me, I thought they were the most little contemptible creatures I had ever beheld. For indeed while I was in that prince's country, I could never endure to look in a glass after my eyes had been accustomed to such prodigious objects, because the comparison gave me so despicable a conceit[7] of myself. The Captain said that while we were at supper he observed me to look at everything with a sort of wonder, and that I often seemed hardly able to contain my laughter; which he knew not well how to take, but imputed it to some disorder in my brain. I answered, it was very true; and I wondered how I could forbear, when I saw his dishes of the size of a silver threepence, a leg of pork hardly a mouthful, a cup not so big as a nutshell; and so I went on, describing the rest of his household stuff and provisions after the same manner. For, although the Queen had ordered a little equipage of all things necessary for me while I was in her service, yet my ideas were wholly taken up with what I saw on every side of me, and I winked at my own littleness, as people do at their own faults. The Captain understood my raillery very well, and merrily replied with the old English proverb, that he doubted[8] my eyes were bigger than my belly, for he did not observe my stomach so good, although I had fasted all day; and continuing in his mirth, protested he would have gladly given an hundred pounds to have seen my closet in the eagle's bill, and afterwards in its fall from so great an height into the sea; which would certainly have been a most astonishing object, worthy to have the description of it transmitted to future ages: and the comparison of Phaeton[9] was so obvious, that he could not forbear applying it, although I did not much admire the conceit.

The Captain having been at Tonquin,[1] was in his return to England driven northeastward to the latitude of 44 degrees, and of longitude 143. But meeting a trade wind two days after I came on board him, we sailed southward a long time, and coasting New Holland[2] kept our course west-southwest, and then south-southwest till we doubled the Cape of Good Hope. Our voyage was very prosperous, but I shall not trouble the reader with a journal of it. The Captain called in at one or two ports, and sent in his longboat for provisions and fresh water; but I never went out of the ship till we came into

---

6. Wondered.
7. Notion.
8. Feared.
9. Son of Helios, the sun god, whose unsuccessful attempt to drive his father's chariot led to his

death, when he lost control and was hurled by Zeus from the sky, falling into the river Eridanus, where he drowned.
1. Tonkin, now in Vietnam.
2. Australia.

the Downs, which was on the third day of June, 1706, about nine months after my escape. I offered to leave my goods in security for payment of my freight; but the Captain protested he would not receive one farthing. We took kind leave of each other, and I made him promise he would come to see me at my house in Redriff. I hired a horse and guide for five shillings, which I borrowed of the Captain.

As I was on the road, observing the littleness of the houses, the trees, the cattle, and the people, I began to think myself in Lilliput. I was afraid of trampling on every traveler I met, and often called aloud to have them stand out of the way, so that I had like to have gotten one or two broken heads for my impertinence.

When I came to my own house, for which I was forced to inquire, one of the servants opening the door, I bent down to go in (like a goose under a gate) for fear of striking my head. My wife ran out to embrace me, but I stooped lower than her knees, thinking she could otherwise never be able to reach my mouth. My daughter kneeled to ask my blessing, but I could not see her till she arose, having been so long used to stand with my head and eyes erect to above sixty foot; and then I went to take her up with one hand by the waist. I looked down upon the servants and one or two friends who were in the house, as if they had been pygmies and I a giant. I told my wife she had been too thrifty; for I found she had starved herself and her daughter to nothing. In short, I behaved myself so unaccountably that they were all of the Captain's opinion when he first saw me, and concluded I had lost my wits. This I mention as an instance of the great power of habit and prejudice.

In a little time I and my family and friends came to a right understanding; but my wife protested I should never go to sea any more, although my evil destiny so ordered that she had not power to hinder me; as the reader may know hereafter. In the meantime I here conclude the second part of my unfortunate voyages.

From *Part 3. A Voyage to Laputa, Balnibarbi, Glubbdubdrib, Luggnagg, and Japan*

* * *

[THE FLYING ISLAND OF LAPUTA][3]

CHAPTER 2. *The humors and dispositions of the Laputans described. An account of their learning. Of the King and his court. The author's reception there. The inhabitants subject to fears and disquietudes. An account of the women.*

At my alighting I was surrounded by a crowd of people, but those who stood nearest seemed to be of better quality. They beheld me with all the marks and circumstances of wonder; neither indeed was I much in their debt, having never till then seen a race of mortals so singular in their shapes, habits, and countenances. Their heads were all reclined to the right, or the

---

3. In the first chapter of part 3 Gulliver starts on his third voyage, but is captured by pirates and set adrift. Just as he is about to despair, a vast flying island appears in the sky, and the inhabitants draw him up with pulleys.

left; one of their eyes turned inward, and the other directly up to the zenith. Their outward garments were adorned with the figures of suns, moons, and stars, interwoven with those of fiddles, flutes, harps, trumpets, guitars, harpsichords, and many more instruments of music, unknown to us in Europe.[4] I observed here and there many in the habits of servants, with a blown bladder fastened like a flail to the end of a short stick, which they carried in their hands. In each bladder was a small quantity of dried pease or little pebbles (as I was afterwards informed). With these bladders they now and then flapped the mouths and ears of those who stood near them, of which practice I could not then conceive the meaning. It seems, the minds of these people are so taken up with intense speculations, that they neither can speak, or attend to the discourses of others, without being roused by some external taction[5] upon the organs of speech and hearing; for which reason those persons who are able to afford it always keep a flapper (the original is *climenole*) in their family, as one of their domestics; nor ever walk abroad or make visits without him. And the business of this officer is, when two or more persons are in company, gently to strike with his bladder the mouth of him who is to speak, and the right ear of him or them to whom the speaker addresseth himself. This flapper is likewise employed diligently to attend his master in his walks, and upon occasion to give him a soft flap on his eyes, because he is always so wrapped up in cogitation, that he is in manifest danger of falling down every precipice, and bouncing his head against every post; and in the streets, of jostling others, or being jostled himself into the kennel.[6]

It was necessary to give the reader this information, without which he would be at the same loss with me, to understand the proceedings of these people, as they conducted me up the stairs to the top of the island, and from thence to the royal palace. While we were ascending, they forgot several times what they were about, and left me to myself, till their memories were again roused by their flappers; for they appeared altogether unmoved by the sight of my foreign habit and countenance, and by the shouts of the vulgar, whose thoughts and minds were more disengaged.

At last we entered the palace, and proceeded into the chamber of presence; where I saw the King seated on his throne, attended on each side by persons of prime quality. Before the throne was a large table filled with globes and spheres, and mathematical instruments of all kinds. His Majesty took not the least notice of us, although our entrance was not without sufficient noise, by the concourse of all persons belonging to the court. But he was then deep in a problem, and we attended at least an hour before he could solve it. There stood by him on each side a young page, with flaps in their hands, and when they saw he was at leisure, one of them gently struck his mouth, and the other his right ear; at which he started like one awaked on the sudden, and looking towards me, and the company I was in, recollected the occasion of our coming, whereof he had been informed before. He spoke some words, whereupon immediately a young man with a flap came up to my side, and flapped me gently on the right ear; but I made signs as well as I could, that

4. The Laputans represent contemporary speculation, deplored by Swift, about abstract theories of science, mathematics, and music. Both the Royal Society and Sir Isaac Newton took an interest in the mathematical basis of music.
5. Touch.
6. Gutter.

I had no occasion for such an instrument; which as I afterwards found gave his Majesty and the whole court a very mean opinion of my understanding. The King, as far as I could conjecture, asked me several questions, and I addressed myself to him in all the languages I had. When it was found that I could neither understand nor be understood, I was conducted by his order to an apartment in his palace (this prince being distinguished above all his predecessors for his hospitality to strangers),[7] where two servants were appointed to attend me. My dinner was brought, and four persons of quality, whom I remembered to have seen very near the King's person, did me the honor to dine with me. We had two courses, of three dishes each. In the first course there was a shoulder of mutton, cut into an equilateral triangle; a piece of beef into a rhomboid; and a pudding into a cycloid. The second course was two ducks, trussed up into the form of fiddles; sausages and pudding resembling flutes and hautboys,[8] and a breast of veal in the shape of a harp. The servants cut our bread into cones, cylinders, parallelograms, and several other mathematical figures.

While we were at dinner, I made bold to ask the names of several things in their language, and those noble persons, by the assistance of their flappers, delighted to give me answers, hoping to raise my admiration of their great abilities, if I could be brought to converse with them. I was soon able to call for bread and drink, or whatever else I wanted.

After dinner my company withdrew, and a person was sent to me by the King's order, attended by a flapper. He brought with him pen, ink, and paper, and three or four books; giving me to understand by signs, that he was sent to teach me the language. We sat together four hours, in which time I wrote down a great number of words in columns, with the translations over against them. I likewise made a shift to learn several short sentences. For my tutor would order one of my servants to fetch something, to turn about, to make a bow, to sit, or stand, or walk, and the like. Then I took down the sentence in writing. He showed me also in one of his books the figures of the sun, moon, and stars, the zodiac, the tropics and polar circles, together with the denominations of many figures of planes and solids. He gave me the names and descriptions of all the musical instruments, and the general terms of art in playing on each of them. After he had left me, I placed all my words with their interpretations in alphabetical order. And thus in a few days, by the help of a very faithful memory, I got some insight into their language.

The word, which I interpret the *Flying* or *Floating Island*, is in the original *Laputa*; whereof I could never learn the true etymology. *Lap* in the old obsolete language signifieth *high*, and *untuh* a *governor*; from which they say by corruption was derived *Laputa*, from *Lapuntuh*. But I do not approve of this derivation, which seems to be a little strained. I ventured to offer to the learned among them a conjecture of my own, that *Laputa* was *quasi Lap outed*; *Lap* signifying properly the dancing of the sunbeams in the sea, and *outed* a wing, which however I shall not obtrude, but submit to the judicious reader.[9]

Those to whom the King had entrusted me, observing how ill I was clad, ordered a tailor to come next morning, and take my measure for a suit of

---

7. George I, a patron of music and science, had filled his court with Hanoverians when he came to England in 1714.

8. Oboes.

9. Gulliver overlooks a likelier etymology: Spanish *la puta,* "the whore."

clothes. This operator did his office after a different manner from those of his trade in Europe. He first took my altitude by a quadrant, and then, with rule and compasses, described the dimensions and outlines of my whole body; all which he entered upon paper, and in six days brought my clothes very ill made, and quite out of shape, by happening to mistake a figure in the calculation. But my comfort was, that I observed such accidents very frequent, and little regarded.

During my confinement for want of clothes, and by an indisposition that held me some days longer, I much enlarged my dictionary; and when I went next to court, was able to understand many things the King spoke, and to return him some kind of answers. His Majesty had given orders that the island should move northeast and by east, to the vertical point over Lagado, the metropolis of the whole kingdom, below upon the firm earth. It was about ninety leagues distant, and our voyage lasted four days and a half. I was not in the least sensible of the progressive motion made in the air by the island. On the second morning, about eleven o'clock, the King himself in person, attended by his nobility, courtiers, and officers, having prepared all their musical instruments, played on them for three hours without intermission, so that I was quite stunned with the noise; neither could I possibly guess the meaning, till my tutor informed me. He said, that the people of their island had their ears adapted to hear the music of the spheres, which always played at certain periods; and the court was now prepared to bear their part in whatever instrument they most excelled.

In our journey towards Lagado, the capital city, his Majesty ordered that the island should stop over certain towns and villages, from whence he might receive the petitions of his subjects. And to this purpose, several packthreads were let down with small weights at the bottom. On these packthreads the people strung their petitions, which mounted up directly like the scraps of paper fastened by schoolboys at the end of the string that holds their kite.[1] Sometimes we received wine and victuals from below, which were drawn up by pulleys.

The knowledge I had in mathematics gave me great assistance in acquiring their phraseology, which depended much upon that science and music; and in the latter I was not unskilled. Their ideas are perpetually conversant in lines and figures. If they would, for example, praise the beauty of a woman, or any other animal, they describe it by rhombs, circles, parallelograms, ellipses, and other geometrical terms; or else by words of art drawn from music, needless here to repeat. I observed in the King's kitchen all sorts of mathematical and musical instruments, after the figures of which they cut up the joints that were served to his Majesty's table.

Their houses are very ill built, the walls bevil, without one right angle in any apartment; and this defect ariseth from the contempt they bear for practical geometry; which they despise as vulgar and mechanic, those instructions they give being too refined for the intellectuals of their workmen; which occasions perpetual mistakes. And although they are dextrous enough upon a piece of paper, in the management of the rule, the pencil, and the divider, yet in the common actions and behavior of life I have not seen a more clumsy,

1. Petitioners, that is, might as well go fly a kite. Throughout this section Swift satirizes the "distance" of George I (who spent much of his time in Hanover) from his British subjects.

awkward, and unhandy people, nor so slow and perplexed in their conceptions upon all other subjects, except those of mathematics and music. They are very bad reasoners, and vehemently given to opposition, unless when they happen to be of the right opinion, which is seldom their case. Imagination, fancy, and invention, they are wholly strangers to, nor have any words in their language by which those ideas can be expressed; the whole compass of their thoughts and mind being shut up within the two forementioned sciences.

Most of them, and especially those who deal in the astronomical part, have great faith in judicial astrology, although they are ashamed to own it publicly. But what I chiefly admired,[2] and thought altogether unaccountable, was the strong disposition I observed in them towards news and politics; perpetually enquiring into public affairs, giving their judgments in matters of state; and passionately disputing every inch of a party opinion. I have indeed observed the same disposition among most of the mathematicians I have known in Europe; although I could never discover the least analogy between the two sciences; unless those people suppose, that because the smallest circle hath as many degrees as the largest, therefore the regulation and management of the world require no more abilities than the handling and turning of a globe. But I rather take this quality to spring from a very common infirmity of human nature, inclining us to be more curious and conceited in matters where we have least concern, and for which we are least adapted either by study or nature.

These people are under continual disquietudes, never enjoying a minute's peace of mind; and their disturbances proceed from causes which very little affect the rest of mortals. Their apprehensions arise from several changes they dread in the celestial bodies. For instance; that the earth, by the continual approaches of the sun towards it, must in course of time be absorbed or swallowed up. That the face of the sun will by degrees be encrusted with its own effluvia,[3] and give no more light to the world. That the earth very narrowly escaped a brush from the tail of the last comet, which would have infallibly reduced it to ashes; and that the next, which they have calculated for one and thirty years hence, will probably destroy us.[4] For, if in its perihelion it should approach within a certain degree of the sun (as by their calculations they have reason to dread), it will conceive a degree of heat ten thousand times more intense than that of red-hot glowing iron; and in its absence from the sun, carry a blazing tail ten hundred thousand and fourteen miles long; through which if the earth should pass at the distance of one hundred thousand miles from the nucleus, or main body of the comet, it must in its passage be set on fire, and reduced to ashes. That the sun daily spending its rays without any nutriment to supply them, will at last be wholly consumed and annihilated; which must be attended with the destruction of this earth, and of all the planets that receive their light from it.

They are so perpetually alarmed with the apprehensions of these and the like impending dangers, that they can neither sleep quietly in their beds, nor have any relish for the common pleasures or amusements of life. When they

2. Wondered at.
3. Sunspots.
4. Halley's comet, some astronomers had feared, might strike the earth on its next appearance (1758). All the disasters that disquiet the Laputans had occurred to English scientists as possible implications of Newtonian theory.

meet an acquaintance in the morning, the first question is about the sun's health, how he looked at his setting and rising, and what hopes they have to avoid the stroke of the approaching comet. This conversation they are apt to run into with the same temper that boys discover in delighting to hear terrible stories of sprites and hobgoblins, which they greedily listen to, and dare not go to bed for fear.

The women of the island have abundance of vivacity; they contemn their husbands, and are exceedingly fond of strangers, whereof there is always a considerable number from the continent below, attending at court, either upon affairs of the several towns and corporations, or their own particular occasions; but are much despised, because they want the same endowments. Among these the ladies choose their gallants: but the vexation is, that they act with too much ease and security; for the husband is always so rapt in speculation, that the mistress and lover may proceed to the greatest familiarities before his face, if he be but provided with paper and implements, and without his flapper at his side.

The wives and daughters lament their confinement to the island, although I think it the most delicious spot of ground in the world; and although they live here in the greatest plenty and magnificence, and are allowed to do whatever they please, they long to see the world, and take the diversions of the metropolis, which they are not allowed to do without a particular license from the King; and this is not easy to be obtained, because the people of quality have found by frequent experience, how hard it is to persuade their women to return from below. I was told that a great court lady, who had several children, is married to the prime minister, the richest subject in the kingdom, a very graceful person, extremely fond of her, and lives in the finest palace of the island, went down to Lagado, on the pretense of health, there hid herself for several months, till the King sent a warrant to search for her, and she was found in an obscure eating-house all in rags, having pawned her clothes to maintain an old deformed footman, who beat her every day, and in whose company she was taken much against her will. And although her husband received her with all possible kindness, and without the least reproach, she soon after contrived to steal down again with all her jewels, to the same gallant, and hath not been heard of since.

This may perhaps pass with the reader rather for an European or English story, than for one of a country so remote. But he may please to consider, that the caprices of womankind are not limited by any climate or nation; and that they are much more uniform than can be easily imagined.

In about a month's time I had made a tolerable proficiency in their language, and was able to answer most of the King's questions, when I had the honor to attend him. His Majesty discovered not the least curiosity to enquire into the laws, government, history, religion, or manners of the countries where I had been; but confined his questions to the state of mathematics, and received the account I gave him with great contempt and indifference, though often roused by his flapper on each side.[5]

5. In the omitted chapters, Gulliver visits countries that show the consequences of modern learning. After an account of the Flying Island, whose power of motion (derived from a giant magnet or lodestone) allows it to dominate the regions below, he descends to Balnibarbi, a once fertile land now ruined by the fanciful projects of impractical scientists. In the Grand Academy of Lagado he meets many professors who are contriving such perverse "improvements" as making clothes from cobwebs or breeding naked sheep. Then he visits the part of the academy devoted to speculative learning.

* * *

[THE ACADEMY OF LAGADO][6]
FROM CHAPTER 5.

The first professor I saw was in a very large room, with forty pupils about him. After salutation, observing me to look earnestly upon a frame, which took up the greatest part of both the length and breadth of the room, he said, perhaps I might wonder to see him employed in a project for improving speculative knowledge by practical and mechanical operations. But the world would soon be sensible[7] of its usefulness, and he flattered himself that a more noble, exalted thought never sprang in any other man's head. Everyone knew how laborious the usual method is of attaining to arts and sciences; whereas by his contrivance the most ignorant person at a reasonable charge, and with a little bodily labor, may write books in philosophy, poetry, politics, law, mathematics, and theology, without the least assistance from genius or

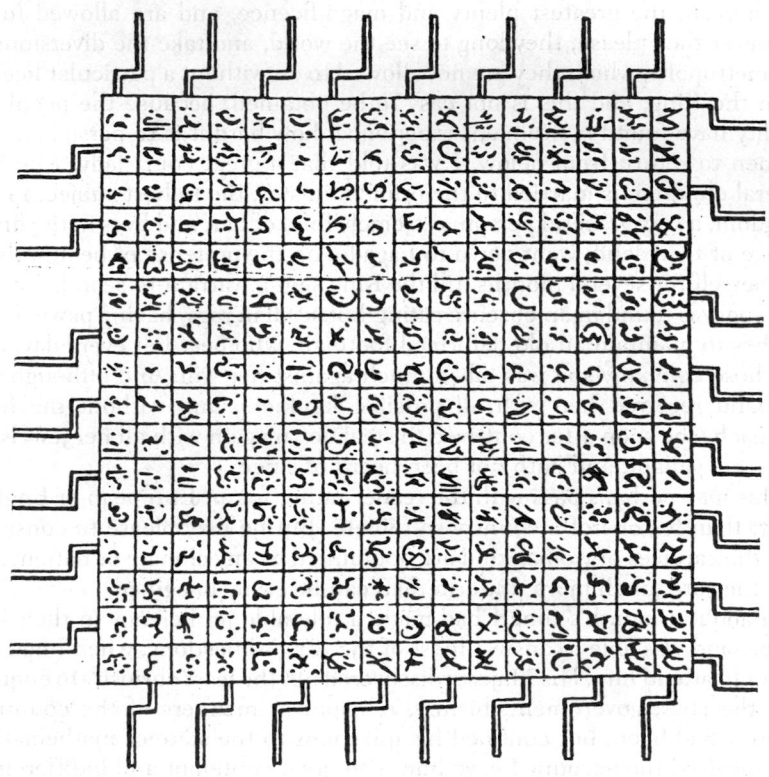

[A PRIMITIVE COMPUTER]

6. The Grand Academy of Lagado satirizes the Royal Society of London, an organization founded in 1662 to encourage the pursuit of scientific knowledge. Some of the projects described by Swift resemble the experiments or speculations of British scientists at the time.
7. Aware.

study. He then led me to the frame, about the sides whereof all his pupils stood in ranks. It was twenty foot square, placed in the middle of the room. The superficies[8] was composed of several bits of wood, about the bigness of a die, but some larger than others. They were all linked together by slender wires. These bits of wood were covered on every square with papers pasted on them; and on these papers were written all the words of their language in their several moods, tenses, and declensions, but without any order. The professor then desired me to observe, for he was going to set his engine at work. The pupils at his command took each of them hold of an iron handle, whereof there were forty fixed round the edges of the frame; and giving them a sudden turn, the whole disposition[9] of the words was entirely changed. He then commanded six and thirty of the lads to read the several lines softly as they appeared upon the frame; and where they found three or four words together that might make part of a sentence, they dictated to the four remaining boys who were scribes. This work was repeated three or four times, and at every turn the engine was so contrived that the words shifted into new places, as the square bits of wood moved upside down.

Six hours a day the young students were employed in this labor; and the professor showed me several volumes in large folio already collected, of broken sentences, which he intended to piece together, and out of those rich materials to give the world a complete body of all arts and sciences; which however might be still improved, and much expedited, if the public would raise a fund for making and employing five hundred such frames in Lagado, and oblige the managers to contribute in common their several[1] collections.

He assured me, that this invention had employed all his thoughts from his youth, that he had emptied the whole vocabulary into his frame, and made the strictest computation of the general proportion there is in books between the numbers of particles, nouns, and verbs, and other parts of speech.

I made my humblest acknowledgments to this illustrious person for his great communicativeness, and promised if ever I had the good fortune to return to my native country, that I would do him justice, as the sole inventor of this wonderful machine; the form and contrivance of which I desired leave to delineate upon paper as in the figure here annexed. I told him, although it were the custom of our learned in Europe to steal inventions from each other, who had thereby at least this advantage, that it became a controversy which was the right owner, yet I would take such caution, that he should have the honor entire without a rival.

We next went to the school of languages, where three professors sat in consultation upon improving that of their own country.[2]

The first project was to shorten discourse by cutting polysyllables into one, and leaving out verbs and participles, because in reality all things imaginable are but nouns.

The other was a scheme for entirely abolishing all words whatsoever; and this was urged as a great advantage in point of health as well as brevity. For it is plain, that every word we speak is in some degree a diminution of our

8. Surface.
9. Arrangement.
1. Separate.
2. Many contemporary scientists had proposed a

philosophical language that would eliminate the treacherous disparity between words and things and thus allow accurate scientific discourse.

lungs by corrosion, and consequently contributes to the shortening of our lives. An expedient was therefore offered, that since words are only names for *things*, it would be more convenient for all men to carry about them such *things* as were necessary to express the particular business they are to discourse on. And this invention would certainly have taken place, to the great ease as well as health of the subject, if the women in conjunction with the vulgar and illiterate had not threatened to raise a rebellion, unless they might be allowed the liberty to speak with their tongues, after the manner of their forefathers. Such constant irreconcilable enemies to science[3] are the common people. However, many of the most learned and wise adhere to the new scheme of expressing themselves by *things*, which hath only this inconvenience attending it, that if a man's business be very great, and of various kinds, he must be obliged in proportion to carry a greater bundle of *things* upon his back, unless he can afford one or two strong servants to attend him. I have often beheld two of those sages almost sinking under the weight of their packs, like pedlars among us, who when they met in the streets would lay down their loads, open their sacks, and hold conversation for an hour together, then put up their implements, help each other to resume their burdens, and take their leave.

But for short conversations a man may carry implements in his pockets and under his arms, enough to supply him, and in his house he cannot be at a loss; therefore the room where company meet who practice this art is full of all *things* ready at hand, requisite to furnish matter for this kind of artificial converse.[4]

Another great advantage proposed by this invention was that it would serve as an universal language to be understood in all civilized nations, whose goods and utensils are generally of the same kind, or nearly resembling, so that their uses might easily be comprehended. And thus, ambassadors would be qualified to treat with foreign princes or ministers of state to whose tongues they were utter strangers.

I was at the mathematical school, where the master taught his pupils after a method scarce imaginable to us in Europe. The proposition and demonstration were fairly written on a thin wafer, with ink composed of a cephalic tincture.[5] This the student was to swallow upon a fasting stomach, and for three days following eat nothing but bread and water. As the wafer digested, the tincture mounted to his brain, bearing the proposition along with it. But the success hath not hitherto been answerable, partly by some error in the *quantum* or composition, and partly by the perverseness of lads, to whom this bolus[6] is so nauseous that they generally steal aside, and discharge it upwards before it can operate; neither have they been yet persuaded to use so long an abstinence as the prescription requires.[7]

* * *

3. Knowledge.
4. The Royal Society had sponsored a collection intended to contain one specimen of every thing in the world.
5. A solution or dye directed toward the head.
6. A large pill. "*Quantum*": amount.
7. In the omitted chapters Gulliver hears projects

for improving politics and offers some of his own. He sails to Glubbdubdrib, the Island of Sorcerers, where he talks with the spirits of the dead; he learns that history is a pack of lies and that humanity has degenerated since ancient times. He is then received by the king of Luggnagg.

[THE STRULDBRUGGS]

CHAPTER 10. *The Luggnaggians commended. A particular description of the struldbruggs, with many conversations between the author and some eminent persons upon that subject.*

The Luggnaggians are a polite[8] and generous people, and although they are not without some share of that pride which is peculiar to all eastern countries, yet they show themselves courteous to strangers, especially such who are countenanced by the court. I had many acquaintance among persons of the best fashion, and being always attended by my interpreter, the conversation we had was not disagreeable.

One day in much good company, I was asked by a person of quality, whether I had seen any of their *struldbruggs* or *immortals*. I said I had not; and desired he would explain to me what he meant by such an appellation, applied to a mortal creature. He told me, that sometimes, although very rarely, a child happened to be born in a family with a red circular spot in the forehead, directly over the left eyebrow, which was an infallible mark that it should never die. The spot, as he described it, was about the compass of a silver threepence, but in the course of time grew larger, and changed its color; for at twelve years old it became green, so continued till five and twenty, then turned to a deep blue; at five and forty it grew coal black, and as large as an English shilling; but never admitted any farther alteration. He said these births were so rare, that he did not believe there could be above eleven hundred *struldbruggs* of both sexes in the whole kingdom, of which he computed about fifty in the metropolis, and among the rest a young girl born about three years ago. That these productions were not peculiar to any family, but a mere effect of chance; and the children of the *struldbruggs* themselves were equally mortal with the rest of the people.

I freely own myself to have been struck with inexpressible delight upon hearing this account: and the person who gave it me happening to understand the Balnibarbian language, which I spoke very well, I could not forbear breaking out into expressions perhaps a little too extravagant. I cried out as in a rapture: Happy nation, where every child hath at least a chance for being immortal! Happy people who enjoy so many living examples of ancient virtue, and have masters ready to instruct them in the wisdom of all former ages! But happiest beyond all comparison are those excellent *struldbruggs*, who being born exempt from that universal calamity of human nature, have their minds free and disengaged, without the weight and depression of spirits caused by the continual apprehension of death. I discovered my admiration that I had not observed any of these illustrious persons at court; the black spot on the forehead being so remarkable a distinction, that I could not have easily overlooked it; and it was impossible that his Majesty, a most judicious prince, should not provide himself with a good number of such wise and able counselors. Yet perhaps the virtue of those reverend sages was too strict for the corrupt and libertine manners of a court. And we often find by experience that young men are too opinionative[9] and volatile to be guided by the

---

8. Refined, cultivated. 9. Speculative, impractical.

sober dictates of their seniors. However, since the King was pleased to allow me access to his royal person, I was resolved upon the very first occasion to deliver my opinion to him on this matter freely, and at large by the help of my interpreter; and whether he would please to take my advice or no, yet in one thing I was determined, that his Majesty having frequently offered me an establishment in this country, I would with great thankfulness accept the favor, and pass my life here in the conversation of those superior beings the *struldbruggs,* if they would please to admit me.

The gentleman to whom I addressed my discourse, because (as I have already observed) he spoke the language of Balnibarbi, said to me with a sort of a smile, which usually ariseth from pity to the ignorant, that he was glad of any occasion to keep me among them, and desired my permission to explain to the company what I had spoke. He did so; and they talked together for some time in their own language, whereof I understood not a syllable, neither could I observe by their countenances what impression my discourse had made on them. After a short silence the same person told me, that his friends and mine (so he thought fit to express himself) were very much pleased with the judicious remarks I had made on the great happiness and advantages of immortal life; and they were desirous to know in a particular manner, what scheme of living I should have formed to myself, if it had fallen to my lot to have been born a *struldbrugg.*

I answered, it was easy to be eloquent on so copious and delightful a subject, especially to me who have been often apt to amuse myself with visions of what I should do if I were a king, a general, or a great lord; and upon this very case I had frequently run over the whole system how I should employ myself, and pass the time if I were sure to live forever.

That, if it had been my good fortune to come into the world a *struldbrugg,* as soon as I could discover my own happiness by understanding the difference between life and death, I would first resolve by all arts and methods whatsoever to procure myself riches: in the pursuit of which, by thrift and management, I might reasonably expect in about two hundred years to be the wealthiest man in the kingdom. In the second place, I would from my earliest youth apply myself to the study of arts and sciences, by which I should arrive in time to excel all others in learning. Lastly, I would carefully record every action and event of consequence that happened in the public, impartially draw the characters of the several successions of princes, and great ministers of state; with my own observations on every point. I would exactly set down the several changes in customs, languages, fashions of dress, diet and diversions. By all which acquirements, I should be a living treasury of knowledge and wisdom, and certainly become the oracle of the nation.

I would never marry after threescore, but live in an hospitable manner, yet still on the saving side. I would entertain myself in forming and directing the minds of hopeful young men, by convincing them from my own remembrance, experience and observation, fortified by numerous examples, of the usefulness of virtue in public and private life. But my choice and constant companions should be a set of my own immortal brotherhood, among whom I would elect a dozen from the most ancient down to my own contemporaries. Where any of these wanted fortunes, I would provide them with convenient lodges round my own estate, and have some of them always at my table, only mingling a few of the most valuable among you mortals, whom length of time would harden me to lose with little or no reluctance, and treat your posterity after the same manner; just as a man diverts himself with the annual succession of pinks and tulips in his garden, without regretting the loss of those which withered the preceding year.

These *struldbruggs* and I would mutually communicate our observations and memorials[1] through the course of time; remark the several gradations by which corruption steals into the world, and oppose it in every step, by giving perpetual warning and instruction to mankind; which, added to the strong influence of our own example, would probably prevent that continual degeneracy of human nature, so justly complained of in all ages.

Add to all this, the pleasure of seeing the various revolutions of states and empires; the changes in the lower and upper world;[2] ancient cities in ruins; and obscure villages become the seats of kings. Famous rivers lessening into shallow brooks; the ocean leaving one coast dry, and overwhelming another; the discovery of many countries yet unknown. Barbarity overrunning the politest nations, and the most barbarous becoming civilized. I should then see the discovery of the longitude, the perpetual motion, the universal medicine,[3] and many other great inventions brought to the utmost perfection.

What wonderful discoveries should we make in astronomy, by outliving and confirming our own predictions, by observing the progress and returns of comets, with the changes of motion in the sun, moon and stars.

I enlarged upon many other topics, which the natural desire of endless life and sublunary happiness could easily furnish me with. When I had ended, and the sum of my discourse had been interpreted as before to the rest of the company, there was a good deal of talk among them in the language of the country, not without some laughter at my expense. At last the same gentleman who had been my interpreter said, he was desired by the rest to set me right in a few mistakes, which I had fallen into through the common imbecility[4] of human nature, and upon that allowance was less answerable for them. That this breed of *struldbruggs* was peculiar to their country, for there were no such people either in Balnibarbi or Japan, where he had the honor to be ambassador from his Majesty, and found the natives in both those kingdoms very hard to believe that the fact was possible; and it appeared from my astonishment when he first mentioned the matter to me, that I received it as a thing wholly new, and scarcely to be credited. That in the two kingdoms above mentioned, where during his residence he had conversed very much, he observed long life to be the universal desire and wish of mankind. That whoever had one foot in the grave was sure to hold back the other as strongly as he could. That the oldest had still hopes of living one day longer, and looked on death as the greatest evil, from which nature always prompted him to retreat; only in this island of Luggnagg the appetite for living was not so eager, from the continual example of the *struldbruggs* before their eyes.

That the system of living contrived by me was unreasonable and unjust, because it supposed a perpetuity of youth, health, and vigor, which no man could be so foolish to hope, however extravagant he might be in his wishes.

1. Memories.
2. Earth and heaven; figuratively, common people and the ruling class. "Revolutions": cycles.
3. The *elixir vitae*, an alchemical formula to pre-

serve life forever, was considered by Swift an impossible dream, like a method for calculating longitude at sea, or a perpetual motion machine.
4. Weakness.

That the question therefore was not whether a man would choose to be always in the prime of youth, attended with prosperity and health; but how he would pass a perpetual life under all the usual disadvantages which old age brings along with it. For although few men will avow their desires of being immortal upon such hard conditions, yet in the two kingdoms before mentioned of Balnibarbi and Japan, he observed that every man desired to put off death for some time longer, let it approach ever so late; and he rarely heard of any man who died willingly, except he were incited by the extremity of grief or torture. And he appealed to me whether in those countries I had traveled, as well as my own, I had not observed the same general disposition.

After this preface he gave me a particular account of the *struldbruggs* among them. He said they commonly acted like mortals, till about thirty years old, after which by degrees they grew melancholy and dejected, increasing in both till they came to fourscore. This he learned from their own confession; for otherwise there not being above two or three of that species born in an age, they were too few to form a general observation by. When they came to fourscore years, which is reckoned the extremity of living in this country, they had not only all the follies and infirmities of other old men, but many more which arose from the dreadful prospect of never dying. They were not only opinionative, peevish, covetous, morose, vain, talkative; but uncapable of friendship, and dead to all natural affection, which never descended below their grandchildren. Envy and impotent desires are their prevailing passions. But those objects against which their envy seems principally directed, are the vices of the younger sort, and the deaths of the old. By reflecting on the former, they find themselves cut off from all possibility of pleasure; and whenever they see a funeral, they lament and repine that others are gone to an harbor of rest, to which they themselves never can hope to arrive. They have no remembrance of anything but what they learned and observed in their youth and middle age, and even that is very imperfect. And for the truth or particulars of any fact, it is safer to depend on common traditions than upon their best recollections. The least miserable among them appear to be those who turn to dotage, and entirely lose their memories; these meet with more pity and assistance, because they want[5] many bad qualities which abound in others.

If a *struldbrugg* happen to marry one of his own kind, the marriage is dissolved of course by the courtesy of the kingdom, as soon as the younger of the two comes to be fourscore. For the law thinks it a reasonable indulgence, that those who are condemned without any fault of their own to a perpetual continuance in the world, should not have their misery doubled by the load of a wife.

As soon as they have completed the term of eighty years, they are looked on as dead in law; their heirs immediately succeed to their estates, only a small pittance is reserved for their support; and the poor ones are maintained at the public charge. After that period they are held incapable of any employment of trust or profit; they cannot purchase land, or take leases, neither are they allowed to be witnesses in any cause, either civil or criminal, not even for the decision of meers[6] and bounds.

At ninety they lose their teeth and hair; they have at that age no distinction of taste, but eat and drink whatever they can get, without relish or appetite.

5. Lack.   6. Boundaries.

The diseases they were subject to still continue without increasing or diminishing. In talking they forget the common appellation of things, and the names of persons, even of those who are their nearest friends and relations. For the same reason they never can amuse themselves with reading, because their memory will not serve to carry them from the beginning of a sentence to the end, and by this defect they are deprived of the only entertainment whereof they might otherwise be capable.

The language of this country being always upon the flux, the *struldbruggs* of one age do not understand those of another; neither are they able after two hundred years to hold any conversation (farther than by a few general words) with their neighbors the mortals; and thus they lie under the disadvantage of living like foreigners in their own country.

This was the account given me of the *struldbruggs*, as near as I can remember. I afterwards saw five or six of different ages, the youngest not above two hundred years old, who were brought to me at several times by some of my friends; but although they were told that I was a great traveler, and had seen all the world, they had not the least curiosity to ask me a question; only desired I would give them *slumskudask*, or a token of remembrance; which is a modest way of begging, to avoid the law that strictly forbids it, because they are provided for by the public, although indeed with a very scanty allowance.

They are despised and hated by all sorts of people; when one of them is born, it is reckoned ominous, and their birth is recorded very particularly; so that you may know their age by consulting the registry, which however hath not been kept above a thousand years past, or at least hath been destroyed by time or public disturbances. But the usual way of computing how old they are, is by asking them what kings or great persons they can remember, and then consulting history; for infallibly the last prince in their mind did not begin his reign after they were fourscore years old.

They were the most mortifying sight I ever beheld; and the women more horrible than the men. Besides the usual deformities in extreme old age, they acquired an additional ghastliness in proportion to their number of years, which is not to be described; and among half a dozen I soon distinguished which was the oldest, although there were not above a century or two between them.

The reader will easily believe, that from what I had heard and seen, my keen appetite for perpetuity of life was much abated. I grew heartily ashamed of the pleasing visions I had formed; and thought no tyrant could invent a death into which I would not run with pleasure from such a life. The King heard of all that had passed between me and my friends upon this occasion, and rallied[7] me very pleasantly; wishing I would send a couple of *struldbruggs* to my own country, to arm our people against the fear of death; but this it seems is forbidden by the fundamental laws of the kingdom; or else I should have been well content with the trouble and expense of transporting them.

I could not but agree, that the laws of this kingdom relating to the *struldbruggs*, were founded upon the strongest reasons, and such as any other country would be under the necessity of enacting in the like circumstances. Otherwise, as avarice is the necessary consequent of old age, those immortals would in time become proprietors of the whole nation, and engross[8] the civil

7. Ridiculed.   8. Absorb, monopolize.

power; which, for want of abilities to manage, must end in the ruin of the public.[9]

* * *

Part 4. A Voyage to the Country of the Houyhnhnms[1]

CHAPTER 1. *The Author sets out as Captain of a ship. His men conspire against him, confine him a long time to his cabin, set him on shore in an unknown land. He travels up into the country. The Yahoos, a strange sort of animal, described. The Author meets two Houyhnhnms.*

I continued at home with my wife and children about five months in a very happy condition, if I could have learned the lesson of knowing when I was well. I left my poor wife big with child, and accepted an advantageous offer made me to be Captain of the *Adventure*, a stout merchantman of 350 tons; for I understood navigation well, and being grown weary of a surgeon's employment at sea, which however I could exercise upon occasion, I took a skillful young man of that calling, one Robert Purefoy, into my ship. We set sail from Portsmouth upon the 7th day of September, 1710; on the 14th we met with Captain Pocock of Bristol, at Tenariff,[2] who was going to the Bay of Campeachy[3] to cut logwood. On the 16th he was parted from us by a storm; I heard since my return that his ship foundered and none escaped, but one cabin boy. He was an honest man and a good sailor, but a little too positive in his own opinions, which was the cause of his destruction, as it hath been of several others. For if he had followed my advice, he might at this time have been safe at home with his family as well as myself.

I had several men died in my ship of calentures,[4] so that I was forced to get recruits out of Barbadoes and the Leeward Islands, where I touched by the direction of the merchants who employed me; which I had soon too much cause to repent, for I found afterwards that most of them had been buccaneers. I had fifty hands on board; and my orders were that I should trade with the Indians in the South Sea, and make what discoveries I could. These rogues whom I had picked up debauched my other men, and they all formed a conspiracy to seize the ship and secure me; which they did one morning, rushing into my cabin, and binding me hand and foot, threatening to throw me overboard, if I offered to stir. I told them I was their prisoner, and would submit. This they made me swear to do, and then unbound me, only fastening one of my legs with a chain near my bed, and placed a sentry at my door with his piece charged, who was commanded to shoot me dead if I attempted my liberty. They sent me down victuals and drink, and took the government of the ship to themselves. Their design was to turn pirates and plunder the Spaniards, which they could not do, till they got more men. But first they resolved to sell the goods in the ship, and then go to Madagascar for recruits, several among them having died since my confinement. They sailed many weeks, and traded with the Indians; but I knew not what course they took,

---

9. In the omitted chapter, Gulliver sails to Japan, where a Dutch ship provides him passage back to Europe.
1. Pronounced *hwin-ims*. The word suggests the neigh characteristic of a horse.
2. Teneriffe, one of the Canary Islands.

3. Campeche, in the Gulf of Mexico.
4. "A distemper peculiar to sailors, in hot climates; wherein they imagine the sea to be green fields, and will throw themselves into it, if not restrained" (Johnson's *Dictionary*).

being kept close prisoner in my cabin, and expecting nothing less than to be murdered, as they often threatened me.

Upon the 9th day of May, 1711, one James Welch came down to my cabin; and said he had orders from the Captain to set me ashore. I expostulated with him, but in vain; neither would he so much as tell me who their new Captain was. They forced me into the longboat, letting me put on my best suit of clothes, which were as good as new, and a small bundle of linen, but no arms except my hanger; and they were so civil as not to search my pockets, into which I conveyed what money I had, with some other little necessaries. They rowed about a league, and then set me down on a strand. I desired them to tell me what country it was; they all swore, they knew no more than myself, but said that the Captain (as they called him) was resolved, after they had sold the lading, to get rid of me in the first place where they discovered land. They pushed off immediately, advising me to make haste, for fear of being overtaken by the tide, and bade me farewell.

In this desolate condition I advanced forward, and soon got upon firm ground, where I sat down on a bank to rest myself, and consider what I had best to do. When I was a little refreshed, I went up into the country, resolving to deliver myself to the first savages I should meet, and purchase my life from them by some bracelets, glass rings, and other toys, which sailors usually provide themselves with in those voyages, and whereof I had some about me. The land was divided by long rows of trees, not regularly planted, but naturally growing; there was great plenty of grass, and several fields of oats. I walked very circumspectly for fear of being surprised, or suddenly shot with an arrow from behind, or on either side. I fell into a beaten road, where I saw many tracks of human feet, and some of cows, but most of horses. At last I beheld several animals in a field, and one or two of the same kind sitting in trees. Their shape was very singular, and deformed, which a little discomposed me, so that I lay down behind a thicket to observe them better. Some of them coming forward near the place where I lay, gave me an opportunity of distinctly marking their form. Their heads and breasts were covered with a thick hair, some frizzled and others lank; they had beards like goats, and a long ridge of hair down their backs, and the fore parts of their legs and feet; but the rest of their bodies were bare, so that I might see their skins, which were of a brown buff color. They had no tails, nor any hair at all on their buttocks, except about the anus; which, I presume Nature had placed there to defend them as they sat on the ground; for this posture they used, as well as lying down, and often stood on their hind feet. They climbed high trees, as nimbly as a squirrel, for they had strong extended claws before and behind, terminating in sharp points, and hooked. They would often spring, and bound, and leap with prodigious agility. The females were not so large as the males; they had long lank hair on their heads, and only a sort of down on the rest of their bodies, except about the anus, and pudenda. Their dugs hung between their forefeet, and often reached almost to the ground as they walked. The hair of both sexes was of several colors, brown, red, black, and yellow. Upon the whole, I never beheld in all my travels so disagreeable an animal, or one against which I naturally conceived so strong an antipathy. So that thinking I had seen enough, full of contempt and aversion, I got up and pursued the beaten road, hoping it might direct me to the cabin of some Indian. I had not gone far when I met one of these creatures full in my way, and coming up directly to me. The ugly monster, when he saw me, distorted several ways every feature of his visage, and stared as at an object he had never seen before; then approaching nearer, lifted up his forepaw, whether out of curiosity or mischief, I could not tell; but I drew my hanger, and gave him a good blow with the flat side of it; for I durst not strike him with the edge, fearing the inhabitants might be provoked against me, if they should come to know that I had killed or maimed any of their cattle. When the beast felt the smart, he drew back, and roared so loud, that a herd of at least forty came flocking about me from the near field, howling and making odious faces; but I ran to the body of a tree, and leaning my back against it, kept them off, by waving my hanger. Several of this cursed brood getting hold of the branches behind, leaped up into the tree, from whence they began to discharge their excrements on my head; however, I escaped pretty well, by sticking close to the stem of the tree, but was almost stifled with the filth, which fell about me on every side.

In the midst of this distress, I observed them all to run away on a sudden as fast as they could; at which I ventured to leave the tree, and pursue the road, wondering what it was that could put them into this fright. But looking on my left hand, I saw a horse walking softly in the field; which my perse-cutors having sooner discovered, was the cause of their flight. The horse started a little when he came near me, but soon recovering himself, looked full in my face with manifest tokens of wonder; he viewed my hands and feet, walking round me several times. I would have pursued my journey, but he placed himself directly in the way, yet looking with a very mild aspect, never offering the least violence. We stood gazing at each other for some time; at last I took the boldness, to reach my hand towards his neck, with a design to stroke it; using the common style and whistle of jockies when they are going to handle a strange horse. But this animal, seeming to receive my civilities with disdain, shook his head, and bent his brows, softly raising up his left forefoot to remove my hand. Then he neighed three or four times, but in so different a cadence, that I almost began to think he was speaking to himself in some language of his own.

While he and I were thus employed, another horse came up; who applying himself to the first in a very formal manner, they gently struck each other's right hoof before, neighing several times by turns, and varying the sound, which seemed to be almost articulate. They went some paces off, as if it were to confer together, walking side by side, backward and forward, like persons deliberating upon some affair of weight; but often turning their eyes towards me, as it were to watch that I might not escape. I was amazed to see such actions and behavior in brute beasts; and concluded with myself that if the inhabitants of this country were endued with a proportionable degree of reason, they must needs be the wisest people upon earth. This thought gave me so much comfort, that I resolved to go forward until I could discover some house or village, or meet with any of the natives, leaving the two horses to discourse together as they pleased. But the first, who was a dapple grey, observing me to steal off, neighed after me in so expressive a tone that I fancied myself to understand what he meant; whereupon I turned back, and came near him, to expect his farther commands; but concealing my fear as much as I could; for I began to be in some pain, how this adventure might terminate; and the reader will easily believe I did not much like my present situation.

The two horses came up close to me, looking with great earnestness upon my face and hands. The grey steed rubbed my hat all round with his right fore hoof, and discomposed it so much that I was forced to adjust it better, by taking it off, and settling it again; whereat both he and his companion (who was a brown bay) appeared to be much surprised; the latter felt the lappet of my coat, and finding it to hang loose about me, they both looked with new signs of wonder. He stroked my right hand, seeming to admire the softness, and color; but he squeezed it so hard between his hoof and his pastern, that I was forced to roar; after which they both touched me with all possible tenderness. They were under great perplexity about my shoes and stockings, which they felt very often, neighing to each other, and using various gestures, not unlike those of a philosopher, when he would attempt to solve some new and difficult phenomenon.

Upon the whole, the behavior of these animals was so orderly and rational, so acute and judicious, that I at last concluded, they must needs be magicians, who had thus metamorphosed themselves upon some design; and seeing a stranger in the way, were resolved to divert themselves with him; or perhaps were really amazed at the sight of a man so very different in habit, feature, and complexion from those who might probably live in so remote a climate. Upon the strength of this reasoning, I ventured to address them in the following manner: "Gentlemen, if you be conjurers, as I have good cause to believe, you can understand any language; therefore I make bold to let your worships know that I am a poor distressed Englishman, driven by his misfortunes upon your coast; and I entreat one of you, to let me ride upon his back, as if he were a real horse, to some house or village, where I can be relieved. In return of which favor, I will make you a present of this knife and bracelet" (taking them out of my pocket). The two creatures stood silent while I spoke, seeming to listen with great attention; and when I had ended, they neighed frequently towards each other, as if they were engaged in serious conversation. I plainly observed, that their language expressed the passions very well, and the words might with little pains be resolved into an alphabet more easily than the Chinese.

I could frequently distinguish the word *Yahoo*,[5] which was repeated by each of them several times; and although it were impossible for me to conjecture what it meant, yet while the two horses were busy in conversation, I endeavored to practice this word upon my tongue; and as soon as they were silent, I boldly pronounced "Yahoo" in a loud voice, imitating, at the same time, as near as I could, the neighing of a horse; at which they were both visibly surprised, and the grey repeated the same word twice, as if he meant to teach me the right accent, wherein I spoke after him as well as I could, and found myself perceivably to improve every time, although very far from any degree of perfection. Then the bay tried me with a second word, much harder to be pronounced; but reducing it to the English orthography, may be spelt thus, *Houyhnhnm*. I did not succeed in this so well as the former, but after two or three farther trials, I had better fortune; and they both appeared amazed at my capacity.

After some farther discourse, which I then conjectured might relate to me, the two friends took their leaves, with the same compliment of striking each

---

5. Perhaps compounded from two expressions of disgust, *yah* and *ugh* (or *hoo*), common in the 18th century.

other's hoof; and the grey made me signs that I should walk before him; wherein I thought it prudent to comply, till I could find a better director. When I offered to slacken my pace, he would cry, "Hhuun, Hhuun"; I guessed his meaning, and gave him to understand, as well as I could that I was weary, and not able to walk faster; upon which, he would stand a while to let me rest.

CHAPTER 2. *The Author conducted by a Houyhnhnm to his house. The house described. The Author's reception. The food of the Houyhnhnms. The Author in distress for want of meat is at last relieved. His manner of feeding in that country.*

Having traveled about three miles, we came to a long kind of building, made of timber, stuck in the ground, and wattled across; the roof was low, and covered with straw. I now began to be a little comforted, and took out some toys, which travelers usually carry for presents to the savage Indians of America and other parts, in hopes the people of the house would be thereby encouraged to receive me kindly. The horse made me a sign to go in first; it was a large room with a smooth clay floor, and a rack and manger extending the whole length on one side. There were three nags, and two mares, not eating, but some of them sitting down upon their hams, which I very much wondered at; but wondered more to see the rest employed in domestic business. The last seemed but ordinary cattle; however this confirmed my first opinion, that a people who could so far civilize brute animals must needs excel in wisdom all the nations of the world. The grey came in just after, and thereby prevented any ill treatment, which the others might have given me. He neighed to them several times in a style of authority, and received answers.

Beyond this room there were three others, reaching the length of the house, to which you passed through three doors, opposite to each other, in the manner of a vista; we went through the second room towards the third; here the grey walked in first, beckoning me to attend.[6] I waited in the second room, and got ready my presents, for the master and mistress of the house; they were two knives, three bracelets of false pearl, a small looking glass and a bead necklace. The horse neighed three or four times, and I waited to hear some answers in a human voice, but I heard no other returns than in the same dialect, only one or two a little shriller than his. I began to think that this house must belong to some person of great note among them, because there appeared so much ceremony before I could gain admittance. But, that a man of quality should be served all by horses, was beyond my comprehension. I feared my brain was disturbed by my sufferings and misfortunes; I roused myself, and looked about me in the room where I was left alone; this was furnished as the first, only after a more elegant manner. I rubbed my eyes often, but the same objects still occurred. I pinched my arms and sides, to awaken myself, hoping I might be in a dream. I then absolutely concluded that all these appearances could be nothing else but necromancy and magic. But I had no time to pursue these reflections; for the grey horse came to the door, and made me a sign to follow him into the third room; where I saw a

---

6. To wait. "Vista": a long, open corridor.

very comely mare, together with a colt and foal, sitting on their haunches, upon mats of straw, not unartfully made, and perfectly neat and clean.

The mare soon after my entrance, rose from her mat, and coming up close, after having nicely observed my hands and face, gave me a most contemptuous look; then turning to the horse, I heard the word Yahoo often repeated betwixt them; the meaning of which word I could not then comprehend, although it were the first I had learned to pronounce; but I was soon better informed, to my everlasting mortification: for the horse beckoning to me with his head, and repeating the word, "Hhuun, Hhuun," as he did upon the road, which I understood was to attend him, led me out into a kind of court, where was another building at some distance from the house. Here we entered, and I saw three of those detestable creatures, which I first met after my landing, feeding upon roots, and the flesh of some animals, which I afterwards found to be that of asses and dogs, and now and then a cow dead by accident or disease. They were all tied by the neck with strong withes, fastened to a beam; they held their food between the claws of their forefeet, and tore it with their teeth.

The master horse ordered a sorrel nag, one of his servants, to untie the largest of these animals, and take him into a yard. The beast and I were brought close together; and our countenances diligently compared, both by master and servant, who thereupon repeated several times the word "Yahoo." My horror and astonishment are not to be described, when I observed, in this abominable animal, a perfect human figure; the face of it indeed was flat and broad, the nose depressed, the lips large, and the mouth wide; but these differences are common to all savage nations, where the lineaments of the countenance are distorted by the natives suffering their infants to lie groveling on the earth, or by carrying them on their backs, nuzzling with their face against the mother's shoulders. The forefeet of the Yahoo differed from my hands in nothing else but the length of the nails, the coarseness and brownness of the palms, and the hairiness on the backs. There was the same resemblance between our feet, with the same differences, which I knew very well, although the horses did not, because of my shoes and stockings; the same in every part of our bodies, except as to hairiness and color, which I have already described.

The great difficulty that seemed to stick with the two horses was to see the rest of my body so very different from that of a Yahoo, for which I was obliged to my clothes, whereof they had no conception; the sorrel nag offered me a root, which he held (after their manner, as we shall describe in its proper place) between his hoof and pastern; I took it in my hand, and having smelled it, returned it to him again as civilly as I could. He brought out of the Yahoo's kennel a piece of ass's flesh, but it smelled so offensively that I turned from it with loathing; he then threw it to the Yahoo, by whom it was greedily devoured. He afterwards showed me a wisp of hay, and a fetlock full of oats; but I shook my head, to signify that neither of these were food for me. And indeed, I now apprehended that I must absolutely starve, if I did not get to some of my own species; for as to those filthy Yahoos, although there were few greater lovers of mankind, at that time, than myself, yet I confess I never saw any sensitive being so detestable on all accounts; and the more I came near them, the more hateful they grew, while I stayed in that country. This the master horse observed by my behavior, and therefore sent the Yahoo back to his kennel. He then put his forehoof to his mouth, at which I was much surprised, although he did it with ease, and with a motion that appeared perfectly natural; and made other signs to know what I would eat; but I could not return him such an answer as he was able to apprehend; and if he had understood me, I did not see how it was possible to contrive any way for finding myself nourishment. While we were thus engaged, I observed a cow passing by; whereupon I pointed to her, and expressed a desire to let me go and milk her. This had its effect; for he led me back into the house, and ordered a mare-servant to open a room, where a good store of milk lay in earthen and wooden vessels, after a very orderly and cleanly manner. She gave me a large bowl full, of which I drank very heartily, and found myself well refreshed.

About noon I saw coming towards the house a kind of vehicle, drawn like a sledge by four Yahoos. There was in it an old steed, who seemed to be of quality; he alighted with his hind feet forward, having by accident got a hurt in his left forefoot. He came to dine with our horse, who received him with great civility. They dined in the best room, and had oats boiled in milk for the second course, which the old horse eat warm, but the rest cold. Their mangers were placed circular in the middle of the room, and divided into several partitions, round which they sat on their haunches upon bosses of straw. In the middle was a large rack with angles answering to every partition of the manger. So that each horse and mare eat their own hay, and their own mash of oats and milk, with much decency and regularity. The behavior of the young colt and foal appeared very modest; and that of the master and mistress extremely cheerful and complaisant to their guest. The grey ordered me to stand by him; and much discourse passed between him and his friend concerning me, as I found by the stranger's often looking on me, and the frequent repetition of the word Yahoo.

I happened to wear my gloves; which the master grey observing, seemed perplexed; discovering signs of wonder what I had done to my forefeet; he put his hoof three or four times to them, as if he would signify, that I should reduce them to their former shape, which I presently did, pulling off both my gloves, and putting them into my pocket. This occasioned farther talk, and I saw the company was pleased with my behavior, whereof I soon found the good effects. I was ordered to speak the few words I understood; and while they were at dinner, the master taught me the names for oats, milk, fire, water, and some others which I could readily pronounce after him, having from my youth a great facility in learning languages.

When dinner was done, the master horse took me aside, and by signs and words made me understand the concern he was in that I had nothing to eat. Oats in their tongue are called *hlunnh*. This word I pronounced two or three times; for although I had refused them at first, yet upon second thoughts, I considered that I could contrive to make a kind of bread, which might be sufficient with milk to keep me alive, till I could make my escape to some other country, and to creatures of my own species. The horse immediately ordered a white mare-servant of his family to bring me a good quantity of oats in a sort of wooden tray. These I heated before the fire as well as I could, and rubbed them till the husks came off, which I made a shift to winnow from the grain; I ground and beat them between two stones, then took water, and made them into a paste or cake, which I toasted at the fire, and eat warm with milk. It was at first a very insipid diet, although common enough in many parts of Europe, but grew tolerable by time; and having been often reduced to hard fare in my life, this was not the first experiment I had made how easily nature is satisfied. And I cannot but observe that I never had one hour's sickness, while I staid in this island. It is true, I sometimes made a shift to catch a rabbit, or bird, by springes[7] made of Yahoos' hairs; and I often gathered wholesome herbs, which I boiled, or eat as salads with my bread; and now and then, for a rarity, I made a little butter, and drank the whey. I was at first at a great loss for salt; but custom soon reconciled the want of it; and I am confident that the frequent use of salt among us is an effect of luxury, and was first introduced only as a provocative to drink; except where it is necessary for preserving of flesh in long voyages, or in places remote from great markets. For we observe no animal to be fond of it but man;[8] and as to myself, when I left this country, it was a great while before I could endure the taste of it in anything that I eat.

This is enough to say upon the subject of my diet, wherewith other travelers fill their books, as if the readers were personally concerned whether we fare well or ill. However, it was necessary to mention this matter, lest the world should think it impossible that I could find sustenance for three years in such a country, and among such inhabitants.

When it grew towards evening, the master horse ordered a place for me to lodge in; it was but six yards from the house, and separated from the stable of the Yahoos. Here I got some straw, and covering myself with my own clothes, slept very sound. But I was in a short time better accommodated, as the reader shall know hereafter, when I come to treat more particularly about my way of living.

CHAPTER 3. *The Author studious to learn the language, the Houyhnhnm his master assists in teaching him. The language described. Several Houyhnhnms of quality come out of curiosity to see the Author. He gives his master a short account of his voyage.*

My principal endeavor was to learn the language, which my master (for so I shall henceforth call him) and his children, and every servant of his house were desirous to teach me. For they looked upon it as a prodigy, that a brute animal should discover such marks of a rational creature. I pointed to everything, and enquired the name of it, which I wrote down in my journal book when I was alone, and corrected my bad accent, by desiring those of the family to pronounce it often. In this employment, a sorrel nag, one of the under servants, was very ready to assist me.

In speaking, they pronounce through the nose and throat, and their language approaches nearest to the High Dutch or German, of any I know in Europe; but is much more graceful and significant. The Emperor Charles V made almost the same observation, when he said, that if he were to speak to his horse, it should be in High Dutch.[9]

The curiosity and impatience of my master were so great, that he spent many hours of his leisure to instruct me. He was convinced (as he afterwards

7. Snares.
8. Gulliver is, of course, in error; many animals require salt.

9. The emperor is supposed to have said that he would speak to his God in Spanish, to his mistress in Italian, and to his horse in German.

told me) that I must be a Yahoo, but my teachableness, civility, and cleanliness astonished him; which were qualities altogether so opposite to those animals. He was most perplexed about my clothes, reasoning sometimes with himself whether they were a part of my body; for I never pulled them off till the family were asleep, and got them on before they waked in the morning. My master was eager to learn from whence I came; how I acquired those appearances of reason, which I discovered in all my actions; and to know my story from my own mouth, which he hoped he should soon do by the great proficiency I made in learning and pronouncing their words and sentences. To help my memory, I formed all I learned into the English alphabet, and writ the words down with the translations. This last, after some time, I ventured to do in my master's presence. It cost me much trouble to explain to him what I was doing; for the inhabitants have not the least idea of books or literature.

In about ten weeks time I was able to understand most of his questions; and in three months could give him some tolerable answers. He was extremely curious to know from what part of the country I came, and how I was taught to imitate a rational creature; because the Yahoos (whom he saw I exactly resembled in my head, hands, and face, that were only visible) with some appearance of cunning, and the strongest disposition to mischief, were observed to be the most unteachable of all brutes. I answered that I came over the sea, from a far place, with many others of my own kind, in a great hollow vessel made of the bodies of trees; that my companions forced me to land on this coast, and then left me to shift for myself. It was with some difficulty, and by the help of many signs, that I brought him to understand me. He replied that I must needs be mistaken, or that I *said the thing which was not.* (For they have no word in their language to express lying or falsehood.) He knew it was impossible that there could be a country beyond the sea, or that a parcel of brutes could move a wooden vessel whither they pleased upon water. He was sure no Houyhnhnm alive could make such a vessel, or would trust Yahoos to manage it.

The word Houyhnhnm, in their tongue, signifies a Horse; and in its etymology, the Perfection of Nature. I told my master that I was at a loss for expression, but would improve as fast as I could; and hoped in a short time I should be able to tell him wonders. He was pleased to direct his own mare, his colt, and foal, and the servants of the family to take all opportunities of instructing me; and every day for two or three hours, he was at the same pains himself. Several horses and mares of quality in the neighborhood came often to our house, upon the report spread of a wonderful Yahoo, that could speak like a Houyhnhnm, and seemed in his words and actions to discover some glimmerings of reason. These delighted to converse with me; they put many questions, and received such answers as I was able to return. By all which advantages, I made so great a progress, that in five months from my arrival, I understood whatever was spoke, and could express myself tolerably well.

The Houyhnhnms who came to visit my master, out of a design of seeing and talking with me, could hardly believe me to be a right Yahoo, because my body had a different covering from others of my kind. They were astonished to observe me without the usual hair or skin, except on my head, face, and hands; but I discovered that secret to my master, upon an accident, which happened about a fortnight before.

I have already told the reader, that every night when the family were gone to bed, it was my custom to strip and cover myself with my clothes; it happened one morning early, that my master sent for me, by the sorrel nag, who was his valet; when he came, I was fast asleep, my clothes fallen off on one side, and my shirt above my waist. I awaked at the noise he made, and observed him to deliver his message in some disorder; after which he went to my master, and in a great fright gave him a very confused account of what he had seen. This I presently discovered; for going as soon as I was dressed, to pay my attendance upon his honor, he asked me the meaning of what his servant had reported; that I was not the same thing when I slept as I appeared to be at other times; that his valet assured him, some part of me was white, some yellow, at least not so white, and some brown.

I had hitherto concealed the secret of my dress, in order to distinguish myself as much as possible, from that cursed race of Yahoos; but now I found it in vain to do so any longer. Besides, I considered that my clothes and shoes would soon wear out, which already were in a declining condition, and must be supplied by some contrivance from the hides of Yahoos, or other brutes; whereby the whole secret would be known. I therefore told my master, that in the country from whence I came, those of my kind always covered their bodies with the hairs of certain animals prepared by art, as well for decency, as to avoid inclemencies of air both hot and cold; of which, as to my own person I would give him immediate conviction, if he pleased to command me; only desiring his excuse, if I did not expose those parts that Nature taught us to conceal. He said, my discourse was all very strange, but especially the last part; for he could not understand why Nature should teach us to conceal what Nature had given. That neither himself nor family were ashamed of any parts of their bodies; but however I might do as I pleased. Whereupon, I first unbuttoned my coat, and pulled it off. I did the same with my waistcoat; I drew off my shoes, stockings, and breeches. I let my shirt down to my waist, and drew up the bottom, fastening it like a girdle about my middle to hide my nakedness.

My master observed the whole performance with great signs of curiosity and admiration. He took up all my clothes in his pastern, one piece after another, and examined them diligently; he then stroked my body very gently, and looked round me several times; after which he said, it was plain I must be a perfect Yahoo; but that I differed very much from the rest of my species, in the whiteness and smoothness of my skin, my want of hair in several parts of my body, the shape and shortness of my claws behind and before, and my affectation of walking continually on my two hinder feet. He desired to see no more; and gave me leave to put on my clothes again, for I was shuddering with cold.

I expressed my uneasiness at his giving me so often the appellation of Yahoo, an odious animal, for which I had so utter an hatred and contempt. I begged he would forbear applying that word to me, and take the same order in his family, and among his friends whom he suffered to see me. I requested likewise, that the secret of my having a false covering to my body might be known to none but himself, at least as long as my present clothing should last; for as to what the sorrel nag his valet had observed, his honor might command him to conceal it.

All this my master very graciously consented to; and thus the secret was kept till my clothes began to wear out, which I was forced to supply by several contrivances, that shall hereafter be mentioned. In the meantime, he desired I would go on with my utmost diligence to learn their language, because he was more astonished at my capacity for speech and reason, than at the figure of my body, whether it were covered or no; adding that he waited with some impatience to hear the wonders which I promised to tell him.

From thenceforward he doubled the pains he had been at to instruct me; he brought me into all company, and made them treat me with civility, because, as he told them privately, this would put me into good humor, and make me more diverting.

Every day when I waited on him, beside the trouble he was at in teaching, he would ask me several questions concerning myself, which I answered as well as I could; and by those means he had already received some general ideas, although very imperfect. It would be tedious to relate the several steps, by which I advanced to a more regular conversation, but the first account I gave of myself in any order and length was to this purpose:

That, I came from a very far country, as I already had attempted to tell him, with about fifty more of my own species; that we traveled upon the seas, in a great hollow vessel made of wood, and larger than his honor's house. I described the ship to him in the best terms I could; and explained by the help of my handkerchief displayed, how it was driven forward by the wind. That, upon a quarrel among us, I was set on shore on this coast, where I walked forward without knowing whither, till he delivered me from the persecution of those execrable Yahoos. He asked me who made the ship, and how it was possible that the Houyhnhnms of my country would leave it to the management of brutes? My answer was that I durst proceed no farther in my relation, unless he would give me his word and honor that he would not be offended; and then I would tell him the wonders I had so often promised. He agreed; and I went on by assuring him, that the ship was made by creatures like myself, who in all the countries I had traveled, as well as in my own, were the only governing, rational animals; and that upon my arrival hither, I was as much astonished to see the Houyhnhnms act like rational beings, as he or his friends could be in finding some marks of reason in a creature he was pleased to call a Yahoo; to which I owned my resemblance in every part, but could not account for their degenerate and brutal nature. I said farther, that if good fortune ever restored me to my native country, to relate my travels hither, as I resolved to do, everybody would believe that I *said the thing which was not,* that I invented the story out of my own head; and with all possible respect to himself, his family, and friends, and under his promise of not being offended, our countrymen would hardly think it probable, that a Houyhnhnm should be the presiding creature of a nation, and a Yahoo the brute.

CHAPTER 4. *The Houyhnhnms' notion of truth and falsehood. The Author's discourse disapproved by his master. The Author gives a more particular account of himself, and the accidents of his voyage.*

My master heard me with great appearances of uneasiness in his countenance; because *doubting* or *not believing* are so little known in this country, that the inhabitants cannot tell how to behave themselves under such circumstances. And I remember in frequent discourses with my master concerning the nature of manhood, in other parts of the world, having occasion to talk of *lying* and *false representation*, it was with much difficulty that he comprehended what I meant; although he had otherwise a most acute judgment. For he argued thus: that the use of speech was to make us understand one another, and to receive information of facts; now if anyone *said the thing which was not*, these ends were defeated; because I cannot properly be said to understand him; and I am so far from receiving information, that he leaves me worse than in ignorance; for I am led to believe a thing *black* when it is *white*, and *short* when it is *long*. And these were all the notions he had concerning the faculty of *lying*, so perfectly well understood, and so universally practiced among human creatures.

To return from this digression; when I asserted that the Yahoos were the only governing animals in my country, which my master said was altogether past his conception, he desired to know, whether we had Houyhnhnms among us, and what was their employment. I told him we had great numbers; that in summer they grazed in the fields, and in winter were kept in houses, with hay and oats, where Yahoo servants were employed to rub their skins smooth, comb their manes, pick their feet, serve them with food, and make their beds. "I understand you well," said my master; "it is now very plain from all you have spoken, that whatever share of reason the Yahoos pretend to, the Houyhnhnms are your masters; I heartily wish our Yahoos would be so tractable." I begged his honor would please to excuse me from proceeding any farther, because I was very certain that the account he expected from me would be highly displeasing. But he insisted in commanding me to let him know the best and the worst; I told him he should be obeyed. I owned that the Houyhnhnms among us, whom we called Horses, were the most generous[1] and comely animal we had; that they excelled in strength and swiftness; and when they belonged to persons of quality, employed in traveling, racing, and drawing chariots, they were treated with much kindness and care, till they fell into diseases, or became foundered in the feet; but then they were sold, and used to all kind of drudgery till they died; after which their skins were stripped and sold for what they were worth, and their bodies left to be devoured by dogs and birds of prey. But the common race of horses had not so good fortune, being kept by farmers and carriers, and other mean people, who put them to greater labor, and feed them worse. I described as well as I could, our way of riding; the shape and use of a bridle, a saddle, a spur, and a whip; of harness and wheels. I added, that we fastened plates of a certain hard substance called iron at the bottom of their feet, to preserve their hoofs from being broken by the stony ways on which we often traveled.

My master, after some expressions of great indignation, wondered how we dared to venture upon a Houyhnhnm's back; for he was sure, that the weakest servant in his house would be able to shake off the strongest Yahoo; or by lying down, and rolling upon his back, squeeze the brute to death. I answered that our horses were trained up from three or four years old to the several uses we intended them for; that if any of them proved intolerably vicious, they were employed for carriages; that they were severely beaten while they were young for any mischievous tricks; that the males, designed

1. Noble.

for the common use of riding or draught, were generally castrated about two years after their birth, to take down their spirits, and make them more tame and gentle; that they were indeed sensible of rewards and punishments; but his honor would please to consider that they had not the least tincture of reason any more than the Yahoos in this country.

It put me to the pains of many circumlocutions to give my master a right idea of what I spoke; for their language doth not abound in variety of words, because their wants and passions are fewer than among us. But it is impossible to express his noble resentment at our savage treatment of the Houyhnhnm race; particularly after I had explained the manner and use of castrating horses among us, to hinder them from propagating their kind, and to render them more servile. He said, if it were possible there could be any country where Yahoos alone were endued with reason, they certainly must be the governing animal, because reason will in time always prevail against brutal strength. But, considering the frame of our bodies, and especially of mine, he thought no creature of equal bulk was so ill-contrived for employing that reason in the common offices of life; whereupon he desired to know whether those among whom I lived resembled me or the Yahoos of his country. I assured him that I was as well shaped as most of my age; but the younger and the females were much more soft and tender, and the skins of the latter generally as white as milk. He said I differed indeed from other Yahoos, being much more cleanly, and not altogether so deformed; but in point of real advantage, he thought I differed for the worse. That my nails were of no use either to my fore or hinder feet; as to my forefeet, he could not properly call them by that name, for he never observed me to walk upon them; that they were too soft to bear the ground; that I generally went with them uncovered, neither was the covering I sometimes wore on them of the same shape, or so strong as that on my feet behind. That I could not walk with any security; for if either of my hinder feet slipped, I must inevitably fall. He then began to find fault with other parts of my body; the flatness of my face, the prominence of my nose, my eyes placed directly in front, so that I could not look on either side without turning my head; that I was not able to feed myself without lifting one of my forefeet to my mouth; and therefore nature had placed those joints to answer that necessity. He knew not what could be the use of those several clefts and divisions in my feet behind; that these were too soft to bear the hardness and sharpness of stones without a covering made from the skin of some other brute; that my whole body wanted a fence against heat and cold, which I was forced to put on and off every day with tediousness and trouble. And lastly, that he observed every animal in his country naturally to abhor the Yahoos, whom the weaker avoided, and the stronger drove from them. So that supposing us to have the gift of reason, he could not see how it were possible to cure that natural antipathy which every creature discovered against us; nor consequently, how we could tame and render them serviceable. However, he would (as he said) debate the matter no farther, because he was more desirous to know my own story, the country where I was born, and the several actions and events of my life before I came hither.

I assured him how extremely desirous I was that he should be satisfied in every point; but I doubted much whether it would be possible for me to explain myself on several subjects whereof his honor could have no conception, because I saw nothing in his country to which I could resemble them.

That however, I would do my best, and strive to express myself by similitudes, humbly desiring his assistance when I wanted proper words; which he was pleased to promise me.

I said, my birth was of honest parents, in an island called England, which was remote from this country, as many days journey as the strongest of his honor's servants could travel in the annual course of the sun. That I was bred a surgeon, whose trade it is to cure wounds and hurts in the body, got by accident or violence. That my country was governed by a female man, whom we called a queen. That I left it to get riches, whereby I might maintain myself and family when I should return. That in my last voyage, I was Commander of the ship and had about fifty Yahoos under me, many of which died at sea, and I was forced to supply them by others picked out from several nations. That our ship was twice in danger of being sunk; the first time by a great storm, and the second, by striking against a rock. Here my master interposed, by asking me, how I could persuade strangers out of different countries to venture with me, after the losses I had sustained, and the hazards I had run. I said, they were fellows of desperate fortunes, forced to fly from the places of their birth, on account of their poverty or their crimes. Some were undone by lawsuits; others spent all they had in drinking, whoring, and gaming; others fled for treason; many for murder, theft, poisoning, robbery, perjury, forgery, coining false money; for committing rapes or sodomy; for flying from their colors, or deserting to the enemy; and most of them had broken prison. None of these durst return to their native countries for fear of being hanged, or of starving in a jail; and therefore were under a necessity of seeking a livelihood in other places.

During this discourse, my master was pleased often to interrupt me. I had made use of many circumlocutions in describing to him the nature of the several crimes, for which most of our crew had been forced to fly their country. This labor took up several days conversation before he was able to comprehend me. He was wholly at a loss to know what could be the use or necessity of practicing those vices. To clear up which I endeavored to give him some ideas of the desire of power and riches; of the terrible effects of lust, intemperance, malice, and envy. All this I was forced to define and describe by putting of cases, and making suppositions. After which, like one whose imagination was struck with something never seen or heard of before, he would lift up his eyes with amazement and indignation. Power, government, war, law, punishment, and a thousand other things had no terms, wherein that language could express them; which made the difficulty almost insuperable to give my master any conception of what I meant; but being of an excellent understanding, much improved by contemplation and converse, he at last arrived at a competent knowledge of what human nature in our parts of the world is capable to perform; and desired I would give him some particular account of that land, which we call Europe, especially, of my own country.

CHAPTER 5. *The Author, at his master's commands, informs him of the state of England. The causes of war among the princes of Europe. The Author begins to explain the English Constitution.*

The reader may please to observe that the following extract of many conversations I had with my master contains a summary of the most material points, which were discoursed at several times for above two years; his honor often desiring fuller satisfaction as I farther improved in the Houyhnhnm tongue. I laid before him, as well as I could, the whole state of Europe; I discoursed of trade and manufactures, of arts and sciences; and the answers I gave to all the questions he made, as they arose upon several subjects, were a fund of conversation not to be exhausted. But I shall here only set down the substance of what passed between us concerning my own country, reducing it into order as well as I can, without any regard to time or other circumstances, while I strictly adhere to truth. My only concern is that I shall hardly be able to do justice to my master's arguments and expressions; which must needs suffer by my want of capacity, as well as by a translation into our barbarous English.

In obedience therefore to his honor's commands, I related to him the Revolution under the Prince of Orange; the long war with France entered into by the said Prince, and renewed by his successor the present queen; wherein the greatest powers of Christendom were engaged, and which still continued. I computed at his request, that about a million of Yahoos might have been killed in the whole progress of it; and perhaps a hundred or more cities taken, and five times as many ships burned or sunk.[2]

He asked me what were the usual causes or motives that made one country to go to war with another. I answered, they were innumerable; but I should only mention a few of the chief. Sometimes the ambition of princes, who never think they have land or people enough to govern; sometimes the corruption of ministers, who engage their master in a war in order to stifle or divert the clamor of the subjects against their evil administration. Difference in opinions hath cost many millions of lives; for instance, whether flesh be bread, or bread be flesh; whether the juice of a certain berry be blood or wine; whether whistling be a vice or a virtue; whether it be better to kiss a post, or throw it into the fire; what is the best color for a coat, whether black, white, red, or grey; and whether it should be long or short, narrow or wide, dirty or clean;[3] with many more. Neither are any wars so furious and bloody, or of so long continuance, as those occasioned by difference in opinion, especially if it be in things indifferent.[4]

Sometimes the quarrel between two princes is to decide which of them shall dispossess a third of his dominions, where neither of them pretend to any right. Sometimes one prince quarreleth with another, for fear the other should quarrel with him. Sometimes a war is entered upon, because the enemy is too strong, and sometimes because he is too weak. Sometimes our neighbors want the things which we have, or have the things which we want; and we both fight, till they take ours or give us theirs. It is a very justifiable cause of war to invade a country after the people have been wasted by famine, destroyed by pestilence, or embroiled by factions amongst themselves. It is justifiable to enter into a war against our nearest ally, when one of his towns lies convenient for us, or a territory of land, that would render our dominions round and compact. If a prince send forces into a nation, where the people

2. Gulliver relates recent English history: the Glorious Revolution (1688–89) and the War of Spanish Succession (1703–13). He greatly exaggerates the casualties in the war.
3. Gulliver refers to the religious controversies of

the Reformation and Counter-Reformation: the doctrine of transubstantiation, the use of music in church services, the veneration of the crucifix, and the wearing of priestly vestments.
4. Of little consequence.

are poor and ignorant, he may lawfully put half of them to death, and make slaves of the rest, in order to civilize and reduce them from their barbarous way of living. It is a very kingly, honorable, and frequent practice, when one prince desires the assistance of another to secure him against an invasion, that the assistant, when he hath driven out the invader, should seize on the dominions himself, and kill, imprison, or banish the prince he came to relieve. Alliance by blood or marriage is a sufficient cause of war between princes; and the nearer the kindred is, the greater is their disposition to quarrel. Poor nations are hungry, and rich nations are proud; and pride and hunger will ever be at variance. For these reasons, the trade of a soldier is held the most honorable of all others: because a soldier is a Yahoo hired to kill in cold blood as many of his own species, who have never offended him, as possibly he can.

There is likewise a kind of beggarly princes in Europe, not able to make war by themselves, who hire out their troops to richer nations for so much a day to each man; of which they keep three fourths to themselves, and it is the best part of their maintenance; such are those in many northern parts of Europe.[5]

"What you have told me," said my master, "upon the subject of war, doth indeed discover most admirably the effects of that reason you pretend to. However, it is happy that the shame is greater than the danger; and that Nature hath left you utterly uncapable of doing much mischief; for your mouths lying flat with your faces, you can hardly bite each other to any purpose, unless by consent. Then, as to the claws upon your feet before and behind, they are so short and tender, that one of our Yahoos would drive a dozen of yours before him. And therefore in recounting the numbers of those who have been killed in battle, I cannot but think that you have *said the thing which is not.*"

I could not forbear shaking my head and smiling a little at his ignorance. And, being no stranger to the art of war, I gave him a description of cannons, culverins, muskets, carabines, pistols, bullets, powder, swords, bayonets, battles, sieges, retreats, attacks, undermines, countermines, bombardments, sea fights; ships sunk with a thousand men; twenty thousand killed on each side; dying groans, limbs flying in the air; smoke, noise, confusion, trampling to death under horses' feet; flight, pursuit, victory; fields strewed with carcasses left for food to dogs, and wolves, and birds of prey; plundering, stripping, ravishing, burning, and destroying. And, to set forth the valor of my own dear countrymen, I assured him that I had seen them blow up a hundred enemies at once in a siege, and as many in a ship; and beheld the dead bodies drop down in pieces from the clouds, to the great diversion of all the spectators.

I was going on to more particulars, when my master commanded me silence. He said, whoever understood the nature of Yahoos might easily believe it possible for so vile an animal, to be capable of every action I had named, if their strength and cunning equaled their malice. But, as my discourse had increased his abhorrence of the whole species, so he found it gave him a disturbance in his mind, to which he was wholly a stranger before. He thought his ears being used to such abominable words, might by degrees admit them with less detestation. That, although he hated the Yahoos of this

---

5. A satiric glance at George I, who, as elector of Hanover, had dealt in this trade.

country, yet he no more blamed them for their odious qualities, than he did a *gnnayh* (a bird of prey) for its cruelty, or a sharp stone for cutting his hoof. But, when a creature pretending to reason could be capable of such enormities, he dreaded lest the corruption of that faculty might be worse than brutality itself. He seemed therefore confident, that instead of reason, we were only possessed of some quality fitted to increase our natural vices; as the reflection from a troubled stream returns the image of an ill-shapen body, not only larger, but more distorted.

He added that he had heard too much upon the subject of war, both in this and some former discourses. There was another point which a little perplexed him at present. I had said that some of our crew left their country on account of being ruined by law: that I had already explained the meaning of the word; but he was at a loss how it should come to pass, that the law which was intended for every man's preservation, should be any man's ruin. Therefore he desired to be farther satisfied what I meant by law, and the dispensers thereof, according to the present practice in my own country; because he thought Nature and Reason were sufficient guides for a reasonable animal, as we pretended to be, in showing us what we ought to do, and what to avoid.

I assured his honor that law was a science wherein I had not much conversed, further than by employing advocates, in vain, upon some injustices that had been done me. However, I would give him all the satisfaction I was able.

I said there was a society of men among us, bred up from their youth in the art of proving by words multiplied for the purpose, that white is black, and black is white, according as they are paid. To this society all the rest of the people are slaves.

"For example. If my neighbor hath a mind to my cow, he hires a lawyer to prove that he ought to have my cow from me. I must then hire another to defend my right; it being against all rules of law that any man should be allowed to speak for himself. Now in this case, I who am the true owner lie under two great disadvantages. First, my lawyer being practiced almost from his cradle in defending falsehood is quite out of his element when he would be an advocate for justice, which as an office unnatural, he always attempts with great awkwardness, if not with ill-will. The second disadvantage is that my lawyer must proceed with great caution, or else he will be reprimanded by the judges, and abhorred by his brethren, as one who would lessen the practice of the law. And therefore I have but two methods to preserve my cow. The first is to gain over my adversary's lawyer with a double fee; who will then betray his client, by insinuating that he hath justice on his side. The second way is for my lawyer to make my cause appear as unjust as he can; by allowing the cow to belong to my adversary; and this if it be skillfully done, will certainly bespeak the favor of the bench.

"Now, your honor is to know that these judges are persons appointed to decide all controversies of property, as well as for the trial of criminals; and picked out from the most dextrous lawyers who are grown old or lazy; and having been biased all their lives against truth and equity, lie under such a fatal necessity of favoring fraud, perjury, and oppression, that I have known some of them to have refused a large bribe from the side where justice lay, rather than injure the faculty,[6] by doing anything unbecoming their nature or their office.

"It is a maxim among these lawyers, that whatever hath been done before may legally be done again; and therefore they take special care to record all the decisions formerly made against common justice and the general reason of mankind. These, under the name of *precedents*, they produce as authorities to justify the most iniquitous opinions; and the judges never fail of directing accordingly.

"In pleading, they studiously avoid entering into the merits of the cause; but are loud, violent, and tedious in dwelling upon all circumstances which are not to the purpose. For instance, in the case already mentioned, they never desire to know what claim or title my adversary hath to my cow; but whether the said cow were red or black; her horns long or short; whether the field I graze her in be round or square; whether she were milked at home or abroad; what diseases she is subject to, and the like. After which they consult precedents, adjourn the cause, from time to time, and in ten, twenty, or thirty years come to an issue.

"It is likewise to be observed, that this society hath a peculiar cant and jargon of their own, that no other mortal can understand, and wherein all their laws are written, which they take special care to multiply; whereby they have wholly confounded the very essence of truth and falsehood, of right and wrong; so that it will take thirty years to decide whether the field, left me by my ancestors for six generations, belong to me, or to a stranger three hundred miles off.

"In the trial of persons accused for crimes against the state, the method is much more short and commendable: the judge first sends to sound the disposition of those in power; after which he can easily hang or save the criminal, strictly preserving all the forms of law."

Here my master interposing said it was a pity that creatures endowed with such prodigious abilities of mind as these lawyers, by the description I gave of them, must certainly be, were not rather encouraged to be instructors of others in wisdom and knowledge. In answer to which, I assured his honor that in all points out of their own trade, they were usually the most ignorant and stupid generation among us, the most despicable in common conversation, avowed enemies to all knowledge and learning; and equally disposed to pervert the general reason of mankind, in every other subject of discourse as in that of their own profession.

CHAPTER 6. *A continuation of the state of England, under Queen Anne. The character of a first minister in the courts of Europe.*

My master was yet wholly at a loss to understand what motives could incite this race of lawyers to perplex, disquiet, and weary themselves by engaging in a confederacy of injustice, merely for the sake of injuring their fellow animals; neither could he comprehend what I meant in saying they did it for hire. Whereupon I was at much pains to describe to him the use of money, the materials it was made of, and the value of the metals; that when a Yahoo

6. Profession.

had got a great store of this precious substance, he was able to purchase whatever he had a mind to; the finest clothing, the noblest houses, great tracts of land, the most costly meats and drinks; and have his choice of the most beautiful females. Therefore since money alone was able to perform all these feats, our Yahoos thought they could never have enough of it to spend or to save, as they found themselves inclined from their natural bent either to profusion or avarice. That the rich man enjoyed the fruit of the poor man's labor, and the latter were a thousand to one in proportion to the former. That the bulk of our people was forced to live miserably, by laboring every day for small wages to make a few live plentifully. I enlarged myself much on these and many other particulars to the same purpose, but his honor was still to seek,[7] for he went upon a supposition that all animals had a title to their share in the productions of the earth; and especially those who presided over the rest. Therefore he desired I would let him know what these costly meats were, and how any of us happened to want[8] them. Whereupon I enumerated as many sorts as came into my head, with the various methods of dressing them, which could not be done without sending vessels by sea to every part of the world, as well for liquors to drink, as for sauces, and innumerable other conveniencies. I assured him, that this whole globe of earth must be at least three times gone round, before one of our better female Yahoos could get her breakfast, or a cup to put it in. He said, "That must needs be a miserable country which cannot furnish food for its own inhabitants." But what he chiefly wondered at, was how such vast tracts of ground as I described, should be wholly without fresh water, and the people put to the necessity of sending over the sea for drink. I replied that England (the dear place of my nativity) was computed to produce three times the quantity of food, more than its inhabitants are able to consume, as well as liquors extracted from grain, or pressed out of the fruit of certain trees, which made excellent drink; and the same proportion in every other convenience of life. But, in order to feed the luxury and intemperance of the males, and the vanity of the females, we sent away the greatest part of our necessary things to other countries, from whence in return we brought the materials of diseases, folly, and vice, to spend among ourselves. Hence it follows of necessity, that vast numbers of our people are compelled to seek their livelihood by begging, robbing, stealing, cheating, pimping, forswearing, flattering, suborning, forging, gaming, lying, fawning, hectoring, voting, scribbling, star gazing, poisoning, whoring, canting, libeling, freethinking, and the like occupations; every one of which terms, I was at much pains to make him understand.

That, wine was not imported among us from foreign countries, to supply the want of water or other drinks, but because it was a sort of liquid which made us merry, by putting us out of our senses; diverted all melancholy thoughts, begat wild extravagant imaginations in the brain, raised our hopes, and banished our fears; suspended every office of reason for a time, and deprived us of the use of our limbs, until we fell into a profound sleep; although it must be confessed, that we always awaked sick and dispirited; and that the use of this liquor filled us with diseases, which made our lives uncomfortable and short.

---

7. Still did not understand.   8. Lack.

But beside all this, the bulk of our people supported themselves by furnishing the necessities or conveniencies of life to the rich, and to each other. For instance, when I am at home and dressed as I ought to be, I carry on my body the workmanship of an hundred tradesmen; the building and furniture of my house employ as many more; and five times the number to adorn my wife.

I was going on to tell him of another sort of people, who get their livelihood by attending the sick; having upon some occasions informed his honor that many of my crew had died of diseases. But here it was with the utmost difficulty that I brought him to apprehend what I meant. He could easily conceive that a Houyhnhnm grew weak and heavy a few days before his death; or by some accident might hurt a limb. But that nature, who worketh all things to perfection, should suffer any pains to breed in our bodies, he thought impossible; and desired to know the reason of so unaccountable an evil. I told him, we fed on a thousand things which operated contrary to each other; that we eat when we were not hungry, and drank without the provocation of thirst; that we sat whole nights drinking strong liquors without eating a bit, which disposed us to sloth, inflamed our bodies, and precipitated or prevented digestion. That, prostitute female Yahoos acquired a certain malady, which bred rottenness in the bones of those who fell into their embraces; that this and many other diseases were propagated from father to son; so that great numbers come into the world with complicated maladies upon them; that it would be endless to give him a catalogue of all diseases incident to human bodies; for they could not be fewer than five or six hundred, spread over every limb, and joint; in short, every part, external and intestine, having diseases appropriated to each. To remedy which, there was a sort of people bred up among us, in the profession or pretense of curing the sick. And because I had some skill in the faculty, I would in gratitude to his honor let him know the whole mystery and method by which they proceed.

Their fundamental is that all diseases arise from repletion; from whence they conclude, that a great evacuation of the body is necessary, either through the natural passage, or upwards at the mouth. Their next business is, from herbs, minerals, gums, oils, shells, salts, juices, seaweed, excrements, barks of trees, serpents, toads, frogs, spiders, dead men's flesh and bones, birds, beasts and fishes, to form a composition for smell and taste the most abominable, nauseous, and detestable, that they can possibly contrive, which the stomach immediately rejects with loathing, and this they call a vomit. Or else from the same storehouse, with some other poisonous additions, they command us to take in at the orifice above or below (just as the physician then happens to be disposed) a medicine equally annoying and disgustful to the bowels; which relaxing the belly, drives down all before it; and this they call a purge, or a clyster. For nature (as the physicians allege) having intended the superior anterior orifice only for the intromission of solids and liquids, and the inferior posterior for ejection, these artists ingeniously considering that in all diseases nature is forced out of her seat; therefore to replace her in it, the body must be treated in a manner directly contrary, by interchanging the use of each orifice; forcing solids and liquids in at the anus, and making evacuations at the mouth.

But, besides real diseases, we are subject to many that are only imaginary, for which the physicians have invented imaginary cures; these have their several names, and so have the drugs that are proper for them; and with these our female Yahoos are always infested.

One great excellency in this tribe is their skill at prognostics, wherein they seldom fail; their predictions in real diseases, when they rise to any degree of malignity, generally portending death, which is always in their power, when recovery is not, and therefore, upon any unexpected signs of amendment, after they have pronounced their sentence, rather than be accused as false prophets, they know how to approve[9] their sagacity to the world by a seasonable dose.

They are likewise of special use to husbands and wives, who are grown weary of their mates; to eldest sons, to great ministers of state, and often to princes.

I had formerly upon occasion discoursed with my master upon the nature of government in general, and particularly of our own excellent constitution, deservedly the wonder and envy of the whole world. But having here accidently mentioned a minister of state, he commanded me some time after to inform him what species of Yahoo I particularly meant by that appellation.

I told him that a first or chief minister of state, whom I intended to describe, was a creature wholly exempt from joy and grief, love and hatred, pity and anger; at least makes use of no other passions but a violent desire of wealth, power, and titles; that he applies his words to all uses, except to the indication of his mind; that he never tells a truth, but with an intent that you should take it for a lie; nor a lie, but with a design that you should take it for a truth; that those he speaks worst of behind their backs are in the surest way to preferment; and whenever he begins to praise you to others or to yourself, you are from that day forlorn. The worst mark you can receive is a promise, especially when it is confirmed with an oath; after which every wise man retires, and gives over all hopes.

There are three methods by which a man may rise to be chief minister: the first is by knowing how with prudence to dispose of a wife, a daughter, or a sister; the second, by betraying or undermining his predecessor; and the third is by a furious zeal in public assemblies against the corruptions of the court. But a wise prince would rather choose to employ those who practice the last of these methods; because such zealots prove always the most obsequious and subservient to the will and passions of their master. That, these ministers having all employments at their disposal, preserve themselves in power by bribing the majority of a senate or great council; and at last by an expedient called an Act of Indemnity[1] (whereof I described the nature to him) they secure themselves from after reckonings, and retire from the public, laden with the spoils of the nation.

The palace of a chief minister is a seminary to breed up others in his own trade; the pages, lackies, and porter, by imitating their master, become ministers of state in their several districts, and learn to excel in the three principal ingredients, of insolence, lying, and bribery. Accordingly, they have a subaltern court paid to them by persons of the best rank; and sometimes by the force of dexterity and impudence, arrive through several gradations to be successors to their lord.

9. Prove.
1. An act passed at each session of Parliament to protect ministers of state who in good faith might have acted illegally.

He is usually governed by a decayed wench, or favorite footman, who are the tunnels through which all graces are conveyed, and may properly be called, in the last resort, the governors of the kingdom.

One day, my master, having heard me mention the nobility of my country, was pleased to make me a compliment which I could not pretend to deserve: that, he was sure, I must have been born of some noble family, because I far exceeded in shape, color, and cleanliness, all the Yahoos of his nation, although I seemed to fail in strength, and agility, which must be imputed to my different way of living from those other brutes; and besides, I was not only endowed with the faculty of speech, but likewise with some rudiments of reason, to a degree, that with all his acquaintance I passed for a prodigy.

He made me observe, that among the Houyhnhnms, the white, the sorrel, and the iron grey were not so exactly shaped as the bay, the dapple grey, and the black; nor born with equal talents of mind, or a capacity to improve them; and therefore continued always in the condition of servants, without ever aspiring to match out of their own race, which in that country would be reckoned monstrous and unnatural.

I made his honor my most humble acknowledgments for the good opinion he was pleased to conceive of me; but assured him at the same time, that my birth was of the lower sort, having been born of plain, honest parents, who were just able to give me a tolerable education; that, nobility among us was altogether a different thing from the idea he had of it; that, our young noblemen are bred from their childhood in idleness and luxury; that, as soon as years will permit, they consume their vigor, and contract odious diseases among lewd females; and when their fortunes are almost ruined, they marry some woman of mean birth, disagreeable person, and unsound constitution, merely for the sake of money, whom they hate and despise. That, the productions of such marriages are generally scrofulous, rickety or deformed children; by which means the family seldom continues above three generations, unless the wife take care to provide a healthy father among her neighbors, or domestics, in order to improve and continue the breed. That a weak diseased body, a meager countenance, and sallow complexion are the true marks of noble blood; and a healthy robust appearance is so disgraceful in a man of quality, that the world concludes his real father to have been a groom or a coachman. The imperfections of his mind run parallel with those of his body; being a composition of spleen, dullness, ignorance, caprice, sensuality, and pride.

Without the consent of this illustrious body, no law can be enacted, repealed, or altered, and these nobles have likewise the decision of all our possessions without appeal.

CHAPTER 7. *The Author's great love of his native country. His master's observations upon the constitution and administration of England, as described by the Author, with parallel cases and comparisons. His master's observations upon human nature.*

The reader may be disposed to wonder how I could prevail on myself to give so free a representation of my own species, among a race of mortals who were already too apt to conceive the vilest opinion of humankind, from that entire congruity betwixt me and their Yahoos. But I must freely confess that the many virtues of those excellent quadrupeds placed in opposite view to human corruptions had so far opened my eyes, and enlarged my understanding, that I began to view the actions and passions of man in a very different light; and to think the honor of my own kind not worth managing;[2] which, besides, it was impossible for me to do before a person of so acute a judgment as my master, who daily convinced me of a thousand faults in myself, whereof I had not the least perception before, and which with us would never be numbered even among human infirmities. I had likewise learned from his example an utter detestation of all falsehood or disguise; and truth appeared so amiable to me, that I determined upon sacrificing everything to it.

Let me deal so candidly with the reader as to confess that there was yet a much stronger motive for the freedom I took in my representation of things. I had not been a year in this country, before I contracted such a love and veneration for the inhabitants, that I entered on a firm resolution never to return to humankind, but to pass the rest of my life among these admirable Houyhnhnms in the contemplation and practice of every virtue; where I could have no example or incitement to vice. But it was decreed by fortune, my perpetual enemy, that so great a felicity should not fall to my share. However, it is now some comfort to reflect that in what I said of my countrymen, I extenuated their faults as much as I durst before so strict an examiner; and upon every article, gave as favorable a turn as the matter would bear. For, indeed, who is there alive that will not be swayed by his bias and partiality to the place of his birth?

I have related the substance of several conversations I had with my master, during the greatest part of the time I had the honor to be in his service; but have indeed for brevity sake omitted much more than is here set down.

When I had answered all his questions, and his curiosity seemed to be fully satisfied; he sent for me one morning early, and commanding me to sit down at some distance (an honor which he had never before conferred upon me), he said he had been very seriously considering my whole story, as far as it related both to myself and my country; that, he looked upon us as a sort of animals to whose share, by what accident he could not conjecture, some small pittance of reason had fallen, whereof we made no other use than by its assistance to aggravate our natural corruptions, and to acquire new ones which nature had not given us. That we disarmed ourselves of the few abilities she had bestowed; had been very successful in multiplying our original wants, and seemed to spend our whole lives in vain endeavors to supply them by our own inventions. That, as to myself, it was manifest I had neither the strength or agility of a common Yahoo; that I walked infirmly on my hinder feet; had found out a contrivance to make my claws of no use or defense, and to remove the hair from my chin, which was intended as a shelter from the sun and the weather. Lastly, that I could neither run with speed, nor climb trees like my brethren (as he called them) the Yahoos in this country.

That our institutions of government and law were plainly owing to our gross defects in reason, and by consequence, in virtue; because reason alone is sufficient to govern a rational creature; which was therefore a character we had no pretense to challenge, even from the account I had given of my own people; although he manifestly perceived, that in order to favor them, I had concealed many particulars, and often *said the thing which was not*.

He was the more confirmed in this opinion, because he observed that I

2. Taking care of.

agreed in every feature of my body with other Yahoos, except where it was to my real disadvantage in point of strength, speed, and activity, the shortness of my claws, and some other particulars where Nature had no part; so, from the representation I had given him of our lives, our manners, and our actions, he found as near a resemblance in the disposition of our minds. He said the Yahoos were known to hate one another more than they did any different species of animals; and the reason usually assigned was the odiousness of their own shapes, which all could see in the rest, but not in themselves. He had therefore begun to think it not unwise in us to cover our bodies, and by that invention, conceal many of our deformities from each other, which would else be hardly supportable. But he now found he had been mistaken; and that the dissensions of those brutes in his country were owing to the same cause with ours, as I had described them. For, if (said he) you throw among five Yahoos as much food as would be sufficient for fifty, they will instead of eating peaceably, fall together by the ears, each single one impatient to have all to itself; and therefore a servant was usually employed to stand by while they were feeding abroad, and those kept at home were tied at a distance from each other. That, if a cow died of age or accident, before a Houyhnhnm could secure it for his own Yahoos, those in the neighborhood would come in herds to seize it, and then would ensue such a battle as I had described, with terrible wounds made by their claws on both sides, although they seldom were able to kill one another, for want of such convenient instruments of death as we had invented. At other times the like battles have been fought between the Yahoos of several neighborhoods without any visible cause; those of one district watching all opportunities to surprise the next before they are prepared. But if they find their project hath miscarried, they return home, and for want of enemies, engage in what I call a civil war among themselves.

That, in some fields of his country, there are certain shining stones of several colors, whereof the Yahoos are violently fond; and when part of these stones are fixed in the earth, as it sometimes happeneth, they will dig with their claws for whole days to get them out, and carry them away, and hide them by heaps in their kennels; but still looking round with great caution, for fear their comrades should find out their treasure. My master said he could never discover the reason of this unnatural appetite, or how these stones could be of any use to a Yahoo; but now he believed it might proceed from the same principle of avarice, which I had ascribed to mankind. That he had once, by way of experiment, privately removed a heap of these stones from the place where one of his Yahoos had buried it, whereupon, the sordid animal missing his treasure, by his loud lamenting brought the whole herd to the place, there miserably howled, then fell to biting and tearing the rest; began to pine away, would neither eat nor sleep, nor work, till he ordered a servant privately to convey the stones into the same hole, and hide them as before; which when his Yahoo had found, he presently recovered his spirits and good humor; but took care to remove them to a better hiding place; and hath ever since been a very serviceable brute.

My master farther assured me, which I also observed myself, that in the fields where these shining stones abound, the fiercest and most frequent battles are fought, occasioned by perpetual inroads of the neighboring Yahoos.

He said it was common when two Yahoos discovered such a stone in a field, and were contending which of them should be the proprietor, a third would take the advantage, and carry it away from them both; which my master would needs contend to have some resemblance with our suits at law; wherein I thought it for our credit not to undeceive him; since the decision he mentioned was much more equitable than many decrees among us; because the plaintiff and defendant there lost nothing beside the stone they contended for; whereas our courts of equity would never have dismissed the cause while either of them had anything left.

My master continuing his discourse said there was nothing that rendered the Yahoos more odious, than their undistinguished appetite to devour everything that came in their way, whether herbs, roots, berries, corrupted flesh of animals, or all mingled together; and it was peculiar in their temper, that they were fonder of what they could get by rapine or stealth at a greater distance, than much better food provided for them at home. If their prey held out, they would eat till they were ready to burst, after which nature had pointed out to them a certain root that gave them a general evacuation.

There was also another kind of root very juicy, but something rare and difficult to be found, which the Yahoos sought for with much eagerness, and would suck it with great delight; it produced the same effects that wine hath upon us. It would make them sometimes hug, and sometimes tear one another; they would howl and grin, and chatter, and reel, and tumble, and then fall asleep in the mud.

I did indeed observe that the Yahoos were the only animals in this country subject to any diseases; which however, were much fewer than horses have among us, and contracted not by any ill treatment they meet with, but by the nastiness and greediness of that sordid brute. Neither has their language any more than a general appellation for those maladies; which is borrowed from the name of the beast, and called *Hnea Yahoo*, or the Yahoo's Evil; and the cure prescribed is a mixture of their own dung and urine, forcibly put down the Yahoo's throat. This I have since often known to have been taken with success, and do here freely recommend it to my countrymen, for the public good, as an admirable specific against all diseases produced by repletion.

As to learning, government, arts, manufactures, and the like, my master confessed he could find little or no resemblance between the Yahoos of that country and those in ours. For he only meant to observe what parity there was in our natures. He had heard indeed some curious Houyhnhnms observe that in most herds there was a sort of ruling Yahoo (as among us there is generally some leading or principal stag in a park) who was always more deformed in body, and mischievous in disposition, than any of the rest. That this leader had usually a favorite as like himself as he could get, whose employment was to lick his master's feet and posteriors, and drive the female Yahoos to his kennel; for which he was now and then rewarded with a piece of ass's flesh. This favorite is hated by the whole herd; and therefore to protect himself, keeps always near the person of his leader. He usually continues in office till a worse can be found; but the very moment he is discarded, his successor, at the head of all the Yahoos in that district, young and old, male and female, come in a body, and discharge their excrements upon him from head to foot. But how far this might be applicable to our courts and favorites, and ministers of state, my master said I could best determine.

I durst make no return to this malicious insinuation, which debased human understanding below the sagacity of a common hound, who hath judgment enough to distinguish and follow the cry of the ablest dog in the pack, without being ever mistaken.

My master told me there were some qualities remarkable in the Yahoos, which he had not observed me to mention, or at least very slightly, in the accounts I had given him of humankind. He said, those animals, like other brutes, had their females in common; but in this they differed, that the she-Yahoo would admit the male while she was pregnant; and that the hes would quarrel and fight with the females as fiercely as with each other. Both which practices were such degrees of infamous brutality, that no other sensitive creature ever arrived at.

Another thing he wondered at in the Yahoos was their strange disposition to nastiness and dirt; whereas there appears to be a natural love of cleanliness in all other animals. As to the two former accusations, I was glad to let them pass without any reply, because I had not a word to offer upon them in defense of my species, which otherwise I certainly had done from my own inclinations. But I could have easily vindicated humankind from the imputation of singularity upon the last article, if there had been any swine in that country (as unluckily for me there were not) which although it may be a sweeter quadruped than a Yahoo, cannot I humbly conceive in justice pretend to more cleanliness; and so his honor himself must have owned, if he had seen their filthy way of feeding, and their custom of wallowing and sleeping in the mud.

My master likewise mentioned another quality, which his servants had discovered in several Yahoos, and to him was wholly unaccountable. He said, a fancy would sometimes take a Yahoo, to retire into a corner, to lie down and howl, and groan, and spurn away all that came near him, although he were young and fat, and wanted neither food nor water; nor did the servants imagine what could possibly ail him. And the only remedy they found was to set him to hard work, after which he would infallibly come to himself. To this I was silent out of partiality to my own kind; yet here I could plainly discover the true seeds of spleen,[3] which only seizeth on the lazy, the luxurious, and the rich; who, if they were forced to undergo the same regimen, I would undertake for the cure.

His Honor had farther observed, that a female Yahoo would often stand behind a bank or a bush, to gaze on the young males passing by, and then appear, and hide, using many antic gestures and grimaces; at which time it was observed, that she had a most offensive smell; and when any of the males advanced, would slowly retire, looking back, and with a counterfeit show of fear, run off into some convenient place where she knew the male would follow her.

At other times, if a female stranger came among them, three or four of her own sex would get about her, and stare and chatter, and grin, and smell her all over; and then turn off with gestures that seemed to express contempt and disdain.

Perhaps my master might refine a little in these speculations, which he had drawn from what he observed himself, or had been told by others; however, I could not reflect without some amazement, and much sorrow, that

3. Hypochondria.

the rudiments of lewdness, coquetry, censure, and scandal, should have place by instinct in womankind.

I expected every moment that my master would accuse the Yahoos of those unnatural appetites in both sexes, so common among us. But Nature it seems hath not been so expert a schoolmistress; and these politer pleasures are entirely the productions of art and reason, on our side of the globe.

CHAPTER 8. *The Author relateth several particulars of the Yahoos. The great virtues of the Houyhnhnms. The education and exercises of their youth. Their general assembly.*

As I ought to have understood human nature much better than I supposed it possible for my master to do, so it was easy to apply the character he gave of the Yahoos to myself and my countrymen; and I believed I could yet make farther discoveries from my own observation. I therefore often begged his honor to let me go among the herds of Yahoos in the neighborhood; to which he always very graciously consented, being perfectly convinced that the hatred I bore those brutes would never suffer me to be corrupted by them; and his honor ordered one of his servants, a strong sorrel nag, very honest and good-natured, to be my guard; without whose protection I durst not undertake such adventures. For I have already told the reader how much I was pestered by those odious animals upon my first arrival. I afterwards failed very narrowly three or four times of falling into their clutches, when I happened to stray at any distance without my hanger. And I have reason to believe, they had some imagination that I was of their own species, which I often assisted myself, by stripping up my sleeves, and shewing my naked arms and breast in their sight, when my protector was with me; at which times they would approach as near as they durst, and imitate my actions after the manner of monkeys, but ever with great signs of hatred; as a tame jackdaw with cap and stockings is always persecuted by the wild ones, when he happens to be got among them.

They are prodigiously nimble from their infancy; however, I once caught a young male of three years old, and endeavored by all marks of tenderness to make it quiet; but the little imp fell a squalling, scratching, and biting with such violence, that I was forced to let it go; and it was high time, for a whole troop of old ones came about us at the noise; but finding the cub was safe (for away it ran) and my sorrel nag being by, they durst not venture near us. I observed the young animal's flesh to smell very rank, and the stink was somewhat between a weasel and a fox, but much more disagreeable. I forgot another circumstance (and perhaps I might have the reader's pardon, if it were wholly omitted) that while I held the odious vermin in my hands, it voided its filthy excrements of a yellow liquid substance, all over my clothes; but by good fortune there was a small brook hard by, where I washed myself as clean as I could; although I durst not come into my master's presence until I were sufficiently aired.

By what I could discover, the Yahoos appear to be the most unteachable of all animals, their capacities never reaching higher than to draw or carry burdens. Yet I am of opinion, this defect ariseth chiefly from a perverse, restive disposition. For they are cunning, malicious, treacherous and revengeful. They are strong and hardy, but of a cowardly spirit, and by consequence insolent, abject, and cruel. It is observed that the red-haired of both sexes are more libidinous and mischievous than the rest, whom yet they much exceed in strength and activity.

The Houyhnhnms keep the Yahoos for present use in huts not far from the house; but the rest are sent abroad to certain fields, where they dig up roots, eat several kinds of herbs, and search about for carrion, or sometimes catch weasels and *luhimuhs* (a sort of wild rat) which they greedily devour. Nature hath taught them to dig deep holes with their nails on the side of a rising ground, wherein they lie by themselves; only the kennels of the females are larger, sufficient to hold two or three cubs.

They swim from their infancy like frogs, and are able to continue long under water, where they often take fish, which the females carry home to their young. And upon this occasion, I hope the reader will pardon my relating an odd adventure.

Being one day abroad with my protector the sorrel nag, and the weather exceeding hot, I entreated him to let me bathe in a river that was near. He consented, and I immediately stripped myself stark naked, and went down softly into the stream. It happened that a young female Yahoo standing behind a bank, saw the whole proceeding; and inflamed by desire, as the nag and I conjectured, came running with all speed, and leaped into the water within five yards of the place where I bathed. I was never in my life so terribly frighted; the nag was grazing at some distance, not suspecting any harm. She embraced me after a most fulsome manner; I roared as loud as I could, and the nag came galloping towards me, whereupon she quitted her grasp, with the utmost reluctancy, and leaped upon the opposite bank, where she stood gazing and howling all the time I was putting on my clothes.

This was matter of diversion to my master and his family, as well as of mortification to myself. For now I could no longer deny that I was a real Yahoo, in every limb and feature, since the females had a natural propensity to me as one of their own species; neither was the hair of this brute of a red color (which might have been some excuse for an appetite a little irregular) but black as a sloe, and her countenance did not make an appearance altogether so hideous as the rest of the kind; for I think, she could not be above eleven years old.

Having already lived three years in this country, the reader I suppose will expect that I should, like other travelers, give him some account of the manners and customs of its inhabitants, which it was indeed my principal study to learn.

As these noble Houyhnhnms are endowed by Nature with a general disposition to all virtues, and have no conceptions or ideas of what is evil in a rational creature; so their grand maxim is to cultivate reason, and to be wholly governed by it. Neither is reason among them a point problematical as with us, where men can argue with plausibility on both sides of a question; but strikes you with immediate conviction; as it must needs do where it is not mingled, obscured, or discolored by passion and interest. I remember it was with extreme difficulty that I could bring my master to understand the meaning of the word "opinion," or how a point could be disputable; because reason taught us to affirm or deny only where we are certain; and beyond our knowledge we cannot do either. So that controversies, wranglings, disputes, and positiveness in false or dubious propositions are evils unknown among the

Houyhnhnms. In the like manner when I used to explain to him our several systems of natural philosophy,[4] he would laugh that a creature pretending to reason should value itself upon the knowledge of other people's conjectures, and in things, where that knowledge, if it were certain, could be of no use. Wherein he agreed entirely with the sentiments of Socrates, as Plato delivers them, which I mention as the highest honor I can do that prince of philosophers. I have often since reflected what destruction such a doctrine would make in the libraries of Europe; and how many paths to fame would be then shut up in the learned world.

Friendship and benevolence are the two principal virtues among the Houyhnhnms; and these not confined to particular objects, but universal to the whole race. For a stranger from the remotest part is equally treated with the nearest neighbor, and wherever he goes, looks upon himself as at home. They preserve decency and civility in the highest degrees, but are altogether ignorant of ceremony. They have no fondness for their colts or foals; but the care they take in educating them proceedeth entirely from the dictates of reason. And I observed my master to show the same affection to his neighbor's issue that he had for his own. They will have it that Nature teaches them to love the whole species, and it is reason only that maketh a distinction of persons, where there is a superior degree of virtue.

When the matron Houyhnhnms have produced one of each sex, they no longer accompany with their consorts, except they lose one of their issue by some casualty, which very seldom happens; but in such a case they meet again; or when the like accident befalls a person whose wife is past bearing, some other couple bestows on him one of their own colts, and then go together a second time, until the mother be pregnant. This caution is necessary to prevent the country from being overburdened with numbers. But the race of inferior Houyhnhnms bred up to be servants is not so strictly limited upon this article; these are allowed to produce three of each sex, to be domestics in the noble families.

In their marriages they are exactly careful to choose such colors as will not make any disagreeable mixture in the breed. Strength is chiefly valued in the male, and comeliness in the female; not upon the account of love, but to preserve the race from degenerating; for, where a female happens to excel in strength, a consort is chosen with regard to comeliness. Courtship, love, presents, jointures, settlements, have no place in their thoughts, or terms whereby to express them in their language. The young couple meet and are joined, merely because it is the determination of their parents and friends; it is what they see done every day; and they look upon it as one of the necessary actions in a reasonable being. But the violation of marriage, or any other unchastity, was never heard of; and the married pair pass their lives with the same friendship and mutual benevolence that they bear to all others of the same species who come in their way, without jealousy, fondness, quarreling, or discontent.

In educating the youth of both sexes, their method is admirable, and highly deserveth our imitation. These are not suffered to taste a grain of oats, except upon certain days, till eighteen years old; nor milk, but very rarely; and in summer they graze two hours in the morning, and as many in the evening,

4. Science.

which their parents likewise observe; but the servants are not allowed above half that time; and a great part of the grass is brought home, which they eat at the most convenient hours when they can be best spared from work.

Temperance, industry, exercise, and cleanliness are the lessons equally enjoined to the young ones of both sexes; and my master thought it monstrous in us to give the females a different kind of education from the males, except in some articles of domestic management; whereby, as he truly observed, one half of our natives were good for nothing but bringing children into the world; and to trust the care of their children to such useless animals, he said was yet a greater instance of brutality.

But the Houyhnhnms train up their youth to strength, speed, and hardiness, by exercising them in running races up and down steep hills, or over hard stony grounds; and when they are all in a sweat, they are ordered to leap over head and ears into a pond or a river. Four times a year the youth of certain districts meet to show their proficiency in running, and leaping, and other feats of strength or agility; where the victor is rewarded with a song made in his or her praise. On this festival the servants drive a herd of Yahoos into the field, laden with hay, and oats, and milk for a repast to the Houyhnhnms; after which these brutes are immediately driven back again, for fear of being noisome to the assembly.

Every fourth year, at the vernal equinox, there is a representative council of the whole nation, which meets in a plain about twenty miles from our house, and continueth about five or six days. Here they inquire into the state and condition of the several districts; whether they abound or be deficient in hay or oats, or cows or Yahoos? And wherever there is any want (which is but seldom) it is immediately supplied by unanimous consent and contribution. Here likewise the regulation of children is settled: as for instance, if a Houyhnhnm hath two males, he changeth one of them with another who hath two females, and when a child hath been lost by any casualty, where the mother is past breeding, it is determined what family in the district shall breed another to supply the loss.

CHAPTER 9. *A grand debate at the general assembly of the Houyhnhnms, and how it was determined. The learning of the Houyhnhnms. Their buildings. Their manner of burials. The defectiveness of their language.*

One of these grand assemblies was held in my time, about three months before my departure, whither my master went as the representative of our district. In this council was resumed their old debate, and indeed, the only debate that ever happened in their country; whereof my master after his return gave me a very particular account.

The question to be debated was whether the Yahoos should be exterminated from the face of the earth. One of the members for the affirmative offered several arguments of great strength and weight, alleging that, as the Yahoos were the most filthy, noisome, and deformed animal which nature ever produced, so they were the most restive and indocile,[5] mischievous, and malicious; they would privately suck the teats of the Houyhnhnms' cows; kill and devour their cats, trample down their oats and grass, if they were

5. Unteachable.

not continually watched; and commit a thousand other extravagancies. He took notice of a general tradition, that Yahoos had not been always in their country, but that many ages ago, two of these brutes appeared together upon a mountain; whether produced by the heat of the sun upon corrupted mud and slime, or from the ooze and froth of the sea, was never known. That these Yahoos engendered, and their brood in a short time grew so numerous as to overrun and infest the whole nation. That the Houyhnhnms to get rid of this evil, made a general hunting, and at last enclosed the whole herd; and destroying the older, every Houyhnhnm kept two young ones in a kennel, and brought them to such a degree of tameness as an animal so savage by nature can be capable of acquiring, using them for draught and carriage. That there seemed to be much truth in this tradition, and that those creatures could not be *ylnhniamshy* (or aborigines of the land) because of the violent hatred the Houyhnhnms as well as all other animals bore them; which although their evil disposition sufficiently deserved, could never have arrived at so high a degree, if they had been aborigines, or else they would have long since been rooted out. That the inhabitants taking a fancy to use the service of the Yahoos, had very imprudently neglected to cultivate the breed of asses, which were a comely animal, easily kept, more tame and orderly, without any offensive smell, strong enough for labor, although they yield to the other in agility of body; and if their braying be no agreeable sound, it is far preferable to the horrible howlings of the Yahoos.

Several others declared their sentiments to the same purpose, when my master proposed an expedient to the assembly, whereof he had indeed borrowed the hint from me. He approved of the tradition, mentioned by the honorable member, who spoke before; and affirmed, that the two Yahoos said to be first seen among them, had been driven thither over the sea; that coming to land, and being forsaken by their companions, they retired to the mountains, and degenerating by degrees, became in process of time much more savage than those of their own species in the country from whence these two originals came. The reason of his assertion was that he had now in his possession a certain wonderful Yahoo (meaning myself) which most of them had heard of, and many of them had seen. He then related to them how he first found me; that my body was all covered with an artificial composure of the skins and hairs of other animals; that I spoke in a language of my own, and had thoroughly learned theirs; that I had related to him the accidents which brought me thither; that when he saw me without my covering, I was an exact Yahoo in every part, only of a whiter color, less hairy and with shorter claws. He added how I had endeavored to persuade him that in my own and other countries the Yahoos acted as the governing, rational animal, and held the Houyhnhnms in servitude; that he observed in me all the qualities of a Yahoo, only a little more civilized by some tincture of reason, which however was in a degree as far inferior to the Houyhnhnm race as the Yahoos of their country were to me; that among other things, I mentioned a custom we had of castrating Houyhnhnms when they were young, in order to render them tame; that the operation was easy and safe; that it was no shame to learn wisdom from brutes, as industry is taught by the ant, and building by the swallow (for so I translate the world *lyhannh*, although it be a much larger fowl). That this invention might be practiced upon the younger Yahoos here, which, besides rendering them tractable and fitter for use, would in an age put an end to the whole species without destroying life. That in the meantime the Houyhnhnms should be exhorted to cultivate the breed of asses, which, as they are in all respects more valuable brutes, so they have this advantage, to be fit for service at five years old, which the other are not till twelve.

This was all my master thought fit to tell me at that time, of what passed in the grand council. But he was pleased to conceal one particular, which related personally to myself, whereof I soon felt the unhappy effect, as the reader will know in its proper place, and from whence I date all the succeeding misfortunes of my life.

The Houyhnhnms have no letters, and consequently, their knowledge is all traditional. But there happening few events of any moment among a people so well united, naturally disposed to every virtue, wholly governed by reason, and cut off from all commerce with other nations, the historical part is easily preserved without burdening their memories. I have already observed that they are subject to no diseases, and therefore can have no need of physicians. However, they have excellent medicines composed of herbs, to cure accidental bruises and cuts in the pastern or frog of the foot by sharp stones, as well as other maims and hurts in the several parts of the body.

They calculate the year by the revolution of the sun and the moon, but use no subdivisions into weeks. They are well enough acquainted with the motions of those two luminaries, and understand the nature of eclipses; and this is the utmost progress of their astronomy.

In poetry they must be allowed to excel all other mortals; wherein the justness of their similes, and the minuteness, as well as exactness of their descriptions, are indeed inimitable. Their verses abound very much in both of these, and usually contain either some exalted notions of friendship and benevolence, or the praises of those who were victors in races and other bodily exercises. Their buildings, although very rude and simple, are not inconvenient, but well contrived to defend them from all injuries of cold and heat. They have a kind of tree, which at forty years old loosens in the root, and falls with the first storm; it grows very straight, and being pointed like stakes with a sharp stone (for the Houyhnhnms know not the use of iron), they stick them erect in the ground about ten inches asunder, and then weave in oat straw, or sometimes wattles, betwixt them. The roof is made after the same manner, and so are the doors.

The Houyhnhnms use the hollow part between the pastern and the hoof of their forefeet as we do our hands, and this with greater dexterity than I could at first imagine. I have seen a white mare of our family thread a needle (which I lent her on purpose) with that joint. They milk their cows, reap their oats, and do all the work which requires hands in the same manner. They have a kind of hard flints, which by grinding against other stones they form into instruments that serve instead of wedges, axes, and hammers. With tools made of these flints, they likewise cut their hay, and reap their oats, which there groweth naturally in several fields. The Yahoos draw home the sheaves in carriages, and the servants tread them in certain covered huts, to get out the grain, which is kept in stores. They make a rude kind of earthen and wooden vessels, and bake the former in the sun.

If they can avoid casualties, they die only of old age, and are buried in the obscurest places that can be found, their friends and relations expressing neither joy nor grief at their departure; nor does the dying person discover the least regret that he is leaving the world, any more than if he were upon returning home from a visit to one of his neighbors; I remember my master having once made an appointment with a friend and his family to come to his house upon some affair of importance; on the day fixed, the mistress and her two children came very late; she made two excuses, first for her husband, who, as she said, happened that very morning to *lhnuwnh*. The word is strongly expressive in their language, but not easily rendered into English; it signifies, *to retire to his first Mother*. Her excuse for not coming sooner was that her husband dying late in the morning, she was a good while consulting her servants about a convenient place where his body should be laid; and I observed she behaved herself at our house, as cheerfully as the rest. She died about three months after.

They live generally to seventy or seventy-five years, very seldom to four-score; some weeks before their death they feel a gradual decay, but without pain. During this time they are much visited by their friends, because they cannot go abroad with their usual ease and satisfaction. However, about ten days before their death, which they seldom fail in computing, they return the visits that have been made by those who are nearest in the neighborhood, being carried in a convenient sledge drawn by Yahoos; which vehicle they use, not only upon this occasion, but when they grow old, upon long journeys, or when they are lamed by any accident. And therefore when the dying Houyhnhnms return those visits, they take a solemn leave of their friends, as if they were going to some remote part of the country, where they designed to pass the rest of their lives.

I know not whether it may be worth observing, that the Houyhnhnms have no word in their language to express anything that is evil, except what they borrow from the deformities or ill qualities of the Yahoos. Thus they denote the folly of a servant, an omission of a child, a stone that cuts their feet, a continuance of foul or unseasonable weather, and the like, by adding to each the epithet of Yahoo. For instance, *hhnm Yahoo, whnaholm Yahoo, ynlhmndwihlma Yahoo,* and an ill-contrived house, *ynholmhnmrohlnw Yahoo.*

I could with great pleasure enlarge farther upon the manners and virtues of this excellent people; but intending in a short time to publish a volume by itself expressly upon that subject, I refer the reader thither. And in the meantime, proceed to relate my own sad catastrophe.

CHAPTER 10. *The Author's economy, and happy life among the Houyhnhnms. His great improvement in virtue, by conversing with them. Their conversations. The Author hath notice given him by his master that he must depart from the country. He falls into a swoon for grief, but submits. He contrives and finishes a canoe, by the help of a fellow servant, and puts to sea at a venture.*

I had settled my little economy to my own heart's content. My master had ordered a room to be made for me after their manner, about six yards from the house; the sides and floors of which I plastered with clay, and covered with rush mats of my own contriving; I had beaten hemp, which there grows wild, and made of it a sort of ticking; this I filled with the feathers of several birds I had taken with springes made of Yahoos' hairs, and were excellent food. I had worked two chairs with my knife, the sorrel nag helping me in the grosser and more laborious part. When my clothes were worn to rags, I made myself others with the skins of rabbits, and of a certain beautiful animal about the same size, called *nnuhnoh*, the skin of which is covered with a fine down. Of these I likewise made very tolerable stockings. I soled my shoes with wood which I cut from a tree, and fitted to the upper leather, and when this was worn out, I supplied it with the skins of Yahoos, dried in the sun. I often got honey out of hollow trees, which I mingled with water, or eat it with my bread. No man could more verify the truth of these two maxims, that *Nature is very easily satisfied;* and, that *Necessity is the mother of invention*. I enjoyed perfect health of body, and tranquility of mind; I did not feel the treachery or inconstancy of a friend, nor the inquiries of a secret or open enemy. I had no occasion of bribing, flattering, or pimping to procure the favor of any great man, or of his minion. I wanted no fence against fraud or oppression; here was neither physician to destroy my body, nor lawyer to ruin my fortune; no informer to watch my words and actions, or forge accusations against me for hire; here were no gibers, censurers, backbiters, pickpockets, highwaymen, housebreakers, attorneys, bawds, buffoons, gamesters, politicians, wits, splenetics, tedious talkers, controvertists, ravishers, murderers, robbers, virtuosos;[6] no leaders or followers of party and faction; no encouragers to vice, by seducement or examples; no dungeons, axes, gibbets, whipping posts, or pillories; no cheating shopkeepers or mechanics; no pride, vanity or affectation; no fops, bullies, drunkards, strolling whores, or poxes; no ranting, lewd, expensive wives; no stupid, proud pedants; no importunate, overbearing, quarrelsome, noisy, roaring, empty, conceited, swearing companions; no scoundrels raised from the dust upon the merit of their vices; or nobility thrown into it on account of their virtues; no lords, fiddlers, judges, or dancing masters.

I had the favor of being admitted to several Houyhnhnms, who came to visit or dine with my master; where his honor graciously suffered me to wait in the room, and listen to their discourse. Both he and his company would often descend to ask me questions, and receive my answers. I had also sometimes the honor of attending my master in his visits to others. I never presumed to speak, except in answer to a question; and then I did it with inward regret, because it was a loss of so much time for improving myself; but I was infinitely delighted with the station of an humble auditor in such conversations, where nothing passed but what was useful, expressed in the fewest and most significant words; where (as I have already said) the greatest decency was observed, without the least degree of ceremony; where no person spoke without being pleased himself, and pleasing his companions; where there was no interruption, tediousness, heat, or difference of sentiments. They have a notion, that when people are met together, a short silence doth much improve conversation; this I found to be true; for during those little intermissions of talk, new ideas would arise in their minds, which very much enlivened the discourse. Their subjects are generally on friendship and benevolence; on order and economy; sometimes upon the visible operations of nature, or ancient traditions; upon the bounds and limits of virtue; upon the unerring rules of reason; or upon some determinations, to be taken at the next great assembly; and often upon the various excellencies of poetry. I

---

6. Savants; those who pursue special interests in the arts or sciences.

may add, without vanity, that my presence often gave them sufficient matter for discourse, because it afforded my master an occasion of letting his friends into the history of me and my country, upon which they were all pleased to descant in a manner not very advantageous to human kind; and for that reason I shall not repeat what they said; only I may be allowed to observe that his honor, to my great admiration, appeared to understand the nature of Yahoos much better than myself. He went through all our vices and follies, and discovered many which I had never mentioned to him; by only supposing what qualities a Yahoo of their country, with a small proportion of reason, might be capable of exerting; and concluded, with too much probability, how vile as well as miserable such a creature must be.

I freely confess, that all the little knowledge I have of any value was acquired by the lectures I received from my master, and from hearing the discourses of him and his friends; to which I should be prouder to listen, than to dictate to the greatest and wisest assembly in Europe. I admired the strength, comeliness, and speed of the inhabitants; and such a constellation of virtues in such amiable persons produced in me the highest veneration. At first, indeed, I did not feel that natural awe which the Yahoos and all other animals bear towards them; but it grew upon me by degrees, much sooner than I imagined, and was mingled with a respectful love and gratitude, that they would condescend to distinguish me from the rest of my species.

When I thought of my family, my friends, my countrymen, or human race in general, I considered them as they really were, Yahoos in shape and disposition, perhaps a little more civilized, and qualified with the gift of speech; but making no other use of reason than to improve and multiply those vices, whereof their brethren in this country had only the share that nature allotted them. When I happened to behold the reflection of my own form in a lake or fountain, I turned away my face in horror and detestation of myself, and could better endure the sight of a common Yahoo than of my own person. By conversing with the Houyhnhnms, and looking upon them with delight, I fell to imitate their gait and gesture, which is now grown into a habit; and my friends often tell me in a blunt way, that I trot like a horse; which, however, I take for a great compliment. Neither shall I disown, that in speaking I am apt to fall into the voice and manner of the Houyhnhnms, and hear myself ridiculed on that account without the least mortification.

In the midst of this happiness, when I looked upon myself to be fully settled for life, my master sent for me one morning a little earlier than his usual hour. I observed by his countenance that he was in some perplexity, and at a loss how to begin what he had to speak. After a short silence, he told me, he did not know how I would take what he was going to say; that, in the last general assembly, when the affair of the Yahoos was entered upon, the representatives had taken offense at his keeping a Yahoo (meaning myself) in his family more like a Houyhnhnm than a brute animal. That he was known frequently to converse with me, as if he could receive some advantage of pleasure in my company; that such a practice was not agreeable to reason or nature, or a thing ever heard of before among them. The assembly did therefore exhort him, either to employ me like the rest of my species, or command me to swim back to the place from whence I came. That the first of these expedients was utterly rejected by all the Houyhnhnms who had ever seen me at his house or their own; for, they alleged, that because I had some rudiments of reason, added to the natural pravity[7] of those animals, it was to be feared, I might be able to seduce them into the woody and mountainous parts of the country, and bring them in troops by night to destroy the Houyhnhnms' cattle, as being naturally of the ravenous kind, and averse from labor.

My master added that he was daily pressed by the Houyhnhnms of the neighborhood to have the assembly's exhortation executed, which he could not put off much longer. He doubted[8] it would be impossible for me to swim to another country; and therefore wished I would contrive some sort of vehicle resembling those I had described to him, that might carry me on the sea; in which work I should have the assistance of his own servants, as well as those of his neighbors. He concluded that for his own part he could have been content to keep me in his service as long as I lived; because he found I had cured myself of some bad habits and dispositions, by endeavoring, as far as my inferior nature was capable, to imitate the Houyhnhnms.

I should here observe to the reader, that a decree of the general assembly in this country is expressed by the word *hnhloayn*, which signifies an exhortation, as near as I can render it; for they have no conception how a rational creature can be compelled, but only advised, or exhorted; because no person can disobey reason without giving up his claim to be a rational creature.

I was struck with the utmost grief and despair at my master's discourse; and being unable to support the agonies I was under, I fell into a swoon at his feet; when I came to myself, he told me that he concluded I had been dead (for these people are subject to no such imbecilities of nature). I answered, in a faint voice, that death would have been too great an happiness; that although I could not blame the assembly's exhortation, or the urgency of his friends; yet in my weak and corrupt judgment, I thought it might consist with reason to have been less rigorous. That I could not swim a league, and probably the nearest land to theirs might be distant above an hundred; that many materials, necessary for making a small vessel to carry me off, were wholly wanting in this country, which, however, I would attempt in obedience and gratitude to his honor, although I concluded the thing to be impossible, and therefore looked on myself as already devoted[9] to destruction. That the certain prospect of an unnatural death was the least of my evils; for, supposing I should escape with life by some strange adventure, how could I think with temper[1] of passing my days among Yahoos, and relapsing into my old corruptions, for want of examples to lead and keep me within the paths of virtue. That I knew too well upon what solid reasons all the determinations of the wise Houyhnhnms were founded, not to be shaken by arguments of mine, a miserable Yahoo; and therefore after presenting him with my humble thanks for the offer of his servants' assistance in making a vessel, and desiring a reasonable time for so difficult a work, I told him I would endeavor to preserve a wretched being; and, if ever I returned to England, was not without hopes of being useful to my own species by celebrating the praises of the renowned Houyhnhnms, and proposing their virtues to the imitation of mankind.

My master in a few words made me a very gracious reply, allowed me the

---

7. Corruption.
8. Feared.

9. Doomed.
1. Equanimity.

space of two months to finish my boat, and ordered the sorrel nag, my fellow servant (for so at this distance I may presume to call him), to follow my instructions, because I told my master that his help would be sufficient, and I knew he had a tenderness for me.

In his company my first business was to go to that part of the coast where my rebellious crew had ordered me to be set on shore. I got upon a height, and looking on every side into the sea, fancied I saw a small island towards the northeast; I took out my pocket glass, and could then clearly distinguish it about five leagues off, as I computed; but it appeared to the sorrel nag to be only a blue cloud; for, as he had no conception of any country besides his own, so he could not be as expert in distinguishing remote objects at sea, as we who so much converse in that element.

After I had discovered this island, I considered no farther; but resolved, it should, if possible, be the first place of my banishment, leaving the consequence to fortune.

I returned home, and consulting with the sorrel nag, we went into a copse at some distance, where I with my knive, and he with a sharp flint fastened very artificially,[2] after their manner, to a wooden handle, cut down several oak wattles about the thickness of a walking staff, and some larger pieces. But I shall not trouble the reader with a particular description of my own mechanics; let it suffice to say, that in six weeks time, with the help of the sorrel nag, who performed the parts that required most labor, I finished a sort of Indian canoe; but much larger, covering it with the skins of Yahoos, well stitched together, with hempen threads of my own making. My sail was likewise composed of the skins of the same animal; but I made use of the youngest I could get, the older being too tough and thick; and I likewise provided myself with four paddles. I laid in a stock of boiled flesh, of rabbits and fowls; and took with me two vessels, one filled with milk, and the other with water.

I tried my canoe in a large pond near my master's house, and then corrected in it what was amiss, stopping all the chinks with Yahoo's tallow, till I found it staunch, and able to bear me and my freight. And when it was as complete as I could possibly make it, I had it drawn on a carriage very gently by Yahoos, to the seaside, under the conduct of the sorrel nag and another servant.

When all was ready, and the day came for my departure, I took leave of my master and lady, and the whole family, my eyes flowing with tears and my heart quite sunk with grief. But his honor, out of curiosity, and perhaps (if I may speak it without vanity) partly out of kindness, was determined to see me in my canoe; and got several of his neighboring friends to accompany him. I was forced to wait above an hour for the tide, and then observing the wind very fortunately bearing towards the island to which I intended to steer my course, I took a second leave of my master; but as I was going to prostrate myself to kiss his hoof, he did me the honor to raise it gently to my mouth. I am not ignorant how much I have been censured for mentioning this last particular. Detractors are pleased to think it improbable that so illustrious a person should descend to give so great a mark of distinction to a creature so inferior as I. Neither have I forgot how apt some travelers are to boast of

2. Artfully.

extraordinary favors they have received. But, if these censurers were better acquainted with the noble and courteous disposition of the Houyhnhnms, they would soon change their opinion. I paid my respects to the rest of the Houyhnhnms in his honor's company; then getting into my canoe, I pushed off from shore.

CHAPTER 11. *The Author's dangerous voyage. He arrives at New Holland, hoping to settle there. Is wounded with an arrow by one of the natives. Is seized and carried by force into a Portuguese ship. The great civilities of the Captain. The Author arrives at England.*

I began this desperate voyage on February 15, 1714/5,[3] at 9 o'clock in the morning. The wind was very favorable; however, I made use at first only of my paddles; but considering I should soon be weary, and that the wind might probably chop about, I ventured to set up my little sail, and thus, with the help of the tide, I went at the rate of a league and a half an hour, as near as I could guess. My master and his friends continued on the shore, till I was almost out of sight; and I often heard the sorrel nag (who always loved me) crying out, *"Hnuy illa nyha maiah Yahoo"* ("Take care of thyself, gentle Yahoo").

My design was, if possible, to discover some small island uninhabited, yet sufficient by my labor to furnish me with necessaries of life, which I would have thought a greater happiness than to be first minister in the politest court of Europe, so horrible was the idea I conceived of returning to live in the society and under the government of Yahoos. For in such a solitude as I desired, I could at least enjoy my own thoughts, and reflect with delight on the virtues of those inimitable Houyhnhnms, without any opportunity of degenerating into the vices and corruptions of my own species.

The reader may remember what I related when my crew conspired against me, and confined me to my cabin, how I continued there several weeks, without knowing what course we took; and when I was put ashore in the longboat, how the sailors told me with oaths, whether true or false, that they knew not in what part of the world we were. However, I did then believe us to be about 10 degrees southward of the Cape of Good Hope, or about 45 degrees southern latitude, as I gathered from some general words I overheard among them, being I supposed to the southeast in their intended voyage to Madagascar. And although this were but little better than conjecture, yet I resolved to steer my course eastward, hoping to reach the southwest coast of New Holland, and perhaps some such island as I desired, lying westward of it. The wind was full west, and by six in the evening I computed I had gone eastward at least eighteen leagues; when I spied a very small island about half a league off, which I soon reached. It was nothing but a rock with one creek, naturally arched by the force of tempests. Here I put in my canoe, and climbing a part of the rock, I could plainly discover land to the east, extending from south to north. I lay all night in my canoe; and repeating my voyage early in the morning, I arrived in seven hours to the southeast point of New Holland. This confirmed me in the opinion I have long entertained, that the maps and charts place this country at least three degrees more to

3. I.e., 1715, by modern dating. The year began on March 25.

the east than it really is; which thought I communicated many years ago to my worthy friend Mr. Herman Moll,[4] and gave him my reasons for it, although he hath rather chosen to follow other authors.

I saw no inhabitants in the place where I landed; and being unarmed, I was afraid of venturing far into the country. I found some shellfish on the shore, and eat them raw, not daring to kindle a fire, for fear of being discovered by the natives. I continued three days feeding on oysters and limpets, to save my own provisions; and I fortunately found a brook of excellent water, which gave me great relief.

On the fourth day, venturing out early a little too far, I saw twenty or thirty natives upon a height, not above five hundred yards from me. They were stark naked, men, women, and children round a fire, as I could discover by the smoke. One of them spied me, and gave notice to the rest; five of them advanced towards me, leaving the women and children at the fire. I made what haste I could to the shore, and getting into my canoe, shoved off; the savages observing me retreat, ran after me; and before I could get far enough into the sea, discharged an arrow, which wounded me deeply on the inside of my left knee. (I shall carry the mark to my grave.) I apprehended the arrow might be poisoned; and paddling out of the reach of their darts (being a calm day) I made a shift to suck the wound, and dress it as well as I could.

I was at a loss what to do, for I durst not return to the same landing place, but stood to the north, and was forced to paddle; for the wind, although very gentle, was against me, blowing northwest. As I was looking about for a secure landing place, I saw a sail to the north northeast, which appearing every minute more visible, I was in some doubt whether I should wait for them or no; but at last my detestation of the Yahoo race prevailed; and turning my canoe, I sailed and paddled together to the south, and got into the same creek from whence I set out in the morning, choosing rather to trust myself among these barbarians than live with European Yahoos. I drew up my canoe as close as I could to the shore, and hid myself behind a stone by the little brook, which, as I have already said, was excellent water.

The ship came within half a league of this creek, and sent out her longboat with vessels to take in fresh water (for the place it seems was very well known), but I did not observe it until the boat was almost on shore; and it was too late to seek another hiding place. The seamen at their landing observed my canoe, and rummaging it all over, easily conjectured that the owner could not be far off. Four of them well armed searched every cranny and lurking hole, till at last they found me flat on my face behind the stone. They gazed a while in admiration at my strange uncouth dress; my coat made of skins, my wooden-soled shoes, and my furred stockings; from whence, however, they concluded I was not a native of the place, who all go naked. One of the seamen in Portuguese bid me rise, and asked who I was. I understood that language very well, and getting upon my feet, said I was a poor Yahoo, banished from the Houyhnhnms, and desired they would please to let me depart. They admired to hear me answer them in their own tongue, and saw by my complexion I must be an European; but were at a loss to know what I meant by Yahoos and Houyhnhnms, and at the same time fell a laughing at my strange tone in speaking, which resembled the neighing of

4. A famous contemporary map maker.

a horse. I trembled all the while betwixt fear and hatred; I again desired leave to depart, and was gently moving to my canoe; but they laid hold on me, desiring to know what country I was of? whence I came? with many other questions. I told them I was born in England, from whence I came about five years ago, and then their country and ours was at peace. I therefore hoped they would not treat me as an enemy, since I meant them no harm, but was a poor Yahoo, seeking some desolate place where to pass the remainder of his unfortunate life.

When they began to talk, I thought I never heard or saw any thing so unnatural; for it appeared to me as monstrous as if a dog or a cow should speak in England, or a Yahoo in Houyhnhnmland. The honest Portuguese were equally amazed at my strange dress, and the odd manner of delivering my words, which however they understood very well. They spoke to me with great humanity, and said they were sure their Captain would carry me *gratis* to Lisbon, from whence I might return to my own country; that two of the seamen would go back to the ship, to inform the Captain of what they had seen, and receive his orders; in the meantime, unless I would give my solemn oath not to fly, they would secure me by force. I thought it best to comply with their proposal. They were very curious to know my story, but I gave them very little satisfaction; and they all conjectured, that my misfortunes had impaired my reason. In two hours the boat, which went laden with vessels of water, returned with the Captain's commands to fetch me on board. I fell on my knees to preserve my liberty; but all was in vain, and the men having tied me with cords, heaved me into the boat, from whence I was taken into the ship, and from thence into the Captain's cabin.

His name was Pedro de Mendez; he was a very courteous and generous person; he entreated me to give some account of myself, and desired to know what I would eat or drink; said I should be used as well as himself, and spoke so many obliging things, that I wondered to find such civilities from a Yahoo. However, I remained silent and sullen; I was ready to faint at the very smell of him and his men. At last I desired something to eat out of my own canoe; but he ordered me a chicken and some excellent wine, and then directed that I should be put to bed in a very clean cabin. I would not undress myself, but lay on the bedclothes; and in half an hour stole out, when I thought the crew was at dinner; and getting to the side of the ship, was going to leap into the sea, and swim for my life, rather than continue among Yahoos. But one of the seamen prevented me, and having informed the Captain, I was chained to my cabin.

After dinner Don Pedro came to me, and desired to know my reason for so desperate an attempt; assured me he only meant to do me all the service he was able; and spoke so very movingly, that at last I descended to treat him like an animal which had some little portion of reason. I gave him a very short relation of my voyage; of the conspiracy against me by my own men; of the country where they set me on shore, and of my five years residence there. All which he looked upon as if it were a dream or a vision; whereat I took great offense; for I had quite forgot the faculty of lying, so peculiar to Yahoos in all countries where they preside, and consequently the disposition of suspecting truth in others of their own species. I asked him whether it were the custom of his country to *say the thing that was not?* I assured him I had almost forgot what he meant by falsehood; and if I had lived a thousand years in Houyhnhnmland, I should never have heard a lie from the meanest servant. That I was altogether indifferent whether he believed me or no; but however, in return for his favors, I would give so much allowance to the corruption of his nature, as to answer any objection he would please to make; and he might easily discover the truth.

The Captain, a wise man, after many endeavors to catch me tripping in some part of my story, at last began to have a better opinion of my veracity. But he added that since I professed so inviolable an attachment to truth, I must give him my word of honor to bear him company in this voyage without attempting anything against my life; or else he would continue me a prisoner till we arrived at Lisbon. I gave him the promise he required; but at the same time protested that I would suffer the greatest hardships rather than return to live among Yahoos.

Our voyage passed without any considerable accident. In gratitude to the Captain I sometimes sat with him at his earnest request, and strove to conceal my antipathy against humankind, although it often broke out; which he suffered to pass without observation. But the greatest part of the day, I confined myself to my cabin, to avoid seeing any of the crew. The Captain had often entreated me to strip myself of my savage dress, and offered to lend me the best suit of clothes he had. This I would not be prevailed on to accept, abhorring to cover myself with anything that had been on the back of a Yahoo. I only desired he would lend me two clean shirts, which having been washed since he wore them, I believed would not so much defile me. These I changed every second day, and washed them myself.

We arrived at Lisbon, Nov. 5, 1715. At our landing, the Captain forced me to cover myself with his cloak, to prevent the rabble from crowding about me. I was conveyed to his own house; and at my earnest request, he led me up to the highest room backwards.[5] I conjured him to conceal from all persons what I had told him of the Houyhnhnms; because the least hint of such a story would not only draw numbers of people to see me, but probably put me in danger of being imprisoned, or burned by the Inquisition. The Captain persuaded me to accept a suit of clothes newly made; but I would not suffer the tailor to take my measure; however, Don Pedro being almost of my size, they fitted me well enough. He accoutered me with other necessaries, all new, which I aired for twenty-four hours before I would use them.

The Captain had no wife, nor above three servants, none of which were suffered to attend at meals; and his whole deportment was so obliging, added to very good human understanding, that I really began to tolerate his company. He gained so far upon me, that I ventured to look out of the back window. By degrees I was brought into another room, from whence I peeped into the street, but drew my head back in a fright. In a week's time he seduced me down to the door. I found my terror gradually lessened, but my hatred and contempt seemed to increase. I was at last bold enough to walk the street in his company, but kept my nose well stopped with rue, or sometimes with tobacco.

In ten days, Don Pedro, to whom I had given some account of my domestic affairs, put it upon me as a point of honor and conscience that I ought to return to my native country, and live at home with my wife and children. He

5. At the rear.

told me there was an English ship in the port just ready to sail, and he would furnish me with all things necessary. It would be tedious to repeat his arguments, and my contradictions. He said it was altogether impossible to find such a solitary island as I had desired to live in; but I might command in my own house, and pass my time in a manner as recluse as I pleased.

I complied at last, finding I could not do better. I left Lisbon the 24th day of November, in an English merchantman, but who was the Master I never inquired. Don Pedro accompanied me to the ship, and lent me twenty pounds. He took kind leave of me, and embraced me at parting; which I bore as well as I could. During this last voyage I had no commerce with the Master, or any of his men; but pretending I was sick kept close in my cabin. On the fifth of December, 1715, we cast anchor in the Downs about nine in the morning, and at three in the afternoon I got safe to my house at Redriff.

My wife and family received me with great surprise and joy, because they concluded me certainly dead; but I must freely confess, the sight of them filled me only with hatred, disgust, and contempt; and the more, by reflecting on the near alliance I had to them. For although since my unfortunate exile from the Houyhnhnm country, I had compelled myself to tolerate the sight of Yahoos, and to converse with Don Pedro de Mendez; yet my memory and imaginations were perpetually filled with the virtues and ideas of those exalted Houyhnhnms. And when I began to consider that by copulating with one of the Yahoo species, I had become a parent of more, it struck me with the utmost shame, confusion, and horror.

As soon as I entered the house, my wife took me in her arms, and kissed me; at which, having not been used to the touch of that odious animal for so many years, I fell in a swoon for almost an hour. At the time I am writing, it is five years since my last return to England. During the first year I could not endure my wife or children in my presence, the very smell of them was intolerable; much less could I suffer them to eat in the same room. To this hour they dare not presume to touch my bread, or drink out of the same cup; neither was I ever able to let one of them take me by the hand. The first money I laid out was to buy two young stone-horses,[6] which I keep in a good stable, and next to them the groom is my greatest favorite; for I feel my spirits revived by the smell he contracts in the stable. My horses understand me tolerably well; I converse with them at least four hours every day. They are strangers to bridle or saddle; they live in great amity with me, and friendship to each other.

CHAPTER 12. *The Author's veracity. His design in publishing this work. His censure of those travelers who swerve from the truth. The Author clears himself from any sinister ends in writing. His native country commended. The right of the crown to those countries described by the Author is justified. The difficulty of conquering them. The Author takes his last leave of the reader; proposeth his manner of living for the future; gives good advice, and concludeth.*

Thus gentle reader, I have given thee a faithful history of my travels for sixteen years, and above seven months; wherein I have not been so studious

6. Stallions.

of ornament as of truth. I could perhaps like others have astonished thee with strange improbable tales; but I rather chose to relate plain matter of fact in the simplest manner and style; because my principal design was to inform, and not to amuse thee.

It is easy for us who travel into remote countries, which are seldom visited by Englishmen or other Europeans, to form descriptions of wonderful animals both at sea and land. Whereas a traveler's chief aim should be to make men wiser and better, and to improve their minds by the bad as well as good example of what they deliver concerning foreign places.

I could heartily wish a law were enacted, that every traveler, before he were permitted to publish his voyages, should be obliged to make oath before the Lord High Chancellor that all he intended to print was absolutely true to the best of his knowledge; for then the world would no longer be deceived as it usually is, while some writers, to make their works pass the better upon the public, impose the grossest falsities on the unwary reader. I have perused several books of travels with great delight in my younger days; but, having since gone over most parts of the globe, and been able to contradict many fabulous accounts from my own observation, it hath given me a great disgust against this part of reading, and some indignation to see the credulity of mankind so impudently abused. Therefore, since my acquaintance were pleased to think my poor endeavors might not be unacceptable to my country, I imposed on myself as a maxim, never to be swerved from, that I would *strictly adhere to truth*; neither indeed can I be ever under the least temptation to vary from it, while I retain in my mind the lectures and example of my noble master, and the other illustrious Houyhnhnms, of whom I had so long the honor to be an humble hearer.

> ——*Nec si miserum Fortuna Sinonem*
> *Finxit, vanum etiam, mendacemque improba finget.*[7]

I know very well how little reputation is to be got by writings which require neither genius nor learning, nor indeed any other talent, except a good memory, or an exact *Journal*. I know likewise, that writers of travels, like dictionary-makers, are sunk into oblivion by the weight and bulk of those who come last, and therefore lie uppermost. And it is highly probable that such travelers who shall hereafter visit the countries described in this work of mine, may be detecting my errors (if there be any) and adding many new discoveries of their own, jostle me out of vogue, and stand in my place, making the world forget that ever I was an author. This indeed would be too great a mortification if I wrote for fame; but, as my sole intention was the PUBLIC GOOD, I cannot be altogether disappointed. For, who can read the virtues I have mentioned in the glorious Houyhnhnms, without being ashamed of his own vices, when he considers himself as the reasoning, governing animal of his country? I shall say nothing of those remote nations where Yahoos preside; amongst which the least corrupted are the Brobdingnagians, whose wise maxims in morality and government it would be our happiness to observe. But I forbear descanting further, and rather leave the judicious reader to his own remarks and applications.

---

7. Nor if Fortune had molded Sinon for misery, will she also in spite mold him as false and lying (Latin; Virgil's *Aeneid* 2.79–80).

I am not a little pleased that this work of mine can possibly meet with no censurers; for what objections can be made against a writer who relates only plain facts that happened in such distant countries, where we have not the least interest with respect either to trade or negotiations? I have carefully avoided every fault with which common writers of travels are often too justly charged. Besides, I meddle not the least with any party, but write without passion, prejudice, or ill-will against any man or number of men whatsoever. I write for the noblest end, to inform and instruct mankind, over whom I may, without breach of modesty, pretend to some superiority, from the advantages I received by conversing so long among the most accomplished Houyhnhnms. I write without any view towards profit or praise. I never suffer a word to pass that may look like a reflection, or possibly give the least offense even to those who are most ready to take it. So that, I hope, I may with justice pronounce myself an Author perfectly blameless; against whom the tribes of answerers, considerers, observers, reflectors, detecters, remarkers will never be able to find matter for exercising their talents.

I confess it was whispered to me that I was bound in duty as a subject of England, to have given in a memorial[8] to a secretary of state, at my first coming over; because, whatever lands are discovered by a subject, belong to the Crown. But I doubt whether our conquests in the countries I treat of would be as easy as those of Ferdinando Cortez over the naked Americans. The Lilliputians, I think, are hardly worth the charge of a fleet and army to reduce them; and I question whether it might be prudent or safe to attempt the Brobdingnagians; or, whether an English army would be much at their ease with the Flying Island over their heads. The Houyhnhnms, indeed, appear not to be so well prepared for war, a science to which they are perfect strangers, and especially against missive weapons. However, supposing myself to be a minister of state, I could never give my advice for invading them. Their prudence, unanimity, unacquaintedness with fear, and their love of their country would amply supply all defects in the military art. Imagine twenty thousand of them breaking into the midst of an European army, confounding the ranks, overturning the carriages, battering the warriors' faces into mummy, by terrible yerks[9] from their hinder hoofs: for they would well deserve the character given to Augustus, *Recalcitrat undique tutus*.[1] But instead of proposals for conquering that magnanimous nation, I rather wish they were in a capacity or disposition to send a sufficient number of their inhabitants for civilizing Europe; by teaching us the first principles of Honor, Justice, Truth, Temperance, public Spirit, Fortitude, Chastity, Friendship, Benevolence, and Fidelity. The names of all which virtues are still retained among us in most languages, and are to be met with in modern as well as ancient authors, which I am able to assert from my own small reading.

But I had another reason which made me less forward to enlarge his majesty's dominions by my discoveries: to say the truth, I had conceived a few scruples with relation to the distributive justice of princes upon those occasions. For instance, a crew of pirates are driven by a storm they know not whither; at length a boy discovers land from the topmast; they go on shore to rob and plunder; they see an harmless people, are entertained with kind-

---

8. Statement of facts for government use.
9. Kicks. "Mummy": pulp.

1. He kicks backward, at every point on his guard (Latin; Horace's *Satires* 2.1.20).

ness, they give the country a new name, they take formal possession of it for the king, they set up a rotten plank or a stone for a memorial, they murder two or three dozen of the natives, bring away a couple more by force for a sample, return home, and get their pardon. Here commences a new dominion acquired with a title by Divine Right. Ships are sent with the first opportunity; the natives driven out or destroyed, their princes tortured to discover their gold; a free license given to all acts of inhumanity and lust; the earth reeking with the blood of its inhabitants: and this execrable crew of butchers employed in so pious an expedition is a *modern colony* sent to convert and civilize an idolatrous and barbarous people.

But this description, I confess, doth by no means affect the British nation, who may be an example to the whole world for their wisdom, care, and justice in planting colonies; their liberal endowments for the advancement of religion and learning; their choice of devout and able pastors to propagate Christianity; their caution in stocking their provinces with people of sober lives and conversations from this the Mother Kingdom; their strict regard to the distribution of justice, in supplying the civil administration through all their colonies with officers of the greatest abilities, utter strangers to corruption: and to crown all, by sending the most vigilant and virtuous governors, who have no other views than the happiness of the people over whom they preside, and the honor of the king their master.

But, as those countries which I have described do not appear to have any desire of being conquered, and enslaved, murdered, or driven out by colonies, nor abound either in gold, silver, sugar, or tobacco, I did humbly conceive they were by no means proper objects of our zeal, our valor, or our interest. However, if those whom it may concern, think fit to be of another opinion, I am ready to depose, when I shall be lawfully called, that no European did ever visit these countries before me. I mean, if the inhabitants ought to be believed.

But, as to the formality of taking possession in my sovereign's name, it never came once into my thoughts; and if it had, yet as my affairs then stood, I should perhaps in point of prudence and self-preservation have put it off to a better opportunity.

Having thus answered the only objection that can be raised against me as a traveler, I here take a final leave of my courteous readers, and return to enjoy my own speculations in my little garden at Redriff; to apply those excellent lessons of virtue which I learned among the Houyhnhnms; to instruct the Yahoos of my own family as far as I shall find them docible animals; to behold my figure often in a glass, and thus if possible habituate myself by time to tolerate the sight of a human creature; to lament the brutality of Houyhnhnms in my own country, but always treat their persons with respect, for the sake of my noble master, his family, his friends, and the whole Houyhnhnm race, whom these of ours have the honor to resemble in all their lineaments, however their intellectuals came to degenerate.

I began last week to permit my wife to sit at dinner with me, at the farthest end of a long table; and to answer (but with the utmost brevity) the few questions I ask her. Yet the smell of a Yahoo continuing very offensive, I always keep my nose well stopped with rue, lavender, or tobacco leaves. And although it be hard for a man late in life to remove old habits, I am not altogether out of hopes in some time to suffer a neighbor Yahoo in my company, without the apprehensions I am yet under of his teeth or his claws.

My reconcilement to the Yahoo kind in general might not be so difficult, if they would be content with those vices and follies only which nature hath entitled them to. I am not in the least provoked at the sight of a lawyer, a pickpocket, a colonel, a fool, a lord, a gamester, a politician, a whoremonger, a physician, an evidence,[2] a suborner, an attorney, a traitor, or the like: this is all according to the due course of things. But when I behold a lump of deformity, and diseases both in body and mind, smitten with *pride*, it immediately breaks all the measures of my patience; neither shall I be ever able to comprehend how such an animal and such a vice could tally together. The wise and virtuous Houyhnhnms, who abound in all excellencies that can adorn a rational creature, have no name for this vice in their language, which hath no terms to express anything that is evil, except those whereby they describe the detestable qualities of their Yahoos, among which they were not able to distinguish this of pride, for want of thoroughly understanding human nature, as it showeth itself in other countries, where that animal presides. But I, who had more experience, could plainly observe some rudiments of it among the wild Yahoos.

But the Houyhnhnms, who live under the government of reason, are no more proud of the good qualities they possess, than I should be for not wanting a leg or an arm, which no man in his wits would boast of, although he must be miserable without them. I dwell the longer upon this subject from the desire I have to make the society of an English Yahoo by any means not insupportable; and therefore I here entreat those who have any tincture of this absurd vice, that they will not presume to appear in my sight.

1726, 1735

A Modest Proposal[1] Ironic title

FOR PREVENTING THE CHILDREN OF POOR PEOPLE IN IRELAND FROM BEING A BURDEN TO THEIR PARENTS OR COUNTRY, AND FOR MAKING THEM BENEFICIAL TO THE PUBLIC

It is a melancholy object to those who walk through this great town[2] or travel in the country, when they see the streets, the roads, and cabin doors, crowded with beggars of the female sex, followed by three, four, or six children, all in rags and importuning every passenger for an alms. These mothers, [he sounds as though he feels sorry for them] instead of being able to work for their honest livelihood, are forced to employ all their time in strolling to beg sustenance for their helpless infants, who, as they grow up, either turn thieves for want of work, or leave their dear

---

2. Witness.

1. *A Modest Proposal* is an example of Swift's favorite satiric devices used with superb effect. Irony (from the deceptive adjective *modest* in the title to the very last sentence) pervades the piece. A rigorous logic deduces ghastly arguments from a premise so quietly assumed that readers assent before they are aware of what that assent implies. Parody, at which Swift is adept, allows him to glance sardonically at the by then familiar figure of the benevolent humanitarian (forerunner of the modern sociologist, social worker, and economic planner) concerned to correct a social evil by means of a theoretically conceived plan. The pro-

poser, as naive as he is apparently logical and kindly, ignores and therefore emphasizes for the reader the enormity of his plan. The whole is an elaboration of a rather trite metaphor: "The English are devouring the Irish." But there is nothing trite about the pamphlet, which expresses in Swift's most controlled style his pity for the oppressed, ignorant, populous, and hungry Catholic peasants of Ireland and his anger at the rapacious English absentee landlords, who were bleeding the country white with the silent approbation of Parliament, ministers, and the crown.
2. Dublin.

persona: made up character
this has a very sinical tone

native country to fight for the Pretender in Spain, or sell themselves to the Barbadoes.[3]

I think it is agreed by all parties that this prodigious number of children in the arms, or on the backs, or at the heels of their mothers, and frequently of their fathers, is in the present deplorable state of the kingdom a very great additional grievance; and therefore whoever could find out a fair, cheap, and easy method of making these children sound, useful members of the commonwealth would deserve so well of the public as to have his statue set up for a preserver of the nation.

But my intention is very far from being confined to provide only for the children of professed beggars; it is of a much greater extent, and shall take in the whole number of infants at a certain age who are born of parents in effect as little able to support them as those who demand our charity in the streets.

As to my own part, having turned my thoughts for many years upon this important subject, and maturely weighed the several schemes of other projectors,[4] I have always found them grossly mistaken in their computation. It is true, a child just dropped from its dam may be supported by her milk for a solar year, with little other nourishment; at most not above the value of two shillings, which the mother may certainly get, or the value in scraps, by her lawful occupation of begging; and it is exactly at one year old that I propose to provide for them in such a manner as instead of being a charge upon their parents or the parish, or wanting food and raiment for the rest of their lives, they shall on the contrary contribute to the feeding, and partly to the clothing, of many thousands.

There is likewise another great advantage in my scheme, that it will prevent those voluntary abortions, and that horrid practice of women murdering their bastard children, alas, too frequent among us, sacrificing the poor innocent babes, I doubt, more to avoid the expense than the shame, which would move tears and pity in the most savage and inhuman breast.

The number of souls in this kingdom[5] being usually reckoned one million and a half, of these I calculate there may be about two hundred thousand couple whose wives are breeders; from which number I subtract thirty thousand couples who are able to maintain their own children, although I apprehend there cannot be so many under the present distresses of the kingdom; but this being granted, there will remain an hundred and seventy thousand breeders. I again subtract fifty thousand for those women who miscarry, or whose children die by accident or disease within the year. There only remain an hundred and twenty thousand children of poor parents annually born. The question therefore is, how this number shall be reared and provided for, which, as I have already said, under the present situation of affairs, is utterly impossible by all the methods hitherto proposed. For we can neither employ them in handicraft or agriculture; we neither build houses (I mean in the country) nor cultivate land. They can very seldom pick up a livelihood by stealing till they arrive at six years old, except where they are of towardly

---

3. James Francis Edward Stuart (1688–1766), the son of James II, was claimant ("Pretender") to the throne of England from which the Glorious Revolution had barred his succession. Catholic Ireland was loyal to him, and Irishmen joined him in his exile on the Continent. Because of the poverty in

Ireland, many Irishmen emigrated to the West Indies and other British colonies in America; they paid their passage by binding themselves to work for a stated period for one of the planters.
4. Devisers of schemes.
5. Ireland.

It is very cost effective. He doesn't think about money or emotion.

parts;[6] although I confess they learn the rudiments much earlier, during which time they can however be looked upon only as probationers, as I have been informed by a principal gentleman in the county of Cavan, who protested to me that he never knew above one or two instances under the ages of six, even in a part of the kingdom so renowned for the quickest proficiency in that art.

I am assured by our merchants that a boy or a girl before twelve years old is no salable commodity; and even when they come to this age they will not yield above three pounds, or three pounds and half a crown at most on the Exchange; which cannot turn to account either to the parents or the kingdom, the charge of nutriment and rags having been at least four times that value.

I shall now therefore humbly propose my own thoughts, which I hope will not be liable to the least objection.

I have been assured by a very knowing American of my acquaintance in London, that a young healthy child well nursed is at a year old a most delicious, nourishing, and wholesome food, whether stewed, roasted, baked, or boiled; and I make no doubt that it will equally serve in a fricassee or a ragout.[7]

I do therefore humbly offer it to public consideration that of the hundred and twenty thousand children, already computed, twenty thousand may be reserved for breed, whereof only one fourth part to be males, which is more than we allow to sheep, black cattle, or swine; and my reason is that these children are seldom the fruits of marriage, a circumstance not much regarded by our savages, therefore one male will be sufficient to serve four females. That the remaining hundred thousand may at a year old be offered in sale to the persons of quality and fortune through the kingdom, always advising the mother to let them suck plentifully in the last month, so as to render them plump and fat for a good table. A child will make two dishes at an entertainment for friends; and when the family dines alone, the fore or hind quarter will make a reasonable dish, and seasoned with a little pepper or salt will be very good boiled on the fourth day, especially in winter.

I have reckoned upon a medium that a child just born will weigh twelve pounds, and in a solar year if tolerably nursed increaseth to twenty-eight pounds.

I grant this food will be somewhat dear, and therefore very proper for landlords, who, as they have already devoured most of the parents, seem to have the best title to the children.

Infant's flesh will be in season throughout the year, but more plentiful in March, and a little before and after. For we are told by a grave author, an eminent French physician,[8] that fish being a prolific diet, there are more children born in Roman Catholic countries about nine months after Lent than at any other season; therefore, reckoning a year after Lent, the markets will be more glutted than usual, because the number of popish infants is at least three to one in this kingdom; and therefore it will have one other collateral advantage, by lessening the number of Papists among us.

I have already computed the charge of nursing a beggar's child (in which

6. Promising abilities.
7. A highly seasoned meat stew.

8. François Rabelais (ca. 1494–1553), a humorist and satirist, by no means grave.

list I reckon all cottagers, laborers, and four fifths of the farmers) to be about two shillings per annum, rags included; and I believe no gentleman would repine to give ten shillings for the carcass of a good fat child, which, as I have said, will make four dishes of excellent nutritive meat, when he hath only some particular friend or his own family to dine with him. Thus the squire will learn to be a good landlord, and grow popular among the tenants; the mother will have eight shillings net profit, and be fit for the work till she produces another child.

Those who are more thrifty (as I must confess the times require) may flay the carcass; the skin of which artificially[9] dressed will make admirable gloves for ladies, and summer boots for fine gentlemen.

As to our city of Dublin, shambles[1] may be appointed for this purpose in the most convenient parts of it, and butchers we may be assured will not be wanting; although I rather recommend buying the children alive, and dressing them hot from the knife as we do roasting pigs.

A very worthy person, a true lover of his country, and whose virtues I highly esteem, was lately pleased in discoursing on this matter to offer a refinement upon my scheme. He said that many gentlemen of this kingdom, having of late destroyed their deer, he conceived that the want of venison might be well supplied by the bodies of young lads and maidens, not exceeding fourteen years of age nor under twelve, so great a number of both sexes in every county being now ready to starve for want of work and service; and these to be disposed of by their parents, if alive, or otherwise by their nearest relations. But with due deference to so excellent a friend and so deserving a patriot, I cannot be altogether in his sentiments; for as to the males, my American acquaintance assured me from frequent experience that their flesh was generally tough and lean, like that of our schoolboys, by continual exercise, and their taste disagreeable; and to fatten them would not answer the charge. Then as to the females, it would, I think with humble submission, be a loss to the public, because they soon would become breeders themselves; and besides, it is not improbable that some scrupulous people might be apt to censure such a practice (although indeed very unjustly) as a little bordering upon cruelty; which I confess, hath always been with me the strongest objection against any project, how well soever intended.

But in order to justify my friend, he confessed that this expedient was put into his head by the famous Psalmanazar,[2] a native of the island Formosa, who came from thence to London above twenty years ago, and in conversation told my friend that in his country when any young person happened to be put to death, the executioner sold the carcass to persons of quality as a prime dainty; and that in his time the body of a plump girl of fifteen, who was crucified for an attempt to poison the emperor, was sold to his Imperial Majesty's prime minister of state, and other great mandarins of the court, in joints from the gibbet, at four hundred crowns. Neither indeed can I deny that if the same use were made of several plump young girls in this town, who without one single groat to their fortunes cannot stir abroad without a chair, and appear at the playhouse and assemblies in foreign fineries which they never will pay for, the kingdom would not be the worse.

---

9. Skillfully.
1. Slaughterhouses.
2. George Psalmanazar (ca. 1679–1763), a famous impostor. A Frenchman, he imposed himself on English bishops, noblemen, and scientists as a Formosan. He wrote an entirely fictitious account of Formosa, in which he described human sacrifices and cannibalism.

150,000 born
- 30,000 well to do
 120,000 to be eaten

A MODEST PROPOSAL / 2477

Some persons of a desponding spirit are in great concern about that vast number of poor people who are aged, diseased, or maimed, and I have been desired to employ my thoughts what course may be taken to ease the nation of so grievous an encumbrance. But I am not in the least pain upon that matter, because it is very well known that they are every day dying and rotting by cold and famine, and filth and vermin, as fast as can be reasonably expected. And as to the younger laborers, they are now in almost as hopeful a condition. They cannot get work, and consequently pine away for want of nourishment to a degree that if at any time they are accidentally hired to common labor, they have not strength to perform it; and thus the country and themselves are happily delivered from the evils to come.

they are diging as fast as you can hope for

I have too long digressed, and therefore shall return to my subject. I think the advantages by the proposal which I have made are obvious and many, as well as of the highest importance.

For first, as I have already observed, it would greatly lessen the number of Papists, with whom we are yearly overrun, being the principal breeders of the nation as well as our most dangerous enemies; and who stay at home on purpose to deliver the kingdom to the Pretender, hoping to take their advantage by the absence of so many good Protestants, who have chosen rather to leave their country than stay at home and pay tithes against their conscience to an Episcopal curate.

Secondly, the poorer tenants will have something valuable of their own, which by law may be made liable to distress,[3] and help to pay their landlord's rent, their corn and cattle being already seized and money a thing unknown.

Thirdly, whereas the maintenance of an hundred thousand children, from two years old and upwards, cannot be computed at less than ten shillings a piece per annum, the nation's stock will be thereby increased fifty thousand pounds per annum, besides the profit of a new dish introduced to the tables of all gentlemen of fortune in the kingdom who have any refinement in taste. And the money will circulate among ourselves, the goods being entirely of our own growth and manufacture.

Fourthly, the constant breeders, besides the gain of eight shillings sterling per annum by the sale of their children, will be rid of the charge of maintaining them after the first year.

Fifthly, this food would likewise bring great custom to taverns, where the vintners will certainly be so prudent as to procure the best receipts for dressing it to perfection, and consequently have their houses frequented by all the fine gentlemen, who justly value themselves upon their knowledge in good eating; and a skillful cook, who understands how to oblige his guests, will contrive to make it as expensive as they please.

Sixthly, this would be a great inducement to marriage, which all wise nations have either encouraged by rewards or enforced by laws and penalties. It would increase the care and tenderness of mothers toward their children, when they were sure of a settlement for life to the poor babes, provided in some sort by the public, to their annual profit instead of expense. We should see an honest emulation among the married women, which of them could bring the fattest child to the market. Men would become as fond of their wives during the time of their pregnancy as they are now of their mares in

---

3. Distraint, i.e., the seizing, through legal action, of property for the payment of debts and other obligations.

foal, their cows in calf, or sows when they are ready to farrow; nor offer to beat or kick them (as is too frequent a practice) for fear of a miscarriage.

Many other advantages might be enumerated. For instance, the addition of some thousand carcasses in our exportation of barreled beef, the propagation of swine's flesh, and improvement in the art of making good bacon, so much wanted among us by the great destruction of pigs, too frequent at our tables, which are no way comparable in taste or magnificence to a well-grown, fat, yearling child, which roasted whole will make a considerable figure at a lord mayor's feast or any other public entertainment. But this and many others I omit, being studious of brevity.

Supposing that one thousand families in this city would be constant customers for infants' flesh, besides others who might have it at merry meetings, particularly weddings and christenings, I compute that Dublin would take off annually about twenty thousand carcasses, and the rest of the kingdom (where probably they will be sold somewhat cheaper) the remaining eighty thousand.

I can think of no one objection that will probably be raised against this proposal, unless it should be urged that the number of people will be thereby much lessened in the kingdom. This I freely own, and it was indeed one principal design in offering it to the world. I desire the reader will observe, that I calculate my remedy for this one individual kingdom of Ireland and for no other that ever was, is, or I think ever can be upon earth. Therefore let no man talk to me of other expedients: of taxing our absentees at five shillings a pound: of using neither clothes nor household furniture except what is of our own growth and manufacture: of utterly rejecting the materials and instruments that promote foreign luxury: of curing the expensiveness of pride, vanity, idleness, and gaming in our women: of introducing a vein of parsimony, prudence, and temperance: of learning to love our country, in the want of which we differ even from Laplanders and the inhabitants of Topinamboo:[4] of quitting our animosities and factions, nor acting any longer like the Jews, who were murdering one another at the very moment their city was taken:[5] of being a little cautious not to sell our country and conscience for nothing: of teaching landlords to have at least one degree of mercy toward their tenants: lastly, of putting a spirit of honesty, industry, and skill into our shopkeepers; who, if a resolution could now be taken to buy only our native goods, would immediately unite to cheat and exact upon us in the price, the measure, and the goodness, nor could ever yet be brought to make one fair proposal of just dealing, though often and earnestly invited to it.[6]

Therefore I repeat, let no man talk to me of these and the like expedients, till he hath at least some glimpse of hope that there will ever be some hearty and sincere attempt to put them in practice.

But as to myself, having been wearied out for many years with offering vain, idle, visionary thoughts, and at length utterly despairing of success, I fortunately fell upon this proposal, which, as it is wholly new, so it hath something solid and real, of no expense and little trouble, full in our own power, and whereby we can incur no danger in disobliging England. For this

4. I.e., even Laplanders love their frozen, infertile country and the savage tribes of Brazil love their jungle more than the Anglo-Irish love Ireland.
5. During the siege of Jerusalem by the Roman emperor Titus, who captured and destroyed the city in 70 C.E., bloody fights broke out between factions of fanatics.
6. Swift himself had made all these proposals in various pamphlets. In editions printed during his lifetime the various proposals were italicized to indicate that Swift is no longer being ironic.

kind of commodity will not bear exportation, the flesh being of too tender a consistence to admit a long continuance in salt, although perhaps I could name a country which would be glad to eat up our whole nation without it.[7]

After all, I am not so violently bent upon my own opinion as to reject any offer proposed by wise men, which shall be found equally innocent, cheap, easy, and effectual. But before something of that kind shall be advanced in contradiction to my scheme, and offering a better, I desire the author or authors will be pleased maturely to consider two points. First, as things now stand, how they will be able to find food and raiment for an hundred thousand useless mouths and backs. And secondly, there being a round million of creatures in human figure throughout this kingdom, whose sole subsistence put into a common stock would leave them in debt two millions of pounds sterling, adding those who are beggars by profession to the bulk of farmers, cottagers, and laborers, with their wives and children who are beggars in effect; I desire those politicians who dislike my overture, and may perhaps be so bold to attempt an answer, that they will first ask the parents of these mortals whether they would not at this day think it a great happiness to have been sold for food at a year old in the manner I prescribe, and thereby have avoided such a perpetual sense of misfortunes as they have since gone through by the oppression of landlords, the impossibility of paying rent without money or trade, the want of common sustenance, with neither house nor clothes to cover them from the inclemencies of the weather, and the most inevitable prospect of entailing the like or greater miseries upon their breed forever.

I profess, in the sincerity of my heart, that I have not the least personal interest in endeavoring to promote this necessary work, having no other motive than the public good of my country, by advancing our trade, providing for infants, relieving the poor, and giving some pleasure to the rich. I have no children by which I can propose to get a single penny; the youngest being nine years old, and my wife past childbearing.

1729

7. I.e., England.

JOSEPH ADDISON *and* SIR RICHARD STEELE
1672–1719   1672–1729

The friendship of Joseph Addison and Richard Steele began when they were schoolboys together in London. Their careers ran parallel courses and brought them for a while into fruitful collaboration. Addison, although charming when among friends, was by nature reserved, calculating, and prudent. Steele was impulsive and rakish when young (but ardently devoted to his beautiful wife), often imprudent, and frequently in want of money. Addison never stumbled in his progress to financial security, a late marriage to a widowed countess, and a successful political career; walking less surely, Steele experienced many vicissitudes and faced serious financial problems during his last years.

Both men attended Oxford, where Addison took his degree, won a fellowship, and earned a reputation for Latin verse; the less scholarly Steele did not stay for a degree but left the university to take a commission in the army. For a while he cut a dashing figure in London, even, to his horror, seriously wounding a man in a duel. Both men enjoyed the patronage of the great Whig magnates; and except during the last four years of Queen Anne's reign, when the Tories were in the ascendancy, they were generously treated. Steele edited and wrote the *London Gazette,* an official newspaper that normally appeared twice a week, listing government appointments and reporting domestic and foreign news—much like a modern paper. He served in Parliament, was knighted by George I, and later became manager of the Theatre Royal, Drury Lane. Addison held more important positions: he was secretary to the lord lieutenant of Ireland and later an undersecretary of state; finally, toward the end of his life, he became secretary of state. Both men wrote plays: Addison's *Cato,* a frigid and very "correct" tragedy, had great success in 1713, and Steele's later plays at Drury Lane (especially *The Conscious Lovers,* 1722) were instrumental in establishing the popularity of sentimental comedy throughout the eighteenth century.

Steele's debts and Addison's loss of office in 1710 drove them to journalistic enterprises, through which they developed one of the most characteristic types of eighteenth-century literature, the periodical essay. Steele's experience as gazetteer had involved him in journalism, and in 1709, when in need of money, he launched the *Tatler* under the pseudonym Isaac Bickerstaff. He sought to attract the largest possible audience: the title was a bid for female readers, and the mixture of news with personal reflections soon became popular in coffeehouses and at breakfast tables. The paper appeared three times a week from April 1709 to January 1711. Steele wrote by far the greater number of *Tatlers,* but Addison contributed helpfully, as did other friends. The *Spectator,* which appeared daily except Sunday from March 1711 to December 1712 (and was briefly resumed by Addison in 1714), was the joint undertaking of the two friends, although it was dominated by Addison. The papers had many imitators in their own day and throughout the rest of the century. There was a *Female Tatler* and a *Female Spectator,* as well as Samuel Johnson's *Rambler* and *Idler* and Oliver Goldsmith's brief *Bee.*

Both Steele and Addison were conscious moralists who not disguise their intention of improving the minds and manners of their readers. The periodical essay they developed is less formal and didactic than the essays of Francis Bacon, less personal than those of Charles Lamb and William Hazlitt in the next century. But it succeeded not only in amusing its audience but in changing it. Moral reform had been in the air since the 1690s, and the new society that was coming into existence (in some degree the creation of Addison and Steele) strove for a balance between the morality and respectability of the old, rather Puritan middle class (which was often narrowly Philistine in taste and outlook) and the wit and grace of the older aristocratic and fashionable class (which, in the previous century, had often been libertine in morals and thought). The new social ideal, fostered by the essayists themselves, stressed moderation, reasonableness, self-control, urbanity, and good taste. Steele's *Tatler* essays applied this ideal to any topic that suggested itself as pleasing or useful: the theater, true breeding as against vulgar manners, education, simplicity in dress, the proper use of Sunday, and so on; and he lightly ridiculed common social types such as the prude, the coquette, the "pretty fellow," and the rake. Addison's best *Tatler* essays initiated his study of eccentric or affected characters, cleverly observed and described with agreeable humor. The *Tatler* quickly won an appreciative audience and when published in book form it continued (like the *Spectator*) to sell throughout the century.

The readers whom Steele had reached and influenced were at hand when the *Spectator* began to appear two months after the last *Tatler.* Steele played a more important role in the paper than Addison had in the *Tatler,* but the *Spectator* is throughout Addisonian. In the second number, Steele introduces us to the members of Mr. Spectator's Club: a man about town, a student of law and literature, a churchman, a soldier, a Tory country squire, and, interestingly enough, a London merchant. As a Whig, Steele sympathized with the new moneyed class in London and evidently intended to pit the merchant Sir Andrew Freeport, the representative of the new order, against the Tory Sir Roger de Coverley, representative of a vanishing order. Addison, however, preferred to present Sir Roger in episodes set in town and in country as an endearing, eccentric character, often absurd but always amiable and innocent. He is a prominent ancestor of a long line of similar characters in fiction during the following two centuries. Addison's scholarly interests broadened the material to include not only social criticism but the popularization of current philosophical and scientific notions; and he wrote important critical papers distinguishing true and false wit, an extended series of Saturday essays evaluating *Paradise Lost,* and an influential series on "the pleasures of the imagination," which treated the aesthetics of visual beauty in nature and art. Altogether, the *Spectator* fulfilled his ambition (see *The Aims of the Spectator,* p. 2492) to be considered an agreeable modern Socrates.

The best description of Addison's prose is Samuel Johnson's in his *Life of Addison:* "His prose is the model of the middle style; on grave subjects not formal, on light occasions not groveling; pure without scrupulosity, and exact without apparent elaboration; always equable, and always easy, without glowing words or pointed sentences." And he concludes: "Whoever wishes to attain an English style, familiar but not coarse, and elegant but not ostentatious, must give his days and nights to the volumes of Addison," a course of study that a good many aspiring writers during the century seem to have undertaken.

THE PERIODICAL ESSAY: MANNERS

STEELE: [The Gentleman; The Pretty Fellow]

From *The Tatler,* No. 21, Saturday, May 28, 1709

Quidquid agunt homines—
——nostri farrago libelli.[1]
—JUVENAL, *Satire* 1.85–86

White's Chocolate House,[2] May 26

A gentleman has writ to me out of the country a very civil letter, and said things which I suppress with great violence to my vanity. There are many terms in my narratives which he complains want explaining, and has therefore desired that, for the benefit of my country readers, I would let him know what I mean by a Gentleman, a Pretty Fellow, a Toast, a Coquette, a Critic, a Wit, and all other appellations of those now in the gayer world, who are in possession of these several characters; together with an account of those who unfortunately pretend to them. I shall begin with him we usually call a Gentleman, or man of conversation.

It is generally thought that warmth of imagination, quick relish of pleasure, and a manner of becoming it, are the most essential qualities for forming this sort of man. But anyone that is much in company will observe that the

---

1. Whatever men do . . . shall form the motley subject of my book (Latin). Steele used this epigraph for all but a few of the first sixty-two *Tatlers.*
2. One of the fashionable chocolate houses, from which Steele, in the earlier numbers of the *Tatler,* dated "accounts of gallantry, pleasure, and entertainment."

height of good breeding is shown rather in never giving offense, than in doing obliging things. Thus, he that never shocks you, though he is seldom entertaining, is more likely to keep your favor than he who often entertains, and sometimes displeases you. The most necessary talent therefore in a man of conversation, which is what we ordinarily intend by a fine gentleman, is a good judgment. He that has this in perfection is master of his companion, without letting him see it; and has the same advantage over men of any other qualifications whatsoever, as one that can see would have over a blind man of ten times his strength.

This is what makes Sophronius the darling of all who converse with him, and the most powerful with his acquaintance of any man in town. By the light of this faculty, he acts with great ease and dispatch among the men of business. All which he performs with so much success that, with as much discretion in life as any man ever had, he neither is, nor appears, cunning. But as he does a good office, if he ever does it, with readiness and alacrity, so he denies what he does not care to engage in, in a manner that convinces you that you ought not to have asked it. His judgment is so good and unerring, and accompanied with so cheerful a spirit, that his conversation is a continual feast, at which he helps some, and is helped by others, in such a manner that the equality of society is perfectly kept up, and every man obliges as much as he is obliged: for it is the greatest and justest skill in a man of superior understanding, to know how to be on a level with his companions. This sweet disposition runs through all the actions of Sophronius, and makes his company desired by women, without being envied by men. Sophronius would be as just as he is, if there were no law; and would be as discreet as he is, if there were no such thing as calumny.

In imitation of this agreeable being, is made that animal we call a Pretty Fellow; who being just able to find out that what makes Sophronius acceptable is a natural behavior, in order to the same reputation, makes his own an artificial one. Jack Dimple is his perfect mimic, whereby he is of course the most unlike him of all men living. Sophronius just now passed into the inner room directly forward: Jack comes as fast after as he can for the right and left looking glass, in which he had but just approved himself by a nod at each, and marched on. He will meditate within for half an hour, till he thinks he is not careless enough in his air, and come back to the mirror to recollect his forgetfulness.* * *

STEELE: [Dueling]

From *The Tatler*, No. 25, Tuesday, June 7, 1709

Quidquid agunt homines——
——nostri farrago libelli.
—JUVENAL, *Satire* 1.85–86

White's Chocolate House, June 6

A letter from a young lady, written in the most passionate terms, wherein she laments the misfortune of a gentleman, her lover, who was lately wounded in a duel, has turned my thoughts to that subject, and inclined me to examine into the causes which precipitate men into so fatal a folly. And as it has been proposed to treat of subjects of gallantry in the article from hence, and no one point in nature is more proper to be considered by the company who frequent this place than that of duels, it is worth our consideration to examine into this chimerical groundless humor, and to lay every other thought aside, until we have stripped it of all its false pretenses to credit and reputation amongst men.

But I must confess, when I consider what I am going about, and run over in my imagination all the endless crowd of men of honor who will be offended at such a discourse, I am undertaking, methinks, a work worthy an invulnerable hero in romance, rather than a private gentleman with a single rapier; but as I am pretty well acquainted by great opportunities with the nature of man, and know of a truth that all men fight against their will, the danger vanishes, and resolution rises upon this subject. For this reason, I shall talk very freely on a custom which all men wish exploded, though no man has courage enough to resist it.

But there is one unintelligible word, which I fear will extremely perplex my dissertation, and I confess to you I find very hard to explain, which is the term "satisfaction." An honest country gentleman had the misfortune to fall into company with two or three modern men of honor, where he happened to be very ill treated; and one of the company, being conscious of his offense, sends a note to him in the morning, and tells him he was ready to give him satisfaction. "This is fine doing," says the plain fellow; "last night he sent me away cursedly out of humor, and this morning he fancies it would be a satisfaction to be run through the body."

As the matter at present stands, it is not to do handsome actions denominates a man of honor; it is enough if he dares to defend ill ones. Thus you often see a common sharper in competition with a gentleman of the first rank; though all mankind is convinced that a fighting gamester is only a pickpocket with the courage of an highwayman. One cannot with any patience reflect on the unaccountable jumble of persons and things in this town and nation, which occasions very frequently that a brave man falls by a hand below that of a common hangman, and yet his executioner escapes the clutches of the hangman for doing it. I shall therefore hereafter consider how the bravest men in other ages and nations have behaved themselves upon such incidents as we decide by combat; and show, from their practice, that this resentment neither has its foundation from true reason or solid fame; but is an imposture, made of cowardice, falsehood, and want of understanding. For this work, a good history of quarrels would be very edifying to the public, and I apply myself to the town for particulars and circumstances within their knowledge, which may serve to embellish the dissertation with proper cuts.[1] Most of the quarrels I have ever known have proceeded from some valiant coxcomb's persisting in the wrong, to defend some prevailing folly, and preserve himself from the ingenuity[2] of owning a mistake.

By this means it is called "giving a man satisfaction" to urge your offense against him with your sword; which puts me in mind of Peter's order to the keeper, in *The Tale of a Tub*:[3] "If you neglect to do all this, damn you and

---

1. Woodcuts or engravings (with a pun).
2. Honorable candor.
3. In Swift's satire, the Roman Church is attacked

in the character of Peter. The passage (slightly misquoted) satirizes the pope's practice of issuing indulgences.

your generation forever: and so we bid you heartily farewell." If the contradiction in the very terms of one of our challenges were as well explained and turned into downright English, would it not run after this manner?

"SIR,

"Your extraordinary behavior last night, and the liberty you were pleased to take with me, makes me this morning give you this, to tell you, because you are an ill-bred puppy, I will meet you in Hyde Park an hour hence; and because you want both breeding and humanity, I desire you would come with a pistol in your hand, on horseback, and endeavor to shoot me through the head to teach you more manners. If you fail of doing me this pleasure, I shall say you are a rascal, on every post in town: and so, sir, if you will not injure me more, I shall never forgive what you have done already. Pray, sir, do not fail of getting everything ready; and you will infinitely oblige,

Sir,

Your most obedient,

humble servant, etc." * * *

STEELE: [The Spectator's Club]

The Spectator, No. 2, Friday, March 2, 1711

——Ast alii sex
Et plures uno conclamant ore.[1]
—JUVENAL, Satire 7.167–68

The first of our society is a gentleman of Worcestershire, of ancient descent, a baronet, his name Sir Roger de Coverley. His great-grandfather was inventor of that famous country-dance which is called after him. All who know the shire are very well acquainted with the parts and merits of Sir Roger. He is a gentleman that is very singular in his behavior, but his singularities proceed from his good sense, and are contradictions to the manners of the world only as he thinks the world is in the wrong. However, this humor creates him no enemies, for he does nothing with sourness or obstinacy; and his being unconfined to modes and forms makes him but the readier and more capable to please and oblige all who know him. When he is in town, he lives in Soho Square. It is said he keeps himself a bachelor by reason he was crossed in love by a perverse, beautiful widow of the next county to him. Before this disappointment, Sir Roger was what you call a fine gentleman, had often supped with my Lord Rochester and Sir George Etherege, fought a duel upon his first coming to town, and kicked Bully Dawson[2] in a public coffeehouse for calling him "youngster." But being ill used by the above-mentioned widow, he was very serious for a year and a half; and though, his temper being naturally jovial, he at last got over it, he grew careless of himself, and never dressed afterwards. He continues to wear a coat and doublet of the same cut that were in fashion at the time of his repulse, which, in his merry humors, he tells us, has been in and out twelve

1. Six more at least join their consenting voice (Latin).
2. Notorious sharper of the period. Rochester

(1647–1680), the poet. Etherege (ca. 1634–1691), playwright, rake, and boon companion of the king and Rochester.

times since he first wore it. 'Tis said Sir Roger grew humble in his desires after he had forgot this cruel beauty, insomuch that it is reported he has frequently offended in point of chastity with beggars and gypsies; but this is looked upon by his friends rather as matter of raillery than truth. He is now in his fifty-sixth year, cheerful, gay, and hearty; keeps a good house both in town and country; a great lover of mankind; but there is such a mirthful cast in his behavior that he is rather beloved than esteemed. His tenants grow rich, his servants look satisfied, all the young women profess love to him, and the young men are glad of his company; when he comes into a house he calls the servants by their names, and talks all the way upstairs to a visit. I must not omit that Sir Roger is a justice of the quorum,[3] that he fills the chair at a quarter-session with great abilities; and, three months ago, gained universal applause by explaining a passage in the Game Act.

The gentleman next in esteem and authority among us is another bachelor, who is a member of the Inner Temple;[4] a man of great probity, wit, and understanding; but he has chosen his place of residence rather to obey the direction of an old humorsome[5] father, than in pursuit of his own inclinations. He was placed there to study the laws of the land, and is the most learned of any of the house in those of the stage. Aristotle and Longinus are much better understood by him than Littleton or Coke.[6] The father sends up, every post, questions relating to marriage articles, leases, and tenures, in the neighborhood; all which questions he agrees with an attorney to answer and take care of in the lump. He is studying the passions themselves, when he should be inquiring into the debates among men which arise from them. He knows the argument of each of the orations of Demosthenes and Tully,[7] but not one case in the reports of our own courts. No one ever took him for a fool, but none, except his intimate friends, know he has a great deal of wit. This turn makes him at once both disinterested and agreeable; as few of his thoughts are drawn from business, they are most of them fit for conversation. His taste of books is a little too just[8] for the age he lives in; he has read all, but approves of very few. His familiarity with the customs, manners, actions, and writings of the ancients makes him a very delicate observer of what occurs to him in the present world. He is an excellent critic, and the time of the play is his hour of business; exactly at five he passes through New Inn, crosses through Russell Court, and takes a turn at Will's[9] till the play begins; he has his shoes rubbed and his periwig powdered at the barber's as you go into the Rose.[1] It is for the good of the audience when he is at a play, for the actors have an ambition to please him.

The person of next consideration is Sir Andrew Freeport, a merchant of great eminence in the city of London, a person of indefatigable industry, strong reason, and great experience. His notions of trade are noble and gen-

3. A county justice of the peace, presiding over quarterly sessions of the court.
4. One of the Inns of Court, where lawyers resided or had their offices and where students studied law.
5. Full of crotchets.
6. In other words, he is more familiar with the laws of literature than those of England. The *Poetics* of Aristotle and the Greek treatise *On the Sublime* (reputedly by Longinus) were in high favor among the critics of the time. Sir Thomas Littleton, 15th-century jurist, was author of a renowned

treatise on *Tenures*. Sir Edward Coke (1552–1634) was the judge and writer whose *Reports* and *Institutes of the Laws of England* (known as *Coke upon Littleton*) have exerted a great influence on the interpretation of English law.
7. Marcus Tullius Cicero.
8. Exact.
9. The coffeehouse in Covent Garden associated with literature and criticism since Dryden had begun to frequent it in the 1660s.
1. A tavern near Drury Lane.

erous, and (as every rich man has usually some sly way of jesting which would make no great figure were he not a rich man) he calls the sea the British Common. He is acquainted with commerce in all its parts, and will tell you that it is a stupid and barbarous way to extend dominion by arms; for true power is to be got by arts and industry. He will often argue that if this part of our trade were well cultivated, we should gain from one nation; and if another, from another. I have heard him prove that diligence makes more lasting acquisitions than valor, and that sloth has ruined more nations than the sword. He abounds in several frugal maxims, among which the greatest favorite is, "A penny saved is a penny got." A general trader of good sense is pleasanter company than a general scholar; and Sir Andrew having a natural unaffected eloquence, the perspicuity of his discourse gives the same pleasure that wit would in another man. He has made his fortunes himself, and says that England may be richer than other kingdoms by as plain methods as he himself is richer than other men; though at the same time I can say this of him, that there is not a point in the compass but blows home a ship in which he is an owner.

Next to Sir Andrew in the clubroom sits Captain Sentry, a gentleman of great courage, good understanding, but invincible modesty. He is one of those that deserve very well, but are very awkward at putting their talents within the observation of such as should take notice of them. He was some years a captain, and behaved himself with great gallantry in several engagements and at several sieges; but having a small estate of his own, and being next heir to Sir Roger, he has quitted a way of life in which no man can rise suitably to his merit who is not something of a courtier as well as a soldier. I have heard him often lament that in a profession where merit is placed in so conspicuous a view, impudence should get the better of modesty. When he has talked to this purpose I never heard him make a sour expression, but frankly confess that he left the world because he was not fit for it. A strict honesty and an even, regular behavior are in themselves obstacles to him that must press through crowds who endeavor at the same end with himself—the favor of a commander. He will, however, in his way of talk, excuse generals for not disposing according to men's desert, or inquiring into it, "for," says he, "that great man who has a mind to help me, has as many to break through to come at me as I have to come at him"; therefore he will conclude that the man who would make a figure, especially in a military way, must get over all false modesty, and assist his patron against the importunity of other pretenders by a proper assurance in his own vindication. He says it is a civil cowardice to be backward in asserting[2] what you ought to expect, as it is a military fear to be slow in attacking when it is your duty. With this candor does the gentleman speak of himself and others. The same frankness runs through all his conversation. The military part of his life has furnished him with many adventures, in the relation of which he is very agreeable to the company; for he is never overbearing, though accustomed to command men in the utmost degree below him; nor ever too obsequious from an habit of obeying men highly above him.

But that our society may not appear a set of humorists[3] unacquainted with

2. Claiming.

3. Eccentrics.

the gallantries and pleasures of the age, we have among us the gallant Will Honeycomb, a gentleman who, according to his years, should be in the decline of his life, but having ever been very careful of his person, and always had a very easy fortune, time has made but very little impression either by wrinkles on his forehead or traces in his brain. His person is well turned, of a good height. He is very ready at that sort of discourse with which men usually entertain women. He has all his life dressed very well, and remembers habits[4] as others do men. He can smile when one speaks to him, and laughs easily. He knows the history of every mode, and can inform you from which of the French king's wenches our wives and daughters had this manner of curling their hair, that way of placing their hoods; whose frailty was covered by such a sort of petticoat, and whose vanity to show her foot made that part of the dress so short in such a year. In a word, all his conversation and knowledge has been in the female world. As other men of his age will take notice to you what such a minister said upon such and such an occasion, he will tell you when the Duke of Monmouth[5] danced at court such a woman was then smitten, another was taken with him at the head of his troop in the Park. In all these important relations, he has ever about the same time received a kind glance or a blow of a fan from some celebrated beauty, mother of the present Lord Such-a-one. If you speak of a young commoner that said a lively thing in the House, he starts up: "He has good blood in his veins; Tom Mirabell begot him, the rogue cheated me in that affair; that young fellow's mother used me more like a dog than any woman I ever made advances to." This way of talking of his very much enlivens the conversation among us of a more sedate turn; and I find there is not one of the company but myself, who rarely speak at all, but speaks of him as of that sort of man who is usually called a well-bred, fine gentleman. To conclude his character, where women are not concerned he is an honest, worthy man.

I cannot tell whether I am to account him whom I am next to speak of as one of our company, for he visits us but seldom; but when he does, it adds to every man else a new enjoyment of himself. He is a clergyman, a very philosophic man, of general learning, great sanctity of life, and the most exact good breeding. He has the misfortune to be of a very weak constitution, and consequently cannot accept of such cares and business as preferments in his function would oblige him to; he is therefore among divines what a chamber-counselor[6] is among lawyers. The probity of his mind and the integrity of his life create him followers, as being eloquent or loud advances others. He seldom introduces the subject he speaks upon; but we are so far gone in years that he observes, when he is among us, an earnestness to have him fall on some divine topic, which he always treats with much authority, as one who has no interest in this world, as one who is hastening to the object of all his wishes and conceives hope from his decays and infirmities. These are my ordinary companions.

---

4. Clothes.
5. The illegitimate son of Charles II, the ill-fated Absalom of Dryden's *Absalom and Achitophel*.

6. A lawyer who gives opinions in private, not in court.

ADDISON: [Sir Roger at Church]

The Spectator, No. 112, Monday, July 9, 1711

'Athanátous mèn prōta theoùs, nómo os diákeitai, Tíma.[1]

—PYTHAGORAS

I am always very well pleased with a country Sunday, and think, if keeping holy the seventh day were only a human institution, it would be the best method that could have been thought of for the polishing and civilizing of mankind. It is certain the country people would soon degenerate into a kind of savages and barbarians were there not such frequent returns of a stated time, in which the whole village meet together with their best faces, and in their cleanliest habits, to converse with one another upon indifferent subjects, hear their duties explained to them, and join together in adoration of the Supreme Being. Sunday clears away the rust of the whole week, not only as it refreshes in their minds the notions of religion, but as it puts both the sexes upon appearing in their most agreeable forms, and exerting all such qualities as are apt to give them a figure in the eye of the village. A country fellow distinguishes himself as much in the churchyard as a citizen does upon the 'Change,[2] the whole parish politics being generally discussed in that place either after sermon or before the bell rings.

My friend Sir Roger, being a good churchman, has beautified the inside of his church with several texts of his own choosing; he has likewise given a handsome pulpit cloth, and railed in the communion table at his own expense. He has often told me that, at his coming to his estate, he found his parishioners very irregular; and that, in order to make them kneel and join in the responses, he gave every one of them a hassock and a Common Prayer book, and at the same time employed an itinerant singing master, who goes about the country for that purpose, to instruct them rightly in the tunes of the Psalms; upon which they now very much value themselves, and indeed outdo most of the country churches that I have ever met.

As Sir Roger is landlord to the whole congregation, he keeps them in very good order, and will suffer nobody to sleep in it besides himself; for if by chance he has been surprised into a short nap at sermon, upon recovering out of it he stands up and looks about him, and if he sees anybody else nodding, either wakes them himself, or sends his servant to them. Several other of the old knight's particularities break out upon these occasions; sometimes he will be lengthening out a verse in the Singing-Psalms half a minute after the rest of the congregation have done with it; sometimes, when he is pleased with the matter of his devotion, he pronounces "Amen" three or four times to the same prayer; and sometimes stands up when everybody else is upon their knees, to count the congregation, or see if any of his tenants are missing.

I was yesterday very much surprised to hear my old friend, in the midst of

---

1. First worship the immortal gods as custom decrees (Greek). The first of the so-called Golden Verses of Pythagoras.

2. The Exchange in London, where merchants met to transact business. "Citizen": i.e., of the City, hence commonly a merchant.

the service, calling out to one John Matthews to mind what he was about, and not disturb the congregation. This John Matthews, it seems, is remarkable for being an idle fellow, and at that time was kicking his heels for his diversion. This authority of the knight, though exerted in that odd manner which accompanies him in all circumstances of life, has a very good effect upon the parish, who are not polite[3] enough to see anything ridiculous in his behavior; besides that the general good sense and worthiness of his character make his friends observe these little singularities as foils that rather set off than blemish his good qualities.

As soon as the sermon is finished, nobody presumes to stir till Sir Roger is gone out of the church. The knight walks down from his seat in the chancel between a double row of his tenants, that stand bowing to him on each side, and every now and then inquires how such an one's wife, or mother, or son, or father do, whom he does not see at church—which is understood as a secret reprimand to the person that is absent.

The chaplain has often told me that upon a catechizing day, when Sir Roger has been pleased with a boy that answers well, he has ordered a Bible to be given him next day for his encouragement, and sometimes accompanies it with a flitch of bacon to his mother. Sir Roger has likewise added five pounds a year to the clerk's place; and, that he may encourage the young fellows to make themselves perfect in the church service, has promised, upon the death of the present incumbent, who is very old, to bestow it according to merit.

The fair understanding between Sir Roger and his chaplain, and their mutual concurrence in doing good, is the more remarkable because the very next village is famous for the differences and contentions that rise between the parson and the squire, who live in a perpetual state of war. The parson is always preaching at the squire, and the squire, to be revenged on the parson, never comes to church. The squire has made all his tenants atheists and tithe-stealers;[4] while the parson instructs them every Sunday in the dignity of his order, and insinuates to them almost in every sermon that he is a better man than his patron. In short, matters are come to such an extremity that the squire has not said his prayers either in public or private this half year; and that the parson threatens him, if he does not mend his manners, to pray for him in the face of the whole congregation.

Feuds of this nature, though too frequent in the country, are very fatal to the ordinary people, who are so used to be dazzled with riches that they pay as much deference to the understanding of a man of an estate as of a man of learning; and are very hardly brought to regard any truth, how important soever it may be, that is preached to them, when they know there are several men of five hundred a year who do not believe it.

---

3. Refined.
4. Farmers who cheat the parson to whom they
are bound to pay annual tithes (i.e., one-tenth of the produce of their farms).

ADDISON: [Sir Roger at the Assizes[1]]

The Spectator, No. 122, Friday, July 20, 1711

Comes jucundus in via pro vehiculo est.[2]
—PUBLILIUS SYRUS, *Fragments*

A man's first care should be to avoid the reproaches of his own heart; his next, to escape the censures of the world. If the last interferes with the former, it ought to be entirely neglected; but otherwise there cannot be a greater satisfaction to an honest mind than to see those approbations which it gives itself seconded by the applauses of the public. A man is more sure of his conduct when the verdict which he passes upon his own behavior is thus warranted and confirmed by the opinion of all that know him.

My worthy friend Sir Roger is one of those who is not only at peace within himself but beloved and esteemed by all about him. He receives a suitable tribute for his universal benevolence to mankind in the returns of affection and good will which are paid him by everyone that lives within his neighborhood. I lately met with two or three odd instances of that general respect which is shown to the good old knight. He would needs carry Will Wimble[3] and myself with him to the county assizes. As we were upon the road, Will Wimble joined a couple of plain men who rid before us, and conversed with them for some time, during which my friend Sir Roger acquainted me with their characters.

"The first of them," says he, "that has a spaniel by his side, is a yeoman[4] of about an hundred pounds a year, an honest man. He is just within the Game Act,[5] and qualified to kill an hare or a pheasant. He knocks down a dinner with his gun twice or thrice a week; and by that means lives much cheaper than those who have not so good an estate as himself. He would be a good neighbor if he did not destroy so many partridges; in short he is a very sensible man, shoots flying,[6] and has been several times foreman of the petty jury.[7]

"The other that rides along with him is Tom Touchy, a fellow famous for taking the law of everybody. There is not one in the town where he lives that he has not sued at a quarter sessions. The rogue had once the impudence to go to law with the widow.[8] His head is full of costs, damages, and ejectments; he plagued a couple of honest gentlemen so long for a trespass in breaking one of his hedges, till he was forced to sell the ground it enclosed to defray the charges of the prosecution. His father left him fourscore pounds a year, but he has cast[9] and been cast so often that he is not now worth thirty. I suppose he is going upon the old business of the willow tree."

As Sir Roger was giving me this account of Tom Touchy, Will Wimble and

1. Periodic sessions of superior courts held by visiting judges throughout England.
2. An agreeable companion upon the road is as good as a coach (Latin). Addison substituted *jucundus* for the original's *facundus* ("eloquent").
3. A character used by Addison to illustrate the injury done to younger sons of gentlemen by not educating them for a profession or to trade.
4. A man who owns and cultivates a small estate. His rank is just below that of gentleman.
5. This law restricted the right to kill game to owners of land whose annual income was £100 or more.
6. A true sportsman, he shoots birds only when they are on the wing.
7. The trial jury of twelve in an ordinary civil or criminal case.
8. The woman whom Sir Roger had loved in his youth. She is frequently mentioned in essays that deal with the old knight.
9. Defeated in a lawsuit.

his two companions stopped short till we came up to them. After having paid their respects to Sir Roger, Will told him that Mr. Touchy and he must appeal to him upon a dispute that arose between them. Will, it seems, had been giving his fellow travelers an account of his angling one day in such a hole; when Tom Touchy, instead of hearing out his story, told him that Mr. Such-an-one, if he pleased, might take the law of him for fishing in that part of the river. My friend Sir Roger heard them both, upon a round trot,[1] and after having paused some time, told them, with an air of a man who would not give his judgment rashly, "that much might be said on both sides." They were neither of them dissatisfied with the knight's determination, because neither of them found himself in the wrong by it. Upon which we made the best of our way to the assizes.

The court was sat before Sir Roger came; but notwithstanding all the justices had taken their places upon the bench, they made room for the old knight at the head of them; who, for his reputation in the country, took occasion to whisper in the judge's ear that he was glad his lordship had met with so much good weather in his circuit. I was listening to the proceedings of the court with much attention, and infinitely pleased with that great appearance and solemnity which so properly accompanies such a public administration of our laws, when, after about an hour's sitting, I observed to my great surprise, in the midst of a trial, that my friend Sir Roger was getting up to speak. I was in some pain for him, till I found he had acquitted himself of two or three sentences, with a look of much business and great intrepidity.

Upon his first rising the court was hushed, and a general whisper ran among the country people that Sir Roger was up. The speech he made was so little to the purpose that I shall not trouble my readers with an account of it; and I believe was not so much designed by the knight himself to inform the court, as to give him a figure in my eye, and keep up his credit in the country.

I was highly delighted, when the court rose, to see the gentlemen of the country gathering about my old friend, and striving who should compliment him most; at the same time that the ordinary people gazed upon him at a distance, not a little admiring his courage that was not afraid to speak to the judge.

In our return home we met with a very odd accident which I cannot forbear relating, because it shows how desirous all who know Sir Roger are of giving him marks of their esteem. When we were arrived upon the verge of his estate, we stopped at a little inn to rest ourselves and our horses. The man of the house had, it seems, been formerly a servant in the knight's family; and to do honor to his old master, had some time since, unknown to Sir Roger, put him up in a signpost before the door; so that the knight's head had hung out upon the road about a week before he himself knew anything of the matter. As soon as Sir Roger was acquainted with it, finding that his servant's indiscretion proceeded wholly from affection and good will, he only told him that he had made him too high a compliment; and when the fellow seemed to think that could hardly be, added, with a more decisive look, that it was too great an honor for any man under a duke; but told him at the same time that it might be altered with a very few touches, and that he himself

1. While trotting briskly.

would be at the charge of it. Accordingly they got a painter, by the knight's directions, to add a pair of whiskers to the face, and by a little aggravation of the features to change it into the Saracen's Head. I should not have known this story had not the innkeeper, upon Sir Roger's alighting, told him in my hearing that his honor's head was brought back last night with the alterations that he had ordered to be made in it. Upon this my friend, with his usual cheerfulness, related the particulars above-mentioned, and ordered the head to be brought into the room. I could not forbear discovering greater expressions of mirth than ordinary upon the appearance of this monstrous face, under which, notwithstanding it was made to frown and stare in a most extraordinary manner, I could still discover a distant resemblance of my old friend. Sir Roger, upon seeing me laugh, desired me to tell him truly if I thought it possible for people to know him in that disguise. I at first kept my usual silence; but upon the knight's conjuring me to tell him whether it was not still more like himself than a Saracen, I composed my countenance in the best manner I could, and replied that much might be said on both sides.

These several adventures, with the knight's behavior in them, gave me as pleasant a day as ever I met with in any of my travels.

THE PERIODICAL ESSAY: IDEAS

ADDISON: [The Aims of the *Spectator*]

The Spectator, No. 10, Monday, March 12, 1711

> *Non aliter quam qui adverso vix flumine lembum*
> *Remigiis subigit, si bracchia forte remisit,*
> *Atque illum in præceps prono rapit alveus amni.*[1]
> —VIRGIL, *Georgics* 1.201–3

It is with much satisfaction that I hear this great city inquiring day by day after these my papers, and receiving my morning lectures with a becoming seriousness and attention. My publisher tells me that there are already three thousand of them distributed every day. So that if I allow twenty readers to every paper, which I look upon as a modest computation, I may reckon about three-score thousand disciples in London and Westminster, who I hope will take care to distinguish themselves from the thoughtless herd of their ignorant and unattentive brethren. Since I have raised to myself so great an audience, I shall spare no pains to make their instruction agreeable, and their diversion useful. For which reasons I shall endeavor to enliven morality with wit, and to temper wit with morality, that my readers may, if possible, both ways find their account in the speculation of the day. And to the end that their virtue and discretion may not be short, transient, intermitting starts of thought, I have resolved to refresh their memories from day to day, till I have recovered them out of that desperate state of vice and folly into which the age is fallen. The mind that lies fallow but a single day sprouts up in

---

1. Like him whose oars can hardly force his boat against the current, if by chance he relaxes his arms, the boat sweeps him headlong down the stream (Latin).

follies that are only to be killed by a constant and assiduous culture. It was said of Socrates that he brought philosophy down from heaven, to inhabit among men; and I shall be ambitious to have it said of me that I have brought philosophy out of closets and libraries, schools and colleges, to dwell in clubs and assemblies, at tea tables and in coffeehouses.

I would therefore in a very particular manner recommend these my speculations to all well-regulated families that set apart an hour in every morning for tea and bread and butter; and would earnestly advise them for their good to order this paper to be punctually served up, and to be looked upon as a part of the tea equipage.

Sir Francis Bacon observes that a well-written book, compared with its rivals and antagonists, is like Moses's serpent, that immediately swallowed up and devoured those of the Egyptians.[2] I shall not be so vain as to think that where *The Spectator* appears the other public prints will vanish; but shall leave it to my reader's consideration whether is it not much better to be let into the knowledge of one's self, than to hear what passes in Muscovy or Poland; and to amuse ourselves with such writings as tend to the wearing out of ignorance, passion, and prejudice, than such as naturally conduce to inflame hatreds, and make enmities irreconcilable?

In the next place, I would recommend this paper to the daily perusal of those gentlemen whom I cannot but consider as my good brothers and allies, I mean the fraternity of spectators who live in the world without having anything to do in it; and either by the affluence of their fortunes or laziness of their dispositions have no other business with the rest of mankind but to look upon them. Under this class of men are comprehended all contemplative tradesmen, titular physicians, fellows of the Royal Society, Templars[3] that are not given to be contentious, and statesmen that are out of business; in short, everyone that considers the world as a theater, and desires to form a right judgment of those who are the actors on it.

There is another set of men that I must likewise lay a claim to, whom I have lately called the blanks of society, as being altogether unfurnished with ideas, till the business and conversation of the day has supplied them. I have often considered these poor souls with an eye of great commiseration, when I have heard them asking the first man they have met with, whether there was any news stirring? and by that means gathering together materials for thinking. These needy persons do not know what to talk of till about twelve o'clock in the morning; for by that time they are pretty good judges of the weather, know which way the wind sits, and whether the Dutch mail[4] be come in. As they lie at the mercy of the first man they meet, and are grave or impertinent all the day long, according to the notions which they have inbibed in the morning, I would earnestly entreat them not to stir out of their chambers till they have read this paper, and do promise them that I will daily instil into them such sound and wholesome sentiments as shall have a good effect on their conversation for the ensuing twelve hours.

But there are none to whom this paper will be more useful than to the female world. I have often thought there has not been sufficient pains taken

2. In *The Advancement of Learning* 2, "To the King." But it was the rod of Aaron, not of Moses, that turned into a devouring serpent (Exodus 7.10–12).

3. Lawyers or students of the law who live or have their offices ("chambers") in the Middle or Inner Temple, one of the Inns of Court.

4. Bringing the latest war news.

in finding out proper employments and diversions for the fair ones. Their amusements seem contrived for them, rather as they are women, than as they are reasonable creatures; and are more adapted to the sex than to the species. The toilet[5] is their great scene of business, and the right adjusting of their hair the principal employment of their lives. The sorting of a suit of ribbons[6] is reckoned a very good morning's work; and if they make an excursion to a mercer's or a toyshop,[7] so great a fatigue makes them unfit for anything else all the day after. Their more serious occupations are sewing and embroidery, and their greatest drudgery the preparation of jellies and sweetmeats. This, I say, is the state of ordinary women; though I know there are multitudes of those of a more elevated life and conversation, that move in an exalted sphere of knowledge and virtue, that join all the beauties of the mind to the ornaments of dress, and inspire a kind of awe and respect, as well as love, into their male beholders. I hope to increase the number of these by publishing this daily paper, which I shall always endeavor to make an innocent if not improving entertainment, and by that means at least divert the minds of my female readers from greater trifles. At the same time, as I would fain give some finishing touches to those which are already the most beautiful pieces in human nature, I shall endeavor to point all those imperfections that are the blemishes, as well as those virtues which are the embellishments, of the sex. In the meanwhile I hope these my gentle readers, who have so much time on their hands, will not grudge throwing away a quarter of an hour in a day on this paper, since they may do it without any hindrance to business.

I know several of my friends and well-wishers are in great pain for me, lest I should not be able to keep up the spirit of a paper which I oblige myself to furnish every day: but to make them easy in this particular, I will promise them faithfully to give it over as soon as I grow dull. This I know will be matter of great raillery to the small wits; who will frequently put me in mind of my promise, desire me to keep my word, assure me that it is high time to give over, with many other little pleasantries of the like nature, which men of a little smart genius cannot forbear throwing out against their best friends, when they have such a handle given them of being witty. But let them remember that I do hereby enter my caveat against this piece of raillery.

ADDISON: [Wit: True, False, Mixed]

The Spectator, No. 62, Friday, March 11, 1711

Scribendi recte sapere est et principium et fons.[1]
—HORACE, *Ars Poetica* 309

Mr. Locke has an admirable reflection upon the difference of wit and judgment, whereby he endeavors to show the reason why they are not always the talents of the same person. His words are as follow: "And hence, perhaps, may be given some reason of that common observation, that men who have

---

5. Dressing table.
6. A set of ribbons to be worn together.
7. A shop where baubles and trifles are sold. "Mercer": a seller of such notions as tape, ribbon, and

fringe.
1. Discernment is the source and fount of writing well (Latin).

a great deal of wit and prompt memories, have not always the clearest judgment, or deepest reason. For wit lying most in the assemblage of ideas, and putting those together with quickness and variety, wherein can be found any resemblance or congruity, thereby to make up pleasant pictures and agreeable visions in the fancy; judgment, on the contrary, lies quite on the other side, in separating carefully one from another, ideas wherein can be found the least difference, thereby to avoid being misled by similitude, and by affinity to take one thing for another. This is a way of proceeding quite contrary to metaphor and allusion; wherein, for the most part, lies that entertainment and pleasantry of wit which strikes so lively on the fancy, and is therefore so acceptable to all people."[2]

This is, I think, the best and most philosophical account that I have ever met with of wit, which generally, though not always, consists in such a resemblance and congruity of ideas as this author mentions. I shall only add to it, by way of explanation, that every resemblance of ideas is not that which we call wit, unless it be such an one that gives delight and surprise to the reader. These two properties seem essential to wit, more particularly the last of them. In order therefore that the resemblance in the ideas be wit, it is necessary that the ideas should not lie too near one another in the nature of things; for where the likeness is obvious, it gives no surprise. To compare one man's singing to that of another, or to represent the whiteness of any object by that of milk and snow, or the variety of its colors by those of the rainbow, cannot be called wit, unless, besides this obvious resemblance, there be some further congruity discovered in the two ideas that is capable of giving the reader some surprise. Thus when a poet tells us, the bosom of his mistress is as white as snow, there is no wit in the comparison; but when he adds, with a sigh, that it is as cold too, it then grows into wit. Every reader's memory may supply him with innumerable instances of the same nature. For this reason, the similitudes in heroic poets, who endeavor rather to fill the mind with great conceptions, than to divert it with such as are new and surprising, have seldom anything in them that can be called wit. Mr. Locke's account of wit, with this short explanation, comprehends most of the species of wit, as metaphors, similitudes, allegories, enigmas, mottoes, parables, fables, dreams, visions, dramatic writings, burlesque, and all the methods of allusion:[3] as there are many other pieces of wit (how remote soever they may appear at first sight from the foregoing description) which upon examination will be found to agree with it.

As true wit generally consists in this resemblance and congruity of ideas, false wit chiefly consists in the resemblance and congruity sometimes of single letters, as in anagrams, chronograms, lipograms,[4] and acrostics; sometimes of syllables, as in echoes and doggerel rhymes; sometimes of words, as in puns and quibbles; and sometimes of whole sentences or poems, cast into the figures of eggs, axes, or altars:[5] nay, some carry the notion of wit so far, as to ascribe it even to external mimicry; and to look upon a man as an ingenious person, that can resemble the tone, posture, or face of another.

As true wit consists in the resemblance of ideas, and false wit in the resem-

2. John Locke's *An Essay Concerning Human Understanding* 2.11.2.
3. Word play; more broadly, any covert or symbolic use of language.
4. A composition omitting all words that contain a certain letter or letters. "Chronogram": phrase in

which certain letters express a date. For example, "LorD haVe MerCIe Vpon Vs"; the capital letters (in Roman numerals) add up to 1666, the *annus mirabilis* of fire, plague, and war.
5. For example, George Herbert's *The Altar* (p. 1597) and *Easter Wings* (p. 1599).

blance of words, according to the foregoing instances; there is another kind of wit which consists partly in the resemblance of ideas, and partly in the resemblance of words; which for distinction's sake I shall call mixed wit. This kind of wit is that which abounds in Cowley, more than in any author that ever wrote. Mr. Waller has likewise a great deal of it. Mr. Dryden is very sparing in it. Milton had a genius much above it. Spenser is in the same class with Milton. The Italians, even in their epic poetry, are full of it. Monsieur Boileau, who formed himself upon the ancient poets, has everywhere rejected it with scorn. If we look after mixed wit among the Greek writers, we shall find it nowhere but in the epigrammatists. There are indeed some strokes of it in the little poem ascribed to Musaeus,[6] which by that, as well as many other marks, betrays itself to be a modern composition. If we look into the Latin writers, we find none of this mixed wit in Virgil, Lucretius, or Catullus; very little in Horace, but a great deal of it in Ovid, and scarce anything else in Martial.

Out of the innumerable branches of mixed wit, I shall choose one instance which may be met with in all the writers of this class. The passion of love in its nature has been thought to resemble fire; for which reason the words fire and flame are made use of to signify love. The witty poets therefore have taken an advantage from the doubtful meaning of the word fire, to make an infinite number of witticisms. Cowley, observing the cold regard of his mistress's eyes,[7] and at the same time their power of producing love in him, considers them as burning-glasses made of ice; and finding himself able to live in the greatest extremities of love, concludes the torrid zone to be habitable. When his mistress has read his letter written in juice of lemon by holding it to the fire, he desires her to read it over a second time by love's flames. When she weeps, he wishes it were inward heat that distilled those drops from the limbec.[8] When she is absent he is beyond eighty, that is, thirty degrees nearer the pole than when she is with him. His ambitious love is a fire that naturally mounts upwards; his happy love is the beams of heaven, and his unhappy love flames of hell. When it does not let him sleep, it is a flame that sends up no smoke; when it is opposed by counsel and advice, it is a fire that rages the more by the wind's blowing upon it. Upon the dying of a tree in which he had cut his loves, he observes that his written flames had burned up and withered the tree. When he resolves to give over his passion, he tells us that one burnt like him for ever dreads the fire. His heart is an Aetna, that instead of Vulcan's shop[9] encloses Cupid's forge in it. His endeavoring to drown his love in wine, is throwing oil upon the fire. He would insinuate to his mistress, that the fire of love, like that of the sun (which produces so many living creatures) should not only warm but beget. Love in another place cooks pleasure at his fire. Sometimes the poet's heart is frozen in every breast, and sometimes scorched in every eye. Sometimes he is drowned in tears, and burnt in love, like a ship set on fire in the middle of the sea.

The reader may observe in every one of these instances, that the poet mixes

---

6. A poem called *Hero and Leander*, attributed to the ancient Greek poet Musaeus, was first published in 1635.
7. In *The Mistress, or Several Copies of Love-Verses* (1647).

8. Alembic, an apparatus used in distilling.
9. Mount Etna was supposed to be the workshop of Vulcan, the Roman god of fire and metalworking.

the qualities of fire with those of love; and in the same sentence speaking of it both as a passion, and as real fire, surprises the reader with those seeming resemblances or contradictions that make up all the wit in this kind of writing. Mixed wit therefore is a composition of pun and true wit, and is more or less perfect as the resemblance lies in the ideas or in the words. Its foundations are laid partly in falsehood and partly in truth: reason puts in her claim for one half of it, and extravagance for the other. The only province therefore for this kind of wit, is epigram, or those little occasional poems that in their own nature are nothing else but a tissue of epigrams. I cannot conclude this head of mixed wit, without owning that the admirable poet out of whom I have taken the examples of it, had as much true wit as any author that ever writ; and indeed all other talents of an extraordinary genius.

It may be expected, since I am upon this subject, that I should take notice of Mr. Dryden's definition of wit; which, with all the deference that is due to the judgment of so great a man, is not so properly a definition of wit, as of good writing in general. Wit, as he defines it, is "a propriety of words and thoughts adapted to the subject."[1] If this be a true definition of wit, I am apt to think that Euclid[2] was the greatest wit that ever set pen to paper: it is certain there never was a greater propriety of words and thoughts adapted to the subject, than what that author has made use of in his elements. I shall only appeal to my reader, if this definition agrees with any notion he has of wit: if it be a true one, I am sure Mr. Dryden was not only a better poet, but a greater wit than Mr. Cowley; and Virgil a much more facetious man than either Ovid or Martial.

Bouhours,[3] whom I look upon to be the most penetrating of all the French critics, has taken pains to show that it is impossible for any thought to be beautiful which is not just, and has not its foundation in the nature of things; that the basis of all wit is truth; and that no thought can be valuable, of which good sense is not the groundwork. Boileau[4] has endeavored to inculcate the same notion in several parts of his writings, both in prose and verse. This is that natural way of writing, that beautiful simplicity, which we so much admire in the compositions of the ancients; and which nobody deviates from, but those who want strength of genius to make a thought shine in its own natural beauties. Poets who want this strength of genius to give that majestic simplicity to nature, which we so much admire in the works of the ancients, are forced to hunt after foreign ornaments, and not to let any piece of wit of what kind soever escape them. I look upon these writers as Goths in poetry, who, like those in architecture, not being able to come up to the beautiful simplicity of the old Greeks and Romans, have endeavored to supply its place with all the extravagances of an irregular fancy. Mr. Dryden makes a very handsome observation on Ovid's writing a letter from Dido to Aeneas, in the following words:[5] "Ovid" (says he, speaking of Virgil's fiction of Dido and Aeneas) "takes it up after him, even in the same age, and makes an ancient heroine of Virgil's new-created Dido; dictates a letter for her just before her death to the ungrateful fugitive; and, very unluckily for himself,

1. Adapted from Dryden's *Apology for Heroic Poetry*.
2. Hellenic mathematician (ca. 300 B.C.E.).
3. Dominique Bouhours (1628–1702), who wrote an *Art of Criticism*.

4. Nicolas Boileau (1636–1711), a famous French neoclassicist, wrote a verse *Art of Poetry* (1674) which was translated by Dryden.
5. From Dryden's dedication to his translation of the *Aeneid* (1697).

is for measuring a sword with a man so much superior in force to him, on the same subject. I think I may be judge of this, because I have translated both. The famous author of the Art of Love[6] has nothing of his own; he borrows all from a greater master in his own profession, and, which is worse, improves nothing which he finds: nature fails him, and being forced to his old shift, he has recourse to witticism. This passes indeed with his soft admirers, and gives him the preference to Virgil in their esteem."

Were not I supported by so great an authority as that of Mr. Dryden, I should not venture to observe, that the taste of most of our English poets, as well as readers, is extremely Gothic. He quotes Monsieur Segrais[7] for a threefold distinction of the readers of poetry: in the first of which he comprehends the rabble of readers, whom he does not treat as such with regard to their quality,[8] but to their numbers and the coarseness of their taste. His words are as follow: "Segrais has distinguished the readers of poetry, according to their capacity of judging, into three classes. [He might have said the same of writers too, if he had pleased.] In the lowest form he places those whom he calls les petits esprits,[9] such things as are our upper-gallery audience in a play-house; who like nothing but the husk and rind of wit, prefer a quibble, a conceit, an epigram, before solid sense and elegant expression: these are mob-readers. If Virgil and Martial stood for parliament-men, we know already who would carry it.[1] But though they make the greatest appearance in the field, and cry the loudest, the best on 't is they are but a sort of French Huguenots, or Dutch boors,[2] brought over in herds, but not naturalized; who have not lands of two pounds per annum in Parnassus, and therefore are not privileged to poll.[3] Their authors are of the same level, fit to represent them on a mountebank's stage, or to be masters of the ceremonies in a bear-garden: yet these are they who have the most admirers. But it often happens, to their mortification, that as their readers improve their stock of sense (as they may by reading better books, and by conversation with men of judgment), they soon forsake them."

I must not dismiss this subject without observing, that as Mr. Locke in the passage above-mentioned has discovered the most fruitful source of wit, so there is another of a quite contrary nature to it, which does likewise branch itself out into several kinds. For not only the resemblance but the opposition of ideas does very often produce wit; as I could show in several little points, turns, and antitheses, that I may possibly enlarge upon in some future speculation.[4]

6. Ovid.
7. Jean Regnauld de Segrais (1624–1701), who had translated Virgil into French, is quoted extensively by Dryden.
8. Social standing.
9. The small minded (French).
1. I.e., the witty Martial would easily defeat the weighty Virgil in an election.

2. Peasants. Huguenots and the Dutch were the largest class of immigrants in England. "On 't": that one can say.
3. Vote. Only freeholders worth £2 a year could go to the polls, and these readers of little taste hold no land in Parnassus (where the Muses live).
4. For such an "enlargement," see Samuel Johnson's remarks on wit in the life of Cowley (p. 2736).

ADDISON: [*Paradise Lost*: General Critical Remarks]

The Spectator, No. 267, Saturday, January 5, 1712

Cedite Romani scriptores, cedite Graii.[1]
—PROPERTIUS, *Elegies* 2.34.65

There is nothing in nature so irksome as general discourses, especially when they turn chiefly upon words. For this reason I shall waive the discussion of that point which was started some years since, Whether Milton's *Paradise Lost* may be called an heroic poem? Those who will not give it that title may call it (if they please) a *divine poem*. It will be sufficient to its perfection, if it has in it all the beauties of the highest kind of poetry; and as for those who allege it is not an heroic poem, they advance no more to the diminution of it, than if they should say Adam is not Aeneas, nor Eve Helen.

I shall therefore examine it by the rules of epic poetry,[2] and see whether it falls short of the *Iliad* or *Aeneid*, in the beauties which are essential to that kind of writing. The first thing to be considered in an epic poem is the fable,[3] which is perfect or imperfect, according as the action which it relates is more or less so. This action should have three qualifications in it. First, it should be but one action. Secondly, it should be an entire action; and thirdly, it should be a great action. To consider the action of the *Iliad*, *Aeneid*, and *Paradise Lost*, in these three several lights. Homer to preserve the unity of his action hastens into the midst of things, as Horace has observed:[4] had he gone up to Leda's egg, or begun much later, even at the rape of Helen, or the investing of Troy, it is manifest that the story of the poem would have been a series of several actions. He therefore opens his poem with the discord of his princes, and with great art interweaves in the several succeeding parts of it, an account of everything material which relates to them and had passed before that fatal dissension. After the same manner Aeneas makes his first appearance in the Tyrrhene seas,[5] and within sight of Italy, because the action proposed to be celebrated was that of his settling himself in Latium.[6] But because it was necessary for the reader to know what had happened to him in the taking of Troy, and in the preceding parts of his voyage, Virgil makes his hero relate it by way of episode[7] in the second and third books of the *Aeneid*. The contents of both which books come before those of the first book in the thread of the story, though for preserving of this unity of action, they follow them in the disposition of the poem. Milton, in imitation of these two great poets, opens his *Paradise Lost* with an infernal council plotting the

---

1. Yield place, ye Roman and ye Grecian writers, yield (Latin).
2. The rules for the conduct of an epic poem—derived out of the poems of Homer and Virgil, the *Poetics* of Aristotle, and the *Art of Poetry* of Horace—had been given their most systematic and complete statement in Père René Le Bossu's *Traité du poème épique* (1675), which was immediately absorbed into English critical thought. Addison writes of *Paradise Lost* with Le Bossu well in sight, but he is no slavish disciple.
3. The plot of a drama or poem.
4. *Art of Poetry*, 147–49. Helen, whose abduction from her husband Menelaus by the Trojan prince

Paris brought on the Trojan War, was the daughter of Leda, who was visited by Zeus in the guise of a swan.
5. That part of the Mediterranean west of Italy, bounded by the islands of Sicily, Sardinia, and Corsica.
6. The kingdom of the Latini, where Aeneas was hospitably received when he landed at the mouth of the Tiber. He married Lavinia, the daughter of King Latinus, and later ruled the kingdom.
7. An incidental narration or digression in an epic that arises naturally from the subject but is separable from the main action.

fall of man, which is the action he proposed to celebrate; and as for those great actions which preceded in point of time, the battle of the angels, and the creation of the world (which would have entirely destroyed the unity of his principal action, had he related them in the same order that they happened), he cast them into the fifth, sixth, and seventh books, by way of episode to this noble poem.

Aristotle himself allows that Homer has nothing to boast of as to the unity of his fable, though at the same time that great critic and philosopher endeavors to palliate this imperfection in the Greek poet, by imputing it in some measure to the very nature of an epic poem. Some have been of opinion that the *Aeneid* labors also in this particular, and has episodes which may be looked upon as excrescences rather than as parts of the action. On the contrary, the poem which we have now under our consideration hath no other episodes than such as naturally arise from the subject, and yet is filled with such a multitude of astonishing incidents that it gives us at the same time a pleasure of the greatest variety, and of the greatest simplicity.

I must observe also that as Virgil, in the poem which was designed to celebrate the original of the Roman Empire, has described the birth of its great rival, the Carthaginian commonwealth, Milton with the like art in his poem on the Fall of Man, has related the fall of those angels who are his professed enemies. Besides the many other beauties in such an episode, its running parallel with the great action of the poem hinders it from breaking the unity so much as another episode would have done that had not so great an affinity with the principal subject. In short, this is the same kind of beauty which the critics admire in the *Spanish Friar, or The Double Discovery,*[8] where the two different plots look like counterparts and copies of one another.

The second qualification required in the action of an epic poem is, that it should be an *entire* action. An action is entire when it is complete in all its parts; or as Aristotle describes it, when it consists of a beginning, a middle, and an end. Nothing should go before it, be intermixed with it, or follow after it, that is not related to it. As on the contrary, no single step should be omitted in that just and regular process which it must be supposed to take from its original to its consummation. Thus, we see the anger of Achilles in its birth, its continuance, and effects; and Aeneas's settlement in Italy, carried on through all the oppositions in his way to it both by sea and land. The action in Milton excels (I think) both the former in this particular: we see it contrived in hell, executed upon earth, and punished by heaven. The parts of it are told in the most distinct manner, and grow out of one another in the most natural method.

The third qualification of an epic poem is its *greatness*. The anger of Achilles was of such consequence that it embroiled the kings of Greece, destroyed the heroes of Troy, and engaged all the gods in factions. Aeneas's settlement in Italy produced the Caesars, and gave birth to the Roman Empire. Milton's subject was still greater than either of the former; it does not determine the fate of single persons or nations, but of a whole species. The united powers of hell are joined together for the destruction of mankind, which they effected in part, and would have completed, had not Omnipotence itself

8. A comedy by Dryden.

interposed. The principal actors are man in his greatest perfection, and woman in her highest beauty. Their enemies are the fallen angels: the Messiah their friend, and the Almighty their protector. In short, everything that is great in the whole circle of being, whether within the verge of nature, or out of it, has a proper part assigned it in this noble poem.

In poetry, as in architecture, not only the whole, but the principal members, and every part of them, should be great. I will not presume to say, that the book of games in the *Aeneid*, or that in the *Iliad*, are not of this nature, nor to reprehend Virgil's simile of the top, and many other of the same nature in the *Iliad*, as liable to any censure in this particular; but I think we may say, without derogating from those wonderful performances, that there is an unquestionable magnificence in every part of *Paradise Lost*, and indeed a much greater than could have been formed upon any pagan system.

But Aristotle, by the greatness of the action, does not only mean that it should be great in its nature, but also in its duration, or in other words, that it should have a due length in it, as well as what we properly call greatness. The just measure of the kind of magnitude, he explains by the following similitude. An animal, no bigger than a mite, cannot appear perfect to the eye, because the sight takes it in at once, and has only a confused idea of the whole, and not a distinct idea of all its parts: if on the contrary you should suppose an animal of ten thousand furlongs in length, the eye would be so filled with a single part of it, that it would not give the mind an idea of the whole. What these animals are to the eye, a very short or a very long action would be to the memory. The first would be, as it were, lost and swallowed up by it, and the other difficult to be contained in it. Homer and Virgil have shown their principal art in this particular; the action of the *Iliad*, and that of the *Aeneid*, were in themselves exceeding short, but are so beautifully extended and diversified by the invention of episodes, and the machinery[9] of gods, with the like poetical ornaments, that they make up an agreeable story sufficient to employ the memory without overcharging it. Milton's action is enriched with such a variety of circumstances that I have taken as much pleasure in reading the contents of his books as in the best invented story I ever met with. It is possible that the traditions on which the *Iliad* and *Aeneid* were built had more circumstances in them than the history of the Fall of Man, as it is related in Scripture. Besides it was easier for Homer and Virgil to dash the truth with fiction, as they were in no danger of offending the religion of their country by it. But as for Milton, he had not only a very few circumstances upon which to raise his poem, but was also obliged to proceed with the greatest caution in everything that he added out of his own invention. And, indeed, notwithstanding all the restraints he was under, he has filled his story with so many surprising incidents, which bear so close an analogy with what is delivered in Holy Writ, that it is capable of pleasing the most delicate reader, without giving offense to the most scrupulous.

The modern critics have collected from several hints in the *Iliad* and *Aeneid* the space of time which is taken up by the action of each of these poems; but as a great part of Milton's story was transacted in regions that lie out of the reach of the sun and the sphere of day, it is impossible to gratify

---

9. The technical term (from *deus ex machina*) in critical theory for the supernatural beings who oversee and intervene in the affairs of the characters in epic poems.

the reader with such a calculation, which indeed would be more curious than instructive; none of the critics, either ancient or modern, having laid down rules to circumscribe the action of an epic poem with any determined number of years, days, or hours.

This Piece of Criticism on Milton's Paradise Lost *shall be carried on in the following Saturdays' papers.*[1]

ADDISON: [On the Scale of Being]

The Spectator, No. 519, October 25, 1712

*Inde hominum pecudumque genus, vitaeque volantum,
Et quae marmoreo fert monstra sub aequore pontus.*[1]
—VIRGIL, *Aeneid* 6.728–29

Though there is a great deal of pleasure in contemplating the material world, by which I mean that system of bodies into which nature has so curiously wrought the mass of dead matter, with the several relations which those bodies bear to one another, there is still, methinks, something more wonderful and surprising in contemplations on the world of life, by which I mean all those animals with which every part of the universe is furnished. The material world is only the shell of the universe: the world of life are its inhabitants.

If we consider those parts of the material world which lie the nearest to us and are, therefore, subject to our observations and inquiries, it is amazing to consider the infinity of animals with which it is stocked. Every part of matter is peopled. Every green leaf swarms with inhabitants. There is scarce a single humor in the body of a man, or of any other animal, in which our glasses[2] do not discover myriads of living creatures. The surface of animals is also covered with other animals which are, in the same manner, the basis of other animals that live upon it; nay, we find in the most solid bodies, as in marble itself, innumerable cells and cavities that are crowded with such imperceptible inhabitants as are too little for the naked eye to discover. On the other hand, if we look into the more bulky parts of nature, we see the seas, lakes, and rivers teeming with numberless kinds of living creatures. We find every mountain and marsh, wilderness and wood, plentifully stocked with birds and beasts, and every part of matter affording proper necessaries and conveniences for the livelihood of multitudes which inhabit it.

The author of *The Plurality of Worlds*[3] draws a very good argument upon this consideration for the peopling of every planet, as indeed it seems very probable from the analogy of reason that, if no part of matter which we are acquainted with lies waste and useless, those great bodies, which are at such a distance from us, should not be desert and unpeopled, but rather that they should be furnished with beings adapted to their respective situations.

1. The series on *Paradise Lost* contains eighteen essays.
1. Thence the race of men and beasts, the life of flying creatures, and the monsters that ocean bears beneath her smooth surface (Latin).
2. Microscopes. "Humor": fluid.
3. Bernard de Fontenelle (1657–1757). This pop- ular book, a series of dialogues between a scientist and a countess concerning the possibility of other inhabited planets and the new astrophysics in general, was published in 1686 in France and was translated in 1688 by both John Glanvill and Aphra Behn.

Existence is a blessing to those beings only which are endowed with perception and is, in a manner, thrown away upon dead matter any further than as it is subservient to beings which are conscious of their existence. Accordingly, we find from the bodies which lie under our observation that matter is only made as the basis and support of animals and that there is no more of the one than what is necessary for the existence of the other.

Infinite Goodness is of so communicative a nature that it seems to delight in the conferring of existence upon every degree of perceptive being. As this is a speculation which I have often pursued with great pleasure to myself, I shall enlarge farther upon it, by considering that part of the scale of beings which comes within our knowledge.

There are some living creatures which are raised but just above dead matter. To mention only that species of shellfish, which are formed in the fashion of a cone, that grow to the surface of several rocks and immediately die upon their being severed from the place where they grow. There are many other creatures but one remove from these, which have no other sense besides that of feeling and taste. Others have still an additional one of hearing; others of smell, and others of sight. It is wonderful to observe by what a gradual progress the world of life advances through a prodigious variety of species before a creature is formed that is complete in all its senses; and, even among these, there is such a different degree of perfection in the sense which one animal enjoys, beyond what appears in another, that, though the sense in different animals be distinguished by the same common denomination, it seems almost of a different nature. If after this we look into the several inward perfections of cunning and sagacity, or what we generally call instinct, we find them rising after the same manner, imperceptibly, one above another, and receiving additional improvements, according to the species in which they are implanted. This progress in nature is so very gradual that the most perfect of an inferior species comes very near to the most imperfect of that which is immediately above it.

The exuberant and overflowing goodness of the Supreme Being, whose mercy extends to all his works, is plainly seen, as I have before hinted, from his having made so very little matter, at least what falls within our knowledge, that does not swarm with life. Nor is his goodness less seen in the diversity than in the multitude of living creatures. Had he only made one species of animals, none of the rest would have enjoyed the happiness of existence; he has, therefore, *specified* in his creation every degree of life, every capacity of being. The whole chasm in nature, from a plant to a man, is filled up with diverse kinds of creatures, rising one over another by such a gentle and easy ascent that the little transitions and deviations from one species to another are almost insensible. This intermediate space is so well husbanded and managed that there is scarce a degree of perception which does not appear in some one part of the world of life. Is the goodness or wisdom of the Divine Being more manifested in this his proceeding?

There is a consequence, besides those I have already mentioned, which seems very naturally deducible from the foregoing considerations. If the scale of being rises by such a regular progress so high as man, we may by a parity of reason[4] suppose that it still proceeds gradually through those beings which

4. A reasonable analogy or equivalence.

are of a superior nature to him, since there is an infinitely greater space and room for different degrees of perfection between the Supreme Being and man than between man and the most despicable insect. This consequence of so great a variety of beings which are superior to us, from that variety which is inferior to us, is made by Mr. Locke[5] in a passage which I shall here set down after having premised that, notwithstanding there is such infinite room between man and his Maker for the creative power to exert itself in, it is impossible that it should ever be filled up, since there will be still an infinite gap or distance between the highest created being and the Power which produced him:

> That there should be more species of intelligent creatures above us than there are of sensible and material below, is probable to me from hence: That in all the visible corporeal world we see no chasms or no gaps. All quite down from us, the descent is by easy steps and a contin- ued series of things that, in each remove, differ very little from the other. There are fishes that have wings and are not strangers to the airy region; and there are some birds that are inhabitants of the water, whose blood is cold as fishes and their flesh so like in taste that the scrupulous are allowed them on fish days. There are animals so near of kin both to birds and beasts that they are in the middle between both: amphibious animals link the terrestrial and aquatic together; seals live at land and at sea, and porpoises have the warm blood and entrails of a hog, not to mention what is confidently reported of mermaids or seamen. There are some brutes that seem to have as much knowledge and reason as some that are called men; and the animal and vegetable kingdoms are so nearly joined that, if you will take the lowest of one and the highest of the other, there will scarce be perceived any great difference between them; and so on, till we come to the lowest and the most inorganical parts of matter, we shall find everywhere that the several species are linked together and differ but in almost insensible degrees. And when we con- sider the infinite power and wisdom of the Maker, we have reason to think that it is suitable to the magnificent harmony of the universe and the great design and infinite goodness of the Architect, that the species of creatures should also, by gentle degrees, ascend upward from us toward his infinite perfection, as we see they gradually descend from us downward; which, if it be probable, we have reason to be persuaded that there are far more species of creatures above us than there are beneath, we being in degrees of perfection much more remote from the infinite being of God than we are from the lowest state of being and that which approaches nearest to nothing. And yet of all those distinct species we have no clear distinct ideas.

In this system of being, there is no creature so wonderful in its nature, and which so much deserves our particular attention, as man, who fills up the middle space between the animal and intellectual nature, the visible and invisible world, and is that link in the chain of beings which has been often termed the *nexus utriusque mundi*.[6] So that he who, in one respect, is asso- ciated with angels and archangels, may look upon a Being of infinite perfec-

5. John Locke, in his *Essay Concerning Human Understanding*, 3.6.12.   6. The binding together of both worlds (Latin).

tion as his father, and the highest order of spirits as his brethren, may, in another respect, say to corruption, "Thou art my father," and to the worm, "Thou art my mother and my sister."[7]

7. Job 17.14.

ALEXANDER POPE
1688–1744

Alexander Pope is the only important writer of his generation who was solely a man of letters. Because he could not, as a Roman Catholic, attend a university, vote, or hold public office, he was excluded from the sort of patronage that was bestowed by statesmen on many writers during the reign of Anne. This disadvantage he turned into a positive good, for the translation of Homer's *Iliad* and *Odyssey*, which he undertook for profit as well as for fame, gave him ample means to live the life of an independent suburban gentleman. After 1718 he lived hospitably in his villa by the Thames at Twickenham (then pronounced *Twit'nam*), entertaining his friends and converting his five acres of land into a diminutive landscape garden. Almost exactly a century earlier, William Shakespeare had earned enough to retire to a country estate at Stratford—but he had been an actor-manager as well as a playwright; Pope was the first English writer to demonstrate that literature alone could be a gainful profession.

Ill health plagued Pope almost from birth. Crippled early by tuberculosis of the bone, he never grew taller than four and a half feet. In later life he suffered from violent headaches and required constant attention from servants. But Pope did not allow his infirmities to hold him back; he was always a master at making the best of what he had. Around 1700 his father, a well-to-do, retired London merchant, moved to a small property at Binfield in Windsor Forest. There, in rural surroundings, young Pope completed his education by reading whatever he pleased, "like a boy gathering flowers in the woods and fields just as they fall in his way"; and there, encouraged by his father, he began to write verse. He was already an accomplished poet in his teens; no English poet has ever been more precocious.

Pope's first striking success as a poet was *An Essay on Criticism* (1711), which brought him Joseph Addison's approval and an intemperate personal attack from the critic John Dennis, who was angered by a casual reference to himself in the poem. *The Rape of the Lock,* both in its original shorter version of 1712 and in its more elaborate version of 1714, proved the author a master not only of metrics and of language but also of witty, urbane satire. In *An Essay on Criticism,* Pope had excelled all his predecessors in writing a didactic poem after the example of Horace; in the *Rape,* he had written the most brilliant mock epic in the language. But there was another vein in Pope's youthful poetry, a tender concern with natural beauty and love. The *Pastorals* (1709), his first publication, and *Windsor Forest* (1713; much of it was written earlier) abound in visual imagery and descriptive passages of ideally ordered nature; they remind us that Pope was an amateur painter. The *Elegy to the Memory of an Unfortunate Lady* and *Eloisa to Abelard,* published in the collected poems of 1717, dwell on the pangs of unhappy lovers (Pope himself never married). And even the long task of translating Homer; the "dull duty" of editing Shakespeare; and in middle age, his preoccupation with ethical and satirical poetry did not make less fine his keen sense of beauty in nature and art.

Pope's early poetry brought him to the attention of literary men, with whom he began to associate in the masculine world of coffeehouse and tavern, where he liked to play the rake. Between 1706 and 1711 he came to know, among many others, William Congreve; William Walsh, the critic and poet; and Richard Steele and Joseph Addison. As it happened, all were Whigs. Pope could readily ignore politics in the excitement of taking his place among the leading wits of the town. But after the fall of the Whigs in 1710 and the formation of the Tory government under Robert Harley (later earl of Oxford) and Henry St. John (later Viscount Bolingbroke) party loyalties bred bitterness among the wits as among the politicians. By 1712, Pope had made the acquaintance of another group of writers, all Tories, who were soon his intimate friends: Jonathan Swift, by then the close associate of Harley and St. John and the principal propagandist for their policies; Dr. John Arbuthnot, physician to the queen, a learned scientist, a wit, and a man of humanity and integrity; John Gay, the poet, who in 1728 was to create *The Beggar's Opera*, the greatest theatrical success of the century; and the poet Thomas Parnell. Through them he became the friend and admirer of Oxford and later the intimate of Bolingbroke. In 1714 this group, at the instigation of Pope, formed a club for satirizing all sorts of false learning. The friends proposed to write jointly the biography of a learned fool whom they named Martinus Scriblerus (Martin the Scribbler), whose life and opinions would be a running commentary on educated nonsense. Some amusing episodes were later rewritten and published as the *Memoirs of Martinus Scriblerus* (1741). The real importance of the club, however, is that it fostered a satiric temper that would be expressed in such mature works of the friends as *Gulliver's Travels*, *The Beggar's Opera*, and *The Dunciad*.

"The life of a wit is a warfare on earth," said Pope, generalizing from his own experience. His very success as a poet (and his astonishing precocity brought him success very early) made enemies who were to plague him in pamphlets, verse satires, and squibs in the journals throughout his entire literary career. He was attacked for his writings, his religion, and his physical deformity. Although he smarted under the jibes of his detractors, he was a fighter who struck back, always giving better than he got. Pope's literary warfare began in 1713, when he announced his intention of translating the *Iliad* and sought subscribers to a deluxe edition of the work. Subscribers came in droves, but the Whig writers who surrounded Addison at Button's Coffee House did all they could to discredit the venture. The eventual success of the first published installment of his *Iliad* in 1715 did not obliterate Pope's resentment against Addison and his "little senate"; and he took his revenge in the damaging portrait of Addison (under the name of Atticus), which was later included in the *Epistle to Dr. Arbuthnot* (1735), lines 193–214. The not unjustified attacks on Pope's edition of Shakespeare (1725) by the learned Shakespeare scholar Lewis Theobald (Pope always spelled and pronounced the name "Tibbald" in his satires), led to Theobald's appearance as king of the dunces in *The Dunciad* (1728). In this impressive poem Pope stigmatized his literary enemies as agents of all that he disliked and feared in the tendencies of his time—the vulgarization of taste and the arts consequent on the rapid growth of the reading public and the development of journalism, magazines, and other popular and cheap publications, which spread scandal, sensationalism, and political partisanship—in short the new commercial spirit of the nation that was corrupting not only the arts but, as Pope saw it, the national life itself.

In the 1730s Pope moved on to philosophical, ethical, and political subjects in *An Essay on Man*, the *Epistles to Several Persons*, and the *Imitations of Horace*. The reigns of George I and George II appeared to him, as to Swift and other Tories, a period of rapid moral, political, and cultural deterioration. The agents of decay fed on the rise of moneyed (as opposed to landed) wealth, which accounted for the political corruption encouraged by Sir Robert Walpole and the court party, and the corruption of all aspects of the national life by a vulgar class of *nouveaux riches*. Pope assumed the role of the champion of traditional values: of right reason, humanistic learning, sound art, good taste, and public virtue. It was fortunate that most of his enemies happened to illustrate various degrees of unreason, pedantry, bad art, vulgar taste, and at best, indifferent morals.

The satirist traditionally deals in generally prevalent evils and generally observable human types, not with particular individuals. So too with Pope; the bulk of his satire can be read and enjoyed without much biographical information. Usually he used fictional or type names, although he most often had an individual in mind—Sappho, Atossa, Atticus, Sporus—and when he named individuals (as he consistently did in *The Dunciad*), his purpose was to raise his victims to emblems of folly and vice. To judge and censure the age, Pope also created the *I* of the satires (not identical with Alexander Pope of Twickenham). This semifictional figure is the detached observer, somewhat removed from the City, town, and court, the centers of corruption; he is the friend of the virtuous, whose friendship for him testifies to his integrity; he is fond of peace, country life, the arts, morality, and truth; and he detests their opposites that flourish in the great world. In such an age, Pope implies, it is impossible for such a man—honest, truthful, blunt—not to write satire.

Pope was a master of style. From first to last, his verse is notable for its rhythmic variety, despite the apparently rigid metrical unit—the heroic couplet—in which he wrote; for the precision of meaning and the harmony (or expressive disharmony) of his language; and for the union of maximum conciseness with maximum complexity. Variety and harmony can be observed in even so short a passage as lines 71–76 of the pastoral *Summer* (1709), lines so lyrical that, in *Semele,* Handel set them to music. In the passage quoted below (as also in the following quotation), only those rhetorical stresses that distort the normal iambic flow of the verse have been marked; internal pauses within the line are indicated by single and double bars, alliteration and assonance by italics.

> Óh déign to visit our *forsaken seats,*
>
> The mossy *fountains* ‖ and the *green* retreats!
>
> Where'er yóu wálk ‖ cóol gáles shall fan the glade,
>
> Trées whére yóu sít ‖ shall crowd into a shade:
>
> Where'er yóu tréad ‖ the blushing *flowers* shall rise,
>
> And all things *flóurish* where yóu túrn your eyes.

Pope has attained metrical variety by the free substitution of trochees and spondees for the normal iambs; he has achieved rhythmic variety by arranging phrases and clauses (units of syntax and logic) of different lengths within single lines and couplets, so that the passage moves with the sinuous fluency of thought and feeling; and he not only has chosen musical combinations of words but has also subtly modulated the harmony of the passage by unobtrusive patterns of alliteration and assonance.

Contrast with this pastoral passage lines 16–25 of the *Epilogue to the Satires, Dialogue* 2 (1738), in which Pope is not making music but imitating actual conversation so realistically that the metrical pattern and the integrity of the couplet and individual line seem to be destroyed (although in fact they remain in place). In a dialogue with a friend who warns him that his satire is too personal, indeed mere libel, the poet-satirist replies:

> Yé státesmen, | priests of one religion all!
>
> Yé trádesmen vile ‖ in army, court, or hall!
>
> Yé réverend atheists. ‖ F. Scandal! | name them, | Who?

P. Why that's the thing you bid me not to do.

Whó stárved a sister, ‖ who foreswore a debt,

Í néver named; ‖ the town's inquiring yet.

The poisoning dame—| F. Yóu méan—| P. I don't—| F. Yóu dó.

P. Sée, nów Í kéep the secret, ‖ and nót yóu!

The bribing statesman—| F. Hóld, ‖ tóo hígh you go.

P. The bribed elector—‖ F. There you stoop tóo lów.

In such a passage the language and rhythms of poetry merge with the language and rhythms of impassioned living speech.

A fine example of Pope's ability to derive the maximum of meaning from the most economic use of language and image is the description of the manor house in which lives old Cotta, the miser (*Epistle to Lord Bathurst,* lines 187–96):

> Like some lone Chartreuse stands the good old Hall,
> Silence without, and fasts within the wall;
> No raftered roofs with dance and tabor sound,
> No noontide bell invites the country round;
> Tenants with sighs the smokeless towers survey,
> And turn the unwilling steeds another way;
> Benighted wanderers, the forest o'er,
> Curse the saved candle and unopening door;
> While the gaunt mastiff growling at the gate,
> Affrights the beggar whom he longs to eat.

The first couplet of this passage associates the "Hall," symbol of English rural hospitality, with the Grande Chartreuse, the monastery in the French Alps, which, although a place of "silence" and "fasts" for the monks, afforded food and shelter to all travelers. Then the dismal details of Cotta's miserly dwelling provide a stark contrast, and the meaning of the scene is concentrated in the grotesque image of the last couplet: the half-starved watchdog and the frightened beggar confronting each other in mutual hunger.

But another sort of variety derives from Pope's respect for the idea that the different kinds of literature have their different and appropriate styles. Thus *An Essay on Criticism,* an informal discussion of literary theory, is written, like Horace's *Art of Poetry* (a similarly didactic poem), in a plain style, the easy language of well-bred talk. *The Rape of the Lock,* "a heroi-comical poem" (that is, a comic poem that treats trivial material in an epic style), employs the lofty heroic language that John Dryden had perfected in his translation of Virgil and introduces amusing parodies of passages in *Paradise Lost;* parodies later raised to truly Miltonic sublimity and complexity by the conclusion of *The Dunciad. Eloisa to Abelard* renders the brooding, passionate voice of its heroine in a declamatory language, given to sudden outbursts and shifts of tone, that recalls the stage. The grave epistles that make up *An Essay on Man,* a philosophical discussion of such majestic themes as the Creator and His creation, the universe, human nature, society, and happiness, are written in a stately forensic language and tone and constantly employ the traditional rhetorical figures. The *Imitations of Horace,* and above all, the *Epistle to Dr. Arbuthnot,* his finest poem "in the Horatian way," reveal Pope's final mastery of the plain style of Horace's epistles and satires and support his image of himself as the heir of the Roman poet. In short, no other poet of the century can equal Pope in the range of his materials, the diversity of his poetic styles, and the wizardry of his technique.

An Essay on Criticism   There is no pleasanter introduction to the canons of taste in the English Augustan age than Pope's *An Essay on Criticism.* As Addison said in his review in *Spectator* 253, it assembles the "most known and most received observations on the subject of literature and criticism." Pope was attempting to do for his time what Horace, in his *Art of Poetry,* and what Nicolas Boileau (French poet of the age of Louis XIV), in his *L'Art Poétique,* had done for theirs. Horace is Pope's model not only for principles of criticism but also for style, especially in the simple, conversational language and the tone of well-bred ease.

In framing his critical creed, Pope did not try for novelty: he wished merely to give to generally accepted doctrines pleasing and memorable expression and make them useful to modern poets. Here one meets the key words of neoclassical criticism: *wit, Nature, ancients, rules,* and *genius. Wit* in the poem is a word of many meanings—a clever remark or the person who makes it, a conceit, liveliness of mind, inventiveness, fancy, genius, a genius, and poetry itself, among others. *Nature* is an equally ambiguous word, meaning not "things out there" or "the outdoors" but most important that which is representative, universal, permanent in human experience as opposed to the idiosyncratic, the individual, the temporary. In line 21, *Nature* comes close to meaning "intuitive knowledge." In line 52, it means that half-personified power manifested in the cosmic order, which in its modes of working is a model for art. The reverence felt by most Augustans for the great writers of ancient Greece and Rome raised the question how far the authority of these *ancients* extended. Were their works to be received as models to be conscientiously imitated? Were the *rules* received from them or deducible from their works to be accepted as prescriptive laws or merely convenient guides? Was individual *genius* to be bound by what has been conventionally held to be *Nature,* by the authority of the *ancients,* and by the legalistic pedantry of *rules*? Or could it go its own way?

In part 1 of the *Essay,* Pope constructs a harmonious system in which he effects a compromise among all these conflicting forces—a compromise that is typically eighteenth century in spirit. Part 2 analyzes the causes of faulty criticism. Part 3 characterizes the good critic and praises the great critics of the past.

An Essay on Criticism

Part 1

'Tis hard to say, if greater want of skill
Appear in writing or in judging ill;
But of the two less dangerous is the offense
To tire our patience than mislead our sense.
5 Some few in that, but numbers err in this,
Ten censure° wrong for one who writes amiss;   judge
A fool might once himself alone expose,
Now one in verse makes many more in prose.
'Tis with our judgments as our watches, none
10 Go just alike, yet each believes his own.
In poets as true genius is but rare,
True taste as seldom is the critic's share;
Both must alike from Heaven derive their light,
These born to judge, as well as those to write.
15 Let such teach others who themselves excel,
And censure freely who have written well.
Authors are partial to their wit, 'tis true,
But are not critics to their judgment too?

Yet if we look more closely, we shall find
20 Most have the seeds of judgment in their mind:
Nature affords at least a glimmering light;
The lines, though touched but faintly, are drawn right.
But as the slightest sketch, if justly traced, ⎫
Is by ill coloring but the more disgraced, ⎬
25 So by false learning is good sense defaced: ⎭
Some are bewildered in the maze of schools,
And some made coxcombs[1] Nature meant but fools.
In search of wit these lose their common sense,
And then turn critics in their own defense:
30 Each burns alike, who can, or cannot write,
Or with a rival's or an eunuch's spite.
All fools have still an itching to deride,
And fain would be upon the laughing side.
If Maevius[2] scribble in Apollo's spite,
35 There are who judge still worse than he can write.
    Some have at first for wits, then poets passed,
Turned critics next, and proved plain fools at last.
Some neither can for wits nor critics pass,
As heavy mules are neither horse nor ass.
40 Those half-learn'd witlings, numerous in our isle,
As half-formed insects on the banks of Nile;[3]
Unfinished things, one knows not what to call,
Their generation's so equivocal:
To tell° them would a hundred tongues require,   *reckon, count*
45 Or one vain wit's, that might a hundred tire.
    But you who seek to give and merit fame,
And justly bear a critic's noble name,
Be sure yourself and your own reach to know,
How far your genius, taste, and learning go;
50 Launch not beyond your depth, but be discreet,
And mark that point where sense and dullness meet.
    Nature to all things fixed the limits fit,
And wisely curbed proud man's pretending wit.
As on the land while here the ocean gains,
55 In other parts it leaves wide sandy plains;
Thus in the soul while memory prevails,
The solid power of understanding fails;
Where beams of warm imagination play,
The memory's soft figures melt away.
60 One science[4] only will one genius fit,
So vast is art, so narrow human wit.
Not only bounded to peculiar arts,
But oft in those confined to single parts.
Like kings we lose the conquests gained before,
65 By vain ambition still to make them more;
Each might his several province well command,

---

1. Superficial pretenders to learning.
2. A silly poet alluded to contemptuously by Virgil
in *Eclogue* 3 and by Horace in *Epode* 10.
3. The ancients believed that many forms of life

were spontaneously generated in the fertile mud of
the Nile.
4. Branch of learning.

Would all but stoop to what they understand.
   First follow Nature, and your judgment frame
By her just standard, which is still the same;
70   Unerring Nature, still divinely bright,
One clear, unchanged, and universal light,
Life, force, and beauty must to all impart,
At once the source, and end, and test of art.
Art from that fund each just supply provides,
75   Works without show, and without pomp presides.
In some fair body thus the informing soul
With spirits feeds, with vigor fills the whole,
Each motion guides, and every nerve sustains;
Itself unseen, but in the effects remains.
80   Some, to whom Heaven in wit has been profuse,
Want as much more to turn it to its use;
For wit and judgment often are at strife,
Though meant each other's aid, like man and wife.
'Tis more to guide than spur the Muse's steed,
85   Restrain his fury than provoke his speed;
The wingèd courser,[5] like a generous° horse,   *spirited, highly bred*
Shows most true mettle when you check his course.
   Those rules of old discovered, not devised,
Are Nature still, but Nature methodized;
90   Nature, like liberty, is but restrained
By the same laws which first herself ordained.
   Hear how learn'd Greece her useful rules indites,
When to repress and when indulge our flights:
High on Parnassus' top her sons she showed,
95   And pointed out those arduous paths they trod;
Held from afar, aloft, the immortal prize,
And urged the rest by equal steps to rise.
Just precepts thus from great examples given,
She drew from them what they derived from Heaven.
100   The generous critic fanned the poet's fire,
And taught the world with reason to admire.
Then criticism the Muse's handmaid proved,
To dress her charms, and make her more beloved:
But following wits from that intention strayed,
105   Who could not win the mistress, wooed the maid;
Against the poets their own arms they turned,
Sure to hate most the men from whom they learned.
So modern 'pothecaries, taught the art
By doctors's bills° to play the doctor's part,   *prescriptions*
110   Bold in the practice of mistaken rules,
Prescribe, apply, and call their masters fools.
Some on the leaves of ancient authors prey,
Nor time nor moths e'er spoiled so much as they.
Some dryly plain, without invention's aid,
115   Write dull receipts[6] how poems may be made.

5. Pegasus, associated with the Muses and poetic inspiration.
6. Formulas for preparing a dish; recipes. Pope

himself wrote an amusing burlesque, *Receipt to Make an Epic Poem*, first published in the *Guardian* 78 (1713).

These leave the sense their learning to display,
And those explain the meaning quite away.
You then whose judgment the right course would steer,
Know well each ancient's proper character;
120 His fable,[7] subject, scope° in every page;　　　　　　*aim, purpose*
Religion, country, genius of his age:
Without all these at once before your eyes,
Cavil you may, but never criticize.
Be Homer's works your study and delight,
125 Read them by day, and meditate by night;
Thence form your judgment, thence your maxims bring,
And trace the Muses upward to their spring.
Still with itself compared, his text peruse;
And let your comment be the Mantuan Muse.
130 When first young Maro[8] in his boundless mind
A work to outlast immortal Rome designed,
Perhaps he seemed above the critic's law,
And but from Nature's fountains scorned to draw;
But when to examine every part he came,
135 Nature and Homer were, he found, the same.
Convinced, amazed, he checks the bold design, ⎫
And rules as strict his labored work confine ⎬
As if the Stagirite[9] o'erlooked each line. ⎭
Learn hence for ancient rules a just esteem;
140 To copy Nature is to copy them.
Some beauties yet no precepts can declare,
For there's a happiness as well as care.[1]
Music resembles poetry, in each ⎫
Are nameless graces which no methods teach, ⎬
145 And which a master hand alone can reach. ⎭
If, where the rules not far enough extend
(Since rules were made but to promote their end)
Some lucky license answers to the full
The intent proposed, that license is a rule.
150 Thus Pegasus, a nearer way to take,
May boldly deviate from the common track.
Great wits sometimes may gloriously offend,
And rise to faults true critics dare not mend;
From vulgar bounds with brave disorder part,
155 And snatch a grace beyond the reach of art,
Which, without passing through the judgment, gains
The heart, and all its end at once attains.
In prospects thus, some objects please our eyes, ⎫
Which out of Nature's common order rise, ⎬
160 The shapeless rock, or hanging precipice. ⎭

---

7. Plot or story of a play or poem.
8. Virgil. He was born in a village adjacent to Mantua in Italy, hence "Mantuan Muse." His epic, the *Aeneid*, was modeled on Homer's *Iliad* and *Odyssey* and was considered to be a refinement on the Greek poems. Thus it could be thought of as a commentary ("comment") on Homer's poems.
9. Aristotle, native of Stagira, from whose *Poetics*

later critics formulated strict rules for writing tragedy and the epic.
1. I.e., no rules ("precepts") can explain ("declare") some beautiful effects in a work of art that can be the result only of inspiration or good luck ("happiness"), not of painstaking labor ("care").

But though the ancients thus their rules invade
(As kings dispense with laws themselves have made)
Moderns, beware! or if you must offend
Against the precept, ne'er transgress its end;
165 Let it be seldom, and compelled by need;
And have at least their precedent to plead.
The critic else proceeds without remorse,
Seizes your fame, and puts his laws in force.
  I know there are, to whose presumptuous thoughts
170 Those freer beauties, even in them, seem faults.[2]
Some figures monstrous and misshaped appear,
Considered singly, or beheld too near,
Which, but proportioned to their light or place,
Due distance reconciles to form and grace.
175 A prudent chief not always must display
His powers in equal ranks and fair array,
But with the occasion and the place comply,
Conceal his force, nay seem sometimes to fly.
Those oft are stratagems which errors seem,
180 Nor is it Homer nods, but we that dream.
  Still green with bays each ancient altar stands
Above the reach of sacrilegious hands,
Secure from flames, from envy's fiercer rage,
Destructive war, and all-involving age.
185 See, from each clime the learn'd their incense bring!
Here in all tongues consenting° paeans ring!   *agreeing, concurring*
In praise so just let every voice be joined,[3]
And fill the general chorus of mankind.
Hail, bards triumphant! born in happier days,
190 Immortal heirs of universal praise!
Whose honors with increase of ages grow,
As streams roll down, enlarging as they flow;
Nations unborn your mighty names shall sound,
And worlds applaud that must not yet be found!
195 Oh, may some spark of your celestial fire,
The last, the meanest of your sons inspire
(That on weak wings, from far, pursues your flights,
Glows while he reads, but trembles as he writes)
To teach vain wits a science little known,
200 To admire superior sense, and doubt their own!

Part 2

  Of all the causes which conspire to blind
Man's erring judgment, and misguide the mind,
What the weak head with strongest bias rules,
Is pride, the never-failing vice of fools.
205 Whatever Nature has in worth denied,
She gives in large recruits° of needful pride;   *supplies*
For as in bodies, thus in souls, we find

---

2. Pronounced *fawts*.   3. Pronounced *jined*.

What wants in blood and spirits, swelled with wind:
Pride, where wit fails, steps in to our defense,
210   And fills up all the mighty void of sense.
If once right reason drives that cloud away,
Truth breaks upon us with resistless day.
Trust not yourself: but your defects to know,
Make use of every friend—and every foe.
215   A little learning is a dangerous thing;
Drink deep, or taste not the Pierian spring.[4]
There shallow draughts intoxicate the brain,
And drinking largely sobers us again.
Fired at first sight with what the Muse imparts,
220   In fearless youth we tempt° the heights of arts,   attempt
While from the bounded level of our mind
Short views we take, nor see the lengths behind;
But more advanced, behold with strange surprise
New distant scenes of endless science rise!
225   So pleased at first the towering Alps we try,
Mount o'er the vales, and seem to tread the sky,
The eternal snows appear already past,
And the first clouds and mountains seem the last;
But, those attained, we tremble to survey
230   The growing labors of the lengthened way,
The increasing prospect tires our wandering eyes,
Hills peep o'er hills, and Alps on Alps arise!
       A perfect judge will read each work of wit
With the same spirit that its author writ:
235   Survey the whole, nor seek slight faults to find
Where Nature moves, and rapture warms the mind;
Nor lose, for that malignant dull delight,
The generous pleasure to be charmed with wit.
But in such lays as neither ebb nor flow,
240   Correctly cold, and regularly low,
That, shunning faults, one quiet tenor keep,
We cannot blame indeed—but we may sleep.
In wit, as nature, what affects our hearts
Is not the exactness of peculiar parts;
245   'Tis not a lip, or eye, we beauty call,
But the joint force and full result of all.
Thus when we view some well-proportioned dome[5]
(The world's just wonder, and even thine, O Rome!),
No single parts unequally surprise,
250   All comes united to the admiring eyes:
No monstrous height, or breadth, or length appear;
The whole at once is bold and regular.
       Whoever thinks a faultless piece to see,
Thinks what ne'er was, nor is, nor e'er shall be.
255   In every work regard the writer's end,
Since none can compass more than they intend;
And if the means be just, the conduct true,

---

4. The spring in Pieria on Mount Olympus, sacred
to the Muses.

5. The dome of St. Peter's, designed by Michelangelo.

Applause, in spite of trivial faults, is due.
As men of breeding, sometimes men of wit,
260   To avoid great errors must the less commit,
Neglect the rules each verbal critic lays,
For not to know some trifles is a praise.
Most critics, fond of some subservient art,
Still make the whole depend upon a part:
265   They talk of principles, but notions prize,
And all to one loved folly sacrifice.
         Once on a time La Mancha's knight,[6] they say,
A certain bard encountering on the way,
Discoursed in terms as just, with looks as sage,
270   As e'er could Dennis,[7] of the Grecian stage;
Concluding all were desperate sots and fools
Who durst depart from Aristotle's rules.
Our author, happy in a judge so nice,
Produced his play, and begged the knight's advice;
275   Made him observe the subject and the plot,
The manners, passions, unities; what not?
All which exact to rule were brought about,
Were but a combat in the lists left out.
"What! leave the combat out?" exclaims the knight.
280   "Yes, or we must renounce the Stagirite."
"Not so, by Heaven!" he answers in a rage,
"Knights, squires, and steeds must enter on the stage."
"So vast a throng the stage can ne'er contain."
"Then build a new, or act it in a plain."
285   Thus critics of less judgment than caprice,
Curious,° not knowing, not exact, but nice,°   laborious/fussy
Form short ideas, and offend in arts
(As most in manners), by a love to parts.
         Some to conceit[8] alone their taste confine,
290   And glittering thoughts struck out at every line;
Pleased with a work where nothing's just or fit,
One glaring chaos and wild heap of wit.
Poets, like painters, thus unskilled to trace
The naked nature and the living grace,
295   With gold and jewels cover every part,
And hide with ornaments their want of art.
True wit is Nature to advantage dressed,
What oft was thought, but ne'er so well expressed;
Something whose truth convinced at sight we find,
300   That gives us back the image of our mind.
As shades more sweetly recommend the light,
So modest plainness sets off sprightly wit;
For works may have more wit than does them good,
As bodies perish through excess of blood.
305   Others for language all their care express,

6. Don Quixote. The story comes not from Cervantes's novel, but from a spurious sequel to it by Don Alonzo Fernandez de Avellaneda.
7. John Dennis (1657–1734), although one of the leading critics of the time, was frequently ridiculed by the wits for his irascibility and pomposity. Pope

apparently did not know Dennis personally, but his jibe at him in part 3 of this poem made him a bitter enemy.
8. Pointed wit, ingenuity and extravagance, or affectation in the use of figures, especially similes and metaphors.

And value books, as women men, for dress.
Their praise is still—the style is excellent;
The sense they humbly take upon content.°   *mere acquiescence*
Words are like leaves; and where they most abound,
310   Much fruit of sense beneath is rarely found.
False eloquence, like the prismatic glass,
Its gaudy colors spreads on every place;[9]
The face of Nature we no more survey,
All glares alike, without distinction gay.
315   But true expression, like the unchanging sun, ⎫
Clears and improves whate'er it shines upon;   ⎬
It gilds all objects, but it alters none.   ⎭
Expression is the dress of thought, and still
Appears more decent as more suitable.
320   A vile conceit in pompous words expressed
Is like a clown° in regal purple dressed: *rustic, boor*
For different styles with different subjects sort,
As several garbs with country, town, and court.
Some by old words to fame have made pretense,
325   Ancients in phrase, mere moderns in their sense.
Such labored nothings, in so strange a style,
Amaze the unlearn'd, and make the learned smile;
Unlucky as Fungoso[1] in the play,   ⎫
These sparks with awkward vanity display   ⎬
330   What the fine gentleman wore yesterday;   ⎭
And but so mimic ancient wits at best,
As apes our grandsires in their doublets dressed.
In words as fashions the same rule will hold,
Alike fantastic if too new or old:
335   Be not the first by whom the new are tried,
Nor yet the last to lay the old aside.
      But most by numbers° judge a poet's song,   *versification*
And smooth or rough with them is right or wrong.
In the bright Muse though thousand charms conspire,
340   Her voice is all these tuneful fools admire,
Who haunt Parnassus but to please their ear, ⎫
Not mend their minds; as some to church repair, ⎬
Not for the doctrine, but the music there.   ⎭
These equal syllables alone require,
345   Though oft the ear the open vowels tire,[2]
While expletives[3] their feeble aid do join,
And ten low words oft creep in one dull line:
While they ring round the same unvaried chimes,
With sure returns of still expected rhymes;
350   Where'er you find "the cooling western breeze,"
In the next line, it "whispers through the trees";
If crystal streams "with pleasing murmurs creep,"

9. A very up-to-date scientific reference. Newton's *Optics*, which dealt with the prism and the spectrum, had been published in 1704, although his theories had been known earlier.
1. A character in Ben Jonson's comedy *Every Man out of His Humor* (1599).

2. In lines 345–57 Pope cleverly contrives to make his own metrics or diction illustrate the faults that he is exposing.
3. Words used merely to achieve the necessary number of feet in a line of verse.

The reader's threatened (not in vain) with "sleep";
Then, at the last and only couplet fraught
355 With some unmeaning thing they call a thought,
A needless Alexandrine[4] ends the song
That, like a wounded snake, drags its slow length along.
Leave such to tune their own dull rhymes, and know
What's roundly smooth or languishingly slow;
360 And praise the easy vigor of a line
Where Denham's strength and Waller's sweetness join.[5]
True ease in writing comes from art, not chance,
As those move easiest who have learned to dance.
'Tis not enough no harshness gives offense,
365 The sound must seem an echo to the sense.
Soft is the strain when Zephyr gently blows,
And the smooth stream in smoother numbers flows;
But when loud surges lash the sounding shore,
The hoarse, rough verse should like the torrent roar.
370 When Ajax strives some rock's vast weight to throw,
The line too labors, and the words move slow;
Not so when swift Camilla scours the plain,
Flies o'er the unbending corn, and skims along the main.
Hear how Timotheus'[6] varied lays surprise,
375 And bid alternate passions fall and rise!
While at each change the son of Libyan Jove°   *Alexander the Great*
Now burns with glory, and then melts with love;
Now his fierce eyes with sparkling fury glow,
Now sighs steal out, and tears begin to flow:
380 Persians and Greeks like turns of nature[7] found
And the world's victor stood subdued by sound!
The power of music all our hearts allow,
And what Timotheus was, is Dryden now.
　　　Avoid extremes; and shun the fault of such
385 Who still are pleased too little or too much.
At every trifle scorn to take offense:
That always shows great pride, or little sense.
Those heads, as stomachs, are not sure the best,
Which nauseate all, and nothing can digest.
390 Yet let not each gay turn thy rapture move;
For fools admire,° but men of sense approve:[8]   *wonder*
As things seem large which we through mists descry,
Dullness is ever apt to magnify.
　　　Some foreign writers, some our own despise;
395 The ancients only, or the moderns prize.
Thus wit, like faith, by each man is applied
To one small sect, and all are damned beside.
Meanly they seek the blessing to confine,

4. A line of verse containing six iambic feet; it is illustrated in the next line.
5. Dryden, whom Pope echoes here, considered Sir John Denham (1615–1669) and Edmund Waller (1606–1687) to have been the principal shapers of the closed pentameter couplet. He had distinguished the "strength" of the one and the "sweet-

ness" of the other.
6. The musician in Dryden's *Alexander's Feast.* Pope retells the story of that poem in the following lines.
7. Alternations of feelings.
8. Judge favorably only after due deliberation.

And force that sun but on a part to shine,
400   Which not alone the southern wit sublimes,°   raises up, purifies
But ripens spirits in cold northern climes;
Which from the first has shone on ages past,
Enlights the present, and shall warm the last;
Though each may feel increases and decays,
405   And see now clearer and now darker days.
Regard not then if wit be old or new,
But blame the false and value still the true.
    Some ne'er advance a judgment of their own,
But catch the spreading notion of the town;
410   They reason and conclude by precedent,
And own stale nonsense which they ne'er invent.
Some judge of authors' names, not works, and then
Nor praise nor blame the writings, but the men.
Of all this servile herd the worst is he
415   That in proud dullness joins with quality,⁹
A constant critic at the great man's board,
To fetch and carry nonsense for my lord.
What woeful stuff this madrigal would be
In some starved hackney sonneteer° or me!   hireling poet
420   But let a lord once own the happy lines,
How the wit brightens! how the style refines!
Before his sacred name flies every fault,
And each exalted stanza teems with thought!
    The vulgar thus through imitation err;
425   As oft the learn'd by being singular;
So much they scorn the crowd, that if the throng
By chance go right, they purposely go wrong.
So schismatics¹ the plain believers quit,
And are but damned for having too much wit.
430   Some praise at morning what they blame at night,
But always think the last opinion right.
A Muse by these is like a mistress used,
This hour she's idolized, the next abused;
While their weak heads like towns unfortified,
435   'Twixt sense and nonsense daily change their side.
Ask them the cause; they're wiser still, they say;
And still tomorrow's wiser than today.
We think our fathers fools, so wise we grow;
Our wiser sons, no doubt, will think us so.
440   Once school divines² this zealous isle o'erspread;
Who knew most sentences³ was deepest read.
Faith, Gospel, all seemed made to be disputed,
And none had sense enough to be confuted.
Scotists and Thomists now in peace remain
445   Amidst their kindred cobwebs in Duck Lane.⁴

9. People of high rank.
1. Those who have divided the church on points of theology. Pope stressed the first syllable, the pronunciation approved by Johnson in his *Dictionary*.
2. The medieval theologians, such as the followers

of Duns Scotus and St. Thomas Aquinas, mentioned below.
3. Allusion to Peter Lombard's *Book of Sentences*, a book esteemed by Scholastic philosophers.
4. Street where publishers' remainders and secondhand books were sold.

If faith itself has different dresses worn,
What wonder modes in wit should take their turn?
Oft, leaving what is natural and fit,
The current folly proves the ready wit;
450 And authors think their reputation safe,
Which lives as long as fools are pleased to laugh.
    Some valuing those of their own side or mind,
Still make themselves the measure of mankind:
Fondly° we think we honor merit then,   *foolishly*
455 When we but praise ourselves in other men.
Parties in wit attend on those of state,
And public faction doubles private hate.
Pride, Malice, Folly against Dryden rose,
In various shapes of parsons, critics, beaux;
460 But sense survived, when merry jests were past;
For rising merit will buoy up at last.
Might he return and bless once more our eyes,
New Blackmores and new Milbourns must arise.[5]
Nay, should great Homer lift his awful head,
465 Zoilus[6] again would start up from the dead.
Envy will merit, as its shade, pursue,
But like a shadow, proves the substance true;
For envied wit, like Sol eclipsed, makes known
The opposing body's grossness, not its own.
470 When first that sun too powerful beams displays,
It draws up vapors which obscure its rays;
But even those clouds at last adorn its way,
Reflect new glories, and augment the day.
    Be thou the first true merit to befriend;
475 His praise is lost who stays till all commend.
Short is the date, alas! of modern rhymes,
And 'tis but just to let them live betimes.
No longer now that golden age appears,
When patriarch wits survived a thousand years:
480 Now length of fame (our second life) is lost,
And bare threescore is all even that can boast;
Our sons their fathers' failing language see,
And such as Chaucer is, shall Dryden be.[7]
So when the faithful pencil has designed
485 Some bright idea of the master's mind,
Where a new world leaps out at his command,
And ready Nature waits upon his hand;
When the ripe colors soften and unite,
And sweetly melt into just shade and light;
490 When mellowing years their full perfection give,
And each bold figure just begins to live,
The treacherous colors the fair art betray,

5. Sir Richard Blackmore, physician and poet, had attacked Dryden for the immorality of his plays; Rev. Luke Milbourn had attacked his translation of Virgil.
6. A Greek critic of the 4th century B.C.E., who wrote a book of carping criticism of Homer.

7. The radical changes that took place in the English language between the death of Chaucer in 1400 and the death of Dryden in 1700 suggested that in another three hundred years Dryden would be unintelligible. Latin seemed the only means of attaining enduring fame.

And all the bright creation fades away!
   Unhappy wit, like most mistaken things,
495 Atones not for that envy which it brings.
In youth alone its empty praise we boast,
But soon the short-lived vanity is lost;
Like some fair flower the early spring supplies,
That gaily blooms, but even in blooming dies.
500 What is this wit, which must our cares employ?
The owner's wife, that other men enjoy;
Then most our trouble still when most admired,
And still the more we give, the more required;
Whose fame with pains we guard, but lose with ease,
505 Sure some to vex, but never all to please;
'Tis what the vicious fear, the virtuous shun,
By fools 'tis hated, and by knaves undone!
   If wit so much from ignorance undergo,
Ah, let not learning too commence its foe!
510 Of old those met rewards who could excel,
And such were praised who but endeavored well;
Though triumphs were to generals only due,
Crowns were reserved to grace the soldiers too.[8]
Now they who reach Parnassus' lofty crown
515 Employ their pains to spurn some others down;
And while self-love each jealous writer rules,
Contending wits become the sport of fools;
But still the worst with most regret commend,
For each ill author is as bad a friend.
520 To what base ends, and by what abject ways,
Are mortals urged through sacred[9] lust of praise!
Ah, ne'er so dire a thirst of glory boast,
Nor in the critic let the man be lost!
Good nature and good sense must ever join;
525 To err is human, to forgive divine.
   But if in noble minds some dregs remain
Not yet purged off, of spleen and sour disdain,
Discharge that rage on more provoking crimes,
Nor fear a dearth in these flagitious° times.   *scandalously wicked*
530 No pardon vile obscenity should find,
Though wit and art conspire to move your mind;
But dullness with obscenity must prove
As shameful sure as impotence in love.
In the fat age of pleasure, wealth, and ease
535 Sprung the rank weed, and thrived with large increase:
When love was all an easy monarch's[1] care,
Seldom at council, never in a war;
Jilts[2] ruled the state, and statesmen farces writ;
Nay, wits had pensions, and young lords had wit;

---

8. To celebrate Roman victories, valiant soldiers were decorated with a variety of crowns.
9. Accursed. The phrase imitates Virgil's *auri sacra famis*, "accursed hunger for gold" (*Aeneid* 3.57).

1. Charles II. The concluding lines of part 2 discuss the corruption of wit and poetry under this monarch.
2. Mistresses of the king.

540   The fair sat panting at a courtier's play,
      And not a mask[3] went unimproved away;
      The modest fan was lifted up no more,
      And virgins smiled at what they blushed before.
      The following license of a foreign reign
545   Did all the dregs of bold Socinus[4] drain;
      Then unbelieving priests reformed the nation,
      And taught more pleasant methods of salvation;
      Where Heaven's free subjects might their rights dispute,
      Lest God himself should seem too absolute;
550   Pulpits their sacred satire learned to spare,
      And Vice admired to find a flatterer there!
      Encouraged thus, wit's Titans braved the skies,
      And the press groaned with licensed blasphemies.
      These monsters, critics! with your darts engage,
555   Here point your thunder, and exhaust your rage!
      Yet shun their fault, who, scandalously nice,
      Will needs mistake an author into vice;
      All seems infected that the infected spy,
      As all looks yellow to the jaundiced eye.

Part 3

560   Learn then what morals critics ought to show,
      For 'tis but half a judge's task, to know.
      'Tis not enough, taste, judgment, learning, join;
      In all you speak, let truth and candor° shine: *kindness, impartiality*
      That not alone what to your sense is due
565   All may allow; but seek your friendship too.
         Be silent always when you doubt your sense;
      And speak, though sure, with seeming diffidence:
      Some positive, persisting fops we know,
      Who, if once wrong, will needs be always so;
570   But you, with pleasure own your errors past,
      And make each day a critic° on the last.   *critique*
         'Tis not enough, your counsel still be true;
      Blunt truths more mischief than nice falsehoods do;
      Men must be taught as if you taught them not,
575   And things unknown proposed as things forgot.
      Without good breeding, truth is disapproved;
      That only makes superior sense beloved.
         Be niggards of advice on no pretense;
      For the worst avarice is that of sense.
580   With mean complacence[5] ne'er betray your trust,
      Nor be so civil as to prove unjust.
      Fear not the anger of the wise to raise;
      Those best can bear reproof, who merit praise.
      'Twere well might critics still this freedom take;

---

3. A woman wearing a mask.
4. The name of two Italian theologians of the 16th century who denied the divinity of Jesus. "Foreign

reign": William III, a Dutchman.
5. Softness of manners; desire of pleasing.

585 But Appius reddens at each word you speak,
  And stares, tremendous! with a threatening eye,
  Like some fierce tyrant in old tapestry.[6]
  Fear most to tax an honorable fool,
  Whose right it is, uncensured to be dull;
590 Such, without wit, are poets when they please,
  As without learning they can take degrees.[7]
  Leave dangerous truths to unsuccessful satyrs,°   *satires*
  And flattery to fulsome dedicators,
  Whom, when they praise, the world believes no more,
595 Than when they promise to give scribbling o'er.
  'Tis best sometimes your censure to restrain,
  And charitably let the dull be vain:
  Your silence there is better than your spite,
  For who can rail so long as they can write?
600 Still humming on, their drowsy course they keep,
  And lashed so long, like tops, are lashed asleep.[8]
  False steps but help them to renew the race,
  As, after stumbling, jades° will mend their pace.   *worn-out horses*
  What crowds of these, impenitently bold,
605 In sounds and jingling syllables grown old,
  Still run on poets, in a raging vein,
  Even to the dregs and squeezings of the brain,
  Strain out the last dull droppings of their sense,
  And rhyme with all the rage of impotence.
610 Such shameless bards we have, and yet 'tis true,
  There are as mad, abandoned critics too.
  The bookful blockhead, ignorantly read,
  With loads of learned lumber° in his head,   *rubbish*
  With his own tongue still edifies his ears,
615 And always listening to himself appears.
  All books he reads, and all he reads assails,
  From Dryden's *Fables* down to Durfey's *Tales*.[9]
  With him, most authors steal their works, or buy;
  Garth did not write his own *Dispensary*.[1]
620 Name a new play, and he's the poet's friend,
  Nay showed his faults—but when would poets mend?
  No place so sacred from such fops is barred,
  Nor is Paul's church more safe than Paul's churchyard:[2]
  Nay, fly to altars; *there* they'll talk you dead:
625 For fools rush in where angels fear to tread.
  Distrustful sense with modest caution speaks, ⎫
  It still looks home, and short excursions makes; ⎬
  But rattling nonsense in full volleys breaks, ⎭

6. "This picture was taken to himself by John Dennis, a furious old critic by profession, who, upon no other provocation, wrote against this Essay and its author, in a manner perfectly lunatic" [Pope's note, 1744]. Pope *did* intend to ridicule Dennis, whose *Appius and Virginia* had failed on the stage in 1709 and who was known for his stare and his use of the word *tremendous* (see line 270).
7. Honorary degrees were granted to unqualified men of rank.
8. Tops "sleep" when they spin so rapidly that they seem not to move.
9. Dryden's *Fables* (1700), a set of translations, were among his most admired works; Thomas D'Urfey's *Tales* (1704) were notorious potboilers.
1. Samuel Garth (1661–1719), who had been accused of plagiarizing his mock-epic poem *The Dispensary* (1699), was admired and defended by Pope.
2. Booksellers' district near St. Paul's Cathedral, whose aisles were used as a place to meet and do business.

And never shocked, and never turned aside,
630 Bursts out, resistless, with a thundering tide.
     But where's the man, who counsel can bestow,
Still pleased to teach, and yet not proud to know?
Unbiased, or° by favor, or by spite: *either*
Not dully prepossessed, nor blindly right;
635 Though learned, well-bred; and though well-bred, sincere;
Modestly bold, and humanly severe:
Who to a friend his faults can freely show,
And gladly praise the merit of a foe?
Blessed with a taste exact, yet unconfined;
640 A knowledge both of books and humankind;
Gen'rous converse;[3] a soul exempt from pride;
And love to praise, with reason on his side?
     Such once were critics; such the happy few,
Athens and Rome in better ages knew.
645 The mighty Stagirite[4] first left the shore,
Spread all his sails, and durst the deeps explore;
He steered securely, and discovered far,
Led by the light of the Maeonian star.[5]
Poets, a race long unconfined, and free,
650 Still fond and proud of savage liberty,
Received his laws; and stood convinced 'twas fit,
Who conquered nature, should preside o'er wit.
     Horace still charms with graceful negligence,
And without method talks us into sense;
655 Will, like a friend, familiarly convey
The truest notions in the easiest° way.   *least formal*
He, who supreme in judgment, as in wit,
Might boldly censure, as he boldly writ,
Yet judged with coolness, though he sung with fire;
660 His precepts teach but what his works inspire.
Our critics take a contrary extreme,
They judge with fury, but they write with fle'me.°   *phlegmatically*
Nor suffers Horace more in wrong translations
By wits, than critics[6] in as wrong quotations.
665 See Dionysius[7] Homer's thoughts refine,
And call new beauties forth from every line!
     Fancy and art in gay Petronius[8] please,
The scholar's learning, with the courtier's ease.
     In grave Quintilian's[9] copious work, we find
670 The justest rules, and clearest method joined:
Thus useful arms in magazines° we place,   *storehouses, arsenals*
All ranged in order, and disposed with grace,

---

3. Well-bred conversation.
4. Aristotle, whose *Poetics* founded the art of literary criticism, was born at Stagira.
5. Homer, who was supposed to have been born in Maeonia.
6. I.e., than by critics. Phrases from Horace's *Art of Poetry* were quoted incessantly by critics.
7. Dionysius of Halicarnassus (1st century B.C.E.)

wrote an important treatise on the artistic arrangement of words.
8. Author of the *Satyricon* (1st century C.E.).
9. Author of the *Institutio Oratoria* (ca. 95 C.E.), a famous treatise on rhetoric. Here as elsewhere, Pope's terms of praise are drawn from the author he is praising.

But less to please the eye, than arm the hand,
Still fit for use, and ready at command.
675   Thee, bold Longinus![1] all the nine° Inspire,   *Muses*
And bless their critic with a poet's fire.
An ardent judge, who, zealous in his trust,
With warmth gives sentence, yet is always just;
Whose own example strengthens all his laws,
680 And is himself that great sublime he draws.
    Thus long succeeding critics justly reigned,
License repressed, and useful laws ordained.
Learning and Rome alike in empire grew;
And arts still followed where her eagles[2] flew;
685 From the same foes, at last, both felt their doom,
And the same age saw learning fall, and Rome.
With tyranny, then superstition joined,
As that the body, this enslaved the mind;
Much was believed, but little understood,
690 And to be dull was construed to be good;
A second deluge learning thus o'errun,
And the monks finished what the Goths begun.[3]
    At length Erasmus, that great, injured name
(The glory of the priesthood, and the shame!),[4]
695 Stemmed the wild torrent of a barb'rous age,
And drove those holy Vandals off the stage.
    But see! each Muse, in Leo's golden days,
Starts from her trance, and trims her withered bays![5]
Rome's ancient Genius, o'er its ruins spread,
700 Shakes off the dust, and rears his reverend head.
Then sculpture and her sister-arts revive;
Stones leaped to form, and rocks began to live;
With sweeter notes each rising temple rung;
A Raphael painted, and a Vida[6] sung.
705 Immortal Vida: on whose honored brow
The poet's bays and critic's ivy grow:
Cremona now shall ever boast thy name,
As next in place to Mantua, next in fame![7]
    But soon by impious arms from Latium[8] chased,
710 Their ancient bounds the banished Muses passed;
Thence arts o'er all the northern world advance,
But critic-learning flourished most in France:
The rules a nation, born to serve, obeys;
And Boileau still in right of Horace sways.[9]
715   But we, brave Britons, foreign laws despised,

1. Supposed author of the influential treatise *On the Sublime* (1st century C.E.), greatly in vogue at the time of Pope.
2. Emblems on the standards of the Roman army.
3. Pope thought that the Scholastic theologians of the Middle Ages were "holy Vandals" who had "sacked" learning as the Goths and Vandals had sacked Rome.
4. Erasmus (1466–1536), the great humanist scholar, was the "glory of the priesthood" because of his goodness and learning and its "shame" because he was persecuted.
5. The wreath of poetry. Leo X, pope from 1513

to 1521, was notable for his encouragement of artists.
6. "M. Hieronymus Vida, an excellent Latin poet, who writ an Art of Poetry in verse. He flourished in the time of Leo the Tenth" [Pope's note]. Raphael (1483–1520) painted many of his greatest works under the patronage of Leo X.
7. Vida came from Cremona, near Mantua, the birthplace of Virgil, his favorite poet.
8. Italy. German and Spanish troops sacked Rome in 1527.
9. Boileau's *L'Art Poétique* (1674) regularized and modernized the lessons of Horace's *Art of Poetry*.

THE RAPE OF THE LOCK / 2525

And kept unconquered—and uncivilized;
Fierce for the liberties of wit, and bold,
We still defied the Romans, as of old.
Yet some there were, among the sounder few
720 Of those who less presumed, and better knew,
Who durst assert the juster ancient cause,
And here restored wit's fundamental laws.
Such was the Muse, whose rules and practice tell,
"Nature's chief masterpiece is writing well."[1]
725 Such was Roscommon,[2] not more learned than good,
With manners gen'rous as his noble blood;
To him the wit of Greece and Rome was known,
And every author's merit, but his own.
Such late was Walsh—the Muse's[3] judge and friend,
730 Who justly knew to blame or to commend;
To failings mild, but zealous for desert;
The clearest head, and the sincerest heart.
This humble praise, lamented shade! receive,
This praise at least a grateful Muse may give:
735 The Muse, whose early voice you taught to sing,
Prescribed her heights, and pruned her tender wing,
(Her guide now lost) no more attempts to rise,
But in low numbers° short excursions tries: *humble verses*
Content, if hence the unlearned their wants may view,
740 The learned reflect on what before they knew:
Careless of censure, nor too fond of fame;
Still pleased to praise, yet not afraid to blame;
Averse alike to flatter, or offend;
Not free from faults, nor yet too vain to mend.

1709   1711

The Rape of the Lock

The Rape of the Lock *The Rape of the Lock* is based on an actual episode
that provoked a quarrel between two prominent Catholic families. Pope's friend John
Caryll, to whom the poem is addressed (line 3), suggested that Pope write it, in the
hope that a little laughter might serve to soothe ruffled tempers. Lord Petre had cut
off a lock of hair from the head of the lovely Arabella Fermor (often spelled "Farmer"
and doubtless so pronounced), much to the indignation of the lady and her relatives.
In its original version of two cantos and 334 lines, published in 1712, *The Rape of
the Lock* was a great success. In 1713 a new version was undertaken against the
advice of Addison, who considered the poem perfect as it was first written. Pope
greatly expanded the earlier version, adding the delightful "machinery" (i.e., the supernatural agents in epic action) of the Sylphs, Belinda's toilet, the card game, and the
visit to the Cave of Spleen in canto 4. In 1717, with the addition of Clarissa's speech
on good humor, the poem assumed its final form.

With delicate fancy and playful wit, Pope elaborated the trivial episode that occa-

---

1. Quoted from an *Essay on Poetry* by John Sheffield, duke of Buckingham (1648–1721), who had
befriended the young Pope.
2. Wentworth Dillon, earl of Roscommon, wrote
the important *Essay on Translated Verse* (1684).

3. The "Muse" here is Pope himself. William
Walsh (1663–1708), whom Dryden once called
"the best critic of our nation," had advised Pope to
work at becoming the first great "correct" poet in
English.

sioned the poem into the semblance of an epic in miniature, the most nearly perfect heroicomical poem in English. The verse abounds in parodies and echoes of the *Iliad,* the *Aeneid,* and *Paradise Lost,* thus constantly forcing the reader to compare small things with great. The familiar devices of epic are observed, but the incidents or characters are beautifully proportioned to the scale of mock epic. The *Rape* tells of war, but it is the drawing-room war between the sexes; it has its heroes and heroines, but they are beaux and belles; it has its supernatural characters ("machinery"), but they are Sylphs (borrowed, as Pope tells us in his engaging dedicatory letter, from Rosicrucian lore)—creatures of the air, the souls of dead coquettes, with tasks appropriate to their nature—or the Gnome Umbriel, once a prude on earth; it has its epic game, played on the "velvet plain" of the card table, its feasting heroes, who sip coffee and gossip, and its battle, fought with the clichés of compliment and conceits, with frowns and angry glances, with snuff and bodkin; it has the traditional epic journey to the underworld—here the Cave of Spleen, emblematic of the ill nature of female hypochondriacs. And Pope creates a world in which these actions take place, a world that is dense with beautiful objects: brocades, ivory and tortoiseshell, cosmetics and diamonds, lacquered furniture, silver teapot, delicate chinaware. It is a world that is constantly in motion and that sparkles and glitters with light, whether the light of the sun or of Belinda's eyes or that light into which the "fluid" bodies of the Sylphs seem to dissolve as they flutter in shrouds and around the mast of Belinda's ship. Though Pope laughs at this world and its creatures—and remembers that a grimmer, darker world surrounds it (3.19–24 and 5.145–48)—he makes us very much aware of its beauty and charm.

The epigraph may be translated, "I was unwilling, Belinda, to ravish your locks; but I rejoice to have conceded this to your prayers" (Martial's *Epigrams* 12.84.1–2). Pope substituted his heroine for Martial's Polytimus. The epigraph is intended to suggest that the poem was published at Miss Fermor's request.

The Rape of the Lock

An Heroi-Comical Poem

Nolueram, Belinda, tuos violare capillos;
sed juvat hoc precibus me tribuisse tuis.
—MARTIAL

TO MRS. ARABELLA FERMOR

MADAM,

It will be in vain to deny that I have some regard for this piece, since I dedicate it to you. Yet you may bear me witness, it was intended only to divert a few young ladies, who have good sense and good humor enough to laugh not only at their sex's little unguarded follies, but at their own. But as it was communicated with the air of a secret, it soon found its way into the world. An imperfect copy having been offered to a bookseller, you had the good nature for my sake to consent to the publication of one more correct; this I was forced to, before I had executed half my design, for the machinery was entirely wanting to complete it.

The machinery, Madam, is a term invented by the critics, to signify that part which the deities, angels, or demons are made to act in a poem; for the ancient poets are in one respect like many modern ladies: let an action be never so trivial in itself, they always make it appear of the utmost importance.

These machines I determined to raise on a very new and odd foundation, the Rosicrucian[1] doctrine of spirits.

I know how disagreeable it is to make use of hard words before a lady; but 'tis so much the concern of a poet to have his works understood, and particularly by your sex, that you must give me leave to explain two or three difficult terms.

The Rosicrucians are a people I must bring you acquainted with. The best account I know of them is in a French book called *Le Comte de Gabalis*,[2] which both in its title and size is so like a novel, that many of the fair sex have read it for one by mistake. According to these gentlemen, the four elements are inhabited by spirits, which they call Sylphs, Gnomes, Nymphs, and Salamanders. The Gnomes or Demons of earth delight in mischief; but the Sylphs, whose habitation is in the air, are the best-conditioned creatures imaginable. For they say, any mortals may enjoy the most intimate familiarities with these gentle spirits, upon a condition very easy to all true adepts, an inviolate preservation of chastity.

As to the following cantos, all the passages of them are as fabulous as the vision at the beginning, or the transformation at the end (except the loss of your hair, which I always mention with reverence). The human persons are as fictitious as the airy ones; and the character of Belinda, as it is now managed, resembles you in nothing but in beauty.

If this poem had as many graces as there are in your person, or in your mind, yet I could never hope it should pass through the world half so uncensured as you have done. But let its fortune be what it will, mine is happy enough, to have given me this occasion of assuring you that I am, with the truest esteem,

MADAM,
Your most obedient, humble servant,
A. POPE

Canto 1

What dire offense from amorous causes springs,
What mighty contests rise from trivial things,
I sing—This verse to Caryll, Muse! is due:
This, even Belinda may vouchsafe to view:
5   Slight is the subject, but not so the praise,
If she inspire, and he approve my lays.
    Say what strange motive, Goddess! could compel
A well-bred lord to assault a gentle belle?
Oh, say what stranger cause, yet unexplored,
10   Could make a gentle belle reject a lord?
In tasks so bold can little men engage,
And in soft bosoms dwells such mighty rage?
    Sol through white curtains shot a timorous ray,
And oped those eyes that must eclipse the day.
15   Now lapdogs give themselves the rousing shake,

---

1. A system of arcane philosophy introduced into England from Germany in the 17th century.

2. By the Abbé de Montfaucon de Villars, published in 1670.

And sleepless lovers, just at twelve, awake:
Thrice rung the bell, the slipper knocked the ground,
And the pressed watch[3] returned a silver sound.
Belinda still her downy pillow pressed,
20 Her guardian Sylph prolonged the balmy rest.
'Twas he had summoned to her silent bed
The morning dream that hovered o'er her head.
A youth more glittering than a birthnight beau[4]
(That even in slumber caused her cheek to glow)
25 Seemed to her ear his winning lips to lay,
And thus in whispers said, or seemed to say:
    "Fairest of mortals, thou distinguished care
Of thousand bright inhabitants of air!
If e'er one vision touched thy infant thought,
30 Of all the nurse and all the priest have taught,
Of airy elves by moonlight shadows seen,
The silver token, and the circled green,[5]
Or virgins visited by angel powers,
With golden crowns and wreaths of heavenly flowers,
35 Hear and believe! thy own importance know,
Nor bound thy narrow views to things below.
Some secret truths, from learned pride concealed,
To maids alone and children are revealed:
What though no credit doubting wits may give?
40 The fair and innocent shall still believe.
Know, then, unnumbered spirits round thee fly,
The light militia of the lower sky:
These, though unseen, are ever on the wing,
Hang o'er the box, and hover round the Ring.[6]
45 Think what an equipage thou hast in air,
And view with scorn two pages and a chair.°   *sedan chair*
As now your own, our beings were of old,
And once enclosed in woman's beauteous mold;
Thence, by a soft transition, we repair
50 From earthly vehicles to these of air.
Think not, when woman's transient breath is fled,
That all her vanities at once are dead:
Succeeding vanities she still regards,
And though she plays no more, o'erlooks the cards.
55 Her joy in gilded chariots, when alive,
And love of ombre,[7] after death survive.
For when the Fair in all their pride expire,
To their first elements[8] their souls retire:
The sprites of fiery termagants in flame

3. A watch that chimes the hour and the quarter hour when the stem is pressed down. "Knocked the ground": summons to a maid.
4. Courtiers wore especially fine clothes on the sovereign's birthday.
5. Rings of bright green grass, which are common in England even in winter, were held to be due to the round dances of fairies. According to popular belief fairies skim off the cream from jugs of milk left standing overnight and leave a coin ("silver token") in payment.
6. The "box" in the theater and the fashionable circular drive ("Ring") in Hyde Park.
7. The popular card game (see n. 8, p. 2534).
8. The four elements out of which all things were believed to have been made were fire, water, earth, and air. One or another of these elements was supposed to be predominant in both the physical and the psychological makeup of each human being. In this context they are spoken of as "humors."

60 Mount up, and take a Salamander's⁹ name.
    Soft yielding minds to water glide away,
    And sip, with Nymphs, their elemental tea.¹
    The graver prude sinks downward to a Gnome,
    In search of mischief still on earth to roam.
65 The light coquettes in Sylphs aloft repair,
    And sport and flutter in the fields of air.
        "Know further yet; whoever fair and chaste
    Rejects mankind, is by some Sylph embraced:
    For spirits, freed from mortal laws, with ease
70 Assume what sexes and what shapes they please.²
    What guards the purity of melting maids,
    In courtly balls, and midnight masquerades,
    Safe from the treacherous friend, the daring spark,
    The glance by day, the whisper in the dark,
75 When kind occasion prompts their warm desires,
    When music softens, and when dancing fires?
    'Tis but their Sylph, the wise Celestials know,
    Though Honor is the word with men below.
        "Some nymphs there are, too conscious of their face,
80 For life predestined to the Gnomes' embrace.
    These swell their prospects and exalt their pride,
    When offers are disdained, and love denied:
    Then gay ideas° crowd the vacant brain,   *showy images*
    While peers, and dukes, and all their sweeping train,
85 And garters, stars, and coronets³ appear,
    And in soft sounds, 'your Grace'° salutes their ear.   *a duchess*
    'Tis these that early taint the female soul,
    Instruct the eyes of young coquettes to roll,
    Teach infant cheeks a bidden blush to know,
90 And little hearts to flutter at a beau.
        "Oft, when the world imagine women stray,
    The Sylphs through mystic mazes guide their way,
    Through all the giddy circle they pursue,
    And old impertinence° expel by new.   *trifle*
95 What tender maid but must a victim fall
    To one man's treat, but for another's ball?
    When Florio speaks, what virgin could withstand,
    If gentle Damon did not squeeze her hand?
    With varying vanities, from every part,
100 They shift the moving toyshop⁴ of their heart;
    Where wigs with wigs, with sword-knots sword-knots strive,
    Beaux banish beaux, and coaches coaches drive.
    This erring mortals levity may call;
    Oh, blind to truth! the Sylphs contrive it all.
105   "Of these am I, who thy protection claim,
    A watchful sprite, and Ariel is my name.
    Late, as I ranged the crystal wilds of air,

9. A lizardlike animal, in antiquity believed to live
in fire. Each element was inhabited by a spirit, as
the following lines explain.
1. Pronounced *tay*.

2. Cf. *Paradise Lost* 1.427–31; this is one of many
allusions to that poem in the *Rape*.
3. Emblems of nobility.
4. A shop stocked with baubles and trifles.

In the clear mirror of thy ruling star
I saw, alas! some dread event impend,
110 Ere to the main this morning sun descend,
But Heaven reveals not what, or how, or where:
Warned by the Sylph, O pious maid, beware!
This to disclose is all thy guardian can:
Beware of all, but most beware of Man!"
115   He said; when Shock,[5] who thought she slept too long,
Leaped up, and waked his mistress with his tongue.
'Twas then, Belinda, if report say true,
Thy eyes first opened on a billet-doux;
Wounds, charms, and ardors were no sooner read,
120 But all the vision vanished from thy head.
        And now, unveiled, the toilet stands displayed,
Each silver vase in mystic order laid.
First, robed in white, the nymph intent adores,
With head uncovered, the cosmetic powers.
125 A heavenly image in the glass appears;
To that she bends, to that her eyes she rears.
The inferior priestess, at her altar's side,
Trembling begins the sacred rites of Pride.
Unnumbered treasures ope at once, and here
130 The various offerings of the world appear;
From each she nicely culls with curious toil,
And decks the goddess with the glittering spoil.
This casket India's glowing gems unlocks,
And all Arabia breathes from yonder box.
135 The tortoise here and elephant unite,
Transformed to combs, the speckled and the white.
Here files of pins extend their shining rows,
Puffs, powders, patches, Bibles,[6] billet-doux.
Now awful Beauty puts on all its arms;
140 The fair each moment rises in her charms,
Repairs her smiles, awakens every grace,
And calls forth all the wonders of her face;
Sees by degrees a purer blush arise,
And keener lightnings quicken in her eyes.
145 The busy Sylphs surround their darling care,
These set the head, and those divide the hair,
Some fold the sleeve, whilst others plait the gown;
And Betty's[7] praised for labors not her own.

Canto 2

Not with more glories, in the ethereal plain,
The sun first rises o'er the purpled main,
Than, issuing forth, the rival of his beams
Launched on the bosom of the silver Thames.
5 Fair nymphs and well-dressed youths around her shone,

---

5. A long-haired poodle, Belinda's lapdog.
6. It has been suggested that Pope intended here
not "Bibles," but "bibelots" (trinkets), but this
interpretation has not gained wide acceptance.
7. Belinda's maid, the "inferior priestess" mentioned in line 127.

But every eye was fixed on her alone.
On her white breast a sparkling cross she wore,
Which Jews might kiss, and infidels adore.
Her lively looks a sprightly mind disclose,
10   Quick as her eyes, and as unfixed as those:
Favors to none, to all she smiles extends;
Oft she rejects, but never once offends.
Bright as the sun, her eyes the gazers strike,
And, like the sun, they shine on all alike.
15   Yet graceful ease, and sweetness void of pride,
Might hide her faults, if belles had faults to hide:
If to her share some female errors fall,
Look on her face, and you'll forget 'em all.
      This nymph, to the destruction of mankind,
20   Nourished two locks which graceful hung behind
In equal curls, and well conspired to deck
With shining ringlets her smooth ivory neck.
Love in these labyrinths his slaves detains,
And mighty hearts are held in slender chains.
25   With hairy springes[8] we the birds betray,
Slight lines of hair surprise the finny prey,
Fair tresses man's imperial race ensnare,
And beauty draws us with a single hair.
      The adventurous Baron the bright locks admired,
30   He saw, he wished, and to the prize aspired.
Resolved to win, he meditates the way,
By force to ravish, or by fraud betray;
For when success a lover's toil attends,
Few ask if fraud or force attained his ends.
35   For this, ere Phoebus rose, he had implored
Propitious Heaven, and every power adored,
But chiefly Love—to Love an altar built,
Of twelve vast French romances, neatly gilt.
There lay three garters, half a pair of gloves,
40   And all the trophies of his former loves.
With tender billet-doux he lights the pyre,
And breathes three amorous sighs to raise the fire.
Then prostrate falls, and begs with ardent eyes
Soon to obtain, and long possess the prize:
45   The powers gave ear, and granted half his prayer,
The rest the winds dispersed in empty air.
      But now secure the painted vessel glides,
The sunbeams trembling on the floating tides,
While melting music steals upon the sky,
50   And softened sounds along the waters die.
Smooth flow the waves, the zephyrs gently play,
Belinda smiled, and all the world was gay.
All but the Sylph—with careful thoughts oppressed,
The impending woe sat heavy on his breast.
55   He summons straight his denizens of air;

8. Snares; pronounced *sprin-jez*.

The lucid squadrons round the sails repair:
Soft o'er the shrouds aërial whispers breathe
That seemed but zephyrs to the train beneath.
Some to the sun their insect-wings unfold,
60 Waft on the breeze, or sink in clouds of gold.
Transparent forms too fine for mortal sight,
Their fluid bodies half dissolved in light,
Loose to the wind their airy garments flew,
Thin glittering textures of the filmy dew,
65 Dipped in the richest tincture of the skies,
Where light disports in ever-mingling dyes,
While every beam new transient colors flings,
Colors that change whene'er they wave their wings.
Amid the circle, on the gilded mast,
70 Superior by the head was Ariel placed;
His purple⁹ pinions opening to the sun,
He raised his azure wand, and thus begun:
    "Ye Sylphs and Sylphids, to your chief give ear!
Fays, Fairies, Genii, Elves, and Daemons, hear!
75 Ye know the spheres and various tasks assigned
By laws eternal to the aërial kind.
Some in the fields of purest ether play,
And bask and whiten in the blaze of day.
Some guide the course of wandering orbs on high,
80 Or roll the planets through the boundless sky.
Some less refined, beneath the moon's pale light
Pursue the stars that shoot athwart the night,
Or suck the mists in grosser air below,
Or dip their pinions in the painted bow,
85 Or brew fierce tempests on the wintry main,
Or o'er the glebe° distill the kindly rain.   cultivated field
Others on earth o'er human race preside,
Watch all their ways, and all their actions guide:
Of these the chief the care of nations own,
90 And guard with arms divine the British Throne.
    "Our humbler province is to tend the Fair,
Not a less pleasing, though less glorious care:
To save the powder from too rude a gale,
Nor let the imprisoned essences exhale;
95 To draw fresh colors from the vernal flowers;
To steal from rainbows e'er they drop in showers
A brighter wash;° to curl their waving hairs,   cosmetic lotion
Assist their blushes, and inspire their airs,
Nay oft, in dreams invention we bestow,
100 To change a flounce, or add a furbelow.
    "This day black omens threat the brightest fair,
That e'er deserved a watchful spirit's care;
Some dire disaster, or by force or slight,
But what, or where, the Fates have wrapped in night:
105 Whether the nymph shall break Diana's¹ law,

---

9. In 18th-century poetic diction the word might
mean bloodred, purple, or simply (as is likely here)
brightly colored. The word derives from Virgil's

Eclogue 9.40, *purpureum*. An example of the Latinate nature of some poetic diction of the period.
1. Diana was the goddess of chastity.

Or some frail china jar receive a flaw,
Or stain her honor, or her new brocade,
Forget her prayers, or miss a masquerade,
Or lose her heart, or necklace, at a ball;
110 Or whether Heaven has doomed that Shock must fall.
Haste, then, ye spirits! to your charge repair:
The fluttering fan be Zephyretta's care;
The drops[2] to thee, Brillante, we consign;
And, Momentilla, let the watch be thine;
115 Do thou, Crispissa,[3] tend her favorite Lock;
Ariel himself shall be the guard of Shock.
     "To fifty chosen Sylphs, of special note,
We trust the important charge, the petticoat;
Oft have we known that sevenfold fence to fail,
120 Though stiff with hoops, and armed with ribs of whale.
Form a strong line about the silver bound,
And guard the wide circumference around.
     "Whatever spirit, careless of his charge,
His post neglects, or leaves the fair at large,
125 Shall feel sharp vengeance soon o'ertake his sins,
Be stopped in vials, or transfixed with pins,
Or plunged in lakes of bitter washes lie,
Or wedged whole ages in a bodkin's[4] eye;
Gums and pomatums shall his flight restrain,
130 While clogged he beats his silken wings in vain,
Or alum styptics with contracting power
Shrink his thin essence like a riveled[5] flower:
Or, as Ixion[6] fixed, the wretch shall feel
The giddy motion of the whirling mill,
135 In fumes of burning chocolate shall glow,
And tremble at the sea that froths below!"
     He spoke; the spirits from the sails descend;
Some, orb in orb, around the nymph extend;
Some thread the mazy ringlets of her hair;
140 Some hang upon the pendants of her ear:
With beating hearts the dire event they wait,
Anxious, and trembling for the birth of Fate.

Canto 3

Close by those meads, forever crowned with flowers,
Where Thames with pride surveys his rising towers,
There stands a structure of majestic frame,
Which from the neighboring Hampton[7] takes its name.
5 Here Britain's statesmen oft the fall foredoom
Of foreign tyrants and of nymphs at home;
Here thou, great Anna! whom three realms obey,

---

2. Diamond earrings. Observe the appropriateness
of the names of the Sylphs to their assigned functions.
3. From Latin *crispere*, "to curl."
4. A blunt needle with a large eye, used for drawing ribbon through eyelets in the edging of
women's garments.

5. To "rivel" is to "contract into wrinkles and cor-
rugations" (Johnson's *Dictionary*).
6. In the Greek myth, he was punished in the
underworld by being bound on an everturning
wheel.
7. Hampton Court, the royal palace, about fifteen
miles up the Thames from London.

Dost sometimes counsel take—and sometimes tea.
Hither the heroes and the nymphs resort,
10 To taste awhile the pleasures of a court;
In various talk the instructive hours they passed,
Who gave the ball, or paid the visit last;
One speaks the glory of the British Queen,
And one describes a charming Indian screen;
15 A third interprets motions, looks, and eyes;
At every word a reputation dies.
Snuff, or the fan, supply each pause of chat,
With singing, laughing, ogling, and all that.
Meanwhile, declining from the noon of day,
20 The sun obliquely shoots his burning ray;
The hungry judges soon the sentence sign,
And wretches hang that jurymen may dine;
The merchant from the Exchange returns in peace,
And the long labors of the toilet cease.
25 Belinda now, whom thirst of fame invites,
Burns to encounter two adventurous knights,
At ombre[8] singly to decide their doom,
And swells her breast with conquests yet to come.
Straight the three bands prepare in arms to join,
30 Each band the number of the sacred nine.
Soon as she spreads her hand, the aërial guard
Descend, and sit on each important card:
First Ariel perched upon a Matadore,
Then each according to the rank they bore;
35 For Sylphs, yet mindful of their ancient race,
Are, as when women, wondrous fond of place.
Behold, four Kings in majesty revered,
With hoary whiskers and a forky beard;
And four fair Queens whose hands sustain a flower,
40 The expressive emblem of their softer power;
Four Knaves in garbs succinct,° a trusty band,   *girded up*
Caps on their heads, and halberts in their hand;
And parti-colored troops, a shining train,
Draw forth to combat on the velvet plain.
45   The skillful nymph reviews her force with care;
"Let Spades be trumps!" she said, and trumps they were.
Now move to war her sable Matadores,
In show like leaders of the swarthy Moors.
Spadillio first, unconquerable lord!
50 Led off two captive trumps, and swept the board.
As many more Manillio forced to yield,
And marched a victor from the verdant field.

8. The game of ombre that Belinda plays against the baron and another young man is too complicated for complete explication here. Pope has carefully arranged the cards so that Belinda wins. The baron's hand is strong enough to be a threat, but the third player's is of little account. The hand is played exactly according to the rules of ombre, and Pope's description of the cards is equally accurate. Each player holds nine cards (line 30). The "Mata-dores" (line 33), when spades are trump, are "Spadillio" (line 49), the ace of spades; "Manillio" (line 51), the two of spades; and "Basto" (line 53), the ace of clubs. Belinda holds all three of these. (For a more complete description of ombre, see *The Rape of the Lock and Other Poems*, ed. Geoffrey Tillotson, in the Twickenham Edition of Pope's poems, vol. 2, Appendix C.)

Him Basto followed, but his fate more hard
Gained but one trump and one plebeian card.
55   With his broad saber next, a chief in years,
The hoary Majesty of Spades appears,
Puts forth one manly leg, to sight revealed,
The rest his many-colored robe concealed.
The rebel Knave, who dares his prince engage,
60   Proves the just victim of his royal rage.
Even mighty Pam,[9] that kings and queens o'erthrew
And mowed down armies in the fights of loo,
Sad chance of war! now destitute of aid,
Falls undistinguished by the victor Spade.
65   Thus far both armies to Belinda yield;
Now to the Baron fate inclines the field.
His warlike amazon her host invades,
The imperial consort of the crown of Spades.
The Club's black tyrant first her victim died,
70   Spite of his haughty mien and barbarous pride.
What boots the regal circle on his head,
His giant limbs, in state unwieldy spread?
That long behind he trails his pompous robe,
And of all monarchs only grasps the globe?
75   The Baron now his Diamonds pours apace;
The embroidered King who shows but half his face,
And his refulgent Queen, with powers combined,
Of broken troops an easy conquest find.
Clubs, Diamonds, Hearts, in wild disorder seen,
80   With throngs promiscuous strew the level green.
Thus when dispersed a routed army runs,
Of Asia's troops, and Afric's sable sons,
With like confusion different nations fly,
Of various habit, and of various dye,
85   The pierced battalions disunited fall
In heaps on heaps; one fate o'erwhelms them all.
The Knave of Diamonds tries his wily arts,
And wins (oh, shameful chance!) the Queen of Hearts.
At this, the blood the virgin's cheek forsook,
90   A livid paleness spreads o'er all her look;
She sees, and trembles at the approaching ill,
Just in the jaws of ruin, and Codille.[1]
And now (as oft in some distempered state)
On one nice trick depends the general fate.
95   An Ace of Hearts steps forth: the King unseen
Lurked in her hand, and mourned his captive Queen.
He springs to vengeance with an eager pace,
And falls like thunder on the prostrate Ace.
The nymph exulting fills with shouts the sky,
100   The walls, the woods, and long canals reply.
O thoughtless mortals! ever blind to fate,

9. The knave of clubs, the highest trump in the   1. The term applied to losing a hand at cards.
game of loo.

Too soon dejected, and too soon elate:
Sudden these honors shall be snatched away,
And cursed forever this victorious day.
For lo! the board with cups and spoons is crowned,   105
The berries crackle, and the mill turns round;[2]
On shining altars of Japan[3] they raise
The silver lamp; the fiery spirits blaze:
From silver spouts the grateful liquors glide,
While China's earth receives the smoking tide.   110
At once they gratify their scent and taste,
And frequent cups prolong the rich repast.
Straight hover round the fair her airy band;
Some, as she sipped, the fuming liquor fanned,
Some o'er her lap their careful plumes displayed,   115
Trembling, and conscious of the rich brocade.
Coffee (which makes the politician wise,
And see through all things with his half-shut eyes)
Sent up in vapors to the Baron's brain
New stratagems, the radiant Lock to gain.   120
Ah, cease, rash youth! desist ere 'tis too late,
Fear the just Gods, and think of Scylla's[4] fate!
Changed to a bird, and sent to flit in air,
She dearly pays for Nisus' injured hair!
But when to mischief mortals bend their will,   125
How soon they find fit instruments of ill!
Just then, Clarissa drew with tempting grace
A two-edged weapon from her shining case:
So ladies in romance assist their knight,
Present the spear, and arm him for the fight.   130
He takes the gift with reverence, and extends
The little engine on his fingers' ends;
This just behind Belinda's neck he spread,
As o'er the fragrant steams she bends her head.
Swift to the Lock a thousand sprites repair,   135
A thousand wings, by turns, blow back the hair,
And thrice they twitched the diamond in her ear,
Thrice she looked back, and thrice the foe drew near.
Just in that instant, anxious Ariel sought
The close recesses of the virgin's thought;   140
As on the nosegay in her breast reclined,
He watched the ideas rising in her mind,
Sudden he viewed, in spite of all her art,
An earthly lover lurking at her heart.
Amazed, confused, he found his power expired,   145
Resigned to fate, and with a sigh retired.
The Peer now spreads the glittering forfex° wide,   *scissors*
To enclose the Lock; now joins it, to divide.

---

2. I.e., coffee is roasted and ground.
3. I.e., small, lacquered tables. "Altars" suggests the ritualistic character of coffee drinking in Belinda's world.
4. Scylla, daughter of Nisus, was turned into a sea bird because, for the sake of her love for Minos of Crete, who was besieging her father's city of Megara, she cut from her father's head the purple lock on which his safety depended. She is not the Scylla of "Scylla and Charybdis."

Even then, before the fatal engine closed,
150 A wretched Sylph too fondly interposed;
Fate urged the shears, and cut the Sylph in twain
(But airy substance soon unites again):
The meeting points the sacred hair dissever
From the fair head, forever and forever!
155 Then flashed the living lightning from her eyes,
And screams of horror rend the affrighted skies.
Not louder shrieks to pitying heaven are cast,
When husbands, or when lapdogs breathe their last;
Or when rich china vessels fallen from high,
160 In glittering dust and painted fragments lie!
"Let wreaths of triumph now my temples twine,"
The victor cried, "the glorious prize is mine!
While fish in streams, or birds delight in air,
Or in a coach and six the British fair,
165 As long as Atalantis[5] shall be read,
Or the small pillow grace a lady's bed,
While visits shall be paid on solemn days,
When numerous wax-lights in bright order blaze,
While nymphs take treats, or assignations give,
170 So long my honor, name, and praise shall live!
"What time would spare, from steel receives its date,
And monuments, like men, submit to fate!
Steel could the labor of the Gods destroy,
And strike to dust the imperial towers of Troy;
175 Steel could the works of mortal pride confound,
And hew triumphal arches to the ground.
What wonder then, fair nymph! thy hairs should feel,
The conquering force of unresisted steel?"

Canto 4

But anxious cares the pensive nymph oppressed,
And secret passions labored in her breast.
Not youthful kings in battle seized alive,
Not scornful virgins who their charms survive,
5 Not ardent lovers robbed of all their bliss,
Not ancient ladies when refused a kiss,
Not tyrants fierce that unrepenting die,
Not Cynthia when her manteau's° pinned awry,   *wrap*
E'er felt such rage, resentment, and despair,
10 As thou, sad virgin! for thy ravished hair.
For, that sad moment, when the Sylphs withdrew
And Ariel weeping from Belinda flew,
Umbriel,[6] a dusky, melancholy sprite
As ever sullied the fair face of light,
15 Down to the central earth, his proper scene,
Repaired to search the gloomy Cave of Spleen.°   *Ill Humor*

5. Delariviere Manley's *New Atalantis* (1709) was
notorious for its thinly concealed allusions to contemporary scandals.
6. The name suggests shade and darkness.

Swift on his sooty pinions flits the Gnome,
And in a vapor reached the dismal dome.
No cheerful breeze this sullen region knows,
20 The dreaded east is all the wind that blows.
Here in a grotto, sheltered close from air,
And screened in shades from day's detested glare,
She sighs forever on her pensive bed,
Pain at her side, and Megrim° at her head.   *headache*
25 Two handmaids wait the throne: alike in place
But differing far in figure and in face.
Here stood Ill-Nature like an ancient maid,
Her wrinkled form in black and white arrayed;
With store of prayers for mornings, nights, and noons,
30 Her hand is filled; her bosom with lampoons.
There Affectation, with a sickly mien,
Shows in her cheek the roses of eighteen,
Practiced to lisp, and hang the head aside,
Faints into airs, and languishes with pride,
35 On the rich quilt sinks with becoming woe,
Wrapped in a gown, for sickness and for show.
The fair ones feel such maladies as these,
When each new nightdress gives a new disease.
A constant vapor⁷ o'er the palace flies,
40 Strange phantoms rising as the mists arise;
Dreadful as hermit's dreams in haunted shades,
Or bright as visions of expiring maids.
Now glaring fiends, and snakes on rolling spires,°   *coils*
Pale specters, gaping tombs, and purple fires;
45 Now lakes of liquid gold, Elysian scenes,
And crystal domes, and angels in machines.⁸
Unnumbered throngs on every side are seen
Of bodies changed to various forms by Spleen.
Here living teapots stand, one arm held out,
50 One bent; the handle this, and that the spout:
A pipkin° there, like Homer's tripod,⁹ walks;   *earthen pot*
Here sighs a jar, and there a goose pie talks;
Men prove with child, as powerful fancy works,
And maids, turned bottles, call aloud for corks.
55 Safe passed the Gnome through this fantastic band,
A branch of healing spleenwort¹ in his hand.
Then thus addressed the Power: "Hail, wayward Queen!
Who rule the sex to fifty from fifteen:
Parent of vapors and of female wit,
60 Who give the hysteric or poetic fit,
On various tempers act by various ways,
Make some take physic, others scribble plays;
Who cause the proud their visits to delay,

7. Emblematic of "the vapors," a fashionable
hypochondria, melancholy, or peevishness.
8. Mechanical devices used in the theaters for
spectacular effects. The catalog of hallucinations
draws on the sensational stage effects popular with
contemporary audiences.

9. In *Iliad* 18.373–77, Vulcan furnishes the gods
with self-propelling "tripods" (three-legged stools).
1. An herb, efficacious against the spleen. Pope
alludes to the golden bough that Aeneas and the
Cumaean sibyl carry with them for protection into
the underworld in *Aeneid* 6.

And send the godly in a pet to pray.
65   A nymph there is that all your power disdains,
And thousands more in equal mirth maintains.
But oh! if e'er thy Gnome could spoil a grace,
Or raise a pimple on a beauteous face,
Like citron-waters[2] matrons' cheeks inflame,
70   Or change complexions at a losing game;
If e'er with airy horns[3] I planted heads,
Or rumpled petticoats, or tumbled beds,
Or caused suspicion when no soul was rude,
Or discomposed the headdress of a prude,
75   Or e'er to costive lapdog gave disease,
Which not the tears of brightest eyes could ease,
Hear me, and touch Belinda with chagrin:°   *ill humor*
That single act gives half the world the spleen."
      The Goddess with a discontented air
80   Seems to reject him though she grants his prayer.
A wondrous bag with both her hands she binds,
Like that where once Ulysses held the winds;[4]
There she collects the force of female lungs,
Sighs, sobs, and passions, and the war of tongues.
85   A vial next she fills with fainting fears,
Soft sorrows, melting griefs, and flowing tears.
The Gnome rejoicing bears her gifts away,
Spreads his black wings, and slowly mounts to day.
      Sunk in Thalestris'[5] arms the nymph he found,
90   Her eyes dejected and her hair unbound.
Full o'er their heads the swelling bag he rent,
And all the Furies issued at the vent.
Belinda burns with more than mortal ire,
And fierce Thalestris fans the rising fire.
95   "O wretched maid!" she spread her hands, and cried
(While Hampton's echoes, "Wretched maid!" replied),
"Was it for this you took such constant care
The bodkin, comb, and essence to prepare?
For this your locks in paper durance bound,
100 For this with torturing irons wreathed around?
For this with fillets strained your tender head,
And bravely bore the double loads of lead?[6]
Gods! shall the ravisher display your hair,
While the fops envy, and the ladies stare!
105 Honor forbid! at whose unrivaled shrine
Ease, pleasure, virtue, all, our sex resign.
Methinks already I your tears survey,
Already hear the horrid things they say,

2. Brandy flavored with orange or lemon peel.
3. The symbol of the cuckold, the man whose wife has been unfaithful to him; here "airy," because they exist only in the jealous suspicions of the husband, the victim of the mischievous Umbriel.
4. Aeolus (later conceived of as god of the winds) gave Ulysses a bag containing all the winds adverse to his voyage home. When his ship was in sight of Ithaca, his companions opened the bag and the storms that ensued drove Ulysses far away (*Odyssey* 10.19ff.).
5. The name is borrowed from a queen of the Amazons, hence a fierce and warlike woman.
6. The frame on which the elaborate coiffures of the day were arranged.

Already see you a degraded toast,
110 And all your honor in a whisper lost!
How shall I, then, your helpless fame defend?
'Twill then be infamy to seem your friend!
And shall this prize, the inestimable prize,
Exposed through crystal to the gazing eyes,
115 And heightened by the diamond's circling rays,
On that rapacious hand forever blaze?
Sooner shall grass in Hyde Park Circus grow,
And wits take lodgings in the sound of Bow;[7]
Sooner let earth, air, sea, to chaos fall,
120 Men, monkeys, lapdogs, parrots, perish all!"
    She said; then raging to Sir Plume repairs,
And bids her beau demand the precious hairs
(Sir Plume of amber snuffbox justly vain,
And the nice conduct of a clouded cane).
125 With earnest eyes, and round unthinking face,
He first the snuffbox opened, then the case,
And thus broke out—"My Lord, why, what the devil!
Z——ds! damn the lock! 'fore Gad, you must be civil!
Plague on 't! 'tis past a jest—nay prithee, pox!
130 Give her the hair"—he spoke, and rapped his box.
    "It grieves me much," replied the Peer again,
"Who speaks so well should ever speak in vain.
But by this Lock, this sacred Lock I swear
(Which never more shall join its parted hair;
135 Which never more its honors shall renew,
Clipped from the lovely head where late it grew),
That while my nostrils draw the vital air,
This hand, which won it, shall forever wear."
He spoke, and speaking, in proud triumph spread
140 The long-contended honors[8] of her head.
    But Umbriel, hateful Gnome, forbears not so;
He breaks the vial whence the sorrows flow.
Then see! the nymph in beauteous grief appears,
Her eyes half languishing, half drowned in tears;
145 On her heaved bosom hung her drooping head,
Which with a sigh she raised, and thus she said:
    "Forever cursed be this detested day,
Which snatched my best, my favorite curl away!
Happy! ah, ten times happy had I been,
150 If Hampton Court these eyes had never seen!
Yet am not I the first mistaken maid,
By love of courts to numerous ills betrayed.
Oh, had I rather unadmired remained
In some lone isle, or distant northern land;
155 Where the gilt chariot never marks the way,
Where none learn ombre, none e'er taste bohea![9]
There kept my charms concealed from mortal eye,

---

7. A person born within sound of the bells of St.
Mary-le-Bow in Cheapside is said to be a cockney.
No fashionable wit would have so vulgar an
address.
8. Ornaments, hence locks; a Latinism.
9. A costly sort of tea.

Like roses that in deserts bloom and die.
What moved my mind with youthful lords to roam?
160 Oh, had I stayed, and said my prayers at home!
'Twas this the morning omens seemed to tell;
Thrice from my trembling hand the patch box[1] fell;
The tottering china shook without a wind,
Nay, Poll sat mute, and Shock was most unkind!
165 A Sylph too warned me of the threats of fate,
In mystic visions, now believed too late!
See the poor remnants of these slighted hairs!
My hands shall rend what e'en thy rapine spares.
These in two sable ringlets taught to break,
170 Once gave new beauties to the snowy neck.
The sister lock now sits uncouth, alone,
And in its fellow's fate foresees its own;
Uncurled it hangs, the fatal shears demands,
And tempts once more thy sacrilegious hands.
175 Oh, hadst thou, cruel! been content to seize
Hairs less in sight, or any hairs but these!"

Canto 5

She said: the pitying audience melt in tears.
But Fate and Jove had stopped the Baron's ears.
In vain Thalestris with reproach assails,
For who can move when fair Belinda fails?
5 Not half so fixed the Trojan[2] could remain,
While Anna begged and Dido raged in vain.
Then grave Clarissa graceful waved her fan;
Silence ensued, and thus the nymph began:
    "Say, why are beauties praised and honored most,
10 The wise man's passion, and the vain man's toast?
Why decked with all that land and sea afford,
Why angels called, and angel-like adored?
Why round our coaches crowd the white-gloved beaux,
Why bows the side box from its inmost rows?
15 How vain are all these glories, all our pains,
Unless good sense preserve what beauty gains;
That men may say when we the front box grace,
'Behold the first in virtue as in face!'
Oh! if to dance all night, and dress all day,
20 Charmed the smallpox, or chased old age away,
Who would not scorn what housewife's cares produce,
Or who would learn one earthly thing of use?
To patch, nay ogle, might become a saint,
Nor could it sure be such a sin to paint.
25 But since, alas! frail beauty must decay,
Curled or uncurled, since locks will turn to gray;

1. To hold the ornamental patches of court plaster worn on the face by both sexes.
2. Aeneas, who forsook Dido at the bidding of the gods, despite her reproaches and the supplications of her sister Anna. Virgil compares him to a steadfast oak that withstands a storm (*Aeneid* 4.437–43).

Since painted, or not painted, all shall fade,
And she who scorns a man must die a maid;
What then remains but well our power to use,
30 And keep good humor still whate'er we lose?
And trust me, dear, good humor can prevail
When airs, and flights, and screams, and scolding fail.
Beauties in vain their pretty eyes may roll;
Charms strike the sight, but merit wins the soul."[3]
35 So spoke the dame, but no applause ensued;
Belinda frowned, Thalestris called her prude.
"To arms, to arms!" the fierce virago cries,
And swift as lightning to the combat flies.
All side in parties, and begin the attack;
40 Fans clap, silks rustle, and tough whalebones crack;
Heroes' and heroines' shouts confusedly rise,
And bass and treble voices strike the skies.
No common weapons in their hands are found,
Like Gods they fight, nor dread a mortal wound.
45 So when bold Homer makes the Gods engage,
And heavenly breasts with human passions rage;
'Gainst Pallas, Mars; Latona, Hermes arms;
And all Olympus rings with loud alarms:
Jove's thunder roars, heaven trembles all around,
50 Blue Neptune storms, the bellowing deeps resound:
Earth shakes her nodding towers, the ground gives way,
And the pale ghosts start at the flash of day!
Triumphant Umbriel on a sconce's[4] height
Clapped his glad wings, and sat to view the fight:
55 Propped on the bodkin spears, the sprites survey
The growing combat, or assist the fray.
While through the press enraged Thalestris flies,
And scatters death around from both her eyes,
A beau and witling perished in the throng,
60 One died in metaphor, and one in song.
"O cruel nymph! a living death I bear,"
Cried Dapperwit, and sunk beside his chair.
A mournful glance Sir Fopling upwards cast,
"Those eyes are made so killing"—was his last.
65 Thus on Maeander's flowery margin lies
The expiring swan, and as he sings he dies.
When bold Sir Plume had drawn Clarissa down,
Chloe stepped in, and killed him with a frown;
She smiled to see the doughty hero slain,
70 But, at her smile, the beau revived again.
Now Jove suspends his golden scales in air,
Weighs the men's wits against the lady's hair;
The doubtful beam long nods from side to side;
At length the wits mount up, the hairs subside.
75 See, fierce Belinda on the Baron flies,
With more than usual lightning in her eyes;

---

3. The speech is a close parody of Pope's own
translation of the speech of Sarpedon to Glaucus,
first published in 1709 and slightly revised in his
version of the *Iliad* (12.371–96).
4. Candlestick fastened on the wall.

Nor feared the chief the unequal fight to try,
Who sought no more than on his foe to die.
　　But this bold lord with manly strength endued,
80　She with one finger and a thumb subdued:
Just where the breath of life his nostrils drew,
A charge of snuff the wily virgin threw;
The Gnomes direct, to every atom just,
The pungent grains of titillating dust.
85　Sudden, with starting tears each eye o'erflows,
And the high dome re-echoes to his nose.
　　"Now meet thy fate," incensed Belinda cried,
And drew a deadly bodkin[5] from her side.
　　(The same, his ancient personage to deck,
90　Her great-great-grandsire wore about his neck,
In three seal rings; which after, melted down,
Formed a vast buckle for his widow's gown:
Her infant grandame's whistle next it grew,
The bells she jingled, and the whistle blew;
95　Then in a bodkin graced her mother's hairs,
Which long she wore, and now Belinda wears.)
　　"Boast not my fall," he cried, "insulting foe!
Thou by some other shalt be laid as low.
Nor think to die dejects my lofty mind:
100　All that I dread is leaving you behind!
Rather than so, ah, let me still survive,
And burn in Cupid's flames—but burn alive."
　　"Restore the Lock!" she cries; and all around
"Restore the Lock!" the vaulted roofs rebound.
105　Not fierce Othello in so loud a strain
Roared for the handkerchief that caused his pain.[6]
But see how oft ambitious aims are crossed,
And chiefs contend till all the prize is lost!
The lock, obtained with guilt, and kept with pain,
110　In every place is sought, but sought in vain:
With such a prize no mortal must be blessed,
So Heaven decrees! with Heaven who can contest?
　　Some thought it mounted to the lunar sphere,
Since all things lost on earth are treasured there.
115　There heroes' wits are kept in ponderous vases,
And beaux' in snuffboxes and tweezer cases.
There broken vows and deathbed alms are found,
And lovers' hearts with ends of riband bound,
The courtier's promises, and sick man's prayers,
120　The smiles of harlots, and the tears of heirs,
Cages for gnats, and chains to yoke a flea,
Dried butterflies, and tomes of casuistry.
　　But trust the Muse—she saw it upward rise,
Though marked by none but quick, poetic eyes
125　(So Rome's great founder to the heavens withdrew,[7]

---

5. Here, an ornamental hairpin shaped like a dagger.
6. *Othello* 3.4.
7. Romulus, the "founder" and first king of Rome, was snatched to heaven in a storm cloud while reviewing his army in the Campus Martius (Livy 1.16).

To Proculus alone confessed in view);
A sudden star, it shot through liquid air,
And drew behind a radiant trail of hair.
Not Berenice's locks first rose so bright,[8]
130 The heavens bespangling with disheveled light.
The Sylphs behold it kindling as it flies,
And pleased pursue its progress through the skies.
    This the beau monde shall from the Mall[9] survey,
And hail with music its propitious ray.
135 This the blest lover shall for Venus take,
And send up vows from Rosamonda's Lake.[1]
This Partridge[2] soon shall view in cloudless skies,
When next he looks through Galileo's eyes;°   telescope
And hence the egregious wizard shall foredoom
140 The fate of Louis, and the fall of Rome.
    Then cease, bright nymph! to mourn thy ravished hair,
Which adds new glory to the shining sphere!
Not all the tresses that fair head can boast
Shall draw such envy as the Lock you lost.
145 For, after all the murders of your eye,
When, after millions slain, yourself shall die:
When those fair suns shall set, as set they must,
And all those tresses shall be laid in dust,
This Lock the Muse shall consecrate to fame,
150 And 'midst the stars inscribe Belinda's name.

1712   1714

Epistle to Miss Blount[1]

On Her Leaving the Town, After the Coronation

    As some fond virgin, whom her mother's care
Drags from the town to wholesome country air,
Just when she learns to roll a melting eye,
And hear a spark,° yet think no danger nigh;   fop, beau
5 From the dear man unwilling she must sever,
Yet takes one kiss before she parts forever:
Thus from the world fair Zephalinda[2] flew,
Saw others happy, and with sighs withdrew;
Not that their pleasures caused her discontent;
10 She sighed not that they stayed, but that she went.
    She went, to plain-work,[3] and to purling brooks,
Old-fashioned halls, dull aunts, and croaking rooks:
She went from opera, park, assembly, play,

---

8. Berenice, the wife of Ptolemy III, dedicated a lock of her hair to the gods to ensure her husband's safe return from war. It was turned into a constellation.
9. A walk laid out by Charles II in St. James's Park (London), a resort for strollers of all sorts.
1. In St. James's Park; associated with unhappy lovers.
2. John Partridge, an astrologer whose annually published predictions had been amusingly satirized by Swift and other wits in 1708.
1. Teresa Blount, sister of Pope's lifelong friend Martha Blount. The "coronation" was that of George I (1714).
2. A fanciful name adopted by Blount.
3. "Needlework, as distinguished from embroidery" (Johnson's *Dictionary*).

To morning walks, and prayers three hours a day;
15   To part her time 'twixt reading and bohea,[4]
To muse, and spill her solitary tea,
Or o'er cold coffee trifle with the spoon,
Count the slow clock, and dine exact at noon;[5]
Divert her eyes with pictures in the fire,
20   Hum half a tune, tell stories to the squire;
Up to her godly garret after seven,
There starve and pray, for that's the way to heaven.
    Some squire, perhaps, you take delight to rack,
Whose game is whist, whose treat a toast in sack;
25   Who visits with a gun, presents you birds,
Then gives a smacking buss, and cries—"No words!"
Or with his hounds comes hollowing from the stable,
Makes love with nods and knees beneath a table;
Whose laughs are hearty, though his jests are coarse,
30   And loves you best of all things—but his horse.
    In some fair evening, on your elbow laid,
You dream of triumphs in the rural shade;
In pensive thought recall the fancied scene,
See coronations rise on every green:
35   Before you pass the imaginary sights
Of lords and earls and dukes and gartered knights,
While the spread fan o'ershades your closing eyes;
Then give one flirt,[6] and all the vision flies.
Thus vanish scepters, coronets, and balls,
40   And leave you in lone woods, or empty walls.
    So when your slave,° at some dear idle time   *Pope*
(Not plagued with headaches or the want of rhyme)
Stands in the streets, abstracted from the crew,
And while he seems to study, thinks of you;
45   Just when his fancy points° your sprightly eyes,   *marks*
Or sees the blush of soft Parthenia[7] rise,
Gay[8] pats my shoulder, and you vanish quite;
Streets, chairs, and coxcombs rush upon my sight;
Vexed to be still in town, I knit my brow,
50   Look sour, and hum a tune—as you may now.

1717

Eloisa to Abelard

Like Ovid's *Sappho to Phaon*, which Pope had translated in his teens, *Eloisa to Abelard* is a heroic epistle: strictly defined, a versified love letter, involving historical persons, which dramatizes the feelings of a woman who has been forsaken. Pope took his subject from one of the most famous affairs of history. Peter Abelard (1079–1142), a brilliant Scholastic theologian, seduced a young girl, his pupil

4. A costly sort of tea.
5. The fashionable hour for dining in London was three or four o'clock. A noon dinner is a sign of old-fashioned rusticity.
6. I.e., opens and closes her fan with a jerk.
7. Martha Blount.
8. John Gay, the poet.

Heloise; eventually she bore him a child, and they were secretly married. Enraged at the betrayal of trust, and what he regarded as the casting off of Heloise, her uncle Fulbert revenged himself by having Abelard castrated. The lovers separated; each of them entered a monastery and went on to a distinguished career in the church. Yet their greatest fame derives from the letters they are supposed to have exchanged late in their lives (some scholars have cast doubt on the authenticity of Heloise's letters). It is this correspondence, made newly popular by French and English translations of the original Latin, that inspired Pope's poem.

The heroic epistle challenges authors in two ways: they must exert historical imagination, projecting themselves into another time and place; and they must enter the mind and passions of a woman, acting her part, and showing everything through her point of view. Historically, Pope draws on his knowledge of Roman Catholic ritual to envelop Eloisa in a rich medieval atmosphere. The dark Gothic convent, situated in an imaginary landscape of grottos, mountains, and pine forests, embodies the eighteenth-century sense of the romantic: fantastic, legendary, and extravagant. Here Eloisa is cloistered, not only physically but mentally, by religious mysticism that surrounds her with a melancholy as palpable as the image of her lover. The greatest triumph of the poem, however, is psychological. In *Eloisa,* for the only time in his career, Pope tells a story wholly through another's voice. Confused and tormented, the heroine tosses between two kinds of love: an erotic passion for the earthly lover whose memory she cannot quell and the divine, chaste love that must content a nun. Abelard and God, within her fantasy, compete for her soul. Pope brings these internal struggles to the surface by externalizing them in bold dramatic rhetoric, formal and intense as an aria in an opera (the poem was long a favorite for reading aloud). Eloisa views herself theatrically, if only because, in the letter, she is trying to make Abelard visualize the pathos of her situation. There is literally no way out for her, and at the end of the poem, she can break the static circle of desire and loneliness only by picturing herself in the peace of death. Yet the high reputation of the work, well into the Romantic era, owes less to its theatrics than to its convincing image of a mind in pain. "If you search for passion," Lord Byron wrote more than a century later, "where is it to be found stronger than in the Epistle from Eloisa to Abelard?"

Eloisa to Abelard

The Argument

Abelard and Eloisa flourished in the twelfth century; they were two of the most distinguished persons of their age in learning and beauty, but for nothing more famous than for their unfortunate passion. After a long course of calamities, they retired each to a several[1] convent, and consecrated the remainder of their days to religion. It was many years after this separation, that a letter of Abelard's to a friend which contained the history of his misfortune, fell into the hands of Eloisa. This awakening all her tenderness, occasioned those celebrated letters (out of which the following is partly extracted)[2] which give so lively a picture of the struggles of grace and nature, virtue and passion.

> In these deep solitudes and awful cells,
> Where heavenly-pensive contemplation dwells,
> And ever-musing melancholy reigns;

---

1. Separate.
2. Pope's source was a highly romanticized

English version of the letters by John Hughes, published in 1713.

What means this tumult in a vestal's[3] veins?
5   Why rove my thoughts beyond this last retreat?
Why feels my heart its long-forgotten heat?
Yet, yet I love!—From Abelard it[4] came,
And Eloisa yet must kiss the name.
    Dear fatal name! rest ever unrevealed,
10 Nor pass these lips in holy silence sealed.
Hide it, my heart, within that close disguise,
Where mixed with God's, his loved idea° lies.   *mental image*
O write it not, my hand—the name appears
Already written—wash it out, my tears!
15 In vain lost Eloisa weeps and prays,
Her heart still dictates, and her hand obeys.
    Relentless walls! whose darksome round contains
Repentant sighs, and voluntary pains:
Ye rugged rocks! which holy knees have worn;
20 Ye grots and caverns shagged with horrid° thorn!   *bristling*
Shrines! where their vigils pale-eyed virgins keep,
And pitying saints, whose statues learn to weep![5]
Tho' cold like you, unmoved, and silent grown,
I have not yet forgot myself to stone.
25 All is not Heaven's while Abelard has part,
Still rebel nature holds out half my heart;
Nor prayers nor fasts its stubborn pulse restrain,
Nor tears, for ages taught to flow in vain.
    Soon as thy letters trembling I unclose,
30 That well-known name awakens all my woes.
Oh name for ever sad! for ever dear!
Still breathed in sighs, still ushered with a tear.
I tremble too, where'er my own I find,
Some dire misfortune follows close behind.
35 Line after line my gushing eyes o'erflow,
Led through a sad variety of woe:
Now warm in love, now withering in my bloom,
Lost in a convent's solitary gloom!
There stern religion quenched the unwilling flame,
40 There died the best of passions, love and fame.
    Yet write, oh write me all, that I may join
Griefs to thy griefs, and echo sighs to thine.
Nor foes nor fortune take this power away.
And is my Abelard less kind than they?
45 Tears still are mine, and those I need not spare,
Love but demands what else were shed in prayer;
No happier task these faded eyes pursue,
To read and weep is all they now can do.
    Then share thy pain, allow that sad relief;
50 Ah, more than share it! give me all thy grief.
Heaven first taught letters for some wretch's aid,
Some banished lover, or some captive maid;

---

3. Nun's. Here, as elsewhere, Eloisa substitutes a pagan form for a Christian; nor is she in fact a virgin (vestal).

4. The letter to which Eloisa is replying.
5. In damp places, stone "weeps" through condensation.

They live, they speak, they breathe what love inspires,
Warm from the soul, and faithful to its fires,
55 The virgin's wish without her fears impart,
Excuse the blush, and pour out all the heart,
Speed the soft intercourse from soul to soul,
And waft a sigh from Indus[6] to the Pole.
   Thou knowest how guiltless first I met thy flame,
60 When love approached me under friendship's name;
My fancy formed thee of angelic kind,
Some emanation of the all-beauteous Mind.[7]
Those smiling eyes, attempering° every ray,   *moderating, assuaging*
Shone sweetly lambent with celestial day:
65 Guiltless I gazed; heaven listened while you sung;
And truths divine came mended from that tongue.[8]
From lips like those what precept failed to move?
Too soon they taught me 'twas no sin to love.
Back through the paths of pleasing sense I ran,
70 Nor wished an angel whom I loved a man.
Dim and remote the joys of saints I see,
Nor envy them, that heaven I lose for thee.
   How oft, when pressed to marriage, have I said,
Curse on all laws but those which love has made!
75 Love, free as air, at sight of human ties,
Spreads his light wings, and in a moment flies.
Let wealth, let honor, wait the wedded dame,
August her deed, and sacred be her fame;
Before true passion all those views remove,°   *depart*
80 Fame, wealth, and honor! what are you to love?
The jealous god, when we profane his fires,
Those restless passions in revenge inspires,
And bids them make mistaken mortals groan,
Who seek in love for aught but love alone.
85 Should at my feet the world's great master fall,
Himself, his throne, his world, I'd scorn 'em all:
Nor Caesar's empress would I deign to prove;°   *try*
No, make me mistress to the man I love;
If there be yet another name more free,
90 More fond than mistress, make me that to thee!
Oh happy state! when souls each other draw,
When love is liberty, and nature, law:
All then is full, possessing, and possessed,
No craving void left aching in the breast:
95 Even thought meets thought ere from the lips it part,
And each warm wish springs mutual from the heart.
This sure is bliss (if bliss on earth there be)
And once the lot of Abelard and me.
   Alas how changed! what sudden horrors rise!
100 A naked lover bound and bleeding lies!
Where, where was Eloise? her voice, her hand,

---

6. A southern constellation.
7. God, conceived (as is proper to a student of philosophy) in Platonic terms.

8. He was her preceptor in philosophy and divinity
[Pope's note].

Her poniard, had opposed the dire command.
Barbarian, stay! that bloody stroke restrain;
The crime was common,° common be the pain.°   *shared / punishment*
105 I can no more; by shame, by rage suppressed,
Let tears, and burning blushes speak the rest.
   Canst thou forget that sad, that solemn day,
When victims at yon altar's foot we lay?
Canst thou forget what tears that moment fell,
110 When, warm in youth, I bade the world farewell?
As with cold lips I kissed the sacred veil,
The shrines all trembled, and the lamps grew pale:
Heaven scarce believed the conquest it surveyed,
And saints with wonder heard the vows I made.
115 Yet then, to those dread altars as I drew,
Not on the Cross my eyes were fixed, but you;
Not grace, or zeal, love only was my call,
And if I lose thy love, I lose my all.
Come! with thy looks, thy words, relieve my woe;
120 Those still at least are left thee to bestow.
Still on that breast enamored let me lie,
Still drink delicious poison from thy eye,
Pant on thy lip, and to thy heart be pressed;
Give all thou canst—and let me dream the rest.
125 Ah no! instruct me other joys to prize,
With other beauties charm my partial[9] eyes,
Full in my view set all the bright abode,
And make my soul quit Abelard for God.
   Ah think at least thy flock deserves thy care,
130 Plants of thy hand, and children of thy prayer.
From the false world in early youth they fled,
By thee to mountains, wilds, and deserts led.
You raised these hallowed walls;[1] the desert smiled,
And paradise was opened in the wild.
135 No weeping orphan saw his father's stores
Our shrines irradiate,[2] or emblaze the floors;
No silver saints, by dying misers given,
Here bribed the rage of ill-requited heaven:
But such plain roofs as piety could raise,
140 And only vocal with the Maker's[3] praise.
In these lone walls (their day's eternal bound)
These moss-grown domes with spiry turrets crowned,
Where awful arches make a noon-day night,
And the dim windows shed a solemn light,
145 Thy eyes diffused a reconciling ray,
And gleams of glory brightened all the day.
But now no face divine contentment wears,
'Tis all blank sadness, or continual tears.

9. Fond; seeing only a part.
1. "He founded the monastery" [Pope's note].
Abelard erected the "Paraclete," a modest oratory
near Troyes, in 1122; seven years later, when the
nunnery of which Heloise was prioress was evicted

from its property, he ceded the lands of the Paraclete to her.
2. Adorn with splendor.
3. God's or Abelard's.

See how the force of others' prayers I try,
150 (O pious fraud of amorous charity!)
But why should I on others' prayers depend?
Come thou, my father, brother, husband, friend!
Ah let thy handmaid, sister, daughter move,
And all those tender names in one, thy love!
155 The darksome pines that o'er yon rocks reclined
Wave high, and murmur to the hollow wind,
The wandering streams that shine between the hills,
The grots that echo to the tinkling rills,
The dying gales that pant upon the trees,
160 The lakes that quiver to the curling breeze;
No more these scenes my meditation aid,
Or lull to rest the visionary⁴ maid.
But o'er the twilight groves and dusky caves,
Long-sounding isles,⁵ and intermingled graves,
165 Black Melancholy sits, and round her throws
A death-like silence, and a dread repose:
Her gloomy presence saddens all the scene,
Shades every flower, and darkens every green,
Deepens the murmur of the falling floods,
170 And breathes a browner horror on the woods.⁶
    Yet here for ever, ever must I stay;
Sad proof how well a lover can obey!
Death, only death, can break the lasting chain;
And here, even then, shall my cold dust remain,
175 Here all its frailties, all its flames resign,
And wait, till 'tis no sin to mix with thine.
    Ah wretch! believed the spouse of God in vain,
Confessed within the slave of love and man.
Assist me, heaven! but whence arose that prayer?
180 Sprung it from piety, or from despair?
Even here, where frozen chastity retires,
Love finds an altar for forbidden fires.
I ought to grieve, but cannot what I ought;
I mourn the lover, not lament the fault;
185 I view my crime, but kindle at the view,
Repent old pleasures, and solicit new;
Now turned to heaven, I weep my past offense,
Now think of thee, and curse my innocence.
Of all affliction taught a lover yet,
190 'Tis sure the hardest science° to forget!   *knowledge*
How shall I lose the sin, yet keep the sense,⁷
And love the offender, yet detest the offense?
How the dear object from the crime remove,
Or how distinguish penitence from love?
195 Unequal task! a passion to resign,

4. Given to visions.
5. Sounds reverberate over water as in the *aisles* of a church.
6. The image of the Goddess Melancholy sitting over the convent, and, as it were, expanding her

dreadful wings over its whole circuit, and diffusing her gloom all around it, is truly sublime, and strongly conceived [Joseph Warton's note].
7. Both perception and sensation.

For hearts so touched, so pierced, so lost as mine.
Ere such a soul regains its peaceful state,
How often must it love, how often hate!
How often hope, despair, resent, regret,
200   Conceal, disdain—do all things but forget.
But let heaven seize it, all at once 'tis fired,
Not touched, but rapt; not wakened, but inspired![8]
Oh come! oh teach me nature to subdue,
Renounce my love, my life, my self—and you.
205   Fill my fond heart with God alone, for he
Alone can rival, can succeed to thee.
      How happy is the blameless vestal's lot!
The world forgetting, by the world forgot.
Eternal sun-shine of the spotless mind!
210   Each prayer accepted, and each wish resigned;
Labor and rest, that equal periods keep;
"Obedient slumbers that can wake and weep;"[9]
Desires composed, affections ever even;
Tears that delight, and sighs that waft to heaven.
215   Grace shines around her with serenest beams,
And whispering angels prompt her golden dreams.
For her the unfading rose of Eden blooms,
And wings of seraphs shed divine perfumes,
For her the Spouse prepares the bridal ring,
220   For her white virgins hymenaeals[1] sing,
To sounds of heavenly harps she dies away,
And melts in visions of eternal day.
      Far other dreams my erring soul employ,
Far other raptures, of unholy joy:
225   When at the close of each sad, sorrowing day,
Fancy restores what vengeance snatched away,
Then conscience sleeps, and leaving nature free,
All my loose soul unbounded springs to thee.
O curst, dear horrors of all-conscious night![2]
230   How glowing guilt exalts the keen delight!
Provoking daemons all restraint remove,
And stir within me every source of love.
I hear thee, view thee, gaze o'er all thy charms,
And round thy phantom glue my clasping arms.
235   I wake—no more I hear, no more I view,
The phantom flies me, as unkind as you.
I call aloud; it hears not what I say;
I stretch my empty arms; it glides away:
To dream once more I close my willing eyes;
240   Ye soft illusions, dear deceits, arise!
Alas, no more!—methinks we wandering go
Through dreary wastes, and weep each other's woe;
Where round some moldering tower pale ivy creeps,

---

8. I.e., when touched, at once rapt; when wakened, at once inspired.
9. From *Description of a Religious House* (1648),
by Richard Crashaw.

1. Wedding hymns. Every nun is the bride of
Christ, her spouse.
2. The night knows everything, and Eloisa is conscious (guiltily aware) all through the night.

And low-browed rocks hang nodding o'er the deeps.
245 Sudden you mount! you beckon from the skies;
Clouds interpose, waves roar, and winds arise.
I shriek, start up, the same sad prospect find,
And wake to all the griefs I left behind.[3]
For thee the fates, severely kind, ordain
250 A cool suspense° from pleasure and from pain;   *suspension*
Thy life a long dead calm of fixed repose;
No pulse that riots, and no blood that glows.
Still as the sea, ere winds were taught to blow,
Or moving spirit bade the waters flow;
255 Soft as the slumbers of a saint forgiven,
And mild as opening gleams of promised heaven.
    Come, Abelard! for what hast thou to dread?
The torch of Venus burns not for the dead.
Nature stands checked; religion disapproves;
260 Even thou art cold—yet Eloisa loves.
Ah hopeless, lasting flames! like those that burn
To light the dead, and warm the unfruitful urn.[4]
    What scenes appear where'er I turn my view?
The dear ideas, where I fly, pursue,
265 Rise in the grove, before the altar rise,
Stain all my soul, and wanton in my eyes!
I waste the matin lamp in sighs for thee,
Thy image steals between my God and me,
Thy voice I seem in every hymn to hear,
270 With every bead I drop too soft a tear.
When from the censer clouds of fragrance roll,
And swelling organs lift the rising soul,
One thought of thee puts all the pomp to flight,
Priests, tapers, temples, swim before my sight:
275 In seas of flame[5] my plunging soul is drowned,
While altars blaze, and angels tremble round.
    While prostrate here in humble grief I lie,
Kind, virtuous drops just gathering in my eye,
While praying, trembling, in the dust I roll,
280 And dawning grace is opening on my soul:
Come, if thou dar'st, all charming as thou art!
Oppose thyself to heaven; dispute° my heart;   *contend for*
Come, with one glance of those deluding eyes
Blot out each bright idea of the skies.
285 Take back that grace, those sorrows, and those tears,
Take back my fruitless penitence and prayers,
Snatch me, just mounting, from the blest abode,
Assist the fiends and tear me from my God!
    No, fly me, fly me! far as pole from pole;
290 Rise Alps between us! and whole oceans roll!
Ah come not, write not, think not once of me,
Nor share one pang of all I felt for thee.
Thy oaths I quit,° thy memory resign,   *absolve*

---

3. Cf. the conclusion to the *Epistle to Miss Blount*
(p. 2545), a comic companion piece to this poem.
4. Perpetual fires were placed in Roman tombs.
5. Love or hell.

Forget, renounce me, hate whate'er was mine.
295   Fair eyes, and tempting looks (which yet I view!)
Long loved, adored ideas! all adieu!
O grace serene! oh virtue heavenly fair!
Divine oblivion of low-thoughted care!
Fresh blooming hope, gay daughter of the sky!
300   And faith, our early immortality!
Enter, each mild, each amicable guest;
Receive, and wrap me in eternal rest!
    See in her cell sad Eloisa spread,
Propped on some tomb, a neighbor of the dead!
305   In each low wind methinks a spirit calls,
And more than echoes talk along the walls.
Here, as I watched the dying lamps around,
From yonder shrine I heard a hollow sound.
"Come, sister, come! (it said, or seemed to say)
310   Thy place is here, sad sister, come away!
Once like thyself, I trembled, wept, and prayed,
Love's victim then, tho' now a sainted maid:
But all is calm in this eternal sleep;
Here grief forgets to groan, and love to weep,
315   Even superstition loses every fear:
For God, not man, absolves our frailties here."
    I come, I come! prepare your roseate bowers,
Celestial palms, and ever-blooming flowers.
Thither, where sinners may have rest, I go,
320   Where flames refined in breasts seraphic glow.
Thou, Abelard! the last sad office pay,
And smooth my passage to the realms of day;
See my lips tremble, and my eyeballs roll,
Suck my last breath, and catch my flying soul!
325   Ah no—in sacred vestments may'st thou stand,
The hallowed taper trembling in thy hand,
Present the Cross before my lifted eye,
Teach me at once, and learn of° me to die.   *from*
Ah then, thy once-loved Eloisa see!
330   It will be then no crime to gaze on me.
See from my cheek the transient roses fly!
See the last sparkle languish in my eye!
Till every motion, pulse, and breath be o'er;
And even my Abelard be loved no more.
335   O death all-eloquent! you only prove
What dust we doat on, when 'tis man we love.
    Then too, when fate shall thy fair frame destroy,
(That cause of all my guilt, and all my joy)
In trance ecstatic may thy pangs be drowned,
340   Bright clouds descend, and angels watch thee round,
From opening skies may streaming glories shine,
And saints embrace thee with a love like mine.
    May one kind grave unite each hapless name,[6]

6. Abelard and Eloisa were interred in the same grave, or in monuments adjoining, in the monastery of the Paraclete [Pope's note].

And graft my love immortal on thy fame!
345 Then, ages hence, when all my woes are o'er,
When this rebellious heart shall beat no more;
If ever chance two wandering lovers brings
To Paraclete's white walls, and silver springs,
O'er the pale marble shall they join their heads,
350 And drink the falling tears each other sheds,
Then sadly say, with mutual pity moved,
"Oh may we never love as these have loved!"
From the full choir when loud Hosannas rise,
And swell the pomp of dreadful sacrifice,[7]
355 Amid that scene if some relenting eye
Glance on the stone where our cold relics lie,
Devotion's self shall steal a thought from heaven,
One human tear shall drop, and be forgiven.
And sure if fate some future bard shall join
360 In sad similitude of griefs to mine,
Condemned whole years in absence to deplore,[8]
And image charms he must behold no more,
Such if there be, who loves so long, so well,
Let him our sad, our tender story tell;
365 The well-sung woes will sooth my pensive ghost;
He best can paint 'em, who shall feel 'em most.

1717

An Essay on Man

Pope's philosophical poem, *An Essay on Man*, is a fragment of an ambitious but never completed scheme for what the poet referred to as his "ethic work," which was to have been a large survey of human nature, society, and morals. The work is dedicated to Henry St. John (pronounced *Sín-jun*), Viscount Bolingbroke (1678–1751), the brilliant, though erratic, secretary of state in the Tory ministry of 1710–14, whom Pope had come to know through Jonathan Swift. After the accession of George I he fled to France, attainted of treason, but was pardoned and allowed to return in 1723. He settled near Pope at Dawley farm and a close friendship developed between the two men. In their conversations Bolingbroke, who fancied himself a philosopher, helped Pope formulate the optimistic system that is expounded in this poem. Yet it is clear that the poem would have been pretty much what it is had the two men never met, for it expresses doctrines widely circulated and generally accepted at the time by enlightened minds throughout Europe. The *Essay* gives memorable expression to ideas about the nature of the universe and our place in it, ideas on which eighteenth-century optimism rested.

Pope's purpose is to "vindicate the ways of God to man," a phrase that consciously echoes *Paradise Lost* 1.26. Like John Milton, Pope faces the problem of the existence of evil in a world presumed to be the creation of a good God. *Paradise Lost* is biblical in content, Christian in doctrine; *An Essay on Man* avoids all specifically Christian doctrines, not because Pope disbelieved them, but because "man," the subject of the poem, includes millions who never heard of Christianity, and Pope is concerned with the universal. Milton tells a mythological story. Pope writes in abstract terms.

The *Essay* is divided into four epistles. In the first Pope asserts the essential order

---

7. The celebration of the Eucharist (mass).
8. Lament. Pope, imagining himself imagined by Eloisa, hints that he too is separated from a loved

one; perhaps Lady Mary Wortley Montagu, who was in Turkey. Pope and Montagu later quarreled, and she appears as Sappho in Epistle 2, *To a Lady*.

and goodness of the universe and the rightness of our place in it. The other epistles deal with how we may emulate in our nature and in society the cosmic harmony revealed in the first epistle. The second seeks to show how we may attain a psychological harmony that can become the basis of a virtuous life through the cooperation of self-love and the passions (both necessary to our complete humanity) with reason, the controller and director. The third is concerned with the individual in society, which, it teaches, was created through the cooperation of self-love (the egoistic drives that motivate us) and social love (our dependence on others, our inborn benevolence). The fourth is concerned with happiness, which lies within the reach of all, for it is dependent on virtue, which becomes possible when—though only when—self-love is transmuted into love of others and love of God. Such, in brief summary, are Pope's main ideas, expressed in many phrases so memorable that they have detached themselves from the poem and become part of daily speech.

From An Essay on Man

TO HENRY ST. JOHN, LORD BOLINGBROKE

Epistle 1. Of the Nature and State of Man, With Respect to the Universe

Awake, my St. John! leave all meaner things
To low ambition, and the pride of kings.
Let us (since life can little more supply
Than just to look about us and to die)
5 Expatiate free° o'er all this scene of man;   *range freely*
A mighty maze! but not without a plan;
A wild, where weeds and flowers promiscuous shoot,
Or garden, tempting with forbidden fruit.
Together let us beat this ample field,
10 Try what the open, what the covert yield;
The latent tracts, the giddy heights, explore
Of all who blindly creep, or sightless soar;
Eye Nature's walks, shoot folly as it flies,
And catch the manners living as they rise;
15 Laugh where we must, be candid° where we can;   *kindly*
But vindicate the ways of God to man.

1. Say first, of God above, or man below,
What can we reason, but from what we know?
Of man, what see we but his station here,
20 From which to reason, or to which refer?
Through worlds unnumbered though the God be known,
'Tis ours to trace him only in our own.
He, who through vast immensity can pierce,
See worlds on worlds compose one universe,
25 Observe how system into system runs,
What other planets circle other suns,
What varied being peoples every star,
May tell why Heaven has made us as we are.
But of this frame the bearings, and the ties,

30   The strong connections, nice dependencies,
      Gradations just, has thy pervading soul
      Looked through? or can a part contain the whole?
          Is the great chain, that draws all to agree,
      And drawn supports, upheld by God, or thee?[1]

35   2. Presumptuous man! the reason wouldst thou find,
      Why formed so weak, so little, and so blind?
      First, if thou canst, the harder reason guess,
      Why formed no weaker, blinder, and no less!
      Ask of thy mother earth, why oaks are made
40   Taller or stronger than the weeds they shade?
      Or ask of yonder argent fields above,
      Why Jove's satellites[2] are less than Jove?
          Of systems possible, if 'tis confessed
      That Wisdom Infinite must form the best,
45   Where all must full or not coherent be,
      And all that rises, rise in due degree;
      Then, in the scale of reasoning life, 'tis plain,
      There must be, somewhere, such a rank as man:
      And all the question (wrangle e'er so long)
50   Is only this, if God has placed him wrong?
          Respecting man, whatever wrong we call,
      May, must be right, as relative to all.
      In human works, though labored on with pain,
      A thousand movements scarce one purpose gain;
55   In God's, one single can its end produce;
      Yet serves to second too some other use.
      So man, who here seems principal alone,
      Perhaps acts second to some sphere unknown,
      Touches some wheel, or verges to some goal;
60   'Tis but a part we see, and not a whole.
          When the proud steed shall know why man restrains
      His fiery course, or drives him o'er the plains;
      When the dull ox, why now he breaks the clod,
      Is now a victim, and now Egypt's god:
65   Then shall man's pride and dullness comprehend
      His actions', passions', being's use and end;
      Why doing, suffering, checked, impelled; and why
      This hour a slave, the next a deity.
          Then say not man's imperfect, Heaven in fault;
70   Say rather, man's as perfect as he ought;
      His knowledge measured to his state and place,
      His time a moment, and a point his space.
      If to be perfect in a certain sphere,[3]
      What matter, soon or late, or here or there?
75   The blest today is as completely so,
      As who began a thousand years ago.

1. For the chain of being, see Addison's *The Spec-*   Pope's giving this word four syllables, as in Latin.
tator 519 (p. 2502) and lines 207–58.   3. I.e., in one's "state and place."
2. In his *Dictionary*, Johnson notes and condemns

3. Heaven from all creatures hides the book of Fate,
All but the page prescribed, their present state:
From brutes what men, from men what spirits know:
80 Or who could suffer being here below?
The lamb thy riot dooms to bleed today,
Had he thy reason, would he skip and play?
Pleased to the last, he crops the flowery food,
And licks the hand just raised to shed his blood.
85 O blindness to the future! kindly given,
That each may fill the circle marked by Heaven:
Who sees with equal eye, as God of all,
A hero perish, or a sparrow fall,
Atoms or systems° into ruin hurled,   solar systems
90 And now a bubble burst, and now a world.
        Hope humbly then; with trembling pinions soar;
Wait the great teacher Death, and God adore!
What future bliss, he gives not thee to know,
But gives that hope to be thy blessing now.
95 Hope springs eternal in the human breast:
Man never is, but always to be blest:
The soul, uneasy and confined from home,
Rests and expatiates in a life to come.
        Lo! the poor Indian, whose untutored mind
100 Sees God in clouds, or hears him in the wind;
His soul proud Science never taught to stray
Far as the solar walk, or milky way;
Yet simple Nature to his hope has given,
Behind the cloud-topped hill, an humbler heaven;
105 Some safer world in depth of woods embraced,
Some happier island in the watery waste,
Where slaves once more their native land behold,
No fiends torment, no Christians thirst for gold!
To be, contents his natural desire,
110 He asks no angel's wing, no seraph's fire;
But thinks, admitted to that equal sky,
His faithful dog shall bear him company.

4. Go, wiser thou! and, in thy scale of sense,
Weigh thy opinion against Providence;
115 Call imperfection what thou fancy'st such,
Say, here he gives too little, there too much;
Destroy all creatures for thy sport or gust,[4]
Yet cry, if man's unhappy, God's unjust;
If man alone engross not Heaven's high care,
120 Alone made perfect here, immortal there:
Snatch from his hand the balance and the rod,
Rejudge his justice, be the God of God!
        In pride, in reasoning pride, our error lies;
All quit their sphere, and rush into the skies.

4. "Sense of tasting" (Johnson's *Dictionary*).

125   Pride still is aiming at the blest abodes,
Men would be angels, angels would be gods.
Aspiring to be gods, if angels fell,
Aspiring to be angels, men rebel:
And who but wishes to invert the laws
130   Of order, sins against the Eternal Cause.

       5. Ask for what end the heavenly bodies shine,
Earth for whose use? Pride answers, " 'Tis for mine:
For me kind Nature wakes her genial power,
Suckles each herb, and spreads out every flower;
135   Annual for me, the grape, the rose renew
The juice nectareous, and the balmy dew;
For me, the mine a thousand treasures brings;
For me, health gushes from a thousand springs;
Seas roll to waft me, suns to light me rise;
140   My footstool earth, my canopy the skies."
       But errs not Nature from this gracious end,
From burning suns when livid deaths descend,
When earthquakes swallow, or when tempests sweep
Towns to one grave, whole nations to the deep?
145   "No," 'tis replied, "the first Almighty Cause
Acts not by partial, but by general laws;
The exceptions few; some change since all began,
And what created perfect?"—Why then man?
If the great end be human happiness,
150   Then Nature deviates; and can man do less?
As much that end a constant course requires
Of showers and sunshine, as of man's desires;
As much eternal springs and cloudless skies,
As men forever temperate, calm, and wise.
155   If plagues or earthquakes break not Heaven's design,
Why then a Borgia, or a Catiline?[5]
Who knows but he whose hand the lightning forms,
Who heaves old ocean, and who wings the storms,
Pours fierce ambition in a Caesar's mind,
160   Or turns young Ammon[6] loose to scourge mankind?
From pride, from pride, our very reasoning springs;
Account for moral, as for natural things:
Why charge we Heaven in those, in these acquit?
In both, to reason right is to submit.
165   Better for us, perhaps, it might appear,
Were there all harmony, all virtue here;
That never air or ocean felt the wind;
That never passion discomposed the mind:
But ALL subsists by elemental strife;
170   And passions are the elements of life.

---

5. The Renaissance Italian family of the Borgias was notorious for its crimes: ruthless lust for power, cruelty, rapaciousness, treachery, and murder (especially by poisoning). Cesare Borgia (1476–1507), son of Pope Alexander VI, is here referred to. Lucius Sergius Catiline (ca. 108–62 B.C.E.), an ambitious, greedy, and cruel conspirator against the Roman state, was denounced in Cicero's famous orations before the senate and in the Forum.
6. Alexander the Great.

The general ORDER, since the whole began,
Is kept in Nature, and is kept in man.

    6. What would this man? Now upward will he soar,
    And little less than angel, would be more;
175 Now looking downwards, just as grieved appears
    To want the strength of bulls, the fur of bears.
    Made for his use all creatures if he call,
    Say what their use, had he the powers of all?
    Nature to these, without profusion, kind,
180 The proper organs, proper powers assigned;
    Each seeming want compènsated of course,
    Here with degrees of swiftness, there of force;
    All in exact proportion to the state;
    Nothing to add, and nothing to abate.
185 Each beast, each insect, happy in its own;
    Is Heaven unkind to man, and man alone?
    Shall he alone, whom rational we call,
    Be pleased with nothing, if not blessed with all?
        The bliss of man (could pride that blessing find)
190 Is not to act or think beyond mankind;
    No powers of body or of soul to share,
    But what his nature and his state can bear.
    Why has not man a microscopic eye?
    For this plain reason, man is not a fly.
195 Say what the use, were finer optics given,
    To inspect a mite, not comprehend the heaven?
    Or touch, if tremblingly alive all o'er,
    To smart and agonize at every pore?
    Or quick effluvia[7] darting through the brain,
200 Die of a rose in aromatic pain?
    If nature thundered in his opening ears,
    And stunned him with the music of the spheres,
    How would he wish that Heaven had left him still
    The whispering zephyr, and the purling rill?
205 Who finds not Providence all good and wise,
    Alike in what it gives, and what it denies?

    7. Far as creation's ample range extends,
    The scale of sensual,° mental powers ascends: sensory
    Mark how it mounts, to man's imperial race,
210 From the green myriads in the peopled grass:
    What modes of sight betwixt each wide extreme,
    The mole's dim curtain, and the lynx's beam:[8]
    Of smell, the headlong lioness between,
    And hound sagacious[9] on the tainted green:
215 Of hearing, from the life that fills the flood,

7. According to the philosophy of Epicurus (adopted by Robert Boyle, the chemist, and other 17th-century scientists), the senses are stirred to perception by being bombarded through the pores by steady streams of "effluvia," incredibly thin and tiny —but material—images of the objects that surround us.
8. One of several early theories of vision held that the eye casts a beam of light that makes objects visible.
9. Quick of scent.

To that which warbles through the vernal wood:
The spider's touch, how exquisitely fine!
Feels at each thread, and lives along the line:
In the nice° bee, what sense so subtly true   exact, accurate
220 From poisonous herbs extracts the healing dew:
How instinct varies in the groveling swine,
Compared, half-reasoning elephant, with thine!
'Twixt that, and reason, what a nice barrier,[1]
Forever separate, yet forever near!
225 Remembrance and reflection how allied;
What thin partitions sense from thought divide:
And middle natures, how they long to join,
Yet never pass the insuperable line!
Without this just gradation, could they be
230 Subjected, these to those, or all to thee?
The powers of all subdued by thee alone,
Is not thy reason all these powers in one?

8. See, through this air, this ocean, and this earth,
All matter quick, and bursting into birth.
235 Above, how high progressive life may go!
Around, how wide! how deep extend below!
Vast Chain of Being! which from God began,
Natures ethereal, human, angel, man,
Beast, bird, fish, insect, what no eye can see,
240 No glass can reach! from Infinite to thee,
From thee to nothing.—On superior powers
Were we to press, inferior might on ours:
Or in the full creation leave a void,
Where, one step broken, the great scale's destroyed:
245 From Nature's chain whatever link you strike,
Tenth or ten thousandth, breaks the chain alike.
    And, if each system in gradation roll
Alike essential to the amazing whole,
The least confusion but in one, not all
250 That system only, but the whole must fall.
Let earth unbalanced from her orbit fly,
Planets and suns run lawless through the sky,
Let ruling angels from their spheres be hurled,
Being on being wrecked, and world on world,
255 Heaven's whole foundations to their center nod,
And Nature tremble to the throne of God:
All this dread ORDER break—for whom? for thee?
Vile worm!—oh, madness, pride, impiety!

9. What if the foot, ordained the dust to tread,
260 Or hand, to toil, aspired to be the head?
What if the head, the eye, or ear repined
To serve mere engines to the ruling Mind?[2]

---

1. Pronounced *ba-réer.*   2. Cf. 1 Corinthians 12.14–26.

Just as absurd, to mourn the tasks or pains,
The great directing MIND of ALL ordains.
265   All are but parts of one stupendous whole,
Whose body Nature is, and God the soul;
That, changed through all, and yet in all the same,
Great in the earth, as in the ethereal frame,
Warms in the sun, refreshes in the breeze,
270 Glows in the stars, and blossoms in the trees,
Lives through all life, extends through all extent,
Spreads undivided, operates unspent,
Breathes in our soul, informs our mortal part,
As full, as perfect, in a hair as heart;
275 As full, as perfect, in vile man that mourns,
As the rapt seraph that adores and burns;
To him no high, no low, no great, no small;
He fills, he bounds, connects, and equals all.

10. Cease then, nor ORDER imperfection name:
280 Our proper bliss depends on what we blame.
Know thy own point: this kind, this due degree
Of blindness, weakness, Heaven bestows on thee.
Submit—In this, or any other sphere,
Secure to be as blest as thou canst bear:
285 Safe in the hand of one disposing Power,
Or in the natal, or the mortal hour.
All Nature is but art, unknown to thee;
All chance, direction, which thou canst not see;
All discord, harmony not understood;
290 All partial evil, universal good:
And, spite of pride, in erring reason's spite,
One truth is clear: Whatever IS, is RIGHT.

From *Epistle 2. Of the Nature and State of Man With Respect to Himself, as an Individual*

1. Know then thyself, presume not God to scan;
The proper study of mankind is Man.
Placed on this isthmus of a middle state,
A being darkly wise, and rudely great:
5 With too much knowledge for the skeptic side,
With too much weakness for the Stoic's pride,
He hangs between; in doubt to act, or rest,
In doubt to deem himself a god, or beast;
In doubt his mind or body to prefer,
10 Born but to die, and reasoning but to err;
Alike in ignorance, his reason such,
Whether he thinks too little, or too much:
Chaos of thought and passion, all confused;
Still by himself abused, or disabused;
15 Created half to rise, and half to fall;

Great lord of all things, yet a prey to all;
Sole judge of truth, in endless error hurled:
The glory, jest, and riddle of the world!

*   *   *

1733

Epistle to Dr. Arbuthnot

Dr. John Arbuthnot (1667–1735), to whom Pope addressed his best-known verse epistle, was distinguished both as a physician and as a man of wit. He had been one of the liveliest members of the Martinus Scriblerus Club, helping his friends create the character and shape the career of the learned pedant whose memoirs the club had undertaken to write.

Pope had long been meditating such a poem, which was to be both an attack on his detractors and a defense of his own character and career. In his usual way, he had jotted down hints, lines, couplets, and fragments over a period of two decades, but the poem might never have been completed had it not been for two events: Arbuthnot, from his deathbed, wrote to urge Pope to continue his abhorrence of vice and to express it in his writings and, during 1733, Pope was the victim of two bitter attacks by "persons of rank and fortune," as the *Advertisement* has it. The *Verses Addressed to the Imitator of Horace* was the work of Lady Mary Wortley Montagu, helped by her friend Lord Hervey (pronounced *Harvey*), a close friend and confidant of Queen Caroline. *An Epistle to a Doctor of Divinity from a Nobleman at Hampton Court* was the work of Lord Hervey alone. Montagu, it must be admitted, had provocation enough, especially in Pope's recent reference to her in *The First Satire of the Second Book of Horace*, lines 83–84, but Hervey had little to complain of beyond occasional covert references to him as "Lord Fanny." At any rate, the two scurrilous attacks goaded Pope into action, and the poem was completed by the end of the summer of 1734.

The epistle is a masterpiece of poetic rhetoric. The very fact that it is addressed to Arbuthnot, a man generally known to be honest and kind, seems to guarantee the integrity of the *I* of the poem and to diminish the moral stature of his enemies. This acquisition of virtue through association, an effective stroke, is supported by every device of persuasive rhetoric—reasonable argument and emotional appeals, subtly suggestive imagery, and superbly controlled shifts in tone and style—which help sway the reader's judgment to the side of the speaker. The poem opens in the flat language of commonplace prose discourse, tinged with a wry humor and a tone of exasperation: "Shut, shut the door, good John! (fatigued, I said)" and as it progresses it rises or falls in language and style according to the emotions that the speaker expresses—anger, contempt, amusement, sarcasm, mock self-pity, indignation, hatred, affection, gratitude, and tenderness—to return at the end to the homely tone of the opening.

It is not clear that Pope intended the poem to be thought of as a dialogue, as it has usually been printed since Warburton's edition of 1751. The original edition, while suggesting interruptions in the flow of the monologue, kept entirely to the form of a letter. The introduction of the friend, who speaks from time to time, converts the original letter into a dramatic dialogue.

Epistle to Dr. Arbuthnot

Advertisement

TO THE FIRST PUBLICATION OF THIS *Epistle*

This paper is a sort of bill of complaint, begun many years since, and drawn up by snatches, as the several occasions offered. I had no thoughts of publishing it, till it pleased some persons of rank and fortune (the authors of *Verses to the Imitator of Horace*, and of an *Epistle to a Doctor of Divinity from a Nobleman at Hampton Court*) to attack, in a very extraordinary manner, not only my writings (of which, being public, the public is judge) but my person, morals, and family, whereof, to those who know me not, a truer information may be requisite. Being divided between the necessity to say something of myself, and my own laziness to undertake so awkward a task, I thought it the shortest way to put the last hand to this epistle. If it have anything pleasing, it will be that by which I am most desirous to please, the truth and the sentiment; and if anything offensive, it will be only to those I am least sorry to offend, the vicious or the ungenerous.

Many will know their own pictures in it, there being not a circumstance but what is true; but I have, for the most part, spared their names, and they may escape being laughed at, if they please.

I would have some of them know, it was owing to the request of the learned and candid friend to whom it is inscribed, that I make not as free use of theirs as they have done of mine. However, I shall have this advantage, and honor, on my side, that whereas, by their proceeding, any abuse may be directed at any man, no injury can possibly be done by mine, since a nameless character can never be found out, but by its truth and likeness. P.

P. Shut, shut the door, good John![1] (fatigued, I said),
Tie up the knocker, say I'm sick, I'm dead.
The Dog Star[2] rages! nay 'tis past a doubt
All Bedlam,[3] or Parnassus, is let out:
5 Fire in each eye, and papers in each hand,
They rave, recite, and madden round the land.
 What walls can guard me, or what shades can hide?
They pierce my thickets, through my grot[4] they glide,
By land, by water, they renew the charge,
10 They stop the chariot, and they board the barge.
No place is sacred, not the church is free;
Even Sunday shines no Sabbath day to me:
Then from the Mint[5] walks forth the man of rhyme,
Happy! to catch me just at dinner time.
15 Is there a parson, much bemused in beer,

---

1. John Serle, Pope's gardener.
2. Sirius, associated with the period of greatest heat (and hence of madness) because it sets with the sun in late summer. August, in ancient Rome, was the season for reciting poetry.
3. Bethlehem Hospital for the insane, in London.
4. The subterranean passage under the road that

separated his house at Twickenham from his garden became, in Pope's hands, a romantic grotto ornamented with shells and mirrors.
5. A place in Southwark where debtors were free from arrest (they could not be arrested anywhere on Sundays).

A maudlin poetess, a rhyming peer,
A clerk foredoomed his father's soul to cross,
Who pens a stanza when he should engross?[6]
Is there who, locked from ink and paper,[7] scrawls
20 With desperate charcoal round his darkened walls?
All fly to Twit'nam,[8] and in humble strain
Apply to me to keep them mad or vain.
Arthur,[9] whose giddy son neglects the laws,
Imputes to me and my damned works the cause:
25 Poor Cornus[1] sees his frantic wife elope,
And curses wit, and poetry, and Pope.
⠀⠀⠀Friend to my life (which did not you prolong,
The world had wanted many an idle song)
What drop or nostrum° can this plague remove?⠀⠀⠀⠀⠀*medicine*
30 Or which must end me, a fool's wrath or love?
A dire dilemma! either way I'm sped,[2]
If foes, they write, if friends, they read me dead.
Seized and tied down to judge, how wretched I!
Who can't be silent, and who will not lie.
35 To laugh were want of goodness and of grace,
And to be grave exceeds all power of face.
I sit with sad civility, I read
With honest anguish and an aching head,
And drop at last, but in unwilling ears,
40 This saving counsel, "Keep your piece nine years."[3]
⠀⠀⠀"Nine years!" cries he, who high in Drury Lane,[4]
Lulled by soft zephyrs through the broken pane,
Rhymes ere he wakes, and prints before term[5] ends,
Obliged by hunger and request of friends:
45 "The piece, you think, is incorrect? why, take it,
I'm all submission, what you'd have it, make it."
⠀⠀⠀Three things another's modest wishes bound,
My friendship, and a prologue, and ten pound.
⠀⠀⠀Pitholeon[6] sends to me: "You know his Grace,
50 I want a patron; ask him for a place."
Pitholeon libeled me—"but here's a letter
Informs you, sir, 'twas when he knew no better.
Dare you refuse him? Curll[7] invites to dine,
He'll write a *Journal*, or he'll turn divine."[8]
55 Bless me! a packet.—" 'Tis a stranger sues,

6. Write out legal documents.
7. Is there some madman who, locked up without ink or paper . . . ?
8. I.e., Twickenham, Pope's villa on the bank of the Thames, a few miles above Hampton Court.
9. Arthur Moore, whose son, James Moore Smythe, dabbled in literature. Moore Smythe had earned Pope's enmity by using in one of his plays some unpublished lines from Pope's *Epistle 2. To a Lady* in spite of Pope's objections.
1. Latin for "horn," the traditional emblem of the cuckold.
2. "Destroyed; killed" (Johnson's *Dictionary*).
3. The advice of Horace in *Art of Poetry* (line 388).
4. I.e., living in a garret in Drury Lane, site of one of the theaters and the haunt of the profligate.

5. One of the four annual periods in which the law courts are in session and with which the publishing season coincided.
6. "A foolish poet of Rhodes, who pretended much to Greek" [Pope's note]. He is Leonard Welsted, who translated Longinus and had attacked and slandered Pope (see line 375).
7. Edmund Curll, shrewd and disreputable bookseller, published pirated works, works falsely ascribed to reputable writers, scandalous biographies, and other ephemera. Pope had often attacked him and had assigned to him a low role in *The Dunciad*.
8. I.e., he will attack Pope in the *London Journal* or write a treatise on theology, as Welsted in fact did.

A virgin tragedy, an orphan Muse."
If I dislike it, "Furies, death, and rage!"
If I approve, "Commend it to the stage."
There (thank my stars) my whole commission ends,
60   The players and I are, luckily, no friends.
Fired that the house reject him, " 'Sdeath, I'll print it,
And shame the fools—Your interest, sir, with Lintot!"[9]
Lintot, dull rogue, will think your price too much.
"Not, sir, if you revise it, and retouch."
65   All my demurs but double his attacks;
At last he whispers, "Do; and we go snacks."°   *shares*
Glad of a quarrel, straight I clap the door,
"Sir, let me see your works and you no more."
   'Tis sung, when Midas' ears began to spring
70   (Midas, a sacred person and a king),
His very minister who spied them first,
(Some say his queen) was forced to speak, or burst.[1]
And is not mine, my friend, a sorer case,
When every coxcomb perks them in my face?
75   A. Good friend, forbear! you deal in dangerous things.
I'd never name queens, ministers, or kings;
Keep close to ears, and those let asses prick;
'Tis nothing——P. Nothing? if they bite and kick?
Out with it, *Dunciad!* let the secret pass,
80   That secret to each fool, that he's an ass:
The truth once told (and wherefore should we lie?)
The queen of Midas slept, and so may I.
   You think this cruel? take it for a rule,
No creature smarts so little as a fool.
85   Let peals of laughter, Codrus! round thee break,
Thou unconcerned canst hear the mighty crack.
Pit, box, and gallery in convulsions hurled,
Thou stand'st unshook amidst a bursting world.
Who shames a scribbler? break one cobweb through,
90   He spins the slight, self-pleasing thread anew:
Destroy his fib or sophistry, in vain;
The creature's at his dirty work again,
Throned in the center of his thin designs,
Proud of a vast extent of flimsy lines.
95   Whom have I hurt? has poet yet or peer
Lost the arched eyebrow or Parnassian sneer?
And has not Colley[2] still his lord and whore?
His butchers Henley? his freemasons Moore?
Does not one table Bavius still admit?
100   Still to one bishop Philips[3] seem a wit?

---

9. Bernard Lintot, publisher of Pope's Homer and other early works.
1. Midas, king of ancient Lydia, had the bad taste to prefer the flute-playing of Pan to that of Apollo, whereupon the god endowed him with ass's ears. It was his barber (not his wife or his minister) who discovered the secret and whispered it into a hole in the earth. The reference to "queen" and "minister" makes it plain that Pope is alluding to George

II, Queen Caroline, and Walpole.
2. Colley Cibber, the laureate. John Henley, known as "Orator" Henley, an independent preacher of marked eccentricity, was popular among the lower orders, especially for his elocution.
3. The "bishop" is Hugh Boulter, bishop of Armagh; he had employed as his secretary Ambrose Philips (1674–1749), whose insipid sim-

Still Sappho[4]——A. Hold! for god's sake—you'll offend.
No names—be calm—learn prudence of a friend.
I too could write, and I am twice as tall;
But foes like these!——P. One flatterer's worse than all.
105 Of all mad creatures, if the learn'd are right,
It is the slaver kills, and not the bite.
A fool quite angry is quite innocent:
Alas! 'tis ten times worse when they repent.

One dedicates in high heroic prose,
110 And ridicules beyond a hundred foes;
One from all Grub Street[5] will my fame defend,
And, more abusive, calls himself my friend.
This prints my letters,[6] that expects a bribe,
And others roar aloud, "Subscribe, subscribe!"[7]
115 There are, who to my person pay their court:
I cough like Horace, and, though lean, am short;
Ammon's great son° one shoulder had too high,   *Alexander the Great*
Such Ovid's nose,[8] and "Sir! you have an eye—"
Go on, obliging creatures, make me see
120 All that disgraced my betters met in me.
Say for my comfort, languishing in bed,
"Just so immortal Maro° held his head":   *Virgil*
And when I die, be sure you let me know
Great Homer died three thousand years ago.

125 Why did I write? what sin to me unknown
Dipped me in ink, my parents', or my own?
As yet a child, nor yet a fool to fame,
I lisped in numbers, for the numbers came.
I left no calling for this idle trade,
130 No duty broke, no father disobeyed.
The Muse but served to ease some friend, not wife,
To help me through this long disease, my life,
To second, Arbuthnot! thy art and care,
And teach the being you preserved, to bear.°   *endure*

135 A. But why then publish? P. Granville the polite,
And knowing Walsh, would tell me I could write;
Well-natured Garth inflamed with early praise,
And Congreve loved, and Swift endured my lays;
The courtly Talbot, Somers, Sheffield, read;
140 Even mitered Rochester would nod the head,
And St. John's self (great Dryden's friends before)
With open arms received one poet more.[9]

---

plicity of manner in poetry earned him the nickname of "Namby-Pamby." Bavius, the bad poet alluded to in Virgil's *Eclogue* 3.
4. Lady Mary Wortley Montagu.
5. A term denoting the whole society of literary, political, and journalistic hack writers.
6. In 1726 Curll had surreptitiously acquired and published without permission some of Pope's letters to Henry Cromwell.
7. To ensure the financial success of a work, the

public was often asked to "subscribe" to it by taking a certain number of copies before printing was undertaken. Pope's Homer was published in this manner.
8. Ovid's family name, Naso, suggests the Latin word *nasus* ("nose"), hence the pun.
9. The purpose of this list is to establish Pope as the successor of Dryden and thus to place him far above his Grub Street persecutors. George Granville, Lord Lansdowne, poet and statesman; Wil-

Happy my studies, when by these approved!
Happier their author, when by these beloved!
145 From these the world will judge of men and books,
Not from the Burnets, Oldmixons, and Cookes.[1]
    Soft were my numbers; who could take offense
While pure description held the place of sense?
Like gentle Fanny's[2] was my flowery theme,
150 A painted mistress, or a purling stream.
Yet then did Gildon draw his venal quill;[3]
I wished the man a dinner, and sat still.
Yet then did Dennis[4] rave in furious fret;
I never answered, I was not in debt.
155 If want provoked, or madness made them print,
I waged no war with Bedlam or the Mint.
    Did some more sober critic come abroad?
If wrong, I smiled; if right, I kissed the rod.
Pains, reading, study are their just pretense,
160 And all they want is spirit, taste, and sense.
Commas and points they set exactly right,
And 'twere a sin to rob them of their mite.
Yet ne'er one sprig of laurel graced these ribalds,
From slashing Bentley down to piddling Tibbalds.[5]
165 Each wight who reads not, and but scans and spells,
Each word-catcher that lives on syllables,
Even such small critics some regard may claim,
Preserved in Milton's or in Shakespeare's name.
Pretty! in amber to observe the forms
170 Of hairs, or straws, or dirt, or grubs, or worms!
The things, we know, are neither rich nor rare,
But wonder how the devil they got there.
    Were others angry? I excused them too;
Well might they rage; I gave them but their due.
175 A man's true merit 'tis not hard to find;
But each man's secret standard in his mind,
That casting weight[6] pride adds to emptiness,
This, who can gratify? for who can guess?
The bard[7] whom pilfered pastorals renown,
180 Who turns a Persian tale for half a crown,

liam Walsh, poet and critic; Sir Samuel Garth, physician and mock-epic poet; William Congreve, the playwright; the statesmen Charles Talbot, duke of Shrewsbury; Lord Sommers; John Sheffield, duke of Buckinghamshire; and Francis Atterbury, bishop of Rochester, had all been associated with Dryden in his later years and had all encouraged the young Pope.
1. Thomas Burnet, John Oldmixon, and Thomas Cooke: Pope identifies them in a note as "authors of secret and scandalous history."
2. John, Lord Hervey, whom Pope satirizes in the character of Sporus (lines 305–33).
3. Charles Gildon, minor critic and scribbler, who, Pope believed, early attacked him at the instigation of Addison; hence "venal quill."
4. John Dennis (see An Essay on Criticism, n. 7, p. 2515).

5. Lewis Theobald (1688–1744), whose minute learning in Elizabethan literature had enabled him to expose Pope's defects as an editor of Shakespeare in 1726. Pope made him king of the Dunces in The Dunciad of 1728. Richard Bentley (1662–1742), the eminent classical scholar, seemed to both Pope and Swift the perfect type of the pedant: he is called "slashing" because, in his edition of Paradise Lost (1732), he had set in square brackets all passages that he disliked on the grounds they had been slipped into the poem without the blind poet's knowledge.
6. The weight that turns the scale; here, the "deciding factor."
7. Ambrose Philips, Pope's rival in pastoral poetry in 1709, when their pastorals were published in Tonson's 6th Miscellany. Philips had also translated some Persian tales (cf. line 100).

Just writes to make his barrenness appear,
And strains from hard-bound brains eight lines a year:
He, who still wanting, though he lives on theft,
Steals much, spends little, yet has nothing left;
185   And he who now to sense, now nonsense leaning,
Means not, but blunders round about a meaning:
And he whose fustian's so sublimely bad,
It is not poetry, but prose run mad:
All these, my modest satire bade translate,
190   And owned that nine such poets made a Tate.[8]
How did they fume, and stamp, and roar, and chafe!
And swear, not Addison himself was safe.
        Peace to all such! but were there one whose fires
True Genius kindles, and fair Fame inspires;
195   Blessed with each talent and each art to please,
And born to write, converse, and live with ease:
Should such a man, too fond to rule alone,
Bear, like the Turk, no brother near the throne;
View him with scornful, yet with jealous eyes,
200   And hate for arts that caused himself to rise;
Damn with faint praise, assent with civil leer,
And without sneering, teach the rest to sneer;
Willing to wound, and yet afraid to strike,
Just hint a fault, and hesitate dislike;
205   Alike reserved to blame or to commend,
A timorous foe, and a suspicious friend;
Dreading even fools; by flatterers besieged,
And so obliging that he ne'er obliged;
Like Cato, give his little senate[9] laws,
210   And sit attentive to his own applause;
While wits and Templars° every sentence raise,   *law students*
And wonder with a foolish face of praise—
Who but must laugh, if such a man there be?
Who would not weep, if Atticus[1] were he?
215   What though my name stood rubric[2] on the walls
Or plastered posts, with claps,° in capitals?   *posters*
Or smoking forth, a hundred hawkers' load,
On wings of winds came flying all abroad?
I sought no homage from the race that write;
220   I kept, like Asian monarchs, from their sight:
Poems I heeded (now berhymed so long)
No more than thou, great George! a birthday song.
I ne'er with wits or witlings passed my days
To spread about the itch of verse and praise;

8. Nahum Tate, poet laureate from 1692 to 1715.
His popular rewriting of Shakespeare's *King Lear*
provided a happy ending; he wrote most of part 2
of *Absalom and Achitophel*. The line refers to the
old adage that it takes nine tailors to make one
man.
9. Addison's tragedy *Cato* had been a sensational
success in 1713. Pope had written the prologue, in
which occurs the line, "While Cato gives his little
senate laws." The satirical reference here is to

Addison in the role of arbiter of taste among his
friends and admirers, mostly Whigs, at Button's
Coffee House. It was these people who had worked
against the success of Pope's Homer.
1. Pope's satiric pseudonym for Addison; Atticus
(109–32 B.C.E.) was a wealthy man of letters and
a friend of Cicero, known as a wise and disinterested man.
2. In red letters.

225   Nor like a puppy daggled through the town
       To fetch and carry sing-song up and down;
       Nor at rehearsals sweat, and mouthed, and cried,
       With handkerchief and orange at my side;
       But sick of fops, and poetry, and prate,
230   To Bufo left the whole Castalian[3] state.
          Proud as Apollo on his forkèd hill,[4]
       Sat full-blown Bufo, puffed by every quill;
       Fed with soft dedication all day long,
       Horace and he went hand in hand in song.
235   His library (where busts of poets dead
       And a true Pindar stood without a head)
       Received of wits an undistinguished race,
       Who first his judgment asked, and then a place:
       Much they extolled his pictures, much his seat,[5]
240   And flattered every day, and some days eat:
       Till grown more frugal in his riper days,
       He paid some bards with port, and some with praise;
       To some a dry rehearsal was assigned,
       And others (harder still) he paid in kind.
245   Dryden alone (what wonder?) came not nigh;
       Dryden alone escaped this judging eye:
       But still the great have kindness in reserve;
       He helped to bury whom he helped to starve.
          May some choice patron bless each gray goose quill!
250   May every Bavius have his Bufo still!
       So when a statesman wants a day's defense,
       Or envy holds a whole week's war with sense,
       Or simple pride for flattery makes demands,
       May dunce by dunce be whistled off my hands!
255   Blessed be the great! for those they take away,
       And those they left me—for they left me Gay;[6]
       Left me to see neglected genius bloom,
       Neglected die, and tell it on his tomb;
       Of all thy blameless life the sole return
260   My verse, and Queensberry weeping o'er thy urn!
       Oh, let me live my own, and die so too!
       ("To live and die is all I have to do")[7]
       Maintain a poet's dignity and ease,
       And see what friends, and read what books I please;
265   Above a patron, though I condescend
       Sometimes to call a minister my friend.
       I was not born for courts or great affairs;
       I pay my debts, believe, and say my prayers,
       Can sleep without a poem in my head,

---

3. The Castalian spring on Mount Parnassus was sacred to Apollo and the Muses. "Bufo": a type of tasteless patron of the arts. (*Bufo* means "toad" in Latin.)
4. Mount Parnassus had two peaks, one sacred to Apollo, one to Bacchus.
5. Estate. Pronounced *sate* and rhymed in next line with "eat" (*ate*).
6. John Gay (1685–1732), author of *The Beggar's*

Opera and other delightful works, dear friend of Swift and Pope. His failure to obtain patronage from the court intensified Pope's hostility to the Whig administration and the queen. Gay spent the last years of his life under the protection of the duke and duchess of Queensberry.
7. A quotation from John Denham's poem *Of Prudence.*

270 Nor know if Dennis be alive or dead.
       Why am I asked what next shall see the light?
       Heavens! was I born for nothing but to write?
       Has life no joys for me? or (to be grave)
       Have I no friend to serve, no soul to save?
275 "I found him close with Swift"—"Indeed? no doubt"
       Cries prating Balbus, "something will come out."
       'Tis all in vain, deny it as I will.
       "No, such a genius never can lie still,"
       And then for mine obligingly mistakes
280 The first lampoon Sir Will or Bubo[8] makes.
       Poor guiltless I! and can I choose but smile,
       When every coxcomb knows me by my style?
           Cursed be the verse, how well soe'er it flow,
       That tends to make one worthy man my foe,
285 Give virtue scandal, innocence a fear,
       Or from the soft-eyed virgin steal a tear!
       But he who hurts a harmless neighbor's peace,
       Insults fallen worth, or beauty in distress,
       Who loves a lie, lame slander helps about,
290 Who writes a libel, or who copies out:
       That fop whose pride affects a patron's name,
       Yet absent, wounds an author's honest fame;
       Who can your merit selfishly approve,
       And show the sense of it without the love;
295 Who has the vanity to call you friend,
       Yet wants the honor, injured, to defend;
       Who tells whate'er you think, whate'er you say,
       And, if he lie not, must at least betray:
       Who to the dean and silver bell can swear,
300 And sees at Cannons what was never there:[9]
       Who reads but with a lust to misapply,
       Make satire a lampoon, and fiction, lie:
       A lash like mine no honest man shall dread,
       But all such babbling blockheads in his stead.
305   Let Sporus[1] tremble—— A. What? that thing of silk,
       Sporus, that mere white curd of ass's milk?[2]
       Satire or sense, alas! can Sporus feel?
       Who breaks a butterfly upon a wheel?
           P. Yet let me flap this bug with gilded wings,
310 This painted child of dirt, that stinks and stings;
       Whose buzz the witty and the fair annoys,
       Yet wit ne'er tastes, and beauty ne'er enjoys;

---

8. Sir William Yonge, Whig politician and poetaster. George Bubb ("Bubo") Dodington, a Whig
patron of letters.
9. Pope's enemies had accused him of satirizing
Cannons, the ostentatious estate of the duke of
Chandos, in his description of Timon's villa in the
Epistle to Burlington. This Pope quite justly
denied. The bell of Timon's chapel was of silver,
and there preached a dean who "never mentions

Hell to ears polite."
1. John, Lord Hervey, effeminate courtier and
confidant of Queen Caroline (see the headnote to
Epistle to Dr. Arbuthnot, p. 2562). The original
Sporus was a boy, whom the emperor Nero publicly married (see Suetonius's life of Nero in The
Twelve Caesars).
2. Drunk by invalids.

So well-bred spaniels civilly delight
In mumbling of the game they dare not bite.
315 Eternal smiles his emptiness betray,
As shallow streams run dimpling all the way.
Whether in florid impotence he speaks,
And, as the prompter breathes, the puppet squeaks;
Or at the ear of Eve,[3] familiar toad,
320 Half froth, half venom, spits himself abroad,
In puns, or politics, or tales, or lies,
Or spite, or smut, or rhymes, or blasphemies.
His wit all seesaw between *that* and *this*,
Now high, now low, now master up, now miss,
325 And he himself one vile antithesis.
Amphibious thing! that acting either part,
The trifling head or the corrupted heart,
Fop at the toilet, flatterer at the board,
Now trips a lady, and now struts a lord.
330 Eve's tempter thus the rabbins[4] have expressed,
A cherub's face, a reptile all the rest;
Beauty that shocks you, parts that none will trust,
Wit that can creep, and pride that licks the dust.
    Not fortune's worshiper, nor fashion's fool,
335 Not lucre's madman, nor ambition's tool,
Not proud, nor servile, be one poet's praise,
That if he pleased, he pleased by manly ways:
That flattery, even to kings, he held a shame,
And thought a lie in verse or prose the same:
340 That not in fancy's maze he wandered long,
But stooped[5] to truth, and moralized his song:
That not for fame, but virtue's better end,
He stood the furious foe, the timid friend,
The damning critic, half approving wit,
345 The coxcomb hit, or fearing to be hit;
Laughed at the loss of friends he never had,
The dull, the proud, the wicked, and the mad;
The distant threats of vengeance on his head,
The blow unfelt, the tear he never shed;
350 The tale revived, the lie so oft o'erthrown,
The imputed trash, and dullness not his own;
The morals blackened when the writings 'scape,
The libeled person, and the pictured shape;[6]
Abuse on all he loved, or loved him, spread,
355 A friend in exile, or a father dead;
The whisper, that to greatness still too near,
Perhaps yet vibrates on his Sovereign's ear—
Welcome for thee, fair virtue! all the past:
For thee, fair virtue! welcome even the last!

---

3. The queen; the allusion is to *Paradise Lost* (4.799–809).
4. Scholars of and authorities on Jewish law and doctrine.

5. The falcon is said to "stoop" to its prey when it swoops down and seizes it in flight.
6. Pope's deformity was frequently ridiculed and occasionally caricatured.

360   A. But why insult the poor, affront the great?
       P. A knave's a knave to me in every state:
       Alike my scorn, if he succeed or fail,
       Sporus at court, or Japhet[7] in a jail,
       A hireling scribbler, or a hireling peer,
365   Knight of the post[8] corrupt, or of the shire,
       If on a pillory, or near a throne,
       He gain his prince's ear, or lose his own.
           Yet soft by nature, more a dupe than wit,
       Sappho° can tell you how this man was bit:°   Montagu / deceived
370   This dreaded satirist Dennis will confess
       Foe to his pride, but friend to his distress:[9]
       So humble, he has knocked at Tibbald's door,
       Has drunk with Cibber, nay, has rhymed for Moore.
       Full ten years slandered, did he once reply?
375   Three thousand suns went down on Welsted's lie.
       To please a mistress one aspersed his life;
       He lashed him not, but let her be his wife.
       Let Budgell charge low Grub Street on his quill,
       And write whate'er he pleased, except his will;[1]
380   Let the two Curlls of town and court,[2] abuse
       His father, mother, body, soul, and muse.
       Yet why? that father held it for a rule,
       It was a sin to call our neighbor fool;
       That harmless mother thought no wife a whore:
385   Hear this, and spare his family, James Moore!
       Unspotted names, and memorable long,
       If there be force in virtue, or in song.
           Of gentle blood (part shed in honor's cause,
       While yet in Britain honor had applause)
390   Each parent sprung——A. What fortune, pray?——P. Their own,
       And better got than Bestia's[3] from the throne.
       Born to no pride, inheriting no strife,
       Nor marrying discord in a noble wife,
       Stranger to civil and religious rage,
395   The good man walked innoxious through his age.
       No courts he saw, no suits would ever try,
       Nor dared an oath,[4] nor hazarded a lie.
       Unlearn'd, he knew no schoolman's subtle art,
       No language but the language of the heart.
400   By nature honest, by experience wise,
       Healthy by temperance, and by exercise;
       His life, though long, to sickness passed unknown,
       His death was instant, and without a groan.

---

7. Japhet Crook, a notorious forger.
8. One who lives by selling false evidence.
9. Pope wrote the prologue to Cibber's *Provoked Husband* (1728) when that play was performed for Dennis's benefit, shortly before the old critic died.
1. Eustace Budgell attacked the *Grub Street Journal* for publishing what he took to be a squib by Pope charging him with having forged the will of Dr. Matthew Tindal.
2. I.e., the publisher and Lord Hervey.

3. Probably the duke of Marlborough, whose vast fortune was made through the favor of Queen Anne. The actual Bestia was a corrupt Roman consul.
4. As a Catholic, Pope's father refused to take the Oaths of Allegiance and Supremacy and the oath against the pope. He thus rendered himself vulnerable to the many repressive anti-Catholic laws then in force.

Oh, grant me thus to live, and thus to die!
405 Who sprung from kings shall know less joy than I.
     O friend! may each domestic bliss be thine!
     Be no unpleasing melancholy mine:
     Me, let the tender office long engage,
     To rock the cradle of reposing age,
410 With lenient arts extend a mother's breath,
     Make languor smile, and smooth the bed of death,
     Explore the thought, explain the asking eye,
     And keep a while one parent from the sky![5]
     On cares like these if length of days attend,
415 May Heaven, to bless those days, preserve my friend,
     Preserve him social, cheerful, and serene,
     And just as rich as when he served a Queen![6]
        A. Whether that blessing be denied or given,
     Thus far was right—the rest belongs to Heaven.

1735

The Dunciad: Book the Fourth The fourth book of *The Dunciad*, Pope's last major work, was originally intended as a continuation of *An Essay on Man*. To Jonathan Swift, the spiritual ancestor of the poem, Pope confided in 1736 that he was at work on a series of epistles on the uses of human reason and learning, to conclude with "a satire against the misapplication of all these, exemplified by pictures, characters, and examples." But the epistles never appeared; instead, the satire grew until it took their place. As Pope surveyed England in his last years, the complex literary and social order that had sustained him seemed to be crumbling. It was a time for desperate measures, for satire. And the means of retribution was at hand, in the structure of Pope's own *Dunciad*, the long work that had already impaled so many enemies.

The first *Dunciad*, published in three books in 1728, is a mock-epic reply to Pope's critics and other petty authors. Its hero and victim, Lewis Theobald, had attacked Pope's edition of Shakespeare (1725); other victims had offended Pope either by personal abuse or simply by ineptitude. Inspired by Dryden's *Mac Flecknoe*, *The Dunciad* celebrates the triumph of the hordes of Grub Street. Indeed, so many obscure hacks were mentioned that a *Dunciad Variorum* (1729) was soon required, in which mock-scholarly notes identify the victims, "since it is only in this monument that they must expect to survive." But a modern reader need not catch every reference to enjoy the dazzling wit of the poem, or the sheer sense of fun with which Pope remakes the London literary world into a tiny insane fairground of his own.

The New Dunciad (1742), however, plays a far more serious game: here Pope takes aim at the rot of the whole social fabric. The satire goes deep, and works at many levels, which for convenience may be divided into four. (1) Politics: From 1721 to 1742 England had been ruled by the Whig supremacy of Robert Walpole, first minister. To Pope and his circle, the immensely powerful Walpole (no friend of poets) seemed a crass and greedy vulgarian, like his monarch George II. It is no accident, in the kingdom of *The Dunciad*, that Dulness personified sits on a throne. (2) Society: Just as the action of the *Aeneid* had been the removal of the empire of Troy to Latium,

---

5. Pope was a tender and devoted son. His mother had died in 1733, and the earliest version of these lines dates from 1731, when the poet was nursing her through a serious illness.

6. Pope alludes to the fact that Arbuthnot, a man of strict probity, left the queen's service no wealthier than when he entered it.

the action of *The Dunciad,* according to Pope, is "the removal of the empire of Dulness from the City of London to the polite world, Westminster"; that is, the abdication of civility in favor of commerce and financial interests. In modern England, authors write for money, and ministers govern for profit; conspicuous consumption (especially the consumption of paper by scribblers) has replaced the old values of the yeoman and the aristocrat. In 1743, Pope revised the original *Dunciad,* substituting the actor and poet laureate Colley Cibber for Theobald as the hero and incorporating *The New Dunciad* as the fourth book (the version printed here). Dulness, he implies, has achieved her final triumph; Cibber is laureate in England. (3) Education: The word *dunce* is derived from the Scholastic philosopher John Duns Scotus (ca. 1265–1308), whose name had come to stand for silly and useless subtlety, logical hairsplitting. Pope, as an heir of the Renaissance, believes that the central subject of education must always be its relevance for human behavior: "The proper study of mankind is Man," and moral philosophy, the relation of individuals to each other and to the world, should be the teacher's first and last concern. By contrast, Dunces waste their time on grammar (words alone) or the "science" of the collector (things alone); they never comprehend that word and thing, like spirit and matter, are essentially dead unless they join. (4) Religion: At its deepest level, the subject of *The Dunciad* is the undoing of God's creation. Many passages from the fourth book echo *Paradise Lost,* and one of Pope's starting places seems to be Satan's threat to return the world to its original darkness, chaos, and ancient night (*Paradise Lost* 2.968–87). *The Dunciad* ends in a great apocalypse, with a yawn that signals the death of *Logos;* as words have become meaningless, so has the whole creation, which the Lord called forth with words. Here Pope invokes, with terrifying intensity, the old idea that God was the first poet, whose poem was the world, and suggests that the sickness of the word has infected all nature. But there is one consolation: out of non-art itself, out of matter without spirit and substance without essence, the poet creates his own final artistic triumph, and makes a poem.

From The Dunciad

From *Book the Fourth*

> Yet, yet a moment, one dim ray of light
> Indulge, dread Chaos, and eternal Night!
> Of darkness visible[1] so much be lent,
> As half to show, half veil the deep intent.
> 5 Ye Powers![2] whose mysteries restored I sing,
> To whom Time bears me on his rapid wing,
> Suspend a while your force inertly strong,
> Then take at once the poet and the song.
>   Now flamed the Dog-star's[3] unpropitious ray,
> 10 Smote every brain, and withered every bay,[4]
> Sick was the sun, the owl forsook his bower,
> The moon-struck prophet felt the madding hour:
> Then rose the seed[5] of Chaos, and of Night,
> To blot out Order, and extinguish Light,
> 15 Of dull and venal a new world to mold,

---

1. Cf. *Paradise Lost* 1.63.
2. Chaos and Night, invoked in place of the Muse, because "the restoration of their empire is the action of the poem" [Pope's note].
3. Sirius, associated with the heat of summer and

the madness of poets (see *Epistle to Dr. Arbuthnot,* line 3, p. 2563).
4. The laurel, whose garlands are bestowed on poets.
5. The Goddess Dulness.

And bring Saturnian days of lead and gold.[6]
    She mounts the throne: her head a cloud concealed,
In broad effulgence all below revealed,
('Tis thus aspiring Dulness ever shines)
20   Soft on her lap her Laureate son[7] reclines.
    Beneath her foot-stool, Science groans in chains,
And Wit dreads exile, penalties and pains.
There foamed rebellious Logic, gagged and bound,
There, stripped, fair Rhetoric languished on the ground;
25   His blunted arms by Sophistry are born,
And shameless Billingsgate[8] her robes adorn.
Morality, by her false guardians drawn,
Chicane in furs, and Casuistry in lawn,[9]
Gasps, as they straighten at each end the cord,
30   And dies, when Dulness gives her Page[1] the word.

*   *   *

[THE EDUCATOR]

135   Now crowds on crowds around the Goddess press,
Each eager to present the first address.[2]
Dunce scorning dunce beholds the next advance,
But fop shows fop superior complaisance.
When lo! a specter[3] rose, whose index-hand
140 Held forth the virtue of the dreadful wand;
His beavered brow a birchen garland wears,[4]
Dropping with infant's blood, and mother's tears.
O'er every vein a shuddering horror runs;
Eton and Winton shake through all their sons.
145 All flesh is humbled, Westminster's bold race[5]
Shrink, and confess the Genius[6] of the place:
The pale boy-Senator yet tingling stands,
And holds his breeches close with both his hands.
    Then thus. "Since Man from beast by words is known,
150 Words are Man's province, words we teach alone.
When reason doubtful, like the Samian letter,[7]
Points him two ways, the narrower is the better.
Placed at the door of learning, youth to guide,
We never suffer it to stand too wide.
155 To ask, to guess, to know, as they commence,

---

6. Saturn ruled during the golden age; the new age of "gold" will be reestablished by the dull and venal.
7. Colley Cibber, the poet laureate.
8. Fishmarket slang, which now covers the noble science of rhetoric.
9. Chicanery (legal trickery) wears the ermine robe of a judge; casuistry wears the linen sleeves of a bishop.
1. Sir Francis Page, a notorious hanging judge; or court page, used to strangle criminals in Turkey; or page of writing on which a dull author "kills" moral sentiments.
2. The goddess, newly enthroned, is receiving petitions and congratulations.
3. The ghost of Dr. Busby, stern headmaster of Westminster School.
4. He wears a hat (beaver) and a garland of birch twigs, used for flogging. "Wand": cane used for beating.
5. Alumni of Westminster School, with a play on the justices and members of Parliament who meet at Westminster Hall.
6. I.e., admit that Dr. Busby is the presiding deity (Genius).
7. The letter Y, which Pythagoras (a native of Samos) used as an emblem of the different roads of virtue and vice.

As fancy opens the quick springs of sense,
We ply the memory, we load the brain,
Bind rebel wit, and double chain on chain,
Confine the thought, to exercise the breath;[8]
160 And keep them in the pale of words till death.
Whate'er the talents, or howe'er designed,
We hang one jingling padlock on the mind:
A poet the first day, he dips his quill;
And what the last? a very poet still.
165 Pity! the charm works only in our wall,
Lost, lost too soon in yonder House or Hall."[9]

* * *

[THE CARNATION AND THE BUTTERFLY]

Then thick as locusts blackening all the ground,
A tribe,[1] with weeds and shells fantastic crowned,
Each with some wondrous gift approached the Power,
400 A nest, a toad, a fungus, or a flower.
But far the foremost, two, with earnest zeal,
And aspect ardent to the throne appeal.
The first thus opened: "Hear thy suppliant's call,
Great Queen, and common mother of us all!
405 Fair from its humble bed I reared this flower,
Suckled, and cheer'd, with air, and sun, and shower,
Soft on the paper ruff its leaves I spread,
Bright with the gilded button tipped its head,
Then throned in glass, and named it CAROLINE:[2]
410 Each maid cried, charming! and each youth, divine!
Did Nature's pencil ever blend such rays,
Such varied light in one promiscuous blaze?
Now prostrate! dead! behold that Caroline:
No maid cries, charming! and no youth, divine!
415 And lo the wretch! whose vile, whose insect lust
Laid this gay daughter of the Spring in dust.
Oh punish him, or to th' Elysian shades
Dismiss my soul, where no carnation fades."
He ceased, and wept. With innocence of mien,
420 The accused stood forth, and thus addressed the Queen.
"Of all th' enameled race,° whose silvery wing   colored insects
Waves to the tepid zephyrs of the spring,
Or swims along the fluid atmosphere,
Once brightest shined this child of heat and air.
425 I saw, and started from its vernal bower
The rising game, and chased from flower to flower.
It fled, I followed; now in hope, now pain;
It stopped, I stopped; it moved, I moved again.

---

8. Students are taught only to recite the classic poets by heart.
9. The House of Commons and Westminster Hall, where law cases were heard. The eloquence learned by rote disappears on occasions for public speaking.

1. The Virtuosi, or amateur scientists and collectors.
2. Queen Caroline, an enthusiastic gardener, is an appropriate choice to lend her name to the perfect carnation.

At last it fixed, 'twas on what plant it pleased,
430 And where it fixed, the beauteous bird° I seized: insect
Rose or carnation was below my care;
I meddle, Goddess! only in my sphere.
I tell the naked fact without disguise,
And, to excuse it, need but show the prize;
435 Whose spoils this paper offers to your eye,
Fair even in death! this peerless Butterfly."
    "My sons!" she answered, "both have done your parts;
Live happy both, and long promote our arts.
But hear a mother, when she recommends
440 To your fraternal care, our sleeping friends.
The common soul, of heaven's more frugal make,
Serves but to keep fools pert, and knaves awake:
A drowsy watchman, that just gives a knock,
And breaks our rest, to tell us what's a clock.[3]
445 Yet by some object every brain is stirred;
The dull may waken to a hummingbird;
The most recluse, discreetly opened, find
Congenial matter in the cockle-kind;[4]
The mind, in metaphysics at a loss,
450 May wander in a wilderness of moss;
The head that turns at super-lunar things,
Poised with a tail, may steer on Wilkins' wings.[5]
    "O! would the Sons of Men once think their eyes
And reason given them but to study *flies!*[6]
455 See Nature in some partial narrow shape,
And let the Author of the whole escape:
Learn but to trifle; or, who most observe,
To wonder at their Maker, not to serve."

*   *   *

[THE TRIUMPH OF DULNESS]

    Then blessing all,[7] "Go children of my care!
580 To practice now from theory repair.
All my commands are easy, short, and full:
My sons! be proud, be selfish, and be dull.
Guard my prerogative, assert my throne:
This nod confirms each privilege your own.
585 The cap and switch be sacred to his Grace;[8]
With staff and pumps[9] the Marquis lead the race;
From stage to stage the licensed[1] Earl may run,
Paired with his fellow-charioteer the sun;

---

3. In the 18th-century, watchmen kept guard in the streets and announced the hours.
4. Cockleshells, popular with collectors, as were hummingbirds and varieties of moss.
5. John Wilkins (1614–1672), one of the founders of the Royal Society, had speculated "that a man may be able to fly, by the application of wings to his own body."
6. Cf. *An Essay on Man* 1.189–96 (p. 2559): "Say what the use, were finer optics given, / To inspect a mite, not comprehend the heaven?"
7. Having conferred her titles, Dulness bids each of the rulers of England to indulge in the triviality closest to his heart.
8. His Grace, a duke who loves horse racing, is to use the cap and switch of a jockey.
9. Footmen, who wore pumps (low-cut shoes for running), were matched in races.
1. The license required by the owner of a stage-coach; also privileged or licentious.

The learned baron butterflies design,
590   Or draw to silk Arachne's subtle line;°   *spiderweb*
The Judge to dance his brother Sergeant[2] call;
The Senator at cricket urge the ball;
The Bishop stow (pontific luxury!)
An hundred souls of turkeys in a pie;[3]
595   The sturdy squire to Gallic masters° stoop,   *French chefs*
And drown his lands and manors in a soup.
Others import yet nobler arts from France,
Teach kings to fiddle, and make senates dance.
Perhaps more high some daring son may soar,[4]
600   Proud to my list to add one monarch more;
And nobly conscious, Princes are but things
Born for First Ministers, as slaves for kings,
Tyrant supreme! shall three estates command,
And MAKE ONE MIGHTY DUNCIAD OF THE LAND!"
605   More she had spoke, but yawned—All Nature nods:
What mortal can resist the yawn of Gods?
Churches and chapels instantly it reached;
(St. James's first, for leaden Gilbert[5] preached)
Then catched the schools; the Hall scarce kept awake;
610   The Convocation gaped,[6] but could not speak:
Lost was the Nation's Sense,° nor could be found,   *Parliament*
While the long solemn unison went round:
Wide, and more wide, it spread o'er all the realm;
Even Palinurus[7] nodded at the helm:
615   The vapor mild o'er each committee crept;
Unfinished treaties in each office slept;
And chiefless armies dozed out the campaign;
And navies yawned for orders on the main.
    O Muse! relate (for you can tell alone,
620   Wits have short memories, and dunces none)
Relate, who first, who last resigned to rest;
Whose heads she partly, whose completely blessed;
What charms could faction, what ambition lull,
The venal quiet, and entrance the dull;
625   'Till drowned was sense, and shame, and right, and wrong—
O sing, and hush the nations with thy song!
· ·
In vain, in vain,—the all-composing Hour
Resistless falls: The Muse obeys the Power.
She comes! she comes![8] the sable throne behold
630   Of Night primeval, and of Chaos old!
Before her, Fancy's gilded clouds decay,

---

2. A lawyer or legislative officer. Formal ceremonies at the Inns of Court are said to have resembled a country dance, "a call of sergeants."
3. According to Pope, a hundred turkeys had been "not unfrequently deposited in one Pye in the Bishopric of Durham."
4. A bold, direct attack on Walpole.
5. Dr. John Gilbert, dean of Exeter.

6. The Convocation, an assembly of clergy consulting on ecclesiastical affairs, had been adjourned since 1717.
7. The pilot of Aeneas's ship; here Walpole.
8. Having triumphed in the contemporary world of affairs, Dulness (like her antitype Christ) has a Second Coming, a prophetic vision in which she extinguishes the light of the arts and sciences.

And all its varying rainbows die away.
Wit shoots in vain its momentary fires,
The meteor drops, and in a flash expires.
635 As one by one, at dread Medea's strain,
The sickening stars fade off the ethereal plain;[9]
As Argus' eyes by Hermes' wand oppressed,
Closed one by one to everlasting rest;[1]
Thus at her felt approach, and secret might,
640 Art after Art goes out, and all is Night.
See skulking Truth to her old cavern fled,[2]
Mountains of casuistry heaped o'er her head!
Philosophy, that leaned on Heaven before,
Shrinks to her second cause,[3] and is no more.
645 Physic[4] of Metaphysic begs defense,
And Metaphysic calls for aid on Sense!
See Mystery[5] to Mathematics fly!
In vain! they gaze, turn giddy, rave, and die.
Religion blushing veils her sacred fires,
650 And unawares Morality expires.
Nor public flame, nor private, dares to shine;
Nor human spark is left, nor glimpse divine!
Lo! thy dread Empire, CHAOS! is restored;
Light dies before thy uncreating word:[6]
655 Thy hand, great Anarch! lets the curtain fall;
And Universal Darkness buries All.

1743

9. In Seneca's *Medea*, the stars obey the curse of
Medea, a magician and avenger.
1. Argus, Hera's hundred-eyed watchman, was
charmed to sleep and slain by Hermes.
2. Alluding to the saying of Democritus, that
Truth lay at the bottom of a deep well [Pope's
note].
3. Science (philosophy) no longer accepts God as
the first cause or final explanation of how all things

came to be; instead, it accepts only the second or
material cause and tries to account for all things
by physical principles alone.
4. Natural science in general.
5. A religious truth known only through divine
revelation.
6. Cf. God's first creating words in Genesis, "Let
there be light."

LADY MARY WORTLEY MONTAGU
1689–1762

In her early teens Lady Mary Pierrepont did something that well-bred young women
were not supposed to do: she secretly taught herself Latin. The act reveals many of
the traits that would also characterize her as a mature woman: curiosity, love of
learning, intelligence, ambition, and independence of mind. The eldest daughter of
a wealthy Whig peer (he later became marquess of Dorchester), she grew up amid a
glittering London circle that included Addison, Steele, Congreve, and later Pope and
Gay. But she was not content to live the life of a dutiful aristocratic daughter. Unlike
most women in her time, she married for love, and when her husband, Edward Wortley Montagu, was appointed ambassador to Constantinople in 1716, she took advan-

tage of the opportunity by traveling through Europe, studying the language and customs of Turkey, and even visiting Turkish harems. She also pioneered in introducing smallpox inoculation to England (her own son and daughter were among the first to be inoculated). Returning home in 1718, she spent unhappy years that included bitter political quarrels with Pope and the gradual failure of her marriage. Then, in middle age, she fell in love with a young Italian author, Francesco Algarotti. In 1739 she traveled to Italy hoping to see him; but the passion that had kindled in their letters was soon quenched when he failed to join her. The rest of her life was passed abroad, in Avignon, Brescia, and Venice. She died soon after her return to London in 1762.

As an author, Montagu is remembered chiefly for her letters. In a century that included many of the great letter writers in English—Gray, Horace Walpole, Cowper, and others—she is one of the greatest. "What fire, what ease, what knowledge of Europe and Asia!" Edward Gibbon commented when her Turkish correspondence was published. But from an early age she had also tried her hand at other literary forms: essays, poems, and even a translated play. In her own time she was especially admired as a poet. When Pope, after their quarrel, gave her the name of "Sappho" (see *Epistle 2. To a Lady*, lines 24–26, p. 2593), he was doubtless betraying the nervousness that most men felt in the presence of intelligent women (the Greek poet Sappho, after all, preferred women to men); yet he was also associating her with the classic author of lyric verse. Montagu's verse, although often casual, reveals the mind of a woman who is not willing to accept the stereotypes imposed on her by men. Like her friend Mary Astell, Montagu puts her trust in education and reason, not in the opinions of others, and she always insists on preserving her freedom of choice. A woman, her poems suggest, need not defer to a man who is less than her equal; she must look to her own satisfaction before she looks to his, and she always has the right to say no. The verse demands respect by virtue of its sexual candor and punishing wit. Like Montagu herself, it is never dull, and at its best it places her in that ideal community defined by E. M. Forster: "Not an aristocracy of power, based upon rank and influence, but an aristocracy of the sensitive, the considerate, and the plucky."

The Lover: A Ballad

> At length, by so much importunity pressed,
> Take, (Molly),[1] at once, the inside of my breast;
> This stupid indifference so often you blame
> Is not owing to nature, to fear, or to shame;
> 5 I am not as cold as a Virgin in lead,[2]
> Nor is Sunday's sermon so strong in my head;
> I know but too well how time flies along,
> That we live but few years and yet fewer are young.
>
> But I hate to be cheated, and never will buy
> 10 Long years of repentance for moments of joy.
> Oh was there a man (but where shall I find
> Good sense and good nature so equally joined?)

1. Molly Skerrett, a friend of Lady Mary, was the mistress of Sir Robert Walpole. The ideal "lover" of the title, however, is not to be identified with any particular person.

2. I.e., an image of the Virgin Mary, either as a leaden statue or as a stained-glass window framed in lead.

Would value his pleasure, contribute to mine,
Not meanly would boast, nor lewdly design,°   plot
15   Not over severe, yet not stupidly vain,
For I would have the power though not give the pain;

No pedant yet learnèd, not rakehelly gay
Or laughing because he has nothing to say,
To all my whole sex obliging and free,
20   Yet never be fond of any but me;
In public preserve the decorums are just,
And show in his eyes he is true to his trust,
Then rarely approach, and respectfully bow,
Yet not fulsomely pert, nor yet foppishly low.

25   But when the long hours of public are past
And we meet with champagne and a chicken at last,
May every fond pleasure that hour endear,
Be banished afar both discretion and fear,
Forgetting or scorning the airs of the crowd
30   He may cease to be formal, and I to be proud,
Till lost in the joy we confess that we live,
And he may be rude, and yet I may forgive.

And that my delight may be solidly fixed,
Let the friend and the lover be handsomely mixed,
35   In whose tender bosom my soul might confide,
Whose kindness can sooth me, whose counsel could guide.
From such a dear lover as here I describe
No danger should fright me, no millions should bribe;
But till this astonishing creature I know,
40   As I long have lived chaste, I will keep myself so.

I never will share with the wanton coquette,
Or be caught by a vain affectation of wit.
The toasters and songsters may try all their art
But never shall enter the pass of my heart.
45   I loathe the lewd rake, the dressed fopling despise;
Before such pursuers the nice° virgin flies;   fastidious
And as Ovid has sweetly in parables told
We harden like trees, and like rivers are cold.[3]

1747

---

3. In Ovid's *Metamorphoses*, Daphne, to escape Apollo, was turned into a laurel, and Arethusa, escaping
Alpheus, became a fountain.

Epistle from Mrs. Yonge to Her Husband[1]

Think not this paper comes with vain pretense
To move your pity, or to mourn th' offense.
Too well I know that hard obdurate heart;
No softening mercy there will take my part,
5 Nor can a woman's arguments prevail,
When even your patron's wise example fails.[2]
But this last privilege I still retain;
Th' oppressed and injured always may complain.
    Too, too severely laws of honor bind
10 The weak submissive sex of womankind.
If sighs have gained or force compelled our hand,
Deceived by art, or urged by stern command,
Whatever motive binds the fatal tie,
The judging world expects our constancy.
15   Just heaven! (for sure in heaven does justice reign,
Though tricks below that sacred name profane)
To you appealing I submit my cause,
Nor fear a judgment from impartial laws.
All bargains but conditional[3] are made;
20 The purchase void, the creditor unpaid;
Defrauded servants are from service free;
A wounded slave regains his liberty.
For wives ill used no remedy remains,
To daily racks condemned, and to eternal chains.
25   From whence is this unjust distinction grown?
Are we not formed with passions like your own?
Nature with equal fire our souls endued,
Our minds as haughty, and as warm our blood;
O'er the wide world your pleasures you pursue, ⎫
30 The change is justified by something new; ⎬
But we must sigh in silence—and be true. ⎭
Our sex's weakness you expose and blame
(Of every prattling fop the common theme),
Yet from this weakness you suppose is due
35 Sublimer virtue than your Cato[4] knew.
Had heaven designed us trials so severe,

---

1. In 1724 the notorious libertine William Yonge, separated from his wife, Mary, discovered that she (like him) had committed adultery. He sued her lover, Colonel Norton, for damages and collected £1,500. Later that year, according to the law of the time, he petitioned the Houses of Parliament for a divorce. The case was tried in public, Mrs. Yonge's love letters were read aloud, and two men testified that they had found her and Norton "together in naked bed." Yonge was granted the divorce, his wife's dowry, and the greater part of her fortune.
    Alhough the *Epistle* is obviously based on this sensational affair, it is also a work of imagination. Like Pope's *Eloisa to Abelard*—to which the author himself called Montagu's attention—it takes the form of a heroic epistle, the passionate outcry of an abandoned woman. The poet, entering into the feelings of Mary Yonge, justifies her conduct with reasons both of the heart and of the head. The objects of her attack include the institution of marriage, which binds wives in "eternal chains"; the double standard of morality, which requires chastity from women but not men; the hypocrisy of society, which condemns the very behavior it secretly lusts after; and the craven greed and cruelty of the husband himself. But 18th-century women seldom dared to speak like this in public, and the *Epistle* was not published until the 1970s.
2. Sir Robert Walpole, William Yonge's friend at court, was rumored to tolerate his own wife's infidelities.
3. Only conditionally.
4. The asceticism and self-discipline of the Roman statesman Cato had been emphasized in Addison's famous tragedy *Cato* (1713).

It would have formed our tempers then to bear.
    And I have borne (oh what have I not borne!)
The pang of jealousy, the insults of scorn.
40 Wearied at length, I from your sight remove,
And place my future hopes in secret love.
In the gay bloom of glowing youth retired,
I quit the woman's joy to be admired,
With that small pension your hard heart allows,
45 Renounce your fortune, and release your vows.
To custom (though unjust) so much is due;
I hide my frailty from the public view.
My conscience clear, yet sensible of shame,
My life I hazard, to preserve my fame.
50 And I prefer this low inglorious state
To vile dependence on the thing I hate—
But you pursue me to this last retreat.
Dragged into light, my tender crime is shown
And every circumstance of fondness known.
55 Beneath the shelter of the law you stand,
And urge my ruin with a cruel hand,
While to my fault thus rigidly severe,
Tamely submissive to the man you fear.[5]
    This wretched outcast, this abandoned wife,
60 Has yet this joy to sweeten shameful life:
By your mean conduct, infamously loose,
You are at once my accuser and excuse.
Let me be damned by the censorious prude
(Stupidly dull, or spiritually lewd),
65 My hapless case will surely pity find
From every just and reasonable mind.
When to the final sentence I submit,
The lips condemn me, but their souls acquit.
    No more my husband, to your pleasures go,
70 The sweets of your recovered freedom know.
Go: court the brittle friendship of the great,
Smile at his board,° or at his levee[6] wait;   *dining table*
And when dismissed, to madam's toilet[7] fly,
More than her chambermaids, or glasses,° lie,   *mirrors*
75 Tell her how young she looks, how heavenly fair,
Admire the lilies and the roses there.
Your high ambition may be gratified,
Some cousin of her own be made your bride,
And you the father of a glorious race
80 Endowed with Ch——l's strength and Low——r's face.[8]

1724   1972

5. I.e., Walpole. Montagu suggests that the whole political establishment of England takes sides against Mary Yonge.
6. Morning reception of visitors.
7. It was fashionable for women like Lady Walpole to receive visitors during the last stages of dressing (their "toilet").
8. General Churchill was rumored to have had an affair with Lady Walpole; Antony Lowther was a notorious gallant. The author implies that William Yonge's next wife may be as untrue as his first. Mary Yonge remarried immediately after her divorce; five years later Yonge himself (whose divorce had made him rich) married the daughter of a baron.

Debating Women: Arguments in Verse

Satires on women are an ancient tradition. In many cultures, male writers have defined the nature of women, distinguished them sharply from men, laughed at their faults, looked into their hearts, and told them how to behave; and female writers such as Christine de Pisan (1363?–1431) have countered by pointing out the virtues of women and the unfairness of men. But the argument intensified in seventeenth- and eighteenth-century Britain. As literacy increased to unprecedented numbers, much of the reading public began to consist of women, whose concerns were addressed directly by Mary Astell and other women as well as by men. New forms of writing— the periodical essay, the conduct book, and above all the novel—developed to give women rules and models for living. But the early eighteenth century was also a great age of satire. Male satirists could not resist the urge to reflect on, or try to reform, women's follies; nor could female satirists resist the urge to reply that men were just as bad or worse and did not know what they were talking about. This led to a lively exchange in which women were not only the subject of the debate but also agents who spoke for themselves.

Jonathan Swift and Alexander Pope, who were lifelong bachelors and friends as well as brilliant satirists, represent two different positions. Swift's misogyny is part of his misanthropy. As a Christian he hates human pride, or the illusion that we can rise above the sinfulness and frailty that are our nature as impure, fallen creatures; and he never misses a chance to shatter that illusion. Hence women, associated romantically with beauty and love, must be dragged down to earth and have their cosmetics rubbed off. To Swift's admirers, this is realism; to his detractors, woman-hating. His focus on bodily functions in works like *The Lady's Dressing Room* has often been ascribed to a personal fixation or frustrated desire, as in Lady Mary Wortley Montagu's counterattack. It might also be regarded as the fury of an idealist when he looks at the world as it is.

Pope was far more comfortable with illusions; when he writes about a lady's dressing room, in *The Rape of the Lock,* it sparkles with glamour. Many readers have thought he had a feminine sensibility. Despite his patronizing attitude toward "female wit"—as in the exchange with Lady Winchilsea—he certainly took a strong interest in female psychology; and his pleasure in delicate things and domestic arrangements appealed to many women. Anne Irwin and Mary Leapor argue with Pope's *Characters of Women,* but they are clearly influenced by the way he sees their world as well as by his poetic style. In this respect his satire might be thought more insidious than Swift's. The sympathy he expresses for women lends plausibility to his analysis of their flaws, and his distinctions between the sexes seem rooted in nature, not merely in custom. Thus Pope's shrewd portraits of the ways that women waste their lives can be very chilling.

Yet women could also write satire. The poets who respond to Swift and Pope poke fun at the smug assumption that men can tell women what women are thinking and feeling. Montagu's parody, one of many answers to Swift's poem, turns the tables on his disgust at the body; here the *man's* body falls short. (Some women agreed that men were Yahoos, though women were not.) Irwin suggests that Pope is the problem, not the solution: because lack of education makes all the difference between women and men, a truly good poet would devote himself to educating women, not to ridiculing faults they cannot help. Similarly, Leapor regards satire of women as blaming the victim; her characters resemble Pope's, but what dooms them is not the bad choices they make but the lack of any good choice in a man's world that turns all their dreams against them. The female satirists in this debate do not belong to any set, nor do they agree with each other's diagnoses. They do agree, however, on one main point: when the ways of women come into question, women must speak for themselves.

JONATHAN SWIFT

The Lady's Dressing Room is the first in a series of "excremental" poems in which Swift looks below the surface of women's allure. If one object of satire is the grossness of Celia, "the goddess," the romantic illusions of Strephon, her disabused lover, are far more absurd.

The Lady's Dressing Room

Five hours (and who can do it less in?)
By haughty Celia spent in dressing,
The goddess from her chamber issues,
Arrayed in lace, brocade, and tissues.
5   Strephon, who found the room was void,
And Betty otherwise employed,
Stole in, and took a strict survey
Of all the litter as it lay;
Whereof, to make the matter clear,
10 An inventory follows here.
    And first a dirty smock appeared,
Beneath the armpits well besmeared.
Strephon, the rogue, displayed it wide,
And turned it round on every side.
15 In such a case few words are best,
And Strephon bids us guess the rest;
But swears how damnably the men lie,
In calling Celia sweet and cleanly.
    Now listen while he next produces
20 The various combs for various uses,
Filled up with dirt so closely fixed,
No brush could force a way betwixt;
A paste of composition rare,
Sweat, dandruff, powder, lead, and hair;
25 A forehead cloth with oil upon't
To smooth the wrinkles on her front;
Here alum flower° to stop the steams   *styptic powder*
Exhaled from sour unsavory streams;

There night-gloves made of Tripsy's hide,
30   Bequeathed by Tripsy when she died,
With puppy water,[1] beauty's help,
Distilled from Tripsy's darling whelp;
Here gallipots° and vials placed,   *small pots*
Some filled with washes, some with paste,
35   Some with pomatum,° paints, and slops,   *pomade*
And ointments good for scabby chops.
Hard by a filthy basin stands,
Fouled with the scouring of her hands;
The basin takes whatever comes,
40   The scraping of her teeth and gums,
A nasty compound of all hues,
For here she spits, and here she spews.
    But oh! it turned poor Strephon's bowels,
When he beheld and smelt the towels,
45   Begummed, bemattered, and beslimed,
With dirt, and sweat, and earwax grimed.
No object Strephon's eye escapes;
Here petticoats in frowzy heaps,
Nor be the handkerchiefs forgot,
50   All varnished o'er with snuff and snot.
The stockings why should I expose,
Stained with the marks of stinking toes,
Or greasy coifs and pinners° reeking,   *nightcaps*
Which Celia slept at least a week in?
55   A pair of tweezers next he found
To pluck her brows in arches round,
Or hairs that sink the forehead low,
Or on her chin like bristles grow.
    The virtues we must not let pass
60   Of Celia's magnifying glass.
When frighted Strephon cast his eye on't,
It showed the visage of a giant—
A glass that can to sight disclose
The smallest worm in Celia's nose,
65   And faithfully direct her nail
To squeeze it out from head to tail;
For catch it nicely by the head,
It must come out alive or dead.
    Why Strephon will you tell the rest?
70   And must you needs describe the chest?
That careless wench! no creature warn her
To move it out from yonder corner,
But leave it standing full in sight,
For you to exercise your spite.
75   In vain the workman showed his wit
With rings and hinges counterfeit
To make it seem in this disguise
A cabinet to vulgar eyes;

---

1. A cosmetic made from the internal organs of a puppy (here from the whelp of Celia's former lapdog).

For Strephon ventured to look in,
80 Resolved to go through thick and thin;
He lifts the lid, there needs no more,
He smelt it all the time before.
    As from within Pandora's box,
When Epimetheus oped the locks,
85 A sudden universal crew
Of human evils upward flew,
He still was comforted to find
That Hope at last remained behind;[2]
So Strephon, lifting up the lid
90 To view what in the chest was hid,
The vapors flew from out the vent,
But Strephon cautious never meant
The bottom of the pan to grope,
And foul his hands in search of Hope.
95 Oh never may such vile machine
Be once in Celia's chamber seen!
Oh may she better learn to keep
"Those secrets of the hoary deep"![3]
    As mutton cutlets, prime of meat,
100 Which though with art you salt and beat,
As laws of cookery require,
And roast them at the clearest fire,
If from adown the hopeful chops
The fat upon a cinder drops,
105 To stinking smoke it turns the flame,
Poisoning the flesh from whence it came,
And thence exhales a greasy stench,
For which you curse the careless wench;
So things which must not be expressed,
110 When plumped into the reeking chest,
Send up an excremental smell
To taint the parts from which they fell,
The petticoats and gown perfume,
And waft a stink round every room.
115   Thus finishing his grand survey,
The swain disgusted slunk away,
Repeating in his amorous fits,
"Oh! Celia, Celia, Celia shits!"
    But Vengeance, goddess never sleeping,
120 Soon punished Strephon for his peeping.
His foul imagination links
Each dame he sees with all her stinks,
And, if unsavory odors fly,
Conceives a lady standing by.
125 All women his description fits,
And both ideas jump like wits,[4]

---

2. Despite the warnings of his brother Prometheus, Epimetheus married Pandora, the first woman (according to Greek mythology). When the box that Zeus had given her was opened, all evils flew out into the world, and only hope remained.
3. *Paradise Lost* 2.891.
4. Coincide; after the proverb "Good wits jump" (i.e., great minds think alike).

By vicious fancy coupled fast,
And still appearing in contrast.
   I pity wretched Strephon, blind
130 To all the charms of womankind.
Should I the queen of love refuse
Because she rose from stinking ooze?[5]
To him that looks behind the scene,
Statira's but some pocky quean.[6]
135 When Celia in her glory shows,
If Strephon would but stop his nose,
Who now so impiously blasphemes
Her ointments, daubs, and paints, and creams,
Her washes, slops, and every clout°   rag
140 With which she makes so foul a rout,
He soon would learn to think like me,
And bless his ravished eyes to see
Such order from confusion sprung,
Such gaudy tulips raised from dung.

1732

5. The goddess Venus rose out of the sea.
6. Strumpet, with a pun on Nathaniel Lee's *Rival*

Queens (1677), a play in which Statira was a heroine.

LADY MARY WORTLEY MONTAGU

Montagu did not like Swift. She objected to his politics (he worked for Tories, she was a Whig), his friendship with Pope (with whom she had bitterly quarreled), his vanity (especially at knowing important people), and his defiant indecency (which she considered not only inappropriate for a clergyman but also a sign of low breeding). Her reply to *The Lady's Dressing Room* mimics its style, but substitutes vulgar names for its mock-pastoral (Betty instead of Celia) and personal pique for its moralistic conclusions.

The Reasons That Induced Dr. Swift
to Write a Poem Called the Lady's Dressing Room

The Doctor in a clean starched band,°   *clerical collar*
His golden snuff box in his hand,
With care his diamond ring displays
And artful shows its various rays,
5 While grave he stalks down ———— Street,
His dearest Betty ———— to meet.
   Long had he waited for this hour,
Nor gained admittance to the bower,
Had joked and punned, and swore and writ,
10 Tried all his gallantry and wit,
Had told her oft what part he bore

In Oxford's[1] schemes in days of yore,
But bawdy, politics, nor satyr[2]
Could move this dull hard-hearted creature.
15 Jenny her maid could taste a rhyme
And grieved to see him lose his time,
Had kindly whispered in his ear,
"For twice two pound you enter here;
My lady vows without that sum
20 It is in vain you write or come."
    The destined offering now he brought
And in a paradise of thought
With a low bow approached the dame
Who smiling heard him preach his flame.
25 His gold she takes (such proofs as these
Convince most unbelieving shes)
And in her trunk rose up to lock it
(Too wise to trust it in her pocket)
And then, returned with blushing grace,
30 Expects the Doctor's warm embrace.
    But now this is the proper place
Where morals stare me in the face
And for the sake of fine expression
I'm forced to make a small digression.
35 Alas for wretched humankind,
With learning mad, with wisdom blind!
The ox thinks he's for saddle fit
(As long ago friend Horace writ)[3]
And men their talents still mistaking,
40 The stutterer fancies his is speaking.
With admiration oft we see
Hard features heightened by toupée,
The beau affects the politician,
Wit is the citizen's[4] ambition,
45 Poor Pope philosophy displays on
With so much rhyme and little reason,
And though he argues ne'er so long
That all is right, his head is wrong.[5]
    None strive to know their proper merit
50 But strain for wisdom, beauty, spirit,
And lose the praise that is their due
While they've the impossible in view.
So have I seen the injudicious heir
To add one window the whole house impair.
55   Instinct the hound does better teach
Who never undertook to preach;
The frighted hare from dogs does run
But not attempts to bear a gun.
Here many noble thoughts occur

---

1. Robert Harley, earl of Oxford, headed the government from 1710 to 1714.
2. Satire (pronounced *say' tir*).
3. *Epistles* 1.14.43.

4. "A townsman; a man of trade; not a gentleman" (Johnson's *Dictionary*).
5. A parody of Pope's *Essay on Man* 1.292, which had just been published.

60 But I prolixity abhor,
And will pursue the instructive tale
To show the wise in some things fail.
    The reverend lover with surprise ⎫
Peeps in her bubbies, and her eyes,   ⎬
65 And kisses both, and tries—and tries. ⎭
The evening in this hellish play,
Beside his guineas thrown away,
Provoked the priest to that degree
He swore, "The fault is not in me.
70 Your damned close stool so near my nose,
Your dirty smock, and stinking toes,
Would make a Hercules as tame
As any beau that you can name."
    The nymph grown furious roared, "By God!
75 The blame lies all in sixty odd,"
And scornful pointing to the door
Cried, "Fumbler, see my face no more."
"With all my heart I'll go away,
But nothing done, I'll nothing pay.
80 Give back the money."—"How," cried she,
"Would you palm such a cheat on me!
For poor four pound to roar and bellow,
Why sure you want some new Prunella?"[6]
"I'll be revenged, you saucy quean"°   strumpet
85 (Replies the disappointed Dean),
"I'll so describe your dressing room
The very Irish shall not come."[7]
She answered short, "I'm glad you'll write,
You'll furnish paper when I shite."

1734

6. A name for a prostitute and a worsted cloth
worn by clergymen.

7. A gibe at the supposed crassness of Irishmen
(like Swift himself).

ALEXANDER POPE

In Pope's *Rape of the Lock* (4.59–62) a gnome invokes the goddess Spleen: "Parent of vapors and of female wit, / Who give the hysteric or poetic fit, / On various tempers act by various ways, / Make some take physic, others scribble plays." Anne Finch, countess of Winchilsea, had written a well-known poem, *The Spleen*, and two plays and thus would have been justified in taking the lines as a personal attack. Instead, she defended women poets in general, as she had in *The Introduction* (p. 2291). Pope's flattering reply maintains that she is better than all other female wits and hence a lonely exception. Such arguments are typical of male poets who patronize women.

Impromptu to Lady Winchilsea

Occasioned by Four Satirical Verses on Women Wits,
in The Rape of the Lock

In vain you boast poetic dames of yore,
And cite those Sapphos[1] we admire no more;
Fate doomed the fall of every female wit,
But doomed it then when first Ardelia[2] writ.
5 Of all examples by the world confessed,
I knew Ardelia could not quote the best,
Who, like her mistress on Britannia's throne,[3]
Fights and subdues in quarrels not her own.
To write their praise you but in vain essay;
10 Even while you write, you take that praise away.
Light to the stars the sun does thus restore,
But shines himself till they are seen no more.

1714?   1741

1. The name of the Greek poet Sappho was used   2. Winchilsea's pen name.
generically for women poets.   3. Queen Anne.

ANNE FINCH, COUNTESS OF WINCHILSEA

Finch and Pope were on friendly terms; he published an abridged version of her
Answer in *Poems on Several Occasions* (1717). Like Pope's *Impromptu*, her reply mixes
flattery with irony. Playfully threatening him with retribution by women, she tops his
myth about female wits with a myth about the destruction of Orpheus, the prototypical male poet. Men make a bad mistake, she advises, when they underestimate
women's powers.

The Answer (To Pope's *Impromptu*)

Disarmed with so genteel an air,
The contest I give o'er,
Yet, Alexander! have a care,
And shock the sex no more.
5 We rule the world our life's whole race,
Men but assume that right;
First slaves to every tempting face,
Then martyrs to our spite.
You of one Orpheus sure have read,
10 Who would like you have writ
Had he in London town been bred,
And polished too his wit;

But he, poor soul, thought all was well,
    And great should be his fame,
15 When he had left his wife in Hell,
    And birds and beasts could tame.[1]
Yet venturing then with scoffing rhymes
    The women to incense,
Resenting heroines of those times
20   Soon punished his offense.
And as through Hebrus rolled his skull
    And harp besmeared with blood,
They clashing, as the waves grew full,
    Still harmonized the flood.[2]
25 But you our follies gently treat,
    And spin so fine the thread,
You need not fear his awkward fate:
    The *Lock* won't cost the head.
Our admiration you command
30   For all that's gone before;
What next we look for at your hand
    Can only raise it more.
Yet soothe the ladies, I advise,
    As me to pride you've wrought;
35 We're born to wit, but to be wise
    By admonitions taught.[3]

1717

1. Orpheus won permission to lead Eurydice, his dead wife, out of Hades, on condition that he not look back; when he did, she was lost forever. His music had power to charm not only animals but trees and stones.
2. Enraged because Orpheus had spurned them,

maenads tore him to pieces. His head and lyre floated down the Hebrus River, making music all the way.
3. This seems deliberately ambiguous: those in need of being taught might be either the ladies or Pope.

ALEXANDER POPE

Epistle 2. To a Lady is one of four poems that Pope grouped together under the title *Epistles to Several Persons* but that have usually been known by the less appropriate title *Moral Essays*. They were conceived as parts of Pope's ambitious "ethic work," of which only the first part, *An Essay on Man,* was completed. *Epistle* 1 treats the characters of men and *Epistle* 2, the characters of women. The other two epistles are concerned with the use of riches, a subject that engaged Pope's attention during the 1730s, because he distrusted the influence on private morals and public life of the rapidly growing wealth of England under the first Hanoverians.

    Epistle 2 combines two literary forms: the satire on women, and the verse letter to a particular person—here Martha Blount (1690–1763), Pope's closest female friend, whose remark in line 2 sets the theme of the poem. The first section (to line 198) sketches a portrait gallery of ladies that illustrates their inconsistency and volatility. As an amateur painter, Pope is fascinated by the problem of catching such contrary types: the affected, the soft-natured, the cunning, the whimsical, the witty, and the silly. The next part of the poem (lines 199–248) develops Pope's favorite theory of the ruling passion—the idea that each person is driven by a single irresistible desire—and argues that women are limited to two passions: love of pleasure and love of power. The final part (line 249 to the end) describes an ideal woman, good-natured, sensible, and well balanced, who is identified with Blount herself.

Like every satire on women, *Epistle* 2 is shaped by stereotypes: women are fickle, frail, and subordinate to men. Yet much of the poem undermines those prejudices by showing the real difficulties of women's lives. "By man's oppression cursed," they waste their talents on trivial pursuits and "die of nothing but a rage to live." The poem shares that restlessness. If women are full of contradictions, so are Pope's couplets, torn between sympathy and satiric bite. The poet finds himself strangely attracted to what he disapproves, and many female readers, then and now, have felt the same way about the poem.

Epistle 2. To a Lady

Of the Characters of Women

Nothing so true as what you once let fall,
"Most women have no characters at all."
Matter too soft a lasting mark to bear,
And best distinguished by black, brown, or fair.

5   How many pictures[1] of one nymph we view,
All how unlike each other, all how true!
Arcadia's countess, here, in ermined pride,
Is, there, Pastora by a fountain side.
Here Fannia, leering on her own good man,

10 And there, a naked Leda with a swan.[2]
Let then the fair one beautifully cry,
In Magdalen's loose hair and lifted eye,
Or dressed in smiles of sweet Cecilia shine,[3]
With simpering angels, palms, and harps divine;

15 Whether the charmer sinner it, or saint it,
If folly grow romantic,° I must paint it.   *extravagant*
    Come then, the colors and the ground[4] prepare!
Dip in the rainbow, trick° her off in air;   *sketch*
Choose a firm cloud, before it fall, and in it

20 Catch, ere she change, the Cynthia[5] of this minute.
    Rufa, whose eye quick-glancing o'er the park,
Attracts each light gay meteor of a spark,°   *beau*
Agrees as ill with Rufa studying Locke,
As Sappho's diamonds with her dirty smock,

25 Or Sappho at her toilet's greasy task,[6]
With Sappho fragrant at an evening masque:
So morning insects that in muck begun,
Shine, buzz, and flyblow[7] in the setting sun.

---

1. Ladies of the 17th and 18th centuries were often painted in the costumes and attitudes of fanciful, mythological, or historical characters.
2. Leda was seduced by Zeus, who approached her in the form of a swan.
3. St. Mary Magdalen and St. Cecilia were often painted in the manner described.
4. The first coatings of paint on the canvas before the figures in the picture are sketched in.
5. One of the names of Diana, goddess of the moon, a notoriously changeable heavenly body.
6. Lady Mary Wortley Montagu, although beautiful as a young woman, became notorious for her slatternly appearance and personal uncleanliness. Both Sappho and Montagu were poets.
7. Deposit their eggs.

How soft is Silia! fearful to offend,
30   The frail one's advocate, the weak one's friend:
To her, Calista proved her conduct nice,
And good Simplicius asks of her advice.
Sudden, she storms! she raves! You tip the wink,
But spare your censure; Silia does not drink.
35   All eyes may see from what the change arose,
All eyes may see—a pimple on her nose.
          Papillia,[8] wedded to her amorous spark,
Sighs for the shades—"How charming is a park!"
A park is purchased, but the fair he sees
40   All bathed in tears—"Oh, odious, odious trees!"
          Ladies, like variegated tulips, show;
'Tis to their changes half their charms we owe;
Their happy spots the nice admirer take,
Fine by defect, and delicately weak.
45   'Twas thus Calypso[9] once each heart alarmed,
Awed without virtue, without beauty charmed;
Her tongue bewitched as oddly as her eyes,
Less wit than mimic, more a wit than wise;
Strange graces still, and stranger flights she had,
50   Was just not ugly, and was just not mad;
Yet ne'er so sure your passion to create,
As when she touched the brink of all we hate.
          Narcissa's[1] nature, tolerably mild,
To make a wash,° would hardly stew a child;   cosmetic lotion
55   Has even been proved to grant a lover's prayer,
And paid a tradesman once to make him stare,
Gave alms at Easter, in a Christian trim,
And made a widow happy, for a whim.
Why then declare good nature is her scorn,
60   When 'tis by that alone she can be borne?
Why pique all mortals, yet affect a name?
A fool to pleasure, yet a slave to fame:
Now deep in Taylor and the *Book of Martyrs*,[2]
Now drinking citron with his Grace and Chartres.[3]
65   Now conscience chills her, and now passion burns;
And atheism and religion take their turns;
A very heathen in the carnal part,
Yet still a sad, good Christian at her heart.
          See Sin in state, majestically drunk;

8. The name comes from Latin for "butterfly."
9. The name is borrowed from the fascinating god-dess who detained Odysseus on her island for seven years after the fall of Troy, thus preventing his return to his kingdom, Ithaca.
1. Type of extreme self-love. Narcissus, a beautiful youth, fell in love with his own image when he saw it reflected in a fountain.
2. John Foxe's *Acts and Monuments*, usually referred to as Foxe's *Book of Martyrs*, was a house-hold book in most Protestant families in the 17th and 18th centuries. A record of the Protestants

who perished for their faith under the persecution of Mary Tudor (1553–58), it was instrumental in keeping anti-Catholic sentiments alive. Jeremy Taylor, 17th-century Anglican divine, whose *Holy Living and Holy Dying* was often reprinted in the 18th century.
3. Francis Chartres was a debauchee often men-tioned by Pope. "His Grace" is usually said to be the duke of Wharton, an old enemy of Swift's and a notorious libertine. "Citron": citron water, brandy flavored with lemon or orange peels.

70 Proud as a peeress, prouder as a punk;°   *harlot*
    Chaste to her husband, frank° to all beside,   *licentious*
    A teeming mistress, but a barren bride.
    What then? let blood and body bear the fault,
    Her head's untouched, that noble seat of thought:
75 Such this day's doctrine—in another fit
    She sins with poets through pure love of wit.
    What has not fired her bosom or her brain?
    Caesar and Tallboy, Charles[4] and Charlemagne.
    As Helluo,[5] late dictator of the feast,
80 The nose of hautgout,[6] and the tip of taste,
    Criticked your wine, and analyzed your meat,
    Yet on plain pudding deigned at home to eat;
    So Philomedé,[7] lecturing all mankind
    On the soft passion, and the taste refined,
85 The address, the delicacy—stoops at once,
    And makes her hearty meal upon a dunce.
        Flavia's a wit, has too much sense to pray;
    To toast our wants and wishes, is her way;
    Nor asks of God, but of her stars, to give
90 The mighty blessing, "while we live, to live."
    Then all for death, that opiate of the soul!
    Lucretia's dagger, Rosamonda's bowl.[8]
    Say, what can cause such impotence of mind?
    A spark too fickle, or a spouse too kind.
95 Wise wretch! with pleasures too refined to please,
    With too much spirit to be e'er at ease,
    With too much quickness ever to be taught,
    With too much thinking to have common thought:
    You purchase pain with all that joy can give,
100 And die of nothing but a rage to live.
        Turn then from wits; and look on Simo's mate,
    No ass so meek, no ass so obstinate:
    Or her, that owns her faults, but never mends,
    Because she's honest, and the best of friends:
105 Or her, whose life the Church and scandal share,
    Forever in a passion, or a prayer:
    Or her, who laughs at hell, but (like her Grace)
    Cries, "Ah! how charming, if there's no such place!"
    Or who in sweet vicissitude appears
110 Of mirth and opium, ratafie[9] and tears,
    The daily anodyne, and nightly draught,
    To kill those foes to fair ones, time and thought.

---

4. "Charles," as F. W. Bateson points out, was a generic name for a footman in the period. "Tall-boy": a crude young man in Richard Brome's comedy *The Jovial Crew* (1641) or the opera adapted from the play (1731).
5. Glutton (Latin).
6. "Anything with a strong relish or strong scent, as overkept venison" (Johnson's *Dictionary*).
7. The name is Pope's adaptation of a Greek epi-

thet meaning "laughter-loving," frequently applied to Aphrodite, the goddess of love.
8. According to tradition, the "fair Rosamonda," mistress of Henry II, was forced by Queen Eleanor to drink poison. Lucretia, violated by Tarquin, committed suicide.
9. "A fine liquor, prepared from the kernels of apricots and spirits" (Johnson's *Dictionary*).

Woman and fool are two hard things to hit,
For true no-meaning puzzles more than wit.
But what are these to great Atossa's[1] mind?
Scarce once herself, by turns all womankind!
Who, with herself, or others, from her birth
Finds all her life one warfare upon earth:
Shines in exposing knaves, and painting fools,
Yet is whate'er she hates and ridicules.
No thought advances, but her eddy brain
Whisks it about, and down it goes again.
Full sixty years the world has been her trade,
The wisest fool much time has ever made.
From loveless youth to unrespected age,
No passion gratified except her rage.
So much the fury still outran the wit,
The pleasure missed her, and the scandal hit.
Who breaks with her, provokes revenge from hell,
But he's a bolder man who dares be well:[2]
Her every turn with violence pursued,
Nor more a storm her hate than gratitude:
To that each passion turns, or soon or late;
Love, if it makes her yield, must make her hate:
Superiors? death! and equals? what a curse!
But an inferior not dependent? worse.
Offend her, and she knows not to forgive;
Oblige her, and she'll hate you while you live:
But die, and she'll adore you—Then the bust
And temple rise—then fall again to dust.
Last night, her lord was all that's good and great;
A knave this morning, and his will a cheat.
Strange! by the means defeated of the ends,
By spirit robbed of power, by warmth of friends,
By wealth of followers! without one distress
Sick of herself through very selfishness!
Atossa, cursed with every granted prayer,
Childless with all her children, wants an heir.
To heirs unknown descends the unguarded store,
Or wanders, Heaven-directed, to the poor.
Pictures like these, dear Madam, to design,
Asks no firm hand, and no unerring line;
Some wandering touches, some reflected light,
Some flying stroke alone can hit 'em right:
For how should equal colors do the knack?[3]
Chameleons who can paint in white and black?
"Yet Chloe sure was formed without a spot—"
Nature in her then erred not, but forgot.
"With every pleasing, every prudent part,
Say, what can Chloe want?"—She wants a heart.
She speaks, behaves, and acts just as she ought;

1. Atossa, daughter of Cyrus, emperor of Persia (d. 529 B.C.E.). If the duchess of Buckinghamshire is alluded to, the name is appropriate, for she was the natural daughter of James II.
2. Be in her favor.
3. Do the trick.

But never, never, reached one generous thought.
Virtue she finds too painful an endeavor,
Content to dwell in decencies forever.
165 So very reasonable, so unmoved,
As never yet to love, or to be loved.
She, while her lover pants upon her breast,
Can mark⁴ the figures on an Indian chest;
And when she sees her friend in deep despair,
170 Observes how much a chintz exceeds mohair.
Forbid it Heaven, a favor or a debt
She e'er should cancel—but she may forget.
Safe is your secret still in Chloe's ear;
But none of Chloe's shall you ever hear.
175 Of all her dears she never slandered one,
But cares not if a thousand are undone.
Would Chloe know if you're alive or dead?
She bids her footman put it in her head.
Chloe is prudent—Would you too be wise?
180 Then never break your heart when Chloe dies.
   One certain portrait may (I grant) be seen,
Which Heaven has varnished out, and made a *Queen:*⁵
The same forever! and described by all
With truth and goodness, as with crown and ball.
185 Poets heap virtues, painters gems at will,
And show their zeal, and hide their want of skill.
'Tis well—but, artists! who can paint or write,
To draw the naked is your true delight.
That robe of quality so struts and swells,
190 None see what parts of Nature it conceals:
The exactest traits of body or of mind,
We owe to models of an humble kind.
If Queensberry⁶ to strip there's no compelling,
'Tis from a handmaid we must take a Helen.
195 From peer or bishop 'tis no easy thing
To draw the man who loves his God, or king:
Alas! I copy (or my draft would fail)
From honest Mah'met or plain Parson Hale.⁷
   But grant, in public men sometimes are shown,
200 A woman's seen in private life alone:
Our bolder talents in full light displayed;
Your virtues open fairest in the shade.
Bred to disguise, in public 'tis you hide;
There, none distinguish 'twixt your shame or pride,
205 Weakness or delicacy; all so nice,
That each may seem a virtue, or a vice.
   In men, we various ruling passions find;
In women, two almost divide the kind;

---

4. Pay attention to.
5. Pope refers as usual to Queen Caroline with disapprobation.
6. The duchess of Queensberry, whom Pope valued because of her kindness to his friend John Gay,

had been a famous beauty.
7. Dr. Stephen Hales, an Anglican clergyman and friend of Pope. Mahomet was a Turkish servant of George I.

Those, only fixed, they first or last obey,
210   The love of pleasure, and the love of sway.
     That, Nature gives; and where the lesson taught
Is but to please, can pleasure seem a fault?
Experience, this; by man's oppression cursed,
They seek the second not to lose the first.
215   Men, some to business, some to pleasure take;
But every woman is at heart a rake;
Men, some to quiet, some to public strife;
But every lady would be queen for life.
     Yet mark the fate of a whole sex of queens!
220   Power all their end, but beauty all the means:
In youth they conquer, with so wild a rage,
As leaves them scarce a subject in their age:
For foreign glory, foreign joy, they roam;
No thought of peace or happiness at home.
225   But wisdom's triumph is well-timed retreat,
As hard a science to the fair as great!
Beauties, like tyrants, old and friendless grown,
Yet hate repose, and dread to be alone,
Worn out in public, weary every eye,
230   Nor leave one sigh behind them when they die.
     Pleasures the sex, as children birds, pursue,
Still out of reach, yet never out of view,
Sure, if they catch, to spoil the toy at most,
To covet flying, and regret when lost:
235   At last, to follies youth could scarce defend,
It grows their age's prudence to pretend;
Ashamed to own they gave delight before,
Reduced to feign it, when they give no more:
As hags hold sabbaths, less for joy than spite,
240   So these their merry, miserable night;[8]
Still round and round the ghosts of beauty glide,
And haunt the places where their honor died.
     See how the world its veterans rewards!
A youth of frolics, an old age of cards;
245   Fair to no purpose, artful to no end,
Young without lovers, old without a friend;
A fop their passion, but their prize a sot;
Alive, ridiculous, and dead, forgot!
     Ah friend! to dazzle let the vain design;
250   To raise the thought, and touch the heart be thine!
That charm shall grow, while what fatigues the Ring[9]
Flaunts and goes down, an unregarded thing:
So when the sun's broad beam has tired the sight,
All mild ascends the moon's more sober light,
255   Serene in virgin modesty she shines,
And unobserved the glaring orb declines.

---

8. I.e., evenings on which ladies entertained guests. "Sabbaths": obscene rites popularly supposed to be held by witches ("hags").
9. The fashionable drive in Hyde Park.

  Oh! blest with temper, whose unclouded ray
  Can make tomorrow cheerful as today;
  She, who can love a sister's charms, or hear
260 Sighs for a daughter with unwounded ear;
  She, who ne'er answers till a husband cools,
  Or, if she rules him, never shows she rules;
  Charms by accepting, by submitting sways,
  Yet has her humor most, when she obeys;
265 Lets fops or fortune fly which way they will;
  Disdains all loss of tickets° or Codille;[1]   *lottery tickets*
  Spleen, vapors, or smallpox, above them all,
  And mistress of herself, though China[2] fall.
   And yet, believe me, good as well as ill,
270 Woman's at best a contradiction still.
  Heaven, when it strives to polish all it can
  Its last best work, but forms a softer man;
  Picks from each sex, to make the favorite blest,
  Your love of pleasure, our desire of rest:
275 Blends, in exception to all general rules,
  Your taste of follies, with our scorn of fools:
  Reserve with frankness, art with truth allied,
  Courage with softness, modesty with pride;
  Fixed principles, with fancy ever new;
280 Shakes all together, and produces—you.
   Be this a woman's fame: with this unblest,
  Toasts live a scorn, and queens may die a jest.
  This Phoebus promised (I forget the year)
  When those blue eyes first opened on the sphere;
285 Ascendant Phoebus watched that hour with care,
  Averted half your parents' simple prayer;
  And gave you beauty, but denied the pelf
  That buys your sex a tyrant o'er itself.
  The generous god, who wit and gold refines,
290 And ripens spirits as he ripens mines,[3]
  Kept dross for duchesses, the world shall know it,
  To you gave sense, good humor, and a poet.

1735, 1744

---

1. The loss of a hand at the card games of ombre or quadrille.
2. Pope refers punningly to the chinaware that fashionable women collected enthusiastically.

3. Phoebus Apollo, as god of poetry "ripens wit"; as god of the sun, he "ripens mines," for respectable scientific theory held that the sun's rays mature precious metals in the earth.

ANNE INGRAM, VISCOUNTESS IRWIN

Lady Anne Howard (ca. 1696–1764) was raised on the Yorkshire estate of her father, third earl of Carlisle; many years later she paid tribute to it and him in a poem, *Castle Howard* (1732). In 1717 she married Richard Ingram, fifth Viscount Irwin; and after he died of smallpox in 1721, she mourned him so long that she was reproached for it in verse by Lady Mary Wortley Montagu. Although the two women were friends, Irwin said that Montagu's "principles are as corrupt as her wit is entertaining"; and Montagu, who liked Irwin's good nature, was also amused by her "vanity and false pretensions." Irwin showed her independence by traveling alone in Holland and France in 1730. Later she served the princess of Wales as a lady-in-waiting, but court life did not satisfy her; Pope's and Addison's works were "antidotes to preserve me from the contagion." In 1737, against the strong opposition of her family, she married Colonel William Douglas; he died in 1748. A young woman who knew her afterward was impressed by her learning and wit: "she wrote poetry, and every body was afraid of her." She died, in 1764, after a party at cards.

An Epistle to Mr. Pope reveals Irwin's keen attention to Pope's work as a whole, not only to his *Characters of Women;* it turns his verse technique as well as many of his principles against him. The sharp antithesis he draws between men and women, as distinct as the two lines of a heroic couplet, is shown to be artificial. In fact both sexes, she argues, want the same thing: love of power motivates them both. If women often trifle away their lives, the reason is poor education; not even Pope has taught them how to live. Irwin provides some positive models. Addressing Pope as an equal, in verse much like his own, she proves that men and women can think alike.

An Epistle to Mr. Pope,

Occasioned by *his* Characters of Women

Nec rude quid prosit video ingenium.[1]

> By custom doomed to folly, sloth and ease,
> No wonder Pope such female triflers sees.
> But would the satirist confess the truth,
> Nothing so like as male and female youth,
> 5 Nothing so like as man and woman old,
> Their joys, their loves, their hates, if truly told.
> Though different acts seem different sex's growth,
> 'Tis the same principle impels them both.
>   View daring men stung with ambition's fire,
> 10 The conquering hero, or the youthful 'squire,
> By different deeds aspire to deathless fame,
> One murthers° man, the other murthers game.   *murders*
> View a fair nymph blest with superior charms,
> Whose tempting form the coldest bosom warms;
> 15 No eastern monarch more despotic reigns
> Than this fair tyrant of the Cyprian plains.[2]
> Whether a crown or bauble we desire,
> Whether to learning or to dress aspire,
> Whether we wait with joy the trumpet's call,
> 20 Or wish to shine the fairest at a ball,
> In either sex the appetite's the same,
> For love of power is still° the love of fame.[3]   *always*
> Women must in a narrow orbit move,

1. Nor can I see what good can come from untrained talent (Latin; Horace's *Art of Poetry* 410).

2. Love. Aphrodite was worshipped on Cyprus.

3. Cf. Pope's *Epistle* 2, lines 207–10.

But power alike both males and females love.
25   What makes the difference then, you may inquire,
Between the hero and the rural 'squire,
Between the maid bred up with courtly care,
Or she who earns by toil her daily fare?
Their power is stinted, but not so their will;
30 Ambitious thoughts the humblest cottage fill;
Far as they can they push their little fame,
And try to leave behind a deathless name.
In education all the difference lies;
Women, if taught, would be as bold and wise
35 As haughty man, improved by art and rules;
Where God makes one, neglect makes twenty fools.
And though *Nugatrixes*° are daily found,   *female triflers*
Flutt'ring *Nugators*° equally abound;   *male triflers*
Such heads are toyshops,[4] filled with trifling ware,
40 And can each folly with each female share.
    A female mind like a rude fallow lies;
No seed is sown, but weeds spontaneous rise.
As well might we expect, in winter, spring,
As land untilled a fruitful crop should bring;
45 As well might we expect Peruvian ore
We should possess, yet dig not for the store.
Culture° improves all fruits, all sorts we find,   *cultivation, tillage*
Wit, judgment, sense—fruits of the human mind.
    Ask the rich merchant, conversant in trade,
50 How nature operates in the growing blade;
Ask the philosopher the price of stocks,
Ask the gay courtier how to manage flocks;
Inquire the dogmas of the learned schools
(From Aristotle down to Newton's rules),
55 Of the rough soldier, bred to boisterous war,
Or one still rougher, a true British tar:
They'll all reply, unpracticed in such laws,
The effect they know, though ignorant of the cause.
The sailor may perhaps have equal parts°   *abilities*
60 With him bred up to sciences and arts;
And he who at the helm or stern is seen,
Philosopher or hero might have been.
The whole in application is comprised,
Reason's not reason, if not exercised;
65 Use, not possession, real good affords;
No miser's rich that dares not touch his hoards.
    Can female youth, left to weak woman's care,
Misled by custom (folly's fruitful heir),
Told that their charms a monarch may enslave,
70 That beauty like the gods can kill or save;
Taught the arcanas,[5] the mysterious art
By ambush dress to catch unwary hearts;

---

4. See Pope's *Rape of the Lock* 1.100 (p. 2529).
5. Profound secrets, as in alchemy. *Arcana* is the

plural of the Latin *arcanum,* but some English
writers added an *s.*

If wealthy born, taught to lisp French and dance,
Their morals left (Lucretius-like) to chance;[6]
75 Strangers to reason and reflection made,
Left to their passions, and by them betrayed;
Untaught the noble end of glorious truth,
Bred to deceive even from their earliest youth;
Unused to books, nor virtue taught to prize;
80 Whose mind a savage waste unpeopled lies,
Which to supply, trifles fill up the void,
And idly busy, to no end employed—
Can these, from such a school, more virtue show,
Or tempting vice treat like a common foe?
85 Can they resist, when soothing pleasure woos;
Preserve their virtue, when their fame° they lose?   reputation
Can they on other themes converse or write,
Than what they hear all day, and dream all night?
Not so the Roman female fame was spread;
90 Not so was Clelia, or Lucretia bred;
Not so such heroines true glory sought;
Not so was Portia, or Cornelia[7] taught.
Portia! the glory of the female race;
Portia! more lovely by her mind than face.
95 Early informed by truth's unerring beam,
What to reject, what justly to esteem.
Taught by philosophy all moral good,
How to repel in youth the impetuous blood,
How her most favorite passions to subdue,
100 And fame through virtue's avenues pursue,
She tries herself, and finds even dolorous pain
Can't the close secret from her breast obtain.
To Cato born, to noble Brutus joined,
She shines invincible in form and mind.
105   No more such generous sentiments we trace
In the gay moderns of the female race,
No more, alas! heroic virtue's shown;
Since knowledge ceased, philosophy's unknown.
No more can we expect our modern wives
110 Heroes should breed, who lead such useless lives.
Would you, who know the arcana of the soul,
The secret springs which move and guide the whole,
Would you, who can instruct as well as please,
Bestow some moments of your darling ease,
115 To rescue woman from this Gothic[8] state,
New passions raise, their minds anew create,

6. The Roman poet Lucretius was known as a materialist and atheist who taught that everything in the world results from the chance convergence of atoms.
7. Famous Roman paragons of virtue. Clelia (or Cloelia), given as a hostage to an enemy, Lars Porsenna, escaped to Rome by swimming the Tiber and was later set free by Porsenna for her bravery. Lucretia was raped by a son of King Tarquin and

committed suicide, kindling a revolt that overthrew the Tarquins. Portia, the daughter of Cato and wife of Brutus, stabbed herself in the thigh to prove she was strong enough to keep her husband's secrets. Cornelia, mother of the Gracchi, was a model of maternal self-sacrifice.
8. Barbaric, as opposed to Greek or Roman. Cf. Pope's Essay on Criticism 3.692 (p. 2524).

> Then for the Spartan virtue[9] we might hope;
> For who stands unconvinced by generous Pope?
> Then would the British fair perpetual bloom,
120 And vie in fame with ancient Greece and Rome.

1736

9. Spartan women were known for their courage and contempt of pleasure.

MARY LEAPOR

A gardener's daughter, Leapor (1722–1746) spent her short life in or near the small town of Brackley in Northamptonshire. When she was ten or eleven "she would often be scribbling," and poetry turned into a consuming interest. One of her poems describes her sitting "whole evenings, reading wicked plays" by candlelight; according to another, she lost employment as a cook-maid because she would not stop writing, even in the kitchen. Passed around the neighborhood, her verse impressed Bridget Freemantle, the daughter of a former Oxford don; she became Leapor's best friend and mentor. Together they planned to publish Leapor's work. A play was sent to Colley Cibber, the impresario and poet laureate, but it was returned stained by wine. Leapor's health was rarely good, and she died of measles at twenty-four; she had never seen any of her poems in print. But Freemantle arranged an edition of Leapor's *Poems upon Several Occasions* (1748), with six hundred subscribers, and it was warmly received. Samuel Richardson admired the "sweetly easy poems" so much that he published a second volume; later, William Cowper thought they showed "more marks of a true poetical talent than I remember to have observed in the verses of any, whether male or female, so disadvantageously circumstanced." Recently Leapor's work has attracted renewed attention for its wit and skill as well its sharp observations about the life of a working-class woman.

The preface to Leapor's *Poems* reports that "the author she most admired was Mr. Pope, whom she chiefly endeavored to imitate." *An Essay on Woman*, like Irwin's epistle, reflects careful study of the *Characters of Women*. But its view of female predicaments is very much darker. If women are living contradictions, as Pope had asserted, the reason is that whatever they are and whatever they do can be turned against them. Beauty will be betrayed, wit will be shunned, and the pursuit of wealth will shrink the soul. Nor is education a practical solution: wisdom makes women envious and men resentful. Leapor's own situation gives her satire bite. As a gardener's daughter, she knows that cultivating the flower of womanhood costs money and does not last; as someone witty, poor, infirm, and unattractive, she sees through romantic myths. But despite its stress on the softness and weakness of women, the verse is strong. This poet never stops fighting against the traps in which she is caught.

An Essay on Woman

> WOMAN—a pleasing but a short-lived flower,
> Too soft for business and too weak for power:
> A wife in bondage, or neglected maid;
> Despised if ugly; if she's fair—betrayed.
> 5 'Tis wealth alone inspires every grace,

And calls the raptures to her plenteous[1] face.
What numbers for those charming features pine,
If blooming acres[2] round her temples twine?
Her lip the strawberry, and her eyes more bright
10 Than sparkling Venus in a frosty night;
Pale lilies fade and, when the fair appears,
Snow turns a negro[3] and dissolves in tears,
And where the charmer treads her magic toe,
On English ground Arabian odors grow;
15 Till mighty Hymen[4] lifts his sceptred rod,
And sinks her glories with a fatal nod,
Dissolves her triumphs, sweeps her charms away,
And turns the goddess to her native clay.
But, Artemisia,[5] let your servant sing
20 What small advantage wealth and beauties bring.
Who would be wise, that knew Pamphilia's fate?
Or who be fair, and joined to Sylvia's mate?
Sylvia, whose cheeks are fresh as early day,
As evening mild, and sweet as spicy May;
25 And yet that face her partial husband tires,
And those bright eyes, that all the world admires.
Pamphilia's wit who does not strive to shun,
Like death's infection or a dog-day's sun?
The damsels view her with malignant eyes,
30 The men are vexed to find a nymph so wise,
And wisdom only serves to make her know
The keen sensation of superior woe.
The secret whisper and the listening ear,
The scornful eyebrow and the hated sneer,
35 The giddy censures of her babbling kind,
With thousand ills that grate a gentle mind,
By her are tasted in the first degree,
Though overlooked by Simplicus and me.
Does thirst of gold a virgin's heart inspire,
40 Instilled by nature or a careful sire?
Then let her quit extravagance and play,
The brisk companion and expensive tea,
To feast with Cordia in her filthy sty
On stewed potatoes or on mouldy pie;
45 Whose eager eyes stare ghastly at the poor,
And fright the beggars from the hated door;
In greasy clouts she wraps her smoky chin,
And holds that pride's a never-pardoned sin.
    If this be wealth, no matter where it falls;
50 But save, ye Muses, save your Mira's[6] walls:
Still give me pleasing indolence and ease,
A fire to warm me and a friend to please.

1. Not only blooming but wealthy.
2. Not only hair but property.
3. Black, when set against the fair one's skin. The hyperbolic comparisons throughout this passage are intentionally ironic, as in Shakespeare's Sonnet 130.
4. The god of marriage.
5. Bridget Freemantle, given the name of an ancient patron of the arts.
6. Leapor's pen name.

Since, whether sunk in avarice or pride,
A wanton virgin or a starving bride,
55 Or wondering crowds attend her charming tongue,
Or deemed an idiot, ever speaks the wrong;
Though nature armed us for the growing ill
With fraudful cunning and a headstrong will,
Yet, with ten thousand follies to her charge,
60 Unhappy woman's but a slave at large.

1751

JOHN GAY
1685–1732

The career of John Gay encompasses most of the ways that a talented but indigent writer of the early eighteenth century could try to make a living: publication, patronage, odd jobs at court, and the theater. After a good education at school in Devon, he went to London at seventeen to try his luck as apprentice to a dealer in silks. Five years later he became secretary to a friend from school, the writer and entrepreneur Aaron Hill, who introduced him to the publishing world and literary circles. Eventually, leading authors in London adopted Gay as a favorite; with Pope, Swift, Arbuthnot, and Thomas Parnell, he founded the Scriblerus Club, famous for its literary satires and practical jokes. Friends like these helped him obtain the patrons and political appointments that supported him. The same Scriblerian influence shaped the mixture of high Virgilian style and rustic humor in his first successful poem, *The Shepherd's Week* (1714), a burlesque pastoral. Here and in his other verse Gay shows off his own special gifts: lightness of touch, a keen eye for homely details, and an irony that exposes the disparity between high poetic expectations and the coarse reality of the way people live. Two years later a mock georgic, *Trivia, or the Art of Walking the Streets of London,* revealed that the town could be as rough as the country, and far more corrupting. Gay's hopes for affluence were blasted by the collapse of South Sea stock in 1721. His popularity and financial security rose to new heights, however, with the phenomenal success of his verse *Fables* (1727; a second set was published posthumously in 1738) and above all *The Beggar's Opera* (1728), which made him rich. But he did not enjoy his prosperity for long. A sequel, *Polly* (1729), was banned from the stage by Walpole; and although the printed version sold very well, the tension may have precipitated the illness that led a few years later to his death.

Audiences have always loved *The Beggar's Opera.* Nothing quite like it had ever been seen on the London stage; when Congreve read the script, he said "It would either take greatly, or be damned confoundedly." On opening night, according to Pope, Gay's friends were anxious, "till we were very much encouraged by overhearing the Duke of Argyle, who sat in the next box to us, say, 'It will do—it must do! I see it in the eyes of them.'" The Duke was right. The play quickly became the talk of the town, it ran for a record sixty-two performances, and during the rest of the century it kept being revived. At first the shock of pleasure must have been sparked by daring thrusts at people and things in the news. Italian opera is one obvious target. Although it was preposterously artificial and costly, with lavish scenery and imported stars, opera had been the rage of fashionable London. Now Gay turned the music over to

beggars, or actors playing thieves and whores, and gave them popular British tunes
to sing instead of showy foreign arias.

On this stage, moreover, the underworld rose to the surface. Crime was a constant,
brutal threat in early eighteenth-century London, and stories about notorious criminals (such as Moll Flanders) poured from the press. In the corrupt legal system, which
rewarded racketeers for informing on (or "peaching") less powerful felons, the line
between those who broke the law and those who enforced it was often smudged.
Jonathan Wild, the "Thief-Taker General of Great Britain and Ireland," became rich
and famous by manipulating this system (before the executioner caught up with him);
he serves as a model for Peachum. By comparison, a forthright highwayman and killer
like Macheath might seem rather gallant. But the electricity of the play comes from
its superimposition of these criminals on heads of state, especially the prime minister,
Robert Walpole. Playgoers recognized Walpole everywhere. In Act 2, scene 10, for
instance, when Peachum and Lockit argue and conspire—"like great statesmen, we
encourage those who betray their friends"—the audience roared at the allusion to
Walpole and Lord Townshend, his ally and brother-in-law (at an early performance,
Walpole himself is said to have won over the crowd by calling for an encore). Spectators saw a picture of their own times on the stage: a society driven by greed, where
everything, including justice and love, was for sale.

Yet *The Beggar's Opera* has lasted beyond its age. The parallel between high life
and low life turned out to be more than a trick; it still rings true when audiences
reflect on those who hold power today. Brecht's and Weill's famous *Threepenny Opera*
adapted Gay's story to the sinister conditions of Germany in the 1920s; gang lords,
fascists, and capitalistic bosses all seem the same. Little people go to jail, the high
ones get away. That worldly and cynical message, seasoned with wit, continues to
make sense to people who compare their ideals of government, society, and law to
things as they are.

Pope's epitaph on Gay, inscribed in Westminster Abbey, begins this way:

> Of manners gentle, of affections mild;
> In wit, a man; simplicity, a child;
> With native humor tempering virtuous rage,
> Formed to delight at once and lash the age.

But Gay's own epitaph is far less pious.

> Life is a jest, and all things show it;
> I thought so once, but now I know it.

The Beggar's Opera

DRAMATIS PERSONAE[1]

Men

PEACHUM	ROBIN OF BAGSHOT
LOCKIT	NIMMING NED
MACHEATH	HARRY PADDINGTON
FILCH	MATT OF THE MINT

1. The names of characters reflect their trades.
Peachum ("peach 'em") is an informer, Lockit a
jailer, Macheath a "son of the heath" or highwayman, Twitcher and Diver pickpockets, Nimming
Ned a thief, Budge a burglar, Trull and Doxy harlots. Dreary ("gory") suggests a cutthroat; Bagshot
Heath was known for highway robberies; Paddington ("pad," a highwayman) was where criminals
were hanged; the Mint was a sanctuary for outlaws.
Trapes and Slammekin are slatterns.

JEMMY TWITCHER   BEN BUDGE
CROOK-FINGERED JACK   BEGGAR
WAT DREARY   PLAYER
CONSTABLES, DRAWER, TURNKEY, ETC.

Women

MRS. PEACHUM	MRS. VIXEN
POLLY PEACHUM	BETTY DOXY
LUCY LOCKIT	JENNY DIVER
DIANA TRAPES	MRS. SLAMMEKIN
MRS. COAXER	SUKY TAWDRY
DOLLY TRULL	MOLLY BRAZEN

Introduction

BEGGAR, PLAYER

BEGGAR   If poverty be a title to poetry, I am sure nobody can dispute mine. I own myself of the Company of Beggars; and I make one at their weekly festivals at St. Giles's. I have a small yearly salary for my catches,[2] and am welcome to a dinner there whenever I please, which is more than most poets can say.

PLAYER   As we live by the Muses, 'tis but gratitude in us to encourage poetical merit wherever we find it. The Muses, contrary to all other ladies, pay no distinction to dress, and never partially mistake the pertness of embroidery for wit, nor the modesty of want for dullness. Be the author who he will, we push his play as far as it will go. So (though you are in want) I wish you success heartily.

BEGGAR   This piece I own was originally writ for the celebrating the marriage of James Chanter and Moll Lay, two most excellent ballad singers. I have introduced the similes that are in all your celebrated operas: the swallow, the moth, the bee, the ship, the flower, etc. Besides, I have a prison scene, which the ladies always reckon charmingly pathetic. As to the parts, I have observed such a nice impartiality to our two ladies, that it is impossible for either of them to take offense.[3] I hope I may be forgiven, that I have not made my opera throughout unnatural, like those in vogue; for I have no recitative.[4] Excepting this, as I have consented to have neither prologue nor epilogue, it must be allowed an opera in all its forms. The piece indeed hath been heretofore frequently represented by ourselves in our great room at St. Giles's, so that I cannot too often acknowledge your charity in bringing it now on the stage.

PLAYER   But I see 'tis time for us to withdraw; the actors are preparing to begin. Play away the overture.

[*Exeunt.*]

---

2. Rounds, in which one singer follows or chases the words of another. St. Giles was a slum named after the patron saint of beggars and lepers.
3. Two famous divas, Faustina and Cuzzoni, had recently feuded on stage.
4. Operatic declamation, midway between singing and speaking.

Act 1

SCENE 1 *Peachum's house*

PEACHUM *sitting at a table with a large book of accounts before him.*

AIR 1.   An old woman clothed in gray[5]

Through all the employments of life
Each neighbor abuses his brother;
Whore and rogue they call husband and wife;
All professions be-rogue one another.
The priest calls the lawyer a cheat,
The lawyer be-knaves the divine;
And the statesman, because he's so great,
Thinks his trade as honest as mine.

A lawyer is an honest employment, so is mine. Like me too he acts in a double capacity, both against rogues and for 'em; for 'tis but fitting that we should protect and encourage cheats, since we live by them.

SCENE 2

PEACHUM, FILCH

FILCH   Sir, Black Moll hath sent word her trial comes on in the afternoon, and she hopes you will order matters so as to bring her off.

PEACHUM   Why, she may plead her belly[6] at worst; to my knowledge she hath taken care of that security. But as the wench is very active and industrious, you may satisfy her that I'll soften the evidence.

FILCH   Tom Gagg, sir, is found guilty.

PEACHUM   A lazy dog! When I took him the time before, I told him what he would come to if he did not mend his hand. This is death without reprieve. I may venture to book him. [*Writes.*] For Tom Gagg, forty pounds.[7] Let Betty Sly know that I'll save her from transportation, for I can get more by her staying in England.

FILCH   Betty hath brought more goods into our lock to-year[8] than any five of the gang; and in truth, 'tis a pity to lose so good a customer.

PEACHUM   If none of the gang take her off,[9] she may, in the common course of business, live a twelve-month longer. I love to let women scape. A good sportsman always lets the hen partridges fly, because the breed of the game depends upon them. Besides, here the law allows us no reward; there is nothing to be got by the death of women—except our wives.

FILCH   Without dispute, she is a fine woman! 'Twas to her I was obliged for my education, and (to say a bold word) she hath trained up more young fellows to the business than the gaming-table.

---

5. The name of the ballad whose tune Peachum sings.
6. Claim to be pregnant, hence not at risk of execution.
7. The reward when informing resulted in execution.
8. This year. "Lock": a house where stolen goods are kept.
9. Inform on her.

PEACHUM   Truly, Filch, thy observation is right. We and the surgeons are
more beholden to women than all the professions besides.[1]

AIR 2.   The bonny gray-eyed morn

FILCH   *'Tis woman that seduces all mankind,*
           By her we first were taught the wheedling arts:
         Her very eyes can cheat; when most she's kind,
           She tricks us of our money with our hearts.
         For her, like wolves by night we roam for prey,
           And practise every fraud to bribe her charms;
         For suits of love, like law, are won by pay,
           And beauty must be fee'd into our arms.

PEACHUM   But make haste to Newgate,[2] boy, and let my friends know what
I intend; for I love to make them easy one way or other.

FILCH   When a gentleman is long kept in suspense, penitence may break
his spirit ever after. Besides, certainty gives a man a good air upon his
trial, and makes him risk another without fear or scruple. But I'll away,
for 'tis a pleasure to be the messenger of comfort to friends in affliction.

SCENE 3

PEACHUM

But 'tis now high time to look about me for a decent execution against
next Sessions.[3] I hate a lazy rogue, by whom one can get nothing 'till he
is hanged. A register of the gang, [*reading*] Crook-fingered Jack. A year
and a half in the service; let me see how much the stock owes to his
industry: one, two, three, four, five gold watches, and seven silver ones.
A mighty clean-handed fellow! Sixteen snuff-boxes, five of them of true
gold. Six dozen of handkerchiefs, four silver-hilted swords, half a dozen
of shirts, three tye-perriwigs, and a piece of broad cloth. Considering
these are only the fruits of his leisure hours, I don't know a prettier
fellow, for no man alive hath a more engaging presence of mind upon
the road. Wat Dreary, alias Brown Will, an irregular dog, who hath an
underhand way of disposing of his goods. I'll try him only for a Sessions
or two longer upon his good behavior. Harry Padington, a poor petty-
larceny rascal, without the least genius; that fellow, though he were to
live these six months, will never come to the gallows with any credit.
Slippery Sam; he goes off the next Sessions, for the villain hath the impudence to have views of following his trade as a tailor, which he calls an
honest employment. Mat of the Mint; listed[4] not above a month ago, a
promising sturdy fellow, and diligent in his way; somewhat too bold and
hasty, and may raise good contributions on the public, if he does not cut
himself short by murder. Tom Tipple, a guzzling soaking sot, who is
always too drunk to stand himself, or to make others stand. A cart[5] is

1. Surgeons treated venereal diseases.
2. The chief London prison.
3. Trials of criminals, held eight times a year.

4. Enlisted.
5. Carriage to the gallows. "Stand": stand still,
when held up.

absolutely necessary for him. Robin of Bagshot, alias Gorgon, alias Bluff
Bob, alias Carbuncle, alias Bob Booty.[6]

SCENE 4

PEACHUM, MRS. PEACHUM

MRS. PEACHUM   What of Bob Booty, husband? I hope nothing bad hath
betided him. You know, my dear, he's a favorite customer of mine. 'Twas
he made me a present of this ring.

PEACHUM   I have set his name down in the black-list, that's all, my dear;
he spends his life among women, and as soon as his money is gone, one
or other of the ladies will hang him for the reward, and there's forty
pound lost to us forever.

MRS. PEACHUM   You know, my dear, I never meddle in matters of death;
I always leave those affairs to you. Women indeed are bitter bad judges
in these cases, for they are so partial to the brave that they think every
man handsome who is going to the camp or the gallows.

AIR 3.   Cold and raw

If any wench Venus's girdle wear,
  Though she be never so ugly;
Lilies and roses will quickly appear,
  And her face look wond'rous smugly.
Beneath the left ear so fit but a cord,
  (A rope so charming a zone is!)
The youth in his cart hath the air of a lord,
  And we cry, "There dies an Adonis!"[7]

But really, husband, you should not be too hard hearted, for you never
had a finer, braver set of men than at present. We have not had a murder
among them all, these seven months. And truly, my dear, that is a great
blessing.

PEACHUM   What a dickens is the woman always a-whimpering about murder for? No gentleman is ever looked upon the worse for killing a man
in his own defense; and if business cannot be carried on without it, what
would you have a gentleman do?

MRS. PEACHUM   If I am in the wrong, my dear, you must excuse me, for
nobody can help the frailty of an over-scrupulous conscience.

PEACHUM   Murder is as fashionable a crime as a man can be guilty of.
How many fine gentlemen have we in Newgate every year, purely upon
that article! If they have wherewithal to persuade the jury to bring it in
manslaughter, what are they the worse for it? So, my dear, have done
upon this subject. Was Captain Macheath here this morning, for the
bank notes he left with you last week?

MRS. PEACHUM   Yes, my dear; and though the bank hath stopped payment,
he was so cheerful and so agreeable! Sure there is not a finer gentleman
upon the road than the Captain! If he comes from Bagshot at any rea-

---

6. This became a nickname for Walpole.
7. Venus's lover. The magic powers of Venus's belt
("girdle"), which could make any woman sexy, are

associated with the rope or belt ("zone") around a
condemned man's neck.

sonable hour he hath promised to make one this evening with Polly and me, and Bob Booty, at a party of quadrille.[8] Pray, my dear, is the Captain rich?

PEACHUM   The Captain keeps too good company ever to grow rich. Marybone and the chocolate-houses[9] are his undoing. The man that proposes to get money by play should have the education of a fine gentleman, and be trained up to it from his youth.

MRS. PEACHUM   Really, I am sorry upon Polly's account the Captain hath not more discretion. What business hath he to keep company with lords and gentlemen? He should leave them to prey upon one another.

PEACHUM   Upon Polly's account! What, a plague, does the woman mean? Upon Polly's account!

MRS. PEACHUM   Captain Macheath is very fond of the girl.

PEACHUM   And what then?

MRS. PEACHUM   If I have any skill in the ways of women, I am sure Polly thinks him a very pretty man.

PEACHUM   And what then? You would not be so mad to have the wench marry him! Gamesters and highwaymen are generally very good to their whores, but they are very devils to their wives.

MRS. PEACHUM   But if Polly should be in love, how should we help her, or how can she help herself? Poor girl, I am in the utmost concern about her.

AIR 4.   Why is your faithful slave disdained?

> If love the virgin's heart invade,
> How, like a moth, the simple maid
>   Still plays about the flame!
> If soon she be not made a wife,
> Her honor's singed, and then for life,
>   She's—what I dare not name.

PEACHUM   Look ye, wife. A handsome wench in our way of business is as profitable as at the bar of a Temple[1] coffee-house, who looks upon it as her livelihood to grant every liberty but one. You see I would indulge the girl as far as prudently we can. In anything but marriage! After that, my dear, how shall we be safe? Are we not then in her husband's power? For a husband hath the absolute power over all a wife's secrets but her own. If the girl had the discretion of a court lady, who can have a dozen young fellows at her ear without complying with one, I should not matter it; but Polly is tinder, and a spark will at once set her on a flame. Married! If the wench does not know her own profit, sure she knows her own pleasure better than to make herself a property![2] My daughter to me should be, like a court lady to a minister of state, a key to the whole gang. Married! If the affair is not already done, I'll terrify her from it, by the example of our neighbors.

MRS. PEACHUM   Mayhap, my dear, you may injure the girl. She loves to imitate the fine ladies, and she may only allow the Captain liberties in the view of interest.

8. A card game.
9. Popular haunts for gambling.
1. London college for lawyers.

2. A husband had legal title to everything his wife possessed.

PEACHUM But 'tis your duty, my dear, to warn the girl against her ruin, and to instruct her how to make the most of her beauty. I'll go to her this moment, and sift her. In the meantime, wife, rip out the coronets and marks of these dozen of cambric handkerchiefs, for I can dispose of them this afternoon to a chap in the City.

SCENE 5

MRS. PEACHUM

Never was a man more out of the way in an argument than my husband! Why must our Polly, forsooth, differ from her sex, and love only her husband? And why must Polly's marriage, contrary to all observation, make her the less followed by other men? All men are thieves in love, and like a woman the better for being another's property.

AIR 5. Of all the simple things we do

A maid is like the golden ore,
Which hath guineas intrinsical in't,
Whose worth is never known, before
It is tried and impressed in the Mint.
A wife's like a guinea in gold,
Stamped with the name of her spouse:
Now here, now there, is bought, or is sold,
And is current in every house.

SCENE 6

MRS. PEACHUM, FILCH

MRS. PEACHUM Come hither, Filch. I am as fond of this child, as though my mind misgave me he were my own. He hath as fine a hand at picking a pocket as a woman, and is as nimble-fingered as a juggler. If an unlucky Session does not cut the rope of thy life, I pronounce, boy, thou wilt be a great man in history. Where was your post last night, my boy?

FILCH I plied at the opera, madam; and considering 'twas neither dark nor rainy, so that there was no great hurry in getting chairs and coaches, made a tolerable hand on't. These seven handkerchiefs, madam.

MRS. PEACHUM Colored ones, I see. They are of sure sale from our warehouse at Redriff among the seamen.

FILCH And this snuffbox.

MRS. PEACHUM Set in gold! A pretty encouragement this to a young beginner.

FILCH I had a fair tug at a charming gold watch. Pox take the tailors for making the fobs so deep and narrow! It stuck by the way, and I was forced to make my escape under a coach. Really, madam, I fear I shall be cut off in the flower of my youth, so that every now and then (since I was pumped)[3] I have thoughts of taking up and going to sea.

MRS. PEACHUM You should go to Hockley in the Hole,[4] and to Marybone,

---

3. When pickpockets were caught, they were doused with water.

4. A place for brutal sports such as bear-baiting.

child, to learn valor. These are the schools that have bred so many brave men. I thought, boy, by this time, thou hadst lost fear as well as shame. Poor lad! How little does he know as yet of the Old Bailey![5] For the first fact I'll insure thee from being hanged; and going to sea, Filch, will come time enough upon a sentence of transportation. But now, since you have nothing better to do, even go to your book, and learn your catechism, for really a man makes but an ill figure in the Ordinary's paper,[6] who cannot give a satisfactory answer to his questions. But, hark you, my lad. Don't tell me a lie; for you know I hate a liar. Do you know of anything that hath passed between Captain Macheath and our Polly?

FILCH   I beg you, madam, don't ask me; for I must either tell a lie to you or to Miss Polly; for I promised her I would not tell.

MRS. PEACHUM   But when the honor of our family is concerned—

FILCH   I shall lead a sad life with Miss Polly, if ever she come to know that I told you. Besides, I would not willingly forfeit my own honor by betraying anybody.

MRS. PEACHUM   Yonder comes my husband and Polly. Come, Filch, you shall go with me into my own room, and tell me the whole story. I'll give thee a glass of a most delicious cordial that I keep for my own drinking.

SCENE 7

PEACHUM, POLLY

POLLY   I know as well as any of the fine ladies how to make the most of myself and of my man too. A woman knows how to be mercenary, though she hath never been in a court or at an assembly.[7] We have it in our natures, papa. If I allow Captain Macheath some trifling liberties, I have this watch and other visible marks of his favor to show for it. A girl who cannot grant some things, and refuse what is most material, will make but a poor hand of her beauty, and soon be thrown upon the common.[8]

AIR 6.   What shall I do to show how much I love her

> Virgins are like the fair flower in its luster,
>   Which in the garden enamels the ground;
> Near it the bees in play flutter and cluster,
>   And gaudy butterflies frolic around.
> But, when once plucked, 'tis no longer alluring,
>   To Covent Garden[9] 'tis sent (as yet sweet),
> There fades, and shrinks, and grows past all enduring,
>   Rots, stinks, and dies, and is trod under feet.

PEACHUM   You know, Polly, I am not against your toying and trifling with a customer in the way of business, or to get out a secret, or so. But if I find out that you have played the fool and are married, you jade you, I'll cut your throat, hussy. Now you know my mind.

5. London's criminal court.
6. First offenders could escape the death sentence by pleading "benefit of clergy" if they passed a literacy test given by the Ordinary or Chaplain of Newgate.
7. A public social affair.
8. Common land; common law; and a name for a prostitute.
9. A market where produce and prostitutes were bought.

SCENE 8

PEACHUM, POLLY, MRS. PEACHUM

AIR 7. Oh London is a fine town

MRS. PEACHUM [*In a very great passion.*]

Our Polly is a sad slut! nor heeds what we have taught her.
I wonder any man alive will ever rear a daughter!
For she must have both hoods and gowns, and hoops to swell her pride,
With scarfs and stays, and gloves and lace; and she will have men beside;
And when she's dressed with care and cost, all-tempting, fine and gay,
As men should serve a cowcumber,[1] *she flings herself away.*
  Our Polly is a sad slut, etc.

You baggage! You hussy! You inconsiderate jade! Had you been hanged, it would not have vexed me, for that might have been your misfortune; but to do such a mad thing by choice! The wench is married, husband.

PEACHUM Married! The Captain is a bold man, and will risk anything for money; to be sure he believes her a fortune. Do you think your mother and I should have lived comfortably so long together, if ever we had been married? Baggage!

MRS. PEACHUM I knew she was always a proud slut; and now the wench hath played the fool and married, because forsooth she would do like the gentry. Can you support the expense of a husband, hussy, in gaming, drinking and whoring? Have you money enough to carry on the daily quarrels of man and wife about who shall squander most? There are not many husbands and wives who can bear the charges of plaguing one another in a handsome way. If you must be married, could you introduce nobody into our family but a highwayman? Why, thou foolish jade, thou wilt be as ill-used, and as much neglected, as if thou hadst married a lord!

PEACHUM Let not your anger, my dear, break through the rules of decency, for the Captain looks upon himself in the military capacity, as a gentleman by his profession. Besides what he hath already, I know he is in a fair way of getting,[2] or of dying; and both these ways, let me tell you, are most excellent chances for a wife. Tell me hussy, are you ruined or no?

MRS. PEACHUM With Polly's fortune, she might very well have gone off to a person of distinction. Yes, that you might, you pouting slut!

PEACHUM What, is the wench dumb? Speak, or I'll make you plead by squeezing out an answer from you. Are you really bound wife to him, or are you only upon liking?[3] [*Pinches her.*]

POLLY Oh! [*Screaming.*]

MRS. PEACHUM How the mother is to be pitied who hath handsome daughters! Locks, bolts, bars, and lectures of morality are nothing to them; they break through them all. They have as much pleasure in cheating a father and mother as in cheating at cards.

PEACHUM Why, Polly, I shall soon know if you are married, by Macheath's keeping from our house.

---

1. Cucumber.
2. Acquiring wealth.
3. On approval.

AIR 8. Grim king of the ghosts

POLLY   *Can love be controlled by advice?*
      Will Cupid our mothers obey?
    Though my heart were as frozen as ice,
      At his flame 'twould have melted away.
    When he kissed me so closely he pressed,
      'Twas so sweet that I must have complied;
    So I thought it both safest and best
      To marry, for fear you should chide.

MRS. PEACHUM   Then all the hopes of our family are gone for ever and ever!

PEACHUM   And Macheath may hang his father and mother-in-law, in hope to get into their daughter's fortune.

POLLY   I did not marry him (as 'tis the fashion) coolly and deliberately for honor or money. But I love him.

MRS. PEACHUM   Love him! Worse and worse! I thought the girl had been better bred. O husband, husband! Her folly makes me mad! My head swims! I'm distracted! I can't support myself—O! [*Faints.*]

PEACHUM   See, wench, to what a condition you have reduced your poor mother! A glass of cordial, this instant. How the poor woman takes it to heart! [POLLY *goes out, and returns with it.*] Ah hussy, now this is the only comfort your mother has left!

POLLY   Give her another glass, sir; my mama drinks double the quantity whenever she is out of order. This, you see, fetches[4] her.

MRS. PEACHUM   The girl shows such a readiness, and so much concern, that I could almost find in my heart to forgive her.

AIR 9. O Jenny, O Jenny, where hast thou been

MRS. PEACHUM   *Oh Polly, you might have toyed and kissed.*
    By keeping men off, you keep them on.
POLLY   *But he so teased me,*
      And he so pleased me,
   What I did, you must have done.

MRS. PEACHUM   Not with a highwayman. You sorry slut!

PEACHUM   A word with you, wife. 'Tis no new thing for a wench to take man without consent of parents. You know 'tis the frailty of woman, my dear.

MRS. PEACHUM   Yes, indeed, the sex is frail. But the first time a woman is frail, she should be somewhat nice[5] methinks, for then or never is the time to make her fortune. After that, she hath nothing to do but to guard herself from being found out, and she may do what she pleases.

PEACHUM   Make yourself a little easy; I have a thought shall soon set all matters again to rights. Why so melancholy, Polly? Since what is done cannot be undone, we must all endeavor to make the best of it.

MRS. PEACHUM   Well, Polly, as far as one woman can forgive another, I forgive thee. Your father is too fond of you, hussy.

POLLY   Then all my sorrows are at an end.

4. Revives.   5. Choosy.

MRS. PEACHUM   A mighty likely speech in troth, for a wench who is just married!

AIR 10.   Thomas, I cannot

POLLY

> I, *like a ship in storms, was tossed,*
> *Yet afraid to put in to land;*
> *For seized in the port the vessel's lost,*
> *Whose treasure is contraband.*
> > *The waves are laid,*
> > *My duty's paid.*
> > O *joy beyond expression!*
> > *Thus, safe ashore,*
> > *I ask no more,*
> *My all is in my possession.*

PEACHUM   I hear customers in t'other room. Go, talk with 'em, Polly; but come to us again as soon as they are gone. But, hark ye, child, if 'tis the gentleman who was here yesterday about the repeating-watch,[6] say, you believe we can't get intelligence of it, till tomorrow, for I lent it to Suky Straddle, to make a figure with it tonight at a tavern in Drury Lane. If t'other gentleman calls for the silver-hilted sword, you know beetle-browed Jemmy hath it on, and he doth not come from Tunbridge till Tuesday night, so that it cannot be had till then.

SCENE 9

PEACHUM, MRS. PEACHUM

PEACHUM   Dear wife, be a little pacified. Don't let your passion run away with your senses. Polly, I grant you, hath done a rash thing.

MRS. PEACHUM   If she had had only an intrigue with the fellow, why the very best families have excused and huddled up a frailty of that sort. 'Tis marriage, husband, that makes it a blemish.

PEACHUM   But money, wife, is the true fuller's earth[7] for reputations, there is not a spot or a stain but what it can take out. A rich rogue nowadays is fit company for any gentleman; and the world, my dear, hath not such a contempt for roguery as you imagine. I tell you, wife, I can make this match turn to our advantage.

MRS. PEACHUM   I am very sensible,[8] husband, that Captain Macheath is worth money, but I am in doubt whether he hath not two or three wives already, and then if he should die in a Session or two, Polly's dower would come into dispute.

PEACHUM   That, indeed, is a point which ought to be considered.

AIR 11.   A soldier and a sailor

> *A fox may steal your hens, sir,*
> *A whore your health and pence, sir,*
> *Your daughter rob your chest, sir,*
> *Your wife may steal your rest, sir,*
> > *A thief your goods and plate.*

---

6. A watch that strikes the hour and quarter-hour when a button is pressed.

7. Clay used for cleaning fabrics.

8. Aware.

> But this is all but picking,
> With rest, pence, chest, and chicken;
> It ever was decreed, sir,
> If lawyer's hand is fee'd, sir,
> He steals your whole estate.

The lawyers are bitter enemies to those in our way. They don't care that anybody should get a clandestine livelihood but themselves.

SCENE 10

MRS. PEACHUM, PEACHUM, POLLY

POLLY   'Twas only Nimming Ned. He brought in a damask window curtain, a hoop-petticoat, a pair of silver candlesticks, a perriwig, and one silk stocking, from the fire that happened last night.

PEACHUM   There is not a fellow that is cleverer in his way, and saves more goods out of the fire than Ned. But now, Polly, to your affair; for matters must not be left as they are. You are married then, it seems?

POLLY   Yes, sir.

PEACHUM   And how do you propose to live, child?

POLLY   Like other women, sir, upon the industry of my husband.

MRS. PEACHUM   What, is the wench turned fool? A highwayman's wife, like a soldier's, hath as little of his pay as of his company.

PEACHUM   And had not you the common views of a gentlewoman in your marriage, Polly?

POLLY   I don't know what you mean, sir.

PEACHUM   Of a jointure,[9] and of being a widow.

POLLY   But I love him, sir. How then could I have thoughts of parting with him?

PEACHUM   Parting with him! Why, that is the whole scheme and intention of all marriage articles. The comfortable estate of widowhood is the only hope that keeps up a wife's spirits. Where is the woman who would scruple to be a wife, if she had it in her power to be a widow whenever she pleased? If you have any views of this sort, Polly, I shall think the match not so very unreasonable.

POLLY   How I dread to hear your advice! Yet I must beg you to explain yourself.

PEACHUM   Secure what he hath got, have him peached the next Sessions, and then at once you are made a rich widow.

POLLY   What, murder the man I love! The blood runs cold at my heart with the very thought of it.

PEACHUM   Fie, Polly! What hath murder to do in the affair? Since the thing sooner or later must happen, I dare say, the Captain himself would like that we should get the reward for his death sooner than a stranger. Why, Polly, the Captain knows that as 'tis his employment to rob, so 'tis ours to take robbers; every man in his business. So that there is no malice in the case.

MRS. PEACHUM   Ay, husband, now you have nicked the matter.[1] To have him peached is the only thing could ever make me forgive her.

9. Property jointly held by a couple, hence inherited by the wife if her husband died.   1. Hit the mark.

AIR 12.   Now Ponder well, ye parents dear

POLLY   *O, ponder well! be not severe;*
               So save a wretched wife!
               For on the rope that hangs my dear
               Depends poor Polly's life.

MRS. PEACHUM   But your duty to your parents, hussy, obliges you to hang
him. What would many a wife give for such an opportunity!

POLLY   What is a jointure, what is widowhood to me? I know my heart. I
cannot survive him.

AIR 13.   Le printemps rappelle aux armes[2]

The turtle[3] thus with plaintive crying,
Her lover dying,
The turtle thus with plaintive crying,
Laments her dove.
Down she drops quite spent with sighing,
Paired in death, as paired in love.

Thus, sir, it will happen to your poor Polly.

MRS. PEACHUM   What, is the fool in love in earnest then? I hate thee for
being particular.[4] Why, wench, thou art a shame to thy very sex.

POLLY   But hear me, mother. If you ever loved—

MRS. PEACHUM   Those cursed playbooks she reads have been her ruin.
One word more, hussy, and I shall knock your brains out, if you have
any.

PEACHUM   Keep out of the way, Polly, for fear of mischief, and consider
of what is proposed to you.

MRS. PEACHUM   Away, hussy. Hang your husband, and be dutiful.

SCENE 11

MRS. PEACHUM, PEACHUM [POLLY *listening.*]

MRS. PEACHUM   The thing, husband, must and shall be done. For the sake
of intelligence[5] we must take other measures, and have him peached the
next Session without her consent. If she will not know her duty, we know
ours.

PEACHUM   But really, my dear, it grieves one's heart to take off a great
man. When I consider his personal bravery, his fine stratagem,[6] how
much we have already got by him, and how much more we may get,
methinks I can't find in my heart to have a hand in his death. I wish you
could have made Polly undertake it.

MRS. PEACHUM   But in a case of necessity—our own lives are in danger.

PEACHUM   Then, indeed, we must comply with the customs of the world,
and make gratitude give way to interest. He shall be taken off.

MRS. PEACHUM   I'll undertake to manage Polly.

PEACHUM   And I'll prepare matters for the Old Bailey.

---

2. The spring calls to arms (French).   5. Secret information.
3. Turtledove.   6. Guile.
4. Attached to one person; freakish.

SCENE 12

POLLY

Now I'm a wretch, indeed. Methinks I see him already in the cart, sweeter and more lovely than the nosegay in his hand! I hear the crowd extolling his resolution and intrepidity! What volleys of sighs are sent from the windows of Holborn,[7] that so comely a youth should be brought to disgrace! I see him at the tree! The whole circle are in tears! Even butchers weep! Jack Ketch[8] himself hesitates to perform his duty, and would be glad to lose his fee, by a reprieve. What then will become of Polly! As yet I may inform him of their design, and aid him in his escape. It shall be so. But then he flies, absents himself, and I bar my self from his dear dear conversation![9] That too will distract me. If he keep out of the way, my papa and mama may in time relent, and we may be happy. If he stays, he is hanged, and then he is lost forever! He intended to lie concealed in my room, 'till the dusk of the evening. If they are abroad, I'll this instant let him out, lest some accident should prevent him.

[*Exit, and returns.*]

SCENE 13

POLLY, MACHEATH

AIR 14. Pretty parrot, say

MACHEATH	*Pretty Polly, say,*
	When I was away,
	Did your fancy never stray
	To some newer lover?
POLLY	*Without disguise,*
	Heaving sighs,
	Doating eyes,
	My constant heart discover.
	Fondly let me loll!
MACHEATH	*O pretty, pretty Poll.*

POLLY   And are *you* as fond as ever, my dear?

MACHEATH   Suspect my honor, my courage, suspect anything but my love. May my pistols misfire, and my mare slip her shoulder while I am pursued, if I ever forsake thee!

POLLY   Nay, my dear, I have no reason to doubt you, for I find in the romance you lent me, none of the great heroes were ever false in love.

AIR 15. Pray, fair one, be kind

MACHEATH	*My heart was so free,*
	It roved like the bee,
	'Till Polly my passion requited;
	I sipped each flower,

7. The street that connects Newgate to the gallows ("tree") at Tyburn.
8. The hangman (after a famous 17th-century executioner).
9. Intimate contact.

I changed every hour,
But here every flower is united.

POLLY   Were you sentenced to transportation, sure, my dear, you could
not leave me behind you—could you?

MACHEATH   Is there any power, any force that could tear me from thee?
You might sooner tear a pension out of the hands of a courtier, a fee
from a lawyer, a pretty woman from a looking glass, or any woman from
quadrille. But to tear me from thee is impossible!

AIR 16.   Over the hills and far away

MACHEATH   *Were I laid on Greenland's coast,*
And in my arms embraced my lass;
Warm amidst eternal frost,
Too soon the half year's night would pass.

POLLY   *Were I sold on Indian soil,*
Soon as the burning day was closed,
I could mock the sultry toil,
When on my charmer's breast reposed.

MACHEATH   *And I would love you all the day,*

POLLY   *Every night would kiss and play,*

MACHEATH   *If with me you'd fondly stray*

POLLY   *Over the hills and far away.*

Yes, I would go with thee. But oh! How shall I speak it? I must be torn
from thee. We must part.

MACHEATH   How? Part?

POLLY   We must, we must. My papa and mama are set against thy life.
They now, even now, are in search after thee. They are preparing evidence against thee. Thy life depends upon a moment.

AIR 17.   Gin thou wert mine awn thing

Oh what pain it is to part!
Can I leave thee, can I leave thee?
Oh what pain it is to part!
Can thy Polly ever leave thee?
But lest death my love should thwart,
And bring thee to the fatal cart,
Thus I tear thee from my bleeding heart!
Fly hence, and let me leave thee.

One kiss and then—one kiss—begone—farewell.

MACHEATH   My hand, my heart, my dear, is so riveted to thine, that I
cannot unloose my hold.

POLLY   But my papa may intercept thee, and then I should lose the very
glimmering of hope. A few weeks, perhaps, may reconcile us all. Shall
thy Polly hear from thee?

MACHEATH   Must I then go?

POLLY   And will not absence change your love?

MACHEATH   If you doubt it, let me stay—and be hanged.

POLLY   Oh how I fear! How I tremble! Go—but when safety will give you
leave, you will be sure to see me again; for 'till then Polly is wretched.

AIR 18. *Oh the broom*

[*Parting, and looking back at each other with fondness; he at one door, she at the other.*]

MACHEATH *The miser thus a shilling sees,*
      Which he's obliged to pay,
      With sighs resigns it by degrees,
      And fears 'tis gone for aye.
POLLY   *The boy, thus, when his sparrow's flown,*
      The bird in silence eyes;
      But soon as out of sight 'tis gone,
      Whines, whimpers, sobs, and cries.

Act 2

SCENE 1 *A tavern near Newgate*

JEMMY TWITCHER, CROOK-FINGERED JACK, WAT DREARY, ROBIN OF BAGSHOT, NIMMING NED, HENRY PADDINGTON, MATT OF THE MINT, BEN BUDGE, *and the rest of the gang, at the table, with wine, brandy, and tobacco*

BEN But prithee, Matt, what is become of thy brother Tom? I have not seen him since my return from transportation.

MATT Poor brother Tom had an accident this time twelve-month, and so clever a made[1] fellow he was, that I could not save him from those flaying rascals the surgeons; and now, poor man, he is among the otamies[2] at Surgeon's Hall.

BEN So it seems, his time was come.

JEMMY But the present time is ours, and nobody alive hath more. Why are the laws levelled at us? Are we more dishonest than the rest of mankind? What we win, gentlemen, is our own by the law of arms and the right of conquest.

JACK Where shall we find such another set of practical philosophers, who to a man are above the fear of death?

WAT Sound men, and true!

ROBIN Of tried courage, and indefatigable industry!

NED Who is there here that would not die for his friend?

HARRY Who is there here that would betray him for his interest?

MATT Show me a gang of courtiers that can say as much.

BEN We are for a just partition of the world, for every man hath a right to enjoy life.

MATT We retrench the superfluities of mankind. The world is avaricious, and I hate avarice. A covetous fellow, like a jackdaw, steals what he was never made to enjoy, for the sake of hiding it. These are the robbers of mankind, for money was made for the free-hearted and generous, and where is the injury of taking from another what he hath not the heart to make use of?

---

1. Well-made. The "accident" was hanging. 2. Skeletons ("anatomies").

JEMMY   Our several stations[3] for the day are fixed. Good luck attend us all. Fill the glasses.

AIR 19.   Fill every glass

MATT   *Fill every glass, for wine inspires us,*
And fires us
With courage, love, and joy.
Women and wine should life employ.
Is there ought else on earth desirous?

CHORUS   *Fill every glass, etc.*

SCENE 2

To them enter MACHEATH

MACHEATH   Gentlemen, well met. My heart hath been with you this hour; but an unexpected affair hath detained me. No ceremony, I beg you.

MATT   We were just breaking up to go upon duty. Am I to have the honor of taking the air with you, sir, this evening upon the heath? I drink a dram now and then with the stagecoachmen in the way of friendship and intelligence; and I know that about this time there will be passengers upon the Western Road, who are worth speaking with.

MACHEATH   I was to have been of that party, but—

MATT   But what, sir?

MACHEATH   Is there any man who suspects my courage?

MATT   We have all been witnesses of it.

MACHEATH   My honor and truth to the gang?

MATT   I'll be answerable for it.

MACHEATH   In the division of our booty, have I ever shown the least marks of avarice or injustice?

MATT   By these questions something seems to have ruffled you. Are any of us suspected?

MACHEATH   I have a fixed confidence, gentlemen, in you all, as men of honor, and as such I value and respect you. Peachum is a man that is useful to us.

MATT   Is he about to play us any foul play? I'll shoot him through the head.

MACHEATH   I beg you, gentlemen, act with conduct and discretion. A pistol is your last resort.

MATT   He knows nothing of this meeting.

MACHEATH   Business cannot go on without him. He is a man who knows the world, and is a necessary agent to us. We have had a slight difference, and till it is accommodated I shall be obliged to keep out of his way. Any private dispute of mine shall be of no ill consequence to my friends. You must continue to act under his direction, for the moment we break loose from him, our gang is ruined.

MATT   As a bawd to a whore, I grant you, he is to us of great convenience.

MACHEATH   Make him believe I have quitted the gang, which I can never

3. Individual posts.

do but with life. At our private quarters I will continue to meet you. A
week or so will probably reconcile us.

MATT Your instructions shall be observed. 'Tis now high time for us to
repair to our several duties; so till the evening at our quarters in Moor-
fields⁴ we bid you farewell.

MACHEATH I shall wish myself with you. Success attend you. [*Sits down
melancholy at the table.*]

AIR 20. March in *Rinaldo*,⁵ with drums and trumpets

MATT   *Let us take the road.*
        Hark! I hear the sound of coaches!
        The hour of attack approaches,
        To your arms, brave boys, and load.
            See the ball I hold!
        Let the chemists⁶ toil like asses,
        Our fire their fire surpasses,
            And turns all our lead to gold.

[*The gang, ranged in the front of the stage, load their pistols, and stick
them under their girdles; then go off singing the first part in chorus.*]

SCENE 3

MACHEATH

What a fool is a fond wench! Polly is most confoundedly bit.⁷ I love
the sex. And a man who loves money might as well be contented with
one guinea, as I with one woman. The town perhaps hath been as much
obliged to me for recruiting it with free-hearted ladies, as to any recruiting officer in the army. If it were not for us and the other gentlemen of
the sword, Drury Lane⁸ would be uninhabited.

AIR 21. Would you have a young virgin

        If the heart of a man is depressed with cares,
        The mist is dispelled when a woman appears;
        Like the notes of a fiddle, she sweetly, sweetly
        Raises the spirits, and charms our ears,
            Roses and lilies her cheeks disclose,
            But her ripe lips are more sweet than those.
                Press her,
                Caress her,
                With blisses,
                Her kisses
        Dissolve us in pleasure, and soft repose.

I must have women. There is nothing unbends the mind like them.
Money is not so strong a cordial for the time. Drawer! [*Enter DRAWER.*]
Is the porter gone for all the ladies, according to my directions?

4. A district known as a "seminary of vice."   7. Taken in.
5. English opera by Handel.   8. Associated with prostitutes.
6. Alchemists.

DRAWER I expect him back every minute. But you know, sir, you sent him as far as Hockley in the Hole, for three of the ladies, for one in Vinegar Yard, and for the rest of them somewhere about Lewkner's Lane. Sure some of them are below, for I hear the bar bell. As they come I will show them up. Coming, coming.

SCENE 4

MACHEATH, MRS. COAXER, DOLLY TRULL, MRS. VIXEN, BETTY DOXY, JENNY DIVER, MRS. SLAMMEKIN, SUKY TAWDRY, *and* MOLLY BRAZEN

MACHEATH Dear Mrs. Coaxer, you are welcome. You look charmingly today. I hope you don't want the repairs of quality, and lay on paint.[9] Dolly Trull! Kiss me, you slut; are you as amorous as ever, hussy? You are always so taken up with stealing hearts, that you don't allow yourself time to steal anything else. Ah Dolly, thou wilt ever be a coquette! Mrs. Vixen, I'm yours, I always loved a woman of wit and spirit; they make charming mistresses, but plaguey wives. Betty Doxy! Come hither, hussy. Do you drink as hard as ever? You had better stick to good wholesome beer; for in troth, Betty, strong waters[1] will in time ruin your constitution. You should leave those to your betters. What! and my pretty Jenny Diver too! As prim and demure as ever! There is not any prude, though ever so high bred, hath a more sanctified look, with a more mischievous heart. Ah! Thou art a dear artful hypocrite. Mrs. Slammekin! As careless and genteel as ever! All you fine ladies, who know your own beauty, affect an undress.[2] But see, here's Suky Tawdry come to contradict what I was saying. Everything she gets one way she lays out upon her back. Why, Suky, you must keep at least a dozen tallymen.[3] Molly Brazen! [*She kisses him.*] That's well done. I love a free-hearted wench. Thou hast a most agreeable assurance, girl, and art as willing as a turtle. But hark! I hear music. The harper is at the door. "If music be the food of love, play on."[4] E'er you seat yourselves, ladies, what think you of a dance? Come in. [*Enter* HARPER.] Play the French tune that Mrs. Slammekin was so fond of.

[*A dance a la ronde in the French manner; near the end of it this song and chorus.*]

AIR 22. Cotillon

MACHEATH   *Youth's the season made for joys,*
             Love is then our duty,
          She alone who that employs,
             Well deserves her beauty.
                Let's be gay,
                While we may,
             Beauty's a flower despised in decay.
CHORUS   *Youth's the season etc.*
MACHEATH   *Let us drink and sport today,*

9. Cosmetics. "Quality": women of high social position.
1. Spirits.

2. Prefer casual clothes.
3. Suppliers of clothes on credit.
4. The opening line of *Twelfth Night*.

> Ours is not tomorrow.
> Love with youth flies swift away,
> Age is nought but sorrow.
> Dance and sing,
> Time's on the wing,
> Life never knows the return of spring.

CHORUS   Let us drink etc.

MACHEATH   Now, pray ladies, take your places. Here, fellow. [*Pays the* HARPER.] Bid the drawer bring us more wine. [*Exit* HARPER.] If any of the ladies choose gin, I hope they will be so free to call for it.

JENNY   You look as if you meant me. Wine is strong enough for me. Indeed, sir, I never drink strong waters, but when I have the colic.

MACHEATH   Just the excuse of the fine ladies! Why, a lady of quality is never without the colic. I hope, Mrs. Coaxer, you have had good success of late in your visits among the mercers.[5]

MRS. COAXER   We have so many interlopers.[6] Yet with industry, one may still have a little picking. I carried a silver flowered lute string and a piece of black padesoy[7] to Mr. Peachum's lock but last week.

MRS. VIXEN   There's Molly Brazen hath the ogle of a rattlesnake. She riveted a linen draper's eye so fast upon her that he was nicked of three pieces of cambric before he could look off.

MOLLY BRAZEN   Oh dear madam! But sure nothing can come up to your handling of laces! And then you have such a sweet deluding tongue. To cheat a man is nothing; but the woman must have fine parts indeed who cheats a woman!

MRS. VIXEN   Lace, madam, lies in a small compass, and is of easy conveyance. But you are apt, madam, to think too well of your friends.

MRS. COAXER   If any woman hath more art than another, to be sure, 'tis Jenny Diver. Though her fellow be never so agreeable, she can pick his pocket as coolly, as if money were her only pleasure. Now that is a command of the passions uncommon in a woman!

JENNY   I never go to the tavern with a man, but in the view of business. I have other hours, and other sort of men, for my pleasure. But had I your address,[8] madam—

MACHEATH   Have done with your compliments, ladies; and drink about. You are not so fond of me, Jenny, as you use to be.

JENNY   'Tis not convenient, sir, to show my fondness among so many rivals. 'Tis your own choice, and not the warmth of my inclination, that will determine you.

AIR 23.   All in a misty morning

> Before the barn door crowing,
> The cock by hens attended,
> His eyes around him throwing,
> Stands for a while suspended.
> Then one he singles from the crew,
> And cheers the happy hen;

---

5. Dealers in fabrics.
6. I.e., competitors in thievery.
7. Expensive silks.
8. Adroitness.

> *With how do you do, and how do you do,*
> *And how do you do again.*

MACHEATH Ah Jenny! Thou art a dear slut.

DOLLY Pray, madam, were you ever in keeping?[9]

SUKY I hope, madam, I ha'nt been so long upon the town, but I have met with some good fortune as well as my neighbors.

DOLLY Pardon me, madam, I meant no harm by the question; 'twas only in the way of conversation.

SUKY Indeed, madam, if I had not been a fool, I might have lived very handsomely with my last friend. But upon his missing five guineas, he turned me off. Now I never suspected he had counted them.

MRS. SLAMMEKIN Who do you look upon, madam, as your best sort of keepers?

DOLLY That, madam, is thereafter as they be.[1]

MRS. SLAMMEKIN I, madam, was once kept by a Jew; and bating[2] their religion, to women they are a good sort of people.

SUKY Now for my part, I own I like an old fellow, for we always make them pay for what they can't do.

MRS. VIXEN A spruce prentice, let me tell you, ladies, is no ill thing, they bleed[3] freely. I have sent at least two or three dozen of them in my time to the plantations.[4]

JENNY But to be sure, sir, with so much good fortune as you have had upon the road, you must be grown immensely rich.

MACHEATH The road, indeed, hath done me justice, but the gaming table hath been my ruin.

AIR 24. When once I lay with another man's wife

JENNY *The gamesters and lawyers are jugglers[5] alike,*
> *If they meddle your all is in danger.*
> *Like gypsies, if once they can finger a souse,[6]*
> *Your pockets they pick, and they pilfer your house,*
> *And give your estate to a stranger.*

A man of courage should never put anything to the risk but his life. These are the tools of a man of honor. Cards and dice are only fit for cowardly cheats, who prey upon their friends. [*She takes up his pistol.* SUKY *takes up the other.*]

SUKY This, sir, is fitter for your hand. Besides your loss of money, 'tis a loss to the ladies. Gaming takes you off from women. How fond could I be of you! But before company, 'tis ill bred.

MACHEATH Wanton hussies!

JENNY I must and will have a kiss to give my wine a zest.

> [*They take him about the neck, and make signs to* PEACHUM *and the constables, who rush in upon him.*]

---

9. A kept mistress.
1. Depends on their behavior.
2. Except for.
3. Spend.

4. The colonies, where convicts were transported.
5. Tricksters.
6. A negligible coin.

SCENE 5

To them, PEACHUM *and constables.*

PEACHUM   I seize you, sir, as my prisoner.

MACHEATH   Was this well done, Jenny? Women are decoy ducks; who can trust them! Beasts, jades, jilts, harpies, furies, whores!

PEACHUM   Your case, Mr. Macheath, is not particular. The greatest heroes have been ruined by women. But, to do them justice, I must own they are a pretty sort of creatures, if we could trust them. You must now, sir, take your leave of the ladies, and if they have a mind to make you a visit, they will be sure to find you at home. The gentleman, ladies, lodges in Newgate. Constables, wait upon the Captain to his lodgings.

AIR 25.   When first I laid siege to my Chloris

MACHEATH   *At the tree I shall suffer with pleasure,*
                    At the tree I shall suffer with pleasure,
                        Let me go where I will,
                        In all kinds of ill,
                    I shall find no such Furies as these are.

PEACHUM   Ladies, I'll take care the reckoning shall be discharged.

[*Exit* MACHEATH, *guarded, with* PEACHUM *and the constables.*]

SCENE 6

The women remain.

MRS. VIXEN   Look ye, Mrs. Jenny, though Mr. Peachum may have made a private bargain with you and Suky Tawdry for betraying the Captain, as we were all assisting, we ought all to share alike.

MRS. COAXER   I think Mr. Peachum, after so long an acquaintance, might have trusted me as well as Jenny Diver.

MRS. SLAMMEKIN   I am sure at least three men of his hanging, and in a year's time too (if he did me justice), should be set down to my account.

DOLLY   Mrs. Slammekin, that is not fair. For you know one of them was taken in bed with me.

JENNY   As far as a bowl of punch or a treat, I believe Mrs. Suky will join with me. As for anything else, ladies, you cannot in conscience expect it.

MRS. SLAMMEKIN   Dear madam—

DOLLY   I would not for the world[7]—

MRS. SLAMMEKIN   'Tis impossible for me—

DOLLY   As I hope to be saved, madam—

MRS. SLAMMEKIN   Nay, then I must stay here all night—

DOLLY   Since you command me.

[*Exeunt with great ceremony.*]

---

7. With exaggerated politeness, each gestures for the other to leave the room first.

SCENE 7 *Newgate*

LOCKIT, *turnkeys*, MACHEATH, *constables*

LOCKIT Noble Captain, you are welcome. You have not been a lodger of mine this year and half. You know the custom, sir. Garnish,[8] Captain, garnish. Hand me down those fetters there.

MACHEATH Those, Mr. Lockit, seem to be the heaviest of the whole set. With your leave, I should like the further pair better.

LOCKIT Look ye, Captain, we know what is fittest for our prisoners. When a gentleman uses me with civility, I always do the best I can to please him. Hand them down I say. We have them of all prices, from one guinea to ten, and 'tis fitting every gentleman should please himself.

MACHEATH I understand you, sir. [*Gives money.*] The fees here are so many, and so exorbitant, that few fortunes can bear the expense of getting off handsomely, or of dying like a gentleman.

LOCKIT Those, I see, will fit the Captain better. Take down the further pair. Do but examine them, sir. Never was better work. How genteelly they are made! They will sit as easy as a glove, and the nicest man in England might not be ashamed to wear them. [*He puts on the chains.*] If I had the best gentleman in the land in my custody, I could not equip him more handsomely. And so, sir, I now leave you to your private meditations.

SCENE 8

MACHEATH

AIR 26. Courtiers, courtiers think it no harm

> Man may escape from rope and gun;
> Nay, some have outlived the doctor's pill;
> Who takes a woman must be undone,
>   That basilisk[9] is sure to kill.
> The fly that sips treacle is lost in the sweets,
> So he that tastes woman, woman, woman,
>   He that tastes woman, ruin meets.

To what a woeful plight have I brought myself! Here must I (all day long, 'till I am hanged) be confined to hear the reproaches of a wench who lays her ruin at my door. I am in the custody of her father, and to be sure if he knows of the matter, I shall have a fine time on't betwixt this and my execution. But I promised the wench marriage. What signifies a promise to a woman? Does not man in marriage itself promise a hundred things that he never means to perform? Do all we can, women will believe us, for they look upon a promise as an excuse for following their own inclinations. But here comes Lucy, and I cannot get from her. Would I were deaf!

---

8. Jailer's fee or bribe.   9. Mythical reptile whose breath and look were fatal.

SCENE 9

MACHEATH, LUCY

LUCY You base man you! How can you look me in the face after what hath passed between us? See here, perfidious wretch, how I am forced to bear about the load of infamy[1] you have laid upon me. O Macheath! Thou hast robbed me of my quiet. To see thee tortured would give me pleasure!

AIR 27. A lovely lass to a friar came

> Thus when a good huswife sees a rat
>   In her trap in the morning taken,
> With pleasure her heart goes pit a pat,
>   In revenge for her loss of bacon.
>   Then she throws him
>   To the dog or cat,
>   To be worried, crushed and shaken.

MACHEATH Have you no bowels,[2] no tenderness, my dear Lucy, to see a husband in these circumstances?
LUCY A husband!
MACHEATH In every respect but the form, and that, my dear, may be said over us at any time. Friends should not insist upon ceremonies. From a man of honor, his word is as good as his bond.
LUCY 'Tis the pleasure of all you fine men to insult the women you have ruined.

AIR 28. 'Twas when the sea was roaring

> How cruel are the traitors,
>   Who lie and swear in jest,
> To cheat unguarded creatures
>   Of virtue, fame, and rest!
> Whoever steals a shilling,
>   Through shame the guilt conceals;
> In love the perjured villain
>   With boasts the theft reveals.

MACHEATH The very first opportunity, my dear (have but patience), you shall be my wife in whatever manner you please.
LUCY Insinuating monster! And so you think I know nothing of the affair of Miss Polly Peachum. I could tear thy eyes out!
MACHEATH Sure Lucy, you can't be such a fool as to be jealous of Polly!
LUCY Are you not married to her, you brute, you?
MACHEATH Married! Very good. The wench gives it out only to vex thee, and to ruin me in thy good opinion. 'Tis true, I go to the house; I chat with the girl, I kiss her, I say a thousand things to her (as all gentlemen do) that mean nothing, to divert myself; and now the silly jade hath set it about that I am married to her, to let me know what she would be at. Indeed, my dear Lucy, these violent passions may be of ill consequence to a woman in your condition.

1. Pregnancy.   2. Pity.

LUCY Come, come, Captain, for all your assurance, you know that Miss
Polly hath put it out of your power to do me the justice you promised
me.

MACHEATH A jealous woman believes everything her passion suggests. To
convince you of my sincerity, if we can find the Ordinary,[3] I shall have
no scruples of making you my wife; and I know the consequence of
having two at a time.

LUCY That you are only to be hanged, and so get rid of them both.

MACHEATH I am ready, my dear Lucy, to give you satisfaction—if you
think there is any in marriage. What can a man of honor say more?

LUCY So then it seems you are not married to Miss Polly.

MACHEATH You know, Lucy, the girl is prodigiously conceited. No man
can say a civil thing to her, but (like other fine ladies) her vanity makes
her think he's her own for ever and ever.

AIR 29. The sun had loosed his weary teams

The first time at the looking-glass
  The mother sets her daughter,
The image strikes the smiling lass
  With self-love ever after.
Each time she looks, she, fonder grown,
  Thinks every charm grows stronger.
But alas, vain maid, all eyes but your own
  Can see you are not younger.

When women consider their own beauties, they are all alike unreasonable in their demands; for they expect their lovers should like them as
long as they like themselves.

LUCY Yonder is my father. Perhaps this way we may light upon the Ordinary, who shall try if you will be as good as your word. For I long to be
made an honest woman.

SCENE 10

PEACHUM, LOCKIT *with an account book*

LOCKIT In this last affair, Brother Peachum, we are agreed. You have
consented to go halves in Macheath.

PEACHUM We shall never fall out about an execution. But as to that article, pray how stands our last year's account?

LOCKIT If you will run your eye over it, you'll find 'tis fair and clearly
stated.

PEACHUM This long arrear[4] of the Government is very hard upon us! Can
it be expected that we should hang our acquaintance for nothing, when
our betters will hardly save theirs without being paid for it. Unless the
people in employment pay better, I promise them for the future, I shall
let other rogues live besides their own.

LOCKIT Perhaps, brother, they are afraid these matters may be carried too
far. We are treated too by them with contempt, as if our profession were
not reputable.

3. Chaplain. 4. Overdue reward money.

PEACHUM   In one respect indeed, our employment may be reckoned dishonest, because, like great statesmen, we encourage those who betray their friends.

LOCKIT   Such language, brother, anywhere else, might turn to your prejudice. Learn to be more guarded, I beg you.

AIR 30.   How happy are we

When you censure the age,
Be cautious and sage,
Lest the courtiers offended should be:
If you mention vice or bribe,
'Tis so pat to all the tribe,
Each cries, "That was leveled at me!"

PEACHUM   Here's poor Ned Clincher's name, I see. Sure, brother Lockit, there was a little unfair proceeding in Ned's case; for he told me in the condemned hold,[5] that for value received, you had promised him a Session or two longer without molestation.

LOCKIT   Mr. Peachum, this is the first time my honor was ever called in question.

PEACHUM   Business is at an end if once we act dishonorably.

LOCKIT   Who accuses me?

PEACHUM   You are warm, brother.

LOCKIT   He that attacks my honor, attacks my livelihood. And this usage, sir, is not to be born.

PEACHUM   Since you provoke me to speak, I must tell you too that Mrs. Coaxer charges you with defrauding her of her information money, for the apprehending of curl-pated Hugh. Indeed, indeed, brother, we must punctually pay our spies, or we shall have no information.

LOCKIT   Is this language to me, sirrah, who have saved you from the gallows, sirrah! [*Collaring each other.*]

PEACHUM   If I am hanged, it shall be for ridding the world of an arrant rascal.

LOCKIT   This hand shall do the office of the halter[6] you deserve, and throttle you—you dog!

PEACHUM   Brother, brother, we are both in the wrong. We shall be both losers in the dispute—for you know we have it in our power to hang each other. You should not be so passionate.

LOCKIT   Nor you so provoking.

PEACHUM   'Tis our mutual interest; 'tis for the interest of the world we should agree. If I said anything, brother, to the prejudice of your character, I ask pardon.

LOCKIT   Brother Peachum, I can forgive as well as resent. Give me your hand. Suspicion does not become a friend.

PEACHUM   I only meant to give you occasion to justify yourself. But I must now step home, for I expect the gentleman about this snuffbox, that Filch nimmed[7] two nights ago in the park. I appointed him at this hour.

5. Prison cell.   7. Stole.
6. Noose.

SCENE 11

LOCKIT, LUCY

LOCKIT Whence come you, hussy?

LUCY My tears might answer that question.

LOCKIT You have then been whimpering and fondling, like a spaniel, over the fellow that hath abused you.

LUCY One can't help love; one can't cure it. 'Tis not in my power to obey you, and hate him.

LOCKIT Learn to bear your husband's death like a reasonable woman. 'Tis not the fashion, nowadays, so much as to affect sorrow upon these occasions. No woman would ever marry, if she had not the chance of mortality for a release. Act like a woman of spirit, hussy, and thank your father for what he is doing.

AIR 31. Of a noble race was Shenkin

LUCY   *Is then his fate decreed, sir?*
          Such a man can I think of quitting?
          When first we met, so moves me yet,
          Oh see how my heart is splitting!

LOCKIT Look ye, Lucy, there is no saving him. So I think you must even do like other widows: buy yourself weeds, and be cheerful.

AIR 32. You'll think e'er many days ensue

          You'll think e'er many days ensue
          This sentence not severe;
          I hang your husband, child, 'tis true,
          But with him hang your care.
          Twang dang dillo dee.

Like a good wife, go moan over your dying husband. That, child, is your duty. Consider, girl, you can't have the man and the money too. So make yourself as easy as you can, by getting all you can from him.

SCENE 12

LUCY, MACHEATH

LUCY Though the Ordinary was out of the way today, I hope, my dear, you will, upon the first opportunity, quiet my scruples. Oh sir! My father's hard heart is not to be softened, and I am in the utmost despair.

MACHEATH But if I could raise a small sum—would not twenty guineas, think you, move him? Of all the arguments in the way of business, the perquisite[8] is the most prevailing. Your father's perquisites for the escape of prisoners must amount to a considerable sum in the year. Money well timed, and properly applied, will do any thing.

8. Tip or bribe.

AIR 33. London ladies

If you at an office solicit your due,
 And would not have matters neglected,
You must quicken the clerk with the perquisite too,
 To do what his duty directed.
Or would you the frowns of a lady prevent,
 She too has this palpable failing,
The perquisite softens her into consent;
 That reason with all is prevailing.

LUCY   What love or money can do shall be done; for all my comfort depends upon your safety.

SCENE 13

LUCY, MACHEATH, POLLY

POLLY   Where is my dear husband? Was a rope ever intended for this neck! Oh let me throw my arms about it, and throttle thee with love! Why dost thou turn away from me? 'Tis thy Polly! 'Tis thy wife!

MACHEATH   Was ever such an unfortunate rascal as I am!

LUCY   Was there ever such another villain!

POLLY   Oh Macheath! Was it for this we parted? Taken! Imprisoned! Tried! Hanged! Cruel reflection! I'll stay with thee 'till death. No force shall tear thy dear wife from thee now. —What means my love? Not one kind word! Not one kind look! Think what thy Polly suffers to see thee in this condition.

AIR 34.   All in the downs

Thus when the swallow, seeking prey,
 Within the sash⁹ is closely pent,
His consort, with bemoaning lay,
 Without sits pining for th' event.
Her chattering lovers all around her skim;
She heeds them not (poor bird!), her soul's with him.

MACHEATH   [*Aside.*] I must disown her. The wench is distracted.

LUCY   Am I then bilked of my virtue? Can I have no reparation? Sure men were born to lie, and women to believe them! Oh villain! Villain!

POLLY   Am I not thy wife? Thy neglect of me, thy aversion to me, too severely proves it. Look on me. Tell me, am I not thy wife?

LUCY   Perfidious wretch!

POLLY   Barbarous husband!

LUCY   Hadst thou been hanged five months ago, I had been happy.

POLLY   And I too. If you had been kind to me 'till death, it would not have vexed me—and that's no very unreasonable request (though from a wife) to a man who hath not above seven or eight days to live.

LUCY   Art thou then married to another? Hast thou two wives, monster?

MACHEATH   If women's tongues can cease for an answer, hear me.

9. Window.

LUCY   I won't. Flesh and blood can't bear my usage.

POLLY   Shall I not claim my own? Justice bids me speak.

AIR 35.   Have you heard of a frolicsome ditty

MACHEATH   *How happy could I be with either,*
                    Were t'other dear charmer away!
                But while you thus tease me together,
                    To neither a word will I say,
                        But tol de rol, etc.

POLLY   Sure, my dear, there ought to be some preference shown to a wife. At least she may claim the appearance of it. He must be distracted with his misfortunes, or he could not use me thus!

LUCY   Oh villain, villain! Thou hast deceived me. I could even inform against thee with pleasure. Not a prude wishes more heartily to have facts[1] against her intimate acquaintance, than I now wish to have facts against thee. I would have her satisfaction, and they should all out.

AIR 36.   Irish trot

POLLY   *I'm bubbled.*[2]

LUCY   *I'm bubbled.*

POLLY   *O how I am troubled!*

LUCY   *Bamboozled, and bit!*

POLLY   *My distresses are doubled.*

LUCY   *When you come to the tree, should the hangman refuse,*
            These fingers, with pleasure, could fasten the noose.

POLLY   *I'm bubbled, etc.*

MACHEATH   Be pacified, my dear Lucy. This is all a fetch[3] of Polly's, to make me desperate with you in case I get off. If I am hanged, she would fain have the credit of being thought my widow. Really, Polly, this is no time for a dispute of this sort; for whenever you are talking of marriage, I am thinking of hanging.

POLLY   And hast thou the heart to persist in disowning me?

MACHEATH   And hast thou the heart to persist in persuading me that I am married? Why, Polly, dost thou seek to aggravate my misfortunes?

LUCY   Really, Miss Peachum, you but expose yourself. Besides, 'tis barbarous in you to worry a gentleman in his circumstances.

AIR 37.

POLLY   *Cease your funning;*
            Force or cunning
        Never shall my heart trapan.[4]
            All these sallies
            Are but malice
        To seduce my constant man.
            'Tis most certain,
            By their flirting
        Women oft have envy shown;

---

1. Incriminating information.   3. Ruse.
2. Cheated.   4. Beguile.

> *Pleased to ruin*
> *Others wooing,*
> *Never happy in their own!*

Decency, madam, methinks might teach you to behave yourself with some reserve with the husband, while his wife is present.

MACHEATH But seriously, Polly, this is carrying the joke a little too far.

LUCY If you are determined, madam, to raise a disturbance in the prison, I shall be obliged to send for the turnkey to show you the door. I am sorry, madam, you force me to be so ill-bred.

POLLY Give me leave to tell you, madam, these forward airs don't become you in the least, madam. And my duty, madam, obliges me to stay with my husband, madam.

AIR 38. Good morrow, gossip Joan

LUCY	*Why how now, Madam Flirt?*
	If you thus must chatter;
	And are for flinging dirt,
	Let's try who best can spatter,
	Madam Flirt!

POLLY	*Why how now, saucy jade?*
	Sure the wench is tipsy!
[To him.]	*How can you see me made*
	The scoff of such a gipsy?
[To her.]	*Saucy jade!*

SCENE 14

LUCY, MACHEATH, POLLY, PEACHUM

PEACHUM Where's my wench? Ah hussy! Hussy! Come you home, you slut; and when your fellow is hanged, hang yourself, to make your family some amends.

POLLY Dear, dear father, do not tear me from him. I must speak; I have more to say to him—Oh! Twist thy fetters about me, that he may not haul me from thee!

PEACHUM Sure all women are alike! If ever they commit the folly, they are sure to commit another by exposing themselves. Away, not a word more. You are my prisoner now, hussy.

AIR 39. Irish howl

POLLY	*No power on earth can e'er divide*
	The knot that sacred love hath tied.
	When parents draw against our mind,
	The true love's knot they faster bind.
	Oh, oh ray, oh Amborah—oh, oh, etc.

[*Holding* MACHEATH, PEACHUM *pulling her.*]

SCENE 15

LUCY, MACHEATH

MACHEATH   I am naturally compassionate, wife, so that I could not use the wench as she deserved; which made you at first suspect there was something in what she said.

LUCY   Indeed, my dear, I was strangely puzzled.

MACHEATH   If that had been the case, her father would never have brought me into this circumstance. No, Lucy, I had rather die than be false to thee.

LUCY   How happy am I, if you say this from your heart! For I love thee so, that I could sooner bear to see thee hanged than in the arms of another.

MACHEATH   But couldst thou bear to see me hanged?

LUCY   O Macheath, I can never live to see that day.

MACHEATH   You see, Lucy, in the account of love you are in my debt, and you must now be convinced that I rather choose to die than be another's. Make me, if possible, love thee more, and let me owe my life to thee. If you refuse to assist me, Peachum and your father will immediately put me beyond all means of escape.

LUCY   My father, I know, hath been drinking hard with the prisoners, and I fancy he is now taking his nap in his own room. If I can procure the keys, shall I go off with thee, my dear?

MACHEATH   If we are together, 'twill be impossible to lie concealed. As soon as the search begins to be a little cool, I will send to thee. 'Till then my heart is thy prisoner.

LUCY   Come then, my dear husband, owe thy life to me. And though you love me not, be grateful. But that Polly runs in my head strangely.

MACHEATH   A moment of time may make us unhappy forever.

AIR 40.   The lass of Patie's mill

LUCY

I like the fox shall grieve,
   Whose mate hath left her side,
Whom hounds, from morn to eve,
   Chase o'er the country wide.
Where can my lover hide?
   Where cheat the weary pack?
If love be not his guide,
   He never will come back!

Act 3

SCENE 1 *Newgate*

LOCKIT, LUCY

LOCKIT   To be sure, wench, you must have been aiding and abetting to help him to this escape.

LUCY   Sir, here hath been Peachum and his daughter Polly, and to be sure they know the ways of Newgate as well as if they had been born and bred in the place all their lives. Why must all your suspicion light upon me?

LOCKIT   Lucy, Lucy, I will have none of these shuffling answers.

LUCY   Well then—if I know anything of him I wish I may be burnt!

LOCKIT   Keep your temper, Lucy, or I shall pronounce you guilty.

LUCY   Keep yours, sir. I do wish I may be burnt. I do. And what can I say more to convince you?

LOCKIT   Did he tip handsomely? How much did he come down with? Come hussy, don't cheat your father, and I shall not be angry with you. Perhaps you have made a better bargain with him than I could have done. How much, my good girl?

LUCY   You know, sir, I am fond of him, and would have given money to have kept him with me.

LOCKIT   Ah Lucy! Thy education might have put thee more upon thy guard, for a girl in the bar of an ale house is always besieged.

LUCY   Dear sir, mention not my education, for 'twas to that I owe my ruin.

AIR 41.   If love's a sweet passion

When young at the bar you first taught me to score,
And bid me be free of my lips, and no more,
I was kissed by the parson, the squire, and the sot;
When the guest was departed, the kiss was forgot.
But his kiss was so sweet, and so closely he pressed,
That I languished and pined 'till I granted the rest.

If you can forgive me, sir, I will make a fair confession, for to be sure he hath been a most barbarous villain to me.

LOCKIT   And so you have let him escape, hussy, have you?

LUCY   When a woman loves, a kind look, a tender word can persuade her to anything. And I could ask no other bribe.

LOCKIT   Thou wilt always be a vulgar slut, Lucy. If you would not be looked upon as a fool, you should never do anything but upon the foot of interest. Those that act otherwise are their own bubbles.[5]

LUCY   But love, sir, is a misfortune that may happen to the most discreet woman, and in love we are all fools alike. Notwithstanding all he swore, I am now fully convinced that Polly Peachum is actually his wife. Did I let him escape (fool that I was!) to go to her? Polly will wheedle herself into his money, and then Peachum will hang him, and cheat us both.

LOCKIT   So I am to be ruined because, forsooth, you must be in love! A very pretty excuse!

LUCY   I could murder that impudent happy strumpet. I gave him his life, and that creature enjoys the sweets of it. Ungrateful Macheath!

AIR 42.   South Sea ballad

My love is all madness and folly,
Alone I lie,
Toss, tumble, and cry,
What a happy creature is Polly!
Was e'er such a wretch as I!

---

5. Dupes.

> *With rage I redden like scarlet,*
> *That my dear inconstant varlet,*
> *Stark blind to my charms,*
> *Is lost in the arms*
> *Of that jilt, that inveigling harlot!*
> *Stark blind to my charms,*
> *Is lost in the arms*
> *Of that jilt, that inveigling harlot!*
> *This, this my resentment alarms.*

LOCKIT   And so, after all this mischief, I must stay here to be entertained with your caterwauling, Mistress Puss! Out of my sight, wanton strumpet! You shall fast and mortify yourself into reason, with now and then a little handsome discipline to bring you to your senses. Go.

SCENE 2

LOCKIT

Peachum then intends to outwit me in this affair; but I'll be even with him. The dog is leaky[6] in his liquor, so I'll ply him that way, get the secret from him, and turn this affair to my own advantage. Lions, wolves, and vultures don't live together in herds, droves, or flocks. Of all animals of prey, man is the only sociable one. Every one of us preys upon his neighbor, and yet we herd together. Peachum is my companion, my friend. According to the custom of the world, indeed, he may quote thousands of precedents for cheating me. And shall not I make use of the privilege of friendship to make him a return?

AIR 43.   Packington's pound

> *Thus gamesters united in friendship are found,*
> *Though they know that their industry all is a cheat;*
> *They flock to their prey at the dice-box's sound,*
> *And join to promote one another's deceit.*
> *But if by mishap*
> *They fail of a chap,[7]*
> *To keep in their hands, they each other entrap.*
> *Like pikes, lank with hunger, who miss of their ends,*
> *They bite their companions, and prey on their friends.*

Now, Peachum, you and I, like honest tradesmen, are to have a fair trial which of us two can overreach the other. Lucy! [*Enter* LUCY] Are there any of Peachum's people now in the house?

LUCY   Filch, sir, is drinking a quartern[8] of strong waters in the next room with Black Moll.

LOCKIT   Bid him come to me.

---

6. A blabbermouth.
7. Customer or sucker.

8. Quarter of a pint.

SCENE 3

LOCKIT, FILCH

LOCKIT Why, boy, thou lookest as if thou wert half starved, like a shotten herring.[9]

FILCH One had need have the constitution of a horse to go through the business. Since the favorite child-getter[1] was disabled by a mishap, I have picked up a little money by helping the ladies to a pregnancy against their being called down to sentence. But if a man cannot get an honest livelihood any easier way, I am sure 'tis what I can't undertake for another Session.

LOCKIT Truly, if that great man should tip off,[2] 'twould be an irreparable loss. The vigor and prowess of a knight-errant never saved half the ladies in distress that he hath done. But, boy, can'st thou tell me where thy master is to be found?

FILCH At his lock, sir, at the Crooked Billet.

LOCKIT Very well. I have nothing more with you. [*Exit* FILCH.] I'll go to him there, for I have many important affairs to settle with him; and in the way of those transactions, I'll artfully get into his secret. So that Macheath shall not remain a day longer out of my clutches.

SCENE 4 *A gaming-house*

MACHEATH *in a fine tarnished coat,* BEN BUDGE, MATT OF THE MINT

MACHEATH I am sorry, gentlemen, the road was so barren of money. When my friends are in difficulties, I am always glad that my fortune can be serviceable to them. [*Gives them money.*] You see, gentlemen, I am not a mere court friend, who professes everything and will do nothing.

AIR 44. Lillibullero

> The modes of the court so common are grown,
>   That a true friend can hardly be met;
> Friendship for interest is but a loan,
>   Which they let out for what they can get.
>   'Tis true, you find
>   Some friends so kind,
> Who will give you good counsel themselves to defend.
>   In sorrowful ditty,
>   They promise, they pity,
> But shift you for money, from friend to friend.

But we, gentlemen, have still honor enough to break through the corruptions of the world. And while I can serve you, you may command me.

BEN It grieves my heart that so generous a man should be involved in such difficulties, as oblige him to live with such ill company, and herd with gamesters.

9. A herring exhausted by spawning.   2. Die.
1. Stud.

MATT See the partiality of mankind! One man may steal a horse, better than another look over a hedge.[3] Of all mechanics,[4] of all servile handi-craftsmen, a gamester is the vilest. But yet, as many of the quality are of the profession, he is admitted amongst the politest company. I wonder we are not more respected.

MACHEATH There will be deep play tonight at Marybone, and conse-quently money may be picked up upon the road. Meet me there, and I'll give you the hint who is worth setting.[5]

MATT The fellow with a brown coat with a narrow gold binding, I am told, is never without money.

MACHEATH What do you mean, Matt? Sure you will not think of meddling with him! He's a good honest kind of a fellow, and one of us.

BEN To be sure, sir, we will put ourselves under your direction.

MACHEATH Have an eye upon the moneylenders. A rouleau,[6] or two, would prove a pretty sort of an expedition. I hate extortion.

MATT Those rouleaus are very pretty things. I hate your bank bills; there is such a hazard in putting them off.[7]

MACHEATH There is a certain man of distinction, who in his time hath nicked me out of a great deal of the ready. He is in my cash,[8] Ben. I'll point him out to you this evening, and you shall draw upon him for the debt. The company are met; I hear the dicebox in the other room. So, gentlemen, your servant. You'll meet me at Marybone.

SCENE 5 *Peachum's Lock*

A table with wine, brandy, pipes, and tobacco

PEACHUM, LOCKIT

LOCKIT The Coronation account,[9] brother Peachum, is of so intricate a nature, that I believe it will never be settled.

PEACHUM It consists indeed of a great variety of articles. It was worth to our people, in fees of different kinds, above ten installments.[1] This is part of the account, brother, that lies open before us.

LOCKIT A lady's tail[2]—of rich brocade—that, I see, is disposed of.

PEACHUM To Mrs. Diana Trapes, the tallywoman, and she will make a good hand on't in shoes and slippers, to trick out young ladies, upon their going into keeping.[3]

LOCKIT But I don't see any article of the jewels.

PEACHUM Those are so well known, that they must be sent abroad. You'll find them entered under the article of exportation. As for the snuffboxes, watches, swords, etc., I thought it best to enter them under their several heads.

LOCKIT Seven and twenty women's pockets[4] complete, with the several things therein contained; all sealed, numbered, and entered.

---

3. I.e., a mere look at a horse can get some people in trouble.
4. Workers who use their hands.
5. Robbing.
6. Rolls of gold coins.
7. Converting them into money.
8. He owes me. "The ready": money.

9. Register of goods stolen during the coronation of George II (1727).
1. Public installations of the new Lord Mayor of London.
2. Train.
3. Becoming mistresses.
4. Purses worn around the waist.

PEACHUM But, brother, it is impossible for us now to enter upon this affair. We should have the whole day before us. Besides, the account of the last half year's plate[5] is in a book by itself, which lies at the other office.

LOCKIT Bring us then more liquor. Today shall be for pleasure, tomorrow for business. Ah brother, those daughters of ours are two slippery hussies. Keep a watchful eye upon Polly, and Macheath in a day or two shall be our own again.

AIR 45. Down in the North Country

What gudgeons[6] are we men!
Every woman's easy prey.
Though we have felt the hook, again
We bite and they betray.

The bird that hath been trapped,
When he hears his calling mate,
To her he flies, again he's clapped
Within the wiry grate.

PEACHUM But what signifies catching the bird, if your daughter Lucy will set open the door of the cage?

LOCKIT If men were answerable for the follies and frailties of their wives and daughters, no friends could keep a good correspondence together for two days. This is unkind of you, brother; for among good friends, what they say or do goes for nothing.

[*Enter a* SERVANT.]

SERVANT Sir, here's Mrs. Diana Trapes wants to speak with you.

PEACHUM Shall we admit her, brother Lockit?

LOCKIT By all means. She's a good customer, and a fine-spoken woman. And a woman who drinks and talks so freely, will enliven the conversation.

PEACHUM Desire her to walk in.

[*Exit* SERVANT.]

SCENE 6

PEACHUM, LOCKIT, MRS. TRAPES

PEACHUM Dear Mrs. Dye, your servant. One may know by your kiss that your gin is excellent.

MRS. TRAPES I was always very curious[7] in my liquors.

LOCKIT There is no perfumed breath like it. I have been long acquainted with the flavor of those lips, han't I, Mrs. Dye?

MRS. TRAPES Fill it up. I take as large draughts of liquor, as I did of love. I hate a flincher in either.

AIR 46. A shepherd kept sheep

In the days of my youth I could bill like a dove, fa, la, la, etc.
Like a sparrow at all times was ready for love, fa, la, la, etc.

5. Silver or gold utensils.
6. Minnows.
7. Choosy.

> *The life of all mortals in kissing should pass,*
> *Lip to lip while we're young—then the lip to the glass, fa, etc.*

But now, Mr. Peachum, to our business. If you have blacks of any kind, brought in of late, mantoes[8]—velvet scarfs, petticoats—let it be what it will, I am your chap. For all my ladies are very fond of mourning.

PEACHUM   Why, look ye, Mrs. Dye, you deal so hard with us that we can afford to give the gentlemen who venture their lives for the goods little or nothing.

MRS. TRAPES   The hard times oblige me to go very near[9] in my dealing. To be sure, of late years I have been a great sufferer by the Parliament—three thousand pounds would hardly make me amends. The Act for destroying the Mint[1] was a severe cut upon our business. 'Till then, if a customer stepped out of the way, we knew where to have her. No doubt you know Mrs. Coaxer. There's a wench now ('till today) with a good suit of clothes of mine upon her back, and I could never set eyes upon her for three months together. Since the Act too against imprisonment for small sums,[2] my loss there too hath been very considerable, and it must be so, when a lady can borrow a handsome petticoat or a clean gown, and I not have the least hank[3] upon her! And o' my conscience, nowadays most ladies take a delight in cheating, when they can do it with safety.

PEACHUM   Madam, you had a handsome gold watch of us t'other day for seven guineas. Considering we must have our profit, to a gentleman upon the road, a gold watch will be scarce worth the taking.

MRS. TRAPES   Consider, Mr. Peachum, that watch was remarkable, and not of very safe sale. If you have any black velvet scarfs, they are a handsome winter wear, and take with most gentlemen who deal with my customers. 'Tis I that put the ladies upon a good foot. 'Tis not youth or beauty that fixes their price. The gentlemen always pay according to their dress, from half a crown to two guineas; and yet those hussies make nothing of bilking of me. Then too, allowing for accidents—I have eleven fine customers now down under the surgeon's hands. What with fees and other expenses, there are great goings-out, and no comings-in, and not a farthing to pay for at least a month's clothing. We run great risks, great risks indeed.

PEACHUM   As I remember, you said something just now of Mrs. Coaxer.

MRS. TRAPES   Yes, sir. To be sure I stripped her of a suit of my own clothes about two hours ago; and have left her as she should be, in her shift, with a lover of hers at my house. She called him upstairs, as he was going to Marybone in a hackney coach. And I hope, for her own sake and mine, she will persuade the Captain to redeem her, for the Captain is very generous to the ladies.

LOCKIT   What Captain?

MRS. TRAPES   He thought I did not know him. An intimate acquaintance of yours, Mr. Peachum. Only Captain Macheath—as fine as a lord.

---

8. Mantles or cloaks. "Blacks": mourning clothes.
9. Niggardly.
1. The status of the Mint district as a sanctuary for outlaws had been undermined by recent stat-

utes.
2. Previous to this Act, someone could be arrested for owing any sum, however small.
3. Hold.

PEACHUM   Tomorrow, dear Mrs. Dye, you shall set your own price upon any of the goods you like. We have at least half a dozen velvet scarfs, and all at your service. Will you give me leave to make you a present of this suit of night-clothes for your own wearing? But are you sure it is Captain Macheath?

MRS. TRAPES   Though he thinks I have forgot him, nobody knows him better. I have taken a great deal of the Captain's money in my time at second hand, for he always loved to have his ladies well dressed.

PEACHUM   Mr. Lockit and I have a little business with the Captain—you understand me—and we will satisfy you for Mrs. Coaxer's debt.

LOCKIT   Depend upon it. We will deal like men of honor.

MRS. TRAPES   I don't inquire after your affairs, so whatever happens, I wash my hands on't. It hath always been my maxim, that one friend should assist another. But if you please, I'll take one of the scarfs home with me. 'Tis always good to have something in hand.

SCENE 7 *Newgate*

LUCY

Jealousy, rage, love, and fear are at once tearing me to pieces. How I am weather-beaten and shattered with distresses!

AIR 47.   One evening, having lost my way

> *I'm like a skiff on the ocean tossed,*
> *Now high, now low, with each billow born,*
> *With her rudder broke, and her anchor lost,*
> *Deserted and all forlorn.*
> *While thus I lie rolling and tossing all night,*
> *That Polly lies sporting on seas of delight!*
> *Revenge, revenge, revenge,*
> *Shall appease my restless sprite.*

I have the ratsbane[4] ready. I run no risk, for I can lay her death upon the gin, and so many die of that naturally that I shall never be called in question. But say I were to be hanged—I never could be hanged for anything that would give me greater comfort than the poisoning that slut.
   [*Enter* FILCH.]

FILCH   Madam, here's our Miss Polly come to wait upon you.

LUCY   Show her in.

SCENE 8

LUCY, POLLY

LUCY   Dear madam, your servant. I hope you will pardon my passion when I was so happy to see you last. I was so overrun with the spleen[5] that I was perfectly out of myself. And really when one hath the spleen, everything is to be excused by a friend.

4. Poison.   5. Fashionable seizure of peevishness or melancholy.

AIR 48.   Now Roger, I'll tell thee, because thou'rt my son

> When a wife's in her pout,
> (As she's sometimes, no doubt!)
> The good husband as meek as a lamb,
> Her vapors[6] to still,
> First grants her her will,
> And the quieting draught is a dram.
> Poor man! And the quieting draught is a dram.

I wish all our quarrels might have so comfortable a reconciliation.

POLLY   I have no excuse for my own behavior, madam, but my misfortunes. And really, madam, I suffer too upon your account.

LUCY   But, Miss Polly, in the way of friendship, will you give me leave to propose a glass of cordial to you?

POLLY   Strong waters are apt to give me the headache. I hope, madam, you will excuse me.

LUCY   Not the greatest lady in the land could have better in her closet,[7] for her own private drinking. You seem mighty low in spirits, my dear.

POLLY   I am sorry, madam, my health will not allow me to accept of your offer. I should not have left you in the rude manner I did when we met last, madam, had not my papa hauled me away so unexpectedly. I was indeed somewhat provoked, and perhaps might use some expressions that were disrespectful. But really, madam, the Captain treated me with so much contempt and cruelty that I deserved your pity rather than your resentment.

LUCY   But since his escape, no doubt all matters are made up again. Ah Polly, Polly! 'Tis I am the unhappy wife, and he loves you as if you were only his mistress.

POLLY   Sure, madam, you cannot think me so happy as to be the object of your jealousy. A man is always afraid of a woman who loves him too well, so that I must expect to be neglected and avoided.

LUCY   Then our cases, my dear Polly, are exactly alike. Both of us indeed have been too fond.

AIR 49.   O Bessy Bell

POLLY
> A curse attends that woman's love,
> Who always would be pleasing.

LUCY
> The pertness of the billing dove,
> Like tickling, is but teasing.

POLLY
> What then in love can woman do?

LUCY
> If we grow fond they shun us.

POLLY
> And when we fly them, they pursue.

LUCY
> But leave us when they've won us.

Love is so very whimsical in both sexes, that it is impossible to be lasting. But my heart is particular, and contradicts my own observation.

POLLY   But really, Mistress Lucy, by his last behavior I think I ought to envy you. When I was forced from him, he did not show the least tenderness. But perhaps he hath a heart not capable of it.

---

6. Ill humor or whims.   7. Small private room.

AIR 50.   Would Fate to me Belinda give

Among the men, coquettes we find,
Who court by turns all womankind;
And we grant all their hearts desired,
When they are flattered, and admired.

The coquettes of both sexes are self-lovers, and that is a love no other whatever can dispossess. I fear, my dear Lucy, our husband is one of those.

LUCY   Away with these melancholy reflections. Indeed, my dear Polly, we are both of us a cup too low. Let me prevail upon you, to accept of my offer.

AIR 51.   Come, sweet lass

Come sweet lass,
Let's banish sorrow
'Till tomorrow;
Come, sweet lass,
Let's take a chirping⁸ glass.
Wine can clear
The vapors of despair,
And make us light as air;
Then drink, and banish care.

I can't bear, child, to see you in such low spirits. And I must persuade you to what I know will do you good. [*Aside.*] I shall now soon be even with the hypocritical strumpet.

SCENE 9

POLLY

All this wheedling of Lucy cannot be for nothing. At this time too, when I know she hates me! The dissembling of a woman is always the forerunner of mischief. By pouring strong waters down my throat, she thinks to pump some secrets out of me. I'll be upon my guard, and won't taste a drop of her liquor, I'm resolved.

SCENE 10

LUCY, *with strong waters.* POLLY

LUCY   Come, Miss Polly.

POLLY   Indeed, child, you have given yourself trouble to no purpose. You must, my dear, excuse me.

LUCY   Really, Miss Polly, you are so squeamishly affected about taking a cup of strong waters as a lady before company. I vow, Polly, I shall take it monstrously ill if you refuse me. Brandy and men (though women love them never so well) are always taken by us with some reluctance—unless 'tis in private.

8. Cheering.

POLLY I protest, madam, it goes against me.—What do I see! Macheath
again in custody! Now every glimmering of happiness is lost. [*Drops the
glass of liquor on the ground.*]

LUCY [*Aside.*] Since things are thus, I'm glad the wench hath escaped; for
by this event, 'tis plain she was not happy enough to deserve to be poisoned.

Hogarth's *The Beggar's Opera* 3.11. Macheath stands at the center, flanked by the women
between whom he cannot choose—"Which way shall I turn me?" His leg irons hold him fast,
his arms are folded. To the left Lucy kneels to Lockit, the jailer who holds the keys, but he
turns away—"let us have no more whimpering or whining." To the right Polly kneels to Peachum, who closes his ears—"Set your heart at rest, Polly. Your husband is to die today." In
the rear, behind Polly, a group of prisoners wait for their cue. But the setting is not so much
a prison as the theater. Spectators are seated on each side of the stage, beneath satyrs; and
overhead a curtain holds the royal arms and two theatrical formulas: *Veluti in Speculum* (even
as in a mirror) and *Utile Dulce* (useful and sweet). Hogarth connects the audience with the
actors, just as *The Beggar's Opera* itself does. Several of the spectators were identified with
real people, including Gay and his producer, John Rich, conferring on the right. But the finest
stroke is the rapt gaze that Polly exchanges with the gentleman on the far right, whose Star
of the Garter identifies him as the duke of Bolton. A satyr points down at him, alerting us to
the talk of the town. At the first night the duke fell in love with Lavinia Fenton, the young
actress acclaimed as Polly; he came back every night, until she became his mistress—as well
as his duchess, two decades later, after his first wife died.

SCENE 11

LOCKIT, MACHEATH, PEACHUM, LUCY, POLLY

LOCKIT Set your heart to rest, Captain. You have neither the chance of
love or money for another escape, for you are ordered to be called down
upon your trial immediately.

PEACHUM Away, hussies! This is not a time for a man to be hampered with his wives. You see, the gentleman is in chains already.

LUCY O husband, husband, my heart longed to see thee; but to see thee thus distracts me!

POLLY Will not my dear husband look upon his Polly? Why hadst thou not flown to me for protection? With me thou hadst been safe.

AIR 52. The last time I went o'er the moor

POLLY	*Hither, dear husband, turn your eyes.*
LUCY	*Bestow one glance to cheer me.*
POLLY	*Think with that look, thy Polly dies.*
LUCY	*O shun me not, but hear me.*
POLLY	*'Tis Polly sues.*
LUCY	*—'Tis Lucy speaks.*
POLLY	*Is thus true love requited?*
LUCY	*My heart is bursting*
POLLY	*—Mine too breaks.*
LUCY	*Must I—*
POLLY	*—Must I be slighted?*

MACHEATH What would you have me say, ladies? You see, this affair will soon be at an end, without my disobliging either of you.

PEACHUM But the settling this point, Captain, might prevent a lawsuit between your two widows.

AIR 53. Tom Tinker's my true love

MACHEATH

Which way shall I turn me? How can I decide?
Wives, the day of our death, are as fond as a bride.
One wife is too much for most husbands to hear,
But two at a time there's no mortal can bear.
This way, and that way, and which way I will,
What would comfort the one, t'other wife would take ill.

POLLY But if his own misfortunes have made him insensible to mine, a father sure will be more compassionate. Dear, dear sir, sink⁹ the material evidence, and bring him off at his trial. Polly upon her knees begs it of you.

AIR 54. I am a poor shepherd undone

When my hero in court appears,
And stands arraigned for his life,
Then think of poor Polly's tears;
For ah! Poor Polly's his wife.
Like the sailor he holds up his hand,
Distressed on the dashing wave.
To die a dry death at land,
Is as bad as a wat'ry grave.
And alas, poor Polly!
Alack, and well-a-day!

9. Suppress.

Before I was in love,
Oh! every month was May.

LUCY   If Peachum's heart is hardened, sure you, sir, will have more compassion on a daughter. I know the evidence is in your power: how then can you be a tyrant to me? [*Kneeling.*]

AIR 55.   Ianthe the lovely

When he holds up his hand arraigned for his life,
Oh think of your daughter, and think I'm his wife!
What are cannons, or bombs, or clashing of swords?
For death is more certain by witnesses' words.
Then nail up their lips, that dread thunder allay;
And each month of my life will hereafter be May.

LOCKIT   Macheath's time is come, Lucy. We know our own affairs, therefore let us have no more whimpering or whining.

AIR 56.   A cobbler there was

Ourselves, like the great, to secure a retreat,
When matters require it, must give up our gang.
And good reason why,
Or, instead of the fry,
Even Peachum and I,
Like poor petty rascals, might hang, hang;
Like poor petty rascals, might hang.

PEACHUM   Set your heart at rest, Polly. Your husband is to die today. Therefore, if you are not already provided, 'tis high time to look about for another. There's comfort for you, you slut.

LOCKIT   We are ready, sir, to conduct you to the Old Bailey.

AIR 57.   Bonny Dundee

MACHEATH   *The charge is prepared; the lawyers are met;*
The judges all ranged (a terrible show!).
I go, undismayed, for death is a debt,
A debt on demand. So take what I owe.
Then farewell my love—dear charmers, adieu.
Contented I die—'tis the better for you.
Here ends all dispute the rest of our lives,
For this way at once I please all my wives.

Now, gentlemen, I am ready to attend you.

SCENE 12

LUCY, POLLY, FILCH

POLLY   Follow them, Filch, to the court. And when the trial is over, bring me a particular account of his behavior, and of everything that happened.

You'll find me here with Miss Lucy. [*Exit* FILCH.] But why is all this music?

LUCY   The prisoners whose trials are put off till next Session are diverting themselves.

POLLY   Sure there is nothing so charming as music, I'm fond of it to distraction. But alas! Now all mirth seems an insult upon my affliction. Let us retire, my dear Lucy, and indulge our sorrows. The noisy crew, you see, are coming upon us.   [*Exeunt.*]

[*A Dance of Prisoners in Chains, etc.*]

SCENE 13 *The condemned hold*

MACHEATH, *in a melancholy posture*

AIR 58.   Happy groves

O cruel, cruel, cruel case!
Must I suffer this disgrace?

AIR 59.   Of all the girls that are so smart

Of all the friends in time of grief,
When threat'ning death looks grimmer,
Not one so sure can bring relief,
As this best friend, a brimmer.[1]   [*Drinks.*]

AIR 60.   Britons strike home

Since I must swing, I scorn, I scorn to wince or whine.   [*Rises.*]

AIR 61.   Chevy Chase

But now again my spirits sink;
I'll raise them high with wine.
                                                 [*Drinks a glass of wine.*]

AIR 62.   To old Sir Simon the King

But valor the stronger grows,
The stronger liquor we're drinking.
And how can we feel our woes,
When we've lost the trouble of thinking?   [*Drinks.*]

AIR 63.   Joy to great Caesar

If thus—A man can die
Much bolder with brandy.
                              [*Pours out a bumper of brandy.*]

___
1. Brimming goblet.

AIR 64. There was an old woman

So I drink off this bumper. And now I can stand the test.
And my comrades shall see, that I die as brave as the best. [Drinks.]

AIR 65. Did you ever hear of a gallant sailor

But can I leave my pretty hussies,
Without one tear, or tender sigh?

AIR 66. Why are mine eyes still flowing

Their eyes, their lips, their busses²
Recall my love. Ah must I die?

AIR 67. Green sleeves

Since laws were made for every degree,
To curb vice in others, as well as me,
I wonder we han't better company,
Upon Tyburn Tree!
But gold from law can take out the sting;
And if rich men like us were to swing,
'Twould thin the land, such numbers to string
Upon Tyburn Tree!

JAILER Some friends of yours, Captain, desire to be admitted. I leave you together.

SCENE 14

MACHEATH, BEN BUDGE, MATT OF THE MINT

MACHEATH For my having broke prison, you see, gentlemen, I am ordered immediate execution. The sheriff's officers, I believe, are now at the door. That Jemmy Twitcher should peach me, I own surprised me! 'Tis a plain proof that the world is all alike, and that even our gang can no more trust one another than other people. Therefore, I beg you, gentlemen, look well to yourselves, for in all probability you may live some months longer.

MATT We are heartily sorry, Captain, for your misfortune. But 'tis what we must all come to.

MACHEATH Peachum and Lockit, you know, are infamous scoundrels. Their lives are as much in your power as yours are in theirs. Remember your dying friend! 'Tis my last request. Bring those villains to the gallows before you, and I am satisfied.

MATT We'll do't.

JAILER Miss Polly and Miss Lucy entreat a word with you.

MACHEATH Gentlemen, adieu.

2. Kisses.

SCENE 15

LUCY, MACHEATH, POLLY

MACHEATH   My dear Lucy, my dear Polly, whatsoever hath passed
  between us is now at an end. If you are fond of marrying again, the best
  advice I can give you, is to ship yourselves off for the West Indies,[3] where
  you'll have a fair chance of getting a husband apiece; or by good luck,
  two or three, as you like best.
POLLY   How can I support this sight!
LUCY   There is nothing moves one so much as a great man in distress.

AIR 68.   All you that must take a leap

LUCY	*Would I might be hanged!*
POLLY	*And I would so too!*
LUCY	*To be hanged with you.*
POLLY	*My dear, with you.*
MACHEATH	*O leave me to thought! I fear! I doubt!*
	I tremble! I droop! See, my courage is out.

[*Turns up the empty bottle.*]

POLLY	*No token of love?*
MACHEATH	*See, my courage is out.*

[*Turns up the empty pot.*]

LUCY	*No token of love?*
POLLY	*Adieu.*
LUCY	*Farewell.*
MACHEATH	*But hark! I hear the toll of the bell.*[4]
CHORUS	*Tol de rol lol, etc.*

JAILER   Four women more, Captain, with a child apiece! See, here they
  come. [*Enter women and children.*]
MACHEATH   What—four wives more! This is too much. Here— tell the
  sheriff's officers I am ready. [*Exit* MACHEATH *guarded.*]

SCENE 16

To them, enter PLAYER *and* BEGGAR

PLAYER   But, honest friend, I hope you don't intend that Macheath shall
  be really executed.
BEGGAR   Most certainly, sir. To make the piece perfect, I was for doing
  strict poetical justice. Macheath is to be hanged; and for the other personages of the drama, the audience must have supposed they were all
  either hanged or transported.
PLAYER   Why then, friend, this is a downright deep tragedy. The catastrophe is manifestly wrong, for an opera must end happily.
BEGGAR   Your objection, sir, is very just, and is easily removed. For you
  must allow that in this kind of drama 'tis no matter how absurdly things

---

3. In the sequel to *The Beggar's Opera*, Polly does
find a husband in the West Indies, where fortunes
could be made.

4. Rung five minutes before the condemned were
taken to Tyburn.

are brought about. So—you rabble there—run and cry a reprieve. Let the prisoner be brought back to his wives in triumph.

PLAYER   All this we must do, to comply with the taste of the town.

BEGGAR   Through the whole piece you may observe such a similitude of manners in high and low life, that it is difficult to determine whether (in the fashionable vices) the fine gentlemen imitate the gentlemen of the road, or the gentlemen of the road the fine gentlemen. Had the play remained as I at first intended, it would have carried a most excellent moral. 'Twould have shown that the lower sort of people have their vices in a degree as well as the rich, and that they are punished for them.[5]

SCENE 17

To them, MACHEATH *with rabble, etc.*

MACHEATH   So, it seems, I am not left to my choice, but must have a wife at last. Look ye, my dears, we will have no controversy now. Let us give this day to mirth, and I am sure she who thinks herself my wife will testify her joy by a dance.

ALL   Come, a dance, a dance.

MACHEATH   Ladies, I hope you will give me leave to present a partner to each of you. And (if I may without offense) for this time, I take Polly for mine. [*To* POLLY.] And for life, you slut, for we were really married. As for the rest—But at present keep your own secret.

A DANCE

AIR 69.   Lumps of pudding

Thus I stand like the Turk, with his doxies around;
From all sides their glances his passion confound;
For black, brown, and fair, his inconstancy burns,
And the different beauties subdue him by turns;
Each calls forth her charms, to provoke his desires;
Though willing to all, with but one he retires.
But think of this maxim, and put off your sorrow,
The wretch of today may be happy tomorrow.

CHORUS   *But think of this maxim, etc.*

FINIS

1728

5. *Unlike* the rich.

WILLIAM HOGARTH
1697–1764

William Hogarth was a Londoner born and bred; the life of the city, both high and low, fills all his work. His early life was hard. When his father, a writer and teacher, failed in business, the family was confined to the area of the Fleet, the debtor's prison. Hogarth never forgot "the cruel treatment" of his father by booksellers, and he resolved to make his living without relying on dealers; he would always be aggressively independent. Apprenticed as an engraver, he trained himself to sketch scenes quickly or catch them in memory. He also learned to paint, studying with the Serjeant Painter to the King, Sir James Thornhill, whose daughter he married (late in life Hogarth himself would become Serjeant Painter). Gradually he won a reputation for portraits and conversation pieces—group portraits in which members of a family or assembly interact in a social situation. But his popular fame was forged by sets of pictures that told a story: *A Harlot's Progress* (1731–32), *A Rake's Progress* (1734–35), and *Marriage A-la-Mode* (1743–45). First Hogarth painted these Modern Moral Subjects (as he called them), then prints were made and sold in large editions. He also found new ways to market and protect his work; a copyright bill to ban cheap imitations of prints was known as "Hogarth's Act." Despite this success, however, his ambition to redefine British standards of art led to frustration. The high regard and high prices for continental old masters were too well entrenched to be undermined. Hogarth did not get prestigious commissions, and his *Analysis of Beauty* (1753), an effort to fix "the fluctuating ideas of taste" by appealing to practical observations, not academic rules, was poorly received. Political and aesthetic controversies embittered his final years.

Writers have always loved Hogarth's satiric art, and many have claimed him as one of their own. Swift, Fielding, and Sterne associated their work with his; Horace Walpole considered him more "a writer of comedy with a pencil" than a painter; Charles Lamb compared him to Shakespeare; and William Hazlitt included him among the great English comic writers. This emphasis may slight Hogarth's importance in the history of art. His attempts to found a British school that looked at life and nature directly, not through a haze of ideas or reverence for the past, and to give pleasure to common people, not only to critics and connoisseurs, opened the eyes of many artists to come. But Hogarth is also a great storyteller, someone to *read*. Like novels and plays, his pictures have plots and morals; they ask us not only to look but also to think. Yet looking and thinking are always intertwined. The mind delights in riddles, according to Hogarth; and as he revised his work he stuffed in more and more clues, like a mystery writer. A feast of interpretation draws the reader in. So many expressive details crowd the pictures, so many keys to character and meaning, that viewers often become obsessed with figuring them out. Even inanimate objects can speak; playwrights rely on words, as Walpole pointed out, but "it was reserved to Hogarth to write a scene of furniture."

The furniture is particularly eloquent in *Marriage A-la-Mode*; note, for example, the fallen chairs in Plates 2 and 6. Hogarth took special pains with this series. The audience at which he aimed, as well as the subject matter, belonged to high society; and the art too is highly refined. A sinuous line weaves through each picture, leading the reader on, and each piece of bric-a-brac carries a message of lavish excess. Yet the story itself is brutally straightforward. A disastrous forced marriage stands at the center: a rich but miserly merchant buys the worthless son of an aristocrat for his restless daughter, and with nothing in common the couple destroy one another. The crisis of values that Hogarth depicts was bringing about radical changes in English life. In the tension between a fading aristocracy, both morally and financially bankrupt, and an upwardly mobile middle class, greedy for power but culturally insecure, the marriage reflects a society that has lost all sense of right and wrong. The artist plays no favorites. The aristocratic Squanderfields are not only vain, effete, and dissipated but also lacking in taste; the wan mythological paintings on their walls are just the sort of pretentious, overpriced art that Hogarth hates. But the vulgar Dutch art on the merchant's walls (in Plate 6) seems even worse, and his daughter falls for every extravagant, spurious fashion (in Plate 4). Nor do the parasites who live off these easy marks offer any hope. Lawyer and doctor, bawd and servant pave the road to ruin. Hogarth's satire warns against the spreading corruption of modern times, when self-interest eats into marriage and old values die. Look hard, he tells the public. These objects make up the world we live in. We might become these people.

Marriage A-la-Mode

Plate 1. *The Marriage Contract.* Lord Squanderfield points to the family tree, going back to William the Conquerer, that his son will bring to the marriage. Coronets are blazed all over the room, from the top of the canopy at the upper left to the side of the prostrate dog on the lower right. The earl, though hobbled by gout, is proud. But he has run out of money: construction has stopped on the Palladian mansion seen through the window. Sitting across from him, a squinting merchant grasps the marriage settlement. Some of the coins and banknotes he has placed on the table have been taken up by a scrawny usurer, who hands the earl a mortgage in return. At the right the betrothed sit back to back, uncaring as the dogs chained to each other below. The vacuous viscount pinches snuff and gazes at himself in a mirror, which ominously reflects the image of lawyer Silvertongue, who sharpens his pen as he bends unctuously over the bride-to-be. Pouting, she twirls her wedding ring in a handkerchief. Disasters from mythology cover the walls. A bombastic portrait of the earl as Jupiter, astride a cannon, dominates the room; and in a candle sconce on the right Medusa glowers over the scene.

Plate 2. *After the Marriage.*   By now the couple are used to ignoring each other. The morning after a spree, the rumpled, exhausted viscount slouches in a chair. His broken sword has dropped on the carpet, and a lapdog sniffs at a woman's cap in his pocket—souvenirs of the night. Lolling and stretching in an unladylike pose, his wife too is half asleep. She has spent the night home but not alone. *Hoyle on Whist* lies before her, cards are scattered on the floor, and the overturned chair, book of music, and violin cases suggest that some player may have departed in haste. A steward carries away a sheaf of bills—only one paid—and the household ledger; a Methodist (*Regeneration* is in his pocket), he petitions heaven to look down on these heathens. Oriental idols decorate the mantel over the fireplace, surmounted by a broken-nosed Roman bust that frowns like the steward and a painting of Cupid playing the bagpipes. On the left, amid the shrubbery of a rococo clock, a cat leers over fish and a Buddha smiles. In the next room, a dozing servant fails to notice that a candle has set fire to a chair. Next to a row of saints, a curtain does not quite cover a bawdy painting from which a naked foot peeps.

Plate 3. *The Scene with the Quack*. The husband has come to this chamber of medical horrors in search of a cure. The pillbox he holds toward the quack has not done its job, and he raises his cane as if with a playful threat. Evidently the little girl who stands between his legs is infected. She dabs a sore on her lip, and her ageless face may hint that she is not as young and pure as she looks. Her cap resembles the cap in Plate 2; she is the husband's mistress. Perhaps the beauty spot on his neck also covers a sore. The bowlegged Monsieur de la Pillule comfortably wipes his glasses; he has seen all this before. Between the two men an angry woman, fortified by a massive hoop skirt, opens a knife. She may be the wife of the quack, defending her man, or else a bawd who resents the charge that her girls are damaged goods. Medical oddities and monstrosities clutter the room, along with portents of death. The viscount's cane points to a cabinet where a wigged head looks at a skeleton that seems to be groping a cadaver; the tripod above evokes a gallows tree. At the far left, in front of a laboratory door, are two of the doctor's inventions: machines for setting bones and uncorking bottles. Their similarity to instruments of torture hints at how useful the doctor's assistance will be.

Plate 4. *The Countess's Levee.* In her bedchamber at rising (*levée*; French), the countess receives some guests and puts on a show. Her husband is now earl (note the coronets), and they have a child (note the rattle on her chair). While a hairdresser curls her locks, she hangs on the words of Silvertongue, who makes himself at home (note his portrait on the upper right wall). Tonight they will be going to a masquerade ball, like the one on the screen he gestures toward; his left hand holds the tickets. At the far right a puffy, bedizened castrato sings, accompanied by a flute. His audience includes a self-absorbed dandy in curl-papers; a man who appreciatively smirks and opens his hand, from which a fan dangles; a snoring husband, holding his riding-crop like a baton; and his enraptured wife, who leans forward as if about to swoon. Unobserved by the others, a black servant, bearing a cup of chocolate, smiles in amazement at these precious airs. At the lower left another black servant, a boy in a turban, grins at gewgaws purchased at an auction. His finger points both to Actaeon's horns, the sign of a cuckold, and to the couple as they arrange their tryst. Wall paintings illustrate unnatural sex: Lot's seduction by his daughters, Jupiter embracing Io, and the rape of Ganymede.

Plate 5. *The Death of the Earl.*   The melodramatic tableau at the center, as the earl totters toward death and the countess kneels to beg forgiveness, imitates paintings of Christ descending from the cross while Mary Magdalen mourns. But the surroundings are sordid. At a house of ill repute, the Turk's Head Bagnio, the countess and Silvertongue have been surprised in bed. The earl has broken in (key and socket on the floor) and drawn his sword, and the lawyer has run him through. As the horrified owner and constable enter, under a watchman's lantern, the killer, still in his nightshirt, flees through a window. A fire, outside the picture on the lower right, casts lurid light on the victim; the shadow of the tongs encircles the murder weapon. Costumed as a nun and friar, the lovers have come from a masquerade, and their discarded masks and clothes show they were in haste. Pills (presumably mercury, prescribed for venereal disease) have spilled from an overturned table on the right, beside an advertisement for the bagnio, a corset, and a bundle of firewood. The portrait of a streetwalker, a squirrel perched on her hand, leers over the countess; on the wall behind the earl an uplifted blade is about to sever a child, in the Judgment of Solomon. At the top left St. Luke, the patron of artists, inscribes these transgressions.

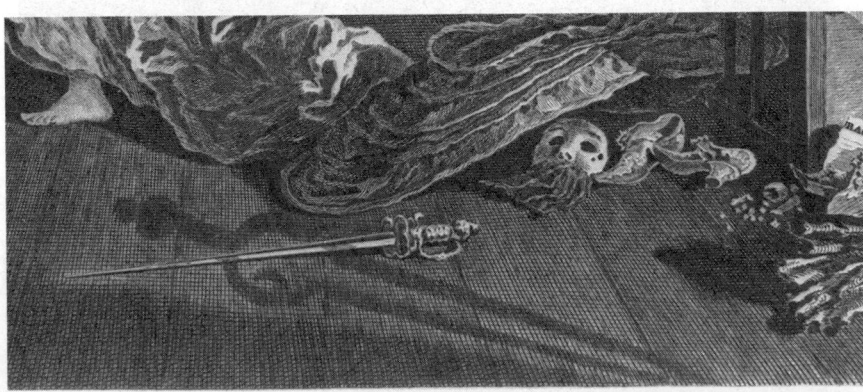

Plate 6. *The Death of the Countess.* "Counseller Silvertongues Last Dying Speech," a paper on the floor announces, and a bottle of laudanum has dropped beside it. News of her lover's execution has driven the countess to poison herself. Slumped in a chair, she is already dead; on the far right a doctor steals away. Her father calmly slides the ring from her finger. This is his house; a window with cobwebs and broken panes opens on London Bridge, in the heart of the City. No luxury here. The furnishings are sparse, the floor is bare, and the dining table holds only one egg and a few leftovers, including a pathetic boar's head from which a starving hound is tearing scraps. The art is equally cheap: a pissing boy, a jumbled still life, a pipe set alight by the glowing nose of a drunk. At the center, beneath a coatrack, a stout apothecary (stomach pump and julep in his pocket) points toward the empty bottle in reproof and pokes the servant who brought it—an idiot wearing a coat many sizes too large, the merchant's hand-me-down. The service staff is completed by a withered old woman who holds out the countess's little child for one last hug and kiss. But the mark on the child's cheek and the brace on its leg imply that disease has passed to the next generation. This noble family will have no heir.

SAMUEL JOHNSON
1709–1784

Samuel Johnson was famous as a talker in his own time, and his conversation (pre-served by James Boswell and others) has been famous ever since. But his wisdom survives above all in his writings: a few superb poems; the grave *Rambler* essays, which established his reputation as a stylist and a moralist; the lessons about life in *Rasselas* and the *Lives of the Poets*; and literary criticism that ranks among the best in English. The virtues of the talk and the writings are the same. They come hot from a mind well stored with knowledge, searingly honest, humane, and quick to seize the unex-pected but appropriate image of truth. Johnson's wit is timeless, for it deals with the great facts of human experience, with hope and happiness and loss and duty and the fear of death. Whatever topic he addresses, whatever the form in which he writes, he holds to one commanding purpose: to see life as it is.

Two examples must suffice here. When Anna Williams wondered why a man should make a beast of himself through drunkenness, Johnson answered that "he who makes a beast of himself gets rid of the pain of being a man." In this reply Williams's tired metaphor is so charged with an awareness of the dark aspects of human life that it comes almost unbearably alive. Such moments characterize Johnson's writings as well. For instance, in reviewing the book of a fatuous would-be philosopher who blandly explained away the pains of poverty by declaring that a kindly providence compensates the poor by making them more hopeful, more healthy, more easily pleased, and less sensitive than the rich, Johnson retorted: "The poor indeed are insensible of many little vexations which sometimes embitter the possessions and pollute the enjoyments of the rich. They are not pained by casual incivility, or mor-tified by the mutilation of a compliment; but this happiness is like that of a malefactor who ceases to feel the cords that bind him when the pincers are tearing his flesh."

Johnson had himself known the pains of poverty. During his boyhood and youth, his father's financial circumstances steadily worsened, so that he was forced to leave Oxford before he had taken a degree. An early marriage to a well-to-do widow, Eliz-abeth ("Tetty") Porter, more than twenty years older than he, enabled him to open a school. But the school failed, and he moved to London to make his way as a writer. The years between 1737, when he first arrived there with his pupil David Garrick (later to become the leading actor of his generation), and 1755, when the publication of the *Dictionary* established his reputation, were often difficult. He supported him-self at first as best he could by doing hack work for the *Gentleman's Magazine*, but gradually his own original writings began to attract attention.

In 1747 Johnson published the *Plan* of his *Dictionary*, and he spent the the next seven years compiling it—although he had expected to finish it in three. When in 1748 Dr. Adams, a friend from Oxford days, questioned his ability to carry out such a work alone so fast and reminded him that the *Dictionary* of the French Academy had needed forty academicians working for forty years, Johnson replied with humor-ous jingoism: "Sir, thus it is. This is the proportion. Let me see; forty times forty is sixteen hundred. As three to sixteen hundred, so is the proportion of an Englishman to a Frenchman."

Johnson's achievement in compiling the *Dictionary* seems even greater when we realize that he was writing some of his best essays and poems during the same period. Although the booksellers who published the *Dictionary* paid him what was then the large sum of £1,575, it was not enough to enable him to support his household, buy materials, and pay the wages of the six assistants whom he employed year by year until the task was accomplished. He therefore had to earn more money by writing. In 1749, his early tragedy *Irene* (pronounced *I-re-nĕ*) was produced at long last by his old friend Garrick, by then the manager of Drury Lane. The play was not a success, although Johnson made some profit from it. In the same year appeared his finest poem, *The Vanity of Human Wishes*. With the *Rambler* (1750–52) and the *Idler* (1758–60), two series of periodical essays, Johnson found a devoted audience, but his pleasure was tempered by the death of his wife in 1752. He never remarried.

Boswell said of the *Rambler* essays that "in no writings whatever can be found more bark and steel [i.e., quinine and iron] for the mind." Moral strength and health; the importance of applying reason to experience; the test of virtue by what we do, not what we say or "feel"; faith in God: these are the centers to which Johnson's moral writings always return. What Johnson uniquely offers us is the quality of his understanding of the human condition, based on wide reading but always ultimately referred to his own passionate and often anguished experience. Such understanding had to be fought for again and again.

Johnson is thought of as the great generalizer, but what gives his generalizations strength is that they are rooted in the particulars of his self-knowledge. He had constantly to fight against what he called "filling the mind" with illusions to avoid the call of duty, his own black melancholy, and the realities of life. The portrait (largely a self-portrait) of Sober in *Idler* 31 is revealing: he occupies his idle hours with crafts and hobbies and has now taken up chemistry—he "sits and counts the drops as they come from his retort, and forgets that, whilst a drop is falling, a moment flies away." So clear a vision is some distance away from the secure ease of the Addisonian essay.

His theme of themes is expressed in the title *The Vanity of Human Wishes*: the dangerous but all-pervasive power of wishful thinking, the feverish intrusion of desires and hopes that distort reality and lead to false expectations. Almost all of Johnson's major writings—verse satire, moral essay, or the prose fable *Rasselas* (1759)—express this theme. In *Rasselas* it is called "the hunger of imagination, which preys upon life," picturing things as one would like them to be, not as they are. The travelers who are the fable's protagonists pursue some formula for happiness; they reflect our naive hope, against the lessons of experience, that one choice of life will make us happy forever.

During this time of great activity, Johnson developed his characteristic style: the rotund periods, proceeding through balanced or parallel words; phrases or clauses moving to carefully controlled rhythms, in language that is characteristically general, often Latinate, and frequently polysyllabic. It is a style at the opposite extreme from Jonathan Swift's simplicity or Joseph Addison's neatness. In Johnson's writings this style never becomes obscure or turgid, for even a very complex sentence reveals—as it should—the structure of the thought, and the learned words are always precisely used. While reading early scientists to collect words for the *Dictionary*, he developed a new vocabulary: for example, *obtund, exuberate, fugacity,* and *frigorific*. But he used many of these strange words in conversation as well as in his writings, often with a peculiarly Johnsonian felicity, describing the operations of the mind with a scientific precision.

After Johnson received his pension in 1762, he no longer had to write for a living, and because he held that "no man but a blockhead" ever wrote for any other reason, he produced as little as he decently could during the last twenty years of his life. His edition of Shakespeare, long delayed, was published in 1765, with a fine preface and fascinating notes. His last important work is the *Lives of the Poets*, which came out in two parts in 1779 and 1781. These biographical and critical prefaces were commissioned by a group of booksellers who had joined together to publish a large collection of the English poets and who wished to give their venture the prestige that Johnson would lend it. The poets to be included (except for four insisted on by Johnson) were selected by the booksellers according to current fashions. Therefore the collection begins with Abraham Cowley and John Milton and ends with Thomas Gray, and it omits such standard poets as Geoffrey Chaucer, Edmund Spenser, Sir Philip Sidney, John Donne, and Andrew Marvell.

In the *Lives of the Poets* and in the earlier *Life of Richard Savage* (1744), Johnson did much to advance the art of biography in England. Biography had long been associated with panegyrics or scandalous memoirs; and therefore Johnson's insistence on truth, even about the subject's defects, and on concrete, often minute, details was a new departure, disliked by many readers. "The biographical part of literature is what I love most," Johnson said, for he found every biography useful in revealing the human nature that all of us share. His insistence on truth in biography (and knowing that Boswell intended to write his life, he insisted that he should write it truthfully) was owing to his conviction that only a truthful work can be trusted to help us with the business of living.

The ideal poet, according to Johnson, has a genius for making the things we see every day seem new. The same might be said of Johnson himself as a critic. He is our great champion, in criticism, of common sense and the common reader. Without denying the right of the poet to flights of imagination, he also insists that poems must make sense, please readers, and help us not only understand the world but cope with it. Johnson holds poems to the truth, as he sees it: the principles of nature, logic, religion, and morality. Not even Shakespeare can be excused when "he sacrifices virtue to convenience" and "seems to write without any moral purpose." Yet Johnson is no worshiper of authority or mere "correctness." As a critic he is always the empiricist, testing theory by practice. His determination to judge literature by its truth to life, not by abstract rules, is perfectly illustrated by his treatment of the doctrine of the three unities in the *Preface* to Shakespeare. Johnson is never afraid to state the obvious, whether the lack of human interest in *Paradise Lost* or Shakespeare's temptation by puns. But at its best, as in the praise of Milton or Shakespeare, his criticism engages some of the deepest questions about literature: why it endures, and how it helps us endure.

The Vanity of Human Wishes   This poem is an imitation of Juvenal's *Satire 10*. Although it closely follows the order and the ideas of the Latin poem, it remains a very personal work, for Johnson has used the Roman Stoic's satire as a means of expressing his own sense of the tragic and comic in human life. He has tried to reproduce in English verse the qualities he thought especially Juvenalian: stateliness, pointed sentences, and declamatory grandeur. The poem is difficult because of the extreme compactness of the style: every line is forced to convey the greatest possible amount of meaning. Johnson's poetic theory demanded that the poet should deal in the general rather than mere particulars, but he certainly did not intend that the general should fade into the abstract: observe, for example, how he makes abstract nouns concrete, active, and dramatic by using them as subjects of active and dramatic verbs: "Hate *dogs* their flight, and Insult *mocks* their end" (line 78). But the difficulty of the poem is also related to its theme, the difficulty of seeing anything clearly on this earth. In a world of blindness and illusion, human beings must struggle to find a point of view that will not deceive them, and a happiness that can last.

The Vanity of Human Wishes

In Imitation of the Tenth Satire of Juvenal

> Let Observation, with extensive view,
> Survey mankind, from China to Peru;
> Remark each anxious toil, each eager strife,
> And watch the busy scenes of crowded life;
> 5 Then say how hope and fear, desire and hate

O'erspread with snares the clouded maze of fate,
Where wavering man, betrayed by venturous pride
To tread the dreary paths without a guide,
As treacherous phantoms in the mist delude,
10 Shuns fancied ills, or chases airy good;
How rarely Reason guides the stubborn choice,
Rules the bold hand, or prompts the suppliant voice;
How nations sink, by darling schemes oppressed,
When Vengeance listens to the fool's request.
15 Fate wings with every wish the afflictive dart,
Each gift of nature, and each grace of art;
With fatal heat impetuous courage glows,
With fatal sweetness elocution flows,
Impeachment stops the speaker's powerful breath,
20 And restless fire precipitates on death.
But scarce observed, the knowing and the bold
Fall in the general massacre of gold;
Wide-wasting pest! that rages unconfined,
And crowds with crimes the records of mankind;
25 For gold his sword the hireling ruffian draws,
For gold the hireling judge distorts the laws;
Wealth heaped on wealth, nor truth nor safety buys,
The dangers gather as the treasures rise.
Let History tell where rival kings command,
30 And dubious title shakes the madded land,
When statutes glean the refuse of the sword,
How much more safe the vassal than the lord;
Low skulks the hind° beneath the rage of power,   *peasant*
And leaves the wealthy traitor[1] in the Tower,
35 Untouched his cottage, and his slumbers sound,
Though Confiscation's vultures hover round.
The needy traveler, serene and gay,
Walks the wild heath, and sings his toil away.
Does envy seize thee? crush the upbraiding joy,
40 Increase his riches and his peace destroy;
New fears in dire vicissitude invade,
The rustling brake° alarms, and quivering shade,   *thicket*
Nor light nor darkness bring his pain relief,
One shows the plunder, and one hides the thief.
45 Yet still one general cry the skies assails,
And gain and grandeur load the tainted gales;
Few know the toiling statesman's fear or care,
The insidious rival and the gaping heir.
Once more, Democritus,[2] arise on earth,
50 With cheerful wisdom and instructive mirth,
See motley life in modern trappings dressed,
And feed with varied fools the eternal jest:
Thou who couldst laugh where Want enchained Caprice,
Toil crushed Conceit, and man was of a piece;

---

1. Johnson first wrote "bonny traitor," recalling the Jacobite uprising of 1745 and the execution of four of its Scot leaders.

2. A Greek philosopher of the late 5th century B.C.E., remembered as the "laughing philosopher" because men's follies only moved him to mirth.

55　Where Wealth unloved without a mourner died;
　　And scarce a sycophant was fed by Pride;
　　Where ne'er was known the form of mock debate,
　　Or seen a new-made mayor's unwieldy state;
　　Where change of favorites made no change of laws,
60　And senates heard before they judged a cause;
　　How wouldst thou shake at Britain's modish tribe,
　　Dart the quick taunt, and edge the piercing gibe?
　　Attentive truth and nature to descry,
　　And pierce each scene with philosophic eye.
65　To thee were solemn toys or empty show
　　The robes of pleasure and the veils of woe:
　　All aid the farce, and all thy mirth maintain,
　　Whose joys are causeless, or whose griefs are vain.
　　　　Such was the scorn that filled the sage's mind,
70　Renewed at every glance on human kind;
　　How just that scorn ere yet thy voice declare,
　　Search every state, and canvass every prayer.
　　　　Unnumbered suppliants crowd Preferment's gate,
　　Athirst for wealth, and burning to be great;
75　Delusive Fortune hears the incessant call,
　　They mount, they shine, evaporate, and fall.
　　On every stage the foes of peace attend,
　　Hate dogs their flight, and Insult mocks their end.
　　Love ends with hope, the sinking statesman's door
80　Pours in the morning worshiper no more;[3]
　　For growing names the weekly scribbler lies,
　　To growing wealth the dedicator flies;
　　From every room descends the painted face,
　　That hung the bright palladium[4] of the place;
85　And smoked in kitchens, or in auctions sold,
　　To better features yields the frame of gold;
　　For now no more we trace in every line
　　Heroic worth, benevolence divine:
　　The form distorted justifies the fall,
90　And Detestation rids the indignant wall.
　　　　But will not Britain hear the last appeal,
　　Sign her foes' doom, or guard her favorites' zeal?
　　Through Freedom's sons no more remonstrance rings,
　　Degrading nobles and controlling kings;
95　Our supple tribes repress their patriot throats,
　　And ask no questions but the price of votes;
　　With weekly libels and septennial ale,[5]
　　Their wish is full to riot and to rail.
　　　　In full-blown dignity, see Wolsey[6] stand,

3. Statesmen gave interviews and received friends
and petitioners at levees, or morning receptions.
4. An image of Pallas Athena, which fell from
heaven and was preserved at Troy. Not until it was
stolen by Diomedes could the city fall to the
Greeks.
5. Ministers and even the king freely bought support by bribing Members of Parliament, who in

turn won elections by buying votes. "Weekly
libels": politically motivated lampoons published in
the weekly newspapers. "Septennial ale": the ale
given away by candidates at parliamentary elections, held at least every seven years.
6. Thomas Cardinal Wolsey (ca. 1475–1530), lord
chancellor and favorite of Henry VIII. Shakespeare
dramatized his fall in Henry VIII.

100 Law in his voice, and fortune in his hand:
To him the church, the realm, their powers consign,
Through him the rays of regal bounty shine;
Turned by his nod the stream of honor flows,
His smile alone security bestows:

105 Still to new heights his restless wishes tower,
Claim leads to claim, and power advances power;
Till conquest unresisted ceased to please,
And rights submitted, left him none to seize.
At length his sovereign frowns—the train of state

110 Mark the keen glance, and watch the sign to hate.
Where'er he turns, he meets a stranger's eye,
His suppliants scorn him, and his followers fly;
At once is lost the pride of awful state,
The golden canopy, the glittering plate,

115 The regal palace, the luxurious board,
The liveried army, and the menial lord.
With age, with cares, with maladies oppressed,
He seeks the refuge of monastic rest.
Grief aids disease, remembered folly stings,

120 And his last sighs reproach the faith of kings.
     Speak thou, whose thoughts at humble peace repine,
Shall Wolsey's wealth, with Wolsey's end be thine?
Or liv'st thou now, with safer pride content,
The wisest justice on the banks of Trent?

125 For why did Wolsey, near the steeps of fate,
On weak foundations raise the enormous weight?
Why but to sink beneath misfortune's blow,
With louder ruin to the gulfs below?
     What gave great Villiers[7] to the assassin's knife,

130 And fixed disease on Harley's closing life?
What murdered Wentworth, and what exiled Hyde,
By kings protected, and to kings allied?
What but their wish indulged in courts to shine,
And power too great to keep or to resign?

135   When first the college rolls receive his name,
The young enthusiast quits his ease for fame;
Through all his veins the fever of renown
Burns from the strong contagion of the gown:
O'er Bodley's dome his future labors spread,

140 And Bacon's[8] mansion trembles o'er his head.
Are these thy views? proceed, illustrious youth,
And Virtue guard thee to the throne of Truth!
Yet should thy soul indulge the generous heat,
Till captive Science yields her last retreat;

7. George Villiers, first duke of Buckingham, favorite of James I and Charles I, was assassinated in 1628. Mentioned in the following lines: Robert Harley, earl of Oxford, chancellor of the exchequer and later lord treasurer under Queen Anne (1710–14), impeached and imprisoned by the Whigs in 1715. Thomas Wentworth, earl of Strafford, intimate and adviser of Charles I, impeached by the Long Parliament and executed in 1641. Edward Hyde, earl of Clarendon ("to kings allied" because his daughter married James, duke of York), lord chancellor under Charles II (impeached in 1667, he fled to the Continent).
8. Roger Bacon (ca. 1214–1294), scientist and philosopher, taught at Oxford, where his study, according to tradition, would collapse when a man greater than he should appear at Oxford. "Bodley's dome": the Bodleian Library, Oxford.

145 Should Reason guide thee with her brightest ray,
And pour on misty Doubt resistless day;
Should no false kindness lure to loose delight,
Nor praise relax, nor difficulty fright;
Should tempting Novelty thy cell refrain,
150 And Sloth effuse her opiate fumes in vain;
Should Beauty blunt on fops her fatal dart,
Nor claim the triumph of a lettered heart;
Should no disease thy torpid veins invade,
Nor Melancholy's phantoms haunt thy shade;
155 Yet hope not life from grief or danger free,
Nor think the doom of man reversed for thee:
Deign on the passing world to turn thine eyes,
And pause a while from letters, to be wise;
There mark what ills the scholar's life assail,
160 Toil, envy, want, the patron,[9] and the jail.
See nations slowly wise, and meanly just,
To buried merit raise the tardy bust.
If dreams yet flatter, once again attend,
Hear Lydiat's life, and Galileo's[1] end.

165   Nor deem, when Learning her last prize bestows,
The glittering eminence exempt from foes;
See when the vulgar 'scapes, despised or awed,
Rebellion's vengeful talons seize on Laud.[2]
From meaner minds, though smaller fines content,
170 The plundered palace or sequestered rent;[3]
Marked out by dangerous parts he meets the shock,
And fatal Learning leads him to the block:
Around his tomb let Art and Genius weep,
But hear his death, ye blockheads, hear and sleep.

175   The festal blazes, the triumphal show,
The ravished standard, and the captive foe,
The senate's thanks, the gazette's pompous tale,
With force resistless o'er the brave prevail.
Such bribes the rapid Greek° o'er Asia whirled,   Alexander the Great
180 For such the steady Romans shook the world;
For such in distant lands the Britons shine,
And stain with blood the Danube or the Rhine;
This power has praise that virtue scarce can warm,
Till fame supplies the universal charm.
185 Yet Reason frowns on War's unequal game,
Where wasted nations raise a single name,
And mortgaged states their grandsires' wreaths regret
From age to age in everlasting debt;
Wreaths which at last the dear-bought right convey
190 To rust on medals, or on stones decay.

9. In the first edition, "garret." For the reason of the change see Boswell's *Life of Johnson* (p. 2762).
1. Galileo (1564–1642), famous astronomer, was imprisoned as a heretic by the Inquisition in 1633; he died blind. Thomas Lydiat (1572–1646), Oxford scholar, died impoverished because of his Royalist sympathies.

2. Appointed archbishop of Canterbury by Charles I, William Laud followed rigorously High Church policies and was executed by order of the Long Parliament in 1645.
3. During the Commonwealth, the estates of many Royalists were pillaged and their incomes confiscated ("sequestered") by the state.

On what foundation stands the warrior's pride?
How just his hopes, let Swedish Charles[4] decide;
A frame of adamant, a soul of fire,
No dangers fright him, and no labors tire;
195   O'er love, o'er fear, extends his wide domain,
Unconquered lord of pleasure and of pain;
No joys to him pacific scepters yield,
War sounds the trump, he rushes to the field;
Behold surrounding kings their powers combine,
200   And one capitulate, and one resign;[5]
Peace courts his hand, but spreads her charms in vain;
"Think nothing gained," he cries, "till naught remain,
On Moscow's walls till Gothic standards fly,
And all be mine beneath the polar sky."
205   The march begins in military state,
And nations on his eye suspended wait;
Stern Famine guards the solitary coast,
And Winter barricades the realms of Frost;
He comes, nor want nor cold his course delay—
210   Hide, blushing Glory, hide Pultowa's day:
The vanquished hero leaves his broken bands,
And shows his miseries in distant lands;
Condemned a needy supplicant to wait,
While ladies interpose, and slaves debate.
215   But did not Chance at length her error mend?
Did no subverted empire mark his end?
Did rival monarchs give the fatal wound?
Or hostile millions press him to the ground?
His fall was destined to a barren strand,
220   A petty fortress, and a dubious hand;
He left the name at which the world grew pale,
To point a moral, or adorn a tale.
    All times their scenes of pompous woes afford,
From Persia's tyrant to Bavaria's lord.[6]
225   In gay hostility, and barbarous pride,
With half mankind embattled at his side,
Great Xerxes comes to seize the certain prey,
And starves exhausted regions in his way;
Attendant Flattery counts his myriads o'er,
230   Till counted myriads soothe his pride no more;
Fresh praise is tried till madness fires his mind,
The waves he lashes, and enchains the wind;
New powers are claimed, new powers are still bestowed,
Till rude resistance lops the spreading god;
235   The daring Greeks deride the martial show,

4. Charles XII of Sweden (1682–1718). Defeated by the Russians at Pultowa (1709), he escaped to Turkey and tried to form an alliance against Russia with the sultan. Returning to Sweden, he attacked Norway and was killed in the attack on Fredrikshald.
5. Frederick IV of Denmark capitulated to Charles in 1700. Augustus II of Poland resigned his throne to Charles in 1704.
6. The Elector Charles Albert caused the War of the Austrian Succession (1740–48) when he contested the crown of the empire with Maria Theresa ("Fair Austria" in line 245). "Persia's tyrant": Xerxes invaded Greece and was totally defeated in the sea battle off Salamis, 480 B.C.E.

And heap their valleys with the gaudy foe;
The insulted sea with humbler thoughts he gains,
A single skiff to speed his flight remains;
The encumbered oar scarce leaves the dreaded coast
240   Through purple billows and a floating host.
    The bold Bavarian, in a luckless hour,
Tries the dread summits of Caesarean power,
With unexpected legions bursts away,
And sees defenseless realms receive his sway;
245   Short sway! fair Austria spreads her mournful charms,
The queen, the beauty, sets the world in arms;
From hill to hill the beacon's rousing blaze
Spreads wide the hope of plunder and of praise;
The fierce Croatian, and the wild Hussar,[7]
250   With all the sons of ravage crowd the war;
The baffled prince in honor's flattering bloom
Of hasty greatness finds the fatal doom;
His foes' derision, and his subjects' blame,
And steals to death from anguish and from shame.
255   Enlarge my life with multitude of days!
In health, in sickness, thus the suppliant prays;
Hides from himself his state, and shuns to know,
That life protracted is protracted woe.
Time hovers o'er, impatient to destroy,
260   And shuts up all the passages of joy;
In vain their gifts the bounteous seasons pour,
The fruit autumnal, and the vernal flower;
With listless eyes the dotard views the store,
He views, and wonders that they please no more;
265   Now pall the tasteless meats, and joyless wines,
And Luxury with sighs her slave resigns.
Approach, ye minstrels, try the soothing strain,
Diffuse the tuneful lenitives[8] of pain:
No sounds, alas! would touch the impervious ear,
270   Though dancing mountains witnessed Orpheus[9] near;
Nor lute nor lyre his feeble powers attend,
Nor sweeter music of a virtuous friend,
But everlasting dictates crowd his tongue,
Perversely grave, or positively wrong.
275   The still returning tale, and lingering jest,
Perplex the fawning niece and pampered guest,
While growing hopes scarce awe the gathering sneer,
And scarce a legacy can bribe to hear;
The watchful guests still hint the last offense,
280   The daughter's petulance, the son's expense,
Improve his heady rage with treacherous skill,
And mold his passions till they make his will.
    Unnumbered maladies his joints invade,
Lay siege to life and press the dire blockade;

7. Hungarian light cavalry.
8. Medicines that relieve pain.

9. A legendary poet who played on the lyre so beautifully that wild beasts were spellbound.

285 But unextinguished avarice still remains,
And dreaded losses aggravate his pains;
He turns, with anxious heart and crippled hands,
His bonds of debt, and mortgages of lands;
Or views his coffers with suspicious eyes,
290 Unlocks his gold, and counts it till he dies.
 But grant, the virtues of a temperate prime
Bless with an age exempt from scorn or crime;
An age that melts with unperceived decay,
And glides in modest innocence away;
295 Whose peaceful day Benevolence endears,
Whose night congratulating Conscience cheers;
The general favorite as the general friend:
Such age there is, and who shall wish its end?
 Yet even on this her load Misfortune flings,
300 To press the weary minutes' flagging wings;
New sorrow rises as the day returns,
A sister sickens, or a daughter mourns.
Now kindred Merit fills the sable bier,
Now lacerated Friendship claims a tear;
305 Year chases year, decay pursues decay,
Still drops some joy from withering life away;
New forms arise, and different views engage,
Superfluous lags the veteran[1] on the stage,
Till pitying Nature signs the last release,
310 And bids afflicted Worth retire to peace.
 But few there are whom hours like these await,
Who set unclouded in the gulfs of Fate.
From Lydia's monarch[2] should the search descend,
By Solon cautioned to regard his end,
315 In life's last scene what prodigies surprise,
Fears of the brave, and follies of the wise!
From Marlborough's eyes the streams of dotage flow,
And Swift[3] expires a driveler and a show.
 The teeming mother, anxious for her race,
320 Begs for each birth the fortune of a face:
Yet Vane could tell what ills from beauty spring;
And Sedley[4] cursed the form that pleased a king.
Ye nymphs of rosy lips and radiant eyes,
Whom Pleasure keeps too busy to be wise,
325 Whom Joys with soft varieties invite,
By day the frolic, and the dance by night;
Who frown with vanity, who smile with art,
And ask the latest fashion of the heart;
What care, what rules your heedless charms shall save,
330 Each nymph your rival, and each youth your slave?

1. A veteran of life, not of war.
2. Croesus, the wealthy and fortunate king, was warned by Solon not to count himself happy until he ceased to live. He lost his crown to Cyrus the Great of Persia.
3. Jonathan Swift, who passed the last four years of his life in utter senility. John Churchill, duke of Marlborough, England's brilliant general during most of the War of the Spanish Succession (1702–13).
4. Catherine Sedley, mistress of James II. Anne Vane, mistress of Frederick, prince of Wales (son of George II).

Against your fame with Fondness Hate combines,
The rival batters, and the lover mines.
With distant voice neglected Virtue calls,
Less heard and less, the faint remonstrance falls;
335 Tired with contempt, she quits the slippery reign,
And Pride and Prudence take her seat in vain.
In crowd at once, where none the pass defend,
The harmless freedom, and the private friend.
The guardians yield, by force superior plied:
340 To Interest, Prudence; and to Flattery, Pride.
Now Beauty falls betrayed, despised, distressed,
And hissing Infamy proclaims the rest.
   Where then shall Hope and Fear their objects find?
Must dull Suspense corrupt the stagnant mind?
345 Must helpless man, in ignorance sedate,
Roll darkling down the torrent of his fate?
Must no dislike alarm, no wishes rise,
No cries invoke the mercies of the skies?
Inquirer, cease; petitions yet remain,
350 Which Heaven may hear, nor deem religion vain.
Still raise for good the supplicating voice,
But leave to Heaven the measure and the choice.
Safe in his power, whose eyes discern afar
The secret ambush of a specious prayer.
355 Implore his aid, in his decisions rest,
Secure, whate'er he gives, he gives the best.
Yet when the sense of sacred presence fires,
And strong devotion to the skies aspires,
Pour forth thy fervors for a healthful mind,
360 Obedient passions, and a will resigned;
For love, which scarce collective man can fill;[5]
For patience sovereign o'er transmuted ill;
For faith, that panting for a happier seat,
Counts death kind Nature's signal of retreat:
365 These goods for man the laws of Heaven ordain,
These goods he grants, who grants the power to gain;
With these celestial Wisdom calms the mind,
And makes the happiness she does not find.

1749

Prologue Spoken by Mr. Garrick[1]

At the Opening of the Theatre Royal, Drury Lane, 1747

   When Learning's triumph o'er her barbarous foes
First reared the stage, immortal Shakespeare rose;
Each change of many-colored life he drew,
Exhausted worlds, and then imagined new:

---

5. Which humankind as a whole can hardly over-
task.
1. David Garrick, the famous actor, had become

joint patentee and manager of Drury Lane Theatre.
Boswell says that this Prologue is unrivaled "for
just and manly dramatic criticism."

5   Existence saw him spurn her bounded reign,
    And panting Time toiled after him in vain.
    His powerful strokes presiding Truth impressed,
    And unresisted Passion stormed the breast.
      Then Jonson came, instructed from the school
10   To please in method and invent by rule;
    His studious patience and laborious art
    By regular approach essayed the heart;
    Cold Approbation gave the lingering bays,
    For those who durst not censure, scarce could praise.[2]
15   A mortal born, he met the general doom,
    But left, like Egypt's kings, a lasting tomb.
      The wits of Charles[3] found easier ways to fame,
    Nor wished for Jonson's art, or Shakespeare's flame;
    Themselves they studied; as they felt, they writ;
20   Intrigue was plot, obscenity was wit.
    Vice always found a sympathetic friend;
    They pleased their age, and did not aim to mend.
    Yet bards like these aspired to lasting praise,
    And proudly hoped to pimp in future days.
25   Their cause was general, their supports were strong,
    Their slaves were willing, and their reign was long:
    Till Shame regained the post that Sense betrayed,
    And Virtue called Oblivion to her aid.
      Then, crushed by rules,[4] and weakened as refined,
30   For years the power of Tragedy declined;
    From bard to bard the frigid caution crept,
    Till Declamation roared while Passion slept;
    Yet still did Virtue deign the stage to tread;
    Philosophy remained though Nature fled;
35   But forced at length her ancient reign to quit,
    She saw great Faustus[5] lay the ghost of Wit;
    Exulting Folly hailed the joyous day,
    And Pantomime and Song confirmed her sway.
      But who the coming changes can presage,
40   And mark the future periods of the stage?
    Perhaps if skill could distant times explore,
    New Behns, new Durfeys,[6] yet remain in store;
    Perhaps where Lear has raved, and Hamlet died,
    On flying cars new sorcerers may ride;[7]
45   Perhaps (for who can guess the effects of chance?)
    Here Hunt may box, or Mahomet[8] may dance.
      Hard is his lot that, here by fortune placed,
    Must watch the wild vicissitudes of taste;
    With every meteor of caprice must play,

2. Cf. Dryden's contrast of Shakespeare and Ben Jonson in *An Essay of Dramatic Poesy* (p. 2117).
3. The comic playwrights of the Restoration period.
4. Cf. Johnson's remarks on the dramatic unities in *The Preface to Shakespeare* (p. 2729).
5. Dr. Faustus at that time was a popular subject for both farce and pantomime.

6. Thomas Durfey (1653–1723) and Aphra Behn (1640–1689) were then regarded as frothy, outmoded playwrights.
7. It was a common complaint that the use of increasingly elaborate stage machinery was subordinating drama to mere spectacle.
8. Mahomet, a tightrope dancer. Edward Hunt, a popular pugilist.

50 And chase the new-blown bubbles of the day.
Ah! let not censure term our fate our choice,
The stage but echoes back the public voice.
The drama's laws, the drama's patrons give,
For we that live to please, must please to live.
55   Then prompt no more the follies you decry,
As tyrants doom their tools of guilt to die;
'Tis yours this night to bid the reign commence
Of rescued Nature and reviving Sense;
To chase the charms of Sound, the pomp of Show,
60 For useful Mirth and salutary Woe;
Bid scenic Virtue form the rising age,
And Truth diffuse her radiance from the stage.

1747

On the Death of Dr. Robert Levet[1]

Condemned to Hope's delusive mine,
   As on we toil from day to day,
By sudden blasts, or slow decline,
   Our social comforts drop away.

5 Well tried through many a varying year,
   See Levet to the grave descend;
Officious,[2] innocent, sincere,
   Of every friendless name the friend.

Yet still he fills Affection's eye,
10   Obscurely wise, and coarsely kind;
Nor, lettered Arrogance, deny
   Thy praise to merit unrefined.

When fainting Nature called for aid,
   And hovering Death prepared the blow,
15 His vigorous remedy displayed
   The power of art without the show.

In Misery's darkest caverns known,
   His useful care was ever nigh,
Where hopeless Anguish poured his groan,
20   And lonely Want retired to die.

No summons mocked by chill delay,
   No petty gain disdained by pride,
The modest wants of every day
   The toil of every day supplied.

1. An unlicensed physician, who lived in Johnson's house for many years and who died in 1782. His practice was among the very poor. Boswell wrote: "He was of a strange grotesque appearance, stiff and formal in his manner, and seldom said a word while any company was present."
2. "Kind, doing good offices" (Johnson's *Dictionary*).

25 His virtues walked their narrow round,
   Nor made a pause, nor left a void;
   And sure the Eternal Master found
   The single talent well employed.[3]

   The busy day, the peaceful night,
30   Unfelt, uncounted, glided by;
   His frame was firm, his powers were bright,
   Though now his eightieth year was nigh.

   Then with no throbbing fiery pain,
   No cold gradations of decay,
35 Death broke at once the vital chain,
   And freed his soul the nearest way.

1783

Translation of Horace, *Odes*, Book 4.7[1]

   The snow dissolved no more is seen,
   The fields, and woods, behold, are green,
   The changing year renews the plain,
   The rivers know their banks again,
5   The spritely nymph and naked grace[2]
   The mazy dance together trace.
   The changing year's successive plan
   Proclaims mortality to man.
   Rough winter's blasts to spring give way,
10   Spring yields to summer's sovereign ray,
   Then summer sinks in autumn's reign,
   And winter chills the world again.
   Her losses soon the moon supplies,
   But wretched man, when once he lies
15   Where Priam[3] and his sons are laid,
   Is naught but ashes and a shade.
   Who knows if Jove who counts our score
   Will toss us in a morning more?
   What with your friend you nobly share
20   At least you rescue from your heir.
   Not you, Torquatus, boast of Rome,
   When Minos once has fixed your doom,[4]
   Or eloquence, or splendid birth,
   Or virtue shall replace on earth.
25   Hippolytus[5] unjustly slain

---

3. In the parable of the talents (Matthew 25.14–30), Jesus suggests that salvation will be granted to those who make good use of their abilities, however small.
1. Johnson composed this translation the month before his death.
2. One of the Three Graces, emblematic of beauty.
3. Last king of Troy, slain with his sons at the end of the Trojan War.
4. Sentence. L. Manlius Torquatus, a friend of Horace and an advocate, is represented as pleading his case before Minos, judge of the dead.
5. Phaedra, wife of Theseus, falsely accused his chaste son Hippolytus of rape. Theseus brought about the death of his son, and even Diana, goddess of chastity, could not restore him.

Diana calls to life in vain,
Nor can the might of Theseus rend
The chains of hell that hold his friend.[6]

1784

Rambler No. 5[1]

[ON SPRING]

TUESDAY, *April* 3, 1750

Et nunc omnis ager, nunc omnis parturit arbos,
Nunc frondent silvae, nunc formosissimus annus.
VIRGIL, *Eclogues* 3.5.56
Now ev'ry field, now ev'ry tree is green;
Now genial nature's fairest face is seen.
ELPHINSTON

Every man is sufficiently discontented with some circumstances of his present state, to suffer his imagination to range more or less in quest of future happiness, and to fix upon some point of time, in which, by the removal of the inconvenience which now perplexes him, or acquisition of the advantage which he at present wants, he shall find the condition of his life very much improved.

When this time, which is too often expected with great impatience, at last arrives, it generally comes without the blessing for which it was desired; but we solace ourselves with some new prospect, and press forward again with equal eagerness.

It is lucky for a man, in whom this temper prevails, when he turns his hopes upon things wholly out of his own power; since he forbears then to precipitate[2] his affairs, for the sake of the great event that is to complete his felicity, and waits for the blissful hour, with less neglect of the measures necessary to be taken in the mean time.

I have long known a person of this temper, who indulged his dream of happiness with less hurt to himself than such chimerical wishes commonly produce, and adjusted his scheme with such address, that his hopes were in full bloom three parts of the year, and in the other part never wholly blasted. Many, perhaps, would be desirous of learning by what means he procured to himself such a cheap and lasting satisfaction. It was gained by a constant practice of referring the removal of all his uneasiness to the coming of the next spring; if his health was impaired, the spring would restore it; if what he wanted was at a high price, it would fall in value in the spring.

The spring, indeed, did often come without any of these effects, but he was always certain that the next would be more propitious; nor was ever convinced that the present spring would fail him before the middle of sum-

6. Pirithous, held prisoner with Theseus in hell.
1. The *Rambler*, almost wholly written by Johnson himself, appeared every Tuesday and Saturday from March 20, 1750, to March 14, 1752—years in which Johnson was writing the *Dictionary*. It is a successor of the *Tatler* and the *Spectator*, but it is much more serious in tone than the earlier peri-

odicals. Johnson's reputation as a moralist and a stylist was established by these essays; because of them Boswell first conceived the ambition to seek Johnson's acquaintance.
2. "To hurry blindly or rashly" (Johnson's *Dictionary*).

mer; for he always talked of the spring as coming till it was past, and when it was once past, everyone agreed with him that it was coming.

By long converse with this man, I am, perhaps, brought to feel immoderate pleasure in the contemplation of this delightful season; but I have the satisfaction of finding many, whom it can be no shame to resemble, infected with the same enthusiasm; for there is, I believe, scarce any poet of eminence, who has not left some testimony of his fondness for the flowers, the zephyrs, and the warblers of the spring. Nor has the most luxuriant imagination been able to describe the serenity and happiness of the golden age, otherwise than by giving a perpetual spring, as the highest reward of uncorrupted innocence.

There is, indeed, something inexpressibly pleasing, in the annual renovation of the world, and the new display of the treasures of nature. The cold and darkness of winter, with the naked deformity of every object on which we turn our eyes, make us rejoice at the succeeding season, as well for what we have escaped, as for what we may enjoy; and every budding flower, which a warm situation brings early to our view, is considered by us as a messenger to notify the approach of more joyous days.

The spring affords to a mind, so free from the disturbance of cares or passions as to be vacant[3] to calm amusements, almost every thing that our present state makes us capable of enjoying. The variegated verdure of the fields and woods, the succession of grateful odors, the voice of pleasure pouring out its notes on every side, with the gladness apparently conceived by every animal, from the growth of his food, and the clemency of the weather, throw over the whole earth an air of gaiety, significantly expressed by the smile of nature.

Yet there are men to whom these scenes are able to give no delight, and who hurry away from all the varieties of rural beauty, to lose their hours, and divert their thoughts by cards, or assemblies, a tavern dinner, or the prattle of the day.

It may be laid down as a position which will seldom deceive, that when a man cannot bear his own company there is something wrong. He must fly from himself, either because he feels a tediousness in life from the equipoise of an empty mind, which, having no tendency to one motion more than another but as it is impelled by some external power, must always have recourse to foreign objects; or he must be afraid of the intrusion of some unpleasing ideas, and, perhaps, is struggling to escape from the remembrance of a loss, the fear of a calamity, or some other thought of greater horror.

Those whom sorrow incapacitates to enjoy the pleasures of contemplation, may properly apply to such diversions, provided they are innocent, as lay strong hold on the attention; and those, whom fear of any future affliction chains down to misery, must endeavor to obviate the danger.

My considerations shall, on this occasion, be turned on such as are burthensome to themselves merely because they want subjects for reflection, and to whom the volume of nature is thrown open, without affording them pleasure or instruction, because they never learned to read the characters.

A French author has advanced this seeming paradox, that *very few men*

3. "At leisure" (Johnson's *Dictionary*).

know how to take a walk; and, indeed, it is true, that few know how to take a walk with a prospect of any other pleasure, than the same company would have afforded them at home.

There are animals that borrow their color from the neighboring body, and, consequently, vary their hue as they happen to change their place. In like manner it ought to be the endeavor of every man to derive his reflections from the objects about him; for it is to no purpose that he alters his position, if his attention continues fixed to the same point. The mind should be kept open to the access of every new idea, and so far disengaged from the predominance of particular thoughts, as easily to accommodate itself to occasional entertainment.

A man that has formed this habit of turning every new object to his entertainment, finds in the productions of nature an inexhaustible stock of materials upon which he can employ himself, without any temptations to envy or malevolence; faults, perhaps, seldom totally avoided by those, whose judgment is much exercised upon the works of art. He has always a certain prospect of discovering new reasons for adoring the sovereign author of the universe, and probable hopes of making some discovery of benefit to others, or of profit to himself. There is no doubt but many vegetables and animals have qualities that might be of great use, to the knowledge of which there is not required much force of penetration, or fatigue of study, but only frequent experiments, and close attention. What is said by the chemists of their darling mercury, is, perhaps, true of everybody through the whole creation, that if a thousand lives should be spent upon it, all its properties would not be found out.

Mankind must necessarily be diversified by various tastes, since life affords and requires such multiplicity of employments, and a nation of naturalists is neither to be hoped, or desired; but it is surely not improper to point out a fresh amusement to those who languish in health, and repine in plenty, for want of some source of diversion that may be less easily exhausted, and to inform the multitudes of both sexes, who are burthened with every new day, that there are many shows which they have not seen.

He that enlarges his curiosity after the works of nature, demonstrably multiplies the inlets to happiness; and, therefore, the younger part of my readers, to whom I dedicate this vernal speculation, must excuse me for calling upon them, to make use at once of the spring of the year, and the spring of life; to acquire, while their minds may be yet impressed with new images, a love of innocent pleasures, and an ardor for useful knowledge; and to remember, that a blighted spring makes a barren year, and that the vernal flowers, however beautiful and gay, are only intended by nature as preparatives to autumnal fruits.

Idler No. 31[1]

[ON IDLENESS]

SATURDAY, *November* 18, 1758

Many moralists have remarked, that Pride has of all human vices the widest dominion, appears in the greatest multiplicity of forms, and lies hid under the greatest variety of disguises; of disguises, which, like the moon's *veil of brightness,* are both *its luster and its shade,*[2] and betray it to others, though they hide it from ourselves.

It is not my intention to degrade Pride from this pre-eminence of mischief, yet I know not whether Idleness may not maintain a very doubtful and obstinate competition.

There are some that profess Idleness in its full dignity, who call themselves the Idle, as Busiris in the play "calls himself the Proud";[3] who boast that they do nothing, and thank their stars that they have nothing to do; who sleep every night till they can sleep no longer, and rise only that exercise may enable them to sleep again; who prolong the reign of darkness by double curtains, and never see the sun but to "tell him how they hate his beams";[4] whose whole labor is to vary the postures of indulgence, and whose day differs from their night but as a couch or chair differs from a bed.

These are the true and open votaries of Idleness, for whom she weaves the garlands of poppies, and into whose cup she pours the waters of oblivion; who exist in a state of unruffled stupidity, forgetting and forgotten; who have long ceased to live, and at whose death the survivors can only say, that they have ceased to breathe.

But Idleness predominates in many lives where it is not suspected; for being a vice which terminates in itself, it may be enjoyed without injury to others; and is therefore not watched like Fraud, which endangers property, or like Pride, which naturally seeks its gratifications in another's inferiority. Idleness is a silent and peaceful quality, that neither raises envy by ostentation, nor hatred by opposition; and therefore nobody is busy to censure or detect it.

As Pride sometimes is hid under humility, Idleness is often covered by turbulence and hurry. He that neglects his known duty and real employment, naturally endeavors to crowd his mind with something that may bar out the remembrance of his own folly, and does any thing but what he ought to do with eager diligence, that he may keep himself in his own favor.

Some are always in a state of preparation, occupied in previous measures, forming plans, accumulating materials, and providing for the main affair. These are certainly under the secret power of Idleness. Nothing is to be expected from the workman whose tools are forever to be sought. I was once told by a great master, that no man ever excelled in painting, who was eminently curious about pencils and colors.

There are others to whom Idleness dictates another expedient, by which

1. Johnson wrote and published the *Idler,* a periodical similar to the *Rambler,* from 1758 until 1760.
2. Quoted from Samuel Butler's *Hudibras*

2. 1.907–08.
3. Edward Young's *Busiris* (1719) 1.1.13.
4. *Paradise Lost* 4.37.

life may be passed unprofitably away without the tediousness of many vacant hours. The art is, to fill the day with petty business, to have always something in hand which may raise curiosity, but not solicitude, and keep the mind in a state of action, but not of labor.

This art has for many years been practiced by my old friend Sober, with wonderful success. Sober is a man of strong desires and quick imagination, so exactly balanced by the love of ease, that they can seldom stimulate him to any difficult undertaking; they have, however, so much power, that they will not suffer him to lie quite at rest, and though they do not make him sufficiently useful to others, they make him at least weary of himself.

Mr. Sober's chief pleasure is conversation; there is no end of his talk or his attention; to speak or to hear is equally pleasing; for he still fancies that he is teaching or learning something, and is free for the time from his own reproaches.

But there is one time at night when he must go home, that his friends may sleep; and another time in the morning, when all the world agrees to shut out interruption. These are the moments of which poor Sober trembles at the thought. But the misery of these tiresome intervals, he has many means of alleviating. He has persuaded himself that the manual arts are undeservedly overlooked; he has observed in many trades the effects of close thought, and just ratiocination. From speculation he proceeded to practice, and supplied himself with the tools of a carpenter, with which he mended his coalbox very successfully, and which he still continues to employ, as he finds occasion.

He has attempted at other times the crafts of the shoemaker, tinman, plumber, and potter; in all these arts he has failed, and resolves to qualify himself for them by better information. But his daily amusement is chemistry. He has a small furnace, which he employs in distillation, and which has long been the solace of his life. He draws oils and waters, and essences and spirits, which he knows to be of no use; sits and counts the drops as they come from his retort, and forgets that, whilst a drop is falling, a moment flies away.

Poor Sober![5] I have often teased him with reproof, and he has often promised reformation; for no man is so much open to conviction as the Idler, but there is none on whom it operates so little. What will be the effect of this paper I know not; perhaps he will read it and laugh, and light the fire in his furnace; but my hope is that he will quit his trifles, and betake himself to rational and useful diligence.

Rasselas   Johnson wrote *Rasselas* in January 1759, during the evenings of one week, a remarkable instance of his ability to write rapidly and brilliantly under the pressure of necessity. His mother lay dying in Lichfield. Her son, famous for his *Dictionary,* was nonetheless oppressed by poverty and in great need of ready money with which to make her last days comfortable, pay her funeral expenses, and settle her small debts. He was paid £100 for the first edition of *Rasselas,* but not in time to attend her deathbed or her funeral.

5. Sober represents aspects of Johnson's own character. He was much given to indolence, and he performed chemical experiments in a small laboratory in his garret.

Rasselas is a philosophical fable cast in the popular form of an Oriental tale, a type of fiction that owed its popularity to the vogue of the *Arabian Nights*, first translated into English in the early eighteenth century. Because the work is a fable, we should not approach it as a novel: psychologically credible characters and a series of intricately involved actions that lead to a necessary resolution and conclusion are not to be found in *Rasselas*. Instead we are meant to reflect on the ideas and to savor the melancholy resonance and intelligence of the stately prose that expresses them. Johnson arranges the incidents of the fable to test a variety of possible solutions to a problem: What choice of life will bring us happiness? (*The Choice of Life* was his working title for the book.) Many ways of life are examined in turn, and each is found wanting. Johnson does not pretend to have solved the problem. Rather, he locates the sources of discontent in a basic principle of human nature: the "hunger of imagination which preys incessantly upon life" (chapter 32) and which lures us to "listen with credulity to the whispers of fancy and pursue with eagerness the phantoms of hope" (chapter 1). The tale is a gentle satire on one of the perennial topics of satirists: the folly of all of us who stubbornly cling to our illusions despite the evidence of experience. *Rasselas* is not all darkness and gloom, for Johnson's theme invites comic as well as tragic treatment, and some of the episodes evoke that laughter of the mind that is the effect of high comedy. In its main theme, however—the folly of cherishing the dream of ever attaining unalloyed happiness in a world that can never wholly satisfy our desires—and in many of the sayings of its characters, especially of the sage Imlac, *Rasselas* expresses some of Johnson's own deepest convictions.

From The History of Rasselas, Prince of Abyssinia

Chapter 1. Description of a Palace in a Valley

Ye who listen with credulity to the whispers of fancy, and pursue with eagerness the phantoms of hope; who expect that age will perform the promises of youth, and that the deficiencies of the present day will be supplied by the morrow—attend to the history of Rasselas, prince of Abyssinia.

Rasselas was the fourth son of the mighty emperor in whose dominions the Father of Waters[1] begins his course; whose bounty pours down the streams of plenty, and scatters over half the world the harvests of Egypt.

According to the custom which has descended from age to age among the monarchs of the torrid zone, Rasselas was confined in a private palace, with the other sons and daughters of Abyssinian royalty, till the order of succession should call him to the throne.

The place which the wisdom or policy of antiquity had destined for the residence of the Abyssinian princes was a spacious valley[2] in the kingdom of Amhara, surrounded on every side by mountains, of which the summits overhang the middle part. The only passage by which it could be entered was a cavern that passed under a rock, of which it has long been disputed whether it was the work of nature or of human industry. The outlet of the cavern was concealed by a thick wood, and the mouth which opened into the valley was closed with gates of iron, forged by the artificers of ancient days, so massy that no man could, without the help of engines, open or shut them.

From the mountains on every side rivulets descended that filled all the

1. The Nile.
2. Johnson had read of the Happy Valley in the Portuguese Jesuit Father Lobo's book on Abyssinia, which he translated in 1735. The description in this and the immediately following paragraphs illustrates Johnson's preference for the "general" over the "particular" (see chap. 10). It owes something to the description of the Garden in *Paradise Lost* 4, and Coleridge's *Kubla Khan* owes something to it.

valley with verdure and fertility, and formed a lake in the middle, inhabited by fish of every species, and frequented by every fowl whom nature has taught to dip the wing in water. This lake discharged its superfluities by a stream, which entered a dark cleft of the mountain on the northern side, and fell with dreadful noise from precipice to precipice till it was heard no more.

The sides of the mountains were covered with trees, the banks of the brooks were diversified with flowers; every blast shook spices from the rocks, and every month dropped fruits upon the ground. All animals that bite the grass, or browse the shrub, whether wild or tame, wandered in this extensive circuit, secured from beasts of prey by the mountains which confined them. On one part were flocks and herds feeding in the pastures, on another all the beasts of chase frisking in the lawns; the sprightly kid was bounding on the rocks, the subtle monkey frolicking in the trees, and the solemn elephant reposing in the shade. All the diversities of the world were brought together, the blessings of nature were collected, and its evils extracted and excluded.

The valley, wide and fruitful, supplied its inhabitants with the necessaries of life, and all delights and superfluities were added at the annual visit which the emperor paid his children, when the iron gate was opened to the sound of music, and during eight days everyone that resided in the valley was required to propose whatever might contribute to make seclusion pleasant, to fill up the vacancies of attention, and lessen the tediousness of time. Every desire was immediately granted. All the artificers of pleasure were called to gladden the festivity; the musicians exerted the power of harmony, and the dancers showed their activity before the princes, in hope that they should pass their lives in this blissful captivity, to which those only were admitted whose performance was thought able to add novelty to luxury. Such was the appearance of security and delight which this retirement afforded, that they to whom it was new always desired that it might be perpetual; and as those on whom the iron gate had once closed were never suffered to return, the effect of longer experience could not be known. Thus every year produced new schemes of delight and new competitors for imprisonment.

The palace stood on an eminence, raised about thirty paces above the surface of the lake. It was divided into many squares or courts, built with greater or less magnificence according to the rank of those for whom they were designed. The roofs were turned into arches of massy stone, joined with a cement that grew harder by time, and the building stood from century to century, deriding the solstitial rains and equinoctial hurricanes, without need of reparation.

This house, which was so large as to be fully known to none but some ancient officers, who successively inherited the secrets of the place, was built as if suspicion herself had dictated the plan. To every room there was an open and secret passage; every square had a communication with the rest, either from the upper stories by private galleries, or by subterranean passages from the lower apartments. Many of the columns had unsuspected cavities, in which a long race of monarchs had reposited their treasures. They then closed up the opening with marble, which was never to be removed but in the utmost exigencies of the kingdom, and recorded their accumulations in a book, which was itself concealed in a tower, not entered but by the emperor, attended by the prince who stood next in succession.

Chapter 2. The Discontent of Rasselas in the Happy Valley

Here the sons and daughters of Abyssinia lived only to know the soft vicissitudes of pleasure and repose, attended by all that were skillful to delight, and gratified with whatever the senses can enjoy. They wandered in gardens of fragrance, and slept in the fortresses of security. Every art was practiced to make them pleased with their own condition. The sages who instructed them told them of nothing but the miseries of public life, and described all beyond the mountains as regions of calamity, where discord was always raging, and where man preyed upon man.

To heighten their opinion of their own felicity, they were daily entertained with songs, the subject of which was the *happy valley*. Their appetites were excited by frequent enumerations of different enjoyments, and revelry and merriment was the business of every hour, from the dawn of morning to the close of even.

These methods were generally successful; few of the princes had ever wished to enlarge their bounds, but passed their lives in full conviction that they had all within their reach that art or nature could bestow, and pitied those whom fate had excluded from this seat of tranquility, as the sport of chance and the slaves of misery.

Thus they rose in the morning and lay down at night, pleased with each other and with themselves; all but Rasselas, who, in the twenty-sixth year of his age, began to withdraw himself from their pastimes and assemblies, and to delight in solitary walks and silent meditation. He often sat before tables covered with luxury, and forgot to taste the dainties that were placed before him; he rose abruptly in the midst of the song, and hastily retired beyond the sound of music. His attendants observed the change, and endeavored to renew his love of pleasure. He neglected their officiousness, repulsed their invitations, and spent day after day on the banks of rivulets sheltered with trees, where he sometimes listened to the birds in the branches, sometimes observed the fish playing in the stream, and anon cast his eyes upon the pastures and mountains filled with animals, of which some were biting the herbage, and some sleeping among the bushes.

This singularity of his humor made him much observed. One of the sages, in whose conversation he had formerly delighted, followed him secretly, in hope of discovering the cause of his disquiet. Rasselas, who knew not that anyone was near him, having for some time fixed his eyes upon the goats that were browsing among the rocks, began to compare their condition with his own.

"What," said he, "makes the difference between man and all the rest of the animal creation? Every beast that strays beside me has the same corporal necessities with myself; he is hungry, and crops the grass, he is thirsty, and drinks the stream, his thirst and hunger are appeased, he is satisfied, and sleeps; he rises again, and he is hungry, he is again fed, and is at rest. I am hungry and thirsty like him, but when thirst and hunger cease, I am not at rest; I am, like him, pained with want, but am not, like him, satisfied with fullness. The intermediate hours are tedious and gloomy; I long again to be hungry that I may again quicken my attention. The birds peck the berries or the corn, and fly away to the groves, where they sit in seeming happiness on the branches, and waste their lives in tuning one unvaried series of sounds.

I likewise can call the lutanist and the singer, but the sounds that pleased me yesterday weary me today, and will grow yet more wearisome tomorrow. I can discover within me no power of perception which is not glutted with its proper pleasure, yet I do not feel myself delighted. Man has surely some latent sense for which this place affords no gratification, or he has some desires distinct from sense, which must be satisfied before he can be happy."

After this he lifted up his head, and seeing the moon rising, walked towards the palace. As he passed through the fields, and saw the animals around him, "Ye," said he, "are happy, and need not envy me that walk thus among you, burthened with myself; nor do I, ye gentle beings, envy your felicity, for it is not the felicity of man. I have many distresses from which ye are free; I fear pain when I do not feel it; I sometimes shrink at evils recollected, and some-times start at evils anticipated. Surely the equity of Providence has balanced peculiar sufferings with peculiar enjoyments."

With observations like these the prince amused himself as he returned, uttering them with a plaintive voice, yet with a look that discovered him to feel some complacence in his own perspicacity, and to receive some solace of the miseries of life from consciousness of the delicacy with which he felt, and the eloquence with which he bewailed them. He mingled cheerfully in the diversions of the evening, and all rejoiced to find that his heart was lightened.

Chapter 3. The Wants of Him That Wants Nothing

On the next day his old instructor, imagining that he had now made him-self acquainted with his disease of mind, was in the hope of curing it by counsel, and officiously sought an opportunity of conference, which the prince, having long considered him as one whose intellects were exhausted, was not very willing to afford. "Why," said he, "does this man thus intrude upon me; shall I be never suffered to forget those lectures which pleased only while they were new, and to become new again must be forgotten?" He then walked into the wood, and composed himself to his usual meditations; when, before his thoughts had taken any settled form, he perceived his pur-suer at his side, and was at first prompted by his impatience to go hastily away; but, being unwilling to offend a man whom he had once reverenced and still loved, he invited him to sit down with him on the bank.

The old man, thus encouraged, began to lament the change which had been lately observed in the prince, and to inquire why he so often retired from the pleasures of the palace, to loneliness and silence. "I fly from plea-sure," said the prince, "because pleasure has ceased to please; I am lonely because I am miserable, and am unwilling to cloud with my presence the happiness of others." "You, sir," said the sage, "are the first who has com-plained of misery in the *happy valley*. I hope to convince you that your com-plaints have no real cause. You are here in full possession of all that the emperor of Abyssinia can bestow; here is neither labor to be endured nor danger to be dreaded, yet here is all that labor or danger can procure or purchase. Look round and tell me which of your wants is without supply; if you want nothing, how are you unhappy?"

"That I want nothing," said the prince, "or that I know not what I want, is the cause of my complaint; if I had any known want, I should have a certain wish; that wish would excite endeavor, and I should not then repine to see the sun move so slowly towards the western mountain, or lament when the day breaks, and sleep will no longer hide me from myself. When I see the kids and the lambs chasing one another, I fancy that I should be happy if I had something to pursue. But, possessing all that I can want, I find one day and one hour exactly like another, except that the latter is still more tedious than the former. Let your experience inform me how the day may now seem as short as in my childhood, while nature was yet fresh and every moment showed me what I never had observed before. I have already enjoyed too much; give me something to desire."

The old man was surprised at this new species of affliction and knew not what to reply, yet was unwilling to be silent. "Sir," said he, "if you had seen the miseries of the world you would know how to value your present state." "Now," said the prince, "you have given me something to desire. I shall long to see the miseries of the world, since the sight of them is necessary to happiness."[3]

* * *

Chapter 6. A Dissertation on the Art of Flying

Among the artists that had been allured into the happy valley, to labor for the accommodation and pleasure of its inhabitants, was a man eminent for his knowledge of the mechanic powers, who had contrived many engines[4] both of use and recreation. By a wheel, which the stream turned, he forced the water into a tower, whence it was distributed to all the apartments of the palace. He erected a pavillion in the garden, around which he kept the air always cool by artificial showers. One of the groves, appropriated to the ladies, was ventilated by fans, to which the rivulet that run through it gave a constant motion; and instruments of soft music were placed at proper distances, of which some played by the impulse of the wind, and some by the power of the stream.

This artist was sometimes visited by Rasselas, who was pleased with every kind of knowledge, imagining that the time would come when all his acquisitions should be of use to him in the open world. He came one day to amuse himself in his usual manner, and found the master busy in building a sailing chariot: he saw that the design was practicable upon a level surface, and with expressions of great esteem solicited its completion. The workman was pleased to find himself so much regarded by the prince, and resolved to gain yet higher honors. "Sir," said he, "you have seen but a small part of what the mechanic sciences can perform. I have been long of opinion, that, instead of the tardy conveyance of ships and chariots, man might use the swifter migration of wings; that the fields of air are open to knowledge, and that only ignorance and idleness need crawl upon the ground."

This hint rekindled the prince's desire of passing the mountains; having seen what the mechanist had already performed, he was willing to fancy that he could do more; yet resolved to inquire further before he suffered hope to afflict him by disappointment. "I am afraid," said he to the artist, "that your imagination prevails over your skill, and that you now tell me rather what

---

3. In chapters 4 and 5, Rasselas dreams about escaping the valley.

4. Machines. "Mechanic powers": the forces that cause things to move.

you wish than what you know. Every animal has his element assigned him; the birds have the air, and man and beasts the earth." "So," replied the mechanist, "fishes have the water, in which yet beasts can swim by nature, and men by art. He that can swim needs not despair to fly: to swim is to fly in a grosser fluid, and to fly is to swim in a subtler. We are only to proportion our power of resistance to the different density of the matter through which we are to pass. You will be necessarily upborn by the air, if you can renew any impulse upon it, faster than the air can recede from the pressure."

"But the exercise of swimming," said the prince, "is very laborious; the strongest limbs are soon wearied; I am afraid the act of flying will be yet more violent, and wings will be of no great use, unless we can fly further than we can swim."

"The labor of rising from the ground," said the artist "will be great, as we see it in the heavier domestic fowls; but, as we mount higher, the earth's attraction, and the body's gravity, will be gradually diminished, till we shall arrive at a region where the man will float in the air without any tendency to fall: no care will then be necessary, but to move forwards, which the gentlest impulse will effect. You, Sir, whose curiosity is so extensive, will easily conceive with what pleasure a philosopher, furnished with wings, and hovering in the sky, would see the earth, and all its inhabitants, rolling beneath him, and presenting to him successively, by its diurnal motion, all the countries within the same parallel. How must it amuse the pendent spectator to see the moving scene of land and ocean, cities and deserts! To survey with equal security the marts of trade, and the fields of battle; mountains infested by barbarians, and fruitful regions gladdened by plenty, and lulled by peace! How easily shall we then trace the Nile through all his passage; pass over to distant regions, and examine the face of nature from one extremity of the earth to the other!"

"All this," said the prince, "is much to be desired, but I am afraid that no man will be able to breathe in these regions of speculation and tranquility. I have been told, that respiration is difficult upon lofty mountains, yet from these precipices, though so high as to produce great tenuity of the air, it is very easy to fall: therefore I suspect, that from any height, where life can be supported, there may be danger of too quick descent."

"Nothing," replied the artist, "will ever be attempted, if all possible objections must be first overcome. If you will favor my project I will try the first flight at my own hazard. I have considered the structure of all volant[5] animals, and find the folding continuity of the bat's wings most easily accommodated to the human form. Upon this model I shall begin my task tomorrow, and in a year expect to tower into the air beyond the malice or pursuit of man. But I will work only on this condition, that the art shall not be divulged, and that you shall not require me to make wings for any but ourselves."

"Why," said Rasselas, "should you envy others so great an advantage? All skill ought to be exerted for universal good; every man has owed much to others, and ought to repay the kindness that he has received."

"If men were all virtuous," returned the artist, "I should with great alacrity teach them all to fly. But what would be the security of the good, if the bad

5. Able to fly.

could at pleasure invade them from the sky? Against an army sailing through the clouds neither walls, nor mountains, nor seas, could afford any security. A flight of northern savages might hover in the wind, and light at once with irresistible violence upon the capital of a fruitful region that was rolling under them. Even this valley, the retreat of princes, the abode of happiness, might be violated by the sudden descent of some of the naked nations that swarm on the coast of the southern sea."

The prince promised secrecy, and waited for the performance, not wholly hopeless of success. He visited the work from time to time, observed its progress, and remarked many ingenious contrivances to facilitate motion, and unite levity with strength. The artist was every day more certain that he should leave vultures and eagles behind him, and the contagion of his confidence seized upon the prince.

In a year the wings were finished, and, on a morning appointed, the maker appeared furnished for flight on a little promontory: he waved his pinions a while to gather air, then leaped from his stand, and in an instant dropped into the lake. His wings, which were of no use in the air, sustained him in the water, and the prince drew him to land, half dead with terror and vexation.[6]

* * *

Chapter 10. Imlac's History Continued. A Dissertation upon Poetry

"Wherever I went, I found that poetry was considered as the highest learning, and regarded with a veneration somewhat approaching to that which man would pay to the angelic nature. And yet it fills me with wonder that, in almost all countries, the most ancient poets are considered as the best: whether it be that every other kind of knowledge is an acquisition gradually attained, and poetry is a gift conferred at once; or that the first poetry of every nation surprised them as a novelty, and retained the credit by consent which it received by accident at first; or whether, as the province of poetry is to describe nature and passion, which are always the same, the first writers took possession of the most striking objects for description and the most probable occurrences for fiction, and left nothing to those that followed them, but transcription of the same events, and new combinations of the same images—whatever be the reason, it is commonly observed that the early writers are in possession of nature, and their followers of art; that the first excel in strength and invention, and the latter in elegance and refinement.

"I was desirous to add my name to this illustrious fraternity. I read all the poets of Persia and Arabia, and was able to repeat by memory the volumes that are suspended in the mosque of Mecca. But I soon found that no man was ever great by imitation. My desire of excellence impelled me to transfer my attention to nature and to life. Nature was to be my subject, and men to be my auditors: I could never describe what I had not seen; I could not hope to move those with delight or terror, whose interests and opinions I did not understand.

"Being now resolved to be a poet, I saw everything with a new purpose;

6. In chapters 7–9, Rasselas comes to know Imlac, a scholar and poet who knows the great world outside the valley and who tells the story of his life.

my sphere of attention was suddenly magnified; no kind of knowledge was to be overlooked. I ranged mountains and deserts for images and resemblances, and pictured upon my mind every tree of the forest and flower of the valley. I observed with equal care the crags of the rock and the pinnacles of the palace. Sometimes I wandered along the mazes of the rivulet, and sometimes watched the changes of the summer clouds. To a poet nothing can be useless. Whatever is beautiful, and whatever is dreadful, must be familiar to his imagination; he must be conversant with all that is awfully vast or elegantly little. The plants of the garden, the animals of the wood, the minerals of the earth, and meteors of the sky, must all concur to store his mind with inexhaustible variety: for every idea[7] is useful for the enforcement or decoration of moral or religious truth; and he who knows most will have most power of diversifying his scenes, and of gratifying his reader with remote allusions and unexpected instruction.

"All the appearances of nature I was therefore careful to study, and every country which I have surveyed has contributed something to my poetical powers."

"In so wide a survey," said the prince, "you must surely have left much unobserved. I have lived till now within the circuit of these mountains, and yet cannot walk abroad without the sight of something which I have never beheld before, or never heeded."

"The business of a poet," said Imlac, "is to examine, not the individual, but the species; to remark general properties and large appearances; he does not number the streaks of the tulip, or describe the different shades in the verdure of the forest. He is to exhibit in his portraits of nature such prominent and striking features as recall the original to every mind, and must neglect the minuter discriminations, which one may have remarked and another have neglected, for those characteristics which are alike obvious to vigilance and carelessness.

"But the knowledge of nature is only half the task of a poet; he must be acquainted likewise with all the modes of life. His character requires that he estimate the happiness and misery of every condition; observe the power of all the passions in all their combinations, and trace the changes of the human mind, as they are modified by various institutions and accidental influences of climate or custom, from the sprightliness of infancy to the despondence of decrepitude. He must divest himself of the prejudices of his age or country; he must consider right and wrong in their abstracted and invariable state; he must disregard present laws and opinions, and rise to general and transcendental[8] truths, which will always be the same. He must, therefore, content himself with the slow progress of his name, contemn the applause of his own time, and commit his claims to the justice of posterity. He must write as the interpreter of nature and the legislator of mankind, and consider himself as presiding over the thoughts and manners of future generations, as a being superior to time and place.

"His labor is not yet at an end; he must know many languages and many sciences; and, that his style may be worthy of his thoughts, must by incessant practice familiarize to himself every delicacy of speech and grace of harmony."

7. Mental image.
8. "General; pervading many particulars" (Johnson's *Dictionary*).

Chapter 11. Imlac's Narrative Continued. A Hint on Pilgrimage

Imlac now felt the enthusiastic fit, and was proceeding to aggrandize his own profession, when the prince cried out: "Enough! thou hast convinced me that no human being can ever be a poet. Proceed with thy narration."

"To be a poet," said Imlac, "is indeed very difficult." "So difficult," returned the prince, "that I will at present hear no more of his labors. Tell me whither you went when you had seen Persia."

"From Persia," said the poet, "I traveled through Syria, and for three years resided in Palestine, where I conversed with great numbers of the northern and western nations of Europe, the nations which are now in possession of all power and all knowledge, whose armies are irresistible, and whose fleets command the remotest parts of the globe. When I compared these men with the natives of our own kingdom, and those that surround us, they appeared almost another order of beings. In their countries it is difficult to wish for anything that may not be obtained; a thousand arts, of which we never heard, are continually laboring for their convenience and pleasure; and whatever their own climate has denied them is supplied by their commerce."

"By what means," said the prince, "are the Europeans thus powerful, or why, since they can so easily visit Asia and Africa for trade or conquest, cannot the Asiatics and Africans invade their coasts, plant colonies in their ports, and give laws to their natural princes? The same wind that carries them back would bring us thither."

"They are more powerful, sir, than we," answered Imlac, "because they are wiser; knowledge will always predominate over ignorance, as man governs the other animals. But why their knowledge is more than ours, I know not what reason can be given, but the unsearchable will of the Supreme Being."

"When," said the prince with a sigh, "shall I be able to visit Palestine, and mingle with this mighty confluence of nations? Till that happy moment shall arrive, let me fill up the time with such representations as thou canst give me. I am not ignorant of the motive that assembles such numbers in that place, and cannot but consider it as the center of wisdom and piety, to which the best and wisest men of every land must be continually resorting."

"There are some nations," said Imlac, "that send few visitants to Palestine; for many numerous and learned sects in Europe concur to censure pilgrimage as superstitious, or deride it as ridiculous."

"You know," said the prince, "how little my life has made me acquainted with diversity of opinions. It will be too long to hear the arguments on both sides; you, that have considered them, tell me the result."

"Pilgrimage," said Imlac, "like many other acts of piety, may be reasonable or superstitious, according to the principles upon which it is performed. Long journeys in search of truth are not commanded. Truth, such as is necessary to the regulation of life, is always found where it is honestly sought. Change of place is no natural cause of the increase of piety, for it inevitably produces dissipation of mind. Yet, since men go every day to view the fields where great actions have been performed, and return with stronger impressions of the event, curiosity of the same kind may naturally dispose us to view that country whence our religion had its beginning; and I believe no man surveys those awful scenes without some confirmation of holy resolutions. That the Supreme Being may be more easily propitiated in one place than in another is the dream of idle superstition, but that some places may operate upon our own minds in an uncommon manner is an opinion which hourly experience will justify. He who supposes that his vices may be more successfully combated in Palestine, will, perhaps, find himself mistaken, yet he may go thither without folly; he who thinks they will be more freely pardoned, dishonors at once his reason and religion."

"These," said the prince, "are European distinctions. I will consider them another time. What have you found to be the effect of knowledge? Are those nations happier than we?"

"There is so much infelicity," said the poet, "in the world that scarce any man has leisure from his own distresses to estimate the comparative happiness of others. Knowledge is certainly one of the means of pleasure, as is confessed by the natural desire which every mind feels of increasing its ideas. Ignorance is mere privation, by which nothing can be produced; it is a vacuity in which the soul sits motionless and torpid for want of attraction; and, without knowing why, we always rejoice when we learn, and grieve when we forget. I am therefore inclined to conclude that if nothing counteracts the natural consequence of learning, we grow more happy as our minds take a wider range.

"In enumerating the particular comforts of life, we shall find many advantages on the side of the Europeans. They cure wounds and diseases with which we languish and perish. We suffer inclemencies of weather which they can obviate. They have engines for the despatch of many laborious works, which we must perform by manual industry. There is such communication between distant places that one friend can hardly be said to be absent from another. Their policy removes all public inconveniences; they have roads cut through their mountains, and bridges laid upon their rivers. And, if we descend to the privacies of life, their habitations are more commodious, and their possessions are more secure."

"They are surely happy," said the prince, "who have all these conveniencies, of which I envy none so much as the facility with which separated friends interchange their thoughts."

"The Europeans," answered Imlac, "are less unhappy than we, but they are not happy. Human life is everywhere a state in which much is to be endured, and little to be enjoyed."[9]

* * *

Chapter 15. The Prince and Princess Leave the Valley, and See Many Wonders

The prince and princess had jewels sufficient to make them rich whenever they came into a place of commerce, which, by Imlac's direction, they hid in their clothes, and, on the night of the next full moon, all left the valley. The princess was followed only by a single favorite, who did not know whither she was going.

They clambered through the cavity, and began to go down on the other side. The princess and her maid turned their eyes towards every part, and, seeing nothing to bound their prospect, considered themselves as in danger of being lost in a dreary vacuity. They stopped and trembled. "I am almost

9. In chapters 12–14, Rasselas and Imac, assisted by Nekayah, Rasselas's sister, succeed in making a tunnel through the mountain.

afraid," said the princess, "to begin a journey of which I cannot perceive an end, and to venture into this immense plain where I may be approached on every side by men whom I never saw." The prince felt nearly the same emotions, though he thought it more manly to conceal them.

Imlac smiled at their terrors, and encouraged them to proceed; but the princess continued irresolute till she had been imperceptibly drawn forward too far to return.

In the morning they found some shepherds in the field, who set milk and fruits before them. The princess wondered that she did not see a palace ready for her reception, and a table spread with delicacies; but, being faint and hungry, she drank the milk and ate the fruits, and thought them of a higher flavor than the products of the valley.

They traveled forward by easy journeys, being all unaccustomed to toil or difficulty, and knowing, that though they might be missed, they could not be pursued. In a few days they came into a more populous region, where Imlac was diverted with the admiration which his companions expressed at the diversity of manners, stations and employments.

Their dress was such as might not bring upon them the suspicion of having any thing to conceal, yet the prince, wherever he came, expected to be obeyed, and the princess was frighted, because those that came into her presence did not prostrate themselves before her. Imlac was forced to observe them with great vigilance, lest they should betray their rank by their unusual behavior, and detained them several weeks in the first village to accustom them to the sight of common mortals.

By degrees the royal wanderers were taught to understand that they had for a time laid aside their dignity, and were to expect only such regard as liberality and courtesy could procure. And Imlac, having, by many admonitions, prepared them to endure the tumults of a port, and the ruggedness of the commercial race, brought them down to the seacoast.

The prince and his sister, to whom every thing was new, were gratified equally at all places, and therefore remained for some months at the port without any inclination to pass further. Imlac was content with their stay, because he did not think it safe to expose them, unpracticed in the world, to the hazards of a foreign country.

At last he began to fear lest they should be discovered, and proposed to fix a day for their departure. They had no pretensions to judge for themselves, and referred the whole scheme to his direction. He therefore took passage in a ship to Suez; and, when the time came, with great difficulty prevailed on the princess to enter the vessel. They had a quick and prosperous voyage, and from Suez traveled by land to Cairo.

Chapter 16. They Enter Cairo, and Find Every Man Happy

As they approached the city, which filled the strangers with astonishment, "This," said Imlac to the prince, "is the place where travelers and merchants assemble from all the corners of the earth. You will here find men of every character and every occupation. Commerce is here honorable. I will act as a merchant, and you shall live as strangers, who have no other end of travel than curiosity. It will soon be observed that we are rich; our reputation will procure us access to all whom we shall desire to know; you will see all the conditions of humanity, and enable yourself at leisure to make your *choice of life.*"

They now entered the town, stunned by the noise, and offended by the crowds. Instruction had not yet so prevailed over habit, but that they wondered to see themselves pass undistinguished along the street, and met by the lowest of the people without reverence or notice. The princess could not at first bear the thought of being leveled with the vulgar,[1] and for some days continued in her chamber, where she was served by her favorite, Pekuah, as in the palace of the valley.

Imlac, who understood traffic,[2] sold part of the jewels the next day, and hired a house, which he adorned with such magnificence that he was immediately considered as a merchant of great wealth. His politeness attracted many acquaintance, and his generosity made him courted by many dependents. His table was crowded by men of every nation, who all admired his knowledge, and solicited his favor. His companions, not being able to mix in the conversation, could make no discovery of their ignorance or surprise, and were gradually initiated in the world as they gained knowledge of the language.

The prince had, by frequent lectures, been taught the use and nature of money; but the ladies could not for a long time comprehend what the merchants did with small pieces of gold and silver, or why things of so little use should be received as equivalent to the necessaries of life.

They studied the language two years, while Imlac was preparing to set before them the various ranks and conditions of mankind. He grew acquainted with all who had anything uncommon in their fortune or conduct. He frequented the voluptuous and the frugal, the idle and the busy, the merchants and the men of learning.

The prince being now able to converse with fluency, and having learned the caution necessary to be observed in his intercourse with strangers, began to accompany Imlac to places of resort, and to enter into all assemblies, that he might make his *choice of life*.

For some time he thought choice needless, because all appeared to him equally happy. Wherever he went he met gaiety and kindness, and heard the song of joy or the laugh of carelessness. He began to believe that the world overflowed with universal plenty, and that nothing was withheld either from want or merit; that every hand showered liberality, and every heart melted with benevolence: "And who then," says he, "will be suffered to be wretched?"

Imlac permitted the pleasing delusion, and was unwilling to crush the hope of inexperience, till one day, having sat awhile silent, "I know not," said the prince, "what can be the reason that I am more unhappy than any of our friends. I see them perpetually and unalterably cheerful, but feel my own mind restless and uneasy. I am unsatisfied with those pleasures which I seem most to court; I live in the crowds of jollity, not so much to enjoy company as to shun myself, and am only loud and merry to conceal my sadness."

"Every man," said Imlac, "may, by examining his own mind, guess what passes in the minds of others; when you feel that your own gaiety is counterfeit, it may justly lead you to suspect that of your companions not to be

1. Ordinary people. 2. Commerce.

sincere. Envy is commonly reciprocal. We are long before we are convinced that happiness is never to be found, and each believes it possessed by others, to keep alive the hope of obtaining it for himself. In the assembly where you passed the last night, there appeared such sprightliness of air, and volatility of fancy, as might have suited beings of an higher order, formed to inhabit serener regions, inaccessible to care or sorrow; yet, believe me, prince, there was not one who did not dread the moment when solitude should deliver him to the tyranny of reflection."

"This," said the prince, "may be true of others, since it is true of me; yet, whatever be the general infelicity of man, one condition is more happy than another, and wisdom surely directs us to take the least evil in the *choice of life.*"

"The causes of good and evil," answered Imlac, "are so various and uncertain, so often entangled with each other, so diversified by various relations, and so much subject to accidents which cannot be foreseen, that he who would fix his condition upon incontestable reasons of preference must live and die inquiring and deliberating."

"But, surely," said Rasselas, "the wise men, to whom we listen with reverence and wonder, chose that mode of life for themselves which they thought most likely to make them happy."

"Very few," said the poet, "live by choice. Every man is placed in his present condition by causes which acted without his foresight, and with which he did not always willingly cooperate; and therefore you will rarely meet one who does not think the lot of his neighbor better than his own."

"I am pleased to think," said the prince, "that my birth has given me at least one advantage over others, by enabling me to determine for myself. I have here the world before me. I will review it at leisure; surely happiness is somewhere to be found."

Chapter 17. The Prince Associates with Young Men of Spirit and Gaiety

Rasselas rose next day, and resolved to begin his experiments upon life. "Youth," cried he, "is the time of gladness: I will join myself to the young men, whose only business is to gratify their desires, and whose time is all spent in a succession of enjoyments."

To such societies he was readily admitted, but a few days brought him back weary and disgusted. Their mirth was without images,[3] their laughter without motive; their pleasures were gross and sensual, in which the mind had no part; their conduct was at once wild and mean; they laughed at order and at law, but the frown of power dejected, and the eye of wisdom abashed them.

The prince soon concluded, that he should never be happy in a course of life of which he was ashamed. He thought it unsuitable to a reasonable being to act without a plan, and to be sad or cheerful only by chance. "Happiness," said he, "must be something solid and permanent, without fear and without uncertainty."

But his young companions had gained so much of his regard by their frankness and courtesy, that he could not leave them without warning and

3. Ideas.

remonstrance. "My friends," said he, "I have seriously considered our manners and our prospects, and find that we have mistaken our own interest. The first years of man must make provision for the last. He that never thinks never can be wise. Perpetual levity must end in ignorance; and intemperance, though it may fire the spirits for an hour, will make life short or miserable. Let us consider that youth is of no long duration, and that in maturer age, when the enchantments of fancy shall cease, and phantoms of delight dance no more about us, we shall have no comforts but the esteem of wise men, and the means of doing good. Let us, therefore, stop, while to stop is in our power: let us live as men who are sometime to grow old, and to whom it will be the most dreadful of all evils not to count their past years but by follies, and to be reminded of their former luxuriance of health only by the maladies which riot has produced."

They stared a while in silence one upon another, and, at last, drove him away by a general chorus of continued laughter.

The consciousness that his sentiments were just, and his intentions kind, was scarcely sufficient to support him against the horror of derision. But he recovered his tranquillity, and pursued his search.

Chapter 18. The Prince Finds a Wise and Happy Man

As he was one day walking in the street, he saw a spacious building which all were, by the open doors, invited to enter: he followed the stream of people, and found it a hall or school of declamation, in which professors read lectures to their auditory. He fixed his eye upon a sage raised above the rest, who discoursed with great energy on the government of the passions. His look was venerable, his action graceful, his pronunciation clear, and his diction elegant. He showed with great strength of sentiment and variety of illustration that human nature is degraded and debased, when the lower faculties predominate over the higher; that when fancy, the parent of passion, usurps the dominion of the mind, nothing ensues but the natural effect of unlawful government, perturbation, and confusion; that she betrays the fortresses of the intellect to rebels, and excites her children to sedition against reason, their lawful sovereign. He compared reason to the sun, of which the light is constant, uniform and lasting; and fancy to a meteor, of bright but transitory luster, irregular in its motion, and delusive in its direction.

He then communicated the various precepts given from time to time for the conquest of passion, and displayed the happiness of those who had obtained the important victory, after which man is no longer the slave of fear, nor the fool of hope; is no more emaciated by envy, inflamed by anger, emasculated by tenderness, or depressed by grief; but walks on calmly through the tumults or the privacies of life, as the sun pursues alike his course through the calm or the stormy sky.

He enumerated many examples of heroes immovable by pain or pleasure, who looked with indifference on those modes or accidents to which the vulgar give the names of good and evil. He exhorted his hearers to lay aside their prejudices, and arm themselves against the shafts of malice or misfortune, by invulnerable patience; concluding that this state only was happiness, and that this happiness was in everyone's power.

Rasselas listened to him with the veneration due to the instructions of a superior being, and, waiting for him at the door, humbly implored the liberty of visiting so great a master of true wisdom. The lecturer hesitated a moment, when Rasselas put a purse of gold into his hand, which he received with a mixture of joy and wonder.

"I have found," said the prince at his return to Imlac, "a man who can teach all that is necessary to be known; who, from the unshaken throne of rational fortitude, looks down on the scenes of life changing beneath him. He speaks, and attention watches his lips. He reasons, and conviction closes his periods. This man shall be my future guide; I will learn his doctrines, and imitate his life."

"Be not too hasty," said Imlac, "to trust or to admire the teachers of morality: they discourse like angels, but they live like men."

Rasselas, who could not conceive how any man could reason so forcibly without feeling the cogency of his own arguments, paid his visit in a few days, and was denied admission. He had now learned the power of money, and made his way by a piece of gold to the inner apartment, where he found the philosopher in a room half darkened, with his eyes misty and his face pale. "Sir," said he, "you are come at a time when all human friendship is useless; what I suffer cannot be remedied, what I have lost cannot be supplied. My daughter, my only daughter, from whose tenderness I expected all the comforts of my age, died last night of a fever. My views, my purposes, my hopes are at an end; I am now a lonely being, disunited from society."

"Sir," said the prince, "mortality is an event by which a wise man can never be surprised; we know that death is always near, and it should therefore always be expected." "Young man," answered the philosopher, "you speak like one that has never felt the pangs of separation." "Have you then forgot the precepts," said Rasselas, "which you so powerfully enforced? Has wisdom no strength to arm the heart against calamity? Consider that external things are naturally variable, but truth and reason are always the same." "What comfort," said the mourner, "can truth and reason afford me? Of what effect are they now, but to tell me that my daughter will not be restored?"

The prince, whose humanity would not suffer him to insult misery with reproof, went away, convinced of the emptiness of rhetorical sound, and the inefficacy of polished periods and studied sentences.[4]

Chapter 19. A Glimpse of Pastoral Life

He was still eager upon the same inquiry; and having heard of a hermit that lived near the lowest cataract of the Nile, and filled the whole country with the fame of his sanctity, resolved to visit his retreat, and inquire whether that felicity which public life could not afford was to be found in solitude; and whether a man whose age and virtue made him venerable could teach any peculiar art of shunning evils, or enduring them.

Imlac and the princess agreed to accompany him, and, after the necessary preparations, they began their journey. Their way lay through fields, where shepherds tended their flocks and the lambs were playing upon the pasture. "This," said the poet, "is the life which has been often celebrated for its innocence and quiet; let us pass the heat of the day among the shepherds'

4. Maxims or moral axioms. "Periods": complete sentences.

tents, and know whether all our searches are not to terminate in pastoral simplicity."

The proposal pleased them, and they induced the shepherds, by small presents and familiar questions, to tell their opinion of their own state. They were so rude and ignorant, so little able to compare the good with the evil of the occupation, and so indistinct in their narratives and descriptions, that very little could be learned from them. But it was evident that their hearts were cankered with discontent; that they considered themselves as condemned to labor for the luxury of the rich, and looked up with stupid malevolence toward those that were placed above them.

The princess pronounced with vehemence that she would never suffer these envious savages to be her companions, and that she should not soon be desirous of seeing any more specimens of rustic happiness; but could not believe that all the accounts of primeval pleasures were fabulous, and was yet in doubt whether life had anything that could be justly preferred to the placid gratifications of fields and woods. She hoped that the time would come, when, with a few virtuous and elegant companions, she could gather flowers planted by her own hand, fondle the lambs of her own ewe, and listen, without care, among brooks and breezes, to one of her maidens reading in the shade.

Chapter 20. The Danger of Prosperity

On the next day they continued their journey, till the heat compelled them to look round for shelter. At a small distance they saw a thick wood, which they no sooner entered than they perceived that they were approaching the habitations of men. The shrubs were diligently cut away to open walks where the shades were darkest; the boughs of opposite trees were artificially interwoven; seats of flowery turf were raised in vacant spaces, and a rivulet, that wantoned along the side of a winding path, had its banks sometimes opened into small basins, and its stream sometimes obstructed by little mounds of stone heaped together to increase its murmurs.

They passed slowly through the wood, delighted with such unexpected accommodations, and entertained each other with conjecturing what, or who, he could be, that, in those rude and unfrequented regions, had leisure and art for such harmless luxury.

As they advanced, they heard the sound of music, and saw youths and virgins dancing in the grove; and, going still further, beheld a stately palace built upon a hill surrounded with woods. The laws of eastern hospitality allowed them to enter, and the master welcomed them like a man liberal and wealthy.

He was skilful enough in appearances soon to discern that they were no common guests, and spread his table with magnificence. The eloquence of Imlac caught his attention, and the lofty courtesy of the princess excited his respect. When they offered to depart he entreated their stay, and was the next day still more unwilling to dismiss them than before. They were easily persuaded to stop, and civility grew up in time to freedom and confidence.

The prince now saw all the domestics cheerful, and all the face of nature smiling round the place, and could not forbear to hope that he should find here what he was seeking; but when he was congratulating the master upon his possessions, he answered with a sigh, "My condition has indeed the appearance of happiness, but appearances are delusive. My prosperity puts my life in danger; the Bassa of Egypt is my enemy, incensed only by my wealth and popularity. I have been hitherto protected against him by the princes of the country; but, as the favor of the great is uncertain, I know not how soon my defenders may be persuaded to share the plunder with the Bassa. I have sent my treasures into a distant country, and, upon the first alarm, am prepared to follow them. Then will my enemies riot in my mansion, and enjoy the gardens which I have planted."

They all joined in lamenting his danger, and deprecating his exile; and the princess was so much disturbed with the tumult of grief and indignation, that she retired to her apartment. They continued with their kind inviter a few days longer, and then went forward to find the hermit.

Chapter 21. The Happiness of Solitude. The Hermit's History

They came on the third day, by the direction of the peasants, to the hermit's cell: it was a cavern in the side of a mountain, over-shadowed with palm-trees; at such a distance from the cataract, that nothing more was heard than a gentle uniform murmur, such as composed the mind to pensive meditation, especially when it was assisted by the wind whistling among the branches. The first rude essay of nature had been so much improved by human labor, that the cave contained several apartments, appropriated to different uses, and often afforded lodging to travelers, whom darkness or tempests happened to overtake.

The hermit sat on a bench at the door, to enjoy the coolness of the evening. On one side lay a book with pens and papers, on the other mechanical instruments of various kinds. As they approached him unregarded, the princess observed that he had not the countenance of a man that had found, or could teach, the way to happiness.

They saluted him with great respect, which he repaid like a man not unaccustomed to the forms of courts. "My children," said he, "if you have lost your way, you shall be willingly supplied with such conveniencies for the night as this cavern will afford. I have all that nature requires, and you will not expect delicacies in a hermit's cell."

They thanked him, and, entering, were pleased with the neatness and regularity of the place. The hermit set flesh and wine before them, though he fed only upon fruits and water. His discourse was cheerful without levity, and pious without enthusiasm.[5] He soon gained the esteem of his guests, and the princess repented of her hasty censure.

At last Imlac began thus: "I do not now wonder that your reputation is so far extended; we have heard at Cairo of your wisdom, and came hither to implore your direction for this young man and maiden in the *choice of life*."

"To him that lives well," answered the hermit, "every form of life is good; nor can I give any other rule for choice, than to remove from all apparent evil."

"He will remove most certainly from evil," said the prince, "who shall

---

5. "A vain belief of private revelation; a vain confidence of divine favor or communication" (Johnson's *Dictionary*).

devote himself to that solitude which you have recommended by your example."

"I have indeed lived fifteen years in solitude," said the hermit, "but have no desire that my example should gain any imitators. In my youth I professed arms, and was raised by degrees to the highest military rank. I have traversed wide countries at the head of my troops, and seen many battles and sieges. At last, being disgusted by the preferment of a younger officer, and feeling that my vigor was beginning to decay, I resolved to close my life in peace, having found the world full of snares, discord, and misery. I had once escaped from the pursuit of the enemy by the shelter of this cavern, and therefore chose it for my final residence. I employed artificers to form it into chambers, and stored it with all that I was likely to want.

"For some time after my retreat, I rejoiced like a tempest-beaten sailor at his entrance into the harbor, being delighted with the sudden change of the noise and hurry of war, to stillness and repose. When the pleasure of novelty went away, I employed my hours in examining the plants which grow in the valley, and the minerals which I collected from the rocks. But that inquiry is now grown tasteless and irksome. I have been for some time unsettled and distracted: my mind is disturbed with a thousand perplexities of doubt, and vanities of imagination, which hourly prevail upon me, because I have no opportunities of relaxation or diversion. I am sometimes ashamed to think that I could not secure myself from vice, but by retiring from the exercise of virtue, and begin to suspect that I was rather impelled by resentment, than led by devotion, into solitude. My fancy riots in scenes of folly, and I lament that I have lost so much, and have gained so little. In solitude, if I escape the example of bad men, I want likewise the counsel and conversation of the good. I have been long comparing the evils with the advantages of society, and resolve to return into the world tomorrow. The life of a solitary man will be certainly miserable, but not certainly devout."

They heard his resolution with surprise, but, after a short pause, offered to conduct him to Cairo. He dug up a considerable treasure which he had hid among the rocks, and accompanied them to the city, on which, as he approached it, he gazed with rapture.

Chapter 22. The Happiness of a Life Led According to Nature

Rasselas went often to an assembly of learned men, who met at stated times to unbend their minds and compare their opinions. Their manners were somewhat coarse, but their conversation was instructive, and their disputations acute, though sometimes too violent, and often continued till neither controvertist remembered upon what question they began. Some faults were almost general among them; everyone was desirous to dictate to the rest, and everyone was pleased to hear the genius or knowledge of another depreciated.

In this assembly Rasselas was relating his interview with the hermit, and the wonder with which he heard him censure a course of life which he had so deliberately chosen, and so laudably followed. The sentiments of the hearers were various. Some were of opinion that the folly of his choice had been justly punished by condemnation to perpetual perseverance. One of the youngest among them, with great vehemence, pronounced him an hypocrite. Some talked of the right of society to the labor of individuals, and considered retirement as a desertion of duty. Others readily allowed that there was a time when the claims of the public were satisfied, and when a man might properly sequester himself, to review his life and purify his heart.

One, who appeared more affected with the narrative than the rest, thought it likely that the hermit would in a few years go back to his retreat, and perhaps, if shame did not restrain, or death intercept him, return once more from his retreat into the world. "For the hope of happiness," said he, "is so strongly impressed that the longest experience is not able to efface it. Of the present state, whatever it be, we feel and are forced to confess the misery; yet when the same state is again at a distance, imagination paints it as desirable. But the time will surely come when desire will be no longer our torment, and no man shall be wretched but by his own fault."

"This," said a philosopher who had heard him with tokens of great impatience, "is the present condition of a wise man. The time is already come when none are wretched but by their own fault. Nothing is more idle than to inquire after happiness, which nature has kindly placed within our reach. The way to be happy is to live according to nature, in obedience to that universal and unalterable law with which every heart is originally impressed; which is not written on it by precept, but engraven by destiny, not instilled by education, but infused at our nativity. He that lives according to nature will suffer nothing from the delusions of hope, or importunities of desire; he will receive and reject with equability of temper, and act or suffer as the reason of things shall alternately prescribe. Other men may amuse themselves with subtle definitions, or intricate ratiocination. Let them learn to be wise by easier means; let them observe the hind of the forest, and the linnet of the grove; let them consider the life of animals, whose motions are regulated by instinct; they obey their guide, and are happy. Let us therefore, at length, cease to dispute, and learn to live; throw away the encumbrance of precepts, which they who utter them with so much pride and pomp do not understand, and carry with us this simple and intelligible maxim, that deviation from nature is deviation from happiness."

When he had spoken, he looked round him with a placid air, and enjoyed the consciousness of his own beneficence. "Sir," said the prince with great modesty, "as I, like all the rest of mankind, am desirous of felicity, my closest attention has been fixed upon your discourse. I doubt not the truth of a position which a man so learned has so confidently advanced. Let me only know what it is to live according to nature."

"When I find young men so humble and so docile," said the philosopher, "I can deny them no information which my studies have enabled me to afford. To live according to nature, is to act always with due regard to the fitness arising from the relations and qualities of causes and effects; to concur with the great and unchangeable scheme of universal felicity; to co-operate with the general disposition and tendency of the present system of things."

The prince soon found that this was one of the sages whom he should understand less as he heard him longer. He therefore bowed and was silent; and the philosopher, supposing him satisfied, and the rest vanquished, rose up and departed with the air of a man that had co-operated with the present system.[6]

* * *

Chapter 26. The Princess Continues Her Remarks upon Private Life

Nekayah, perceiving her brother's attention fixed, proceeded in her narrative.

"In families where there is or is not poverty, there is commonly discord. If a kingdom be, as Imlac tells us, a great family, a family likewise is a little kingdom, torn with factions and exposed to revolutions. An unpracticed observer expects the love of parents and children to be constant and equal; but this kindness seldom continues beyond the years of infancy: in a short time the children become rivals to their parents. Benefits are allayed[7] by reproaches, and gratitude debased by envy.

"Parents and children seldom act in concert; each child endeavors to appropriate the esteem or fondness of the parents, and the parents, with yet less temptation, betray each other to their children. Thus, some place their confidence in the father, and some in the mother, and by degrees the house is filled with artifices and feuds.

"The opinions of children and parents, of the young and the old, are naturally opposite, by the contrary effects of hope and despondence, of expectation and experience, without crime or folly on either side. The colors of life in youth and age appear different, as the face of nature in spring and winter. And how can children credit the assertions of parents, which their own eyes show them to be false?

"Few parents act in such a manner as much to enforce their maxims by the credit of their lives. The old man trusts wholly to slow contrivance and gradual progression; the youth expects to force his way by genius, vigor, and precipitance. The old man pays regard to riches, and the youth reverences virtue. The old man deifies prudence; the youth commits himself to magnanimity and chance. The young man, who intends no ill, believes that none is intended, and therefore acts with openness and candor; but his father, having suffered the injuries of fraud, is impelled to suspect, and too often allured to practice it. Age looks with anger on the temerity of youth, and youth with contempt on the scrupulosity[8] of age. Thus parents and children, for the greatest part, live on to love less and less; and, if those whom nature has thus closely united are the torments of each other, where shall we look for tenderness and consolation?"

"Surely," said the prince, "you must have been unfortunate in your choice of acquaintance: I am unwilling to believe that the most tender of all relations is thus impeded in its effects by natural necessity."

"Domestic discord," answered she, "is not inevitably and fatally necessary, but yet is not easily avoided. We seldom see that a whole family is virtuous; the good and evil cannot well agree, and the evil can yet less agree with one another. Even the virtuous fall sometimes to variance, when their virtues are

---

6. In chapters 23–25, Rasselas examines court life; and Nekayah, domestic life. She reports her findings to him.
7. To allay is "to join any thing to another, so as

to abate its predominant qualities" (Johnson's *Dictionary*).
8. "Fear of acting in any manner" (Johnson's *Dictionary*).

of different kinds, and tending to extremes. In general, those parents have most reverence who most deserve it; for he that lives well cannot be despised.

"Many other evils infest private life. Some are the slaves of servants whom they have trusted with their affairs. Some are kept in continual anxiety to the caprice of rich relations, whom they cannot please, and dare not offend. Some husbands are imperious, and some wives perverse; and, as it is always more easy to do evil than good, though the wisdom or virtue of one can very rarely make many happy, the folly or vice of one may often make many miserable."

"If such be the general effect of marriage," said the prince, "I shall for the future think it dangerous to connect my interest with that of another, lest I should be unhappy by my partner's fault."

"I have met," said the princess, "with many who live single for that reason; but I never found that their prudence ought to raise envy. They dream away their time without friendship, without fondness, and are driven to rid them-selves of the day, for which they have no use, by childish amusements, or vicious delights. They act as beings under the constant sense of some known inferiority that fills their minds with rancor, and their tongues with censure. They are peevish at home, and malevolent abroad; and, as the outlaws of human nature, make it their business and their pleasure to disturb that soci-ety which debars them from its privileges. To live without feeling or exciting sympathy, to be fortunate without adding to the felicity of others, or afflicted without tasting the balm of pity, is a state more gloomy than solitude; it is not retreat but exclusion from mankind. Marriage has many pains, but cel-ibacy has no pleasures."

"What then is to be done?" said Rasselas; "the more we inquire, the less we can resolve. Surely he is most likely to please himself that has no other inclination to regard."[9]

* * *

Chapter 29. The Debate on Marriage Continued

"The good of the whole," says Rasselas, "is the same with the good of all its parts. If marriage be best for mankind it must be evidently best for indi-viduals, or a permanent and necessary duty must be the cause of evil, and some must be inevitably sacrificed to the convenience of others. In the esti-mate which you have made of the two states, it appears that the incommod-ities of a single life are, in a great measure, necessary and certain, but those of the conjugal state accidental and avoidable.

"I cannot forbear to flatter myself that prudence and benevolence will make marriage happy. The general folly of mankind is the cause of general complaint. What can be expected but disappointment and repentance from a choice made in the immaturity of youth, in the ardor of desire, without judgment, without foresight, without inquiry after conformity of opinions, similarity of manners, rectitude of judgment, or purity of sentiment.

"Such is the common process of marriage. A youth and maiden meeting by chance, or brought together by artifice, exchange glances, reciprocate civilities, go home, and dream of one another. Having little to divert atten-

9. In chapters 27–29, Rasselas reports on the unhappiness of court life, and he and Nekayah debate whether marriage leads to happiness or misery.

tion, or diversify thought, they find themselves uneasy when they are apart, and therefore conclude that they shall be happy together. They marry, and discover what nothing but voluntary blindness had before concealed; they wear out life in altercations, and charge nature with cruelty.

"From those early marriages proceeds likewise the rivalry of parents and children: the son is eager to enjoy the world before the father is willing to forsake it, and there is hardly room at once for two generations. The daughter begins to bloom before the mother can be content to fade, and neither can forbear to wish for the absence of the other.

"Surely all these evils may be avoided by that deliberation and delay which prudence prescribes to irrevocable choice. In the variety and jollity of youthful pleasures life may be well enough supported without the help of a partner. Longer time will increase experience, and wider views will allow better opportunities of inquiry and selection: one advantage, at least, will be certain; the parents will be visibly older than their children."

"What reason cannot collect," said Nekayah, "and what experiment has not yet taught, can be known only from the report of others. I have been told that late marriages are not eminently happy. This is a question too important to be neglected, and I have often proposed it to those, whose accuracy of remark, and comprehensiveness of knowledge, made their suffrages[1] worthy of regard. They have generally determined that it is dangerous for a man and woman to suspend their fate upon each other, at a time when opinions are fixed, and habits are established; when friendships have been contracted on both sides, when life has been planned into method, and the mind has long enjoyed the contemplation of its own prospects.

"It is scarcely possible that two traveling through the world under the conduct of chance should have been both directed to the same path, and it will not often happen that either will quit the track which custom has made pleasing. When the desultory levity of youth has settled into regularity, it is soon succeeded by pride ashamed to yield, or obstinacy delighting to contend. And even though mutual esteem produces mutual desire to please, time itself, as it modifies unchangeably the external mien, determines likewise the direction of the passions, and gives an inflexible rigidity to the manners. Long customs are not easily broken: he that attempts to change the course of his own life very often labors in vain; and how shall we do that for others which we are seldom able to do for ourselves?"

"But surely," interposed the prince, "you suppose the chief motive of choice forgotten or neglected. Whenever I shall seek a wife, it shall be my first question, whether she be willing to be led by reason?"

"Thus it is," said Nekayah, "that philosophers are deceived. There are a thousand familiar[2] disputes which reason never can decide; questions that elude investigation, and make logic ridiculous; cases where something must be done, and where little can be said. Consider the state of mankind, and inquire how few can be supposed to act upon any occasions, whether small or great, with all the reasons of action present to their minds. Wretched would be the pair above all names of wretchedness, who should be doomed to adjust by reason every morning all the minute detail of a domestic day.

"Those who marry at an advanced age will probably escape the encroach-

1. Opinions.　　　　　　　　　　2. Domestic.

ments of their children; but, in diminution of this advantage, they will be likely to leave them, ignorant and helpless, to a guardian's mercy: or, if that should not happen, they must at least go out of the world before they see those whom they love best either wise or great.

"From their children, if they have less to fear, they have less also to hope, and they lose, without equivalent, the joys of early love, and the convenience of uniting with manners pliant and minds susceptible of new impressions, which might wear away their dissimilitudes by long cohabitation, as soft bodies, by continual attrition, conform their surfaces to each other.

"I believe it will be found that those who marry late are best pleased with their children, and those who marry early with their partners."

"The union of these two affections," said Rasselas, "would produce all that could be wished. Perhaps there is a time when marriage might unite them, a time neither too early for the father, nor too late for the husband."

"Every hour," answered the princess, "confirms my prejudice in favor of the position so often uttered by the mouth of Imlac, 'That nature sets her gifts on the right hand and on the left.' Those conditions, which flatter hope and attract desire, are so constituted that, as we approach one, we recede from another. There are goods so opposed that we cannot seize both, but, by too much prudence, may pass between them at too great a distance to reach either. This is often the fate of long consideration; he does nothing who endeavors to do more than is allowed to humanity. Flatter not yourself with contrarieties of pleasure. Of the blessings set before you make your choice, and be content. No man can taste the fruits of autumn, while he is delighting his scent with the flowers of the spring: no man can, at the same time, fill his cup from the source and from the mouth of the Nile."[3]

* * *

Chapter 31. They Visit the Pyramids

The resolution being thus taken, they set out the next day. They laid tents upon their camels, being resolved to stay among the pyramids till their curiosity was fully satisfied. They traveled gently, turned aside to everything remarkable, stopped from time to time and conversed with the inhabitants, and observed the various appearances of towns ruined and inhabited, of wild and cultivated nature.

When they came to the great pyramid, they were astonished at the extent of the base, and the height of the top. Imlac explained to them the principles upon which the pyramidal form was chosen for a fabric intended to coextend its duration with that of the world; he showed that its gradual diminution gave it such stability as defeated all the common attacks of the elements, and could scarcely be overthrown by earthquakes themselves, the least resistible of natural violence. A concussion that should shatter the pyramid would threaten the dissolution of the continent.

They measured all its dimensions, and pitched their tents at its foot. Next day they prepared to enter its interior apartments, and having hired the common guides, climbed up to the first passage, when the favorite of the princess, looking into the cavity, stepped back and trembled. "Pekuah," said the prin-

3. In chapter 30, Imlac proposes a visit to the pyramids.

cess, "of what art thou afraid?" "Of the narrow entrance," answered the lady, "and of the dreadful gloom. I dare not enter a place which must surely be inhabited by unquiet souls. The original possessors of these dreadful vaults will start up before us, and perhaps shut us in forever." She spoke, and threw her arms round the neck of her mistress.

"If all your fear be of apparitions," said the prince, "I will promise you safety. There is no danger from the dead; he that is once buried will be seen no more."

"That the dead are seen no more," said Imlac, "I will not undertake to maintain, against the concurrent and unvaried testimony of all ages, and of all nations. There is no people, rude or learned, among whom apparitions of the dead are not related and believed. This opinion, which perhaps prevails as far as human nature is diffused, could become universal only by its truth; those that never heard of one another would not have agreed in a tale which nothing but experience can make credible. That it is doubted by single cavilers can very little weaken the general evidence; and some who deny it with their tongues confess it by their fears.

"Yet I do not mean to add new terrors to those which have already seized upon Pekuah. There can be no reason why specters should haunt the pyramid more than other places, or why they should have power or will to hurt innocence and purity. Our entrance is no violation of their privileges; we can take nothing from them, how then can we offend them?"

"My dear Pekuah," said the princess, "I will always go before you, and Imlac shall follow you. Remember that you are the companion of the princess of Abyssinia."

"If the princess is pleased that her servant should die," returned the lady, "let her command some death less dreadful than enclosure in this horrid cavern. You know I dare not disobey you; I must go if you command me, but if I once enter, I never shall come back."

The princess saw that her fear was too strong for expostulation or reproof, and, embracing her, told her that she should stay in the tent till their return. Pekuah was yet not satisfied, but entreated the princess not to pursue so dreadful a purpose as that of entering the recesses of the pyramid. "Though I cannot teach courage," said Nekayah, "I must not learn cowardice, nor leave at last undone what I came hither only to do."

Chapter 32. They Enter the Pyramid

Pekuah descended to the tents, and the rest entered the pyramid. They passed through the galleries, surveyed the vaults of marble, and examined the chest in which the body of the founder is supposed to have been reposited. They then sat down in one of the most spacious chambers to rest a while before they attempted to return.

"We have now," said Imlac, "gratified our minds with an exact view of the greatest work of man, except the wall of China.

"Of the wall it is very easy to assign the motive. It secured a wealthy and timorous nation from the incursions of barbarians, whose unskillfulness in arts made it easier for them to supply their wants by rapine than by industry, and who from time to time poured in upon the habitations of peaceful commerce, as vultures descend upon domestic fowl. Their celerity and fierceness made the wall necessary, and their ignorance made it efficacious.

"But for the pyramids, no reason has ever been given adequate to the cost and labor of the work. The narrowness of the chambers proves that it could afford no retreat from enemies, and treasures might have been reposited at far less expense with equal security. It seems to have been erected only in compliance with that hunger of imagination which preys incessantly upon life, and must be always appeased by some employment. Those who have already all that they can enjoy must enlarge their desires. He that has built for use till use is supplied, must begin to build for vanity, and extend his plan to the utmost power of human performance, that he may not be soon reduced to form another wish.

"I consider this mighty structure as a monument of the insufficiency of human enjoyments. A king, whose power is unlimited, and whose treasures surmount all real and imaginary wants, is compelled to solace, by the erection of a pyramid, the satiety of dominion and tastelessness of pleasures, and to amuse the tediousness of declining life by seeing thousands laboring without end, and one stone, for no purpose, laid upon another. Whoever thou art, that, not content with a moderate condition, imaginest happiness in royal magnificence, and dreamest that command or riches can feed the appetite of novelty with perpetual gratifications, survey the pyramids, and confess thy folly!"[4]

* * *

Chapter 40. The History of a Man of Learning

They returned to Cairo, and were so well pleased at finding themselves together, that none of them went much abroad. The prince began to love learning, and one day declared to Imlac, that he intended to devote himself to science,[5] and pass the rest of his days in literary solitude.

"Before you make your final choice," answered Imlac, "you ought to examine its hazards, and converse with some of those who are grown old in the company of themselves. I have just left the observatory of one of the most learned astronomers in the world, who has spent forty years in unwearied attention to the motions and appearances of the celestial bodies, and has drawn out his soul in endless calculations. He admits a few friends once a month to hear his deductions and enjoy his discoveries. I was introduced as a man of knowledge worthy of his notice. Men of various ideas and fluent conversation are commonly welcome to those whose thoughts have been long fixed upon a single point, and who find the images of other things stealing away. I delighted him with my remarks, he smiled at the narrative of my travels, and was glad to forget the constellations, and descend for a moment into the lower world.

"On the next day of vacation I renewed my visit, and was so fortunate as to please him again. He relaxed from that time the severity of his rule, and permitted me to enter at my own choice. I found him always busy, and always

4. In chapters 33–39, Pekuah—while her friends are in the pyramid—is abducted by a troop of Arabs. The chief is tempted to keep her, but even-

tually accepts a ransom and returns her unharmed.
5. Knowledge.

glad to be relieved. As each knew much which the other was desirous of learning, we exchanged our notions with great delight. I perceived that I had every day more of his confidence, and always found new cause of admiration in the profundity of his mind. His comprehension is vast, his memory capacious and retentive, his discourse is methodical, and his expression clear.

"His integrity and benevolence are equal to his learning. His deepest researches and most favorite studies are willingly interrupted for any opportunity of doing good by his counsel or his riches. To his closest retreat, at his most busy moments, all are admitted that want his assistance: 'For though I exclude idleness and pleasure, I will never,' says he, 'bar my doors against charity. To man is permitted the contemplation of the skies, but the practice of virtue is commanded.'"

"Surely," said the princess, "this man is happy."

"I visited him," said Imlac, "with more and more frequency, and was every time more enamored of his conversation: he was sublime without haughtiness, courteous without formality, and communicative without ostentation. I was at first, great princess, of your opinion, thought him the happiest of mankind, and often congratulated him on the blessing that he enjoyed. He seemed to hear nothing with indifference but the praises of his condition, to which he always returned a general answer, and diverted the conversation to some other topic.

"Amidst this willingness to be pleased, and labor to please, I had quickly reason to imagine that some painful sentiment pressed upon his mind. He often looked up earnestly towards the sun, and let his voice fall in the midst of his discourse. He would sometimes, when we were alone, gaze upon me in silence with the air of a man who longed to speak what he was yet resolved to suppress. He would often send for me with vehement injunctions of haste, though, when I came to him, he had nothing extraordinary to say. And sometimes, when I was leaving him, he would call me back, pause a few moments and then dismiss me.

Chapter 41. The Astronomer Discovers[6] the Cause of his Uneasiness

"At last the time came when the secret burst his reserve. We were sitting together last night in the turret of his house, watching the emersion of a satellite of Jupiter. A sudden tempest clouded the sky, and disappointed our observation. We sat a while silent in the dark, and then he addressed himself to me in these words: 'Imlac, I have long considered thy friendship as the greatest blessing of my life. Integrity without knowledge is weak and useless, and knowledge without integrity is dangerous and dreadful. I have found in thee all the qualities requisite for trust, benevolence, experience, and fortitude. I have long discharged an office which I must soon quit at the call of nature, and shall rejoice in the hour of imbecility[7] and pain to devolve it upon thee.'

"I thought myself honored by this testimony, and protested that whatever could conduce to his happiness would add likewise to mine.

"'Hear, Imlac, what thou wilt not without difficulty credit. I have possessed for five years the regulation of weather, and the distribution of the

---

6. Reveals.

7. Feebleness.

seasons: the sun has listened to my dictates, and passed from tropic to tropic by my direction; the clouds, at my call, have poured their waters, and the Nile has overflowed at my command; I have restrained the rage of the dog-star, and mitigated the fervors of the crab.[8] The winds alone, of all the elemental powers, have hitherto refused my authority, and multitudes have perished by equinoctial tempests which I found myself unable to prohibit or restrain. I have administered this great office with exact justice, and made to the different nations of the earth an impartial dividend of rain and sunshine. What must have been the misery of half the globe, if I had limited the clouds to particular regions, or confined the sun to either side of the equator?'

Chapter 42. *The Opinion of the Astronomer Is Explained and Justified*

"I suppose he discovered in me, through the obscurity of the room, some tokens of amazement and doubt, for, after a short pause, he proceeded thus:

" 'Not to be easily credited will neither surprise nor offend me; for I am, probably, the first of human beings to whom this trust has been imparted. Nor do I know whether to deem this distinction a reward or punishment; since I have possessed it I have been far less happy than before, and nothing but the consciousness of good intention could have enabled me to support the weariness of unremitted vigilance.'

" 'How long, Sir', said I, 'has this great office been in your hands?'

" 'About ten years ago,' said he, 'my daily observations of the changes of the sky led me to consider, whether, if I had the power of the seasons, I could confer greater plenty upon the inhabitants of the earth. This contemplation fastened on my mind, and I sat days and nights in imaginary dominion, pouring upon this country and that the showers of fertility, and seconding every fall of rain with a due proportion of sunshine. I had yet only the will to do good, and did not imagine that I should ever have the power.

" 'One day as I was looking on the fields withering with heat, I felt in my mind a sudden wish that I could send rain on the southern mountains, and raise the Nile to an inundation. In the hurry of my imagination I commanded rain to fall, and, by comparing the time of my command, with that of the inundation, I found that the clouds had listened to my lips.'

" 'Might not some other cause,' said I, 'produce this concurrence? the Nile does not always rise on the same day.'

" 'Do not believe,' said he with impatience, 'that such objections could escape me: I reasoned long against my own conviction, and labored against truth with the utmost obstinacy. I sometimes suspected myself of madness, and should not have dared to impart this secret but to a man like you, capable of distinguishing the wonderful from the impossible, and the incredible from the false.'

" 'Why, Sir,' said I, 'do you call that incredible, which you know, or think you know, to be true?'

" 'Because,' said he, 'I cannot prove it by any external evidence; and I know too well the laws of demonstration to think that my conviction ought to

---

8. The fourth sign of the zodiac (Cancer). "The dogstar": Sirius was supposed to cause the heat ("dog days") of summer.

influence another, who cannot, like me, be conscious of its force. I therefore shall not attempt to gain credit by disputation. It is sufficient that I feel this power, that I have long possessed, and every day exerted it. But the life of man is short, the infirmities of age increase upon me, and the time will soon come when the regulator of the year must mingle with the dust. The care of appointing a successor has long disturbed me; the night and the day have been spent in comparisons of all the characters which have come to my knowledge, and I have yet found none so worthy as thyself.

Chapter 43. The Astronomer Leaves Imlac His Directions

" 'Hear therefore, what I shall impart, with attention, such as the welfare of a world requires. If the task of a king be considered as difficult, who has the care only of a few millions, to whom he cannot do much good or harm, what must be the anxiety of him, on whom depends the action of the elements, and the great gifts of light and heat!—Hear me therefore with attention.

" 'I have diligently considered the position of the earth and sun, and formed innumerable schemes in which I changed their situation. I have sometimes turned aside the axis of the earth, and sometimes varied the ecliptic of the sun: but I have found it impossible to make a disposition by which the world may be advantaged; what one region gains, another loses by any imaginable alteration, even without considering the distant parts of the solar system with which we are unacquainted. Do not, therefore, in thy administration of the year, indulge thy pride by innovation; do not please thyself with thinking that thou canst make thyself renowned to all future ages, by disordering the seasons. The memory of mischief is no desirable fame. Much less will it become thee to let kindness or interest prevail. Never rob other countries of rain to pour it on thine own. For us the Nile is sufficient.'

"I promised that when I possessed the power, I would use it with inflexible integrity, and he dismissed me, pressing my hand. 'My heart,' said he, 'will be now at rest, and my benevolence will no more destroy my quiet: I have found a man of wisdom and virtue, to whom I can cheerfully bequeath the inheritance of the sun.' "

The prince heard this narration with very serious regard, but the princess smiled, and Pekuah convulsed herself with laughter. "Ladies," said Imlac, "to mock the heaviest of human afflictions is neither charitable nor wise. Few can attain this man's knowledge, and few practice his virtues; but all may suffer his calamity. Of the uncertainties of our present state, the most dreadful and alarming is the uncertain continuance of reason."

The princess was recollected, and the favorite was abashed. Rasselas, more deeply affected, inquired of Imlac, whether he thought such maladies of the mind frequent, and how they were contracted.

Chapter 44. The Dangerous Prevalence[9] of Imagination

"Disorders of intellect," answered Imlac, "happen much more often than superficial observers will easily believe. Perhaps, if we speak with rigorous

9. Predominance.

exactness, no human mind is in its right state. There is no man whose imagination does not sometimes predominate over his reason, who can regulate his attention wholly by his will, and whose ideas will come and go at his command. No man will be found in whose mind airy notions do not sometimes tyrannize, and force him to hope or fear beyond the limits of sober probability. All power of fancy over reason is a degree of insanity; but while this power is such as we can control and repress, it is not visible to others, nor considered as any depravation of the mental faculties; it is not pronounced madness but when it comes ungovernable, and apparently influences speech or action.

"To indulge the power of fiction, and send imagination out upon the wing, is often the sport of those who delight too much in silent speculation. When we are alone we are not always busy; the labor of excogitation is too violent to last long; the ardor of inquiry will sometimes give way to idleness or satiety. He who has nothing external that can divert him must find pleasure in his own thoughts, and must conceive himself what he is not; for who is pleased with what he is? He then expatiates in boundless futurity, and culls from all imaginable conditions that which for the present moment he should most desire, amuses his desires with impossible enjoyments, and confers upon his pride unattainable dominion. The mind dances from scene to scene, unites all pleasures in all combinations, and riots in delights which nature and fortune, with all their bounty, cannot bestow.

"In time, some particular train of ideas fixes the attention; all other intellectual gratifications are rejected; the mind, in weariness or leisure, recurs constantly to the favorite conception, and feasts on the luscious falsehood, whenever she is offended with the bitterness of truth. By degrees the reign of fancy is confirmed; she grows first imperious, and in time despotic. Then fictions begin to operate as realities, false opinions fasten upon the mind, and life passes in dreams of rapture or of anguish.

"This, sir, is one of the dangers of solitude, which the hermit has confessed not always to promote goodness, and the astronomer's misery has proved to be not always propitious to wisdom."

"I will no more," said the favorite, "imagine myself the queen of Abyssinia. I have often spent the hours which the princess gave to my own disposal, in adjusting ceremonies and regulating the court; I have repressed the pride of the powerful, and granted the petitions of the poor; I have built new palaces in more happy situations, planted groves upon the tops of mountains, and have exulted in the beneficence of royalty, till, when the princess entered, I had almost forgotten to bow down before her."

"And I," said the princess, "will not allow myself any more to play the shepherdess in my waking dreams. I have often soothed my thoughts with the quiet and innocence of pastoral employments, till I have in my chamber heard the winds whistle, and the sheep bleat; sometimes freed the lamb entangled in the thicket, and sometimes with my crook encountered the wolf. I have a dress like that of the village maids, which I put on to help my imagination, and a pipe on which I play softly, and suppose myself followed by my flocks."

"I will confess," said the prince, "an indulgence of fantastic delight more dangerous than yours. I have frequently endeavored to image the possibility of a perfect government, by which all wrong should be restrained, all vice reformed, and all the subjects preserved in tranquility and innocence. This thought produced innumerable schemes of reformation, and dictated many useful regulations and salutary edicts. This has been the sport, and sometimes the labor, of my solitude; and I start, when I think with how little anguish I once supposed the death of my father and my brothers."

"Such," says Imlac, "are the effects of visionary schemes; when we first form them, we know them to be absurd, but familiarize them by degrees, and in time lose sight of their folly."

Chapter 45. They Discourse with an Old Man

The evening was now far past, and they rose to return home. As they walked along the bank of the Nile, delighted with the beams of the moon quivering on the water, they saw at a small distance an old man, whom the prince had often heard in the assembly of the sages. "Yonder," said he, "is one whose years have calmed his passions, but not clouded his reason. Let us close the disquisitions of the night by inquiring what are his sentiments of his own state, that we may know whether youth alone is to struggle with vexation, and whether any better hope remains for the latter part of life."

Here the sage approached and saluted them. They invited him to join their walk, and prattled a while, as acquaintance that had unexpectedly met one another. The old man was cheerful and talkative, and the way seemed short in his company. He was pleased to find himself not disregarded, accompanied them to their house, and, at the prince's request, entered with them. They placed him in the seat of honor, and set wine and conserves before him.

"Sir," said the princess, "an evening walk must give to a man of learning like you pleasures which ignorance and youth can hardly conceive. You know the qualities and the causes of all that you behold, the laws by which the river flows, the periods in which the planets perform their revolutions. Everything must supply you with contemplation, and renew the consciousness of your own dignity."

"Lady," answered he, "let the gay and the vigorous expect pleasure in their excursions; it is enough that age can obtain ease. To me the world has lost its novelty; I look round, and see what I remember to have seen in happier days. I rest against a tree, and consider that in the same shade I once disputed upon the annual overflow of the Nile with a friend who is now silent in the grave. I cast my eyes upward, fix them on the changing moon, and think with pain on the vicissitudes of life. I have ceased to take much delight in physical truth; for what have I to do with those things which I am soon to leave?"

"You may at least recreate[1] yourself," said Imlac, "with the recollection of an honorable and useful life, and enjoy the praise which all agree to give you."

"Praise," said the sage with a sigh, "is to an old man an empty sound. I have neither mother to be delighted with the reputation of her son, nor wife to partake the honors of her husband. I have outlived my friends and my rivals. Nothing is now of much importance; for I cannot extend my interest beyond myself. Youth is delighted with applause, because it is considered as

---

1. Refresh.

the earnest of some future good, and because the prospect of life is far extended; but to me, who am now declining to decrepitude, there is little to be feared from the malevolence of men, and yet less to be hoped from their affection or esteem. Something they may yet take away, but they can give me nothing. Riches would now be useless, and high employment would be pain. My retrospect of life recalls to my view many opportunities of good neglected, much time squandered upon trifles, and more lost in idleness and vacancy. I leave many great designs unattempted, and many great attempts unfinished. My mind is burthened with no heavy crime, and therefore I compose myself to tranquility; endeavor to abstract my thoughts from hopes and cares which, though reason knows them to be vain, still try to keep their old possession of the heart; expect,[2] with serene humility, that hour which nature cannot long delay; and hope to possess, in a better state, that happiness which here I could not find, and that virtue which here I have not attained."

He arose and went away, leaving his audience not much elated with the hope of long life. The prince consoled himself with remarking that it was not reasonable to be disappointed by this account; for age had never been considered as the season of felicity, and if it was possible to be easy in decline and weakness, it was likely that the days of vigor and alacrity might be happy; that the noon of life might be bright, if the evening could be calm.

The princess suspected that age was querulous and malignant, and delighted to repress the expectations of those who had newly entered the world. She had seen the possessors of estates look with envy on their heirs, and known many who enjoy pleasure no longer than they can confine it to themselves.

Pekuah conjectured that the man was older than he appeared, and was willing to impute his complaints to delirious dejection; or else supposed that he had been unfortunate, and was therefore discontented. "For nothing," said she, "is more common than to call our own condition the condition of life."

Imlac, who had no desire to see them depressed, smiled at the comforts which they could so readily procure to themselves, and remembered that, at the same age, he was equally confident of unmingled prosperity, and equally fertile of consolatory expedients. He forbore to force upon them unwelcome knowledge, which time itself would too soon impress. The princess and her lady retired; the madness of the astronomer hung upon their minds, and they desired Imlac to enter upon his office, and delay next morning the rising of the sun.[3]

*　　*　　*

Chapter 48. Imlac Discourses on the Nature of the Soul

"What reason," said the prince, "can be given, why the Egyptians should thus expensively preserve those carcasses which some nations consume with fire, others lay to mingle with the earth, and all agree to remove from their sight, as soon as decent rites can be performed?"

2. Await.
3. In chapters 46 and 47, Nekayah, Pekuah, and Rasselas befriend the astronomer and gradually wean him from madness. In search of diversion, all of them visit the catacombs.

"The original of ancient customs," said Imlac, "is commonly unknown; for the practice often continues when the cause has ceased; and concerning superstitious ceremonies it is vain to conjecture; for what reason did not dictate reason cannot explain. I have long believed that the practice of embalming arose only from tenderness to the remains of relations or friends, and to this opinion I am more inclined, because it seems impossible that this care should have been general: had all the dead been embalmed, their repositories must in time have been more spacious than the dwellings of the living. I suppose only the rich or honorable were secured from corruption, and the rest left to the course of nature.

"But it is commonly supposed that the Egyptians believed the soul to live as long as the body continued undissolved, and therefore tried this method of eluding death."

"Could the wise Egyptians," said Nekayah, "think so grossly of the soul? If the soul could once survive its separation, what could it afterwards receive or suffer from the body?"

"The Egyptians would doubtless think erroneously," said the astronomer, "in the darkness of heathenism, and the first dawn of philosophy. The nature of the soul is still disputed amidst all our opportunities of clearer knowledge: some yet say, that it may be material, who, nevertheless, believe it to be immortal."

"Some," answered Imlac, "have indeed said that the soul is material, but I can scarcely believe that any man has thought it, who knew how to think; for all the conclusions of reason enforce the immateriality of mind, and all the notices of sense and investigations of science concur to prove the unconsciousness of matter.

"It was never supposed that cogitation is inherent in matter, or that every particle is a thinking being. Yet if any part of matter be devoid of thought, what part can we suppose to think? Matter can differ from matter only in form, density, bulk, motion, and direction of motion: to which of these, however varied or combined, can consciousness be annexed? To be round or square, to be solid or fluid, to be great or little, to be moved slowly or swiftly one way or another, are modes of material existence, all equally alien from the nature of cogitation. If matter be once without thought, it can only be made to think by some new modification, but all the modifications which it can admit are equally unconnected with cogitative powers."

"But the materialists," said the astronomer, "urge that matter may have qualities with which we are unacquainted."

"He who will determine," returned Imlac, "against that which he knows, because there may be something which he knows not; he that can set hypothetical possibility against acknowledged certainty, is not to be admitted among reasonable beings. All that we know of matter is, that matter is inert, senseless and lifeless; and if this conviction cannot be opposed but by referring us to something that we know not, we have all the evidence that human intellect can admit. If that which is known may be overruled by that which is unknown, no being, not omniscient, can arrive at certainty."

"Yet let us not," said the astronomer, "too arrogantly limit the Creator's power."

"It is no limitation of omnipotence," replied the poet, "to suppose that one thing is not consistent with another, that the same proposition cannot be at once true and false, that the same number cannot be even and odd, that cogitation cannot be conferred on that which is created incapable of cogitation."

"I know not," said Nekayah, "any great use of this question. Does that immateriality, which, in my opinion, you have sufficiently proved, necessarily include eternal duration?"

"Of immateriality," said Imlac, "our ideas are negative, and therefore obscure. Immateriality seems to imply a natural power of perpetual duration as a consequence of exemption from all causes of decay: whatever perishes, is destroyed by the solution of its contexture,[4] and separation of its parts; nor can we conceive how that which has no parts, and therefore admits no solution, can be naturally corrupted or impaired."

"I know not," said Rasselas, "how to conceive anything without extension: what is extended must have parts, and you allow, that whatever has parts may be destroyed."

"Consider your own conceptions," replied Imlac, "and the difficulty will be less. You will find substance without extension. An ideal form is no less real than material bulk: yet an ideal form has no extension. It is no less certain, when you think on a pyramid, that your mind possesses the idea of a pyramid, than that the pyramid itself is standing. What space does the idea of a pyramid occupy more than the idea of a grain of corn? or how can either idea suffer laceration? As is the effect such is the cause; as thought is, such is the power that thinks; a power impassive and indiscerptible."[5]

"But the Being," said Nekayah, "whom I fear to name, the Being which made the soul, can destroy it."

"He, surely, can destroy it," answered Imlac, "since, however unperishable, it receives from a superior nature its power of duration. That it will not perish by any inherent cause of decay, or principle of corruption, may be shown by philosophy; but philosophy can tell no more. That it will not be annihilated by him that made it, we must humbly learn from higher authority."

The whole assembly stood a while silent and collected. "Let us return," said Rasselas, "from this scene of mortality. How gloomy would be these mansions of the dead to him who did not know that he shall never die; that what now acts shall continue its agency, and what now thinks shall think on for ever. Those that lie here stretched before us, the wise and the powerful of ancient times, warn us to remember the shortness of our present state: they were, perhaps, snatched away while they were busy, like us, in the choice of life."

"To me," said the princess, "the choice of life is become less important; I hope hereafter to think only on the choice of eternity."

They then hastened out of the caverns, and, under the protection of their guard, returned to Cairo.

Chapter 49. The Conclusion, in Which Nothing Is Concluded

It was now the time of the inundation of the Nile: a few days after their visit to the catacombs, the river began to rise.

They were confined to their house. The whole region being under water

4. Dissolution of its structure.   5. Not to be separated.

gave them no invitation to any excursions, and being well supplied with materials for talk, they diverted themselves with comparisons of the different forms of life which they had observed, and with various schemes of happiness which each of them had formed.

Pekuah was never so much charmed with any place as the convent of St. Anthony, where the Arab restored her to the princess, and wished only to fill it with pious maidens, and to be made prioress of the order; she was weary of expectation and disgust,[6] and would gladly be fixed in some unvariable state.

The princess thought that, of all sublunary things, knowledge was the best: she desired first to learn all sciences, and then purposed to found a college of learned women, in which she would preside, that, by conversing with the old and educating the young, she might divide her time between the acquisition and communication of wisdom, and raise up for the next age models of prudence, and patterns of piety.

The prince desired a little kingdom, in which he might administer justice in his own person, and see all the parts of government with his own eyes; but he could never fix the limits of his dominion, and was always adding to the number of his subjects.

Imlac and the astronomer were contented to be driven along the stream of life, without directing their course to any particular port.

Of these wishes that they had formed, they well knew that none could be obtained. They deliberated a while what was to be done, and resolved, when the inundation should cease, to return to Abyssinia.[7]

1759

Rambler No. 4

[ON FICTION]

Saturday, *March* 31, 1750

Simul et jucunda et idonea dicere vitae.
—HORACE, *Art of Poetry*, 334
And join both profit and delight in one.
—CREECH

The works of fiction with which the present generation seems more particularly delighted are such as exhibit life in its true state, diversified only by accidents that daily happen in the world, and influenced by passions and qualities which are really to be found in conversing with mankind.

This kind of writing may be termed, not improperly, the comedy of romance, and is to be conducted nearly by the rules of comic poetry. Its province is to bring about natural events by easy means, and to keep up curiosity without the help of wonder: it is therefore precluded from the machines[1] and expedients of the heroic romance, and can neither employ

---

6. Aversion.
7. Probably not, as is often suggested, to the Happy Valley, which the travelers earlier fled as a prison. Presumably the travelers return, with whatever wisdom they have gained but also with their cherished illusions, to share the common destiny of humankind.
1. The technical term in neoclassical critical theory for the supernatural agents who intervene in human affairs in epic and tragedy.

giants to snatch away a lady from the nuptial rites, nor knights to bring her back from captivity; it can neither bewilder its personages in deserts, nor lodge them in imaginary castles.

I remember a remark made by Scaliger upon Pontanus,[2] that all his writings are filled with the same images; and that if you take from him his lilies and his roses, his satyrs and his dryads, he will have nothing left that can be called poetry. In like manner, almost all the fictions of the last age will vanish if you deprive them of a hermit and a wood, a battle and a shipwreck.

Why this wild strain of imagination found reception so long in polite and learned ages, it is not easy to conceive; but we cannot wonder that while readers could be procured, the authors were willing to continue it; for when a man had by practice gained some fluency of language, he had no further care than to retire to his closet, let loose his invention, and heat his mind with incredibilities; a book was thus produced without fear of criticism, without the toil of study, without knowledge of nature, or acquaintance with life.

The task of our present writers is very different; it requires, together with that learning which is to be gained from books, that experience which can never be attained by solitary diligence, but must arise from general converse and accurate observation of the living world. Their performances have, as Horace expresses it, *plus oneris quanto veniae minus*,[3] little indulgence, and therefore more difficulty. They are engaged in portraits of which everyone knows the original, and can detect any deviation from exactness of resemblance. Other writings are safe, except from the malice of learning, but these are in danger from every common reader; as the slipper ill executed was censured by a shoemaker who happened to stop in his way at the Venus of Apelles.[4]

But the fear of not being approved as just copiers of human manners is not the most important concern that an author of this sort ought to have before him. These books are written chiefly to the young, the ignorant, and the idle, to whom they serve as lectures of conduct, and introductions into life. They are the entertainment of minds unfurnished with ideas, and therefore easily susceptible of impressions; not fixed by principles, and therefore easily following the current of fancy; not informed by experience, and consequently open to every false suggestion and partial account.

That the highest degree of reverence should be paid to youth, and that nothing indecent should be suffered to approach their eyes or ears, are precepts extorted by sense and virtue from an ancient writer by no means eminent for chastity of thought.[5] The same kind, though not the same degree, of caution, is required in everything which is laid before them, to secure them from unjust prejudices, perverse opinions, and incongruous combinations of images.

In the romances formerly written, every transaction and sentiment was so remote from all that passes among men that the reader was in very little danger of making any applications to himself; the virtues and crimes were equally beyond his sphere of activity; and he amused himself with heroes

2. Julius Caesar Scaliger (1484–1558) criticized the Latin poems of the Italian poet Jovianus Pontanus (1426–1503).
3. *Epistles* 2.1.170.
4. According to Pliny the Younger (*Naturalis Historia* 35.85), the Greek painter Apelles of Kos (4th century B.C.E.) corrected the drawing of a sandal after hearing a shoemaker criticize it as faulty, but when the flattered artisan dared to find fault with the drawing of a leg, the artist bade him "stick to his last."
5. Juvenal's *Satires* 14.1–58.

and with traitors, deliverers and persecutors, as with beings of another species, whose actions were regulated upon motives of their own, and who had neither faults nor excellencies in common with himself.

But when an adventurer is leveled with the rest of the world, and acts in such scenes of the universal drama as may be the lot of any other man, young spectators fix their eyes upon him with closer attention, and hope, by observing his behavior and success, to regulate their own practices when they shall be engaged in the like part.

For this reason these familiar histories may perhaps be made of greater use than the solemnities of professed morality, and convey the knowledge of vice and virtue with more efficacy than axioms and definitions. But if the power of example is so great as to take possession of the memory by a kind of violence, and produce effects almost without the intervention of the will, care ought to be taken that when the choice is unrestrained, the best examples only should be exhibited; and that which is likely to operate so strongly should not be mischievous or uncertain in its effects.

The chief advantage which these fictions have over real life is that their authors are at liberty, though not to invent, yet to select objects, and to cull from the mass of mankind those individuals upon which the attention ought most to be employed; as a diamond, though it cannot be made, may be polished by art, and placed in such situation as to display that luster which before was buried among common stones.

It is justly considered as the greatest excellency of art to imitate nature; but it is necessary to distinguish those parts of nature which are most proper for imitation: greater care is still required in representing life, which is so often discolored by passion or deformed by wickedness. If the world be promiscuously[6] described, I cannot see of what use it can be to read the account; or why it may not be as safe to turn the eye immediately upon mankind as upon a mirror which shows all that presents itself without discrimination.

It is therefore not a sufficient vindication of a character that it is drawn as it appears, for many characters ought never to be drawn; nor of a narrative that the train of events is agreeable to observation and experience, for that observation which is called knowledge of the world will be found much more frequently to make men cunning than good. The purpose of these writings is surely not only to show mankind, but to provide that they may be seen hereafter with less hazard; to teach the means of avoiding the snares which are laid by Treachery for Innocence, without infusing any wish for that superiority with which the betrayer flatters his vanity; to give the power of counteracting fraud without the temptation to practice it; to initiate youth by mock encounters in the art of necessary defense, and to increase prudence without impairing virtue.

Many writers, for the sake of following nature, so mingle good and bad qualities in their principal personages that they are both equally conspicuous; and as we accompany them through their adventures with delight, and are led by degrees to interest ourselves in their favor, we lose the abhorrence of their faults because they do not hinder our pleasure, or perhaps regard them with some kindness for being united with so much merit.

There have been men indeed splendidly wicked, whose endowments threw

6. Indiscriminately.

a brightness on their crimes, and whom scarce any villainy made perfectly detestable because they never could be wholly divested of their excellencies; but such have been in all ages the great corrupters of the world, and their resemblance ought no more to be preserved than the art of murdering without pain.

Some have advanced, without due attention to the consequences of this notion, that certain virtues have their correspondent faults, and therefore that to exhibit either apart is to deviate from probability. Thus men are observed by Swift to be "grateful in the same degree as they are resentful." This principle, with others of the same kind, supposes man to act from a brute impulse, and pursue a certain degree of inclination without any choice of the object; for, otherwise, though it should be allowed that gratitude and resentment arise from the same constitution of the passions, it follows not that they will be equally indulged when reason is consulted; yet, unless that consequence be admitted, this sagacious maxim becomes an empty sound, without any relation to practice or to life.

Nor is it evident that even the first motions to these effects are always in the same proportion. For pride, which produces quickness of resentment, will obstruct gratitude by unwillingness to admit that inferiority which obligation implies; and it is very unlikely that he who cannot think he receives a favor will acknowledge or repay it.

It is of the utmost importance to mankind that positions of this tendency should be laid open and confuted; for while men consider good and evil as springing from the same root, they will spare the one for the sake of the other, and in judging, if not of others at least of themselves, will be apt to estimate their virtues by their vices. To this fatal error all those will contribute who confound the colors of right and wrong, and, instead of helping to settle their boundaries, mix them with so much art that no common mind is able to disunite them.

In narratives where historical veracity has no place, I cannot discover why there should not be exhibited the most perfect idea of virtue; of virtue not angelical, nor above probability (for what we cannot credit, we shall never imitate), but the highest and purest that humanity can reach, which, exercised in such trials as the various revolutions of things shall bring upon it, may, by conquering some calamities and enduring others, teach us what we may hope, and what we can perform. Vice (for vice is necessary to be shown) should always disgust; nor should the graces of gaiety, nor the dignity of courage, be so united with it as to reconcile it to the mind. Wherever it appears, it should raise hatred by the malignity of its practices, and contempt by the meanness of its stratagems: for while it is supported by either parts or spirit, it will be seldom heartily abhorred. The Roman tyrant was content to be hated if he was but feared;[7] and there are thousands of the readers of romances willing to be thought wicked if they may be allowed to be wits. It is therefore to be steadily inculcated that virtue is the highest proof of understanding, and the only solid basis of greatness; and that vice is the natural consequence of narrow thoughts; that it begins in mistake, and ends in ignominy.

---

7. The Emperor Tiberius (see Suetonius's *Lives of the Caesars*).

Rambler No. 60

[BIOGRAPHY]

Saturday, *October* 13, 1750

—*Quid sit pulchrum, quid turpe, quid utile, quid non,*
Plenius ac melius Chrysippo et Crantore dicit.
—HORACE, *Epistles,* 1.2. 3–4

> Whose works the beautiful and base contain,
> Of vice and virtue more instructive rules,
> Than all the sober sages of the schools.

—FRANCIS

All joy or sorrow for the happiness or calamities of others is produced by an act of the imagination, that realizes the event, however fictitious, or approximates it, however remote, by placing us, for a time, in the condition of him whose fortune we contemplate; so that we feel, while the deception lasts, whatever motions would be excited by the same good or evil happening to ourselves.

Our passions are therefore more strongly moved, in proportion as we can more readily adopt the pains or pleasure proposed to our minds, by recognizing them as once our own, or considering them as naturally incident to our state of life. It is not easy for the most artful writer to give us an interest in happiness or misery, which we think ourselves never likely to feel, and with which we have never yet been made acquainted. Histories of the downfall of kingdoms, and revolutions of empires, are read with great tranquility; the imperial tragedy pleases common auditors only by its pomp of ornament, and grandeur of ideas; and the man whose faculties have been engrossed by business, and whose heart never fluttered but at the rise or fall of stocks, wonders how the attention can be seized, or the affections agitated, by a tale of love.

Those parallel circumstances, and kindred images to which we readily conform our minds, are, above all other writings, to be found in narratives of the lives of particular persons; and therefore no species of writing seems more worthy of cultivation than biography, since none can be more delightful or more useful, none can more certainly enchain the heart by irresistible interest, or more widely diffuse instruction to every diversity of condition.

The general and rapid narratives of history, which involve a thousand fortunes in the business of a day, and complicate innumerable incidents in one great transaction, afford few lessons applicable to private life, which derives its comforts and its wretchedness from the right or wrong management of things, which nothing but their frequency makes considerable, *Parva si non fiunt quotidie,* says Pliny,[1] and which can have no place in those relations which never descend below the consultation of senates, the motions of armies, and the schemes of conspirators.

I have often thought that there has rarely passed a life of which a judicious and faithful narrative would not be useful. For, not only every man has in the mighty mass of the world great numbers in the same condition with himself, to whom his mistakes and miscarriages, escapes and expedients,

---

1. Pliny the Younger's *Epistles* 3.1. Johnson translates the phrase in the preceding clause.

would be of immediate and apparent use; but there is such an uniformity in the state of man, considered apart from adventitious and separable decorations and disguises, that there is scarce any possibility of good or ill, but is common to humankind. A great part of the time of those who are placed at the greatest distance by fortune, or by temper, must unavoidably pass in the same manner; and though, when the claims of nature are satisfied, caprice, and vanity, and accident, begin to produce discriminations and peculiarities, yet the eye is not very heedful or quick, which cannot discover the same causes still[2] terminating their influence in the same effects, though sometimes accelerated, sometimes retarded, or perplexed by multiplied combinations. We are all prompted by the same motives, all deceived by the same fallacies, all animated by hope, obstructed by danger, entangled by desire, and seduced by pleasure.

It is frequently objected to relations of particular lives, that they are not distinguished by any striking or wonderful vicissitudes. The scholar who passed his life among his books, the merchant who conducted only his own affairs, the priest whose sphere of action was not extended beyond that of his duty, are considered as no proper objects of public regard, however they might have excelled in their several stations, whatever might have been their learning, integrity, and piety. But this notion arises from false measures of excellence and dignity, and must be eradicated by considering, that in the esteem of uncorrupted reason, what is of most use is of most value.

It is, indeed, not improper to take honest advantages of prejudice, and to gain attention by a celebrated name; but the business of the biographer is often to pass slightly over those performances and incidents, which produce vulgar greatness, to lead the thoughts into domestic privacies, and display the minute details of daily life, where exterior appendages are cast aside, and men excel each other only by prudence and by virtue. The account of Thuanus[3] is, with great propriety, said by its author to have been written, that it might lay open to posterity the private and familiar character of that man, *cujus ingenium et candorem ex ipsius scriptis sunt olim semper miraturi,* whose candor and genius will to the end of time be by his writings preserved in admiration.

There are many invisible circumstances which, whether we read as inquirers after natural or moral knowledge, whether we intend to enlarge our science, or increase our virtue, are more important than public occurrences. Thus Sallust, the great master of nature, has not forgot, in his account of Catiline,[4] to remark that *his walk was now quick, and again slow,* as an indication of a mind revolving something with violent commotion. Thus the story of Melancthon[5] affords a striking lecture on the value of time, by informing us that when he made an appointment, he expected not only the hour, but the minute to be fixed, that the day might not run out in the idleness of suspense; and all the plans and enterprises of De Witt are now of less importance to the world, than that part of his personal character, which represents him as careful of his health, and negligent of his life.[6]

But biography has often been allotted to writers who seem very little

2. Always.
3. Jacques-Auguste de Thou (1553–1617), an important French historian, of whom Nicholas Rigault wrote a brief biography, a sentence of which Johnson quotes and translates below.
4. Sallust, a Roman historian of the 1st century

B.C.E., wrote an account of Catiline's conspiracy against the Roman state.
5. Camerarius wrote a life of Melancthon, a German theologian of the 16th century.
6. Sir William Temple, characterizing the Dutch statesman John De Witt.

acquainted with the nature of their task, or very negligent about the performance. They rarely afford any other account than might be collected from public papers, but imagine themselves writing a life when they exhibit a chronological series of actions or preferments; and so little regard the manners or behavior of their heroes, that more knowledge may be gained of a man's real character, by a short conversation with one of his servants, than from a formal and studied narrative, begun with his pedigree, and ended with his funeral.

If now and then they condescend to inform the world of particular facts, they are not always so happy as to select the most important. I know not well what advantage posterity can receive from the only circumstance by which Tickell has distinguished Addison from the rest of mankind, the irregularity of his pulse:[7] nor can I think myself overpaid for the time spent in reading the life of Malherbe, by being enabled to relate, after the learned biographer,[8] that Malherbe had two predominant opinions; one, that the looseness of a single woman might destroy all her boast of ancient descent; the other, that the French beggars made use very improperly and barbarously of the phrase *noble gentleman,* because either word included the sense of both.

There are, indeed, some natural reasons why these narratives are often written by such as were not likely to give much instruction or delight, and why most accounts of particular persons are barren and useless. If a life be delayed till interest and envy are at an end, we may hope for impartiality, but must expect little intelligence;[9] for the incidents which give excellence to biography are of a volatile and evanescent kind, such as soon escape the memory, and are rarely transmitted by tradition. We know how few can portray a living acquaintance, except by his most prominent and observable particularities, and the grosser features of his mind; and it may be easily imagined how much of this little knowledge may be lost in imparting it, and how soon a succession of copies will lose all resemblance of the original.

If the biographer writes from personal knowledge, and makes haste to gratify the public curiosity, there is danger lest his interest, his fear, his gratitude, or his tenderness, overpower his fidelity, and tempt him to conceal, if not to invent. There are many who think it an act of piety to hide the faults or failings of their friends, even when they can no longer suffer by their detection; we therefore see whole ranks of characters adorned with uniform panegyric, and not to be known from one another, but by extrinsic and casual circumstances. "Let me remember," says Hale, "when I find myself inclined to pity a criminal, that there is likewise a pity due to the country."[1] If we owe regard to the memory of the dead, there is yet more respect to be paid to knowledge, to virtue, and to truth.

7. From Thomas Tickell's preface to Addision's *Works* (1721).
8. The life of the French poet François de Malherbe (1555–1628) was written by Honorat de Racan.
9. Information.
1. From Gilbert Burnet's *Life and Death of Sir Matthew Hale* (1682).

A Dictionary of the English Language   Before Johnson, no standard dictionary of the English language existed. The lack had troubled speakers of English for some time, both because Italian and French academies had produced major dictionaries of their own tongues and because, in the absence of any authority, English seemed likely to change utterly from one generation to another. Many eighteenth-century authors feared that their own language would soon become obsolete: as Alexander Pope wrote in *An Essay on Criticism,*

> Our sons their fathers' failing language see,
> And such as Chaucer is, shall Dryden be.

A dictionary could help retard such change, and commercially it would be a book that everyone would need to buy. In 1746 a group of London publishers commissioned Johnson, still an unknown author, to undertake the project. He hoped to finish it in three years; it took him nine. But the quantity and quality of work he accomplished, aided only by six part-time assistants, made him famous as "Dictionary Johnson." The *Dictionary* remained a standard reference book for one hundred years.

Johnson's achievement is notable in three respects: its size (forty thousand words), the wealth of illustrative quotations, and the excellence of the definitions. No earlier English dictionary rivaled the scope of Johnson's two large folio volumes. About 114,000 quotations, gathered from the best English writers from Sidney to the eighteenth century, exemplify the usage of words as well as their meanings. Above all, it was the definitions, however, that established the authority of Johnson's *Dictionary.* A small selection is only too likely to concentrate on a few amusing or notorious definitions, but the great majority are full, clear, and totally free from eccentricity. Indeed, many of them are still repeated in modern dictionaries. Language, Johnson knew, cannot be fixed once and for all; many of the words he defines have radically changed meaning since the eighteenth century. Yet Johnson did more than any person of his time to preserve the ideal of a standard English.

From A Dictionary of the English Language

From *Preface*

*   *   *

A large work is difficult because it is large, even though all its parts might singly be performed with facility; where there are many things to be done, each must be allowed its share of time and labor, in the proportion only which it bears to the whole; nor can it be expected that the stones which form the dome of a temple should be squared and polished like the diamond of a ring.

Of the event of this work, for which, having labored it with so much application, I cannot but have some degree of parental fondness, it is natural to form conjectures. Those who have been persuaded to think well of my design will require that it should fix our language, and put a stop to those alterations which time and chance have hitherto been suffered to make in it without opposition. With this consequence I will confess that I flattered myself for a while;[1] but now begin to fear that I have indulged expectation which neither

---

1. Johnson's *Plan* (1747) had called for "a dictionary by which the pronunciation of our language may be fixed, and its attainment facilitated; by which its purity may be preserved, its use ascertained, and its duration lengthened."

reason nor experience can justify. When we see men grow old and die at a certain time one after another, from century to century, we laugh at the elixir that promises to prolong life to a thousand years; and with equal justice may the lexicographer be derided, who being able to produce no example of a nation that has preserved their words and phrases from mutability, shall imagine that his dictionary can embalm his language and secure it from corruption and decay, that it is in his power to change sublunary nature, or clear the world at once from folly, vanity, and affectation.

With this hope, however, academies have been instituted, to guard the avenues of their languages, to retain fugitives, and repulse intruders; but their vigilance and activity have hitherto been vain; sounds are too volatile and subtle for legal restraints; to enchain syllables, and to lash the wind, are equally the undertakings of pride, unwilling to measure its desires by its strength. The French language has visibly changed under the inspection of the academy;[2] the style of Amelot's translation of father Paul is observed by Le Courayer to be *un peu passé*;[3] and no Italian will maintain that the diction of any modern writer is not perceptibly different from that of Boccace, Machiavel, or Caro.[4]

Total and sudden transformations of a language seldom happen; conquests and migrations are now very rare: but there are other causes of change, which, though slow in their operation, and invisible in their progress, are perhaps as much superior to human resistance as the revolutions of the sky, or intumescence[5] of the tide. Commerce, however necessary, however lucrative, as it depraves the manners, corrupts the language; they that have frequent intercourse with strangers, to whom they endeavor to accommodate themselves, must in time learn a mingled dialect, like the jargon which serves the traffickers[6] on the Mediterranean and Indian coasts. This will not always be confined to the exchange, the warehouse, or the port, but will be communicated by degrees to other ranks of the people, and be at last incorporated with the current speech.

There are likewise internal causes equally forcible. The language most likely to continue long without alteration would be that of a nation raised a little, and but a little, above barbarity, secluded from strangers, and totally employed in procuring the conveniencies of life; either without books, or, like some of the Mahometan countries, with very few: men thus busied and unlearned, having only such words as common use requires, would perhaps long continue to express the same notions by the same signs. But no such constancy can be expected in a people polished by arts, and classed by subordination, where one part of the community is sustained and accommodated by the labor of the other. Those who have much leisure to think, will always be enlarging the stock of ideas, and every increase of knowledge, whether real or fancied, will produce new words, or combinations of words. When the mind is unchained from necessity, it will range after convenience;

---

2. The French academy, founded to purify the French language, had produced a dictionary in 1694; but revisions were necessary within a few years.

3. A bit old-fashioned (French). Le Courayer's translation (1736) of Father Paolo Sarpi's *History of the Council of Trent* superseded Amelot's (1683).

4. Like Boccaccio (1313–1375) and Machiavelli (1469–1527), Annibale Caro (1507–1566) was a classic Italian stylist whose work had preceded the dictionary published in 1612 by the Italian academy.

5. Swelling.

6. Traders.

when it is left at large in the fields of speculation, it will shift opinions; as any custom is disused, the words that expressed it must perish with it; as any opinion grows popular, it will innovate speech in the same proportion as it alters practice.

As by the cultivation of various sciences, a language is amplified, it will be more furnished with words deflected from their original sense; the geometrician will talk of a courtier's zenith, or the eccentric virtue of a wild hero, and the physician of sanguine expectations and phlegmatic delays.[7] Copiousness of speech will give opportunities to capricious choice, by which some words will be preferred, and others degraded; vicissitudes of fashion will enforce the use of new, or extend the signification of known terms. The tropes[8] of poetry will make hourly encroachments, and the metaphorical will become the current sense: pronunciation will be varied by levity or ignorance, and the pen must at length comply with the tongue; illiterate writers will at one time or other, by public infatuation, rise into renown, who, not knowing the original import of words, will use them with colloquial licentiousness, confound distinction, and forget propriety. As politeness increases, some expressions will be considered as too gross and vulgar for the delicate, others as too formal and ceremonious for the gay and airy; new phrases are therefore adopted, which must, for the same reasons, be in time dismissed. Swift, in his petty treatise on the English language,[9] allows that new words must sometimes be introduced, but proposes that none should be suffered to become obsolete. But what makes a word obsolete, more than general agreement to forbear it? and how shall it be continued, when it conveys an offensive idea, or recalled again into the mouths of mankind, when it has once by disuse become unfamiliar, and by unfamiliarity unpleasing.

There is another cause of alteration more prevalent than any other, which yet in the present state of the world cannot be obviated. A mixture of two languages will produce a third distinct from both, and they will always be mixed, where the chief part of education, and the most conspicuous accomplishment, is skill in ancient or in foreign tongues. He that has long cultivated another language, will find its words and combinations crowd upon his memory; and haste or negligence, refinement or affectation, will obtrude borrowed terms and exotic expressions.

The great pest of speech is frequency of translation. No book was ever turned from one language into another, without imparting something of its native idiom; this is the most mischievous and comprehensive innovation; single words may enter by thousands, and the fabric of the tongue continue the same, but new phraseology changes much at once; it alters not the single stones of the building, but the order[1] of the columns. If an academy should be established for the cultivation of our style, which I, who can never wish to see dependence multiplied, hope the spirit of English liberty will hinder or destroy, let them, instead of compiling grammars and dictionaries, endeavor with all their influence to stop the license of translators, whose

---

7. "Sanguine" and "phlegmatic" once referred only to the physiological predominance of blood or phlegm. "Zenith" (the point of the sky directly overhead) and "eccentric" (deviating from the center) were originally astronomical and geometrical terms.

8. "A change of a word from its original signification" (Johnson's *Dictionary*).
9. *A Proposal for Correcting, Improving, and Ascertaining the English Tongue* (1712). "Petty": little.
1. Architectural mode (Doric, etc.), which determines the style and proportions of columns.

idleness and ignorance, if it be suffered to proceed, will reduce us to babble a dialect of France.

If the changes that we fear be thus irresistible, what remains but to acquiesce with silence, as in the other insurmountable distresses of humanity? It remains that we retard what we cannot repel, that we palliate what we cannot cure. Life may be lengthened by care, though death cannot be ultimately defeated: tongues, like governments, have a natural tendency to degeneration; we have long preserved our constitution, let us make some struggles for our language.

In hope of giving longevity to that which its own nature forbids to be immortal, I have devoted this book, the labor of years, to the honor of my country, that we may no longer yield the palm of philology without a contest to the nations of the continent. The chief glory of every people arises from its authors: whether I shall add anything by my own writings to the reputation of English literature, must be left to time. Much of my life has been lost under the pressures of disease; much has been trifled away; and much has always been spent in provision for the day that was passing over me; but I shall not think my employment useless or ignoble, if by my assistance foreign nations, and distant ages, gain access to the propagators of knowledge, and understand the teachers of truth; if my labors afford light to the repositories of science, and add celebrity to Bacon, to Hooker, to Milton, and to Boyle.[2]

When I am animated by this wish, I look with pleasure on my book, however defective; and deliver it to the world with the spirit of a man that has endeavored well. That it will immediately become popular I have not promised to myself: a few wild blunders and risible absurdities, from which no work of such multiplicity was ever free, may for a time furnish folly with laughter, and harden ignorance in contempt; but useful diligence will at last prevail, and there never can be wanting some who distinguish desert;[3] who will consider that no dictionary of a living tongue ever can be perfect, since while it is hastening to publication, some words are budding, and some falling away; that a whole life cannot be spent upon syntax and etymology, and that even a whole life would not be sufficient; that he, whose design includes whatever language can express, must often speak of what he does not understand; that a writer will sometimes be hurried by eagerness to the end, and sometimes faint with weariness under a task, which Scaliger compares to the labors of the anvil and the mine;[4] that what is obvious is not always known, and what is known is not always present; that sudden fits of inadvertency will surprise vigilance, slight avocations[5] will reduce attention, and casual eclipses of the mind will darken learning; and that the writer shall often in vain trace his memory at the moment of need, for that which yesterday he knew with intuitive readiness, and which will come uncalled into his thoughts tomorrow.

In this work, when it shall be found that much is omitted, let it not be forgotten that much likewise is performed; and though no book was ever spared out of tenderness to the author, and the world is little solicitous to

2. Leading physicist and chemist (1627–1691). "Science": knowledge. Richard Hooker wrote *The Laws of Ecclesiastical Polity* (1594–97), a famous defense of the Church of England.
3. Merit.

4. Joseph Justus Scaliger (1540–1609), a great scholar and lexicographer, wrote Latin verses suggesting that criminals should be condemned to lexicography.
5. Whatever calls one aside.

know whence proceeded the faults of that which it condemns; yet it may gratify curiosity to inform it, that the *English Dictionary* was written with little assistance of the learned, and without any patronage of the great;[6] not in the soft obscurities of retirement, or under the shelter of academic bowers, but amidst inconvenience and distraction, in sickness and in sorrow: and it may repress the triumph of malignant criticism to observe, that if our language is not here fully displayed, I have only failed in an attempt which no human powers have hitherto completed. If the lexicons of ancient tongues, now immutably fixed, and comprised in a few volumes, be yet, after the toil of successive ages, inadequate and delusive; if the aggregated knowledge and cooperating diligence of the Italian academicians did not secure them from the censure of Beni;[7] if the embodied critics of France, when fifty years had been spent upon their work, were obliged to change its economy,[8] and give their second edition another form, I may surely be contented without the praise of perfection, which, if I could obtain, in this gloom of solitude, what would it avail me? I have protracted my work till most of those whom I wished to please have sunk into the grave,[9] and success and miscarriage are empty sounds: I therefore dismiss it with frigid tranquility, having little to fear or hope from censure or from praise.

[SOME DEFINITIONS: A SMALL ANTHOLOGY][1]

ANTHO'LOGY. *n.*
1. A collection of flowers.
To CANT. *v.*
    To talk in the jargon of particular professions, or in any kind of formal affected language, or with a peculiar and studied tone of voice.
> Men *cant* endlessly about *materia forma;* and hunt chimeras by rules of art, or dress up ignorance in words of bulk or sound, which may stop up the mouth of inquiry.—*Glanville's Scepsis Scientifica.*

ENTHU'SIASM. *n.*
1. A vain belief of private revelation; a vain confidence of divine favor or communication.
> *Enthusiasm* is founded neither on reason nor divine revelation, but rises from the conceits of a warmed or overweening brain.—*Locke.*

GE'NIUS. *n.*
1. The protecting or ruling power of men, places, or things.
>   And as I awake, sweet music breathe,
> Sent by some spirit to mortals good,
> Or th' unseen *genius* of the wood.—*Milton.*

2. A man endowed with superior faculties.
3. Mental power or faculties.
4. Disposition of nature by which anyone is qualified for some peculiar employment.
5. Nature; disposition.

6. See Johnson's letter to Lord Chesterfield in Boswell's *Life of Johnson* (p. 2760).
7. Paolo Beni's *L'Anticrusca* (1612) violently attacked the first edition of the *Vocabolario* (the Italian dictionary).
8. Organization.
9. Johnson's wife had died three years earlier.
1. Johnson's definitions include etymologies and illustrative quotations, some of which are omitted in this selection.

IMA'GINATION. *n.*

1. Fancy; the power of forming ideal pictures; the power of representing things absent to one's self or others.
2. Conception; image in the mind; idea.
3. Contrivance; scheme.

LEXICO'GRAPHER. *n.*

A writer of dictionaries; a harmless drudge, that busies himself in tracing the original, and detailing the signification of words.

MELANCHO'LY. *n.*

1. A disease, supposed to proceed from a redundance of black bile.
2. A kind of madness, in which the mind is always fixed on one object.
3. A gloomy, pensive, discontented temper.

NA'TURE. *n.*

1. An imaginary being supposed to preside over the material and animal world.

    Thou, *nature*, art my goddess; to thy law
      My services are bound.—*Shakespeare.*

2. The native state or properties of anything, by which it is discriminated from others.
3. The constitution of an animated body.
4. Disposition of mind; temper.
5. The regular course of things.
6. The compass of natural existence.
7. Natural affection, or reverence; native sensations.
8. The state or operation of the material world.
9. Sort; species.
10. Sentiments or images adapted to nature, or comfortable to truth and reality.
11. Physics; the science which teaches the qualities of things.

    Nature and *nature's* laws lay hid in night,
      God said, Let Newton be, and all was light.—*Pope.*

NE'TWORK. *n.*

Anything reticulated or decussated, at equal distances, with interstices between the intersections.

OATS. *n.*

A grain, which in England is generally given to horses, but in Scotland supports the people.

PA'STERN. *n.*

1. The knee of an horse.[2]

PA'TRON. *n.*

1. One who countenances, supports, or protects. Commonly a wretch who supports with insolence, and is paid with flattery.

PE'NSION. *n.*

An allowance made to anyone without an equivalent. In England it is generally understood to mean pay given to a state hireling for treason to his country.[3]

---

2. "A lady once asked him how he came to define *Pastern* the *knee* of a horse: instead of making an elaborate defense, as she expected, he at once answered, 'Ignorance, Madam, pure ignorance' " (Boswell).

3. In 1762 Johnson was awarded a pension, but he did not revise the definition in later editions.

SA'TIRE. *n.*

    A poem in which wickedness or folly is censured. Proper *satire* is distinguished, by the generality of the reflections, from a *lampoon*, which is aimed against a particular person; but they are too frequently confounded.

TO'RY. *n.*

    One who adheres to the ancient constitution of the state, and the apostolical hierarchy of the church of England, opposed to a whig.

        The knight is more a *tory* in the country than the town, because it
    more advances his interest.—*Addison.*

WHIG. *n.*

2. The name of a faction.

        Whoever has a true value for church and state, should avoid the
    extremes of *whig* for the sake of the former, and the extremes of tory on
    the account of the latter.—*Swift.*

WIT. *n.*

1. The powers of the mind; the mental faculties; the intellects. This is the original signification.

2. Imagination; quickness of fancy.

3. Sentiments produced by quickness of fancy.

4. A man of fancy.

5. A man of genius.

6. Sense; judgment.

7. In the plural. Sound mind; intellect not crazed.

8. Contrivance; stratagem; power of expedients.

1755

The Preface to Shakespeare

This is the finest piece of Shakespeare criticism in the eighteenth century; it culminates a critical tradition that began with John Dryden's remarks on Shakespeare and continued as the plays were edited by Nicholas Rowe, Alexander Pope, Lewis Theobald, and William Warburton. Johnson addresses the standard topics: Shakespeare is the poet of nature, not learning; the creator of characters who spring to life; and a writer whose works express the full range of human passions. But the *Preface* also takes a fresh look not only at the plays but at the first principles of criticism. Resisting "bardolatry"—uncritical worship of Shakespeare—Johnson points out his faults as well as his virtues, yet finds that his truth to life, or "just representations of general nature," surpasses that of all other modern writers. The *Preface* is most original when it attacks the long-standing critical reverence for the unities of time and place. What seems real on the stage, Johnson argues, does not depend on artificial rules but on what the mind is willing to imagine.

    Johnson's edition of Shakespeare also contained footnotes and brief introductions to each of the plays. Reprinted here are his afterwords on *Twelfth Night* and *King Lear.*

From The Preface to Shakespeare

[SHAKESPEARE'S EXCELLENCE. GENERAL NATURE]

    That praises are without reason lavished on the dead, and that the honors due only to excellence are paid to antiquity, is a complaint likely to be always continued by those who, being able to add nothing to truth, hope for eminence from the heresies of paradox; or those who, being forced by disappointment upon consolatory expedients, are willing to hope from posterity what the present age refuses, and flatter themselves that the regard which is yet denied by envy will be at last bestowed by time.

Antiquity, like every other quality that attracts the notice of mankind, has undoubtedly votaries that reverence it not from reason but from prejudice. Some seem to admire indiscriminately whatever has been long preserved, without considering that time has sometimes cooperated with chance; all perhaps are more willing to honor past than present excellence; and the mind contemplates genius through the shades of age, as the eye surveys the sun through artificial opacity. The great contention of criticism is to find the faults of the moderns and the beauties of the ancients. While an author is yet living we estimate his powers by his worst performance; and when he is dead we rate them by his best.

To works, however, of which the excellence is not absolute and definite, but gradual and comparative; to works not raised upon principles demonstrative and scientific, but appealing wholly to observation and experience, no other test can be applied than length of duration and continuance of esteem. What mankind have long possessed they have often examined and compared; and if they persist to value the possession, it is because frequent comparisons have confirmed opinion in its favor. As among the works of nature no man can properly call a river deep or a mountain high, without the knowledge of many mountains and many rivers; so in the productions of genius, nothing can be styled excellent till it has been compared with other works of the same kind. Demonstration[1] immediately displays its power and has nothing to hope or fear from the flux of years; but works tentative and experimental must be estimated by their proportion to the general and collective ability of man, as it is discovered in a long succession of endeavors. Of the first building that was raised, it might be with certainty determined that it was round or square, but whether it was spacious or lofty must have been referred to time. The Pythagorean scale of numbers[2] was at once discovered to be perfect; but the poems of Homer we yet know not to transcend the common limits of human intelligence, but by remarking that nation after nation, and century after century, has been able to do little more than transpose his incidents, new name his characters, and paraphrase his sentiments.

The reverence due to writings that have long subsisted arises, therefore, not from any credulous confidence in the superior wisdom of past ages, or gloomy persuasion of the degeneracy of mankind, but is the consequence of acknowledged and indubitable positions, that what has been longest known has been most considered, and what is most considered is best understood.

The poet of whose works I have undertaken the revision may now begin to assume the dignity of an ancient and claim the privilege of established fame and prescriptive veneration. He has long outlived his century, the term commonly fixed as the test of literary merit.[3] Whatever advantages he might once derive from personal allusions, local customs, or temporary opinions, have for many years been lost; and every topic of merriment or motive of sorrow which the modes of artificial life afforded him now only obscure the

1. "The highest degree of deducible or argumental evidence" (Johnson's *Dictionary*).
2. Pythagoras discovered the ratios that determine the principal intervals of the musical scale.
3. Horace's *Epistles* 2.1.39.

scenes which they once illuminated. The effects of favor and competition are at an end; the tradition of his friendships and his enmities has perished; his works support no opinion with arguments nor supply any faction with invectives; they can neither indulge vanity nor gratify malignity; but are read without any other reason than the desire of pleasure, and are therefore praised only as pleasure is obtained; yet, thus unassisted by interest or passion, they have passed through variations of taste and changes of manners, and, as they devolved from one generation to another, have received new honors at every transmission.

But because human judgment, though it be gradually gaining upon certainty, never becomes infallible, and approbation, though long continued, may yet be only the approbation of prejudice or fashion, it is proper to inquire by what peculiarities of excellence Shakespeare has gained and kept the favor of his countrymen.

Nothing can please many, and please long, but just representations of general nature. Particular manners can be known to few, and therefore few only can judge how nearly they are copied. The irregular combinations of fanciful invention may delight awhile by that novelty of which the common satiety of life sends us all in quest; but the pleasures of sudden wonder are soon exhausted, and the mind can only repose on the stability of truth.

Shakespeare is, above all writers, at least above all modern writers, the poet of nature, the poet that holds up to his readers a faithful mirror of manners and of life. His characters are not modified by the customs of particular places, unpracticed by the rest of the world; by the peculiarities of studies or professions, which can operate but upon small numbers; or by the accidents of transient fashions or temporary opinions: they are the genuine progeny of common humanity, such as the world will always supply and observation will always find. His persons act and speak by the influence of those general passions and principles by which all minds are agitated and the whole system of life is continued in motion. In the writings of other poets a character is too often an individual: in those of Shakespeare it is commonly a species.

It is from this wide extension of design that so much instruction is derived. It is this which fills the plays of Shakespeare with practical axioms and domestic wisdom. It was said of Euripides[4] that every verse was a precept; and it may be said of Shakespeare that from his works may be collected a system of civil and economical prudence. Yet his real power is not shown in the splendor of particular passages, but by the progress of his fable[5] and the tenor of his dialogue; and he that tries to recommend him by select quotations will succeed like the pedant in Hierocles[6] who, when he offered his house to sale, carried a brick in his pocket as a specimen.

It will not easily be imagined how much Shakespeare excels in accommodating his sentiments to real life but by comparing him with other authors. It was observed of the ancient schools of declamation that the more diligently they were frequented, the more was the student disqualified for the world, because he found nothing there which he should ever meet in any other

---

4. The Greek tragic poet (ca. 480–406 B.C.E.). The observation is Cicero's.
5. Plot. "The series or contexture of events which constitute a poem epic or dramatic" (Johnson's *Dictionary*).
6. Hierocles of Alexandria, a Greek philosopher of the 5th century C.E.

place. The same remark may be applied to every stage but that of Shake-speare. The theater, when it is under any other direction, is peopled by such characters as were never seen, conversing in a language which was never heard, upon topics which will never arise in the commerce of mankind. But the dialogue of this author is often so evidently determined by the incident which produces it, and is pursued with so much ease and simplicity, that it seems scarcely to claim the merit of fiction, but to have been gleaned by diligent selection out of common conversation and common occurrences.

Upon every other stage the universal agent is love, by whose power all good and evil is distributed and every action quickened or retarded. To bring a lover, a lady, and a rival into the fable; to entangle them in contradictory obligations, perplex them with oppositions of interest, and harass them with violence of desires inconsistent with each other; to make them meet in rap-ture, and part in agony; to fill their mouths with hyperbolical joy and out-rageous sorrow; to distress them as nothing human ever was distressed; to deliver them as nothing human ever was delivered, is the business of a mod-ern dramatist. For this, probability is violated, life is misrepresented, and language is depraved. But love is only one of many passions; and as it has no great influence upon the sum of life, it has little operation in the dramas of a poet who caught his ideas from the living world and exhibited only what he saw before him. He knew that any other passion, as it was regular or exorbitant, was a cause of happiness or calamity.

Characters thus ample and general were not easily discriminated and pre-served; yet perhaps no poet ever kept his personages more distinct from each other. I will not say with Pope that every speech may be assigned to the proper speaker,[7] because many speeches there are which have nothing char-acteristical; but perhaps though some may be equally adapted to every per-son, it will be difficult to find that any can be properly transferred from the present possessor to another claimant. The choice is right when there is reason for choice.

Other dramatists can only gain attention by hyperbolical or aggravated characters, by fabulous and unexampled excellence or depravity, as the writ-ers of barbarous romances invigorated the reader by a giant and a dwarf; and he that should form his expectations of human affairs from the play or from the tale would be equally deceived. Shakespeare has no heroes; his scenes are occupied only by men, who act and speak as the reader thinks that he should himself have spoken or acted on the same occasion; even where the agency is supernatural, the dialogue is level with life. Other writers disguise the most natural passions and most frequent incidents so that he who con-templates them in the book will not know them in the world: Shakespeare approximates[8] the remote, and familiarizes the wonderful; the event which he represents will not happen, but, if it were possible, its effects would prob-ably be such as he has assigned; and it may be said that he has not only shown human nature as it acts in real exigencies, but as it would be found in trials to which it cannot be exposed.

This therefore is the praise of Shakespeare, that his drama is the mirror of life; that he who has mazed his imagination in following the phantoms

---

7. In the preface to his edition of Shakespeare's plays (1725).

8. Brings near.

which other writers raise up before him, may here be cured of his delirious ecstasies by reading human sentiments in human language, by scenes from which a hermit may estimate the transactions of the world, and a confessor predict the progress of the passions.

[SHAKESPEARE'S FAULTS. THE THREE DRAMATIC UNITIES]

Shakespeare with his excellencies has likewise faults, and faults sufficient to obscure and overwhelm any other merit. I shall show them in the proportion in which they appear to me, without envious malignity or superstitious veneration. No question can be more innocently discussed than a dead poet's pretensions to renown; and little regard is due to that bigotry which sets candor[9] higher than truth.

His first defect is that to which may be imputed most of the evil in books or in men. He sacrifices virtue to convenience, and is so much more careful to please than to instruct that he seems to write without any moral purpose. From his writings indeed a system of social duty may be selected, for he that thinks reasonably must think morally, but his precepts and axioms drop casually from him; he makes no just distribution of good or evil, nor is always careful to show in the virtuous a disapprobation of the wicked; he carries his persons indifferently through right and wrong, and at the close dismisses them without further care, and leaves their examples to operate by chance. This fault the barbarity of his age cannot extenuate; for it is always a writer's duty to make the world better, and justice is a virtue independent on time or place.

The plots are often so loosely formed that a very slight consideration may improve them, and so carelessly pursued that he seems not always fully to comprehend his own design. He omits opportunities of instructing or delighting which the train of his story seems to force upon him, and apparently rejects those exhibitions which would be more affecting for the sake of those which are more easy.

It may be observed that in many of his plays the latter part is evidently neglected. When he found himself near the end of his work, and in view of his reward, he shortened the labor to snatch the profit. He therefore remits his efforts where he should most vigorously exert them, and his catastrophe is improbably produced or imperfectly represented.

He had no regard to distinction of time or place, but gives to one age or nation, without scruple, the customs, institutions, and opinions of another, at the expense not only of likelihood but of possibility. These faults Pope has endeavored, with more zeal than judgment, to transfer to his imagined interpolators. We need not wonder to find Hector quoting Aristotle, when we see the loves of Theseus and Hippolyta combined with the Gothic mythology of fairies.[1] Shakespeare, indeed, was not the only violator of chronology, for in the same age Sidney, who wanted not the advantages of learning, has, in his *Arcadia*, confounded the pastoral with the feudal times, the days of innocence, quiet, and security with those of turbulence, violence, and adventure.

In his comic scenes he is seldom very successful when he engages his

9. Kindness.
1. In *Troilus and Cressida* 2.2.166 and in *Midsummer Night's Dream*, respectively.

characters in reciprocations of smartness and contests of sarcasm; their jests are commonly gross, and their pleasantry licentious; neither his gentlemen nor his ladies have much delicacy, nor are sufficiently distinguished from his clowns by any appearance of refined manners. Whether he represented the real conversation of his time is not easy to determine: the reign of Elizabeth is commonly supposed to have been a time of stateliness, formality, and reserve; yet perhaps the relaxations of that severity were not very elegant. There must, however, have been always some modes of gaiety preferable to others, and a writer ought to choose the best.

In tragedy his performance seems constantly to be worse as his labor is more. The effusions of passion, which exigence forces out, are for the most part striking and energetic; but whenever he solicits his invention, or strains his faculties, the offspring of his throes is tumor,[2] meanness, tediousness, and obscurity.

In narration he affects a disproportionate pomp of diction and a wearisome train of circumlocution, and tells the incident imperfectly in many words which might have been more plainly delivered in few. Narration in dramatic poetry is naturally tedious, as it is unanimated and inactive, and obstructs the progress of the action; it should therefore always be rapid and enlivened by frequent interruption. Shakespeare found it an encumbrance, and instead of lightening it by brevity, endeavored to recommend it by dignity and splendor.

His declamations or set speeches are commonly cold and weak, for his power was the power of nature; when he endeavored, like other tragic writers, to catch opportunities of amplification and, instead of inquiring what the occasion demanded, to show how much his stores of knowledge could supply, he seldom escapes without the pity or resentment of his reader.

It is incident to him to be now and then entangled with an unwieldy sentiment which he cannot well express, and will not reject; he struggles with it awhile, and, if it continues stubborn, comprises it in words such as occur, and leaves it to be disentangled and evolved[3] by those who have more leisure to bestow upon it.

Not that always where the language is intricate the thought is subtle, or the image always great where the line is bulky; the equality of words to things is very often neglected, and trivial sentiments and vulgar[4] ideas disappoint the attention, to which they are recommended by sonorous epithets and swelling figures.

But the admirers of this great poet have most reason to complain when he approaches nearest to his highest excellence, and seems fully resolved to sink them in dejection and mollify them with tender emotions by the fall of greatness, the danger of innocence, or the crosses of love. What he does best, he soon ceases to do. He is not long soft and pathetic without some idle conceit or contemptible equivocation. He no sooner begins to move than he counteracts himself; and terror and pity, as they are rising in the mind, are checked and blasted by sudden frigidity.

A quibble[5] is to Shakespeare what luminous vapors are to the traveler: he follows it at all adventures; it is sure to lead him out of his way, and sure to

2. Inflated grandeur, false magnificence.
3. Unfolded.
4. "Mean; low; being of the common rate" (John-

son's *Dictionary*).
5. Pun.

engulf him in the mire. It has some malignant power over his mind, and its fascinations are irresistible. Whatever be the dignity or profundity of his disquisitions, whether he be enlarging knowledge or exalting affection, whether he be amusing[6] attention with incidents, or enchaining it in suspense, let but a quibble spring up before him, and he leaves his work unfinished. A quibble is the golden apple for which he will always turn aside from his career[7] or stoop from his elevation. A quibble, poor and barren as it is, gave him such delight that he was content to purchase it by the sacrifice of reason, propriety, and truth. A quibble was to him the fatal Cleopatra for which he lost the world, and was content to lose it.

It will be thought strange that in enumerating the defects of this writer, I have not yet mentioned his neglect of the unities; his violation of those laws which have been instituted and established by the joint authority of poets and critics.

For his other deviations from the art of writing, I resign him to critical justice without making any other demand in his favor than that which must be indulged to all human excellence: that his virtues be rated with his failings. But from the censure which this irregularity may bring upon him I shall, with due reverence to that learning which I must oppose, adventure to try how I can defend him.

His histories, being neither tragedies nor comedies, are not subject to any of their laws; nothing more is necessary to all the praise which they expect than that the changes of action be so prepared as to be understood; that the incidents be various and affecting, and the characters consistent, natural, and distinct. No other unity is intended, and therefore none is to be sought.

In his other works he has well enough preserved the unity of action. He has not, indeed, an intrigue regularly perplexed and regularly unraveled: he does not endeavor to hide his design only to discover it, for this is seldom the order of real events, and Shakespeare is the poet of nature: but his plan has commonly what Aristotle requires,[8] a beginning, a middle, and an end; one event is concatenated with another, and the conclusion follows by easy consequence. There are, perhaps, some incidents that might be spared, as in other poets there is much talk that only fills up time upon the stage; but the general system makes gradual advances, and the end of the play is the end of expectation.

To the unities of time and place he has shown no regard; and perhaps a nearer view of the principles on which they stand will diminish their value and withdraw from them the veneration which, from the time of Corneille,[9] they have very generally received, by discovering that they have given more trouble to the poet than pleasure to the auditor.

The necessity of observing the unities of time and place arises from the supposed necessity of making the drama credible. The critics hold it impossible that an action of months or years can be possibly believed to pass in three hours; or that the spectator can suppose himself to sit in the theater

<hr />

6. "To entertain with tranquility; to fill with thoughts that engage the mind, without distracting it" (Johnson's *Dictionary*).
7. Course of action; the ground on which a race is run. In Greek legend Atalanta refused to marry any man who could not defeat her in a foot race. Hippomenes won her by dropping, as he ran, three

of the golden apples of the Hesperides, which she paused to pick up.
8. *Poetics* 7.
9. Pierre Corneille (1606–1684), the French playwright, discussed the unities in his *Discours des trois unités* (1660).

while ambassadors go and return between distant kings, while armies are levied and towns besieged, while an exile wanders and returns, or till he whom they saw courting his mistress shall lament the untimely fall of his son. The mind revolts from evident falsehood, and fiction loses its force when it departs from the resemblance of reality.

From the narrow limitation of time necessarily arises the contraction of place. The spectator who knows that he saw the first act at Alexandria cannot suppose that he sees the next at Rome, at a distance to which not the dragons of Medea[1] could, in so short a time, have transported him; he knows with certainty that he has not changed his place; and he knows that place cannot change itself, that what was a house cannot become a plain, that what was Thebes can never be Persepolis.

Such is the triumphant language with which a critic exults over the misery of an irregular poet, and exults commonly without resistance or reply. It is time, therefore, to tell him by the authority of Shakespeare that he assumes, as an unquestionable principle, a position which, while his breath is forming it into words, his understanding pronounces to be false. It is false that any representation is mistaken for reality; that any dramatic fable in its materiality was ever credible or, for a single moment, was ever credited.

The objection arising from the impossibility of passing the first hour at Alexandria and the next at Rome supposes that when the play opens the spectator really imagines himself at Alexandria, and believes that his walk to the theater has been a voyage to Egypt, and that he lives in the days of Antony and Cleopatra. Surely he that imagines this may imagine more. He that can take the stage at one time for the palace of the Ptolemies may take it in half an hour for the promontory of Actium. Delusion, if delusion be admitted, has no certain limitation; if the spectator can be once persuaded that his old acquaintances are Alexander and Caesar, that a room illuminated with candles is the plain of Pharsalia or the bank of Granicus, he is in a state of elevation above the reach of reason or of truth, and from the heights of empyrean poetry may despise the circumscriptions of terrestrial nature. There is no reason why a mind thus wandering in ecstasy should count the clock, or why an hour should not be a century in that calenture[2] of the brain that can make the stage a field.

The truth is that the spectators are always in their senses, and know, from the first act to the last, that the stage is only a stage, and that the players are only players. They came to hear a certain number of lines recited with just gesture and elegant modulation. The lines relate to some action, and an action must be in some place; but the different actions that complete a story may be in places very remote from each other; and where is the absurdity of allowing that space to represent first Athens, and then Sicily, which was always known to be neither Sicily nor Athens but a modern theater?

By supposition, as place is introduced, time may be extended; the time required by the fable elapses, for the most part, between the acts; for, of so much of the action as is represented, the real and poetical duration is the same. If, in the first act, preparations for war against Mithridates are represented to be made in Rome, the event of the war may, without absurdity,

---

1. According to legend, Medea fled the scene of her crimes in a chariot drawn by dragons.
2. A delirium produced by tropical heat, which causes sailors to leap into the sea under the delusion that it is a green field.

be represented, in the catastrophe, as happening in Pontus; we know that there is neither war nor preparation for war; we know that we are neither in Rome nor Pontus, that neither Mithridates nor Lucullus are before us. The drama exhibits successive imitations of successive actions; and why may not the second imitation represent an action that happened years after the first, if it be so connected with it that nothing but time can be supposed to intervene? Time is, of all modes of existence, most obsequious[3] to the imagination; a lapse of years is as easily conceived as a passage of hours. In contemplation we easily contract the time of real actions, and therefore willingly permit it to be contracted when we only see their imitation.

It will be asked how the drama moves if it is not credited. It is credited with all the credit due to a drama. It is credited, whenever it moves, as a just picture of a real original; as representing to the auditor what he would himself feel if he were to do or suffer what is there feigned to be suffered or to be done. The reflection that strikes the heart is not that the evils before us are real evils, but that they are evils to which we ourselves may be exposed. If there be any fallacy, it is not that we fancy the players, but that we fancy ourselves, unhappy for a moment; but we rather lament the possibility than suppose the presence of misery, as a mother weeps over her babe when she remembers that death may take it from her. The delight of tragedy proceeds from our consciousness of fiction; if we thought murders and treasons real, they would please no more.

Imitations produce pain or pleasure, not because they are mistaken for realities, but because they bring realities to mind. When the imagination is recreated[4] by a painted landscape, the trees are not supposed capable to give us shade or the fountains coolness; but we consider how we should be pleased with such fountains playing beside us and such woods waving over us. We are agitated in reading the history of *Henry the Fifth*; yet no man takes his book for the field of Agincourt. A dramatic exhibition is a book recited with concomitants that increase or diminish its effect. Familiar comedy is often more powerful on the theater than in the page; imperial tragedy is always less. The humor of Petruchio may be heightened by grimace; but what voice or what gesture can hope to add dignity or force to the soliloquy of Cato?[5]

A play read affects the mind like a play acted. It is therefore evident that the action is not supposed to be real; and it follows that between the acts a longer or shorter time may be allowed to pass, and that no more account of space or duration is to be taken by the auditor of a drama than by the reader of a narrative, before whom may pass in an hour the life of a hero or the revolutions of an empire.

Whether Shakespeare knew the unities and rejected them by design or deviated from them by happy ignorance, it is, I think, impossible to decide and useless to inquire. We may reasonably suppose that, when he rose to notice, he did not want[6] the counsels and admonitions of scholars and critics, and that he at last deliberately persisted in a practice which he might have begun by chance. As nothing is essential to the fable but unity of action, and

---

3. "Obedient; compliant" (Johnson's *Dictionary*).
4. Delighted.
5. In Addison's tragedy *Cato* (5.1), the hero soliloquizes on immortality shortly before committing

suicide. Petruchio is the hero of Shakespeare's comedy *The Taming of the Shrew*.
6. Lack.

as the unities of time and place arise evidently from false assumptions, and, by circumscribing the extent of the drama, lessen its variety, I cannot think it much to be lamented that they were not known by him, or not observed: nor, if such another poet could arise, should I very vehemently reproach him that his first act passed at Venice and his next in Cyprus.[7] Such violations of rules merely positive[8] become the comprehensive genius of Shakespeare, and such censures are suitable to the minute and slender criticism of Voltaire.

> Non usque adeo permiscuit imis
> Longus summa dies, ut non, si voce Metelli
> Serventur leges, malint a Caesare tolli.[9]

Yet when I speak thus slightly of dramatic rules, I cannot but recollect how much wit and learning may be produced against me; before such authorities I am afraid to stand: not that I think the present question one of those that are to be decided by mere authority, but because it is to be suspected that these precepts have not been so easily received but for better reasons than I have yet been able to find. The result of my inquiries, in which it would be ludicrous to boast of impartiality, is that the unities of time and place are not essential to a just drama, that though they may sometimes conduce to pleasure, they are always to be sacrificed to the nobler beauties of variety and instruction; and that a play written with nice observation of critical rules is to be contemplated as an elaborate curiosity, as the product of superfluous and ostentatious art, by which is shown rather what is possible than what is necessary.

He that without diminution of any other excellence shall preserve all the unities unbroken deserves the like applause with the architect who shall display all the orders of architecture in a citadel without any deduction for its strength; but the principal beauty of a citadel is to exclude the enemy, and the greatest graces of a play are to copy nature and instruct life.* * *

[TWELFTH NIGHT]

This play is in the graver part elegant and easy, and in some of the lighter scenes exquisitely humorous. Ague-cheek is drawn with great propriety, but his character is, in a great measure, that of natural fatuity, and is therefore not the proper prey of a satirist. The soliloquy of Malvolio is truly comick; he is betrayed to ridicule merely by his pride. The marriage of Olivia, and the succeeding perplexity, though well enough contrived to divert on the stage, wants credibility, and fails to produce the proper instruction required in the drama, as it exhibits no just picture of life.

[KING LEAR]

The tragedy of Lear is deservedly celebrated among the dramas of Shakespeare. There is perhaps no play which keeps the attention so strongly fixed;

---

7. As is the case in Othello.
8. Arbitrary; not natural.
9. Lucan's Pharsalia 3.138–40: "The course of time has not wrought such confusion that the laws would not rather be trampled on by Caesar than saved by Metellus."

which so much agitates our passions and interests our curiosity. The artful involutions[1] of distinct interests, the striking opposition of contrary characters, the sudden changes of fortune, and the quick succession of events, fill the mind with a perpetual tumult of indignation, pity, and hope. There is no scene which does not contribute to the aggravation of the distress or conduct of the action, and scarce a line which does not conduce to the progress of the scene. So powerful is the current of the poet's imagination, that the mind, which once ventures within it, is hurried irresistibly along.

On the seeming improbability of Lear's conduct it may be observed, that he is represented according to histories at that time vulgarly[2] received as true. And perhaps if we turn our thoughts upon the barbarity and ignorance of the age to which this story is referred, it will appear not so unlikely as while we estimate Lear's manners by our own. Such preference of one daughter to another, or resignation of dominion on such conditions, would be yet credible, if told of a petty prince of Guinea or Madagascar. Shakespeare, indeed, by the mention of his earls and dukes, has given us the idea of times more civilized, and of life regulated by softer manners; and the truth is, that though he so nicely discriminates, and so minutely describes the characters of men, he commonly neglects and confounds the characters of ages, by mingling customs ancient and modern, English and foreign.

My learned friend Mr. Warton, who has in the *Adventurer* very minutely criticized this play,[3] remarks, that the instances of cruelty are too savage and shocking, and that the intervention of Edmund destroys the simplicity of the story. These objections may, I think, be answered, by repeating that the cruelty of the daughters is an historical fact, to which the poet has added little, having only drawn it into a series by dialogue and action. But I am not able to apologize with equal plausibility for the extrusion of Gloucester's eyes, which seems an act too horrid to be endured in dramatic exhibition, and such as must always compel the mind to relieve its distress by incredulity. Yet let it be remembered that our author well knew what would please the audience for which he wrote.

The injury done by Edmund to the simplicity of the action is abundantly recompensed by the addition of variety, by the art with which he is made to co-operate with the chief design, and the opportunity which he gives the poet of combining perfidy with perfidy, and connecting the wicked son with the wicked daughters, to impress this important moral, that villainy is never at a stop, that crimes lead to crimes, and at last terminate in ruin.

But though this moral be incidentally enforced, Shakespeare has suffered the virtue of Cordelia to perish in a just cause, contrary to the natural ideas of justice, to the hope of the reader, and, what is yet more strange, to the faith of chronicles. Yet this conduct is justified by the Spectator, who blames Tate for giving Cordelia success and happiness in his alteration, and declares that in his opinion, "the tragedy has lost half its beauty."[4] Dennis has remarked, whether justly or not, that to secure the favorable reception of *Cato*, "the town was poisoned with much false and abominable criticism,"[5]

1. Entanglements.
2. Popularly.
3. Joseph Warton (1722–1800) contributed several papers to Johnson's periodical *The Adventurer*; Nos. 113, 116, and 122 discuss *King Lear*.
4. Addison, *Spectator* 40. During the 18th century, *King Lear* was regularly performed with a happy ending, in the adaptation by Nahum Tate.
5. John Dennis, "Remarks upon *Cato, a Tragedy*" (1713). Dennis implies that Addison excuses the lack of poetic justice in *Lear* to justify the absence of poetic justice in his own play, *Cato*.

and that endeavors had been used to discredit and decry poetical justice. A play in which the wicked prosper, and the virtuous miscarry, may doubtless be good, because it is a just representation of the common events of human life: but since all reasonable beings naturally love justice, I cannot easily be persuaded, that the observation of justice makes a play worse; or, that if other excellencies are equal, the audience will not always rise better pleased from the final triumph of persecuted virtue.

In the present case the public has decided. Cordelia, from the time of Tate, has always retired with victory and felicity. And, if my sensations could add anything to the general suffrage, I might relate, that I was many years ago so shocked by Cordelia's death, that I know not whether I ever endured to read again the last scenes of the play till I undertook to revise them as an editor.

1765

FROM LIVES OF THE POETS

From Cowley[1]

[METAPHYSICAL WIT]

Wit, like all other things subject by their nature to the choice of man, has its changes and fashions, and at different times takes different forms. About the beginning of the seventeenth century appeared a race of writers that may be termed the metaphysical poets,[2] of whom in a criticism on the works of Cowley it is not improper to give some account.

The metaphysical poets were men of learning, and to show their learning was their whole endeavor; but, unluckily resolving to show it in rhyme, instead of writing poetry they only wrote verses, and very often such verses as stood the trial of the finger better than of the ear; for the modulation was so imperfect that they were only found to be verses by counting the syllables.

If the father of criticism[3] has rightly denominated poetry *tekhnē mimētikè, an imitative art,* these writers will without great wrong lose their right to the name of poets, for they cannot be said to have imitated anything: they neither copied nature nor life; neither painted the forms of matter nor represented the operations of intellect.

Those however who deny them to be poets allow them to be wits. Dryden confesses of himself and his contemporaries that they fall below Donne in wit, but maintains that they surpass him in poetry.[4]

If wit be well described by Pope as being "that which has been often thought, but was never before so well expressed,"[5] they certainly never

1. Abraham Cowley (1618–1667) was much admired during the middle of the 17th century. His reputation began to decline before 1700, but he was remembered as a writer of false wit, especially in his love poems *The Mistress.*
2. Presumably Johnson took this now common designation from a hint in Dryden's *A Discourse Concerning the Original and Progress of Satire.* Dryden condemned Donne because "he affects the

metaphysics . . . and perplexes the minds of the fair sex with nice speculations of philosophy, when he should engage their hearts, and entertain them with the softnesses of love" (*Essays,* ed. W. P. Ker, 2.19).
3. Aristotle in his *Poetics.*
4. *A Discourse . . . of Satire* (Ker 2.102).
5. *An Essay on Criticism,* lines 297–98.

attained nor ever sought it, for they endeavored to be singular in their thoughts, and were careless of their diction. But Pope's account of wit is undoubtedly erroneous; he depresses it below its natural dignity, and reduces it from strength of thought to happiness of language.

If by a more noble and more adequate conception that be considered as wit which is at once natural and new, that which though not obvious is, upon its first production, acknowledged to be just; if it be that which he that never found it, wonders how he missed; to wit of this kind the metaphysical poets have seldom risen. Their thoughts are often new, but seldom natural; they are not obvious, but neither are they just;[6] and the reader, far from wondering that he missed them, wonders more frequently by what perverseness of industry they were ever found.

But wit, abstracted from its effects upon the hearer, may be more rigorously and philosophically considered as a kind of *discordia concors;*[7] a combination of dissimilar images, or discovery of occult resemblances in things apparently unlike. Of wit, thus defined, they have more than enough. The most heterogeneous ideas are yoked by violence together; nature and art are ransacked for illustrations, comparisons, and allusions; their learning instructs, and their subtlety surprises; but the reader commonly thinks his improvement dearly bought, and, though he sometimes admires, is seldom pleased.

From this account of their compositions it will be readily inferred that they were not successful in representing or moving the affections. As they were wholly employed on something unexpected and surprising, they had no regard to that uniformity of sentiment which enables us to conceive and to excite the pains and the pleasure of other minds: they never inquired what on any occasion they should have said or done, but wrote rather as beholders than partakers of human nature; as beings looking upon good and evil, impassive and at leisure; as Epicurean deities making remarks on the actions of men and the vicissitudes of life, without interest and without emotion. Their courtship was void of fondness and their lamentation of sorrow. Their wish was only to say what they hoped had been never said before.

Nor was the sublime more within their reach than the pathetic; for they never attempted that comprehension and expanse of thought which at once fills the whole mind, and of which the first effect is sudden astonishment, and the second rational admiration. Sublimity is produced by aggregation, and littleness by dispersion. Great thoughts are always general, and consist in positions not limited by exceptions, and in descriptions not descending to minuteness. It is with great propriety that subtlety, which in its original import means exility[8] of particles, is taken in its metaphorical meaning for nicety of distinction. Those writers who lay on the watch for novelty could have little hope of greatness; for great things cannot have escaped former observation. Their attempts were always analytic: they broke every image into fragments, and could no more represent by their slender conceits and labored particularities the prospects of nature or the scenes of life, than he who

6. Exact, proper.
7. A harmonious discord (Latin). Johnson is himself being witty in using this phrase, a familiar philosophical concept denoting the general harmony of God's creation despite its manifold and often contradictory particulars.
8. Thinness, smallness.

dissects a sunbeam with a prism can exhibit the wide effulgence of a summer noon.

What they wanted however of the sublime they endeavored to supply by hyperbole;[9] their amplification had no limits: they left not only reason but fancy behind them, and produced combinations of confused magnificence that not only could not be credited, but could not be imagined.

Yet great labor directed by great abilities is never wholly lost: if they frequently threw away their wit upon false conceits, they likewise sometimes struck out unexpected truth: if their conceits were farfetched, they were often worth the carriage.[1] To write on their plan it was at least necessary to read and think. No man could be born a metaphysical poet, nor assume the dignity of a writer by descriptions copied from descriptions, by imitations borrowed from imitations, by traditional imagery and hereditary similes, by readiness of rhyme and volubility of syllables.

1779

From Milton[1]

[*LYCIDAS*]

One of the poems on which much praise has been bestowed is *Lycidas;* of which the diction is harsh,[2] the rhymes uncertain, and the numbers unpleasing. What beauty there is, we must therefore seek in the sentiments and images. It is not to be considered as the effusion of real passion; for passion runs not after remote allusions and obscure opinions. Passion plucks no berries from the myrtle and ivy, nor calls upon Arethuse and Mincius, nor tells of "rough satyrs and fauns with cloven heel." Where there is leisure for fiction there is little grief.

In this poem there is no nature, for there is no truth; there is no art, for there is nothing new. Its form is that of a pastoral, easy, vulgar, and therefore disgusting:[3] whatever images it can supply are long ago exhausted; and its inherent improbability always forces dissatisfaction on the mind. When Cowley tells of Hervey that they studied together, it is easy to suppose how much he must miss the companion of his labors and the partner of his discoveries;[4] but what image of tenderness can be excited by these lines!

> We drove afield, and both together heard
> What time the grayfly winds her sultry horn,
> Battening our flocks with the fresh dews of night.

We know that they never drove afield, and that they had no flocks to batten; and though it be allowed that the representation may be allegorical, the true

9. An image heightened beyond reality.
1. In the *Life of Addison,* Johnson wrote: "A simile may be compared to lines converging at a point, and is more excellent as the lines approach from greater distance."
1. Johnson's treatment of Milton as man and poet gave great offense to many ardent Miltonians in his own day and damaged his reputation as a critic in the following century. He did not admire Milton's character, and he detested his politics and religion. But no one has praised *Paradise Lost* more handsomely. Especially offensive in the 19th century was his attack on *Lycidas.* Johnson disliked modern pastorals, recognizing that the tradition had been worn threadbare. His views on the genre may be read in *Rambler* no. 36 and no. 37.
2. This notorious word does not mean "unmelodious," but "strained, forced, affected, or labored."
3. I.e., displeasing, because its stale conventionality made it "vulgar" by putting it within the reach of the many.
4. Cowley's *On the Death of Mr. William Hervey* (1656).

meaning is so uncertain and remote that it is never sought because it cannot be known when it is found.

Among the flocks and copses and flowers appear the heathen deities, Jove and Phoebus, Neptune and Aeolus, with a long train of mythological imagery, such as a college easily supplies. Nothing can less display knowledge or less exercise invention than to tell how a shepherd has lost his companion and must now feed his flocks alone, without any judge of his skill in piping; and how one god asks another god what is become of Lycidas, and how neither god can tell. He who thus grieves will excite no sympathy; he who thus praises will confer no honor.

This poem has yet a grosser fault. With these trifling fictions are mingled the most awful and sacred truths, such as ought never to be polluted with such irreverent combinations. The shepherd likewise is now a feeder of sheep, and afterwards an ecclesiastical pastor, a superintendent of a Christian flock. Such equivocations are always unskillful; but here they are indecent,[5] and at least approach to impiety, of which, however, I believe the writer not to have been conscious.

Such is the power of reputation justly acquired that its blaze drives away the eye from nice examination. Surely no man could have fancied that he read *Lycidas* with pleasure had he not known its author.

[*L'ALLEGRO, IL PENSEROSO*]

Of the two pieces, *L'Allegro* and *Il Penseroso,* I believe opinion is uniform; every man that reads them, reads them with pleasure. The author's design is not, what Theobald[6] has remarked, merely to show how objects derived their colors from the mind, by representing the operation of the same things upon the gay and the melancholy temper, or upon the same man as he is differently disposed; but rather how, among the successive variety of appearances, every disposition of mind takes hold on those by which it may be gratified.

The *cheerful* man hears the lark in the morning; the *pensive* man hears the nightingale in the evening. The *cheerful* man sees the cock strut, and hears the horn and hounds echo in the wood; then walks "not unseen" to observe the glory of the rising sun or listen to the singing milkmaid, and view the labors of the plowman and the mower; then casts his eyes about him over scenes of smiling plenty, and looks up to the distant tower, the residence of some fair inhabitant: thus he pursues rural gaiety through a day of labor or of play, and delights himself at night with the fanciful narratives of superstitious ignorance.

The *pensive* man at one time walks "unseen" to muse at midnight, and at another hears the sullen curfew. If the weather drives him home he sits in a room lighted only by "glowing embers"; or by a lonely lamp outwatches the North Star to discover the habitation of separate souls, and varies the shades of meditation by contemplating the magnificent or pathetic scenes of tragic and epic poetry. When the morning comes, a morning gloomy with rain and wind, he walks into the dark trackless woods, falls asleep by some murmuring

5. Unbecoming, lacking in decorum.
6. Lewis Theobald (1688–1744), the editor of Shakespeare and the enemy of Pope.

water, and with melancholy enthusiasm expects some dream of prognostication or some music played by aerial performers.

Both Mirth and Melancholy are solitary, silent inhabitants of the breast that neither receive nor transmit communication: no mention is therefore made of a philosophical friend or a pleasant companion. The seriousness does not arise from any participation of calamity, nor the gaiety from the pleasures of the bottle.

The man of *cheerfulness* having exhausted the country tries what "towered cities" will afford, and mingles with scenes of splendor, gay assemblies, and nuptial festivities; but he mingles a mere spectator as, when the learned comedies of Jonson or the wild dramas of Shakespeare are exhibited, he attends the theater.

The *pensive* man never loses himself in crowds, but walks the cloister or frequents the cathedral. Milton probably had not yet forsaken the Church.

Both his characters delight in music; but he seems to think that cheerful notes would have obtained from Pluto a complete dismission of Eurydice, of whom solemn sounds only procured a conditional release.

For the old age of Cheerfulness he makes no provision; but Melancholy he conducts with great dignity to the close of life. His Cheerfulness is without levity, and his Pensiveness without asperity.

Through these two poems the images are properly selected and nicely distinguished, but the colors of the diction seem not sufficiently discriminated. I know not whether the characters are kept sufficiently apart. No mirth can, indeed, be found in his melancholy; but I am afraid that I always meet some melancholy in his mirth. They are two noble efforts of imagination.

[*PARADISE LOST*]

Those little pieces may be dispatched without much anxiety; a greater work calls for greater care. I am now to examine *Paradise Lost*, a poem which, considered with respect to design, may claim the first place, and with respect to performance the second, among the productions of the human mind.

By the general consent of critics the first praise of genius is due to the writer of an epic poem, as it requires an assemblage of all the powers which are singly sufficient for other compositions. Poetry is the art of uniting pleasure with truth, by calling imagination to the help of reason. Epic poetry undertakes to teach the most important truths by the most pleasing precepts, and therefore relates some great event in the most affecting manner. History must supply the writer with the rudiments of narration, which he must improve and exalt by a nobler art, must animate by dramatic energy, and diversify by retrospection and anticipation; morality must teach him the exact bounds and different shades of vice and virtue; from policy and the practice of life he has to learn the discriminations of character and the tendency of the passions, either single or combined; and physiology must supply him with illustrations and images. To put these materials to poetical use is required an imagination capable of painting nature and realizing fiction. Nor is he yet a poet till he has attained the whole extension of his language, distinguished all the delicacies of phrase, and all the colors of words, and learned to adjust their different sounds to all the varieties of metrical modulation.

Bossu is of opinion that the poet's first work is to find a *moral,* which his fable is afterwards to illustrate and establish.[7] This seems to have been the process only of Milton: the moral of other poems is incidental and consequent; in Milton's only it is essential and intrinsic. His purpose was the most useful and the most arduous: "to vindicate the ways of God to man";[8] to show the reasonableness of religion, and the necessity of obedience to the Divine Law.

To convey this moral there must be a *fable,* a narration artfully constructed, so as to excite curiosity and surprise expectation. In this part of his work Milton must be confessed to have equaled every other poet. He has involved in his account of the Fall of Man the events which preceded, and those that were to follow it: he has interwoven the whole system of theology with such propriety that every part appears to be necessary, and scarcely any recital is wished shorter for the sake of quickening the progress of the main action.

The subject of an epic poem is naturally an event of great importance. That of Milton is not the destruction of a city, the conduct of a colony, or the foundation of an empire. His subject is the fate of worlds, the revolutions of heaven and of earth; rebellion against the Supreme King raised by the highest order of created beings; the overthrow of their host and the punishment of their crime; the creation of a new race of reasonable creatures; their original happiness and innocence, their forfeiture of immortality, and their restoration to hope and peace.

Great events can be hastened or retarded only by persons of elevated dignity. Before the greatness displayed in Milton's poem all other greatness shrinks away. The weakest of his agents are the highest and noblest of human beings, the original parents of mankind; with whose actions the elements consented; on whose rectitude or deviation of will depended the state of terrestrial nature and the condition of all the future inhabitants of the globe.

Of the other agents in the poem, the chief are such as it is irreverence to name on slight occasions. The rest were lower powers;

> of which the least could wield
> Those elements, and arm him with the force
> Of all their regions;[9]

powers which only the control of Omnipotence restrains from laying creation waste, and filling the vast expanse of space with ruin and confusion. To display the motives and actions of beings thus superior, so far as human reason can examine them or human imagination represent them, is the task which this mighty poet has undertaken and performed.

In the examination of epic poems much speculation is commonly employed upon the *characters.* The characters in the *Paradise Lost* which admit of examination are those of angels and of man; of angels good and evil, of man in his innocent and sinful state.

Among the angels the virtue of Raphael is mild and placid, of easy condescension and free communication; that of Michael is regal and lofty, and,

---

7. Père le Bossu wrote a treatise on the epic poem, *Traité du Poëme Épique,* 1675, much admired during the late 17th and early 18th centuries.
8. Milton wrote "justify," not "vindicate" (*Paradise*

Lost 1.26). It was Pope, in *An Essay on Man* 1.16, who used "vindicate."
9. *Paradise Lost* 6.221.

as may seem, attentive to the dignity of his own nature. Abdiel and Gabriel appear occasionally, and act as every incident requires; the solitary fidelity of Abdiel is very amiably painted.[1]

Of the evil angels the characters are more diversified. To Satan, as Addison observes, such sentiments are given as suit "the most exalted and most depraved being."[2] Milton has been censured by Clarke for the impiety which sometimes breaks from Satan's mouth. For there are thoughts, as he justly remarks, which no observation of character can justify, because no good man would willingly permit them to pass, however transiently, through his own mind.[3] To make Satan speak as a rebel, without any such expressions as might taint the reader's imagination, was indeed one of the great difficulties in Milton's undertaking, and I cannot but think that he has extricated himself with great happiness. There is in Satan's speeches little that can give pain to a pious ear. The language of rebellion cannot be the same with that of obedience. The malignity of Satan foams in haughtiness and obstinacy; but his expressions are commonly general, and no otherwise offensive than as they are wicked.

The other chiefs of the celestial rebellion are very judiciously discriminated in the first and second books; and the ferocious character of Moloch appears, both in the battle and the council, with exact consistency.

To Adam and Eve are given during their innocence such sentiments as innocence can generate and utter. Their love is pure benevolence and mutual veneration; their repasts are without luxury and their diligence without toil. Their addresses to their Maker have little more than the voice of admiration and gratitude. Fruition left them nothing to ask, and Innocence left them nothing to fear.

But with guilt enter distrust and discord, mutual accusation, and stubborn self-defense; they regard each other with alienated minds, and dread their Creator as the avenger of their transgression. At last they seek shelter in his mercy, soften to repentance, and melt in supplication. Both before and after the Fall the superiority of Adam is diligently sustained.

Of the *probable* and the *marvelous*,[4] two parts of a vulgar epic poem which immerge the critic in deep consideration, the *Paradise Lost* requires little to be said. It contains the history of a miracle, of Creation and Redemption; it displays the power and the mercy of the Supreme Being: the probable therefore is marvelous, and the marvelous is probable. The substance of the narrative is truth; and as truth allows no choice, it is, like necessity, superior to rule. To the accidental or adventitious parts, as to every thing human, some slight exceptions may be made. But the main fabric is immovably supported.

It is justly remarked by Addison[5] that this poem has, by the nature of its subject, the advantage above all others, that it is universally and perpetually interesting. All mankind will, through all ages, bear the same relation to Adam and to Eve, and must partake of that good and evil which extend to themselves.

Of the *machinery*, so called from *theòs apò mēkhanēs*,[6] by which is meant the occasional interposition of supernatural power, another fertile topic of

---

1. *Paradise Lost* 5.803ff.
2. *Spectator* 303.
3. John Clarke's *Essay upon Study* (1731).
4. Actions in an epic poem that are wonderful because they exceed the probable.

5. *Spectator* 273.
6. Aristotle's *Poetics* 15.10. *Deus ex machina*, the intervention of supernatural powers into the affairs of humans.

critical remarks, here is no room to speak, because every thing is done under the immediate and visible direction of Heaven; but the rule is so far observed that no part of the action could have been accomplished by any other means.

Of *episodes*[7] I think there are only two, contained in Raphael's relation of the war in heaven and Michael's prophetic account of the changes to happen in this world. Both are closely connected with the great action; one was necessary to Adam as a warning, the other as a consolation.

To the completeness or *integrity* of the design nothing can be objected; it has distinctly and clearly what Aristotle requires, a beginning, a middle, and an end. There is perhaps no poem of the same length from which so little can be taken without apparent mutilation. Here are no funeral games, nor is there any long description of a shield. The short digressions at the beginning of the third, seventh, and ninth books might doubtless be spared; but superfluities so beautiful who would take away? or who does not wish that the author of the *Iliad* had gratified succeeding ages with a little knowledge of himself? Perhaps no passages are more frequently or more attentively read than those extrinsic paragraphs; and since the end of poetry is pleasure, that cannot be unpoetical with which all are pleased.

The questions, whether the action of the poem be strictly *one*,[8] whether the poem can be properly termed *heroic*, and who is the hero, are raised by such readers as draw their principles of judgment rather from books than from reason. Milton, though he entitled *Paradise Lost* only a "poem," yet calls it himself "heroic song."[9] Dryden, petulantly and indecently, denies the heroism of Adam because he was overcome; but there is no reason why the hero should not be unfortunate except established practice, since success and virtue do not go necessarily together. Cato is the hero of Lucan, but Lucan's authority will not be suffered by Quintilian to decide. However, if success be necessary, Adam's deceiver was at last crushed; Adam was restored to his Maker's favor, and therefore may securely resume his human rank.

After the scheme and fabric of the poem must be considered its component parts, the sentiments, and the diction.

The *sentiments*, as expressive of manners or appropriated to characters, are for the greater part unexceptionably just. Splendid passages containing lessons of morality or precepts of prudence occur seldom. Such is the original formation of this poem that as it admits no human manners till the Fall, it can give little assistance to human conduct. Its end is to raise the thoughts above sublunary cares or pleasures. Yet the praise of that fortitude, with which Abdiel maintained his singularity of virtue against the scorn of multitudes, may be accommodated to all times; and Raphael's reproof of Adam's curiosity after the planetary motions, with the answer returned by Adam, may be confidently opposed to any rule of life which any poet has delivered.[1]

The thoughts which are occasionally called forth in the progress are such as could only be produced by an imagination in the highest degree fervid and active, to which materials were supplied by incessant study and unlimited curiosity. The heat of Milton's mind might be said to sublimate his learning,

---

7. Incidental but related narratives within an epic poem. Johnson is citing *Paradise Lost* 5.577ff. and 11.334ff.
8. I.e., a single action dealing with a single char-
acter.
9. *Paradise Lost* 9.25.
1. *Paradise Lost* 8.65ff.

to throw off into his work the spirit of science,[2] unmingled with its grosser parts.

He had considered creation in its whole extent, and his descriptions are therefore learned. He had accustomed his imagination to unrestrained indulgence, and his conceptions therefore were extensive. The characteristic quality of his poem is sublimity. He sometimes descends to the elegant, but his element is the great. He can occasionally invest himself with grace; but his natural port is gigantic loftiness. He can please when pleasure is required; but it is his peculiar power to astonish.

He seems to have been well acquainted with his own genius, and to know what it was that Nature had bestowed upon him more bountifully than upon others; the power of displaying the vast, illuminating the splendid, enforcing the awful, darkening the gloomy, and aggravating the dreadful: he therefore chose a subject on which too much could not be said, on which he might tire his fancy without the censure of extravagance.

*　*　*

The defects and faults of *Paradise Lost,* for faults and defects every work of man must have, it is the business of impartial criticism to discover. As in displaying the excellence of Milton I have not made long quotations, because of selecting beauties there had been no end, I shall in the same general manner mention that which seems to deserve censure; for what Englishman can take delight in transcribing passages, which, if they lessen the reputation of Milton, diminish in some degree the honor of our country?

*　*　*

The plan of *Paradise Lost* has this inconvenience, that it comprises neither human actions nor human manners. The man and woman who act and suffer are in a state which no other man or woman can ever know. The reader finds no transaction in which he can be engaged, beholds no condition in which he can by any effort of imagination place himself; he has, therefore, little natural curiosity or sympathy.

We all, indeed, feel the effects of Adam's disobedience; we all sin like Adam, and like him must all bewail our offenses; we have restless and insidious enemies in the fallen angels, and in the blessed spirits we have guardians and friends; in the Redemption of mankind we hope to be included: in the description of heaven and hell we are surely interested, as we are all to reside hereafter either in the regions of horror or of bliss.

But these truths are too important to be new: they have been taught to our infancy; they have mingled with our solitary thoughts and familiar conversation, and are habitually interwoven with the whole texture of life. Being therefore not new they raise no unaccustomed emotion in the mind: what we knew before, we cannot learn; what is not unexpected, cannot surprise.

Of the ideas suggested by these awful scenes, from some we recede with reverence, except when stated hours require their association; and from others we shrink with horror, or admit them only as salutary inflictions, as counterpoises to our interests and passions. Such images rather obstruct the career of fancy than incite it.

2. Knowledge.

Pleasure and terror are indeed the genuine sources of poetry; but poetical pleasure must be such as human imagination can at least conceive, and poetical terror such as human strength and fortitude may combat. The good and evil of Eternity are too ponderous for the wings of wit; the mind sinks under them in passive helplessness, content with calm belief and humble adoration.

Known truths however may take a different appearance, and be conveyed to the mind by a new train of intermediate images. This Milton has undertaken, and performed with pregnancy and vigor of mind peculiar to himself. Whoever considers the few radical positions which the Scriptures afforded him will wonder by what energetic operation he expanded them to such extent and ramified them to so much variety, restrained as he was by religious reverence from licentiousness of fiction.

Here is a full display of the united force of study and genius; of a great accumulation of materials, with judgment to digest and fancy to combine them: Milton was able to select from nature or from story, from ancient fable or from modern science, whatever could illustrate or adorn his thoughts. An accumulation of knowledge impregnated his mind, fermented by study and exalted by imagination.

* * *

But original deficience cannot be supplied. The want of human interest is always felt. *Paradise Lost* is one of the books which the reader admires and lays down, and forgets to take up again. None ever wished it longer than it is. Its perusal is a duty rather than a pleasure. We read Milton for instruction, retire harassed and overburdened, and look elsewhere for recreation; we desert our master, and seek for companions.

* * *

Dryden remarks that Milton has some flats among his elevations.[3] This is only to say that all the parts are not equal. In every work one part must be for the sake of others; a palace must have passages, a poem must have transitions. It is no more to be required that wit should always be blazing than that the sun should always stand at noon. In a great work there is a vicissitude[4] of luminous and opaque parts, as there is in the world a succession of day and night. Milton, when he has expatiated in the sky, may be allowed sometimes to revisit earth; for what other author ever soared so high or sustained his flight so long?

* * *

The highest praise of genius is original invention. Milton cannot be said to have contrived the structure of an epic poem, and therefore owes reverence to that vigor and amplitude of mind to which all generations must be indebted for the art of poetical narration, for the texture of the fable, the variation of incidents, the interposition of dialogue, and all the stratagems that surprise and enchain attention. But of all the borrowers from Homer Milton is perhaps the least indebted. He was naturally a thinker for himself,

3. Preface to *Sylvae*; see W. P. Ker (ed.), *Essays*   4. Change.
1.268.

confident of his own abilities and disdainful of help or hindrance; he did not refuse admission to the thoughts or images of his predecessors, but he did not seek them. From his contemporaries he neither courted nor received support; there is in his writings nothing by which the pride of other authors might be gratified or favor gained, no exchange of praise or solicitation of support. His great works were performed under discountenance and in blindness, but difficulties vanished at his touch; he was born for whatever is arduous; and his work is not the greatest of heroic poems, only because it is not the first.

1779

From Pope

[POPE'S INTELLECTUAL CHARACTER. POPE AND DRYDEN COMPARED]

Of his intellectual character, the constituent and fundamental principle was good sense, a prompt and intuitive perception of consonance and propriety. He saw immediately, of his own conceptions, what was to be chosen, and what to be rejected; and, in the works of others, what was to be shunned, and what was to be copied.

But good sense alone is a sedate and quiescent quality, which manages its possessions well, but does not increase them; it collects few materials for its own operations, and preserves safety, but never gains supremacy. Pope had likewise genius; a mind active, ambitious, and adventurous, always investigating, always aspiring; in its widest searches still longing to go forward, in its highest flights still wishing to be higher; always imagining something greater than it knows, always endeavoring more than it can do.

To assist these powers, he is said to have had great strength and exactness of memory. That which he had heard or read was not easily lost; and he had before him not only what his own meditation suggested, but what he had found in other writers that might be accommodated to his present purpose.

These benefits of nature he improved by incessant and unwearied diligence; he had recourse to every source of intelligence, and lost no opportunity of information; he consulted the living as well as the dead; he read his compositions to his friends, and was never content with mediocrity when excellence could be attained. He considered poetry as the business of his life, and however he might seem to lament his occupation, he followed it with constancy: to make verses was his first labor, and to mend them was his last.

From his attention to poetry he was never diverted. If conversation offered anything that could be improved, he committed it to paper; if a thought, or perhaps an expression more happy than was common, rose to his mind, he was careful to write it; an independent distich was preserved for an opportunity of insertion, and some little fragments have been found containing lines, or parts of lines, to be wrought upon at some other time.

He was one of those few whose labor is their pleasure; he was never elevated to negligence, nor wearied to impatience; he never passed a fault unamended by indifference, nor quitted it by despair. He labored his works first to gain reputation, and afterwards to keep it.

Of composition there are different methods. Some employ at once memory and invention, and, with little intermediate use of the pen, form and polish large masses by continued meditation, and write their productions only when, in their own opinion, they have completed them. It is related of Virgil[1] that his custom was to pour out a great number of verses in the morning, and pass the day in retrenching exuberances and correcting inaccuracies. The method of Pope, as may be collected from his translation, was to write his first thoughts in his first words, and gradually to amplify, decorate, rectify, and refine them.

With such faculties and such dispositions, he excelled every other writer in *poetical prudence;* he wrote in such a manner as might expose him to few hazards. He used almost always the same fabric of verse; and, indeed, by those few essays which he made of any other, he did not enlarge his reputation. Of this uniformity the certain consequence was readiness and dexterity. By perpetual practice, language had in his mind a systematical arrangement; having always the same use for words, he had words so selected and combined as to be ready at his call. This increase of facility he confessed himself to have perceived in the progress of his translation.

But what was yet of more importance, his effusions were always voluntary, and his subjects chosen by himself. His independence secured him from drudging at a task, and laboring upon a barren topic: he never exchanged praise for money, nor opened a shop of condolence or congratulation. His poems, therefore, were scarce ever temporary. He suffered coronations and royal marriages to pass without a song, and derived no opportunities from recent events, nor any popularity from the accidental disposition of his readers. He was never reduced to the necessity of soliciting the sun to shine upon a birthday, of calling the Graces and Virtues to a wedding, or of saying what multitudes have said before him. When he could produce nothing new, he was at liberty to be silent.

His publications were for the same reason never hasty. He is said to have sent nothing to the press till it had lain two years under his inspection: it is at least certain that he ventured nothing without nice examination. He suffered the tumult of imagination to subside, and the novelties of invention to grow familiar. He knew that the mind is always enamored of its own productions, and did not trust his first fondness. He consulted his friends, and listened with great willingness to criticism; and, what was of more importance, he consulted himself, and let nothing pass against his own judgment.

He professed to have learned his poetry from Dryden, whom, whenever an opportunity was presented, he praised through his whole life with unvaried liberality; and perhaps his character may receive some illustration, if he be compared with his master.

Integrity of understanding and nicety of discernment were not allotted in a less proportion to Dryden than to Pope. The rectitude of Dryden's mind was sufficiently shown by the dismission of his poetical prejudices, and the rejection of unnatural thoughts and rugged numbers. But Dryden never desired to apply all the judgment that he had. He wrote, and professed to write, merely for the people; and when he pleased others, he contented himself. He spent no time in struggles to rouse latent powers; he never attempted

---

1. By Suetonius, in his brief life of the poet.

to make that better which was already good, nor often to mend what he must have known to be faulty. He wrote, as he tells us, with very little consideration; when occasion or necessity called upon him, he poured out what the present moment happened to supply, and, when once it had passed the press, ejected it from his mind; for when he had no pecuniary interest, he had no further solicitude.

Pope was not content to satisfy; he desired to excel, and therefore always endeavored to do his best: he did not court the candor,[2] but dared the judgment of his reader, and, expecting no indulgence from others, he showed none to himself. He examined lines and words with minute and punctilious observation, and retouched every part with indefatigable diligence, till he had left nothing to be forgiven.

For this reason he kept his pieces very long in his hands, while he considered and reconsidered them. The only poems which can be supposed to have been written with such regard to the times as might hasten their publication were the two satires of *Thirty-Eight*; of which Dodsley[3] told me that they were brought to him by the author, that they might be fairly copied. "Almost every line," he said, "was then written twice over; I gave him a clean transcript, which he sent some time afterwards to me for the press, with almost every line written twice over a second time."

His declaration, that his care for his works ceased at their publication, was not strictly true. His parental attention never abandoned them; what he found amiss in the first edition, he silently corrected in those that followed. He appears to have revised the *Iliad,* and freed it from some of its imperfections; and the *Essay on Criticism* received many improvements after its first appearance. It will seldom be found that he altered without adding clearness, elegance, or vigor. Pope had perhaps the judgment of Dryden; but Dryden certainly wanted the diligence of Pope.

In acquired knowledge, the superiority must be allowed to Dryden, whose education was more scholastic, and who before he became an author had been allowed more time for study, with better means of information. His mind has a larger range, and he collects his images and illustrations from a more extensive circumference of science. Dryden knew more of man in his general nature, and Pope in his local manners. The notions of Dryden were formed by comprehensive speculation, and those of Pope by minute attention. There is more dignity in the knowledge of Dryden, and more certainty in that of Pope.

Poetry was not the sole praise of either; for both excelled likewise in prose; but Pope did not borrow his prose from his predecessor. The style of Dryden is capricious and varied, that of Pope is cautious and uniform; Dryden obeys the motions of his own mind, Pope constrains his mind to his own rules of composition; Dryden is sometimes vehement and rapid; Pope is always smooth, uniform, and gentle. Dryden's page is a natural field, rising into inequalities, and diversified by the varied exuberance of abundant vegetation; Pope's is a velvet lawn, shaven by the scythe, and leveled by the roller.

Of genius, that power which constitutes a poet; that quality without which judgment is cold and knowledge is inert; that energy which collects, combines, amplifies, and animates; the superiority must, with some hesitation,

---

2. Kindness, sweetness of temper.   3. Robert Dodsley, the publisher.

be allowed to Dryden. It is not to be inferred that of this poetical vigor Pope had only a little, because Dryden had more; for every other writer since Milton must give place to Pope; and even of Dryden it must be said that if he has brighter paragraphs, he has not better poems. Dryden's performances were always hasty, either excited by some external occasion, or extorted by domestic necessity; he composed without consideration, and published without correction. What his mind could supply at call, or gather in one excursion, was all that he sought, and all that he gave. The dilatory caution of Pope enabled him to condense his sentiments, to multiply his images, and to accumulate all that study might produce, or chance might supply. If the flights of Dryden therefore are higher, Pope continues longer on the wing. If of Dryden's fire the blaze is brighter, of Pope's the heat is more regular and constant. Dryden often surpasses expectation, and Pope never falls below it. Dryden is read with frequent astonishment, and Pope with perpetual delight.

This parallel will, I hope, when it is well considered, be found just; and if the reader should suspect me, as I suspect myself, of some partial fondness for the memory of Dryden, let him not too hastily condemn me; for meditation and inquiry may, perhaps, show him the reasonableness of my determination.

1781

JAMES BOSWELL
1740–1795

The discovery of a vast number of James Boswell's personal papers (believed until 1925 to have been destroyed by his literary executors) has made it possible to know the author of *The Life of Samuel Johnson* better, perhaps, than we can know any other person, dead or living. His published letters and journals have made modern readers aware of the serious and absurd, the charming and repellent sides of his character. At twenty-three, when he met Johnson, he had already trained himself to listen, to observe, and to remember until he found time to set it all down in writing. Only very rarely, it seems, did he ever take notes of conversations while they were in progress, which might have inhibited the speakers. His unusual memory and disciplined art enabled him to re-create and vividly preserve the many "scenes" that distinguish his journals as they do the *Life*.

Boswell was the elder son of Alexander Boswell of Auchinleck (pronounced *Affléck*) in Ayrshire, a judge who bore the courtesy title of Lord Auchinleck. As a member of an ancient family and heir to its large estate, Boswell was in the technical sense of the term a gentleman, with entrée into the best circles of Edinburgh and London. By temperament he was unstable, emotionally and sexually skittish. After attending the universities of Edinburgh and Glasgow and studying law in Holland, he made the grand tour of Europe; in Switzerland he met and succeeded in captivating the two foremost French men of letters, Jean-Jacques Rousseau and Voltaire. He visited the beleaguered hero of Corsica, General Pasquale de Paoli, whose revolt against Genoa seemed to European liberals to embody all the civic and military virtues of Republican Rome. Upon returning to England, Boswell wrote *An Account of Cor-*

sica (1768). It was promptly translated into Dutch, German, French, and Italian, and its young author found himself with a modest European reputation.

By 1769, Boswell was established in what was to prove a successful law practice in Edinburgh and had married his cousin, Margaret Montgomerie. But he kept his ties to London and Johnson. In 1773 he persuaded Johnson to join him in a tour of the Highlands and the Hebrides. Almost every aspect of the adventure should have made it impossible. Johnson, far from young and after years of sedentary city living, found himself astride a horse in wild country or in open boats in autumn weather. As a devout Anglican, he was an outspoken enemy of the Presbyterian church. As a lover of London, he was a stranger to the primitive life of the Highlands. Moreover, for many years he had half-jestingly, half-seriously, made Scots the butt of his wit. But such were Boswell's social tact and Johnson's vigor and curiosity that the tour was a great success. Johnson's *Journey to the Western Isles of Scotland* (1775) is a thoughtful account of the way that people live in the Hebrides (though some Scots were offended). Boswell's *Journal of a Tour to the Hebrides* (1785), a preliminary study for the *Life,* is a lively and entertaining diary, approved, at least in part, by Johnson himself.

In 1788, four years after Johnson's death, Boswell abandoned his Scottish practice, moved to London, was admitted to the English bar (but never actually practiced), and often depressed and drunken, began the *Life.* Fortunately he had the help and encouragement of the distinguished literary scholar Edmond Malone, without whose guidance he might never have finished his task.

Boswell had an overwhelming amount of material to deal with: his own journals, all of Johnson's letters that he could find, Johnson's voluminous writings, and every scrap of information that his friends would furnish—all of which had to be collected, verified, and somehow reduced to unity. The *Life* is a record not of Johnson alone but of literary England during the last half of the century. But Boswell wrote with his eye on the object, and that object was Samuel Johnson, toward whom such eminent persons as Sir Joshua Reynolds, Edmund Burke, Oliver Goldsmith, Lord Chesterfield—even the king himself—always face. Individual episodes are designed to reveal the great protagonist in a variety of aspects, and the world that Boswell created and populated is sustained by the vitality of his hero.

Boswell's gift is not only narrative but also dramatic. A gifted mimic, he often writes like a theatrical improviser, creating scenes with living people and playing simultaneously the roles of contriver of the dialogue, director of the plot, actor in the drama, and applauding audience—for Boswell kept an eye on his own performance. The quintessence of Boswell as both a social genius and a literary artist is to be found in his description of his visit to Voltaire: "I placed myself by him. I touched the keys in unison with his imagination. I wish you had heard the music."

Although the Johnson of popular legend is largely Boswell's creation, there was much in his life about which Boswell had no firsthand knowledge. At their first meeting, Johnson was fifty-four, a widower, already established as "Dictionary" Johnson and the author of the *Rambler,* and pensioned by the crown. Boswell knew nothing at firsthand of the long, hard years during which Johnson made his way painfully up from obscurity to fame. Hence the *Life* is the portrait of a sage. Its chief glory is conversation: the talk of a man who has experienced broadly, read widely, and observed and reflected on his observations; whose ideas are constantly brought to the test of experience; and whose experience is habitually transmuted into ideas. The book is as large as life and as human as its central character.

From Boswell on the Grand Tour

[BOSWELL INTERVIEWS VOLTAIRE][1]

And whence do I now write to you, my friend?[2] From the château of Monsieur de Voltaire. I had a letter for him from a Swiss colonel at The Hague. I came hither Monday and was presented to him. He received me with dignity and that air of a man who has been much in the world which a Frenchman acquires in perfection. I saw him for about half an hour before dinner. He was not in spirits. Yet he gave me some brilliant sallies. He did not dine with us, and I was obliged to post away immediately after dinner, because the gates of Geneva shut before five and Ferney is a good hour from town. I was by no means satisfied to have been so little time with the monarch of French literature. A happy scheme sprung up in my adventurous mind. Madame Denis, the niece of Monsieur de Voltaire, had been extremely good to me. She is fond of our language. I wrote her a letter in English begging her interest to obtain for me the privilege of lodging a night under the roof of Monsieur de Voltaire, who, in opposition to our sun, rises in the evening. I was in the finest humor and my letter was full of wit. I told her, "I am a hardy and a vigorous Scot. You may mount me to the highest and coldest garret. I shall not even refuse to sleep upon two chairs in the bedchamber of your maid. I saw her pass through the room where we sat before dinner." I sent my letter on Tuesday by an express. It was shown to Monsieur de Voltaire, who with his own hand wrote this answer in the character of Madame Denis: "You will do us much honor and pleasure. We have few beds. But you will (*shall*) not sleep on two chairs. My uncle, though very sick, hath guessed at your merit. I know it better; for I have seen you longer." * * *

I returned yesterday to this enchanted castle. The magician appeared a very little before dinner. But in the evening he came into the drawing room in great spirits. I placed myself by him. I touched the keys in unison with his imagination. I wish you had heard the music. He was all brilliance. He gave me continued flashes of wit. I got him to speak English, which he does in a degree that made me now and then start up and cry, "Upon my soul this is astonishing!" When he talked our language he was animated with the soul of a Briton. He had bold flights. He had humor. He had an extravagance; he had a forcible oddity of style that the most comical of our *dramatis personae* could not have exceeded. He swore bloodily, as was the fashion when he was in England.[3] He hummed a ballad; he repeated nonsense. Then he talked of our Constitution with a noble enthusiasm. I was proud to hear this from the mouth of an illustrious Frenchman. At last we came upon religion. Then did

1. Voltaire was the name assumed by François-Marie Arouet (1694–1778), the most famous French writer of his generation. Playwright, poet, satirist, philosopher, enemy of the church, and irrepressible ironist, he (after a stormy career) was living in splendor at his château at Ferney near the border of Switzerland and France, just outside Geneva. His housekeeper and mistress was his niece Marie-Louise Denis. He and Jean-Jacques Rousseau, whom Boswell had just visited and flattered, were deadly enemies.
2. This passage is taken from a letter, dated

December 28, 1764, written to Boswell's closest friend, a young clergyman named William Temple.
3. In 1726, to avoid imprisonment because of a quarrel with a nobleman, Voltaire had gone into exile in England, where he remained for three years, meeting many distinguished English writers and statesmen and learning to admire the British Constitution and the English principle of religious toleration. His *Lettres philosophiques sur les Anglais* (1734) expressed his admiration of English institutions and indirectly criticized France.

he rage. The company went to supper. Monsieur de Voltaire and I remained in the drawing room with a great Bible before us; and if ever two mortal men disputed with vehemence, we did. Yes, upon that occasion he was one individual and I another. For a certain portion of time there was a fair opposition between Voltaire and Boswell. The daring bursts of his ridicule confounded my understanding. He stood like an orator of ancient Rome. Tully[4] was never more agitated than he was. He went too far. His aged frame trembled beneath him. He cried, "Oh, I am very sick; my head turns round," and he let himself gently fall upon an easy chair. He recovered. I resumed our conversation, but changed the tone. I talked to him serious and earnest. I demanded of him an honest confession of his real sentiments. He gave it me with candor and with a mild eloquence which touched my heart. I did not believe him capable of thinking in the manner that he declared to me was "from the bottom of his heart." He expressed his veneration—his love—of the Supreme Being, and his entire resignation to the will of Him who is all-wise. He expressed his desire to resemble the Author of Goodness by being good himself. His sentiments go no farther. He does not inflame his mind with grand hopes of the immortality of the soul. He says it may be, but he knows nothing of it. And his mind is in perfect tranquility. I was moved; I was sorry. I doubted his sincerity. I called to him with emotion, "Are you sincere? are you really sincere?" He answered "Before God, I am." Then with the fire of him whose tragedies have so often shone on the theater of Paris, he said, "I suffer much. But I suffer with patience and resignation; not as a Christian—but as a man."

Temple, was not this an interesting scene? Would a journey from Scotland to Ferney have been too much to obtain such a remarkable interview? * * *

1764   1928

From The Life of Samuel Johnson, LL.D.

[PLAN OF THE *LIFE*]

* * * Had Dr. Johnson written his own life, in conformity with the opinion which he has given, that every man's life may be best written by himself;[1] had he employed in the preservation of his own history, that clearness of narration and elegance of language in which he has embalmed so many eminent persons, the world would probably have had the most perfect example of biography that was ever exhibited. But although he at different times, in a desultory manner, committed to writing many particulars of the progress of his mind and fortunes, he never had persevering diligence enough to form them into a regular composition. Of these memorials a few have been preserved; but the greater part was consigned by him to the flames, a few days before his death.

As I had the honor and happiness of enjoying his friendship for upwards of twenty years; as I had the scheme of writing his life constantly in view; as he was well apprised of this circumstance, and from time to time obligingly satisfied my inquiries, by communicating to me the incidents of his early years; as I acquired a facility in recollecting, and was very assiduous in recording, his conversation, of which the extraordinary vigor and vivacity constituted one of the first features of his character; and as I have spared no pains in obtaining materials concerning him, from every quarter where I could discover that they were to be found, and have been favored with the most liberal communications by his friends; I flatter myself that few biographers have entered upon such a work as this with more advantages; independent of literary abilities, in which I am not vain enough to compare myself with some great names who have gone before me in this kind of writing. * * *

Instead of melting down my materials into one mass, and constantly speaking in my own person, by which I might have appeared to have more merit in the execution of the work, I have resolved to adopt and enlarge upon the excellent plan of Mr. Mason, in his *Memoirs of Gray*.[2] Wherever narrative is necessary to explain, connect, and supply, I furnish it to the best of my abilities; but in the chronological series of Johnson's life, which I trace as distinctly as I can, year by year, I produce, wherever it is in my power, his own minutes, letters, or conversation, being convinced that this mode is more lively, and will make my readers better acquainted with him than even most of those were who actually knew him, but could know him only partially; whereas there is here an accumulation of intelligence from various points, by which his character is more fully understood and illustrated.

Indeed I cannot conceive a more perfect mode of writing any man's life than not only relating all the most important events of it in their order, but interweaving what he privately wrote, and said, and thought; by which mankind are enabled as it were to see him live, and to "live o'er each scene"[3] with him, as he actually advanced through the several stages of his life. Had his other friends been as diligent and ardent as I was, he might have been almost entirely preserved. As it is, I will venture to say that he will be seen in this work more completely than any man who has ever yet lived.

And he will be seen as he really was; for I profess to write, not his panegyric, which must be all praise, but his Life; which, great and good as he was, must not be supposed to be entirely perfect. To be as he was, is indeed subject of panegyric enough to any man in this state of being; but in every picture there should be shade as well as light, and when I delineate him without reserve, I do what he himself recommended, both by his precept and his example. * * *

I am fully aware of the objections which may be made to the minuteness on some occasions of my detail of Johnson's conversation, and how happily it is adapted for the petty exercise of ridicule, by men of superficial understanding and ludicrous fancy; but I remain firm and confident in my opinion, that minute particulars are frequently characteristic, and always amusing, when they relate to a distinguished man. I am therefore exceedingly unwilling that anything, however slight, which my illustrious friend thought it worth his while to express, with any degree of point, should perish. * * *

Of one thing I am certain, that considering how highly the small portion which we have of the table-talk and other anecdotes of our celebrated writers is valued, and how earnestly it is regretted that we have not more, I am

---

2. William Mason, poet and dramatist, published his life of Thomas Gray in 1774.

3. Pope's *Prologue* to Addison's *Cato*, line 4.

justified in preserving rather too many of Johnson's sayings, than too few; especially as from the diversity of dispositions it cannot be known with certainty beforehand, whether what may seem trifling to some, and perhaps to the collector himself, may not be most agreeable to many; and the greater number that an author can please in any degree, the more pleasure does there arise to a benevolent mind. * * *

[JOHNSON'S EARLY YEARS. MARRIAGE AND LONDON]

[1709] Samuel Johnson was born at Lichfield, in Staffordshire, on the 18th of September, N.S.,[4] 1709; and his initiation into the Christian Church was not delayed; for his baptism is recorded, in the register of St. Mary's parish in that city, to have been performed on the day of his birth. His father is there styled *Gentleman*, a circumstance of which an ignorant panegyrist has praised him for not being proud; when the truth is, that the appellation of Gentleman, though now lost in the indiscriminate assumption of *Esquire*, was commonly taken by those who could not boast of gentility. His father was Michael Johnson, a native of Derbyshire, of obscure extraction, who settled in Lichfield as a bookseller and stationer. His mother was Sarah Ford, descended of an ancient race of substantial yeomanry in Warwickshire. They were well advanced in years when they married, and never had more than two children, both sons; Samuel, their first-born, who lived to be the illustrious character whose various excellence I am to endeavor to record, and Nathanael, who died in his twenty-fifth year.

Mr. Michael Johnson was a man of a large and robust body, and of a strong and active mind; yet, as in the most solid rocks veins of unsound substance are often discovered, there was in him a mixture of that disease, the nature of which eludes the most minute inquiry, though the effects are well known to be a weariness of life, an unconcern about those things which agitate the greater part of mankind, and a general sensation of gloomy wretchedness. From him then his son inherited, with some other qualities, "a vile melancholy," which in his too strong expression of any disturbance of the mind, "made him mad all his life, at least not sober." Michael was, however, forced by the narrowness of his circumstances to be very diligent in business, not only in his shop, but by occasionally resorting to several towns in the neighborhood, some of which were at a considerable distance from Lichfield. At that time booksellers' shops in the provincial towns of England were very rare, so that there was not one even in Birmingham, in which town old Mr. Johnson used to open a shop every market day. He was a pretty good Latin scholar, and a citizen so creditable as to be made one of the magistrates of Lichfield; and, being a man of good sense, and skill in his trade, he acquired a reasonable share of wealth, of which however he afterwards lost the greatest part, by engaging unsuccessfully in a manufacture of parchment. He was a zealous highchurch man and royalist, and retained his attachment to the unfortunate house of Stuart, though he reconciled himself, by casu-

---

4. New Style. In 1752, Great Britain adopted the Gregorian calendar, introduced in 1582 by Pope Gregory XIII, to correct the accumulated inaccuracies of Julius Caesar's calendar, which had been in use since 46 B.C.E. By 1752, the error amounted to eleven days. Dates before September 2, 1752, must, therefore, be corrected by adding eleven days or by using the Julian date, followed by "O.S." (Old Style).

istical arguments of expediency and necessity, to take the oaths imposed by the prevailing power. * * *

Johnson's mother was a woman of distinguished understanding. I asked his old schoolfellow, Mr. Hector,[5] surgeon of Birmingham, if she was not vain of her son. He said, "She had too much good sense to be vain, but she knew her son's value." Her piety was not inferior to her understanding; and to her must be ascribed those early impressions of religion upon the mind of her son, from which the world afterwards derived so much benefit. He told me that he remembered distinctly having had the first notice of Heaven, "a place to which good people went," and hell, "a place to which bad people went," communicated to him by her, when a little child in bed with her; and that it might be the better fixed in his memory, she sent him to repeat it to Thomas Jackson, their manservant; he not being in the way, this was not done; but there was no occasion for any artificial aid for its preservation. * * *

[1728] That a man in Mr. Michael Johnson's circumstances should think of sending his son to the expensive University of Oxford, at his own charge, seems very improbable. The subject was too delicate to question Johnson upon. But I have been assured by Dr. Taylor[6] that the scheme never would have taken place had not a gentleman of Shropshire, one of his schoolfellows, spontaneously undertaken to support him at Oxford, in the character of his companion; though, in fact, he never received any assistance whatever from that gentleman.

He, however, went to Oxford, and was entered a Commoner of Pembroke College on the 31st of October, 1728, being then in his nineteenth year.

The Reverend Dr. Adams,[7] who afterwards presided over Pembroke College with universal esteem, told me he was present, and gave me some account of what passed on the night of Johnson's arrival at Oxford. On that evening, his father, who had anxiously accompanied him, found means to have him introduced to Mr. Jorden, who was to be his tutor. * * *

His father seemed very full of the merits of his son, and told the company he was a good scholar, and a poet, and wrote Latin verses. His figure and manner appeared strange to them; but he behaved modestly and sat silent, till upon something which occurred in the course of conversation, he suddenly struck in and quoted Macrobius; and thus he gave the first impression of that more extensive reading in which he had indulged himself.

His tutor, Mr. Jorden, fellow of Pembroke, was not, it seems, a man of such abilities as we should conceive requisite for the instructor of Samuel Johnson, who gave me the following account of him. "He was a very worthy man, but a heavy man, and I did not profit much by his instructions. Indeed, I did not attend him much. The first day after I came to college I waited upon him, and then stayed away four. On the sixth, Mr. Jorden asked me why I had not attended. I answered I had been sliding in Christ Church meadow. And this I said with as much *nonchalance* as I am now talking to you. I had no notion that I was wrong or irreverent to my tutor." BOSWELL: "That, Sir, was great fortitude of mind." JOHNSON: "No, Sir; stark insensibility." * * *

5. Edmund Hector, a lifelong friend of Johnson.
6. A well-to-do clergyman, who had been John-son's schoolfellow in Lichfield.

7. The Reverend William Adams, D. D., elected master of Pembroke in 1775.

[1729] The "morbid melancholy," which was lurking in his constitution, and to which we may ascribe those particularities and that aversion to regular life, which, at a very early period, marked his character, gathered such strength in his twentieth year as to afflict him in a dreadful manner. While he was at Lichfield, in the college vacation of the year 1729, he felt himself overwhelmed with an horrible hypochondria, with perpetual irritation, fretfulness, and impatience; and with a dejection, gloom, and despair, which made existence misery. From this dismal malady he never afterwards was perfectly relieved; and all his labors, and all his enjoyments, were but temporary interruptions of its baleful influence. He told Mr. Paradise[8] that he was sometimes so languid and inefficient that he could not distinguish the hour upon the town-clock. * * *

To Johnson, whose supreme enjoyment was the exercise of his reason, the disturbance or obscuration of that faculty was the evil most to be dreaded. Insanity, therefore, was the object of his most dismal apprehension; and he fancied himself seized by it, or approaching to it, at the very time when he was giving proofs of a more than ordinary soundness and vigor of judgment. That his own diseased imagination should have so far deceived him, is strange; but it is stranger still that some of his friends should have given credit to his groundless opinion, when they had such undoubted proofs that it was totally fallacious; though it is by no means surprising that those who wish to depreciate him should, since his death, have laid hold of this circumstance, and insisted upon it with very unfair aggravation. * * *

Dr. Adams told me that Johnson, while he was at Pembroke College, "was caressed and loved by all about him, was a gay and frolicsome fellow, and passed there the happiest part of his life." But this is a striking proof of the fallacy of appearances, and how little any of us know of the real internal state even of those whom we see most frequently; for the truth is, that he was then depressed by poverty, and irritated by disease. When I mentioned to him this account as given me by Dr. Adams, he said, "Ah, Sir, I was mad and violent. It was bitterness which they mistook for frolic. I was miserably poor, and I thought to fight my way by my literature and my wit; so I disregarded all power and all authority." * * *

[1734] In a man whom religious education has secured from licentious indulgences, the passion of love, when once it has seized him, is exceedingly strong; being unimpaired by dissipation, and totally concentrated in one object. This was experienced by Johnson, when he became the fervent admirer of Mrs. Porter, after her first husband's death. Miss Porter told me that when he was first introduced to her mother, his appearance was very forbidding: he was then lean and lank, so that his immense structure of bones was hideously striking to the eye, and the scars of the scrofula were deeply visible. He also wore his hair,[9] which was straight and stiff, and separated behind: and he often had, seemingly, convulsive starts and odd gesticulations, which tended to excite at once surprise and ridicule. Mrs. Porter was so much engaged by his conversation that she overlooked all these external disadvantages, and said to her daughter, "This is the most sensible man that I ever saw in my life."

8. John Paradise, a member of the Essex Head Club, which Johnson founded in 1783.

9. I.e., he wore no wig.

[*1735*] Though Mrs. Porter was double the age of Johnson, and her person and manner, as described to me by the late Mr. Garrick,[1] were by no means pleasing to others, she must have had a superiority of understanding and talents, as she certainly inspired him with a more than ordinary passion; and she having signified her willingness to accept of his hand, he went to Lichfield to ask his mother's consent to the marriage, which he could not but be conscious was a very imprudent scheme, both on account of their disparity of years and her want of fortune. But Mrs. Johnson knew too well the ardor of her son's temper, and was too tender a parent to oppose his inclinations.

I know not for what reason the marriage ceremony was not performed at Birmingham; but a resolution was taken that it should be at Derby, for which place the bride and bridegroom set out on horseback, I suppose in very good humor. But though Mr. Topham Beauclerk[2] used archly to mention Johnson's having told him, with much gravity, "Sir, it was a love marriage on both sides," I have had from my illustrious friend the following curious account of their journey to church upon the nuptial morn:

9th July: "Sir, she had read the old romances, and had got into her head the fantastical notion that a woman of spirit should use her lover like a dog. So, Sir, at first she told me that I rode too fast, and she could not keep up with me; and, when I rode a little slower, she passed me, and complained that I lagged behind. I was not to be made the slave of caprice; and I resolved to begin as I meant to end. I therefore pushed on briskly, till I was fairly out of her sight. The road lay between two hedges, so I was sure she could not miss it; and I contrived that she should soon come up with me. When she did, I observed her to be in tears." * * *

[*1737*] Johnson now thought of trying his fortune in London, the great field of genius and exertion, where talents of every kind have the fullest scope and the highest encouragement. It is a memorable circumstance that his pupil David Garrick went thither at the same time, with intention to complete his education, and follow the profession of the law, from which he was soon diverted by his decided preference for the stage.[3] * * *

[*1744*] * * * He produced one work this year, fully sufficient to maintain the high reputation which he had acquired. This was *The Life of Richard Savage*;[4] a man of whom it is difficult to speak impartially without wondering that he was for some time the intimate companion of Johnson; for his character was marked by profligacy, insolence, and ingratitude: yet, as he undoubtedly had a warm and vigorous, though unregulated mind, had seen life in all its varieties, and been much in the company of the statesmen and wits of his time, he could communicate to Johnson an abundant supply of

1. David Garrick (1717–1779), the most famous actor of his day. In 1736 he was one of Johnson's three pupils in an unsuccessful school at Edial.
2. Pronounced *bo-clare*. A descendant of Charles II and the actress Nell Gwynn, he was brilliant and dissolute.
3. Johnson had hoped to complete his tragedy *Irene* and to get it produced, but this was not accomplished until Garrick staged it in 1749. Meanwhile Johnson struggled against poverty, at first as a writer and translator for Edward Cave's *Gentleman's Magazine*. He gradually won recognition but was never financially secure until he was pensioned in 1762. Garrick succeeded in the the-

ater much more rapidly than did Johnson in literature.
4. Richard Savage, poet, courted and gained notoriety by claiming to be the illegitimate son of Earl Rivers and the countess of Macclesfield, whose husband had divorced her because of her unfaithfulness with Rivers. Savage publicized his claim and persecuted his alleged mother. Johnson and many others believed Savage's story and resented what they considered the lady's inhumanity. Savage was a gifted man, but he lived in poverty as a hack writer, although he was long assisted by Pope and others. He died in a debtor's prison in Bristol in 1743.

such materials as his philosophical curiosity most eagerly desired; and as Savage's misfortunes and misconduct had reduced him to the lowest state of wretchedness as a writer for bread, his visits to St. John's Gate[5] naturally brought Johnson and him together.

It is melancholy to reflect that Johnson and Savage were sometimes in such extreme indigence that they could not pay for a lodging; so that they have wandered together whole nights in the streets. Yet in these almost incredible scenes of distress, we may suppose that Savage mentioned many of the anecdotes with which Johnson afterwards enriched the life of his unhappy companion, and those of other poets.

He told Sir Joshua Reynolds that one night in particular, when Savage and he walked round St. James's Square for want of a lodging, they were not at all depressed by their situation; but in high spirits and brimful of patriotism, traversed the square for several hours, inveighed against the minister, and "resolved they would *stand by their country.*" * * *

[1752] That there should be a suspension of his literary labors during a part of the year 1752[6] will not seem strange when it is considered that soon after closing his *Rambler,* he suffered a loss which, there can be no doubt, affected him with the deepest distress. For on the 17th of March, O.S., his wife died. * * *

The following very solemn and affecting prayer was found, after Dr. Johnson's decease, by his servant, Mr. Francis Barber, who delivered it to my worthy friend the Reverend Mr. Strahan, Vicar of Islington, who at my earnest request has obligingly favored me with a copy of it, which he and I compared with the original:

"April 26, 1752, being after 12 at night of the 25th.

"O Lord! Governor of heaven and earth, in whose hands are embodied and departed spirits, if thou hast ordained the souls of the dead to minister to the living, and appointed my departed wife to have care of me, grant that I may enjoy the good effects of her attention and ministration, whether exercised by appearance, impulses, dreams or in any other manner agreeable to thy government. Forgive my presumption, enlighten my ignorance, and however meaner agents are employed, grant me the blessed influences of thy holy Spirit, through Jesus Christ our Lord. Amen." * * *

One night when Beauclerk and Langton[7] had supped at a tavern in London, and sat till about three in the morning, it came into their heads to go and knock up Johnson, and see if they could prevail on him to join them in a ramble. They rapped violently at the door of his chambers in the Temple,[8] till at last he appeared in his shirt, with his little black wig on the top of his head, instead of a nightcap, and a poker in his hand, imagining, probably, that some ruffians were coming to attack him. When he discovered who they

---

5. Where Cave published the *Gentleman's Magazine.*
6. Johnson's important works written before the publication of the *Dictionary* are the poems *London* (1738) and *The Vanity of Human Wishes* (1749), the *Life of Savage* (1744), and the essays that made up his periodical *The Rambler* (1750–52).

7. Bennet Langton. As a boy he so much admired the *Rambler* that he sought Johnson's acquaintance. They became lifelong friends.
8. Because Johnson lived in Inner Temple Lane between 1760 and 1765, the "frisk" could not have taken place in the year of his wife's death, where Boswell, for his own convenience, placed it.

were, and was told their errand, he smiled, and with great good humor agreed to their proposal: "What, is it you, you dogs! I'll have a frisk with you." He was soon dressed, and they sallied forth together into Covent Garden, where the greengrocers and fruiterers were beginning to arrange their hampers, just come in from the country. Johnson made some attempts to help them; but the honest gardeners stared so at his figure and manner and odd interference, that he soon saw his services were not relished. They then repaired to one of the neighboring taverns, and made a bowl of that liquor called *Bishop*,[9] which Johnson had always liked; while in joyous contempt of sleep, from which he had been roused, he repeated the festive lines,

> Short, O short then be thy reign,
> And give us to the world again![1]

They did not stay long, but walked down to the Thames, took a boat, and rowed to Billingsgate. Beauclerk and Johnson were so well pleased with their amusement that they resolved to persevere in dissipation for the rest of the day: but Langton deserted them, being engaged to breakfast with some young ladies. Johnson scolded him for "leaving his social friends, to go and sit with a set of wretched *un-idea'd* girls." Garrick being told of this ramble, said to him smartly, "I heard of your frolic t' other night. You'll be in the *Chronicle*." Upon which Johnson afterwards observed, "*He* durst not do such a thing. His *wife* would not *let* him!" * * *

[THE LETTER TO CHESTERFIELD]

[1754] Lord Chesterfield,[2] to whom Johnson had paid the high compliment of addressing to his Lordship the *Plan* of his *Dictionary*, had behaved to him in such a manner as to excite his contempt and indignation. The world has been for many years amused with a story confidently told, and as confidently repeated with additional circumstances, that a sudden disgust was taken by Johnson upon occasion of his having been one day kept long in waiting in his Lordship's antechamber, for which the reason assigned was that he had company with him; and that at last, when the door opened, out walked Colley Cibber;[3] and that Johnson was so violently provoked when he found for whom he had been so long excluded, that he went away in a passion, and never would return. I remember having mentioned this story to George Lord Lyttelton, who told me he was very intimate with Lord Chesterfield; and holding it as a well-known truth, defended Lord Chesterfield, by saying, that Cibber, who had been introduced familiarly by the back stairs, had probably not been there above ten minutes. It may seem strange even to entertain a doubt concerning a story so long and so widely current, and thus implicitly adopted, if not sanctioned, by the authority which I have mentioned; but Johnson himself assured me that there was not the least

9. A drink made of wine, sugar, and either lemon or orange.
1. Misquoted from Lansdowne's *Drinking Song to Sleep*.
2. Philip Dormer Stanhope, earl of Chesterfield (1694–1773), statesman, wit, man of fashion. His *Letters*, written for the guidance of his natural son, are famous for their worldly good sense and for their expression of the ideal of an 18th-century gentleman.
3. Colley Cibber (1671–1757), playwright, comic actor, and (after 1730) poet laureate. A fine actor but a very bad poet, Cibber was a constant object of ridicule by the wits of the town. Pope made him king of the Dunces in the *Dunciad* of 1743.

foundation for it. He told me that there never was any particular incident which produced a quarrel between Lord Chesterfield and him; but that his Lordship's continued neglect was the reason why he resolved to have no connection with him. When the *Dictionary* was upon the eve of publication, Lord Chesterfield, who, it is said, had flattered himself with expectations that Johnson would dedicate the work to him, attempted, in a courtly manner, to soothe, and insinuate himself with the sage, conscious, as it should seem, of the cold indifference with which he had treated its learned author; and further attempted to conciliate him, by writing two papers in *The World,* in recommendation of the work; and it must be confessed that they contain some studied compliments, so finely turned, that if there had been no previous offense, it is probable that Johnson would have been highly delighted. Praise, in general, was pleasing to him; but by praise from a man of rank and elegant accomplishments, he was peculiarly gratified. * * *

This courtly device failed of its effect. Johnson, who thought that "all was false and hollow,"[4] despised the honeyed words, and was even indignant that Lord Chesterfield should, for a moment, imagine that he could be dupe of such an artifice. His expression to me concerning Lord Chesterfield, upon this occasion, was, "Sir, after making great professions, he had, for many years, taken no notice of me; but when my *Dictionary* was coming out, he fell a-scribbling in *The World* about it. Upon which, I wrote him a letter expressed in civil terms, but such as might show him that I did not mind what he said or wrote, and that I had done with him."

This is that celebrated letter of which so much has been said, and about which curiosity has been so long excited, without being gratified. I for many years solicited Johnson to favor me with a copy of it, that so excellent a composition might not be lost to posterity. He delayed from time to time to give it me; till at last in 1781, when we were on a visit at Mr. Dilly's,[5] at Southill in Bedfordshire, he was pleased to dictate it to me from memory. He afterwards found among his papers a copy of it, which he had dictated to Mr. Baretti,[6] with its title and corrections, in his own handwriting. This he gave to Mr. Langton; adding that if it were to come into print, he wished it to be from that copy. By Mr. Langton's kindness, I am enabled to enrich my work with a perfect transcript of what the world has so eagerly desired to see.

TO THE RIGHT HONORABLE THE EARL OF CHESTERFIELD

February 7, 1755

MY LORD,

I have been lately informed, by the proprietor of *The World,* that two papers, in which my Dictionary is recommended to the public, were written by your Lordship. To be so distinguished, is an honor, which, being very little accustomed to favors from the great, I know not well how to receive, or in what terms to acknowledge.

---

4. *Paradise Lost* 2.112.
5. Southill was the country home of Charles and Edward Dilly, publishers. The firm published all of Boswell's serious works and shared in the publi-

cation of Johnson's *Lives of the Poets* (1779–81).
6. Giuseppe Baretti, an Italian writer and lexicographer whom Johnson introduced into his circle.

When, upon some slight encouragement, I first visited your Lordship, I was overpowered, like the rest of mankind, by the enchantment of your address; and could not forbear to wish that I might boast myself *Le vainqueur du vainqueur de la terre*[7]—that I might obtain that regard for which I saw the world contending; but I found my attendance so little encouraged that neither pride nor modesty would suffer me to continue it. When I had once addressed your Lordship in public, I had exhausted all the art of pleasing which a retired and uncourtly scholar can possess. I had done all that I could; and no man is well pleased to have his all neglected, be it ever so little.

Seven years, my Lord, have now passed since I waited in your outward rooms, or was repulsed from your door; during which time I have been pushing on my work through difficulties of which it is useless to complain, and have brought it, at last, to the verge of publication, without one act of assistance, one word of encouragement, or one smile of favor. Such treatment I did not expect, for I never had a patron before.

The shepherd in Virgil grew at last acquainted with Love, and found him a native of the rocks.[8]

Is not a patron, my Lord, one who looks with unconcern on a man struggling for life in the water, and, when he has reached ground, encumbers him with help? The notice which you have been pleased to take of my labors, had it been early, had been kind; but it has been delayed till I am indifferent, and cannot enjoy it; till I am solitary, and cannot impart it; till I am known, and do not want it. I hope it is no very cynical asperity not to confess obligations where no benefit has been received, or to be unwilling that the public should consider me as owing that to a patron which Providence has enabled me to do for myself.

Having carried on my work thus far with so little obligation to any favorer of learning, I shall not be disappointed though I should conclude it, if less be possible, with less; for I have been long wakened from that dream of hope in which I once boasted myself with so much exultation, my Lord, your Lordship's most humble, most obedient servant,

SAM. JOHNSON.

"While this was the talk of the town," says Dr. Adams, in a letter to me, "I happened to visit Dr. Warburton,[9] who finding that I was acquainted with Johnson, desired me earnestly to carry his compliments to him, and to tell him that he honored him for his manly behavior in rejecting these condescensions of Lord Chesterfield, and for resenting the treatment he had received from him, with a proper spirit. Johnson was visibly pleased with this compliment, for he had always a high opinion of Warburton. Indeed, the force of mind which appeared in this letter was congenial with that which Warburton himself amply possessed."

---

7. The conqueror of the conqueror of the earth (French). From the first line of Scudéry's epic *Alaric* (1654).
8. *Eclogues* 8.44.

9. William Warburton, bishop of Gloucester, friend and literary executor of Pope, editor of Pope and Shakespeare, theological controversialist.

There is a curious minute circumstance which struck me, in comparing the various editions of Johnson's imitations of Juvenal. In the tenth satire, one of the couplets upon the vanity of wishes even for literary distinction stood thus:

> Yet think what ills the scholar's life assail,
> Toil, envy, want, the *garret*, and the jail.

But after experiencing the uneasiness which Lord Chesterfield's fallacious patronage made him feel, he dismissed the word *garret* from the sad group, and in all the subsequent editions the line stands

> Toil, envy, want, the *patron*, and the jail.

[*1762*] The accession of George the Third to the throne of these kingdoms[1] opened a new and brighter prospect to men of literary merit, who had been honored with no mark of royal favor in the preceding reign. His present Majesty's education in this country, as well as his taste and beneficence, prompted him to be the patron of science and the arts; and early this year Johnson, having been represented to him as a very learned and good man, without any certain provision, his Majesty was pleased to grant him a pension of three hundred pounds a year. The Earl of Bute,[2] who was then Prime Minister, had the honor to announce this instance of his Sovereign's bounty, concerning which many and various stories, all equally erroneous, have been propagated: maliciously representing it as a political bribe to Johnson, to desert his avowed principles, and become the tool of a government which he held to be founded in usurpation. I have taken care to have it in my power to refute them from the most authentic information. Lord Bute told me that Mr. Wedderburne, now Lord Loughborough, was the person who first mentioned this subject to him. Lord Loughborough told me that the pension was granted to Johnson solely as the reward of his literary merit, without any stipulation whatever, or even tacit understanding that he should write for administration. His Lordship added that he was confident the political tracts which Johnson afterwards did write, as they were entirely consonant with his own opinions, would have been written by him though no pension had been granted to him.[3] * * *

[A MEMORABLE YEAR: BOSWELL MEETS JOHNSON]

[*1763*] This is to me a memorable year; for in it I had the happiness to obtain the acquaintance of that extraordinary man whose memoirs I am now writing; an acquaintance which I shall ever esteem as one of the most fortunate circumstances in my life. * * *

Mr. Thomas Davies the actor, who then kept a bookseller's shop in Russel Street, Covent Garden, told me that Johnson was very much his friend, and came frequently to his house, where he more than once invited me to meet

---

1. In 1760.
2. An intimate friend of George III's mother, he early gained an ascendancy over the young prince and was largely responsible for the king's autocratic views. He was hated in England both as a favorite and as a Scot.

3. Johnson's few political pamphlets in the 1770s invariably supported the policies of the crown. The best known is his answer to the American colonies, *Taxation No Tyranny* (1775). His dislike of the Americans was in large part due to the fact they owned slaves.

him; but by some unlucky accident or other he was prevented from coming to us. * * *

At last, on Monday the 16th of May, when I was sitting in Mr. Davies's back parlor, after having drunk tea with him and Mrs. Davies, Johnson unexpectedly came into the shop; and Mr. Davies having perceived him through the glass door in the room in which we were sitting, advancing towards us— he announced his awful approach to me, somewhat in the manner of an actor in the part of Horatio, when he addresses Hamlet on the appearance of his father's ghost, "Look, my Lord, it comes." I found that I had a very perfect idea of Johnson's figure, from the portrait of him painted by Sir Joshua Reynolds soon after he had published his *Dictionary*, in the attitude of sitting in his easy chair in deep meditation, which was the first picture his friend did for him, which Sir Joshua very kindly presented to me, and from which an engraving has been made for this work. Mr. Davies mentioned my name, and respectfully introduced me to him. I was much agitated; and recollecting his prejudice against the Scotch, of which I had heard much, I said to Davies, "Don't tell where I come from."—"From Scotland," cried Davies roguishly. "Mr. Johnson," said I, "I do indeed come from Scotland, but I cannot help it." I am willing to flatter myself that I meant this as light pleasantry to soothe and conciliate him, and not as an humiliating abasement at the expense of my country. But however that might be, this speech was somewhat unlucky; for with that quickness of wit for which he was so remarkable, he seized the expression "come from Scotland," which I used in the sense of being of that country; and, as if I had said that I had come away from it, or left it, retorted, "That, Sir, I find, is what a very great many of your countrymen cannot help." This stroke stunned me a good deal; and when we had sat down, I felt myself not a little embarrassed, and apprehensive of what might come next. He then addressed himself to Davies: "What do you think of Garrick? He has refused me an order for the play for Miss Williams,[4] because he knows the house will be full, and that an order would be worth three shillings." Eager to take any opening to get into conversation with him, I ventured to say, "O Sir, I cannot think Mr. Garrick would grudge such a trifle to you." "Sir," said he, with a stern look, "I have known David Garrick longer than you have done: and I know no right you have to talk to me on the subject." Perhaps I deserved this check; for it was rather presumptuous in me, an entire stranger, to express any doubt of the justice of his animadversion upon his old acquaintance and pupil. I now felt myself much mortified, and began to think that the hope which I had long indulged of obtaining his acquaintance was blasted. And, in truth, had not my ardor been uncommonly strong, and my resolution uncommonly persevering, so rough a reception might have deterred me forever from making any further attempts. Fortunately, however, I remained upon the field not wholly discomfited. * * *

I was highly pleased with the extraordinary vigor of his conversation, and regretted that I was drawn away from it by an engagement at another place. I had, for a part of the evening, been left alone with him, and had ventured to make an observation now and then, which he received very civilly; so that

4. Mrs. Anna Williams (1706–1783), a blind poet and friend of Mrs. Johnson. She continued to live in Johnson's house after his wife's death and habit- ually sat up to make tea for him whenever he came home.

I was satisfied that though there was a roughness in his manner, there was no ill nature in his disposition. Davies followed me to the door, and when I complained to him a little of the hard blows which the great man had given me, he kindly took upon him to console me by saying, "Don't be uneasy. I can see he likes you very well."

A few days afterwards I called on Davies, and asked him if he thought I might take the liberty of waiting on Mr. Johnson at his chambers in the Temple. He said I certainly might, and that Mr. Johnson would take it as a compliment. So upon Tuesday the 24th of May, after having been enlivened by the witty sallies of Messieurs Thornton, Wilkes, Churchill, and Lloyd,[5] with whom I had passed the morning, I boldly repaired to Johnson. His chambers were on the first floor of No. 1, Inner Temple Lane, and I entered them with an impression given me by the Reverend Dr. Blair,[6] of Edinburgh, who had been introduced to him not long before, and described his having "found the giant in his den"; an expression, which, when I came to be pretty well acquainted with Johnson, I repeated to him, and he was diverted at this picturesque account of himself. Dr. Blair had been presented to him by Dr. James Fordyce.[7] At this time the controversy concerning the pieces published by Mr. James Macpherson, as translations of *Ossian*, was at its height.[8] Johnson had all along denied their authenticity; and, what was still more provoking to their admirers, maintained that they had no merit. The subject having been introduced by Dr. Fordyce, Dr. Blair, relying on the internal evidence of their antiquity, asked Dr. Johnson whether he thought any man of a modern age could have written such poems? Johnson replied, "Yes, Sir, many men, many women, and many children." Johnson, at this time, did not know that Dr. Blair had just published a dissertation, not only defending their authenticity, but seriously ranking them with the poems of Homer and Virgil; and when he was afterwards informed of this circumstance, he expressed some displeasure at Dr. Fordyce's having suggested the topic, and said, "I am not sorry that they got thus much for their pains. Sir, it was like leading one to talk of a book when the author is concealed behind the door."

He received me very courteously; but, it must be confessed that his apartment, and furniture, and morning dress, were sufficiently uncouth. His brown suit of clothes looked very rusty; he had on a little old shriveled unpowdered wig, which was too small for his head; his shirt neck and knees of his breeches were loose; his black worsted stockings ill drawn up; and he had a pair of unbuckled shoes by way of slippers. But all these slovenly particularities were forgotten the moment that he began to talk. Some gentlemen, whom I do not recollect, were sitting with him; and when they went away, I also rose; but he said to me, "Nay, don't go." "Sir," said I, "I am afraid that I intrude upon you. It is benevolent to allow me to sit and hear you." He seemed pleased with this compliment, which I sincerely paid him, and

5. Robert Lloyd, poet and essayist. Bonnell Thornton, journalist. Charles Churchill, satirist. For Wilkes see p. 2772, n. 9. The four were bound together by a common love of wit and dissipation. Boswell enjoyed their company in 1763.
6. The Reverend Hugh Blair (1718–1800), Scottish divine and professor of rhetoric and *belles lettres* at the University of Edinburgh.
7. A Scottish preacher.

8. Macpherson had imposed on most of his contemporaries, Scottish and English, by convincing them of the genuineness of prose poems that he had concocted but that he claimed to have translated from the original Gaelic of Ossian, a blind epic poet of the 3rd century. The vogue of the poems both in Europe and in America was enormous.

answered, "Sir, I am obliged to any man who visits me." I have preserved the following short minute of what passed this day:

"Madness frequently discovers itself merely by unnecessary deviation from the usual modes of the world. My poor friend Smart showed the disturbance of his mind by falling upon his knees, and saying his prayers in the street, or in any other unusual place. Now although, rationally speaking, it is greater madness not to pray at all than to pray as Smart did, I am afraid there are so many who do not pray, that their understanding is not called in question."

Concerning this unfortunate poet, Christopher Smart, who was confined in a madhouse, he had, at another time, the following conversation with Dr. Burney:[9] BURNEY. "How does poor Smart do, Sir; is he likely to recover?" JOHNSON. "It seems as if his mind had ceased to struggle with the disease; for he grows fat upon it." BURNEY. "Perhaps, Sir, that may be from want of exercise." JOHNSON. "No, Sir; he has partly as much exercise as he used to have, for he digs in the garden. Indeed, before his confinement, he used for exercise to walk to the ale house; but he was *carried* back again. I did not think he ought to be shut up. His infirmities were not noxious to society. He insisted on people praying with him; and I'd as lief pray with Kit Smart as anyone else. Another charge was that he did not love clean linen; and I have no passion for it."—Johnson continued. "Mankind have a great aversion to intellectual labor; but even supposing knowledge to be easily attainable, more people would be content to be ignorant than would take even a little trouble to acquire it."

Talking of Garrick, he said, "He is the first man in the world for sprightly conversation."

When I rose a second time he again pressed me to stay, which I did. * * *

[GOLDSMITH. SUNDRY OPINIONS. JOHNSON MEETS HIS KING]

As Dr. Oliver Goldsmith will frequently appear in this narrative, I shall endeavor to make my readers in some degree acquainted with his singular character. He was a native of Ireland, and a contemporary with Mr. Burke[1] at Trinity College, Dublin, but did not then give much promise of future celebrity. He, however, observed to Mr. Malone,[2] that "though he made no great figure in mathematics, which was a study in much repute there, he could turn an ode of Horace into English better than any of them." He afterwards studied physic[3] at Edinburgh, and upon the Continent; and I have been informed, was enabled to pursue his travels on foot, partly by demanding at universities to enter the lists as a disputant, by which, according to the custom of many of them, he was entitled to the premium of a crown, when luckily for him his challenge was not accepted; so that, as I once observed to Dr. Johnson, he *disputed* his passage through Europe. He then came to England, and was employed successively in the capacities of an usher[4] to an academy, a corrector of the press, a reviewer, and a writer for a newspaper. He had sagacity enough to cultivate assiduously the acquain-

9. Dr. Charles Burney (1726–1814), historian of music and father of the novelist and diarist Frances Burney, whom Johnson befriended in his old age.
1. Edmund Burke (1729–1797), statesman, orator, and political philosopher.
2. Edmond Malone (1741–1812), distinguished editor and literary scholar, He helped Boswell in the writing and publication of the *Life*.
3. Medicine.
4. An assistant teacher; then a disagreeable and ill-paid job.

tance of Johnson, and his faculties were gradually enlarged by the contemplation of such a model. To me and many others it appeared that he studiously copied the manner of Johnson, though, indeed, upon a smaller scale.

At this time I think he had published nothing with his name, though it was pretty generally known that *one Dr. Goldsmith* was the author of *An Enquiry into the Present State of Polite Learning in Europe,* and of *The Citizen of the World,* a series of letters supposed to be written from London by a Chinese. No man had the art of displaying, with more advantage as a writer, whatever literary acquisitions he made. *"Nihil quod tetigit non ornavit."*[5] His mind resembled a fertile, but thin soil. There was a quick, but not a strong vegetation, of whatever chanced to be thrown upon it. No deep root could be struck. The oak of the forest did not grow there; but the elegant shrubbery and the fragrant parterre[6] appeared in gay succession. It has been generally circulated and believed that he was a mere fool in conversation; but, in truth, this has been greatly exaggerated. He had, no doubt, a more than common share of that hurry of ideas which we often find in his countrymen, and which sometimes produces a laughable confusion in expressing them. He was very much what the French call *un étourdi,*[7] and from vanity and an eager desire of being conspicuous wherever he was, he frequently talked carelessly without knowledge of the subject, or even without thought. His person was short, his countenance coarse and vulgar, his deportment that of a scholar awkwardly affecting the easy gentleman. Those who were in any way distinguished, excited envy in him to so ridiculous an excess that the instances of it are hardly credible. When accompanying two beautiful young ladies with their mother on a tour in France, he was seriously angry that more attention was paid to them than to him; and once at the exhibition of the *Fantoccini* in London, when those who sat next him observed with what dexterity a puppet was made to toss a pike, he could not bear that it should have such praise, and exclaimed with some warmth, "Pshaw! I can do it better myself." * * *

I had as my guests this evening at the Mitre Tavern, Dr. Johnson, Dr. Goldsmith, Mr. Thomas Davies, Mr. Eccles, an Irish gentleman, for whose agreeable company I was obliged to Mr. Davies, and the Reverend Mr. John Ogilvie,[8] who was desirous of being in company with my illustrious friend, while I, in my turn, was proud to have the honor of showing one of my countrymen upon what easy terms Johnson permitted me to live with him. * * *

Mr. Ogilvie was unlucky enough to choose for the topic of his conversation the praises of his native country. He began with saying that there was very rich land round Edinburgh. Goldsmith, who had studied physic there, contradicted this, very untruly, with a sneering laugh. Disconcerted a little by this, Mr. Ogilvie then took new ground, where, I suppose, he thought himself perfectly safe; for he observed that Scotland had a great many noble wild prospects. JOHNSON. "I believe, Sir, you have a great many. Norway, too, has noble wild prospects; and Lapland is remarkable for prodigious noble wild prospects. But, Sir, let me tell you, the noblest prospect which a Scotchman

---

5. He touched nothing that he did not adorn (Latin). From Johnson's epitaph for Goldsmith's monument in Westminster Abbey.

6. A flower garden with beds laid out in patterns.
7. One who acts without thought.
8. An eminent Scottish divine.

ever sees, is the highroad that leads him to England!" This unexpected and pointed sally produced a roar of applause. After all, however, those who admire the rude grandeur of nature cannot deny it to Caledonia. * * *

At night Mr. Johnson and I supped in a private room at the Turk's Head Coffeehouse, in the Strand. "I encourage this house," said he, "for the mistress of it is a good civil woman, and has not much business.

"Sir, I love the acquaintance of young people; because, in the first place, I don't like to think myself growing old. In the next place, young acquaintances must last longest, if they do last; and then, Sir, young men have more virtue than old men: they have more generous sentiments in every respect. I love the young dogs of this age: they have more wit and humor and knowledge of life than we had; but then the dogs are not so good scholars. Sir, in my early years I read very hard. It is a sad reflection, but a true one, that I knew almost as much at eighteen as I do now. My judgment, to be sure, was not so good; but I had all the facts. I remember very well, when I was at Oxford, an old gentleman said to me, 'Young man, ply your book diligently now, and acquire a stock of knowledge; for when years come upon you, you will find that poring upon books will be but an irksome task.'" * * *

He again insisted on the duty of maintaining subordination of rank. "Sir, I would no more deprive a nobleman of his respect than of his money. I consider myself as acting a part in the great system of society, and I do to others as I would have them to do to me. I would behave to a nobleman as I should expect he would behave to me, were I a nobleman and he Sam. Johnson. Sir, there is one Mrs. Macaulay[9] in this town, a great republican. One day when I was at her house, I put on a very grave countenance, and said to her, 'Madam, I am now become a convert to your way of thinking. I am convinced that all mankind are upon an equal footing; and to give you an unquestionable proof, Madam, that I am in earnest, here is a very sensible, civil, well-behaved fellow citizen, your footman; I desire that he may be allowed to sit down and dine with us.' I thus, Sir, showed her the absurdity of the leveling doctrine. She has never liked me since. Sir, your levelers wish to level *down* as far as themselves; but they cannot bear leveling *up* to themselves. They would all have some people under them; why not then have some people above them?" * * *

At supper this night he talked of good eating with uncommon satisfaction. "Some people," he said, "have a foolish way of not minding, or pretending not to mind, what they eat. For my part, I mind my belly very studiously, and very carefully; for I look upon it that he who does not mind his belly will hardly mind anything else." He now appeared to me *Jean Bull philosophe,*[1] and he was, for the moment, not only serious but vehement. Yet I have heard him, upon other occasions, talk with great contempt of people who were anxious to gratify their palates; and the 206th number of his *Rambler* is a masterly essay against gulosity.[2] His practice, indeed, I must acknowledge, may be considered as casting the balance of his different opinions upon this subject; for I never knew any man who relished good eating more than he did. When at table, he was totally absorbed in the business of the moment; his looks seemed riveted to his plate; nor would he, unless when in very high

9. Catharine Macaulay, at this time much in the public eye as a female historian and a propounder of libertarian and egalitarian ideas.

1. I.e., John Bull (the typical hard-headed Englishman) in the role of philosopher.
2. Greediness.

company, say one word, or even pay the least attention to what was said by others, till he had satisfied his appetite, which was so fierce, and indulged with such intenseness, that while in the act of eating, the veins of his forehead swelled, and generally a strong perspiration was visible. To those whose sensations were delicate, this could not but be disgusting; and it was doubtless not very suitable to the character of a philosopher, who should be distinguished by self-command. But it must be owned that Johnson, though he could be rigidly *abstemious*, was not a *temperate* man either in eating or drinking. He could refrain, but he could not use moderately. He told me that he had fasted two days without inconvenience, and that he had never been hungry but once. They who beheld with wonder how much he eat upon all occasions when his dinner was to his taste, could not easily conceive what he must have meant by hunger; and not only was he remarkable for the extraordinary quantity which he eat, but he was, or affected to be, a man of very nice discernment in the science of cookery. * * *

[1767] In February, 1767, there happened one of the most remarkable incidents of Johnson's life, which gratified his monarchical enthusiasm, and which he loved to relate with all its circumstances, when requested by his friends. This was his being honored by a private conversation with his Majesty, in the library at the Queen's house. He had frequently visited those splendid rooms and noble collection of books, which he used to say was more numerous and curious than he supposed any person could have made in the time which the King had employed. Mr. Barnard, the librarian, took care that he should have every accommodation that could contribute to his ease and convenience, while indulging his literary taste in that place; so that he had here a very agreeable resource at leisure hours.

His Majesty having been informed of his occasional visits, was pleased to signify a desire that he should be told when Dr. Johnson came next to the library. Accordingly, the next time that Johnson did come, as soon as he was fairly engaged with a book, on which, while he sat by the fire, he seemed quite intent, Mr. Barnard stole round to the apartment where the King was, and, in obedience to his Majesty's commands, mentioned that Dr. Johnson was then in the library. His Majesty said he was at leisure, and would go to him; upon which Mr. Barnard took one of the candles that stood on the King's table, and lighted his Majesty through a suite of rooms, till they came to a private door into the library, of which his Majesty had the key. Being entered, Mr. Barnard stepped forward hastily to Dr. Johnson, who was still in a profound study, and whispered him, "Sir, here is the King." Johnson started up, and stood still. His Majesty approached him, and at once was courteously easy.

His Majesty began by observing that he understood he came sometimes to the library; and then mentioning his having heard that the Doctor had been lately at Oxford, asked him if he was not fond of going thither. To which Johnson answered that he was indeed fond of going to Oxford sometimes, but was likewise glad to come back again. The King then asked him what they were doing at Oxford. Johnson answered, he could not much commend their diligence, but that in some respects they were mended, for they had put their press under better regulations, and were at that time printing Polybius. He was then asked whether there were better libraries at Oxford or Cambridge. He answered, he believed the Bodleian was larger than any they had at Cambridge; at the same time adding, "I hope, whether we have more books or not than they have at Cambridge, we shall make as good use of them as they do." Being asked whether All Souls or Christ Church library was the largest, he answered, "All Souls library is the largest we have, except the Bodleian." "Aye," said the King, "that is the public library."

His Majesty inquired if he was then writing anything. He answered, he was not, for he had pretty well told the world what he knew, and must now read to acquire more knowledge. The King, as it should seem with a view to urge him to rely on his own stores as an original writer, and to continue his labors, then said "I do not think you borrow much from anybody." Johnson said he thought he had already done his part as a writer. "I should have thought so too," said the King, "if you had not written so well."—Johnson observed to me, upon this, that "No man could have paid a handsomer compliment; and it was fit for a king to pay. It was decisive." When asked by another friend, at Sir Joshua Reynolds's, whether he made any reply to this high compliment, he answered, "No, Sir. When the King had said it, it was to be so. It was not for me to bandy civilities with my sovereign." Perhaps no man who had spent his whole life in courts could have shown a more nice and dignified sense of true politeness than Johnson did in this instance. * * *

[FEAR OF DEATH]

[1769] When we were alone, I introduced the subject of death, and endeavored to maintain that the fear of it might be got over. I told him that David Hume said to me, he was no more uneasy to think he should *not be* after this life, than that he *had not been* before he began to exist. JOHNSON. "Sir, if he really thinks so, his perceptions are disturbed; he is mad: if he does not think so, he lies. He may tell you, he holds his finger in the flame of a candle, without feeling pain; would you believe him? When he dies, he at least gives up all he has." BOSWELL. "Foote,[3] Sir, told me, that when he was very ill he was not afraid to die." JOHNSON. "It is not true, Sir. Hold a pistol to Foote's breast, or to Hume's breast, and threaten to kill them, and you'll see how they behave." BOSWELL. "But may we not fortify our minds for the approach of death?" Here I am sensible I was in the wrong, to bring before his view what he ever looked upon with horror; for although when in a celestial frame, in his *Vanity of Human Wishes*, he has supposed death to be "kind Nature's signal for retreat," from this stage of being to "a happier seat," his thoughts upon this awful change were in general full of dismal apprehensions. His mind resembled the vast amphitheater, the Colosseum at Rome. In the center stood his judgment, which, like a mighty gladiator, combated those apprehensions that, like the wild beasts of the arena, were all around in cells, ready to be let out upon him. After a conflict, he drove them back into their dens; but not killing them, they were still assailing him. To my question, whether we might not fortify our minds for the approach of death, he answered, in a passion, "No, Sir, let it alone. It matters not how a man dies, but how he lives. The act of dying is not of importance, it lasts so short a time." He added (with an earnest look), "A man knows it must be so, and submits. It will do him no good to whine."

3. Samuel Foote, actor and dramatist, famous for his wit and his skill in mimicry.

I attempted to continue the conversation. He was so provoked that he said, "Give us no more of this"; and was thrown into such a state of agitation that he expressed himself in a way that alarmed and distressed me; showed an impatience that I should leave him, and when I was going away, called to me sternly, "Don't let us meet tomorrow." * * *

[OSSIAN. "TALKING FOR VICTORY"]

MR. BOSWELL TO DR. JOHNSON

Edinburgh, Feb. 2, 1775.

* * * As to Macpherson, I am anxious to have from yourself a full and pointed account of what has passed between you and him. It is confidently told here that before your book[4] came out he sent to you, to let you know that he understood you meant to deny the authenticity of Ossian's poems; that the originals were in his possession; that you might have inspection of them, and might take the evidence of people skilled in the Erse language; and that he hoped, after this fair offer, you would not be so uncandid[5] as to assert that he had refused reasonable proof. That you paid no regard to his message, but published your strong attack upon him; and then he wrote a letter to you, in such terms as he thought suited to one who had not acted as a man of veracity. * * *

What words were used by Mr. Macpherson in his letter to the venerable sage, I have never heard; but they are generally said to have been of a nature very different from the language of literary contest. Dr. Johnson's answer appeared in the newspapers of the day, and has since been frequently republished; but not with perfect accuracy. I give it as dictated to me by himself, written down in his presence, and authenticated by a note in his own handwriting, *This, I think, is a true copy.*

MR. JAMES MACPHERSON,

I received your foolish and impudent letter. Any violence offered me I shall do my best to repel; and what I cannot do for myself, the law shall do for me. I hope I shall never be deterred from detecting what I think a cheat, by the menaces of a ruffian.

What would you have me retract? I thought your book an imposture; I think it an imposture still. For this opinion I have given my reasons to the public, which I here dare you to refute. Your rage I defy. Your abilities, since your Homer, are not so formidable; and what I hear of your morals inclines me to pay regard not to what you shall say, but to what you shall prove. You may print this if you will.

SAM. JOHNSON.

Mr. Macpherson little knew the character of Dr. Johnson if he supposed that he could be easily intimidated; for no man was ever more remarkable for personal courage. He had, indeed, an awful dread of death, or rather, "of something after death"; and what rational man, who seriously thinks of quit-

---

4. Johnson's *Journey to the Western Islands* (1775), in which he had publicly expressed his views on the Ossianic poems.
5. Unfair, malicious.

ting all that he has ever known, and going into a new and unknown state of being, can be without that dread? But his fear was from reflection; his courage natural. His fear, in that one instance, was the result of philosophical and religious consideration. He feared death, but he feared nothing else, not even what might occasion death. Many instances of his resolution may be mentioned. One day, at Mr. Beauclerk's house in the country, when two large dogs were fighting, he went up to them, and beat them till they separated; and at another time, when told of the danger there was that a gun might burst if charged with many balls, he put in six or seven, and fired it off against a wall. Mr. Langton told me that when they were swimming together near Oxford, he cautioned Dr. Johnson against a pool which was reckoned particularly dangerous; upon which Johnson directly swam into it. He told me himself that one night he was attacked in the street by four men, to whom he would not yield, but kept them all at bay, till the watch came up, and carried both him and them to the roundhouse.[6] In the playhouse at Lichfield, as Mr. Garrick informed me, Johnson having for a moment quitted a chair which was placed for him between the side-scenes, a gentleman took possession of it, and when Johnson on his return civilly demanded his seat, rudely refused to give it up; upon which Johnson laid hold of it, and tossed him and the chair into the pit. Foote, who so successfully revived the old comedy, by exhibiting living characters, had resolved to imitate Johnson on the stage, expecting great profits from his ridicule of so celebrated a man. Johnson being informed of his intention, and being at dinner at Mr. Thomas Davies's the bookseller, from whom I had the story, he asked Mr. Davies what was the common price of an oak stick; and being answered six-pence, "Why then, Sir," said he, "give me leave to send your servant to purchase me a shilling one. I'll have a double quantity; for I am told Foote means to *take me off*, as he calls it, and I am determined the fellow shall not do it with impunity." Davies took care to acquaint Foote of this, which effectually checked the wantonness of the mimic. Mr. Macpherson's menaces made Johnson provide himself with the same implement of defense; and had he been attacked, I have no doubt that, old as he was, he would have made his corporal prowess be felt as much as his intellectual. * * *

[1776] I mentioned a new gaming club, of which Mr. Beauclerk had given me an account, where the members played to a desperate extent. JOHNSON. "Depend upon it, Sir, this is mere talk. *Who* is ruined by gaming? You will not find six instances in an age. There is a strange rout made about deep play: whereas you have many more people ruined by adventurous trade, and yet we do not hear such an outcry against it." THRALE.[7] "There may be few people absolutely ruined by deep play; but very many are much hurt in their circumstances by it." JOHNSON. "Yes, Sir, and so are very many by other kinds of expense." I had heard him talk once before in the same manner; and at Oxford he said, he wished he had learnt to play at cards. The truth, however, is that he loved to display his ingenuity in argument; and therefore

6. "The constable's prison, in which disorderly persons, found in the street, are confined" (Johnson's *Dictionary*).
7. Johnson met Henry Thrale, the wealthy brewer, and his charming wife, Hester, in 1765. Thereafter he was domesticated as much as he wished to be at their house at Streatham near London. There

he enjoyed the good things of life, as well as the companionship of Mrs. Thrale and her children. Henry Thrale died in 1781. His widow's marriage to Gabriel Piozzi, an Italian musician, in 1784, caused Johnson to quarrel with her and darkened the last months of his life.

would sometimes in conversation maintain opinions which he was sensible
were wrong, but in supporting which, his reasoning and wit would be most
conspicuous. He would begin thus: "Why, Sir, as to the good or evil of card
playing——" "Now," said Garrick, "he is thinking which side he shall take."
He appeared to have a pleasure in contradiction, especially when any opinion
whatever was delivered with an air of confidence; so that there was hardly
any topic, if not one of the great truths of religion and morality, that he might
not have been incited to argue, either for or against. Lord Elibank[8] had the
highest admiration of his powers. He once observed to me, "Whatever opinion Johnson maintains, I will not say that he convinces me; but he never fails
to show me that he has good reasons for it." I have heard Johnson pay his
Lordship this high compliment: "I never was in Lord Elibank's company
without learning something." * * *

[DINNER WITH WILKES]

My worthy booksellers and friends, Messieurs Dilly in the Poultry, at
whose hospitable and well-covered table I have seen a greater number of
literary men than at any other, except that of Sir Joshua Reynolds, had invited
me to meet Mr. Wilkes[9] and some more gentlemen on Wednesday, May 15.
"Pray," said I, "let us have Dr. Johnson."—"What, with Mr. Wilkes? not for
the world," said Mr. Edward Dilly, "Dr. Johnson would never forgive me."—
"Come," said I, "if you'll let me negotiate for you, I will be answerable that
all shall go well." DILLY. "Nay, if you will take it upon you, I am sure I shall
be very happy to see them both here."

Notwithstanding the high veneration which I entertained for Dr. Johnson,
I was sensible that he was sometimes a little actuated by the spirit of contradiction, and by means of that I hoped I should gain my point. I was persuaded that if I had come upon him with a direct proposal, "Sir, will you
dine in company with Jack Wilkes?" he would have flown into a passion, and
would probably have answered, "Dine with Jack Wilkes, Sir! I'd as soon dine
with Jack Ketch."[1] I therefore, while we were sitting quietly by ourselves at
his house in an evening, took occasion to open my plan thus: "Mr. Dilly, Sir,
sends his respectful compliments to you, and would be happy if you would
do him the honor to dine with him on Wednesday next along with me, as I
must soon go to Scotland." JOHNSON. "Sir, I am obliged to Mr. Dilly. I will
wait upon him——" BOSWELL. "Provided, Sir, I suppose, that the company
which he is to have, is agreeable to you." JOHNSON. "What do you mean, Sir?
What do you take me for? Do you think I am so ignorant of the world as to
imagine that I am to prescribe to a gentleman what company he is to have

8. Prominent in Scottish literary circles. Johnson,
who admired him, had visited him on his tour of
Scotland with Boswell in 1773.
9. John Wilkes (1727–1797) was obnoxious to the
Christian and Tory Johnson in every way. He was
profane and dissolute, and his personal life was a
public scandal. For more than a decade he had
been notorious as a courageous, resourceful, and
finally victorious opponent of the arbitrary and
tyrannical policies of the king and his ministers
and had been the envenomed critic of Lord Bute,

to whom Johnson owed his pension. When Johnson met him he had totally defeated his enemies,
had served as lord mayor, and was again a Member
of Parliament, a post from which he had been
expelled and driven into exile as an outlaw in 1764.
Boswell had found Wilkes a gay and congenial
companion in Italy in 1764.
1. After the public hangman Jack Ketch died in
1686, his name became the common designation
of all those who filled that office.

at his table?" BOSWELL. "I beg your pardon, Sir, for wishing to prevent you from meeting people whom you might not like. Perhaps he may have some of what he calls his patriotic[2] friends with him." JOHNSON. "Well, Sir, and what then? What care I for his *patriotic friends*? Poh!" BOSWELL. "I should not be surprised to find Jack Wilkes there." JOHNSON. "And if Jack Wilkes *should* be there, what is that to *me*, Sir? My dear friend, let us have no more of this. I am sorry to be angry with you; but really it is treating me strangely to talk to me as if I could not meet any company whatever, occasionally." BOSWELL. "Pray forgive me, Sir: I meant well. But you shall meet whoever comes, for me." Thus I secured him, and told Dilly that he would find him very well pleased to be one of his guests on the day appointed.

Upon the much-expected Wednesday, I called on him about half an hour before dinner, as I often did when we were to dine out together, to see that he was ready in time, and to accompany him. I found him buffeting his books, as upon a former occasion, covered with dust, and making no preparation for going abroad. "How is this, Sir?" said I. "Don't you recollect that you are to dine at Mr. Dilly's?" JOHNSON. "Sir, I did not think of going to Dilly's: it went out of my head. I have ordered dinner at home with Mrs. Williams." BOSWELL. "But, my dear Sir, you know you were engaged to Mr. Dilly, and I told him so. He will expect you, and will be much disappointed if you don't come." JOHNSON. "You must talk to Mrs. Williams about this."

Here was a sad dilemma. I feared that what I was so confident I had secured would yet be frustrated. He had accustomed himself to show Mrs. Williams such a degree of humane attention as frequently imposed some restraint upon him; and I knew that if she should be obstinate, he would not stir. I hastened downstairs to the blind lady's room, and told her I was in great uneasiness, for Dr. Johnson had engaged to me to dine this day at Mr. Dilly's, but that he had told me he had forgotten his engagement, and had ordered dinner at home. "Yes, Sir," said she, pretty peevishly, "Dr. Johnson is to dine at home."—"Madam," said I, "his respect for you is such that I know he will not leave you unless you absolutely desire it. But as you have so much of his company, I hope you will be good enough to forgo it for a day; as Mr. Dilly is a very worthy man, has frequently had agreeable parties at his house for Dr. Johnson, and will be vexed if the Doctor neglects him today. And then, Madam, be pleased to consider my situation; I carried the message, and I assured Mr. Dilly that Dr. Johnson was to come, and no doubt he has made a dinner, and invited a company, and boasted of the honor he expected to have. I shall be quite disgraced if the Doctor is not there." She gradually softened to my solicitations, which were certainly as earnest as most entreaties to ladies upon any occasion, and was graciously pleased to empower me to tell Dr. Johnson that all things considered, she thought he should certainly go. I flew back to him, still in dust, and careless of what should be the event, "indifferent in his choice to go or stay";[3] but as soon as I had announced to him Mrs. Williams' consent, he roared, "Frank, a clean

2. In Tory circles the word had come to be used ironically of those who opposed the government. The "patriots" considered themselves the defenders of the ancient liberties of the English. They included the partisans of both Wilkes and the American colonists.

3. Addison's *Cato* 5.1.40. Boswell cleverly adapts to his own purpose Cato's words, "Indifferent in his choice to sleep or die."

shirt," and was very soon dressed. When I had him fairly seated in a hackney coach with me, I exulted as much as a fortune hunter who has got an heiress into a post chaise with him to set out for Gretna Green.[4]

When we entered Mr. Dilly's drawing room, he found himself in the midst of a company he did not know. I kept myself snug and silent, watching how he would conduct himself. I observed him whispering to Mr. Dilly, "Who is that gentleman, Sir?"—"Mr. Arthur Lee."—JOHNSON. "Too, too, too" (under his breath), which was one of his habitual mutterings. Mr. Arthur Lee could not but be very obnoxious to Johnson, for he was not only a *patriot* but an *American*.[5] He was afterwards minister from the United States at the court of Madrid. "And who is the gentleman in lace?"—"Mr. Wilkes, Sir." This information confounded him still more; he had some difficulty to restrain himself, and taking up a book, sat down upon a window seat and read, or at least kept his eye upon it intently for some time, till he composed himself. His feelings, I dare say, were awkward enough. But he no doubt recollected his having rated me for supposing that he could be at all disconcerted by any company, and he, therefore, resolutely set himself to behave quite as an easy man of the world, who could adapt himself at once to the disposition and manners of those whom he might chance to meet.

The cheering sound of "Dinner is upon the table," dissolved his reverie, and we *all* sat down without any symptom of ill humor. There were present, beside Mr. Wilkes, and Mr. Arthur Lee, who was an old companion of mine when he studied physic at Edinburgh, Mr. (now Sir John) Miller, Dr. Lettsom, and Mr. Slater the druggist. Mr. Wilkes placed himself next to Dr. Johnson, and behaved to him with so much attention and politeness that he gained upon him insensibly. No man eat more heartily than Johnson, or loved better what was nice and delicate. Mr. Wilkes was very assiduous in helping him to some fine veal. "Pray give me leave, Sir—It is better here—A little of the brown—Some fat, Sir—A little of the stuffing—Some gravy—Let me have the pleasure of giving you some butter—Allow me to recommend a squeeze of this orange—or the lemon, perhaps, may have more zest."—"Sir, Sir, I am obliged to you, Sir," cried Johnson, bowing, and turning his head to him with a look for some time of "surly virtue," but, in a short while, of complacency.

Foote being mentioned, Johnson said, "He is not a good mimic." One of the company added, "A merry Andrew, a buffoon." JOHNSON. "But he has wit too, and is not deficient in ideas, or in fertility and variety of imagery, and not empty of reading; he has knowledge enough to fill up his part. One species of wit he has in an eminent degree, that of escape. You drive him into a corner with both hands; but he's gone, Sir, when you think you have got him—like an animal that jumps over your head. Then he has a great range for wit; he never lets truth stand between him and a jest, and he is sometimes mighty coarse. Garrick is under many restraints from which Foote is free." WILKES. "Garrick's wit is more like Lord Chesterfield's." JOHNSON. "The first time I was in company with Foote was at Fitzherbert's. Having no

---

4. A village just across the Scottish border where runaway couples were married by the local innkeeper or the blacksmith.
5. Johnson was extremely hostile to the rebelling American colonists. On one occasion he said, "I

am willing to love all mankind, except an American." Lee had been educated in England and Scotland, and had recently been admitted to the English bar. He had been a loyal supporter of Wilkes.

good opinion of the fellow, I was resolved not to be pleased; and it is very difficult to please a man against his will. I went on eating my dinner pretty sullenly, affecting not to mind him. But the dog was so very comical, that I was obliged to lay down my knife and fork, throw myself back upon my chair, and fairly laugh it out. No, Sir, he was irresistible. He upon one occasion experienced, in an extraordinary degree, the efficacy of his powers of entertaining. Amongst the many and various modes which he tried of getting money, he became a partner with a small-beer[6] brewer, and he was to have a share of the profits for procuring customers amongst his numerous acquaintance. Fitzherbert was one who took his small beer; but it was so bad that the servants resolved not to drink it. They were at some loss how to notify their resolution, being afraid of offending their master, who they knew liked Foote much as a companion. At last they fixed upon a little black boy, who was rather a favorite, to be their deputy, and deliver their remonstrance; and having invested him with the whole authority of the kitchen, he was to inform Mr. Fitzherbert, in all their names, upon a certain day, that they would drink Foote's small beer no longer. On that day Foote happened to dine at Fitzherbert's, and this boy served at table; he was so delighted with Foote's stories, and merriment, and grimace, that when he went downstairs, he told them, 'This is the finest man I have ever seen. I will not deliver your message. I will drink his small beer.' "

Somebody observed that Garrick could not have done this. WILKES. "Garrick would have made the small beer still smaller. He is now leaving the stage; but he will play Scrub[7] all his life." I knew that Johnson would let nobody attack Garrick but himself, as Garrick once said to me, and I had heard him praise his liberality; so to bring out his commendation of his celebrated pupil, I said, loudly, "I have heard Garrick is liberal." JOHNSON. "Yes, Sir, I know that Garrick has given away more money than any man in England that I am acquainted with, and that not from ostentatious views. Garrick was very poor when he began life; so when he came to have money, he probably was very unskillful in giving away, and saved when he should not. But Garrick began to be liberal as soon as he could; and I am of opinion, the reputation of avarice which he has had, has been very lucky for him, and prevented his having many enemies. You despise a man for avarice, but do not hate him. Garrick might have been much better attacked for living with more splendor than is suitable to a player: if they had had the wit to have assaulted him in that quarter, they might have galled him more. But they have kept clamoring about his avarice, which has rescued him from much obloquy and envy."

Talking of the great difficulty of obtaining authentic information for biography, Johnson told us, "When I was a young fellow I wanted to write the Life of Dryden, and in order to get materials, I applied to the only two persons then alive who had seen him; these were old Swinney,[8] and old Cibber. Swinney's information was no more than this, that at Will's Coffeehouse Dryden had a particular chair for himself, which was set by the fire in winter, and was then called his winter chair; and that it was carried out for him to the balcony in summer, and was then called his summer chair. Cibber could

---

6. Weak beer, served in the servants' hall.
7. The servant of Squire Sullen in George Farquhar's Beaux' Stratagem, a favorite role of Garrick.
8. Owen Mac Swinney, a playwright.

tell no more but that he remembered him a decent old man, arbiter of critical disputes at Will's. You are to consider that Cibber was then at a great distance from Dryden, had perhaps one leg only in the room, and durst not draw in the other." BOSWELL. "Yet Cibber was a man of observation?" JOHNSON. "I think not." BOSWELL. "You will allow his *Apology* to be well done." JOHNSON. "Very well done, to be sure, Sir. That book is a striking proof of the justice of Pope's remark:

> Each might his several province well command,
> Would all but stoop to what they understand."[9]

BOSWELL. "And his plays are good." JOHNSON. "Yes; but that was his trade; *l'esprit du corps:* he had been all his life among players and play writers. I wondered that he had so little to say in conversation, for he had kept the best company, and learnt all that can be got by the ear. He abused Pindar to me, and then showed me an ode of his own, with an absurd couplet, making a linnet soar on an eagle's wing. I told him that when the ancients made a simile, they always made it like something real."

Mr. Wilkes remarked that "among all the bold flights of Shakespeare's imagination, the boldest was making Birnam Wood march to Dunsinane;[1] creating a wood where there never was a shrub; a wood in Scotland! ha! ha! ha!" And he also observed, that "the clannish slavery of the Highlands of Scotland was the single exception to Milton's remark of 'The mountain nymph, sweet Liberty,'[2] being worshiped in all hilly countries."—"When I was at Inverary," said he, "on a visit to my old friend, Archibald, Duke of Argyle, his dependents congratulated me on being such a favorite of his Grace. I said, 'It is then, gentlemen, truly lucky for me; for if I had displeased the Duke, and he had wished it, there is not a Campbell among you but would have been ready to bring John Wilkes's head to him in a charger. It would have been only

> Off with his head! So much for Aylesbury.'[3]

I was then member for Aylesbury." * * *

Mr. Arthur Lee mentioned some Scotch who had taken possession of a barren part of America, and wondered why they should choose it. JOHNSON. "Why, Sir, all barrenness is comparative. The *Scotch* would not know it to be barren." BOSWELL. "Come, come, he is flattering the English. You have now been in Scotland, Sir, and say if you did not see meat and drink enough there." JOHNSON. "Why yes, Sir; meat and drink enough to give the inhabitants sufficient strength to run away from home." All these quick and lively sallies were said sportively, quite in jest, and with a smile, which showed that he meant only wit. Upon this topic he and Mr. Wilkes could perfectly assimilate; here was a bond of union between them, and I was conscious that as both of them had visited Caledonia, both were fully satisfied of the strange narrow ignorance of those who imagine that it is a land of famine. But they amused themselves with persevering in the old jokes. When I claimed a superiority for Scotland over England in one respect, that no man can be arrested there for a debt merely because another swears it against

---

9. *An Essay on Criticism* 1.66–67.
1. *Macbeth* 5.5.30–52.
2. *L'Allegro,* line 36.

3. "Off with his head! So much for Buckingham." A line in Cibber's version of Shakespeare's *Richard III.* "Charger": platter.

him; but there must first be the judgment of a court of law ascertaining its justice; and that a seizure of the person, before judgment is obtained, can take place only if his creditor should swear that he is about to fly from the country, or, as it is technically expressed, is *in meditatione fugae:* WILKES. "That, I should think, may be safely sworn of all the Scotch nation." JOHNSON (to Mr. Wilkes). "You must know, Sir, I lately took my friend Boswell and showed him genuine civilized life in an English provincial town. I turned him loose at Lichfield, my native city, that he might see for once real civility: for you know he lives among savages in Scotland, and among rakes in London." WILKES. "Except when he is with grave, sober, decent people like you and me." JOHNSON (smiling). "And we ashamed of him."

They were quite frank and easy. Johnson told the story of his asking Mrs. Macaulay to allow her footman to sit down with them, to prove the ridiculousness of the argument for the equality of mankind; and he said to me afterwards, with a nod of satisfaction, "You saw Mr. Wilkes acquiesced." * * *

This record, though by no means so perfect as I could wish, will serve to give a notion of a very curious interview, which was not only pleasing at the time, but had the agreeable and benignant effect of reconciling any animosity and sweetening any acidity, which in the various bustle of political contest, had been produced in the minds of two men, who, though widely different, had so many things in common—classical learning, modern literature, wit, and humor, and ready repartee—that it would have been much to be regretted if they had been forever at a distance from each other.

Mr. Burke gave me much credit for this successful "negotiation"; and pleasantly said that there was nothing to equal it in the whole history of the *Corps Diplomatique.* * * *

[DREAD OF SOLITUDE]

[*1777*] I talked to him of misery being "the doom of man" in this life, as displayed in his *Vanity of Human Wishes.* Yet I observed that things were done upon the supposition of happiness; grand houses were built, fine gardens were made, splendid places of public amusement were contrived, and crowded with company. JOHNSON. "Alas, Sir, these are all only struggles for happiness. When I first entered Ranelagh,[4] it gave an expansion and gay sensation to my mind, such as I never experienced anywhere else. But, as Xerxes wept when he viewed his immense army, and considered that not one of that great multitude would be alive a hundred years afterwards, so it went to my heart to consider that there was not one in all that brilliant circle that was not afraid to go home and think; but that the thoughts of each individual there, would be distressing when alone." * * *

["A BOTTOM OF GOOD SENSE." BET FLINT. "CLEAR YOUR MIND OF CANT"]

[*1781*] Talking of a very respectable author, he told us a curious circumstance in his life, which was that he had married a printer's devil.[5] REYNOLDS. "A printer's devil, Sir! Why, I thought a printer's devil was a creature with a

---

4. Pleasure gardens in Chelsea, where concerts were held, fireworks displayed, and food and drink sold.

5. Apprentice in a print shop.

black face and in rags." JOHNSON. "Yes, Sir. But I suppose, he had her face washed, and put clean clothes on her." Then looking very serious, and very earnest: "And she did not disgrace him; the woman had a bottom of good sense." The word *bottom* thus introduced was so ludicrous when contrasted with his gravity, that most of us could not forbear tittering and laughing; though I recollect that the Bishop of Killaloe kept his countenance with perfect steadiness, while Miss Hannah More[6] slyly hid her face behind a lady's back who sat on the same settee with her. His pride could not bear that any expression of his should excite ridicule, when he did not intend it; he therefore resolved to assume and exercise despotic power, glanced sternly around, and called out in a strong tone, "Where's the merriment?" Then collecting himself, and looking awful, to make us feel how he could impose restraint, and as it were searching his mind for a still more ludicrous word, he slowly pronounced, "I say the *woman* was *fundamentally* sensible"; as if he had said, "hear this now, and laugh if you dare." We all sat composed as at a funeral. * * *

He gave us an entertaining account of Bet Flint, a woman of the town, who, with some eccentric talents and much effrontery, forced herself upon his acquaintance. "Bet," said he, "wrote her own Life in verse, which she brought to me, wishing that I would furnish her with a Preface to it" (laughing). "I used to say of her that she was generally slut and drunkard; occasionally, whore and thief. She had, however, genteel lodgings, a spinnet on which she played, and a boy that walked before her chair. Poor Bet was taken up on a charge of stealing a counterpane, and tried at the Old Bailey. Chief Justice ———, who loved a wench, summed up favorably, and she was acquitted. After which Bet said, with a gay and satisfied air, 'Now that the counterpane is *my own*, I shall make a petticoat of it.' " * * *

[1783] I have no minute of any interview with Johnson till Thursday, May 15, when I find what follows: BOSWELL. "I wish much to be in Parliament, Sir." JOHNSON. "Why, Sir, unless you come resolved to support any administration, you would be the worse for being in Parliament, because you would be obliged to live more expensively." BOSWELL. "Perhaps, Sir, I should be the less happy for being in Parliament. I never would sell my vote, and I should be vexed if things went wrong." JOHNSON. "That's cant,[7] Sir. It would not vex you more in the house than in the gallery: public affairs vex no man." BOSWELL. "Have not they vexed yourself a little, Sir? Have not you been vexed by all the turbulence of this reign, and by that absurd vote of the House of Commons, 'That the influence of the Crown has increased, is increasing, and ought to be diminished?' " JOHNSON. "Sir, I have never slept an hour less, nor eat an ounce less meat. I would have knocked the factious dogs on the head, to be sure; but I was not *vexed*." BOSWELL. "I declare, Sir, upon my honor, I did imagine I was vexed, and took a pride in it; but it *was*, perhaps, cant; for I own I neither ate less, nor slept less." JOHNSON. "My dear friend, clear your *mind* of cant. You may *talk* as other people do: you may say to a man, 'Sir, I am your most humble servant.' You are *not* his most humble servant. You may say, 'These are bad times; it is a melancholy thing to be reserved to such times.' You don't mind the times. You tell a man, 'I

---

6. Blue-stocking and religious writer (1745–1833), one of the promoters of the Sunday School movement.

7. "A whining pretension to goodness in formal and affected terms" (Johnson's *Dictionary*).

am sorry you had such bad weather the last day of your journey, and were so much wet.' You don't care sixpence whether he is wet or dry. You may *talk* in this manner; it is a mode of talking in society: but don't *think* foolishly." * * *

[JOHNSON PREPARES FOR DEATH]

My anxious apprehensions at parting with him this year proved to be but too well founded; for not long afterwards he had a dreadful stroke of the palsy, of which there are very full and accurate accounts in letters written by himself, to show with what composure of mind, and resignation to the Divine Will, his steady piety enabled him to behave. * * *

Two days after he wrote thus to Mrs. Thrale:

"On Monday, the 16th, I sat for my picture, and walked a considerable way with little inconvenience. In the afternoon and evening I felt myself light and easy, and began to plan schemes of life. Thus I went to bed, and in a short time waked and sat up, as has been long my custom, when I felt a confusion and indistinctness in my head, which lasted, I suppose, about half a minute. I was alarmed, and prayed God that however he might afflict my body, he would spare my understanding. This prayer, that I might try the integrity of my faculties, I made in Latin verse. The lines were not very good, but I knew them not to be very good: I made them easily, and concluded myself to be unimpaired in my faculties.

"Soon after I perceived that I had suffered a paralytic stroke, and that my speech was taken from me. I had no pain, and so little dejection in this dreadful state, that I wondered at my own apathy, and considered that perhaps death itself, when it should come, would excite less horror than seems now to attend it.

"In order to rouse the vocal organs, I took two drams. Wine has been celebrated for the production of eloquence. I put myself into violent motion, and I think repeated it; but all was vain. I then went to bed and strange as it may seem, I think, slept. When I saw light, it was time to contrive what I should do. Though God stopped my speech, he left me my hand; I enjoyed a mercy which was not granted to my dear friend Lawrence,[8] who now perhaps overlooks me as I am writing, and rejoices that I have what he wanted. My first note was necessarily to my servant, who came in talking, and could not immediately comprehend why he should read what I put into his hands.

"I then wrote a card to Mr. Allen,[9] that I might have a discreet friend at hand, to act as occasion should require. In penning this note, I had some difficulty; my hand, I knew not how nor why, made wrong letters. I then wrote to Dr. Taylor to come to me, and bring Dr. Heberden; and I sent to Dr. Brocklesby, who is my neighbor.[1] My physicians are very friendly, and give me great hopes; but you may imagine my situation. I have so far recovered my vocal powers as to repeat the Lord's Prayer

8. Dr. Thomas Lawrence, president of the Royal College of Physicians and Johnson's own doctor, had died paralyzed shortly before this was written.
9. Edmund Allen, a printer, Johnson's landlord
and neighbor.
1. These two physicians attended Johnson on his deathbed.

with no very imperfect articulation. My memory, I hope, yet remains as it was; but such an attack produces solicitude for the safety of every faculty." * * *

[1784] To Mr. Henry White, a young clergyman, with whom he now formed an intimacy, so as to talk to him with great freedom, he mentioned that he could not in general accuse himself of having been an undutiful son. "Once, indeed," said he, "I was disobedient; I refused to attend my father to Uttoxeter market. Pride was the source of that refusal, and the remembrance of it was painful. A few years ago, I desired to atone for this fault; I went to Uttoxeter in very bad weather, and stood for a considerable time bareheaded in the rain, on the spot where my father's stall used to stand. In contrition I stood, and I hope the penance was expiatory."

"I told him," says Miss Seward,[2] "in one of my latest visits to him, of a wonderful learned pig, which I had seen at Nottingham; and which did all that we have observed exhibited by dogs and horses. The subject amused him. 'Then,' said he, 'the pigs are a race unjustly calumniated. *Pig* has, it seems, not been wanting to *man,* but *man* to *pig.* We do not allow *time* for his education, we kill him at a year old.' Mr. Henry White, who was present, observed that if this instance had happened in or before Pope's time, he would not have been justified in instancing the swine as the lowest degree of groveling instinct.[3] Dr. Johnson seemed pleased with the observation, while the person who made it proceeded to remark that great torture must have been employed, ere the indocility of the animal could have been subdued. 'Certainly,' said the Doctor; 'but,' turning to me, 'how old is your pig?' I told him, three years old. 'Then,' said he, 'the pig has no cause to complain; he would have been killed the first year if he had not been *educated,* and protracted existence is a good recompense for very considerable degrees of torture.' "

[JOHNSON FACES DEATH]

As Johnson had now very faint hopes of recovery, and as Mrs. Thrale was no longer devoted to him, it might have been supposed that he would naturally have chosen to remain in the comfortable house of his beloved wife's daughter,[4] and end his life where he began it. But there was in him an animated and lofty spirit, and however complicated diseases might depress ordinary mortals, all who saw him, beheld and acknowledged the *invictum animum Catonis.*[5] Such was his intellectual ardor even at this time that he said to one friend, "Sir, I look upon every day to be lost, in which I do not make a new acquaintance"; and to another, when talking of his illness, "I will be conquered; I will not capitulate." And such was his love of London, so high a relish had he of its magnificent extent, and variety of intellectual entertainment, that he languished when absent from it, his mind having become quite luxurious from the long habit of enjoying the metropolis; and, therefore, although at Lichfield, surrounded with friends, who loved and revered him, and for whom he had a very sincere affection, he still found

2. Anna Seward, "the Swan of Lichfield," a poet.
3. *An Essay on Man* 1.221.
4. Lucy Porter.

5. The unconquered soul of Cato (Latin). An adaptation of a phrase in Horace's *Odes* 2.1.24.

that such conversation as London affords, could be found nowhere else. These feelings, joined, probably, to some flattering hopes of aid from the eminent physicians and surgeons in London, who kindly and generously attended him without accepting fees, made him resolve to return to the capital. * * * Death had always been to him an object of terror; so that, though by no means happy, he still clung to life with an eagerness at which many have wondered. At any time when he was ill, he was very much pleased to be told that he looked better. An ingenious member of the Eumelian Club[6] informs me that upon one occasion when he said to him that he saw health returning to his cheek, Johnson seized him by the hand and exclaimed, "Sir, you are one of the kindest friends I ever had." * * *

Dr. Heberden, Dr. Brocklesby, Dr. Warren, and Dr. Butter, physicians, generously attended him, without accepting any fees, as did Mr. Cruikshank, surgeon; and all that could be done from professional skill and ability was tried, to prolong a life so truly valuable. He himself, indeed, having, on account of his very bad constitution, been perpetually applying himself to medical inquiries, united his own efforts with those of the gentlemen who attended him; and imagining that the dropsical collection of water which oppressed him might be drawn off by making incisions in his body, he, with his usual resolute defiance of pain, cut deep, when he thought that his surgeon had done it too tenderly.

About eight or ten days before his death, when Dr. Brocklesby paid him his morning visit, he seemed very low and desponding, and said, "I have been as a dying man all night." He then emphatically broke out in the words of Shakespeare:

> "Canst thou not minister to a mind diseased;
> Pluck from the memory a rooted sorrow,
> Raze out the written troubles of the brain,
> And with some sweet oblivious antidote
> Cleanse the stuffed bosom of that perilous stuff
> Which weighs upon the heart?"

To which Dr. Brocklesby readily answered, from the same great poet:

> "Therein the patient
> Must minister to himself."[7]

Johnson expressed himself much satisfied with the application. * * *

Amidst the melancholy clouds which hung over the dying Johnson, his characteristical manner showed itself on different occasions.

When Dr. Warren, in the usual style, hoped that he was better; his answer was, "No, Sir; you cannot conceive with what acceleration I advance towards death."

A man whom he had never seen before was employed one night to sit up with him. Being asked next morning how he liked his attendant, his answer was, "Not at all, Sir: the fellow's an idiot; he is as awkward as a turnspit[8] when first put into the wheel, and as sleepy as a dormouse."

Mr. Windham[9] having placed a pillow conveniently to support him, he

---

6. A club to which Boswell and Reynolds belonged.
7. *Macbeth* 5.3.40–46.
8. A dog kept to turn the roasting-spit by running

within a tread-wheel connected to it (*NED*).
9. William Windham, one of Johnson's younger friends, later a Member of Parliament.

thanked him for his kindness, and said, "That will do—all that a pillow can do." * * *

Johnson, with that native fortitude, which, amidst all his bodily distress and mental sufferings, never forsook him, asked Dr. Brocklesby, as a man in whom he had confidence, to tell him plainly whether he could recover. "Give me," said he, "a direct answer." The Doctor having first asked him if he could bear the whole truth, which way soever it might lead, and being answered that he could, declared that, in his opinion, he could not recover without a miracle. "Then," said Johnson, "I will take no more physic, not even my opiates; for I have prayed that I may render up my soul to God unclouded." In this resolution he persevered, and, at the same time, used only the weakest kinds of sustenance. Being pressed by Mr. Windham to take somewhat more generous nourishment, lest too low a diet should have the very effect which he dreaded, by debilitating his mind, he said, "I will take anything but inebriating sustenance."

The Reverend Mr. Strahan,[1] who was the son of his friend, and had been always one of his great favorites, had, during his last illness, the satisfaction of contributing to soothe and comfort him. That gentleman's house, at Islington, of which he is Vicar, afforded Johnson, occasionally and easily, an agreeable change of place and fresh air; and he attended also upon him in town in the discharge of the sacred offices of his profession.

Mr. Strahan has given me the agreeable assurance that, after being in much agitation, Johnson became quite composed, and continued so till his death.

Dr. Brocklesby, who will not be suspected of fanaticism, obliged me with the following account:

> "For some time before his death, all his fears were calmed and absorbed by the prevalence of his faith, and his trust in the merits and *propitiation* of Jesus Christ." * * *

Johnson having thus in his mind the true Christian scheme, at once rational and consolatory, uniting justice and mercy in the Divinity, with the improvement of human nature, previous to his receiving the Holy Sacrament in his apartment, composed and fervently uttered this prayer:

> "Almighty and most merciful Father, I am now as to human eyes, it seems, about to commemorate, for the last time, the death of thy Son Jesus Christ, our Saviour and Redeemer. Grant, O Lord, that my whole hope and confidence may be in his merits, and thy mercy; enforce and accept my imperfect repentance; make this commemoration available to the confirmation of my faith, the establishment of my hope, and the enlargement of my charity; and make the death of thy Son Jesus Christ effectual to my redemption. Have mercy upon me, and pardon the multitude of my offenses. Bless my friends; have mercy upon all men. Support me, by thy Holy Spirit, in the days of weakness, and at the hour of death; and receive me, at my death, to everlasting happiness, for the sake of Jesus Christ. Amen."

---

1. The Reverend George Strahan (pronounced *Strawn*), who later published Johnson's *Prayers and Meditations*.

Having * * * made his will on the 8th and 9th of December, and settled all his worldly affairs, he languished till Monday, the 13th of that month, when he expired, about seven o'clock in the evening, with so little apparent pain that his attendants hardly perceived when his dissolution took place. * * *

1791

FRANCES BURNEY
1752–1840

People have often made the mistake of underestimating Frances Burney. In person, as in her writing, she seemed a proper, self-effacing lady. Many readers still call her "Fanny," as if familiarity could make her harmless. But she saw through such poses. Sir Joshua Reynolds said that "if he was conscious to himself of any trick, or any affectation, there is nobody he should so much fear as this little Burney!" And Samuel Johnson teased her by claiming that "your shyness, & slyness, & pretending to know nothing, never took *me* in, whatever you may do with others. *I* always knew you for a *toadling!*" (according to legend, little toads may look submissive but actually carry poison). Although her writing crackles with humor, it can be relentless—and sometimes cruel—in exposing bad manners or a selfish heart.

She learned quite young how to hide in a crowd. Devoted daughter of Charles Burney, a popular teacher and historian of music, Frances grew up in a large family that gave her many opportunities to study character and mix discreetly in society. Her first novel, *Evelina, or A Young Lady's Entrance into the World* (1778), was written in secret and published anonymously. But delighted readers, including Johnson, Burke, and Hester Thrale, soon found her out and sang her praises; and a second novel, *Cecilia* (1782), confirmed her reputation. Her home life was less happy, however; she and her stepmother disliked each other, and she fell in love with a young clergyman who never got around to proposing. In 1786, to please her father, she accepted a place as a lady-in-waiting at court, where the paralyzing etiquette and lack of independence tormented her for the next five years, until she finally managed to resign. At forty-one she married a French émigré, General Alexandre Gabriel-Jean-Baptiste d'Arblay. Despite the disapproval of her father—d'Arblay was penniless, Catholic, and politically liberal—the marriage was happy. Madame d'Arblay soon bore a son, and her novel *Camilla* (1796) brought in good money. When she joined her husband in France, in 1802, the Napoleonic wars prevented them from returning to England for ten years; the pain of an outcast dominates her last novel, *The Wanderer, or Female Difficulties* (1814). But she never stopped writing, producing a doctored version of her father's *Memoirs* (1832) and more of the diaries and letters that, edited after her death by a niece, made her famous again.

Burney wrote all her life—not only novels and plays but perpetual letters and journals, recording whatever she saw for friends and family as well as herself. Even the most informal pages display her gifts: a knack for catching character, a wonderful ear for dialogue, wry humor, and a swift pace that carries the reader along from moment to moment. Her special subject is embarrassment—often her own. In scenes like her flight from the king, where she is torn between opposite notions of the right thing to do, shame and comedy mingle. But these trepidations can also be incredibly painful, as in her gripping account of a mastectomy. Despite her propriety, Burney looks at the world and its institutions with the clear eyes of an outsider, aware of the gaps between what people say and what they do. She frees herself to write with utter honesty by pretending, at first, that nobody is going to read her. But her private thoughts are reported so fully and faithfully that, in the end, every reader can share them.

From The Journal and Letters

[FIRST JOURNAL ENTRY]

Poland Street, London, March 27, 1768[1]

To have some account of my thoughts, manners, acquaintance & actions, when the hour arrives in which time is more nimble than memory, is the reason which induces me to keep a journal: a journal in which I must confess my *every* thought, must open my whole heart! But a thing of this kind ought to be addressed to somebody—I must imagine myself to be talking—talking to the most intimate of friends—to one in whom I should take delight in confiding, & remorse in concealment: but who must this friend be?—to make choice of one to whom I can but *half* rely, would be to frustrate entirely the intention of my plan. The only one I could wholly, totally confide in, lives in the same house with me, & not only never *has*, but never *will*, leave me one secret *to* tell her.[2] To whom, then, *must* I dedicate my wonderful, surprising & interesting adventures?—to *whom* dare I reveal my private opinion of my nearest relations? the secret thoughts of my dearest friends? my own hopes, fears, reflections & dislikes?—Nobody!

To Nobody, then, will I write my journal! since to Nobody can I be wholly unreserved—to Nobody can I reveal every thought, every wish of my heart, with the most unlimited confidence, the most unremitting sincerity to the end of my life! For what chance, what accident can end my connections with Nobody? No secret *can* I conceal from No—body, & to No—body can I be *ever* unreserved. Disagreement cannot stop our affection, time itself has no power to end our friendship. The love, the esteem I entertain for Nobody, No-body's self has not power to destroy. From Nobody I have nothing to fear, the secrets sacred to friendship, Nobody will not reveal, when the affair is doubtful, Nobody will not look towards the side least favorable—.

I will suppose you, then, to be my best friend; tho' God forbid you ever should! my dearest companion—& a romantick girl, for mere oddity may perhaps be more sincere—more *tender*—than if you were a friend in propria personæ[3]—in as much as imagination often exceeds reality. In your breast my errors may create pity without exciting contempt; may raise your compassion, without eradicating your love.

From this moment, then, my dear girl—but why, permit me to ask, must a *female* be made Nobody? Ah! my dear, what were this world good for, *were* Nobody a female? And now I have done with *preambulation*.

---

1. This is the first page of Burney's first journal, begun when she was fifteen.
2. Burney's younger sister, Susanna. In 1773, when Burney spent the summer away from home,

she began a journal for her sister, and continued it off and on until 1800, when Susanna died.
3. In your own person.

[MR. BARLOW'S PROPOSAL]

May 28, 1775

About 2 o'clock, while I was dawdling in the study, & waiting for an opportunity to speak, we heard a rap at the door—& soon after, John came up, & said "A gentleman is below, who asks for Miss Burney,—Mr. Barlow."[4]

I think I was never more mad in my life—to have taken pains to avoid a private conversation so highly disagreeable to me, & at last to be forced into it at so unfavorable a juncture,—for I had now 2 letters from him, both unanswered & consequently open to his conjectures. I exclaimed "Lord!—how provoking! what shall I do?"

My father looked uneasy & perplexed:—he said something about not being hasty, which I did not desire him to explain, but only said as I left the room—

"Well, I must soon tell him I *have* answered his letter, & so send one tomorrow, & let him think it kept at the post office." In this determination, I went down stairs.—I saw my mother pass into the back parlor; which did not add to the *graciousness* of my reception of poor Mr. Barlow, who I found alone in the parlor. I was not sorry that none of the family were there, as I now began to seriously dread any protraction of this affair.

He came up to me, & with an air of *tenderness* & satisfaction, began some anxious enquiries about my health, but I interrupted him with saying "I fancy, sir, You have not received a letter I have written to you—I—"

"A letter?—no, ma'am!"

"You will have it, then, tomorrow, sir."

We were both silent for a minute or two, when he said, "In consequence, I presume, ma'am, of the one I—"

"Yes, sir!" cried I.

"And pray—ma'am—Miss Burney!—may I—beg to ask the contents? that is—the—the—" he could not go on.

"Sir—I—it was only—it was merely—in short, you will see it tomorrow."

"But if you would favor me with the contents now, I could perhaps answer it at once?"

"Sir, it requires no answer!"

A second silence ensued. I was really distressed myself to see *his* distress, which was very apparent. After some time, he stammered out something of *hoping*—& *beseeching*,—which, gathering more firmness, I announced—"I am much obliged to you, sir, for the great opinion you are pleased to have of me—but I should be sorry you should lose any more time upon my account—as I have no thoughts at all of changing my situation."

He seemed to be quite overset: having, therefore, so freely explained myself, I then asked him to sit down, & began to talk of the weather. When he had a little recovered himself, he drew a chair close to me, & began making most ardent professions of respect & regard, & so forth. I interrupted him, as soon as I could, & begged him to rest satisfied with my answer.

"*Satisfied?*" repeated he—"my dear ma'am—is that possible?"

4. Thomas Barlow had met Burney early in May and immediately wrote to declare that he loved and admired her. She did not reciprocate his feelings: "his language is stiff & uncommon, he has a great desire to please, but no elegance of manners; neither, though he may be very worthy, is he at all agreeable." Her family, however, approved of the match and encouraged her to accept him.

"Perhaps, sir," said I, "I ought to make some apologies for not answering your first letter—but really, I was so much surprised—upon so short an acquaintance."

He then began making excuses for having written but as to *short acquaintance,* he owned it was a reason for *me*—but for *him*—fifty years could not have more convinced him of my &c &c.

"You have taken a sudden, & far too partial idea of my character," answered I. "If you look round among your older acquaintance, I doubt not but you will very soon be able to make a better choice."

He shook his head: "I have seen, Madam, a great many ladies, it is true—but never—"

"You do me much honor," cried I, "but I must desire you would take no further trouble about me—for I have not, at present, the slightest thoughts of ever leaving this house."

"*At present?*" repeated he, eagerly,—"no, I would not expect it—I would not *wish* to precipitate—but in future—"

"Neither now or ever, sir," returned I, "have I any view of changing my situation."

"But surely—surely this can never be! so severe a resolution—you cannot mean it—it would be wronging all the world!"

"I am extremely sorry, sir, that you did not receive my letter—because it might have saved you this trouble."

He looked very much mortified, & said, in a dejected voice—"If there is any thing in me—in my connections—or in my situation in life—which you wholly think unworthy of you—& beneath you—or if my character or disposition meet with your disapprobation—I will immediately forgo all—I will not—I would not—"

"No, indeed, sir," cried I, "I have neither seen or heard any thing of your character that was to your disadvantage—& I have no doubts of your worthiness—"

He thanked me, & seemed reassured; but renewed his solicitations in the most urgent manner. He repeatedly begged my permission to acquaint my family of the state of his affairs, & to abide by their decision—but I would not let him say two words following upon that subject. I told him that the answer I had written was a final one, & begged him to take it as such.

He remonstrated very earnestly. "This is the severest decision!—I am persuaded, madam, you cannot be so cruel?—Surely you must allow that the *social state* is what we were all meant for?—that we were created for one another?—that to form such a resolution is contrary to the design of our being?—"

"All this may be true,—" said I;—"I have nothing to say in contradiction to it—but you know there are many odd characters in the world—& I am one of them."

"O no, no, no,—that can never be!—but is it possible you can have so bad an opinion of the married state? It seems to me the *only* state for happiness!—"

"Well, sir, *you* are attached to the married life—*I* am to the single—therefore, *every man in his humor*[5]—do *you* follow *your* opinion,—& let *me* follow *mine.*"

5. Title of a play (1598) by Ben Jonson.

"But surely—is not this—*singular?*—"

"I give you leave, sir," cried I, laughing, "to think me singular—odd—queer—nay, even whimsical, if you please."

"But, my *dear* Miss Burney, only—"

"I entreat you, sir, to take my answer—you really pain me by being so urgent.—"

"That would not I do for the world!—I only beg you to suffer me—perhaps in future—"

"No, indeed; I shall never change—I do assure you you will find me very obstinate!"

He began to lament his own destiny. I grew extremely tired of saying so often the same thing;—but I could not absolutely turn him out of the house, & indeed he seemed so dejected & unhappy, that I made it my study to soften my refusal as much as I could without leaving room for future expectation.

About this time, my mother came in. We both rose.—I was horridly provoked at my situation—

"I am only come in for a letter," cried she,—"pray don't let me disturb you.—" & away she went.

Very obliging indeed!

She was no sooner gone, than Mr. Barlow began again the same story, & seemed determined not to give up his cause. He hoped, at least, that I would allow him to enquire after my health?—

"I must beg you, sir, to send me no more letters."

He seemed much hurt.

"You had better, sir, think of me no more—if you study your own happiness—"

"I *do* study my own happiness—more than I have ever had any probability of doing before—!"

"You have made an unfortunate choice, sir; but you will find it easier to forget it than you imagine. You have only to suppose I was not at Mr. Burney's on May Day—& it was a mere chance my being there—& then you will be—"

"But if I *could*—could I also forget seeing you at old Mrs. Burney's?—and if I did—can I forget that I see you now?—"

"O yes!—in 3 months time you may forget you ever knew me. You will not find it so difficult a task as you suppose."

"You have heard, ma'am, of an old man being growed young?—perhaps you believe *that?*—But you will not deny me leave to sometimes see you?—"

"My father, sir, is seldom,—hardly ever, indeed, at home—"

"I have never seen the Doctor—but I hope he would not refuse me permission to enquire after your health? I have no wish without his consent."

"Though I acknowledge myself to be *singular*, I would not have you think me either *affected* or *trifling*,—& therefore I must assure you that I am *fixed* in the answer I have given you; *unalterably* fixed."

*   *   *

He then took his leave:—returned back—took leave—returned again:—he had then a new petition, for then I took a more formal leave of him, expressing my good wishes for his welfare, in a sort of way that implied I expected never to see him again—he would fain have taken a more *tender* leave of me,—but I repulsed him with great surprise & displeasure. I did not, however, as he was so terribly sorrowful, refuse him my hand, which he had made sundry vain attempts to take in the course of our conversation; when I withdrew it, as I did presently, I rang the bell, to prevent him again returning from the door.

Though I was really sorry for the unfortunate & misplaced attachment which this young man professes for me, yet I could almost have *jumped* for joy when he was gone, to think that the affair was thus finally over.

Indeed I think it hardly possible for a woman to be in a more irksome situation, than when rejecting an honest man who is all humility, respect & submission, & who throws himself & his fortune at her feet.

* * *

The next day—a day the remembrance of which will be never erased from my memory—my father first spoke to me *in favor* of Mr. Barlow! & desired me not to be *peremptory* in the answer I was going to write.

I scarce made any answer—I was terrified to death—I felt the utter impossibility of resisting not merely my father's *persuasion*, but even his *advice*.—I felt, too, that I had no *argumentative* objections to make to Mr. Barlow, his character—disposition—situation—I knew nothing against—but O!—I felt he was no companion for my heart!—I wept like an infant—eat nothing—seemed as if already married—& passed the whole day in more misery than, merely on my own account, I ever did before in my life,—except upon the loss of my own beloved mother—& ever revered & most dear grandmother!

After supper, I went into the study, while my dear father was alone, to wish him good night, which I did as cheerfully as I could, though pretty evidently in dreadful uneasiness. When I had got to the door, he called me back, & asked me concerning a new mourning gown I had bought for the mourning of Queen Caroline[6]—he desired to know what it would come to, & as our allowance for clothes is not *sumptuous*, said he would assist Sukey & me, which he accordingly did, & affectionately embraced me, saying "I wish I could do more for thee, Fanny!" "O sir!—" cried I—"*I* wish for nothing!—only let me live with you!—"—"My life!" cried he, kissing me kindly, "Thee shalt live with me for ever, if thee wilt! Thou canst not think I meant to get rid of thee?"

"I could not, sir! I could not!" cried I, "I could not outlive such a thought—" I saw his dear eyes full of tears! a mark of his tenderness which I shall never forget!

"God knows"—continued he—"I wish not to part with my girls!—they are my greatest comfort!—only—do not be too hasty!—"

Thus relieved, restored to future hopes, I went to bed as light, happy & thankful as if escaped from destruction.[7]

---

6. A period of general mourning had been ordered after the death of George III's sister Caroline, the queen of Denmark.

7. Burney wrote Barlow a letter of refusal, and her father never mentioned him again.

["DOWN WITH HER, BURNEY!"]

Streatham, September 15, 1778[8]

I was then looking over the Life of Cowley, which he had himself given me to read, at the same time that he gave to Mrs. Thrale that of Waller.— They are now *printed*, though they will not be *published* for some time. But he bid me put it away.—"Do," cried he, "put away that now, & *prattle* with us;—I can't make this little Burney prattle,—& I am *sure* she prattles well.— but I shall teach her another lesson than to sit thus silent, before I have done with her."

"To *talk*," cried I, "is the *only* lesson I shall be backward to learn from you, sir."

"You shall give me," cried he, "a discourse 'pon the passions,—come, begin!—tell us the necessity of regulating them, watching over, & curbing them!—Did you ever read Norris's *Theory of Love?*"[9]

F.B. No, Sir.

Dr. J. Well, it is worth your reading. He will make you see that *inordinate* love is the root of all evil: inordinate love of *wealth*, brings on avarice; of *wine*, brings on intemperance;—of *power*, brings on cruelty;—& so on,—he deduces from *inordinate love* all human frailty.

Mrs. T. Tomorrow, sir, Mrs. Montagu[1] dines here! & then you will have talk enough.

Dr. Johnson began to seesaw, with a countenance strongly expressive of *inward fun*,—&, after enjoying it some time in silence, he suddenly, & with great animation, turned to me, & cried "*Down* with her, Burney!—*down* with her!—spare her not! attack her, fight her, & *down* with her at once!—*You* are a *rising* wit,—*she* is at the *top*,—& when *I* was beginning the world, & was nothing & nobody, the joy of my life was to fire at all the established wits!—& then, every body loved to hallow[2] me on;—but there is no game *now*, & *now*, every body would be glad to see me *conquered*: but *then*, when I was *new*,—to vanquish the great ones was all the delight of my poor little dear soul!—So at her, Burney!—at her, & *down* with her!"

O how we all hollowed![3] By the way, I must tell you that Mrs. Montagu is in very great estimation here, even with Dr. Johnson himself, when others do not praise her *improperly*: Mrs. Thrale ranks her as the *first of women*, in the literary way.

I should have told you, that Miss Gregory, daughter of the Gregory who wrote the letters, or *Legacy* of advice,[4] lives with Mrs. Montagu, & was invited to accompany her.

"Mark, now," said Dr. Johnson, "if I *contradict* her tomorrow; I am determined, let her say what she will, that I will *not* contradict her."

Mrs. T. Why, to be sure, Sir, you *did* put her a little out of countenance last

8. *Evelina* was published in January 1778 and enthusiastically received. After her authorship became known, Burney was invited to Streatham Park, the country house of Hector and Hester Lynch Thrale. Johnson spent much of his time there and was then writing his *Lives of the Poets*. He and Hester Thrale became fond of each other.

9. The Reverend John Norris had published *The Theory and Regulation of Love* in 1688.

1. Elizabeth Montagu, known as "Queen of the Blues" (or bluestockings), a group of intellectual women, was probably the most respected literary woman in England; she had written the famous *Essay on Shakespear* (1769).

2. A cry inciting hunters to the chase.

3. "To shout; to hoot" (Johnson's *Dictionary*).

4. John Gregory, *A Father's Legacy to His Daughters* (1774).

time she came,—yet you were neither rough, nor cruel, nor ill-natured,—
but still, when a lady *changes color*, we imagine her feelings are not quite
composed.

Dr. J. Why, madam, I won't answer that I sha'n't contradict her again, if she
provokes me as she did then; but a *less* provocation I will withstand. I believe
I am not high in her good graces already, & I begin (added he, laughing
heartily) to tremble for my admission into her new house! I doubt I shall
never see the inside of it!

Mrs. Montagu is building a most superb house.

Mrs. T. O, I warrant you! she *fears* you, indeed, but that, you know, is nothing
uncommon: & dearly I love to hear your *disquisitions*,—for certainly she is
the first woman, for literary knowledge, in England,—& if in *England* I hope
I may say in the *world!*

Dr. J. I believe you may, Madam. She diffuses more knowledge in her conversation than any woman I know,—or, indeed, *almost* any man.

Mrs. T. I declare *I* know *no* man equal to her, take away yourself & Burke,
for *that* art.—And *you*, who love magnificence, won't quarrel with her, as
everybody else does, for her love of finery.

Dr. J. No, I shall not quarrel with her upon that topic. (then, looking earnestly at *me*) "Nay," he added, "it's very handsome."

"What, sir?" cried I, amazed.

"Why your cap:—I have looked at it some time, & I like it much. It has
not that vile *bandeau*⁵ across it, which I have so often cursed."

Did you ever hear any thing so strange? *Nothing* escapes him. My Daddy
Crisp⁶ is not more minute in his attentions: nay, I think he is even *less* so.

Mrs. T. Well, sir, that bandeau you quarreled with was worn by every woman
at court the last Birth Day,⁷—& I observed that *all* the men found fault with
it.

Dr. J. The truth is,—women,—take them in general,—have *no* idea of
grace!—Fashion is *all* they think of;—I don't mean Mrs. Thrale & Miss Burney, when I talk of *women!*—*they* are goddesses!—& therefore I except them.

Mrs. T. Lady Ladd never wore the bandeau, & said she never would, because
it is unbecoming.

Dr. J. (*laughing*) Did not she? then is Lady Ladd a charming woman, & I
have yet hopes of entering into engagements with her!

Mrs. T. Well, as to that, I can't say,—but, to be sure, the only similitude *I*
have yet discovered in you, *is* in *size: there* you agree mighty well.

Dr. J. Why if *any* body could have worn the bandeau, it must have been Lady
Ladd, for there is *enough* of her to carry it off; but *you* are too *little* for any
thing ridiculous; that which seems *nothing* upon a Patagonian,⁸ will become
very *conspicuous* upon a Lilliputian; & of *you* there is so little in *all*, that one
single absurdity would swallow up *half* of you.

Some time after,—when we had all been a few minutes wholly silent, he
turned to me, & said "Come, Burney,—shall you & I *study our parts* against⁹
Mrs. Montagu comes?"

---

5. A narrow headband.
6. Samuel Crisp, an old family friend, had been a
mentor to Burney.
7. June 4, the king's birthday.

8. The Indians of Patagonia, whose average height
was more than six feet, were commonly thought to
be giants.
9. Before.

How would you be entertained, my dear Susy, if I could give you the *manner*, as well as *matter*, of the conversation of this greatest of men.

[A YOUNG AND AGREEABLE INFIDEL]

Bath, June 1780

Miss W—— is young and pleasing in her appearance, not pretty but agree-able in her face, and soft, gentle, and well-bred in her manners. Our con-versation, for some time, was upon the common Bath topics; but when Mrs. Lambart left us—called to receive more company—we went insensibly into graver matters.

As I soon found, by the looks and expressions of this young lady, that she was of a peculiar cast, I left all choice of subjects to herself, determined quietly to follow as she led; and very soon, and I am sure I know not how, we had for topics the follies and vices of mankind, and, indeed, she spared not for lashing them. The women she rather excused than defended, laying to the door of the men their faults and imperfections; but the men, she said, were all bad—all, in one word, and without exception, sensualists!

I stared much at a severity of speech for which her softness of manner had so ill-prepared me; and she, perceiving my surprise, said,

"I am sure I ought to apologize for speaking my opinion to you—you, who have so just and so uncommon a knowledge of human nature. I have long wished ardently to have the honor of conversing with you; but your party has, altogether, been regarded as so formidable, that I have not had courage to approach it."

I made—as what could I do else?—disqualifying speeches, and she then led to discoursing of happiness and misery: the latter she held to be the invariable lot of us all; and "one word," she added, "we have in our language, and in all others, for which there is never any essential necessity, and that is—*pleasure!*" And her eyes filled with tears as she spoke.

"How you amaze me!" cried I; "I have met with misanthropes before, but never with so complete a one; and I can hardly think I hear right when I see how young you are!"

She then, in rather indirect terms, gave me to understand that she was miserable at home, and in very direct terms, that she was wretched abroad; and openly said, that to affliction she was born, and in affliction she must die, for that the world was so vilely formed as to render happiness impossible for its inhabitants.

There was something in this freedom of repining that I could by no means approve, and, as I found by all her manner that she had a disposition to even respect whatever I said, I now grew very serious, and frankly told her that I could not think it consistent with either truth or religion to cherish such notions.

"One thing," answered she, "there is, which I believe might make me happy, but for that I have no inclination: it is an amorous disposition; but that I do not possess. I can make myself no happiness by intrigue."

"I hope not, indeed!" cried I, almost confounded by her extraordinary notions and speeches; "but, surely, there are worthier objects of happiness attainable!"

"No, I believe there are not, and the reason the men are happier than us, is because they are more sensual!"

"I would not think such thoughts," cried I, clasping my hands with an involuntary vehemence, "for worlds!"

The Misses C—— then interrupted us, and seated themselves next to us; but Miss W—— paid them little attention at first, and soon after none at all; but, in a low voice, continued her discourse with me, recurring to the same subject of happiness and misery, upon which, after again asserting the folly of ever hoping for the former, she made this speech:

"There may be, indeed, one moment of happiness, which must be the finding one worthy of exciting a passion which one should dare own to himself. That would, indeed, be a moment worth living for! but that can never happen—I am sure not to me—the men are so low, so vicious, so worthless! No, there is not one such to be found!"

What a strange girl! I could do little more than listen to her, from surprise at all she said.

"If, however," she continued, "I had your talents I could, bad as this world is, be happy in it. There is nothing, there is nobody I envy like you. With such resources as yours there can never be *ennui*; the mind may always be employed, and always be gay! Oh, if I could write as you write!"

"Try," cried I, "that is all that is wanting: try, and you will soon do much better things!"

"O no! I have tried, but I cannot succeed."

"Perhaps you are too diffident. But is it possible you can be serious in so dreadful an assertion as that you are never happy? Are you sure that some real misfortune would not show you that your present misery is imaginary?"

"I don't know," answered she, looking down, "perhaps it is so,—but in that case 'tis a misery so much the harder to be cured."

"You surprise me more and more," cried I; "is it possible you can so rationally see the disease of a disordered imagination, and yet allow it such power over your mind?"

"Yes, for it is the only source from which I draw any shadow of felicity. Sometimes when in the country, I give way to my imagination for whole days, and then I forget the world and its cares, and feel some enjoyment of existence."

"Tell me what is then your notion of felicity? Whither does your castle-building carry you?"

"O, quite out of the world—I know not where, but I am surrounded with sylphs, and I forget everything besides."

"Well, you are a most extraordinary character, indeed; I must confess I have seen nothing like you!"

"I hope, however, I shall find something like myself, and, like the magnet rolling in the dust, attract some metal as I go."

"That you may attract what you please, is of all things the most likely; but if you wait to be happy for a friend resembling yourself, I shall no longer wonder at your despondency."

"Oh!" cried she, raising her eyes in ecstasy, "could I find such a one!— male or female—for sex would be indifferent to me. With such a one I would go to live directly."

I half laughed, but was perplexed in my own mind whether to be sad or merry at such a speech.

"But then," she continued, "after making, should I lose such a friend, I would not survive."

"Not survive?" repeated I, "what can you mean?"

She looked down, but said nothing.

"Surely you cannot mean," said I, very gravely indeed, "to put a violent end to your life."

"I should not," said she, again looking up, "hesitate a moment."

I was quite thunderstruck, and for some time could not say a word; but when I did speak, it was in a style of exhortation so serious and earnest, I am ashamed to write it to you, lest you should think it too much.

She gave me an attention that was even respectful, but when I urged her to tell me by what right she thought herself entitled to rush unlicensed on eternity, she said, "By the right of believing I shall be extinct." I really felt horror-struck.

"Where, for heaven's sake," I cried, "where have you picked up such dreadful reasoning?"

"In Hume," said she; "I have read his *Essays*[1] repeatedly."

"I am sorry to find they have power to do so much mischief; you should not have read them, at least till a man equal to Hume in abilities had answered him. Have you read any more infidel writers?"

"Yes, Bolingbroke,[2] the divinest of all writers."

"And do you read nothing upon the right side?"

"Yes, the Bible, till I was sick to death of it, every Sunday evening to my mother."

"Have you read Beattie[3] on the Immutability of Truth?"

"No."

"Give me leave then to recommend it to you. After Hume's *Essays* you ought to read it. And even for lighter reading, if you were to look at Mason's 'Elegy on Lady Coventry,'[4] it might be of no disservice to you."

This was the chief of our conversation, which indeed made an impression upon me I shall not easily get rid of. A young and agreeable infidel is even a shocking sight, and with her romantic, flighty, and unguarded turn of mind, what could happen to her that could give surprise?

Poor misguided girl!

[ENCOUNTERING THE KING]

Kew Palace, Monday February 2, 1789

What an adventure had I this morning! one that has occasioned me the severest personal terror I ever experienced in my life.

---

1. The edition of David Hume's *Essays* published in 1777, the year after his death, included two essays previously suppressed: *Of Suicide*, which argues that suicide is not a transgression, and *Of the Immortality of the Soul*, which argues that immortality is unlikely and cannot be proved.
2. The philosophical *Letters, or Essays, addressed to Alexander Pope* (1754) by Henry St. John, Vis-count Bolingbroke, advocate a religion and ethics based on nature rather than on the teachings of the established church.
3. James Beattie's *Essay on Truth* (1770) attempts a refutation of Hume and other "infidels."
4. Burney quotes eight lines on immortality from William Mason's elegy *On the Death of a Lady* (1760).

Sir Lucas Pepys still persisting that exercise and air were absolutely necessary to save me from illness, I have continued my walks, varying my gardens from Richmond to Kew, according to the accounts I received of the movements of the king. For this I had her majesty's permission, on the representation of Sir Lucas.

This morning, when I received my intelligence of the king from Dr. John Willis,[5] I begged to know where I might walk in safety? "In Kew gardens," he said, "as the king would be in Richmond."

"Should any unfortunate circumstance," I cried, "at any time, occasion my being seen by his majesty, do not mention my name, but let me run off without call or notice."

This he promised. Everybody, indeed, is ordered to keep out of sight.

Taking, therefore, the time I had most at command, I strolled into the gardens. I had proceeded, in my quick way, nearly half the round, when I suddenly perceived, through some trees, two or three figures. Relying on the instructions of Dr. John, I concluded them to be workmen and gardeners; yet tried to look sharp, and in so doing, as they were less shaded, I thought I saw the person of his majesty!

Alarmed past all possible expression, I waited not to know more, but turning back, ran off with all my might. But what was my terror to hear myself pursued!—to hear the voice of the king himself loudly and hoarsely calling after me, "Miss Burney! Miss Burney!"

I protest I was ready to die. I knew not in what state he might be at the time; I only knew the orders to keep out of his way were universal; that the queen would highly disapprove any unauthorized meeting, and that the very action of my running away might deeply, in his present irritable state, offend him. Nevertheless, on I ran, too terrified to stop, and in search of some short passage, for the garden is full of little labyrinths, by which I might escape.

The steps still pursued me, and still the poor hoarse and altered voice rang in my ears:—more and more footsteps resounded frightfully behind me,— the attendants all running, to catch their eager master, and the voices of the two Doctor Willises loudly exhorting him not to heat himself so unmercifully.

Heavens, how I ran! I do not think I should have felt the hot lava from Vesuvius—at least not the hot cinders—had I so run during its eruption. My feet were not sensible that they even touched the ground.

Soon after, I heard other voices, shriller, though less nervous, call out "Stop! stop! stop!"

I could by no means consent; I knew not what was purposed, but I recollected fully my agreement with Dr. John that very morning, that I should decamp if surprised, and not be named.

My own fears and repugnance, also, after a flight and disobedience like this, were doubled in the thought of not escaping; I knew not to what I might be exposed, should the malady be then high, and take the turn of resentment. Still, therefore, on I flew; and such was my speed, so almost incredible to relate or recollect, that I fairly believe no one of the whole party could have overtaken me, if these words, from one of the attendants, had not reached me: "Doctor Willis begs you to stop!"

5. In 1788, two years after Burney joined the court, George III began to have fits of delirium or madness (today diagnosed as porphyria, a hereditary disease). He was kept in isolation at Kew, under the control of two physicians, Francis and John Willis.

"I cannot! I cannot!" I answered, still flying on, when he called out "You must, ma'am; it hurts the king to run."

Then, indeed, I stopped—in a state of fear really amounting to agony. I turned round, I saw the two doctors had got the king between them, and three attendants of Dr. Willis's were hovering about. They all slackened their pace, as they saw me stand still; but such was the excess of my alarm, that I was wholly insensible to the effects of a race which, at any other time, would have required an hour's recruit.[6]

As they approached, some little presence of mind happily came to my command; it occurred to me that, to appease the wrath of my flight, I must now show some confidence. I therefore faced them as undauntedly as I was able, only charging the nearest of the attendants to stand by my side.

When they were within a few yards of me, the king called out, "Why did you run away?"

Shocked at a question impossible to answer, yet a little assured by the mild tone of his voice, I instantly forced myself forward, to meet him, though the internal sensation, which satisfied me this was a step the most proper to appease his suspicions and displeasure, was so violently combated by the tremor of my nerves, that I fairly think I may reckon it the greatest effort of personal courage I have ever made.

The effort answered: I looked up, and met all his wonted benignity of countenance, though something still of wildness in his eyes. Think, however, of my surprise, to feel him put both his hands round my two shoulders, and then kiss my cheek!

I wonder I did not really sink, so exquisite was my affright when I saw him spread out his arms! Involuntarily, I concluded he meant to crush me; but the Willises, who have never seen him till this fatal illness, not knowing how very extraordinary an action this was from him, simply smiled and looked pleased, supposing, perhaps, it was his customary salutation!

I believe, however, it was but the joy of a heart unbridled, now, by the forms and proprieties of established custom and sober reason. To see any of his household thus by accident, seemed such a near approach to liberty and recovery, that who can wonder it should serve rather to elate than lessen what yet remains of his disorder!

He now spoke in such terms of his pleasure in seeing me, that I soon lost the whole of my terror; astonishment to find him so nearly well, and gratification to see him so pleased, removed every uneasy feeling, and the joy that succeeded, in my conviction of his recovery, made me ready to throw myself at his feet to express it.

What a conversation followed! When he saw me fearless, he grew more and more alive, and made me walk close by his side, away from the attendants, and even the Willises themselves, who, to indulge him, retreated. I own myself not completely composed, but alarm I could entertain no more.

Everything that came uppermost in his mind he mentioned; he seemed to have just such remains of his flightiness as heated his imagination without deranging his reason, and robbed him of all control over his speech, though nearly in his perfect state of mind as to his opinions.

6. Renewal of strength.

What did he not say!—He opened his whole heart to me,—expounded all his sentiments, and acquainted me with all his intentions.

The heads of his discourse I must give you briefly, as I am sure you will be highly curious to hear them, and as no accident can render of much consequence what a man says in such a state of physical intoxication. He assured me he was quite well—as well as he had ever been in his life; and then inquired how I did, and how I went on? and whether I was more comfortable? If these questions, in their implication, surprised me, imagine how that surprise must increase when he proceeded to explain them! He asked after the coadjutrix,[7] laughing, and saying "Never mind her!—don't be oppressed—I am your friend! don't let her cast you down!—I know you have a hard time of it—but don't mind her!"

Almost thunderstruck with astonishment, I merely curtsied to his kind "I am your friend," and said nothing.

Then presently he added, "Stick to your father—stick to your own family— let them be your objects."

How readily I assented!

Again he repeated all I have just written, nearly in the same words, but ended it more seriously: he suddenly stopped, and held me to stop too, and putting his hand on his breast, in the most solemn manner, he gravely and slowly said, "I will protect you!—I promise you that—and therefore depend upon me!"

I thanked him; and the Willises, thinking him rather too elevated,[8] came to propose my walking on. "No, no, no!" he cried, a hundred times in a breath; and their good humor prevailed, and they let him again walk on with his new companion.

He then gave me a history of his pages, animating almost into a rage, as he related his subjects of displeasure with them, particularly with Mr. Ernst, who he told me had been brought up by himself. I hope his ideas upon these men are the result of the mistakes of his malady.

Then he asked me some questions that very greatly distressed me, relating to information given him in his illness, from various motives, but which he suspected to be false, and which I knew he had reason to suspect; yet was it most dangerous to set anything right, as I was not aware what might be the views of their having been stated wrong. I was as discreet as I knew how to be, and I hope I did no mischief; but this was the worst part of the dialogue.

He next talked to me a great deal of my dear father, and made a thousand inquiries concerning his "History of Music." This brought him to his favorite theme, Handel;[9] and he told me innumerable anecdotes of him, and particularly that celebrated tale of Handel's saying of himself, when a boy, "While that boy lives, my music will never want a protector." And this, he said, I might relate to my father. Then he ran over most of his oratorios, attempting to sing the subjects of several airs and choruses, but so dreadfully hoarse that the sound was terrible.

7. Co-worker. Mrs. Schwellenberg, a German who had long served the queen, was keeper of the robes and tyrannized Burney, who was assistant keeper.
8. Heated or exhilarated.
9. From childhood George III had been a devotee of George Frederick Handel (1685–1759), the great German-English composer. George III, who loved German music, took a keen interest in Charles Burney's pioneering work, *A General History of Music*; the third and fourth volumes were just about to be published.

Dr. Willis, quite alarmed at this exertion, feared he would do himself harm, and again proposed a separation. "No! no! no!" he exclaimed, "not yet; I have something I must just mention first."

Dr. Willis, delighted to comply, even when uneasy at compliance, again gave way. The good king then greatly affected me. He began upon my revered old friend, Mrs. Delany;[1] and he spoke of her with such warmth—such kindness! "She was my friend!" he cried, "and I loved her as a friend! I have made a memorandum when I lost her—I will show it you."

He pulled out a pocketbook, and rummaged some time, but to no purpose. The tears stood in his eyes—he wiped them, and Dr. Willis again became very anxious. "Come, sir," he cried, "now do you come in and let the lady go on her walk,—come, now you have talked a long while, so we'll go in,—if your majesty pleases."

"No, no!" he cried, "I want to ask her a few questions;—I have lived so long out of the world, I know nothing!"

This touched me to the heart. * * * He then told me he was very much dissatisfied with several of his state officers, and meant to form an entire new establishment. He took a paper out of his pocketbook, and showed me his new list.

This was the wildest thing that passed; and Dr. John Willis now seriously urged our separating; but he would not consent; he had only three more words to say, he declared, and again he conquered.

He now spoke of my father, with still more kindness, and told me he ought to have had the post of master of the band,[2] and not that little poor musician Parsons, who was not fit for it: "But Lord Salisbury," he cried, "used your father very ill in that business, and so he did me! However, I have dashed out his name, and I shall put your father's in,—as soon as I get loose again!"

This again—how affecting was this!

"And what," cried he, "has your father got, at last? nothing but that poor thing at Chelsea?[3] O fie! fie! fie! But never mind! I will take care of him! I will do it myself!" Then presently he added, "As to Lord Salisbury, he is out already, as this memorandum will show you, and so are many more. I shall be much better served; and when once I get away, I shall rule with a rod of iron!"

This was very unlike himself, and startled the two good doctors, who could not bear to cross him, and were exulting at my seeing his great amendment, but yet grew quite uneasy at his earnestness and volubility.

Finding we now must part, he stopped to take leave, and renewed again his charges about the coadjutrix. "Never mind her!" he cried, "depend upon me! I will be your friend as long as I live!—I here pledge myself to be your friend!" And then he saluted[4] me again just as at the meeting, and suffered me to go on.

What a scene! how variously was I affected by it! but, upon the whole, how inexpressibly thankful to see him so nearly himself—so little removed from recovery!

---

1. Mary Delany, a kind old woman regarded by Burney as the "pattern of a perfect fine lady," had died the previous year.
2. Charles Burney had expected to be appointed master of the king's band in 1786, but the lord chamberlain, Lord Salisbury, appointed William Parsons instead, against the king's wishes.
3. The post of organist at Chelsea College.
4. Kissed.

[A MASTECTOMY]

Paris, March 22, 1812[5]

Separated as I have now so long—long been from my dearest father—brothers—sisters—nieces, & native friends, I would spare, at least, their kind hearts any grief for me but what they must inevitably feel in reflecting upon the sorrow of such an absence to one so tenderly attached to all her first and forever so dear & regretted ties—nevertheless, if they should hear that I have been dangerously ill from any hand but my own, they might have doubts of my perfect recovery which my own alone can obviate. And how can I hope they will escape hearing what has reached Seville to the south, and Constantinople to the east? from both I have had messages—yet nothing could urge me to this communication till I heard that M. de Boinville had written it to his wife, without any precaution, because in ignorance of my plan of silence.[6] Still I must hope it may never travel to my dearest father—But to you, my beloved Esther, who, living more in the world, will surely hear it ere long, to you I will write the whole history, certain that, from the moment you know any evil has befallen me your kind kind heart will be constantly anxious to learn its extent, & its circumstances, as well as its termination.

About August, in the year 1810, I began to be annoyed by a small pain in my breast, which went on augmenting from week to week, yet, being rather heavy than acute, without causing me any uneasiness with respect to the consequences: Alas, *"what was the ignorance?"* The most sympathizing of partners, however, was more disturbed: not a start, not a wry face, not a movement that indicated pain was unobserved, & he early conceived apprehensions to which I was a stranger. He pressed me to see some surgeon; I revolted from the idea, & hoped, by care & warmth, to make all succor unnecessary. Thus passed some months, during which Madame de Maisonneuve, my particularly intimate friend, joined with M. d'Arblay to press me to consent to an examination. I thought their fears groundless, and could not make so great a conquest over my repugnance. I relate this false confidence, now, as a warning to my dear Esther—my sisters & nieces, should any similar sensations excite similar alarm. M. d'A. now revealed his uneasiness to another of our kind friends, Mme. de Tracy, who wrote to me a long & eloquent letter upon the subject, that began to awaken very unpleasant surmises; & a conference with her ensued, in which her urgency & representations, aided by her long experience of disease, & most miserable existence by art, subdued me, and, most painfully & reluctantly, I ceased to object, & M. d'A. summoned a physician—M. Bourdois? Maria will cry;—No, my dear Maria, I would not give your beau frere[7] that trouble; not him, but Dr. Jouart, the physician of Miss Potts. Thinking but slightly of my statement, he gave me some directions that produced no fruit—on the contrary, I grew worse, & M. d'A. now would take no denial to my consulting M. Dubois, who had already attended & cured me in an abscess of which Maria, my dearest Esther, can give you the history. M. Dubois, the most celebrated

---

5. Burney (now Madame d'Arblay) sent this letter to Esther Burney, her sister, describing an operation performed the previous September.
6. Because Chastel de Boinville's wife was English, it was likely that news of the illness would spread to the Burney family in England.
7. Brother-in-law. Maria (or Marianne), Esther Burney's daughter, had married Antoine Bourdois, whose brother was a prominent French physician.

surgeon of France, was then appointed accoucheur to the empress, & already lodged in the Tuilleries,[8] & in constant attendance: but nothing could slacken the ardor of M. d'A. to obtain the first advice. Fortunately for his kind wishes, M. Dubois had retained a partial regard for me from the time of his former attendance, &, when applied to through a third person, he took the first moment of liberty, granted by a *promenade* taken by the empress, to come to me. It was now I began to perceive my real danger. M. Dubois gave me a prescription to be pursued for a month, during which time he could not undertake to see me again, & pronounced nothing—but uttered so many charges to me to be tranquil, & to suffer no uneasiness, that I could not but suspect there was room for terrible inquietude. My alarm was increased by the nonappearance of M. d'A. after his departure. They had remained together some time in the book room, & M. d'A. did not return— till, unable to bear the suspense, I begged him to come back. He, also, sought then to tranquilize me—but in words only; his looks were shocking! his features, his whole face displayed the bitterest woe. I had not, therefore, much difficulty in telling myself what he endeavored not to tell me—that a small operation would be necessary to avert evil consequences!—Ah, my dearest Esther, for this I felt no courage—my dread & repugnance, from a thousand reasons *besides* the pain, almost shook all my faculties, &, for some time, I was rather confounded & stupified than affrighted.—Direful, however, was the effect of this interview; the pains became quicker & more violent, & the hardness of the spot affected increased. I took, but vainly, my prescription, & every symptom grew more serious. At this time, M. de Narbonne spoke to M. d'A. of a surgeon of great eminence, M. Larrey, who had cured a polon- oise[9] lady of his acquaintance of a similar malady; &, as my horror of an operation was insuperable, M. de Narbonne strongly recommended that I should have recourse to M. Larrey. I thankfully caught at any hope; & another friend of M. d'A. gave the same counsel at the same instant, which other, M. Barbier Neuville, has an influence irresistible over this M. Larrey, to whom he wrote the most earnest injunction that he would use every exer- tion to rescue me from what I so much dreaded. M. Larrey came, though very unwillingly, & full of scruples concerning M. Dubois; nor would he give me his services till I wrote myself to state my affright at the delay of atten- dance occasioned by the present high office & royal confinement of M. Dubois, & requesting that I might be made over to M. Larrey. An answer such as might be expected arrived, & I was now put upon a new *regime,* & animated by the fairest hopes.—M. Larrey has proved one of the worthiest, most disinterested, & singularly excellent of men, endowed with real genius in his profession, though with an ignorance of the world & its usages that induces a *naïveté* that leads those who do not see him thoroughly to think him not alone simple, but weak. They are mistaken; but his attention & thoughts having exclusively turned one way, he is hardly awake any other. His directions seemed all to succeed, for though I had still cruel seizures of terrible pain, the fits were shorter & more rare, & my spirits revived, & I went out almost daily, & quite daily received in my apartment some friend or intimate acquaintance, contrarily to my usual mode of *sauvagerie*[1]—and what friends have I found! what kind, consoling, zealous friends during all

8. The royal palace in Paris. "Accoucheur": obste- trician.
9. Polish. Dominique-Jean Larrey, "Napoleon's

surgeon," is still remembered for his courage on the battlefield and his innovative procedures.
1. Unsociability.

this painful period! In fine, I was much better, & every symptom of alarm abated. My good M. Larrey was enchanted, yet so anxious, that he forced me to see le Docteur Ribe, the first anatomist, he said, in France, from his own fear lest he was under any delusion, from the excess of his desire to save me. I was as rebellious to the first visit of this famous anatomist as Maria will tell you I had been to that of M. Dubois, so odious to me was this sort of process: however, I was obliged to submit: & M. Ribe confirmed our best hopes———Here, my dearest Esther, I must grow brief, for my theme becomes less pleasant—Sundry circumstances, too long to detail, combined to counteract all my flattering expectations, & all the skill, & all the cares of my assiduous & excellent surgeon. * * * A physician was now called in, Dr. Moreau, to hear if he could suggest any new means: but Dr. Larrey had left him no resources untried. A formal consultation now was held, of Larrey, Ribe, & Moreau—&, in fine, I was formally condemned to an operation by all three. I was as much astonished as disappointed—for the poor breast was no where discolored, & not much larger than its healthy neighbor. Yet I felt the evil to be deep, so deep, that I often thought if it could not be dissolved, it could only with life be extirpated. I called up, however, all the reason I possessed, or could assume, & told them—that if they saw no other alternative, I would not resist their opinion & experience:—the good Dr. Larrey, who, during his long attendance had conceived for me the warmest friendship, had now tears in his eyes; from my dread he had expected resistance. He proposed again calling in M. Dubois. * * *—M. Dubois behaved extremely well, no pique intervened with the interest he had professed in my well-doing, & his conduct was manly & generous. It was difficult still to see him, but he appointed the earliest day in his power for a general & final consultation. I was informed of it only on the same day, to avoid useless agitation. He met here Drs. Larrey, Ribe, & Moreau. The case, I saw, offered uncommon difficulties, or presented eminent danger, but, the examination over, they desired to consult together. I left them—what an half hour I passed alone!—M. d'A. was at his office. Dr. Larrey then came to summon me. He did not speak, but looked very like my dear brother James, to whom he has a personal resemblance that has struck M. d'A. as well as myself. I came back, & took my seat, with what calmness I was able. All were silent, & Dr. Larrey, I saw, hid himself nearly behind my sofa. My heart beat fast: I saw all hope was over. I called upon them to speak. M. Dubois then, after a long & unintelligible harangue, from his own disturbance, pronounced my doom. I now saw it was inevitable, and abstained from any further effort. They received my formal consent, & retired to fix a day.

All hope of escaping this evil being now at an end, I could only console or employ my mind in considering how to render it less dreadful to M. d'A. M. Dubois had pronounced "il faut s'attendre à souffrir. Je ne veux pas vous trompez—Vous souffrirez—vous souffrirez *beaucoup*!—"[2] M. Ribe had *charged* me to cry! to withhold or restrain myself might have seriously bad consequences, he said. M. Moreau, in echoing this injunction, inquired whether I had cried or screamed at the birth of Alexander—Alas, I told him, it had not been possible to do otherwise; Oh then, he answered, there is no fear!—What terrible inferences were here to be drawn! I desired, therefore,

---

2. You must expect to suffer. I do not want to deceive you—you will suffer—you will suffer *greatly* (French). Operations were then performed without anesthetics.

that M. d'A. might be kept in ignorance of the day till the operation should be over. To this they agreed, except M. Larrey, with high approbation; M. Larrey looked dissentient, but was silent. M. Dubois protested he would not undertake to act, after what he had seen of the agitated spirits of M. d'A. if he were present; nor would he suffer me to know the time myself over night. I obtained with difficulty a promise of 4 hours warning, which were essential to me for sundry regulations.

From this time, I assumed the best spirits in my power, *to meet the coming blow;*—& support my too sympathizing partner. They would let me make no preparations, refusing to inform me what would be necessary; I have known, since, that Madame de Tessé, an admirable old friend of M. d'A, now mine, equally, & one of the first of her sex, in any country, for uncommon abilities, & nearly universal knowledge, had insisted upon sending all that might be necessary, & of keeping me in ignorance. M. d'A filled a closet with charpie,[3] compresses, & bandages—All that to *me* was owned, as wanting, was an armchair & some towels.—Many things, however, joined to the depth of my pains, assured me the business was not without danger. I therefore made my will—unknown, to this moment, to M. d'A. * * *

After sentence thus passed, I was in hourly expectation of a summons to execution; judge, then, my surprise to be suffered to go on full 3 weeks in the same state! M. Larrey from time to time visited me, but pronounced nothing, & was always melancholy. At length, M. d'A. was told that he waited himself for a summons! & that, a formal one, & in writing! *I* could not give one; a *consent* was my utmost effort. But poor M. d'A. wrote a desire that the operation, if necessary, might take place without further delay. In my own mind, I had all this time been persuaded there were hopes of a cure; why else, I thought, let me know my doom thus long? But here I must account for this apparently useless, & therefore cruel measure, though I only learnt it myself 2 months afterwards. M. Dubois had given his opinion that the evil was too far advanced for any remedy; that the cancer was already internally declared;[4] that I was inevitably destined to that most frightful of deaths, & that an operation would but accelerate my dissolution. Poor M. Larrey was so deeply affected by this sentence, that—as he has lately told me—he regretted to his soul ever having known me, & was upon the point of demanding a commission to the furthest end of France in order to force me into other hands. I had said, however, he remembered, once, that I would far rather suffer a quick end without, than a lingering life with this dreadfullest of maladies; he finally, therefore, considered it might be possible to save me by the trial, but that without it my case was desperate, & resolved to make the attempt. Nevertheless, the responsibility was too great to rest upon his own head entirely; & therefore he waited the formal summons.— In fine, one morning—the last of September, 1811, while I was still in bed, & M. d'A. was arranging some papers for his office—I received a letter written by M. de Lally to a journalist, in vindication of the honored memory of his father against the assertions of Madame du Deffand.[5] I read it aloud to my Alexanders,[6] with tears of admiration & sympathy, & then sent it by Alex to its excellent author, as I had promised the preceding evening. I then

---

3. Linen for surgical dressings.
4. Malignant. This diagnosis was probably incorrect.
5. M. de Lally's father had been executed for trea-

son in 1766; some letters written at the time by Mme du Deffand, who agreed with the verdict, were published in Paris in 1811.
6. Husband and son.

dressed, aided, as usual for many months, by my maid, my right arm being condemned to total inaction; but not yet was the grand business over, when another letter was delivered to me—another, indeed!—'twas from M. Larrey, to acquaint me that at 10 o'clock he should be with me, properly accompanied, & to exhort me to rely as much upon his sensibility & his prudence, as upon his dexterity & his experience; he charged to secure the absence of M. d'A.; & told me that the young physician who would deliver me this *announce*, would prepare for the operation, in which he must lend his aid; & also that it had been the decision of the consultation to allow me but two hours notice.—Judge, my Esther, if I read this unmoved!—yet I had to disguise my sensations & intentions from M. d'A.!—Dr. Aumont, the messenger & terrible herald, was in waiting; M. d'A. stood by my bed side; I affected to be long reading the note, to gain time for forming some plan, & such was my terror of involving M. d'A. in the unavailing wretchedness of witnessing what I must go through, that it conquered every other, & gave me the force to act as if I were directing some third person. * * * Sundry necessary works & orders filled up my time entirely till one o'clock. When all was ready——but Dr. Moreau then arrived, with news that M. Dubois could not attend till three. Dr. Aumont went away—& the coast was clear. This, indeed, was a dreadful interval. I had no longer any thing to do—I had only to think—TWO HOURS thus spent seemed never-ending. I would fain have written to my dearest father—to you, my Esther—to Charlotte, James, Charles—Amelia Lock—but my arm prohibited me. I strolled to the salon—I saw it fitted with preparations, & I recoiled—But I soon returned; to what effect disguise from myself what I must so soon know?—yet the sight of the immense quantity of bandages, compresses, sponges, lint——made me a little sick.—I walked backwards & forwards till I quieted all emotion, & became, by degrees, nearly stupid—torpid, without sentiment or consciousness;—& thus I remained till the clock struck three. A sudden spirit of exertion then returned—I defied my poor arm, no longer worth sparing, & took my long banished pen to write a few words to M. d'A.—& a few more for Alex, in case of a fatal result. These short billets I could only deposit safely, when the cabriolets[7]—one—two—three—four—succeeded rapidly to each other in stopping at the door. Dr. Moreau instantly entered my room, to see if I were alive. He gave me a wine cordial, & went to the salon. I rang for my maid & nurses—but before I could speak to them, my room, without previous message, was entered by 7 men in black, Dr. Larrey, M. Dubois, Dr. Moreau, Dr. Aumont, Dr. Ribe, & a pupil of Dr. Larrey, & another of M. Dubois. I was now awakened from my stupor—& by a sort of indignation—Why so many? & without leave?—But I could not utter a syllable. M. Dubois acted as commander in chief. Dr. Larrey kept out of sight; M. Dubois ordered a bedstead into the middle of the room. Astonished, I turned to Dr. Larrey, who had promised that an armchair would suffice; but he hung his head, & would not look at me. Two *old mattresses* M. Dubois then demanded, & an old sheet. I now began to tremble violently, more with distaste & horror of the preparations even than of the pain. These arranged to his liking, he desired me to mount the bedstead. I stood suspended, for a moment, whether I should not abruptly escape—I looked at the door, the windows—I felt desperate—but it was only

7. Carriages.

for a moment, my reason then took the command, & my fears & feelings struggled vainly against it. I called to my maid—she was crying, & the two nurses stood, transfixed, at the door. "Let those women all go!" cried M. Dubois. This order recovered me my voice—"No," I cried, "let them stay! *qu'elles restent!*" This occasioned a little dispute, that re-animated me. The maid, however, & one of the nurses ran off—I charged the other to approach, & she obeyed. M. Dubois now tried to issue his commands *en militaire*,[8] but I resisted all that were resistible—I was compelled, however, to submit to taking off my long robe de chambre,[9] which I had meant to retain—Ah, then, how did I think of my sisters!—not one, at so dreadful an instant, at hand, to protect—adjust—guard me—I regretted that I had refused Mme de Maisonneuve–Mme Chastel—no one upon whom I could rely—my departed angel![1]—how did I think of her!—how did I long—long for my Esther—my Charlotte!—My distress was, I suppose, apparent, though not my wishes, for M. Dubois himself now softened, & spoke soothingly. "Can *you*," I cried, "feel for an operation that, to *you*, must seem so trivial?"—"Trivial?" he repeated—taking up a bit of paper, which he tore, unconsciously, into a million of pieces, "*oui—c'est peu de chose—mais—*"[2] he stammered, & could not go on. No one else attempted to speak, but I was softened myself, when I saw even M. Dubois grow agitated, while Dr. Larrey kept always aloof, yet a glance showed me he was pale as ashes. I knew not, positively, then, the immediate danger, but everything convinced me danger was hovering about me, & that this experiment could alone save me from its jaws. I mounted, therefore, unbidden, the bedstead—& M. Dubois placed me upon the mattress, & spread a cambric handkerchief upon my face. It was transparent, however, & I saw, through it, that the bedstead was instantly surrounded by the 7 men & my nurse. I refused to be held; but when, bright through the cambric, I saw the glitter of polished steel—I closed my eyes. I would not trust to convulsive fear the sight of the terrible incision. A silence the most profound ensued, which lasted for some minutes, during which, I imagine, they took their orders by signs, & made their examination—Oh what a horrible suspension!—I did not breathe—& M. Dubois tried vainly to find any pulse. This pause, at length, was broken by Dr. Larrey, who, in a voice of solemn melancholy, said "Qui me tiendra ce sein?—"[3]

No one answered; at least not verbally; but this aroused me from my passively submissive state, for I feared they imagined the whole breast infected—feared it too justly—for, again through the cambric, I saw the hand of M. Dubois held up, while his forefinger first described a straight line from top to bottom of the breast, secondly a cross, & thirdly a circle; intimating that the WHOLE was to be taken off. Excited by this idea, I started up, threw off my veil, &, in answer to the demand "Qui me tiendra ce sein?" cried "C'est moi, monsieur!"[4] & I held my hand under it, & explained the nature of my sufferings, which all sprang from one point, though they darted into every part. I was heard attentively, but in utter silence, & M. Dubois then re-placed me as before, &, as before, spread my veil over my face. How vain, alas, my representation! immediately again I saw the fatal finger describe the

---

8. In military fashion. Most of the attending physicians had been army surgeons.
9. Dressing gown.
1. Susanna, Burney's favorite sister, had died in

1800.
2. Yes—it is not much—but— (French).
3. Who will hold this breast for me? (French).
4. *I* will! (French).

cross—& the circle. Hopeless, then, desperate, & self-given up, I closed once more my eyes, relinquishing all watching, all resistance, all interference, & sadly resolute to be wholly resigned.

My dearest Esther, & all my dears to whom she communicates this doleful ditty, will rejoice to hear that this resolution once taken, was firmly adhered to, in defiance of a terror that surpasses all description, & the most torturing pain. Yet—when the dreadful steel was plunged into the breast—cutting through veins—arteries—flesh—nerves—I needed no injunctions not to restrain my cries. I began a scream that lasted uninterruptedly during the whole time of the incision—& I almost marvel that it rings not in my ears still! so excruciating was the agony. When the wound was made, & the instrument was withdrawn, the pain seemed undiminished, for the air that suddenly rushed into those delicate parts felt like a mass of minute but sharp & forked poniards,[5] that were tearing the edges of the wound—but when again I felt the instrument—describing a curve—cutting against the grain, if I may so say, while the flesh resisted in a manner so forcible as to oppose & tire the hand of the operator, who was forced to change from the right to the left—then, indeed, I thought I must have expired. I attempted no more to open my eyes,—they felt as if hermetically shut, & so firmly closed, that the eyelids seemed indented into the cheeks. The instrument this second time withdrawn, I concluded the operation over. Oh no! presently the terrible cutting was renewed—& worse than ever, to separate the bottom, the foundation of this dreadful gland from the parts to which it adhered. Again all description would be baffled—yet again all was not over.—Dr. Larrey rested but his own hand, &—Oh heaven!—I then felt the knife rackling[6] against the breast bone—scraping it!—This performed, while I yet remained in utterly speechless torture, I heard the voice of Mr. Larrey (all others guarded a dead silence) in a tone nearly tragic, desire every one present to pronounce if any thing more remained to be done. The general voice was Yes—but the finger of Mr. Dubois—which I literally *felt* elevated over the wound, though I saw nothing, & though he touched nothing, so indescribably sensitive was the spot—pointed to some further requisition[7]—& again began the scraping!—and, after this, Dr. Moreau thought he discerned a peccant atom—and still, & still, M. Dubois demanded atom after atom. My dearest Esther, not for days, not for weeks, but for months I could not speak of this terrible business without nearly again going through it! I could not *think* of it with impunity! I was sick, I was disordered by a single question—even now, 9 months after it is over, I have a headache from going on with the account! & this miserable account, which I began 3 months ago, at least, I dare not revise, nor read, the recollection is still so painful.

To conclude, the evil was so profound, the case so delicate, & the precautions necessary for preventing a return so numerous, that the operation, including the treatment & the dressing, lasted 20 minutes! a time, for sufferings so acute, that was hardly supportable. However, I bore it with all the courage I could exert, & never moved, nor stopped them, nor resisted, nor remonstrated, nor spoke—except once or twice, during the dressings, to say "Ah Messieurs! que je vous plains!—"[8] for indeed I was sensible to the feeling

---

5. Daggers.
6. Raking (?).
7. Necessity. Surgical practice of the time dictated

that "the whole diseased structure" be cut out, no matter how long or painful the operation.
8. How I pity you! (French).

concern with which they all saw what I endured, though my speech was principally—*very* principally meant for Dr. Larrey. Except this, I uttered not a syllable, save, when so often they recommenced, calling out "Avertissez moi,[9] Messieurs! avertissez moi!—" Twice, I believe, I fainted; at least, I have two total chasms in my memory of this transaction, that impede my tying together what passed. When all was done, & they lifted me up that I might be put to bed, my strength was so totally annihilated, that I was obliged to be carried, & could not even sustain my hands & arms, which hung as if I had been lifeless; while my face, as the nurse has told me, was utterly colorless. This removal made me open my eyes—& I then saw my good Dr. Larrey, pale nearly as myself, his face streaked with blood, & its expression depicting grief, apprehension, & almost horror.

When I was in bed, my poor M. d'Arblay—who ought to write you himself his own history of this morning—was called to me—& afterwards our Alex.—

[M. D'ARBLAY'S POSTSCRIPT]

No! No my dearest & ever more dear friends, I shall not make a fruitless attempt. No language could convey what I felt in the deadly course of these seven hours. Nevertheless, every one *of you, my dearest dearest friends*, can guess, must even know it. Alexander had no less feeling, but showed more fortitude. He, perhaps, will be more able to describe to you, nearly at least, the torturing state of my poor heart & soul. Besides, I must own, to you, that these details which were, till just now, quite unknown to me, have almost killed me, & I am only able to thank God that this more than half angel has had the sublime courage to deny herself the comfort I might have offered her, to spare me, not the sharing of her excruciating pains, that was impossible, but the witnessing so terrific a scene, & perhaps the remorse to have rendered it more tragic. For I don't flatter myself I could have got through it—I must confess it.

Thank heaven! She is now surprisingly well, & in good spirits, & we hope to have many many still happy days. May that of peace soon arrive, and enable me to embrace better than with my pen my beloved & ever ever more dear friends of the town & country. Amen. Amen![1]

9. Give me warning! (French).
1. The wound healed without infection. Burney returned to England later in 1812 and lived for twenty-eight years.

Slavery and Freedom

In the early 1660s, when the events in Behn's *Oroonoko* are supposed to have taken place, England had just entered the slave trade. Ships took slaves from the West African coast (Guinea) to Surinam and Barbados, and later to Jamaica, in exchange for sugar. The trade grew quickly. In 1713 Great Britain was awarded the contract (*asiento*) to export slaves to the Spanish Indies. This was a risky business, but profits could be immense. Bristol, then Liverpool, developed into prosperous slave ports, trading manufactured goods to Africa for human cargo, which crossed the Atlantic on ships that returned to England with sugar and money. By the 1780s, when Britain shipped a third of a million slaves to the New World, the national economy depended on the trade.

The human cost was terrible. Although slavery was not new to Africa, the Middle Passage—the deadly voyage across the Atlantic—made it something unfamiliar, brutal, unendurable. Torn from their homes, slaves were often packed into tiny, spaces, with barely enough food, drink, and air to keep them alive. The former slave Olaudah Equiano, writing about his own experience, describes such a crossing. Those who survived to work on Caribbean sugar plantations were driven so hard that new shiploads were constantly needed to replace the dead (the situation was different in North America, where slaves lived on to reproduce and grow in numbers). Renamed and cut off from their roots, black people came to be identified merely by the color of their skin. It was convenient for owners to view them as less than human.

The loss of humanity rebounded on Britain as well. The English had long regarded themselves as a people uniquely devoted to liberty, guaranteed by Magna Carta since 1215. "*Britons* never will be slaves," James Thomson boasted in *Rule, Britannia*. But British rule meant slavery for others. The deep contradictions of this position were reflected in the political philosophy of John Locke and in William Blackstone's commentaries on English law. Though Locke maintained that all men were born free, he had himself invested in the slave trade and drafted *The Fundamental Constitutions of Carolina* (1669), which granted absolute power over slaves. And though Blackstone wrote that "a slave or negro, the moment he lands in England, falls under the protection of the laws" and thus becomes a freeman, he later added another clause: "though the master's right to his service may probably still continue" (1769). Some Britons, like James Boswell, argued that slavery had uplifted negroes by introducing them to Christianity and civilization. But other Britons were troubled and ashamed. Humanitarian feelings grew in strength throughout the later eighteenth century. The exchange of letters between the black writer Ignatius Sancho and the novelist Laurence Sterne displays their mutual sympathy for slaves. The cruel trade in victims, they thought, was a libel on human nature.

By the 1780s a wave of abolitionist fervor swept through Great Britain, led by the Quakers and, in Parliament, by William Wilberforce (1759–1833). Many poets, including William Cowper, joined the campaign. Despite a conservative backlash against the French Revolution, a bill abolishing the British slave trade became law in 1807. That did not, of course, put an end to illegal trade, let alone to slavery itself. The conflict between boasts of liberty and the enslavement of human beings passed from Britain to America, where its consequences would be written in blood. Yet the eighteenth century, which witnessed the high tide of the slave trade, also gave rise to the ideals of freedom, equality, and human rights that led to its doom.

IGNATIUS SANCHO *and* LAURENCE STERNE

Born on a slave ship, Ignatius Sancho (1729–1780) was brought to England as a child. His owners, three sisters in Greenwich, named him Sancho after Don Quixote's squire. At twenty he ran away to work as a butler in the household of the duke and duchess of Montagu. There he became a man of refinement, well versed in music, painting, and theater as well as writing, and he made the acquaintance of eminent people. Garrick once considered casting him as Othello or Oroonoko; Gainsborough painted his portrait; and Johnson may have intended to write his life. In 1773 he set up a grocery shop, specializing in tobacco. When his letters were published in 1782, two years after his death, one reviewer wrote that the book "presents to us the naked effusions of a negroe's heart, and shews it glowing with the finest philanthropy, and the purest affections."

In 1766 Sancho wrote a letter to Laurence Sterne (1713–1768), a clergyman whose brilliant and whimsical novel *The Life and Opinions of Tristram Shandy, Gentleman* had made a sensation when its first two volumes were published in 1759. Sterne was a country pastor who preached in York, a name he adopted—with a nod to Shakespeare—in publishing *The Sermons of Mr. Yorick* (Parson Yorick is also a character in *Tristram Shandy* and the narrator of Sterne's last novel, *A Sentimental Journey*). One of the sermons had especially touched Sancho because of its pity for slaves. In asking Sterne to write more on this topic, Sancho also imitates his style, in which frequent dashes express a mind always in motion and bursting with spontaneous feelings.

IGNATIUS SANCHO: A Letter to Laurence Sterne

July 21, 1766

Reverend Sir,

It would be an insult on your humanity (or perhaps look like it) to apologize for the liberty I am taking.—I am one of those people whom the vulgar and illiberal call "*Negurs*."—The first part of my life was rather unlucky, as I was placed in a family who judged ignorance the best and only security for obedience.—A little reading and writing I got by unwearied application.—The latter part of my life has been—thro' God's blessing, truly fortunate, having spent it in the service of one of the best families in the kingdom.—My chief pleasure has been books.—Philanthropy I adore.—How very much, good Sir, am I (amongst millions) indebted to you for the character of your amiable uncle Toby!—I declare, I would walk ten miles in the dog-days, to shake hands with the honest corporal.[1]—Your Sermons have touch'd me to the heart, and I hope have amended it, which brings me to the point.—In your tenth discourse, page seventy-eight, in the second volume—is this very affecting passage—"Consider how great a part of our species—in all ages down to this—have been trod under the feet of cruel and capricious tyrants, who would neither hear their cries, nor pity their distresses.—Consider slavery—what it is—how bitter a draught—and how many millions are made to drink it!"[2]—Of all my favorite authors, not one has drawn a tear in favor of

---

1. In *Tristram Shandy*, Corporal Trim is the orderly of Tristram's uncle Toby, a retired army officer who is memorably innocent and gentle.

2. From Sterne's sermon on Job in *The Sermons of Mr. Yorick* (1760).

my miserable black brethren—excepting yourself, and the humane author of *Sir George Ellison*.[3]—I think you will forgive me;—I am sure you will applaud me for beseeching you to give one half-hour's attention to slavery, as it is at this day practised in our West Indies.—That subject, handled in your striking manner, would ease the yoke (perhaps) of many—but if only of one—Gracious God!—what a feast to a benevolent heart!—and, sure I am, you are an epicurean in acts of charity.—You, who are universally read, and as universally admired—you could not fail—Dear Sir, think in me you behold the uplifted hands of thousands of my brother Moors.[4]—Grief (you pathetically observe) is eloquent;—figure to yourself their attitudes;—hear their supplicating addresses!—alas!—you cannot refuse.—Humanity must comply—in which hope I beg permission to subscribe myself,

Reverend Sir, &c.

IGN. SANCHO

LAURENCE STERNE: Reply to Sancho

July 27, 1766

There is a strange coincidence, Sancho, in the little events (as well as in the great ones) of this world: for I had been writing a tender tale of the sorrows of a friendless poor negro-girl, and my eyes had scarce done smarting with it, when your letter of recommendation in behalf of so many of her brethren and sisters, came to me—but why *her brethren?*—or your's, Sancho! any more than mine? It is by the finest tints, and most insensible gradations, that nature descends from the fairest face about St. James's,[1] to the sootiest complexion in Africa: at which tint of these, is it, that the ties of blood are to cease? and how many shades must we descend lower still in the scale, 'ere mercy is to vanish with them?—but 'tis no uncommon thing, my good Sancho, for one half of the world to use the other half of it like brutes, & then endeavor to make 'em so. For my own part, I never look *Westward* (when I am in a pensive mood at least) but I think of the burdens which our brothers and sisters are *there* carrying—& could I ease their shoulders from one ounce of 'em, I declare I would set out this hour upon a pilgrimage to Mecca for their sakes—which by the by, Sancho, exceeds your walk of ten miles, in about the same proportion, that a visit of humanity should one of mere form—however if you meant my Uncle Toby, more—he is your debtor.

If I can weave the tale I have wrote into the work I'm about—'tis at the service of the afflicted—and a much greater matter; for in serious truth, it casts a sad shade upon the world, that so great a part of it, are and have been so long bound in chains of darkness & in chains of misery; and I cannot but

---

3. In the first part of Sarah Scott's utopian novel, *The History of Sir George Ellison* (1766), the hero marries a woman in Jamaica who owns many slaves. Although she regards them as less than human, he treats them with sympathy and kindness; educates them; converts them to Christianity; and sets up a model plantation, which is so

prosperous that the condition of slaves improves throughout the island.
4. "A negro; a black-a-moor" (Johnson's *Dictionary*).
1. London's royal palace, next to a park where people of fashion went to be seen.

both respect & felicitate you, that by so much laudable diligence you have broke the one—& that by falling into the hands of so good and merciful a family, Providence has rescued you from the other.

And so, good hearted Sancho! adieu! & believe me, I will not forget your letter.

Yrs
L. Sterne

LAURENCE STERNE: *From* Tristram Shandy

Volume 9, Chapter 6[1]

When *Tom,* an'[2] please your honor, got to the shop, there was nobody in it, but a poor negro girl, with a bunch of white feathers slightly tied to the end of a long cane, flapping away flies—not killing them.—'Tis a pretty picture! said my uncle *Toby*—she had suffered persecution, *Trim,* and had learnt mercy—[3]

—She was good, an' please your honor, from nature as well as from hardships; and there are circumstances in the story of that poor friendless slut that would melt a heart of stone, said *Trim;* and some dismal winter's evening, when your honor is in the humor, they shall be told you with the rest of *Tom's* story, for it makes a part of it—

Then do not forget, *Trim,* said my uncle *Toby.*

A Negro has a soul? an' please your honor, said the Corporal (doubtingly).

I am not much versed, Corporal, quoth my uncle *Toby,* in things of that kind; but I suppose, God would not leave him without one, any more than thee or me—

—It would be putting one sadly over the head of another, quoth the Corporal.

It would so; said my uncle *Toby.* Why then, an' please your honor, is a black wench to be used worse than a white one?

I can give no reason, said my uncle *Toby*—

—Only, cried the Corporal, shaking his head, because she has no one to stand up for her—

—'Tis that very thing, *Trim,* quoth my uncle *Toby,*—which recommends her to protection—and her brethren with her; 'tis the fortune of war which has put the whip into our hands *now*—where it may be hereafter, heaven knows!—but be it where it will, the brave, *Trim!* will not use it unkindly.

—God forbid, said the Corporal.

Amen, responded my uncle *Toby,* laying his hand upon his heart.

1767

---

1. This is the chapter that Sterne had been writing when Sancho's letter arrived. Corporal Trim is telling a story about his brother Tom, who has just gone to a sausage shop in Lisbon.
2. If it.

3. Uncle Toby would not harm a fly: "go poor devil, get thee gone, why should I hurt thee?—This world surely is wide enough to hold both thee and me" (*Tristram Shandy* 2.12).

IGNATIUS SANCHO: Letter to Jack Wingrave[1]

1778

In some one of your letters which I do not recollect—you speak (with honest indignation) of the treachery and chicanery of the natives.—My good friend, you should remember from whom they learnt those vices:—The first Christian visitors found them a simple, harmless people—but the cursed avidity for wealth urged these first visitors (and all the succeeding ones) to such acts of deception—and even wanton cruelty—that the poor ignorant natives soon learnt to turn the knavish and diabolical arts—which they too soon imbibed—upon their teachers.

I am sorry to observe that the practice of your country (which as a resident I love—and for its freedom, and for the many blessings I enjoy in it, shall ever have my warmest wishes, prayers, and blessings): I say it is with reluctance that I must observe your country's conduct has been uniformly wicked in the East—West-Indies—and even on the coast of Guinea.—The grand object of English navigators—indeed of all Christian navigators—is money— money—money—for which I do not pretend to blame them—Commerce was meant by the goodness of the Deity to diffuse the various goods of the earth into every part—to unite mankind in the blessed chains of brotherly love, society, and mutual dependence:—the enlightened Christian should diffuse the riches of the gospel of peace, with the commodities of his respective land—Commerce attended with strict honesty, and with religion for its companion, would be a blessing to every shore it touched at.—In Africa, the poor wretched natives—blessed with the most fertile and luxuriant soil—are rendered so much the more miserable for what Providence meant as a blessing:—the Christians' abominable traffic for slaves—and the horrid cruelty and treachery of the petty kings—encouraged by their Christian customers— who carry them strong liquors, to inflame their national madness—and powder and bad fire-arms, to furnish them with the hellish means of killing and kidnapping.—But enough—it is a subject that sours my blood—and I am sure will not please the friendly bent of your social affections.—I mentioned these only to guard my friend against being too hasty in condemning the knavery of a people who, bad as they may be—possibly—were made worse by their Christian visitors.

---

1. Jack Wingrave, the son of a London bookseller, went to India to make his fortune. He wrote his father some letters from Bombay which were shown to Sancho. Here are two extracts: "I have introduced myself to Mr. G——, who behaved very friendly in giving me some advice, which was very necessary, as the inhabitants, who are chiefly blacks, are a set of canting, deceitful people, and of whom one must have great caution" (1776). "I am now thoroughly convinced, that the account which Mr. G—— gave me of the natives of this country is just and true, that they are a set of deceitful people, and have not such a word as gratitude in their language, neither do they know what it is—and as to their dealings in trade, they are like unto Jews" (1777).

SAMUEL JOHNSON

Samuel Johnson detested slavery and the owners of slaves. Once, "in company with some very grave men at Oxford, his toast was, 'Here's to the next insurrection of the Negroes in the West Indies,' " and in his pamphlet *Taxation No Tyranny* (1775), he put the American rebels down with a devastating question: "How is it that we hear the loudest yelps for liberty among the drivers of Negroes?" Although slavery had been abolished in England in 1772, serfdom still existed in Scotland, and the British remained heavily involved in the slave trade. In 1777 a black slave, Joseph Knight, sued for freedom from the Scottish master he had escaped. On his behalf Johnson dictated this argument to Boswell.

[A Brief to Free a Slave]

It must be agreed that in most ages many countries have had part of their inhabitants in a state of slavery; yet it may be doubted whether slavery can ever be supposed the natural condition of man. It is impossible not to conceive that men in their original state were equal; and very difficult to imagine how one would be subjected to another but by violent compulsion. An individual may, indeed, forfeit his liberty by a crime; but he cannot by that crime forfeit the liberty of his children. What is true of a criminal seems true likewise of a captive. A man may accept life from a conquering enemy on condition of perpetual servitude; but it is very doubtful whether he can entail[1] that servitude on his descendants; for no man can stipulate without commission for another. The condition which he himself accepts, his son or grandson perhaps would have rejected. If we should admit, what perhaps may with more reason be denied, that there are certain relations between man and man which may make slavery necessary and just,[2] yet it can never be proved that he who is now suing for his freedom ever stood in any of those relations. He is certainly subject by no law, but that of violence, to his present master,[3] who pretends no claim to his obedience, but that he bought him from a merchant of slaves, whose right to sell him never was examined. It is said that, according to the constitutions of Jamaica, he was legally enslaved; these constitutions are merely positive;[4] and apparently injurious to the rights of mankind, because whoever is exposed to sale is condemned to slavery without appeal; by whatever fraud or violence he might have been originally brought into the merchant's power. In our own time princes have been sold, by wretches to whose care they were entrusted, that they might have an European education; but when once they were brought to a market in the plantations, little would avail either their dignity or their wrongs. The laws of Jamaica afford a Negro no redress. His color is considered as a sufficient testimony against him. It is to be lamented that moral right should ever give way to political convenience. But if temptations of interest are sometimes too strong for human virtue, let us at least retain a virtue where there is no

---

1. Settle unalterably.
2. Boswell, who strongly disagreed with Johnson's "prejudice" against slavery, argued that "to abolish a *status*, which in all ages GOD has sanctioned, and man has continued, would not only be *robbery* to

an innumerable class of our fellow subjects; but it would be extreme cruelty to the African savages."
3. Knight had been kidnapped as a child.
4. Arbitrarily instituted (opposed to *natural* laws).

temptation to quit it. In the present case there is apparent right on one side, and no convenience on the other. Inhabitants of this island can neither gain riches nor power by taking away the liberty of any part of the human species. The sum of the argument is this:—No man is by nature the property of another: The defendant is, therefore, by nature free: The rights of nature must be some way forfeited before they can be justly taken away: That the defendant has by any act forfeited the rights of nature we require to be proved; and if no proof of such forfeiture can be given, we doubt not but the justice of the court will declare him free.[5]

1777   1792

5. Knight was set free by the Scottish court.

OLAUDAH EQUIANO

The Interesting Narrative of the Life of Olaudah Equiano, or Gustavus Vassa, the African, Written by Himself, published in 1789, is the classic story of an eighteenth-century African's descent into slavery and rise to freedom. Raised in an Ibo village (in modern Nigeria), Olaudah Equiano (ca. 1745–1797) was kidnapped by African raiders and sold into slavery. He survived the horrors of the Middle Passage to the New World, where an English naval officer bought him to serve as a cabin boy and renamed him Gustavus Vassa, after a sixteenth-century Swedish hero who freed his people from the Danes (such names concealed the status of a slave, because slavery was frowned on by the British Navy). During years at sea, as well as a period at a London school, Equiano acquired a basic education. He was also baptized, which many slaves expected to make them free. But his hopes were cruelly disappointed when, after six years' service, he was suddenly sold and shipped to the West Indies. There a Quaker merchant, Robert King, purchased him, employed him as a clerk and seaman, and eventually allowed him, in 1766, to buy his freedom. Equiano went back to England, working first as a hairdresser and later voyaging all over the world, even taking part in an effort to find a passage to India by way of the North Pole. In the 1780s he became involved in the abolitionist movement. The story of his life was an important contribution to that movement, not only for its explicit arguments against the slave trade but also for its demonstration that someone born in Africa could be humane, intelligent, a good Christian, and a free and eloquent British subject. The book went through many editions and made Equiano famous. He married an Englishwoman, fathered two daughters, and died in London in 1797.

The *Life of Equiano* combines several literary genres. It is a captivity narrative, a spiritual autobiography, a travel memoir, an adventure story, and an abolitionist tract. The early chapters describe the healthy, cheerful, and virtuous life of Africans, contrasted with European inhumanity, and the later chapters show how much a black man can achieve, when given a chance. Equiano does not disguise the strains of his position as he is pulled between different identities and different worlds. His main purpose, however, is clearly to force his readers to face the ordeals a slave must endure—to live in his skin. If *Oroonoko* taught Europeans to sympathize with Africans, Equiano taught them that a black man could speak for himself.

From The Interesting Narrative of the Life of Olaudah Equiano, or Gustavus Vassa, the African, Written by Himself

[THE MIDDLE PASSAGE][1]

The first object which saluted my eyes when I arrived on the coast was the sea, and a slave ship, which was then riding at anchor, and waiting for its cargo. These filled me with astonishment, which was soon converted into terror when I was carried on board. I was immediately handled and tossed up to see if I were sound by some of the crew; and I was now persuaded that I had gotten into a world of bad spirits, and that they were going to kill me. Their complexions too differing so much from ours, their long hair, and the language they spoke, (which was very different from any I had ever heard) united to confirm me in this belief. Indeed such were the horrors of my views and fears at the moment, that, if ten thousand worlds had been my own, I would have freely parted with them all to have exchanged my condition with that of the meanest slave in my own country. When I looked round the ship too and saw a large furnace of copper boiling, and a multitude of black people of every description chained together, every one of their countenances expressing dejection and sorrow, I no longer doubted of my fate; and, quite overpowered with horror and anguish, I fell motionless on the deck and fainted. When I recovered a little I found some black people about me, who I believe were some of those who brought me on board, and had been receiving their pay; they talked to me in order to cheer me, but all in vain. I asked them if we were not to be eaten by those white men with horrible looks, red faces, and loose hair. They told me I was not; and one of the crew brought me a small portion of spirituous liquor in a wine glass; but, being afraid of him, I would not take it out of his hand. One of the blacks therefore took it from him and gave it to me, and I took a little down my palate, which, instead of reviving me, as they thought it would, threw me into the greatest consternation at the strange feeling it produced, having never tasted any such liquor before. Soon after this the blacks who brought me on board went off, and left me abandoned to despair. I now saw myself deprived of all chance of returning to my native country, or even the least glimpse of hope of gaining the shore, which I now considered as friendly; and I even wished for my former slavery in preference to my present situation, which was filled with horrors of every kind, still heightened by my ignorance of what I was to undergo. I was not long suffered to indulge my grief; I was soon put down under the decks, and there I received such a salutation in my nostrils as I had never experienced in my life; so that, with the loathsomeness of the stench, and crying together, I became so sick and low that I was not able to eat, nor had I the least desire to taste any thing. I now wished for the last friend, death, to relieve me; but soon, to my grief, two of the white men offered me eatables; and, on my refusing to eat, one of them held me fast by the hands, and laid me across I think the windlass, and tied my feet, while the other flogged me severely. I had never experienced any thing of this kind

---

1. After his kidnapping, young Equiano passes from one African master to another. The last of these, a merchant, treats him like a member of the family, until one morning the boy is suddenly wakened and hurried away to the seacoast.

before; and although, not being used to the water, I naturally feared that element the first time I saw it, yet nevertheless, could I have got over the nettings,[2] I would have jumped over the side, but I could not; and, besides, the crew used to watch us very closely who were not chained down to the decks, lest we should leap into the water; and I have seen some of these poor African prisoners most severely cut for attempting to do so, and hourly whipped for not eating. This indeed was often the case with myself. In a little time after, amongst the poor chained men, I found some of my own nation, which in a small degree gave ease to my mind. I inquired of these what was to be done with us; they gave me to understand we were to be carried to these white people's country to work for them. I then was a little revived, and thought, if it were no worse than working, my situation was not so desperate: but still I feared I should be put to death, the white people looked and acted, as I thought, in so savage a manner; for I had never seen among any people such instances of brutal cruelty; and this not only shewn towards us blacks, but also to some of the whites themselves. One white man in particular I saw, when we were permitted to be on deck, flogged so unmercifully with a large rope near the foremast, that he died in consequence of it; and they tossed him over the side as they would have done a brute. This made me fear these people the more; and I expected nothing less than to be treated in the same manner. I could not help expressing my fears and apprehensions to some of my countrymen: I asked them if these people had no country, but lived in this hollow place (the ship): they told me they did not, but came from a distant one. "Then," said I, "how comes it in all our country we never heard of them?" They told me because they lived so very far off. I then asked where were their women? had they any like themselves? I was told they had: "and why," said I, "do we not see them?" they answered, because they were left behind. I asked how the vessel could go? they told me they could not tell; but that there were cloths put upon the masts by the help of the ropes I saw, and then the vessel went on; and the white men had some spell or magic they put in the water when they liked in order to stop the vessel. I was exceedingly amazed at this account, and really thought they were spirits. I therefore wished much to be from amongst them, for I expected they would sacrifice me: but my wishes were vain; for we were so quartered that it was impossible for any of us to make our escape. While we stayed on the coast I was mostly on deck; and one day, to my great astonishment, I saw one of these vessels coming in with the sails up. As soon as the whites saw it, they gave a great shout, at which we were amazed; and the more so as the vessel appeared larger by approaching nearer. At last she came to an anchor in my sight, and when the anchor was let go I and my countrymen who saw it were lost in astonishment to observe the vessel stop; and were now convinced it was done by magic. Soon after this the other ship got her boats out, and they came on board of us, and the people of both ships seemed very glad to see each other. Several of the strangers also shook hands with us black people, and made motions with their hands, signifying I suppose we were to go to their country; but we did not understand them. At last, when the ship we were in had got in all her cargo, they made ready with many fearful noises, and we were all put under deck, so that we could not

2. A network of small ropes around the ship kept slaves from jumping overboard.

see how they managed the vessel. But this disappointment was the least of my sorrow. The stench of the hold while we were on the coast was so intolerably loathsome, that it was dangerous to remain there for any time, and some of us had been permitted to stay on the deck for the fresh air; but now that the whole ship's cargo were confined together, it became absolutely pestilential. The closeness of the place, and the heat of the climate, added to the number in the ship, which was so crowded that each had scarcely room to turn himself, almost suffocated us. This produced copious perspirations, so that the air soon became unfit for respiration, from a variety of loathsome smells, and brought on a sickness among the slaves, of which many died, thus falling victims to the improvident avarice, as I may call it, of their purchasers. This wretched situation was again aggravated by the galling of the chains, now become insupportable; and the filth of the necessary tubs,[3] into which the children often fell, and were almost suffocated. The shrieks of the women, and the groans of the dying, rendered the whole a scene of horror almost inconceivable. Happily perhaps for myself I was soon reduced so low here that it was thought necessary to keep me almost always on deck; and from[4] my extreme youth I was not put in fetters. In this situation I expected every hour to share the fate of my companions, some of whom were almost daily brought upon deck at the point of death, which I began to hope would soon put an end to my miseries. Often did I think many of the inhabitants of the deep much more happy than myself. I envied them the freedom they enjoyed, and as often wished I could change my condition for theirs. Every circumstance I met with served only to render my state more painful, and heighten my apprehensions, and my opinion of the cruelty of the whites. One day they had taken a number of fishes; and when they had killed and satisfied themselves with as many as they thought fit, to our astonishment who were on the deck, rather than give any of them to us to eat as we expected, they tossed the remaining fish into the sea again, although we begged and prayed for some as well as we could, but in vain; and some of my countrymen, being pressed by hunger, took an opportunity, when they thought no one saw them, of trying to get a little privately; but they were discovered, and the attempt procured them some very severe floggings.

One day, when we had a smooth sea and moderate wind, two of my wearied countrymen who were chained together (I was near them at the time), preferring death to such a life of misery, somehow made through the nettings and jumped into the sea; immediately another quite dejected fellow, who, on account of his illness, was suffered to be out of irons, also followed their example; and I believe many more would very soon have done the same if they had not been prevented by the ship's crew, who were instantly alarmed. Those of us that were the most active were in a moment put down under the deck, and there was such a noise and confusion amongst the people of the ship as I never heard before, to stop her, and get the boat out to go after the slaves. However two of the wretches were drowned, but they got the other, and afterwards flogged him unmercifully for thus attempting to prefer death to slavery. In this manner we continued to undergo more hardships than I can now relate, hardships which are inseparable from this accursed trade. Many a time we were near suffocation from the want of fresh air, which we

3. Latrines. 4. Because of.

were often without for whole days together. This, and the stench of the necessary tubs, carried off many. During our passage I first saw flying fishes, which surprised me very much: they used frequently to fly across the ship, and many of them fell on the deck. I also now first saw the use of the quadrant; I had often with astonishment seen the mariners make observations with it, and I could not think what it meant. They at last took notice of my surprise; and one of them, willing to increase it, as well as to gratify my curiosity, made me one day look through it. The clouds appeared to me to be land, which disappeared as they passed along. This heightened my wonder; and I was now more persuaded than ever that I was in another world, and that every thing about me was magic. At last we came in sight of the island of Barbados,[5] at which the whites on board gave a great shout, and made many signs of joy to us. We did not know what to think of this; but as the vessel drew nearer we plainly saw the harbor, and other ships of different kinds and sizes; and we soon anchored amongst them off Bridge Town. Many merchants and planters now came on board, though it was in the evening. They put us in separate parcels,[6] and examined us attentively. They also made us jump, and pointed to the land, signifying we were to go there. We thought by this we should be eaten by these ugly men, as they appeared to us; and, when soon after we were all put down under the deck again, there was much dread and trembling among us, and nothing but bitter cries to be heard all the night from these apprehensions, insomuch that at last the white people got some old slaves from the land to pacify us. They told us we were not to be eaten, but to work, and were soon to go on land, where we should see many of our country people. This report eased us much; and sure enough, soon after we were landed, there came to us Africans of all languages. We were conducted immediately to the merchant's yard, where we were pent up altogether like so many sheep in a fold, without regard to sex or age. As every object was new to me, every thing I saw filled me with surprise. What struck me first was that the houses were built with stories, and in every other respect different from those in Africa; but I was still more astonished on seeing people on horseback. I did not know what this could mean; and indeed I thought these people were full of nothing but magical arts. While I was in this astonishment one of my fellow prisoners spoke to a countryman of his about the horses, who said they were the same kind they had in their country. I understood them, though they were from a distant part of Africa, and I thought it odd I had not seen any horses there; but afterwards, when I came to converse with different Africans, I found they had many horses amongst them, and much larger than those I then saw. We were not many days in the merchant's custody before we were sold after their usual manner, which is this:—On a signal given (as the beat of a drum) the buyers rush at once into the yard where the slaves are confined, and make a choice of that parcel they like best. The noise and clamor with which this is attended, and the eagerness visible in the countenances of the buyers, serve not a little to increase the apprehensions of the terrified Africans, who may well be supposed to consider them as the ministers of that destruction to which they think themselves devoted.[7] In this manner, without scruple, are relations and friends

---

5. The easternmost Caribbean island, then an important center for the trade of sugar and slaves.

6. Groups sorted to be sold as one lot.
7. Doomed.

separated, most of them never to see each other again. I remember in the vessel in which I was brought over, in the men's apartment, there were several brothers, who, in the sale, were sold in different lots; and it was very moving on this occasion to see and hear their cries at parting. O, ye nominal Christians! might not an African ask you, learned you this from your God, who says unto you, Do unto all men as you would men should do unto you? Is it not enough that we are torn from our country and friends to toil for your luxury and lust of gain? Must every tender feeling be likewise sacrificed to your avarice? Are the dearest friends and relations, now rendered more dear by their separation from their kindred, still to be parted from each other, and thus prevented from cheering the gloom of slavery with the small comfort of being together and mingling their sufferings and sorrows? Why are parents to lose their children, brothers their sisters, or husbands their wives? Surely this is a new refinement in cruelty, which, while it has no advantage to atone for it, thus aggravates distress, and adds fresh horrors even to the wretchedness of slavery.

* * *

[A FREE MAN][8]

Every day now brought me nearer my freedom, and I was impatient till we proceeded again to sea, that I might have an opportunity of getting a sum large enough to purchase it. I was not long ungratified; for, in the beginning of the year 1766, my master bought another sloop, named the *Nancy*, the largest I had ever seen. She was partly laden, and was to proceed to Philadelphia; our Captain had his choice of three, and I was well pleased he chose this, which was the largest; for, from his having a large vessel, I had more room, and could carry a larger quantity of goods with me. Accordingly, when we had delivered our old vessel, the *Prudence*, and completed the lading of the *Nancy*, having made near three hundred per cent, by four barrels of pork I brought from Charlestown, I laid in as large a cargo as I could, trusting to God's providence to prosper my undertaking. With these views I sailed for Philadelphia. On our passage, when we drew near the land, I was for the first time surprised at the sight of some whales, having never seen any such large sea monsters before; and as we sailed by the land one morning I saw a puppy whale close by the vessel; it was about the length of a wherry boat, and it followed us all the day till we got within the Capes. We arrived safe and in good time at Philadelphia, and I sold my goods there chiefly to the Quakers. They always appeared to be a very honest discreet sort of people, and never attempted to impose on me; I therefore liked them, and ever after chose to deal with them in preference to any others.

One Sunday morning while I was here, as I was going to church, I chanced to pass a meeting house. The doors being open, and the house full of people, it excited my curiosity to go in. When I entered the house, to my great surprise, I saw a very tall woman standing in the midst of them, speaking in an audible voice something which I could not understand. Having never seen

8. Frustrated in his hope to be set free in England, Equiano is shipped to Montserrat, a British colony in the Leeward Islands of the West Indies. Robert King, a prosperous Quaker merchant from Philadelphia, buys him, treats him kindly, and values him as a reliable worker. By being useful to a friendly sea captain, Thomas Farmer, Equiano has opportunities to travel and trade goods for money. Eventually King promises to let him purchase his freedom for his original cost: forty pounds sterling.

anything of this kind before, I stood and stared about me for some time, wondering at this odd scene. As soon as it was over I took an opportunity to make inquiry about the place and people, when I was informed they were called Quakers.[9] I particularly asked what that woman I saw in the midst of them had said, but none of them were pleased to satisfy me; so I quitted them, and soon after, as I was returning, I came to a church crowded with people; the church-yard was full likewise, and a number of people were even mounted on ladders, looking in at the windows. I thought this a strange sight, as I had never seen churches, either in England or the West Indies, crowded in this manner before. I therefore made bold to ask some people the meaning of all this, and they told me the Rev. Mr. George Whitfield[1] was preaching. I had often heard of this gentleman, and had wished to see and hear him; but I had never before had an opportunity. I now therefore resolved to gratify myself with the sight, and I pressed in amidst the multitude. When I got into the church I saw this pious man exhorting the people with the greatest fervor and earnestness, and sweating as much as I ever did while in slavery on Montserrat beach. I was very much struck and impressed with this; I thought it strange I had never seen divines exert themselves in this manner before, and I was no longer at a loss to account for the thin congregations they preached to.

When we had discharged our cargo here, and were loaded again, we left this fruitful land once more, and set sail for Montserrat. My traffic had hitherto succeeded so well with me, that I thought, by selling my goods when we arrived at Montserrat, I should have enough to purchase my freedom. But, as soon as our vessel arrived there, my master came on board, and gave orders for us to go to St. Eustatia,[2] and discharge our cargo there, and from thence proceed for Georgia. I was much disappointed at this; but thinking, as usual, it was of no use to murmur at the decrees of fate, I submitted without repining, and we went to St. Eustatia. After we had discharged our cargo there we took in a live cargo, as we call a cargo of slaves. Here I sold my goods tolerably well; but, not being able to lay out all my money in this small island to as much advantage as in many other places, I laid out only part, and the remainder I brought away with me neat.[3] We sailed from hence for Georgia, and I was glad when we got there, though I had not much reason to like the place from my last adventure in Savannah;[4] but I longed to get back to Montserrat and procure my freedom, which I expected to be able to purchase when I returned. As soon as we arrived here I waited on my careful doctor, Mr. Brady, to whom I made the most grateful acknowledgments in my power for his former kindness and attention during my illness.

While we were here an odd circumstance happened to the Captain and me, which disappointed us both a good deal. A silversmith, whom we had brought to this place some voyages before, agreed with the Captain to return with us to the West Indies, and promised at the same time to give the Captain

---

9. Quaker meetings are not led by clergy; any male or female worshiper who felt inspired by God could rise to speak.

1. Whitefield (1714–1770), a famous evangelist who helped found Methodism, was in Britain, not Philadelphia, in 1766. It is possible that Equiano had heard him preach the previous year, in Savannah, Georgia. Equiano's later conversion to Meth-

odism will become a dominant theme of his life story.

2. An island in the Netherlands Antilles (West Indies).

3. Intact.

4. The year before, a drunken slave owner and his servant had beaten Equiano so brutally that he nearly died.

a great deal of money, having pretended to take a liking to him, and being, as we thought, very rich. But while we stayed to load our vessel this man was taken ill in a house where he worked, and in a week's time became very bad. The worse he grew the more he used to speak of giving the Captain what he had promised him, so that he expected something considerable from the death of this man, who had no wife or child, and he attended him day and night. I used also to go with the Captain, at his own desire, to attend him; especially when we saw there was no appearance of his recovery; and, in order to recompense me for my trouble, the Captain promised me ten pounds, when he should get the man's property. I thought this would be of great service to me, although I had nearly money enough to purchase my freedom, if I should get safe this voyage to Montserrat. In this expectation I laid out above eight pounds of my money for a suit of superfine clothes to dance with at my freedom, which I hoped was then at hand. We still continued to attend this man, and were with him even on the last day he lived, till very late at night, when we went on board. After we were got to bed, about one or two o'clock in the morning, the Captain was sent for, and informed the man was dead. On this he came to my bed, and, waking me, informed me of it, and desired me to get up and procure a light, and immediately go to him. I told him I was very sleepy, and wished he would take somebody else with him, or else, as the man was dead, and could want no farther attendance, to let all things remain as they were till next morning. "No, no," said he, "we will have the money tonight, I cannot wait till tomorrow; so let us go." Accordingly I got up and struck a light, and away we both went and saw the man as dead as we could wish. The Captain said he would give him a grand burial, in gratitude for the promised treasure; and desired that all the things belonging to the deceased might be brought forth. Among others, there was a nest of trunks of which he had kept the keys whilst the man was ill, and when they were produced we opened them with no small eagerness and expectation; and as there were a great number within one another, with much impatience we took them one out of the other. At last, when we came to the smallest, and had opened it, we saw it was full of papers, which we supposed to be notes; at the sight of which our hearts leapt for joy; and that instant the Captain, clapping his hands, cried out, "Thank God, here it is." But when we took up the trunk, and began to examine the supposed treasure and long-looked-for bounty, (alas! alas! how uncertain and deceitful are all human affairs!) what had we found! While we were embracing a substance we grasped an empty nothing. The whole amount that was in the nest of trunks was only one dollar and a half; and all that the man possessed would not pay for his coffin. Our sudden and exquisite joy was now succeeded by as sudden and exquisite pain; and my Captain and I exhibited, for some time, most ridiculous figures—pictures of chagrin and disappointment! We went away greatly mortified, and left the deceased to do as well as he could for himself, as we had taken so good care of him when alive for nothing. We set sail once more for Montserrat, and arrived there safe; but much out of humor with our friend the silversmith. When we had unladen the vessel, and I had sold my venture, finding myself master of about forty-seven pounds, I consulted my true friend, the Captain, how I should proceed in offering my master the money for my freedom. He told me to come on a certain morning, when he and my master would be at breakfast together. Accordingly, on that morning I went, and met the Captain there, as he had appointed. When I went in I made my obeisance to my master, and with my money in my hand, and many fears in my heart, I prayed him to be as good as his offer to me, when he was pleased to promise me my freedom as soon as I could purchase it. This speech seemed to confound him; he began to recoil; and my heart that instant sank within me. "What," said he, "give you your freedom? Why, where did you get the money? Have you got forty pounds sterling?" "Yes, sir," I answered. "How did you get it?" replied he. I told him, very honestly. The Captain then said he knew I got the money very honestly and with much industry, and that I was particularly careful. On which my master replied, I got money much faster than he did; and said he would not have made me the promise he did if he had thought I should have got money so soon. "Come, come," said my worthy Captain, clapping my master on the back, "Come, Robert" (which was his name), "I think you must let him have his freedom; you have laid your money out very well; you have received good interest for it all this time, and here is now the principal at last. I know Gustavus has earned you more than an hundred a-year, and he will still save you money, as he will not leave you:—Come, Robert, take the money." My master then said, he would not be worse than his promise; and, taking the money, told me to go to the Secretary at the Register Office, and get my manumission[5] drawn up. These words of my master were like a voice from heaven to me: in an instant all my trepidation was turned into unutterable bliss; and I most reverently bowed myself with gratitude, unable to express my feelings, but by the overflowing of my eyes, while my true and worthy friend, the Captain, congratulated us both with a peculiar degree of heartfelt pleasure. As soon as the first transports of my joy were over, and that I had expressed my thanks to these my worthy friends in the best manner I was able, I rose with a heart full of affection and reverence, and left the room, in order to obey my master's joyful mandate of going to the Register Office. As I was leaving the house I called to mind the words of the Psalmist, in the 126th Psalm, and like him, "I glorified God in my heart, in whom I trusted." These words had been impressed on my mind from the very day I was forced from Deptford[6] to the present hour, and I now saw them, as I thought, fulfilled and verified. My imagination was all rapture as I flew to the Register Office, and in this respect, like the apostle Peter[7] (whose deliverance from prison was so sudden and extraordinary, that he thought he was in a vision), I could scarcely believe I was awake. Heavens! who could do justice to my feelings at this moment! Not conquering heroes themselves, in the midst of a triumph—Not the tender mother who had just regained her long-lost infant, and presses it to her heart—Not the weary hungry mariner, at the sight of the desired friendly port—Not the lover, when he once more embraces his beloved mistress, after she had been ravished from his arms!— All within my breast was tumult, wildness, and delirium! My feet scarcely touched the ground, for they were winged with joy, and, like Elijah, as he rose to Heaven,[8] they "were with lightning sped as I went on." Every one I met I told of my happiness, and blazed about the virtue of my amiable master and captain.

---

5. Release from slavery.
6. The port near London from which Equiano was sold by his English master.

7. Acts, chap. xii, ver. 9 [Equiano's note].
8. 2 Kings 2.11.

When I got to the office and acquainted the Register with my errand he congratulated me on the occasion, and told me he would draw up my manumission for half price, which was a guinea. I thanked him for his kindness; and having received it and paid him, I hastened to my master to get him to sign it, that I might be fully released. Accordingly he signed the manumission that day, so that, before night, I who had been a slave in the morning, trembling at the will of another, was become my own master, and completely free. I thought this was the happiest day I had ever experienced; and my joy was still heightened by the blessings and prayers of the sable race, particularly the aged, to whom my heart had ever been attached with reverence.

As the form of my manumission has something peculiar in it, and expresses the absolute power and dominion one man claims over his fellow, I shall beg leave to present it before my readers at full length:

Montserrat.—To all men unto whom these presents shall come: I Robert King, of the parish of St. Anthony in the said island, merchant, send greeting: Know ye, that I the aforesaid Robert King, for and in consideration of the sum of seventy pounds current money of the said island,[9] to me in hand paid, and to the intent that a negro man-slave, named Gustavus Vassa, shall and may become free, have manumitted, emancipated, enfranchised, and set free, and by these presents do manumit, emancipate, enfranchise, and set free, the aforesaid negro man-slave, named Gustavus Vassa, for ever, hereby giving, granting, and releasing unto him, the said Gustavus Vassa, all right, title, dominion, sovereignty, and property, which, as lord and master over the aforesaid Gustavus Vassa, I had, or now I have, or by any means whatsoever I may or can hereafter possibly have over him the aforesaid negro, for ever. In witness whereof I the above-said Robert King have unto these presents set my hand and seal, this tenth day of July, in the year of our Lord one thousand seven hundred and sixty-six.

ROBERT KING

Signed, sealed, and delivered in the presence of Terrylegay, Montserrat.

Registered the within manumission at full length, this eleventh day of July, 1766, in liber D.[1]

TERRYLEGAY, REGISTER.

In short, the fair as well as black people immediately styled me by a new appellation, to me the most desirable in the world, which was Freeman, and at the dances I gave my Georgia superfine blue clothes made no indifferent appearance, as I thought.

*   *   *

1789

9. The equivalent of forty pounds in British money.

1. Book or register D.

JAMES THOMSON
1700–1748

Thomson, the first and most popular nature poet of the century, did not see London until he was twenty-five years old. He grew up in the picturesque border country of Roxboroughshire in Scotland and, after studying divinity in Edinburgh, went to London in 1725, bringing with him, in addition to a memory well stored with images of the external world, the earliest version of his descriptive poem *Winter* in 405 lines of blank verse. Published in 1726, it soon became popular. Thomson went on to publish *Summer* (1727), *Spring* (1728), and *Autumn* in the first collected edition of *The Seasons* (1730), to which he added the *Hymn to the Seasons*. During the next sixteen years, because of constant revisions and additions, the poem grew in length to 5,541 lines. *The Seasons* continued to be popular well into the Romantic period; between 1730 and 1800 it was printed fifty times. Thomson's last poem, *The Castle of Indolence* (1748), is a witty imitation of Spenser; it moves from a playful portrait of the idleness of the poet and his friends to a celebration of industry and progress.

The Seasons set the fashion for the poetry of natural description. Generations of readers learned to look at the external world through Thomson's eyes and with the emotions that he had taught them to feel. The *eye* dominates the literature of external nature during the eighteenth century as the *imagination* was to do in the poetry of William Wordsworth. And Thomson amazed his readers by his capacity to see: the general effects of light and cloud and foliage or the particular image of a leaf tossed in the gale or the slender feet of a robin or the delicate film of ice at the edge of a brook. He tries to view each season from every perspective, as it might be perceived by a bird in the sky or by the tiniest insect, by God or a painter or Milton or Sir Isaac Newton (whom Thomson commemorated in a popular ode). As the poem grew, it became an *omnium gatherum* of contemporary ideas and interests: natural history; ideas about the nature of man and society, primitive and civilized; the conception of created nature as a source of religious experience, as an object of religious veneration, and as a continuing revelation of a Creator whose presence fills the world.

From The Seasons

From *Autumn*

[EVENING AND NIGHT][1]

The western sun withdraws the shortened day;
And humid evening, gliding o'er the sky,
In her chill progress, to the ground condensed
1085   The vapors throws. Where creeping waters ooze,
Where marshes stagnate, and where rivers wind,
Cluster the rolling fogs, and swim along
The dusky-mantled lawn. Meanwhile the moon,
Full-orbed and breaking through the scattered clouds,
1090   Shows her broad visage in the crimsoned east.
Turned to the sun direct, her spotted disk

---

1. This passage, like many in *The Seasons*, went through extensive revisions. The opening lines on the harvest moon shining through fog (1082–1102) originally belonged to *Winter*; the descriptions of the aurora borealis (1108–37) and wildfire (1150–64) first appeared in *Summer*. Scientific and visionary, divine and human perspectives are contrasted and join together in an intricate harmony.

(Where mountains rise, umbrageous dales descend,
And caverns deep, as optic tube[2] descries)
A smaller earth, gives all his blaze again,
1095   Void of its flame, and sheds a softer day.
Now through the passing cloud she seems to stoop,
Now up the pure cerulean rides sublime.
Wide the pale deluge° floats, and streaming mild   *moonlight*
O'er the skied[3] mountain to the shadowy vale,
1100   While rocks and floods reflect the quivering gleam,
The whole air whitens with a boundless tide
Of silver radiance trembling round the world.
     But when, half blotted from the sky, her light
Fainting, permits the starry fires to burn
1105   With keener luster through the depth of heaven;
Or quite extinct her deadened orb appears,
And scarce appears, of sickly beamless white;
Oft in this season, silent from the north
A blaze of meteors[4] shoots—ensweeping first
1110   The lower skies, they all at once converge
High to the crown[5] of heaven, and, all at once
Relapsing quick, as quickly reascend,
And mix and thwart,° extinguish and renew,   *cross*
All ether coursing[6] in a maze of light.
1115   From look to look, contagious through the crowd,
The panic runs, and into wondrous shapes
The appearance throws—armies in meet° array,   *fitting*
Thronged with aerial spears and steeds of fire;
Till, the long lines of full-extended war
1120   In bleeding fight commixed, the sanguine flood
Rolls a broad slaughter o'er the plains of heaven.
As thus they scan the visionary scene,
On all sides swells the superstitious din,
Incontinent; and busy frenzy talks
1125   Of blood and battle; cities overturned,
And late at night in swallowing earthquake sunk,
Or hideous wrapped in fierce ascending flame;
Of sallow famine, inundation, storm;
Of pestilence, and every great distress;
1130   Empires subversed,° when ruling fate has struck   *overthrown*
The unalterable hour; even nature's self
Is deemed to totter on the brink of time.
Not so the man of philosophic eye
And inspect sage:[7] the waving brightness he
1135   Curious surveys, inquisitive to know
The causes and materials, yet unfixed,[8]
Of this appearance beautiful and new.

2. Telescope. Observation of the moon had revealed shadows ("umbrageous dales"), hence an irregular surface.
3. I.e., seeming to touch the sky.
4. Not meteors as we think of them, but the aurora borealis, or northern lights (multicolored, streaming pulses of light in the upper atmosphere). The aurora had often been associated with cosmic battles, in both literature and popular superstition.
5. The corona or central ring of the aurora.
6. Running through all the upper sky.
7. Wise examination.
8. Unexplained by science.

Now black and deep the night begins to fall,
A shade immense! Sunk in the quenching gloom,
1140 Magnificent and vast, are heaven and earth.
Order confounded lies, all beauty void,
Distinction lost, and gay variety
One universal blot—such the fair power
Of light to kindle and create the whole.
1145 Drear is the state of the benighted wretch
Who then bewildered wanders through the dark
Full of pale fancies and chimeras[9] huge;
Nor visited by one directive ray
From cottage streaming or from airy hall.
1150 Perhaps, impatient as he stumbles on,
Struck from the root of slimy rushes, blue
The wildfire[1] scatters round, or, gathered, trails
A length of flame deceitful o'er the moss;
Whither decoyed by the fantastic blaze,
1155 Now lost and now renewed, he sinks absorbed,
Rider and horse, amid the miry gulf—
While still, from day to day, his pining wife
And plaintive children his return await,
In wild conjecture lost. At other times,
1160 Sent by the better genius of the night,
Innoxious,° gleaming on the horse's mane,   *harmless*
The meteor[2] sits, and shows the narrow path
That winding leads through pits of death, or else
Instructs him how to take the dangerous ford.

1165   The lengthened night elapsed, the morning shines
Serene, in all her dewy beauty bright,
Unfolding fair the last autumnal day.
And now the mounting sun dispels the fog;
The rigid hoarfrost melts before his beam;
1170 And, hung on every spray, on every blade
Of grass, the myriad dewdrops twinkle round.

1730

Ode: Rule, Britannia[1]

I

When *Britain* first, at heaven's command,
    Arose from out the azure main°   *open ocean*
This was the charter of the land,
    And guardian angels sung *this* strain:

---

9. Imaginary monsters.
1. Will-o'-the-wisp, or ignis fatuus, a flitting phos-
phorescent light thought to kindle from the gas of
decaying swamp grasses ("slimy rushes").
2. The ignis lambens, or St. Elmo's fire, a halo of
light that shines on the tips of certain objects dur-

ing electrical storms.
1. This famous patriotic song, set to music by Thomas Arne, was composed for *Alfred* (1740), a
masque in honor of the prince of Wales. It was
originally sung by an actor dressed as an ancient
bard, accompanied by a British harp.

> "Rule, *Britannia*, rule the waves;
> Britons never will be slaves."

2

> The nations, not so blest as thee,
> Must, in their turns, to tyrants fall:
> While thou shalt flourish great and free,
> The dread and envy of them all.
> "Rule," etc.

3

> Still more majestic shalt thou rise,
> More dreadful, from each foreign stroke:
> As the loud blast that tears the skies,
> Serves but to root thy native oak.
> "Rule," etc.

4

> Thee haughty tyrants ne'er shall tame:
> All their attempts to bend thee down
> Will but arouse thy generous flame;
> But work their woe, and thy renown.
> "Rule," etc.

5

> To thee belongs the rural reign;
> Thy cities shall with commerce shine:
> All thine shall be the subject main,
> And every shore it circles thine.
> "Rule," etc.

6

> The Muses, still° with freedom found,   *always*
> Shall to thy happy coast repair:
> Blest isle! with matchless beauty crowned,
> And manly hearts to guard the fair.
> "Rule, *Britannia*, rule the waves;
> Britons never will be slaves."

1740   1745–46

THOMAS GRAY
1716–1771

The man who wrote the English poem best known and most loved by those whom
Samuel Johnson called "the common reader" was oddly enough a scholarly recluse

who lived the quiet life of a university professor in the stagnant atmosphere of mid-eighteenth-century Cambridge. He was educated at Eton, where he made his first intimate friends—Richard West; Thomas Ashton; and Horace Walpole, the son of the prime minister. After a little over four years at Cambridge he left without a degree to make the grand tour of France and Italy as Walpole's guest. The death of West in 1742 was a crucial event for Gray, who, having quarreled with Walpole, felt keenly the loss of this gifted and congenial friend. The Eton ode and possibly some of the stanzas of the *Elegy Written in a Country Churchyard* are associated with memories of West.

After 1742 Gray returned to Cambridge, pursuing his studies and indulging his tastes for the then-little-known fields of pre-Elizabethan poetry and old Welsh and Norse literature. He seldom left Cambridge except to read in the newly opened British Museum or to go in the summer to the Lake District or to Scotland in search of the sublime and beautiful in nature. He wrote slowly and carefully and published very little. The solitary, brooding speaker of the Eton ode and the *Elegy* may be a dramatic projection of Gray himself. The later poems, including two grandiloquent Pindaric odes, *The Progress of Poesy* (1754) and *The Bard* (1757), are accomplished literary exercises. But the living Gray is to be sought in his correspondence, where his genial humor, shy affection, and wide intellectual interests are revealed in some of the most delightful letters of an age that made letter writing into an art.

Although Gray never knew William Collins, he shared his fondness for Edmund Spenser and the early John Milton. The melancholy of Collins's *Ode to Evening* is that of the opening stanzas of the *Elegy,* and in both poems mood and landscape mutually sustain each other. Gray joined his contemporaries in the search for a new style, at once intimate and prophetic. Yet he wrote often in a highly artificial diction and a distorted word order (see the first four stanzas of the Eton ode, for example), for he held that "the language of the age is never the language of poetry," a heresy that earned him the harsh criticism of William Wordsworth in his Preface to *Lyrical Ballads*.

The *Elegy* stands alone in Gray's work: it is his one poem that belongs to world literature. It speaks to our common humanity through an art so subtle that one can know the poem for many years before becoming aware of its scores of echoes from other poems, its complex organization, and its balance of Latinate phrases with living English speech. If to express perennial feelings is to be classic, then the *Elegy* is one of our true classics. Johnson, no friend of Gray's poetry in general, long ago said the final word on this aspect of the poem:

> The Churchyard abounds with images which find a mirror in every mind, and with sentiments to which every bosom returns an echo. The four stanzas beginning "Yet even these bones" are to me original: I have never seen the notions in any other place; yet he that reads them here, persuades himself that he has always felt them. Had Gray written often thus, it had been vain to blame, and useless to praise him.

Ode on a Distant Prospect of Eton College

Anthrōpos ikanē prophasis eis tò dustukheīn.[1]

MENANDER

Ye distant spires, ye antique towers,
    That crown the watery glade,

---

1. I am a man: sufficient reason for being miserable (Greek).

Where grateful Science° still adores   *Learning*
    Her Henry's holy shade;[2]
5 And ye, that from the stately brow
Of Windsor's heights the expanse below
    Of grove, of lawn, of mead survey,
Whose turf, whose shade, whose flowers among
Wanders the hoary Thames along
10   His silver-winding way.

Ah happy hills, ah pleasing shade,
    Ah fields beloved in vain,
Where once my careless childhood strayed,
    A stranger yet to pain!
15 I feel the gales, that from ye blow,
A momentary bliss bestow,
    As waving fresh their gladsome wing,
My weary soul they seem to soothe,
And, redolent of joy and youth,
20   To breathe a second spring.

Say, Father Thames, for thou hast seen
    Full many a sprightly race
Disporting on thy margent° green   *margin, bank*
    The paths of pleasure trace,
25 Who foremost now delight to cleave
With pliant arm thy glassy wave?
    The captive linnet which enthrall?°   *imprison*
What idle progeny succeed[3]
To chase the rolling circle's° speed,   *hoop's*
30   Or urge the flying ball?

While some on earnest business bent
    Their murmuring labors ply
'Gainst graver hours, that bring constraint
    To sweeten liberty:
35 Some bold adventurers disdain
The limits of their little reign,
    And unknown regions dare descry:
Still as they run they look behind,
They hear a voice in every wind,
40   And snatch a fearful joy.

Gay hope is theirs by fancy fed,
    Less pleasing when possessed;
The tear forgot as soon as shed,
    The sunshine of the breast:
45 Theirs buxom° health of rosy hue,   *zestful, jolly*
Wild wit, invention ever new,
    And lively cheer of vigor born;
The thoughtless day, the easy night,

2. Henry VI founded Eton in 1440.   3. I.e., follow in succession Gray's generation.

The spirits pure, the slumbers light,
50   That fly the approach of morn.

Alas, regardless of their doom,
    The little victims play!
No sense have they of ills to come,
    Nor care beyond today.
55 Yet see how all around 'em wait
The ministers of human fate,
    And black Misfortune's baleful train!
Ah, show them where in ambush stand
To seize their prey the murderous band!
60   Ah, tell them they are men!

These shall the fury Passions tear,
    The vultures of the mind,
Disdainful Anger, pallid Fear,
    And Shame that skulks behind;
65 Or pining Love shall waste their youth,
Or Jealousy with rankling tooth,
    That inly gnaws the secret heart,
And Envy wan, and faded Care,
Grim-visaged comfortless Despair,
70   And Sorrow's piercing dart.

Ambition this shall tempt to rise,
    Then whirl the wretch from high,
To bitter Scorn a sacrifice,
    And grinning Infamy.
75 The stings of Falsehood those shall try,
And hard Unkindness' altered eye,
    That mocks the tear it forced to flow;
And keen Remorse with blood defiled,
And moody Madness laughing wild
80   Amid severest woe.

Lo, in the vale of years beneath
    A grisly troop are seen,
The painful family of Death,
    More hideous than their queen:
85 This racks the joints, this fires the veins,
That every laboring sinew strains,
    Those in the deeper vitals rage:
Lo, Poverty, to fill the band,
That numbs the soul with icy hand,
90   And slow-consuming Age.

To each his sufferings: all are men,
    Condemned alike to groan;
The tender for another's pain,
    The unfeeling for his own.
95 Yet ah! why should they know their fate?

Since sorrow never comes too late,
    And happiness too swiftly flies.
Thought would destroy their paradise.
No more; where ignorance is bliss,
100   'Tis folly to be wise.

1742   1747

Ode on the Death of a Favorite Cat[1]

Drowned in a Tub of Goldfishes

'Twas on a lofty vase's side,
Where China's gayest art had dyed
    The azure flowers that blow;°   bloom
Demurest of the tabby kind,
5   The pensive Selima reclined,
    Gazed on the lake below.

Her conscious tail her joy declared;
The fair round face, the snowy beard,
    The velvet of her paws,
10 Her coat, that with the tortoise vies,
Her ears of jet, and emerald eyes,
    She saw; and purred applause.

Still had she gazed; but 'midst the tide
Two angel forms were seen to glide,
15   The genii of the stream:
Their scaly armor's Tyrian° hue   purple
Through richest purple to the view
    Betrayed a golden gleam.

The hapless nymph with wonder saw:
20 A whisker first and then a claw,
    With many an ardent wish,
She stretched in vain to reach the prize.
What female heart can gold despise?
    What cat's averse to fish?

25 Presumptuous maid! with looks intent
Again she stretched, again she bent,
    Nor knew the gulf between.
(Malignant Fate sat by and smiled)
The slippery verge her feet beguiled,
30   She tumbled headlong in.

Eight times emerging from the flood
She mewed to every watery god,

---

1. Selima, one of Horace Walpole's cats, had recently drowned in a china cistern. Gray wrote this memorial at Walpole's request.

Some speedy aid to send.
No dolphin came, no nereid° stirred: *sea nymph*
35 Nor cruel Tom, nor Susan[2] heard.
A favorite has no friend!

From hence, ye beauties, undeceived,
Know, one false step is ne'er retrieved,
And be with caution bold.
40 Not all that tempts your wandering eyes
And heedless hearts is lawful prize;
Nor all that glisters gold.

1747   1748

Elegy Written in a Country Churchyard

The curfew tolls the knell of parting day,
The lowing herd wind slowly o'er the lea,
The plowman homeward plods his weary way,
And leaves the world to darkness and to me.

5   Now fades the glimmering landscape on the sight,
And all the air a solemn stillness holds,
Save where the beetle wheels his droning flight,
And drowsy tinklings lull the distant folds;

Save that from yonder ivy-mantled tower
10   The moping owl does to the moon complain
Of such, as wandering near her secret bower,
Molest her ancient solitary reign.

Beneath those rugged elms, that yew tree's shade,
Where heaves the turf in many a moldering heap,
15   Each in his narrow cell forever laid,
The rude° forefathers of the hamlet sleep.   *untaught*

The breezy call of incense-breathing Morn,
The swallow twittering from the straw-built shed,
The cock's shrill clarion, or the echoing horn,°   *hunter's horn*
20   No more shall rouse them from their lowly bed.

For them no more the blazing hearth shall burn,
Or busy housewife ply her evening care;
No children run to lisp their sire's return,
Or climb his knees the envied kiss to share.

25   Oft did the harvest to their sickle yield,
Their furrow oft the stubborn glebe° has broke;   *soil, turf*

2. "Tom" and "Susan" are servants' names.

How jocund did they drive their team afield!
How bowed the woods beneath their sturdy stroke!

Let not Ambition mock their useful toil,
30   Their homely joys, and destiny obscure;
Nor Grandeur hear with a disdainful smile
The short and simple annals of the poor.

The boast of heraldry,° the pomp of power,   *noble birth*
And all that beauty, all that wealth e'er gave,
35   Awaits alike the inevitable hour.
The paths of glory lead but to the grave.

Nor you, ye proud, impute to these the fault,
If Memory o'er their tomb no trophies[1] raise,
Where through the long-drawn aisle and fretted[2] vault
40   The pealing anthem swells the note of praise.

Can storied urn[3] or animated° bust   *lifelike*
Back to its mansion call the fleeting breath?
Can Honor's voice provoke° the silent dust,   *call forth*
Or Flattery soothe the dull cold ear of Death?

45   Perhaps in this neglected spot is laid
Some heart once pregnant with celestial fire;
Hands that the rod of empire might have swayed,
Or waked to ecstasy the living lyre.

But Knowledge to their eyes her ample page
50   Rich with the spoils of time did ne'er unroll;
Chill Penury repressed their noble rage,
And froze the genial current of the soul.

Full many a gem of purest ray serene,
The dark unfathomed caves of ocean bear:
55   Full many a flower is born to blush unseen,
And waste its sweetness on the desert air.

Some village Hampden,[4] that with dauntless breast
The little tyrant of his fields withstood;
Some mute inglorious Milton here may rest,
60   Some Cromwell guiltless of his country's blood.

The applause of listening senates to command,
The threats of pain and ruin to despise,
To scatter plenty o'er a smiling land,
And read their history in a nation's eyes,

---

1. An ornamental or symbolic group of figures
depicting the achievements of the deceased.
2. Decorated with intersecting lines in relief.
3. A funeral urn with an epitaph or pictured story
inscribed on it.

4. John Hampden (1594–1643), who, both as a
private citizen and as a Member of Parliament,
zealously defended the rights of the people against
the autocratic policies of Charles I.

65 Their lot forbade: nor circumscribed alone
    Their growing virtues, but their crimes confined;
Forbade to wade through slaughter to a throne,
    And shut the gates of mercy on mankind,

The struggling pangs of conscious truth to hide,
70   To quench the blushes of ingenuous shame,
Or heap the shrine of Luxury and Pride
    With incense kindled at the Muse's flame.

Far from the madding crowd's ignoble strife,
    Their sober wishes never learned to stray;
75 Along the cool sequestered vale of life
    They kept the noiseless tenor of their way.

Yet even these bones from insult to protect
    Some frail memorial still erected nigh,
With uncouth rhymes and shapeless sculpture decked,[5]
80   Implores the passing tribute of a sigh.

Their name, their years, spelt by the unlettered Muse,
    The place of fame and elegy supply:
And many a holy text around she strews,
    That teach the rustic moralist to die.

85 For who to dumb Forgetfulness a prey,
    This pleasing anxious being e'er resigned,
Left the warm precincts of the cheerful day,
    Nor cast one longing lingering look behind?

On some fond breast the parting soul relies,
90   Some pious drops the closing eye requires;
Even from the tomb the voice of Nature cries,
    Even in our ashes live their wonted fires.

For thee, who mindful of the unhonored dead
    Dost in these lines their artless tale relate;
95 If chance, by lonely contemplation led,
    Some kindred spirit shall inquire thy fate,

Haply some hoary-headed swain may say,
    "Oft have we seen him at the peep of dawn
Brushing with hasty steps the dews away
100   To meet the sun upon the upland lawn.

"There at the foot of yonder nodding beech
    That wreathes its old fantastic roots so high,
His listless length at noontide would he stretch,
    And pore upon the brook that babbles by.

---

5. Cf. "the storied urn or animated bust" dedicated inside the church to "the proud" (line 41).

105   "Hard by yon wood, now smiling as in scorn,
      Muttering his wayward fancies he would rove,
    Now drooping, woeful wan, like one forlorn,
      Or crazed with care, or crossed in hopeless love.

    "One morn I missed him on the customed hill,
110   Along the heath and near his favorite tree;
    Another came; nor yet beside the rill,
      Nor up the lawn, nor at the wood was he;

    "The next with dirges due in sad array
      Slow through the churchway path we saw him borne.
115   Approach and read (for thou canst read) the lay,
      Graved on the stone beneath yon aged thorn."

The Epitaph

Here rests his head upon the lap of Earth
    A youth to Fortune and to Fame unknown.
Fair Science° frowned not on his humble birth,   Learning
120   *And Melancholy marked him for her own.*

Large was his bounty, and his soul sincere,
    Heaven did a recompense as largely send:
He gave to Misery all he had, a tear,
    He gained from Heaven ('twas all he wished) a friend.

125   *No farther seek his merits to disclose,*
    Or draw his frailties from their dread abode
(There they alike in trembling hope repose),
    The bosom of his Father and his God.

ca. 1742–50   1751

WILLIAM COLLINS
1721–1759

William Collins was born in Chichester and was educated at Winchester and Oxford. Coming up to London from the university, he tried to establish himself as an author, but he was given rather to planning than to writing books. He came to know Samuel Johnson, who later remembered him affectionately as a man of learning who "loved fairies, genii, giants, and monsters" and who "delighted to rove through the meanders of enchantment." In 1746 Collins published his *Odes on Several Descriptive and Allegorical Subjects*, his part in an undertaking, with his friend Joseph Warton, to create a new poetry, more lyrical and fanciful than that of Alexander Pope's generation. Collins's *Odes* are addressed to personified abstractions (Fear, Pity, the Passions), which are imagined as vivid presences that overwhelm the poet as he calls them to life. In form these poems represent a new version of the Great or Cowleian

Ode (see headnote to Ben Jonson's Cary-Morison ode," p. 1409); Collins returns to Pindar's regularity of structure. But the originality of the *Odes* lies in their intensity of vision, which risks obscurity in quest of the sublime.

Because of this obscurity, the volume was not much liked. Inheriting some money, the poet traveled for a while, but fits of depression gradually deepened into total debility. He spent his last years in Chichester, forgotten by all but a small circle of loyal friends. As the century progressed he gained in reputation. The Romantics admired his poems and felt akin to him as they did to Thomas Chatterton and Robert Burns. The *Ode to Evening*, which combines a chaste and cool classicism with a delicate feeling for landscape and mood, is one of the delightful poems of the century.

Ode Written in the Beginning of the Year 1746

> How sleep the brave[1] who sink to rest
> By all their country's wishes blest!
> When Spring, with dewy fingers cold,
> Returns to deck their hallowed mold,
> 5 She there shall dress a sweeter sod
> Than Fancy's feet have ever trod.
>
> By fairy hands their knell is rung,
> By forms unseen their dirge is sung;
> There Honor comes, a pilgrim gray,
> 10 To bless the turf that wraps their clay,
> And Freedom shall awhile repair,
> To dwell a weeping hermit there!

1746

Ode on the Poetical Character
This ode, long disregarded, has lately been elevated in critical estimation, for it is now seen as an early, dramatic engagement with one of the central concerns of the Romantic age—the origin and role of the creative imagination and, indeed, of the poet himself.

In the strophe an analogy is drawn between the *cestus*, or girdle of Venus, which only the chaste can wear, and the cest of Fancy, or the creative imagination. In the epode the action of the creation of the world is presented as an act of the divine imagination. Inspired by God, Fancy gives birth to another sublime creation, the spirit of poetry.

In the antistrophe, John Milton is regarded as the type of poet true enough to wear the girdle of Fancy. Collins pictures himself pursuing the "guiding steps" (line 71) of Milton, as of Edmund Spenser (in the strophe)—both poet-prophets. He retreats from the elegant school of Edmund Waller (and, by implication, that of Alexander Pope)— "In vain" (line 72), however, for he lives in an uninspired age.

---

1. Collins is presumably thinking of those who lost their lives defending England in 1745, when the Scotch Jacobites, led by Bonnie Prince Charlie, penetrated to within 127 miles of London.

Ode on the Poetical Character

Strophe

As once, if not with light regard,
I read aright that gifted bard
(Him whose school above the rest
His loveliest Elfin Queen has blest),[1]
5 One, only one, unrivaled fair
Might hope the magic girdle wear,
At solemn tourney hung on high,
The wish of each love-darting eye;[2]
Lo! to each other nymph in turn applied,
10   As if, in air unseen, some hovering hand,
Some chaste and angel-friend to virgin-fame,
    With whispered spell had burst the starting band,
It left unblest her loathed dishonored side;
    Happier, hopeless fair, if never
15   Her baffled hand with vain endeavor
Had touched that fatal zone° to her denied!   *girdle*
Young Fancy thus, to me divinest name,
    To whom, prepared and bathed in Heaven
    The cest of amplest power is given:
20   To few the godlike gift assigns,
    To gird their blest, prophetic loins,[3]
And gaze her visions wild, and feel unmixed her flame!

Epode

The band, as fairy legends say,
Was wove on that creating day,
25 When He,[4] who called with thought to birth
Yon tented sky, this laughing earth,
And dressed with springs, and forests tall,
And poured the main engirting all,
Long by the loved Enthusiast[5] wooed,
30 Himself in some diviner mood,
Retiring, sate with her alone,
And placed her on his sapphire throne;
The whiles, the vaulted shrine around,
Seraphic wires were heard to sound,
35 Now sublimest triumph swelling,
Now on love and mercy dwelling;
And she, from out the veiling cloud,
Breathed her magic notes aloud:
And thou, thou rich-haired Youth of Morn,[6]
40 And all thy subject life was born!

1. Edmund Spenser.
2. *The Faerie Queene* 4.5 tells of the contest of many beautiful ladies for the girdle of Venus.
3. Pronounced *lines.*
4. God, on the day of creation.

5. I.e., Fancy; literally, "enthusiast" means "one possessed by a god."
6. Apollo, god of the sun and of poetry, associated with the archetypal poet.

The dangerous Passions kept aloof,
Far from the sainted growing woof:
But near it sate ecstatic Wonder,
Listening the deep applauding thunder:
45 And Truth, in sunny vest arrayed,
By whose the tarsel's° eyes were made;   *falcon's*
All the shadowy tribes of Mind,
In braided dance their murmurs joined,
And all the bright uncounted Powers
50 Who feed on Heaven's ambrosial flowers.
Where is the bard, whose soul can now
Its high presuming hopes avow?
Where he who thinks, with rapture blind,
This hallow'd work[7] for him designed?

Antistrophe

55 High on some cliff, to Heaven up-piled,
Of rude access, of prospect wild,
Where, tangled round the jealous steep,
Strange shades o'erbrow the valleys deep,
And holy Genii guard the rock,
60 Its glooms embrown, its springs unlock,
While on its rich ambitious head,
An Eden, like his° own, lies spread: *Milton's*
I view that oak, the fancied glades among,
By which as Milton lay, his evening ear,
65 From many a cloud that dropped ethereal dew,
Nigh sphered in Heaven its native strains could hear:
On which that ancient trump he reached was hung;
    Thither oft, his glory greeting,
    From Waller's[8] myrtle shades retreating,
70 With many a vow from Hope's aspiring tongue,
My trembling feet his guiding steps pursue;
    In vain—such bliss to one alone,°   *Milton*
    Of all the sons of soul was known,
    And Heaven, and Fancy, kindred powers,
75   Have now o'erturned the inspiring bowers,
Or curtained close such scene from every future view.

1746

Ode to Evening[1]

If aught of oaten stop, or pastoral song,
May hope, chaste Eve, to soothe thy modest ear,
    Like thy own solemn springs,

---

7. The girdle of Fancy.
8. Edmund Waller (1606–1687). The myrtle is the symbol of love poetry; Waller's poetry is thought of as trivial compared with Milton's grandeur.

1. Collins borrowed the metrical structure and the rhymeless lines of this ode from Milton's translation of Horace, *Odes* 1.5 (1673). The text printed here is based on the revised version, published in Dodsley's *Miscellany* (1748).

Thy springs and dying gales,
5 O nymph reserved, while now the bright-haired sun
Sits in yon western tent, whose cloudy skirts,
    With brede° ethereal wove,   *embroidery*
    O'erhang his wavy bed:
Now air is hushed, save where the weak-eyed bat,
10 With short shrill shriek flits by on leathern wing,
    Or where the beetle winds
    His small but sullen horn,
As oft he rises 'midst the twilight path,
Against the pilgrim borne in heedless hum:
15   Now teach me, maid composed,
    To breathe some softened strain,
Whose numbers,° stealing through thy darkening vale,   *measures*
May not unseemly with its stillness suit,
    As, musing slow, I hail
20   Thy genial loved return!
For when thy folding-star² arising shows
His paly circlet, at his warning lamp
    The fragrant Hours, and elves
    Who slept in flowers the day,
25 And many a nymph who wreaths her brows with sedge,
And sheds the freshening dew, and, lovelier still,
    The pensive Pleasures sweet,
    Prepare thy shadowy car.
Then lead, calm vot'ress, where some sheety lake
30 Cheers the lone heath, or some time-hallowed pile
    Or upland fallows gray
    Reflect its last cool gleam.
But when chill blustering winds, or driving rain,
Forbid my willing feet, be mine the hut
35   That from the mountain's side
    Views wilds, and swelling floods,
And hamlets brown, and dim-discovered spires,
And hears their simple bell, and marks o'er all
    Thy dewy fingers draw
40   The gradual dusky veil.
While Spring shall pour his showers, as oft he wont,
And bathe thy breathing tresses, meekest Eve;
    While Summer loves to sport
    Beneath thy lingering light;
45 While sallow Autumn fills thy lap with leaves;
Or Winter, yelling through the troublous air,
    Affrights thy shrinking train,
    And rudely rends thy robes;
So long, sure-found beneath the sylvan shed,
50 Shall Fancy, Friendship, Science, rose-lipped Health,
    Thy gentlest influence own,
    And hymn thy favorite name!

1746, 1748

---

2. The evening star, which signals the hour for herding the sheep into the sheepfold.

Ode on the Death of Mr. Thomson[1]

1

In yonder grave a Druid[2] lies
    Where slowly winds the stealing wave!
The year's best sweets shall duteous rise
    To deck its poet's sylvan grave![3]

2

5   In yon deep bed of whispering reeds
    His airy harp[4] shall now be laid,
That he, whose heart in sorrow bleeds,
    May love through life the soothing shade.

3

Then maids and youths shall linger here,
10   And while its sounds at distance swell,
Shall sadly seem in pity's ear
    To hear the woodland pilgrim's knell.

4

Remembrance oft shall haunt the shore
    When Thames in summer wreaths is dressed,
15   And oft suspend the dashing oar
    To bid his gentle spirit rest!

5

And oft as ease and health retire
    To breezy lawn or forest deep,
The friend shall view yon whitening spire,[5]
20   And mid the varied landscape weep.

6

But thou, who own'st that earthy bed,
    Ah! what will every dirge avail?
Or tears, which love and pity shed
    That mourn beneath the gliding sail!

7

25   Yet lives there one, whose heedless eye
    Shall scorn thy pale shrine glimmering near?

1. James Thomson died in 1748 and was buried in the parish church of Richmond, a village on the Thames near London. Collins memorializes the poet, who was his friend, both by imagining a visit to his grave and by filling his own verses with reminiscences of Thomson's poetry.
2. I.e., Thomson himself. The Druids, an order of priests in ancient Britain, had been idealized by Thomson as poet-philosophers of nature. Druidic circles like Stonehenge remain standing in England, and Collins's *Ode* itself might be said to have a circular form (the same beginning and ending).
3. The year pays tribute to Thomson because he wrote *The Seasons*.
4. Thomson had helped to popularize the Aeolian harp, which is played by the wind.
5. Richmond Church, seen from the water.

With him, sweet bard, may fancy die,
And joy desert the blooming year.

8

But thou, lorn stream, whose sullen tide
30   No sedge-crowned sisters[6] now attend,
Now waft me from the green hill's side,
Whose cold turf hides the buried friend!

9

And see, the fairy valleys fade,
Dun night has veiled the solemn view!
35   —Yet once again, dear parted shade,
Meek nature's child, again adieu!

10

The genial meads,° assigned to bless   *fostering meadows*
Thy life, shall mourn thy early doom,
Their hinds° and shepherd girls shall dress   *peasants*
40   With simple hands thy rural tomb.

11

Long, long, thy stone and pointed[7] clay
Shall melt the musing Briton's eyes,
"O! vales and wild woods," shall he say,
"In yonder grave your Druid lies!"

1749

6. Naiads, or river nymphs, supposed to have deserted the Thames since Thomson's death.

7. I.e., pointed out to visitors.

CHRISTOPHER SMART
1722–1771

In 1756 Christopher Smart, who had won prizes at Pembroke College, Cambridge, as a scholar and poet and was known in London as a wit and bon vivant, was seized by religious mania: "a preternatural excitement to prayer," according to Hester Thrale, "which he held it as a duty not to control or repress." If Smart had been content to pray in private, his life might have ended as happily as it began, but he insisted on kneeling down in the streets, in parks, and in assembly rooms. He became a public nuisance, and the public took its revenge. For most of the next seven years Smart was confined, first in St. Luke's hospital, then in a private madhouse. There, severed from his wife, his children, and his friends, he began to write a bold new sort of poetry: vivid, concise, abrupt, syntactically daring. Few of his contemporaries noticed it. After Smart's release from the madhouse (1763) he fell into debt—he had always been profligate—and his *Translation of the Psalms of David* (1765) and *Hymns for the Amusement of Children* (1770) were almost completely ignored. He died, forgotten, in a debtor's prison. But in the nineteenth century his reputation revived, and since the publication of *Jubilate Agno* in 1939 his poems have become newly famous.

The work of Smart's great period (1759–65) resembles nothing else in English. Its sources lie partly in the classics, especially Horace (whom Smart translated both in verse and prose), but far more in the Old Testament. Above all, the spirit that informs the poetry is praise and celebration, an intense vision of the divine presence shining through ordinary life. Smart believed that the world had been called into being solely to pay homage to its Maker; the function of a human being, and the poet most of all, was to be "minister of praise at large," to provide a voice of prayer for the whole creation. Thus the hero of his masterpiece, *A Song to David* (1763), is not only king but psalmist of Israel, the inspired man and poet, possessed by the spirit of the Lord, who orders and blesses everything that exists. Such poets, like the first Creator, strive to construct a microcosm in which every element—word, image, and number—fits into one grand design. The stanzas of *A Song to David* are organized in groups of three and seven (divine numbers), and separate stanzas are devoted to each of David's twelve virtues, the seven days of creation, the ten commandments, the four seasons, the five senses, and finally, in a mighty climax, the five degrees in which David excelled. To critics who accused the poem of incoherence, Smart properly replied that its chief fault, if any, was "the *exact* REGULARITY and METHOD with which it is conducted." At its best, however, the poem transports its reader into that state of adoration "Where ask is have, where seek is find, / Where knock is open wide," a state of prayer that acknowledges no division between desire and its fulfillment or God and His worshiper.

From Jubilate Agno[1]

[MY CAT JEOFFRY]

For I will consider my Cat Jeoffry.
For he is the servant of the Living God duly and daily serving him.
For at the first glance of the glory of God in the East[2] he worships in his way.
For is this done by wreathing his body seven times round with elegant quickness.
5   For then he leaps up to catch the musk, wch is the blessing of God upon his prayer.
For he rolls upon prank[3] to work it in.
For having done duty and received blessing he begins to consider himself.
For this he performs in ten degrees.
For first he looks upon his fore-paws to see if they are clean.
10 For secondly he kicks up behind to clear away there.
For thirdly he works it upon stretch with the fore-paws extended.

1. *Jubilate Agno (Rejoice in the Lamb)*, written a few lines at a time during Smart's confinement in a madhouse from 1759 to 1763, is (1) a record of his daily life and thoughts; (2) the notebook of a scholar, crammed with puns and obscure learning, which sets out elaborate correspondences between the world of the Bible and modern England; and (3) a personal Testament or book of worship, antiphonally arranged in lines beginning alternately with *Let* and *For*, which seeks to join the material and spiritual universes in one unending prayer. It has also come to be recognized, since first being published in 1939 by W. F. Stead, as a poem—a poem unique in English for its ecstatic sense of the presence of the Divine Spirit. The most famous passage describes Smart's cat, Jeoffry, his only companion during the years of confinement: "For I am possessed of a cat, surpassing in beauty, from whom I take occasion to bless Almighty God." At once a real cat, lovingly observed in all its frisks, and visible evidence of the providential plan, Jeoffry celebrates the Maker, as all things do, in his very being.

2. The sunrise.

3. Prankishly.

For fourthly he sharpens his paws by wood.
For fifthly he washes himself.
For Sixthly he rolls upon wash.
15 For Seventhly he fleas himself, that he may not be interrupted upon the
        beat.
For Eighthly he rubs himself against a post.
For Ninthly he looks up for his instructions.
For Tenthly he goes in quest of food.
For having consider'd God and himself he will consider his neighbor.
20 For if he meets another cat he will kiss her in kindness.
For when he takes his prey he plays with it to give it a chance.
For one mouse in seven escapes by his dallying.
For when his day's work is done his business more properly begins.
For he keeps the Lord's watch in the night against the adversary.
25 For he counteracts the powers of darkness by his electrical skin & glaring
        eyes.
For he counteracts the Devil, who is death, by brisking about the life.
For in his morning orisons he loves the sun and the sun loves him.
For he is of the tribe of Tiger.
For the Cherub Cat is a term of the Angel Tiger.[4]
30 For he has the subtlety and hissing of a serpent, which in goodness he sup-
        presses.
For he will not do destruction if he is well-fed, neither will he spit without
        provocation.
For he purrs in thankfulness, when God tells him he's a good Cat.
For he is an instrument for the children to learn benevolence upon.
For every house is incomplete without him & a blessing is lacking in the
        spirit.
35 For the Lord commanded Moses concerning the cats at the departure of the
        Children of Israel from Egypt.[5]
For every family had one cat at least in the bag.
For the English Cats are the best in Europe.
For he is the cleanest in the use of his fore-paws of any quadrupede.
For the dexterity of his defence is an instance of the love of God to him
        exceedingly.
40 For he is the quickest to his mark of any creature.
For he is tenacious of his point.
For he is a mixture of gravity and waggery.
For he knows that God is his Saviour.
For there is nothing sweeter than his peace when at rest.
45 For there is nothing brisker than his life when in motion.
For he is of the Lord's poor and so indeed is he called by benevolence per-
        petually—Poor Jeoffry! poor Jeoffry! the rat has bit thy throat.
For I bless the name of the Lord Jesus that Jeoffry is better.
For the divine spirit comes about his body to sustain it in compleat cat.
For his tongue is exceeding pure so that it has in purity what it wants in
        music.
50 For he is docile and can learn certain things.
For he can set up with gravity which is patience upon approbation.

---

4. As a cherub is a small angel, so a cat is a small
tiger.

5. No cats are mentioned in the Bible.

For he can fetch and carry, which is patience in employment.
For he can jump over a stick which is patience upon proof positive.
For he can spraggle upon waggle⁶ at the word of command.
55 For he can jump from an eminence into his master's bosom.
For he can catch the cork and toss it again.
For he is hated by the hypocrite and miser.
For the former is afraid of detection.
For the latter refuses the charge.
60 For he camels his back to bear the first notion of business.
For he is good to think on, if a man would express himself neatly.
For he made a great figure in Egypt for his signal services.
For he killed the Icneumon-rat very pernicious by land.⁷
For his ears are so acute that they sting again.
65 For from this proceeds the passing quickness of his attention.
For by stroking of him I have found out electricity.
For I perceived God's light about him both wax and fire.
For the Electrical fire is the spiritual substance, which God sends from
        heaven to sustain the bodies both of man and beast.
For God has blessed him in the variety of his movements.
70 For, though he cannot fly, he is an excellent clamberer.
For his motions upon the face of the earth are more than any other quad-
        rupede.
For he can tread to all the measures upon the music.
For he can swim for life.
For he can creep.

1759–63   1939

A Song to David¹

> David the son of Jesse said, and the man who was raised up on
> high, the anointed of the God of Jacob, and the sweet psalmist of
> Israel, said, "The Spirit of the Lord spake by me, and His Word was
> in my tongue."
>
>   —2 SAMUEL 23.1,2

1

O Thou, that sit'st upon a throne,
With harp of high majestic tone,   [*Invocation*]
        To praise the King of kings;
And voice of heaven-ascending swell,
5 Which, while its deeper notes excel,
        Clear, as a clarion, rings:

2

To bless each valley, grove and coast,
And charm the cherubs to the post

---

6. He can sprawl when his master waggles a finger
or stick.
7. The Ichneumon, which resembles a weasel,
was venerated and domesticated by the ancient

Egyptians.
1. For the first edition of the poem, Smart supplied a summary of the argument, here reprinted
as a running series of marginal glosses.

Of gratitude in throngs;
10　To keep the days on Zion's mount,
And send the year to his account,
　　With dances and with songs:

3

O Servant of God's holiest charge,
The minister of praise at large,
15　　Which thou may'st now receive;
From thy blessed mansion hail and hear,
From topmost eminence appear
　　To this the wreath I weave.[2]

4

Great, valiant, pious, good, and clean,
20　Sublime, contemplative, serene,
　　Strong, constant, pleasant, wise!
Bright effluence of exceeding grace;
Best man!—the swiftness and the race,
　　The peril, and the prize!

[The excellence and lus-
ter of David's character
in twelve points of view;]

5

25　Great—from the luster of his crown,
From Samuel's horn[3] and God's renown,
　　Which is the people's voice;
For all the host from rear to van,
Applauded and embraced the man—
30　　The man of God's own choice.

[proved from the history
of his life]

6

Valiant—the word, and up he rose—
The fight—he triumphed o'er the foes,
　　Whom God's just laws abhor;
And armed in gallant faith he took
35　Against the boaster,[4] from the brook,
　　The weapons of the war.

7

Pious—magnificent and grand;
'Twas he the famous temple planned:
　　(The seraph in his soul)[5]
40　Foremost to give the Lord his dues,
Foremost to bless the welcome news,
　　And foremost to condole.

2. David, a king among mortals, and now an angel in heaven, serves the King of kings by praising Him with music, which keeps the world below in tune; Smart, in turn, sings the praises of David, the poet's intermediary with God.
3. "Then Samuel took the horn of oil, and anointed him in the midst of his brethren: and the

spirit of the Lord came upon David from that day forward" (1 Samuel 16.13).
4. Goliath, whom David slew with a stone from the brook.
5. According to 1 Chronicles 28, David's plan for the Temple in Jerusalem was directly inspired by the Lord's "seraph" within him.

8

Good—from Jehudah's genuine vein,
From God's best nature good in grain,[6]
    His aspect and his heart;
To pity, to forgive, to save,
Witness En-gedi's conscious cave,
    And Shimei's blunted dart.[7]

9

Clean—if perpetual prayer be pure,
And love, which could itself inure
    To fasting and to fear—
Clean in his gestures, hands, and feet,
To smite the lyre, the dance complete,
    To play the sword and spear.

10

Sublime—invention ever young,
Of vast conception, towering tongue,
    To God the eternal theme;
Notes from yon exaltations caught,
Unrivaled royalty of thought,
    O'er meaner strains supreme.

11

Contemplative—on God to fix
His musings, and above the six
    The sabbath-day he blessed;
'Twas then his thoughts self-conquest pruned,
And heavenly melancholy tuned,
    To bless and bear the rest.

12

Serene—to sow the seeds of peace,
Remembering, when he watched the fleece,
    How sweetly Kidron purled[8]—
To further knowledge, silence vice,
And plant perpetual paradise
    When God had calmed the world.

13

Strong—in the Lord, who could defy
Satan, and all his powers that lie
    In sempiternal night;
And hell, and horror, and despair

---

6. In background and substance; Judah, David's tribe, was the tribe of kings.
7. In a cave in En-gedi, David spared Saul, who had wanted to kill him (1 Samuel 24); though Shimei threw stones and curses at him, David later refused to take his life (2 Samuel 16, 19).
8. As a young man, David kept his father's sheep near Kidron, a brook that borders the district of Jerusalem; later, fleeing his own son Absalom, he crossed Kidron into the wilderness.

Were as the lion and the bear[9]
        To his undaunted might.

14

Constant—in love to God The Truth,
80 Age, manhood, infancy, and youth—
        To Jonathan his friend
Constant, beyond the verge of death;
And Ziba, and Mephibosheth,
        His endless fame attend.[1]

15

85 Pleasant—and various as the year;
Man, soul, and angel, without peer,
        Priest, champion, sage and boy;
In armor, or in ephod[2] clad,
His pomp, his piety was glad;
90   Majestic was his joy.

16

Wise—in recovery from his fall,
Whence rose his eminence o'er all,
        Of all the most reviled;
The light of Israel in his ways,
95 Wise are his precepts, prayer and praise,
        And counsel to his child.[3]

17

His muse, bright angel of his verse,
Gives balm for all the thorns that pierce,
        For all the pangs that rage;
100 Blessed light, still gaining on the gloom,
The more than Michal of his bloom,
        The Abishag of his age.[4]

*[He consecrates his
genius for consolation
and edification]*

18

He sung of God—the mighty source
Of all things—the stupendous force
105   On which all strength depends;
From whose right arm, beneath whose eyes,
All period, power, and enterprise
        Commences, reigns, and ends.

*[The subjects he made
choice of—the Supreme
Being;]*

9. As a shepherd, David slew a lion and a bear with the help of the Lord, as later he slew Goliath (1 Samuel 17).
1. Jonathan's son Mephibosheth was restored to Saul's land by David and was attended by Saul's servant Ziba.
2. Vestment of a Hebrew priest.

3. The Proverbs and Psalms were supposed to be intended by David for his son Solomon.
4. More than Michal, his first wife, or Abishag, who ministered to him in old age, David's consolation is his muse, which gives balm for his sorrow as the Holy Spirit for Christ's.

19

Angels—their ministry and meed,
110 Which to and fro with blessings speed,
    Or with their citterns wait;
Where Michael with his millions[5] bows,
Where dwells the seraph and his spouse,
    The cherub and her mate.

[angels;]

20

115 Of man—the semblance and effect
Of God and Love—the Saint elect
    For infinite applause—
To rule the land, and briny broad,
To be laborious in his laud,
120   And heroes in his cause.

[men of renown;]

21

The world—the clustering spheres he made,
The glorious light, the soothing shade,
    Dale, champaign, grove, and hill;
The multitudinous abyss,
125 Where secrecy remains in bliss,
    And wisdom hides her skill.

*[the works of nature in
all directions, either particularly or collectively
considered]*

22

Trees, plants, and flowers—of virtuous root;
Gem[6] yielding blossom, yielding fruit,
    Choice gums and precious balm;
130 Bless ye the nosegay in the vale,
And with the sweeteners of the gale
    Enrich the thankful psalm.

23

Of fowl—e'en every beak and wing
Which cheer the winter, hail the spring,
135   That live in peace or prey;
They that make music, or that mock,
The quail, the brave domestic cock,
    The raven, swan, and jay.

24

Of fishes—every size and shape,
140 Which nature frames of light escape,
    Devouring man to shun:
The shells are in the wealthy deep,
The shoals[7] upon the surface leap,
    And love the glancing sun.

---

5. God's legions, commanded by the archangel Michael. "Citterns": guitars.

6. Bud. "Virtuous": potent, medicinal.
7. Schools of fish.

25

145 Of beasts—the beaver plods his task;
While the sleek tigers roll and bask,
    Nor yet the shades arouse;
Her cave the mining coney[8] scoops;
Where o'er the mead the mountain stoops,
150   The kids exult and browse.

26

Of gems—their virtue and their price,
Which hid in earth from man's device,
    Their darts of luster sheathe;
The jasper of the master's stamp,[9]
155 The topaz blazing like a lamp
    Among the mines beneath.

27

Blessed was the tenderness he felt
When to his graceful harp he knelt,
    And did for audience call;
160 When Satan with his hand he quelled,
And in serene suspense he held
    The frantic throes of Saul.[1]

*[He obtains power over
infernal spirits,]*

28

His furious foes no more maligned
As he such melody divined,
165   And sense and soul detained;
Now striking strong, now soothing soft,
He sent the godly sounds aloft,
    Or in delight refrained.

*[and the malignity of his
enemies;]*

29

When up to heaven his thoughts he piled,
170 From fervent lips fair Michal smiled,
    As blush to blush she stood;
And chose herself the queen, and gave
Her utmost from her heart, "so brave,
    And plays his hymns so good."[2]

*[wins the heart of
Michal]*

30

175 The pillars of the Lord are seven,
Which stand from earth to topmost heaven;
    His wisdom drew the plan;
His Word accomplished the design,

*[Shows that the pillars
of knowledge are the
monuments of God's
works in the first week]*

8. Rabbit.
9. Jasper is used to make seals or signets of authority; hid in earth, it signifies no authority but God's.
1. When Saul was oppressed by an evil spirit,
David cured him by playing on the harp (1 Samuel

16).
2. Though intended by her father Saul to be a
"snare" to David, Michal fell in love with him, as
her speech (invented by Smart) indicates.

From brightest gem to deepest mine,
180   From Christ enthroned to man.[3]

31

Alpha, the cause of causes, first
In station, fountain, whence the burst
    Of light, and blaze of day;[4]
Whence bold attempt, and brave advance,
185 Have motion, life, and ordinance,
    And heaven itself its stay.[5]

32

Gamma supports the glorious arch
On which angelic legions march,
    And is with sapphires paved;
190 Thence the fleet clouds are sent adrift,
And thence the painted folds, that lift
    The crimson veil, are waved.[6]

33

Eta with living sculpture breathes,
With verdant carvings, flowery wreathes
195   Of never-wasting bloom:
In strong relief his goodly base
All instruments of labor grace,
    The trowel, spade, and loom.

34

Next Theta stands to the Supreme—
200 Who formed, in number, sign,[7] and scheme,
    The illustrious lights that are;
And one addressed[8] his saffron robe,
And one, clad in a silver globe,
    Held rule with every star.[9]

35

205 Iota's tuned to choral hymns
Of those that fly, while he that swims
    In thankful safety lurks;
And foot, and chapitre,[1] and niche,
The various histories enrich
210   Of God's recorded works.

3. The seven pillars of the house of wisdom, referred to in Proverbs, are associated by the Masons with the building of the first Temple, erected by Solomon in Jerusalem according to divine order. Smart believed that both Proverbs and the Temple had been planned by David. In the following seven stanzas, each pillar is conflated with one of the days of Creation and with a Greek letter that represents one of the names of God. The implicit suggestion is that David, the greatest of poets and leaders, resembles the Creator, who called the universe into being with a Word.

4. On the first day God called forth light.
5. Support.
6. The firmament, created on the second day, is compared to the oracle of the Temple, which holds the Ark of the Covenant.
7. Constellation.
8. Put on.
9. The sun, with the moon and stars, was created on the fourth day.
1. Capital of a pillar. The abundance of fish and fowl, created on the fifth day, is compared to the rich decorations of the Temple (1 Kings 7).

36

Sigma presents the social droves,
With him that solitary roves,
    And man of all the chief;
Fair on whose face, and stately frame,
215   Did God impress his hallowed name,
    For ocular belief.

37

OMEGA! GREATEST and the BEST,
Stands sacred to the day of rest,
    For gratitude and thought;
220   Which blessed the world upon his pole,
And gave the universe his goal,
    And closed the infernal draught.[2]

38

O DAVID, scholar of the Lord!
Such is thy science, whence reward
    And infinite degree;[3]
225   O strength, O sweetness, lasting ripe!
God's harp thy symbol, and thy type[4]
    The lion and the bee!

39

There is but one who ne'er rebelled,
230   But One by passion unimpelled,
    By pleasure unenticed;
He from himself his semblance sent,
Grand object of his own content,
And saw the God in CHRIST.

[An exercise upon the decalogue]

40

235   "Tell them, I am," JEHOVA said
To Moses; while earth heard in dread,
    And smitten to the heart,
At once above, beneath, around,
All Nature, without voice or sound,
240   Replied, "O Lord, THOU ART."

41

Thou art—to give and to confirm,
For each his talent and his term;
    All flesh thy bounties share:
Thou shalt not call thy brother fool;

2. The completed structure of the house of God (the world) shuts out the currents of hell.
3. Elevation, rank.
4. Emblem. Theologically, a type is something in the Old Testament that prefigures some Christian truth. The lion and the bee, emblemizing the union of strength with sweetness (Judges 14), prefigure David, and David himself prefigures Christ, although, as the next stanza explains, no one can equal Him, because God is His own type. Stanzas 38 and 49 frame a ten-string "harp," the center of the poem, in which each of the Ten Commandments is interpreted according to the new Law of Christ's teachings.

245 The porches[5] of the Christian school
　　Are meekness, peace, and prayer.

42

Open, and naked of offense,
Man's made of mercy, soul, and sense;
　　God armed the snail and wilk;[6]
250 Be good to him that pulls thy plough;
Due food and care, due rest, allow
　　For her that yields thee milk.

43

Rise up before the hoary head,
And God's benign commandment dread,
255 　　Which says thou shalt not die;
"Not as I will, but as thou wilt,"[7]
Prayed He whose conscience knew no guilt;
　　With whose blessed pattern vie.

44

Use all thy passions!—love is thine,
260 And joy, and jealousy[8] divine,
　　Thine hope's eternal fort,
And care thy leisure to disturb,
With fear concupiscence to curb,
　　And rapture to transport.

45

265 Act simply, as occasion asks;
Put mellow wine in seasoned casks;
　　Till not with ass and bull:
Remember thy baptismal bond;
Keep from commixtures foul and fond,
270 　　Nor work thy flax with wool.

46

Distribute: pay the Lord his tithe,
And make the widow's heart-strings blithe;
　　Resort with those that weep;
As you from all and each expect,
275 For all and each thy love direct,
　　And render as you reap.

47

The slander and its bearer spurn,
And propagating praise sojourn
　　To make thy welcome last;
280 Turn from old Adam to the New;[9]

---

5. Porticos where ancient philosophers debated.
6. Shellfish (the whelk).
7. Matthew 26.39. Christ exemplifies the fifth commandment by submitting to his Father's will.
8. Devotion.

9. Christ. As elsewhere in this section, Smart interprets the commandment positively, less as a warning against bearing false witness than as encouragement to bear witness to truth.

By hope futurity pursue;
    Look upwards to the past.

48
Control thine eye, salute success,
Honor the wiser, happier bless,
285   And for thy neighbor feel;
Grutch not of mammon and his leaven,[1]
Work emulation up to heaven
    By knowledge and by zeal.

49
O DAVID, highest in the list
290 Of worthies, on God's ways insist,
    The genuine word repeat.[2]
Vain are the documents of men,
And vain the flourish of the pen
    That keeps the fool's conceit.

50
295 Praise above all—for praise prevails;
Heap up the measure, load the scales,
    And good to goodness add:
The generous soul her Savior aids,
But peevish obloquy degrades;
300   The Lord is great and glad.

*[The transcendent virtue
of praise and adoration]*

51
For ADORATION all the ranks
Of angels yield eternal thanks,
    And DAVID in the midst;
With God's good poor, which, last and least
305 In man's esteem, thou to thy feast,
    O blessed bride-groom, bidst.

52
For ADORATION seasons change,
And order, truth, and beauty range,
    Adjust, attract, and fill:
310 The grass the polyanthus checks;[3]
And polished porphyry reflects,
    By the descending rill.

*[An exercise upon the
seasons, and the right
use of them]*

53
Rich almonds color to the prime
For ADORATION; tendrils climb,
315   And fruit-trees pledge their gems;
And Ivis[4] with her gorgeous vest
Builds for her eggs her cunning nest,
    And bell-flowers bow their stems.

---

1. Do not begrudge the wealthy man his rise.
2. Psalm 119 [Smart's note].
3. Checkers.
4. Humming-bird [Smart's note].

54

With vinous syrup cedars spout;
320 From rocks pure honey gushing out,
    For ADORATION springs:
All scenes of painting crowd the map
Of nature; to the mermaid's pap
    The scalèd infant clings.

55

325 The spotted ounce and playsome cubs
Run rustling 'mongst the flowering shrubs,
    And lizards feed[5] the moss;
For ADORATION beasts embark,[6]
While waves upholding halcyon's ark[7]
330   No longer roar and toss.

56

While Israel sits beneath his fig,[8]
With coral root and amber sprig
    The weaned adventurer[9] sports;
Where to the palm the jasmin cleaves,
335 For ADORATION 'mong the leaves
    The gale his peace reports.

57

Increasing days their reign exalt,
Nor in the pink and mottled vault
    The opposing spirits tilt;[1]
340 And, by the coasting reader spied,
The silverlings and crusions[2] glide
    For ADORATION gilt.

58

For ADORATION ripening canes
And cocoa's[3] purest milk detains
345   The western pilgrim's staff;
Where rain in clasping boughs inclosed,
And vines with oranges disposed,
    Embower the social laugh.

59

Now labor his reward receives,
350 For ADORATION counts his sheaves
    To peace, her bounteous prince;

5. Eat. "Ounce": lynx.
6. There is a large quadruped that preys upon fish, and provides himself with a piece of timber for that purpose, with which he is very handy [Smart's note].
7. The kingfisher's nest was supposed to calm the sea by floating on it.
8. According to Micah 4.4, "they shall sit every man under his vine and his fig tree; and none shall make them afraid." As spring turns into summer, so mankind shall mature into peace.
9. Child.
1. Clouds clash together.
2. Tarpon and carp. "Coasting": floating in a boat.
3. Coconut's.

The nectarine his strong tint imbibes,
And apples of ten thousand tribes,
　　And quick[4] peculiar quince.

60

355　The wealthy crops of whitening rice,
'Mongst thyine[5] woods and groves of spice,
　　For ADORATION grow;
And, marshalled in the fencèd land,
The peaches and pomegranates stand,
360　　Where wild carnations blow.

61

The laurels with the winter strive;
The crocus burnishes alive
　　Upon the snow-clad earth:
For ADORATION myrtles stay
365　To keep the garden from dismay,
　　And bless the sight from dearth.

62

The pheasant shows his pompous neck;
And ermine, jealous of a speck[6]
　　With fear eludes offense:
370　The sable, with his glossy pride,
For ADORATION is descried,
　　Where frosts the wave condense.

63

The cheerful holly, pensive yew,
And holy thorn,[7] their trim renew;
375　　The squirrel hoards his nuts:
All creatures batten o'er their stores,
And careful nature all her doors
　　For ADORATION shuts.

64

For ADORATION, DAVID's psalms
380　Lift up the heart to deeds of alms;
　　And he, who kneels and chants,
Prevails his passions to control,
Finds meat and medicine to the soul,
　　Which for translation[8] pants.

65

385　For ADORATION, beyond match,
The scholar[9] bulfinch aims to catch

　　　　　　　　　　　　　　[An exercise upon the
　　　　　　　　　　　　　　senses, and how to
　　　　　　　　　　　　　　subdue them]

4. Pungent.
5. A precious wood mentioned in Revelation.
6. Suspicious of distant things.
7. Hawthorn.
8. Transference to heaven.
9. Imitative (the bullfinch can learn a tune).

The soft flute's ivory touch;
And careless on the hazel spray,
The daring redbreast keeps at bay
390   The damsel's greedy clutch.

66

For ADORATION, in the skies,
The Lord's philosopher espies
        The Dog, the Ram, and Rose;
The planet's ring, Orion's sword;
395 Nor is his greatness less adored
        In the vile worm that glows.

67

For ADORATION on the strings[1]
The western breezes work their wings,
        The captive ear to sooth—
400 Hark! 'tis a voice—how still, and small[2]—
That makes the cataracts to fall,
        Or bids the sea be smooth.

68

For ADORATION, incense comes
From bezoar, and Arabian gums;
405   And from the civet's[3] fur.
But as for prayer, or ere it faints,
Far better is the breath of saints
        Than galbanum and myrrh.[4]

69

For ADORATION from the down
410 Of damasins to the anana's crown,[5]
        God sends to tempt the taste;
And while the luscious zest invites
The sense, that in the scene delights,
        Commands desire be chaste.

70

415 For ADORATION, all the paths
Of grace are open, all the baths
        Of purity refresh;
And all the rays of glory beam
To deck the man of God's esteem,
420   Who triumphs o'er the flesh.

71

For ADORATION, in the dome
Of Christ the sparrows find an home,

1. Aeolian harp [Smart's note]. It is played by the wind.
2. In 1 Kings 19.11–12, the Lord does not speak in the wind but in "a still small voice."
3. Civet cat's. "Bezoar": a medicinal lump that forms in the stomachs of some animals.
4. Gum resins used in incense.
5. Pineapple's tuft. "Damesins": plums.

And on his olives perch:
The swallow also dwells with thee,
425 O man of God's humility,
  Within his Savior CHURCH.

72

Sweet is the dew that falls betimes,   *[An amplification in five*
And drops upon the leafy limes;   *degrees,]*
  Sweet Hermon's fragrant air:[6]
430 Sweet is the lily's silver bell,
And sweet the wakeful tapers smell
  That watch for early prayer.

73

Sweet the young nurse with love intense,
Which smiles o'er sleeping innocence;
435   Sweet when the lost arrive:
Sweet the musician's ardor beats,
While his vague[7] mind's in quest of sweets,
  The choicest flowers to hive.

74

Sweeter in all the strains of love,
440 The language of thy turtle dove,
  Paired to thy swelling chord;
Sweeter with every grace endued,
The glory of thy gratitude,
  Respired unto the Lord.

75

445 Strong is the horse upon his speed;
Strong in pursuit the rapid glede,[8]
  Which makes at once his game:
Strong the tall ostrich on the ground;
Strong through the turbulent profound
450   Shoots xiphias[9] to his aim.

76

Strong is the lion—like a coal
His eyeball—like a bastion's mole
  His chest against the foes:
Strong the gier-eagle[1] on his sail,
455 Strong against tide, the enormous whale
  Emerges, as he goes.

77

But stronger still, in earth and air,
And in the sea, the man of prayer;
  And far beneath the tide;

---

6. The dew of Hermon, a mountain in Syria, is
associated with Zion's dew in Psalm 133.
7. Wandering.

8. Hawk.
9. The swordfish [Smart's note].
1. Vulture. "Mole": fortified wall.

460 And in the seat to faith assigned,
　　Where ask is have, where seek is find,
　　　Where knock is open wide.

78

Beauteous the fleet before the gale;
Beauteous the multitudes in mail,
465　　Ranked arms and crested heads:
Beauteous the garden's umbrage mild,
Walk, water, meditated wild,[2]
　　And all the bloomy beds.

79

Beauteous the moon full on the lawn;
470 And beauteous, when the veil's withdrawn,
　　The virgin to her spouse:
Beauteous the temple decked and filled,
When to the heaven of heavens they build
　　Their heart-directed vows.

80

475 Beauteous, yea beauteous more than these,
The shepherd king upon his knees,
　　For his momentous trust;
With wish of infinite conceit,
For man, beast, mute,[3] the small and great,
480　　And prostrate dust to dust.

81

Precious the bounteous widow's mite;
And precious, for extreme delight,
　　The largess from the churl:[4]
Precious the ruby's blushing blaze,
485 And alba's[5] blest imperial rays,
　　And pure cerulean pearl.

82

Precious the penitential tear;
And precious is the sigh sincere,
　　Acceptable to God:
490 And precious are the winning flowers,
In gladsome Israel's feast of bowers,[6]
　　Bound on the hallowed sod.

83

More precious that diviner part
Of David, even the Lord's own heart,

2. Artificial wild place within a garden or park.
3. Fish. "Conceit": conception.
4. Samuel 25:18 [Smart's note]. Against the will of Nabal, a churlish rich man, his wife, Abigail, gave largess to David.
5. Revelation 2:17 [Smart's note]. A white stone, given to the church triumphant.
6. The Feast of Tabernacles, or Sukkoth, celebrated in arbors (see Leviticus 23.39–43).

495 Great, beautiful, and new:
In all things where it was intent,
In all extremes, in each event,
Proof[7]—answering true to true.

84

Glorious the sun in mid career;
500 Glorious the assembled fires appear;
Glorious the comet's train:
Glorious the trumpet and alarm;
Glorious the almighty stretched-out arm;
Glorious the enraptured main:

85

505 Glorious the northern lights astream;
Glorious the song, when God's the theme;
Glorious the thunder's roar:
Glorious hosanna from the den;
Glorious the catholic amen;
510 Glorious the martyr's gore:

86

Glorious—more glorious is the crown
Of Him, that brought salvation down
By meekness, called thy Son;
Thou that stupendous truth believed,
515 And now the matchless deed's achieved,
DETERMINED, DARED, and DONE.

1759–63   1939

[which is wrought up to this conclusion, That the best poet which ever lived was thought worthy of the highest honor which possibly can be conceived, as the Savior of the World was ascribed to his house, and called his son in the body.]

7. Meeting the test.

OLIVER GOLDSMITH
ca. 1730–1774

Oliver Goldsmith was born in Ireland, the son of an Anglican clergyman whose geniality he inherited and whose improvidence he imitated. He was early disfigured by smallpox and grew up ugly of face, ungraceful of figure, and in his early years apparently stupid and certainly idle. Nonetheless, he was sent to Trinity College, Dublin, as a sizar—i.e., a student who did menial jobs for well-to-do undergraduates—and there he took his A.B. in 1749. After several false starts in choosing a career, he was sent by a generous uncle to study medicine at the University of Edinburgh. Instead of taking a degree, he wandered for a while on the Continent, visiting Holland, France, Italy, and Switzerland. A romanticized account of this journey can be read in the story of George Primrose in Goldsmith's novel, *The Vicar of Wakefield* (1766). He returned to England in 1756 with a mysteriously acquired M.D. and tried in vain to support himself as a physician among the poor in the borough of Southwark. After serving for a while as an usher in a school, he drifted into the profession of hack writer for Ralph Griffiths, the proprietor of the *Monthly Review,* and later worked for and with the benevolent publisher John Newbery. He first attracted attention by the short book *An Inquiry into the Present State of Polite Learning in Europe* (1759), in which he traced what he considered to be the decline of the fine arts in mid-eighteenth-century Europe to the lack of enlightened patronage and to the malign influence of criticism and scholarship. Soon he became a famous author and an intimate of the brilliant circle around Samuel Johnson. Although his writings brought in a great deal of money, his habitual extravagance and generosity kept him always in debt. He died owing the then prodigious sum (for a man whose only source of income was writing) of £2,000.

The variety and excellence of Goldsmith's work are astonishing. His easy and pleasant prose style, his abundant humor, his shrewd observations of character and scene have made his essays constantly popular. His gift for the comedy of character and situation enabled him to achieve in his two plays, *The Good-Natured Man* (1768) and *She Stoops to Conquer* (1773), a sort of hearty and mirthful comedy—unspoiled by the fashionable sentimentality of the moment—that is unique in the century. His two important poems, *The Traveler, or A Prospect of Society* (1764) and *The Deserted Village,* are distinguished for the unforced grace of their couplets and for an air of simplicity that is far from simple to achieve.

The Deserted Village[1]

Sweet Auburn! loveliest village of the plain,
Where health and plenty cheered the laboring swain,
Where smiling spring its earliest visit paid,
And parting summer's lingering blooms delayed:
5   Dear lovely bowers of innocence and ease,
Seats of my youth, when every sport could please,
How often have I loitered o'er thy green,
Where humble happiness endeared each scene;
How often have I paused on every charm,
10   The sheltered cot,° the cultivated farm,   *cottage*
The never-failing brook, the busy mill,
The decent church that topped the neighboring hill,
The hawthorn bush, with seats beneath the shade,
For talking age and whispering lovers made;
15   How often have I blessed the coming day,
When toil remitting lent its turn to play,
And all the village train, from labor free,
Led up their sports beneath the spreading tree,
While many a pastime circled in the shade,
20   The young contending as the old surveyed;
And many a gambol frolicked o'er the ground,

---

1. *The Deserted Village* is an idealization of English rural life, mingled with poignant memories of the poet's own youth in Lissoy, Ireland. Goldsmith was seriously concerned about the effects of the agricultural revolution then in progress, which was being hastened by Enclosure Acts. Either for the sake of more profitable farming or to create vast private parks and landscape gardens, arable land was being "enclosed"—i.e., taken out of the hands of small proprietors—thus displacing yeoman farmers who, like their ancestors, had lived for generations in small villages, grazing their cattle on common land and raising food on small hold-ings. The only alternative available to many such people was to seek employment in the city or to migrate to America. In the poem, Goldsmith opposes "luxury" (the increase of wealth, the growth of cities, and the costly country estates of great noblemen and wealthy merchants) to "rural virtue" (the old agrarian economy that supported a sturdy population of independent peasants). His poem is thus at once a nostalgic lament for a doomed way of life and a denunciation of what he regarded as the corrupting, destructive force of new wealth.

And sleights of art and feats of strength went round;
And still as each repeated pleasure tired,
Succeeding sports the mirthful band inspired;
25 The dancing pair that simply sought renown,
By holding out to tire each other down;
The swain mistrustless of his smutted face,
While secret laughter tittered round the place;
The bashful virgin's sidelong looks of love,
30 The matron's glance that would those looks reprove:
These were thy charms, sweet village! sports like these,
With sweet succession, taught even toil to please;
These round thy bowers their cheerful influence shed,
These were thy charms—But all these charms are fled.
35   Sweet smiling village, loveliest of the lawn,
Thy sports are fled, and all thy charms withdrawn;
Amidst thy bowers the tyrant's hand is seen,
And desolation saddens all thy green:
One only master grasps the whole domain,
40 And half a tillage stints thy smiling plain;
No more thy glassy brook reflects the day,
But choked with sedges, works its weedy way;
Along thy glades, a solitary guest,
The hollow-sounding bittern guards its nest;
45 Amidst thy desert walks the lapwing flies,
And tires their echoes with unvaried cries.
Sunk are thy bowers, in shapeless ruin all,
And the long grass o'ertops the moldering wall;
And trembling, shrinking from the spoiler's hand,
50 Far, far away thy children leave the land.
    Ill fares the land, to hastening ills a prey,
Where wealth accumulates, and men decay;
Princes and lords may flourish, or may fade;
A breath can make them, as a breath has made;
55 But a bold peasantry, their country's pride.
When once destroyed, can never be supplied.
    A time there was, ere England's griefs began,
When every rood° of ground maintained its man;   *quarter acre*
For him light labor spread her wholesome store,
60 Just gave what life required, but gave no more:
His best companions, innocence and health;
And his best riches, ignorance of wealth.
    But times are altered; Trade's unfeeling train
Usurp the land and dispossess the swain;
65 Along the lawn, where scattered hamlets rose,
Unwieldy wealth, and cumbrous pomp repose;
And every want to opulence allied,
And every pang that folly pays to pride.
These gentle hours that plenty bade to bloom,
70 Those calm desires that asked but little room,
Those healthful sports that graced the peaceful scene,
Lived in each look, and brightened all the green;
These far departing seek a kinder shore,

And rural mirth and manners are no more.
75 Sweet Auburn! parent of the blissful hour,
Thy glades forlorn confess the tyrant's power.
Here, as I take my solitary rounds,
Amidst thy tangling walks, and ruined grounds,
And, many a year elapsed, return to view
80 Where once the cottage stood, the hawthorn grew,
Remembrance wakes with all her busy train,
Swells at my breast, and turns the past to pain.
     In all my wanderings round this world of care,
In all my griefs—and God has given my share—
85 I still had hopes my latest hours to crown,
Amidst these humble bowers to lay me down;
To husband out life's taper at the close,
And keep the flame from wasting by repose.
I still had hopes, for pride attends us still,
90 Amidst the swains to show my book-learned skill,
Around my fire an evening group to draw,
And tell of all I felt, and all I saw;
And, as an hare whom hounds and horns pursue,
Pants to the place from whence at first she flew,
95 I still had hopes, my long vexations past,
Here to return—and die at home at last.
     O blest retirement, friend to life's decline,
Retreats from care that never must be mine,
How happy he who crowns in shades like these,
100 A youth of labor with an age of ease;
Who quits a world where strong temptations try,
And, since 'tis hard to combat, learns to fly!
For him no wretches, born to work and weep,
Explore the mine, or tempt the dangerous deep;
105 No surly porter stands in guilty state
To spurn imploring famine from the gate;
But on he moves to meet his latter end,
Angels around befriending virtue's friend;
Bends to the grave with unperceived decay,
110 While Resignation gently slopes the way;
And, all his prospects brightening to the last,
His Heaven commences ere the world be passed!
     Sweet was the sound when oft at evening's close,
Up yonder hill the village murmur rose;
115 There, as I passed with careless steps and slow,
The mingling notes came softened from below;
The swain responsive as the milkmaid sung,
The sober herd that lowed to meet their young,
The noisy geese that gabbled o'er the pool,
120 The playful children just let loose from school;
The watchdog's voice that bayed the whispering wind,
And the loud laugh that spoke the vacant° mind;   *idle, carefree*
These all in sweet confusion sought the shade,
And filled each pause the nightingale had made.
125 But now the sounds of population fail,

No cheerful murmurs fluctuate in the gale,
No busy steps the grass-grown footway tread,
For all the bloomy flush of life is fled.
All but yon widowed, solitary thing
130 That feebly bends beside the plashy° spring;   *boggy*
She, wretched matron, forced, in age, for bread,
To strip the brook with mantling cresses spread,
To pick her wintry faggot from the thorn,
To seek her nightly shed, and weep till morn;
135 She only left of all the harmless train,
The sad historian of the pensive plain.
      Near yonder copse, where once the garden smiled,
And still where many a garden flower grows wild,
There, where a few torn shrubs the place disclose,
140 The village preacher's modest mansion rose.
A man he was, to all the country dear,
And passing rich with forty pounds a year;
Remote from towns he ran his godly race,
Nor e'er had changed, nor wished to change his place;
145 Unpracticed he to fawn, or seek for power,
By doctrines fashioned to the varying hour;
Far other aims his heart had learned to prize,
More skilled to raise the wretched than to rise.
His house was known to all the vagrant train,
150 He chid their wanderings, but relieved their pain;
The long-remembered beggar was his guest,
Whose beard descending swept his aged breast;
The ruined spendthrift, now no longer proud,
Claimed kindred there, and had his claims allowed;
155 The broken soldier, kindly bade to stay,
Sate by his fire, and talked the night away;
Wept o'er his wounds, or tales of sorrow done,
Shouldered his crutch, and showed how fields were won.
Pleased with his guests, the good man learned to glow,
160 And quite forgot their vices in their woe;
Careless their merits, or their faults to scan,
His pity gave ere charity began.
      Thus to relieve the wretched was his pride,
And even his failings leaned to Virtue's side;
165 But in his duty prompt at every call,
He watched and wept, he prayed and felt, for all.
And, as a bird each fond endearment tries,
To tempt its new-fledged offspring to the skies,
He tried each art, reproved each dull delay,
170 Allured to brighter worlds, and led the way.
      Beside the bed where parting life was laid,
And sorrow, guilt, and pain, by turns dismayed,
The reverend champion stood. At his control,
Despair and anguish fled the struggling soul;
175 Comfort came down the trembling wretch to raise,
And his last faltering accents whispered praise.
      At church, with meek and unaffected grace,

His looks adorned the venerable place;
Truth from his lips prevailed with double sway,
180   And fools, who came to scoff, remained to pray.
The service past, around the pious man,
With steady zeal each honest rustic ran;
Even children followed with endearing wile,
And plucked his gown, to share the good man's smile.
185   His ready smile a parent's warmth expressed,
Their welfare pleased him, and their cares distressed;
To them his heart, his love, his griefs were given,
But all his serious thoughts had rest in Heaven.
As some tall cliff that lifts its awful form,
190   Swells from the vale, and midway leaves the storm,
Though round its breast the rolling clouds are spread,
Eternal sunshine settles on its head.
     Beside yon straggling fence that skirts the way,
With blossomed furze unprofitably gay,
195   There, in his noisy mansion, skilled to rule,
The village master taught his little school;
A man severe he was, and stern to view,
I knew him well, and every truant knew;
Well had the boding tremblers learned to trace
200   The day's disasters in his morning face;
Full well they laughed with counterfeited glee,
At all his jokes, for many a joke had he;
Full well the busy whisper circling round,
Conveyed the dismal tidings when he frowned;
205   Yet he was kind, or if severe in aught,
The love he bore to learning was in fault;[2]
The village all declared how much he knew;
'Twas certain he could write, and cipher too;
Lands he could measure, terms and tides[3] presage,
210   And even the story ran that he could gauge.[4]
In arguing too, the parson owned his skill,
For even though vanquished, he could argue still;
While words of learned length, and thundering sound,
Amazed the gazing rustics ranged around;
215   And still they gazed, and still the wonder grew,
That one small head could carry all he knew.
     But past is all his fame. The very spot
Where many a time he triumphed, is forgot.
Near yonder thorn, that lifts its head on high,
220   Where once the signpost caught the passing eye,
Low lies that house where nut-brown draughts inspired,
Where graybeard Mirth and smiling Toil retired,
Where village statesmen talked with looks profound,
And news much older than their ale went round.
225   Imagination fondly stoops to trace
The parlor splendors of that festive place:

2. Because the *l* was silent, *fault* and *aught* rhymed perfectly.
3. Feasts and seasons in the church year. "Terms": dates on which rent, wages, etc. were due and tenancy began or ended.
4. Measure the content of casks and other vessels.

The whitewashed wall, the nicely sanded floor,
The varnished clock that clicked behind the door;
The chest contrived a double debt to pay,
230   A bed by night, a chest of drawers by day;
The pictures placed for ornament and use,
The twelve good rules, the royal game of goose;[5]
The hearth, except when winter chilled the day,
With aspen boughs, and flowers, and fennel gay,
235   While broken teacups, wisely kept for show,
Ranged o'er the chimney, glistened in a row.
    Vain transitory splendors! Could not all
Reprieve the tottering mansion from its fall!
Obscure it sinks, nor shall it more impart
240   An hour's importance to the poor man's heart;
Thither no more the peasant shall repair
To sweet oblivion of his daily care;
No more the farmer's news, the barber's tale,
No more the woodman's ballad shall prevail;
245   No more the smith his dusky brow shall clear,
Relax his ponderous strength, and lean to hear;
The host himself no longer shall be found
Careful to see the mantling bliss[6] go round;
Nor the coy maid, half willing to be pressed,
250   Shall kiss the cup to pass it to the rest.
    Yes! let the rich deride, the proud disdain,
These simple blessings of the lowly train,
To me more dear, congenial to my heart,
One native charm, than all the gloss of art;
255   Spontaneous joys, where nature has its play,
The soul adopts, and owns their first-born sway;
Lightly they frolic o'er the vacant mind,
Unenvied, unmolested, unconfined.
But the long pomp, the midnight masquerade,
260   With all the freaks of wanton wealth arrayed,
In these, ere triflers half their wish obtain,
The toiling pleasure sickens into pain;
And, even while fashion's brightest arts decoy,
The heart distrusting asks, if this be joy.
265   Ye friends to truth, ye statesmen, who survey
The rich man's joys increase, the poor's decay,
'Tis yours to judge how wide the limits stand
Between a splendid and an happy land.
Proud swells the tide with loads of freighted ore,
270   And shouting Folly hails them from her shore;
Hoards, even beyond the miser's wish abound,
And rich men flock from all the world around.
Yet count our gains. This wealth is but a name
That leaves our useful products still the same.
275   Not so the loss. The man of wealth and pride

5. A game in which counters were moved on a board, according to the throw of the dice. "The twelve good rules" of conduct, attributed to Charles I, were printed in a broadside that was often seen on the walls of taverns.
6. Foaming bliss, i.e., foaming ale.

Takes up a space that many poor supplied;
Space for his lake, his park's extended bounds,
Space for his horses, equipage, and hounds;
The robe that wraps his limbs in silken sloth
280   Has robbed the neighboring fields of half their growth;
His seat, where solitary sports are seen,
Indignant spurns the cottage from the green;
Around the world each needful product flies,
For all the luxuries the world supplies.
285   While thus the land adorned for pleasure all
In barren splendor feebly waits the fall.
      As some fair female unadorned and plain,
Secure to please while youth confirms her reign,
Slights every borrowed charm that dress supplies,
290   Nor shares with art the triumph of her eyes:
But when those charms are past, for charms are frail,
When time advances, and when lovers fail,
She then shines forth, solicitous to bless,
In all the glaring impotence of dress:
295   Thus fares the land, by luxury betrayed;
In nature's simplest charms at first arrayed;
But verging to decline, its splendors rise,
Its vistas strike, its palaces surprise;
While scourged by famine from the smiling land,
300   The mournful peasant leads his humble band;
And while he sinks without one arm to save,
The country blooms—a garden, and a grave.
      Where then, ah where, shall Poverty reside,
To 'scape the pressure of contiguous Pride?
305   If to some common's fenceless limits strayed,
He drives his flock to pick the scanty blade,
Those fenceless fields the sons of wealth divide,
And even the bare-worn common is denied.
      If to the city sped—What waits him there?
310   To see profusion that he must not share;
To see ten thousand baneful arts combined
To pamper luxury, and thin mankind;
To see those joys the sons of pleasure know,
Extorted from his fellow creature's woe.
315   Here, while the courtier glitters in brocade,
There the pale artist° plies the sickly trade;   *artisan*
Here, while the proud their long-drawn pomps display,
There the black gibbet glooms beside the way.
The dome where Pleasure holds her midnight reign,
320   Here, richly decked, admits the gorgeous train;
Tumultuous grandeur crowds the blazing square,
The rattling chariots clash, the torches glare.
Sure scenes like these no troubles e'er annoy!
Sure these denote one universal joy!
325   Are these thy serious thoughts?—Ah, turn thine eyes
Where the poor houseless shivering female lies.
She once, perhaps, in village plenty blest,
Has wept at tales of innocence distressed;

Her modest looks the cottage might adorn,
330 Sweet as the primrose peeps beneath the thorn;
Now lost to all; her friends, her virtue fled,
Near her betrayer's door she lays her head,
And pinched with cold, and shrinking from the shower,
With heavy heart deplores that luckless hour,
335 When idly first, ambitious of the town,
She left her wheel° and robes of country brown.   *spinning wheel*
    Do thine, sweet Auburn, thine, the loveliest train,
Do thy fair tribes participate her pain?
Even now, perhaps, by cold and hunger led,
340 At proud men's doors they ask a little bread!
    Ah, no. To distant climes, a dreary scene,
Where half the convex world intrudes between,
Through torrid tracts with fainting steps they go,
Where wild Altama[7] murmurs to their woe.
345 Far different there from all that charmed before,
The various terrors of that horrid shore;
Those blazing suns that dart a downward ray,
And fiercely shed intolerable day;
Those matted woods where birds forget to sing,
350 But silent bats in drowsy clusters cling;
Those poisonous fields with rank luxuriance crowned,
Where the dark scorpion gathers death around;
Where at each step the stranger fears to wake
The rattling terrors of the vengeful snake;
355 Where crouching tigers wait their hapless prey,[8]
And savage men, more murderous still than they;
While oft in whirls the mad tornado flies,
Mingling the ravaged landscape with the skies.
Far different these from every former scene,
360 The cooling brook, the grassy-vested green,
The breezy covert of the warbling grove,
That only sheltered thefts of harmless love.
    Good Heaven! what sorrows gloomed that parting day,
That called them from their native walks away;
365 When the poor exiles, every pleasure past,
Hung round their bowers, and fondly looked their last,
And took a long farewell, and wished in vain
For seats like these beyond the western main;
And shuddering still to face the distant deep,
370 Returned and wept, and still returned to weep.
The good old sire, the first prepared to go
To new-found worlds, and wept for other's woe.
But for himself, in conscious virtue brave,
He only wished for worlds beyond the grave.
375 His lovely daughter, lovelier in her tears,
The fond companion of his helpless years,
Silent went next, neglectful of her charms,
And left a lover's for a father's arms.
With louder plaints the mother spoke her woes,

---

7. The Altamaha River in Georgia.   8. Not the Asiatic tiger, but the puma.

380   And blessed the cot where every pleasure rose;
      And kissed her thoughtless babes with many a tear,
      And clasped them close in sorrow doubly dear;
      Whilst her fond husband strove to lend relief
      In all the silent manliness of grief.
385   O luxury! Thou cursed by Heaven's decree,
      How ill exchanged are things like these for thee!
      How do thy portions, with insidious joy,
      Diffuse their pleasures only to destroy!
      Kingdoms, by thee, to sickly greatness grown,
390   Boast of a florid vigor not their own.
      At every draught more large and large they grow,
      A bloated mass of rank unwieldy woe;
      Till sapped their strength, and every part unsound,
      Down, down they sink, and spread a ruin round.
395   Even now the devastation is begun,
      And half the business of destruction done;
      Even now, methinks, as pondering here I stand,
      I see the rural Virtues leave the land.
      Down where yon anchoring vessel spreads the sail,
400   That idly waiting flaps with every gale,
      Downward they move, a melancholy band,
      Pass from the shore, and darken all the strand.
      Contented Toil, and hospitable Care,
      And kind connubial Tenderness are there;
405   And Piety, with wishes placed above,
      And steady Loyalty, and faithful Love:
      And thou, sweet Poetry, thou loveliest maid,
      Still° first to fly where sensual joys invade;   *always*
      Unfit in these degenerate times of shame,
410   To catch the heart, or strike for honest fame;
      Dear charming Nymph, neglected and decried,
      My shame in crowds, my solitary pride;
      Thou source of all my bliss, and all my woe,
      That found'st me poor at first, and keep'st me so;
415   Thou guide by which the nobler arts excel,
      Thou nurse of every virtue, fare thee well.
      Farewell, and O! where'er thy voice be tried
      On Torno's cliffs, or Pambamarca's side,[9]
      Whether where equinoctial fervors glow,
420   Or winter wraps the polar world in snow,
      Still let thy voice, prevailing over time,
      Redress the rigors of the inclement clime;
      Aid slighted truth, with thy persuasive strain
      Teach erring man to spurn the rage of gain;
425   Teach him that states of native strength possessed,
      Though very poor, may still be very blest;
      That Trade's proud empire hastes to swift decay,
      As ocean sweeps the labored mole[1] away;

9. The river Torne in Sweden falls into the Gulf of Bothnia. Pambamarca is a mountain in Ecua-dor.
1. The laboriously built breakwater.

While self-dependent power can time defy,
430　　As rocks resist the billows and the sky.[2]

1770

2. Johnson composed the last four lines of the poem.

GEORGE CRABBE
1754–1832

George Crabbe survived through the Romantic period, but his first successful poem is very much a part of eighteenth-century literature. Born to poverty in a small, decayed Suffolk seaport, Aldeburgh, he was apprenticed to a surgeon, but found it impossible to earn a living by practicing in his native village. In 1780 he went to London and succeeded neither in finding a patron nor in securing literary employment until, reduced to desperate straits, he sent an appeal to Edmund Burke, who recognized his merit and gave him timely help. Through Burke's influence *The Library* was published; Samuel Johnson agreed to correct *The Village*; and Crabbe was ordained a minister in the Anglican Church. His appointment as chaplain to the duke of Rutland enabled him to marry the woman to whom he had long been engaged.

After 1785 he published nothing until 1807, when *The Parish Register* appeared. It was followed by *The Borough* (1810), *Tales* (1812), and *Tales of the Hall* (1819). In these poems, which won the admiration of William Wordsworth, Sir Walter Scott, and Lord Byron, Crabbe continued his vein of realism and developed his powers for narrative and characterization. *The Village* was widely read and admired despite its sometimes flat and stilted language. But its unrelieved realism and gloom set it sharply apart from conventional poems on rural life during the century. Indeed, it is an angry, scornful reply to the sentimental cult of rural simplicity, innocence, and happiness. It glances at the unrealities of pastoral conventions and systematically answers Oliver Goldsmith's charming idealization of villagers and their life in *The Deserted Village*. Crabbe knew the degrading effect of hopeless poverty, he had observed rural vice, and he knew the gulf that sometimes separated the landed gentry from their laboring tenants. Out of recollections of Aldeburgh and the neighboring seacoast, he fashioned a setting for his poem in which a niggardly nature seems the only proper background for the penury of the people who inhabit it. The accuracy of the details created a poetry of the ugly and the barren that is at variance with the long tradition of natural description from James Thomson to William Cowper.

From The Village

Book 1

The village life, and every care that reigns
O'er youthful peasants and declining swains;
What labor yields, and what, that labor past,
Age, in its hour of languor, finds at last;
5　　What forms the real picture of the poor,
Demand a song—the Muse can give no more.

Fled are those times when, in harmonious strains,
The rustic poet praised his native plains.
No shepherds now, in smooth altérnate verse,
10 Their country's beauty or their nymphs' rehearse;
Yet still for these we frame the tender strain,
Still in our lays fond Corydons[1] complain,
And shepherds' boys their amorous pains reveal,
The only pains, alas! they never feel.
15 On Mincio's banks, in Caesar's bounteous reign,
If Tityrus found the Golden Age again,
Must sleepy bards the flattering dream prolong,
Mechanic echoes of the Mantuan song?[2]
From Truth and Nature shall we widely stray,
20 Where Virgil, not where Fancy, leads the way?
Yes, thus the Muses sing of happy swains,
Because the Muses never knew their pains.
They boast their peasants' pipes; but peasants now
Resign their pipes and plod behind the plow;
25 And few, amid the rural tribe, have time
To number syllables, and play with rhyme;
Save honest Duck,[3] what son of verse could share
The poet's rapture, and the peasant's care?
Or the great labors of the field degrade,
30 With the new peril of a poorer trade?
From this chief cause these idle praises spring,
That themes so easy few forbear to sing;
For no deep thought the trifling subjects ask:
To sing of shepherds is an easy task.
35 The happy youth assumes the common strain,
A nymph his mistress, and himself a swain;
With no sad scenes he clouds his tuneful prayer,
But all, to look like her, is painted fair.
I grant indeed that fields and flocks have charms
40 For him that grazes or for him that farms;
But when amid such pleasing scenes I trace
The poor laborious natives of the place,
And see the midday sun, with fervid ray,
On their bare heads and dewy temples play;
45 While some, with feebler heads and fainter hearts,
Deplore their fortune, yet sustain their parts:
Then shall I dare these real ills to hide
In tinsel trappings of poetic pride?
No; cast by Fortune on a frowning coast,
50 Which neither groves nor happy valleys boast;
Where other cares than those the Muse relates,
And other shepherds dwell with other mates;
By such examples taught, I paint the cot,°   cottage

---

1. "Corydon" is a stock name for a shepherd in pastorals, used by both Theocritus and Virgil.
2. Virgil was born near Mantua, in Italy, not far from the river Mincius. Tityrus is one of the speakers in Virgil's *Eclogues* 1.

3. Stephen Duck (1705–1756), the "Thresher Poet," was a self-educated agricultural laborer whose verses attracted attention and finally won him the patronage of Queen Caroline.

As Truth will paint it, and as bards will not:
55 Nor you, ye poor, of lettered scorn complain,
To you the smoothest song is smooth in vain;
O'ercome by labor, and bowed down by time,
Feel you the barren flattery of a rhyme?
Can poets soothe you, when you pine for bread,
60 By winding myrtles round your ruined shed?
Can their light tales your weighty griefs o'erpower,
Or glad with airy mirth the toilsome hour?
        Lo! where the heath, with withering brake grown o'er,
Lends the light turf that warms the neighboring poor;
65 From thence a length of burning sand appears,
Where the thin harvest waves its withered ears;
Rank weeds, that every art and care defy,
Reign o'er the land, and rob the blighted rye:
There thistles stretch their prickly arms afar,
70 And to the ragged infant threaten war;
There poppies, nodding, mock the hope of toil;
There the blue bugloss paints the sterile soil;
Hardy and high, above the slender sheaf,
The slimy mallow waves her silky leaf;
75 O'er the young shoot the charlock throws a shade,
And clasping tares cling round the sickly blade;
With mingled tints the rocky coasts abound,
And a sad splendor vainly shines around.
So looks the nymph whom wretched arts adorn,
80 Betrayed by man, then left for man to scorn;
Whose cheek in vain assumes the mimic rose,
While her sad eyes the troubled breast disclose;
Whose outward splendor is but folly's dress,
Exposing most, when most it gilds distress.
85   Here joyless roam a wild amphibious race,
With sullen woe displayed in every face;
Who far from civil arts and social fly,
And scowl at strangers with suspicious eye.
        Here too the lawless merchant of the main
90 Draws from his plow the intoxicated swain;
Want only claimed the labor of the day,
But vice now steals his nightly rest away.
        Where are the swains, who, daily labor done,
With rural games played down the setting sun;
95 Who struck with matchless force the bounding ball,
Or made the ponderous quoit obliquely fall;
While some huge Ajax, terrible and strong,
Engaged some artful stripling of the throng,
And fell beneath him, foiled, while far around
100 Hoarse triumph rose, and rocks returned the sound?
Where now are these?—Beneath yon cliff they stand,
To show the freighted pinnace where to land;[4]
To load the ready steed with guilty haste;

4. Smuggling was common on the East Anglian coast.

To fly in terror o'er the pathless waste;
105 Or, when detected in their straggling course,
To foil their foes by cunning or by force;
Or yielding part (which equal knaves demand)
To gain a lawless passport[5] through the land.
Here, wandering long amid these frowning fields,
110 I sought the simple life that Nature yields;
Rapine and Wrong and Fear usurped her place,
And a bold, artful, surly, savage race;
Who, only skilled to take the finny tribe,
The yearly dinner, or septennial bribe,[6]
115 Wait on the shore, and, as the waves run high,
On the tossed vessel bend their eager eye,
Which to their coast directs its venturous way;
Theirs, or the ocean's, miserable prey.
As on their neighboring beach yon swallows stand,
120 And wait for favoring winds to leave the land,
While still for flight the ready wing is spread:
So waited I the favoring hour, and fled;
Fled from these shores where guilt and famine reign,
And cried, "Ah! hapless they who still remain;
125 Who still remain to hear the ocean roar,
Whose greedy waves devour the lessening shore;
Till some fierce tide, with more imperious sway,
Sweeps the low hut and all it holds away;
When the sad tenant weeps from door to door,
130 And begs a poor protection from the poor!"
But these are scenes where Nature's niggard hand
Gave a spare portion to the famished land;
Hers is the fault, if here mankind complain
Of fruitless toil and labor spent in vain.
135 But yet in other scenes, more fair in view,
Where Plenty smiles—alas! she smiles for few—
And those who taste not, yet behold her store,
Are as the slaves that dig the golden ore, $\Big\}$
The wealth around them makes them doubly poor.
140 Or will you deem them amply paid in health,
Labor's fair child, that languishes with wealth?
Go, then! and see them rising with the sun,
Through a long course of daily toil to run;
See them beneath the dog star's raging heat,
145 When the knees tremble and the temples beat;
Behold them, leaning on their scythes, look o'er
The labor past, and toils to come explore;
See them alternate suns and showers engage,
And hoard up aches and anguish for their age;
150 Through fens and marshy moors their steps pursue,
When their warm pores imbibe the evening dew;
Then own that labor may as fatal be

---

5. License to import or travel.
6. Paid to electors by candidates for election to Parliament. Because parliaments must be elected at least every seven years, the bribes are "septennial."

To these thy slaves, as thine excess to thee.
   Amid this tribe too oft a manly pride
155 Strives in strong toil the fainting heart to hide;
There may you see the youth of slender frame
Contend, with weakness, weariness, and shame;
Yet, urged along, and proudly loath to yield,
He strives to join his fellows of the field;
160 Till long-contending nature droops at last,
Declining health rejects his poor repast,
His cheerless spouse the coming danger sees,
And mutual murmurs urge the slow disease.
   Yet grant them health, 'tis not for us to tell,
165 Though the head droops not, that the heart is well;
Or will you praise that homely, healthy fare,
Plenteous and plain, that happy peasants share?
Oh! trifle not with wants you cannot feel,
Nor mock the misery of a stinted meal,
170 Homely, not wholesome; plain, not plenteous; such
As you who praise would never deign to touch.
   Ye gentle souls, who dream of rural ease,
Whom the smooth stream and smoother sonnet please;
Go! if the peaceful cot your praises share,
175 Go, look within, and ask if peace be there:
If peace be his—that drooping weary sire,
Or theirs, that offspring round their feeble fire;
Or hers, that matron pale, whose trembling hand
Turns on the wretched hearth the expiring brand!
180   Nor yet can Time itself obtain for these
Life's latest comforts, due respect and ease:
For yonder see that hoary swain, whose age
Can with no cares except his own engage;
Who, propped on that rude staff, looks up to see
185 The bare arms broken from the withering tree,
On which, a boy, he climbed the loftiest bough,
Then his first joy, but his sad emblem now.
   He once was chief in all the rustic trade;
His steady hand the straightest furrow made;
190 Full many a prize he won, and still is proud
To find the triumphs of his youth allowed.
A transient pleasure sparkles in his eyes;
He hears and smiles, then thinks again and sighs;
For now he journeys to his grave in pain;
195 The rich disdain him, nay, the poor disdain;
Altérnate masters now their slave command,[7]
Urge the weak efforts of his feeble hand;
And, when his age attempts its task in vain,
With ruthless taunts, of lazy poor complain.
200   Oft may you see him, when he tends the sheep,
His winter charge, beneath the hillock weep;
Oft hear him murmur to the winds that blow

---

7. Paupers were sent to do odd jobs for anyone who wanted them.

O'er his white locks and bury them in snow,
When, roused by rage and muttering in the morn
205 He mends the broken hedge with icy thorn:
    "Why do I live, when I desire to be
At once from life and life's long labor free?
Like leaves in spring, the young are blown away,
Without the sorrows of a slow decay;
210 I, like yon withered leaf, remain behind,
Nipped by the frost, and shivering in the wind;
There it abides till younger buds come on,
As I, now all my fellow swains are gone;
Then, from the rising generation thrust,
215 It falls, like me, unnoticed to the dust.
    "These fruitful fields, these numerous flocks I see,
Are others' gain, but killing cares to me:
To me the children of my youth are lords,
Cool in their looks, but hasty in their words:
220 Wants of their own demand their care; and who
Feels his own want and succors others too?
A lonely, wretched man, in pain I go,
None need my help, and none relieve my woe;
Then let my bones beneath the turf be laid,
225 And men forget the wretch they would not aid!"
    Thus groan the old, till, by disease oppressed,
They taste a final woe, and then they rest.
    Theirs is yon house that holds the parish poor,
Whose walls of mud scarce bear the broken door;
230 There, where the putrid vapors, flagging, play,
And the dull wheel hums doleful through the day—
There children dwell, who know no parents' care;
Parents, who know no children's love, dwell there!
Heartbroken matrons on their joyless bed,
235 Forsaken wives, and mothers never wed;
Dejected widows with unheeded tears,
And crippled age with more than childhood fears;
The lame, the blind, and, far the happiest they!
The moping idiot and the madman gay.
240 Here too the sick their final doom receive,
Here brought, amid the scenes of grief, to grieve,
Where the loud groans from some sad chamber flow,
Mixed with the clamors of the crowd below;
Here, sorrowing, they each kindred sorrow scan,
245 And the cold charities of man to man:
Whose laws indeed for ruined age provide,
And strong compulsion plucks the scrap from pride;
But still that scrap is bought with many a sigh,
And pride embitters what it can't deny.
250   Say ye, oppressed by some fantastic woes,
Some jarring nerve that baffles your repose;
Who press the downy couch, while slaves advance
With timid eye to read the distant glance;
Who with sad prayers the weary doctor tease,

255 To name the nameless ever-new disease;
Who with mock patience dire complaints endure,
Which real pain, and that alone, can cure—
How would ye bear in real pain to lie,
Despised, neglected, left alone to die?
260 How would ye bear to draw your latest breath,
Where all that's wretched paves the way for death?
    Such is that room which one rude beam divides,
And naked rafters form the sloping sides;
Where the vile bands that bind the thatch are seen,
265 And lath and mud are all that lie between,
Save one dull pane, that, coarsely patched, gives way
To the rude tempest, yet excludes the day.
Here, on a matted flock, with dust o'erspread,
The drooping wretch reclines his languid head;
270 For him no hand the cordial cup applies,
Or wipes the tear that stagnates in his eyes;
No friends with soft discourse his pain beguile,
Or promise hope till sickness wears a smile.
    But soon a loud and hasty summons calls,
275 Shakes the thin roof, and echoes round the walls.
Anon, a figure enters, quaintly neat,
All pride and business, bustle and conceit;
With looks unaltered by these scenes of woe,
With speed that, entering, speaks his haste to go,
280 He bids the gazing throng around him fly,
And carries fate and physic in his eye:
A potent quack, long versed in human ills,
Who first insults the victim whom he kills;
Whose murderous hand a drowsy Bench protect,[8]
285 And whose most tender mercy is neglect.
    Paid by the parish for attendance here,
He wears contempt upon his sapient sneer;
In haste he seeks the bed where Misery lies,
Impatience marked in his averted eyes;
290 And, some habitual queries hurried o'er,
Without reply, he rushes on the door.
His drooping patient, long inured to pain,
And long unheeded, knows remonstrance vain;
He ceases now the feeble help to crave
295 Of man; and silent sinks into the grave.
    But ere his death some pious doubts arise,
Some simple fears, which "bold bad" men despise:
Fain would he ask the parish priest to prove
His title certain to the joys above;
300 For this he sends the murmuring nurse, who calls
The holy stranger to these dismal walls;
And doth not he, the pious man, appear,
He, "passing rich with forty pounds a year"?[9]

8. Crabbe, who had practiced medicine among the poor of Aldeburgh, well knew the indifference of the local magistrates ("the drowsy Bench") to the incompetence and callousness of the physician hired by the parish to attend its paupers.
9. Cf. Goldsmith's *Deserted Village*, line 142 (p. 2861).

Ah! no; a shepherd of a different stock,
305 And far unlike him, feeds this little flock:
A jovial youth, who thinks his Sunday's task
As much as God or man can fairly ask;
The rest he gives to loves and labors light,
To fields the morning, and to feasts the night;
310 None better skilled the noisy pack to guide,
To urge their chase, to cheer them or to chide;
A sportsman keen, he shoots through half the day,
And, skilled at whist, devotes the night to play.
Then, while such honors bloom around his head,
315 Shall he sit sadly by the sick man's bed,
To raise the hope he feels not, or with zeal
To combat fears that e'en the pious feel?
    Now once again the gloomy scene explore, ⎫
Less gloomy now; the bitter hour is o'er,   ⎬
320 The man of many sorrows sighs no more.—   ⎭
Up yonder hill, behold how sadly slow
The bier moves winding from the vale below;
There lie the happy dead, from trouble free,
And the glad parish pays the frugal fee.
325 No more, O Death! thy victim starts to hear
Churchwarden stern, or kingly overseer;
No more the farmer claims his humble bow,
Thou art his lord, the best of tyrants thou!
    Now to the church behold the mourners come,
330 Sedately torpid and devoutly dumb;
The village children now their games suspend,
To see the bier that bears their ancient friend:
For he was one in all their idle sport,
And like a monarch ruled their little court;
335 The pliant bow he formed, the flying ball,
The bat, the wicket, were his labors all;
Him now they follow to his grave, and stand
Silent and sad, and gazing, hand in hand;
While bending low, their eager eyes explore
340 The mingled relics of the parish poor.
The bell tolls late, the moping owl flies round,
Fear marks the flight and magnifies the sound;
The busy priest, detained by weightier care,
Defers his duty till the day of prayer;
345 And, waiting long, the crowd retire distressed,
To think a poor man's bones should lie unblessed.

1780–83   1783

WILLIAM COWPER
1731–1800

There are no saner poems in the language than William Cowper's, yet they were written by a man who was periodically insane and who, for forty years, lived day to day with the possibility of madness. One form that his madness took was a conviction that he was damned for having committed the unforgivable sin, the "sin against the Holy Ghost." When he recovered from his first attack, in which he had attempted suicide, he was persuaded by his physician that this conviction was a delusion, and he embraced the doctor's own hopeful Evangelical creed, an inner assurance of divine mercy. From then on, a refugee from life, he found shelter first, in 1765, in the pious family of the Evangelical clergyman Morley Unwin, and after Unwin's death, with his widow, Mary Unwin, who gave him exactly the sort of loving shelter that he needed. They were never separated until her death in 1796. The move of Mary Unwin and Cowper from Huntington to Olney (pronounced *Own-y*) in 1765 brought them under the influence of the strenuous and fervent Evangelical clergyman John Newton, author of "Amazing Grace." With him Cowper wrote the famous *Olney Hymns,* still familiar to Methodists and other Nonconformists. But a second attack of madness, in 1773, not only frustrated his planned marriage to Mary Unwin but left him for the rest of his life with the assurance that he had been cast out by God and was inevitably damned. He never again attended services, and the main purpose of his life thereafter was to divert his mind from numb despair by every possible innocent device. He gardened, he kept pets, he walked, he wrote letters (some of the best of the century), he conversed, he read—and he wrote poetry. When it was published, it brought him a measure of fame that his modest nature could never have hoped for.

Cowper's major work is *The Task* (1785), undertaken at the bidding—hence the title—of Lady Austen, a friend who, when he complained that he had no subject, directed him to write about the sofa in his parlor. It began with a mock-heroic account of the development of the sofa from a simple stool, but it grew into a long meditative poem of more than five thousand lines. The poet describes in his murmuring voice his small world of country, village, garden, and parlor, and from time to time he glances toward the great world to condemn cities and worldliness, war and slavery, luxury and corruption. The tone is muted, the sensibility delicate, the language on the whole precise and clear, and the technique masterful. Cowper does not strive to be great, yet his contemporaries recognized their own concerns in his pious and humorous musings. Blake, Wordsworth, and Coleridge felt close to him; and in the nineteenth century his verse appealed especially to women. His introspective nature poetry and nonconforming hymns foreshadow Emily Dickinson.

From The Task

From *Book 1*

[A LANDSCAPE DESCRIBED. RURAL SOUNDS]

150   Thou[1] knowest my praise of nature most sincere,
        And that my raptures are not conjured up
        To serve occasions of poetic pomp,
        But genuine, and art partner of them all.
        How oft upon yon eminence our pace

1. Mary Unwin.

155 Has slackened to a pause, and we have borne
The ruffling wind, scarce conscious that it blew,
While admiration, feeding at the eye,
And still unsated, dwelt upon the scene.
Thence with what pleasure have we just discerned
160 The distant plow slow moving, and beside
His laboring team, that swerved not from the track,
The sturdy swain diminished to a boy!
Here Ouse,[2] slow winding through a level plain
Of spacious meads with cattle sprinkled o'er,
165 Conducts the eye along its sinuous course
Delighted. There, fast rooted in their bank,
Stand, never overlooked, our favorite elms,
That screen the herdsman's solitary hut;
While far beyond, and overthwart the stream
170 That, as with molten glass, inlays the vale,
The sloping land recedes into the clouds;
Displaying on its varied side the grace
Of hedgerow beauties numberless, square tower,
Tall spire, from which the sound of cheerful bells
175 Just undulates upon the listening ear,
Groves, heaths, and smoking villages, remote.
Scenes must be beautiful, which, daily viewed,
Please daily, and whose novelty survives
Long knowledge and the scrutiny of years—
180 Praise justly due to those that I describe.
   Nor rural sights alone, but rural sounds,
Exhilarate the spirit, and restore
The tone of languid Nature. Mighty winds,
That sweep the skirt of some far-spreading wood
185 Of ancient growth, make music not unlike
The dash of ocean on his winding shore,
And lull the spirit while they fill the mind;
Unnumbered branches waving in the blast,
And all their leaves fast fluttering, all at once.
190 Nor less composure waits upon the roar
Of distant floods, or on the softer voice
Of neighboring fountain, or of rills that slip
Through the cleft rock, and, chiming as they fall
Upon loose pebbles, lose themselves at length
195 In matted grass, that with a livelier green
Betrays the secret of their silent course.
Nature inanimate employs sweet sounds,
But animated nature sweeter still,
To soothe and satisfy the human ear.
200 Ten thousand warblers cheer the day, and one
The livelong night: nor these alone, whose notes
Nice-fingered art[3] must emulate in vain,
But cawing rooks, and kites that swim sublime

2. The village of Olney, where Cowper and Mary
Unwin were living, is situated on the river Ouse.

3. Refined skill, such as that of a flutist imitating
the nightingale's song.

In still repeated circles, screaming loud,
205 The jay, the pie, and even the boding owl
That hails the rising moon, have charms for me.
Sounds inharmonious in themselves and harsh,
Yet heard in scenes where peace forever reigns,
And only there, please highly for their sake.

[CRAZY KATE]

There often wanders one, whom better days
535 Saw better clad, in cloak of satin trimmed
With lace, and hat with splendid ribband bound.
A servingmaid was she, and fell in love
With one who left her, went to sea, and died.
Her fancy followed him through foaming waves
540 To distant shores; and she would sit and weep
At what a sailor suffers; fancy, too,
Delusive most where warmest wishes are,
Would oft anticipate his glad return,
And dream of transports she was not to know.
545 She heard the doleful tidings of his death—
And never smiled again! And now she roams
The dreary waste; there spends the livelong day,
And there, unless when charity forbids,
The livelong night. A tattered apron hides,
550 Worn as a cloak, and hardly hides, a gown
More tattered still; and both but ill conceal
A bosom heaved with never-ceasing sighs.
She begs an idle pin of all she meets,
And hoards them in her sleeve; but needful food,
555 Though pressed with hunger oft, or comelier clothes,
Though pinched with cold, asks never.—Kate is crazed!

From *Book* 3

[THE STRICKEN DEER]

I was a stricken deer, that left the herd
Long since; with many an arrow deep infixed
110 My panting side was charged, when I withdrew
To seek a tranquil death in distant shades.
There was I found by one who had himself
Been hurt by the archers. In his side he bore,
And in his hands and feet, the cruel scars.
115 With gentle force soliciting[4] the darts,
He drew them forth, and healed, and bade me live.
Since then, with few associates, in remote
And silent woods I wander, far from those
My former partners of the peopled scene;
120 With few associates, and not wishing more.
Here much I ruminate, as much I may,

---

4. "To endeavor to draw out by the use of gentle force" (*NED*).

With other views of men and manners now
Than once, and others of a life to come.
I see that all are wanderers, gone astray
125 Each in his own delusions; they are lost
In chase of fancied happiness, still wooed
And never won. Dream after dream ensues;
And still they dream that they shall still succeed,
And still are disappointed. Rings the world
130 With the vain stir. I sum up half mankind
And add two-thirds of the remaining half,
And find the total of their hopes and fears
Dreams, empty dreams.

From *Book 4*

[THE WINTER EVENING: A BROWN STUDY]

Come evening once again, season of peace,
Return sweet evening, and continue long!
245 Methinks I see thee in the streaky west,
With matron-step slow-moving, while the night
Treads on thy sweeping train; one hand employed
In letting fall the curtain of repose
On bird and beast, the other charged for man
250 With sweet oblivion of the cares of day;
Not sumptuously adorned, nor needing aid
Like homely featured night, of clustering gems;
A star or two just twinkling on thy brow
Suffices thee; save that the moon is thine
255 No less than hers, not worn indeed on high
With ostentatious pageantry, but set
With modest grandeur in thy purple zone,[5]
Resplendent less, but of an ampler round.[6]
Come then and thou shalt find thy votary calm,
260 Or make me so. Composure is thy gift.
And whether I devote thy gentle hours
To books, to music, or the poet's toil,
To weaving nets for bird-alluring fruit;
Or twining silken threads round ivory reels
265 When they command whom man was born to please;[7]
I slight thee not, but make thee welcome still.
   Just when our drawing rooms begin to blaze
With lights by clear reflection multiplied
From many a mirror, in which he of Gath,
270 Goliath,[8] might have seen his giant bulk
Whole without stooping, towering crest and all,
My pleasures too begin. But me perhaps
The glowing hearth may satisfy awhile

5. Encircling band. Evening is seen both as a personified goddess, whose "zone" is her royal belt, and as a natural phenomenon, where the "zone" is a stripe of color in the sky.
6. The moon looks larger at evening, when just

over the horizon, than at night, when it is higher and brighter.
7. I.e., women.
8. Goliath, the giant of Gath slain by David (1 Samuel 17.19–51).

With faint illumination that uplifts
275 The shadow to the ceiling, there by fits
Dancing uncouthly to the quivering flame.
Not undelightful is an hour to me
So spent in parlor twilight; such a gloom
Suits well the thoughtful or unthinking mind,
280 The mind contemplative, with some new theme
Pregnant, or indisposed alike to all.
Laugh ye, who boast your more mercurial powers
That never feel a stupor, know no pause,
Nor need one. I am conscious,° and confess,   conscious of
285 Fearless, a soul that does not always think.
Me oft has fancy ludicrous and wild
Soothed with a waking dream of houses, towers,
Trees, churches, and strange visages expressed
In the red cinders, while with poring eye
290 I gazed, myself creating what I saw.
Nor less amused have I quiescent watched
The sooty films that play upon the bars,[9]
Pendulous and foreboding, in the view
Of superstition prophesying still,
295 Though still deceived, some stranger's near approach.[1]
'Tis thus the understanding takes repose
In indolent vacuity of thought,
And sleeps and is refreshed. Meanwhile the face
Conceals the mood lethargic with a mask
300 Of deep deliberation, as° the man   as if
Were tasked to his full strength, absorbed and lost.
Thus oft reclined at ease, I lose an hour
At evening, till at length the freezing blast
That sweeps the bolted shutter, summons home
305 The recollected powers, and snapping short
The glassy threads with which the fancy weaves
Her brittle toys, restores me to myself.
How calm is my recess, and how the frost,
Raging abroad, and the rough wind, endear
310 The silence and the warmth enjoyed within.
I saw the woods and fields at close of day,
A variegated show; the meadows green,
Though faded; and the lands where lately waved
The golden harvest, of a mellow brown,
315 Upturned so lately by the forceful share.°   plowshare
I saw far off the weedy fallows[2] smile
With verdure not unprofitable, grazed
By flocks fast feeding and selecting each
His favorite herb; while all the leafless groves
320 That skirt the horizon wore a sable hue,
Scarce noticed in the kindred dusk of eve.
Tomorrow brings a change, a total change!

9. The grate of a fireplace.
1. The piece of soot that often flaps on the bars of a grate was called a "stranger" and was supposed to portend an unexpected visitor. Cf. lines 272–310 with Coleridge's *Frost at Midnight*.
2. Plowed but unseeded land.

Which even now, though silently performed
And slowly, and by most unfelt, the face
325 Of universal nature undergoes.
Fast falls a fleecy shower. The downy flakes,
Descending and with never-ceasing lapse,[3]
Softly alighting upon all below,
Assimilate all objects. Earth receives
330 Gladly the thickening mantle, and the green
And tender blade that feared the chilling blast,
Escapes unhurt beneath so warm a veil.

1785

The Castaway

Obscurest night involved the sky,
    The Atlantic billows roared,
When such a destined wretch as I,
    Washed headlong from on board,
5 Of friends, of hope, of all bereft,
His floating home forever left.

No braver chief[1] could Albion boast
    Than he with whom he went,
Nor ever ship left Albion's coast,
10   With warmer wishes sent.
He loved them both, but both in vain,
Nor him beheld, nor her again.

Not long beneath the whelming brine,
    Expert to swim, he lay;
15 Nor soon he felt his strength decline,
    Or courage die away;
But waged with death a lasting strife,
Supported by despair of life.

He shouted; nor his friends had failed
20   To check the vessel's course,
But so the furious blast prevailed,
    That, pitiless perforce,
They left their outcast mate behind,
And scudded still before the wind.

25 Some succor yet they could afford;
    And, such as storms allow,
The cask, the coop, the floated cord,
    Delayed not to bestow.

3. Gentle downward glide.
1. George, Lord Anson (1697–1762), in whose *Voyage* (1748), Cowper, years before writing this poem, had read the story of the sailor washed overboard in a storm.

But he (they knew) nor ship, nor shore,
30   Whate'er they gave, should visit more.

Nor, cruel as it seemed, could he
        Their haste himself condemn,
Aware that flight, in such a sea,
        Alone could rescue them;
35   Yet bitter felt it still to die
        Deserted, and his friends so nigh.

He long survives, who lives an hour
        In ocean, self-upheld;
And so long he, with unspent power,
40   His destiny repelled;
And ever, as the minutes flew,
Entreated help, or cried, "Adieu!"

At length, his transient respite past,
        His comrades, who before
45   Had heard his voice in every blast,
        Could catch the sound no more.
For then, by toil subdued, he drank
The stifling wave, and then he sank.

No poet wept him; but the page
50   Of narrative sincere,
That tells his name, his worth, his age,
        Is wet with Anson's tear.
And tears by bards or heroes shed
Alike immortalize the dead.

55   I therefore purpose not, or dream,
        Descanting on his fate,
To give the melancholy theme
        A more enduring date:
But misery still delights to trace
60   Its semblance in another's case.

No voice divine the storm allayed,
        No light propitious shone,
When, snatched from all effectual aid,
        We perished, each alone;
65   But I beneath a rougher sea,
And whelmed in deeper gulfs than he.

1799   1803

POPULAR BALLADS

The English and Scottish popular ballads were originally narrative poems transmitted orally and only rarely recorded in some manuscript or song book until systematic efforts were made to collect and publish them in the late eighteenth and nineteenth centuries. It is, therefore, difficult to fit them into an anthology divided into historical periods because their anonymity and oral provenance resist periodization. The earlier collectors chose to believe that their material was very old. Among the first, Bishop Percy (1729–1811), whose literary interest in ballads was awakened by his chance discovery of a seventeenth-century manuscript in which a number of them had been copied down, called his three-volume collection *Reliques of Ancient English Poetry* (1765). There is no evidence, however, that any but a handful of the surviving ballads are older than the seventeenth century. Percy's followers, notably Sir Walter Scott, whose *Minstrelsy of the Scottish Border* (1802–03) enjoyed a great success, went to the living sources of the ballads and set them down on paper at the dictation of the people among whom the old poems were still being recited and sung. Oral tradition survives longest in regions remote from urbanization and written culture. Many of the best English ballads derive from the border regions between the Scottish Highlands and Lowlands and between Scotland and England, from where they were exported to America, where they continued to flourish on the Appalachian frontier.

The distinctive quality shared by most popular ballads is spareness: the narrative style typically strips the story down to a few objective and dramatic scenes. Ballads are apt to deal only with the culminating incident or climax of a plot, to describe that event with intense compression, to put the burden of narration on allusive monologue or dialogue, and to avoid editorial comment. The force of the ballad often depends on what is *not* told directly, which must be inferred from dialogue and action.

Oral poetry depends on regular meter and heavy use of formulaic expressions. The narrative progresses by stanzas that are often linked by repetition. The most common stanza form, called ballad stanza, is a quatrain rhyming *abcb* in which the *a* and *c* lines usually have four beats and the *b* lines, three (as in *Sir Patrick Spens*). Alternatively, a ballad may be arranged in couplets (*The Three Ravens*). Ballads are known to have been recited, but the stanzaic and formulaic quality of many of them is enhanced by the fact that they are also songs, set to simple, haunting melodies. The practice of using refrains (as in *The Three Ravens*) and other kinds of repetition probably lent the ballad one of its most impressive qualities, for while the actual narratives are tightly compressed, ballads rarely develop in an unbroken line. The reader—originally, the hearer—is constantly made to pause by a repeated phrase or even by nonsense syllables, which retard the action in a suspenseful way. The progress to a foreknown, foredoomed conclusion is paradoxically made to seem more inevitable, more urgent, by such relaxations of narrative tension.

Some of the best ballads have as their subject a tragic incident—often a murder or accidental death, at times involving supernatural elements. These motifs are part of the common legacy of European folklore, and many of the English and Scottish ballads have their counterparts in other languages. To this class belong, among the selections here, *The Three Ravens, Lord Randall, The Wife of Usher's Well, Bonny Barbara Allan,* and—although not in its present form—*Sir Patrick Spens*.

A few ballads go back to incidents recorded elsewhere. *The Bonny Earl of Murray* laments the political murder of a popular sixteenth-century Scots noble. *Sir Patrick Spens*, scholars have conjectured, may be based on a historical incident of the end of the thirteenth century. The publication of ballads in the eighteenth century by Bishop Percy and others helped to inspire literary imitations such as those by William Wordsworth and Samuel Coleridge in the *Lyrical Ballads*. The adoption by these Romantic poets of what they conceived to be the simple and natural style of the folk had at the time political as well as literary implications. During the 1960s the American antiwar and civil rights movements inspired original ballads by performers like Bob Dylan and by African American poets like Dudley Randall. Thus protesters at different periods of time have taken over the style and manner of this seemingly timeless poetry.

Ballad collectors found that basically the same poem appeared in various versions in different manuscripts or was rendered differently by different performers. Thus when one speaks of *Sir Patrick Spens*, one is actually speaking of a number of poems that tell the same story in slightly or widely different words. F. J. Child, in the great collection *English and Scottish Popular Ballads*, prints multiple versions. The numbers under which Child lists each of the ballads printed here and the provenance of the particular version are given in the footnotes to individual titles. Spelling has been modernized; most of the northernisms in the originals have been retained.

Lord Randall[1]

"Oh where ha'e ye been, Lord Randall my son?
O where ha'e ye been, my handsome young man?"
  "I ha'e been to the wild wood: mother, make my bed soon,
  For I'm weary wi' hunting, and fain° wald° lie   *gladly / would*
    down."

5 "Where gat ye your dinner, Lord Randall my son?
Where gat ye your dinner, my handsome young man?"
  "I dined wi' my true love: mother, make my bed soon,
  For I'm weary wi' hunting, and fain wald lie down."

"What gat ye to your dinner, Lord Randall my son?
10 What gat ye to your dinner, my handsome young man?"
  "I gat eels boiled in broo:° mother, make my bed soon,   *broth*
  For I'm weary wi' hunting and fain wald lie down."

"What became of your bloodhounds, Lord Randall my son?
What became of your bloodhounds, my handsome young man?"
15   "O they swelled and they died: mother, make my bed soon,
  For I'm weary wi' hunting and fain wald lie down."

"O I fear ye are poisoned, Lord Randall my son!
O I fear ye are poisoned, my handsome young man!"
  "Oh yes, I am poisoned: mother, make my bed soon,
20 For I'm sick at the heart, and I fain wald lie down."

Bonny Barbara Allan[2]

It was in and about the Martinmas° time,   *November 11*
  When the green leaves were a-fallin';
That Sir John Graeme in the West Country
  Fell in love with Barbara Allan.

---

1. Child, no. 12. From Scott (1803).   2. Child, no. 84. From a miscellany (1740).

5   He sent his man down through the town
     To the place where she was dwellin':
    "O haste and come to my master dear,
     Gin° ye be Barbara Allan."   *if*

    O hooly,° hooly rase° she up,   *gently/rose*
10   To the place where he was lyin',
    And when she drew the curtain by:
     "Young man, I think you're dyin'."

    "O it's I'm sick, and very, very sick,
     And 'tis a' for Barbara Allan."
15   "O the better for me ye sal° never be,   *shall*
     Though your heart's blood were a-spillin'.

    "O dinna ye mind,[3] young man," said she,
     "When ye the cups were fillin',
    That ye made the healths gae° round and round,   *go*
20   And slighted Barbara Allan?"

    He turned his face unto the wall,
     And death with him was dealin':
    "Adieu, adieu, my dear friends all,
     And be kind to Barbara Allan."

25   And slowly, slowly, rase she up,
     And slowly, slowly left him;
    And sighing said she could not stay,
     Since death of life had reft° him.   *deprived*

    She had not gane° a mile but twa,°   *gone/two*
30   When she heard the dead-bell knellin',
    And every jow° that the dead-bell ga'ed°   *stroke/made*
     It cried, "Woe to Barbara Allan!"

    "O mother, mother, make my bed,
     O make it soft and narrow:
35   Since my love died for me today,
     I'll die for him tomorrow."

The Wife of Usher's Well[4]

There lived a wife at Usher's Well,
    And a wealthy wife was she;
She had three stout and stalwart sons,
    And sent them o'er the sea.

---

3. Don't you remember.
4. Child, no. 79. From Scott (1802), from the recitation of an old woman.

5   They hadna' been a week from her,
      A week but barely ane,°   *one*
   When word came to the carlin° wife   *old*
      That her three sons were gane.°   *gone*

   They hadna' been a week from her,
10   A week but barely three,
   When word came to the carlin wife
      That her sons she'd never see.

   "I wish the wind may never cease
      Nor fashes° in the flood,   *disturbances*
15   Till my three sons come hame° to me,   *home*
      In earthly flesh and blood."

   It fell about the Martinmas,°   *November 11*
      When nights are long and mirk,°   *dark*
   The carlin wife's three sons came hame,
20   And their hats were o' the birk.⁵

   It neither grew in sike° nor ditch,   *field*
      Nor yet in ony sheugh,°   *furrow*
   But at the gates o' Paradise
      That birk grew fair eneugh.

25   "Blow up the fire, my maidens,
      Bring water from the well:
   For a' my house shall feast this night,
      Since my three sons are well."

   And she has made to them a bed,
30   She's made it large and wide,
   And she's ta'en her mantle her about,
      Sat down at the bedside.

   Up then crew the red, red cock,
      And up and crew the gray.
35   The eldest to the youngest said,
      " 'Tis time we were away."⁶

   The cock he hadna' crawed but once,
      And clapped his wings at a',
   When the youngest to the eldest said,
40   "Brother, we must awa'.°   *away*

   "The cock doth craw, the day doth daw,°   *dawn*
      The channerin'° worm doth chide: *fretting*
   Gin° we be missed out o' our place,   *if*
      A sair pain we maun bide.⁷

---

5. Birch: those returning from the dead were thought to wear vegetation on their heads.
6. The dead must return to their graves at cock-
crow.
7. A sore pain we must abide.

well
cow house

45 "Fare ye weel,° my mother dear,
    Fareweel to barn and byre.°
    And fare ye weel, the bonny lass
    That kindles my mother's fire."

The Three Ravens[8]

There were three ravens sat on a tree,
   Down a down, hay down, hay down
There were three ravens sat on a tree,
   With a down
5 There were three ravens sat on a tree,
They were as black as they might be,
   With a down, derry, derry, derry, down, down.[9]

The one of them said to his mate,
"Where shall we our breakfast take?"

10 "Down in yonder green field
There lies a knight slain under his shield.

"His hounds they lie down at his feet,
So well they can their master keep.

"His hawks they fly so eagerly,°   *fiercely*
15 There's no fowl° dare him come nigh."   *bird*

Down there comes a fallow° doe,   *red-brown*
As great with young as she might go.° *walk*

She lifted up his bloody head,
And kissed his wounds that were so red.

20 She got him up upon her back,
And carried him to earthen lake.°   *pit*

She buried him before the prime;[1]
She was dead herself ere evensong time.

God send every gentleman
25 Such hawks, such hounds, and such a lemman.° *mistress*

Sir Patrick Spens[2]

The king sits in Dumferline town,
    Drinking the blude-reid° wine: *bloodred*

---

8. Child, no. 26. From a song book (1611).
9. The following stanzas take the same pattern
with the repetition of the first line and the refrains.

1. The first hour of the morning.
2. Child, no. 58. From Percy (1765).

"O whar will I get a guid sailor
    To sail this ship of mine?"

5 Up and spak an eldern° knicht,   *ancient*
    Sat at the king's richt knee:
"Sir Patrick Spens is the best sailor
    That sails upon the sea."

The king has written a braid° letter   *broad*
10   And signed it wi' his hand,
And sent it to Sir Patrick Spens,
    Was walking on the sand.

The first line that Sir Patrick read,
    A loud lauch° lauched he;   *laugh*
15 The next line that Sir Patrick read,
    The tear blinded his ee.°   *eye*

"O wha° is this has done this deed,   *who*
    This ill deed done to me,
To send me out this time o' the year,
20   To sail upon the sea?

"Make haste, make haste, my mirry men all,
    Our guid ship sails the morn."
"O say na° sae,° my master dear,   *not/so*
    For I fear a deadly storm.

25 "Late late yestre'en I saw the new moon
    Wi' the auld° moon in her arm,   *old*
And I fear, I fear, my dear master,
    That we will come to harm."

O our Scots nobles were richt laith°   *loath*
30   To weet° their cork-heeled shoon,°   *wet/shoes*
But lang owre° a' the play were played   *ere*
    Their hats they swam aboon.°   *above*

O lang, lang may their ladies sit,
    Wi' their fans into their hand,
35 Or e'er they see Sir Patrick Spens
    Come sailing to the land.

O lang, lang may the ladies stand,
    Wi' their gold kembs° in their hair,   *combs*
Waiting for their ain° dear lords,   *own*
40   For they'll see thame na mair.°   *more*

    Half o'er,° half o'er to Aberdour   *halfway over*
    It's fifty fadom° deep,   *fathoms*

And there lies guid Sir Patrick Spens,
Wi' the Scots lords at his feet.

The Bonny Earl of Murray[3]

Ye Highlands and ye Lawlands,°   *Lowlands*
O where have you been?
They have slain the Earl of Murray,
And they laid him on the green.

5   "Now wae° be to thee, Huntly,[4]   *woe*
And wherefore did you sae?°   *so*
I bade you bring him wi' you,
But forbade you him to slay."

He was a braw° gallant,   *brave*
10   And he rid° at the ring;[5]   *rode*
And the bonny Earl of Murray,
O he might have been a king.

He was a braw gallant,
And he played at the ba';°   *ball*
15   And the Bonny Earl of Murray
Was the flower amang them a'.

He was a braw gallant,
And he played at the glove;[6]
And the bonny Earl of Murray,
20   O he was the queen's love.

O lang will his lady
Look o'er the Castle Down,
Ere she see the Earl of Murray
Come sounding° through the town.   *blowing horns*

---

3. Child, no. 181. From a miscellany (1750).
4. Huntly, who slew Murray in 1592, had been
ordered by King James VI of Scotland (the speaker
of this stanza) to arrest the earl.

5. The "ring" was a hanging ring that mounted
knights tried to impale on their spears.
6. Either the goal in a race or a lady's favor.

Poems in Process

In all ages some poets have claimed that their poems were not willed but were inspired, whether by a muse, by divine visitation, or by sudden emergence from the author's unconscious mind. But as the poet Richard Aldington has remarked, "genius is not enough; one must also work." The working manuscripts of the greatest writers show that, however involuntary the origin of a poem, vision was usually followed by laborious revision before the work achieved the seeming inevitability of its final form.

Milton is the first major English author for whom we possess drafts of poems indubitably written in his own hand; the excerpt below from his manuscript of *Lycidas* shows the extent to which he worked over and expanded his initial attempts. It is no surprise to find Pope, one of the most meticulous of craftsmen, working and reworking his drafts, and radically enlarging *The Rape of the Lock* even after the success that attended its first printed version. But the manuscript of Samuel Johnson's greatest poem, *The Vanity of Human Wishes*, discovered in the 1940s, is a surprise, for it shows that this neoclassic writer who, in his critical theory, regarded poetry as primarily an art of achieving preconceived ends by tested means in fact composed with even greater speed and assurance than the Romantic Byron, who liked to represent himself to his readers as dashing off his verses with unreflecting ease. In the manuscript of Gray's *Elegy Written in a Country Churchyard* we find that the poet, by late afterthought, converted a relatively simple elegiac meditation into a longer and much more complex apologia for his chosen way of life. In all these selections we look on as poets, no matter how rapidly they achieve a result they are willing to let stand, carry on their inevitably tentative efforts to meet the multiple requirements of meaning, syntax, meter, sound pattern, and the constraints imposed by a chosen stanza. And because these are all very good poets, the seeming conflict between the necessities of significance and form results not in the distortion but in the perfecting of the poetic statement.

Our transcriptions from the poets' drafts attempt to reproduce, as accurately as the change from script to print will allow, the appearance of the manuscript page. A poet's first attempt at a line or phrase is reproduced in larger type, the revisions in smaller type. The line numbers that are used to identify an excerpt are those of the final form of the complete poem, as reprinted in this anthology. The marginal numbers beside the extract from *The Vanity of Human Wishes* are Johnson's own additions.

SELECTED BIBLIOGRAPHY

Autograph Poetry in the English Language, 2 vols., 1973, compiled by P. J. Croft, reproduces and transcribes one or more pages of manuscript in the poet's own hand, from the 14th century to the present time; volume 1 includes many of the poets represented in this volume of *The Norton Anthology of English Literature*, from John Skelton to George Crabbe. Books that discuss the process of poetic composition and revision, with examples from manuscripts and printed versions, are Charles D. Abbott, ed., *Poets at Work*, 1948; Phyllis Bartlett, *Poems in Process*, 1951; A. F. Scott, *The Poet's Craft*, 1957. In *Word for Word. A Study of Authors' Alterations*, 1965, Wallace Hildick analyzes the composition of prose fiction, as well as poems.

JOHN MILTON
From Lycidas[1]

[*Lines 1–14*][2]

yet once more O ye laurells and once more

ye myrtl's browne wth Ivie never sere

I come to pluck yor berries harsh and crude

~~before the mellowing yeare~~ and wth forc't fingers rude

~~and crop yor young~~ shatter yor leaves before ye mellowing yeare

bitter constraint, and sad occasion deare

compells me to disturbe yor season due

for ~~young~~ Lycidas is dead, dead ere his prime

young Lycidas and hath not left his peere

who would ∧^{not} sing for Lycidas he well knew

himselfe to sing & build the loftie rime

he must not flote upon his watrie beare

unwept, and welter to the parching wind

without the meed of some melodious teare

[*Lines 56–63*]

ay mee I fondly dreame

~~had yee~~ bin there, ~~for~~ what could that have don?

~~what could the golden hayrd Calliope~~

for her inchaunting son —————————

~~when shee beheld (the gods farre sighted bee)~~

~~his goarie scalpe rowle downe the Thracian lee~~

*whome universal nature
might lament
~~and heaven and hel deplore~~
~~when his divine head downe~~
the streame was sent
downe the Swift Hebrus to the
Lesbian shore.*

[THE THIRD AND FOLLOWING LINES ARE REWRITTEN ON A SEPARATE PAGE]

*what could the muse her selfe that Orpheus bore
the muse her selfe for her inchanting son

~~for her inchanting son~~

whome universal nature ~~might~~^{did} lament

when by the rout that made the hideous roare

*goarie his ~~divine~~^{gorie} visage down the streame was sent

downe the swift Hebrus to ye Lesbian shoare.

---

1. Transcribed from a manuscript of fifty pages in the library of Trinity College, Cambridge. Among the poems written in Milton's own hand are *Lycidas, Comus,* seven sonnets, and several other short poems. The manuscript has been photographically reproduced, with printed transcriptions, by W. Aldis Wright, *Facsimile of the Manuscript of Milton's Minor Poems* (Cambridge, England, 1899).

2. This draft is written on a separate page of the manuscript, which also contains drafts of the passages, "What could the muse her selfe" and "Bring the rathe primrose," transcribed below.

[*Lines 132–53*]

Returne Alpheus the dred voice is past
   that shrunk thy streams, returne Sicilian Muse
   and call the vales and bid them hither cast
   thire bells, and flowrets of a thousand hues
   yee vallies low where the mild wispers use

   of shades, and wanton winds, and goshing brooks ✳

   on whose fresh lap the swart starre sparely looks   ✳ sparely faintly

   bring hither all yoʳ quaint enamel'd eyes ✳ throw
   that on the greene terfe suck the honied showrs

   and purple all the ground wᵗʰ vernal flowrs
   —————————— Bring the rathe &c.[3]
   to strew the laureat herse where Lycid' lies
   for so to interpose a little ease
   ✳ fraile
   let our sad thoughts dally wᵗʰ false surmise ✳ fraile

[LINES 142–50 ARE DRAFTED ON A SEPARATE PAGE, AS FOLLOWS]

   Bring the rathe primrose that unwedded dies
   collu colouring the pale cheeke of uninjoyd love
   and that sad floure that stroue
   to write his owne woes on the vermeil graine

   next adde Narcissus yᵗ still weeps in vaine

   the woodbine and yᵉ pancie freak't wᵗʰ jet
   the glowing violet
   the cowslip wan that hangs his pensive head
   and every bud that sorrows liverie weares

   with
   let Daffadillies fill thire cups teares
   bid Amaranthus all his beautie shed
   to strew the laureat herse &c.

   Bring the rathe primrose that forsaken dies
   the tufted crowtoe and pale Gessamin

   ye
   the white pinke, and pansie freakt wᵗʰ jet
   the glowing violet

   the well-attired woodbine
   the muske rose and the garish columbine ——

   wᵗʰ cowslips wan that hang the pensive head
   ✳ weare ✳ weares
   and every flower that sad escutcheon beares imbroidrie beares

   &
   2 let daffadillies fill thire cups wᵗʰ teares
   1 bid Amaranthus all his beauties shed
   to strew &c.

3. I.e., Milton plans to insert here the passage that follows, lines 142–50.

ALEXANDER POPE

From The Rape of the Lock[1]

[1712 Version: Canto 1, Lines 1–24]

WHAT dire Offence from Am'rous Causes springs,
What mighty Quarrels rise from Trivial Things,
 I sing—This Verse to C—l, Muse! is due;
This, ev'n *Belinda* may vouchsafe to view:
Slight is the Subject, but not so the Praise,
If she inspire, and He approve my Lays.
 Say what strange Motive, Goddess! cou'd compel
A well-bred *Lord* t'assault a gentle *Belle?*
Oh say what stranger Cause, yet unexplor'd,
Cou'd make a gentle *Belle* reject a *Lord?*
And dwells such Rage in *softest Bosoms* then?
And lodge such daring Souls in *Little Men?*
 Sol thro' white Curtains did his Beams display,
And op'd those Eyes which brighter shine than they;
Shock just had giv'n himself the rowzing Shake,
And Nymphs prepar'd their *Chocolate* to take;
Thrice the wrought Slipper knock'd against the Ground,
And striking Watches the tenth Hour resound.
Belinda rose, and 'midst attending Dames
Launch'd on the Bosom of the silver *Thames:*
A Train of well-drest Youths around her shone,
And ev'ry Eye was fix'd on her alone;
On her white Breast a sparking *Cross* she wore,
Which *Jews* might kiss, and Infidels adore.

[Revised Version: Canto 1, Lines 1–22]

WHAT dire Offence from am'rous Causes springs,
What mighty Contests rise from trivial Things,
 I sing—This Verse to *Caryll*, Muse! is due;
This, ev'n *Belinda* may vouchsafe to view:
Slight is the Subject, but not so the Praise,
If She inspire, and He approve my Lays.
 Say what strange Motive, Goddess! cou'd compel
A well-bred *Lord* t'assault a gentle *Belle?*
Oh say what stranger Cause, yet unexplor'd,
Cou'd make a gentle *Belle* reject a *Lord?*

1. The first version of *The Rape of the Lock,* published 1712, consisted of two cantos and a total of 334 lines. Two years later, in 1714, Pope published an enlarged version of five cantos and 794 lines, in which he added the supernatural "machinery" of the Sylphs and Gnomes as well as a number of mock-epic episodes. The excerpts reprinted here show how Pope revised and expanded passages that he retained from the first version of the poem. The revised version includes changes that Pope added in later editions of the enlarged text of 1714.

In Tasks so bold, can Little Men engage,
And in soft Bosoms dwells such mighty Rage?
   Sol thro' white Curtains shot a tim'rous Ray,
And op'd those Eyes that must eclipse the Day;
Now Lapdogs give themselves the rowzing Shake,
And sleepless Lovers, just at Twelve, awake:
Thrice rung the Bell, the Slipper knock'd the Ground,
And the press'd Watch return'd a silver Sound.
Belinda still her downy Pillow prest,
Her Guardian *Sylph* prolong'd the balmy Rest.
'Twas he had summon'd to her silent Bed
The Morning-Dream that hover'd o'er her Head.

[Revised Version: Canto 2, Lines 1–8]

Not with more Glories, in th' Etherial Plain,
   The Sun first rises o'er the purpled Main,
   Than issuing forth, the Rival of his Beams
Launch'd on the Bosom of the Silver *Thames.*
Fair Nymphs, and well-drest Youths around her shone,
But ev'ry Eye was fix'd on her alone.
On her white Breast a sparkling *Cross* she wore,
Which *Jews* might kiss, and Infidels adore.

From An Essay on Man[1]

[From the First Manuscript]

we ourselves

1. Learn ~~then thyself,~~ not God presume to scan,
But
  ~~And~~ know, the Study of Mankind is <u>Man.</u>
Plac'd on this <u>Isthmus</u> of a Middle State,
A Being <u>darkly wise,</u> & <u>rudely great.</u>
With too much <u>knowledge</u> for the <u>Sceptic</u> side,
And too much <u>Weakness</u> for a <u>Stoic's</u> Pride,
He hangs between, uncertain where to rest;
Whether to deem himself a <u>God</u> or <u>Beast;</u>
Whether his <u>Mind</u> or <u>Body</u> to prefer,
Born but to <u>die,</u> & reas'ning but to <u>err;</u>
his
Alike in <u>Ignorance,</u> (~~that~~ Reason such)
~~Who~~   ~~who thinks~~
Whether he thinks too <u>little</u> or too <u>much</u>:
Chaos of <u>Thought</u> & <u>Passion,</u> all confus'd,
Still by <u>himself</u> abus'd & dis-abus'd:

1. Two of Pope's holograph manuscripts of *An Essay on Man* have survived. The earlier one is at the Pierpont Morgan Library in New York. The second one, at the Houghton Library, Harvard, was evidently intended as a fair copy for printing; but Pope, who was an inveterate reviser, intro-duced some last-minute changes. The passage transcribed here from each of these manuscripts is Pope's famed description of man's "middle state" in the great chain of being; in the published version, it opens Epistle 2, lines 1–18.

Created half to <u>rise</u>, & half to <u>fall</u>;
Great <u>Lord</u> of all things, yet a <u>prey</u> to all;
Sole <u>Judge</u> of <u>Truth</u>, in endless <u>Error</u> hurl'd;
The <u>Glory</u>, <u>Jest</u>, and <u>Riddle</u> of the World.

[*From the Second Manuscript*]²

~~Incipit I~~ Know
~~Incipit III~~ ~~Learn~~ we ourselves, not God presume to scan,
The only Science Convinc'd,
 ~~But know~~, the Study of Mankind is Man;
 (Plac'd on this Isthmus of a Middle State,
 A Being darkly wise, and rudely great;
 With too much Knowledge for the Sceptic side,
  With
 ~~And~~ too much Weakness for a Stoic's Pride,
    in doubt to act or
 He hangs between, ~~uncertain where to~~ rest,
     Part of
 Whether ⌐o deem himself a‸God or Beast;
  In doubt
 Whether his Mind, or Body to prefer.
  ~~This born~~ ~~that~~
 Born but to die, and reas'ning but to err;
 Alike in Ignorance, his Reason such,
  Whether he thinks or too much.
~~Who thinks~~ too little, ~~or who thinks too much:~~
 Chaos of Thought and Passion, all confus'd,
 Still by himself abus'd and dis-abus'd:
 Created half to rise, and half to fall;
 Great Lord of all things, yet a prey to all;
 Sole Judge of Truth, in endless error hurl'd;
 The Glory, Jest, and Riddle of the World!

2. In this version of the manuscript, Pope inserted some marginal glosses. In the right-hand margin (next to the line beginning "Learn we ourselves . . ."), he wrote, "Of Man, as an Individual," while next to the line beginning "Plac'd on this Isthmus . . . ," he wrote, "His Middle Nature." And in the left-hand margin, a little below the line beginning "With too much knowledge . . . ," he wrote, "His Powers, and Imperfections."

SAMUEL JOHNSON

Johnson told Boswell in 1766 that when composing verses "I have generally had them in my mind, perhaps fifty at a time, walking up and down in my room; and then I have written them down, and often, from laziness, have written only half lines. . . . I remember I wrote a hundred lines of *The Vanity of Human Wishes* in a day." When the first manuscript draft of this poem turned up in the 1940s among Boswell's papers at Malahide Castle, it supported Johnson's account, for it had been written and corrected in haste, with only sparse punctuation; also the second half of each line had been filled out, obviously from memory, at some time after the writing of the first half, in a darker ink. In the transcriptions from this manuscript (which is in the collection of Mary Hyde, Somerville, New Jersey), the half-lines and emendations that Johnson added to his initial draft are printed in boldface type.

The draft was written on the right-hand pages of a small homemade pocket book;

some words in the added half-line, impinging on the right margin of the page, had to be completed above or below the line. The two added lines, "See Nations slowly wise . . . the tardy Bust," were written on the blank left-hand page, at the place where they were to be inserted. The numeration of every tenth line was added by Johnson in the manuscript and incorporates these two additional lines.

Johnson published the poem in 1749 and revised it for a second publication in 1755, when it achieved the final form printed in the selections from Johnson, above. It was in 1755 that Johnson introduced his most famous emendation, when, after his disillusionment with Lord Chesterfield as literary patron, he substituted in line 162 the word "patron" for "garret": "Toil, envy, want, the patron, and the jail."

From The Vanity of Human Wishes

[*Lines 135–64*]

When first the College Rolls receive his nam^e
The young Enthusiast quits his ease for fame

Quick fires his breast
~~Each act betrays~~ the fever of renown
Caught from the strong Contagion of the Gown
On Isis banks he waves, from noise withdrawn
140 In sober state th' imaginary Lawn
O'er Bodley's Dome his future Labours spread
And Bacon's Mansion trembles o'er his head.
Are these thy views, proceed illustrious Youth
And Virtue guard thee to the throne of Trut^h
Yet should thy ~~fate~~ Soul indulge the gen'rous
                                                  Heat
Till Captive Science yields her last Retreat
Should Reason guide thee with her brightest Ray
And pour on misty Doubt resistless day
Should no false kindness lure to loose delight
150 Nor Praise relax, nor difficulty fright
Should tempting Novelty thy cell refrain
                                                  vain
And Sloth's bland opiates shed their fumes in
sShould Beuty blunt on fops her fatal dart
Nor claim the triumph of a letter'd heart
~~S Nor~~ Should no Disease thy torpid veins invade
Nor Melancholys Spectres haunt thy Shade
                hope
Yet ~~dream~~ not Life from Grief or Danger free,
Nor think the doom of Man revers'd for thee
Deign   passing   to
~~Turn~~ on the world ~~awhile~~ turn thine eyes
160 And pause awhile from Learning to be wise
There mark what ill the Scholar's life assail
                the
Toil envy Want ~~a~~ Garret and the Jayl
                Dreams
If ~~Hope~~ yet flatter once again attend
Hear Lydiats life and Galileo's End.

See Nations slowly wise, and meanly just,
To buried merit raise the tardy Bust.

THOMAS GRAY

There are three manuscript versions of the *Elegy* in Gray's handwriting. The one reproduced here in part is the earliest of these, preserved at Eton College, England; Gray entitled it "Stanzas wrote in a Country Church-Yard."

It is evident that Gray originally intended to conclude his poem at the end of the fifth stanza transcribed below. At some later time he bracketed off the last four stanzas, introduced a transitional stanza that incorporated the last two lines of the original conclusion, and then went on to write a new and much enlarged conclusion to the poem, which includes the closing "Epitaph." A comparison with the final version of the *Elegy*, above, will show that the author deleted some of these added stanzas, and also made a number of verbal changes, in his published texts of the poem.

From Elegy Written in a Country Churchyard

[*Lines 69–128*]

The struggleing/ Pangs of conscious Truth to hide,
To quench the Blushes of ingenuous Shame,
^{crown}
And at the Shrine of Luxury & Pride
^{With}   ^{by}
~~Burn~~ Incense hallowd in the Muse's Flame.
^{kindled at}

The thoughtless World to Majesty may bow
Exalt the brave, & idolize Success
But more to Innocence their Safety owe
Than Power & Genius e'er conspired to bless

And thou, who mindful of the unhonour'd Dead
^{eir}
Dost in these notes thy\artless Tale relate
By Night & lonely Contemplation led
To linger in the gloomy Walks of Fate

Hark how the sacred Calm, that broods around
Bids ev'ry fierce tumultuous Passion cease
In still small Accents whisp'ring from the Ground
A grateful Earnest of eternal Peace

No more with Reason & thyself at Strife
Give anxious Cares & endless Wishes room
But thro' the cool sequester'd Vale of Life
Pursue the silent Tenour of thy Doom.

Far from the madding Crowd's ignoble Strife;
Their sober Wishes never knew to stray:
Along the cool sequester'd Vale of Life
^{noiseless}
They kept the silent Tenour of their Way.

Yet even these Bones from Insult to protect
Some frail Memorial still erected nigh

With
~~In~~-uncouth Rhime, & shapeless Sculpture deckt
Implores the passing Tribute of a Sigh.

Their Name, their Years, spelt by th' unletter'd Muse
The Place of Fame, & Epitaph supply,
And many a holy Text around she strews
That teach the rustic Moralist to die.

For who to dumb Forgetfulness a Prey
This pleasing anxious Being e'er resign'd;
Left the warm Precincts of the chearful Day,
Nor cast one longing lingring Look behind?

On some fond Breast the parting Soul relies,
Some pious Drops the closing Eye requires:
Even from the Tomb the Voice of Nature cries,
And buried Ashes glow with social Fires
  For Thee, who mindful &c: as above.[1]

If chance that e'er some pensive Spirit more,
By sympathetic Musings here delay'd,
With vain, tho' kind, Enquiry shall explore
Thy once-loved Haunt, this long-deserted Shade.

Haply some hoary-headed Swain shall say,[2]
Oft have we seen him at the Peep of Dawn
With hasty Footsteps brush the Dews away
On the high Brow of yonder hanging Lawn
Him have we seen the Green-wood Side along,
While o'er the Heath we hied, our Labours done,
Oft as the Woodlark piped her farewell Song
With whistful Eyes pursue the setting Sun.
                spreading   nodding
Oft at the Foot of yonder hoary Beech
That wreathes its old fantastic Roots so high
His listless Length at Noontide would he stretch,
And pore upon the Brook that babbles by.
  With Gestures quaint now smileing as in Scorn,
         wayward fancies   ~~loved~~ would he
  Mutt'ring his fond Conceits he ~~wont to~~ rove:
    drooping,
  Now woeful wan, ~~he droop'd,~~ as one forlorn
  Or crazed with Care, or cross'd in hopeless Love.
    One Morn we miss'd him on th' accustom'd Hill,
    Along the   near
    By the Heath-~~side,~~ & at his fav'rite Tree.
    Another came, nor yet beside the Rill,
            by
    Nor up the Lawn, nor at the Wood was he.

---

1. I.e., Gray indicates that the second bracketed stanza, above, is to be inserted here, except that the opening "And thou" is to be altered to "For Thee."

2. At this point in the manuscript Gray ceases to leave a space between the stanzas. The first edition of 1751, at Gray's request, was printed without such spaces. They were, however, inserted in later editions printed during Gray's lifetime.

~~There scatter'd oft, the earliest~~
The next with Dirges meet in sad Array
       by
Slow thro the Church-way Path we saw him born
Approach & read, for thou can'st read the Lay
  Graved carved   yon
Wrote on the Stone beneath that ancient Thorn

                      Year
There scatter'd oft the earliest of y^e ~~Spring~~
         showers of
By Hands unseen are frequent Vi'lets found
  Redbreast
The Robin loves to build & warble there,
And little Footsteps lightly print the Ground.

Here rests his Head upon the Lap of Earth[3]
A Youth to Fortune & to Fame unknown
Fair Science frown'd not on his humble Birth
And Melancholy mark'd him for her own

Large was his Bounty & his Heart sincere;
Heaven did a Recompence as largely send.
He gave to Mis'ry all he had, a Tear.
He gain'd from Heav'n, 'twas all he wish'd, a Friend

No farther seek his Merits to disclose,
  think
Nor seek to draw them from their dread Abode
(His Frailties there in trembling Hope repose)
The Bosom of his Father & his God.

3. These last three stanzas (which Gray in the first edition of 1751 labeled "The Epitaph") are written in the right-hand margin, with the page turned crosswise.

Selected Bibliographies

The Selected Bibliographies consist of a list of Suggested General Readings on English literature, followed by bibliographies for each of the literary periods in this volume. For ease of reference, the authors within each period are arranged in alphabetical order. Entries for certain classes of writings (e.g., "Literature of the Sacred") are included, in alphabetical order, within the listings for individual authors.

SUGGESTED GENERAL READINGS

Histories of England and of English Literature

New research and new perspectives have made even the most distinguished of the comprehensive, general histories written in past generations seem outmoded. Innovative research in social, cultural, and political history has made it difficult to write a single, coherent account of England from the Middle Ages to the present, let alone to accommodate in a unified narrative the complex histories of Scotland, Ireland, and Wales. Readers who wish to explore the historical matrix out of which the works of literature collected in this anthology emerged are advised to consult the studies of particular periods listed in the appropriate sections of this bibliography. The multivolume *Oxford History of England* is useful, as are the three-volume *Peoples of the British Isles: A New History*, ed. Stanford Lehmberg, 1992, and the nine-volume *Cambridge Cultural History of Britain*, ed. Boris Ford, 1992. Albert Baugh et al., *A Literary History of England*, rev. 1967, remains a convenient source of factual materials about authors, works, and chronology. Given the cultural centrality of London, readers may find Roy Porter's *London: A Social History*, 1994, valuable. Similar observations may be made about literary history. In the light of such initiatives as women's studies, new historicism, and postcolonialism, the range of authors deemed most significant has expanded in recent years, along with the geographical and conceptual boundaries of literature in English. Attempts to capture in a unified account the great sweep of literature from *Beowulf* to late last night have largely given way to studies of individual genres, carefully delimited time periods, and specific authors. For these more focused accounts, see the listings by period.

Among the large-scale literary surveys, *The Cambridge Guide to Literature in English*, 1993, is useful, as is *The Penguin History of Literature*. The *Feminist Companion to Literature in English*, ed. Virginia Blain, Isobel Grundy, and Patricia Cle-

ments, 1990, is an important resource, and the editorial materials in *The Norton Anthology of Literature by Women*, 2nd ed., 1996, ed. Sandra M. Gilbert and Susan Gubar, constitute a concise history and set of biographies of women authors since the Middle Ages. *Annals of English Literature, 1475–1950*, rev. 1961, lists important publications year by year, together with the significant literary events for each year. David Daiches, *A Critical History of English Literature*, 2 vols., rev. 1970, provides a running literary appreciation.

Helpful treatments and surveys of English meter, rhyme, and stanza forms are Paul Fussell Jr., *Poetic Meter and Poetic Form*, rev. 1979; Donald Wesling, *The Chances of Rhyme: Device and Modernity*, 1980; Derek Attridge, *The Rhythms of English Poetry*, 1982; Charles O. Hartman, *Free Verse: An Essay in Prosody*, 1983; John Hollander, *Vision and Resonance: Two Senses of Poetic Form*, rev. 1985; and Robert Pinsky, *The Sounds of Poetry: A Brief Guide*, 1998.

On the development of the novel as a form, see Ian Watt, *The Rise of the Novel*, 1957; *The Columbia History of the British Novel*, ed. John Richetti, 1994; and Margaret Doody, *The True Story of the Novel*, 1996. On women novelists and readers, see Nancy Armstrong, *Desire and Domestic Fiction: A Political History of the Novel*, 1987; and Catherine Gallagher, *Nobody's Story: The Vanishing Acts of Women Writers in the Marketplace, 1670–1820*, 1994.

On the history of playhouse design, see Richard Leacroft, *The Development of the English Playhouse: An Illustrated Survey of Theatre Building in England from Medieval to Modern Times*, 1988. For a survey of the plays that have appeared on these and other stages, see Allardyce Nicoll, *British Drama*, rev. 1962, and the eight-volume *Revels History of Drama in English*, gen. eds. Clifford Leech and T. W. Craik, 1975–83.

On some of the key intellectual currents that are at once reflected in and shaped by English literature, Arthur T. Lovejoy's classic studies *The Great*

Chain of Being, 1936, and Essays in the History of Ideas, 1948, remain valuable, along with such works as Lovejoy and George Boas, Primitivism and Related Ideas in Antiquity, 1935; Ernst Kantowicz, The King's Two Bodies: A Study in Medieval Political Theology, 1957, new ed. 1997; Richard Popkin, The History of Skepticism from Erasmus to Descartes, 1960; M. H. Abrams, Natural Supernaturalism: Tradition and Revolution in Romantic Literature, 1971; and Michel Foucault, Madness and Civilization: A History of Insanity in the Age of Reason, Eng. trans. 1965, and The Order of Things: An Archaeology of the Human Sciences, Eng. trans. 1970.

Reference Works

The single most important tool for the study of literature in English is the Oxford English Dictionary, 2nd ed., 1989, also available on CD-ROM. The OED is written on historical principles: that is, it attempts not only to describe current word use but also to record the history and development of the language from its origins before the Norman conquest to the present. It thus provides, for familiar as well as archaic and obscure words, the widest possible range of meanings and uses, organized chronologically and illustrated with quotations. Beyond the OED there are many other valuable dictionaries, such as The American Heritage Dictionary, The Oxford Dictionary of Etymology, and an array of reference works from The Cambridge Encyclopedia of the English Language, ed. David Crystal, 1995, to guides to specialized vocabularies, slang, regional dialects, and the like.

There is a steady flow of new editions of most major and many minor writers in English, along with a ceaseless outpouring of critical appraisals and scholarship. The MLA International Bibliography (also on line) is the best way to keep abreast of the most recent work and to conduct bibliographic searches. The New Cambridge Bibliography of English Literature ed. George Watson, 1969–77, updated shorter ed. 1981, is a valuable guide to the huge body of earlier literary criticism and scholarship. A Guide to English and American Literature, ed. F. W. Bateson and Harrison Meserole, rev. 1976, is a selected list of editions, as well as scholarly and critical treatments. Further bibliographical aids are described in Arthur G. Kennedy, A Concise Bibliography for Students of English, rev. 1972; Richard D. Altick and Andrew Wright, Selective Bibliography for the Study of English and American Literature rev. 1979, and James L. Harner, Literary Research Guide, rev. 1998.

For compact biographies of English authors, see the multivolume Dictionary of National Biography, ed. Leslie Stephen and Sidney Lee, 1885–1900, with supplements that carry the work to 1980; condensed biographies will be found in the Concise Dictionary of National Biography, 2 parts (1920, 1988). Handy reference books of authors, works, and various literary terms and allusions are The Oxford Companion to the Theatre, Phyllis Hartnoll,

rev. 1990; Princeton Encyclopedia of Poetry and Poetics, ed. Alex Preminger and others, rev. 1993; and The Oxford Companion to English Literature, ed. Margaret Drabble, rev. 1998. Low-priced handbooks that define and illustrate literary concepts and terms are The Penguin Dictionary of Literary Terms and Literary Theory, ed. J. A. Cuddon, 1991; W. F. Thrall and Addison Hibbard, A Handbook to Literature, ed. C. Hugh Holman, rev. 1992; Critical Terms for Literary Study, ed. Frank Lentricchia and Thomas McLaughlin, rev. 1995; and M. H. Abrams, A Glossary of Literary Terms, rev. 1992. On Greek and Roman background, see G. M. Kirkwood, A Short Guide to Classical Mythology, 1959; The Oxford Classical Dictionary, rev. 1996; and The Oxford Companion to Classical Literature, ed. M. C. Howatson and Ian Chilvers, rev. 1993.

Literary Criticism and Theory

Three volumes of the Cambridge History of Literary Criticism have been published, 1989–: Classical Criticism, ed. George A. Kennedy; The Eighteenth Century, ed. H. B. Nisbet and Claude Rawson; and From Formalism to Poststructuralism, ed. Raman Selden. See also M. H. Abrams, The Mirror and the Lamp: Romantic Theory and the Critical Tradition, 1953; William K. Wimsatt and Cleanth Brooks, Literary Criticism: A Short History, 1957; George Watson, The Literary Critics, 1962; René Wellek, A History of Modern Criticism: 1750–1950, 9 vols., 1955–1993; Frank Lentricchia, After the New Criticism, 1980; and Redrawing the Boundaries: The Transformation of English and American Literary Studies, ed. Stephen Greenblatt and Giles Gunn, 1992. Raman Selden, Peter Widdowson, and Peter Brooker have written A Reader's Guide to Contemporary Literary Theory, 1997.

The following is a selection of books in literary criticism that have been notably influential in shaping modern approaches to English literature and literary forms: Lionel Trilling, The Liberal Imagination, 1950; T. S. Eliot, Selected Essays, 3rd ed. 1951, and On Poetry and Poets, 1957; Erich Auerbach, Mimesis: The Representation of Reality in Western Literature, 1953; William Empson, Seven Types of Ambiguity, 3rd ed. 1953; William K. Wimsalt, The Verbal Icon, 1954; Northrop Frye, Anatomy of Criticism, 1957; Wayne C. Booth, The Rhetoric of Fiction, 1961, rev. ed. 1983; W. J. Bate, The Burden of the Past and the English Poet, 1970; Harold Bloom, The Anxiety of Influence, 1973; and Paul de Man, Allegories of Reading, 1979.

René Wellek and Austin Warren, Theory of Literature, rev. 1970, is a useful introduction to the variety of scholarly and critical approaches to literature up to the time of its publication. Jonathan Culler's Literary Theory: A Very Short Introduction, 1997, discusses recurrent issues and debates. Modern feminist literary criticism was fashioned by such works as Particia Meyers Spacks, The Female Imagination, 1975; Ellen Moers, Literary Women, 1976; Elaine Showalter, A Literature of Their Own, 1977; and Sandra Gilbert and Susan Gubar, The Mad-

woman in the Attic, 1979. More recent studies include Jane Gallop, *The Daughter's Seduction: Feminism and Psychoanalysis*, 1982; Gayatri Chakravorty Spivak, *In Other Worlds: Essays in Cultural Politics*, 1987; Sandra Gilbert and Susan Gubar, *No Man's Land: The Place of the Woman Writer in the Twentieth Century*, 2 vols., 1988–89; Barbara Johnson, *A World of Difference*, 1989; Judith Butler, *Gender Trouble*, 1990; and the critical views sampled in Elaine Showalter, *The New Feminist Criticism*, 1985; *Feminist Literary Theory: A Reader*, ed. Mary Eagleton, 2nd ed., 1995; and *Feminisms: An Anthology of Literary Theory and Criticism*, ed. Robyn R. Warhol and Diane Price Herndl, 2nd ed. 1997. Gay and lesbian studies and criticism are represented in *The Lesbian and Gay Studies Reader*, ed. Henry Abelove, Michele Barale, and David Halperin, 1993, and by such books as Eve Sedgwick, *Between Men: English Literature and Male Homosocial Desire*, 1985, and *Epistemology of the Closet*, 1990; Diana Fuss, *Essentially Speaking: Feminism, Nature, and Difference*, 1989; and Gregory Woods, *A History of Gay Literature: The Male Tradition*, 1998. Convenient introductions to structuralist literary criticism include Robert Scholes, *Structuralism in Literature: An Introduction*, 1974, and Jonathan Culler, *Structuralist Poetics*, 1975. The poststructuralist challenges to this approach are discussed in Jonathan Culler, *On Deconstruction*, 1982; Fredric Jameson, *Poststructuralism; or the Cultural Logic of Late Capitalism*, 1991; John

McGowan, *Postmodernism and Its Critics*, 1991; and *Beyond Structuralism*, ed. Wendell Harris, 1996. New historicism is represented in Stephen Greenblatt, *Learning to Curse*, 1990, and in the essays collected in *The New Historicism*, ed. Harold Veeser, 1989, and *New Historical Literary Study: Essays on Reproducing Texts, Representing History*, ed. Jeffrey N. Cox and Larry J. Reynolds, 1993. The related social and historical dimension of texts is discussed in Jerome McGann, *Critique of Modern Textual Criticism*, 1983, and D. F. McKenzie, *Bibliography and Sociology of Texts*, 1986. Characteristic of new historicism is an expansion of the field of literary interpretation extended still further in cultural studies; for a broad sampling of the range of interests, see *The Cultural Studies Reader*, ed. Simon During, 1993, and *A Cultural Studies Reader: History, Theory, Practice*, ed. Jessica Munns and Gita Rajan, 1997. This expansion of the field is similarly reflected in postcolonial studies: see *The Post-Colonial Studies Reader*, ed. Bill Ashcroft, Gareth Griffiths, and Helen Tiffin, 1995, and such influential books as Ranajit Guha and Gayatri Chakravorti Spivak, *Selected Subaltern Studies*, 1988; Edward Said, *Culture and Imperialism*, 1993; and Homi Bhabha, *The Location of Culture*, 1994.

Anthologies representing a range of recent approaches include *Modern Criticism and Theory*, ed. David Lodge, 1988, and *Contemporary Literary Criticism*, ed. Robert Con Davis and Ronald Schlieffer, rev. 1998.

THE MIDDLE AGES

Scholarship during this era has been divided into the same three periods as in the General Introduction: Anglo-Saxon England, Anglo-Norman England, and Middle English Literature of the Fourteenth and Fifteenth Centuries. A reference book for the whole era is Joseph Strayer et al., *Dictionary of the Middle Ages*, 1982–.

Anglo-Saxon England

D. Whitelock, *The Beginnings of English Society*, 1952, provides concise historical background for the literature of the period. The most detailed history is F. M. Stenton's authoritative *Anglo-Saxon England*, 3rd ed., 1971. Also highly informative are P. Hunter Blair, *An Introduction to Anglo-Saxon England*, 1956, and *Roman Britain and Early England, 55 B.C.–A.D. 871*, 1963. The classic study of the culture of the primitive Germanic peoples is H. M. Chadwick, *The Heroic Age*, 1912. For those who wish to sample basic historical documents of the period, there is available the translation by G. N. Garmonsway of *The Anglo-Saxon Chronicle*, 1953. *The Age of Bede*, ed. D. H. Farmer, rev. 1983, and *Alfred the Great*, ed. S. Keynes and M. Lapidge, 1983, contain texts documenting two crucial periods of Anglo-Saxon history. Bede's *Ecclesiastical History of the English People* is

translated and edited by B. Colgrave and R. A. B. Mynors, 1969. For studies of Bede, see G. H. Brown, *Bede, the Venerable*, 1987, and J. M. Wallace-Hadrill, *Bede's Ecclesiastical History of the English People: A Historical Commentary*, 1993. A lavishly and finely illustrated introduction to Anglo-Saxon England is *The Anglo-Saxons*, ed. J. Campbell, 1982. C. Fell, *Women in Anglo-Saxon England*, 1984, is pertinent to women's studies. The journal *Anglo-Saxon England* is devoted to all aspects of the history and culture of the period.

All the surviving poetry in Old English is contained in the six volumes edited by G. P. Krapp and E. V. K. Dobbie, *The Anglo-Saxon Poetic Records*, 1931–53, but the absence of glossaries makes this edition difficult for nonspecialists. Excellent texts of the shorter poems translated in this anthology are contained in J. C. Pope, *Seven Old English Poems*, 1966, rev. 1981. The standard text of *Beowulf and the Fight of Finnsburg* is F. Klaeber's 3rd ed., 1950; C. L. Wrenn's edition, *Beowulf, with the Finnsburg Fragment*, rev. W. F. Bolton, 1973, rev. 1988, is very useful; H. D. Chickering Jr. has made a dual-language edition with extensive commentary, and G. B. Jack has prepared *Beowulf: A Student Edition*, 1994. There are individual editions of *The Dream of the Rood* by M. Swanton, 1970; of *The Wanderer* by T. P. Dunning and A. J. Bliss, 1969. *The Wanderer* and *The Wife's Lament* are included in *The Old English Elegies: A Critical Edition and Genre Study*, ed. A. L. Klinck, 1992. Modern English translations of many of the Old English poems have been published under various titles by R. K. Gordon, C. W. Kennedy, M. Alexander, S. A. J. Bradley, and K. Crossley-Holland. Many translations of *Beowulf* are available. E. T. Donaldson's translation is used in *Beowulf*, A Norton Critical Edition, ed. J. F. Tuso, 1975.

General discussions of Old English literature will be found in Vol. 1 of the *Cambridge History of English Literature*; S. B. Greenfield and D. G. Calder, *New Critical History of Old English Literature*, 1986; C. L. Wrenn, *A Study of Old English Literature*; M. Alexander, *Old English Literature*, 1983; and *The Cambridge Companion to Old English Literature*, ed. M. Godden and M. Lapidge, 1991.

Some useful studies and collections devoted exclusively to Old English poetry are S. B. Greenfield, *The Interpretation of Old English Poems*, 1972; T. A. Shippey, *Old English Verse*, 1972; J. B. Bessinger Jr. and S. J. Kahrl, *Essential Articles for the Study of Old English Poetry*, 1977; D. A. Pearsall, *Old and Middle English Poetry*, 1977; B. C. Raw, *The Art and Background of Old English Poetry*, 1978; *Old English Poetry: Essays on Style*, ed. D. G. Calder, 1979; *The Old English Elegies*, ed. M. Green, 1983; S. B. Greenfield, *Hero and Exile: The Art of Old English Poetry*, 1989; *De Gustibus*, ed. J. M. Foley et al., 1992; *Heroic Poetry in the Anglo-Saxon Period*, ed. H. Damico and J. Leyerle, 1993; *Companion to Old English Poetry*, ed. H. Aertsen and R. H. Bremmer Jr., 1994; and *Old English Shorter Poems: Basic Readings*, ed. K. O'Brien O'Keeffe, 1994.

General collections of essays on Old English literature include *Old English Literature in Context*, ed. J. D. Niles, 1980; *Literature and Learning in Anglo-Saxon England*, ed. M. Lapidge and H. Gneuss, 1985; *Modes of Interpretation in Old English Literature*, ed. P. R. Brown et al., 1986; F. C. Robinson, *The Tomb of Beowulf and Other Essays on Old English*, 1993; and *Studies in English Language and Literature*, ed. M. J. Toswell and E. M. Tyler, 1996.

Some studies of special topics in Old English literature are J. Chance, *Woman as Hero in Old English Literature*, 1986; *New Readings on Women in Old English Literature*, ed. Helen Damico and A. H. Olsen, 1990; A. J. Frantzen, *Desire for Origins: New Language, Old English, and Teaching the Tradition*, 1990; *The Battle of Maldon AD 991*, ed. D. Scragg, 1991; *Class and Gender in Early English Literature*, ed. B. J. Harwood and G. R. Overing, 1994; and *Holy Men, Holy Women: Old English Prose Saints' Lives and Their Contexts*, ed. P. Szarmach, 1996.

Beowulf

Essential backgrounds to the study of the poem are provided by R. W. Chambers, *Beowulf: An Introduction to the Study of the Poem*, 3rd ed., with a supplement by C. L. Wrenn, 1959; and a wide-ranging overview of *Beowulf* scholarship is furnished by *A Beowulf Handbook*, ed. R. E. Bjork and J. D. Niles, 1997. Important critical studies of the poem are found in D. Whitelock, *The Audience of Beowulf*, 1951; A. G. Brodeur, *The Art of Beowulf*, 1959; E. B. Irving Jr., *A Reading of Beowulf*, 1968, *Introduction to Beowulf*, 1969, and *Rereading Beowulf*, 1990; T. A. Shippey, *Beowulf*, 1978; J. D. Niles, *Beowulf: The Poem and Its Tradition*, 1983; G. Clark, *Beowulf*, 1990; J. W. Earl, *Thinking about Beowulf*, 1994; J. M. Hill, *The Cultural World in Beowulf*, 1995; and C. R. Davis, *Beowulf and the Demise of Germanic Legend in England*, 1996.

For anthologies of criticism, see *The Beowulf Poet*, ed. D. K. Fry, 1968; *Beowulf*, A Norton Critical Edition, ed. J. Tuso, 1975; *Interpretations of Beowulf*, ed. R. D. Fulk, 1991; and *Beowulf: Basic Readings*, ed. P. S. Baker, 1995. Special mention should be made of J. R. R. Tolkien's famous lecture, *Beowulf, the Monsters and the Critics*, 1937, reprinted in the anthologies of Fry and Fulk.

Anglo-Norman England

For accounts of the Norman conquest and its historical consequences, see C. Brooke, *From Alfred to Henry III, 871–1272*, 2 vols., 1961; R. A. Brown, *The Normans*, 1984; A. L. Poole, *From Domesday Book to Magna Carta*, 1955; P. Stafford, *A Political and Social History of England in the Tenth and Eleventh Centuries*, 1989; and F. M. Powicke, *The Thirteenth Century, 1216–1307*, 1953. The *Peterborough Chronicle*, a continuation of the *Anglo-Saxon Chronicle* to the year 1154, relates events from the point of view of English monks and can be read in translation in *The Anglo-Saxon Chronicle: a Revised Translation*, ed. by D. Whitelock with D. C. Douglas and S. I. Tucker, 1961, rev. 1965.

Studies of historical writing within the period itself, including the legendary histories of the kings of Britain, are J. S. P. Tatlock, *The Legendary History of Britain*, 1950; R. W. Hanning, *The Vision of History in Early Britain: From Gildas to Geoffrey of Monmouth*, 1966; and M. Otter, *Inventiones: Fiction and Referentiality in Twelfth-Century Historical Writing*.

On **Geoffrey of Monmouth**, in addition to the texts mentioned above, see the translation of his *History of the Kings of Britain* by Lewis Thorpe, 1966; R. W. Leckie Jr., *The Passage of Dominion: Geoffrey of Monmouth and the Periodization of Insular History in the Twelfth Century*, 1981; and M. J. Curley, *Geoffrey of Monmouth*, 1994. The *Brut* of **Layamon** is available in translations by D. G. Bzdyl, 1989; Rosamund Allen, 1992; and in an edition of the Middle English text with facing translation, notes, and commentary by W. R. J. Barron and S. C. Weinberg, 1989. The Arthurian sections of Wace's *Roman de Brut*, translated by Judith Weiss, and of Layamon in Allen's translation are printed together as *The Life of King Arthur*, 1997.

M. D. Legge, *Anglo-Norman Literature and Its Background*, 1963, is the standard history. The lais of **Marie de France** have been translated by R. H. Hanning and J. Ferrante, 1978, and by G. S. Burgess and K. Busby, 1986. For background and critical interpretations of Marie de France's works, see E. J. Mickel, *Marie de France*, 1974; P. M. Clifford, *Marie de France, Lais*, 1982; and G. S. Burgess, *The Lais of Marie de France*, 1987.

R. M. Wilson's *Early Middle English Literature* focuses primarily on this period. Vol. 1 of the *Oxford History of English Literature*, by J. A. W. Bennett and D. Gray, *Middle English Literature*, 1986, which goes up to 1400 (exclusive of Chaucer), contains excellent discussions of early Middle English texts. Selections of texts from this era with a valuable introduction to the language and annotations are contained in the anthology edited by J. A. W. Bennett and G. V. Smithers, *Early Middle English Verse and Prose*, 2nd ed, 1968. The *Ancrene Riwle* (Anchoresses' rule) is available in a modern translation by Mary Salu, 1963. For a study of the work, called by its variant title *Ancrene Wisse* (Anchoresses' guide), and related early Middle English texts, see B. Millett with G. B. Jack and Y. Wada, *Ancrene Wisse, the Katherine Group, and the Wooing Group*, 1996. For a fine essay on the language and culture of the work, see J. R. R. Tolkien, "*Ancrene Wisse* and *Hali Meidenhad*" in *Essays and Studies*, 14.104–26, 1929. See also the commentary in *Medieval English Prose for Women*, ed. B. Millett and J. Wogan-Browne, 1990, from which the translation printed in this anthology is taken.

Translations of Old Irish literature are available by T. Kinsella in *The Táin from the Irish Epic Táin Bó Cuailnge*, 1969, from which **Exile of the Sons of Uisliu** is taken, and by Jeffrey Gantz, *Early Irish Myths and Sagas*, 1981. For background, see K. H. Jackson, *The Oldest Irish Tradition: A Window on the Iron Age*, 1964; K. McCone, *Pagan Past and Christian Present in Early Irish Literature*, 1990; and J. E. Caerwyn Williams and P. K. Ford, *The Irish Literary Tradition*, 1992.

Llud and Lleuelys is taken from P. K. Ford's translation, *The Mabinogi and Other Medieval Welsh Tales*, 1977. Jeffrey Gantz has also translated the *Mabinogion*, 1976, with a useful introduction, bibliography, and commentary on individual selections. On Welsh literature in general, see K. Jackson, *Language and History in Early Britain*, 1953, and *A Guide to Welsh Literature*, vol. 1, ed. A. O. H. Jarman and G. R. Hughes, 1976. Specific commentary on the *Mabinogion* may be found in S. Davies, *The Four Branches of The Mabinogi*, 1993; C. Matthews, *Mabon and the Mysteries of Britain: An Exploration of The Mabinogion*, 1987; P. MacCana, *The Mabinogi*, 1992; and W. J. Gruffyd, *Folklore and Myth in The Mabinogion*, 1994.

For discussions of the Arthurian materials in Geoffrey of Monmouth, Wace, Marie de France, Layamon, and the *Mabinogi*, see chaps. 4 and 8 to 11 in *Arthurian Literature in the Middle Ages*, ed. R. S. Loomis, 1959.

Middle English Literature of the Fourteenth and Fifteenth Centuries

Histories of the period include G. Holmes, *The Later Middle Ages, 1272–1485*, 1962; M. McKisack, *The Fourteenth Century, 1307–99*, 1959; and E. F. Jacob, *The Fifteenth Century*, 1961. Accounts of life and society during this period are provided by G. G. Coulton in *Chaucer and His England*, 1908, *The Medieval Scene*, 1930, and *Medieval Panorama*, 1938; E. Rickert, *Chaucer's World*, 1948; G. M. Trevelyan, *Chaucer's England and the Early Tudors*, vol. 1 of *The Illustrated English Social History*, 1949; and M. Keen, *English Society in the Later Middle Ages*, 1990. See also the picture books listed under Chaucer. J. Huizinga has written a famous account of the culture and spirit of the late fourteenth to fifteenth centuries, formerly translated as *The Waning of the Middle Ages*, 1924, now available in a fuller text under the more accurate title, *The Autumn of the Middle Ages*, trans. R. J. Payton and U. Mammitzsch, 1996. F. R. H. Du Boulay complements and qualifies Huizinga in *An Age of Ambition*, 1970. Chaps. 6 to 10 in E. Auerbach's *Mimesis: The Representation of Reality in Western Literature*, trans. by W. R. Trask, 1953, although it does not deal with works in this anthology, gives penetrating insights into the reading of medieval texts. C. S. Lewis, *The Discarded Image: An Introduction to Medieval and Renaissance Literature*, 1964, seeks to restore for modern readers the perspective and sensibilities of the earlier age.

For general discussion of late Middle English literature, see the *The Oxford History of English Literature*: J. A. W. Bennett and D. Gray, *Middle English Literature*, 1986, vol. 1, part 2 (up to 1400, exclusive of Chaucer); H. S. Bennett, *Chaucer and the Fifteenth Century*, vol. 2, part 1, 1947, and E. K. Chambers, *English Literature at the Close of the Middle Ages*, vol. 2, part 2, 1954; also D. A. Pearsall, *Old and Middle English Poetry*, 1977; J. A. Burrow, *Middle English Literature and Its Background*, 1982; and D. S. Brewer, *English Gothic Literature*, 1983.

Critical works devoted to more than one author or genre in the period are G. Kane, *Middle English Literature*, 1951 (chapters on the romances, the religious lyrics, and *Piers Plowman*); J. A. Burrow, *Ricardian Poetry: Chaucer, Gower, Langland, and the Gawain Poet*, 1971; C. Muscatine, *Poetry and Crisis in the Age of Chaucer*, 1972; A. C. Spearing, *Medieval Dream Poetry*, 1976, and *Readings in Medieval Poetry*, 1987; T. Turville-Petre, *The Alliterative Revival*, 1977; *Medieval Literature: Chaucer and the Alliterative Tradition*, vol. 1 of *The New Pelican Guide to English Literature*, ed. Boris Ford, 1982; D. Despres, *Ghostly Sights: Visual Meditation in Late-Medieval Literature*, 1989; S. Justice, *Writing and Rebellion: England in 1381*, 1994; and G. Margherita, *The Romance of Origins: Language and Sexual Difference in Middle English Literature*, 1994. *Middle English Survey: Critical Essays*, ed. E. Vasta, 1965, contains commentary on Langland, *Gawain*, and drama.

For the Middle English language, see Helge Kökeritz, *A Guide to Chaucer's Pronunciation*, 1954; David Burnley, *A Guide to Chaucer's Language*, 1983; and J. A. Burrow and T. Turville-Petre, *A Book of Middle English*, 1996.

The standard bibliography is *A Manual of the Writings in Middle English, 1050–1500*, 6 vols., ed. J. B. Severs, A. E. Hartung, et al., 1967–80, which is based on and supersedes the *Manual* of J. E. Wells, 1916, with nine supplements through 1945.

Geoffrey Chaucer

The standard edition of Chaucer's writing is *The Riverside Chaucer*, 3rd ed., ed. L. D. Benson et al., 1987, based on F. N. Robinson's edition. E. Talbot Donaldson, *Chaucer's Poetry*, 2nd ed., 1975, from which are taken the selections printed here, is helpful to the nonspecialist, as are John H. Fisher, *The Complete Poetry and Prose of Geoffrey Chaucer*, 2nd ed., 1989, and V. A. Kolve and Glending Olson, *The Canterbury Tales: Nine Tales and The "General Prologue,"* Norton Critical Edition, 1989. Vivid presentations of Chaucer in the background of fourteenth-century England are found in D. S. Brewer, *Chaucer and His World*, 1978, which is beautifully illustrated, and *A New Introduction to Chaucer*, 2nd ed., 1998. Pictorial companions to Chaucer's works, especially the *Canterbury Tales*, include R. S. Loomis, *A Mirror of Chaucer's World*, 1965, Maurice Hussey, *Chaucer's World*, 1967, Ian Serraillier, *Chaucer and His World*, 1968, and Roger Hart, *English Life in Chaucer's Day*, 1973.

The raw material for Chaucer's biography is contained in *Chaucer Life-Records*, ed. M. M. Crow and C. C. Olson, 1966. D. R. Howard, *Chaucer: His Life, His Works, His World*, 1987, and D. A. Pearsall, *The Life of Geoffrey Chaucer*, 1992, contain extensive background and interpretation. For succinct accounts of the sources and literary background of Chaucer's works, see R. D. French, *A Chaucer Handbook*, 2nd ed., 1947; reproductions of many of the known sources of the *Canterbury Tales* are contained in *Sources and Analogues of Chaucer's Canterbury Tales*, ed. W. F. Bryan and Germaine Dempster, 1941, 1958. Useful literary materials are collected in R. P. Miller, *Chaucer: Sources and Backgrounds*, 1977. Muriel Bowden, *A Commentary on the General Prologue to the Canterbury Tales*, 1948, provides a wealth of background information on the individual Canterbury pilgrims; see also Jill Mann, *Chaucer and Medieval Estates Satire*, 1973. Various aspects of Chaucer's work are treated by a number of scholars in *Chaucer and Chaucerians*, ed. D. S. Brewer, 1966; *Geoffrey Chaucer (Writers and Their Background)*, ed. D. S. Brewer, 1974; *Companion to Chaucer Studies*, ed. Beryl Rowland, rev. 1979; and *The Cambridge Chaucer Companion*, ed. Piero Boitani and Jill Mann, 1986.

For literary criticism on both *The Canterbury Tales* and other works by Chaucer, the following contain stimulating discussions: G. L. Kittredge, *Chaucer and His Poetry*, 1915; J. L. Lowes, *Geoffrey Chaucer and the Development of His Genius*, 1934; C. Muscatine, *Chaucer and the French Tradition*, 1957; W. C. Curry, *Chaucer and the Medieval Sciences*, rev. 1960; R. O. Payne, *The Key of Remembrance*, 1963; M. Hussey, A. C. Spearing, and J. Winny, *An Introduction to Chaucer*, 1965; E. T. Donaldson, *Speaking of Chaucer*, 1970; T. Ross, *Chaucer's Bawdy*, 1972; D. S. Brewer, *Chaucer*, 3rd ed., 1973; P. Elbow, *Oppositions in Chaucer*, 1975; A. David, *The Strumpet Muse: Art and Morals in Chaucer's Poetry*, 1976; R. Burlin, *Chaucerian Fiction*, 1977; G. Kane, *Chaucer*, 1984; S. Knight, *Geoffrey Chaucer*, 1986; D. Wallace, *Chaucerian Polity: Absolutist Lineages and Associational Forms in England and Italy*, 1997; and R. P. McGerr, *Chaucer's Open Book: Resistance to Closure in Medieval Discourse*, 1998.

Criticism that deals mainly with *The Canterbury Tales* and with earlier commentary on it includes P. Ruggiers, *The Art of The Canterbury Tales*, 1964; D. R. Howard, *The Idea of The Canterbury Tales*, 1976; T. Lawler, *The One and the Many in The Canterbury Tales*, 1980; D. Pearsall, *The Canterbury Tales*, 1985; C. D. Benson, *Chaucer's Drama of Style: Poetic Variety in The Canterbury Tales*, 1986; W. Wetherbee, *Geoffrey Chaucer: The Canterbury Tales*, 1989; H. M. Leicester Jr., *The Disenchanted Self: Representing the Subject in The Canterbury Tales*, 1990; S. Crane, *Gender and Romance in Chaucer's Canterbury Tales*, 1994; and H. Cooper, *The Canterbury Tales*, Oxford Guides to Chaucer, 2nd ed., 1996.

D. W. Robertson's *A Preface to Chaucer*, 1962, is a learned and stimulating introduction to the reading of Chaucer in the light of medieval aesthetic doctrines. V. A. Kolve, *Chaucer and the Imagery of Narrative*, 1984, relates the first five of the *Canterbury Tales* to medieval art. Several recent books stress the importance of oral delivery, performance, and storytelling in the *Canterbury Tales*: Betsy Bowden, *Chaucer Aloud*, 1987; Carl Lindahl, *Earnest Games: Folkloric Patterns in The Canterbury Tales*, 1987; L. M. Koff, *Chaucer and the Art of Storytelling*, 1988; and J. M. Ganim, *Chaucerian Theatricality*, 1990. The following studies relate Chaucer's works to their social and historical background: Paul Strohm, *Social Chaucer*, 1989; Peggy Knapp, *Chaucer and the Social Contest*, 1990; Peter Brown and Andrew Butcher, *The Age of Saturn: Literature and History in The Canterbury Tales*, 1991; and Lee Patterson, *Chaucer and the Subject of History*, 1991. A pioneer feminist study of Chaucer is Carolyn Dinshaw, *Chaucer's Sexual Poetics*, 1989; see also E. T. Hansen, *Chaucer and the Fictions of Gender*, 1992.

The following are collections of critical essays: *Chaucer: Modern Essays in Criticism*, ed. E. C. Wagenknecht, 1959; *Chaucer Criticism: The Canterbury Tales*, ed. R. J. Schoeck and J. Taylor, 1960; *Discussions of The Canterbury Tales*, ed. C. J. Owen, 1961; *Geoffrey Chaucer: A Critical Anthology*, ed. J. A. Burrow, 1969; and *Geoffrey Chaucer* Contemporary Studies in Literature, ed. G. D. Economou,

1975. See also the prefatory remarks on individual works and tales in *The Riverside Chaucer* and the commentary in E. Talbot Donaldson's anthology, cited above.

Perhaps the most reliable glossary is that edited by Norman Davis et al., 1979. The standard bibliographies are E. P. Hammond, *Chaucer: A Bibliographical Manual*, 1908; D. D. Griffith, *Bibliography of Chaucer*, 1955; W. R. Crawford, *1954–63*, 1967; L. Y. Baird, *1964–73*, 1977; and L. Y. Baird-Lange and H. Schnutgen, *1974–85*, 1988. Two very useful annotated bibliographies are by Mark Allen and J. H. Fisher, *The Essential Chaucer*, 1987, and John Leyerle and Anne Quick, *Chaucer: A Bibliographical Introduction*, 1986. *Studies in the Age of Chaucer*, the journal of The New Chaucer Society, publishes a current bibliography as well as articles on Chaucer and other medieval literature. See also Caroline Spurgeon, *Five Hundred Years of Chaucer Criticism and Allusion, 1357–1900*, 1925.

Everyman
See entries under **Mystery Plays; Everyman**.

Robert Henryson
The Poems of Robert Henryson, ed. D. Fox, 1980 and 1987, is the standard edition. *The Moral Fables of Aesop*, ed. G. D. Copen, 1987, has a facing page prose translation. For background and criticism, see J. MacQueen, *Robert Henryson: A Study of the Major Poems*, 1967, and D. Gray, *Robert Henryson*, 1979.

Julian of Norwich
The standard Middle English text with a wealth of commentary is *A Book of Showings to the Anchoress Julian of Norwich*, 2 vols., ed. Edmund Colledge and James Walsh, 1978. The editors' translation is published as *Julian of Norwich: Showings*, 1978; another translation of the long text by Clifton Walters is published under the title *Revelations of Divine Love*, 1966. Another edition of the long text, ed. G. R. Crampton, 1994, published for TEAMS (Consortium for the Teaching of the Middle Ages) is designed for students.

General studies of mystical writing in England and on the Continent are W. Riehle, *The Middle English Mystics*, trans. B. Standring, 1981; *An Introduction to the Medieval Mystics of Europe*, ed. P. Szarmach, 1984; A. K. Warren, *Anchorites and their Patrons in Medieval England*, 1985; F. Beer, *Women and Mystical Experience in the Middle Ages*, 1992; S. Beckwith, *Christ's Body: Identity, Culture, and Society in Late Medieval Writings*, 1993; and D. Aers and L. Staley, *The Powers of the Holy: Religion, Politics, and Gender in Late Medieval English Culture*, 1996. Studies helpful to understanding the mystical thought of Julian of Norwich are B. Pelphrey, *Christ Our Mother*, 1989, and D. N. Baker, *Julian of Norwich's Showing: From Vision to Book*, 1994.

Margery Kempe
The standard Middle English text of *The Book of Margery Kempe* is that of S. B. Meech and H. E. Allen, 1940. Another edition, ed. L. Staley, 1996, for TEAMS (Consortium for the Teaching of Middle English) is designed for students. Barry Windeatt has made a translation, 1985, with notes and a helpful introduction. For general studies of mystical writings, see under Julian of Norwich. Studies of Kempe are C. W. Atkinson, *Mystic and Pilgrim: The Book and the World of Margery Kempe*, 1983; K. Lochrie, *Margery Kempe and Translations of the Flesh*, 1991; *Margery Kempe: A Book of Essays*, S. McEntire, ed., 1992; and L. S. Johnson, *Margery Kempe's Dissenting Fictions*, 1994. Gibson, cited under **Mystery Plays**, provides background on Kempe's region and includes a chapter on Kempe.

William Langland
The most handy edition is A. V. C. Schmidt, *The Vision of Piers Plowman: A Complete Edition of the B-Text*, 1978. W. W. Skeat, *The Vision of William Concerning Piers the Plowman . . .*, 2 vols., 1886, gives all three versions side by side; the commentary and notes in volume 2 remain invaluable. The Athlone edition, based on all extant manuscripts, has the A text, ed. G. Kane, 1960, the B text, ed. Kane and E. T. Donaldson, 1975, and the C text, ed. Kane and G. H. Russell, 1997. J. A. W. Bennett's edition of the first eight passus of the B text, 1972, is very useful, as is D. A. Pearsall's edition of the C text, 1978. The selections here are taken from E. T. Donaldson's *Piers Plowman: An Alliterative Verse Translation*, 1990. A literal prose translation is J. F. Goodridge, *Langland: Piers the Ploughman*, rev. 1966. The best general account of the poem is in chap. 4 and 5 of R. W. Chambers, *Man's Unconquerable Mind*, 1939; see also Kane's chapter in *Middle English Literature. A Companion to Piers Plowman*, ed. J. A. Alford, 1988, has essays and extensive bibliographies on many aspects of the poem. Book-length studies helpful to the student as well as the specialist include R. W. Frank, *Piers Plowman and the Scheme of Salvation*, 1957; Elizabeth Salter, *Piers Plowman: An Introduction*, 1962; E. D. Kirk, *The Dream Thought of Piers Plowman*, 1972; David Aers, *Piers Plowman and Christian Allegory*, 1975; James Simpson, *Piers Plowman: An Introduction to the B-Text*, 1990; J. A. Burrow, *Langland's Fictions*, 1993; J. Wittig, *William Langland Revisited*, 1997; and S. Justice and K. Kerby-Fulton, *Written Work: Langland, Labor, and Authorship*, 1997. Collections of critical essays have been made by Edward Vasta, *Interpretations of Piers Plowman*, 1968; R. J. Blanch, *Style and Symbolism in Piers Plowman*, 1969; and S. S. Hussey, *Piers Plowman: Critical Approaches*, 1969. Useful background material has been collected by Jeanne Krochalis and Edward Peters in *The World of Piers Plowman*, 1975. F. R. H. DuBoulay, *The England of Piers Plowman*, 1991, places the poem in its historical and cultural setting.

Sir Thomas Malory
The Winchester manuscript of Malory's *Morte Darthur*, with full commentary and valuable discussion,

is given in Eugène Vinaver's *The Works of Sir Thomas Malory*, 3 vols., 2nd ed., 1967; the one-volume edition, 2nd ed., Oxford, 1970, contains the text only. The Caxton version is most readily available in *Caxton's Malory*, ed. J. W. Spisak, 1983. Vinaver, *Malory*, 1929, surveys Malory's life and career; see also, P. J. C. Field, *The Life and Times of Sir Thomas Malory*, 1993. Guides to Malory are B. Dillon, *A Malory Handbook*, 1978; Terence McCarthy, *An Introduction to Malory*, rev. ed., 1991; and E. Archibald and A. S. G. Edwards, *A Companion to Malory*, 1996. A number of critical problems in Malory's work, especially its unity, are discussed in three collections of essays by various scholars: *Essays on Malory*, ed. J. A. W. Bennett, 1963, *Malory's Originality*, ed. by R. M. Lumianski, 1964, and *Studies in Malory*, ed. J. W. Spisak, 1985. Other studies of Malory and the *Morte Darthur* include Mark Lambert, *Malory: Style and Vision in Le Morte Darthur*, 1975; L. D. Benson, *Malory's Morte Darthur*, 1976; and Felicity Riddy, *Sir Thomas Malory*, 1987.

For reference books and discussions of the development and of the political and social significance of the Arthurian tradition in England, see R. S. Loomis, *The Development of Arthurian Romance*, 1963; S. Knight, *Arthurian Literature and Society*, 1983; *The Arthurian Handbook*, ed. N. J. Lacy and G. Ashe, 2nd ed., 1998; *The New Arthurian Encyclopedia*, ed. N. J. Lacy, 1991; *Approaches to Teaching the Arthurian Tradition*, ed. M. Fries and J. Watson, 1992; *Culture and the King: the Social Implications of the Arthurian Legend*, ed. M. Schichtman and J. Carley, 1994; *Arthurian Women: A Casebook*, ed. T. Fenster, 1996; and *King Arthur: A Casebook*, ed. E. D. Kennedy, 1996.

Middle English Lyrics

The best selections of Middle English lyrics are *Medieval English Lyrics: A Critical Anthology*, ed. R. T. Davies, 1963; *Middle English Lyrics, A Norton Critical Edition*, ed. M. S. Luria and R. L. Hoffman, 1974; *The Oxford Book of Medieval English Verse*, ed. Celia and Kenneth Sisam, 1970; *English Lyrics before 1500*, ed. Theodore Silverstein, 1971. For criticism see A. K. Moore, *The Secular Lyric in Middle English*, 1951; Kane's chapter in *Middle English Literature*; Stephen Manning, *Wisdom and Number*, 1962; Rosemary Woolf, *The English Religious Lyric in the Middle Ages*, 1968; and D. Gray, *Themes and Images in the Medieval English Religious Lyric*, 1972.

For general studies of English and Continental lyric poetry, see P. Dronke, *The Medieval Lyric*, 3rd ed., 1996, and *Vox Feminae: Studies in Medieval Woman's Song*, ed. J. F. Plummer, 1981.

Mystery Plays; Everyman

E. K. Chambers's classic *The Medieval Stage*, 1905, remains a mine of information, although its views about the evolution of medieval drama are no longer accepted. A new understanding and appreciation of medieval drama begins with O. B. Hardison, *Christian Rite and Christian Drama in the Middle Ages*, 1965; and for the mysteries, with V. A. Kolve, *The Play Called Corpus Christie*, 1966. Rosemary Woolf, *The English Mystery Plays*, 1972, makes detailed comparisons among the extant plays. Individual cycles are studied by Peter Travis in *Dramatic Design in the Chester Cycle*, 1982, and by Martin Stevens in *Four Middle English Mystery Cycles: Textual, Contextual, and Critical Interpretations*, 1987. G. M. Gibson fills in the social and religious background in *The Theater of Devotion: East Anglian Drama and Society in the Late Middle Ages*, 1989. Good selections of Middle English plays are presented by A. C. Cawley, *Everyman and Medieval Miracle Plays*, 1960; by D. M. Bevington, *Medieval Drama*, 1975; and by Peter Happé, *The English Mystery Plays*, 1975. Cawley, *The Wakefield Pageants in the Towneley Cycle*, 1958, has a discussion of the work of the "Wakefield Master" whose hand is seen in the *Second Shepherds' Play*. A collection of critical essays has been made by Jerome Taylor and A. H. Nelson in *Medieval English Drama*, 1972. *Approaches to Teaching Medieval Drama*, ed. Richard Emmerson, 1990, contains essays by many hands and makes up a nontechnical survey of current opinion. For commentary on *Everyman*, see the introduction to A. C. Cawley's 1961 edition and Robert Potter's comprehensive *The English Morality Play: Origins, History, and Influence of a Dramatic Tradition*, 1975.

Sir Gawain and the Green Knight

The standard Middle English edition of the poem is by J. R. R. Tolkien and E. V. Gordon, rev. Norman Davis, 1967. Easier to use are the editions by R. A. Waldron, 1970, rev. for *The Poems of the Pearl Manuscript*, 1978; and by J. A. Burrow, 1972. For a guide to the poems in the manuscript, see A. Putter, *An Introduction to the Gawain-Poet*, 1996, and *A Companion to the Gawain Poet*, ed. D. S. Brewer and J. Gibson, 1997. Discussions of various aspects of the poem appear in Marie Borroff, *Sir Gawain and the Green Knight: A Stylistic and Metrical Study*, 1962; L. D. Benson, *Art and Tradition in Sir Gawain and the Green Knight*, 1965; J. A. Burrow, *A Reading of Sir Gawain and the Green Knight*, 1965; A. C. Spearing, *The Gawain Poet: A Critical Study*, 1971; And W. Clein, *Concepts of Chivalry in Sir Gawain and the Green Knight*, 1984.

Collections of essays have been compiled by R. J. Blanch, *Sir Gawain and Pearl*, 1966, and *Text and Matter: New Critical Perspectives of the Pearl-Poet*, 1991 D. Fox, *Twentieth-Century Interpretations of Sir Gawain and the Green Knight*, 1968; and D. R. Howard and C. K. Zacher, *Critical Studies of Sir Gawain and the Green Knight*, 1968.

THE SIXTEENTH CENTURY

Some important books on society and culture in early modern England are Lawrence Stone, *The Crisis of the Aristocracy, 1558–1641*, 1965, and *The Family, Sex and Marriage in England, 1500–1800*, 1979; Keith Thomas, *Religion and the Decline of Magic*, 1971; J. A. Sharpe, *Early Modern England: A Social History*, 1987; P. G. Emmison, *Elizabethan Life: Disorder*, 1970; David Cressy, *Literacy and the Social Order: Reading and Writing in Tudor and Stuart England*, 1980, and *Birth, Marriage, and Death: Ritual, Religion, and the Life-Cycle in Tudor and Stuart England*, 1997; Keith Wrightson, *English Society, 1580–1680*, 1982; Peter Clark, *The English Alehouse: A Social History, 1200–1830*, 1983; Peter Laslett, *The World We Have Lost, Further Explored*, 1984; Paul Slack, *The Impact of Plague in Tudor and Stuart England*, 1985; Mervyn James, *Society, Politics, and Culture: Studies in Early Modern England*, 1986; Susan Amussen, *An Ordered Society: Gender and Class in Early Modern England*, 1988; Felicity Heal, *Hospitality in Early Modern England*, 1990; Ian Archer, *The Pursuit of Stability: Social Relations in Elizabethan London*, 1991; Illana Ben-Amos, *Adolescence and Youth in Early Modern England*, 1994; Ronald Hutton, *The Rise and Fall of Merry England: The Ritual Year 1400–1700*, 1994; Lena Orlin, *Private Matters and Public Culture in Post-Reformation England*, 1994; and Kim Hall, *Things of Darkness: Economies of Race and Gender in Early Modern England*, 1995.

Useful general studies of the history of the period include J. B. Black, *The Reign of Elizabeth, 1558–1603*, 2nd ed., 1959; G. R. Elton, *England under the Tudors*, 1955, and *Reform and Reformation: England, 1509–1559*, 1977; Conrad Russell, *The Crisis of Parliaments: English History, 1509–1660*, 1971; and John Guy, *Tudor England*, 1988. Political theory in the period is surveyed in Quentin Skinner, *The Foundations of Modern Political Thought*, 2 vols., 1978; and there is an important analysis of the theory of kingship in E. H. Kantorowicz, *The King's Two Bodies*, 1957. Exploration and military history are treated in G. Mattingly, *The Armada*, 1959, and J. A. Williamson, *The Age of Drake*, 4th ed., 1960. For church history and religion, see John Bossy, *The English Catholic Community, 1570–1850*, 1979; Patrick Collinson, *The Religion of Protestants: The Church in English Society, 1559–1625*, 1982, and *The Birthpangs of Protestant England: Religious and Cultural Change in the Sixteenth and Seventeenth Centuries*, 1988; Peter Lake, *Anglicans and Puritans?*, 1988; Debora Shuger, *Habits of Thought in the English Renaissance: Religion, Politics, and the Dominant Culture*, 1990; Eamon Duffy, *The Stripping of the Altars: Traditional Religion in England c. 1400–c. 1580*, 1992; Christopher Haigh, *English Reformations: Religion, Politics, and Society under the Tudors*,

1993; and James Shapiro, *Shakespeare and the Jews*, 1996.

Life at court is described in David Starkey, *The English Court: From the Wars of the Roses to the Civil War*, 1987. Patronage and courtiership, with special reference to literature, are analyzed in David Javitch, *Poetry and Courtliness in Renaissance England*, 1976; *Patronage in the Renaissance*, ed. Guy Fitch Lytle and Stephen Orgel, 1981; and Frank Whigham, *Ambition and Privilege: The Social Tropes of Elizabethan Courtesy Theory*, 1984. On publishing and the book trade, see H. S. Bennett, *English Books and Readers, 1475–1557*, 1952, and *English Books and Readers, 1558–1603*, 1965; Elizabeth L. Eisenstein, *The Printing Press as an Agent of Change*, 2 vols., 1979; and Adrian Johns, *The Nature of the Book: Print and Knowledge in the Making*, 1998.

Several classic studies define the Renaissance in terms of humanism, imitation of the ancients, and individual achievement: Jacob Burckhardt, *The Civilization of the Renaissance*, 1878, rev. 1944; Douglas Bush, *The Renaissance and English Humanism*, 1939; E. M. W. Tillyard, *The Elizabethan World Picture*, 1943; *The Renaissance Philosophy of Man*, ed. Ernst Cassirer et al., 1948; Erwin Panofsky, *Renaissance and Renascences in Western Art*, 2 vols., 1960; and Paul O. Kristeller, *Renaissance Thought*, 2 vols., 1961, 1965. Revisionist analyses by new historicist and cultural materialist critics focus on the interaction of institutions, ideology, and the conditions of cultural production in the social construction of persons and literary texts. Some seminal studies are Stephen Greenblatt, *Renaissance Self-Fashioning*, 1980; *Representing the English Renaissance*, ed. S. Greenblatt, 1988; Richard Helgerson, *Self-Crowned Laureates: Spenser, Jonson, Milton and the Literary System*, 1983, and *Forms of Nationhood: The Elizabethan Writing of England*, 1992; Annabel Patterson, *Censorship and Interpretation: The Conditions of Writing and Reading in Early Modern England*, 1984; Peter Stallybrass and Allon White, *The Politics and Poetics of Transgression*, 1986; and Richard Halpern, *The Poetics of Primitive Accumulation: English Renaissance Culture and the Genealogy of Capital*, 1991. (Others on the theater and on Shakespeare are noted in appropriate sections.)

Science and medicine in this period are discussed in Antonia Mclean, *Humanism and the Rise of Science in Tudor England*, 1972; Roy Porter, *Disease, Medicine and Society in England 1550–1860*, 1987; Thomas Laqueur, *Making Sex: Body and Gender from the Greeks to Freud*, 1990; and Jonathan Sawday, *The Body Emblazoned: Dissection and the Human Body in Renaissance Culture*, 1995. Education is the subject of T. W. Baldwin, *William Shakespere's Small Latine and Lesse Greeke*, 2 vols., 1944, and Kenneth Charlton, *Education in Renais-*

sance England, 1965. On logic and rhetoric see W. S. Howell, *Logic and Rhetoric in England, 1500–1700*, 1956; Sister Miriam Joseph, *Rhetoric in Shakespeare's Time*, 1962; Frances Yates, *The Art of Memory*, 1966; and Victoria Kahn, *Rhetoric and Skepticism in the Renaissance*, 1985.

Some books on Renaissance art and architecture are Marcus Whiffin, *An Introduction to Elizabethan and Jacobean Architecture*, 1952; J. Buxton, *Elizabethan Taste*, 1963; Roy Strong, *The English Icon: Elizabethan and Jacobean Portraiture*, 1969, and *The Cult of Elizabeth: Elizabethan Portraiture and Pageantry*, 1977; Mark Girouard, *Life in the English Country House*, 1978; John King, *Tudor Royal Iconography: Literature and Art in an Age of Religious Crisis*, 1989; Lucy Gent, *Picture and Poetry, 1560–1620*, 1981; and Norman K. Farmer, *Poets and the Visual Arts in Renaissance England*, 1984. Renaissance iconology and emblem books often illuminate literary imagery; important studies are Erwin Panofsky, *Studies in Iconology*, 1939; Rosemary Freeman, *English Emblem Books*, 1948; Jean Seznec, *The Survival of the Pagan Gods*, trans. B. F. Sessions, 1963. The attack on religious images is treated by John Phillips, *The Reformation of Images: Destruction of Art in England, 1535–1660*, 1971; and Ernest B. Gilman, *Iconoclasm and Poetry in the English Reformation*, 1986.

For Tudor music and musicians in relation to poetry see M. C. Boyd, *Elizabethan Music and Music Criticism*, 1940; E. H. Fellowes, *English Madrigal Verse*, rev. 1967; John Stevens, *Music and Poetry in the Early Tudor Court*, 1961, rpt. 1979; David Price, *Patrons and Musicians of the English Renaissance*, 1981; and Winifred Meynard, *Elizabethan Lyric Poetry and Its Music*, 1986. John Hollander studies music as symbol in *The Untuning of the Sky: Ideas of Music in English Poetry, 1500–1700*, 1961; and Paula Johnson analyzes structural affinities of the two art forms in *Form and Transformation in Music and Poetry of the English Renaissance*, 1975.

Useful anthologies of Elizabethan literary criticism are G. G. Smith, *Elizabethan Critical Essays*, 2 vols., 1904, and O. B. Hardison Jr., *English Literary Criticism: The Renaissance*, 1963. Important studies of Renaissance literary theory and criticism include Rosamond Tuve, *Elizabethan and Metaphysical Imagery*, 1947; Baxter Hathaway, *Marvels and Commonplaces: Renaissance Literary Criticism*, 1968; Don C. Allen, *Mysteriously Meant: The Rediscovery of Pagan Symbolism and Allegorical Interpretation in the Renaissance*, 1970; S. K. Heninger, *Touches of Sweet Harmony: Pythagorean Cosmology and Renaissance Poetics*, 1974; Margaret W. Ferguson, *Trials of Desire: Renaissance Defenses of Poetry*, 1983; and Arthur Kinney, *Humanist Poetics*, 1986.

Some distinguished historical and critical accounts of Renaissance literature include Hallett Smith, *Elizabethan Poetry: A Study in Conventions, Meaning, and Expression*, 1952, rpt. 1968; C. S. Lewis, *English Literature in the Sixteenth Century, Excluding Drama*, 1954; Douglas Bush, *Mythology*

and the Renaissance Tradition in English Poetry, rev. 1963; Rosalie Colie, *The Resources of Kind: Genre-Theory in the Renaissance*, 1973; Thomas M. Greene, *The Light in Troy: Imitation and Discovery in Renaissance Poetry*, 1982; Alan Sinfield, *Literature in Protestant England, 1560–1660*, 1983; and David Norbrook, *Poetry and Politics in the English Renaissance*, 1984. Important studies of particular Renaissance genres and kinds include J. W. Lever, *The Elizabethan Love Sonnet*, 1956; Alvin Kernan, *The Cankered Muse: Satire of the English Renaissance*, 1959; Lily B. Campbell, *Divine Poetry and Drama in Sixteenth-Century England*, 1959; Angus Fletcher, *Allegory: The Theory of a Symbolic Mode*, 1964; Douglas L. Peterson, *The English Lyric from Wyatt to Donne*, 1966; *Seventeenth-Century Prose*, ed. Stanley Fish, 1971; Patricia Parker, *Inescapable Romance*, 1979; Anne Ferry, *The "Inward" Language: Sonnets of Wyatt, Sidney, Shakespeare, and Donne*, 1983; Janel Mueller, *The Native Tongue and the Word: Developments in English Prose Style, 1380–1580*, 1984; Peter Sacks, *The English Elegy: Studies in the Genre from Spenser to Yeats*, 1985; Susanne Wofford, *The Choice of Achilles: The Ideology of Figure in the Epic*, 1992; Arthur Marotti, *Manuscript, Print, and the English Renaissance Lyric*, 1995; and Paul Alpers, *What Is Pastoral?*, 1996.

Important studies of stage history, audiences, and the development of dramatic forms include E. K. Chambers, *The Elizabethan Stage*, 4 vols., 1923; Allardyce Nicoll, *British Drama*, rev. 1962; *Revels History of Drama in English*, 8 vols., 1978–83; Muriel D. Bradbrook, *A History of Elizabethan Drama*, 6 vols., 1935–76; F. T. Bowers, *Elizabethan Revenge Tragedy, 1578–1642*, 1940; Glynne Wickham, *Early English Stages, 1300–1660*, 3 vols., 1959–81; Richard Leacroft, *The Development of the English Playhouse*, 1973; David Bevington, *From "Mankind" to Marlowe*, 1962; Stephen Orgel, *The Illusion of Power: Political Theater in the English Renaissance*, 1975, and *Impersonations: The Performance of Gender in Shakespeare's England*, 1996; Ann Jennalie Cook, *The Privileged Playgoers of Shakespeare's London: 1576–1642*, 1981; Andrew Gurr, *Playgoing in Shakespeare's London*, 1987; and Leeds Barroll, *Politics, Plague, and Shakespeare's Theater*, 1991. Some important studies of drama in relation to contemporary politics and ideology are David Bevington, *Tudor Drama and Politics*, 1968; Robert Weiman, *Shakespeare and the Popular Tradition in the Theater*, 1967, rpt. 1987; Jonas Barish, *The Antitheatrical Prejudice*, 1981; Jonathan Dollimore, *Radical Tragedy: Religion, Ideology and Power in the Drama of Shakespeare and his Contemporaries*, 1984; Catherine Belsey, *The Subject of Tragedy: Identity and Difference in Renaissance Drama*, 1985; Jean-Christophe Agnew, *Worlds Apart: The Market and the Theatre in Anglo-American Thought, 1550–1750*, 1986; Steven Mullaney, *The Place of the Stage*, 1988; Katharine Maus, *Inwardness and Theater in the English Renaissance*, 1995; and Louis Montrose, *The Pur-*

pose of Playing: Shakespeare and the Cultural Politics of the Elizabethan Theatre, 1996.

The many recent studies of the status of women in early modern England have a distinguished precursor in Alice Clark, *Working Life of Women in the Seventeenth Century*, 1919. On the situation of women in the Renaissance and the achievements of women writers, see Joan Kelly-Gadol, "Did Women Have a Renaissance?" in *Becoming Visible: Women in European History*, ed. R. Bridenthal and C. Koonz, 1977; Ian Maclean, *The Renaissance Notion of Women*, 1980; *Beyond Their Sex: Learned Women of the European Past*, ed. Patricia H. Labalme, 1980; Retha M. Warnicke, *Women of the English Renaissance and Reformation*, 1983; Linda Woodbridge, *Women and the English Renaissance: Literature and the Nature of Womankind, 1540–1640*, 1984; *Rewriting the Renaissance: The Discourses of Sexual Difference in Early Modern Europe*, ed. Margaret Ferguson et al., 1986; Elaine Beilin, *Redeeming Eve: Women Writers of the English Renaissance*, 1987; *The Renaissance Englishwoman in Print: Counterbalancing the Canon*, ed. Anne M. Haselkorn and Betty S. Travitsky, 1990; Constance Jordan, *Renaissance Feminism: Literary Texts and Political Models*, 1990; and Patricia Crawford, *Women and Religion in England, 1500–1720*, 1993. A useful anthology is *The Paradise of Women: Writings by Englishwomen of the Renaissance*, ed. Betty Travitsky, 1981; see also Randall Martin, *Women Writers in Renaissance England*, 1997. On male homosexuality in the period, see Alan Bray, *Homosexuality in Renaissance England*, 1982, and Bruce Smith, *Homosexual Desire in Shakespeare's England*, 1991.

An invaluable tool for the study of early modern literature is the *Oxford English Dictionary*, 2nd ed., 1989, now also on CD-ROM. Also useful are Morris Tilley, *A Dictionary of the Proverbs in England in the Sixteenth and Seventeenth Centuries*, 1950; Richard Jones, *The Triumph of the English Language*, 1953; Richard Lanham, *A Handlist of Rhetorical Terms*, 1968; James Hencke, *Courtesans and Cuckolds: A Glossary of Renaissance Dramatic Bawdy (Exclusive of Shakespeare)*, 1979; Fausto Cercignani, *Shakespeare's Works and Elizabethan Pronunciation*, 1981; Eric Partridge, *Shakespeare's Bawdy*, 3rd ed., 1991; and Charles Barber, *Early Modern English*, rev. ed., 1997.

Roger Ascham

The Whole Works of Roger Ascham, 3 vols., ed. J. A. Giles, 1864–65, rpt. 1965, remains standard, although it omits some theological works and letters. The standard, annotated edition of *The Scholemaster* is by John E. B. Mayor, 1863, rpt. 1967. Lawrence V. Ryan edited *The Schoolmaster* in modern spelling, 1967; he also wrote a useful biographical and critical study, *Roger Ascham*, 1963. Ascham studies are surveyed in *English Literary Renaissance* [hereafter *ELR*] 10 (1980): 300–10, and in Jerome S. Dees, *Sir Thomas Elyot and Roger Ascham: A Reference Guide*, 1981.

Thomas Campion

The standard edition (including a biography) is Percival Vivian, *Campion's Works*, 1909, rpt. 1960. Campion's English works, with a selection from his Latin poetry, are edited by Walter R. Davis, 1967, who also published a biographical and critical study, *Thomas Campion*, 1987. Other studies include E. Lowbury et al., *Thomas Campion, Poet, Composer, Physician*, 1970; John Hollander, "The Case of Campion," in *Vision and Resonance: Two Senses of Poetic Form*, 1975, 71–90; Muriel T. Eldridge, *Thomas Campion: His Poetry and Music*, 1977; Stephen Ratcliffe, *Campion: On Song*, 1981; David Lindley, *Thomas Campion*, 1986; and Christopher Wilson, *Words and Notes Coupled Lovingly Together: Thomas Campion, A Critical Study*, 1989. Recent studies are surveyed in *ELR* 4 (1974): 404–11 and 16 (1986): 253–56.

Samuel Daniel

The only complete edition is *Complete Works in Verse and Prose*, 5 vols., ed. A. B. Grosart, 1885–96, rpt. 1963; a new edition, by John Pitcher, is currently in preparation. A. C. Sprague edited *Poems and A Defense of Rhyme*, 1930, rpt. 1965. Some useful studies are Joan Rees, *Samuel Daniel, A Critical and Biographical Study*, 1964; Cecil Seronsy, *Samuel Daniel*, 1967; and Arthur F. Marotti, "'Love is not Love': Elizabethan Sonnet Sequences and the Social Order," *ELH* 49 (1982): 396–428. Recent studies are surveyed in *ELR* 24 (1994): 489–502.

Michael Drayton

The standard edition is by J. W. Hebel, 5 vols., 1931–41, rpt. 1961; there is a useful selected edition by John Buxton, 1953. The standard biography is B. H. Newdigate, *Michael Drayton and his Circle*, 1941, rpt. 1961. Critical studies include J. A. Berthelot, *Michael Drayton*, 1967; R. F. Hardin, *Michael Drayton and the Passing of Elizabethan England*, 1973; and Jean R. Brink, *Michael Drayton Revisited*, 1990. There are valuable discussions of Drayton in Richard Helgerson, *Forms of Nationhood*, 1992, and Claire McEachern, *The Poetics of English Nationhood, 1590–1612*, 1996.

Queen Elizabeth I

There is no complete edition of Queen Elizabeth's writings. *The Poems of Queen Elizabeth I*, ed. Leicester Bradner, 1964, prints several of her poems and verse translations. The most inclusive edition of her letters is by G. B. Harrison, 1935; and George P. Rice Jr. prints twenty-one of her speeches in *The Public Speaking of Queen Elizabeth: Selections from her Official Addresses*, 1951, rpt. 1966. Frances Teague surveys Elizabeth's life and writings, and prints a selection of her works, in *Women Writers of the Renaissance and Reformation*, ed. Katharina M. Wilson, 1987; Marc Shell edits and provides an extended commentary on one of her religious translations in *Elizabeth's Glass*, 1993. The standard biography remains J. E. Neale, *Queen Elizabeth I*, 1934, rpt. 1967. Maria Perry has a documentary biography, *The Word of a Prince: The Life of Elizabeth I from Contemporary Documents*, 1990. The queen's significance as political and cultural presence is treated by Frances Yates, *Astraea: The Imperial Theme*, 1975; Marie Axton, *The Queen's Two Bodies: Drama and the Elizabethan Succession*, 1977; Phillippa Berry, *Of Chastity and Power: Elizabethan Literature and the Unmarried Queen*, 1989; and Carole Levin, *"The Heart and Stomach of a King": Elizabeth I and the Politics of Sex and Power*, 1994. Susan Bassnett, *Elizabeth I: A Feminist Perspective*, 1988, approaches the queen's career through her writings; Susan Frye, *Elizabeth I: The Competition for Representation*, 1993, studies Elizabeth's construction of her power within a patriarchal society. *ELR* 23 (1993): 345–54 and 24 (1994): 234–36 survey recent studies of Elizabeth.

John Foxe

There is no standard edition of Foxe's collected works. The most useful modern edition of *The Acts and Monuments* is by Stephen R. Cattley, 8 vols., 1837–41, revised by Josiah Pratt, 1877, and rpt. 1965. The best account of Foxe's life is J. F. Mozley's *John Foxe and His Book*, 1940, rpt. 1970. A more recent study of the life and works is W. Wooden, *John Foxe*, 1983. On Foxe's significance, see William Haller, *The Elect Nation: The Meaning and Relevance of Foxe's Book of Martyrs*, 1963; V. Olson, *John Foxe and the Elizabethan Church*, 1973; and discussions in John King, *English Reformation Literature*, 1982. For a discussion of Foxe's role in the shaping of English nationalism, see Richard Helgerson, *Forms of Nationhood*, 1992. A survey of recent studies is in *ELR* 11 (1981): 224–32. See also entries under **Literature of the Sacred**.

George Gascoigne

John W. Cunliffe edited the *Complete Works*, 2 vols., 1907–10, rpt. 1969. The standard edition of Gascoigne's poems, *A Hundreth Sundrie Flowres*, is by C. T. Prouty, 1942, as is a major study of his life and works, *George Gascoigne, Elizabethan Courtier, Soldier, and Poet*, 1942, rpt. 1966. Important literary studies include Ivor Winters, "The 16th Century Lyric in England," rpt. in *Elizabethan Poetry*, ed. Paul Alpers, 1967; Richard Helgerson in *The Elizabethan Prodigals*, 1976; and Richard McCoy, "Gascoigne's 'Poemata Castrata': The Wages of Courtly Success," *Criticism* 27 (1985): 29–55. Recent studies are surveyed in *ELR* 3 (1973): 322–27.

Arthur Golding

Ovid's Metamorphoses: The Arthur Golding Translation was edited by John F. Nims, 1965; it is analyzed in Gordon Braden, *The Classics and English Renaissance Poetry: Three Case Studies*, 1978. The only general study is L. T. Golding's biographical/critical account, *An Elizabethan Puritan*, 1937.

Fulke Greville

Most of Greville's literary works are in *The Poems and Dramas of Fulke Greville, First Lord Brooke*, 2 vols., ed. Geoffrey Bullough, 1939, rpt. 1945; G. A. Wilkes edited the other philosophical poems, *The Remains, Being Poems of Monarchy and Religion*, 1965; Greville's *Prose Works*, including his *Life of Sir Philip Sidney*, were edited by John Gouws, 1986. There are editions of *Selected Poems* by Thom Gunn, 1968, and Neil Powell, 1990, and of *Selected Writings* by Joan Rees, 1973. The major biography is by Ronald A. Rebholz, 1971; there is also a critical biography by Joan Rees, 1971. Important critical studies are Richard Waswo, *The Fatal Mirror: Themes and Techniques in the Poetry of Fulke Greville*, 1972, and C. H. Howard, *Fulke Greville*, 1980. Scholarship is surveyed in P. J. Klemp, *Fulke Greville and Sir John Davies: A Reference Guide*, 1985.

Thomas Hariot

Hariot's *Report on Virginia* is handsomely edited, with illustrations first published in the 1590 edition, by Paul Hulton, 1972. The *Report* was included in Richard Hakluyt's collection, *The Principal Navigations, Voyages, Traffics, and Discoveries*, 1598–1600, ed. in 12 vols., Glasgow, 1903–05, 8: 348–86. See George B. Parks, *Richard Hakluyt and the English Voyages*, 1928. Useful biographical studies are Muriel Rukeyser, *The Traces of Thomas Hariot*, 1971, and James W. Shirley, *Thomas Hariot, a Biography*, 1983. Stephen Greenblatt analyzes the cultural response to Hariot's report in "Invisible Bullets: Renaissance Authority and Its Subversion," *Glyph* 8 (1981): 40–61; the work is also examined by Shannon Miller in *Invested with Meaning: The Raleigh Circle in the New World*, 1998. See also entries under **The Wider World**.

Mary (Sidney) Herbert, Countess of Pembroke

Margaret P. Hannay et al. edited the *Collected Works*, 2 vols., 1998; there is an important edition of *The Psalms of Sir Philip Sidney and the Countess of Pembroke*, ed J. C. A. Rathmell, 1963. Margaret P. Hannay has written the only literary biography, *Philip's Phoenix*, 1990. Mary Herbert is also one of the three writers treated in Kim Walker, *Women Writers of the English Renaissance*, 1996. Other important studies are Gary Waller, *Mary Sidney, Countess of Pembroke: A Critical Study of Her Writings and Literary Milieu*, 1979, and Mary Ellen Lamb, *Gender and Authorship in the Sidney Circle*, 1990. Recent studies are surveyed in *ELR* 14 (1984): 426–37 and 24 (1994): 237–38.

Sir Thomas Hoby

Hoby's *Book of the Courtier* was edited by Walter Raleigh, 1900, rpt. 1967. Hoby's diary, *The Booke of the Travaile and Lief of Me*, was edited by E. Powell, 1902. Castiglione's *Il Cortegiano* received a fine modern translation by C. S. Singleton in 1959. The significance of the work is discussed in Wayne A. Rebhorn, *Courtly Performances*, 1978; *Castiglione: The Ideal and the Real in Renaissance Culture*, ed. Robert W. Hanning and David Rosand, 1983; Frank Whigham, *Ambition and Privilege*, 1984; and Peter Burke, *The Fortunes of the "Courtier": The European Reception of Castiglione's "Cortegiano,"* 1995.

Richard Hooker

Hooker's *Works* are edited by G. Edelen et al., 5 vols., 1977–90; the first four volumes include the

Laws. Arthur Stephen McGrade published a handy, useful edition of the Preface and Books 1 and 8 in 1989. Isaac Walton wrote a *Life* of Hooker in 1665; it is reprinted in *The Lives of John Donne, Sir Henry Wotton, Richard Hooker, George Herbert, and Robert Sanderson*, ed. George Saintsbury, 1927, rpt. 1956. There is a brief modern treatment of Hooker's life and works by Arthur Pollard, 1966. Some important studies are C. J. Sisson, *The Judicious Marriage of Mr. Hooker and the Birth of "The Laws of Ecclesiastical Polity,"* 1940; E. T. Davies, *The Political Ideas of Richard Hooker*, 1946; *Studies in Richard Hooker*, ed. W. Speed Hill, 1972; R. K. Faulkner, *Richard Hooker and the Politics of a Christian England*, 1981; and *Richard Hooker and the Construction of Christian Community*, ed. Arthur S. McGrade, 1997, which includes a selected bibliography. See also entries under **Literature of the Sacred**.

Literature of the Sacred
Debora Shuger's *The Renaissance Bible: Scholarship, Sacrifice, and Subjectivity*, 1994, is a brilliant analysis of the place of Scripture in a wide range of early modern discourses. Studies of the English Bible include John Coolidge, *The Pauline Renaissance in England: Puritanism and the Bible*, 1970; David Daiches, *The King James Version of the English Bible*, 1968; F. F. Bruce, *History of the Bible in English*, 1978; and A. C. Partridge, *English Biblical Translation*, 1973. William Tyndale's doctrinal treatises were edited by Henry Walter in 1848; there is a modern biography of Tyndale by David Daniell, 1994, and an account of his psychological and literary power in Stephen Greenblatt, *Renaissance Self-Fashioning*, 1980. William Bouwsma, *John Calvin: A Sixteenth-Century Portrait*, 1988, is a fine introduction to the life and thought of the reformer. There is a selection from Anne Askew's examination in *The Paradise of Women*, ed. Betty Travitsky, 1981, and an analysis of her challenge to authority in Elaine Beilin, *Redeeming Eve*, 1987. A complete edition of John Foxe's *Acts and Monuments*, 8 vols., was edited by Stephen R. Cattley, 1837–41, and revised by Josiah Pratt, 1877, rpt. 1965. John Booty edited the 1559 version of the Book of Common Prayer in 1976; Booty also edited *The Godly Kingdom of Tudor England*, 1981, a useful collection of essays on the prayer book, the Book of Homilies, and other Reformation texts. Ronald Bond edited *"Certain Sermons or Homilies" (1547)* and *"A Homily against Disobedience and Wilful Rebellion" (1570)*, 1987. There is a major biography of Thomas Cranmer by Diarmaid MacCulloch, 1996. See also entries under **Foxe**, **Hooker**, and **Southwell**.

John Lyly
The *Complete Works* are edited by R. Warwick Bond, 3 vols., 1902; an important edition and analysis of *Euphues* is by M. W. Croll and H. Clemons, 1916. Significant studies include Jonas Barish, "The prose-style of Lyly," *ELH* 23 (1956): 14–35; G. K. Hunter, *The Humanist as Courtier*, 1962; Joseph W. Houppert, *John Lyly*, 1975; Richard Hel-

gerson in *The Elizabethan Prodigals*, 1976; Devon L. Hodges in *Renaissance Fictions of Anatomy*, 1985; Paul Salzman, *English Prose Fiction, 1558–1700: A Critical History*, 1985; and R. W. Maslen, *Elizabethan Fictions*, 1997. Recent studies are surveyed in *ELR* 22 (1992): 435–50 and 25 (1995): 258–59.

Christopher Marlowe
Fredson Bowers has edited the *Complete Works*, 2 vols., 1973, rev. 1981; R. H. Case has a modern-spelling edition, 6 vols., 1930–33, rpt. 1966; of Roma Gill's projected three-volume edition, the first two volumes appeared in 1987. W. W. Greg edited parallel texts of the two versions of *Dr. Faustus* in 1950; the two versions have also been edited by David Bevington and Eric Rasmussen, 1993; and Roma Gill edited the A text (our copy text for *Faustus*) in 1989. Stephen Orgel edited *The Complete Poems and Translations of Christopher Marlowe*, 1971. For Marlowe's biography see John Bakeless, *The Tragicall History of Christopher Marlowe*, 2 vols., 1942, and Charles Nicholl, *The Reckoning: The Murder of Christopher Marlowe*, 1992. Valuable critical studies include Harry Levin, *The Overreacher*, 1952; Douglas Cole, *Suffering and Evil in the Plays of Christopher Marlowe*, 1962; *Two Renaissance Mythmakers: Christopher Marlowe and Ben Jonson*, ed. Alvin B. Kernan, 1977; *Marlowe: The Critical Heritage*, ed. Millar McLure, 1979; Clifford Leech, *Christopher Marlowe: Poet for the Stage*, 1986; Simon Shepherd, *Marlowe and the Politics of Elizabethan Theatre*, 1986; *Christopher Marlowe*, in the series "Modern Critical Views," ed. Harold Bloom, 1986; C. L. Barber, *Creating Elizabethan Tragedy: the Theater of Marlowe and Kyd*, 1988. *Christopher Marlowe's "Doctor Faustus,"* in "Modern Critical Interpretations," ed. Harold Bloom, 1988; and *Christopher Marlowe and English Renaissance Culture*, ed. Darryll Grantley and Peter Roberts, 1996. For *Hero and Leander*, Louis L. Martz's facsimile of the first edition, 1972, has an important introduction. On the genre, see William Keach, *Elizabeth Erotic Narratives*, 1977; and Clark Hulse, *Metamorphic Verse: The Elizabethan Minor Epic*, 1981. Recent studies are surveyed in *ELR* 7 (1977): 382–99 and 18 (1988): 329–42.

Sir Thomas More
The *Yale Edition of the Complete Works of St. Thomas More*, 15 vols., 1963–97, is standard. Vol. 4 of this edition is *Utopia*, ed. Edward L. Surtz, S.J., and J. H. Hexter, 1965; it includes a wealth of information and commentary. Our text is based on the translation in *Utopia*, ed. George M. Logan and Robert M. Adams, 1989, an edition intended for students. Logan, Adams, and Clarence H. Miller edited *Utopia: Latin Text and English Translation*, 1995. Both editions include evaluative guides to Utopian scholarship. Adams's Norton Critical Edition, rev. 1992, includes background readings and a selection of the best criticism on *Utopia*. More's *Richard III* is vol. 3 of the Yale edition, ed. Richard S. Sylvester, 1963, but is most conveniently read in Sylvester's English-only edition, *The History of King*

Richard III and Selections from the English and Latin Poems, 1976. The biography by More's son-in-law William Roper is published in *Two Early Tudor Lives*, ed. Sylvester and Davis P. Harding, 1962. R. M. Chambers's eminently readable *Thomas More*, 1935, long the standard modern biography, is now superseded by the two most recent ones, Richard Marius, *Thomas More*, 1984, and Peter Ackroyd, *The Life of Thomas More*, 1998. The psychobiographical essay in Stephen Greenblatt's *Renaissance Self-Fashioning from More to Shakespeare*, 1980, has been influential, as has Alistair Fox's overview of the life and works, *Thomas More: History and Providence*, 1983. Influential books on *Utopia* include Hexter's brilliant *More's "Utopia": The Biography of an Idea*, 1952, rpt. with an epilogue 1965, and rewritten in his section of the introduction to the Yale *Utopia*; Surtz, *The Praise of Pleasure: Philosophy, Education, and Communism in More's Utopia*, 1957; Logan, *The Meaning of More's "Utopia,"* 1983; and Dominic Baker's synthesis, *More's "Utopia,"* 1991. *Essential Articles for the Study of Thomas More*, ed. Sylvester and G. P. Marc'hadour, 1977, reprints many valuable articles. Recent studies are surveyed by Albert J. Geritz, *Thomas More: An Annotated Bibliography of Criticism, 1935–1997*, 1998.

Thomas Nashe
The standard edition, 5 vols., is by R. W. McKerrow, rev. F. P. Wilson, 1958; there are selected editions by Stanley Wells, 1965, and J. B. Steane, 1972. Charles Nicholl has written *A Cup of News: The Life of Thomas Nashe*, 1984. Useful critical studies include G. R. Hibbard, *Thomas Nashe: A Critical Introduction*, 1962; Jonathan V. Crewe, *Unredeemed Rhetoric: Thomas Nashe and the Scandal of Authorship*, 1982; Stephen S. Hilliard, *The Singularity of Thomas Nashe*, 1986; Lorna Hutson, *Thomas Nashe in Context*, 1989; and Peter Holbrook, *Literature and Degree in Renaissance England: Nashe, Bourgeois Tragedy, Shakespeare*, 1994. *ELR* 25 (1995): 261–64 reviews recent studies.

Sir Walter Ralegh
The collected edition is by William Oldys and Thomas Birch, 8 vols., 1829, rpt. 1965; the standard edition of the poems is by A. M. C. Latham, rev. 1950; a useful edition is *Selected Writings*, ed. Gerard Hammond, 1984. *The Discoverie of the Large, Rich and Bewtiful Empyre of Guiana* has been newly edited, with much contextual and interpretive material, by Neil L. Whitehead, 1997. Biographies include Willard M. Wallace, *Sir Walter Raleigh*, 1959, and Stephen Coote, *A Play of Passion*, 1993. Noteworthy studies include David B. Quinn, *Ralegh and the British Empire*, 1947, rpt. 1962; E. A. Strathmann, *Sir Walter Ralegh, A Study in Elizabethan Skepticism*, 1951; Philip Edwards, *Sir Walter Ralegh*, 1953, rpt. 1976; F. J. Levy in *Tudor Historical Thought*, 1967; Stephen Greenblatt, *Sir Walter Ralegh*, 1973; and Shannon Miller, *Invested with Meaning: The Raleigh Circle in the New World*, 1998. For guides to scholarship, see Jerry L. Mills, *Sir Walter Ralegh: A Reference Guide*, 1986, and Christopher Armitage, *Sir Walter Ralegh, An Annotated Bibliography*, 1987. See also entries under **The Wider World**.

William Shakespeare
Important editions of *Twelfth Night* include the Variorum (H. H. Furness, ed., 1901); the Arden (J. M. Lothan and T. W. Craik, eds., 1975); and the Oxford (Roger Warren and Stanley Wells, eds., 1994). Important editions of *King Lear* include the Variorum (H. H. Furness, ed., 1880); the Arden (Reginald Foakes, ed., 1997); and the New Cambridge (Jay Halio, ed., 1992). *The Complete King Lear, 1608–1623*, ed. Michael Warren, 1989, is a valuable resource for textual study. *The Norton Shakespeare*, ed. Stephen Greenblatt et al., 1997, presents the quarto and Folio texts of *King Lear* on facing pages, and the two versions are discussed in *The Division of the Kingdoms*, ed. Gary Taylor and Michael Warren, 1983. Significant studies of *Twelfth Night* are assembled by Walter King ("Twentieth Century Interpretations"), 1968; Stanley Wells ("Critical Essays"), 1986; Harold Bloom ("Modern Critical Interpretations"), 1987; and Barbara Everett ("New Casebooks"), 1996. The play is treated in the context of Shakespearean comedy by C. L. Barber, *Shakespeare's Festive Comedy*, 1959; Northrop Frye, *A Natural Perspective*, 1965; Linda Bamber, *Comic Women, Tragic Men*, 1982; Edward Berry, *Shakespeare's Comic Rites*, 1984; and William Carroll, *The Metamorphoses of Shakespearean Comedy*, 1985. Among the many great essays on *King Lear* are those in A. C. Bradley, *Shakespearean Tragedy*, 1904; J. V. Cunningham, *Woe or Wonder*, 1951; Jan Kott, *Shakespeare Our Contemporary*, 1967; Stephen Booth, *"King Lear," "Macbeth," Indefinition, and Tragedy*, 1983; and Stanley Cavell, *Disowning Knowledge*, 1987. Significant essays on the play are assembled by Janet Adelman ("Twentieth Century Interpretations"), 1978; Harold Bloom ("Modern Critical Interpretations"), 1987; Kiernan Ryan ("New Casebooks"), 1993; and Jay Halio ("Critical Essays"), 1996.

The objects of obsessive critical attention for centuries, Shakespeare's plays have recently been studied from new historicist, feminist, psychoanalytic, and deconstructive perspectives, among others. The range may be sampled in such collections as *Representing Shakespeare: New Psychoanalytic Essays*, ed. Murray Schwartz and Coppelia Kahn, 1980; *Alternative Shakespeares*, ed. John Drakakis, 1985; *Shakespeare and the Question of Theory*, ed. Patricia Parker and Geoffrey Hartman, 1985; *Shakespeare Reproduced*, ed. Jean Howard and M. O'Connor, 1987; *Political Shakespeare*, ed. Jonathan Dollimore and Alan Sinfield, 1994; and in such books as Lisa Jardine, *Still Harping on Daughters*, 1983; Marjorie Garber, *Shakespeare's Ghost Writers*, 1987; Stephen Greenblatt, *Shakespearean Negotiations*, 1988; Margreta de Grazia, *Shakespeare Verbatim*, 1991; Janet Adelman, *Suf-*

focating Mothers, 1992; Valerie Traub, *Desire and Anxiety*, 1992; and Harry Berger Jr., *Making Trifles of Terrors*, 1997. Notable performance studies include Marvin Rosenberg, *The Masks of Lear*, 1972; David Bevington, *Action Is Eloquence*, 1984; Michael Goldman, *Acting and Action in Shakespearean Tragedy*, 1985; Peter Donaldson, *Shakespearean Films, Shakespearean Directors*, 1990; and *Shakespeare, the Movie*, ed. Lynda Boose and Richard Burt, 1997.

Hyder Rollins's Variorum edition of the sonnets, 2 vols., 1944, summarizes many commentaries and problems; Stephen Booth's edition, 1977, presents a facsimile of the first edition and a modernized text on facing pages, with elaborate commentary; see, likewise, the Arden Edition (K. Duncan-Jones, ed., 1997) and Helen Vendler, *The Art of Shakespeare's Sonnets*, 1997. Noteworthy criticism of the sonnets and poems includes Stephen Booth, *An Essay on Shakespeare's Sonnets*, 1969; Joel Fineman, *Shakespeare's Perjured Eye: The Invention of Poetic Subjectivity in the Sonnets*, 1986; Heather Dubrow, *Captive Victors: Shakespeare's Narrative Poems and Sonnets*, 1987; Bruce Smith, *Homosexual Desire in Shakespeare's England*, 1991; and Margreta de Grazia, "The Scandal of Shakespeare's Sonnets," in *Shakespeare Survey* 46 (1994): 35–49.

The life and works are treated by E. K. Chambers, *William Shakespeare: A Study of Facts and Problems*, 2 vols., 1930. S. Schoenbaum's important biographical research is recorded in *William Shakespeare: A Documentary Life*, 1975, and *A Compact Documentary Life*, 1977. Some useful aids to scholarship are Geoffrey Bullough, *Narrative and Dramatic Sources of Shakespeare*, 8 vols., 1957–75, and *A New Companion to Shakespeare Studies*, ed. Kenneth Muir and S. Schoenbaum, 1971, rpt. 1976.

Sir Philip Sidney

Oxford editions are standard for everything except the correspondence: the poetry is edited by William A. Ringler Jr., 1962; the *Old Arcadia* by Jean Robertson, 1973; the *New Arcadia* by Victor Skretkowicz, 1987; and the *Miscellaneous Prose* (including the *Defense*) by Katherine Duncan-Jones and Jan Van Dorsten, 1973. Sidney's letters are found in *The Prose Works of Sir Philip Sidney*, 4 vols., ed. Albert Feuillerat, 1912, rpt. 1962, 3: 75–184. There are valuable editions of the *Defense* by Geoffrey Shepherd, 1965, and Van Dorsten, 1966. Maurice Evans edited *The Countess of Pembroke's Arcadia* (the 1593 composite version) in 1977. Useful volumes of selected works are those by David Kalstone, 1970; Duncan-Jones for the Oxford English Authors series, 1989; Catherine Bates (poetry), 1994; and Elizabeth P. Watson, 1997. The earliest biography was by Sidney's friend Fulke Greville, 1652; it is included in *Greville's Prose Works*, ed. John Gouws, 1986. The standard modern biography is Duncan-Jones, *Sir Philip Sidney: Courtier Poet*, 1991. Modern studies of the life and works are John Buxton, *Sir Philip Sidney and the English Renais-*

sance, 1954, rpt. 1964; James M. Osborn, *Young Philip Sidney*, 1972; and A. C. Hamilton, *Sir Philip Sidney: A Study of His Life and Works*, 1977. Some important critical studies are Walter R. Davis and Richard Lanham, *Sidney's Arcadia*, 1965; David Kalstone, *Sidney's Poetry: Contexts and Interpretations*, 1965; Neil L. Rudenstine, *Sidney's Poetic Development*, 1967; Andrew Weiner, *Sir Philip Sidney and the Poetics of Protestantism*, 1978; Richard C. McCoy, *Sir Philip Sidney: Rebellion in Arcadia*, 1979; Stephen Greenblatt, "Murdering Peasants: Status, Genre, and the Representation of Rebellion," in *Representations* 1 (1983): 1–29; Joan Rees, *Sir Philip Sidney and "Arcadia,"* 1991; Roland Greene in *Post-Petrarchism*, 1991; and Blair Worden, *The Sound of Virtue: Philip Sidney's "Arcadia" and Elizabethan Politics*, 1996. Dennis Kay edited *Sir Philip Sidney: An Anthology of Modern Criticism*, 1987. *Sidney in Retrospect: Selections from "English Literary Renaissance,"* ed. Arthur F. Kinney, 1988, reprints articles and reviews of recent scholarship from a leading Renaissance journal. Recent studies of *Arcadia* are surveyed in *ELR* 26 (1996): 173–81.

John Skelton

The comprehensive edition is Alexander Dyce, *Poetical Works*, 2 vols., 1843, rpt. 1965; the standard edition for the English poems is by John Scattergood, 1983. There are also useful editions by Philip Henderson, rev. 1964, and Robert Kinsman, 1969. Biographical studies include H. L. R. Edwards, *Skelton: The Life and Times of an Early Tudor Poet*, 1949; Maurice Pollet, *John Skelton: Poet of Tudor England*, 1971; and Greg Walter, *John Skelton and the Politics of the 1520s*, 1988. Noteworthy critical studies include Arthur R. Heiserman, *Skelton and Satire*, 1961; Stanley Fish, *John Skelton's Poetry*, 1965; Arthur F. Kinney, *John Skelton, Priest as Poet: Seasons of Discovery*, 1987; and Richard Halpern, *The Poetics of Primitive Accumulation*, 1991. Anthony S. G. Edwards edited *Skelton: The Critical Heritage*, 1981. *ELR* 20 (1990): 505–16 surveys recent scholarship.

Robert Southwell

The standard edition of Southwell's poetry, by James H. McDonald and Nancy Pollard Brown, 1967, includes a biographical account. There is also a biography by Christopher Devlin, *Life of Robert Southwell, Poet and Martyr*, 1956, and an overview of the life and works by F. W. Brownlow, 1996. Important studies include P. Janelle, *Robert Southwell the Writer*, 1935; Louis L. Martz, in *The Poetry of Meditation*, rev. 1962; Helen C. White in *Tudor Books of Saints and Martyrs*, 1963; and A. D. Cousins, *The Catholic Religious Poets from Southwell to Crashaw*, 1991. John Bossy, *The English Catholic Community, 1570–1850*, 1976, provides a good introduction to the dangerous world of the Catholic recusants and their missionary priests. *ELR* 13 (1983): 221–27 contains a review of recent studies. See also entries under **Literature of the Sacred**.

Edmund Spenser

Edwin A. Greenlaw et al. edited a ten-volume Variorum edition, *The Works of Edmund Spenser,* 1932–49. Important editions of *The Faerie Queene* are by A. C. Hamilton, 1977, and Thomas P. Roche Jr., 1978; William A. Oram et al. edited *The Yale Edition of the Shorter Poems of Edmund Spenser,* 1989. The chief biography is *The Life of Edmund Spenser* by Alexander Judson, 1945. Two recent overviews of the life and works are Gary Waller, *Edmund Spenser, A Literary Life,* 1994, and Oram, *Edmund Spenser,* 1997. Important critical studies include C. S. Lewis, *The Allegory of Love,* 1936; Paul J. Alpers, *The Poetry of "The Faerie Queene,"* 1967; Isabel MacCaffrey, *Spenser's Allegory: The Anatomy of Imagination,* 1975; James Nohrnberg, *The Analogy of "The Faerie Queene,"* 1976; Michael O'Connell, *Mirror and Veil: The Historical Dimension of Spenser's "Faerie Queene,"* 1977; Jonathan Goldberg, *Endlesse Worke: Spenser and the Structure of Discourse,* 1981; John Guillory, *Poetic Authority: Spenser, Milton, and Literary History,* 1983; Harry Berger Jr., *Revisionary Play: Studies in the Spenserian Dynamics,* 1988; John N. King, *Spenser's Poetry and the Reformation Tradition,* 1990; Theresa M. Krier, *Gazing on Secret Sights: Spenser, Classical Imitation, and the Decorums of Vision,* 1990; Richard Rambuss, *Spenser's Secret Career,* 1993; Gordon Teskey, *Allegory, Materialism, Violence,* 1994; Lauren Silberman, *Transforming Desire: Erotic Knowledge in Books III and IV of "The Faerie Queene,"* 1995; and Willy Maley, *Salvaging Spenser: Colonialism, Culture, and Identity,* 1997. Hamilton edited *Essential Articles for the Study of Edmund Spenser,* 1972. A wide range of criticism is reprinted in Hugh Maclean and Anne Lake Prescott's Norton Critical Edition, *Edmund Spenser's Poetry,* rev. 1993. Mihoko Suzuki edited a collection of recent *Critical Essays on Edmund Spenser,* 1996; a parallel collection, issued the same year, is *Edmund Spenser,* ed. Andrew Hadfield. A collection that students may find intriguing is *Approaches to Teaching Spenser's "Faerie Queene,"* ed. David L. Miller and Alexander Dunlop, 1994. *The Spenser Encyclopedia,* ed. Hamilton et al., 1990, is an invaluable aid. The best guides to recent work are the bibliographies in the encyclopedia and the selected bibliography, with annotations, in Oram's *Edmund Spenser.*

Henry Howard, Earl of Surrey

The complete edition is by F. M. Padelford, 1928, rpt. 1966; Emrys Jones's excellent selected edition, 1964, is widely used. *Tottel's Miscellany* is edited by Hyder E. Rollins, 2 vols., rev. 1965. E. R. Casady's biography, 1938, rpt. 1966, and W. R. Sessions's study of the life and works, 1986, bear the same title, *Henry Howard, Earl of Surrey.* Noteworthy critical studies are Walter R. Davis, "Contexts in Surrey's Poetry," *ELR* 4 (1974): 40–55; the chapters on Surrey in Alastair Fowler, *Conceitful Thought: The Interpretation of English Renaissance Poems,* 1975, and Jonathan Crewe, *Trials of Authorship: Anterior Forms and Poetic Reconstruction from Wyatt to Shakespeare,* 1990, and those on Wyatt

and Surrey in Maurice Evans, *English Poetry in the Sixteenth Century,* rev. 1967; Susanne Woods, *Natural Emphasis: English Versification from Chaucer to Dryden,* 1984; A. C. Spearing, *Medieval to Renaissance in English Poetry,* 1985; and Elizabeth Heale, *Wyatt, Surrey and Early Tudor Poetry,* 1998. Scholarship is surveyed in Clyde W. Jentoft, *Sir Thomas Wyatt and Henry Howard, Earl of Surrey: A Reference Guide,* 1980. Reviews of recent studies are in *ELR* 19 (1989): 389–401 and 28 (1998): 307.

Isabella Whitney

A facsimile of *A Sweet Nosegay* and *The Copy of a Letter,* with an introduction by Richard Panofsky, was published in 1982. There is an excellent edition of the "Will and Testament" by Betty Travitsky, in *ELR* 10 (1980): 76–94. Critical studies include Ann Rosalind Jones, "Nets and Bridles: Early Modern Conduct Books and Sixteenth-Century Women's Lyrics," in *The Ideology of Conduct,* ed. Nancy Armstrong and Leonard Tennenhouse, 1987; Elaine Beilin, "Writing Public Poetry: Humanism and the Woman Writer," in *Modern Language Quarterly* 51 (1990): 249–71; Wendy Wall, "Isabella Whitney and the Female Legacy," in *ELH* 58 (1991): 35–62; and Patricia Phillippy, "The Maid's Lawful Liberty," in *Modern Philology* 95 (1998): 439–62.

The Wider World

Richard Hakluyt's great collection *The Principal Navigations Voyages Traffiques and Discoveries of the English Nation* was reprinted in twelve volumes, 1903–05; many of the individual texts have been edited in the series published by the Hakluyt Society. Studies of early modern literature of exploration include Stephen Greenblatt, *Marvelous Possessions: The Wonder of the New World,* 1991; *New World Encounters* (1993), ed. Greenblatt; Anthony Grafton, *New Worlds, Ancient Texts: The Power of Tradition and the Shock of Discovery,* 1992; and Jeffrey Knapp, *An Empire Nowhere: England, America, and Literature from "Utopia" to "The Tempest,"* 1995. See also entries under **Hariot** and **Ralegh**.

Sir Thomas Wyatt

The most useful edition is by Kenneth Muir and Patricia Thomson, *Collected Poems,* 1969; others are by Richard C. Harrier, 1975; Joost Daalder, 1975; and R. A. Rebholz, 1978. *Tottel's Miscellany* is edited by Hyder E. Rollins, 2 vols., rev. 1965. Letters and life records are included in Muir's biography, 1963; Thomson treats both life and works in *Sir Thomas Wyatt and His Background,* 1964; a more recent, slighter treatment is Stephen M. Foley, *Sir Thomas Wyatt,* 1990. Critical studies include E. M. W. Tillyard, *The Poetry of Sir Thomas Wyatt,* 1929, rpt. 1949; Raymond Southall, *The Courtly Maker,* 1964; Elizabeth W. Pomeroy, *The Elizabethan Miscellanies: Their Development and Conventions,* 1973; Stephen Greenblatt, *Renaissance Self-Fashioning,* 1980; Thomas M. Greene, *The Light in Troy: Imitation and Discovery in Renaissance Poetry,* 1982; and Barbara L. Estrin, *Laura: Uncovering Gender and Genre in Wyatt,*

Donne, and Marvell, 1994. Since the sixteenth century, Wyatt and Surrey have often been discussed in tandem: for some modern instances, see **Surrey**.

Thomson edited *Wyatt: The Critical Heritage*, 1974. Reviews of recent studies arc in *ELR* 19 (1989): 226–46 and 28 (1998): 307–09.

THE EARLY SEVENTEENTH CENTURY

The journal *English Literary Renaissance (ELR)* publishes recent studies of individual sixteenth- and seventeenth-century authors and of some literary topics, on an ongoing basis; they are updated periodically. In its winter issue, annually, the journal *Studies in English Literature* publishes "Recent Studies in the English Renaissance," evaluating the past year's publications. These journals regularly carry important new articles on seventeenth-century topics, as do *English Literary History, Representations, The Seventeenth Century, Seventeenth Century News, Renaissance Studies, John Donne Journal, Milton Studies*, and *Milton Quarterly*.

Politics, Society, and Political Thought

Some general histories of the seventeenth century or some part of it are Christopher Hill, *The Century of Revolution*, 1961; Barry Coward, *The Stuart Age: A History of England, 1603–1714*, 1980; Derek Hirst, *Authority and Conflict: England, 1603–58*, 1986; and Austin Woolrych, *Commonwealth to Protectorate*, 1982. Interpretation of the causes and progress of the English revolution is a contested issue. A series of books by Christopher Hill emphasizes political, social, and ideological conflict: *Puritanism and Revolution*, 1958; *The World Turned Upside Down: Radical Ideas During the English Revolution*, 1972; and *The Experience of Defeat*, 1984. The "revisionist" view sees this event not as a revolution but as an accidental consequence of politicians' incompetence: it is represented by J. S. Morrill, *Seventeenth-Century Britain, 1603–1714*, 1980; and Conrad Russell, *The Causes of the English Civil War*, 1990, and *Unrevolutionary England, 1603–1642*, 1990. Recent efforts to revise the revisionists include J. P. Sommerville, *Politics and Ideology in England, 1603–1640*, 1986; *Conflict in Early Stuart England: Studies in Religion and Politics, 1603–1642*, ed. Richard Cust and Ann Hughes, 1989, and *Reviving the English Revolution: Reflections and Elaborations on the Work of Christopher Hill*, ed. Geoff Eley and William Hunt, 1988. The complex place of religion, both as doctrine and cultural force, is explored in William Haller, *The Rise of Puritanism*, 1938; Keith Thomas, *Religion and the Decline of Magic: Popular Beliefs in Sixteenth- and Seventeenth-Century England*, 1971; Patrick Collinson, *The Religion of Protestants: The Church in English Society, 1559–1625*, 1982, and *The Birthpangs of Protestant England*, 1986; and David Underdown, *Revel, Riot, and Rebellion: Popular Politics and Culture in England, 1603–1660*, 1985. Suggestive essays on the interrelation of events, religion, and culture are collected in *Culture and Politics in Early Stuart England*, ed. Kevin Sharpe and Peter Lake, 1993.

English society in the seventeenth century was analyzed by the German sociologist Max Weber in a very influential essay, 1904–05, emphasizing the importance of the Protestant doctrine of the calling or vocation for the aspiring capitalist class; that thesis was further developed by R. H. Tawney in *Religion and the Rise of Capitalism*, 1926, but it has been much disputed, notably by II. R. Trevor-Roper. Peter Laslett's book, *The World We Have Lost*, 3rd. ed., 1984, helps in imagining what life was like in a preindustrial society. Studies of early modern society of special interest to students of literature include Lawrence Stone, *The Family, Sex and Marriage in England, 1500–1800*, 1977; Keith Wrightson, *English Society, 1580–1680*, 1982, Susan Amussen, *An Ordered Society: Gender and Class in Early Modern England*, 1988; and Alan Bray, *Homosexuality in Renaissance England*, 1982. Elizabeth Eisenstein, *The Printing Press as an Agent of Change*, 2 vols., 1979, bears directly on the production and transmission of literature. A general study of schools and education in the period is K. Charlton, *Education in Renaissance England*, 1965.

Helpful accounts of political thought in the seventeenth century are found in J. G. A. Pocock's seminal works, *The Ancient Constitution and the Feudal Law*, rev. 1987, and *The Machiavellian Moment: Florentine Political Thought and the Atlantic Republican Tradition*, 1975, as well as in Quentin Skinner, *The Foundations of Modern Political Thought*, 2 vols., 1978, and Richard Tuck, *Philosophy and Government, 1572–1651*, 1993. A useful collection of political treatises in the period has been edited by David Wootton, *Divine Right and Democracy: An Anthology of Political Writing in Stuart England*, 1986. J. H. Burns has edited essays included in *The Cambridge History of Political Thought, 1450–1700*, 1991.

Literature, Culture, and Politics

Several studies focus on the intellectual and cultural milieu of the period as it affects literature. Inherited views of the universe based on hierarchy, order, and analogy, which were still prevalent in poetic imagery, are set forth in E. M. W. Tillyard's concise though oversimplified account, *The Elizabethan World Picture*, 1943. Studies focusing on the challenge of the new science include Rupert Hall, *The Scientific Revolution, 1500–1800*, 1954; William R. Shea, *Galileo's Intellectual Revolution*, 1972; Hans Blumenberg, *The Genesis of the Copernican World*, 1987; and Barbara Shapiro, *Probability and Certainty in Seventeenth-Century England*, 1983. Some sense of the still-powerful influence of the occult—alchemy, magic, hermeticism, and the like—may be gleaned from Wayne Shumaker, *The Occult Sciences in the Renaissance*, 1972. C. A. Patrides and Raymond Waddington have edited a useful collection of essays on various facets of seventeenth-century society and culture, *The Age of Milton: Backgrounds to Seventeenth-Century Literature*, 1980. More focused studies of intellectual currents include Debora Shuger, *Habits of Thought in the English Renaissance: Religion, Politics, and the Dominant Culture*, 1990; Victoria Kahn, *Machiavellian Rhetoric: From the Counter-Reformation to Milton*, 1994; and John Rogers, *The Matter of Revolution: Science, Poetry, and Politics in the Age of Milton*, 1996. A fine brief account of court culture in the Jacobean and Caroline eras is by Graham Parry, *The Golden Age Restor'd: The Culture of the Stuart Court, 1603–1642*, 1981.

Studies of seventeenth-century literature in relation to political and cultural forces include James Turner, *The Politics of Landscape: Rural Scenery and Society in English Poetry, 1630–1660*, 1979; Annabel Patterson, *Censorship and Interpretation: The Conditions of Writing and Reading in Early Modern England*, 1984; Graham Parry, *Seventeenth Century Poetry: The Social Context*, 1985; Leah Marcus, *The Politics of Mirth: Jonson, Herrick, Milton, Marvell*, 1986; and David Norbrook, *Poetry and Politics in the English Renaissance*, 1984. Several collections of essays treat particular topics and writers in these terms: *The Muses' Common-Weale: Poetry and Politics in the Seventeenth Century*, ed. Claude Summers and Ted-Larry Pebworth, 1988; *The Politics of Discourse: The Literature and History of Seventeenth-Century England*, ed. Kevin Sharpe and Steven Zwicker, 1987; *Patronage, Politics, and Literary Traditions in England, 1558–1658*, ed. Cedric Brown, 1993; and *Religion and Culture in Renaissance England*, ed. C. McEachern and D. Shuger, 1997.

Analyses focusing especially on the Jacobean era are Jonathan Goldberg, *James I and the Politics of Literature: Jonson, Shakespeare, Donne and Their Contemporaries*, 1983; Curtis Perry, *The Making of Jacobean Culture*, 1987; and an important collection of essays edited by Linda Levy Peck, *The Mental World of the Jacobean Court*, 1991. Kevin Sharpe has edited essays pertaining to the Caroline era, *Criticism and Compliment: The Politics of Literature in the England of Charles I*, 1987. Studies treating the literature and culture of the revolutionary era focus on Milton, Marvell, and several royalist poets and prose writers, including Michael Wilding, *Dragon's Teeth: Literature in the English Revolution*, 1987; Nigel Smith, *Literature and Revolution in England, 1640–1660*, 1994, which treats the political uses of various genres; Steven Zwicker, *Lines of Authority: Politics and English Culture, 1649–1689*, 1993; and essays edited by Thomas Healy and Jonathan Sawday, *Literature and the English Civil War*, 1990. Works that attend especially to royalist writers are Raymond Anselment, *Loyalist Resolve: Patient Fortitude in the English Civil War*, 1988; Lois Potter, *Secret Rites and Secret Writing: Royalist Literature, 1641–1660*, 1989; and *Classic and Cavalier: Essays on Jonson and the Sons of Ben*, ed. Claude J. Summers and Ted-Larry Pebworth, 1982.

David Norbrook has written an impressive, wide-ranging study of writers who contributed to the emergence of republican thought and culture in England before and during the revolution, *Writing the English Republic: Poetry, Rhetoric and Politics, 1627–1660*, 1999. Joad Raymond has studied the emergence of the newspaper during the revolutionary era in *The Invention of the Newspaper: English Newsbooks 1641–1649*, 1996. Nigel Smith has analyzed the rhetoric and assumptions about language of the revolution's radicals—Quakers, Ranters, Diggers—in *Perfection Proclaimed: Language and Literature in English Radical Religion, 1640–1660*, 1989.

Genre, Style, and Poetics

Valuable perspectives on literary history, the literary institution, and aspects of style in the period are provided in several works. J. E. Spingarn has edited a collection of literary criticism, *Critical Essays of the Seventeenth Century*, reissued, 1957. An illuminating and elegant brief account of the place and uses of genre is supplied by Rosalie Colie in *The Resources of Kind: Genre-Theory in the Renaissance*, 1973. Although the category of Metaphysical poets has generally lost its usefulness, Earl Miner's three volumes provide important surveys of the literature of the era: *The Metaphysical Mode from Donne to Cowley*, 1969; *The Cavalier Mode from Jonson to Cotton*, 1971; and *The Restoration Mode from Milton to Dryden*, 1974. George Parfitt has provided a single-volume survey, *English Poetry of the Seventeenth Century*, 1985. Barbara K. Lewalski, *Protestant Poetics and the Seventeenth-Century Religious Lyric*, 1979, treats the effect of Protestant theology, sermon theory, and devotional practices on poetics and religious poetry, especially Donne, Herbert, Vaughan, and Traherne. Diane McColley has explored the relationship between the poetic language of several major poets and the music of the period in *Poetry and Music in Seventeenth-Century England*, 1997. An important collection of essays that reconsiders canonical poets of period in the light of poststructuralist theory is *Soliciting Interpretation: Literary Theory and Seventeenth-Century Poetry*, ed. Elizabeth D. Harvey and Katharine E. Maus, 1990.

The styles, varieties, and rhetoric of seventeenth-century prose are treated in several important studies: Maurice Croll, in *Style, Rhetoric, and Rhythm: Essays*, ed. J. M. Patrick et al., 1966; Stanley Fish, *Self-Consuming Artifacts: The Experience of Seventeenth-Century Literature*, 1972 (Bacon, Burton, Browne, Milton, Bunyan); Joan Webber, *The Eloquent I: Style and Self in Seventeenth-Century Prose*, 1968; and Roger Pooley, *English Prose of the Seventeenth Century, 1590–1700*, 1992. In *Paradoxia Epidemica*, 1966, Rosalie Colie studied the pervasiveness of paradox in texts of all kinds throughout the century.

Important studies of particular genres in relation to seventeenth-century culture include Rosemary Freeman, *English Emblem Books*, 1948; Paul

Delany, *British Autobiography in the Seventeenth Century*, 1969; Ellen Z. Lambert, *Placing Sorrow: A Study of Pastoral Elegy*, 1976; Anthony Low, *Love's Architecture: Devotional Modes in Seventeenth-Century English Poetry*, 1978, and *The Georgic Revolution*, 1985; Paul Salzman, *English Prose Fiction 1558–1700: A Critical History*, 1985; Heather DuBrow, *The Happier Eden: The Politics of Marriage in the Stuart Epithalamium*, 1990; Alastair Fowler, *The Country-House Poem*. 1994; and Amy Boesky, *Founding Fictions: Utopias in Early Modern England*, 1996. Some of the many studies of drama in the Stuart era are Brian Gibbons, *Jacobean City Comedy: A Study of Satiric Plays by Jonson, Marston, and Middleton*, 1968; Margot Heinemann, *Puritanism and Theatre: Thomas Middleton and Opposition Drama Under the Early Stuarts*, 1980; Albert Tricomi, *Anticourt Drama in England, 1603–1642*, 1989; and Richard Strier ed., et al., *The Theatrical City: Culture, Theater, and Politics in London, 1576–1649*, 1995.

Women's Roles and Writing

An important recovery effort is under way in publishing and studying hitherto unknown or little-studied works by early modern women, sometimes highlighting gender issues, sometimes attending to women's self-constructions as patrons and authors, sometimes addressing aesthetic and stylistic matters. Some anthologies of writing by women in (or including) the seventeenth century are *The Paradise of Women*, ed. Betty Travitsky, 1981; *First Feminists: British Women Writers, 1578–1799*, ed. Moira Ferguson, 1985; *Kissing the Rod: An Anthology of Seventeenth-Century Women's Verse*, ed. Germaine Greer et al., 1988; *Women Writers of the Seventeenth Century*, ed. Katharina Wilson and Frank J. Warnke, 1989; and *Her Own Life: Autobiographical Writings by Seventeenth-Century Englishwomen*, ed. Elspeth Graham et al., 1989. An annotated bibliography by Hilda Smith and Susan Cardinale, *Women and the Literature of the Seventeenth Century*, 1900, gives a brief account of all the works by or about women listed in Donald Wing's *Short-Title Catalogue of English books published between 1641 and 1700*. Elaine Hobby in *Virtue of Necessity: English Women's Writing, 1649–88*, 1988, discusses women writers and their several genres, with bibliography. Other important bibliographical resources are Mary Thomas Crane, "Women and the Early Modern Canon: Recent Editions of Works by English Women, 1500–1500," *Renaissance Quarterly* 51 (1998); and recent studies of seventeenth-century women writers by Elizabeth Hageman and Sara Jayne Steen, in *ELR* 14 (1984), 18 (1988), and 24 (1994). Anthologies of texts that illuminate the place of women and women writers in seventeenth-century society are *Half Humankind: Contexts and Texts of the Controversy about Women in England, 1540–1640*, ed. K. Henderson and B. McManus, 1985, and *Daughters, Wives, and Widows: Writings By Men About Women and Marriage in England, 1500–1640*, ed. Joan L. Klein,

1992. Antonia Fraser has written a lively social history of women throughout the century, with many vignettes of particular lives, *The Weaker Vessel*, 1984.

Some important studies and collections of essays on women, writing, and gender in the period are Linda Woodbridge, *Women and the English Renaissance: Literature and the Nature of Womenkind, 1540–1620*, 1984; *Women in English Society, 1500–1800*, ed. Mary Prior, 1985; *Rewriting the Renaissance: The Discourses of Sexual Difference in Early Modern England*, ed. Margaret Ferguson, Maureen Quilligan, and Nancy Vickers, 1986; and Margaret J. M. Ezell, *The Patriarch's Wife: Literary Evidence and the History of the Family*, 1987. Some of the women writers included in this anthology (Lanyer, Speght, Cary, Wroth, Trapnall, Philips, and Cavendish) are treated by Elaine Beilin in *Redeeming Eve: Women Writers of the English Renaissance*, 1987; by Sara Mendelson in *The Mental World of Stuart Women*, 1987; by Tina Krontiris in *Oppositional Voices: Women as Writers and Translators of Literature in the English Renaissance*, 1991; by Barbara K. Lewalski in *Writing Women in Jacobean England*, 1993; and by Louise Schleiner in *Tudor and Stuart Women Writers*, 1994. Phyllis Mack, *Visionary Women: Ecstatic Prophecy in Seventeenth-Century England*, 1992, highlights the emergence of prophecy as a genre for women, especially during the revolution; a complementary study by Bonnelyn Y. Kunze is *Margaret Fell and the Rise of Quakerism*, 1994. Useful collections of essays discussing various women writers are *Ambiguous Realities: Women in the Middle Ages and Renaissance*, ed. Carole Levin and Jeanie Watson, 1987; *The Renaissance Englishwoman in Print: Counterbalancing the Canon*, ed. Anne M. Haselkorn and Travitsky, 1990; Jean Brink, *Privileging Gender in Early Modern England*, 1993; *Women and Literature in Britain, 1500–1700*, ed. Helen Wilcox, 1996; and *Representing Women in Renaissance England*, ed. Claude J. Summers and Ted-Larry Pebworth, 1997.

Francis Bacon

The standard edition remains *The Works of Francis Bacon* (English and Latin), 14 vols., ed. James Spedding, Robert Ellis, and Douglas Heath, 1858–74. A fine edition of the essays is that of Michael Kiernan, *The Essayes or Counsels, Civill and Morall*, 1985. There is a good edition of *The Advancement of Learning* and *The New Atlantis* by Arthur Johnson, 1974. Anthony Quinton, in *Francis Bacon*, 1980, provides a useful introduction to the man and his work. Charles Williams, *Bacon*, 1933, rpt. 1971, is a classic study. A recent trend in Bacon studies has been to emphasize his powers as a persuasive imaginative writer. Studies in that vein include Brian Vickers, *Francis Bacon and Renaissance Prose*, 1968; Lisa Jardine, *Francis Bacon: Discovery and the Art of Discourse*, 1974; and John C. Briggs, *Francis Bacon and the Rhetoric of Nature*, 1989. Some important articles on Bacon were edited by Brian

Vickers, *Essential Articles for the Study of Francis Bacon*, 1968, and by William A. Sessions, *Francis Bacon Revisited*, 1996. Recent studies are surveyed in *ELR* 17 (1987): 351–71.

Sir Thomas Browne

The standard complete edition remains *The Works of Sir Thomas Browne*, 4 vols., ed. Geoffrey Keynes, 1964. A handy annotated *Religio Medici* was published in 1963 by James Winny; L. C. Martin edited *Religio Medici and Other Works* in 1964; C. A. Patrides edited *Sir Thomas Browne: The Major Works*, 1977, with a good introduction and bibliography. Important studies include F. L. Huntley, *Sir Thomas Browne: A Biographical and Critical Study*, 1962; Leonard Nathanson, *The Strategy of Truth*, 1967; Jonathan Post, *Sir Thomas Browne*, 1987; and Anne Drury Hall, *Ceremony and Civility in English Renaissance Prose*, 1991. Patrides edited a collection of essays, *Approaches to Sir Thomas Browne* (1982). Recent studies are surveyed in *ELR* 39 (1989): 118–29.

Robert Burton

A scholarly edition of the *Anatomy of Melancholy* in four volumes has been prepared by Thomas C. Faulkner et al., 1989–98. Holbrook Jackson published a handy edition of that work in 1972, with paraphrases or translations of the Latin and Greek quotations, a glossary, and Burton's footnotes. The classic modern study of melancholy is Raymond Kilbansky, Erwin Panofsky, and Fritz Saxl, *Saturn and Melancholy*, 1964. Also useful is Bridget Gelbert Lyons, *Voices of Melancholy: Studies in Literary Treatments of Melancholy in Renaissance England*, 1971. A good general introduction to Burton's life and writing is Michael J. O'Connell, *Robert Burton*, 1986. Critical studies include Lawrence Babb, *Sanity in Bedlam*, 1959, rpt. 1977; Devon Hodges, *Renaissance Fictions of Anatomy*, 1985; and Patricia Vicari, *The View from Minerva's Tower: Learning and Imagination in the Anatomy of Melancholy*, 1989. Recent studies are surveyed in *ELR* 17 (1987): 243–51.

Thomas Carew

The edition by Rhodes Dunlap, *The Poems of Thomas Carew*, 1949, contains all the poems, Carew's single masque, and a note on musical settings for his poems. Edward Selig published a study of Carew in 1958, *The Flourishing Wreath: A Study of Thomas Carew*; and Lynn Sadler a Twayne biography, *Thomas Carew*, in 1979. There are useful essays on Carew in collections noted above: by Diana Benet in *The Muses' Common-Weale: Poetry and Politics in the Seventeenth Century*, ed. Claude Summers and Ted-Larry Pebworth, 1988, and by Kevin Sharpe in *The Politics of Discourse*, 1987, and *Criticism and Compliment*, 1987. Recent studies are surveyed in *ELR* (1977): 245–48.

Elizabeth Cary, Lady Falkland

There is a facsimile edition of the *The Tragedy of Mariam*, 1613, prepared by A. C. Dunstan and W. W. Greg. Margaret Ferguson and Barry Weller have edited that work, together with a near-contemporary biography, *The Tragedy of Mariam: The Fair Queen of Jewry* with *The Lady Falkland her Life by One of her Daughters*, 1994. The history usually attributed to Cary, *The History of the Life, Reign, and Death of Edward II*, is included in *Renaissance Women: The Plays of Elizabeth Cary; The Poems of Aemilia Lanyer*, ed. Diane Purkiss, 1994. The only biography is by Kenneth Murdock, *The Sun at Noon: Three Biographical Sketches*, 1939. Some important essays are Margaret Ferguson, "The Spectre of Resistance," in *Staging the Renaissance: Reinterpretations of Elizabethan and Jacobean Drama*, ed. David Kastan and Peter Stallybrass, 1991, and Maureen Quilligan, "Staging Gender: William Shakespeare and Elizabeth Cary," *Sexuality and Gender in Early Modern Europe: Institutions, Texts, Images*, ed. James Grantham Turner, 1993.

Margaret Cavendish, Duchess of Newcastle

Kate Lilley has edited *Margaret Cavendish: The Description of a New World Called The Blazing World and Other Writings*, 1992; *The Blazing World* is also included in Paul Salzman's *Anthology of Seventeenth-Century Fiction*, 1991, and he discusses that work in his *English Prose Fiction*, 1985, as does Amy Boesky in *Founding Fictions: Utopias in Early Modern England*, 1996. Two of Cavendish's books have been reprinted in facsimile, *Sociable Letters*, 1969, and *Poems and Fancies*, 1972. There are selections in *Women Writers of the Seventeenth Century*, ed. Katharina Wilson and Frank J. Warnke, and in *Kissing the Rod: An Anthology of Seventeenth-Century Women's Verse* ed. Germaine Greer et al., 1988. Ann Shaver has edited plays by Cavendish in *Convent of Pleasure and Other Plays*, 1999. The best biography is by Kathleen Jones, *A Glorious Fame: The Life of Margaret Cavendish, Duchess of Newcastle, 1623–1673*, 1988. There are substantial scholarly treatments of Cavendish in Hilda Smith, *Reason's Disciples: Seventeenth-Century English Feminists*, 1982; Sara Mendelson, *The Mental World of Stuart Women*, 1987; and Mary Beth Rose, *Women in the Middle Ages and Renaissance*, 1986. Some useful articles are Catherine Gallagher, "Embracing the Absolute: The Politics of the Female Subject in Seventeenth-Century England," in *Genders* 1 (1988): 24–29, and Eve Keller, "Producing Petty Gods: Margaret Cavendish's Critique of Experimental Science," in *English Literary History* 64 (1997): 447–71.

Edward Hyde, Earl of Clarendon

The standard edition is *The History of the Rebellion and Civil Wars in England*, 6 vols., 1888, rpt. 1992. Clarendon's autobiography, *The Life of Edward, Earl of Clarendon*, 12 vols., was published in 1759. In 1978 Gertrude Huehns edited a useful volume of selections from the *History* and the *Life*. In 1983 George Miller published a Twayne biography, *Edward Hyde, Earl of Clarendon*. Some important studies are Brian Wormald, *Clarendon: Politics, Historiography and Religion, 1640–1660*, 1951; French R. Fogle and H. R. Trevor-Roper, *Milton and Clarendon*, 1965; R. W. Harris, *Clarendon and the English Revolution*, 1983; and Richard Ollard, *Clarendon and His Friends*, 1987.

Abiezer Coppe

All of Coppe's writings between 1648 and 1651, including both *Fiery Flying Rolls*, are included in *A Collection of Ranter Writings from the Seventeenth Century*, 1983, ed. Nigel Smith, which also has a useful introductory essay on the Ranters. Indispensable authorities on the Ranters and other radical groups are A. L. Morton, *The World of the Ranters*, 1970, and Christopher Hill, *The World Turned Upside Down*, 1972. In *Perfection Proclaimed: Language and Literature in English Radical Religion*, 1989, Smith has analyzed the language of Ranter and other radical texts.

Abraham Cowley

Cowley's English *Poems* were edited by A. R. Waller, 1905; his *Essays and Other Prose Writings* by A. B. Gough in 1915. The first two volumes of a projected six-volume complete edition, edited by Thomas Calhoun et al., appeared in 1989. Samuel Johnson's "Life of Cowley," in his *Lives of the Poets*, 1779–81 was influential in setting terms for analyzing poetic style in Cowley, Donne, and other poets critics have labeled Metaphysical. A biography by A. H. Nethercot, *The Muses' Hannibal*, appeared in 1931. Three useful studies are R. B. Hinman, *Abraham Cowley's World of Order*, 1960; J. Taaffe, *Abraham Cowley*, 1972; and David Trotter, *The Poetry of Abraham Cowley*, 1979. Recent studies are surveyed in *ELR* 6 (1976): 466–75.

Richard Crashaw

The standard edition is *The Works of Richard Crashaw*, 2nd ed., ed. L. C. Martin, 1957; George W. Williams edited the *Complete Poetry* in 1970, rpt. 1974. Two studies that relate Crashaw's life to the historical and religious milieu of the period are Paul Parrish, *Richard Crashaw*, 1980, and Thomas Healy, *Richard Crashaw*, 1986. Influential studies of Crashaw's baroque style and Counter-Reformation poetics are Austin Warren, *Richard Crashaw: A Study in Baroque Sensibility*, 1939; George Williams, *Image and Symbol in the Sacred Poetry of Richard Crashaw*, 1963; Robert Peterson, *The Art of Ecstasy: Teresa, Bernini, and Crashaw*, 1970; and Anthony Raspa, *The Emotive Image: Jesuit Poetics in the English Renaissance*, 1983. Louise Schleiner examines the influence of contemporary song on Crashaw's prosody in *The Living Lyre in English Verse: From Elizabeth through the Restoration*, 1984. Two useful collections of essays are *Essays on Richard Crashaw*, ed. Robert M. Cooper, 1979, and *New Perspectives on the Life and Art of Richard Crashaw*, ed. John R. Roberts, 1990. Recent studies are reviewed in *ELR* 21 (1991): 425–45.

John Donne

The two-volume edition of Donne's *Poems* edited by H. J. C. Grierson, 1912, is still important, although we now have newer Oxford editions of Donne's several genres: *The Divine Poems*, ed. Helen Gardner, 1952, rev. 1978; *The Elegies and the Songs and Son-*

nets, ed. Gardner, 1965; *The Satires, Epigrams, and Verse Letters*, ed. Wesley Milgate, 1967; and *The Epithalamions, Anniversaries, and Epicedes*, ed., Milgate, 1978. George Potter and Evelyn Simpson have edited *The Sermons of John Donne*, 10 vols., 1953–62. Donne's meditations were edited by Anthony Raspa, *John Donne: Devotions upon Emergent Occasions*, 1975. There are several single-volume editions of the English poems, one by C. A. Patrides, 1985, rpt. 1994, and another by A. L. Clements, 1966, rev. 1992. A *Donne Variorum* edition is in progress, 1995–, under the general editorship of Gary Stringer; Vol. 6, *Anniversaries and Epicedes*, and Vol. 8, *Epigrams, Epithalamions, Epitaphs, etc.* have been published. The first biography of Donne was by Izaak Walton, 1640. R. C. Bald's *John Donne: A Life*, 1970, is the standard biography. John Carey, *John Donne: Life, Mind, and Art*, 1981, offers a challenging account of the psychological and social factors influencing Donne's life choices and his poetry. Arthur Marotti, *John Donne: Coterie Poet*, 1986, locates Donne in his social milieu and places his poems in relation to the various audiences they addressed.

T. S. Eliot's essay "The Varieties of Metaphysical Poets," in *Selected Essays, 1917–1932*, 1932, rpt. 1969, was influential in setting terms for analyzing Donne over several decades; Cleanth Brook's reading of "The Canonization" in his *Well Wrought Urn*, 1947, is a classic of the New Criticism. Donne is discussed in many accounts of the period—Earl Miner, *The Metaphysical Mode from Donne to Cowley*, 1969; Barbara K. Lewalski, *Protestant Poetics and the Seventeenth-Century Religious Lyric*, 1979; and Jonathan Goldberg, *James I and the Politics of Literature*, 1983—and has invited several valuable individual studies: Donald Guss, *John Donne: Petrarchist*, 1966; Murray Roston, *The Soul of Wit*, 1974; Lewalski, *Donne's Anniversaries and the Poetry of Praise*, 1973; Stevie Davies, *Reassessing John Donne*, 1986; Terry Sherwood, *Fulfilling the Circle*, 1986; Meg Lota Brown, *Donne and the Politics of Conscience*, 1995. Many significant critical essays are collected in *John Donne: Essays in Celebration*, ed. A. J. Smith, 1972; *John Donne: The Critical Heritage*, ed. Smith, 1975–1996; *John Donne and the Seventeenth-Century Metaphysical Poets*, ed. Harold Bloom, 1986; *The Eagle and the Dove: Reassessing John Donne*, ed. Claude J. Summers and Ted-Larry Pebworth, 1986; and *Critical Essays on John Donne*, ed. Arthur Marotti, 1994.

Lady Ann Halkett

Halkett's *Memoirs* were edited by John Loftis in 1979. She is discussed in Antonia Fraser, *The Weaker Vessel*, 1984; in Margaret Bottrall, *Every Man a Phoenix: Studies in Seventeenth-Century Autobiography*, 1958; and in Mary Beth Rose, *Women in the Middle Ages and Renaissance*, 1986.

George Herbert

The standard edition is *The Works of George Herbert*, ed. F. E. Hutchinson, rev. 1945; C. A. Patrides edited a compact edition of *The English Poems*, 1974. Izaak Walton wrote a contemporary *Life of*

George Herbert, 1670; there are modern ones by Amy Charles, *A Life of George Herbert*, 1977, and by Stanley Stewart, *George Herbert*, 1986. Besides the general studies mentioned in the general bibliography for the period, several important critical books on Herbert deal with the interrelation of his religion and his art: Rosemund Tuve, *A Reading of George Herbert*, 1952; Joseph Summers, *George Herbert: His Religion and His Art*, 1954; Stanley Fish, *The Living Temple: George Herbert and Catechizing*, 1978; Diana Benet, *Secretary of Praise: The Poetic Vocation of George Herbert*, 1984; Chana Bloch, *Spelling the Word: George Herbert and the Bible*, 1985; Terry Sherwood, *Herbert's Prayerful Art*, 1989; Richard Strier, *Love Known: Theology and Experience in George Herbert's Poetry*, 1983; and Gene E. Veith, *Reformation Spirituality: The Religion of George Herbert*, 1985. Helen Vendler, in *The Poetry of George Herbert*, 1975, focuses on Herbert's exquisite art. Michael Schoenfeldt, in *Prayer and Power: George Herbert and Renaissance Courtship*, 1991, explores the interdependence of social and religious discourse, to advance a cultural poetics of Herbert's lyrics. There are several essay collections all or partly on Herbert: *"Too Rich to Clothe the Sunne": Essays on George Herbert*, ed. Claude Summers and Ted-Larry Pebworth, 1980; *"Bright Shoots of Everlastingness": The Seventeenth-Century Religious Lyric*, ed. Summers and Pebworth, 1987; and *George Herbert: The Critical Heritage*, ed. C. A. Patrides, 1983. Recent studies are surveyed in *ELR* 18 (1988): 460–75.

Robert Herrick

The standard edition is by L. C. Martin, *Robert Herrick: Poems*, 1965. J. Max Patrick also edited the *Complete Poetry of Robert Herrick* in 1963. There are biographical accounts by Roger Rollin, *Robert Herrick*, 1966, and George W. Scott, *Robert Herrick*, 1974. Important critical studies include Robert Deming, *Ceremony and Art: Robert Herrick's Poetry*, 1974; Leigh DeNeef, *"This Poetic Liturgie": Robert Herrick's Ceremonial Mode*, 1974; Ann Baynes Coiro, *Robert Herrick's Hesperides and the Epigram Book Tradition*, 1988; as well as essays by Leah Marcus in *The Politics of Mirth*, 1986, and by Aschah Guibbory in *The Muses' Common-Weale: Poetry and Politics in the Seventeenth Century*, ed. Claude Summers and Ted-Larry Pebworth, 1988. A collection of essays edited by Roger Rollin and J. Max Patrick, *Trust to Good Verses: Herrick Tercentenary Essays*, appeared in 1978. Recent studies are surveyed in *ELR* 3 (1973): 462–71.

Thomas Hobbes

The classic edition is by Sir William Molesworth, the *English Works* in eleven volumes, the *Opera Philosophica* in five, 1839–45. A useful student's edition of the *Leviathan* is by C. P. Macpherson, 1968. A delightful seventeenth-century biographical sketch is in John Aubrey's *Brief Lives*. Recent biographies include Mariam Reik, *The Golden Lands of Thomas Hobbes*, 1977, and Arnold Rogow, *Thomas Hobbes: Radical in the Service of Reason*,

1986. Important studies of Hobbes' thought and rhetoric include Michael Oakeshott, *Hobbes on Civil Association*, 1975; David Johnston, *The Rhetoric of Leviathan: Thomas Hobbes and the Politics of Cultural Transformation*, 1986; Charles Catalupo, *A Literary Leviathan: Thomas Hobbes' Masterpiece of Language*, 1991; and Richard Tuck, *Hobbes*, 1989. Samuel I. Mintz in *The Hunting of Leviathan*, 1962, recounts the often amusing seventeenth-century reactions to Hobbes' thought.

Lucy Hutchinson

The best edition of Hutchinson's *Memoir of the Life of Colonel Hutchinson, with a Fragment of Autobiography*, is by N. W. Keeble, 1995. David Norbrook has published and discussed twenty-three of her poems preserved in a manuscript in the Nottinghamshire archives, in "Lucy Hutchinson's 'Elegies' and the Situation of the Republican Woman Writer (with text)," in *ELR* 27 (1997): 468–521. He has also published and discussed a poem almost certainly by her on Oliver Cromwell: "Lucy Hutchinson versus Edmund Waller: An Unpublished Reply to Waller's *A Panegyrick to my Lord Protector*," in *The Seventeenth Century* 11 (1996): 61–86. Her translation of Lucretius' *De Rerum Natura* has been edited by Hugh de Quehen, 1996. Useful studies of Hutchinson's writing include Keeble, "'The Colonel's Shadow': Lucy Hutchinson, Women's Writing and the Civil War," in *Literature and the English Civil War*, ed. Healy and Sawday, 1990; and Sandra Findley and Elaine Hobby, *1642: Literature and Power in the Seventeenth Century*, ed. Francis Barker et al., 1981.

Ben Jonson

A monumental edition of Jonson's *Works* was edited by C. H. Herford and Percy and Evelyn Simpson, 11 vols., 1925–52. The Yale edition and the paperback series known as the New Mermaids provide good modernized and annotated versions of the major plays (one play to a volume). Robert M. Adams has edited *Ben Jonson's Plays and Masques*, 1979, with critical essays. Stephen Orgel has edited *The Complete Masques*, 1969. Handy editions of the verse are by W. B. Hunter, *The Complete Poetry of Ben Jonson*, 1963, and George Parfitt, *Ben Jonson: The Complete Poems*, 1975. There is an edition of *Timber* by Ralph Walker, 1953. David Riggs has written a fine biography, *Ben Jonson: A Life*, 1989.

Important critical studies include Alexander Leggatt, *Ben Jonson: His Vision and His Art*, 1981; Richard Helgerson, *Self-Crowned Laureates: Spenser, Jonson, Milton and the Literary System*, 1983; Katherine E. Maus, *Ben Jonson and the Roman Frame of Mind*, 1984; Robert N. Watson, *Ben Jonson's Parodic Strategy: Literary Imperialism in the Comedies*, 1987; George Rowe, *Distinguishing Jonson*, 1988; Jonathan Haynes, *The Social Relations of Jonson's Theater*, 1992; and Richard Burt, *Licensed by Authority: Ben Jonson and the Discourses of Censorship*, 1993. Works that deal especially with Jonson's poetry are Sara Van den Berg, *The Action of Ben Jonson's Poetry*, 1987, and Robert C. Evans,

Ben Jonson and the Poetics of Patronage, 1989. Don E. Wayne, *Penshurst: The Semiotics of Place and the Poetics of History*, 1984, locates Jonson's poem in its social and architectural context; Raymond Williams, *The Country and the City*, 1973, places it within a broad social history of movements affecting agriculture and the land.

Stuart court masques, and Jonson's major contribution to them, are analyzed in two essay collections: *The Court Masque*, ed. David Lindley, 1984, and *The Politics of the Stuart Court Masque*, ed. David Bevington and Peter Holbrook, 1998, and by Orgel in *The Illusion of Power: Political Theater in the English Renaissance*, 1975. The fascinating reproduction of drawings and designs for the masques, published by Orgel and Roy Strong in *Inigo Jones: The Theatre of the Stuart Court*, 2 vols., 1973, gives some sense of what masques looked like in presentation. Collections of critical essays on Jonson include *Classic and Cavalier: Essays on Jonson and the Sons of Ben*, ed. Claude J. Summers and Ted-Larry Pebworth, 1982; *Ben Jonson: A Collection of Critical Essays*, ed. Jonas A. Barish, 1963; and *New Perspectives on Ben Jonson*, ed. James Hirsh, 1997.

Aemilia Lanyer

Susanne Woods has edited *The Poems of Aemelia Lanyer: Salve Deus Rex Judaeorum*, 1993, and has also analyzed her life and works in *Lanyer: A Renaissance Woman Poet*, 1999. The important collection of essays edited by Marshall Grossman, *Aemilia Lanyer: Gender, Genre, and the Canon*, 1998, includes a valuable annotated bibliography. There are chapters on Lanyer in Elaine Beilin, *Redeeming Eve: Women Writers of the English Renaissance*, 1987; Tina Krontiris, *Oppositional Voices: Women as Writers and Translators of Literature in the English Renaissance*, 1991; Barbara K. Lewalski, *Writing Women in Jacobean England*, 1993; and Louise Schleiner, *Tudor and Stuart Women Writers*, 1994. Other notable essays include Mary Ellen Lamb, "Patronage and Class in Aemilia Lanyer's *Salve Deus Rex Judaeorum*," in *Women, Writing, and the Reproduction of Culture*, ed. Jane Donaworth et al., 1999, and Wendy Wall, "The Body of Christ, Aemilia Lanyer's Passion," in her volume, *The Imprint of Gender: Authorship and Publication in the English Renaissance*, 1993.

John Lilburne

The major writings of Lilburne are available in William Haller's three-volume collection, *Tracts on Liberty in the Puritan Revolution, 1638–1647*, 1934, and in *The Leveller Tracts*, ed. Haller and Godfrey Davies, 1944. There are two biographies: M. A. Gibb, *John Lilburne, The Leveller*, 1947, and Pauline Gregg, *Free-Born John*, 1961. Lilburne's activities and writings are discussed in several studies dealing with polemic in the revolution: Haller, *Liberty and Reformation in the Puritan Revolution*, 1955; Christopher Hill, *The World Turned Upside Down*, 1972; G. E. Aylmer, *The Levellers in the English Revolution*, 1975; Thomas Corns, *Unclois-*

tered Virtue: English Political Literature, 1640–1660, 1992; Nigel Smith, *Literature and Revolution in England, 1640–1660*, 1994; and Sharon Achinstein, *Milton and the Revolutionary Reader*, 1994.

Richard Lovelace

C. H. Wilkinson edited the *Poems*, 1930, rpt. 1968. Manfred Weidhorn published a biography, *Richard Lovelace*, 1970; and both the life and works are treated in Cyril Hartmann, *The Cavalier Spirit and Its Influence on the Life and Work of Richard Lovelace (1618–1658)*, 1925. Commentary can be found in Earl Miner, *The Cavalier Mode from Jonson to Cotton*, 1971; in Raymond Anselment, "'Stone Walls' and 'Iron Bars': Richard Lovelace and Seventeenth-Century Prison Literature," in *Renaissance and Reformation* 17 (1993); and in two essay collections edited by Claude J. Summers and Ted-Larry Pebworth: *Classic and Cavalier: Essays on Jonson and the Sons of Ben*, 1982, and *The Wit of Seventeenth-Century Poetry*, 1995. Recent studies are reviewed in *ELR* 7 (1977): 248–52.

Andrew Marvell

The standard edition is *The Poems and Letters of Andrew Marvell*, ed. H. M. Margoliouth, 1927; rev. Pierre Legouis and E. E. Duncan-Jones, 2 vols., 1971. His Restoration prose satires, *The Rehearsal Transpros'd* (2 parts), are edited by D. I. B. Smith, 1971. There are handy editions of Marvell's *Complete Poetry* by George de F. Lord, 1968, rpt. 1984, and Elizabeth Story Donno, 1972. Biographical studies include John Dixon Hunt, *Andrew Marvell: His Life and Writings*, 1978; Patsy Griffin, *The Modest Ambition of Andrew Marvell: A Study of Marvell and His Relation to Lovelace, Fairfax, Cromwell, and Milton*, 1995; and Thomas Wheeler, *Andrew Marvell Revisited*, 1996. Influential studies of his political attitudes and writing in connection with his poetry include John M. Wallace, *Destiny His Choice: The Loyalism of Andrew Marvell*, 1968; Annabel Patterson, *Marvell and the Civic Crown*, 1978; Warren Chernaik, *The Poet's Time: Politics and Religion in the Work of Marvell*, 1983; *The Political Identity of Andrew Marvell*, ed. Conal Condren and A. D. Cousins, 1990; and the important essay by David Norbrook, "Horatian Ode," in *Literature and the English Civil War*, ed. Thomas Healy and Jonathan Sawday, 1990. Important analyses of Marvell's poetic art include Rosalie Colie's elegant and learned study, *'My Ecchoing Song': Andrew Marvell's Poetry of Criticism*, 1970; Donald Friedman, *Marvell's Pastoral Art*, 1970; Patrick Cullen, *Spenser, Marvell, and Renaissance Pastoral*, 1970; Robert Wilcher, *Andrew Marvell*, 1985; and Christine Rees, *The Judgment of Marvell*, 1989. Donno has edited *Andrew Marvell: The Critical Heritage*, 1978. Important essays dealing with Marvell are included in various tercentenary tributes: *Tercentenary Essays in Honor of Andrew Marvell*, ed. Kenneth Friedenreich, 1977; *Approaches to Marvell*, ed. C. A. Patrides, 1978; and *Andrew Marvell: Essays on the Tercentenary of His Death*, ed. R. L. Brett, 1979. Others are in *Politics of Discourse: The*

John Milton

Literature and History of Seventeenth-Century England, ed. Kevin Sharpe and Steven Zwicker, 1987; in Leah Marcus, Politics of Mirth: Jonson, Herrick, Milton, Marvell, 1986; and in Zwicker, Lines of Authority: Politics and English Culture, 1649–1689, 1993.

The Columbia Milton, The Works of John Milton, 18 vols., ed. F. A. Patterson, et al., 1931–40, with its invaluable two-volume index, is the only complete edition of all the poetry and prose, English and Latin. The Yale edition, Complete Prose Works of John Milton, 8 vols., ed. Don M. Wolfe et al., 1953–82, supplies excellent historical introductions to all the prose. The single-volume edition, Complete Poems and Major Prose, by Merritt Y. Hughes, 1957, is still useful; The Riverside Milton, ed. Roy Flannagan, 1998, contains all the poetry and much of the English prose, with updated introductions and bibliography. John Leonard's paperback, John Milton: The Complete Poems, 1998, supplies a good text and useful notes; the Longman edition is in two volumes: John Carey, John Milton: Complete Shorter Poems, 1972, rev. 1997, and Paradise Lost, ed. Alastair Fowler, 1966, rev. 1998. For the prose, C. A. Patrides's paperback edition, John Milton: Selected Prose, 1985, offers a judicious selection. Three volumes of the Variorum Commentary on the Poems of John Milton, ed. Douglas Bush, et al., 1970–75, have been published, but the volume on Paradise Lost is still in process.

The standard biography is William Riley Parker, Milton: A Biography, 2 vols., 1968. David Masson's, The Life of John Milton, 6 vols. plus index, 1859–91, is still a treasure trove of information about the poet and the period. Christopher Hill's Milton and the English Revolution, 1977, has spearheaded an ongoing effort to locate Milton more precisely among his revolutionary contemporaries. Cedric C. Brown's brief biography, John Milton: A Literary Life, 1995, offers a useful introduction to the man and his works. Milton is psychoanalyzed by William Kerrigan in The Sacred Complex: On the Psychogenesis of Paradise Lost, 1983. The five volumes of J. Milton French's The Life Records of John Milton, 1949–58, rpt. 1966, gather much primary material for the life. Gordon Campbell, A Milton Chronology, 1997, reexamines, records, and adds to these materials. Aids to the study of Milton include the nine-volume Milton Encyclopedia, ed. William Hunter et al., 1978–83, with bibliographies and updates in Vol. 9, and The Cambridge Companion to Milton, ed. Dennis Danielson, 1989, rev. 1999.

Valuable critical studies that address all or some considerable part of Milton's career and writing include the following: Kerrigan, The Prophetic Milton, 1974; Louis L. Martz, Milton: Poet of Exile, 1980; Christopher Kendrick, Milton: A Study in Ideology and Form, 1986; Marshall Grossman, "Authors to Themselves": Milton and the Revelation of History, 1987; Catherine Belsey, John Milton: Language, Gender, Power, 1988; Joan Bennett,

Reviving Liberty: Radical Christian Humanism in Milton's Great Poems, 1989; Loewenstein, Milton and the Drama of History, 1990; John T. Shawcross, John Milton: The Self and the World, 1993; Sharon Achinstein, Milton and the Revolutionary Reader, 1994; Laura Lunger Knoppers, Historicizing Milton: Spectacle, Power, and Poetry in Restoration England, 1994; Lana Cable, Carnal Rhetoric: Milton's Iconoclasm and the Poetics of Desire, 1995; John Rumrich, Milton Unbound: Controversy and Reinterpretation, 1996; and David Norbrook, Writing the English Republic: Poetry, Rhetoric, and Politics, 1627–1660, 1999.

Various approaches to Milton over the centuries can be sampled in two volumes edited by Shawcross, Milton: The Critical Heritage, 1628–1731, 1970, and Milton, 1732–1801: The Critical Heritage, 1972; in The Romantics on Milton, ed. Joseph Wittreich, 1970; and in Milton: A Collection of Critical Essays, ed. Louis L. Martz, 1966. Useful essay collections include Mary Nyquist and Margaret Ferguson, Re-Membering Milton: Essays on the Texts and Traditions, 1988; Milton in Italy, ed. Mario Di Cesare, 1991; John Milton, ed. Annabel Patterson, 1992; Literary Milton: Text, Pretext, Context, ed. Diana Benet and Michael Lieb, 1994; Of Poetry and Politics: New Essays on Milton and His World, ed. Paul G. Stanwood, 1995; Milton and Republicanism, ed. David Armitage, Armand Himy, and Quentin Skinner, 1995; Arenas of Conflict: Milton and the Unfettered Mind, ed. Kristin McColgan and Charles Durham, 1997; and Stephen B. Dobranski and John P. Rumrich, Milton and Heresy, 1998. Milton's views of women and various feminist issues are addressed in several of these collections, and centrally in Diane McColley, Milton's Eve, 1983; James Grantham Turner, One Flesh: Paradisal Marriage and Sexual Relations in the Age of Milton, 1987; Joseph Wittreich, Feminist Milton, 1987; and Milton and the Idea of Woman, ed. Julia M. Walker, 1988.

Stella Revard has written an excellent account of Milton's shorter poems, including the Latin poems, Milton and the Tangles of Neaera's Hair: The Making of the 1645 Poems, 1997. Rosamond Tuve, Images and Themes in Five Poems by Milton, 1957, can still illuminate Milton's most important shorter poems. Brown treats Milton's Comus and "Lycidas" in their social and political contexts in John Milton's Aristocratic Entertainments, 1985. Patrides has edited a useful collection of essays, Milton's Lycidas: The Tradition and the Poem, rev. 1983; and that poem is at the center of Joseph A Wittreich, Visionary Poetics: Milton's Tradition and His Legacy, 1980. Milton's prose is discussed in several important books and essays: Arthur Barker, Milton and the Puritan Dilemma, 1641–1660, 1942; Thomas A. Kranides, The Fierce Equation: A Study of Milton's Decorum, 1964; Joan Webber, The Eloquent I: Style and Self in Seventeenth-Century Prose, 1968; Stanley Fish, Self-Consuming Artifacts, 1972; Keith W. Staveley, The Politics of Milton's Prose Style, 1975; Achievements of the Left Hand, ed. Michael Lieb and Shawcross, 1974; Thomas N. Corns, *The Development of Milton's Prose Style*, 1982; and *Politics, Poetics, and Hermeneutics in Milton's Prose*, ed. David Loewenstein and James G. Turner, 1990.

Modern criticism of *Paradise Lost* still engages with issues of interpretation and generic tradition raised in C. S. Lewis, *A Preface to Paradise Lost*, 1942; C. M. Bowra, *From Virgil to Milton*, 1945; and William Empson's provocative attack on the figure of God in the poem, *Milton's God*, rev. 1965. A classic study of Milton's theology in reference to the epic is Maurice Kelley, *This Great Argument: A Study of Milton's De Doctrina Christiana as a Gloss upon Paradise Lost*, 1941; Dennis R. Danielson, *Milton's Good God: A Study in Literary Theodicy*, 1982, revisits that issue. Some important earlier critical books include Joseph Summers, *The Muse's Method: An Introduction to Paradise Lost*, 1962; Christopher Ricks, *Milton's Grand Style*, 1963; Northrop Frye, *The Return to Eden*, 1966; and Fish's very influential reader response criticism, *Surprised by Sin: The Reader in Paradise Lost*, 1967. Collections of critical essays include *Approaches to Paradise Lost*, ed. Patrides, 1968, and *New Essays on Paradise Lost*, ed. Thomas Kranidas, 1969. Concerns in some recent criticism are indicated by the titles: J. M. Evans, *Paradise Lost and the Genesis Tradition*, 1968; Lieb, *The Dialectics of Creation: Patterns of Birth and Regeneration in Paradise Lost*, 1970; John R. Knott, *Milton's Pastoral Vision*, 1971; John Steadman, *Epic and Tragic Structure in Paradise Lost*, 1976; Joan Webber, *Milton and His Epic Tradition*, 1979; Murray Roston, *Milton and the Baroque*, 1980; Maureen Quilligan, *Milton's Spenser: The Politics of Reading*, 1983; Stevie Davies, *Images of Kingship in Paradise Lost*, 1983; Barbara K. Lewalski, *Paradise Lost and the Rhetoric of Literary Forms*, 1985; David Quint, *Epic and Empire: Politics and Generic Form from Virgil to Milton*, 1993; Jason Rosenblatt, *Torah and Law in Paradise Lost*, 1994; and J. Martin Evans, *Milton's Imperial Epic: Paradise Lost and the Discourse of Colonialism*, 1996. Placing Milton's epic in relation to relevant visual traditions is the burden of a beautifully illustrated book by Roland M. Frye, *Milton's Imagery and the Visual Arts: Iconographic Traditions in the Epic Poems*, 1978; and of a broader study by Diane McColley, *A Gust for Paradise: Milton's Eden and the Visual Arts*, 1993.

Milton's brief epic, *Paradise Regained*, is the subject of Lewalski, *Milton's Brief Epic: The Genre, Meaning, and Art of Paradise Regained*, 1966; the poem is treated at some length in Loewenstein, *Milton and the Drama of History*; Knoppers, *Historicizing Milton*; Quint, *Epic and Empire*; Mary Ann Radzinowicz, *Milton's Epics and the Book of Psalms*, 1989; *Calm of Mind*, ed. Joseph Wittreich, 1971; and *The Prison and the Pinnacle*, ed. Balachandra Rajan, 1972, which also contain essays on *Samson Agonistes*. Some important works dealing with Milton's tragedy, *Samson Agonistes*, include William R. Parker, *Milton's Debt to Greek Tragedy in Samson Agonistes*, 1937; Anthony Low, *The Blaze of Noon:*

A Reading of Samson Agonistes, 1974; and with reference to competing traditions of interpreting the Samson story, in Wittreich, *Interpreting Samson Agonistes*, 1986. Radzinowicz, *Toward Samson Agonistes: The Growth of Milton's Mind*, 1978, treats themes and concerns in all his writing as leading toward his great tragedy. In 1987 Patrides provided the very useful *Annotated Critical Bibliography of John Milton*.

Martha Moulsworth

An edition of Moulsworth's poem, transcribed from the manuscript at Yale (Osborn MS fb 150) has been edited, with annotations, analysis, and contextual discussion, by Robert C. Evans and Barbara Wiedemann, *"My Name Was Martha": A Renaissance Woman's Autobiographical Poem*, 1993. Other criticism is collected in *"The Muses females Are": Martha Moulsworth and Other Women Writers of the English Renaissance*, ed. Evans and Anne C. Little, 1995. Studies of contemporary women's autobiography include Sara H. Mendleson, "Stuart Women's Diaries and Occasional Memoirs," in *Women in English Society, 1500–1800*, ed. Mary Prior, 1985, and *Her Own Life: Autobiographical Writings by Seventeenth-Century Englishwomen*, ed. Elspeth Graham et al., 1989.

Katherine Philips

Patrick Thomas has edited *The Collected Works of Katherine Philips: The Matchless Orinda*, 1993. Her translations of Corneille and other French works were edited by Ruth Little, 1991. There are two biographies: Philip W. Souer, *The Matchless Orinda*, 1931, and Patrick Thomas, *Katherine Philips*, 1988. Useful critical studies include Harriette Andreadis, "The Sapphic-Platonics of Katherine Philips, 1632–1664," in *Signs* 15 (1989): 34–60; Elizabeth Hageman, "Katherine Philips: The Matchless Orinda," in *Women Writers of the Renaissance and Reformation*, ed. Katharina M. Wilson, 1987; and Arlene Stiebel, "Subversive Sexuality: Masking the Erotic in Poems by Katherine Philips and Aphra Behn," in *Renaissance Discourses of Desire*, ed. Claude J. Summers and Ted-Larry Pebworth, 1993.

Rachel Speght

Barbara K. Lewalski has edited *A Mouzell for Melastomus* and *Mortalities Memorandum, with a Dream Prefixed*, in *The Polemics and Poems of Rachel Speght*, 1996. Other tracts in the Jacobean controversy about women are included in *The Women's Sharp Revenge: Five Women's Pamphlets from the Renaissance*, ed. Simon Shepherd, 1985, and *Half Humankind: Contexts and Texts of the Controversy about Women in England, 1540–1640*, ed. Katherine Henderson and Barbara McManus, 1985. Speght is discussed in Linda Woodbridge, *Women and the English Renaissance: Literature and the Nature of Womankind, 1540–1620*, 1984; Ann Rosalind Jones, *The Renaissance Englishwoman in Print: Counterbalancing the Canon*, ed. Anne M.

Haselkorn and Betty Travitsky, 1990; and Lewalski, *Writing Women in Jacobean England*, 1993.

Sir John Suckling

Suckling's plays and poems have been edited by L. A. Beurline and Thomas Clayton, *The Works of John Suckling*, 2 vols, 1971. Charles L. Squier published a compact life and works, *John Suckling*, 1978. A useful article is Michael P. Parker, " 'All are not born (Sir) to the Bay': 'Jack' Suckling, 'Tom' Carew, and the Making of a Poet," in *ELR* 12 (1982): 341–68. Suckling is discussed in Earl Miner, *The Cavalier Mode from Jonson to Cotton*, 1971; Joseph H. Summers, *The Heirs of Donne and Jonson*, 1970; George Parfitt, *English Poetry of the Seventeenth Century*, 1985; and *Classic and Cavalier: Essays on Jonson and the Sons of Ben*, ed. Claude Summers and Ted-Larry Pebworth, 1982. Recent studies are surveyed in *ELR* 7 (1977).

Thomas Traherne

The standard edition is *Thomas Traherne: Centuries, Poems, and Thanksgivings*, 2 vols., ed. H. M. Margoliouth, rev. 1972. There is a biography by Gladys Wade, *Thomas Traherne*, 1944, and a Twayne life and works by Malcolm Day, *Thomas Traherne*, 1983. Significant critical studies include A. L. Clements, *The Mystical Poetry of Thomas Traherne*, 1969; Stanley Stewart, *The Expanded Voice: The Art of Thomas Traherne*, 1970; Sharon Seelig, *The Shadow of Eternity: Belief and Structure in Herbert, Vaughan, and Traherne*, 1981; and Graham Dowell, *Enjoying the World: The Rediscovery of Thomas Traherne*, 1990. Recent studies are surveyed in *ELR* 4 (1974): 189–96.

Henry Vaughan

The standard edition is *The Works of Henry Vaughan*, ed. L. C. Martin, rev. 1957; French Fogle edited the *Complete Poetry* in 1964, and Alan Rudrum did so in 1976. F. E. Hutchinson published a biography in 1947, *Henry Vaughan: a Life and Interpretation*. Critical studies include E. C. Pettit, *Of Paradise and Light*, 1960; James D. Simmonds, *Masques of God*, 1972; Thomas O. Calhoun, *Henry Vaughan: The Achievement of "Silex Scintillans,"* 1981; and Noel K. Thomas, *Henry Vaughan: Poet of Revelation*, 1986. Jonathan Post's *Henry Vaughan: The Unfolding Vision*, 1982, offers a comprehensive overview. Alan Rudrum edited *Essential Articles for the Study of Henry Vaughan* in 1987. Recent studies are surveyed in *ELR* 4 (1974).

Edmund Waller

The only complete edition is by G. Thorn-Drury, 1893, rpt. 1968. Jack G. Gilbert published a Twayne biography, *Edmund Waller*, in 1979. Critical studies include A. W. Alison, *Toward an Augustan Poetic*, 1962; W. L. Chernaik, *The Poetry of Limitation*, 1968; and A. B. Chambers, *Andrew Marvell and Edmund Waller: Seventeenth-Century Praise and Restoration Satire*, 1991. Recent studies are surveyed in *ELR* 7 (1977): 255–58.

Izaak Walton

Geoffrey Keynes edited a handy edition of all Walton's works in 1929. *The Compleat Angler, 1653–1676*, was edited by Jonquil Bevan, 1983. P. G. Stanwood has written a Twayne life and works, *Izaak Walton*, 1998. The *Life of Donne* is discussed in Judith H. Anderson's *Biographical Truth: The Representation of Historical Persons in Tudor-Stuart Writing*, 1984. Important critical studies include David Novarr, *The Making of Walton's Lives*, 1958; John R. Cooper, *The Art of "The Compleat Angler,"* 1968; Earl Miner, *The Cavalier Mode: from Jonson to Cotton, 1971*; Michael Wilding, *Dragon's Teeth: Literature in the English Revolution*, 1987; and Steven Zwicker, *Lines of Authority: Politics and English Culture, 1649–1689*, 1993. Recent studies are reviewed in *ELR* 17 (1987).

John Webster

F. L. Lucas edited the *Complete Works*, 4 vols., 1927, rpt. 1967, and re-edited *The Duchess of Malfi* and *The White Devil* in 1959. The Revels Plays edition of *The Duchess of Malfi*, ed. John Russell Brown, 1964, includes much interesting material; a new edition of Webster's *Selected Plays* is by Jonathan Dollimore and Alan Sinfield, 1983. There is a biography by M. C. Bradbrook, *John Webster: Citizen and Dramatist*, 1980. Book-length studies of *The Duchess of Malfi* include Clifford Leech, *Webster: The Duchess of Malfi*, 1963, and Joyce Peterson, *Curs'd Example: "The Duchess of Malfi" and Commonweal Tragedy*, 1978; *Malfi* is treated along with *Othello, King Lear*, and *The White Devil* in Dympna Callahan, *Women and Gender in Renaissance Tragedy*, 1989. General critical studies include Ralph Berry, *The Art of John Webster*, 1972; Charles R. Forker, *Skull Beneath the Skin: The Achievement of John Webster*, 1986; Lee Bliss, *The World's Perspective: John Webster and the Jacobean Drama*, 1983; and Christina Luckyi, *A Winter's Snake: Dramatic Form in the Tragedies of John Webster*, 1989. Don D. Moore surveys criticism in *The Critical Heritage: John Webster*, 1981; and R. B. Heldworth reprints selected essays in *Webster: "The White Devil" and "The Duchess of Malfi,"* 1975. Recent studies are surveyed in *ELR* 12 (1982): 369–75.

Gerrard Winstanley

The most nearly complete edition is *The Writings of Gerrard Winstanley*, ed. George H. Sabine, 1941, rpt. 1965. Christopher Hill's selections, *"The Law of Freedom" and Other Writings of Gerard Winstanley*, 1973, rev. 1983, includes an excellent introduction. The best biographical account is still in David Petegorsky, *Left-Wing Democracy in the English Civil War*, 1940; Winstanley also figures prominently in Christopher Hill, *The World Turned Upside Down*, 1972. His ideas and writing are analyzed by T. Wilson Hayes in *Winstanley the Digger*, 1979; by George A. Shulman in *Radicalism and Reverence: The Political Thought of Gerrard Winstanley*, 1989, and by Nigel Smith in *Perfection Pro-*

claimed: Language and Literature in English Radical Religion, 1640–1660, 1989.

Lady Mary Wroth
Josephine Roberts edited *Poems,* 1983, and also *The First Part of The Countess of Montgomery's Urania,* 1995. Part II of the *Urania* is being published from the manuscript in the Newberry Library. There is a modernized edition of *Poems* edited by R. E. Pritchard, 1996. Wroth's pastoral drama, *Love's Victory,* was edited by Michael Brennan, 1988. There are biographical accounts in Roberts' introductions, and in Kim Walker, *Women Writers of the English Renaissance,* 1996. Critical studies include May Nelson Paulissen, *The Love Sonnets of Lady Mary Wroth: A Critical Introduction,* 1982; Gary Waller,

The Sidney Family Romance: Mary Wroth, William Herbert, and the Early Modern Construction of Gender, 1993; and Naomi Miller, *Changing the Subject: Mary Wroth and Figurations of Gender in Early Modern England,* 1996. Miller and Waller have also edited a collection of essays, *Reading Mary Wroth: Representing Alternatives in Early Modern England,* 1991. Wroth's works are also treated by Maureen Quilligan in *Unfolded Tales: Essays on Renaissance Romance,* ed. George Logan and Gordon Teskey, 1989; by several hands in *The Renaissance English-woman in Print: Counterbalancing the Canon,* ed. Anne M. Haselkorn and Betty Travitsky, 1990; and in Barbara K. Lewalski, *Writing Women in Jacobean England,* 1993. Recent studies are surveyed in *ELR* 18 (1988) and 24 (1994).

THE RESTORATION AND THE EIGHTEENTH CENTURY

In recent decades, historians have placed less emphasis on stories about the ruling classes and their political conflicts and more on the economic and social forces that shape the lives of ordinary people. A good example of this approach is *The Peoples of the British Isles: A New History,* 3 vols., 1992; volume 2, by T. W. Heyck, covers the period from 1688 to 1870. A fuller account is provided by J. R. Jones, *Country and Court; England, 1658–1714,* 1978; W. A. Speck, *Stability and Strife: England, 1714–1760,* 1977; and Ian Christie, *Wars and Revolutions: Britain, 1760–1815,* 1982. Linda Colley, *Britons,* 1992, studies the forging of a new national identity. J. H. Plumb, *England in the Eighteenth Century,* 1950, describes the structure of society, and Roy Porter, *English Society in the Eighteenth Century,* rev. 1990, is a mine of information. John Brewer, *The Pleasures of the Imagination,* 1997, is a wide-ranging history of popular culture. The life and manners of the age are surveyed in *Johnson's England,* 2 vols., ed. A. S. Turberville, 1933; Dorothy Marshall, *English People in the Eighteenth Century,* 1956; and R. B. Schwartz, *Daily Life in Johnson's England,* 1983. *The Birth of a Consumer Society,* 1982, by Neil McKendrick, Brewer, and J. H. Plumb, traces the rise of modern commercialization in the eighteenth century. Useful guides to the historical and cultural contexts of literature include A. R. Humphreys, *The Augustan World,* 1954; Donald Greene, *The Age of Exuberance,* 1970; *The Eighteenth Century,* ed. Pat Rogers, 1978; and James Sambrook, *The Eighteenth Century, 1700–1789,* 2nd ed., 1993.

On the intellectual background of the period, Sir Leslie Stephen, *History of English Thought in the Eighteenth Century,* 2 vols., 1876, remains valuable; so do A. O. Lovejoy, *The Great Chain of Being,* 1942, and *Essays in the History of Ideas,* 1948. Basil Willey, *The Eighteenth Century Background,* 1940, studies ideas about nature, and Keith Thomas, *Man and the Natural World,* 1983, shows the development of a modern sensibility between 1500 and

1800. Gordon Rupp, *Religion in England, 1688–1791,* 1986, is dependable. Volumes 4 to 6 of F. C. Coplestone, *History of Philosophy,* 1960, deal with the period from Descartes to Kant; Peter Gay, *The Enlightenment: An Interpretation,* 2 vols., 1969, forcefully defends the philosophers of the Age of Reason. Paul Hazard, *The European Mind, 1680–1715,* 1953, and *European Thought in the Eighteenth Century,* 1954, trans. from French by J. L. May, are readable surveys of intellectual movements on the Continent as well as in England. J. W. Johnson, *The Formation of English Neo-Classical Thought,* 1967, and J. M. Levine, *The Battle of the Books: History and Literature in the Augustan Age,* 1991, study the ways that writers came to terms with the past. Burton Feldman and R. D. Richardson, *The Rise of Modern Mythology 1680–1860,* 1972, and Gerald Newman, *The Rise of English Nationalism,* 1987, deal with important new directions of thought. Steven Shapin, *The Scientific Revolution,* 1996, is a brief clear survey. Valuable studies of the influence of scientific ideas include R. F. Jones, *Ancients and Moderns,* 1936; Marjorie Nicolson, *Newton Demands the Muse,* 1946, and *Science and the Imagination,* 1956; and W. P. Jones, *The Rhetoric of Science,* 1966. Myra Reynolds, *The Learned Lady in England, 1650–1760,* 1920, still useful, should be supplemented by Sylvia Myers, *The Bluestocking Circle,* 1990. Sensibility, a set of new ideas and feelings associated especially with women, is the subject of several good books, including Jean Hagstrum, *Sex and Sensibility,* 1970; Janet Todd, *Sensibility: An Introduction,* 1986; John Mullan, *Sentiment and Sociability,* 1988; and G. J. Barker-Benfield, *The Culture of Sensibility,* 1992. Changes in the literary marketplace are illuminated by Pat Rogers, *Grub Street,* 1972; Paula McDowell, *The Women of Grub Street,* 1998; Mark Rose, *Authors and Owners: The Invention of Copyright,* 1993; and Dustin Griffin, *Literary Patronage in England, 1650–1800,* 1996. Martin Price, *To the Palace of Wisdom: Studies in Order and Energy from*

Dryden to Blake, 1964; Paul Fussell, *The Rhetorical World of Augustan Humanism*, 1965; W. J. Bate, *The Burden of the Past and the English Poet*, 1970; John Sitter, *Literary Loneliness in Mid-Eighteenth-Century England*, 1982; Howard Weinbrot, *Britannia's Issue: The Rise of British Literature from Dryden to Ossian*, 1993; and Stuart Sherman, *Telling Time: Clocks, Diaries, and English Diurnal Form, 1660–1785*, 1996, are all thoughtful and stimulating studies that relate ideas to literary art.

Good surveys of the literature of the age include George Sherburn, "The Restoration and Eighteenth Century," in *A Literary History of England*, ed. A. C. Baugh, rev. 1967, and *Dryden to Johnson*, ed. Roger Lonsdale, rev. 1987, vol. 4 of the Sphere History of Literature. Far more detailed are three volumes of the *Oxford History of English Literature*: James Sutherland, *English Literature of the Late Seventeenth Century*, 1969; Bonamy Dobrée, *English Literature in the Early Eighteenth Century, 1700–1740*, 1959; and John Butt and Geoffrey Carnall, *English Literature in the Mid-Eighteenth Century*, 1979. On women writers they need to be supplemented by Janet Todd, *A Dictionary of British and American Women Writers, 1660–1800*, 1985.

Among books that deal with a single literary mode, James Sutherland, *A Preface to Eighteenth-Century Poetry*, 1948, is a deft introduction, and Eric Rothstein, *Restoration and Eighteenth-Century Poetry, 1660–1780*, 1981, is a fresh, informative survey. Other useful studies include Ian Jack, *Augustan Satire*, 1952; Earl Miner, *The Restoration Mode from Milton to Dryden*, 1974; Rachel Trickett, *The Honest Muse*, 1974; Margaret Doody, *The Daring Muse*, 1985; and Robert Griffin, *Wordsworth's Pope*, 1995. Anne Williams, *Prophetic Strain*, 1984, and Richard Feingold, *Moralized Song*, 1989, both stress the lyricism of eighteenth-century poems. Two anthologies edited by Roger Lonsdale, *The New Oxford Book of Eighteenth Century Verse*, 1984, and *Eighteenth-Century Women Poets*, 1989, have sparked an interest in neglected poems about daily life; Joyce Fullard has edited *Eighteenth-Century Women Poets 1660–1800*, 1990; and David Fairer and Christine Gerrard have edited an annotated anthology, *Eighteenth-Century Poetry*, 1999.

On drama, a good introduction is R. W. Bevis, *English Drama: Restoration and Eighteenth Century, 1660–1789*, 1988. Fuller accounts appear in Allardyce Nicoll, *A History of Restoration Drama 1660–1700*, *A History of Early Eighteenth-Century Drama, 1700–1750*, and *A History of Late Eighteenth-Century Drama, 1750–1800*, rev. 1952; and *The Revels History of Drama in English*, Vol. 5, *1660–1750*, 1976, and Vol. 6, *1750–1880*, 1975. An invaluable store of detailed information is *The London Stage, 1660–1800*, 11 vols., 1960–68, the critical introductions of which have been gathered in five paperback books. Six of the most important plays of the period, together with critical commentary and background material on theaters, staging, and audience, are edited by Scott McMillin in a Norton Critical Edition, *Restoration and Eigh-teenth-Century Comedy*, 2nd ed., 1997. Two collections, *Restoration Dramatists*, ed. Earl Miner, 1966, and *Restoration Drama*, ed. John Loftis, 1966, provide essays in criticism by various writers; Loftis has also analyzed *Comedy and Society from Congreve to Fielding*, 1959. Walter Graham has surveyed *English Literary Periodicals*, 1930. Letter writing was an important eighteenth-century genre, discussed in *The Familiar Letter in the Eighteenth Century*, ed. Howard Anderson, P. B. Daghlian, and Irvin Ehrenpreis, 1966, and Bruce Redford, *The Converse of the Pen*, 1987. Another important genre, history writing, is examined in Karen O'Brien, *Narratives of Enlightenment*, 1997. D. A. Stauffer, *English Biography before 1700*, 1930, and *The Art of Biography in Eighteenth-Century England*, 2 vols., 1941, are standard surveys; William H. Epstein, *Recognizing Biography*, 1987, is a challenging theoretical study. Bunyan figures prominently in two books on autobiography: John N. Morris, *Versions of the Self*, 1966, and Felicity Nussbaum, *The Autobiographical Subject*, 1989. Patricia Spacks, *Imagining a Self*, 1976, discusses conceptions of personal identity in eighteenth-century autobiographies and novels.

The Cambridge Companion to the Eighteenth-Century Novel, ed. John Richetti, 1996, is a good general survey. E. A. Baker, *The History of the English Novel*, vols. 3–5, 1930–34, assembles many details. A. D. McKillop, *The Early Masters of English Fiction*, 1956, and Clive Probyn, *English Fiction of the Eighteenth Century, 1700–1789*, 1987, offer good introductions to major novelists. Ian Watt, *The Rise of the Novel*, 1957, an influential study of Defoe, Richardson, and Fielding, set off a long discussion that has been joined by Jane Spencer, *The Rise of the Woman Novelist*, 1986; Michael McKeon, *The Origins of the English Novel*, 1987; Nancy Armstrong, *Desire and Domestic Fiction*, 1987; J. Paul Hunter, *Before Novels*, 1990; Homer O. Brown, *Institutions of the English Novel from Defoe to Scott*, 1997; and William B. Warner, *Licensing Entertainment*, 1998. Interesting studies of special aspects of fiction include Lennard Davis, *Factual Fictions*, 1983; Terry Castle, *Masquerade and Civilization*, 1986; John Bender, *Imagining the Penitentiary*, 1987; Carol Kay, *Political Constructions*, 1988; and Catherine Gallagher, *Nobody's Story*, 1994, which has chapters on *Oroonoko* and Frances Burney.

The most comprehensive account of eighteenth-century criticism is vol. 4 of *The Cambridge History of Literary Criticism*, ed. H. B. Nisbet and Claude Rawson, 1997. J. E. Spingarn, *Critical Essays of the Seventeenth Century*, vols. 2 and 3, 1908 (the preface is still useful), and Scott Elledge, *Eighteenth-Century Critical Essays*, 2 vols., 1961, are valuable collections. R. S. Crane's "Neo-Classical Criticism," in *A Dictionary of World Literature*, ed. J. T. Shipley, 1943, has not been surpassed. A survey of major critical movements is provided by James Engell, *Forming the Critical Mind: Dryden to Coleridge*, 1989. René Wellek, *A History of Modern Criticism*

1750–1950, vol. 1, 1955, and W. K. Wimsatt and Cleanth Brooks, *Literary Criticism: A Short History*, 1957, review important issues of theory and aesthetics. Raymond Williams, *Keywords: A Vocabulary of Culture and Society*, 1983, examines the changing meanings of critical terms. A feminist perspective is offered by Marilyn Williamson, *Raising Their Voices: British Women Writers, 1650–1750*, 1990. The issues explored by Samuel H. Monk's classic study, *The Sublime*, 1935, have been taken up by many later critics, among them David Morris, *The Religious Sublime*, 1972, and Steven Knapp, *Personification and the Sublime*, 1985. The theory of satire has also been a perennial source of interest, most recently in John Sitter, *Arguments of Augustan Wit*, 1991, and Dustin Griffin, *Satire: A Critical Reintroduction*, 1994. Though primarily concerned with Romantic theory, M. H. Abrams, *The Mirror and the Lamp*, 1953, delves deeply into eighteenth-century critical ideas.

The relation of literature to other arts has been the subject of many instructive studies. Jean Hagstrum, *The Sister Arts*, 1958, compares paintings with poems; John Dixon Hunt, *The Figure in the Landscape*, 1977, deals with poetry, painting, and gardening; and Richard Wendorf, *The Elements of Life*, 1990, compares biography with portrait-painting. Lawrence Lipking discusses the first histories of the arts in *The Ordering of the Arts in Eighteenth-Century England*, 1970; Ronald Paulson, *Breaking and Remaking*, 1989, explores aesthetic practice from 1700 to 1820; and Murray Roston analyzes *Changing Perspectives in Literature and the Visual Arts 1650–1820*, 1990. B. Sprague Allen, *Tides of English Taste 1619–1800*, 2 vols., 1937, on architecture, gardening, and decoration, and Sir Kenneth Clark, *The Gothic Revival*, 2nd ed., 1950, on architecture, chronicle significant changes in style.

Good collections of criticism have been edited by James L. Clifford, *Eighteenth-Century English Literature: Modern Essays in Criticism*, 1959, and Leopold Damrosch, *Modern Essays on Eighteenth-Century Literature*, 1988. Essays that explore new theoretical approaches are collected by Felicity Nussbaum and Laura Brown, *The New Eighteenth Century*, 1987. *Studies in English Literature* devotes its summer issue to the Restoration and the eighteenth century and includes an article reviewing important work published in the preceding year. Finally, for elaborate bibliographies and reviews of eighteenth-century studies, the student may consult the bibliography of English literature, 1660–1800, that has appeared annually since 1926 in *Philological Quarterly* and, since 1976, in yearly volumes, *The Eighteenth Century: A Current Bibliography*.

Joseph Addison and Sir Richard Steele

There is no scholarly edition of the collected works. Donald F. Bond's editions of *The Spectator*, 5 vols., 1965, and *The Tatler*, 3 vols., 1987, are both superb. *The Commerce of Everyday Life*, ed. Erin Mackie, 1998, provides cultural contexts for selected essays. John Stephens has edited *The Guardian*, 1982. *The Letters of Joseph Addison* was edited by Walter Graham, 1941. Peter Smithers, *The Life of Joseph Addison*, 1968, is the standard biography. Edward and Lillian Bloom survey Addison's views of society in *Joseph Addison's Sociable Animal*, 1971. Calhoun Winton, *Captain Steele: The Early Career of Richard Steele*, 1964, and *Sir Richard Steele, M. P.: The Later Career*, 1970, compose a fine biography. Rae Blanchard has edited Steele's *Correspondence*, 1941, *Tracts and Pamphlets*, 1944, *Occasional Verse*, 1952, and other lesser works. The *Plays* have been edited by Shirley S. Kenny, 1971. Richmond P. Bond has analyzed *The Tatler: The Making of a Literary Journal*, 1971.

Mary Astell

Bridget Hill edited selected writings in *The First English Feminist*, 1986, and Patricia Springborg has edited *Political Writings*, 1996, and *A Serious Proposal to the Ladies*, 1997. Ruth Perry, *The Celebrated Mary Astell*, 1986, is a fine biography that puts Astell in the context of her times; it supersedes Florence M. Smith's pioneering *Mary Astell*, 1912. Hilda L. Smith, *Reason's Disciples*, 1982, includes a good section on Astell.

Aphra Behn

Janet Todd has edited *The Works of Aphra Behn*, 7 vols., 1992–96. The Norton Critical Edition of *Oroonoko*, ed. Joanna Lipking, 1997, includes relevant historical backgrounds and criticism. The paucity of reliable facts about Behn's life prevents any biography from being authoritative, but Maureen Duffy, *The Passionate Shepherdess*, 1977, is worth reading, and Janet Todd, *The Secret Life of Aphra Behn*, 1997, is full of interesting speculations and fresh information. Wylie Sypher, *Guinea's Captive Kings*, 1942, puts *Oroonoko* in the context of antislavery literature. Mary Ann O'Donnell, *Aphra Behn: An Annotated Bibliography*, 1986, is a thorough review of primary and secondary sources through 1985.

James Boswell

Modern revaluations of Boswell began with the publication of *The Private Papers of James Boswell from Malahide Castle*, ed. Geoffrey Scott and Frederick A. Pottle, 18 vols., 1928–34. Pottle described the history of the papers in *Pride and Negligence*, 1981. A trade edition of Boswell's *Journals*, 14 vols., 1950–89, has valuable introductions and notes. The *Letters*, ed. C. B. Tinker, 2 vols., 1924, need to be supplemented by the recovered *Correspondence of James Boswell*, 1966–97, of which seven volumes have been published. The best edition of the *Life of Johnson* is L. F. Powell's revision of G. B. Hill's edition, 6 vols., 1934–64. A good one-volume edition by R. W. Chapman and J. D. Fleeman, 1982, is available in paperback.

F. A. Pottle, *James Boswell, The Earlier Years, 1740–1769*, 1966, and Frank Brady, *James Boswell, The Later Years, 1769–1795*, 1984, are the two halves of the standard biography, judicious and well informed. Pottle, *The Literary Career of James Boswell*, 1929, and Mary Hyde, *The Impossible Friendship: Boswell and Mrs. Thrale*, 1972, are both useful. B. H. Bronson, "Boswell's Boswell," in *Johnson and Boswell*, 1944, is a wise and sympathetic study; and J. L. Smith-Dampier, *Who's Who in Boswell?*, 1935, is a helpful guide through the *Life of Johnson*. Greg Clingham has edited a collection of essays, *New Light on Boswell*, 1991.

John Bunyan

Bunyan was a prolific writer: Part II of *The Pilgrim's Progress*, dealing with the journey of Christian's wife and children, appeared in 1684; *The Life and Death of Mr. Badman* in 1680; *The Holy War* in 1682. But these major works form only a small part of all his writings.

Christopher Hill, *A Tinker and a Poor Man: John Bunyan and His Church, 1628–1688*, 1989, is a vigorous, informative life. The critical edition of *The Pilgrim's Progress* is by J. B. Wharey, 1928, revised by Roger Sharrock, 1960; Sharrock has also edited *Grace Abounding to the Chief of Sinners*, 1962, and, with James Forrest, *The Holy War*, 1980, and *The Life and Death of Mr. Badman*, 1988. Interesting modern studies include G. B. Harrison, *John Bunyan: A Study in Personality*, 1928; Henri A. Talon, *John Bunyan, The Man and His Work*, 1951, a translation from the French; U. Milo Kaufmann, *The Pilgrim's Progress and Traditions in Puritan Meditation*, 1966; and a collection of essays edited by N. H. Keeble, *John Bunyan: Conventicle and Parnassus*, 1988.

Frances Burney

The *Diary and Letters* were first edited in a truncated version by Charlotte Barrett, Burney's niece, 7 vols., 1842–46. The original texts of *The Journals and Letters of Fanny Burney (Madame d'Arblay), 1791–1840*, 12 vols., have been superbly edited by Joyce Hemlow et al., 1972–84. Several volumes of *The Early Journals and Letters of Fanny Burney, 1768–1791*, which will eventually fill ten or twelve volumes, have been edited by Lars Troide et al., 1988–94. There is no standard edition of the novels, but Peter Sabor has edited *The Complete Plays of Frances Burney*, 2 vols., 1995. Joyce Hemlow wrote the standard biography, *The History of Fanny Burney*, 1958, and Margaret Doody's critical biography, *Frances Burney: The Life in the Works*, 1988, is lively and thought provoking.

Samuel Butler

Materials for a full-length biography of Butler do not exist; George Wasserman, *Samuel "Hudibras" Butler*, 1989, summarizes what is known. Of editions of *Hudibras*, Zachary Grey's, 2 vols., 1744, is still useful for its illustrative notes; the best modern edition is John Wilders's, 1967. *Characters*, ed. C. W. Daves, 1970, and *Prose Observations*, ed. Hugh de Quehen, 1979, are invaluable for studying Butler's opinions; René Lamar has edited *Satires and Miscellaneous Poetry and Prose*, 1928. E. A. Richards, *Hudibras in the Burlesque Tradition*,

1937, is useful. Ian Jack, *Augustan Satire*, 1952, and Blandford Parker, *The Triumph of Augustan Poetics*, 1998, include excellent essays on Butler.

William Collins

The *Works* of Collins, which amount only to one slim volume, have been well edited by Richard Wendorf and Charles Ryskamp, 1979. Lonsdale's edition (see **Gray**) has copious notes. P. L. Carver, *The Life of a Poet*, 1967, is the fullest biography. Wendorf, *William Collins and Eighteenth-Century English Poetry*, 1981, is a fine critical study.

William Congreve

Congreve's *Complete Works* were edited by Montague Summers, 4 vols., 1923; a new edition is forthcoming. Herbert Davis edited the *Plays*, 1967. The best biography is J. C. Hodges, *William Congreve the Man*, 1941. Julie S. Peters analyzes the relation of plays to texts in *Congreve, the Drama, and the Printed Word*, 1990. Maximilian Novak's *William Congreve*, 1971, Harold Love's *Congreve*, 1975, and Arthur Hoffman, *Congreve's Comedies*, 1993, are good critical introductions. Early criticism of Congreve has been collected by Alexander Lindsay and Howard Erskine-Hill, 1989. More recent criticism is abundant in books on Restoration drama—for example, T. H. Fujimura, *The Restoration Comedy of Wit*, 1952; N. N. Holland, *The First Modern Comedies*, 1959; Ian Donaldson, *The World Upside Down: Comedy from Jonson to Fielding*, 1970; Harriet Hawkins, *Likenesses of Truth in Elizabethan and Restoration Drama*, 1972; Robert Hume, *The Development of English Drama in the Late Seventeenth Century*, 1976; and Derek Hughes, *English Drama 1660–1700*, 1996.

William Cowper

The *Poems*, 3 vols., have been expertly edited by John D. Baird and Charles Ryskamp, 1980–95. James Sambrook's edition of *The Task and Selected Other Poems*, 1994, has useful notes. James King and Ryskamp have edited Cowper's *Letters and Prose Writings*, 5 vols., 1979–86, and one volume of *Selected Letters*, 1989. King, *William Cowper: A Biography*, 1986, is the best full life; Ryskamp's fine *William Cowper of the Inner Temple, Esq.*, 1959, ends in 1768. Useful critical studies include Morris Golden, *In Search of Stability: The Poetry of William Cowper*, 1960; Vincent Newey, *Cowper's Poetry*, 1982; Martin Priestman, *Cowper's Task*, 1983; and the last chapter of Donald Davie, *The Eighteenth-Century Hymn in England*, 1993.

George Crabbe

Crabbe's biography was written by his son, George, in 1834. It has been reedited by E. M. Forster, 1932, and by Edmund Blunden, 1947. *The Complete Poetical Works*, ed. Norma Dalrymple-Champneys and Arthur Pollard, 3 vols., 1988, is the standard edition. Howard Mills has edited *Tales (1812) and Other Selected Poems*, 1967; and T. C. Faulkner edited *Selected Letters and Journals*, 1985. Lilian Haddakin, *The Poetry of Crabbe*, 1955; Oliver Sigworth, *Nature's Sternest Painter*, 1965; Peter

New, *George Crabbe's Poetry*, 1976; and Frank Whitehead, *George Crabbe: A Reappraisal*, 1995, are essays in criticism.

Daniel Defoe

Paula Backscheider, *Daniel Defoe: His Life*, 1989, is a comprehensive, up-to-date biography. James Sutherland has written a good short life, *Defoe*, 1950, and a critical study, *Daniel Defoe*, 1971. As P. N. Furbank and W. R. Owens stress in *The Canonisation of Daniel Defoe*, 1988, and in their *Critical Bibliography of Daniel Defoe*, 1998, too little is known about what Defoe actually wrote, and there is no good scholarly edition of the works. The *Letters* were edited by George Healey, 1955. Most books on the early English novel contain significant chapters on Defoe; see especially, Robert Mayer, *History and the Early English Novel*, 1997. Full-length studies include John Richetti, *Daniel Defoe*, 1987 (a good brief survey), and *Defoe's Narratives*, 1975; Maximilian Novak, *Economics and the Fiction of Daniel Defoe*, 1962, and *Defoe and the Nature of Man*, 1963; G. A. Starr, *Defoe and Casuistry*, 1971; Peter Earle, *The World of Defoe*, 1976; and Ian Bell, *Defoe's Fiction*, 1985.

Three of Defoe's novels are in the Norton Critical Editions series: *Moll Flanders*, ed. Edward Kelley, 1974; *Robinson Crusoe*, ed. Michael Shinagel, rev. 1993; and *A Journal of the Plague Year*, ed. Paula Backscheider, 1992.

John Dryden

James A. Winn's *John Dryden and His World*, 1987, is the best biography. G. R. Noyes's edition of the *Poetical Works*, 2nd ed., 1950, includes a good biographical sketch; and Samuel Johnson's *Life of Dryden* is still worth reading. A fine scholarly edition of the *Works*, launched in 1956, under the general editorship first of E. N. Hooker, then H. T. Swedenberg, and lately Alan Roper, has reached twenty volumes. Keith Walker has edited a useful selected *Works*, 1987. The poems have been edited by James Kinsley, 4 vols., 1958, and the essays by W. P. Ker, 2 vols., 1900, and George Watson, 2 vols., 1962. Paul Hammond's new edition of the poems has useful notes; the first two volumes appeared in 1995.

Mark Van Doren, *John Dryden: A Study of His Poetry*, 1920, remains valuable for its fresh critical responses, as do T. S. Eliot's brief studies, *Homage to John Dryden*, 1924, and *John Dryden the Poet, the Dramatist, and the Critic*, 1932. Important modern criticism includes Arthur Hoffman, *John Dryden's Imagery*, 1962; Alan Roper, *Dryden's Poetic Kingdoms*, 1965; and Earl Miner, *Dryden's Poetry*, 1967. David Hopkins, *John Dryden*, 1986, is a good introduction. Steven Zwicker has studied *Politics and Language in Dryden's Poetry*, 1984. The standard work on Dryden's philosophical and religious ideas is Philip Harth, *Contexts of Dryden's Thought*, 1968, and Harth has also analyzed the politics of *Absalom and Achitophel* in *Pen for a Party*, 1993. Robert Hume analyzes *Dryden's Criticism*, 1970; Edward Pechter, *Dryden's Classical Theory of Literature*, 1975; and John C. Aden brings together

The Critical Opinions of John Dryden, A Dictionary, 1963, under convenient headings. James Winn has edited *Critical Essays on John Dryden*, 1997.

Olaudah Equiano

A facsimile of the first edition of the *Interesting Narrative* was published by Paul Edwards, 2 vols., 1969. Equiano's later revisions of the *Narrative* and other writings have been edited, with useful notes, by Vincent Carretta, 1995. Carretta includes Equiano as well as other eighteenth-century black authors in a good anthology, *Unchained Voices*, 1996. Angelo Costanzo, *Surprising Narrative: Olaudah Equiano and the Beginnings of Black Autobiography*, 1987; Keith Sandiford, *Measuring the Moment: Strategies of Protest in Eighteenth-Century Afro-English Writing*, 1988; and Peter Fryer, *Staying Power: The History of Black People in Britain*, 1984, place Equiano amid the debates of his time.

Anne Finch, Countess of Winchilsea

Myra Reynolds added a long biographical introduction to her valuable edition of the *Poems*, 1903, which needs to be supplemented by *The Anne Finch Wellesley Manuscript Poems*, ed. Barbara McGovern and Charles Hinnant, 1998. McGovern has written a good critical biography, *Anne Finch and Her Poetry*, 1992. Hinnant, *The Poetry of Anne Finch*, 1994, is an essay in interpretation.

John Gay

David Nokes, *John Gay: A Profession of Friendship*, 1995, is an up-to-date life. Vinton Dearing and Charles Beckwith have edited Gay's *Poetry and Prose*, 2 vols., 1974; John Fuller, the *Dramatic Works*, 2 vols., 1983; and C. F. Burgess, the *Letters*, 1966. W. E. Schultz, *Gay's "Beggar's Opera,"* 1923, and Calhoun Winton, *John Gay and the London Theatre*, 1993, provide useful historical information. Critical studies include Sven Armens, *John Gay, Social Critic*, 1954, and *John Gay and the Scriblerians*, ed. Peter Lewis and Nigel Wood, 1988.

Oliver Goldsmith

The *Collected Works of Oliver Goldsmith*, ed. Arthur Friedman, 5 vols., 1966, is standard. The best biography is Ralph M. Wardle, *Oliver Goldsmith*, 1957. Kathleen C. Balderston edited the *Collected Letters*, 1928. The notes in Lonsdale's edition of the *Poems* (see **Gray**) are valuable. Ricardo Quintana, *Oliver Goldsmith*, 1967, and Peter Dixon, *Oliver Goldsmith Revisited*, 1991, are useful critical surveys. Andrew Swarbrick has edited a collection of essays, *The Art of Oliver Goldsmith*, 1984. Raymond Williams, *The Country and the City*, 1973, includes an influential section on *The Deserted Village*.

Thomas Gray

The poems of Gray, Collins, and Goldsmith have been edited, with informative notes, by Roger Lonsdale, 1969. The standard edition of Gray's *Works* remains that of Edmund Gosse, 4 vols., rev. 1902–6; of the *Correspondence*, that of Paget Toynbee and Leonard Whibley, 3 vols., 1935; of the poems, that of H. W. Starr and J. R. Hendrickson, 1966. R. W. Ketton-Cremer, *Thomas Gray*, 1955, is the best biography. Among critical studies, Henry Weinfield, *The Poet without a Name: Gray's Elegy and the Problem of History*, 1991, is thoughtful and searching, and B. Eugene McCarthy, *Thomas Gray: The Progress of a Poet*, 1997, is a good general introduction. *From Sensibility to Romanticism*, ed. F. W. Hilles and Harold Bloom, 1965, includes studies of the *Elegy* by Ian Jack, B. H. Bronson, and Frank Brady.

William Hogarth

The standard, comprehensive critical biography is Ronald Paulson, *Hogarth*, 3 vols., 1991–93. Jenny Uglow, *Hogarth: A Life and a World*, 1997, is perceptive and lively. Paulson has edited *Hogarth's Graphic Works*, 2 vols., 1970, as well as *The Analysis of Beauty*, 1998. The paintings are catalogued by R. B. Beckett, *Hogarth*, 1949, and the drawings by A. P. Oppé, *The Drawings of William Hogarth*, 1948. Sean Shesgreen has edited *Engravings by Hogarth*, 1973, in a generous and inexpensive format. *Hogarth on High Life*, 1970, illuminates *Marriage A-la-Mode* with the famous eighteenth-century commentaries by Georg Christoph Lichtenberg, translated and edited by Arthur Wensinger with W. B. Coley. David Bindman, *Hogarth*, 1981, is a good brief introduction to the art, and Bindman and Scott Wilcox have edited *Among the Whores and Thieves*, 1997, a collection of essays on Hogarth and *The Beggar's Opera*.

Anne Irwin

There is no edition of Irwin's poems, and only a smattering of biographical information is in print. Her long poem *Castle Howard*, 1732, describes her father's estate. "An Epistle to Mr. Pope" was published in the *Gentleman's Magazine* in 1736. Irwin's response to Pope is briefly considered by Valerie Rumbold, *Women's Place in Pope's World*, 1989, and by Claudia Thomas, *Alexander Pope and His Eighteenth-Century Women Readers*, 1994.

Samuel Johnson

Others among Johnson's friends besides Boswell wrote of him: notably, Hester Lynch Thrale Piozzi, whose *Anecdotes* (1786) have been edited, along with William Shaw's *Anecdotes*, by Arthur Sherbo, 1974; Sir John Hawkins, whose *Life* (1787) has been edited and abridged by Bertram H. Davis, 1961; and Frances Burney (Mme D'Arblay), from whose diary C. B. Tinker extracted the Johnsonian passages in *Dr. Johnson and Fanny Burney*, 1911. Pat Rogers, *The Samuel Johnson Encyclopedia*, 1996, is a handy source of information. James L. Clifford, *Young Sam Johnson*, 1955, and *Dictionary Johnson*, 1979, are well-informed studies of the early and middle years that supplement Boswell's rather sketchy account of Johnson's life before their meeting in 1763. There are fine modern biographies by John Wain, 1975, and W. J. Bate, 1977.

The best collected edition of Johnson's *Works* appeared as long ago as 1825. It is being replaced by an excellent scholarly edition, published by Yale, that has been coming out irregularly since 1958. The poems have been edited by D. N. Smith and E. L. McAdam, 2nd ed. rev. by J. D. Fleeman, 1974. G. B. Hill's editions of *Johnsonian Miscellanies*, 2 vols., 1897, and *The Lives of the Poets*, 3 vols., 1905, are still worth consulting for their fine notes. Bruce Redford's edition of the *Letters*, 5 vols., 1992–94, is superb. The *Dictionary* is available on CD-ROM, ed. Anne McDermott, 1996.

Robert DeMaria, *The Life of Samuel Johnson*, 1993, and Lawrence Lipking, *Samuel Johnson: The Life of an Author*, 1998, offer critical overviews of Johnson's literary career. Thomas Woodman, *A Preface to Samuel Johnson*, 1993, and *The Cambridge Companion to Samuel Johnson*, ed. Greg Clingham, 1997, are useful guides. Among critical introductions, W. J. Bate, *The Achievement of Samuel Johnson*, 1955, is inspiring, and Paul Fussell, *Samuel Johnson and the Life of Writing*, 1971, is lively. Good specialized studies include W. K. Wimsatt, *The Prose Style of Samuel Johnson*, 1941; Donald J. Greene, *The Politics of Samuel Johnson*, 2nd ed., 1990; Carey McIntosh, *The Choice of Life: Samuel Johnson and the World of Fiction*, 1973; Robert Folkenflik, *Samuel Johnson, Biographer*, 1978; Nicholas Hudson, *Samuel Johnson and Eighteenth-Century Thought*, 1988; and John Cannon, *Samuel Johnson and the Politics of Hanoverian England*, 1994. Joseph E. Brown collected *The Critical Opinions of Samuel Johnson*, 1926. Jean Hagstrum's fine study of *Samuel Johnson's Literary Criticism*, 1952, has been complemented by Leopold Damrosch, *The Uses of Johnson's Criticism*, 1976, and G. F. Parker, *Johnson's Shakespeare*, 1989. DeMaria, *Johnson's Dictionary and the Language of Learning*, 1986, looks at the range of ideas gathered by Johnson, and Allen Reddick has studied *The Making of Johnson's Dictionary, 1746–1773*, rev. 1996. J. L. Clifford and D. J. Greene's survey and bibliography of critical studies, rev. 1970, was updated through 1985 by Greene and J. A. Vance, 1987.

Mary Leapor

There is no modern edition of Leapor's work; the standard source remains *Poems upon Several Occasions*, 2 vols., 1748–51. The only full-length study is Richard Greene, *Mary Leapor: A Study in Eighteenth-Century Women's Poetry*, 1993. Donna Landry puts Leapor among eighteenth-century laboring-class women poets in *The Muses of Resistance*, 1990, and Betty Rizzo places her in the contexts of her time in "Molly Leapor: An Anxiety for Influence," in *The Age of Johnson* 4 (1991). Claudia Thomas (see **Irwin**) analyzes Leapor's relation to Pope.

John Locke

P. H. Nidditch has edited the standard edition of *An Essay concerning Human Understanding*, 1975. Maurice Cranston, *John Locke*, 1957, is a good biography. John Yolton, *Locke: An Introduction*, 1985 and *The Cambridge Companion to Locke*, ed. Vere Chappell, 1994, survey the range of his thought. John Jenkins, *Understanding Locke*, 1983, and Ian Harris, *The Mind of John Locke*, 1994, are strenuous accounts of his ideas.

Lady Mary Wortley Montagu

Isobel Grundy's full-scale biography, *Lady Mary Wortley Montagu: Comet of the Enlightenment*, 1999, adds much information to Robert Halsband's elegant *Life of Lady Mary Wortley Monagu*, 1956. Halsband also edited *The Complete Letters*, 3 vols., 1965–67; *Selected Letters*, 1970; and with Grundy, *Essays and Poems and Simplicity, a Comedy*, 2nd ed., 1993. Grundy has edited the *Romance Writings*, 1996.

Sir Isaac Newton

The Norton Critical Edition of Newton, ed. I. Bernard Cohen and Richard Westfall, 1995, includes texts and commentaries that reflect his various interests. Cohen's edition of *Papers and Letters on Natural Philosophy*, 1978, has a good introduction to Newton's optics by Thomas Kuhn. The *Correspondence*, 7 vols., was edited by H. W. Turnbull et al., 1959–77. Two fine biographies, Westfall, *Never at Rest*, 1980, and A. Rupert Hall, *Isaac Newton: Adventurer in Thought*, 1992, offer an introduction to Newton's ideas as well as his life.

Samuel Pepys

The standard edition of *The Diary of Samuel Pepys*, 11 vols., ed. Robert Latham and William Matthews, 1970–83, includes a companion and index. Latham has also edited a good one-volume selection, *The Shorter Pepys*, 1985. J. R. Tanner's lectures, reprinted as *Samuel Pepys and the Royal Navy*, 1920, helped call attention to the serious work of Pepys's life. The fullest biography is Arthur Bryant, *Samuel Pepys*, 3 vols., 1933–38. A good popular biography is Richard Ollard, *Pepys*, 1984. Stuart Sherman analyzes Pepys's use of the diary in *Telling Time*, 1996.

Alexander Pope

There is no reliable complete edition of Pope's works. Although defective in many respects, the Victorian edition by Whitwell Elwin and J. W. Courthope, 10 vols., 1871–89, must still be consulted (with caution). The excellent Twickenham Edition of the poems, 11 vols., 1939–67, a cooperative undertaking by several scholars (under John Butt), includes valuable introductory and critical materials and notes. A convenient selection in a single volume, with selected notes, omits the translations of Homer. *The Prose Works* have been edited in 2 vols., by Norman Ault, 1936, and Rosemary Cowler, 1986.

Maynard Mack, *Alexander Pope: A Life*, 1986, is a full and sympathetic biography. George Sherburn, *Early Career of Alexander Pope*, 1934, and Mack, *The Garden and the City*, 1969, on Pope's later career, are valuable studies. David Foxon, *Pope and the Early Eighteenth-Century Book Trade*, 1991, and Brean Hammond, *Professional Imaginative Writing in England, 1670–1740*, 1997, treat Pope's concern with the business of publication. Howard

Erskine-Hill has described *The Social Milieu of Alexander Pope*, 1975, and Valerie Rumbold examined *Women's Place in Pope's World*, 1989. Sherburn's edition of the *Correspondence*, 5 vols., 1956, is standard. R. H. Griffith, *Alexander Pope: A Bibliography*, 2 vols., 1962, is a detailed list of Pope's writings.

A good critical introduction to the poems is Geoffrey Tillotson, *On the Poetry of Pope*, 2nd ed., 1950; and Tillotson, *Pope and Human Nature*, 1958, throws light on a difficult subject. David B. Morris, *Alexander Pope: The Genius of Sense*, 1984, offers fine criticism of individual poems. Reuben A. Brower, *Alexander Pope: The Poetry of Allusion*, 1959, is an enlightening study of Pope's lifelong habit of adapting phrases, images, and ideas from earlier poets, especially those of classical antiquity. Much information is gathered up in Robert W. Rogers, *The Major Satires of Alexander Pope*, 1955. Austin Warren, *Alexander Pope as Critic and Humanist*, 1929, is dated but still useful. Aubrey Williams has analyzed *Pope's Dunciad*, 1955, and John Sitter, *The Poetry of Pope's Dunciad*, 1971. Several essays on Pope are included in Maynard Mack, *Collected in Himself*, 1982. Mack has also edited *Essential Articles for the Study of Alexander Pope*, 1964, and with James Winn, *Pope: Recent Essays*, 1980. *The Enduring Legacy*, ed. G. S. Rousseau and Pat Rogers, 1988, collects new essays on Pope, and Bran Hammond has edited *Pope*, 1996, a critical reader.

Popular Ballads

The great ballad collection is that of F. J. Child, *The English and Scottish Popular Ballads*, 1882, more available in the somewhat abridged edition by H. C. Sargent and G. L. Kittredge, 1904. Selections will be found in *The Faber Book of Ballads*, ed. M. J. C. Hodgart, 1965, and *The Oxford Book of Ballads*, ed. James Kinsley, 1969. For general discussion, see F. B. Gummere, *The Popular Ballads*, 1907; G. H. Gerould, *The Ballad of Tradition*, 1932; W. J. Entwistle, *European Balladry*, 1939; M. J. C. Hodgart, *The Ballads*, 1950; and David Buchan, *The Ballad and the Folk*, 1972.

Matthew Prior

The complete critical edition of Prior is *Literary Works*, ed. H. B. Wright and M. K. Spears, 2 vols., 1971. The older and less complete edition in two volumes by A. R. Waller, 1905, 1907, is useful. F. M. Rippy, *Matthew Prior*, 1986, is a good brief survey. The best biography is Charles K. Eves, *Matthew Prior, Poet and Diplomatist*, 1939.

John Wilmot, Second Earl of Rochester

There are good editions of the complete works, by Frank Ellis, 1994, and of the poems, by David Vieth, 1968, and Keith Walker, 1984. Since Vivian de Sola Pinto's biography, *Enthusiast in Wit*, 1962, new source materials have been added by John Adlard, *The Debt to Pleasure*, 1974, and Jeremy Treglown's edition of the *Letters*, 1980. Dustin Griffin, *Satires against Man*, 1973; David Farley-Hills, *Rochester's Poetry*, 1978; and Marianne Thormählen, *Roches-*

ter: *The Poems in Context*, 1993, are good critical studies. A collection of *Critical Essays*, 1988, was edited by Vieth.

Ignatius Sancho

Most information about Sancho derives from Joseph Jekyll's preface to *Letters of the Late Ignatius Sancho, an African*, 2 vols., 1782. That preface is included in a fine modern edition by Paul Edwards and Polly Rewt, *The Letters of Ignatius Sancho*, 1994. Sancho's musical compositions have been collected in a facsimile edition by Josephine Wright, 1981. A series of essays, *Ignatius Sancho: An African Man of Letters*, 1997, derive from an exhibition at the National Portrait Gallery in London. Sandiford and Fryer (see **Equiano**) provide a context for Sancho.

Christopher Smart

The standard edition is Smart's *Poetical Works*, ed. Karina Williamson and Marcus Walsh, 6 vols., 1980–96. There is a useful one-volume selection by R. E. Brittain, 1950. On the life, Christopher Devlin, *Poor Kit Smart*, 1961, should be supplemented by Arthur Sherbo, *Christopher Smart, Scholar of the University*, 1967. Betty Rizzo and Robert Mahony have edited *The Annotated Letters of Christopher Smart* (1991). Good critical studies are Moira Dearnley, *The Poetry of Christopher Smart*, 1968, and Harriet Guest, *A Form of Sound Words: The Religious Poetry of Christopher Smart*, 1989. Geoffrey Hartman includes interesting essays on Smart and Collins in *Beyond Formalism*, 1970, and *The Fate of Reading*, 1975.

Sir Richard Steele

See **Joseph Addison and Sir Richard Steele.**

Laurence Sterne

The standard biography is Arthur Cash, *Laurence Sterne*, 2 vols., 1975–86. Lewis P. Curtis edited the letters, 1935, and wrote *The Politics of Laurence Sterne*, 1929. A scholarly edition of the works has been in progress since 1978, ed. Melvyn New et al.; the first three volumes are devoted to *Tristram Shandy*, the following two to sermons. The Norton Critical Edition of *Tristram Shandy*, ed. Howard Anderson, 1980, includes important critical essays. Full-length studies of *Tristram Shandy* include a good introduction by Max Byrd, 1985, and William Holtz, *Image and Immortality*, 1970, which draws interesting connections between Sterne and Hogarth. Gardner Stout's edition of *A Sentimental Journey*, 1967, is excellent.

Jonathan Swift

Irvin Ehrenpreis's standard, comprehensive biography, *Swift: The Man, His Works, and the Age*, consists of three volumes: *Mr. Swift and His Contemporaries*, 1962, *Dr. Swift*, 1967, and *Dean Swift*, 1983. J. A. Downie, *Jonathan Swift, Political Writer*, 1984, and David Nokes, *Jonathan Swift, A Hypocrite Reversed*, 1985, are good introductions to

the life and writings. Louis A. Landa, *Swift and the Church of Ireland*, 1954, is a valuable special study.

The standard edition of the poems is by Sir Harold Williams, 2 vols., 1937, rev., 1958. Pat Rogers's edition of Swift's *Complete Poems*, 1983, is reliable and less expensive. Herbert Davis has edited the prose works in fourteen volumes, 1939–68. Swift's *Correspondence* was edited by Williams, 5 vols., 1963–65. Other distinguished editions include Davis, *The Drapier's Letters*, 1935; Williams, *Journal to Stella*, 2 vols., 1948; A. C. Guthkelch and D. Nichol Smith, *A Tale of a Tub*, 2nd ed., 1958; and Frank H. Ellis, *A Discourse of the Contests and Dissentions between the Nobles and the Commons in Athens and Rome*, 1967. For the Norton Critical Editions series, Robert Greenberg has edited *Gulliver's Travels*, rev. 1971, and with W. B. Piper, *The Writings of Jonathan Swift*, 1973.

Among the abundant critical studies, the student should find especially helpful Ricardo Quintana, *The Mind and Art of Jonathan Swift*, 1936, and *Swift: An Introduction*, 1955. Arthur Case, *Four Essays on Gulliver's Travels*, Herbert Davis, *Jonathan Swift: Essays on his Satire and Other Studies*, 1964; C. J. Rawson, *Gulliver and the Gentle Reader*, 1973; and Robert Phiddian, *Swift's Parodies*, 1995, are all useful. After long neglect, Swift's poems have attracted a wealth of criticism; some of the best has been collected by David Vieth, *Essential Articles for the study of Jonathan Swift's Poetry*, 1984. Three books by Robert C. Elliott, *The Power of Satire*, 1960, *The Shape of Utopia*, 1970, and *The Literary Persona*, 1982, contain interesting chapters on Swift; so do Edward Said, *The World, the Text, and the Critic*, 1983, and Carol Houlihan Flynn, *The Body in Swift and Defoe*, 1990. Two good collections of essays are *Jonathan Swift: A Critical Anthology*, ed. Denis Donoghue, 1971, and *The Character of Swift's Satire*, ed. C. J. Rawson, 1983.

James Thomson

The standard biography is James Sambrook, *James Thomson, 1740–1748: A Life*, 1991. A. D. McKillop edited Thomson's *Letters and Documents*, 1958, which contains much about Thomson's friends and literary circle, and *The Castle of Indolence and Other Poems*, 1961. There are good notes in Sambrook's edition of *The Seasons and The Castle of Indolence*, 1972, and Sambrook has edited scholarly texts of *The Seasons*, 1981, and *Liberty, The Castle of Indolence, and Other Poems*, 1986. McKillop, *The Background of Thomson's Seasons*, 1942, is valuable. Ralph Cohen, *The Art of Discrimination*, 1964, uses responses to *The Seasons* to illustrate the development of critical theory; and Cohen has added a critical study, *The Unfolding of the Seasons*, 1970. Patricia M. Spacks, *The Poetry of Vision*, 1966, contains chapters on Thomson, Collins, Gray, Smart, and Cowper. John Barrell, *English Literature in History 1730–80*, 1983, examines the social implications of Thomson's poems.

Geographic Nomenclature: England, Great Britain, The United Kingdom

The British Isles refers to the prominent group of islands off the northwest coast of Europe, especially to the two largest, **Great Britain** and **Ireland**. At present these comprise two sovereign states: **The Republic of Ireland**, or **Eire**, and **The United Kingdom of Great Britain and Northern Ireland**—known for short as **The United Kingdom** or **The U.K.** Most of the smaller islands are part of **The U.K.** but a few, like the **Isle of Man** and the tiny **Channel Islands**, are very largely independent. **The U.K.** is often loosely referred to as "**Britain**" or "**Great Britain**" and is sometimes simply called "**England**." The latter usage, though technically inaccurate and occasionally confusing, is common among Englishmen as well as foreigners, though, for obvious reasons, it is rarely heard among the inhabitants of the other countries of **The U.K.—Scotland, Wales,** and **Northern Ireland** (sometimes called **Ulster**). England is by far the most populous part of the kingdom, as well as the seat of its capital, London.

From the first to the fifth century C.E. most of what is now **England** and **Wales** was a province of the Roman Empire called **Britain** (in Latin, **Britannia**). After the fall of Rome, much of the island was invaded and settled by peoples from northern Germany and Denmark speaking what we now call Old English. They are collectively known as the Anglo-Saxons, and the word **England** is related to the first element of their name. By the time of the Norman Conquest (1066) most of the kingdoms founded by the Anglo-Saxons and subsequent Viking invaders had coalesced into the kingdom of **England**, which, in the latter Middle Ages, conquered and largely absorbed the neighboring Celtic kingdom of **Wales**. In 1603 James VI of **Scotland** inherited the island's other throne as James I of **England**, and for the next hundred years—except for the brief period of Puritan rule—**Scotland** and **England** (with **Wales**) were two kingdoms under a single king. In 1707 the Act of Union welded them together as **The United Kingdom of Great Britain**, which, upon the incorporation of **Ireland** in 1801, became **The United Kingdom of Great Britain and Ireland**. With the division of Ireland and the establishment of **The Irish Free State** after World War I, this name was modified to its present form. In 1949 **The Irish Free State** became **The Republic of Ireland**; and in 1997 **Scotland** voted to restore the separate parliament it had relinquished in 1707, without, however, ceasing to be part of **The United Kingdom**.

The **British Isles** are further divided into counties, which in **Great Britain** are also known as shires. This word, with its vowel shortened in pronunciation, forms the suffix in the names of many counties, such as **Yorkshire, Wiltshire, Somersetshire**.

The Latin names **Britannia (Britain), Caledonia (Scotland),** and **Hibernia (Ireland)** are sometimes used in poetic diction; so too is **Britain**'s ancient Celtic name, **Albion**. Because of its accidental resemblance to *albus* (Latin for "white"), **Albion** is especially associated with the chalk cliffs which seem to gird much of the English coast like defensive walls.

The British Empire took its name from **The British Isles** because it was created not only by the **English** but by the **Irish, Scots,** and **Welsh**, as well as by civilians and servicemen from other constituent countries of the Empire.

British Money

Since 1971, British money has been calculated on the decimal system, with 100 pence to the pound; the pound has fluctuated from a bit more than 2 American dollars to virtual parity—whatever dollars may be worth. Before 1971, the pound consisted of 20 shillings, each containing 12 pence, making 240 pence to the pound. In paper money the change has not been great; 5- and 10-pound notes constitute the mass of bills under both the old and the new systems; nowadays, in addition, 20- and 50-pound notes have been added. But in the smaller coinage the change has been considerable and the simplification remarkable. Most notable is the abolition of the shilling, which goes into retirement now with the mark (worth in its day two-thirds of a pound or 13 shillings 4 pence) and the angel (once 10 shillings but replaced by the 10-shilling note, now in its turn abolished). The guinea, an oddity of the old currency, amounted to a pound and a shilling; though it has not been minted since 1813, a very few quality items or prestige awards (like horse races) may still be quoted in guineas. Colloquially, a pound was (and is) called a quid; a shilling a bob; sixpence a tanner; a penny, half-penny, or farthing, a copper. The common signs were £ for pound, s. for shilling, d. for a penny (from Latin *denarius*). A sum would normally be written £2.19.3, i.e., 2 pounds, 19 shillings, 3 pence. In Joyce's *Ulysses*, that is Leopold Bloom's budget for June 16, 1904. In new currency, it would be about £2.96.

Old	New
1 pound note	1 pound coin (or note in Scotland)
10 shilling (half-pound note)	50 pence
5 shilling (crown)	
	20 pence
2½ shilling (half crown)	
2 shilling (florin)	10 pence
1 shilling	5 pence
6 pence	
2½ pence	1 penny
2 pence	
1 penny	
½ penny	
¼ penny (farthing)	

What the pound was worth at any point in history is ever easy to state. In the first part of the twentieth century, 1 pound equaled about 5 American dollars; but those dollars bought three or four times what they would today. Historians sometimes attempt to calculate the value of the pound in terms of the goods and services it would purchase, but these too vary radically with special circumstances such as wars and poor harvests. Nevertheless, it is clear that money used to be worth much more than it is now. In the early sixteenth century, according to Hugh Latimer, people would say, "Oh, he's a rich man, he's worth £500." Four centuries later, Virginia Woolf argued that £500 a year (along with a room of one's own) was the bare minimum necessary for a woman to be able to write. Whatever Latimer meant by "rich," or Woolf by "necessary," it is clear that the value of the pound had declined drastically over this period, as it has continued to do in the course of the twentieth century. In Britain today, a worker on minimum wage earns more than £500 a month, an income associated with severe poverty.

In the Anglo-Saxon period, the silver penny was the biggest coin in general circulation; 4 of them would buy a sheep. Peasants and craftsmen before the Black Death of the fourteenth century made at most 2 or 3 pence a day—an annual income of £3 or £4; after the onset of the plague, wages nearly doubled, due to the shortage of laborers. Throughout the medieval period, kings and commoners worried less about inflation than about the debasement of the silver currency. In 1124, dozens of mint-masters had their right hands chopped off on Christmas Day for issuing inferior coinage. In the early sixteenth century, under Henry VIII and his son Edward VI, the silver content of coins fell as low as 25 percent. Elizabeth I considered the revaluation of the silver coinage to be one of her greatest achievements as queen. Nevertheless, her reign was marked by sustained inflation of prices, caused in part by the influx of gold and silver from the New World, and in part by the rising population.

In the Elizabethan era, admission to the public theaters cost a penny for those who stood throughout the performance. Playwrights were paid about £6 for each play, so to make a living a writer had to be prolific (or, like Shakespeare, own shares in the theater company). In the same period, 40 pounds a year in independent income (generally rent from lands) was the minimum requirement for a justice of the peace; it marked the threshold of gentry status and was also the sum fixed by King James I at which a man could be forced to accept knighthood (paying a fee to the crown). In 1661, following further inflation, Samuel Pepys calculated his worth at a modest £650 just after he had begun working for the navy; five years later, that good bourgeois was worth more than £6000, and his annual income was about £3000. Of course, he was working for most of this income. Pepys was a rising official and would become a very important one; but he never achieved a title or even knighthood because the smell of commerce had never been washed from his money by possession of land.

Various writers provide examples of the incomes of rich and poor in the eighteenth and nineteenth centuries. Joseph Andrews (in Fielding's novel, published 1742) worked as a footman in the house of Lady Booby for £8 a year; in addition, he got his room, board, and livery, plus the occasional tip. Among the comfortable classes, Mr. Bennet of Jane Austen's *Price and Prejudice* (1813) enjoyed an income of £2000 a year (with a family of five nonearning females to support), while Mr. Darcy had close to £10,000, nearing the level of the aristocracy. In his deepest degradation David Copperfield (of Dickens's 1850 novel) worked in the warehouse of Murdstone & Grinby for 6 or 7 shillings a week (£15 to £18 a year). Mr. Murdstone paid extra for his lodging and laundry, but even so the boy was bitterly impoverished, though he had only himself to feed. When his father died, his mother was thought to be pretty well taken care of with £105 a year, less than £9 per month. Even in 1888, Annie Besant reports workers in Bryant and May's match factory made 4 to 9 shillings a week and paid for their own lodging—this, in the words of Ada Nield Chew, was not a living wage, but "a lingering, dying wage." Far removed from this world is Jack Worthing in Wilde's comedy *The Importance of Being Earnest* (1895), who receives £7000 or £8000 a year from investments and has a country house with about fifteen hundred acres attached to it, though it yields no income worth talking about.

While incomes have risen enormously over the centuries, and the value of the pound declined accordingly, the gap between rich and poor has remained. So too has the gap between the country and the city: London has always been very expensive, and elsewhere a small income goes further. To a large extent, one's position in terms of class and geography determines not only what money can buy but what it means.

We have only to contrast Jack Worthing's vague estimate of his income with the factory workers' exact sense of the value of a shilling. As Woolf acknowledged, having a purse with the power "to breed ten-shilling notes automatically," changes one's view of money and of the world. Perhaps it is because British currency has been so important in shaping people's views of themselves and their society that many Britons are reluctant to let it go. The question of whether the United Kingdom should relinquish the pound and the penny to join the single European currency (the Euro) is a matter of fierce and prolonged debate. For some, the pound, far more than the flag, is an enduring symbol of the nation. Whether or not one holds this view, it can at least be said that over the centuries the pound has undergone as many crises and transformations as the nation itself.

The British Baronage

The English monarchy is in principle hereditary, though at times during the Middle Ages the rules were subject to dispute. In general, authority passes from father to eldest surviving son, from daughters in order of seniority if there is no son, to a brother if there are no children, and in default of direct descendants to collateral lines (cousins, nephews, nieces) in order of closeness. There have been breaks in the order of succession (1066, 1399, 1688), but so far as possible the usurpers have always sought to paper over the break with a legitimate, i.e., a hereditary claim. When a queen succeeds to the throne and takes a husband, he does not become king unless he is in the line of blood succession; rather, he is named prince consort, as Albert was to Victoria. He may father kings, but is not one himself.

The original Saxon nobles were the king's thanes, ealdormen, or earls, who provided the king with military service and counsel in return for booty, gifts, or landed estates. William the Conqueror, arriving from France, where feudalism was fully developed, considerably expanded this group. In addition, as the king distributed the lands of his new kingdom, he also distributed dignities to men who became known collectively as "the baronage." "Baron" in its root meaning signifies simply "man," and barons were the king's men. As the title was common, a distinction was early made between greater and lesser barons, the former gradually assuming loftier and more impressive titles. The first English "duke" was created in 1337; the title of "marquess," or "marquis" (pronounced "markwis"), followed in 1385, and "viscount" ("vyekount") in 1440. Though "earl" is the oldest title of all, it now comes between a marquess and a viscount in order of dignity and precedence, and the old term "baron" now designates a rank just below viscount. "Baronets" were created in 1611 as a means of raising revenue for the crown (the title could be purchased for about £1000); they are marginal nobility and do not sit in the House of Lords.

Kings and queens are addressed as "Your Majesty," princes and princesses as "Your Highness," the other hereditary nobility as "My Lord" or "Your Lordship." Peers receive their titles either by inheritance (like Lord Byron, the sixth baron of that line) or from the monarch (like Alfred Lord Tennyson, created first Baron Tennyson by Victoria). The children, even of a duke, are commoners unless they are specifically granted some other title or inherit their father's title from him. A peerage can be forfeited by act of attainder, as for example when a lord is convicted of treason; and, when forfeited, or lapsed for lack of a successor, can be bestowed on another family. Thus Robert Cecil was made in 1605 first earl of Salisbury in the third creation, the first creation dating from 1149, the second from 1337, the title having been in abeyance since 1539. Titles descend by right of succession and do not depend on tenure of land; thus, a title does not always indicate where a lord dwells or holds power. Indeed, noble titles do not always refer to a real place at all. At Prince Edward's marriage in 1999, the queen created him earl of Wessex, although the old kingdom of Wessex has had no political existence since the Anglo-Saxon period, and the name was all but forgotten until it was resurrected by Thomas Hardy as the setting of his novels. (This is perhaps but one of many ways in which the world of the aristocracy increasingly resembles the realm of literature.)

The king and queen Prince and princess	(These are all of the royal line.)
Duke and duchess Marquess and marchioness Earl and countess Viscount and viscountess Baron and baroness Baronet and lady	(These may or may not be of the royal line, but are ordinarily remote from the succession.)

Scottish peers sat in the parliament of Scotland, as English peers did in the parliament of England, till at the Act of Union (1707) Scots peers were granted sixteen seats in the English House of Lords, to be filled by election. Similarly, Irish peers, when the Irish parliament was abolished in 1801, were granted the right to elect twenty-eight of their number to the House of Lords in Westminster. (Now that the Republic of Ireland is a separate nation, of course, this no longer applies.) The House of Lords still retains some power to influence or delay legislation. But this upper house is now being reformed. All or most of the hereditary peers are to be expelled, while recipients of nonhereditary Life Peerages will remain and vote as before.

Below the peerage the chief title of honor is "knight." Knighthood, which is not hereditary, is generally a reward for services rendered. A knight (Sir John Black) is addressed, using his first name, as "Sir John"; his wife, using the last name, is "Lady Black"—unless she is the daughter of an earl or nobleman of higher rank, in which case she will be "Lady Arabella." The female equivalent of a knight bears the title of "Dame."

Though the word itself comes from the Anglo-Saxon *cniht*, there seems to be some doubt as to whether knighthood amounted to much before the arrival of the Normans. The feudal system required military service as a condition of land tenure, and a man who came to serve his king at the head of an army of tenants required a title of authority and badges of identity—hence the title of knighthood and the coat of arms. During the Crusades, when men were far removed from their land (or had even sold it in order to go on crusade), more elaborate forms of fealty sprang up that soon expanded into orders of knighthood. The Templars, Hospitallers, Knights of the Teutonic Order, Knights of Malta, and Knights of the Golden Fleece were but a few of these companionships; not all of them were available at all times in England.

Gradually, with the rise of centralized government and the decline of feudal tenures, military knighthood became obsolete, and the rank largely honorific; sometimes, as under James I, it degenerated into a scheme of the royal government for making money. For hundreds of years after its establishment in the fourteenth century, the Order of the Garter was the only English order of knighthood, an exclusive courtly companionship. Then, during the late seventeenth, the eighteenth, and the nineteenth centuries, a number of additional orders were created, with names such as the Thistle, Saint Patrick, the Bath, Saint Michael and Saint George, plus a number of special Victorian and Indian orders. They retain the terminology, ceremony, and dignity of knighthood, but the military implications are vestigial.

Although the British Empire now belongs to history, appointments to the Order of the British Empire continue to be conferred for services to that empire at home or abroad. Such honors (commonly referred to as "gongs") are granted by the monarch in her New Year's and Birthday lists, but the decisions are now made by the government in power. In recent years there have been efforts to popularize and democratize the dispensation of honors, with recipients including rock stars and actors. But this does not prevent large sectors of British society from regarding both knighthood and the peerage as largely irrelevant to modern life.

The Royal Lines of England and Great Britain

England

SAXONS AND DANES

Egbert, king of Wessex	802–839
Ethelwulf, son of Egbert	839–858
Ethelbald, son of Ethelwulf	858–860
Ethelbert, second son of Ethelwulf	860–866
Ethelred I, third son of Ethelwulf	866–871
Alfred the Great, fourth son of Ethelwulf	871–899
Edward the Elder, son of Alfred	899–924
Athelstan the Glorious, son of Edward	924–940
Edmund I, third son of Edward	940–946
Edred, fourth son of Edward	946–955
Edwy the Fair, son of Edmund	955–959
Edgar the Peaceful, second son of Edmund	959–975
Edward the Martyr, son of Edgar	975–978 (murdered)
Ethelred II, the Unready, second son of Edgar	978–1016
Edmund II, Ironside, son of Ethelred II	1016–1016
Canute the Dane	1016–1035
Harold I, Harefoot, natural son of Canute	1035–1040
Hardecanute, son of Canute	1040–1042
Edward the Confessor, son of Ethelred II	1042–1066
Harold II, brother-in-law of Edward	1066–1066 (died in battle)

HOUSE OF NORMANDY

William I the Conqueror	1066–1087
William II, Rufus, third son of William I	1087–1100 (shot from ambush)
Henry I, Beauclerc, youngest son of William I	1100–1135

HOUSE OF BLOIS

Stephen, son of Adela, daughter of William I	1135–1154

HOUSE OF PLANTAGENET

Henry II, son of Geoffrey Plantagenet by Matilda, daughter of Henry I	1154–1189
Richard I, Coeur de Lion, son of Henry II	1189–1199
John Lackland, son of Henry II	1199–1216
Henry III, son of John	1216–1272
Edward I, Longshanks, son of Henry III	1272–1307
Edward II, son of Edward I	1307–1327
Edward III of Windsor, son of Edward II	1327–1377
Richard II, grandson of Edward III	1377–1400

HOUSE OF LANCASTER

Henry IV, son of John of Gaunt, son of Edward III	1399–1413
Henry V, Prince Hal, son of Henry IV	1413–1422
Henry VI, son of Henry V	1422–1471 (deposed)

HOUSE OF YORK

Edward IV, great-great-grandson of Edward III	1461–1483
Edward V, son of Edward IV	1483–1483 (murdered)
Richard III, Crookback	1483–1485 (died in battle)

HOUSE OF TUDOR

Henry VII, married daughter of Edward IV	1485–1509
Henry VIII, son of Henry VII	1509–1547
Edward VI, son of Henry VIII	1547–1553
Mary I, "Bloody," daughter of Henry VIII	1553–1558
Elizabeth I, daughter of Henry VIII	1558–1603

HOUSE OF STUART

James I (James VI of Scotland)	1603–1625
Charles I, son of James I	1625–1649 (executed)

COMMONWEALTH & PROTECTORATE

Council of State	1649–1653
Oliver Cromwell, Lord Protector	1653–1658
Richard Cromwell, son of Oliver	1658–1660 (resigned)

HOUSE OF STUART (RESTORED)

Charles II, son of Charles I	1660–1685
James II, second son of Charles I	1685–1688

(INTERREGNUM, 11 DECEMBER 1688 TO 13 FEBRUARY 1689)

William III of Orange, by Mary, daughter of Charles I	1685–1701
and Mary II, daughter of James II	–1694
Anne, second daughter of James II	1702–1714

Great Britain

HOUSE OF HANOVER

George I, son of Elector of Hanover and Sophia, granddaughter of James I	1714–1727
George II, son of George I	1727–1760
George III, grandson of George II	1760–1820
George IV, son of George III	1820–1830
William IV, third son of George III	1830–1837
Victoria, daughter of Edward, fourth son of George III	1837–1901

HOUSE OF SAXE-COBURG AND GOTHA

Edward VII, son of Victoria	1901–1910

HOUSE OF WINDSOR (NAME ADOPTED 17 JULY 1917)

George V, second son of Edward VII	1910–1936
Edward VIII, eldest son of George V	1936–1936 (abdicated)
George VI, second son of George V	1936–1952
Elizabeth II, daughter of George VI	1952–

Religions in England

Religious distinctions and denominations are important in British social history, hence deeply woven into the nation's literature. The numerous (over three hundred) British churches and sects divide along a scale from high to low, depending on the amount of authority they give to the church or the amount of liberty they concede to the individual conscience. At one end of the scale is the Roman Catholic Church, asserting papal infallibility, universal jurisdiction, and the supreme importance of hierarchy as guide and intercessor. For political and social reasons, Catholicism struck deep roots in Ireland but in England was the object of prolonged, bitter hatred on the part of Protestants from the Reformation through the nineteenth century. The Established English (Anglican) Episcopal church has been the official national church since the sixteenth century; it enjoys the support (once direct and exclusive, now indirect and peripheral) of the national government. Its creed is defined by Thirty-Nine Articles, but these are intentionally vague, so there are numerous ways of adhering to the Church of England. Roughly and intermittently, the chief classes of Anglicans have been known as High Church (with its highest portion calling itself Anglo-Catholic); Broad Church, or Latitudinarian (when they get so broad that they admit anyone believing in God, they may be known as Deists, or some may leave the church altogether and be known as Unitarians); and Low Church, whose adherents may stay in the English church and yet come close to shaking hands with Presbyterians or Methodists. These various groups may be arranged, from the High down to the Low Church, in direct relation to the amount of ritual each prefers and in the degree of authority conceded to the upper clergy—and in inverse relation to the importance ascribed to a saving faith directly infused by God into an individual conscience.

All English Protestants who decline to subscribe to the English established church are classed as Dissenters or Nonconformists; for a time in the sixteenth and seventeenth centuries, they were also known as Puritans. (Nowadays, though Puritanism has less distinct theological meaning, it marks a distinct character type; because of his passionate emphasis on individual conscience and moral economy, Bernard Shaw was a prototypical Puritan.) The Presbyterians model their church government on that established by John Calvin in the Swiss city of Geneva. It has no bishops, and therefore is more democratic for the clergy; but it gains energy by associating lay elders with clergymen in matters of social discipline and tends to be strict with the ungodly. From its first reformation the Scottish Kirk was fixed on the Presbyterian model. During the civil wars of the seventeenth century, a great many sects sprang up on the left wing of the Presbyterians, most of them touched by Calvinism but some rebelling against it; a few of these still survive. The Independents became our modern Congregationalists; the Quakers are still Quakers, as Baptists are still Baptists, though multiply divided. But many of the sects flourished and perished within the space of a few years. Among these now vanished groups were the Shakers (though a few groups still exist in America), the Seekers, the Ranters, the Anabaptists, the Muggletonians, the Fifth Monarchy Men, the Family of Love, the Sweet Singers of Israel, and many others, forgotten by all except scholars. During the eighteenth and nineteenth centuries, new sects arose, supplanting old ones; the Methodists, under John and Charles Wesley, became numerous and important, taking root particularly in Wales. (The three "subject" nationalities, Ireland, Scotland, and Wales, thus turned three different ways to avoid the Anglican church.) With the passage of time a small number of Swedenborgians sprang up, followers of the Swedish mystic Emanuel Swedenborg—to be followed by the Plymouth Brethren, Christian Scientists, Jehovah's Witnesses, and countless other nineteenth-century groups. All these sects constantly grow, shrink, split, and occasionally disappear as they succeed or fail in attracting new converts.

Within the various churches and sects, independent of them all but amazingly persistent, there has always survived a stream of esoteric or hermetic thought—a belief in occult powers, and sometimes in magic also, exemplified by the pseudo-sciences of astrology and alchemy but taking many other forms as well. From the mythical Egyptian seer Hermes Trismegistus through Paracelsus, Cornelius Agrippa, Giordano Bruno, Jakob Boehme, the society of Rosicrucians, and a hundred other shadowy figures, the line can be traced to William Blake and William Butler Yeats, who both in their different ways brought hermetic Protestantism close to its ultimate goal, a mystic church of a single consciousness, poised within its mind-elaborated cosmos.

Christianity is not, of course, the only religion present on the British Isles. The few Jews in medieval England were regarded as resident aliens, as were those in other European countries. In 1290 all English Jews who refused baptism were expelled from the kingdom, and officially, there were no Jews living in England between that time and the mid-1650s, when Cromwell encouraged Jewish merchants to settle in London. A considerable number of east European Jews emigrated to England in the first half of the twentieth century (many as refugees), but the country's Jewish population as a whole remains quite small (less than half a million). Hardly any Muslims or Hindus lived in the U.K. before the dissolution of the Empire shortly after World War II. Today both religions have a large and growing representation among ex-colonial immigrants and their children.

Poetic Forms and
Literary Terminology

Systematic literary theory and criticism in English began in the sixteenth century, at a time when the standard education for upper-class students emphasized the study of the classical languages and literatures. As a consequence, the English words that were introduced to describe meter, figures of speech, and literary genres often derive from Latin and Greek roots.

RHYTHM AND METER

Verse is generally distinguished from prose as a more compressed and more regularly rhythmic form of statement. This approximate truth underlines the importance of **meter** in poetry, as the means by which rhythm is measured and described.

In Latin and Greek, meter was established on a **quantitative** basis, by the regular alternation of long and short syllables (that is, syllables classified according to the time taken to pronounce them). Outside of a few experiments (and the songs of Thomas Campion), this system has never proved congenial to Germanic languages such as English, which distinguish, instead, between **stressed** and **unstressed,** or accented and unaccented syllables. Two varieties of accented stress may be distinguished. On the one hand, there is the natural stress pattern of words themselves; *sýllable* is accented on the first syllable, *deplórable* on the second, and so on. Then there is the sort of stress that indicates rhetorical emphasis. If the sentence "You went to Greece?" is given a pronounced accent on the last word, it implies "Greece (of all places)?" If the accent falls on the first word, it implies "you (of all people)?" The meter of poetry—that is, its rhythm—is ordinarily built up out of a regular recurrence of accents, whether established as **word accents** or **rhetorical accents;** once started, it has (like all rhythm) a tendency to persist in the reader's mind.

The unit that is repeated to give steady rhythm to a poem is called a **foot;** in English it usually consists of accented and unaccented syllables in one of five fairly simple patterns:

The **iambic foot** (or **iamb**) consists of an unstressed followed by a stressed syllable, as in *uníte, repeát,* or *insíst.* Most English verse falls naturally into the iambic pattern.

The **trochaic foot** (**trochee**) inverts this order; it is a stressed followed by an unstressed syllable—for example, *únit, réaper,* or *ínstant.*

The **anapestic foot (anapest)** consists of two unstressed syllables followed by a stressed syllable, as in *intercéde, disarránged,* or *Cameróon.*

The **dactylic foot (dactyl)** consists of a stressed syllable followed by two unstressed syllables, as in *Wáshington, Écuador,* or *ápplejack.*

The **spondaic foot (spondee)** consists of two successive stressed syllables, as in *heartbreak, headline,* or *Kashmir.*

In all the examples above, word accent and the quality of the metrical foot coincide exactly. But the metrical foot may well consist of several words, or, on the other hand, one word may well consist of several metrical feet. *Phótolithógraphy* consists of two dactyls in a single word; *dárk and with spóts on it,* though it consists of six words rather than one, is also two dactyls. When we read a piece of poetry with the intention of discovering its underlying metrical pattern, we are said to **scan** it—that is, we go through it line by line, indicating by conventional signs which are the accented and which the unaccented syllables within the feet. We also count the number of feet in each line; a line is, formally, also called a **verse** (from Latin *versus,* which means one "row" of metrical feet). Verse lengths are conventionally described in terms derived from the Greek:

Monometer: one foot (of rare occurrence)
Dimeter: two feet (also rare)
Trimeter: three feet
Tetrameter: four feet
Pentameter: five feet
Hexameter: six feet (six iambic feet make what is called an **Alexandrine**)
Heptameter: seven feet (also rare)

Samuel Johnson wrote a little parody of simpleminded poets which can be scanned this way:

> Ĭ pút mў hát ŭpón mў héad
> Ănd wálked ĭntó thĕ Stránd
> Ănd thére Ĭ mét ănóthĕr mán
> Whŏse hát wăs ín hĭs hánd.

The poem is iambic in rhythm, alternating tetrameter and trimeter in the length of the verse-lines. The fact that it scans so nicely is, however, no proof that it is good poetry. Quite the contrary. Many of poetry's most subtle effects are achieved by establishing an underlying rhythm and then varying it by means of a whole series of devices, some dramatic and expressive, others designed simply to lend variety and interest to the verse. A well-known sonnet of Shakespeare's (*116*) begins,

> Let me not to the marriage of true minds
> Admit impediments. Love is not love
> Which alters when it alteration finds,
> Or bends with the remover to remove.

It is possible to read the first line of this poem as mechanical iambic pentameter:

Lĕt mé nŏt tó thĕ márriăge óf trŭe mińds

But of course nobody ever reads it that way, except to make a point; read with normal English accent and some sense of what it is saying, the line would form a pattern something like this:

Lét mĕ nŏt tŏ thĕ márriăge ŏf trúe mińds

which is neither pentameter nor in any way iambic. The second line is a little more iambic, but, read expressively also falls short of pentameter:

Ădmít ĭmpédĭmeňts. Lóve ĭs nŏt lóve

Only in the third and fourth lines of the sonnet do we get verses that read as five iambic feet.

The fact is that perfectly regular metrical verse is easy to write and dull to read. Among the devices in common use for varying too regular a pattern are the insertion of a trochaic foot among iambics, especially at the opening of a line, where the soft first syllable of the iambic foot often needs stiffening (see line 1 of the sonnet above); the more or less free addition of extra unaccented syllables; and the use of **caesura,** or strong grammatical pause within a line (conventionally indicated, in scanning, by the sign ||). The second line of the sonnet above is a good example of caesura:

Admit impediments. || Love is not love

The strength of the caesura, and its placing in the line, may be varied to produce striking variations of effect. More broadly, the whole relation between the poem's sound- and rhythm-patterns and its pattern as a sequence of assertions (phrases, clauses, sentences) may be manipulated by the poet. Sometimes the statements fit neatly within the lines, so that each line ends with a strong mark of punctuation; they are then known as **end-stopped lines.** Sometimes the sense flows over the ends of the lines, creating **run-on lines;** this process is also known, from the French, as **enjambment** (literally, "straddling").

End-stopped lines (Marlowe, *Hero and Leander*, lines 45–48):

> So lovely fair was Hero, Venus' nun,
> As Nature wept, thinking she was undone,
> Because she took more from her than she left
> And of such wondrous beauty her bereft.

Run-on lines (Keats, *Endymion* 1.89–93):

> Full in the middle of this pleasantness
> There stood a marble altar, with a tress
> Of flowers budded newly; and the dew
> Had taken fairy fantasies to strew
> Daisies upon the sacred sward, . . .

Following the example of such poets as Blake, Rimbaud, and Whitman, many twentieth-century poets have undertaken to write what is called **free** verse—that is, verse which has neither a fixed metrical foot nor (consequently) a fixed number of feet in its lines, but which depends for its rhythm on a pattern of cadences, or the rise and fall of the voice in utterance, or the pattern indicated to the reader's eye by the breaks between the verse lines. As in traditional versification, free verse is printed in short lines instead of with the continuity of prose; it differs from such versification, however, by the fact that its stressed syllables are not organized into a regular metric sequence.

SENSE AND SOUND

The words of which poetic lines—whether free or traditional—are composed cause them to have different sounds and produce different effects. Polysyllables, being pronounced fast, often cause a line to move swiftly; monosyllables, especially when heavy and requiring distinct accents, may cause it to move heavily, as in Milton's famous line (*Paradise Lost* 2.621):

> Rocks, caves, lakes, fens, bogs, dens, and shades of death

Poetic assertions are often dramatized and reinforced by means of **alliteration**—that is, the use of several nearby words or stressed syllables beginning with the same consonant. When Shakespeare writes (*Sonnet 64*),

> Ruin hath taught me thus to ruminate
> That Time will come and take my love away,

the alliterative *r*'s and rich internal echoes of the first line contrast with the sharp anxiety and directness of the alliterative *t*'s in the second. When Dryden starts *Absalom and Achitophel* with the couplet,

> In pious times, ere priestcraft did begin,
> Before polygamy was made a sin,

the satiric undercutting is strongly reinforced by the triple alliteration that links "*p*ious" with "*p*riestcraft" and "*p*olygamy."

Assonance, or repetition of the same or similar vowel sounds within a passage (usually in accented syllables), also serves to enrich it, as in two lines from Keats's *Ode on Melancholy*:

> For shade to shade will come too drowsily,
> And drown the wakeful anguish of the soul.

It is clear that the round, hollow tones of "drowsily," repeated in "drown" and darkening to the full *o*-sound of "soul," have much to do with the effect of the passage. A related device is **consonance**, or the repetition of a pattern of consonants with changes in the intervening vowels—for example: *linger, longer, languor; rider, reader, raider, ruder.*

The use of words that seem to reproduce the sounds they designate (known as **onomatopoeia**) has been much attempted, from Virgil's galloping horse—

Quadrupedante putrem sonitu quatit ungula campum—

through Tennyson's account, in *The Princess*, of

The moan of doves in immemorial elms,
And murmuring of innumerable bees—

to many poems in the present day.

RHYME AND STANZA

Rhyme consists of a repetition of accented sounds in words, usually those falling at the end of verse lines. If the rhyme sound is the very last syllable of the line (*rebound, sound*), the rhyme is called **masculine**; if the accented syllable is followed by an unaccented syllable (*hounding, bounding*), the rhyme is called **feminine**. Rhymes amounting to three or more syllables, like forced rhymes, generally have a comic effect in English, and have been freely used for this purpose, e.g., by Byron (*intellectual, henpecked-you-all*). Rhymes occurring within a single line are called **internal**; for instance, the Mother Goose rhyme "Mary, Mary, quite contrary," or from Coleridge's *Ancient Mariner* ("We were the first that ever burst / Into that silent sea"). **Eye rhymes** are words used as rhymes that look alike but actually sound different (for example, *alone, done; remove, love*); **off rhymes** (sometimes called **partial, imperfect,** or **slant rhymes**) are occasionally the result of pressing exigencies or lack of skill, but are also, at times, used deliberately by modern poets for special effects. For instance, a poem by Wilfred Owen (*Strange Meeting*) contains such paired words (which Owen called "pararhymes") as *years / yours* or *tigress / progress.*

Blank verse is unrhymed iambic pentameter; until the recent advent of free verse, it was the only unrhymed measure to achieve general popularity in English. Though first used by the earl of Surrey in translating Virgil's *Aeneid*, blank verse was during the sixteenth century employed primarily in plays; *Paradise Lost* was one of the first nondramatic poems in English to use it. But Milton's authority and his success were so great that during the eighteenth and nineteenth centuries blank verse came to be used for a great variety of discursive, descriptive, and philosophical poems—besides remaining the standard metrical form for epics. Thomson's *Seasons*, Cowper's *Task*, Wordsworth's *Prelude*, and Tennyson's *Idylls of the King* were all written in blank verse.

A **stanza** is a recurring unit of a poem, consisting of a number of verses. Certain poems (for example, Dryden's *Alexander's Feast*) have stanzas comprising a variable number of verses, of varying lengths. Others are more regular, and are identified by particular names.

The simplest form of stanza is the **couplet**; it is two lines rhyming together. A single couplet considered in isolation is sometimes called a **distich**; when it expresses a complete thought, ending with a terminal mark of punctuation such as a semicolon or period, it is called a **closed couplet.** The development of very regular end-stopped couplets, their use in so-called heroic tragedies, and their consequent acquisition of the name **heroic couplets** took place for the most part during the mid-seventeenth century. The heroic couplet was the principal form in English neoclassical poems.

Another traditional and challenging form of couplet is the **tetrameter, or four-beat couplet.** All rhymed couplets are hard to manage without monotony; and since, in addition, a four-beat line is hard to divide by caesura without splitting it into two tick-tock dimeters, tetrameter couplets have posed a perpetual challenge to poets, and still provide an admirable finger-exercise for aspiring versifiers. An instance of tetrameter couplets managed with marvelous variety, complexity, and expressiveness is Marvell's *To His Coy Mistress*:

> Thou by the Indian Ganges' side
> Shouldst rubies find; I by the tide
> Of Humber would complain. I would
> Love you ten years before the Flood,
> And you should, if you please, refuse
> Till the conversion of the Jews.

English has not done much with rhymes grouped in threes, but has borrowed from Italian the form known as **terza rima,** in which Dante composed his *Divine Comedy*. This form consists of linked groups of three rhymes according to the following pattern: *aba bcb cdc ded*, etc. Shelley's *Ode to the West Wind* is composed in stanzas of *terza rima*, the poem as a whole ending with a couplet.

Quatrains are stanzas of four lines; the lines usually rhyme alternately, *abab*, or in the second and fourth lines, *abcb*. When they alternate tetrameter and trimeter lines, as in Johnson's little poem about men in hats (above), or as in *Sir Patrick Spens*, they are called **ballad stanza.** Dryden's *Annus Mirabilis* and Gray's *Elegy Written in a Country Churchyard* are in **heroic quatrains;** these rhyme alternately *abab*, and employ five-stress iambic verse throughout. Tennyson used for *In Memoriam* a tetrameter quatrain rhymed *abba*, and FitzGerald translated *The Rubáiyát of Omar Khayyám* into a pentameter quatrain rhymed *aaba*; but these forms have not been widely adopted.

Chaucer's *Troilus and Criseide* is the premier example in English of **rhyme royal,** a seven-line iambic pentameter stanza consisting essentially of a quatrain dovetailed onto two couplets, according to the rhyme scheme *ababbcc* (the fourth line serves both as the final line of the quatrain and as the first line of the first couplet). Closely akin to rhyme royal, but differentiated by an extra *a*-rhyme between the two *b*-rhymes, is **ottava rima,** that is, an eight-line stanza rhyming *abababcc*. As its name suggests, ottava rima is of Italian origin; it was first used in English by Wyatt. Its final couplet, being less prepared for than in rhyme royal, and usually set off as a separate verbal unit, is capable of manifesting a witty snap, for which Byron found good use in *Don Juan*.

The longest and most intricate stanza generally used for narrative purposes in English is that devised by Edmund Spenser for *The Faerie Queene*. The **Spenserian stanza** has nine lines rhyming *ababbcbcc*; the first eight lines are pentameter, the last line an Alexandrine. Slow-moving, intricate of pattern, and very demanding in its rhyme scheme (the *b*-sound recurs four times, the *c*-sound three), the Spenserian stanza has nonetheless appealed widely to poets who seek a rich and complicated metrical form. Keats's *Eve of St. Agnes* and Shelley's *Adonais* are brilliantly successful nineteenth-century examples of its use.

The **sonnet,** originally a stanza of Italian origin that has developed into an independent lyric form, is usually defined nowadays as fourteen lines of iambic pentameter. None of the elements in this definition is absolute and in earlier centuries there were sonnets in hexameters (the first of Sidney's *Astrophil and Stella*), and sonnets of as many as twenty lines (Milton's *On the New Forcers of Conscience*). Most, however, approximate the definition. Most Elizabethan sonnets dealt with love; and some poets, like Sidney, Spenser, and Shakespeare, imitated Petrarch in grouping together their sonnets dealing with a particular lady or situation. The term for these gatherings is **sonnet sequences;** the extent to which they tell a sequential story, and the extent to which such stories are autobiographical, vary greatly. Since Elizabethan times, the sonnet has been applied to a wide range of subject matters—religious, political, satiric, moral, and philosophic.

In blank verse or irregularly rhymed verse, where stanzaic divisions do not exist or are indistinct, the poetry sometimes falls into **verse paragraphs,** which are in effect divisions of sense like prose paragraphs. This division can be clearly seen in Milton's *Lycidas* and *Paradise Lost*. An intermediate form, clearly stanzaic but with stanzas of varying patterns of line-length and rhyme, is illustrated by Spenser's *Epithalamion*; in this instance, the division into stanzas is reinforced by a **refrain,** which is simply a line repeated at the end of each stanza. Ballads also customarily have refrains; for example, the refrain of *Lord Randall* is

> mother, make my bed soon,
> For I'm weary wi' hunting, and fain wald lie down.

FIGURATIVE LANGUAGE

The act of bringing words together into rich and vigorous poetic lines is complex and demanding, chiefly because so many variables require control. There is the "thought" of the lines, their verbal texture, their emotional resonance, the developing perspective of the reader—all these to be managed at once. One of the poet's chief resources toward this end is figurative language. Here, as in matters of meter, one may distinguish a great variety of devices, some of which we use in everyday speech without special awareness of their names and natures. When we say someone eats "like a horse" or "like a bird," we are using a **simile,** that is, a comparison marked out by a specific word of likening—"like" or "as." When we omit the word of comparison but imply a likeness—as in the sentence "That hog has guzzled all the champagne"—we are making use of **metaphor.** The **epic simile,** frequent in epic poetry, is an extended simile in which the thing compared is described as an object in its own right, beyond its point of likeness with the main subject. Milton starts to compare Satan to Leviathan, but concludes his simile with the story of a sailor who moored his ship by mistake, one night, to a whale (*Paradise Lost* 1.200–208). Metaphors and similes have been distinguished according to their special effects; they may be, for instance, violent, comic, degrading, decorative, or ennobling.

When we speak of "forty head of cattle" or ask someone to "lend a hand" with a job, we are using **synecdoche,** a figure that substitutes the part for the whole. When we speak of a statement coming "from the White House," or a man much interested in "the turf," (that is, the race-course), we are using **metonymy,** or the substitution of one term for another with which it is closely associated. **Antithesis** is a device for placing opposing ideas in grammatical parallel, as, for example, in the following passage from Alexander Pope's *Rape of the Lock* (5.25–30), where there are more examples of antithesis than there are lines:

> But since, alas! frail beauty must decay,
> Curled or uncurled, since locks will turn to gray;
> Since painted, or not painted, all shall fade,
> And she who scorns a man must die a maid;
> What then remains but well our power to use,
> And keep good humor still whate'er we lose?

Irony is a verbal device that implies an attitude quite different from (and often opposite to) that which is literally expressed. In Pope's *The Rape of the Lock* (4.131–32), after poor Sir Plume has stammered an incoherent request to return the stolen lock of hair, the Baron answers ironically:

> "It grieves me much," replied the Peer again,
> "Who speaks so well should ever speak in vain."

And when Donne "proves," in *The Canonization,* that he and his mistress are going to found a new religion of love, he seems to be inviting us to take a subtly ironic attitude toward religion as well as love.

Because it is easy to see through, **hyperbole,** or willful exaggeration, is a favorite device of irony—which is not to say that it may not be "serious" as well. When she hears that a young man is "dying for love" of her, a sensible young woman does not accept this statement literally, but it may convey a serious meaning to her nonetheless. The **pun,** or play on words (known to the learned, sometimes, as **paronomasia**), may also be serious or comic in intent; witness, for example, the famous series of puns on Donne's name in his *Hymn to God the Father.* **Oxymoron** is a conjunction of two terms that in ordinary use are contraries or incompatible—for instance, Milton's famous description of hell as containing "darkness visible" (*Paradise Lost* 1.63). A **paradox** is a statement that seems absurd but turns out to have rational meaning after all, usually in some unexpected sense; Donne speaks of fear being great courage and high valor (*Satire* 3, line 16), and turns out to mean that fear of God is greater courage than any earthly bravery. A **conceit** is a far-fetched and unusually elaborate comparison. Writing in the fourteenth century, the Italian poet Petrarch popularized a great number of conceits handy for use in love poetry, and readily adapted by his English imitators. Wyatt, for example, is using **Petrarchan conceits** when he compares love to a warrior, or the lover's state to that of a storm-tossed ship; and a hundred other sonneteers developed the themes of the lady's stony heart, incendiary glances, and so forth. On the other hand, the **metaphysical conceit** was a more intellectualized, many-leveled comparison, giving a strong sense of the poet's ingenuity in overcoming obstacles—for instance, Donne's comparison of separated lovers to the legs of a compass (A *Valediction: Forbidding Mourning*) or Herbert's comparison of devotion to a pulley, in the poem of that name.

Personification (or in the term derived from Latin **prosopopoeia**) is the attribution of human qualities to an inanimate object (for example, the Sea) or an abstract concept (Freedom); a special variety of it is called (in a term of John Ruskin's invention) the **pathetic fallacy**. When we speak of leaves "dancing" or a lake "smiling," we attribute human traits to nonhuman objects. Ruskin thought this was false and therefore "morbid"; modern criticism tends to view the practice as artistically and morally neutral. A more formal and abstract variety of personification is **allegory,** in which a narrative (such as *Pilgrim's Progress*) is constructed by representing general concepts (Faithfulness, Sin, Despair) as persons who act out the plot. A **fable** (like Chaucer's *The Nun's Priest's Tale*) represents beasts behaving like humans; a **parable** is a brief story, or simply an observation, with strong moral application; and an **exemplum** is a story told to illustrate a point in a sermon.

A special series of devices, nearly obsolete today, used to be available to poets who could count on readers trained in the classics. These were the devices of **classical allusion**—that is, reference to the mythology (stories about the actions of gods and other supernatural beings) of the Greeks and Romans. In their simplest form, the classic **myths** used to provide a repertoire of agreeable stage properties, and a convenient shorthand for expressing emotional attitudes. Picturesque creatures like centaurs, satyrs, and sphinxes, heroes and heroines like Hector and Helen, and the whole pantheon of Olympic deities could be used to make ready reference to a great many aspects of human nature. One does not have to explain the problems of a man who is "cleaning the Augean stables"; if he is afflicted with an "Achilles' heel," or is assailing "Hydra-headed difficulties," his state is clear. These descriptive phrases, making **allusion** to mythological stories, suggest in a phrase situations that would normally require cumbersome explanations. But because it used to be taken for granted that the classical mythology was the common possession of all educated readers, the classic myths entered into English literature as early as Chaucer. In poets like Spenser and Milton, classical allusion becomes a kind of enormously learned game, in which the poet seeks to make his points as indirectly as possible. For instance, Spenser writes in the *Epithalamion*, lines 328–29:

> Lyke as when Jove with fayre Alcmena lay,
> When he begot the great Tirynthian groome.

The mere mention of Alcmena in the first line suggests, to the informed reader, Hercules, the son of Jupiter (Jove) by Alcmena. Spenser's problem in the second line is to find a way of referring to him that is neither redundant nor heavy-handed. "Tirynthian" reminds the reader of Hercules' long connection with the city of Tiryns, stretching our minds (as it were) across his whole career; and "groome" compresses references to a man-child, a servant, and a bridegroom, all of which apply to different aspects of Hercules' history. Thus, far from simply avoiding redundancy, Spenser has enriched, for the reader who possesses the classical information, the whole texture of his verse, thought, and feeling.

SCHOOLS

Literary scholars and critics often group together in **schools** writers who share stylistic traits or thematic concerns. Whether they considered themselves a group doesn't much matter; although in some cases—for example, the Imagists or the Beat poets—the writers themselves have identified themselves as belonging to a group. None of the **Romantic poets** knew they were being romantic, although Hazlitt, Shelley, and other writers of the time recognized shared features that they called "the spirit of the age." The followers of Spenser are known as **Spenserians**; they knew they admired and to some extent wrote like Spenser, but didn't realize that made them a group. **Cavalier** poets are set decisively apart from **Metaphysical** poets, though pretty surely none of the two-dozen-odd men involved knew that was what they were. And so with the **Gothic novelists,** and the so-called **Graveyard School** of the eighteenth century; these schools are generally grouped, defined, and named by scholars and critics after the event.

Intellectual affinities have led some writers to be classified under the names of the philosophical schools of Greece and Rome. These are chiefly the **Epicureans,** who specify that the aim of life and the source of value is pleasure; the **Stoics,** who emphasize stern virtue and the dignified endurance of what cannot be avoided; and the **Skeptics,** who doubt that anything can be known for certain. These categories are useful as capsule descriptions, but they aren't very tidy, as they are omissive, overlap one another, and cut across other categories. Dryden is an author strongly tinged with skepticism, but many of his poems suggest an unabashed epicureanism. *The Vanity of Human Wishes*, by Samuel Johnson, is the classic poem in English of stoic philosophy, but it also expresses a particularly strong coloring of Christian humanism.

TERMS OF LITERARY ART

The following section defines frequently used literary terms, especially frequently used terms that are closely related or tend to be mistaken for each other.

Allegory, Symbol, Emblem, Type. Allegory is a narrative in which the agents, and sometimes also the setting, are personified concepts or character-types, and the plot represents a doctrine or thesis. John Bunyan's *Pilgrim's Progress*, for example, allegorizes the Christian doctrine of salvation by narrating how the character named Christian, warned by Evangelist, flees the City of Destruction and makes his laborious way to the Celestial City; en route he meets such characters as Faithful and the Giant Despair, and passes through places like the Slough of Despond and Vanity Fair. A literary **symbol** is the representation of an object or event which has a further range of reference beyond itself. Examples of sustainedly symbolic poems are William Blake's *The Sick Rose* and William Butler Yeats's *Sailing to Byzantium*. In the sixteenth and seventeenth centuries, an **emblem** was an enigmatic picture of a physical object, to which was attached a motto and a verse explaining its significance. In present-day usage, an emblem is any object which is widely understood to signify an abstract concept; thus a dove is an emblem of peace, and a cross, of Christianity. In what was once a widespread Christian mode of biblical interpretation, a **type** was a person or event in the Old Testament which was regarded as historically real, but also as "prefiguring" a person or event in the New Testament. Thus Adam was often said to be a type of Christ, and the act of Moses in liberating the children of Israel was said to prefigure Christ in freeing men from Satan.

Baroque and **Mannerist** are terms imported into literary study from the history of art, and applied by analogy. Michelangelo is a **baroque** artist; he holds great masses in powerful dynamic tension, his style is heavily ornamented and restless. In these respects he is sometimes compared to Milton. El Greco is a **mannerist,** whose gaunt and distorted figures often seem to be laboring under great spiritual stress, whose light seems to be focused in spots against a dark background. He has been compared to Donne. Analogies of this sort are occasionally suggestive, but can readily deteriorate into parallels that are forced and nominal rather than substantial.

Bathos. See **Pathos,** the **Sublime,** and **Bathos.**

Burlesque and **Mock Heroic** differ in that the former makes its subject ludicrous by directly cutting it down, the latter by inflating it. In Pope's mock-heroic *Dunciad,* the figure of Dulness (Colley Cibber) is given inappropriately heroic dimensions; in Butler's burlesque *Hudibras,* the knightly hero is characterized by low and vulgar attributes, and persistently engages in inappropriately low behavior. Burlesque contributed to the development of the English novel; and during the nineteenth century, when formal drama tended to be stagy and melodramatic, a vigorous burlesque stage flourished in England, making fun of the classics. See **Imitation** and **Parody.**

Catastrophe and **Catharsis.** The **catastrophe** is the conclusion of a play; the word means "down-turning," and is usually applied only to tragedies, in which a frequent kind of catastrophe is the death of the protagonist. (A term for the precipitating final scene that applies both to tragedy and to comedy is **denouement,** which in French means "unknotting.") **Catharsis** in Greek signifies "purgation" or "purification." In Aristotle's *Poetics,* the special effect of tragedy is the "catharsis" of the "emotions of pity and fear" that have been aroused in the audience by the events of the drama.

Chiasmus and **Zeugma.** **Chiasmus** is an inversion of the word order in two parallel phrases, as in John Denham's *Cooper's Hill*: "Strong without rage, without o'erflowing full." **Zeugma** is the use of a single verb or adjective to control two nouns, as in Pope's *The Rape of the Lock*: "Or stain her honor, or her new brocade."

Classic and **Neoclassic.** See **Gothic, Classic, Neoclassic.**

Convention and **Tradition.** **Conventions** are agreed-upon artistic procedures peculiar to an art form. None of Shakespeare's contemporaries spoke blank verse in everyday life, but characters in his plays do, and the audience accepts it—as the audience at an opera accepts that characters will sing arias to express their feelings. A **tradition** consists of beliefs, attitudes, and ways of representing things that is widely shared by writers over a span of time; it generally includes a number of conventions.

Didactic poetry is designed to teach a branch of knowledge, or to embody in fictional form a moral, religious, or philosophical doctrine. The term is not derogatory. John Milton's *Paradise Lost*, for example, can be called didactic, insofar as it is organized, as Milton claimed in his invocation, to "assert Eternal Providence / And justify the ways of God to men." In the eighteenth century, a number of poets wrote didactic poems called **georgics** (modeled on the Roman Virgil's *Georgics* on rural life and farming), which described such applied arts as making cider or running a sugar plantation.

Dramatic irony and **Dramatic monologue** are quite different literary modes. In **dramatic irony** a stage character says something that has one meaning for him, but quite another for the audience who possesses relevant knowledge that the speaker lacks. The **dramatic monologue** is a form that was perfected by Robert Browning in such poems as *My Last Duchess* and *The Bishop Orders His Tomb*. In it, the poetic speaker unintentionally reveals to the reader his character and temperament by what he says, usually to another person whose presence we infer from the utterance of the speaker.

Eclogue. See **Pastorals.**

Emblem. See **Allegory, Symbol, Emblem, Type.**

Epigram, Epigraph, Epitaph. An **epigram** is a short, witty statement in verse or prose. One of Oscar Wilde's characters remarks, "I can resist everything, except temptation." An **epigraph** is an apposite quotation placed at the beginning of a book or a section of it. An **epitaph** is a brief statement about someone who has died; usually, it is intended to be inscribed on a tombstone.

Eulogy and **Elegy.** The **eulogy** is a work of praise, in prose or poetry, for a person either very distinguished or recently dead. In its usual modern sense, an **elegy** is a formal, and usually long, poetic lament for someone who has died. In an extended sense, the term is also used to designate poems on the transience of earthly things (such as the Old English *The Seafarer*) or poetic meditations on mortality (such as Thomas Gray's *Elegy Written in a Country Churchyard*).

Euphemism and **Euphuism.** **Euphemism,** or "fine speech," is a verbal device for avoiding an unpleasant concept or expression, as when, instead of saying a person "died," we say he "passed away." Euphues was the hero of a prose romance (published 1579–80) by John Lyly; his adventures are recounted in a mannered style full of puns, alliteration, and antithetical "points." Under the name of **Euphuism** this courtly style enjoyed a brief vogue in the Elizabethan era.

Fancy and **Imagination.** The distinction between these two mental powers was central to the literary theory of S. T. Coleridge. **Fancy** (a word directly derived by contraction from "fantasy") was defined by Coleridge as the power of combining several known properties into new combinations; **imagination,** on the other hand, was the faculty of using such properties to create an integral whole that is entirely new.

Folios, Quartos, etc., are terms used to specify the size of book pages. To make a **folio,** a sheet of paper (14" × 20" or larger) is folded just once (producing thereby four pages); **quartos** are folded twice (producing eight pages). Shakespeare's plays were first printed in quartos (often in several different editions), but when they were collected together, in 1623, they appeared as the First Folio edition.

Genre, Decorum. A **genre** is an established literary form or type, such as stage comedy, the picaresque novel, the epic, the sonnet. Works belonging to a certain genre tend to represent certain characters and events, and to seek a similar effect. **Decorum,** in literary criticism—where it was a central concept from the Renaissance through the eighteenth century—designates the requirement that there should be a propriety, or fitness, in the way that the character, actions, and style are matched to each other in a particular genre. Low characters, actions, and style, for example, were thought appropriate for satire, while epic demanded characters of high estate, engaged in great actions, and speaking in an appropriately high style.

Gothic, Classic, Neoclassic. These terms are used to distinguish prominent tendencies in literature and the other arts. The term **Gothic** originally referred to the Goths, an early Germanic tribe, then came to signify "medieval." In the eighteenth century "Gothic" connoted primitive and irregular work, possessing the qualities of the relatively barbaric North. **Gothic novels** were a very popular type of prose fiction, inaugurated by Horace Walpole's *Castle of Otranto* (1764), usually set in a medieval castle, which aimed to evoke chilling terror from their readers. **Classic** implies lucid, rational, and orderly works, such as are usually attributed to the writers and thinkers in the classic era of the Greeks and Romans. **Neoclassic**— a term often applied to the period in England from 1660 through most of the eighteenth century—implies an ideal of life, art, and thought deliberately modeled on Greek and Roman examples.

Heroic poems, Heroic drama, Heroic couplets. Because they concentrate on the figure of a typical hero (Achilles, Aeneas), epic poems were frequently called "**heroic.**" Trying to transfer epic grandeur to the stage, playwrights of the Restoration period wrote what was called **heroic drama,** but usually achieved only grandiosity. The stately iambic pentameter couplets in which they made their characters speak became known as **heroic couplets.**

Humor. See **Wit** and **Humor.**

Humors and **Temperaments** are psychological terms used by Renaissance writers. It was believed that every person's constitution contained four basic humors: the **choleric** (bile), the **sanguine** (blood), the **phlegmatic** (phlegm), and the **melancholy** (black bile). The **temperament,** or mixture, of these four humors was held to determine both a person's physical condition and a person's type of character. When a particular humor predominated, it pushed the character in that direction: choler = anger; sanguine = geniality; phlegm = cold torpor; and melancholy = gloomy self-absorption.

Imagination. See **Fancy** and **Imagination.**

Imitation and **Parody** are forms in which a literary work refers back to a predecessor. In the eighteenth century, an "imitation" was a poem that deliberately echoed an older work, but adapted it to subject matter in the writer's own era, usually with a satirical aim directed against that subject matter; Alexander Pope, for example, wrote a number of satires on contemporary life that he entitled *Imitations of Horace*. A **parody** imitates the characteristic style and other features of a particular literary work—or else of a particular literary type—but in such a way as to satirize that work, by making it either amusing or ridiculous. *Northanger Abbey* (1818) by Jane Austen was a good-humored parody of the popular horror-narratives known as gothic novels. (See **Burlesque** and **Gothic**.)

Irony, Sarcasm. **Irony** and **sarcasm** are both ways of saying one thing but implying something sharply different, often opposite; they differ, however, in the way they go about doing so. **Sarcasm** is a broad and taunting form of using apparent praise in order in fact to denigrate. The patriarch Job is bitterly sarcastic when he replies to his would-be comforters (12.2), "No doubt but ye are the people, and wisdom shall die with you." On the other hand, Jane Austen, in the first sentence of *Pride and Prejudice*, overstates the case just enough to make it drily **ironic** when she writes, "It is a truth universally acknowledged, that a single man in possession of a good fortune, must be in want of a wife." (See **Irony**, in the section "Figurative Language," above.)

Legend. See **Myth** and **Legend**.

Logic. See **Rhetoric** and **Logic**.

Masque. The **Masque**, which flourished during the reigns of Elizabeth I, James I, and Charles I, was an elaborate court entertainment that combined poetic drama, music, song, dance, and splendid costumes and settings. For a discussion of the English masque, see the introduction to Jonson's *Pleasure Reconciled to Virtue*.

Myth and **Legend.** **Myths** are hereditary narratives that purport to account, in supernatural terms, for why the world is as it is, and why people act as they do; they also often provide the rules by which people conduct their lives. Myths often spring up to explain rituals, the original meanings of which have been forgotten. A system of related myths is called a **mythology**—a body of supernatural narratives believed to be true by a particular cultural group. The term "myth" is frequently extended to a set of supernatural narratives that are developed by individual poets such as William Blake and W. B. Yeats. Three great mythologies that have been exploited by poets long after they ceased to be believed are the classical (Greek and Roman), the Celtic, and the Germanic. A **legend** is an old and popularly repeated story, of which the protagonist is not supernatural, but a human being. If a hereditary story concerns supernatural beings who are not gods, and the story is not part of a systematic mythology, it is usually classified as a **folktale**.

Naturalism. See **Realism** and **Naturalism**.

Neo-Classic. See **Gothic, Classic, Neoclassic**.

Novel. See **Romance, Novel**.

Ode. A long lyric poem serious in subject and treatment, written in an elevated style and, usually, in an elaborate stanza. See the discussion of English odes in the headnote to Jonson's *Ode on Cary and Morison*.

Pastoral, Eclogue, and **Pastoral Elegy.** **Pastorals** (from the Latin word for "shepherd") are deliberately conventional poems that project a cultivated poet's nostalgic image of the peace and simplicity of the life of shepherds and other rural folk in an idealized natural setting. The form was estab-

2958 / Poetic Forms and Literary Terminology

lished by the Greek poet Theocritus in the third century B.C.E.; it is sometimes also called an **eclogue,** which was the title that the Roman poet
Virgil gave to his collection of pastorals. The pastorals by Theocritus and
later classical poets often included a poem in which a shepherd mourns
the death of a fellow shepherd; from these poems developed the highly
conventional **pastoral elegy,** a type that includes such great laments as
Milton's *Lycidas* and Shelley's *Adonais*. *Lycidas* is also an example of the
extension of the classical pastoral to a Christian range of reference, by
way of the use of the term "pastor" (shepherd) for a parish priest or minister and the frequent representation of Christ as "the Good Shepherd."

Pathos, the Sublime, and Bathos. In Greek, **pathos** signified deep feeling,
especially suffering; in modern criticism, it is used in a more limited way
to signify a scene or passage designed to evoke the feelings of pity or
sympathetic sorrow from an audience. An example is the passage in which
King Lear is briefly reunited with his daughter Cordelia, beginning

> Pray, do not mock me.
> I am a very foolish fond old man . . .

In the first century the Greek rhetorician Longinus wrote a treatise *On
the Sublime*, in which he proposed that sublimity ("loftiness") is the
greatest of stylistic qualities in literature; the effect of the sublime on the
reader is *elestasis* ("transport"). In 1757 Edmund Burke published a highly
influential treatise on *The Sublime and Beautiful*, in which he distinguished the sublime from the beautiful, not as a stylistic quality, but as
the representation of objects that are vast, obscure, and powerful, which
evoke from the reader a "delightful horror" that combines pleasure and
terror. **Bathos** (Greek for "depth") was used by Pope, in a parodic parallel
to Longinus' "sublime," to signify an unintentional descent in literature,
when an author, straining to be passionate or elevated, overshoots the
mark and falls into the trivial or the ridiculous.

Poetic diction, Poetic license, Poetic justice. Poetic diction denotes a
distinctive language used by a poet which is not current in the discourse
of the age; an example is the deliberately archaic language of Spenser's
The Faerie Queene. In modern critical discussion, the term is applied especially to the style of eighteenth-century poets who, according to the reigning principle of decorum (see **Decorum**), believed that a poet must adapt
the level of his diction to the dignity of the high genres of epic, tragedy,
and ode. The results were such phrases as "the finny tribe" for "fish" and
"the bleating kind" for "sheep." **Poetic license** designates the freedom of
a poet or other literary writer to depart, for special effects, from the norms
of common discourse and of literal or historical truth. Examples: the use
of archaic words, meter, and rhyme, and the use of other literary conventions. (See **Convention**.) **Poetic justice** was coined by Thomas Rymer, in
the later seventeenth century, to denote his claim that a narrative or drama
should, at the end, distribute rewards and punishments in proportion to
the virtues and vices of each character. No important critic since Rymer
has adopted this doctrine, except in a highly qualified way.

Quarto. See Folios, Quartos.

Realism and **Naturalism** are both terms applied to prose fictions that aim at a faithful representation of actual existence; they differ, however, in the aspects of that existence that they represent and in the manner in which they represent them. The realistic novel attempts to give the effect of representing ordinary life as it commonly occurs. Realistic novelists such as George Eliot in England and William Dean Howells in America present everyday characters experiencing ordinary events, rendered in great detail. **Naturalism,** which the French novelist Émile Zola developed in the 1870s and later, is based on the philosophy that a human being is merely a higher-order animal, whose character and behavior are determined by heredity and environment. Zola, followed by such later naturalistic novelists as the Americans Frank Norris and Theodore Dreiser, typically represents characters who inherit such compulsive instincts as greed and the sexual drive and are shaped by the social and economic forces of family, class, and the milieu into which they are born. Naturalistic novelists also often display an almost medical candor in describing human activities and bodily functions largely unmentioned in earlier fiction.

Rhetoric and **Logic.** **Rhetoric** was developed by Greek and Roman theorists as the art of using all available means of persuading an audience, either by speech or in writing; it had a great influence on literary criticism in the Renaissance and through the eighteenth century. Rhetorical theorists developed a detailed analysis of figures of speech, largely as effective means to the overall aim of persuasion. In the present century, however, the analysis of such figures has been excerpted from this rhetorical context and made an independent and central concern of language theorists and literary critics. See **Figurative language.** **Logic** is the study of the principles of reasoning. Logic may be used to persuade an audience, but it does not, like rhetoric, avail itself of all means of persuasion, emotional as well as rational; instead, logic limits itself to a concern with the formal procedures of reasoning from sound premises to valid conclusions.

Romance and **Novel.** Medieval **romances** were verse narratives of adventure, usually about a knightly hero on a quest to gain a lady's favor, who encounters both natural tribulations and supernatural marvels. The term "romance" has since come to be opposed to realism (see **Realism** and **Naturalism**) and is applied to prose fictions that represent characters and events which are more picturesque, fantastic, adventurous, or heroic than one encounters in ordinary life. The **novel,** as distinguished from the prose romance, undertakes to be a more realistic representation of common life and social relationships and tends to avoid the fantastic, the fabulous, and the realm of high derring-do. (See **Realism.**)

Sarcasm. See **Irony, Sarcasm.**

Satire designates literary forms which diminish or derogate a subject by making it ridiculous and by evoking toward it amusement, or scorn, or indignation. In **formal satire,** such as Alexander Pope's *Moral Essays*, the satire is accomplished in a direct, first-person address, either to the audience or to a listener within the work. **Indirect satire** is not a direct address, but is cast in the form of a fictional narrative, as in Swift's *Gulliver's Travels* or Byron's *Don Juan*. For a discussion of the backgrounds of English satire, see the introduction to Donne's *Satire 3*.

Sublime. See **Pathos, the Sublime,** and **Bathos.**

Symbol. See **Allegory, Symbol, Emblem, Type.**

Tradition. See **Convention** and **Tradition.**

Type. See **Allegory, Symbol, Emblem, Type.**

Wit and **Humor,** in their present use, designate elements in a literary work which are designed to amuse or to excite mirth in the reader or audience. **Wit,** through the seventeenth century, had a broad range of meanings, including general intelligence, mental acuity, and ingenuity in literary invention, especially in a brilliant and paradoxical style. From this last application there derived the most common present use of "wit" to denote a kind of verbal expression that is brief, deft, and contrived to produce a shock of comic surprise; a characteristic form of wit, in this sense, is the epigram. (See **Epigram.**) **Humor** goes back to the ancient theory of the four humors and the application of the term "humorous" to a comically eccentric character who has an imbalance of the humors in his or her temperament. (See **Humors** and **Temperament.**) As we now use the word, **humor** is ascribed both to a comic utterance and to the comic appearance or behavior of a literary character. A humorous utterance, unlike a witty utterance, need not be intended to be comic by the speaker, and is not cast in the neat epigrammatic form of a witty saying. In Shakespeare's *Twelfth Night,* for example, Malvolio's utterances, as well as his appearance and behavior, are all found humorous by the audience, but his utterances are never witty and are humorous despite his own very solemn intentions.

Zeugma. See **Chiasmus** and **Zeugma.**

THE UNIVERSE ACCORDING TO PTOLEMY

Ptolemy was a Roman astronomer of Greek descent, born in Egypt during the second century C.E.; after his death, for nearly fifteen hundred years his account of the design of the universe was accepted as standard. During that long period, the basic pattern underwent many detailed modifications and was fitted out with many astrological and pseudoscientific trappings. But in essence Ptolemy's followers agreed in portraying the earth as the center of the universe, with the sun, planets, and fixed stars set in transparent spheres orbiting around it. In this scheme of things, as modified for Christian usage, Hell was usually placed under the earth's surface at the center of the cosmic globe, while Heaven, the abode of the blessed spirits, was in the outermost, uppermost circle, the empyrean. But in 1543 the Polish astronomer Copernicus proposed an alternative hypothesis—that the earth rotates around the sun, not vice versa; and despite theological opposition, observations with the new telescope and careful mathematical calculations insured ultimate acceptance of the new view.

The map of the Ptolemaic universe represented here is a simplified version of a diagram in Peter Apian's *Cosmography* (1584). In such a diagram, the Firmament is the sphere which contained the fixed stars; the Crystalline Sphere, which contained no heavenly bodies, is a late innovation, included to explain certain anomalies in the observed movement of the heavenly bodies; and the Prime Mover is the sphere which, itself put into motion by God, imparts rotation around the earth to all the other spheres.

Milton, writing in mid-seventeenth century, made use of two universes. The Copernican universe, though he alludes to it, was too large, formless, and unfamiliar to serve as the setting for the war between Heaven and Hell in *Paradise Lost.* He therefore adopted as his setting the Ptolemaic cosmos, but placed Heaven well outside this smaller earth-centered universe, Hell far beneath it, and assigned the vast middle space to Chaos.

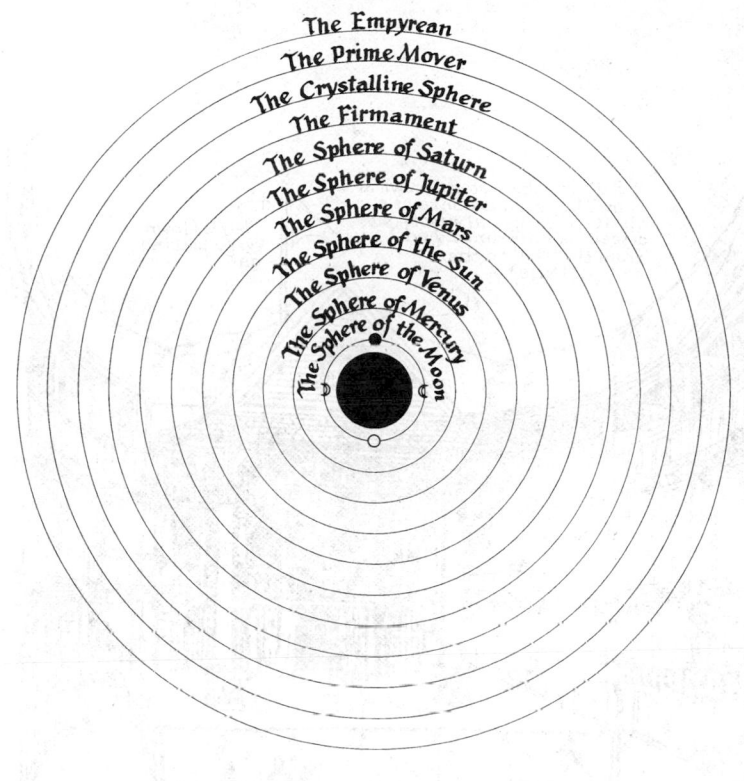

The Empyrean
The Prime Mover
The Crystalline Sphere
The Firmament
The Sphere of Saturn
The Sphere of Jupiter
The Sphere of Mars
The Sphere of the Sun
The Sphere of Venus
The Sphere of Mercury
The Sphere of the Moon

A LONDON PLAYHOUSE OF SHAKESPEARE'S TIME

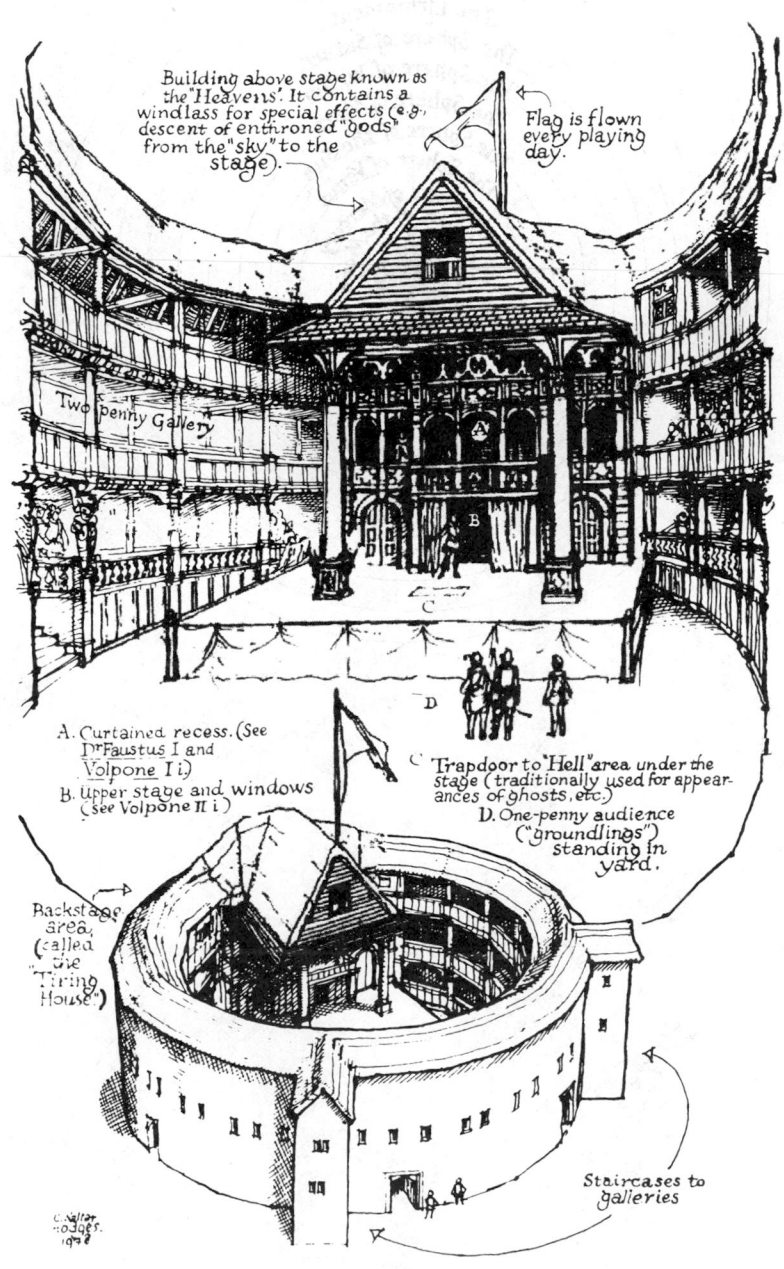

Building above stage known as the "Heavens". It contains a windlass for special effects (e.g. descent of enthroned "gods" from the "sky" to the stage).

Flag is flown every playing day.

Two Penny Gallery

A. Curtained recess. (See Dr Faustus I and Volpone I i)

B. Upper stage and windows (see Volpone II i)

C. Trapdoor to "Hell" area under the stage (traditionally used for appearances of ghosts, etc.)

D. One-penny audience ("groundlings") standing in yard.

Backstage area (called the "Tiring House")

Staircases to galleries

C. Walter Hodges. 1948

PERMISSIONS ACKNOWLEDGMENTS

Ancrene Riwle: Excerpt (ca. 1200 words) from MEDIEVAL ENGLISH PROSE FOR WOMEN, edited by Bella Millett and Jocelyn Wogan-Browne (1990). Reprinted by permission of Oxford University Press.

Beowulf: A new translation by Seamus Heaney. Copyright © 2000 by Seamus Heaney. Reprinted with permission of W. W. Norton & Company, Inc.

Aphra Behn: *The Complete Text of* OROONOKO, edited by Joanna Lipking. Copyright © 1993 by Joanna Lipking and W. W. Norton & Company, Inc. Reprinted by permission of W. W. Norton & Company, Inc.

James Boswell: *Boswell Interviews Voltaire* from BOSWELL ON THE GRAND TOUR: GERMANY AND SWITZERLAND, 1764, edited by F. A. Pottle. Reprinted with the permission of Edinburgh University Press.

Frances Burney: *First Journal Entry* (ca. 800 words), from THE EARLY JOURNALS AND LETTERS OF FANNY BURNEY, VOL. 1, edited by Lars E. Troide (1988). *Rejection of Mr. Barlow's Marriage Proposal* (ca. 3200 words), from THE EARLY JOURNALS AND LETTERS OF FANNY BURNEY, VOL. 2, edited by Lars E. Troide (1990). Reprinted by permission of Oxford University Press. *"Down with Her, Burney!"* from THE EARLY JOURNALS AND LETTERS OF FANNY BURNEY, VOL. 3, edited by Lars E. Troide & Stewart J. Cooke. *Mastectomy,* from THE JOURNALS AND LETTERS OF FANNY BURNEY, VOL. 6, edited by Joyce Hemlow. Reprinted with the permission of McGill–Queen's University Press Ltd.

Margaret Lucas Cavendish: Extracts from THE BLAZING WORLD are taken from Margaret Cavendish, Duchess of Newcastle, THE DESCRIPTION OF A NEW WORLD CALLED THE BLAZING WORLD AND OTHER WRITINGS, edited by Kate Lilley (London: Pickering & Chatto). Reprinted by permission of the publisher.

Geoffrey Chaucer: All excerpts are from CHAUCER'S POETRY: AN ANTHOLOGY FOR THE MODERN READER, 2nd ed. by E. T. Donaldson. Copyright © 1958, 1975 by John Wiley & Sons, Inc. Reprinted by permission of Addison Wesley Longman Educational Publishers, Inc.

Queen Elizabeth: *On Monsieur's Departure* from THE POEMS OF QUEEN ELIZABETH I, edited by Leicester Bradner. Copyright © 1964 by Brown University. Reprinted by permission of the University Press of New England. *Letter to Sir Amyes Paulet* and *Letter to Henry III, King of France* from THE LETTERS OF QUEEN ELIZABETH, edited by G. B. Harrison (Cassell, 1935). Reprinted by permission of David Higham Associates. *The Golden Speech* from THE PUBLIC SPEAKING OF QUEEN ELIZABETH: SELECTIONS FROM HER OFFICIAL ADDRESSES, edited by George P. Rice, Jr. (AMS Press, 1966). Reprinted with the permission of AMS Press, Inc.

Sir Gawain: Complete text of SIR GAWAIN AND THE GREEN KNIGHT: A New Verse Translation by Marie Boroff, translator. Copyright © 1967 by W. W. Norton & Company, Inc. Reprinted by permission of W. W. Norton & Company, Inc.

Thomas Gray: From the manuscript of *Elegy Written in a Country Churchyard.* Transcribed by kind permission of the Provost and Fellows of Eton College.

Stephen Greenblatt et al.: Footnotes to *King Lear* by Stephen Greenblatt, copyright © 1997 by W. W. Norton & Company, Inc., from THE NORTON SHAKESPEARE: BASED ON THE OXFORD EDITION, edited by Stephen Greenblatt et al. Reprinted by permission of W. W. Norton & Company, Inc.

Robert Henryson: *The Cock and the Fox* from ROBERT HENRYSON: THE POEMS, edited by Denton Fox (1987). Reprinted by permission of Oxford University Press.

William Hogarth: *Marriage A-la-Mode,* 1745, Plates 1–6, and *Beggar's Opera,* William Blake's engraving of the Hogarth illustration, 1795, reproduced by permission of the Print Collection, Miriam and Ira D. Wallach Division of Art, Prints and Photographs, The New York Public Library, Astor, Lenox and Tilden Foundations.

Robert Herrick: *How the Roses Came Red* by Robert Herrick, from BEN JONSON AND THE CAVALIER POETS: A Norton Critical Edition by Hugh Maclean, editor. Copyright © 1974 by W. W. Norton & Company, Inc. Reprinted by permission of W. W. Norton & Company, Inc.

Samuel Johnson: Excerpt from the manuscript of *The Vanity of Human Wishes.* Reprinted with permission.

Ben Jonson: *The Masque of Blackness* (ca. 3600 words), from COURT MASQUES: JACOBEAN AND CAROLINE ENTERTAINMENTS, 1605–1640, edited by David Lindley (1995). Reprinted by permission of Oxford University Press.

Julian of Norwich: Excerpts reprinted from Julian of Norwich, A BOOK OF SHOWINGS, edited by Edmund Colledge and James Walsh, by permission of the publisher. Copyright © 1978 by the Pontifical Institute of Mediaeval Studies, Toronto.

Margery Kempe: Excerpts from THE BOOK OF MARGERY KEMPE, edited by Meech and Allen. Reprinted by permission of The Council of the Early English Text Society.

William Langland: Excerpts from PIERS PLOWMAN: An Alliterative Verse Translation, translated by E. Talbot Donaldson. Translation copyright © 1990 by W. W. Norton & Company, Inc. Reprinted by permission of W. W. Norton & Company, Inc.

Layamon: Excerpts from Layamon's BRUT translated by Rosamund Allen. Reprinted by permission of The Orion Publishing Group Ltd. on behalf of the publisher, Everyman.

The Mabinogi: From THE MABINOGI AND OTHER WELSH TALES by Patrick Ford. Copyright © 1977 by the Regents of the University of California. Reprinted by permission of the University of California Press.

Index